Dictionnaire technique anglais

French Technical Dictionary

Routledge
Dictionnaire technique anglais
French Technical Dictionary

VOLUME 2

ANGLAIS–FRANÇAIS
ENGLISH–FRENCH

ROUTLEDGE

Reference

London and New York

First published 1994
by Routledge
11 New Fetter Lane, London EC4P 4EE

Simultaneously published in the USA and Canada
by Routledge
29 West 35th Street, New York, NY 10001

Conversion tables adapted from *Dictionary of Scientific Units*, H. G. Jerrard and
D. B. McNeill, London: Chapman & Hall, 1992.

Typeset in Monotype Times, Helvetica Neue and Bauer Bodoni
by Routledge

Printed in Great Britain by TJ Press (Padstow), Cornwall

Printed on acid-free paper

British Library Cataloguing-in-Publication Data
A catalogue record for this book is available from the British Library

Library of Congress Cataloging-in-Publication Data
Applied for

ISBNs:
Vol 1 French–English 0–415–11224–9
Vol 2 English–French 0–415–11225–7
2-volume set 0–415–05670–5

Table des matières/Contents

Direction éditoriale/Editorial staff

Direction rédactionnelle/General Editor
Yves Arden

Chef de projet/Managing Editor
Neil Clements

Direction de collection/Programme Management
Flavia Hodges   **Sinda López**
Wendy Morris   **Elizabeth Handford**

Etude de marché/Market Research
Judith Watts   **Rachel Miller**
Jane Gardner   **Nadia Lovell**
Susanne Jordans   **Perdita Geier**
Rebecca Moy

Informatique/Systems
George Allard   **Julian Zinovieff**
Simon Thompson   **Phoebe Bright**
Michael Al-Nassir

Secrétariat/Administration
Gemma Marren   **Kristoffer Blegvad**
Hazel Egerton   **Jessica Ramage**

Rédaction/Subeditorial
Martin Barr

Production/Production
Nigel Marsh

Collaborateurs et lexicographes/
Contributors and lexicographers

Collaborateurs/Contributors

Réjane Amery

Yves Arden

Josephine Bacon

John P. Bryon

Michael Carpenter

Anna Cordon

Maguy Couette

Elisabeth Coyne

P. J. Doyle

J. V. Drazil

Bill Duffin

James Dunster

Christopher Freeland

Crispin Geoghegan

Susan Green

Freda Klipstein

C. A. Lagall

David Larcher

Virginia Lester

Pamela Mayorcas

James Millard

Charles Polley

Michael Rawson

Louis Rioual

Tom Williams

Stephen Wilson

Stewart Wittering

Lexicographes/Lexicographers

Tom Bartlett

Hazel Curties

Charles Denroche

Anna Howes

Duncan Marshall

Valerie Smith

John Williams

Spécialistes consultés/
Specialist consultants

Chris Buchanan
Abbey Road Studios

Gérard Mercier
Air France

Maryline Grellier
Apple France

Hélène Mateescu
Association Française de Normalisation

Jean-Jacques Bisson
AT&T/NCR

Alain de Kermoysan
Automobiles Citroën

Patrick Leggatt
anciennement /formerly BBC Engineering
Information Department

John Camm
British Ceramic Research Limited

A.J. Wardle
British Coal Corporation

Annick Piant
Centre Audiovisuel Simone de Beauvoir

Dr Gilles Pinay
Centre d'Ecologie des Systèmes Fluviaux

Dr Bertrand Fritz
Dr Christine Mosser
Centre de Géochimie de la Surface

Jean-Louis Astor
Centre National d'Etudes Spatiales

Dr Nicole Kurtz-Newell
Centre National de la Recherche Scientifique

Prof. Roland Triay
Centre de Physique Théorique/Université de
Provence

Dr Christian Voltolini
Centre de Recherches Nucléaires

Dr Francis Saupé
Centre de Recherches Pétrographiques et
Géochimiques

Dr Frank Roux
Centre de Recherches en Physique de
l'Environnement Terrestre et Planétaire

Juliette Kohiyama
Charbonnages de France

Ronald Ridout
Chartered Institute of Building

Hans Bamert
Chemins de Fer Fédéraux Suisses

Gerald Cameron
Ciba-Geigy Limited

Christine Nunes
Compagnie Générale Maritime

Philippe Chambin
CREAR

Kevin Colcomb-Heiliger
Department of Transport
Marine Pollution
Control Unit

Héloïse Neefs
Dictionnaires Hachette

Ripple Linant
Elf Aquitaine Production

Nicolette Walshe
Energy Technology Support Unit

Bertrand Humbert
France 2

Josette Mell
France Télécom

Colin Andrews
Gambica

Marie-Dominique Agay
Sandra Buder
GRETA Alpes Dauphiné

Dr Gilles Zumbach
Harvard University

Prof. Michael Worthington
Imperial College London

Ray Griffiths
Institut Français pour l'Exploitation de la Mer

Dr Gilbert Binder
Institut National Polytechnique de
Grenoble/Université Joseph Fourrier

Jean-Pierre Michel
Institut National Polytechnique de Lorraine

Philip Maylor
Brian Patterson
Institute of Data Processing Management

J. E. H. Leach
Institute of Energy

Celia Kirby
D. B. Smith
Institute of Hydrology

J. H. Durran
Institute of Mathematics and its Applications

Dr Peter Collar
Institute of Oceanographic Sciences

Christopher Wolfe
Institute of Physics

Malcolm Horlick
Institute of Refrigeration

Chris Murphy
Institute of Wastes Management

Derek Chapman
Malcolm J. Raven
Institution of Gas Engineers

Don Goodsell
Institution of Mechanical Engineers

Michael White
anciennement/formerly International Maritime
Organization

Jean-Pierre Portier
Isabelle Prat
IRFIP

Dr Norman Borrett
Dr Michael Clode
Janine Lajudie
King's College London

Peter Sutherst
Kodak Limited

Dr Michel Vauclin
Laboratoire d'Etude des Transferts en
Hydrologie et Environnement

R. N. Avis
Lafarge Réfractaires Monolithiques

François Ducellier
Lesieur Alimentaire/Céréol

J. E. Lunn
Locomotive & Carriage Institution

Bernard Agnard
Georges Dive
Matra Défense

Jacques Siméon
Météo France

Dave Farlow
Michelin Tyre plc

Kevin Murphy
Mineralogical Society

Jean-Marie Massin
Ministère de l'Environnement

Thierry Berthaux
Ministère de l'Industrie
et du Commerce Extérieur

Claude Lannoy
Moulinex

Gill Wilkinson
National Radiological Protection Board

Gillian Strachan-Gray
Optical Information Council

Dr Graham Moore
Diana Deavin
Pira International

Dr Jim Smith
Prince Edward Island Food Technology Centre

Patrick Pigault
Régie Autonome des Transports Parisiens

Jean-Marc Pelletier
Renault Automation

R. G. Lee
anciennement/formerly Royal Military College
of Science

D. J. Elliott
Rubber Consultants

Jean-Louis Richard
Saunier Duval Electricité

Philippe de La Cotardière
Société Astronomique de France

Prof. Antoine Chaigne
Société Française d'Acoustique

Paul Dinsdale
Society of Dyers and Colourists

Phil Thompson
Andrew Melvin
Gwyneth Hughes
Texaco Limited

Michel Baeckelandt
Thomson-CSF

Dr Alan Williams
Université de Genève

Dr Minh-Tâm Tran
Université de Lausanne

Dr Bernard Junod
Université de Neuchâtel

Simon Achenbaum
Université de Paris V

Prof. Georges Calas
Université de Paris VII

Dr Alain Mauffret
Université Pierre et Marie Curie/Groupe
d'Etude de la Marge Continentale

Dr Roger Marchand
Dr Odile Merdrignac
Université de Rennes I

Michel Deblock
Université des Sciences et Technologies de Lille

Prof. Yves Gourinard
Université de Toulouse III

Mark Hempsell
University of Bristol

Dr Philippe Sarda
University of Cambridge

Elizabeth Fraser
University of Edinburgh

Dr John A Elliott
University of Manchester Institute of Science
and Technology

Line Fiquet
Witco

Nous tenons aussi particulièrement à exprimer nos remerciements à ceux et celles qui nous ont apporté leur concours lors de la rédaction de ce dictionnaire:

Serge Bouchval

John Chillingworth

Catherine Maryan Green

Jason Miles

We are also particularly indebted to the following people for their assistance during the compilation of this dictionary:

Dr Jacqueline Mitton

Thomas Stengel

John W. Thristan

Suzy Vergez

Préface/Preface

Les deux facteurs qui nous ont permis de créer un dictionnaire technique bilingue totalement nouveau, posant des normes nouvelles, sont un système de base de données et une méthode de compilation parfaitement adaptés aux résultats souhaités.

La sortie de ce dictionnaire dans les délais et conformément aux critères prévus imposait la compilation d'une base de données spécifique extrêmement sophistiquée. Au début du projet, nous avons soigneusement étudié tous les systèmes de développement de dictionnaire existants. Aucun n'étant suffisamment flexible, nous avons opté pour le développement intégral d'un nouveau système, totalement adapté à nos exigences.

Ce système a pour caractéristique essentielle d'être conçu comme une base de données relationnelle: dans chaque langue, les termes sont stockés dans des fichiers séparés, tandis que d'autres fichiers ne se composent que de liens. Les liens entre les termes de fichiers de langues séparés représentent des traductions et nous permettent de gérer de manière très sophistiquée différents types d'équivalences de traduction 'un à plusieurs' et 'plusieurs à un'. Les liens entre les différents termes d'un même fichier de langue représentent des renvois, eux-mêmes de différents types: synonymes, antonymes, variantes orthographiques, variantes géographiques et abréviations.

La base de données a été créée en trois phases principales: tout d'abord, les termes et leurs traductions ont été sélectionnés par une équipe de traducteurs professionnels, ayant une connaissance pratique approfondie du domaine concerné et intéressés par la compilation et la diffusion de la terminologie. Ces termes regroupés ont ensuite été approuvés dans les différents pays par des spécialistes techniques de haut niveau, ayant pour mission de garantir l'actualité et la précision des termes, ainsi que l'étendue des sujets traités. Enfin, chaque fichier de langue a été contrôlé par des lexicographes des pays concernés, chargés de veiller au respect des variantes géographiques. Dans chaque langue, les formes et l'orthographe (anglaises ou américaines, canadiennes, suisses ou belges) sont

The two factors that have enabled us to create a completely new bilingual technical dictionary that sets new standards in its field are the database system and the method of compilation.

It would not have been possible to compile this dictionary within a realistic timescale, and to the standard that we have achieved, without the use of a highly sophisticated, custom-designed database. During the initial planning stages we looked closely at all the dictionary development systems then available, but concluded that none was sufficiently flexible for our purposes. As a result, we have had a completely unique system developed to our own specifications.

Its most significant feature is that it is designed as a relational database: term records for each language are held in separate files, with further files consisting only of link records. Links between terms in different language files represent translations and enable us to handle, in a sophisticated way, various types of one-to-many and many-to-one translation equivalences. Links between terms within a single language file represent cross-references, themselves of a wide variety of types: synonyms, antonyms, spelling variants, geographical variants and abbreviations.

The content of the database for this dictionary was created in three principal phases: the terms and their translations were originally solicited from a panel of professional translators with current practical experience of a narrowly defined specialist subject area and an interest in the collection and dissemination of terminology; the terms in each language were then vetted by native-speaker subject specialists working at the leading edge of the respective technology in order to ensure their currency, the accuracy of explanations, and the adequacy of coverage. Finally, each language file was reviewed by regional editors to ensure worldwide coverage of usage. British and North American forms and spellings are clearly labelled and distinguished, and careful attention is also paid to Canadian, Swiss and Belgian French.

The creation and editing of the database of terms was, however, only the first stage in the

clairement identifiées.

La création et la vérification de la base de données terminologique n'ont cependant représenté que la première étape de la constitution du dictionnaire. La distinction entre les langues cible et source n'étant pas significative au niveau de la base de données, nous avons dû, pour la version imprimée, mettre les données en forme pour obtenir des volumes français–anglais et anglais–français séparés. Les données ont alors été traitées par un logiciel permettant de produire deux séquences alphabétiques, des mots-clés français avec leurs traductions anglaises – et vice versa – avec, dans chaque cas, indication de l'imbrication des composants, de l'ordre des traductions, du style des renvois de différents types, et d'autres fonctions, selon un algorithme complexe.

A ce stade, le texte mis en forme a été vérifié par une équipe de lexicographes expérimentés, qui avaient pour mission d'éliminer les doublons et les incohérences, de vérifier les informations et les explications contextuelles, et de supprimer les termes soit trop généraux, soit trop spécialisés pour être inclus dans un dictionnaire de 'technique générale'.

Cette méthodologie nous a permis d'établir des normes de contrôle de qualité extrêmement élevées et d'éliminer le manque d'homogénéité dont souffrent généralement les dictionnaires 'techniques généraux' compilés par des individus isolés ou de petites équipes, et d'offrir à nos clients un dictionnaire bilingue spécialisé d'un type entièrement nouveau.

Les éditeurs

making of the dictionary. Within the database the distinction between source and target languages is not meaningful, but for this printed dictionary it has been necessary to format the data to produce separate French–English and English–French volumes. The data were processed by a further software module to produce two alphabetic sequences, of French headwords with English translations and vice versa, each displaying the nesting of compounds, ordering of translations, style for cross-references of different types, and other features according to a complex algorithm.

At this stage the formatted text was edited by a team of experienced lexicographers whose task it was to eliminate duplication or inconsistency; edit the contextual information and explanations; and remove terms that were on the one hand too general, or on the other, too specialized for inclusion in a 'general technical' dictionary.

This phased method of working has enabled us to set extremely high standards of quality control, and eliminate the idiosyncrasy often characteristic of 'general technical' dictionaries compiled by individuals or small teams, with the result that we can claim this to be an entirely new type of specialist bilingual dictionary.

The Publisher

Caractéristiques du dictionnaire/
Features of the dictionary

Les principales caractéristiques de ce dictionnaire sont mentionnées ci-contre dans les éclatés. Pour une explication détaillée de chacune de ces caractéristiques et pour tirer le meilleur parti de votre dictionnaire, reportez-vous aux pages xxi–xxiii.

The main features of the dictionary are highlighted in the text extracts on the opposite page. For a more detailed explanation of each of these features and information on how to get the most out of the dictionary, see pages xxv–xxvii.

Signification de l'abréviation indiquée pour le terme anglais ainsi que pour la traduction française	**COLR** *abbr* *(connected line identification restriction)* TELECOM RILC *(restriction de l'identification de la ligne connectée)*	The abbreviation is expanded in both French and English
	columbite *n* CHEM niobite *f*	
Domaines en ordre alphabétique indiquant la traduction appropriée à chaque domaine	**column** *n* COMP, DP, ELECTRON colonne *f*, MINING affût-colonne *m*, PRINT colonne *f*, rubrique *f*; ~ **box** *n* PROD ENG *founding* châssis à colonnes *m*; ~ **charge** *n* MINING charge de colonne *f*; ~ **loudspeaker** *n* RECORDING haut-parleur à colonne *f*	Subject area labels given in alphabetical order show appropriate translation
	columnar: ~ **basalt** *n* GEOL orgue basaltique *m*; ~ **charge** *n* MINING charge de colonne *f*; ~ **crystal** *n* METALL cristal colonnaire *m*; ~ **jointing** *n* GEOL prismation *f*, prismation basaltique *f*	
Dans les cas où l'abréviation prend un sens différent selon le domaine, le sens est donné après le domaine correspondant	**COM** *abbr* COMP *(computer output on microfilm)* sortie ordinateur sur microfilm *f*, TELECOM *(continuation of message)* suite de message *f*	When the meaning of an abbreviation differs according to area it follows the subject area label
	coma *n* ELECTRON, PHOTO, PHYS coma *m*; ~ **aberration** *n* ASTRON *of reflecting telescope* aberration de coma *f*; ~ **fail** *n* ASTRON *of comet* chevelure cométaire *f*	
	Coma: ~ **Berenices** *n* ASTRON Chevelure de Bérénice *f*	
	comagmatic *adj* GEOL comagmatique	
Genre de chaque nom indiqué pour la traduction française	**comb**[1] *n* TEXTILES peigne *m*; ~ **filter** *n* ELECTRON filtre en peigne *m*; ~ **filtering** *n* ELECTRON filtrage par filtre en peigne *m*	Genders are indicated at French noun translations
	comb[2] *vt* TEXTILES peigner	
	combat: ~ **aircraft** *n* MILIT avion de combat *m*; ~ **helicopter** *n* AERONAUT hélicoptère armé *m*	
	combed[1] *adj* TEXTILES peigné	
	combed:[2] ~ **top** *n* TEXTILES ruban peigné *m*; ~ **wool fabric** *n* TEXTILES tissu peigné *m*; ~ **yarn** *n* TEXTILES fil peigné *m*	
Contextes fournissant des informations supplémentaires pour faciliter la sélection de la traduction exacte	**combination** *n* AERONAUT *helicopters* conjugaison *f*, CHEM *action* combinaison *f*, *product* combiné *m*, COMP, DP, MATH combinaison *f*; ~ **bulk carrier** *n* TRANSP navire combiné *m*, transport combiné minerai-vrac-pétrole *m*; ~ **chuck** *n* MECH ENG mandrin à combinaisons *m*; ~ **lathe** *n* MECH ENG tour à combinaisons *m*; ~ **lock** *n* CONST serrure à combinaisons *f*; ~	Contexts give supplementary information to help locate the right translation
Termes composés imbriqués en ordre alphabétique sous le premier élément	**microphone** *n* RECORDING microphone combiné *m*; ~ **pliers** *n pl* MECH ENG *press tools* pinces à combinaisons *f pl*; ~ **run** *n* PRINT tirage *m*; ~ **sound** *n* ACOUSTICS son de combinaison *m*; ~ **surface gage** *n* (AmE), ~ **surface gauge** *n* (BrE) MECH ENG trusquin à combinaisons *m*; ~ **tap assembly** *n* MECH ENG robinetterie mélangeur *f*; ~ **tone** *n* ACOUSTICS son résultant *m*; ~ **tools** *n pl* MECH ENG *press tools* outillages multiples *m pl*	Compound terms are nested alphabetically at the first element
Informations complètes sur les variantes américaines et anglaises suivies de codes géographiques	**combinational:** ~ **circuit** *n* (AmE) *(cf combinatorial circuit)* COMP, ELECTRON circuit combinatoire *m* **combinatorial:** ~ **analysis** *n* MATH analyse combinatoire *f*; ~ **circuit** *n* (BrE) *(cf combinational circuit)* COMP circuit combinatoire *m*, ELECTRON circuit combinatoire *m*, circuit logique combinatoire *m*; ~ **logic** *n* ELECTRON logique combinatoire *f*	British English and American English variants are given in full and followed by regional labels
	combinatorics *n* MATH *study of configurations* combinatoire *f*, combinatorique *f*	
	combine *vt* COMP, DP combiner, MECH ENG *multicylinder engine output diagrams* rankiniser	
Deux-points indiquant un mot dépourvu de valeur technique et introduisant un mot composé	**combined:** ~ **bending shrinking and welding machine** *n* MECH ENG machine à refouler souder couder et contre-couder *f*; ~ **braking** *n* RAIL *vehicles* freinage mixte *m*; ~ **cargo and passenger liner** *n* TRANSP cargo mixte *m*; ~ **cargo and passenger ship** *n* TRANSP cargo mixte passagers-marchandises *m*; ~ **diagram** *n* MECH ENG *engine output* diagramme rankinisé *m*; ~ **distribution frame** *n*	A colon introduces a compound where the headword has no technical value
Abréviation du terme donnée à l'entrée pour la forme intégrale	*(CDF)* TELECOM répartiteur mixte *m*; ~ **drill and countersink** *n* MECH ENG foret à centrer *m*	Abbreviation of the term is given at the full form entry

Comment utiliser ce dictionnaire

Domaines traités

Ce dictionnaire est un ouvrage technique 'général' qui couvre l'ensemble des nouvelles technologies et des connaissances scientifiques sur lesquelles elles reposent. Il comporte une importante base terminologique extraite des disciplines traditionnelles comme la mécanique, le bâtiment, l'électro-technique, l'électronique appliquée, ainsi que les nouvelles technologies comme les sources d'énergie renouvelable, la sécurité appliquée et l'assurance de la qualité.

Sélection des termes

Les termes qu'il contient se rapportent au vocabulaire de base de chaque discipline, et ont été minutieusement vérifiés par des spécialistes de haut niveau, chargés de veiller à l'exactitude et à l'actualité des termes anglais et français; à la parfaite correspondance des termes, et à la cohérence de l'ensemble.

Nous avons également veillé à n'inclure que des termes véritablement techniques, à l'exclusion de tout vocabulaire général dépourvu de valeur technique. Nous avons cependant inclus le vocabulaire technique de base dans son intégralité, bien que certains termes puissent également figurer dans des dictionnaires généraux. Nous avons eu pour principe de donner les traductions préférées par les spécialistes bien qu'il y ait souvent d'autres variantes possibles.

Classement des termes

Tous les termes sont classés par ordre alphabétique. Les termes composés apparaissent sous leur premier élément, quelle que soit la structure sémantique de l'ensemble.

Termes ignorés

Les termes anglais qui ne sont pas pris en compte lors du classement sont les suivants:

a, all, an, and, any, anybody, anyone, anything, anywhere, are, be, by, during, each, every, everybody, everyone, everything, everywhere, for, from, here, if, in, is, it, no, nobody, no-one, nor, not, nothing, nowhere, of, off, on, or, out, over, so, some, somebody, someone, something, somewhere, the, that, then, there, they, thing, this, to, too, under, very, where, while, who, with

Les locutions ou les syntagmes figurent sous le premier élément. Dans les listes imbriquées, la forme simple est remplacée par un 'tilde' (~). Exemple:

airborne:[2] **~ acoustical noise** *n* SAFETY bruit acoustique aérien *m*; **~ collision avoidance system** *n* AERONAUT système anticollision embarqué *m*; **~ dust** *n* SAFETY poussières aériennes *f pl*, poussières en suspension dans l'air *f pl*

Lorsque ce premier élément est un mot-vedette ayant un ou plusieurs sens techniques, les mots composés suivent la forme simple et sont classés par ordre alphabétique. Exemple:

bronze[2] *n* CHEM bronze *m*, COLOURS pigment bronze *m*, pigment de bronze *m*; **~ guide bush** *n* MECH ENG bague de guidage en bronze *f*; **~ lacquer** *n* COLOURS vernis à bronzer *m*; **~ pigment** *n* COLOURS bronze en poudre *m*, pigment de bronze *m*

Si le premier élément n'est pas traduit, ses composants sont précédés de deux-points. Exemple:

swipe: ~ card *n* TELECOM carte à mémoire *f*

Ordre des termes

Les locutions ou termes comportant des traits-d'union sont entrés en ordre alphabétique, et suivent donc les locutions ou termes ayant le même premier élément. Exemple:

broken:[2] **~ circuit** *n* ELEC ENG circuit ouvert *m*; **~ country** *n* CONST pays accidenté *m*, pays tourmenté *m*; **~ end** *n* TEXTILES casse *f*; **~ ice** *n* REFRIG glace concassée *f*; **~ line** *n* GEOM ligne brisée *f*; **~ ore** *n* MINING minerai abattu *m*, minerai broyé *m*; **~ rice** *n* FOOD TECH brisure de riz *f*; **~ rock** *n* COAL TECH menu de concassage *m*; **~ seed** *n* C&G bouillon crevé *m*; **~ stone** *n* CONST pierre cassée *f*; **~ white line** *n* CONST *road marking* ligne blanche discontinue *f*; **~ working** *n* COAL TECH abattage *m*, chantier accidenté *m*, déhouillement des piliers *m*, dépilage des piliers *m*, enlèvement des piliers *m*
broken-backed *adj* NAUT *ship* arqué
broken-down: ~ timber *n* CONST bois débité *m*

Les articles (*a, an, the*), et la préposition *of* ne sont pas pris en compte lors du tri. Exemple:

beginning: ~ **of call demand** n TELECOM début de la demande d'appel m; ~ **of life** n NUCLEAR of core début de vie m; ~ **of message** n (BOM) COMP, TELECOM début de message m

Lorsque des composants ont de nombreuses imbrications, des repères en marge facilitent la recherche. Exemple:

air:[2]

▊**~ n** ~ **nozzle** n COAL TECH éjecteur de ventilation m, MECH ENG ajutage m;

▊**~ o** ~ **outlet** n MECH ENG évacuation d'air f, of blower sortie du vent f; ~ **oven** n P&R equipment étuve à l'air chaud f;

▊**~ p** ~ **passage** n MECH ENG passage d'air m, MINING conduit m; ~ **passageway** n MINING conduit m; ~ **permeability** n HEAT ENG, PRINT perméabilité à l'air f

Les abréviations et acronymes en majuscules figurent après les termes de même forme en minuscules. Exemple:

age[1] n GEOL, PETR âge m; ~ **dating** n GEOL datation f; ~ **hardening** n CRYSTALL, METALL, P&R durcissement par vieillissement m, PROP MAT durcissement structural m, SPRINGS durcissement structural m, vieillissement par écrouissage m; ~ **of the universe** n ASTRON âge de l'univers m
age[2] vt METALL, PAPER TECH vieillir, THERMOD metals mûrir, tremper, vieillir
AGE abbr (allyl glycidyl ether) P&R éther allylglycidique m

Les termes contenant des chiffres ou des symboles sont classés comme s'ils étaient écrits en lettres. Exemple:

three-cylinder: ~ **engine** n MECH ENG machine à trois cylindres f
three-D: ~ **log** n PETR diagraphie de densité variable f
three-dimensional[1] adj PHYS tridimensionnel, PROP MAT à trois dimensions

Homographes

Chaque terme est accompagné d'une abréviation indiquant sa fonction grammaticale. La liste complète de ces abréviations figure page xxix.

Un terme ayant plusieurs fonctions grammaticales figure sous une entrée séparée pour chaque fonction. Ces entrées se distinguent par un chiffre en exposant qui suit immédiatement le mot-vedette. La séquence est la suivante: abréviation, adjectif, adverbe, nom, verbe, suivie des fonctions moins fréquentes. Exemple:

bubbling[1] adj PHYS bouillonnant
bubbling[2] n C&G bouillonnage m, OCEANOG pétillement de la mer m, PAPER TECH cloquage m, PHYS barbotage m, bouillonnement m

Ordre des traductions

Chaque terme est accompagné d'une ou plusieurs abréviations indiquant le domaine auquel il se rapporte. La liste complète de ces abréviations figure pages xxxi–xxxii.

Lorsqu'un terme est utilisé dans plusieurs disciplines, il est suivi des abréviations appropriées, en ordre alphabétique.

Lorsqu'un terme est traduit de la même manière dans différentes disciplines, la traduction figure après la liste des abréviations. Exemple:

ammeter n ELEC, ELEC ENG, LAB EQUIP electric current, PHYS, TV, VEHICLES electrical system ampèremètre m

Lorsqu'un terme peut se traduire de différentes façons selon les disciplines, sa traduction figure après chaque abréviation ou série d'abréviations. Exemple:

branch[1] n COMP of circuit branche f, of programme branchement m, CONST metal piece at end of hose lance f, lance à eau f, plumbing branchement m, embranchement m, DP branchement m, of circuit branche f

Informations complémentaires

Le genre de chaque nom est indiqué. Pour les expressions ou termes composés, le genre est celui du terme dans son ensemble (c'est-à-dire de son mot-vedette), et non celui de l'élément final. Exemple:

data ~ **switching exchange** n (DSE) COMP, TELECOM centre de commutation de données m

Dans de très nombreux cas, des informations complémentaires expliquent l'utilisation du terme concerné. Exemple:

(a) le sujet ou l'objet typique d'un verbe, par exemple:

set[2] n CINEMAT décor m, plateau m, COMP ensemble m, jeu m, CONST in concrete prise f, nail set chasse-clou m, chasse-pointe m, pousse-pointe m, of pile avant-pieu m, rivet set bouterolle f, chasse-rivet m, street paving pavé m, pavé en granit m, DP ensemble m, jeu m, ELEC ENG of machines groupe m, GEOL of beds ensemble m

(b) les noms typiques utilisés avec un adjectif, par exemple:

air-cooled[1] adj ELEC equipment refroidi par l'air

(c) les mots indiquant la référence d'un nom, par exemple:

belly[1] n C&G of shaft furnace ventre m, CONST of wall bombement m, NAUT of sail, boat creux m, ventre m

(d) un domaine plus limité que celui indiqué par l'abréviation, par exemple:

scrambler *n* SPACE *communications*, TELECOM embrouilleur *m*

(e) une paraphrase ou un équivalent d'ordre général, par exemple:

bank[1] *n* PRINT table à papier *f*, *newspaper headline* gros titre *m*

Lorsqu'un terme peut donner lieu à différentes traductions, des informations contextuelles indiquent également la traduction appropriée. Exemple:

stringer *n* CONST longeron *m*, longrine *f*, poutre de rive *f*, sommier *m*, *of roof truss* entrait *m*, tirant d'une ferme de comble *m*, MINING cordon *m*, crin *m*, filet *m*, veinule *f*, NAUT *boatbuilding* gouttière *f*, hiloire *f*, serre *f*, RAIL longrine *f*, SPACE *spacecraft* lisse *f*; **~ angle** *n* NAUT *shipbuilding* cornière de gouttière *f*; **~ head** *n* PETR première passe *f*

Renvois

Les variantes linguistiques (entre l'anglais et l'américain ou entre le français de France, du Canada, de Suisse et de Belgique) sont toujours indiquées. Tous les termes non universels sont accompagnés de la mention typique. La liste complète de ces mentions figure à la page xxxii.

En cas de variantes lexicales, les informations les concernant – et notamment les traductions et renvois à d'autres formes régionales – sont fournies systématiquement à chaque entrée. Exemple:

Bowden: **~ cable** *n* *(cf brake cable)* MECH, VEHICLES *on clutch, brake* câble Bowden *m*
brake:[1] **~ cable** *n* *(cf Bowden cable)* MECH, VEHICLES câble de frein *m*

Lorsque les variantes orthographiques ne sont pas différenciées par région ou par pays, la forme la moins courante renvoie à la forme dominante. Les informations complètes figurent uniquement sous cette entrée. Exemple:

tire *n* (AmE) *see tyre*

Les variantes géographiques, tant orthographiques que lexicales, sont indiquées intégralement lorsqu'il s'agit de traductions. Exemple:

braked: **~ car** *n* (AmE) *(cf braked wagon)* RAIL *vehicles* wagon freiné *m*; **~ wagon** *n* (BrE) *(cf braked car)* RAIL *vehicles* wagon freiné *m*

Les abréviations et leurs formes intégrales figurent dans le corps principal du dictionnaire, classées par ordre alphabétique. Les informations complètes – et notamment leurs traductions et les renvois à leur abréviation ou à leur forme intégrale, le cas échéant – sont indiquées pour chaque entrée. Exemple:

CAI *abbr* *(computer-assisted instruction)* COMP IAO *(instruction assistée par ordinateur)* *f*

binary:[2] **~ phase shift keying** *n* *(BPSK)* TELECOM modulation par déplacement de phase bivalente *f* *(MDPB)*

La liste alphabétique des abréviations contenues dans ce dictionnaire figure à la fin de ce volume.

Dans certains cas, les antonymes ou termes contraires sont également spécifiés. Les informations complètes figurent sous chaque entrée. Exemple:

high-pass: **~ filter** *n* *(cf low-pass filter)* COMP, DP, ELEC, ELECTRON, PHYS, RECORDING, TELECOM, TV filtre passe-haut *m*
low-pass: **~ filter** *n* *(cf high-pass filter)* COMP, DP, ELEC, ELECTRON, PHYS, RECORDING, TELECOM, TV filtre passe-bas *m*.

Using the dictionary

Range of coverage

This is one volume (the English–French volume) of a general technical dictionary that covers the whole range of modern technology and the scientific knowledge that underlies it. It contains a broad base of terminology drawn from traditional areas of technology such as mechanical engineering, construction, electrical and electronic engineering, but also includes the vocabulary of newly prominent subject areas such as fuelless energy sources, safety engineering and quality assurance.

Selection of terms

We have aimed to include the essential vocabulary of each subject area, and the material has been checked by leading subject experts to ensure that both the English and the French terms are accurate and current, that the translations are valid equivalents, and that there are no gaps in coverage.

We have been careful about including only genuine technical terms and not allowing general vocabulary with no technical value. At the same time, we have entered the core vocabulary of technical discourse in its totality, although some of these items may also be found in general dictionaries. Although other variant translations would be permissible in a particular subject area, we have given the term most widely preferred by specialists in the area.

Placement of terms

All terms are ordered alphabetically, beginning with their first element. Compound terms are never entered under their second or third element, regardless of the semantic structure of the unit.

Stoplists

Terms in English are not entered under the following elements:

a, all, an, and, any, anybody, anyone, anything, anywhere, are, be, by, during, each, every, everybody, everyone, everything, everywhere, for, from, here, if, in, is, it, no, nobody, no-one, nor, not, nothing, nowhere, of, off, on, or, out, over, so, some, somebody, someone, something, somewhere, the, that, then, there, they, thing, this, to, too, under, very, where, while, who, with

Open compounds consisting of more than one element are listed at their first element. In these nested listings, the simple form is replaced by a swung dash (~). For example:

airborne:[2] ~ **acoustical noise** n SAFETY bruit acoustique aérien m; ~ **collision avoidance system** n AERONAUT système anticollision embarqué m; ~ **dust** n SAFETY poussières aériennes f pl, poussières en suspension dans l'air f pl

When this first element is itself a headword with one or more technical senses, compounds follow the simple form in alphabetical order. For example:

bronze[2] n CHEM bronze m, COLOURS pigment bronze m, pigment de bronze m; ~ **guide bush** n MECH ENG bague de guidage en bronze f; ~ **lacquer** n COLOURS vernis à bronzer m; ~ **pigment** n COLOURS bronze en poudre m, pigment de bronze m

If the first element is not itself translated, a colon (:) precedes the compounds. For example:

swipe: ~ **card** n TELECOM carte à mémoire f

Ordering of terms

Hyphenated and solid compounds are entered in alphabetical sequence, and will thus follow a nest of open compounds with the same first element. For example

broken:[2] ~ **circuit** n ELEC ENG circuit ouvert m; ~ **country** n CONST pays accidenté m, pays tourmenté m; ~ **end** n TEXTILES casse f; ~ **ice** n REFRIG glace concassée f; ~ **line** n GEOM ligne brisée f; ~ **ore** n MINING minerai abattu m, minerai broyé m; ~ **rice** n FOOD TECH brisure de riz f; ~ **rock** n COAL TECH menu de concassage m; ~ **seed** n C&G bouillon crevé m; ~ **stone** n CONST pierre cassée f; ~ **white line** n CONST road marking ligne blanche discontinue f; ~ **working** n COAL TECH abattage m, chantier accidenté m, déhouillement des piliers m, dépilage des piliers m, enlèvement des piliers m
broken-backed adj NAUT ship arqué
broken-down: ~ **timber** n CONST bois débité m

Articles (a, an, the) and the preposition of are ignored in determining the sequence of nested open compounds. For example:

beginning: ~ **of call demand** *n* TELECOM début de la demande d'appel *m*; ~ **of life** *n* NUCLEAR *of core* début de vie *m*; ~ **of message** *n* *(BOM)* COMP, TELECOM début de message *m*

In the case of very long nests of compounds, marginal markers have been used to make it easy to find a term more quickly. For example:

air: [2]

~ **n** ~ **nozzle** *n* COAL TECH éjecteur de ventilation *m*, MECH ENG ajutage *m*;

~ **o** ~ **outlet** *n* MECH ENG évacuation d'air *f*, *of blower* sortie du vent *f*; ~ **oven** *n* P&R *equipment* étuve à l'air chaud *f*;

~ **p** ~ **passage** *n* MECH ENG passage d'air *m*, MINING conduit *m*; ~ **passageway** *n* MINING conduit *m*; ~ **permeability** *n* HEAT ENG, PRINT perméabilité à l'air *f*

Abbreviations and acronyms written in upper case appear after vocabulary words of the same form written in lower case. For example:

age[1] *n* GEOL, PETR âge *m*; ~ **dating** *n* GEOL datation *f*; ~ **hardening** *n* CRYSTALL, METALL, P&R durcissement par vieillissement *m*, PROP MAT durcissement structural *m*, SPRINGS durcissement structural *m*, vieillissement par écrouissage *m*; ~ **of the universe** *n* ASTRON âge de l'univers *m*
age[2] *vt* METALL, PAPER TECH vieillir, THERMOD *metals* mûrir, tremper, vieillir
AGE *abbr* *(allyl glycidyl ether)* P&R éther allylglycidique *m*

Terms containing figures and symbols are alphabetized according to the usual expansion in reading aloud. For example:

three-cylinder: ~ **engine** *n* MECH ENG machine à trois cylindres *f*
three-D: ~ **log** *n* PETR diagraphie de densité variable *f*
three-dimensional[1] *adj* PHYS tridimensionnel, PROP MAT à trois dimensions

Homographs

Every term is accompanied by a label indicating its part of speech. For a complete list of these labels and their expansions, please see xxix.

A term that has more than one part of speech is listed in a separate entry for each. Such entries are distinguished by a raised number immediately following the headword. The sequence is abbreviation, adjective, adverb, noun, verb, followed by less frequent parts of speech. For example:

bubbling[1] *adj* PHYS bouillonnant
bubbling[2] *n* C&G bouillonnage *m*, OCEANOG pétillement de la mer *m*, PAPER TECH cloquage *m*, PHYS barbotage *m*, bouillonnement *m*

Ordering of translations

Every term is accompanied by one or more labels indicating the technological area in which it is used. For a complete list of these labels and their expansions, please see pages xxi–xxii.

Where the same term is used in more than one technological area, multiple labels are given as appropriate. These labels appear in alphabetical order.

Where a term has the same translation in more than one technological area, this translation is given after the sequence of labels. For example:

ammeter *n* ELEC, ELEC ENG, LAB EQUIP *electric current*, PHYS, TV, VEHICLES *electrical system* ampèremètre *m*

Where a term has different translations according to the technological area in which it is used, the appropriate translation is given after each label or set of labels. For example:

branch[1] *n* COMP *of circuit* branche *f*, *of programme* branchement *m*, CONST *metal piece at end of hose* lance *f*, lance à eau *f*, *plumbing* branchement *m*, embranchement *m*, DP branchement *m*, *of circuit* branche *f*

Supplementary information

When the French translation is a noun, the relevant gender is shown. In the case of compound terms this is the gender of the term as a whole (that is, its noun head) rather than the final element. For example:

data ~ **switching exchange** *n* *(DSE)* COMP, TELECOM centre de commutation de données *m*

In very many cases additional data is given about a term in order to show how it is used. Such contextual information can be:

(a) the typical subject or object of a verb, for example:

set[2] *n* CINEMAT décor *m*, plateau *m*, COMP ensemble *m*, jeu *m*, CONST *in concrete* prise *f*, *nail set* chasse-clou *m*, chasse-pointe *m*, pousse-pointe *m*, *of pile* avant-pieu *m*, *rivet set* bouterolle *f*, chasse-rivet *m*, *street paving* pavé *m*, pavé en granit *m*, DP ensemble *m*, jeu *m*, ELEC ENG *of machines* groupe *m*, GEOL *of beds* ensemble *m*

(b) typical nouns used with an adjective, for example:

air-cooled[1] *adj* ELEC *equipment* refroidi par l'air

(c) words indicating the reference of a noun, for example:

belly[1] *n* C&G *of shaft furnace* ventre *m*, CONST *of wall* bombement *m*, NAUT *of sail, boat* creux *m*, ventre *m*

(d) a narrower subject area than indicated by the label, for example:

scrambler *n* SPACE *communications*, TELECOM embrouilleur *m*

(e) a paraphrase or broad equivalent

bank[1] *n* PRINT table à papier *f*, *newspaper headline* gros titre *m*

When various different translations apply in the same subject area, contextual information is also used to show which translation is appropriate in different circumstances. For example:

stringer *n* CONST longeron *m*, longrine *f*, poutre de rive *f*, sommier *m*, *of roof truss* entrait *m*, tirant d'une ferme de comble *m*, *of stairway* limon *m*, MINING cordon *m*, crin *m*, filet *m*, veinule *f*, NAUT *boatbuilding* gouttière *f*, hiloire *f*, serre *f*, RAIL longrine *f*, SPACE *spacecraft* lisse *f*; **~ angle** *n* NAUT *shipbuilding* cornière de gouttière *f*; **~ head** *n* PETR première passe *f*

Cross-references

All terms not universally applicable are accompanied by a regional label. Both British and North American terms are fully covered. Translations which are restricted to Belgium, Canada, France or Switzerland are also followed by the relevant regional label. For a complete list of these labels and their expansions, please see page xxxiii.

In the case of lexical variants, full information – including translations and cross-references to other regional forms – is given at each entry. For example:

Bowden: **~ cable** *n* *(cf brake cable)* MECH, VEHICLES *on clutch, brake* câble Bowden *m*

brake:[1] **~ cable** *n* *(cf Bowden cable)* MECH, VEHICLES câble de frein *m*

In the case of spelling variants not differentiated by region, the less common form is cross-referred to the dominant form. Full information is given at that entry only. For example:

tire *n* (AmE) *see tyre*

Geographical variants, both spelling and lexical, are given in full when they are translations. For example:

braked: **~ car** *n* (AmE) *(cf braked wagon)* RAIL *vehicles* wagon freiné *m*; **~ wagon** *n* (BrE) *(cf braked car)* RAIL *vehicles* wagon freiné *m*

Both abbreviations and their full forms are entered in the main body of the dictionary in alphabetical sequence. Full information – including translations and cross-references to the full form or abbreviation as appropriate – is given at each entry. For example:

CAI *abbr (computer-assisted instruction)* COMP IAO *(instruction assistée par ordinateur) f*

binary:[2] **~ phase shift keying** *n (BPSK)* TELECOM modulation par déplacement de phase bivalente *f (MDPB)*

Abbreviations are also listed in a separate alphabetical sequence at the back of this volume, to allow browsing in cases where the exact form of the abbreviation is not known.

Where appropriate, mention is made of antonyms or opposing terms. Full information is given at each entry. For example:

high-pass: **~ filter** *n (cf low-pass filter)* COMP, DP, ELEC, ELECTRON, PHYS, RECORDING, TELECOM, TV filtre passe-haut *m*

low-pass: **~ filter** *n (cf high-pass filter)* COMP, DP, ELEC, ELECTRON, PHYS, RECORDING, TELECOM, TV filtre passe-bas *m*.

Catégories grammaticales/
Parts of speech

abbrev	abbreviation	abréviation
adj	adjective	adjectif
adv	adverb	adverbe
f	feminine	féminin
f pl	feminine plural	féminin pluriel
m	masculine	masculin
m pl	masculine plural	masculin pluriel
n	noun	nom
n pl	noun plural	nom pluriel
phr	phrase	locution
pref	prefix	préfixe
prep	preposition	préposition
vi	intransitive verb	verbe intransitif
vt	transitive verb	verbe transitif
vti	transitive and intransitive verb	verbe transitif et intransitif

Marques déposées

Nous avons fait le maximum pour faire suivre de la mention appropriée les termes que nous estimons protégés par un dépôt de marque. Néanmoins, l'absence ou la présence de cette mention est sans effet sur leur statut légal.

Registered trademarks

Every effort has been made to label terms which we believe constitute trademarks. The legal status of these, however, remains unchanged by the presence or absence of any such label.

(TM)	registered trademark	marque déposée (MD)

Domaines/Subject labels

ACOUSTICS	Acoustics	Acoustique
AERONAUT	Aeronautics	Aéronautique
ASTRON	Astronomy	Astronomie
AUTO	Automotive Engineering	Génie automobile
C&G	Ceramics and Glass	Céramique et verre
CHEM	Chemistry	Chimie
CHEM TECH	Chemical Technology Processes	Génie chimique
CINEMAT	Cinematography	Cinématographie
COAL TECH	Coal Technology	Technologie du charbon
COATINGS	Coatings Technology	Revêtements
COLOURS	Colours Technology	Couleurs
COMP	Computer Technology	Ordinateurs
CONST	Construction	Construction
CONTROL	Control Technology	Contrôle et automatisation
CRYSTALL	Crystallography	Cristallographie
DETERGENTS	Detergents	Détergents
DP	Data Processing	Informatique
ELEC ENG	Electrical Engineering	Electrotechnique
ELECTR	Electricity	Electricité
ELECTRON	Electronic Engineering	Electronique industrielle
FLUID PHYS	Fluid Physics	Physique des fluides
FOOD TECH	Food Technology	Alimentation
FUELLESS	Fuelless Energy Sources	Sources d'énergie renouvelable
GAS TECH	Gas Technology	Technologie du gaz
GEOL	Geology	Géologie
GEOM	Geometry	Géométrie
GEOPHYS	Geophysics	Géophysique
HEAT ENG	Heat Engineering Components	Appareils de chauffage
HEATING	Heating Equipment	Installations de chauffage
HYDR EQUIP	Hydraulic Equipment	Matériel hydraulique
HYDROL	Hydrology	Hydrologie
INSTRUMENT	Instrumentation	Instrumentation
LAB EQUIP	Laboratory Equipment	Equipement de laboratoire
MAR POLL	Marine Pollution	Pollution de la mer
MATH	Mathematics	Mathématiques
MECH	Mechanics	Mécanique
MECH ENG	Mechanical Engineering	Construction mécanique
METALL	Metallurgy	Métallurgie
METEO	Meteorology	Météorologie
METR	Metrology	Métrologie
MILIT	Military Technology	Armement et défense
MINERAL	Mineralogy	Minéralogie
MINING	Mining	Exploitation minière
NAUT	Water Transport Engineering	Transport par voie d'eau
NUCLEAR	Nuclear Technology	Energie nucléaire
OCEANOG	Oceanography	Océanographie
OPTICS	Optics	Optique

P&R	Plastics and Rubber	Plastiques et caoutchouc
PACKAGING	Packaging	Emballage
PAPER TECH	Paper Technology	Papeterie
PART PHYS	Particle Physics	Physique des particules
PATENTS	Patents and Trademarks	Brevets et marques de fabrique
PETR	Petrology	Pétrologie
PETR TECH	Petroleum Technology	Technologie du pétrole
PHOTO	Photography	Photographie
PHYS	Physics	Physique
POLLUTION	Pollution	Pollution
PRINT	Printing	Imprimerie
PROD ENG	Production Engineering	Gestion de la production
PROP MAT	Properties of Materials	Propriétés des matériaux
QUALITY	Quality assurance	Assurance de la qualité
RAD PHYS	Radiation Physics	Physique des rayonnements
RAIL	Railway Engineering	Chemins de fer
RECORDING	Recording Engineering	Enregistrement
RECYCLING	Recycling	Recyclage
REFRIG	Refrigeration	Réfrigération
SAFETY	Safety Engineering	Sécurité
SPACE	Space Technology	Technologie spatiale
SPRINGS	Springs	Ressorts
TELECOM	Telecommunications	Télécommunications
TESTING	Testing	Essais
TEXTILES	Textiles	Textile
THERMOD	Thermodynamics	Thermodynamique
TRANSP	Transport	Transport
TV	Television	Télévision
VEHICLES	Vehicle Components	Pièces détachées pour véhicules
WATER SUPP	Water supply engineering	Distribution de l'eau
WAVE PHYS	Wave Physics	Physique ondulatoire

Codes géographiques/
Geographic codes

	Variantes d'anglais	**Varieties of English**
(AmE)	anglais américain	American English
(BrE)	anglais britannique	British English
(Can)	anglais canadien	Canadian English

	Variantes de français	**Varieties of French**
(Belg)	Belgique	Belgium
(Can)	Canada	Canada
(Fra)	France	France
(Sui)	Suisse	Switzerland

A

A *abbr (amp, ampere)* ELEC, ELEC ENG, METR, PHYS A *(ampère)*

A4: ~ **size** *n* PRINT *international size paper* format A4 *m*; ~ **wave** *n* PRINT onde A4 *f*

AA *n (aggregate abrasion value)* CONST coefficient d'abrasion de gravier *m*

AAL[1] *abbr (ATM adaptation layer)* TELECOM couche d'adaptation AAL *f*

AAL:[2] ~ **protocol control information** *n (AAL-PCI)* TELECOM information de contrôle du protocole AAL *f*; ~ **service data unit** *n (AAL-SDU)* TELECOM unité de données de service AAL *f*

Aalenian *adj* GEOL aalénien

AAL-PCI *abbr (AAL protocol control information)* TELECOM information de contrôle du protocole AAL *f*

AAL-SDU *abbr (AAL service data unit)* TELECOM unité de données de service AAL *f*

A-associate response *n (AARE)* TELECOM réponse A-associate

AARE *abbr (A-associate response)* TELECOM réponse A-associate *f*

aback *adj* NAUT à contre

abacus *n* COMP abaque *m*; ~ **major** *n* MINING abaque *m*

abaft[1] *adv* NAUT sur l'arrière, à l'arrière

abaft[2] *prep* NAUT sur l'arrière de, à l'arrière de

abandon[1] *vt* PATENTS abandonner

abandon:[2] ~ **ship** *vi* NAUT abandonner le navire, quitter le navire, évacuer le navire

abandoned: ~ **workings** *n pl* MINING chantier abandonné *m*

abandonment: ~ **of ship** *n* NAUT abandon du navire *m*, délaissement du navire *m*

abate *vi* NAUT *wind, weather* diminuer, mollir, s'abattre

abatement *n* PRINT abattement *m*, réduction sur facture *f*

abattoir *n* REFRIG abattoir *m*

Abbé: ~ **number** *n* PHYS *constringence* nombre d'Abbé *m*; ~ **refractometer** *n* PHYS réfractomètre d'Abbé *m*; ~ **theory** *n* PHYS *of image formation* théorie d'Abbé *f*; ~ **value** *n* C&G nombre d'Abbé *m*

abbreviated: ~ **dialing** *n* (AmE), ~ **dialling** *n* (BrE) TELECOM composition abrégée *f*, numérotation abrégée *f*; ~ **number** *n* TELECOM numéro abrégé *m*; ~ **precision approach path indicator** *n* AERONAUT indicateur de trajectoire d'approche de précision simplifié *m*; ~ **visual approach slope indicator system** *n* AERONAUT indicateur visuel de pente d'approche simplifié *m*

abeam *adv* NAUT, SPACE par le travers

abelian *adj* MATH abélien

aberration *n* ASTRON *of starlight*, METALL, OPT, WAVE PHYS aberration *f*

abietate *n* CHEM abiétate *m*

abietic: ~ **acid** *n* PAPER TECH acide abiétique *m*

ability *n* PROP MAT aptitude *f*

ablated: ~ **ion** *n* NUCLEAR ion ablati *m*

ablating: ~ **cone** *n* SPACE *missile warheads* cône d'abla-tion *m*, cône érodable *m*; ~ **momentum** *n* NUCLEAR impulsion d'ablation *f*

ablation *n* COMP *optical recording*, HYDROL ablation *f*, NUCLEAR processus d'ablation et compression *m*, PHYS ablation *f*; ~ **shield** *n* SPACE *spacecraft* bouclier ablatif *m*

ablative[1] *adj* SPACE *spacecraft* ablatif

ablative:[2] ~ **cooling** *n* SPACE *spacecraft* refroidissement par ablation *m*; ~ **method recording** *n* OPT enregistre-ment par ablation *m*

ablaze *adj* THERMOD en feu, *with light* resplendissant

abnormal: ~ **pressure** *n* GEOL, PETR TECH *geology* pres-sion anormale *f*, pression de formation anormale positive *f*; ~ **structure** *n* METALL structure anormale *f*; ~ **termination** *n* COMP fin anormale *f*

abort[1] *n* COMP abandon *m*

abort[2] *vt* COMP abandonner, faire avorter, SPACE aban-donner, avorter, faire long feu, interrompre, échouer

aborted: ~ **takeoff** *n* AERONAUT arrêt au décollage *m*, décollage interrompu *m*

above:[1] ~ **ground** *adj* MINING au jour, du jour, superfi-ciel, à la surface

above:[2] ~ **ground** *adv* COAL TECH en surface

above-ground: ~ **workers** *n pl* MINING ouvriers du jour *m pl*

abradant *n* COAL TECH, PROP MAT abrasif *m*

abrade *vt* MECH user par abrasion, PAPER TECH user, user par abrasion, PROP MAT user

abraded: ~ **yarn** *n* TEXTILES fil abrasé *m*

abrading: ~ **wheel** *n* PROD ENG meule à user *f*

Abraham: ~ **momentum** *n* NUCLEAR impulsion d'Abra-ham *f*

abraser *n* PAPER TECH abrasimètre *m*

abrasion *n* COAL TECH abrasion *f*, GEOL abrasion *f*, érosion *f*, HYDROL, MECH, MECH ENG, P&R, PAPER TECH, PRINT, PROD ENG, PROP MAT abrasion *f*; ~ **factor** *n* MECH *materials* taux d'abrasion *m*, taux d'usure *m*; ~ **fretting corrosion** *n* MECH corrosion due à l'usure par frottement *f*; ~ **resistance** *n* P&R, PAPER TECH, PROP MAT résistance à l'abrasion *f*; ~ **resistance index** *n* P&R indice d'abrasion *m*, indice d'abrasion de Taber *m*; ~ **test** *n* MECH ENG essai abrasif *m*, PRINT essai de résis-tance au frottement *m*; ~ **tester** *n* MECH *materials*, P&R, PAPER TECH abrasimètre *m*

abrasion-proof *adj* COATINGS antiusure, résistant à l'a-brasion, MECH *materials* résistant à l'abrasion

abrasion-resistant[1] *adj* PRINT résistant à l'abrasion

abrasion-resistant:[2] ~ **coating** *n* COATINGS couche résis-stante à l'abrasion *f*

abrasive[1] *adj* COAL TECH, MECH *materials*, PAPER TECH, PRINT, PROD ENG, PROP MAT, SAFETY abrasif

abrasive[2] *n* COAL TECH, MECH *materials*, PAPER TECH, PROD ENG, PROP MAT, SAFETY abrasif *m*; ~ **belt** *n* C&G *for grinding glass*, MECH ENG bande abrasive *f*; ~ **cloth** *n* MECH ENG toile abrasive *f*; ~ **coating** *n* COATINGS enrobage aux abrasifs *m*; ~ **cutoff machine** *n* MECH ENG *machine tool* tronçonneuse à meule *f*; ~ **disc** *n* (BrE) MECH ENG disque abrasif *m*; ~ **disk** *n* (AmE) *see* *abrasive disc*; ~ **dust** *n* SAFETY poussières abrasives *f pl*; ~ **flap wheel** *n* MECH ENG meule à lamelles abrasives *f*; ~ **material** *n* PAPER TECH abrasif *m*; ~ **paper** *n* ELEC *for cleaning* papier abrasif *m*, MECH *tools* papier abrasif *m*, papier-émeri *m*, PRINT papier abrasif *m*; ~ **sheet** *n* MECH ENG feuille abrasive *f*; ~ **shot** *n* MECH *surface treatment* grenaille abrasive *f*; ~ **wear** *n* CONST usure abrasive *f*, P&R usure par abrasion *f*; ~ **wheel** *n* MECH *tools*, MECH ENG, SAFETY meule *f*; ~ **wheels regulations** *n pl* SAFETY *wheel condition, speed, marking, use and storage* règlements de sécurité des meules abrasives *m pl*

abrasiveness *n* COAL TECH abrasivité *f*, PAPER TECH pouvoir abrasif *m*, PRINT abrasion *f*

abreast *adv* NAUT par le travers

abridged: ~ **edition** *n* PRINT édition abrégée *f*

abrupt: ~ **junction** *n* ELECTRON *p-n junction* jonction abrupte *f*

ABS *n* *(acrylonitrile-butadiene-styrene)* P&R styrène-acrylonitrile-butadiène *m*

abscissa *n* DP abscisse *f*, MATH axe des abscisses *m*, axe des x *m*

abscissic *adj* CHEM abscisique

absence *n* ACOUSTICS *of harmonics*, SPACE *of convection* absence *f*

absent: ~ **reflection** *n* CRYSTALL *from diffraction patterns* extinction *f*, réflexions absentes *f pl*; ~ **subscriber** *n* TELECOM abonné absent *m*; ~ **subscriber service** *n* TELECOM service des abonnés absents *m*

absinth *n* CHEM absinthe *f*

absinthole *n* CHEM thuyone *m*

absolute[1] *adj* CHEM, COMP, DP absolu

absolute:[2] ~ **activity** *n* PHYS activité absolue *f*; ~ **address** *n* COMP adresse absolue *f*; ~ **alcohol** *n* CHEM alcool absolu *m*, alcool enhydre *m*; ~ **capacity** *n* TRANSP capacité possible *f*; ~ **code** *n* COMP code absolu *m*; ~ **error** *n* COMP erreur absolue *f*; ~ **gain** *n* SPACE *communications* gain isotrope *m*; ~ **humidity** *n* HEAT ENG, HYDROL *of ground, soil*, METEO *of air*, PHYS humidité absolue *f*; ~ **loader** *n* COMP chargeur absolu *m*; ~ **magnitude** *n* ASTRON magnitude absolue *f*; ~ **measuring system** *n* ELECTRON système de mesure absolue *m*; ~ **motion** *n* PHYS mouvement absolu *m*; ~ **movement** *n* CHEM mouvement absolu *m*; ~ **permeability** *n* ELEC *magnetism* perméabilité absolue *f*, ELEC ENG perméabilité magnétique absolue *f*, PETR, TESTING perméabilité absolue *f*; ~ **permittivity** *n* ELEC *electrical field*, ELEC ENG permittivité absolue *f*; ~ **potential** *n* ELEC potentiel absolu *m*; ~ **pressure** *n* REFRIG pression absolue *f*; ~ **range** *n* MILIT rayon d'action absolu *m*; ~ **refractive index** *n* RAD PHYS indice de réfraction absolu *m*; ~ **scale of temperature** *n* CHEM échelle K *f*, échelle absolue *f*; ~ **speed variation** *n* ELEC *electrical machine* variation absolue de la vitesse de rotation *f*; ~ **stability** *n* TELECOM stabilité absolue *f*; ~ **stop signal** *n* RAIL carré *m*; ~ **system** *n* TESTING *coil arrangements* système absolu *m*; ~ **temperature** *n* CHEM, PHYS température absolue *f*, REFRIG température absolue *f*, température thermodynamique *f*, THERMOD température absolue *f*; ~ **threshold** *n* TV *of luminance* seuil absolu *m*; ~ **vacuum** *n* REFRIG vide absolu *m*; ~ **value** *n* CHEM, COMP, MATH valeur absolue *f*; ~ **velocity** *n* MECH vitesse absolue *f*; ~ **viscosity** *n* PROP MAT viscosité absolue *f*; ~ **water velocity** *n* FUELLESS vitesse absolue de l'eau *f*; ~ **zero** *n* CHEM zéro absolu *m*, FOOD TECH température absolue *f*, PHYS, REFRIG, THERMOD zéro

absolu *m*

absorb *vt* COAL TECH, MECH ENG, PAPER TECH absorber

absorbable *adj* PAPER TECH, PROP MAT absorbable

absorbance *n* PHYS, RAD PHYS absorbance *f*

absorbed: ~ **dose** *n* PHYS, RAD PHYS *of ionizing radiation* dose absorbée *f*; ~ **dose rate** *n* PHYS débit de dose absorbée *m*; ~ **energy** *n* METALL, RAD PHYS énergie absorbée *f*

absorbency *n* PACKAGING, PAPER TECH pouvoir absorbant *m*; ~ **value** *n* PAPER TECH coefficient d'absorption *m*

absorbent[1] *adj* CHEM absorbant *m*, absorptif, PAPER TECH, PROP MAT absorbant; ~ **of water** *adj* PROP MAT avide d'eau

absorbent[2] *n* COAL TECH, MECH *materials*, PAPER TECH, POLLUTION, PROP MAT absorbant *m*; ~ **belt skimmer** *n* POLLUTION récupérateur à bande absorbante *m*; ~ **paper** *n* PRINT papier absorbant *m*

absorber *n* CHEM TECH vase d'absorption *m*, PAPER TECH absorbeur *m*, PETR TECH *refinery* colonne d'absorption *f*, REFRIG *of liquid refrigerant* absorbeur *m*; ~ **element bundle** *n* NUCLEAR faisceau d'éléments absorbants *m*; ~ **finger** *n* NUCLEAR doigt absorbant *m*; ~ **member** *n* NUCLEAR élément absorbant *m*; ~ **plate** *n* FUELLESS plaque absorbeur *f*, NUCLEAR plaque absorbante *f*; ~ **rod** *n* NUCLEAR crayon absorbant *m*; ~ **trap** *n* CHEM TECH piège à absorption *m*; ~ **tube** *n* CHEM TECH tube absorbant *m*

absorbing: ~ **capacity** *n* MECH *materials* pouvoir absorbant *m*; ~ **well** *n* WATER SUPP puits absorbant *m*

absorbtiveness *n* PAPER TECH pouvoir absorbant *m*

absorptance *n* PHYS *absorption factor* absorptance *f*, facteur d'absorption *m*

absorptiometer *n* PAPER TECH absorptiomètre *m*

absorptiometry *n* NUCLEAR absorptiométrie *f*

absorption *n* CHEM TECH, COAL TECH, ELEC ENG, FOOD TECH absorption *f*, HYDROL imbibition *f*, OPT, P&R, PAPER TECH, PETR, RAD PHYS *radio and optical wavebands* absorption *f*; ~ **band** *n* PHYS, RAD PHYS bande d'absorption *f*; ~ **capacity** *n* PAPER TECH porosité *f*; ~ **cell** *n* CHEM TECH vase d'absorption *m*; ~ **circuit** *n* ELEC circuit d'absorption *m*; ~ **coefficient** *n* PHYS, RAD PHYS coefficient d'absorption *m*; ~ **column** *n* CHEM TECH colonne d'absorption *f*, tour d'absorption *f*, COAL TECH colonne d'absorption *f*, PAPER TECH tour d'absorption *f*, PETR TECH *refinery* colonne d'absorption *f*; ~ **cooling** *n* FUELLESS refroidissement absorbant *m*; ~ **correction** *n* CRYSTALL correction d'absorption *f*; ~ **cross-section** *n* RAD PHYS *of atom* coupe transversale d'absorption *f*; ~ **current** *n* ELEC courant d'absorption *m*; ~ **edge** *n* CRYSTALL *X-ray spectra* limite d'absorption *f*, seuil d'absorption *m*, NUCLEAR discontinuité d'absorption *f*; ~ **factor** *n* ACOUSTICS facteur d'absorption *m*, PAPER TECH absorptivité *f*, TELECOM facteur d'absorption *m*; ~ **filter** *n* CINEMAT, INSTRUMENT filtre d'absorption *m*; ~ **filtering** *n* RECORDING filtrage par absorption *m*; ~ **ink test** *n* PRINT essai de porosité à l'encre *m*; ~ **in the soil** *n* WATER SUPP absorption par le sol *f*; ~ **of ionizing radiation** *n* RAD PHYS absorption de rayonnement ionisant *f*; ~ **of light** *n* RAD PHYS absorption de lumière *f*; ~ **line** *n* ASTRON, PHYS raie d'absorption *f*; ~ **loss** *n* ELEC ENG, TV perte par absorption *f*; ~ **peak** *n* ELEC ENG pic d'absorption *m*; ~ **plant** *n* PETR TECH installation de récupération de l'essence *f*, SAFETY installation d'absorption *f*; ~ **of**

radiation *n* WAVE PHYS absorption de rayonnement *f*; ~ **range** *n* PAPER TECH spectre d'absorption *m*; ~ **rate** *n* PAPER TECH coefficient d'absorption *m*; ~ **refrigerating cycle** *n* REFRIG cycle de réfrigération à absorption *m*; ~ **refrigerating installation** *n* MECH ENG installation frigorifique à absorption *f*; ~ **refrigeration machine** *n* REFRIG machine frigorifique à absorption *f*; ~ **refrigeration system** *n* REFRIG système frigorifique à absorption *m*; ~ **refrigerator** *n* REFRIG réfrigérateur à absorption *m*; ~ **silencer** *n* SAFETY amortisseur de bruit à absorption *m*; ~ **spectroanalysis** *n* RAD PHYS analyse d'absorption par spectrophotométrie *f*; ~ **spectrometer** *n* LAB EQUIP *analytical instrument* spectromètre d'absorption *m*; ~ **spectrometry** *n* TELECOM spectrométrie d'absorption *f*; ~ **spectrophotometer** *n* RAD PHYS spectrophotomètre d'absorption *m*; ~ **spectroscopy** *n* PHYS spectroscopie par absorption *f*, RAD PHYS spectroscopie d'absorption *f*; ~ **spectrum** *n* PHYS, RAD PHYS, SPACE spectre d'absorption *m*; ~ **tester** *n* PAPER TECH absorptiomètre *m*; ~ **tower** *n* CHEM TECH, COAL TECH, FOOD TECH *for drying purposes* colonne d'absorption *f*, tour d'absorption *f*, PAPER TECH tour d'absorption *f*, PETR TECH colonne d'absorption *f*; ~ **tube** *n* LAB EQUIP *glassware* tube absorbeur *m*; ~ **vessel** *n* CHEM TECH vase d'absorption *m*

absorption-type: ~ **refrigerator** *n* THERMOD réfrigérateur à absorption *m*

absorptive[1] *adj* PAPER TECH, PROP MAT absorbant

absorptive:[2] ~ **attenuator** *n* ELECTRON atténuateur à absorption *m*, TELECOM affaiblisseur à absorption *m*, atténuateur à absorption *m*; ~ **capacity** *n* HYDROL *of well* capacité d'absorption *f*, porosité efficace *f*, PACKAGING capacité d'absorption *f*, PAPER TECH *of paper and cardboard* porosité *f*; ~ **dielectric** *n* ELEC diélectrique à absorption *m*; ~ **modulator** *n* ELECTRON modulateur à absorption *m*

absorptiveness *n* PAPER TECH absorptivité *f*

absorptivity *n* PAPER TECH, TV absorptivité *f*

abstract[1] *adj* COMP, DP abstrait

abstract[2] *n* COMP résumé *m*, PATENTS abrégé *m*; ~ **data type** *n* DP type abstrait *m*, type abstrait de données *m*; ~ **symbol** *n* DP symbole abstrait *m*; ~ **syntax notation one** *n* (*ASN1*) TELECOM notation de syntaxe abstraite numéro un *f*; ~ **topological principle** *n* GEOM principe topologique abstrait *m*

abstract[3] *vt* CHEM extraire, COMP, DP résumer

abstraction *n* DP abstraction *f*

abundance *n* PHYS abondance *f*; ~ **pattern** *n* GEOL spectre d'abondance *m*; ~ **ratio of isotopes** *n* NUCLEAR rapport des teneurs isotopiques *m*, PART PHYS rapport isotopique *m*

aburton: ~ **stowage** *adv* NAUT arrimage en breton *m*, arrimage en travers *m*

abuse *n* PATENTS abus *m*

abut[1] *vt* CONST *carpentry* abouter

abut[2] *vi* CONST *carpentry* s'abouter

abutment *n* CONST *architecture* butée *f*, culée *f*, *carpentry* aboutement *m*

abutting: ~ **joint** *n* CONST assemblage en about *m*, joint en about *m*, PETR TECH *pipeline* assemblage en about *m*

abyssal: ~ **cone** *n* OCEANOG cône sous-marin *m*; ~ **hill** *n* OCEANOG colline abyssale *f*; ~ **pass** *n* OCEANOG goulet abyssal *m*; ~ **plain** *n* GEOL plaine abyssale *f*, GEOPHYS fond océanique *m*, OCEANOG, PETR plaine abyssale *f*; ~ **spit** *n* OCEANOG flèche abyssale *f*

Ac (*actinium*) CHEM Ac (*actinium*)

AC[1] *abbr* (*alternating current*) ELEC, ELEC ENG, ELECTRON, PHYS, RECORDING, TELECOM, TV CA (*courant alternatif*)

AC:[2] ~ **ammeter** *n* ELEC ENG ampèremètre alternatif *m*, ampèremètre pour courant alternatif *m*; ~ **amplifier** *n* ELECTRON amplificateur de courant alternatif *m*; ~ **armature relay** *n* ELEC ENG relais à armature à courant alternatif *m*; ~ **bias** *n* RECORDING polarisation en courant alternatif *f*; ~ **capacitor** *n* ELEC ENG condensateur pour courant alternatif *m*; ~ **circuit** *n* ELEC ENG circuit à courant alternatif *m*; ~ **contactor** *n* PROD ENG contacteur CA *m*; ~ **discharge** *n* ELEC ENG décharge en courant alternatif *f*; ~ **electromotive force** *n* ELEC ENG force électromotrice alternative *f*; ~ **excitation** *n* ELEC ENG excitation par un courant alternatif *f*; ~ **generation** *n* ELEC ENG génération de courant alternatif *f*; ~ **generator** *n* ELEC ENG générateur de courant alternatif *m*; ~ **input** *n* ELEC ENG entrée alternative *f*, entrée en courant alternatif *f*; ~ **Josephson effect** *n* ELECTRON effet Josephson alternatif *m*; ~ **line** *n* ELEC ENG ligne à courant alternatif *f*; ~ **load** *n* ELEC ENG charge à courant alternatif *f*; ~ **machine** *n* ELEC ENG machine électrique à courant alternatif *f*, machine à courant alternatif *f*; ~ **magnetic biasing** *n* TV polarisation magnétique par courant alternatif *f*; ~ **marker** *n* NAUT (*anticollision marker*) marqueur anticollision *m*; ~ **meter** *n* ELEC ampèremètre alternatif *m*, appareil de mesure pour CA *m*; ~ **motor** *n* ELEC moteur à courant alternatif *m*, ELEC ENG moteur électrique à courant alternatif *m*, moteur à courant alternatif *m*, PHYS moteur à courant alternatif *m*; ~ **operation** *n* ELEC ENG fonctionnement en courant alternatif *m*; ~ **output** *n* ELEC ENG sortie alternative *f*, sortie en courant alternatif *f*; ~ **potentiometer** *n* ELEC potentiomètre à courant alternatif *m*; ~ **power** *n* ELEC ENG énergie en courant alternatif *f*, PROD ENG alimentation secteur *f*; ~ **power line** *n* ELEC ENG ligne de transport d'énergie à courant alternatif *f*; ~ **power system** *n* SPACE *spacecraft* alimentation en courant alternatif *f*; ~ **relay** *n* ELEC ENG relais à courant alternatif *m*; ~ **resistance** *n* ELEC ENG résistance en courant alternatif *f*; ~ **servomotor** *n* ELEC ENG servomoteur à courant alternatif *m*; ~ **source** *n* ELEC ENG source alternative *f*, source de courant alternatif *f*; ~ **switching** *n* ELEC ENG commutation de courant alternatif *f*; ~ **voltmeter** *n* ELEC ENG voltmètre alternatif *m*, voltmètre pour courant alternatif *m*

academy: ~ **aperture** *n* CINEMAT fenêtre standard *f*; ~ **mask** *n* CINEMAT cache normalisé *m*

acanthicone *n* MINERAL acanthikon *m*, akanthicone *m*

acanthite *n* MINERAL acanthite *f*

ACC *abbr* CONTROL (*adaptive control constraint*) commande ACC *f* (*contrainte de commande adaptative*), TV (*automatic chrominance control*) CAC (*contrôle automatique de chrominance*)

accelerate *vt* PAPER TECH, PHYS accélérer, PROD ENG accélérer, *combustion by a blower* activer

accelerated[1] *adj* PHYS accéléré

accelerated:[2] ~ **ageing test** *n* (BrE) P&R essai de vieillissement accéléré *m*; ~ **aging test** *n* (AmE) *see accelerated ageing test*; ~ **commutation** *n* ELEC commutation accélérée *f*; ~ **creep** *n* METALL fluage accéléré *m*; ~ **filtration** *n* CHEM TECH, FOOD TECH filtration accélérée *f*; ~ **freeze-drying** *n* (*AFD*) FOOD TECH lyophilisation accélérée *f*; ~ **motion** *n* MECH mouvement accéléré *m*; ~ **storage test** *n* PACKAGING essai accéléré d'emmagasinage *m*; ~ **testing** *n* TESTING essai rapide *m*; ~ **weathering test** *n* P&R essai de vieillissement accéléré aux intempéries *m*

accelerate-stop: ~ **distance** *n* AERONAUT distance d'accélération-arrêt *f*; ~ **distance available** *n* AERONAUT distance utilisable pour l'accélération-arrêt *f*; ~ **distance required** *n* AERONAUT distance nécessaire pour l'accélération-arrêt *f*

accelerating *n* PAPER TECH accélérateur; ~ **agent** *n* PAPER TECH accélérateur *m*; ~ **anode** *n* ELEC ENG anode accélératrice *f*, anode d'accélération *f*, RAD PHYS anode accélératrice *f*; ~ **chamber** *n* CHEM TECH chambre d'accélération *f*; ~ **electrode** *n* NUCLEAR électrode accélératrice *f*; ~ **force** *n* PHYS, SPACE force d'accélération *f*; ~ **period** *n* CHEM TECH période d'accélération *f*; ~ **tube** *n* CHEM TECH tube d'accélération *m*; ~ **voltage** *n* ELEC *charged particles*, ELEC ENG tension accélératrice *f*, tension d'accélération *f*

acceleration *n* MECH, PAPER TECH, PHYS, SPACE *due to gravity*, VEHICLES accélération *f*; ~ **control unit** *n* AERONAUT contrôle d'accélération *m*; ~ **detector** *n* AERONAUT détecteur d'accélération *m*; ~ **device** *n* TRANSP tapis accélérateur pour piétons *m*; ~ **jet** *n* AUTO gicleur de pompe *m*; ~ **lane** *n* CONST *roads* voie d'accélération *f*, TRANSP rampe d'accès *f*; ~ **relay** *n* ELEC relais d'accélération *m*; ~ **time** *n* COMP temps d'accélération *m*, PAPER TECH temps de montée en vitesse *m*

accelerative *adj* PAPER TECH accélérateur

accelerator *n* (*cf gas pedal*) AUTO (BrE) pédale d'accélérateur *f*, CHEM TECH accélérateur *m*, CINEMAT bain accélérateur *m*, CONST *concrete mixing* accélérateur de prise *m*, ELEC ENG, FOOD TECH, MECH *vehicles* (BrE), NAUT *engine, boat building*, P&R *vulcanization process*, PART PHYS, SPACE, TELECOM, VEHICLES (BrE) *carburettor* accélérateur *m*; ~ **breeder** *n* NUCLEAR accélérateur surrégénérateur *m*; ~ **card** *n* COMP carte accélératrice *f*; ~ **cavities** *n pl* PART PHYS *part of the LEP installation* cavités accélératrices *f pl*; ~ **jet** *n* VEHICLES *carburettor* gicleur d'accélération *m*, gicleur de reprise *m*; ~ **linkage** *n* TRANSP timonérie d'accélérateur *f*, VEHICLES *carburettor* timonerie d'accélérateur *f*; ~ **molten salt breeder** *n* NUCLEAR accélérateur surrégénérateur au sel fondu *m*; ~ **pedal** *n* (BrE) (*cf gas pedal*) VEHICLES *carburettor* pédale d'accélérateur *f*; ~ **physicist** *n* PART PHYS physicien des accélérateurs *m*; ~ **pump** *n* VEHICLES *carburettor* pompe d'accélération *f*, pompe de reprise *f*

accelerator-driven: ~ **light water reactor** *n* NUCLEAR réacteur à eau légère excité par accélérateur *m*

accelerometer *n* AERONAUT, ELEC ENG, MECH, PAPER TECH, PETR, PHYS accéléromètre *m*

accent *n* PRINT accent *m*; ~ **light** *n* CINEMAT éclairage d'appoint *m*

accented: ~ **letter** *n* PRINT lettre accentuée *f*

accentuate *vt* PRINT accentuer, mettre en relief, souligner

acceptable: ~ **quality level** *n* (*AQL*) QUALITY niveau de qualité acceptable *m* (*NQA*)

acceptance *n* MECH *contracts* recette *f*, QUALITY acceptation *f*, agrément *m*, réception *f*, SPACE réception *f*; ~ **angle** *n* CINEMAT angle d'ouverture *m*, ELEC ENG, ELECTRON, OPT angle d'admission *m*, PRINT angle de mesure *m*, TELECOM angle d'admission *m*; ~ **of a beam** *n* NUCLEAR réception du faisceau *f*; ~ **certificate**

n QUALITY certificat d'acceptation *m*, certificat de réception *m*; ~ **criterion** *n* SPACE *spacecraft* critère d'acceptation *m*; ~ **firing test** *n* SPACE essai de réception à chaud *m*; ~ **flight** *n* AERONAUT, TRANSP vol de réception *m*; ~ **inspection** *n* CONTROL, MECH ENG, QUALITY contrôle de réception *m*; ~ **report** *n* MECH *contracts* procès-verbal de recette *m*; ~ **specification** *n* QUALITY spécification de réception *f*; ~ **test** *n* COAL TECH, COMP essai de réception *m*, NAUT essai de recette *m*, PROP MAT preuve de réception *f*, SPACE essai de réception *m*, TELECOM essai de qualification *m*, essai de recette *m*, essai de réception *m*, test de recette *m*; ~ **testing** *n* MECH *contracts* essai de recette *m*; ~ **test sheet** *n* PROD ENG fiche de contrôle *f*; ~ **trial** *n* AERONAUT vol de réception *m*, NAUT *ship* essai de recette *m*

accepted: ~ **stock** *n* PACKAGING stock contrôlé *m*, PAPER TECH pâte acceptée *f*, pâte épurée *f*

acceptor *n* CHEM *atom, molecule*, COMP *semiconductors*, ELEC *induction, circuit*, ELECTRON accepteur *m*; ~ **atom** *n* ELECTRON, PHYS atome accepteur *m*; ~ **circuit** *n* ELEC *induction* circuit de résonance *m*; ~ **impurity** *n* ELECTRON impureté acceptrice *f*; ~ **level** *n* ELECTRON niveau accepteur *m*, niveau d'énergie accepteur *m*; ~ **resonance** *n* ELEC *AC circuit* résonance des tensions *f*

access[1] *n* COAL TECH, COMP, SPACE *spacecraft*, TELECOM accès *m*; ~ **arm** *n* COMP bras d'accès *m*; ~ **burst signal** *n* TELECOM salve de signaux d'accès *f*; ~ **channel** *n* TELECOM voie d'accès *f*; ~ **charge rate** *n* TELECOM tarif d'accès *m*; ~ **circuit** *n* TELECOM circuit d'accès *m*; ~ **concentrator** *n* TELECOM concentrateur de voies asynchrones *m*; ~ **connection element** *n* (*ACE*) TELECOM élément de connexion d'accès *m*; ~ **control** *n* TELECOM contrôle d'accès *m*; ~ **control list** *n* TELECOM liste de contrôle d'accès *f*; ~ **door** *n* AERONAUT porte d'accès *f*; ~ **line** *n* COMP ligne d'accès *f*; ~ **link** *n* (*AL*) TELECOM liaison d'accès *f*; ~ **list** *n* COMP liste des habilitations *f*; ~ **matrix** *n* TELECOM chercheur d'opérateur *m*; ~ **method** *n* COMP méthode d'accès *f*; ~ **mode** *n* COMP mode d'accès *m*; ~ **network** *n* TELECOM réseau d'accès *m*; ~ **node** *n* TELECOM noeud d'accès *m*; ~ **number** *n* TELECOM numéro d'accès *m*; ~ **panel** *n* AERONAUT panneau d'accès *m*, SPACE *spacecraft* écoutille d'accès *f*; ~ **path** *n* COMP chemin d'accès *m*; ~ **port** *n* NUCLEAR *of refuelling machine* regard d'accès *m*, TELECOM point d'accès *m*; ~ **ramp** *n* CONST, TRANSP rampe d'accès *f*; ~ **road** *n* (AmE) (*cf slip road*) TRANSP route d'accès *f*, voie d'accès *f*, voie de ralentissement *f*; ~ **road census** *n* (AmE) (*cf slip road census*) TRANSP comptage des accès *m*; ~ **road control** *n* (AmE) (*cf slip road control*) TRANSP régulation des accès *f*; ~ **road count** *n* (AmE) (*cf slip road count*) TRANSP comptage des accès *m*; ~ **road metering** *n* (AmE) (*cf slip road metering*) TRANSP régulation des rampes d'accès *f*; ~ **speed** *n* ELEC ENG vitesse d'accès *f*; ~ **subsystem** *n* TELECOM *radio paging* sous-système d'accès *m*; ~ **time** *n* COMP, ELEC ENG, OPT, PRINT temps d'accès *m*; ~ **to platforms** *n* RAIL accès aux quais *m*; ~ **unit** *n* (*AU*) TELECOM unité d'accès *f*

access[2] *vt* COMP accéder à

accessibility *n* MECH, QUALITY accessibilité *f*

accessible: ~ **coast** *n* NAUT côte abordable *f*; ~ **resource base** *n* FUELLESS base des ressources accessibles *f*

accessory: ~ **drive** *n* AERONAUT prise d'entraînement des accessoires *f*; ~ **gearbox** *n* AERONAUT boîte de commande d'accessoires *f*; ~ **shoe** *n* CINEMAT porte-accessoire *m*, PHOTO griffe à accessoires *f*, griffe-support *f*

accident: ~ **advisory sign** *n* TRANSP signal avertisseur d'accident *m*; ~ **at work** *n* CONST accident du travail *m*; ~ **data reporting** *n* AERONAUT compte rendu de données d'accident *m*; ~ **detector** *n* TRANSP détecteur d'accidents *m*; ~ **prevention** *n* SAFETY prévention des accidents *f*; ~ **prevention advertising signs** *n pl* SAFETY panneaux de signalisation contre les accidents *m pl*

accidental: ~ **alteration** *n* ACOUSTICS altération accidentelle *f*; ~ **braking** *n* RAIL *vehicles* freinage intempestif *m*; ~ **discharge** *n* MAR POLL rejet accidentel *m*, POLLUTION rejet accidentel *m*, échappement accidentel *m*

accidentally *adv* SAFETY accidentellement, par hasard

accident-prone *adj* SAFETY prédisposé aux accidents

accidents: ~ **to workers** *n pl* SAFETY accidents au personnel ouvrier *m pl*, accidents du travail *m pl*

acclimatization *n* HEAT ENG, METEO acclimatation *f*

acclimatize[1] *vt* METEO acclimater

acclimatize[2] *vi* METEO s'acclimater

acclimatized *adj* PROP MAT acclimaté

accommodation *n* MECH *construction site* logement *m*, MECH eng aménagement *m*, NAUT *boatbuilding* aménagement *m*, locaux d'habitation *m pl*, logement *m*; ~ **ladder** *n* NAUT coupée *f*, échelle de commandement *f*, échelle de coupée *f*; ~ **plan** *n* NAUT plan d'aménagement *m*; ~ **platform** *n* PETR TECH *offshore* plate-forme d'hébergement *f*; ~ **rig** *n* PETR TECH *offshore* plate-forme d'hébergement *f*

accordance *n* MECH ENG conformité *f*

accordion: ~ **fold** *n* PAPER TECH pliure accordéon *f*, PRINT pli zigzag *m*, pliure accordéon *f*

accountability *n* TELECOM imputabilité *f*

accounting: ~ **file** *n* COMP fichier de statistiques *m*; ~ **machine** *n* COMP machine comptable *f*; ~ **ratio** *n* CONST coût de l'unité d'oeuvre *m*

accretion *n* ASTRON accrétion *f*, METEO accrétion *f*, *groundwater* alimentation *f*, WATER SUPP *of sediment* accrétion *f*, engraissement *m*; ~ **disc** *n* (BrE) ASTRON disque d'accrétion *m*; ~ **disk** *n* (AmE) *see accretion disc*; ~ **flow** *n* ASTRON flux d'accrétion *m*; ~ **of matter** *n* ASTRON accrétion de matière *f*; ~ **rate** *n* ASTRON taux d'accrétion *m*

accretionary: ~ **prism** *n* GEOL prisme d'accrétion *m*

accumulating: ~ **counter** *n* ELECTRON compteur progressif *m*

accumulation *n* METEO *of snow, ice* accumulation *f*

accumulator *n* COMP, ELEC, ELEC ENG, HYDR EQUIP, NAUT *electrics*, PAPER TECH, PHYS accumulateur *m*, REFRIG accumulateur tampon *m*, bouteille tampon *f*, réservoir tampon *m*, vase tampon *f*, VEHICLES accumulateur *m*, batterie *f*; ~ **battery** *n* TELECOM batterie d'accumulateurs *f*; ~ **box** *n* PAPER TECH cuve d'accumulateur *f*; ~ **cell** *n* AUTO élément de batterie *m*, ELEC, ELECTRON élément d'accumulateur *m*; ~ **charge** *n* ELEC charge d'accumulateur *f*; ~ **discharge** *n* ELEC décharge d'accumulateur *f*; ~ **plate** *n* ELEC plaque d'accumulateur *f*; ~ **railcar** *n* TRANSP automotrice à accumulateurs *f*; ~ **register** *n* COMP, DP registre de cumul *m*; ~ **tank** *n* PAPER TECH accumulateur *m*, PETR TECH réservoir d'emmagasinage *m*

accuracy *n* COMP exactitude *f*, précision *f*, MECH exactitude *f*, précision *f*, MECH ENG précision *f*, METR, PHYS exactitude *f*, justesse *f*, précision *f*; ~ **of measurement** *n* METR exactitude de mesure *f*; ~ **of parallel gears** *n* MECH ENG précision des engrenages parallèles *f*; ~ **of**

ship's position *n* NAUT *navigation* précision de point *f*; ~ **test** *n* MECH ENG essai de précision *m*

accurate[1] *adj* MECH exact, précis, METR exact, juste, PHYS exact, juste, précis

accurate:[2] ~ **print registration** *n* PACKAGING repérage exact de l'impression *m*; ~ **reproduction** *n* PHOTO rendu correct *m*

accurately *adv* METR exactement, justement

ACD *abbr* (*automatic call distributor*) TELECOM distributeur automatique d'appels *m*

ACE *abbr* (*access connection element*) TELECOM élément de connexion d'accès *m*

acetal[1] *adj* FOOD TECH acétal

acetal[2] *n* P&R acétal *m*

acetaldehyde *n* FOOD TECH acétaldéhyde *m*

acetanilide *n* CHEM acétanilide *m*

acetate *n* CHEM, FOOD TECH, PRINT, TEXTILES acétate *m*; ~ **adhesive** *n* PACKAGING adhésif avec acétate *m*; ~ **base** *n* PRINT support d'acétate *m*; ~ **film** *n* CINEMAT pellicule support acétate *f*, PACKAGING film d'acétate *m*; ~ **glue** *n* PACKAGING colle à base d'acétate *f*; ~ **laminate** *n* PACKAGING laminé d'acétate *m*; ~ **proof** *n* PRINT *reproduction proof* cello *m*

acetic[1] *adj* CHEM acétique

acetic:[2] ~ **acid** *n* FOOD TECH *preserving and confectionery*, P&R acide acétique *m*; ~ **acid bacterium** *n* FOOD TECH bactérie acétique *f*; ~ **anhydride** *n* FOOD TECH anhydride acétique *m*; ~ **fermentation** *n* FOOD TECH fermentation acétique *f*

acetification *n* CHEM acétification *f*

acetify *vt* CHEM acétifier

acetin *n* CHEM acétine *f*

acetobacter *n* FOOD TECH acétobacter *m*

acetoin *n* FOOD TECH acétine *f*

acetolysis *n* CHEM, FOOD TECH acétolyse *f*

acetone *n* CHEM, FOOD TECH, P&R *solvent*, PRINT acétone *f*; ~ **extract** *n* P&R *test* extrait à l'acétone *m*; ~ **lacquer** *n* COLOURS vernis à l'acétone *m*; ~ **resin** *n* P&R, PACKAGING résine acétonique *f*

acetonitrile *n* CHEM acétonitrile *m*

acetonuria *n* CHEM acétonurie *f*

acetophenone *n* CHEM acétophénone *f*

acetoxy- *pref* CHEM acétoxy-

acetoxyl *n* FOOD TECH groupe acétoxyle *m*

acetyl *n* PAPER TECH acétyle *m*; ~ **cellulose lacquer** *n* COLOURS vernis acétocellulosique *m*, vernis à l'acétylcellulose *m*; ~ **group** *n* CHEM groupe acétyle *m*; ~ **iodide** *n* CHEM iodure d'acétyle *m*; ~ **value** *n* P&R *chemical property* indice d'acétyle *m*

acetylate *vt* PAPER TECH acétyler

acetylation *n* PAPER TECH acétylation *f*

acetylene *n* CHEM, CONST, GAS TECH, PAPER TECH, PROD ENG, SAFETY acétylène *m*; ~ **blowpipe** *n* CONST chalumeau acétylénique *m*, chalumeau à acétylène *m*; ~ **bottle** *n* SAFETY bouteille d'acétylène *f*; ~ **cutting** *n* MECH coupage à l'acétylène *m*; ~ **cylinder** *n* PROD ENG *tools* bouteille d'acétylène *f*; ~ **generator** *n* CHEM TECH, CONST *welding*, GAS TECH générateur d'acétylène *m*; ~ **lamp** *n* CONST lampe à acétylène *f*

acetylenic *adj* CHEM acétylénique

acetylide *n* CHEM acétylure *m*

acetylsalicylic *adj* CHEM acétylsalicylique

achievable: ~ **availability** *n* PROD ENG disponibilité réalisable *f*; ~ **burn-up** *n* NUCLEAR combustion massique réalisable *f*

achondrites *n pl* ASTRON achondrites *f pl*

achrematite *n* MINERAL achrématite *f*

achroite *n* MINERAL achroïte *f*

achromat *n* PHYS achromat *m*, objectif achromatique *m*

achromatic[1] *adj* PHYS, PRINT achromatique

achromatic:[2] ~ **color** *n* (AmE) *see achromatic colour*; ~ **color removal** *n* (AmE) *see achromatic colour removal*; ~ **colour** *n* (BrE) PRINT couleur achromatique *f*; ~ **colour removal** *n* (BrE) PRINT technique de stabilisation de la couleur *f*; ~ **doublet** *n* PHYS doublet achromatique *m*; ~ **fringes** *n pl* PHYS franges achromatiques *f pl*; ~ **lens** *n* ASTRON *of a telescope*, PHOTO objectif achromatique *m*, PHYS lentille achromatique *f*, objectif achromatique *m*, PRINT objectif achromatique *m*; ~ **quartz fluoride lens** *n* INSTRUMENT lentille achromatique en quartz-fluorine *f*; ~ **telescope** *n* ASTRON télescope achromatique *m*

ACI *abbr (automatic car identification)* TRANSP identification automatique des wagons *f*

acicular[1] *adj* METALL aciculaire, PROP MAT aiguillé

acicular:[2] ~ **crystal** *n* PROP MAT cristal aciculaire *m*

aciculate *adj* PROP MAT aiguillé

aciculated *adj* PROP MAT aiguillé

aciculiform *adj* PROP MAT aiguillé

aciculite *n* MINERAL aciculite *f*

acid *n* CHEM, FOOD TECH, PAPER TECH, TEXTILES acide *m*; ~ **acceptor** *n* P&R *compounding ingredient* accepteur d'acide *m*; ~ **aerosol** *n* POLLUTION aérosol acide *m*; ~ **badging** *n* C&G gravure au cachet *f*; ~ **bath** *n* PAPER TECH, PHOTO bain acide *m*; ~ **chloride** *n* CHEM chlorure d'acide *m*, FOOD TECH acide chlorhydrique *m*; ~ **colors** *n pl* (AmE), ~ **colours** *n pl* (BrE) PRINT couleurs acides *f pl*; ~ **concentration** *n* POLLUTION concentration acide *f*, concentration en acides *f*; ~ **content** *n* PACKAGING teneur en acide *f*; ~ **deposit** *n* POLLUTION dépôt d'acides *m*; ~ **determination** *n* PAPER TECH dosage de l'acidité *m*; ~ **dipping** *n* CHEM TECH décapage au bain acidulé *m*; ~ **dye** *n* CHEM, TEXTILES colorant acide *m*; ~ **earth** *n* POLLUTION planète acide *f*; ~ **egg** *n* CHEM TECH monte-acides *m pl*; ~ **elevator** *n* CHEM TECH monte-acides *m pl*; ~ **embossing** *n* C&G matage à l'acide *m*; ~ **etching** *n* C&G gravure à l'acide *f*; ~ **fallout** *n* POLLUTION dépôt acide *m*, dépôt d'acides *m*, retombées acides *f pl*; ~ **fixing bath** *n* CHEM TECH fixage acide *m*, PHOTO bain fixateur acide *m*; ~ **fog** *n* POLLUTION brouillard acide *m*; ~ **hardening bath** *n* PHOTO bain d'arrêt durcissant *m*; ~ **hydrometer** *n* AUTO *car maintenance* pèse-acide *m*; ~ **lake** *n* POLLUTION lac acide *m*, lac acidifié *m*; ~ **level** *n* AUTO niveau d'électrolyte *m*, CONST niveau d'acidité *m*; ~ **loading** *n* POLLUTION charge acide *f*; ~ **mark** *n* C&G tache d'acide *f*; ~ **neutralizing capacity** *n (ANC)* POLLUTION capacité de neutralisation des acides *f (CNA)*, potentiel de neutralisation de l'acide *m* (PNA), pouvoir neutralisant des acides *m* (PNA); ~ **number** *n* PETR TECH indice d'acidité *m*; ~ **particle** *n* POLLUTION particule acide *f*; ~ **pickling technology** *n* NUCLEAR technologie du décapage chimique *f*; ~ **plant** *n* PAPER TECH atelier de préparation de la lessive *m*; ~ **polishing** *n* C&G polissage à l'acide *m*; ~ **pollution** *n* POLLUTION dépôts acides *m pl*, précipitations acides *f pl*; ~ **precipitation** *n* POLLUTION précipitations acides *f pl*; ~ **prepickling** *n* NUCLEAR prédécapage à l'acide *m*; ~ **process** *n* PAPER TECH procédé acide *m*; ~ **radical** *n* CHEM radical acide *m*; ~ **rain** *n* GAS TECH pluie acide *f*, POLLUTION pluies acides *f pl*, précipitations acides *f pl*; ~ **rain zone** *n* POLLUTION zone de précipitations acides

f, zone de retombées acides *f*; ~ **recovery plant** *n* PETR TECH installation de récupération de l'acide *f*; ~ **resist** *n* PRINT réserve à l'acide *f*; ~ **resistance** *n* P&R résistance aux acides *f*; ~ **rock** *n* GEOL roche acide *f*, roche de type acide *f*; ~ **runoff** *n* POLLUTION ruissellement acide *m*; ~ **salt** *n* FOOD TECH sel acide *m*; ~ **shock** *n* POLLUTION choc acide *m*; ~ **size** *n* PRINT colle acide *f*; ~ **snow** *n* POLLUTION neige acide *f*; ~ **solution** *n* FOOD TECH solution acide *f*; ~ **stop bath** *n* CINEMAT, PHOTO bain d'arrêt acide *m*; ~ **strength** *n* CHEM force d'un acide *f*; ~ **stress** *n* POLLUTION agression acide *f*, stress acide *m*, stress d'acidité *m*; ~ **tester** *n* PAPER TECH acidomètre *m*; ~ **tolerance** *n* POLLUTION résistance à l'acidité *f*, tolérance à l'acidité *f*; ~ **value** *n* FOOD TECH indice d'acide *m*, valeur d'acidité *f*, P&R, PAPER TECH indice d'acide *m*; ~ **vat** *n* PAPER TECH cuve d'acide *f*; ~ **wash** *n* PAPER TECH lavage à l'eau acidulée *m*; ~ **washing** *n* PAPER TECH lavage à l'acide *m*; ~ **water** *n* POLLUTION eau acide *f*; ~ **well treatment** *n (AWT)* PETR TECH acidification *f*

acid-etched: ~ **frosted glass** *n* C&G verre givré à l'acide *m*

acid-free[1] *adj* PAPER TECH, PRINT sans acide

acid-free:[2] ~ **glue** *n* PHOTO colle neutre *f*; ~ **paper** *n* PACKAGING, PAPER TECH papier non acide *m*, PRINT papier neutre *m*, papier sans acide *m*

acidic[1] *adj* CHEM, PETR TECH acide

acidic:[2] ~ **area** *n* POLLUTION centre d'acidité *m*, zone de précipitations acides *f*, zone de retombées acides *f*; ~ **chloride** *n* CHEM chlorure acide *m*; ~ **particle** *n* POLLUTION particule acide *f*; ~ **precursor** *n* POLLUTION polluant acidifiant *m*, précurseur acide *m*, précurseur d'acides *m*; ~ **rain** *n* POLLUTION pluies acides *f pl*, précipitations acides *f pl*; ~ **rock** *n* CHEM roche acide *f*, GEOL roche acide *f*, roche de type acide *f*

acidiferous *adj* CHEM, PAPER TECH, PROP MAT acidifère

acidifiable *adj* CHEM, PAPER TECH acidifiable

acidification *n* CHEM, CHEM TECH, HYDROL, PAPER TECH, POLLUTION acidification *f*

acidified: ~ **lake** *n* POLLUTION lac acidifié *m*

acidifier *n* CHEM acidificateur *m*, PAPER TECH acidifiant *m*, TEXTILES acidificateur *m*, bac à acidifier *m*

acidify[1] *vt* CHEM, FOOD TECH, PAPER TECH, POLLUTION, TEXTILES acidifier

acidify[2] *vi* CHEM s'acidifier

acidifying[1] *adj* PAPER TECH acidifiant, POLLUTION acidifiant, acidogène

acidifying:[2] ~ **agent** *n* TEXTILES acidificateur *m*; ~ **beck** *n* TEXTILES bac à acidifier *m*

acidimeter *n* CHEM acidimètre *m*, pèse-acide *m*, CHEM TECH, PAPER TECH acidimètre *m*

acidimetric *adj* CHEM, PAPER TECH acidimétrique

acidimetry *n* CHEM, CHEM TECH, PAPER TECH acidimétrie *f*

acidity *n* CHEM, HYDROL, PAPER TECH, POLLUTION acidité *f*, PRINT degré d'acidité *m*, PROP MAT acidité *f*; ~ **level** *n* POLLUTION niveau d'acidité *m*

acidization *n* PETR TECH acidification *f*

acidize *vt* PAPER TECH acidifier

acidizer *n* PETR TECH acidifiant *m*

acidizing *n* PETR traitement acide *m*

acidless *adj* PACKAGING sans acide

acidolysis *n* FOOD TECH acidolyse *f*

acidometer *n* CHEM acidimètre *m*

acid-proof[1] *adj* PAPER TECH, PRINT résistant aux acides,

PROP MAT antiacide

acid-proof:[2] ~ **coat** n COLOURS peinture résistant aux acides f; ~ **enamel** n COATINGS vernis résistant aux acides m, COLOURS vernis antiacide m; ~ **lining** n COATINGS revêtement résistant aux acides m; ~ **paper** n PRINT papier résistant aux acides m; ~ **protective gloves** n pl SAFETY gants protecteurs antiacides m pl; ~ **varnish** n PACKAGING vernis résistant aux acides m

acid-resistant adj PACKAGING résistant aux acides, POLLUTION tolérant à l'acide, PRINT résistant aux acides

acid-resisting: ~ **covering** n SAFETY revêtement résistant aux acides m; ~ **paint** n CONST peinture antiacide f

acid-stressed adj POLLUTION agressé par la pollution acide

acidulate vt CHEM, FOOD TECH aciduler

acidulated adj CHEM acidulé

aciform adj CHEM aciculiforme, aciforme

ACK abbr (acknowledgement) COMP, DP, TELECOM AR (accusé de réception)

acknowledge[1] n DP accusé de réception m; ~ **character** n COMP caractère accusé de réception m

acknowledge[2] vt COMP recognize, DP reconnaître; ~ **receipt of** vt COMP accuser réception de

acknowledge:[3] ~ **a signal** vi NAUT faire l'aperçu

acknowledged: ~ **information transfer service** n (AITS) TELECOM service de transfert d'informations avec accusé de réception m

acknowledgement n (ACK) COMP, DP, TELECOM accusé de réception m (AR); ~ **request** n TELECOM demande d'accusé de réception f; ~ **signal** n TELECOM signal d'accusé de réception m

aclinic: ~ **line** n GEOPHYS ligne aclinique f

Acme: ~ **thread** n MECH ENG filetage Acmé m; ~ **thread tap** n MECH ENG taraud fileté Acme m

acmite n MINERAL acmite f

ACO abbr (adaptive control optimization) CONTROL optimisation de la commande adaptative f

aconitase n CHEM aconitase f

aconitate n CHEM aconitate m

aconitic adj CHEM aconitique

aconitine n FOOD TECH aconitine f

AC-operated: ~ **service** adj PROD ENG service CA m

acorn: ~ **nut** n AERONAUT écrou borgne m, écrou à portée sphérique m; ~ **tube** n ELECTRON tube-gland m

acouphene n ACOUSTICS acouphène m

acoustic[1] adj RECORDING acoustique

acoustic:[2] ~ **absorption** n RECORDING absorption acoustique f; ~ **absorption coefficient** n PHYS facteur d'absorption acoustique m; ~ **absorption loss** n RECORDING perte acoustique par absorption f; ~ **admittance** n ACOUSTICS, ELEC ENG admittance acoustique f; ~ **amplifier** n RECORDING amplificateur acoustique m; ~ **antenna** n TELECOM antenne acoustique f; ~ **attenuation** n ELECTRON atténuation acoustique f; ~ **attenuation constant** n ELECTRON constante d'atténuation acoustique f; ~ **blanket** n SPACE spacecraft revêtement antibruit m; ~ **boards** n pl SAFETY plaques d'insonorisation f pl; ~ **branch** n PHYS solid state theory branche acoustique f; ~ **capacitance** n ACOUSTICS élasticité acoustique f; ~ **carrier** n ELECTRON porteuse acoustique f; ~ **channel** n OCEANOG chenal acoustique m, chenal sonore m; ~ **coloring** n (AmE), ~ **colouring** n (BrE) RECORDING coloration acoustique f; ~ **compliance** n RECORDING capacitance acoustique f; ~ **coupler** n COMP, ELECTRON coupleur

acoustique m; ~ **coupling** n ELECTRON, TELECOM couplage acoustique m; ~ **current meter** n OCEANOG courantomètre acoustique m; ~ **delay line** n COMP, ELECTRON ligne à retard acoustique f; ~ **diffraction** n ACOUSTICS diffraction acoustique f; ~ **dispersion** n ACOUSTICS dispersion acoustique f; ~ **efficiency** n RECORDING rendement acoustique m; ~ **emission** n NUCLEAR émission acoustique f; ~ **enclosure** n ACOUSTICS enceinte acoustique f; ~ **energy** n ELEC ENG énergie acoustique f; ~ **feedback** n RECORDING réaction acoustique f; ~ **fencing** n CONST protection antibruit f; ~ **filter** n ACOUSTICS, ELECTRON, MECH ENG, RECORDING filtre acoustique m; ~ **flat** n RECORDING panneau acoustique m; ~ **frequency** n ELECTRON, RECORDING fréquence acoustique f; ~ **generator** n MECH ENG génératrice de signaux acoustiques f; ~ **impedance** n ACOUSTICS, ELEC ENG, PETR, PHYS, RECORDING impédance acoustique f; ~ **inertance** n PHYS inertance acoustique f; ~ **insulating materials** n pl POLLUTION matériaux d'isolation acoustique m pl; ~ **interferometer** n ACOUSTICS interféromètre acoustique m; ~ **isolation** n ACOUSTICS isolation acoustique f; ~ **log** n PETR TECH exploration diagraphie acoustique f; ~ **mass** n ACOUSTICS masse acoustique f; ~ **modem** n DP modem acoustique m; ~ **noise** n TELECOM bruit acoustique m; ~ **oscillation** n ACOUSTICS oscillation acoustique f; ~ **perspective** n RECORDING perspective sonore f; ~ **pick-up** n RECORDING capteur acoustique m, lecteur acoustique m; ~ **plaster** n COATINGS enduit acoustique m; ~ **pressure** n RECORDING pression acoustique f, SPACE spacecraft pression sonore f; ~ **propagation constant** n ACOUSTICS constante de propagation acoustique f; ~ **pulse** n ELECTRON impulsion acoustique f; ~ **radiometer** n ACOUSTICS radiomètre acoustique m; ~ **reactance** n ACOUSTICS, ELEC ENG, PHYS réactance acoustique f; ~ **resistance** n ACOUSTICS résistance acoustique f; ~ **resonator** n ELECTRON résonateur acoustique m; ~ **scattering** n RECORDING diffusion acoustique f; ~ **screen** n RECORDING écran acoustique m; ~ **sensor** n ELECTRON capteur acoustique m; ~ **shielding** n RECORDING blindage acoustique m; ~ **signal** n ELECTRON, MECH ENG signal acoustique m; ~ **signal generator** n MECH ENG génératrice de signaux acoustiques f; ~ **spectrum** n RECORDING spectre acoustique m; ~ **stiffness** n ACOUSTICS, PHYS raideur acoustique f; ~ **system** n ACOUSTICS système acoustique m; ~ **testing room** n MECH ENG chambre d'essai acoustique f; ~ **tile** n RECORDING panneau acoustique m; ~ **transmission line** n ELEC ENG ligne de transmission acoustique f; ~ **trauma** n ACOUSTICS trauma sonore m; ~ **velocity level** n ACOUSTICS niveau de vitesse acoustique m; ~ **velocity log** n FUELLESS étalonnage de la vitesse de son m; ~ **vibration** n ACOUSTICS vibration acoustique f; ~ **wave** n ELEC ENG onde acoustique f; ~ **waveband** n OCEANOG chenal acoustique m; ~ **wave filter** n ELECTRON filtre à ondes acoustiques m; ~ **wave propagation** n ELEC ENG propagation acoustique f, propagation des ondes acoustiques f; ~ **well logging** n PETR TECH exploration diagraphie acoustique f

acoustical: ~ **design** n RECORDING étude acoustique f; ~ **field** n ACOUSTICS champ acoustique m; ~ **log** n GEOPHYS diagramme acoustique m; ~ **spectrum** n ACOUSTICS spectre acoustique m; ~ **test** n SAFETY essai acoustique m

acoustically-coupled: ~ **modem** n DP modem à couplage

acoustique *m*

acoustics *n* PHYS, RECORDING, SAFETY acoustique *f*

acoustoelectric: **~ effect** *n* TELECOM effet électroacoustique *m*

acousto-optic: **~ effect** *n* OPT effet acousto-optique *m*; **~ modulation** *n* ELECTRON modulation acousto-optique *f*; **~ modulator** *n* ELECTRON, OPT modulateur acousto-optique *m*; **~ processor** *n* ELECTRON processeur acousto-optique *m*

acousto-optical: **~ modulator** *n* ELECTRON, OPT modulateur acousto-optique *m*

acquisition *n* SPACE acquisition *f*; **~ of attitude** *n* SPACE *spacecraft* acquisition d'attitude *f*; **~ of normal mode** *n* SPACE *spacecraft* acquisition du mode normal *f*; **~ of orbit** *n* SPACE *spacecraft* mise sur orbite *f*

acre *n* METR acre *f*

acrid: **~ odor** *n* (AmE), **~ odour** *n* (BrE) POLLUTION odeur âcre *f*

acridine: **~ dye** *n* COLOURS colorant d'acridine *m*

acrolein *n* AERONAUT, PROP MAT acroléine *f*

acrometer *n* METR oléomètre *m*

acronym *n* COMP, DP acronyme *m*

across:[1] **~ flats** *adj* MECH ENG entre plats, sur plats

across:[2] **~ the bow** *adv* NAUT à travers de l'avant; **~ the page** *adv* PRINT au travers de la page

across-the-line: **~ motor** *n* ELEC moteur à démarrage direct *m*; **~ starter** *n* ELEC démarreur direct *m*

across-track: **~ error** *n* SPACE erreur transversale *f*

acrylate *n* P&R acrylate *m*

acrylated: **~ epoxy resin** *n* P&R *paints, adhesives, plastics* résine époxyde acrylée *f*

acrylic[1] *adj* CONST, MECH *materials*, TEXTILES acrylique

acrylic[2] *n* CONST, TEXTILES acrylique *m*; **~ acid** *n* PROP MAT acide acrylique *m*; **~ fiber** *n* (AmE), **~ fibre** *n* (BrE) PROP MAT fibre acrylique *f*; **~ paint** *n* CONST peinture acrylique *f*; **~ plastic** *n* PACKAGING plastique acrylique *m*; **~ resin** *n* MECH *materials, plastics*, P&R *coatings, adhesives*, PACKAGING résine acrylique *f*; **~ resin coating** *n* COATINGS enduction par résine acrylique *f*, plaxage *m*; **~ rubber** *n* PACKAGING caoutchouc acrylique *m*; **~ size** *n* TEXTILES colle acrylique *f*; **~ tester** *n* PACKAGING contrôleur acrylique *m*

acrylonitrile *n* CHEM acrylonitrile *m*; **~ rubber** *n* P&R, PROD ENG *materials* caoutchouc de nitrile acrylique *m*

acrylonitrile-butadiene-styrene *n* *(ABS)* P&R styrène-acrylonitrile-butadiène *m*

ACSE *abbr* *(association control service element)* TELECOM élément de service de commande d'association *m*, élémentde service de contrôle d'association *m*

act: **~ as** *vt* CONST se porter comme; **~ upon** *vt* PHYS agir sur, solliciter

Act *n* SAFETY (BrE) loi *f*

acted: **~ upon by a force** *phr* PHYS sollicité par une force

actin *n* FOOD TECH actine *f*

acting: **~ area** *n* CINEMAT plateau *m*

actinic[1] *adj* PHOTO, PHYS, PRINT actinique

actinic:[2] **~ light** *n* CINEMAT lumière actinique *f*, RAD PHYS radiation actinique *f*; **~ radiation** *n* RAD PHYS radiation actinique *f*

actinide *n* PHYS actinide *m*; **~ element** *n* RAD PHYS élément actinide *m*; **~ series** *n* RAD PHYS série d'actinides *f*

actinides *n pl* CHEM, RAD PHYS actinides *m pl*

actinism *n* PHYS actinisme *m*

actinium *n* *(Ac)* CHEM actinium *m* *(Ac)*; **~ series** *n* RAD

PHYS famille de l'actinium *f*

actinolite *n* MINERAL actinote *f*

actinometer *n* ASTRON, PHYS, RAD PHYS *to measure intensity of radiation* actinomètre *m*

actinometry *n* METEO, PHYS, RAD PHYS actinométrie *f*

actinon *n* CHEM actinon *m*

actinote *n* MINERAL actinote *f*

action *n* MECH action *f*, effet *m*, fonctionnement *m*, MECH ENG intervention *f*, PHYS action *f*; **~ entry** *n* COMP *decision table* entrée des procédures autorisées *f*; **~ outline** *n* CINEMAT découpage technique *m*; **~ signal** *n* CONTROL signal d'action *m*; **~ still** *n* CINEMAT photo de travail *f*; **~ turbine** *n* HYDR EQUIP turbine à action directe *f*, turbine à impulsion *f*, turbine à libre déviation *f*; **~ of viscosity between wall and fluid** *n* FLUID PHYS effet de viscosité entre la paroi et le fluide *m*

activate:[1] **~ button** *n* CONTROL bouton de déclenchement *m*

activate[2] *vt* COAL TECH, PAPER TECH activer

activated: **~ carbon** *n* CHEM charbon actif *m*, charbon activé *m*, GAS TECH, HYDROL *sewage* charbon actif *m*, P&R *filler* charbon activé *m*, PAPER TECH carbone activé *m*, WATER SUPP charbon actif *m*; **~ carbon black** *n* P&R *pigment, filler* noir de carbone activé *m*; **~ carbon filter** *n* HYDROL filtre à charbon actif *m*, NUCLEAR filtre à charbon *m*; **~ charcoal** *n* CHEM charbon activé *m*, FOOD TECH charbon actif *m*, P&R *filler* charbon activé *m*, PROP MAT charbon actif *m*; **~ charcoal bed** *n* NUCLEAR lit de charbon de bois activé *m*; **~ charcoal filter** *n* PROP MAT filtre à charbon activé *m*; **~ complex** *n* METALL complexe activé *m*; **~ molecule** *n* RAD PHYS molécule activée *f*; **~ recycled sludge** *n* HYDROL *sewage* boue recyclée et active *f*; **~ return sludge** *n* HYDROL boue recyclée et active *f*; **~ sludge** *n* HYDROL *sewage*, POLLUTION, RECYCLING boue activée *f*; **~ sludge process** *n* WATER SUPP procédé d'épuration par boues activées *m*, procédé des boues activées *m*; **~ sludge tank** *n* HYDROL *sewage* bassin d'activation *m*; **~ sludge treatment plant** *n* HYDROL *sewage* station d'épuration à boues actives *f*; **~ state** *n* METALL état activé *m*; **~ zinc oxide** *n* P&R *filler, activator* oxyde de zinc activé *m*

activating: **~ agent** *n* COAL TECH agent activant *m*

activation *n* COAL TECH, HYDROL, METALL, PAPER TECH activation *f*, RAD PHYS déclenchement *m*, TELECOM *alarms* activation *f*; **~ analysis** *n* PHYS analyse par activation *f*; **~ area** *n* METALL aire d'activation *f*; **~ comprising three successive levels of decision** *n* RAD PHYS déclenchement comprenant trois niveaux de décision successifs *m*; **~ energy** *n* CRYSTALL, METALL, NUCLEAR, PROP MAT énergie d'activation *f*, RAD PHYS énergie de déclenchement *f*; **~ entropy** *n* METALL entropie d'activation *f*; **~ log** *n* PETR TECH *exploration* diagraphie par activation *f*; **~ logging** *n* PETR diagraphie activation *f*; **~ parameter** *n* METALL paramètre d'activation *f*

activator *n* CHEM, COAL TECH, ELEC ENG, P&R *compounding ingredient* activateur *m*, PAPER TECH activeur *m*

active[1] *adj* COMP, DP, ELEC ENG actif

active:[2] **~ air defence** *n* (BrE) MILIT défense aérienne active *f*; **~ air defense** *n* (AmE) *see active air defence* **~ band-pass filter** *n* ELECTRON filtre passe-bande actif *m*; **~ bandstop filter** *n* ELECTRON filtre coupe-bande actif *m*; **~ beacon collision avoidance system** *n* AERONAUT système radar anticollision actif *m*; **~ carbon absorption** *n* POLLUTION absorption sur charbon actif *f*; ~ **chlorine** *n* DETERGENTS, PAPER TECH chlore actif *m*; ~ **circuit** *n* PHYS circuit actif *m*; ~ **coils** *n pl* SPRINGS spires actives *f pl*; ~ **component** *n* ELEC composante active *f*, ELEC ENG composant actif *m*, composante active *f*, PHYS composante active *f*, TELECOM composant active *m*; ~ **control** *n* SPACE *spacecraft* contrôle actif *m*; ~ **current** *n* ELEC courant actif *m*, courant watté *m*, PHYS courant actif *m*; ~ **development** *n* PROD ENG développement en cours *m*; ~ **dipole** *n* ELEC ENG dipôle actif *m*; ~ **dope** *n* PROP MAT base active *f*; ~ **earth pressure** *n* COAL TECH poussée active des terres *f*; ~ **effluent holdup tank** *n* NUCLEAR réservoir de stockage des effluents *m*; ~ **effluent system** *n* NUCLEAR système des effluents radioactifs *m*; ~ **element** *n* ELEC ENG élément actif *m*; ~ **emanation** *n* NUCLEAR émanation *f*; ~ **energy** *n* ELEC *of system* énergie active *f*; ~ **energy meter** *n* ELEC compteur d'énergie active *m*; ~ **equalizer** *n* RECORDING égaliseur actif *m*; ~ **field period** *n* TV temps utile de trame *m*; ~ **filler** *n* P&R charge active *f*; ~ **filter** *n* ELECTRON filtre actif *m*; ~ **filtering** *n* ELECTRON filtrage actif *m*; ~ **galaxy** *n* ASTRON galaxie active *f*; ~ **guidance** *n* SPACE *spacecraft* guidage actif *m*; ~ **impeder** *n* ELEC *component* dipôle actif *m*; ~ **infrared detector** *n* TRANSP détecteur à infrarouge actif *m*; ~ **integrator** *n* ELECTRON intégrateur actif *m*; ~ **laser medium** *n* OPT milieu actif laser *m*, TELECOM milieu laser *m*; ~ **lattice** *n* NUCLEAR coeur *m*; ~ **layer** *n* ELECTRON couche active *f*; ~ **length** *n* NUCLEAR *of fuel element* longueur active *f*; ~ **line** *n* ELECTRON ligne de balayage *f*, TV ligne active *f*; ~ **load** *n* ELEC, ELEC ENG charge active *f*; ~ **margin** *n* GEOL *cordillera or island-arc type* marge active *f*; ~ **material** *n* ELEC ENG matière active *f*; ~ **medium** *n* PROP MAT milieu actif *m*; ~ **microwave integrated circuit** *n* ELECTRON circuit intégré hyperfréquence actif *m*; ~ **mine** *n* MINING mine en activité *f*; ~ **mirror** *n* NUCLEAR miroir actif *m*; ~ **mixer** *n* MECH ENG mélangeur actif *m*; ~ **motor vehicle safety** *n* TRANSP sécurité active des véhicules automobiles *f*; ~ **network** *n* ELEC ENG réseau actif *m*, réseau électrique actif *m*; ~ **notch filter** *n* ELECTRON filtre coupe-bande à bande étroite actif *m*; ~ **potential** *n* ELEC tension active *f*; ~ **power** *n* ELEC puissance active *f*, ELEC ENG *consumed by semiconductor memory* puissance en activité *f*, *of active component of AC circuit* puissance active *f*, PHYS puissance active *f*; ~ **power meter** *n* ELEC appareil de mesure de puissance active *m*; ~ **power relay** *n* ELEC relais de puissance active *m*; ~ **pressure** *n* MECH, MECH ENG pression effective *f*; ~ **processor** *n* TELECOM processeur actif *m*; ~ **pull-up device** *n* ELECTRON *transistor* dispositif actif d'excursion haute *m*; ~ **quadripole** *n* ELEC ENG quadripôle actif *m*; ~ **region** *n* ELECTRON *of semiconductor substrate* zone active *f*; ~ **runway** *n* AERONAUT piste en service *f*; ~ **satellite** *n* SPACE *spacecraft* satellite actif *m*; ~ **sensor** *n* SPACE capteur actif *m*; ~ **solar system** *n* FUELLESS système solaire actif *m*; ~ **solvent** *n* PACKAGING solvant actif *m*; ~ **star** *n* DP *networks* étoile active *f*; ~ **supervisor** *n* TELECOM *packet switching* superviseur actif *m*; ~ **surface** *n* PROP MAT surface active *f*; ~ **suspension** *n* TRANSP suspension active *f*; ~ **system** *n* ACOUSTICS système actif *m*; ~ **test loop** *n* NUCLEAR boucle active *f*, boucle d'essai active *f*; ~ **threat** *n* TELECOM menace active *f*; ~ **transducer** *n* ELEC, ELEC ENG transducteur actif *m*; ~ **volcano** *n* GEOL volcan en activité *m*; ~ **voltage** *n* ELEC *alternating current*, ELEC ENG, PHYS tension active *f*; ~ **water** *n* WATER SUPP eau corrosive *f*

activity *n* COMP, DP, PHYS activité *f*; ~ **coefficient** *n* PHYS coefficient d'activité *m*, facteur d'activité *m*; ~ **factor** *n* SPACE *communications* facteur d'activité *m*, taux d'activité *m*; ~ **inventory** *n* NUCLEAR inventaire en radioactivité *m*; ~ **overvoltage** *n* SPACE *spacecraft* suractivation *f*

AC-to-DC: ~ **conversion** *n* ELEC ENG conversion alternatif-continu *f*, conversion ca-cc *f*, conversion d'alternatif en continu *f*; ~ **converter** *n* ELEC ENG convertisseur alternatif-continu *m*, convertisseur ca-cc *m*, convertisseur de courant alternatif en courant continu *m*

actomyosin *n* FOOD TECH actomyosine *f*

actual: ~ **aperture** *n* CINEMAT ouverture efficace *f*; ~ **current** *n* ELEC courant actif *m*, courant watté *m*; ~ **evapotranspiration** *n* HYDROL évapotranspiration réelle *f*; ~ **flight path** *n* AERONAUT trajectoire de vol réelle *f*; ~ **horsepower** *n* MECH puissance effective en chevaux *f*, MECH ENG cheval effectif *m*, puissance au frein en chevaux *f*, puissance effective en chevaux *f*, puissance en chevaux-vapeur effectifs *f*; ~ **horsepower-hour** *n* MECH cheval heure effectif *m*; ~ **parameter** *n* COMP paramètre réel *m*; ~ **power** *n* MECH puissance effective *f*; ~ **running speed** *n* MECH vitesse effective de marche *f*; ~ **size** *n* MECH ENG, PROD ENG vraie grandeur *f*; ~ **state** *n* NUCLEAR état réel *m*; ~ **value** *n* PRINT valeur réelle *f*; ~ **weight** *n* PRINT *paper* grammage réel *m*

actuate *vt* MECH actionner, commander, déclencher, MECH ENG actionner, activer, enclencher, PRINT *machine* activer, lancer, mettre en oeuvre

actuating: ~ **plate** *n* AERONAUT palette de manoeuvre *f*; ~ **rod** *n* AERONAUT bielle d'attaque *f*, bielle de commande *f*, bielle vérin *f*; ~ **signal** *n* NUCLEAR signal de mise en action *m*; ~ **transfer function** *n* CONTROL fonction de transfert de commande *f*

actuation *n* AERONAUT commande *f*, SPACE sollicitation *f*

actuator *n* AERONAUT vérin *m*, COMP actionneur *m*, DP actionneur *m*, déclencheur *m*, mécanisme de commande *m*, mécanisme de positionnement *m*, ELEC *transducer* actionneur *m*, ELEC ENG actionneur *m*, organe d'exécution *m*, organe de puissance *m*, MECH actionneur *m*, TRANSP vérin *m*; ~ **attachment** *n* MECH ENG raccordement de servomoteurs *m*; ~ **control valve** *n* AERONAUT distributeur de servodyne *m*; ~ **disc** *n* (BrE) AERONAUT disque sustentateur *m*; ~ **disk** *n* (AmE) *see actuator disc*

ACU *abbr* (*automatic calling unit*) COMP, DP EAA (*équipement d'appel automatique*)

acuity: ~ **projector** *n* INSTRUMENT projecteur *m*

acutance *n* PHOTO netteté des contours *f*

acute: ~ **angle** *n* GEOM angle aigu *m*; ~ **effect** *n* POLLUTION effet aigu *m*; ~ **triangle** *n* GEOM triangle aigu *m*

acute-angled *adj* GEOM acutangle

acute-angular *adj* GEOM actangulaire

acuteness *n* GEOM *of an angle* acuité *f*

ACV *abbr* (*air cushion vehicle*) TRANSP véhicule à coussin d'air *m*

acyclic[1] *adj* CHEM acyclique

acyclic:[2] ~ **dynamo** *n* ELEC dynamo unipolaire *f*; ~ **generator** *n* ELEC dynamo unipolaire *f*

acyl *n* CHEM acyle *m*; ~ **chloride** *n* PROP MAT chlorure d'acyle *m*; ~ **group** *n* PROP MAT groupe acyle *m*

acylate *vt* CHEM acyler

acylation *n* CHEM acylation *f*

ad: ~ **face** *n* PRINT caractère d'annonce *m*

adamantine: ~ **luster** n (AmE), ~ **lustre** n (BrE) MINERAL éclat adamantin m; ~ **spar** n MINERAL corindon adamantin m

adamine n MINERAL adamine f

adamite n MINERAL adamine f

adamsite n MINERAL adamsite f

adapt: ~ **to space conditions** vt SPACE spacecraft spatialibiliser

adaptable: ~ **operation** n GAS TECH exploitation modulable f

adaptation n PRINT of a text adaptation f

adaptive[1] adj COMP, CONTROL, DP, MECH adaptatif

adaptive:[2] ~ **antenna** n TELECOM antenne adaptative f; ~ **channel allocation** n COMP affectation adaptable de voies f; ~ **coding** n TELECOM codage adaptatif m; ~ **control** n CONTROL, ELEC ENG commande adaptative f; ~ **control constraint** n (ACC) CONTROL contrainte de commande adaptative f (commande ACC); ~ **control electronics** n pl CONTROL asservissement électronique auto-adaptable m; ~ **control optimization** n (ACO) CONTROL optimisation de la commande adaptative f; ~ **control system** n DP système autocommandé m, ELEC ENG système asservi adaptatif m, MECH système de commande adaptative m; ~ **delay equalizer** n CONTROL correcteur adaptatif de phase m, correcteur adaptatif de temps de propagation m; ~ **differential pulse code modulation** n (ADPCM) TELECOM modulation par impulsion et codage différentiels adaptatifs f (MICDA); ~ **equalization** n ELEC ENG égalisation adaptative f, égalisation autoadaptative f; ~ **filter** n ELECTRON filtre adaptatif m; ~ **filtering** n COMP, TELECOM filtrage adaptatif m; ~ **process** n COMP processus adaptatif m; ~ **regulating system** n CONTROL système de réglage à auto-adaptation m; ~ **routing** n DP acheminement adaptatif m; ~ **signal processing** n ELECTRON traitement adaptatif des signaux m; ~ **speed control** n CONTROL commande adaptative de la vitesse f; ~ **sweep** n ELECTRON balayage adaptatif m; ~ **system** n COMP, CONTROL système adaptatif m; ~ **tuning** n ELECTRON accord adaptatif m

adaptor n COMP, DP, ELEC connector, ELEC ENG, LAB EQUIP glassware, MECH adaptateur m, MECH ENG adaptateur m, adapteur m, répartiteur m, TELECOM, TEXTILES adaptateur m; ~ **plate** n MECH ENG to fit a chuck faux plateau m; ~ **ring** n CINEMAT anneau intermédiaire m, PHOTO bague d'adaptation f

ADC abbr COMP (analog-to-digital converter), ELECTRON (analog-to-digital converter, analogue-to-digital converter), PHYS (analogue-to-digital converter, analog-to-digital converter), TELECOM (analog-to-digital converter, analogue-to-digital converter) CAN (convertisseur analogique-numérique)

add[1] n COMP addition f

add[2] vt COMP ajouter, MATH additionner; ~ **and delete** vt PRINT ajouter et effacer, retoucher; ~ **thin space** vt PRINT text justification ajouter une espace fine

ADD abbr (address prompt) TELECOM incitation d'adressage f

add-and-divide: ~ **principle** n ELECTRON frequency synthesis principe d'addition et de division m

add-drop: ~ **multiplexer** n TELECOM multiplexeur insertion-extraction m

added:[1] ~ **loop** n SPRINGS anneau rapporté m

added:[2] **no** ~ **sugar** phr FOOD TECH sans addition de sucre

added-on: ~ **component** n SPACE spacecraft élément rapporté m

addend n COMP cumulateur m

addendum n MECH ENG gear saillie f, PRINT addendum m, ajout m; ~ **circle** n MECH ENG cercle de couronne m, cercle de tête m, cercle extérieur m; ~ **flank** n MECH ENG gears flanc de saillie m

adder n COMP, ELECTRON additionneur m, TV circuit mélangeur m

add-in: ~ **board** n ELECTRON carte d'extension f

adding: ~ **counter** n ELECTRON compteur progressif m; ~ **network** n ELEC circuit circuit additionneur m

addition n MATH addition f, MECH ENG addition f, adjonction f, ajout m; ~ **polymer** n P&R polymère d'addition m; ~ **polymerization** n P&R process polymérisation d'addition f

additional[1] adj MECH ENG complémentaire, supplémentaire, PRINT additionnel, supplémentaire

additional:[2] ~ **charge** n PRINT coût supplémentaire m; ~ **feature** n PATENTS caractéristique additionnelle f; ~ **keyboard** n PRINT clavier auxiliaire m; ~ **tank** n SPACE spacecraft réservoir additionnel m

additive[1] adj MATH additif

additive[2] n CHEM additif m, adjuvant m, DETERGENTS, FOOD TECH, MECH materials additif m, P&R additif m, adjuvant m, PETR TECH additif m, PRINT agent additif m, PROP MAT additif m, produit d'addition m; ~ **color** n (AmE) see additive colour; ~ **color printer** n (AmE) see additive colour printer; ~ **color process** n (AmE) see additive colour process; ~ **color system** n (AmE) see additive colour system; ~ **color theory** n (AmE) see additive colour theory; ~ **colour** n (BrE) COLOURS couleur additive f, couleur d'addition f; ~ **colour printer** n (BrE) CINEMAT tireuse par synthèse additive f; ~ **colour process** n (BrE) CINEMAT procédé couleur par synthèse additive m, PHOTO procédé par synthèse additive des couleurs m; ~ **colour system** n (BrE) CINEMAT procédé en couleur par synthèse additive m; ~ **colour theory** n (BrE) PRINT théorie additive de couleur f; ~ **lamphouse** n CINEMAT lanterne de tireuse additive f; ~ **method** n CINEMAT, ELECTRON méthode additive f; ~ **mixing** n ELECTRON conversion additive f; ~ **noise** n TELECOM bruit additif m; ~ **primaries** n pl CINEMAT couleurs primaires additives f pl, PRINT couleurs primaires dans la synthèse additive f pl; ~ **printer** n CINEMAT tireuse additive f; ~ **process** n ELECTRON procédé additif m; ~ **synthesis** n PHOTO mélange des couleurs par addition de lumière m, PRINT synthèse additive f

additive-free adj FOOD TECH sans additif

add-on: ~ **edit** n TV montage en assemblage m; ~ **memory** n COMP extension mémoire f; ~ **to the packaging** n PACKAGING ajouté à l'emballage m

address[1] n COMP, PRINT adresse f ~ **bus** n COMP, DP bus d'adresses m; ~ **code** n CINEMAT code temporel m; ~ **format** n COMP format d'adresse m; ~ **generation** n COMP calcul d'adresse m, génération d'adresses f; ~ **label** n PACKAGING étiquette pour l'adresse f; ~ **mapping** n COMP conversion d'adresses f; ~ **presentation restricted indicator** n TELECOM indicateur de restriction de divulgation d'adresse m; ~ **prompt** n (ADD) TELECOM incitation d'adressage f; ~ **register** n COMP registre d'adresse m; ~ **space** n COMP espace d'adressage m; ~ **stencil** n PACKAGING stencil pour l'adresse m; ~ **which pulses on and off** n PROD ENG adresse dont les changements d'état sont temporisés de 1 à 0 f

address[2] vt COMP adresser, CONST a project appréhender

addressable[1] *adj* COMP adressable

addressable:[2] **~ location** *n* COMP position adressable *f*

addressee *n* COMP destinataire *m*

addressing *n* COMP, TELECOM adressage *m*; **~ system** *n* COMP système d'adressage *m*

Addressograph *n* (TM) PRINT machine à adresser *f*

add-subtract: **~ time** *n* COMP temps d'addition ou de soustraction *m*

adduct *n* CHEM composé d'addition *m*

adduction *n* CHEM, HYDROL adduction *f*

adelpholite *n* MINERAL adelpholite *f*, adelpholithe *f*

adenine *n* CHEM, FOOD TECH adénine *f*

adenosine *n* CHEM adénosine *f*; **~ triphosphate** *n* FOOD TECH triphosphate d'adénosine *m*

ADF *abbr* (*automatic direction finding*) AERONAUT, TELECOM radiogoniométrie automatique *f*

adhere *vi* P&R, PACKAGING, PAPER TECH adhérer

adherence *n* PACKAGING, PAPER TECH adhérence *f*

adherend *n* P&R *adhesives* pièce à coller *f*, surface à coller *f*

adherent *adj* PAPER TECH adhérent

adhering: **~ nappe** *n* HYDROL nappe adhérente *f*

adherometer *n* P&R *instrument* adhésiomètre *m*

adhesion *n* COAL TECH, CONST adhérence *f*, P&R *of adhesive* adhérence *f*, adhésion *f*, PAPER TECH, RAIL *of wheels to rails* adhérence *f*; **~ coefficient** *n* AUTO coefficient d'adhérence *m*; **~ promoter** *n* P&R *adhesives* promoteur d'adhésion *m*; **~ railcar** *n* TRANSP automotrice à adhérence *f*; **~ strength test** *n* MECH ENG essai d'adhérence *m*; **~ system** *n* TRANSP système de guidage par adhérence *m*; **~ test** *n* P&R essai d'adhérence *m*

adhesive[1] *adj* P&R adhésif, PACKAGING collant, PAPER TECH adhésif

adhesive[2] *n* MECH *materials*, P&R, PRINT adhésif *m*, PROD ENG adhésif *m*, colle *f*; **~ applicator** *n* PACKAGING applicateur de colle *m*; **~ coating** *n* COATINGS couche adhésive *f*, PRINT couche adhésive *f*, enduction adhésive *f*; **~ disc** *n* (BrE) PACKAGING disque adhésif *m*; **~ disk** *n* (AmE) *see adhesive disc*; **~ film** *n* COATINGS couche mince de colle *f*, film adhésif *m*, PACKAGING couche mince de colle *f*; **~ fumes** *n pl* SAFETY vapeurs de colle *f pl*; **~ insulating tape** *n* ELEC ENG ruban isolant *m*; **~ machine** *n* PACKAGING machine d'encollage *f*; **~ shear strength** *n* P&R résistance au cisaillement *f*; **~ side** *n* PACKAGING côté adhésif *m*; **~ strength** *n* P&R force d'adhésion *f*; **~ surface** *n* PAPER TECH surface d'adhérence *f*; **~ tape** *n* ELEC ENG ruban isolant *m*, MECH *materials*, P&R, PACKAGING ruban adhésif *m*; **~ varnish** *n* COLOURS vernis adhésif *m*, vernis collant *m*

adhesiveness *n* PAPER TECH, PROP MAT adhésivité *f*

adiabatic[1] *adj* FLUID PHYS, MECH, PHYS, THERMOD adiabatique

adiabatic:[2] **~ change** *n* THERMOD changement adiabatique *m*; **~ coefficient** *n* THERMOD rapport des chaleurs spécifiques *m*; **~ compression** *n* FLUID PHYS, THERMOD compression adiabatique *f*; **~ curve** *n* PHYS, THERMOD courbe adiabatique *f*; **~ demagnetization** *n* PHYS démagnétisation adiabatique *f*, désaimantation adiabatique *f*; **~ efficiency** *n* PHYS, THERMOD rendement adiabatique *m*; **~ expansion** *n* PHYS dilatation adiabatique *f*, THERMOD détente adiabatique *f*; **~ invariant** *n* PHYS invariant adiabatique *m*; **~ lapse rate** *n* AERONAUT gradient adiabatique *m*, THERMOD vitesse adiabatique *f*; **~ pressure drop** *n* AERONAUT, FLUID PHYS détente adiabatique *f*; **~ process** *n* THERMOD transformation adiabatique *f*; **~ shockwave** *n* SPACE *spacecraft* onde de choc adiabatique *f*; **~ sound waves** *n pl* WAVE PHYS ondes sonores adiabatiques *f pl*; **~ system** *n* THERMOD système adiabatique *m*; **~ temperature gradient** *n* FLUID PHYS gradient de température adiabatique *m*; **~ transformation** *n* METALL transformation adiabatique *f*; **~ wall** *n* PHYS paroi adiabatique *f*

adiabatically *adv* FLUID PHYS, PHYS, THERMOD adiabatiquement

adiabatism *n* THERMOD adiabatisme *m*

adinole *n* GEOL adinole *f*

adipic[1] *adj* CHEM adipique

adipic:[2] **~ ester** *n* P&R ester adipique *m*

adipocerite *n* PHYS adipocérite *f*

adit *n* COAL TECH, MINING galerie à flanc de coteau *f*

adjacence *n* GEOM adjacence *f*

adjacency *n* GEOM adjacence *f*

adjacent[1] *adj* GEOM adjacent

adjacent:[2] **~ angles** *n pl* GEOM angles adjacents *m pl*; **~ bed effect** *n* PETR effet d'épontes *m*; **~ channel** *n* TV canal adjacent *m*; **~ channel interference** *n* RECORDING interférence de canal adjacent *f*; **~ channel rejection ratio** *n* TELECOM sélectivité pour la voie adjacente *f*; **~ channel selectivity** *n* TELECOM sélectivité vis à vis de la voie adjacente *f*; **~ coil** *n* ELEC ENG bobine voisine *f*; **~ sides** *n pl* GEOM côtés adjacents *m pl*; **~ waters** *n pl* OCEANOG eaux adjacentes *f pl*

adjust[1] *vt* CONST *levelling instrument* régler, MECH ajuster, mettre, régler, METR *microscope* mettre au point, NAUT *compass* compenser, PAPER TECH *shade* corriger, PRINT caler, PROD ENG *data table* dimensionner, SAFETY ajuster; **~ focus** *vt* CINEMAT faire la mise au point

adjust[2] *vi* PROD ENG *control* agir sur

adjustable[1] *adj* CONTROL, MECH, MECH ENG ajustable, réglable; **~ at will** *adj* MECH ENG librement réglable, réglable à volonté

adjustable:[2] **~ adaptor** *n* MECH ENG *for multispindle heads* douille de réglage *f*; **~ aperture** *n* PHYS diaphragme réglable *m*; **~ axle** *n* RAIL essieu mobile *m*; **~ blade reamer** *n* MECH ENG alésoir réglable *m*, alésoir à lames mobiles *m*, alésoir à lames rapportées *m*; **~ capacitor** *n* ELEC condensateur variable *m*, ELEC ENG condensateur ajustable *m*; **~ ceramic capacitor** *n* ELEC ENG condensateur céramique ajustable *m*; **~ core** *n* ELEC ENG noyau magnétique réglable *m*, noyau réglable *m*; **~ curtain wall** *n* C&G mur-rideau *m*; **~ discharge pump** *n* MECH ENG pompe à débit réglable *f*, pompe à débit variable *f*; **~ edge doctor blade** *n* PRINT racle à arêtes réglables *f*; **~ eyepiece** *n* CINEMAT, PHOTO oculaire réglable *m*; **~ gib** *n* MECH ENG lardon réglable *m*; **~ hacksaw frame** *n* MECH ENG monture réglable de scie à métaux *f*; **~ inductance** *n* ELEC inductance réglable *f*; **~ inductance coil** *n* ELEC bobine de réactance réactive *f*; **~ lens holder** *n* CINEMAT montage réglable *m*; **~ lens hood barrel** *n* CINEMAT soufflet réglable de contre-jour *m*; **~ nozzle** *n* MECH ENG buse réglable *f*, buse à débit variable *f*; **~ pitch propeller** *n* AERONAUT hélice à pas réglable *f*; **~ reamer** *n* MECH ENG alésoir expansible *m*, alésoir réglable *m*, alésoir à lames mobiles *m*, alésoir à lames rapportées *m*; **~ rear-view mirror** *n* VEHICLES rétroviseur orientable *m*; **~ resistor** *n* ELEC résistance variable *f*, ELEC ENG résistance ajustable *f*, résistance à collier *f*; **~ screw die** *n* SPRINGS coussinet de filière *m*; **~ short circuit** *n* ELEC ENG court-circuit réglable *m*, PHYS *waveguide* piston de court-circuit *m*, plongeur *m*; **~ shutter** *n* CINEMAT obturateur réglable *m*; **~ spanner** *n*

(BrE) *(cf adjustable spanner wrench, adjustable wrench)* MECH, MECH ENG, VEHICLES clé à molette *f*; ~ **speed motor** *n* ELEC moteur à vitesse réglable *m*, MECH moteur à vitesse variable *m*; ~ **stilt** *n* MINING allonge réglable pour pied de cadre *f*; ~ **stop** *n* CINEMAT, MECH, MECH ENG butée réglable *f*; ~ **submersion weir** *n* POLLUTION déversoir à immersion réglable *m*; ~ **transformer** *n* ELEC transformateur variable *m*; ~ **tripod** *n* METR trépied à coulisse *m*, pied à trois branches coulissantes *m*, trépied à coulisse *m*; ~ **trip setting** *n* PROD ENG courant de déclenchement réglable *m*; ~ **varying speed motor** *n* ELEC moteur à vitesse réglable et variable *m*; ~ **voltage divider** *n* ELEC diviseur de tension d'ajustement *m*; ~ **wrench** *n* (AmE) *(cf adjustable spanner)* MECH, MECH ENG, VEHICLES clé à molette *f*

adjusted *adj* PAPER TECH bien équilibré

adjuster *n* PAPER TECH régleur *m*

adjusting[1] *adj* CONTROL ajustable, de réglage, réglable, MECH ENG de réglage

adjusting[2] *n* PAPER TECH mise au point *f*; ~ **button** *n* CONTROL bouton de réglage *m*; ~ **circuit** *n* ELEC ENG circuit de compensation *m*; ~ **device** *n* CONTROL dispositif d'ajustage *m*, dispositif de réglage *m*, organe de réglage *m*, régleur d'ajustage *m*; ~ **gib** *n* MECH ENG lardon de réglage *m*; ~ **knob** *n* CONTROL bouton de réglage *m*, GEOPHYS bouton de mise au point *m*, bouton de réglage *m*, MECH bouton de réglage *m*; ~ **lever** *n* CONTROL levier de manoeuvre *m*; ~ **mechanism** *n* CONTROL organe de réglage *m*; ~ **motor** *n* CONTROL servomoteur *m*; ~ **nut** *n* CONTROL écrou de calage *m*, écrou de réglage *m*, écrou tendeur *m*; ~ **plate** *n* CONTROL plaque de réglage *f*; ~ **potentiometer** *n* AERONAUT potentiomètre de réglage *m*; ~ **rheostat** *n* CONTROL rhéostat d'ajustage *m*; ~ **ring** *n* CONTROL bague de réglage *f*; ~ **screw** *n* CONTROL vis calante *f*, vis d'ajustage *f*, vis régulatrice *f*, vis calante *f*, vis de réglage *f*, MECH, MECH ENG, PRINT, PROD ENG vis de réglage *f*; ~ **sleeve** *n* AUTO *motor* douille *f*, *steering* manchon de réglage *m*; ~ **spindle** *n* CONTROL broche de réglage *f*, tige de réglage *f*; ~ **telescope** *n* INSTRUMENT lunette d'approche de mise au point *f*; ~ **valve** *n* GAS TECH vanne de régulation *f*; ~ **voltage** *n* ELEC tension de réglage *f*

adjustment *n* CONTROL ajustage *m*, mise au point *f*, réglage *m*, CRYSTALL ajustement *m*, réglage *m*, ELECTRON, MECH ENG calage *m*, réglage *m*, METR ajustage *m*, *of a balance* ajustement *m*, PAPER TECH mise au point *f*, PRINT réglage *m*; ~ **button** *n* CONTROL bouton de réglage *m*; ~ **circuit** *n* CONTROL circuit de mise au point *m*; ~ **device** *n* CONTROL dispositif d'ajustage *m*, dispositif de réglage *m*; ~ **indicator** *n* CONTROL mécanisme indicateur de réglage *m*; ~ **instructions** *n pl* CONTROL instructions de réglage *f pl*; ~ **knob** *n* PHOTO bouton de mise au point *m*; ~ **nut** *n* CONTROL écrou de calage *m*, écrou de réglage *m*, écrou tendeur *m*; ~ **screw** *n* CONTROL vis calante *f*, vis d'ajustage *f*, vis régulatrice *f*, vis de calante *f*, vis de réglage *f*; ~ **spanner** *n* (BrE) *(cf adjustment wrench)* CONTROL clé de réglage *f*; ~ **spring** *n* CONTROL ressort de réglage *m*; ~ **of the stroke without stopping the machine** *n* MECH ENG réglage de la course pendant la marche de la machine *m*; ~ **washer** *n* CONTROL rondelle d'ajustage *f*; ~ **wrench** *n* (AmE) *(cf adjustment spanner)* CONTROL clé de réglage *f*

adjuvant *n* COAL TECH additif *m*, adjuvant *m*

administration: ~ **building** *n* MINING bâtiment administratif *m*

administrative: ~ **area** *n* CONST circonscription administrative *f*, section administrative *f*; ~ **processor** *n* TELECOM calculateur de gestion *m*; ~ **unit** *n* (AU) TELECOM unité administrative *f* (UAD); ~ **unit group** *n* TELECOM GUA, groupe d'unités administratives *m*

admiral *n* NAUT amiral *m*

Admiralty: ~ **chart** *n* (BrE) NAUT carte hydrographique *f*

admissible: ~ **claim** *n* PATENTS revendication autorisée *f*; ~ **interrupting current** *n* ELEC *circuit breaker* courant admissible de coupure *m*

admission: ~ **valve** *n* MECH ENG soupape d'admission *f*

admittance *n* ELEC *AC circuit*, ELEC ENG, PHYS admittance *f*

admix *n* C&G retour des déchets *m*

admixture *n* CONST *concrete mixing* adjuvant *m*, P&R *ingredient* mélange additionnel *m*, TEXTILES mélange *m*

adobe *n* C&G brique crue *f*

adornment *n* PRINT ornement *m*

ADP *abbr (automatic data processing)* COMP traitement automatique de données *m*

ADPCM[1] *abbr (adaptive differential pulse code modulation)* TELECOM MICDA *(modulation par impulsion et codage différentiels adaptatifs)*

ADPCM:[2] ~ **decoder** *n* TELECOM décodeur MICDA *m*; ~ **encoder** *n* TELECOM codeur MICDA *m*

adrift[1] *adj* NAUT en dérive, à la dérive

adrift[2] *adv* NAUT en dérive, à la dérive

adsorb *vt* COAL TECH adsorber

adsorbable *adj* CHEM qui peut être absorbé

adsorbent *n* CHEM adsorbant *m*, FOOD TECH agent adsorbant *m*

adsorber *n* GAS TECH adsorbeur *m*

adsorption *n* CHEM, COAL TECH, FOOD TECH, HYDROL, P&R, PROP MAT, WATER SUPP adsorption *f*; ~ **heat** *n* NUCLEAR chaleur d'adsorption *f*; ~ **isotherm** *n* NUCLEAR isotherme d'adsorption *f*; ~ **trap** *n* NUCLEAR piège à absorption *m*

ad-stack *n* PRINT colonne des petites annonces classées *f*

ADT *abbr (average daily traffic)* TRANSP débit journalier moyen

adularia *n* MINERAL adulaire *f*

adulterant *n* FOOD TECH adultérant *m*

adulterate *vt* FOOD TECH adultérer

adulterated *adj* FOOD TECH adultéré, falsifié

advance[1] *n* ASTRON *of perihelion* avance *f*, CINEMAT *picture in relation to sound* décalage image *m*, décalage son *m*, COAL TECH, ELEC *phase*, MECH ENG, PHYS *of perihelion*, VEHICLES *ignition* avance *f*; ~ **angle** *n* ELEC angle d'avance *m*; ~ **ball** *n* ACOUSTICS patin *m*; ~ **booking charter** *n* AERONAUT vol affrété avec réservation à l'avance *m*; ~ **classification track** *n* RAIL voie de sous-triage *f*; ~ **copy** *n* PRINT copie d'avance *f*; ~ **diameter ratio** *n* AERONAUT *propeller* paramètre de similitude *m*; ~ **information** *n* TRANSP information prédictive *f*; ~ **mechanism** *n* VEHICLES *ignition* dispositif d'avance *m*, variateur d'avance *m*; ~ **mining** *n* MINING exploitation en avant *f*; ~ **purchase excursion fare** *n* *(APEX fare)* AERONAUT tarif excursion avec achat anticipé *m*; ~ **termination** *n* PROD ENG réalisation anticipée *f*; ~ **warning sign** *n* CONTROL signal avancé *m*

advance:[2] ~ **the throttle** *vi* AERONAUT mettre les gaz

advanced: ~ **airborne fire support system** *n* AERONAUT système aérien d'appui feu avancé *m*; ~ **fuel cycle** *n*

NUCLEAR cycle à combustible avancé *m*; ~ **passenger train** *n (APT)* RAIL train expérimental à grande vitesse *m*, train à grande vitesse *m (TGV)*; ~ **signal processing** *n* ELECTRON traitement élaboré des signaux *m*; ~ **technology** *n* COMP, DP technologie de pointe *f*

advancing: ~ **blade** *n* AERONAUT pale avançante *f*; ~ **blade concept** *n* AERONAUT *rotary winged aircraft* concept de pale avançante *m*; ~ **blade concept helicopter** *n* TRANSP hélicoptère ABC *m*; ~ **face** *n* COAL TECH front d'avancement *m*

advantage *n* PATENTS avantage *m*; ~ **factor** *n* NUCLEAR facteur d'avantage *m*

advection *n* METEO, PHYS advection *f*

advertise *vi* PRINT passer une annonce

advertisement *n* PRINT annonce *f*; ~ **layout** *n* PRINT maquette de composition des annonces *f*; ~ **page** *n* PRINT page d'annonces *f*

advertising: ~ **department** *n* PRINT service des annonces *m*; ~ **photography** *n* PHOTO photographie publicitaire *f*; ~ **slot** *n* TV créneau publicitaire *m*

advise: ~ **duration and charge** *n* TELECOM indication verbale des éléments de taxation *f*

advisory: ~ **diversion** *n* TRANSP déviation recommandée *f*; ~ **message** *n* TRANSP message recommandé *m*

adze *n* CONST doloire *f*, herminette *f*

AE *abbr (application entry)* TELECOM entité d'application *f*

aegirine *n* MINERAL aegirine *f*, aegyrine *f*

aegirite *n* MINERAL aegirine *f*, aegyrine *f*

aegyrite *n* MINERAL aegirine *f*, aegyrine *f*

aenigmatite *n* MINERAL aenigmatite *f*

aeolian *adj* GEOL *erosion*, PETR éolien

aerate *vt* COAL TECH aérer, ventiler, CONST aérer, FOOD TECH aérer, battre en neige, foisonner, ventiler, PRINT *paper* aérer, déramer, RECYCLING aérer

aerated: ~ **mud** *n* PETR boue allégée *f*, PETR TECH boue allégée *f*, boue aérée *f*

aeration *n* COAL TECH aérage *m*, aération *f*, CONST, HYDROL *sewage* aération *f*, PACKAGING ventilation d'air *f*, RECYCLING aération *f*; ~ **basin** *n* WATER SUPP bassin d'aération *m*; ~ **tank** *n* RECYCLING bassin d'aération *m*; ~ **time** *n* HYDROL *sewage* temps de contact *m*

aerator *n* AERONAUT aérateur *m*, bouche de soufflage *f*, bouche de ventilation individuelle *f*, RECYCLING aérateur *m*; ~ **muffler** *n* (AmE) *(cf aerator silencer)* AERONAUT silencieux de soufflage *m*; ~ **silencer** *n* (BrE) *(cf aerator muffler)* AERONAUT silencieux de soufflage *m*

aeraulics *n* GAS TECH aéraulique *f*

aerial[1] *adj* AERONAUT aérien

aerial[2] *n* NAUT *radio, radar*, PHYS *antenna*, TELECOM, TV, VEHICLES antenne *f*; ~ **cable** *n* ELEC ENG, TELECOM câble aérien *m*; ~ **camera** *n* CINEMAT caméra pour prise de vue aérienne *f*; ~ **collision** *n* AERONAUT abordage aérien *m*, collision aérienne *f*, collision en vol *f*; ~ **conveyor** *n* PACKAGING transporteur aérien *m*; ~ **directivity** *n* TV directivité d'antenne *f*; ~ **efficiency** *n* TV coefficient de rayonnement de l'antenne *m*; ~ **fog** *n* CINEMAT voile atmosphérique *m*; ~ **gain** *n* PHYS, TV gain d'antenne *m*; ~ **guideway** *n* TRANSP voie en surélévation *f*, voie surélevée *f*; ~ **image** *n* CINEMAT image virtuelle *f*; ~ **image animation** *n* CINEMAT animation avec image virtuelle *f*; ~ **insulated cable** *n* ELEC câble aérien isolé *m*; ~ **lead** *n* TV descente d'antenne *f*; ~ **line** *n* ELEC *supply network* ligne aérienne *f*; ~ **mapping camera** *n* PHOTO chambre de photogrammétrie aérienne *f*; ~ **mast** *n* NAUT pylône d'antenne *m*, TELECOM, TV mât d'antenne *m*; ~ **matching** *n* TELECOM adaptation d'impédance *f*; ~ **motion picture survey** *n* TRANSP étude par procédé aérocinématographique *f*; ~ **photographic survey** *n* GEOL photogrammétrie aérienne *f*; ~ **photography** *n* PHOTO prise de vues aériennes *f*; ~ **reconnaissance** *n* MAR POLL observation aérienne *f*; ~ **resistance** *n* PHYS résistance d'antenne *f*; ~ **shot** *n* CINEMAT plan tourné en vol *m*; ~ **surveillance** *n* MAR POLL surveillance aérienne *f*; ~ **survey** *n* AERONAUT levé aérien *m*, TRANSP étude par photographies aériennes *f*; ~ **terminal** *n* TV borne d'antenne *f*

aerification *n* CHEM aérification *f*

aerobatics *n* AERONAUT acrobaties aériennes *f pl*

aerobic[1] *adj* FOOD TECH *bacteria* aérobe, aérobie, HYDROL *sewage*, RECYCLING aérobie

aerobic[2] *n* FOOD TECH aérobie *m*; ~ **digester** *n* RECYCLING digesteur aérobie *m*; ~ **digestion** *n* RECYCLING digestion aérobie *f*; ~ **fermentation** *n* FOOD TECH fermentation aérobie *f*; ~ **sludge digestion** *n* WATER SUPP digestion aérobie des boues *f*

aerobiology *n* METEO aérobiologie *f*

aerobiosis *n* RECYCLING aérobiose *f*

aerobrake *vi* SPACE *spacecraft* exécuter un freinage aérodynamique

aerobridge *n* AERONAUT passerelle télescopique *f*

aerobus *n* TRANSP aérobus *m*

aerodrome *n* (BrE) AERONAUT aérodrome *m*

aerodynamic[1] *adj* PHYS, TRANSP aérodynamique

aerodynamic:[2] ~ **axis** *n* NAUT *ship design* axe de poussée *m*; ~ **balance** *n* AERONAUT balance aérodynamique *f*; ~ **braking** *n* SPACE *spacecraft* freinage aérodynamique *m*; ~ **center** *n* (AmE), ~ **centre** *n* (BrE) AERONAUT foyer d'un profil aérodynamique *m*, NAUT *ship design* centre de poussée *m*; ~ **coefficient** *n* SPACE coefficient aérodynamique *m*; ~ **control surface** *n* SPACE gouverne aérodynamique *f*; ~ **drag** *n* TRANSP résistance aérodynamique *f*; ~ **efficiency** *n* AERONAUT finesse aérodynamique *f*; ~ **factor** *n* AERONAUT coefficient aérodynamique *m*; ~ **form** *n* VEHICLES forme aérodynamique *f*; ~ **heating** *n* SPACE *spacecraft* échauffement cinétique *m*; ~ **lag** *n* AERONAUT retard aérodynamique *m*; ~ **lift** *n* TRANSP portance aérodynamique *f*; ~ **load** *n* AERONAUT charge aérodynamique *f*; ~ **mast** *n* NAUT mât profilé *m*; ~ **missile** *n* MILIT missile aérodynamique *m*; ~ **noise** *n* AERONAUT bruit de cellule *m*; ~ **power** *n* FUELLESS puissance aérodynamique *f*; ~ **pressure** *n* AERONAUT poussée aérodynamique *f*; ~ **shape** *n* VEHICLES forme aérodynamique *f*, profil aérodynamique *m*; ~ **twist** *n* AERONAUT torsion aérodynamique *f*

aerodynamical: ~ **levitation** *n* TRANSP résistance aérodynamique *f*

aerodynamics *n* METEO, NAUT *boat design*, PHYS, TRANSP aérodynamique *f*

aerodynamic-type: ~ **air cushion vehicle** *n* TRANSP aéroglisseur à sustentation aérodynamique *m*

aeroelasticity *n* FUELLESS *wind power*, NUCLEAR aéroélasticité *f*

aeroembolism *n* OCEANOG aéroembolisme *m*

aerofoil *n* (BrE) AERONAUT profil aérodynamique *m*, FUELLESS plan de sustentation *m*, NAUT *ship, boat design* plan à profilé d'aile *m*, surface portante *f*; ~ **chord** *n* (BrE) AERONAUT corde de profil *f*; ~ **de-icing** *n* (BrE) AERONAUT dégivrage planeur *m*; ~ **de-icing valve** *n* (BrE) AERONAUT vanne de dégivrage planeur *f*;

~ **fan** *n* (BrE) REFRIG ventilateur à aubes profilées *m*; ~ **hull** *n* (BrE) NAUT coque à ailes aériennes *f*

aeroglide *n* TRANSP goulotte à coussin d'air *f*

aerograph *n* PRINT aérographe *m*

aerography *n* C&G aérographie *f*

aerolite *n* ASTRON aérolithe *m*, SPACE météorite pierreuse *f*

aerology *n* METEO aérologie *f*

aeromagnetic[1] *adj* GEOL aéromagnétométrique, PETR aéromagnétique, magnétique aéroporté

aeromagnetic:[2] ~ **survey** *n* GEOL levé aéromagnétique *m*; ~ **train** *n* TRANSP train aéromagnétique *m*

aerometer *n* PAPER TECH, PHYS aéromètre *m*

aerometry *n* PAPER TECH, PHYS aérométrie *f*

aeronautical: ~ **chart** *n* (BrE) *(cf sectional chart)* AERONAUT carte aéronautique *f*; ~ **fixed circuit** *n* AERONAUT circuit fixe aéronautique *m*; ~ **fixed network** *n* (AmE) *(cf aeronautical fixed service)* AERONAUT service fixe aéronautique *m*; ~ **fixed service** *n* (BrE) *(cf aeronautical fixed network, aeronautical fixed system)* AERONAUT service fixe aéronautique *m*; ~ **fixed station** *n* AERONAUT station fixe aéronautique *f*; ~ **fixed system** *n* (AmE) *(cf aeronautical fixed service)* AERONAUT service fixe aéronautique *m*; ~ **fixed telecommunication network** *n* AERONAUT réseau du service fixe des télécommunications aéronautiques *m*; ~ **information circular** *n* AERONAUT circulaire d'information aéronautique *f*; ~ **information service** *n* AERONAUT service d'information aéronautique *m*; ~ **meteorological station** *n* AERONAUT station météorologique aéronautique *f*; ~ **mobile satellite service** *n* SPACE *communications* service mobile aéronautique par satellite *m*; ~ **radio navigation service** *n* AERONAUT service de radionavigation aéronautique *m*; ~ **register** *n* AERONAUT registre aéronautique *m*; ~ **route chart** *n* AERONAUT carte de navigation *f*, routier aéronautique *m*

aeronautics *n* AERONAUT, TRANSP navigation aérienne *f*

aeronomy *n* SPACE aéronomie *f*

aeroplane *n* (BrE) AERONAUT avion *m*; ~ **mass ratio** *n* (BrE) AERONAUT paramètre de masse de l'avion *m*; ~ **tow launch** *n* (BrE) TRANSP remorquage *m*

aeropulse *n* TRANSP pulsoréacteur *m*

aerosite *n* MINERAL aérosite *f*

aeroslides *n pl* MECH ENG *handling equipment* glissières pneumatiques *f pl*, glissières à coussin d'air *f pl*

aerosol *n* METEO, PACKAGING, PHYS, POLLUTION, PROP MAT aérosol *m*; ~ **and dust measuring and analysis apparatus** *n* SAFETY appareils de mesure et d'analyse pour aérosols et poussières *m pl*; ~ **can** *n* PACKAGING boîte aérosol *f*; ~ **cap** *n* PACKAGING capsule d'aérosol *f*; ~ **container** *n* MECH ENG bombe *f*, boîte aérosol *f*, PACKAGING emballage aérosol *m*; ~ **packing** *n* PACKAGING emballage aérosol *m*; ~ **propellant** *n* PETR TECH gaz propulseur *m*; ~ **spray container** *n* MECH ENG boîte de pulvérisateur par pression *f*; ~ **valve** *n* PACKAGING clapet d'aérosol *m*

aerospace[1] *adj* SPACE aérospatial

aerospace:[2] ~ **medicine** *n* SPACE médecine aérospatiale *f*

aerospatial *adj* SPACE aérospatial

aerostatics *n* METEO aérostatique *f*

aerostatic-type: ~ **air cushion vehicle** *n* TRANSP aéroglisseur à sustentation aérostatique *m*

aerothermodynamic: ~ **duct** *n* TRANSP statoréacteur *m*

aerotow: ~ **flight** *n* AERONAUT, TRANSP vol à la remorque *m*

aerotrain *n* TRANSP aérotrain *m*

AES *abbr (Auger electron spectroscopy)* PHYS spectroscopie électronique Auger *f*

aeschynite *n* MINERAL aeschynite *f*, eschynite *f*

aesculin *n* CHEM aesculine *f*

aethogen *n* CHEM éthogène *m*

AF *abbr (audio frequency)* ACOUSTICS, ELECTRON, RECORDING, TELECOM, WAVE PHYS audiofréquence *f*, fréquence audible *f*

AFC *abbr (automatic frequency control)* CONTROL, ELEC, ELECTRON, PHYS, PROD ENG, RECORDING, TELECOM, TV CAF *(contrôle automatique de fréquence)*

AFD *abbr (accelerated freeze-drying)* FOOD TECH lyophilisation accélérée *f*

affiliate *n* TV station satellite *f*

affine: ~ **geometry** *n* GEOM géométrie affine *f*; ~ **transformation** *n* METALL transformation affine *f*

affinity *n* CHEM affinité *f*

affluent: ~ **stream** *n* HYDROL ruisseau affluent *m*

affusion *n* CHEM affusion *f*

AFI *abbr (authority and format identifier)* TELECOM identificateur d'autorité et de format *m*

aflatoxin *n* FOOD TECH *phytopathology* aflatoxine *f*

aft[1] *adv* NAUT, SPACE à l'arrière

aft[2] *n* NAUT arrière *m*; ~ **bay** *n* WATER SUPP arrière-bief *m*, bief d'aval *m*; ~ **gate** *n* WATER SUPP *of canal lock* porte d'aval *f*; ~ **perpendicular** *n* NAUT *ship design* perpendiculaire arrière *f*; ~ **rake** *n* NAUT élancement arrière *m*; ~ **section** *n* NAUT *of ship* section arrière *f*; ~ **stay** *n* NAUT *of standing rigging* étai arrière *m*

after:[1] ~ **ageing** *adj* (BrE) P&R après vieillissement; ~ **aging** *adj* (AmE) *see after ageing*

after:[2] ~ **sales service** *n* CONST, QUALITY service après vente *m*; ~ **sales servicing** *n* QUALITY soutien après vente *m*

afterblow *n* PROD ENG *steel manufacture* sursoufflage *m*

afterbody *n* SPACE *spacecraft* arrière-corps *m*, partie solidaire du satellite après séparation *f*

afterburner *n* AERONAUT, MECH ENG postcombustion *f*, NUCLEAR *of incinerator* four à postcombustion *m*, PROP MAT chambre de postcombustion *f*, THERMOD *of jet engine* brûleur de postcombustion *m*, chambre de postcombustion *f*, TRANSP dispositif de réchauffe *m*, postbrûleur *m*, VEHICLES *of engine* dispositif de postcombustion *m*, tuyère de postcombustion *f*

afterburning *n* THERMOD postcombustion *f*, réchauffe *f*

aftercooler *n* HEAT ENG radiateur secondaire *m*

afterdamp *n* MINING *gas* mofette *f*

afterdeck *n* NAUT arrière-pont *m*, dunette *f*, gaillard arrière *m*, plage arrière *f*, pont arrière *m*, pont de gaillard arrière *m*, pont de la dunette *m*

afterdryer *n* PAPER TECH postsécheur *m*

aftereffect *n* PHYS, RAD PHYS rémanence *f*

afterglow *n* COMP persistance lumineuse *f*, ELECTRON persistance *f*, NAUT *radar* rémanence *f*, PAPER TECH incandescence résiduelle *f*, RAD PHYS *radiative decay* dernières lueurs *f pl*, SPACE traînée lumineuse *f*, THERMOD incandescence résiduelle *f*, TV persistance *f*, phosphorescence *f*, traînage *m*

afterheat *n* AERONAUT chaleur rémanente *f*, chaleur résiduelle *f*; ~ **release** *n* NUCLEAR dégagement de chaleur résiduelle *m*

afterimage *n* CINEMAT persistance *f*, TV traînage *m*

after-shrinkage *adj* PACKAGING après rétrécissement

AFV *abbr (armoured fighting vehicle, armored fighting vehicle)* MILIT véhicule blindé de combat *m*

afwillite n MINERAL afwillite f
Ag (silver) CHEM Ag (argent)
against: ~ **the grain** adv PRINT en sens travers; ~ **the light** adv CINEMAT, PHOTO contre-jour; ~ **text** adv PRINT face texte
agalite n MINERAL, PAPER TECH agalite f, PRINT poudre d'amiante f
agalmatolite n MINERAL agalmatolite f, agalmatolithe f, koréite f
agaphite n MINERAL agaric fossile m, agaric minéral m, agarice f
agar: ~ **slant** n FOOD TECH gélose inclinée f
agar-agar n FOOD TECH agar m, agar-agar m, gélose f
agaric: ~ **mineral** n MINERAL agaric fossile m, agaric minéral m, agarice f
agate n C&G, MINERAL agate f; ~ **line** n PRINT ligne agate f; ~ **mortar** n CHEM, PROP MAT mortier d'agate m; ~ **ware** n C&G articles en agate m pl
agaty adj MINERAL agaté
AGC abbr (automatic gain control) CONTROL CAG (contrôle automatique de gain), ELECTRON CAG (commande automatique de gain), GEOPHYS CAG (contrôle automatique de gain), RECORDING réglage automatique du gain m, TELECOM CAG (commande automatique de gain)
age[1] n GEOL, PETR âge m; ~ **dating** n GEOL datation f; ~ **hardening** n CRYSTALL, METALL, P&R durcissement par vieillissement m, PROP MAT durcissement structural m, SPRINGS durcissement structural m, vieillissement par écrouissage m; ~ **of the universe** n ASTRON âge de l'univers m
age[2] vt METALL, PAPER TECH vieillir, THERMOD metals mûrir, tremper, vieillir
AGE abbr (allyl glycidyl ether) P&R éther allylglycidique m
aged adj PROP MAT, THERMOD vieilli
ageing n (BrE) C&G of glass, thermometer pourrissage m, CINEMAT of film stock, CONST, CRYSTALL of alloy, ELEC of equipment vieillissement m, FOOD TECH bakery, milling maturation f, P&R of coatings, PACKAGING maturation f, vieillissement m, PAPER TECH, PRINT vieillissement m, REFRIG of meat maturation f, TELECOM vieillissement m; ~ **room** n (BrE) REFRIG chambre de maturation f; ~ **study** n (BrE) SPACE étude de vieillissement f; ~ **test** n (BrE) PACKAGING essai de la maturation m
ageing-resistant adj (BrE) PACKAGING résistant au vieillissement
agency n AERONAUT organisme m, PROP MAT, TEXTILES agence f
agene n FOOD TECH agène m
agent n CHEM, COAL TECH, TEXTILES agent m
agglomerate[1] n GEOL brèche volcanique à gros fragments f, PETR agglomérat m
agglomerate[2] vti CHEM TECH, COAL TECH, PAPER TECH agglomérer
agglomerated adj PAPER TECH aggloméré
agglomerating: ~ **plant** n CHEM TECH installation d'agglomération f
agglomeration n CHEM TECH, P&R pigments, fillers, PAPER TECH agglomération f
agglomerative adj PAPER TECH agglomératif
agglutinate[1] vt CHEM TECH agglutiner, joindre avec de la colle
agglutinate[2] vi CHEM s'agglutiner
agglutination n CHEM, CHEM TECH, FOOD TECH agglutina-

tion f
agglutinative adj CHEM TECH agglutinant, collant, PROP MAT agglutinant
agglutinin n FOOD TECH agglutinine f
aggradation n WATER SUPP aggradation f, atterrissement m
aggradational: ~ **deposit** n WATER SUPP couche alluvionnaire f
aggrade vt GEOL alluvionner
aggregate[1] n C&G, COAL TECH agrégat m, CONST agrégat m, gravier m, gravier à béton m, METALL, PRINT, PROP MAT agrégat m; ~ **abrasion value** n (AA) CONST coefficient d'abrasion de gravier m; ~ **cooling** n REFRIG refroidissement des agrégats m; ~ **crushing value** n CONST coefficient d'écrasement de gravier m; ~ **output** n PROD ENG rendement d'ensemble m, rendement total m; ~ **scraper** n TRANSP benne racleuse f; ~ **signal** n TELECOM signal composite m; ~ **stripping** n CONST bitumen défrichage m, désenrobage m; ~ **stripping test** n CONST essai de désenrobage m
aggregate[2] vi GEOL s'agglomérer, s'agréger
aggression n HYDROL agressivité f
aggressive: ~ **water** n HYDROL, WATER SUPP eau aggressive f
aging n (AmE) see ageing
aging-resistant adj (AmE) see ageing-resistant
agitate vt CHEM TECH agiter, brasser, remuer, PAPER TECH agiter, PHOTO, PRINT agiter, remuer
agitating: ~ **machine** n CHEM TECH agitateur m, brasseur m; ~ **mixer** n CHEM TECH agitateur mélangeur m, mélangeur agitateur m, mélangeur brasseur m; ~ **vessel** n CHEM TECH bac à agitation m
agitator n CHEM TECH agitateur m, brasseur m, COAL TECH, FOOD TECH, MECH ENG, PAPER TECH, PETR TECH agitateur m
agonic: ~ **line** n GEOPHYS isogone f, ligne agonique f
agreed: ~ **spillover** n TV of satellite window débordement toléré m
agreement: ~ **residual** n NUCLEAR facteur R m
agricolite n MINERAL agricolite f, agricolithe f
agricultural: ~ **machine** n MECH machine agricole f
agrobusiness n FOOD TECH EEC agroindustrie f
aground[1] adj NAUT au plain, au plein, au sec, échoué
aground[2] adv NAUT au plain, au plein, au sec
ahead[1] adj SPACE frontal
ahead[2] adv NAUT de l'avant, devant, en avant, sur l'avant, SPACE en avant
ahull[1] adj NAUT à la cape sèche
ahull[2] adv NAUT à la cape sèche
AI abbr COMP (artificial intelligence), TELECOM (artificial intelligence) IA (intelligence artificielle), TELECOM (articulation index) IN (indice de netteté)
AIA abbr (audio indicate active) TELECOM indication audio active f
aids: ~ **to navigation** n pl NAUT aides à la navigation f pl
aigrette n GEOPHYS aigrette f
aiguille n MINING blasting needle aiguille f, épinglette f
aikinite n MINERAL aikinite f
aileron n AERONAUT aileron m; ~ **control** n AERONAUT commande de gauchissement f; ~ **control wheel** n AERONAUT volant d'aileron m; ~ **deflection** n AERONAUT braquage d'ailerons m; ~ **follow-up** n AERONAUT transmetteur de gauchissement m; ~ **position indicator** n AERONAUT indicateur de position de gauchissement m
AIM abbr (audio indicate muted) TELECOM indication

audio muette *f*

ainalite *n* MINERAL ainalite *f*

air:[1] **on ~** *adj* TV sur l'antenne, à l'antenne

air:[2]

~ b ~ **bag** *n* AUTO sac gonflable *m*; ~ **bar** *n* PRINT barre soufflante *f*, barre à air *f*; ~ **base** *n* TRANSP base aérienne *f*; ~ **bearing** *n* CINEMAT roulement sur coussin d'air *m*; ~ **bell** *n* C&G, CINEMAT bulle d'air *f*, PAPER TECH soufflette *f*; ~ **blade** *n* PAPER TECH lame d'air *f*; ~ **blast** *n* COAL TECH déflagration aérienne *f*, MINING chasse d'air *f*, PROP MAT jet d'air *m*; ~ **blast breaker** *n* ELEC *circuit breaker* disjoncteur pneumatique *m*, disjoncteur à air comprimé *m*, disjoncteur à soufflage d'air *m*; ~ **blast burner** *n* MECH ENG brûleur à courant d'air *m*; ~ **blast circuit breaker** *n* ELEC ENG disjoncteur pneumatique *m*, disjoncteur à air comprimé *m*; ~ **blast cooling** *n* REFRIG refroidissement par jet d'air *m*, refroidissement par soufflerie *m*; ~ **blast freezer** *n* REFRIG congélateur à air forcé *m*; ~ **blast freezing** *n* REFRIG congélation ventilée *f*; ~ **blasting** *n* PROP MAT jets d'air *m pl*; ~ **blast labeling** *n* (AmE), ~ **blast labelling** *n* (BrE) PACKAGING étiquetage par air soufflé *m*; ~ **blast refining** *n* METALL, PROP MAT affinage au vent *m*; ~ **blast switch** *n* ELEC *circuit breaker* disjoncteur à air comprimé *m*, disjoncteur à soufflage d'air *m*; ~ **blast transformer** *n* ELEC transformateur à refroidissement par l'air soufflé *m*; ~ **bleed valve** *n* AERONAUT soupape de prélèvement d'air *f*, FOOD TECH *vacuum processing* soupape d'évacuation d'air *f*; ~ **blowing** *n* MECH ENG soufflerie *f*, ventilation forcée *f*; ~ **bottle** *n* HEAT ENG *hot water heating systems* accumulateur aérohydraulique *m*; ~ **box** *n* MECH ENG boîte à air *f*, boîte à vent *f*, réservoir d'air *m*, MINING caisson d'aérage *m*, PETR TECH boîte à air *f*, caisson d'aérage *m*; ~ **brake** *n* AERONAUT aérofrein *m*, MECH *vehicles* frein à air comprimé *m*, MECH ENG frein pneumatique *m*, frein à air comprimé *m*, VEHICLES frein pneumatique *m*; ~ **brake hose** *n* MECH ENG tuyauterie souple d'alimentation de frein pneumatique *f*, P&R tuyau de frein à air *m*; ~ **brattice** *n* MINING cloison d'aérage *f*; ~ **breaker** *n* ELEC *switch* disjoncteur à air *m*, disjoncteur à coupuredans l'air *m*; ~ **break switch** *n* ELEC ENG disjoncteur pneumatique *m*; ~ **breather** *n* PROD ENG reniflard *m*; ~ **breathing engine** *n* AERONAUT moteur aérobie *m*; ~ **bridge** *n* AERONAUT passerelle téléscopique *f*; ~ **bubble** *n* PHYS, PRINT bulle d'air *f*; ~ **bubble bag** *n* PACKAGING sac avec bulles d'air *m*; ~ **bubble cushioning** *n* PACKAGING amortissement avec bulles d'air *m*; ~ **bubble wrap** *n* PACKAGING emballage avec bulles d'air *m*;

~ c ~ **capacitor** *n* ELEC, PHYS condensateur à air *m*; ~ **cargo** *n* PACKAGING cargaison d'avion *f*; ~ **cell** *n* ELEC ENG pile à dépolarisation par l'air *f*; ~ **cell diesel engine** *n* AUTO moteur diesel à chambre d'accumulation *m*; ~ **charging valve** *n* AERONAUT clapet de gonflage *m*; ~ **chuck** *n* MECH ENG, PRINT mandrin pneumatique *m*; ~ **circuit breaker** *n* ELEC *switch* disjoncteur à air *m*, disjoncteur à coupure dans l'air *m*; ~ **classification** *n* FOOD TECH séparation par air *f*; ~ **cleaner** *n* COAL TECH épurateur d'air *m*, MECH ENG, VEHICLES *carburettor* filtre à air *m*, épurateur d'air *m*; ~ **cleaning** *n* COAL TECH épuration de l'air *f*; ~ **clutch** *n* MECH ENG embrayage pneumatique *m*; ~ **column loudspeaker** *n* RECORDING haut-parleur à colonne d'air *m*; ~ **combat simulator** *n* MILIT simulateur de combat aérien *m*; ~ **compressor** *n* AUTO compresseur

de frein *m*, HYDR EQUIP, LAB EQUIP, MECH, MECH ENG compresseur d'air *m*; ~ **compressor set** *n* MECH ENG groupe de compresseur d'air *m*; ~ **conditioner** *n* AUTO climatiseur *m*, MECH ENG conditionneur d'air *m*, VEHICLES climatiseur *m*; ~ **conditioning** *n* HEATING climatisation *f*, conditionnement d'air *m*, MECH ENG climatisation *f*, conditionnement d'air *m*, METEO, PAPER TECH, REFRIG climatisation *f*, SAFETY conditionnement d'air *m*; ~ **conditioning installations** *n pl* SAFETY installations de conditionnement d'air *f pl*; ~ **conditioning master valve** *n* MECH ENG vanne de climatisation *f*; ~ **conditioning plant** *n* HEATING, REFRIG installation de conditionnement d'air *f*; ~ **conditioning unit** *n* REFRIG climatiseur *m*, conditionneur d'air *m*; ~ **conduction** *n* ACOUSTICS conduction aérienne *f*; ~ **conduit** *n* MECH ENG conduit d'air *m*, conduit à vent *m*; ~ **connection** *n* MECH ENG raccord d'air *m*; ~ **coolant** *n* NUCLEAR air de refroidissement *m*, aéroréfrigérant *m*; ~ **cooler** *n* NUCLEAR aéroréfrigérant *m*, réfrigérant atmosphérique *m*, REFRIG refroidisseur à air *m*; ~ **cooling** *n* AUTO, ELEC ENG refroidissement par l'air *m*, MECH ENG ventilation d'air frais *f*; ~ **core** *n* ELEC ENG noyau à air *m*; ~ **core inductance** *n* ELEC bobine sans noyau de fer *f*; ~ **core transformer** *n* ELEC transformateur sans noyau de fer *m*, ELEC ENG transformateur sans fer *m*, transformateur sans noyau *m*, transformateur sans noyau magnétique *m*, transformateur à air *m*; ~ **core winding** *n* SPACE *spacecraft* bobinage sans fer *m*, bobinage à air *m*; ~ **correction jet** *n* AUTO ajutage d'automaticité *m*; ~ **corridor** *n* AERONAUT couloir aérien *m*; ~ **course** *n* NAUT *shipbuilding* virure d'aération *f*; ~ **cross bleed valve** *n* AERONAUT clapet d'intercommunication d'air *m*; ~ **cure** *n* P&R vulcanisation en étuve *f*; ~ **curtain** *n* HEATING, REFRIG, TRANSP rideau d'air *m*; ~ **curtain installation** *n* SAFETY *for open doors* installation de rideaux d'air chaud *f*; ~ **cushion** *n* AERONAUT coussin d'air *m*, matelas d'air *m*, MECH ENG *handling equipment*, NAUT *hovercraft*, TRANSP coussin d'air *m*; ~ **cushion levitation** *n* TRANSP sustentation par coussin d'air *f*; ~ **cushion restraint system** *n* TRANSP coussin d'air à gonflage instantané *m*; ~ **cushion vehicle** *n* NAUT aéroglisseur *m*, véhicule sur coussin d'air *m*, TRANSP véhicule à coussin d'air *m*; ~ **cycle refrigeration machine** *n* REFRIG machine frigorifique à air *f*; ~ **cylinder** *n* MECH *systems* bouteille d'air *f*, MECH ENG vérin pneumatique *m*, PRINT rouleau pneumatique *m*;

~ d ~ **dashpot** *n* AERONAUT amortisseur pneumatique *m*; ~ **data computer** *n* AERONAUT centrale aérodynamique *f*; ~ **date** *n* TV date de passage à l'antenne *f*; ~ **defence** *n* MILIT DCA, défense contre avions *f*; ~ **defence gun** *n* MILIT canon contre-avion *m*; ~ **dehumidifiers** *n pl* SAFETY déshumidificateurs d'air *m pl*; ~ **dielectric** *n* ELEC diélectrique à air *m*; ~ **diffuser** *n* REFRIG diffuseur d'air *m*; ~ **discharge** *n* MECH *systems* échappement d'air *m*; ~ **discharge nozzle** *n* MECH tubulure d'échappement d'air *f*, PAPER TECH docteur à lame d'air *m*; ~ **doctor dampening system** *n* PRINT système de mouillage à lame d'air *m*; ~ **door** *n* MINING porte d'aérage *f*; ~ **draft** *n* (AmE) *see air draught*; ~ **drain** *n* NUCLEAR mise à l'air *f*, purge de l'air *f*, soutirage *m*; ~ **drain valve** *n* NUCLEAR purgeur d'air *m*, venteuse *f*; ~ **draught** *n* (BrE) NAUT *ship design* tirant d'air *m*; ~ **drill** *n* MECH *tools* perforateur pneumatique *m*, MECH ENG perceuse pneumatique *f*; ~ **drilling** *n* PETR forage à l'air *m*, PETR TECH forage à l'air

comprimé *m*; ~ **dryer** *n* PRINT sécheur à air *m*; ~ **drying**
n PRINT séchage à l'air *m*; ~ **duct** *n* COAL TECH, HEATING
conduite d'air *f*, MECH ENG conduite d'air *f*, manche à
air *f*, REFRIG conduite d'air *f*, gaine d'air *f*; ~ **ducting** *n*
MECH ENG adduction d'air *f*;

~ e ~ **embolism** *n* OCEANOG aéroembolisme *m*; ~
engine *n* MECH ENG machine pneumatique *f*, moteur
pneumatique *m*; ~ **eraser** *n* PRINT pistolet sableur *m*; ~
exchanger *n* PAPER TECH aérateur *m*; ~ **exhaust** *n* PETR
TECH conduite d'évacuation d'air *f*; ~ **exhauster** *n*
OCEANOG exhausteur *m*;

~ f ~ **ferry** *n* AERONAUT bac aérien *m*; ~ **film system** *n*
TRANSP système à film d'air *m*; ~ **filter** *n* AUTO, CHEM
TECH, COAL TECH, HEAT ENG, VEHICLES *carburet-*
tor filtre à air *m*; ~ **fit to breathe** *n* SAFETY air respirable
m; ~ **float dryer** *n* PAPER TECH sécherie à feuille aéroportée *f*; ~ **flooding** *n* PETR TECH injection d'air
comprimé *f*; ~ **flotation** *n* POLLUTION flottaison *f*; ~
flotation dryer *n* PRINT sécheur à coussins d'air *m*; ~
flue *n* PROD ENG *of furnace* carneau à air *m*, *vent hole*
aspiral *m*; ~ **fog** *n* CINEMAT voile d'oxydation *m*; ~
freight *n* AERONAUT, PACKAGING fret aérien *m*; ~ **fric-**
tion *n* SPACE *spacecraft* frottement de l'air *m*; ~ **friction**
heating *n* SPACE *spacecraft* échauffement cinétique *m*;
~ **furnace** *n* HEATING four à réverbère *m*;

~ g ~ **gage** *n* (AmE) *see air gauge*; ~ **gap** *n* ELEC
capacitor, transformer, ELEC ENG *magnetic or electric*
circuit entrefer *m*, intervalle d'air *m*, PETR TECH intervalle d'air *m*, PHYS *electromagnet* entrefer *m*, TRANSP
hovercraft intervalle de fuite d'air *m*; ~ **gap coil** *n* ELEC
bobine avec espace d'air *f*; ~ **gap induction** *n* ELEC *coil*
induction dans l'entrefer *f*; ~ **gap protector** *n* ELEC
safety parafoudre à éclateur *m*; ~ **gas** *n* GAS TECH gaz
d'air *m*; ~ **gauge** *n* (BrE) MECH ENG, METR manomètre
à air *m*; ~ **gun exploration method** *n* GEOPHYS méthode
du canon à air *f*;

~ h ~ **hammer** *n* MECH *tools* marteau pneumatique *m*;
~ **heater** *n* HEATING réchauffeur d'air *m*, MECH ENG
appareil de chauffage d'air *m*, aérotherme *m*, réchauffeur d'air *m*, PAPER TECH réchauffeur d'air *m*; ~
hoist *n* MECH ENG appareil de levage pneumatique *m*,
treuil pneumatique *m*, PETR TECH, PROD ENG treuil à
air comprimé *m*; ~ **hole** *n* PROD ENG *flaw in casting*
soufflure *f*, *vent* aspiral *m*, soupirail *m*, trou d'évent
m, évent *m*; ~ **hose** *n* CONST *compressed air* tuyau d'air
comprimé *m*, MECH flexible à air comprimé *m*, MECH
ENG tuyauterie flexible d'alimentation en air *f*, MINING
flexible d'air *m*; ~ **humidifier** *n* SAFETY humidificateur
d'air *m*; ~ **humidity** *n* THERMOD degré hygrométrique
de l'air *m*, humidité atmosphérique *f*;

~ i ~ **impingement** *n* PRINT point d'impact de l'air *m*;
~ **infiltration loss** *n* HEATING perte d'infiltration de l'air
f; ~ **injection compressor** *n* HYDR EQUIP compresseur à
injection d'air *m*, compresseur à injection pneumatique *m*; ~ **injection reactor** *n* *(AIR)* TRANSP réacteur à
injection d'air *m*; ~ **injector** *n* MECH ENG injecteur d'air
m; ~ **inlet** *n* C&G amenée d'air de soufflage *f*, MECH ENG
admission d'air *f*, arrivée d'air *f*, entrée d'air *f*, prise
d'air *f*, *of* blower arrivée du vent *f*; ~ **inlet cock** *n* MECH
ENG robinet d'admission d'air *m*; ~ **inlet nozzle** *n* MECH
ENG buse d'insufflation d'air *f*; ~ **inlet pipe** *n* MECH ENG
tuyau d'arrivée d'air *m*; ~ **inlet purifier** *n* PROD ENG
épurateur d'arrivée d'air *m*; ~ **inlet valve** *n* MECH ENG
soupape de purge d'air *f*; ~ **input well** *n* PETR TECH
puits d'injection d'air *m*; ~ **insulation** *n* ELEC isolation
à l'air *f*, ELEC ENG isolation par air *f*; ~ **intake** *n* MECH

ENG admission d'air *f*, prise d'air *f*, NAUT prise d'air *f*;
~ **intake pressure** *n* AERONAUT pression d'admission
d'air *f*; ~ **intake valve** *n* AERONAUT vanne d'admission
d'air *f*;

~ j ~ **jack** *n* MECH ENG vérin pneumatique *m*; ~ **jet**
coater *n* PAPER TECH coucheuse à lame d'air *f*; ~ **jet**
labeling *n* (AmE), ~ **jet labelling** *n* (BrE) PACKAGING
étiquetage par jet d'air *m*; ~ **jig** *n* COAL TECH bac à air
comprimé *m*, jig pneumatique *m*;

~ k ~ **knife** *n* P&R *coating equipment* lame d'air *f*,
racle à air comprimé *f*, PAPER TECH lame d'air *f*, PRINT
couteau d'air *m*, lame d'air *f*; ~ **knife coated paper** *n*
PAPER TECH papier couché à lame d'air *m*; ~ **knife**
coater *n* PAPER TECH coucheuse à lame d'air *f*; ~ **knife**
coating *n* PAPER TECH couchage par lame d'air *m*;

~ l ~ **leg** *n* MINING pousseur pneumatique *m*, poussoir pneumatique *m*; ~ **level** *n* CONST *instrument*
niveau à bulle d'air *m*;

~ m ~ **main** *n* MECH ENG canalisation principale d'adduction d'air *f*; ~ **mass** *n* FUELLESS *solar power* masse
d'air *f*; ~ **mass classification** *n* METEO classification des
masses d'air *f*; ~ **meter** *n* MECH ENG compteur de débit
d'air *m*; ~ **moisture** *n* COAL TECH humidité d'air *f*; ~
monitor *n* TV moniteur d'antenne *m*, moniteur de
retour antenne *m*, moniteur final *m*; ~ **motor** *n* AERO-
NAUT moteur pneumatique *m*, MECH ENG machine
pneumatique *f*, moteur pneumatique *m*;

~ n ~ **nozzle** *n* COAL TECH éjecteur de ventilation *m*,
MECH ENG ajutage *m*;

~ o ~ **outlet** *n* MECH ENG évacuation d'air *f*, *of blower*
sortie du vent *f*; ~ **oven** *n* P&R *equipment* étuve à l'air
chaud *f*;

~ p ~ **passage** *n* MECH ENG passage d'air *m*, MINING
conduit *m*; ~ **passageway** *n* MINING conduit *m*; ~
permeability *n* HEAT ENG, PRINT perméabilité à l'air *f*; ~
photo interpretation *n* COAL TECH interprétation photographique aérienne *f*; ~ **pin block** *n* MECH ENG
Monotype caster vérin pneumatique *m*; ~ **pipe** *n* MECH
ENG conduite d'air *f*, tuyau d'air *m*, MINING *ventilation*
buse *f*, canal *m*, canard *m*; ~ **pipeline** *n* MECH ENG
canalisation d'air *f*; ~ **piston** *n* MECH ENG piston pneumatique *m*, piston à air *m*, *of Monotype machine* vérin
pneumatique *m*; ~ **pocket** *n* AERONAUT poche d'air *f*; ~
pollutant *n* POLLUTION polluant atmosphérique *m*,
polluant de l'air *m*; ~ **polluting substance** *n* POLLUTION
polluant atmosphérique *m*; ~ **pollution** *n* POLLUTION
pollution atmosphérique *f*, pollution de l'air *f*, SAFETY
pollution de l'air *f*; ~ **pollution control** *n* POLLUTION
contrôle de la pollution atmosphérique *m*; ~ **pollution**
emission *n* POLLUTION émission de polluants atmosphériques *f*; ~ **pollution episode** *n* POLLUTION épisode
de pollution atmosphérique *m*, épisode de pollution
météorologique *m*; ~ **pollution incident** *n* POLLUTION
incident de pollution atmosphérique *m*; ~ **preheater** *n*
MECH ENG appareil de préchauffage d'air *m*; ~ **pres-**
sure *n* MECH ENG pression d'air *f*, pression
pneumatique *f*; ~ **pressure brake** *n* AUTO frein à air
comprimé *m*; ~ **pressure gage** *n* (AmE), ~ **pressure**
gauge *n* (BrE) PETR TECH manomètre à air *m*; ~
pressure relief duct *n* RAIL rameau de pistonnement
m; ~ **pressure switch** *n* CONTROL interrupteur à pression d'air *m*; ~ **propeller** *n* TRANSP hélice aérienne *f*; ~
pulse *n* PETR onde aérienne *f*, vague d'air *f*, énergie
acoustique *f*; ~ **pump** *n* MECH ENG, PHYS pompe à air *f*;
~ **pump exhaust pipe** *n* MECH ENG tuyau d'évacuation
d'une pompe à air *m*; ~ **pump lubricator** *n* MECH ENG

lubrificateur de pompe à air *m*; ~ **pump throttle** *n* MECH ENG robinet de freinage d'une pompe à air *m*, régulateur de débit d'une pompe à air *m*; ~ **purger** *n* PACKAGING purgeur d'air *m*; ~ **purification and deodorization equipment** *n* SAFETY équipement de purification et de désodorisation de l'air *m*; ~ **purity** *n* POLLUTION pureté de l'air *f*;

~ q ~ **quality** *n* TV qualité antenne *f*;

~ r ~ **ratio** *n* AUTO rapport lambda *m*; ~ **reactor** *n* ELEC inductance à air *f*, réactance à air *f*; ~ **receiver** *n* MECH ENG réservoir d'air *m*, *of air compressor* ballon d'air comprimé *m*, réservoir d'air comprimé *m*; ~ **refractive index** *n* WAVE PHYS indice de réfraction de l'air *m*; ~ **refrigeration cycle** *n* REFRIG cycle frigorifique à air *m*; ~ **regulator** *n* MECH ENG *of gas burner* virole d'air de combustion *f*; ~ **reheater** *n* MECH ENG réchauffeur d'air *m*; ~ **renewal** *n* AERONAUT renouvellement de l'air *m*; ~ **repressuring** *n* PETR TECH *oil field* remise en pression par air comprimé *f*; ~ **reservoir** *n* MINING caisson d'aérage *m*; ~ **roll** *n* PAPER TECH rouleau souffleur *m*; ~ **route facilities** *n pl* AERONAUT installations et services de route aérienne *f pl*;

~ s ~ **sample** *n* SAFETY échantillon d'air *m*; ~ **sampling techniques** *n pl* SAFETY techniques d'échantillonnage de l'air *f pl*; ~ **scoop** *n* AERONAUT bossette d'entrée d'air *f*, entrée d'air *f*, ouïe d'admission *f*, ouïe d'entrée d'air *f*, prise d'air *f*, MECH ENG manche à air *f*; ~ **screen blow gun** *n* PROD ENG *production, maintenance* soufflette à écran d'air *f*; ~ **scrubber** *n* MINING laveur d'air *m*; ~ **search radar** *n* NAUT *navy* radar de veille air *m*; ~ **separation** *n* CHEM TECH séparation de l'air *f*, FOOD TECH *of fractions* séparation par air *f*, turboséparation *f*; ~ **separator** *n* MECH ENG séparateur d'air *m*; ~ **shaft** *n* MINING puits d'aérage *m*, puits de ventilation *m*; ~ **shed** *n* POLLUTION bassin atmosphérique *m*, bassin d'air *m*; ~ **shower** *n* ASTRON gerbe de rayons cosmiques *f*, PAPER TECH rampe de soufflage d'air *f*; ~ **sniffing valve** *n* MECH ENG clapet d'aspiration d'air *m*; ~ **squeegee** *n* CINEMAT essoreuse par succion *f*; ~ **stack** *n* MINING cheminée d'aérage *f*; ~ **stairs** *n* AERONAUT *aircraft* escalier intégré *m*; ~ **starter** *n* MECH ENG démarreur pneumatique *m*; ~ **supply** *n* AERONAUT adduction d'air *f*;

~ t ~ **tank** *n* NAUT *of ship* caisson de flottabilité *m*, caisson à air *m*, réservoir de flottabilité *m*, PETR TECH caisson d'air *m*; ~ **tap** *n* MECH ENG robinet d'air *m*; ~ **taxi** *n* AERONAUT taxi aérien *m*; ~ **terminal** *n* TRANSP aérogare *f*; ~ **terminal device** *n* REFRIG bouche d'air *f*; ~ **traffic** *n* TRANSP trafic aérien *m*; ~ **traffic control** *n* AERONAUT contrôle de la circulation aérienne *m*, contrôle du trafic aérien *m*, CONTROL contrôle de la circulation aérienne *m*, TRANSP contrôle du trafic aérien *m*; ~ **traffic control center** *n* (AmE), ~ **traffic control centre** *n* (BrE) AERONAUT centre de contrôle de la circulation aérienne *m*; ~ **traffic control clearance** *n* AERONAUT autorisation du contrôle de la circulation aérienne *f*; ~ **traffic controller** *n* AERONAUT aiguilleur du ciel *m*, contrôleur de la circulation aérienne *m*, CONTROL contrôleur de la circulation aérienne *m*, contrôleur du trafic aérien *m*; ~ **traffic control service** *n* AERONAUT service du contrôle de la circulation aérienne *m*; ~ **traffic pattern** *n* AERONAUT réseau de circulation aérienne *m*; ~ **transformer** *n* ELEC transformateur à air *m*; ~ **transport** *n* AERONAUT, TRANSP transport aérien *m*; ~ **treatment** *n* REFRIG traitement de l'air *m*; ~ **trimmer capacitor** *n* ELEC ENG condensateur ajustable à air *m*; ~ **turbine** *n* MECH ENG turbine atmosphérique *f*, turbine à air *f*; ~ **turn** *n* PRINT barre de retournement *f*, courbe à coussin d'air *f*, dispositif de retournement aéroporté *m*;

~ u ~ **unfit for respiration** *n* SAFETY air impropre à la respiration *m*;

~ v ~ **valve** *n* FUELLESS obturateur d'air *m*, ventouse d'aération *f*, MECH ENG clapet d'air *m*, soupape d'air *f*, *of tyre* valve de gonflage *f*; ~ **variable capacitor** *n* ELEC ENG condensateur variable à air *m*; ~ **velocity** *n* HEATING vitesse de l'air *f*; ~ **vent** *n* MECH ENG trou d'aération *m*, évent *m*, NAUT hublot d'aération *m*, NUCLEAR purgeur d'air *m*, venteuse *f*, PETR TECH robinet à air *m*, PRINT aération *f*; ~ **vent pin** *n* MECH ENG pièce rapportée d'évacuation d'air *f*; ~ **vent valve** *n* AERONAUT clapet de mise à l'air libre *m*, MECH ENG soupape d'arrivée d'air *f*, soupape de purge d'air *f*

air[3] *vt* NAUT *hold, bilges* aérer, SAFETY aérer, sécher, TV diffuser, faire passer à l'antenne, transmettre, émettre

AIR *abbr (air injection reactor)* TRANSP réacteur à injection d'air *m*

air-and-sea *adj* NAUT *forces* aéronaval

airborne[1] *adj* TRANSP aéroporté

airborne:[2] ~ **acoustical noise** *n* SAFETY bruit acoustique aérien *m*; ~ **collision avoidance system** *n* AERONAUT système anticollision embarqué *m*; ~ **dust** *n* SAFETY poussières aériennes *f pl*, poussières en suspension dans l'air *f pl*; ~ **dust concentration** *n* SAFETY concentration des poussières en suspension dans l'air *f*; ~ **earth station** *n* SPACE *communications* station terrienne embarquée *f*; ~ **laser** *n* ELECTRON laser embarqué *m*; ~ **marker balloon** *n* MILIT ballon marqueur aéroporté *m*; ~ **noise** *n* MECH ENG bruit aérien *m*, SAFETY *emitted by machine tools* bruit transmis par l'air *m*; ~ **particles** *n pl* METEO particules en suspension dans l'air *f pl*; ~ **proximity warning indicator** *n* AERONAUT avertisseur de proximité aéroporté *m*; ~ **radar** *n* TELECOM radar aéroporté *m*; ~ **remote sensing** *n* MAR POLL télédétection aéroportée *f*; ~ **survey** *n* GEOL prospection aéroportée *f*; ~ **television** *n* TV stratovision *f*

airbrush *n* P&R lame d'air *f*, racle à air comprimé *f*, PACKAGING, PAPER TECH lame d'air *f*, PHOTO, PRINT aérographe *m*; ~ **coater** *n* PAPER TECH coucheuse à lame d'air *f*

airbrushing *n* PRINT travail à l'aérographe *m*

airbus *n* TRANSP airbus *m*

aircheck *n* TV enregistrement témoin *m*; ~ **tape** *n* TV enregistrement témoin d'une émission simultané antenne *m*

air-condition *vt* HEATING, REFRIG climatiser

air-cool *vt* THERMOD refroidir par l'air

air-cooled[1] *adj* ELEC *equipment* refroidi par l'air, MECH ENG refroidi à l'air, à refroidissement à l'air, PAPER TECH, PRINT refroidi à l'air, THERMOD refroidi par l'air, à refroidissement par l'air

air-cooled:[2] ~ **air conditioning unit** *n* REFRIG climatiseur à condenseur à air *m*; ~ **compressor** *n* REFRIG compresseur refroidi par air *m*; ~ **condenser** *n* HEAT ENG condenseur à refroidissement *m*, REFRIG condenseur à air *m*; ~ **engine** *n* VEHICLES moteur à refroidissement par air *m*; ~ **motor** *n* MECH ENG moteur refroidi à l'air *m*; ~ **surface condenser** *n* MECH ENG surface de condensation refroidie à l'air *f*; ~ **system** *n* MECH ENG système à refroidissement d'air *m*; ~ **transformer** *n* ELEC transformateur refroidi par l'air *m*, transformateur à air *m*; ~ **tube** *n* ELECTRON tube refroidi par air *m*

air-cooling: ~ **installation** n MECH ENG installation de refroidissement d'air f

aircraft n AERONAUT avion m, aéronef m; ~ **axis** n AERONAUT axe d'aéronef m; ~ **balance** n AERONAUT centrage m; ~ **behavior** n (AmE), ~ **behaviour** n (BrE) AERONAUT comportement d'un avion m; ~ **call sign** n AERONAUT indicatif d'appel d'aéronef m; ~ **carrier** n NAUT, TRANSP porte-avions m; ~ **category** n AERONAUT aéronef m, catégorie d'aéronef f; ~ **classification** n AERONAUT numéro de classification d'aéronef m; ~ **effectivity** n AERONAUT validité avion f; ~ **electrical system** n (AmE) (cf aircraft mains) AERONAUT réseau électrique de bord m; ~ **engine emissions** n pl AERONAUT émissions de moteurs d'aviation f pl; ~ **equipment** n AERONAUT équipement de bord m; ~ **icing indicator** n AERONAUT indicateur de givrage d'aéronef m; ~ **identification** n AERONAUT identification d'un aéronef f; ~ **lift** n TRANSP ascenseur d'avions m; ~ **light** n AERONAUT feu d'aéronef m; ~ **mains** n pl (BrE) (cf aircraft electrical system) AERONAUT réseau électrique de bord m; ~ **maintenance engineer** n AERONAUT mécanicien d'entretien avions m, mécanicien d'entretien d'aéronefs m; ~ **maintenance mechanic** n AERONAUT mécanicien d'entretien avions m, mécanicien d'entretien d'aéronefs m; ~ **maintenance rating** n AERONAUT qualification entretien d'aéronef f; ~ **movement** n AERONAUT mouvement d'aéronef m; ~ **noise monitoring** n CONTROL contrôle du bruit des avions m; ~ **overhaul rating** n AERONAUT qualification révisions d'aéronef f; ~ **tail unit** n AERONAUT queue de l'avion f; ~ **tractor** n TRANSP remorqueur d'avion m; ~ **tug** n TRANSP remorqueur d'avion m; ~ **with powered lift** n AERONAUT avion à aile propulsive m

aircraft-kilometer: ~ **performed** n (AmE) AERONAUT aéronef-kilomètre réalisé m

aircraft-kilometre: ~ **performed** n (BrE) AERONAUT aéronef-kilomètre réalisé m

air-depolarized: ~ **battery** n ELEC ENG pile à dépolarisation par l'air f

airdraulic: ~ **gun** n AUTO car maintenance pistolet oléopneumatique m

air-dried adj FOOD TECH, PACKAGING, PAPER TECH, PRINT paper séché à l'air

airdrome n (AmE) see aerodrome

airdrop vt TRANSP parachuter

air-dry:[1] ~ **mass** n PAPER TECH of pulp masse sèche à l'air f; ~ **paper** n PRINT papier séché à l'air m; ~ **pulp** n PAPER TECH, PRINT pâte séchée à l'air f

air-dry[2] vt PAPER TECH sécher à l'air

air-entrained: ~ **concrete** n CONST béton avec occlusion d'air m, béton occlu m

air-entraining: ~ **admixture** n CONST concrete agent entraîneur d'air m, entraîneur d'air m

air-filed: ~ **flight plan** n AERONAUT plan de vol déposé en vol m

airflow n AERONAUT débit d'air m, écoulement d'air m, CONST courant d'air m, flux d'air m, FLUID PHYS courant d'air m, écoulement d'air m, MECH ENG courant d'air m, SPACE écoulement aérodynamique m; ~ **rate** n HEATING débit d'air m; ~ **sensor** n AUTO débitmètre d'air m

airfoil n (AmE) see aerofoil

airframe n PRINT châssis pneumatique m ~ **bonding lead** n AERONAUT fil de métallisation m; ~ **reference plane** n AERONAUT plan de référence structure m

air-fuel: ~ **ratio** n TRANSP rapport air-combustible m

airglow n ASTRON lueur de l'atmosphère f

air-gun n GEOPHYS canon à air comprimé m, PETR canon à air m

air-hardened: ~ **steel** n SPRINGS acier trempé à l'air m

airhead n MINING airage m, galerie d'aérage f, voie d'air f

airheading n MINING airage m, galerie d'aérage f, voie d'air f

air-impermeable: ~ **clothing material** n SAFETY tissu pour vêtements imperméables à l'air m

airlift n TRANSP transport aérien m; ~ **pump** n CHEM TECH pompe élévatoire f

airline n AERONAUT compagnie aérienne f, entreprise de transport aérien f, transporteur aérien m, C&G bulle capillaire f, MECH ENG canalisation d'air f, PAPER TECH conduite d'air f, TRANSP câble aérien m, ligne aérienne f; ~ **pressure regulator** n MECH ENG réducteur de pression pour air comprimé m

airliner n AERONAUT avion de ligne m

airlock n AERONAUT poche d'air f, FLUID PHYS in pipe bouchon d'air m, MINING sas d'aérage m, sas à air m, PRINT sas à air m, vanne à air f, REFRIG, SAFETY entry-exit sas à air m, SPACE spacecraft sas de communication m, TRANSP bouchon de vapeur m, WATER SUPP of caisson sas à air m, écluse f; ~ **feeder** n PAPER TECH distributeur à tambour alvéolé m; ~ **system** n NUCLEAR système de sas m

airmail n AERONAUT, TRANSP poste aérienne f; ~ **paper** n PAPER TECH, PRINT papier avion m

air-no-fuel: ~ **vent valve** n AERONAUT clapet de mise à l'air libre étanche au carburant m

air-oil: ~ **actuator** n PROD ENG échangeur de pression air-huile m

air-operated: ~ **chuck** n MECH ENG mandrin pneumatique m; ~ **gage** n (AmE), ~ **gauge** n (BrE) METR calibre de préréglage m, calibre pneumatique m; ~ **position switch** n PROD ENG interrupteur de position pneumatique m; ~ **valve grinder** n AUTO car maintenance rodoir pneumatique de soupapes m

air-or-oil: ~ **cooling** n THERMOD transformers refroidissement par circulation d'huile m

airplane n (AmE) see aeroplane

airport n AERONAUT aéroport m; ~ **charge** n AERONAUT redevance d'aéroport f, taxe aéroportuaire f; ~ **manager** n AERONAUT directeur de l'aéroport m; ~ **security committee** n AERONAUT comité de sûreté d'aéroport m; ~ **traffic** n AERONAUT trafic d'aéroport m

airproof adj PAPER TECH imperméable à l'air

air-propelled: ~ **hovercraft** n TRANSP aéroglisseur à propulsion marine m

airscrew n TRANSP hélice aérienne f

air-sea: ~ **rescue** n MILIT sauvetage des naufragés d'un désastre aérien m, NAUT sauvetage air-mer m, sauvetage aérien en mer m, sauvetage aéromaritime m; ~ **rescue equipment** n MILIT dispositif de sauvetage pour aviateurs naufragés m

airspace n AERONAUT espace aérien m, MINING chambre à air f, in shot hole chambre d'air f; ~ **insulation** n HEAT ENG isolation par lame d'air f; ~ **restriction** n AERONAUT réglementation de l'espace aérien f

airspeed n AERONAUT vitesse anémométrique f, vitesse propre f; ~ **indicator** n AERONAUT anémomètre m, badin m, indicateur de vitesse relative m, PAPER TECH aéromètre m, TRANSP anémomètre m

airstream: ~ **separation** n AERONAUT décollement des filets d'air m

airtight *adj* MECH étanche à l'air, MECH ENG, NAUT hermétique, étanche à l'air, PACKAGING hermétique, PAPER TECH imperméable à l'air, PETR TECH étanche à l'air, PHYS hermétique, imperméable à l'air, étanche à l'air

airtime *n* TELECOM temps d'émission *m*, TV créneau horaire *m*, heure d'émission *f*, temps d'antenne *m*

air-to-air: ~ **heat exchanger** *n* MECH ENG échangeur de chaleur d'air *m*; ~ **refueling** *n* (AmE), ~ **refuelling** *n* (BrE) MILIT ravitaillement air-air *m*

airwave *n* PETR onde aérienne *f*, WAVE PHYS *radio* onde hertzienne *f*

airway *n* AERONAUT route aérienne *f*, MINING airage *m*, conduit *m*, galerie d'aérage *f*, voie d'air *f*; ~ **bill** *n* AERONAUT lettre de transport aérien *f*, TRANSP connaissement aérien *m*, lettre de transport aérien *f*

airworthiness *n* AERONAUT aptitude au vol *f*, navigabilité *f*, tenue au vol *f*, valeur aéronautique *f*

airworthy *adj* AERONAUT en état de navigabilité

Airy: ~ **disc** *n* (BrE) ASTRON tache Airy *f*, PHYS disque d'Airy *m*, tache d'Airy *f*; ~ **disk** *n* (AmE) *see Airy disc*

AIS *abbr (alarm indication signal)* TELECOM SIA *(signal d'indication d'alarme)*, SNA *(signal de neutralisation d'alarme)*

AITS *abbr (acknowledged information transfer service)* TELECOM service de transfert d'informations avec accusé de réception *m*

akanticone *n* MINERAL acanthikon *m*, akanthicone *m*

akerite *n* PETR akérite *f*

åkermanite *n* MINERAL akermanite *f*

Al *(aluminium, aluminum)* CHEM Al *(aluminium)*

AL *abbr (access link)* TELECOM liaison d'accès *f*

alabaster *n* MINERAL albâtre *m* ~ **glass** *n* C&G verre d'albâtre *m*

alalite *n* MINERAL alalite *f*

alanine *n* CHEM alanine *f*

alarm *n* MECH ENG alarme *f*, avertisseur *m*, SAFETY alarme *f*, alerte *f*, *indicator* avertisseur *m*, signal d'alarme *m*, sirène *f*; ~ **and logging system** *n* SAFETY *for industrial application* système d'alarme et d'enregistrement *m*; ~ **bell** *n* ELEC sonnette d'alarme *f*, PAPER TECH avertisseur *m*, SAFETY sonnerie d'alarme *f*; ~ **call** *n* TELECOM réveil automatique *m*, réveil téléphonique *m*; ~ **card** *n* TELECOM carte d'alarme *f*; ~ **circuit** *n* TELECOM circuit d'alarme *m*; ~ **flashing light** *n* SAFETY lampe d'alarme clignotante *f*; ~ **function** *n* TELECOM fonction d'alarme *f*; ~ **fuse** *n* ELEC fusible de signalisation *m*; ~ **gage** *n* (AmE), ~ **gauge** *n* (BrE) MECH ENG instrument de mesure à avertisseur *m*; ~ **indication lamp** *n* TELECOM voyant d'indication d'alarme *m*; ~ **indication signal** *n (AIS)* TELECOM signal d'indication d'alarme *m (SIA)*, signal de neutralisation d'alarme *m (SNA)*; ~ **printout facility** *n* TELECOM édition des alarmes *f*; ~ **relay** *n* ELEC relais avertisseur *m*; ~ **setting** *n* TELECOM seuil de déclenchement des alarmes *m*; ~ **signal** *n* CONTROL, NAUT *emergency radio call* signal d'alarme *m*; ~ **switch** *n* CONTROL interrupteur d'alarme *m*; ~ **system** *n* SAFETY système avertisseur *m*; ~ **thermometer** *n* MECH ENG thermomètre avertisseur *m*; ~ **whistle** *n* MECH ENG sifflet avertisseur *m*; ~ **whistle signal** *n* HYDR EQUIP indicateur à sifflet d'alarme *m*

alaskaite *n* MINERAL alaskaïte *f*

alaskite *n* PETR alaskite *f*

alban *n* CHEM cristal blanc *m*

albedo *n* ASTRON, GEOPHYS, METEO, SPACE albédo *m*; ~ **features** *n pl* ASTRON taches d'albédo *f pl*

albertite *n* MINERAL albertite *f*

Albian *n* GEOL albien *m*

albite *n* C&G, MINERAL albite *f*

albumen *n* FOOD TECH albumen *m*; ~ **process** *n* PHOTO procédé à l'albumine *m*

albumenized: ~ **paper** *n* PAPER TECH papier albuminé *m*, PRINT papier papier glacé albumineux *m*

albumin *n* CHEM, FOOD TECH albumine *f*

albuminate *n* CHEM, FOOD TECH albuminate *m*

albuminoid *adj* CHEM albuminoïde

albumose *n* CHEM, FOOD TECH albumose *f*

alcohol *n* CHEM, P&R, PRINT, TEXTILES alcool *m*; ~ **ink** *n* PRINT encre à l'alcool *f*; ~ **thermometer** *n* REFRIG thermomètre à alcool *m*

alcoholate *n* CHEM alcoolat *m*

alcoholic[1] *adj* FOOD TECH alcoolisé

alcoholic:[2] ~ **fermentation** *n* FOOD TECH fermentation alcoolique *f*

alcohol-proof: ~ **printing** *n* PRINT impression résistant à l'alcool *f*

alcoholysis *n* CHEM *of ester* alcoolyse *f*

aldehyde *n* CHEM, FOOD TECH, P&R *chemical compound* aldéhyde *m*; ~ **acid** *n* CHEM, FOOD TECH acide-aldéhyde *m*

aldehydic *adj* CHEM aldéhydique

alder *n* PAPER TECH aulne *m*, aune *m*

aldohexose *n* CHEM, FOOD TECH aldohexose *m*

aldol *n* CHEM aldol *m*

aldose *n* CHEM, FOOD TECH aldose *m*

aldosterone *n* FOOD TECH aldostérone *f*

ALDP *abbr (axial plasma deposition)* TELECOM déposition axiale *f*

alee[1] *adj* NAUT sous le vent

alee[2] *adv* NAUT sous le vent

A-leg *n* TELECOM conducteur de pointe *m*, fil de pointe *m*

ALEPH: ~ **experiment** *n* PART PHYS expérience ALEPH *f*

alerting *n* TELECOM alerte *f*

alexandrite *n* MINERAL alexandrite *f*

alfa *n* PRINT alfa *m*

algae *n pl* HYDROL, PETR algues *f pl*

algal: ~ **bloom** *n* OCEANOG poussée phytoplanctonique *f*; ~ **destruction** *n* HYDROL lutte contre les algues *f*; ~ **growth potential** *n* HYDROL potentiel de croissance des algues *m*; ~ **limestone** *n* PETR calcaire à algues *m*; ~ **mat** *n* OCEANOG goémon d'épave *m*

algebra *n* COMP, MATH algèbre *f*

algebraic[1] *adj* MATH algébrique

algebraic:[2] ~ **geometry** *n* GEOM géométrie algébrique *f*

Algerian: ~ **onyx** *n* MINERAL onyx calcaire *m*, onyx d'Algérie *m*

algicide[1] *adj* HYDROL algicide

algicide[2] *n* HYDROL algicide *m*

alginate *n* P&R alginate *m*

alginic: ~ **acid** *n* FOOD TECH acide alginique *m*

algoculture *n* OCEANOG algoculture *f*

algodonite *n* MINERAL algodonite *f*

Algol *n* ASTRON Algol *f*

algology *n* OCEANOG algologie *m*

algorithm *n* COMP, MATH, SPACE *communications* algorithme *m*

algorithmic[1] *adj* COMP, DP algorithmique

algorithmic:[2] ~ **language** *n* COMP langage algorithmique *m*

alias *n* COMP nom alternatif *m*, DP alias *m*

aliased: ~ **frequency** *n* ELECTRON fréquence de repliement *f*; ~ **signal** *n* ELECTRON signal à spectre replié *m*; ~

spectrum *n* ELECTRON spectre de repliement *m*

aliasing *n* COMP *graphics* crénelage *m*, ELECTRON repliement du spectre *m*; ~ **error** *n* PETR pli déversé *m*

alidade *n* CONST alidade *f*, INSTRUMENT alidade *f*, graphomètre *m*, NAUT alidade *f*

align *vt* CINEMAT, CONST aligner, MECH ENG aligner, faire coïncider, PHOTO centrer, PRINT aligner, parangonner

aligned *adj* MECH ENG aligné

aligning: ~ **plug** *n* ELEC ENG téton de centrage *m*

alignment *n* CONST *ground plan* alignement *m*, tracé *m*, MECH alignement *m*, lignage *m*, NAUT *coastal navigation* alignement *m*, PRINT alignement *m*, contrecollage *m*, parangonnage *m*, TELECOM *of frame* verrouillage *m*; ~ **fault** *n* TELECOM défaut d'alignement *m*; ~ **frame** *n* PETR ligneur *m*; ~ **mark** *n* PRINT repère d'alignement *m*; ~ **pin** *n* MECH goujon d'assemblage *m*; ~ **tape** *n* TV bande d'étalonnage *f*; ~ **telescope** *n* INSTRUMENT lunette d'alignement *f*

align-reaming: ~ **box** *n* AERONAUT palier d'alignement *m*, palier à alignement *m*

aliphatic[1] *adj* PETR TECH aliphatique

aliphatic:[2] ~ **hydrocarbon** *n* CHEM, P&R hydrocarbure aliphatique *m*; ~ **polyamine** *n* P&R *adhesives, coatings* polyamine aliphatique *f*; ~ **solvent** *n* PETR TECH solvant aliphatique *m*

alive *adj* ELEC *circuit*, ELEC ENG sous tension

alkali *n* CHEM alcali *m*, COAL TECH alcalin *m*, PAPER TECH, PETR TECH, TEXTILES alcali *m*; ~ **cellulose** *n* PAPER TECH alcali cellulose *m*; ~ **content** *n* DETERGENTS teneur en alcalis *f*; ~ **feldspar** *n* PETR feldspath alcalin *m*; ~ **halide** *n* CRYSTALL halogénure alcalin *m*; ~ **metal** *n* METALL métal alcalin *m*; ~ **resistance** *n* P&R résistance aux alcalis *f*; ~ **treatment** *n* DETERGENTS lavage alcalin *m*

alkalic *adj* GEOL *mineral or igneous suite* alcalin

alkali-fast *adj* DETERGENTS résistant aux alcalis

alkalimeter *n* FOOD TECH, PAPER TECH alcalimètre *m*

alkalimetry *n* CHEM, DETERGENTS alcalimétrie *f*

alkaline[1] *adj* CHEM, GEOL *mineral or igneous suite*, HYDROL alcalin

alkaline:[2] ~ **battery** *n* ELEC ENG pile alcaline *f*; ~ **cell** *n* ELEC ENG pile alcaline *f*; ~ **cleaning** *n* DETERGENTS dégraissage alcalin *m*; ~ **medium-level radioactive waste** *n* NUCLEAR déchets alcalins d'activité intermédiaire *m pl*; ~ **photocell** *n* PHOTO cellule photoélectrique à métal alcalin *f*; ~ **solution** *n* DETERGENTS lessive alcaline *f*; ~ **storage battery** *n* ELEC, ELEC ENG batterie alcaline *f*, batterie d'accumulateurs alcalins *f*; ~ **storage cell** *n* ELEC ENG accumulateur alcalin *m*, accumulateur à électrolyte alcalin *m*, pile alcaline *f*, élément de batterie alcaline *m*

alkaline-earth: ~ **element** *n* PROP MAT élément alcalino-terreux *m*; ~ **metal** *n* METALL, PROP MAT métal alcalino-terreux *m*

alkaline-resistant: ~ **lining** *n* SAFETY *for industrial plants* revêtement résistant aux alcalins *m*

alkalinity *n* CHEM, DETERGENTS, HYDROL, PAPER TECH, POLLUTION, PROP MAT alcalinité *f*

alkalinize *vt* CHEM alcaliniser

alkali-proof[1] *adj* DETERGENTS, PACKAGING, PAPER TECH, PROP MAT résistant aux alcalis

alkali-proof:[2] ~ **paper** *n* PACKAGING papier résistant aux alcalis *m*

alkali-soluble *adj* DETERGENTS soluble en milieu alcalin

alkalization *n* CHEM alcalinisation *f*, alcalisation *f*

alkalize *vti* HYDROL alcaliser

alkaloid *n* CHEM alcaloïde *m*

alkane *n* CHEM, DETERGENTS alcane *m*; ~ **sulfonate** *n* (AmE), ~ **sulphonate** *n* (BrE) DETERGENTS alcane sulfonate *m*

alkanes *n pl* PETR TECH alcanes *m pl*

alkaptone *n* CHEM alcaptone *f*

alkene *n* CHEM alcène *m*, DETERGENTS alcoylène *m*, alcène *m*, alkylène *m*, hydrocarbure éthylénique *m*, PETR TECH alcène *m*

alkenyl *adj* CHEM alcényle

alkoxide *n* CHEM alcoxyde *m*, alkoxyde *m*

alkoxy- *pref* CHEM alcoxy-, alkoxy-

alkyd *n* CHEM alkyd *m*; ~ **resin** *n* P&R *paint binder* résine alkyde *f*; ~ **resin varnish** *n* COATINGS vernis à base de résines alkydes *m*

alkyl *n* CHEM, DETERGENTS, PETR TECH alcoyle *m*, alkyle *m*, PROP MAT alcoyle *m*; ~ **benzene** *n* DETERGENTS alkylbenzène *m*; ~ **halide** *n* PROP MAT halogénure d'alcoyle *m*, halogénure d'alkyle *m*; ~ **sulfonic acid** *n* (AmE), ~ **sulphonic acid** *n* (BrE) DETERGENTS acide alcanesulfonique *m*

alkylamine *n* DETERGENTS alcoylamine *f*, alkylamine *f*

alkylaromatics *n pl* PETR TECH alkylaromatiques *m pl*

alkylation *n* CHEM *process*, DETERGENTS alkylation *f*, PROP MAT alcoylation *f*; ~ **plant** *n* DETERGENTS installation d'alkylation *f*; ~ **unit** *n* DETERGENTS installation d'alkylation *f*

alkylene *n* CHEM alcoylène *m*, alkylène *m*, DETERGENTS alcoylène *m*, alcène *m*, alkylène *m*, hydrocarbure éthylénique *m*

alkyne *n* CHEM *compound* alcyne *m*

alkynes *n pl* PETR TECH alcynes *m pl*

allactite *n* MINERAL allactite *f*

allagite *n* MINERAL allagite *f*

Allan's: ~ **link motion** *n* MECH ENG distribution par système d'Allan *f*

allanite *n* MINERAL allanite *f*

allantoin *n* CHEM allantoïne *f*

all-around: ~ **swing crane** *n* (AmE) *see all-round swing crane*

all-capacitor: ~ **filtering** *n* ELECTRON filtrage par capacité seule *m*

all-cargo: ~ **aircraft** *n* AERONAUT avion de transport exclusif de fret *m*, avion tout-cargo *m*, aéronef tout-cargo *m*; ~ **carrier** *n* AERONAUT transporteur exclusif de fret *m*; ~ **charter flight** *n* AERONAUT vol affrété tout-cargo *m*; ~ **load factor** *n* AERONAUT coefficient de remplissage tout-cargo *m*; ~ **service** *n* AERONAUT service tout-cargo *m*

all-current: ~ **motor** *n* (AmE) *(cf all-mains motor)* ELEC moteur universel *m*

allelotropic *adj* CHEM allélotropique

allemontite *n* MINERAL allemontite *f*

Allen: ~ **key** *n* (BrE) *(cf Allen wrench)* MECH ENG *tool* clé mâle *f*, clé pour vis à six-pans creux *f*, PRINT clé Allen mâle *f*, VEHICLES *tool* clé hexagonale coudée *f*; ~ **screw** *n* PRINT vis Allen à tête hexagonale *f*; ~ **valve** *n* MECH ENG tiroir d'Allen *m*, tiroir à canal *m*; ~ **wrench** *n* (AmE) *(cf Allen key)* MECH ENG clé mâle *f*, clé pour vis à six-pans creux *f*, PRINT clé Allen mâle *f*, VEHICLES *tool* clé hexagonale coudée *f*

Allen's: ~ **loop test** *n* ELEC essai de boucle Allen *m*

Allende: ~ **meteorite** *n* ASTRON météorite Allende *f*

allene *n* CHEM *compound* allène *m*

alleviation: ~ **factor** *n* AERONAUT facteur d'atténuation *m*

alleyway *n* NAUT *boat building* coursive *f*

all-freight: ~ **service** *n* AERONAUT service exclusif de fret *m*, vol de transport exclusif de fret *m*

all-gear: ~ **head** *n* MECH ENG poupée de tour à boîte de vitesse intégrée *f*; ~ **single-pulley drive** *n* MECH ENG transmission par poulie unique et boîte de vitesse intégrée *f*

all-geared: ~ **headstock** *n* MECH ENG poupée de tour à boîte de vitesse intégrée *f*

all-glass: ~ **fiber** *n* (AmE), ~ **fibre** *n* (BrE) TELECOM fibre de verre *f*; ~ **optical fiber** *n* (AmE), ~ **optical fibre** *n* (BrE) ELEC ENG fibre optique verre-verre *f*

alligator: ~ **clamp** *n* CINEMAT pince crocodile *f*; ~ **clip** *n* ELEC *connection*, ELEC ENG, MECH ENG pince crocodile *f*; ~ **wrench** *n* MECH ENG clé crocodile *f*

alligatoring *n* AERONAUT formation de frisures *f*, peinture craquelée *f*, P&R *rubber defect* peau de crocodile *f*

all-in: ~ **ballast** *n* CONST madrague *f*, tout-venant *m*; ~ **tariff** *n* ELEC *supply* tarif pour usages multiples *m*

all-insulated: ~ **switch** *n* ELEC disjoncteur à boîtier isolant *m*

all-mail: ~ **service** *n* AERONAUT vol de transport exclusif de poste *m*

all-mains: ~ **motor** *n* (BrE) *(cf all-current motor)* ELEC moteur universel *m*

allocate *vt* COMP allouer, attribuer, DP affecter, allouer, attribuer

allocated: ~ **frequency** *n* TV fréquence affectée *f*; ~ **stock** *n* PROD ENG stock réservé *m*

allocation *n* COMP, DP affectation *f*, attribution *f*, PROD ENG affectation *f*, allocation *f*, réservation *f*

allochem *n* GEOL allochem *m*

allochroite *n* MINERAL allochroïte *f*

allochthon *n* GEOL allochtone *m*

allochthonous[1] *adj* PETR allochtone

allochthonous:[2] ~ **matter** *n* POLLUTION matière allochtone *f*, matière organique allochtone *f*

allomorphite *n* MINERAL allomorphite *f*

allopalladium *n* MINERAL allopalladium *m*

allophane *n* MINERAL allophane *f*

all-optical: ~ **switching system** *n* TELECOM système de commutation tout-optique *m*

all-or-nothing: ~ **control** *n* CONTROL commande tout-ou-rien *f*; ~ **relay** *n* ELEC, ELEC ENG relais tout-ou-rien *m*

allotment *n* PROD ENG affectation *f*, allocation *f*, réservation *f*

allotriomorphic *adj* GEOL *texture*, PETR allotriomorphe

allotrope *n* CHEM *of element* forme allotropique *f*

allotropic *adj* CHEM, CRYSTALL allotropique

allotropy *n* CHEM allotropie *f*, allotropisme *m*, CRYSTALL allotropie *f*

allow: ~ **to breed** *vt* PROD ENG *blast furnace fire* laisser couver

allowable: ~ **landing mass** *n* AERONAUT masse admissible à l'atterrissage *f*; ~ **load** *n* AERONAUT charge offerte *f*, ELEC *equipment* charge admissible *f*; ~ **takeoff mass** *n* AERONAUT masse admissible au décollage *f*

allowance *n* MECH surépaisseur *f*, MECH ENG *machining* tolérance d'usinage *f*, PROD ENG critère d'acceptation *m*, provision *f*, tolérance *f*; ~ **for machining** *n* PROD ENG *founding* surépaisseur pour usinage *f*; ~ **for shrinkage** *n* MECH ENG prévision de serrage *f*

allowed: ~ **electron dipole transitions** *n pl* RAD PHYS transitions permises du dipôle électrique *f pl*; ~ **energy band** *n* RAD PHYS bande d'énergie permise *f*; ~ **spectrum** *n* NUCLEAR spectre permis *m*; ~ **transition** *n* PHYS

transition permise *f*

alloy[1] *n* CHEM *metals*, PAPER TECH, PROD ENG alliage *m*; ~ **carbide** *n* METALL carbure allié *m*; ~ **diode** *n* ELECTRON diode à jonction par alliage *f*; ~ **junction** *n* ELECTRON jonction par alliage *f*; ~ **junction transistor** *n* ELECTRON transistor à jonction par alliage *m*; ~ **steel** *n* PROP MAT acier allié *m*

alloy[2] *vt* CHEM allier

alloyed: ~ **steel** *n* COAL TECH acier allié *m*

alloying: ~ **element** *n* PROP MAT élément d'alliage *m*; ~ **method** *n* ELECTRON méthode d'alliage *f*

all-pass: ~ **filter** *n* ELECTRON filtre passe-tout *m*

all-plastic: ~ **fiber** *n* (AmE), ~ **fibre** *n* (BrE) TELECOM fibre plastique *f*; ~ **optical fiber** *n* (AmE), ~ **optical fibre** *n* (BrE) ELEC ENG fibre optique plastique-plastique *f*

all-purpose: ~ **adhesive** *n* PACKAGING colle à usages multiples *f*; ~ **trailer** *n* TRANSP remorque polyvalente *f*

all-rag: ~ **paper** *n* PAPER TECH papier de chiffons *m*, papier pur chiffon *m*, pur chiffon *m*

all-round: ~ **light** *n* NAUT feu d'horizon *m*; ~ **swing crane** *n* (BrE) CONST grue pivotante *f*, grue à rotation complète *f*

all-silica: ~ **fiber** *n* (AmE), ~ **fibre** *n* (BrE) TELECOM fibre de silice *f*

all-solid: ~ **state** *adj* ELECTRON entièrement transistorisé

all-speed: ~ **aileron** *n* TRANSP aileron intérieur *m*

all-tantalum: ~ **capacitor** *n* ELEC ENG condensateur tout tantale *m*

all-terrain: ~ **vehicle** *n* *(AT vehicle)* TRANSP, véhicule tout-terrain *m*

alluaudite *n* MINERAL alluaudite *f*

all-up: ~ **weight** *n* *(AUW)* TRANSP poids total en charge *m*

alluvial: ~ **areas** *n pl* CONST aires d'alluvions *f pl*; ~ **bed** *n* WATER SUPP canal alluvial *m*, lit alluvial *m*; ~ **cone** *n* HYDROL cône d'alluvion *m*, WATER SUPP cône d'éboulis *m*; ~ **deposit** *n* OCEANOG dépôt alluvial *m*, WATER SUPP dépôt alluvionnaire *m*; ~ **mining** *n* MINING gisements alluvionnaires *m pl*, minière *f*, placer *m*; ~ **nappe** *n* HYDROL nappe alluviale *f*; ~ **plain** *n* WATER SUPP plaine alluviale *f*

alluviation *n* OCEANOG atterrissement *m*

alluvium *n* OCEANOG alluvion *f*, lais *m*, lais de la mer *m*, PETR alluvion *f*

all-watt: ~ **motor** *n* ELEC moteur à phases compensées *m*

all-weather: ~ **helicopter** *n* AERONAUT hélicoptère tous-temps *m*; ~ **operations** *n pl* AERONAUT exploitation tous-temps *f*; ~ **search aircraft** *n* MILIT avion de recherche tous-temps *m*

allyl *n* CHEM allyle *m*; ~ **alcohol** *n* CHEM alcool allylique *m*; ~ **glycidyl ether** *n* *(AGE)* P&R *epoxy resin* éther allylglycidique *m*

almandine *n* MINERAL almandin *m*

almandite *n* MINERAL almandin *m*

Almen: ~ **test strip** *n* SPRINGS éprouvette Almen *f*

alnoeite *n* MINERAL alnoeite *f*

alnoite *n* MINERAL alnoeite *f*

ALOHA: ~ **system** *n* TELECOM système ALOHA *m*

aloin *n* CHEM aloïne *f*

along: ~ **the line of strike** *adv* MINING en direction; ~ **the strike** *adv* MINING en direction

alongshore *adv* NAUT le long de la côte

alongside[1] *adv* NAUT *ship or quay* bord à bord, à couple

alongside[2] *prep* NAUT *ship or quay* bord à bord avec, le long de, le long du bord de, à côté de, à couple de

along-track: ~ **error** *n* SPACE erreur longitudinale *f*

alpha: ~ **cellulose** *n* PAPER TECH alpha-cellulose *f*; ~ **decay** *n* PART PHYS, PHYS désintégration alpha *f*; ~ **device** *n* NUCLEAR dispositif alpha *m*; ~ **disintegration energy** *n* PHYS énergie de désintégration alpha *f*; ~ **elimination mechanism** *n* RAD PHYS *ionizing radiation* mécanisme d'élimination alpha *m*; ~ **emitter** *n* PHYS, RAD PHYS émetteur alpha *m*; ~ **ionization gas analyzer** *n* NUCLEAR analyseur de gaz à ionisation alpha *m*; ~ **particle** *n* ASTRON, ELEC, PART PHYS, PHYS, RAD PHYS particule alpha *f*; ~ **profile** *n* OPT profil d'indice à loi en puissance *m*, profil à loi en puissance *m*; ~ **ray** *n* PHYS rayon alpha *m*; ~ **ray spectrometry** *n* RAD PHYS spectrométrie à rayons alpha *f*; ~ **wrap** *n* TV *tape path* enroulement *m*, guidage alpha *m*

alphabet *n* DP alphabet *m*

alphabetic[1] *adj* DP alphabétique

alphabetic:[2] ~ **code** *n* DP code alphabétique *m*

alphageometric: ~ **display** *n* TELECOM affichage alpha-géométrique *m*

alphamosaic *adj* DP alphamosaïque

alphanumeric[1] *adj* DP alphanumérique

alphanumeric:[2] ~ **character** *n* DP caractère alphanumérique *m*; ~ **code** *n* DP code alphanumérique *m*; ~ **display** *n* TELECOM affichage alphanumérique *m*; ~ **pager** *n* TELECOM récepteur alphanumérique *m*; ~ **sort** *n* COMP tri alphanumérique *m*

alquifou *n* MINERAL alquifoux *m*, galène *m*

alquifoux *n* MINERAL alquifoux *m*, galène *m*

ALS *abbr* TELECOM *(automatic laser shutdown)* coupure automatique du laser *f*, TELECOM *(application layer structure)* structure en couches d'application *f*

alstonite *n* MINERAL alstonite *f*

altaite *n* MINERAL altaïte *f*

altazimuth: ~ **mounting** *n* ASTRON, INSTRUMENT monture altazimutale *f*

altazimuthal: ~ **mount** *n* ASTRON monture altazimutale *f*

alterable: ~ **optical memory** *n* OPT mémoire optique effaçable *f*

alteration *n* ACOUSTICS altération *f*; ~ **of course** *n* NAUT *navigation* changement de cap *m*, changement de route *m*, SPACE changement de cap *m*, changement de direction *m*

alternate: ~ **action switch** *n* ELEC ENG inverseur à point milieu *m*; ~ **current motor** *n* PHYS moteur à courant alternatif *m*; ~ **exterior angles** *n pl* GEOM angles alternes-externes *m pl*; ~ **interior angles** *n pl* GEOM angles alternes-internes *m pl*; ~ **landing site** *n* SPACE terrain d'atterrissage de dégagement *m*; ~ **mark inversion** *n (AMI)* TELECOM signal bipolaire alternant *m*; ~ **mode** *n* ELECTRON mode alterné *m*; ~ **routing** *n* PROD ENG gamme de remplacement *f*; ~ **speech service** *n* TELECOM *ISDN* service mixte parole *m*

alternating[1] *adj* ELEC, MECH ENG alternatif

alternating:[2] ~ **burst** *n* TV salve alternante *f*; ~ **colored lights** *n pl* (AmE), ~ **coloured lights** *n pl* (BrE) NAUT feux alternatifs *m pl*, feux mixtes *m pl*; ~ **component** *n* ELEC *alternating current* composante alternative *f*; ~ **current** *n (AC)* ELEC, ELEC ENG, ELECTRON, PHYS, RECORDING, TELECOM, TV courant alternatif *m (CA)*; ~ **current arc** *n* ELEC arc en courant alternatif *m*; ~ **current balancer** *n* ELEC compensateur de courant alternatif *m*, égaliseur de courant alternatif *m*; ~ **current bridge** *n* ELEC *measurement* pont en courant alternatif *m*, PHYS pont alternatif *m*, TESTING pont de courant alternatif *m*; ~ **current circuit** *n* ELEC circuit de

courant alternatif *m*; ~ **current component** *n* ELEC composante alternative d'un courant *f*; ~ **current coupler** *n* TELECOM coupleur alternatif *m*; ~ **current field** *n* ELEC *electromagnetism* champ de courant alternatif *m*; ~ **current generator** *n* ELEC alternateur *m*; ~ **current hum** *n* ELEC *of amplifier* bruit de courant alternatif *m*; ~ **current machine** *n* ELEC, ELEC ENG machine à courant alternatif *f*; ~ **current motor** *n* ELEC moteur à courant alternatif *m*, ELEC ENG moteur électrique à courant alternatif *m*, moteur à courant alternatif *m*; ~ **current network** *n* ELEC réseau à courant alternatif *m*, ELEC ENG réseau électrique à courant alternatif *m*, réseau à courant alternatif *m*; ~ **current output** *n* ELEC ENG sortie alternative *f*, sortie en courant alternatif *f*; ~ **current relay** *n* ELEC relais à courant alternatif *m*; ~ **current servomotor** *n* ELEC ENG servomoteur à courant alternatif *m*; ~ **current source** *n* ELEC ENG source alternative *f*, source de courant alternatif *f*; ~ **current supply** *n* ELEC alimentation à courant alternatif *f*; ~ **current transmission line** *n* ELEC *supply network* ligne de transport à courant alternatif *f*; ~ **current voltmeter** *n* ELEC voltmètre pour courant alternatif *m*; ~ **electric field** *n* ELEC ENG champ électrique alternatif *m*; ~ **electromotive force** *n* ELEC force électromotrice appliquée *f*; ~ **field** *n* ELEC ENG champ alternatif *m*; ~ **flux** *n* ELEC *electromagnetism* flux alternatif *m*, flux alterné *m*; ~ **magnetic field** *n* ELEC ENG champ magnétique alternatif *m*; ~ **motion** *n* MECH ENG mouvement alternatif *m*, mouvement alterné *m*, va-et-vient *m*; ~ **quantity** *n* TESTING grandeur alternative *f*; ~ **saw** *n* MECH ENG scie à mouvement alternatif *f*; ~ **voltage** *n* ELEC, ELEC ENG tension alternative *f*

alternation *n* MECH ENG alternance *f*, alternation *f*; ~ **of a movement** *n* MECH ENG alternation d'un mouvement *f*

alternative: ~ **current generator** *n* PHYS alternateur *m*, génératrice à courant alternatif *f*; ~ **route** *n* TELECOM voie d'acheminement détourné *f*; ~ **routing** *n* TELECOM acheminement détourné *m*; ~ **test method** *n (ATM)* OPT méthode de mesure de remplacement *f*, méthode possible pour les mesures *f*

alternator *n* ELEC *generator*, ELEC ENG, FUELLESS *hydroelectricity, windpower* alternateur *m*, PHYS alternateur *m*, génératrice à courant alternatif *f*, VEHICLES *electrical system* dynamo *f*; ~ **field voltage** *n* ELEC tension d'excitation d'alternateur *f*

altimeter *n* AERONAUT, GEOPHYS, PHYS, SPACE, TRANSP altimètre *m*; ~ **setting** *n* AERONAUT calage altimétrique *m*, réglage altimétrique *m*

altimetry *n* PHYS altimétrie *f*

altitude *n* GEOM, NAUT *celestial navigation* hauteur *f*, PHYS altitude *f*, hauteur *f*, élévation *f*, SPACE altitude *f*, hauteur *f*, site *m*; ~ **controller** *n* AERONAUT contrôleur d'altitude *m*; ~ **corrector** *n* AUTO correcteur altimétrique *m*; ~ **of optimum rainfall** *n* METEO altitude de l'optimum pluvial *f*

altocumulus *n* AERONAUT, METEO altocumulus *m*

altostratus *n* AERONAUT, METEO altostratus *m*

ALU *abbr (arithmetic and logic unit)* COMP ULA *(unité arithmétique et logique)*

alum *n* CHEM, MINERAL alun *m*, PAPER TECH alun *m*, alun des papetiers *m*, PRINT agent durcissant *m*, alun *m*

alumian *n* MINERAL alumiane *f*

alumina *n* CHEM alumine *f*, oxyde d'aluminium *m*, MINERAL, PAPER TECH alumine *f*; ~ **content** *n* COAL TECH teneur en alumine *f*

aluminate[1] *n* CHEM aluminate *m*, aluminiate *m*

aluminate² *vt* CHEM aluminer, aluner, PAPER TECH aluminer

alumination *n* CHEM alunage *m*, PAPER TECH aluminage *m*

aluminiferous *adj* CHEM aluminifère, alunifère

aluminite *n* MINERAL aluminite *f*

aluminium *n* (BrE) *(Al)* CHEM aluminium *m (Al)*; ~ **alloy** *n* (BrE) MECH ENG *for solid bearings*, PROP MAT alliage d'aluminium *m*; ~ **anode** *n* (BrE) ELEC ENG anode en aluminium *f*; ~ **bottle** *n* (BrE) PACKAGING bouteille en aluminium *f*; ~ **bronze** *n* (BrE) MECH *materials* bronze d'aluminium *m*; ~ **can** *n* (BrE) NUCLEAR gaine en alumine *f*, PACKAGING boîte d'aluminium *f*; ~ **can bank** *n* (BrE) RECYCLING conteneur de boîtes en aluminium *m*; ~ **capsule** *n* (BrE) PACKAGING capsule d'aluminium *f*; ~ **chlorohydrate** *n* (BrE) HYDROL hydrate de chlorure d'aluminium *m*; ~ **conductor** *n* (BrE) ELEC conducteur en aluminium *m*; ~ **electrolytic capacitor** *n* (BrE) ELEC ENG condensateur électrochimique à l'aluminium *m*, condensateur électrolytique à l'aluminium *m*, condensateur à l'aluminium *m*; ~ **foil** *n* (BrE) FOOD TECH feuille d'aluminium *f*, papier d'aluminium *m*, HEAT ENG feuille d'aluminium *f*, PACKAGING feuille mince d'aluminium *f*, PAPER TECH papier d'aluminium *m*; ~ **garnet** *n* (BrE) MINERAL grenat alumineux *m*; ~ **gate** *n* (BrE) ELECTRON grille en aluminium *f*; ~ **hydroxide** *n* (BrE) HYDROL, P&R *filler* hydroxyde d'aluminium *m*; ~ **oxide** *n* (BrE) CHEM alumine *f*, oxyde d'aluminium *m*; ~ **pellet** *n* (BrE) NUCLEAR pastille d'aluminium *f*; ~ **sheet** *n* (BrE) PACKAGING feuille d'aluminium *f*; ~ **silicate** *n* (BrE) DETERGENTS silicate d'aluminium *m*, silico-aluminate *m*; ~ **silicate fibre** *n* (BrE) HEAT ENG fibre de silicate d'aluminium *f*; ~ **sulphate** *n* (BrE) HYDROL sulfate d'aluminium *m*; ~ **tape** *n* (BrE) PACKAGING ruban d'aluminium *m*; ~ **tube** *n* (BrE) PACKAGING tube d'aluminium *m*

aluminium-coated *adj* (BrE) COATINGS aluminé

aluminium-killed: ~ **steel** *n* (BrE) MECH *materials* acier calmé à l'aluminium *m*

aluminized: ~ **screen** *n* ELECTRON écran aluminisé *m*; ~ **Teflon** *n* (TM) SPACE *spacecraft* Téflon aluminisé *m* (MD)

aluminosilicate *n* CHEM, MINERAL aluminosilicate *m*; ~ **brick** *n* HEATING *furnace lining* brique d'aluminosilicate *f*

aluminothermic: ~ **welding** *n* MECH soudure par aluminothermie *f*

aluminous *adj* CHEM alumineux

aluminum *n* (AmE) *see aluminium*

aluminum-coated *adj* (AmE) *see aluminium-coated*

aluminum-killed: ~ **steel** *n* (AmE) *see aluminium-killed steel*

alunite *n* MINERAL alunite *f*

alunogen *n* MINERAL alunite *f*

alurgite *n* MINERAL alurgite *f*

alveolar: ~ **dolomite** *n* GEOL *geological formation* cargneule *f*, carnieule *f*

alvite *n* MINERAL alvite *f*

alychne *n* TV plan de luminance zéro *m*

Am *(americium)* CHEM Am *(américium)*

AM¹ *abbr (amplitude modulation)* COMP, ELECTRON, RECORDING, TV MA *(modulation d'amplitude)*

AM:² ~ **carrier** *n* ELECTRON porteuse AM *f*; ~ **noise** *n* ELECTRON bruit modulé en amplitude *m*; ~ **signal** *n* ELECTRON signal modulé en amplitude *m*

amalgam *n* CHEM *of metal and mercury*, COAL TECH, MINERAL amalgame *m*; ~ **barrel** *n* COAL TECH amalgamateur *m*

amalgamate *vt* COAL TECH amalgamer

amalgamating: ~ **table** *n* COAL TECH table d'amalgamation *f*

amalgamation *n* COAL TECH amalgamation *f*; ~ **plate** *n* COAL TECH plaque d'amalgamation *f*

amalgamator *n* COAL TECH, MECH ENG amalgamateur *m*

amarine *n* CHEM amarine *f*

amateur: ~ **radio service** *n* TELECOM service radio d'amateur *m*

amausite *n* MINERAL amausite *f*

Amazon: ~ **stone** *n* MINERAL amazonite *f*

amazonite *n* MINERAL amazonite *f*

amber *n* MINERAL ambre *m*; ~ **varnish** *n* COATINGS vernis au succin *m*

amberoid *n* MINERAL ambroïne *f*

ambience: ~ **track** *n* CINEMAT silence modulé *m*

ambient¹ *adj* REFRIG ambiant

ambient:² ~ **air** *n* POLLUTION, REFRIG air ambiant *m*; ~ **emission standard** *n* POLLUTION *air* limite de nuisance *f*, norme relative aux émissions atmosphériques *f*; ~ **fluid** *n* FLUID PHYS fluide ambiant *m*; ~ **light** *n* CINEMAT lumière ambiante *f*; ~ **noise** *n* RECORDING son ambiant *m*, TELECOM bruit ambiant *m*; ~ **pollutant concentration** *n* POLLUTION concentration locale d'un polluant *f*; ~ **quality standard** *n* POLLUTION *of air* limite de nuisance *f*, norme relative à la qualité de l'air ambiant *f*; ~ **radioactivity** *n* RAD PHYS radioactivité ambiante *f*; ~ **temperature** *n* GAS TECH, HEATING, METALL, METR, PACKAGING, PHYS, THERMOD température ambiante *f*

ambiguity: ~ **resolution** *n* SPACE *communications* levée d'ambiguïté *f*

amblygonite *n* MINERAL amblygonite *f*

ambrain *n* CHEM ambréine *f*

ambrite *n* MINERAL ambrite *f*, ambérite *f*

ambroid *n* MINERAL ambroïne *f*

ambulance *n* TRANSP ambulance *f*; ~ **installation** *n* AERONAUT installation de transport sanitaire *f*; ~ **station** *n* SAFETY poste de secours *m*

amend *vt* MECH ENG modifier, rectifier

amendment *n* MECH ENG amendement *m*, rectificatif *m*, PATENTS modification *f*; ~ **file** *n* COMP fichier des mouvements *m*; ~ **record** *n* COMP modificatif *m*

American: ~ **National Pipe Taper** *n* MECH ENG filetage conique de tuyauterie à norme américaine *m*; ~ **National Standards Institute** *n* *(ANSI)* TELECOM Institut américain de normalisation *m (ANSI)*; ~ **NPT** *n* MECH ENG filetage conique de tuyauterie à norme américaine *m*; ~ **Standard Code for Information Interchange** *n* *(ASCII)* COMP, DP, PRINT ASCII

americium *n* *(Am)* CHEM américium *m (Am)*

amesite *n* MINERAL amésite *f*

amethyst *n* MINERAL améthyste *f*

AMI *abbr (alternate mark inversion)* TELECOM signal bipolaire alternant *m*

amiant *n* MINERAL amiante *m*

amianthinite *n* MINERAL amianthinite *f*

amianthus *n* MINERAL amiante *m*

amic: ~ **acid** *n* CHEM amide d'acide *m*

Amici: ~ **prism** *n* PHYS *direct vision prism* prisme en toit *m*, prisme à vision directe *m*

amide *n* CHEM *compound, group*, DETERGENTS, P&R amide *m*; ~ **hardener** *n* P&R *adhesives, coatings* durcissant amidique *m*, durcisseur amidique *m*

amidine *n* CHEM amidine *f*

amidogen *n* CHEM amidogène *m*

amidships *adv* NAUT au centre du navire, au milieu du navire

amination *n* CHEM amination *f*

amine *n* DETERGENTS, P&R amine *f*

amine-cured: ~ **epoxy** *n* P&R *adhesives, coatings* époxyde à durcissement aminique *m*

amine-curing: ~ **agent** *n* P&R *adhesives, coatings* durcissant aminique *m*, durcisseur aminique *m*

amino: ~ **acid** *n* CHEM acide aminé *m*, amino acide *m*, FOOD TECH acide aminé *m*; ~ **resin** *n* P&R *coatings, adhesives* amino résine *f*, aminoplaste *f*, résine amino *f*

amino- *pref* CHEM amino-

aminoazo *adj* CHEM azoamidé, azoaminé

ammeter *n* ELEC, ELEC ENG, LAB EQUIP *electric current,* PHYS, TV, VEHICLES *electrical system* ampèremètre *m*

ammine *n* CHEM ammine *f*

ammiolite *n* MINERAL ammiolite *f*

ammonal *n* CHEM ammonal *m*

ammonia *n* CHEM ammoniac *m*, ammoniaque *f*, DETERGENTS, ELECTRON ammoniaque *f*, HYDROL ammoniac *m*, PAPER TECH ammoniaque *f*, POLLUTION ammoniac *m*, SPACE ammoniaque *f*; ~ **alum** *n* CHEM, PAPER TECH alun ammoniacal *m*; ~ **carboy** *n* DETERGENTS bonbonne d'ammoniaque *f*; ~ **dynamite** *n* MINING explosif nitraté *m*; ~ **gas** *n* DETERGENTS, HYDROL gaz ammoniac *m*; ~ **hydrate** *n* PAPER TECH solution aqueuse d'ammoniaque *f*; ~ **maser** *n* ELECTRON maser à l'ammoniaque *m*

ammoniacal *adj* CHEM ammoniacal

ammonical: ~ **hydroxide** *n* PAPER TECH solution aqueuse d'ammoniaque *f*; ~ **water** *n* PAPER TECH eau ammoniacale *f*

ammonite *n* GEOL *palaeontology* ammonite *f*

ammonium *n* CHEM ammonium *m*; ~ **chloride** *n* CHEM chlorure d'ammonium *m*; ~ **hydroxide** *n* PETR TECH ammoniaque *f*; ~ **nitrate fuel oil** *n (ANFO)* MINING nitrate d'ammonium et fuel-oil *m*, nitrate-fioul *m*, nitrate-fuel *m*, nitrate-huile *m*; ~ **perchlorate** *n* SPACE *spacecraft* perchlorate d'ammonium *m*

ammonolysis *n* PROP MAT ammonolyse *f*

ammunition *n* MILIT munitions *f pl*; ~ **box** *n* MILIT coffre à munitions *m*; ~ **depot** *n* MILIT dépôt de munitions *m*; ~ **dump** *n* MILIT dépôt de munitions *m*

amorphism *n* CHEM amorphie *f*, amorphisme *m*

amorphous[1] *adj* CHEM, COAL TECH, CRYSTALL amorphe, GEOL amorphe, non cristallin

amorphous:[2] ~ **layer** *n* ELECTRON couche amorphe *f*; ~ **semiconductor** *n* ELECTRON semi-conducteur amorphe *m*; ~ **silicon** *n* ELECTRON silicium amorphe *m*; ~ **structure** *n* P&R structure amorphe *f*; ~ **substrate** *n* ELECTRON substrat amorphe *m*

amount: ~ **of substance** *n* PHYS quantité de matière *f*

amp *n (A, ampere)* ELEC, ELEC ENG, METR, PHYS ampere

amp: ~ **rating** *n* PROD ENG intensité nominale *f*

amperage *n* ELEC *current* intensité du courant *f*, ELEC ENG ampérage *m*

ampere *n (A, amp)* ELEC, ELEC ENG, METR, PHYS ampère *m*; ~ **balance** *n* ELEC balance électrodynamique *f*; ~ **conductor** *n* ELEC ampère-conducteur *m*; ~ **density** *n* ELEC *of current* densité de courant *f*; ~ **turn** *n* METR ampère tour *m*

Ampère's: ~ **law** *n* PHYS théorème d'Ampère *m*; ~ **rule** *n* ELEC *electromagnetism* règle d'Ampère *f*; ~ **theorem** *n* ELEC théorème d'Ampère *m*

ampere-hour *n* ELEC *quantity*, PHYS ampère-heure *m*; ~ **capacity** *n* PHOTO ampérage *m*

Ampère-Laplace: ~ **theorem** *n* ELEC théorème d'Ampère-Laplace *m*

ampere-second *n* ELEC ampère-seconde *m*

ampere-turn *n* ELEC *of winding*, PHYS ampère-tour *m*

Amperian: ~ **current** *n* PHYS courant ampérien *m*

ampersand *n* PRINT esperluète *f*

amphibian[1] *adj* NAUT amphibie

amphibian[2] *n* NAUT voiture amphibie *f*

amphibious: ~ **armored car** *n* (AmE), ~ **armoured car** *n* (BrE) MILIT auto blindée amphibie *f*; ~ **tank** *n* MILIT char d'assaut amphibie *m*; ~ **vehicle** *n* MILIT véhicule amphibie *m*

amphibole *n* CHEM, MINERAL amphibole *f*

amphibolic *adj* MINERAL amphibolique

amphiboliferous *adj* MINERAL amphibolifère

amphibolite *n* PETR amphibolite *f*

amphiboloid *adj* MINERAL amphiboloïde

amphiphilic[1] *adj* DETERGENTS amphiphile

amphiphilic:[2] ~ **compound** *n* DETERGENTS composé amphiphile *m*

amphitalite *n* MINERAL amphitalite *f*

amphodelite *n* MINERAL amphodélite *f*

ampholyte *n* CHEM ampholyte *m*

amphoteric[1] *adj* CHEM, DETERGENTS amphotère

amphoteric:[2] ~ **compound** *n* DETERGENTS composé amphotère *m*

amplidyne *n* ELEC ENG amplidyne *f*

amplification *n* ELEC *of signal*, ELECTRON, RECORDING amplification *f*; ~ **factor** *n* ELECTRON coefficient d'amplification *m*, RECORDING facteur d'amplification *m*; ~ **ratio** *n* RECORDING rapport d'amplification *m*

amplified: ~ **circuit** *n* TELECOM circuit amplifié *m*; ~ **handset** *n* TELECOM combiné téléphonique à écoute amplifiée *m*

amplifier *n* COMP, DP, ELEC, ELECTRON amplificateur *m*, NAUT *radar* ampli *m*, amplificateur *m*, PHYS, RECORDING, TELECOM, WAVE PHYS amplificateur *m*; ~ **chip** *n* ELECTRON puce amplificatrice *f*; ~ **circuit** *n* ELECTRON montage amplificateur *m*; ~ **class** *n* ELECTRON classe d'un amplificateur *f*; ~ **gain** *n* ELECTRON, PHYS gain d'un amplificateur *m*; ~ **noise** *n* ELECTRON bruit de l'amplificateur *m*; ~ **stage** *n* ELECTRON étage amplificateur *m*; ~ **tube** *n* ELECTRON tube amplificateur *m*

amplify *vt* COMP, DP, ELECTRON, WAVE PHYS amplifier

amplifying[1] *adj* ELEC amplificateur

amplifying:[2] ~ **circuit** *n* ELECTRON montage amplificateur *m*; ~ **stage** *n* RECORDING étage d'amplification *m*; ~ **transistor** *n* ELECTRON transistor amplificateur *m*

amplitron *n* ELECTRON, PHYS amplitron *m*

amplitude *n* ACOUSTICS, ASTRON *of star*, COMP, ELEC *wave*, ELECTRON, FUELLESS *tidal power*, NAUT *of celestial body*, PHYS, RECORDING, WAVE PHYS amplitude *f*; ~ **adjustment** *n* ELECTRON réglage de l'amplitude *m*; ~ **calibration** *n* ELECTRON calibrage de l'amplitude *m*; ~ **calibrator** *n* ELECTRON calibrateur d'amplitude *m*; ~ **control** *n* WAVE PHYS réglage d'amplitude *m*; ~ **corrector** *n* TV correcteur d'amplitude *m*; ~ **demodulation** *n* ELECTRON démodulation d'amplitude *f*; ~ **distortion** *n* ELECTRON, PHYS, RECORDING, TELECOM, WAVE PHYS distorsion d'amplitude *f*; ~ **equalizer** *n* TELECOM égaliseur d'amplitude *m*; ~ **frequency distortion** *n* RECORDING distorsion d'amplitude non linéaire *f*; ~ **gate** *n* ELECTRON porte de sélection d'amplitude *f*; ~

information *n* ELECTRON information d'amplitude *f*; ~ **limiter** *n* ELECTRON limiteur d'amplitude *m*; ~ **limiter circuit** *n* TV circuit d'écrêtage *m*, limiteur *m*; ~ **modulation** *n* COMP *(AM)*, ELEC *wave*, ELECTRON *(AM)*, PHYS, RECORDING *(AM)*, TELECOM, TV *(AM)*, WAVE PHYS modulation d'amplitude *f*; ~ **modulation noise** *n* RECORDING bruit de modulation d'amplitude *m*; ~ **modulator** *n* ELECTRON modulateur d'amplitude *m*; ~ **probability distribution** *n* *(APD)* TELECOM distribution de probabilité des amplitudes *f*, répartition de probabilité des amplitudes *f*; ~ **resonance** *n* PHYS résonance d'amplitude *f*; ~ **response** *n* ELECTRON réponse en amplitude *f*; ~ **response curve** *n* ELECTRON courbe de réponse en amplitude *f*; ~ **shift keying** *n* ELECTRON modulation par sauts d'amplitude *f*; ~ **spectrum** *n* PETR spectre d'amplitude *m*, WAVE PHYS spectre d'amplitudes *m*; ~ **threshold** *n* ELECTRON seuil d'amplitude *m*

amplitude-amplitude: ~ **distortion** *n* ELECTRON distorsion d'amplitude *f*; ~ **response** *n* ELECTRON réponse amplitude-amplitude *f*

amplitude-frequency: ~ **distortion** *n* ELECTRON distorsion amplitude-fréquence *f*; ~ **response** *n* ELECTRON réponse amplitude-fréquence *f*; ~ **response curve** *n* ELECTRON courbe de réponse amplitude-fréquence *f*

amplitude-modulated[1] *adj* ELECTRON modulé en amplitude

amplitude-modulated:[2] ~ **carrier** *n* ELECTRON porteuse modulée en amplitude *f*

AM-PM: ~ **conversion coefficient** *n* SPACE *communications* coefficient de conversion AM-PM *m*; ~ **transfer coefficient** *n* SPACE *communications* coefficient de transfert AM-PM *m*

ampoule *n* C&G, LAB EQUIP *glassware*, PACKAGING ampoule *f*; ~ **box** *n* PACKAGING boîte pour ampoules *f*

ampule *n* (AmE) *see ampoule*

amyl *n* CHEM, PAPER TECH amyle *m* ~ **acetate** *n* P&R *solvent*, PAPER TECH acétate d'amyle *m*; ~ **alcohol** *n* PAPER TECH alcool amylique *m*

amylaceous *adj* FOOD TECH farineux, PAPER TECH amylacé

amylic *adj* PAPER TECH amylique

amylopectin *n* TEXTILES amylopectine *f*

anabatic: ~ **front** *n* *(cf katabatic front)* METEO front anabatique *m*

anachromatic: ~ **lens** *n* PHOTO objectif anachromatique *m*

anaerobe *n* FOOD TECH *microorganism*, HYDROL, OCEANOG, RECYCLING anaérobie *f*

anaerobic[1] *adj* FOOD TECH *microorganism* anaérobique, HYDROL *sewage* anaérobie, anaérobique, RECYCLING anaérobie

anaerobic:[2] ~ **adhesive** *n* P&R adhésif anaérobie *m*; ~ **decomposition** *n* HYDROL *sewage* décomposition anaérobie *f*, dégradation anaérobie *f*, RECYCLING décomposition anaérobie *f*; ~ **digestion** *n* RECYCLING digestion anaérobie *f*; ~ **treatment** *n* RECYCLING traitement anaérobie *m*

anaerobiosis *n* RECYCLING anaérobiose *f*

anaerobium *n* (AmE) *see anaerobe*

anaglyph: ~ **process** *n* CINEMAT système anaglyphe *m*

Anaglypta *n* COATINGS papier peint anagIyptique *m*

anaglyptic: ~ **wallpaper** *n* COATINGS papier peint anaglyptique *m*

analog (AmE), **analogue** (BrE)[1] *adj* ELEC ENG, ELECTRON, COMP, DP, PETR, TELECOM analogique

analog (AmE), **analogue** (BrE):[2] ~ **actuator** *n* ELEC ENG actionneur analogique *m*; ~ **ammeter** *n* ELEC ENG ampèremètre analogique *m*; ~ **bipolar integrated circuit** *n* ELECTRON circuit intégré bipolaire analogique *m*; ~ **board** *n* ELECTRON carte analogique *f*; ~ **calculation** *n* COMP calcul analogique *m*; ~ **call processor** *n* TELECOM calculateur analogique *m*; ~ **carrier system** *n* COMP, DP système à porteuse analogique *m*; ~ **channel** *n* COMP, DP voie analogique *f*; ~ **chip** *n* ELECTRON puce analogique *f*; ~ **circuit** *n* ELEC ENG circuit analogique *m*, ELECTRON circuit analogique *m*, montage analogique *m*, TELECOM circuit analogique *m*; ~ **circuit design** *n* ELECTRON conception des circuits analogiques *f*; ~ **comparator** *n* ELECTRON comparateur analogique *m*; ~ **data** *n* ELECTRON données analogiques *f pl*; ~ **delay line** *n* TV ligne à retard analogique *f*; ~ **device** *n* TELECOM appareil analogique *m*; ~ **filter** *n* ELECTRON filtre analogique *m*; ~ **filtering** *n* ELECTRON filtrage analogique *m*; ~ **gate** *n* ELECTRON porte analogique *f*; ~ **incremental system** *n* COMP système analogique relatif *m*; ~ **information** *n* ELECTRON information analogique *f*; ~ **integrated circuit** *n* ELECTRON circuit intégré analogique *m*; ~ **interface** *n* TELECOM interface analogique *f*; ~ **line driver** *n* COMP amplificateur d'attaque de ligne *m*; ~ **measuring instrument** *n* ELEC instrument de mesure analogique *m*, METR appareil de mesure analogique *m*; ~ **measuring system** *n* COMP système de mesures analogique *m*; ~ **meter** *n* ELEC ENG appareil indicateur analogique *m*; ~ **modulation** *n* ELECTRON, PHYS modulation analogique *f*; ~ **output** *n* INSTRUMENT sortie analogique *f*; ~ **private wire** *n* TELECOM liaison spécialisée tous-usages *f*; ~ **quantity** *n* COMP, DP quantité analogique *f*; ~ **recording** *n* TELECOM enregistrement analogique *m*; ~ **shift register** *n* COMP, DP registre à décalage analogique *m*; ~ **signal** *n* COMP, ELECTRON, PHYS, TELECOM signal analogique *m*; ~ **signal generator** *n* ELECTRON générateur de signaux analogiques *m*; ~ **signal processing** *n* ELECTRON traitement analogique des signaux *m*; ~ **switching system** *n* TELECOM système de commutation analogique *m*; ~ **system** *n* TELECOM système analogique *m*; ~ **transmission** *n* TELECOM transmission analogique *f*; ~ **videodisk** *n* OPT vidéodisque analogique *m*; ~ **voltmeter** *n* ELEC ENG voltmètre analogique *m*

analogous: ~ **pole** *n* CRYSTALL *pyroelectricity* pôle analogue *m*

analog-to-digital (AmE), **analogue-to-digital** (BrE)[1] *adj* *(A-to-D)* TV analogique-numérique

analog-to-digital (AmE), **analogue-to-digital** (BrE):[2] ~ **conversion** *n* ELEC conversion analogique-numérique *f*, ELECTRON numérisation *f*, RECORDING conversion analogique-numérique *f*; ~ **converter** *n* (BrE) *(ADC)* ELECTRON convertisseur analogique-numérique *m*, numériseur *m*, PHYS, TELECOM convertisseur analogique-numérique *m* *(CAN)*

analysis *n* CHEM analyse *f*, essai *m*, COAL TECH analyse *f*, MECH ENG analyse *f*, étude *f*, QUALITY, TEXTILES, WATER SUPP analyse *f*; ~ **error** *n* COAL TECH erreur d'analyse *f*; ~ **laboratory** *n* COAL TECH laboratoire d'analyse *m*; ~ **sample** *n* COAL TECH échantillon d'essai *m*; ~ **of variance** *n* *(ANOVA)* COMP analyse de la variance *f*

analyst *n* CHEM analyste *m*, essayeur *m*

analytic[1] *adj* CHEM analytique

analytic:[2] ~ **projector** *n* CINEMAT appareil de projection d'analyse *m*

analytical[1] *adj* CHEM analytique

analytical:[2] ~ **balance** *n* LAB EQUIP balance sensible *f*, PHYS balance d'analyse *f*; ~ **engine** *n* COMP machine analytique *f*; ~ **geometry** *n* GEOM géométrie analytique *f*; ~ **mechanics** *n* PHYS mécanique analytique *f*

analyze *vt* CHEM analyser, essayer

analyzer *n* COMP, DP analyseur syntaxique *m*, ELECTRON, METALL, PHYS, TELECOM analyseur *m*

analyzing: ~ **projector** *n* CINEMAT appareil de projection pour étude de mouvement *m*

anamesite *n* PETR anamésite *f*

anamorphic[1] *adj* CINEMAT anamorphoseur, anamorphosé

anamorphic:[2] ~ **lens** *n* CINEMAT objectif anamorphoseur *m*, INSTRUMENT lentille anamorphosique *f*, PHOTO anamorphoseur *m*; ~ **print** *n* CINEMAT copie anamorphosée *f*; ~ **squeeze** *n* CINEMAT coefficient d'anamorphose *m*; ~ **system** *n* CINEMAT système anamorphoseur *m*

anamorphoser *n* CINEMAT objectif anamorphoseur *m*

anamorphosing: ~ **printing** *n* CINEMAT tirage optique anamorphosé *m*

anamorphosis *n* TELECOM anamorphose *f*

anastigmat *n* PHOTO, PHYS anastigmat *m*; ~ **lens** *n* PHOTO objectif anastigmat *m*

anastigmatic: ~ **lens** *n* CINEMAT objectif anastigmatique *m*, PHOTO objectif anastigmat *m*, objectif anastigmatique *m*, objectif stigmatique *m*

anatexis *n* GEOL anatexie *f*

anatto *n* FOOD TECH anatto *m*

ANC *abbr (acid neutralizing capacity)* POLLUTION CNA *(capacité de neutralisation des acides)*, PNA *(potentiel de neutralisation de l'acide, pouvoir neutralisant des acides)*

ancestor *n* DP *of a node* ancêtre *m*

anchor[1] *n* CONST *building* ancre *f*, MECH ancrage *m*, NAUT ancre *f*; ~ **arm** *n* NAUT bras d'ancre *m*; ~ **bearing** *n* NAUT relèvement du mouillage *m*; ~ **bill** *n* NAUT bec d'ancre *m*; ~ **bolt** *n* CONST, MECH, MECH ENG boulon d'ancrage *m*, PAPER TECH boulon de scellement *m*; ~ **boss** *n* NAUT bossoir d'ancre *m*; ~ **buoy** *n* NAUT bouée d'ancre *f*; ~ **buoy rope** *n* NAUT orin d'ancre *m*; ~ **cable attachment** *n* NAUT étalingure *f*; ~ **chain** *n* NAUT chaîne d'ancre *f*, chaîne de mouillage *f*; ~ **deck** *n* NAUT pont de teugue *m*, teugue *f*; ~ **fluke** *n* NAUT oreille d'ancre *f*; ~ **ice** *n* OCEANOG glace de fond *f*; ~ **light** *n* NAUT *mooring* feu de mouillage *m*; ~ **nut** *n* MECH ENG écrou pression *m*, écrou à patte de scellement *m*, écrou à river *m*; ~ **plate** *n* COAL TECH plaque d'ancrage *f*; ~ **post** *n* CONST poteau d'ancrage *m*; ~ **ring** *n* NAUT cigale d'ancre *f*, organeau d'ancre *m*; ~ **rod** *n* COAL TECH tige d'ancrage *f*; ~ **shackle** *n* NAUT organeau *m*; ~ **stock** *n* NAUT jas d'ancre *m*; ~ **watch** *n* MILIT *naval* quart au mouillage *m*; ~ **well** *n* NAUT puits à ancre *m*

anchor[2] *vt* CONST *floor joist*, NAUT *ship* ancrer, SPACE *spacecraft* ancrer, fixer

anchor[3] *vi* NAUT mouiller; ~ **in the roads** *vi* NAUT ancrer en rade

anchorage *n* NAUT mouillage *m*; ~ **block** *n* CONST massif d'ancrage *m*; ~ **system** *n* NUCLEAR système d'ancrage *m*

anchoring *n* CONST ancrage *m*, SPACE *spacecraft* ancrage *m*, fixation *f*; ~ **bolt** *n* CONST boulon d'ancrage *m*; ~ **ground** *n* NAUT mouillage *m*; ~ **plate** *n* CONST plaque d'ancrage *f*; ~ **tower** *n* ELEC *supply network* pylône de haubanage *m*, pylône à haubans *m*

ancillaries *n pl* PRINT périphériques *m pl*, équipements auxiliaires *m pl*

ancillary[1] *adj* PROD ENG auxiliaire, SPACE *spacecraft* auxiliaire, de servitude

ancillary:[2] ~ **equipment** *n* MECH matériel auxiliaire *m*

AND: ~ **circuit** *n* ELECTRON circuit ET *m*; ~ **gate** *n* COMP, ELECTRON, PHYS porte ET *f*; ~ **operation** *n* COMP opération ET *f*

Anderson: ~ **bridge** *n* ELEC *circuit* pont d'Anderson *m*

andesite *n* PETR andésite *f*

andesitic *adj* PETR andésitique

andradite *n* MINERAL mélanite *f*

Andromeda *n* ASTRON Andromède *f*; ~ **galaxy** *n* ASTRON galaxie d'Andromède *f*

anechoic: ~ **room** *n* ACOUSTICS salle anéchoïque *f*, PHYS chambre sourde *f*, salle sourde *f*

anelasticity *n* METALL, PHYS anélasticité *f*

anemograph *n* METEO anémographe *m*

anemometer *n* FUELLESS *tidal power*, HYDROL, LAB EQUIP, METEO, NAUT, PAPER TECH, PHYS anémomètre *m*

anemometric *adj* PAPER TECH anémométrique

anemometry *n* METEO, PHYS anémométrie *f*

aneroid: ~ **altimeter** *n* AERONAUT altimètre anéroïde *m*; ~ **barometer** *n* AERONAUT, LAB EQUIP, METEO, PHYS baromètre anéroïde *m*

anethole *n* CHEM anéthole *m*

aneurin *n* CHEM aneurine *f*, thiamine *f*

ANFO *abbr (ammonium nitrate fuel oil)* MINING nitrate d'ammonium et fuel-oil *m*, nitrate-fioul *m*, nitrate-fuel *m*, nitrate-huile *m*

angiographic: ~ **examination table** *n* INSTRUMENT table d'angiographie *f*

angiography *n* INSTRUMENT angiographie *f*

angle[1] *n* CINEMAT angle *m*, approche *f*, champ *m*, CONST cornière *f*, cornières *f pl*, fers cornières *m pl*, fers d'angle *m pl*, équerre *f*, GEOM angle *m*, MECH ENG cornière *f*, NAUT angle de braquage *m*, shipbuilding cornière *f*, PHYS *of contact* angle *m*, *of deviation* angle *m*; ~ **of acceptance** *n* NUCLEAR *of ions* angle d'entrée *m*; ~ **of advance** *n* AUTO angle de calage *m*, avance à l'allumage *f*, MECH ENG avance angulaire *f*; ~ **of arrival** *n* TELECOM angle d'arrivée *m*; ~ **of attack** *n* PHYS angle d'incidence *m*; ~ **of attack indicator** *n* AERONAUT indicateur d'incidence *m*; ~ **bar** *n* PAPER TECH lame coudée de platine *f*, PRINT barre de retournement *f*; ~ **box** *n* PRINT boîte de renvoi d'angle *f*; ~ **box wrench** *n* MECH ENG *tool* clé en tube *f*; ~ **brace** *n* CONST aisselier *m*; ~ **bracket** *n* CONST potence angulaire *f*, potence cornière *f*, potence d'assemblage *f*, *shafting* chaise en bout *f*, équerre-applique *f*, MECH cornière de renforcement *f*, équerre de fixation *f*, MECH ENG équerre *f*; ~ **of brush lag** *n* ELEC *of motor brush* angle de décalage *m*; ~ **of clearance** *n* PROD ENG *of machine tool* angle d'incidence *m*; ~ **of contact** *n* PROD ENG angle de contact *m*, angle de contingence *m*; ~ **of coverage** *n* CINEMAT angle de convergence *m*; ~ **cut** *n* PAPER TECH coupe diagonale *f*; ~ **of cutoff** *n* CINEMAT angle d'obturation *m*; ~ **cutter** *n* MECH *tools* pince coupante diagonale *f*, MECH ENG *of milling machine* fraise d'angle *f*, fraise à chanfreiner *f*; ~ **cutting** *n* PAPER TECH coupe losange *f*; ~ **of departure** *n* TELECOM angle de départ *m*; ~ **of dip** *n* PHYS inclinaison *f*, inclinaison magnétique *f*; ~ **drive** *n* MECH entraînement à renvoi d'angle *m*; ~ **of elevation** *n* GEOM angle d'élévation *m*, TELECOM angle de site *m*; ~ **error** *n* METR erreur d'angle *f*; ~ **fishplate** *n* (BrE) *(cf applying of angle joint bar)* RAIL éclisse cornière *f*, éclisse à patin *f*; ~ **fishplating** *n* (BrE) *(cf applying of angle joint bars)* RAIL éclissage angulaire *m*; ~ **of friction** *n* COAL TECH, CONST, PHYS, PROD ENG angle de frottement *m*; ~ **of hade** *n* GEOL angle d'inclinaison *m*; ~ **of heel** *n* NAUT *ship, boat design* angle de gîte *m*; ~ **of incidence** *n* CINEMAT, FUELLESS, OPT, PHYS *aerodynamics*, PROD ENG, TELECOM, WAVE PHYS angle d'incidence *m*; ~ **of inclination** *n* PROD ENG angle d'inclinaison *m*, inclinaison *f*; ~ **in radians** *n* GEOM angle en radians *m*; ~ **iron** *n* CONST cornière *f*, fer cornière *m*, fer d'angle *m*, fer en L *m*, fer en équerre *m*, équerre *f*; ~ **iron joint** *n* CONST assemblage à cornières *m*; ~ **joint** *n* CONST assemblage d'angle *m*; ~ **of keying** *n* MECH ENG angle de calage *m*; ~ **of lag** *n* ELEC *of motor brush* angle de retard *m*; ~ **of lap** *n* MECH ENG *of slide valve* angle de recouvrement *m*; ~ **of lead** *n* ELEC *of motor brush* angle de décalage *m*, MECH ENG *of slide valve* angle d'avance à l'admission *m*; ~ **of loll** *n* NAUT *ship design* angle d'équilibre instable *m*, angle de gîte permanente *m*; ~ **of magnetic declination** *n* PHYS déclinaison magnétique *f*; ~ **of magnetic inclination** *n* PHYS inclinaison magnétique *f*; ~ **mark** *n* PRINT repère d'angle *m*; ~ **measurement** *n* METR mesure d'angle *f*; ~ **meter** *n* METR anglomètre *m*; ~ **modulation** *n* ELECTRON modulation angulaire *f*; ~ **of nip** *n* COAL TECH angle de prise *m*; ~ **of obliquity** *n* MECH ENG *gearing* angle de pression *m*; ~ **of overlap** *n* ELEC *of rectifier* angle d'empiètement *m*; ~ **peeling test** *n* P&R *for adhesives* essai de pelage angulaire *m*; ~ **of phase difference** *n* ELEC *alternating current* déphasage *m*, ELEC ENG angle de déphasage *m*; ~ **pin** *n* MECH ENG *diecasting die* doigt de démoulage *m*; ~ **of pitch** *n* C&G, NAUT angle de tangage *m*; ~ **plate** *n* MECH ENG porte-équerre *m*, METR *box* équerre d'angle *f*; ~ **of precession** *n* FUELLESS angle de précession *m*; ~ **of prerelease** *n* MECH ENG angle d'avance à l'échappement *m*, avance angulaire à l'échappement *f*; ~ **of pressure** *n* MECH ENG *gears* angle de pression *m*; ~ **of pull** *n* MECH angle de traction *m*, NAUT *of rope* angle de tire *m*; ~ **rafter** *n* CONST arêtier *m*; ~ **of rake** *n* CINEMAT angle horizontal de projection *m*, MECH ENG *of cutting tool* angle de dégagement *m*; ~ **of reflection** *n* PHYS, WAVE PHYS angle de réflexion *m*; ~ **of refraction** *n* PHYS angle de réfraction *m*; ~ **of relief** *n* MECH ENG *of a cutting tool* angle d'incidence *m*; ~ **of repose** *n* CONST *materials* talus naturel *m*, PACKAGING angle de frottement *m*; ~ **section** *n* MECH cornière *f*; ~ **sensor** *n* MECH détecteur de position angulaire *m*; ~ **shot** *n* CINEMAT plan incliné *m*, plan oblique *m*; ~ **of sight** *n* MILIT *artillery* angle de tir *m*, TELECOM angle de site *m*; ~ **of stall** *n* AERONAUT angle de décrochage *m*; ~ **steel** *n* MECH *materials* cornière d'acier *f*; ~ **of taper** *n* MECH *tools* angle de conicité *m*; ~ **tie** *n* CONST aisselier *m*; ~ **of tilt** *n* CINEMAT angle d'inclinaison *m*; ~ **of traction** *n* MECH angle de traction *m*; ~ **of twist** *n* MECH *of wire rope* angle de commettage *m*; ~ **of view** *n* CINEMAT angle d'observation *m*, angle de vue *m*; ~ **of wing setting** *n* AERONAUT angle de calage de la voilure *m*

angle[2] *vt* PAPER TECH angler

angled[1] *adj* PROD ENG coudé

angled:[2] ~ **column** *n* PHOTO *of enlarger* colonne inclinée *f*; ~ **column head** *n* PRINT titre de colonne incliné *m*; ~ **core slide** *n* MECH ENG *injection moulds* coulisseau incliné *m*; ~ **drill** *n* MINING sondeuse à couronne *f*; ~ **key** *n* MECH ENG *tool* clé mâle coudée *f*; ~ **open socket spanner** *n* (BrE) MECH ENG *tool* clé à pipes débouchées

f; ~ **open socket wrench** *n* MECH ENG *tool* clé à pipes débouchées *f*; ~ **socket spanner** *n* (BrE) MECH ENG *tool* clé à pipes *f*; ~ **socket wrench** *n* MECH ENG *tool* clé à pipes *f*

angledozer *n* CONST angledozer *m*, bouteur biais *m*

angling *n* PRINT mise des trames selon le bon angle *f*; ~ **error** *n* PRINT erreur d'implantation des trames *f*

angstrom *n* METR, PRINT angstroem *m*, angström *m*

Ångström: ~ **unit** *n* FOOD TECH unité Ångström *f*

angular[1] *adj* GEOM, MECH angulaire

angular:[2] ~ **ball bearing** *n* MECH roulement à billes à contact oblique *m*; ~ **deviation** *n* ELEC ENG écart angulaire *m*; ~ **diameter** *n* SPACE diamètre angulaire *m*; ~ **disconformity** *n* GEOL discordance angulaire *f*; ~ **displacement** *n* ELEC *alternating current* déphasage *m*; ~ **displacement sensitivity** *n* AERONAUT *between two directions or axes* sensibilité d'écart angulaire *f*; ~ **distortion** *n* CINEMAT distorsion angulaire *f*; ~ **frequency** *n* ELEC, ELEC ENG, PHYS, RAD PHYS, WAVE PHYS fréquence angulaire *f*; ~ **grooved-and-tongued joint** *n* CONST assemblage à grain-d'orge *m*, assemblage à rainure et languette *m*, joint refeuillé *m*; ~ **kinetic energy** *n* MECH ENG énergie cinétique angulaire *f*; ~ **lead** *n* MECH ENG avance angulaire à l'admission *f*; ~ **magnification** *n* PHYS grandissement angulaire *m*; ~ **meshing** *n* MECH *gears* attaque angulaire *f*; ~ **milling cutter** *n* MECH *tool* fraise conique *f*; ~ **misalignment loss** *n* OPT, TELECOM perte par désalignement angulaire *f*, perte par inclinaison axiale *f*; ~ **momentum** *n* AERONAUT moment cinétique *m*, ASTRON moment angulaire *m*, MECH moment cinétique *m*, PART PHYS moment angulaire *m*, PHYS moment angulaire *m*, moment cinétique *m*; ~ **pitch rate** *n* AERONAUT vitesse angulaire de tangage *f*; ~ **prerelease** *n* MECH ENG avance angulaire à l'échappement *f*; ~ **pulsing** *n* ACOUSTICS pulsation angulaire *f*; ~ **resolution** *n* ASTRON résolution angulaire *f*; ~ **roller bearing** *n* MECH roulement à rouleaux obliques *m*; ~ **roll rate** *n* AERONAUT vitesse angulaire de roulis *f*; ~ **rotation** *n* SPRINGS rotation de l'arc *f*; ~ **rotor speed** *n* AERONAUT vitesse angulaire de rotation de rotor *f*; ~ **separation** *n* TELECOM séparation angulaire *f*; ~ **three-axis rate sensor** *n* AERONAUT boîte de gyromètre pour pilote automatique *f*, détecteur angulaire trois axes *m*, détecteur à trois axes *m*; ~ **unconformity** *n* GEOL discordance angulaire *f*; ~ **velocity** *n* ELEC ENG, FUELLESS, MECH ENG, PHYS, SPACE vitesse angulaire *f*; ~ **velocity of precession** *n* FUELLESS vitesse angulaire de précession *f*; ~ **velocity rate sensor** *n* AERONAUT détecteur de vitesse angulaire *m*; ~ **viewfinder** *n* CINEMAT viseur coudé *m*; ~ **yaw rate** *n* AERONAUT vitesse angulaire de lacet *f*

angulometer *n* METR anglomètre *m*

anhydration *n* CHEM, PAPER TECH *drying* anhydrisation *f*

anhydride *n* CHEM, DETERGENTS, PAPER TECH anhydride *m*; ~ **hardener** *n* P&R *resins, adhesives, coatings* durcisseur anhydrique *m*, durcisseur anhydrique *m*

anhydrite *n* GAS TECH, PETR, PETR TECH anhydrite *f*

anhydrous[1] *adj* CHEM, FOOD TECH, PAPER TECH, PETR TECH anhydre

anhydrous:[2] ~ **ammonia** *n* PETR TECH ammoniac anhydre *m*

anilide *n* CHEM anilide *f*

aniline *n* PAPER TECH aniline *f*; ~ **dye** *n* COLOURS colorant d'aniline *m*, PHOTO couleur à base d'aniline *f*; ~ **formaldehyde resin** *n* PACKAGING résine d'aniline-formaldéhyde *f*; ~ **print** *n* PRINT copie à l'aniline *f*; ~ **printing** *n* PACKAGING flexographie *f*; ~ **value** *n* P&R *chemical properties* point d'aniline *m*

anilox: ~ **roll** *n* PRINT rouleau anilox *m*, rouleau encreur tramé *m*

animal: ~ **fat** *n* FOOD TECH graisse animale *f*; ~ **glue** *n* P&R *adhesives* colle animale *f*, colle de peau *f*, PAPER TECH, PRINT colle animale *f*; ~ **protein factor** *n* FOOD TECH protéine animale spécifique *f*; ~ **size** *n* COLOURS colle animale *f*; ~ **starch** *n* FOOD TECH glycogène *m*

animate *vt* CINEMAT animer

animated: ~ **cartoon** *n* CINEMAT dessin animé *m*; ~ **film** *n* CINEMAT film d'animation *m*

animation: ~ **backlight** *n* CINEMAT éclairage par transparence *m*; ~ **bench** *n* CINEMAT banc d'animation *m*, table d'animation *f*; ~ **camera** *n* CINEMAT caméra d'animation *f*; ~ **cell** *n* CINEMAT cellule d'animation *f*; ~ **director** *n* CINEMAT chef animateur *m*, réalisateur de dessin animé *m*

animator *n* CINEMAT intervalliste *m*

anion *n* CHEM, COAL TECH, ELEC, ELEC ENG, FOOD TECH, PHYS, RAD PHYS anion *m*; ~ **exchanger** *n* COAL TECH échangeur d'anion *m*

anionic[1] *adj* CHEM, COAL TECH anionique

anionic:[2] ~ **detergent** *n* DETERGENTS détergent anionique *m*; ~ **exchanger** *n* DETERGENTS échangeur d'anions *m*, échangeur d'ions anioniques *m*; ~ **surface active agent** *n* DETERGENTS agent de surface anionique *m*

anionotropy *n* CHEM anionotropie *f*

anisaldehyde *n* CHEM aldéhyde anisique *m*

anisentropic *adj* THERMOD anisentropique

Anisian *n* GEOL *stratigraphy* anisien *m*

anisidine *n* CHEM anisidine *f*

anisochronous[1] *adj* COMP, DP anisochrone

anisochronous:[2] ~ **transmission** *n* DP transmission anisochrone *f*

anisoelastic[1] *adj* SPACE *gyroscopes* anisoélastique

anisoelastic:[2] ~ **drift** *n* SPACE *gyroscopes* dérive anisoélastique *f*

anisoelasticity *n* SPACE anisoélasticité *f*; ~ **factor** *n* SPACE *gyroscopes* facteur d'anisoélasticité *m*

anisole *n* CHEM, FOOD TECH *flavouring agent* anisol *m*

anisotropic[1] *adj* ASTRON, CRYSTALL, OPT *electromagnetic waves*, P&R, PROP MAT, TELECOM anisotrope

anisotropic:[2] ~ **fibers** *n pl* (AmE), ~ **fibres** *n pl* (BrE) PROP MAT fibres anisotropes *f pl*; ~ **material** *n* PROP MAT, TEXTILES matière anisotrope *f*

anisotropy *n* CRYSTALL, GEOL, PROP MAT anisotropie *f* ~ **of turbulence** *n* FLUID PHYS anisotropie de la turbulence *f*

ankerite *n* MINERAL ankérite *f*

annaline *n* PAPER TECH annaline *f*

annatto *n* FOOD TECH annatto *m*

anneal[1] *n* THERMOD recuit *m*, revenu *m*

anneal[2] *vt* C&G, MECH *process* recuire

anneal[3] *vi* THERMOD *metals* faire un recuit

annealed[1] *adj* CRYSTALL, THERMOD recuit; ~ **under gas** *adj* THERMOD recuit en atmosphère contrôlée

annealed:[2] ~ **steel** *n* PAPER TECH acier recuit *m*

annealing *n* C&G recuisson *f*, CRYSTALL, ELECTRON, HEATING, METALL recuit *m*, THERMOD recuit *m*, revenu *m*; ~ **bath** *n* THERMOD bain de recuit *m*; ~ **furnace** *n* C&G four de recuisson *m*, MECH *process*, NUCLEAR four de recuit *m*, THERMOD *cast iron* four de recuisson *m*, four de recuit *m*; ~ **kiln** *n* C&G carcasse de recuisson *f*; ~ **lehr** *n* C&G *for flat glass* galerie de recuisson *f*, *for plate glass*

stracou *m*; ~ **lehr with rollers** *n* C&G *for flat glass* étenderie à rouleaux *f*; ~ **range** *n* C&G intervalle de recuisson *m*; ~ **schedule** *n* C&G programme thermique *m*

annex: ~ **block** *n* (AmE), **annexe block** *n* (BrE) MECH ENG cartouche annexe *f*

annihilation *n* PART PHYS annihilation *f*, PHYS annihilation *f*, dématérialisation *f*; ~ **photon** *n* RAD PHYS photon d'annihilation *m*; ~ **radiation** *n* RAD PHYS rayonnement d'annihilation *m*

annotation *n* DP annotation *f*

announcement: ~ **machine** *n* TELECOM machine parlante *f*

annual: ~ **capacity factor** *n* FUELLESS facteur de capacité de rendement annuelle *m*; ~ **evaporation** *n* WATER SUPP évaporation annuelle *f*; ~ **flood** *n* WATER SUPP crue annuelle *f*; ~ **flow** *n* WATER SUPP abondance annuelle *f*, débit annuel *m*; ~ **load** *n* WATER SUPP charge annuelle *f*; ~ **mean water level** *n* WATER SUPP niveau moyen annuel *m*; ~ **natural background radiation** *n* RAD PHYS radiation annuelle de fond *f*; ~ **parallax** *n* ASTRON *of celestial body* parallaxe annuelle *f*; ~ **runoff** *n* WATER SUPP écoulement annuel *m*

annular[1] *adj* ASTRON, GEOM, MECH, SPACE *spacecraft* annulaire

annular:[2] ~ **air gap** *n* NUCLEAR *between fuel and can* carapace d'air annulaire *f*; ~ **bit** *n* PETR TECH trépan annulaire *m*; ~ **borer** *n* MINING sondeuse à couronne *f*; ~ **bushing** *n* C&G filière annulaire *f*; ~ **channel** *n* NUCLEAR canal annulaire *m*; ~ **core** *n* NUCLEAR *of reactor* coeur annulaire *m*; ~ **crack** *n* C&G *in bottle finish* casse annulaire *f*; ~ **drainage** *n* WATER SUPP drainage annulaire *m*; ~ **film boiling** *n* NUCLEAR ébullition par film annulaire *f*; ~ **fuel element** *n* NUCLEAR élément combustible annulaire *m*; ~ **gap** *n* NUCLEAR passage annulaire *m*; ~ **gear** *n* MECH ENG couronne dentée *f*; ~ **kiln** *n* C&G four annulaire *m*; ~ **magnet** *n* PHYS aimant torique *m*, TV bague-aimant circulaire *f*; ~ **resonator** *n* ELECTRON cavité résonnante annulaire *f*; ~ **saw** *n* MECH ENG scie circulaire *f*; ~ **solar eclipse** *n* ASTRON éclipse solaire annulaire *f*; ~ **space** *n* GAS TECH espace annulaire *m*, PETR TECH *of well* annulaire *m*, espace annulaire *m*

annulus *n* AERONAUT chambre annulaire *f*, collecteur annulaire *m*, ASTRON couronne planétaire *f*, GEOM anneau *m*, PETR espace annulaire *m*, PETR TECH *of well* annulaire *m*, espace annulaire *m*, SPACE *spacecraft* chambre annulaire *f*

annunciator *n* ELEC ENG annonciateur *m*, SPACE *spacecraft* panneau indicateur *m*; ~ **panel** *n* PROD ENG panneau avertisseur *m*

anode *n* CHEM, ELEC anode *f*, ELEC ENG anode *f*, pôle positif *m*, NAUT *shipbuilding*, PHYS, TV anode *f*; ~ **characteristic** *n* ELEC ENG caractéristique d'anode *f*; ~ **circuit** *n* ELEC ENG circuit anodique *m*, circuit de l'anode *m*; ~ **circuit breaker** *n* ELEC disjoncteur anodique *m*; ~ **current** *n* ELEC ENG courant anodique *m*; ~ **drop** *n* GAS TECH chute anodique *f*; ~ **modulation** *n* ELECTRON modulation par l'anode *f*, modulation par la plaque *f*; ~ **ray** *n* RAD PHYS rayon d'anode *m*; ~ **rays** *n pl* ELEC ENG ions positifs d'anode *m pl*; ~ **saturation** *n* ELEC ENG saturation de courant anodique *f*; ~ **voltage** *n* ELEC ENG tension anodique *f*, tension appliquée à l'anode *f*, tension de l'anode *f*

anodic[1] *adj* ELEC anodique

anodic:[2] ~ **coat** *n* COATINGS couche anodique *f*; ~ **coating**

n COATINGS revêtement anodique *m*

anodize *vt* CHEM, NAUT anodiser

anodized: ~ **aluminium plate** *n* (BrE) PRINT plaque d'aluminium anodisée *f*; ~ **aluminum plate** *n* (AmE) *see anodized aluminium plate*

anomalistic: ~ **month** *n* ASTRON mois anomalistique *m*; ~ **year** *n* ASTRON année anomalistique *f*

anomalous: ~ **dispersion** *n* PHYS dispersion anomale *f*; ~ **scattering** *n* CRYSTALL diffusion anomale *f*; ~ **Zeeman effect** *n* PHYS effet Zeeman anomal *m*

anomaly *n* ASTRON *angular distance*, GEOL, PETR anomalie *f*

anomer *n* CHEM anomère *m*

anorogenic *adj* GEOL *tectonic setting* anorogénique

anorthite *n* C&G anorthite *f*

anorthosite *n* PETR anorthosite *f*

ANOVA *abbr* (*analysis of variance*) COMP analyse de la variance *f*

ANPN *abbr* (*army navy performance number system*) TRANSP *fuel rating octane* système ANPN *m*

ANSI *abbr* (*American National Standards Institute*) TELECOM ANSI (*Institut américain de normalisation*)

answer: ~ **print** *n* CINEMAT copie d'étalonnage *f*, première copie *f*; ~ **signal** *n* TELECOM signal de réponse *m*

answerback *n* TELECOM indicatif *m*

answering: ~ **pennant** *n* NAUT *international code of signals* flamme aperçue *f*, pavillon aperçu *m*; ~ **service** *n* TELECOM service des abonnés absents *m*

antacid *n* CHEM antiacide *m*

antagonistic: ~ **torque** *n* AERONAUT couple antagoniste *m*

antenna *n* NAUT *radio, radar*, PHYS, SPACE *communications*, VEHICLES *accessory* antenne *f*; ~ **array** *n* ASTRON réseau d'antennes *m*, SPACE groupement d'antennes *m*, réseau d'antennes *m*; ~ **gain** *n* SPACE *communications* gain d'antenne *m*; ~ **mast** *n* NAUT pylône d'antenne *m*; ~ **pointing loss** *n* TELECOM affaiblissement dû au pointage de l'antenne *m*; ~ **system** *n* SPACE groupement d'antennes *m*

anthracene *n* CHEM anthracine *f*, anthracène *m*; ~ **dyes** *n pl* CHEM colorants anthracéniques *m pl*; ~ **oil** *n* CHEM huile anthracénique *f*

anthracite *n* COAL TECH anthracite *m*; ~ **coal** *n* COAL TECH anthracite *m*

anthragallol *n* CHEM anthragallol *m*

anthropic: ~ **principle** *n* ASTRON principe anthropique *m*

anthropogenic: ~ **acidification** *n* POLLUTION acidification anthropique *f*, acidification anthropogène *f*

anti-abrasion: ~ **coating** *n* CINEMAT couche anti-abrasive *f*, couche de protection *f*; ~ **layer** *n* COATINGS couche anti-abrasive *f*

anti-acid: ~ **film** *n* COATINGS couche antiacide *f*

anti-adhesive: ~ **paper** *n* PACKAGING papier de séparation *m*

anti-air: ~ **camouflage equipment** *n* MILIT ensemble de camouflage contre les attaques aériennes *m*

anti-aliasing *n* COMP anticrénelage *m*, ELECTRON antirepliement du spectre *m*, TV antialiassage *m*, antirepliement *m*; ~ **filter** *n* ELECTRON filtre antirepliement du spectre *m*; ~ **filtering** *n* ELECTRON filtrage par filtre antirepliement de spectre *m*

antiarmor: ~ **warhead** *n* (AmE), **antiarmour warhead** *n* (BrE) MILIT obus perforant *m*

antibaryon *n* PART PHYS antibaryon *m*

antiblocking: ~ **agent** *n* P&R *adhesives* agent antiblocant *m*; ~ **system** *n* AUTO dispositif antiblocage *m*

antibonding: ~ **atomic orbital** *n* RAD PHYS orbitale antiliante atomique *f*; ~ **electron** *n* RAD PHYS électron antiliant *m*; ~ **molecular orbital** *n* RAD PHYS orbitale antiliante moléculaire *f*

anticaking: ~ **agent** *n* FOOD TECH agent antimottant *m*, produit anti-agglomérant *m*

anticapillary: ~ **course** *n* CONST *road construction* couche anticapillaire *f*

anticatalyst *n* FOOD TECH anticatalyseur *m*

anticathode *n* ELEC *in X-ray tube*, PHYS anticathode *f*

antichlor *n* CHEM, PAPER TECH antichlore *m*

anticipated: ~ **operating conditions** *n pl* AERONAUT conditions d'utilisation prévues *f pl*

anticlinal[1] *adj* GAS TECH anticlinal

anticlinal:[2] ~ **trap** *n* PETR TECH piège anticlinal *m*

anticline *n* GEOL, PETR TECH anticlinal *m*

anticlinorium *n* GEOL anticlinorium *m*

anticlockwise: ~ **rotation** *n* MECH rotation dans le sens antihoraire *f*

anticlutter: ~ **control** *n* NAUT *radar* dispositif antiécho parasite *m*

anticoincidence *n* ELECTRON anticoïncidence *f*; ~ **circuit** *n* PHYS circuit à anticoïncidence *m*

anticollision: ~ **light** *n* AERONAUT feu anticollision *m*; ~ **marker** *n* (*AC marker*) NAUT marqueur anticollision *m*

anticorrosion: ~ **additive** *n* PETR TECH additif anticorrosion *m*; ~ **agent** *n* PAPER TECH anticorrosion *f*, PETR TECH *in petrol* additif anticorrosion *m*; ~ **coating** *n* NUCLEAR revêtement anticorrosion *m*; ~ **oil** *n* PROD ENG huile de protection *f*; ~ **paint** *n* COATINGS peinture antirouille *f*; ~ **paper** *n* PACKAGING papier anticorrosif *m*

anticorrosive[1] *adj* MECH *materials* anticorrosif

anticorrosive[2] *n* PAPER TECH, PRINT anticorrosion *f*; ~ **coating** *n* P&R *paint* peinture anticorrosive *f*; ~ **film** *n* PACKAGING pellicule anticorrosive *f*; ~ **paint** *n* COLOURS peinture anticorrosion *f*; ~ **primer** *n* COLOURS primaire anticorrosion *m*

anticyclogenesis *n* METEO anticyclogenèse *f*

anticyclone *n* METEO anticyclone *m*

anticyclonic[1] *adj* METEO anticyclonique

anticyclonic[2] *n* METEO anticyclonique; ~ **circulation** *n* METEO circulation anticyclonique *f*; ~ **generation** *n* METR développement d'un anticyclone *m*, formation d'un anticyclone *f*; ~ **growth** *n* METEO formation d'un anticyclone *f*; ~ **rotation** *n* METEO rotation anticyclonique *f*

antidazzle[1] *adj* SAFETY antiéblouissement

antidazzle:[2] ~ **glass** *n* C&G verre antiéblouissement *m*; ~ **glasses** *n pl* INSTRUMENT lunettes protectrices contre l'éblouissement *f pl*; ~ **visor** *n* VEHICLES *accessory* écran antiéblouissant *m*

antideflection: ~ **roll** *n* PAPER TECH rouleau antiflexion *m*

antidive: ~ **fork** *n* VEHICLES *of motorcycle* fourche anti-plongée *f*; ~ **suspension** *n* VEHICLES *of motorcycle* suspension anti-plongée *f*

antidote *n* CHEM antidote *m*, contrepoison *m*, SAFETY antidote *m*

antidust: ~ **filter** *n* GAS TECH filtre dépoussiéreur *m*

anti-enzyme *n* FOOD TECH antienzyme *f*

antiferromagnetic *adj* PHYS antiferromagnétique

antiferromagnetism *n* ELEC, PHYS antiferromagnétisme *m*

antiflare *n* PRINT antireflet *m*

antiflash: ~ **varnish** *n* COLOURS vernis antiflash *m*

antiflicker: ~ **blade** n CINEMAT pale d'antiscintillement f

antiflooding: ~ **agent** n P&R *for paints* agent antiflottation m

antifoam[1] *adj* PACKAGING antimousse

antifoam[2] n PAPER TECH antimousse m; ~ **agent** n PETR TECH antimoussant m

antifoaming: ~ **agent** n COAL TECH, P&R *coatings, adhesives*, PRINT agent antimousse m

antifog: ~ **film** n PACKAGING film antibuée m

antifogging: ~ **agent** n CINEMAT, PHOTO réactif antivoile m

antifouling: ~ **composition** n COATINGS peinture marine antisalissure f; ~ **paint** n COATINGS peinture marine antisalissure f, NAUT *ship maintenance*, P&R peinture antifouling f

antifreeze n AERONAUT, AUTO antigel m, CONST produit antigélif m, VEHICLES antigel m; ~ **agent** n REFRIG antigel m; ~ **paper** n PAPER TECH papier antigel m

antifreezing *adj* AERONAUT incongelable, non congelable

antifret: ~ **plate** n SPACE *spacecraft* plaquette antiusure f

antifriction[1] *adj* MECH, MECH ENG antifriction

antifriction[2] n PAPER TECH antifriction m; ~ **bearing** n MECH ENG *roller bearing*, PROD ENG palier antifriction m; ~ **lining** n MECH ENG alliage antifriction m, garniture antifriction f

antifroth n CHEM, PAPER TECH antimousse m

anti-G[1] *adj* SPACE antigravité

anti-G:[2] ~ **suit** n SPACE combinaison anti-g f

antigas: ~ **shelter** n MILIT abri antigaz m

antigen n CHEM antigène m

antiglare n CINEMAT antireflet m; ~ **coating** n TELECOM revêtement antireflet m; ~ **glasses** n pl INSTRUMENT lunettes protectrices contre l'éblouissement f pl; ~ **visor** n VEHICLES *accessory* écran antiéblouissant m

antigravity *adj* SPACE antigravité

antihalation: ~ **backing** n COATINGS, PHOTO, PRINT couche antihalo f; ~ **layer** n CINEMAT couche antihalo f

antihalo: ~ **layer** n PHOTO couche antihalo f

anti-icing n SPACE *spacecraft* antigivrage m; ~ **system** n SPACE dispositif antigivrage m

anti-interference *adj* ELEC *protection* antiparasite

antiknock: ~ **additive** n AUTO antidétonant m, POLLUTION additif antidétonant m; ~ **agent** n VEHICLES *in fuel* additif antidétonant m

antilock: ~ **brake system** n VEHICLES système antibloquant m, système antibloquant de roue m; ~ **system** n VEHICLES *of brakes* système antibloquant m

antilocking: ~ **system** n VEHICLES système antiblocage m

antilogarithm n MATH antilogarithme m

antilogous: ~ **pole** n CRYSTALL *pyroelectricity* pôle antilogue m

antimatter n PART PHYS, PHYS antimatière f

antimonial *adj* CHEM antimonial

antimoniate n CHEM antimoniate m

antimonic *adj* CHEM antimonique, stibique

antimonide n CHEM antimoniure m

antimonite n CHEM antimonite m

antimony n CHEM antimoine m, PRINT stibine f

antineutrino n PART PHYS antineutrino m

antineutron n PHYS antineutron m

antinodal: ~ **line** n ACOUSTICS ligne ventrale f

antinode n ACOUSTICS ventre m, ELEC antinoeud m, ventre m, ventre d'onde antinoeud m, PHYS, WAVE PHYS ventre d'onde antinoeud m

antinoise[1] *adj* ACOUSTICS antibruit

antinoise:[2] ~ **soft rubber lining** n SAFETY revêtement en caoutchouc mou antibruit m

anti-offset: ~ **spray** n PRINT antimaculeur m

antioxidant[1] *adj* PACKAGING antiozone

antioxidant[2] n FOOD TECH antioxydant m, P&R *compounding ingredient* antioxydant m, antioxygène m, PRINT antioxydant m

antiparallel[1] *adj* GEOM antiparallèle

antiparallel:[2] ~ **arrangement** n ELEC ENG montage tête-bêche m; ~ **connection** n ELEC connexion antiparallèle f

antiparticle n PART PHYS, PHYS antiparticule f

antipersonnel: ~ **mine** n MILIT mine antipersonnel f

antiperthite n MINERAL antiperthite f

antiphase[1] *adv* TV en antiphase

antiphase:[2] ~ **boundary** n CRYSTALL limite d'antiphase f, paroi d'antiphase f

antipodes n pl GEOM antipodes m pl

antipollution *adj* AUTO, MECH non-polluant

antiproton n PART PHYS, PHYS antiproton m

antipulse: ~ **flask** n GAS TECH ballon antipulsatoire m

antiquark n PART PHYS, PHYS antiquark m

antique: ~ **drawn glass** n C&G verre antique étiré m; ~ **face** n PRINT caractères gothiques m pl; ~ **finish** n PRINT fini brut m; ~ **glass** n C&G *formed from cylinders* verre antique m

antiredepositing n DETERGENTS antiredéposition f

antiredeposition: ~ **agent** n DETERGENTS agent antiredéposition m

antireflecting: ~ **treatment** n C&G application de couche antireflet f

antireflection: ~ **coating** n C&G couche antiréfléchissante f, CINEMAT couche antireflet f, COATINGS couche antireflet f, couche antiréfléchissante f, OPT, PHOTO couche antireflet f, SPACE *spacecraft* traitement antireflet m, TELECOM couche antireflet f

antireflective: ~ **coating** n COATINGS application d'antireflet f, revêtement par couches antiréfléchissantes m, TELECOM revêtement antiréfléchissant m

antireset: ~ **wind-up** n PROD ENG antiemballement m

antiresonance n ACOUSTICS, ELECTRON antirésonance f

antiresonant: ~ **circuit** n AERONAUT circuit bouchon m, ELECTRON circuit antirésonnant m, PHYS circuit antirésonnant m, circuit bouchon m

antiroll: ~ **bar** n AERONAUT barre de stabilisateur f, AUTO barre antiroulis f, MECH barre stabilisatrice f, VEHICLES *suspension* barre stabilisatrice f, barre de stabilisateur m

antirolling: ~ **device** n NAUT dispositif antiroulis m

antirot *adj* PACKAGING résistant à la pourriture

antirust[1] *adj* MECH *materials* antirouille

antirust[2] n PAPER TECH antirouille f; ~ **coating** n COATINGS couche antirouille f; ~ **paint** n COATINGS peinture antirouille f; ~ **paper** n PACKAGING, PAPER TECH papier antirouille m

antirusting: ~ **primer** n COLOURS primaire antirouille m

antisatellite: ~ **laser** n ELECTRON laser antisatellite m

antiscorching: ~ **agent** n P&R agent antigrilleur m, retardeur de grillage m

antiscratch: ~ **solution** n CINEMAT traitement contre les rayures m, traitement permafilm m

antiseize *adj* MECH antigrippant

antisettling *adj* P&R *additive* antidépôt

antishrink: ~ **treatment** n TEXTILES traitement antirétrécissement m

antishrinkage: ~ **admixture** n CONST produit antiretrait *m*

antisidetone *adj* TELECOM affaiblissant le signal local

antiskating *n* ACOUSTICS dispositif antidérapant *m*, RECORDING antiripage *m*

antiskid: ~ **braking system** *n* AUTO dispositif antienrayeur intégral *m*, dispositif antipatinage *m*; ~ **device** *n* VEHICLES *brake system* antidérapeur *m*, antienrayeur *m*; ~ **unit** *n* AERONAUT dispositif antidérapant *m*

antiskinning: ~ **agent** *n* P&R *paints* agent antipeau *m*, PRINT agent antipeau *m*

antislide: ~ **pad** *n* PROD ENG coussin anticoulissant *m*, coussin antidérapant *m*

antislip: ~ **material floor covering** *n* SAFETY matériaux antidérapants pour revêtement de sol *m pl*; ~ **operating lever clamp** *n* PROD ENG goupille antidérapante du levier de commande *f*

antispattering: ~ **agent** *n* FOOD TECH *food-processing machinery* agent antiéclaboussant *m*

antispill: ~ **bottle** *n* PACKAGING bouteille qui ne répand pas *f*

antisplash: ~ **head** *n* LAB EQUIP *distillation* soupape de Gockel *f*

antistain: ~ **agent** *n* CINEMAT agent inhibiteur de voile coloré *m*

antistaling: ~ **agent** *n* FOOD TECH agent retardant le rassissement *m*, antirassissant *m*

antistatic[1] *adj* CINEMAT, ELEC *materials*, PHOTO antistatique

antistatic:[2] ~ **agent** *n* DETERGENTS, P&R *additive, treatment* agent antistatique *m*, TEXTILES agent antistatique *m*, produit antistatique *m*; ~ **backing** *n* PHOTO support antistatique *m*; ~ **finishing** *n* PROP MAT finissage antistatique *m*; ~ **footwear** *n* SAFETY chaussures antistatiques *f pl*; ~ **mat** *n* COMP tapis antistatique *m*; ~ **materials** *n pl* SAFETY matériaux antistatiques *m pl*; ~ **protection** *n* MECH ENG protection contre les charges électrostatiques *f*; ~ **protective clothing** *n* SAFETY vêtements de protection antistatiques *m pl*; ~ **rubber** *n* P&R caoutchouc antistatique *m*; ~ **spray** *n* COMP enduit antistatique *m*

antistiction: ~ **oscillator** *n* ELECTRON oscillateur d'activation *m*

antistorm: ~ **glazing** *n* C&G vitrage antiouragan *m*

antisubmarine: ~ **defence** *n* (BrE) NAUT *naval* défense anti-sous-marine *f*; ~ **defense** *n* (AmE) *see antisubmarine defence*; ~ **helicopter** *n* AERONAUT hélicoptère anti-sous-marin *m*

antisurge: ~ **baffle** *n* AERONAUT cloison antiballast *f*; ~ **valve** *n* AERONAUT relais hydraulique *m*

antisymmetric: ~ **wave function** *n* PHYS fonction d'onde antisymétrique *f*

antitamper: ~ **cover** *n* PROD ENG capot de plombage *m*

antitank: ~ **grenade** *n* MILIT grenade antichar *f*; ~ **gun** *n* MILIT canon antichar *m*; ~ **helicopter** *n* AERONAUT hélicoptère antichar *m*; ~ **mine** *n* MILIT mine antichar *f*

antitarnish: ~ **paper** *n* PAPER TECH papier antiternissure *m*

antitheft[1] *adj* PACKAGING, QUALITY, SAFETY antivol

antitheft:[2] ~ **ignition lock** *n* AUTO coupe-contact antivol *m*

antithetic: ~ **fault** *n* GEOL faille antithétique *f*

antitorque: ~ **device** *n* AERONAUT dispositif anticouple *m*; ~ **propeller** *n* AERONAUT hélice anticouple *f*; ~ **rotor** *n* TRANSP rotor de queue *m*

antitrades *n pl* NAUT contre-alizés *m pl*

antivacuum: ~ **valve** *n* FUELLESS *hydroelectricity* aérateur pour la conduite forcée *m*

antivibration: ~ **table** *n* LAB EQUIP plateau antivibratoire *m*

Antlia *n* ASTRON Antlia *f*, Machine pneumatique *f*

antozonite *n* MINERAL antozonite *f*

anvil *n* MECH *tools* enclume *f*, MECH ENG enclume *f*, *of micrometer* butée *f*, MINING, PRINT enclume *f*; ~ **block** *n* MECH ENG billot d'enclume *m*, *of power hammer* chabotte *f*; ~ **die** *n* MECH ENG matrice inférieure *f*, porte-matrice *m*; ~ **vice** *n* (BrE) MECH ENG étau à enclumette *m*; ~ **vise** *n* (AmE) *see anvil vice*

AOCS *abbr* (*attitude and orbit control system*) SPACE système de commande d'attitude et d'orbite *m*

AOQ *abbr* (*average outgoing quality*) QUALITY QMAC (*qualité moyenne après contrôle*)

AOQL *n* (*average outgoing quality limit*) QUALITY LQMAC (*limite de qualité moyenne après contrôle*)

apastron *n* ASTRON, SPACE apoastre *m*

apatelite *n* MINERAL apatélite *f*

apatite *n* MINERAL apatite *f*

APC *abbr* (*automatic phase control*) ELECTRON, TV contrôle automatique de phase *m*

APD *abbr* ELECTRON (*avalanche photodiode*) photodiode à avalanche *f*, OPT (*avalanche photodiode*) photodiode à avalanche *f*, TELECOM (*amplitude probability distribution*) distribution de probabilité des amplitudes *f*, répartition de probabilité des amplitudes *f*, TELECOM (*avalanche photodiode*) photodiode à avalanche *f*

APDU *abbr* (*application protocol data unit*) TELECOM unité de données du protocole d'application *f*

aperiodic *adj* ELEC *galvanometer*, ELECTRON *circuit*, PHYS apériodique

aperture *n* ASTRON *lens, mirror*, COMP ouverture *f*, CONST *building* baie *f*, DP, MECH ouverture *f*, MECH ENG lumière *f*, ouverture *f*, passage *m*, PAPER TECH orifice *m*, PHOTO *of lens* diaphragme *m*, PHYS diaphragme *m*, ouverture *f*, PRINT *of diaphragm or lens*, SPACE *communications*, TELECOM, TV ouverture *f* ~ **angle** *n* CINEMAT angle d'ouverture *m*; ~ **antenna** *n* TELECOM antenne type ouverture rayonnante *f*, antenne à ouverture *f*; ~ **card** *n* DP carte à fenêtre *f*; ~ **diaphragm** *n* METALL diaphragme d'ouverture *m*; ~ **distortion** *n* ELECTRON distorsion d'ouverture *f*; ~ **grill** *n* (AmE), ~ **grille** *n* (BrE) ELECTRON masque à fentes *m*; ~ **guide** *n* CINEMAT barrette de guidage *f*; ~ **mask** *n* ELECTRON masque perforé *m*, TV masque d'ombre *m*; ~ **plate** *n* CINEMAT plaque de centrage *f*, plaque de couloir *f*, platine de fenêtre *f*; ~ **preselector** *n* PHOTO présélecteur de diaphragme *m*; ~ **ratio** *n* CINEMAT rapport de format *m*; ~ **ring** *n* CINEMAT, PHOTO bague de diaphragme *f*; ~ **scale** *n* PHOTO échelle des diaphragmes *f*; ~ **stop** *n* PHYS ouverture du diaphragme *f*; ~ **synthesis** *n* ASTRON synthèse d'ouverture *f*; ~ **top slide** *n* INSTRUMENT coulisseau du diaphragme d'ouverture *m*, curseur du diaphragme d'ouverture *m*

aperture-setting: ~ **lever** *n* PHOTO bouton de réglage de l'ouverture *m*, bouton de réglage du diaphragme *m*; ~ **ring** *n* PHOTO bague de commande du diaphragme *f*

apex *n* COAL TECH apex *m*, orifice de pointe *m*, GEOM *of cone* sommet *m*, MINING tête *f*, *of lode* faîte *m*, sommet *m*, PAPER TECH sommet *m*, SPACE apex *m*, sommet *m*

APEX: ~ **fare** *n* (*advance purchase excursion fare*) AERONAUT tarif excursion avec achat anticipé *m*

aphanesite *n* MINERAL aphanésite *f*, aphanèse *f*

aphanite *n* PETR aphanite *f*

aphanitic *adj* GEOL *texture* aphanitique

aphelion *n* ASTRON, PHYS, SPACE aphélie *m*

aphrite *n* MINERAL aphrite *f*

aphrizite *n* MINERAL aphrizite *f*

aphrodite *n* MINERAL aphrodite *f*

aphrosiderite *n* MINERAL aphrosidérite *f*

aphthalose *n* MINERAL aphtalose *f*, aphthalose *f*, aphthitalite *f*

aphthitalite *n* MINERAL aphtalose *f*, aphthalose *f*, aphthitalite *f*

aphthonite *n* MINERAL aphthonite *f*

aphyric *adj* GEOL *texture* aphanitique, aphyrique

API: ~ gravity *n* PETR, PETR TECH densité API *f*

apiin *n* CHEM apiine *f*

apionol *n* CHEM apionol *m*

apjohnite *n* MINERAL apjohnite *f*

aplanatic: ~ lens *n* PHOTO objectif aplanat *m*

aplite *n* PETR aplite *f*

aplome *n* MINERAL aplome *m*

apnea *n* (AmE), apnoea *n* (BrE) OCEANOG apnée *f*

apoapsis *n* ASTRON apside *f*

apochromat *n* CINEMAT objectif apochromatique *m*

apochromatic[1] *adj* PRINT apochromatique

apochromatic:[2] ~ correction *n* PHOTO correction apochromatique *f*; ~ lens *n* PHOTO objectif apochromatique *m*

apodization *n* ELECTRON mise à longueur *f*

apogee *n* ASTRON, PHYS, SPACE *spacecraft* apogée *m*; ~ maneuver *n* (AmE), ~ manoeuvre *n* (BrE) SPACE *spacecraft* manoeuvre d'apogée *f*; ~ motor *n* SPACE *spacecraft* moteur d'apogée *m*

Apollo: ~ programme of moon exploration *n* (BrE) ASTRON programme Apollo d'exploration de la Lune *m*; ~ program of moon exploration *n* (AmE) *see Apollo programme of moon exploration*

apophyllite *n* MINERAL apophyllite *f*

apostilb *n* METR apostilb *m*

apostrophe *n* PRINT *punctuation mark* apostrophe *f*

apothem *n* GEOM apothème *m*

apotome *n* ACOUSTICS apotome *f*

apparatus *n* LAB EQUIP appareil *m*, MECH ENG appareil *m*, dispositif *m*, équipement *m*, PAPER TECH dispositif *m*, PHOTO attirail *m*, *of photographer* attirail *m* ~ charge rate *n* TELECOM tarif des terminaux *m*; ~ dew point *n* REFRIG point de rosée équivalent *m*

apparel *n* TEXTILES habillement *m*, vêtement *m*

apparent: ~ altitude *n* NAUT *sextant* hauteur apparente *f*; ~ density *n* COAL TECH densité apparente *f*, masse volumique apparente *f*,P&R densité apparente *f*, PAPER TECH *of board* masse volumique apparente *f*, *of paper* masse volumique apparente *f*; ~ diffusion coefficient *n* PROP MAT coefficient de diffusion apparente *m*; ~ energy *n* ELEC énergie apparente *f*; ~ energy meter *n* ELEC compteur d'énergie apparente *m*; ~ horizon *n* ASTRON horizon apparent *m*, horizon visible *m*; ~ magnitude *n* ASTRON magnitude apparente *f*; ~ pitch *n* MECH ENG *of screw* pas apparent *m*; ~ porosity *n* C&G porosité ouverte *f*; ~ power *n* ELEC, ELEC ENG, PHYS puissance apparente *f*; ~ power meter *n* ELEC compteur de puissance apparente *m*; ~ resistivity *n* PETR résistivité apparente *f*; ~ specific gravity *n* PAPER TECH densité apparente *f*; ~ time *n* ASTRON temps apparent *m*; ~ utilization of oxygen *n* OCEANOG UAO, utilisation apparente d'oxygène *f*; ~ velocity *n* GEOPHYS vitesse

apparente *f*; ~ water table *n* WATER SUPP surface d'eau perchée *f*; ~ wind *n* NAUT *navigation* vent apparent *m*

appeal *n* PATENTS recours *m*

appearance *n* PAPER TECH *of paper*, TESTING aspect *m*; ~ cover *n* COATINGS revêtement décoratif *m*

appendix *n* PRINT *layout* annexe *f*, appendice *m*

Applegate: ~ diagram *n* ELECTRON *klystrons* diagramme d'Applegate *m*

Appleton: ~ layer *n* GEOPHYS, PHYS couche F *f*, couche d'Appleton *f*

appliance *n* MECH ENG appareil *m*, dispositif *m*, engin *m*, équipement *m*, PROD ENG appareil *m*, dispositif *m*

applicant *n* PATENTS demandeur *m*, déposant *m*

application[1] *n* COMP application *f*, MECH application *f*, demande *f*, dépôt *m*, PATENTS demande *f*; ~ appliance label *n* TELECOM étiquette verte *f*; ~ association *n* TELECOM association d'application *f*; ~ considerations *n* PROD ENG applications possibles *f pl*; ~ context *n* TELECOM contexte d'application *m*; ~ entry *n* (AE) TELECOM entité d'application *f*; ~ layer *n* DP, TELECOM *open systems interconnection* couche d'application *f*; ~ layer structure *n* (ALS) TELECOM structure en couches d'application *f*; ~ level gateway *n* TELECOM passerelle de niveau application *f*; ~ of microprocessors to gaging systems *n* (AmE), ~ of microprocessors to gauging systems *n* (BrE) MECH ENG utilisation des microprocesseurs dans les systèmes de calibrage *f*; ~ package *n* COMP, DP progiciel d'application *m*; ~ program *n* COMP programme d'application *m*; ~ protocol data unit *n* (APDU) TELECOM unité de données du protocole d'application *f*; ~ rate *n* CONST couverture *f*, taux d'application *m*, MAR POLL taux d'épandage *m*; ~ reference *n* TELECOM référence d'application *f*; ~ roller *n* PACKAGING rouleau d'application *m*; ~ service element *n* (ASE) TELECOM élément de service d'application *m*; ~ service object *n* (ASO) TELECOM objet de service d'application *m*; ~ software *n* COMP logiciel d'application *m*

application:[2] ~ is pending *phr* PATENTS demande est en instance

application-oriented: ~ language *n* COMP langage orienté application *m*

applications: ~ processor *n* TELECOM serveur *m*

application-specific: ~ integrated circuit *n* (ASIC) COMP circuit spécifique à une application *m*

applicative: ~ language *n* COMP langage fonctionnel *m*

applicator: ~ head *n* PACKAGING *for labels* tête d'application *f*; ~ roll *n* PAPER TECH rouleau enducteur *m*

applied: ~ chemistry *n* CHEM chimie appliquée *f*; ~ electromagnetic force *n* PHYS force électromotrice appliquée *f*; ~ emf *n* PHYS force électromotrice appliquée *f*; ~ research *n* POLLUTION recherche appliquée *f*; ~ stress *n* METALL contrainte appliquée *f*; ~ thermodynamics *n* MECH ENG thermodynamique appliquée *f*; ~ thread *n* C&G fil rapporté *m*

apply[1] *vt* CINEMAT *emulsion* couler, COATINGS *glue* enduire, ELEC ENG *voltage*, MECH appliquer; ~ for *vt* PATENTS demander, déposer, PROD ENG *permit* demander; ~ power to *vt* ELEC ENG mettre sous tension

apply:[2] ~ the brake *vi* VEHICLES freiner, serrer le frein; ~ vacuum *vi* PAPER TECH faire le vide

applying: ~ of angle joint bar *n* (AmE) *(cf angle fishplate)* RAIL éclisse cornière *f*, éclisse à patin *f*; ~ of angle joint bars *n* (AmE) *(cf angle fishplating)* RAIL éclissage angulaire *m*; ~ of emergency joint bars *n* (AmE) *(cf emergency fishplating)* RAIL éclissage de fortune *m*; ~ **of joint bars** *n* (AmE) (*cf fishplating*) RAIL éclissage *m*

apportion *vt* PROD ENG répartir

apportionment *n* PATENTS répartition *f*

appraisal: ~ **cost** *n* QUALITY coût d'évaluation *m*; ~ **drilling** *n* PETR TECH forage de délinéation *m*; ~ **well** *n* PETR puits d'estimation *m*, puits d'évaluation *m*, PETR TECH puits de délinéation *m*

apprenticeship *n* PROD ENG apprentissage *m*

approach[1] *n* AERONAUT *of aircraft* présentation *f*, CONST *means of access* abord *m*, accès *m*, NAUT *to land* abord *m*, SPACE approche *f*, rapprochement *m*; ~ **channel** *n* NAUT chenal d'accès *m*, chenal d'approche *m*; ~ **chart** *n* AERONAUT carte d'approche *f*; ~ **clearance** *n* AERONAUT autorisation d'approche *f*; ~ **control** *n* AERONAUT contrôle d'approche *m*; ~ **control office** *n* AERONAUT bureau de contrôle d'approche *m*; ~ **control rating** *n* AERONAUT qualification de contrôle d'approche *f*; ~ **control service** *n* AERONAUT service de contrôle d'approche *m*; ~ **elevation guidance** *n* AERONAUT guidage en site d'approche *m*; ~ **end of runway** *n* AERONAUT entrée de piste *f*; ~ **fix** *n* AERONAUT repère d'approche *m*; ~ **flow** *n* PAPER TECH courant de pâte *m*; ~ **funnel** *n* AERONAUT trouée d'approche *f*; ~ **guidance** *n* SPACE guidage en phase d'approche *m*; ~ **idling conditions** *n pl* AERONAUT ralenti de prise de terrain *m*; ~ **light beacon** *n* AERONAUT phare d'approche *m*; ~ **lighting system** *n* AERONAUT balisage lumineux d'approche *m*; ~ **noise measurement point** *n* AERONAUT point de mesure du bruit à l'approche *m*; ~ **path** *n* AERONAUT alignement en approche *m*, axe en approche *m*, chenal d'approche *m*, trajectoire en approche *f*; ~ **phase** *n* AERONAUT phase d'approche *f*; ~ **point** *n* AERONAUT repère d'approche *m*; ~ **procedure** *n* SPACE procédure d'approche *f*; ~ **reference noise measurement point** *n* AERONAUT point de référence de détermination du bruit en approche *m*; ~ **sequence** *n* AERONAUT séquence d'approche *f*; ~ **speed** *n* AERONAUT, SPACE, TRANSP vitesse d'approche *f*; ~ **time** *n* AERONAUT temps d'approche *m*

approach[2] *vt* MINING approcher de, arriver à

approaches *n pl* OCEANOG abords *m pl*

approach-locked: ~ **route** *n* RAIL itinéraire enclenché à l'approche *m*

appropriate: ~ **airworthiness requirement** *n* AERONAUT règlement applicable de navigabilité *m*

approval *n* AERONAUT, PROD ENG homologation *f*, QUALITY approbation *f*, homologation *f*, validation *f*, VEHICLES homologation *f*; ~ **certificate** *n* AERONAUT certificat d'homologation *m*; ~ **cost** *n* QUALITY coût d'homologation *m*; ~ **period** *n* QUALITY période d'homologation *f*; ~ **print** *n* CINEMAT copie d'étalonnage *f*; ~ **sign** *n* METR *after inspection* signe d'approbation *m*; ~ **standard** *n* QUALITY norme d'homologation *f*; ~ **system** *n* QUALITY système d'homologation *m*; ~ **test** *n* QUALITY, SPACE, TESTING essai d'homologation *m*; ~ **testing** *n* QUALITY essai d'homologation *m*

approve *vt* AERONAUT homologuer, QUALITY approuver, homologuer, SAFETY agréer, approuver

approved: ~ **first aid certificate** *n* SAFETY certificat agréé de premiers secours *m*; ~ **footwear** *n* SAFETY chaussures agréées *f pl*; ~ **organization** *n* QUALITY organisme agréé *m*; ~ **safety area** *n* SAFETY zone de sécurité agréée *f*; ~ **safety lamp** *n* COAL TECH lampe de sûreté agréée *f*

approximate[1] *adj* MATH approximatif

approximate:[2] ~ **execution time** *n* PROD ENG estimation du temps d'exécution *f*; ~ **weight** *n* PACKAGING poids approximatif *m*

approximation *n* MATH approximation *f*; ~ **error** *n* TELECOM erreur d'approximation *f*; ~ **to the nearest millimeter** *n* (AmE), ~ **to the nearest millimetre** *n* (BrE) MATH approximation au millimètre près *f*

appulse *n* ASTRON appulse *m*

apron *n* CONST tablier *m*, *of culvert* radier *m*, HYDROL *of dam* radier *m*, NAUT *boatbuilding* contre-étrave *f*, PAPER TECH tablier *m*, PRINT feuille de tête *f*, tablier *m*, PROD ENG tablier *m*, *conveyor belt* bande souple de transport *f*, courroie transporteuse *f*, toile transporteuse *f*, SAFETY *article of dress* tablier *m*, TRANSP *of aircraft* aire d'évolution *f*; ~ **applicator** *n* C&G courroie d'ensimage *f*; ~ **board** *n* PAPER TECH support de tablier *m*; ~ **conveyor** *n* CONST *civil engineering* sauterelle *f*, MECH ENG *continuous handling equipment* transporteur à palettes métalliques *m*, PACKAGING transporteur à plateaux *m*, TRANSP sauterelle *f*; ~ **floodlight** *n* ELEC *lighting* projecteur en nappe *m*; ~ **of a lathe** *n* tablier d'un tour *m*; ~ **lip** *n* PAPER TECH contre-lèvre *f*; ~ **management service** *n* AERONAUT service de gestion d'aire de trafic *m*; ~ **taxiway** *n* AERONAUT voie de circulation d'aire de trafic *f*, TRANSP piste de roulement *f*

aprotic: ~ **solvent** *n* CHEM solvant aprotique *m*

APS *abbr* (*automatic protection switching*) TELECOM commutation automatique sur liaison de réserve *f*, commutation de protection automatique *f*

apse *n* ASTRON apside *f*

apsis *n* ASTRON apside *f*

APT *abbr* COMP (*automatic programming tool*) programme de commande automatique *m*, RAIL (*advanced passenger train*) TGV (*train à grande vitesse*)

Aptian *n* GEOL *stratigraphy* aptien *m*

Apus *n* ASTRON Oiseau de Paradis *m*

apyrous *adj* CHEM apyre

AQL *abbr* (*acceptable quality level*) QUALITY NQA (*niveau de qualité acceptable*)

aqua: ~ **regia** *n* CHEM eau régale *f*

aquaculture *n* OCEANOG aquaculture *f*, aquiculture *f*

aquaculturist *n* OCEANOG aquaculteur *m*

aquafer *n* HYDROL aquifère *m*, strate perméable *f*

aqualung *n* OCEANOG scaphandre autonome *m*

aquamarine *n* MINERAL aiguemarine *f*

aquanaut *n* OCEANOG aquanaute *m*, océanaute *m*

aquaplane *n* OCEANOG hydroglisseur *m*

aquaplaning *n* AERONAUT aquaplanage *m*, hydroplanage *m*, effet d'hydroglisseur *m*, AUTO aquaplanage *m*

Aquarius *n* ASTRON Verseau *m*

aquatic[1] *adj* HYDROL aquatique

aquatic:[2] ~ **acidification** *n* POLLUTION acidification des eaux *f*, acidification hydrique *f*; ~ **life** *n* WATER SUPP vie aquatique *f*; ~ **pollutant** *n* WATER SUPP polluant aquatique *m*; ~ **system** *n* WATER SUPP système aquatique *m*

aqueduct *n* CONST, FUELLESS, HYDROL, WATER SUPP aqueduc *m*

aqueous[1] *adj* FLUID PHYS, PAPER TECH, PETR TECH, PROP MAT, WATER SUPP aqueux

aqueous:[2] ~ **effluent** *n* POLLUTION effluent aqueux *m*; ~ **ink** *n* PRINT encre à l'eau *f*; ~ **phase** *n* COAL TECH phase aqueuse *f*

aquiclude *n* WATER SUPP aquiclude *f*

aquiculture *n* WATER SUPP aquiculture *f*

aquifer *n* FUELLESS niveau aquifère *m*, GAS TECH nappe aquifère *f*, HYDROL aquifère *m*, couche perméable *f*, strate perméable *f*, WATER SUPP couche aquifère *f*; ~ **recharge** *n* HYDROL alimentation de la nappe souterraine *f*

aquiferous *adj* HYDROL, WATER SUPP aquifère

aquifuge *n* GEOL formation aquifuge *f*, formation hydrophobe *f*, WATER SUPP aquifuge *m*, couche imperméable *f*

Aquila *n* ASTRON Aigle *m*

aquitard *n* WATER SUPP aquitard *m*

Ar *(argon)* CHEM Ar *(argon)*

Ara *n* ASTRON Autel *m*

arabinose *n* CHEM arabinose *m*

arabitol *n* CHEM arabitol *m*

arachic *adj* CHEM arachique

arachidonic: ~ **acid** *n* FOOD TECH acide arachidonique *m*

arachis: ~ **oil** *n* FOOD TECH huile d'arachide *f*

araeometer *n* HYDROL, PETR TECH, PHYS aréomètre *m*

araeometry *n see areometry*

aragonite *n* MINERAL, PETR aragonite *f*

aramid *n* P&R aramide *m*

Ar-Ar: ~ **step heating method** *n* GEOL technique de datation 39-Ar/40-Ar par paliers de température *f*

arbitrary: ~ **constant** *n* PHYS constante arbitraire *f*; ~ **signs** *n pl* PRINT symboles typographiques inhabituels *m pl*

arbor *n* CHEM arbre de Diane *m*, MECH ENG arbre *m*, broche *f*, mandrin *m*; ~ **press** *n* MECH ENG presse à mandriner *f*; ~ **support** *n* MECH ENG *of milling machine* support d'arbre porte-fraise *m*

arc[1] *n* CINEMAT *light* arc *m*, lampe à arc *f*, ELEC *discharge*, ELEC ENG, GEOM *of circle* arc *m*; ~ **back** *n* ELEC ENG retour d'arc *m*; ~ **brazing** *n* PROD ENG brassage à l'arc *m*; ~ **breaker** *n* ELEC éclateur pare-étincelles *m*, ELEC ENG bobine d'extinction *f*, électro-aimant de soufflage *m*; ~ **carbon** *n* CINEMAT charbon pour arc *m*; ~ **of contact** *n* MECH ENG *of belt* angle d'enroulement *m*; ~ **current** *n* ELEC courant d'arc *m*; ~ **cutter** *n* MECH ENG fraise pour profil courbe *f*; ~ **cutting** *n* CONST, PROD ENG coupage à l'arc *m*; ~ **discharge** *n* ELEC amorçage d'arc *m*, décharge d'arc *f*, ELEC ENG, GAS TECH décharge d'arc *f*; ~ **discharge tube** *n* ELEC ENG tube à décharge d'arc *m*; ~ **discharge without transfer** *n* GAS TECH décharge d'arc sans transfert *f*; ~ **discharge with transfer** *n* GAS TECH décharge d'arc avec transfert *f*; ~ **extinction** *n* ELEC extinction d'arc *f*; ~ **feed** *n* CINEMAT avancement des charbons *m*; ~ **feed control** *n* CINEMAT réglage des charbons *m*; ~ **furnace** *n* HEATING, MECH ENG four à arc *m*; ~ **furnace direct** *n* HEATING four à arc direct *m*; ~ **furnace for steel melting** *n* MECH ENG four à arc de fusion d'acier *m*; ~ **heater** *n* MECH ENG réchauffeur à arc *m*; ~ **heating** *n* ELEC ENG chauffage par arc électrique *m*; ~ **ignition** *n* CINEMAT, ELEC, ELEC ENG amorçage d'arc *m*; ~ **jet engine** *n* MECH ENG réacteur à arc *m*; ~ **lamp** *n* ELEC *lighting* lampe à arc *f*; ~ **lamp carbon** *n* MECH ENG charbon pour lampes à arc *m*; ~ **light** *n* ELEC lumière à arc *f*; ~ **minute** *n* PHYS minute d'angle *f*, minute d'arc *f*; ~ **over** *n* ELEC, ELEC ENG contournement par un arc *m*; ~ **pitch** *n* MECH ENG *of gearwheel* pas circonférentiel *m*, pas circulaire *m*; ~ **projector** *n* CINEMAT projecteur à arc *m*; ~ **quench chamber** *n* ELEC ENG boîte d'extinction d'arc *f*; ~ **quenching** *n* ELEC ENG extinction d'arc *f*; ~ **rectifier** *n* CINEMAT redresseur pour lampe à arc *m*, ELEC ENG redresseur à arc *m*; ~ **regulator** *n* ELEC *lamp* régulateur d'arc *m*; ~ **rheostat** *n* ELEC rhéostat d'arc *m*; ~ **saw** *n* NUCLEAR scie à arc *f*; ~ **spectrum** *n* PHYS spectre d'arc *m*; ~ **striking** *n* ELEC amorçage d'arc *m*; ~ **suppression** *n* ELEC ENG soufflage d'arc *m*; ~ **suppression coil** *n* ELEC ENG *relay* bobine d'extinction *f*, ELEC ENG bobine de soufflage *f*; ~ **welder** *n* MECH soudeur à l'arc *m*; ~ **welding** *n* CONST, ELEC *application*, MECH soudage à l'arc *m*, PROD ENG soudage à l'arc électrique *m*, THERMOD soudage à l'arc *m*; ~ **welding electrode** *n* ELEC *application* électrode de soudage à arc *f*; ~ **welding machine** *n* MECH machine de soudage à l'arc *f*; ~ **width** *n* CINEMAT écartement des charbons *m*

arc[2] *vt* CINEMAT amorcer

arc[3] *vi* ELEC ENG cracher, projeter des étincelles

arcade *n* CONST arcade *f*

arcanite *n* MINERAL arcanite *f*

arch[1] *n* C&G *of glass-making pot* arcade *f*, CONST arc *m*, cintre *m*, voûte *f*, *of bridge* arche *f*, *structure* arceau *m*, voûte *f*, MINING estau *m*, stock *m*, PAPER TECH *boiler furnace* voûte *f*; ~ **brick** *n* CONST brique à couteau *f*; ~ **dam** *n* CONST, WATER SUPP barrage voûte *m*; ~ **of discharge** *n* CONST *architecture* arc de décharge *m*, arc en décharge *m*; ~ **panel** *n* CONST panneau de voûte *m*; ~ **pillar** *n* MINING pilier de voûte *m*; ~ **stone** *n* CONST claveau *m*, vousseau *m*, voussoir *m*

arch[2] *vt* CONST, MINING arquer, cintrer, voûter

arch[3] *vi* MINING se voûter

Archaean *n* GEOL *stratigraphy* archéen *m*

Archean *n* GEOL *stratigraphy* archéen *m*

arched[1] *adj* CONST cintré, en arc, en cintre, voûté

arched:[2] ~ **beam bridge** *n* CONST pont en arc *m*; ~ **tile** *n* CONST tuile canal *f*, tuile creuse *f*

Archie's: ~ **formula** *n* PETR formule d'Archie *f*

Archimedean: ~ **screw** *n* HYDR EQUIP vis d'Archimède *f*, vis élévatoire *f*

Archimedes': ~ **principle** *n* PHYS principe d'Archimède *m*, théorème d'Archimède *m*; ~ **screw** *n* HYDR EQUIP vis d'Archimède *f*, vis élévatoire *f*

arching *n* CONST *of roof* cintrage *m*, MINING arc-boutement en voûte *m*

archipelagic: ~ **passage** *n* OCEANOG passage archipélagique *m*

archipelago *n* NAUT, OCEANOG archipel *m*

architecture *n* COMP architecture *f*

archival: ~ **film** *n* CINEMAT film d'archives *m*; ~ **paper** *n* PAPER TECH papier pour documents de longue conservation *m*

archive[1] *n* DP archive *f*

archive[2] *vt* DP archiver

archived: ~ **file** *n* DP fichier archive *m*

archiving *n* DP archivage *m*

arcing *n* ELEC ENG amorçage d'arc *m*, PROD ENG arc *m*, PROP MAT allumage *m*; ~ **contact** *n* ELEC *of circuit breaker* contact d'arc *m*; ~ **time** *n* ELEC *of pole, fuse, switch* durée d'arc *f*

ardennite *n* MINERAL ardennite *f*

are *n* METR are *m*

area *n* COMP zone *f*, CONST *of building* aire *f*, *superficial extent* superficie *f*, surface *f*, étendue superficielle *f*, *tract of country* circonscription *f*, région *f*, zone *f*, étendue *f*, *tract of property* domaine *m*, DP zone *f*, GEOM *of circle*, MATH aire *f*, PAPER TECH superficie *f*, surface *f*; ~ **broadcasting** *n* TRANSP radiodiffusion régionale *f*; ~ **broadcasting station** *n* TRANSP émetteur zonal *m*; ~ **code** *n* TELECOM indicatif de zone *m*, indicatif interurbain *m*; ~ **control** *n* TRANSP macrorégulation *f*; ~ **of deep weathering** *n* CONST zone de terrain profondément altérée *f*; ~ **emission source** *n* POLLUTION source diffuse *f*, source étendue *f*; ~ **of influence** *n* WATER SUPP zone d'influence *f*; ~ **rule** *n* AERONAUT loi des aires *f*; ~ **traffic information** *n* TRANS-P information routière régionale *f*

arecaine *n* CHEM arécaïne *f*

arenaceous *adj* FUELLESS *rocks* arénacé

arendalite *n* MINERAL arendalite *f*

areometer *n* HYDROL, PETR TECH, PHYS aréomètre *m*

areometry *n* HYDROL, PHYS aréométrie *f*

arfvedsonite *n* MINERAL arfvedsonite *f*

argentic *adj* CHEM argentique

argentiferous *adj* MINERAL argentifère

argentine *n* COLOURS couleur argentée *f*

argentite *n* CHEM, MINERAL argentite *f*

argentopyrite *n* MINERAL argentopyrite *f*

argil *n* CONST argile de potier *f*, argile à poterie *f*

argillaceous *adj* FUELLESS *rocks* argileux

argillite *n* PETR argilite *f*

arginase *n* CHEM arginase *f*

arginine *n* CHEM arginine *f*

argol *n* CHEM tartre brut *m*

argon *n* *(Ar)* CHEM argon *m (Ar)*; ~ **arc welding** *n* PROD ENG soudage à l'argon *m*; ~ **gas blanket** *n* NUCLEAR couverture d'argon *f*; ~ **gas laser** *n* RAD PHYS laser à argon *m*; ~ **laser** *n* ELECTRON laser à argon *m*

Argos: ~ **transmitter** *n* OCEANOG *environmental research* émetteur Argos *m*

argument *n* COMP, MATH *of complex number, function* argument *m*

argyric *adj* CHEM argyrique

argyrite *n* MINERAL argentite *f*

argyrodite *n* MINERAL argyrodite *f*

argyropyrite *n* MINERAL argyropyrite *f*

argyrythrose *n* MINERAL pyrargyrite *f*

arheic *adj* WATER SUPP aréique

Aries *n* ASTRON Bélier *m*, double étoile *f*

Aristoxene: ~ **comma** *n* ACOUSTICS comma d'Aristoxène *m*

Aristoxene-Zarlin: ~ **scale** *n* ACOUSTICS gamme d'Aristoxène-Zarlin *f*

arithmetic *n* COMP, DP, MATH arithmétique *f*; ~ **and logic unit** *n* *(ALU)* COMP unité arithmétique et logique *f* *(ULA)*; ~ **capability** *n* PROD ENG fonctions mathématiques *f pl*; ~ **circuit** *n* ELECTRON circuit arithmétique *m*; ~ **function** *n* PROD ENG fonction mathématique *f*; ~ **instruction** *n* COMP instruction arithmétique *f*; ~ **mean** *n* COMP, MATH moyenne arithmétique *f*; ~ **operation** *n* COMP opération arithmétique *f*; ~ **operator** *n* COMP opérateur arithmétique *m*; ~ **shift** *n* COMP décalage arithmétique *m*; ~ **unit** *n* *(AU)* COMP unité arithmétique *f*

arizonite *n* MINERAL arizonite *f*

arkansite *n* MINERAL arkansite *f*

arkose *n* C&G grès feldspathique *m*, GEOL, PETR arkose *f*

arksutite *n* MINERAL arksutite *f*

arm[1] *n* INSTRUMENT potence *f*, NAUT *of anchor*, PAPER TECH, PETR bras *m*; ~ **elevator** *n* PAPER TECH élévateur-basculeur *m*; ~ **of an epicyclic train** *n* MECH ENG levier porte-train d'un système d'engrenage épicycloïdal *m*; ~ **rocker** *n* MECH ENG *of engine* levier de commande *m*; ~ **signal** *n* CONTROL signal à bras *m*, sémaphore *m*; ~ **swinger** *n* CINEMAT machiniste de grue *m*

arm[2] *vt* COMP armer

ARMA *abbr* *(autoregressive moving average)* COMP

moyenne mobile autorégressive *f*

armament *n* NAUT armement *m*

armature *n* ELEC *of machine* armature *f*, induit *m*, ELEC ENG armature *f*, *of dynamo, alternator* induit *m*, PHYS armature *f*; ~ **bar** *n* ELEC *of machine* , ELEC ENG barre d'induit *f*; ~ **casing** *n* ELEC ENG blindage d'induit *m*; ~ **circuit** *n* ELEC *of machine* circuit d'induit *m*; ~ **coil** *n* ELEC *of machine* , ELEC ENG bobine d'induit *f*; ~ **conductor** *n* ELEC *of machine* conducteur d'induit *m*; ~ **control** *n* ELEC *of machine* commande par tension d'induit *f*; ~ **core** *n* ELEC *of motor, generator* , ELEC ENG noyau d'induit *m*; ~ **current** *n* ELEC *of machine* , ELEC ENG courant d'induit *m*; ~ **end connections** *n pl* ELEC *of machine* connexion frontale d'induit *f*; ~ **end plate** *n* ELEC *of machine* plaque extrême d'induit *f*; ~ **field** *n* ELEC *of machine* champ d'induit *m*; ~ **induction** *n* ELEC *of machine* induction dans l'induit *f*; ~ **iron** *n* ELEC ENG fer d'induit *m*; ~ **reactance** *n* ELEC *of machine* réactance d'induit *f*; ~ **reaction** *n* ELEC *of machine* , ELEC ENG réaction d'induit *f*; ~ **reaction compensation** *n* ELEC ENG compensation de la réaction d'induit *f*; ~ **reaction-excited machine** *n* ELEC *motor* moteur à réaction d'induit *m*; ~ **relay** *n* ELEC ENG relais à armature *m*, relais à palette *m*; ~ **resistance** *n* ELEC *of machine* résistance d'induit *f*, ELEC ENG résistance d'induit *f*; ~ **shaft** *n* ELEC *of machine* arbre porte-enduit *m*; ~ **spider** *n* ELEC *of machine* étoile d'induit *f*, ELEC ENG croisillon d'induit *m*; ~ **tester** *n* ELEC appareil d'essai d'induit *m*; ~ **tooth** *n* ELEC *of machine* dent d'induit *f*; ~ **winding** *n* ELEC *of machine* enroulement d'induit *m*, ELEC ENG bobinage d'induit *m*, enroulement d'induit *m*

armature-controlled: ~ **motor** *n* ELEC moteur à commande de tension d'induit *m*

armor *n* (AmE) *see* armour

armor-clad *adj* (AmE) *see* armour-clad

armored *adj* (AmE) *see* armoured

armor-piercing: ~ **bullet** *n* (AmE) *see* armour-piercing bullet

armour *n* (BrE) ELEC *cable conductor* armure *f*, ELEC ENG blindage *m*, *of cable* armature *f*, armure *f*, cuirasse *f*, MILIT blindage *m*, blindés *m pl* ~ **clamp** *n* (BrE) ELEC *of cable* bride de câble armé *f*; ~ **plate** *n* (BrE) CONST plaque de blindage *f*, tôle de blindage *f*, MECH plaque de blindage *f*; ~ **plate mill** *n* (BrE) PROD ENG laminoir à blindage *m*; ~ **wire** *n* (BrE) OPT *of optical cable* fil d'armure *m*

armour-clad *adj* (BrE) ELEC ENG blindé

armoured[1] *adj* (BrE) ELEC *cable* armé, TELECOM blindé

armoured:[2] ~ **battery** *n* (BrE) TRANSP batterie blindée *f*; ~ **cable** *n* (BrE) ELEC ENG câble armé *m*, MECH ENG câble armé *m*, câble ayant une armature métallique *m*, câble protégé par une gaine en fils métalliques *m*, TELECOM câble blindé *m*; ~ **capillary** *n* (BrE) PROD ENG tube capillaire blindé *m*; ~ **car** *n* (BrE) MILIT auto blindée *f*; ~ **face conveyor** *n* (BrE) MINING convoyeur blindé de taille *m*; ~ **fighting vehicle** *n* (BrE) *(AFV)* MILIT véhicule blindé de combat *m*; ~ **glass** *n* (BrE) C&G verre blindé *m*, CONST verre armé *m*; ~ **hose** *n* (BrE) CONST tuyau armé *m*, tuyau protégé *m*; ~ **reconnaissance car** *n* (BrE) MILIT auto blindée de reconnaissance *f*; ~ **train** *n* (BrE) MILIT train blindé *m*

armour-piercing: ~ **bullet** *n* (BrE) MILIT balle perforante *f*

armrest *n* VEHICLES *of seat* accoudoir *m*

arms: ~ **rack** *n* MILIT râtelier d'armes *m*

arm-type: ~ **brush holder** *n* ELEC *of electrical machine* porte-balais en levier *m*

army: ~ **navy performance number system** *n (ANPN)* TRANSP *fuel rating, octane* système ANPN *m*

aromatic[1] *adj* PETR TECH aromatique

aromatic:[2] ~ **compound** *n* FOOD TECH, PETR TECH, PROP MAT composé aromatique *m*; ~ **hydrocarbon** *n* CHEM, P&R *chemical compound* hydrocarbure aromatique *m*; ~ **series** *n* CHEM série aromatique *f*

aromaticity *n* CHEM aromaticité *f*

aromatization *n* CHEM, PROP MAT aromatisation *f*

aromatize *vt* CHEM aromatiser

ARPA *abbr (automatic radar plotting aid)* NAUT *radar* aide de pointage radar automatique *f*

arpeggio *n* ACOUSTICS arpège *m*

arquerite *n* MINERAL arquérite *f*

arrangement *n* ELEC ENG montage *m*, MECH ENG arrangement *m*, dispositif *m*, disposition *f*, *of workshop* aménagement *m*

array *n* ASTRON ensemble d'antenne *m*, DP, MATH *of figures* tableau *m*, PETR réseau *m*, TELECOM matrice *f* ~ **antenna** *n* SPACE, TELECOM antenne réseau *f*; ~ **blanket** *n* FUELLESS nappe de capteurs solaires *f*, nappe de photopiles *f*; ~ **interconnection** *n* COMP, DP interconnexion matricielle *f*; ~ **processor** *n* COMP processeur matriciel *m*

arrest *n* NAUT *of boat* saisie *f*

arrester *n* ELEC ENG limiteur de surtension *m*, parafoudre *m*

arrhenite *n* MINERAL arrhénite *f*

Arrhenius: ~ **equation** *n* CHEM équation d'Arrhénius *f*

arris *n* C&G angle saillant *m*

arrissed: ~ **edge** *n* C&G joint arête abattue *m*

arrow *n* CONST *surveying peg* fiche *f*

arrowhead *n* CONST langue d'aspic *f*, tête de flèche *f*, PACKAGING *for closing device* flèche *f*; ~ **drill** *n* MECH ENG foret à langue d'aspic *m*, mèche plate *f*; ~ **wing** *n* TRANSP voilure en flèche *f*

arrowroot *n* FOOD TECH *for thickening* arrow-root *m*, fécule de marante *f*

arse *n* MECH ENG *of pulley bloc* élément fixe *m*

arsenate *n* CHEM arséniate *m*

arseniate *n* CHEM arséniate *m*

arsenic *n (As)* CHEM arsenic *m (As)*; ~ **implantation** *n* ELECTRON implantation d'arsenic *f*; ~ **trioxide** *n* CHEM arsenic blanc *m*

arsenide *n* CHEM arséniure *m*

arseniferous *adj* MINERAL arsénifère

arseniopleite *n* MINERAL arséniopléite *f*

arseniosiderite *n* MINERAL arséniosidérite *f*

arsenite *n* CHEM arsénite *m*, MINERAL arsénite *m*, arsénolite *f*

arseniuretted *adj* CHEM *hydrogen* arsénié

arsenolite *n* MINERAL arsénite *m*, arsénolite *f*

arsenopyrite *n* MINERAL arsénopyrite *f*

arsine *n* CHEM arsine *f*

arson *n* SAFETY incendie criminel *m*

art: ~ **canvas** *n* PRINT toile de relieur *f*; ~ **insert** *n* PRINT encart de luxe *m*, encart en quadrichromie *m*; ~ **metalwork** *n* CONST *railings, gates* serrurerie d'art *f*; ~ **paper** *n* PAPER TECH, PRINT papier couché *m*; ~ **of printing** *n* PRINT art typographique *m*

artboard *n* PRINT carte couchée *f*

arterial: ~ **drainage** *n* WATER SUPP assainissement agricole *m*; ~ **highway** *n* TRANSP grand axe *m*, grande route *f*; ~ **railroad** *n* (AmE) *(cf arterial railway)* TRANSP grande ligne de chemin de fer *f*; ~ **railway** *n* (BrE) *(cf arterial railroad)* TRANSP grande ligne de chemin de fer *f*; ~ **road** *n* TRANSP route de sortie *f*; ~ **system** *n* WATER SUPP réseau ramifié *m*

artesian[1] *adj* PETR TECH, WATER SUPP artésien

artesian:[2] ~ **water** *n* COAL TECH eau artésienne *f*; ~ **well** *n* HYDROL fontaine jaillissante *f*, puits jaillissant *m*, WATER SUPP puits artésien *m*, puits foré *m*

articulated[1] *adj* MECH, TRANSP articulé

articulated:[2] ~ **absorber** *n* NUCLEAR absorbeur articulé *m*; ~ **blade** *n* AERONAUT *of helicopter* pale articulée *f*; ~ **bus** *n* TRANSP autobus articulé *m*; ~ **car** *n* TRANSP voiture articulée *f*; ~ **coupling** *n* TRANSP attelage articulé *m*; ~ **diving suit** *n* OCEANOG scaphandre articulé *m*; ~ **lorry** *n* (BrE) *(cf articulated truck, tractor-trailer truck)* VEHICLES camion articulé *m*, camion semi-remorque *m*; ~ **railcar** *n* TRANSP automotrice articulée *f*; ~ **rotor** *n* AERONAUT *of helicopter* rotor articulé *m*; ~ **ship** *n* TRANSP navire articulé *m*; ~ **stinger** *n* PETR rampe articulée *f*; ~ **train** *n* TRANSP train articulé *m*; ~ **tramcar** *n* TRANSP automotrice articulée *f*; ~ **tramway** *n* TRANSP tramway articulé *m*; ~ **trolleybus** *n* TRANSP trolleybus articulé *m*; ~ **truck** *n* (AmE) *(cf articulated lorry)* VEHICLES camion articulé *m*, camion semi-remorque *m*

articulated-type: ~ **moving pavement** *n* (BrE) *(cf articulated-type moving sidewalk)* TRANSP trottoir roulant articulé *m*; ~ **moving sidewalk** *n* (AmE) *(cf articulated-type moving pavement)* TRANSP trottoir roulant articulé *m*

articulation: ~ **index** *n* ACOUSTICS indice d'articulation *m*, TELECOM indice de netteté *m*

articifer *n* MECH ENG dépanneur *m*, mécanicien ajusteur *m*, spécialiste très hautement qualifié *m*, MILIT *technician* artificier *m*

artificial[1] *adj* PAPER TECH artificiel

artificial:[2] ~ **acidification** *n* POLLUTION acidification artificielle *f*, acidification expérimentale *f*; ~ **ageing** *n* (BrE) PROD ENG vieillissement accéléré *m*, THERMOD *metals* durcissement par précipitation *m*, maturation artificielle *f*, vieillissement accéléré *m*; ~ **aging** *n* (AmE) *see artificial ageing*; ~ **bait** *n* OCEANOG leurre *m*; ~ **delay system** *n* RECORDING système à retard artificiel *m*; ~ **ear** *n* ACOUSTICS oreille artificielle *f*; ~ **feel failure detector** *n* AERONAUT détection de panne de sensation musculaire *f*; ~ **fiber** *n* (AmE), ~ **fibre** *n* (BrE) PROP MAT fibre artificielle *f*; ~ **filament** *n* PROP MAT fil artificiel *m*; ~ **gravity** *n* SPACE gravité artificielle *f*; ~ **horizon** *n* AERONAUT, SPACE, TRANSP horizon artificiel *m*; ~ **intelligence** *n (AI)* COMP, TELECOM intelligence artificielle *f (IA)*; ~ **lake** *n* WATER SUPP lac de barrage *m*; ~ **leather** *n* PAPER TECH similicuir *m*; ~ **light color film** *n* (AmE), ~ **light colour film** *n* (BrE) CINEMAT film couleur type lumière artificielle *m*, PHOTO film couleur lumière artificielle *m*; ~ **light photography** *n* PHOTO photographie à la lumière artificielle *f*; ~ **mastoid** *n* ACOUSTICS mastoïde artificiel *m*; ~ **mouth** *n* ACOUSTICS bouche artificielle *f*; ~ **noise** *n* SPACE, TELECOM bruit artificiel *m*; ~ **nuclear reaction** *n* NUCLEAR réaction nucléaire induite *f*; ~ **port** *n* NAUT port artificiel *m*; ~ **radioactivity** *n* PHYS, RAD PHYS radioactivité artificielle *f*; ~ **recharge** *n* HYDROL *of aquifer* alimentation artificielle *f*, recharge artificielle *f*; ~ **reef** *n* OCEANOG récif artificiel *m*; ~ **resin** *n* PROP MAT résine synthétique *f*; ~ **satellite** *n* ASTRON, TELECOM satellite artificiel *m*; ~ **ventilation** *n* SAFETY aérage artificiel *m*; ~ **voice** *n* ACOUSTICS voix artificielle *f*; ~ **weathering** *n*

P&R *test* exposition aux intempéries artificielles *f*

artificially: ~ **age** *vt* THERMOD durcir par précipitation, traiter par maturation artificielle, tremper; ~ **roughen** *vt* NUCLEAR rendre rugueux artificiellement

artificially-aged *adj* THERMOD trempé mûri

artillery *n* MILIT artillerie *f*; ~ **fire** *n* MILIT tir d'artillerie *m*; ~ **park** *n* MILIT parc d'artillerie *m*; ~ **spotter** *n* MILIT avion d'observation *m*

Artinskian *adj* GEOL *stratigraphy* artinskien

artist's: ~ **proof** *n* PRINT épreuve d'artiste *f*

artistic: ~ **porcelain** *n* C&G porcelaine artistique *f*; ~ **pottery** *n* C&G poterie artistique *f*

artpull *n* PRINT épreuve sur papier couché *f*

artwork *n* PRINT illustrations et maquette *f pl*

aryl *n* CHEM aryle *f*

arylamine *n* CHEM arylamine *f*

as:[1] ~ **cast** *adj* PROD ENG brut de coulée, brut de fonderie, brut de fonte; ~ **forged** *adj* PROD ENG brut de forge; ~ **required** *adj* PROD ENG à la demande; ~ **rolled** *adj* PROD ENG brut de laminage; ~ **stamped** *adj* PROD ENG brut d'estampage; ~ **welded** *adj* PROD ENG soudure non traitée thermiquement

as:[2] ~ **cast structure** *n* METALL, PROP MAT structure de coulée *f*; ~ **sintered hard metal pellet** *n* MECH ENG noyau brut en métal dur *m*

As *(arsenic)* CHEM As *(arsenic)*

asbestos *n* C&G amiante *m*, CHEM, MECH asbeste *m*, MINERAL asbeste *m*, P&R *filler*, PAPER TECH, PRINT amiante *m*, SAFETY, TEXTILES amiante *m*, asbeste *m*; ~ **board** *n* PAPER TECH carton d'amiante *m*; ~ **cement** *n* CONST, PAPER TECH amiante-ciment *m*; ~ **control in the workplace** *n* SAFETY contrôle de l'amiante à l'usine *m*; ~ **mat** *n* TEXTILES plaque d'amiante *f*; ~ **millboard** *n* CONST carton d'asbeste *m*; ~ **powder** *n* PAPER TECH poudre d'amiante *f*; ~ **roll disc** *n* (BrE) C&G rondelle d'amiante *f*; ~ **roll disk** *n* (AmE) *see asbestos roll disc*; ~ **sheet** *n* PAPER TECH feuille d'amiante *f*; ~ **sheeting** *n* CONST feuilles d'amiante *f pl*, feuilles d'asbeste *f pl*; ~ **string** *n* CONST ficelle d'amiante *f*, ficelle d'asbeste *f*; ~ **thread** *n* CONST ficelle d'amiante *f*; ~ **twine** *n* CONST ficelle d'amiante *f*; ~ **washer** *n* MECH ENG rondelle en amiante *f*; ~ **wool** *n* NUCLEAR laine d'amiante *f*

asbestos-free: ~ **insulating plates** *n pl* SAFETY plaques d'isolation sans amiante *f pl*; ~ **protective clothing** *n* SAFETY vêtements de protection contre la chaleur sans amiante *m pl*

asbestosis *n* CONST asbestose *f*

asbestos-plaited: ~ **packing** *n* CONST corde d'amiante *f*, corde d'asbeste *f*

asbolane *n* MINERAL asbolane *f*, asbolite *f*

asbolite *n* MINERAL asbolane *f*, asbolite *f*

ASC *abbr (automatic sequence control)* CONTROL contrôle automatique à séquence *m*, vérification automatique *f*

ascaricide *n* CHEM ascaricide *m*

ascender *n* PRINT *of character* hampe *f*, partie montante *f*

ascenders *n pl* PRINT ascendantes *f pl*

ascending: ~ **letter** *n* PRINT lettre montante *f*; ~ **node** *n* SPACE noeud ascendant *m*; ~ **sort** *n* COMP, DP tri ascendant *m*

ascent *n* OCEANOG *diving* remontée *f*, retour en surface *m*; ~ **stage** *n* SPACE *spacecraft* étage de montée *m*

ascepticone: ~ **necrosis** *n* OCEANOG astéonécrose dysbarique *f*

aschistic *adj* PETR aschiste

ASCII[1] *abbr (American Standard Code for Information Interchange)* COMP, DP, PRINT ASCII

ASCII:[2] ~ **code** *n* COMP, DP, PRINT code ASCII *m*

ascorbic *adj* CHEM ascorbique

ASE *abbr* TELECOM *(application service element)* élément de service d'application *m*, TRANSP *(automatic stabilization equipment)* stabilisateur automatique *m*, système de stabilisation artificielle *m*

aseptic[1] *adj* FOOD TECH, PACKAGING aseptique

aseptic:[2] ~ **engineering** *n* SAFETY technique aseptique *f*; ~ **filling** *n* FOOD TECH *food-processing machinery* conditionnement aseptique *m*, remplissage aseptique *m*, PACKAGING remplissage stérilisé *m*; ~ **packaging** *n* PACKAGING emballage stérilisé *m*; ~ **room clothing** *n* SAFETY vêtements pour salles aseptisées *m pl*

ash *n* P&R, PAPER TECH, POLLUTION, THERMOD cendre *f*, cendres *f pl*; ~ **bin** *n* PROD ENG cendrier *m*; ~ **box** *n* HEATING boîte à cendre *f*; ~ **content** *n* FOOD TECH taux de cendres *m*, teneur en cendres *f*, PAPER TECH, PROD ENG teneur en cendres *f*; ~ **dump** *n* PROD ENG dépôt des cendres *m*; ~ **pit** *n* PROD ENG cendrier *m*

ashen: ~ **light** *n* ASTRON *on moon, on dark side of Venus* lumière cendrée *f*

ash-free *adj* POLLUTION cendres exclues *f pl*

ashless[1] *adj* PAPER TECH sans cendres

ashless:[2] ~ **filter paper** *n* FOOD TECH, LAB EQUIP *filtration* papier-filtre sans cendres *m*; ~ **paper** *n* PAPER TECH papier sans cendres *m*

ashore[1] *adj* NAUT à terre

ashore[2] *adv* NAUT à terre

ASIC *abbr (application-specific integrated circuit)* COMP circuit spécifique à une application *m*

askarel *n* ELEC ENG askarel *m*, diphényle chloriné *m*

askew *adj* PRINT déviant de la ligne centrale, en biais

asmanite *n* MINERAL asmanite *f*

ASME: ~ **code** *n* MECH code ASME *m*

ASN1 *abbr (abstract syntax notation one)* TELECOM notation de syntaxe abstraite numéro un *f*

ASO *abbr (application service object)* TELECOM objet de service d'application *m*

aspartame *n* FOOD TECH aspartame *m*

aspartic[1] *adj* CHEM aspartique

aspartic:[2] ~ **acid** *n* FOOD TECH acide aspartique *m*

aspatron *n* NUCLEAR pile atomique transportable *f*

aspect: **off** ~ *n* RAIL *of mechanical signal* signal effacé *m*; ~ **ratio** *n* AERONAUT *of wing* allongement *m*, CINEMAT rapport de format *m*, rapport largeur-hauteur de l'image *m*, COMP rapport de cadrage *m*, ELEC ENG format de l'image *m*, rapport largeur-hauteur *m*, MECH rapport d'élancement *m*, PHYS allongement *m*, TRANSP rapport longueur-largeur *m*; ~ **ratio adjustment** *n* TV ajustage de format *m*

asperolite *n* MINERAL aspérolite *f*

asphalt *n* CONST, MINERAL, PETR TECH asphalte *m*; ~ **boiler** *n* CONST chaudière de bitumier *f*; ~ **concrete** *n* CONST béton asphaltique *m*, béton bitumineux *m*; ~ **paper** *n* PAPER TECH papier bitumé *m*; ~ **plant** *n* CONST *civil engineering* centrale d'enrobage *f*; ~ **surfacing** *n* CONST pavage asphaltique *m*, tapis asphaltique *m*; ~ **tanking** *n* CONST *basement waterproofing* revêtement asphaltique *m*; ~ **varnish** *n* COLOURS laque à l'asphalte *f*, vernis à l'asphalte *m*

asphaltene *n* MINERAL asphaltène *m*

asphalter *vt* CONST asphalter, bitumer, bituminer

asphalting *n* CONST asphaltage *m*, bitumage *m*

asphaltite *n* MINERAL asphaltite *f*

asphalt-spreading: ~ **machine** n (AmE) *(cf road metal-spreading machine)* TRANSP épandeur-régleur-dameur m

aspheric: ~ **corrector plate** n TV lentille asphérique correctrice f

aspherical: ~ **lens** n CINEMAT objectif asphérique m

aspidolite n MINERAL aspidolite f

aspirated: ~ **psychrometer** n REFRIG psychromètre ventilé m

aspiration n PAPER TECH aspiration f; ~ **psychrometer** n REFRIG psychromètre à aspiration m; ~ **pump** n HYDR EQUIP pompe aspirante f, pompe suceuse f

aspirator n LAB EQUIP *glassware* flacon tubulé m, PROD ENG aspirateur m

aspiring: ~ **pump** n HYDR EQUIP pompe aspirante f, pompe suceuse f, MECH ENG machine pneumatique f, pompe aspirante f, pompe d'évacuation d'air f

ASR abbr *(automatic send-receive)* COMP téléimprimeur émetteur-récepteur m, DP appareil émetteur-récepteur m, émetteur-récepteur automatique m

assault: ~ **rifle** n MILIT fusil d'assaut m

assay n CHEM analyse f, dosage m, essai m; ~ **balance** n CHEM balance d'essai f; ~ **furnace** n CHEM four d'essai m, HEATING fourneau d'essai m; ~ **grade** n COAL TECH teneur f; ~ **office** n CHEM bureau d'essais m, COAL TECH laboratoire d'analyse m; ~ **sample** n CHEM échantillon à doser m; ~ **value** n COAL TECH teneur f

assayer n CHEM essayeur m

assaying n CHEM analyse f, essai m

assemble:[1] ~ **edit** n TV montage en assemblage m; ~ **to order** n PROD ENG assemblage à la commande m

assemble[2] vt COMP assembler, CONST assembler, monter, PAPER TECH *machine* monter, PRINT assembler, monter

assemble:[3] ~ **edit** vi CINEMAT prémonter

assembler n COMP assembleur m; ~ **directive** n COMP directive d'assemblage f

assembling n MECH ENG assemblage m, PAPER TECH *of machine* montage m; ~ **bolt** n MECH ENG boulon d'assemblage m

assembly n CINEMAT prémontage m, COMP assemblage m, CONST montage m, ELEC, GAS TECH assemblage m, MECH assemblage m, ensemble m, MECH ENG, PRINT assemblage m, VEHICLES ensemble m, montage m; ~ **area** n NAUT *for on-board emergency* zone de rassemblement f; ~ **building** n SPACE halle d'assemblage f; ~ **coefficient** n PROD ENG coefficient de montage m; ~ **drawing** n MECH plan d'assemblage m, MECH ENG plan d'ensemble m; ~ **hall** n NAUT *shipbuilding* nef de montage f, salle de montage f; ~ **jig** n MECH ENG banc d'assemblage m, gabarit de montage m; ~ **language** n COMP langage d'assemblage m; ~ **line** n MECH, MECH ENG chaîne de montage f, NAUT *shipbuilding* chaîne de montage f, *shipbuilding* ligne de montage f, PACKAGING, PROD ENG chaîne de montage f; ~ **line inspection** n CONTROL contrôle d'assemblage m, contrôle du montage à la chaîne m; ~ **list** n PROD ENG nomenclature de montage f; ~ **pitch** n NUCLEAR pas inter-assemblage m; ~ **plan** n MECH ENG schéma de montage m; ~ **point** n TRANSP point de départ m; ~ **robot** n MECH robot d'assemblage m; ~ **sheet** n PROD ENG nomenclature de montage f; ~ **shop** n MECH atelier d'assemblage m; ~ **tools** n pl MECH ENG outils de manoeuvre m pl

assess vt QUALITY estimer, TEXTILES évaluer; ~ **the distribution** vt MECH ENG *of carbides in tool steels* évaluer la répartition

assessed: ~ **quality** n QUALITY qualité estimée f

assessment n MECH ENG estimation f, expertise f, évaluation f, QUALITY estimation f; ~ **of reliability** n QUALITY évaluation de la fiabilité f

assign vt COMP, DP affecter, allouer, attribuer

assignable: ~ **cause** n QUALITY cause attribuable f

assigned: ~ **flight path** n AERONAUT trajectoire de vol assignée f

assignee n PATENTS cessionnaire m

assignment n PATENTS cession f, SPACE *of frequency* affectation f, assignation f; ~ **map** n TELECOM carte d'assignation f; ~ **message** n TELECOM message d'assignation m; ~ **statement** n COMP, DP instruction d'affectation f

assignor n PATENTS cédant m

assistance n MECH ENG aide f, SAFETY aide f, assistance f, secours m

assistant: ~ **driller** n PETR aide foreur m

associated: ~ **gain** n ELECTRON gain au minimum du bruit m; ~ **gas** n GAS TECH, PETR TECH gaz associé m; ~ **liquid** n PETR TECH liquide associé m; ~ **mark** n PATENTS marque associée f

association n CHEM, TELECOM association f; ~ **control service element** n *(ACSE)* TELECOM élément de service de commande d'association m, élément de service de contrôle d'association m; ~ **initiator** n TELECOM demandeur de l'association m

associative: ~ **addressing** n COMP adressage associatif m; ~ **memory** n COMP mémoire associative f; ~ **processor** n TELECOM processeur associatif m; ~ **storage** n (AmE) *(cf associative store)* COMP mémoire associative f; ~ **store** n (BrE) *(cf associative storage)* COMP mémoire associative f

assortment n PROD ENG assortiment m

assumption: ~ **analysis** n PROD ENG analyse hypothétique f

assured: ~ **water supply** n WATER SUPP provision d'eau assurée f

astable: ~ **circuit** n ELECTRON circuit astable m, montage astable m; ~ **multivibrator** n ELECTRON multivibrateur astable m

A-stage: ~ **resin** n P&R résine à l'état A f, résol à l'état A m

astatic[1] adj PHYS astatique

astatic:[2] ~ **ammeter** n ELEC ampèremètre astatique m; ~ **galvanometer** n ELEC ENG, PHYS galvanomètre astatique m; ~ **microphone** n RECORDING microphone antidirectionnel m, microphone omnidirectionnel m; ~ **voltmeter** n ELEC voltmètre astatique m

astatine n *(At)* CHEM astate m *(At)*

astatki n PETR astaki m

asterism n ASTRON astérisme m, constellation f

astern adv NAUT en arrière, vers l'arrière, à l'arrière

asteroid n ASTRON, SPACE astéroïde m; ~ **belt** n ASTRON ceinture d'astéroïdes f; ~ **nomenclature** n ASTRON nomenclature des astéroïdes f

asthenosphere n GEOL, PETR asthénosphère f

asthma: ~ **paper** n PAPER TECH papier antiasthmatique m

astigmatic n PHYS astigmatique m

astigmatism n PHYS, TV astigmatisme m

astragal n CONST *moulding* astragale m

astrakanite n MINERAL astrakanite f

astrionics n SPACE électronique spatiale f

astro: ~ **fix** n SPACE point astronomique m

astrobiology *n* ASTRON astrobiologie *f*
astrochemistry *n* ASTRON astrochimie *f*
astrocompass *n* SPACE *guidage* astrocompas *m*
astrodrome *n* SPACE astrodrome *m*
astrodynamics *n* SPACE astrodynamique *f*
astrograph *n* ASTRON *for taking wide-angle photographs* astrographe *m*
astrolabe *n* ASTRON *to measure altitude* astrolabe *m*
astrometric: ~ **binary** *n* ASTRON binaire astrométrique *m*
astrometry *n* ASTRON, SPACE astrométrie *f*
astronaut *n* SPACE astronaute *m*, spationaute *m*
astronavigation *n* NAUT navigation astronomique *f*
astronomer *n* ASTRON, SPACE astronome *m*
astronomic: ~ **longitude** *n* SPACE longitude astronomique *f*; ~ **unit** *n* (*AU*) ASTRON unité astronomique *f* (*UA*)
astronomical: ~ **camera** *n* PHOTO chambre d'astrophotographie *f*; ~ **navigation** *n* NAUT navigation astronomique *f*; ~ **position** *n* NAUT point astronomique *m*; ~ **telescope** *n* INSTRUMENT lunette astronomique *f*, télescope astronomique *m*, PHYS lunette astronomique *f*; ~ **tide** *n* OCEANOG marée astronomique *f*; ~ **unit** *n* (*AU*) ASTRON unité astronomique *f* (*UA*)
astrophotography *n* ASTRON astrophotographie *f*
astrophyllite *n* MINERAL astrophyllite *f*
astrophysics *n* ASTRON, SPACE astrophysique *f*
asymmetric[1] *adj* COMP, DP, GEOM, MATH asymétrique
asymmetric:[2] ~ **circuit** *n* ELEC circuit asymétrique *m*; ~ **suspension** *n* TRANSP *monorail* suspension asymétrique *f*
asymmetrical[1] *adj* GEOM asymétrique, SPRINGS dissymétrique
asymmetrical:[2] ~ **circuit** *n* ELEC circuit asymétrique *m*; ~ **deflection** *n* TV balayage asymétrique *m*; ~ **leaf** *n* SPRINGS lame dissymétrique *f*; ~ **trapezoidal screw thread** *n* MECH ENG *artillery-type* filetage trapézoïdal asymétrique *m*
asymmetry *n* CHEM asymétrie *f*, MATH asymétrie *f*, dissymétrie *f*
asymptomatic: ~ **approximation** *n* TELECOM approximation asymptomatique *f*
asymptomatical: ~ **approximation** *n* TELECOM approximation asymptomatique *f*
asymptote *n* GEOM, MATH asymptote *f*
asymptotic *adj* GEOM asymptotique
asynchronism *n* PHYS asynchronisme *m*
asynchronous[1] *adj* COMP, DP, ELEC, PHYS asynchrone, TV asynchrone, non synchrone
asynchronous:[2] ~ **alternator** *n* ELEC ENG alternateur asynchrone *m*; ~ **channel adaptor** *n* COMP adaptateur de canal asynchrone *m*; ~ **circuit** *n* COMP, TELECOM circuit asynchrone *m*; ~ **generator** *n* ELEC alternateur asynchrone *m*; ~ **linear induction motor** *n* TRANSP moteur linéaire asynchrone *m*; ~ **link** *n* ELEC *of two AC systems* liaison asynchrone *f*; ~ **machine** *n* ELEC ENG machine asynchrone *f*; ~ **modem** *n* ELECTRON modem asynchrone *m*, modem pour transmission asynchrone *m*; ~ **motor** *n* ELEC, ELEC ENG, RAIL *vehicles*, TRANSP moteur asynchrone *m*; ~ **operation** *n* ELEC *of motor* fonctionnement asynchrone *m*; ~ **port** *n* TELECOM accès en mode asynchrone *m*, point d'accès asynchrone *m*; ~ **running** *n* ELEC marche asynchrone *f*; ~ **sound** *n* CINEMAT son désynchronisé *m*, son non synchrone *m*; ~ **time-division multiplexing** *n* (*ATDM*) TELECOM multiplexage temporel asynchrone *m*; ~

transmission *n* COMP, DP transmission asynchrone *f*, TELECOM transmission non synchrone *f*
asynchronous: ~ **transfer mode** *n* (*ATM*) TELECOM Transfert temporel asynchrone *m* (*TTA*)
at:[1] ~ **sea level** *adj* METEO *maritime* au niveau de la mer
at:[2] ~ **the far end** *adv* TELECOM chez le destinataire; ~ **grade** *adv* CONST de niveau; ~ **the near end** *adv* TELECOM *telex* chez l'émetteur; ~ **sea** *adv* NAUT en mer, sur mer; ~ **water level** *adv* WATER SUPP à fleur d'eau
at:[3] ~ **the rate of** *prep* METR à raison de; ~ **right angles to** *prep* GEOM perpendiculaire à
at:[4] **be** ~ **grade** *vi* CONST *physical geography* posséder sa courbe de lit, posséder sa pente-limite, posséder son profil d'équilibre
At (*astatine*) CHEM At (*astate*)
AT: ~ **vehicle** *n* (*all-terrain vehicle*) TRANSP, véhicule tout-terrain *m*
atacamite *n* MINERAL atacamite *f*
atactic[1] *adj* CHEM *polymers*, PROP MAT *polymers* atactique
atactic:[2] ~ **polymer** *n* P&R polymère atactique *m*
ATC *abbr* RAIL (*automatic train control*) contrôle automatique des trains *m*, TRANSP (*air traffic control*) contrôle du trafic aérien *m*
ATDM *abbr* (*asynchronous time division multiplexing*) TELECOM multiplexage temporel asynchrone *m*
ATE *abbr* (*automatic test equipment*) COMP matériel de test automatique *m*
atelestite *n* MINERAL atélestite *f*
atelite *n* MINERAL atélite *f*
athermal *adj* CHEM athermal
athermancy *n* PHYS athermanéité *f*
athodyd *n* AERONAUT *ramjet*, TRANSP statoréacteur *m*
athwartships *adv* NAUT en travers, par le travers, transversalement
ATK *abbr* (*aviation turbine kerosene*) PETR TECH carburéacteur *m*
atlasite *n* MINERAL atlasite *f*
ATM[1] *abbr* COMP (*automatic teller machine*) guichet automatique de banque *m*, OPT (*alternative test method*) *optical fibres* méthode de mesure de remplacement *f*, TELECOM (*asynchronous transfer mode*) TTA (*transfert temporel asynchrone*)
ATM:[2] ~ **adaptation layer** *n* (*AAL*) TELECOM couche d'adaptation AAL *f*; ~ **service data unit** *n* (*ATM-SDU*) TELECOM unité de données de service ATM *f*
atmolysis *n* CHEM atmolyse *f*
atmos: ~ **track** *n* RECORDING bande effets sonores *f*
atmosphere *n* ASTRON, METEO, PHYS atmosphère *f*
atmospheric[1] *adj* METEO, PHYS atmosphérique
atmospheric:[2] ~ **absorption** *n* METEO, RAD PHYS absorption atmosphérique *f*; ~ **acidity** *n* POLLUTION acidité de l'air *f*; ~ **agent** *n* PETR TECH agent atmosphérique *m*; ~ **brake** *n* MECH ENG frein à air comprimé *m*; ~ **burner** *n* THERMOD brûleur atmosphérique *m*; ~ **chemical process** *n* POLLUTION processus chimique atmosphérique *m*; ~ **chemistry** *n* POLLUTION chimie atmosphérique *f*, chimie de l'atmosphère *f*; ~ **concentration** *n* POLLUTION concentration atmosphérique *f*; ~ **conditions** *n pl* METEO, NAUT *radio propagation* conditions atmosphériques *f pl*, PROP MAT conditions atmosphériques *f pl*, état atmosphérique *m*; ~ **degassing** *n* HYDROL dégazement atmosphérique *m*; ~ **disturbance** *n* METEO perturbation atmosphérique *f*; ~ **electric field** *n* GEOPHYS champ électrique atmosphérique *m*; ~ **electricity** *n* GEOPHYS, METEO électricité atmosphérique *f*; ~ **fall-**

out n POLLUTION apport atmosphérique m, dépôt atmosphérique m, retombées atmosphériques f pl; **~ haze** n PHOTO voile atmosphérique m; **~ hyperbare** n OCEANOG ambiance hyperbare f; **~ interference** n GEOPHYS parasites atmosphériques m pl; **~ inversion** n POLLUTION inversion atmosphérique f; **~ lifetime** n POLLUTION durée de vie dans l'atmosphère f, vie atmosphérique f; **~ line** n PHYS ligne atmosphérique f; **~ load** n POLLUTION charge atmosphérique f, charge de polluants atmosphériques f; **~ loading** n POLLUTION charge atmosphérique f, charge de polluants atmosphériques f; **~ noise** n ELECTRON bruit atmosphérique m, RECORDING bruit d'ambiance m, SPACE bruit atmosphérique m; **~ obscurity** n POLLUTION obscurité atmosphérique f; **~ phenomenon** n POLLUTION phénomène atmosphérique m; **~ pollution** n POLLUTION pollution atmosphérique f; **~ pressure** n GAS TECH, METEO, PHYS pression atmosphérique f, PROP MAT pression extérieure f; **~ radiation** n METEO rayonnement atmosphérique m; **~ re-entry** n SPACE rentrée dans l'atmosphère f; **~ refiner** n PAPER TECH raffineur atmosphérique m; **~ refraction** n ASTRON of light réfraction atmosphérique f; **~ scrubbing** n POLLUTION lavage atmosphérique m; **~ sulfur** n (AmE), **~ sulphur** n (BrE) POLLUTION soufre atmosphérique m; **~ tide** n GEOPHYS marée atmosphérique f; **~ window** n ASTRON, PHYS, RAD PHYS fenêtre atmosphérique f

atmospherics n pl ELEC ENG parasites atmosphériques m pl, ELECTRON brouillage m, bruit atmosphérique m, parasites atmosphériques m pl, GEOPHYS parasites atmosphériques m pl, SPACE bruit atmosphérique m

ATM-SDU abbr (ATM service data unit) TELECOM unité de données de service ATM f

ATO abbr (automatic train operation) TRANSP commande automatique des trains f

A-to-D adj (analog-to-digital, analogue-to-digital) TV analogique-numérique

atoll n NAUT, OCEANOG atoll m

atom n COMP, DP, PART PHYS, PHYS atome m

atom-atom: **~ collision** n NUCLEAR collision atome-atome f

atomic[1] adj CHEM, PART PHYS, PHYS atomique

atomic:[2] **~ absorption analysis** n RAD PHYS spectrophotometry analyse par absorption atomique f; **~ absorption spectrometer** n LAB EQUIP analysis spectromètre d'absorption atomique m; **~ absorption spectrophotometer** n RAD PHYS chemical analysis spectrophotomètre d'absorption atomique m; **~ absorption spectroscopy** n CHEM analysis, PHYS spectroscopie par absorption atomique f; **~ air-to-air rocket** n MILIT fusée air-air à charge atomique f; **~ beam** n NUCLEAR faisceau atomique m; **~ beam diffraction** n NUCLEAR diffraction des faisceaux atomiques f; **~ beam frequency standard** n NUCLEAR étalon de fréquence atomique m; **~ bomb** n NUCLEAR bombe atomique f; **~ clock** n PHYS, TELECOM horloge atomique f; **~ coordinates** n pl CRYSTALL coordonnées atomiques f pl; **~ core** n NUCLEAR coeur de l'atome m; **~ cross section** n NUCLEAR section atomique efficace f; **~ density** n RAD PHYS densité atomique f; **~ displacement** n METALL déplacement atomique m; **~ energy control** n CONTROL contrôle de l'énergie atomique m; **~ energy level** n NUCLEAR niveau énergétique d'un atome m; **~ fluorescence analysis** n RAD PHYS spectrometry analyse par fluorescence atomique f; **~ gas**

laser n ELECTRON laser atomique m, laser à gaz atomique m; **~ heat capacity** n RAD PHYS chaleur spécifique atomique f; **~ hydrogen maser** n ELECTRON maser à hydrogène atomique m; **~ hydrogen welding** n NUCLEAR soudage à l'hydrogène atomique m; **~ interspace** n NUCLEAR espace entre les atomes m; **~ line width** n PART PHYS largeur de raie atomique f; **~ mass** n CHEM of element, PART PHYS of element masse atomique f; **~ mass unit** n PART PHYS, PHYS unité de masse atomique f; **~ nucleus** n NUCLEAR, PART PHYS noyau atomique m; **~ number** n CHEM of element, PART PHYS, PHYS nombre atomique m, numéro atomique m; **~ orbital** n CHEM orbitale atomique f, PART PHYS orbitale d'un atome f, PHYS orbitale atomique f; **~ physicist** n PART PHYS physicien de l'atome m; **~ physics** n PHYS physique atomique f; **~ pile** n NUCLEAR, PHYS pile atomique f; **~ polarization** n RAD PHYS polarisation atomique f; **~ radiation** n NUCLEAR rayonnement atomique m; **~ radius** n CHEM, NUCLEAR rayon atomique m; **~ research** n NUCLEAR recherche atomique f; **~ rocket** n MILIT roquette à charge atomique f, NUCLEAR fusée atomique f; **~ scattering** n NUCLEAR diffusion atomique f; **~ scattering factor** n CRYSTALL facteur de diffusion atomique m; **~ shuffling** n METALL réajustement atomique m; **~ spectroscopy** n RAD PHYS spectroscopie atomique f; **~ spectrum** n NUCLEAR, PHYS spectre atomique m; **~ state** n NUCLEAR état atomique m; **~ structure** n PART PHYS structure atomique f; **~ test** n MILIT essai nucléaire m; **~ time** n ASTRON temps atomique m; **~ trunk** n NUCLEAR tronc de l'atome m; **~ uranium vapor** n (AmE), **~ uranium vapour** n (BrE) NUCLEAR vapeur d'uranium atomique f; **~ vapor method** n (AmE), **~ vapour method** n (BrE) NUCLEAR of laser isotope separation méthode de vapeur atomique f; **~ volume** n NUCLEAR volume atomique m; **~ weapon** n MILIT arme atomique f; **~ weight** n CHEM of element masse atomique relative f, poids atomique m, PART PHYS, PHYS masse atomique relative f; **~ weight unit** n (AWU) NUCLEAR unité de masse atomique chimique f, unité de poids atomique f (UPA)

ATOMIC abbr (automatic train operation by mini computer) RAIL conduite automatique des trains par mini-ordinateur f

atomicity n CHEM, COMP, DP, PHYS atomicité f

atomistic: **~ structure** n NUCLEAR of matter structure atomistique f

atomization n CHEM of liquid, NUCLEAR, PETR TECH atomisation f

atomize vt CHEM atomiser, PAPER TECH pulvériser

atomizer n CHEM TECH atomiseur m, diffuseur champignon m, pulvérisateur m, vaporisateur m, LAB EQUIP, PACKAGING, PAPER TECH pulvérisateur m; **~ injection nozzle** n CHEM TECH cône de diffuseur m, cône de pulvérisateur m; **~ nozzle** n CHEM TECH alésage de diffuseur m

atomizing: **~ burner** n THERMOD brûleur atomiseur m, brûleur à évaporation m; **~ cone** n CHEM TECH cône de projection m; **~ nozzle** n FOOD TECH buse d'atomisation f; **~ oil burner** n HEAT ENG brûleur à vaporisation de fuel m; **~ process** n CHEM TECH atomisation f

atonal: **~ space** n ACOUSTICS écart atonal m

atopite n MINERAL atopite f

ATP abbr (BrE) (automatic train protection) RAIL PAT (protection automatique de trains)

atropic adj CHEM atropique

attach *vt* COMP attacher, connecter, DP attacher, connecter, relier, MECH ENG accoupler, fixer, *trailer to tractor* atteler, PAPER TECH, SPACE fixer

attached: ~ **eddies** *n pl* FLUID PHYS tourbillons liés *m pl*

attaching: ~ **gun** *n* PACKAGING pistolet de fixation *m*; ~ **part** *n* MECH ENG élément de fixation *m*

attachment *n* COAL TECH accessoire *m*, adhésion *f*, fixation *f*, COMP, DP connexion *f*, raccordement *m*, INSTRUMENT instrument auxiliaire *m*, MECH ENG *coupling* accessoire *m*, fixation *f*, élément de liaison *m*, PROD ENG *for machine* accessoire *m*, RAIL attelage *m*, SPACE fixation *f*; ~ **fitting** *n* MECH ENG ferrule de fixation *f*; ~ **link** *n* MECH ENG manille d'attelage *f*

attack *n* ACOUSTICS, COAL TECH attaque *f*; ~ **angle** *n* AERONAUT incidence *f*, MINING angle d'attaque *m*; ~ **helicopter** *n* MILIT hélicoptère avec armement lourd *m*; ~ **time** *n* RECORDING temps d'attaque *m*

attacked: ~ **by acids** *adj* POLLUTION attaqué par les acides

attacolite *n* MINERAL attacolite *f*

attapulgite *n* MINERAL, PETR attapulgite *f*, PETR TECH attapulgite *f*, *drilling* attapulgite *f*

attended: ~ **operation** *n* COMP exploitation sous surveillance *f*, DP exploitation sous surveillance *f*, fonctionnement sous surveillance *m*

attenuate *vt* ELECTRON, RECORDING atténuer

attenuating: ~ **element** *n* ELECTRON élément atténuateur *m*; ~ **filter** *n* RECORDING filtre atténuateur *m*

attenuation *n* COMP atténuation *f*, ELEC *of signal* , ELECTRON, OPT affaiblissement *m*, atténuation *f*, PETR atténuation *f*, PHYS, RECORDING affaiblissement *m*, atténuation *m*, SPACE *communications*, TELECOM *transmission*, TV affaiblissement *m*, WAVE PHYS atténuation *f*; ~ **band** *n* ELECTRON *filters* bande atténuée *f*; ~ **coefficient** *n* ACOUSTICS affaiblissement linéique *m*, ELECTRON coefficient d'atténuation *m*, OPT affaiblissement linéique *m*, PHYS affaiblissement linéique *m*, coefficient d'affaiblissement *m*, coefficient d'atténuation *m*, TELECOM affaiblissement linéique *m*; ~ **constant** *n* ELECTRON constante d'atténuation *f*, OPT, PHYS constante d'affaiblissement *f*; ~ **contour** *n* ELECTRON gabarit de filtrage *m*, gabarit de filtre *m*; ~ **distortion** *n* ELECTRON, PHYS *frequency* distorsion d'affaiblissement *f*, RECORDING distorsion d'atténuation *f*; ~ **factor** *n* RECORDING coefficient d'affaiblissement *m*

attenuation-limited: ~ **operation** *n* OPT, TELECOM fonctionnement limité par l'affaiblissement *m*

attenuator *n* ELECTRON affaiblisseur *m*, atténuateur *m*, RECORDING atténuateur *m*, SPACE amortisseur *m*, TELECOM affaiblisseur *m*, atténuateur *m*; ~ **diode** *n* ELECTRON diode d'atténuation *f*

attitude *n* SPACE *of spacecraft* attitude *f*, orientation *f*; ~ **acquisition** *n* SPACE *of spacecraft* acquisition d'attitude *f*; ~ **and orbit control system** *n* *(AOCS)* SPACE système de commande d'attitude et d'orbite *m*; ~ **control** *n* AERONAUT stabilisation d'orientation *f*; ~ **control unit** *n* SPACE *of spacecraft* centrale de commande d'attitude *f*, chaîne de pilotage *f*; ~ **reference unit** *n* SPACE *of spacecraft* centrale de référence d'attitude *f*; ~ **sensor** *n* SPACE capteur d'attitude *m*

atto- *pref* METR atto-

attract *vi* PHYS *reciprocally* s'attirer

attraction *n* PHYS, SPACE attraction *f*, gravitation *f*

attractive[1] *adj* PHYS attractif

attractive:[2] ~ **effect** *n* TRANSP effet des forces attractives

m; ~ **force** *n* ELEC *electromagnetism*, PHYS force d'attraction *f*

attribute *n* COMP, DP, TELECOM attribut *m*

attrition *n* C&G, COAL TECH attrition *f*, CONST attrition *f*, usure par frottement *f*, MECH ENG usure *f*, PAPER TECH usure par frottement *f*, PRINT attrition *f*, usure par frottement *f*; ~ **mill** *n* PAPER TECH affleureuse *f*; ~ **test** *n* MECH ENG essai d'abrasion *m*

Atwater: ~ **factor** *n* FOOD TECH *nutrition* facteur Atwater *m*; ~ **table** *n* FOOD TECH *nutrition* table Atwater *f*

Atwood's: ~ **machine** *n* PHYS machine d'Atwood *f*

A-type: ~ **color film** *n* (AmE), ~ **colour film** *n* (BrE) CINEMAT pellicule couleur pour lumière artificielle *f*; ~ **facsimile** *n* PRINT fac-similé à éléments d'intensité constante *m*

Au *(gold)* CHEM Au *(or)*

AU *abbr* ASTRON *(astronomical unit, astronomic unit)* UA *(unité astronomique)*, COMP *(arithmetic unit)* unité arithmétique *f*, TELECOM *(administrative unit)* UAD *(unité administrative)*, TELECOM *(access unit)* unité d'accès *f*

audibility: ~ **meter** *n* RECORDING audimètre *m*

audible: ~ **alarm** *n* CONTROL signal avertisseur acoustique *m*, TELECOM alarme sonore *f*; ~ **emergency evacuation signal** *n* SAFETY signal sonore d'évacuation d'urgence *m*; ~ **frequency range** *n* ACOUSTICS domaine des fréquences audibles *m*; ~ **machmeter** *n* AERONAUT machmètre audible *m*; ~ **runout indicator** *n* CINEMAT indicateur sonore de fin de bobine *m*; ~ **signal** *n* CONTROL signal acoustique *m*, RECORDING signal sonore *m*, TELECOM signal acoustique *m*, signal sonore *m*; ~ **spectrum** *n* RECORDING spectre audible *m*; ~ **warning** *n* CONTROL signal avertisseur acoustique *m*; ~ **warning system** *n* PACKAGING système d'avertissement sonore *m*

audience: ~ **rating** *n* TV indice d'écoute *m*

audio[1] *adj* COMP, DP, ELECTRON audio, RECORDING acoustique *f*, audio, sonore

audio:[2] ~ **amplifier** *n* ELECTRON amplificateur audiofréquence *m*, RECORDING amplificateur basse fréquence *m*; ~ **attenuator** *n* ELECTRON atténuateur basse fréquence *m*; ~ **band** *n* RECORDING gamme de fréquences acoustiques *f*; ~ **bearer service** *n* TELECOM service de circuit commuté audio *m*, service support CCBNT type audio *m*, service support audiofréquence *m*; ~ **CD player** *n* OPT lecteur audionumérique *m*, lecteur de disque audionumérique *m*; ~ **channel** *n* RECORDING canal audio *m*, canal son *m*, voie audio *f*, voie son *f*, TV canal son *m*; ~ **check** *n* CONTROL contrôle d'écoute *m*; ~ **compact disc** *n* (BrE) OPT disque audionumérique *m*, disque compact audio *m*, disque compact audionumérique *m*; ~ **compact disc player** *n* (BrE) OPT lecteur audionumérique *m*, lecteur de disque audionumérique *m*; ~ **compact disk** *n* (AmE) *see audio compact disc*; ~ **compact disk player** *n* (AmE) *see audio compact disc player*; ~ **console** *n* RECORDING console son *f*; ~ **control engineer** *n* RECORDING ingénieur du son *m*; ~ **control room** *n* RECORDING régie son *f*; ~ **cue** *n* RECORDING repère son *m*; ~ **drop-out** *n* RECORDING drop audio *m*; ~ **feedback** *n* RECORDING effet Larsen *m*; ~ **feedback circuit** *n* TV retour d'écoute *m*; ~ **filter** *n* ELECTRON filtre audiofréquence *m*; ~ **frequency** *n* *(AF)* ACOUSTICS, ELECTRON, RECORDING, TELECOM, WAVE PHYS audiofréquence *f*, fréquence audible *f*; ~ **frequency amplifier** *n* ELECTRON amplificateur audiofréquence *m*, RECORDING amplificateur de fréquences audibles *m*; ~ **frequency band** *n* RECORDING bande de fréquences audibles *f*; ~ **frequency oscillator** *n* ELECTRON oscillateur audiofréquence *m*; ~ **frequency range** *n* RAD PHYS gamme des fréquences audibles *f*; ~ **frequency signal** *n* RECORDING signal de fréquences audibles *m*; ~ **frequency signal generator** *n* ELECTRON générateur audiofréquence *m*, générateur de signaux à audiofréquence *m*; ~ **head** *n* RECORDING tête sonore *f*; ~ **indicate active** *n* (*AIA*) TELECOM indication audio active *f*; ~ **indicate muted** *n* (*AIM*) TELECOM indication audio muette *f*; ~ **input** *n* RECORDING entrée son *f*; ~ **level meter** *n* RECORDING appareil de mesure du niveau des audiofréquences *m*; ~ **loop** *n* TELECOM boucle audio *f*; ~ **modulation** *n* ELECTRON modulation basse fréquence *f*; ~ **oscillator** *n* RAD PHYS générateur à basse fréquence *m*; ~ **playback** *n* TV reproduction de son *f*; ~ **power amplifier** *n* ELECTRON amplificateur de puissance basse fréquence *m*; ~ **record** *n* TV enregistrement de son *m*; ~ **response** *n* CONTROL réponse acoustique *f*, ELECTRON réponse vocale *f*; ~ **response unit** *n* COMP répondeur vocal *m*, DP répondeur vocal *m*, unité à réponse vocale *f*; ~ **signal** *n* CONTROL signal audio *m*, ELECTRON signal audio *m*, signal audiofréquence *m*; ~ **signal input level** *n* RECORDING niveau d'entrée du signal audiofréquence *m*; ~ **splitter** *n* TELECOM diviseur audiofréquence *m*; ~ **tape machine** *n* TV magnétophone *m*; ~ **track** *n* CINEMAT piste sonore *f*, TV piste audio *f*, piste sonore *f*; ~ **track 1** *n* TV piste sonore 1 *f*, piste sonore de programme 1 *f*

audiogram *n* ACOUSTICS audiogramme *m*

audiometer *n* ACOUSTICS, WAVE PHYS audiomètre *m*

audiometric: ~ **booth** *n* RECORDING cabine audiométrique *f*; ~ **room** *n* ACOUSTICS cabine audiométrique *f*

audiometry *n* ACOUSTICS audiométrie *f*, RECORDING audiométrie *f*, phonométrie *f*

audio-videotex *n* TELECOM audiovidéographie *f*

audit *n* QUALITY audit *m*, enquête *f*, TELECOM audit *m*; ~ **of inspection procedure** *n* METR vérification d'une procédure de contrôle *f*; ~ **trail** *n* COMP, DP piste de contrôle *f*, PROD ENG journal de vérification *m*, TELECOM enregistrement d'audit *m*

auditee *n* QUALITY audité *m*

auditorium *n* RECORDING auditorium *m*

auditory: ~ **perspective** *n* RECORDING perspective auditive *f*; ~ **sensation area** *n* ACOUSTICS aire d'audition *f*; ~ **signals** *n pl* SAFETY signaux auditifs *m pl*

augelite *n* MINERAL augélite *f*

augen: ~ **structure** *n* GEOL structure lenticulaire oeillée *f*

augend *n* COMP cumulande *m*

auger *n* COAL TECH tarière *f*, CONST *for wood* laceret *m*, tarière *f*, MINING *boring* tarière *f*; ~ **bit** *n* MECH ENG *drilling device* tarière *f*; ~ **gimlet** *n* CONST foret *m*, perçoir *m*, queue-de-cochon *f*, vrille *f*

Auger: ~ **effect** *n* PHYS, RAD PHYS effet Auger *m*; ~ **electron** *n* PHYS, RAD PHYS électron Auger *m*; ~ **electron spectroscopy** *n* CHEM, PHYS spectroscopie électronique Auger *f*; ~ **yield** *n* PHYS rendement Auger *m*

augite *n* MINERAL augite *f*

augmented: ~ **interval** *n* ACOUSTICS intervalle augmenté *m*

aulacogen *n* GEOL aulacogène *m*

aural: ~ **flutter** *n* ACOUSTICS papillotement auditif *m*; ~ **harmonic** *n* ACOUSTICS harmonique subjectif *m*; ~ **null loop** *n* TRANSP antenne radiogoniométrique *f*

auralite *n* MINERAL auralite *f*

aurichalcite *n* MINERAL aurichalcite *f*

auriferous[1] *adj* MINERAL, MINING aurifère

auriferous:[2] ~ **pyrites** *n* MINERAL pyrite aurifère *f*

Auriga *n* ASTRON *constellation* Cocher *m*

aurocyanide *n* CHEM aurocyanure *m*

aurora *n* ASTRON, GEOPHYS, SPACE aurore *f* ~ **australis** *n* ASTRON aurore australe *f*, GEOPHYS aurore australis *f*, METEO, NAUT aurore australe *f*; ~ **borealis** *n* ASTRON, GEOPHYS, METEO, NAUT aurore boréale *f*; ~ **polaris** *n* NAUT aurore polaire *f*

auroral: ~ **belt** *n* GEOPHYS zone des aurores polaires *f*; ~ **light** *n* ASTRON lumière à l'aurore *f*; ~ **zone** *n* SPACE zone aurorale *f*; ~ **zone ionized layers** *n pl* ASTRON couches ionisées de la zone aurorale *f pl*

aurous *adj* CHEM aureux

austenitic[1] *adj* PROP MAT austénitique

austenitic:[2] ~ **stainless steel** *n* MECH ENG acier inoxydable austénitique *m*; ~ **steel** *n* MECH acier austénitique *m*; ~ **structure** *n* SPRINGS structure austénitique *f*

authenticate *vt* QUALITY authentifier, certifier

authentication *n* COMP, DP, QUALITY, TELECOM authentification *f*; ~ **code** *n* DP code d'authentification *m*; ~ **exchange** *n* TELECOM échange d'authentification *m*; ~ **information** *n* TELECOM information d'authentification *f*; ~ **procedure** *n* TELECOM authentification *f*

authigenesis *n* GEOL *of sedimentary rocks* authigenèse *f*

authigenic *adj* PETR authigène

author's: ~ **alterations** *n pl* PRINT corrections d'auteur *f pl*

authority *n* PATENTS autorisation *f*, PROD ENG organisme officiel *m*; ~ **and format identifier** *n* (*AFI*) TELECOM identificateur d'autorité et de format *m*

authorization *n* COMP, DP autorisation *f*, PATENTS autorisation *f*, pouvoir *m*, PROD ENG confirmation *f*, TELECOM autorisation *f*; ~ **information** *n* TELECOM informations d'autorisation *f pl*; ~ **information qualifier** *n* TELECOM qualificatif des informations d'autorisation *m*

auto: ~ **stop and rewind** *n* PHOTO *of camera* arrêt et rebobinage automatique *m*; ~ **winding** *n* PHOTO *of camera* avance automatique *f*

autocatalysis *n* CHEM *process* autocatalyse *f*

autocatalytic: ~ **effect** *n* METALL autocatalyse *f*, réaction en chaîne *f*

autochart *n* COMP générateur de diagramme *m*

autochthon *n* GEOL autochtone *m*

autochtonal *adj* PETR autochtone

autochtonous[1] *adj* PETR autochtone, POLLUTION autochtonal, autochtone

autochtonous:[2] ~ **matter** *n* POLLUTION matière autochtone *f*

autoclastic *adj* GEOL bréchique

autoclave *n* C&G, CHEM, COAL TECH, FOOD TECH *food-processing machinery*, LAB EQUIP *heat, pressure* autoclave *m*

autocollimator *n* INSTRUMENT lunette à autocollimation *f*, METR *for angle measurement* autocollimateur *m*

autocorrelation *n* ELECTRON, TELECOM autocorrélation *f*; ~ **function** *n* PETR fonction d'autocorrélation *f*

autocue *n* TV prompteur *m*, télésouffleur *m*

autodefrost *n* REFRIG dégivrage automatique *m*

autodyne *n* ELECTRON montage autodyne *m*

auto-editing *n* TV montage automatique *m*

auto-equalization *n* ELECTRON, TV égalisation automatique *f*

autofeathering n AERONAUT *of propeller* mise en drapeau automatique f

autofocus n CINEMAT, PHOTO *of camera* mise au point automatique f; **~ window** n PHOTO *of camera* fenêtre de mise au point automatique f

autogenous[1] adj COAL TECH, MECH ENG *welding* autogène

autogenous:[2] **~ mill** n COAL TECH autobroyeur m; **~ milling** n COAL TECH autobroyage m

autogiro n *see autogyro*

autographic: **~ ink** n COLOURS encre hectographique f, encre à autocopier f

autogyro n AERONAUT, TRANSP autogyre m

auto-ignition n AERONAUT auto-allumage m, VEHICLES *engine* allumage spontané m, auto-allumage m

auto-ionization n PHYS auto-ionisation f

auto-iris n CINEMAT diaphragme automatique m

autoland n TRANSP système d'atterrissage automatique m

autoload n COMP chargement automatique m

autolysis n FOOD TECH *of cell* autolyse f

automanual: **~ switchboard** n TELECOM pupitre automatique m, pupitre de commande automatique m

automate vt COMP, CONST automatiser, CONTROL automatiser, rendre automatique, DP automatiser

automated[1] adj PROD ENG automatisé

automated:[2] **~ personal rapid transit** n TRANSP transport en commun individualisé m

automatic[1] adj COMP, DP, MECH automatique

automatic:[2]

~ a **~ ADC** n TELECOM indication automatique verbale des éléments de taxation f; **~ adjustment to light intensity** n SAFETY réglage automatique en fonction de l'intensité de la lumière m; **~ advance** n CONTROL avance automatique f, dispositif d'avance automatique m; **~ advance device** n CONTROL dispositif d'avance automatique m; **~ alarm** n CONTROL avertisseur automatique m; **~ alternative routing** n CONTROL changement de voie automatique m; **~ amplitude control** n CONTROL commande automatique de volume f; **~ application of the brakes** n CONTROL application automatique des freins f; **~ approach control** n AERONAUT contrôle automatique d'approche m; **~ arc welding** n MECH ENG soudage à arc automatique m; **~ assembly machine** n MECH ENG machine pour assemblage automatique f; **~ assembly work** n PACKAGING assemblage automatique m; **~ attempt** n TELECOM tentative automatique f;

~ b **~ blade-folding system** n AERONAUT *of helicopter* dispositif de repliage automatique de pales m; **~ blowout preventer** n PETR TECH bloc obturateur automatique m; **~ brake** n VEHICLES frein automatique m; **~ braking system** n CONTROL système de freinage automatique m; **~ brightness control** n CONTROL, TV contrôle automatique de luminance m; **~ burette** n LAB EQUIP *analysis* burette automatique f;

~ c **~ call distributor** n *(ACD)* TELECOM distributeur automatique d'appels m; **~ calling unit** n *(ACU)* COMP, DP unité d'appel automatique f, équipement d'appel automatique m *(EAA)*; **~ call transfer** n TELECOM renvoi automatique m (Can), transfert automatique m; **~ capper** n PACKAGING capsulatrice automatique f; **~ car identification** n (AmE) *(ACI, automatic wagon identification)* TRANSP identification automatique des wagons f; **~ changeover** n ELEC *switch* commutation automatique f, TELECOM passage

automatique m; **~ check** n COMP, DP vérification automatique f; **~ choke** n AUTO starter automatique m; **~ chrominance control** n *(ACC)* TV contrôle automatique de chrominance m *(CAC)*; **~ chucking lathe** n MECH ENG tour automatique pour le travail en mandrin m; **~ circuit recloser** n ELEC *switch* réenclencheur automatique m; **~ clutch** n VEHICLES embrayage automatique m; **~ collation** n PACKAGING assemblage automatique m; **~ control** n CONST commande automatique f, CONTROL asservissement m, autoguidage m, commande automatique f, contrôle automatique m, direction automatique f, régulation automatique f, ELEC automatisme m, commande automatique f, réglage automatique m, MECH ENG, PACKAGING commande automatique f; **~ control assembly** n NUCLEAR ensemble de réglage automatique m; **~ control device** n CONTROL dispositif de commande automatique m; **~ control equipment** n PETR TECH appareil de réglage automatique m; **~ control functions** n pl CONTROL fonctions automatiques de contrôle f pl; **~ control of headway** n TRANSP commande automatique de l'espacement entre les véhicules f; **~ controller** n CONTROL dispositif d'asservissement m; **~ control switch** n CONTROL, ELEC *relay* relais ampèremétrique m; **~ control system** n CONTROL système d'asservissement m, système de réglage et de commande m, PROD ENG système d'automatisme m; **~ copying lathe** n MECH ENG tour automatique à copier m; **~ coupling** n RAIL *vehicles*, TRANSP attelage automatique m; **~ credit card service** n TELECOM service automatique de cartes de crédit m; **~ crossfeed range** n PROD ENG plage d'avance transversale automatique f; **~ current controller** n ELEC *relay* relais ampèremétrique m; **~ cutout switch** n ELEC, SAFETY interrupteur automatique m; **~ cutter** n C&G chariot de découpe m;

~ d **~ data conversion** n COMP, DP conversion automatique de données f; **~ data processing** n COMP, DP *(ADP)* traitement automatique de données m; **~ decurling** n PACKAGING dévrillement automatique m; **~ device** n TELECOM appareil automatique m; **~ dialing** n (AmE), **~ dialling** n (BrE) TELECOM sélection automatique f; **~ direction** n CONTROL direction automatique f; **~ direction finder** n AERONAUT radiocompas m, radiogoniomètre automatique m, TRANSP radiocompas automatique m; **~ direction finding** n *(ADF)* AERONAUT, TELECOM radiogoniométrie automatique f; **~ disconnection** n CONTROL déclenchement automatique m, désembrayage automatique m; **~ down feed** n MECH ENG *machine tools* avance automatique en plongée f;

~ e **~ editing** n TV montage automatique m; **~ enlarger** n PHOTO agrandisseur à mise au point automatique m; **~ error correction** n AERONAUT, TELECOM correction automatique des erreurs f; **~ expansion gear** n MECH ENG détente automatique f; **~ exposure** n PHOTO réglage automatique de la durée de pose m;

~ f **~ feed** n MECH ENG *of cutting tool* alimentation automatique f, amenage automatique m, avance automatique f, PETR TECH *of bit* avance automatique f, avancement automatique m, *of material* alimentation forcée f; **~ feeder** n PROD ENG charge automatique f; **~ feeding** n C&G alimentation automatique f; **~ feeding system** n PACKAGING système d'alimentation automatique m; **~ film-threading** n CINEMAT chargement automatique de pellicule m; **~ fire alarm** n CONST commande automatique d'incendie *f*, contrôleur d'incendie *m*, SAFETY alarme automatique d'incendie *f*, contrôleur d'incendie *m*; ~ **fire detection system** *n* SAFETY système automatique de détection d'incendie *m*; ~ **fire-extinguishing system** *n* CONTROL système automatique d'extinction des incendies *m*; ~ **fire-fighting system** *n* SAFETY *using atomized water* installation fixe d'extinction automatique *f*; ~ **fire sprinkler** *n* NAUT extincteur automatique d'incendie *m*; ~ **firing unit** *n* MILIT unité de tir automatique *f*; ~ **flame guard** *n* CONTROL contrôleur de flammes *m*; ~ **flexible bag-filling machine** *n* PACKAGING machine automatique pour remplir les sacs flexibles *f*; ~ **flight control system** *n* AERONAUT système de contrôle de vol automatique *m*; ~ **focusing** *n* PHOTO mise au point automatique *f*; ~ **forming** *n* C&G formage automatique *m*; ~ **frequency control** *n* *(AFC)* CONTROL contrôle automatique de fréquence *m* *(CAF)*, ELEC réglage automatique de la fréquence *m*, ELECTRON, PHYS, PROD ENG commande automatique de fréquence *f* *(CAF)*, RECORDING contrôle automatique de fréquence *m* *(CAF)*, TELECOM commande automatique de fréquence *f* *(CAF)*, TV contrôle automatique de fréquence *m* *(CAF)*;

~ g ~ **gain control** *n* *(AGC)* CONTROL contrôle automatique de gain *m* *(CAG)*, ELECTRON antifading *m*, commande automatique de gain *f*, GEOPHYS contrôle automatique de gain *m* *(CAG)*, RECORDING réglage automatique du gain *m*, TELECOM commande automatique de gain *f* *(CAG)*; ~ **gain monitoring** *n* CONTROL contrôle automatique de gain *m*; ~ **gear lever** *n* (BrE) *(cf automatic gearshift)* VEHICLES rétrogradation automatique *f*; ~ **gearshift** *n* (AmE) *(cf automatic gear lever)* VEHICLES rétrogradation automatique *f*; ~ **governor** *n* FUELLESS régulateur automatique *m*; ~ **guidance system** *n* ELEC ENG asservissement *m*; ~ **gun** *n* MILIT canon automatique *m*, canon automoteur *m*;

~ h ~ **highway** *n* (AmE) *(cf automatic motorway)* TRANSP autoroute automatique *f*;

~ i ~ **ignition** *n* GAS TECH allumage automatique *m*; ~ **infringement recorder** *n* TRANSP enregistreur automatique d'infraction *m*; ~ **intercept system** *n* TELECOM système d'interception automatique *m*; ~ **isolating valve** *n* PETR TECH vanne de sectionnement automatique *f*;

~ j ~ **jump** *n* PRINT coupure automatique *f*;

~ l ~ **laser shutdown** *n* *(ALS)* TELECOM coupure automatique du laser *f*; ~ **lathe** *n* MECH tour automatique *m*; ~ **level control** *n* AUTO correcteur d'assiette *m*; ~ **level regulator** *n* CONTROL régulateur automatique de niveau *m*; ~ **light signals** *n pl* RAIL *at level crossing* SAL, signalisation automatique lumineuse *f*; ~ **loading system** *n* PHOTO système de chargement automatique *m*; ~ **load transfer** *n* ELEC *supply* enclenchement automatique de réserve *m*; ~ **location registration of ships** *n* TELECOM relèvement et enregistrement automatiques de la position des navires *m*;

~ m ~ **message switching center** *n* (AmE), ~ **message switching centre** *n* (BrE) TELECOM centre automatique de commutation de messages *m*; ~ **microscope camera** *n* INSTRUMENT appareil de microscope automatique *m*; ~ **monitoring** *n* CONTROL contrôle automatique *m*; ~ **motorway** *n* (BrE) *(cf automatic highway)* TRANSP autoroute automatique *f*; ~ **movements being put into operation at the same time** *n pl* SAFETY embrayage simultané de mouvements automatiques *m*;

~ n ~ **numbering equipment** *n* TELECOM émetteur à numérotation automatique *m*;

~ o ~ **oil burner** *n* HEAT ENG brûleur automatique à mazout à jet sous pression *m*; ~ **operation** *n* CONST marche automatique *f*;

~ p ~ **page numbering** *n* COMP foliotage automatique *m*; ~ **pagination** *n* PRINT foliotage automatique *m*, pagination automatique *f*; ~ **peak limiter** *n* TV limiteur automatique de crête *m*, limiteur automatique de crête du blanc *m*; ~ **phase control** *n* ELECTRON contrôle automatique de phase *m*, ELECTRON commande automatique de phase *f*, TV contrôle automatique de phase *m*; ~ **pilot** *n* AERONAUT, NAUT, SPACE, TRANSP pilote automatique *m*; ~ **pirn change** *n* TEXTILES changement automatique de canette *m*; ~ **pressing** *n* C&G pressage automatique *m*; ~ **printer** *n* PHOTO tireuse automatique *f*; ~ **programming tool** *n* *(APT)* COMP programme de commande automatique *m*; ~ **protection switching** *n* *(APS)* TELECOM commutation automatique sur liaison de réserve *f*, commutation de protection automatique *f*; ~ **punch** *n* DP *for tape* perforateur automatique *m*;

~ r ~ **radar plotting aid** *n* *(ARPA)* NAUT aide de pointage radar automatique *f*; ~ **rammer** *n* MILIT *artillery* refouloir automatique *m*; ~ **ramp down** *n* PROD ENG système d'arrêt progressif automatique *m*; ~ **recall** *n* TELECOM rappel automatique *m*; ~ **recording level control** *n* RECORDING contrôle automatique du niveau d'enregistrement *m*; ~ **regulation** *n* MECH ENG régulation automatique *f*; ~ **regulator** *n* CONTROL régulateur automatique *m*, MECH ENG autorégulateur *m*, régulateur automatique *m*; ~ **release** *n* MECH ENG desserrage automatique *m*; ~ **repair** *n* TEXTILES réparation automatique *f*; ~ **report generation** *n* PROD ENG génération automatique de messages *f*; ~ **reset** *n* ELEC *control* retour automatique *m*; ~ **rewinder** *n* PHOTO rembobineuse automatique *f*; ~ **roaming** *n* TELECOM repérage automatique des déplacements *m*; ~ **running and braking control** *n* TRANSP commande automatique de marche et de freinage *f*;

~ s ~ **sampler** *n* COAL TECH échantillonneur automatique *m*; ~ **sampling** *n* PROD ENG, QUALITY échantillonnage automatique *m*; ~ **screen printing** *n* TEXTILES impression au cadre automatique *f*; ~ **screw machine** *n* MECH tour à décolleter automatique *m*; ~ **selectivity control** *n* CONTROL contrôle automatique de sélectivité *m*; ~ **send-receive** *n* *(ASR)* COMP téléimprimeur émetteur-recepteur *m*, DP appareil émetteur-recepteur *m*, émetteur-récepteur automatique *m*; ~ **sensitivity control** *n* CONTROL contrôle automatique de sensitivité *m*; ~ **sequence control** *n* *(ASC)* CONTROL contrôle automatique à séquence *m*, vérification automatique *f*; ~ **sewage flow regulator** *n* HYDROL régulateur automatique de débit des eaux usées *m*; ~ **side and bottom loading machine** *n* PACKAGING machine automatique pour chargement latéral et par le fond *f*; ~ **slide changer** *n* PHOTO passe-vues automatique *m*; ~ **speed checker** *n* MECH ENG limiteur de vitesse automatique *m*; ~ **speed control** *n* TRANSP régulation automatique de la vitesse *f*; ~ **speed control device** *n* AUTO régulateur automatique de vitesse *m*; ~ **spur gear cutting machine** *n* MECH ENG machine automatique à tailler les engrenages à denture droite *f*; ~ **stabilization equipment** *n* *(ASE)*

TRANSP stabilisateur automatique *m*, système de stabilisation artificielle *m*; ~ **starting unit** *n* AERONAUT boîtier de démarrage *m*; ~ **stop** *n* RECORDING arrêt automatique *m*; ~ **switch** *n* ELEC commutateur automatique *m*; ~ **switchboard** *n* TELECOM pupitre automatique *m*, pupitre de commande automatique *m*; ~ **switching** *n* ELEC ENG commutation automatique *f*, TRANSP aiguillage automatique *m*; ~ **system** *n* SPACE *spacecraft* automatisme *m*;

~ **t** ~ **telephone exchange** *n* TELECOM central téléphonique automatique *m*; ~ **telephone switching** *n* ELEC ENG commutation téléphonique automatique *f*; ~ **teller** *n* CONTROL guichet libre-service *m*; ~ **teller machine** *n* *(ATM)* COMP guichet automatique de banque *m*; ~ **test equipment** *n* *(ATE)* COMP matériel de test automatique *m*; ~ **timer** *n* PHOTO déclencheur automatique *m*; ~ **titration** *n* LAB EQUIP *analysis* titration automatique *f*; ~ **tracking** *n* ASTRON *of telescope* , NAUT *radar* poursuite automatique *f*; ~ **traffic light signals** *n pl* RAIL *at level crossing* SAR, signalisation automatique routière *f*; ~ **train control** *n* RAIL contrôle automatique des trains *m*, TRANSP commande automatique des trains *f*; ~ **train monitoring** *n* RAIL contrôle automatique de la marche *m*; ~ **train operation** *n* *(ATO)* TRANSP commande automatique des trains *f*; ~ **train operation by mini computer** *n* *(ATOMIC)* RAIL conduite automatique des trains par mini-ordinateur *f*; ~ **train protection** *n* *(ATP)* RAIL protection automatique de trains *f* *(PAT)*; ~ **transmission** *n* AUTO boîte automatique *f*, transmission automatique *f*, MECH, TELECOM transmission automatique *f*, VEHICLES boîte automatique *f*, transmission automatique *f*; ~ **transportation system** *n* TRANSP système de transport automatique *m*; ~ **tripping** *n* CONTROL déclenchement automatique *m*, désembrayage automatique *m*; ~ **trunk working** *n* TELECOM *telephone* exploitation interurbaine automatique *f*;

~ **u** ~ **uncoupling of rolling stock** *n* TRANSP dételage automatique des wagons *m*;

~ **v** ~ **vacuum brake** *n* MECH ENG frein à vide automatique *m*; ~ **valve** *n* PETR TECH, REFRIG vanne automatique *f*; ~ **vehicle identification** *n* *(AVI)* TRANSP identification automatique des véhicules *f*; ~ **vehicle location** *n* *(AVL)* TELECOM localisation automatique des véhicules *f*; ~ **verification** *n* QUALITY *of quantitative data* analyse routinière *f*; ~ **voltage control** *n* ELEC réglage automatique de la tension *m*; ~ **volume compression** *n* RECORDING compression automatique de volume *f*; ~ **volume control** *n* CONTROL *(AVC)* commande automatique de volume *f* *(CAV)*, ELEC ENG *radio* antifading *m*, ELEC ENG *(AVC) radio*, OPT *(AVC)*, PHYS *(AVC)* commande automatique de volume *f* *(CAV)*;

~ **w** ~ **wagon identification** *n* (BrE) *(cf automatic car identification)* TRANSP identification automatique des wagons *f*; ~ **weather station** *n* METEO station météorologique automatique *f*; ~ **white balance** *n* TV balance automatique du blanc *m*

automatically-closing *adj* CONTROL autoserrant, à fermeture automatique

automatically-controlled[1] *adj* CONTROL autorégulateur, autorégulé

automatically-controlled:[2] ~ **crossing signal** *n* CONTROL signalisateur à commande automatique de traversée *m*; ~ **signaling device** *n* (AmE), ~ **signalling device** *n* (BrE) CONTROL signalisateur à commande automat-

ique *m*

automatic-tripping: ~ **equipment** *n* CONTROL déclencheur automatique *m*

automation *n* COMP automatisation *f*, CONST automation *f*, automatisation *f*, DP, MECH ENG, NAUT, PROD ENG, SPACE automatisation *f*

automatize *vt* CONST automatiser

automaton *n* COMP, DP automate *m*

autometamorphism *n* FUELLESS autométamorphisme *m*

automobile[1] *adj* TRANSP automobile

automobile[2] *n* AUTO, TRANSP, VEHICLES automobile *f*, voiture *f*

automodulation *n* TELECOM automodulation *f*

automorphic *adj* GEOL *texture* automorphe, idiomorphe, PETR automorphe

automorphous *adj* PETR automorphe

automotive[1] *adj* TRANSP automobile

automotive:[2] ~ **industry** *n* PROD ENG industrie de l'automobile *f*

autonomous[1] *adj* SPACE *spacecraft* autonome

autonomous:[2] ~ **submersible** *n* OCEANOG robot sous-marin *m*

autonomy *n* SPACE *of spacecraft* autonomie *f*

auto-oxidation *n* CHEM auto-oxydation *f*

autopaster *n* PRINT dérouleur à collage automatique *m*

autopilot *n* AERONAUT bloc de pilotage *m*, pilote automatique *m*, NAUT pilote automatique *m*, SPACE autoguidage *m*, pilote automatique *m*, TRANSP pilote automatique *m*; ~ **control unit** *n* AERONAUT boîte de commande de pilote automatique *f*; ~ **disengagement** *n* AERONAUT débrayage de pilote automatique *m*; ~ **disengage push button** *n* AERONAUT poussoir de débrayage rapide *m*; ~ **engagement** *n* AERONAUT embrayage de pilote automatique *m*; ~ **pitch sensitivity system** *n* AERONAUT double sensibilité *f*; ~ **turn knob** *n* AERONAUT bouton de virage *m*

autopositioning: ~ **unit** *n* AERONAUT système d'autopositionnement *m*

autoradiography *n* PHYS, RAD PHYS autoradiographie *f*

autoradiolysis *n* RAD PHYS autoradiolyse *f*

autoreclosing: ~ **system** *n* PRINT système à réenclenchement automatique *m*

autoregression *n* COMP autorégression *f*

autoregressive: ~ **moving average** *n* *(ARMA)* COMP moyenne mobile autorégressive *f*

autoregulating *adj* CONTROL autorégulé

autoreverse *n* CINEMAT marche en continu *f*

autorotation: ~ **flight** *n* AERONAUT vol en autorotation *m*; ~ **transition time** *n* AERONAUT délai de passage en autorotation *m*

autorotative: ~ **flight** *n* AERONAUT *of helicopter* fonctionnement en autogyre *m*

autosampler *n* LAB EQUIP *analysis* échantillonneur automatique *m*

autoservo: ~ **mode** *n* TV mode d'asservissement automatique *m*

autosynchronization *n* TELECOM autosynchronisation *f*

autothermic: ~ **piston** *n* AUTO piston autothermique *m*

autothrottle *n* AERONAUT automanette *f*

autotracking *n* SPACE poursuite automatique *f*, TV centrage automatique des têtes *m*

autotransformer *n* ELEC ENG, PHYS autotransformateur *m*; ~ **starter** *n* ELEC *of motor* autotransformateur de démarrage *m*

autotroph *n* FOOD TECH autotrophe *m*

autoxidation *n* FOOD TECH autoxydation *f*

autunite *n* MINERAL autunite *f*

AUW *abbr (all-up weight)* TRANSP poids total en charge *m*

auxiliary[1] *adj* MECH ENG auxiliaire

auxiliary:[2] **~ boiler** *n* HEATING chaudière auxiliaire *f*; **~ boiler feeder** *n* HYDR EQUIP machine d'alimentation *f*, petit cheval alimentaire *m*; **~ close-up lens** *n* CINEMAT bonnette *f*; **~ contact** *n* ELEC ENG contact auxiliaire *m*; **~ contact accessory** *n* ELEC, PROD ENG contact auxiliaire en accessoire *m*; **~ contact deck** *n* PROD ENG bloc additif *m*; **~ cut** *n* C&G coupe de desserrage *f*; **~ electrode** *n* C&G électrode d'appoint *f*; **~ engine** *n* MECH ENG moteur auxiliaire *m*, NAUT machine auxiliaire *f*; **~ engine sailing ship** *n* NAUT navire mixte *m*; **~ jet** *n* VEHICLES *of carburettor* gicleur auxiliaire *m*; **~ machinery** *n* NAUT apparaux auxiliaires *m pl*; **~ memory** *n* COMP mémoire auxiliaire *f*; **~ mirror** *n* PHOTO miroir auxiliaire *m*; **~ motor** *n* ELEC moteur auxiliaire *m*, MECH ENG machine auxiliaire *f*; **~ parachute** *n* MILIT parachute auxiliaire *m*; **~ power unit** *n* AERONAUT groupe auxiliaire de puissance *m*, générateur auxiliaire de bord *m*; **~ rotor** *n* AERONAUT *of helicopter* rotor auxiliaire *m*; **~ service position** *n* TELECOM position terminale *f*; **~ servocontrol** *n* MECH ENG servocommande auxiliaire *f*; **~ shoe** *n* PHOTO contacteur supplémentaire *m*; **~ spring** *n* SPRINGS ressort compensateur *m*; **~ storage** *n* (AmE) *(cf auxiliary store)* COMP mémoire auxiliaire *f*, mémoire de sauvegarde *f*; **~ store** *n* (BrE) *(cf auxiliary storage)* COMP mémoire auxiliaire *f*, mémoire de sauvegarde *f*; **~ switch** *n* ELEC interrupteur auxiliaire *m*, PROD ENG contact auxiliaire *m*, TELECOM commutateur auxiliaire *m*; **~ switching point** *n* TELECOM point de commutation auxiliaire *m*; **~ switching unit** *n* TELECOM commutateur auxiliaire *m*; **~ telescope** *n* ASTRON chercheur *m*; **~ track** *n* RAIL voie de secours *f*; **~ transformer** *n* ELEC transformateur auxiliaire *m*; **~ valve** *n* MECH ENG clapet de détente *m*, tiroir d'expansion *m*, tiroir de détente *m*; **~ vessel** *n* NAUT navire auxiliaire *m*, navire-annexe *m*

auxochrome *n* CHEM auxochrome *m*

availability *n* COMP, DP, TELECOM disponibilité *f*; **~ indicator** *n* CONTROL signal de disponibilité *m*

available[1] *adj* QUALITY disponible

available:[2] **~ heat** *n* THERMOD chaleur efficace *f*, chaleur utile *f*; **~ inventory** *n* PROD ENG stock disponible *m*; **~ light** *n* CINEMAT lumière ambiante *f*; **~ list** *n* COMP liste libre *f*; **~ power** *n* ELEC *supply*, FUELLESS, MECH ENG, RECORDING *of amplifier*, TELECOM puissance disponible *f*; **~ power gain** *n* RECORDING gain en puissance disponible *m*; **~ stock** *n* PROD ENG stock disponible *m*; **~ time** *n* COMP temps disponible *m*; **~ train path** *n* RAIL sillon de train *m*

avalanche *n* ELEC ENG, METEO avalanche *f*; **~ breakdown** *n* ELEC *of semiconductor diode*, ELECTRON claquage par avalanche *m*; **~ diode** *n* ELECTRON, PHYS diode à avalanche *f*; **~ gain** *n* ELECTRON gain d'avalanche *m*; **~ photodiode** *n* (APD) ELECTRON, OPT, TELECOM photodiode à avalanche *f*; **~ transit-time diode** *n* PHYS diode à avalanche à temps de transit *f*; **~ voltage** *n* ELEC tension d'avalanche *f*

avalent *adj* CHEM avalent

avalite *n* MINERAL avalite *f*

AVC *abbr (automatic volume control)* CONTROL, ELEC ENG, OPT, PHYS CAV *(commande automatique de volume)*

avenin *n* CHEM avénine *f*, avénéine *f*

avenine *n* CHEM avénine *f*, avénéine *f*

aventurine *n* C&G verre aventurine *m*; **~ feldspar** *n* MINERAL feldspath aventurine *m*; **~ quartz** *n* MINERAL quartz aventurine *f*

average[1] *adj* PHYS moyen

average[2] *n* MATH, PHYS moyenne *f*; **~ adjuster** *n* NAUT *insurance* répartiteur d'avarie *m*; **~ annual daily traffic** *n* (AADT) TRANSP débit journalier moyen d'une année *m*; **~ annual flow** *n* HYDROL débit moyen annuel *m*, module annuel *m*; **~ bits per sample** *n* TELECOM nombre moyen des bits par échantillon *m*; **~ castings** *n pl* PROD ENG pièces moyennes *f pl*; **~ characteristic flow** *n* HYDROL débit moyen caractéristique *m*; **~ circulation** *n* PRINT diffusion moyenne *f*; **~ cladding diameter** *n* OPT, TELECOM diamètre moyen de la gaine *m*; **~ consumption of water** *n* HYDROL consommation d'eau moyenne *f*; **~ core diameter** *n* OPT, TELECOM diamètre moyen du coeur *m*; **~ crossing rate** *n* TELECOM fréquence moyenne de passage à zéro *f*; **~ daily flow** *n* HYDROL débit journalier moyen *m*; **~ daily output** *n* FUELLESS, PROD ENG rendement journalier moyen *m*; **~ daily traffic** *n* (ADT) TRANSP débit journalier moyen *m*; **~ delay per vehicle** *n* TRANSP retard moyen par véhicule *m*; **~ density** *n* TRANSP densité moyenne *f*; **~ deviation** *n* ELEC écart moyen *m*, MATH écart moyen *m*, écart type *m*; **~ distribution diagram** *n* HYDROL diagramme moyen de distribution *m*; **~ journey time** *n* TRANSP temps de parcours moyen *m*; **~ life** *n* PHYS durée de vie moyenne *f*, vie moyenne *f*; **~ load** *n* ELEC charge moyenne *f*; **~ mean temperature** *n* REFRIG température moyenne *f*; **~ monthly flow** *n* HYDROL débit moyen mensuel *m*; **~ outgoing quality** *n* (AOQ) QUALITY qualité moyenne après contrôle *f* (QMAC); **~ outgoing quality limit** *n* (AOQL) QUALITY limite de qualité moyenne après contrôle *f* (LQMAC); **~ output** *n* THERMOD rendement moyen *m*; **~ overall travel speed** *n* TRANSP moyenne des vitesses de parcours *f*; **~ power** *n* TELECOM puissance moyenne *f*; **~ running speed** *n* PRINT vitesse moyenne de production *f*, TRANSP vitesse moyenne de marche *f*; **~ sound power per unit area** *n* ACOUSTICS puissance surfacique acoustique moyenne *f*; **~ speech power** *n* ACOUSTICS puissance vocale moyenne *f*; **~ speed including stoppages** *n* PROD ENG vitesse commerciale *f*; **~ spot speed** *n* TRANSP moyenne des vitesses instantanées *f*; **~ steady state pressure** *n* MECH ENG *in closed circuit* pression moyenne en régime permanent *f*; **~ stopped time** *n* TRANSP temps moyen d'attente *m*; **~ time interval** *n* TRANSP intervalle moyen entre véhicules *m*; **~ value** *n* ELEC, PHYS valeur moyenne *f*; **~ vehicle length** *n* TRANSP longueur moyenne des véhicules *f*; **~ wind speed** *n* FUELLESS vitesse moyenne du vent *f*; **~ workload** *n* TEXTILES charge de travail moyenne *f*; **~ yearly flow** *n pl* HYDROL débit de l'année moyenne *m pl*

average:[3] **~ in turbulent flow** *vi* FLUID PHYS faire des moyennes sur les écoulements turbulents

AVI *abbr (automatic vehicle identification)* TRANSP identification automatique des véhicules *f*

aviation: **~ fuel** *n* PETR TECH essence aviation *f*, TRANSP carburéacteur *m*; **~ turbine kerosene** *n* (ATK) PETR TECH carburéacteur *m*

avionics *n* AERONAUT avionique *f*, aéroélectronique *f*, SPACE électronique aérospatiale *f*, TRANSP électronique appliquée aux avions *f*, électronique aérospatiale *f*

AVL *abbr (automatic vehicle location)* TELECOM localisation automatique des véhicules *f*

avoiding: ~ **line** *n* RAIL raquette *f*

avoir: ~ **de la main** *vi* PRINT bulk

avoirdupois: ~ **weight** *n* METR poids avoirdupoids *m*

awarding: ~ **of costs** *n* PATENTS fixation des frais *f*

awaruite *n* MINERAL awaruite *f*

awash *adv* NAUT à fleur d'eau

awl *n* CONST alêne *f*, poinçon *m*

awning *n* NAUT *sun* taud *m*

AWT *abbr (acid well treatment)* PETR TECH acidification *f*

AWU *abbr (atomic weight unit)* NUCLEAR UPA *(unité de poids atomique)*

ax *n* (AmE) **axe** *n* (BrE) CONST hache *f* ~ **head** *n* CONST tête de hache *f*

axial[1] *adj* GEOM, PAPER TECH axial

axial:[2] ~ **actuator** *n* SPACE *of spacecraft* actionneur axial *m*; ~ **armature** *n* ELEC *of electrical machine* induit axial *m*; ~ **blower** *n* SAFETY soufflante axiale *f*; ~ **clearance** *n* MECH jeu axial *m*; ~ **compressor** *n* AERONAUT, MECH compresseur axial *m*; ~ **culmination** *n* GEOL culmination d'un pli *f*; ~ **cylindrical roller bearing** *n* MECH ENG roulement à rouleaux cylindriques axiaux *m*; ~ **deposition** *n* C&G dépôt axial *m*; ~ **depression** *n* GEOL dépression axiale *f*, ensellement *m*; ~ **displacement** *n* TV décalage axial des têtes *m*; ~ **efficiency** *n* ACOUSTICS efficacité axiale *f*; ~ **flow** *n* AERONAUT flux axial *m*, écoulement axial *m*, VEHICLES *of engine* flux axial *m*; **flow fan** *n* HEAT ENG ventilateur axial *m*; ~ **flow lift fan** *n* TRANSP ventilateur axial *m*; ~ **flow pump** *n* MECH ENG pompe à écoulement axial *f*, MINING pompe à flux axial *f*; ~ **flow turbine** *n* HYDR EQUIP turbine hélicoïdale *f*, turbine parallèle *f*; ~ **height** *n* SPRINGS hauteur axiale *f*; ~ **interference** *n* OPT interférométrie axiale *f*; ~ **interference microscopy** *n* OPT, TELECOM microscopie axiale interférentielle *f*; ~ **interferometry** *n* OPT interférométrie axiale *f*; ~ **line** *n* GEOM axe *m*; ~ **load fatigue testing** *n* MECH ENG essai de fatigue sous charge axiale *m*; ~ **loading** *n* METALL chargement axial *m*; ~ **magnification** *n* PHYS grandissement axial *m*; ~ **period** *n* SPACE période axiale *f*; ~ **piston pump** *n* MECH pompe à pistons axiaux *f*; ~ **plane** *n* GEOL *of fold* plan axial *m*; ~ **plane cleavage** *n* GEOL clivage ardoisier axial *m*; ~ **plane foliation** *n* GEOL schistosité de fracturation *f*; ~ **plasma deposition** *n (ALDP)* TELECOM déposition axiale *f*; ~ **propagation coefficient** *n* OPT, TELECOM exposant linéique de propagation longitudinale *m*; ~ **pump** *n* MECH ENG pompe hélicoïde *f*; ~ **radial bearing** *n* INSTRUMENT monture à déplacement *f*; ~ **radius** *n* OPT rayon axial *m*; ~ **ratio** *n* CRYSTALL rapport des axes *m*, SPACE taux d'ellipticité *m*; ~ **ray** *n* OPT, TELECOM rayon axial *m*; ~ **rift zone** *n* GEOL *mid-ocean or in continental rift valley* fossé médian *m*, zone axiale *f*; ~ **scanning** *n* OPT lecture par la tache centrale *f*; ~ **shield** *n* NUCLEAR écran axial *m*; ~ **slab interferometry** *n* TELECOM interférométrie axiale *f*; ~ **symmetry** *n* GEOM symétrie axiale *f*; ~ **thrust bearing** *n* MECH ENG butée à billes *f*; ~ **trace** *n* GEOL trace de l'axe *f*; ~ **velocity** *n* FUELLESS vitesse axiale *f*; ~ **velocity sensor** *n* SPACE *spacecraft* capteur de vitesse axiale *m*; ~ **ventilator** *n* SAFETY ventilateur axial *m*

axially:[1] ~ **symmetric** *adj* CRYSTALL axisymétrique

axially:[2] ~ **collapsing steering column** *n* TRANSP colonne de direction télescopique *f*

axinite *n* MINERAL axinite *f*

axiom *n* GEOM, MATH axiome *m*

axiomatic *adj* GEOM axiomatique

axis *n* CRYSTALL, GEOM axe *m*, MECH *of couple* axe *m*, *of wheel, of pulley* axe *m*, METEO *of depression* axe *m*, PAPER TECH ligne d'axe *f*, PHYS axe *m*; ~ **of an anticyclone** *n* METEO axe d'anticyclone *m*, axe de haute pression *m*; ~ **of commutation** *n* ELEC *of electrical machine* axe de commutation *m*; ~ **of declination** *n* ASTRON axe de déclinaison *m*; ~ **of inertia** *n* MECH axe d'inertie *m*; ~ **of oscillation** *n* PHYS axe d'oscillation *m*; ~ **of projection** *n* CINEMAT axe de projection *m*; ~ **of revolution** *n* MECH axe de révolution *m*; ~ **of rotation** *n* ASTRON, MECH axe de rotation *m*; ~ **of symmetry** *n* CRYSTALL, GEOM, MECH ENG axe de symétrie *m*

axle *n* CONST essieu *m*, PAPER TECH axe *m*, VEHICLES *transmission* essieu *m*; ~ **box** *n* (BrE) *(cf journal box)* RAIL *vehicles* boîte d'essieu *f*; ~ **bush** *n* VEHICLES *transmission* coussinet d'axe *m*, douille d'axe *f*; ~ **bushing** *n* VEHICLES *transmission* coussinet d'axe *m*; ~ **cap** *n* AUTO chapeau de moyeu *m*; ~ **casing** *n* VEHICLES *transmission* carter d'essieu *m*; ~ **crank** *n* MECH ENG coude d'essieu *m*, manivelle d'essieu *f*; ~ **fit** *n* MECH ENG calage d'essieu *m*; ~ **flange** *n* VEHICLES *of wheels* flasque de l'essieu *m*; ~ **guide** *n* RAIL *vehicles* bielle de changement de marche *f*; ~ **guide stay** *n* RAIL *vehicles* entretoise de plaque de garde *f*; ~ **housing** *n* VEHICLES carter d'essieu *m*; ~ **lathe** *n* MECH ENG tour à essieux *m*; ~ **load** *n* CONST charge par essieu *f*, poids d'essieu *m*; ~ **pulley** *n* CONST *hardware* poulie de renvoi à pont *f*, renvoi à pont *m*; ~ **ratio** *n* VEHICLES *rear axle assembly* rapport de pont *m*; ~ **seat** *n* MECH ENG portée de calage de l'essieu *f*; ~ **shaft** *n* VEHICLES *transmission* arbre de roue *m*

Az-El: ~ **mount** *n* ASTRON, SPACE monture Azimut-Elévation *f*, monture Azimut-Site *f*

azelaic *adj* CHEM azélaïque

azeotrope *n* CHEM mélange azéotrope *m*, REFRIG azéotrope *m*

azeotropic[1] *adj* CHEM azéotropique

azeotropic:[2] ~ **distillation** *n* FOOD TECH distillation azéotrope *f*; ~ **mixture** *n* FOOD TECH azéotrope *m*, REFRIG mélange azéotropique *m*; ~ **point** *n* REFRIG point azéotrope *m*, point d'azéotropie *m*

azeotropy *n* REFRIG azéotropie *f*

AZERTY: ~ **keyboard** *n* COMP, DP clavier AZERTY *m*

azide *n* CHEM azoture *m*

azimino[1] *adj* CHEM azimidé

azimino:[2] ~ **compound** *n* CHEM azimide *m*

azimuth *n* ASTRON, CONST *surveying*, NAUT *navigation*, PETR, PHYS, SPACE, TV azimut *m*; ~ **adjustment** *n* TV réglage d'azimut *m*; ~ **angle** *n* FUELLESS angle azimutal *m*; ~ **bearing** *n* OCEANOG gisement azimutal *m*; ~ **coarse motion clamp** *n* INSTRUMENT vis de blocage du réglage approximatif d'azimut *f*; ~ **compass** *n* NAUT compas azimutal *m*, compas de relèvement *m*; ~ **deviation** *n* RECORDING déviation en azimut *f*; ~ **distortion** *n* TV distorsion d'azimut *f*; ~ **gyro** *n* SPACE *of spacecraft* gyro d'azimut *m*; ~ **loss** *n* TV perte par déréglage d'azimut *f*; ~ **stabilization** *n* NAUT *radar* stabilisation en azimut *f*; ~ **thrust** *n* SPACE *of spacecraft* poussée axiale *f*

azimuthal: ~ **control** *n* AERONAUT commande cyclique *f*; ~ **quantum number** *n* PHYS nombre quantique du moment cinétique orbital *m*, nombre quantique orbital *m*, RAD PHYS nombre quantique azimutal *m*

azo: ~ **dye** *n* CHEM colorant azoïque *m*

azobenzene *n* CHEM azobenzène *m*
azobenzoic *adj* CHEM azobenzoïque
azoic: ~ dye *n* TEXTILES colorant azoïque *m*
azorite *n* MINERAL azorite *f*
azulene *n* CHEM azulène *m*

azulin *n* CHEM azuline *f*
azulmin *n* CHEM azulmine *f*
azurite *n* MINERAL azurite *f*

B

b *abbr (barn)* PART PHYS b *(barn)*

B *(boron)* CHEM B *(bore)*

B&W *abbr (black and white)* PRINT noir et blanc *m*

B/H: ~ **loop** *n* ELEC *magnetism* boucle d'hystérésis magnétique *f*

B3ZS *abbr (bipolar code with three-zero substitution)* TELECOM code bipolaire avec substitution de trois zéros *m*

Ba *(barium)* CHEM Ba *(baryum)*

BA: ~ **screw thread** *n (British Association screw thread)* MECH ENG filetage British Association *m*

Babbitt's: ~ **metal** *n* METALL métal Babbitt *m*

babbitted: ~ **cast-iron bearings** *n pl* MECH ENG coussinets en fonte garnis d'un alliage antifriction *m pl*, paliers régulés *m pl*

Babcock: ~ **plan** *n* TELECOM plan de Babcock *m*

Babinet: ~ **compensator** *n* PHYS compensateur Babinet *m*

Babinet's: ~ **principle** *n* PHYS théorème de Babinet *m*

babingtonite *n* MINERAL babingtonite *f*

baby *n* CINEMAT projecteur spot de 500 watts *m*, projecteur spot de 750 watts *m*; ~ **dryer** *n* PAPER TECH embarqueur *m*, sécheur embarqueur *m*; ~ **press** *n* PAPER TECH rouleau leveur sur forme ronde *m*; ~ **tripod** *n* CINEMAT petit trépied *m*

bacat: ~ **ship** *n (cf barge-aboard-catamaran ship)* TRANSP navire porteur de type catamaran *m*

bacca: ~ **box smoother** *n* MECH ENG lissoir à champignon *m*

bacillus *n* FOOD TECH bacille *m*

back:[1] *n* CONST *of arch* extrados *m*, MECH ENG dos *m*, MINING amont-pendage *m*, PACKAGING *of ticket*, PAPER TECH verso *m*, PHOTO *of camera* arrière *m*, corps d'arrière *m*; ~ **adjustment** *n* PHOTO *of bellows unit* noix de réglage arrière *f*; ~ **azimuth guidance** *n* AERONAUT *navigation* guidage en azimut arrière *m*; ~ **balance** *n* MECH ENG contrepoids arrière *m*; ~ **beam** *n* TEXTILES ensouple primaire *f*; ~ **boiler** *n* MECH ENG *for hot water* petite chaudière *f*; ~ **center** *n* (AmE), ~ **centre** *n* (BrE) MECH ENG *of lathe* contre-pointe d'un tour *f*, pointe de la poupée mobile *f*; ~ **contact** *n* ELEC *relay* contact de repos *m*; ~ **cover** *n* PHOTO *of camera* dos *m*; ~ **cover release** *n* PHOTO *of camera* dispositif de verrouillage du dos *m*; ~ **cylinder cover** *n* HYDR EQUIP arrière de cylindre *m*, MECH ENG *of horizontal stationary engine* fond de cylindre *m*; ~ **diffusion** *n* NUCLEAR rétrodiffusion *f*; ~ **diffusion loss** *n* NUCLEAR perte due à la diffusion inverse *f*; ~ **eddy** *n* HYDROL courant de retour *m*, courant rétrograde *m*; ~ **edge margin** *n* PRINT blanc de gorge *m*, marge centrale *f*; ~ **electromotive force** *n (bemf)* ELEC, ELEC ENG, PHYS force contre-électromotrice *f (fcém)*; ~ **emf** *n (bemf)* ELEC, ELEC ENG, PHYS force contre-électromotrice *f (fcém)*; ~ **finish** *n* COATINGS apprêt envers *m*; ~ **focus** *n* CINEMAT tirage arrière *m*; ~ **folding** *n* PRINT plissement en retour *m*; ~ **freight** *n* NAUT fret de retour *m*; ~ **gap** *n* ACOUSTICS entrefer arrière *m*, RECORDING contre-entrefer *m*, entrefer secondaire *m*, TV entrefer arrière *m*; ~ **gear** *n*

MECH ENG engrenage inverseur de mouvement *m*, marche arrière *f*; ~ **gutter** *n* PRINT blanc de couture *m*; ~ **iron** *n* CONST *of plane* contre-fer *m*; ~ **label** *n* PACKAGING étiquette au verso *f*; ~ **lens** *n* INSTRUMENT lentille arrière *f*; ~ **lining** *n* PRINT papier garniture *m*, *of book* doublure du dos *f*; ~ **loader** *n* CONST rétrochargeuse *f*; ~ **margin** *n* PRINT blanc de couture *m*; ~ **marks** *n pl* PRINT indices de collationnement *m pl*; ~ **observation** *n* CONST *levelling* coup arrière *m*; ~ **panel layout** *n* PROD ENG gabarit d'installation *m*; ~ **porch** *n* TV palier arrière *m*; ~ **porch clamping** *n* TV clamping sur le palier arrière *m*; ~ **pressure** *n* C&G pression différentielle au tapis *f*, HYDR EQUIP, PAPER TECH, PRINT contre-pression *f*; ~ **pressure valve** *n* HYDR EQUIP clapet de retenue *m*, soupape de retenue *f*; ~ **printing** *n* PRINT impression en retiration *f*; ~ **projection** *n* CINEMAT projection arrière *f*, projection par transparence *f*; ~ **projection screen** *n* CINEMAT écran pour projection par transparence *m*; ~ **puppet** *n* MECH ENG contre-pointe *f*, contre-poupée *f*, poupée mobile *f*; ~ **reaction** *n* NUCLEAR réaction inverse *f*; ~ **reef** *n* GEOL zone en arrière du récif *f*; ~ **reflection method** *n* CRYSTALL méthode de réflexion en retour *f*, méthode de rétroréflexion *f*; ~ **rounding** *n* PRINT arrondissure et endossure *f*; ~ **run** *n* CINEMAT, TV marche arrière *f*; ~ **saw** *n* CONST scie à dos *f*, scie à tenon *f*; ~ **sheet** *n* MECH ENG *of fire box* plaque arrière *f*; ~ **signal** *n* ELECTRON signal de retour *m*; ~ **speed** *n* MECH ENG engrenage inverseur de mouvement *m*, marche arrière *f*; ~ **splice** *n* NAUT cul de porc *m*; ~ **spotfacing** *n* MECH ENG chambrage arrière *m*, lamage arrière *m*; ~ **stope** *n* CONST gradin renversé *m*, maintenage *m*; ~ **stress** *n* METALL contrainte en retour *f*; ~ **surface** *n* C&G *of drawn glass sheet* côté four *m*; ~ **tension** *n* RECORDING tension de retenue *f*; ~ **thrusting** *n* GEOL rétrocharriage *m*; ~ **timing** *n* TV compte à rebours *m*; ~ **title** *n* PRINT *of book* titre au dos *m*; ~ **titration** *n* CHEM titrage en retour *m*; ~ **tube sheet** *n* MECH ENG plaque tubulaire de foyer *f*; ~ **tweel** *n* C&G registre obturateur *m*; ~ **wall photovoltaic cell** *n* ELEC ENG cellule photovoltaïque à couche postérieure *f*; ~ **weld** *n* PROD ENG soudure de soutien *f*

back:[2] *vt* MECH ENG *drill, tap* dépouiller, NAUT *anchor* empenneler, *sail* masquer, PAPER TECH soutenir, PRINT endosser; ~ **off** *vt* MECH ENG *give clearance, relieve* dégager, usiner une dépouille, *milling cutter* dépouiller; ~ **titrate** *vt* CHEM titrer en retour; ~ **up** *vt* COMP sauvegarder, PRINT habiller, imprimer au verso

back:[3] ~ **off** *vi* PROD ENG *control* réduire l'effet de la commande; ~ **up** *vi* COMP faire une copie de sauvegarde, RAIL *vehicles* refouler

back-and-forth: ~ **motion** *n* MECH ENG mouvement d'avance et de recul *m*; ~ **printing** *n* CINEMAT tirage aller-et-retour *m*

back-arc: ~ **basin** *n* GEOL, OCEANOG bassin arrière-arc *m*

backblowing *n* WATER SUPP *of well* chasse par reflux *f*, décolmatage *m*

backbone: ~ **bus** *n* DP bus principal *m*

backcoating *n* TEXTILES enduction envers *f*

back-connected *adj* ELEC *switch* avec prise arrière
back-discharge: ~ **car** *n* (AmE) *(cf back-discharge wagon)* RAIL *vehicles* wagon à déversement arrière *m*; ~ **wagon** *n* (BrE) *(cf back-discharge car, rear dump car)* RAIL *vehicles* wagon à déversement arrière *m*
backed-off: ~ **cutter** *n* MECH ENG fraise dégagée *f*; ~ **teeth** *n pl* MECH ENG *of gear or a rack* dents dégagées *f pl*, denture dégagée *f*
back-end: ~ **plate** *n* MECH ENG panneau arrière *m*
backfall *n* PAPER TECH saut de pile *m*
backfill[1] *n* COAL TECH matériau de remblai *m*, CONST remblai *m*, POLLUTION remblai *m*, remblayage *m*
backfill[2] *vt* CONST remblayer
backfiller *n* CONST *civil engineering*, TRANSP remblayeuse *f*
backfire *n* CONST *welding* claquement *m*, retour de flamme *m*, VEHICLES *engine* pétarade *f*, retour de flamme *m*; ~ **antenna** *n* SPACE antenne rétrodirective *f*
backflow *n* HYDR EQUIP *of boiler water* refoulement *m*, retour d'eau *m*, WATER SUPP reflux *m*
backflushing *n* NUCLEAR rétrolavage *m*
background *n* PHOTO arrière-plan *m*, PRINT arrière-plan *m*, fond *m*, historique *m*; ~ **absorption** *n* RAD PHYS *spectrometry* fond spectral *m*; ~ **art** *n* PATENTS état de la technique antérieure *m*; ~ **blur** *n* PHOTO flou du fond de l'image *m*; ~ **concentration** *n* POLLUTION concentration ambiante *f*, concentration de fond *f*; ~ **film** *n* CINEMAT positif pour transparence *m*; ~ **gas** *n (BG)* PETR TECH *drilling* fond gazeux *m*; ~ **intensity** *n* CRYSTALL *X-rays* fond continu *m*; ~ **level** *n* POLLUTION niveau de fond *m*, niveau de pollution naturelle *m*; ~ **light** *n* CINEMAT éclairage de fond *m*; ~ **negative** *n* CINEMAT négatif pour transparence *m*; ~ **noise** *n* ACOUSTICS, ELECTRON, GEOPHYS, PHYS bruit de fond *m*, RECORDING bruit de fond *m*, bruit parasite *m*, SPACE *communications* bruit de fond *m*, TELECOM bruit de fond *m*, bruit parasite *m*, TESTING bruit de fond *m*; ~ **pollution** *n* POLLUTION pollution de base *f*; ~ **processing** *n* COMP, DP traitement d'arrière-plan *m*; ~ **program** *n* COMP programme d'arrière-plan *m*; ~ **radiation** *n* ASTRON rayonnement de fond *m*, PHYS rayonnement ambiant *m*, rayonnement de fond *m*, RAD PHYS bruit de fond *m*, radiation de fond *f*; ~ **vorticity** *n* FLUID PHYS tourbillonnement de fond *m*
backhand: ~ **welding** *n* MECH, PROD ENG soudage en arrière *m*
backhead *n* MECH ENG contre-pointe *f*, contre-poupée *f*, poupée mobile *f*
backhoe *n* MAR POLL pelle excavatrice mécanique *f*, pelle rétrocaveuse *f*, tractopelle *f*; ~ **loader** *n* CONST *roadbuilding* chargeuse-pelle *f*, chargeuse-pelleteuse *f*, TRANSP chargeuse-pelleteuse *f*
backhole *n* MINING trou de couronne *m*, trou de toit *m*
backing *n* AERONAUT *of seat* dosseret *m*, COATINGS sous-couche *f*, MECH ENG renforcement *m*, renfort *m*, NAUT *of wind* recul *m*, PACKAGING renforcement *m*, support *m*, PAPER TECH soutien *m*, PRINT *of book, plate, blanket* garnissage du dos *m*, sous-habillage *m*, RAIL *vehicles* refoulement *m*, TEXTILES renforcement *m*, *of book* endossure *f*; ~ **bar** *n* AERONAUT contre-bouterolle *f*; ~ **fabric** *n* TEXTILES *lining* tissu de doublure *m*; ~ **movement** *n* RAIL *vehicles* manoeuvre de rebroussement *f*, manoeuvre de refoulement *f*; ~ **paper** *n* PHOTO papier de protection *m*, PRINT papier siliconé servant de support aux adhésifs *m*; ~ **pass** *n* PROD ENG *welding* passe de soutien *f*; ~ **plate** *n* MECH ENG contre-plaque *f*,

VEHICLES *brakes* plateau de frein *m*; ~ **removal** *n* CINEMAT élimination de la dorsale *f*; ~ **roll** *n* PAPER TECH rouleau de soutien *m*; ~ **roller** *n* PRINT rouleau de contrepression *m*, rouleau support *m*; ~ **roller gap** *n* PRINT *machines* dégagement du rouleau-support *m*; ~ **sheet** *n* PRINT feuille d'habillage *f*, manille *f*; ~ **signal** *n* RAIL signal de refoulement *m*; ~ **storage** *n* (AmE) *(cf backing store)* COMP mémoire auxiliaire *f*, mémoire de sauvegarde *f*; ~ **store** *n* (BrE) COMP mémoire auxiliaire *f*, COMP mémoire de sauvegarde *f*; ~ **tape** *n* DP bande de sauvegarde *f*; ~ **up** *n* HYDR EQUIP *of tail water* reflux *m*, PRINT garnissage au dos *m*, retiration *f*; ~ **wire** *n* PAPER TECH toile de soutien *f*
backing-off *n* MECH ENG *machining* détalonnage *m*, *relief, clearance* dégagement *m*, dépouille *f*; ~ **lathe** *n* MECH ENG tour à détalonner *m*
backlash *n* CINEMAT, MECH jeu *m*, MECH ENG *of gear* jeu *m*, jeu de transmission d'un engrenage *m*, jeu à l'inversion du mouvement *m*, MINING *of explosion* contrecoup *m*, répercussion *f*, NAUT *radar* effet de rayonnage *m*, PRINT jeu mécanique *m*, SPACE *communications* jeu d'entraînement *m*, jeu de denture *m*, VEHICLES *transmission* jeu d'engrènement *m*; ~ **error** *n* AERONAUT *in altimeter* erreur de jeu *f*
backlight[1] *n* CINEMAT lumière de décrochement *f*, éclairage à contre-jour *m*
backlight[2] *vt* PHOTO éclairer à contre-jour
backlighting *n* ELEC ENG éclairage par l'arrière *m*
backlit[1] *adj* CINEMAT, PHOTO à contre-jour
backlit:[2] ~ **push button** *n* PROD ENG bouton-poussoir lumineux *m*
backlog *n* MECH retard de fabrication *m*, PROD ENG arrière de fabrication *m*; ~ **of orders** *n* PROD ENG carnet de commandes *m*, commandes en cours *f pl*
backnut *n* PRINT contre-écrou *m*
backpack: ~ **radio** *n* MILIT poste de radio portatif *m*
backplane *n* COMP face arrière *f*, ELECTRON fond de panier *m*, PROD ENG fond de panier *m*, panneau arrière *m*
backplate *n* ELECTRON *of camera tubes* plaque collectrice *f*, MECH ENG faux plateau *m*, TV contre-électrode *f*
backrest *n* AUTO dossier *m*, MECH ENG *of lathe* lunette de tour *f*, VEHICLES *of seat* dossier *m*
backrush *n* OCEANOG flot de retour *m*
backscatter[1] *n* SPACE rétrodiffusion *f*; ~ **effect** *n* NUCLEAR effet de rétrodiffusion *m*; ~ **error** *n* NUCLEAR erreur par diffusion sur le support *f*; ~ **gage** *n* (AmE), ~ **gauge** *n* (BrE) NUCLEAR *density, thickness* jaugeage à rétrodiffusion *m*, mesure à rétrodiffusion *f*; ~ **peak** *n* RAD PHYS *gamma radiation* pic de rétrodiffusion *m*
backscatter[2] *vti* OPT rétrodiffuser
backscattered: ~ **light beam method** *n* ACOUSTICS méthode du faisceau lumineux réfléchi *f*
backscatterer *n* NUCLEAR matière rétrodiffusante *f*, rétrodiffuseur *m*
backscattering *n* ELECTRON, OPT rétrodiffusion *f*, RAD PHYS *of radiation* diffusion rétrograde *f*, rétrodiffusion *f*, SPACE, TELECOM rétrodiffusion *f*; ~ **factor** *n* SPACE facteur de rétrodiffusion *m*; ~ **technique** *n* OPT réflectométrie optique dans le domaine temporel *f*, technique de rétrodiffusion *f*, TELECOM méthode de rétrodiffusion *f*
backset *n* HYDR EQUIP refoulement *m*, retour au point de départ *m*
backshore *n* OCEANOG arrière-plage *f*

backside *n* PAPER TECH *of paper machine* côté transmission *m*, PRINT arrière *m*, dos *m*, verso *m*; ~ **batt** *n* TEXTILES nappe envers *f*; ~ **coating** *n* CINEMAT enduit dorsal *m*

backsight *n* CONST *levelling*, MINES coup arrière *m*

backspace[1] *n* COMP caractère espace arrière *m*, espace arrière *m*, PRINT espacement arrière *m*, retour-arrière *m*; ~ **character** *n* DP caractère de retour arrière *m*

backspace[2] *vi* COMP, DP reculer d'un espace

backstay *n* NAUT *standing rigging* galhauban *m*, pataras *m*

backstep: ~ **sequence** *n* PROD ENG *welding* séquence à pas de pèlerin *f*

backstop *n* PRINT butée arrière *f*

back-to-back[1] *adj* CONST adossé, dos-à-dos, PROD ENG dos-à-dos

back-to-back[2] *n* TEXTILES dos-à-dos *m*; ~ **arrangement** *n* ELEC ENG *capacitors* montage en opposition *m*, *of diodes* montage tête-bêche *m*; ~ **commercials** *n pl* TV spots successifs *m pl*, écrans publicitaires successifs *m pl*

backtrack *vi* AERONAUT remonter la piste

backtracking *n* COMP, DP recherche en arrière *f*

backup[1] *adj* COMP de réserve, de sauvegarde, de secours, DP de sauvegarde, sauvegarde, de secours, secours

backup[2] *n* COMP, DP reprise en secours *f*, ELEC ENG dispositif de secours *m*, PETR TECH *drilling* blocage à la clé *m*, PRINT, PROD ENG sauvegarde *f*; ~ **battery** *n* PROD ENG pile de maintien de la mémoire *f*, pile de secours *f*; ~ **bearing** *n* SPACE *spacecraft* palier de secours *m*; ~ **circuit** *n* PROD ENG circuit de secours *m*; ~ **communication** *n* PROD ENG communication de redondance *f*, communication en redondance *f*; ~ **configuration** *n* PROD ENG configuration de redondance *f*; ~ **light** *n* VEHICLES feu de recul *m*; ~ **line** *n* PETR TECH câble de clé *m*, PROD ENG mode de redondance *m*; ~ **post** *n* PETR TECH point fixe de clé *m*; ~ **power** *n* PROD ENG alimentation de secours *f*; ~ **power supply** *n* ELEC ENG, TELECOM alimentation de secours *f*; ~ **processor** *n* PROD ENG processeur secondaire *m*; ~ **reactor** *n* NUCLEAR système d'arrêt complémentaire *m*; ~ **roll** *n* C&G rouleau fixe *m*; ~ **service** *n* TRANSP service d'appoint *m*; ~ **signal** *n* RAIL signal de refoulement *m*; ~ **supervisor** *n* TELECOM superviseur de secours *m*; ~ **switch** *n* CONTROL interrupteur de secours *m*, PROD ENG interrupteur de redondance *m*

Backus: ~ **normal form** *n* COMP forme normale de Backus *f*

backward[1] *adv* PROD ENG en amont

backward[2] *n* PROD ENG amont *m*; ~ **diode** *n* ELECTRON diode inverse *f*, diode unitunnel *f*; ~ **explicit congestion notification** *n* *(BECN)* TELECOM notification d'encombrement explicite émise vers l'arrière *f*; ~ **flight** *n* AERONAUT vol vers l'arrière *m*; ~ **input signal** *n* TELECOM signal d'entrée vers l'arrière *m*; ~ **interworking telephony event** *n* TELECOM événement téléphonique d'interfonctionnement vers l'arrière *m*; ~ **motion** *n* MECH ENG marche rétrograde *f*, mouvement de recul *m*, recul *m*, PRINT mouvement arrière *m*, mouvement de recul *m*; ~ **movement** *n* MECH ENG marche rétrograde *f*, mouvement de recul *m*, recul *m*; ~ **scheduling** *n* PROD ENG chargement amont *m*, chargement au plus tard *m*, jalonnement amont *m*, jalonnement au plus tard *m*; ~ **signal** *n* CONTROL signal vers l'arrière *m*; ~ **sort** *n* COMP tri descendant *m*, tri en ordre décroissant *m*, DP tri descendant *m*; ~ **stroke** *n*

MECH ENG course de recul *f*; ~ **takeoff** *n* AERONAUT *of helicopter* décollage arrière *m*; ~ **wave** *n* ELEC ENG *transmission line* onde réfléchie *f*, *travelling wave tube* onde inverse *f*, onde progressive inverse *f*, onde régressive *f*; ~ **wave guide** *n* TELECOM tube à onde régressive *m*; ~ **wave oscillator** *n* *(BWO)* ELECTRON oscillateur à onde régressive *m*, tube oscillateur à onde régressive *m*, PHYS carcinotron O *m*, TELECOM oscillateur à onde rétrograde *m*; ~ **wave tube** *n* ELECTRON, PHYS tube à onde régressive *m*; ~ **welding** *n* PROD ENG soudage à droite *m*

backward-and-forward: ~ **motion** *n* MECH ENG mouvement d'avance et de recul *m*

backwash *n* HYDROL remous *m*, OCEANOG flot de retour *m*, ressac *m*; ~ **tank** *n* NUCLEAR réservoir de rétrolavage *m*; ~ **water** *n* HYDROL eau de lavage *f*, WATER SUPP eau de rinçage *f*

backwashing *n* HYDROL *water treatment* lavage par retour de courant *m*

backwater *n* HYDROL bras mort *m*, PAPER TECH eau de retour *f*, WATER SUPP remous *m*, *of canal* sous-biez *m*; ~ **effect** *n* FUELLESS effet d'eau arrêtée *m*

backwind:[1] ~ **handle** *n* CINEMAT manivelle de rebobinage *f*

backwind[2] *vi* CINEMAT rebobiner

bacteria: ~ **bed** *n* RECYCLING, WATER SUPP lit bactérien *m*; ~ **propagation tank** *n* FOOD TECH *fermentation* vase clos pour la multiplication des bactéries *m*

bacterial: ~ **bed** *n* HYDROL lit bactérien *m*; ~ **count** *n* WATER SUPP numération bactérienne *f*

bactericidal *adj* FOOD TECH, HYDROL bactéricide

bactericide *n* CHEM, FOOD TECH, HYDROL bactéricide *m*

bacteriological: ~ **oven** *n* LAB EQUIP étuve bactériologique *f*; ~ **warfare** *n* MILIT guerre bactériologique *f*

bacteriolysis *n* FOOD TECH bactériolyse *f*

bacteriophage *n* FOOD TECH bactériophage *m*, phage *m*

bacteriostat *n* FOOD TECH bactériostatique *m*

bacteriotoxin *n* CHEM bactériotoxine *f*

bacterium *n* HYDROL, RECYCLING bactérie *f*

bad: ~ **air** *n* MINING air vicié *m*, mauvais air *m*; ~ **annealing** *n* C&G mauvais recuit *m*; ~ **break** *n* PRINT mauvaise coupure de ligne *f*, mauvaise césure *f*; ~ **contact** *n* ELEC ENG faux contact *m*; ~ **ground** *n* CONST mauvais terrain *m*, mauvaise condition de terrain *f*; ~ **weather zone** *n* METEO zone de mauvais temps *f*; ~ **work** *n* PROD ENG malfaçon *f*; ~ **workmanship** *n* PROD ENG malfaçon *f*

badge[1] *n* C&G écusson *m*, DP badge *m*; ~ **plate** *n* PROD ENG *boiler test plate* timbre *m*; ~ **reader** *n* DP lecteur de badge *m*

badge[2] *vt* PROD ENG *boiler* timbrer

badging *n* C&G marquage *m*

baffle[1] *n* ACOUSTICS enceinte acoustique *f*, écran acoustique *m*, C&G déflecteur de la gaine d'étirage *m*, CHEM TECH, CONST *for deflecting walls or gases* chicane *f*, déflecteur *m*, MECH ENG chicane *f*, déflecteur *m*, sourdine *f*, tôle de séparation *f*, MINING tôle de séparation *f*, NUCLEAR, PAPER TECH chicane *f*, RECORDING baffle *m*, VEHICLES *silencer* chicane *f*; ~ **boards** *n pl* CONST planches en chicane *f pl*; ~ **brick** *n* CONST culot *m*; ~ **collector** *n* POLLUTION dépoussiéreur à chicane *m*; ~ **hole** *n* C&G orifice de remplissage du moule *m*; ~ **mark** *n* C&G couture de fond ébaucheur *f*; ~ **muffler** *n* (AmE) *(cf baffle silencer)* AUTO silencieux à chicanes *m*; ~ **plate** *n* C&G fond ébaucheur *m*, CHEM TECH déflecteur à chicanes *m*, tôle-chicane *f*, CONST chicane *f*; ~ **plates**

n pl REFRIG chicanes *f pl*, cloisonnage *m*, déflecteurs *m pl*; ~ **ring** *n* PETR TECH anneau de retenue *m*; ~ **silencer** *n* (BrE) *(cf baffle muffler)* AUTO silencieux à chicanes *m*; ~ **tube** *n* CHEM TECH tuyau de refroidissement des gaz *m*; ~ **wall** *n* PAPER TECH mur déflecteur *m*

baffle² *vt* CHEM TECH étrangler, MINING *firedamp* noyer

baffle-type: ~ **separator** *n* CHEM TECH séparateur à chicanes *m*

baffling: ~ **wind** *n* METEO brise folle *f*

bag¹ *n* COAL TECH sac *m*, MINING *containing gas or water* poche *f*, sac *m*, PACKAGING *large* sac *m*, *small* sachet *m*, POLLUTION élément filtrant *m*, PRINT sac *m*, sachet *m*; ~ **conveyor** *n* TRANSP bande transporteuse pour sacs *f*; ~ **factory** *n* PACKAGING usine de fabrication de sacs *f*; ~ **filling** *n* PACKAGING remplissage de sacs *m*; ~ **filling machine** *n* PACKAGING machine pour remplir les sacs *f*; ~ **filter** *n* COAL TECH filtre à manche *m*; ~ **holder** *n* PACKAGING porte-sac *m*; ~ **in box** *n* PRINT bag-in-box *m*; ~ **in a box packaging** *n* PACKAGING emballage d'un sachet dans une boîte *m*; ~ **in a can** *n* PACKAGING sachet dans une boîte métallique *m*; ~ **loading machine** *n* PACKAGING machine pour charger les sacs *f*; ~ **opener** *n* PACKAGING dispositif d'ouverture de sachets *m*; ~ **packaging** *n* PACKAGING emballage en sacs *m*; ~ **paper** *n* PACKAGING papier pour sacs *m*; ~ **placing system** *n* PACKAGING système de positionnement de sachets *m*; ~ **reel** *n* PACKAGING rouleau de sacs *m*; ~ **rolling** *n* PROD ENG enroulage des poches *m*; ~ **sealing equipment** *n* PACKAGING équipement pour la fermeture des sacs *m*; ~ **staple** *n* PACKAGING agrafe pour sac *f*; ~ **stitcher** *n* PRINT machine à coudre les sacs *f*; ~ **stitching machine** *n* PACKAGING machine à coudre les sacs *f*

bag² *vt* FOOD TECH ensacher

bagasse: ~ **roller** *n* FOOD TECH cylindre à bagasse *m*

baggage: ~ **car** *n* (AmE) *(cf luggage van)* RAIL, TRANSP fourgon à bagages *m*; ~ **compartment** *n* (AmE) *(cf luggage compartment)* TRANSP soute à bagages *f*; ~ **loader** *n* TRANSP véhicule de manipulation des bagages *m*; ~ **retrieval** *n* TRANSP délivrance des bagages *f*; ~ **room** *n* (AmE) *(cf luggage compartment)* TRANSP compartiment à bagages *m*; ~ **terminal** *n* TRANSP terminal des bagages *m*

bagging *n* PACKAGING ensachement *m*; ~ **machine** *n* PACKAGING ensacheuse *f*

baghouse *n* COAL TECH chambre de filtration *f*, POLLUTION dépoussiéreur à tissu filtrant *m*

bagmaker *n* PACKAGING fabricant de sacs *m*

bag-making: ~ **machine** *n* PACKAGING machine pour fabriquer les sacs *f*

baikalite *n* MINERAL baïkalite *f*

bail¹ *n* PROD ENG anse *f*

bail² *vt* FLUID PHYS puiser, vider; ~ **out** *vt* FLUID PHYS puiser, vider, NAUT *boat* assécher, vider, écoper

bail:³ ~ **out** *vi* AERONAUT sauter en parachute

bailer *n* NAUT écope *f*, PETR bailer *m*

Bailey: ~ **bridge** *n* CONST, MILIT pont Bailey *m*

bailing *n* PETR puisage *m*; ~ **tank** *n* WATER SUPP cuffat d'épuisement *m*

bainite *n* METALL, SPRINGS bainite *f*

bainitic: ~ **ferrite** *n* METALL ferrite bainitique *f*

bait *n* C&G amorce d'étirage *f*

baiting *n* OCEANOG dos *m*, petit dos *m*

Bajocian *adj* GEOL *stratigraphy* bajocien

bake:¹ ~ **and UV-irradiation test** *n* C&G *for laminated glass* essai d'échauffement et d'irradiation UV *m*

bake² *vt* C&G *clay* cuire, PROD ENG *core, mould* étuver, TEXTILES cuire, THERMOD *in furnace* cuire, étuver

baked: ~ **enamel** *n* COATINGS vernis-émail *m*, COLOURS laque au four *f*, émail au four *m*; ~ **glass painting** *n* COLOURS peinture sur verre *f*; ~ **sand** *n* PROD ENG *founding* sable d'étuve *m*, sable recuit *m*, sable étuvé *m*

bakelite *n* ELEC *insulation*, P&R *plastics* bakélite *f*

bakery: ~ **concentrate** *n* FOOD TECH concentré de produit de boulangerie *m*

baking *n* C&G, P&R *paint* cuisson *f*, PROD ENG *of bricks* cuisson *f*, cuite *f*, *of cores* étuvage *m*, étuvement *m*, TEXTILES cuisson *f*; ~ **enamel** *n* COLOURS laque au four *f*, émail au four *m*, PROD ENG émail au four *m*; ~ **fault** *n* FOOD TECH défaut de cuisson *m*, défaut des produits cuits au four *m*; ~ **loss** *n* FOOD TECH perte à la cuisson *f*; ~ **process** *n* PRINT *of plate* processus de cuisson *m*; ~ **quality** *n* FOOD TECH *milling* qualité boulangère *f*, valeur boulangère *f*, valeur de panification *f*; ~ **sheet** *n* FOOD TECH plaque à four *f*; ~ **soda** *n* FOOD TECH bicarbonate de sodium *m*; ~ **varnish** *n* PROP MAT vernis séchant au four *m*

balance¹ *n* LAB EQUIP *analysis* balance *f*, *light chemical balance for precision work* trébuchet *m*, METR *of spring or lever type* peson *m*, *scales* balance *f*, PAPER TECH équilibre *m*, PHYS *instrument* balance *f*, *state* équilibre *m*, PRINT équilibre *m*, PROD ENG *of stock* quantité restante *f*, reste *m*, solde *m*, RECORDING balance *f*; ~ **arm** *n* AERONAUT balancier *m*; ~ **bar** *n* WATER SUPP *of lock gate* balancier *m*, flèche *f*; ~ **beam** *n* MECH ENG fléau de balance *m*, METR fléau de balance *m*, verge de balance *f*; ~ **bob** *n* MINING *of pump spear rod* balancier à contrepoids *m*, contre-balancier *m*; ~ **bridge** *n* CONST pont à bascule *m*; ~ **brush** *n* LAB EQUIP *analysis* pinceau pour balance *m*; ~ **chain** *n* MECH ENG chaîne d'équilibrage *f*, chaîne de contrepoids *f*; ~ **coil** *n* ELEC bobine d'équilibrage *f*; ~ **control** *n* RECORDING contrôle d'équilibrage de niveau *m*; ~ **crank** *n* MECH ENG manivelle d'équilibrage *f*, manivelle à contrepoids *f*; ~ **engineer** *n* RECORDING ingénieur du son *m*; ~ **gear** *n* MECH ENG différentiel *m*, engrenage différentiel *m*; ~ **horn** *n* AERONAUT bec de compensation *m*; ~ **lever** *n* MECH ENG levier d'équilibrage *m*, levier à bascule *m*; ~ **point** *n* AERONAUT point d'équilibre *m*; ~ **pressure** *n* REFRIG pression d'équilibre *f*; ~ **relay** *n* ELEC relais balancé *m*; ~ **signal** *n* CONTROL signal équilibré *m*; ~ **step** *n* CONST *stair building* marche balancée *f*, marche balançante *f*; ~ **stripe** *n* CINEMAT piste de compensation *f*; ~ **tab** *n* AERONAUT compensateur d'évolution *m*, fletteur d'équilibrage *m*, tab automatique de compensation *m*, volet de compensation *m*; ~ **tank** *n* REFRIG réservoir d'équilibre *m*; ~ **washer** *n* AERONAUT rondelle d'équilibrage *f*; ~ **weight** *n* AERONAUT masse d'équilibrage *f*, MECH, MECH ENG contrepoids *m*; ~ **wheel** *n* CINEMAT volant de compensation *m*

balance² *vt* PAPER TECH équilibrer

balance:³ **be out of** ~ *vi* METR présenter un balourd

balanced: ~ **aileron** *n* AERONAUT aileron compensé *m*; ~ **amplifier** *n* ELECTRON amplificateur symétrique *m*, RECORDING amplificateur équilibré *m*; ~ **armature loudspeaker** *n* RECORDING haut-parleur à armature équilibrée *m*; ~ **armature unit** *n* ELEC *motor* moteur équilibré *m*; ~ **bridge interferometer switch** *n* TELECOM coupleur Mach-Zehnder *m*; ~ **circuit** *n* RECORDING circuit symétrique *m*; ~ **control surface** *n* AERONAUT gouverne compensée *f*; ~ **current** *n* ELEC ENG courant équilibré *m*; ~ **disc valve** *n* (BrE) FUELLESS *dams* vanne

papillon *f*; ~ **disk valve** *n* (AmE) *see balanced disc valve*; ~ **error** *n* DP erreur centrée *f*; ~ **field length** *n* AERONAUT longueur de piste équivalente *f*; ~ **flow** *n* REFRIG flux équilibré *m*; ~ **grading group** *n* TELECOM *traffic* groupement de lignes à trafic équilibré *m*; ~ **input** *n* ELEC ENG entrée symétrique *f*; ~ **line** *n* ELEC *supply* artère d'alimentation *f*, ligne équilibrée *f*, ELEC ENG ligne de transmission équilibrée *f*, ligne équilibrée *f*, RECORDING ligne symétrique *f*; ~ **load** *n* ELEC ENG charge équilibrée *f*; ~ **mixer** *n* ELEC ENG mélangeur symétrique *m*, mélangeur équilibré *m*, ELECTRON mélangeur symétrique *m*; ~ **modulator** *n* ELECTRON modulateur équilibré *m*; ~ **network** *n* ELEC *supply*, ELEC ENG réseau équilibré *m*; ~ **rudder** *n* NAUT gouvernail compensé *m*; ~ **slide valve** *n* MECH ENG distributeur équilibré *m*, tiroir compensé *m*, tiroir équilibré *m*; ~ **tension block** *n* MECH ENG contrepoids de maintien de la tension *m*; ~ **valve** *n* FUELLESS vanne équilibrée *f*, HYDR EQUIP clapet équilibré *m*
balancer *n* ELEC ENG compensateur *m*
balancing *n* AERONAUT, AUTO, NUCLEAR, PAPER TECH, PHYS *alternating current bridge*, TELECOM équilibrage *m*; ~ **machine** *n* MECH ENG machine à équilibrer *f*; ~ **magnetic stripe** *n* TV piste magnétique de compensation *f*; ~ **motion** *n* MECH ENG mouvement alterné *m*, mouvement basculant *m*; ~ **network** *n* ELEC ENG réseau d'équilibrage *m*; ~ **piston** *n* HYDR EQUIP piston compensateur *m*, piston équilibreur *m*; ~ **relay** *n* ELEC relais différentiel *m*; ~ **resistor** *n* ELEC résistance d'équilibrage *f*; ~ **weight** *n* MECH masselotte d'équilibrage *f*
balas: ~ **ruby** *n* MINERAL rubis-balais *m*
balata *n* P&R balata *m*; ~ **belt** *n* MECH ENG courroie balata *f*
balcony *n* C&G balcon *m*
bald: ~ **tire** *n* (AmE), ~ **tyre** *n* (BrE) VEHICLES pneumatique lisse *m*, pneumatique usé *m*
bale[1] *n* PACKAGING balle *f*, PAPER TECH balle de pâte *f*, TEXTILES balle *f*; ~ **hoop** *n* PACKAGING ruban pour balles *m*; ~ **loader** *n* TRANSP chargeur de balles *m*
bale[2] *vt* PACKAGING mettre en balle
bale:[3] ~ **out** *vt see bail*[2]
baling: ~ **press** *n* PACKAGING presse à faire les balles *f*, PAPER TECH presse à balles *f*
balk *n* (AmE) *see baulk*
ball[1] *n* CONST *float* flotteur *m*, MECH ENG articulation à rotule *f*, rotule *f*, *of bearing* bille de roulement *f*, *of governor* boule de régulateur *f*, *of pendulum* lentille de balancier *f*, lentille de pendule *f* ~ **and socket** *n* PHOTO, PRINT rotule *f*; ~ **and socket head** *n* CINEMAT, PHOTO tête à rotule *f*; ~ **and socket joint** *n* MECH articulation sphérique *f*, MECH ENG accouplement à rotule *m*, articulation à rotule *f*, joint à rotule sphérique *m*, PRINT joint à rotule *m*; ~ **bearing** *n* MECH, MECH ENG, VEHICLES roulement à billes *m*; ~ **bearing cage** *n* MECH ENG cage à billes *f*; ~ **bearing guideway** *n* MECH ENG glissière à billes *f*; ~ **bearing plummet block** *n* MECH ENG palier à billes *m*; ~ **bearing race** *n* VEHICLES bague de roulement à billes *f*; ~ **bearing reactor** *n* MECH ENG butée à billes *f*; ~ **bearing roller** *n* PROD ENG galet à bille *m*; ~ **bushing** *n* MECH ENG douille à billes *f*; ~ **cage** *n* MECH ENG cage à billes *f*; ~ **check valve** *n* NUCLEAR soupape d'arrêt à boulet *f*; ~ **circulating lead screw** *n* MECH ENG vis-mère à billes *f*; ~ **circulating nut** *n* MECH ENG écrou à billes *m*; ~ **clay** *n* GEOL, PETR TECH argile plastique *f*; ~ **cock** *n* CONST flotteur sphérique *m*,

robinet à flotteur *m*, MECH ENG robinet à flotteur *m*; ~ **coupling** *n* NUCLEAR dispositif d'accouplement à bille *m*; ~ **cup** *n* MECH ENG coupelle de rotule *f*; ~ **end** *n* MECH ENG embout sphérique *m*; ~ **gage** *n* (AmE), ~ **gauge** *n* (BrE) METR jauge à billes *f*; ~ **governor** *n* MECH ENG régulateur centrifuge *m*, régulateur de Watt *m*, régulateur à boules *m*; ~ **inner race** *n* MECH ENG bague intérieure de roulement *f*; ~ **joint** *n* MECH ENG articulation à rotule *f*, PAPER TECH joint sphérique *m*, VEHICLES *in steering* articulation sphérique *f*, joint à rotule *m*, rotule *f*; ~ **joint cage** *n* MECH ENG cage de rotule *f*; ~ **knob** *n* MECH ENG bouton sphérique *m*, poignée sphérique *f*; ~ **lock** *n* MECH ENG *tools* retenue à bille *f*; ~ **lock retainer** *n* MECH ENG *for punches* porte-poinçon à bille *m*; ~ **lock round punch** *n* MECH ENG poinçon cylindrique à démontage rapide *m*; ~ **mill** *n* C&G broyeur à boulets *m*, CHEM TECH broyeur à billes *m*, broyeur à boules *m*, broyeur à boulets *m*, COAL TECH broyeur mixeur *m*, broyeur à billes *m*, broyeur à boulets *m*, FOOD TECH *machinery* broyeur à boulets *m*, broyeur à son *m*, moulin à galets *m*, LAB EQUIP broyeur à boulets *m*, MINING *ore-dressing, mineral processing* broyeur à boulets *m*, moulin à boulets *m*, P&R *equipment* broyeur à billes *m*, broyeur à boules *m*, moulin à billes *m*, PAPER TECH raffineur à boulets *m*; ~ **milling** *n* COAL TECH broyage à boulets *m*; ~ **nut** *n* NUCLEAR écrou sphérique *m*; ~ **pad** *n* MECH ENG patin à billes *m*; ~ **pane** *n* MECH ENG *of hammer* panne bombée *f*, panne sphérique *f*; ~ **pean** *n* MECH ENG *of hammer* panne bombée *f*, panne sphérique *f*; ~ **peen** *n* MECH ENG *of hammer* panne bombée *f*, panne sphérique *f*; ~ **race** *n* MECH ENG bague de roulement *f*, chemin de roulement pour billes *m*, PRINT cage à billes *f*; ~ **register** *n* MECH ENG dispositif de positionnement des billes *m*; ~ **screw** *n* MECH ENG vis à billes *f*; ~ **socket seat** *n* MECH ENG siège de rotule *m*; ~ **stage microscope** *n* INSTRUMENT microscope à surplatine hémisphérique *m*; ~ **stop** *n* MECH ENG butée à billes *f*; ~ **thrust bearing** *n* MECH ENG, PAPER TECH butée à billes *f*; ~ **valve** *n* HYDR EQUIP clapet à bille *m*, robinet à flotteur *m*, MECH robinet à tournant sphérique *m*, MECH ENG clapet à bille *m*, robinet sphérique *m*, *float-type* soupape à flotteur *f*, PAPER TECH soupape à boulet *f*; ~ **vein** *n* MINING filon nodulaire *m*, filon à nodules *m*
ball[2] *vt* COAL TECH bouleter
ballast:[1] **in** ~ *adv* NAUT *ship* sur lest
ballast[2] *n* AERONAUT lest *m*, CONST ballast *m*, *for making concrete* blocaille *f*, ELEC ENG ballast *m*, lest *m*, NAUT *boat building* lest *m*, RAIL, TRANSP ballast *m*; ~ **keel** *n* NAUT *boat building* lest *m*, quille lestée *f*; ~ **resistor** *n* ELEC, ELEC ENG résistance ballast *f*; ~ **retainer** *n* RAIL murette garde-ballast *f*; ~ **screening** *n* RAIL criblage du ballast *m*; ~ **tank** *n* NAUT *ships and submarines* ballast *m*, caisse de ballast *f*
ballasting *n* CONST *material* ballast *m*, ballastage *m*; ~ **circuit** *n* ELEC ENG circuit de protection *m*
ballastless: ~ **track** *n* TRANSP voie sans ballast *f*
ball-ended: ~ **linkage** *n* MECH ENG embiellage à embout sphérique *m*
balling *n* COAL TECH bouletage *m*; ~ **drum** *n* COAL TECH tambour bouleteur *m*
ballistic[1] *adj* SPACE balistique
ballistic:[2] ~ **galvanometer** *n* ELEC, PHYS galvanomètre balistique *m*; ~ **missile** *n* ELECTRON *defence*, MILIT missile balistique *m*, SPACE engin balistique *m*, missile balistique *m*; ~ **path** *n* SPACE trajectoire balistique *f*; ~

trajectory *n* SPACE trajectoire balistique *f*

ballistics *n* SPACE *mechanics* balistique *m*

balloon *n* CHEM *flask* ballon *m*, PRINT bulle *f*; ~ **release station** *n* SPACE station de lâchage de ballons *f*, station lâcheuse de ballons *f*; ~ **surfacing** *n* OCEANOG remontée en ballon *f*; ~ **system** *n* MILIT *airborne parachutist training* ballon *m*; ~ **tire** *n* (AmE), ~ **tyre** *n* (BrE) AUTO pneu ballon *m*

ballooning *n* NUCLEAR *of fuel* ballonnement *m*, OCEANOG remontée en ballon *f*; ~ **instability** *n* NUCLEAR instabilité de ballonnement *f*

Balmer: ~ **series** *n* PHYS série Balmer *f*; ~ **series line** *n* PART PHYS *in atomic spectrum* raie de la série de Balmer *f*

Balmer's: ~ **formula** *n* PHYS formule de Balmer *f*

baltimorite *n* MINERAL baltimorite *f*

baluster *n* CONST balustre *m*

balustrade *n* CONST balustrade *f*, garde-corps *m*, rampe *f*

bamboo *n* C&G bambou *m*; ~ **effect** *n* NUCLEAR *ridge formation* effet bambou *m*; ~ **pulp** *n* PAPER TECH pâte de bambou *f*

banana: ~ **handling terminal** *n* TRANSP terminal à bananes *m*; ~ **jack** *n* ELEC ENG douille banane *f*; ~ **orbit** *n* NUCLEAR trajectoire banane *f*; ~ **plug** *n* CINEMAT, ELEC ENG fiche banane *f*, PHOTO fiche à ressort *f*; ~ **regime** *n* NUCLEAR régime banane *m*; ~ **trajectory** *n* NUCLEAR trajectoire banane *f*

Banbury: ~ **mixer** *n* P&R *equipment* mélangeur Banbury *m*

band[1] *n* COAL TECH barre *f*, COMP bande *f*, CONST *round chimney shaft, kiln* bande *f*, frette *f*, DP bande *f*, MECH ENG bandage *m*, *machine belt* courroie de transmission *f*, PHYS bande *f*, PRINT bandage *m*, bande *f*, bandeau *m*, ceinture *f*, nerf *m*; ~ **brake** *n* MECH frein à bande *m*, MECH ENG frein à bande *m*, frein à sangle *m*; ~ **chain** *n* CONST *surveying* chaîne à ruban d'acier *f*; ~ **clutch** *n* MECH ENG embrayage à bande *m*; ~ **conveyor** *n* PACKAGING transporteur à bande *m*, PROD ENG transporteur à courroie *m*, transporteur à toile sans fin *m*; ~ **coupling** *n* MECH ENG accouplement à bande *m*; ~ **heater** *n* MECH ENG *injection moulds* collier chauffant *m*; ~ **iron** *n* PACKAGING cercle en feuillard *m*; ~ **label** *n* PACKAGING étiquette-bande *f*; ~ **model** *n* METALL modèle des bandes *m*; ~ **pressure level** *n* RECORDING niveau de pression sélectif *m*; ~ **printer** *n* COMP imprimante à courroie *f*, DP imprimante à bande *f*; ~ **pulley** *n* MECH ENG poulie à courroie *f*, poulie à sangle *f*; ~ **sealer** *n* PACKAGING soudeuse en continu *f*; ~ **sealing** *n* PACKAGING soudage en continu *m*; ~ **separation** *n* ELECTRON sélection de bande *f*; ~ **spectrum** *n* PHYS, RAD PHYS spectre de bandes *m*; ~ **structure** *n* PROP MAT structure de bandes *f*; ~ **tape** *n* CONST chaîne à ruban d'acier *f*; ~ **theory** *n* PHYS théorie des bandes *f*; ~ **theory of solids** *n* RAD PHYS théorie des bandes d'état solide *f*; ~ **wheel** *n* MECH ENG volant de scie à ruban *m*

band[2] *vt* MECH ENG fretter

bandage *vt* PRINT *forme* envelopper d'un film protecteur

banded[1] *adj* GEOL lité, rubané, zoné, PETR zoné

banded:[2] ~ **structure** *n* METALL structure bandée *f*, PROP MAT structure en bandes *f*

banderole *n* PACKAGING banderole *f*

banding *n* C&G bordure *f*, MECH ENG courroie de transmission *f*, PACKAGING cerclage *m*, TV effet de bande *m*;

~ **machine** *n* PACKAGING bandeuse *f*; ~ **on hue** *n* TV effet de bande sur la teinte *m*; ~ **on noise** *n* TV effet de bande sur le bruit *m*; ~ **on saturation** *n* TV effet de bande sur la saturation *m*

band-limit *vi* ELECTRON réduire la largeur de bande

band-limited: ~ **channel** *n* DP canal à bande réduite *m*; ~ **signal** *n* ELECTRON signal à bande réduite *m*

bandoliered: ~ **component** *n* ELEC ENG composant en bande *m*

band-pass *n* PETR passe-bande *m*; ~ **amplifier** *n* ELECTRON amplificateur accordé *m*, RECORDING amplificateur passe-bande *m*; ~ **filter** *n* (*BPF*) COMP, DP, ELEC, ELECTRON, PHYS, RECORDING, TELECOM, TV filtre passe-bande *m* (*FPB*); ~ **filtering** *n* ELECTRON filtrage par filtre passe-bande *m*; ~ **filter shaping** *n* ELECTRON mise au gabarit par filtre passe-bande *f*

band-rejection: ~ **filter** *n* COMP filtre coupe-bande *m*, filtre d'arrêt *m*, filtre stop-bande *m*, SPACE *communications* filtre de bande *m*

bands *n pl* WAVE PHYS *due to interference* franges d'interférence *f pl*; ~ **of the spectrum** *n pl* WAVE PHYS bandes spectrales *f pl*

band-saw *n* MECH ENG scie à ruban *f*; ~ **brazing apparatus** *n* MECH ENG appareil à braser les scies à ruban *m*; ~ **brazing sharpening and setting machine** *n* MECH ENG machine à braser à affûter et à avoyer les lames de scies à ruban *f*; ~ **pulley** *n* MECH ENG volant de scie à ruban *m*

band-sawing: ~ **machine** *n* MECH ENG scie à ruban *f*

bandspread *n* RAD PHYS étalement de bande *m*

bandstop: ~ **filter** *n* COMP filtre coupe-bande *m*, filtre d'arrêt *m*, filtre stop-bande *m*, ELECTRON filtre coupe-bande *m*, RECORDING filtre bouchon *m*, TESTING filtre bande *m*; ~ **filtering** *n* ELECTRON filtrage par filtre coupe-bande *m*

bandwidth *n* COMP, ELECTRON largeur de bande *f*, OPT *optical fibre* bande passante *f*, largeur de bande *f*, PHYS, RAD PHYS, RECORDING *of recorded signal*, SPACE *communications*, TELECOM largeur de bande *f*, TV bande passante *f*, largeur de bande *f*; ~ **compression** *n* ELECTRON compression de bande *f*, TV compression de bande passante *f*; ~ **expansion** *n* ELECTRON expansion de bande *f*

bandwidth-limited: ~ **operation** *n* OPT, TELECOM fonctionnement limité par la largeur de bande *m*

banger *n* PAPER TECH chasse-pâte *f*

banjo: ~ **bolt** *n* MECH ENG boulon à oeil *m*, *hollow bolt* boulon creux de raccord *m*; ~ **union** *n* MECH ENG raccord banjo *m*

banjo-type: ~ **housing** *n* VEHICLES *rear axle* pont banjo *m*

bank[1] *n* AERONAUT inclinaison transversale *f*, pente latérale *f*, COAL TECH remblai *m*, CONST *of canal, road, railway, of cut* berge *f*, talus *m*, *of earth* banquette *f*, berme *f*, talus *m*, *of sand, rock* banc *m*, ELEC ENG *group of capacitors, oscillators* batterie *f*, *of buttons, contacts* rangée *f*, ELECTRON *of filters* batterie *f*, HYDROL *of pond* rive *f*, *of river, lake* berge *f*, bord *m*, rive *f*, MINING *auriferous gravels* lit continu *m*, *landing* accrochage du jour *m*, recette d'à haut *f*, recette d'à jour *f*, *working face* front *m*, front d'abattage *m*, front d'attaque *m*, front de taille *m*, NAUT banc *m*, haut-fond *m*, berge *f*, bord *m*, rive *f*, OCEANOG *sea bed* banc *m*, basse *f*, PHOTO *of lights* batterie *f*, rampe lumineuse *f*, PRINT table à papier *f*, *newspaper headline* gros titre *m*, RAIL rampe *f*, RECYCLING conteneur de collecte *m*;

~ **of capacitors** n ELEC ENG batterie de condensateurs f;
~ **of cells** n COAL TECH banc de cellules m; ~ **clearance
angle** n MECH ENG angle d'incidence arrière m; ~
contact n TELECOM broche f; ~ **of dryers** n PAPER TECH
sécherie à cylindres sécheurs superposés f; ~ **of lights** n
CINEMAT batterie de projecteurs f; ~ **paper** n PRINT
papier machine à écrire m; ~ **of RAMs** n ELEC ENG
batterie de RAMs f; ~ **of relays** n PROD ENG ensemble
de relais m; ~ **switching** n COMP commutation de blocs
mémoire f; ~ **winding** n ELEC coil enroulement rangé m
bank² vt CONST amasser, amonceler, entasser, mettre en
tas, of bank or mound endiguer, terrasser; ~ **up** vt
MINING endiguer, remblayer, terrasser; ~ **up with earth**
vt CONST wall terrasser
bank³ vi AERONAUT virer, CONST of heap or pile s'amasser, s'amonceler, s'entasser, se mettre en tas, MINING
atterrir, SPACE spacecraft virer; ~ **up** vi CONST s'amasser, s'amonceler, s'entasser, se mettre en tas, METEO
clouds s'amonceler
bank-and-pitch: ~ **indicator** n (BrE) (cf turn-and-bank
indicator) AERONAUT indicateur d'inclinaison longitudinale et latérale m
banked:¹ ~ **up** adj THERMOD fire, blast furnace feu en
veilleuse, feu four, feu fourneau
banked:² ~ **configuration** n NUCLEAR of rod configuration en grappes f; ~ **winding** n ELEC coil enroulement
rangé m, ELEC ENG bobinage extra-plat m
banket n MINING banket m, conglomérat aurifère m
bankhead n MINING carreau de mine m
banking n MINING cage atterrissage m, RAIL vehicles
marche en pousse f, TRANSP dévers m; ~ **locomotive** n
(BrE) (cf pusher locomotive) RAIL locomotive de
pousse f, locomotive de renfort en queue f
banknote: ~ **paper** n (BrE) (cf onionskin paper) PAPER
TECH papier pour billet de banque m
banquette n CONST banquette f, berme f
bar¹ n COAL TECH, CONST of catch for gate latch clenche f,
clenchette f, HYDROL at entrance to harbour, at mouth
of river barre f, MECH ENG of foundry flask barrette f,
traverse f, METR bar m, MINES barre f, MINING rock drill
mounting affût m, NAUT geography barre f, OCEANOG
poulier m, PAPER TECH lame f, PETR TECH unit of
pressure, PHYS bar m, TEXTILES strap bride f, streaki-
ness barre f; ~ **armature** n ELEC of machine induit à
barres m; ~ **bolt** n CONST boulon de scellement à crans
m; ~ **chamfering tool** n MECH ENG outil à chanfreiner
m; ~ **channeler** n (AmE), ~ **channeller** n (BrE) MINING
quarrying trancheuse f; ~ **chart** n COMP, MATH graphique à barres m, histogramme m; ~ **chuck** n MECH ENG
machine tools mandrin à pince pour la prise de barres
m; ~ **coal-cutting machine** n MINING haveuse à barre
coupante f; ~ **coater** n P&R enduiseuse avec barre
d'application f; ~ **code** n DP, PACKAGING, PRINT, TELE-
COM code barres m, code à barres m; ~ **code labeling
system** n (AmE), ~ **code labelling system** n (BrE)
PACKAGING système d'étiquetage avec code à barres
m; ~ **code label printer** n PACKAGING imprimeur d'étiquettes code à barres m; ~ **code pen** n DP crayon de
code à barres m; ~ **code reader** n PACKAGING lecteur
de code à barres m; ~ **code scanner** n COMP scanner de
code à barres m, DP lecteur de code à barres m; ~ **code
scanner and decoder logic** n PACKAGING logique de
lecture d'étiquetage avec code à barres f; ~ **facing tool**
n MECH ENG outil à dresser m; ~ **frame** n TEXTILES boîte
des barres f; ~ **generator** n TV générateur de mire de
barres m; ~ **hanger** n MECH ENG accrochage à barre m,

suspension à barre f; ~ **holes** n pl MECH ENG of capstan
logement de barre m; ~ **magnet** n PHYS aimant droit m,
barreau aimanté m; ~ **mill** n MECH ENG laminoir à
barres m, train de laminage d'aciers marchands m; ~
pattern n TV mire de barres f; ~ **screen** n HYDROL
sewage grille f, MECH ENG grille à barreaux f; ~ **shear** n
MECH ENG cisaille à barres f; ~ **shearing machine** n
MECH ENG machine à cisailler les barres f; ~ **shears** n pl
MECH ENG cisaille de mise à longueur des barres f; ~
turning tool n MECH ENG outil à charioter m; ~ **weir** n
WATER SUPP barrage à barreaux m; ~ **winding** n ELEC
armature enroulement à barres m
bar² vt HYDR EQUIP steam engine mettre en service
barbed: ~ **bolt** n CONST boulon de scellement à crans m; ~
wire n CONST fil de fer barbelé m, ronce f, ronce
artificielle f, MILIT fil de fer barbelé m; ~ **wire entanglement** n MILIT réseau de fil de fer barbelé m; ~ **wire nail** n
CONST clou barbelé m
barbiturate n CHEM barbiturate m, barbiturique m
barbituric¹ adj CHEM barbiturique
barbituric:² ~ **acid** n CHEM acide barbiturique m
Bardeen-Cooper-Schrieffer: ~ **theory** n (BCS theory)
ELECTRON, PHYS of super conductivity théorie BCS f
bare¹ adj ELEC ENG nu, PROD ENG dénudé
bare² n CONST pureau m, échantillon m; ~ **boat charter** n
NAUT, PETR TECH shipping affrètement en coque nue
m; ~ **conductor** n ELEC conducteur nu m; ~ **drain wire** n
ELEC, PROD ENG fil de masse nu m; ~ **hull** n AERONAUT
coque nue f; ~ **light** n CINEMAT lumière non tamisée f,
lumière non tramée f; ~ **metal** n METALL base d'alliage
f, métal de base m; ~ **particle** n NUCLEAR particule nue
f; ~ **reactor** n NUCLEAR réacteur nu m; ~ **wire** n ELEC
ENG fil non isolé m, fil nu m, TELECOM fil nu m
barefaced: ~ **tenon** n CONST tenon bâtard m, tenon
éhonté m
barefoot: ~ **completion** n PETR complétion en trou ouvert f
barge n NAUT allège f, barge f, chaland m, deuxième
canot m, gabare f, péniche f, PETR barge f, chaland m,
ponton m, TRANSP allège f, chaland m, gabare f,
péniche remorquée f; ~ **carrier** n NAUT type of ship
porte-barges m, TRANSP navire porte-chalands m,
porte-barges m; ~ **container** n TRANSP conteneur flottant m
barge-aboard-catamaran: ~ **ship** n (cf bacat ship)
TRANSP navire conteneur du type catamaran m, navire porteur de type catamaran m
barge-carrying: ~ **ship** n TRANSP navire porte-barges m
bargee n (BrE) (cf bargeman) NAUT on working barge
batelier m, marinier de chaland m, TRANSP marinier
de chaland m
bargeman n (AmE) (cf bargee) NAUT on working barge
batelier m, marinier de chaland m, TRANSP marinier
de chaland m
baric adj CHEM barytique
baring n MINING décapelage m, découverture f, dépouillement m, PAPER TECH barre espacée f
barite n MINERAL baryte f, PETR baryte f, spath pesant m
BARITT: ~ **diode** n (barrier injection transit time) PHYS
diode BARITT f
barium n (Ba) CHEM baryum m (Ba); ~ **chromate
pigment** n COLOURS pigment au chromate de baryum
m; ~ **monosulfite** n (AmE), ~ **monosulphite** n (BrE)
PRINT blanc permanent m
bark n PAPER TECH écorce f; ~ **boiler** n PAPER TECH
chaudière à écorces f; ~ **burner** n PAPER TECH chau-

dière à écorces *f*; ~ **power boiler** *n* PAPER TECH chaudière à écorces *f*; ~ **press** *n* PAPER TECH presse à écorces *f*; ~ **schooner** *n* (AmE) *see barque schooner*

barked: ~ **timber** *n* CONST bois pelard *m*

barker *n* PAPER TECH écorceuse *f*

barkevikite *n* MINERAL barkévicite *f*

Barkhausen: ~ **effect** *n* PHYS effet Barkhausen *m*

barking *n* PAPER TECH écorçage *m*; ~ **drum** *n* PAPER TECH tambour écorceur *m*

Barlow: ~ **lens** *n* ASTRON oculaire Barlow *m*

Barlow's: ~ **wheel** *n* PHYS roue de Barlow *f*

barn *n (b)* METR, PHYS barn *m (b)*

Barnard's: ~ **star** *n* ASTRON étoile Barnard *f*

barndoor *n* CINEMAT volet réglable *m*

Barnett: ~ **effect** *n* PHYS effet Barnett *m*

barney *n* CINEMAT couverture insonorisante pour caméra *f*

barnhardite *n* MINERAL barnhardite *f*

barnhardtite *n* MINERAL barnhardtite *f*

barodiffusion *n* NUCLEAR diffusion sous pression *f*, piézodiffusion *f*

barograph *n* LAB EQUIP barographe *m*, METEO barographe *m*, baromètre enregistreur *m*, NAUT, PHYS *recording barometer* barographe *m*, baromètre enregistreur *m*

barometer *n* LAB EQUIP, METEO, NAUT, PHYS baromètre *m*; ~ **reading** *n* NAUT hauteur barométrique *f*

barometric[1] *adj* PHYS barométrique

barometric:[2] ~ **altitude controller** *n* AERONAUT centrale baro-altimétrique *f*; ~ **column** *n* PAPER TECH colonne barométrique *f*; ~ **controller** *n* AERONAUT régulateur altimétrique *m*; ~ **height of pressure** *n* METEO hauteur barométrique *f*; ~ **leg** *n* PAPER TECH colonne barométrique *f*; ~ **maximum** *n* METEO région de haute pression *f*; ~ **pressure** *n* METEO pression barométrique *f*; ~ **switch** *n* AERONAUT commutateur barométrique *m*; ~ **trough** *n* METEO creux barométrique *m*

barometrical: ~ **variation** *n* METEO tendance barométrique *f*

baroscope *n* PHYS baroscope *m*

barostat *n* AERONAUT barostat *m*

barothermograph *n* PHYS barothermographe *m*

barotrauma *n* ACOUSTICS barotraumatisme *m*

barque: ~ **schooner** *n* (BrE) TRANSP trois-mâts goélette à huniers *m*

barracks *n pl* CONST baraque *f*, baraquement *m*, caserne *f*, MILIT baraquement *m*

barrage *n* CONST, HYDROL barrage *m*, MILIT *artillery* tir de barrage *m*, OCEANOG barrage *m*

barrandite *n* MINERAL barrandite *f*

barred: ~ **spiral galaxies** *n pl* ASTRON galaxies spirales barrées *f pl*

barrel *n* CONST *of Archimedean screw* canon *m*, *of key* canon *m*, *of lock* canon *m*, canon d'entrée de clé *m*, *of screw* tige *f*, FOOD TECH *machinery* baril *m*, barrique *f*, caque *f*, fût *m*, tonneau *m*, HYDR EQUIP *of cylinder, steam cylinder, hydraulic actuator* corps *m*, LAB EQUIP *of stopcock* canon *m*, MECH canon *m*, tambour *m*, MECH ENG *of boiler* corps cylindrique *m*, *of centre punch* canon de guidage *m*, *of capstan* cloche *f*, *of crab winch* tambour *m*, *of pump* barillet *m*, corps *m*, cylindre *m*, *of rolling mill* table *f*, *of the tailstock of* a lathe fourreau *m*, *of the headstock of a lathe* fourreau *m*, PETR baril *m*, TRANSP baril *m*, fût *m*; ~ **amalgamation** *n* PROD ENG amalgamation au tonneau *f*; ~ **bolt** *n* CONST *locksmithing* verrou à coquille *m*; ~ **buoy** *n* NAUT

navigation marks bouée tonne *f*; ~ **cam** *n* MECH ENG came cylindrique *f*; ~ **distortion** *n* CINEMAT, PHOTO, PHYS distorsion en barillet *f*; ~ **finishing** *n* PROD ENG polissage au tonneau *m*; ~ **key** *n* (AmE) *(cf pipe key)* CONST clef forée *f*; ~ **mixer** *n* FOOD TECH mélangeur à tonneau *m*; ~ **nipple** *n* MECH ENG *pipe fitting* double mamelon *m*; ~ **oil equivalent** *n (BOE)* PETR TECH *petrol* baril équivalent pétrole *m*; ~ **plating** *n* PROD ENG revêtement électrolytique à cuve rotative *m*; ~ **plotter** *n* (BrE) *(cf drum plotter)* COMP traceur à tambour *m*; ~ **printer** *n* (BrE) *(cf drum printer)* COMP, DP imprimante à tambour *f*; ~ **roller bearing** *n* MECH ENG roulement à rouleaux barriques *m*; ~ **spring** *n* SPRINGS ressort à barillet *m*; ~ **vault** *n* CONST berceau *m*

barrel-shaped: ~ **roller bearing** *n* MECH ENG roulement à rouleaux bombés *m*

Barremian *adj* GEOL *stratigraphy* barrémien

barren[1] *adj* COAL TECH, GEOL, MINING stérile

barren:[2] ~ **gangue** *n* COAL TECH gangue stérile *f*; ~ **ground** *n* MINING déblais de mine *m pl*, déchets *m pl*, rebuts *m pl*, stériles *m pl*; ~ **solution** *n* COAL TECH jus stérile *m*

barrette: ~ **file** *n* MECH ENG lime à barrettes *f*, lime à biseau *f*

barretter *n* ELEC *voltage stabilizer* barretter *m*, ELEC ENG barretter *m*, résistance ballast *f*, PHYS barretter *m*

barricade[1] *n* CONST barricade *f*, SAFETY barricade *f*, barrière *f*, obstacle *m*, SPACE merlon *m*

barricade[2] *vt* CONST, SAFETY barricader

barrier *n* CONST barrière *f*, MINING *stopping* arrêt-barrage *m*; ~ **beach** *n* GEOL cordon littoral *m*; ~ **film** *n* PACKAGING pellicule barrière *f*; ~ **grid** *n* ELECTRON grille d'arrêt *f*; ~ **grid storage tube** *n* ELECTRON tube à mémoire à grille *m*, tube à mémoire à grille d'arrêt *m*; ~ **layer** *n* ELECTRON couche d'arrêt *f*, OPT couche barrière *f*, POLLUTION couche-barrage *f*, TELECOM couche d'arrêt *f*; ~ **layer cell** *n* ELEC ENG cellule à couche d'arrêt *f*; ~ **material** *n* PACKAGING matériel barrière *m*; ~ **packaging** *n* PACKAGING conditionnement sous matériaux barrière *m*; ~ **reef** *n* OCEANOG récif-barrière *m*

barriness *n* TEXTILES barre *f*; ~ **in the weft** *n* TEXTILES barre de trame *f*

barrow *n* CONST brouette *f*, MINING halde *f*, halde de déblais *f*, halde de déchets *f*, TRANSP *luggage handling* chariot *m*

barrowful *n* CONST brouettée *f*

barrowing *n* CONST brouettage *m*

barrowload *n* CONST brouettée *f*

Bartlett: ~ **force** *n* NUCLEAR force de Bartlett *f*

bar-type: ~ **pickup base** *n* NUCLEAR capteur en forme de tige *m*; ~ **transformer** *n* ELEC transformateur en barres *m*

barycenter *n* (AmE), **barycentre** *n* (BrE) ASTRON, MATH *centre of mass* barycentre *m*, SPACE barycentre *m*, centre de masse *m*

barylite *n* MINERAL barylite *f*

baryon *n* PART PHYS, PHYS baryon *m* ~ **number** *n* PART PHYS, PHYS nombre baryonique *m*

barysphere *n* GEOPHYS barysphère *f*, nifé *m*, noyau terrestre *m*

barytes *n* C&G, CHEM, MINERAL baryte *f*, P&R *pigment* baryte *f*, spath lourd *m*, PETR TECH *drilling* baryte *f*, spath lourd *m*, spath pesant *m*

barytocalcite *n* MINERAL barytocalcite *f*

barytocelestine *n* MINERAL barytocélestine *f*

barytocelestite *n* MINERAL barytocélestine *f*
basal[1] *adj* GEOL basal
basal:[2] **~ plane** *n* METALL plan de base *m*, PROP MAT plan basal *m*; **~ slip** *n* METALL glissement basal *m*
basalt *n* GEOL, MINERAL, PETR, PROP MAT basalte *m*; **~ glass** *n* PETR basalte vitreux *m*, tachylite *f*
basaltic: ~ columns *n pl* GEOL orgues basaltiques *m pl*
basaltine *n* MINERAL basaltine *f*
basan *n* PRINT basane *f*
basanite *n* PETR basanite *f*
bascule *n* MECH ENG bascule *f*; **~ bridge** *n* CONST pont à bascule *m*
base:[1] **~ down** *adj* CINEMAT culot en bas
base[2] *n* C&G *of neck* base du col *f*, CHEM base *f*, CINEMAT *of film* support *m*, COMP base *f*, CONST *architecture* base *f*, fondement *m*, soubassement *m*, *block to receive fitting* bloc encastré *m*, embase *f*, patère *f*, *surveying* ligne d'opérations *f*, point fixé *m*, ELEC ENG *of electrode* base *f*, ELECTRON substrat *m*, *electronic tube* culot *m*, GEOM base *f*, INSTRUMENT embase *f*, pied *m*, socle-support *m*, MATH *as logarithm* base *f*, MECH ENG *of machine* bâti *m*, NUCLEAR, PHYS *of transistor* base *f*, PRINT semelle *f*, RECORDING *of tape* support *m*, TELECOM base *f*; **~ address** *n* COMP adresse de base *f*; **~ address register** *n* COMP registre d'adresse de base *m*; **~ cation** *n* POLLUTION cation basique *m*; **~ check** *n* AERONAUT petite visite *f*; **~ circle** *n* MECH ENG *of involute gear* cercle de base *m*; **~ coat** *n* P&R couche de fond *f*, première couche *f*, PROD ENG couche inférieure *f*; **~ contact** *n* ELEC ENG contact de base *m*; **~ course** *n* CONST *road construction* couche de base *f*; **~ cup** *n* PACKAGING coupelle *f*, embase *f*; **~ density** *n* CINEMAT densité de support *f*; **~ design** *n* NUCLEAR conception de base *f*; **~ diffusion** *n* ELECTRON *transistors* diffusion de la base *f*; **~ displacement** *n* COMP déplacement à la base *m*; **~ doping** *n* ELECTRON *transistors* dopage de la base *m*; **~ drive** *n* ELECTRON attaque de la base *f*; **~ drive signal** *n* ELECTRON signal appliqué à la base *m*; **~ electrode** *n* ELEC ENG électrode de base *f*; **~ failure** *n* COAL TECH rupture du sol *f*, CONST fracture de base *f*, rupture de base *f*, tassement *m*; **~ of figure** *n* GEOM base d'une figure *f*; **~ film** *n* TV support de bande *m*; **~ flow** *n* HYDROL *rate* débit de base *m*, écoulement de base *m*; **~ flow effect** *n* SPACE effet de culot *m*; **~ fog** *n* PHOTO voile de fond *m*; **~ frame** *n* NUCLEAR base *f*, châssis *m*, support *m*, support de base *m*; **~ glass** *n* C&G verre de base *m*; **~ impurities** *n pl* ELECTRON impuretés de la base *f pl*; **~ load boiler** *n* NUCLEAR chaudière de base *f*; **~ modulation** *n* ELECTRON modulation par la base *f*; **~ of operations** *n* PROD ENG base d'opérations *f*; **~ paper** *n* PAPER TECH papier de base *m*, papier support *m*, PRINT papier de base *m*, papier support *m*, support *m*; **~ of plummer block** *n* MECH ENG embase de palier *f*, semelle de palier *f*; **~ power** *n* NUCLEAR puissance de creux *f*; **~ region** *n* ELECTRON zone de la base *f*; **~ resistance** *n* ELEC ENG résistance de la base *f*; **~ scratch** *n* PHOTO rayure sur le support *f*; **~ station** *n* MILIT, TELECOM station de base *f*; **~ station controller** *n* TELECOM contrôleur de station de base *m*; **~ tint** *n* PRINT fond *m*, fond coloré *m*, grisé *m*, tramé *m*; **~ unit** *n* *(BU)* TELECOM coeur de chaîne *m*; **~ of verification** *n* CONST *triangulation* base de contrôle *f*; **~ volume** *n* TRANSP débit de base *m*; **~ wall** *n* CONST *architecture* mur de soubassement *m*; **~ washer** *n* MECH ENG rondelle de montage *f*; **~ widening** *n* ELECTRON épaississement de la base *m*; **~ width** *n* ELECTRON

épaisseur de la base *f*
base[3] *vi* PRINT *plate* préparer la gomme
baseband *n* COMP, ELECTRON, TELECOM, TV bande de base *f*; **~ modem** *n* COMP modem courte distance *m*, modem en bande de base *m*, TELECOM modem en bande de base *m*; **~ response function** *n* OPT, TELECOM fonction de réponse en bande de base *f*; **~ signal** *n* ELECTRON signal en bande de base *m*; **~ transfer function** *n* OPT, TELECOM fonction de transfert en bande de base *f*
baseboard *n* (AmE) *(cf skirting board)* CONST filet d'embase *m*, plinthe *f*, PHOTO margeur d'agrandisseur *m*, plateau de l'agrandisseur *m*
base-centered: ~ lattice *n* (AmE), **base-centred lattice** *n* (BrE) METALL réseau centré sur base *m*
baseline *n* CONST *surveying* base *f*, base d'opérations *f*, ligne d'opérations *f*, INSTRUMENT repère de ligne de marche *m*, NAUT *ship design, navigation* droit de hauteur *m*, ligne de base *f*, tracé de la quille hors membres *m*, PRINT ligne de base *f*; **~ inspection** *n* MECH état zéro *m*; **~ shift** *n* PETR changement de la ligne de base *m*
basement *n* GEOL socle *m*, PAPER TECH sous-sol *m*, PETR socle *m*, soubassement *m*; **~ complex** *n* GEOL socle métamorphique *m*; **~ wall** *n* CONST *architecture* mur de soubassement *m*
baseness *n* MINING *of ore* basse teneur *f*, faible teneur *f*, pauvreté *f*
baseplate *n* CINEMAT embase *f*, CONST plaque d'assise *f*, plaque de base *f*, plaque de fondation *f*, sole *f*, taque d'assise *f*, taque de soubassement *f*, INSTRUMENT base *f*, embase *f*, plaque de fixation *f*, socle *m*, MECH plaque d'embase *f*, MECH ENG plaque de base *f*, plaque de montage *f*, PAPER TECH plaque de fondation *f*; **~ for fine blanking** *n* MECH ENG *die set* plaque porte-matrice pour découpage fin *f*
base-to-mobile: ~ relay *n* TELECOM relais de passage *m*
basher *n* CINEMAT projecteur flood 500 watts *m*
basic[1] *adj* CHEM *salt, process* basique
basic:[2] **~ access** *n* TELECOM accès de base *m*; **~ amplifier** *n* ELECTRON amplificateur propre *m*; **~ bit rate** *n* TELECOM débit de base *m*; **~ call charge** *n* TELECOM frais de base *m pl*; **~ capacity** *n* TRANSP capacité de base *f*; **~ circuit diagram** *n* NUCLEAR schéma des connexions de base *m*; **~ coding** *n* COMP, DP codage de base *m*; **~ color** *n* (AmE), **~ colour** *n* (BrE) PAPER TECH colorant basique *m*; **~ coding** COMP, DP codage de base *m*; **~ dye** *n* CHEM, PAPER TECH, TEXTILES colorant basique *m*; **~ failure** *n* AERONAUT défaillance intrinsèque de base *f*; **~ fiber** *n* (AmE), **~ fibre** *n* (BrE) C&G fibre de base *f*; **~ frame alignment** *n* *(BFA)* TELECOM verrouillage de trame de base *m*; **~ frequency** *n* ELECTRON fréquence de base *f*, fréquence fondamentale *f*, TV fréquence fondamentale *f*; **~ group** *n* ELEC ENG groupe de base *m*, TELECOM groupe primaire *m*; **~ instrument flight trainer** *n* AERONAUT entraîneur primaire de vol aux instruments *m*; **~ legislation** *n* SAFETY législation de fond *f*; **~ lining** *n* METALL, PROP MAT garnissage basique *m*; **~ linkage** *n* COMP, DP liaison de base *f*; **~ open-hearth furnace** *n* C&G four Martin basique *m*; **~ petrochemicals** *n pl* PETR produits pétrochimiques de base *m pl*; **~ pig iron** *n* PROP MAT fonte phosphore *f*; **~ rack** *n* MECH ENG *gears* crémaillère de référence *f*; **~ rate access** *n* *(BRA)* TELECOM accès au débit de base *m*; **~ rate service** *n* TELECOM service au débit de base *m*; **~ triangle** *n* METALL triangle de base *m*; **~ weight** *n* PRINT *paper* poids de base *m*, poids spécifique *m*

BASIC *abbr (beginner's all-purpose symbolic instruction code)* COMP, DP BASIC
basicity *n* CHEM, PROP MAT basicité *f*
basification *n* CHEM désacidification *f*
basify *vt* CHEM rendre basique
basin *n* C&G, COAL TECH, GEOL, HYDROL bassin *m*, LAB EQUIP bassin *m*, *evaporation* capsule *f*, *glassware* cuvette *f*, PETR TECH bassin *m*, PROD ENG *of table* cuve *f*, WATER SUPP bassin *m*, cuvette *f*, vasque *f*
basin-and-range: ~ **structure** *n* GEOL structure à horsts et dépressions tectoniques *f*
basis: ~ **vector** *n* PHYS vecteur de base *m*; ~ **weight** *n* PAPER TECH grammage *m*
basket *n* SPACE nacelle *f*; ~ **centrifuge** *n* COAL TECH centrifugeuse à bol perforé *f*; ~ **coil** *n* ELEC ENG bobinage en fond de panier *m*; ~ **handle arch** *n* CONST arc en anse de panier *m*, voûte en anse de panier *f*, *of bridge* arche en anse de panier *f*; ~ **trap** *n* OCEANOG caseyeur *m*
basketweave: ~ **packing** *n* C&G empilage en tressage de panier *m*
Basov: ~ **diagram** *n* NUCLEAR diagramme de Basov *m*
bass *n* ACOUSTICS basse *f*, OCEANOG bourriche *f*, RECORDING grave *m*; ~ **boost** *n* ELECTRON renforcement des graves *m*; ~ **compensation** *n* RECORDING compensation des basses *f*; ~ **control** *n* CONTROL régulateur des graves *m*, RECORDING contrôle des basses *m*; ~ **cut** *n* RECORDING coupure des basses *f*; ~ **cut filter** *n* RECORDING filtre coupe-basses *m*; ~ **reflex enclosure** *n* RECORDING enceinte à basse réflexe *f*; ~ **response** *n* RECORDING réponse des basses *f*
bastard: ~ **cut** *n* MECH ENG *of file, rasp* taille bâtarde *f*; ~ **double** *n* PRINT fausses-doubles *f pl*; ~ **file** *n* MECH *tools* lime bâtarde *f*; ~ **pitch** *n* MECH ENG *of screw* pas bâtard *m*; ~ **size** *n* PAPER TECH format bâtard *m*, format hors norme *m*; ~ **title** *n* PRINT faux titre *m*
bastite *n* MINERAL bastite *f*
bastnaesite *n* MINERAL bastnaésite *f*
basyl *n* CHEM base oxygénée *f*
basyle *n* CHEM base oxygénée *f*
bat *n* CONST briqueton *m*; ~ **bolt** *n* CONST boulon de scellement à crans *m*
batardeau *n* CONST *cofferdam* bâtardeau *m*
batch[1] *n* C&G *of bricks* cuite *f*, *of glass-making raw materials* composition *f*, CINEMAT fabrication *f*, lot *m*, COMP, DP lot *m*, FOOD TECH batch *m*, charge *f*, fournée *f*, lot *m*, MECH lot *m*, P&R charge *f*, fournée *f*, PAPER TECH batée *f*, mélange de matières premières *m*, PETR TECH lot *m*, PRINT assortiment *m*, *computing* ensemble *m*, groupe *m*, lot *m*, PROD ENG gâchée *f*, lot *m*, série *f*, TELECOM lot *m*, TEXTILES passe de teinture *f*, TRANSP lot *m*; ~ **card** *n* PROD ENG ticket de mélange *m*; ~ **charger** *n* C&G enfourneuse *f*; ~ **code** *n* PACKAGING code de lot *m*; ~ **composition** *n* C&G formule de composition *f*; ~ **control** *n* CONTROL contrôle de lot *m*; ~ **crust** *n* C&G croûte de composition *f*; ~ **digester** *n* PAPER TECH lessiveur en discontinu *m*; ~ **distillation** *n* NUCLEAR distillation discontinue *f*; ~ **dust** *n* C&G volage *m*; ~ **extraction** *n* NUCLEAR extraction en discontinu *f*; ~ **file** *n* COMP fichier de commandes *m*, fichier séquentiel *m*; ~ **formula** *n* C&G formule de composition *f*; ~ **freezer** *n* FOOD TECH *food-processing machinery* congélateur discontinu *m*; ~ **fuel loading** *n* NUCLEAR *of reactor* chargement en discontinu *m*; ~ **furnace** *n* CHEM TECH four intermittent *m*, THERMOD four discontinu *m*, four à paquets *m*; ~ **house** *n* C&G

atelier de composition *m*; ~ **melting line** *n* (AmE) *(cf silica scum line)* C&G cordon de silice *m*; ~ **meltout line** *n* C&G cordon de silice *m*; ~ **mix** *n* CONST dosage volumétrique *m*, gâchis à centrale *m*; ~ **mixer** *n* C&G mélangeur *m*, CHEM TECH mélangeur en discontinu *m*, FOOD TECH *food-processing machinery* mélangeur discontinu *m*; ~ **mixing** *n* C&G mélange de la composition *m*; ~ **mode** *n* PROD ENG traitement automatique *m*, traitement différé *m*; ~ **number** *n* CONST, PACKAGING numéro de lot *m*; ~ **pile** *n* C&G borne *f* (Bel), motte *f* (Fra); ~ **plant** *n* CONST centrale à gâchage *f*, installation à trémies doseuses *f*; ~ **process** *n* PROD ENG production par lots *f*; ~ **processing** *n* CHEM TECH traitement intermittent *m*, COMP, DP traitement par lots *m*, PAPER TECH procédé discontinu *m*, PRINT traitement par lots *m*, traitement séquentiel *m*; ~ **pulper** *n* PAPER TECH triturateur en discontinu *m*; ~ **reactor** *n* NUCLEAR réacteur à chargement en discontinu *m*; ~ **roll** *n* PAPER TECH bobine en bout de machine *f*; ~ **sampling** *n* PROD ENG prélèvement par lots *m*; ~ **stone** *n* C&G infondu *m*; ~ **tabbing** *n* PACKAGING identification d'un lot *f*; ~ **test** *n* PROD ENG essai par lots *m*; ~ **total** *n* COMP, DP total de contrôle *m*; ~ **tower** *n* C&G tour de composition *f*; ~ **wetting** *n* C&G humidification de la composition *f*
batch:[2] ~ **off** *vi* CHEM TECH enlever du malaxeur
batch-free *adj* C&G fondu
batching: ~ **tank** *n* NUCLEAR réservoir de préparation *m*
batch-type: ~ **freezer** *n* REFRIG congélateur discontinu *m*, congélateur à crème glacée *m*
batchwise: ~ **operation** *n* CHEM TECH, FOOD TECH opération discontinue *f*
bath *n* C&G *of glass tank furnace*, CINEMAT *of chemicals*, PRINT, TEXTILES bain *m*; ~ **atmosphere** *n* C&G gaz protecteur *m*
batholic *n* GEOPHYS batholite *m*
batholith *n* PETR batholite *m*
bathometer *n* OCEANOG, PHYS bathomètre *m*, bathymètre *m*
Bathonian *adj* GEOL *stratigraphy* bathonien
bathymeter *n* OCEANOG, PHYS bathomètre *m*, bathymètre *m*
bathymetric: ~ **chart** *n* NAUT *navigation* carte bathymétrique *f*
bathymetry *n* FUELLESS, NAUT, OCEANOG bathymétrie *f*
bathyscaph *n* OCEANOG bathyscaphe *m*
bathysphere *n* OCEANOG bathysphère *f*
bathytachymetry *n* OCEANOG bathycélérimétrie *f*
bathythermograph *n* OCEANOG bathythermographe *m*
bathythermography *n* OCEANOG bathythermographie *f*
bathythermy *n* OCEANOG bathythermie *f*
batt *n* TEXTILES nappe *f*; ~ **anchorage** *n* TEXTILES accrochage de la nappe *m*; ~ **anchorage testing device** *n* TEXTILES dispositif test d'accrochage *m*
batten[1] *n* CINEMAT latte *f*, CONST *carpentry, steelwork* liteau *m*, réglette *f*, *roofing* carrelet *m*, *slate lath* latte volige *f*, volige *f*, MECH ENG éclisse *f*, NAUT *sail, cargo handling* latte *f*; ~ **pocket** *n* NAUT *of sail* gaine de latte *f*, étui de latte *m*
batten[2] *vt* CONST voliger; ~ **down** *vt* NAUT *hatches* condamner
battening *n* CONST voligeage *m*
batter[1] *n* C&G *of wall* adossement *m*, CONST *of wall* fruit *m*, talus *m*
batter[2] *vt* CONST damer, taluter, MECH ENG mater
batter[3] *vi* CONST donner du fruit à

battering n CONST of ditch talutage m, upsetting refoulement m

battery n AUTO, CHEM batterie f, COMP accumulateur m, ELEC collection of cells batterie f, single cell pile f, ELEC ENG accumulateur m, batterie f, ELECTRON batterie d'accumulateurs f, HYDR EQUIP accumulateur m, MECH ENG batterie f, of rolls, cylinders batterie f, jeu m, train m, MINING plancher de manoeuvre m, stamps batterie f, NAUT electricity accumulateur m, electrics, guns batterie f, PAPER TECH accumulateur m, PHOTO batterie f, PHYS accumulateur m, batterie f, pile f, REFRIG accumulateur tampon m, bouteille tampon f, réservoir tampon m, vase tampon f, SPACE spacecraft accumulateur m, batterie f, TELECOM batterie d'accumulateurs f, pile f, VEHICLES accumulateur m, batterie f; ~ **assembly** n PROD ENG ensemble pile m; ~ **backup** n ELEC ENG alimentation de secours par batterie f, PROD ENG pile de sauvegarde f; ~ **belt** n CINEMAT batterie de ceinture f; ~ **box** n AUTO coffre de batterie m, PAPER TECH cuve d'accumulateur f; ~ **bus** n TRANSP autobus à accumulateur m; ~ **cable** n CINEMAT câble de batterie m; ~ **cell** n AUTO élément de batterie m, ELEC of accumulator élément d'accumulateur m, ELEC ENG cellule de batterie f, élément d'accumulateur m, SPACE spacecraft élément d'accumulateur m, élément électrochimique m; ~ **chamber** n PHOTO logement de pile m; ~ **chamber cover** n PHOTO of camera couvercle du logement de la pile m; ~ **changeover relay** n AUTO coupleur de batteries m; ~ **charge** n ELEC charge d'accumulateur f, ELEC ENG charge de batterie f; ~ **charger** n ELEC ENG, PHOTO, TRANSP chargeur de batterie m; ~ **charging** n SPACE spacecraft charge des accumulateurs f; ~ **check** n CINEMAT contrôle de charge de batterie m; ~ **clip** n ELEC ENG pince à batterie f; ~ **compartment cover** n PHOTO couvercle du logement de la pile m; ~ **condition** n TELECOM état des batteries m; ~ **cradle** n AUTO support de batterie m; ~ **discharge** n ELEC décharge d'accumulateur f, SPACE spacecraft décharge des accumulateurs f; ~ **drain** n SPACE spacecraft débit d'accumulateurs f; ~ **drive** n CINEMAT entraînement par batterie m; ~ **exchange point** n TRANSP station d'échange de batteries f; ~ **fuse** n MINING amorce de quantité f, amorce à fil f; ~ **grip** n PHOTO poignée à piles f; ~ **holder** n PROD ENG logement de pile m; ~ **house** n MINING ore-stamping atelier des bocards m; ~ **housing** n ELEC, PROD ENG porte-piles m; ~ **ignition** n AUTO allumage par batterie m; ~ **jar** n C&G bac d'accumulateur m; ~ **loading point** n TRANSP station-service batterie f; ~ **load switch** n CONTROL disjoncteur de batterie m, interrupteur de charge m; ~ **low LED** n PROD ENG DEL seuil bas de pile f; ~ **master switch** n AUTO robinet de batterie m; ~ **operation** n ELEC ENG alimentation par pile f, fonctionnement sur pile m; ~ **pack** n CINEMAT bloc de batteries m, PHOTO accumulateur m, PROD ENG bloc porte-piles m, ensemble porte-piles m; ~ **plate** n AUTO plaque de batterie f, ELEC ENG plaque d'accumulateur f, plaque de batterie f; ~ **of rolls** n MECH ENG mill train de cylindres de laminage m, train de laminage m; ~ **switch** n CONTROL disjoncteur de batterie m, interrupteur de charge m, PHOTO interrupteur de batterie m; ~ **terminal** n AUTO, ELEC ENG, PHOTO borne de batterie f; ~ **terminal pliers** n pl MECH ENG tool pince à cosse de batterie f; ~ **transfer bus** n SPACE spacecraft bus de transfert d'énergie m; ~ **truck** n TRANSP camion à accumulateur m; ~ **vehicle** n ELEC ENG véhicule à batterie m

battery-powered[1] adj CINEMAT, ELEC ENG alimenté par batterie

battery-powered:[2] ~ **electric vehicle** n TRANSP véhicule électrique à accumulateur m; ~ **flash unit** n PHOTO flash électronique à accumulateur m; ~ **moped** n TRANSP bicyclette électrique f; ~ **viewer** n PHOTO visionneuse à pile sèche f

batting: ~ **down** n TV fonçage des noirs m

battle: ~ **cruiser** n NAUT croiseur de bataille m; ~ **sight** n MILIT on gun hausse de combat f

battledore n C&G planche f

baud n COMP, DP, PRINT baud m; ~ **rate** n COMP, DP vitesse de transmission en bauds f

baulite n PETR baulite f

baulk n (BrE) CONST timber bois équarri m, forte pièce de bois équarri f, forte pièce équarrie f, poutre f, tronc d'arbre équarri m

Baum: ~ **box** n COAL TECH bac de type Baum m; ~ **jig** n COAL TECH bac à air comprimé m, bac à pistonnage de type Baum m; ~ **washbox** n COAL TECH bac à air comprimé m

Baumé: ~ **scale** n FOOD TECH, PHYS hydrometry échelle Baumé f

bauxite n C&G, CHEM, MINERAL, PETR bauxite f

BAW abbr (bulk acoustic wave) ELEC ENG onde acoustique en volume f

bay n CONST civil engineering travée f, recess alcôve f, empochement m, FUELLESS, HYDROL baie f, MECH in workshop travée f, NAUT geography baie f, SPACE soute f, TELECOM baie f; ~ **bolt** n CONST boulon de scellement à crans m

Bayard-Alpert: ~ **ionization gage** n (AmE), ~ **ionization gauge** n (BrE) NUCLEAR manomètre à ionisation Bayard-Alpert m

Bayes': ~ **theorem** n MATH formule de Bayes f, formule de la probabilité des causes f

bay-mouth: ~ **bar** n OCEANOG barre littorale f

bayonet n ELEC ENG baïonnette f; ~ **base** n ELEC ENG, PHOTO culot à baïonnette m; ~ **cap** n ELEC of light bulb culot à baïonnette m; ~ **cap finish** n C&G bague de baïonnette f; ~ **catch** n MECH, PACKAGING verrouillage à baïonnette m; ~ **closure** n NUCLEAR of coolant channel emboîtement à baïonnette m; ~ **coupling** n ELEC ENG verrouillage par baïonnette m; ~ **fitting** n CONST of light bulb douille à baïonnette f; ~ **joint** n ELEC joint à baïonnette m; ~ **lamp holder** n ELEC douille à baïonnette f; ~ **mount** n CINEMAT, PHOTO monture à baïonnette f; ~ **socket** n CINEMAT, ELEC light, PHOTO douille à baïonnette f

Bazin's: ~ **formula** n HYDR EQUIP formule de Bazin f

BBD abbr (bucket brigade device) ELEC ENG, TELECOM dispositif de transfert à la chaîne m

BC abbr PETR TECH (bit change) drilling changement d'outil m, TELECOM (bearer channel) voie porteuse f, voie support f, TELECOM (broadcast) émission f

bcc: ~ **lattice** n CRYSTALL réseau ccc m

BCD abbr (binary-coded decimal) COMP DCB (décimal codé binaire)

B-channel n TELECOM information channel canal B m; ~ **virtual circuit service** n TELECOM service CVB m, service de circuit virtuel sur canal B m

BCS: ~ **theory** n (Bardeen-Cooper-Schrieffer theory) ELECTRON of superconductivity, PHYS théorie BCS f

BCU abbr (big close up) CINEMAT très gros plan m

BDC abbr (bottom dead center, bottom dead centre) MECH PMB (point mort bas)

Be *(beryllium)* CHEM Be *(béryllium)*

beach[1] *n* GEOL, NAUT *geography, shiphandling* plage *f*; ~ **berm** *n* GEOL gradin de plage *m*, terrasse de plage *f*; ~ **buggy** *n* TRANSP chariot des dunes *m*; ~ **cusp** *n* OCEANOG croissant de plage *m*; ~ **fishing** *n* OCEANOG pêche à pied *f*; ~ **growth** *n* OCEANOG crue de plage *f*; ~ **ridge** *n* OCEANOG cordon littoral *m*, crête de plage *f*, levée de plage *f*; ~ **rock** *n* GEOL dépôt de plage induré *m*, OCEANOG grès de plage *m*; ~ **seine** *n* OCEANOG lampara *m*, senne de plage *f*

beach[2] *vt* NAUT échouer volontairement

beaching: ~ **leg** *n* NAUT béquille *f*

beacon[1] *n* CONST *surveying* balise *f*, NAUT *navigation marks* balise *f*, *on coast* fanal *m*, RAIL, SPACE balise *f*, TRANSP phare *m*; ~ **generator** *n* SPACE *spacecraft* générateur de balise *m*

beacon[2] *vt* CONST baliser

beaconing *n* CONST balisage *m*, balisement *m*

bead[1] *n* C&G *in fiberizing glass* goutte *f*, *of glass* perle *f*, *on bottle* contre-bague *f*, COMP tore magnétique *m*, CONST *joinery* baguette *f*, MECH *welding* cordon de soudure *m*, MECH ENG boule *f*, bourrelet *m*, PROD ENG *moulder's tool* gouge *f*, VEHICLES *of tyre* talon *m*; ~ **core** *n* AUTO tringle de talon *f*; ~ **down** *n* C&G perle descendue *f* (Bel), rupture totale due à la goutte *f* (Fra); ~ **polymerization** *n* NUCLEAR polymérisation en perles *f*; ~ **tool** *n* PROD ENG *moulder's tool* gouge *f*

bead:[2] ~ **over** *vt* CONST rabattre la collerette de

beaded[1] *adj* PROD ENG perlé

beaded:[2] ~ **bevel** *n* C&G biseau avec olives *m*; ~ **chain** *n* MECH ENG chaînette à boules *f*; ~ **esker** *n* GEOL esker en chapelet *m*; ~ **extrusion** *n* MECH ENG profilé à boudin *m*; ~ **screen** *n* CINEMAT, PHOTO écran perlé *m*

beak: ~ **iron** *n* MECH ENG bigorne *f*

beaker *n* C&G, CHEM, FOOD TECH bécher *m*, vase *m*, LAB EQUIP *glassware*, PAPER TECH bécher *m*; ~ **holder** *n* LAB EQUIP pince à bécher *f*; ~ **with spout** *n* LAB EQUIP *glassware* bécher à bec *m*

beaker-type: ~ **container** *n* PROD ENG récipient style bécher *m*

beam[1] *n* CINEMAT faisceau *m*, rayon *m*, CONST *small* poutre *f*, solive *f*, CRYSTALL, ELECTRON *unidirectional flux* faisceau *m*, GAS TECH poutre *f*, MECH ENG poutre *f*, *of machine* balancier *m*, METR *of balance or scale* fléau *m*, NAUT *ship, lighthouse* bau *m*, faisceau *m*, largeur *f*, *transverse member of ship's frame* barrot *m*, PART PHYS *of particles* faisceau *m*, PHYS *girder* poutre *f*, *of particles* faisceau *m*, PRINT faisceau lumineux *m*, poutre *f*, RAD PHYS *of radiation* faisceau *m*, faisceau de rayonnement *m*, SPACE *communications*, TELECOM faisceau *m*, TEXTILES ensouple *f*, TV faisceau *m*; ~ **alignment** *n* TV alignement du faisceau *m*, centrage de faisceau *m*; ~ **and scales** *n* METR balance à fléau *f*; ~ **angle** *n* ELECTRON angle d'ouverture du faisceau *m*, angle de radiation *m*, ouverture angulaire du faisceau *f*; ~ **attenuation** *n* ELECTRON atténuation du faisceau *f*; ~ **balance** *n* METR balance à fléau *f*; ~ **blanking** *n* ELECTRON, TV suppression du faisceau *f*; ~ **bracket** *n* NAUT *shipbuilding* gousset de barrot *m*, gousset de pont *m*; ~ **caliper** *n* (AmE) *see beam calliper*; ~ **caliper gage** *n* (AmE) *see beam calliper gauge*; ~ **calliper** *n* (BrE) METR calibre à coulisse *m*, compas à coulisse *m*, mesure à coulisse *f*, pied à coulisse *m*, équerre à coulisse *f*; ~ **calliper gauge** *n* (BrE) METR calibre à coulisse *m*, compas à coulisse *m*, mesure à coulisse *f*, pied à coulisse *m*, équerre à coulisse *f*; ~ **capture** *n*

AERONAUT prise d'un faisceau *f*; ~ **compasses** *n pl* METR *with adjusting screw* compas à verge *m*; ~ **cutoff** *n* TV coupure du faisceau *f*; ~ **diameter** *n* OPT diamètre d'un faisceau *m*; ~ **divergence** *n* OPT, TELECOM divergence *f*; ~ **dividers** *n pl* MECH ENG *tool* compas à verge *m*; ~ **drive** *n* MECH ENG commande par balancier *f*; ~ **dyeing** *n* TEXTILES teinture sur ensouple *f*; ~ **dyeing machine** *n* TEXTILES appareil à teindre sur ensouple *m*; ~ **engine** *n* MECH ENG machine à balancier *f*; ~ **fixed at one end** *n* MECH ENG poutre encastrée à une extrémité *f*; ~ **focusing** *n* ELECTRON focalisation du faisceau *f*; ~ **forming** *n* ELECTRON formation du faisceau *f*; ~ **gate** *n* TV blocage du faisceau *m*; ~ **hook** *n* PROD ENG *of foundry beam* crochet de balancier *m*; ~ **impact point** *n* TV point d'impact du faisceau *m*; ~ **injection** *n* NUCLEAR injection de faisceau *f*; ~ **intercept** *n* AERONAUT attaque d'un faisceau *f*; ~ **jitter** *n* TV fluctuation du faisceau *f*; ~ **knee** *n* NAUT *shipbuilding* gousset de barrot *m*, gousset de pont *m*; ~ **lead** *n* ELECTRON chips patte de puce *f*; ~ **lead chip** *n* ELECTRON puce à pattes *f*; ~ **lead device** *n* ELECTRON composant à conducteurs poutres *m*, composant à pattes *m*; ~ **loading** *n* TV charge du faisceau *f*; ~ **model** *n* RAD PHYS *atomic nucleus* modèle de faisceaux *m*; ~ **pattern** *n* TV figure d'interférence *f*; ~ **plasma interaction** *n* NUCLEAR interaction faisceau-plasma *f*; ~ **power** *n* ELECTRON puissance du faisceau *f*; ~ **power density** *n* ELECTRON densité de puissance du faisceau *f*; ~ **pulser** *n* NUCLEAR *for bursts of photons* hacheur de faisceau *m*, système de pulsation de faisceau *m*; ~ **reactor** *n* NUCLEAR réacteur à faisceau sorti *m*; ~ **return** *n* TV retour du faisceau *m*; ~ **reversing lens** *n* TV optique inverseuse de faisceau *f*; ~ **scales** *n pl* METR balance à fléau *f*; ~ **scanning** *n* ELECTRON balayage par faisceau *m*; ~ **sea** *n* NAUT houle par le travers *f*, mer de travers *f*; ~ **shaft** *n* TEXTILES axe d'ensouple *m*; ~ **shaping** *n* ELECTRON mise en forme du faisceau *f*; ~ **signal** *n* ELECTRON signal du faisceau *m*; ~ **splitter** *n* CINEMAT, OPT diviseur du faisceau *m*, PRINT assemblage de prismes diffractant la lumière *m*, TV diviseur du faisceau *m*; ~ **splitting** *n* ELECTRON division de faisceau *f*; ~ **support** *n* METR *of delicate balance* fourchette *f*, trébuchet *m*; ~ **switching** *n* SPACE *communications* commutation de faisceaux *f*; ~ **tilt** *n* TV *of aerial system* inclinaison du diagramme *f*; ~ **well** *n* PETR TECH puits à balancier *m*; ~ **width** *n* ELECTRON, OPT largeur du faisceau *f*

beam[2] *vt* ELECTRON *emit* rayonner, rayonner en faisceau, émettre

beamed: ~ **yarn** *n* C&G fil sur ensouple *m*

beamer *n* TEXTILES machine d'ensouplage *f*

beaming *n* TEXTILES mise sur ensouple *f*

beam-positioning: ~ **magnet** *n* TV aimant de convergence *m*; ~ **system** *n* TV système déflecteur du faisceau *m*

beams *n pl* CONST poutrage *m*, poutraison *f*, solivage *m*

beam-splitting: ~ **prism** *n* CINEMAT prisme diviseur *m*; ~ **prisms** *n pl* INSTRUMENT prismes de déviation *m pl*; ~ **system** *n* CINEMAT système de division de faisceau *m*, système de prisme diviseur *m*

beam-to-beam: ~ **sizing** *n* TEXTILES encollage de chaînes sectionnelles *m*

bean *n* PETR duse *f*

bear[1] *n* C&G loup *m*, PROD ENG carcas *m*, cochon *m*, loup *m*

bear[2] *vt* MECH ENG supporter; ~ **down on** *vt* NAUT *sailing* courir sur

bear:³ ~ **away** *vi* NAUT *sailing* abattre, laisser arriver, laisser porter; ~ **down** *vi* NAUT *sailing* foncer; ~ **stock-holding costs** *vi* TEXTILES supporter les coûts des stocks

bearded: ~ **needle frame** *n* TEXTILES bâti des aiguilles à bec *m*

bearding *n* TV filage *m*

bearer *n* MECH ENG *of rolling mill* cage de laminoir *f*, colonne de laminoir *f*, MINING *timbering* porteuse *f*, PRINT cordon de cylindre *m*, porteur *m*, PROD ENG *of grate bars of furnace* barreau dormant *m*, sommier *m*; ~ **bracket** *n* PROD ENG *of grate* galoche *f*; ~ **capacity** *n* TELECOM capacité du support *f*; ~ **channel** *n* (*BC*) TELECOM voie porteuse *f*, voie support *f*; ~ **cradle** *n* PROD ENG *of grate* galoche *f*; ~ **height** *n* PRINT creux du cylindre *m*; ~ **service** *n* TELECOM service support *m*; ~ **set** *n* MINING cadre porteur *m*

bearers *n pl* PRINT métal mort *m*

bearer-to-bearer *n* PRINT cordon-sur-cordon *m*

bearing *n* CONST orientation *f*, ELEC *of machine* palier *m*, GEOL azimut *m*, MECH coussinet *m*, palier *m*, MECH ENG coussinet *m*, *of shaft, axle* palier *m*, roulement *m*, MINING *of lode, mine level* direction *f*, orientation *f*, NAUT *navigation* relèvement *m*, PAPER TECH roulement *m*, PRINT coussinet *m*, palier *m*, roulement *m*, PROD ENG *of core print* porte-noyau *m*, portée *f*, portée de noyau *f*, portée de remmoulage *f*,   RAIL coussinet *m*, VEHICLES coussinet *m*, palier *m*, tourillon *m*; ~ **and power transfer assembly** *n* (*BAPTA*) SPACE *spacecraft* mécanisme d'entraînement du générateur solaire *m*; ~ **axle box** *n* (BrE) (*cf bearing journal box*) RAIL *vehicles* boîte d'essieu à coussinets *f*; ~ **block** *n* MECH ENG palier *m*; ~ **bracket** *n* PROD ENG support de coussinet *m*; ~ **bush** *n* MECH ENG coussinet *m*; ~ **cage** *n* MECH ENG cage de roulement *f*; ~ **cap** *n* AUTO chapeau de palier *m*, MECH ENG chapeau de palier *m*, couvercle de palier *m*; ~ **capacity** *n* COAL TECH charge maximale *f*, portance *f*, CONST *of pile* capacité portante *f*; ~ **compass** *n* NAUT *navigation* compas de relèvement *m*; ~ **end** *n* MECH ENG *of shaft, axle* portée d'arbre *f*, portée d'axe *f*; ~ **housing** *n* PAPER TECH logement de palier *m*; ~ **journal box** *n* (AmE) (*cf bearing axle box*) RAIL boîte d'essieu à coussinets *f*; ~ **lined with antifriction metal** *n* MECH ENG palier garni d'alliage antifriction *m*; ~ **lining** *n* MECH garniture de coussinet *f*; ~ **lubrication system** *n* PROD ENG système de graissage des paliers *m*; ~ **marker** *n* NAUT *radar* alidade *f*; ~ **materials** *n pl* MECH ENG matériaux pour paliers *m pl*; ~ **pad** *n* MECH patin de palier de butée *m*; ~ **plate** *n* MECH ENG *disc-shaped* disque d'appui *m*; ~ **point** *n* MECH ENG point d'appui *m*; ~ **race** *n* MECH ENG bague de roulement *f*; ~ **rail** *n* TRANSP rail porteur *m*; ~ **RTD** *n* PROD ENG PTC pour paliers *m*; ~ **surface** *n* MECH ENG palier *m*, portée *f*, surface de frottement *f*, surface frottante *f*, surface portante *f*, SPRINGS *of spring* surface d'appui *f*

bearings *n pl* CONST *of several faces of building* orientations *f pl*, *situation with respect to points of compass* orientation *f*, MECH ENG paliers *m pl*, METR *of a balance* chape *f*, PRINT paliers *m pl*

beat¹ *n* ACOUSTICS battement *m*, AERONAUT *of engine* battement régulier *m*, ELECTRON, PHYS battement *m*; ~ **frequency** *n* ELECTRON, PHYS, RECORDING fréquence de battement *f*; ~ **frequency oscillator** *n* (*BFO*) AERONAUT oscillateur à battement de fréquence *m*, ELECTRON oscillateur de battement *m*, PHYS oscilla-

teur hétérodyne *m*, RECORDING oscillateur à battement de fréquence *m*, TELECOM oscillateur à battement *m*, TV oscillateur hétérodyne *m*; ~ **frequency wavemeter** *n* WAVE PHYS ondemètre hétérodyne *m*; ~ **note** *n* WAVE PHYS son de battement *m*; ~ **note detector** *n* ELECTRON détecteur de battement *m*; ~ **note pitch** *n* WAVE PHYS hauteur du son de battement *f*; ~ **signal** *n* ELECTRON signal de battement *m*

beat² *vt* ELECTRON battre, PAPER TECH raffiner, TEXTILES *carpet* battre

beat³ *vi* NAUT *sailing* louvoyer

beatability *n* PAPER TECH aptitude au raffinage *f*

beaten *adj* PAPER TECH raffiné

beater *n* CONST *platelayer's* batte des chemins de fer *f*, bourroir *m*, pioche à bourrer *f*, pioche à tasser et pointue *f*, *plumber's mallet* batte *f*, batte-plate *f*, rabattoir *m*, PAPER TECH pile raffineuse *f*; ~ **bar** *n* PAPER TECH lame de pile *f*; ~ **plate** *n* PAPER TECH platine de pile *f*; ~ **roll** *n* PAPER TECH cylindre de pile raffineuse *m*

beater-breaker *n* PAPER TECH broyeur *m*, pile désagrégeante *f*

beating *n* ELECTRON battement *m*, PAPER TECH raffinage *m*, PROD ENG *into shape* battage *m*, emboutissage *m*; ~ **hammer** *n* MECH ENG marteau-batte *m*; ~ **pick** *n* CONST *platelayer's* batte des chemins de fer *f*, bourroir *m*, pioche à bourrer *f*

Beaufort: ~ **scale** *n* METEO, NAUT échelle Beaufort *f*

beaumontage *n* PROD ENG *iron putty* mastic de fonte *m*

beaumontite *n* PETR beaumontite *f*

beauty: ~ **quark** *n* PART PHYS, PHYS quark de beauté *m*

becket *n* NAUT *ropes* ganse *f*, patte *f*, patte de ris *f*, petite erse *f*; ~ **bend** *n* NAUT *knot* noeud d'écoute *m*

Beckmann: ~ **rearrangement** *n* CHEM *of ketoxime* réarrangement Beckmann *m*; ~ **thermometer** *n* PHYS thermomètre de Beckmann *m*

BECN *abbr* (*backward explicit congestion notification*) TELECOM notification d'encombrement explicite émise vers l'arrière *f*

become: ~ **effective** *vi* MECH ENG entrer en vigueur, prendre effet

becquerel *n* (*Bq*) METR, PHYS, RAD PHYS becquerel *m* (*Bq*)

Becquerel: ~ **effect** *n* ELEC *electrolytic cell* effet Becquerel *m*

bed¹ *n* COAL TECH couche *f*, CONST assise *f*, fondation *f*, lit *m*, gisement *m*, gîte *m*, masse *f*, GEOL couche *f*, niveau *m*, strate *f*, HYDROL *of river* lit *m*, *of watercourse* bas *m*, bas-fond *m*, mouille *f*, MECH ENG banc *m*, *of machine tool* bâti *m*, OCEANOG souille *f*, PETR TECH *geology* litage *m*, PRINT *liquid* solution de gomme adragante *f*, *of press* lit *m*, marbre *m*; ~ **bars** *n pl* MECH ENG *of lathe* tirants de bâti *m pl*; ~ **of clay** *n* CONST couche d'argile *f*; ~ **gage** *n* (AmE), ~ **gauge** *n* (BrE) METEO *measuring* table de mesure *f*; ~ **knife** *n* PAPER TECH contre-lame *f*; ~ **lathe** *n* MECH ENG tour à bâti *m*; ~ **load** *n* GEOL charge de fond *f*; ~ **load transport** *n* HYDROL charriage de fond *m*, transport de fond *m*; ~ **roll** *n* PAPER TECH rouleau support *m*; ~ **sequence** *n* COAL TECH succession des couches *f*; ~ **sizes** *n pl* TEXTILES dimensions des lits *f pl*

bed² *vt* CONST *foundations* asseoir; ~ **in** *vt* PROD ENG *founding* fixer; ~ **out** *vt* CONST *masonry* appareiller, appliquer, cimenter, maçonner

bed:³ ~ **in a gun** *vi* MILIT *artillery* asseoir une pièce

bedding *n* ELEC *cable* matelas *m*, MILIT *artillery* assise *f*, PETR stratification *f*; ~ **in** *n* PROD ENG moulage en fosse *m*; ~ **mortar** *n* CONST couche de mortier *f*, joint d'assise *m*, mortier de pose *m*; ~ **surface** *n* CONST surface d'assise *f*

bedplate *n* CONST plaque d'appui *f*, plaque d'assise *f*, plaque de fondation *f*, MECH ENG *of engine* plaque de base *f*, NAUT *of engine* plaque de fondation *f*, PAPER TECH platine de pile *f*, PETR TECH *offshore drilling* plaque de base *f*, PROD ENG *of loam mould* assise *f*; ~ **box** *n* PAPER TECH boîte à platine *f*

bedrock *n* PETR TECH soubassement *m*, WATER SUPP bed-rock *m*

bed-type: ~ **surfacing and boring lathe** *n* MECH ENG tour en l'air sur banc *m*

beef *n* GEOL filons de calcite fibreux *m pl*

beehive: ~ **kiln** *n* C&G four à ruche *m*; ~ **oven** *n* PROD ENG *coking* four à ruche *m*

beep: ~ **switch** *n* AERONAUT *on cycle stick* interrupteur pas-à-pas *m*; ~ **tone** *n* CINEMAT bip *m*

beeper: ~ **trim** *n* AERONAUT *of helicopter* rappel de manche *m*

beer: ~ **cooler** *n* REFRIG refroidisseur à bière *m*

beetle *n* CONST *paviour's rammer* marteau *m*; ~ **head** *n* CONST tête de marteau *f*

before: ~ **and after study** *n* TRANSP étude avant-après *f*

beginner's: ~ **all-purpose symbolic instruction code** *n* *(BASIC)* COMP *programming language*, DP BASIC

beginning: ~ **of call demand** *n* TELECOM début de la demande d'appel *m*; ~ **of life** *n* NUCLEAR *of core* début de vie *m*; ~ **of message** *n* *(BOM)* COMP, TELECOM début de message *m*; ~ **of tape** *n* *(BOT)* COMP, DP début de bande *m*

beginning-of-tape: ~ **marker** *n* DP marqueur de début de bande *m*

behavior *n* (AmE), **behaviour** *n* (BrE) CONST *of structure*, MAR POLL *of oil slick*, PRINT comportement *m*

beheaded: ~ **river** *n* WATER SUPP rivière capturée *f*

behenic *adj* CHEM béhénique

beidellite *n* MINERAL beidellite *f*

bel *n* ACOUSTICS, ELEC ENG, PHYS, RAD PHYS bel *m*

belay *vt* NAUT *rope* amarrer

belaying: ~ **cleat** *n* NAUT taquet de tournage *m*; ~ **pin** *n* NAUT *deck equipment* cabillot *m*

bell *n* PROD ENG *of blast furnace* cloche *f*, PROP MAT *blast furnace* cône *m*; ~ **buoy** *n* NAUT *navigation marks* bouée sonore à cloche *f*; ~ **centering punch** *n* (AmE), ~ **centring punch** *n* (BrE) MECH ENG poinçon à cloche de centrage *m*; ~ **character** *n* DP caractère de sonnerie *m*; ~ **chuck** *n* MECH ENG *of lathe* mandrin à mors étagés *m*; ~ **code signaling** *n* (AmE), ~ **code signalling** *n* (BrE) RAIL signalisation par cloches *f*; ~ **cone** *n* C&G cône creux *m*; ~ **crank** *n* AERONAUT *helicopter* guignol *m*, guignol d'angle *m*, MECH ENG levier coudé *m*, renvoi de sonnette *m*; ~ **crank block** *n* MECH ENG relais mécanique *m*; ~ **crank system** *n* MECH système à genouillère *m*; ~ **furnace** *n* PROD ENG four à cloche *m*; ~ **gear** *n* MECH ENG pignon cloche *m*; ~ **jar** *n* C&G *for clock* globe de pendule *m*, CHEM, LAB EQUIP *glassware* cloche *f*; ~ **mouth** *n* MECH ENG, SPACE *spacecraft* buse d'entrée *f*; ~ **push** *n* CONTROL bouton de sonnerie *m*; ~ **transformer** *n* ELEC, ELEC ENG transformateur de sonnerie *m*; ~ **valve** *n* HYDR EQUIP robinet à cloche *m*; ~ **wire** *n* ELEC ENG fil de sonnerie *m*

Bell: ~ **operating company** *n* (TM) *(BOC)* TELECOM compagnie opératrice Bell *f* (MD)

bellhousing *n* PROD ENG carter en cloche *m*

bellow *n* PROD ENG soufflet *m*; ~ **expansion joint** *n* MECH ENG compensateur de dilatation à soufflet *m*, joint à soufflet *m*, joint glissant *m*; ~ **valve** *n* MECH ENG soupape à soufflet *f*

bellows *n* CINEMAT, MECH, MECH ENG, PHOTO soufflet *m*, PROD ENG soufflet *m*; ~ **attachment** *n* PHOTO porte-objectif à soufflet *m*; ~ **covering** *n* PHOTO gaine de soufflet *f*; ~ **extension** *n* PHOTO tirage du soufflet *m*; ~ **frame** *n* PHOTO cadre de soufflet *m*; ~ **pump** *n* LAB EQUIP pompe à soufflet *f*; ~ **seal** *n* SPACE *spacecraft* joint à soufflet *m*; ~ **shutter** *n* PHOTO obturateur à soufflet *m*; ~ **valve** *n* MECH ENG soupape à soufflet *f*, REFRIG vanne à soufflet *f*

bellows-type: ~ **folding camera** *n* PHOTO appareil photographique à soufflet *m*; ~ **pressure switch** *n* PROD ENG pressostat à soufflet *m*

bell-shaped: ~ **curve** *n* GEOM courbe en forme de cloche *f*, MATH courbe de Gauss *f*, courbe en forme de cloche *f*, courbe gaussienne *f*; ~ **distribution curve** *n* MATH courbe normale de répartition *f*; ~ **insulator** *n* ELEC ENG isolateur à cloche *m*

bell-type: ~ **armature** *n* ELEC *generator, motor* induit en cloche *m*

belly[1] *n* C&G *of shaft furnace* ventre *m*, CONST *of wall* bombement *m*, NAUT *of sail, boat* creux *m*, ventre *m*, PROD ENG ventre *m*, *of flask* bouge *f*; ~ **landing** *n* AERONAUT atterrissage sur le ventre *m*, atterrissage train rentré *m*; ~ **pipe** *n* PROD ENG *blast furnace* porte-vent *m*, tuyau porte-vent *m*

belly[2] *vi* CONST bomber; ~ **out** *vi* CONST bomber

belonite *n* MINERAL bélonite *f*

below[1] *adj* NAUT en bas; ~ **decks** *adj* NAUT dans l'entrepont, en bas, à l'intérieur du navire

below[2] *adv* NAUT dans l'entrepont, en bas, à l'intérieur du navire, *on ship* dans l'entrepont, en bas, à l'intérieur du navire

below-ground workers *n pl* MINING ouvriers du fond *m pl*

below-cloud: ~ **scavenging** *n* POLLUTION entraînement *m*, lessivage *m*

belshazzar *n* C&G balthazar *m*

belt *n* MECH ceinture *f*, courroie *f*, tapis *m*, MECH ENG courroie de transmission *f*, PAPER TECH, PRINT, PROD ENG *of machine* courroie *f*, VEHICLES *cooling* courroie *f*, *safety* ceinture *f*; ~ **bolt** *n* PROD ENG boulon de courroie *m*, boulon pour courroies *m*; ~ **cleaner** *n* MINING nettoyeur de bande *m*; ~ **conveyor** *n* MECH ENG *material handling* bande transporteuse *f*, MINING transporteur à bande *m*, transporteur à courroie *m*, PACKAGING transporteur à bande *m*, PAPER TECH convoyeur à courroie *m*, fourchette de débrayage *f*, PROD ENG transporteur à courroie *m*, transporteur à toile sans fin *m*; ~ **conveyor with carrying idlers** *n* MECH ENG transporteur à courroie muni de rouleaux porteurs *m*; ~ **drive** *n* MECH entraînement par courroie *m*, MECH ENG marche à la volée *f*, PAPER TECH commande par courroie *f*, PROD ENG commande par courroie *f*, transmission par courroie *f*; ~ **dryer** *n* CHEM TECH sécheur pour bandes transporteuses *m*; ~ **fastener** *n* PAPER TECH attache de courroie *f*, PROD ENG attache par courroies *f*; ~ **feeder** *n* CHEM TECH alimentateur à courroie *m*; ~ **fork** *n* PROD ENG débrayage *m*, débrayeur *m*, embrayeur *m*, fourche de débrayage *f*, fourche de manoeuvre de courroie *f*; ~ **freezing** *n* REFRIG *on conveyor belt* congélation sur bande *f*; ~ **friction** *n* MECH ENG friction de courroie de transmission *f*; ~ **guard** *n* MECH ENG carter de courroie *m*,

SAFETY *machine tools* cache-courroie *m*, capot couvre-courroie *m*; ~ **idler** *n* AUTO tendeur de courroie *m*, PROD ENG galet de renvoi *m*, galet guide *m*, poulie-guide *f*, *tightening pulley* galet tendeur *m*, poulie de tension *f*, rouleau de tension *m*; ~ **lace** *n* PROD ENG lanière pour courroie *f*; ~ **lacing** *n* PROD ENG *steel* agrafes à griffes pour courroies *f pl*; ~ **marks** *n pl* C&G marques de tapis *f pl*; ~ **mounter** *n* PROD ENG crochet pour la pose des courroies *m*, monte-courroie *m*, perche *f*; ~ **pinch** *n* NUCLEAR striction en bande *f*; ~ **press** *n* PRINT presse à bandes de type Cameron *f*; ~ **printer** *n* COMP imprimante à bande *f*, DP imprimante à courroie *f*; ~ **pulley** *n* PROD ENG poulie à courroie *f*; ~ **pump** *n* PROD ENG pompe à commande par courroie *f*, pompe à courroie *f*; ~ **rivet** *n* PROD ENG rivet pour courroie *m*; ~ **shifter** *n* PROD ENG *with wooden handle* crochet pour la pose des courroies *m*, monte-courroie *m*; ~ **shipper** *n* PROD ENG *with wooden handle* crochet pour la pose des courroies *m*, monte-courroie *m*, perche *f*; ~ **skimmer** *n* MAR POLL récupérateur à bande *m*, récupérateur à courroie *m*, écrémeur à bande *m*, POLLUTION récupérateur à bande *m*, récupérateur à courroie *m*; ~ **stress** *n* MECH ENG contrainte de courroie de transmission *f*; ~ **tension** *n* MECH ENG tension de courroie de transmission *f*

belt-driven[1] *adj* PROD ENG commandé par courroie

belt-driven:[2] ~ **pump** *n* PROD ENG pompe à commande par courroie *f*, pompe à courroie *f*

belt-fed *adj* CHEM TECH alimenté par courroie

belting *n* MECH ENG courroies *f pl*, PROD ENG courroies *f pl*, courroies de transmission *f pl*

belt-type: ~ **moving pavement** *n* (BrE) *(cf belt-type moving sidewalk)* TRANSP trottoir roulant à bande continue *m*; ~ **moving sidewalk** *n* (AmE) *(cf belt-type moving pavement)* TRANSP trottoir roulant à bande continue *m*; ~ **sling** *n* SAFETY courroie *f*

bemf *abbr* ELEC ENG *(back electromotive force, back emf)*, ELECTR *(back emf, back electromotive force)*, PHYS *(back electromotive force, back emf)* fcém *(force contre-électromotrice)*

Ben: ~ **Day** *n* PRINT benday *m*, fond tramé *m*

bench *n* CONST *banquette* banquette *f*, berme *f*, *worktable* banc *m*, établi *m*, LAB EQUIP *furniture* paillasse *f*, OCEANOG plate-forme littorale *f*; ~ **blasting** *n* MINING abattage par pans *m*, sautage par pans *m*; ~ **board** *n* NUCLEAR pupitre de commande debout *m*; ~ **cloth** *n* C&G toile de scellage *f*; ~ **drill** *n* MECH, MECH ENG perceuse d'établi *f*; ~ **drilling machine** *n* MECH ENG perceuse d'établi *f*; ~ **grinder** *n* MECH ENG *machine tool* touret électrique *m*; ~ **height** *n* MINING hauteur du gradin *f*; ~ **hole** *n* MINING trou d'abattage *m*; ~ **lathe** *n* MECH, MECH ENG tour d'établi *m*; ~ **molding machine** *n* (AmE), ~ **moulding machine** *n* (BrE) PROD ENG machine à mouler d'établi *f*; ~ **pillar drilling machine** *n* MECH ENG perceuse d'établi à colonne *f*; ~ **plane** *n* CONST mouchette *f*, rabot d'établi *m*, varlope *f*, varlope des bennes *f*; ~ **rammer** *n* PROD ENG *moulder's* fouloir d'établi *m*; ~ **screw** *n* CONST vis d'établi *f*; ~ **seat** *n* VEHICLES banquette *f*; ~ **shears** *n pl* CONST cisailles d'établi *f pl*; ~ **stake** *n* CONST tasseau d'établi *m*; ~ **stop** *n* CONST crochet pour établis de menuisiers *m*; ~ **time** *n* FOOD TECH temps de préparation *m*; ~ **vice with clamp** *n* (BrE) CONST étau à agrafes d'établi *m*, étau à griffes pour établi *m*; ~ **vise with clamp** *n* (AmE) *see bench vice with clamp*; ~ **work** *n* CINEMAT tournage par animation *m*

benchmark[1] *n* COMP point de repère *m*, test de performance *m*, CONST *surveying* point de repère *m*, point fixé *m*, repère *m*, repère de position *m*, DP point d'essai *m*, test de performance *m*, MECH point de repère *m*

benchmark[2] *vt* COMP, DP évaluer les performances de

benchmarking *n* COMP, DP mise au banc d'essai *f*, évaluation des performances *f*

bench-type: ~ **shaping machine** *n* MECH ENG étau-limeur d'établi *m*

bend[1] *n* C&G pli *m*, CONST *pipe elbow* coude *m*, courbe *f*, pièce coudée *f*, tuyau coudé *m*, ELEC ENG *of fibre optics* courbure *f*, *waveguides* coude *m*, HYDROL *of river* méandre *m*, MECH ENG coude *m*, NAUT *of river, channel, pipe* coude *m*, courbure *f*; ~ **angle** *n* PROD ENG angle de cintrage *m*; ~ **coupling** *n* MECH ENG *pipe fitting* raccord coudé *m*; ~ **radius** *n* PROD ENG rayon de cintrage *m*; **under ~** *n* MECH ENG coude *m*, PETR concavité *f*

bend[2] *vt* CONST *branch* ployer, *flex* fléchir, plier, ployer, *osier* plier, *piece of wood* arquer, cintrer, courber, *pipe* cintrer, NAUT *cable to anchor* étalinguer, *rope* frapper, *sail* enverguer, PAPER TECH fléchir, PROD ENG arquer, cintrer, courber, *bar of iron* couder

bend[3] *vi* CONST arquer, se courber, se plier, se couder, se ployer, PROD ENG se couder; ~ **under a load** *vi* CONST *beam* courber sous une charge

bender *n* PRINT coudeuse de plaques *f*

bending *n* C&G *of flat glass* bombage *m*, *of tubing* pliage *m*, CONST *of wood* courbement *m*, courbure *f*, MECH flexion *f*, OPT courbure *f*, PAPER TECH flexion *f*, PROD ENG pliage *m*, profilé plié *m*, SPACE flexion *f*, SPRINGS *of loop* pliage *m*; ~ **circumferential stress** *n* NAUT *shipbuilding* contrainte circonférentielle de flexion *f*; ~ **die** *n* MECH ENG *press tools* outillage de pliage pour presse *m*; ~ **loss** *n* ELEC ENG *fibre optics* perte de courbure *f*; ~ **machine** *n* MECH ENG machine à cintrer *f*; ~ **mold** *n* (AmE) *see bending mould*; ~ **moment** *n* MECH ENG, NAUT *ship design* moment de flexion *m*, PHYS couple de flexion *m*, couple fléchissant *m*, PROD ENG moment de flexion *m*, SPRINGS couple de flexion *m*; ~ **mould** *n* (BrE) C&G moule conformateur *m*; ~ **press** *n* MECH ENG cintreuse *f*, machine à rouler *f*, presse à cintrer *f*; ~ **radius** *n* MECH ENG rayon de cintrage *m*, PROD ENG rayon de pliage *m*, SPRINGS rayon de courbure *m*; ~ **roll** *n* MECH ENG cylindre à cintrer *m*; ~ **roller** *n* C&G *for forming flat glass* rouleau plieur *m*; ~ **stiffness tester** *n* PAPER TECH flexiomètre *m*; ~ **strength** *n* NUCLEAR, PAPER TECH résistance à la flexion *f*; ~ **stress** *n* MECH contrainte de flexion *f*, P&R effort de flexion *m*, tension de pliage *f*, SPRINGS contrainte de flexion *f*; ~ **test** *n* PRINT essai de pliage *m*; ~ **tester** *n* P&R *instrument* machine pour essais de flexion *f*; ~ **vibrations** *n pl* RAD PHYS vibrations de déformation *f pl*

Bendix: ~ **starter** *n* (TM) VEHICLES démarreur Bendix *m* (MD)

Bendix-type: ~ **starter** *n* (TM) AUTO démarreur Bendix *m* (MD)

bends *n* NAUT *diving illness* maladie des plongeurs *f*, OCEANOG maladie de décompression *f*, PETR TECH *personnel safety* aérémie *f*, mal des caissons *m*

bend-up: ~ **lock washer** *n* MECH ENG rondelle Grower *f*, rondelle de blocage *f*, rondelle de freinage à lamelle *f*

beneficiation *n* C&G enrichissement *m*

Benioff: ~ **plane** *n* GEOL plan de Benioff *m*; ~ **zone** *n* FUELLESS *geothermal resources* zone Benioff *f*

bent[1] *adj* C&G penché

bent:[2] ~ **finish** n C&G bague penchée f; ~ **glass** n C&G verre bombé m; ~ **neck** n C&G col penché m; ~ **spanner** n (cf bent wrench) (BrE) MECH ENG clé coudée f; ~ **tool** n MECH ENG lathe outil coudé m; ~ **wrench** n (AmE) (cf bent spanner)

benthonic adj GEOL benthonique

bent-nose: ~ **pliers** n pl MECH ENG pince à becs coudés f

bentonite n COAL TECH, CONST bentonite f, DETERGENTS smectite f, MINERAL, PETR, PETR TECH drilling, PROP MAT bentonite f

benzaldehyde n CHEM benzaldéhyde m

benzaldoxime n CHEM benzaldoxime f

benzamide n CHEM benzamide m

benzanilide n CHEM benzanilide m

benzene n CHEM, PETR TECH benzène m; ~ **hexachloride** n FOOD TECH hexachlorure de benzène m; ~ **ring** n CHEM noyau benzénique m

benzenoid adj CHEM benzénoïde

benzidine n CHEM benzidine f

benzil n CHEM benzile m

benzo: ~ **dyestuff** n COLOURS colorant benzoïque m

benzoate n CHEM benzoate m

benzohydrol n CHEM benzohydrol m

benzoic[1] adj CHEM benzoïque

benzoic:[2] ~ **acid** n FOOD TECH acide benzoïque m

benzoin n CHEM benzoïne f

benzol n CHEM benzol m

benzole n CHEM benzol m

benzonaphthol n CHEM benzonaphtol m

benzonitrile n CHEM benzonitrile m

benzophenone n CHEM benzophénone f

benzopyrene n CHEM benzopyrène m

benzoquinone n CHEM benzoquinone f

benzoyl: ~ **chloride** n CHEM chlorure de benzoyle m; ~ **peroxide** n FOOD TECH peroxyde d'acétylbenzoyle m, peroxyde de benzoyle m, P&R polyesters lucidol m, peroxyde de benzoyle m

benzyl: ~ **alcohol** n CHEM alcool benzylique m; ~ **cinnamate** n FOOD TECH cinnamate de benzyle m

benzyne n CHEM benzyne m

BER abbr (binary error rate, bit error rate) COMP, ELECTRON, TELECOM TEB (taux d'erreurs binaires, taux d'erreurs sur les bits)

bergmannite n MINERAL bergmannite f

berkelium n (Bk) CHEM berkélium m (Bk)

Berlin: ~ **eye** n SPRINGS oeil de Berlin m, oeil épaulé m

berm n COAL TECH berme f, CONST civil engineering banquette f, berme f, OCEANOG berme f, gradins de plage m pl; ~ **ditch** n WATER SUPP contre-fossé m, fossé de berge m

Berne: ~ **key** n RAIL clé de Berne f; ~ **rectangle** n RAIL rectangle de Berne m

Bernoulli's: ~ **equation** n FLUID PHYS équation de Bernoulli f; ~ **theorem** n PHYS théorème de Bernoulli m

berth[1] n NAUT crew cadre m, passengers couchette f

berth[2] vt NAUT shiphandling accoster, amener à quai

berth[3] vi NAUT mooring aborder à quai, se ranger à quai

berthierite n MINERAL berthiérite f

berthing n NAUT abordage à quai m, accostage m, SPACE accostage m

bertrandite n MINERAL bertrandite f

beryl n C&G émeraude f, CHEM, MINERAL béryl m

beryllia n C&G glucine f

beryllium n (Be) CHEM béryllium m (Be); ~ **content meter** n NUCLEAR teneurmètre en béryllium m; ~ **copper casting** n MECH ENG fonte en cuivre au béryllium f;

~ **copper die** n MECH ENG matrice en cuivre au béryllium f; ~ **moderated reactor** n NUCLEAR réacteur modéré au béryllium m; ~ **prospecting meter** n NUCLEAR ensemble de prospection de béryllium m; ~ **reflected reactor** n NUCLEAR réacteur à réflecteur de béryllium m

beryllonite n MINERAL béryllonite f

berzelianite n MINERAL berzélianite f, berzéliite f

Bessemer: ~ **converter** n HEATING steel manufacture cornue Bessemer f, MECH ENG, PROD ENG convertisseur Bessemer m; ~ **iron** n PROD ENG fer Bessemer m; ~ **pig** n PROD ENG fonte Bessemer f; ~ **process** n PROD ENG procédé Bessemer m; ~ **steel** n PROD ENG acier Bessemer m

best:[1] ~ **climb angle** n AERONAUT angle optimal de montée m; ~ **coal** n COAL TECH charbon en morceaux m

best:[2] ~ **before** phr PACKAGING à consommer avant

beta: ~ **backscatter gage** n (AmE), ~ **backscatter gauge** n (BrE) NUCLEAR indicateur à radioélément à rétrodiffusion bêta m; ~ **decay** n PART PHYS désintégration bêta moins f, PHYS désintégration bêta f; ~ **density gage** n (AmE), ~ **density gauge** n (BrE) NUCLEAR densimètre bêta m; ~ **disintegration energy** n PHYS énergie de désintégration bêta f; ~ **emission** n RAD PHYS rayonnement bêta m; ~ **emitter** n PHYS émetteur bêta m; ~ **particle** n ELEC, NUCLEAR, PART PHYS, PHYS particule bêta f; ~ **particle absorption analysis** n RAD PHYS analyse par absorption des rayons bêta f; ~ **particle backscattering analysis** n RAD PHYS analyse par rétrodiffusion des rayons bêta f; ~ **radiation** n RAD PHYS radiation bêta f; ~ **ray** n ELEC radiation, NUCLEAR, PHYS rayon bêta m; ~ **ray spectrum** n PHYS spectre des rayons bêta m, RAD PHYS spectre bêta m; ~ **stability island** n NUCLEAR îlot de stabilité bêta m; ~ **test** n COMP, DP essai bêta m, essai pilote m; ~ **version** n COMP version bêta f

beta-amylase n FOOD TECH bêta-amylase f

betatron n NUCLEAR, PHYS bêtatron m, RAD PHYS accélérateur à induction m, bêtatron m

Bethe-Goldstone: ~ **equation** n NUCLEAR équation de Bethe-Goldstone f

between:[1] ~ **decks** adv NAUT dans l'entrepont

between:[2] ~ **decks** n NAUT entrepont m

between:[3] ~ **comfort and discomfort** phr SAFETY entre le confort et la gêne

between-the-lens: ~ **filter** n CINEMAT filtre central m; ~ **shutter** n PHOTO obturateur au diaphragme m

beudantine n MINERAL beudantine f

beudantite n MINERAL beudantite f

bevel[1] n C&G, INSTRUMENT, MECH, MECH ENG, METR biseau m; ~ **cutter** n MECH ENG fraise d'angle f; ~ **edge** n MECH ENG biseau m, bord biseauté m; ~ **gear** n MECH engrenage conique m, MECH ENG engrenage conique m, pignon conique m; ~ **gear drive** n MECH ENG transmission par engrenages coniques f, transmission par pignons coniques f; ~ **gear housing** n AERONAUT helicopter trompette de roue conique f; ~ **gearing** n AUTO couple conique m, couronne dentée f, MECH ENG engrenage d'angle m; ~ **gear set** n VEHICLES rear axle couple conique m; ~ **gears with straight and spiral tooth system** n pl MECH ENG engrenages coniques à denture droite et hélicoïdale m pl; ~ **joint** n CONST joint en biseau m, MECH ENG assemblage en coupe d'onglets m, joint biseauté m; ~ **protractor** n METR sauterelle graduée f; ~ **ring** n MECH ENG engrenage conique m, roue conique f; **~ ring flared stub shaft** n AERONAUT *helicopter* trompette de roue conique f; **~ square** n METR angloir m, fausse équerre f, sauterelle f; **~ wheel** n MECH ENG roue d'angle f

bevel[2] vt INSTRUMENT biseauter, PROD ENG *of mirror* biseau m

beveled: ~ chisel n (AmE) *(see bevelled chisel)*; **~ washer** n (AmE) *(see beveled washer)*

bevel-edged: ~ flat n MECH ENG fer biseauté m, outil biseauté m

bevel-headed: ~ bolt n CONST *of lock* boulon à tête en biseau m

beveling n (AmE) *see bevelling*

bevelled: ~ chisel n (BrE) MECH ENG ciseau biseauté m; **~ washer** n (BrE) MECH ENG rondelle biseautée f

bevelling n (BrE) C&G biseautage m, CONST chanfreinage m, INSTRUMENT biseautage m, PETR chanfreinage m **~ machine** n (BrE) MECH ENG *machine tool* machine à biseauter f; **~ tool** n (BrE) INSTRUMENT biseautoir m

beverage: ~ dispenser n REFRIG distributeur de boissons m

beyond: ~ repair adj MECH ENG irréparable

bezel n PROD ENG collerette f

bezier n PRINT bezier m

BFA $abbr$ *(basic frame alignment)* TELECOM verrouillage de trame de base m

BFO $abbr$ *(beat frequency oscillator)* TELECOM oscillateur à battements m

B-format: ~ video recorder n TV magnétoscope un pouce B m

BG $abbr$ *(background gas)* PETR TECH *while drilling* fond gazeux m

BHA $abbr$ FOOD TECH *(butylated hydroxyanisole)* BHA m *(hydroxyanisol butylé)*, PETR TECH *(bottom hole assembly)* bas de garniture m

BHP $abbr$ *(brake horsepower)* MECH ENG, PROD ENG cheval effectif m, puissance au frein en chevaux f, puissance effective en chevaux f, puissance en chevaux-vapeur effectifs f, TRANSP puissance au frein f

BHT $abbr$ *(butylated hydroxytoluene)* FOOD TECH BHT *(hydroxytoluène butylé)*

Bi *(bismuth)* CHEM Bi *(bismuth)*

biacid n CHEM biacide m

bias[1] n COAL TECH erreur systématique f, COMP polarisation f, DP biais m, polarisation f, écart m, ELEC ENG polarisation f, MATH biais m, RECORDING polarisation f, TV polarisation magnétique f, prémagnétisation f; **~ battery** n ELEC ENG pile de polarisation f; **~ circuit** n ELEC ENG circuit de polarisation m; **~ frequency** n RECORDING fréquence de polarisation f; **~ generator** n ELEC ENG générateur de polarisation m; **~ oscillator** n ELECTRON, RECORDING oscillateur de polarisation m; **~ ply** n TEXTILES nappe de carcasse en diagonale f; **~ ply tire** n (AmE) *(cf crossply tyre)* VEHICLES pneu diagonal m, pneu à carcasse diagonale m, pneumatique diagonal m; **~ resistor** n ELEC ENG, PHYS résistance de polarisation f; **~ source** n ELEC ENG source de polarisation f; **~ trap** n RECORDING piège de polarisation m; **~ voltage** n PHYS tension de polarisation f; **~ winding** n ELEC ENG enroulement de polarisation m

bias[2] vt ELEC ENG polariser

biased[1] adj PHYS polarisé

biased:[2] **~ exponent** n DP *floating point notation* caractéristique f; **~ relay** n ELEC, ELEC ENG relais polarisé m

biasing n RECORDING polarisation f, TV polarisation f, prémagnétisation f; **~ current** n TV courant de préma-

gnétisation m

biatomic: ~ gas n GAS TECH gaz diatomique m

biaxial[1] adj CRYSTALL, MATH biaxe

biaxial:[2] **~ cable** n ELEC, PROD ENG câble biaxial m; **~ loading** n METALL chargement biaxial m; **~ orientation** n P&R *plastic film* orientation biaxiale f

biaxially-oriented: ~ film n P&R *plastic film* feuille à orientation biaxiale f

bib n CONST robinet m; **~ nozzle** n CONST *of bib cock* ajutage de robinet m; **~ tap** n MECH ENG robinet à bec courbe m

bibcock n CONST robinet m, MECH ENG robinet à bec courbe m

bible: ~ paper n PAPER TECH papier bible m

bibliometer n PAPER TECH capillarimètre m

bicarbonate n CHEM bicarbonate m; **~ of soda** n CHEM, DETERGENTS, FOOD TECH bicarbonate de sodium m

Bickford: ~ fuse n MINING bickford m, cordeau Bickford m

BiCMOS: ~ transistor n COMP transistor bipolaire CMOS m

bicolored adj (AmE), **bicoloured** adj (BrE) COLOURS bicolore, de deux couleurs

biconcave: ~ lens n INSTRUMENT, PHYS lentille biconcave f

biconical: ~ antenna n TELECOM antenne biconique f

biconvex: ~ lens n INSTRUMENT, PHYS lentille biconvexe f

bicrystal n METALL bicristal m

bicycle: ~ nipple adjusters n pl TRANSP tendeurs de nipples m pl; **~ pump** n TRANSP pompe à vélo f; **~ tools** n pl TRANSP outils pour bicyclettes m pl

bicyclic adj CHEM bicyclique

bid n COMP tentative de prise f, DP *in telephony* demande de ligne f, MECH *contracts* soumission f, TELECOM tentative de prise f

bidirectional[1] adj COMP, DP bidirectionnel, TELECOM bidirectionnel, bilatéral

bidirectional:[2] **~ block transfer** n PROD ENG transfert en bloc bidirectionel m; **~ counter** n ELECTRON compteur bidirectionnel m; **~ coupler** n ELEC ENG coupleur bidirectionnel m; **~ flow** n COMP transfert bilatéral m, DP transfert bidirectionnel m; **~ I/O module group** n PROD ENG groupe de modules d'E/S à communication bidirectionnelle m; **~ microphone** n ACOUSTICS, RECORDING microphone bidirectionnel m; **~ network** n ELEC ENG réseau bilatéral m, réseau électrique bilatéral m; **~ refueling** n (AmE), **~ refuelling** n (BrE) NUCLEAR rechargement bidirectionnel m; **~ switch** n ELEC ENG interrupteur bidirectionnel m; **~ transducer** n ELEC ENG transducteur bilatéral m; **~ wind vane** n METEO anémomètre bidirectionnel m

bi-drum: ~ boiler n HEATING chaudière à deux ballons f

bieberite n MINERAL biebérite f

bi-ergol: ~ technology n TRANSP technologie biergol f

bifilar[1] adj ELEC *winding*, PHYS bifilaire

bifilar:[2] **~ electrometer** n ELEC électromètre bifilaire m; **~ suspension** n ELEC *of instrument*, PHYS suspension bifilaire f; **~ winding** n ELEC *of inductor* bobinage bifilaire m

bifocal: ~ glasses n pl INSTRUMENT lunettes bifocales f pl, lunettes à double foyer f pl; **~ lens** n C&G verre à double foyer m, INSTRUMENT lentille bifocale f, verre à double foyer m

bifurcated: ~ mating contact n ELEC, PROD ENG contact jumelé à pression m; **~ movable contact** n PROD ENG contact mobile à double portée m; **~ rivet** n MECH ENG rivet à corps fendu *m*, rivet à deux pointes *m*, PROD ENG rivet bifurqué *m*

bifurcation *n* TRANSP marque de bifurcation *f*

big ~ close up *n (BCU)* CINEMAT très gros plan *m*; **~ end** *n* AUTO, VEHICLES *connecting rod* tête de bielle *f*; **~ end bearing** *n* AUTO, VEHICLES *connecting rod* coussinet de tête de bielle *m*; **~ hole** *n* PETR TECH *drilling* forage en grand diamètre *m*

Big: ~ Bang *n* ASTRON Big Bang *m*; SPACE Big Bang *m*, explosion cosmologique initiale *f*, explosion primordiale *f*; **~ Bang radiation** *n* SPACE *astronomy* rayonnement fossile *m*; **~ Bang theory** *n* PHYS théorie d'explosion cosmogonique initiale *f*, théorie d'explosion cosmogonique primitive *f*; **~ Dipper** *n* (AmE) ASTRON Grand Chariot *m*

bight *n* NAUT *of rope* anse *f*, balant *m*

biguanide *n* CHEM biguanide *m*

bilateral: ~ amplifier *n* ELECTRON amplificateur bilatéral *m*; **~ transducer** *n* ELEC ENG transducteur bilatéral *m*

bildstein *n* MINERAL bildstein *m*

bile: ~ acid *n* CHEM acide biliaire *m*

bilevel: ~ operation *n* ELEC ENG fonctionnement à deux niveaux *m*, fonctionnement à deux niveaux de puissance *m*

bilge *n* NAUT bouchain *m*, fond de cale *m*; **~ blower** *n* NAUT aérateur de cale *m*; **~ keel** *n* NAUT *shipbuilding* quille de roulis *f*; **~ plate** *n* NAUT *shipbuilding* tôle de bouchain *f*; **~ plating** *n* NAUT *shipbuilding* bordé de bouchain *m*; **~ pump** *n* NAUT pompe de cale *f*; **~ shore** *n* NAUT *shipbuilding* accore de bouchain *f*; **~ strake** *n* NAUT *shipbuilding* virure de bouchain *f*; **~ stringer** *n* NAUT *shipbuilding* serre de bouchain *f*; **~ water** *n* NAUT eau de cale *f*

bilirubin *n* CHEM bilirubine *f*

bill: ~ of health *n* NAUT *ship's papers* patente de santé *f*; **~ of lading** *n* NAUT *ship's papers*, PETR TECH *shipping* connaissement *m*; **~ of material** *n* PROD ENG nomenclature *f*

billblade *n* PRINT billblade *f*, encolleuse *f*

billet: ~ shears *n pl* MECH ENG cisaille à billettes *f*

Billet: ~ split lens *n* PHYS bilentille de Billet *f*

billetting: ~ rolls *n pl* MECH ENG laminoir à billettes *m*, train à billettes *m*

billiard: ~ ball collision *n* NUCLEAR collision élastique *f*

billing *n* TELECOM facturation *f*; **~ center** *n* (AmE), **~ centre** *n* (BrE) TELECOM centre de facturation *m*

billion *n* MATH milliard *m*

billow *n* NAUT *of sea* lame *f*

billyboy: ~ dolly *n* CINEMAT chariot de travelling sur pneumatiques *m*

bimetal: ~ piston *n* AUTO piston bimétal *m*; **~ plate** *n* PRINT plaque bimétallique *f*

bimetallic: ~ contact *n* ELEC ENG contact bimétallique *m*; **~ element** *n* REFRIG bilame métallique *f*; **~ strip** *n* ELEC *in thermostat, thermometer* bilame métallique *f*, lame bimétallique *f*, PHYS bilame métallique *f*; **~ switch** *n* ELEC interrupteur bimétallique *m*; **~ wire** *n* ELEC ENG fil à âme d'acier *m*

bimodal: ~ bus *n* TRANSP autobus bimodal *m*

bimolecular *adj* CHEM bimoléculaire

bin *n* CINEMAT *for film offcuts* bac à chutes *m*, chutier *m*, MECH trémie *f*, PACKAGING casier *m*, PRINT corbeille *f*, PROD ENG *in store* casier *m*; **~ liner** *n* PACKAGING sac en plastique pour casier *m*

binary[1] *adj* CHEM, DP, ELECTRON, MATH, METALL binaire

binary:[2] **~ adder** *n* COMP, ELECTRON additionneur binaire

m; **~ addition** *n* ELECTRON addition binaire *f*; **~ alloy** *n* PROP MAT alliage binaire *m*; **~ arithmetic** *n* COMP, ELECTRON arithmétique binaire *f*; **~ chop** *n* COMP, DP recherche binaire *f*; **~ circuit** *n* ELECTRON circuit binaire *m*; **~ code** *n* DP code binaire *m*; **~ coding** *n* TELECOM codage binaire *m*; **~ column** *n* COMP, DP colonne binaire *f*; **~ command language** *n* PROD ENG langage de gestion binaire *m*; **~ counter** *n* COMP, ELECTRON compteur binaire *m*; **~ delay line** *n* TV ligne à retard binaire *f*; **~ digit** *n* COMP, DP chiffre binaire *m*; **~ divider** *n* ELECTRON diviseur binaire *m*; **~ division** *n* ELECTRON division binaire *f*; **~ dump** *n* COMP vidage binaire *m*; **~ engine** *n* MECH ENG machine thermique combinée *f*; **~ error rate** *n (BER)* COMP, ELECTRON, TELECOM taux d'erreurs binaires *m*, taux d'erreurs sur les bits *m (TEB)*; **~ heat engine** *n* MECH ENG machine thermique combinée *f*; **~ image** *n* SPACE, TELECOM image binaire *f*; **~ logic** *n* COMP logique binaire *f*; **~ modulation** *n* TELECOM modulation binaire *f*; **~ multiplication** *n* ELECTRON multiplication binaire *f*; **~ multiplier** *n* ELECTRON, TELECOM multiplicateur binaire *m*; **~ notation** *n* COMP, DP notation binaire *f*; **~ number** *n* MECH ENG chiffre binaire *m*; **~ operation** *n* COMP opération binaire *f*; **~ pair** *n* ELECTRON bascule binaire *f*; **~ phase shift keying** *n (BPSK)* TELECOM modulation par déplacement de phase bivalente *f (MDPB)*; **~ pulsar** *n* ASTRON pulsar binaire *m*; **~ representation** *n* DP représentation binaire *f*; **~ scaler** *n* ELECTRON diviseur par deux *m*, échelle binaire *f*, échelle de comptage binaire *f*, échelle de deux *f*; **~ search** *n* COMP, DP recherche binaire *f*; **~ search procedure** *n* TELECOM procédure de recherche par division binaire *f*; **~ sequence** *n* COMP, DP, TELECOM séquence binaire *f*; **~ signal** *n* COMP, DP, ELECTRON, TELECOM signal binaire *m*; **~ sort** *n* COMP tri binaire *m*; **~ star** *n* ASTRON étoile binaire *f*; **~ subtraction** *n* ELECTRON soustraction binaire *f*; **~ subtractor** *n* ELECTRON soustracteur binaire *m*; **~ synchronous communication** *n (BSC, BISYNC)* COMP transmission binaire synchrone *f*; **~ system** *n* DP système binaire *m*; **~ tree** *n* COMP arbre binaire *m*

binary-coded: ~ decimal *n (BCD)* COMP, PRINT décimal codé binaire *m*; **~ octal** *n* PROD ENG octal codé binaire *m*; **~ signal** *n* ELECTRON signal codé en binaire *m*

binaural[1] *adj* ACOUSTICS binaural

binaural:[2] **~ sound system** *n* RECORDING système d'enregistrement binaural *m*

bind[1] *vt* COMP associer, fixer, CONST *lash* attacher, *stones with mortar, to tie* lier, *two ends of scaffold board border, frotter, two wires* ligaturer, PRINT brocher

bind[2] *vi* CONST se caler, se gripper, se taler, serrer

binder *n* C&G liant *m*, CONST *civil engineering* agglomérant *m*, liant *m*, *masonry* coincement *m*, coinçage *m*, *of double floor* solive *f*, tie, *fastening* attache *f*, *to effect cohesion* liant *m*, GEOL ciment *m*, liant *m*, P&R *paint* liant *m*, PACKAGING ficeleuse *f*, PRINT liant *m*, véhicule *m*, RECORDING *of particles on tape*, SPACE *spacecraft*, TV liant *m*; **~ agent** *n* PROP MAT liant *m*; **~ course** *n* CONST couche de liaison *f*; **~ heater** *n* CONST chauffe-liant *m*

bindery *n* PRINT reliure *f*

binding *n* AERONAUT *of engine* grippage *m*, COAL TECH, MECH ENG colmatage *m*, METALL liaison *f*, WATER SUPP colmatage *m*; **~ agent** *n* CHEM TECH agglutinant *m*, FOOD TECH agglomérant *m*, agglutinant *m*, liant *m*, MAR POLL agglomérant *m*; **~ beam** *n* CONST moise *f*, parre *m*, poutre *f*, ventrier *f*; ~ **closure** *n* PACKAGING fermeture avec ligature *f*; ~ **energy** *n* CHEM, CRYSTALL, PART PHYS *of nucleus*, RAD PHYS énergie de liaison *f*; ~ **energy curve** *n* NUCLEAR courbe de l'énergie de liaison *f*; ~ **head screw** *n* PROD ENG vis à tête plate *f*; ~ **machine** *n* PACKAGING ficeleuse *f*; ~ **post** *n* ELEC ENG borne à écrou *f*; ~ **pulley** *n* MECH ENG galet tendeur *m*, poulie tendeuse *f*, rouleau tendeur *m*; ~ **stone** *n* CONST *masonry* pierre de clavage *f*, voussoir *m*; ~ **thread** *n* PRINT fil à brocher *m*

binnacle *n* NAUT *housing for compass* habitacle *m*; ~ **compass** *n* NAUT compas d'habitacle *m*

binocular[1] *adj* PHYS binoculaire

binocular:[2] ~ **head** *n* INSTRUMENT tube binoculaire *m*; ~ **microscope** *n* INSTRUMENT, LAB EQUIP *instrument* microscope binoculaire *m*; ~ **refractometer** *n* INSTRUMENT réfractomètre binaire *m*

binoculars *n pl* ASTRON, INSTRUMENT, MILIT, NAUT, PHYS jumelles *f pl*; ~ **with light intensification** *n pl* ASTRON jumelles à intensificateur de lumière *f pl*

binomial *n* MATH binôme *m*; ~ **coefficient** *n* MATH coefficient binomial *m*; ~ **distribution** *n* MATH loi binomiale *f*, PHYS distribution binomiale *f*; ~ **theorem** *n* MATH formule de Newton *f*, formule du binôme de Newton *f*

biocatalyst *n* PROP MAT biocatalyseur *m*

biocenosis *n* POLLUTION biocénose *f*

biochemical: ~ **oxygen demand** *n* (*BOD*) FOOD TECH, HYDROL *sewage* demande biochimique d'oxygène *f* (*DBO*), PETR TECH demande biologique d'oxygène *f* (*DBO*), POLLUTION demande biochimique d'oxygène *f* (*DBO*); ~ **tracer** *n* POLLUTION traceur biochimique *m*

bioclastic *adj* GEOL bioclastique

biodegradability *n* RECYCLING biodégradabilité *f*

biodegradable[1] *adj* POLLUTION, PROP MAT, RECYCLING biodégradable

biodegradable:[2] ~ **packaging** *n* RECYCLING emballage biodégradable *m*; ~ **plastic** *n* RECYCLING plastique biodégradable *m*; ~ **substance** *n* POLLUTION substance biodégradable *f*

biodegradation *n* DETERGENTS, HYDROL *sewage*, MAR POLL, PACKAGING, POLLUTION biodégradation *f*, dégradation biologique *f*, PROP MAT, RECYCLING biodégradation *f*

biofilter *n* POLLUTION biofiltre *m*

biogas *n* GAS TECH biogaz *m*

biogenic[1] *adj* PETR TECH *formation of hydrocarbons* biogénique

biogenic:[2] ~ **rock** *n* PETR roche biogénique *f*; ~ **sedimentation** *n* GEOL sédimentation biogénique *f*

biogeochemical: ~ **cycling** *n* GEOL cycle biogéochimique *m*

bioglass *n* C&G bioverre *m*

bioindicator *n* POLLUTION bio-indicateur *m*, indicateur biologique *m*

biological: ~ **agent** *n* POLLUTION agent biologique *m*, PROP MAT agent antimicrobien *m*; ~ **effect** *n* RAD PHYS effet biologique *m*; ~ **effects** *n pl* SAFETY effets biologiques *m pl*; ~ **equilibrium** *n* POLLUTION équilibre écologique *m*; ~ **filter** *n* CHEM TECH lit bactérien *m*, lit percolateur *m*; ~ **hazard** *n* SAFETY risque biologique *m*; ~ **indicator** *n* HYDROL, POLLUTION indicateur biologique *m*; ~ **oxidation** *n* HYDROL *sewage* oxydation biologique *f*; ~ **protection cooling system** *n* NUCLEAR système de refroidissement de la protection biologi-

que *m*; ~ **purification** *n* HYDROL *sewage* épuration biologique *f*; ~ **shield** *n* NUCLEAR bouclier biologique *m*, protection biologique *f*, écran biologique *m*; ~ **sludge** *n* HYDROL *sewage* boues biologiques *f pl*; ~ **treatment** *n* POLLUTION traitement biologique *m*; ~ **water treatment** *n* WATER SUPP traitement biologique de l'eau *m*

biomass *n* FUELLESS, GAS TECH, HYDROL *sewage* biomasse *f*

biomicrite *n* PETR biomicrite *f*

bio-oxidation: ~ **ditch** *n* HYDROL *sewage* fossé d'oxydation *m*, fossé serpent *m*

biophysics *n* PHYS biophysique *f*

biorotor *n* HYDROL *sewage* rotor à tambour biologique *m*

biose *n* CHEM biose *m*

biosparite *n* PETR biosparite *f*

biosphere *n* METEO biosphère *f*, POLLUTION biosphère *f*, écosphère *f*

biostratigraphy *n* GEOL biostratigraphie *f*

biostrome *n* GEOL biostrome *m*

biosynthesis *n* CHEM biosynthèse *f*

biotechnology *n* FOOD TECH biotechnologie *f*

biotin *n* FOOD TECH biotine *f*

biotite[1] *adj* PETR biotite

biotite[2] *n* C&G mica magnésien *m*, MINERAL biotite *f*

Biot-Savart: ~ **law** *n* PHYS loi de Biot et Savart *f*

bioturbation *n* GEOL bioturbation *f*

biozone *n* GEOL *biostratigraphic unit* biozone *f*

BIP *abbr* (*bit interleaved parity*) TELECOM parité d'entrelacement des bits *f*

BIP-8 *abbr* (*bit interleaved parity 8, bit interleaved parity order 8*) TELECOM parité 8 à entrelacement de bits *f*, parité entrelacée bit d'ordre 8 *f*

bipack *n* CINEMAT bipack *m*, tirage en surimpression *m*

biphase[1] *adj* ELEC *current* diphasé

biphase:[2] ~ **current** *n* ELEC courant diphasé *m*

biphasic: ~ **flow** *n* GAS TECH écoulement biphasique *m*

biphenyl *n* CHEM diphényle *m*

bipolar[1] *adj* COMP, ELEC *motor*, PHYS bipolaire

bipolar:[2] ~ **amplifier** *n* ELECTRON amplificateur bipolaire *m*; ~ **code** *n* TELECOM code bipolaire *m*; ~ **code with three-zero substitution** *n* (*B3ZS*) TELECOM code bipolaire avec substitution de trois zéros *m*; ~ **cutout switch** *n* CONTROL interrupteur bipolaire *m*; ~ **diode** *n* ELECTRON diode à jonction classique *f*; ~ **electrode** *n* ELEC électrode bipolaire *f*; ~ **integrated circuit** *n* COMP circuit intégré bipolaire *m*, ELECTRON circuit bipolaire *m*, circuit intégré bipolaire *m*; ~ **line** *n* ELEC *supply* ligne bipolaire *f*; ~ **logic** *n* ELECTRON logique bipolaire *f*; ~ **machine** *n* ELEC machine bipolaire *f*; ~ **outflow** *n* ASTRON écoulement bipolaire *m*; ~ **power supply** *n* ELEC ENG alimentation bipolaire *f*; ~ **power transistor** *n* ELECTRON transistor bipolaire de puissance *m*; ~ **signal** *n* TELECOM signal bipolaire *m*; ~ **technology** *n* ELECTRON technique bipolaire *f*; ~ **transistor** *n* COMP transistor bipolaire *m*, ELECTRON transistor bipolaire *m*, transistor du type bipolaire *m*, PHYS, TELECOM transistor bipolaire *m*; ~ **winding** *n* ELEC *machine* enroulement bipolaire *m*

bipropellant *n* SPACE biergol *m*, diergol *m*

BIP-X *abbr* (*bit interleaved parity-X*) TELECOM parité X à entrelacement de bits *f*

biquinary[1] *adj* DP biquinaire

biquinary:[2] ~ **code** *n* DP code biquinaire *m*

bird: ~ **cage** *n* C&G aiguille *f*; ~ **strike hazard** *n* AERONAUT péril aviaire *m*, risque aviaire *m*

bird's: ~ **nest** *n* C&G nid *m*

birefringence *n* OPT, RAD PHYS biréfringence *f*

birefringent[1] *adj* CRYSTALL, OPT biréfringent

birefringent:[2] ~ **filter** *n* ASTRON filtre biréfringent *m*; ~ **medium** *n* OPT milieu biréfringent *m*

birth *n* ASTRON *of star* naissance *f*

bis-azo: ~ **dye** *n* CHEM colorant diazoïque *m*

biscuit: ~ **dipper** *n* C&G trempeur de biscuit *m*; ~ **ware** *n* C&G biscuit *m*

biscuit-baked: ~ **porcelain** *n* C&G dégourdi *m*

biscuit-fired: ~ **porcelain** *n* C&G dégourdi *m*

B-ISDN[1] *abbr (broadband integrated services digital network, broadband ISDN)* TELECOM RNIS-LB *(réseau numérique avec intégration des services à large bande)*; ~ **PBX** *abbr* TELECOM autocommutateur privé pour le RNIS-LB *m*

B-ISDN:[2] ~ **network termination** *n (NT-LB)* TELECOM terminaison de réseau pour le RNIS-LB *f*; ~ **network termination 1** *n (NT1-LB)* TELECOM terminaison de réseau 1 pour le RNIS-LB *f*; ~ **network termination 2** *n (NT2-LB)* TELECOM terminaison de réseau 2 pour le RNIS-LB *f*; ~ **service** *n* TELECOM service RNIS à large bande *m*; ~ **terminal adaptor** *n (TA-LB)* TELECOM adaptateur de terminal pour le RNIS-LB *m*; ~ **terminal equipment** *n (TE-LB)* TELECOM équipement terminal pour le RNIS-LB *m*

bisect *vt* GEOM couper en deux parties égales, diviser en deux parties égales

bisecting *adj* GEOM bissecteur

bisection *n* GEOM *of angle* bissection *f*

bisector *n* GEOM bissectrice *f*

bisilicate *n* CHEM métasilicate *m*

bismite *n* MINERAL bismite *f*

bismuth *n (Bi)* CHEM bismuth *m (Bi)*

bismuthate *n* CHEM bismuthate *m*

bismuthine *n* MINERAL bismuthine *f*

bismuthinite *n* MINERAL bismuthine *f*

bismuthite *n* MINERAL bismuthite *f*

bismutite *n* MINERAL bismuthite *f*

bisphenol: ~ **A** *n* P&R *raw material* bisphénol A *m*, diphénol A *m*

bistability *n* TELECOM bistabilité *f*

bistable[1] *adj* COMP, ELECTRON, PHYS bistable

bistable:[2] ~ **circuit** *n* ELECTRON circuit bistable *m*; ~ **multivibrator** *n* ELECTRON multivibrateur bistable *m*; ~ **relay** *n* ELEC ENG relais bistable *m*

bisulfate *n* (AmE) *see* bisulphate

bisulfide *n* (AmE) *see* bisulphide

bisulfite *n* (AmE) *see* bisulphite

bisulphate *n* (BrE) CHEM bisulfate *m*

bisulphide *n* (BrE) CHEM bisulfure *m*

bisulphite *n* (BrE) CHEM bisulfite *m*

BISYNC *abbr (binary synchronous communication)* COMP transmission binaire synchrone *f*

bit *n* COMP bit *m*, chiffre binaire *m*, CONST *cutting blade of plane* tranchant de lame *m*, *of key* panneton *m*, *of soldering iron* fer à souder *m*, fleuret *m*, DP bit *m*, chiffre binaire *m*, ELECTRON *binary digital* bit *m*, MECH ENG *of brace, drill* foret *m*, mèche *f*, *of tool* embout de vissage *m*, PETR bit *m*, outil de forage *m*, PETR TECH *drilling* outil *m*, trépan *m*, PRINT bit *m*, TELECOM bit *m*, élément binaire *m*, nombre binaire *m* ~ **bearing** *n* PETR palier de trépan *m*; ~ **brace** *n* MECH ENG vilebrequin *m*; ~ **breaker** *n* PETR TECH *drilling* débloqueur *m*; ~ **change** *n (BC)* PETR TECH *drilling* changement d'outil

m; ~ **controlling instruction** *n* PROD ENG instruction de positionnement de bit *f*; ~ **density** *n* DP densité binaire *f*, densité de bits *f*, PETR bit densité *m*; ~ **error rate** *n (BER)* COMP, ELECTRON, TELECOM taux d'erreurs binaires *m*, taux d'erreurs sur les bits *m (TEB)*; ~ **examining** *n* PROD ENG test de bits *m*; ~ **examining instruction** *n* PROD ENG instruction de test de bits *f*; ~ **holder** *n* MECH ENG mandrin de perceuse *m*, porte-foret *m*, porte-mèche *m*; ~ **interleaved parity** *n (BIP)* TELECOM parité d'entrelacement des bits *f*; ~ **interleaved parity 8** *n (BIP-8)* TELECOM parité 8 à entrelacement de bits *f*, parité entrelacée bit d'ordre 8 *f*; ~ **interleaved parity order 8** *n (BIP-8)* TELECOM parité 8 à entrelacement de bits *f*, parité entrelacée bit d'ordre 8 *f*; ~ **interleaved parity-X** *n (BIP-X)* TELECOM parité X à entrelacement de bits *f*; ~ **load** *n* PETR charge sur l'outil *f*, charge sur la mèche *f*, charge sur le foret *f*, charge sur le trépan *f*; ~ **location** *n* PROD ENG emplacement de bit *m*; ~ **map** *n* COMP représentation binaire *f*, DP mode point *m*; ~ **mapping** *n* ELECTRON représentation binaire *f*; ~ **parallel transfer** *n* COMP, DP transfert en parallèle par bit *m*; ~ **pattern** *n* DP configuration binaire *f*; ~ **position** *n* COMP, DP position du bit *f*; ~ **rate** *n* COMP, DP débit binaire *m*, débit en bits *m*, SPACE *communications* débit numérique *m*, TELECOM débit binaire *m*; ~ **serial transfer** *n* COMP, DP transfert en série par bits *m*; ~ **shift register** *n* PROD ENG registre de décalage binaire *m*; ~ **slice** *n* ELECTRON puce partielle *f*; ~ **slice processor** *n* COMP processeur en tranches *m*; ~ **stock** *n* MECH ENG vilebrequin *m*; ~ **stock drill** *n* MECH ENG foret de vilebrequin *m*, mèche de vilebrequin *f*; ~ **stream** *n* COMP train de bits *m*, DP flot binaire *m*; ~ **string** *n* COMP, DP chaîne binaire *f*, chaîne de bits *f*, ELECTRON suite binaire *f*; ~ **stuffing** *n* COMP insertion de bits *f*; ~ **switch** *n* TELECOM commutateur de bits *m*; ~ **wear** *n* PETR TECH usure d'outil *f*; ~ **weight** *n* PETR poids de l'outil *m*, poids de la mèche *m*, poids du foret *m*, poids du trépan *m*

bit-by-bit: ~ **encoding** *n* TELECOM codage bit à bit *m*

bite[1] *n* CONST pénétration *f*

bite[2] *vt* CONST avaser, enfoncer, gratter, *of screw* mordre, MECH ENG faire pénétrer les dents dans, mordre dans; ~ **into** *vt* MECH ENG *object* faire pénétrer les dents dans, mordre dans

bite[3] *vi* CONST *of screw* mordre, NAUT *of anchor* prendre fond

biting *n* MECH ENG mordant *m*, *of rolling mill* mordant *m*

bit-mapped: ~ **font** *n* DP fonte matricielle *f*

bitone: ~ **ink** *n* COLOURS encre double-ton *f*

bits: ~ **per inch** *n pl (BPI)* COMP bits par pouce *m pl*; ~ **per second** *n (BPS)* COMP bits par seconde *m pl (BPS)*

bitt *n* NAUT bitte *f*, bollard *m*

bitter: ~ **end** *n* NAUT *of cable* extrémité *f*

Bitter: ~ **magnet** *n* PHYS aimant de Bitter *m*; ~ **pattern** *n* PHYS figures de Bitter *f pl*

bittern *n* CHEM eaux mères *f pl*

bitumen *n* CONST, ELEC *insulation*, MECH ENG, P&R *raw material*, PETR bitume *m*, PETR TECH bitume *m*, goudron *m*; ~ **coating** *n* COATINGS revêtement de bitume *m*; ~ **emulsion** *n* CONST, MECH ENG émulsion de bitume *f*; ~ **pipe coating** *n* MECH ENG revêtement de bitume pour tubes *m*

bitumen-coated: ~ **paper** *n* PACKAGING papier revêtu de bitume *m*

bituminization *n* CONST bitumage *m*, bitumation *f*, bitu-

minisation *f*
bituminize *vt* CONST asphalter, bitumer, bituminer, bituminiser
bituminized[1] *adj* CONST bituminé, bitumé
bituminized:[2] ~ **paper** *n* CONST papier bituminé *m*
bituminous[1] *adj* CONST bitumineux
bituminous:[2] ~ **coal** *n* COAL TECH charbon bitumineux *m*; ~ **membrane** *n* CONST membrane bitumineuse *f*; ~ **paint** *n* COLOURS, CONST, P&R peinture bitumineuse *f*; ~ **shale** *n* GEOL schiste bitumineux *m*
bivalence *n* CHEM bivalence *f*
bivalent *adj* CHEM bivalent
bixin *n* FOOD TECH bixine *f*
Bjernim: ~ **association theory of ions** *n* RAD PHYS théorie de Bjernim de l'association des ions *f*
Bk *(berkelium)* CHEM Bk *(berkélium)*
BL: ~ **Lacertae** *n pl* ASTRON BL-Lacs *m pl*
black[1] *n* PRINT absence totale de réflexion *f*, noir *m*; ~ **absorber rod** *n* NUCLEAR crayon absorbant noir *m*; ~ **and white** *n (B&W)* PRINT noir et blanc *m*; ~ **and white film** *n* CINEMAT pellicule monochrome *f*, pellicule noir et blanc *f*; ~ **and white television** *n* TV télévision en noir et blanc *f*; ~ **body** *n* CINEMAT, PHYS, PRINT, RAD PHYS, SPACE *communications*, TV corps noir *m*; ~ **body radiation** *n* ASTRON, PHYS rayonnement du corps noir *m*, RAD PHYS radiation de corps noir *f*; ~ **body radiator** *n* RAD PHYS radiateur intégral *m*; ~ **body temperature** *n* PHYS température de rayonnement du corps noir *f*; ~ **box** *n* AERONAUT, COMP boîte noire *f*, INSTRUMENT boîte noire *f*, enregistreur de trajectoire de vol *m*, enregistreur de vol *m*; ~ **chert** *n* GEOL *graphitic microquartzite* phtanite *f*; ~ **clipper** *n* TV écrêteur de noir *m*; ~ **cobalt ocher** *n* (AmE), ~ **cobalt ochre** *n* (BrE) MINERAL cobalt oxydé noir *m*; ~ **compression** *n* TV compression des noirs *f*, tassement des noirs *m*; ~ **crush** *n* TV compression des noirs *f*, noircissement des gris *m*; ~ **diamond** *n* MINERAL diamant noir *m*; ~ **dwarf** *n* ASTRON naine noire *f*; ~ **finishing** *n* PROD ENG brunissage galvanique *m*; ~ **hole** *n* ASTRON, PHYS, SPACE trou noir *m*; ~ **ice** *n* METEO glace noire *f*; ~ **iron oxide** *n* COLOURS oxyde de fer noir *m*; ~ **iron sand** *n* PROD ENG sable noir ferrugineux *m*; ~ **japan** *n* COLOURS laque à l'asphalte *f*, vernis à l'asphalte *m*; ~ **lead** *n* COLOURS graphite *m*, plombinage *m*; ~ **lead crucible** *n* PROD ENG creuset de plombagine *m*, creuset en mine de plomb *m*; ~ **leader** *n* CINEMAT amorce noire *f*; ~ **letter** *n* PRINT lettre gothique *f*; ~ **level** *n* TV niveau de noir *m*; ~ **level frequency** *n* TV fréquence du niveau de noir *f*; ~ **lift** *n* TV décollement du noir *m*; ~ **light** *n* PRINT lumière noire *f*; ~ **liquor** *n* HYDROL eau noire *f*, PAPER TECH liqueur noire *f*; ~ **peak** *n* TV crête du noir *f*; ~ **porch** *n* TV palier du noir *m*; ~ **printer** *n* PRINT film noir *m*, plaque du noir *f*, squelette noir *m*; ~ **shading** *n* TV voile *m*; ~ **shale** *n* GEOL ampélite *f*, black shale *m*; ~ **spacing** *n* CINEMAT amorce noire *f*; ~ **speck** *n* C&G pierre noire *f*; ~ **squall** *n* OCEANOG grain noir *m*; ~ **stain** *n* C&G noir pour grisaille *m*; ~ **staining** *n* C&G cémentation en noir *f*; ~ **start-up** *n* NUCLEAR *of nuclear plant* démarrage autonome *m*; ~ **stretch** *n* TV étalement des noirs *m*; ~ **tellurium** *n* MINERAL tellure auroplombifère *m*; ~ **tide** *n* MAR POLL, POLLUTION marée noire *f*; ~ **varnish** *n* COLOURS laque noire *f*; ~ **water** *n* POLLUTION eau usée *f*
black:[2] ~ **out** *vt* CINEMAT décrocher, fermer dans un fondu, noircir
blacken *vt* THERMOD *with heat* carboniser, noircir
blackened *adj* THERMOD *with heat* carbonisé, noirci

blackening *n* C&G noircissement *m*, PAPER TECH plombage *m*, PROD ENG *foundry facing* noircissage *m*, noircissement *m*
blacking *n* PROD ENG *foundry facing* noircissement *m*; ~ **bag** *n* PROD ENG *founding* sac à noir *m*
blackout *n* TELECOM silence radio *m*; ~ **curtain** *n* TEXTILES rideau d'obscurcissement *m*
blacksmith *n* MECH ENG forgeron *m*, maréchal-ferrant *m*
blacksmith's: ~ **bellow** *n* MECH ENG soufflet de forge *m*; ~ **forge** *n* MECH ENG atelier de forgeron *m*, forge artisanale *f*; ~ **hammer** *n* MECH ENG marteau de forgeron *m*; ~ **shop** *n* MECH ENG atelier de forgeron *m*; ~ **tongs** *n pl* MECH ENG tenaille de forgeron *f*
blackwall: ~ **hitch** *n* NAUT gueule-de-loup *f*
blackwash *n* COATINGS enduit de noir *m*, PROD ENG *founding* noir d'étuve *m*, noir de couche *m*
black-white: ~ **monitoring** *n* TV contrôle noir-blanc *m*
bladder: ~ **tank** *n* AERONAUT *flexible* réservoir souple *m*
blade *n* AERONAUT *of helicopter* pale *f*, CONST *of bulldozer* lame *f*, HYDR EQUIP *of turbine* aube *f*, pale *f*, MECH lame *f*, MECH ENG lame *f*, *of fan* aile *f*, ailette *f*, aube *f*, pale *f*, NAUT *of propeller* aile *f*, ailette *f*, aube *f*, pale *f*, PAPER TECH lame *f*, REFRIG *of fan* pale *f*, SPACE *spacecraft* ailette *f*, aube *f*; ~ **aerodynamic center** *n* (AmE), ~ **aerodynamic centre** *n* (BrE) AERONAUT *helicopter* foyer de la pale *m*; ~ **and slot drive** *n* AERONAUT entraînement à tournevis *m*; ~ **angle** *n* AERONAUT angle du pas *m*; ~ **angle of attack** *n* AERONAUT incidence de la pale *f*; ~ **angle check gage** *n* (AmE), ~ **angle check gauge** *n* (BrE) AERONAUT vérificateur d'angle de pale *m*; ~ **aspect ratio** *n* AERONAUT allongement de la pale *m*; ~ **attachment fitting** *n* AERONAUT *of helicopter* ferrure d'attache de la pale *f*; ~ **balance** *n* AERONAUT équilibrage des pales *m*; ~ **balance weight** *n* AERONAUT *of helicopter* masse d'équilibrage de pale *f*; ~ **bit** *n* PETR TECH trépan à lames *m*; ~ **center of pressure** *n* (AmE), ~ **centre of pressure** *n* (BrE) AERONAUT centre de poussée de la pale *m*; ~ **chord** *n* AERONAUT corde de la pale *f*; ~ **coater** *n* PAPER TECH coucheuse à lame *f*; ~ **coating** *n* PAPER TECH couchage à la lame *m*, PRINT couchage à la lame *m*, couchage à la racle *m*; ~ **control system** *n* AERONAUT *of helicopter* dispositif de commande de pale *m*; ~ **cross-section** *n* AERONAUT section de la pale *f*; ~ **cuff** *n* AERONAUT ferrure de pied de pale *f*; ~ **depth** *n* AERONAUT profondeur de pale *f*; ~ **distortion** *n* AERONAUT *of helicopter* déformation de la pale *f*; ~ **duct** *n* AERONAUT *of helicopter* conduit de pale *m*; ~ **efficiency factor** *n* AERONAUT facteur d'efficacité de la pale *m*; ~ **flapping angle** *n* AERONAUT *of helicopter* angle de battement de pale *m*; ~ **folder** *n* PRINT plieuse à lame *f*; ~ **folding** *n* AERONAUT *of helicopter* repliage de la pale *m*; ~ **folding hinge** *n* AERONAUT *of helicopter* articulation de repliage des pales *f*; ~ **holder** *n* MECH ENG porte-lame *m*; ~ **leading edge** *n* AERONAUT *of helicopter* bord d'attaque de pale *m*; ~ **life** *n* AERONAUT durée de vie de la pale *f*; ~ **lift** *n* AERONAUT *of helicopter* portance de la pale *f*; ~ **lift coefficient** *n* AERONAUT *of helicopter* coefficient de portance de pale *m*; ~ **loading** *n* AERONAUT *of helicopter* charge de pale *f*; ~ **lower surface** *n* AERONAUT *of helicopter* intrados de la pale *m*; ~ **materials** *n pl* FUELLESS matériaux composant des ailes *m pl*, matériaux composant des pales *m pl*; ~ **moment of inertia** *n* AERONAUT *of helicopter* moment d'inertie de la pale *m*; ~ **pitch** *n* FUELLESS *turbines* pas de l'aubage *m*; ~ **pitch angle** *n* AERONAUT angle d'attaque de pale *m*,

angle d'incidence de pale *m*, angle de pas de pale *m*; ~
pitch change hinge *n* AERONAUT *of helicopter* articulation de pas *f*; ~ **pitch change rod** *n* AERONAUT *of helicopter* biellette de commande de pas *f*; ~ **pitch control compensator** *n* AERONAUT *of helicopter* compensateur de commande de pas *m*; ~ **pitch indicator** *n* AERONAUT indicateur de pas des pales *m*; ~ **pitch reversal** *n* TRANSP inversion du pas de l'hélice *f*; ~ **pitch setting** *n* AERONAUT *of helicopter* réglage du pas des pales *m*; ~ **pitch transmitter** *n* AERONAUT *of helicopter* transmetteur de pas *m*; ~ **pitch variation** *n* AERONAUT variation du pas de la pale *f*; ~ **pocket** *n* AERONAUT *of helicopter* caisson de pale *m*; ~ **profile** *n* AERONAUT profil de pale *m*; ~ **quantity** *n* FUELLESS nombre d'ailes *m*, nombre de pales *m*; ~ **radius** *n* AERONAUT rayon de pale *m*; ~ **retention strap** *n* AERONAUT lame de retenue de pale *f*; ~ **root** *n* AERONAUT pied d'aube *m*, talon d'aube *m*; ~ **setting** *n* AERONAUT *of helicopter* réglage de pale *m*; ~ **setting angle** *n* AERONAUT angle de calage de pale *m*; ~ **shank** *n* AERONAUT *of helicopter* extrémité de pied de pale *f*; ~ **shutter** *n* CINEMAT obturateur à pales *m*; ~ **slap** *n* AERONAUT *of helicopter* claquement de pales *m*; ~ **sleeve** *n* AERONAUT *of helicopter* manchon de pale *m*; ~ **spacing system** *n* AERONAUT *of helicopter* câble d'équipartition *m*, système de calage des aubes *m*; ~ **span axis** *n* AERONAUT *of helicopter* axe de la pale *m*; ~ **speed** *n* FUELLESS vitesse des aubes *f*, vitesse des pales *f*; ~ **spindle** *n* AERONAUT *of helicopter* fusée de pale *f*; ~ **spring** *n* MECH ENG ressort plat *m*; ~ **stall** *n* AERONAUT *of helicopter* décrochage des pales *m*; ~ **stop** *n* AERONAUT *of helicopter* butée de pale *f*; ~ **sweep** *n* AERONAUT déport dans le plan de rotation *m*; ~ **tilt** *n* AERONAUT *of helicopter* angle de calage de pale *m*, déport dans l'avancement *m*; ~ **tip** *n* AERONAUT bout de pale *m*; ~ **tip cap** *n* AERONAUT *of helicopter* saumon de pale *m*; ~ **tip fairing** *n* AERONAUT *of helicopter* carénage de bout de pale *m*; ~ **tip loss factor** *n* AERONAUT *of helicopter* facteur de perte en bout de pale *m*; ~ **tip nozzle** *n* AERONAUT *of helicopter* tuyère d'extrémité de pale *f*; ~ **tip stall** *n* AERONAUT *helicopter* décrochage de bout de pale *m*; ~ **tip vortex** *n* AERONAUT *of helicopter* tourbillon d'extrémité de pale *m*; ~ **tracking** *n* AERONAUT *of helicopter* alignement des pales *m*; ~ **trailing edge** *n* AERONAUT bord de fuite de pale *m*; ~ **trim tab** *n* AERONAUT *of helicopter* tab de réglage d'incidence de pale *m*; ~ **upper surface** *n* AERONAUT *of helicopter* extrados de la pale *m*; ~ **width ratio** *n* AERONAUT *of helicopter* allongement de pale *m*
blade-twisting: ~ **moment** *n* AERONAUT moment de torsion de la pale *m*
blading *n* MECH ailettage de turbine *m*, aubage *m*
blanch *vt* FOOD TECH blanchir, faire cuire à demi
bland: ~ **formula** *n* PROD ENG bon de mélange *m*
blank[1] *adj* COMP, DP blanc, vierge
blank[2] *n* COMP, DP caractère blanc *m*, caractère espace *m*, MECH bride aveugle *f*, flan *m*, PRINT blanc *m*, zone non imprimée *f*, PROD ENG flan *m*, ébauche *f*, *metal* pièce brute d'usinage *f*; ~ **cartridge** *n* MILIT cartouche à blanc *f*; ~ **circle** *n* MECH ENG *gearing* cercle de tête *m*, cercle extérieur *m*; ~ **cracking** *n* C&G ouverture de l'ébaucher *f*; ~ **door** *n* CONST porte aveugle *f*, porte fausse *f*; ~ **flange** *n* MECH ENG bride pleine *f*; ~ **glass** *n* C&G verre non décoré *m*; ~ **groove** *n* ACOUSTICS sillon blanc *m*; ~ **liner** *n* PETR TECH *drilling* colonne perdue non crépinée *f*, tube perdu non crépiné *m*; ~ **magnetic tape** *n* TV bande magnétique vierge *f*; ~ **medium** *n* DP

support vierge *m*; ~ **mold** *n* (AmE) *see blank mould*; ~ **mold seam** *n* (AmE) *see blank mould seam*; ~ **mold turnover** *n* (AmE) *see blank mould turnover*; ~ **mould** *n* (BrE) C&G moule ébaucheur *m*; ~ **mould seam** *n* (BrE) C&G couture ébaucheur *f*; ~ **mould turnover** *n* (BrE) C&G renversement de l'ébaucheur *m*; ~ **nut** *n* PROD ENG écrou non taraudé *m*; ~ **printing** *n* PRINT impression en blanc *f*; ~ **seam** *n* C&G couture ébaucheur *f*; ~ **table** *n* C&G plateau des ébaucheurs *m*; ~ **tear** *n* C&G pli d'ébauche *m*; ~ **test** *n* PRINT essai en blanc *m*; ~ **ticket** *n* PACKAGING étiquette vierge *f*; ~ **transfer** *n* C&G transfert de l'ébauche *m*; ~ **trimmings** *n pl* PRINT chutes non imprimées *f pl*; ~ **wall** *n* CONST mur aveugle *m*; ~ **washer** *n* MECH ENG rondelle d'obturation *f*; ~ **window** *n* CONST fenêtre aveugle *f*
blank[3] *vt* PROD ENG masquer; ~ **off** *vt* PROD ENG obturer
blank-and-burst: ~ **message** *n* TELECOM message neutralisation-salve *m*
blanked: ~ **beam** *n* ELECTRON faisceau supprimé *m*
blanked-off: ~ **channel** *n* TELECOM voie neutralisée *f*
blanket[1] *n* C&G nappe *f*, PRINT blanchet *m*, SPACE *spacecraft* couverture *f*, matelas *m*, TEXTILES couverture *f*; ~ **charger** *n* C&G enfourneuse en tapis *f*; ~ **cylinder** *n* PRINT cylindre blanchet *m*; ~ **feed** *n* C&G enfournement en nappe *m*; ~ **gas** *n* NUCLEAR gaz de couverture *m*; ~ **reprocessing circuit** *n* NUCLEAR circuit de traitement de matières fertiles *m*; ~ **separation plant** *n* NUCLEAR installation de séparation des matières fertiles *f*; ~ **washer** *n* PRINT dispositif de lavage des blanchets *m*
blanket[2] *vt* NUCLEAR garnir d'une couverture
blanketing *n* PETR TECH *production safety* inertage *m*
blanket-to-blanket *adj* PRINT blanchet-blanchet
blanket-type: ~ **insulant** *n* REFRIG isolant en matelas souple *m*
blank-fed *adj* PRINT alimenté en blanc
blanking *n* ELECTRON suppression du faisceau *f*, PROD ENG découpage à la presse *m*, TV effacement *m*, suppression *f*; ~ **and sync signal** *n* TV signal de suppression et de synchronisation *m*; ~ **and sync signal mixer** *n* TV mélangeur de mesure *m*; ~ **circuit** *n* TV circuit de suppression *m*; ~ **cover** *n* AERONAUT bouchon obturateur *m*; ~ **cover for air-cooling unit outlet** *n* AERONAUT obturateur d'évacuation d'air re-froidisseur *m*; ~ **cover for fin air scoop** *n* AERONAUT obturateur d'entrée d'air dérivé *m*; ~ **die** *n* MECH ENG *for small intricate processes* matrice de poinçonnage *f*, *press tools* outillage de découpage de flan *m*; ~ **effect** *n* AERONAUT ombre aérodynamique *f*; ~ **generator** *n* ELECTRON générateur d'impulsions de suppression *m*; ~ **interval** *n* TV intervalle de suppression *m*; ~ **level** *n* TV niveau de suppression *m*; ~ **operations** *n pl* MECH ENG *to produce blanks* ébauchage *m*; ~ **plate** *n* AERONAUT plaque obturatrice *f*, plaquette d'obturation *f*; ~ **plug** *n* PROD ENG obturateur plug *m*; ~ **press** *n* MECH ENG presse d'ébauchage *f*, presse de découpage *f*, presse à découper *f*; ~ **pulse** *n* TV impulsion de suppression *f*; ~ **signal** *n* ELECTRON, TV signal de suppression *m*; ~ **voltage** *n* TV tension de suppression *f*
blast[1] *n* AERONAUT souffle *m*, PROD ENG courant d'air *m*, SPACE *spacecraft* souffle *m*; ~ **fence** *n* AERONAUT *barrier* barrière antisouffle *f*, écran anti-souffle *m*, écran pare-souffle *m*; ~ **forming** *n* P&R *plastics* formage par soufflage *m*; ~ **freezing** *n* FOOD TECH congélation sous courant d'air *f*; ~ **furnace** *n* C&G haut-fourneau *m*, COAL TECH haut-fourneau conventionnel *m*, HEATING,

MECH ENG, PROD ENG, THERMOD haut-fourneau *m*; ~ **furnace campaign** *n* PROD ENG campagne de haut-fourneau *f*; ~ **furnace cement** *n* CONST ciment de haut-fourneau *m*; ~ **furnace for coke** *n* PROD ENG haut-fourneau au coke *m*; ~ **furnace gas** *n* PROD ENG gaz de haut-fourneau *m*, gaz pauvre de haut-fourneau *m*; ~ **furnace slag** *n* PROD ENG laitiers de hauts fourneaux *m pl*, scories de hauts fourneaux *f pl*; ~ **gage** *n* (AmE) *see blast gauge*; ~ **gate** *n* PROD ENG registre de réglage du vent *m*, vanne de réglage de vent *f*;~ **gauge** *n* (BrE) PROD ENG indicateur de pression de vent *m*; ~ **hole** *n* MINING chambre de mine *f*, fourneau de mine *m*, mine *f*, trou de mine *m*, forage *m*, sondage *m*, troude sonde *m*, trou *m*; ~ **main** *n* PROD ENG *of furnace, cupola* conduite de vent *f*; ~ **nozzle** *n* PROD ENG tuyère *f*, *at end of blowpipe* buse *f*, busillon *m*; ~ **on the horn** *n* CONTROL appel de klaxon *m*, appel de trompe *m*; ~ **pipe** *n* PROD ENG *of blower* porte-vent *m*, tube porte-vent *m*; ~ **preheater** *n* THERMOD *metals* réchauffeur d'air *m*; ~ **pressure** *n* PROD ENG pression du vent *f*; ~ **shelter** *n* COAL TECH abri *m*

blast[2] *vt* COAL TECH, CONST abattre à l'explosif, fragmenter par explosif; ~ **by heating** *vt* COAL TECH étonner

blasted: ~ **stone** *n* COAL TECH débris de rocher *m*

blaster *n* COAL TECH préposé au tir *m*, MINING *machine* exploseur *m*

blasting *n* COAL TECH abattage *m*, minage *m*, CONST minage *m*, MINING abattage par explosifs *m*, abattage à l'explosif *m*, minage *m*, sautage *m*, tir de mines *m*, tirage *m*; ~ **cap** *n* MINING amorce *f*, détonateur de mine *m*; ~ **charge** *n* MINING charge explosive *f*; ~ **foreman** *n* CONST, MINING boutefeu *m*; ~ **fuse** *n* MINING mèche de sûreté *f*, mèche lente *f*; ~ **gelatine** *n* MINING dynamite gomme *f*, gomme *f*, gélatine explosive *f*; ~ **machine** *n* MINING exploseur *m*; ~ **pattern** *n* MINING plan de tir *m*

blastoff *n* SPACE *spacecraft* mise à feu *f*

blastomylonite *n* GEOL blastomylonite *f*

blazar *n* ASTRON blazar *m*

blaze[1] *n* THERMOD *fire* feu *m*, flambée *f*, flamme *f*, incendie *m*, *of light* torrent de lumière *m*

blaze:[2] ~ **up** *vi* THERMOD s'embraser, s'enflammer

blazed: ~ **grating** *n* PHYS réseau en échelette *m*

blazing[1] *adj* TEXTILES flamboyant, THERMOD *fire* ardent

blazing:[2] ~ **fire** *n* CONST feu d'enfer *m*

bleach:[1] ~ **liquor** *n* PROD ENG solution de chlorure de calcium *f*

bleach[2] *vt* CHEM blanchir, décolorer, CINEMAT blanchir, FOOD TECH *flour*, PACKAGING décolorer, PAPER TECH, PRINT blanchir, TEXTILES décolorer; ~ **out** *vt* PHOTO blanchir

bleached: ~ **flour** *n* FOOD TECH *baking, milling* farine blanche *f*, farine blanchie *f*; ~ **lined board** *n* PAPER TECH *folding boxboard* carton blanchi *m*; ~ **pulp** *n* PACKAGING cellulose blanchie *f*, PAPER TECH pâte blanchie *f*

bleacher *n* PAPER TECH pile blanchisseuse *f*

bleaching[1] *n* CHEM blanchiment *m*, décoloration *f*, DETERGENTS blanchiment *m*, décoloration *f*, blanchissage *m*, PAPER TECH blanchiment *m*, PRINT blanchiment *m*, décoloration *f*; ~ **agent** *n* DETERGENTS agent de blanchiment *m*, agent décolorant *m*, chlorure décolorant *m*, FOOD TECH agent de blanchiment *m*, décolorant *m*, produit blanchissant *m*, TEXTILES *chloride* décolorant *m*; ~ **bath** *n* CINEMAT, PHOTO bain de blanchiment *m*; ~ **chest** *n* PAPER TECH cuvier de

blanchiment *m*; ~ **clay** *n* C&G terre à blanchir *f*; ~ **earth** *n* DETERGENTS argile smectique décolorante *f*, terre décolorante *f*; ~ **lime** *n* DETERGENTS chaux chlorée *f*, chlorure de chaux *m*, hypochlorite de chaux *m*; ~ **liquor** *n* PAPER TECH solution de blanchiment *f*; ~ **powder** *n* DETERGENTS chaux chlorée *f*, chlorure de chaux *m*, hypochlorite de chaux *m*, FOOD TECH poudre à blanchir *f*, PAPER TECH chlorure de chaux *m*; ~ **tower** *n* PAPER TECH tour de blanchiment *f*; ~ **washer** *n* PAPER TECH pile blanchisseuse *f*

bleaching[2] *vt* FOOD TECH *baking and milling* blanchiment *m*

bleaching-resistant *adj* COLOURS résistant à la décoloration

bleed[1] *n* PRINT fond perdu *m*, impression à fonds perdus *f*; ~ **elbow** *n* MECH ENG coude de piquage *m*; ~ **flow** *n* PROD ENG débit de purge *m*; ~ **off** *n* PRINT impression à fonds perdus *f*; ~ **plug** *n* MECH ENG bouchon de purge *m*; ~ **printing** *n* PRINT impression à fonds perdus *f*; ~ **screw** *n* MECH ENG vis-bouchon d'un orifice de purge *f*; ~ **valve** *n* AUTO purgeur *m*, MECH ENG clapet de purge *m*, robinet de purge *m*, PETR TECH vanne de purge *f*

bleed[2] *vt* CINEMAT effilocher, franger, MECH soutirer, MECH ENG purger; ~ **down** *vt* PETR purger; ~ **off** *vt* COAL TECH purger, PETR décomprimer, TEXTILES dégorger

bleed[3] *vi* P&R *of paint* dégorger

bleeder *n* ELEC ENG charge stabilisatrice *f*; ~ **resistor** *n* ELEC ENG résistance stabilisatrice *f*; ~ **screw** *n* AUTO vis de purge *f*; ~ **winding** *n* ELEC enroulement dérivé *m*, enroulement en dérivation *m*

bleeder-type: ~ **condenser** *n* REFRIG condenseur à purgeur *m*

bleeding *n* MECH soutirage *m*, MECH ENG *of brakes* purge *f*, NUCLEAR mise à l'air *f*, purge de l'air *f*, soutirage *m*, PETR TECH purge *f*, PRINT *of pigments into paper* dégorgement *m*; ~ **cock** *n* WATER SUPP robinet de purge *m*; ~ **valve** *n* WATER SUPP robinet de purge *m*; ~ **whites** *n pl* TV coulées de blancs *f pl*

bleed-off *n* REFRIG purge *f*

bleep[1] *n* CINEMAT bip *m*

bleep[2] *vi* NAUT *of radio, satellite signal* faire bip-bip

B-leg *n* TELECOM conducteur de nuque *m*, fil de nuque *m*

blemish *n* FOOD TECH anomalie *f*, défaut *m*, défectuosité *f*

blend[1] *n* P&R, PAPER TECH, TEXTILES mélange *m*; ~ **ratio** *n* TEXTILES pourcentage de mélange *m*

blend[2] *vt* MECH ENG *industrial activity, residential areas* imbriquer, P&R combiner, mélanger, PAPER TECH, TEXTILES mélanger

blende *n* MINERAL blende *f*, PROP MAT hornblende *f*

blender *n* C&G, P&R *equipment*, PAPER TECH mélangeur *m*

blending *n* PROD ENG *founding* coupage *m*, RAIL *vehicles* conjugaison *f*; ~ **agent** *n* PROP MAT diluant *m*; ~ **chest** *n* PAPER TECH cuvier de mélange *m*; ~ **plant** *n* PETR TECH installation de mélange *f*

blendous *adj* PROD ENG blendeux

blendy *adj* PROD ENG blendeux

blibe *n* C&G bouillon élongé *m*

blimp[1] *n* CINEMAT caisson insonore *m*

blimp[2] *vt* CINEMAT insonoriser

blimped: ~ **camera** *n* CINEMAT caméra autosilencieuse *f*

blind[1] *adj* SPACE aveugle

blind[2] *n* MECH obturateur *m*, VEHICLES *of radiator* rideau d'obstruction *m*; ~ **alley** *n* CONST cul-de-sac *m*, passage sans issue *m*; ~ **angle** *n* AERONAUT angle mort *m*; ~ **arch** *n* CONST *architecture* fausse arche *f*, fausse voûte *f*; ~ **auction** *n* PETR TECH enchères sous plis fermés *f pl*; ~ **blocking** *n* PRINT estampage *m*, gaufrage *m*, gaufrage à sec *m*; ~ **door** *n* CONST fausse porte *f*; ~ **drainage area** *n* WATER SUPP bassin fermé *m*; ~ **drill roll** *n* PAPER TECH rouleau à trous borgnes *m*; ~ **embossing** *n* PRINT estampage *m*, gaufrage à sec *m*, tracé *m*; ~ **flange** *n* MECH ENG bride d'obturation *f*, bride pleine *f*; ~ **flight** *n* AERONAUT vol sans visibilité *m*; ~ **hole** *n* CONST trou borgne *m*, PROP MAT borgne *m*; ~ **image** *n* PRINT surface imprimante repoussant l'encre *f*; ~ **keyboard** *n* PRINT clavier aveugle *m*; ~ **landing** *n* AERONAUT atterrissage sans visibilité *m*; ~ **level** *n* MINING galerie en cul-de-sac *f*; ~ **navigation** *n* SPACE navigation sans visibilité *f*; ~ **pit** *n* CONST puits borgne *m*; ~ **rivet** *n* MECH ENG rivet aveugle *m*; ~ **roaster** *n* PROD ENG four à moufle *m*; ~ **sector without traffic rights** *n* AERONAUT, TRANSP tronçon de route sans droits de trafic *m*; ~ **shaft** *n* CONST puits borgne *m*; ~ **stud bolt** *n* MECH ENG prisonnier *m*; ~ **thrust** *n* GEOL chevauchement aveugle *m*; ~ **wall** *n* CONST façade borgne *f*, mur borgne *m*, mur masqué *m*, mur orbe *m*; ~ **washer** *n* MECH ENG rondelle d'obturation *f*, rondelle pleine *f*; ~ **window** *n* CONST fausse fenêtre *f*; ~ **workings** *n pl* CONST chantier d'exploitation borgne *m*; ~ **zone** *n* PETR zone aveugle *f*, zone morte *f*

blinding *n* PROD ENG *of screen, sieve* engorgement *m*; ~ **concrete** *n* CONST béton de propreté *m*, béton maigre *m*, forme en béton *f*

blink *vi* COMP *of graphic display* clignoter

blinker *n* PRINT clignotant *m*, VEHICLES clignotant *m*, clignoteur *m*

blinking *n* COMP clignotement *m*; ~ **light** *n* PRINT lumière clignotante *f*, SPACE feu clignotant *m*

blip *n* TELECOM réponse *f*; ~ **tone** *n* CINEMAT mille *m*

blister *n* AERONAUT *of helicopter* coupole *f*, C&G bouillon *m*, NAUT *GRP construction, paint* bulle *f*, cloque *f*, P&R cloque *f*, PAPER TECH bulle *f*, cloque *f*, PRINT blister *m*, cloque *f*, PROD ENG cloque *f*, *air bubble in casting* soufflure *f*, TESTING cloque *f*; ~ **card** *n* PACKAGING carte thermoformée *f*; ~ **edge and foil machine** *n* PACKAGING machine pour emballage thermoformé avec aluminium mince *f*; ~ **pack** *n* PACKAGING emballage thermoformé *m*, habillage transparent *m*, PRINT blister *m*, coquille de plastique *f*; ~ **packaging machine** *n* PACKAGING machine pour emballage thermoformé *f*; ~ **packing line** *n* PACKAGING chaîne d'emballage thermoformé *f*; ~ **pack tooling** *n* MECH ENG outils pour emballages sous feuilles plastiques *m pl*; ~ **sealer** *n* PACKAGING fermeture pour emballage thermoformé *f*

blistering *n* PAPER TECH cloquage *m*, soufflette *f*, PRINT cloquage *m*; ~ **test** *n* TESTING essai de cloquage *m*

blizzard *n* METEO blizzard *m*

bloach *n* C&G tache de jour *f*

bloating *n* OCEANOG saurissage *m*, PAPER TECH boursouflure *f*

block[1] *n* C&G tête du diamant *f*, COAL TECH bloc *m*, CONST *of land* parcelle *f*, MECH ENG *of anvil* billot *m*, table *f*, *wedge* cale *f*, NAUT *pulley* poulie *f*, PETR TECH *prospecting and production licence* bloc *m*, PRINT bloc *m*, cliché typographique *m*, cliché *m*, cliché à dorer *m*, PROD ENG cale *f*, SPACE *of ice* bloc *m*; ~ **and tackle** *n* MECH ENG moufle *m*, palan *m*; ~ **capitals** *n pl* PRINT lettres capitales bâton *f pl*; ~ **carriage** *n* MECH ENG *of*

overhead travelling crane chariot de palan *m*; ~ **chain** *n* MECH ENG chaîne à maillons plats *f*; ~ **check** *n* CONTROL contrôle par bloc *m*; ~ **coding** *n* TELECOM codage par blocs *m*; ~ **compaction** *n* COMP compression de blocs *f*; ~ **compression** *n* COMP compression de blocs *f*; ~ **copolymer** *n* P&R copolymère en masse *m*; ~ **diagram** *n* COMP schéma fonctionnel *m*, ELEC ENG schéma fonctionnel synoptique *m*, MECH ENG schéma de principe *m*, TELECOM schéma synoptique *m*; ~ **dropping indicator** *n* TELECOM indicateur d'abandon de bloc *m*; ~ **error rate** *n* COMP taux d'erreurs sur les blocs *m*; ~ **faulting** *n* GEOL compartimentage *m*, faille de bloc *f*; ~ **grease** *n* MECH ENG graisse consistante *f*; ~ **headway** *n* RAIL distance *f*; ~ **lava** *n* GEOL lave blocailleuse *f*; ~ **length** *n* COMP longueur de bloc *f*; ~ **letters** *n pl* PRINT lettres de titrage *f pl*, lettres majuscules écrites à la main *f pl*; ~ **number** *n* PETR TECH numéro de bloc *m*; ~ **polymer** *n* DETERGENTS copolymère block *m*; ~ **polymerization** *n* DETERGENTS polymérisation en masse *f*, PROP MAT copolymérisation en bloc *f*; ~ **print** *n* PRINT cliché typographique *m*; ~ **printing** *n* PRINT impression de titres par dorure à chaud *f*, impression typographique *f*, typographie *f*, TEXTILES impression à la planche *f*; ~ **quantization** *n* TELECOM quantification des blocs *f*; ~ **salt cake** *n* (BrE) *(cf salt cake)* FOOD TECH sulfate de sodium commercial *m*; ~ **section** *n* RAIL canton de block *m*; ~ **sensor** *n* PROD ENG détecteur carré *m*; ~ **shear test** *n* MECH ENG essai de cisaillement par compression *m*; ~ **signal locked** *n* RAIL blocage à l'aubinage *m*; ~ **size** *n* COMP longueur de bloc *f*, ~ **sort** *n* COMP tri par bloc *m*; ~ **speed** *n* AERONAUT vitesse commerciale *f*, TRANSP vitesse commerciale *f*, vitesse de cale à cale *f*; ~ **structure** *n* COMP structure de bloc *f*; ~ **system** *n* RAIL block *m*, cantonnement *m*, système de bloc *m*; ~ **terminal** *n* TELECOM boîte de raccordement *f*, rosace de raccordement *f*, *on subscriber's telephone* boîte d'entrée *f*; ~ **time** *n* AERONAUT temps bloc *m*; ~ **tin** *n* PROD ENG étain en saumon *m*; ~ **train** *n* RAIL *vehicles* train-bloc *m*; ~ **transfer** *n* COMP, DP transfert de blocs *m*, transfert par blocs *m*; ~ **transfer read** *n* PROD ENG transfert en bloc lecture *m*; ~ **transfer write** *n* PROD ENG transfert en bloc écriture *m*; ~ **transmission** *n* TELECOM transmission en bloc *f*

block[2] *vt* MECH ENG bloquer, caler, NAUT *harbour* bloquer; ~ **out** *vt* PRINT masquer

blockade[1] *n* NAUT *of harbour* blocus *m*

blockade[2] *vt* NAUT bloquer

blockage: ~ **effects** *n pl* TELECOM effets de blocage *m pl*

blocked: ~ **impedance** *n* ELEC ENG impédance statique *f*; ~ **reactance** *n* ELEC ENG réactance statique *f*

blocked-out: ~ **halftone** *n* PRINT simili détourée *f*

blockhouse *n* MILIT blockhaus *m*

blocking *n* COAL TECH blocage *m*, COMP groupage *m*, ELEC ENG *of conduction* blocage *m*, P&R adhérence de contact *f*, blocage *m*, PROD ENG colmatage *m*, TELECOM blocage *m*, TV blocage *m*, bourrage *m*, WATER SUPP colmatage *m*; ~ **anticyclone** *n* METEO anticyclone de blocage *m*; ~ **board** *n* MINING écoin *m*; ~ **capacitor** *n* ELEC condensateur d'arrêt *m*, ELEC ENG condensateur de liaison *m*, PHYS condensateur d'arrêt *m*, condensateur de blocage *m*; ~ **device** *n* ELEC ENG dispositif de blocage *m*; ~ **loss** *n* SPACE *communications* perte par effet de masque *f*; ~ **network** *n* ELEC ENG réseau avec blocage *m*, TELECOM réseau à blocage *m*; ~ **oscillator** *n* ELECTRON oscillateur bloqué *m*, PHYS oscillateur de blocage *m*; ~ **period** *n* ELEC ENG période de blocage *f*; ~

state *n* ELECTRON état bloqué *m*; ~ **temperature** *n* GEOL température de blocage *f*, température de fermeture *f*

blockmaking *n* PRINT clicherie typographique *f*, fabrication de clichés pour la reliure *f*, photogravure typographique *f*

blockout *n* PRINT détourage *m*

blocks *n pl* PETR TECH *of tackle* mouflage *m*

block-shaped: ~ **fuel element** *n* NUCLEAR bloc de combustible *m*, élément en forme de bloc *m*

block-structured: ~ **language** *n* COMP langage à structure de blocs *m*

block-to-block: ~ **time** *n* AERONAUT temps bloc *m*

block-type: ~ **element-fueled high temperature reactor** *n* (AmE), ~ **element-fuelled high temperature reactor** *n* (BrE) NUCLEAR réacteur à haute température à éléments *m*; ~ **insulant** *n* REFRIG bloc isolant *m*

blodite *n* MINERAL bloedite *f*

blood: ~ **albumin** *n* FOOD TECH albumine de sang *f*, sérum-albumine *m*; ~ **bank** *n* REFRIG banque de sang *f*; ~ **black** *n* FOOD TECH charbon de sang *m*, noir animal *m*; ~ **transfusion equipment** *n* SAFETY matériel de transfusion du sang *m*

bloodstone *n* MINERAL jaspe sanguin *m*

bloom *n* C&G *due to formation of sulphate during annealing* voile *m*, *stain* impression *f*, FOOD TECH efflorescence *f*, givre *m*, P&R *plastics, paints, rubber* efflorescence *f*; ~ **shears** *n pl* MECH ENG cisaille à blooms *f*

bloomed[1] *adj* C&G bleuté

bloomed:[2] ~ **lens** *n* CINEMAT objectif traité *m*, PHOTO lentille traitée *f*, objectif bleui *m*, objectif fluoruré *m*, PHYS objectif bleuté *m*, objectif à revêtement antiréfléchissant *m*

blooming *n* C&G application de couche antireflet *f*, CINEMAT traitement antireflet *m*, COATINGS revêtement par couches antiréfléchissantes *m*, PHOTO bleutage *m*, fluoration *f*; ~ **mill** *n* MECH ENG laminoir à blooms *m*, train ébaucheur *m*; ~ **roll** *n* MECH ENG cylindre de laminoir à blooms *m*

bloop[1] *n* CINEMAT bruit de collure dans le son *m*, claque de collage *f*, RECORDING bruit de raccord de la piste sonore *m*; ~ **lamp** *n* RECORDING *film* lampe d'effaçage du raccord de la piste sonore *f*; ~ **punch** *n* RECORDING *film* trou d'effaçage du raccord de la piste sonore *m*

bloop[2] *vt* CINEMAT zaponner

blooping *n* RECORDING *film* effaçage du raccord de la piste sonore *m*; ~ **ink** *n* CINEMAT zapon liquide *m*; ~ **notch** *n* CINEMAT encoche sonore *f*; ~ **patch** *n* RECORDING *film* enduit d'effaçage de raccord de la piste sonore *m*; ~ **tape** *n* RECORDING *film* ruban d'effaçage du raccord de la piste sonore *m*

blotch *n* TEXTILES tache *f*

blotter: ~ **material** *n* CONST *asphalting* matériau absorbant *m*

blotting: ~ **paper** *n* PAPER TECH papier buvard *m*

blow[1] *n* METALL soufflage *m*, PAPER TECH souffure *f*, PROD ENG *air hole in casing* bouillon *m*, souffure *f*, *emission of current of air* soufflage *m*; ~ **ball** *n* LAB EQUIP poire *f*; ~ **bending test** *n* MECH ENG essai de flexion au choc *m*; ~ **fill seal system** *n* PACKAGING système de remplissage en soufflant combiné avec fermeture *m*; ~ **head** *n* C&G tête de soufflage *f*; ~ **mold** *n* (AmE) *see blow mould*; ~ **molding** *n* (AmE) *see blow moulding*; ~ **mould** *n* (BrE) MECH ENG *for plastics* moule de soufflage pour plastiques *m*; ~ **moulding** *n* P&R *process* soufflage *m*, PACKAGING extrusion par

soufflage *f*; ~ **roll** *n* PAPER TECH rouleau souffleur *m*; ~ **table** *n* C&G plateau des finisseurs *m*; ~ **valve** *n* HYDR EQUIP clapet de décharge *m*, clapet de surpression *m*

blow[2] *vt* PAPER TECH souffler, PROD ENG *cupola* souffler, *fire* souffler, SPACE *spacecraft* chasser; ~ **down** *vt* WATER SUPP purger; ~ **in** *vt* PROD ENG *blast furnace* mettre en feu, mettre à feu; ~ **off** *vt* WATER SUPP purger; ~ **up** *vt* CINEMAT gonfler, PHOTO agrandir

blow:[3] ~ **up** *vi* SPACE exploser

blow-and-blow: ~ **process** *n* C&G procédé soufflé-soufflé *m*

blowback *n* AUTO explosion au carburateur *f*, retour au carburateur *m*, C&G refoulement *m*

blowdown[1] *n* HEAT ENG *boilers* débourbage *m*, WATER SUPP purge sous pression *f*; ~ **accident** *n* NUCLEAR accident de dépressurisation *m*; ~ **pressurization** *n* SPACE *spacecraft* pressurisation non-régulée *f*; ~ **valve** *n* HEAT ENG *boilers* vanne de purge *f*

blowdown[2] *vt* HEAT ENG *boilers* débourber

blower *n* AUTO soufflante *f*, C&G souffleur *m*, FOOD TECH *food-processing machinery* soufflante *f*, MECH soufflante *f*, ventilateur *m*, METEO *for snow* chasse-neige *m*, PAPER TECH *exhaust* ventilateur souffant *m*, PROD ENG soufflerie *f*, souffleur *m*, *engine for blast furnace* machine soufflante *f*, soufflante *f*, *force fan* ventilateur *m*, ventilateur soufflant *m*, REFRIG *of fan* soufflante *f*, VEHICLES *in cooling system* soufflante *f*, soufflerie *f*; ~ **brush** *n* CINEMAT pinceau soufflant *m*, PHOTO blaireau pour épousseter *m*; ~ **cock** *n* PROD ENG robinet de souffleur *m*; ~ **wheel** *n* MECH ENG rotor de ventilateur *m*

blowhole *n* OCEANOG trou souffleur *m*, PROD ENG soufflure *f*

blowing *n* C&G soufflage *m*, FOOD TECH *of tins, cans* bombement *m*, PROD ENG soufflage *m*; ~ **agent** *n* P&R *compounding* agent de gonflement *m*; ~ **crown** *n* C&G couronne de soufflage *f*; ~ **engine** *n* PROD ENG machine soufflante *f*, soufflante *f*, soufflet *m*; ~ **in** *n* PROD ENG *blast furnace* mise en feu *f*, mise à feu *f*; ~ **out** *n* PROD ENG *blast furnace* mise hors feu *f*; ~ **ring** *n* C&G couronne de soufflage *f*

blowlamp *n* CONST *brazing* lampe à braser *f*, *soldering* lampe à braser *f*, CONST *paint-burning* lampe à souder *f*, HEAT ENG, MECH ENG chalumeau *m*

blown:[1] ~ **ashore** *adj* NAUT poussé à la côte; ~ **out to sea** *adj* NAUT poussé au large; **not ~ up** *adj* C&G mal rendu (Fra), non moulé (Bel)

blown:[2] ~ **bottle** *n* PACKAGING bouteille soufflée *f*; ~ **fiber** *n* (AmE), ~ **fibre** *n* (BrE) TELECOM câble soufflé *m*; ~ **film** *n* P&R *plastics* feuille soufflée *f*; ~ **fire** *n* PROD ENG feu poussé *m*; ~ **fuse** *n* ELEC ENG fusible fondu *m*, fusible sauté *m*; ~ **fuse indicator** *n* PROD ENG voyant de fusible fusé *m*; ~ **glass** *n* PROD ENG verre soufflé *m*; ~ **glass tube** *n* LAB EQUIP tube en verre soufflé *m*; ~ **sheet** *n* (AmE) *(cf cylinder glass)* C&G verre en cylindres *m*

blown-flap *n* AERONAUT *boundary layer control* volet soufflé *m*; ~ **system** *n* AERONAUT système de volets soufflés *m*

blow-off *n* COAL TECH soufflage *m*; ~ **valve** *n* REFRIG soupape de purge *f*, soupape purgeur *f*

blow-out *vt* PROD ENG *blast furnace* mettre hors feu

blowout *n* COAL TECH soufflage *m*, PETR, PETR TECH, POLLUTION éruption *f*, SPACE *communications* extinction *f*; ~ **coil** *n* ELEC ENG bobine de soufflage *f*; ~ **fuse** *n* ELEC ENG dispositif de protection contre les claquages *m*; ~ **preventer** *n* *(BOP)* CONTROL bloc obturateur de puits *m (BOP)*, vanne d'éruption *f*, GAS TECH bloc d'obturation de puits *m (BOP)*, OCEANOG bloc obturateur de puits *m (BOP)*, PETR bloc d'obturation de puits *m (BOP)*, PETR TECH bloc obturateur *m*, bloc obturateur de puits *m, (BOP)* obturateur *m*

blowpipe *n* C&G canne *f*, CONST *welding*, MECH ENG chalumeau *m*, PROD ENG *of tuyere* porte-vent *m*

blowpiping *n* CONST travail du chalumeau *m*

blowtorch *n* CONST, MECH ENG chalumeau *m*

blowup *n* CINEMAT gonflage *m*, PRINT agrandissement photographique *m*; ~ **ascent** *n* OCEANOG décompression explosive *f*; ~ **printing** *n* CINEMAT tirage optique par agrandissement *m*

blue:[1] ~ **adder** *n* TV circuit mélangeur pour le bleu *m*; ~ **beam** *n* ELECTRON faisceau bleu *m*, TV faisceau pour le bleu *m*; ~ **beam magnet** *n* TV aimant du faisceau bleu *m*; ~ **black level** *n* TV niveau minimal du bleu *m*; ~ **brittleness** *n* METALL fragilité au bleu *f*; ~ **clay** *n* C&G argile bleue *f*; ~ **glaze pigment** *n* COLOURS pigment bleuté *m*; ~ **gun** *n* TV canon du bleu *m*; ~ **key** *n* PRINT faux décalque bleu *m*, film du cyan *m*, épreuve *f*; ~ **litmus paper** *n* CHEM papier de tournesol bleu *m*; ~ **moon** *n* ASTRON lune bleue *f*; ~ **peak level** *n* TV niveau maximal du signal bleu *m*; ~ **pot** *n* PROD ENG creuset de plombagine *m*, creuset en graphite *m*, creuset en mine de plomb *m*, creuset en plombagine *m*; ~ **primary** *n* TV bleu primaire *m*; ~ **printer** *n* PRINT film du bleu *m*, plaque du bleu *f*; ~ **quark** *n* PHYS quark bleu *m*; ~ **quartz** *n* MINERAL quartz bleu *m*; ~ **reflectance factor** *n* PAPER TECH facteur de réflectance dans le bleu *m*; ~ **sapphire** *n* MINERAL saphir bleu *m*; ~ **schist** *n* GEOL schiste bleu *m*, schiste à glaucophane *m*; ~ **screen grid** *n* TV grille-écran bleue *f*; ~ **screen process** *n* CINEMAT procédé fond bleu *m*; ~ **shift** *n* ASTRON décalage spectral vers le bleu *m*; ~ **signal** *n* ELECTRON signal bleu *m*; ~ **silica gel** *n* PACKAGING gel de silice bleue *m*; ~ **spar** *n* MINERAL lazulite *f*; ~ **stars** *n pl* ASTRON étoiles bleues *f pl*; ~ **tourmaline** *n* MINERAL tourmaline bleue *f*; ~ **vitriol** *n* CHEM couperose bleue *f*, sulfate de cuivre *m*, vitriol bleu *m*

blue[2] *vt* PRINT azurer

Blue: ~ **Peter** *n* NAUT *signal flag* pavillon de départ *m*, pavillon de partance *m*

blue-green: ~ **laser** *n* ELECTRON laser bleu-vert *m*

blueground *n* GEOL brèche diamantifère *f*

blueprint *n* CONST bleu *m*, MECH ENG tirage *m*, PRINT épreuve *f*, PROD ENG bleu *m*, épreuve en traits blancs sur fond bleu *f*, TEXTILES bleu tirage *m*

bluestone *n* CHEM couperose bleue *f*, sulfate de cuivre *m*, vitriol bleu *m*

bluff *n* CONST escarpement *m*, NAUT *geography* falaise à pic *f*, OCEANOG accore *f*, microfalaise *f*

bluff-bowed *adj* NAUT *ship* à proue renflée

blunt[1] *adj* MECH ENG, PRINT émoussé

blunt[2] *vt* MECH ENG, PRINT émousser

blur: ~ **pan** *n* CINEMAT panoramique filé *m*

blurred: ~ **image** *n* PHYS image floue *f*

blurring *n* CINEMAT flou d'image *m*

blushing *n* P&R *paint* nuageage *m*, PRINT voile au magenta *m*

board:[1] **off** - *adj* ELECTRON hors carte, non incorporé à la carte

board[2] *n* COMP carte *f*, CONST *notice board* écriteau *m*, *timber* ais *m*, planche *f*, ELECTRON carte imprimée *f*, NAUT *of ship* bord *m*, PAPER TECH carton *m*, PRINT carte *f*, carton *m*, tablette graphique *f*, PROD ENG *of*

bellows flasque *m*, plateau *m*, TELECOM *switchboard* tableau *m*; ~ **felt** *n* PAPER TECH feutre preneur pour carton *m*; ~ **for pressing** *n* PAPER TECH carton pour emboutissage *m*; ~ **locking tab** *n* PROD ENG languette de verrouillage des cartes *f*; ~ **machine** *n* PAPER TECH machine à carton *f*; ~ **mill** *n* PACKAGING carton gris *m*

board[3] *vt* CONST *cover with boards* garnir de planches, parqueter, planchéier

board[4] *vi* NAUT *ship* aborder, accoster, aller à bord de, monter à bord de

boarding *n* AERONAUT embarquement *m*, CONST cloison de planches *f*, garniture de planches *f*, planches *f pl*, planchéiage *m*, NAUT *of ship* abordage *m*, embarquement *m*, TEXTILES mise en forme *f*; ~ **bridge** *n* AERONAUT passerelle télescopique *f*; ~ **party** *n* NAUT *of inspectors, pirates* détachement d'abordage *m*, détachement de visite *m*; ~ **platform** *n* TRANSP quai d'embarquement *m*

board-level: ~ **modem** *n* ELECTRON modem sur carte *m*

board-type: ~ **insulant** *n* REFRIG isolant en panneau *m*

boat *n* CONST *of travelling cradle* échafaud itinérant *m*, échafaud volant *m*, échafaudage volant *m*, échelle suspendue *f*, LAB EQUIP *analysis* coupelle *f*, MAR POLL navire *m*, NAUT barque *f*, bateau *m*, canot *m*, embarcation *f*, navire *m*, OCEANOG navire *m*, PROD ENG *founding* bouchon *m*, bouchon d'obturation de trou de coulée *m*, tampon *m*, TRANSP bateau *m*, navire *m*; ~ **carriage** *n* TRANSP remorque à bateaux *f*; ~ **chock** *n* NAUT *shipbuilding* chantier d'embarcation *m*; ~ **deck** *n* NAUT, TRANSP pont des embarcations *m*; ~ **drill** *n* NAUT exercice d'embarcation *m*, manoeuvres des embarcations *f pl*; ~ **elevator** *n* TRANSP ascenseur à bateaux *m*; ~ **fall** *n* NAUT garant de bossoir *m*; ~ **hook** *n* NAUT gaffe *f*; ~ **house** *n* TRANSP hangar à bateaux *m*; ~ **launching crane** *n* TRANSP bossoir d'embarcation *m*; ~ **lift** *n* TRANSP ascenseur à bateaux *m*; ~ **slings** *n pl* NAUT pattes d'embarcation *f pl*; ~ **stations** *n pl* NAUT *in emergency* postes d'embarcation *m pl*; ~ **tackle** *n* NAUT garant de bossoir *m*; ~ **tank** *n* TRANSP sas *m*; ~ **trailer** *n* TRANSP remorque à bateaux *f*

boat's: ~ **heading** *n* NAUT cap *m*, ligne de foi *f*

boatload *n* NAUT *of cargo* batelée *f*, *of passengers* plein bateau *m*

boatman *n* NAUT batelier *m*

boatswain *n* NAUT bosco *m*, maître d'équipage *m*

boatswain's: ~ **chair** *n* NAUT chaise de gabier *f*

bob *n* CONST *of plumb line* plomb *m*, METR *of steelyard* poids *m*, poids curseur *m*, poire *f*, PROD ENG *of beam engine* balancier *m*

bobbin *n* C&G roquet *m*, CINEMAT noyau *m*, ELEC ENG bobine isolateur *f*, MECH ENG, TEXTILES bobine *f*

bobierrite *n* MINERAL bobierrite *f*

bobstay *n* NAUT *standing rigging* sous-barbe *f*

BOC *abbr* (*Bell operating company*) (TM) TELECOM compagnie opératrice Bell *f* (MD)

BOD *abbr* (*biochemical oxygen demand*) FOOD TECH, HYDROL *sewage*, PETR TECH, POLLUTION DBO (*demande biochimique d'oxygène*)

body *n* C&G pâte *f*, HYDROL *of ore* corps *m*, massif *m*, INSTRUMENT corps *m*, tube *m*, NAUT *of ship* carène *f*, PHOTO *of camera* boîtier *m*, PRINT *of character* corps *m*, *of ink* consistance *f*, PROD ENG *of rolling mill* roll table *f*, *of water, petroleum* nappe *f*, RAIL *vehicles* caisse *f*, TELECOM corps *m*, TEXTILES *of fabric* fond *m*, VEHICLES caisse *f*, carrosserie *f*, WATER SUPP *of carriage, wagon* caisse *f*; ~ **at rest** *n* MECH corps au repos *m*; ~ **brace** *n* CINEMAT pied de poitrine *m*; ~ **filler** *n* VEHICLES mastic pour carrosserie *m*; ~ **force** *n* METALL force volumique *f*; ~ **free length** *n* SPRINGS *of coil spring* longueur libre du corps *f*; ~ **gasket** *n* PROD ENG joint d'étanchéité *m*; ~ **icing** *n* REFRIG glaçage au sein du chargement *m*; ~ **in motion** *n* MECH corps en mouvement *m*, mobile *m*; ~ **in white** *n* VEHICLES coque *f*; ~ **matter** *n* PRINT composition *f*; ~ **mold** *n* (AmE), ~ **mould** *n* (BrE) C&G corps de moule *m*; ~ **plan** *n* MECH ENG *ship design* plan des formes *m*, vertical du plan des formes *m*; ~ **of the print** *n* TEXTILES fond d'impression *m*; ~ **section** *n* NAUT *ship design* couple de tracé *m*; ~ **shell** *n* VEHICLES coque *f*; ~ **size** *n* PRINT corps de caractère *m*; ~ **tube** *n* INSTRUMENT tube électronique *m*, tube à claire-voie *m*; ~ **type** *n* PRINT caractère *m*, caractère principal *m*; ~ **waves** *n pl* GEOL ondes sismiques *f pl*

body-centered:[1] ~ **cubic** *adj* (AmE) *see body-centred cubic*

body-centered:[2] ~ **cubic lattice** *n* (AmE) CRYSTALL *see body-centered cubic lattice*; ~ **lattice** *n* (AmE) *see body-centred lattice*

body-centred:[1] ~ **cubic** *adj* (BrE) CHEM cubique centré

body-centred:[2] ~ **cubic lattice** *n* (BrE) réseau cubique centré *m*; ~ **lattice** *n* (BrE) METALL réseau centré *m*

bodying *n* PRINT *of ink* action d'épaissir *f*; ~ **agent** *n* PRINT agent épaississant *m*

body-transmitted: ~ **vibration hazard** *n* SAFETY risque dû aux vibrations transmises par des objets *m*

BOE *abbr* (*barrel oil equivalent*) PETR TECH baril équivalent pétrole *m*

boehmite *n* MINERAL boehmite *f*

bog: ~ **butter** *n* COAL TECH beurre de tourbière *m*; ~ **peat** *n* COAL TECH tourbe de marais *f*

boggy *adj* COAL TECH marécageux

boghead *n* COAL TECH boghead *m*

bogie *n* (*cf trailer, truck*) CONST, MECH ENG, RAIL *vehicles*, VEHICLES *trailer* bogie *m*; ~ **bolster** *n* (*cf truck bolster*) RAIL *vehicles* traverse danseuse *f*; ~ **frame** *n* (*cf bogie truck frame*) RAIL *vehicles* châssis de bogie *m*; ~ **kiln** *n* HEATING four à sole mobile *m*; ~ **open self-discharge wagon** *n* (BrE) (*cf truck open self-discharge car*) TRANSP wagon ouvert autodéchargeur à bogies *m*; ~ **pin** *n* (BrE) (*cf truck pin*) VEHICLES *trailer* pivot de bogie *m*; ~ **pivot** *n* (BrE) (*cf truck pivot*) VEHICLES *trailer* pivot de bogie *m*; ~ **truck** *n* (AmE) (*cf bogie*) RAIL *vehicles* bogie *m*; ~ **truck frame** *n* (AmE) (*cf bogie frame*) RAIL *vehicles* châssis de bogie *m*; ~ **wagon with swivelling roof** *n* (BrE) (*cf truck car with swiveling roof*) TRANSP wagon à bogies à toit pivotant *m*

Bohemian: ~ **crystal** *n* C&G cristal de Bohème *m*

Bohr: ~ **magneton** *n* PHYS, RAD PHYS magnéton de Bohr *m*; ~ **radius** *n* PHYS rayon de Bohr *m*

Bohr-Sommerfeld: ~ **model** *n* PHYS modèle Bohr-Sommerfeld *m*

boil[1] *n* COAL TECH boulance *f*; ~ **in bag** *n* PACKAGING sac de cuisson *m*; ~ **period** *n* PROD ENG *Bessemer process* période de décarburation *f*, période des flammes *f*

boil[2] *vt* PHYS bouillir, THERMOD bouillir, faire bouillir, *bring to boil* amener à ébullition; ~ **down** *vt* FOOD TECH concentrer par ébullition, réduire par ébullition, évaporer

boil:[3] ~ **away** *vi* THERMOD réduire, ébouillir; ~ **fast** *vi* THERMOD bouillir fort, bouillir à gros bouillons; ~ **over** *vi* THERMOD déborder; ~ **slowly** *vi* THERMOD bouil-

lir à petits bouillons

boilable: ~ **pouch** *n* PACKAGING sachet de cuisson *m*

boiled: ~ **linseed oil** *n* CHEM huile de lin cuite *f*; ~ **starch** *n* FOOD TECH empois d'amidon *m*

boiler *n* CHEM chaudière *f*, FOOD TECH *food-processing machinery* bouilleur *m*, chaudière *f*, HYDR EQUIP, MECH, MECH ENG, NAUT *engine* chaudière *f*, PAPER TECH lessiveur *m*, PHYS, RAIL *vehicles* chaudière *f*, REFRIG *used to drive off refrigerant* chaudière *f*, générateur *m*, THERMOD chaudière *f*; ~ **alarm** *n* HYDR EQUIP alarme de chaudière *f*; ~ **capacity** *n* HEATING puissance de chaudière *f*; ~ **coal** *n* COAL TECH charbon à vapeur *m*; ~ **efficiency** *n* HEATING rendement de chaudière *m*; ~ **emergency float** *n* HYDR EQUIP flotteur d'alarme de chaudière *m*; ~ **explosion** *n* HYDR EQUIP, SAFETY explosion de chaudière *f*; ~ **feeding** *n* HYDR EQUIP alimentation de chaudière *f*; ~ **feed pump** *n* HEATING pompe alimentaire de chaudière *f*; ~ **feed water** *n* PETR TECH eau d'alimentation de chaudière *f*; ~ **fittings** *n pl* HYDR EQUIP accessoires de chaudière *m pl*, accessoires de générateur *m pl*, organes accessoires de chaudière *m pl*, PROD ENG accessoires de chaudières *m pl*, organes accessoires de chaudière *m pl*; ~ **float** *n* HYDR EQUIP flotteur de chaudière *m*; ~ **flue** *n* HYDR EQUIP cheminée de chaudière *f*; ~ **front** *n* HYDR EQUIP façade de chaudière *f*; ~ **furnace** *n* HYDR EQUIP foyer de chaudière *m*; ~ **grate** *n* HEATING grille de chaudière *f*; ~ **house** *n* HEATING halle des chaudières *f*, HYDR EQUIP chaufferie *f*; ~ **inspection** *n* SAFETY visite de la chaudière *f*; ~ **jacket** *n* HYDR EQUIP caisson de chaudière *m*, revêtement isolant de chaudière *m*, chemisage extérieur de chaudière *m*; ~ **jacketing** *n* HYDR EQUIP revêtement de chaudière *m*; ~ **lagging** *n* HYDR EQUIP enveloppe isolante *f*; ~ **pipe shaping mandrel** *n* HYDR EQUIP mandrin conformateur de tubes de chaudière *m*; ~ **plate** *n* HYDR EQUIP tôle de chaudronnerie *f*; ~ **rivet** *n* HYDR EQUIP rivet de chaudière *m*, rivet de chaudronnerie *m*; ~ **room** *n* HEATING salle des chaudières *f*, HYDR EQUIP chaufferie *f*, salle de chauffe *f*; ~ **scale** *n* DETERGENTS, FOOD TECH *food-processing machinery* tartre *m*, HYDR EQUIP dépôt *m*, entartrage *m*, incrustation *f*, tartre *m*; ~ **scaling hammer** *n* HYDR EQUIP marteau à détartrer les chaudières *m*; ~ **shell** *n* HYDR EQUIP corps de chaudière *m*; ~ **stay** *n* MECH ENG entretoise de chaudière *f*; ~ **stay screwing tap** *n* MECH ENG taraud pour fileter l'entretoise de chaudière *m*; ~ **test plate** *n* HYDR EQUIP timbre de chaudière *m*; ~ **tube** *n* MECH ENG tube de chaudière *m*; ~ **tube expander** *n* HYDR EQUIP tube de dilatation *m*; ~ **water treatment** *n* HEATING traitement des eaux de chaudière *m*; ~ **works** *n pl* HYDR EQUIP atelier de chaudronnerie *m*, chaudronnerie *f*

boiler-cleaning: ~ **compound** *n* HEATING *water treatment* désincrustant *m*

boilermaker *n* HYDR EQUIP, MECH chaudronnier *m*

boilermaking *n* HEATING grosse chaudronnerie *f*, HYDR EQUIP chaudronnerie *f*

boiler-scaling: ~ **appliance** *n* RAIL *vehicles* désincrustant *m*, désincrusteur de chaudière *m*

boilersmith *n* HYDR EQUIP chaudronnier *m*

boiling[1] *adj* PHYS, THERMOD bouillant

boiling[2] *n* CHEM bouillonnement *m*, ébullition *f*, CHEM TECH, FOOD TECH ébullition *f*, PAPER TECH lessivage *m*, PHYS, REFRIG ébullition *f*; ~ **assembly** *n* NUCLEAR élément combustible à eau bouillant-surchauffé *m*; ~ **bed** *n* NUCLEAR lit bouillant *m*; ~ **fermentation** *n* CHEM

TECH fermentation par ébullition *f*; ~ **flask** *n* CHEM TECH ballon *m*; ~ **heavy water-moderated reactor** *n* NUCLEAR réacteur d'ébullition modéré à l'eau lourde *m*; ~ **plate** *n* CHEM TECH plaque chauffante *f*; ~ **point** *n* FOOD TECH point d'ébullition *m*, P&R *of solvent* point d'ébullition *m*, température d'ébullition *f*, PHYS point d'ébullition *m*, température de vaporisation *f*, THERMOD point d'ébullition *m*; ~ **range** *n* P&R *of solvent* intervalle d'ébullition *m*, PETR TECH *fractional distillation* plage d'ébullition *f*; ~ **reactor** *n* NUCLEAR réacteur à fluide bouillant *m*, réacteur à l'ébullition *m*; ~ **water reactor** *n (BWR)* PHYS réacteur à eau bouillante *m*

Bok: ~ **globule** *n* ASTRON globule de Bok *m*

bold[1] *adj* PRINT *typeface* gras

bold:[2] ~ **face** *n* PRINT caractères gras *m*; ~ **print** *n* DP impression en caractères gras *f*; ~ **shore** *n* OCEANOG accore *f*; ~ **type** *n* PRINT *typeface* caractères gras *m pl*, PROD ENG attribut gras *m*

boleite *n* MINERAL boléite *f*

bolide *n* ASTRON bolide *m*

bollard *n* NAUT bollard *m*, borne d'attache *f*, TRANSP borne *f*

bolometer *n* ASTRON, ELEC ENG, PHYS, REFRIG, SPACE bolomètre *m*

bolster *n* CONST *of chisel* ciseau à la charrue *m*, hachard *m*, *of knife* mitre *f*, MECH ENG porte-matrice *m*; ~ **plate** *n* MECH ENG *injection moulds* plaque porte-empreinte *f*

bolt[1] *n* CONST *of lock* pêne *m*, *sliding bar for fastening door* verrou *m*, verrou à coulisse *m*, MECH ENG boulon *m*, goupille filetée *f*, PROD ENG boulon *m*, VEHICLES boulon *m*, goujon *m*; ~ **circle** *n* PROD ENG cercle de boulonnage *m*, cercle de perçage *m*; ~ **cropper** *n* MECH ENG *tool*, NAUT coupe-boulons *m*; ~ **cutter** *n* MECH, MECH ENG coupe-boulons *m*; ~ **forging machine** *n* PROD ENG *for making bolts, rivets, spikes* frappeuse *f*, machine à frapper *f*; ~ **header** *n* PROD ENG boulonnière *f*; ~ **hole** *n* MECH ENG trou de boulon *m*, trou lisse *m*, trou taraudé *m*; ~ **mounting** *n* PROD ENG montage par boulons *m*; ~ **rope** *n* NAUT ralingue *f*; ~ **tongs** *n pl* PROD ENG tenaille pour boulons *f*

bolt[2] *vt* CONST *secure* boulonner, verrouiller, *sift* bluter, *fasten* cheviller, MECH *secure* boulonner

bolted: ~ **connection** *n* SPACE *spacecraft* assemblage boulonné *m*; ~ **joint** *n* MECH ENG assemblage par boulons *m*

bolthead *n* LAB EQUIP matras *m*, MECH, MECH ENG tête de boulon *f*; ~ **flask** *n* (BrE) *(cf matrass)* LAB EQUIP *glassware* ballon à col court *m*

bolting *n* CONST *sifting* blutage *m*, MECH ENG *securing* boulonnage *m*, verrouillage *m*, SAFETY *securing* boulonnage *m*, scellement *m*, scellement par boulons *m*, verrouillage *m*; ~ **cloth** *n* C&G toile à bluter *f*; ~ **fabric** *n* TEXTILES tissu pour tamisage *m*

bolt-screwing: ~ **and nut-tapping machine** *n* PROD ENG machine pour le taraudage des tiges et des écrous *f*, machine à tarauder les tiges et les écrous *f*

Boltzmann: ~ **constant** *n* PHYS, SPACE *communications* constante de Boltzmann *f*; ~ **equation** *n* RAD PHYS *particle conservation* équation de Boltzmann *f*

BOM *abbr (beginning of message)* COMP, TELECOM début de message *m*

bomb: ~ **bay** *n* MILIT soute à bombes *f*; ~ **calorimeter** *n* PHYS bombe calorimétrique *f*; ~ **disposal team** *n* MILIT équipe de désamorçage de bombes *f*; ~ **rack** *n* MILIT *on aircraft* lance-bombes *m*

bombardment *n* GAS TECH, MILIT bombardement *m*

bombing *n* MILIT bombardement *m*; ~ **area** *n* MILIT zone de bombardement *f*

bombsight *n* MILIT *on aircraft* viseur de bombardement *m*

bond[1] *n* C&G liant *m*, CHEM liaison *f*, CONST appareil *m*, parpaing *m*, *of steel to concrete in RC* adhérence *f*, *tie, fastening* attache *f*, lien *m*, CRYSTALL liaison *f*, NUCLEAR *of fuel and can* joint *m*, liaison *f*, P&R liaison *f*, PETR TECH *chemistry* liaison chimique *f*, PRINT accrochage *m*, encollage *m*, liant *m*, lien *m*, PROD ENG liant *m*, *of emery wheel* agglutinant *m*; ~ **angle** *n* CRYSTALL angle de liaison *m*; ~ **energy** *n* METALL énergie de liaison *f*; ~ **length** *n* CRYSTALL longueur de liaison *f*; ~ **separation** *n* P&R *adhesives, rubber* décollage *m*, décollement *m*; ~ **stone** *n* CONST parpaing *m*; ~ **strength** *n* CRYSTALL force de liaison *f*, énergie de liaison *f*, P&R *adhesives, rubber* force d'adhérence *f*, résistance d'adhésion *f*

bond[2] *vt* CONST liaisonner, *masonry* appareiller, *masonry joint* liaisonner, MECH coller, PACKAGING lier

bond[3] *vi* REFRIG ensimer

bonded[1] *adj* C&G encollé

bonded:[2] ~ **abrasive products** *n pl* MECH ENG produits abrasifs agglomérés *m pl*; ~ **area** *n* NAUT *of port* zone sous douane *f*; ~ **goods** *n pl* PETR TECH *commerce* marchandises sous douane *f pl*; ~ **masonry** *n* CONST maçonnerie en liaison *f*; ~ **mat** *n* C&G mat overlay *m*; ~ **metal** *n* PROP MAT tôle composée *f*; ~ **seal** *n* PACKAGING fermeture hermétique collée *f*; ~ **steel plate** *n* CONST tôle collée *f*; ~ **thread** *n* TEXTILES fil ensimé *m*; ~ **value** *n* NAUT valeur en douane *f*; ~ **warehouse** *n* NAUT entrepôt en douane *m*

bonder *n* CONST parpaing *m*

bonding *n* CONST *building* liaison *f*, *masonry* appareillage *m*, MECH collage *m*, NAUT *GRP construction* liaison *f*, P&R *adhesives* adhérence *f*, adhésion *f*, collage *m*, PROD ENG collage *m*, métallisation *f*, PROP MAT liaison *f*, REFRIG ensimage *m*, SPACE *spacecraft* métallisation *f*; ~ **agent** *n* P&R *adhesives* adhésif *m*, liant *m*, PACKAGING colle *f*; ~ **angle** *n* PROD ENG équerre de métallisation *f*; ~ **gun** *n* MECH ENG pistolet à colle *m*; ~ **jumper** *n* ELEC ENG conducteur de métallisation *m*, PROD ENG tresse de mise à la masse *f*, tresse de métallisation *f*; ~ **layer** *n* COATINGS couche adhésive *f*, couche de liage *f*; ~ **material** *n* NUCLEAR liaison *f*, PROP MAT liant *m*; ~ **pad** *n* ELECTRON *of semiconductor* pastille de contact *f*; ~ **property** *n* PROP MAT propriété liante *f*; ~ **resistance** *n* PROP MAT résistance d'adhésion *f*; ~ **strap** *n* SPACE *spacecraft* conducteur de mise à la masse *m*, tresse de mise à la masse *f*; ~ **strip** *n* PROD ENG bande de métallisation *f*, jarretière de masse *f*; ~ **strut** *n* PROD ENG borne de métallisation *f*; ~ **tab** *n* PROD ENG patte de métallisation *f*; ~ **test** *n* PACKAGING essai de collage *m*, PROD ENG essai d'adhérence *m*

bone:[1] ~ **dry** *adj* PAPER TECH sec absolu, TEXTILES sec à l'absolu

bone:[2] ~ **ash** *n* C&G cendre d'os *f*, CHEM cendre d'os *f*, claire de coupelle *f*; ~ **bank** *n* REFRIG banque d'os *f*; ~ **china** *n* C&G porcelaine tendre anglaise *f*; ~ **coal** *n* COAL TECH charbon barré *m*; ~ **conduction** *n* ACOUSTICS conduction osseuse *f*; ~ **glue** *n* TEXTILES osséine *f*; ~ **taint** *n* REFRIG *due to poor cooling of meat* altération en profondeur *f*; ~ **vibrator** *n* ACOUSTICS ossivibrateur *m*

bone[3] *vt* CONST *surveying* niveler

boning *n* CONST *of road between two points* nivellement *m*; ~ **rod** *n* CONST *surveying* nivelette *f*; ~ **stick** *n* CONST *surveying* nivelette *f*

bonnet *n* AUTO (BrE) *(cf hood)* capot *m*, MINING *timbering* écoin *m*, NAUT *of funnel* chapeau *m*, couvercle *m*, VEHICLES capot-moteur *m*; ~ **catch** *n* (BrE) *(cf hood catch)* VEHICLES attache capot *f*; ~ **lock** *n* (BrE) *(cf hood lock)* AUTO dispositif de fermeture du capot *m*

bonneted: ~ **lamp** *n* CONST lampe avec chapeau *f*

book:[1] ~ **capacitor** *n* ELEC condensateur pliant *m*; ~ **case** *n* PRINT boîte *f*, emboîtage *m*; ~ **faces** *n pl* PRINT caractères d'édition *m pl*; ~ **fonts** *n pl* PRINT polices de caractères d'édition *f pl*; ~ **ink** *n* COLOURS encre labeur *f*

book:[2] ~ **a call** *vi* TELECOM réserver une communication

bookbinder *n* PRINT relieur *m*

bookbinder's: ~ **brass** *n* PRINT cuivre jaune *m*; ~ **needle** *n* PRINT aiguille de relieur *f*

bookbinding *n* PRINT reliure *f*; ~ **board** *n* PAPER TECH carton pour reliure *m*

booked: ~ **call** *n* TELECOM appel réservé *m*

bookplate *n* PRINT ex-libris *m*

Boolean[1] *adj* DP booléen

Boolean:[2] ~ **algebra** *n* COMP, DP algèbre de Boole *f*, MATH algèbre booléenne *f*; ~ **operator** *n* COMP, DP opérateur booléen *m*; ~ **type** *n* COMP, DP type booléen *m*, type logique *m*; ~ **value** *n* COMP, DP valeur booléenne *f*; ~ **variable** *n* COMP, DP variable booléenne *f*

boom[1] *n* CINEMAT perche *f*, CONST chapeau *m*, plate-bande *f*, *of crane* flèche *f*, volée *f*, MAR POLL barrage flottant *m*, barrière flottante *f*, MECH *lifting gear* flèche *f*, NAUT barrage flottant *m*, barre flottante *f*, bout-dehors *m*, bôme *f*, estacade flottante *m*, NUCLEAR flèche *f*, porte-à-faux *m*, PETR TECH barrage *m*, SPACE *spacecraft* flèche *f*, perche *f*; ~ **arm** *n* CINEMAT flèche *f*; ~ **dolly** *n* CINEMAT grue *f*; ~ **guy** *n* NAUT retenue de bôme *f*; ~ **mike** *n* CINEMAT micro sur perche *m*; ~ **operator** *n* CINEMAT perchiste *m*; ~ **pack** *n* MAR POLL barrage en conteneur *m*, ~ **plate** *n* CONST *of built-up girder* chapeau *m*, plate-bande *f*; ~ **retrieval** *n* MAR POLL récupération de barrage *f*; ~ **shot** *n* CINEMAT plan à partir d'une grue *m*; ~ **towing** *n* MAR POLL chalutage de barrage flottant *m*, remorquage de barrage flottant *m*; ~ **vang** *n* NAUT *of yacht* hale-bas de bôme *m*

boom[2] ~ **out** *vi* NAUT tangonner

boomer *n* RECORDING haut-parleur de graves *m*

boomerang *n* FLUID PHYS *for study of air currents* boomerang *m*

boom-laying: ~ **configuration** *n* MAR POLL configuration de pose de barrage *f*

boost:[1] ~ **charge** *n* TRANSP charge rapide *f*; ~ **pressure** *n* AERONAUT *excess pressure* pression de suralimentation *f*, surpression d'admission *f*, SPACE *spacecraft* pression de suralimentation *f*, TRANSP surpression d'admission *f*; ~ **pump** *n* SPACE *spacecraft* pompe de gavage *f*, pompe de suralimentation *f*

boost[2] *vt* ELEC ENG survolter, ELECTRON amplifier, MECH accélérer, gaver, renforcer, SPACE *spacecraft* accélérer, suralimenter; ~ **productivity** *vt* TEXTILES augmenter la productivité

booster *n* ELEC survolteur *m*, ELEC ENG dévolteur *m*, *positive* survolteur *m*, ELECTRON amplificateur *m*, MINING booster *m*, relais d'amorçage *m*, SPACE pousseur *m*, premier étage *m*, propulseur d'accélération *m*, propulseur d'appoint *m*, VEHICLES *car component* suramplificateur *m*; ~ **battery** *n* TRANSP batterie de renfort *f*, batterie de traction *f*; ~ **coil** *n* TRANSP bobine de démarrage *f*; ~ **compressor** *n* REFRIG précompres-

seur *m*; ~ **control** *n* TRANSP servocommande *f*; ~ **dynamo** *n* ELEC dynamo auxiliaire *f*; ~ **element** *n* NUCLEAR élément de dopage *m*, élément de surréactivité *m*; ~ **generator** *n* ELEC dynamo auxiliaire *f*; ~ **heating system** *n* FUELLESS *solar, geothermal* chaufferie d'appoint *f*; ~ **light** *n* CINEMAT lumière d'appoint *f*; ~ **mill** *n* FUELLESS installation booster *f*; ~ **platform** *n* PETR TECH *pipelines* plate-forme de surpression *f*, station-relais *f*; ~ **pump** *n* MECH pompe d'accélération *f*, pompe de gavage *f*, pompe relais *f*, MECH ENG pompe d'appoint *f*, pompe de gavage *f*, pompe de suralimentation *f*, PETR TECH surpresseur *m*, TRANSP pompe de gavage *f*, pompe de suralimentation *f*; ~ **rod** *n* NUCLEAR barre de dopage *f*, barre de surréactivité *f*; ~ **station** *n* PETR station de pompage *f*, TV relais de diffusion *m*; ~ **transformer** *n* ELEC transformateur survolteur *m*, ELEC ENG *negative* transformateur dévolteur *m*, *positive* transformateur survolteur *m*; ~ **ventilation fan** *n* MINING ventilateur amplificateur *m*; ~ **voltage** *n* TV tension de récupération *f*, tension élévatrice *f*

boosting: ~ **regulator** *n* SPACE *spacecraft* régulateur survolteur *m*, régulateur élévateur *m*, régulateur élévateur de tension *m*; ~ **station** *n* HYDROL station de relèvement *f*

boot[1] *n* *(cf trunk)* AERONAUT soufflet de protection *m*, AUTO (BrE) coffre *m*, coffre à bagages *m*, C&G pipe de cueillage *f*, CONST dauphin *m*, TRANSPORT (BrE) coffre à bagages *m*, VEHICLES (BrE) coffre *m*; ~ **area** *n* PROD ENG zone d'initialisation *f*; ~ **handle** *n* (BrE) *(cf trunk handle)* VEHICLES poignée du coffre *f*; ~ **lid** *n* (BrE) *(cf trunk lid)* VEHICLES porte du coffre *f*; ~ **topping** *n* NAUT *boat building* bande de flottaison *f*, exposant de charge *m*

boot[2] *vt* COMP amorcer

bootable: ~ **disc** *n* (BrE) ELECTRON disque amorçable *m*; ~ **disk** *n* (AmE) *see bootable disc*

Boötes *n* ASTRON Bouvier *m*

booth *n* CINEMAT cabine *f*, PRINT cabine *f*, stand *m*

bootleg *n* TV piratage *m*

bootstrap[1] *n* COMP, PRINT amorce *f*, TV circuit autoélévateur *m* ~ **system** *n* REFRIG système bouclé *m*

bootstrap[2] *vt* COMP amorcer

bootstrapping *n* COMP amorçage *m*

BOP *abbr* *(blowout preventer)* CONTROL, GAS TECH, OCEANOG, PETR, PETR TECH BOP *(bloc obturateur de puits)*

boracite *n* MINERAL boracite *f*

borane *n* CHEM borane *m*

borate *n* CHEM borate *m*

borax *n* C&G, CHEM borax *m*, DETERGENTS borax *m*, tétraborate de sodium *m*, MINERAL borax *m*; ~ **bead** *n* CONST perle de borax *f*; ~ **lake** *n* DETERGENTS lac borique *m*

borazon *n* CHEM borazon *m*

Borda: ~ **mouthpiece** *n* HYDR EQUIP ajutage rentrant de Borda *m*

border *n* C&G bord de feuille *m*, PRINT bordure *f*; ~ **irrigation** *n* WATER SUPP irrigation par surverse *f*

bore[1] *n* AUTO alésage *m*, C&G débouchage *m*, FUELLESS *water power* mascaret *m*, HYDROL barre d'eau *f*, mascaret *m*, mascaret *m*, MECH ENG alésage *m*, âme *f*, MINING forage *m*, percement *m*, sondage *m*, NAUT *of river* mascaret *m*, OCEANOG barre *f*, mascaret *m*, seiche *f*, VEHICLES *of engine, cylinder* alésage *m*; ~ **bit** *n* CONST *earth-boring* foret *m*, perçoir *m*, trépan *m*; ~ **gage** *n*

(AmE), ~ **gauge** *n* (BrE) METR calibre d'alésage *m*; ~ **rod** *n* CONST rallonge *f*, tige de sonde *f*

bore² *vt* CONST percer, MECH aléser, forer, MECH ENG aléser, MINING forer, percer, PROD ENG *hole* aléser, TESTING sonder; ~ **out** *vt* PROD ENG *hole* aléser

bore³ *vi* CONST faire des sondages, faire un trou de sondage, forer, pratiquer un trou de sonde, MINING faire des forages, faire des sondages, pratiquer un trou de sonde; ~ **against water** *vi* MINING percer aux eaux accumulées; ~ **for water** *vi* WATER SUPP faire des sondages pour trouver de l'eau

bored: ~ **and plain plates** *n pl* MECH ENG plaques alésées et simples *f pl*; ~ **well** *n* HYDROL puits tubé *m*, WATER SUPP puits foré *m*

borehole *n* COAL TECH trou de forage *m*, CONST coup de sonde *m*, forage *m*, sondage *m*, trou de sonde *m*, GAS TECH trou de sonde *m*, GEOL trou de forage *m*, trou de sondage *m*, GEOPHYS trou de sondage *m*, HYDROL forage de captage *m*, MINING chambre de mine *f*, fourneau de mine *m*, mine *f*, trou de mine *m*, forage *m*, sondage *m*, trou de sonde *m*, PETR sondage *m*, trou de sonde *m*; ~ **effect** *n* PETR effet de trou *m*; ~ **logging** *n* GEOPHYS diagraphie du trou de sondage *f*; ~ **logging equipment** *n* GEOPHYS équipement de carottage *m*; ~ **pump** *n* CONST pompe de sondage *f*, WATER SUPP pompe de forage *f*

boreholing *n* CONST forage *m*, sondage *m*; ~ **plant** *n* CONST installation de sondage *f*, matériel de forage *m*

borer *n* MINING perforateur mécanique *m*, perforatrice mécanique *f*, sonde *f*, *rock drilling, earth boring* burin *m*, fleuret *m*, foreuse *f*, perforateur *m*, perforatrice *f*, pistolet *m*, sondeuse *f*; ~ **bit** *n* PETR TECH trépan pour sondage percutant *m*

boric¹ *adj* CHEM borique

boric:² ~ **acid** *n* C&G, CHEM acide borique *m*; ~ **acid blender** *n* NUCLEAR réservoir de mélange d'acide borique *m*; ~ **oxide** *n* C&G anhydride borique *m*

boride *n* CHEM borure *m*

boring *n* COAL TECH forage *m*, CONST percement *m*, perçage *m*, GAS TECH percement *m*, MECH ENG alésage *m*, MINING percement *m*, percée *f*, perforage *m*, perforation *f*, sondage *m*, *act of making hole* forage *m*, PROD ENG alésage *m*, percement *m*, percée *f*; ~ **against water** *n* WATER SUPP percement aux eaux *m*, percée aux eaux *f*; ~ **and turning mill** *n* MECH ENG tour vertical *m*; ~ **bar** *n* MECH ENG barre d'alésage *f*; ~ **bit** *n* CONST *mortising* amorçoir *m*, dégorgeoir *m*, ébauchoir *m*, ébauchoir à mortaises *m*; ~ **by percussion** *n* CONST sondage par battage *m*; ~ **by percussion with rods** *n* CONST sondage par battage à la tige *m*; ~ **by rotation** *n* CONST forage par rodage *m*, sondage par rodage *m*; ~ **by shot drills** *n* CONST sondage à la grenaille d'acier *m*; ~ **chisel** *n* MINING trépan *m*; ~ **contractor** *n* CONST entrepreneur de sondages *m*; ~ **cutter** *n* MECH ENG outil à aléser *m*; ~ **head** *n* MECH ENG chariot d'alésage *m*, dispositif d'alésage *m*, MINING trépan composé *m*; ~ **machine** *n* MECH, MECH ENG aléseuse *f*, MINING foreuse *f*, sonde *f*, sondeuse *f*; ~ **mill** *n* MECH aléseuse-fraiseuse *f*; ~ **out** *n* PROD ENG alésage *m*; ~ **plant** *n* MINING installation de sondage *f*, matériel de forage *m*; ~ **rod** *n* CONST rallonge *f*, tige de sonde *f*; ~ **site** *n* CONST emplacement de forage *m*, emplacement de sondage *m*; ~ **spindle** *n* MECH, MECH ENG *of machine* broche d'alésage *f*; ~ **tool** *n* MECH ENG outil d'alésage *m*, *for roughing* outil d'ébauchage *m*, *for finishing* outil de finition *m*, MINING outil de forage *m*, outil de sondage

m, outil foreur *m*; ~ **with the bit** *n* CONST sondage au trépan *m*

borings *n pl* COAL TECH copeaux de forage *m pl*

borneol *n* CHEM bornéol *m*

bornite *n* MINERAL bornite *f*

bornyl *n* CHEM bornyle *m*; ~ **acetate** *n* CHEM acétate de bornyle *m*; ~ **alcohol** *n* CHEM bornéol *m*

borofluoride *n* CHEM borofluorure *m*

boron *n (B)* CHEM bore *m (B)*; ~ **fiber** *n* (AmE), ~ **fibre** *n* (BrE) PROP MAT fibre de bore *f*

boronated: ~ **steel absorber** *n* NUCLEAR *in spent fuel pit* puits en tôle d'acier au bore *m*

borosilicate *n* CHEM borosilicate *m*; ~ **glass** *n* C&G, HEAT ENG, LAB EQUIP verre borosilicaté *m*

borrow *n* CONST *material* emprunt *m*, PROD ENG retenue *f*; ~ **pit** *n* COAL TECH fouille *f*, CONST zone d'emprunt *f*

bort *n* MINING *drilling* carbonado *m*, diamant noir *m*, PROD ENG *for polishing* bort *m*, égrisé *m*

Bose-Einstein: ~ **condensation** *n* PHYS condensation de Bose-Einstein *f*, condensation statistique de Bose-Einstein *f*; ~ **distribution** *n* PHYS distribution de Bose-Einstein *f*; ~ **statistics** *n pl* PHYS statistiques de Bose-Einstein *f pl*

bosh *n* C&G baquet *m*

boson *n* PART PHYS, PHYS boson *m*

boss *n* C&G *of plano-convex lens* bosse *f*, MECH ENG bossage *m*, bosse *f*, protubérance *f*, renflement *m*, saillie *f*, portée *f*, *of crank* moyeu *m*, MINING *of ore stamp* bosseyeuse *f*, tête *f*, PROD ENG *on casting* renflement *m*, VEHICLES *of wheel hub* bossage *m*; ~ **grip** *n* CINEMAT chef machiniste *m*

bosshead *n* LAB EQUIP *clamp* noix *f*

bossing: ~ **mallet** *n* CONST *plumber's* batte *f*, batte-plate *f*, rabattoir *m*

BOT¹ *abbr* (*beginning of tape*) COMP, DP début de bande *m*

BOT:² ~ **marker** *n* COMP, DP marqueur de début de bande *m*

both: ~ **justified** *adj* (*BT*) PRINT justifié à droite et à gauche

both-way: ~ **circuit** *n* TELECOM circuit mixte *m*, circuit à double sens *m*; ~ **group** *n* TELECOM faisceau mixte *m*, faisceau à double sens *m*; ~ **line** *n* TELECOM ligne mixte *f*, ligne à double sens *f*

botryogen *n* MINERAL botryogène *m*

botryoidal *adj* MINERAL botryoïde

bott *n* PROD ENG *founding* bouchon *m*, bouchon d'obturation de trou de coulée *m*, tampon *m*; ~ **stick** *n* PROD ENG *founding* porte-tampon *m*

bottle *n* LAB EQUIP flacon *m*; ~ **bank** *n* RECYCLING conteneur de collecte de verre usé *m*; ~ **cap** *n* PACKAGING capsule de bouteille *f*; ~ **capsule** *n* PACKAGING capsule de bouteille *f*; ~ **carrier** *n* PACKAGING panier à bouteilles *m*; ~ **closure** *n* PACKAGING fermeture de bouteille *f*; ~ **cooler** *n* REFRIG refroidisseur de bouteilles *m*; ~ **deposit** *n* PACKAGING consignation *f*; ~ **filler** *n* FOOD TECH embouteilleuse *f*, remplisseuse de bouteilles *f*, soutireuse à bouteilles *f*; ~ **glass** *n* C&G verre à bouteilles *m*; ~ **industry** *n* C&G industrie du verre d'emballage *f*; ~ **jack** *n* MECH ENG vérin à bouteille *m*; ~ **jacket** *n* PACKAGING gaine pour bouteille *f*; ~ **leak detector** *n* PACKAGING indicateur de fuite sur bouteille *m*; ~ **screw** *n* NAUT *rigging* ridoir *m*; ~ **sleeve** *n* PACKAGING manchon pour bouteille *m*; ~ **stopper** *n* PACKAGING fermeture de bouteille *f*; ~ **unscrambler** *n* PACKAGING machine rangeuse de bouteilles *f*; ~ **was-**

her *n* FOOD TECH laveuse de bouteille *f*, machine à rincer les bouteilles *f*; **~ with molded neck** *n* (AmE), **~ with moulded neck** *n* (BrE) LAB EQUIP *glassware* flacon à col moulé *m*

bottle-capping: ~ machine *n* PACKAGING machine pour encapsuler les bouteilles *f*

bottle-casing: ~ machine *n* C&G capsuleuse de bouteilles *f*

bottle-closing: ~ machine *n* PACKAGING machine à boucher les bouteilles *f*

bottle-corking: ~ machine *n* PACKAGING bouche-bouteilles *m*

bottled[1] *adj* FOOD TECH embouteillé, en bocal

bottled:[2] **~ gas** *n* GAS TECH, THERMOD gaz en bouteille *m*; **~ liquefied petroleum gas** *n* GAS TECH gaz liquéfié conditionné *m*

bottleneck *n* MECH goulot d'étranglement *m*, PACKAGING col de bouteille *m*, PRINT goulot d'étranglement *m*, PROD ENG goulet d'étranglement *m*, goulot d'étranglement *m*, point d'embouteillage *m*, TRANSP goulot d'étranglement *m*

bottle-packing: ~ machine *n* PACKAGING machine d'emballage pour bouteilles *f*

bottle-rinsing: ~ machine *n* PACKAGING machine à rincer les bouteilles *f*

bottle-sealing: ~ machine *n* PACKAGING machine à boucher les bouteilles *f*

bottle-type: ~ liquid cooler *n* REFRIG refroidisseur à bouteille *m*

bottle-washing: ~ machine *n* PACKAGING machine à rincer les bouteilles *f*

bottling: ~ line *n* PACKAGING chaîne de mise en bouteilles *f*; **~ machine** *n* FOOD TECH *food-processing machinery* embouteilleuse *f*, remplisseuse de bouteilles *f*, soutireuse à bouteilles *f*, PACKAGING machine pour la mise en bouteilles *f*; **~ tank** *n* FOOD TECH tank de soutirage *m*

bottom[1] *n* COAL TECH *of coal seam* mur *m*, CONST *of hill* bas *m*, base *f*, pied *m*, *of valley* fond *m*, HYDROL *of basin, reservoir* fond *m*, MINING *of mine shaft, borehole* fond *m*, *of working* aval pendage *m*, OCEANOG lit *m*, mouille *f*, PRINT bas *m*, fond *m*, partie inférieure *f*; **~ block** *n* C&G bloc de sole *m*; **~ brass** *n* MECH ENG coussinet *m*, coussinet inférieur *m*, demi-coussinet inférieur *m*; **~ cementing plug** *n* PETR TECH bouchon de cimentation inférieur *m*; **~ charge** *n* MINING charge de pied *f*; **~ coder** *n* PACKAGING dispositif codeur de fond *m*; **~ culvert** *n* WATER SUPP pertuis de fond *m*; **~ current** *n* OCEANOG, WATER SUPP courant de fond *m*; **~ dead center** *n* (AmE), **~ dead centre** *n* (BrE) *(BDC)* MECH point mort bas *m* *(PMB)*; **~ deposit** *n* WATER SUPP vase de fond *f*; **~ die** *n* PROD ENG *of power hammer* anse *f*, tas *m*, tas inférieur *m*; **~ dyeing** *n* COLOURS teinture de fond *f*; **~ filling** *n* PACKAGING remplissage par le fond *m*; **~ fitting** *n* NUCLEAR *nozzle* raccord inférieur *m*; **~ flange** *n* CONST aile inférieure *f*, semelle inférieure *f*, *of I section* membrane inférieure *f*; **~ flap** *n* PACKAGING trappe de fond *f*; **~ flow** *n* WATER SUPP courant de fond *m*; **~ flue** *n* HEAT ENG carneau de sole *m*; **~ fold** *n* PACKAGING pli de fond *m*; **~ glass** *n* C&G verre résiduel dans le pot *m*; **~ heat** *n* C&G chaleur de fond *f*; **~ hole** *n* MINING *blasting* mine de relevage *f*, PETR TECH fond de sondage *m*, fond de trou *m*, *of well* fond du puits *m*; **~ hole assembly** *n* *(BHA)* PETR TECH appareil de fond de puits *m*, bas de garniture *m*; **~ hole conditions** *n pl* PETR TECH conditions de fond *f pl*; **~ hole pressure** *n*

PETR pression de fond *f*; **~ ice** *n* OCEANOG glace de fond *f*; **~ level** *n* MINING galerie de fond *f*, voie de fond *f*, *horizontal plane* niveau de fond *m*, étage du fond *m*; **~ lighting** *n* CINEMAT éclairage par transparence *m*; **~ outlet** *n* HYDROL *dams*, WATER SUPP vidange de fond *f*; **~ pallet** *n* PROD ENG *of power hammer* tas *m*, tas inférieur *m*; **~ part** *n* PROD ENG *of flask* corps *m*, dessous *m*; **~ paving** *n* C&G dallage de sol *m*; **~ pillar** *n* MINING massif de protection de puits *m*, pilier de protection de puits *m*; **~ plate** *n* CONST plaque de dessous *f*, plaque de fond *f*, plaque inférieure *f*, PROD ENG *of loam mould* armature du dessous *f*, plaque de fond *f*; **~ plating** *n* NAUT *boat building* bordé de fond *m*; **~ pouring** *n* PROD ENG *founding* coulée en source *f*, coulée en source directe *f*; **~ press** *n* PAPER TECH presse inférieure *f*; **~ profile** *n* OCEANOG profil bathymétrique *m*; **~ quark** *n* PART PHYS quark de beauté *m*, PHYS quark bottom *m*; **~ rail** *n* CONST *of doorframe, sash frame* traverse basse *f*, traverse du bas *f*; **~ ripples** *n pl* HYDROL rides de fond *f pl*; **~ road** *n* MINING voie de fond *f*; **~ road bridge** *n* CONST pont à tablier inférieur *m*; **~ roll** *n* PROD ENG *rolling mill* cylindre du dessous *m*, cylindre femelle *m*; **~ shot** *n* MINING *blasting* coup de relevage *m*; **~ spool box** *n* CINEMAT carter récepteur *m*; **~ sprocket** *n* CINEMAT tambour denté inférieur *m*; **~ structure** *n* AERONAUT baquet *m*, *of helicopter* barque *f*; **~ surge** *n* OCEANOG lame de fond *f*; **~ swage** *n* PROD ENG dessous d'étampe *m*, sous-étampe pour fers ronds *f*, étampe de dessous *f*; **~ tear** *n* C&G arraché *m*; **~ topography** *n* OCEANOG topographie sous-marine *f*; **~ transport** *n* HYDROL charriage de fond *m*; **~ water** *n* OCEANOG eau de fond *f*; **~ workings** *n pl* MINING chantier du fond *m*; **~ yeast** *n* FOOD TECH levure basse *f*

bottom[2] *vt* OCEANOG *net* caler

bottom[3] *vi* MINING *placer-working* atteindre le bedrock, rencontrer

bottom-blown: ~ oxygen converter *n* PROP MAT convertisseur soufflé à l'oxygène au sol *m*

bottomer: ~ slab *n* REFRIG plaque de durcissement des fonds *f*

bottom-folding: ~ and seaming machine *n* PACKAGING machine à plier et à jointurer *f*

bottom-hole *adj* PETR TECH au fond d'un puits

bottoming: ~ indicator *n* AERONAUT *aviation* jauge d'enfoncement *f*; **~ tap** *n* MECH ENG taraud finisseur *m*

bottom-poured: ~ steel *n* PROP MAT acier coulé par le fond *m*

bottoms *n* FOOD TECH *fermentation*, PETR TECH résidu *m*

bottomset: ~ beds *n pl* GEOL couches de fond *f pl*, couches deltaïques de fond *f pl*

bottom-up: ~ methodology *n* COMP méthodologie ascendante *f*

botulinum: ~ cook *n* FOOD TECH stérilisation force 10 *f*

botulism *n* FOOD TECH botulisme *m*

boudinage *n* GEOL boudinage *m*

Bouguer: ~ anomaly *n* GEOL, GEOPHYS anomalie de Bouguer *f*; **~ correction** *n* GEOPHYS correction de Bouguer *f*, réduction de Bouguer *f*

boulangerite *n* MINERAL boulangérite *f*

boulder *n* COAL TECH bloc *m*, CONST caillou *m*, galet *m*, gros galet *m*, PETR bloc *m*; **~ clay** *n* COAL TECH, GEOL *glacial deposit* argile à blocaux *f*; **~ soil** *n* COAL TECH sol à blocs *m*

boulet *n* COAL TECH boulette *f*

bounce: ~ board *n* CINEMAT panneau réflecteur *m*; **~ lighting** *n* CINEMAT éclairage indirect *m*, éclairage par réflexion m

bounced: ~ **landing** n AERONAUT rebondissement à l'atterrissage m

bound:[1] ~ **for** adj NAUT ship en partance pour, en route pour, à destination de

bound:[2] ~ **book** n PRINT livre relié m; ~ **electron** n PART PHYS électron lié m; ~ **mode** n OPT mode de propagation m, mode guidé m, mode lié m, TELECOM mode guidé m, mode lié m; ~ **water** n FOOD TECH eau liée f, PETR eau de constitution f

boundary n ASTRON of black hole surface f, CONST borne f, délimitation f, frontière f, limite f, GEOL bord m, bordure f, limite f, METALL joint m, limite f; ~ **dimensions** n pl MECH ENG overall size dimensions d'encombrement f pl; ~ **fault** n GEOL faille bordière f; ~ **fence** n CONST clôture de bornage f; ~ **film** n COATINGS couche de limite f, couche de séparation f, couche mitoyenne f; ~ **layer** n AERONAUT couche limite f, COATINGS couche de limite f, couche mitoyenne f, FLUID PHYS, FUELLESS, MECH hydraulics, OCEANOG, PHYS fluid flow couche limite f, PRINT couche limite f, couche supérieure f, REFRIG couche limite f; ~ **layer control** n TRANSP contrôle de la couche limite m; ~ **layer formation** n FLUID PHYS formation de la couche limite f; ~ **layer separation** n FLUID PHYS décollement de la couche limite m; ~ **layer stability** n FLUID PHYS stabilité de la couche limite f; ~ **light** n AERONAUT balise d'extrémité f; ~ **line** n CONST démarcation f, ligne frontière f; ~ **lubrication** n AERONAUT graissage à film d'huile m; ~ **mark** n CONST borne f; ~ **pillar** n MINING investison m, massif de protection m; ~ **post** n CONST poteau de bornage m; ~ **stone** n CONST borne f, pierre bornale f, pierre de bornage f; ~ **wall** n CONST mur de clôture m

boundstone n GEOL, PETR calcaire construit m

Bourdon: ~ **gage** n (AmE), ~ **gauge** n (BrE) PETR TECH tube de Bourdon m, PHYS manomètre de Bourdon m

bournonite n MINERAL bournonite f

bouton n CONTROL bouton m

bow n CONST anse f, compas-balustre m, of key anneau m, of padlock branche f, MECH ENG archet m, NAUT foremost end of ship avant m, bossoir m, proue f, étrave f, PROD ENG handle of foundry ladle anse f, RAIL vehicles archet m; ~ **anchor** n NAUT ancre de bossoir f, ancre principale f; ~ **and biais** n TEXTILES centrage et bias m; ~ **and warp** n (AmE) (cf warped sheet) C&G tôle f; ~ **calipers** n pl (AmE), ~ **callipers** n pl (BrE) CONST compas sphérique m; ~ **chock** n NAUT shipbuilding galoche d'avant f; ~ **compass** n CONST compas à balustre m, compas-balustre m, MECH ENG compas à balustre m; ~ **compasses** n pl CONST compas à balustre m, compas-balustre m, MECH ENG compas à balustre m; ~ **dividers** n pl CONST compas-balustre à pointes sèches m; ~ **drill** n MECH ENG foret à archet m; ~ **entrance** n NAUT boat design formes de l'avant f pl; ~ **fender** n NAUT deck equipment défense d'étrave f; ~ **handle** n PROD ENG of foundry ladle anse f; ~ **hanger** n PROD ENG appareil de suspension à arc m, arc de suspension m; ~ **lathe** n MECH ENG tour à archet m, touret m; ~ **shock** n ASTRON front d'onde de choc m, SPACE choc avant m; ~ **spring** n NAUT mooring amarre en belle f; ~ **spring compasses** n pl CONST compas-balustre à pincettes m; ~ **stopper** n NAUT deck fittings stoppeur m; ~ **thruster** n NAUT propulsion propulseur avant m, propulseur d'étrave m; ~ **wave** n AERONAUT onde de choc amont f, NAUT lame d'étrave f, vague d'étrave f

Bowden: ~ **cable** n (cf brake cable) MECH, VEHICLES on clutch, brake câble Bowden m

bowed: ~ **roll** n PAPER TECH rouleau brisé m

bowenite n MINERAL bowénite f

bowl n COAL TECH bol m, cuve f, METR of balance or scales bassin m, plat m, plateau m, PROD ENG bac m; ~ **centrifuge** n COAL TECH centrifugeuse à bol plein f; ~ **classifier** n COAL TECH classificateur à coupe m; ~ **mill crusher** n COAL TECH broyeur bowl-mill m

bowline n NAUT mooring amarre debout de l'avant f, bouline f, noeud de chaise m

bowlingite n MINERAL bowlingite f

bowser n AERONAUT, SPACE avitailleur m

bowsprit n NAUT beaupré m

bowstring: ~ **bridge** n CONST bow-string m, pont bow-string m; ~ **girder** n CONST poutre bow-string f

box[1] n CONST keeper of lock bolt gâche f, PRINT cadre m, PROD ENG moulding flask châssis m, châssis de fonderie m, châssis de moulage m, TRANSP container boîte f, in garage stalle f; ~ **and pin** n MINING for drill rod boîte et vis f; ~ **camera** n PHOTO chambre box f; ~ **casting** n MECH ENG moulage en châssis m; ~ **connecting rod end** n MECH ENG tête de bielle à cage fermée f; ~ **coupling** n MECH ENG accouplement à manchon m; ~ **culvert** n CONST dalot m, ponceau avec dalles m; ~ **die** n PRINT découpe f, emporte-pièce m, plaque flexo pour l'impression du carton f; ~ **fold** n GEOL pli coffré m; ~ **frame** n MECH ENG machine tools bâti en caisson m; ~ **furnace** n HEATING four armoire m; ~ **girder** n CONST poutre en caisson f, poutre en tôle section rectangulaire f, poutre tubulaire f, poutre-caisson f; ~ **gutter** n CONST building chéneau encaissé m, gouttière f; ~ **kiln** n HEATING four armoire m; ~ **lock** n CONST serrure de coffre f; ~ **lug** n PROD ENG borne tubulaire f; ~ **molding** n (AmE), ~ **moulding** n (BrE) PROD ENG moulage en châssis m; ~ **nut** n MECH ENG écrou à chapeau m; ~ **pallet** n PACKAGING palette-caisse f, with side walls palette-caisse f; ~ **pallet with mesh** n PACKAGING palette-caisse à claire-voie f; ~ **pass** n PROD ENG rolling mill cannelure carrée f; ~ **pin** n MECH ENG goujon de centrage m; ~ **relay** n ELEC relais tabatière m; ~ **screw** n CONST filière à bois f; ~ **section track girder** n TRANSP poutre porteuse à section rectangulaire f; ~ **spanner** n (BrE) (cf box wrench) MECH, MECH ENG clef à douille f; ~ **staple** n CONST lock staple gâche f, palâtre m; ~ **switch** n ELEC interrupteur à boîte m; ~ **tilts** n pl PRINT box-tilts m pl, compensateurs m pl, embarreurs m pl; ~ **wagon** n (BrE) (cf boxcar) RAIL wagon couvert m; ~ **wipe** n CINEMAT volet carré m; ~ **wrench** n (AmE) (cf box spanner) MECH, MECH ENG clef à douille f; ~ **yard** n PROD ENG foundry parc à châssis m

box[2] vt CONST tenon in mortise emboîter

box:[3] ~ **the compass** vi NAUT réciter la rose des vents

boxcar n (AmE) (cf box wagon) RAIL wagon couvert m; ~ **pulse** n ELECTRON impulsion longue f, impulsion rectangulaire allongée f

boxed: ~ **head** n PRINT titre encadré m

box-end: ~ **connecting rod** n MECH ENG bielle avec tête à cage fermée f

box-erecting: ~ **machine** n PACKAGING machine pour assembler les boîtes f

box-filling: ~ **machine** n PACKAGING machine pour remplir les boîtes f

box-girder: ~ **bridge** n CONST pont à poutres en caisson m

boxing *n* CONST *of mortises and tenons* emboîtement *m*; ~ **machine** *n* PACKAGING machine pour la mise en boîtes *f*

box-making: ~ **machine** *n* PACKAGING machine pour fabriquer les boîtes *f*

box-spun: ~ **yarn** *n* TEXTILES fil filé sur système centrifuge *m*

box-type: ~ **stiffener** *n* AERONAUT caisson raidisseur *m*; ~ **structure** *n* AERONAUT caisson *m*

Boyle: ~ **temperature** *n* PHYS température de Boyle-Mariotte *f*

Boyle's: ~ **law** *n* PHYS loi de Boyle-Mariotte *f*, loi de Mariotte *f*

BPF *abbr* (*band-pass filter*) COMP, DP, ELEC, ELECTRON, PHYS, RECORDING, TELECOM, TV FPB (*filtre passe-bande*)

BPS *abbr* (*bits per second*) COMP BPS (*bits par seconde*)

BPSK *abbr* (*binary phase shift keying*) TELECOM MDPB (*modulation par déplacement de phase bivalente*)

Bq *abbr* (*becquerel*) METR, PHYS, RAD PHYS Bq (*becquerel*)

Br (*bromine*) CHEM Br (*brome*)

BRA *abbr* (*basic rate access*) TELECOM accès au débit de base *m*

brace[1] *n* AERONAUT croisillon *m*, COAL TECH étai *m*, CONST arc-boutant *m*, contrefiche *f*, cliquet *m*, rochet *m*, croisillon *m*, décharge *f*, écharpe *f*, moise *f*, vilebrequin *m*, *strut* entretoise *f*, HYDR EQUIP, MECH entretoise *f*, MECH ENG bretelle *f*, renfort *m*, MINING plancher de manoeuvre *m*, SPACE *spacecraft* entretoise *f*; ~ **bit** *n* MECH ENG mèche de vilebrequin *f*; ~ **head** *n* MINING manche de manoeuvre *m*, manivelle *f*, tourne-à-gauche *m*; ~ **key** *n* MINING manche de manoeuvre *m*, manivelle *f*, tourne-à-gauche *m*; ~ **strut** *n* MECH ENG contrefiche *f*

brace[2] *vt* CONST moiser, *banks of cut* étrésillonner, *beam* armer, *framing* entretoiser, MECH ENG entretoiser, étrésillonner, NAUT *yard* brasser; ~ **against wind pressure** *vt* CONST *roof, truss* contreventer; ~ **together** *vt* CONST moiser ensemble

braces *n pl* CONST *of system of shoring* moises *f pl*

brachistochrone *n* GEOM brachystocrone *f*

bracing *n* C&G *of tank blocks* ancrage *m*, CONST *strengthening* renforcement *m*, renforçage *m*, *strutting* entretoisement *m*, étrésillonnement *m*, *trussing* armature *f*; ~ **against wind pressure** *n* CONST contreventement *m*; ~ **truss** *n* MECH ENG membrure *f*

bracket[1] *n* CONST *support* applique *f*, console *f*, potence *f*, ELEC ENG *for electric light* applique *f*, HYDR EQUIP *for supporting boiler* support *m*, équerre de fixation *f*, MECH chaise *f*, console *f*, support *m*, MECH ENG console *f*, étrier *m*, MINING plancher de manoeuvre *m*, NAUT *shipbuilding* gousset *m*, PRINT parenthèse *f*; ~ **crab** *n* MINING treuil d'applique *m*; ~ **hanger** *n* MINING *shafting* chaise console *f*, chaise-applique *f*, palier à potence *m*

bracket[2] *vt* PRINT mettre entre crochets

brackets *n pl* PRINT accolades *f pl*, crochets *m pl*

Brackett: ~ **series** *n* PHYS série de Brackett *f*

brackish *adj* CONST *water* salée, saumâtre, FOOD TECH *pickling*, GEOL *fauna, sedimentary environment*, HYDROL, OCEANOG *water*, WATER SUPP *water* saumâtre; ~ **marl and limestone** *n* GEOL caillasse

brad *n* CONST *slender nail* cheville *f*, goupille *f*, pointe *f*

bradawl *n* CONST chasse-clou *m*, chasse-pointe *m*

bradenhead: ~ **cap for the casing** *n* PETR TECH *drilling*

bouchon de tête de tubage *m*

Bradford: ~ **breaker** *n* COAL TECH trommel rotatif Bradford *m*

Bragg: ~ **angle** *n* CRYSTALL angle de Bragg *m*; ~ **cell** *n* CRYSTALL cristal de Bragg *m*, ELEC ENG cellule de Bragg *f*; ~ **indices** *n pl* CRYSTALL indices de Bragg *m pl*; ~ **reflection** *n* CRYSTALL réflexion de Bragg *f*

Bragg's: ~ **law** *n* CRYSTALL condition de Bragg *f*, équation de Bragg *f*

braid[1] *n* C&G, ELEC *cable* tresse *f*, ELEC ENG *copper-wire shielding* tresse de blindage *f*, *insulation of electric wire* tresse *f*, TEXTILES tresse *f*

braid[2] *vt* ELEC ENG tresser

braided: ~ **hose** *n* P&R tuyau tressé *m*; ~ **river** *n* GEOL rivière en tresse *f*; ~ **stream** *n* PETR chevelure hydrographique *f*; ~ **wire** *n* ELEC ENG tresse ronde *f*

braiding *n* ELEC ENG guipage *m*, HYDROL *of river* partage *m*, TEXTILES tresse *f*; ~ **technique** *n* TEXTILES technique de tressage *f*

brailer *n* OCEANOG *net* haveneau *m*, épuisette *f*; ~ **boom** *n* NAUT *fishing* corne de salabarde *f*

brain: ~ **train** *n* TRANSP train robot *m*

braise *vt* FOOD TECH faire cuire à l'étuvée

brake[1] *n* AUTO, MECH, MECH ENG, PAPER TECH, VEHICLES frein *m*; ~ **anchor plate** *n* AUTO plateau de frein *m*; ~ **application** *n* RAIL *vehicles* serrage du frein *m*; ~ **band** *n* AUTO sangle de frein *f*, MECH, MECH ENG bande de frein *f*, VEHICLES *clutch* bande de frein *f*, ruban de frein *m*; ~ **bleeder unit** *n* AUTO purge des freins *f*; ~ **block** *n* MECH ENG, RAIL *vehicles*, VEHICLES *of cycle* sabot de frein *m*; ~ **cabin** *n* RAIL vigie de frein *f*; ~ **cable** *n* (*cf Bowden cable*) MECH, VEHICLES câble de frein *m*; ~ **caliper** *n* (AmE); ~ **calliper** *n* (BrE) MECH étrier de frein *m*; ~ **cam** *n* AUTO, MECH came de frein *f*; ~ **carrier plate** *n* AUTO plateau support de segments *m*; ~ **chute** *n* SPACE parachute-frein *m*; ~ **clearance** *n* AUTO écartement des garnitures *m*; ~ **compensator** *n* VEHICLES palonnier de frein *m*, égalisateur du système de freinage *m*; ~ **connecting rod** *n* VEHICLES tige de frein *f*, tringle de tirage de frein *f*; ~ **crank** *n* MECH ENG manivelle de frein à vis *f*; ~ **cylinder** *n* AUTO, MECH ENG, VEHICLES cylindre de frein *m*; ~ **disc** *n* (BrE) MECH, VEHICLES disque de frein *m*; ~ **disk** *n* (AmE) *see brake disc*; ~ **drum** *n* MECH, MECH ENG, VEHICLES tambour de frein *m*; ~ **dynamo** *n* ELEC *generator* dynamo dynamométrique *f*, dynamo-frein *f*; ~ **effort** *n* TRANSP force de freinage *m*; ~ **fade** *n* VEHICLES *of brake pad lining* fading des freins *m*; ~ **failure** *n* TRANSP incident de frein *m*; ~ **flange** *n* RAIL *vehicles* flasque de frein *f*; ~ **fluid** *n* AUTO, MECH ENG liquide de frein *m*, VEHICLES fluide des freins *m*, liquide de frein *m*; ~ **fluid reservoir** *n* AUTO réservoir pour liquide de freins *m*; ~ **fluid tank** *n* MECH ENG réservoir de liquide de freins *m*; ~ **force** *n* MECH ENG effort de freinage *m*; ~ **horsepower** *n* (*BHP*) MECH ENG, PROD ENG cheval effectif *m*, puissance au frein en chevaux *f*, puissance effective en chevaux *f*, puissance en chevaux-vapeur effectifs *f*, TRANSP puissance au frein *f*; ~ **horsepower hour** *n* MECH ENG, PROD ENG cheval heure effectif *m*; ~ **hose** *n* VEHICLES flexible de frein *m*, tuyau de frein *m*; ~ **hose coupling head** *n* RAIL *vehicles* tête d'accouplement de frein *f*; ~ **housing** *n* AUTO carter du frein *m*; ~ **jaw** *n* MECH ENG mâchoire de frein *f*; ~ **lever** *n* MECH ENG levier de freinage *m*, RAIL *vehicles* levier de frein *m*; ~ **line** *n* AUTO conduite de frein *f*, VEHICLES canalisation de frein *f*, tuyauterie de frein *f*; ~ **lining** *n* C&G fourrure de frein *f*, MECH, MECH

ENG, VEHICLES garniture de frein *f*; ~ **lining wear indicator** *n* AUTO témoin d'usure de plaquettes de frein *m*; ~ **linkage** *n* MECH ENG tringlerie de frein *f*, VEHICLES timonerie de frein *f*; ~ **master cylinder** *n* AUTO, VEHICLES maître-cylindre de frein *m*; ~ **mean-effective pressure** *n* AERONAUT pression moyenne efficace au frein *f*; ~ **motor** *n* ELEC moteur de frein *m*; ~ **pad** *n* AUTO, MECH, VEHICLES plaquette de frein *f*; ~ **parachute** *n* TRANSP parachute de queue *m*; ~ **pedal** *n* AUTO, VEHICLES pédale de frein *f*; ~ **pitch** *n* TRANSP pas de freinage *m*; ~ **plate** *n* VEHICLES plateau de frein *m*; ~ **power** *n* MECH ENG puissance de freinage *f*; ~ **power distributor** *n* AUTO répartiteur de freinage *m*; ~ **pressure** *n* AUTO pression de freinage *f*; ~ **pressure regulator** *n* MECH ENG limiteur-régleur de freinage *m*; ~ **reaction** *n* TRANSP réaction au freinage *f*; ~ **release** *n* RAIL *vehicles* desserrage du frein *m*; ~ **release spring** *n* AUTO ressort de rappel des segments de frein *m*; ~ **rigging** *n* RAIL *vehicles* timonerie de frein *f*; ~ **ring** *n* MECH ENG bague de freinage *f*; ~ **rod** *n* VEHICLES tige de frein *f*, tringle de tirage de frein *f*; ~ **screw handle** *n* RAIL *vehicles* manivelle de frein à vis *f*; ~ **servo** *n* VEHICLES servo de frein *m*; ~ **shaft** *n* VEHICLES arbre de frein *m*; ~ **shield** *n* AUTO plateau de frein *m*; ~ **shoe** *n* AUTO, MECH segment de frein *m*, MECH ENG sabot de frein *m*, VEHICLES *drum brake* mâchoire de frein *f*, segment de frein *m*; ~ **strap** *n* MECH ENG bande de frein *f*, sangle de frein *f*; ~ **system** *n* MECH ENG circuit de freinage *m*, VEHICLES système de freinage *m*; ~ **test** *n* MECH ENG essai de freinage *m*; ~ **testing** *n* CONST essai de freinage *m*; ~ **torque** *n* AERONAUT couple de freinage *m*; ~ **turbine air cycle** *n* REFRIG cycle à air à turbodétendeur *m*; ~ **valve** *n* RAIL *vehicles* indicateur de frein *m*, robinet de freinage *m*, soupape de freinage *f*; ~ **warning light** *n* VEHICLES témoin de frein *m*; ~ **wheel cylinder** *n* AUTO cylindre de roue *m*

brake[2] *vi* VEHICLES freiner, serrer

braked: ~ **car** *n* (AmE) *(cf braked wagon)* RAIL *vehicles* wagon freiné *m*; ~ **wagon** *n* (BrE) *(cf braked car)* RAIL *vehicles* wagon freiné *m*; ~ **weight percentage** *n* RAIL pourcentage de poids-frein *m*

brakeman *n* RAIL *vehicles* freineur *m*, serre-frein *m*

brakeman's: ~ **cabin** *n* RAIL *vehicles* guérite *f*, guérite de frein *f*

brakes: ~ **off** *n* RAIL *vehicles* desserrage *m*

braking *n* MECH freinage *m*, RAIL enrayage *m*, freinage *m*; ~ **airscrew** *n* TRANSP hélice de freinage *f*; ~ **deceleration** *n* TRANSP décélération de freinage *f*; ~ **distance** *n* AUTO distance d'arrêt *f*, TRANSP distance d'arrêt du véhicule *f*; ~ **distance less brake lag distance** *n* TRANSP distance de freinage *f*; ~ **governor** *n* TRANSP régulateur de freinage *m*; ~ **pitch** *n* AERONAUT *of helicopter* pas de freinage *m*; ~ **power** *n* TRANSP puissance au frein *f*; ~ **resistance** *n* TRANSP résistance de freinage *f*; ~ **shield** *n* SPACE bouclier de freinage *m*; ~ **system** *n* MECH ENG système de freinage *m*; ~ **time** *n* TRANSP temps de serrage des freins *m*; ~ **to a stop** *n* TRANSP freinage d'arrêt *m*

bran: ~ **finisher** *n* FOOD TECH brosse à son *f*

branch[1] *n* COMP *of circuit* branche *f*, *of programme* branchement *m*, CONST *metal piece at end of hose* lance *f*, lance à eau *f*, *plumbing* branchement *m*, embranchement *m*, DP branchement *m*, *of circuit* branche *f*, *of programme* branchement *m*, ELEC *of supply network* dérivation *f*, ELEC ENG *of network* branche *f*, ELECTRON *in programme execution* branchement *m*, *of circuit* dérivation *f*, PHYS *of circuit* branche *f*; ~ **box** *n* ELEC *connection* boîte de dérivation *f*; ~ **circuit** *n* PROD ENG circuit de dérivation *m*; ~ **circuit protective device** *n* PROD ENG dispositif de protection du circuit de dérivation *m*; ~ **close** *n* PROD ENG fermeture de branche *f*; ~ **close instruction** *n* PROD ENG instruction de fermeture de branche *f*; ~ **end** *n* PROD ENG fin de branche *f*; ~ **group** *n* PROD ENG ensemble de branches *m*; ~ **instruction** *n* COMP instruction de branchement *f*; ~ **line** *n* ELEC *supply network* dérivation *f*, RAIL ligne secondaire *f*, voie d'embranchement *f*; ~ **open** *n* PROD ENG ouverture de branche *f*; ~ **open instruction** *n* PROD ENG instruction d'ouverture de branche *f*; ~ **pipe** *n* CONST *metal piece at end of hose* lance *f*, lance à eau *f*, *plumbing* branchement *m*, embranchement *m*, MECH *hydraulics* piquage *m*, WATER SUPP lance d'arrosage *f*, *for extinguishing fire* lance d'incendie *f*, lance à incendie *f*; ~ **point** *n* COMP point de branchement *m*, ELECTRON *in circuit* point de dérivation *m*, *in programme* point de branchement *m*; ~ **sewer** *n* WATER SUPP collecteur secondaire *m*; ~ **start** *n* PROD ENG début de branche *m*; ~ **terminal** *n* ELEC *connection* borne de dérivation *f*; ~ **warehouse** *n* PROD ENG entrepôt décentralisé *m*

branch[2] *vt* COMP brancher, *of programme* aiguiller, CONST brancher, embrancher, *one pipe on another* embrancher, piquer, DP brancher, *of programme* aiguiller; ~ **off** *vt* CONST brancher, embrancher

branch[3] *vi* CONST s'embrancher, se ramifier; ~ **off** *vi* CONST s'embrancher, se ramifier

branched[1] *adj* CHEM ramifié

branched:[2] ~ **chain** *n* CHEM chaîne ramifiée *f*; ~ **polymer** *n* P&R polymère ramifié *m*

branching *n* PHYS branchement *m*, WATER SUPP branchement *m*, embranchement *m*, ramification *f*; ~ **condition** *n* PROD ENG condition de branche *f*; ~ **filter** *n* ELECTRON *in programme* filtre d'aiguillage *m*; ~ **instruction** *n* PROD ENG instruction de branches *f*; ~ **ratio** *n* PHYS rapport d'embranchement *m*, rapport de branchement *m*

branding: ~ **iron** *n* PACKAGING fer à marquer à chaud *m*

brandisite *n* MINERAL brandisite *f*

brasilin *n* CHEM brésiline *f*

brass *n* ELEC, MECH *materials* laiton *m*, MECH ENG cuivre jaune *m*, laiton *m*, PROD ENG, PROP MAT laiton *m*; ~ **foundry** *n* CONST cuivrerie *f*, fonderie de cuivre *f*, robinetterie *f*; ~ **insert ring** *n* PROD ENG bague rapportée en laiton *f*; ~ **rod** *n* FUELLESS *in windmill pump* tige de laiton *f*; ~ **round head woodscrew** *n* CONST vis à bois en laiton à tête ronde *f*; ~ **screw** *n* MECH ENG vis en laiton *f*; ~ **smith** *n* CONST robinetier *m*; ~ **solder** *n* CONST brasure *f*, soudure au cuivre *f*; ~ **type** *n* PRINT caractère en cuivre *m*; ~ **wire** *n* CONST fil de laiton *m*; ~ **wire gauze** *n* CONST toile en fil de laiton *f*

brass-finisher's: ~ **lathe** *n* CONST tour de robinetterie *m*, tour à cuivre *m*

brassing *n* CONST laitonnage *m*

brassworking: ~ **tools** *n pl* PROD ENG *of lathe* outils de tour au cuivre *m pl*

brassworks *n pl* CONST cuivrerie *f*

brattice *n* MINING cloison *f*; ~ **cloth** *n* MINING toiles d'aérage *f pl*

braunite *n* MINERAL braunite *f*

Bravais: ~ **lattice** *n* CRYSTALL réseau de Bravais *m*

braze:[1] ~ **welding** *n* CONST soudo-brasage *m*

braze[2] *vi* MECH, MECH ENG, PROD ENG, THERMOD braser

brazeability *n* MECH ENG aptitude au brasage *f*

brazed *adj* THERMOD brasé, soudé au laiton

brazed-on: ~ **tips** *n pl* MECH ENG mises rapportées *f pl*

brazier: ~ **head rivet** *n* PROD ENG rivet à tête chaudron-née *m*, rivet à tête goutte de suif *m*

Brazilian: ~ **ruby** *n* MINERAL rubis du Brésil *m*

brazing *n* CONST, HEATING brasage *m*, PROD ENG brasage *m*, brasement *m*, soudo-brasure *f*, SAFETY brasage *m*, brasement *m*, soudure forte *f*, SPACE brasage par fusion *m*, THERMOD brasage *m*; ~ **blowpipe** *n* CONST chalumeau braseur *m*; ~ **flux** *n* CONST flux de brasage *m*; ~ **hazard** *n* SAFETY risque du brasage *m*; ~ **lamp** *n* PROD ENG lampe à braser *f*; ~ **solder** *n* PROD ENG brasure *f*, soudure au cuivre *f*, SAFETY brasure *f*

breach *n* WATER SUPP brèche *f*; ~ **of the safety rules** *n* SAFETY infraction aux règles de sécurité *f*

breached: ~ **anticline** *n* GEOL anticlinal à coeur érodé *m*

bread: ~ **grain** *n* FOOD TECH céréales panifiables *f pl*; ~ **improver** *n* FOOD TECH *commercial bakery* améliorant de boulangerie *m*; ~ **texture** *n* FOOD TECH alvéolage du pain *m*, porosité du pain *f*, texture aérée du pain *f*

breadboard *n* COMP maquette *f*; ~ **model** *n* ELEC ENG montage d'essai *m*

breadth *n* NAUT *ship design*, PAPER TECH largeur *f*

break[1] *n* COAL TECH cassure *f*, rupture *f*, COMP interrup-tion *f*, CONST *of curb roof* brisis *m*, curbature *f*, *of hinge* brisure *f*, PAPER TECH rupture *f*, PRINT coupure *f*, PROD ENG ouverture *f*, repos *m*, TEXTILES cassé de fil *f*; ~ **bulk** *n* TRANSP marchandises non unitisées *f pl*; ~ **character** *n* PROD ENG caractère d'interruption *m*; ~ **contact** *n* ELEC *relay* contact de repos *m*, contact de rupture *m*, contact à ouverture *m*, ELEC ENG contact de repos *m*, contact repos *m*, PROD ENG contact repos *m*; ~ **distance** *n* ELEC ENG distance d'ouverture *f*; ~ **joint** *n* CONST joint brisé *m*; ~ **line** *n* PRINT fin d'alinéa *f*, ligne de coupure *f*; ~ **roller** *n* FOOD TECH *milling and baking* cylindre de broyage *m*, cylindre de pulvérisation *m*, cylindre désagrégeur *m*; ~ **stone** *n* WATER SUPP cail-loutis *m*, pierraille *f*; ~ **tailings** *n pl* FOOD TECH *milling and baking* déchets de broyage *m pl*, refus de broyage *m*; ~ **thrust** *n* GEOL faille inverse sur un flanc de pli *f*; ~ **time** *n* ELEC *relay* durée de coupure *f*, ELEC ENG instant d'ouverture *m*

break[2] *vt* CHEM *emulsion* défaire, COMP interrompre, CONST casser, concasser, fragmenter, morceler, *a lock* fracturer, ELEC ENG *circuit* couper, mettre hors circuit, ouvrir, rompre, NAUT *flag* déferler, hisser, SAFETY briser; ~ **coal** *vt* COAL TECH faire du charbon; ~ **down** *vt* CINEMAT *negative prior to assembly* dédoubler, CONST *timber* abattre, débiter, MINING *ore* abattre; ~ **edges** *vt* MECH abattre les arêtes; ~ **off** *vt* (BrE) *(cf cap)* C&G croquer; ~ **open** *vt* CONST *door*, SAFETY enfoncer; ~ **out again** *vt* SAFETY raviver; ~ **up** *vt* CONST fragmenter, morceler; ~ **with a pick** *vt* CONST *ground* ouvrir au pic, piocher

break[3] *vi* CONST se briser, se casser, se fracturer, se rompre, se fragmenter, se morceler, NAUT *wave* défer-ler; ~ **down** *vi* CONST *mechanical failure*, TEXTILES tomber en panne; ~ **for colors** *vi* (AmE), ~ **for colours** *vi* (BrE) PRINT analyser les couleurs, sélectionner les couleurs; ~ **out** *vi* PROD ENG *run from mould* couler, SAFETY *fire* éclater; ~ **out again** *vi* SAFETY se raviver; ~ **up** *vi* CONST se fragmenter, se morceler

breakage *n* MINING *of ore* fragmentation *f*, morcelle-ment *m*; ~ **rate** *n* PAPER TECH, TEXTILES taux de casse *m*

breakaway: ~ **prop** *n* CINEMAT accessoire brisable *m*; ~

starting current *n* ELEC courant initial de démarrage *m*

break-before-make: ~ **switch** *n* TV commutateur de séquence repos-travail *m*

break-break: ~ **contact** *n* ELEC relais double repos *m*

breakdown[1] *adj* PHYS d'amorçage, disruptif

breakdown[2] *n* CHEM décomposition *f*, CONST *details of accounts* sous-détail *m*, *mechanical failure* panne *f*, CONTROL interruption *f*, interruption de marche *f*, interruption de service *f*, ELEC *of dielectric* claquage *m*, ELEC ENG *of insulator, p-n junction* claquage *m*, percement *m*, *of machine* panne *m*, ELECTRON *of gas tube* amorçage *m*, *of insulation* claquage *m*, GEOL *of mineral, rock* décomposition *f*, MECH ENG incident de non-fonctionnement *m*, panne *f*, NUCLEAR désassem-blage *m*, P&R *electrical* claquage *m*, *physics, chemistry* dégradation *f*, PHYS décomposition *f*, *failure* défail-lance *f*, défaut *m*, panne *f*, *interruption of supply* coupure *f*, *of insulation* amorçage *m*, claquage *m*, PROD ENG décomposition *f*, *division* découpe *f*, MATH répartition au moyen d'une formule *f*, SAFETY *of ma-chine* panne *f*, TELECOM panne *f*, *of network* coupure *f*; ~ **car** *n* (AmE) *(cf breakdown wagon)* RAIL wagon de secours *m*; ~ **gang** *n* CONST équipe de secours *f*; ~ **operator** *n* CINEMAT *cutting negatives* dédoubleur *m*; ~ **voltage** *n* ELEC *of dielectric* tension de claquage *f*, tension disruptive *f*, ELEC ENG potentiel disruptif *m*, *of gas tube* tension d'amorçage *f*, *of insulator, p-n junc-tion* tension de claquage *f*, tension disruptive *f*, MECH ENG tension de claquage *f*, PHYS tension d'amorçage *f*, tension de claquage *f*, tension de rupture *f*, TELECOM tension d'amorçage *f*; ~ **wagon** *n* (BrE) *(cf breakdown car)* RAIL wagon de secours *m*

breaker *n* AUTO rupteur *m*, CHEM TECH broyeur *m*, MECH ENG *crushing or grinding machine* broyeur *m*, concas-seur *m*, NAUT *in sea* brisant *m*, OCEANOG brisant *m*, coup de mer *m*, houle déferlante *f*, vague déferlante *f*, PAPER TECH broyeur *m*; ~ **board** *n* MAR POLL panneau de disjoncteur *m*; ~ **contact** *n* VEHICLES *of ignition* contact de rupture *m*; ~ **point** *n* CONST aiguille *f*, fleuret *m*; ~ **spring** *n* AUTO ressort de rupteur *m*; ~ **stack** *n* PAPER TECH lisse *f*, lisse intermédiaire *f*; ~ **steel** *n* CONST aiguille *f*, casseur *m*; ~ **strip** *n* REFRIG entretoise isolante *f*; ~ **triggering** *n* AUTO déclenchement par rupteur *m*

breakerless: ~ **triggering** *n* AUTO déclenchement sans rupteur *m*

breakeven: ~ **point** *n* TEXTILES seuil de rentabilité *m*

break-free[1] *adj* TELECOM *power supply* sans coupure

break-free:[2] ~ **switch** *n* CONTROL interrupteur instanta-né *m*, interrupteur à rupture brusque *m*

break-induced: ~ **current** *n* ELEC ENG extracourant de rupture *m*

breaking *n* CHEM TECH broyage *m*, cassure *f*, CONST *of lock* fracture *f*, *of ore, stone* cassage *m*, concassage *m*, MINING *of ore* abattage *m*, OCEANOG *of wave* déferle-ment *m*, PAPER TECH broyage *m*; ~ **arc** *n* ELEC ENG arc de rupture *m*; ~ **capacity** *n* ELEC *of switch, fuse* pouvoir de coupure *m*, pouvoir de rupture *m*, puissance de coupure *f*, puissance de rupture *f*, ELEC ENG pouvoir de coupure *m*; ~ **of a circuit** *n* ELEC ENG mise hors circuit *f*, ouverture d'un circuit *f*; ~ **current** *n* ELEC *of relay* courant de rupture *m*; ~ **down** *n* C&G *of pot* casse *f*, COAL TECH abattage *m*, concassage *m*, débitage *m*, CONST *of logs, of timber* débit *m*, débitage *m*; ~ **ground** *n* MINING abattage *m*; ~ **in** *n* (AmE) *(cf running in)* MECH ENG rodage *m*; ~ **length** *n* TEXTILES point de rupture *m*, résistance kilométrique *f*; ~ **load** *n* COAL TECH, MECH, MECH ENG, NAUT *of rope, chain, etc*, PACKAGING, PAPER TECH charge de rupture *f*; ~ **pattern** *n* MECH *materials* faciès de rupture *m*; ~ **point** *n* MECH limite de rupture *f*; ~ **shot** *n* MINING tir avec bouchon *m*, *blasting* mine d'empiétage *f*; ~ **strength** *n* MECH *materials*, P&R résistance à la rupture *f*, TEXTILES module de résistance *m*; ~ **strength tester** *n* PAPER TECH dynamomètre de traction *m*; ~ **stress** *n* MECH, MECH ENG contrainte de rupture *f*; ~ **test** *n* MECH *materials* essai de rupture *m*; ~ **wave** *n* OCEANOG brisant *m*, coup de mer *m*, houle déferlante *f*, vague déferlante *f*

breaking-down: ~ **roll** *n* MECH ENG *roll* cylindre dégrossisseur *m*, cylindre ébaucheur *m*

breaking-in *n* MECH rodage *m*; ~ **hole** *n* MINING *blasting* mine d'empiétage *f*; ~ **shot** *n* MINING tir avec bouchon *m*, *blasting* mine d'empiétage *f*

breaking-off: ~ **of base** *n* C&G décutage *m*

breaking-up *n* CONST fragmentation *f*, morcellement *m*, HYDROL *of ice in rivers* débâcle *f*, MECH dislocation *f*, dissociation *f*

break-of-slope *n* GEOL rupture de pente *f*

break-out *n* MECH ENG percée *f*, PETR TECH *drilling* déblocage *m*, dévissage *m*, PROD ENG *of molten iron from blast furnace* chat *m*, *of molten metal from mould* coulage *m*, coulure *f*, *of molten slag from blast furnace* pissée *f*; ~ **box** *n* CINEMAT répartiteur *m*

breakpoint *n* COMP point de rupture *m*, PROD ENG seuil *m*; ~ **chlorination** *n* HYDROL chloration au point optimal *f*

breakthrough *n* CONST *tunnelling* percement *m*, MINING boyau de mine *m*, PRINT *paper and ink* transpercement *m*, TELECOM *land mobile* brouillage *m*; ~ **point** *n* COAL TECH point de fuite *m*

breakwater *n* CONST brise-lame *m*, digue *f*, NAUT brise-lames *m*, môle *m*, OCEANOG, WATER SUPP brise-lames *m*

breast *n* COAL TECH taille *f*; ~ **box** *n* PAPER TECH caisse d'arrivée de pâte *f*; ~ **drill** *n* MECH ENG perceuse à main *f*, perceuse à main à conscience *f*, vilebrequin à conscience *m*; ~ **face** *n* MINING front *m*, front d'abattage *m*, front d'attaque *m*, front de taille *m*; ~ **hole** *n* MINING trou de front *m*, PROD ENG trou à laitier *m*; ~ **line** *n* NAUT *mooring* amarre traversière *f*, traversière *f*; ~ **roll** *n* PAPER TECH rouleau de tête *m*; ~ **roller** *n* PRINT rouleau d'entrée *m*, rouleau de front *m*; ~ **summer** *n* CONST linteau *m*, poitrail *m*; ~ **wall** *n* C&G piédroit *m*, CONST *breast-high wall* mur d'appui *m*, mur de parapet *m*, *retaining wall* mur de revêtement *m*, mur de terrasse *m*; ~ **wheel** *n* HYDR EQUIP roue à aubes *f*

breasting: ~ **parapet** *n* HYDR EQUIP rambarde *f*

breastplate *n* MECH ENG conscience de perceuse *f*

breathable: ~ **air** *n* SAFETY air respirable *m*

breather *n* AUTO, MECH ENG, PROD ENG reniflard *m*, VEHICLES *of engine crankcase* reniflard de carter *m*; ~ **pipe** *n* AUTO reniflard *m*

breath-holding *n* OCEANOG apnée *f*

breathing: ~ **apparatus** *n* COAL TECH, OCEANOG, PETR TECH *personnel safety* appareil respiratoire *m*, SAFETY appareil respiratoire *m*, respirateur *m*; ~ **mixture** *n* OCEANOG mélange respiratoire *m*

breccia *n* ASTRON, PETR brèche *f*

breech *n* MILIT culasse *f*; ~ **cover** *n* MILIT couvre-culasse *m*; ~ **screw** *n* MILIT vis de culasse *f*

breechblock *n* MILIT bloc de culasse *m*

breeches: ~ **buoy** *n* NAUT *for rescue* bouée culotte *f*; ~ **joint** *n* ELEC *cable connection* dérivation en Y *f*, dérivation tangente *f*; ~ **pipe** *n* MECH culotte *f*, tuyau à fourche *m*, MECH ENG, PROD ENG culotte *f*

breeching *n* PROD ENG *of boiler* culottes de la cheminée *f pl*; ~ **piece** *n* PROD ENG *Y pipe connection* raccord à culotte *m*

breed *vi* PROD ENG couver

breeder *n* SPACE surrégénérateur *m*; ~ **reactor** *n* NUCLEAR, PHYS réacteur surrégénérateur *m*

breeding: ~ **cycle** *n* NUCLEAR cycle surrégénérateur *m*; ~ **process** *n* NUCLEAR surrégénération *f*; ~ **process efficiency** *n* NUCLEAR rendement de surrégénération *m*; ~ **section** *n* NUCLEAR *of fuel rod* section de surrégénération *f*

breeze *n* COAL TECH braise *f*, METEO brise *f*

breezeway *n* TV palier intermédiaire *m*

breezing *n* C&G grainette *f*

breithauptite *n* MINERAL breithauptite *f*

bremsstrahlung *n* PHYS, RAD PHYS bremsstrahlung *f*, rayonnement de freinage *m*; ~ **source** *n* NUCLEAR source de rayonnement de freinage *f*

bressummer *n* CONST linteau *m*, poitrail *m*

breunnerite *n* MINERAL breunérite *f*

brewer's: ~ **grain** *n* FOOD TECH *fermentation* drèche de brasserie *f*

brewing *n* FOOD TECH brasserie *f*; ~ **industry** *n* FOOD TECH secteur brassicole *m*; ~ **liquor** *n* FOOD TECH *fermentation* eau de brassage *f*

Brewster: ~ **incidence** *n* PHYS incidence brewstérienne *f*

Brewster's: ~ **angle** *n* OPT angle de Brewster *m*

brewsterite *n* MINERAL brewstérite *f*

brick[1] *n* C&G, CONST brique *f*; ~ **and tile machine** *n* C&G machine pour la fabrication des briques et des tuiles *f*; ~ **arch** *n* CONST *of furnace or firebox* arc en briques *m*, voûte en briques *f*; ~ **arch bearer** *n* CONST sommier de voûte en briques *m*; ~ **clay** *n* CONST argile à briques *f*; ~ **field** *n* CONST briqueterie *f*; ~ **kiln** *n* CONST four à briques *m*; ~ **molding machine** *n* (AmE), ~ **moulding machine** *n* (BrE) C&G presse à façonner les briques *f*; ~ **pavement** *n* CONST carrelage *m*, carrelage en briques *m*, pavage en briques *m*; ~ **paving** *n* CONST carrelage *m*, carrelage en briques *m*, pavage en briques *m*; ~ **trowel** *n* CONST truelle *f*, truelle à mortier *f*; ~ **wall** *n* CONST mur en briques *m*; ~ **works** *n pl* C&G briqueterie *f*

brick[2] *vt* CONST briqueter, garnir de briques, maçonner; ~ **up** *vt* CONST briqueter, garnir de briques, maçonner

brickearth *n* CONST terre *f*, terre à briques *f*

bricked: ~ **up core** *n* CONST *loam-moulding* noyau maçonné *m*

bricklayer *n* CONST briqueteur *m*, maçon *m*, ouvrier maçon *m*

bricklayer's: ~ **trowel** *n* CONST truelle *f*, truelle à mortier *f*

brickwork *n* C&G maçonnerie *f*, CONST briquetage *m*, maçonnage *m*, maçonnerie *f*, maçonnerie de brique *f*

bridge[1] *n* C&G barrage fixe *m*, COMP pont *m*, CONST *of travelling crane; over river, road* pont *m*, DP, ELEC, INSTRUMENT, MECH ENG pont *m*, NAUT *of ship* baignoire *f*, passerelle *f*, passerelle de commandement *f*, PROD ENG *fire bridge of furnace* autel *m*, pont *m*, TELECOM dérivation *f*; ~ **amplifier** *n* ELECTRON amplificateur de pont *m*; ~ **arm** *n* INSTRUMENT branche du pont *f*; ~ **balancing** *n* ELEC ENG équilibrage du pont *m*; ~ **castle** *n* NAUT *shipbuilding* château *m*; ~ **circuit** *n* ELEC montage en pont *m*, ELEC ENG circuit en pont *m*, montage en pont *m*, pont *m*, réseau en pont *m*; ~ **connection** *n* ELEC *in circuit* montage en pont *m*; ~ **crane** *n* CONST pont-grue *m*; ~ **deck** *n* NAUT plage arrière *f*; ~ **deflective recorder** *n* CONST enregistreur de flèche de pont *m*; ~ **house** *n* NAUT *of ship* rouf-passerelle *m*; ~ **keeper** *n* NAUT *of opening bridge* pontier *m*; ~ **plate** *n* CONST *back support of grate-bars* plaque d'autel *f*, MECH ENG *injection moulds* plaque d'arrêt *f*; ~ **rail** *n* CONST rail en U *m*, rail à pont *m*; ~ **reamer** *n* MECH ENG alésoir de chaudronnerie *m*; ~ **rectifier** *n* ELEC redresseur en pont *m*, ELEC ENG pont-redresseur *m*, redresseur en pont *m*; ~ **resistance** *n* ELEC résistance de pont *f*; ~ **truss** *n* CONST ferme de pont *f*; ~ **unbalance technique** *n* TESTING technique de dissymétrie de pont *f*; ~ **under railroad** *n* (AmE) *(cf bridge under railway)* TRANSP passage supérieur de chemin de fer *m*; ~ **under railway** *n* (BrE) *(cf bridge under railroad)* TRANSP passage supérieur de chemin de fer *m*; ~ **with diminished arches** *n* CONST pont à arches surbaissées *m*; ~ **with equal bays** *n* CONST pont à travées égales *m*

bridge[2] *vt* CONST *span* croiser, traverser, *valley* franchir; ~ **over** *vt* CONST *valley* franchir

bridged *adj* PROD ENG ponté

bridged-H: ~ **network** *n* ELEC ENG *quadripole* réseau en H ponté *m*

bridged-T: ~ **network** *n* ELEC ENG *quadripole* réseau en T ponté *m*

bridge-layer: ~ **tank** *n* MILIT char poseur de ponts *m*

bridging *n* CONST *strutting between floor joists* entretoises *f pl*, liernes *f pl*, étrésillons *m pl*; ~ **amplifier** *n* RECORDING amplificateur ponté *m*; ~ **contact** *n* ELEC ENG contact à chevauchement *m*, contact à court-circuit *m*; ~ **piece** *n* CONST entretoise *f*, lierne *f*, sous-poutre *f*, étrésillon *m*; ~ **shot** *n* CINEMAT plan de transition *m*, plan raccord *m*; ~ **tank** *n* MILIT *to cross antitank ditches* pont-char *m*

bridle *n* NAUT *of rope or chain for towing, anchoring* patte d'oie *f*, PETR bride *f*; ~ **chain** *n* MINING *for mine cage* chaîne de sûreté *f*; ~ **joint** *n* CONST assemblage à embrèvements anglais *m*, assemblage à embrèvements séparés par un plat joint *m*, chevronnage à tenon *m*, joint anglais *m*

brief *n* PROD ENG dossier *m*

Briet-Wigner: ~ **resonance** *n* NUCLEAR résonance de Briet et Wigner *f*, résonance à un niveau *f*

Brigg's: ~ **pipe thread** *n* MECH ENG filetage de tube au pas Briggs *m*, filetage de tube au pas standard américain *m*

bright[1] *adj* OPT lumineux, TEXTILES brillant; ~ **all over** *adj* MECH ENG *tool* poli partout

bright:[2] ~ **annealed wire** *n* MECH ENG fil recuit blanc *m*; ~ **annealing** *n* HEATING recuit blanc *m*; ~ **bolt** *n* MECH ENG boulon décolleté *m*, vis décolletée *f*; ~ **coal** *n* COAL TECH charbon de terre *m*; ~ **color** *n* (AmE), ~ **colour** *n* (BrE) PROP MAT couleur éclatante *f*; ~ **etching** *n* C&G gravure lisse *f*; ~ **field** *n* METALL fond clair *m*; ~ **field illumination** *n* PHYS éclairage à fond clair *m*; ~ **field image** *n* CRYSTALL image en champ clair *f*; ~ **fringe** *n* PHYS frange brillante *f*; ~ **gold** *n* C&G or brillant *m*; ~ **hard-drawn wire** *n* MECH ENG fil étiré dur *m*; ~ **level** *n* TV niveau de blanc *m*; ~ **line viewfinder** *n* PHOTO viseur à cadre lumineux *m*; ~ **silver** *n* C&G argent brillant *m*

brightening *n* PROD ENG brillantage *m*

brightness *n* ASTRON *of star, planet* éclat *m*, ELECTRON brillance *f*, luminosité *f*, OPT brillance *f*, luminance *f*, luminance énergétique *f*, PAPER TECH blancheur *f*,

PHYS luminosité *f*, PRINT brillance *f*, brillant *m*, TV luminosité *f*; ~ **control** *n* TV commande de luminosité *f*, réglage de luminosité *m*, régulateur de luminance *m*; ~ **curve** *n* TV courbe de luminosité *f*; ~ **modulation** *n* ELECTRON modulation de luminosité *f*; ~ **range** *n* PHOTO intervalle de luminosité *m*; ~ **ratio** *n* CINEMAT rapport des luminances *m*, TV rapport de luminosité *m*; ~ **value** *n* TV facteur de luminosité *m*; ~ **variation** *n* ASTRON variation d'éclat *f*

brilliance *n* ELECTRON brillance *f*

brilliant: ~ **cutting** *n* C&G taille à la roue *f*; ~ **polish** *n* PROD ENG poli éclatant *m*; ~ **varnish** *n* COLOURS vernis brillant *m*, vernis de laque *m*

Brillouin: ~ **zone** *n* METALL, PHYS zone de Brillouin *f*

brim: ~ **capacity** *n* C&G capacité à ras-bord *f*

brine *n* CHEM, GAS TECH saumure *f*, HYDROL eau salée *f*, saumure *f*, NUCLEAR saumure *f*, solution saline *f*, OCEANOG eaux-mères *f pl*, saumure *f*, REFRIG saumure *f*; ~ **cooler** *n* REFRIG refroidisseur à saumure *m*; ~ **cooling** *n* FOOD TECH réfrigération par saumure *f*, saumurage *m*; ~ **cooling system** *n* NUCLEAR circuit de refroidissement de saumure *m*; ~ **droplet** *n* NUCLEAR gouttelette de saumure *f*; ~ **drum** *n* REFRIG tube accumulateur de saumure *m*; ~ **fermentation** *n* OCEANOG anchoitage *m*; ~ **header** *n* REFRIG collecteur de saumure *m*; ~ **line** *n* REFRIG conduite de saumure *f*; ~ **pickling** *n* OCEANOG anchoitage *m*, saumurage *m*; ~ **pump** *n* REFRIG pompe à saumure *f*; ~ **return tank** *n* REFRIG réservoir à retour de saumure *m*; ~ **sparge** *n* REFRIG aspersion de saumure *f*; ~ **spray** *n* REFRIG pulvérisation de saumure *f*; ~ **tank** *n* REFRIG bac à saumure *m*

Brinell: ~ **ball test** *n* MECH ENG mesure de dureté Brinell par empreinte de bille *f*; ~ **hardness** *n* MECH *materials* dureté Brinell *f*; ~ **hardness number** *n* MECH ENG degré de dureté Brinell *m*; ~ **hardness testing machine** *n* MECH ENG machine d'essais de dureté Brinell *f*; ~ **test** *n* MECH ENG essai Brinell *m*

brinelling *n* MECH ENG billage *m*

bring:[1] ~ **the air bubble to the center of its run** *vt* (AmE), ~ **the air bubble to the centre of its run** *vt* (BrE) CONST *levelling* amener la bulle d'air entre ses repères, appeler la bulle d'air entre ses repères; ~ **into position for use** *vt* PROD ENG *drill* mettre au point; ~ **to the surface** *vt* MINING monter au jour, remonter au jour, remonter à la surface; ~ **up** *vt* PRINT mettre en valeur, rehausser, remonter, soulever, RECORDING *sound* monter; ~ **up to date** *vt* MECH ENG mettre à jour

bring:[2] ~ **down the face** *vi* MINING effectuer la tombée de front de taille; ~ **up** *vi* NAUT *moor* mouiller

briny *adj* HYDROL saumâtre

briquette *n* C&G briquette de composition *f*, COAL TECH aggloméré *m*, briquette *f*

brisance *n* MINING brisance *f*

British: ~ **Association screw thread** *n* *(BA screw thread)* MECH ENG filetage British Association *m*; ~ **Standard fine screw thread** *n* *(BSF screw thread)* MECH ENG filetage fin norme britannique *m*; ~ **Standard parallel pipe thread** *n* *(BSP)* MECH ENG filetage cylindrique de tuyauterie à norme britannique *m*; ~ **Standard Pipe Taper** *n* *(BSPT)* MECH ENG filetage conique de tuyauterie à norme britannique *m*; ~ **Standards Specification** *n* *(BSS)* MECH ENG norme britannique *f*; ~ **Standard Whitworth thread** *n* *(BSW thread)* MECH ENG filetage Whitworth *m*, filetage normal anglais *m*, pas Whitworth *m*, filetage Whitworth norme britannique *m*; ~ **Thermal Unit** *n* *(BTU, BThU)* METR calorie Britannique *f*

brittle[1] *adj* CRYSTALL fragile, GEOL *deformation* cassant, MECH *materials* cassant, fragile, METALL fragile, P&R cassant, fragile, PAPER TECH cassant, PROP MAT cassant, friable

brittle:[2] ~ **crack** *n* NUCLEAR fissure fragile *f*; ~ **ductile transition** *n* NUCLEAR transition fragile-ductile *f*; ~ **failure** *n* NUCLEAR défaut fragile *m*; ~ **fiber** *n* (AmE), ~ **fibre** *n* (BrE) PROP MAT fibre fragile *f*; ~ **fracture** *n* CRYSTALL rupture fragile *f*, MECH *materials* rupture de fragilité *f*, METALL rupture fragile *f*, SPRINGS rupture à fragilité *f*; ~ **fracture resistance** *n* METALL résistance à la rupture fragile *f*; ~ **fracture transition temperature** *n* MECH *materials* température de transition de rupture *f*; ~ **metal** *n* PROP MAT métal cassant *m*; ~ **reinforcement** *n* PROP MAT *ceramics* renforcement fragile *m*

brittleness *n* C&G, CRYSTALL, METALL, P&R fragilité *f*, PROP MAT fragilité *f*, frangibilité *f*

Brix: ~ **scale** *n* FOOD TECH échelle de Brix *f*

broach[1] *n* CONST *pin of lock* broche *f*, MECH ENG alésoir *m*, équarrissoir *m*

broach[2] *vt* MECH ENG aléser, équarrir

broach[3] *vi* NAUT partir au lof, partir au tapis, tomber en travers

broaching *n* MECH, MECH ENG brochage *m*, MINING battage au large *m*, entaillage des épontes *m*; ~ **bit** *n* MINING *boring* alésoir *m*; ~ **machine** *n* MECH machine à brocher *f*, MECH ENG brocheuse *f*, machine à brocher *f*; ~ **tool** *n* MECH broche *f*

broad:[1] **on a ~ reach** *adv* NAUT *sailing* au grand largue

broad:[2] ~ **flange girder** *n* CONST poutre à larges ailes *f*; ~ **irrigation** *n* HYDROL irrigation par ruissellement *f*, WATER SUPP irrigation par aspersion *f*; ~ **pulse** *n* TV impulsion de demi-ligne *f*

broadband[1] *adj* TV large bande

broadband:[2] ~ **aerial** *n* TV antenne à large bande *f*; ~ **amplifier** *n* ELECTRON amplificateur à large bande *m*; ~ **crosspoint** *n* TELECOM point de commutation large bande *m*; ~ **integrated services digital network** *n* *(B-ISDN)* TELECOM réseau numérique avec intégration des services à large bande *m* *(RNIS-LB)*; ~ **ISDN** *n* *(B-ISDN)* TELECOM RNIS à large bande *m* *(RNIS-LB)*; ~ **ISDN service** *n* TELECOM service RNIS à large bande *m*; ~ **noise** *n* RECORDING bruit à large bande *m*; ~ **switch** *n* TELECOM commutateur à large bande *m*; ~ **switching network** *n* TELECOM réseau de connexion à large bande *m*

broadcast[1] *n* DP diffusion *f*, TELECOM *(BC)* émission *f*, TV diffusion *f*, émission *f*; ~ **mode** *n* DP mode de diffusion *m*; ~ **quality** *n* TV qualité antenne *f*; ~ **signaling virtual channel** *n* (AmE), ~ **signalling virtual channel** *n* (BrE) *(BSVC)* TELECOM voie virtuelle diffusée de signalisation *f*; ~ **standard** *n* TV norme de diffusion *f*; ~ **transmitter** *n* TELECOM émetteur de radiodiffusion *m*; ~ **videographics** *n pl* TV télétexte *m*

broadcast[2] *vt* TELECOM diffuser, TV diffuser, transmettre, émettre, WAVE PHYS *radio* diffuser

broadcasting *n* SPACE *communications* diffusion *f*, radiodiffusion *f*, télédiffusion *f*, TELECOM diffusion *f*, radiodiffusion *f*, télédiffusion *f*, TV diffusion *f*, télédiffusion *f*; ~ **network** *n* TV réseau de diffusion *m*, réseau de télédistribution *m*; ~ **right** *n* TV droit d'antenne *m*, droit de diffusion *m*; ~ **satellite** *n* SPACE *communications* satellite de radiodiffusion *m*, TV satellite de diffusion *m*; ~ **satellite service** *n* SPACE *communica-*

tions service de radiodiffusion par satellite *m*; ~ **station** *n* TV station d'émission *f*, station émettrice *f*; ~ **times** *n pl* TV heures d'antenne *f pl*

broad-crested: ~ **weir** *n* WATER SUPP déversoir sur seuil *m*, déversoir à crête épaisse *m*

broad-gage: ~ **railroad** *n* (AmE) *(cf broad-gauge railway)* RAIL chemin de fer à voie large *m*

broad-gauge: ~ **railway** *n* (BrE) *(cf broad-gage railroad)* RAIL chemin de fer à voie large *m*

broadloom: ~ **carpet** *n* TEXTILES tapis en grande largeur *m*

broadsheet *n* PRINT feuille plein format *f*

broadside *n* PRINT côté plat *m*, format horizontal *m*; ~ **antenna** *n* SPACE *communications* antenne à rayonnement transversal *f*; ~ **array antenna** *n* TELECOM antenne à rayonnement transversal *f*; ~ **page** *n* PRINT grand format journal *m*

brocade *n* TEXTILES brocart *m*

brocatel *n* MINERAL brocatelle *f*

brocatello *n* MINERAL brocatelle *f*

brochantite *n* MINERAL brochantite *f*

broke *n* PAPER TECH cassés de fabrication *m pl*

broken[1] *adj* NAUT *mooring line, boom* cassé, rompu, TELECOM *conductor* interrompu

broken:[2] ~ **circuit** *n* ELEC ENG circuit ouvert *m*; ~ **country** *n* CONST pays accidenté *m*, pays tourmenté *m*; ~ **end** *n* TEXTILES casse *f*; ~ **ice** *n* REFRIG glace concassée *f*; ~ **line** *n* GEOM ligne brisée *f*; ~ **ore** *n* MINING minerai abattu *m*, minerai broyé *m*; ~ **rice** *n* FOOD TECH brisure de riz *f*; ~ **rock** *n* COAL TECH menu de concassage *m*; ~ **seed** *n* C&G bouillon crevé *m*; ~ **stone** *n* CONST pierre cassée *f*; ~ **white line** *n* CONST *road marking* ligne blanche discontinue *f*; ~ **working** *n* COAL TECH abattage *m*, chantier accidenté *m*, déhouillement des piliers *m*, dépilage des piliers *m*, enlèvement des piliers *m*

broken-backed *adj* NAUT *ship* arqué

broken-down: ~ **timber** *n* CONST bois débité *m*

bromal *n* CHEM bromal *m*

bromargyrite *n* MINERAL bromargyrite *f*

bromate *n* CHEM bromate *m*

bromelain *n* FOOD TECH broméline *f*

bromic *adj* CHEM bromique

bromide *n* CHEM, DETERGENTS, PHOTO bromure *m*; ~ **paper** *n* PHOTO papier au gélatino-bromure *m*, PRINT papier bromure *m*; ~ **print** *n* PRINT bromure *m*

bromine *n* *(Br)* CHEM brome *m* *(Br)*

bromite *n* MINERAL bromargyrite *f*

bromlite *n* MINERAL bromlite *f*

bromoacetic *adj* CHEM bromoacétique

bromoacetone *n* CHEM bromoacétone *m*

bromobenzene *n* CHEM bromobenzène *m*

bromoform *n* CHEM bromoforme *m*

bromoil: ~ **print** *n* PHOTO oléobromie *f*

bromophenol *n* CHEM bromophénol *m*

bromyrite *n* MINERAL bromargyrite *f*

bronze:[1] ~ **chromate finished** *adj* PROD ENG chromaté au bronze

bronze[2] *n* CHEM bronze *m*, COLOURS pigment bronze *m*, pigment de bronze *m*; ~ **guide bush** *n* MECH ENG bague de guidage en bronze *f*; ~ **lacquer** *n* COLOURS vernis à bronzer *m*; ~ **pigment** *n* COLOURS bronze en poudre *m*, pigment de bronze *m*; ~ **powder** *n* COLOURS, PRINT poudre de bronze *f*; ~ **varnish** *n* COLOURS vernis à bronzer *m*; ~ **welding** *n* CONST soudo-brasage *m*

bronzing *n* PRINT bronzage *m*; ~ **tincture** *n* COLOURS teinture à bronzer *f*

bronzite *n* MINERAL bronzite *f*

brook *n* HYDROL ru *m*

Brookfield: ~ viscosity *n* P&R viscosité Brookfield *f*

brookite *n* MINERAL brookite *f*

broom *n* CONST brosse *f*

brow *n* CONST *of hill* front *m*, MINING plan incliné automoteur *m*

brown: ~ coal *n* COAL TECH lignite *m*; **~ coal gas** *n* GAS TECH gaz de lignite *m*; **~ dwarf** *n* ASTRON naine brune *f*; **~ haematite** *n* (BrE) CHEM hématite brune *f*, limonite *f*; **~ hematite** *n* (AmE) *see brown haematite*; **~ iron ore** *n* CHEM hématite brune *f*, limonite *f*; **~ mechanical pulp** *n* PAPER TECH pâte mécanique brune *f*; **~ mechanical pulp board** *n* PAPER TECH carton bois brun *m*, carton de pâte mécanique brune *m*; **~ mixed pulp board** *n* PAPER TECH carton de pâte brune mixte *m*; **~ print** *n* PRINT ozalid *m*, épreuve *f*; **~ spar** *n* MINERAL spath brunissant *m*; **~ tourmaline** *n* MINERAL tourmaline brune *f*

Brownian: ~ motion *n* PHYS, RAD PHYS mouvement brownien *m*; **~ movement** *n* PHYS, RAD PHYS *molecular* mouvement brownien *m*

browning *n* COLOURS teinture pour caramel *f*

brownout *n* ELEC ENG baisse de tension *f*, creux de tension *m*, microcoupure *f*, PROD ENG baisse de tension *f*

browse *vt* COMP, DP parcourir, survoler

brucine *n* CHEM, FOOD TECH brucine *f*

brucite *n* MINERAL brucite *f*

Brückner: ~ cycle *n* METEO cycle de Brückner *m*

bruise *n* C&G coup *m*, FOOD TECH meurtrissure *f*, talure *f*

brush *n* AUTO balais *m pl*, charbon de contact *m*, CONST brosse *f*, brushwood broussailles *f pl*, ELEC *in machine* balai *m*, ELEC ENG balai *m*, frotteur *m*, LAB EQUIP *for cleaning tubes* goupillon *m*, MECH *tools, electrics* balai *m*, brosse *f*, pinceau *m*, PAPER TECH brosse *f*, PROD ENG *of carbon* balai *m*; **~ angle** *n* ELEC *for machine* angle d'inclinaison des balais *m*; **~ coater** *n* PAPER TECH coucheuse à brosses *f*; **~ coating** *n* COATINGS peinture à la brosse *f*, PAPER TECH couchage par brosses *m*, couchage à la brosse *m*; **~ contact resistance** *n* ELEC *in machine* résistance de contact des balais *f*; **~ discharge** *n* ELEC *in machine* aigrette lumineuse *f*, ELEC ENG décharge en aigrette *f*, effluve *m*, PHYS effluve *m*; **~ dyeing** *n* COLOURS teinture à la brosse *f*; **~ glazing** *n* PAPER TECH lustrage par brosse *m*; **~ holder** *n* ELEC *in machine*, ELEC ENG porte-balais *m*; **~ lifting device** *n* ELEC *in machine* lève-balai *m*; **~ lines** *n pl* C&G peignage fin *m*; **~ marks** *n pl* C&G traces de pinceau *f pl*; **~ plating** *n* COATINGS galvanoplastie au tampon *f*; **~ polishing** *n* PAPER TECH lustrage par brosse *m*; **~ polishing machine** *n* PAPER TECH brosseuse pour couché *f*; **~ position** *n* ELEC ENG position des balais *m*; **~ proof** *n* PRINT morasse *f*, épreuve à la brosse *f*; **~ rocker** *n* ELEC ENG dispositif de décalage des balais *m*; **~ rod** *n* ELEC ENG porte-balais *m*; **~ selector** *n* ELEC *in machine* sélecteur de balai *m*; **~ sparking** *n* ELEC *in machine* crachement aux balais *m*; **~ spring** *n* ELEC ENG ressort de balai *m*; **~ washer** *n* TEXTILES laveur à la brosse *m*; **~ yoke** *n* ELEC *in motor, generator* armature de porte-balais *f*

brush-coated: ~ paper *n* PAPER TECH papier couché à la brosse *m*

brushed *adj* MECH *surface* mat

brushing *n* TEXTILES grattage *m*

brushite *n* MINERAL brushite *f*

brushless: ~ DC motor *n* (*brushless direct current motor*) ELEC ENG moteur à courant continu sans collecteur *m*; **~ direct current motor** *n* (*brushless DC motor*) ELEC ENG moteur à courant continu sans collecteur *m*; **~ generator** *n* ELEC *in machine* génératrice sans balais *f*; **~ motor** *n* ELEC moteur sans balai *m*

brush-type: ~ DC motor *n* (*brush-type direct current motor*) ELEC ENG moteur à courant continu à collecteur *m*; **~ direct current motor** *n* (*brush-type DC motor*) ELEC ENG moteur à courant continu à collecteur *m*

brute *n* CINEMAT *arc lamp* projecteur à arc 10.000 watts *m*

BS *abbr* (*backspace*) COMP caractère espace arrière *m*, espace arrière *m*

BSC *abbr* (*binary synchronous communication*) COMP transmission binaire synchrone *f*

BSF: ~ screw thread *n* (*British Standard fine screw thread*) MECH ENG filetage fin norme britannique *m*

B-sizes *n pl* PRINT *international paper sizes* formats B *m pl*

BSP *abbr* (*British Standard parallel pipe thread*) MECH ENG filetage cylindrique de tuyauterie à norme britannique *m*

BSPT *abbr* (*British Standard pipe thread*) MECH ENG filetage conique de tuyauterie à norme britannique *m*

BSS *abbr* (*British Standards Specification*) MECH ENG norme britannique *f*

B-stage: ~ resin *n* P&R résine à l'état B *f*, résitole à l'état B *m*

B-star *n* ASTRON étoile B *f*

BSVC *abbr* (*broadcast signalling virtual channel, broadcast signaling virtual channel*) TELECOM voie virtuelle diffusée de signalisation *f*

BSW: ~ thread *n* (*British Standard Whitworth thread*) MECH ENG filetage Whitworth *m*, filetage normal anglais *m*, pas Whitworth *m*

BT *abbr* (*both justified*) PRINT justifié à droite et à gauche

BThU *abbr* (*British thermal unit*) METR calorie Britannique *f*

BTU *abbr* (*British thermal unit*) METR calorie Britannique *f*

BU *abbr* (*base unit*) TELECOM coeur de chaîne *m*

bubble[1] *n* C&G, CHEM TECH, COAL TECH, P&R *plastics, paints defect*, PAPER TECH bulle *f*, PHYS bouillon *m*, bulle *f*; **~ barriers** *n pl* MAR POLL barrage à bulles d'air *m*; **~ cap** *n* FOOD TECH *packaging* cloche de barbotage *f*, NUCLEAR calotte à barbotage *f*, cloche de barbotage *f*, PETR TECH *refinery* calotte de barbotage *f*; **~ chamber** *n* PART PHYS, PHYS chambre à bulles *f*; **~ detector** *n* OCEANOG détecteur de bulles *m*; **~ film** *n* PACKAGING film à bulles *m*; **~ flowmeter** *n* LAB EQUIP *flow of gases* débitmètre à bulle de savon *m*; **~ gage** *n* (AmE), **~ gauge** *n* (BrE) CHEM TECH débitmètre à bulle de gaz *m*; **~ hood** *n* NUCLEAR calotte à barbotage *f*, cloche de barbotage *f*; **~ jet printer** *n* PRINT imprimante à bulle *f*; **~ level** *n* MECH *tools* niveau à bulle *m*; **~ memory** *n* ELEC ENG mémoire à bulles magnétiques *f*; **~ model** *n* METALL modèle de bulles *m*; **~ nut** *n* CONST *of levelling instrument* vis de réglage de la bulle *f*; **~ pack** *n* PACKAGING emballage coque *m*; **~ point pressure** *n* PETR pression de bulle *f*; **~ sort** *n* COMP tri par permutation *m*; **~ test** *n* PAPER TECH essai de cloquage *m*; **~ tray** *n* CHEM TECH plateau de barbotage *m*; **~ tray column** *n* CHEM TECH colonne à plateaux de barbotage *f*; **~ tube** *n* CONST fiole *f*, fiole d'arpentage *f*; **~ type** *n*

TEXTILES tissu bouillonné *m*

bubble^2 *vi* PAPER TECH faire des bulles; ~ **through** *vi* PHYS barboter

bubble-coated: ~ **paper** *n* PAPER TECH papier couché mousse *m*

bubbler *n* C&G bouillonneur *m*, PHYS barboteur *m*

bubbling^1 *adj* PHYS bouillonnant

bubbling^2 *n* C&G bouillonnage *m*, OCEANOG pétillement de la mer *m*, PAPER TECH cloquage *m*, PHYS barbotage *m*, bouillonnement *m*

Buchmann: ~ **and Meyer pattern** *n* ACOUSTICS méthode du faisceau lumineux réfléchi *f*

Buchner: ~ **flask** *n* LAB EQUIP *for filtration* fiole à vide *f*; ~ **funnel** *n* LAB EQUIP *for filtration* entonnoir de Buchner *m*

bucholzite *n* MINERAL bucholzite *f*

buck *n* (AmE) C&G chevalet *m*, CONST chevalet de scieur *m*

buck-boost: ~ **regulator** *n* SPACE *spacecraft* régulateur abaisseur-élévateur *m*, régulateur survolteur-dévolteur *m*

bucket *n* COMP compartiment *m*, CONST *for aerial ropeway* seau au benne à câble *m*, *of crane* benne *f*, *of elevator, dredge* auget *m*, chapelet *m*, godet *m*, *pail* baquet *m*, seau *m*, seille *f*, FUELLESS *of turbine* auge *f*, HYDR EQUIP, LAB EQUIP *container* seau *m*, MAR POLL *containing dispersants, slung under helicopter* cuve *f*, MECH *of turbine* auget de turbine *m*, MINING *hoisting bucket* benne *f*, cuffat *m*, tonne *f*, WATER SUPP *of water wheel* auge *f*, auget *m*; ~ **angle** *n* FUELLESS *hydroelectricity, turbines* angle d'auge *m*; ~ **brigade device** *n* (*BBD*) ELEC ENG, TELECOM *shift register* dispositif de transfert à la chaîne *m*; ~ **chain** *n* CONST *dredge, elevator* chaîne à augets *f*, chaîne à godets *f*; ~ **chain excavator** *n* MINING excavatrice à godets *f*; ~ **conveyor** *n* CONST convoyeur à godets *m*, transporteur à godets *m*; ~ **dredger** *n* CONST drague à chapelets *f*, drague à godets *f*, NAUT drague à godets *f*, WATER SUPP excavateur à godets *m*; ~ **drogue** *n* NAUT drogue à godet *f*; ~ **elevator** *n* CONST élévateur à chapelets *m*, élévateur à godets *m*; ~ **excavator** *n* CONST excavateur à godets *m*; ~ **ladder** *n* CONST *of dredge* élinde *f*; ~ **pump** *n* HYDR EQUIP noria *f*, MECH ENG élévateur à godets *m*; ~ **seat** *n* VEHICLES baquet *m*; ~ **velocity** *n* FUELLESS vitesse d'auge *f*; ~ **wheel** *n* CONST roue à augets *f*, roue à godets *f*; ~ **wheel excavator** *n* MINING excavatrice à roue *f*; ~ **with drop bottom** *n* CONST benne à fond mobile *f*

bucketful *n* CONST seau plein *m*

bucketless: ~ **system** *n* PROD ENG système non compartimenté *m*

buckeye: ~ **drophead coupling** *n* RAIL *vehicles* attelage à l'américaine *m*

bucking: ~ **bar** *n* AERONAUT contre-bouterolle *f*; ~ **circuit** *n* ELEC circuit de tarage *m*; ~ **coil** *n* ELEC ENG enroulement de compensation *m*; ~ **regulator** *n* SPACE *spacecraft* régulateur abaisseur *m*, régulateur dévolteur *m*

buckle^1 *n* C&G pli *m*, CINEMAT bourrage *m*, gondolage *m*, MECH ENG *of leaf spring, of strap* boucle *f*, bride *f*, distorsion *f*, flambage *m*, gauchissement *m*, voile *m*, PETR, PROP MAT *strength of materials* flambement *m*; ~ **arrester** *n* PETR limiteur de flambement *m*; ~ **detector** *n* PETR détecteur de flambement *m*; ~ **folder machine** *n* PRINT plieuse à poches *f*; ~ **trip** *n* CINEMAT interrupteur automatique *m*

buckle^2 *vt* MECH ENG déformer, fausser, gauchir, voiler

buckle^3 *vi* MECH *materials*, SPRINGS flamber

buckling *n* GEOL gauchissement *m*, plissotement *m*, MECH *materials* flambement *m*, MECH ENG *distorting strap* boucle *f*, bride *f*, distorsion *f*, flambage *m*, gauchissement *m*, voile *m*, NUCLEAR *of rod, fuel cladding* flabage *m*, gauchissement *m*, voile voilage *m*, PHOTO *of photographic emulsion* cintrage *m*, PROD ENG *defect in casting* déformation *f*, flexion *f*, gauchissement *m*, *of boilerplate* déjettement *m*, voilure *f*, PROP MAT *strength of materials* flambement *m*; ~ **load** *n* MECH *materials* charge de flambement *f*

buckram *n* PRINT bougran *m*

buckstay *n* C&G poteau d'ancrage *m*

buddle *n* MINING buddle *m*

buff:^{1} ~ **wheel** *n* PROD ENG disque en buffle *m*

buff^2 *vt* PROD ENG polir

buffer^1 *n* CHEM tampon *m*, COMP tampon *m*, ELEC ENG tampon *m*, MECH, MECH ENG butoir *m*, P&R *pH control* tampon *m*, PRINT tampon *m*, zone de stockage temporaire *f*, *computer, printer* mémoire tampon *f*, RAIL butoir *m*, heurtoir *m*, tampon *m*, TV *fibre cable* circuit intermédiaire *m*, tampon *m*; ~ **action** *n* CHEM tamponnage *m*, tamponnement *m*, DETERGENTS tamponnage *m*; ~ **amplifier** *n* ELECTRON, RECORDING amplificateur séparateur *m*; ~ **battery** *n* ELEC ENG, TRANSP batterie tampon *f*; ~ **beam** *n* RAIL *vehicles* traverse porte-tampons *f*; ~ **circuit** *n* ELECTRON circuit tampon *m*; ~ **dynamo** *n* ELEC *generator* dynamo tampon *f*; ~ **memory** *n* ELEC ENG mémoire tampon *f*, TELECOM mémoire intermédiaire *f*; ~ **register** *n* COMP registre tampon *m*; ~ **salt** *n* FOOD TECH tampon *m*; ~ **solution** *n* FOOD TECH, PROD ENG *chroming* solution tampon *f*; ~ **stage** *n* PROD ENG état intermédiaire *m*, état séparateur *m*; ~ **stop** *n* RAIL butoir *m*, heurtoir *m*; ~ **stop block** *n* RAIL heurtoir-frein *m*, *vehicles* heurtoir glissant *m* (Fra), heurtoir patinant *m* (Bel); ~ **tank** *n* GAS TECH capacité tampon *f*

buffer^2 *vt* CHEM tamponner, COMP mettre en mémoire tampon, tamponner, ranger en mémoire tampon

buffered: ~ **fiber** *n* (AmE), ~ **fibre** *n* (BrE) OPT fibre gainée *f*; ~ **input/output** *n* COMP entrée/sortie tamponnée *f*

buffering *n* COMP mise en mémoire tampon *f*, tamponnage *m*, rangement en mémoire tampon *m*, DP rangement en mémoire tampon *m*, OPT *optical fibre* gainage *m*, revêtement secondaire *m*; ~ **agent** *n* CINEMAT agent tampon *m*

buffet *n* SPACE secousse *f*, turbulence *f*; ~ **car** *n* (AmE) (*cf buffet coach*) RAIL *vehicles* voiture-bar *f*, voiture-buffet *f*; ~ **coach** *n* (BrE) (*cf buffet car*) RAIL *vehicles* voiture-bar *f*, voiture-buffet *f*

buffeting *n* AERONAUT battement de vibration *m*, flottement *m*, secousses *f pl*, tremblement *m*, SPACE battement de vibration *m*, flottement *m*

buffing *n* PROD ENG lustrage *m*, PROP MAT polissage *m*; ~ **gear** *n* RAIL appareil de choc *m*, appareil de tamponnement *m*; ~ **wheel** *n* PROD ENG disque à polir *m*

bufotoxin *n* CHEM bufotoxine *f*

bug *n* COMP bogue *f*, erreur *f*, PRINT *computers* erreur *f*, *typography* insecte *m*, puce *f*, punaise *f*

buggy *n* COAL TECH wagonnet *m*, TRANSP chariot des dunes *m*

build *vt* CONST édifier, *house* bâtir, construire, PRINT *page* monter; ~ **up** *vt* CONST *girder* composer

builder *n* CONST constructeur *m*, *building contractor* entrepreneur *m*, entrepreneur de bâtiments *m*, entrepreneur de constructions *m*, *worker* bâtisseur *m*, constructeur de bâtiments *m*

builder's: ~ **certificate** *n* NAUT *of ship* certificat de construction *m*

builders': ~**hardware** *n* CONST serrurerie de bâtiment *f*; ~ **hardware merchant** *n* CONST serrurier en bâtiment *m*; ~ **timber** *n* CONST bois de construction *m*

building *n* CONST *edifice* bâtiment *m*, construction *f*, MINING *pack wall* mur de remblai *m*, muretin de remblai *m*, muretin en pierres sèches *m*, PROD ENG *mantle of blast furnace* chemise extérieure *f*, enveloppe extérieure *f*; ~ **berth** *n* NAUT *shipbuilding* cale de construction *f*; ~ **line** *n* CONST ligne de construction *f*; ~ **materials** *n pl* CONST matériaux de construction *m pl*; ~ **penetration loss** *n* TELECOM affaiblissement dû à la pénétration dans les bâtiments *m*; ~ **freezing** *n* CONST *loam-moulding* couronne de renfort *f*; ~ **slip** *n* NAUT *shipbuilding* cale de construction *f*; ~ **stone** *n* CONST maçonnerie de pierres *f*, pierre équarrie *f*, pierre de construction *f*, pierre de taille *f*, pierre taillée *f*, pierre à bâtir *f*; ~ **trade** *n* CONST industrie du bâtiment *f*

built-in[1] *adj* ELEC ENG incorporé, MECH, MECH ENG encastré, incorporé, intégré

built-in:[2] ~ **beam** *n* MECH ENG poutre encastrée *f*; ~ **charger** *n* TRANSP chargeur embarqué *m*; ~ **exposure meter** *n* PHOTO cellule incorporée *f*; ~ **filter** *n* CINEMAT filtre incorporé *m*; ~ **function** *n* COMP fonction intrinsèque *f*; ~ **light meter** *n* CINEMAT cellule incorporée *f*; ~ **microphone** *n* RECORDING microphone incorporé *m*; ~ **modem** *n* DP modem incorporé *m*; ~ **motor** *n* ELEC ENG moteur incorporé *m*; ~ **tank** *n* MECH ENG réservoir intégré *m*

built-up: ~ **crank** *n* MECH ENG manivelle en plusieurs pièces *f*; ~ **edge** *n* MECH ENG *tools* arête rapportée *f*; ~ **girder** *n* CONST poutre composée *f*, poutre en tôles *f*, poutre à âme pleine *f*

bulb *n* C&G olive *f*, CINEMAT ampoule *f*, lampe *f*, ELEC ampoule *f*, ELEC ENG lampe *f*, *lamp* ampoule *f*, LAB EQUIP *blowing ball* poire *f*, MECH ENG *light* bulbe *m*; ~ **alternator** *n* ELEC alternateur bulbe *m*, générateur bulbe *m*; ~ **edge** *n* C&G bourrelet *m*; ~ **generator** *n* ELEC alternateur bulbe *m*, générateur bulbe *m*; ~ **plate** *n* MECH *materials* tôle larmée *f*

bulbous: ~ **bow** *n* NAUT *boat building* étrave à bulbe *f*

bulb-type: ~ **temperature switch** *n* PROD ENG thermostat de type à sonde *m*

bulge[1] *n* CONST *of wall* bombement *m*, ventre *m*, MECH ENG bombure *f*, renflement *m*

bulge[2] *vi* CONST bomber, faire ventre, pousser au vide, pousser en dehors, se bomber, tirer au vide, boucler, MECH ENG gonfler, se bomber

bulged: ~ **finish** *n* C&G bague gonflée *f*; ~ **wall** *n* CONST mur bombé *m*, mur bouclé *m*

bulging *n* CONST bombement *m*, poussée au vide *f*; ~ **wall** *n* CONST muraille qui pousse *f*

bulk:[1] **in** ~ *adv* COAL TECH, TRANSP en vrac

bulk[2] *n* C&G, CONST *of stone* volume *m*, MECH encombrement *m*, NAUT *cargo* charge *f*, chargement arrimé *m*, PAPER TECH bouffant *m*, PHYS encombrement *m*, grandeur *f*, grosseur *f*, PRINT bouffant *m*, indice de bouffant *m*, indice de main *m*, *paper* main *f*, volume *m*, TEXTILES gonflant *m*; ~ **acoustic wave** *n* *(BAW)* ELEC ENG onde acoustique en volume *f*; ~ **carrier** *n* NAUT *vessel* navire pour le transport en vrac *m*, vraquier *m*, TRANSP vraquier *m*; ~ **cement** *n* CONST

ciment en vrac *m*; ~ **channel** *n* ELECTRON *buried channel, transistors* canal enterré *m*; ~ **concentration** *n* PROP MAT concentration nominale *f*; ~ **container with gravity discharge** *n* TRANSP conteneur à pulvérulents à vidange par gravité *m*; ~ **container with pressure discharge** *n* TRANSP conteneur à pulvérulents à vidange par air pulsé *m*; ~ **density** *n* C&G densité apparente *f*, COAL TECH masse volumique apparente *f*, P&R, PETR TECH densité apparente *f*, PRINT apparente *f*, densité *f*, PROP MAT densité apparente *f*; ~ **deposition** *n* POLLUTION dépôt brut *m*, dépôt global *m*, retombées globales *f pl*; ~ **diffusion** *n* METALL diffusion volumique *f*; ~ **eraser** *n* RECORDING effaceur total *m*, TV démagnétiseur *m*, effaceur *m*; ~ **film** *n* PHOTO film au mètre *m*, film en vrac *m*; ~ **film loader** *n* PHOTO bobineuse *f*; ~ **flotation** *n* COAL TECH flottation collective *f*; ~ **freezing** *n* REFRIG congélation en vrac *f*; ~ **goods** *n pl* PACKAGING marchandises en vrac *f pl*; ~ **index** *n* PRINT bouffant *m*, indice de bouffant *m*, indice de main *m*; ~ **lifetime** *n* ELECTRON *buried channel, transistors* durée de vie en profondeur *f*; ~ **material** *n* COAL TECH matériau en vrac *m*; ~ **of material** *n* PROP MAT coeur du matériau *m*; ~ **memory** *n* COMP mémoire de grande capacité *f*, mémoire de masse *f*; ~ **modulus** *n* PETR module de volume *m*, PHYS module d'élasticité cubique *m*, module de compression *m*; ~ **modulus of elasticity** *n* MECH ENG module de masse d'élasticité *m*; ~ **oil circuit breaker** *n* ELEC disjoncteur à bain d'huile *m*; ~ **properties** *n pl* ELECTRON propriétés en profondeur *f pl*; ~ **property** *n* METALL propriété en volume *f*; ~ **resistivity** *n* ELEC ENG résistivité en profondeur *f*; ~ **semiconductor** *n* ELECTRON semi-conducteur massif *m*, semi-conducteur non épitaxié *m*; ~ **ship train** *n* TRANSP train océanique *m*; ~ **solids handling technology** *n* MECH ENG technologie de manutention des matériaux en vrac *f*; ~ **transport** *n* PACKAGING transport de matières en vrac *m*; ~ **volume** *n* PETR, PROP MAT volume apparent *m*; ~ **wafer** *n* ELECTRON plaquette non épitaxiée *f*; ~ **wave oscillator** *n* ELECTRON oscillateur à ondes en volume *m*; ~ **wave resonator** *n* ELECTRON résonateur à ondes en volume *m*

bulk[3] *vt* WATER SUPP gonfler

bulk[4] *vi* PAPER TECH avoir de la main

bulkhead *n* MECH cloison *f*, cloison étanche *f*, MECH ENG cloison *f*, NAUT *shipbuilding* cloison *f*, couple de construction *m*, SPACE *spacecraft* cloison *f*; ~ **coupling** *n* MECH ENG *pipe fitting* joint cloison *m*; ~ **plan** *n* NAUT *ship design* plan des cloisons *m*; ~ **plate** *n* NAUT *shipbuilding* tôle de bouchain *f*; ~ **stiffener** *n* NAUT *shipbuilding* montant de cloison *m*, raidisseur de cloison *m*

bulking *n* CONST gonflement *m*, *expansion of earth when excavated* foisonnement *m*, RECYCLING *of sludge* gonflement *m*; ~ **index** *n* *(cf specific index)* PRINT bouffant *m*, indice de bouffant *m*, indice de main *m*; ~ **paper** *n* PAPER TECH papier bouffant *m*; ~ **thickness** *n* PAPER TECH épaisseur moyenne d'une feuille en liasse *f*

bulky[1] *adj* PAPER TECH bouffant

bulky:[2] ~ **group** *n* CHEM groupe encombrant *m*; ~ **paper** *n* PAPER TECH papier qui a du corps *m*; ~ **waste** *n* RECYCLING déchets encombrants *m pl*, déchets monstres *m pl*

bull *n* PROD ENG anse *f*; ~ **block** *n* MECH ENG banc à tréfiler les gros fils *m*; ~ **handle** *n* PROD ENG anse *f*; ~ **ladle** *n* MECH ENG poche de coulée *f*, PROD ENG *foun-*

ding poche à armature fixe et à anse démontable *f*; ~ **pump** *n* MINING pompe à maîtresse-tige *f*

bullbar *n* AUTO pare-buffle *m*

bulldog: ~ **casing spear** *n* MINING navette *f*

bulldozer *n* CONST bouteur *m*, bulldozer *m*, MINING bouteur *m*, TRANSP bouteur *m*, bulldozer *m*

bulldozing *n* CONST fragmentation de gros blocs de minerai au moyen de petits *f*

bullet *n* PRINT puce typographique *f*, signe typographique *m*

bulletin: ~ **board** *n* COMP, TELECOM tableau d'affichage *m*

bulletproof[1] *adj* MILIT à l'épreuve des balles

bulletproof:[2] ~ **jacket** *n* MILIT gilet de protection pareballes *m*; ~ **vest** *n* MILIT gilet de protection pare-balles *m*

bullhead: ~ **rivet** *n* CONST rivet à tête fraisée et goutte de suif *m*

bullheaded: ~ **rail** *n* RAIL *track* rail à double champignon *m*; ~ **rivet** *n* CONST rivet à tête fraisée et goutte de suif *m*

bullion *n* C&G boudine *f*, METALL métal précieux en barres *m*, métal précieux en lingots *m*

bulwark: ~ **rail** *n* NAUT *shipbuilding* lisse *f*

bulwarks *n pl* NAUT pavois *m*

bump:[1] ~ **exposure** *n* PRINT exposition secondaire *f*

bump:[2] ~ **up** *vt* CINEMAT, TV gonfler

bump[3] *vi* CHEM *boiling liquid* cogner

bumper *n* (BrE) AUTO, *(cf fender)* MECH *(cf fender)* pare-chocs *m*, RAIL *(cf damper)* on wagon or coach tampon *m*, VEHICLES *(cf fender)* body pare-chocs *m*; ~ **rod** *n* MECH ENG *die casting die* butée d'éjection *f*

bumping *n* CHEM *of boiling liquid* cognement *m*, soubresaut *m*; ~ **hammer** *n* MECH ENG *tool* postillon *m*; ~ **screen** *n* PROD ENG crible à secousse *m*; ~ **table** *n* PROD ENG table à secousses *f*; ~ **tray** *n* PROD ENG plateau à secousses *m*

bumpkin *n* NAUT bout-dehors *m*

bumpless: ~ **transfer** *n* PROD ENG transfert sans heurts *m*

bunched: ~ **cable** *n* (BrE) *(cf bundled cable)* ELEC câble groupé *m*, ELEC ENG câble à plusieurs conducteurs *m*; ~ **conductor** *n* (BrE) *(cf bundled conductor)* ELEC *for cable* âme tordonnée *f*

buncher: ~ **resonator** *n* ELECTRON cavité d'entrée *f*, cavité résonnante d'entrée *f*; ~ **space** *n* ELECTRON *of klystron* espace de modulation *m*

bunching *n* AERONAUT *air traffic control* concentration *f*, ELECTRON *of klystron* groupement des électrons en paquets *m*; ~ **space** *n* ELECTRON *of klystron* espace de groupement *m*

bunchy *adj* MINING poché

bundle[1] *n* C&G nappe *f*, OPT faisceau *m*, PACKAGING botte *f*, RAIL *of rails* paquet *m*, TELECOM *of fibres* faisceau *m*; ~ **corner rod** *n* NUCLEAR crayon d'angle *m*; ~ **tier** *n* PRINT fardeleuse-ficeleuse *f*

bundle[2] *vt* PAPER TECH embotteler, mettre en botte, PROD ENG grouper, placer ensemble

bundled: ~ **cable** *n* (AmE) *(cf bunched cable)* ELEC câble groupé *m*, ELEC ENG câble à plusieurs conducteurs *m*; ~ **conductor** *n* (AmE) *(cf bunched conductor)* ELEC *for cable* âme tordonnée *f*; ~ **software** *n* COMP logiciel fourni en bundle *m*

bundle-tying: ~ **machine** *n* PACKAGING machine à lier les bottes *f*

bundle-type: ~ **machine** *n* PRINT fardeleuse *f*

bundling: ~ **machine** *n* PACKAGING machine pour mettre en bottes *f*; ~ **press** *n* PAPER TECH presse à emballer *f*

bung *n* FOOD TECH *fermentation* bouchon *m*, LAB EQUIP

closure, PROD ENG bonde *f*; ~ **of saggars** *n* C&G pile de cassettes *f*

bunghole *n* FOOD TECH *fermentation* bonde de bouchon *f*, PROD ENG trou de bonde *m*

bunging: ~ **up** *n* PROD ENG *of blast furnace, cupola* engorgement *m*

bunk *n* NAUT banette *f*, couchette *f*

bunker[1] *n* COAL TECH soute *f*, CONST trémie *f*, MAR POLL soute *f*, MINING *for ore* caisson *m*, case *f*, coffre *m*, réservoir *m*, NAUT soute *f*; ~ **C** *n* AERONAUT fuel de soute *m*; ~ **car** *n* MINING berline accumulatrice *f*; ~ **C fuel** *n* MAR POLL fuel lourd pour soutes *m*; ~ **coal** *n* COAL TECH charbon de soute *m*; ~ **conveyor** *n* MINING convoyeur accumulateur *m*; ~ **fuels** *n pl* MAR POLL fuels de soutes *m pl*; ~ **oils** *n pl* TRANSP combustibles pour soutes *m pl*; ~ **system** *n* MINING trémie *f*; ~ **tank** *n* POLLUTION soute *f*; ~ **vibrator** *n* MINING vibreur de silo *m*

bunker[2] *vt* NAUT charbonner

bunkering *n* NAUT mazoutage *m*, soutage *m*

Bunsen: ~ **burner** *n* LAB EQUIP *heating* bec Bunsen *m*; ~ **cell** *n* ELEC pile de Bunsen *f*

bunsenine *n* MINERAL bunsénine *f*

bunsenite *n* MINERAL bunsénite *f*

bunter *n* PETR TECH *geology* buntsandstein *m*

Bunter *n* PETR Bunter *m*

buoy[1] *n* NAUT *navigation marks*, PETR bouée *f*; ~ **line** *n* NAUT orin *m*; ~ **rope** *n* NAUT *for anchor* orin *m*; ~ **tender** *n* NAUT baliseur *m*

buoy[2] *vt* NAUT *navigation marks* baliser, marquer

buoyancy *n* AERONAUT flottabilité *f*, poussée hydrostatique *f*, FLUID PHYS flottabilité *f*, poussée d'Archimède *f*, poussée *f*, HYDR EQUIP flottabilité *f*, NAUT flottabilité *f*, poussée *f*, poussée hydrostatique *f*, PHYS poussée *f*, *of fluid* flottabilité *f*, poussée d'Archimède *f*; ~ **compensator** *n* OCEANOG bouée-fenzi *f*; ~ **curve** *n* NAUT *ship design* courbe de flottabilité *f*; ~ **force** *n* FLUID PHYS force d'Archimède *f*; ~ **tank** *n* NAUT *ship, floating booms* caisson de flottabilité *m*, caisson à air *m*, réservoir de flottabilité *m*

buoyant *adj* NAUT flottable, porteur

buratite *n* MINERAL buratite *f*

burette *n* CHEM burette *f*, éprouvette graduée *f*, LAB EQUIP *analysis* burette *f*; ~ **stand** *n* LAB EQUIP *support* support de burettes *m*

burgee *n* C&G sable usé *m*, NAUT *triangular flag* guidon *m*

Burgers: ~ **circuit** *n* METALL circuit de Burgers *m*; ~ **vector** *n* CRYSTALL vecteur de Burgers *m*

burglar: ~ **alarm** *n* SAFETY alarme antieffraction *f*, dispositif antieffraction *m*, système avertisseur anti-effraction *m*

burglar-proof *adj* SAFETY *lock* antivol

burglary *n* SAFETY cambriolage *m*

burial *n* PETR TECH enfouissement *m*; ~ **metamorphism** *n* GEOL métamorphisme général *m*

buried[1] *adj* ELECTRON *channel* enterré

buried:[2] ~ **channel CCD** *n* ELECTRON CCD à canaux enterrés *m*; ~ **loop** *n* TRANSP boucle noyée dans la chaussée *f*; ~ **pipeline** *n* GAS TECH canalisation enterrée *f*; ~ **topography** *n* GEOL paléorelief enfoui *m*

burn[1] *n* CINEMAT reflet gênant *m*, PRINT *of plate* brûlure *f*, insolation *f*, SAFETY *of person* brûlure *f*, TV rémanence d'image *f*; ~ **cut** *n* MINING bouchon canadien *m*; ~ **mark** *n* C&G piqûre *f*; ~ **pit** *n* PETR fosse creusée en terre *f*; ~ **time** *n* MILIT durée de propulsion *f*

burn[2] *vt* PROD ENG cuire, THERMOD brûler, calciner, griller, incinérer, mettre en flamme; ~ **in** *vt* CINEMAT *of timecode*, TV incruster; ~ **off** *vt* THERMOD *paint* nettoyer par le feu, *waste gas* brûler à la torche, torcher
burn[3] *vi* THERMOD brûler, être en flammes
burned: ~ **brick** *n* CONST brique cuite *f*; ~ **sand** *n* PROD ENG *founding* sable brûlé *m*, sable de râperie *m*, sable gris *m*
burner *n* GAS TECH brûleur *m*, chalumeau *m*, HEAT ENG brûleur *m*, LAB EQUIP *heating* bec *m*, PRINT brûleur *m*, TELECOM chalumeau *m*, THERMOD brûleur *m*; ~ **block** *n* C&G bloc de brûleur *m*; ~ **brick** *n* HEATING brique de brûleur *f*, brique réfractaire *f*; ~ **can** *n* SPACE chambre de combustion *f*; ~ **outlet port** *n* C&G brûleur côté fumées *m*
burn-in *n* PROD ENG déverminage *m*, SPACE *testing* rodage *m*
burning[1] *adj* THERMOD ardent, brûlant, en flammes
burning[2] *n* C&G cuisson *f*, PROD ENG coulée sur métal *f*, soudure par la fonte liquide *f*, *baking* cuisson *f*, cuite *f*, THERMOD brûlage *m*, calcination *f*, cuisson *f*, grillage *m*, incinération *f*, combustion *f*; ~ **agent** *n* MAR POLL agent de combustion *m*; ~ **behavior** *n* (AmE), ~ **behaviour** *n* (BrE) SAFETY *fire research* comportement au feu *m*; ~ **coal** *n* COAL TECH charbon ardent *m*; ~ **heat** *n* THERMOD chaleur ardente *f*; ~ **house** *n* PROD ENG *kiln* four de grillage *m*, four à griller *m*; ~ **mirror** *n* INSTRUMENT miroir ardent *m*, miroir concave *m*; ~ **reflector** *n* INSTRUMENT miroir ardent *m*, miroir concave *m*; ~ **surface-to-throat area ratio** *n* SPACE facteur de serrage *m*
burning-in *n* PRINT cuisson *f*
burning-off *n* C&G coupé-rebrûlé *m*; ~ **and edge-melting machine** *n* (BrE) *(cf remelting machine)* C&G coupeuse-rebrûleuse *f*
burnish *vt* C&G *tinfoil* aviver
burnisher *n* C&G brunissoir *m*
burnishing *n* C&G brunissage *m*, MECH brunissage *m*, polissage *m*, PRINT, PROD ENG, PROP MAT brunissage *m*; ~ **gold** *n* C&G or à brunir *m*; ~ **silver** *n* C&G argent à polir *m*
burnout *n* SPACE arrêt par épuisement *m*, *spacecraft* extinction par épuisement *f*, THERMOD *aeronautics flameout* extinction de la flamme dans la chambre de combustion *f*; ~ **velocity** *n* SPACE *spacecraft* vitesse en fin de combustion *f*
burnt[1] *adj* PROD ENG calciné, THERMOD brûlé, calciné, carbonisé, incinéré, noirci
burnt:[2] ~ **clay** *n* C&G argile cuite *f*; ~ **contact** *n* VEHICLES *ignition system* contact brûlé *m*; ~ **earthenware** *n* C&G terre cuite *f*; ~ **mold** *n* (AmE), ~ **mould** *n* (BrE) C&G moule brûlé *m*; ~ **sugar coloring** *n* (AmE), ~ **sugar colouring** *n* (BrE) COLOURS teinture pour caramel *f*; ~ **valve** *n* VEHICLES *in engine* soupape grillée *f*
burnt-in: ~ **time code** *n* TV code temporel incrusté *m*
burnup *n* NUCLEAR épuisement spécifique *m*; ~ **fraction** *n* NUCLEAR taux de combustion *m*
burr *n* MECH barbe *f*, bavure *f*, MECH ENG barbe *f*, *rough edge* bavure *f*, *tool* fraise-lime *f*, PROD ENG *fin on casting* balcon *m*, balène *f*, balètre *f*, bavure *f*, ébarbure *f*, *rough edge* barbe *f*, *scale on casting* balèvre *f*, barbure *f*
burring: ~ **reamer** *n* MECH ENG *burr remover* fraise ébarbeuse *f*
Burrus: ~ **diode** *n* OPT, TELECOM diode de Burrus *f*
burst[1] *n* COMP *of errors*, DP *of errors*, MILIT *of machine*

gun fire rafale *f*, NUCLEAR bouffée *f*, PAPER TECH perforation *f*, éclatement *m*, SPACE, TELECOM salve *f*, TEXTILES éclatement *m*, TV impulsion de synchronisation *f*, salve *f*; ~ **amplifier** *n* ELECTRON, TV amplificateur de salve *m*; ~ **can** *n* NUCLEAR système de détection de rupture de gaine *m*; ~ **error correcting capability** *n* TELECOM capacité de correction des paquets d'erreur *f*; ~ **factor** *n* PAPER TECH indice d'éclatement *m*; ~ **gate** *n* TV porte déclenchant la synchronisation de la sous-porteuse *f*; ~ **index** *n* PAPER TECH indice d'éclatement *m*; ~ **locked oscillator** *n* TV oscillateur asservi à la salve de référence *m*; ~ **mode** *n* COMP mode continu *m*; ~ **phase** *n* TV phase de sous-porteuse de synchronisation couleur *f*; ~ **ratio** *n* PAPER TECH indice d'éclatement *m*; ~ **separator** *n* TV séparateur de synchronisation couleur *m*; ~ **slug** *n* NUCLEAR système de détection de rupture de gaine *m*; ~ **tester** *n* PAPER TECH perforamètre *m*, éclatomètre *m*; ~ **value** *n* PAPER TECH indice d'éclatement *m*; ~ **word** *n* SPACE *communications* mot particulier *m*
burst[2] *vt* CONST faire crever, faire éclater, *pipe* crever
burst[3] *vi* COMP, MECH, MECH ENG, PAPERtech éclater; ~ **its bank** *vi* HYDROL *of river* déborder, passer par-dessus ses berges
burster *n* COMP rupteur *m*
bursters *n pl* ASTRON sources à sursauts *f pl*
bursting *n* CONST crevaison *f*, éclatement *m*, PRINT éclatement *m*; ~ **disc** *n* (BrE) MECH diaphragme d'éclatement *m*; ~ **disk** *n see bursting disc*; ~ **pressure** *n* C&G, PACKAGING, PAPER TECH pression d'éclatement *f*; ~ **shot** *n* MINING *blasting* mine d'empiétage *f*; ~ **strength** *n* P&R, PACKAGING, PAPER TECH, TEXTILES résistance à l'éclatement *f*
bursting-off *n* C&G détachage par soufflage au mince *m*
bury: ~ **barge** *n* PETR TECH *for sub-sea pipeline* barge d'ensouillage *f*
bus *n* COMP, DP artère *f*, DP, ELEC ENG bus *m*, SPACE *spacecraft* bus *m*, liaison *f*, plate-forme *f*, TELECOM bus *m*, TV voie de commutation *f*; ~ **arbitrator** *n* TELECOM arbitre de bus *m*; ~ **bay** *n* TRANSP zone d'arrêt d'autobus *f*; ~ **choke** *n* PROD ENG inductance de lissage de bus *f*; ~ **configuration** *n* TELECOM interconnexion par bus *f*; ~ **discharge board** *n* PROD ENG carte de décharge du bus *f*; ~ **driver** *n* TRANSP conducteur d'autobus *m*; ~ **duct plug-in unit** *n* ELEC *connection* prise pour jeux de barres *f*; ~ **interface** *n* COMP, DP interface de bus *f*; ~ **lane** *n* TRANSP couloir réservé aux bus *m*; ~ **lane equipped with guiding device** *n* TRANSP voie d'autobus équipée d'un système de guidage *f*; ~ **line** *n* ELEC ligne d'accès *f*, ligne omnibus *f*; ~ **network** *n* COMP, DP réseau de type bus *m*; ~ **on railroad car** *n* (AmE) *(cf bus on railway wagon)* TRANSP autobus sur wagon de chemin de fer *m*; ~ **on railroad tracks** *n* (AmE) *(cf bus on railway tracks)* TRANSP autobus sur voie de chemin de fer *m*; ~ **on railway tracks** *n* (BrE) *(cf bus on railroad tracks)* TRANSP autobus sur voie de chemin de fer *m*; ~ **on railway wagon** *n* (BrE) *(cf bus on railroad car)* TRANSP autobus sur wagon de chemin de fer *m*; ~ **shelter** *n* TRANSP aubette *f*; ~ **terminator** *n* COMP, DP terminaison de bus *f*; ~ **topology** *n* COMP, DP topologie en bus *f*
busbar *n* COMP, DP bus *m*, ELEC *connection* barre omnibus *f*, jeu de barres *m*, ELEC ENG barre bus *f*, bus d'alimentation *m*, MECH ENG barre omnibus *f*, rail collecteur *m*, TELECOM barre d'alimentation *f*, bus *m*; ~ **coupler** *n* ELEC *switch* commutateur de bouclage *m*;

~ **sectionalizing switch** n ELEC sectionneur de barres m; ~ **system** n ELEC *connection* jeu de barres m

bush n MECH ENG bague f, douille f, manchon m, palier m

bushel n FOOD TECH *milling and baking*, METR boisseau m

bushing n C&G filière f, MECH coussinet m, douille f, MECH ENG bague f, douille f, manchon m, palier m, *mechanical component* douille lisse f, RAIL fourrure f, fourrure mécanique f; ~ **assembly** n C&G filière f (Bel), four-filière m (Fra); ~ **blower** n C&G soufflerie f souffleur m

business: ~ **aircraft** n AERONAUT avion d'affaires m; ~ **communication system** n TELECOM installation de communication d'entreprises f; ~ **forms printing** n PRINT impression en continu f; ~ **graphics** n PRINT infographie d'entreprise f, infographie de gestion f; ~ **system** n TELECOM installation de communication d'entreprises f; ~ **traffic** n TRANSP trafic commercial m

bus-mouse: ~ **adaptor** n COMP, DP interface de souris-bus f

bustamite n MINERAL bustamite f

buster: ~ **shot** n MINING tir avec bouchon m, *blasting* mine d'empiétage f

busting: ~ **shot** n MINING *blasting* mine d'empiétage f

bustle: ~ **pipe** n PROD ENG *of blast furnace* conduite circulaire de vent f

bustline n TEXTILES buste m; ~ **ruffle** n TEXTILES pince à poitrine f

busway: ~ **for rapid transit** n TRANSP système d'autobus express sur voie réservée m

busy: ~ **hour** n TELECOM heure chargée f; ~ **number** n TELECOM numéro occupé m; ~ **period** n TELECOM période d'occupation totale f; ~ **signal** n COMP signal d'occupation m; ~ **state** n TELECOM état d'occupation m; ~ **status** n TELECOM état d'occupation m

butadiene n CHEM, PETR TECH butadiène m; ~ **acrylonitrile rubber** n P&R caoutchouc butadiène acrylonitrile m; ~ **rubber** n P&R caoutchouc butadiène m; ~ **styrene copolymer** n PETR TECH copolymère butadiène-styrène m

butane n CHEM, PETR TECH butane m; ~ **carrier** n PETR TECH, TRANSP butanier m; ~ **tanker** n PETR TECH *shipping*, TRANSP butanier m

butanol n CHEM butanol m

butanone n P&R *solvent* butanone f

butenal n CHEM butenal m

butene n CHEM butylène m, butène m

butt n CONST charnière f, *carpentry* about m, MECH aboutement m, MECH ENG *of connecting rod* tête f, NAUT *shipbuilding* about m; ~ **cock** n CONST cannelle f, robinet pour fûts m; ~ **contact** n ELEC *of relay* contact à pression directe m; ~ **coupling** n MECH ENG accouplement à manchon m; ~ **end** n CONST *carpentry* about m; ~ **end splicer** n CINEMAT colleuse bout à bout f; ~ **hinge** n CONST charnière f; ~ **joint** n CONST *plumbing* noeud de jonction m, *square joint* assemblage à plat m, assemblage à plat joint m, joint à plat m, MECH ENG jonction bout à bout f, PROD ENG *riveting* assemblage à franc-bord m, *welding* joint bout à bout m, joint d'about m, joint à franc-bord m; ~ **plate** n MECH couvre-joint m; ~ **riveting** n PROD ENG rivetage à bande de recouvrement m, rivure à couvre-joint f, rivure à franc-bord f, rivure à éclisser f; ~ **seal** n PROD ENG joint en bout m, soudure f; ~ **seam welding** n PROD ENG soudage bout à bout m; ~ **strap** n MECH couvre-joint m, PROD ENG bande de

recouvrement f, couvre-joint m; ~ **strap joint** n PROD ENG assemblage à couvre-joints m; ~ **strip** n PROD ENG bande de recouvrement f, couvre-joint m; ~ **weld** n MECH ENG soudure bout à bout f, PROD ENG soudure en bout f, soudure par encollage f, soudure par rapprochement f; ~ **welding** n CONST soudage en bout m, MECH soudage bout à bout m, soudage en bout m, soudage à franc-bord m, PROD ENG soudage par rapprochement m, soudure par encollage f; ~ **welding machine** n PROD ENG machine à souder par rapprochement f

butt-and-strap: ~ **hinge** n CONST penture à T f

butter: ~ **coloring** n (AmE), ~ **colouring** n (BrE) COLOURS colorant pour beurre m; ~ **oil** n FOOD TECH butteroil m, huile de beurre f

butterfly n AUTO papillon des gaz m; ~ **damper** n HEAT ENG registre pivotant m, REFRIG registre à papillon m; ~ **nut** n CONST papillon m, écrou papillon m, écrou à ailettes m; ~ **screw** n CONST vis ailée f, vis à ailettes f, MECH ENG vis ailée f, vis à oreilles f; ~ **throttle valve** n HYDR EQUIP robinet de freinage m; ~ **valve** n FUELLESS *dams*, HYDR EQUIP vanne papillon f, MECH ENG vanne papillon f, *fast closing* vanne papillon à fermeture rapide f

Butterworth: ~ **filter** n ELECTRON, PHYS filtre de Butterworth m

butting n CONST *carpentry* aboutement m

butt-joint vt CONST abouter

buttock: ~ **lines** n pl NAUT *shipbuilding* sections longitudinales f pl

buttocks n pl NAUT *shipbuilding* sections longitudinales f pl

button n CONST bouton m, taquet m, ELEC ENG, PETR bouton m, TELECOM touche f; ~ **fastener** n PROD ENG *for machine belts* bouton pour courroies m; ~ **head bolt** n CONST boulon à tête en goutte de suif m, MECH ENG boulon à tête de goutte-de-suif m; ~ **head rivet** n PROD ENG rivet à tête bombée m, rivet à tête en arc de cercle m, rivet à tête en goutte-de-suif m

buttress[1] n CONST *of wall, bridge* contrefort m, éperon m; ~ **dam** n CONST barrage à contreforts m; ~ **screw thread** n MECH ENG *asymmetrical thread* filetage trapézoïdal m; ~ **thread** n CONST *screws* filet de vis trapézoïdal m

buttress[2] vt CONST arc-bouter

buttressing n CONST étayage m

butyl: ~ **acetate** n P&R *solvent* acétate de butyle m; ~ **alcohol** n DETERGENTS alcool butylique m; ~ **ether** n FOOD TECH éther butylique m; ~ **phthalate** n P&R *plasticizer* phtalate de dibutyle m; ~ **rubber** n P&R butyl m, butyl-caoutchouc m

butylated: ~ **hydroxyanisole** n (BHA) FOOD TECH hydroxyanisol butylé m (BHA); ~ **hydroxytoluene** n (BHT) FOOD TECH hydroxytoluène butylé m (BHT)

butylene n DETERGENTS butylène m, butène m

butyraldehyde n CHEM butyraldéhyde m

butyrate n CHEM butyrate m

butyric[1] adj CHEM butyrique

butyric:[2] ~ **acid** n FOOD TECH acide butyrique m

butyrin n CHEM butyrine f

butyrite n COAL TECH butyrellite f

buy-back: ~ **price** n PETR TECH *commerce* prix de rachat m

buzz n TRANSP bourdonnement m; ~ **track** n RECORDING piste d'alignement sonore f, piste sonore de bourdonnement f

buzzer *n* ELEC ENG, PRINT, TELECOM ronfleur *m*, vibreur sonore *m*, TRANSP vibreur sonore *m*

B-wind *n* CINEMAT enroulement B *m*

BWO *abbr (backward wave oscillator)* TELECOM OOR *(oscillateur à ondes rétrogrades)*

BWR *abbr (boiling water reactor)* PHYS réacteur à eau bouillante *m*

B-Y: **~ axis** *n* TV axe B-Y *m*; **~ signal** *n* TV signal B-Y *m*

bypass[1] *adj* PHYS en dérivation

bypass[2] *adv* PHYS en dérivation

bypass[3] *n* COAL TECH dérivation *f*, CONST *road* déviation *f*, ELEC *circuit*, GAS TECH bypass *m*, dérivation *f*, HYDR EQUIP dérivation *f*, MECH ENG bypass *m*, dérivation *f*, PETR TECH *drilling* bipasse *m*, bypass *m*, dérivation *f*, PROD ENG dérivation *f*, TRANSP voie de rocade *f*; **~ anode** *n* ELEC ENG anode de shuntage *f*; **~ bore** *n* AUTO orifice de progression *m*; **~ capacitor** *n* PHYS condensateur de découplage *m*, condensateur de dérivation *m*; **~ engine** *n* AERONAUT moteur bypass *m*, moteur à double flux *m*, moteur à dérivation *m*, turboréacteur double flux *m*, THERMOD *fanjet or turbofan engine* turboréacteur à double flux *m*, TRANSP réacteur à double flux *m*, turboréacteur à double flux *m*; **~ line** *n* TRANSP itinéraire de dégagement *m*; **~ oil cleaner** *n* AUTO filtre à huile en dérivation *m*; **~ ratio** *n* AERONAUT *turbojet, turbofan* taux de dilution *m*; **~ road** *n* TRANSP route de dégagement *f*; **~ switch** *n* ELEC disjoncteur de shuntage *m*; **~ valve** *n* LAB EQUIP vanne de dérivation *f*

bypassable: **~ traffic** *n* TRANSP trafic de transit *m*

bypassing *n* PETR dérivation *f*

bypath *n* CONST faux fuyant *m*, route transversale *f*

by-product *n* CHEM produit secondaire *m*, *of reaction* sous-produit *m*, COAL TECH, MECH ENG, PETR TECH sous-produit *m*, POLLUTION dérivé *m*, PROD ENG produit secondaire *m*, sous-produit *m*; **~ gas** *n* GAS TECH gaz de four à coke *m*

byroad *n* CONST faux fuyant *m*, route transversale *f*

byssolite *n* MINERAL byssolite *f*

byte *n* DP octet *m*; **~ designation** *n* PROD ENG identification de l'octet *f*; **~ machine** *n* COMP machine octale *f*; **~ switch** *n* TELECOM commutateur d'octets *m*

bytownite *n* MINERAL bytownite *f*

byway *n* CONST chemin détourné *m*, faux fuyant *m*, route transversale *f*

C

c *abbr (centi-)* METR c *(centi-)*

C¹ *abbr* ELEC *(coulomb)*, ELEC ENG *(coulomb)* C *(coulomb)*, METR *(Celsius)* C *(Celsius)*, METR *(centigrade)* C *(centigrade)*, METR *(coulomb)*, PHYS *(coulomb)* C *(coulomb)*

C² *(carbon)* CHEM C *(carbone)*

Ca *(calcium)* CHEM Ca *(calcium)*

CA: ~ **packaging** *n* PACKAGING conditionnement sous atmosphère contrôlée *m*

cab *n* CONST *of crane* cabine *f*, TRANSP cabine *f*, cabine circulante *f*, VEHICLES *body* cabine *f*; ~ **and pillar distribution service** *n* TELECOM système des points de répartition primaire et secondaire *m*; ~ **signal** *n* RAIL *vehicles* signalisation en cabine *f*; ~ **signaling** *n* (AmE), ~ **signalling** *n* (BrE) TRANSP installation de répétition des signaux en cabine *f*

cabal: ~ **glass** *n* C&G verre cabal *m*

cabin *n* AERONAUT cabine *f*, CONST *of crane* cabine *f*, guérite *f*, NAUT *accommodation* cabine *f*, *navy* chambre *f*, RAIL *vehicles* cabine *f*, cabine de conduite *f*, SPACE *spacecraft* cabine *f*, habitacle *m*; ~ **altimeter** *n* AERONAUT altimètre de cabine *m*; ~ **altitude** *n* AERONAUT altitude cabine *f*, altitude fictive *f*; ~ **attendants** *n pl* AERONAUT personnel commercial de bord *m*; ~ **baggage** *n* AERONAUT bagages de cabine *m pl*; ~ **class** *n* TRANSP deuxième classe *f*; ~ **conveyor** *n* TRANSP trottoir roulant à cabines *m*; ~ **crew** *n* AERONAUT PNC, personnel navigant commercial *m*, équipage commercial *m*; ~ **cruiser** *n* NAUT bateau de plaisance *m*; ~ **differential pressure** *n* AERONAUT pression différentielle de cabine *f*; ~ **differential pressure gage** *n* (AmE), ~ **differential pressure gauge** *n* (BrE) AERONAUT manomètre de pression différentielle de cabine *m*; ~ **floor** *n* AERONAUT plancher cabine *m*; ~ **headroom** *n* NAUT hauteur sous barrots *f*; ~ **layout** *n* AERONAUT aménagement cabine *m*; ~ **pressure** *n* AERONAUT, SPACE *spacecraft* pression de cabine *f*; ~ **pressurization** *n* AERONAUT gonflage cabine *m*, pressurisation cabine *f*; ~ **pulley cradle** *n* TRANSP train de galets de la cabine *m*; ~ **services** *n pl* AERONAUT servitudes passagers *f pl*; ~ **sole** *n* NAUT *shipbuilding* plancher *m*; ~ **sole reinforcement** *n* NAUT *shipbuilding* varangue *f*; ~ **system on rail** *n* TRANSP système à cabine sur rail *m*; ~ **telephone** *n* AERONAUT téléphone de cabine *m*; ~ **temperature** *n* AERONAUT température de cabine *f*; ~ **temperature indicator** *n* AERONAUT indicateur de température de cabine *m*

cabinet *n* MECH armoire *f*, habillage *m*, P&R *curing of coatings and plastics* étuve *f*, TELECOM armoire *f*, armoire de sous-répartiteur *f*, point de distribution primaire *m*; ~ **loudspeaker** *n* RECORDING enceinte de haut-parleur *f*; ~ **radiation** *n* TELECOM rayonnement par les coffrets *m*; ~ **shell** *n* REFRIG cuve extérieure *f*

cabinetmaker *n* CONST menuisier *m*, ébéniste *m*

cabinetmaking *n* CONST ébénisterie *f*

cabinetwork *n* CONST ébénisterie *f*

cabin-type: ~ **moving pavement** *n* (BrE) *(cf cabin-type moving sidewalk)* TRANSP trottoir roulant à cabines

m; ~ **moving sidewalk** *n* (AmE) *(cf cabin-type moving pavement)* TRANSP trottoir roulant à cabines *m*

cable *n* COMP, ELEC *conductor*, ELEC ENG câble *m*, MECH cordage *m*, câble *m*, NAUT *communications* câble *m*, encablure *f*, P&R *rubber, plastics*, PETR, RECORDING, TELECOM, VEHICLES *electrical system, controls* câble *m*; ~ **angle indicator** *n* NAUT indicateur d'angle de câble *m*; ~ **assembly** *n* OPT, TELECOM câble assemblé *m*; ~ **box** *n* ELEC *connection* boîte à câble *f*, manchon de câble *m*, ELEC ENG boîte de raccordement *f*; ~ **bundle** *n* ELEC ENG faisceau de câbles *m*; ~ **chain** *n* MINING chaîne-câble *f*, câble-chaîne *m*, NAUT câble-chaîne *m*; ~ **clamp** *n* ELEC ENG collier de câble *m*, porte-câble *m*, MECH, MECH ENG collier de serrage *m*; ~ **clinch** *n* NAUT étalingure *f*; ~ **clip** *n* ELEC *fixing* collier de câble *m*, VEHICLES *electrical system, controls* cosse-câble de serrage *f*, serre-câble *m*; ~ **communications** *n pl* TELECOM télécommunications par câble *f pl*; ~ **compensation circuit** *n* TV circuit de compensation de câble *m*; ~ **conduit** *n* ELEC ENG caniveau pour câbles *m*, conduit de câbles *m*; ~ **connector** *n* ELEC connection raccord des câbles *m*, ELEC ENG connecteur de câbles *m*; ~ **conveyor** *n* PAPER TECH convoyeur à câble *m*; ~ **core** *n* ELEC ENG, P&R *rubber, plastics* âme de câble *f*; ~ **coupling** *n* ELEC ENG couplage de câbles *m*; ~ **covering** *n* ELEC ENG, P&R *rubber, plastics* enveloppe de câble *f*; ~ **cutter** *n* SPACE *spacecraft* coupe-câble *m*; ~ **defect** *n* ELEC ENG défaut de câble *m*; ~ **detector** *n* ELEC appareil chercheur de câble *m*; ~ **distribution point** *n* ELEC ENG point de montée de câble *m*; ~ **distributor** *n* ELEC ENG distributeur de câble *m*; ~ **drilling** *n* PETR forage au câble *m*; ~ **drilling bit** *n* PETR TECH trépan de forage au câble *m*; ~ **drum** *n* CONST enrouleur *m*, ELEC tambour de câble *m*, ELEC ENG touret *m*, touret pour câbles *m*, OCEANOG touret *m*, PACKAGING tambour de câble *m*; ~**duct** *n* ELEC ENG caniveau pour câbles *m*, tuyau de câble *m*; ~ **end** *n* ELEC extrémité de câble *f*, ELEC ENG embout de câble *m*, extrémité de câble *f*, MINING *attached to cage* patte du câble *f*; ~ **ferry** *n* TRANSP bac à chaîne *m*, bac à câble *m*; ~ **fitting** *n* ELEC ENG garniture de câble *f*; ~ **form** *n* ELEC ENG forme de câble *f*; ~ **gage** *n* (AmE), ~ **gauge** *n* (BrE) ELEC ENG jauge pour câble *f*; ~ **grease** *n* ELEC ENG graisse à câble *f*; ~ **guide** *n* VEHICLES *electrical system, control* guidage de câbles *m*; ~ **harness** *n* ELEC ENG peigne de câble *m*; ~ **head** *n* ELEC ENG tête de câble *f*; ~ **insulation** *n* ELEC, ELEC ENG isolation de câble *f*; ~ **insulator** *n* ELEC ENG isolateur pour câble *m*; ~ **isolator** *n* ELEC ENG sectionneur de câble *m*; ~ **joint** *n* ELEC *connection* jonction de câbles *f*, TELECOM épissure *f*; ~ **jointer** *n* TELECOM soudeur *m*, épisseur *m*; ~ **junction** *n* ELEC ENG jonction de câbles *f*; ~ **junction box** *n* ELEC *connection* boîte de jonction de câbles *f*; ~ **laying** *n* ELEC *supply*, ELEC ENG pose de câbles *f*; ~ **link** *n* TV liaison par câble *f*; ~ **locator** *n* ELEC appareil chercheur de câble *m*, détecteur de câble *m*; ~ **locker** *n* NAUT puits à chaînes *m*; ~ **loss** *n* ELEC ENG pertes dues au câble *f pl*; ~ **lug** *n* ELEC ENG cosse de câble *f*; ~ **manhole** *n* ELEC *supply* chambre à câbles *f*, puits à câbles *m*; ~ **network** *n* ELEC ENG réseau de câbles *m*; ~ **pair** *n* COMP câble bifilaire *m*, ELEC ENG paire de conducteurs *f*; ~ **rack** *n* ELEC ENG étagère à câbles *f*; ~ **railway** *n* MECH ENG, TRANSP funiculaire fixe à câble *m*; ~ **reel** *n* PACKAGING bobine de câble *f*, PETR touret pour flexibles *m*; ~ **release** *n* PHOTO déclencheur métallique *m*; ~ **release socket** *n* PHOTO prise de déclencheur souple *f*; ~ **repeater** *n* ELEC ENG répéteur sur câble *m*; ~ **run** *n* ELEC *supply* chemin de câble *m*, tracé de câble *m*; ~ **screen** *n* ELEC *conductor* écran d'un câble *m*; ~ **section** *n* ELEC ENG section de câble *f*; ~ **shaft** *n* ELEC ENG puits à câbles *m*; ~ **sheath** *n* ELEC ENG enveloppe de câble *f*; ~ **sheathing** *n* P&R revêtement de câble *m*; ~ **sheath stripper** *n* MECH ENG *tool* outil à dégainer les câbles *m*; ~ **ship** *n* NAUT câblier *m*, navire câblier *m*, TELECOM navire câblier *m*; ~ **splicing** *n* ELEC épissure de câble *f*; ~ **sprinter** *n* PRINT pince à dénuder *f*; ~ **storage hold** *n* TELECOM cuve de stockage de câble *f*; ~ **support** *n* TRANSP pylône de téléphérique *m*; ~ **suspension wire** *n* ELEC ENG fil porte-câble *m*; ~ **television network** *n* TELECOM réseau de télévision par câbles *m*; ~ **television system** *n* TELECOM système CATV *m*, système de télévision par câbles *m*; ~ **tensioner** *n* ELEC ENG serre-câble *m*; ~ **terminal box** *n* CINEMAT tête de câble *f*; ~ **termination** *n* ELEC *connection* extrémité de câble *f*; ~ **transmission** *n* TV transmission par câble *f*; ~ **trench** *n* ELEC *supply* tranchée de câble *f*; ~ **trough** *n* ELEC ENG caniveau pour câbles *m*; ~ **weight** *n* AERONAUT masse de câblage *f*, masse de tierçage *f*; ~ **winch** *n* ELEC ENG treuil de câble *m*, TRANSP treuil à câble *m*

cable's: ~ **length** *n* NAUT encablure *f*

cablecast *n* TV diffusion par câble *f*, télédistribution *f*

cabled: ~ **home** *n* TV foyer câblé *m*, foyer raccordé *m*; ~ **network** *n* TV réseau câblé *m*

cablegram *n* ELEC ENG télégramme par câble *m*

cable-handling: ~ **system** *n* ELEC ENG dispositif de manutention de câbles *m*

cable-laid *adj* NAUT *rope* commis en aussière, commis en grelin

cable-laying: ~ **ship** *n* NAUT câblier *m*

cable-stayed: ~ **bridge** *n* CONST pont à câbles *m*, pont à hauban *m*

cableway *n* TRANSP téléphérique *m*

cabling *n* ELEC *supply*, ELEC ENG, TELECOM câblage *m*

caboose *n* (AmE) *(cf guard's van)* RAIL *vehicles* fourgon *m*

cabotage *n* TRANSP navigation côtière *f*

cab-over-engine *n* VEHICLES *body* cabine avancée *f*

cabrerite *n* MINERAL cabrérite *f*

cabriolet *n* VEHICLES *vehicle type* cabriolet *m*

cache *n* COMP mémoire cache *f*; ~ **memory** *n* COMP mémoire cache *f*

cacholong *n* MINERAL cacholong *m*

cacoxenite *n* MINERAL cacorcénite *f*

CAD *abbr (computer-aided design)* COMP, ELEC, MECH, PRINT, PROD ENG, TELECOM CAO *(conception assistée par ordinateur)*

cadastral: ~ **survey** *n* CONST carte cadastrale *f*, plan cadastral *m*

cadaverine *n* CHEM cadavérine *f*

CADCAM *abbr (computer-aided design and manufacture)* COMP, PROD ENG CFAO *(conception et fabrication assistées par ordinateur)*

cadmium *n (Cd)* CHEM cadmium *m (Cd)*; ~ **blende** *n* MINERAL greenockite *f*; ~ **cell** *n* ELEC pile cadmium *f*; ~

nickel cell *n* ELEC ENG accumulateur cadmium-nickel *m*; ~ **ocher** *n* (AmE), ~ **ochre** *n* (BrE) MINERAL greenockite *f*; ~ **sulfide cell** *n* (AmE), ~ **sulphide cell** *n* (BrE) ELEC pile à sulfure de cadmium *f*

cadmium-plated *adj* MECH cadmié

Caelum *n* ASTRON Burin *m*

caesium *n* (BrE) *(Cs)* CHEM césium *m (Cs)*; ~ **beam resonator** *n* (BrE) ELECTRON résonateur à jet de césium *m*; ~ **cathode** *n* (BrE) ELEC ENG cathode au césium *f*; ~ **clock** *n* (BrE) SPACE *communications* horloge au césium 133 *f*; ~ **phototube** *n* (BrE) ELECTRON phototube au césium *m*

caesium-doped: ~ **glass** *n* (BrE) SPACE *spacecraft* verre dopé au césium *m*

caffeic[1] *adj* CHEM caféique

caffeic:[2] ~ **acid** *n* FOOD TECH acide caféique *m*

caffeine *n* CHEM caféine *f*

caffetannic *adj* CHEM cafétannique

cage:[1] ~ **armature** *n* ELEC *generator, motor* induit à barres *m*; ~ **guides** *n pl* MINING coulantage *m*, coulants *m pl*, guidage *m*, guides *m pl*, guidonnage *m*; ~ **relay** *n* ELEC ENG relais à cage *m*; ~ **rotor** *n* ELEC ENG rotor à cage *m*; ~ **sheets** *n pl* MINING clichages *m pl*, taquets *m pl*; ~ **shuts** *n pl* MINING clichages *m pl*, taquets *m pl*; ~ **slides** *n pl* MINING coulantage *m*, coulants *m pl*, guidage *m*, guides *m pl*, guidonnage *m*; ~ **winding system** *n* MINING installation d'extraction par cages *f*, installation d'extraction par cages à berlines *f*

cage[2] *vt* MINING encager

CAI *abbr (computer-assisted instruction)* COMP IAO *(instruction assistée par ordinateur) f*

Cainozoic *adj* GEOL *stratigraphy* cénozoïque

caisson *n* CONST caisson *m*, NAUT bateau-porte *m*, caisson *m*, caisson à air *m*, flotteur de relevage *m*, WATER SUPP caisson *m*; ~ **disease** *n* NAUT, OCEANOG maladie de décompression *f*; ~ **master** *n* OCEANOG ATS, agent technique de saturation *m*, chef de caisson *m*; ~ **worker** *n* OCEANOG tubiste *m*

cake[1] *n* C&G *in glass fibre manufacture* gâteau *m*, PROD ENG *loam moulding* motte de recouvrement *f*

cake[2] *vt* CHEM TECH grumeler

cake[3] *vi* FOOD TECH se grumeler, se mettre en grumeaux

cake-dyed *adj* TEXTILES teint en gâteau

caking *n* FOOD TECH agglomération *f*, agglutination *f*, concrétation *f*, concrétion *f*, solidification *f*, P&R *pigment, filler* agglutination *f*; ~ **coal** *n* COAL TECH charbon agglutinant *m*

CAL *abbr (computer-assisted learning)* EAO COMP *(enseignement assisté par ordinateur)*

calamine *n* MINERAL calamine *f*

calamite *n* MINERAL calamite *f*

calandria *n* CHEM TECH appareil à cuire à faisceau tubulaire *m*, calandre *f*

calaverite *n* MINERAL calavérite *f*

calc-alkaline *adj* GEOL *igneous rock or suite* calco-alcalin

calcarenite *n* GEOL calcarénite *f*

calcareous[1] *adj* CHEM, GEOL calcaire

calcareous:[2] ~ **dolomite** *n* GEOL dolomie calcaire *f*; ~ **grits** *n pl* GEOL sables calcaréo-siliceux *m pl*; ~ **ooze** *n* GEOL boue calcaire *f*, vase calcaire *f*; ~ **sandstone** *n* GEOL grès calcaire *m*; ~ **tufa** *n* GEOL travertin calcaire *m*, tuf *m*

calcic *adj* CHEM, GEOL calcique

calciferol *n* CHEM calciférol *m*

calciferous *adj* CHEM calcarifère, GEOL calcifère

calcify *vt* CHEM calcifier

calcimine n COLOURS peinture à la colle f

calcin n HYDR EQUIP encrassage des chaudières m

calcination n CHEM frittage m, COAL TECH calcination f

calcine vt CHEM, COAL TECH calciner

calcined: ~ magnesia n P&R compounding ingredient magnésie calcinée f

calcining n CHEM frittage m, HEATING calcination f; ~ kiln n COAL TECH four de grillage m

calciocelestine n MINERAL calciocélestite f

calcioferrite n MINERAL calcioferrite f

calciothorite n MINERAL calciothorite f

calcite n GEOL spath calcaire m, MINERAL, PETR calcite f

calcitic: ~ dolomite n GEOL dolomie calcaire f

calcium n (Ca) CHEM calcium m (Ca); ~ carbide n CHEM carbure de calcium m; ~ carbonate n FOOD TECH milling carbonate de calcium m; ~ chloride n CHEM, FOOD TECH chlorure de calcium m; ~ naphthenate n P&R paints, polyesters naphténate de calcium m; ~ pantothenate n FOOD TECH pantothénate de calcium m; ~ petroleum sulfanates n pl (AmE), ~ petroleum sulphanates n pl (BrE) PETR TECH sulfanates de calcium m pl; ~ phosphate n FOOD TECH phosphate de calcium m; ~ silicate n DETERGENTS silicate de calcium m; ~ sulfate n (AmE), ~ sulphate n (BrE) FOOD TECH sulfate de calcium m

calco-silicate: ~ hornfels n GEOL cornéenne calco-silicatée f

calcrete n GEOL encroûtement calcaire m

calc-schist n GEOL metamorphosed marl calcschiste m

calculable: ~ capacitor n PHYS condensateur calculable m

calculate vt MATH calculer

calculating: ~ machine n COMP machine à calculer f

calculation n MATH calcul m

calculator n COMP additionneuse f, calculatrice f, machine à calculer f, ELECTRON calculatrice f, MATH calculateur m, calculatrice f, machine à calculer f

calculus n MATH calcul m; ~ of variations n MATH calcul des variations m

caldera n GEOL volcanic feature caldeira f

caledonite n MINERAL calédonite f

calender[1] n P&R calandre f, PACKAGING machine to finish smooth paper satineuse f, PAPER TECH, PRINT, TEXTILES calandre f; ~ bowl n PAPER TECH rouleau de calandre m; ~ bowl paper n PAPER TECH papier pour rouleaux de calandre m; ~ roll n PAPER TECH rouleau de calandre m; ~ stack n PAPER TECH lisse f; ~ unit n PACKAGING ensemble de calandrage m; ~ water box n PAPER TECH caisse à eau de rouleau de calandre f

calender[2] vt P&R calandrer

calendered: ~ film n P&R plastics feuille calandrée f; ~ paperboard n PAPER TECH papier carton calandré m

calendering n P&R operation, PAPER TECH calandrage m

calf: ~ binding n PRINT reliure en veau pleine f; ~ leather n PRINT veau m; ~ vellum n PRINT parchemin de veau m

caliber n (AmE) see calibre

calibrate vt LAB EQUIP, PAPER TECH calibrer, PHYS calibrer, graduer, étalonner, PRINT measure calibrer

calibrated: ~ airspeed n AERONAUT vitesse corrigée f; ~ dial n PROD ENG cadran gradué m; ~ measure n PROP MAT éprouvette graduée f; ~ measure tube n PROP MAT éprouvette graduée f; ~ valve n MECH ENG clapet taré m; ~ watershed n POLLUTION bassin calibré m, bassin jaugé m, bassin versant calibré m

calibrating: ~ transformer n NUCLEAR convertisseur d'é-talonnage m, transformateur d'étalonnage m

calibration n COAL TECH calibrage m, COMP, ELEC étalonnage m, ELECTRON calibrage m, of measurement device étalonnage m, LAB EQUIP instrument, glassware, MECH ENG, METR étalonnage m, NUCLEAR calibrage m, jaugeage m, étalonnage m, PAPER TECH, PETR TECH metrology, drilling étalonnage m, PRINT calibrage m, PROD ENG calibrage m, tarage m, étalonnage m, PROP MAT, RAD PHYS, RECORDING of microphone, SPACE étalonnage m; ~ accuracy n PROP MAT précision d'étalonnage f; ~ chart n COMP table d'étalonnage f; ~ flight n AERONAUT vol d'étalonnage m; ~ flume n WATER SUPP canal d'étalonnage m; ~ instrument n INSTRUMENT instrument d'étalonnage m, instrument étalon m; ~ module n AERONAUT module de réglage m; ~ pressure n AERONAUT pression de déclenchement f; ~ ring n NAUT radar cercle de distance fixe m; ~ service n METR service étalonnage m; ~ signal n ELECTRON signal de calibrage m; ~ tail n PETR queue d'étalonnage f, queue de calibrage f; ~ test n AERONAUT essai d'étalonnage m, vérification d'étalonnage f; ~ value n PROP MAT valeur d'étalon f; ~ weight n LAB EQUIP poids étalon m

calibrator n ELECTRON calibrateur m, dispositif de calibrage m

calibre n (BrE) PETR calibre m, étalon m

calico n PRINT calicot m; ~ mop n PROD ENG disque en drap m

California: ~ Bearing Ratio n (CBR) CONST essai de poinçonnement m

californium n (Cf) CHEM californium m (Cf)

caliper[1] n (AmE) see calliper

caliper:[2] ~ gage vt (AmE) see calliper gauge

calipers n pl (AmE) see callipers

call[1] n COMP appel m, TELECOM appel m, communication f ~ acceptance signal n TELECOM signal d'acceptation d'appel m; ~ accounting device n TELECOM taxeur m; ~ attempt n TELECOM tentative d'appel f; ~ barring n TELECOM interdiction d'appel f; ~ bell n ELEC ENG sonnerie f, sonnerie d'appel f; ~ button n ELEC ENG electric bell touche d'appel f; ~ by name n COMP appel par nom m; ~ by reference n COMP appel par référence m; ~ by value n COMP appel par valeur m; ~ charge n TELECOM frais de communication m pl; ~ charge rate n TELECOM tarif du trafic m, tarification f; ~ charges n pl TELECOM prix des communications m; ~ charging equipment n TELECOM équipement de facturation m, équipement de taxation m; ~ control n (CC) TELECOM traitement d'appel m; ~ control agent n (CCA) TELECOM agent de traitement d'appel m; ~ data recording n (CDR) TELECOM enregistrement des données d'appel m; ~ detail recording n (CDR) TELECOM enregistrement des données d'appel m; ~ distributor n TELECOM distributeur d'appel m; ~ diversion n TELECOM renvoi d'appel m; ~ diverter n TELECOM dispositif de renvoi m; ~ duration n TELECOM durée de la communication f; ~ flow n TELECOM flux du trafic m; ~ forwarding may occur indicator n TELECOM indicateur de prolongement d'appel possible m; ~ handling n TELECOM traitement d'appels m; ~ held n TELECOM mise en garde f; ~ hold n TELECOM mise en garde f; ~ holding n TELECOM mise en garde f; ~ identification n TELECOM identification d'appel f; ~ identity n TELECOM identité d'appel f; ~ indicating device n TELECOM récepteur d'appel m; ~ instruction n COMP instruction d'appel f; ~ interception n TELECOM interception d'appel *f*; ~ **logging** *n* TELECOM relevé des communications *m*; ~ **metering** *n* TELECOM comptage des appels *m*; ~ **modification completed message** *n* (*CMC*) TELECOM message de modification d'appel effectuée *m* (*MAE*); ~ **modification reject message** *n* (*CMRJ*) TELECOM message de refus de modification d'appel *m* (*MAR*); ~ **modification request message** *n* (*CMR*) TELECOM demande de modification d'appel *f* (*MAD*); ~ **origin** *n* TELECOM provenance *f*; ~ **portability** *n* TELECOM déplacement en cours de communication *m*, portabilité *f*; ~ **processor** *n* (*CP*) TELECOM calculateur *m*, processeur de traitement des appels *m*; ~ **queueing facility** *n* TELECOM mise en attente *f*; ~ **reference** *n* TELECOM référence d'appel *f*; ~ **register** *n* (*CR*) TELECOM compteur d'appels *m*, registre d'appels *m*; ~ **retrieval** *n* TELECOM reprise *f*; ~ **sender** *n* TELECOM robot d'appels *m*; ~ **sequence** *n* TELECOM séquence d'appel *f*; ~ **setup** *n* TELECOM établissement des communications *m*; ~ **setup delay** *n* TELECOM durée d'établissement d'une communication *f*; ~ **setup packet** *n* TELECOM paquet d'appel *m*; ~ **setup phase** *n* TELECOM phase d'établissement de la communication *f*; ~ **sheet** *n* CINEMAT fiche de prévision de tournage *f*; ~ **sign** *n* NAUT *radio* indicatif d'appel *m*; ~ **store** *n* TELECOM mémoire temporaire *f*; ~ **success rate** *n* TELECOM taux d'aboutissement des appels *m*; ~ **trace** *n* TELECOM identification d'appel *f*; ~ **transfer** *n* TELECOM transfert d'appel *m*; ~ **waiting** *n* (*CW*) TELECOM appel en instance *m*; ~ **waiting indication** *n* TELECOM signal d'appel en instance *m*; ~ **waiting signal** *n* TELECOM indication d'appel en instance *f*

call² *vt* TELECOM téléphoner à

callainite *n* MINERAL callaïnite *f*

call-barring: ~ **equipment** *n* TELECOM discriminateur *m*

call-down *n* C&G arrêt de fabrication *m*

called: ~ **line identification** *n* TELECOM identification de la ligne appelée *f*, TELECOM (*CDLI*) identification de la ligne du demandé *f*; ~ **number display** *n* TELECOM affichage du numéro appelé *m*; ~ **party** *n* TELECOM correspondant *m*, demandé *m*; ~ **station identity** *n* (*CSI*) TELECOM identité de la station demandée *f*; ~ **subscriber identification** *n* (*CSI*) TELECOM identification de l'abonné demandé *f*; ~ **telephone** *n* TELECOM téléphone appelé *m*

caller *n* TELECOM demandeur *m*

calling: ~ **channel** *n* TELECOM *land mobile* voie d'appel *f*; ~ **indicator** *n* TELECOM indicateur d'appel *m*; ~ **lamp** *n* TELECOM lampe d'appel *f*; ~ **line** *n* TELECOM ligne appelante *f*; ~ **line identification** *n* (*CLI*) TELECOM identification de la ligne appelante *f* (*ILA*); ~ **line identification display** *n* (*CLID*) TELECOM présentation de l'identification de la ligne appelante *f* (*PILA*); ~ **line identification presentation** *n* (*CLIP*) TELECOM présentation de l'identification de la ligne appelante *f* (*PILA*); ~ **line identification restriction** *n* TELECOM secret de l'identité du demandeur *m*, TELECOM restriction de l'identification de la ligne appelante *f*; ~ **party address request indicator** *n* TELECOM indicateur de demande d'adresse du demandeur *m*; ~ **party address response indicator** *n* TELECOM indicateur de réponse à une demande d'adresse du demandeur *m*; ~ **party category request indicator** *n* TELECOM indicateur de demande de catégorie du demandeur *m*; ~ **party category response indicator** *n* TELECOM indicateur de réponse à une demande de catégorie du demandeur *m*; ~ **party number incom-**

plete indicator *n* TELECOM indicateur de numéro du demandeur incomplet *m*; ~ **sequence** *n* COMP séquence d'appel *f*; ~ **signal** *n* TELECOM indicatif d'appel *m*; ~ **telephone** *n* TELECOM téléphone appelant *m*

call-in-progress: ~ **cost information** *n* TELECOM indication de coût en temps réel *f*

calliper *n* (BrE) AUTO étrier *m*, MECH pied à coulisse *m*, étrier de frein *m*, MECH ENG calibre *m*, PAPER TECH calibre *m*, épaisseur du papier *f*, PRINT épaisseur précise du papier *f*, VEHICLES *of brake* étrier *m*; ~ **calender** *n* (BrE) PAPER TECH laminoir *m*; ~ **compasses** *n pl* (BrE) METR compas de calibre *m*; ~ **gauge** *n* (BrE) MECH ENG pied à coulisse *m*; ~ **log** *n* (BrE) PETR diamétreur *m*, PETR TECH diagraphie de diamétrage *f*; ~ **square** *n* (BrE) MECH ENG équerre à coulisse *f*

callipers *n pl* (BrE) C&G galet de calibrage *m*, LAB EQUIP pied à coulisse *m*, METR compas de calibre *m*, pieds à coulisse *m pl*, *beam, digital* calibres *m pl*

callout *n* PRINT appel de note *m*, légende *f*

Callovian *adj* GEOL callovien

call-queued *adj* TELECOM mis en attente

calls *n pl* TELECOM trafic *m*; ~ **per second** *n pl* (*CS*) TELECOM appels par seconde *m pl*

calm¹ *adj* HYDROL, METEO calme

calm² *n* HYDROL *marine* calme *m*; ~ **sea** *n* OCEANOG bonace *f*

calomel *n* CHEM, MINERAL calomel *m*; ~ **electrode** *n* ELEC pile calomel *f*

caloric¹ *adj* THERMOD calorique

caloric:² ~ **conductibility** *n* THERMOD *thermal conductibility* conductibilité thermique *f*; ~ **content** *n* THERMOD capacité calorifique *f*; ~ **power** *n* THERMOD pouvoir calorifique *m*, puissance calorifique *f*, rendement calorique *m*

calorie *n* FOOD TECH, PHYS, THERMOD calorie *f*

calorific¹ *adj* PHYS calorifique, PROD ENG calorifiant, calorifique, échauffant, THERMOD calorifique, thermogène

calorific:² ~ **balance** *n* THERMOD *heat balance, thermal balance* bilan calorifique *m*; ~ **output** *n* THERMOD *heat output* rendement calorifique *m*; ~ **power** *n* THERMOD pouvoir calorifique *m*; ~ **value** *n* HEAT ENG, PETR TECH *fuel analysis* pouvoir calorifique *m*, PHYS, THERMOD valeur calorifique *f*

calorifier *n* HEAT ENG *heat transfer* serpentin réchauffeur *m*, MECH ENG calorifieur *m*

calorimeter *n* CHEM, LAB EQUIP *heat measurement*, MECH ENG, PART PHYS *in particle detectors*, PHYS, REFRIG, THERMOD calorimètre *m*; ~ **assembly** *n* RAD PHYS *particle radiation detection* ensemble du calorimètre *m*

calorimetric¹ *adj* CHEM calorimétrique

calorimetric:² ~ **bomb** *n* LAB EQUIP *heat measurement* bombe calorimétrique *f*; ~ **thermometer** *n* THERMOD thermomètre calorimétrique *m*

calorimetry *n* CHEM, PHYS, REFRIG, THERMOD calorimétrie *f*

calyx: ~ **drill** *n* MINING sondeuse à couronne à dents d'acier *f*

cam *n* AUTO came *f*, CINEMAT came *f*, excentrique *m*, MECH came *f*, MECH ENG bossage *m*, came *f*, excentrique *m*, VEHICLES *engine* came *f*; ~ **action** *n* MECH ENG levée de came *f*; ~ **angle** *n* AUTO angle de came *m*, avance à l'admission *f*; ~ **cleat** *n* NAUT *boat equipment* taquet coinceur *m*; ~ **contour** *n* AERONAUT profil de came *m*; ~ **follower** *n* AERONAUT galet suiveur *m*, palpeur *m*, MECH contre-came *f*, MECH ENG galet suiveur *m*; ~ **following** *n* VEHICLES *engine* poussoir *m*, taquet *m*; ~ **lobe** *n* AERONAUT, AUTO, VEHICLES bossage de came *m*; ~ **measuring equipment** *n* METR arbres à came *m pl*; ~ **profile** *n* VEHICLES *engine* profil de came *m*; ~ **shape** *n* MECH profil de came *m*; ~ **switch** *n* ELEC contrôleur à cames *m*

CAM *abbr (computer-aided manufacturing)* COMP, ELEC, TELECOM FAO *(fabrication assistée par ordinateur)*

camber[1] *n* ACOUSTICS inclinaison latérale *f*, AERONAUT *runway* bombement *m*, CONST cambre *f*, cambrure *f*, *of piece of wood* cambrure *f*, *of road* bombement *m*, NAUT *shipbuilding* bouge *f*, tonture *f*, OCEANOG cambrure *f*, PAPER TECH bombé *m*, VEHICLES *road, wheel* carrossage *m*; ~ **bar** *n* PAPER TECH barre déplisseuse *f*

camber[2] *vt* CONST bomber, cambrer

camber[3] *vi* CONST bomber, se bomber, se cambrer

cambered: ~ **deck** *n* NAUT *boatbuilding* pont cambré *m*; ~ **suction box** *n* PAPER TECH caisse aspirante bombée *f*

cambering *n* CONST bombement *m*, cambrage *m*; ~ **parallelism** *n* SPRINGS parallélisme des cambrages *m*

Cambrian *adj* GEOL cambrien

Cambridge: ~ **ring** *n* COMP anneau de Cambridge *m*

CAMC *abbr (customer access maintenance centre, customer access maintenance center)* TELECOM centre de maintenance des accès client *m*

camcorder *n* TV camescope *m*

camel *n* NAUT caisson à air *m*, chameau *m*, flotteur de relevage *m*

Camelopardalis *n* ASTRON Girafe *f*

cameo *n* C&G gemme *f*

camera *n* CHEM chambre noire *f*, CINEMAT caméra *f*, INSTRUMENT caméra *f*, chambre photographique *f*, PHOTO appareil *m*, appareil de prise de vue *m*, appareil photographique *m*, PHYS appareil *m*, caméra *f*, PRINT caméra *f*, objectif *m*, TV caméra *f*; ~ **angle** *n* CINEMAT angle de prise de vue *m*; ~ **body** *n* CINEMAT corps d'appareil de prise de vue *m*; ~ **boom** *n* CINEMAT grue de caméra *f*; ~ **bracket** *n* CINEMAT support de caméra *m*; ~ **car** *n* CINEMAT voiture travelling *f*; ~ **channel** *n* TV voie de caméra *f*; ~ **control unit** *n (CCU)* TV dispositif de réglage de caméra *m*, téléréglage de caméra *m*, voie de caméra *f*; ~ **crew** *n* CINEMAT équipe caméra *f*, équipe de prise de vues *f*, équipe image *f*; ~ **director** *n* CINEMAT opérateur réalisateur *m*; ~ **drive** *n* CINEMAT système d'entraînement de caméra *m*; ~ **equipment** *n* CINEMAT matériel de prise de vues *m*; ~ **extension** *n* PHOTO tirage de la chambre *m*; ~ **front** *n* PHOTO corps avant *m*; ~ **gate** *n* CINEMAT fenêtre d'exposition *f*; ~ **line-up** *n* TV réglage de la caméra *m*; ~ **log** *n* CINEMAT rapport image *m*; ~ **lucida** *n* PHOTO caméra lucida *f*, chambre claire *f*; ~ **matching** *n* TV réglage des caméras *m*, équilibrage des caméras *m*; ~ **monitor** *n* TV moniteur de caméra *m*, viseur électronique *m*, écran témoin *m*; ~ **mount** *n* CINEMAT support de caméra *m*, PHOTO support de chambre *m*; ~ **movement** *n* CINEMAT jeu de caméra *m*; ~ **opticals** *n pl* CINEMAT trucages réalisés à la prise de vues *m pl*; ~ **original** *n* CINEMAT original tourné *m*; ~ **prompting system** *n* TV téléprompteur *m*, télésouffleur *m*; ~ **report** *n* CINEMAT rapport image *m*; ~ **signal** *n* TV signal de caméra *m*, signal vidéo *m*; ~ **slate** *n* CINEMAT claquette image *f*; ~ **speed** *n* CINEMAT vitesse de prise de vues *f*; ~ **speed checker** *n* CINEMAT tachymètre *m*; ~ **stand** *n* PHOTO pied photographique *m*; ~ **switching** *n* TV commuta-

tion des caméras *f*; ~ **tape** *n* CINEMAT chatterton *m*; ~ **test** *n* CINEMAT essai caméra *m*; ~ **tube** *n* ELECTRON tube analyseur *m*, TV tube de caméra *m*, tube image *m*; ~ **viewpoint** *n* CINEMAT cadrage *m*; ~ **with built-in exposure meter** *n* PHOTO appareil à photomètre incorporé *m*; ~ **with collapsible mount** *n* PHOTO appareil à monture rentrante *m*; ~ **with coupled exposure meter** *n* PHOTO appareil à cellule couplée *m*; ~ **with coupled rangefinder** *n* PHOTO appareil à télémètre couplé *m*; ~ **with detachable reflex viewfinder** *n* PHOTO appareil à visée reflex amovible *m*; ~ **with diaphragm shutter** *n* PHOTO chambre à obturateur central *f*; ~ **with interchangeable lens** *n* PHOTO appareil à optique interchangeable *m*; ~ **with long bellows extension** *n* PHOTO chambre à long tirage *f*; ~ **with mirror-reflex focusing** *n* PHOTO appareil à visée reflex *m*; ~ **with rising and swinging front** *n* PHOTO appareil muni de décentrement *m*; ~ **with short bellows extension** *n* PHOTO chambre à court tirage *f*

cameraman *n* CINEMAT cadreur *m*, cameraman *m*, opérateur *m*, TV cadreur *m*

camera-ready[1] *adj* PRINT prêt pour la photogravure

camera-ready:[2] ~ **copy** *n (CRC)* PRINT copie prête à la reproduction *f*, document prêt *m*

camouflage: ~ **paint** *n* COLOURS peinture de camouflage *f*; ~ **supports** *n pl* MILIT supports pour filet de camouflage *m pl*; ~ **system** *n* MILIT système de camouflage *m*

campaign *n* C&G *of glass furnace* campagne *f*, PROD ENG *of furnace* campagne *f*, roulement *m*

Campanian *adj* GEOL campanien

Campbell-Stokes: ~ **recorder** *n* FUELLESS dispositif enregistreur Campbell-Stokes *m*

camper *n* VEHICLES caravane de camping *f*

camphane *n* CHEM camphane *m*

camphene *n* CHEM camphène *m*

camphol *n* CHEM bornéol *m*, camphol *m*

camphor *n* CHEM camphre *m*; ~ **oil** *n* CHEM huile camphrée *f*

camphorate *n* CHEM camphorate *m*

camphorated *adj* CHEM camphré

camphoric *adj* CHEM camphorique

camping: ~ **gas** *n* PETR TECH gaz en bouteille *m*

campylite *n* MINERAL campylite *f*

camshaft *n* AUTO, MECH arbre à cames *m*, MECH ENG arbre à cames *m*, *prefabricated* arbre à cames préfabriqué *m*, NAUT *engine*, VEHICLES *engine* arbre à cames *m*; ~ **bushing** *n* AUTO bague d'arbre à cames *f*; ~ **clearance** *n* AUTO jeu de réglage des culbuteurs *m*; ~ **controller** *n* ELEC *switch* commutateur à cames *m*; ~ **drive** *n* AUTO commande de la distribution *f*; ~ **drive chain** *n* VEHICLES *engine* chaîne d'entraînement d'arbre à cames *f*, chaîne de distribution *f*; ~ **gear** *n* MECH ENG *machine tools* roue d'arbre à cames *f*; ~ **gears** *n pl* MECH ENG pignons d'arbres à cames *m pl*; ~ **grinding machine** *n* MECH ENG machine à rectifier les arbres à cames *f*

can[1] *n* PROD ENG burette *f*; ~ **bank** *n* RECYCLING conteneur de boîtes de conserve à recycler *m*; ~ **buoy** *n* NAUT *navigation mark* bouée cylindrique *f*, bouée plate *f*, bouéetonne *f*; ~ **closing machine** *n (AmE) (cf tin closing machine)* PACKAGING machine pour fermer les boîtes *f*; ~ **delabeling** *n (AmE)*, ~ **delabelling** *n (BrE)* PACKAGING désétiquetage de boîte *m*; ~ **filling line** *n (AmE) (cf tin filling line)* PACKAGING chaîne de remplissage de boîtes *f*; ~ **packing machine** *n (AmE) (cf tin packing machine)* PACKAGING machine d'emballage de boîtes *f*; ~ **relabeling** *n* (AmE), ~ **relabelling** *n* (BrE) PACKAGING réétiquetage de boîtes *m*; ~ **sealing compound** *n* (AmE) *(cf tin sealing compound)* PACKAGING composition de fermeture pour boîtes *f*

can² *vt* CINEMAT mettre en boîte, PACKAGING mettre en conserve

Canadian: ~ **Switched Network** *n (CSN)* TELECOM réseau commuté canadien *m (RCC)*

canal *n* C&G *of sheet-glass tank furnace* , NAUT *waterway* canal *m*; ~ **boat** *n* NAUT péniche *f*; ~ **entrance** *n* TRANSP entrée du canal *f*; ~ **lock** *n* WATER SUPP écluse *f*, écluse de canal *f*; ~ **lock-gate** *n* WATER SUPP porte d'écluse *f*, porte d'écluse de canal *f*, écluse *f*; ~ **ray** *n* PHYS rayon canal *m*; ~ **ray analysis** *n* NUCLEAR analyse par rayons positifs *f*; ~ **ray discharge** *n* NUCLEAR décharge en rayons canaux *f*; ~ **transport** *n* NAUT batellerie *f*

canalize *vt* WATER SUPP canaliser

canard-wing: ~ **aircraft** *n* AERONAUT avion à voilure canard *m*

cancelation *n* (AmE), **cancellation** *n* (BrE) PATENTS *of entry* radiation *f*

Cancer *n* ASTRON Cancer *m*

cancrinite *n* MINERAL cancrinite *f*

candel: ~ **coal** *n* COAL TECH charbon mat *m*

candela *n (cd)* ELEC ENG, METR, OPT, PHYS candela *m (cd)*

candite *n* MINERAL candite *f*

candle: ~ **power** *n* PHOTO intensité lumineuse mesurée en bougies *f*

cane: ~ **juice** *n* FOOD TECH jus sucré *m*, vesou *m*; ~ **sugar** *n* CHEM, FOOD TECH sucre de canne *m*

Canes: ~ **Venatici** *n pl* ASTRON Chiens de Chasse *m pl*

can-filling: ~ **machine** *n* (AmE) *(cf tin-filling machine)* PACKAGING machine pour remplir les boîtes *f*

Canis: ~ **Major** *n* ASTRON Canis major *m*; ~ **Minor** *n* ASTRON Canis minor *m*, Petit Chien *m*

canister *n* PACKAGING boîte métallique *f*

canless: ~ **fuel assembly** *n* NUCLEAR assemblage combustible sans boîtier *m*

cannage *n* TEXTILES cannage *m*

canned¹ *adj* (AmE) *(cf tinned)* FOOD TECH mis en boîte, mis en conserve

canned:² ~ **food** *n* (AmE) *(cf tinned food)* PACKAGING alimentation en boîte *f*; ~ **motor** *n* MECH *hydraulics* moteur à rotor noyé *m*

cannel: ~ **coal** *n* COAL TECH charbon mat *m*

canning *n* FOOD TECH appertisation *f*, mise en boîte *f*, mise en conserve par autoclavage *f*; ~ **jar** *n* (AmE) *(cf preserving jar)* C&G bocal à conserves *m*; ~ **tooling** *n* MECH ENG *press tools* outillage pour mise en boîte *m*

Cannizzaro: ~ **reaction** *n* CHEM réaction de Cannizzaro *f*

cannon: ~ **plug** *n* CINEMAT prise cannon *f*

canoe *n* TV canal de bande *m*; ~ **fold** *n* GEOL pli synclinal en forme d'auge *m*, synclinal coffré *m*; ~ **stern** *n* NAUT *boatbuilding* arrière à canoë *m*

canola: ~ **oil** *n* FOOD TECH huile de colza *f*

canonical: ~ **distribution** *n* PHYS distribution canonique *f*; ~ **ensemble** *n* PHYS ensemble canonique *m*; ~ **equations** *n pl* PHYS équations canoniques *f pl*

canopy *n* AERONAUT verrière *f*, voilure de parachutage *f*, voilure de parachute *f*, NAUT taud *m*

cant¹ *n* CONST dévers *m*, inclinaison *f*, MECH ENG chanfrein *m*, RAIL dévers *m*, surhaussement *m*; ~ **file** *n* MECH ENG lime biseautée *f*

cant² *vt* NAUT *swing round, heel- ship* faire abattre, faire éviter, mettre à la bande

cant:³ ~ **over** *vi* NAUT *ship* gîter, prendre du gîte

cantharadine *n* CHEM cantharadine *f*

cantilever¹ *adj* CONST, PHYS, RAIL cantilever

cantilever² *n* CONST, MECH ENG encorbellement *m*, PAPER TECH porte-à-faux *m*; ~ **beam** *n* CONST poutre cantilever *f*, poutre en porte-à-faux *f*, PHYS poutre-console *f*; ~ **bridge** *n* CONST pont cantilever *m*, pont console *m*, pont en encorbellement *m*, pont à poutres à consoles *m*; ~ **loaded at free end** *n* CONST *strength of materials* poutre encastrée à une extrémité et chargée à l'autre *f*; ~ **retaining wall** *n* CONST mur de soutènement cantilever *m*, mur de soutènement-encorbellement *m*; ~ **wing** *n* AERONAUT voilure en porte-à-faux *f*

cantilevered¹ *adj* MECH en porte-à-faux, encastré

cantilevered:² ~ **Fourdrinier** *n* PAPER TECH table plate en porte-à-faux *f*

cantilevering *n* CONST *bridges* encorbellement *m*

cantonite *n* MINERAL cantonite *f*

canvas:¹ **under** ~ *adj* NAUT sous voile

canvas² *n* NAUT *sails* toile *f*, voile *f*, PRINT *bookbinder* canevas *m*, gaze *f*, TEXTILES toile *f*; ~ **brattice** *n* CONST cloison en toile grossière *f*; ~ **filter** *n* MINING *amalgam* manche en toile à voile *f*; ~ **table** *n* MINING toile de triage *f*

canyon *n* NUCLEAR *for irradiated fuel treatment* canyon *m*, enceinte *f*

caoutchouc *n* CHEM caoutchouc *m*, gomme élastique *f*

cap¹ *n* C&G calotte *f*, CONST *blasting* amorce *f*, capsule *f*, détonateur *m*, *of pile* chapeau *m*, *of sheerlegs* calotte *f*, coiffe *f*, *well-boring* obturateur *m*, ELEC ENG capuchon *m*, chapeau *m*, embout *m*, *of electric lamp* culot *m*, GEOL bouchon *m*, HYDR EQUIP *of steam chest* couvercle *m*, *of valve* chapeau *m*, opercule *m*, MECH chapeau *m*, couvercle *m*, MINING chapeau *m*, *blasting* détonateur *m*, PETR amorce *f*, capsule *f*, dernière passe *f*, détonateur *m*, PHOTO capuchon protecteur *m*, *for camera lens* bouchon *m*, PRINT capsule *f*, couvercle *m*, TEXTILES coiffe *f*; ~ **and pin insulator** *n* ELEC ENG chaîne d'isolateurs suspendus *f*; ~ **and rod insulator** *n* ELEC ENG isolateur capot et tige *m*; ~ **nut** *n* MECH écrou à chapeau *m*, MECH ENG écrou borgne *m*; ~ **piece** *n* MINING chapeau *m*; ~ **rock** *n* FUELLESS morts-terrains *m pl*, GEOL *of deposit or reservoir* chapeau *m*, roche couverture *f*, toit *m*, PETR roche couverture *f*, PETR TECH couverture *f*; ~ **sealing** *n* PACKAGING fermeture avec capsule *f*; ~ **sealing compound** *n* PACKAGING composition pour fermeture avec capsule *f*; ~ **sealing equipment** *n* PACKAGING équipement pour fermeture avec capsule *m*; ~ **spinning frame** *n* TEXTILES métier à filer à cloches *m*; ~ **still** *n* WATER SUPP *of sluice gate* chapeau *m*

cap² *vt* C&G croquer, CONST *ridge of roof* couronner, *well* coiffer, obturer; ~ **up** *vt* CINEMAT *lens* couvrir

CAP *abbr* *(controlled atmosphere packaging)* PACKAGING conditionnement sous atmosphère contrôlée *m*

capability *n* QUALITY aptitude *f*, capabilité *f*, TELECOM capacité *f*; ~ **approval** *n* QUALITY homologation d'aptitude *f*

capable: ~ **of detonation** *adj* MINING détonant, explosible

capacitance *n* ELEC, ELEC ENG, PHYS, TELECOM capacité *f*; ~ **box** *n* ELEC ENG boîte de capacités *f*; ~ **bridge** *n* ELEC pont de mesure de capacité *m*; ~ **coupling** *n* ELEC ENG couplage capacitif *m*, liaison par capacité *f*; ~ **disc** *n* (BrE) OPT disque capacitif *m*, vidéodisque analogique m, vidéodisque capacitif m; ~ **disk** n (AmE) *see capacitance disc*; ~ **meter** n ELEC ENG capacimètre m; ~ **relay** n ELEC relais capacitif m; ~ **sensing** n OPT lecture capacitive f; ~ **tolerance** n PROD ENG tolérance sur la capacité f

capacitive: ~ **component** n ELEC composante capacitive f; ~ **coupling** n ELEC, TELECOM couplage capacitif m; ~ **feedback** n ELEC ENG réaction capacitive f, rétroaction capacitive f; ~ **load** n ELEC AC circuit, ELEC ENG, TELECOM charge capacitive f; ~ **reactance** n ELEC AC circuit réactance capacitive f, ELEC ENG capacitance f, réactance de capacité f, PHYS réactance capacitive f; ~ **resistance** n ELEC ENG résistance capacitive f; ~ **tuning** n ELEC ENG accord capacitif m, accord par variation de capacité m; ~ **voltage divider** n ELEC ENG diviseur capacitif m, diviseur de tension capacitif m

capacitor n AUTO, COMP condensateur m, ELEC capaciteur m, condensateur m, ELEC ENG condensateur m, LAB EQUIP *electrical apparatus* capaciteur m, MECH ENG, PAPER TECH, PHYS, TELECOM, TV, VEHICLES *ignition* condensateur m; ~ **bank** n ELEC ENG batterie de condensateurs f; ~ **discharge** n ELEC ENG décharge d'un condensateur f; ~ **film** n ELEC lamelle pour condensateur f; ~ **ignition** n AUTO allumage classique m, allumage par capacité m, allumage électrostatique m; ~ **leakage current** n ELEC ENG courant de fuite d'un condensateur m; ~ **microphone** n RECORDING microphone à condensateur m; ~ **motor** n ELEC ENG moteur à condensateur m; ~ **plate** n ELEC plaque de condensateur f; ~ **plates** n pl PHYS armatures f pl; ~ **reactance** n ELEC ENG réactance d'un condensateur f; ~ **start-and-run motor** n ELEC moteur à condensateur à deux capacités m; ~ **start motor** n ELEC moteur à condensateur m, ELEC ENG moteur à condensateur m, moteur à démarrage par condensateur m; ~ **start-run motor** n ELEC ENG moteur à condensateur permanent m; ~ **store** n COMP mémoire à condensateur f; ~ **tissue paper** n PAPER TECH papier pour condensateur m

capacity n COMP, CONST capacité f, DP capacité f, capacité de mémoire f, ELEC ENG capacité f, MECH ENG capacité f, capacité électrique f, contenance f, METR *of micrometer* ouverture f, NUCLEAR *of plant* capacité f, PROD ENG *productive power* capacité f, rendement m, REFRIG *ability* capacité f, *load* charge f, VEHICLES *engine* cylindrée f, WATER SUPP *output of pump* débit m; ~ **bridge** n ELEC *of circuit* pont de capacité m; ~ **clause** n AERONAUT clause de capacité f; ~ **control** n AERONAUT contrôle de capacité m, REFRIG *of refrigerant* réglage de la puissance m; ~ **controller** n REFRIG *of refrigerant* régulateur de puissance m; ~ **factor** n (AmE) *(cf load factor)* PETR TECH taux de charge m; ~ **of output** n PROD ENG *of fan* pouvoir débitant m; ~ **plan** n NAUT *of cargo ship* plan des volumes m; ~ **reducer** n REFRIG *of refrigerant* réducteur de puissance m; ~ **requirement planning** n PROD ENG calcul des charges m, planification des capacités f; ~ **of a road** n TRANSP capacité d'écoulement f; ~ **under prevailing conditions** n TRANSP capacité momentanée f

cape n NAUT, OCEANOG cap m

capillarimeter n COAL TECH capillarimètre m

capillarity n CHEM, COAL TECH, CONST, PETR TECH, PHYS capillarité f; ~ **breaking layer** n COAL TECH couche anticapillaire f

capillary[1] adj MECH ENG capillaire

capillary:[2] ~ **action** n FLUID PHYS effet capillaire m; ~ **conductivity** n HYDROL conductivité capillaire f; ~

crack n NUCLEAR tapure f; ~ **diffusion** n HYDROL diffusion capillaire f; ~ **filling** n MECH ENG raccord capillaire m; ~ **flowmeter** n LAB EQUIP *liquid flow* débitmètre capillaire m; ~ **fringe** n HYDROL frange capillaire f; ~ **fusion** n NUCLEAR fusion capillaire f; ~ **instability** n FLUID PHYS *of fluid jet* instabilité capillaire f; ~ **molding** n (AmE), ~ **moulding** n (BrE) PROD ENG moulage capillaire m; ~ **rise** n COAL TECH remontée capillaire f, PAPER TECH ascension capillaire f; ~ **rise tester** n PAPER TECH capillarimètre m; ~ **soil water** n HYDROL eau capillaire du sol f; ~ **solder fitting** n MECH ENG *for copper tubes* raccord à braser pour capillarité m; ~ **tube** n LAB EQUIP *glassware*, PETR TECH, PHYS tube capillaire m; ~ **viscometer** n CHEM, LAB EQUIP *liquid flow* viscomètre capillaire m, viscosimètre capillaire m; ~ **viscosimeter** n CHEM, LAB EQUIP *liquid flow* viscomètre capillaire m, viscosimètre capillaire m; ~ **water** n COAL TECH, HYDROL eau capillaire f; ~ **wave** n OCEANOG onde capillaire f, vague capillaire f, vaguelette f, PHYS vague capillaire f; ~ **waves** n pl OCEANOG ondes de capillarité f pl

capillary-type: ~ **temperature switch** n PROD ENG thermostat de type à tube capillaire m

capital n PRINT capitale f; ~ **cost** n QUALITY coût d'investissement m; ~ **letter** n PRINT capitale f, majuscule f

capper n (AmE) *(cf cutoff man)* C&G croqueur m, PACKAGING machine à capsuler f

capping n MINING chapeau de filon m, PACKAGING capsulation f, WATER SUPP morts-terrains m; ~ **shutter** n CINEMAT obturateur secondaire m

capric adj CHEM caprique

Capricornus n ASTRON Capricorne m

caproic adj CHEM caproïque

caproin n CHEM caproïne f

caprolactam n CHEM, PROP MAT caprolactame m

caproyl n CHEM caproyle m

capryl n CHEM capryle m

caprylic adj CHEM caprylique

capsaicin n CHEM capsaïcine f

capsicin n CHEM capsicine f

capsize[1] vt NAUT chavirer

capsize[2] vi NAUT capoter, chavirer

capsizing n NAUT capotage m

capstan n ACOUSTICS, CINEMAT, DP, ELEC ENG, MECH, MECH ENG, NAUT, RECORDING, TV cabestan m; ~ **drive** n RECORDING entraînement de cabestan m, TV commande à cabestan f; ~ **drum** n NAUT poupée de cabestan f; ~ **lathe** n MECH ENG tour à revolver m; ~ **motor control** n CINEMAT commande du servomoteur de cabestan f; ~ **pit** n CONST puits à cabestan m; ~ **screw** n CONST vis à oeil f, vis à tête romaine f; ~ **servo** n CINEMAT, RECORDING servomoteur du cabestan m; ~ **servolock** n CINEMAT asservissement du cabestan m; ~ **tach lamp** n CINEMAT lampe de tachymètre du cabestan f

capstan-headed: ~ **screw** n CONST vis à oeil f, vis à tête romaine f

capsule n MINING *blasting* capsule f, SPACE *of spacecraft* capsule spatiale f

captain n AERONAUT commandant de bord m, NAUT capitaine de vaisseau m; ~ **call** n AERONAUT appel commandant de bord m

captation: ~ **drag** n TRANSP traînée de captation f

caption n CINEMAT légende f, titre m, PACKAGING, PRINT légende f; ~ **generator** n TV générateur de titres m; ~ **roller** n CINEMAT déroulant titre m; ~ **scanner** n TV analyseur de titres *m*, caméra titre *f*; ~ **stand** *n* TV banc titre *m*

captive[1] *adj* MECH imperdable

captive:[2] ~ **crosshead terminal screw** *n* PROD ENG borne à vis cruciforme *f*; ~ **flight** *n* SPACE *spacecraft* vol captif *m*, vol porté *m*; ~ **head terminal** *n* ELEC *connection* borne à prisonnier *f*; ~ **screw** *n* MECH ENG vis imperdable *f*

capture[1] *n* PHYS *nuclear*, SPACE *of satellite* capture *f*, WATER SUPP *of ground water* captage *m*; ~ **cross-section** *n* PETR capture coupe transversale *f*, section de capture *f*; ~ **effect** *n* ELECTRON effet d'étouffement *m*, TELECOM effet de capture *m*; ~ **range** *n* ELECTRON plage de synchronisation *f*; ~ **unit** *n* PETR capture unitaire *f*

capture[2] *vt* AERONAUT *beam* crocheter

car *n* *(cf wagon)* AUTO automobile *f*, voiture *f*, COAL TECH, MINING wagonnet *m*, RAIL (AmE) wagon *m*, TRANSP chariot *m*, TRANSP (AmE) *railways* wagon *m*, VEHICLES automobile *f*, voiture *f*; ~ **accessories** *n pl* VEHICLES accessoires d'auto *m pl*, accessoires de voiture *m pl*, accessoires pour automobile *m pl*; ~ **body tooling** *n* MECH ENG outillage destiné aux carrosseries automobiles *m*; ~ **clamp** *n* AUTO *car maintenance* serre-joints *m*; ~ **deck** *n* TRANSP pont des voitures *m*; ~ **distributor's office** *n* RAIL groupe de répartition *m*; ~ **elevator** *n* (AmE) *(cf wagon lift, wagon hoist)* RAIL *vehicles* monte-wagon *m*; ~ **ferry** *n* NAUT bac à voitures *m*, ferry-boat pour voitures *m*, transbordeur pour voitures *m*, TRANSP transbordeur pour voitures *m*; ~ **for internal yard use** *n* (AmE) *(cf wagon for internal yard use)* RAIL wagon de brouettage *m*; ~ **heater** *n* HEATING chauffage de voiture *m*; ~ **ladle** *n* PROD ENG *founding* poche montée sur wagonnet *f*, poche à chariot *f*; ~ **polish** *n* COATINGS vernis d'automobile *m*; ~ **pool** *n* TRANSP covoiturage *m*; ~ **pooling** *n* TRANSP covoiturage *m*; ~ **repair shop** *n* (AmE) *(cf workshop)* RAIL atelier de réparation de wagons *m*; ~ **shed** *n* (AmE) *(cf wagon shed)* RAIL dépôt de wagons *m*; ~ **sleeper train** *n* RAIL train autos-couchettes *m*; ~ **telephone** *n* TRANSP téléphone de voiture *m*

caramel *n* COLOURS teinture pour caramel *f*; ~ **sugar** *n* (AmE) *(cf caramelized sugar)* FOOD TECH sucre caramélisé *m*

caramelized: ~ **sugar** *n* (BrE) *(cf caramel sugar)* FOOD TECH sucre caramélisé *m*

carat *n* METR carat *m*; ~ **fine** *n* METR carat de fin *m*

caravan *n* (BrE) *(cf trailer, house trailer, trailer)* TRANSP caravane *f*, VEHICLES caravane de camping *f*

carbamate *n* CHEM carbamate *m*

carbamic *adj* CHEM carbamique

carbamyl *n* CHEM carbamyle *m*

carbamyle *n* CHEM carbamyle *m*

carbanil *n* CHEM carbanile *m*

carbanilide *n* CHEM diphénylurée *f*

carbanion *n* CHEM carbanion *m*

carbazide *n* CHEM carbazide *m*

carbazole *n* CHEM carbazol *m*, carbazole *m*

carbene *n* CHEM carbène *m*

carbide *n* CHEM carbure *m*, MECH *materials* carbure métallique *m*, PROP MAT carbure *m*; ~ **cracking** *n* METALL fissuration de carbures *f*; ~ **formation** *n* METALL formation de carbures *f*; ~ **grains** *n pl* PROP MAT grains de carbure *m pl*; ~ **tips** *n pl* MECH ENG plaquettes en carbures métalliques *f pl*; ~ **tool** *n* MECH ENG outil au carbure *m*

carbide-tipped: ~ **hole saw** *n* MECH ENG trépan carbure

m; ~ **tool** *n* MECH outil à plaquette carbure *m*, MECH ENG outil à mise rapportée en carbure *m*

carbinol *n* CHEM carbinol *m*

carbocyclic *adj* CHEM carbocyclique

carbohydrase *n* CHEM, FOOD TECH carbohydrase *f*

carbohydrate *n* CHEM hydrate de carbone *m*, FOOD TECH glucide *m*, hydrate de carbone *m*; ~ **size** *n* TEXTILES colle à l'hydrate de carbone *f*

carbolic *adj* CHEM carbolique, phéniqué

carbon *n* *(C)* CHEM carbone *m* *(C)*; ~ **14 analysis** *n* RAD PHYS analyse de carbone 14 *f*; ~ **advancing** *n* CINEMAT avancement des charbons *m*; ~ **arc** *n* ELEC, ELEC ENG arc à charbon *m*; ~ **arc lamp** *n* ELEC *illumination* lampe à arc de charbon *f*; ~ **arc welding** *n* PROD ENG soudage à l'arc à électrodes de carbone *m*; ~ **bisulfide** *n* (AmE), ~ **bisulphide** *n* (BrE) *(cf carbon disulphide)* CHEM anhydride sulfocarbonique *m*; ~ **black** *n* P&R *pigment, filler*, PETR TECH noir de carbone *m*; ~ **brick** *n* HEATING *refractory material* brique de carbone *f*; ~ **brush** *n* ELEC *motor, generator* balai en charbon *m*, ELEC ENG balai *m*, balai en charbon *m*, MECH ENG balai au carbone *m*; ~ **burning** *n* NUCLEAR combustion du carbone *f*; ~ **composition resistor** *n* ELEC ENG résistance agglomérée *f*; ~ **contact** *n* ELEC contact en charbon *m*; ~ **content** *n* PROP MAT teneur en carbone *f*; ~ **cycle** *n* ASTRON, FOOD TECH cycle du carbone *m*; ~ **dating** *n* RAD PHYS analyse de carbone 14 *f*; ~ **dioxide** *n* CHEM acide carbonique *m*, gaz carbonique *m*, COAL TECH dioxyde de carbone *m*, MECH ENG anhydride carbonique *m*, gaz carbonique *m*; ~ **dioxide fire extinguisher** *n* SAFETY extincteur d'incendie à dioxyde de carbone *m*; ~ **dioxide greenhouse effect** *n* POLLUTION effet de serre dû au dioxyde de carbone *m*, effet de serre dû au gaz carbonique *m*; ~ **dioxide laser** *n* ELECTRON laser à gaz carbonique *m*; ~ **dioxide snow** *n* REFRIG neige carbonique *f*; ~ **disulfide** *n* (AmE) *see carbon disulphide*; ~ **disulphide** *n* (BrE) *(cf carbon bisulphide, carbon disulfide)* CHEM anhydride sulfocarbonique *m*, FOOD TECH sulfure de carbone *m*; ~ **electrode** *n* ELEC *cell* électrode de charbon *f*; ~ **fiber** *n* (AmE) *see carbon fibre*; ~ **fiber felt** *n* (AmE) *see carbon fibre felt*; ~ **fiber reinforced plastic** *n* (AmE) *see carbon fibre reinforced plastic*; ~ **fiber tool** *n* (AmE) *see carbon fibre tool*; ~ **fibre** *n* (BrE) P&R *filler*, PROP MAT, SPACE *of spacecraft* fibre de carbone *f*; ~ **fibre felt** *n* (BrE) SPACE *of spacecraft* feutre de carbone *m*; ~ **fibre reinforced plastic** *n* (BrE) P&R matière plastique renforcée par fibre de carbone *f*; ~ **fibre tool** *n* (BrE) MECH ENG outil en fibre de carbone *m*; ~ **filament lamp** *n* ELEC ENG lampe à filament de charbon *f*; ~ **film** *n* ELEC ENG couche de carbone *f*; ~ **film resistor** *n* ELEC ENG résistance à couche de carbone *f*; ~ **holder** *n* CINEMAT porte-charbon *m*; ~ **holder lamp** *n* ELEC ENG porte-charbon *m*; ~ **mass transfer** *n* NUCLEAR transfert de masse du carbone *m*; ~ **microphone** *n* ACOUSTICS, RECORDING microphone à cartouche de charbon *m*; ~ **monoxide** *n* CHEM oxyde de carbone *m*, COAL TECH monoxyde de carbone *m*, MECH ENG oxyde de carbone *m*, POLLUTION monoxyde de carbone *m*, oxyde de carbone *m*, VEHICLES *exhaust* monoxyde de carbone *m*; ~ **monoxide filter** *n* SAFETY filtre à oxyde de carbone *m*; ~ **monoxide filter self-rescue** *n* SAFETY respirateur *m*; ~ **monoxide laser** *n* ELECTRON laser à oxyde de carbone *m*; ~ **paper** *n* PAPER TECH, PRINT papier carbone *m*; ~ **replica** *n* NUCLEAR *electron microscopy* réplique au carbone *f*; ~ **resistor** *n* ELEC résistance carbone *f*, ELEC ENG résistance au carbone *f*, PHYS *composition* résistance au charbon *f*, résistance carbone *f*; ~ **star** *n* ASTRON étoile C *f*; ~ **steel** *n* COAL TECH, MECH *materials*, MECH ENG acier au carbone *m*, NUCLEAR acier au carbone *m*, acier noir *m*; ~ **steel dust** *n* COAL TECH poussière d'acier au carbone *f*; ~ **steel tool** *n* MECH ENG tube en acier au carbone *m*; ~ **tetrachloride** *n* CHEM tétrachlorure de carbone *m*; ~ **tissue** *n* PRINT papier charbon *m*

carbonaceous[1] *adj* CHEM charbonneux, GEOL, PROP MAT carboné

carbonaceous:[2] ~ **chondrite** *n* ASTRON chondrite charbonneuse *f*; ~ **shale** *n* GEOL schiste charbonneux *m*

carbonado *n* MINERAL carbonado *m*

carbonatation *n* CHEM, GEOL carbonatation *f*

carbonate[1] *n* CHEM, DETERGENTS carbonate *m*; ~ **alkalinity** *n* HYDROL alcalinité de carbonate *f*; ~ **hardness** *n* HYDROL dureté carbonatée *f*; ~ **platform** *n* GEOL plate-forme carbonatée *f*

carbonate[2] *vt* CHEM carbonater

carbonated *adj* FOOD TECH gazeux, GEOL carbonaté

carbonation *n* CHEM, GEOL, HYDROL carbonatation *f*

carbon-free *adj* METALL, PROP MAT exempt de carbone

carbonic[1] *adj* CHEM carbonique

carbonic:[2] ~ **acid equilibrium** *n* HYDROL équilibre calco-carbonate *m*

carboniferous[1] *adj* MINERAL carbonifère

carboniferous[2] *n* PETR TECH *geological period* carbonifère *m*

carbonization *n* COAL TECH carbonification *f*, carbonisation *f*, houillification *f*

carbonize[1] *vt* COAL TECH carboniser, charbonner, houillifier, THERMOD carboniser

carbonize[2] *vi* COAL TECH se carboniser, se charbonner

carbonized[1] *adj* COAL TECH charbonné

carbonized:[2] ~ **forms** *n pl* PAPER TECH papiers pour formulaires carbonés *m pl*

carbonizing: ~ **base paper** *n* PAPER TECH papier pour support carboné *m*

carbonless[1] *adj* PRINT sans carbone

carbonless:[2] ~ **copy paper** *n* PAPER TECH, PRINT papier autocopiant *m*; ~ **copy paper forms** *n pl* PAPER TECH formulaires non carbonés *m pl*

carbonyl[1] *adj* PROP MAT carbonyle

carbonyl[2] *n* CHEM carbonyle *m*; ~ **chloride** *n* CHEM acide chlorocarbonique *m*, chlorure de carbonyle *m*, phosgène *m*; ~ **sulfide** *n* (AmE), ~ **sulphide** *n* (BrE) POLLUTION carbone sulfuré *m*, oxysulfure de carbone *m*, sulfure de carbonyle *m*

Carborundum *n* CHEM Carborundum *m* (MD), MECH ENG Carborundum *m* (MD), carbure de silicium *m*; ~ **wheel** *n* PROD ENG meule en Carborundum *f* (MD)

carbostyril *n* CHEM carbostyryle *m*

carboxyl *n* CHEM carboxyle *m*

carboxylate *n* CHEM carboxylate *m*

carboxylated *adj* P&R *chemical* carboxylé

carboxylic *adj* CHEM carboxylique

carboxymethyl: ~ **cellulose** *n* DETERGENTS,, FOOD TECH, P&R carboxyméthylcellulose *f*

carboy *n* C&G dame-jeanne *f*, FOOD TECH bonbonne *f*, dame-jeanne *f*, LAB EQUIP *glassware* bonbonne *f*

carbro: ~ **color print** *n* (AmE), ~ **colour print** *n* (BrE) PHOTO épreuve trichrome par le procédé carbro *f*; ~ **printing** *n* PHOTO ozobromie *f*

carburet *vt* CHEM carburer

carburetor *n* (AmE) *see* carburettor

carburettor *n* (BrE) AUTO, C&G, MECH *vehicles*, MECH ENG, NAUT *engine*, VEHICLES *fuel supply* carburateur *m*; ~ **barrel** *n* (BrE) AUTO corps de carburateur *m*; ~ **control cable** *n* (BrE) AUTO câble d'accélérateur *m*; ~ **engine** *n* (BrE) AUTO moteur à carburateur *m*; ~ **float** *n* (BrE) VEHICLES flotteur de carburateur *m*; ~ **float chamber** *n* (BrE) VEHICLES chambre de flotteur de carburateur *f*, cuve à niveau constant de carburateur *f*; ~ **jacket** *n* (BrE) AUTO réchauffeur de combustible *m*; ~ **linkage** *n* (BrE) AUTO tringlerie de gaz *f*, VEHICLES timonerie de carburateur *f*; ~ **needle** *n* (BrE) VEHICLES aiguille de carburateur *f*, pointeau de carburateur *m*

carburizing *n* HEATING, MECH ENG cémentation au carbone *f*; ~ **furnace** *n* MECH ENG four de cémentation *m*

carbylamine *n* CHEM carbylamine *f*

carcass *n* CONST *carpentry*, ELEC ENG *of electric motor*, TEXTILES carcasse *f*; ~ **chilling** *n* REFRIG ressuage réfrigéré *m*, réfrigération primaire des carcasses *f*; ~ **dressing percentage** *n* FOOD TECH *butchery* rendement à l'abattage *m*; ~ **yield** *n* FOOD TECH *butchery* performance à l'abattage *f*, rendement en carcasse *m*, rendement à l'abattage *m*, rendement à l'habillage *m*

carcinogen *n* CHEM cancérigène *m*, substance carcinogène *f*, FOOD TECH carcinogène *m*

carcinogenic[1] *adj* CHEM cancérigène, cancérogène, carcinogène

carcinogenic:[2] ~ **substance** *n* SAFETY substance cancérigène *f*, substance cancérogène *f*

carcinotron *n* (TM) ELECTRON carcinotron *m* (MD), TELECOM carcinotron *m* (MD), oscillateur à ondes rétrogrades *m*

card[1] *n* DP, ELECTRON carte *f*, TEXTILES carde *f*; ~ **bed** *n* DP chemin de cartes *m*; ~ **cage** *n* DP panier à cartes *m*; ~ **clothing** *n* TEXTILES habillage de carde *m*; ~ **column** *n* DP colonne de carte *f*; ~ **cutting** *n* TEXTILES mise en carte de dessin jacquard *f*; ~ **deck** *n* DP jeu de cartes *m*; ~ **feed** *n* DP mécanisme d'alimentation *m*, mécanisme d'alimentation en cartes *m*; ~ **hopper** *n* DP magasin d'alimentation de cartes *m*; ~ **jam** *n* DP bourrage de cartes *m*; ~ **module** *n* ELECTRON module sur carte *m*; ~ **molding** *n* (AmE), ~ **moulding** *n* (BrE) PROD ENG *founding* moulage sur plaque-modèle *m*; ~ **punch** *n* DP perforateur de cartes *m*; ~ **reader** *n* DP lecteur de cartes *m*, TELECOM lecam *m*, lecteur de cartes *m*; ~ **row** *n* DP ligne de carte *f*; ~ **system** *n* DP système à cartes *m*

card[2] *vt* TEXTILES carder

cardamom: ~ **oil** *n* FOOD TECH essence de cardamome *f*

cardan *n* AERONAUT accouplement à cardan *m*; ~ **coupling** *n* MECH ENG cardan *m*; ~ **joint** *n* MECH joint à la Cardan *m*; ~ **shaft** *n* AUTO arbre à cardan longitudinal *m*, MECH arbre cardan *m*

Cardan's: ~ **suspension** *n* MECH ENG suspension à la cardan *f*

cardboard *n* PRINT carton *m*; ~ **backing** *n* PACKAGING support de carton *m*; ~ **machine** *n* PACKAGING cartonneuse *f*; ~ **packaging** *n* PACKAGING emballage en carton *m*; ~ **tray** *n* PACKAGING barquette en carton *f*; ~ **tube** *n* PACKAGING tube en carton *m*

carded: ~ **packaging** *n* PACKAGING conditionnement sous carte *m*; ~ **pattern** *n* PROD ENG *founding* plaque porte-modèle *f*, plaque-modèle *f*

Cardew: ~ **voltmeter** *n* ELEC voltmètre Cardew *m*

cardinal: ~ **number** *n* MATH nombre cardinal *m*; ~ **points** *n pl* ASTRON, NAUT *of compass*, PHYS points cardinaux *m pl*; ~ **system** *n* NAUT *navigation marks* système cardinal *m*

carding *n* TEXTILES cardage *m*

cardioid *n* MECH ENG cardioïde *f*; ~ **diagram** *n* RECORDING diagramme cardioïde *m*; ~ **microphone** *n* ACOUSTICS, RECORDING microphone cardioïde *m*

card-operated: ~ **payphone** *n* TELECOM cabine à cartes *f*

cardphone *n* TELECOM cabine à cartes *f*, publiphone à cartes *m*

cardroom *n* TEXTILES carderie *f*

care *n* SAFETY *charge, responsibility* charge *f*, TEXTILES entretien *m*; ~ **of flammable stores** *n* SAFETY conservation des matériaux inflammables *f*; ~ **of health** *n* SAFETY soin d'hygiène *m*; ~ **labeling** *n* (AmE), ~ **labelling** *n* (BrE) TEXTILES étiquetage d'entretien *m*

careen[1] *vt* NAUT abattre en carène, mettre en carène, se coucher

careen[2] *vti* NAUT caréner

careening *n* NAUT carénage *m*; ~ **grid** *n* NAUT grille de carénage *f*

carene *n* CHEM carène *m*

caret *n* PRINT *proof correction mark* lambda *m*, signe d'omission *m*

cargo *n* AERONAUT fret *m*, NAUT cargaison *f*, chargement *m*, SPACE *spacecraft* cargaison *f*; ~ **and passenger ship** *n* NAUT navire mixte *m*; ~ **barge** *n* TRANSP péniche remorquée *f*; ~ **bay** *n* SPACE *spacecraft* soute *f*; ~ **boom** *n* NAUT corne de charge *f*; ~ **capacity** *n* NAUT *ship design* port en lourd *m*; ~ **carrier support** *n* AERONAUT *helicopter* plateau porte-charge *m*; ~ **compartment** *n* AERONAUT soute *f*; ~ **compartment door** *n* AERONAUT porte de soute *f*; ~ **compartment equipment** *n* AERONAUT aménagement fixe de soute *m*, aménagement fixe des soutes *m*; ~ **crane** *n* NAUT *shipbuilding* grue de chargement *f*; ~ **derrick** *n* NAUT *shipbuilding* mât de charge *m*; ~ **gear** *n* NAUT *shipbuilding* apparaux de charge *m pl*, apparaux de levage *m pl*; ~ **handling** *n* AERONAUT manutention du fret *f*, NAUT manutention de la cargaison *f*; ~ **handling berth** *n* TRANSP installation de manutention de marchandises *f*; ~ **hatch** *n* NAUT panneau de chargement *m*, panneau de déchargement *m*, SPACE *spacecraft* écoutille de soute *f*; ~ **hatchway** *n* TRANSP panneau de chargement *m*; ~ **helicopter** *n* TRANSP hélicoptère de transport *m*; ~ **hold** *n* SPACE *spacecraft* soute *f*, TRANSP soute *f*, *ship* cale *f*; ~ **hook** *n* NAUT crochet de levage *m*; ~ **manifest** *n* AERONAUT liste du fret *f*, manifeste de marchandises *m*, NAUT manifeste de cargaison *m*; ~ **officer** *n* NAUT officier chargé des marchandises *m*; ~ **plan** *n* NAUT plan de cargo *m*; ~ **plane** *n* AERONAUT avion cargo *m*; ~ **port** *n* NAUT *shipbuilding* sabord de chargement *m*; ~ **pump** *n* MAR POLL, NAUT *tanker* pompe de cargaison *f*; ~ **release hook** *n* AERONAUT *helicopter* crochet délesteur de fret *m*; ~ **satellite** *n* SPACE cargo satellite *m*; ~ **ship** *n* NAUT cargo *m*, navire de charge *m*, TRANSP cargo *m*; ~ **sling** *n* AERONAUT *helicopter* délesteur de charges *m*, élingue de chargement *f*, élingue defret *f*; ~ **space** *n* TRANSP *trucks* compartiment à marchandises *m*; ~ **swing** *n* AERONAUT *helicopter* élingue balançoire *f*; ~ **tank** *n* POLLUTION citerne de cargaison *f*; ~ **terminal** *n* AERONAUT aérogare de fret *f*, TRANSP gare de fret *f*; ~ **warehouse** *n* TRANSP aérogare de fret *f*; ~ **winch** *n* NAUT treuil de chargement *m*, treuil de levage *m*, TRANSP treuil de chargement *m*

Carina *n* ASTRON Carène *f*

carinated: ~ **propeller** *n* TRANSP hélice carénée *f*

carload *n* (AmE) *(cf wagonload)* RAIL wagon complet *m*, TRANSP *rail* charge complète *f*

CARM *abbr (chemical agent resisting material)* MILIT matériel résistant aux produits chimiques *m*

carmine *n* FOOD TECH carmin *m*; ~ **lacquer** *n* COLOURS laque carmine *f*

carminic *adj* CHEM carminique

carnallite *n* MINERAL carnallite *f*

carnauba: ~ **wax** *n* FOOD TECH cire de carnauba *f*

carnet *n* CINEMAT carnet de douane *m*

Carnian *adj* GEOL carnien

carnitine *n* CHEM carnitine *f*

Carnot: ~ **cycle** *n* HEATING, PHYS, THERMOD cycle de Carnot *m*; ~ **engine** *n* PHYS machine de Carnot *f*

Carnot's: ~ **theorem** *n* PHYS théorème de Carnot *m*

carnotite *n* MINERAL carnotite *f*

carob *n* FOOD TECH caroube *f*

carone *n* CHEM carone *f*

carotene *n* CHEM, FOOD TECH carotène *m*

carousel: ~ **structure** *n* SPACE *communications* structure à carrousel *f*

carpenter *n* CONST charpentier *m*

carpenter's: ~ **gage** *n* (AmE), ~ **gauge** *n* (BrE) CONST troussequin *m*, trusquin *m*

carpenters': ~ **bench** *n* CONST banc de charpentier *m*, établi de charpentier *m*; ~ **joint** *n* CONST assemblages de charpente *m pl*

carpentry *n* CONST charpente en bois *f*, charpenterie *f*

carpet *n* CONST *road* couche de roulement *f*; ~ **cleaner** *n* DETERGENTS dégraissant pour tapis *m*; ~ **shampoo** *n* DETERGENTS dégraissant pour tapis *m*; ~ **underlay** *n* TEXTILES thibaude *f*; ~ **yarn** *n* TEXTILES fil de tapis *m*

carpholite *n* MINERAL carpholite *f*

carrageen *n* FOOD TECH carrhagénine *m*, mousse d'Irlande *f*, mousse perlée *f*

carriage *n* DP, MECH, MECH ENG chariot *m*, MILIT *of gun* affût de canon *m*, PACKAGING port *m*, PRINT chariot *m*, transporteur *m*, PROD ENG port *m*, RAIL voiture *f*, wagon *m*, TRANSP chariot *m*, port *m*; ~ **A** *n* PRINT *containing motor* motrice *f*, TRANSP *containing motor* motrice *f*, voiture de tête *f*; ~ **by sea** *n* PACKAGING transport maritime *m*; ~ **key** *n* RAIL carré de Berne *m*; ~ **planing machine** *n* MECH ENG raboteuse à table mobile *f*; ~ **return** *n (CR)* COMP caractère de retour chariot *m*, retour de chariot *m*; ~ **spring** *n* MECH ENG ressort de voiture *m*

carrick: ~ **bend** *n* NAUT *knot* noeud de carrick *m*

carrier *n* COMP, DP porteuse *f*, support *m*, ELECTRON courant porteur *m*, onde porteuse *f*, porteuse *f*, PHYS *electric charge* porteur *m*, *wave* porteuse *f*, PRINT *personnel* porteur *m*, *transmission of data* onde porteuse *f*, PROD ENG transporteur *m*, PROP MAT support *m*, RECORDING, SPACE *communications*, TELECOM porteuse *f*, TEXTILES transporteur *m*, TV porteuse *f*; ~ **acquisition** *n* ELECTRON accrochage de la porteuse *m*; ~ **amplifier** *n* ELECTRON amplificateur à courant porteur *m*; ~ **analysis** *n* NUCLEAR analyse par entraîneur *f*; ~ **balance** *n* TV équilibrage de la sous-porteuse couleur *m*; ~ **bandwidth** *n* ELECTRON largeur de bande de la porteuse *f*; ~ **bed** *n* PETR drain *m*, roche réservoir *f*; ~ **box** *n* PACKAGING boîte pour emplettes *f*; ~ **car** *n* (AmE) *(cf carrier wagon)* RAIL wagon porteur *m*; ~ **detect** *n (CD)* ELECTRON, TELECOM détection de porteuse *f*; ~ **difference system** *n* TV réception par battements *f*; ~ **frequency** *n* COMP fréquence porteuse *f*, DP fréquence d'onde porteuse *f*, fréquence porteuse *f*, ELECTRON, TELECOM, TV fréquence porteuse *f*; ~ **frequency offset** *n* TELECOM décalage des fréquences porteuses *m*; ~ **frequency oscillator** *n* ELECTRON oscillateur à fréquence porteuse *m*, NUCLEAR *chromatography* gaz vecteur *m*, POLLUTION, PROP MAT gaz porteur *m*; ~ **generation** *n* ELECTRON génération de la porteuse *f*; ~ **group alarm** *n* *(CGA)* TELECOM alarme de groupe de voies *f*; ~ **level** *n* ELECTRON niveau de la porteuse *m*; ~ **mobility** *n* PHYS mobilité des porteurs *f*; ~ **modulation** *n* ELECTRON modulation de porteuse *f*; ~ **noise** *n* ELECTRON bruit de la porteuse *m*; ~ **reinsertion operator** *n* ELECTRON oscillateur de régénération de la porteuse *m*; ~ **repeater** *n* ELECTRON répéteur *m*; ~ **sense multiple access** *n* *(CSMA)* TELECOM accès multiple par détection de porteuse *m* *(CSMA)*; ~ **sense multiple access with collision detection** *n* *(CSMA-CD)* COMP, DP, ELECTRON accès multiple par détection de porteuse avec détection de collision *m* *(CSMA-CD)*; ~ **sense signal** *n* TELECOM signal de détection de porteuse *m*; ~ **sense system** *n* TELECOM système de détection de porteuse *m*; ~ **shipborne helicopter** *n* AERONAUT hélicoptère embarqué *m*; ~ **signal** *n* COMP, DP signal de porteuse *m*; ~ **suppression** *n* ELECTRON, TELECOM suppression de la porteuse *f*; ~ **wagon** *n* (BrE) *(cf carrier car)* RAIL wagon porteur *m*; ~ **wave** *n* NAUT *radio f*, PHYS onde porteuse *f*, TV onde porteuse *f*, porteuse *f*, WAVE PHYS onde porteuse *f*; ~ **wave generator** *n* WAVE PHYS génératrice de l'onde porteuse *f*; ~ **wave modulation** *n* WAVE PHYS modulation d'onde porteuse *f*

carrier-borne: ~ **aircraft** *n* MILIT avion embarqué *m*

carrier-to-interface: ~ **ratio** *n* *(CIR)* TELECOM rapport porteuse/brouillage *m*

carrier-to-intermodulation: ~ **noise density ratio** *n* TELECOM rapport porteuse-densité de bruit d'intermodulation *m*

carrier-to-noise: ~ **density ratio** *n* TELECOM rapport porteuse-densité de bruit *m*; ~ **ratio** *n* RECORDING rapport de la porteuse sur le bruit *m*

carrier-to-receiver: ~ **thermal-no-noise ratio** *n* TELECOM rapport porteuse-bruit thermique du récepteur *m*

carrot: ~ **wedge** *n* MECH ENG broche conique *f*

carry[1] *n* COMP *arithmetic*, DP *arithmetic*, ELECTRON *arithmetic* report *m*; ~ **digit** *n* COMP, DP retenue *f*; ~ **level** *n* PROD ENG niveau normal de stockage *m*; ~ **look-ahead** *n* COMP, DP report parallèle *m*

carry[2] *vt* COMP retenir, CONST porter, *road* pousser, DP retenir, MECH ENG appuyer, soutenir, supporter, tenir, PAPER TECH porter, TELECOM *traffic* véhiculer, écouler, TEXTILES transporter, WATER SUPP canal conduire; ~ **out to sea** *vt* HYDROL entraîner au large

carry-in *n* C&G mise à l'arche *f*

carrying *n* TEXTILES transport *m*; ~ **axle** *n* MECH ENG essieu porteur *m*, RAIL *vehicles* essieu porteur d'avant *m*; ~ **bar** *n* PAPER TECH barre porteuse *f*; ~ **bogie** *n* RAIL bogie porteur *m*; ~ **capacity** *n* FUELLESS *pipe* capacité *f*, MECH *vehicles* charge utile *f*, MECH ENG capacité de charge *f*, PACKAGING capacité de transport *f*; ~ **handle** *n* INSTRUMENT poignée *f*, MECH poignée de transport *f*, PACKAGING poignée de manutention *f*, poignée de transport *f*; ~ **idler** *n* MECH ENG rouleau porteur *m*; ~ **medium** *n* PRINT liant *m*; ~ **out** *n* PATENTS mise en oeuvre *f*; ~ **roller** *n* C&G rouleau porteur *m*; ~ **wheel** *n* TRANSP roue porteuse *f*

carrying-in: ~ **fork** *n* C&G fourche pour mise à l'arche *f*

carry-off *n* NUCLEAR *of corrosion products* entraînement *m*

carry-over *n* C&G entraînement de poussières *m*

CARS *abbr* *(coherent anti-Stokes Raman scattering)* PHYS DRASC *(diffusion Raman anti-Stokes cohérente)*

Carson's: ~ **rule bandwidth** *n* SPACE *communications* bande de Carson *f*

cart *n* (AmE) *(cf truck)* CONST bogie *m*

Cartesian: ~ **coordinate** *n* CONST, MATH, PHYS coordonnée cartésienne *f*; ~ **coordinate system** *n* ELECTRON système de coordonnées cartésiennes *m*; ~ **geometry** *n* GEOM géométrie cartésienne *f*; ~ **product** *n* DP produit cartésien *m*

carton: ~ **compact** *n* PAPER TECH carton compact *m*; ~ **dosing machine** *n* PACKAGING machine à doser les cartons *f*; ~ **erector and closer** *n* PACKAGING machine pour dresser et fermer les cartons *f*; ~ **filler** *n* PACKAGING remplisseuse de cartons *f*

cartoner *n* PACKAGING encartonneuse *f*

cartoning: ~ **machine** *n* PACKAGING encartonneuse *f*

cartoon *n* CINEMAT dessin animé *m*

cartridge *n* DP, MINING *explosive*, PHOTO cartouche *f*, PRINT cartouche *f*, cassette *f*, TV cartouche *f*; ~ **belt** *n* MILIT ceinture cartouchière *f*; ~ **brass** *n* MECH ENG laiton à cartouches *m*; ~ **case** *n* MILIT douille de cartouche *f*; ~ **depot** *n* MILIT cartoucherie *f*; ~ **drive** *n* DP unité à cartouche *f*; ~ **factory** *n* MILIT cartoucherie *f*; ~ **filter** *n* MECH ENG, VEHICLES filtre à cartouche *m*; ~ **for indexable inserts** *n* MECH ENG *cutting tools* cartouche à plaquette amovible *f*; ~ **fuse** *n* ELEC, ELEC ENG fusible à cartouche *m*; ~ **heater** *n* MECH ENG *injection moulds* cartouche chauffante *f*; ~ **loading** *n* DP chargement de cartouche *m*; ~ **paper** *n* PACKAGING papier de mise en cartes *m*, PRINT papier en cartouche *m*; ~ **pen** *n* PRINT stylo à cartouche *m*; ~ **recorder** *n* INSTRUMENT enregistreur à cartouche *m*; ~ **relief valve** *n* PROD ENG limiteur de pression à cartouche *m*; ~ **tape** *n* RECORDING bande en cartouche *f*; ~ **tape recorder** *n* RECORDING magnétophone à cassette *m*

carving: ~ **machine** *n* PROD ENG machine à sculpter *f*; ~ **tool** *n* PROD ENG outil de sculpteur *m*

CAS *abbr* *(channel-associated signalling, channel-associated signaling)* TELECOM signalisation canal par canal *f*

cascadable: ~ **counter** *n* COMP compteur en cascade *m*

cascade[1] *n* COAL TECH, ELEC ENG *series connection*, HYDROL cascade *f*; ~ **aerator** *n* HYDROL aérateur à cascades *m*; ~ **amplifier** *n* ELECTRON amplificateur en cascade *m*, amplificateur à plusieurs étages *m*; ~ **arrangement** *n* ELEC ENG montage en cascade *m*; ~ **blades** *n pl* AERONAUT grille d'aubes *f*; ~ **connection** *n* ELEC ENG *series connection* connexion en cascade *f*, couplage en cascade *m*, NUCLEAR *networks, electronics* connexion en cascade *f*; ~ **control** *n* CONTROL régulation en cascade *f*; ~ **controller** *n* CONTROL régulateur en cascade *m*; ~ **furnace** *n* HEATING four à cascade *m*; ~ **milk cooler** *n* REFRIG refroidisseur à lait par ruissellement *m*; ~ **mill** *n* COAL TECH broyeur à cascade *m*; ~ **printer** *n* CINEMAT tireuse multiple *f*; ~ **process** *n* RAD PHYS processus cascade *m*; ~ **set** *n* ELEC ENG groupe en cascade *m*; ~ **vanes** *n pl* AERONAUT grille d'aubes *f*; ~ **washing** *n* PHOTO *of prints* lavage en cascade *m*

cascade[2] *vt* ELEC ENG monter en cascade

cascaded: ~ **carry** *n* ELECTRON *arithmetic* report en cascade *m* cascading: ~ **counters** n pl PROD ENG compteurs en cascade m pl; ~ **timer** n PROD ENG temporisateur en cascade m

case[1] n AERONAUT carter réacteur m, CONST of lock boîte f, coffre m, MECH boîtier m, coffret m, étui m, MECH ENG boîte f, caisson m, carter m, carter d'engrenage m, couvre-engrenages m, gaine protectrice contre les accidents f, METR of balance of precision cage f, PRINT casse f, for book couverture f, SPACE of spacecraft enveloppe f, VEHICLES tools trousse f; ~ **depth** n MECH ENG profondeur de cémentation f; ~ **hardening** n MECH process, MECH ENG cémentation f; ~ **law** n PATENTS jurisprudence f; ~ **lining paper** n PACKAGING papier de revêtement pour caisses m; ~ **loader** n PACKAGING machine à encaisser f; ~ **maker** n PRINT machine à faire les emboîtages f; ~ **packing** n PACKAGING mise en caisse f; ~ **packing and unpacking of ampoules machine** n PACKAGING machine pour emballer et déballer les ampoules f; ~ **statement** n COMP instruction de cas f

case[2] vt CONST well, borehole cuveler, tuber

case:[3] **in ~ of fire** phr SAFETY en cas d'incendie

CASE abbr (computer-aided software engineering) COMP ingénierie logicielle assistée par ordinateur f

cased: ~ **beam** n CONST steel beam poutre encastrée f; ~ **book** n PRINT livre cartonné m; ~ **hollow ware** n C&G verre creux doublé m; ~ **well** n HYDROL puits revêtu m, puits tubé m

case-erecting: ~ **filling and closing machine** n PACKAGING machine pour dresser remplir et fermer les cartons f

case-hardened: ~ **steel** n MECH materials acier cémenté m

casein n CHEM, FOOD TECH, P&R caséine f; ~ **acid** n FOOD TECH caséine acide f; ~ **glue** n FOOD TECH colle à base de caséine f; ~ **hydrolysate** n FOOD TECH hydrolysat de caséine m; ~ **paint** n COLOURS peinture à la caséine f

caseinate: ~ **gum** n FOOD TECH colle à base de caséine f

casement n C&G châssis à verre m, CONST fenêtre ordinaire f, fenêtre à battants f; ~ **cloth** n TEXTILES tissu pour rideaux de fenêtre m; ~ **fastener** n CONST agrafe f, fermeture simple f, crochet pour tenir la fenêtre ouvert m; ~ **window** n CONST fenêtre ordinaire f, vantail de fenêtre m

case-sealing: ~ **machine** n PACKAGING machine pour fermer les caisses f

cashew: ~ **nut oil** n P&R paint binder huile d'acajou f

cashey: ~ **box** n C&G pontil à boîte m

casing n C&G chemise f, CINEMAT boîtier m, carter m, CONST around door, window bâti m, bâti dormant m, huisserie f, ELEC of motor carter m, FOOD TECH for sausages boyau m, GAS TECH cuvelage m, HYDR EQUIP of centrifuge pump corps m, of fan carter m, of turbine corps de turbine m, MECH boîtier m, gaine f, tubage m, MECH ENG gears carter m, carter d'engrenage m, couvre-engrenages m, gaine protectrice contre les accidents f, NAUT light capot m, coffrage m, PETR tubage m, PETR TECH cuvelage m, wells, drilling tube m, PRINT boîte f, coffret m, emboîtage m, enveloppe f, REFRIG carrosserie f, SPACE of spacecraft enveloppe structurale f, VEHICLES engine, transmission carter m; ~ **clamp** n CONST for lowering well casing collier de retenue m, frein de retenue m, PETR TECH wells, drilling anneau de retenue m; ~ **cutter** n CONST coupe-tubage m; ~ **elevator** n CONST élévateur de tubage m; ~ **expander** n CONST élargisseur m; ~ **grab** n CONST accroche-tube m; ~ **hanger** n PETR dispositif de suspension de liner m, dispositif de suspension de tubage m; ~ **head** n CONST tête de tubage f, tête de tube f, PETR TECH tête de puits f; ~ **head gasoline** n PETR TECH essence de dégasolinage f; ~ **lift** n CONST élévateur de tubage m; ~ **line** n CONST colonne de tubage f, colonne de tubes f; ~ **packer** n CONST garniture étanche pour tubage f; ~ **perforation** n PETR TECH wells, drilling perforation du cuvelage f; ~ **pipe** n MINING boring tube perforateur m, WATER SUPP tubage d'un puits m; ~ **set** n PETR TECH wells, drilling sabot de cuvelage m; ~ **shoe** n GAS TECH sabot de cuvelage m; ~ **spear** n CONST arrache-tuyau m

casing-in n PRINT emboîtage m, endossure f, reliure f; ~ **machine** n PRINT machine à emboîter f

Cassegrain: ~ **aerial** n PHYS antenne Cassegrain f; ~ **antenna** n SPACE communications antenne Cassegrain f; ~ **telescope** n ASTRON, PHYS télescope Cassegrain m

cassette n CINEMAT, DP cassette f, OPT optical disc enveloppe de protection f, PHOTO, RECORDING, TV cassette f; ~ **compartment** n RECORDING logement de cassette m; ~ **loading** n CINEMAT chargement par cassette m; ~ **recorder** n INSTRUMENT enregistreur de cassette m; ~ **tape recorder** n RECORDING enregistreur à cassette m, magnétophone à cassette m

cassia: ~ **oil** n FOOD TECH essence de cannelle de Chine f

Cassini: ~ **division** n ASTRON of Saturn's rings division Cassini f

Cassiopeia n ASTRON Cassiopée f

cassiterite n MINERAL cassitérite f

cast[1] adj PROD ENG coulé, fondu, moulé, venu de fonte, venu à la coulée

cast[2] n C&G, PROD ENG coulée f; ~ **bronze** n MECH materials bronze coulé m; ~ **coating** n PAPER TECH, PRINT couchage au glacis m; ~ **film** n P&R feuille mince coulée f; ~ **gate** n PROD ENG founding coulée f, jet de coulée m, trou de coulée m; ~ **glass** n C&G verre coulé m; ~ **house** n PROD ENG blast furnace halle de coulée f; ~ **iron** n MECH materials, MECH ENG, PAPER TECH fonte f; ~ **nail** n CONST clou fondu m; ~ **scrap** n PROD ENG bocage de fonte m, débris de fonte m, déchets de fonderie m pl, scraps de fonderie m pl, vieilles fontes f pl; ~ **steel** n PAPER TECH, PROD ENG acier moulé m

cast[3] vt C&G plate glass couler, MECH ENG couler, fondre, mouler, NAUT abattre, PAPER TECH fondre, PROD ENG ingot couler, iron mouler, lathe bed faire venir de fonte, fondre, jeter; ~ **in open sand** vt PROD ENG couler à découvert; ~ **off** vt NAUT mooring lines larguer, PRINT calibrer

cast:[4] **be ~** vi PROD ENG se couler, se mouler, venir de fonte, venir à la coulée, être fondu, être moulé NAUT virer, PROD ENG se mouler; ~ **anchor** vi NAUT jeter l'ancre; ~ **off** vi NAUT ship démarrer

castable n C&G béton réfractaire m

cast-coated adj PAPER TECH couché à haut brillant

castellated: ~ **head fastener** n MECH ENG élément de fixation à tête à créneaux m; ~ **nut** n CONST écrou crénelé m, écrou à créneaux m, MECH ENG écrou crénelé m

caster n PRINT fondeuse f, PROD ENG person couleur m, fondeur m, swivelling roller, wheel galet pivotant m, roulette f, swivelling, roller roulette f

casting n C&G plate glass coulée f, refractories coulage m, MECH materials pièce moulée f, MECH ENG pièce de fonderie f, P&R pièce coulée f, moulding process coulée f, PAPER TECH pièce moulée f, PRINT caractère de

plomb *m*, pièce de fonderie *f*, PROD ENG coulage *m*,
fonte *f*, jet *m*, ingot coulée *f*, *metals* moulage *m*, *object
cast in mould* coulé *m*, pièce *f*, pièce coulée *f*, pièce de
fonderie *f*, pièce de fonte *f*, pièce fondue *f*, pièce
moulée *f*, PROP MAT pièce moulée *f*; ~ **box** *n* PAPER
TECH moule *m*, PROD ENG *moulding flask* châssis *m*,
châssis de fonderie *m*, châssis de moulage *m*; ~ **crane** *n*
C&G pont verseur *m*; ~ **in molds** *n* (AmE), ~ **in moulds**
n (BrE) PROD ENG coulage dans les moules *m*; ~ **ladle**
n PROD ENG *foundry* poche *f*, poche de coulée *f*, poche
de fonderie *f*, poche à fonte *f*; ~ **lip** *n* C&G lèvre de
coulée *f*; ~ **machine** *n* PAPER TECH fondeuse *f*; ~ **mold** *n*
(AmE), ~ **mould** *n* (BrE) MECH ENG, P&R moule   pour
moulage par coulée *m*; ~ **on** *n* PROD ENG *founding*
coulée sur métal *f*, soudure par la fonte liquide *f*; ~
pattern *n* MECH *materials* modèle de fonderie *m*; ~ **pit** *n*
PROD ENG *iron foundry* fosse de coulée *f*, *steel works*
bassin *m*, bassin de coulée *m*; ~ **roller** *n* C&G rouleau
lamineur *m*; ~ **scar** *n* C&G cicatrice de coulée *f*; ~ **slip** *n*
C&G barbotine de coulage *f*; ~ **table** *n* C&G table de
coulée *f*; ~ **temperature** *n* PROP MAT température de
coulée *f*; ~ **template** *n* PAPER TECH gabarit à cire *m*; ~
unit *n* C&G lamineuse *f*

cast-in-place: ~ **pile** *n* COAL TECH pieu moulé dans le
sol *m*

cast-iron: ~ **elbow** *n* CONST coude en fonte *m*; ~ **joint** *n*
CONST assemblage de la fonte *m*; ~ **pipe** *n* CONST
conduit en fonte *m*, tuyau de fonte *m*; ~ **pipeline** *n*
MECH ENG tuyauterie en fonte *f*

castle: ~ **nut** *n* CONST écrou crénelé *m*,   écrou à créneaux *m*, MECH ENG écrou à créneaux *m*

castor *n* MECH ENG roulette pivotante *f*, *machine tool
accessory* roue pivotante *f*; ~ **oil** *n* P&R *paint binder*
huile de ricin *f*

castorin *n* CHEM castorine *f*

cat: ~ **cracker** *n* PETR TECH unité de craquage catalytique *f*; ~ **whisker** *n* PROD ENG tige souple à ressort *f*; ~
whisker head *n* PROD ENG tête à tige souple à ressort *f*

CAT *abbr (computer-aided testing)* COMP vérification
assistée par ordinateur *f*

cat's: ~ **eye** *n* (TM) C&G cataphote *m*, CONST catadioptre *m*, oeil-de-chat *m*, MINERAL oeil-de-chat *m*; ~ **eye
quartz** *n* MINERAL quartz oeil-de- chat *m*; ~ **paw** *n*
NAUT *on surface of water* fraîcheur *f*, gueule-de-raie *f*,
risette *f*, risée *f*; ~ **whisker transistor** *n* ELECTRON
transistor à pointes *m*

cataclasis *n* GEOL cataclase *f*

cataclysm *n* GEOL cataclysme *m*

catadioptric[1] *adj* PHYS catadioptrique

catadioptric[2] *n* ASTRON catadioptrique

catalase *n* CHEM, FOOD TECH catalase *f*

catalog *n* (AmE), **catalogue** *n* (BrE) COMP, DP catalogue *m*, répertoire *m*; ~ **number** *n* PROD ENG référence *f*

catalysis *n* CHEM, FOOD TECH, PROP MAT catalyse *f*

catalyst *n* CHEM, GAS TECH, NAUT *boatbuilding material*,
P&R, PETR TECH, PROP MAT, TEXTILES, VEHICLES *exhaust system* catalyseur *m*; ~ **activity** *n* PROP MAT
activité du catalyseur *f*; ~ **bed** *n* NUCLEAR lit catalytique *m*; ~ **poison** *n* POLLUTION poison de catalyseur *m*

catalytic[1] *adj* CHEM catalytique

catalytic:[2] ~ **bomb** *n* CHEM TECH bombe catalytique *f*; ~
converter *n* (BrE) *(cf catalytic muffler)* AUTO pot
catalytique *m*, POLLUTION, TRANSP, VEHICLES convertisseur catalytique *m*; ~ **cracking** *n* CHEM *of heavy
oil*, PETR TECH craquage catalytique *m*; ~ **cracking
plant** *n* PETR TECH unité de craquage catalytique *f*; ~

muffler *n* (AmE) *(cf catalytic converter)* AUTO, POL-
LUTION pot catalytique *m*, TRANSP, VEHICLES
convertisseur catalytique *m*; ~ **poison** *n* CHEM TECH
inhibiteur catalytique *m*; ~ **process** *n* POLLUTION procédé catalytique *m*; ~ **reaction** *n* GAS TECH réaction
catalytique *f*; ~ **reactor** *n* CHEM TECH, PROP MAT
réacteur catalytique *m*; ~ **reduction process** *n* PROP
MAT réduction catalytique *f*; ~ **reforming** *n* PETR TECH,
PROP MAT reformage catalytique *m*

catalyze *vt* CHEM, P&R catalyser

catalyzed: ~ **deuterium reaction** *n* NUCLEAR réaction de
deutérium catalysée *f*

catalyzer *n* CHEM catalyseur *m*

catamaran *n* NAUT, TRANSP catamaran *m*; ~ **dredge** *n*
WATER SUPP drague en catamaran *f*

catapleiite *n* MINERAL catapléite *f*

catapleite *n* MINERAL catapléite *f*

cataract *n* C&G *glassworker*, COAL TECH, WATER SUPP
cataracte *f*

catastrophic: ~ **failure** *n* ELEC ENG défaillance catastro-
phique *f*

catch *n* CONST *fastener* clenche *f*, loqueteau *m*, MECH
loquet *m*, verrou *m*, MECH ENG cliquet de verrouillage
m, cran d'arrêt *m*, crochet de verrouillage *m*, doigt
d'accrochage *m*, MINING *landing dog* clichage *m*, taquet *m*, OCEANOG capture *f*, prise *f*; ~ **basin** *n* WATER
SUPP puisard *m*; ~ **feeder** *n* WATER SUPP canal d'irrigation *m*; ~ **index** *n* OCEANOG capacité de capture *f*,
indice de capture *m*; ~ **light** *n* CINEMAT lumière pour
éclairer les yeux *f*; ~ **pan** *n* C&G bac à calcin *m*; ~ **per
unit effort** *n* *(CUE)* OCEANOG capture par unité d'effort *f*, prise par unité d'effort *f*; ~ **pin** *n* MECH ENG
mentonnet *m*, *of lathe catch plate* doigt d'entraînement *m*, pivot d'entraînement *m*, toc d'entraînement
m, RAIL *vehicles* pivot d'entraînement *m*; ~ **pit** *n* CONST
road drainage puisard *m*; ~ **plate** *n* MECH ENG plaque
d'accrochage *f*, *lathe* mandrin à toc *m*, plateau
pousse-toc *m*, plateau-toc *m*; ~ **points** *n pl* RAIL aiguille de déraillement *f*; ~ **quota** *n* OCEANOG quota *m*

catchability: ~ **coefficient** *n* OCEANOG capacité de capture *f*, coefficient de capturabilité *m*, indice de
capture *m*, possibilité de capture *f*

catcher: ~ **cavity** *n* ELECTRON *klystron* cavité résonnante
de sortie *f*; ~ **space** *n* ELECTRON *klystron* espace d'excitation *m*

catching *n* WATER SUPP captage *m*, captation *f*

catchline *n* PRINT accroche *f*, slogan accroche *m*

catchment *n* WATER SUPP captage *m*, captation *f*; ~ **area**
n CONST, FUELLESS bassin versant *m*, HYDROL *impluvium* bassin hydrographique *m*; ~ **area response lag** *n*
HYDROL délai de réponse d'un bassin versant *m*; ~
basin *n* HYDROL bassin de drainage *m*, bassin versant
m, impluvium *m*, réservoir de retenue d'eau *m*, WA-
TER SUPP bassin hydrographique *m*

catchpot *n* PETR TECH *piping, refinery* pot de purge *m*

catechol *n* CHEM catéchine *f*

catecholamine *n* CHEM catéchinamine *f*

catechutannic *adj* CHEM catéchutannique

category *n* PATENTS catégorie *f*

catenary[1] *adj* GEOM caténaire

catenary[2] *n* GEOM arc en chaînette *m*, chaînette *f*, courbe
en chaînette *f*, MECH, NAUT *chain* chaînette *f*, PHYS,
RAIL caténaire *f*; ~ **support** *n* RAIL poteau caténaire *m*

catenation *n* CHEM *chain formation* enchaînement *m*

catenoid *n* GEOM caténoïde *f*

catergol *n* SPACE *spacecraft* catergol *m*

caterpillar n MILIT *on tank* chenille f; ~ **grinder** n PAPER
TECH défibreur à chaîne m; ~ **hauling scraper** n
TRANSP décapeuse f, décapeuse sur chenilles f; ~ **trac-
tor** n MILIT tracteur à chenilles m

cathartic adj CHEM cathartique

cathead n MECH ENG manchon de centrage m, PETR
poupée de cabestan f

cathedral: ~ **glass** n C&G verre cathédrale m

cathepsin n CHEM cathepsine f

cathetometer n LAB EQUIP, PHYS cathétomètre m

cathode n ELEC, ELEC ENG, PHYS, TV cathode f; ~ **beam** n
ELECTRON faisceau cathodique m; ~ **circuit** n ELEC ENG
circuit cathodique m; ~ **dark space** n ELEC ENG zone
obscure cathodique f; ~ **disintegration** n ELEC ENG
destruction de la cathode f; ~ **drop** n GAS TECH chute
cathodique f; ~ **follower** n ELEC ENG montage catho-
dyne m, PHYS montage à cathode asservie m; ~ **glow** n
PHYS lueur cathodique f; ~ **modulation** n ELECTRON
modulation par la cathode f; ~ **ray** n ELECTRON, PHYS
rayon cathodique m, RAD PHYS rayon de cathode m,
TV rayon cathodique m; ~ **ray beam** n TV faisceau de
rayons cathodiques m; ~ **ray direction finder** n TELE-
COM radiogoniomètre à tube cathodique m; ~ **ray
oscilloscope** n ELECTRON, PHYS oscilloscope à rayons
cathodiques m, RAD PHYS oscilloscope à rayons de
cathode m; ~ **ray screen** n TELECOM écran cathodique
m; ~ **ray tube** n (CRT) COMP, ELEC *display*, ELECTRON,
PRINT, SAFETY, TV tube à rayons cathodiques m
(TRC); ~ **screen** n TV écran cathodique m; ~ **spot** n
ELEC ENG tache cathodique f; ~ **sputtering** n ELEC ENG,
METALL pulvérisation cathodique f

cathodic: ~ **etching** n METALL attaque cathodique f; ~
oxide coating n COATINGS revêtement de protection
cathodique m; ~ **protection** n COAL TECH, HYDROL
protection cathodique f

cathodoluminescence n ELEC ENG, PHYS cathodoluminescence f

cation n CHEM, ELEC, HYDROL, PHYS, RAD PHYS cation m;
~ **denudation rate** n POLLUTION TAC, TDC, taux
d'appauvrissement en cations m, taux d'élimination
des cations m, taux de dénudation des cations m; ~
exchange n HYDROL échange de cations m; ~ **exchange capacity** n (CEC) GEOL, PETR TECH capacité
d'échange cationique f (CEC), POLLUTION capacité
d'échange cationique f, pouvoir d'échange cationique m; ~ **exchanger** n COAL TECH échangeur
cationique m

cationic adj CHEM *group, compound*, COAL TECH,
HYDROL cationique

cattle: ~ **car** n (AmE) (*cf cattle wagon*) RAIL wagon à
bestiaux m; ~ **grid** n CONST *on roads* saut de mouton m;
~ **truck** n TRANSP camion à bestiaux m; ~ **wagon** n
(BrE) (*cf cattle car*) RAIL wagon à bestiaux m

catwalk n CONST, MECH passerelle f, NUCLEAR galerie
d'accès f, passerelle f

Cauer: ~ **filter** n PHYS filtre de Cauer m

cauldron n MINING cloche f, PROD ENG chaudron m

caulk vt MECH ENG, NAUT *boatbuilding, maintenance*
calfater, PROD ENG mater, matir, matter

caulked: ~ **joint** n NAUT joint calfaté m

caulker n MECH ENG, NAUT calfat m

caulking n MECH calfatage m, matage m, MECH ENG,
NAUT calfatage m, PROD ENG calfatage m, matage m; ~
chisel n PROD ENG matoir m, mattoir m; ~ **hammer** n
MECH ENG marteau à mater m, PROD ENG marteau à
mater m, marteau-matoir m; ~ **iron** n MECH ENG calfait

m, NAUT burin m, calfait m, PROD ENG matoir m,
mattoir m; ~ **mallet** n MECH ENG marteau à mater m

cause:[1] ~ **value** n TELECOM valeur de la cause f

cause:[2] ~ **to subside** vt CONST affaisser, faire baisser,
faire effondrer, ébouler

causeway n CONST levée f, NAUT chaussée f

caustic[1] adj CHEM caustique

caustic[2] n CHEM, PHYS caustique m; ~ **alkali** n DETER-
GENTS alcali caustique m; ~ **curve** n PHYS courbe
caustique f; ~ **potash** n DETERGENTS potasse caustique
f; ~ **soda** n CHEM soude f, soude caustique f, DETER-
GENTS soude caustique f; ~ **surface** n PHYS surface
caustique f

causticity n CHEM causticité f

causticize vt CHEM caustifier

caution: ~ **label** n PACKAGING étiquette d'avertissement
f; ~ **signal** n RAIL signal d'avertissement m

CAV[1] abbr (*constant angular velocity*) COMP, OPT vitesse angulaire constante f

CAV:[2] ~ **disc** n (BrE) OPT disque à vitesse angulaire
constante m; ~ **disk** n (AmE) *see CAV disc*

caved[1] adj GEOL effondré, éboulé

caved:[2] ~ **area** n MINING région effondrée f, éboule-
ments m pl, éboulis m

Cavendish: ~ **experiment** n PHYS expérience de Cavendish f

cavernous adj GEOL caverneux

caving n MINING effondrement m, tombée f, éboulement
m, écrasée f, PETR éboulement m, PETR TECH *drilling*
retombée f; ~ **in** n MINING effondrement m, tombée f,
éboulement m, écrasée f

cavitate vi PROD ENG caviter

cavitating adj MECH *hydraulics* cavitant

cavitation n CONST, FLUID PHYS, FUELLESS, MECH *hydraulics*, METALL, PETR TECH *inside pump*, PHYS cavitation
f; ~ **failure** n METALL rupture par cavitation f

cavity n COAL TECH, CONST, ELECTRON, GAS TECH, ME-
TALL cavité f, MINING cavité f, creux m, espace creux
m, *containing gas or water* poche f, sac m, NUCLEAR
caverne cavité f, PETR, PHYS, PROP MAT cavité f; ~ **filler**
n ELECTRON filtre à cavités m; ~ **insert** n MECH ENG
injection moulds empreinte rapportée f; ~ **magnetron**
n ELECTRON, PHYS magnétron à cavités m; ~ **mirror** n
INSTRUMENT miroir de la cavité m; ~ **oscillator** n
ELECTRON oscillateur à cavité m; ~ **plate** n MECH ENG
plaque porte-empreinte f; ~ **resonance** n ELECTRON
résonance dans une cavité f; ~ **resonance effect** n
RECORDING effet de cavité résonante m; ~ **resonator** n
ELECTRON, OPT, PHYS cavité résonnante f, TELECOM
cavité optique résonnante f, cavité résonnante f, cavité résonnante f, résonateur de cavité m, TV cavité
résonnante f

CAW abbr (*channel address word*) COMP mot d'adresse
de canal m

cay n OCEANOG caye f

CB[1] abbr (*citizen's band*) TELECOM bande de fréquence
banalisée f, bande de fréquence publique f

CB:[2] ~ **switchboard** n (*cf central battery switchboard*)
TELECOM commutateur à batterie centrale m

CBDS abbr (*connectionless broadband data service*) TE-
LECOM service de données à haut débit en mode non
connecté m

CBL abbr (*cement bond log*) PETR TECH diagraphie
d'adhésivité f, diagraphie d'adhésivité du ciment f

CBO abbr (*continuous bit stream oriented*) TELECOM
train de bits en continu m

CBR *abbr (California Bearing Ratio)* CONST essai de poinçonnement *m*

Cc *abbr (cirrocumulus)* METEO Cc *(cirro-cumulus)*

CC[1] *abbr* TELECOM *(control channel)* canal de commande *m*, TELECOM *(connect confirm)* confirmation de connexion *f*, TELECOM *(country code)* indicatif du pays *m*, TELECOM *(call control)* traitement d'appel *m*

CC:[2] **~ filter** *n (colour compensating filter)* CINEMAT filtre compensateur de couleurs *m*

CCA *abbr (call control agent)* TELECOM agent de traitement d'appel *m*

CCD[1] *abbr (charge-coupled device)* ASTRON, COMP, ELEC ENG, ELECTRON, PHYS, TELECOM, TV CCD *(dispositif à couplage de charge)*

CCD:[2] **~ filter** *n* ELECTRON filtre intégré à CCD *m*, filtre à CCD *m*; **~ signal processing** *n* ELECTRON traitement de signaux par circuit à CCD *m*

CCIR *abbr (International Radio Consultative Committee)* TELECOM CCIR *(Comité consultatif international des radiocommunications)*

CCITT *abbr (International Telegraph and Telephone Consultative Committee)* TELECOM CCITT *(Comité consultatif international télégraphique et téléphonique)*

C-compiler *n* COMP compilateur C *m*

CCTV *abbr (closed-circuit television)* TV télévision en circuit fermé *f*

CCU *abbr (camera control unit)* TV dispositif de réglage de caméra *m*, téléréglage de caméra *m*, voie de caméra *f*

CCW *n (counterclockwise)* MECH ENG SCAM, SIH *(sens contraire des aiguilles d'une montre, sens inverse horaire)*

cd *abbr (candela)* ELEC ENG, METR, OPT, PHYS cd *(candela)*

Cd *(cadmium)* CHEM Cd *(cadmium)*

CD[1] *abbr* COMP *(compact disk)* disque audionumérique *m*, disque compact *m*, COMP *(collision detection)* détection de collisions *f*, DP *(compact disk)* disque compact *m*, DP *(collision detection)* détection de collisions *f*, ELECTRON *(carrier detect)* détection de porteuse *f*, OPT *(compact disc, compact disk)*, RECORDING *(compact disc, compact disk)* disque compact *m*, TELECOM *(collision detection)* détection de collisions *f*, TELECOM *(carrier detect)* détection de porteuse *f*

CD:[2] **~ audio disc** *n* (BrE) OPT disque compact audio *m*, disque compact audionumérique *m*; **~ audio disk** *n* (AmE) *see CD audio disc* **~ audio player** *n* OPT lecteur audionumérique *m*, lecteur de disque audionumérique *m*; **~ drive** *n* OPT lecteur de disque compact *m*

CDF *abbr* MATH *(cumulative distribution function)* fonction de répartition *f*, TELECOM *(combined distribution frame)* répartiteur mixte *m*

CD-I *abbr (compact disc-interactive, compact disk-interactive)* OPT disque compact interactif *m*

CDLI *abbr (called line identification)* TELECOM identification de la ligne du demandé *f*

CDM *abbr* TELECOM *(code-division multiplexing)* MRC *(multiplexage par répartition de code)*, TELECOM *(companded delta modulation)* modulation delta avec compression-extension *f*

CDMA *abbr (code-division multiple access)* SPACE communications AMRC *(accès multiple par répartition en code)*

CDO *abbr* TELECOM *(community dial office)* central automatique local *m*, TELECOM *(connect data overflow)* débordement de données de connexion *m*

CDR *abbr* SPACE *(critical design review)* revue critique de définition *f*, TELECOM *(call data recording, call detail recording)* enregistrement des données d'appels *m*

CD-ROM[1] *abbr* COMP *(compact disk- read only memory)*, DP *(compact disk-read only memory)*, OPT *(compact disk-read only memory, compact disc-read only memory)* CD-ROM *(disque compact ROM)*

CD-ROM:[2] **~ disc drive** *n* (BrE) OPT unité de disque CD-ROM *f*; **~ disk drive** *n* (AmE) *see CD- ROM disc drive* **~ drive** *n* OPT unité de disque CD-ROM *f*; **~ player** *n* OPT lecteur de CD-ROM *m*

CDU *abbr (crude distillation unit)* PETR TECH unité de distillation au brut *f*

Ce *(cerium)* CHEM Ce *(cérium)*

CE *abbr* TELECOM *(common equipment)* matériel commun *m*, organe commun *m*, TELECOM *(channel equipment)* matériel de canaux *m*, matériel de voies *m*, équipement de canaux *m*, TELECOM *(connection element)* élément de connexion *m*

cease[1] *n* TELECOM *telephone line* résiliation *f*; **~ sending signal** *n* CONTROL signal d'arrêt d'émission *m*

cease:[2] **~ work** *vi* MINING arrêter les travaux, suspendre l'exploitation

ceased: ~ subscriber *n* TELECOM abonné résiliateur *m*

CEB *abbr (consecutive error block)* TELECOM bloc erroné consécutif *m*

CEC *abbr (cation exchange capacity)* GEOL, PETR TECH, POLLUTION CEC *(capacité d'échange cationique)*

cedrene *n* CHEM cédrène *m*

cedrol *n* CHEM cédrol *m*

ceiling *n* AERONAUT, METEO plafond *m*; **~ altitude** *n* SPACE *spacecraft* altitude de plafond *m*; **~ baffle** *n* RECORDING baffle de plafond *m*; **~ coil** *n* REFRIG élément plafonnier *m*; **~ diffuser** *n* REFRIG diffuseur plafonnier *m*; **~ fitting** *n* ELEC *lighting* plafonnier *m*; **~ joist** *n* CONST solive de plafond *f*; **~ rose** *n* ELEC, ELEC ENG rosace de plafond *f*; **~ switch** *n* CONTROL interrupteur de plafond *m*; **~ tile** *n* CONST *building* dalle de plafond *f*

ceilometer *n* AERONAUT célomètre *m*, télémètre de nuages *m*, télémètre de plafond *m*, télémètre de plafond de nuages *m*

celadonite *n* MINERAL céladonite *f*

celestial[1] *adj* ASTRON céleste, NAUT astronomique

celestial:[2] **~ atlas** *n* ASTRON atlas céleste *m*; **~ axis** *n* ASTRON axe céleste *m*; **~ body** *n* ASTRON, SPACE astre *m*, corps céleste *m*; **~ equator** *n* ASTRON équateur céleste *m*; **~ guidance** *n* SPACE guidage stellaire *m*; **~ horizon** *n* ASTRON horizon céleste *m*; **~ longitude** *n* SPACE longitude céleste *f*; **~ mechanics** *n pl* ASTRON, SPACE mécanique céleste *f*; **~ navigation** *n* AERONAUT navigation astrale *f*, navigation astronomique *f*, NAUT navigation astronomique *f*; **~ poles** *n pl* ASTRON pôles célestes *m pl*; **~ sphere** *n* ASTRON sphère céleste *f*

celestine *n* MINERAL célestin *m*, célestine *f*

celestite *n* MINERAL célestin *m*, célestine *f*

cell *n* CINEMAT, COAL TECH, COMP, DP cellule *f*, ELEC *supply* pile *f*, ELEC ENG cellule *f*, *of battery* élément *m*, INSTRUMENT barillet *m*, LAB EQUIP *analysis* cuve *f*, PRINT alvéole *f*, cellule *f*, SPACE *spacecraft* cellule *f*, TELECOM *land mobile* cellule *f*, pile *f*; **~ boundary** *n* TELECOM frontière d'une cellule *f*; **~ definition** *n* PRINT taille de l'alvéole *f*; **~ flare** *n* CINEMAT reflet sur cellule *m*; **~ loss priority** *n (CLP)* TELECOM priorité de perte de cellule *f*; **~ parameters** *n pl* CRYSTALL paramètres de maille *m pl*; **~ polarization** *n* ELEC ENG polarisation *f*, polarisation d'une pile *f*; **~ shape** *n* PRINT forme de l'alvéole *f*; **~ side** *n* CINEMAT côté support *m*

cellar *n* PETR cave *f*; **~ deck** *n* PETR pont inférieur *m*

cellophane: ~ film *n* PACKAGING film de cellophane *m*

cellular[1] *adj* AERONAUT alvéolaire, PROP MAT cellulaire, cellulaire toéton

cellular:[2] **~ array** *n* ELECTRON matrice cellulaire *f*; **~ bottom** *n* NAUT *shipbuilding* fond cellulaire *m*; **~ cofferdam** *n* HYDROL batardeau cellulaire *m*; **~ container ship** *n* TRANSP navire porte-conteneurs cellulaire *m*; **~ dolomite** *n* GEOL cargneule *f*, carnieule *f*; **~ glass** *n* HEAT ENG verre cellulaire *m*; **~ logic** *n* ELECTRON logique cellulaire *f*; **~ network** *n* TELECOM réseau cellulaire *m*; **~ plastic** *n* P&R plastique alvéolaire *m*, plastique expansé *m*, REFRIG plastique alvéolaire *m*; **~ radio** *n* COMP, DP radiotéléphonie cellulaire *f*; **~ rubber** *n* HEAT ENG, REFRIG caoutchouc cellulaire *m*; **~ structure** *n* TELECOM structure cellulaire *f*; **~ system** *n* TELECOM système cellulaire *m*, système multicellulaire *m*, système à cellules *m*; **~ technique** *n* TELECOM système à cellules *m*

cellular-dendritic: ~ structure *n* PROP MAT structure cellulaire-dendritique *f*

celluloid *n* CHEM celluloïd *m*, CINEMAT celluloïd *m*, nitrate de cellulose *m*, PACKAGING celluloïd *m*

cellulose *n* CHEM, P&R, PACKAGING, PROP MAT cellulose *f*; **~ acetate** *n* P&R acétate de cellulose *m*; **~ acetate base** *n* CINEMAT support en acétate de cellulose *m*; **~ acetate film** *n* PACKAGING pellicule d'acétocellulose *f*; **~ acetobutyrate** *n* P&R acétobutyrate de cellulose *m*; **~ lacquer** *n* COLOURS peinture cellulosique *f*, vernis cellulosique *m*; **~ nitrate** *n* P&R nitrate de cellulose *m*; **~ nitrate base** *n* CINEMAT support en nitrate de cellulose *m*; **~ paint** *n* P&R peinture cellulosique *f*; **~ triacetate** *n* P&R triacétate de cellulose *m*; **~ triacetate base** *n* CINEMAT support en triacétate de cellulose *m*

cellulosic *adj* CHEM, TEXTILES cellulosique

Celsius[1] *adj (C)* METR Celsius *(C)*

Celsius:[2] **~ temperature** *n* PHYS température Celsius *f*, PROD ENG température en valeur Celsius *f*

cement[1] *n* C&G, CHEM ciment *m*, CINEMAT colle pour film *f*, pathéine *f*, CONST agglomérant *m*, mortar ciment *m*, GEOL *of sedimentary rock* ciment *m*, P&R ciment *m*, adhésif *m*, colle *f*, PROP MAT ciment *m*; **~ bond log** *n (CBL)* PETR TECH diagraphie d'adhésivité *f*, diagraphie d'adhésivité du ciment *f*; **~ concrete** *n* CONST béton de ciment *m*; **~ dust** *n* CONST poussière de ciment *f*; **~ injection process** *n* CONST procédé d'injection de ciment *m*; **~ kiln** *n* C&G four à ciment *m*; **~ maker** *n* CONST cimentier *m*; **~ manufacturer** *n* CONST cimentier *m*; **~ marl** *n* CONST marne à ciment *f*; **~ mill** *n* CONST broyeur à ciment *m*; **~ paint** *n* COLOURS couleur pour ciment *f*; **~ plug** *n* PETR TECH bouchon de ciment *m*; **~ slurry** *n* CONST coulis de ciment *m*; **~ splice** *n* CINEMAT collure à la pathéine *f*; **~ splicer** *n* CINEMAT colleuse à pathéine *f*; **~ stabilization** *n* CONST stabilisation au ciment *f*; **~ stone** *n* CONST calcaire à ciment *m*; **~ works** *n pl* C&G fabrique de ciment *f*, CONST cimenterie *f*

cement[2] *vt* C&G, CONST *mortar* cimenter

cementation *n* CONST *with mortar* cimentation *f*, NUCLEAR injection de ciment *f*, PETR, PETR TECH cimentation *f*; **~ factor** *n* PETR facteur de cimentation

m; **~ furnace** *n* HEATING four de cimentation *m*; **~ process** *n* CONST *mortar* procédé de cimentage *m*

cemented: ~ glass *n* C&G verre collé *m*; **~ lenses** *n pl* C&G lentilles collées *f pl*

cementing[1] *adj* CONST *mortar* cimentaire

cementing[2] *n* CONST *mortar* cimentage *m*, cimentation *f*, PETR, PETR TECH cimentation *f*; **~ material** *n* CONST matière cimentaire *f*, matière de cimentation *f*; **~ plug** *n* PETR TECH bouchon de cimentation *m*; **~ string** *n* PETR TECH colonne de cimentation *f*

cementite *n* PROP MAT cémentite *f*

cemf *abbr (counter-electromotive force, counter emf)* ELEC ENG, ELECTR, PHYS fcém *(force contre-électromotrice)*

cenomanian *adj* GEOL *stratigraphy* cénomanien

censured: ~ test *n* SPACE essai censuré *m*

Centaurus *n* ASTRON Centaure *f*

center *n* (AmE) *see* centre

centerboard *n* (AmE) *see* centreboard

centered: ~ system *n* (AmE) *see* centred system

centerfold *n* (AmE) *see* centrefold

centering *n* (AmE) *see* centring

centerless: ~ grinder *n* (AmE) *see* centreless grinder; **~ grinding** *n* (AmE) *see* centreless grinding; **~ precision grinding** *n* (AmE) *see* centreless precision grinding

center-to-center[1] *adj* (AmE) *see* centre-to-centre

center-to-center:[2] **from ~** *adv* (AmE) *see* from centre-to-centre

centi- *pref (c)* METR centi-*(c)*

centiare *n* METR centiare *m*

centigrade *adj (C)* METR centigrade *(C)*

centigram *n* (AmE), **centigramme** *n* (BrE) METR centigramme *m*

centiliter *n* (AmE), **centilitre** *n* (BrE) METR centilitre *m*

centimeter *n* (AmE) *see* centimetre

centimeter-gram-second *n* (AmE) *see* centimetre-gramme-second

centimetre *n* (BrE) METR centimètre *m* **~ waves** *n pl* (BrE) PHYS ondes centimétriques *f pl*

centimetre-gramme-second *n* (BrE) *(CGS)* METR centimètre-gramme-seconde *m (CGS)*; **~ system** *n* (BrE) METR système centimètre-gramme-seconde *m*

centinormal *adj* CHEM centinormal

centipoise *n* P&R centipoise *m*

centner *n* METR *weight of metal* quintal *m*

central: ~ battery switchboard *n (cf CB switchboard)* TELECOM commutateur à batterie centrale *m*; **~ buffer coupling** *n* TRANSP attelage à tampon central *m*; **~ charging equipment** *n* TELECOM équipement de taxation centralisée *m*; **~ claw** *n* CINEMAT griffe centrale *f*; **~ column** *n* PHOTO *of tripod* colonne centrale *f*; **~ control** *n* TELECOM unité centrale *f*; **~ control room** *n* TV régie *f*; **~ exchange** *n* TELECOM commutateur urbain *m*; **~ exchange switch** *n* (BrE) *(cf central office switch)* TELECOM commutateur public *m*; **~ exchange trunk** *n* (BrE) *(cf central office trunk)* TELECOM ligne réseau *f*; **~ focusing wheel** *n* INSTRUMENT molette de mise au point *f*; **~ force** *n* PHYS force centrale *f*; **~ gangway** *n* TRANSP couloir central *m*; **~ heating** *n* CONST, HEATING, THERMOD chauffage central *m*; **~ heating boiler** *n* HEATING chaudière de chauffage central *f*; **~ limit theorem** *n* MATH théorème de la limite centrée *m*; **~ load-bearing element** *n* OPT *optical cable* porteur central *m*; **~ locking** *n* MECH ENG serre-tube à chaînes *m*, VEHICLES serre-tube à chaînes *m*, *doors* condamnation centrale *f*, verrouillage centralisé *m*; **~**

office switch *n* (AmE) *(cf central exchange switch)* TELECOM commutateur public *m*; ~ **office trunk** *n* (AmE) *(cf central exchange trunk)* TELECOM ligne réseau *f*; ~ **power plant** *n* ELEC ENG centrale de force motrice *f*, centrale génératrice *f*; ~ **processing unit** *n* *(CPU)* COMP unité centrale *f*, unité centrale de traitement *f*, DP, TELECOM unité centrale *f* *(UC)*; ~ **processor** *n* COMP processeur central *m*, TELECOM calculateur central *m*; ~ **pulse distributor** *n* TELECOM distributeur rapide *m*; ~ **refrigerating plant** *n* REFRIG installation centrale de froid *f*; ~ **splitter edge** *n* FUELLESS *turbines* arête centrale *f*; ~ **station** *n* GAS TECH station centrale *f*; ~ **strength member** *n* OPT *optical cable* porteur central *m*; ~ **switching unit** *n* TELECOM commutateur urbain *m*; ~ **vacuum cleaning system** *n* SAFETY système centralisé d'aspiration *m*

centralized[1] *adj* COMP centralisé

centralized:[2] ~ **control system** *n* TELECOM autocommutateur électronique à commande centralisée *m*, système à commande centralisée *m*; ~ **lubricating system** *n* MECH ENG système de lubrification centralisé *m*; ~ **operation** *n* COMP opération centralisée *f*; ~ **routing** *n* COMP, DP routage centralisé *m*; ~ **system** *n* TELECOM système à commande centralisée *m*; ~ **traffic division system** *n* TELECOM système à coeur réparti universel *m*

centralizer *n* PETR TECH centreur *m*

centre *n* (BrE) CONST charpente de cintre *f*, cintre *m*, GEOM centre *m*, MECH ENG *lathe* centre *m*, pointe *f*, PACKAGING *tube on which paper is reeled* mandrin *m*, TELECOM centre *m*; ~ **bearing** *n* (BrE) AUTO palier intermédiaire *m*; ~ **bearing plate** *n* (BrE) MECH ENG culot *m*, grain d'acier *m*; ~ **bit** *n* (BrE) MECH ENG mèche à centre *f*, mèche à trois pointes *f*; ~ **bit for bit stock** *n* (BrE) MECH ENG foret à centre *m*, foret à queue carrée *m*, mèche à centre *f*, mèche à queue carrée *f*; ~ **brace bit** *n* (BrE) MECH ENG foret à centre *m*, foret à queue carrée *m*, mèche à centre *f*, mèche à queue carrée *f*; ~ **of buoyancy** *n* (BrE) HYDROL centre de poussée *m*, NAUT *boatbuilding* centre de carène *m*, centre de poussée *m*; ~ **casting** *n* (BrE) RAIL crapaudine *f*; ~ **clipping** *n* (BrE) RECORDING limiteur central *m*; ~ **core** *n* (BrE) MINING *of rock to be removed* stross central *m*; ~ **of curvature** *n* (BrE) GEOM, PHYS, RAD PHYS *of lens, mirror* centre de courbure *m*; ~ **cut** *n* (BrE) MINING *blasting* fossé central *m*; ~ **cut hole** *n* (BrE) MINING *blasting* mine d'empiétage *f*; ~ **of displacement** *n* (BrE) HYDROL centre de poussée *m*; ~ **distance** *n* (BrE) MECH ENG distance des centres *f*; ~ **drill** *n* (BrE) MECH ENG foret à centrer *m*, mèche à centrer *f*; ~ **engine** *n* (BrE) AUTO moteur au centre *m*; ~ **finder** *n* METEO *measuring* équerre à centrer à téton *f*; ~ **of flotation** *n* (BrE) NAUT *ship design* centre de gravité de la flottaison *m*; ~ **folding tubing** *n* (BrE) PACKAGING tube avec pli central *m*; ~ **frequency** *n* (BrE) ELECTRON fréquence centrale *f*; ~ **girder** *n* (BrE) NAUT *shipbuilding* support central *m*; ~ **of gravity** *n* (BrE) CONST centre de gravité *m*, MECH ENG centre de gravité *m*, centre de masse *m*, NAUT *ship design*, PHYS, SPACE *spacecraft* centre de gravité *m*; ~ **hole** *n* (BrE) MECH ENG centre *m*, trou de centrage *m*; ~ **hole with protecting chamfer** *n* (BrE) MECH ENG centre avec chanfrein de protection *m*; ~ **hung window** *n* (BrE) CONST *pivoted horizontally* fenêtre basculante *f*, fenêtre à bascule *f*; ~ **of impact** *n* (BrE) MECH centre de percussion *m*; ~ **of inertia** *n* (BrE) MECH, PHYS centre

d'inertie *m*; ~ **key** *n* (BrE) MECH ENG *for removing drills from sockets* broche de déchassage *f*; ~ **knife edge** *n* (BrE) METR *balance* couteau central *m*, couteau du fléau *m*; ~ **of lateral resistance** *n* (BrE) NAUT *ship design* centre de dérive *m*; ~ **lathe** *n* (BrE) MECH ENG tour entre-pointes *m*, tour à pointes *m*; ~ **line** *n* (BrE) MECH axe *m*, ligne médiane *f*, MECH ENG axe *m*, axe principal *m*, NAUT *ship design, motion* axe de roulis *m*, axe longitudinal *m*, PROD ENG trait de centre *m*, SPACE axe longitudinal *m*; ~ **line bulkhead** *n* (BrE) NAUT *ship design* cloison axiale *f*; ~ **line of rudderstock** *n* (BrE) NAUT *ship design* axe de la mèche du gouvernail *m*; ~ **of low pressure** *n* (BrE) METEO centre de basse pression *m*, centre dépressionnaire *m*; ~ **of mass** *n* (BrE) MECH barycentre *m*, PHYS, SPACE *spacecraft* centre de masse *m*; ~ **of mass coordinates** *n pl* (BrE) PHYS repère barycentrique *m*; ~ **of mass system** *n* (BrE) MECH système du centre de masse *m*; ~ **of motion** *n* (BrE) MECH centre fixe *m*; ~ **of oscillation** *n* (BrE) PHYS centre d'oscillation *m*; ~ **panel** *n* (BrE) AERONAUT panneau central *m*; ~ **of percussion** *n* (BrE) PHYS centre de percussion *m*; ~ **pin** *n* (BrE) MECH ENG *of turntable* pivot central *m*; ~ **plate** *n* (BrE) NAUT *boatbuilding* dérive *f*, RAIL crapaudine *f*; ~ **point** *n* (BrE) MECH ENG *of centre bit* pivot *m*, téton *m*; ~ **pop** *n* (BrE) MECH ENG pointeau *m*, pointeau de mécanicien *m*, PROD ENG coup de pointeau *m*; ~ **of pressure** *n* (BrE) AERONAUT *aerodynamics* centre de poussée *m*, centre de pression *m*, PHYS centre de poussée *m*; ~ **punch** *n* (BrE) MECH poinçon de centrage *m*, MECH ENG pointeau *m*, pointeau de mécanicien *m*; ~ **punch mark** *n* (BrE) PROD ENG coup de pointeau *m*; ~ **rail** *n* (BrE) TRANSP rail central *m*, rail de guidage *m*; ~ **rest** *n* (BrE) MECH ENG *of lathe* lunette *f*; ~ **stable relay** *n* (BrE) ELEC relais à repos central *m*; ~ **of symmetry** *n* (BrE) CRYSTALL centre de symétrie *m*; ~ **tap** *n* (BrE) *(CT)* ELEC *transformer* prise médiane *f*; ~ **of thrust** *n* (BrE) SPACE *spacecraft* centre de poussée *m*; ~ **track** *n* (BrE) RECORDING piste DIN *f*, piste centrale *f*; ~ **track time code** *n* (BrE) RECORDING code temporel à piste centrale *m*; ~ **of waterplane area** *n* (BrE) NAUT *ship design* centre de gravité de la flottaison *m*; ~ **of wind pressure** *n* (BrE) NAUT *ship design* centre vélique *m*; ~ **wind reel** *n* (BrE) PAPER TECH enrouleuse à entraînement axial *f*; ~ **wing section** *n* (BrE) AERONAUT plan central *m*, section centrale de voilure *f*, voilure médiane *f*

centreboard *n* (BrE) NAUT *boatbuilding* dérive *f*

centred: ~ **system** *n* (BrE) PHYS *optics* système centré *m*

centrefold *n* (BrE) PRINT pli médian *m*

centreless: ~ **grinder** *n* (BrE) MECH rectifieuse sans centre *f*; ~ **grinding** *n* (BrE) MECH ENG rectification sans centre *f*; ~ **precision grinding** *n* (BrE) MECH ENG rectification sans centre *f*

centre-to-centre[1] *adj* (BrE) MECH ENG centre à centre, entre-axe

centre-to-centre:[2] **from** ~ *adv* (BrE) MECH ENG d'axe en axe, entre-axe

Centrex: ~ **system** (TM) *n* TELECOM système Centrex *m* (MD)

centrifiner *n* PAPER TECH dépastilleur *m*

centrifugal[1] *adj* CHEM TECH, MECH, PHYS centrifuge

centrifugal[2] *n* CHEM TECH essoreuse séparatrice *f*, séparateur centrifuge *m*; ~ **acceleration** *n* AERONAUT accélération centrifuge *f*; ~ **advance mechanism** *n* AUTO mécanisme d'avance centrifuge *m*, VEHICLES *ignition* dispositif d'avance centrifuge *m*; ~ **and vacuum governor** *n* AERONAUT régulateur à force centrifuge et dépression *m*; ~ **casting** *n* C&G moulage par centrifugation *m*, PROD ENG moulage centrifuge *m*; ~ **cleaner** *n* CHEM TECH épurateur à force centrifuge *m*; ~ **clutch** *n* AUTO, VEHICLES embrayage centrifuge *m*; ~ **compressor** *n* MECH ENG compresseur centrifuge *m*; ~ **contact governor** *n* CONTROL régulateur centrifuge à contact *m*; ~ **contact regulator** *n* CONTROL régulateur centrifuge à contact *m*; ~ **crusher** *n* CHEM TECH broyeur centrifuge *m*, broyeur giratoire *m*, concasseur centrifuge *m*, concasseur giratoire *m*; ~ **drawing** *n* C&G étirage centrifuge *m*; ~ **dryer** *n* CHEM TECH dessiccateur centrifuge *m*, hydroextracteur *m*, COAL TECH essoreuse centrifuge *f*; ~ **exhauster** *n* CHEM TECH aspirateur centrifuge *m*; ~ **extractor** *n* NUCLEAR extracteur centrifuge *m*; ~ **fan** *n* HEAT ENG, REFRIG ventilateur centrifuge *m*; ~ **filter** *n* COAL TECH, MECH ENG filtre centrifuge *m*; ~ **flow fan** *n* TRANSP ventilateur centrifuge *m*; ~ **force** *n* FLUID PHYS, PHYS, POLLUTION, SPACE *spacecraft* force centrifuge *f*; ~ **force sizer** *n* CHEM TECH séparateur à force centrifuge *m*; ~ **hydroextrator** *n* CHEM TECH dessiccateur centrifuge *m*, hydroextracteur *m*; ~ **machine** *n* CHEM TECH centrifugeur *m*, centrifugeuse *f*; ~ **mass** *n* MECH masse d'inertie *f*; ~ **pump** *n* CHEM TECH, MAR POLL, MECH ENG, REFRIG pompe centrifuge *f*; ~ **regulator** *n* CONTROL régulateur centrifuge *m*; ~ **relay** *n* ELEC relais centrifuge *m*; ~ **separator** *n* CHEM TECH essoreuse séparatrice *f*, séparateur centrifuge *m*; ~ **skimmer** *n* MAR POLL récupérateur centrifuge *m*, écrémeur centrifuge *m*, écrémeur à action centrifuge *m*; ~ **supercharger** *n* AUTO compresseur centrifuge *m*; ~ **switch** *n* MECH ENG contacteur centrifuge *m*

centrifugally: ~ **operated** *adj* FUELLESS à contrôle centrifuge

centrifugation *n* CHEM centrifugation *f*, CHEM TECH essorage *m*, HYDROL *sewage*, WATER SUPP centrifugation *f*

centrifuge[1] *n* CHEM centrifugeur *m*, CHEM TECH centrifugeuse *f*, LAB EQUIP *separation* centrifugeur *m*, MECH centrifugeuse *f*, P&R centrifugeuse *f*, essoreuse *f*, PHYS centrifugeuse *f*; ~ **bucket** *n* LAB EQUIP *separation* godet de centrifugeur *m*; ~ **drive** *n* MECH ENG transmission pour centrifuge *f*; ~ **mill** *n* CHEM TECH broyeur centrifuge *m*; ~ **rotor** *n* LAB EQUIP *separation* rotor à godets de centrifugeur *m*; ~ **screen** *n* CHEM TECH épurateur centrifuge *m*; ~ **switch** *n* CONTROL interrupteur centrifuge *m*; ~ **tube** *n* LAB EQUIP *separation* tube à centrifugeur *m*

centrifuge[2] *vt vi* CHEM TECH centrifuger, essorer à la machine centrifuge, COAL TECH, P&R centrifuger

centrifuged: ~ **latex** *n* P&R latex centrifugé *m*

centrifuging *n* COAL TECH centrifugation *f*

centring *n* (BrE) CONST charpente de cintre *f*, cintre *m*, MECH, MECH ENG centrage *m*; ~ **bridge** *n* (BrE) PROD ENG simbleau *m*; ~ **bush** *n* (BrE) MECH ENG bague de centrage *f*, canon de centrage *m*; ~ **control** *n* (BrE) TV réglage de cadrage *m*; ~ **lathe** *n* (BrE) MECH ENG tour entre-pointes *m*, tour à pointes *m*; ~ **lens with ruled cross** *n* (BrE) C&G verre de centrage muni d'un réticule *m*; ~ **machine** *n* (BrE) MECH ENG machine à centrer *f*; ~ **nut** *n* (BrE) MECH ENG écrou de centrage *m*; ~ **pin** *n* (BrE) MECH ENG centreur *m*, tige de repérage *f*, téton de centrage *m*; ~ **ring** *n* (BrE) TV bague de centrage *f*; ~ **rod** *n* (BrE) MECH ENG tige de centrage *f*;

~ **screw** *n* (BrE) MECH ENG vis de centrage *f*; ~ **sleeve** *n* (BrE) MECH ENG douille de centrage *f*; ~ **suction holder** *n* (BrE) INSTRUMENT support de centrage *m*; ~ **wedge** *n* (BrE) PRINT coin de centrage *m*

centripetal[1] *adj* PHYS centripète

centripetal:[2] ~ **acceleration** *n* AERONAUT accélération centripète *f*; ~ **filter** *n* MECH ENG filtre centripète *m*; ~ **force** *n* PHYS force centripète *f*

centroid[1] *adj* GEOM centroïde

centroid[2] *n* PHYS barycentre *m*

Centronics: ~ **interface** *n* (TM) PRINT *computers* interface Centronics *f* (MD)

centrosphere *n* GEOPHYS barysphère *f*, nifé *m*, noyau terrestre *m*

centrosymmetric *adj* CRYSTALL centrosymétrique

cephalopod *n* GEOL céphalopode *m*

cephalosporin *n* CHEM céphalosporine *f*

Cepheid *n* ASTRON Céphéide *f*

Cepheus *n* ASTRON Céphée *f*

cepstrum *n* ELECTRON cepstre *m*

CEQ *abbr* (*customer equipment*) TELECOM équipement d'usager *m*

ceramic *n* C&G, CHEM *substance* céramique *f*; ~ **art** *n* C&G art céramique *m*; ~ **capacitor** *n* ELEC, ELEC ENG, PHYS, TELECOM condensateur céramique *m*; ~ **chip capacitor** *n* ELEC ENG condensateur pastille céramique *m*; ~ **coating** *n* COATINGS enduit céramique de surface *m*, revêtement céramique de surface *m*; ~ **color** *n* (AmE), ~ **colour** *n* (BrE) COLOURS couleur pour céramique *f*; ~ **cylinder microphone** *n* RECORDING microphone céramique cylindrique *m*; ~ **fiber** *n* (AmE), ~ **fibre** *n* (BrE) HEATING fibre céramique *f*; ~ **glaze** *n* C&G glaçure céramique *f*; ~ **industry** *n* C&G industrie céramique *f*; ~ **insulating material** *n* ELEC ENG isolateur céramique *m*; ~ **insulator** *n* ELEC isolateur céramique *m*; ~ **kiln** *n* C&G four céramique *m*; ~ **machine** *n* C&G machine pour la céramique *f*; ~ **matrix** *n* C&G, PROP MAT matrice de céramique *f*; ~ **pavement slab** *n* C&G carreau de carrelage céramique *m*; ~ **slip gage** *n* (AmE), ~ **slip gauge** *n* (BrE) MECH ENG cale étalon en céramique *f*; ~ **tile** *n* GAS TECH plaquette céramique *f*; ~ **transfer** *n* C&G décalcomanie pour porcelaine *f*; ~ **wall tile** *n* C&G carreau de revêtement céramique *m*

ceramist *n* C&G céramiste *m*

ceramoplastics *n* PROP MAT céramo-plastiques *m pl*

cerargyrite *n* MINERAL cérargyrite *f*

cerasin *n* CHEM cérasine *f*

cerealin *n* CHEM céréaline *f*

cerealose *n* CHEM céréalose *m*

Cerenkov: ~ **counter** *n* ASTRON, RAD PHYS compteur Cerenkov *m*; ~ **detector** *n* RAD PHYS détecteur Cerenkov *m*; ~ **radiation** *n* PHYS, RAD PHYS rayonnement Cerenkov *m*

cererite *n* MINERAL cérite *f*, cérérite *f*

ceresin *n* CHEM cérésine *f*

ceresine *n* CHEM cérésine *f*

ceric *adj* CHEM cérique

cerin *n* CHEM, MINERAL cérine *f*

ceri-rouge *n* C&G ceri-rouge *m*

cerite *n* MINERAL cérite *f*, cérérite *f*

cerium *n* (*Ce*) CHEM cérium *m* (*Ce*)

cermet *n* MECH *tools* composé métallo-céramique *m*

CERN *abbr* (*European Organization for Nuclear Research*) PART PHYS CERN (*Conseil européen pour la recherche nucléaire*)

cerolite *n* MINERAL kérolite *f*

cerotic *adj* CHEM cérotique

cerous *adj* CHEM céreux

certificate *n* PATENTS certificat *m*; **~ of airworthiness** *n* AERONAUT certificat de navigabilité *m*; **~ of compliance** *n* QUALITY certificat de conformité *m*; **~ of conformity** *n* MECH ENG, QUALITY certificat de conformité *m*; **~ of registration** *n* AERONAUT certificat d'immatriculation *m*, NAUT *of ship* acte d'immatriculation *m*; **~ of registry** *n* NAUT lettre de mer *f*, *French ship* acte de francisation *m*; **~ of seaworthiness** *n* NAUT certificat de navigabilité *m*

certification *n* COMP, DP certification *f*, QUALITY authentification *f*, certification *f*, VEHICLES *regulations* homologation *f*; **~ body** *n* QUALITY organisme d'homologation *m*; **~ mark** *n* PATENTS marque de certification *f*; **~ organisation** *n* QUALITY organisme de certification *m*; **~ system** *n* QUALITY système de certification *m*; **~ test** *n* AERONAUT épreuve d'homologation *f*, GAS TECH essai de certification *m*; **~ weight** *n* AERONAUT masse totale *f*

certified: ~ company *n* QUALITY entreprise certifiée *f*, société certifiée *f*

certify *vt* AERONAUT *as airworthy*, QUALITY certifier

ceruleum *n* CHEM céruléum *m*

ceruse *n* CHEM céruse *f*

cerusite *n* MINERAL cérusite *f*

cerussite *n* MINERAL cérusite *f*

cervantite *n* MINERAL cervantite *f*

cerylic *adj* CHEM cérylique

cesium *n* (AmE) *see* caesium

cesium-doped: ~ glass *n* (AmE) *see* caesium-doped glass

cesspit *n* WATER SUPP fosse d'aisance *f*, puisard *m*

cesspool *n* WATER SUPP fosse d'aisance *f*, puisard *m*

cetane *n* CHEM cétane *m*

Cetus *n* ASTRON Baleine *f*

cetyl *n* CHEM cétyle *m*

cevadine *n* CHEM vératrine *f*

ceylanite *n* MINERAL ceylanite *f*, ceylonite *f*

ceylonite *n* MINERAL ceylanite *f*, ceylonite *f*

Cf *(californium)* CHEM Cf *(californium)*

CF *abbr (control function)* TELECOM fonction de commande *f*

CFC *abbr (chlorofluorocarbon)* PACKAGING, POLLUTION CFC *(hydrocarbure chlorofluoré)*

C-format: ~ videotape recorder *n* TV magnétoscope enregistreur format un pouce C *m*

CG *abbr (connection gas)* PETR TECH bouchon d'ajout de tige *m*

CGA *abbr* COMP *(colour graphics adaptor, color graphics adaptor)* carte graphique couleur *f*, TELECOM *(carrier group alarm)* alarme de groupe de voies *f*

CGS[1] *abbr (centimetre-gramme-second, centimeter-gram-second)* METR CGS *(centimètre-gramme-seconde)*

CGS:[2] **~ system** *n* METR système CGS *m*

chabasite *n* MINERAL chabasite *f*

chabazite *n* MINERAL chabazite *f*

chad *n* DP confetti *m*

chafer *n* TEXTILES tissu croisé *m*

chaff *n* FOOD TECH *milling* balle *f*, glume *f*

chafing *n* NAUT *sails* ragage *m*, NUCLEAR écorçage *m*; **~ plate** *n* MECH ENG plaque de friction *f*, plaque de frottement *f*; **~ strip** *n* AERONAUT bande de frottement *f*

chain[1] *n* CHEM, COMP, DP, GEOL, MECH chaîne *f*, MECH

ENG chaîne *f*, chaînette *f*, METR *measurement* chaîne *f*, chaînée *f*, portée *f*, NAUT, TEXTILES, VEHICLES *timing, transmission* chaîne *f*; **~ and sprocket drive** *n* AUTO entraînement par chaîne *m*; **~ and sprocket wheels** *n pl* MECH ENG roues et poulies à chaînes *f pl*; **~ block** *n* MECH *lifting gear* palan à chaîne *m*, MECH ENG moufle *m*, *sheave* moufle à chaîne *m*; **~ bolt** *n* MECH ENG boulon de chaîne *m*; **~ bridge** *n* CONST pont suspendu à chaînes *m*; **~ cable** *n* MECH ENG câble-chaîne *m*, NAUT *mooring* chaîne *f*; **~ coal-cutting machine** *n* MINING haveuse à chaîne *f*; **~ code** *n* COMP code à enchaînement *m*; **~ conveyor** *n* MECH ENG transporteur à chaîne *m*; **~ coupling** *n* MECH ENG attelage à chaîne *m*; **~ drive** *n* MECH entraînement par chaîne *m*, transmission par chaîne *f*, MECH ENG commande par chaîne *f*, transmission par chaîne *f*, VEHICLES *transmission, motorcycles* entraînement à chaîne *m*; **~ elevator** *n* (AmE) *(cf chain lift)* MECH ENG élévateur à chaîne *m*; **~ ferry** *n* TRANSP bac à câble *m*; **~ formation** *n* CHEM *compounds* enchaînement *m*; **~ gear** *n* MECH ENG engrenage à chaîne *m*; **~ grab** *n* NAUT *on windlass* barbotin *m*; **~ grate** *n* MECH ENG grille à chaîne *f*; **~ grinder** *n* PAPER TECH défibreur à chaînes *m*; **~ guard** *n* MECH ENG protège-chaîne *m*, VEHICLES *transmission, motorcycles* garde-chaîne *m*; **~ guide** *n* MECH ENG *of pulley block*, VEHICLES *engine* guide-chaîne *m*; **~ haulage** *n* COAL TECH extraction par chaîne *f*; **~ hoist** *n* MECH ENG treuil à chaîne *m*; **~ ladder** *n* CONST échelle en chaîne *f*; **~ length** *n* P&R longueur de chaîne *f*; **~ lever** *n* MECH ENG levier à chaîne *m*; **~ lift** *n* (BrE) *(cf chain elevator)* MECH ENG élévateur à chaîne *m*; **~ link** *n* VEHICLES *transmission, motorcycles* maillon de chaîne *m*; **~ locker** *n* NAUT puits à chaînes *m*; **~ mail garments** *n pl* SAFETY vêtements à cotte de mailles *m pl*; **~ maker** *n* PROD ENG *person* chaînier *m*, chaîniste *m*; **~ pin** *n* MINING fiche *f*; **~ pipe spanner** *n* (BrE) MECH ENG clé serre-tubes à chaîne *f*; **~ pipe wrench** *n* MECH ENG clé serre-tubes à chaîne *f*, clé à chaîne pour tubes *f*, pinces serre-tubes à chaîne *f pl*; **~ plate** *n* NAUT *rigging* cadène *f*; **~ printer** *n* (AmE) *(cf train printer)* COMP imprimante à train de caractères *f*, COMP imprimante à chaîne *f*; **~ pulley** *n* MECH ENG roue à chaîne *f*; **~ pulley block** *n* MECH ENG *block and tackle* palan à chaîne *m*; **~ pump** *n* MECH élévateur à chaîne *m*, WATER SUPP pompe à chapelet *f*, pompe à chaîne *f*; **~ reacting amount** *n* NUCLEAR quantité critique *f*; **~ reaction** *n* MECH ENG, METALL, PHYS, RAD PHYS *fission* réaction en chaîne *f*; **~ saw** *n* MECH ENG scie à chaîne *f*, *for wood* tronçonneuse *f*; **~ scraper** *n* HYDROL *sewage* racleur à chaînes sans fin *m*; **~ sheave** *n* MECH ENG roue à chaîne *f*, *cupped* poulie à empreintes *f*, roue à empreintes *f*; **~ sling** *n* PROD ENG, SAFETY chaîne de suspension *f*; **~ sprocket** *n* MECH ENG renvoi de chaîne *m*; **~ tensioner** *n* VEHICLES *transmission, motorcycles* tendeur de chaîne *m*; **~ tightener** *n* PAPER TECH tendeur de chaîne *m*; **~ vice** *n* (BrE) MECH ENG *for tubes* étau à chaîne *m*; **~ vise** *n* (AmE) *see chain vice*; **~ wheel** *n* MECH ENG roue à chaîne *f*; **~ winding** *n* ELEC ENG enroulement en chaîne *m*

chain[2] *vt* CONST *surveying* chaîner

chainage *n* CONST chaînage *m*

chaincase *n* SAFETY couvercle *m*, protection de chaîne *f*, VEHICLES *transmission, motorcycles* carter de chaîne *m*

chain-driven *adj* MECH ENG actionné par chaîne, à commande par chaîne

chained: ~ file *n* COMP fichier chaîné *m*; **~ list** *n* COMP liste chaînée *f*

chaining *n* COMP, CONST chaînage *m*; ~ **search** *n* COMP, DP recherche par chaînage *f*

chainman *n* CONST *surveying* chaîneur *m*, porte-chaîne *m*

chain-oiled: ~ **bearing** *n* MECH ENG palier à graissage automatique par chaîne *m*

chainsmith *n* PROD ENG *person* chaînetier *m*, chaînier *m*, chaîniste *m*

chair *n* C&G banc de verrier *m*; ~ **arm** *n* C&G bardelle *f*; ~ **lift** *n* TRANSP télésiège *m*

chalcanthite *n* MINERAL chalcanthite *f*, cyanose *f*, cyanosite *f*

chalcedony *n* MINERAL calcédoine *f*

chalcedonyx *n* MINERAL calcédonix *m*

chalcocite *n* MINERAL chalcocite *f*

chalcogenide: ~ **glass** *n* C&G verre de chalcogénure *m*

chalcolite *n* MINERAL chalcolite *f*

chalcomenite *n* MINERAL chalcoménite *f*

chalcone *n* CHEM chalcone *f*

chalcophanite *n* MINERAL chalcophanite *f*

chalcophilous *adj* PROP MAT chalcophile

chalcophyllite *n* MINERAL chalcophyllite *f*

chalcopyrite *n* MINERAL chalcopyrite *f*

chalcopyrrhotine *n* MINERAL chalcopyrrhotite *f*

chalcopyrrhotite *n* MINERAL chalcopyrrhotite *f*

chalcosiderite *n* MINERAL chalcosidérite *f*

chalcosine *n* MINERAL chalcocite *f*

chalcostibite *n* MINERAL chalcostibite *f*

chalcotrichite *n* MINERAL chalcotrichite *f*

chaldron *n* METR mesure à charbon *f*, mesure à coke *f*

chalk *n* C&G chaux *f*, GEOL craie *f*; ~ **formation** *n* WATER SUPP karst *m*; ~ **marl** *n* CONST craie bleue *f*, craie marneuse *f*, GEOL craie marneuse *f*, marne calcaire *f*; ~ **strata** *n* CONST couche de craie *f*, strate de craie *f*

chalking *n* P&R *coating* farinage *m*, PRINT crayeuse *f*, impression poudreuse *f*

chalkomorphite *n* MINERAL chalcomorphite *f*

chalky *adj* GEOL crayeux

chalybite *n* MINERAL chalybite *f*

Chamaeleon *n* ASTRON Caméléon *m*

chamber *n* CHEM, MECH chambre *f*, MECH ENG *of injector* chambre *f*, cheminée *f*, mélangeur *m*, MINING taille *f*, *blasting* chambre de mine *f*, fourneau de mine *m*, mine *f*, trou de mine *m*, WATER SUPP *of canal lock* chambre *f*, chambre d'écluse *f*, chambre des portes *f*, coffre *m*, sas *m*; ~ **acid** *n* CHEM TECH acide de chambre *m*; ~ **ascent** *n* AERONAUT montée en caisson *f*; ~ **crystals** *n pl* CHEM TECH cristaux de chambre *m pl*; ~ **process** *n* CHEM TECH procédé des chambres *m*

chambered: ~ **core** *n* PROD ENG *founding* noyau chambré *m*; ~ **eccentric** *n* MECH ENG excentrique évidé *m*; ~ **hole** *n* MINING *blasting* mine chambrée *f*

chambering *n* MINING sautage en pochées *m*, sautage par mines pochées *m*

chamber-type: ~ **vacuum sealing** *n* PACKAGING chambre pour fermeture hermétique *f*

chambray *n* TEXTILES batiste *f*, batiste de Cambrai *f*

chamfer[1] *n* CONST chanfrein *m*; ~ **stop** *n* CONST *joinery* arrêt de chanfrein *m*

chamfer[2] *vt* CONST chanfreiner, MECH ENG chanfreiner, écorner, PRINT chanfreiner

chamfered[1] *adj* SPRINGS chanfreiné

chamfered:[2] ~ **end** *n* SPRINGS bout chanfreiné *m*; ~ **joint** *n* CONST assemblage en onglet *m*, assemblage à onglet *m*, joint à chanfrein *m*, onglet d'encadrement *m*

chamfering *n* CONST, PETR chanfreinage *m*

chamois *n* CONST, PROD ENG chamois *m*, peau de chamois *f*

chamosite *n* MINERAL chamoisite *f*

chamotte *n* C&G chamotte *f*

champagne: ~ **finish** *n* C&G bague champenoise *f*

chandelier *n* C&G, ELEC *lighting* lustre *m*

Chandler: ~ **wobble** *n* ASTRON oscillation de Chandler *f*

Chandrasekhar: ~ **limit** *n* ASTRON limite de Chandrasekhar *f*

change[1] *n* PHYS changement *m*; ~ **dump** *n* COMP, DP vidage *m*; ~ **feed box** *n* MECH ENG *machine tools* boîte de changement d'avance *f*; ~ **file** *n* COMP fichier des mouvements *m*; ~ **gear** *n* MECH ENG engrenage de rechange *m*; ~ **hook** *n* MECH ENG crochet double *m*, crochet à ancre *m*, crochet à tête de bélier *m*, tête de bélier *f*; ~ **order** *n* MECH modification *f*; ~ **record** *n* COMP enregistrement mouvement *m*; ~ **speed gear** *n* MECH ENG changement de vitesse *m*; ~ **of state** *n* PHYS, THERMOD changement d'état *m*; ~ **tape** *n* COMP bande des mouvements *f*; ~ **wheel** *n* MECH ENG *for screw-cutting lathe* roue de filetage *f*, roue de rechange *f*, roue à fileter *f*, *gearing* roue de rechange *f*

change[2] *vt* NAUT *course* changer; ~ **over** *vt* CINEMAT *of projectors* commuter

change:[3] ~ **over from gear-drive to belt-drive** *vi* MECH ENG passer de la marche par engrenages à la marche à la volée

changeable *adj* METEO variable

change-of-gage: ~ **station** *n* (AmE), **change-of-gauge station** *n* (BrE) RAIL gare de contact entre lignes d'écartement différent *f*

changeover *n* TV enchaînement *m*; ~ **cue** *n* CINEMAT marque de fin de bobine *f*, marque de passage *f*, TV marque de passage *f*, top d'enchaînement *m*; ~ **procedure** *n* PACKAGING procédé pour changer d'un système à un autre *m*; ~ **relay** *n* ELEC relais de commutation *m*, relais inverseur *m*, ELEC ENG relais à contacts inverseurs *m*; ~ **switch** *n* ELEC commutateur *m*, ELEC ENG, NAUT inverseur *m*; ~ **to stand-by** *n* TELECOM passage normal-secours *m*; ~ **valve** *n* PROD ENG vanne d'inversion *f*

changing: ~ **bag** *n* CINEMAT manchon noir *m*, pantalon *m*, sac de chargement *m*, PHOTO manchon chargeur *m*

channel[1] *n* COMP canal *m*, voie *f*, CONST canal *m*, chenal *m*, rigole *f*, *U section* fer en U *m*, *drainage* canal de vidange *m*, caniveau *m*, DP canal *m*, voie *f*, ELEC ENG canal *m*, *telephony* voie *f*, FUELLESS canal *m*, chenal *m*, GEOL, HYDROL *watercourse* chenal *m*, MECH fer en U *m*, profilé en U *m*, NAUT, OCEANOG canal *m*, chenal *m*, RECORDING canal *m*, voie *f*, SPACE canal *m*, canal de prise de vue *m*, TELECOM canal *m*, voie *f*, TV canal *m*, chaîne *f*, voie *f*, WATER SUPP chenal *m*; ~ **address word** *n* COMP, DP *(CAW)* mot d'adresse de canal *m*; ~ **allocation** *n* TV allocation des canaux *f*; ~ **allocation time** *n* TELECOM durée d'attribution des canaux *f*; ~ **amplifier** *n* TV amplificateur de voie *m*; ~ **balancing** *n* RECORDING équilibrage des voies *m*; ~ **bandwidth** *n* TV bande passante de canal *f*, largeur de bande de canal *f*; ~ **bed** *n* WATER SUPP couche de gravier *f*; ~ **capacity** *n* COMP capacité d'une voie *f*, DP débit de canal *m*, TELECOM capacité de canal *f*; ~ **command word** *n* COMP, DP mot de commande du canal *m*; ~ **configuration** *n* NUCLEAR *of MHD generator* configuration du type canal *f*; ~ **control** *n* TELECOM commande de voie

f; **~ doping** *n* ELECTRON dopage du canal *m*; **~ efficiency** *n* TELECOM efficacité des canaux *f*; **~ equipment** *n* *(CE)* TELECOM matériel de canaux *m*, matériel de voies *m*, équipement de canaux *m*; **~ fill** *n* GEOL alluvions sédimentées dans les chenaux *f pl*; **~ filter** *n* ELECTRON filtre de voie *m*; **~ induction furnace** *n* HEATING four à induction à canal *m*; **~ iron** *n* CONST *U section* fer en U *m*, *square section* fer carrelé *m*; **~ lag** *n* GEOL couche de gravier *f*; **~ loading** *n* TELECOM charge des canaux *f*; **~ markings** *n pl* TRANSP balisage d'un chenal *m*; **~ marks** *n pl* TRANSP marques de balisage *f pl*; **~ modulation** *n* ELECTRON modulation du canal *f*; **~ noise** *n* ELECTRON bruit de la voie *m*; **~ occupancy** *n* TELECOM degré d'occupation des voies *m*; **~ phasing** *n* RECORDING mise en phase des voies *f*; **~ sample** *n* COAL TECH échantillon d'entaille *m*; **~ selector** *n* TELECOM sélecteur de canal *m*; **~ selector switch** *n* RECORDING, TV sélecteur de canal *m*; **~ separation** *n* RECORDING contrôle de piste *m*, séparation entre canaux *f*; **~ spacing** *n* COMP distance intercanal *f*, écart intervoie *m*, DP distance intercanal *f*, espacement des canaux *m*, écart intervoie *m*, TV espacement entre canaux *m*; **~ status table** *n* COMP, DP table d'état des canaux *f*; **~ status word** *n* COMP, DP mot d'état de canal *m*; **~ stopper** *n* ELEC ENG anneau de garde *m*; **~ track** *n* TRANSP voie en forme de double L *f*; **~ using lower sideband** *n* TV canal inversé *m*; **~ using upper sideband** *n* TV canal direct *m*; **~ vocoder** *n* TELECOM codeur à fréquences vocales de voies *m*
channel[2] *vt* CONST canneler, raviner, FUELLESS canaliser, GEOL creuser, raviner; **~ out** *vt* PROD ENG évider
channel-associated: **~ signaling** *n* (AmE), **~ signalling** *n* (BrE) *(CAS)* TELECOM signalisation canal par canal *f*
channeler *n* (AmE) *see channeller*
channeling *n* (AmE) *see channelling*
channelization *n* TRANSP canalisation *f*
channeller *n* (BrE) MINING *machine* trancheuse *f*
channelling *n* (BrE) FUELLESS *dams, geothermal power* canalisation *f*, PROD ENG *grooving* cannelure *f*, TELECOM découpage en voies *m*, multiplexage *m*
channels: in ~ *adj* FLUID PHYS dans les canaux
channelway *n* WATER SUPP chenal de cours d'eau *m*
chaos: ~ theory *n* MATH théorie du chaos *f*
chapelet *n* WATER SUPP chapelet hydraulique *m*, pompe à chapelet *f*, pompe à godets *f*
chaplet *n* PROD ENG *founding* support *m*
chaps *n pl* MECH ENG *of vice* mâchoires *f pl*
char *vt* COAL TECH charboniser, charbonner
character *n* DP caractère *m*; **~ code** *n* DP code de caractère *m*; **~ count** *n* PRINT calibrage *m*; **~ coupling switch** *n* TELECOM commutateur caractère par caractère *m*; **~ generator** *n* COMP, DP, ELECTRON générateur de caractères *m*, TV synthétiseur d'écriture *m*; **~ outline** *n* COMP, DP contour d'un caractère *m*; **~ pitch** *n* PRINT chasse du caractère *f*; **~ printer** *n* COMP imprimante caractère par caractère *f*; **~ reader** *n* COMP lecteur de caractères *m*; **~ reading vision system** *n* PACKAGING système visuel de lecture de caractères *m*; **~ recognition** *n* COMP, DP reconnaissance de caractères *f*; **~ set** *n* DP jeu de caractères *m*; **~ string** *n* DP, PRINT chaîne de caractères *f*; **~ subset** *n* DP jeu partiel de caractères *m*; **~ switch** *n* TELECOM commutateur de caractères *m*; **~ tracer** *n* INSTRUMENT enregistreur de caractéristiques *m*; **~ type** *n* COMP, DP type de caractère *m*; **~ width** *n* PRINT chasse du caractère *f*
characteristic *n* DP, ELECTRON, MATH caractéristique *f*,

MECH ENG caractéristique *f*, caractéristique *f*, propriété *f*, QUALITY caractéristique *f*, caractère *m*, TELECOM caractéristique *f*; **~ admittance** *n* ELEC *alternating current* admittance caractéristique *f*; **~ curve** *n* ACOUSTICS courbe sensitométrique *f*, CINEMAT *of emulsion* courbe caractéristique *f*, courbe sensitométrique *f*, ELEC courbe caractéristique *f*, ELECTRON caractéristique *f*, courbe caractéristique *f*, PHOTO courbe de sensibilité *f*, PHYS, SPACE courbe caractéristique *f*; **~ efficiency** *n* ACOUSTICS efficacité caractéristique *f*; **~ equation** *n* SPACE équation caractéristique *f*; **~ floodwater flow rate** *n* HYDROL débit caractéristique de crue *m*, débit caractéristique maximal *m*; **~ flow** *n* HYDROL débit caractéristique *m*; **~ frequency** *n* RAD PHYS fréquence caractéristique *f*; **~ impedance** *n* ELEC ENG, PHYS impédance caractéristique *f*; **~ low water flow rate** *n* HYDROL débit caractéristique d'étiage *m*; **~ shape** *n* MECH ENG *of roughness profile* motifs caractéristiques *m pl*; **~ X-ray spectrum** *n* RAD PHYS spectre caractéristique rayons X *m*
characterizing: **~ portion** *n* PATENTS partie caractérisante *f*
character-oriented: **~ machine** *n* DP machine fonctionnant en mode caractère *f*
characters: **~ per inch** *n pl (CPI)* PRINT caractères par pouce *m pl*; **~ per second** *n pl (CPS)* COMP, PRINT caractères par seconde *m pl (CPS)*
charcoal *n* CHEM, COAL TECH charbon de bois *m*; **~ duff** *n* COAL TECH menu de charbon de bois *m*; **~ filter** *n* LAB EQUIP *filtration* filtre à charbon de bois *m*
charge[1] *n* C&G composition *f*, ELEC *capacitor*, ELEC ENG charge *f*, MINING *blasting* charge *f*, charge de mine *f*, PART PHYS charge électrique *f*, TELECOM charge *f*, taxe *f*; **~ amplifier** *n* ELECTRON amplificateur de charge *m*; **~ area** *n* NUCLEAR aire de chargement *f*; **~ of batch without cullet** *n* C&G enfournement sans calcin *m* (Fra), enfournement toute composition *m* (Bel); **~ build-up** *n* ELEC ENG accumulation de charges *f*; **~ carrier** *n* ELEC ENG porteur *m*, porteur de charge *m*, SPACE *spacecraft* porteur de charge *m*; **~ chamber** *n* PROD ENG *of reverbatory furnace* laboratoire *m*; **~ cloud** *n* RAD PHYS nuage de charge *m*; **~ density** *n* ELEC *capacitor*, PHYS, RAD PHYS *of particle* densité de charge *f*; **~ discharge cycle** *n* TRANSP cycle de charge-décharge *m*; **~ face** *n* NUCLEAR aire de chargement *f*; **~ hand** *n* PROD ENG chef d'équipe *m*; **~ indicator** *n* NAUT *batteries* indicateur de charge *m*; **~ injection device** *n* *(CID)* TELECOM dispositif à injection de charge *m*; **~ leakage** *n* ELEC *capacitor* fuite électrique *f*; **~ mass ratio** *n* PHYS charge massique *f*; **~ multiplet** *n* RAD PHYS multiplet de charge *m*; **~ neutralization** *n* ELEC *electrostatics* neutralisation de charge *f*; **~ parity symmetry** *n* RAD PHYS symétrie charge-parité *f*; **~ pump** *n* ELEC ENG pompe à charge *f*; **~ rate** *n* TELECOM niveau de tarification *m*, taxation *f*; **~ storage** *n* ELEC ENG conservation de charges électriques *f*; **~ storage diode** *n* ELECTRON diode à coupure brusque *f*; **~ storage tube** *n* ELECTRON tube à mémoire *m*; **~ stratification** *n* TRANSP stratification de la charge *f*; **~ transfer** *n* NUCLEAR transfert de charge *m*; **~ transfer band** *n* RAD PHYS bande de transfert de charge *f*; **~ transfer device** *n (CTD)* ELEC ENG, PHYS, SPACE, TELECOM dispositif à transfert de charges *m (DTC)*
charge[2] *vt* PROD ENG, THERMOD *furnace* enfourner; **~ at** *vt* TELECOM tarifer à; **~ by friction** *vt* PHYS électriser par

frottement; **~ the call to** *vt* TELECOM imputer les taxes à

chargecard *n* TELECOM carte pastel *f*

charge-coupled: **~ device** *n (CCD)* ASTRON, COMP, ELEC ENG, ELECTRON, PHYS, TELECOM, TV circuit CCD *m*, dispositif à couplage de charge *m (CCD)*; **~ device camera** *n* PACKAGING caméra pour mémoire ccd *f*

charged: **~ particle** *n* ELEC ENG, PART PHYS, POLLUTION particule chargée *f*; **~ particle activation analysis** *n* RAD PHYS analyse par activation aux particules chargées *f*; **~ particle beam** *n* ELECTRON faisceau de particules chargées *m*; **~ particle radiography** *n* NUCLEAR radiographie aux particules chargées *f*

charge-metering: **~ converter** *n* TELECOM CG, convertisseur de gestion *m*

charger *n* ELECTRON chargeur *m*, PROD ENG *furnace filler* chargeur *m*, enfourneur *m*

charging *n* C&G enfournement *m*, ELEC ENG charge *f*, MINING chargement *m*, PROD ENG *putting into furnace* enfournage *m*, enfournement *m*, enfournée *f*; **~ circuit** *n* ELEC *battery, accumulator, etc* circuit de charge *m*; **~ connection** *n* REFRIG raccord de chargement *m*; **~ cullet only** *n* C&G enfournement de calcin *m* (Fra), enfournement tout groisil *m* (Bel); **~ current** *n* ELEC *battery, accumulator, etc* courant de charge *m*; **~ door** *n* PROD ENG *furnace* porte de chargement *f*, porte à enfournage *f*; **~ end** *n* C&G enfournement *m*; **~ equipment** *n* TELECOM équipement de facturation *m*, équipement de taxation *m*; **~ hole** *n* PROD ENG *of cupola* gueulard *m*; **~ information** *n* TELECOM information de taxation *f*; **~ machine** *n* PROD ENG *furnace* chargeuse *f*, enfourneuse *f*, machine à charger *f*; **~ platform** *n* PROD ENG *furnace* plate-forme de chargement *f*, pont de chargement *m*; **~ point** *n* TRANSP poste de charge *m*; **~ rectifier** *n* ELEC *battery, accumulator* redresseur de charge d'accumulateurs *m*; **~ regulator** *n* SPACE *spacecraft* régulateur de charge *m*; **~ scaffold** *n* PROD ENG plate-forme de chargement *f*, pont de chargement *m*; **~ station** *n* ELEC ENG *accumulator, battery* poste de charge *m*; **~ voltage** *n* ELEC *accumulator, battery* tension de charge *f*

Charles's: **~ law** *n* PHYS loi de Charles *f*

charm *n* PHYS charme *m*; **~ quark** *n* PART PHYS quark charmé *m*

charmed: **~ quark** *n* PHYS quark charmé *m*

charmonium *n* PHYS charmonium *m*

Charpy: **~ impact test** *n* MECH *materials* essai de résilience Charpy *m*, METALL essai de résilience au mouton de Charpy *m*; **~ impact tester** *n* P&R *instrument* essai de choc Charpy *m*; **~ test** *n* PHYS essai Charpy *m*, essai de choc sur éprouvette à entaille de V *m*; **~ V-notch impact specimen** *n* NUCLEAR éprouvette Charpy V *f*, éprouvette à entaille en V *f*; **~ V-notch test** *n* MECH *materials* essai Charpy sur éprouvette à entaille en V *m*

charred *adj* CHEM carbonisé

charring *n* CHEM carbonisation *f*, CONST carbonisage *m*, flambage *m*

chart[1] *n* NAUT *map* carte marine *f*, PHYS abaque *m*, diagramme *m*, graphique *m*, PRINT carte *f*, graphique *m*, tableau *m*; **~ correction** *n* NAUT *navigation* amélioration de la carte *f*; **~ datum** *n* NAUT *navigation* niveau de réduction des sondes *m*, zéro des cartes *m*; **~ recorder** *n* INSTRUMENT enregistreur de diagrammes *m*, LAB EQUIP enregistreur *m*, registreux *m*; **~ strip** *n* ELEC *recorder* bande enregistreuse *f*, bande pour l'en-

registrement *f*; **~ table** *n* NAUT table à cartes *f*

chart[2] *vt* NAUT *navigation, hydrography* hydrographier, porter, porter sur une carte

charted: **~ depth** *n* NAUT *navigation* profondeur indiquée sur la carte *f*

charter[1] *n* NAUT affrètement *m*, nolisage *m*; **~ company** *n* AERONAUT, NAUT compagnie d'affrètement *f*; **~ party** *n* NAUT affrètement *m*, charte-partie *f*, contrat d'affrètement *m*, PETR TECH charte-partie *f*

charter[2] *vt* AERONAUT fréter, NAUT *boat* affréter, fréter

charterage *n* NAUT affrètement *m*

charterer *n* NAUT affréteur *m*

chartering *n* NAUT affrètement *m*; **~ broker** *n* NAUT courtier d'affrètement *m*

charterworthiness *n* AERONAUT admissibilité à l'affrètement *f*

chartroom *n* NAUT *boatbuilding* cabine des cartes *f*, chambre de navigation *f*, chambre des cartes *f*

chase[1] *n* PRINT châssis *m*, châssis de montage *m*, châssis à négatif *m*

chase[2] *vt* MECH ENG *screw cutting* peigner, MINING *seam* tracer, PROD ENG *rivets* repasser

chaser *n* MECH ENG *screw cutting* peigne *m*, peigne à fileter *m*; **~ die screwing stock** *n* MECH ENG filière à peignes *f*

chasing *n* MECH ENG *screw cutting* peignage *m*; **~ lathe** *n* MECH ENG tour à repousser *m*; **~ machine** *n* MECH ENG machine à fileter au peigne *f*

chassis *n* VEHICLES châssis *m*; **~ cab** *n* VEHICLES châssis-cabine *m*; **~ member** *n* VEHICLES longeron de châssis *m*

chat: **~ roller** *n* COAL TECH broyeur *m*

chatoyant *adj* MINERAL chatoyant

chatter:[1] **~ mark** *n* GEOL *glacial erosion* coup de gouge *m*

chatter[2] *vi* C&G coudre, MECH ENG cliqueter, PROD ENG brouter

chattering *n* PROD ENG broutage *m*, broutement *m*

chauffage *n* HYDR EQUIP chemisage extérieur de chaudière *m*

chauffer *n* PROD ENG poêle à flamber *m*

chaulmoogra *n* CHEM *oil* chaulmoogra *m*

chavibetol *n* CHEM chavibétol *m*

chavicol *n* CHEM chavicol *m*

cheap: **~ call** *n* TELECOM tarif bleu nuit *m*; **~ call rate** *n* TELECOM tarif bleu *m*

Chebyshev: **~ filter** *n* ELECTRON, PHYS filtre de Chebyshev *m*

check[1] *n* C&G glaçure *f*, COMP, DP contrôle *m*, vérification *f*, MECH ENG visite *f*, vérification *f*, PACKAGING vérification *f*, REFRIG, SPACE contrôle *m*; **~ analysis** *n* CHEM analyse contradictoire *f*; **~ assay** *n* CHEM analyse contradictoire *f*; **~ bit** *n* ELECTRON bit de contrôle *m*; **~ character** *n* COMP, DP caractère de contrôle *m*; **~ digit** *n* COMP, DP chiffre de contrôle *m*; **~ digit verifier** *n* CONTROL contrôleur d'indicatif numérique *m*; **~ out system** *n* SPACE équipement de contrôle *m*; **~ print** *n* CINEMAT copie zéro *f*; **~ sample** *n* CHEM échantillon de contrôle *m*, échantillon témoin *m*, COAL TECH échantillon témoin *m*; **~ sequence** *n* TELECOM séquence de contrôle *f*; **~ switch** *n* ELEC commutateur du point de mesure *m*; **~ valve** *n* AUTO soupape d'arrêt *f*, soupape de non-retour *f*, FUELLESS clapet de non-retour *m*, MECH *hydraulics* clapet anti-retour *m*, MECH ENG clapet anti-retour *m*, clapet de non-retour *m*, soupape d'arrêt de retenue *f*, PAPER TECH vanne d'arrêt *f*, SPACE *craft* clapet anti-retour *m*, VEHICLES *lubrication* clapet de non-retour *m*, WATER SUPP clapet de retenue

m, retour d'eau *m*, soupape de retenue à clapet *f*; ~
weighing *n* PACKAGING vérification du poids *f*
check² *vt* CINEMAT vérifier, COMP vérifier, CONST,
CONTROL contrôler, DP, METR vérifier, NAUT *naval*
choquer, contrôler, PROD ENG *speed* modérer, SAFETY
vérifier
checked: ~ **finish** *n* C&G bague incisée *f*
checker¹ *n* PROD ENG *tallyman* contrôleur *m*, gouver-
neur *m*, marqueur *m*, pointeur *m*; ~ **brick** *n* C&G
brique d'empilage *f*; ~ **chamber** *n* C&G chambre de
régénération *f*; ~ **pattern** *n* C&G dessin de trempe *m*; ~
plate *n* (AmE) *see chequer plate*
checker² *vt* (AmE) *see chequer*
checkerboard: ~ **signal** *n* CONTROL signal des barres
verticales et horizontales *m*
checkerboarding *n* CINEMAT montage en A et B *m*
checkered: ~ **plate** *n* (AmE) *see chequered plate*
checkering *n* (AmE) *see chequering*
checking *n* PACKAGING vérification *f*, PAPER TECH
contrôle *m* ~ **apparatus** *n* PACKAGING appareil de
vérification *m*; ~ **fixture** *n* MECH ENG *machine tools*
montage de vérification *m*
checklist *n* MECH ENG liste de vérification *f*
checknut *n* MECH ENG contre-écrou *m*
checkout *n* NUCLEAR *of nuclear power plant* remise *f*
checkpoint *n* COMP point de contrôle *m*, SPACE point de
vérification *m*; ~ **recovery** *n* COMP relance sur point de
contrôle *f*
checkrail *n* CONST *railway* contre-rail *m*, RAIL *track* rail
de guidage *m*
checks *n pl* TEXTILES carreaux *m pl*
checkshot *n* PETR TECH sismosondage *m*
checksum *n* COMP total de contrôle *m*, ELECTRON
somme de contrôle *f*
checkweigher *n* PACKAGING balance de vérification *f*
cheek *n* MECH ENG, NAUT *of block* joue *f*, PROD ENG *of
flask* chape *f*, chape de châssis *f*; ~ **block** *n* NAUT *deck
fittings* galoche *f*
cheeks *n pl* CONST *of mortise* joues *f pl*, MECH ENG *of
lathe* flasques *m pl*, *of pulley block* joues *f pl*, *of vice*
mors *m*, mâchoires *f pl*, MINING *of lode* parois *f pl*
cheese *n* TEXTILES bicône *m*; ~ **adaptor** *n* TEXTILES tube
adaptateur *m*; ~ **drying room** *n* REFRIG hâloir à fromage *m*; ~ **head fastener** *n* MECH ENG élément de
fixation à tête cylindrique *m*; ~ **head rivet** *n* CONST
rivet à tête cylindrique *m*; ~ **head screw** *n* CONST,
MECH, PROD ENG vis à tête cylindrique *f*; ~ **tube** *n*
TEXTILES tube support *m*
chelate¹ *n* CHEM, DETERGENTS chélate *m*, HYDROL noyau
chélaté *m*; ~ **formation** *n* NUCLEAR chélation séquestration *f*
chelate² *vt* CHEM chélater
chelating *n* HYDROL traitement chélatant *m*; ~ **agent** *n*
CHEM chélateur *m*, DETERGENTS agent chélateur *m*,
HYDROL agent chélatant *m*
chelation *n* CHEM chélation *f*, HYDROL traitement chélatant *m*, NUCLEAR chélation séquestration *f*
chemical¹ *adj* CHEM, TEXTILES chimique
chemical:² ~ **agent** *n* POLLUTION, TEXTILES agent chimique *m*; ~ **agent resisting material** *n (CARM)*   MILIT
matériel résistant aux produits chimiques *m*; ~ **analysis** *n* COAL TECH analyse chimique *f*; ~ **atomic mass
unit** *n* NUCLEAR unité de masse atomique chimique *f*,
unité de poids atomique *f*; ~ **balance** *n* LAB EQUIP
analysis balance de laboratoire *f*, PHYS balance chimique *f*; ~ **bond** *n* CRYSTALL, PETR TECH liaison

chimique *f*; ~ **burn** *n* SAFETY brûlure chimique *f*; ~ **coal
cleaning** *n* POLLUTION nettoyage chimique du charbon *m*, épuration chimique du charbon *f*; ~ **coating** *n*
NUCLEAR revêtement par voie chimique *m*; ~ **component** *n* GEOL composant chimique *m*; ~ **decanning** *n*
NUCLEAR pelage dégainage chimique *m*; ~ **decladding**
n NUCLEAR pelage dégainage chimique *m*; ~ **development** *n* PHOTO développement chimique *m*; ~ **
dosimetry** *n* RAD PHYS dosimétrie chimique *f*; ~ **drains**
n pl NUCLEAR drains chimiques *m pl*; ~ **durability** *n* C&G
durabilité chimique *f*; ~ **evolution** *n* ASTRON *of galaxy,
star* évolution chimique *f*; ~ **fogging** *n* CINEMAT voile
chimique *m*; ~ **grouting and freezing** *n* MINING durcissement par produits chimiques et congélation *m*; ~
hardening *n* METALL durcissement chimique *m*; ~ **hazard** *n* SAFETY risque chimique *m*; ~ **intensification** *n*
PHOTO renforcement chimique *m*; ~ **laser** *n* ELECTRON
laser chimique *m*, laser à pompage chimique *m*; ~
leavening *n* FOOD TECH *baking* levure chimique *f*, levée
de pâte par agents chimiques *f*, poudre à lever *f*; ~ **machining** *n* MECH usinage par voie chimique *m*; ~ **milling**
n PROD ENG usinage chimique *m*; ~ **oxygen demand** *n
(COD)* CHEM *sewage*, HYDROL, POLLUTION demande
chimique d'oxygène *f (DCO)*; ~ **plant** *n* CHEM TECH
usine chimique *f*; ~ **polishing** *n* METALL polissage
chimique *m*; ~ **potential** *n* PHYS potentiel chimique *m*;
~ **precipitation** *n* HYDROL *sewage* précipitation chimique *f*; ~ **pulp** *n* PAPER TECH pâte chimique *f*, PRINT
pâte chimique *f*, pâte de bois chimique *f*; ~ **purification** *n* HYDROL *sewage* épuration chimique *f*; ~ **
reprocessing plant** *n* NUCLEAR installation de retraitement chimique *f*; ~ **resistance** *n* C&G durabilité chimique *f*, P&R résistance chimique *f*; ~ **rocket engine** *n*
MECH ENG moteur-fusée chimique *m*; ~ **sedimentation**
n GEOL sédimentation chimique *f*; ~ **stability** *n* COAL
TECH stabilité chimique *f*; ~ **stabilization** *n* HYDROL
sewage stabilisation chimique *f*; ~ **tanker** *n* NAUT
chimiquier *m*; ~ **treatment** *n* COAL TECH traitement
chimique *m*; ~ **vapor deposition** *n* (AmE), ~ **vapour
deposition** *n* (BrE) *(CVD)* ELECTRON, OPT, TELECOM
dépôt chimique en phase vapeur *m (DCV)*; ~ **water
treatment** *n* WATER SUPP traitement chimique de l'eau
m; ~ **weathering** *n* GEOL *of rocks* altération chimique *f*,
altération météorique *f*, PETR altération chimique *f*; ~
wood pulp *n* PRINT pâte chimique *f*, pâte de bois *f*,
pâte de bois chimique *f*
chemically:¹ ~ **resistant** *adj* PACKAGING résistant aux
attaques chimiques
chemically:² ~ **neutral oil** *n* PETR TECH huile chimique-
ment neutre *f*
chemically-resistant: ~ **glass** *n* C&G verre résistant aux
attaques chimiques *m*
chemical-resistant: ~ **coating** *n* COATINGS couche résistante aux attaques chimiques *f*, enduit résistant aux
attaques chimiques *m*
chemicals *n pl* PAPER TECH produits chimiques *m pl*
chemico-analytical *adj* CHEM chimico-analytique
chemico-electrical *adj* CHEM chimico-électrique
chemicometallurgical *adj* CHEM chimico-métallurgique,
métallochimique
chemicometallurgy *n* CHEM métallochimie *f*
chemicomineralogical *adj* CHEM chimico-minéralogi-
que
chemicophysical *adj* CHEM chimico-physique
chemicothermomechanical pulp *n* PAPER TECH pâte
chemico-thermomécanique de copeaux *f*

chemiluminescence *n* PHYS, RAD PHYS chimiolumines-
cence *f*

chemonuclear: ~ **fuel reactor** *n* NUCLEAR réacteur de
radiochimie *m*

chemotherapy *n* CHEM chimiothérapie *f*

chenille: ~ **fabric** *n* TEXTILES tissu chenillé *m*; ~ **yarn** *n*
TEXTILES fil chenillé *m*

chequer:[1] ~ **plate** *n* (BrE) PROD ENG plaque striée *f*, tôle
striée *f*

chequer[2] *vt* (BrE) PROD ENG guillocher, strier

chequered: ~ **plate** *n* (BrE) PROD ENG plaque striée *f*,
tôle striée *f*

chequering *n* (BrE) PROD ENG guillochure *f*, strie *f*,
striure *f*

cherry: ~ **coal** *n* COAL TECH agglomérant par frittage *m*,
houille demi-grasse *f*

cherrying: ~ **attachment** *n* MECH ENG *machine tools* appareil à fraiser les angles et les axes *m*

chert *n* GEOL chert *m*; ~ **nodule** *n* GEOL chaille *f*

cherty: ~ **beds** *n* GEOL couches à chailles *f pl*, couches à
chert *f pl*, silexites *f pl*; ~ **limestone** *n* GEOL calcaire
siliceux *m*, meulière *f*; ~ **marl** *n* GEOL marne à silex *f*

chessylite *n* CHEM azurite *f*, chessylite *f*, MINERAL chessylite *f*

chest *n* C&G cachon *m*, PAPER TECH cuvier *m*; ~ **freezer** *n*
REFRIG coffre congélateur *m*

chestpod *n* CINEMAT pied de poitrine *m*

chevron *n* MECH ENG chevron *m*; ~ **fold** *n* GEOL pli en
accordéon *m*, pli en chevron *m*; ~ **notch** *n* NUCLEAR
entaille en V *f*; ~ **runner bars** *n pl* C&G chevrons *m pl*

chevron-cut: ~ **gears** *n pl* MECH ENG taille d'engrenage
en chevrons *f*

Chezy's: ~ **formula** *n* HYDROL formule de Chézy *f*

chiaroscuro *n* CINEMAT clair-obscur *m*

chiastolite *n* MINERAL chiastolite *f*

chief: ~ **building authority** *n* CONST autorité accordant
des permis de construire *f*; ~ **cameraman** *n* CINEMAT
chef opérateur *m*; ~ **designer** *n* CONST chef de bureau
d'études *m*; ~ **engineer** *n* CONST ingénieur en chef *m*,
maître d'oeuvre *m*, NAUT *aboard ship* chef mécanicien
m; ~ **erecting engineer** *n* CONST ingénieur-technicien
de montage *m*; ~ **factor** *n* PROD ENG facteur majeur *m*;
~ **petty officer** *n* NAUT *navy* premier maître *m*; ~
superintendent engineer *n* CONST conducteur de
chantiers *m*, maître de chantier *m*

childproof: ~ **finish** *n* C&G bague de sécurité enfants *f*

childrenite *n* MINERAL childrénite *f*

child-resistant: ~ **closure** *n* PACKAGING fermeture de
protection pour enfants *f*; ~ **packaging** *n* PACKAGING
emballage de protection pour enfants *m*

chileite *n* MINERAL chiléite *f*

chill:[1] ~ **casting** *n* PROD ENG *action of casting* fonte en
coquille *f*, moulage en coquille *m*, *object cast* moulage en fonte trempée *m*, pièce coulée en coquille *f*,
pièce fondue en coquille *f*; ~ **hardening** *n* PROD ENG
founding trempe en coquille *f*; ~ **mark** *n* (BrE) *(cf chill
wrinkle)* C&G frisure *f*; ~ **mold** *n*, ~ **mould** *n* (BrE)
PROD ENG *founding* coquille *f*; ~ **permanent adhesive** *n*
PACKAGING colle permanente résistante à la réfrigération *f*; ~ **proofing** *n* REFRIG stabilité au froid *f*, tenue
au froid *f*; ~ **roll** *n* P&R *equipment* cylindre refroidisseur *m*, rouleau refroidisseur *m*, PRINT rouleau
refroidisseur *m*; ~ **room** *n* REFRIG chambre de réfrigération *f*, chambre réfrigérée *f*; ~ **wrinkle** *n* (AmE) *(cf
chill mark)* C&G frisure *f*

chill[2] *vt* MECH refroidir brusquement, tremper, PROD

ENG coquiller, tremper, tremper en coquille; ~ **harden**
vt PROD ENG coquiller, tremper, tremper en coquille

chill[3] *vti* REFRIG refroidir, réfrigérer, THERMOD refroidir

chilled[1] *adj* FOOD TECH réfrigéré, THERMOD refroidi

chilled:[2] ~ **cast iron** *n* PROD ENG fonte trempée *f*; ~ **goods**
n PACKAGING produits réfrigérés *m*; ~ **iron** *n* PROD ENG
fonte trempée *f*; ~ **iron casting** *n* PROD ENG moulage
en fonte trempée *m*, pièce coulée en coquille *f*, pièce
fondue en coquille *f*; ~ **iron roll** *n* PROD ENG cylindre en
fonte trempée *m*; ~ **shot** *n* PROD ENG grenaille d'acier
trempé *f*

chilling[1] *adj* REFRIG réfrigérant

chilling[2] *n* C&G refroidissement rapide *m*, P&R *process*
refroidissement *m*, PROD ENG *founding* trempe en
coquille *f*, REFRIG refroidissement *m*, refroidissement
brusque *m*, THERMOD refroidissement *m*; ~ **injury** *n*
REFRIG *to beer* trouble au froid *m*, *to food* accident
causé par refroidissement brusque *m*, accident causé
par réfrigération *m*, dommage causé par refroidissement brusque *m*, dommage causé par réfrigération
m; ~ **process** *n* REFRIG réfrigération primaire *f*; ~
tower *n* PRINT tour de refroidissement *f*

chimney *n* CONST cheminée *f*, tuyau de cheminée *m*, HEAT ENG cheminée *f*, MINING cheminée *f*,
trompe évasée *f*, *chute raise* fendue *f*, PROD ENG
cheminée *f*; ~ **cooler** *n* CONST réfrigérant à cheminée
m; ~ **effect** *n* HEAT ENG effet de cheminée *m*; ~ **flue** *n*
CONST tuyau de cheminée *m*; ~ **stack** *n* CONST cheminée *f*, cheminée d'usine *f*, souche de cheminée *f*; ~
valve *n* PROD ENG *hot blast stove, blast furnace* vanne
de cheminée *f*

china *n* C&G porcelaine *f*; ~ **borer** *n* C&G perceur de
porcelaine *m*; ~ **caster** *n* C&G mouleur en porcelaine
m; ~ **clay** *n* C&G terre à porcelaine *f*, GEOL, MINERAL,
P&R *pigment, filler* kaolin *m*; ~ **clay quarry** *n* C&G
carrière de terre à porcelaine *f*; ~ **clay washing** *n* C&G
laverie de kaolin *f*; ~ **decoration** *n* C&G décoration de
porcelaine *f*; ~ **insulator** *n* C&G isolateur en porcelaine
m; ~ **ornamentation** *n* C&G pastillage *m*; ~ **painter** *n*
C&G peintre sur porcelaine *m*; ~ **painting** *n* C&G peinture sur porcelaine *f*; ~ **piercer** *n* C&G perceur de
porcelaine *m*; ~ **thrower** *n* C&G tourneur de porcelaine *m*

China: ~ **water** *n* COATINGS encre de Chine *f*

chinagraph *n* CINEMAT crayon gras *m*

chine *n* AERONAUT quille d'angle *f*; ~ **tire** *n* (AmE), ~ **tyre**
n (BrE) AERONAUT *motor* pneu à bavette *m*

Chinese: ~ **blue** *n* C&G bleu de faïence *m*; ~ **ink** *n*
COLOURS encre de Chine *f*; ~ **lacquer** *n* COLOURS laque
d'orient *f*

chiolite *n* MINERAL chiolite *f*

chip:[1] **off** ~ *adj* ELECTRON hors puce, non incorporé à la
puce; **on** ~ *adj* ELECTRON incorporé à la puce

chip[2] *n* C&G écaille *f*, COMP microprocesseur *m*, puce *f*,
CONST *of stone* écaille *f*, éclat *m*, *of wood, metal*
copeau *m*, DP microprocesseur *m*, ELEC microprocesseur *m*, puce *f*, ELECTRON microplaquette *f*,
microprocesseur *m*, pastille *f*, plaquette *f*, puce *f*,
MECH *of wood, metal* copeau *m*, MECH ENG microprocesseur *m*, PAPER TECH copeau *m*, PRINT extrémité
acérée de pointure *f*, microprocesseur *m*, puce *f*, PROD
ENG *of wood, metal* copeau *m*, éclat *m*, SPACE bribe *f*,
microprocesseur *m*, TELECOM *signal* circuit intégré *m*,
puce *f*, élément *m*; ~ **area** *n* ELECTRON surface de la
puce *f*; ~ **breaker** *n* MECH ENG *machine tools* brise-co-
peaux *m*; ~ **card** *n* COMP carte à puce *f*; ~ **carrier** *n*

ELECTRON porte-puce *m*; ~ **complexity** *n* ELECTRON complexité de la puce *f*; ~ **design** *n* ELECTRON conception des puces *f*; ~ **layout** *n* ELECTRON tracé de la puce *m*; ~ **rate** *n* TELECOM débit des éléments *m*; ~ **refining** *n* PAPER TECH raffinage de copeaux *m*; ~ **removal** *n* MECH ENG *machining* enlèvement de copeaux *m*; ~ **set** *n* ELECTRON jeu de puces *m*

chip³ *vt* CONST *with cold chisel* buriner, ébarber, PROD ENG *whittle* tailler par éclats

chip-and-wire: ~ **hybrid circuit** *n* ELECTRON circuit hybride à puces nues connectées par fils *m*

chipboard *n* PACKAGING, PAPER TECH, PRINT carton gris *m*

chipped: ~ **corner** *n* C&G écorné *m*; ~ **edge** *n* C&G encoche *f*; ~ **ice** *n* REFRIG glace en copeaux *f*

chipper *n* CONST burineur *m*, ébarbeur *m*, PAPER TECH coupeuse de copeaux *f*, coupeuse à bois *f*; ~ **knife** *n* PAPER TECH couteau de coupeuse *m*

chipping *n* C&G rognage *m*, CONST *of stone* écaille *f*, éclat *m*, *of wood, metal* copeau *m*, PROD ENG *of wood, metal* copeau *m*, éclat *m*, *with cold chisel* burinage *m*, PROP MAT écaillage *m*; ~ **chisel** *n* PROD ENG *cross cut* bec d'âne *m*, burin bédane *m*, bédane *m*, bédane à froid *m*, *flat* burin *m*, *round-nosed* burin grain-d'orge *m*, dégorgeoir *m*, gouge pleine *f*; ~ **hammer** *n* PROD ENG marteau à buriner *m*, marteau à piquer les soudures *m*; ~ **tool** *n* C&G pince à fionner *f*; ~ **to the weight** *n* C&G découpe et mise au poids *f*

chippings *n pl* COAL TECH sédiments de forage *m pl*

chips: ~ **exhaust installation** *n* SAFETY *for milling machines* installation d'aspiration de copeaux *f*

chiral *adj* CHEM chiral, possédant le pouvoir rotatoire

chirality *n* CRYSTALL, PROP MAT chiralité *f*

chirp *n* COMP signal sonore *m*; ~ **modulation** *n* SPACE *communications* modulation de fréquence linéaire *f*

chirping *n* TELECOM fluctuation de longueur d'onde *f*

chisel *n* CONST *for wood, stone* ciseau *m*, MECH *tools* burin *m*, MECH ENG gouge pleine *f*, MINING *earth-boring bit* ciseau *m*, trépan *m*, *hand drill, borer* burin *m*, fleuret *m*, pistolet *m*, PROD ENG *for metal* burin *m*, ciseau *m*; ~ **bit** *n* MINING *boring* trépan *m*, trépan tranchant *m*, trépan à biseau *m*, PETR TECH trépan trancheur *m*, trépan à biseau *m*; ~ **marking** *n* MECH ENG marquage au burin *m*; ~ **which binds** *n* CONST *in groove* ciseau qui se grippe *m*

chisel-and-point: ~ **pick** *n* CONST pioche à bec plat et pointu *f*

chiseler *n* (AmE) *see* chiseller

chiseling *n* (AmE) *see* chiselling

chiseller *n* (BrE) PROD ENG *person* burineur *m*, ciseleur *m*

chiselling *n* (BrE) PROD ENG burinage *m*, ciselure *f*

chitin *n* CHEM chitine *f*

chitosamine *n* CHEM chitosamine *f*

chiviatite *n* MINERAL chiviatite *f*

chloanthite *n* MINERAL chloanthite *f*

chloracetate *n* CHEM chloracétate *m*

chloracetic *adj* CHEM chloracétique

chloral *n* CHEM chloral *m*

chloralamide *n* CHEM chloralamide *m*

chloralbenzene *n* CHEM chloralbenzène *m*

chloralbutol *n* CHEM chloralbutol *m*

chloralformate *n* CHEM chloralformiate *m*

chloralhydrate *n* CHEM hydrate de chloral *m*

chloralose *n* CHEM chloralose *m*

chloranil *n* CHEM chloranile *m*

chlorastrolite *n* MINERAL chlorastrolite *f*

chlorate *n* CHEM chlorate *m* ~ **explosive** *n* MINING cheddite *f*, explosif chloraté *m*

chloric¹ *adj* CHEM chlorique

chloric:² ~ **acid** *n* FOOD TECH acide chlorhydrique *m*

chloride *n* CHEM, COAL TECH, PROP MAT chlorure *m*; ~ **glass** *n* C&G verre de chlorure *m*; ~ **of lime bleaching** *n* DETERGENTS blanchiment au chlorure de chaux *m*; ~ **paper** *n* PHOTO papier au chlorure d'argent *m*

chlorinate *vt* CHEM chlorurer, HYDROL chlorer

chlorinated¹ *adj* DETERGENTS, HYDROL chloré

chlorinated:² ~ **lime** *n* DETERGENTS chaux chlorée *f*, chlorure de chaux *m*, hypochlorite de chaux *m*, FOOD TECH chaux chlorée *f*, chlorure de chaux *m*; ~ **polyethylene** *n* P&R polyéthylène chloré *m*; ~ **polyvinyl chloride** *n* P&R chlorurede polyvinyle chloré *m*; ~ **rubber** *n* P&R caoutchouc chloré *m*; ~ **water** *n* HYDROL, PROD ENG eau chlorée *f*

chlorination *n* CHEM chloration *f*, chloruration *f*, DETERGENTS chlorage *m*, HYDROL chloration *f*; ~ **tank** *n* HYDROL bassin de chloration *m*; ~ **vessel** *n* HYDROL bassin de chloration *m*

chlorine *n* (*Cl*) CHEM chlore *m* (*Cl*); ~ **bleaching agent** *n* DETERGENTS chlorure décolorant *m*; ~ **contact chamber** *n* HYDROL bassin de chloration *m*; ~ **demand** *n* HYDROL demande en chlore *f*

chlorine-ammonia: ~ **process** *n* HYDROL traitement aux chloramines *m*

chlorine-fast *adj* DETERGENTS solide au chlore

chlorite *n* CHEM, COAL TECH, MINERAL, PETR TECH chlorite *f*; ~ **spar** *n* MINERAL chloritoïde *f*

chloritoid *n* MINERAL chloritoïde *f*

chlorocalcite *n* MINERAL chlorocalcite *f*

chlorofibers *n pl* (AmE), **chlorofibres** *n pl* (BrE) TEXTILES chlorofibres *f pl*

chlorofluorocarbon *n* (*CFC*) PACKAGING chlorofluorocarbone *m* (*CFC*), POLLUTION hydrocarbure chlorofluoré *m* (*CFC*)

chlorohydrin *n* CHEM chlorohydrine *f*

chloromelanite *n* MINERAL chloromélanite *f*

chloropal *n* MINERAL chloropale *f*

chlorophane *n* MINERAL chlorophane *f*

chlorophenol *n* CHEM chlorophénol *m*

chlorophyll *n* CHEM chlorophylle *f*

chloropicrin *n* CHEM chloropicrine *f*

chloroplatinate *n* CHEM chloroplatinate *m*

chloroprene *n* CHEM chlorobutadiène *m*, chloroprène *m* ~ **rubber** *n* P&R caoutchouc chloroprène *m*

chlorospinel *n* MINERAL chlorospinelle *m*

chlorosulfonated *adj* (AmE) *see* chlorosulphonated

chlorosulfonation *n* (AmE) *see* chlorosulphonation

chlorosulphonated *adj* (BrE) DETERGENTS chlorosulfoné

chlorosulphonation *n* (BrE) DETERGENTS chlorosulfonation *f*

chlorous *adj* CHEM chloreux

chock¹ *n* MECH *vehicles* cale *f*, NAUT *shipbuilding* cale *f*, clef *f*, clé *f*, PROD ENG *of rolling mill* chaise *f*, empoise *f*, *scotch, stopping block* cale *f*

chock² *vt* PROD ENG *scotch* caler

chocolate: ~ **coating** *n* FOOD TECH enrobage au chocolat *m*; ~ **coating machine** *n* FOOD TECH *food-processing* machine à enrober le chocolat *f*; ~ **mousse** *n* MAR POLL *weathered oil*, POLLUTION mousse au chocolat *f*

choke¹ *n* AUTO enrichisseur *m*, C&G col trop étroit *m*, ELEC *inductor* bobine d'arrêt *f*, bobine de choc *f*, ELEC

ENG bobine d'arrêt *f*, *waveguides* piège *m*, MECH *vehicles* enrichisseur *m*, starter *m*, volet d'air *m*,OCEANOG dispnée *f*, PETR duse *f*, PETR TECH *pipelines* duse *f*, orifice calibre *m*, TELECOM piège *m*, VEHICLES *carburettor* starter *m*, volet de départ *m*; ~ **circuit** *n* ELEC circuit de réactance *m*; ~ **coil** *n* ELEC *inductor* bobine d'arrêt *f*, bobine de choc *f*, ELEC ENG bobine d'arrêt *f*; ~ **feed** *n* ELEC *supply* alimentation par bobine *f*; ~ **flange** *n* ELEC ENG bride à piège *f*; ~ **input filter** *n* ELEC ENG filtre à inductance en tête *m*; ~ **plunger** *n* ELEC ENG piston à piège *m*

choke[2] *vt* PROD ENG boucher, engorger, obstruer

choke[3] *vi* PROD ENG s'engorger, s'obstruer, se boucher

choked: ~ **nozzle** *n* AERONAUT tuyère en régime sonique *f*

choker: ~ **plate** *n* AUTO volet de départ *m*; ~ **valve** *n* COAL TECH vanne d'étranglement *f*

choking *n* AERONAUT amortissement *m*, amorçage *m*, PROD ENG engorgement *m*, obstruction *f*

cholate *n* CHEM cholate *m*

cholecystography *n* INSTRUMENT cholécystographie *f*

cholesteric[1] *adj* CHEM cholestérique

cholesteric[2] ~ **phase** *n* CRYSTALL phase cholestérique *f*

cholesterol *n* CHEM, FOOD TECH cholestérol *m*

cholic *adj* CHEM cholique

choline *n* FOOD TECH choline *f*

cholinergic *adj* CHEM cholinergique

cholinesterase *n* CHEM cholinestérase *f*

chondrarsenite *n* MINERAL chondroarsénite *f*

chondrin *n* CHEM chondrine *f*

chondrite *n* ASTRON chondrite *f*

chondritic *adj* GEOL chondritique

chondrodite *n* MINERAL chondrodite *f*

chop *vt* ELECTRON découper

chopped: ~ **mode** *n* ELECTRON mode de balayage découpé *m*; ~ **signal** *n* ELECTRON signal découpé *m*; ~ **strand** *n* C&G fibre coupée *f*; ~ **strand mat** *n* C&G mat à fils coupés *m*, NAUT *GRP construction* mat de verre *m*, P&R *glass fibre reinforced resin* mat en fibre de verre à fils coupés *m*

chopper *n* AERONAUT découpeur *m*, hachoir *m*, relais modulateur *m*, vibreur *m*, écrêteur *m*, ELECTRON découpeur *m*, PAPER TECH coupeuse à bois *f*; ~ **amplifier** *n* ELECTRON amplificateur à découpage *m*; ~ **circuitry** *n* SPACE *spacecraft* électronique à découpage *f*; ~ **fold** *n* PRINT pli d'équerre *m*; ~ **fold blade** *n* PRINT lame du pli d'équerre *f*

chopper-stabilized: ~ **amplifier** *n* ELECTRON amplificateur stabilisé par découpage *m*

choppiness *n* OCEANOG clapotis *m*

chopping: ~ **bit** *n* MINING *earth boring* trépan tranchant *m*, trépan à biseau *m*

choppy: ~ **sea** *n* NAUT, OCEANOG clapot *m*

chops *n pl* MECH ENG *of joiner's vice* mâchoires *f pl*

chord *n* ACOUSTICS accord *m*, AERONAUT profondeur d'aile *f*, FUELLESS, GEOM *of curve* corde *f*; ~ **line** *n* FUELLESS ligne de corde *f*; ~ **member** *n* AERONAUT *of truss* longeron *m*

chordal: ~ **thickness** *n* AERONAUT *gears* épaisseur rectiligne *f*

christianite *n* MINERAL christianite *f*

Christmas: ~ **tree** *n* PETR arbre de Noël *m*, tête d'éruption *f*

chroma *n* PRINT composante de la chromatologie *f*, couleur *f*, teinte *f*, TV chrominance *f*; ~ **control** *n* TV réglage de chrominance *m*, réglage de saturation de la

couleur *m*; ~ **delay** *n* TV retard de chrominance *m*; ~ **flutter** *n* TV scintillement de chrominance *m*; ~ **pilot** *n* TV fréquence pilote de sous-porteuse de chrominance *f*

chromakey *n* (AmE) *(cf colour separation overlay)*

chromate *n* CHEM chromate *m*

chromatic[1] *adj* PHOTO, PHYS, TV chromatique

chromatic:[2] ~ **aberration** *n* ASTRON *telescope lens*, PHOTO, PHYS aberration chromatique *f*; ~ **balance** *n* TV équilibre chromatique *m*; ~ **color** *n* (AmE), ~ **colour** *n* (BrE) COLOURS couleur chromatique *f*; ~ **component** *n* TV composante chromatique *f*; ~ **coordinates** *n pl* PHYS coordonnées chromatiques *f pl*; ~ **dispersion** *n* OPT dispersion chromatique *f*; ~ **distortion** *n* OPT distorsion intramodale *f*, TELECOM distorsion par dispersion *f*; ~ **flicker** *n* TV papillotement chromatique *m*; ~ **resolving power** *n* PHYS pouvoir chromatique de résolution *m*; ~ **scale** *n* ACOUSTICS gamme chromatique *f*; ~ **semitone** *n* ACOUSTICS demi-ton chromatique *m*; ~ **spectrum** *n* PHOTO spectre *m*; ~ **splitting** *n* TV division chromatique *f*

chromaticity *n* TV chromaticité *f*; ~ **aberration** *n* TV aberration chromatique *f*, erreur de teinte *f*; ~ **coordinates** *n pl* PHYS coordonnées de chromaticité *f pl*; ~ **diagram** *n* TV triangle des couleurs *m*

chromatography *n* CHEM *analysis* chromatographie *f*; ~ **column** *n* LAB EQUIP colonne à chromatographie *f*; ~ **papers** *n pl* LAB EQUIP papiers pour chromatographie *m pl*; ~ **tank** *n* LAB EQUIP cuve pour chromatographie *f*

chromatospherical: ~ **eruption** *n* ASTRON éruption chromosphérique *f*

chrome:[1] ~ **green** *adj* C&G vert de chrome

chrome[2] *n* CHEM chrome *m*; ~ **alum** *n* CHEM alun de chrome *m*; ~ **color** *n* (AmE), ~ **colour** *n* (BrE) COLOURS couleur de chrome *f*; ~ **dioxide tape** *n* TV bande au chrome *f*, bande magnétique à haute coercivité *f*, bande à enduit en bioxyde de chrome *f*; ~ **intensifier** *n* PHOTO renforçateur à sel de chrome *m*; ~ **ocher** *n* (AmE), ~ **ochre** *n* (BrE) MINERAL ocre de chrome *f*; ~ **ore** *n* C&G minéral de chrome *m*; ~ **strip** *n* VEHICLES baguette chromée *f*

chrome[3] *vt* CHEM TECH chromer

chromic[1] *adj* CHEM chromique

chromic:[2] ~ **oxide** *n* C&G oxyde de chrome *m*; ~ **oxide pigment** *n* COLOURS pigment de chrome *m*

chrominance *n* ELECTRON chrominance *f*; ~ **amplifier** *n* ELECTRON amplificateur de chrominance *m*; ~ **bandwidth** *n* TV bande passante de la chrominance *f*; ~ **carrier output** *n* TV niveau de sortie de chrominance *m*; ~ **component** *n* TV composante de chrominance *f*; ~ **demodulator** *n* TV démodulateur couleur *m*; ~ **phase** *n* TV phase de chrominance *f*; ~ **signal** *n* (AmE) CONTROL signal de chrominance *m*, signal de couleur *m*, ELECTRON, SPACE *communications*, TV signal de chrominance *m*; ~ **subcarrier** *n* ELECTRON sous-porteuse de chrominance *f*, TV sous-porteuse couleur *f*, sous-porteuse de chrominance *f*; ~ **subcarrier demodulation** *n* ELECTRON démodulation de la sous-porteuse de chrominance *f*; ~ **subcarrier demodulator** *n* ELECTRON démodulateur de la sous-porteuse de chrominance *m*; ~ **subcarrier modulation** *n* ELECTRON modulation de sous-porteuse de chrominance *f*; ~ **subcarrier modulator** *n* ELECTRON modulateur de sous-porteuse de chrominance *m*; ~ **subcarrier oscillator** *n* ELECTRON oscillateur de régénération *m*; ~ **subcarrier reference** *n* TV sous-porteuse couleur de référence *f*; ~ **subcarrier signal** *n* TV signal de la sous-porteuse couleur *m*

chromite *n* C&G chromite *f*, MINERAL chromite *f*, sidérochrome *m*

chromium *n (Cr)* CHEM chrome *m (Cr)*; ~ **deposit** *n* COATINGS couche de chrome *f*; ~ **plating** *n* PROP MAT, VEHICLES chromage *m*

chromizing *n* PROP MAT chromage *m*, chromatisation *f*

chromogen *n* CHEM chromogène *m*

chromophoric *adj* CHEM chromophorique

chromosphere *n* ASTRON, SPACE chromosphère *f*

chromotropic *adj* CHEM chromotropique

chromous *adj* CHEM chromeux

chronic: ~ **effect** *n* POLLUTION effet chronique *m*

chronograph *n* INSTRUMENT enregistreur de temps *m*

chronology *n* SPACE *of launching* chronologie *f*

chronometer *n* LAB EQUIP, NAUT, PHYS chronomètre *m*; ~ **rate** *n* NAUT *navigation* marche du chronomètre *f*

chronostratigraphic: ~ **division** *n* GEOL découpage chronostratigraphique *m*; ~ **unit** *n* GEOL unité chronostratigraphique *f*

chrysene *n* CHEM chrysène *m*

chrysoberyl *n* MINERAL chrysobéryl *m*

chrysocolla *n* MINERAL chrysocolle *f*

chrysoidine *n* CHEM chrysoïdine *f*

chrysolite *n* MINERAL chrysolite *f*, chrysolithe *f*

chrysophanic *adj* CHEM chrysophanique

chrysoprase *n* MINERAL chrysoprase *f*

chrysotile *n* MINERAL chrysotile *m*

chuck[1] *n* MECH *tools* mandrin de serrage *m*, MECH ENG *of lathe* chuck *m*, mandrin *m*, plateau *m*, MINING porte-outil *m*; ~ **adaptor** *n* MECH ENG arbre de montage pour mandrin *m*; ~ **back** *n* MECH ENG *of lathe* contre-plateau pour le montage des mandrins *m*, faux plateau de montage des mandrins *m*; ~ **block** *n* C&G monture de roulette *f*; ~ **bushing** *n* MECH ENG douille porte-outil *f*; ~ **face** *n* MECH ENG *machine tools* face d'appui *f*; ~ **faceplate dogs** *n pl* MECH ENG poupées à pompe *f pl*; ~ **guard** *n* MECH ENG *machine tools* capot couvre-mandrin *m*, protecteur de mandrin *m*; ~ **plate** *n* MECH ENG plateau *m*

chuck[2] *vt* MECH ENG monter, *part* mandriner

chucking *n* MECH *tools* blocage *m*, mandrinage *m*, serrage *m*, MECH ENG montage en l'air *m*; ~ **between centers** *n* (AmE), ~ **between centres** *n* (BrE) MECH ENG *lathe* montage entre pointes *m*; ~ **reamer** *n* MECH ENG alésoir en bout *m*, alésoir à queue *m*

chuffing *n* SPACE *spacecraft* halètement *m*, instabilité de combustion *f*

chugging *n* NUCLEAR chocage *m*, ronflement *m*, SPACE choquage *m*, ronflement *m*

chunk: ~ **glass** *n* C&G bloc *m*

churn[1] *n* FOOD TECH baratte *f*; ~ **drill** *n* MINING *boring* sonde percutante *f*, PETR TECH trépan pour sondage au câble *m*; ~ **drill bit** *n* MINING trépan batteur *m*; ~ **drilling** *n* MINING sondage de battage *m*, sondage percutant *m*; ~ **milk cooler** *n* REFRIG refroidisseur à lait en bidons *m*

churn[2] *vt* FOOD TECH agiter, baratter, PROD ENG *founding* pomper

churning *vt* FOOD TECH barattage *m*

chute *n* C&G goulotte d'amenée des billes *f*, COAL TECH cheminée à charbon *f*, CONST couloir *m*, entonnoir *m*, rigole *f*, MECH goulotte *f*, MINING cheminée *f*, fendue *f*, SPACE *spacecraft* parachute *m*, rampe d'évacuation *f*; ~ **door** *n* MINING trappe de cheminée *f*; ~ **gate** *n* CONST,

MINING trappe de cheminée *f*; ~ **hang-up** *n* MINING ancrage *m*, bourrage *m*, engorgement *m*, obstruction *f*; ~ **spillway** *n* FUELLESS *dams* canal à forte pente *m*

Ci *abbr* METEO *(cirrus)* Ci *(cirrus)*, PHYS *(curie)*, RAD PHYS *(curie)* curie *m*

CI *abbr* TELECOM *(conversation impossible)* conversation impossible *f*, TELECOM *(concatenation indication)* indication de concaténation *f*

CID *abbr* TELECOM *(charge injection device)* dispositif à injection de charge *m*, TELECOM *(consecutive identical digits)* symboles identiques consécutifs *m pl*

CIF *abbr (cost insurance freight)* PROD ENG coût assurance fret *m*

cigar: ~ **antenna** *n* SPACE *communications* antenne cigare *f*

CIM *abbr (computer-integrated manufacturing)* COMP productique intégrée *f*

CIME *abbr (customer installation maintenance entities)* TELECOM entité de maintenance d'installation de client *f*

Cimmerian: ~ **orogeny** *n* PETR TECH orogénie cimmérienne *f*; ~ **unconformity** *n* PETR TECH orogénie cimmérienne *f*

cimolite *n* MINERAL cimolite *f*

cinch *n* TV glissement des spires de bande *m*

cinching *n* TV glissement des spires de bande *m*

cinchonia *n* CHEM cinchonine *f*

cinchonidine *n* CHEM cinchonidine *f*

cinchonin *n* CHEM cinchonine *f*

cinder *n* PROD ENG *forge* cale batittures *f pl*, martelures *f pl*, paille de fer *f*, scorie de forge *f*, écailles *f pl*, *slag* crasse *f*, laitier *m*, scorie *f*; ~ **bank** *n* PROD ENG *slag heap* crassier *m*; ~ **bed** *n* PROD ENG lit de mâchefer *m*; ~ **chute** *n* PROD ENG tuyau de vidange des escarbilles *m*; ~ **cone** *n* GEOL cône de cendres *m*, cône de scories *m*; ~ **notch** *n* PROD ENG orifice de coulée du laitier *m*, trou de la scorie *m*, trou à crasse *m*, trou à laitier *m*; ~ **pit** *n* PROD ENG cendrure *f*; ~ **pocket** *n* PROD ENG tuyau de vidange des escarbilles *m*; ~ **wool** *n* PROD ENG coton minéral *m*, laine de la salamandre *f*, laine de scorie *f*, poil de scorie *m*

cinema: ~ **projector** *n* (BrE) *(cf movie projector)* ELEC *lighting* projecteur ciné *m*

Cinemascope *n* (TM) CINEMAT Cinémascope *m* (MD)

cinematographer *n* CINEMAT cinéaste *m*

cinemicrography *n* CINEMAT microcinématographie *f*

cineol *n* CHEM cinéol *m*

cineolic *adj* CHEM cinéolique

cineradiography *n* CINEMAT cinéradiographie *f*

Cinerama *n* (TM) CINEMAT Cinérama *m* (MD)

cinex: ~ **strip** *n* CINEMAT test d'étalonnage *m*

cinnabar *n* CHEM cinabre *m*, mercure sulfuré *m*, MINERAL cinabre *m*

cinnamate *n* CHEM cinnamate *m*

cinnamic *adj* CHEM cinnamique

cinnamyle *n* CHEM cinnamyle *m*

cinnoline *n* CHEM cinnoline *f*

CIP *abbr (cleaning in place)* FOOD TECH *food-processing machinery* nettoyage en place *m*

ciphertext *n* TELECOM cryptogramme *m*

CIR *abbr* TELECOM *(committed information rate)* débit d'information garanti *m*, TELECOM *(carrier-to-interface ratio)* rapport porteuse/brouillage *m*

Circinus *n* ASTRON Compas *m*

circle: ~ **of confusion** *n* CINEMAT cercle de confusion *m*, PHOTO cercle de confusion *m*, tache de diffusion *f*; ~ **of**

least confusion n PHOTO cercle de moindre aberration m, pseudoimage f; ~ wipe n CINEMAT fondu en iris m

circling: ~ approach n AERONAUT approche indirecte f, tour de piste en approche m; ~ guidance light n AERONAUT feu de guidage sur circuit m

circlip n MECH circlip m, MECH ENG frein d'axe m, VEHICLES engine anneau de retenue m, anneau élastique m; ~ pliers n pl MECH ENG pince à circlip f

circuit n COMP circuit m, ELEC circuit m, montage m, ELECTRON, PHYS circuit m; in ~ n ELEC, TELECOM en circuit m; ~ analysis n ELEC ENG analyse des circuits f; ~ availability n TELECOM maritime satellite disponibilité d'un circuit f; ~ board n ELECTRON carte imprimée f; ~ breaker n CINEMAT disjoncteur m, CONST electricity coupe-circuit m, CONTROL coupe-circuit m, interrupteur à coupure m, ELEC switch commutateur disjoncteur m, disjoncteur m, interrupteur m, ELEC ENG disjoncteur m, disjoncteur du circuit m, interrupteur m; ~ closer n ELEC ENG commutateur conjoncteur m, conjoncteur m; ~ delay n ELECTRON temps de propagation m; ~ design n ELEC ENG, ELECTRON conception des circuits f; ~ diagram n ELEC schéma des connexions m, ELEC ENG schéma de circuit m, TV schéma de câblage m; ~ element n ELEC ENG, ELECTRON, PHYS élément de circuit m; ~ group n TELECOM faisceau de circuits m; ~ group query message n (CQM) TELECOM message d'interrogation de groupe de circuits m (IGD); ~ group query response message n (CQR) TELECOM message de réponse à une interrogation de groupe de circuits m (IGR); ~ integration n ELECTRON intégrationedes circuits f; ~ mode bearer service n TELECOM service support en mode circuit m, service support à commutation de circuits m; ~ noise n ELECTRONbruit de ligne m; ~ power requirement n ELEC, PROD ENG consommation de circuit f; ~ state indicator n TELECOM indicateur d'état de circuit m; ~ switch n ELECTRON commutateur de circuits m; ~ switching n (CS) COMP, DP, ELECTRON commutation de circuits f; ~ switching center n (AmE), switching centre n (BrE) TELECOM centre de commutation de circuits m; ~ switching network n TELECOM réseau à commutation de circuits m; ~ switching system n TELECOM système à commutation de circuits m; ~ switching unit n TELECOM commutateur de circuits m; ~ theory n ELEC ENG théorie des circuits f

circuit-switched: ~ exchange n TELECOM commutateur de circuits m; ~ network n COMP, DP, TELECOM réseau à commutation de circuits m

circular: ~ aperture n PHYS ouverture circulaire f; ~ arc n GEOM arc de cercle m; ~ blast aim n PROD ENG blast furnace conduite circulaire de vent f; ~ combing machine n TEXTILES machine peigneuse circulaire f; ~ cut file n MECH ENG lime-fraiseuse à main f; ~ diamond cutting apparatus n MECH ENG tourette f; ~ die set n MECH ENG centre pillar bloc à colonnes rondes m; ~ diestock n MECH ENG porte-filière m; ~ gear n MECH ENG engrenage cylindrique m; ~ gearing n MECH ENG engrenage cylindrique m; ~ level n INSTRUMENT niveau sphérique m; ~ measure n GEOM mesure circulaire f; ~ milling attachment n MECH ENG appareil à fraiser circulairement m; ~ motion n PHYS mouvement circulaire m; ~ orbit n SPACE orbite circulaire f; ~ pitch n MECH gears pas circulaire m, MECH ENG gearing pas circonférentiel m, pas circulaire m; ~ points at infinity n pl GEOM points circulaires dans l'infinité m pl; ~ polarization n PHYS, TELECOM polarisation circu-

laire f; ~ polarization of light n RAD PHYS polarisation circulaire de la lumière f; ~ protractor n GEOM rapporteur circulaire m; ~ reflector n INSTRUMENT réflecteur à armilles m; ~ saw n MECH ENG blade disque-scie m, lame de scie circulaire f, scie circulaire f; ~ scan n ELECTRON balayage circulaire m; ~ screwing die n MECH ENG filière ronde de filetage f; ~ shafts n pl MECH ENG arbres cylindriques m pl; ~ shift n COMP, DP, ELECTRON décalage circulaire m; ~ slide valve n HYDR EQUIP distributeur à tiroir coulissant m, distributeur à tiroir rotatif m; ~ thickness n MECH ENG gears épaisseur curviligne f; ~ vibrating screen n COAL TECH crible à vibrations circulaires m; ~ waveguide n ELEC ENG, PHYS guide d'ondes circulaire m; ~ waves n pl WAVE PHYS ondes circulaires f pl

circularization n SPACE of orbit circularisation f

circularize vt SPACE orbit circulariser

circular-knitted: ~ fabric n TEXTILES tricot circulaire m

circularly-polarized: ~ wave n ACOUSTICS, PHYS onde polarisée circulairement f

circulate: ~ in opposite directions vi PART PHYS of beams circuler en sens opposés

circulating: ~ ball lead screw n MECH ENG vis-mère à billes f; ~ ball spindle n MECH ENG broche à billes circulantes f; ~ boiler n HYDR EQUIP chaudière à circulation f; ~ fan n REFRIG ventilateur brasseur d'air m; ~ load n COAL TECH charge circulante f; ~ pump n HEAT ENG central heating accélérateur m, HYDR EQUIP pompe de circulation f; ~ shift register n PROD ENG registre à décalage bouclé m; ~ system n MECH ENG lubrication système de circulation m

circulation n PETR TECH drilling mud, PHYS vector field, WATER SUPP circulation f; ~ pump n FOOD TECH food processing, REFRIG pompe de circulation f

circulator n SPACE communications, TELECOM waveguide circulateur m

circumaural: ~ earphone n ACOUSTICS écouteur circumaural m

circumcenter n (AmE), circumcentre n (BrE) GEOM centre du cercle circonscrit m

circumcircle n GEOM cercle circonscrit m

circumference n GEOM circonférence f

circumferential: ~ register n PRINT repérage circonférentiel m; ~ speed n AERONAUT vitesse périphérique f; ~ stress n METALL contrainte circonférentielle f

circumnavigation n TRANSP circumnavigation f

circumpolar[1] adj TRANSP circumpolaire

circumpolar:[2] ~ stars n pl ASTRON étoiles circumpolaires f pl

circumscribe vt GEOM circonscrire

circumscribed: ~ circle n GEOM cercle circonscrit m

circumstellar: ~ discs n (BrE) ASTRON disques circumstellaires m pl; ~ disks n pl (AmE) see circumstellar discs

cirrocumulus n (Cc) METEO cirro-cumulus m (Cc)

cirrolite n MINERAL cirrolite f

cirrostratus n (Cs) METEO cirro-stratus m (Cs)

cirrus n (Ci) METEO cirrus m (Ci)

cis adj CHEM cis

CISC abbr (complex instruction set computer) COMP ordinateur à jeu d'instructions complexe m

cislunar adj ASTRON cislunaire

cissing n P&R coating defect formation de cratères f, rampage m

cistern n WATER SUPP citerne f, réservoir m, réservoir à eau m

cis-trans *adj* CHEM cis-trans
citation *n* PATENTS citation *f*
cite *vt* PATENTS citer
citizen's: ~ **band** *n (CB)* TELECOM bande de fréquence banalisée *f*, bande de fréquence publique *f*
citral *n* CHEM citral *m*
citrate *n* CHEM citrate *m*
citric[1] *adj* CHEM citrique
citric:[2] ~ **acid** *n* DETERGENTS, FOOD TECH acide citrique *m*
citrine *n* MINERAL citrine *f*, quartz citrine *m*; ~ **color** *n* (AmE), ~ **colour** *n* (BrE) COLOURS couleur citron *f*; ~ **quartz** *n* MINERAL citrine *f*, quartz citrine *m*
citronella *n* FOOD TECH essence de citronelle *f*; ~ **oil** *n* FOOD TECH essence de citronelle *f*
citronellal *n* CHEM citronellal *m*
citronyl *n* CHEM citronyle *f*
citrulline *n* CHEM citrulline *f*
city: ~ **gas** *n* (AmE) *(cf mains gas)* GAS TECH gaz de ville *m*; ~ **terminal** *n* AERONAUT terminal *m*; ~ **water** *n* (AmE) *(cf mains water)* HYDROL eau de ville *f*
civetone *n* CHEM civettone *f*
civil: ~ **defence** *n* (BrE) MILIT défense passive *f*; ~ **defense** *n* (AmE) *see civil defence* ~ **engineer** *n* CONST ingénieur civil *m*; ~ **engineering** *n* CONST génie civil *m*
Cl *(chlorine)* CHEM Cl *(chlore)*
CL *abbr (connectionless)* TELECOM en mode non connecté, sans connexion
clack *n* MECH ENG clapet *m*; ~ **box** *n* MECH ENG boîte à clapet *f*, chapelle *f*; ~ **valve** *n* HYDR EQUIP clapet *m*, MECH ENG clapet *m*, soupape à clapet *f*
clad: ~ **fuel clearance** *n* NUCLEAR jeu combustible-gaine *m*; ~ **pressure vessel** *n* MECH ENG réservoir à pression vêtu *m*; ~ **steel** *n* PROP MAT acier plaqué *m*
cladding *n* MECH *welding* placage par soudage *m*, OPT *optical fibre* gaine *f*, gaine optique *f*, PHYS *optical fibre* gaine optique *f*, SPACE *spacecraft* gainage *m*, placage *m*, revêtement *m*, TELECOM gaine *f*; ~ **center** *n* (AmE), ~ **centre** *n* (BrE) OPT *optical fibre*, TELECOM centre de la gaine *m*; ~ **diameter** *n* OPT diamètre de la gaine *m*; ~ **diameter tolerance** *n* OPT tolérance sur le diamètre de la gaine *f*; ~ **material** *n* NUCLEAR matière de gaine *f*, matériau de gainage *m*; ~ **mode** *n* OPT, TELECOM mode de gaine *m*; ~ **mode stripper** *n* OPT, TELECOM extracteur de modes de gaine *m*; ~ **temperature limit** *n* NUCLEAR température limite de la gaine *f*; ~ **tolerance field** *n* OPT, TELECOM domaine de tolérance de la gaine *m*
claim[1] *n* MINING claim *m*, concession *f*
claim[2] *vt* PATENTS revendiquer
claire *n* OCEANOG claire *f*
Claisen: ~ **condensation** *n* CHEM *reaction* condensation de Claisen *f*; ~ **flask** *n* CHEM TECH flacon de Claisen *m*
clam: ~ **pack** *n* PACKAGING dispositif de serrage *m*; ~ **shell bucket dredger** *n* CONST drague à mâchoires *f*
clamp[1] *n* ELEC *cable* bride *f*, LAB EQUIP *support* pince *f*, MECH pièce de serrage *f*, MECH ENG attache *f*, serre-fils *m*, bride *f*, bride de serrage *f*, clameaux *m pl*, clampe *f*, crampon *m*, happe *f*, presse *f*, serre-joint *m*, *for rubber tubes* pince *f*, *of levelling instrument* pince d'arrêt *f*, MINING *boring* agrafe de manoeuvre *f*, OCEANOG foène *f*, PAPER TECH agrafe *f*, PHOTO support à pinces *m*, PROD ENG bride *f*, clameaux *m pl*, clampe *f*, TRANSP *wheel clamping* sabot de Denver *m*, VEHICLES collier *m*; ~ **course** *n* CONST couche imperméable *f*; ~ **pin** *n* PROD ENG goupille de blocage *f*; ~ **pulse generator** *n* TV générateur d'impulsions de clamp *m*,

générateur d'impulsions de verrouillage *m*; ~ **screw** *n* PROD ENG vis d'arrêt *f*, vis de blocage *f*; ~ **slot** *n* MECH ENG rainure de bridage *f*; ~ **washer** *n* PROD ENG rondelle de serrage *f*; ~ **with jaws** *n* LAB EQUIP *support* pince à mâchoires *f*
clamp[2] *vt* CONST *levelling instrument* caler, MECH bloquer, serrer, PROD ENG bloquer, serrer avec une bride; ~ **together** *vt* PROD ENG *pipes* brider
clamped[1] *adj* PRODUCTION bloqué, bridé; ~ **in off-state** *adj* PROD ENG bloqué en état de désactivation
clamped:[2] ~ **capacitance** *n* RECORDING capacitance à l'état bloqué *f*, contrôle de pistage *m*; ~ **pipe connection** *n* MECH ENG tuyauterie bridée *f*
clamped:[3] **be** ~ *vi* PROD ENG se bloquer, se brider
clamping *n* ELECTRON fixation de niveau *f*, MECH blocage *m*, serrage *m*, PROD ENG blocage *m*, bridage *m*, calage *m*, RECORDING blocage *m*, TV clamp *m*, verrouillage du niveau *m*; ~ **band** *n* MECH ENG bande de protection de collier de serrage *f*; ~ **circuit** *n* ELECTRON circuit de fixation de niveau *m*, TV circuit de clamp *m*, circuit de verrouillage *m*; ~ **diode** *n* ELECTRON diode de fixation de niveau *f*, diode de niveau *f*, PHYS diode de verrouillage *f*; ~ **dog** *n* PROD ENG *of timber clip, log carriage, log-sawing machine* griffe *f*; ~ **fixture** *n* MECH ENG *machine tools* montage de bridage *m*; ~ **force** *n* PACKAGING force de serrage *f*; ~ **handle** *n* MECH ENG *of lathe* griffe de blocage *f*; ~ **lever** *n* MECH ENG levier de serrage *m*; ~ **mechanism** *n* MECH ENG blocage *m*; ~ **pin** *n* PROD ENG broche à mâchoires *f*; ~ **pulses** *n pl* TV impulsions de clamp *f pl*, impulsions de verrouillage *f pl*; ~ **reflector** *n* PHOTO réflecteur à pince *m*; ~ **ring** *n* PACKAGING bague de serrage *f*; ~ **screw** *n* PROD ENG vis d'arrêt *f*, vis de blocage *f*
clamp-on-type: ~ **amp probe** *n* PROD ENG ampèremètre à pinces *m*
clamshell: ~ **blister** *n* PACKAGING blister double coque *m*; ~ **bucket** *n* CONST benne automatique *f*, benne piocheuse *f*, benne preneuse *f*, benne à demi-coquelle *f*
clap: ~ **sill** *n* WATER SUPP busc *m*, seuil d'écluse *m*
Clapeyron's: ~ **equation** *n* PHYS formule de Clapeyron *f*
clapper *n* HYDR EQUIP soupape à clapet *f*, MECH ENG clapet plat *m*, RECORDING clap *m*; ~ **board** *n* CINEMAT clap *m*, claquette *f*; ~ **person** *n* CINEMAT clapiste *m*; ~ **seat** *n* MECH ENG siège de clapet *m*; ~ **valve** *n* HYDR EQUIP clapet *m*, soupape à clapet *f*
clarification *n* CHEM, COAL TECH, QUALITY clarification *f*; ~ **plant** *n* WATER SUPP installation de clarification *f*
clarified: ~ **butter** *n* FOOD TECH beurre clarifié *m*
clarifier *n* FOOD TECH agent clarifiant *m*, clarifiant *m*, HYDROL bassin de décantation *m*, clarificateur *m*
clarify *vt* CHEM clarifier, CHEM TECH clarifier, débourber, purifier, COAL TECH clarifier, FOOD TECH *butter, liquid* clarifier, *wine* coller
clarifying[1] *adj* CHEM clarificateur
clarifying:[2] ~ **basin** *n* PETR TECH bassin de clarification *m*
clarite *n* MINERAL clarite *f*
clarity *n* TELECOM audibilité *f*
clarkeite *n* MINERAL clarkéite *f*
clarity *n* MINERAL clarkéite *f*
clashing *n* TELECOM *land mobile* collision *f*
clasp[1] *n* MECH ENG agrafe *f*, fermoir *m*; ~ **brake** *n* TRANSP frein à mâchoires *m*; ~ **nut** *n* MECH ENG écrou de vis-mère *m*
clasp[2] *vt* MECH ENG agrafer
clasp[3] *vi* MECH ENG s'agrafer
class *n* COMP, CRYSTALL *of crystals*, DP classe *f*, MECH

ENG catégorie *f*, classe *f*, PATENTS classe *f*; ~ **A amplifier** *n* ELECTRON, PHYS amplificateur classe A *m*; ~ **of accuracy** *n* METR classe de précision *f*; ~ **A evaporating pan** *n* HYDROL bac de classe A *m*

classic: ~ **thermodynamics** *n* THERMOD thermodynamique classique *f*

classical: ~ **radius** *n* PHYS *of electron* rayon classique *m*

classification *n* ASTRON, QUALITY classification *f*, RAIL *vehicles* triage *m*; ~ **detector** *n* TRANSP détecteur de classification *m*; ~ **of ship** *n* NAUT *insurance* cote d'un navire *f*; ~ **siding** *n* RAIL *vehicles*, TRANSP voie de triage *f*; ~ **society** *n* NAUT *insurance* société de classification *f*; ~ **system** *n* QUALITY système de classification *m*; ~ **track** *n* TRANSP voie de triage *f*; ~ **of type design** *n* PRINT classification des caractères *f*; ~ **yard** *n* RAIL, TRANSP chantier de triage *m*; ~ **yard tower** *n* TRANSP poste de butte *m*

classifier *n* C&G classeur *m*, CHEM TECH, COAL TECH classificateur *m*

classify *vt* CHEM TECH classer, trier, tamiser, COAL TECH, QUALITY classer

classifying: ~ **drum** *n* CHEM TECH tambour cribleur *m*, trommel classeur *m*

clast *n* GEOL claste *m*, constituant détritique *m*, élément détritique *m*

clastic[1] *adj* GEOL clastique

clastic:[2] ~ **rocks** *n* GEOL roche clastique *f*, roche détritique *f*, sédiment détritique *m*; ~ **terrigenous rock** *n* GEOL roche clastique terrigène *f*

clathrate: ~ **compound** *n* CHEM composé d'insertion *m*

claudetite *n* MINERAL claudétite *f*

claused: ~ **bill of lading** *n* NAUT connaissement avec réserves *m*

Clausius: ~ **statement** *n* PHYS énoncé de Clausius *m*

Clausius-Mosotti: ~ **formula** *n* PHYS formule de Clausius-Mosotti *f*

clausthalite *n* MINERAL clausthalite *f*

claw[1] *n* CINEMAT griffe *f*, CONST nail pied-de-biche *m*, pied- de-chèvre *m*, pince *f*; ~ **bar** *n* CONST pied-de-biche *m*, pince à pied-de-biche *f*; ~ **carriage** *n* CINEMAT chariot porte-griffe *m*; ~ **clutch** *n* MECH ENG embrayage à griffes *m*, manchon d'embrayage à dents *m*; ~ **feed system** *n* CINEMAT système d'entraînement à griffe *m*; ~ **hammer** *n* CONST marteau à dent *m*; ~ **movement** *n* CINEMAT mouvement à griffe *m*

claw:[2] ~ **off** *vi* NAUT *sailing* remonter au vent

clay *n* C&G, CHEM argile *f*, COAL TECH argile *f*, sol d'argile *m*, CONST, GAS TECH, GEOL, PETR TECH argile *f*; ~ **base mud** *n* PETR TECH boue argileuse *f*, boue à l'argile *f*; ~ **brick** *n* C&G brique crue *f*; ~ **coating** *n* PRINT couchage à l'argile *m*; ~ **composition** *n* C&G composition à base d'argile *f*; ~ **content** *n* COAL TECH teneur en argile *f*; ~ **crucible** *n* C&G creuset en terre réfractaire *m*; ~ **cutter** *n* C&G épée coupe-argiles *f*; ~ **dust** *n* C&G argile en poudre *f*; ~ **flowage** *n* GEOL argilocinèse *f*; ~ **industry** *n* C&G industrie céramique *f*; ~ **kneader** *n* C&G malaxeur d'argile *m*; ~ **kneading machine** *n* C&G machine à pétrir la glaise *f*; ~ **loam** *n* CONST terreau argileux *m*; ~ **marl** *n* WATER SUPP marne argileuse *f*; ~ **mass** *n* C&G pâte céramique *f*; ~ **mill** *n* C&G moulin à préparer l'argile *m*; ~ **mineral** *n* COAL TECH minéral des argiles *m*; ~ **mining** *n* MINING exploitation de l'argile *f*, extraction de l'argile *f*; ~ **mixer** *n* C&G malaxeur d'argile *m*; ~ **mixing machine** *n* C&G machine à mélanger la glaise *f*; ~ **mortar** *n* C&G mortier de terre *m*; ~ **parting** *n* MINING gore *m*; ~ **pipe** *n* C&G pipe en terre glaise *f*; ~ **pit** *n* MINING carrière d'argile *f*, glaisière *f*; ~ **plate press** *n* C&G presse pour plaques en argile *f*; ~ **powder** *n* C&G argile en poudre *f*; ~ **press** *n* C&G presse à l'argile *f*; ~ **rollers** *n pl* C&G laminoir à l'argile *m*; ~ **silt** *n* WATER SUPP limon argileux *m*; ~ **slip** *n* PAPER TECH lait de kaolin *m*; ~ **soil** *n* COAL TECH sol d'argile *m*; ~ **suspension** *n* WATER SUPP suspension argileuse *f*; ~ **tamping** *n* CONST bourre d'argile *f*; ~ **wetting** *n* C&G détrempage de l'argile *m*; ~ **worker** *n* C&G céramiste *m*; ~ **working machine** *n* C&G machine à travailler la terre glaise *f*

clay-coated *adj* PRINT surfacé au kaolin

claying: ~ **bar** *n* PETR TECH trépan sec *m*

claystone *n* GEOL argilite *f*

clay-with-flints *n* GEOL argile à silex *f*

clayworks *n* C&G usine à l'argile *f*

CLCP *abbr (connectionless convergence protocol)* TELECOM protocole de convergence du mode non connecté *m*

cleading *n* HYDR EQUIP bordage *m*

clean:[1] ~ **air act** *n* POLLUTION loi sur la lutte contre la pollution atmosphérique *f*; ~ **air car** *n* TRANSP voiture non polluante *f*, voiture propre *f*; ~ **air device** *n* SAFETY *environmental cleanliness* dispositif de purification de l'air *m*; ~ **bill of lading** *n* NAUT connaissement net *m*, connaissement sans réserve *m*; ~ **coal** *n* COAL TECH charbon pur sans cendre et sec *m*; ~ **configuration** *n* AERONAUT avion lisse *m*, configuration lisse *f*; ~ **cut** *n* C&G coupe franche *f*; ~ **proof** *n* PRINT bonne épreuve *f*; ~ **rain** *n* POLLUTION pluie normale *f*, pluie ordinaire *f*, pluie propre *f*, pluie pure *f*, précipitations naturelles *f pl*, précipitations normales *f pl*; ~ **room** *n* ELECTRON, LAB EQUIP salle blanche *f*, PACKAGING local dépoussiéré *m*, REFRIG salle blanche *f*, SPACE chambre propre *f*; ~ **snow** *n* POLLUTION neige normale *f*, neige propre *f*; ~ **space** *n* REFRIG espace à empoussièrage contrôlé *m*; ~ **technology** *n* POLLUTION technologie propre *f*; ~ **water** *n* WATER SUPP eau propre *f*, eau pure *f*

clean[2] *vt* COAL TECH purifier, PAPER TECH nettoyer, PROD ENG dessabler, *file* dégraisser, *fire* nettoyer, éclaircir, *fire tubes* ramoner; ~ **off** *vt* CONST *carpentry* replanir; ~ **out** *vt* PROD ENG curer, débourber, nettoyer, épurer; ~ **up** *vt* CONST *wood* blanchir, MINING *gold from plates* récolter, PROD ENG *casting on emery wheel* blanchir, RECYCLING assainir

cleanable: ~ **air filter** *n* HEAT ENG filtre à air nettoyable *m*

cleaned: ~ **coal** *n* COAL TECH charbon épuré *m*; ~ **gas** *n* GAS TECH gaz épuré *m*

cleaner *n* CHEM détersif *m*, MINING *boreholes* curette *f*, PAPER TECH épurateur *m*, PROD ENG *founding* dessableur *m*, *moulder's tool* crochet à talon *m*, SAFETY nettoyeur *m*, WATER SUPP *boring* curette *f*; ~ **cell** *n* COAL TECH cellule relaveuse *f*; ~ **jig** *n* COAL TECH table de repassage *f*

cleaning *n* PAPER TECH épuration *f*, PROD ENG *boiler tubes* ramonage *m*, *castings* dessablage *m*, nettoyage *m*; ~ **agent** *n* DETERGENTS produit de nettoyage *m*; ~ **barrel** *n* PROD ENG tambour dessableur *m*, tonneau à dessabler *m*; ~ **brush** *n* PRINT brosse à nettoyer *f*; ~ **door** *n* PROD ENG regard de nettoyage *m*; ~ **equipment** *n* SAFETY *for gases* séparateurs aérauliques *m pl*; ~ **fluid** *n* INSTRUMENT liquide de dégraissage *m*, produit de nettoyage *m*; ~ **hole** *n* PROD ENG regard de nettoyage *m*; ~ **in place** *n* *(CIP)* FOOD TECH *food processing* nettoyage en place *m*; ~ **machine** *n* PROD ENG machine à nettoyer *f*, nettoyeuse *f*; ~ **material** *n*

DETERGENTS produit de nettoyage *m*; ~ **off** *n* CONST *carpentry* replanissage *m*; ~ **out** *n* WATER SUPP curage *m*, débourbage *m*; ~ **pit** *n* PROD ENG fosse à piquer le feu *f*, fosse à visiter *f*; ~ **shop** *n* PROD ENG *founding* atelier de dessablage *m*; ~ **tools** *n pl* MINING *drilling shot holes* outils de curage *m pl*

cleanness: ~ **value** *n* SPRINGS indice de pureté *m*

cleans *n* COAL TECH charbon pur sans cendre et sec *m*

cleanse *vt* WATER SUPP assainir, curer, débourber, *river* curer

cleansing *n* WATER SUPP assainissement *m*, curage *m*, débourbage *m*

cleanup *n* MAR POLL nettoyage *m*, PROD ENG nettoyage *m*, *of piece of work* mise au net *f*, mise au net *f*, RECYCLING assainissement *m*, WATER SUPP *sluices* nettoyage *m*; ~ **technique** *n* MAR POLL technique d'élimination *f*, technique de nettoyage *f*

cleanwork: ~ **station** *n* REFRIG poste de travail propre *m*

clear[1] *adj* PROP MAT débarrassé

clear:[2] ~ **air turbulence** *n* AERONAUT turbulence en air clair *f*, turbulence en ciel clair *f*; ~ **base** *n* CINEMAT support transparent *m*; ~ **binder** *n* TV *magnetic tape* liant clair *m*; ~ **channel capability** *n* TELECOM service de transfert sans restriction *m*, service support transparent *m*; ~ **etching** *n* C&G gravure lisse *f*; ~ **etching bath** *n* C&G bain de gravure lisse *m*; ~ **frit** *n* C&G fritte transparente *f*; ~ **ice** *n* REFRIG glace transparente *f*; ~ **leader** *n* CINEMAT amorce transparente *f*; ~ **light** *n* RAIL panneau à claire-voie *m*; ~ **pond** *n* COAL TECH bassin de décantation *m*; ~ **request** *n* COMP, DP demande de libération *f*; ~ **request packet** *n* TELECOM *ISDN* paquet de demande de libération *m*; ~ **sixty-four service** *n* TELECOM service de circuit commuté en canal B transparent *m*; ~ **speech** *n* TELECOM *land mobile* conversation en clair *f*; ~ **spot** *n* C&G tache claire *f*; ~ **text** *n* TELECOM texte en clair *m*; ~ **to zero** *n* COMP, DP remise à zéro *f*; ~ **transmission** *n* TELECOM transmission en clair *f*; ~ **varnish** *n* COLOURS vernis incolore *m*; ~ **water** *n* WATER SUPP eau claire *f*, eau limpide *f*; ~ **weather** *n* NAUT temps clair *m*; ~ **zone** *n* COMP, DP zone vide *f*

clear[3] *vt* COMP, DP effacer, MINING *fall* déblayer, relever, *working face* déblayer, NAUT *anchor* dégager, parer, PROD ENG *drill* dégager, dépouiller; ~ **away** *vt* CONST *sand bank* déblayer; ~ **out** *vt* CONST *earth, rubbish* déblayer, évacuer

clear[4] *vi* PROD ENG se dégager

clearance *n* AERONAUT *of propeller, wing* garde *f*, COMP, DP *security* habilitation *f*, ELEC ENG intervalle *m*, HYDR EQUIP dégagement *m*, jeu *m*, MECH dégagement *m*, espacement *m*, jeu *m*, MECH ENG chasse *f*, garde *f*, jeu de tolérance *m*, tolérance *f*, écartement *m*, *gearing* jeu *m*, *relief of backing off* dégagement *m*, dépouille *f*, MINING hauteur de sécurité *f*, NAUT *customs* dédouanement *m*, NUCLEAR espace libre *m*, PROD ENG jeu *m*, *negative lap of slide valve* découvert *m*, recouvrement négatif *m*, PROP MAT jeu *m*; ~ **angle** *n* MECH ENG *machine tools* angle d'incidence *m*; ~ **circle** *n* MECH ENG *gearing* cercle limite *m*; ~ **hole** *n* MECH ENG *for threaded bolt for shaft* trou de passage *m*; ~ **level** *n* COMP, DP niveau d'habilitation *m*; ~ **line** *n* MECH ENG *straight gearing* ligne limite *f*; ~ **period** *n* TRANSP intervalle de dégagement *m*; ~ **space** *n* HYDR EQUIP dégagement *m*, jeu *m*

cleared *adj* AERONAUT *for takeoff* autorisé

clearer *n* MECH ENG *tools* curette *f*

clearing *n* COMP, DP effacement *m*, MINING *of falls* déblaiement *m*, relèvement *m*; ~ **and grubbing** *n* CONST *site clearance* débroussaillement *m*; ~ **away** *n* PROD ENG *rubbish* enlèvement *m*; ~ **bath** *n* CINEMAT bain de clarification *m*; ~ **the cage** *n* MINING décagement *m*, déchargement de la cage *m*; ~ **operations** *n pl* CONST travaux de déblaiement *m pl*, travaux de relèvement *m pl*; ~ **procedure** *n* TELECOM procédure de libération *f*; ~ **time** *n* PRINT temps nécessaire à une fonction pour opérer *m*

clearness *n* WATER SUPP *of water* clarté *f*, limpidité *f*

clearscan *n* NAUT *radar* réglage automatique des antiretours *m*

clearview: ~ **screen** *n* NAUT hublot tournant *m*

clearway *n* MECH ENG trouée dégagée *f*

cleat *n* CONST *wood* languette *f*, tasseau *m*, éclisse d'assemblage *f*, MECH ENG peigne *m*, tasseau *m*, *for rope* taquet *m*, NAUT *deck equipment* taquet *m*

cleavage *n* CRYSTALL clivage *m*, GEOL clivage *m*, schistosité *f*, METALL clivage *m*; ~ **crack** *n* METALL fissure de clivage *f*; ~ **facet** *n* METALL facette de clivage *f*; ~ **plane** *n* CHEM *of crystal* plan de clivage *m*

cleaved: ~ **glass** *n* C&G verre clivé *m*

cleaver *n* CONST *for wood* bâche *f*, merlin *m*

cleaving *n* CONST clivage *m*, fendage *m*, refente *f*; ~ **saw** *n* CONST scie à refendre *f*

cleft *n* OCEANOG crevasse *f*; ~ **water** *n* COAL TECH eau de fissure *f*; ~ **weld** *n* PROD ENG soudure à gueule-de-loup *f*; ~ **welding** *n* PROD ENG soudure à gueule-de-loup *f*

clerestory: ~ **roof** *n* RAIL *vehicles* pavillon à lanterneau *m*

cleveite *n* MINERAL clévéite *f*

clevis *n* MECH chape *f*, étrier *m*, MECH ENG chape *f*, *safety hook, spring hook, clip hook* crochet de sûreté *m*, crochet à ressort *m*, mousqueton *m*, *shackle, U bolt with pin or screw* maillon d'attache *m*, maillon de jonction *m*, manille d'assemblage *f*; ~ **bolt** *n* MECH ENG boulon de chape *m*; ~ **link** *n* MECH ENG triangle à chape *m*; ~ **pin** *n* MECH ENG axe de chape *m*, *without head* axe d'articulation *m*

clew *n* NAUT *on sails* point d'écoute *m*

CLI *abbr (calling line identification)* TELECOM ILA *(identification de la ligne appelante)*

click *n* ACOUSTICS claquement *m*, MECH ENG *horology* chien *m*, cliquet *m*, doigt d'encliquetage *m*, déclic *m*, détente *f*; ~ **footage counter** *n* CINEMAT compteur à cliquet *m*; ~ **stop** *n* CINEMAT repère sur diaphragme *m*, PHOTO cran d'immobilisation *m*; ~ **track** *n* RECORDING bande rythmo-son *f*, piste métronome *f*; ~ **wheel** *n* MECH ENG roue à chien *f*, roue à cliquet *f*, roue à rochet *f*

CLID *abbr (calling line identification display, CLIP)* TELECOM PILA *(présentation de l'identification de la ligne appelante)*

client *n* COMP, DP client *m*

client/server *n* COMP client/serveur *m*

cliff *n* NAUT falaise *f*

climagram *n* METEO climagramme *m*

climate *n* METEO climat *m*; ~ **environment** *n* METEO milieu climatique *m*

climatic: ~ **anomaly** *n* METEO anomalie climatique *f*; ~ **chamber** *n* PACKAGING chambre avec conditionnement de l'air *f*, salle avec conditionnement d'air *f*, salle climatisée *f*, REFRIG chambre climatique *f*; ~ **conditions** *n pl* PACKAGING conditions climatiques *f pl*; ~ **detector** *n* TRANSP détecteur climatique *m*; ~

graph *n* METEO carte climatique *f*, climagramme *m*; ~ **hazards** *n pl* SAFETY hasards climatiques *m pl*; ~ **protection** *n* SAFETY protection climatique *f*; ~ **test** *n* PACKAGING, SPACE essai climatique *m*

climatogram *n* METEO climagramme *m*

climatology *n* METEO climatologie *f*

climb[1] *n* AERONAUT, CRYSTALL *of dislocation*, PROP MAT montée *f*; ~ **corridor** *n* AERONAUT couloir de montée *m*; ~ **cruise** *n* AERONAUT croisière ascendante *f*; ~ **gradient** *n* AERONAUT pente aérodynamique *f*, pente de montée *f*; ~ **mechanism** *n* CRYSTALL, PROP MAT mécanisme de montée *m*; ~ **out** *n* AERONAUT montée au décollage *f*, montée initiale *f*; ~ **performance** *n* AERONAUT performance ascensionnelle *f*; ~ **phase** *n* AERONAUT phase de montée *f*; ~ **setting** *n* AERONAUT régime de montée *m*; ~ **turn** *n* AERONAUT virage en montée *m*

climb[2] *vi* SPACE *spacecraft* monter

climbing: ~ **lane** *n* CONST voie d'ascente *f*; ~ **speed** *n* AERONAUT vitesse ascensionnelle *f*, vitesse de montée *f*, SPACE vitesse ascensionnelle *f*

clinch:[1] ~ **rivet** *n* MECH ENG rivet à clin *m*

clinch[2] *vt* NAUT *chain* étalinguer, PROD ENG river

clinched[1] *adj* PRODUCTION rivé

clinched:[2] **be** ~ *vi* PROD ENG se river

cling: ~ **film** *n* PACKAGING pellicule autocollante *f*

clinker *n* CHEM TECH brique vitrifiée *f*, CONST clinker *m*, PROD ENG mâchefer *m*, scorie *f*, *iron slag* crasse de fonte *f*; ~ **brick** *n* C&G brique hollandaise *f*; ~ **cement** *n* C&G laitier de ciment *m*

clinker-built *adj* NAUT *boatbuilding* bordé à clin

clinkstone *n* PROD ENG phonolite *f*

clinochlore *n* MINERAL clinochlore *m*

clinoclase *n* MINERAL clinoclase *f*, clinoclasite *f*

clinoclasite *n* MINERAL clinoclase *f*, clinoclasite *f*

clinohedrite *n* MINERAL clinoédrite *f*

clinohumite *n* MINERAL clinohumite *f*

clinometer *n* COAL TECH clinomètre *m*, CONST clinomètre *m*, inclinomètre *m*, GEOL clinomètre *m*, GEOPHYS clinomètre *m*, indicateur de pente *m*, METR clinomètre *m*; ~ **alidade** *n* INSTRUMENT alidade à éclimètre *f*

clinometry *n* CONST clinométrie *f*

clinozoisite *n* MINERAL clinozoïsite *f*

clintonite *n* MINERAL clintonite *f*

clip[1] *n* CINEMAT *video* clip *m*, LAB EQUIP *for rubber tubing* pince *f*, *on stage of microscope* valet *m*, MECH attache *f*, pince *f*, MECH ENG agrafe *f*, attache *f*, griffe *f*, griffe de serrage *f*, pince *f*, serre *f*, virole *f*, TEXTILES pince *f*; ~ **art item** *n* PRINT image clip art *f*; ~ **band** *n* PACKAGING bande de serrage par pince *f*; ~ **frame** *n* TEXTILES rame à pinces *f*; ~ **gage** *n* (AmE), ~ **gauge** *n* (BrE) METALL extensomètre à lames *m*; ~ **hook** *n* MECH ENG *sister hook* croc à ciseaux *m*, *spring hook, safety hook* crochet de sûreté *m*, crochet à ressort *m*, mousqueton *m*; ~ **stenter** *n* TEXTILES rame à pinces *f*

clip[2] *vt* ELEC ENG *signal* écrêter, PACKAGING attacher avec une pince, PROD ENG *shear* cisailler

clip-on: ~ **carrier** *n* PACKAGING agrippe-col *m*; ~ **instrument** *n* ELEC appareil de mesure à pince *m*; ~ **refrigerating unit** *n* REFRIG groupe frigorifique amovible *m*

clipped: ~ **wing** *n* TRANSP voilure tronquée *f*

clipper *n* AERONAUT écrêteur *m*, ELECTRON limiteur d'amplitude *m*, RECORDING, TV écrêteur *m*; ~ **amplifier** *n* ELECTRON, TV amplificateur limiteur *m*; ~ **circuit** *n* ELECTRON circuit d'écrêtage *m*; ~ **diode** *n* ELECTRON

diode écrêteuse *f*; ~ **dryerfelt** *n* TEXTILES machine à poser les agrafes pour jonction *f*

clipping *n* COMP, DP détourage *m*, RECORDING écrêtage *m*; ~ **level** *n* ELECTRON, TV niveau d'écrêtage *m*

clique *n* TELECOM clique *f*

CLIR *abbr (calling line identification restriction)* TELECOM RILA *(restriction de l'identification de la ligne appelante)*

CLLM *abbr (consolidated link-layer management message)* TELECOM message de gestion de couche liaison consolidé *m*

CLNP *abbr (connectionless network layer protocol)* TELECOM protocole de couche réseau sans connexion *m*

CLNS *abbr (connectionless network layer service)* TELECOM service de couche réseau sans connexion *m*

clock[1] *n* COMP, DP horloge *f*, ELECTRON cadenceur *m*, rythmeur *m*; ~ **circuit** *n* ELECTRON circuit d'horloge *m*; ~ **cycle** *n* COMP, DP, ELECTRON cycle d'horloge *m*; ~ **face reference** *n* AERONAUT localisation horaire *f*; ~ **frequency** *n* ELECTRON fréquence d'horloge *f*; ~ **period** *n* ELECTRON période d'horloge *f*; ~ **pulse** *n* COMP, DP, ELECTRON impulsion d'horloge *f*; ~ **rate** *n* COMP, DP fréquence d'horloge *f*, PROD ENG temporisation *f*; ~ **recovery** *n* SPACE *communications* remise à l'heure *f*; ~ **register** *n* COMP, DP registre d'horloge *m*; ~ **relay** *n* ELEC *switch* commutateur minuterie *m*, commutateur temporisé *m*; ~ **screw plate** *n* PROD ENG filière d'horlogerie *f*; ~ **signal** *n* CONTROL, ELECTRON signal d'horloge *m*; ~ **spring machine** *n* SPRINGS machine à ressort-moteur *m*; ~ **track** *n* COMP, DP piste de synchronisation *f*, RECORDING piste horaire *f*

clock[2] *vt* CINEMAT minuter, ELECTRON cadencer, rythmer

clocked: ~ **circuit** *n* ELECTRON circuit cadencé *m*; ~ **flip-flop** *n* ELECTRON bascule synchrone *f*, bascule synchronisée *f*

clocking *n* COMP, DP synchronisation *f*, ELECTRON cadencement *m*, rythmage *m*, synchronisation *f*; ~ **sequence** *n* ELECTRON séquence de cadencement *f*

clockwise[1] *adj (CW)* ELEC ENG dans le sens horaire

clockwise:[2] ~ **rotation** *n* MECH rotation dans le sens horaire *f*

clockwise-rotating *adj* FOOD TECH *food processing* dextrogyre

clockwork *n* MECH mouvement d'horlogerie *m*; ~ **camera** *n* CINEMAT caméra avec moteur à ressort *f*

clod *n* CONST motte *f*

clog[1] *vt* MECH ENG, PAPER TECH obstruer, PROD ENG *chock up* encrasser, WATER SUPP *obstruct* boucher, colmater, obturer

clog[2] *vi* PROD ENG s'encrasser; ~ **up** *vi* PROD ENG s'envaser, se colmater

clogged[1] *adj* MECH ENG bouché

clogged:[2] ~ **felt** *n* C&G feutre empâté *m*; ~ **head** *n* TV tête magnétique encrassée *f*

clogging *n* COAL TECH, MECH ENG colmatage *m*, MINING *of chute* ancrage *m*, bourrage *m*, engorgement *m*, obstruction *f*, PAPER TECH obstruction *f*, PROD ENG encrassement *m*, WATER SUPP colmatage *m*, engorgement *m*

clone *n* COMP, DP, PHYS clone *m*

cloning *n* PHYS clonage *m*

Clos: ~ **network** *n* TELECOM réseau de Clos *m*

close:[1] **on a** ~ **reach** *adv* NAUT *sailing* au petit largue

close:[2] ~ **annealing** *n* HEATING recuit en caisse *m*; ~ **buttress** *n* CONST contrefort *m*, éperon *m*; ~ **cell foam** *n*

PACKAGING mousse avec cellules fermées *f*; ~ **coils** *n pl* SPRINGS spires serrées *f pl*; ~ **coil spring** *n* MECH ENG ressort de rappel *m*; ~ **couple** *n* CONST *building* ferme à tirant *f*; ~ **couple truss** *n* CONST ferme à tirant *f*; ~ **coupling** *n* COMP, ELEC *inductance* couplage serré *m*; ~ **down** *n* COMP *program* fermeture *f*, DP *program* arrêt *m*; ~ **frequency signals** *n pl* ELECTRON signaux à fréquences proches *m pl*; ~ **joint** *n* PROD ENG joint étanche *m*; ~ **lathing** *n* PROD ENG lattage jointif *m*, lattis jointif *m*; ~ **medium shot** *n* CINEMAT plan américain *m*, plan moyen approché *m*; ~ **packing** *n* CRYSTALL empilement compact *m*; ~ **piling** *n* CONST palplanches jointives *f pl*; ~ **sets** *n pl* MINING cadres jointifs *m pl*; ~ **sliding fit** *n* MECH ENG ajustement glissant juste *m*; ~ **spiral spring** *n* MECH ENG ressort de rappel *m*; ~ **string** *n* CONST *stair building* limon droit *m*, limon à l'escalier *m*; ~ **supervision** *n* SAFETY contrôle attentif *m*, surveillance minutieuse *f*; ~ **talking efficiency** *n* ACOUSTICS efficacité paraphonique *f*; ~ **talking microphone** *n* RECORDING microphone de proximité *m*; ~ **timbering** *n* MINING boisage jointif *m*, boisage serré *m*; ~ **tolerance spacer** *n* MECH ENG entretoise calibrée *f*; ~ **wound coil** *n* SPRINGS spire jointive *f*

close³ *vt* CONST *road* barrer, ELEC ENG fermer, mettre en circuit, PROD ENG *mould* fermer, *plate* serrer, *rivet* refouler, *tube* fermer; ~ **down** *vt* CINEMAT *diaphragm* diaphragmer; ~ **up** *vt* MECH ENG obturer, PRINT gagner, rapprocher

closed¹ *adj* GEOM, MATH *curves, intervals, topological spaces* fermé, *surfaces* clos

closed:² ~ **and ground end** *n* SPRINGS *of coil* extrémité fermée meulée *f*, spire terminale rapprochée et meulée *f*; ~ **and ground tapered end** *n* SPRINGS *of coil* spire terminale amincie rapprochée et meulée *f*; ~ **and sealed cooling system** *n* AUTO circuit de refroidissement à réservoir d'expansion *m*; ~ **box girder** *n* TRANSP poutre porteuse fermée *f*; ~ **butt joint** *n* PROD ENG *welding* joint d'about sans espace *m*; ~ **cell** *n* P&R cellule fermée *f*; ~ **chain** *n* CHEM chaîne fermée *f*; ~ **circuit** *n* COAL TECH, ELEC, ELEC ENG, MECH ENG, PHYS circuit fermé *m*; ~ **coil** *n* SPRINGS spire rapprochée *f*; ~ **coil armature** *n* ELEC *generator, motor* induit à circuit fermé *m*; ~ **container** *n* TRANSP conteneur fermé *m*; ~ **curve** *n* GEOM courbe fermée *f*; ~ **cycle cooling system** *n* NUCLEAR système caloporteur à cycle fermé *m*, système de refroidissement àcycle fermé *m*; ~ **cycle gas turbine** *n* TRANSP turbine à gaz à circuit fermé *f*; ~ **cycle hot air turbine** *n* TRANSP turbine à air chaud et à circuit fermé *f*; ~ **demand** *n* PROD ENG demande fermée *f*, demande soldée *f*; ~ **diaphragm** *n* ACOUSTICS chambre de compression *f*; ~ **end** *n* SPRINGS *of coil* spire terminale rapprochée *f*; ~ **fuel cycle** *n* NUCLEAR cycle fermé de combustibles *m*; ~ **interval** *n* MATH intervalle fermé *m*; ~ **locker** *n* NAUT *accommodation* équipet cloisonné *m*; ~ **loop** *n* AERONAUT boucle fermée *f*, ELEC *circuit* boucle fermée *f*, circuit fermé *m*, ELECTRON boucle fermée *f*, SPRINGS anneau fermé *m*; ~ **pass** *n* PROD ENG*rolling mill* cannelure emboîtée *f*, cannelure fermée *f*; ~ **position** *n* ELEC *relay* position de fermeture *f*, position fermée *f*; ~ **pot** *n* C&G pot couvert *m*; ~ **ring** *n* CHEM *structure* cycle fermé *m*; ~ **sea** *n* OCEANOG mer fermée *f*; ~ **servoloop** *n* CONTROL boucle d'asservissement fermée *f*; ~ **shell** *n* PHYS *atom* couche remplie *f*; ~ **slot armature** *n* ELEC *generator motor* induit à canaux fermés *m*, induit à trous *m*; ~ **system** *n* *(cf open*

system) THERMOD système fermé *m*; ~ **throat wind tunnel** *n* PHYS soufflerie à veine guidée *f*; ~ **turbine chamber** *n* HYDR EQUIP, PROD ENG bâche fermée *f*, enveloppe *f*, huche *f*; ~ **universe** *n* ASTRON univers fermé *m*; ~ **user group** *n* *(CUG)* COMP, DP circuit fermé d'usagers *m*, groupe fermé d'usagers *f* *(GFU)*, TELECOM groupe fermé d'abonnés *m*, groupe fermé d'usagers *m* *(GFU)*; ~ **vessel** *n* LAB EQUIP *glassware* vase clos *m*; ~ **work** *n* MINING exploitation souterraine *f*

closed-cell: ~ **cellular plastic** *n* P&R mousse de plastique à alvéoles fermées *f*; ~ **foamed plastic** *n* REFRIG plastique cellulaire à cellules fermées *f*

closed-circuit: ~ **grinding** *n* COAL TECH broyage en circuit fermé *m*; ~ **television** *n* *(CCTV)* TV télévision en circuit fermé *f*; ~ **voltage** *n* ELEC ENG tension en circuit fermé *f*

closed-cup: ~ **flash point** *n* P&R *test* point d'éclair à vase clos *m*

closed-face: ~ **calender** *n* PAPER TECH calandre à bâti fermé *f*

closed-loop: ~ **control** *n* CONTROL commande à boucle fermée *f*, contrôle à cycle fermé *m*, ELECTRON asservissement *m*; ~ **control system** *n* ELECTRON système asservi *m*; ~ **drive** *n* RECORDING entraînement en boucle fermée *m*; ~ **feedback** *n* PROD ENG retour en boucle fermée *m*; ~ **gain** *n* ELECTRON gain en boucle fermée *m*; ~ **position control** *n* CONTROL régulation en boucle fermée de position *f*; ~ **traffic control system** *n* TRANSP circuit de régulation *m*

close-fit: ~ **thread** *n* MECH ENG filetage à ajustement serré *m*

close-hauled *adj* NAUT *sailing* au plus près

close-packed: ~ **lattice** *n* METALL réseau compact *m*; ~ **plane** *n* PROP MAT plan d'empilement compact *m*; ~ **structure** *n* CRYSTALL structure compacte *f*

closest: ~ **approach distance** *n* NAUT *radar navigation* distance minimale de croisement *f*; ~ **point of approach** *n* NAUT *radar navigation* point de rapprochement maximum *m*

closet *n* C&G closet *m*

close-timbered: ~ **level** *n* MINING galerie à boisage jointif *f*, galerie à boisage serré *f*

close-up *n* CINEMAT gros plan *m*; **very** ~ *n* CINEMAT extrême gros plan *m*, plan très rapproché *m*; ~ **attachment** *n* CINEMAT, PHOTO bonnette d'approche *f*; ~ **lens** *n* INSTRUMENT lentille d'approche *f*

closing *n* PROD ENG *of works* chômage *m*, fermeture *f*; ~ **contact** *n* ELEC *relay* contact travail *m*; ~ **credits** *n pl* CINEMAT génériques de fin *m pl*; ~ **machine** *n* PACKAGING machine de fermeture *f*; ~ **operation** *n* ELEC *relay* clôture *f*, fermeture *f*; ~ **panel** *n* MECH ENG panneau de fermeture *m*; ~ **speed** *n* ELEC *relay* vitesse de réponse *f*, NAUT *navigation* vitesse de rapprochement *f*; ~ **time** *n* ELEC *relay* durée de fermeture *f*

closure *n* C&G *of bottle* agrafe *f*, CHEM *of ring*, ELEC ENG *electric circuit*, GEOL, PACKAGING fermeture *f*; ~ **production line** *n* PACKAGING chaîne de production pour fermetures *f*; ~ **rail** *n* RAIL *track* rail de raccord *m*

clot *vi* PAPER TECH former des matons

cloth *n* TEXTILES tissu *m*; ~ **polisher** *n* C&G polissoir en drap *m*; ~ **turnout** *n* TEXTILES production de tissu *f*

cloth-centered: ~ **board** *n* (AmE) *see* cloth-centred board ~ **paper** *n* (AmE) *see* cloth-centred paper

cloth-centred: ~ **board** *n* (BrE) PAPER TECH carton entre-deux fils *m*, carton entre-deux toiles *m*; ~ **paper** *n*

(BrE) PAPER TECH papier entre-deux fils *m*, papier entre-deux toiles *m*

clothing *n* HYDR EQUIP chemisage *m*, enveloppe *f*, garniture *f*, PAPER TECH habillage *m*, SAFETY vêtements *m pl*; ~ **plate** *n* HYDR EQUIP tôle d'enveloppe extérieure *f*

cloth-lined: ~ **paper** *n* PAPER TECH papier entoilé *m*

clotting *n* CHEM coagulation *f*, floculation *f*, FOOD TECH caillage *m*, grumelage *m*, épaississement *m*

cloud:[1] ~ **amount** *n* METEO couverture nuageuse *f*, nébulosité *f*; ~ **chamber** *n* WAVE PHYS *for detecting radiation* chambre à nuages *f*; ~ **collision warning system** *n* TRANSP système d'avertissement de nuages et de collision *m*; ~ **cover** *n* AERONAUT, METEO couverture nuageuse *f*, NAUT *weather* nébulosité *f*; ~ **formation** *n* METEO formation de nuages *f*; ~ **layer** *n* SPACE couche nuageuse *f*; ~ **point** *n* DETERGENTS point de trouble *m*, température de trouble *f*, REFRIG point de trouble *m*; ~ **pulse** *n* ELEC ENG *charge storage tubes* impulsion de charge d'espace *f*; ~ **system** *n* METEO système nuageux *m*

cloud:[2] ~ **over** *vi* METEO se couvrir de nuages

cloudbase *n* AERONAUT plafond nuageux *m*, METEO base nuageuse *f*; ~ **measuring instrument** *n* AERONAUT télémètre de nuages *m*, télémètre de plafond *m*

cloudburst *n* METEO rafale de pluie *f*, trombe d'eau *f*

cloudiness *n* GAS TECH turbidité *f*

clouding *n* TV effets d'ombre *m pl*, voile électronique *m*

cloudy[1] *adj* WATER SUPP terne, trouble

cloudy:[2] ~ **formation** *n* PAPER TECH épair irrégulier *m*

clout: ~ **nail** *n* MECH ENG clou ardoise *m*

clove: ~ **hitch** *n* NAUT *knot* noeud de cabestan *m*

CLP *abbr (cell loss priority)* TELECOM priorité de perte de cellule *f*

CLS *abbr (connectionless server)* TELECOM serveur en mode non connecté *m*

CLSF *abbr (connectionless service function)* TELECOM fonction de service sans connexion *f*

club:[1] ~ **car** *n* RAIL *vehicles* voiture-salon *f*

club[2] *vi* NAUT *mooring* dériver sur son ancre

clump *n* PRINT plomb d'encrier *m*

clupeine *n* CHEM clupéine *f*

cluster[1] *n* ASTRON *of galaxies, of stars* amas *m*, groupe *m*, COMP, DP grappe *f*, MECH ENG groupe *m*, noeud *m*, *of gear wheels* train *m*, équipage *m*, *of springs* faisceau *m*, PROD ENG barillet *m*, faisceau *m*, grappe *f*, PROP MAT, SPACE *of galaxies* amas *m*, TEXTILES assemblage *m*, TRANSP barillet *m*, faisceau *m*; ~ **controller** *n* COMP, DP contrôleur de grappe *m*; ~ **formation** *n* METALL formation d'amas *f*, PROP MAT formation de cluster *f*; ~ **indicator light** *n* PROD ENG *electricity* voyant multilampes *m*; ~ **spring** *n* MECH ENG faisceau *m*

cluster:[2] ~ **together** *vi* GEOL *particles* s'agglomérer, s'agréger

clustered *adj* TRANSP en grappe

clustering *n* METALL agglomération *f*, formation d'amas *f*, PROP MAT formation d'amas *f*

clutch *n* AUTO embrayage *m*, CINEMAT accouplement *m*, embrayage *m*, MECH embrayage *m*, MECH ENG *coupling* embrayage *m*, manchon d'embrayage *m*, *gripping device* griffe *f*, griffe de serrage *f*, *transmission* embrayage *m*, NAUT *engine* embrayage *m*, PAPER TECH embrayage à mâchoires *m*, VEHICLES embrayage *m*; ~ **cable** *n* AUTO câble de commande d'embrayage *m*, VEHICLES câble Bowden *m*, câble de pédale de débrayage *m*; ~ **casing** *n* VEHICLES carter d'embrayage *m*; ~ **clearance** *n* AUTO garde d'embrayage *f*; ~ **collar** *n*

MECH ENG collier d'embrayage *m*; ~ **coupling** *n* MECH ENG accouplement à débrayage *m*; ~ **disc** *n* (BrE) AUTO, VEHICLES disque d'embrayage *m*; ~ **disk** *n* (AmE) *see clutch disc*; ~ **drive plate** *n* VEHICLES disque menant d'embrayage *m*, disque moteur d'embrayage *m*, plateau d'appui d'embrayage *m*; ~ **drum** *n* AUTO, MECH ENG tambour d'embrayage *m*; ~ **fork** *n* AUTO fourchette d'embrayage *f*, MECH ENG embrayeur *m*; ~ **gear** *n* AUTO pignon entraîneur *m*; ~ **housing** *n* AUTO carter d'embrayage *m*; ~ **lining** *n* AUTO, MECH garniture d'embrayage *f*, MECH ENG garniture de disque d'embrayage *f*, VEHICLES garniture de friction *f*; ~ **linkage** *n* VEHICLES commande de l'embrayage *f*; ~ **master cylinder** *n* AUTO maître-cylindre d'embrayage *m*; ~ **output cylinder** *n* AUTO cylindre récepteur *m*; ~ **pedal** *n* VEHICLES pédale d'embrayage *f*; ~ **pedal clearance** *n* AUTO garde à la pédale d'embrayage *f*; ~ **pedal push rod** *n* VEHICLES tringle de pédale de débrayage *f*; ~ **pedal release lever** *n* AUTO levier de débrayage *m*; ~ **pick-off** *n* AERONAUT détecteur d'embrayage *m*; ~ **plate** *n* VEHICLES disque d'embrayage *m*, *automatic gear change* disque d'accouplement *m*; ~ **pressure plate** *n* MECH ENG plateau de pression d'embrayage *m*; ~ **release bearing** *n* VEHICLES butée de débrayage *f*; ~ **release fork** *n* VEHICLES fourchette de débrayage *f*; ~ **rod** *n* VEHICLES tige d'embrayage *f*; ~ **shaft** *n* AUTO arbre d'embrayage *m*, VEHICLES arbre primaire *m*; ~ **slave cylinder** *n* AUTO servodébrayage *m*; ~ **sleeve** *n* AUTO crabot *m*; ~ **slip** *n* AUTO patinage de l'embrayage *m*, VEHICLES glissement de l'embrayage *m*, patinage de l'embrayage *m*; ~ **spring** *n* MECH ENG, SPRINGS, VEHICLES ressort d'embrayage *m*; ~ **throwout** *n* AUTO débrayage *m*

clutter *n* ELECTRON *radar* fouillis *m*, NAUT *radar* brouillage radar *m*, écho parasite *m*, SPACE fouillis d'écho *m*, TELECOM écho parasite *m*; ~ **filter** *n* ELECTRON *radar* filtre antifouillis *m*

CLV *abbr (constant linear velocity)* COMP, OPT vitesse linéaire constante *f*

Clyburn: ~ **wrench** *n* MECH ENG clé à molette façon Clyburn *f*, clé à molette à une seule mâchoire mobile *f*

Cm *(curium)* CHEM Cm *(curium)*

CM *abbr* COMP, DP *(configuration management)* contrôle de configuration *m*, TELECOM *(conditionally mandatory)* PO *(partiellement obligatoire)*, TELECOM *(connection matrix)* matrice de connexion *f*

CMB *abbr (CRC message bloc)* TELECOM bloc de messages pour le contrôle du CRC *m*

CMC *abbr (carboxymethyl cellulose)* DETERGENTS, FOOD TECH *(carboxymethyl cellulose)*, P&R *(carboxymethyl cellulose)* carboxyméthylcellulose *f*, TELECOM *(call modification completed message)* MAE *(message de modification d'appel effectuée)*

CMI *abbr (coded mark inversion)* TELECOM code CMI *m*

CMIP *abbr (common management information protocol)* TELECOM protocole commun d'information de gestion *m*

CMIPM *abbr (common management information protocol machine)* TELECOM machine du protocole commun de transfert d'informations de gestion *f*

CMIS *abbr (common management information service)* TELECOM service commun d'information de gestion *m*, service commun de transfert d'informations de gestion *m*

CMISE[1] *abbr (common management information service element)* TELECOM élément de service commun d'information de gestion *m*, élément de service commun de transfert d'informations de gestion *m*

CMISE:[2] ~ **service provider** *n* TELECOM fournisseur du service CMISE *m*; ~ **service user** *n* TELECOM utilisateur du service CMISE *m*

CMOS[1] *abbr (compatible metal-oxide semiconductor)* COMP MOS complémentaire *m*, semi- conducteur à oxyde métallique complémentaire *m*

CMOS:[2] ~ **crosspoint** *n* TELECOM point de connexion CMOS *m*; ~ **logic** *n* ELECTRON logique CMOS *f*; ~ **RAM memory module** *n* PROD ENG module mémoire RAM CMOS *m*; ~ **transistor** *n* ELECTRON transistor CMOS *m*

C-mount *n* CINEMAT monture C *f*; ~ **adaptor** *n* CINEMAT intermédiaire monture C *m*

CMR *abbr (call modification request message)* TELECOM MAD *(demande de modification d'appel)*

CMRJ *abbr (call modification reject message)* TELECOM MAR *(message de refus de modification d'appel)*

C-n *abbr (container-n)* TELECOM conteneur-n *m*

CN *abbr (customer network)* TELECOM réseau client *m*

CNC: ~ **cylindrical grinder** *n* MECH ENG *machine tools* machine à rectifier cylindriquement CNC *f*; ~ **production internal grinding machine** *n* MECH ENG *machine tools* machine à rectifier les intérieurs à CNC pour travaux de série *f*; ~ **surface grinder** *n* MECH ENG *machine tools* machine CNC à rectifier les surfaces planes *f*

CNC-controlled *adj (computerized numerical control)* MECH ENG *machine tools* à commande numérique par ordinateur

Co *(cobalt)* CHEM Co *(cobalt)*

CO₂: ~ **laser** *n* ELECTRON laser à CO$_2$ *m*

coacervate *n* CHEM coacervat *m*

coacervation *n* CHEM coacervation *f*

coach *n* RAIL voiture *f*, TRANSP autocar *m*, car long courrier *m*; ~ **bolt** *n* MECH ENG boulon carrossier *m*; ~ **class** *n* TRANSP deuxième classe *f*; ~ **screw** *n* MECH ENG vis de carrosserie *f*; ~ **wrench** *n* MECH ENG clé anglaise *f*, clé de voiture *f*

coachroof *n* NAUT *boatbuilding* rouf *m*

coagulant *n* CHEM TECH coagulant *m*, HYDROL agent de précipitation *m*, coagulant *m*

coagulate *vt* CHEM TECH conglutiner, faire cailler, se coaguler

coagulated *adj* CHEM TECH caillé

coagulating *n* FOOD TECH caillage *m*, coagulation *f*, grumelage *m*; ~ **agent** *n* P&R agent coagulant *m*; ~ **bath** *n* CHEM TECH bain de coagulation *m*

coagulation *n* CHEM coagulation *f*, CHEM TECH coagulation *f*, floculation *f*, HEAT ENG *boiler water treatment* floculation *f*, HYDROL, P&R coagulation *f*; ~ **liquid** *n* CHEM TECH liquide de coagulation *m*

coagulum *n* P&R coagulum *m*

coal[1] *n* COAL TECH charbon *m*, charbon de terre *m*, houille *f*, GEOL charbon *m*, houille *f*; ~ **and stone breaker** *n* MINING concasseur de charbon et de pierre *m*; ~ **ash** *n* COAL TECH cendre de houille *f*; ~ **backing** *n* COAL TECH coltinage du charbon *m*; ~ **basin** *n* COAL TECH bassin charbonnier *m*, bassin houiller *m*, GEOL bassin houiller *m*; ~ **basket** *n* COAL TECH couffe à charbon *f*, manne à charbon *m*, panier à charbon *m*; ~ **bean** *n* COAL TECH menu de houille brut *m*; ~ **bed** *n* COAL TECH assise houillère *f*, couche de charbon *f*, couche de houille *f*, gisement houiller *m*, gîte houiller *m*, lit de houille *m*; ~ **belt** *n* COAL TECH sillon houiller

m, traînée houillère *f*; ~ **breaker** *n* COAL TECH concasseur à charbon *m*; ~ **bunker** *n* COAL TECH soute à charbon *f*, MINING silo de charbon *m*, RAIL soute à charbon *f*; ~ **chute** *n* COAL TECH cheminée à charbon *f*, couloir à charbon *m*; ~ **cracker** *n* COAL TECH concasseur à charbon *m*; ~ **crusher** *n* COAL TECH autobroyeur *m*; ~ **cutter** *n* COAL TECH déhouilleuse *f*, haveuse *f*, houilleuse *f*, MINING déhouilleuse *f*, haveuse *f*, houilleuse *f*, haveur *m*; ~ **deposit** *n* COAL TECH dépôt houiller *m*, gisement houiller *m*, gîte houiller *m*; ~ **dressing** *n* COAL TECH préparation mécanique du charbon *f*; ~ **drift** *n* COAL TECH fendue *f*; ~ **drill** *n* COAL TECH perforatrice au charbon *f*; ~ **dust** *n* COAL TECH charbon pulvérisé *m*, poussier *m*, poussier de houille *m*, poussière de charbon *f*, pulvérin *m*, POLLUTION poussière de charbon *f*, PROP MAT charbon pulvérisé *m*; ~ **extraction** *n* COAL TECH extraction de charbon de la houille *f*; ~ **field** *n* COAL TECH district houiller *m*, région carbonifère *f*; ~ **formation** *n* COAL TECH formation houillère *f*; ~ **gas** *n* COAL TECH gaz de houille *m*, GAS TECH gaz d'éclairage *m*, gaz de houille *m*; ~ **gasification** *n* PETR TECH gazéification de la bouteille *f*; ~ **getting** *n* COAL TECH abattage *m*; ~ **liquefaction** *n* PETR TECH liquéfaction de la houille *f*, liquéfaction du charbon *f*; ~ **measure** *n* MINING gisement houiller *m*; ~ **measures** *n pl* MINING formation carbonifère *f*, formation houillère *f*, terrain carbonifère *m*, terrain houiller *m*, étage houiller *m*; ~ **mine** *n* COAL TECH charbonnage *m*, houillère *f*, mine de charbon *f*, mine de houille *f*, MINING charbonnage *m*, houillère *f*, mine *f*, mine de charbon *f*, mine de houille *f*; ~ **mining** *n* COAL TECH charbonnage *m*, exploitation de la houille *f*, exploitation du charbon *f*; ~ **mining explosive** *n* COAL TECH explosif couche *m*; ~ **naphtha** *n* COAL TECH naphta de charbon *m*; ~ **oil** *n* COAL TECH huile de houille *f*, huile de pierre *f*, huile de roche *f*, naphta minéral *m*, naphte minéral *m*, naphta natif *m*, naphte natif *m*, pétrole *m*; ~ **pick** *n* COAL TECH pic à charbon *m*, pic à la veine *m*; ~ **pillar** *n* COAL TECH pilier de charbon *m*; ~ **pit** *n* COAL TECH fosse *f*; ~ **powder** *n* COAL TECH charbon pulvérisé *m*; ~ **preparation** *n* COAL TECH préparation mécanique du charbon *f*; ~ **road** *n* COAL TECH galerie au charbon *f*; ~ **seam** *n* COAL TECH couche de houille *f*, gisement houiller *m*, gîte houiller *m*; ~ **ship** *n* COAL TECH bateau charbonnier *m*, minéralier *m*, charbonnier *m*, NAUT navire charbonnier *m*; ~ **sizer** *n* MINING calibreur *m*; ~ **slack** *n* COAL TECH charbon menu *m*, charbonnaille *f*, menu *m*; ~ **slake** *n* COAL TECH menu *m*; ~ **sludge** *n* COAL TECH charbon limoneux *m*; ~ **tar** *n* COAL TECH coaltar *m*, goudron de gaz *m*, goudron de houille *m*; ~ **tar dye** *n* COLOURS couleur de goudron *f*; ~ **tar naphtha** *n* COAL TECH huile de houille *f*; ~ **tar pitch** *n* COAL TECH poix de houille *f*; ~ **wall** *n* COAL TECH front de taille du charbon *m*; ~ **washer** *n* COAL TECH lavoir à charbon *m*; ~ **washery** *n* COAL TECH lavoir à charbon *m*; ~ **wharf** *n* TRANSP quai de charbonnage *m*; ~ **winning** *n* COAL TECH abattage *m*; ~ **yard** *n* COAL TECH chantier de houille *m*, parc à charbon *m*

coal[2] *vt* COAL TECH alimenter en charbon, approvisionner en charbon, faire du charbon

coal-bearing[1] *adj* COAL TECH carbonifère

coal-bearing:[2] ~ **rock** *n* MINING formation carbonifère *f*, formation houillère *f*, terrain carbonifère *m*, terrain houiller *m*, étage houiller *m*

coal-cutting: ~ **machine** *n* MINING déhouilleuse *f*, haveuse f, houilleuse f

coalesce vi CHEM se combiner, se fusionner

coalescence n METEO coalescence f

coalface n COAL TECH front de taille du charbon m; ~ **system** n MINING matériel en taille m

coal-fired[1] adj COAL TECH chauffé au charbon

coal-fired:[2] ~ **boiler** n HEATING chaudière à charbon f

coal-handling: ~ **plant** n COAL TECH appareil de manutention de charbon m

coalification n COAL TECH houillification f

co-altitude n SPACE distance zénithale f

coalworks n COAL TECH, MINING siège de charbonnage m

coaming n AERONAUT hiloire de protection f, surbau m, NAUT shipbuilding, boatbuilding hiloire f, surbau m

Coanda: ~ **effect** n FLUID PHYS flow behaviour adhérence à la paroi f, effet Coanda m

coarse[1] adj GEOL of grain size gros, grossier, MECH ENG brut

coarse:[2] ~ **adjustment** n ELEC accord gros m, réglage approximatif m, INSTRUMENT bouton de déplacement rapide m, bouton de mise au point m; ~ **adjustment screw** n INSTRUMENT vis macrométrique f; ~ **aggregate** n CONST agrégat gros m, gravier grossier m, gravier à béton m; ~ **batt** n TEXTILES nappage grossier m; ~ **concentration mill** n MINING ore atelier de travail des grenailles et sables m; ~ **count** n TEXTILES gros titre m; ~ **crusher** n COAL TECH concasseur primaire m, MINING broyeur des gros m; ~ **crushing** n COAL TECH concassage grossier m, MINING broyage grossier m; ~ **crushing mill** n CHEM TECH installation de concassage grossier f; ~ **feed** n MECH ENG machine tools avance rapide f; ~ **filter** n WATER SUPP filtre gros m; ~ **grain** n CINEMAT, METALL gros grain m, MINING grain grossier m, gros grain m; ~ **grain image** n PHOTO image à forte granulation f; ~ **gravelly sand** n CONST sable gros avec cailloux m; ~ **grinding** n COAL TECH broyage primaire m; ~ **groove** n ACOUSTICS sillon large m; ~ **mesh screen** n COAL TECH crible à grosses mailles m; ~ **ore** n MINING gros m pl; ~ **pitch** n AERONAUT of propeller grand pas m, MECH ENG grand pas taraudage m; ~ **pitch screw** n CONST vis à pas rapide f; ~ **pottery** n C&G poterie commune f; ~ **regulator** n CONTROL régulateur grossier m; ~ **sand** n GEOL sable grossier m, MINING sable grossier m, ore dressing gros sables m pl; ~ **sand middlings** n pl MINING ore dressing grenailles f pl; ~ **sands** n MINING ore dressing gros sables m pl; ~ **scanning** n TV analyse approximative f; ~ **screen** n COAL TECH crible à grosses mailles m, PRINT grosse trame f, trame grossière f; ~ **silt** n GEOL limon grossier m; ~ **soil** n COAL TECH sol à grains grossiers m; ~ **solder** n PROD ENG soudure maigre f; ~ **texture** n GEOL granulométrie grossière f; ~ **thread** n MECH ENG nuts, bolts pas large m; ~ **trommel** n MINING trommel des gros m; ~ **yarn** n TEXTILES fil grossier m

coarse-grained adj GEOL, METALL à gros grain

coarsening n METALL, PROP MAT grossissement m

coarsening-up: ~ **sequence** n GEOL séquence négative f

coast[1] n GEOL côte f, littoral m, rivage m, HYDROL maritime, NAUT geography côte f; ~ **battery** n MILIT batterie côtière f; ~ **Earth station** n NAUT navigation by satellite station terrienne côtière f

coast[2] vi NAUT caboter, VEHICLES rouler en roue libre

coastal[1] adj GEOL côtier, littoral, HYDROL, NAUT côtier

coastal:[2] ~ **artillery** n MILIT artillerie côtière f; ~ **chart** n NAUT carte de navigation côtière f; ~ **cruiser** n TRANSP voilier de croisière m; ~ **defence** n (BrE) HYDROL protection côtière f, MILIT, NAUT défense côtière f; ~ **defense** n (AmE) see coastal defence ~ **deposit** n WATER SUPP dépôt côtier m; ~ **erosion** n HYDROL ablation de terre ferme f; ~ **fisherman-farmer** n OCEANOG marin-paysan m; ~ **fishery** n OCEANOG pêche côtière f; ~ **navigation** n HYDROL maritime, NAUT merchant navy cabotage m, navigation côtière f, OCEANOG navigation côtière f; ~ **plain** n GEOL plaine côtière f, plaine littorale f; ~ **platform** n OCEANOG plate-forme littorale f; ~ **ridge** n OCEANOG bourrelet de rive m; ~ **ring road** n CONST rocade littorale f; ~ **river** n WATER SUPP rivière côtière f; ~ **shipping** n HYDROL navigation côtière f; ~ **station** n TELECOM station côtière f; ~ **station identity** n TELECOM identité de station côtière f; ~ **trade** n HYDROL cabotage m, NAUT cabotage m, commerce caboteur m; ~ **vessel** n TRANSP caboteur m; ~ **waters** n pl HYDROL eaux adjacentes aux côtes f pl, NAUT eaux territoriales f pl, OCEANOG eaux côtières f pl; ~ **zone** n GEOL domaine côtier m

coaster n NAUT bateau caboteur m, caboteur m, cabotier m, TRANSP caboteur m

coastguard n NAUT garde de côtes f

coasting: ~ **lugger** n NAUT fishing chasse-marée m; ~ **trade** n NAUT merchant navy cabotage m; ~ **vessel** n TRANSP caboteur m

coastline n GEOL ligne de côte f, littoral m, rivage m, HYDROL rivage m, NAUT littoral m, OCEANOG trait de côte m

coast-to-stop n PROD ENG arrêt en roue libre m

coastwise: ~ **trade** n NAUT merchant navy cabotage m

coat[1] n CONST roads couche f, enduit m, P&R, PAPER TECH, PRINT couche f, PROD ENG voile m, PRODUCTION, SPACE couche f; ~ **of paint** n COATINGS couche de peinture f; ~ **of varnish** n COATINGS couche de laque f, couche de vernis f, enduit de laque m, laque f

coat[2] vt CINEMAT emulsion enduire, COATINGS coucher, enduire, enrober, revêtir, whitewash, distemper badigeonner, with wax cirer, enduire de cire, with slip engober, with gum engommer, with rubber enrober, with lead plomber, FOOD TECH napper, P&R enduire, revêtir; ~ **lenses** vt COATINGS revêtir d'une couche antireflet

coated[1] adj COATINGS bleuté, chargé, enduit, recouvert, revêtu, traité, FOOD TECH in breadcrumbs pané

coated:[2] ~ **abrasive** n MECH ENG abrasif appliqué m; ~ **back** n PRINT dos couché m; ~ **board** n COATINGS carton couché m; ~ **electrode** n MECH welding électrode enrobée f; ~ **fabric** n COATINGS, P&R, PROP MAT tissu enduit m; ~ **fiber** n (AmE), ~ **fibre** n (BrE) PROP MAT fibre enrobée f; ~ **folding board** n PAPER TECH carton couché pour boîtes pliantes m; ~ **front** n PRINT face couchée f; ~ **glass** n C&G verre à couche m; ~ **lens** n CINEMAT objectif traité m, COATINGS objectif bleuté m, objectif traité m, INSTRUMENT lentille antireflet f, lentille à couche antireflet f, PHOTO lentille traitée f, PHYS objectif bleuté m, objectif à revêtement antiréfléchissant m; ~ **paper** n COATINGS papier collé m, papier couché m, papier enduit m, PACKAGING papier encollé m, papier enduit m, PAPER TECH, PRINT papier couché m; ~ **synthetic paper** n PACKAGING papier enduit de matière synthétique m; ~ **tape** n RECORDING bande enduite f; ~ **thickness measurement** n MECH ENG mesure de l'épaisseur des revêtements f; ~ **web** n PRINT bande couchée f; ~ **wire** n COATINGS fil enrobé m

coater n COATINGS coucheuse f, machine à enduire f,

PAPER TECH coucheuse *f*; ~ **pan** *n* COATINGS cuvette de coucheuse *f*; ~ **trough** *n* COATINGS cuvette de coucheuse *f*

coating *n* CINEMAT couchage *m*, traitement de surface optique *m*, CONST chape *f*, couverture *f*, enrobage *m*, enveloppe *f*, revêtement *m*, P&R *paints, adhesives* couchage *m*, enduction *f*, enduit *m*, revêtement *m*, PACKAGING enduit *m*, recouvrement *m*, PAPER TECH couchage *m*, PETR revêtement *m*, PHYS *optical fibre* protection *f*, revêtement *m*, PROD ENG action de couvrir *f*, enduction *f*, enduisage *m*, revêtement *m*, couchage *m*, couche *f*, croûte *f*, efflorescence *f*, enduit *m*, enrobage *m*, enduit *m*, *act* revêtement *m*, PROP MAT revêtement *m*, TEXTILES enducteur *m*; ~ **base paper** *n* PAPER TECH support de couche *m*; ~ **color** *n* (AmE), ~ **colour** *n* (BrE) COATINGS pâte de couchage *f*, solution de couchage *f*, PAPER TECH sauce de couchage *f*; ~ **compound** *n* PACKAGING composition pour enduire *f*; ~ **drum** *n* COATINGS tambour à laquer *m*; ~ **film** *n* COATINGS couche d'enduit *f*, film d'enduit *m*, pellicule de vernis *f*, pellicule protectrice *f*; ~ **finish** *n* COATINGS apprêt par enduction *m*; ~ **head** *n* CINEMAT tête d'émulsionnage *f*; ~ **line supplier** *n* PRINT fournisseur de lignes de couchage *m*; ~ **machine** *n* COATINGS coucheuse *f*, machine à enduire *f*, machine à revêtir *f*, P&R enduiseuse *f*, machine à enduire *f*, PACKAGING machine à enduire *f*, PAPER TECH coucheuse *f*; ~ **material** *n* COATINGS matériau de recouvrement *m*; ~ **mix** *n* PRINT *paper* mélange de couchage *m*, sauce *f*; ~ **mixture** *n* PAPER TECH bain de couche *m*; ~ **pan** *n* PRINT bassine de couchage *f*; ~ **paper** *n* PRINT papier doublure *m*; ~ **powder** *n* COATINGS poudre pour revêtement électrostatique *f*; ~ **property** *n* COATINGS pouvoir couvrant *m*; ~ **roller system** *n* COATINGS rouleau à vernis *m*; ~ **sheet** *n* COATINGS tôle de coffrage *f*; ~ **slip** *n* COATINGS pâte de couchage *f*, solution de couchage *f*; ~ **thickness** *n* COATINGS épaisseur de revêtement *f*, P&R *paints, adhesives* épaisseur de la couche *f*, PACKAGING épaisseur de l'enduit *f*; ~ **thickness measurement apparatus** *n* METR appareil pour mesurer l'épaisseur de films *m*; ~ **trough** *n* - COATINGS cuvette de coucheuse *f*; ~ **unit** *n* PRINT groupe de couchage *m*, groupe de pelliculage *m*, groupe de vernissage *m*; ~ **varnish** *n* COATINGS vernis de barrière de finition *m*, vernis de finition *m*; ~ **wax** *n* COATINGS cire d'enduction *f*, cire d'enrobage *f*, cire à enduire *f*; ~ **weight** *n* PRINT grammage de la couche *m*, poids de la couche *m*

coax *n* COMP, ELEC, ELEC ENG, PHYS, RECORDING, TELECOM, TV câble coaxial *m*

coaxial[1] *adj* ELEC ENG, GEOM coaxial

coaxial:[2] ~ **antenna** *n* TELECOM antenne coaxiale *f*; ~ **attenuator** *n* ELECTRON atténuateur coaxial *m*; ~ **cable** *n* COMP, ELEC, ELEC ENG, PHYS, RECORDING, TELECOM, TV câble coaxial *m*; ~ **cavity** *n* ELECTRON cavité coaxiale *f*; ~ **connector** *n* ELEC ENG connecteur coaxial *m*, prise coaxiale *f*; ~ **diode** *n* ELECTRON diode coaxiale *f*; ~ **filter** *n* ELECTRON filtre coaxial *m*; ~ **fixed load** *n* ELEC ENG charge coaxiale fixe *f*; ~ **helicopter** *n* AERONAUT, TRANSP hélicoptère à rotors coaxiaux *m*; ~ **line** *n* ELEC ENG, PHYS, RECORDING, TELECOM ligne coaxiale *f*; ~ **line system** *n* TELECOM système de ligne coaxiale *m*; ~ **load** *n* ELEC ENG charge coaxiale *f*; ~ **loudspeaker** *n* ACOUSTICS, RECORDING haut-parleur coaxial *m*; ~ **magnetron** *n* ELECTRON magnétron coaxial *m*; ~ **pair** *n* ELEC ENG paire coaxiale *f*; ~ **pair cable** *n* ELEC ENG câble à paires coaxiales *m*; ~ **phase shifter** *n* ELEC ENG déphaseur coaxial *m*; ~ **propeller** *n* TRANSP hélice coaxiale *f*; ~ **resonator** *n* ELECTRON résonateur coaxial *m*

cob *n* CONST torchis *m*; ~ **brick** *n* C&G brique crue *f*; ~ **coal** *n* COAL TECH gailleterie *f*, gaillette *f*

cobalamin *n* CHEM cobalamine *f*

cobalt *n* (*Co*) CHEM cobalt *m* (*Co*); ~ **bloom** *n* MINERAL érythrite *f*; ~ **bottle** *n* C&G bouteille à cobalt *f*; ~ **chloride** *n* C&G chlorure de cobalt *m*; ~ **color** *n* (AmE), ~ **colour** *n* (BrE) COLOURS couleur au cobalt *f*; ~ **glance** *n* MINERAL cobaltite *f*; ~ **naphthenate** *n* P&R *paints, polyesters* naphténate de cobalt *m*; ~ **60 gamma irradiation** *n* NUCLEAR irradiation gamma au cobalt 60 *f*; ~ **60 irradiation plant** *n* NUCLEAR installation d'irradiation au cobalt 60 *f*

cobaltammine *n* CHEM cobaltammine *f*, cobaltiammine *f*, cobaltoammine *f*

cobaltic *adj* CHEM cobaltique

cobaltine *n* MINERAL cobaltite *f*

cobaltite *n* MINERAL cobaltite *f*

cobble *n* GEOL caillou *m*, galet *m*, petit bloc *m*, petit caillou *m*, petit galet *m*

cobbles *n pl* COAL TECH gailleterie *f*, gaillette *f*

cobweb: ~ **gun** *n* CINEMAT machine à produire des toiles d'araignée *f*

cocaine *n* CHEM cocaïne *f*

coccolite *n* MINERAL coccolite *f*

coccolith *n* GEOL coccolithe *f*

co-channel: ~ **interference** *n* RECORDING interférence entre canaux *f*, TV interférence par canal commun *f*; ~ **reuse distance** *n* TELECOM *land mobile* distance de réutilisation des fréquences dans une même voie *f*

cochineal *n* FOOD TECH cochenille *f*, rouge de cochenille *m*

cochlear: ~ **microphonic effect** *n* ACOUSTICS effet microphonique cochléaire *m*

cock[1] *n* CONST *tap* robinet *m*, LAB EQUIP *glassware* boisseau *m*, robinet *m*, MECH *hydraulics* robinet *m*, NAUT *sea* vanne *f*; ~ **brass** *n* CONST bronze pour robinetterie *m*; ~ **key** *n* CONST clef de robinet *f*; ~ **metal** *n* CONST bronze pour robinetterie *m*

cock[2] *vt* CINEMAT *shutter*, PHOTO *shutter* armer

cocking: ~ **lever** *n* PHOTO levier d'armement *m*; ~ **ring** *n* PHOTO bague d'armement *f*

cockle *n* PRINT défaut provenant de la fabrication du papier *m*; ~ **finish** *n* PAPER TECH crispage *m*, fini crispé *m*

cockled: ~ **surface** *n* C&G moutonnage *m*

cockle-finished: ~ **paper** *n* PAPER TECH pelure d'oignon *f*

cockpit *n* AERONAUT habitacle *m*, poste d'équipage *m*, poste pilote *m*, poste de pilotage *m*, NAUT, SPACE *spacecraft* cockpit *m*, poste de pilotage *m*, TRANSP habitacle *m*; ~ **drainage** *n* NAUT vidange du cockpit *f*; ~ **light** *n* AERONAUT feu de cockpit *m*; ~ **temperature indicator** *n* AERONAUT indicateur de température du poste pilote *m*; ~ **voice recorder** *n* AERONAUT enregistreur de conversation *m*, enregistreur de conversation de poste de pilotage *m*

cocks: ~ **and fittings** *n pl* CONST robinetterie *f*

cocoa: ~ **mass** *n* FOOD TECH masse de cacao *f*, pâte de cacao *f*

coconut: ~ **cream** *n* FOOD TECH crème de noix de coco *f*; ~ **oil** *n* FOOD TECH graisse de copra *f*, huile de copra *f*

co-current: ~ **line** *n* OCEANOG ligne cofluctuale *f*

cod: ~ **liver oil** *n* FOOD TECH huile de foie de morue *f*

COD *abbr* *(chemical oxygen demand)* CHEM, HYDROL, POLLUTION DCO *(demande chimique d'oxygène)*

code[1] *n* COMP, DP, ELECTRON, PRINT code *m*, TELECOM *dialling* indicatif *m*, *transmission* code *m*; ~ **conversion** *n* COMP, DP conversion de code *f*; ~ **converter** *n* ELEC ENG convertisseur de code *m*, transcodeur *m*; ~ **extension** *n* DP changement de code *m*; ~ **extension character** *n* DP caractère de changement de code *m*; ~ **flag** *n* NAUT *signals* pavillon du code *m*; ~ **number** *n* CINEMAT *on film* numéro de bord *m*; ~ **string** *n* PRINT chaîne de codes *f*; ~ **violation** *n* *(CV)* TELECOM violation de code *f*

code[2] *vt* TV chiffrer, coder

codec *n* *(coder/decoder)* COMP, ELECTRON, TELECOM codec *m*

coded: ~ **mark inversion** *n* *(CMI)* TELECOM code CMI *m*; ~ **transmission** *n* TELECOM transmission codée *f*

code/decode: ~ **system** *n* TRANSP système de codage/décodage *m*

code-division: ~ **multiple access** *n* *(CDMA)* SPACE *communications* accès multiple par répartition en code *m* *(AMRC)*; ~ **multiplexing** *n* *(CDM)* TELECOM multiplexage par répartition de code *m* *(MRC)*

codeine *n* CHEM codéine *f*

coder *n* DP, ELECTRON, TELECOM codeur *m*, TV codeur *m*, dispositif de codage *m*

coder/decoder *n* *(codec)* COMP, ELECTRON, TELECOM codeur/décodeur *m* *(codec)*

coding *n* COMP programmation *f*, ELECTRON, TELECOM codage *m*; ~ **device** *n* TRANSP dispositif de codage *m*; ~ **error** *n* COMP erreur de programmation *f*, ELECTRON erreur de codage *f*; ~ **scheme** *n* ELECTRON procédé de codage *m*; ~ **standard** *n* TELECOM norme de codage *f*; ~ **theory** *n* COMP, DP théorie de codage *f*; ~ **type** *n* TELECOM type de codage *m*

coefficient *n* ELEC, HYDR EQUIP, MATH, PHYS coefficient *m*, PROD ENG facteur multiplicateur *m*; ~ **of abundance** *n* WATER SUPP coefficient d'abondance *m*; ~ **of capacitance** *n* PHYS coefficient de capacité *m*; ~ **of capture** *n* OCEANOG coefficient de capturabilité *m*; ~ **of consolidation** *n* COAL TECH coefficient de consolidation *m*; ~ **of coupling** *n* ELEC *inductor*, PHYS coefficient de couplage *m*; ~ **of drainage** *n* HYDROL coefficient de tarissement *m*; ~ **of efficiency** *n* MECH, PHYS coefficient d'effet utile *m*; ~ **of efflux** *n* HYDR EQUIP coefficient de décharge *m*, coefficient de perte *m*; ~ **of elasticity** *n* METALL, P&R, PROP MAT coefficient d'élasticité *m*; ~ **of expansion** *n* CONST, MECH, P&R coefficient de dilatation *m*; ~ **of fineness** *n* NAUT *ship design* coefficient de finesse *m*, coefficient de remplissage *m*; ~ **of friction** *n* CONST, MECH coefficient de frottement *m*, METR facteur de frottement *m*, P&R coefficient de friction *m*, coefficient de frottement *m*, PHYS coefficient de frottement *m*; ~ **of haze** *n* POLLUTION coefficient de transmission *m*; ~ **of induction** *n* PHYS coefficient d'influence *m*; ~ **of infiltration** *n* HYDROL coefficient d'infiltration *m*; ~ **of magnetic dispersion** *n* ELEC coefficient de dispersion magnétique *m*; ~ **of mutual induction** *n* ELEC coefficient d'induction mutuelle *m*; ~ **of permeability** *n* COAL TECH, HYDROL coefficient de perméabilité *m*; ~ **of potential** *n* PHYS coefficient de potentiel *m*; ~ **of reduction** *n* NAUT *scantlings* coefficient de réduction *m*; ~ **of roughness** *n* HYDROL coefficient de rugosité *m*; ~ **of run-off** *n* HYDROL coefficient d'écoulement *m*; ~ **of safety** *n* PROD ENG facteur de sécurité *m*; ~ **of thermal conduction** *n* PHYS coefficient de conductibilité thermique *m*; ~ **of thermal conductivity** *n* MECH, P&R coefficient de conductibilité thermique *m*; ~ **of thermal insulance** *n* PHYS coefficient d'isolation thermique *m*; ~ **of torque** *n* FUELLESS coefficient de couple de rotation *m*; ~ **of usable groundwater** *n* HYDROL coefficient de ruissellement utile *m*

coelostat *n* ASTRON coelostat *m*

coenzyme *n* FOOD TECH coenzyme *f*

coercive: ~ **field strength** *n* ELEC *magnetism* force coercitive *f*; ~ **force** *n* ELEC *magnetism* force coercitive *f*, ELEC ENG champ coercible *m*, METALL, PHYS force coercitive *f*; ~ **intensity** *n* ELEC *magnetism* force coercitive *f*

coercivity *n* PHYS champ coercitif *m*, coercivité *f*, PROP MAT force coercitive *f*, RECORDING coercivité *f*, force coercitive *f*, TV champ coercitif *m*, coercivité *f*

coeval *adj* GEOL contemporain

co-extruded: ~ **film** *n* PACKAGING pellicule avec extrusions en couches multiples *f*

coffer[1] *n* WATER SUPP *chamber of lock on canal* chambre *f*, coffre *m*, sas *m*

coffer[2] *vt* MINING coffrer

cofferdam *n* CONST *civil engineering*, HYDROL, WATER SUPP batardeau *m*

coffering *n* WATER SUPP coffrage *m*

cog[1] *n* MECH dent *f*, doigt *m*, MECH ENG alluchon *m*, *tooth* dent *f*; ~ **and round** *n* MECH ENG engrenage à fuseaux *m*, engrenage à lanterne *m*; ~ **belt** *n* MECH ENG courroie à créneaux *f*, VEHICLES *timing* courroie crantée *f*, courroie dentée *f*; ~ **rail** *n* MECH ENG crémaillère *f*; ~ **railroad** *n* (AmE) *(cf cog railway)* TRANSP chemin de fer à crémaillère *m*; ~ **railway** *n* (BrE) *(cf cog railroad)* TRANSP chemin de fer à crémaillère *m*

cog[2] *vt* MECH ENG *scotch, chock* caler, *tooth* denter, endenter

cogged[1] *adj* MECH denté

cogged:[2] ~ **belt timing** *n* AUTO distribution par courroie crantée *f*

cogging: ~ **mill** *n* PROD ENG laminoir à blooms *m*, laminoir à grosses sections *m*, train blooming *m*, train à blooms *m*

cogwheel *n* MECH ENG rouage *m*, roue d'engrenage *f*, roue dentée *f*, roue à dents *f*, rouet *m*; ~ **ore** *n* MINERAL bournonite *f*

cohere *vi* GEOL s'agglomérer

coherence *n* ELECTRON, OPT, PROP MAT, WAVE PHYS *of laser beam* cohérence *f*; ~ **area** *n* OPT aire de cohérence *f*; ~ **bandwidth** *n* TELECOM *land mobile* largeur de bande de cohérence *f*; ~ **length** *n* OPT, PHYS, TELECOM longueur de cohérence *f*; ~ **time** *n* OPT, PHYS, TELECOM durée de cohérence *f*

coherent[1] *adj* ELECTRON, OPT cohérent

coherent:[2] ~ **anti-Stokes Raman scattering** *n* *(CARS)* PHYS diffusion Raman anti-Stokes cohérente *f* *(DRASC)*; ~ **area** *n* OPT, TELECOM aire de cohérence *f*; ~ **boundary** *n* METALL interface cohérente *f*, jointure cohérente *f*; ~ **detection** *n* ELECTRON détection cohérente *f*, détection de phase cohérente *f*; ~ **interface** *n* METALL interface cohérente *f*; ~ **light** *n* ELECTRON *lasers*, TELECOM, WAVE PHYS *waves in phase* lumière cohérente *f*; ~ **monochromatic beam** *n* RAD PHYS faisceau monochromatique cohérent *m*; ~ **noise** *n* GEOPHYS bruit cohérent *m*, bruit organisé *m*, RECORDING bruit cohérent *m*; ~ **oscillator** *n* ELECTRON oscillateur cohérent *m*; ~ **particle** *n* METALL particule cohérente *f*; ~ **phase shift keying** *n (CPSK)* TELECOM modulation par déplacement de phase cohérente *f (MDPC)*; ~ **pulse radar** *n* RAD PHYS radar à impulsions synchronisées *m*; ~ **radiation** *n* OPT, TELECOM rayonnement cohérent *m*; ~ **signal processing** *n* ELECTRON traitement cohérent des signaux *m*; ~ **transmission** *n* TELECOM transmission cohérente *f*; ~ **waves** *n pl* PHYS ondes cohérentes *f pl*

cohesion *n* COAL TECH, CONST, PHYS cohésion *f*; ~ **pile** *n* COAL TECH pieu à cohésion *m*

cohesive[1] *adj* CONST cohésif

cohesive:[2] ~ **energy** *n* METALL énergie de cohésion *f*; ~ **force** *n* PHYS force de cohésion *f*; ~ **soil** *n* COAL TECH sol cohésif *m*, sol résistant *m*

cohobate *vt* CHEM cohober

cohobation *n* CHEM cohobation *f*

coil[1] *n* CONST *piping* tuyau serpentin *m*, ELEC *inductance*, ELEC ENG bobine *f*, HEAT ENG *heat exchangers* serpentin *m*, MECH bobine *f*, rouleau *m*, MECH ENG spire *f*, NAUT *of rope* glène *f*, PACKAGING rouleau *m*, PAPER TECH galette *f*, PHYS bobine *f*, PROD ENG *of wire* botte *f*, couronne *f*, rouleau *m*, SPRINGS rouleau *m*, *steel strip* botte *f*, *wire* bobine *f*, couronne *f*, spire *f*, VEHICLES *ignition* bobine *f*; ~ **arrangement** *n* TESTING réseau de bobine *m*; ~ **clutch** *n* MECH ENG embrayage à enroulement *m*, embrayage à spirale *m*; ~ **coating** *n* P&R couchage sur bande *m*; ~ **core** *n* ELEC noyau de bobine *m*; ~ **diameter** *n* SPRINGS diamètre d'enroulement *m*, diamètre de la spire *m*; ~ **form** *n* ELEC ENG carcasse de bobine *f*; ~ **header** *n* REFRIG *of evaporating coil* collecteur de la batterie *m*; ~ **length** *n* TESTING longueur de bobine *f*; ~ **loading** *n* ELEC ENG pupinisation *f*; ~ **pitch** *n* ELEC pas d'enroulement *m*; ~ **Q- factor** *n* ELEC facteur Q de bobine *m*; ~ **section** *n* ELEC section de bobine *f*; ~ **spring** *n* AUTO ressort hélicoïdal *m*, MECH ressort à boudin *m*, MECH ENG ressort en spirale *m*, SPRINGS ressort en hélice *m*, ressort hélicoïdal *m*, VEHICLES *suspension* ressort hélicoïdal *m*; ~ **spring clutch** *n* AUTO embrayage à ressort *m*; ~ **voltage code** *n* PROD ENG lettre de code correspondant à la tension de la bobine *f*; ~ **winding** *n* ELEC bobinage *m*

coil[2] *vt* NAUT *rope* enrouler, gléner, lover, rouler, PROD ENG bobiner

coiled[1] *adj* SPRINGS enroulé

coiled:[2] ~ **coil filament** *n* ELEC *light bulb* filament bispiral *m*; ~ **coil lamp** *n* ELEC *light bulb* lampe à double boudinage *f*; ~ **spring** *n* MECH ENG ressort en spirale *m*; ~ **spring-type straight pin** *n* MECH ENG goupille élastique spiralée *f*

coiler *n* PROD ENG bobinoir *m*

coiling *n* PROD ENG bobinage *m*, enroulage *m*, enroulement *m*, enroulement en couronne *m*; ~ **machine** *n* SPRINGS machine à enrouler *f*; ~ **tolerance** *n* SPRINGS tolérance d'enroulement *f*

coil-loaded: ~ **cable** *n* ELEC ENG câble pupinisé *m*, câble à charge discontinue *m*

coil-to-coil: ~ **insulation** *n* ELEC *transformer* isolation entre bobines *f*

coin: ~ **box relay** *n* ELEC relais d'encaissement *m*; ~ **slot operator** *n* PROD ENG tête à encoche *f*; ~ **slot selector switch** *n* PROD ENG sélecteur à tête à encoche *m*

coincidence: ~ **circuit** *n* ELECTRON, PHYS circuit à coïncidence *m*; ~ **effect** *n* RECORDING effet de coïncidence *m*

coining: ~ **dies** *n pl* MECH ENG outillage de frappe de formage *m*

coin-operated: ~ **payphone** *n* TELECOM cabine à pièces *f*

coir *n* NAUT *ropes* coco *m*

coke[1] *n* CHEM, COAL TECH, THERMOD coke *m*; ~ **basket** *n* COAL TECH panier à coke *m*; ~ **bed** *n* COAL TECH lit de coke *m*; ~ **blast furnace** *n* PROD ENG haut fourneau au coke *m*; ~ **breaker** *n* COAL TECH casse-coke *m*; ~ **column** *n* COAL TECH colonne de coke *f*; ~ **dust** *n* COAL TECH poussière de coke *f*; ~ **fork** *n* COAL TECH fourche à coke *f*; ~ **mill** *n* COAL TECH broyeur à coke *m*; ~ **oven** *n* C&G, HEATING, MINING, PROD ENG four à coke *m*

coke[2] *vt* COAL TECH cokéfier, transformer en coke

coke-cooling: ~ **tower** *n* MINING tour de charbon à coke *f*, tour à fines *f*

coked: ~ **coal dust** *n* MINING croûtes de coke *f pl*

coke-fired *adj* PROD ENG chauffé au coke

coke-quenching: ~ **tower** *n* MINING tour d'extinction du coke *f*

coking[1] *adj* COAL TECH cokéfiant

coking[2] *n* COAL TECH cokéfaction *f*, transformation en coke *f*; ~ **coal** *n* COAL TECH charbon à coke *m*; ~ **cracking** *n* COAL TECH craquage avec fixation du coke *m*; ~ **duff** *n* COAL TECH menu coke *m*; ~ **plant** *n* HEAT ENG, MINING cokerie *f*; ~ **plate** *n* PROD ENG *of furnace* plaque d'avant- foyer *f*, sole *f*

colchiceine *n* CHEM colchicéine *f*

colchicine *n* CHEM colchicine *f*

colcothar *n* CHEM colcotar *m*

cold[1] *adj* REFRIG, THERMOD froid

cold[2] *n* REFRIG froid *m*, THERMOD froid *m*, froideur *f*; ~ **bending** *n* MECH cintrage à froid *m*, pliage à froid *m*; ~ **blast valve** *n* PROD ENG *blast stove, blast furnace* vanne à vent froid *f*; ~ **bond** *n* THERMOD joint collé à froid *m*; ~ **bonding** *n* THERMOD collage à froid *m*; ~ **brittleness** *n* REFRIG, THERMOD fragilité au froid *f*; ~ **casting** *n* THERMOD moulage à froid *m*; ~ **cathode** *n* ELEC ENG cathode froide *f*; ~ **cathode counter tube** *n* ELECTRON tube compteur à cathode froide *m*; ~ **cathode tube** *n* ELECTRON tube à cathode froide *m*; ~ **chain** *n* REFRIG chaîne de refroidissement *f*, chaîne frigorifique *f*, chaîne froide *f*; ~ **chamber** *n* REFRIG armoire réfrigérée *f*, chambre froide *f*, enceinte réfrigérée *f*; ~ **chisel** *n* MECH ENG bédane à froid *m*; ~ **clamping** *n* SPRINGS bridage à froid *m*; ~ **content** *n* COAL TECH quantité de froid *f*; ~ **creep** *n* (*cf hot creep*) THERMOD fluage à froid *m*; ~ **curing** *n* THERMOD durcissement à froid *m*; ~ **cut varnish** *n* COATINGS vernis fait à froid *m*; ~ **dark matter** *n* ASTRON matière noire froide *f*; ~ **dimpling process** *n* MECH ENG embrèvement à froid *m*; ~ **drawing** *n* MECH étirage à froid *m*, SPRINGS tréfilage à froid *m*; ~ **dyeing** *n* COLOURS teinture à froid *f*; ~ **emission** *n* ELEC ENG émission à froid *f*; ~ **end coating** *n* C&G traitement à froid *m*; ~ **flow** *n* MECH *materials*, P&R fluage à froid *m*; ~ **forging** *n* THERMOD forgeage à froid *m*; ~ **forging dies** *n pl* MECH ENG outillage de forgeage froid *m*; ~ **forming** *n* MECH façonnage à froid *m*; ~ **front** *n* (*cf warm front*) METEO front froid *m*; ~ **gas system** *n* SPACE *spacecraft* système de stabilisation par gaz froid *m*; ~ **glueing system** *n* PACKAGING système d'encollage à froid *m*; ~ **hobbing** *n* MECH ENG matriçage à froid *m*; ~ **injury** *n* REFRIG *food* accident dû au froid *m*; ~ **junction** *n* ELEC *thermocouple* soudure froide *f*, ELEC ENG jonction de référence *f*, soudure froide *f*; ~ **light** *n* CINEMAT lumière froide *f*; ~ **low-density nebula** *n* ASTRON, SPACE nébuleuse froide de faible densité *f*; ~ **mirror reflector** *n* CINEMAT réflecteur miroir à lumière froide *m*; ~ **mix** *n* CONST *asphalting* enrobage à froid *m*, mélange à froid *m*; ~ **mold** *n* (AmE) *see* **cold mould**; ~ **molded wood** *n* (AmE) *see* cold moulded wood; ~ **molding** *n* (AmE) *see* cold moulding; ~ **mould** *n* (BrE) C&G plis de froid *m pl*; ~ **moulded wood** *n* (BrE) NAUT *boatbuilding* bois moulé *m*; ~ **moulding** *n* (BrE) P&R moulage à froid *m*; ~ **presetting** *n* SPRINGS préconformation à froid *f*; ~ **pressure welding** *n* CONST soudage par pression à froid *m*, soudage à froid *m*, MECH soudage à froid *m*; ~ **prestressing** *n* SPRINGS précontrainte à froid *f*, stabilisation à froid *f*; ~ **resistance** *n* ELEC ENG résistance à froid *f*; ~ **riveting** *n* CONST rivetage à froid *m*; ~ **rolling** *n* THERMOD laminage à froid *m*; ~ **saw** *n* MECH ENG scie à froid *f*; ~ **section** *n* AERONAUT *of jet engine* partie froide d'un réacteur *f*; ~ **shortening** *n* REFRIG raccourcissement dû au froid *m*; ~ **shot** *n* PROD ENG *founding* goulotte froide *f*, gouttes froides *f pl*, reprise *f*; ~ **shrink fit** *n* MECH ENG ajustement à froid *m*; ~ **shrink fitting** *n* REFRIG assemblage par contraction frigorifique *m*; ~ **shut** *n* PROD ENG *founding* reprise *f*; ~ **stabilization** *n* REFRIG *of wine* stabilisation du froid *f*; ~ **start** *n* COMP lancement à froid *m*, THERMOD *vehicles* démarrage à froid *m*, départ à froid *m*; ~ **start device** *n* VEHICLES *engines, carburettors* dispositif de démarrage à froid *m*; ~ **start lamp** *n* ELEC *lighting* lampe à amorçage à froid *f*; ~ **static base** *n* REFRIG dessous froid statique *m*; ~ **storage** *n* FOOD TECH *packaging* entreposage frigorifique *m*, entreposage à froid *m*, entrepôt de surgélation *m*, SAFETY entrepôt frigorifique *m*; ~ **storage injury** *n* FOOD TECH *packaging* altération due au froid *f*; ~ **storage room** *n* REFRIG chambre de stockage frigorifique *f*; ~ **storage ship** *n* NAUT navire frigorifique *m*, REFRIG centrale froide *f*; ~ **store** *n* MECH ENG entrepôt frigorifique *m*, REFRIG centrale froide *f*; ~ **store complex** *n* REFRIG complexe frigorifique *m*; ~ **strength** *n* (*cf* hot strength) THERMOD résistance à froid *f*; ~ **surface** *n* C&G plis de froid *m pl*; ~ **trap** *n* REFRIG piège froid *m*; ~ **water down-welling zone** *n* OCEANOG zone source *f*; ~ **working** *n* PROD ENG *blast furnace* allure froide *f*, SPRINGS écrouissage *m*

cold:[3] ~ **cure** *vt* THERMOD *resins, adhesives, plastics* durcir à froid; ~ **draw** *vt* THERMOD étirer à froid; ~ **harden** *vt* THERMOD durcir à froid; ~ **roll** *vt* THERMOD *metals* laminer à froid

cold-bond *vt* THERMOD coller à froid

cold-coiled[1] *adj* SPRINGS enroulé à froid

cold-coiled:[2] ~ **cylindrical spring** *n* SPRINGS ressort hélicoïdal cylindrique enroulé à froid *m*

cold-cured *adj* THERMOD durci à froid

cold-drawn *adj* THERMOD étiré à froid

cold-forge *vt* THERMOD forger à froid

cold-forged *adj* THERMOD forgé à froid

cold-form *vt* THERMOD former à froid

cold-formed[1] *adj* SPRINGS façonné à froid, formé à froid

cold-formed:[2] ~ **compression spring** *n* SPRINGS ressort de compression formé à froid *m*

cold-hardened *adj* SPRINGS écroui

cold-rolled[1] *adj* THERMOD laminé à froid

cold-rolled:[2] ~ **joist** *n* (*CRJ*) THERMOD poutre laminée à froid *f*

coldroom *n* MECH ENG, REFRIG, THERMOD chambre frigorifique *f*, chambre froide *f*

coldseal *n* PRINT scellé à froid *m*; ~ **coating** *n* PRINT couchage à froid *m*

cold-set: ~ **ink** *n* COLOURS encre cold-set *f*, encre pour photocomposition *f*, encre séchant à froid *f*

cold-setting *n* P&R *adhesives* durcissage à froid *m*; ~ **adhesive** *n* P&R adhésif durcissant à froid *m*; ~ **glue** *n* P&R colle durcissante à froid *f*

cold-shear *vt* MECH ENG cisailler à froid

cold-smoked *adj* FOOD TECH fumé à froid

cold-wound: ~ **spring** *n* SPRINGS ressort enroulé à froid *m*

colemanite *n* MINERAL colémanite *f*

COLI *abbr* (*connected line identification*) TELECOM identification de la ligne connectée *f*

colics *n* OCEANOG colique des scaphandriers *f*

coliform: ~ **bacterium** *n* FOOD TECH bactérie coliforme *f*

collagen *n* CHEM, FOOD TECH collagène *m*

collapse[1] *n* CONST effondrement *m*, tombée *f*, écrasée *f*, écroulement *m*, GEOL affaissement *m*, effondrement *m*, MINING *of ground* effondrement *m*, tombée *f*, éboulement *m*, écrasée *f*; ~ **depth** *n* OCEANOG profondeur de destruction *f*

collapse[2] *vi* ASTRON *stars* s'effondrer, GEOL s'affaisser, s'effondrer, s'ébouler

collapsed: ~ **matter** *n* ASTRON matière effondrée *f*

collapsible[1] *adj* MECH ENG télescopable

collapsible:[2] ~ **and reusable packaging system** *n* PACKAGING système d'emballage pliable pouvant être réutilisé *m*; ~ **antenna** *n* SPACE *communications* antenne pliante *f*; ~ **bit** *n* PETR TECH trépan à effacement *m*; ~ **boat** *n* NAUT bateau pliant *m*; ~ **bottle** *n* PHOTO *for developer* flacon souple *m*; ~ **core** *n* MECH ENG *injection moulding* noyau escamotable *m*; ~ **finder** *n* PHOTO viseur pliant *m*; ~ **freight container** *n* TRANSP conteneur repliable *m*; ~ **gate** *n* CONST grille démontable *f*, grille extensible *f*; ~ **section** *n* TRANSP zone déformable *f*; ~ **stand** *n* CINEMAT pied pliant *m*; ~ **steering column** *n* AUTO colonne de direction cédant sous l'impact *f*; ~ **take-up core** *n* CINEMAT noyau récepteur rétractable *m*; ~ **tube** *n* PACKAGING tube souple *m*; ~ **water hose** *n* MECH ENG tuyau d'eau écrasable *m*

collapsing *n* MECH ENG aplatissement *m*, écrasement *m*

collar[1] *n* C&G *Danner tube drawing process* bague de manchon *f*, CONST *head piece, cap of set* chapeau *m*, colain *m*, MECH collerette *f*, collier *m*, virole *f*, MECH ENG bague *f*, bride *f*, entrait retroussé *m*, faux entrait *m*, *building* entrait retroussé *m*, faux entrait *m*, *of axle* champignon *m*, collet *m*, heurtequin *m*, talon *m*, *on coupling* frette *f*, *on shaft* collier *m*, frette *f*, *tools* corset *m*, PETR manchon *m*, PRINT collerette *f*; ~ **beam** *n* MECH ENG *building* entrait retroussé *m*, faux entrait *m*; ~ **beam truss** *n* CONST ferme à faux entrait *f*; ~ **grab** *n* MINING *boring* agrafe de collets *f*; ~ **joint** *n* MECH ENG assemblage à collier *m*; ~ **plate** *n* MECH ENG *lathe steady rest* lunette *f*; ~ **roof** *n* CONST comble retroussé *m*, toit avec entrait *m*; ~ **tie** *n* MECH ENG *building* entrait retroussé *m*, faux entrait *m*; ~ **truss** *n* CONST ferme à faux entrait *f*

collar[2] *vt* MECH ENG baguer, fretter

collared: ~ **coupling** *n* MECH ENG manchon à frettes *m*

collargol *n* CHEM collargol *m*

collate *vt* COMP, DP interclasser, PRINT collationner

collating: ~ **marks** *n pl* PRINT indices de collationnement *m pl*; ~ **press** *n* PRINT assembleuse *f*; ~ **sequence** *n* COMP ordre d'interclassement *m*, DP séquence de classement *f*; ~ **system** *n* PACKAGING système d'assemblage *m*; ~ **transit tray** *n* PACKAGING plateau d'assemblage *m*

collation *n* COMP, DP interclassement *m*

collator *n* COMP, DP interclasseuse *f*, PRINT assembleuse f, collator m

collect:[1] ~ call n (AmE) (cf reverse charge call) TELE-COM appel en PCV m, appel à frais virés m (Can); ~ cylinder n PRINT cylindre accumulateur m; ~ run n PRINT sortie en accumulation f

collect[2] vt WATER SUPP water capter, réunir

collecting: ~ agent n COAL TECH agent collecteur m; ~ ditch n WATER SUPP fossé collecteur m; ~ electrode n POLLUTION électrode collectrice f; ~ pit n CONST puisard m, puits collecteur m; ~ reagent n COAL TECH réactif collecteur m; ~ vat n MINING bac collecteur m, cuve collectrice f

collection n ELEC ENG of current captation f, MAR POLL of oil ramassage m, récupération f, PROD ENG rassemblement m, regroupement m, WATER SUPP of water captage m; ~ and delivery n RAIL camionnage m; ~ basin n MAR POLL of oil bassin collecteur m; ~ device n MAR POLL appareil de ramassage m, système de ramassage m; ~ tray n PAPER TECH bacholle f

collective: ~ aerial n TELECOM antenne collective f; ~ antenna n TELECOM antenne collective f; ~ bell crank n AERONAUT helicopters guignol additionnel m, guignol de pas général m; ~ excitation n RAD PHYS particle interaction excitation collective f; ~ mark n PATENTS marque collective f; ~ model n PHYS nuclear modèle collectif m; ~ pitch n AERONAUT helicopters pas collectif m, pas général m; ~ pitch angle n AERONAUT helicopters pas général m; ~ pitch anticipator n AERONAUT helicopters déphaseur de régulation rotor par le pas général m; ~ pitch control n AERONAUT helicopters commande de pas général f; ~ pitch follow up n AERONAUT helicopters détecteur embrayable m; ~ pitch indicator n AERONAUT helicopters indicateur de pas général m; ~ pitch lever n AERONAUT helicopters levier de pas général m, manche de pas général m; ~ pitch switch n AERONAUT helicopters interrupteur de pas général m; ~ pitch synchronizer n AERONAUT helicopters combinateur de pas général et cyclique m; ~ protection shelter n MILIT chemical warfare abri collectif souple m; ~ protective system n MILIT chemical warfare système souple de protection collective m

collector n COAL TECH collecteur m, ELEC ENG commutator f, of dynamo- electric machine collecteur m, PHYS of transistor, TELECOM, TRANSP collecteur m; ~ contact n ELEC ENG contact du collecteur m; ~ doping n ELECTRON dopage du collecteur m; ~ efficiency n FUELLESS rendement de capteur m; ~ electrode n ELEC ENG électrode collectrice f; ~ motor n ELEC ENG moteur à collecteur m; ~ region n ELEC ENG aire du collecteur f, zone du collecteur f; ~ ring n ELEC ENG anneau collecteur m, MECH ENG anneau collecteur m, barre collectrice f; ~ shoe n ELEC of commutator frotteur m, sabot m, ELEC ENG railways frotteur m; ~ tilt angle n FUELLESS angle d'inclinaison de récepteur m; ~ well n HYDROL puits de captage d'eau brute m

collet n MECH ENG collet m, machine tools bague de serrage f, pince américaine f, VEHICLES of engine, valve clavette f

collico n TRANSP conteneur collico m

collide vi NAUT ship aborder

collidin n CHEM collidine f

collidine n CHEM collidine f

collier n COAL TECH houilleur m, NAUT charbonnier m, navire charbonnier m

colliery n COAL TECH houillère f, siège de charbonnage m, MINING charbonnage m, houillère f, mine f, mine de charbon f, mine de houille f

colligative adj CHEM colligatif

collimate vt ASTRON, ELECTRON, INSTRUMENT collimater

collimated: ~ beam n ELECTRON faisceau collimaté m; ~ lens n PHOTO lentille collimatée f; ~ light n FUELLESS lumière collimatée f; ~ point source n NUCLEAR source ponctuelle centrée f

collimating: ~ fault n PHOTO défaut de collimation m

collimation n ASTRON, ELECTRON, INSTRUMENT, OPT collimation f

collimator n ASTRON, CINEMAT, INSTRUMENT, PHOTO, PHYS, TELECOM collimateur m

collinear[1] adj GEOM colinéaire

collinear:[2] ~ laser spectroscopy n RAD PHYS spectroscopie laser colinéaire f

collinearity n GEOM colinéarité f

collision n COAL TECH, COMP, DP collision f, NAUT of ships abordage m, SAFETY collision f, tamponnement m, TRANSP collision f; ~ avoidance aids n pl NAUT safety aides antiabordage f pl; ~ course n NAUT navigation cap de collision m, SPACE spacecraft trajectoire de collision f; ~ density n RAD PHYS densité des collisions f; ~ detection n (CD) COMP, DP, TELECOM détection de collisions f; ~ energy n PART PHYS énergie de collision f; ~ experiment n PART PHYS expérience de collision f; ~ integral n RAD PHYS Boltzmann equation intégrale des collisions f; ~ ionization n RAD PHYS ionisation par choc f; ~ test n TRANSP essai de choc m; ~ warning system n SPACE spacecraft avertisseur de collision m; ~ wave n MINING explosions onde prolongée f

collocated: ~ concentrator n TELECOM concentrateur d'abonnés local m

collodion n CHEM collodion m; ~ plate n PHOTO plaque au collodion f; ~ process n PRINT procédé au collodion m, procédé au collodion humide m

colloid n C&G, CHEM, COAL TECH, FOOD TECH, HYDROL, P&R colloïde m; ~ disperse system n POLLUTION dispersion colloïdale f; ~ mill n FOOD TECH broyeur pour colloïdes m; ~ propulsion n SPACE spacecraft propulsion colloïdale f

colloidal[1] adj CHEM colloïdal

colloidal:[2] ~ mud n PETR TECH boue colloïdale f; ~ silica n DETERGENTS dioxyde de silicium colloïdal m, silice colloïdale f

colloxylin n CHEM colloxyline f

collyrite n MINERAL collyrite f

colon: ~ bacillus n HYDROL colibacille m

colophene n CHEM colophène m

colophonite n MINERAL colophonite f

colophony n CHEM colophane f

color[1] n (AmE) see colour

color[2] vt (AmE) PAPER TECH colorer

coloradoite n MINERAL coloradoïte f

color-corrected lens n (AmE) see colour-corrected lens

colored[1] adj (AmE) see coloured

colored:[2] ~ clay n (AmE) see coloured clay; ~ edge n (AmE) see coloured edge; ~ glass n (AmE) see coloured glass; ~ lake n (AmE) see coloured lake; ~ light signal n (AmE) see coloured light signal; ~ pigment n (AmE) see coloured pigment, colouring pigment; ~ strapping n (AmE) see coloured strapping

colorfast adj (AmE) see colourfast

colorfastness n (AmE) see colourfastness

colorful adj (AmE) see colourful

colorimeter n CHEM, HYDROL, LAB EQUIP analysis, P&R,

PAPER TECH, PHYS, RAD PHYS colorimètre *m*

colorimetric: ~ **pyrometer** *n* THERMOD pyromètre chromatique *m*

colorimetry *n* CHEM, PHYS, RAD PHYS, WATER SUPP colorimétrie *f*

coloring *n* (AmE) *see colouring*

colorless[1] *adj* (AmE) *see colourless*

colorless:[2] ~ **flux** *n* (AmE) *see colourless flux* ~ **glass** *n* (AmE) *see colourless glass*

colors *n pl* (AmE) *see colours*

colorwork *n* (AmE) *see colourwork*

colour[1] *n* (BrE) CHEM *paint* couleur *f*, FOOD TECH colorant *m*, MINING, PAPER TECH, PRINT, TELECOM, TEXTILES couleur *f* ~ **adaptor** *n* (BrE) COMP carte couleur *f*; ~ **analysis** *n* (BrE) TV analyse de couleur *f*; ~ **analyzer** *n* (BrE) CINEMAT thermocolorimètre *m*, PHOTO analyseur couleur *m*; ~ **automatic time base corrector** *n* (BrE) TV correcteur automatique de base de temps couleur *m*; ~ **background generator** *n* (BrE) TV générateur de fond coloré *m*; ~ **balance** *n* (BrE) CINEMAT équilibre des couleurs *m*, PHOTO harmonisation des couleurs *f*; ~ **bar** *n* (BrE) TV barre colorée *f*, barre de couleur *f*; ~ **bar generator** *n* (BrE) TV générateur de barres couleurs *m*; ~ **bar test pattern** *n* (BrE) TV mire de barres couleurs *f*; ~ **break-up** *n* (BrE) TV décomposition de couleurs *f*; ~ **burst** *n* (BrE) TV impulsion de synchronisation couleur *f*, salve couleur *f*, salve de référence *f*; ~ **cap** *n* (BrE) PROD ENG *for push button* cabochon de couleur *m*; ~ **cast** *n* (BrE) CINEMAT dominante colorée *f*, PHOTO dominante de couleur *f*; ~ **change** *n* (BrE) C&G changement de teinte *m*; ~ **chart** *n* (BrE) PRINT nuancier de couleurs *m*, TV charte chromatique *f*; ~ **chart and grey scale** *n* (BrE) CINEMAT charte de couleurs et gamme de gris *f*; ~ **code letter** *n* (BrE) PROD ENG lettre de code de couleur *f*; ~ **compensating filter** *n* (BrE) *(CC filter)* CINEMAT filtre compensateur de couleurs *m*; ~ **control** *n* (BrE) CONTROL *television* régulateur de couleur *m*; ~ **conversion filter** *n* (BrE) CINEMAT filtre de conversion de couleur *m*; ~ **coordinates** *n pl* (BrE) RAD PHYS coordonnées colorimétriques *f pl*; ~ **correction** *n* (BrE) TV correction colorimétrique *f*, correction d'erreur de chrominance *f*; ~ **correction filter** *n* (BrE) CINEMAT filtre correcteur *m*, ELECTRON filtre de correction de chrominance *m*; ~ **decoder** *n* (BrE) TV décodeur couleur *m*; ~ **densitometer** *n* (BrE) PAPER TECH densitomètre *m*; ~ developer *n* (BrE) PHOTO révélateur chromogène *m*; ~ **development** *n* (BrE) PHOTO développement chromogène *m*; ~ **difference** *n* (BrE) TV différence couleur *f*; ~ **difference signal** *n* (BrE) TV signal de différence couleur *f*; ~ **display** *n* (BrE) AERONAUT affichage en couleur *m*, COMP, DP affichage en couleur *m*, écran couleur *m*, SPACE affichage en couleur *m*; ~ **dupe print** *n* (BrE) CINEMAT copie inversible couleur *f*; ~ **error** *n* (BrE) TV erreur chromatique *f*, erreur de phase de sous-porteuse couleur *f*; ~ **fastness** *n* (BrE) COLOURS, P&R solidité de la couleur *f*, solidité de teinte *f*; ~ **field** *n* (BrE) TV trame à couleurs *f*; ~ **field corrector** *n* (BrE) TV aimant d'uniformisation de la trame de couleurs *m*; ~ **film analyzer** *n* (BrE) CINEMAT analyseur couleur *m*; ~ **form** *n* (BrE) PRINT forme en couleur *f*, forme pour impression en couleur *f*; ~ **formulation** *n* (BrE) COLOURS formulation de couleur *f*; ~ **framing** *n* (BrE) TV synchronisation des trames couleurs *f*; ~ **fringing** *n* (BrE) TV frange couleur *f*; ~ **gate** *n* (BrE) TV porte de

signal couleur *f*; ~ **gradation** *n* (BrE) COLOURS étalonnage des couleurs *m*; ~ **graphics** *n* (BrE) COMP graphiques couleurs *m*; ~ **graphics adaptor** *n* (BrE) *(CGA)* COMP carte graphique couleur *f*; ~ **head** *n* (BrE) CINEMAT, PHOTO tête couleur *f*; ~ **hue** *n* (BrE) COLOURS nuance *f*; ~ **index** *n* (BrE) ASTRON indice de couleur *m*; ~ **indicators of dose** *n pl* (BrE) RAD PHYS *radioactivity* indicateurs de dose à couleurs *m pl*; ~ **key** *n* (BrE) PRINT barre de contrôle *f*, charte des couleurs *f*, film de sélection *m*; ~ **kill** *n* (BrE) TV suppresseur de chrominance *m*; ~ **lightness** *n* (BrE) PRINT valeur chromatique d'une couleur *f*; ~ **limit** *n* (BrE) COLOURS limite de couleur *f*, limite de teinte *f*; ~ **lock** *n* (BrE) TV verrouillage du signal couleur *m*; ~ **map** *n* (BrE) COMP, DP carte des couleurs *f*; ~ **match** *n* (BrE) COLOURS concordance des couleurs *f*, conformité des couleurs *f*; ~ **matching** *n* (BrE) CINEMAT équilibrage colorimétrique *m*, étalonnage couleur *m*, COLOURS contretypage *m*, PRINT correspondance des couleurs *f*; ~ **metallography** *n* (BrE) METALL métallographie en couleurs *f*; ~ **mix** *n* (BrE) C&G mélange colorant *m*, COLOURS mélange de couleurs *m*; ~ **mixing** *n* (BrE) COLOURS *operation* mélange de couleurs *m*; ~ **mixture** *n* (BrE) COLOURS *result* mélange de couleurs *m*; ~ **modulator** *n* (BrE) TV modulateur couleur *m*; ~ **noise** *n* (BrE) TV bruit de chrominance *m*; ~ **palette** *n* (BrE) COMP, DP palette de couleurs *f*; ~ **phase** *n* (BrE) TV angle de phase du signal de chrominance *m*, phase couleur *f*; ~ **phase diagram** *n* (BrE) TV diagramme de phase de couleur *m*; ~ **photography** *n* (BrE) PHOTO photo couleur *f*, photographie en couleur *f*; ~ **picture** *n* (BrE) PHOTO image en couleur *f*; ~ **print** *n* (BrE) PHOTO copie en couleurs *f*; ~ **printing machine** *n* (BrE) PRINT machine pour l'impression en couleurs *f*; ~ **printing process** *n* (BrE) PHOTO chromotypie *f*; ~ **processing** *n* (BrE) CINEMAT traitement couleur *m*; ~ **processing chemicals** *n pl* (BrE) PHOTO produits chimiques pour développement couleur *m pl*; ~ **pyrometer** *n* (BrE) RAD PHYS pyromètre à couleurs *m*; ~ **reference signal** *n* (BrE) TV signal de référence couleur *m*; ~ **rendition** *n* (BrE) CINEMAT rendu des couleurs *m*; ~ **response** *n* (BrE) CINEMAT sensibilité chromatique *f*; ~ **reversal film** *n* (BrE) CINEMAT pellicule couleur inversible *f*, PHOTO film en couleur inversible *m*; ~ **reversal intermediate** *n* (BrE) CINEMAT internégatif couleur *m*; ~ **reversal process** *n* (BrE) PHOTO procédé d'inversion des couleurs *m*; ~ **sampling frequency** *n* (BrE) RAD PHYS fréquence de commutation des couleurs *f*; ~ **sampling rate** *n* (BrE) TV fréquence de commutation de couleurs *f*; ~ **sampling sequence** *n* (BrE) TV séquence de commutation de couleurs *f*; ~ **saturation** *n* (BrE) ELECTRON saturation des couleurs *f*; ~ **screen** *n* (BrE) PHOTO écran orthochromatique *m*, PRINT écran en couleurs *m*; ~ **separation** *n* (BrE) CINEMAT extraction *f*, sélection des couleurs *f*, PRINT sélection des couleurs *f*, TV analyse chromatique *f*, séparation chromatique *f*, sélection des couleurs *f*; ~ **separation filter** *n* (BrE) CINEMAT, PHOTO filtre de sélection *m*; ~ **separation negative** *n* (BrE) PHOTO négatif de sélection trichrome *m*; ~ **separation overlay** *n* (BrE) *(cf chromakey)* TV mixage de signaux d'image à activation électronique *m*; ~ **shift** *n* (BrE) PRINT glissement *m*, modification de la couleur *f*; ~ **signal** *n* (BrE) *(cf chrominance signal)* CONTROL signal de chrominance *m*, signal de couleur *m*, TV signal chromatique *m*,

signal de chrominance *m*, signal de couleur *m*; ~
splitter *n* (BrE) CINEMAT miroir dichroïque *m*; ~
streaks *n pl* (BrE) C&G traînées colorées *f pl*; ~
strength *n* (BrE) P&R *paint, pigments* pouvoir colorant *m*; ~ **striking** *n* (BrE) C&G développement de
couleur *m*; ~ **subcarrier** *n* (BrE) TV sous-porteuse de
chrominance *f*; ~ **sync signal** *n* (BrE) TV signal de
synchronisation couleur *m*; ~ **synthesizer** *n* (BrE) TV
générateur de couleur *m*; ~ **television** *n* (BrE) TV
télévision couleur *f*; ~ **temperature** *n* (BrE) CINEMAT
température de couleur *f*; ~ **temperature meter** *n*
(BrE) CINEMAT, PHOTO thermocolorimètre *m*; ~ **threshold** *n* (BrE) TV seuil de différence couleur *m*; ~ **timer**
n (BrE) CINEMAT étalonneur couleur *m*; ~ **tone** *n* (BrE)
P&R *paint* nuance *f*; ~ **triangle** *n* (BrE) PHYS triangle
des couleurs *m*; ~ **video signal** *n* (BrE) CONTROL signal
complet en couleur *m*; ~ **wheel** *n* (BrE) TEXTILES
palette de couleurs *f*

colour[2] *vt* (BrE) PAPER TECH colorer

colour-corrected: ~ **lens** *n* (BrE) PHOTO objectif corrigé
chromatiquement *m*

coloured *n* (BrE) TELECOM coloré; ~ **clay** *n* (BrE) C&G
engobe *m*; ~ **edge** *n pl* (BrE) PRINT tranche de couleur
f; ~ **glass** *n* (BrE) C&G verre de couleur *m*; ~ **lake** *n*
(BrE) COLOURS laque colorée *f*; ~ **light signal** *n* (BrE)
RAIL panneau- signal à oculaire mobile coloré *m*; ~
pigment *n* (BrE) COLOURS pigment coloré *m*; ~ **strapping** *n* (BrE) PACKAGING bande colorée *f*

colourfast *adj* (BrE) COLOURS grand teint, solide à la
lumière, PACKAGING teinture solide, TEXTILES grand
teint

colourfastness *n* (BrE) P&R solidité de couleur *f*

colourful *adj* (BrE) COLOURS de couleur vive, de couleur
éclatante

colouring *n* (BrE) COLOURS mélange de couleurs *m*,
FOOD TECH colorant *m*; ~ **agent** *n* (BrE) C&G colorant
m, COLOURS colorant *m*, matière colorante *f*, matière
tinctoriale *f*; ~ **body** *n* (BrE) COLOURS corps colorant
m; ~ **matter** *n* (BrE) COLOURS colorant *m*, matière
colorante *f*, matière tinctoriale *f*, PRINT pigment *m*; ~
pigment *n* (BrE) COLOURS pigment coloré *m*; ~ **power**
n (BrE) COLOURS pouvoir colorant *m*; ~ **substance** *n*
(BrE) COLOURS matière colorante *f*, matière tinctoriale *f*; ~ **value** *n* (BrE) COLOURS pouvoir colorant *m*

colourless[1] *adj* (BrE) COLOURS, FOOD TECH incolore,
non coloré

colourless:[2] ~ **flux** *n* (BrE) C&G fondant incolore *m*; ~
glass *n* (BrE) C&G verre incolore *m*

colours *n pl* (BrE) NAUT *flag* couleurs *f pl*

colourwork *n* (BrE) PRINT travail en couleurs *m*

COLP *abbr (connected line identification presentation)*
TELECOM PILC *(présentation de l'identification de la
ligne connectée)*

Colpitts: ~ **oscillator** *n* ELECTRON oscillateur Colpitts *m*

COLR *abbr (connected line identification restriction)*
TELECOM RILC *(restriction de l'identification de la
ligne connectée)*

Columba *n* ASTRON Colombe *f*

columbite *n* CHEM niobite *f*

column *n* COMP, DP, ELECTRON colonne *f*, MINING affût-
colonne *m*, PRINT colonne *f*, rubrique *f*; ~ **box** *n* PROD
ENG *founding* châssis à colonnes *m*; ~ **charge** *n* MINING
charge de colonne *f*; ~ **loudspeaker** *n* RECORDING
haut-parleur à colonne *m*

columnar: ~ **basalt** *n* GEOL orgue basaltique *m*; ~ **charge**
n MINING charge de colonne *f*; ~ **crystal** *n* METALL

cristal colonnaire *m*; ~ **jointing** *n* GEOL prismation *f*,
prismation basaltique *f*

column-type: ~ **drilling machine** *n* MECH ENG machine à
percer sur colonne *f*

colures *n pl* ASTRON colures *m pl*

COM *abbr* COMP *(computer output on microfilm)* sortie
ordinateur sur microfilm *f*, TELECOM *(continuation of
message)* suite de message *f*

coma *n* ELECTRON, PHOTO, PHYS coma *m*; ~ **aberration** *n*
ASTRON *of reflecting telescope* aberration de coma *f*; ~
fail *n* ASTRON *of comet* chevelure cométaire *f*

Coma: ~ **Berenices** *n* ASTRON Chevelure de Bérénice *f*

comagmatic *adj* GEOL comagmatique

comb[1] *n* TEXTILES peigne *m*; ~ **filter** *n* ELECTRON filtre en
peigne *m*; ~ **filtering** *n* ELECTRON filtrage par filtre en
peigne *m*

comb[2] *vt* TEXTILES peigner

combat: ~ **aircraft** *n* MILIT avion de combat *m*; ~
helicopter *n* AERONAUT hélicoptère armé *m*

combed[1] *adj* TEXTILES peigné

combed:[2] ~ **top** *n* TEXTILES ruban peigné *m*; ~ **wool
fabric** *n* TEXTILES tissu peigné *m*; ~ **yarn** *n* TEXTILES fil
peigné *m*

combination *n* AERONAUT *helicopters* conjugaison *f*,
CHEM *action* combinaison *f*, *product* combiné *m*,
COMP, DP, MATH combinaison *f*; ~ **bulk carrier** *n*
TRANSP navire combiné *m*, transport combiné minerai-vrac-pétrole *m*; ~ **chuck** *n* MECH ENG mandrin à
combinaisons *m*; ~ **lathe** *n* MECH ENG tour à combinaisons *m*; ~ **lock** *n* CONST serrure à combinaisons *f*; ~
microphone *n* RECORDING microphone combiné *m*; ~
pliers *n pl* MECH ENG *press tools* pinces à combinaisons
f pl; ~ **run** *n* PRINT tirage *m*; ~ **sound** *n* ACOUSTICS son
de combinaison *m*; ~ **surface gage** *n* (AmE), ~ **surface
gauge** *n* (BrE) MECH ENG trusquin à combinaisons *m*;
~ **tap assembly** *n* MECH ENG robinetterie mélangeur *f*;
~ **tone** *n* ACOUSTICS son résultant *m*; ~ **tools** *n pl* MECH
ENG *press tools* outillages multiples *m pl*

combinational *n* (AmE) *(cf combinatorial circuit)* COMP, ELECTRON circuit combinatoire *m*

combinatorial: ~ **analysis** *n* MATH analyse combinatoire
f; ~ **circuit** *n* (BrE) *(cf combinational circuit)* COMP
circuit combinatoire *m*, ELECTRON circuit combinatoire *m*, circuit logique combinatoire *m*; ~ **logic** *n*
ELECTRON logique combinatoire *f*

combinatorics *n* MATH *study of configurations* combinatoire *f*, combinatorique *f*

combine *vt* COMP, DP combiner, MECH ENG *multicylinder
engine output diagrams* rankiniser

combined: ~ **bending shrinking and welding machine** *n*
MECH ENG machine à refouler souder couder et
contrecouder *f*; ~ **braking** *n* RAIL *vehicles* freinage
mixte *m*; ~ **cargo and passenger liner** *n* TRANSP cargo
mixte *m*; ~ **cargo and passenger ship** *n* TRANSP cargo
mixte passagers-marchandises *m*; ~ **diagram** *n* MECH
ENG *engine output* diagramme rankinisé *m*; ~ **distribution frame** *n (CDF)* TELECOM répartiteur mixte *m*; ~
drill and countersink *n* MECH ENG foret à centrer *m*; ~
flow turbine *n* HYDR EQUIP turbine américaine *f*, turbine hélico-centripète *f*, turbine mixte *f*; ~ **grinder and
sieve** *n* PROD ENG broyeur-tamiseur *m*; ~ **heat and
power station** *n* THERMOD centrale combinée *f*; ~
local-toll system *n* TELECOM système mixte local et
transit *m*; ~ **mark** *n* PATENTS marque combinée *f*; ~
packaging *n* PACKAGING emballage composé *m*; ~
parallel vice *n* (BrE) MECH ENG *for drilling machines*

étau-plateau *m*; ~ **parallel vise** *n* (AmE) *see combined parallel vice*; ~ **print** *n* CINEMAT copie image et son *f*, copie standard *f*; ~ **sewer** *n* HYDROL réseau unitaire *m*, système unitaire *m*, égout conjoint *m*; ~ **sewer system** *n* WATER SUPP réseau d'assainissement mixte *m*, système unitaire d'assainissement *m*; ~ **sights** *n pl* MILIT *of gun* hausses combinées *f pl*; ~ **stamping forging shearing and punching machine** *n* MECH ENG machine à étamper forger cisailler et poinçonner *f*; ~ **stoping** *n* MINING abattage combiné *m*; ~ **sulfur** *n* (AmE), ~ **sulphur** *n* (BrE) P&R soufre combiné *m*; ~ **surfacing planing molding and slot-mortising machine** *n* (AmE), ~ **surfacing planing moulding and slot-mortising machine** *n* (BrE) MECH ENG machine combinée à dégauchir raboter moulurer et mortaiser *f*; ~ **vessel** *n* TRANSP navire combiné *m*; ~ **water** *n* WATER SUPP eau de constitution *f*

combiner *n* TELECOM combineur *m*; ~ **circuit** *n* ELECTRON circuit mélangeur *m*

combing: ~ **machine** *n* TEXTILES peigneuse *f*

combining: ~ **circuit** *n* TELECOM circuit combinateur *m*, circuit combinatoire *m*, TV circuit combinateur *m*; ~ **cone** *n* MECH ENG *of injector* convergent *m*, tuyère convergente *f*; ~ **nozzle** *n* MECH ENG *of injector* ajutage convergent *m*, convergent *m*, tuyère convergente *f*; ~ **tube** *n* MECH ENG *of injector* convergent *m*, tuyère convergente *f*

combo *n* PRINT combinaison d'images *f*

comb-shaped: ~ **electrode** *n* SPACE *spacecraft* électrode en forme de peigne *f*

combust *vi* MINING *explosively* déflagrer

combustibility *n* PACKAGING, SAFETY combustibilité *f*, THERMOD combustibilité *f*, inflammabilité *f*

combustible[1] *adj* CHEM comburable, THERMOD combustible, inflammable

combustible[2] *n* THERMOD *fuel* combustible *m*, substance combustible *f*; ~ **fossil fuels** *n pl* POLLUTION matériaux combustibles *m pl*; ~ **fossils** *n pl* POLLUTION énergies fossiles combustibles *f pl*; ~ **gas** *n* GAS TECH gaz combustible *m*; ~ **material** *n* POLLUTION matériau combustible *m*, SAFETY matière combustible *f*, matériaux combustibles *m pl*; ~ **waste** *n* POLLUTION déchets combustibles *m pl*

combustibles *n pl* COAL TECH combustibles *m pl*

combustion *n* CHEM, P&R, SAFETY, THERMOD combustion *f*; ~ **air** *n* THERMOD air de combustion *m*; ~ **analysis** *n* THERMOD analyse par incinération *f*; ~ **axial gas fan** *n* MECH ENG ventilateur axial à gaz de combustion *m*; ~ **boat** *n* LAB EQUIP *analysis* nacelle à combustion *f*; ~ **chamber** *n* AUTO, HEATING, HYDR EQUIP *of steam boiler furnace*, MECH ENG *of engine*, NAUT *of engine*, SPACE *spacecraft*, THERMOD *piston engines*, VEHICLES *of engine* chambre de combustion *f*; ~ **chamber annular case** *n* AERONAUT enveloppe annulaire de la chambre de combustion *f*; ~ **control** *n* NAUT *engines* contrôle de chauffe *m*; ~ **deposit** *n* THERMOD *in engines, flues* résidu de combustion *m*; ~ **efficiency** *n* SPACE *spacecraft* rendement de combustion *m*, THERMOD efficacité de combustion *f*, rendement de combustion *m*, taux d'efficacité de combustion *m*; ~ **energy** *n* THERMOD énergie de combustion *f*; ~ **engine** *n* TRANSP moteur à combustion *m*; ~ **engineering** *n* THERMOD technique de combustion *f*; ~ **gas** *n* SPACE *spacecraft* gaz de combustion *m*; ~ **heat** *n* THERMOD chaleur de combustion *f*; ~ **index** *n* THERMOD indice de combustion *m*; ~ **instability** *n* THERMOD

instabilité de combustion *f*; ~ **prechamber** *n* TRANSP préchambre de combustion *f*; ~ **residue** *n* POLLUTION imbrûlés *m pl*; ~ **starter** *n* AERONAUT démarreur à combustion *m*

combustive *adj* CHEM comburant, combustible

combustor *n* SPACE *spacecraft* chambre de combustion *f*

come: ~ **back to the center of its run** *vi* (AmE), ~ **back to the centre of its run** *vi* (BrE) CONST *air bubble in levelling instrument* revenir entre ses repères; ~ **into gear** *vi* MECH ENG engrener, s'embrayer, s'engrener; ~ **to** *vi* NAUT *shiphandling* lofer; ~ **to a standstill** *vi* MECH ENG s'arrêter

comeback *n* C&G, THERMOD réchauffage *m*, réchauffe *f*

comenic *adj* CHEM coménique

comet *n* ASTRON comète *f*, PRINT comète *f*, défaut d'impression formant une trace allongée *m*, SPACE comète *f*; ~ **core** *n* ASTRON noyau de comète *m*, SPACE coeur de comète *m*, noyau de comète *m*; ~ **origins** *n pl* ASTRON origines des comètes *f pl*; ~ **shockwave** *n* ASTRON onde de choc de la comète *f*; ~ **tar** *n* ASTRON traînée lumineuse de comète *f*

comet's: ~ **head** *n* ASTRON tête de la comète *f*

cometary: ~ **nebula** *n* ASTRON, SPACE nébuleuse cométaire *f*; ~ **orbit** *n* ASTRON orbite de comète *f*; ~ **tail** *n* ASTRON queue cométaire *f*, queue de la comète *f*

comfort: ~ **cooling** *n* REFRIG rafraîchissement pour le confort *m*

comforter *n* TEXTILES édredon *m*

coming: ~ **and going** *n* TEXTILES va-et-vient *m*; ~ **into gear** *n* MECH ENG embrayage *m*, engrenage *m*; ~ **out of hole** *n* PETR TECH remontée du train de tiges *f*

comingled: ~ **yarn** *n* TEXTILES fil texturé par assemblage *m*

comma *n* ACOUSTICS comma *m*, PRINT virgule *f*

commag *n* CINEMAT copie standard son magnétique *f*

command:[1] **not under** ~ *adj* (NUC) NAUT *shiphandling* non-manoeuvrable, pas maître de sa manoeuvre

command[2] *n* COMP commande *f*, instruction *f*, ordre *m*; ~ **and control center** *n* (AmE), ~ **and control centre** *n* (BrE) NAUT *of ship* centre de contrôle et de commandement *m*; ~ **and control system** *n* (*CSM*) COMP système de commande et contrôle *m*; ~ **and service module** *n* (*CSM*) SPACE module de commande et de service *m*; ~ **buffer** *n* PROD ENG registre tampon des commandes *m*; ~ **channel** *n* SPACE canal de télécommande *m*, voie de télécommande *f*; ~ **Earth station** *n* SPACE station terrienne de télécommande *f*; ~ **language** *n* COMP langage de contrôle *m*; ~ **link** *n* SPACE chaîne de commande *f*; ~ **module** *n* SPACE *spacecraft* module de commande *m*; ~ **prompt** *n* COMP, DP message d'attente d'une commande *m*; ~ **receiver** *n* SPACE récepteur d'ordres *m*; ~ **ship** *n* NAUT *navy* navire amiral *m*; ~ **signal** *n* CONTROL signal de pilotage *m*; ~ **system** *n* COMP système de commande *m*; ~ **window** *n* COMP fenêtre de commande *f*

command-driven: ~ **interface** *n* COMP interface à déclenchement par commande *f*

commander *n* NAUT *navy* capitaine de frégate *m*, SPACE *spacecraft* commandant de bord *m*

commensurable *adj* MATH commensurable

comment *n* COMP, PAPER TECH *in synchronous data link*, PRINT *in synchronous data link* commentaire *m*; ~ **line** *n* PROD ENG ligne d'observations *f*

commentary: ~ **track** *n* CINEMAT bande commentaire *f*, RECORDING piste commentaire *f*

commercial: ~ **amplifier** *n* ELECTRON amplificateur civil *m;* ~ **coal** *n* COAL TECH charbon marchand *m;* ~ **coefficiency** *n* PROD ENG coefficient d'effet utile *m,* coefficient de rendement *m,* rendement industriel *m;* ~ **computing** *n* COMP, DP informatique de gestion *f;* ~ **condensing unit** *n* REFRIG groupe frigorifique commercial *m;* ~ **electric vehicle** *n* TRANSP véhicule utilitaire électrique *m;* ~ **field** *n* PETR TECH gisement rentable *m;* ~ **language** *n* COMP, DP langage de gestion *m;* ~ **mass** *n* TESTING, TEXTILES masse commerciale *f;* ~ **moisture regain** *n* TESTING, TEXTILES reprise commerciale d'humidité *f;* ~ **photography** *n* PHOTO publicité photographique *f;* ~ **port** *n* NAUT port de commerce *m;* ~ **power frequency** *n* ELEC ENG fréquence industrielle *f;* ~ **press** *n* PRINT machine de labeur *f;* ~ **printing** *n* PRINT labeur *m;* ~ **standard** *n* PROD ENG étalon industriel *m;* ~ **traffic** *n* TRANSP trafic commercial *m;* ~ **type** *n* PRINT caractères de labeur *m pl;* ~ **vehicle** *n* VEHICLES véhicule utilitaire *m;* ~ **water** *n* HYDROL eau commerciale *f,* eau pour usage commerciaux *f*

comminution *n* CHEM TECH broyage *m,* comminution *f,* fragmentation *f,* NUCLEAR broyage *m,* pulvérisation *f*

comminutor *n* HYDROL *sewage* broyeur *m*

commission:[1] **in** ~ *adj* NAUT *ship* en commission

commission[2] *vt* CONST mettre en service

commissioned: ~ **work** *n* PROD ENG prestation *f,* travail en régie *m*

commissioning *n* CONST, PROD ENG mise en service *f;* ~ **test** *n* TELECOM essai de mise en service *m*

commit: ~ **to silicon** *vt* ELECTRON convertir en circuit intégré monolithique

commitment *n* PROD ENG engagement *m,* implication *f*

committed: ~ **information rate** *n* (*CIR*) TELECOM débit d'information garanti *m*

commodity: ~ **group** *n* PACKAGING groupe d'articles de commerce *m*

commodore *n* NAUT *navy* chef d'escadre *m*

common *n* PROD ENG masse *f;* ~ **aerial** *n* TELECOM antenne collective *f;* ~ **anode connection** *n* ELEC ENG montage à anode commune *m;* ~ **area** *n* COMP, DP zone commune *f;* ~ **base amplifier** *n* ELECTRON amplificateur à base commune *m;* ~ **base connection** *n* ELEC ENG montage à base commune *m;* ~ **base transistor** *n* ELECTRON transistor monté en base commune *m;* ~ **battery switchboard** *n* TELECOM commutateur à batterie centrale *m;* ~ **branch** *n* ELEC *supply,* ELEC ENG branche mutuelle *f;* ~ **carrier** *n* NAUT *satellite communications* onde porteuse *f,* PRINT réseau officiel de télétransmission *m,* TRANSP transporteur *m,* TV porteuse commune *f;* ~ **cathode** *n* ELEC ENG cathode commune *f;* ~ **cause of accidents** *n* SAFETY cause courante d'accidents *f;* ~ **channel signaling** *n* (AmE), ~ **channel signalling** *n* (BrE) TELECOM signalisation par canal sémaphore *f,* signalisation sémaphore *f;* ~ **clay** *n* C&G limon *m;* ~ **collector amplifier** *n* ELECTRON amplificateur à collecteur commun *m;* ~ **collector connection** *n* ELEC ENG montage à collecteur commun *m;* ~ **control equipment** *n* TELECOM organes communs *m pl;* ~ **control switching system** *n* TELECOM système à commande centrale *m;* ~ **control system** *n* TELECOM système à commande centralisée *m;* ~ **crossing** *n* RAIL coeur de croisement *m;* ~ **depth point** *n* GEOL point miroir commun *m,* PETR point commun de profondeur *m,* point miroir commun *m;* ~ **difference** *n* MATH différence commune *f;* ~ **drain amplifier** *n* ELECTRON amplificateur à drain commun *m;* ~ **drain connection**

n ELEC ENG montage à drain commun *m;* ~ **drain transistor** *n* ELECTRON transistor monté en drain commun *m;* ~ **emitter amplifier** *n* ELECTRON amplificateur à émetteur commun *m;* ~ **emitter connection** *n* ELEC ENG montage à émetteur commun *m;* ~ **emitter transistor** *n* ELECTRON transistor monté en émetteur commun *m;* ~ **equipment** *n* (*CE*) TELECOM matériel commun *m,* organe commun *m;* ~ **fuse** *n* MINING cordeau Bickford *m,* fusée de sûreté *f,* mèche de sûreté *f,* mèche ordinaire *f,* étoupille de sûreté *f;* ~ **gate amplifier** *n* ELECTRON amplificateur à grille commune *m;* ~ **gate connection** *n* ELEC ENG montage à grille commune *m;* ~ **gate transistor** *n* ELECTRON transistor monté en grille commune *m;* ~ **highway** *n* TELECOM tronc commun *m;* ~ **injury in the workplace** *n* SAFETY blessure courante sur les lieux de travail *f;* ~ **logarithm** *n* MATH logarithme à base 10 *m;* ~ **management information protocol** *n* (*CMIP*) TELECOM protocole commun d'information de gestion *m;* ~ **management information protocol machine** *n* (*CMIPM*) TELECOM machine du protocole commun de transfert d'informations de gestion *f;* ~ **management information service** *n* (*CMIS*) TELECOM service commun d'information de gestion *m,* service commun de transfert d'informations de gestion *m;* ~ **management information service element** *n* (*CMISE*) TELECOM élément de service commun d'information de gestion *m,* élément de service commun de transfert d'informations de gestion *m;* ~ **mode** *n* ELECTRON *differential amplifiers* mode commun *m;* ~ **mode gain** *n* ELECTRON gain en mode commun *m;* ~ **mode rejection** *n* ELECTRON réjection du mode commun *f;* ~ **mode rejection ratio** *n* ELECTRON rapport de réjection en mode commun *m;* ~ **mode signal** *n* ELECTRON signal de mode commun *m;* ~ **mode voltage** *n* ELEC ENG tension de mode commun *f;* ~ **normal** *n* MECH ENG normale commune *f, to curves of teeth in contact* ligne de poussée *f,* ligne de pression *f,* normale commune des profils *f,* normale de contact *f;* ~ **properties of electromagnetic waves** *n pl* RAD PHYS propriétés communes des ondes électromagnétiques *f pl;* ~ **quality** *n* PROD ENG qualité ordinaire *f;* ~ **rafter** *n* CONST chevron intermédiaire *m;* ~ **ratio** *n* MATH raison *f;* ~ **reactance** *n* ELEC *inductors* induction mutuelle *f;* ~ **repair tools** *n pl* MECH ENG outils de réparation courants *m pl;* ~ **return** *n* TELECOM retour commun *m;* ~ **scaffold** *n* CONST échafaud de maçon *m,* échafaud ordinaire *m,* échafaud simple *m;* ~ **source amplifier** *n* ELECTRON amplificateur à source commune *m;* ~ **source transistor** *n* ELECTRON transistor monté en source commune *m;* ~ **store** *n* TELECOM mémoire commune *f;* ~ **wire** *n* PROD ENG fil de neutre *m,* fil de neutre de terre *m*

communicating: ~ **vessels** *n pl* LAB EQUIP vases communicants *m pl*

communication *n* PATENTS notification *f;* ~ **channel** *n* COMP, DP voie de communication *f;* ~ **link** *n* COMP liaison *f,* ligne de communication *f,* DP liaison de communication *f;* ~ **medium** *n* COMP, DP support de communication *m;* ~ **network** *n* COMP réseau de communication *m,* réseau de transmission *m,* DP réseau de communication *m,* réseau de transmission *m;* ~ **satellite** *n* SPACE (*COMSAT*) satellite de télécommunications *m;* ~ **server** *n* COMP, DP serveur de communication *m;* ~ **services** *n pl* (*CS*) TELECOM services de communication *m pl;* ~ **software** *n* COMP logiciel de communications *m;* ~ **system** *n* COMP, DP système de communication *m*; ~ **theory** *n* COMP, DP théorie de la communication *f*

communications *n pl* COMP, DP communications *f pl*; ~ **agreement** *n* TELECOM accord d'échange *m*; ~ **cable** *n* ELEC ENG câble de télécommunications *m*; ~ **circuit** *n* ELEC ENG circuit de télécommunications *m*; ~ **filter** *n* ELECTRON filtre de télécommunications *m*; ~ **line** *n* ELEC ENG ligne de télécommunications *f*; ~ **processor** *n* TELECOM processeur de communications *m*; ~ **research centre** *n* (*CRC*) TELECOM centre de recherche sur les communications *m*; ~ **satellite** *n* (*COMSAT*) NAUT satellite de communications *m*; ~ **signal** *n* ELECTRON signal de télécommunications *m*

community: ~ **aerial** *n* TELECOM antenne pour la réception communautaire *f*, TV antenne collective *f*; ~ **antenna** *n* TELECOM antenne pour la réception communautaire *f*, TV antenne collective *f*; ~ **broadcasting** *n* TV radiotélévision communautaire *f*; ~ **dial office** *n* (*CDO*) TELECOM central automatique local *m*; ~ **sewage works** *n* WATER SUPP station d'épuration collective *f*

commutating: ~ **pole** *n* ELEC pôle de commutation *m*; ~ **winding** *n* ELEC enroulement de commutation *m*

commutation *n* ELEC ENG, MATH commutation *f*

commutative *adj* MATH commutatif

commutator *n* ELEC commutateur *m*, ELEC ENG collecteur *m*, collecteur mécanique *m*, *remote measurement* scruteur *m*, TRANSP *electric vehicles* collecteur *m*; ~ **bar** *n* ELEC, ELEC ENG lame de collecteur *f*; ~ **brush** *n* ELEC balai *m*; ~ **DC motor** *n* ELEC ENG moteur à courant continu à collecteur *m*; ~ **direct current motor** *n* ELEC ENG moteur à courant continu à collecteur *m*; ~ **motor** *n* ELEC, ELEC ENG, TRANSP moteur à collecteur *m*; ~ **ring** *n* ELEC bague de collecteur *f*; ~ **segment** *n* ELEC lame de collecteur *f*, ELEC ENG segment du collecteur *m*; ~ **sparking** *n* ELEC crachement aux balais *m*; ~ **switch** *n* ELEC commutateur de sens de marche *m*

commutator-type: ~ **frequency converter** *n* ELEC *converter* convertisseur de fréquence à collecteur *m*

commuter: ~ **traffic** *n* TRANSP trafic habitation travail *m*

comopt *n* CINEMAT copie standard son optique *f*

comp *n* PRINT compositeur *m*

compact[1] *adj* MECH ENG de faible encombrement

compact:[2] ~ **audio disc** *n* (BrE) OPT disque audionumérique *m*, disque compact audio *m*, disque compact audionumérique *m*; ~ **audio disk** *n* (AmE) *see compact audio disc*; ~ **cassette** *n* RECORDING cassette compacte *f*; ~ **CNC universal cylindrical grinding machine** *n* MECH ENG *machine tools* rectifieuse cylindrique universelle compacte à CNC *f*; ~ **disc** *n* (BrE) (*CD*) OPT, RECORDING disque compact *m*; ~ **disc-interactive** *n* (BrE) (*CD-I*) OPT disque compact interactif *m*; ~ **disc-read only memory** *n* (BrE) (*CD-ROM*) OPT disque compact ROM *m* (*CD-ROM*); ~ **disk** *n* COMP (*CD*) disque audionumérique *m*, disque compact *m*, DP (*CD*), OPT, recording *see compact disc*; ~ **disk-interactive** *n* (AmE) *see compact disc-interactive*; ~ **disk-read only memory** *n* COMP (*CD-ROM*), DP (*CD-ROM*), OPT *see compact disc-read only memory* disque compact ROM *m* ~ **immersion tube** *n* GAS TECH tube immergé compact *m*; ~ **medium** *n* PROP MAT milieu compact *m*; ~ **music disc** *n* (BrE) OPT disque audionumérique *m*, disque compact audio *m*, disque compact audionumérique *m*; ~ **music disc drive** *n* (BrE) OPT lecteur audionumérique *m*, lecteur de disque audionumérique *m*; ~ **music disc**

player *n* (BrE) OPT lecteur audionumérique *m*, lecteur de disque audionumérique *m*; ~ **music disk** *n* (AmE) *see compact music disc*; ~ **music disk drive** *n* (AmE) *see compact music disc drive*; ~ **music disk player** *n* (AmE) *see compact music disc player*

compact[3] *vt* PROD ENG compacter

compacted: ~ **apparent density** *n* CHEM TECH masse volumique après tassement *f*; ~ **conductor** *n* ELEC *cable* âme compacte *f*, âme rétreinte *f*; ~ **thickness** *n* CONST épaisseur compactée *f*

compaction *n* COAL TECH compactage *m*, COMP compaction *f*, compression *f*, CONST compactage *m*, serrage *m*, DP compaction *f*, compression *f*, GEOL compaction *f*, tassement *m*, PETR TECH compaction *f*, PROP MAT compactage *m*; ~ **disequilibrium** *n* PETR TECH *clays, shales* sous-compaction *f*; ~ **piling** *n* COAL TECH battage de pieux par compaction *m*, empilement par compaction *m*; ~ **trend** *n* PETR TECH *clays, shales* droite de compaction *f*

companded: ~ **delta modulation** *n* (*CDM*) TELECOM modulation delta avec compression-extension *f*; ~ **signal** *n* ELECTRON signal à compansion *m*

compander *n* COMP, DP compresseur-expanseur *m*, ELECTRON companseur *m*, compresseur-expanseur *m*, RECORDING système à compression- expansion *m*, SPACE *communications*, TELECOM compresseur- extenseur *m*

companding *n* ELECTRON compansion *f*, SPACE *communications*, TELECOM compression-extension *f*

companion: ~ **chip** *n* ELECTRON puce auxiliaire *f*; ~ **source** *n* ELECTRON générateur auxiliaire *m*

companionway *n* NAUT échelle de descente *f*; ~ **hatch** *n* NAUT *shipbuilding* panneau de descente *m*; ~ **ladder** *n* NAUT échelle de descente *f*; ~ **post** *n* NAUT *boatbuilding* montant d'entrée du roof *m*

comparative: ~ **dyeing** *n* COLOURS teinture de comparaison *f*; ~ **system** *n* TESTING *coil arrangements* système comparatif *m*; ~ **test** *n* PHYS essai comparatif *m*

comparator *n* COMP, DP, ELECTRON, METR, PHYS, TELECOM comparateur *m*; ~ **circuit** *n* ELECTRON circuit comparateur *m*; ~ **densitometer** *n* CINEMAT densitomètre comparateur *m*

compare:[1] ~ **signal** *n* CONTROL signal de comparaison *m*

compare[2] *vt* COMP, DP comparer

comparison: ~ **circuit** *n* TELECOM comparateur *m*

compartment *n* COAL TECH cellule *f*, COMP compartiment *m*, MECH ENG case *f*, logement *m*, REFRIG compartiment *m*; ~ **case** *n* PACKAGING carton avec compartiments *m*; ~ **mill** *n* COAL TECH broyeur à compartiments *m*

compartmental: ~ **model** *n* TELECOM modèle à cases *m*, modèle à compartiments *m*

compartmentalization *n* COMP, DP cloisonnement *m*

compartmentation *n* MINING *of shaft* compartimentage *m*, NAUT *naval architecture* compartimentage *m*

compartmented: ~ **insert** *n* PACKAGING compartiment emboîtable *m*; ~ **tray** *n* PACKAGING plateau alvéolé *m*

compass *n* AERONAUT, CONST, GEOPHYS boussole *f*, METR compas *m*, MILIT boussole *f*, NAUT *navigation*, PHYS, SPACE boussole *f*, compas *m*; ~ **bearing** *n* AERONAUT relèvement au compas *m*, GEOL azimut *m*, relèvement au compas *m*, NAUT *navigation* relèvement au compas *m*; ~ **bowl** *n* PHYS cuvette de boussole *f*; ~ **card** *n* INSTRUMENT graduation *f*, NAUT rose des vents *f*, rose du compas *f*; ~ **compensating** *n* AERONAUT compensation de compas *f*; ~ **compensation base** *n*

AERONAUT aire de compensation de compas *f*; ~ **dial** *n* NAUT cadran du compas *m*; ~ **error** *n* NAUT *navigation* variation *f*; ~ **heading** *n* AERONAUT cap au compas *m*, NAUT *navigation* cap au compas *m*; ~ **input** *n* NAUT *radar* données introduites du compas *f pl*; ~ **lens** *n* C&G verre pour boussoles *m*; ~ **locator** *n* AERONAUT radiobalise *f*; ~ **meridian line** *n* INSTRUMENT ligne méridienne *f*; ~ **needle** *n* NAUT *navigation* aiguille aimantée *f*, PHYS aiguille de boussole *f*; ~ **plane** *n* CONST rabot cintré *m*; ~ **repeater** *n* NAUT répétiteur de compas *m*; ~ **saw** *n* CONST scie à guichet *f*, scie à tourner *f*; ~ **survey** *n* MINING levé de plan à la boussole *m*, levé à la boussole *m*; ~ **variation** *n* NAUT déclinaison magnétique locale *f*

compasses *n* GEOM compas *m*, MECH ENG compas *m*, paire de compas *f*, METR compas *m*; ~ **with pencil point** *n pl* MECH ENG compas à porte-crayon *m*; ~ **with pen point** *n pl* MECH ENG compas à tire-ligne *m*

compatibility *n* COMP, DP, MECH ENG, P&R, PROD ENG, QUALITY, TV *of format* compatibilité *f*

compatible[1] *adj* COMP, DP, QUALITY compatible

compatible:[2] ~ **groove modulation** *n* ACOUSTICS gravure universelle *f*; ~ **logic** *n* ELECTRON logique compatible *f*; ~ **metal-oxide semiconductor** *n* (*CMOS*) COMP semi-conducteur à oxyde métallique complémentaire *m*; ~ **MOS** *n* COMP MOS complémentaire *m*

compensate[1] *vt* NAUT *compass*, PHYS compenser, SAFETY *for injuries received* verser des indemnités, *indemnify* dédommager; ~ **for damage** *vt* PATENTS dédommager

compensate:[2] ~ **for wear** *vi* MECH compenser l'usure, rattraper l'usure, rattraper le jeu

compensated: ~ **amplifier** *n* ELECTRON amplificateur à très large bande *m*; ~ **brake rigging** *n* RAIL *vehicles* timonerie de frein compensé *f*; ~ **foundation** *n* COAL TECH fondation compensée *f*; ~ **induction motor** *n* ELEC moteur asynchrone compensé *m*; ~ **motor** *n* ELEC moteur compensé *m*; ~ **pendulum** *n* PHYS pendule compensateur *m*; ~ **semiconductor** *n* ELEC ENG semi-conducteur condensé *m*

compensating: ~ **beam** *n* MECH ENG *equalizer* balancier *m*, balancier de répartition *m*, balancier de suspension *m*; ~ **buffer** *n* RAIL appareil de choc compensateur *m*; ~ **circuit** *n* ELEC circuit de compensation *m*; ~ **coupling** *n* MECH ENG accouplement élastique *m*, manchon d'accouplement élastique *m*, manchon élastique *m*; ~ **current** *n* ELEC courant compensateur *m*; ~ **developer** *n* PHOTO révélateur compensateur *m*; ~ **filter** *n* PHOTO filtre compensateur *m*; ~ **gear** *n* MECH ENG différentiel *m*, engrenage différentiel *m*; ~ **jet** *n* VEHICLES *carburettors* gicleur compensateur *m*; ~ **reservoir** *n* WATER SUPP bassin de compensation *m*; ~ **spool** *n* PROD ENG tiroir de compensation *m*; ~ **voltage** *n* ELEC tension compensatrice *f*

compensation *n* ELEC ENG, ELECTRON, PHYS compensation *f*, SAFETY dédommagement *m*, *for accident* dommages-intérêts *m pl*; ~ **basin** *n* HYDROL bassin de compensation *m*, bassin de retenue *m*; ~ **circuit** *n* TELECOM circuit de compensation *m*; ~ **current** *n* OCEANOG courant de compensation *m*; ~ **depth** *n* OCEANOG profondeur de compensation *f*; ~ **for wear** *n* MECH compensation de l'usure *f*, rattrapage de jeu *m*, rattrapage de l'usure *m*; ~ **reservoir** *n* HYDROL réservoir de compensation *m*; ~ **theorem** *n* ELEC, PHYS théorème de compensation *m*; ~ **winding** *n* ELEC ENG enroulement de compensation *m*

compensator *n* ELEC *alternating current circuits* compensateur *m*, ELEC ENG compensateur *m*, montage compensateur *m*, ELECTRON, PHYS compensateur *m*

competing: ~ **demands** *n pl* PROD ENG demandes concurrentes *f pl*

competition: ~ **growth** *n* METALL croissance concourante *f*

competitive: ~ **edge** *n* PROD ENG esprit de compétition *m*

compilation *n* COMP compilation *f*; ~ **time** *n* COMP durée de compilation *f*

compile *vt* COMP compiler

compiler *n* COMP, TELECOM compilateur *m*; ~ **diagnostic** *n* COMP diagnostic du compilateur *m*; ~ **directive** *n* COMP directive de compilateur *f*

compiler-compiler *n* COMP compilateur de compilateur *m*

complement *n* COMP, DP, ELECTRON complément *m*

complementarity *n* COMP, DP correspondance *f*

complementary: ~ **angle** *n* GEOM angle complémentaire *m*; ~ **code** *n* TELECOM code complémentaire *m*; ~ **color** *n* (AmE), ~ **colour** *n* (BrE) PHOTO couleur complémentaire *f*; ~ **I/O addressing** *n* PROD ENG adressage d'E/S complémentaire *m*; ~ **input rack** *n* PROD ENG rack d'entrée complémentaire *m*; ~ **matte** *n* CINEMAT contre-cache *m*; ~ **outputs** *n pl* ELECTRON sorties complémentaires *f pl*; ~ **pair** *n* ELECTRON paire complémentaire *f*; ~ **set** *n* MATH ensemble complémentaire *m*; ~ **transistors** *n pl* ELECTRON transistors complémentaires *m pl*

complete: ~ **combustion** *n* GAS TECH combustion complète *f*; ~ **diversion** *n* TRANSP déviation totale de circulation *f*; ~ **purification** *n* NUCLEAR épuration fine *f*; ~ **synchronization signal** *n* CONTROL signal complet de synchronisation *m*

complete-assembly *adj* MECH ENG assemblé et équipé

completely: ~ **stable layer** *n* METEO couche absolument stable *f*

completion *n* CONST réception provisoire *f*, PETR TECH *of well* complétion *f*; ~ **time** *n* CONST délai d'exécution *m*

complex *n* GEOL complexe *m*, ensemble *m*; ~ **admittance** *n* ELEC *alternating current circuits*, PHYS admittance complexe *f*; ~ **fraction** *n* MATH double fraction *f*; ~ **impedance** *n* ELEC *alternating current circuits*, ELEC ENG, PHYS impédance complexe *f*; ~ **instruction set computer** *n* (*CISC*) COMP ordinateur à jeu d'instructions complexe *m*; ~ **number** *n* DP, MATH nombre complexe *m*; ~ **ore** *n* COAL TECH minerai complexe *m*; ~ **permeability** *n* ELEC *alternating current circuits* perméabilité complexe *f*; ~ **power** *n* ELEC puissance complexe *f*; ~ **refractive index** *n* PHYS indice de réfraction complexe *m*; ~ **signal** *n* ELECTRON signal complexe *m*; ~ **tone** *n* ACOUSTICS son complexe *m*; ~ **type** *n* COMP, DP type complexe *m*; ~ **wave** *n* TELECOM onde complexe *f*; ~ **waveform** *n* ELEC *alternating current* forme d'onde complexe *f*

complexing: ~ **agent** *n* NUCLEAR agent complexant *m*

complexity *n* COMP, DP complexité *f*

complexometric: ~ **titration** *n* CHEM titration complexométrique *f*

compliance *n* ACOUSTICS souplesse *f*, QUALITY conformité *f*; ~ **test** *n* QUALITY essai de conformité *m*

component[1] *adj* MECH ENG composant, constituant, constitutif

component[2] *n* COAL TECH composant *m*, ELEC *of force, current* composante *f*, *part* composant *m*, ELECTRON composante *f*, *element of functional set* composant *m*, MECH composante *f*, MECH ENG organe *m*, NUCLEAR *of subsystem* composant *m*, PHYS *of vector* composante *f*, PROD ENG composant *m*, organe *m*, TELECOM composant *m*; ~ **cooling filter** *n* NUCLEAR filtre du circuit intermédiaire *m*; ~ **data element separator** *n* TELECOM séparateur d'éléments de données constitutifs *m*; ~ **density** *n* ELECTRON densité de composants *f*; ~ **failure** *n* PROD ENG défaillance du matériel *f*; ~ **identification marker** *n* PROD ENG repère de fonction des composants *m*; ~ **layout** *n* ELECTRON disposition des composants *f*; ~ **level** *n* ELECTRON niveau des composants *m*; ~ **manufacturer** *n* PROD ENG accessoiriste *m*; ~ **procurement** *n* SPACE *spacecraft* approvisionnement des composants *m*; ~ **selection** *n* SPACE *spacecraft* choix des composants *m*; ~ **side** *n* TELECOM côté composant *m*; ~ **spacing** *n* PROD ENG espacement entre les éléments constitutifs *m*

compose *vt* PRINT composer

composing: ~ **machine** *n* PRINT machine à composer *f*; ~ **stick** *n* PRINT compositeur *m*

composite[1] *adj* PROP MAT composite

composite[2] *n* METALL composite *m*, P&R *article* matériau composite *m*; ~ **absorber** *n* NUCLEAR absorbeur composite *m*; ~ **aircraft** *n* AERONAUT avion combiné *m*; ~ **cable** *n* ELEC ENG câble composite *m*; ~ **check print** *n* CINEMAT copie "O" standard *f*; ~ **color signal** *n* (AmE), ~ **colour signal** *n* (BrE) TV signal couleur complet *m*, signal couleur composite *m*; ~ **container** *n* PACKAGING récipient composite *m*; ~ **dike** *n* (AmE); ~ **dyke** *n* (BrE) GEOL *igneous intrusion* filon intrusif composite *m*; ~ **filter** *n* RECORDING filtre composé *m*; ~ **girder** *n* CONST poutre composée *f*, poutre mixte *f*; ~ **lens** *n* PHOTO objectif à lentilles multiples *m*; ~ **log** *n* GEOL colonne stratigraphique *f*; ~ **loudspeaker** *n* RECORDING haut-parleur composé *m*; ~ **mark** *n* PATENTS marque combinée *f*; ~ **material** *n* SPACE *spacecraft* matériau composite *m*; ~ **number** *n* MATH nombre composé *m*; ~ **pass band** *n* ELECTRON bande passante résultante *f*; ~ **pile** *n* COAL TECH pieu combiné *m*; ~ **print** *n* CINEMAT copie standard *f*; ~ **sample** *n* COAL TECH, QUALITY échantillon composite *m*; ~ **shot** *n* CINEMAT plan cache-contrecache *m*, plan multi-images *m*; ~ **signal** *n* ELECTRON, TV signal composite *m*; ~ **signal coding** *n* TELECOM codage de signal composite *m*; ~ **sill** *n* GEOL *igneous intrusion* filon-couche composé *m*; ~ **synchronization signal** *n* CONTROL, TV signal de synchronisation complet *m*, signal de synchronisation composite *m*; ~ **video signal** *n* TV signal vidéo complet *m*, signal vidéo composite *m*; ~ **volcano** *n* GEOL volcan composé *m*; ~ **wave** *n* TELECOM onde composite *f*

composites *n pl* PROP MAT matériaux composites *m pl*

composition *n* CHEM, MECH *of forces* composition *f*, NUCLEAR composition initiale *f*, PAPER TECH *paper, board*, PRINT composition *f*

compositor *n* PRINT compositeur *m*

composting *n* POLLUTION *sewage* compostage *m*

compound *n* CHEM combiné *m*, composé *m*, P&R mélange *m*, PROD ENG enduit *m*, mélange *m*; ~ **blowpipe** *n* PROD ENG chalumeau oxhydrique *m*; ~ **clarification** *n* HYDROL *sewage* décantation composée *f*; ~ **compression** *n* MECH ENG *of air* compression étagée *f*; ~ **compressor** *n* NUCLEAR compresseur à plusieurs étages *m*; ~ **dies** *n pl* MECH ENG *press tools* outillages composés pour presses *m pl*; ~ **engine** *n* MECH ENG machine compound *f*; ~ **expansion engine** *n* MECH ENG moteur compound *m*, moteur à expansion compound *m*; ~ **gage** *n* (AmE), ~ **gauge** *n* (BrE) REFRIG manovacuomètre *m*; ~ **girder** *n* CONST poutre composée *f*, poutre conjuguée *f*; ~ **helicopter** *n* AERONAUT gyrodyne *m*, hélicoptère combiné *m*, TRANSP hélicoptère combiné *m*; ~ **lever** *n* MECH ENG levier double *m*; ~ **magnet** *n* PHYS faisceau aimanté *m*; ~ **microscope** *n* INSTRUMENT, PHYS microscope composé *m*; ~ **modulation** *n* ELECTRON modulation successive *f*; ~ **motion** *n* MECH mouvement composé *m*; ~ **motor** *n* ELEC moteur compound *m*, moteur à excitation compound *m*, moteur à excitation mixte *m*, ELEC ENG moteur à excitation compound *m*; ~ **nucleus** *n* NUCLEAR, PHYS, RAD PHYS noyau composé *m*; ~ **oil** *n* PROD ENG huile compoundée *f*; ~ **pendulum** *n* PHYS pendule composé *m*, pendule pesant *m*; ~ **screw** *n* MECH ENG *differential* vis différentielle *f*, *right-and-left screw* vis à pas contraires *f*; ~ **signal** *n* CONTROL signal composé *m*; ~ **slide rest** *n* MECH ENG support à chariot à double coulisse *m*, support à chariot à mouvement longitudinal et transversal *m*; ~ **state** *n* NUCLEAR état composé *m*, état intermédiaire *m*; ~ **statement** *n* COMP, DP instruction composée *f*; ~ **table** *n* MECH ENG *drilling machine* plateau à double coulisse *m*, table à double coulisse *f*; ~ **tide** *n* OCEANOG onde composée *f*; ~ **tool holder** *n* MECH ENG porte-outil à double coulisse *m*; ~ **twinning** *n* METALL maclage composé *m*; ~ **wedge** *n* MINING coin multiple *m*; ~ **winding** *n* ELEC *direct current*, ELEC ENG enroulement compound *m*; ~ **winding motor** *n* ELEC ENG moteur compound *m*

compounding *n* ELEC ENG compoundage *m*

compound-slotted: ~ **worktable** *n* MECH ENG table porte-pièces à rainures à double coulisse *f*

compound-wound: ~ **motor** *n* ELEC moteur compound *m*

comprehensive: ~ **treatment plant** *n* WATER SUPP station d'oxydation totale *f*

compress *vt* COMP, CONST, DP comprimer

compressed: ~ **air** *n* CONST, MECH ENG, MINING air comprimé *m*; ~ **air conditioning unit** *n* CONST *civil engineering* ensemble pour conditionnement d'air comprimé *m*; ~ **air cylinder** *n* MECH ENG cylindre à air comprimé *m*; ~ **air drill** *n* MECH ENG perforateur pneumatique *m*, perforatrice à air comprimé *f*; ~ **air engine** *n* MECH ENG machine à air comprimé *f*, moteur à air comprimé *m*; ~ **air equipment** *n* MECH ENG outillage à air comprimé *m*; ~ **air line** *n* MECH ENG canalisation d'air comprimé *f*; ~ **air lubricator** *n* MECH ENG lubrificateur à air comprimé *m*; ~ **air motor** *n* MINING moteur à air comprimé *m*; ~ **air socket** *n* MECH ENG douille à air comprimé *f*; ~ **air system** *n* MECH ENG transmission à air comprimé *f*; ~ **digital transmission** *n* TELECOM transmission numérique avec compression *f*; ~ **fitting** *n* MECH ENG *pipes* raccord de compression *m*; ~ **nuclear matter** *n* NUCLEAR matière nucléaire comprimée *f*; ~ **pulse width** *n* ELECTRON largeur de l'impulsion comprimée *f*; ~ **signal** *n* ELECTRON signal comprimé *m*; ~ **speech** *n* ELECTRON parole comprimée *f*; ~ **steel shafting** *n* MECH ENG arbres de transmission en acier comprimé *m pl*; ~ **video level** *n* TV niveau vidéo comprimé *m*

compressibility *n* FLUID PHYS, HEAT ENG, METALL, PAPER TECH, PHYS compressibilité *f*; ~ **coefficient** *n* COAL TECH, PHYS coefficient de compressibilité *m*; ~ **curve** *n* THERMOD courbe de compressibilité *f*; ~ **drag** *n* AERO-

NAUT traînée de compressibilité f; ~ **effects** $n\ pl$ AERO-NAUT effets de compressibilité $m\ pl$; ~ **factor** n PETR, THERMOD facteur de compressibilité m; ~ **of gases** n THERMOD compressibilité des gaz f; ~ **modulus** n COAL TECH module de déformation volumique m

compressible: ~ **flow** n FLUID PHYS écoulement compressible m

compressing: ~ **fan** n MECH ENG ventilateur foulant m, ventilateur positif m, ventilateur soufflant m, PRODUCTION ventilateur foulant m, ventilateur positif m

compression n COMP compaction f, compression f, CONST compression f, DP compaction f, compression f, ELECTRON compression f, HYDR EQUIP compression f, phase de compression f, MECH ENG *of spring* flèche f, *of seal* écrasement m, NUCLEAR *of plasma*, P&R, PHYS, PROP MAT, RECORDING, REFRIG, WAVE PHYS *of sound waves* compression f; ~ **chamber** n AUTO chambre de compression f, COAL TECH caisson de pistonnage m, HYDR EQUIP, PETR TECH *diving* chambre de compression f; ~ **cock** n HYDR EQUIP robinet de compression m; ~ **curve** n COAL TECH courbe de compression f; ~ **damage** n PACKAGING endommagement causé par la compression m; ~ **driver** n RECORDING moteur à compression m; ~ **filter** n ELECTRON filtre de compression d'impulsions f; ~ **ignition engine** n MECH ENG moteur à allumage par compression m; ~ **index** n COAL TECH indice de compression m; ~ **installation** n GAS TECH installation de compression f; ~ **modulus** n P&R module de compression m; ~ **mold** n (AmE) *see compression mould*; ~ **molding** n (AmE) *see compression moulding*; ~ **molding machine** n (AmE) *see compression moulding machine*; ~ **mould** n (BrE) MECH ENG *for rubber* moule pour compression m, *for thermosetting* moule pour compression thermodurcissable m; ~ **moulding** n (BrE) C&G moulage à la presse m, P&R, PACKAGING moulage par compression m; ~ **moulding machine** n (BrE) P&R machine à mouler par compression f; ~ **period** n HYDR EQUIP phase de compression f; ~ **plant** n THERMOD réfrigérateur m; ~ **point** n HYDR EQUIP point de compression m; ~ **pump** n HYDR EQUIP pompe de compression f; ~ **ratio** n ELECTRON rapport de compression m, MECH ENG rapport de compression m, taux de compression m, RECORDING facteur de compression m, REFRIG taux de compression m, THERMOD *motors* rapport volumétrique m, VEHICLES *engines* taux de compression m; ~ **refrigerating cycle** n REFRIG cycle frigorifique à compression m; ~ **refrigerator** n MECH ENG réfrigérateur à compresseur m, THERMOD réfrigérateur à compression m; ~ **ring** n VEHICLES *engines, pistons* segment de compression m; ~ **set** n P&R déformation permanente par sollicitation de compression f, rémanence par compression f; ~ **side** n SPRINGS face comprimée f; ~ **spring** n HYDR EQUIP, SPRINGS ressort de compression m; ~ **stage** n MECH ENG étage de compression m; ~ **strength** n MECH *materials*, PACKAGING résistance à la compression f; ~ **stress** n MECH *materials*, METALL, PACKAGING contrainte de compression f; ~ **stroke** n AUTO, THERMOD *motors*, VEHICLES *engines* course de compression f; ~ **system** n REFRIG système à compression m; ~ **test** n COAL TECH essai de compression m, essai de consolidation m, MECH *materials*, METALL, PACKAGING essai de compression m; ~ **tester** n PAPER TECH compressomètre m; ~ **test machine** n PACKAGING machine à essais de compression f

compressional: ~ **wave** n ACOUSTICS onde de compression f, GEOL onde de compression f, onde longitudinale f, RECORDING onde de compression f

compressive: ~ **behavior** n (AmE), ~ **behaviour** n (BrE) PROP MAT comportement en compression m; ~ **force** n MECH ENG effort de compression m; ~ **strain** n GEOL déformation causée par la compression f, MECH *materials* déformation sous compression f; ~ **strength** n P&R résistance à la compression f

compressometer n COAL TECH compressiomètre m, PAPER TECH compressomètre m

compressor n CONST compresseur m, compresseur d'air m, ELECTRON, GAS TECH, LAB EQUIP, MECH, MECH ENG, PAPER TECH, PETR TECH, RECORDING, REFRIG compresseur m, VEHICLES *engines* compresseur m, suralimenteur m; ~ **air bleed** n MECH ENG prélèvement d'air d'un compresseur m; ~ **blade** n AERONAUT aube du compresseur f, pale du compresseur f; ~ **rotor** n AERONAUT *helicopters* mobile du compresseur m; ~ **stall** n AERONAUT *turbine engines* calage du compresseur m, pompage du compresseur m; ~ **stator** n AERONAUT stator compresseur m; ~ **surge** n AERONAUT pompage du compresseur m; ~ **terminal box** n REFRIG boîte à borne du compresseur f

compressor-expander n TELECOM compresseur-extenseur m

Compton: ~ **continuum** n RAD PHYS distribution Compton f, fond Compton m; ~ **effect** n PHYS effet Compton m, RAD PHYS diffusion Compton f, effet Compton m; ~ **scattering** n PHYS diffusion Compton f; ~ **wavelength** n NUCLEAR *of electron, other particle*, PHYS, RAD PHYS longueur d'onde Compton f

compulsory: ~ **licence** n (BrE) PATENTS licence obligatoire f; ~ **license** n (AmE) *see compulsory licence*

Compur: ~ **shutter** n PHOTO obturateur Compur m

computation n COMP, DP calcul m; ~ **of center of gravity** n (AmE), ~ **of centre of gravity** n (BrE) AERONAUT détermination du centrage f

computer n COMP, DP calculateur m, ordinateur m, ELEC ordinateur m; ~ **animation** n CINEMAT, COMP animation par ordinateur f, TV animation assistée par ordinateur f; ~ **art** n COMP graphisme informatique m; ~ **bank** n COMP batterie d'ordinateurs m, TELECOM batterie d'ordinateurs f; ~ **family** n COMP, DP famille d'ordinateurs f; ~ **graphics** n COMP, DP, TV infographie f; ~ **interface** n TELECOM interface informatique f; ~ **literacy** n COMP ordinatique f, DP connaissances en informatique $f\ pl$; ~ **logic** n COMP, DP logique de calculateur f; ~ **network** n COMP, DP, TELECOM réseau d'ordinateurs m; ~ **network architecture** n COMP architecture de réseau informatique f, DP architecture de réseau informatisé f; ~ **output on microfilm** n COMP *(COM)* sortie ordinateur sur microfilm f; ~ **science** n COMP, DP informatique f; ~ **security** n COMP, DP sécurité informatique f; ~ **system** n DP, ELEC, TELECOM système informatique m; ~ **technology** n COMP technologie informatique f

computer-aided[1] *adj* COMP assisté par ordinateur

computer-aided:[2] ~ **design** n *(CAD)* COMP, ELEC, MECH, PRINT, PROD ENG, TELECOM conception assistée par ordinateur f *(CAO)*; ~ **design and manufacture** n *(CADCAM)* COMP, PROD ENG conception et fabrication assistées par ordinateur f *(CFAO)*; ~ **manufacturing** n *(CAM)* COMP, ELEC, TELECOM fabrication assistée par ordinateur f *(FAO)*; ~ **software engineering** n *(CASE)* COMP ingénierie logicielle assistée par ordinateur *f*; ~ **testing** *n (CAT)* COMP vérification assistée par ordinateur *f*

computer-assisted[1] *adj* COMP assisté par ordinateur

computer-assisted:[2] ~ **instruction** *n (CAI)* COMP instruction assistée par ordinateur *f (IAO)*; ~ **learning** *n (CAL)* COMP enseignement assisté par ordinateur *m (EAO)*; ~ **translation** *n* COMP traduction assistée par ordinateur *f*; ~ **typesetting** *n* PRINT composition assistée par ordinateur *f*

computer-based[1] *adj* PROD ENG automatisé

computer-based:[2] ~ **training** *n* TELECOM enseignement assisté par ordinateur *m*

computer-controlled[1] *adj* PROD ENG contrôlé par ordinateur, TELECOM piloté par informatique

computer-controlled:[2] ~ **all-relay interlocking unit** *n* RAIL PRCI, poste à relais à commande informatique *m*

computer-integrated: ~ **manufacturing** *n (CIM)* COMP productique intégrée *f*

computerized[1] *adj* PROD ENG automatisé; ~ **numerical control** *adj (CNC- controlled)* MECH ENG à commande numérique par ordinateur

computerized:[2] ~ **integrated management** *n* CONTROL gestion intégrée automatisée *f*; ~ **interlocking system** *n* RAIL système d'enclenchement informatisé *m*; ~ **management** *n* CONTROL gestion informatisée *f*; ~ **signal box** *n* RAIL PAI, poste d'aiguillage informatisé *m*

computer-PABX: ~ **interface** *n (CPI)* TELECOM interface PABX-serveur *f*

computing *n* COMP, DP calcul *m*, informatique *f*; ~ **device** *n* COMP, DP équipement de calcul *m*; ~ **facility** *n* COMP installation de calcul *f*, DP installation informatique *f*

COMSAT *abbr (communications satellite)* NAUT satellite de communication *m*

CON *abbr (concentrator)* TELECOM concentrateur *m*

concatenate *vt* COMP chaîner, concaténer, enchaîner, DP chaîner, enchaîner

concatenation *n* COMP, DP concaténation *f*, ELEC ENG concaténation *f*, enchaînement *m*, ELECTRON enchaînement *m*, PRINT chaînage de données de commandes répétitives *m*, concaténation *f*, TELECOM concaténation *f*; ~ **indication** *n (CI)* TELECOM indication de concaténation *f*

concave *n* COAL TECH concave *m*; ~ **bow** *n* C&G bateau *m*; ~ **grating** *n* PHYS *of Rowland* réseau concave *m*; ~ **lens** *n* CINEMAT lentille concave *f*, INSTRUMENT lentille concave *f*, lentille divergente *f*, lentille à bord épais *f*, PHOTO lentille concave *f*; ~ **mirror** *n* INSTRUMENT miroir concave *m*, miroir grossissant *m*, PHYS miroir concave *m*; ~ **side** *n* SPRINGS face concave *f*; ~ **surface** *n* GEOM surface concave *f*; ~ **weld** *n* NUCLEAR soudure concave *f*

concave-convex: ~ **lens** *n* INSTRUMENT verre concave-convexe *m*

concealed[1] *adj* GEOL masqué

concealed:[2] ~ **signal** *n* RAIL signal masqué *m*

concentrate[1] *n* COAL TECH, FOOD TECH concentré *m*

concentrate[2] *vt* CHEM TECH, COAL TECH, FOOD TECH concentrer

concentrated[1] *adj* FOOD TECH concentré

concentrated:[2] ~ **sludge** *n* COAL TECH boue concentrée *f*

concentrates: ~ **box** *n* MINING *ore dressing* boîte à concentrés *f*

concentrating: ~ **mirror** *n* INSTRUMENT miroir concentrateur *m*; ~ **reflector** *n* INSTRUMENT miroir réflecteur

m, réflecteur de concentration *m*; ~ **table** *n* COAL TECH table de concentration *f*

concentration *n* COAL TECH, ELECTRON concentration *f*, P&R concentration *f*, teneur *f*; ~ **basin** *n* OCEANOG bassin de concentration *m*; ~ **cell** *n* ELEC pile de concentration *f*; ~ **column** *n* CHEM TECH colonne de concentration *f*, tour de concentration *f*; ~ **mortar** *n* MINING *stamp mill* mortier avec paroi postérieure droite *m*, mortier sans amalgamation intérieure *m*; ~ **network** *n* TELECOM réseau de concentration *m*; ~ **overvoltage** *n* SPACE *spacecraft* surconcentration *f*; ~ **ratio** *n* COAL TECH, FUELLESS taux de concentration *m*; ~ **stage** *n* TELECOM étage de concentration *m*

concentrator *n* COMP, ELECTRON, FUELLESS, HEATING concentrateur *m*, MINING appareil de concentration *m*, concentrateur *m*, *ore dressing* atelier d'enrichissement *m*, PAPER TECH épaississeur *m*, TELECOM concentrateur *m*

concentric[1] *adj* MECH concentrique

concentric:[2] ~ **circle** *n* GEOM cercle concentrique *m*; ~ **conductor** *n* ELEC *cable conductor* âme concentrique *f*; ~ **control button** *n* CONTROL bouton-poussoir concentrique *m*; ~ **dike** *n* (AmE), ~ **dyke** *n* (BrE) GEOL *igneous intrusion* filon intrusif annulaire *m*; ~ **folds** *n pl* GEOL plis parallèles *m pl*; ~ **Fresnel lens** *n* INSTRUMENT lentille Fresnel plane *f*; ~ **groove** *n* RECORDING sillon concentrique *m*; ~ **loading** *n* CONST chargement concentrique *m*; ~ **magazine** *n* CINEMAT chargeur co-axial *m*; ~ **optical cable** *n* OPT câble classique *m*, câble à structure classique *m*; ~ **pipe** *n* GAS TECH tube concentrique *m*; ~ **track** *n* OPT piste concentrique *f*; ~ **winding** *n* ELEC *machine, transformer* enroulement concentrique *m*

concentrically-stranded: ~ **circular conductor** *n* ELEC *cable conductor* âme circulaire câblée à couches concentriques *f*

concentricity *n* MECH concentricité *f*; ~ **tolerance** *n* MECH tolérance d'excentration *f*

conceptual *adj* COMP, DP conceptuel

concertina: ~ **fold** *n* PRINT pli accordéon *m*, pli zigzag *m*

concession *n* PETR TECH concession *f*

conche *vt* FOOD TECH *cocoa* concher

conching *vt* FOOD TECH conchage *m*

conchoidal: ~ **fracture** *n* C&G fracture conchoïdale *f*, CRYSTALL cassure conchoïdale *f*

conclusive: ~ **evidence** *n* PATENTS preuve entière *f*

concord *n* ACOUSTICS accord *m*

concordance *n* OCEANOG *tidal* concordance *f*, concordance de marée *f*

concourse *n* HYDROL affluence *f*, TRANSP hall de gare *m*

concrete[1] *n* C&G béton *m*, CONST béton *m*, concret *m*; ~ **apron** *n* HYDROL *dam* radier en béton *m*; ~ **base** *n* GEOPHYS plaque de béton *f*; ~ **batching and mixing plant** *n* CONST centrale à béton *f*; ~ **block** *n* C&G, CONST bloc de béton *m*; ~ **breaker** *n* CONST brise-béton *m*, marteau brise-béton *m*; ~ **coating** *n* COATINGS vernis pour le béton *m*, COLOURS peinture pour béton *f*, PETR revêtement béton *m*; ~ **durability** *n* CONST durabilité du béton *f*; ~ **enamel** *n* COLOURS peinture pour béton *f*; ~ **lining** *n* CONST revêtement en béton *m*; ~ **masonry** *n* CONST aggloméré de béton *m*, maçonnerie de béton *f*; ~ **mixer** *n* CONST *civil engineering* bétonneuse *f*, bétonnière *f*; ~ **pile** *n* COAL TECH pieu en béton *m*; ~ **pipe** *n* CONST buse en béton *f*, tuyau en béton *m*; ~ **platform** *n* PETR TECH *offshore operations* plate-forme en béton *f*; ~ **ring** *n* CONST anneau de béton *m*; ~ **roofing tile** *n*

CONST tuile de béton *f*; ~ **saw** *n* CONST coupe-béton *f*, scie à béton *f*; ~ **scraper** *n* TRANSPbenne racleuse *f*; ~ **sleeper** *n* (BrE) *(cf concrete tie)* CONST *railway* traverse béton *f*; ~ **structure** *n* CONST ouvrage en béton *m*, structure en béton *f*; ~ **tie** *n* (AmE) *(cf concrete sleeper)* CONST *railway* traverse béton *f*; ~ **work** *n* CONST bétonnage *m*

concrete[2] *vt* CONST *cover with concrete* bétonner, *form into a mass* concréfier

concreting *n* CONST bétonnage *m*; ~ **train** *n* RAIL *vehicles* train de bétonnage *m*

concretion *n* GEOL, PETR concrétion *f*

concurrent[1] *adj* COMP concurrent, DP concurrent, simultané

concurrent:[2] ~ **execution** *n* COMP exécution concurrente *f*; ~ **lines** *n pl* GEOM lignes concourantes *f pl*; ~ **processing** *n* COMP traitement concurrent *m*, DP, ELECTRON traitement simultané *m*

concussion: ~ **table** *n* MECH ENG table à secousses *f*

condensable[1] *adj* CHEM *gas*, PHYS condensable

condensable:[2] ~ **gas** *n* GAS TECH gaz condensable *m*

condensate[1] *n* CHEM TECH condensat *m*, GAS TECH gaz à condensat *m*, HEAT ENG, PETR TECH condensat *m*, REFRIG eau de dégivrage *f*, THERMOD condensat *m*; ~ **gas** *n* GAS TECH gaz à condensat *m*; ~ **gas reservoir** *n* PETR réservoir à gaz de condensation *m*; ~ **line** *n* REFRIG conduite de condensation *f*; ~ **pump** *n* CHEM TECH pompe d'extraction des condensats *f*; ~ **well** *n* PETR puits à condensat *m*

condensate[2] *vt* PACKAGING condenser

condensation *n* C&G *of double glazing*, CHEM, CHEM TECH, CONST, HEAT ENG, HYDROL, PACKAGING, PHYS, REFRIG, THERMOD condensation *f*; ~ **by injection** *n* CHEM TECH condensation par injection *f*; ~ **by surface cooling** *n* CHEM TECH condensation par refroidissement de la surface *f*; ~ **calorimeter** *n* CHEM TECH calorimètre à condensation *m*; ~ **column** *n* CHEM TECH colonne de condensation *f*; ~ **hygrometer** *n* CHEM TECH hygromètre à condensation *m*; ~ **nucleus** *n* METEO, POLLUTION noyau de condensation *m*; ~ **nucleus counter** *n* POLLUTION compteur de noyaux de condensation *m*; ~ **polymer** *n* P&R polymère de condensation *m*; ~ **polymerization** *n* P&R *process* polymérisation par condensation *f*; ~ **trail** *n* AERONAUT traînée de condensation *f*; ~ **trap** *n* CHEM TECH piège de condensation *m*

condense *vt* CHEM, CHEM TECH, GAS TECH, THERMOD condenser

condensed[1] *adj* PHYS, THERMOD condensé

condensed:[2] ~ **face** *n* PRINT caractère étroit *m*; ~ **ring** *n* CHEM noyau condensé *m*; ~ **sequence** *n* GEOL série condensée *f*; ~ **system** *n* CHEM TECH système de noyaux condensés *m*

condenser *n* CHEM condenseur *m*, *still condenser* réfrigérant *m*, CHEM TECH condenseur *m*, CINEMAT condensateur *m*, COAL TECH condenseur *m*, ELEC *component*, ELEC ENG condensateur *m*, HEAT ENG condenseur *m*, LAB EQUIP condenseur *m*, *electrical apparatus* condensateur *m*, *glassware* réfrigérant *m*, PAPER TECH condenseur *m*, PETR TECH condenseur *m*, PROD ENG *electrics* condensateur *m*, REFRIG condenseur *m*, VEHICLES *ignition* condensateur *m*; ~ **adjustment knob** *n* INSTRUMENT vis de réglage du condensateur *f*; ~ **discharge exploder** *n* MINING exploseur à condensateur *m*; ~ **heat** *n* REFRIG chaleur évacuée au condenseur *f*; ~ **lamp** *n* PHOTO lampe à condensateur *f*; ~ **lens** *n* CINEMAT lentille condensatrice *f*; ~ **microphone** *n* ACOUSTICS microphone à condensateur *m*, RECORDING microphone électrostatique *m*, microphone à condensateur *m*; ~ **system** *n* PHOTO *enlargers* système de condensateur *m*

condensing *n* TELECOM *of information* compactage *m*; ~ **lens** *n* INSTRUMENT lentille antérieure *f*, lentille de champ *f*, lentille frontale *f*, PHOTO optique de condensateur *f*; ~ **plant** *n* CHEM TECH installation de condensation *f*; ~ **pressure** *n* REFRIG pression de condensation *f*; ~ **trap** *n* LAB EQUIP *glassware* piège-condenseur *m*; ~ **turbine** *n* HEATING turbine à condensation *f*; ~ **unit** *n* REFRIG groupe compresseur-condenseur *m*

condition[1] *n* COMP, DP condition *f*; **off** ~ *n* PROD ENG condition fausse *f*; **on** ~ *n* PROD ENG condition vraie *f*; ~ **instruction** *n* PROD ENG instruction conditionnelle *f*; ~ **monitoring** *n* CONTROL contrôle d'état *m*

condition[2] *vt* COAL TECH, PROD ENG conditionner

conditional[1] *adj* COMP, DP conditionnel

conditional:[2] ~ **branch** *n* COMP branchement conditionnel *m*; ~ **expression** *n* COMP, DP expression conditionnelle *f*; ~ **instability** *n* METEO instabilité conditionnelle *f*; ~ **instruction** *n* COMP instruction conditionnelle *f*; ~ **jump** *n* COMP saut conditionnel *m*; ~ **protection** *n* PATENTS protection conditionnelle *f*

conditionally:[1] ~ **mandatory** *adj (CM)* TELECOM partiellement obligatoire *(PO)*

conditionally:[2] ~ **toll denied** *n (CTD)* TELECOM blocage partiel de l'accès à l'interurbain *m*; ~ **unstable unsaturated layer** *n* METEO couche conditionnellement instable non saturée *f*

condition-based: ~ **maintenance** *n* QUALITY entretien à base de conditions *m*

conditioned *adj* TEXTILES conditionné

conditioning *n* C&G, COAL TECH, P&R *process*, PAPER TECH *of temperature humidity* conditionnement *m*, POLLUTION *of waste* conditionnement et traitement *m*, PRINT mise en condition *f*; ~ **instruction** *n* PROD ENG instruction des conditions d'entrée *f*; ~ **tank** *n* COAL TECH conditionneur *m*; ~ **zone** *n* C&G zone de braise *f*

conditions: ~ **for dynamic similarity of two flows** *n pl* FLUID PHYS conditions pour la similitude dynamique de deux écoulements *f pl*

conductance *n* ELEC, ELEC ENG, PHYS, PRINT, TELECOM conductance *f*; ~ **bridge** *n* ELEC *measurement* pont de mesure de conductance *m*; ~ **cell** *n* LAB EQUIP *analysis* cellule de conductance *f*

conducted: ~ **spurious emission** *n* TELECOM rayonnement parasite par conduction *m*

conductimetric: ~ **titration** *n* CHEM titration conductimétrique *f*

conducting[1] *adj* ELEC conducteur, conductible, PETR TECH, PROP MAT conducteur

conducting:[2] ~ **state** *n* ELECTRON état conducteur *m*; ~ **zone** *n* ELEC ENG zone conductrice *f*, zone de conduction *f*

conduction *n* CONST, ELEC ENG, HEATING conduction *f*, HYDROL adduction *f*, amenée *f*, PHYS conduction *f*; ~ **angle** *n* ELEC ENG angle de conduction *m*; ~ **band** *n* PHYS bande de conduction *f*, RAD PHYS bande de conductivité *f*; ~ **charge** *n* PHYS charge de conduction *f*; ~ **current** *n* ELEC, PHYS courant de conduction *m*; ~ **heater** *n* MECH ENG conducteur chauffant *m*; ~ **pump** *n* ELEC ENG pompe à conduction *f*

conductive[1] *adj* PROP MAT conducteur

conductive:[2] ~ **grease** *n* SPACE *spacecraft* graisse conductrice *f*; ~ **lacquer** *n* COATINGS vernis conducteur *m*; ~ **varnish** *n* COATINGS vernis conducteur *m*

conductivity *n* ELEC conductibilité *f*, conductivité électrique *f*, ELEC ENG conductibilité *f*, conductivité *f*, P&R, PETR conductivité *f*, PHYS conductibilité *f*, conductivité *f*, RECORDING, TELECOM, WATER SUPP conductivité *f*; ~ **meter** *n* LAB EQUIP *analysis* conductimètre *m*; ~ **modulation** *n* ELECTRON modulation de conductivité *f*

conductor *n* ELEC conducteur *m*, *cable conductor* âme *f*, ELEC ENG, PETR TECH *electrical, thermal*, PHYS conducteur *m*, RAIL *person* agent d'accompagnement de train *m*, TELECOM conducteur *m*; ~ **pipe** *n* MINING *boring* conducteur tubulaire *m*, tube conducteur *m*, tube-guide *m*; ~ **rail** *n* ELEC rail conducteur *m*, rail de contact *m*, troisième rail *m*, ELEC ENG rail de contact *m*, TRANSP rail conducteur *m*; ~ **screen** *n* ELEC *cable conductor* écran sur âme *m*; ~ **wire** *n* ELEC ENG fil conducteur *m*

conduit *n* CONST conduit *m*, conduite *f*, tuyau de conduite *m*, ELEC *supply* canalisation *f*, conduit *m*, tube d'installation *m*, tube-gaine pourcâbles *m*, ELEC ENG conduit de câbles *m*, FUELLESS conduite *f*, PROD ENG goulotte *f*, WATER SUPP canalisation *f*, conduite *f*; ~ **box** *n* ELEC ENG boîte de connexions *f*; ~ **capacity** *n* FUELLESS capacité de conduite *f*; ~ **entry** *n* PROD ENG entrée de câble *f*; ~ **hub** *n* PROD ENG raccord de conduit *m*; ~ **pipe** *n* CONST conduit *m*, conduite *f*, tuyau de conduite *m*

condurrite *n* MINERAL condurrite *f*

cone *n* C&G cône *m*, ELECTRON *of cathodic tube* , GEOM, MATH cône *m*, MECH ENG cône *m*, cône de transmission *m*, cône de vitesse *m*, cône-poulie *f*, poire *f*, poulie étagée *f*, poulie à gradins *f*, PROD ENG *blast furnace* cloche de gueulard *f*, cône *m*, PROP MAT *blast furnace* cône *m*, RECORDING *of loudspeaker* membrane *f*, SPACE, TEXTILES cône *m*, TV cône *m*, robe *f*; ~ **and socket joint** *n* LAB EQUIP *glassware* raccord à rodage mâle et femelle *m*; ~ **bit** *n* MECH ENG *tool* foret conique *m*, PETR TECH trépan à cônes *m*; ~ **classifier** *n* COAL TECH cône classeur *m*, PROD ENG *for ore* classeur conique *m*; ~ **clutch** *n* AUTO, MECH ENG, VEHICLES embrayage à cône *m*; ~ **countersink** *n* MECH ENG fraise angulaire *f*; ~ **crusher** *n* COAL TECH concasseur à cône *m*; ~ **cut** *n* MINING bouchon conique *m*; ~ **delta** *n* GEOL cône de déjections *m*; ~ **drive** *n* MECH ENG *friction cone drive* commande par cônes de friction *f*; ~ **drum** *n* MECH ENG tambour conique *m*; ~ **for overhead motion** *n* MECH ENG contre-cône *m*, cône de renvoi *m*; ~ **gear** *n* MECH ENG commande par cônes de friction *f*; ~ **head rivet** *n* CONST *steeple head* rivet à tête conique *m*, rivet à tête en pointe de diamant *m*, *truncated cone, pan head* rivet à tête tronconique *m*; ~ **light** *n* ELEC projecteur intensif *m*; ~ **loudspeaker** *n* RECORDING haut-parleur conique *m*; ~ **pliers** *n pl* MECH ENG pinces à cônes *f pl*; ~ **pulley** *n* MECH ENG cône *m*, cône de transmission *m*, cône de vitesse *m*, cône-poulie *m*, poire *f*, poulie étagée *f*, poulie à gradins *f*; ~ **pulley drive** *n* MECH ENG commande par cône *f*, commande parcône-poulie *f*; ~ **resonance** *n* RECORDING résonance de la membrane *f*; ~ **of revolution** *n* GEOM cône de révolution *m*; ~ **sampler** *n* COAL TECH échantillonneur conique *m*; ~ **separator** *n* COAL TECH cône séparateur *m*; ~ **sheave** *n* MECH ENG cône à corde

m; ~ **sheet** *n* GEOL *igneous intrusion* complexe intrusif annulaire *m*; ~ **of silence** *n* MECH ENG cône de silence *m*; ~ **tube** *n* TEXTILES cône support *m*; ~ **union body** *n* MECH ENG bicône *m*; ~ **valve** *n* HYDR EQUIP soupape à opercule conique *f*; ~ **wheel** *n* MECH ENG roue conique *f*

coned: ~ **end** *n* SPRINGS *of spring coil* extrémité queue de cochon meulée *f*, extrémité réduite *f*

confectionery: ~ **mold** *n* (AmE), ~ **mould** *n* (BrE) MECH ENG moule pour la confiserie *m*

conference: ~ **bridge** *n* TELECOM pont de conférence *m*; ~ **call** *n* TELECOM conférence *f*, conférence téléphonique *f*; ~ **call chairman** *n* TELECOM maître de conférence *m*; ~ **call chairperson** *n* TELECOM maître de conférence *m*; ~ **network** *n* TV téléconférence *f*

confidence: ~ **interval** *n* COMP, MATH *statistics* intervalle de confiance *m*

confidentiality *n* TELECOM confidentialité *f*

configuration *n* COMP, DP, ELECTRON, SPACE configuration *f*, TELECOM interconnexion *f*; ~ **control** *n* PROD ENG contrôle de conformité *m*; ~ **management** *n* *(CM)* COMP, DP contrôle de configuration *m*; ~ **plug** *n* PROD ENG connecteur de configuration *m*; ~ **space** *n* GEOM, PHYS espace de configuration *m*

configurational: ~ **entropy** *n* METALL entropie de configuration *f*

configure *vt* COMP configurer

confined: ~ **aquifer** *n* WATER SUPP aquifère captif *m*; ~ **ground water** *n* COAL TECH, WATER SUPP nappe captive *f*; ~ **space** *n* SAFETY espace confiné *m*, espace restreint *m*

confinement *n* GEOL, MINING, PETR TECH, PHYS confinement *m*

confirm[1] *n* TELECOM confirmation *f*, confirmation primitive *f*

confirm[2] *vt* TELECOM confirmer

confirmation *n* TELECOM confirmation *f*

confirmed: ~ **service** *n* TELECOM service avec confirmation *m*, service confirmé *m*

conflict: ~ **point** *n* TRANSP point de conflit *m*

conflicting: ~ **traffic flows** *n* TRANSP flux de circulation en conflit *m pl*

confluence *n* HYDROL, WATER SUPP confluent *m*

conform *vt* CINEMAT, TV conformer; ~ **in shape to** *vt* PROD ENG épouser, épouser la forme de

conformal: ~ **antenna** *n* SPACE *communications* antenne conformée *f*

conformance *n* COMP, DP conformité *f*; ~ **statement** *n* PROD ENG déclaration de conformité *f*

conformer *n* CINEMAT monteur négatif *m*

conformity *n* GEOL, PETR TECH concordance *f*, QUALITY conformité *f*; ~ **test** *n* QUALITY essai de conformité *m*

confused: ~ **sea** *n* NAUT *weather* mer agitée *f*, OCEANOG mer croisée *f*

confusion: ~ **cone** *n* AERONAUT cône de confusion *m*; ~ **message** *n* TELECOM message d'incohérence *m*

congeal[1] *vt* PROP MAT figer

congeal[2] *vi* PROP MAT prendre

congealing: ~ **point** *n* FLUID PHYS point de congélation *m*, PROP MAT point de solidification *m*

congealment *n* PROP MAT congélation *f*

congelation *n* PROP MAT congélation *f*

congestion *n* COAL TECH engorgement *m*, TELECOM encombrement *m*

conglomerate *n* CONST aggloméré *m*, conglomérat *m*, FUELLESS conglomérat *m*, GEOL conglomérat *m*, poudingue *m*

congruence: ~ **arithmetic** *n* MATH arithmétique des congruences *f*

congruent[1] *adj* MATH congru, congruent

congruent:[2] ~ **triangle** *n* GEOM triangle congruent *m*

Coniacian *adj* GEOL coniacien

conic *adj* TEXTILES de forme conique

conical: ~ **beaker** *n* LAB EQUIP *glassware* vase conique *m*; ~ **buoy** *n* NAUT *navigation marks* bouée conique *f*; ~ **clamping connection** *n* MECH ENG *pipe fitting* raccord de serrage conique *m*; ~ **flask** *n* LAB EQUIP *glassware* fiole conique *f*; ~ **gear** *n* MECH ENG engrenage conique *m*, engrenage d'angle *m*; ~ **ground glass point** *n* LAB EQUIP *glassware* raccord à rodage conique *m*; ~ **horn** *n* ACOUSTICS pavillon conique *m*; ~ **mill** *n* COAL TECH broyeur conique *m*; ~ **projection** *n* GEOM projection conique *f*, projection de forme conique *f*; ~ **reinforced rim** *n* C&G bord renforcé *m*; ~ **shaft end** *n* MECH ENG bout d'arbre conique *m*; ~ **shell** *n* SPACE *spacecraft* virole conique *f*; ~ **sieve** *n* FOOD TECH chinois *m*; ~ **snoot** *n* CINEMAT capuchon conique *m*; ~ **spacer** *n* MECH ENG entretoise conique *f*; ~ **spring** *n* SPRINGS ressort conique *m*; ~ **surface** *n* GEOM surface conique *f*

conics *n* GEOM coniques *f pl*

coniferin *n* CHEM coniférine *f*

coniine *n* CHEM coniine *f*, conine *f*

conine *n* CHEM coniine *f*, conine *f*

coning *n* AERONAUT *helicopter* mise en cône *f*; ~ **angle** *n* AERONAUT *helicopter* angle de conicité *m*, conicité *f*, conicité du rotor *f*; ~ **tool female** *n* MECH ENG fraise ébarbeuse femelle *f*; ~ **tool male** *n* MECH ENG fraise ébarbeuse mâle *f*

conjoined: ~ **pitches** *n pl* ACOUSTICS degrés conjoints *m pl*

conjugate[1] *adj* GEOM conjugué

conjugate[2] *n* MATH conjugué *m*; ~ **branch** *n* ELEC ENG branche conjuguée *f*; ~ **impedances** *n pl* ACOUSTICS impédances conjuguées *f pl*; ~ **jointing** *n* GEOL système de deux ensembles de diaclases symétriques *m*; ~ **plane** *n* METALL, PHYS plan conjugué *m*; ~ **points** *n pl* PHYS points conjugués *m pl*; ~ **slip** *n* METALL glissement conjugué *m*

conjugated *adj* CHEM *compound, bond*, MATH conjugué

conjugation *n* CHEM *compound, bond* conjugation *f*

conjunction *n* ASTRON, COMP, DP, ELECTRON conjonction *f*

conn *vt* NAUT *piloting* faire gouverner

connate: ~ **water** *n* GEOL eau connée *f*, eau de constitution *f*, eau fossile *f*, HYDROL eau connée *f*, PETR eau fossile *f*

connect:[1] ~ **and disconnect signaling** *n* (AmE), ~ **and disconnect signalling** *n* (BrE) TELECOM signalisation de connexion et déconnexion *f*; ~ **confirm** *n* (CC) TELECOM confirmation de connexion *f*; ~ **data overflow** *n* (CDO) TELECOM débordement de données de connexion *m*; ~ **time** *n* COMP, DP temps de connexion *m*

connect[2] *vt* CINEMAT brancher, raccorder, COMP brancher, connecter, relier, établir une liaison, DP brancher, connecter, relier, ELEC ENG monter, *communications* mettre en communication, *device* brancher, connecter, raccorder, *several components* relier, PAPER TECH accoupler, PHYS brancher, connecter, raccorder, relier, PROD ENG connecter, embrayer, joindre, raccorder, relier, réunir; ~ **in parallel** *vt* ELEC ENG monter en parallèle; ~ **in series** *vt* ELEC ENG monter en série; ~ **up** *vt* ELEC ENG raccorder

connect[3] *vi* DP établir une liaison

connect:[4] ~ **data set to line** *phr* TELECOM connectez le poste de données sur la ligne

connected[1] *adj* ELEC *circuit* branché, en circuit, raccordé, MECH ENG branché, lié, PHYS branché, raccordé, relié; ~ **in parallel** *adj* ELEC ENG, PHYS monté en parallèle; ~ **in series** *adj* ELEC ENG, PHYS monté en série; ~ **to earth** *adj* (BrE) *(cf connected to ground)* ELEC ENG mis à la terre, mise à la masse; ~ **to the electrical network** *adj* (AmE) *(cf connected to the mains)* ELEC *installation* branché sur le secteur; ~ **to ground** *adj* (AmE) *(cf connected to earth)* ELEC ENG mis à la terre, mise à la masse; ~ **to the mains** *adj* (BrE) *(cf connected to the electrical network)* ELEC *installation* branché sur le secteur

connected:[2] ~ **line identification** *n* (COLI) TELECOM identification de la ligne connectée *f*; ~ **line identification presentation** *n* (COLP) TELECOM présentation de l'identification de la ligne connectée *f* (PILC); ~ **line identification restriction** *n* (COLR) TELECOM restriction de l'identification de la ligne connectée *f* (RILC); ~ **line identity request indicator** *n* TELECOM indicateur de demande d'identité de la ligne connectée *m*; ~ **network** *n* ELEC *supply* réseau connecté *m*

connecting: ~ **brake lever rods** *n pl* MECH ENG bielle de connexion pour levier de frein *f*; ~ **cable** *n* CINEMAT câble de connexion *m*, ELEC ENG câble de liaison *m*; ~ **cord** *n* PHOTO câble de raccordement *m*; ~ **dimensions** *n pl* MECH ENG dimensions d'encombrement *f pl*; ~ **dimensions of chucks** *n pl* MECH ENG dimensions d'encombrement des mandrins *f pl*; ~ **flange** *n* SPACE *spacecraft* bride de liaison *f*; ~ **lead** *n* ELEC ENG conducteur de connexion *m*; ~ **link** *n* MECH ENG *shackle of clevis* manille d'assemblage *f*, *split mending link* fausse maille *f*; ~ **rod** *n* AERONAUT arbre de relais *m*, bielle élastique *f*, AUTO, MECH bielle *f*, MECH ENG bielle *f*, bielle de liaison *f*, NAUT, RAIL *vehicles*, VEHICLES *engine* bielle *f*; ~ **rod bearing** *n* AUTO *car* coussinet de bielle *m*; ~ **rod big end** *n* AUTO tête de bielle *f*, MECH ENG grosse tête de bielle *f*, tête de bielle *f*; ~ **rod cap** *n* AUTO chapeau de bielle *m*; ~ **rod end** *n* MECH ENG tête de bielle *f*; ~ **rod of infinite length** *n* MECH ENG bielle de longueur infinie *f*; ~ **rod little end** *n* MECH ENG petite tête de bielle *f*, pied de bielle *m*; ~ **rod shank** *n* AUTO corps de bielle *m*; ~ **rod small end** *n* AUTO, VEHICLES *engine* pied de bielle *m*; ~ **scene** *n* CINEMAT scène de liaison *f*; ~ **screw** *n* MECH ENG vis d'assemblage *f*; ~ **shaft** *n* AERONAUT arbre de relais *m*; ~ **skirt** *n* SPACE *spacecraft* jupe de liaison *f*; ~ **terminal** *n* ELEC *of cable, connection* borne de jonction *f*; ~ **train** *n* RAIL *vehicles* train en correspondance *m*; ~ **tunnel** *n* SPACE *spacecraft* sas de communication *m*; ~ **twin yoke** *n* AERONAUT jumelle de liaison *f*; ~ **wire** *n* ELEC ENG fil de connexion *m*

connection *n* COMP connexion *f*, CONST association *f*, embrayage *m*, joint *m*, reliage *m*, réunion *f*, *union of wires, tubes* connexion *f*, raccord *m*, DP connexion *f*, ELEC *circuit* raccordement *m*, ELEC ENG montage *m*, *of conductors* branchement *m*, connexion *f*, raccordement *m*, GAS TECH jonction *f*, MECH ENG articulation *f*, raccordement *m*, *connecting rod* bielle *f*, PHYS branchement *m*, raccordement *m*, TELECOM *established call* chaîne de connexion *f*; ~ **between two shafts** *n* MECH ENG communication entre deux puits *f*; ~ **box** *n* ELEC ENG boîte de raccordement *f*; ~ **diagram** *n* ELEC ENG

schéma de branchement *m*; **~ element** *n (CE)* TELE-
COM élément de connexion *m*; **~ gas** *n (CG)* PETR
TECH bouchon d'ajout de tige *m*; **~ matrix** *n (CM)*
TELECOM matrice de connexion *f*; **~ overhead** *n* TELE-
COM résidu de connexion *m*; **~ port** *n* MECH ENG orifice
de raccordement *m*; **~ request** *n (CR)* TELECOM demande de connexion *f*; **~ strip** *n* TELECOM barrette de
connexion *f*; **~ to earth** *n* (BrE) *(cf connection to
ground)* ELEC ENG mise à la masse *f*, mise à la terre *f*; **~
to ground** *n* (AmE) *(cf connection to earth)* ELEC ENG
mise à la masse *f*, mise à la terre *f*
connectionless[1] *adj (CL)* TELECOM en mode non
connecté, sans connexion
connectionless:[2] **~ bearer service** *n* TELECOM service
support sans connexion *m*; **~ broadband data service**
n (CBDS) TELECOM service de données à haut débit
en mode non connecté *m*; **~ convergence protocol** *n
(CLCP)* TELECOM protocole de convergence du
mode non connecté *m*; **~ mode network service** *n*
TELECOM service de couche réseau sans connexion *m*;
~ mode transmission *n* TELECOM transmission en
mode sans connexion *f*; **~ network layer protocol** *n
(CLNP)* TELECOM protocole de couche réseau sans
connexion *m*; **~ network layer service** *n (CLNS)*
TELECOM service de couche réseau sans connexion *m*;
~ server *n (CLS)* TELECOM serveur en mode non
connecté *m*; **~ service function** *n (CLSF)* TELECOM
fonction de service sans connexion *f*
connection-oriented: **~ mode network service** *n
(CONS)* TELECOM service de réseau avec connexion
m; **~ network layer protocol** *n (CONP)* TELECOM
protocole de couche réseau en mode connexion *m*
connection-related: **~ function** *n (CRF)* TELECOM fonction liée à la connexion *f*
connections *n pl* CONST *pipes* raccord de tuyau *m*,
tuyauterie *f*
connective *n* COMP, DP connectif *m*
connectivity *n* COMP, DP connectivité *f*
connector *n* CINEMAT connecteur *m*, prise *f*, raccord *m*,
COMP, ELEC ENG connecteur *m*, LAB EQUIP *glassware*
raccord *m*, TELECOM connecteur *m*, VEHICLES attelage
m; **out ~** *n* TELECOM connecteur de sortie *m*; **~ socket** *n*
ELEC ENG socle de connecteur *m*; **~ socket for trailer** *n*
AUTO, ELEC prise pour remorque *f*
conning: **~ tower** *n* NAUT *submarine* kiosque *m*
CONP *abbr (connection-oriented network layer protocol)* TELECOM protocole de couche réseau en mode
connexion *m*
CONS *abbr (connection-oriented mode network service)*
TELECOM service de réseau avec connexion *m*
conscience *n* PROD ENG *breastplate* conscience *f*, estomac *m*, palette à forer *f*, planchette *f*, plaque
conscience *f*, plastron *m*
consecutive[1] *adj* COMP, DP consécutif
consecutive:[2] **~ error block** *n (CEB)* TELECOM bloc
erroné consécutif *m*; **~ identical digits** *n pl (CID)*
TELECOM symboles identiques consécutifs *m pl*
conservation *n* PETR TECH, SAFETY conservation *f*; **~ of
angular momentum** *n* ASTRON conservation du moment angulaire *f*; **~ of brightness** *n* OPT conservation
de la luminance *f*; **~ of charge** *n* PHYS conservation de
charge *f*; **~ of energy** *n* PHYS conservation de l'énergie
f; **~ of mass** *n* PHYS conservation de la masse *f*; **~ of
momentum** *n* PHYS conservation de quantité de mouvement *f*; **~ of parity** *n* PHYS conservation de la parité *f*;
~ of radiance *n* OPT, TELECOM conservation de la

luminance *f*
conservative: **~ estimate** *n* PROD ENG appréciation réservée *f*, estimation prudente *f*, évaluation prudente *f*; **~
force** *n* PHYS force conservatrice *f*; **~ plate-margin** *n*
GEOL marge passive *f*, zone de décrochement entre
deux plaques lithosphériques *f*
consigned: **~ component** *n* PROD ENG composant fourni *m*
consignment *n* PROD ENG arrivage *m*
consignor *n* PROD ENG expéditeur *m*
consistency *n* COAL TECH consistance *f*, COMP, DP cohérence *f*, FOOD TECH consistance *f*, PAPER TECH densité
de la pâte *f*, PRINT fiabilité *f*, fidélité *f*; **~ check** *n*
CONTROL contrôle d'homogénéité *m*, contrôle d'uniformité *m*; **~ index** *n* COAL TECH indice de consistance
m; **~ regulator** *n* PAPER TECH régulateur de densité *m*
console *n* AERONAUT banquette *f*, COMP, DP console *f*,
ELEC *control* pupitre *m*, NAUT *electronic equipment*
pupitre *m*, pupitre de commande *m*; **~ air conditioning
unit** *n* REFRIG climatiseur mural *m*
consolidate *vt* PROD ENG concentrer
consolidated: **~ link-layer management message** *n
(CLLM)* TELECOM message de gestion de couche
liaison consolidé *m*
consolidation *n* COAL TECH, PETR consolidation *f*,
TRANSP groupage *m*; **~ test** *n* COAL TECH essai de
consolidation *m*
consonance *n* ACOUSTICS consonance *f*
constant[1] *adj* PHYS constant
constant[2] *n* COMP, DP, MATH, PHYS constante *f*; **~ amplitude mechanical reading** *n* ACOUSTICS enregistrement
mécanique à amplitude constante *m*; **~ amplitude
modulation** *n* ELECTRON modulation d'amplitude
constante *f*; **~ angular velocity** *n (CAV)* COMP *of disk
rotation*, OPT vitesse angulaire constante *f*; **~ angular
velocity disc** *n* (BrE) OPT disque à vitesse angulaire
constante *m*; **~ angular velocity disk** *n* (AmE) *see
constant angular velocity disc* **~ bit rate** *n* TELECOM
débit binaire constant *m*, débit constant *m*; **~ boiling
mixture** *n* CHEM mélange à point d'ébullition
constante *m*; **~ current** *n* ELEC ENG courant constant
m; **~ current dynamo** *n* ELEC *generator* dynamo à
courant constant *f*; **~ current modulation** *n* ELECTRON
modulation à courant constant *f*; **~ current oscillator**
n ELECTRON oscillateur à courant constant *m*; **~ current transformer** *n* ELECENG transformateur à courant
constant *m*; **~ delay line** *n* ELECTRON ligne à retard
constant *f*; **~ differential pressure** *n* AERONAUT isosur-
pression *f*; **~ duty** *n* ELEC *equipment* marche continue
f, régime permanent *m*; **~ failure rate period** *n* QUALITY
période de défaillance à taux constant *f*; **~ field** *n* ELEC
champ continu *m*; **~ flow pump** *n* MECH ENG pompe à
débit constant *f*; **~ linear velocity** *n (CLV)* COMP, OPT
vitesse linéaire constante *f*; **~ linear velocity disc** *n*
(BrE) OPT disque à vitesse linéaire constante *m*; **~
linear velocity disk** *n* (AmE) *see constant linear velocity disc*; **~ line number operation** *n* TV opération à
constance du nombre de ligne *f*; **~ load** *n* ELEC *machine*
charge constante *f*, charge continue *f*; **~ mesh** *n* AUTO
gearbox, VEHICLES *gearbox* prise constante *f*; **~ motor
torque** *n* PROD ENG moteur à couple torque *m*; **~
percentage band width filter** *n* ELECTRON filtre à
bande passante relative constante *m*; **~ phase** *n* OPT
phase constante *f*; **~ pressure operation** *n* SPACE
spacecraft fonctionnement à pression constante *m*; **~
rate** *n* TELECOM taux constant *m*; **~ speed** *n* TRANSP

vitesse constante *f*; ~ **speed belt head** *n* PROD ENG *lathe* poupée à monopoulie *f*; ~ **speed drive** *n* MECH ENG entraînement à vitesse constante *m*; ~ **speed propeller** *n* AERONAUT hélice à vitesse constante *f*; ~ **speed pulley** *n* PROD ENG monopoulie *f*; ~ **temperature oven** *n* HEATING, LAB EQUIP étuve à température constante *f*; ~ **velocity mechanical reading** *n* ACOUSTICS enregistrement mécanique à vélocité constante *m*; ~ **velocity recording** *n* RECORDING enregistrement à vitesse constante *m*; ~ **velocity universal joint** *n* VEHICLES *drive shaft* joint homocinétique *m*; ~ **voltage** *n* ELEC ENG tension constante *f*; ~ **voltage dynamo** *n* ELEC *generator* dynamo à tension constante *f*; ~ **voltage source** *n* ELEC, ELEC ENG source à tension constante *f*; ~ **voltage transformer** *n* PROD ENG transformateur régulateur *m*; ~ **volume sampling** *n (CVS)* POLLUTION échantillonnage à volume constant *m*

constantan *n* ELEC *thermocouple* constantan *m*

constellation *n* ASTRON constellation *f*

constitute: ~ **an infringement** *vt* PATENTS constituer une contrefaçon

constitutive: ~ **alteration** *n* ACOUSTICS altération constitutive *f*

constraint *n* COMP, DP contrainte *f*

constricted: ~ **node** *n* METALL noeud pincé *m*

constriction *n* METALL constriction *f*; ~ **energy** *n* METALL énergie de pincement *f*

constringence *n* PHYS *Abbé number* constringence *f*

construct *vt* CONST bâtir, construire, établir

constructed: ~ **limestone** *n* GEOL calcaire construit *m*, calcaire récifal *m*

construction *n* CONST *edifice*, GEOM construction *f*; ~ **joint** *n* CONST joint de construction *m*; ~ **nozzle** *n* SPACE indice de construction *m*; ~ **plan** *n* CONST plan d'ensemble *m*, plan de l'ouvrage *m*, plan de montage *m*; ~ **program** *n* (AmE), ~ **programme** *n* (BrE) CONST calendrier d'exécution *m*, délai d'exécution *m*; ~ **schedule** *n* CONST calendrier d'exécution *m*, liste d'exécution *f*; ~ **sheet** *n* NAUT *shipbuilding* feuille gabarit *f*; ~ **site** *n* CONST chantier *m*, travaux de construction *m pl*; ~ **time** *n* CONST délai *m*; ~ **waterline** *n* NAUT *shipbuilding* flottaison à la construction *f*; ~ **work** *n* CONST travaux de construction *m pl*; ~ **yard** *n* NAUT *boatbuilding* chantier de construction *m*

constructional: ~ **defect** *n* CONST vice de construction *m*; ~ **features** *n* NAUT *shipbuilding* caractéristique de construction *f*

constructive: ~ **interference** *n* PHYS, WAVE PHYS interférence constructive *f*; ~ **plate margin** *n* GEOL marge active *f*, marge de plaque lithosphérique en accrétion *f*

consulting: ~ **engineer** *n* PROD ENG ingénieur-conseil *m*

consumable: ~ **electrode** *n* CONST *welding* électrode fusible *f*, PROP MAT électrode à consommer *f*

consumer *n* GAS TECH consommateur *m*; ~ **awareness** *n* TEXTILES prise de conscience du consommateur *f*; ~ **electronic equipment** *n* ELEC ENG matériel électronique grand public *m*; ~ **electronics** *n* ELEC ENG électronique grand public *f*; ~ **goods** *n pl* PACKAGING produits de consommation *m pl*; ~ **goods sector** *n* PACKAGING secteur des produits de consommation *m*

consumption *n* MECH, VEHICLES *of fuel* consommation *f*; ~ **deviation** *n* PROD ENG écart de consommation *m*; ~ **of smoke** *n* COAL TECH fumivorité *f*; ~ **water** *n* WATER SUPP eau de consommation *f*

contact *n* ELEC *relay, switch*, ELEC ENG contact *m*, GEOL surface de contact *f*; ~ **adhesive** *n* P&R adhésif de contact *m*, colle de contact *f*, PACKAGING colle de contact *f*; ~ **aerator** *n* HYDROL *sewage* aérateur par contact *m*; ~ **angle** *n* COAL TECH angle de contact *m*; ~ **arrangement** *n* ELEC ENG disposition des contacts *f*; ~ **aureole** *n* GEOL *metamorphic* auréole de contact *f*, auréole métamorphique *f*; ~ **blade** *n* ELEC *relay* couteau de coupure *m*; ~ **block** *n* ELEC ENG plot *m*; ~ **bounce** *n* ELEC *relay*, PROD ENG rebondissement de contacts *m*; ~ **breaker** *n* NAUT *electrics* interrupteur *m*, VEHICLES rupture de contact *f*; ~ **breaker point** *n* (BrE) *(cf points)* AUTO vis platinée *f*; ~ **button** *n* CONTROL, ELEC ENG bouton de contact *m*; ~ **chatter** *n* AUTO, ELEC *relay* rebondissement de contacts *m*; ~ **column** *n* HYDROL *sewage* colonne de mise en contact *f*; ~ **continuity** *n* ELEC, PROD ENG continuité de contact *f*; ~ **detector** *n* TRANSP détecteur à contact *m*; ~ **emf** *n* ELEC *between two metals* contact potentiel différence *m*, force électromotrice de contact *f*, PHYS force électromotrice de contact *f*; ~ **fault** *n* ELEC ENG défaut de contact *m*; ~ **flight** *n* AERONAUT vol à vue du sol *m*; ~ **freezer** *n* REFRIG congélateur par contact *m*; ~ **freezing** *n* REFRIG congélation par contact *f*; ~ **gap** *n* AUTO écartement des vis platinées *m*, ELEC *relay* écartement des contacts *m*; ~ **hardening** *n* REFRIG *for ice cream* durcissement par contact *m*; ~ **heater** *n* MECH ENG conducteur chauffant *m*; ~ **histogram** *n* ELEC, PROD ENG histogramme d'état des contacts *m*; ~ **icing** *n* REFRIG glaçage direct *m*; ~ **lens** *n* C&G verre de contact *m*, INSTRUMENT, OPT lentille de contact *f*; ~ **lithography** *n* ELECTRON gravure avec masque en contact *f*, gravure en contact *f*; ~ **log** *n* PETR TECH diagraphie de contact *f*, diagraphie de résistivité *f*; ~ **mask** *n* ELECTRON masque en contact *m*; ~ **masking** *n* ELECTRON masquage par contact *m*; ~ **material** *n* ELEC, PROD ENG matière de contact *f*; ~ **metamorphism** *n* GEOL métamorphisme de contact *m*; ~ **metasomatism** *n* GEOL métasomatose de contact *f*; ~ **microphone** *n* ACOUSTICS, RECORDING microphone à contact *m*; ~ **molding** *n* (AmE), ~ **moulding** *n* (BrE) C&G moulage au contact *m*; ~ **negative** *n* PHOTO négatif par contact *m*; ~ **noise suppression** *n* PROD ENG antiparasitage *m*; ~ **pin** *n* ELEC ENG broche de contact *f*; ~ **point** *n* AERONAUT contact *m*; ~ **point file** *n* MECH ENG *tool* lime contact *f*; ~ **potential** *n* ELEC *between two metals* force électromotrice de contact *f*, potentiel de contact *m*; ~ **print** *n* CINEMAT copie tirée par contact *f*, PHOTO, PRINT épreuve par contact *f*; ~ **printer** *n* CINEMAT matipo *f*, tireuse par contact *f*, PHOTO tireuse pour la copie par contact *f*; ~ **printing** *n* PHOTO tirage par contact *m*; ~ **printing frame** *n* PHOTO châssis-presse *m*; ~ **profile meter** *n* MECH ENG profilomètre d'état de surface à contact *m*; ~ **rail** *n* TRANSP rail de contact *m*; ~ **ramp** *n* RAIL contact fixe de voie *m*, crocodile *m*; ~ **rating** *n* ELEC ENG courant admissible *m*; ~ **resistance** *n* ELEC *between 2 metals*, ELEC ENG résistance de contact *f*; ~ **scanning** *n* COMP balayage par contact *m*; ~ **set** *n* VEHICLES *ignition* jeu de contacts *m*; ~ **spring** *n* ELEC *relay* ressort de contact *m*, WATER SUPP source de contact *f*; ~ **surface** *n* PROP MAT surface de contact *f*; ~ **twin** *n* CRYSTALL macle de contact *f*, macle de juxtaposition *f*; ~ **window** *n* ELEC ENG fenêtre de contact *f*

contact-discontact: ~ **regulator** *n* CONTROL régulateur conjoncteur-disjoncteur *m*

contactless: ~ **pickup** *n* ELEC capteur sans contact *m*; ~ **support vehicle** *n* TRANSP véhicule à sustentation sans contact *m*; ~ **transistorized ignition** *n* AUTO allumage transistorisé sans rupteur *m*

contactor *n* ELEC *relay*, ELEC ENG contacteur *m*; ~ **starter** *n* ELEC *machine* démarreur à contacteur *m*; ~ **with auxiliary adder desk** *n* ELEC contacteur avec blocs instantanés *m*; ~ **with overload relay** *n* ELEC, PROD ENG contacteur avec relais de protection thermique à bilames *m*; ~ **with timer adder desk** *n* ELEC contacteur avec blocs additifs temporisés *m*

container *n* COAL TECH, PACKAGING, TELECOM, TRANSP conteneur *m*; ~ **berth** *n* TRANSP terminal pour conteneurs *m*; ~ **board box** *n* PACKAGING boîte en carton pour conteneur *f*; ~ **capsule** *n* TRANSP cabine-conteneur *f*; ~ **car** *n* (AmE) (*cf container wagon*) TRANSP wagon porte-conteneur *m*; ~ **carrier lorry** *n* (BrE) (*cf container carrier truck*) TRANSPORT camion porte-conteneur *m*; ~ **carrier truck** *n* (AmE) (*cf container carrier lorry*) TRANSP camion porte- conteneur *m*; ~ **destuffing** *n* TRANSP dépotage *m*; ~ **glass** *n* C&G verre d'emballage *m*; ~ **lighter** *n* TRANSP barge porte-conteneurs *f*; ~ **rinsing equipment** *n* PACKAGING équipement pour rincer les conteneurs *m*; ~ **ship** *n* NAUT porte-conteneurs *m*, TRANSP navire porte-conteneurs *m*; ~ **station** *n* TRANSP gare à conteneurs *f*; ~ **stripping** *n* TRANSP dépotage *m*; ~ **terminal** *n* TRANSP terminal à conteneurs *m*; ~ **transport ship** *n* (*CTS*) TRANSP navire porte-conteneurs *m*; ~ **unpacking** *n* TRANSP dépotage *m*; ~ **wagon** *n* (BrE) (*cf container car*) TRANSP wagon porte-conteneur *m*; ~ **wharf** *n* TRANSP quai à conteneurs *m*; ~ **with fixed wheels** *n* TRANSP conteneur à roues fixes *m*; ~ **with opening top** *n* TRANSP conteneur à toit ouvrant *m*

containerization *n* PACKAGING, TRANSP conteneurisation *f*

containerize *vt* PACKAGING mettre en conteneur, TRANSP conteneuriser

containerized: ~ **lighter aboard ship system** *n* (*CLASS*) TRANSP système CLASS *m*

container-n *n* (*C-n*) TELECOM *synchronous digital hierarchy* conteneur-n *m*

containment *n* PHYS confinement *m*; ~ **boom** *n* PETR TECH barrage antipollution *m*

contaminant: ~ **determination** *n* QUALITY *food* détermination de l'élément contaminant *f*, détermination de la contamination *f*

contaminate *vt* COAL TECH contaminer

contaminated: ~ **mud** *n* PETR TECH boue contaminée *f*

contamination *n* CHEM, COAL TECH, HYDROL, NUCLEAR *radioactive* contamination *f*, PROP MAT pollution *f*, QUALITY *food*, SPACE *spacecraft* contamination *f*; ~ **fallout** *n* POLLUTION retombées de polluants *f pl*; ~ **meter** *n* MILIT *nuclear warfare* contaminamètre *m*, SAFETY compteur de contamination *m*

contemporaneous: ~ **fault** *n* GEOL faille syngénétique *f*

content *n* COAL TECH teneur *f*, COMP contenu *m*, CONST *of field* contenance *f*, DP contenu *m*, METALL teneur *f*, MINING *of specified part* teneur *f*, titre *m*, P&R, PAPER TECH teneur *f*, PATENTS *of abstract*, TELECOM contenu *m*, TEXTILES contenu *m*, pourcentage *m*

content-addressable: ~ **memory** *n* COMP mémoire associative *f*; ~ **storage** *n* (AmE) (*cf content-addressable store*) COMP mémoire associative *f*; ~ **store** *n* (BrE) (*cf content- addressable storage*) mémoire associative *f*

contention *n* COMP conflit d'accès *m*, contention *f*, DP, ELECTRON, TELECOM *land mobile* conflit d'accès *m*; ~

control *n* TELECOM *land mobile* limitation des collisions *f*

contents: ~ **declaration** *n* PACKAGING déclaration du contenu *f*; ~ **directory** *n* COMP, DP répertoire de programmes *m*

context *n* COMP, DP contexte *m*; ~ **switching** *n* COMP, DP changement de contexte *m*

context-free *adj* COMP, DP indépendant du contexte

context-sensitive *adj* COMP, DP contextuel

contiguous[1] *adj* COMP, DP, GEOM contigu

contiguous:[2] ~ **angles** *n pl* GEOM angles adjacents *m pl*; ~ **waters** *n pl* OCEANOG eaux adjacentes *f pl*; ~ **zone** *n* OCEANOG zone contiguë *f*

continental: ~ **accretion** *n* GEOL accroissement *m*, accrétion continentale *f*; ~ **air** *n* METEO air continental *m*; ~ **anticyclone** *n* METEO anticyclone continental *m*; ~ **borderland** *n* OCEANOG bordure continentale *f*; ~ **climate** *n* METEO climat continental *m*; ~ **drift** *n* GEOL dérive des continents *f*; ~ **fringe** *n* OCEANOG bordure continentale *f*; ~ **margin** *n* OCEANOG bordure continentale *f*, marge continentale *f*; ~ **mass** *n* GEOPHYS socle continental *m*; ~ **plate** *n* GEOL plaque continentale *f*, GEOPHYS plateau continental *m*; ~ **platform** *n* GEOL onland, GEOPHYS plate-forme continentale *f*; ~ **rise** *n* GEOL, OCEANOG glacis continental *m*; ~ **shelf** *n* GEOL plate-forme continentale *f*, GEOPHYS marge continentale *f*, NAUT *geography*, OCEANOG plate-forme continentale *f*, plateau continental *m*, PETR TECH plateau continental *m*; ~ **shelf waters** *n pl* OCEANOG eaux continentales *f pl*; ~ **shield** *n* GEOL bouclier continental *m*; ~ **slope** *n* GEOL, GEOPHYS talus continental *m*, OCEANOG pente continentale *f*, talus *m*, PETR TECH talus continental *m*; ~ **terrace** *n* OCEANOG terrasse continentale *f*

contingency: ~ **plan** *n* MAR POLL plan d'urgence *m*

continual: ~ **mechanical twinning** *n* METALL maclage mécanique continu *m*

continuation: ~ **of message** *n* (*COM*) TELECOM suite de message *f*; ~ **sheets** *n pl* PRINT feuilles de suite *f pl*

continuity: ~ **check** *n* CONTROL contrôle de continuité *m*; ~ **control** *n* TV contrôle de déroulement *m*, régie finale *f*; ~ **editing** *n* CINEMAT montage en continu *m*; ~ **equation** *n* PHYS équation de continuité *f*; ~ **fault** *n* TELECOM défaut de continuité *m*; ~ **log** *n* TV conducteur d'émission *m*; ~ **sheet** *n* CINEMAT rapport pour montage *m*, rapport scripte *m*; ~ **studio** *n* RECORDING studio *m*; ~ **switch** *n* ELEC commutateur à contactage progressif *m*; ~ **test** *n* ELEC *circuit* contrôle de continuité *m*, essai de continuité *m*; ~ **tester** *n* ELEC appareil de contrôle de continuité *m*

continuity-discontinuity *n* TESTING continuité- discontinuité *f*

continuous[1] *adj* COMP, DP continu

continuous:[2] ~ **access public transport system** *n* TRANSP système de transport en commun à accès continu *m*; ~ **adjustment** *n* ELECTRON réglage continu *m*; ~ **automatic train control** *n* TRANSP transmission linéaire des commandes *f*; ~ **beam** *n* CONST poutre continue *f*, ELECTRON faisceau continu *m*; ~ **beam modulation** *n* TV modulation continue du faisceau *f*; ~ **belt** *n* PROD ENG courroie sans fin *f*; ~ **bit stream oriented** *n* (*CBO*) TELECOM train de bits en continu *m*; ~ **casting** *n* C&G, MECH *materials*, PROP MAT coulée continue *f*; ~ **chart recorder** *n* INSTRUMENT enregistreur sur bande *m*, enregistreur à papier déroulant *m*;~ **control** *n* COMP réglage continu *m*; ~ **cooker** *n* FOOD TECH autoclave continu *m*; ~ **counting station** *n* TRANSP poste de comptage permanent *m*; ~ **cross bonding** *n* ELEC *shield bonding* permutation continue *f*; ~ **current** *n* ELEC ENG courant continu *m*, courant non pulsé *m*; ~ **digester** *n* PAPER TECH lessiveur en continu *m*; ~ **drawing process** *n* C&G étirage continu *m*; ~ **duty** *n* ELEC *equipment* régime continu *m*, service continu *m*; ~ **dyeing** *n* COLOURS teinture en continu *f*; ~ **fiber** *n* (AmE), ~ **fibre** *n* (BrE) METALL fibre continue *f*; ~ **filament** *n* C&G fibre textile continue *f*; ~ **flood** *n* HYDROL torrent permanent *m*, torrent persistant *m*; ~ **forms** *n pl* (AmE) *(cf continuous stationery)* COMP papier en continu *m*; ~ **freeze-drying** *n* REFRIG lyophilisation continue *f*; ~ **freezer** *n* REFRIG congélateur continu *m*; ~ **grinder** *n* PAPER TECH défibreur en continu *m*; ~ **grinder and polisher** *n* C&G douci-poli continu *m*; ~ **high flow** *n* HYDROL torrent persistant *m*; ~ **kiln** *n* HEATING four continu *m*; ~ **laser** *n* ELECTRON laser continu *m*; ~ **laser action** *n* ELECTRON effet laser continu *m*; ~ **laser beam** *n* ELECTRON faisceau laser continu *m*; ~ **load** *n* ELEC charge continue *f*, charge permanente *f*; ~ **loading** *n* ELEC ENG charge continue *f*, charge répartie *f*, krarupisation *f*; ~ **loop** *n* CINEMAT boucle sans fin *f*; ~ **loop projector** *n* CINEMAT appareil de projection à boucle sans fin *m*; ~ **mechanical handling equipment** *n* MECH ENG engins de manutention continue *m pl*; ~ **motion weight filling** *n* PACKAGING remplissage par poids continu *m*; ~ **oscillation** *n* ELECTRON oscillation entretenue *f*; ~ **output** *n* ELEC *generator* puissance continue *f*; ~ **polisher** *n* C&G appareil de polissage continu *m*; ~ **power output** *n* RECORDING puissance de sortie en mode continu *f*; ~ **precipitation** *n* METALL précipitation continue *f*; ~ **presence detector** *n* TRANSP détecteur d'occupation *m*; ~ **printer** *n* PACKAGING tireuse en continu *f*; ~ **processing machine** *n* PHOTO machine de développement continu *f*; ~ **production** *n* PROD ENG production en continu *f*; ~ **production line** *n* PACKAGING chaîne de production à marche continue *f*; ~ **rating** *n* ELEC *generator, motor* puissance nominale continue *f*; ~ **recirculation lehr** *n* C&G arche à recyclage *f*; ~ **ringing bell** *n* ELEC ENG sonnerie continue *f*; ~ **run** *n* CINEMAT fonctionnement en continu *m*, marche continue *f*; ~ **sampling** *n* QUALITY échantillonnage continu *m*; ~ **saw** *n* MECH ENG scie continue *f*; ~ **signal** *n* ELECTRON signal continu *m*; ~ **slab** *n* CONST dalle continue *f*, plancher continu *m*; ~ **spectrum** *n* ACOUSTICS, ELECTRON, PHYS, RAD PHYS, SPACE spectre continu *m*; ~ **spun yarn** *n* TEXTILES fil filé sur système continu *m*; ~ **stationery** *n* (BrE) *(cf continuous forms, continuous-feed paper)* COMP, PRINT papier en continu *m*; ~ **strand mat** *n* C&G mat à fils continus *m*, P&R *glass fibre* mat à fils de verre *m*; ~ **surface** *n* RAIL plan continu *m*; ~ **thread** *n (ct)* PACKAGING vis préfiletée *f*; ~ **thread cap** *n* PACKAGING capsule à vis préfiletée *f*; ~ **thread closure** *n* PACKAGING capsule à vis préfiletée *f*; ~ **tone** *n* PRINT ton continu *m*; ~ **tone- controlled squelch system** *n (CTCSS)* TELECOM dispositif silencieux à commande par tonalité *m*, silencieux de sous-porteuse *m*; ~ **transport** *n* TRANSP transport continu *m*; ~ **transportation system** *n* TRANSP système de transport continu *m*; ~ **tuning** *n* ELECTRON accord continu *m*; ~ **vulcanization** *n* P&R *process* vulcanisation en continu *f*; ~ **wave** *n* ELEC ENG *(CW)*, RECORDING, TV, WAVE PHYS *(CW)* onde entretenue *f*; ~ **wave laser** *n* WAVE PHYS laser à onde continue *m*; ~ **wave radar** *n* NAUT

radar à ondes entretenues *m*; ~ **wave radar detector** *n* TRANSP radar routier à ondes continues *m*; ~ **wave ultrasonic detector** *n* TRANSP détecteur à ultrasons à ondes continues *m*; ~ **web product** *n* PRINT produit en bande continue *m*; ~ **welded rail** *n* RAIL barre longue *f*, RAIL *(CWR)* long rail soudé *m (LRS)*; ~ **white line** *n* CONST *road marking* ligne continue *f*; ~ **yarn** *n* TEXTILES fil continu *m*

continuous-feed: ~ **head** *n* MECH ENG *machine tools* plateau porte-chariot à avance continue *m*; ~ **paper** *n* (AmE) *(cf continuous stationery)* COMP papier en continu *m*

continuously: ~ **adjustable** *adj* ELECTRON à réglage continu

continuously-loaded: ~ **cable** *n* ELEC ENG *telephone* câble krarupisé *m*, câble à charge continue *m*

continuously-tunable: ~ **filter** *n* RECORDING filtre à accord continu *m*; ~ **oscillator** *n* ELECTRON oscillateur à accord continu *m*

continuously-variable: ~ **attenuator** *n* ELECTRON atténuateur à variation continue *m*

conti-snap *n* PRINT conti-snap *m*, recollage sur bande pour impression en continu *f*

contorted: ~ **beds** *n pl* GEOL couches déformées *f pl*, couches plissées *f pl*

contour *n* CONST *of dome* contour *m*, *of pillar* contour *m*, GEOL courbe de niveau *f*; ~ **effect** *n* ACOUSTICS effet de contournement *m*; ~ **follower** *n* MECH ENG profilomètre *m*; ~ **fringes** *n pl* PHYS franges de contour *f pl*; ~ **generation** *n* PROD ENG génération de contours *f*; ~ **grinding** *n* PROD ENG contourage *m*; ~ **grip** *n* CINEMAT poignée anatomique *f*; ~ **interval** *n* GEOL équidistance *f*; ~ **line** *n* CONST *surveying*, GEOL courbe de niveau *f*; ~ **map** *n* CONST carte en courbes de niveau *f*; ~ **map of a radio source** *n* ASTRON carte d'émission radio *f*; ~ **measuring equipment** *n* METR machine de mesure des profils *f*

contoured: ~ **beam antenna** *n* SPACE *communications* antenne à empreinte modelée *f*

contouring *n* PROP MAT fraisage par contourage *m*

contract:[1] ~ **blister packaging service** *n* PACKAGING service contractuel d'emballage thermoformé *m*; ~ **boring** *n* MINING *soft rock, large diameter holes* forage à l'entreprise *m*; ~ **drilling** *n* MINING forage à l'entreprise *m*; ~ **packaging** *n* PACKAGING emballage contractuel *m*; ~ **pegging** *n* PROD ENG gestion à l'affaire *f*; ~ **price** *n* PROD ENG prix forfaitaire *m*; ~ **work** *n* PROD ENG travail au forfait *m*, travail à l'entreprise *m*

contract[2] *vi* PHYS se contracter, se resserrer, se rétrécir, TEXTILES se contracter

contractancy *n* COAL TECH contractabilité *f*

contractant: ~ **soil** *n* COAL TECH sol contractable *m*

contracted: ~ **section** *n* HYDR EQUIP section de contraction *f*; ~ **weir** *n* WATER SUPP déversoir à contraction *m*

contractibility *n* COAL TECH contractabilité *f*

contractible: ~ **soil** *n* COAL TECH sol contractable *m*

contractile *adj* TEXTILES contractile

contracting: ~ **state** *n* PATENTS état contractant *m*

contraction *n* HYDROL *of river bed* étrécissement *m*, MECH ENG retrait *m*, MINING *of vein, lode* resserrement *m*, serrement *m*, serrée *f*, étranglement *m*, étranglement de terre *m*, étreinte *f*, PHYS contraction *f*, rétrécissement *m*, TEXTILES contraction *f*, embuvage *m*; ~ **coefficient** *n* FUELLESS, HYDR EQUIP, MECH ENG coefficient de contraction *m*; ~ **crack** *n* PROD ENG *founding* tapure *f*; ~ **due to cold** *n* THERMOD contraction due au froid *f*; ~ **joint** *n* CONST joint de contraction *m*; ~ **rule** *n* PROD ENG *founding* mètre à retrait *m*

contractor *n* CONST *person* entrepreneur *m*, QUALITY titulaire du contrat *m*

contralode *n* MINING croiseur *m*, filon croiseur *m*

contrast *n* CINEMAT facteur de contraste *m*, OPT, PHYS contraste *m*; ~ **control** *n* CINEMAT réglage du contraste *m*, CONTROL contrôle du contraste *m*, TV réglage du contraste *m*; ~ **effect** *n* TV effet de contraste *m*; ~ **medium injector** *n* INSTRUMENT appareil pour injection de produits de contraste *m*; ~ **ratio** *n* CINEMAT facteur de contraste *m*, PAPER TECH opacité de contraste *f*, TV rapport de contraste *m*; ~ **reduction** *n* PHOTO atténuation de contraste *f*

contrasting: ~ **phase microscope** *n* INSTRUMENT microscope à contraste de phase *m*

contrasty *adj* CINEMAT contrasté

contravene: ~ **regulations** *vi* SAFETY contrevenir aux règlements

contrivance *n* MECH ENG combinaison *f*

control:[1] **under** ~ *adj* CONTROL, MECH ENG sous contrôle

control[2] *n* COMP commande *f*, contrôle *m*, CONTROL commande *f*, régulation *f*, pilotage *m*, ELEC commande *f*, contrôle *m*, réglage *m*, ELECTRON, PAPER TECH contrôle *m*, SPACE commande *f*, contrôle *m*, régulation *f*, TELECOM, TEXTILES contrôle *m*, VEHICLES commande *f*; ~ **and display unit** *n* SPACE coffret de commande et de visualisation *m*, système de commande et de visualisation *m*; ~ **and safety device** *n* HEATING dispositif de régulation et de sécurité *m*; ~ **arm** *n* CINEMAT levier de commande *m*, TV manette de commande *f*, manette de guidage *f*, VEHICLES *suspension* bras de suspension *m*; ~ **assay** *n* CHEM essai contradictoire *m*, COAL TECH analyse de contrôle *f*; ~ **band** *n* CINEMAT bande de réglage *f*; ~ **barrier** *n* CONST barrière de contrôle *f*; ~ **bit** *n* COMP, DP bit de contrôle *m*; ~ **board** *n* ELEC tableau de commande *m*; ~ **box** *n* MECH ENG boîte de commande *f*; ~ **burst** *n* SPACE *communications* salve de commande *f*; ~ **bus** *n* COMP bus de commande *m*, DP bus de contrôle *m*; ~ **button** *n* CONTROL bouton de commande *m*; ~ **cable** *n* MECH ENG câble de commande *m*; ~ **center** *n* (AmE), ~ **centre** *n* (BrE) PROD ENG centre de décision *m*, RAIL PC, poste de commande *m*, SPACE centre de commande *m*, centre de direction *m*, TV régie *f*; ~ **channel** *n* (*CC*) TELECOM canal de commande *m*; ~ **character** *n* COMP caractère de commande *m*, caractère de contrôle *m*, DP caractère de contrôle *m*; ~ **characteristic** *n* ELEC ENG caractéristique de commande *f*; ~ **chart** *n* QUALITY carte de contrôle *f*; ~ **circuit** *n* CINEMAT, COMP circuit de commande *m*, CONTROL circuit de commande *m*, circuit-pilote *m*, ELEC circuit de commande *m*, circuit de contrôle *m*, REFRIG circuit de contrôle *m*, TELECOM circuit de commande *m*; ~ **column** *n* AERONAUT levier de commande *m*, manche à balai *m*; ~ **column boss** *n* AERONAUT tête de manche pilote *f*; ~ **column whip** *n* AERONAUT entraînement de manche *m*; ~ **console** *n* ELEC pupitre de commande *m*, pupitre de contrôle *m*, TV pupitre de commande *m*, pupitre de régie *m*; ~ **cubicle** *n* RECORDING cabine de contrôle *f*; ~ **damper** *n* AERONAUT amortisseur de commande *m*; ~ **data** *n* COMP, DP données de contrôle *f pl*; ~ **deck** *n* TV module de commande *m*; ~ **desk** *n* INSTRUMENT pupitre de commande *m*; ~ **device** *n* CONTROL appareil de commande *m*; ~ **discrepancy switch** *n* ELEC commutateur de commande et d'accusé de réception *m*; ~

driving *n* COAL TECH creusement contrôlé *m*; ~ **dynamo** *n* ELEC *generator* dynamo pilote *f*; ~ **electrode** *n* ELEC ENG électrode de commande *f*; ~ **equipment** *n* PROD ENG, TELECOM équipement de commande *m*; ~ **of exposure to fumes from welding and brazing** *n* SAFETY contrôle d'exposition aux vapeurs de soudage et brasage *m*; ~ **field** *n* COMP, DP zone de contrôle *f*; ~ **film band** *n* CINEMAT bande correctrice *f*; ~ **flow** *n* COMP, DP flux de commande *m*; ~ **of flow** *n* TRANSP *on roadway* régulation du débit *f*; ~ **frequency** *n* TV fréquence pilote *f*; ~ **function** *n* (*CF*) TELECOM fonction de commande *f*; ~ **fuse** *n* PROD ENG fusible de protection *m*; ~ **gear** *n* ELEC appareil de commande *m*, ELEC ENG appareil de commande *m*, appareil de contrôle *m*; ~ **gearing ratio** *n* AERONAUT rapport de démultiplication de commande *m*; ~ **grid** *n* ELEC ENG *of control electrode* grille de commande *f*, *of electron gun* wehnelt *m*; ~ **gyro** *n* AERONAUT *helicopter* gyroscope de commande *m*; ~ **key** *n* COMP, DP touche de commande *f*; ~ **knob** *n* CINEMAT bouton de commande *m*, bouton de réglage *m*, CONTROL, ELEC bouton de commande *m*; ~ **lever** *n* AERONAUT, MINING levier de commande *m*; ~ **lever quadrant** *n* AERONAUT secteur de manette *m*; ~ **light** *n* CINEMAT lampe témoin *f*; ~ **limit** *n* QUALITY limite de contrôle *f*; ~ **loudspeaker** *n* RECORDING haut-parleur de contrôle *m*; ~ **malfunction** *n* PROD ENG mauvais fonctionnement du système de commande *m*; ~ **memory** *n* TELECOM mémoire de commande *f*; ~ **of minimum headway** *n* TRANSP régulation des espacements minimaux entre véhicules *f*; ~ **panel** *n* AERONAUT tableau de bord *m*, COMP panneau de commande *m*, CONST tableau de commande *m*, DP panneau de commande *m*, MECH tableau de commande *m*, NAUT *of instruments* tableau de bord *m*, SPACE tableau de commande *m*, TEXTILES panneau de contrôle *m*; ~ **pedestal** *n* AERONAUT pylône central *m*; ~ **piston** *n* MECH ENG piston de commande *m*; ~ **plane** *n* AERONAUT plan de pilotage *m*; ~ **potentiometer** *n* ELEC ENG potentiomètre de réglage *m*; ~ **program** *n* (AmE), ~ **programme** *n* (BrE) TRANSP programme de régulation *m*; ~ **register** *n* COMP, DP registre de contrôle *m*; ~ **relay** *n* ELEC relais de commande *m*; ~ **reversal** *n* AERONAUT inversion de commande *f*; ~ **rocket** *n* SPACE *spacecraft* fusée de pilotage *f*; ~ **rod** *n* AERONAUT bielle de commande *f*, AUTO tige de crémaillère *f*, PHYS barre de commande *f*, barre de contrôle *f*; ~ **rod resonance** *n* AERONAUT *helicopter* résonance de bielle de commande *f*; ~ **room** *n* ELEC salle de commandes *f*, NAUT *of ship* poste de commande *m*, RECORDING cabine de contrôle *f*, régie *f*, TV régie *f*, régie de studio *f*, salle de régie *f*; ~ **room window** *n* TV baie de la régie *f*; ~ **rotor** *n* AERONAUT servorotor *m*; ~ **routine** *n* COMP superviseur *m*, DP sous-programme de gestion *m*; ~ **screen** *n* INSTRUMENT moniteur *m*; ~ **sector** *n* AERONAUT *air traffic* secteur de contrôle *m*; ~ **sequence** *n* COMP, DP séquence d'exécution *f*; ~ **signal** *n* CONTROL, ELECTRON, TV signal de commande *m*; ~ **size** *n* COAL TECH maille de contrôle *f*; ~ **stage** *n* AERONAUT étage de commande *m*; ~ **stick** *n* AERONAUT levier de commande *m*, manche à balai *m*; ~ **strip** *n* CINEMAT bande témoin *f*; ~ **surface** *n* AERONAUT, PHYS *aerodynamics* gouverne *f*; ~ **surface angle** *n* AERONAUT angle de braquage des gouvernes *m*; ~ **surface locking** *n* AERONAUT blocage de gouverne *m*; ~ **switch** *n* ELEC commutateur de commande *m*, ELEC ENG commutateur de commande *m*, sélecteur de contrôle *m*; ~ **system** *n* AERONAUT système de commande *m*, CONTROL système de commande *m*, système de contrôle *m*, ELEC système de contrôle *m*, système de réglage *m*, TELECOM système de commande *m*, unité de commande *f*, TEXTILES système de contrôle *m*; ~ **tag** *n* PACKAGING étiquette de contrôle *f*; ~ **tape** *n* DP bande pilote *f*, *numerical control* bande de commande *f*; ~ **technique** *n* CONTROL technique de commande *f*; ~ **terminal** *n (CT)* TELECOM terminal de commande *m*; ~ **total** *n* COMP, DP total de contrôle *m*; ~ **tower** *n* AERONAUT, TRANSP tour de contrôle *f*; ~ **of toxicity at work** *n* SAFETY contrôle de toxicité à l'usine *m*; ~ **track** *n* ACOUSTICS trace pilote *f*, RECORDING piste d'asservissement *f*, piste de contrôle *f*, TV piste d'asservissement *f*, piste de commande *f*, piste de contrôle *f*; ~ **track signal** *n* RECORDING, TV signal d'asservissement *m*; ~ **track time code** *n* RECORDING, TV piste d'asservissement temporel *f*; ~ **transformer** *n* ELEC ENG synchrotransformateur *m*; ~ **tweel** *n* C&G écran plongeant *m*, CINEMAT bande témoin *f*; ~ **unit** *n* CINEMAT bloc de commande *m*, COMP unité de contrôle *f*, CONTROL régulateur *m*, unité de contrôle *f*, DP unité de contrôle *f*, ELEC unité de commande *f*, unité de contrôle *f*, ELEC ENG unité de commande *f*, MECH ENG boîte de commande *f*, PRINT unité de contrôle *f*, TELECOM organe de commande *m*, organe de gestion *m*, unité de commande *f*; ~ **valve** *n* GAS TECH vanne de régulation *f*, HYDR EQUIP distributeur de commande *m*, MECH vanne de régulation *f*, vanne-pilote *f*; ~ **van** *n* CINEMAT camion régie *m*; ~ **voltage** *n* PROD ENG tension de commande *f*; ~ **wedge** *n* CINEMAT bande témoin *f*; ~ **weir** *n* WATER SUPP déversoir de réglage *m*; ~ **word** *n* COMP, DP mot de commande *m*

control[3] *vt* COMP commander, contrôler, CONTROL contrôler, SPACE contrôler, réguler, TELECOM commander

controllability *n* AERONAUT *aircraft* maniabilité *f*, manoeuvrabilité *f*

controllable *adj* CONTROL contrôlable

controllable-pitch: ~ **propeller** *n* NAUT hélice à pas variable *f*

controlled:[1] ~ **atmosphere packed** *adj* FOOD TECH conditionné sous atmosphère contrôlée

controlled:[2] ~ **airspace** *n* AERONAUT *instrument, visual* espace aérien contrôlé *m*; ~ **atmosphere** *n* HEATING atmosphère contrôlée *f*; ~ **atmosphere packaging** *n (CAP)* PACKAGING conditionnement sous atmosphère contrôlée *m*, emballage sous atmosphère contrôlée *m*; ~ **carrier modulation** *n* ELECTRON modulation à taux constant *f*; ~ **combustion system** *n* TRANSP système de combustion contrôlée *m*; ~ **conditions** *n pl* PROP MAT conditions contrôlées *f pl*, état contrôlé *m*; ~ **crossing** *n* CONTROL passage réglementé *m*; ~ **delay lock** *n* TV verrouillage retardé *m*; ~ **dumping** *n* POLLUTION décharge contrôlée *f*, dépôt contrôlé de déchets *m*, RECYCLING décharge contrôlée *f*; ~ **emission toilet** *n* RAIL *vehicles* toilette étanche *f*; ~ **environment storage system** *n* PACKAGING système d'emmagasinage sous conditions climatiques contrôlées *m*; ~ **flight** *n* AERONAUT vol contrôlé *m*; ~ **frequency** *n* ELECTRON fréquence commandée *f*; ~ **oscillator** *n* ELECTRON oscillateur commandé *m*; ~ **outlet** *n* MECH ENG sortie asservie *f*; ~ **pressure** *n* MECH ENG pression réglée *f*; ~ **slip differential** *n* MECH, VEHICLES différentiel à glissement contrôlé *m*; ~ **spillway** *n*

WATER SUPP évacuateur avec vanne *m*; ~ **spin** *n* AERONAUT vrille déclenchée *f*; ~ **temperature** *n* HEAT ENG température contrôlée *f*; ~ **tipping** *n* RECYCLING décharge contrôlée *f*; ~ **transfer** *n (TFC)* TELECOM transfert sous contrôle *m*; ~ **variable** *n* ELEC ENG grandeur réglée *f*

controller *n* COMP contrôleur *m*, CONTROL contrôleur *m*, régulateur *m*, système de régulation *m*, DP contrôleur *m*, ELEC ENG régisseur *m*, MECH ENG, OPT *optical discs* contrôleur *m*, PROD ENG automate *m*, SPACE contrôleur *m*; ~ **layout** *n* PROD ENG gabarit d'installation de l'automate *m*

controls: ~ **and indicating** *n pl* AERONAUT commandes et contrôles *f pl*

convected: ~ **heat** *n* THERMOD chaleur transportée par convection *f*

convection *n* CONST, FLUID PHYS, HEATING, PETR TECH *liquids, gases*, PHYS, THERMOD convection *f*; ~ **cooler** *n* THERMOD refroidisseur à convection *m*; ~ **cooling** *n* THERMOD refroidissement par convection *m*; ~ **current** *n* C&G, ELEC ENG, PHYS, THERMOD courant de convection *m*; ~ **dryer** *n* THERMOD séchoir à convection *m*; ~ **drying** *n* THERMOD séchage par convection *m*; ~ **heat** *n* THERMOD chaleur de convection *f*; ~ **heat transfer coefficient** *n* HEAT ENG coefficient de convection *m*; ~ **oven** *n* HEATING, THERMOD four à air chaud *m*; ~ **superheater** *n* HEATING surchauffeur à convection *m*

convective[1] *adj* HEATING, THERMOD convectif, par convection

convective:[2] ~ **exchange** *n* GAS TECH échange convectif *m*; ~ **flow** *n* FLUID PHYS écoulement convectif *m*; ~ **turbulence** *n* AERONAUT turbulence de convection *f*

convector *n* THERMOD convecteur *m*; ~ **heater** *n* THERMOD convecteur *m*, radiateur à convection *m*

conventional: ~ **cable** *n* OPT câble classique *m*, câble à structure classique *m*; ~ **gas** *n* GAS TECH gaz mixte *m*; ~ **milling** *n* MECH ENG fraisage normal *m*; ~ **moisture regain** *n* TESTING, TEXTILES reprise conventionnelle d'humidité *f*; ~ **takeoff and landing aircraft** *n (CTOL aircraft)* AERONAUT avion à décollage et atterrissage ordinaires *m (ADAO)*; ~ **transportable pallet** *n* PACKAGING palette transportable classique *f*

convergence: ~ **assembly** *n* TV bloc de convergence *m*; ~ **circuit** *n* TV circuit de convergence *m*; ~ **error** *n* TV erreur de convergence *f*; ~ **sublayer** *n (CS)* TELECOM sous-couche de convergence *f*; ~ **sublayer protocol data unit** *n (CSPDU)* TELECOM unité de données du protocole de la sous-couche convergence *f*

convergent[1] *adj* GEOM, OPT, PHYS convergent

convergent:[2] ~ **beam** *n* OPT faisceau convergent *m*; ~ **lens** *n* INSTRUMENT lentille convergente *f*, lentille convexe *f*, lentille à bord mince *f*; ~ **lines** *n pl* GEOM lignes convergentes *f pl*; ~ **margin** *n* GEOL marge active *f*; ~ **sequence** *n* MATH suite convergente *f*

converging: ~ **lens** *n* CINEMAT lentille convergente *f*, INSTRUMENT lentille convergente *f*, lentille convexe *f*, lentille à bord mince *f*, PHYS lentille convergente *f*; ~ **power** *n* WAVE PHYS *of lens* puissance convergente *f*

conversation: ~ **impossible** *n (CI)* TELECOM conversation impossible *f*

conversational[1] *adj* COMP, DP conversationnel

conversational:[2] ~ **frequencies** *n pl* ACOUSTICS fréquences conversationnelles *f pl*; ~ **mode** *n* COMP, DP mode conversationnel *m*

converse *adj* MECH ENG réciproque

conversion n COMP, DP conversion f; ~ **coating** n - COATINGS couche de conversion f; ~ **conductance** n ELEC ENG pente de conversion f; ~ **degree** n TRANSP taux de conversion m; ~ **of electricity** n ELEC supply network conversion d'énergie électrique f, transportation d'énergie électrique f; ~ **electron** n RAD PHYS électron de conversion m; ~ **filter** n CINEMAT filtre de conversion m; ~ **frequency** n ELECTRON fréquence de l'oscillateur local f; ~ **gain** n ELECTRON gain de conversion m; ~ **layer** n COLOURS couche de conversion f; ~ **machinery** n PACKAGING machinerie de conversion f; ~ **oil** n PETR TECH huile de conversion f; ~ **oscillator** n ELECTRON oscillateur local m; ~ **pig** n PROD ENG fonte d'affinage f; ~ **rate** n ELECTRON vitesse de conversion f; ~ **table** n METR table de conversion f; ~ **voltage gain** n ELEC ENG gain en tension du changeur de fréquence m

convert vt COMP, DP, ELEC ENG convertir, PAPER TECH transformer; ~ **to diesel** vt TRANSP diéséliser

converted: ~ **top** n TEXTILES ruban converti m

converter n CINEMAT, ELEC convertisseur m, ELEC ENG changeur de fréquence m, convertisseur m, ELECTRON, FOOD TECH machinery, HEATING convertisseur m, PAPER TECH transformateur de papier m, TELECOM convertisseur m, VEHICLES automatic transmission convertisseur de couple m; ~ **cabinet** n TELECOM armoire de conversion f; ~ **chip** n ELECTRON puce de convertisseur f; ~ **gas** n DETERGENTS fumée de convertisseurs f; ~ **pig** n PROD ENG fonte d'affinage f; ~ **set** n ELEC groupe convertisseur m; ~ **station** n ELEC transformer poste de conversion m, station de conversion f; ~ **tube** n INSTRUMENT tube convertisseur m

convertible n VEHICLES vehicle type cabriolet m; ~ **hood** n VEHICLES toit décapotable m; ~ **top** n VEHICLES toit décapotable m

converting n PAPER TECH transformation f; ~ **pot** n PROD ENG cementation furnace caisse de cémentation f; ~ **station** n ELEC transformer poste de conversion m, station de conversion f

convertiplane n AERONAUT avion convertible m

convex: ~ **bow** n C&G contre-bateau m; ~ **immersions of closed surfaces** n pl GEOM immersions convexes des surfaces fermées f pl; ~ **lens** n INSTRUMENT lentille convergente f, lentille convexe f, lentille à bord mince f, PHOTO lentille convexe f; ~ **mirror** n INSTRUMENT, PHYS miroir convexe m; ~ **optical tool** n C&G balle f; ~ **programming** n COMP programmation convexe f; ~ **side** n SPRINGS face convexe f; ~ **surface** n GEOM surface convexe f

convey: ~ **power** vi MECH ENG transporter la force motrice

conveyor n CONST convoyeur m, transporteur à vis m, tapis roulant m, MINING convoyeur m, PACKAGING, PAPER TECH transporteur m, PROD ENG convoyeur m; ~ **belt** n CONST, MECH bande transporteuse f, MECH ENG courroie transporteuse f, MINING courroie transporteuse f, transporteur à bande m, transporteur à courroie m, PROD ENG bande souple de transport f, courroie transporteuse f, toile transporteuse f, TEXTILES courroie transporteuse f, TRANSP transporteur à bande m; ~ **belt lehr** n C&G arche à tapis f; ~ **belt skimmer** n POLLUTION récupérateur à bande transporteuse m; ~ **belt with a textile carcass** n MECH ENG courroie transporteuse à carcasse textile f; ~ **chain** n MECH ENG chaîne convoyeuse f; ~ **drive** n MINING tête mobile de convoyeur f; ~ **for silvering** n C&G

convoyeur d'argenture m; ~ **handling system** n PACKAGING système transporteur de manutention m; ~ **road** n COAL TECH voie de taille f; ~ **system** n CONST système de transporteur à bandes m

convolute: ~ **lamination** n GEOL lamination contournée f

convolution n ELECTRON convolution f, MECH ENG enroulement m, enroulement spire m, PETR convolution f; ~ **code** n TELECOM code de convolution m; ~ **product** n ELECTRON produit de convolution m

convolutional: ~ **code** n TELECOM code de convolution m; ~ **coding** n TELECOM codage convolutif m; ~ **filter** n ELECTRON filtre à convolution m; ~ **filtering** n ELECTRON filtrage par convolution m

convolutive: ~ **code** n TELECOM code convolutif m

convolver n ELECTRON convoluteur m

convolvulin n CHEM convolvuline f

convoy[1] n NAUT navy convoi m

convoy[2] vt NAUT navy convoyer, escorter

cook vt THERMOD cuire, lessiver

cook-chill: ~ **meal** n FOOD TECH plat cuisiné réfrigéré m

cooked adj FOOD TECH apprêté, préparé

cooker n PAPER TECH lessiveur m, THERMOD appareil de cuisson m, réchaud m

cooking n PAPER TECH cuisson f, lessivage m, THERMOD cuisson f

cool[1] adj THERMOD froid

cool:[2] ~ **water inlet** n INSTRUMENT arrivée d'eau froide f

cool[3] vti PAPER TECH, REFRIG, TEXTILES, THERMOD refroidir; ~ **down** vti C&G refroidir

coolant n CONST building fluide caloporteur m, MECH ENG in machine tools huile de coupe f, in refrigerators fluide de refroidissement m, liquide réfrigérant m, PHYS fluide de refroidissement m, PROP MAT réfrigérant m, REFRIG fluide frigoporteur m, VEHICLES in engine réfrigérant m

cooled adj THERMOD refroidi

cooler n HEAT ENG, MECH ENG refroidisseur m, NUCLEAR of ancillary systems refroidisseur m, réfrigérant m, PAPER TECH refroidisseur m, PETR TECH réfrigérant m, PROD ENG boîte réfrigérante f, manchon de refroidissement m, refroidisseur m, REFRIG refroidisseur m, évaporateur m, THERMOD refroidisseur m; ~ **cock** n PROD ENG robinet d'arrosage m

cooling n C&G, GAS TECH refroidissement m, MECH ENG refroidissement m, machine tools arrosage m, PACKAGING réfrigérant m, REFRIG, TEXTILES refroidissement m; ~ **age** n GEOL âge de refroidissement m; ~ **agent** n PACKAGING réfrigérant m; ~ **air** n MECH ENG air de refroidissement m; ~ **and conveying unit** n MECH ENG machine tool, MINING unité de refroidissement et de convoiement f; ~ **basin** n PROD ENG cuve de refroidissement f; ~ **bath** n REFRIG bain de refroidissement m; ~ **battery** n REFRIG batterie frigorifique f; ~ **cavity** n NUCLEAR puits de désactivation m; ~ **coil** n GAS TECH serpentin de refroidissement m, NUCLEAR serpentin m, of ventilation system batterie de refroidissement f, REFRIG of condenser serpentin refroidisseur m; ~ **cylinder** n PAPER TECH cylindre refroidisseur m; ~ **down** n REFRIG opération de refroidissement f; ~ **duct** n MECH ENG canal de ventilation m; ~ **equipment** n MECH ENG appareil de réfrigération m, TEXTILES équipement de refroidissement m; ~ **fan** n AUTO ventilateur m, CINEMAT, VEHICLES ventilateur de refroidissement m; ~ **fin** n AERONAUT ailette f, ailette de refroidissement f, MECH ENG, NUCLEAR ailette de refroidissement f; ~ **flap** n AERONAUT volet de refroidissement m; ~ **load** n

REFRIG charge calorifique *f*; ~ **medium** *n* POLLUTION fluide réfrigérant *m*, REFRIG agent de refroidissement *m*; ~ **mixture** *n* REFRIG mélange réfrigérant *m*; ~ **oil** *n* MECH ENG serpentin réfrigérant *m*; ~ **pond** *n* WATER SUPP bassin de réfrigération *m*, étang de refroidissement *m*; ~ **range** *n* REFRIG *of liquid, before and after cooling* amplitude de refroidissement *f*; ~ **rib** *n* CINEMAT ailette de refroidissement *f*; ~ **section** *n* FOOD TECH zone de refroidissement *f*; ~ **spirals** *n pl* MECH ENG *injection moulds* pièce rapportée de refroidissement *f*; ~ **system** *n* AUTO circuit de refroidissement *m*, CONST, ELEC *machine* système de refroidissement *m*, POLLUTION dispositif de réfrigération *m*, TEXTILES refroidisseur *m*, système de refroidissement *m*; ~ **tank** *n* CINEMAT cuve de refroidissement *f*; ~ **to low temperature** *n* THERMOD réfrigération *f*; ~ **tower** *n* CHEM TECH tour de réfrigération *f*, CONST, HEAT ENG tour de refroidissement *f*, MECH ENG tour de réfrigération *f*, MINING château de réfrigération *m*, PROD ENG réfrigérant à cheminée *m*, tour de refroidissement *f*, REFRIG tour de refroidissement *f*, THERMOD *industrial, of power station* réfrigérant atmosphérique *m*, réfrigérant à cheminée *m*; ~ **tube** *n* MECH ENG tube de refroidissement *m*; ~ **tunnel** *n* FOOD TECH tunnel de réfrigération *m*, REFRIG tunnel de refroidissement *m*; ~ **turbine** *n* MECH ENG turbine de réfrigération *f*; ~ **water pipe** *n* MECH ENG conduite d'eau de refroidissement *f*; ~ **zone** *n* C&G zone de refroidissement *f*

cooling-down: ~ **period** *n* C&G braise *f*, NUCLEAR durée de désactivation *f*

coolness *n* THERMOD froideur *f*

Cooper: ~ **pairs** *n pl* PHYS paires de Cooper *f pl*

cooperative: ~ **emission** *n* METALL émission coopérative *f*; ~ **phenomenon** *n* PHYS phénomène coopératif *m*

coordinate *n* COMP, DP, MATH, PHYS coordonnée *f*; ~ **axes** *n pl* GEOM axes des coordonnées *m pl*; ~ **boring and milling machine** *n* MECH ENG perceuse et fraiseuse à coordonnées *f*; ~ **geometry** *n* GEOM géométrie des coordonnées *f*; ~ **linkage** *n* METALL liaison homopolaire *f*; ~ **measuring machine** *n* METR machine à mesurer en coordonnées *f*; ~ **system** *n* PHYS repère *m*, système de coordonnées *m*; ~ **transformation** *n* ELECTRON transformation de coordonnées *f*

coordinates *n pl* CONST *surveying* coordonnées *f pl*

coordinating: ~ **gap** *n* ELEC *spark* éclateur de sûreté *m*

coordination: ~ **area** *n* SPACE zone de coordination *f*; ~ **number** *n* CHEM indice de coordination *m*, nombre de coordination *m*, CRYSTALL coordinence *f*, nombre de coordination *m*, METALL nombre de coordination *m*

co-owner: ~ **of private siding** *n* RAIL coembranché *m*

cop *n* C&G cops *m*

copal: ~ **varnish** *n* COLOURS vernis copal *m*

copaline *n* MINERAL copaline *f*

copalite *n* MINERAL copaline *f*

cop-dyed *adj* COLOURS teint sur bobines

cope[1] *n* PROD ENG *of loam mould* chape *f*, dessus *m*, *top part of moulding flask* dessus de châssis *m*; ~ **ring** *n* PROD ENG *founding* armature du dessus *f*

cope[2] *vt* CONST *architecture* chaperonner, *stones* cliver

copiapite *n* MINERAL copiapite *f*

copilot *n* AERONAUT copilote *m*

coping *n* CONST *architecture* chaperon *m*, couronnement *m*, WATER SUPP *of side walls of lock* couronnement *m*

coplanar[1] *adj* GEOM coplanaire

coplanar:[2] ~ **cartridge** *n* ACOUSTICS cassette coplanaire

f; ~ **forces** *n pl* PHYS forces coplanaires *f pl*; ~ **waveguide** *n* PHYS ligne coplanaire *f*

copolar: ~ **attenuation** *n* SPACE *communications* affaiblissement copolaire *m*; ~ **pattern** *n* SPACE *communications* diagramme copolaire *m*

copolymer *n* CHEM, P&R, PETR TECH, PROP MAT, TEXTILES copolymère *m*

copolymerization *n* P&R, PROP MAT copolymérisation *f*

copper *n (Cu)* CHEM cuivre *m (Cu)*; ~ **alloy bush** *n* MECH ENG bague en alliage de cuivre *f*; ~ **asbestos gasket** *n* AUTO, MECH ENG joint métalloplastique *m*; ~ **bit** *n* PROD ENG *of soldering iron* cuivre *m*, portegoutte *m*, soudoir *m*; ~ **braid** *n* PROD ENG toron de cuivre *m*, tresse de cuivre *f*; ~ **braid shielding** *n* ELEC *cable* écran en tresse de cuivre *m*; ~ **cable** *n* TELECOM câble à conducteur de cuivre *m*; ~ **conductor** *n* ELEC *cable* âme en cuivre *f*; ~ **lap** *n* PROD ENG rodoir en cuivre rouge *m*; ~ **light** *n* C&G verre monté cuivre *m*; ~ **loss** *n* ELEC *transformer*, ELEC ENG, PHYS perte dans le cuivre *f*; ~ **mine** *n* MINING mine de cuivre *f*; ~ **nickel** *n* MINERAL arsennickel *m*; ~ **profiles** *n pl* PROP MAT profilés de cuivre *m pl*; ~ **pyrites** *n* MINERAL pyrite de cuivre *f*, PROP MAT chalcopyrite *f*; ~ **rivet** *n* CONST rivet en cuivre rouge *m*; ~ **sheets** *n pl* CONST feuilles de cuivre *f pl*, planches en cuivre rouge *f pl*, tôle de cuivre *f*; ~ **staining** *n* C&G cémentation au cuivre *f*; ~ **sulfate** *n* (AmE), ~ **sulphate** *n* (BrE) CHEM couperose bleue *f*, sulfate de cuivre *m*, PHOTO sulfate de cuivre *m*; ~ **test cell** *n* RAD PHYS cellule d'essai en cuivre *f*; ~ **uranite** *n* NUCLEAR chalcolite *f*, torbernite *f*, uranophyllite *f*; ~ **wire** *n* CONST, ELEC *conductor* fil de cuivre *m*; ~ **works** *n pl* PROD ENG *for treatment of ores* cuivrerie *f*, *foundry* fonderie de cuivre *f*

copperas *n* CHEM couperose *f*

copperasine *n* MINERAL copperasine *f*

copper-bearing *adj* MINING cuprifère

copper-clad *adj* ELEC *cable* cuivré

copper-colored *adj* (AmE),

copper-coloured *adj* (BrE) COLOURS de couleur cuivre

coppered: ~ **wire** *n* CONST fil cuivré *m*

coppering *n* C&G cuivrage *m*

copper-oxide: ~ **rectifier** *n* ELEC ENG redresseur à l'oxyde de cuivre *m*

copperplate *n* PRINT plaque de cuivre *f*; ~ **engraving ink** *n* COLOURS encre pour gravure sur cuivre *f*, encre taille-douce *f*; ~ **printing paper** *n* PRINT papier pour impression hélio *m*; ~ **printing press** *n* PRINT presse hélio *f*

copper-plated: ~ **cylinder** *n* PRINT cylindre cuivré *m*

coprecipitation *n* NUCLEAR coprécipitation *f*

coprocessor *n* COMP coprocesseur *m*

coprolite *n* GEOL coprolite *m*

coprostanol *n* CHEM coprostérine *f*

copy[1] *n* COMP, DP copie *f*, PRINT copie *f*, manuscrit *m*, exemplaire *m*, TV copie *f*; ~ **camera** *n* PHOTO chambre-laboratoire *f*; ~ **fitting** *n* PRINT calibrage de la copie *m*, organisation de la copie *f*; ~ **frame** *n* PRINT porte-documents *m*; ~ **milling** *n* MECH ENG fraisage par reproduction *m*; ~ **milling lathe** *n* MECH ENG *machine tool* tour à reproduire *m*; ~ **milling machine** *n* MECH ENG fraiseuse par copiage *f*, fraiseuse par reproduction *f*, *machine tool* fraiseuse à reproduire *f*; ~ **punch press** *n* MECH ENG poinçonneuse à copier *f*; ~ **stand** *n* CINEMAT banc de reproduction *m*, PHOTO support de reproduction *m*

copy[2] *vt* COMP, DP, PRINT copier

copy-in n DP transfert en entrée m

copying: ~ **attachment** n MECH ENG *machine tools* dispositif de reproduction m; ~ **attachments for lathes** n pl MECH ENG dispositifs de copiage pour tours m pl; ~ **attachments for milling machines** n pl MECH ENG dispositifs à reproduire pour fraiseuses m pl; ~ **ink** n COLOURS encre à copier f; ~ **lathe** n MECH ENG tour à copier m, tour à singer m, tour à touche m; ~ **lathe tool** n MECH ENG outil de tour à reproduire m; ~ **stand** n PHOTO banc de reproduction m; ~ **unit** n MECH ENG *machine tool* appareil à reproduire m

copy-out n DP transfert en sortie m

coquille n C&G coquille lunetterie f

coquina: ~ **limestone** n GEOL lumachelle f

coracite n MINERAL, NUCLEAR coracite f

coral n GEOL corail m, polypier m, OCEANOG récif corallien m; ~ **reef** n GEOL récif corallien m, OCEANOG barrière corallienne f, récif corallien m; ~ **ridge** n OCEANOG échine corallienne f

coralline adj GEOL corallien

corbel n C&G, CONST *architecture* corbeau m

cord n C&G corde f, ELEC *cable* cordon m, MECH ENG cordon m, lanière f, TELECOM dicorde m, TEXTILES cordon m, câble m; ~ **carpet** n TEXTILES tapis de corde m; ~ **circuit** n TELECOM dicorde m; ~ **switch** n ELEC interrupteur à fil souple m; ~ **switchboard** n TELECOM tableau commutateur à cordons m; ~ **of wood** n METR cordée de bois f

cordage n NAUT *rigging* cordage m, filin m

cordierite n C&G, MINERAL cordiérite f

cordless: ~ **power drill** n MECH ENG *tool* perceuse autonome à batterie f; ~ **power screwdriver** n MECH ENG *tool* visseuse autonome à batterie f; ~ **switchboard** n TELECOM tableau commutateur sans cordons m, *office* standard à clefs m, *switchroom* commutateur manuel sans cordons m; ~ **sync** n CINEMAT synchronisation sans fil f; ~ **telephone** n TELECOM poste téléphonique sans cordon m, téléphone sans fil m

cordon: ~ **line** n TRANSP ligne cordon f; ~ **line survey** n TRANSP enquête cordon f

cord-to-coating: ~ **bond test** n MECH ENG essai d'adhérence des câbles dans l'enrobage m

corduroy n TEXTILES velours côtelé m

cordwood n CONST bois de stère m

core[1] n CINEMAT noyau m, *of carbon arc* mèche f, COMP tore m, tore magnétique m, CONST *building* matériau de remplissage m, *concrete testing* carotte f, *dam* moule à noyau m, noyau m, *of screw* noyau m, *town planning* coeur m, noyau m, ELEC conducteur isolé m, *machine transformer* circuit magnétique m, noyau m, ELEC *cable* âme f, ELEC ENG *magnetic, relay, etc* noyau m, *magnetic memory* tore m, *of fibre optic cable* coeur m, *of wire rope, cable* âme f, GEOL *of fold* coeur m, GEOPHYS barysphère f, nifé m, noyau terrestre m, HYDROL *of dam* noyau m, MINING *of drill* carotte f, carotte-témoin f, témoin m, NAUT *of rope* mèche f, âme f, NUCLEAR *of flow* noyau m, *of reactor* coeur m, OPT *optical fibre* coeur m, *optical cable* jonc m, PACKAGING *of spool* âme f, PAPER TECH mandrin m, PETR TECH carotte f, PHYS *magnet* noyau m, *of cable* âme f, *optical fibre, reactor* coeur m, PROD ENG *of crushing roll* noyau m, SPACE coeur m, noyau m, TELECOM coeur m, TEXTILES *of magnet* âme f; ~ **analysis** n PETR TECH analyse des carottes f; ~ **arbor** n PROD ENG *founding* axe de noyau m; ~ **area** n OPT zone de coeur f, REFRIG *of air conditioning grill* section totale

f, TELECOM zone de coeur f; ~ **average burn-up** n NUCLEAR combustion massique moyenne du coeur f; ~ **barrel** n MINING tube carottier m, PETR TECH carottier m, PROD ENG *founding* lanterne f; ~ **bit** n MINING découpeur de carottes m, découpeur de témoins m, trépan carottier m, trépan découpeur m, PETR TECH trépan carottier m; ~ **board** n PROD ENG *founding* planche à noyaux f; ~ **borer** n MINING *soft rock and large diameter holes* foreuse à témoins f, sonde à carottes f, sondeuse à carottes f; ~ **box** n PROD ENG *founding* boîte à noyaux f; ~ **box-boring machine** n PROD ENG machine à aléser les boîtes à noyaux f; ~ **breaker** n MINING cloche à échantillon f, emporte-pièce m, extracteur m; ~ **carriage** n PROD ENG *founding* chariot d'étuve à noyaux m; ~ **casting** n PROD ENG *founding* coulage à noyaux m; ~ **catcher** n MINING cloche à échantillon f, extracteur m, NUCLEAR cendrier m, récupérateur du coeur m; ~ **center** n (AmE), ~ **centre** n (BrE) OPT, TELECOM centre du coeur m; ~ **coolant flow rate** n NUCLEAR débit de refroidissement du coeur par réfrigérant m; ~ **cutter** n MINING découpeur de carottes m, découpeur de témoins m, trépan carottier m, trépan découpeur m; ~ **diameter** n OPT diamètre du coeur m; ~ **diameter tolerance** n OPT, TELECOM tolérance sur le diamètre du coeur f; ~ **drill** n MECH ENG foret-aléseur m, MINING foreuse à témoins f, sonde à carottes f, sondeuse à carottes f, PETR TECH carottier m; ~ **drill carbide tipped for concrete** n MECH ENG *tool* trépan carbure pour béton m; ~ **drilling** n PETR carottage m; ~ **driver** n MECH ENG *mortising machine* mèche f; ~ **dump** n DP vidage mémoire m; ~ **extractor** n MINING cloche à échantillon f, emporte-pièce m, extracteur m; ~ **flooding train** n NUCLEAR noyage du coeur m; ~ **grid** n PROD ENG *founding* armature de noyau f; ~ **grid structure** n NUCLEAR grille du coeur f, sommier du coeur m; ~ **head plug unit** n NUCLEAR bouchon du couvercle de coeur m; ~ **iron** n PROD ENG *founding* armature de noyau f; ~ **laminations** n pl ELEC ENG tôles du noyau f pl; ~ **lathe** n PROD ENG *founding* tour à noyaux m; ~ **lifter** n MINING cloche à échantillon f, extracteur m, découpeur de carottes m, découpeur de témoins m, trépan carottier m, trépan découpeur m; ~ **loss** n ELEC *transformer* perte dans le noyau f, PHYS perte dans le fer f; ~ **making** n PROD ENG *founding* confection des noyaux f, noyauterie f; ~ **nail** n CONST clou pour noyaux m; ~ **oven** n PROD ENG étuve à noyaux f; ~ **pin** n PROD ENG noyau m; ~ **plane** n ELEC ENG plan de tore m; ~ **plate** n MECH ENG *injection mould* contre-plaque dévêtisseuse f, PROD ENG *founding* plaque à noyaux f; ~ **plunger** n MINING cloche à échantillon f, emporte-pièce m, extracteur m; ~ **print** n PROD ENG *founding* portée de noyau f, portée de remmoulage f; ~ **pusher** n MINING cloche à échantillon f, emporte-pièce m, extracteur m; ~ **rack** n PROD ENG *founding* support à noyaux m; ~ **sample** n COAL TECH, GAS TECH carotte f, MINING carotte f, carotte-témoin f, carotte-échantillon f, PETR échantillon de carotte m; ~ **sampling** n CONST carottage m, échantillon carotte m; ~ **sand** n PROD ENG *founding* sable pour noyautage m, sable à noyaux m; ~ **screen** n ELEC *cable conductor* écran sur enveloppe isolante m; ~ **slicer** n PETR carottière latérale f; ~ **slide retaining plate** n MECH ENG plaque de rappel fermeture f; ~ **stock** n PROD ENG *founding* boîte à noyaux f; ~ **storage** n (AmE) *(cf core store)* COMP mémoire à tores f; ~ **store** n (BrE) *(cf* *core storage)* COMP mémoire à tores *f*; ~ **stove** *n* PROD ENG *founding* étuve à noyaux *f*; ~ **test** *n* ELEC *machine* essai de circuit magnétique *m*; ~ **tolerance field** *n* OPT, TELECOM domaine de tolérance du coeur *m*; ~ **trans- former** *n* ELEC ENG transformateur à noyau *m*; ~ **trestle** *n* PROD ENG *founding* tréteau de noyauteur *m*; ~ **tube** *n* MINING tube carottier *m*, PROD ENG *founding* tube à noyaux *m*

core² *vt* GEOL carotter, PROD ENG *in castings* noyauter, *set cores* renmouler; ~ **out** *vt* PROD ENG *in castings* noyauter; ~ **up** *vt* PROD ENG renmouler

core-blowing: ~ **machine** *n* MECH ENG machine à souffler les noyaux *f*

core-cladding: ~ **concentricity error** *n* OPT, TELECOM erreur de concentricité coeur-gaine *f*; ~ **interface** *n* OPT interface coeur-gaine *f*; ~ **ratio** *n* TELECOM rapport coeur-gaine *m*

cored: ~ **casting** *n* PROD ENG pièce à noyaux *f*; ~ **pas- sage** *n* MECH ENG évidement de noyautage *m*; ~ **solder** *n* ELEC *connections* soudure enrobée *f*

coreless: ~ **armature** *n* ELEC induit sans noyau *m*; ~ **induction furnace** *n* HEATING four à induction sans noyau *m*, four à induction à creuset *m*

corer *n* PETR TECH carottier *m*

core-reference: ~ **surface concentricity error** *n* OPT, TELECOM erreur de concentricité coeur-surface de ré- férence *f*

core-type: ~ **transformer** *n* ELEC transformateur à co- lonnes *m*, transformateur à noyau *m*, ELEC ENG transformateur à fer *m*, transformateur à noyau ma- gnétique *m*

coring *n* MECH ENG nodulation *f*, PETR, PETR TECH carottage *m*, PROD ENG *in castings* noyautage *m*, *set- ting cores* renmoulage *m*, renmoulage de noyaux *m*; ~ **machine** *n* PROD ENG *founding* machine à noyauter *f*; ~ **out** *n* PROD ENG *in castings* noyautage *m*; ~ **tool** *n* PETR TECH carottier *m*; ~ **up** *n* PROD ENG *setting cores* renmoulage *m*, renmoulage de noyaux *m*

Coriolis: ~ **acceleration** *n* MECH, SPACE accélération de Coriolis *f*; ~ **effect** *n* FLUID PHYS *rotating fluids* effet de la force de Coriolis *m*; ~ **force** *n* FLUID PHYS, METEO, PHYS force de Coriolis *f*

cork *n* CONST liège *m*, LAB EQUIP *closure* bouchon de liège *m*, *stopper* bouchon *m*, bouchon de bouteille *m*, bouchon en liège *m*, REFRIG *for insulating* liège *m*; ~ **borer** *n* LAB EQUIP *tool* perce-bouchon *m*; ~ **finish** *n* C&G bague pour bouchage liège *f*; ~ **polishing** *n* C&G polissage au liège *m*; ~ **washer** *n* MECH ENG rondelle de liège *f*

corkage *n* (AmE) *(cf bore)* C&G débouchage *m*

corking: ~ **machine** *n* PACKAGING bouche-bouteilles *m*; ~ **plug** *n* PACKAGING bouchon *m*

corkscrew: ~ **antenna** *n* TELECOM antenne hélicoïdale *f*; ~ **rule** *n* ELEC *electromagnetism*, ELEC ENG, PHYS règle de tire-bouchon *f*; ~ **set** *n* SPRINGS mise en tire- bou- chon *f*, vrillage *m*; ~ **stairs** *n pl* CONST escalier en escargot *m*, escalier en limaçon *m*, escalier en spi- rale *m*, escalier en vis *m*, escalier hélicoïdal *m*, escalier tournant *m*

corner: ~ **band** *n* CONST équerre d'angle *f*; ~ **block** *n* C&G bloc d'angle *m*; ~ **cut** *n* PRINT découpe en coin *f*; ~ **detail** *n* TV netteté des coins *f*; ~ **loss** *n* TELECOM perte en courbe *f*; ~ **loudspeaker** *n* RECORDING haut-parleur d'angle *m*; ~ **mounts** *n pl* PHOTO *for prints* coins gommés *m pl*; ~ **pillar** *n* CONST montant d'angle *m*, poteau cornier *m*, poteau d'angle *m*; ~ **post** *n* CONST

montant d'angle *m*, poteau cornier *m*, poteau d'angle *m*; ~ **reinforcement** *n* PACKAGING renforcement des coins *m*; ~ **rod** *n* NUCLEAR crayon d'angle *m*; ~ **slick** *n* PROD ENG *founding* lissoir équerre *m*; ~ **smoother** *n* PROD ENG *founding* lissoir équerre *m*; ~ **stapling** *n* PACKAGING agrafage sur coin *m*; ~ **stapling machine** *n* PACKAGING agrafeuse sur coins *f*; ~ **stub** *n* PRINT talon d'angle *m*; ~ **tile** *n* CONST tuile cornière *f*

corner-rounding: ~ **cutters** *n pl* MECH ENG fraises pour congés *f pl*

cornice *n* CONST *architecture* corniche *f*

corollary *n* MATH corollaire *m*

coromant: ~ **cut** *n* MINING bouchon coromant *m*

corona *n* ASTRON couronne *f*, PHYS effluve en couronne *m*; ~ **discharge** *n* ELEC *high tension* effluve en couronne *m*, effluve électrique *m*, ELEC ENG décharge en cou- ronne *f*, décharge par effet corona *f*, GAS TECH décharge couronne *f*, P&R décharge corona *f*, PHYS décharge corona *f*, décharge par effet corona *f*; ~ **effect** *n* ELEC *discharge*, ELEC ENG effet corona *m*, effet couronne *m*; ~ **resistance** *n* P&R résistance à l'effet corona *f*

Corona: ~ **Australis** *n* ASTRON Couronne australe *f*; ~ **Borealis** *n* ASTRON Couronne boréale *f*

coronagraph *n* ASTRON coronographe *m*; ~ **body** *n* AS- TRON corps de coronographe *m*

coronal: ~ **emission line** *n* RAD PHYS *solar* raie spectrale de la couronne solaire *f*

coronene *n* CHEM coronène *m*

coronograph: ~ **exposure** *n* ASTRON pose de corono- graphe *f*

corral *vt* MAR POLL *oil slick* encercler

correct: ~ **manual lifting techniques** *n pl* SAFETY techni- ques de soulèvement manuel correct *f pl*

corrected: ~ **data** *n* COMP donnée corrigée *f*; ~ **result** *n* METR *of assumed systematic errors* résultat corrigé *m*; ~ **stress** *n* SPRINGS contrainte corrigée *f*

correcting: ~ **lens** *n* PHOTO lentille correctrice *f*; ~ **optics** *n* OPT lentille collimatrice *f*; ~ **plate** *n* INSTRUMENT miroir de déviation *m*

correction *n* ACOUSTICS, COMP correction *f*, MECH ENG rectificatif *m*, PATENTS correction *f*; ~ **factor** *n* METR facteur de correction *m*; ~ **factor for induced drag** *n* AERONAUT facteur de correction de la traînée induite *m*; ~ **filter** *n* PHOTO filtre compensateur *m*; ~ **lens** *n* PHOTO lentille correctrice *f*; ~ **maneuver** *n* (AmE), ~ **manoeuvre** *n* (BrE) SPACE manoeuvre de correction *f*; ~ **signal** *n* CONTROL signal de correction *m*

corrective: ~ **action** *n* QUALITY action corrective *f*; ~ **maintenance** *n* COMP dépannage *m*; ~ **measure** *n* TELECOM remède *m*

correctness *n* METR *of balance* justesse *f*

corrector: ~ **circuit** *n* TV circuit compensateur *m*, circuit correcteur *m*; ~ **magnet** *n* NAUT *compass* aimant de compensation *m*

correlated *adj* ELECTRON, PHYS corrélé

correlation *n* COMP correspondance *f*, DP correspon- dance *f*, corrélation *f*, ELECTRON, FLUID PHYS, MATH, PHYS, TELECOM corrélation *f*; ~ **coefficient** *n* COMP, DP, FLUID PHYS coefficient de corrélation *m*; ~ **function** *n* ELECTRON fonction de corrélation *f*

correlative: ~ **phase shift keying** *n* TELECOM manipula- tion corrélative par déplacement de phase *f*

correlator *n* ELECTRON, TELECOM corrélateur *m*

correspondence *n* ACOUSTICS correspondance *f*; ~ **ana- lysis** *n* MATH analyse des correspondances *f*; ~

envelope *n* PAPER TECH enveloppe postale *f*, pochette postale *f*; ~ **pocket** *n* PAPER TECH enveloppe postale *f*, pochette postale *f*; ~ **principle** *n* PHYS principe de correspondance *m*

corresponding: ~ **angles** *n pl* GEOM angles correspondants *m pl*

corridor: ~ **control** *n* TRANSP régulation des couloirs de circulation *f*

corrodent *n* CHEM corrodant *m*, corrosif *m*

corrodibility *n* NUCLEAR sensibilité à la corrosion *f*

corrodible *adj* CHEM corrodable, oxydable

corrosion *n* C&G altération *f*, CHEM, COAL TECH, PETR TECH, QUALITY, VEHICLES corrosion *f*; ~ **fatigue** *n* METALL fatigue de corrosion *f*; ~ **fatigue crack** *n* NUCLEAR fissure de fatigue due à la corrosion *f*; ~ **inhibitor** *n* AUTO additif anticorrosif *m*, liquide anticorrosion *m*, PAPER TECH anticorrosion *f*, PROP MAT agent anticorrosion *m*, SPACE *communications* inhibiteur de corrosion *m*; ~ **nodule** *n* NUCLEAR *fuel element failure* nodule de corrosion *m*; ~ **pickling** *n* NUCLEAR décapage par corrosion *m*; ~ **prevention** *n* PACKAGING mesures anticorrosives *f pl*; ~ **preventive** *n* PACKAGING agent anticorrosif *m*; ~ **preventive paper** *n* PACKAGING papier anticorrosif *m*; ~ **resistance** *n* CONST, P&R, PROP MAT résistance à la corrosion *f*

corrosion-resistant[1] *adj* PROP MAT anticorrosion

corrosion-resistant:[2] ~ **stainless steel fasteners** *n pl* MECH ENG éléments de fixation en acier inoxydable résistant à la corrosion *m pl*

corrosive[1] *adj* SAFETY corrosif

corrosive:[2] ~ **atmosphere** *n* PROD ENG atmosphère corrosive *f*; ~ **substance** *n* SAFETY substance corrosive *f*; ~ **water** *n* WATER SUPP eau corrosive *f*

corrugated[1] *adj* MECH ENG, PAPER TECH ondulé

corrugated:[2] ~ **board** *n* PACKAGING, PAPER TECH carton ondulé *m*; ~ **board box** *n* PACKAGING boîte de carton ondulé *f*; ~ **board with broadly spaced flutes** *n* PACKAGING carton ondulé avec cannelures espacées *m*; ~ **board with narrowly spaced flutes** *n* PACKAGING carton ondulé avec cannelures serrées *m*; ~ **cardboard** *n* PACKAGING carton ondulé *m*, papier ondulé *m*, PAPER TECH carton ondulé *m*; ~ **expansion joint** *n* NUCLEAR compensateur à tube ondulé *m*, joint glissant à tube ondulé *m*; ~ **fiberboard** *n* (AmE), ~ **fibreboard** *n* (BrE) PACKAGING carton ondulé *m*; ~ **glass** *n* C&G verre ondulé *m*; ~ **iron** *n* CONST tôle ondulée *f*, tôle ondulée en fer *f*; ~ **jaws** *n pl* MINING *rock crusher* mâchoires cannelées *f pl*; ~ **paper** *n* PACKAGING papier ondulé *m*; ~ **products** *n pl* PACKAGING produits en carton ondulé *m pl*; ~ **roll** *n* PROD ENG cylindre cannelé *m*, cylindre à cannelures *m*; ~ **sheet iron** *n* CONST tôle ondulée en fer *f*; ~ **tube compensator** *n* NUCLEAR compensateur à tube ondulé *m*, joint glissant à tube ondulé *m*; ~ **wired glass** *n* C&G verre ondulé armé *m*

corrugating: ~ **medium** *n* PAPER TECH papier à canneler pour carton ondulé *m*

corrugation *n* C&G drapage *m*, PAPER TECH ondulation *f*, PRINT défaut du papier *m*, ondulation *f*

corrugator *n* PAPER TECH machine à onduler *f*

corrupt:[1] ~ **file** *n* COMP fichier altéré *m*

corrupt[2] *vt* COMP altérer, DP corrompre

corruption *n* COMP altération *f*, DP altération *f*, corruption *f*

corsite *n* PETR corsite *f*

corticoid *n* CHEM corticoïde *m*

corticosteroid *n* CHEM corticostéroïde *m*

corticosterone *n* CHEM corticostérone *f*

corticotrophic *adj* CHEM corticotrope

corticotrophin *n* CHEM corticotrophine *f*, corticotropine *f*

corticotropic *adj* CHEM corticotrope

corticotropin *n* CHEM corticotrophine *f*, corticotropine *f*

cortisone *n* CHEM cortisone *f*

corundellite *n* MINERAL corundellite *f*

corundophilite *n* MINERAL corundophilite *f*, corundophyllite *f*

corundum *n* C&G, MINERAL corindon *m*; ~ **wheel** *n* PROD ENG meule en corindon *f*

Corvus *n* ASTRON Corbeau *m*

corynite *n* MINERAL corynite *f*

cos *n* (*cosine*) GEOM cos *m* (*cosinus*)

cosalite *n* MINERAL cosalite *f*

cosec *n* (*cosecant*) GEOM cosec *f* (*cosécante*)

cosecant *n* (*cosec*) GEOM cosécante *f* (*cosec*)

coset: ~ **deposits** *n pl* GEOL sédiments à stratification inclinée dans la direction du cou *m pl*

cosine *n* (*cos*) COMP, CONST *trigonometry*, GEOM, MATH cosinus *m* (*cos*); ~ **emission law** *n* OPT loi de Lambert *f*, loi du cosinus de Lambert *f*; ~ **equalizer** *n* TV égaliseur en cosinus *m*; ~ **tables** *n pl* GEOM tables du cosinus *f pl*; ~ **wave** *n* GEOM onde cosinusoïdale *f*

cosmic[1] *adj* ASTRON cosmique

cosmic:[2] ~ **background radiation** *n* PHYS *microwaves* rayonnement cosmologique *m*, rayonnement universel *m*; ~ **gas and dust** *n* ASTRON gaz et poussière cosmiques *m*; ~ **noise** *n* SPACE bruit cosmique *m*; ~ **radiation** *n* SPACE rayonnement cosmique *m*; ~ **ray** *n* ASTRON rayon cosmique *m*; ~ **ray background** *n* RAD PHYS fond de rayons cosmiques *m*; ~ **ray detector** *n* ASTRON détecteur des rayons cosmiques *m*; ~ **rays** *n pl* PHYS rayonnement cosmique *m*; ~ **shower** *n* SPACE averse cosmique *f*; ~ **space** *n* SPACE espace extra-atmosphérique *m*; ~ **velocity** *n* SPACE vitesse cosmique *f*; ~ **year** *n* ASTRON année cosmique *f*

cosmochemistry *n* ASTRON cosmochimie *f*

cosmodrome *n* SPACE base de lancement *f*, cosmodrome *m*

cosmogony *n* ASTRON, SPACE cosmogonie *f*

cosmography *n* ASTRON, SPACE cosmographie *f*

cosmological: ~ **expansion** *n* ASTRON expansion cosmologique *f*

cosmology *n* ASTRON, SPACE cosmologie *f*

cosmonaut *n* SPACE astronaute *m*, cosmonaute *m*, spationaute *m*

Cosmos *n* ASTRON Cosmos *m*; ~ **satellites** *n pl* ASTRON satellites Cosmos *m pl*

cossyrite *n* MINERAL cossyrite *f*

cost *n* PROD ENG prix coûtant *m*, prix de fabrication *m*, prix de fabrique *m*, prix de revient *m*; ~ **center** *n* (AmE), ~ **centre** *n* (BrE) PROD ENG centre de coûts *m*, centre de frais *m*; ~ **insurance freight** *n* (*CIF*) PROD ENG coût assurance fret *m*; ~ **price** *n* PROD ENG prix coûtant *m*, prix de fabrication *m*, prix de fabrique *m*, prix de revient *m*; ~ **reduction in mechanical assembly** *n* MECH ENG réduction des coûts du montage mécanique *f*; ~ **of space** *n* PACKAGING prix de revient de la surface *m*; ~ **variance** *n* PROD ENG écart de coût *m*

Costas: ~ **loop** *n* TELECOM boucle de Costas *f*

cost-effective[1] *adj* PROD ENG rentable

cost-effective:[2] ~ **maintenance** *n* PROD ENG entretien d'une bonne efficacité économique *m*

costs *n pl* PATENTS frais *m pl*

cot[1] *abbr* *(cotangent)* CONST cot *f (cotangente)*

cot[2] *n (cotangent)* GEOM cot *f (cotangente)*

cotangent *n (cot)* CONST *trigonometry*, GEOM cotangente *f (cot)*

cotidal[1] *adj* GEOPHYS cotidal

cotidal:[2] ~ **line** *n* GEOPHYS ligne cotidale *f*

cotter[1] *n* MECH ENG clavette *f*; ~ **bolt** *n* MECH ENG boulon à clavette *m*; ~ **file** *n* MECH ENG fendante *f*; ~ **pin** *n* MECH goupille fendue *f*, MECH ENG, NAUT goupille *f*; ~ **slot** *n* MECH ENG lumière pour fixation *f*; ~ **stud bolt** *n* MECH ENG prisonnier à clavette *m*

cotter[2] *vt* MECH ENG claveter

cottered: ~ **joint** *n* CONST agrafe à clavette *f*, assemblage par clavette en coin *m*

cottering *n* MECH ENG clavetage *m*

cotton *n* TEXTILES coton *m*; ~ **asbestos** *n* NUCLEAR laine d'amiante *f*; ~ **braid** *n* ELEC ENG, TEXTILES tresse de coton *f*; ~ **condenser spinning** *n* TEXTILES filature de coton condenseur *f*; ~ **insulation** *n* ELEC isolation en coton *f*; ~ **linter** *n* P&R *filler* bourre de coton *f*; ~ **spinning** *n* TEXTILES filature de coton *f*; ~ **waste** *n* PROD ENG bourre de coton *f*, déchet de coton *m*; ~ **yarn** *n* TEXTILES fil de coton *m*

Cotton: ~ **balance** *n* PHYS balance de Cotton *f*

cotton-covered *adj* ELEC ENG *wire* guipé de coton

Cotton-Mouton: ~ **effect** *n* PHYS effet Cotton-Mouton *m*

cottonseed: ~ **oil** *n* FOOD TECH huile de coton *f*, huile de graine de coton *f*

cotunnite *n* MINERAL cotunnite *f*

couch:[1] ~ **mark** *n* PRINT défaut du papier provenant du rouleau coucheur *m*; ~ **press** *n* PAPER TECH presse coucheuse *f*; ~ **roll jacket** *n* PAPER TECH manchon de presse humide *m*

couch[2] *vt* PAPER TECH coucher

Couette: ~ **flow** *n* FLUID PHYS écoulement de Couette *m*

coulomb *n (C)* ELEC *unit*, ELEC ENG, METR, PHYS coulomb *m (C)*; ~ **energy** *n* RAD PHYS *electron interaction* énergie coulombienne *f*

Coulomb: ~ **gage** *n* (AmE) *see Coulomb gauge*; ~ **repulsion** *n* PHYS répulsion coulombienne *f*

Coulomb's: ~ **law** *n* ELEC *electrostatics*, PHYS loi de Coulomb *f*; ~ **theorem** *n* ELEC *electric field*, PHYS théorème de Coulomb *m*; ~ **torsion balance** *n* PHYS balance de torsion de Coulomb *f*

coulombmeter *n* ELEC coulombmètre *m*, coulomètre *m*

coulometer *n* ELEC ENG coulombmètre *m*, coulomètre *m*

coumalic *adj* CHEM coumalique

coumalin *n* CHEM coumaline *f*

coumaline *n* CHEM coumaline *f*

coumaran *n* CHEM coumaranne *m*

coumarane *n* CHEM coumaranne *m*

coumaric *adj* CHEM coumarique

coumarin *n* CHEM coumarine *f*

coumarine *n* CHEM coumarine *f*

coumarone: ~ **resin** *n* P&R résine de coumarone *f*

count *n* TEXTILES titre du fil *m*

countdown *n* SPACE *spacecraft* compte à rebours *m*; ~ **counter** *n* ELECTRON décompteur *m*

counter *n* COMP, DP compteur *m*, ELECTRON compteur *m*, dispositif de comptage *m*, MECH ENG *meter* compteur *m*, MINING costresse *f*, galerie costresse *f*, *counter lode* croiseur *m*, filon croiseur *m*, NAUT *shipbuilding* voûte *f*, TELECOM compteur *m*; ~ **address** *n* PROD ENG instruction de comptage *f*; ~ **circuit** *n* ELECTRON circuit de comptage *m*; ~ **driving motion** *n* MECH ENG renvoi *m*, renvoi de mouvement *m*, transmission in-

termédiaire *f*, transmission secondaire *f*; ~ **emf** *n (cemf)* ELEC, ELEC ENG, PHYS force contre-électromotrice *f (fcém)*; ~ **gangway** *n* MINING coistresse *f*, costresse *f*, galerie costresse *f*; ~ **gear** *n* MECH ENG *countermotion* renvoi *m*, renvoi de mouvement *m*, transmission intermédiaire *f*, transmission secondaire *f*, *geared countershaft* engrenage de renvoi *m*; ~ **key light** *n* CINEMAT lumière de décrochement *f*; ~ **lath** *n* CONST *building* contre-latte *f*; ~ **level** *n* MINING coistresse *f*, costresse *f*, galerie costresse *f*; ~ **tube** *n* ELECTRON tube compteur *m*; ~ **tube probe** *n* NUCLEAR tube compteur sonde *m*

counteracting: ~ **force** *n* MECH ENG force antagoniste *f*

counterbalance[1] *n* AERONAUT compensation *f*; ~ **carriage** *n* MINING *inclined planes* chariot de contrepoids *m*

counterbalance[2] *vt* MECH contrebalancer, équilibrer

counterbalanced: ~ **drilling spindle** *n* MECH ENG arbre porte-foret équilibré *m*; ~ **lever** *n* MECH ENG levier équilibré par contrepoids *m*

counterbalancing: ~ **rope** *n* MINING *hoisting* contre-câble d'équilibre *m*

counterbore[1] *n* MECH ENG chambrage *m*, outil à lamer *m*, suralésage *m*, *drill* foret à téton cylindrique *m*; ~ **with detachable pilot** *n* MECH ENG outil à lamer à pilote amovible *m*; ~ **with solid pilot** *n* MECH ENG outil à lamer à pilote fixe *m*

counterbore[2] *vt* MECH ENG chambrer, réaléser

counterbore[3] *vi* PROD ENG suraléser

counterboring *n* MECH chambrage *m*

counterclockwise *n (CCW)* MECH ENG sens contraire des aiguilles d'une montre *m*, sens inverse horaire *m (SCAM)*; ~ **rotation** *n* MECH, PROD ENG rotation dans le sens antihoraire *f*

countercurrent *n* CHEM contre-courant *m*, ELEC ENG courant opposé *m*, HYDROL, OCEANOG contre-courant *m*; ~ **classifier** *n* COAL TECH classeur à courant ascendant *m*; ~ **diffusion plant** *n* NUCLEAR installation de diffusion à travers un gaz *f*

counter-electromotive: ~ **force** *n (cemf)* ELEC, ELEC ENG, PHYS force contre-électromotrice *f (fcém)*

counterflange *n* MECH, NUCLEAR contre-bride *f*

counterflooding *n* NAUT équilibrage *m*

counterflow *n* COAL TECH contre-courant *m*; ~ **classifier** *n* COAL TECH classificateur à contre-courant *m*; ~ **heat exchanger** *n* FOOD TECH échangeur à contre-courant *m*, REFRIG échangeur thermique à contre-courant *m*

counterlode *n* MINING croiseur *m*, filon croiseur *m*

countermatte *n* CINEMAT contre-cache *m*

countermotion *n* MECH ENG renvoi *m*, renvoi de mouvement *m*, transmission intermédiaire *f*, transmission secondaire *f*

counterplate *n* MECH ENG contre-plaque *f*

counterpoise: ~ **bridge** *n* CONST pont à bascule *m*, pont à contrepoint *m*

counterpunch[1] *n* MECH ENG contre-poinçon *m*

counterpunch[2] *vt* MECH ENG contre-poinçonner

counter-revolving: ~ **axial fan** *n* TRANSP soufflante axiale contrarotative *f*

counter-rotating: ~ **propellers** *n* TRANSP hélices contrarotatives *f pl*

countershaft *n* AUTO arbre intermédiaire *m*, MECH ENG arbre de renvoi *m*, axe secondaire *m*, arbre intermédiaire *m*, arbre secondaire *m*, renvoi *m*, renvoi de mouvement *m*, transmission intermédiaire *f*, trans-

mission secondaire *f*; ~ **and accessories** *n pl* MECH
ENG renvoi *m*, renvoi de mouvement *m*, transmission
intermédiaire *f*, transmission secondaire *f*; ~ **cone** *n*
MECH ENG contre-cône *m*, cône de renvoi *m*; ~ **for floor**
n MECH ENG renvoi de mouvement se fixant au sol *m*,
transmission intermédiaire se fixant au sol *f*, transmission secondaire se fixant au sol *f*; ~ **gear** *n* AUTO
car pignon d'arbre intermédiaire *m*, VEHICLES pignon
récepteur *m*

countershafting *n* MECH ENG renvois de mouvement *m*
pl, transmission intermédiaire *f*, transmission secondaire *f*

countershot *n* CINEMAT contre-champ *m*

countersink[1] *n* MECH ENG fraise *f*, fraise à fraiser les
trous *f*, outil à chanfreiner *m*, PROD ENG fraisure *f*; ~
bit *n* MECH ENG fraise *f*, fraise à fraiser les trous *f*; ~ **for
60 degrees angle** *n* MECH ENG outil à chanfreiner à
angle de 60 degrés au sommet *m*

countersink[2] *vt* MECH ENG fraiser

countersinking *n* MECH ENG fraisage *m*

counterstern *n* NAUT *boatbuilding* arrière en tableau *m*,
arrière à tableau *m*, arrière à voûte *m*

counterstream: ~ **line** *n* HYDR EQUIP contre-courant *m*

countersunk: ~ **buttonhead rivet** *n* CONST rivet à tête
fraisée et goutte de suif *m*; ~ **fastener** *n* MECH ENG
élément de fixation à tête fraisée *m*; ~ **head bolt** *n*
CONST boulon à tête fraisée *m*; ~ **head rivet** *n* CONST
rivet à tête fraisée *m*; ~ **head screw** *n* CONST, MECH vis
à tête fraisée *f*; ~ **hole** *n* MECH ENG fraisure *f*, PROD ENG
trou fraisé *m*; ~ **mount** *n* PHOTO *camera lens* monture
rentrante *f*; ~ **nut** *n* NUCLEAR écrou conique *m*; ~
riveting *n* CONST rivure prisonnière *f*, rivure prisonnière fraisée *f*; ~ **screw** *n* MECH ENG vis à tête noyée *f*; ~
setting *n* PHOTO *camera lens* monture rentrante *f*; ~
woodscrew *n* CONST vis à bois à tête plate fraisée *f*, vis
à bois à tête plate rayée *f*

countersunk-headed: ~ **bolt** *n* CONST boulon à tête fraisée *m*

countertest *n* MECH ENG contre-essai *m*

countertop: ~ **machine** *n* PACKAGING machine pour
utilisation sur comptoir *f*

counterweight *n* CONST, INSTRUMENT, MECH, MECH ENG
contrepoids *m*, RECORDING *of record player arm*
contrepoids d'équilibrage *m*

counting *n* ELECTRON comptage *m*; ~ **device** *n* PACKA-
GING dispositif pour compter *m*; ~ **rate** *n* ELECTRON
cadence de comptage *f*, taux de comptage *m*; ~ **station**
n TRANSP poste de comptage *m*

country: ~ **code** *n (CC)* TELECOM indicatif du pays *m*; ~
rocks *n pl* GEOL roches intercalaires *f pl*, MINING
roches encaissantes *f pl*, terrain encaissant *m*

count-up: ~ **counter** *n* ELECTRON compteur progressif
m; ~ **done bit** *n* PROD ENG bit de fin de comptage *m*

couplability *n* RAIL *vehicles* divisibilité *f*

couple[1] *n* ELEC ENG, MECH ENG, PHYS couple *m*; ~ **roof** *n*
CONST comble à deux longspans sans fermes *m*, toit
batière *m*, toit en dos d'âne *m*

couple[2] *vt* ELEC ENG accoupler, coupler, MINING *drill
rods* emmancher, PAPER TECH accoupler, RAIL accoupler, *cars, coaches* atteler; ~ **in parallel** *vt* ELEC ENG
monter en parallèle

coupled:[1] ~ **circuit** *n* ELEC, ELEC ENG circuit couplé *m*; ~
engines *n pl* MECH ENG machines couplées *f pl*; ~
exposure meter *n* PHOTO cellule couplée au diaphragme *f*; ~ **lid-base bottle tray** *n* PACKAGING
cartonnage combiné pour bouteilles *m*; ~ **modes** *n pl*

OPT, SPACE, TELECOM modes couplés *m pl*; ~ **oscillators** *n pl* PHYS oscillateurs couplés *m pl*; ~ **rangefinder**
n PHOTO télémètre couplé avec l'objectif *m*; ~ **speed
and F-stop setting** *n* PHOTO diaphragme couplé à
l'obturateur *m*; ~ **systems** *n pl* PHYS systèmes couplés *m pl*

coupled:[2] **be** ~ *vi* ELEC ENG s'accoupler, être accouplé
ELECTRON couplé

coupler *n* ACOUSTICS coupleur *m*, CINEMAT connecteur
m, copulant *m*, coupleur *m*, COMP, ELEC ENG, MECH
ENG, TELECOM coupleur *m*; ~ **connector** *n* ELEC prise
mobile de connecteur *f*; ~ **development** *n* CINEMAT
développement chromogène *m*; ~ **loss** *n* OPT, TELE-
COM affaiblissement de coupleur *m*; ~ **plug and socket
connection** *n* ELEC prise mâle et femelle *f*; ~ **socket
connector** *n* ELEC prise mobile de connecteur *f*

coupling *n* AERONAUT *mechanical* accouplement *m*, asservissement *m*, flector *m*, CHEM, COMP couplage *m*,
ELEC *connection, induction* accouplement *m*, couplage
m, ELEC ENG accouplement *m*, couplage *m*, *waveguides* liaison *f*, MECH accouplement *m*, MECH ENG
articulation *f*, *device* emmanchement *m*, joint *m*,
manchon *m*, raccord *m*, *two shafts* accouplement *m*,
manchonnage *m*, NAUT *of engine* accouplement *m*,
PHYS couplage *m*, RAIL *vehicles* attelage *m*, TELECOM
couplage *m*, VEHICLES *electrical system* raccord *m*,
trailer attelage *m*; ~ **agent** *n* P&R *paint binder, fillers*
copulant *m*; ~ **between stages** *n* ELECTRON liaison
entre étages *f*; ~ **blanking plug** *n* PROD ENG obtura-
teur-raccord *m*; ~ **box** *n* MECH ENG accouplement *m*,
manchon *m*, manchon d'accouplement *m*, manchon
d'assemblage *m*, manchon de couplage *m*, manchonnage *m*; ~ **buffer** *n* AERONAUT palet d'accouplement
m; ~ **capacitor** *n* ELEC, PHYS condensateur de couplage
m; ~ **coil** *n* ELEC bobine de couplage *f*; ~ **constant** *n*
NUCLEAR *of interaction*, PHYS constante de couplage *f*;
~ **cover** *n* AERONAUT *helicopter* boîtier de cloche *m*; ~
efficiency *n* OPT, TELECOM rendement de couplage *m*;
~ **flange** *n* MECH bride d'accouplement *f*; ~ **hook** *n*
MECH ENG crochet d'attelage *m*, RAIL *vehicles* crochet
de traction *m*; ~ **hose** *n* RAIL boyau d'accouplement
m; ~ **impedance** *n* ELEC impédance de couplage *f*; ~
link *n* MECH ENG manille d'attelage *f*; ~ **loop** *n* ELEC ENG
boucle de couplage *f*; ~ **loss** *n* OPT perte de couplage *f*,
TELECOM affaiblissement de couplage *m*, perte de
couplage *f*; ~ **nut** *n* MECH ENG écrou de raccord *m*; ~
pin *n* MECH ENG boulon d'attelage *m*, *for trailer* cheville d'attelage *f*; ~ **resistance** *n* ELEC résistance de
couplage *f*; ~ **ring** *n* MECH ENG bague d'entraînement *f*,
virole de raccordement *f*; ~ **rod** *n* RAIL *vehicles* bielle
d'accouplement *f*, bielle de connexion *f*; ~ **sleeve** *n*
MECH couvercle *m*, MECH ENG collier de jonction *m*,
manche d'accouplement *m*, manchon de raccordement *m*, *pipe fitting* manchon d'accouplement *m*; ~
spigot with thread *n* MECH ENG *die set* pigeonneau
fileté *m*; ~ **transformer** *n* ELEC transformateur de
couplage *m*, ELEC ENG transformateur de liaison *m*; ~
tube *n* MECH ENG tube de raccordement *m*

course[1] *n* AERONAUT parcours *m*, route *f*, C&G *of bricks
or blocks* assise *f* (Fra), tas *m* (Bel), CONST *masonry*
assise *f*, *of road* couche *f*, HYDROL *of river* cours *m*,
tracé *m*, MINING *of lode* direction *f*, NAUT *navigation*
cap *m*, PHYS *of experiment* marche *f*, SPACE cap *m*,
route *f*, TEXTILES rangée de mailles *f*; ~ **alignment** *n*
AERONAUT *instrument landing system* réglage de l'alignement de piste *m*; ~ **angle** *n* AERONAUT angle de cap

m, angle de route *m*; ~ **blip pulse** *n* TELECOM impulsion de repérage de cap *f*; ~ **of face stitches** *n* TEXTILES rangée de mailles endroit *f*; ~ **indicator** *n* AERONAUT conservateur de cap *m*, NAUT *navigation* indicateur de cap *m*; ~ **indicator selector** *n* AERONAUT indicateur sélecteur de course *m*; ~ **line** *n* AERONAUT *instrument landing system* alignement de piste *m*, axe de radioalignement *m*; ~ **made good** *n* NAUT *navigation* route fond *f*; ~ **of ore** *n* MINING colonne couchée *f*, filon horizontalement allongé *m*; ~ **of reverse stitches** *n* TEXTILES rangée de mailles envers *f*; ~ **selector** *n* AERONAUT sélecteur de mode de fonctionnement *m*, sélecteur de route *m*; ~ **through the water** *n* NAUT *navigation* route en surface *f*; ~ **to steer** *n* NAUT *navigation* route au compas *f*; ~ **tracer** *n* AERONAUT traceur de route *m*

course:[2] **be on** ~ *vi* NAUT suivre le cap fixé

courses: ~ **per minute** *n pl* TEXTILES rangées à la minute *f pl*

course-up[1] *adj* NAUT *radar* cap en haut

course-up[2] *adv* NAUT *radar* cap en haut

courseware *n* COMP didactitiel *m*

coursing *n* MINING aménagement du courant d'air *m*; ~ **the air** *n* MINING aménagement du courant d'air *m*; ~ **bubble** *n* COAL TECH bulle ascendante *f*

courtesy: ~ **ensign** *n* NAUT *flags* pavillon de courtoisie *m*; ~ **flag** *n* NAUT fanion de courtoisie *m*

Couvinian *adj* GEOL couvinien

covalence *n* CHEM covalence *f*, NUCLEAR covalence *f*, valence homopolaire *f*

covalency *n* CHEM covalence *f*, NUCLEAR covalence *f*, valence homopolaire *f*

covalent[1] *adj* CHEM covalent

covalent:[2] ~ **bond** *n* CRYSTALL liaison covalente *f*, liaison homopolaire *f*, METALL liaison covalente *f*

covariance *n* COMP covariance *f*

cove *n* NAUT *geography* anse *f*, OCEANOG anse *f*, petite baie *f*

covelline *n* MINERAL covellite *f*

covellite *n* MINERAL covellite *f*

cover[1] *n* CONST *welt* bande de recouvrement *f*, couvrejoint *m*, fourrure *f*, GEOL couverture *f*, HYDR EQUIP *steam cylinder* couvercle *m*, fond de cylindre à vapeur *m*, INSTRUMENT chape *f*, pièce de recouvrement *f*, MECH cache *m*, capot *m*, couvercle *m*, MECH ENG bâche de protection *f*, cache de protection *m*, capot *m*, couvercle *m*, housse *f*, carter *m*, carter d'engrenage *m*, couvre- engrenages *m*, gaine protectrice contre les accidents *f*, PRINT couverture *f*, SAFETY couverture *f*, gaine *f*, TEXTILES couverture *f*, VEHICLES enveloppe *f*; ~ **cap** *n* NUCLEAR voûte du couvercle *f*; ~ **gas** *n* NUCLEAR gaz de couverture *m*; ~ **gas discharge line** *n* NUCLEAR conduite de décharge du gaz de couverture *f*; ~ **glass** *n* C&G couvre-objet *m*, LAB EQUIP *microscopy* lamelle couvre-objet *f*; ~ **glass gage** *n* (AmE), ~ **glass gauge** *n* (BrE) C&G calibre pour lamelles couvre-objet *m*; ~ **plate** *n* FUELLESS *of collector* couvercle *m*, MECH ENG plaque de fermeture *f*, tôle de fermeture *f*, NUCLEAR dalle de couverture *f*, plaque supérieure *f*, toit-dalle *m*; ~ **slab** *n* NUCLEAR dalle de couverture *f*, plaque supérieure *f*, toit-dalle *m*; ~ **slip** *n* C&G couvre-objet *m*, INSTRUMENT, LAB EQUIP *microscopy* lamelle couvre-objet *f*; ~ **strip** *n* MECH ENG couvre-joint *m*; ~ **strip of root rib** *n* AERONAUT *helicopter* piétage *m*; ~ **tile** *n* C&G dalle *f*, C&G brique couvre-goulotte *f*

cover[2] *vt* PHYS couvrir, parcourir

coverage *n* TELECOM couverture *f*; ~ **area** *n* SPACE zone de couverture *f*

covercoat *n* C&G décalcomanie *f*

covered[1] *adj* ELEC *conductor*, ELEC ENG guipé

covered:[2] ~ **car** *n* (AmE) *(cf covered wagon)* RAIL *vehicles* wagon couvert *m*; ~ **container** *n* TRANSP conteneur fermé *m*; ~ **electrode** *n* CONST *welding* électrode enrobée *f*; ~ **pot** *n* C&G pot couvert *m*; ~ **wagon** *n* (BrE) *(cf covered car)* RAIL *vehicles* wagon couvert *m*; ~ **yarn** *n* TEXTILES fil guipé *m*

covering *n* CONST *over pit top* fermeture *f*, panneau de couverture *m*, PHOTO *of camera* gainage *m*, gainerie *f*; ~ **board** *n* NAUT *shipbuilding* plat-bord *m*; ~ **fire** *n* MILIT tir de couverture *m*; ~ **paint** *n* P&R peinture couvrante *f*; ~ **plate** *n* PROD ENG *founding* plaque de recouvrement *f*, *welt* bande de recouvrement *f*, couvre-joint *m*, fourrure *f*; ~ **power** *n* P&R *paint* pouvoir couvrant *m*

COW *abbr (crude oil washing)* PETR TECH lavage au brut des citernes *m*

cowcatcher *n* RAIL *vehicles* chasse-bestiaux *m*

cowl *n* AERONAUT *motor* auvent *m*, capot moteur *m*, CONST *of chimney* capote *f*, mitre *f*, HEAT ENG *of chimney* capuchon *m*, MECH capot *m*; ~ **flap** *n* AERONAUT *of engine, gill* volet de capot *m*

cowling *n* AERONAUT capotage *m*

Cowper: ~ **stove** *n* C&G appareil Cowper *m*

CP *abbr (call processor)* TELECOM processeur de traitement des appels *m*

CPI *abbr* PRINT *(characters per inch)* caractères par pouce *m pl*, TELECOM *(computer-PBX interface)* interface PABX-serveur *f*

CPM *abbr (critical path method)* COMP méthode du chemin critique *f*

CPS *abbr (characters per second)* COMP, PRINT CPS *(caractères par seconde)*

CPSK *abbr (coherent phase shift keying)* TELECOM MDPC *(modulation par déplacement de phase cohérente)*

CPT: ~ **theorem** *n* PHYS théorème PCT *m*

CPU *abbr (central processing unit)* COMP, DP, TELECOM UC *(unité centrale)*

CPVC *abbr (critical pigment volume concentration)* COATINGS *paint* CVCP *(concentration volumique critique de pigment)*

CQM *abbr (circuit group query message)* TELECOM IGD *(message d'interrogation de groupe de circuits)*

CQR[1] *abbr (circuit group query response message)* TELECOM IGR *(message de réponse à une interrogation de groupe de circuits)*

CQR:[2] ~ **anchor** *n* NAUT *mooring* ancre CQR *f*, ancre charrue *f*

Cr *(chromium)* CHEM Cr *(chrome)*

CR *abbr* COMP *(carriage return)* caractère de retour chariot *m*, retour de chariot *m*, TELECOM *(call register)* compteur d'appels *m*, registre d'appels *m*, TELECOM *(connection request)* demande de connexion *f*

crab[1] *n* CINEMAT chariot-grue *m*, MECH *lifting gear* chariot de pont roulant *m*, NUCLEAR chariot *m*, treuil roulant *m*, PROD ENG *hoisting* treuil *m*; ~ **angle** *n* AERONAUT angle de crabe *m*; ~ **dolly** *n* CINEMAT chariot omnidirectionnel *m*, chariot-crabe *m*; ~ **winch** *n* PROD ENG treuil à bras *m*, treuil à manivelle *m*

crab[2] *vi* CINEMAT se déplacer latéralement

Crab: ~ **nebula** *n* ASTRON, SPACE nébuleuse du Crabe *f*; ~ **pulsar** *n* ASTRON pulsar du Crabe *m*

crabbing *n* NAUT *of ship* déplacement latéral *m*

crack[1] *n* COAL TECH gerçure *f*, CONST faille *f*, CRYSTALL crique *f*, fissure *f*, GEOL faille *f*, MECH *materials* crique *f*, fente *f*, fissure *f*, METALL, TEXTILES fissure *f*; ~ **arrest temperature** *n* METALL température d'arrêt de fissuration *f*; ~ **branching** *n* METALL ramification de fissures *f*; ~ **detector** *n* MECH ENG, NUCLEAR détecteur de fissures *m*; ~ **extension force** *n* METALL taux de restitution d'énergie *m*; ~ **formation** *n* METALL formation de fissure *f*; ~ **initiation** *n* METALL initialisation de la fissure *f*; ~ **nucleation** *n* METALL nucléation de fissure *f*; ~ **opening displacement** *n* NUCLEAR décalage de l'ouverture de fissure *m*, déplacement de l'ouverture de fissure *m*; ~ **opening stretch** *n* NUCLEAR décalage de l'ouverture de fissure *m*, déplacement de l'ouverture de fissure *m*; ~ **propagation rate** *n* NUCLEAR vitesse de propagation des fissures *f*; ~ **resistance** *n* P&R résistance au craquelage *f*; ~ **test** *n* MECH ENG essai de fissibilité *m*; ~ **tip** *n* METALL tête de fissure *f*; ~ **velocity** *n* METALL vitesse de fissuration *f*

crack[2] *vi* CRYSTALL claquer, craquer, PROP MAT s'effriter

cracked *adj* MECH *materials* fendu, fissuré, fêlé, PROP MAT crevassé

cracker *n* COAL TECH concasseur à charbon *m*

cracking *n* C&G croquage à pédale *m*, CONST *of concrete*, MECH *materials* fissuration *f*, P&R *fault* craquelage *m*, PETR TECH craquage *m*, PROP MAT craquelage *m*, QUALITY fissuration *f*; ~ **coal** *n* C&G charbon à détacher *m*; ~ **open** *n* MECH ENG *of valve* décollement *m*; ~ **plant** *n* PETR TECH installation de craquage *f*; ~ **ring** *n* C&G anneau à détacher *m*; ~ **tool** *n* C&G grugeoir *m*

cracking-off *n* C&G détachage au fer *m*

crackle[1] *n* ACOUSTICS grésillement *m*, RECORDING crépitement *m*

crackle[2] *vi* CHEM fuser

crackled: ~ **finish** *n* PROD ENG fini vermiculé *m*; ~ **glass** *n* C&G verre craquelé *m*

crack-off: ~ **iron** *n* (AmE) *(cf wetting-off iron)* C&G fer à détacher *m*

cradle *n* CINEMAT berceau *m*, support d'objectif *m*, CONST *hanging scaffold* échafaud volant *m*, échafaudage volant *m*, INSTRUMENT bride de fixation *f*, MECH, MECH ENG *tooling* berceau *m*, MINING palier *m*, plancher volant *m*, échafaudage volant *m*, *ore dressing* berceau *m*, cradle *m*, NAUT *for storage or transport of boat* ber *m*, ber de transport *m*, berceau *m*; ~ **dynamo** *n* ELEC *generator* alternateur pilote à aimants permanents *m*; ~ **gear head** *n* CINEMAT tête à manivelle *f*; ~ **head** *n* CINEMAT tête à bascule *f*; ~ **iron** *n* CONST étrier d'échafaudage *m*; ~ **mount** *n* ASTRON monture à berceau *f*; ~ **mounting** *n* MILIT affût à berceau *m*; ~ **rocker** *n* MINING berceau *m*, cradle *m*; ~ **stirrup** *n* CONST étrier d'échafaudage *m*

craft *n* NAUT *boat* embarcation *f*, SPACE engin *m*, véhicule *m*; ~ **porcelain** *n* C&G porcelaine artistique *f*; ~ **pottery** *n* C&G poterie artistique *f*

cramp[1] *n* CONST *carpenter's* clameaux *m pl*, clampe *f*, crochet d'assemblage *m*, happe *f*, *for stonework* agrafe *f*, crampon *m*, happe *f*, MECH ENG *G cramp, C cramp* bride *f*, bride de serrage *f*, bride à capote *f*, happe *f*, presse *f*, presse à coller *f*, serre-joint *m*; ~ **iron** *n* CONST *carpenter's* clameaux *m pl*, clampe *f*, crochet d'assemblage *m*, happe *f*, *for stonework* agrafe *f*, crampon *m*, happe *f*; ~ **iron with stone hook** *n* CONST agrafe à scellement *f*, crampon à scellement *m*; ~ **with**

turned-down ends *n* CONST agrafe à talon *f*

cramp[2] *vt* MECH ENG cramponner

cramping *n* TV contraction d'image *f*

cranage *n* MECH ENG *in workshop* pont roulant *m*; ~ **up to 20 tonnes capacity** *n* MECH ENG pont roulant de 20 tonnes *m*

cranch *n* MINING massif de protection *m*

crane *n* CINEMAT, CONST *travelling*, MECH *lifting gear*, NAUT *dockyard, cargo vessel* grue *f*; ~ **barge** *n* PETR TECH barge de levage *f*; ~ **helicopter** *n* AERONAUT hélicoptèregrue *m*; ~ **hook** *n* CONST crochet de grue *m*, crochet de levage *m*; ~ **jib** *n* MECH *lifting gear* flèche de grue *f*; ~ **ladle** *n* PROD ENG *founding* poche de coulée suspendue *f*, poche pour grues *f*; ~ **operator** *n* CINEMAT, NAUT grutier *m*; ~ **rail** *n* CONST rail de translation *m*

craneman *n* CONST grutier *m*, machiniste de grue *m*

crank[1] *n* MECH manivelle *f*, MECH ENG coude *m*, *of axle of locomotive* manivelle *f*, VEHICLES *engine* manivelle *f*; ~ **and connecting rod system** *n* MECH ENG système bielle-manivelle *m*; ~ **arm** *n* AUTO bras de manivelle *m*, MECH ENG bras de manivelle *m*, corps de manivelle *m*; ~ **bearing** *n* MECH ENG palier-manivelle *m*; ~ **blasting machine** *n* MINING exploseur à manivelle *m*; ~ **cheek** *n* MECH ENG bras de manivelle *m*, corps de manivelle *m*; ~ **handle** *n* RAIL *vehicles* manivelle *f*; ~ **link** *n* PROD ENG biellette *f*; ~ **shaping machine** *n* MECH ENG étau-limeur à commande par bielle *m*

crank[2] *vt* AERONAUT *reactor* lancer

crankcase *n* MECH carter moteur *m*, VEHICLES *engine* carter de vilebrequin *m*; ~ **bottom half** *n* AUTO demi-carter inférieur *m*; ~ **breather** *n* VEHICLES *engine* reniflard de carter *m*; ~ **heater** *n* REFRIG résistance de chauffage de carter *f*; ~ **top half** *n* AUTO demi-carter supérieur *m*; ~ **ventilation** *n* VEHICLES *engine* ventilation de carter *f*

crank-drive: ~ **slotting machine** *n* MECH ENG mortaiseuse à bielle et à manivelle *f*

cranked: ~ **facing tool** *n* MECH ENG outil coudé à dresser les faces *m*; ~ **finishing tool** *n* MECH ENG outil à dresser les angles *m*; ~ **knife tool** *n* MECH ENG outil couteau coudé *m*; ~ **knife tool for copy turning** *n* MECH ENG outil couteau coudé à charioter arrondi *m*; ~ **link** *n* MECH ENG *chain* maillon à crémaillère *m*; ~ **link transmission chain** *n* MECH ENG chaîne de transmission à maillons coudés *f*; ~ **round nose and turning tool** *n* MECH ENG outil coudé à charioter arrondi *m*; ~ **spanner** *n* (BrE) MECH ENG clé coudée *f*; ~ **tool** *n* MECH ENG *metal turning* crochet *m*, outil à crochet *m*; ~ **turning and facing tool** *n* MECH ENG outil coudé à charioter *m*

crank-end *n* MECH ENG *horizontal stationary engine* AV *m*, avant *m*; ~ **of cylinder** *n* MECH ENG *horizontal stationary engine* AV-cylindre *m*, avant-cylindre *m*; ~ **dead center** *n* (AmE), ~ **dead centre** *n* (BrE) MECH ENG admission avant *f*, point mort AV *m*; ~ **release** *n* MECH ENG échappement AV *m*

cranking *n* AERONAUT *piston engine* brassage *m*, dégommage *m*, engin de dégommage *m*, ventilation du réacteur *f*

crankpath *n* MECH ENG chemin suivi par le bouton de manivelle *m*

crankpin *n* AUTO, MECH maneton *m*, MECH ENG *of engine crank* bouton de manivelle *m*, maneton de manivelle *m*, tourillon de manivelle *m*, *of hand crank* soie de manivelle *f*, VEHICLES *engine* maneton *m*

crankshaft *n* AUTO vilebrequin *m*, MECH arbre-manivelle *m*, vilebrequin *m*, MECH ENG arbre coudé *m*, arbre à manivelle *m*, arbre à vilebrequin *m*, arbre-manivelle *m*, vilebrequin *m*, jonc de manivelle *m*, NAUT *engine*, VEHICLES *engine* vilebrequin *m*; ~ **alignment gage** *n* (AmE), ~ **alignment gauge** *n* (BrE) MECH ENG jauge d'alignement pour vilebrequin *f*; ~ **bearing** *n* AUTO palier de vilebrequin *m*, *car* coussinet de palier *m*, VEHICLES *engine* palier de vilebrequin *m*; ~ **bearing cap** *n* AUTO *car* chapeau de palier *m*; ~ **front end** *n* AUTO nez de vilebrequin *m*; ~ **gear** *n* AUTO *car* pignon de distribution *m*

crankweb *n* AUTO masse d'équilibrage *f*, MECH ENG bras de manivelle *m*, corps de manivelle *m*

crash[1] *n* COMP incident *m*, panne *f*, écrasement *m*, DP incident *m*, écrasement *m*; ~ **barrier** *n* SAFETY glissière de sécurité *f*, TRANSP barrière d'arrêt *f*; ~ **landing** *n* AERONAUT, SPACE atterrissage en catastrophe *m*; ~ **numbering** *n* PRINT numérotation par pression *f*; ~ **perforation** *n* PRINT perforation en liasses épaisses *f*; ~ **printing** *n* PRINT impression avec formes en relief et forte pression *f*, repiquage avec formes en relief et forte pression *m*; ~ **switch** *n* AERONAUT interrupteur de crash *m*

crash[2] ~ **into** *vt* SAFETY tamponner

crash[3] *vi* SPACE s'écraser

crate *n* PACKAGING caisse à claire-voies *f*, *bottle* casier *m*; ~ **liners** *n pl* PAPER TECH papier pour doublage de caisse *m*; ~ **pallet** *n* TRANSP palette caisse cadrée *f*

crater *n* ASTRON, GEOL, MINING, P&R *paint defect*, SPACE cratère *m*; ~ **cut** *n* MINING bouchon à tir de cratère *m*, tir de cratère *m*; ~ **drip** *n* (BrE) *(cf top tin)* C&G goutte d'étain en cratère *f*

Crater *n* ASTRON Coupe *f*

cratered: ~ **terrain** *n* ASTRON terrain couvert de cratères *m*

cratering *n* ASTRON formation de cratères *f*

craton *n* GEOL craton *m*

craunch *n* MINING massif de protection *m*

crawfoot *n* CINEMAT araignée *f*

crawl *n* CINEMAT générique déroulant *m*; ~ **title machine** *n* CINEMAT dérouleur pour générique *m*

crawler *n* MECH *vehicles* transporteur à chenilles *m*; ~ **base** *n* MINING élément sur chenilles *m*; ~ **dragline excavator** *n* CONST *civil engineering* dragline sur patins *f*, dragline à chenilles *m*; ~ **tracks** *n pl* MECH ENG chenilles *f pl*

crawling *n* ELEC ENG accrochage *m*, P&R *paint defect* ridage *m*, TV filage *m*, formation de rayures *f*

craze[1] *n* TEXTILES engouement *m*

craze[2] *vi* C&G se fendiller

crazing *n* CONST craquelure *f*, craquelé *m*, crique *f*, P&R *surface defect* craquelure *f*, fendillement *m*

CRC[1] *abbr* CONTROL *(cyclic redundancy check)*, ELECTRON *(cyclic redundancy check)* CRC *(contrôle de redondance cyclique)*, PRINT *(camera-ready copy)* copie prête à la reproduction *f*, document prêt *m*, TELECOM *(communications research centre)* centre de recherche sur les communications *m*

CRC[2] *n* *(cyclical redundancy check)* COMP CRC *(contrôle de redondance cyclique)*; ~ **message bloc** *n* *(CMB)* TELECOM bloc de messages pour le contrôle du CRC *m*

cream: ~ **separator** *n* FOOD TECH écrémeuse *f*; ~ **of tartar** *n* CHEM bitartrate de potasse *m*, crème de tartre *f*, FOOD TECH crème de tartre *f*

creamed: ~ **latex** *n* P&R latex crémé *m*

creaming *n* P&R *operation* crémage *m*; ~ **agent** *n* P&R agent de crémage *m*

crease[1] *n* PAPER TECH faux pli *m*, PRINT pli marqué mais non replié *m*, TEXTILES pli *m*; ~ **and glueing machine** *n* PACKAGING machine à plier et à coller *f*; ~ **recovery** *n* TEXTILES défroissabilité *f*; ~ **resistance** *n* TEXTILES infroissabilité *f*

crease[2] *vt* PACKAGING plier, TEXTILES plisser

crease[3] *vi* TEXTILES se froisser

creaser *n* PRINT molette de marquage du pli *f*

crease-resist: ~ **finish** *n* TEXTILES apprêt d'infroissabilité *m*

crease-resistant: ~ **finish** *n* COATINGS apprêt anti-froisse *m*

creasing: ~ **and scoring machine** *n* PACKAGING machine à plier et à entailler *f*

create[1] *vt* COMP, DP créer

create:[2] ~ **a draft** *vi* (AmE), ~ **a draught** *vi* (BrE) MECH ENG provoquer un appel d'air, provoquer un tirage

credentials *n pl* TELECOM justificatif d'identité *m*

credit: ~ **card call** *n* TELECOM appel carte de crédit *m*; ~ **indicator** *n* TELECOM indicateur de crédit *m*

credits *n pl* CINEMAT générique *m*

creek *n* NAUT anse *f*, crique *f*, ruisseau *m*, OCEANOG calanque *f*

creel *n* OCEANOG caseyeur *m*, TEXTILES cantre *m*; ~ **fishing** *n* OCEANOG caseyage *m*

creep[1] *n* CHEM grimpement *m*, COAL TECH, CONST *of concrete*, CRYSTALL fluage *m*, GAS TECH fluage *m*, suintement *m*, HEAT ENG, MECH *materials* fluage *m*, MINING boursouflement *m*, gonflement *m*, montée *f*, P&R creep *m*, fluage *m*, PETR TECH *pipeline* cheminement *m*, PROD ENG *of belt* glissement *m*, PROP MAT fluage *m*; ~ **properties** *n pl* MECH *materials* caractéristiques de fluage *f pl*; ~ **rate** *n* PROP MAT vitesse de fluage *f*; ~ **resistance** *n* P&R résistance au creep *f*, résistance au fluage *f*, PROP MAT résistance au fluage *f*; ~ **resistance test** *n* TESTING essai de résistance au cheminement *m*; ~ **rupture** *n* SPRINGS rupture par fluage *f*; ~ **rupture elongation** *n* METALL allongement de rupture par fluage *m*; ~ **strain** *n* METALL déformation par fluage *f*; ~ **strength** *n* COAL TECH, METALL résistance au fluage *f*; ~ **test** *n* C&G essai de décrépitation *m*, SPRINGS essai de fluage *m*

creep[2] *vi* MINING gonfler, se boursoufler

creeper: ~ **chain** *n* MINING *haulage* chaîne traînante *f*

creeping[1] *adj* GEOL prograde

creeping:[2] ~ **motion** *n* FLUID PHYS écoulement rampant *m*; ~ **motion equation** *n* FLUID PHYS *viscous flow* équation des mouvements rampants *f*

cremator *n* HEATING four crématoire *m*

crenulation *n* GEOL crénulation *f*, micropli *m*

creosote *n* CHEM créosote *f*

crepe *n* CHEM *rubber*, TEXTILES crêpe *m*; ~ **paper** *n* PACKAGING, PAPER TECH papier crêpé *m*; ~ **rubber** *n* P&R caoutchouc-crêpe *m*

creped *adj* PAPER TECH, TEXTILES crêpé

creping *n* PAPER TECH crêpage *m*

crescent: ~ **moon** *n* ASTRON croissant de lune *m*

crescent-shaped *adj* GEOM en croissant, en forme de croissant

cresol: ~ **resin** *n* P&R résine crésolique *f*

crest *n* CONST crête *f*, *of roof* couronnement *m*, faîtage *m*, faîte *m*, FUELLESS *of dams* couronnement *m*, GEOL axe *m*, *of anticline* crête *f*, HYDROL *of dam* couronnement *m*, *of wave* crête *f*, WATER SUPP *of dam, weir* crête *f*, seuil *m*; ~ **factor** *n* ELEC ENG facteur de crête *m*; ~ **height** *n* FUELLESS hauteur du couronnement *f*; ~ **line** *n* OCEANOG ligne de crête *f*; ~ **province** *n* OCEANOG étage des crêtes *m*; ~ **tile** *n* CONST tuile faîtière *f*

Cretaceous: ~ **period** *n* GEOL, PETR TECH crétacé *m*

crevice *n* COAL TECH gerçure *f*

crew[1] *n* AERONAUT équipage *m*, CINEMAT équipe *f*, NAUT *of boat* équipage *m*, PETR TECH équipe *f*, PROD ENG *shift of staff* poste *m*, équipe *f*, SPACE *of spacecraft* équipage *m*; ~ **compartment** *n* AERONAUT habitacle *m*, poste d'équipage *m*, poste de pilotage *m*; ~ **door** *n* AERONAUT porte de l'équipage *f*; ~ **list** *n* NAUT *ship's papers* rôle d'équipage *m*; ~ **operating manual** *n* AERONAUT manuel de l'équipage *m*; ~ **station** *n* AERONAUT poste d'équipage *m*

crew[2] *vt* NAUT armer d'un équipage

crew[3] *vi* NAUT servir d'équipier

crew's: ~ **quarters** *n pl* NAUT poste d'équipage *m*

crewmate *n* SPACE *spacecraft* coéquipier *m*

CRF *abbr* TELECOM *(connection-related function)* fonction liée à la connexion *f*, TELECOM *(virtual channel connection)* fonction liée à la connexion sur les VC *f*, TELECOM *(virtual path connection-related function)* fonction liée à la connexion sur les VP *f*

CRI: ~ **print** *n* CINEMAT copie tirée d'internégatif *f*

crib *n* MINING *shaft sinking frame, curb* cadre porteur *m*, cadre à oreilles *m*, roue *f*, rouet *m*, roulisse *f*, trousse *f*, PROD ENG encoffrement en charpente *m*

cribble *n* COAL TECH crible à grosses mailles *m*, PROD ENG crible *m*

cribwork *n* PROD ENG encoffrement en charpente *m*

crichtonite *n* MINERAL crichtonite *f*

cricket: ~ **dolly** *n* CINEMAT chariot Elemack *m*

crime: ~ **prevention devices** *n pl* SAFETY appareils pour la lutte contre le crime *m pl*, appareils pour la prévention des infractions *m pl*

crimp[1] *n* C&G croquage *m*, PRINT réduction *f*, TEXTILES frisure *f*; ~ **lock** *n* PRINT griffage *m*; ~ **paper cup** *n* PACKAGING gobelet en papier froncé *m*; ~ **terminal lug** *n* ELEC ENG cosse à sertir *f*

crimp[2] *vt* MECH, MINING, PACKAGING sertir, PRINT gaufrer, griffer, plisser, réduire, PROD ENG sertir par replis, TEXTILES friser

crimped: ~ **connection** *n* ELEC ENG connexion sertie *f*; ~ **fiber** *n* (AmE), ~ **fibre** *n* (BrE) TEXTILES fibre frisée *f*; ~ **yarn** *n* TEXTILES fil moussé *f*

crimper *n* C&G fletteur *m*

crimping *n* MINING sertissage *m*, PRINT griffage *m*, PROD ENG sertissage *m*; ~ **bush** *n* MECH ENG bague de sertissage *f*; ~ **pliers** *n pl* MECH ENG pince à sertir *f*; ~ **tool** *n* ELEC, MECH pince à sertir *f*, MECH ENG outil de sertissage *m*; ~ **washer** *n* MECH ENG rondelle de sertissage *f*

crimp-on: ~ **closure** *n* PACKAGING fermeture sertie *f*

crimson:[1] ~ **lake** *n* COLOURS laque de cochenille *f*, laque pourpre *f*

crimson[2] *vt* COLOURS teindre en cramoisi

cringle *n* NAUT *sail* cosse *f*

crinkle: ~ **washer** *n* MECH ENG rondelle à ressort *f*

crinkled *adj* PROD ENG *finish* granité

crinoidal: ~ **limestone** *n* GEOL calcaire à crinoïdes *m*

crisp[1] *adj* TEXTILES *linen* apprêté, *paper* raide

crisp:[2] ~ **handle** *n* TEXTILES toucher nerveux *m*; ~ **linen** *n* TEXTILES tissu apprêté *m*; ~ **paper-like finish** *n* TEXTILES fini sec *m*

cristobalite *n* MINERAL cristobalite *f*

criterion *n* COMP, DP critère *m*; ~ **of failure** *n* MECH critère de ruine *m*

critical[1] *adj* CHEM, PHYS, QUALITY critique

critical:[2] ~ **altitude** *n* AERONAUT altitude de rétablissement *f*; ~ **amount** *n* NUCLEAR quantité critique *f*; ~ **off-amount** *n* NUCLEAR différence à la masse critique *f*; ~ **angle** *n* CHEM, OPT, PETR angle limite *m*, PHYS *of refraction* angle de réfraction limite *m*, anglelimite *m*, TELECOM angle limite *m*; ~ **backing pressure** *n* MECH ENG *of vacuum pump* pression critique de refoulement *f*; ~ **band** *n* ACOUSTICS, RECORDING bande critique *f*; ~ **constant** *n* CHEM constante critique *f*; ~ **crack length** *n* METALL longueur critique de fissure *f*; ~ **damping** *n* ELEC ENG, PETR, PHYS amortissement critique *m*; ~ **defect** *n* QUALITYdéfaut critique *m*; ~ **density** *n* ASTRON, TRANSP *traffic* densité critique *f*; ~ **density of matter in the universe** *n* ASTRON densité critiquede la matière dans l'Univers *f*; ~ **design review** *n (CDR)* SPACE revue critique de définition *f*; ~ **diameter** *n* MINING diamètre critique *m*; ~ **distance** *n* PETR distance critique *f*; ~ **engine** *n* AERONAUT *airworthiness* moteur critique *m*; ~ **engine inoperative** *n* AERONAUT moteur critique hors de fonctionnement *m*; ~ **event** *n* PROD ENG *of slide valve* phase de distribution *f*, phase de marche du tiroir *f*; ~ **field** *n* ELEC ENG champ critique *m*, *of magnetron* induction critique *f*; ~ **flicker frequency** *n* TV fréquence critique de scintillement *f*, fréquence de papillotement critique *f*; ~ **fracture stress** *n* METALL contrainte critique de rupture *f*; ~ **frequency** *n* SPACE *communications*, TELECOM fréquence critique *f*; ~ **growth rate** *n* PROP MAT vitesse critique de croissance *f*; ~ **heat flow** *n* NUCLEAR crise d'ébullition *f*, échauffement critique *m*; ~ **heat flux** *n* PROD ENG densité de flux thermique critique *f*; ~ **isotherm** *n* CHEM isotherme critique *f*; ~ **mass** *n* PHYS masse critique *f*; ~ **path** *n* COMP, CONST *planning*, DP chemin critique *m*; ~ **path analysis** *n* TEXTILES analyse des flux critiques *f*; ~ **path method** *n* COMP *(CPM)* méthode du chemin critique *f*; ~ **pigment volume concentration** *n (CPVC)* COATINGS *paint* concentration volumique critique de pigment *f (CVCP)*; ~ **point** *n* PHYS point critique *m*; ~ **power unit** *n* AERONAUT groupe motopropulseur critique *m*, groupe motopropulseur le plus défavorable *m*; ~ **pressure** *n* HEAT ENG, PHYS pression critique *f*; ~ **reaction** *n* RAD PHYS réaction critique *f*; ~ **resistance** *n* ELEC résistance critique *f*; ~ **resolved shear stress** *n* PROP MAT macrolimite élastique critique *f*; ~ **resource** *n* COMP, DP ressource critique *f*; ~ **section** *n* COMP, DP section critique *f*; ~ **shear strain** *n* METALL cisaillement critique *m*; ~ **speed** *n* AERONAUT, MECH, SPACE, TRANSP *traffic* vitesse critique *f*; ~ **stress** *n* METALL contrainte critique *f*; ~ **temperature** *n* HEAT ENG, PETR TECH, PHYS, REFRIG température critique *f*, THERMOD température critique *f*, température d'ignition *f*; ~ **temperature curve** *n* THERMOD courbe des températures critiques *f*; ~ **temperature range** *n* THERMOD domaine des températures critiques *m*;~ **value** *n* SPRINGS valeur à titre impératif *f*; ~ **velocity** *n* PHYS vitesse critique *f*; ~ **voltage** *n* ELEC, ELEC ENG tension critique *f*; ~ **volume** *n* HEAT ENG volume critique *m*; ~ **water level** *n* WATER SUPP niveau critique d'eau *m*; ~ **wavelength** *n* PHYS *waveguide* longueur d'onde de coupure *f*; ~ **wing** *n* AERONAUT *airworthiness* aile critique *f*

criticality *n* QUALITY gravité *f*, niveau de risque *m*; ~ **analysis** *n* QUALITY analyse du niveau de risque *f*

crizzle *n* C&G craquelure *f*

crizzled: ~ **finish** *n* C&G bague sale *f*

CRJ *abbr (cold-rolled joist)* THERMOD poutre laminée à froid *f*

crocein *n* CHEM crocéine *f*

crocidolite *n* MINERAL crocidolite *f*

crocin *n* CHEM crocine *f*

crockery: ~ **maker** *n* C&G faïencier *m*; ~ **ware** *n* C&G poterie *f*

crocodile *n* MINING crocodile *m*, RAIL contact fixe de voie *m*, crocodile *m*; ~ **clip** *n* ELEC *connection*, MECH ENG pince crocodile *f*; ~ **squeezer** *n* PROD ENG *for puddled iron* macque *f*, maque *f*, presse à macquer *f*

crocoisite *n* MINERAL crocoïte *f*

crocoite *n* MINERAL crocoïte *f*

croconic *adj* CHEM croconique

crocus: ~ **cloth** *n* MECH ENG toile émeri fine *f*

cronstedtite *n* MINERAL cronstedtite *f*

crooked: ~ **hole** *n* PETR sondage dévié *m*

Crookes: ~ **dark space** *n* ELECTRON zone obscure de Crookes *f*, PHYS espace de Crookes *m*, espace sombre cathodique *m*; ~ **glass** *n* C&G verre de Crookes *m*; ~ **tube** *n* ELECTRON tube de Crookes *m*

crop:[1] ~ **end** *n* PROD ENG *of iron or steel bar* bout affranchi *m*, chute de barre *f*, SPRINGS embase *f*; ~ **load** *n* COAL TECH charge d'un broyeur *f*

crop[2] *vt* CINEMAT recadrer, serrer, PRINT cadrer, couper, TEXTILES *hair* tondre

crop-dusting *n* AERONAUT poudrage des récoltes *m*, pulvérisation agricole *f*, saupoudrage de cultures *m*

cropped *adj* TEXTILES coupé court

cropping *n* PRINT cadrage *m*, TV réduction du plan d'image *f*

cross[1] *n* CONST *pipe connection* croix *f*, té double *m*, *surveying* équerre *f*, équerre d'arpenteur *f*; ~ **assembler** *n* COMP assembleur croisé *m*; ~ **assembly** *n* COMP assemblage croisé *m*; ~ **bearer** *n* PROD ENG *of furnace grate* sommier transversal *m*; ~ **bevel** *n* C&G biseau croisé *m*; ~ **bombardment** *n* RAD PHYS recoupement par bombardement *m*; ~ **color noise** *n* (AmE), ~ **colour noise** *n* (BrE) TV diachromie *f*; ~ **compilation** *n* COMP compilation croisée *f*; ~ **compiler** *n* COMP compilateur croisé *m*; ~ **coupling** *n* ELEC ENG *in symmetric assemblies* rétrocouplage *m*, *inductive coupling* couplage parasite *m*, *of waves* couplage transversal *m*; ~ **direction** *n* PAPER TECH, PRINT sens travers *m*; ~ **drift** *n* MINING recoupe *f*, viaille *f*, volée *f*; ~ **drive** *n* MINING recoupe *f*, viaille *f*, volée *f*; ~ **driving** *n* MINING percement de recoupes *m*; ~ **entry** *n* MINING recoupe *f*; ~ **field bias** *n* RECORDING polarisation à champ transversal *f*; ~ **file** *n* PROD ENG feuille-de-sauge *f*, lime double demi-ronde *f*, lime feuille-de-sauge *f*; ~ **grain** *n* PRINT sens travers *m*; ~ **grinding** *n* PAPER TECH défibrage transversal *m*; ~ **hair** *n* CINEMAT croix de centrage *f*, COMP, DP réticule *m*, PRINT curseur en croix *m*, réticule *m*; ~ **hatching** *n* MECH ENG hachure *f*; ~ **hatch pattern** *n* CINEMAT mire quadrillée *f*; ~ **modulation** *n* ELECTRON transmodulation *f*, TV intermodulation *f*, transmodulation *f*; ~ **perforation** *n* PRINT perforation transversale *f*; ~ **products** *n pl* ELECTRON produits d'intermodulation *m pl*; ~ **recess for screw** *n* MECH ENG empreinte cruciforme pour vis *f*; ~ **ripple** *n* OCEANOG revolin *m*; ~ **section** *n* CONST *of road* profil en travers *m*, profil transversal *m*, GEOL coupe *f*, MECH ENG coupe *f*, coupe en travers *f*, coupe transversale *f*, profil *m*, profil en travers *m*, profil

transversal *m*, section *f*, section transversale *f*, METALL section transversale *f*, NAUT *shipbuilding* coupe transversale *f*, section droite *f*, PAPER TECH coupe transversale *f*, PHYS *scattering* coupe *f*, section efficace *f*, PROD ENG coupe transversale *f*, profil *m*, section *f*, section transversale *f*, PROP MAT section *f*, TEXTILES section transversale *f*, WATER SUPP *of stream, canal, open channel* section *f*; ~ **section density** *n* NUCLEAR section macroscopique efficace *f*; ~ **section iron** *n* PROD ENG *rolled section* fer en croix *m*; ~ **spring** *n* NAUT *mooring* amarre en belle *f*, SPRINGS ressort en crosse *m*; ~ **stone** *n* GEOL, MINING croisette *f*, pierre de croix *f*; ~ **tie** *n* (AmE) *(cf sleeper)* NAUT *shipbuilding* tôle entretoise *f*, RAIL traverse *f*; ~ **tube boiler** *n* HEATING chaudière à bouilleurs croisés *f*; ~ **union** *n* MECH ENG raccord en croix *m*; ~ **vein** *n* GEOL filon croiseur *m*, MINING croiseur *m*, filon croiseur *m*, veine transversale *f*; ~ **wall** *n* CONST *building* mur de refend *m*, refend *m*; ~ **web** *n* PRINT sens transversal de la bande *m*; ~ **wind** *n* AERONAUT vent latéral *m*; ~ **wires** *n pl* ASTRON fils du réticule *m pl*

cross[2] *vt* CONST *from one side to other* franchir, passer, traverser, *roads* se croiser, GEOL croiser, recouper, traverser, PROD ENG *screw thread* fausser; ~ **the bows** *vt* NAUT *of ship* couper la route; ~ **drive** *vt* MINING recouper; ~ **hatch** *vt* PROD ENG hachurer

cross-banding *n* PROP MAT glissement transversal *m*

crossbar *n* AERONAUT palonnier *m*, *approach lighting system* barre transversale de feux *f*, CONST traverse *f*, MECH ENG barrette *f*, PROD ENG *of bed of lathe* nervure d'entretoisage *f*, *of foundry* flask barrette *f*, traverse *f*, RAIL *vehicles* entretoise *f*; ~ **exchange** *n* TELECOM autocommutateur crossbar *m*; ~ **selector** *n* ELEC ENG sélecteur à barres croisées *f*; ~ **system** *n* TELECOM système crossbar *m*, système de connexion électromécanique *m*

crossbeam *n* CONST traverse *f*, NAUT *shipbuilding* barrotin *m*

cross-bedding *n* GEOL stratification entrecroisée *f*

crossbit *n* PETR TECH trépan en croix *m*

crossbond *n* RAIL connexion transversale de rail *f*

crossbonding *n* ELEC *shield bonding* permutation *f*

cross-border: ~ **system** *n* TELECOM *land mobile* réseau transfrontalier *m*

crossbrace *n* NAUT *shipbuilding* étrier *m*

crossbreak *n* C&G casse en travers *f*

cross-channel *adj* NAUT transmanche

cross-connect: ~ **cabinet** *n* TELECOM armoire de sous-répartiteur *f*; ~ **unit** *n* TELECOM brasseur *m*

cross-correlation *n* ELECTRON intercorrélation *f*; ~ **function** *n* ELECTRON fonction d'intercorrélation *f*, PETR fonction de crosscorrélation *f*

cross-correlator *n* ELECTRON intercorrélateur *m*

cross-country: ~ **lorry** *n* (BrE) *(cf cross-country truck)* TRANSP camion tout-terrain *m*; ~ **truck** *n* (AmE) *(cf cross-country lorry)* TRANSP camion tout-terrain *m*

crosscurve *n* NAUT *ship design* courbe de stabilité *f*, courbe pantocarène *f*

crosscut[1] *n* PROD ENG coupe en travers *f*, MECH ENG bec d'âne *m*, burin bédane *m*, bédane *m*, bédane à froid *m*, MINING bouveau *m*, bovette *f*, bowette *f*, galerie au rocher *f*, MINING travers-banc *m*; ~ **chisel** *n* PROD ENG *engineer's* bec d'âne *m*, bédane *m*; ~ **file** *n* PROD ENG lime à double taille *f*, lime à taille croisée *f*; ~ **saw** *n* PROD ENG scie de travers *f*, scie passe-partout *f*, scie à couper en travers *f*, *reciprocating* scie alternative à tronçonner *f*; ~ **saw hazard** *n* SAFETY risque inhérent à l'emploi de scies passe-partout *m*; ~ **tooth** *n* PROD ENG *of saw* dent pour couper en travers *f*, dent triangulaire *f*

crosscut² *vt* PROD ENG *with saw* couper en travers, scier en travers

crosscut³ *vi* GEOL, MINING percer en travers-banc

crosscutting¹ *adj* GEOL sécant

crosscutting² *n* CINEMAT montage alterné *m*, MINING exploitation par ouvrages en travers *f*, percement en travers- banc *m*, travers-banc *m*

cross-dye *vt* TEXTILES surteindre

crossed: ~ **ends** *n pl* TEXTILES fils croisés *m pl*; ~ **field** *n* TELECOM champ croisé *m*; ~ **field amplifier** *n* ELECTRON, TELECOM amplificateur à champs croisés *m*; ~ **field tube** *n* ELECTRON, PHYS tube à champs croisés *m*; ~ **Nicols** *n pl* PHYS nicols croisés *m pl*

cross-esterification *n* CHEM transestérification *f*

cross-fade *n* ACOUSTICS, CINEMAT, RECORDING fondu enchaîné *m*

crossfall *n* CONST *roads* pente transversale *f*

crossfeed *n* MECH ENG *machine tools* avance transversale *f*; ~ **line** *n* AERONAUT canalisation d'intercommunication *f*, tuyauterie d'intercommunication *f*

crossfire *n* MILIT feu croisé *m*

cross-fired: ~ **furnace** *n* C&G four à brûleurs transversaux *m*

crossflow *n* TRANSP écoulement d'air transversal *m*, VEHICLES *engine* flux transversal *m*; ~ **fan** *n* HEAT ENG ventilateur à courant transversal *m*; ~ **heat exchanger** *n* REFRIG échangeur thermique à courants croisés *m*; ~ **radiator** *n* AUTO radiateur à débit horizontal *m*

cross-fold *n* GEOL pli transverse *m*

cross-garnet: ~ **hinge** *n* CONST penture à T *f*

cross-girth *n* MECH ENG *of bed of lathe* nervure d'entretoisage *f*

crosshead *n* MECH crosse de piston *f*, PHYS *tensile test machine* traverse *f*; ~ **block** *n* MECH ENG coulisseau de crosse *m*; ~ **body** *n* MECH ENG coulisseau de crosse *m*; ~ **displacement rate** *n* PHYS vitesse de déplacement traverse *f*; ~ **engine** *n* NAUT moteur à crosses *m*; ~ **gib** *n* MECH ENG patin de la crosse *m*, semelle de la crosse *f*; ~ **guide** *n* MECH ENG glissière de crosse *f*, guide de la tête de piston *m*; ~ **pin** *n* MECH ENG tourillon de crosse *m*, tourillon de la tête de piston *m*; ~ **of piston** *n* PROD ENG crosse de piston *f*, crossette de piston *f*, tête de piston *f*; ~ **shoe** *n* MECH ENG patin de la crosse *m*, semelle de la crosse *f*; ~ **slipper** *n* MECH ENG patin de la crosse *m*, semelle de la crosse *f*; ~ **terminal screw** *n* PROD ENG borne à vis cruciforme *f*; ~ **with 4-bar guide** *n* MECH ENG tête de piston guidée par quatre glissières *f*

crossheading *n* MINING galerie transversale *f*, traverse *f*, recoupe *f*, viaille *f*, volée *f*, recoupe d'aérage *f*

crossing *n* NAUT *sea* traversée *f*; ~ **the line** *n* NAUT passage de la ligne *m*; ~ **timber** *n* RAIL traverse d'aiguille *f*; ~ **time** *n* NAUT durée de la traversée *f*

crossite *n* MINERAL crossite *f*

cross-link¹ *n* CHEM liaison croisée *f*, *polymer* réticule *m*, P&R lien réticulé *m*

cross-link² *vt* P&R réticuler

cross-linkage *n* CHEM *polymer* réticulation *f*

cross-linking *n* CHEM *polymer* réticulation *f*; ~ **agent** *n* P&R agent de réticulation *m*

crosslode *n* MINING croiseur *m*, filon croiseur *m*, veine transversale *f*

cross-magnetizing: ~ **effect** *n* ELEC aimantation par induction *f*

cross-member *n* RAIL entretoise *f*, VEHICLES *body* traverse *f*

cross-over *vt* RAIL *points* franchir

crossover *n* CONST *railway* traverse *f*, RAIL *of overhead wires* caténaire *f*, diagonale *f*, *of points* traversée *f*, *of tracks* communication *f*, communication de voies *f*, interpénétration *f*, TV point de convergence *m*, recouvrement *m*; ~ **area** *n* ELECTRON zone de transition *f*; ~ **between curved track** *n* RAIL communication enroulée *f*; ~ **between curved tracks** *n* RAIL liaison de voies en courbe *f*; ~ **distortion** *n* RECORDING distorsion de recoupement *f*; ~ **frequency** *n* RECORDING fréquence de recoupement *f*; ~ **network** *n* RECORDING circuit de recoupement *m*

cross-pane: ~ **hammer** *n* CONST marteau à panne en travers *m*

cross-peen: ~ **hammer** *n* CONST marteau à panne en travers *m*; ~ **sledgehammer** *n* CONST marteau à devant panne en travers *m*

crosspiece *n* CONST entretoise *f*, traverse *f*, NAUT *shipbuilding* traversin *m*, WATER SUPP *of lock gate* entretoise *f*

crossplot *n* PETR trace croisée *f*

cross-plugging *n* RECORDING interconnexion *f*

crossply: ~ **tire** *n* (AmE), ~ **tyre** *n* (BrE) P&R pneu classique *m*, pneu diagonal *m*, pneumatique classique *m*, pneumatique diagonal *m*, VEHICLES pneu classique *m*, pneu diagonal *m*, pneu à carcasse diagonale *m*, pneumatique diagonal *m*

crosspoint *n* TELECOM point de connexion *m*

cross-polar: ~ **pattern** *n* SPACE *communications* diagramme contrapolaire *m*

cross-recessed: ~ **pan head screw** *n* MECH ENG vis à tête cylindrique bombée large à empreinte cruciforme *f*

cross-reeded: ~ **glass** *n* C&G verre à cannelures croisées *m*

cross-riveting *n* see cross-rivetting

crossroads *n* CONST carrefour *m*

cross-sectional: ~ **drawing** *n* NAUT *ship design* plan transversal *m*

cross-slide *n* MECH ENG *machine tools* chariot transversal *m*, *of tail stock* semelle *f*

cross-slip *n* CRYSTALL déviation *f*, glissement transversal *m*, METALL glissement croisé *m*, PROP MAT glissement dévié *m*; ~ **mechanism** *n* PROP MAT mécanisme de glissement dévié *m*

cross-staff *n* CONST équerre *f*, équerre d'arpenteur *f*; ~ **head** *n* CONST *surveying* équerre *f*, équerre d'arpenteur *f*

crosstail: ~ **hinge** *n* CONST penture à T *f*

crosstailed: ~ **hinge** *n* CONST penture à T *f*

crosstalk *n* ACOUSTICS, COMP, DP, PHYS diaphonie *f*, RECORDING diaphonie *f*, intermodulation *f*, TELECOM, TV diaphonie *f*; ~ **meter** *n* RECORDING diaphonomètre *m*; ~ **rejection** *n* RECORDING réjection d'intermodulation *f*; ~ **unit** *n* RECORDING unité de mesure d'intermodulation *f*

cross-track: ~ **error** *n* NAUT *navigation by satellite, radar* écart de route transversal *m*; ~ **recording** *n* RECORDING réenregistrement interpiste *m*

cross-traverse *n* PROD ENG *lathe work* avance transversale *f*, chariotage transversal *m*

crosstree *n* NAUT *rigging* barre de flèche *f*

crosswind: ~ **landing** *n* AERONAUT atterrissage par vent de travers *m*

crosswise[1] *adv* PRINT dans le sens travers, transversalement dans la plieuse

crosswise:[2] ~ **ribs** *n pl* TEXTILES côtes sans trame *f pl*; ~ **veneer splicing machine** *n* MECH ENG machine à jointer les placages transversalement *f*

crotonaldehyde *n* CHEM aldéhyde crotonique *m*, butenal *m*

crotonique *adj* CHEM crotonique

crotylic *adj* CHEM crotylique

crow *n* CONST levier *m*, pince *f*, pince à levier *f*

crowbar *n* CONST levier *m*, pince *f*, pince à levier *f*, ELEC ENG protecteur à thyristor *m*, protection par thyristor *f*, thyristor de protection *m*, MECH *tools* pied-de-biche *m*

crowd: ~ **safety** *n* SAFETY sécurité du public *f*

crowdion *n* METALL crowdion *m*

crowfoot *n* CINEMAT araignée *f*

crown *n* C&G voûte *f*, CONST *of arch* sommet *m*, MECH tête *f*, MECH ENG *engines* corps *m*, MINING *mine level timbering* chapeau *m*, NAUT *of anchor* diamant *m*, PAPER TECH bombé de presse *m*, PETR TECH *of derrick* sommet *m*, PROD ENG *of anvil* aire *f*, table *f*, *of crown-faced pulley* bombement *m*, *of furnace* couronne *f*; ~ **and pinion** *n* VEHICLES *transmission, differential* couple conique *m*; ~bearer *n* MINING *timbering* porteuse *f*; ~ **bit** *n* PETR TECH trépan à couronne *m*; ~ **block** *n* PETR, PETR TECH moufle fixe *m*, PROD ENG *of derrick* traverse du haut *f*; ~ **closure** *n* PACKAGING capsule-couronne *f*; ~ **cork** *n* PACKAGING capsule-couronne *f*; ~ **cup** *n* PACKAGING capsule-couronne *f*; ~ **drop** *n* C&G goutte de voûte *f*; ~ **finish** *n* C&G bague couronne *f*; ~ **gate** *n* WATER SUPP *of canal lock* porte d'amont *f*; ~ **glass** *n* C&G verre en plateaux *m*; ~ **glass lens** *n* C&G lentille en crown-glass *f*; ~ **piece** *n* MINING *mine level timbering* chapeau *m*; ~ **post** *n* CONST *of roof truss* poinçon *m*; ~ **process** *n* C&G soufflage en plateaux *m*; ~ **pulley** *n* PROD ENG *derrick* molette *f*; ~ **tile** *n* CONST *arched* tuile canal *f*, tuile creuse *f*, *flat* tuile plate *f*; ~ **tree** *n* MINING flandre *f*; ~ **wheel** *n* AUTO couronne de différentiel *f*, grande couronne *f*, MECH ENG roue de champ *f*, VEHICLES *transmission, differential* couronne de différentiel *f*; ~ **wheel and pinion** *n* VEHICLES *transmission, differential* couple conique *m*

crowned: ~ **pulley** *n* PROD ENG poulie bombée *f*, poulie en dos d'âne *f*

crown-face: ~ **pulley** *n* PROD ENG poulie bombée *f*, poulie en dos d'âne *f*

crowning *n* CONST *architecture* couronnement *m*, PROD ENG *of crowning pulley* bombement *m*; ~ **pulley** *n* PROD ENG poulie bombée *f*, poulie en dos d'âne *f*

CRT[1] *abbr* *(cathode ray tube)* COMP, ELEC, ELECTRON, PRINT, SAFETY, TV TRC *(tube à rayons cathodiques)*

CRT:[2] ~ **controller** *n* ELECTRON régisseur de tube cathodique *m*

crucible *n* CHEM creuset *m*, pot *m*, HEATING, LAB EQUIP *container* creuset *m*, PROD ENG pot *m*, *of blast furnace* creuset *m*, ouvrage *m*, THERMOD creuset *m*; ~ **furnace** *n* LAB EQUIP *heating* four à creuset *m*, PROD ENG four potager *m*, four à creuset *m*, THERMOD four à creuset *m*; ~ **tongs** *n pl* LAB EQUIP pince à creuset *f*

cruciform: ~ **head fastener** *n* MECH ENG vis à empreinte cruciforme *f*

crude[1] *adj* CHEM, COAL TECH brut

crude:[2] **in the ~ state** *adv* PROD ENG à l'état brut

crude[3] *n* PETR TECH brut *m*, pétrole brut *m*; ~ **assay** *n* PETR TECH titrage du brut *m*; ~ **carrier** *n* MAR POLL navire pétrolier *m*, NAUT *ship* transporteur de brut *m*, POLLUTION navire pétrolier *m*; ~ **distillation unit** *n* *(CDU)* PETR TECH unité de distillation au brut *f*; ~ **fiber** *n* *(AmE)*, ~ **fibre** *n* *(BrE)* FOOD TECH fibre de cellulose *f*, matière cellulosique *f*; ~ **oil** *n* MAR POLL, PETR pétrole brut *m*, PETR TECH brut *m*, pétrole brut *m*, POLLUTION pétrole brut *m*; ~ **oil analysis** *n* PETR TECH analyse de l'huile brute *f*, analyse du pétrole brut *f*; ~ **oil tanker** *n* PETR TECH pétrolier *m*; ~ **oil washing** *n* *(COW)* PETR TECH lavage au brut des citernes *m*; ~ **ore** *n* COAL TECH minerai brut *m*; ~ **protein** *n* FOOD TECH protéine brute *f*; ~ **rubber** *n* P&R caoutchouc brut *m*

cruise[1] *n* AERONAUT, NAUT croisière *f*; ~ **climb** *n* AERONAUT croisière ascendante *f*, montée en régime de croisière *f*; ~ **climb drift up** *n* AERONAUT croisière ascendante *f*, montée en régime de croisière *f*; ~ **control** *n* VEHICLES *driving* régulateur de présélecteur de vitesse constante *m*, régulateur de vitesse constante *m*; ~ **control device** *n* TRANSP régulation de vitesse *f*; ~ **descent** *n* AERONAUT *drift down* croisière descendante *f*, descente progressive *f*; ~ **missile** *n* MILIT, NAUT *navy* missile de croisière *m*; ~ **ship** *n* NAUT bateau de croisière *m*, navire de croisière *m*

cruise[2] *vi* NAUT croiser, être en croisière

cruiser *n* NAUT *navy* croiseur de bataille *m*, yacht de croisière *m*, TRANSP yacht de croisière *m*; ~ **stern** *n* NAUT *boatbuilding* arrière de croiseur *m*

cruising: ~ **altitude** *n* AERONAUT altitude de croisière *f*; ~ **cutter** *n* NAUT aviso de croisière *m*; ~ **power** *n* AERONAUT régime de croisière *m*; ~ **range** *n* SPACE autonomie *f*; ~ **speed** *n* AERONAUT vitesse de croisière *f*, NAUT vitesse de croisière *f*, vitesse de marche *f*

crumb: ~ **elasticity** *n* FOOD TECH *of centre of bread* résilience de la mie *f*, élasticité de la mie *f*; ~ **firmness** *n* FOOD TECH *of centre of bread* fermeté de la mie *f*; ~ **formation** *n* FOOD TECH *of centre of bread* formation de la mie *f*; ~ **structure** *n* MECH ENG structure grumeleuse *f*; ~ **texture** *n* FOOD TECH *of centre of bread* texture de la mie *f*

crumble *vi* CONST *walls* s'effriter; ~ **on exposure to the air** *vi* PROP MAT se déliter par exposition à l'air; ~ **to powder** *vi* PROP MAT se déliter en poudre

crumbling *n* PROP MAT effritement *m*

crumple:[1] ~ **zone** *n* AUTO zone déformable *f*

crumple[2] *vt* PAPER TECH froisser

crumpling *n* PAPER TECH froissement *m*

crush:[1] ~ **barrier** *n* SAFETY barrière de sécurité *f*; ~ **belt** *n* GEOL zone de broyage tectonique *f*; ~ **breccia** *n* GEOL brèche de friction *f*, mylonite *f*; ~ **conglomerate** *n* GEOL conglomérat de friction *m*; ~ **resistance** *n* TEXTILES résistance à l'écrasement *f*; ~ **rock** *n* GEOL mylonite *f*

crush[2] *vt* COAL TECH, CONST broyer, concasser, FOOD TECH broyer, pilonner, écraser, égruger, PAPER TECH, TEXTILES écraser

crushed: ~ **aggregate** *n* COAL TECH roche concassée *f*; ~ **ice** *n* REFRIG glace broyée *f*; ~ **material** *n* COAL TECH menu de concassage *m*, CONST matériaux de concassage *m pl*; ~ **ore** *n* MINING minerai broyé *m*, égrugeures de minerai *f pl*; ~ **stone** *n* CONST cailloutis *m*, pierres concassées *f pl*

crusher *n* COAL TECH broyeur *m*, broyeur-concasseur *m*, concasseur *m*, CONST broyeur *m*, concasseur *m*, MECH ENG molette à dresser *f*, PROD ENG broyeur *m*, concasseur *m*; **~ ball** *n* CHEM TECH élément concasseur *m*; **~ gage** *n* (AmE), **~ gauge** *n* (BrE) MECH jauge d'écrasement *f*; **~ jaw** *n* CHEM TECH mâchoire de concasseur *f*; **~ roll** *n* CHEM TECH cylindre broyeur *m*, rouleau concasseur *m*, PROD ENG cylindre broyeur *m*

crushing *n* COAL TECH autobroyage *m*, concassage *m*, CONST *concrete test cubes* écrasement *m*, MINING, P&R *process* broyage *m*, PAPER TECH écrasé *m*, SAFETY *machinery hazards*, TEXTILES écrasement *m*; **~ bowl** *n* CHEM TECH corps du broyeur *m*; **~ efficiency** *n* COAL TECH efficacité de concassage *f*; **~ ejection** *n* SAFETY écrasement éjection *m*; **~ machine** *n* CHEM TECH appareil de fragmentation *m*, machine de concassage *f*; **~ machine for ice** *n* MECH ENG broyeur pour glace *m*; **~ mill** *n* CHEM TECH, PAPER TECH broyeur *m*; **~ plant** *n* CHEM TECH installation de broyage primaire *f*, COAL TECH installation de concassage *f*; **~ power** *n* SAFETY *of machine* force d'écrasement *f*; **~ resistance** *n* PAPER TECH résistance à l'écrasement *f*; **~ roll** *n* CHEM TECH broyeur à cylindres *m*, MECH ENG *for screw threads* rouleau broyeur *m*, PROD ENG *for crushing materials, ores* cylindre broyeur *m*, *ore mill* broyeur à cylindres *m*, moulin à cylindres *m*; **~ test** *n* TESTING essai d'écrasement *m*

crushproof: **~ safety bonnet** *n* (BrE) *(cf crushproof safety hood)* TRANSP *lorries* arceau de sécurité *m*; **~ safety hood** *n* (AmE) *(cf crushproof safety bonnet)* TRANSP *trucks* arceau de sécurité *m*

crush-resistant *adj* TEXTILES infroissable

crust *n* GEOL écorce *f*, PETR croûte terrestre *f*; **~ freezing** *n* REFRIG *shell freezing* congélation superficielle *f*

crutch *n* NAUT *support for boom* croissant *m*; **~ handle** *n* PROD ENG béquille *f*, manche à béquille *m*; **~ key** *n* CONST clé à douille *f*, tête *f*, PROD ENG *of cock* béquille *f*

Crux *n* ASTRON croix du Sud *f*

cryobiology *n* REFRIG cryobiologie *f*

cryobranding *n* REFRIG cryomarquage *m*

cryocooling *n* REFRIG cryorefroidissement *m*

cryoetching *n* REFRIG cryodécapage *m*

cryogenic[1] *adj* PHYS, SPACE, THERMOD cryogénique

cryogenic:[2] **~ fluid** *n* REFRIG fluide cryogénique *m*; **~ fuel** *n* SPACE *spacecraft* ergol cryotechnique *m*; **~ liquid** *n* MECH ENG liquide cryogénique *m*; **~ memory** *n* COMP mémoire cryogénique *f*; **~ pressure vessel** *n* MECH ENG réservoir cryogénique à pression *m*; **~ propellant** *n* SPACE *spacecraft* ergol cryotechnique *m*; **~ refrigerator** *n* REFRIG cryoréfrigérateur *m*; **~ stage** *n* SPACE *spacecraft* étage cryotechnique *m*; **~ tank** *n* SPACE *spacecraft* réservoir cryogénique *m*

cryogenically: **~ treated** *adj* MECH ENG traité cryogéniquement

cryogenics *n* PHYS cryogénie *f*, cryotechnique *f*, REFRIG cryogénie *f*, SPACE cryogénie *f*, cryotechnique *f*, THERMOD cryogénie *f*

cryolite *n* C&G cryolithe *f*, CHEM cryolite *f*, cryolithe *f*, MINERAL cryolithe *f*

cryology *n* REFRIG cryologie *f*

cryomagnetism *n* REFRIG cryomagnétisme *m*

cryomedicine *n* REFRIG cryomédicine *f*

cryophysics *n* PHYS, REFRIG cryophysique *f*

cryopump *n* SPACE *spacecraft* pompe cryotechnique *f*

cryoscopy *n* REFRIG cryoscopie *f*

cryostat *n* CONTROL cryostat *m*, LAB EQUIP, PHYS, PROP MAT, SPACE cryostat *m*

cryostatic: **~ temperature control** *n* CONTROL cryostat *m*

cryosurgery *n* REFRIG cryochirurgie *f*

cryotechnic: **~ arm** *n* SPACE bras cryotechnique *m*

cryotron *n* ELEC ENG cryotron *m*

cryptanalysis *n* COMP cryptanalyse *f*, DP analyse cryptographique *f*, cryptanalyse *f*, TELECOM analyse cryptographique *f*

cryptographic[1] *adj* SPACE *communications* cryptographique

cryptographic:[2] **~ check value** *n* TELECOM valeur de contrôle cryptographique *f*

cryptography *n* COMP, DP, SPACE *communications*, TELECOM cryptographie *f*

cryptosteady: **~ pressure exchanger** *n* TRANSP échangeur de pression atmosphérique *m*

crystal *n* C&G, CHEM, CRYSTALL, ELECTRON cristal *m*; **~ axes** *n pl* CRYSTALL axes cristallins *m pl*; **~ checker** *n* CINEMAT vérificateur pour quartz *m*; **~ chemistry** *n* PROP MAT cristallochimie *f*; **~ control** *n* AERONAUT pilotage piézo-électrique *m*, CINEMAT, RECORDING pilotage par quartz *m*; **~ defect** *n* QUALITY défaut cristallin *m*, imperfection cristalline *f*; **~ diode** *n* ELECTRON diode à cristal *f*; **~ face** *n* CRYSTALL face cristalline *f*; **~ field** *n* RAD PHYS champ cristallin *m*; **~ field splitting energy** *n* RAD PHYS énergie de séparation du champ cristallin *f*; **~ filter** *n* ELECTRON filtre à quartz *m*, TELECOM filtre à cristal *m*; **~ frequency** *n* ELECTRON fréquence d'oscillation du quartz *f*; **~ frequency drift** *n* ELECTRON dérive de la fréquence du quartz *f*; **~ glass** *n* C&G verre sonore *m*; **~ growth** *n* CRYSTALL, METALL croissance cristalline *f*; **~ holder** *n* ELECTRON support de quartz *m*; **~ ice** *n* REFRIG glace cristalline *f*; **~ ladder filter** *n* ELECTRON filtre en échelle à quartz *m*; **~ laser** *n* ELECTRON laser à cristal *m*; **~ lattice** *n* CRYSTALL réseau cristallin *m*; **~ lattice filter** *n* ELECTRON filtre à quartz en treillis *m*; **~ liquid display** *n* TELECOM écran à cristaux liquides *m*; **~ microphone** *n* RECORDING microphone piézoélectrique *m*, microphone à cristal *m*; **~ motor** *n* CINEMAT moteur à quartz *m*; **~ network** *n* PROP MAT réseau cristallin *m*; **~ oscillator** *n* ELEC oscillateur à cristal *m*, ELECTRON oscillateur à quartz *m*, RAD PHYS oscillateur cristallin *m*; **~ plasticity** *n* METALL plasticité cristalline *f*; **~ resonator** *n* ELECTRON résonateur à quartz *m*; **~ sheet glass** *n* (AmE) *(cf thick sheet glass)* C&G verre épais *m*; **~ spectrometer** *n* RAD PHYS radiodiffractomètre *m*; **~ state** *n* PROP MAT état cristallin *m*; **~ structure** *n* COAL TECH, CRYSTALL, METALL, PROP MAT structure cristalline *f*; **~ symmetry** *n* CRYSTALL symétrie cristalline *f*; **~ sync** *n* CINEMAT pilotage par quartz *m*; **~ system** *n* CRYSTALL système cristallin *m*; **~ time base** *n* ELECTRON base de temps pilotée par quartz *f*; **~ tuff** *n* GEOL *pyroclastic rock* roche pyroclastique à cristaux *f*

crystallin *adj* C&G cristallin

crystalline[1] *adj* CHEM, CRYSTALL, PROP MAT cristallin

crystalline:[2] **~ basement** *n* GEOL socle cristallin *m*; **~ fracture** *n* METALL rupture cristalline *f*, rupture à grains *f*; **~ limestone** *n* GEOL calcaire cristallin *m*

crystallite *n* CRYSTALL cristallite *f*

crystallization *n* CRYSTALL, P&R *process* cristallisation *f*; **~ basin** *n* CHEM TECH cristallisoir *m*; **~ point** *n* CHEM TECH point de cristallisation *m*

crystallize: **~ out** *vi* CHEM TECH cristalliser

crystallizer *n* CHEM TECH, PROP MAT cristallisoir *m*

crystallizing: **~ dish** *n* LAB EQUIP *glassware* cristallisoir *m*; **~ pond** *n* CHEM TECH bassin de cristallisation *m*

crystallographic[1] *adj* PROP MAT cristallographique

crystallographic:[2] ~ **plane** n INSTRUMENT miroir d'un cristal m; ~ **slip** n METALL, PROP MAT glissement cristallographique m

crystallography n METALL cristallographie f

Cs[1] abbr (cirrostratus) METEO Cs (cirro-stratus)

Cs[2] (caesium, cesium) CHEM Cs (césium)

CS abbr COMP (circuit switching), DP (circuit switching), ELECTRON (circuit switching) commutation de circuits f, TELECOM (calls per second) appels par seconde m pl, TELECOM (communication services) services de communication m pl, TELECOM (convergence sublayer) sous-couche de convergence f

C-shaped: ~ **frame** n INSTRUMENT bâti en C m, bâti en col m

CSI abbr TELECOM (called subscriber identification) identification de l'abonné demandé f, (called station identity) identité de la station demandée f

CSM abbr COMP (command and control system) système de commande et contrôle m, SPACE (command and service module) module de commande et de service m

CSMA abbr (carrier sense multiple access) TELECOM CSMA (accès multiple par détection de porteuse)

CSMA-CD abbr (carrier sense multiple access with collision detection) COMP, DP, ELECTRON CSMA-CD (accès multiple par détection de porteuse avec détection de collision)

CSN abbr (Canadian Switched Network) TELECOM RCC (réseau commuté canadien)

CSPDU abbr (convergence sublayer protocol data unit) TELECOM unité de données du protocole de la sous-couche convergence f

C-stage: ~ **resin** n P&R résine à l'état C f

ct abbr (continuous thread) PACKAGING vis préfiletée f

CT abbr ELEC (center tap, centre tap) prise médiane f, TELECOM (container) conteneur m, TELECOM (control terminal) terminal de commande m

CTCSS abbr (continuous tone-controlled squelch system) TELECOM dispositif silencieux à commande par tonalité m, silencieux de sous-porteuse m

CTD abbr ELEC ENG (charge transfer device), PHYS (charge transfer device), SPACE (charge transfer device), TELECOM (charge transfer device) DTC (dispositif à transfert de charges), TELECOM (conditionally toll denied) blocage partiel de l'accès à l'interurbain m

CTOL: ~ **aircraft** n (conventional takeoff and landing aircraft) AERONAUT ADAO (avion à décollage et atterrissage ordinaires)

CTS abbr (container transport ship) TRANSP navire porte-conteneurs m

Cu[1] abbr (cumulus) METEO Cu (cumulus)

Cu[2] (copper) CHEM Cu (cuivre)

cubage n COAL TECH houage m, METR cubage m

cubanite n MINERAL cubanite f

cube[1] n GEOM, MATH cube m; ~ **problem** n GEOM problème du cube m

cube[2] vt MATH cuber, élever au cube

cubebin n CHEM cubébine f

cubic[1] adj CRYSTALL cubique

cubic:[2] ~ **boron nitride** n MECH ENG nitrure de bore m; ~ **boron nitride grinding-wheel** n MECH ENG meule au nitrure de bore f, meule à base de nitrure de bore f; ~ **boron nitride saw** n MECH ENG scie à base de nitrure de bore f; ~ **capacity** n MECH vehicles cylindrée f, NAUT of stowage area capacité volumétrique f; ~ **centimeter** n (AmE), ~ **centimetre** n (BrE) METR centimètre cube

m; ~ **decimeter** n (AmE), ~ **decimetre** n (BrE) METR décimètre cube m; ~ **expansion coefficient** n PHYS coefficient de dilatation volumique m; ~ **expansivity** n PHYS coefficient de dilatation volumique m; ~ **foot** n METR, PETR TECH pied cube m; ~ **inch** n METR pouce cube m; ~ **measure** n METR mesure de volume f; ~ **measurement** n METR of solids cubage m; ~ **meter** n (AmE), ~ **metre** n (BrE) MATH, METR mètre cube m; ~ **octahedron** n GEOM cuboctaèdre m; ~ **system** n METALL système cubique m; ~ **yard** n METR yard cube m

cubical: ~ **distortion** n METALL distorsion cubique f; ~ **expansion** n METALL dilatation cubique f

cubicite n MINERAL cubizite f

cuboid n GEOM cuboïde m

cue[1] n CINEMAT marque f, repère m, RECORDING repère m, TV indication de départ f, signal d'avertissement m; ~ **dot** n RECORDING repère m; ~ **light** n TV lampe de signalisation f, rouge antenne m, voyant d'antenne m; ~ **mark** n CINEMAT, RECORDING marque de passage f; ~ **mike** n RECORDING micro d'ordres m; ~ **print** n CINEMAT copie de projection marquée pour doublage f; ~ **screen** n TV écran de repérage m; ~ **sheet** n TV conduite d'émission f, feuille de minutage f, feuille de service f; ~ **track** n TV piste d'ordres f, piste de repérage f; ~ **track address codes** n TV piste d'ordres f

cue[2] vi CINEMAT donner le départ

CUE abbr (catch per unit effort) OCEANOG CPUE (prise par unité d'effort)

cueing n ACOUSTICS repérage m

cuer n TV opérateur de prompteur m

CUG abbr (closed user group) COMP, DP, TELECOM GFU (groupe fermé d'usagers)

cull vt COAL TECH, MINING ore-dressing scheider; ~ **by hand** vt COAL TECH scheider

cullet n C&G calcin m; ~ **catcher** n C&G drapeau m; ~ **chute** n C&G goulotte à calcin f; ~ **crush** n C&G spliures f pl; ~ **crusher** n C&G concasseur à calcin m

culling n COAL TECH épierrage m

culm n C&G fraisil m, COAL TECH menu de charbon m

cultivator n CONST gardening extirpateur m

culture: ~ **plate** n LAB EQUIP bacteriology plaque pour culture f

culvert n CONST, HYDROL ponceau m

cumaldehyde n CHEM aldéhyde cuminique m

cumarin n CHEM cumarine f

cumene n CHEM cumène m

cumengeite n MINERAL cumengéite f

cumengite n MINERAL cumengéite f

cumic adj CHEM cuminique

cummingtonite n MINERAL cummingtonite f

cumulative: ~ **discharge** n FUELLESS débit cumulatif m; ~ **distribution diagram** n HYDROL diagramme de distribution cumulé m; ~ **distribution function** n (CDF) MATH fonction de répartition f; ~ **toxic effect** n POLLUTION effet toxique cumulatif m; ~ **working time** n PROD ENG temps de travail cumulé m

cumulo-dome n GEOL cumulo-dôme m, tholoïde m

cumulo-volcano n GEOL cumulo-volcan m

cumulus n (Cu) METEO cumulus m (Cu); ~ **congestus** n METEO cumulus congestus m; ~ **humilis** n METEO cumulus humilis m

cumyl n CHEM cumyle m

cup n LAB EQUIP of barometer cuvette f, P&R paints, instrument godet m; ~ **chuck** n MECH ENG mandrin à gobelet m; ~ **head bolt** n MECH ENG vis à métaux à tête bombée f; ~ **head rivet** n CONST rivet à tête hémisphérique *m*, rivet à tête ronde *m*; ~ **joint** *n* PROD ENG joint à calotte sphérique *m*, joint à genou *m*, joint à rotule *m*, joint à rotule sphérique *m*, jointure sphérique *f*; ~ **leather** *n* PROD ENG cuir embouti *m*; **in** ~ **powder filling machine** *n* PACKAGING remplisseuse de poudre en godets *f*; ~ **washer** *n* MECH ENG rondelle cuvette *f*; ~ **wheel** *n* PROD ENG *emery wheel* meule boisseau *f*, meule à noyau rentrant *f*

cup-and-ball: ~ **joint** *n* PROD ENG joint à calotte sphérique *m*, joint à genou *m*, joint à rotule *m*, joint à rotule sphérique *m*, jointure sphérique *f*

cup-and-cone *n* PROD ENG *blast furnace* cup et cône *m*; ~ **fracture** *n* METALL rupture en cône et coupe *f*

cupel *n* CHEM coupelle *f*, têt de coupellation *m*

cupola *n* COAL TECH cubilot *m*, GEOL *igneous intrusive structure* coupole *f*, dôme *m*, HEATING *furnace* dôme *m*, PROD ENG cubilot *m*, RAIL *vehicles* guérite *f*, guérite de frein *f*; ~ **furnace** *n* C&G, PROD ENG cubilot *m*; ~ **with receiver** *n* PROD ENG cubilot à avant-creuset *m*

cupped: ~ **chain sheave** *n* PROD ENG poulie à empreintes *f*, roue à empreintes *f*

cupping *n* RECORDING *of tape* bombement *m*, concavité *f*; ~ **glass** *n* C&G ventouse *f*

cuprammonium *n* CHEM, TEXTILES cuprammonium *m*

cuprate *n* CHEM cuprate *m*

cupreous *adj* CHEM cuivreux

cupric[1] *adj* CHEM cuprique

cupric:[2] ~ **sulfate** *n* (AmE), ~ **sulphate** *n* (BrE) PRINT sulfate de cuivre *m*

cupride *n* CHEM cupride *m*

cuprite *n* MINERAL cuprite *f*

cuproapatite *n* MINERAL cuproapatite *f*

cuprodescloizite *n* MINERAL cuprodescloizite *f*

cupromagnesite *n* MINERAL cupromagnésite *f*

cupromanganese *n* CHEM cupromanganèse *m*

cuproplumbite *n* MINERAL cuproplumbite *f*

cuproscheelite *n* MINERAL cuproscheelite *f*

cuprotungstite *n* MINERAL cuprotungstite *f*

cuprous *adj* CHEM cuivreux

curb *n* C&G collerette de la cuvette d'avant-corps *f*, CONST bordure *f*, bordure de trottoir *f*, *building* panne de brisis *f*, MINING cadre porteur *m*, cadre à oreilles *m*, roue *f*, rouet *m*, roulisse *f*, trousse *f* ~ **plate** *n* CONST *building* panne de brisis *f*; ~ **ring** *n* MINING *in mine shaft* gargouille *f*; ~ **roof** *n* CONST comble brisé *m*, comble à la Mansard *m*, comble à la française *m*; ~ **stone** *n* CONST bordure *f*, bordure de trottoir *f*

curbed: ~ **chain** *n* PROD ENG chaîne en S *f*, chaîne torse *f*

curcumine *n* CHEM curcumine *f*

curd *n* FOOD TECH *cheesemaking* caillebotte *f*, caillé *m*; ~ **cheese** *n* FOOD TECH fromage blanc *m*

cure[1] *n* P&R cuisson *f*, durcissement *m*; ~ **period** *n* CONST délai de cure *m*

cure[2] *vt* FOOD TECH affiner, maturer, caquer, P&R durcir, polymériser, vulcaniser, TEXTILES polymériser

cured: ~ **malt** *n* FOOD TECH *distillation* malt touraillé *m*

curie *n* (*Ci*) PHYS, RAD PHYS curie *m* (*Ci*)

Curie: ~ **constant** *n* PHYS, RAD PHYS *in Curie's law* constante de Curie *f*; ~ **point** *n* ELEC *paramagnetism*, PETR, REFRIG point de Curie *m*; ~ **temperature** *n* PHYS, RAD PHYS température de Curie *f*

Curie's: ~ **law** *n* PETR, PHYS, RAD PHYS loi de Curie *f*

Curie-Weiss: ~ **law** *n* PHYS, RAD PHYS loi de Curie-Weiss *f*

curing *n* MECH *materials*, NAUT *of resin, GRP construction* polymérisation *f*, OCEANOG saurissage *m*, P&R

cuisson *f*, durcissement *m*, vulcanisation *f*, TEXTILES polymérisation *f*; ~ **agent** *n* P&R *adhesives, coatings* agent de durcissement *m*; ~ **cellar** *n* REFRIG *for meat* chambre de salaison *f*; ~ **compound** *n* CONST produit de cure *m*; ~ **membrane** *n* CONST membrane de cure *f*; ~ **oven** *n* TEXTILES four de polymérisation *m*; ~ **time** *n* P&R durée de vulcanisation *f*, temps de cuisson *m*, temps de durcissement *m*; ~ **tunnel** *n* CONST tunnel d'étuvage *m*

curium *n* (*Cm*) CHEM curium *m* (*Cm*); ~ **series** *n* RAD PHYS *radioactive series* famillede curium *f*

curl[1] *n* ELECTRON *of vector*, FLUID PHYS *of vector* rotationnel *m*, PACKAGING vrillage *m*, PAPER TECH roulage du papier *m*, tuilage *m*, PHYS *vector field* curl *m*, rotationnel *m*, PRINT cintrage *m*, déformation *f*, gode *m*, RECORDING *of tape* frisure *f*, TEXTILES boucle *f*; ~ **corresponding to vorticity** *n* FLUID PHYS *fluid motion equations* rotationnel correspondant au tourbillon *m*; ~ **field** *n* ELEC ENG champ tourbillonnaire *m*

curl[2] *vt* PAPER TECH, TEXTILES rouler

curled: ~ **edge** *n* C&G festonnage *m* (Fra), serpentage *m* (Bel)

curling *n* PAPER TECH roulage du papier *m*, tuilage *m*, TEXTILES roulottage *m*

current *n* ELEC courant *m*, ELEC ENG courant *m*, intensité *f*, courant secteur *m*, HYDROL ligne de courant *f*, *maritime* courant *m*, écoulement de l'eau *m*, NAUT *navigation, tides* courant *m*, PHYS courant *m*, intensité *f*; ~ **adaptor** *n* (AmE) *(cf mains adaptor)* ELEC ENG adaptateur secteur *m*; ~ **amplification** *n* ELECTRON, RECORDING amplification de courant *f*; ~ **amplifier** *n* ELEC, ELECTRON amplificateur de courant *m*; ~ **antinode** *n* ELEC ENG ventre de courant *m*; ~ **balance** *n* ELEC balance de courant *f*, balance électrodynamique *f*, PHYS balance de courant *f*; ~ **balance relay** *n* ELEC relais de balance électrodynamique *m*; ~ **bedding** *n* GEOL stratification de courant *f*; ~ **chart** *n* NAUT *navigation* carte des courants *f*; ~ **collector** *n* ELEC ENG prise de courant *f*, RAIL *vehicles* capteur de courant *m*; ~ **contactor control** *n* CONTROL commande par relais ampèremétriques *f*, commande à contacteurs *f*; ~ **control** *n* ELEC ENG commande d'intensité *f*, commande de courant *f*; ~ **core** *n* OCEANOG noyau de courant *m*; ~ **density** *n* ELEC, ELEC ENG, GEOPHYS, METALL, PHYS densité de courant *f*; ~ **differential protection** *n* ELEC protection différentielle de courant *f*; ~ **direction** *n* ELEC ENG sens du courant *m*; ~ **distribution** *n* ELEC distribution de courant *f*; ~ **divider** *n* ELEC *circuit* diviseur de courant *m*; ~ **drift** *n* TELECOM dérive de courant *f*; ~ **element** *n* PHYS élément de courant *m*; ~ **feedback** *n* ELEC ENG contre-réaction de courant *f*; ~ **fluctuation** *n* ELEC variation de courant *f*; ~ **frequency** *n* (AmE) *(cf mains frequency)* ELEC *supply*, ELEC ENG fréquence de réseau *f*; ~ **gain** *n* ELECTRON, PHYS gain en courant *m*; ~ **generator** *n* ELEC ENG, PHYS générateur de courant *m*; ~ **input** *n* ELEC ENG courant absorbé *m*, intensité absorbée *f*; ~ **intensity** *n* ELEC ENG intensité du courant *f*; ~ **lead** *n* ELEC ENG amenée de courant *f*; ~ **limiter** *n* ELEC limiteur de courant *m*, ELEC ENG limiteur d'intensité *m*, limiteur de courant *m*; ~ **limiting** *n* ELEC ENG limitation de courant *f*, limitation de l'intensité du courant *f*; ~ **loop** *n* PHYS boucle de courant *f*; ~ **meter** *n* FUELLESS courantomètre *m*, HYDR EQUIP compteur de débit *m*, HYDROL moulinet *m*, NAUT *oceanography* courantomètre *m*, WATER SUPP courantomètre *m*, moulinet *m*; ~ **modulation** *n* ELECTRON modulation d'intensité *f*; ~ **noise** *n* (AmE) *(cf mains noise)* RECORDING bruit de courant *m*; ~ **output** *n* ELEC ENG courant débité *m*, intensité du courant débité *f*, sortie en courant *f*; ~ **overload switch** *n* CONTROL interrupteur à maximum de courant *m*; ~ **path** *n* ELEC ENG trajet du courant *m*; ~ **peak** *n* ELEC crête de courant *f*, pic de courant *m*; ~ **pulse** *n* ELEC ENG impulsion de courant *f*; ~ **ramp** *n* PROD ENG rampe de courant *f*; ~ **rate** *n* NAUT *sea* vitesse du courant *f*; ~ **rating** *n* PROD ENG courant nominal *m*; ~ **rectifier** *n* (AmE) *(cf mains rectifier)* ELEC redresseur de secteur *m*; ~ **regulation** *n* CONTROL régulation du courant *f*, ELEC *control* réglage de courant *m*, ELEC ENG régulation d'intensité *f*; ~ **regulator** *n* ELEC *control* rhéostat régulateur d'intensité *m*, ELEC ENG régulateur d'intensité *m*; ~ **relay** *n* ELEC relais de courant *m*, ELEC ENG relais d'intensité *m*; ~ **requirement** *n* ELEC, PROD ENG consommation en courant *f*; ~ **reverser** *n* ELEC inverseur de pôles *m*; ~ **ripple** *n* ELEC ENG ondulation *f*, ondulation du courant *f*, GEOL ride de courant *f*; ~ **rose** *n* OCEANOG rose des courants *f*; ~ **sensing** *n* ELEC ENG détection de courant *f*; ~ **set** *n* NAUT *sea* direction du courant *f*; ~ **sink** *n* ELEC ENG récepteur de courant *m*; ~ **source** *n* ELEC ENG générateur de courant *m*, source de courant *f*, PHYS source de courant *f*; ~ **state of the art** *n* TELECOM état actuel de la technique *m*; ~ **stream** *n* OCEANOG veine de courant *f*; ~ **strength** *n* ELEC ENG intensité du courant *f*; ~ **surge** *n* ELEC ENG pointe de courant *f*; ~ **switch** *n* (AmE) *(cf mains switch)* CONTROL interrupteur d'alimentation *m*, ELEC commutateur de secteur *m*, interrupteur d'alimentation *m*, ELEC ENG interrupteur d'alimentation *m*; ~ **testing meter** *n* ELEC ENG instrument de mesure *m*; ~ **transformation ratio** *n* ELEC *transformer* rapport de transformation de courant *m*; ~ **transformer** *n* (AmE) *(cf mains transformer)* ELEC *supply, electronics* transformateur d'alimentation *m*, transformateur de courant *m*, ELEC ENG transformateur d'intensité *m*, transformateur de courant *m*, transformateur secteur *m*, ELECTRON transformateur d'alimentation *m*

current-carrying: ~ **capacity** *n* ELEC *line* capacité de charge *f*, intensité admissible de courant *f*; ~ **coil** *n* PHYS bobine parcourue par un courant *f*

current-collecting: ~ **brush** *n* ELEC ENG balai *m*

current-conducting: ~ **pin** *n* PROD ENG lamelle porte-courant *f*

current-controlled: ~ **device** *n* ELEC ENG dispositif commandé en courant *m*; ~ **oscillator** *n* ELECTRON oscillateur commandé en courant *m*

current-limiting: ~ **circuit breaker** *n* ELEC disjoncteur limiteur de courant *m*; ~ **fuse link** *n* ELEC fusible limiteur de courant *m*; ~ **inductor** *n* ELEC inductance limiteuse de courant *f*; ~ **reactor** *n* ELEC réactance de limitation de courant *f*, ELEC ENG inductance de protection *f*

current-mode: ~ **logic** *n* ELEC ENG logique à couplage en courant *f*

current-sensing: ~ **resistor** *n* ELEC ENG résistance de détection de courant *f*

current-voltage: ~ **characteristic** *n* ELEC ENG, SPACE *spacecraft* caractéristique courant-tension *f*

cursor *n* COMP, DP, PRINT curseur *m*; ~ **control** *n* CONTROL régulateur à curseur *m*; ~ **control regulator** *n* CONTROL régulateur à curseur *m*; ~ **hit** *n* PROD ENG manoeuvre du curseur *f*; ~ **key** *n* COMP touche de commande du curseur *f*, DP touche du curseur *f*

curtain *n* C&G *Foucault process* pont fixe *m*, TEXTILES rideau *m*; ~ **boom** *n* MAR POLL barrage rideau *m*; ~ **coater** *n* P&R coucheuse par rideau liquide *f*; ~ **coating** *n* C&G émaillage rideau *m*; ~ **coating machine** *n* MECH ENG machine à vernir par rideaux *f*; ~ **of fire** *n* MILIT *artillery* tir de barrage *m*; ~ **loop** *n* TEXTILES embrasse *f*; ~ **wall** *n* CONST mur-rideau *m*

curtain-coated: ~ **paper** *n* PAPER TECH papier couché par voile *m*

curtaining *n* P&R *paint* frisage *m*

curvature *n* GEOM *of trajectory*, MATH, PHYS courbure *f*; ~ **and twisting test** *n* TESTING essai de courbure et vrillage *m*; ~ **correction factor** *n* SPRINGS facteur de correction de flèche de la contrainte *m*; ~ **of field** *n* CINEMAT, PHYS courbure de champ *f*; ~ **of surfaces** *n* GEOM courbure des surfaces *f*

curve[1] *n* CONST *of arch* cintre *m*, GEOM, MATH courbe *f*; ~ **of contact** *n* MECH ENG *gearing* courbe de contact *f*; ~ **factor** *n* FUELLESS facteur de courbe *m*; ~ **widening** *n* CONST surlargeur *f*, surlargeur de courbe *f*

curve[2] *vt* PROD ENG galber

curved[1] *adj* GEOM courbe

curved:[2] ~ **approach** *n* AERONAUT approche courbe *f*; ~ **azimuth approach path** *n* AERONAUT trajectoire d'approche courbe en azimut *f*; ~ **common crossing** *n* RAIL coeur de croisement courbe *m*; ~ **line** *n* GEOM courbe *f*, ligne courbe *f*; ~ **space time** *n* ASTRON espace-temps courbe *m*; ~ **spanner** *n* MECH ENG clé cintrée en S *f*, clé en S *f*; ~ **step** *n* CONST *stairbuilding* marche cintrée *f*, marche courbe *f*; ~ **vane** *n* HYDR EQUIP aube *f*, pale incurvée *f*

curved-worm: ~ **gear** *n* MECH ENG engrenage globoïde *m*, engrenage à vis globique *m*, engrenage à vis sans fin globique *m*, engrenage à vis à filets convergents *m*

curvilinear[1] *adj* GEOM curviligne

curvilinear:[2] ~ **coordinate** *n* PHYS abscisse curviligne *f*

cushion[1] *n* HYDR EQUIP *of steam in cylinder* tampon *m*, MECH ENG bande de protection de collier de serrage *f*; ~ **borne** *n* TRANSP suspension sur coussin *f*; ~ **car** *n* (AmE) *(cf cushion wagon)* RAIL *vehicles* wagon à attelage souple *m*; ~ **distortion** *n* CINEMAT distorsion en coussinet *f*; ~ **gas** *n* GAS TECH gaz coussin *m*; ~ **spring** *n* VEHICLES *of clutch* plaquette de progressivité *f*; ~ **wagon** *n* (BrE) *(cf cushion car)* RAIL wagon à attelage souple *m*

cushion[2] *vt* HYDR EQUIP amortir

cushioning *n* PROD ENG amortissement *m*; ~ **product** *n* PACKAGING article de tamponnage *m*

cusp *n* ASTRON corne *f*, METALL *on dislocation* crochet *m*

custom: ~ **calling service** *n* TELECOM service confort *m*; ~ **chip** *n* COMP puce à la demande *f*, ELECTRON puce personnalisée *f*; ~ **form** *n* PRINT formulaire personnalisé *m*; ~ **large-scale integration** *n* ELECTRON haute intégration personnalisée *f*; ~ **manufacture** *n* PROD ENG fabrication à la commande *f*, production à la commande *f*; ~ **production** *n* PROD ENG fabrication à la commande *f*, production à la commande *f*

custom-designed[1] *adj* ELECTRON personnalisé

custom-designed:[2] ~ **chip** *n* ELECTRON puce spécialement conçue *f*

customer: ~ **access maintenance center** *n* (AmE), ~ **access maintenance centre** *n* (BrE) *(CAMC)* TELECOM centre de maintenance des accès client *m*; ~ **equipment** *n* *(CEQ)* TELECOM équipement d'usager *m*; ~ **installation maintenance entities** *n* *(CIME)* TE-

LECOM entité de maintenance d'installation de client *f*; ~ **network** *n (CN)* TELECOM réseau client *m*; ~ **order servicing** *n* PROD ENG gestion des commandes de clients *f*; ~ **premises equipment** *n* TELECOM équipement local d'abonnés *m*

customer's: ~ **model** *n* MECH ENG maquette du client *f*

customerization *n* PROD ENG adaptation client *f*

customization *n* ELECTRON personnalisation *f*, PROD ENG adaptation à l'usager *f*, particularisation *f*

customize *vt* TEXTILES faire sur mesure

customized *adj* ELECTRON personnalisé, PRINT standardisé

custom-made *adj* PACKAGING fait sur demande, PRINT sur mesure

custom-ordered *adj* TEXTILES tissé à la demande

customs: ~ **clearance** *n* NAUT dédouanement *m*; ~ **patrol boat** *n* NAUT vedette de la douane *f*

cusum: ~ **chart** *n* QUALITY *statistics* carte à somme cumulée *f*

cut:[1] ~ **off** *abbr* HYDR EQUIP *admission of steam* couper

cut:[2] ~ **from bar** *adj* PROD ENG *bolts, nuts and screws* décolleté dans la barre; ~ **from the solid** *adj* PROD ENG *gears* taillé dans la masse; ~ **from the solid banks** *adj* PROD ENG *gears* taillé dans la masse; ~ **on the bias** *adj* TEXTILES coupé dans le biais

cut[3] *n* C&G taille *f*, CINEMAT chute *f*, COAL TECH coupe *f*, CONST *open excavation, cutting, trench* déblai *m*, excavation *f*, fouille *f*, saignée *f*, tranchée *f*, MECH *tools* passe *f*, MECH ENG *of machine tool* coupe *f*, passe *f*, MINING *holing* coupe *f*, coupure *f*, havage *m*, PROD ENG *of file, rasp* entaille *f*, taille *f*; ~ **and cover** *n* CONST *tunnels* creusement en tranchées *m*; ~ **and cover method** *n* CONST *tunnels* méthode de coupe et de couverture *f*; ~ **and paste** *n* PRINT couper-coller; ~ **chain incline** *n* MINING plan à double effet avec chaîne à deux bouts *m*; ~ **end** *n* CONST *of timber* bout rejeté *m*; ~ **film** *n* PHOTO film coupé au format *m*; ~ **gears** *n pl* MECH ENG engrenages taillés *m pl*, engrenages taillés à la machine *m pl*; ~ **glass** *n* C&G verre creux taillé *m*; ~ **hole** *n* MINING mine d'empiétage *f*, ouverture de bouchon *f*, trou de bouchon *m*; ~ **negative** *n* CINEMAT négatif monté *m*; ~ **oil** *n* PETR TECH huile contenant de l'eau *f*, huile partiellement émulsionnée *f*; ~ **pieces** *n pl* SAFETY pièces coupées *f pl*; ~ **sizes** *n pl* C&G mesures fixes *f pl*; ~ **slide** *n* TV diapositive de transition *f*; ~ **stone** *n* CONST *for building* pierre de taille *f*; ~ **string** *n* CONST *stair building* crémaillère *f*, limon à crémaillère *m*, limon à l'anglaise *m*; ~ **wall string** *n* CONST *stair building* fausse crémaillère *f*, faux limon à crémaillère *m*

cut[4] *vt* CINEMAT monter, *light* couper, CONST *veneers* trancher, MECH *tools* couper, tailler, MINING *coal* abattre, P&R *viscosity* couper, PRINT massicoter, PROD ENG *rack, teeth of file* tailler; ~ **down a shaft** *vt* MINING élargir un puits; ~ **to** *vt* CINEMAT passer à; ~ **to the required length** *vt* PROD ENG *tube* couper à la longueur voulue; ~ **up** *vt* CONST abattre, débiter; ~ **with a jig** *vt* SAFETY *routing* détourage à gabarit *m*

cut:[5] ~ **a landing** *vi* MINING déblayer une chambre d'accrochage, escaver une recette; ~ **a lode** *vi* MINING recouper un filon; ~ **a plat** *vi* MINING déblayer une chambre d'accrochage, escaver une recette; ~ **a station** *vi* MINING déblayer une chambre d'accrochage, escaver une recette

cutaway: ~ **shot** *n* CINEMAT plan de coupe *m*; ~ **view** *n* MECH ENG vue coupée *f*

cutback *n* CONST *bitumen* bitume fluxé *m*, brai de pétrole fluxé *m*, TEXTILES réduction de production *f*; ~ **fiber technique** *n* (AmE), ~ **fibre technique** *n* (BrE) OPT méthode de la fibre coupée *f*; ~ **technique** *n* TELECOM méthode de la fibre coupée *f*

cut-in: ~ **wind speed** *n* FUELLESS vitesse du vent en entrée *f*

cutoff[1] *n* CINEMAT cache dans fenêtre de prise de vue *m*, perte d'image *f*, ELEC ENG coupure *f*, *conduction in electron tube* blocage *m*, HYDR EQUIP arrêt *m*, fermeture *f*, PRINT coupe *f*, PROD ENG fin d'exercice *f*, fin de période *f*, *flow-off gate* déversoir *m*, déversoir *m*, TV *of electronic signal* coupure *f*, WATER SUPP bras mort *m*, délaissé *m*, coupure de méandre *f*, méandre recoupé *m*; ~ **cock** *n* CONST robinet d'isolement *m*; ~ **current** *n* ELEC *circuit breaker* courant de coupure *m*; ~ **device** *n* HYDR EQUIP robinet *m*, *for stopping admission of steam to cylinder* robinet d'arrêt *m*, vanne *f*; ~ **ditch** *n* CONST fossé de crête *m*; ~ **frequency** *n* ACOUSTICS, ELEC, ELECTRON, PHYS, RECORDING, TELECOM fréquence de coupure *f*; ~ **grade** *n* COAL TECH teneur limite *f*; ~ **man** *n* (BrE) *(cf capper)* C&G croqueur *m*; ~ **plate** *n* HYDR EQUIP opercule *m*; ~ **point** *n* HYDR EQUIP phase de détente de la vapeur *f*; ~ **relay** *n* ELEC relais de coupure *m*; ~ **signal** *n* CONTROL signal de coupure *m*; ~ **switch** *n* CINEMAT interrupteur *m*; ~ **trench** *n* OCEANOG, WATER SUPP *dam* parafouille *m*; ~ **valve** *n* CONST arrêt de débit *m*, soupape d'arrêt *f*; ~ **wall** *n* WATER SUPP *dam* parafouille *m*; ~ **wavelength** *n* OPT *of single mode optical fibre*, PHYS *waveguide* longueur d'onde de coupure *f*, TELECOM longueur d'onde critique *f*, longueur d'onde de coupure *f*; ~ **wheel** *n* MECH ENG meule à tronçonner *f*

cutoff[2] *vt* C&G *edges of glass* découper, PROD ENG *sever with tool* couper, décolleter, découper, trancher, tronçonner

cutout[1] *n* C&G tirette *f*, ELEC ENG coupe-circuit *m*, MECH découpe *f*, MECH ENG *machining* échancrure *f*, évidement *m*, PRINT détourage *m*, RAIL sectionneur *m*; ~ **device** *n* SAFETY appareil coupe-circuit *m*, dispositif de disjonction *m*; ~ **photograph** *n* PHOTO image découpée *f*; ~ **relay** *n* CONTROL interrupteur de retour *m*; ~ **switch** *n* ELEC disjoncteur *m*, interrupteur *m*; ~ **wind speed** *n* FUELLESS vitesse du vent en sortie *f*

cutout[2] *vt* CONTROL interrompre, MECH ENG isoler, *machine tools* détourer, échancrer, PROD ENG découper

cut-staple: ~ **spun** *adj* TEXTILES filé de fibres coupées

cut-stone: ~ **quarry** *n* CONST carrière de pierre de taille *f*

cutter *n* CONST *of stone, wood* tailleur *m*, MECH *tools* outil de coupe *m*, MECH ENG molette *f*, molette coupante *f*, *gear-cutting machine* couteau *m*, *of machine or instrument* lame *f*, MINING *person* haveur *m*, soucheveur *m*, souscheveur *m*, NAUT *class of vessel* cotre *m*, PRINT lame de coupe *f*, massicot *m*; ~ **adaptor** *n* MECH ENG *machine tools* arbre de montage pour fraises *m*; ~ **arbor** *n* MECH ENG *milling machine* broche porte-fraise *f*; ~ **arm** *n* COAL TECH barre porte-couteau *f*; ~ **bar** *n* MECH ENG *for boring machine* machine à aléser *f*, *for lathe* porte-lame pour tour *m*, *machine tool work* meneur *m*; ~ **blade** *n* C&G couteau *m*; ~ **chain** *n* COAL TECH chaîne porte-couteau *f*; ~ **dredger** *n* NAUT drague coupeuse *f*; ~ **head** *n* CONST *tunnelling* tête de cavottier *f*, tête de coupe *f*, MECH ENG tête porte-fraise *f*, MINING trépan composé *m*; ~ **loader** *n* COAL TECH haveuse ripante *f*; ~ **mandrel** *n* MECH ENG mandrin porte-outil *m*; ~ **spindle** *n* MECH ENG mandrin porte-outil *m*; ~ **wheel** *n* MECH ENG molette *f*, molette coupante *f*; ~ **with hub** *n* MECH ENG fraise à moyeu *f*; ~ **with shank** *n* MECH ENG fraise à manche *f*; ~ **with tapped hole** *n* MECH ENG fraise à trou taraudé *f*; ~ **wound** *n* SAFETY blessure causée par une fraise *f*

cutter's: ~ **bay** *n* C&G loge de coupeur *f*; ~ **lath** *n* C&G règle de coupeur *f*; ~ **pliers** *n pl* C&G pince de croqueur *f*; ~ **straight edge** *n* C&G règle de coupeur *f*; ~ **table** *n* C&G table de découpe *f*; ~ **table ruler** *n* C&G règle graduée *f*

cutting[1] *adj* GEOL sécant

cutting[2] *n* C&G découpe *f*, COAL TECH havage *m*, CONST *trench* coupure *f*, excavation *f*, tranchée *f*, MINING *holing* coupe *f*, coupure *f*, havage *m*, PAPER TECH coupe *f*, PROD ENG *chip* copeau *m*, rognure *f*, *gearwheel teeth* taille *f*, *metal by oxygen jet* coupe *f*, découpage *m*, RAIL tranchée *f*, *fixed works* voie en tranchée *f*, TEXTILES coupe confection *f*, petit échantillon *m*; ~ **angle** *n* FOOD TECH angle de coupe *m*, angle du tranchant *m*, MECH ENG *machine tool* angle de coupe *m*; ~ **bit** *n* COAL TECH fleuret *m*, MINING *boring* trépan tranchant *m*, trépan à biseau *m*; ~ **blowpipe** *n* CONST chalumeau coupeur *m*, chalumeau oxycoupeur *m*; ~ **copy** *n* CINEMAT copie de montage *f*, copie de travail *f*; ~ **diamond** *n* C&G diamant *m*; ~ **die** *n* PAPER TECH emporte-pièce *m*; ~ **drift** *n* MECH ENG mandrin taillé *m*; ~ **driftpin** *n* MECH ENG mandrin taillé *m*; ~ **edge** *n* CONST *of tool* arête tranchante *f*, coupant *m*, tranchant *m*, CONST *of tool* fil tranchant *m*, MECH *tools* arête de coupe *f*, MECH ENG arête tranchante *f*, fil *m*, tranchant *m*, taillant *m*, TEXTILES arête tranchante *f*; ~ **edge chipping** *n* PROP MAT effritement de l'arête de coupe *m*; ~ **fluid** *n* PROD ENG liquide de coupure *m*; ~ **frame** *n* C&G tour de tailleur *m*; ~ **gage** *n* (AmE), ~ **gauge** *n* (BrE) CONST *joiner's* trusquin à couper *m*; ~ **head** *n* MINING tête d'abattage *f*; ~ **loss** *n* C&G perte à la découpe *f*; ~ **machine** *n* MINING haveur *m*; ~ **nippers** *n pl* CONST pinces coupantes *f pl*, tenailles coupantes *f pl*, tenailles à mors coupants *f pl*; ~ **off the edges** *n* C&G découpe des bords *f*; ~ **oil** *n* MECH ENG huile de coupe *f*; ~ **pliers** *n pl* CONST pince cisailleuse *f*, pince-cisaille *f*; ~ **point** *n* CINEMAT point de coupe *m*; ~ **shop** *n* C&G atelier de découpe *m* (Fra), magasin de découpe *m* (Bel); ~ **speed** *n* MECH ENG vitesse de coupe *f*; ~ **stroke** *n* MECH ENG *machine tool work* course utile *f*; ~ **stylus** *n* ACOUSTICS burin de gravure *m*; ~ **teeth** *n* CONST dents de coupe *f pl*; ~ **tool** *n* MECH outil de coupe *m*, MECH ENG outil coupant *m*; ~ **torch** *n* MECH ENG chalumeau à découper *m*; ~ **veneers** *n pl* CONST tranchage des feuilles de placage *m*; ~ **wheel** *n* C&G meule de taille *f*, MECH ENG molette coupante *f*

cutting-in *n* MECH ENG enclenchement *m*

cutting-off *n* CONST *heads of piles* arasement *m*, recépage *m*, HYDR EQUIP *admission of steam* coupure *f*, PROD ENG *gates* coupage *m*, *of piece of iron at one operation* tranchage *m*, *severing with tool* décolletage *m*, découpage *m*, tranchage *m*, tronçonnage *m*, tronçonnement *m*; ~ **and forming lathe** *n* MECH ENG tour à revolver pour le décolletage et le façonnage *m*; ~ **lathe** *n* MECH ENG tour à tronçonner *m*; ~ **pieces** *n* PROD ENG *from tube* tronçonnage *m*; ~ **slide** *n* MECH ENG chariot à tronçonner *m*; ~ **tool** *n* MECH ENG *lathe* outil à tronçonner *m*; ~ **wheel** *n* MECH ENG meule à tronçonner *f*

cuttings *n pl* COAL TECH sédiments de forage *m pl*, PETR déblais *m pl*, débris de forage *m*, PETR TECH déblais *m*

pl; ~ **gas** *n* PETR TECH gaz occlus *m*; ~ **removal** *n* PETR TECH évacuation des déblais *f*

cut-to-length[1] *adj* PROD ENG coupé à la longueur

cut-to-length:[2] ~ **line** *n* PROD ENG ligne coupée à longueur *f*

cutwater *n* CONST *of bridge pier* bec *m*

CV *abbr* (*code violation*) TELECOM violation de code *f*

CVD *abbr* (*chemical vapor deposition, chemical vapour deposition*) ELECTRON, OPT, TELECOM DCV (*dépôt chimique en phase vapeur*)

CVS *abbr* (*constant volume sampling*) POLLUTION échantillonnage à volume constant *m*

CW[1] *abbr* ELEC ENG (*clockwise*) dans le sens horaire, ELEC ENG (*continuous wave*) onde entretenue *f*, TELECOM (*call waiting*) appel en instance *m*, WAVE PHYS (*continuous wave*) onde entretenue *f*

CW:[2] ~ **gas laser** *n* ELECTRON laser à gaz à émission continue *m*; ~ **laser** *n* ELECTRON laser continu *m*, laser à faisceau continu *m*, laser à émission continue *m*; ~ **laser beam** *n* ELECTRON faisceau laser diode *m*; ~ **laser diode** *n* ELECTRON diode laser à émission continue *f*; ~ **signal** *n* ELEC ENG signal en ondes entretenues *m*

CWR *abbr* (*continuous welded rail*) RAIL LRS (*long rail soudé*)

C-wrench *n* (BrE) MECH ENG *tool* clé à ergots *f*

cyamelid *n* CHEM cyamélide *m*

cyamelide *n* CHEM cyamélide *m*

cyanacetic *adj* CHEM cyanacétique

cyanamide *n* CHEM cyanamide *m*

cyanate *n* CHEM cyanate *m*

cyanic *adj* CHEM cyanique

cyanidation *n* COAL TECH cyanuration *f*

cyanide *n* CHEM cyanure *m*; ~ **process** *n* CHEM procédé de cyanuration *m*

cyanite *n* MINERAL cyanite *f*, disthène *m*

cyanization *n* CHEM *of organic matter* cyanuration *f*

cyanogen *n* CHEM cyanogène *m*

cyanotrichite *n* MINERAL cyanotrichite *f*

cybernetics *n* COMP, SPACE cybernétique *f*

cyclamate *n* CHEM cyclamate *m*

cycle *n* ACOUSTICS, COMP, DP, ELEC, ELEC ENG cycle *m*, MECH ENG période *f*, P&R cycle *m*, PETR période *f*, REFRIG cycle *m*; ~ **counting** *n* PROD ENG inventaire cyclique *m*, inventaire tournant *m*; ~ **of intervals** *n* ACOUSTICS cycle d'intervalles *m*; ~ **path** *n* TRANSP piste cyclable *f*; ~ **split adjustment** *n* TRANSP *traffic control* division du cycle *f*; ~ **stealing** *n* COMP, DP vol de cycle *m*; ~ **time** *n* COMP temps de cycle *m*, DP durée d'un cycle *f*, temps de cycle *m*; ~ **track** *n* CONST piste cyclable *f*

cyclic[1] *adj* CHEM, PETR TECH cyclique

cyclic:[2] ~ **block codes** *n pl* TELECOM codes de blocs cycliques *m pl*; ~ **code** *n* TELECOM code cyclique *m*; ~ **control step** *n* AERONAUT *helicopter* échelon de commande cyclique *m*; ~ **flapping angle** *n* AERONAUT *helicopter* angle de battement cyclique *m*; ~ **inventory** *n* PROD ENG inventaire tournant *m*; ~ **noise** *n* ACOUSTICS bruit rythmique *m*; ~ **pitch** *n* AERONAUT *helicopter* pas cyclique *m*; ~ **pitch control** *n* AERONAUT *helicopter* commande cyclique de pas *f*; ~ **pitch control stick** *n* AERONAUT *helicopter* manche de commande de pas *m*; ~ **pitch servo trim** *n* AERONAUT *helicopter* servo régulateur de pas cyclique *m*; ~ **pitch stick** *n* AERONAUT *helicopter* manche cyclique *m*, manche de commande de pas *m*; ~ **redundancy check** *n* COMP, CONTROL contrôle de redondance cyclique *m*,

DP décalage circulaire *m*, ELECTRON contrôle de redondance cyclique *m*, MATH contrôle cyclique de la superfluité *m*; ~ **redundancy code** *n* TELECOM code de redondance cyclique *m*; ~ **sedimentation** *n* GEOL sédimentation rythmique avec séquences *f*; ~ **shift** *n* COMP, DP décalage circulaire *m*; ~ **stick** *n* AERONAUT *helicopter* manche cyclique *m*, manche de commande de pas *m*; ~ **universe** *n* ASTRON univers cyclique *m*

cyclical: ~ **redundancy check** *n* (*CRC*) COMP contrôle de redondance cyclique *m* (*CRC*)

cycling *n* AERONAUT *helicopter* période de régulation *f*, GEOL recyclage *m*; ~ **thermoresistor** *n* AERONAUT *helicopter* sonde de cyclage *f*

cyclization *n* CHEM *reaction, process* cyclisation *f*

cycloaliphatic: ~ **amine** *n* P&R *curing* amine cycloaliphatique *f*

cycloalkane *n* PETR TECH cyclane *m*, cycloalcane *m*

cycloalkene *n* PETR TECH cyclène *m*

cyclogyro *n* AERONAUT hélicoplane *m*

cyclohexane *n* PETR TECH cyclohéxane *m*

cycloid *n* GEOM cycloïde *f*

cycloidal: ~ **gear** *n* MECH engrenage cycloïdal *m*

cyclone *n* COAL TECH, FOOD TECH cyclone *m*, METEO cyclone *m*, dépression *f*, PETR TECH *dust and sand separator*, POLLUTION cyclone *m*; ~ **furnace** *n* C&G, HEATING four cyclone *m*; ~ **recovery skimmer** *n* POLLUTION récupérateur à vortex *m*

cyclonic: ~ **circulation** *n* METEO circulation cyclonique *f*; ~ **rotation** *n* METEO rotation cyclonique *f*

cycloolefin *n* PETR TECH cyclooléfine *f*

cycloparaffin *n* PETR TECH cycloparaffine *f*

cyclopean: ~ **concrete** *n* CONST béton cyclopéen *m*; ~ **concrete gravity dam** *n* HYDROL barrage poids en béton cyclopéen *m*

cyclopic: ~ **barrage** *n* WATER SUPP barrage cyclopéen *m*

cyclorama *n* CINEMAT cyclorama *m*

cyclothem *n* GEOL cyclothème *m*, séquence sédimentaire rythmique *f*

cyclotron *n* ELEC ENG, PART PHYS, PHYS cyclotron *m*; ~ **frequency** *n* PHYS fréquence de cyclotron *f*, gyrofréquence *f*; ~ **radiation** *n* RAD PHYS radiation de cyclotron *f*; ~ **safety** *n* RAD PHYS sécurité de cyclotron *f*

cyclotronic: ~ **resonance** *n* TELECOM résonance cyclotronique *f*

cylinder *n* AUTO cylindre *m*, C&G *in production of rolled plate* canon *m*, COMP *disk drive*, DP *disk drive*, GEOM cylindre *m*, MECH *air systems* bouteille *f*, cylindre *m*, MINING, NAUT *of engine* cylindre *m*, P&R *of calendar, coater* cylindre *m*, rouleau *m*, *of press* cylindre *m*, PAPER TECH forme ronde *f*, PROD ENG vérin *m*, *of pump* barillet *m*, corps *m*, VEHICLES *of engine* cylindre *m*; ~ **bank angling** *n* AUTO angle d'ouverture *m*, inclinaison des cylindres *f*; ~ **barrel** *n* MECH ENG fût de cylindre *m*, tube pour vérin *m*, PROD ENG, VEHICLES *of engine* corps de cylindre *m*; ~ **block** *n* AUTO bloc-cylindres *m*; ~ **boiler** *n* HYDR EQUIP chaudière cylindrique *f*; ~ **bore** *n* MECH ENG alésage de vérin *m*; ~ **cam** *n* PROD ENG came à cylindre *f*, came à tambour *f*; ~ **capacity** *n* AUTO cylindrée *f*; ~ **casing** *n* PROD ENG tôle d'enveloppe du corps du cylindre *f*; ~ **cock** *n* CONST purgeur *m*, robinet de purge *m*, robinet purgeur *m*; ~ **cover** *n* PROD ENG fond de cylindre *m*, plateau de cylindre *m*; ~ **flange** *n* VEHICLES *of engine* semelle de cylindre *f*; ~ **gasket** *n* REFRIG joint de culasse *m*; ~ **glass** *n* (BrE) (*cf blown sheet*) C&G verre

en cylindres *m*; ~ **head** *n* AUTO culasse *f*, HYDR EQUIP *back* fond *m*, MECH ENG fond *m*, plateau *m*, NAUT *of engine* culasse *f*, PROD ENG fond de cylindre *m*, plateau de cylindre *m*, REFRIG, VEHICLES *of engine* culasse *f*; ~ **head bolt** *n* AUTO boulon de culasse *m*; ~ **head gasket** *n* AUTO, VEHICLES *of engine* joint de culasse *m*; ~ **head stud** *n* MECH ENG vis de culasse *f*; ~ **jacket** *n* PROD ENG enveloppe de cylindre *f*; ~ **lagging** *n* PROD ENG revêtement calorifique du corps du cylindre *m*; ~ **liner** *n* AUTO, MECH chemise *f*, VEHICLES *of engine* chemise de cylindre *f*; ~ **lock** *n* PROD ENG sélecteur clé *m*; ~ **lock operator** *n* PROD ENG sélecteur à clé *m*; ~ **machine** *n* PAPER TECH machine à forme ronde *f*; ~ **mold** *n* (AmE), ~ **mould** *n* (BrE) PAPER TECH forme ronde *f*; ~ **piston rod** *n* MECH ENG piston de vérin *m*; ~ **poppet head** *n* PROD ENG *of lathe* contre-pointe à fourreau *f*; ~ **printing machine** *n* PRINT machine à imprimer à cylindre *f*; ~ **process** *n* C&G soufflage en cylindres *m*; ~ **rheostat** *n* ELEC *resistance* rhéostat cylindrique *m*; ~ **rod** *n* MECH ENG tige de vérin *f*; ~ **sizing machine** *n* TEXTILES encolleuse à tambour *f*; ~ **sleeve** *n* AUTO chemise de cylindre *f*; ~ **tailstock** *n* PROD ENG *of lathe* contre-pointe à fourreau *f*; ~ **wall** *n* AUTO, VEHICLES *of engine* paroi de cylindre *f*; ~ **wrench** *n* PROD ENG clef pour tuyaux *f*, clef à fer creux *f*, clef à tubes *f*, serre-tubes *m*

cylinder-drawing: ~ **process** *n* C&G étirage mécanique en cylindres *m*

cylinder-drying: ~ **machine** *n* TEXTILES machine à tambour *f*

cylindrical[1] *adj* GEOL cylindrique

cylindrical:[2] ~ **abrasive sheet** *n* MECH ENG manchon abrasif cylindrique *m*; ~ **capacitor** *n* PHYS condensateur cylindrique *m*; ~ **coordinates** *n pl* PHYS coordonnées cylindriques *f pl*; ~ **flue boiler** *n* HYDR EQUIP chaudière à foyer cylindrique *f*; ~ **gage** *n* (AmE), ~ **gauge** *n* (BrE) PROD ENG *external* bague *f*, calibre à bague *m*, *internal* bouchon *m*, calibre à bouchon *m*; ~ **gear pair** *n* AUTO engrenage cylindrique *m*; ~ **gears** *n pl* MECH ENG engrenages cylindriques *m pl*; ~ **gears for heavy engineering** *n pl* MECH ENG engrenages cylindriques de grosse mécanique *m pl*; ~ **grinder** *n* MECH rectifieuse cylindrique *f*; ~ **grinding** *n* MECH, MECH ENG rectification cylindrique *f*; ~ **helical compression spring** *n* SPRINGS ressort hélicoïdal cylindrique de compression *m*; ~ **helical extension spring** *n* SPRINGS ressort hélicoïdal cylindrique de traction *m*; ~ **helical spring** *n* SPRINGS ressort hélicoïdal cylindrique *m*; ~ **helix** *n* SPRINGS hélix cylindrique *m*; ~ **irradiator** *n* NUCLEAR *of irradiation rig* irradiateur cylindrique *m*; ~ **lens** *n* INSTRUMENT lentille cylindrique *f*; ~ **mouthpiece** *n* HYDR EQUIP ajutage cylindrique *m*; ~ **pin** *n* MECH ENG goupille cylindrique *f*; ~ **reflecting antenna** *n* TELECOM antenne à réflecteur cylindrique *f*; ~ **roller bearing** *n* MECH ENG roulement à rouleaux cylindriques *m*; ~ **rotor machine** *n* ELEC machine à rotor cylindrique *f*; ~ **shell** *n* SPACE *spacecraft* virole cylindrique *f*; ~ **solid of revolution** *n* GEOM *geometrical shape* cylindre de révolution *m*; ~ **spring** *n* PROD ENG ressort cylindrique *m*; ~ **wave** *n* ACOUSTICS onde cylindrique *f*; ~ **whisker** *n* PROP MAT fil monocristallin cylindrique *m*; ~ **winding** *n* ELEC *coil* enroulement à bobines concentriques *m*

cylindroconic *adj* PROD ENG cylindroconique

cymene *n* CHEM cymène *m*

cymogene *n* PETR cymogène *m*

cymophane *n* MINERAL chrysobéryl *m*
cyprine *n* MINERAL cyprine *f*

cytisine *n* CHEM cytisine *f*, uléxine *f*

D

d *abbr (deci)* METR déci

da *abbr (deca-)* METR da *(déca)*

dabber *n* PROD ENG *of loamplate or loam mould* broche *f*

DAC *abbr* COMP *(digital-to-analog converter)*, ELECTRON *(digital-to-analog converter, digital-to-analogue converter)*, TV *(digital-to-analog converter, digital-to-analogue converter)* CNA *(convertisseur numérique-analogique)*

dacite *n* PETR dacite *f*

Dacron *n* (TM) NAUT *sailcloth* tergal *m* (MD)

daggerboard *n* NAUT dérive *f*

daguerreotype *n* PHOTO daguerréotype *m*

dailies *n pl* CINEMAT production journalière *f*, rushes *m pl*

daily: **~ consumption** *n* WATER SUPP consommation journalière *f*; **~ specific consumption** *n* HYDROL consommation journalière par habitant *f*; **~ use** *n* PROD ENG rotation journalière *f*; **~ water flow** *n* WATER SUPP débit journalier *m*

dairy: **~ plant** *n* FOOD TECH laiterie *f*, usine laitière *f*; **~ produce** *n* FOOD TECH produit laitier *m*; **~ product** *n* FOOD TECH produit laitier *m*

daisy: **~ chain** *n* ELECTRON chaîne d'éléments *f*, PROD ENG connexion en guirlande *f*; **~ chain bus** *n* COMP, DP bus de chaînage en guirlande *m*, bus en chaîne *m*

daisywheel *n* COMP, DP, PRINT marguerite *f*; **~ printer** *n* COMP, DP, PRINT imprimante à marguerite *f*

dalton *n* RAD PHYS dalton *m*

Dalton's: **~ law** *n* PHYS *of partial pressures* loi de Dalton *f*, loi du mélange des gaz *f*

dam[1] *n* CONST barrage *m*, FUELLESS barrage *m*, digue *f*, HYDROL barrage *m*, MINING *in abandoned shaft* plate-curve *f*, *in a mine level* serrage *m*, estouffée *f*, NAUT barrage *m*, digue *f*, PROD ENG *of blast furnace* dame *f*, WATER SUPP arrêt-barrage *m*, barrage *m*, WATER SUPP *across shallow water* digue *f* **~ plate** *n* PROD ENG *of blast furnace* dame *f*, gentilhomme *m*

dam[2] *vt* MINING endiguer, terrasser, WATER SUPP barrer, endiguer

damage[1] *n* NAUT *to ship* avarie *f*, PATENTS, QUALITY dommage *m*; **~ assessment** *n* NAUT *insurance* constat d'avaries *m*

damage[2] *vt* SAFETY *internal or external organs, respiratory system, etc* abîmer

damaged[1] *adj* TELECOM *cable* endommagé

damaged:[2] **~ car** *n* (AmE) *(cf damaged wagon)* RAIL wagon avarié *m*; **~ fuel assembly** *n* NUCLEAR assemblage combustible détérioré *m*; **~ wagon** *n* (BrE) *(cf damaged car)* RAIL wagon avarié *m*; **~ yarn** *n* C&G fil endommagé *m*

damming *n* WATER SUPP barrage *m*, endigage *m*, endiguement *m*

damourite *n* MINERAL damourite *f*

damp[1] *adj* PAPER TECH humide

damp[2] *n* MINING mofette *f*; **~ fog** *n* METEO brouillard mouillant *m*; **~ sheet** *n* MINING arrêt-barrage d'eau *m*; **~ streak** *n* PAPER TECH traînée humide *f*

damp[3] *vt* ELEC *oscillation*, ELEC ENG amortir

damped[1] *adj* PHYS amorti

damped:[2] **~ oscillation** *n* ELECTRON, RECORDING oscillation amortie *f*; **~ sinusoidal quantity** *n* ELEC ENG grandeur sinusoïdale amortie *f*; **~ vibrations** *n pl* WAVE PHYS vibrations amorties *f pl*

dampener *n* PAPER TECH humecteuse *f*

dampening *n* METALL amortissement *m*, PAPER TECH humectage *m*; **~ etch** *n* PRINT solution de mouillage *f*

damper *n* ACOUSTICS silencieux *m*, AUTO amortisseur de vibrations *m*, CONST *of furnace, chimney* registre *m*, ELEC ENG dispositif d'amortissement *m*, HEAT ENG registre *m*, MECH ENG dispositif amortisseur *m*, PROD ENG *of superheater* étouffoir *m*, RAIL *on wagon or coach* tampon *m*, REFRIG *in air conditioning duct* registre *m*, SPACE, VEHICLES *suspension* amortisseur *m*; **~ coil** *n* SPRINGS spire d'amortissement *f*

damping *n* COMP, ELEC *of oscillation*, ELEC ENG amortissement *m*, PAPER TECH humectage *m*, PETR, PHYS, PROP MAT, TV amortissement *m*; **~ capacitor** *n* ELEC ENG condensateur d'amortissement *m*; **~ coefficient** *n* PHYS coefficient d'amortissement *m*; **~ coil** *n* ELEC, ELEC ENG bobine d'amortissement *f*, SPRINGS spire d'amortissement *f*; **~ device** *n* MECH ENG dispositif amortisseur *m*; **~ down** *n* PROD ENG *of blast furnace* bouchage pour arrêt momentané *m*; **~ factor** *n* ELEC *of oscillation* facteur d'amortissement *m*, PHYS décrément *m*; **~ moment** *n* AERONAUT moment d'amortissement *m*; **~ resistance** *n* PHYS résistance d'amortissement *f*; **~ resistor** *n* ELEC résistance d'amortissement *f*; **~ roll** *n* PACKAGING rouleau mouilleur *m*

dampness *n* PAPER TECH humidité *f*

damp-proof: **~ course** *n* CONST *building* couche d'isolement *f*, couche isolante imperméable *f*, lit isolant *m*

danaide *n* HYDR EQUIP siège branlant *m*

danaite *n* MINERAL danaïte *f*

danalite *n* MINERAL danalite *f*

danburite *n* MINERAL danburite *f*

dance *vt* CONST *step* balancer, faire balancer, faire le balancement

dancing: **~ seat** *n* HYDR EQUIP *of valve* siège branlant *m*; **~ sleeper** *n* (BrE) *(cf dancing tie)* RAIL traverse danseuse *f*; **~ step** *n* CONST *stair-building* marche balancée *f*, marche balançante *f*; **~ tie** *n* (AmE) *(cf dancing sleeper, pumping sleeper)* RAIL traverse danseuse *f*

dandy: **~ roll** *n* PACKAGING filigraneur *m*, PAPER TECH rouleau filigraneur *m*, rouleau égoutteur *m*

Danforth: **~ anchor** *n* NAUT ancre à bascule *f*

danger[1] *n* SAFETY danger *m*; **~ area** *n* SAFETY zone dangereuse *f*; **~ point** *n* SAFETY cote d'alerte *f*; **~ signal** *n* CONTROL signal d'alarme *m*, signal de détresse *m*, SAFETY signal de danger *m*; **~ zone** *n* SAFETY zone dangereuse *f*

danger:[2] **be a ~ to** *vt* SAFETY constituer un danger pour, être un danger pour

dangerous: **~ environment** *n* RAD PHYS *radioactive* milieu hostile *m*; **~ goods** *n pl* AERONAUT, PACKAGING marchandises dangereuses *f pl*; **~ materials** *n pl* SAFETY matières dangereuses *f pl*; ~ **substance** *n* SAFETY substance dangereuse *f*

Danian *adj* GEOL *stratigraphy* danien

Danish: ~ **seine** *n* OCEANOG senne danoise *f*

dannemorite *n* MINERAL dannemorite *f*

danny: ~ **neck** *n* C&G arrachement au col *m*

DAO *abbr (deasphalted oil)* PETR TECH huile désasphaltée *f*

daphnetin *n* CHEM daphnétine *f*

daphnin *n* CHEM daphnine *f*

daphnite *n* MINERAL daphnite *f*

darcy *n* HYDROL darcy *m*

dark: ~ **cloud of molecular hydrogen** *n* ASTRON nuage sombre d'hydrogène moléculaire *m*; ~ **conduction** *n* ELEC ENG conduction d'obscurité *f*; ~ **current** *n* ELEC ENG courant d'obscurité *m*, intensité du courant d'obscurité *f*, OPT, PHYS, TELECOM courant d'obscurité *m*; ~ **field image** *n* CRYSTALL image en champ sombre *f*; ~ **filter** *n* INSTRUMENT filtre protecteur contre le rayonnement du soleil *m*; ~ **fringe** *n* PHYS frange sombre *f*; ~ **glass** *n* C&G verre sombre *m*; ~ **ground illumination** *n* PHYS éclairage sur fond obscur *m*; ~ **halo** *n* ASTRON halo noir *m*; ~ **matter** *n* ASTRON matière noire *f*; ~ **nebula** *n* ASTRON, SPACE nébuleuse noire *f*, nébuleuse obscure *f*; ~ **resistance** *n* ELEC ENG, NUCLEAR *of photocell* résistance d'obscurité *f*; ~ **shade** *n* TEXTILES coloris foncé *m*; ~ **slide** *n* PHOTO châssis séparé *m*; ~ **tone** *n* COLOURS teinte sombre *f*

dark-colored *adj* (AmE), **dark-coloured** *adj* (BrE) GEOL mélanocrate, sombre

darken *vt* NAUT *ship* masquer, naviguer à feux masqués

darkening *n* C&G noircissement *m* ~ **index** *n* C&G indice de noircissement *m*

dark-field: ~ **illumination** *n* PHYS éclairage sur fond obscur *m*

dark-line: ~ **spectrum** *n* SPACE spectre d'absorption *m*

darkness *n* ASTRON obscurité *f*

darkroom *n* CINEMAT chambre noire *f*, labo *m*, PHOTO chambre noire *f*, laboratoire obscur *m*; ~ **lighting** *n* CINEMAT éclairage inactinique *m*; ~ **timer** *n* PHOTO compte-pose *m*

dark-trace: ~ **screen** *n* ELECTRON écran à trace foncé *m*

darn *vt* TEXTILES *clothes* raccommoder, *socks* repriser

darning *n* TEXTILES raccommodage *m*, reprise *f*; ~ **needle** *n* TEXTILES aiguille à repriser *f*; ~ **stitch** *n* TEXTILES point de reprise *m*; ~ **wool** *n* TEXTILES laine à repriser *f*

d'Arsonval: ~ **galvanometer** *n* ELEC ENG galvanomètre de d'Arsonval

dart: ~ **impact test** *n* C&G essai de choc à torpille *m*

darting: ~ **flame** *n* THERMOD *welding* dard de chalumeau *m*

dash *n* PRINT tiret *m*

dashboard *n* AUTO planche de bord *f*, VEHICLES tableau d'instruments *m*, tablier *m*

dashing: ~ **vessel** *n* NUCLEAR amortisseur *m*

dashpot *n* MECH amortisseur à air *m*, dashpot *m*, MECH ENG dashpot *m*, NUCLEAR amortisseur *m*, TRANSP amortisseur à fluide *m*, VEHICLES amortisseur du papillon *m*, amortisseur à fluide *m*; ~ **valve** *n* MECH ENG soupape d'amortisseur de choc *f*

DAT *abbr* COMP *(digital audio tape)* bande audio-numérique *f*, COMP *(dynamic address translation)* traduction dynamique d'adresse *f*, RECORDING *(digital audio tape)* cassette numérique *f*

data *n* ASTRON données *f pl*, COMP, DP, ELECTRON données *f pl*, informations *f pl*, GEOL, QUALITY, SPACE,

TESTING données *f pl*;

■ **a** ~ **abstraction** *n* COMP, DP abstraction de données *f*; ~ **acquisition** *n* COMP, DP, ELECTRON acquisition de données *f*; ~ **aggregate** *n* COMP, DP agrégat de données *m*; ~ **amplifier** *n* ELECTRON amplificateur de mesure *m*; ~ **array** *n* COMP ensemble de données *m*;

■ **b** ~ **burst** *n* SPACE *communications* paquet de données *m*; ~ **bus** *n* COMP, DP, SPACE *communications* bus de données *m*;

■ **c** ~ **capture** *n* COMP, DP saisie de données *f*; ~ **carrier** *n* COMP, DP support d'informations *m*, support de données *m*, TELECOM porteuse de données *f*; ~ **carrier detect** *n (DCD)* TELECOM détection de porteuse de données *f*; ~ **carrier failure detector** *n* TELECOM détecteur d'interruption de la porteuse de données *m*; ~ **cartridge** *n* DP cartouche de données *f*; ~ **chaining** *n* COMP, DP chaînage de données *m*; ~ **channel** *n* COMP, DP voie de données *f*; ~ **channel multiplexer** *n* COMP, DP multiplexeur de données *m*; ~ **channel received line signal** detector *n* TELECOM détecteur du signal de ligne reçu sur la voie de données *m*; ~ **circuit terminal equipment** *n (DCE)* TELECOM équipement terminal de circuit de données *m (ETCD)*; ~ **circuit terminating equipment** *n* TELECOM équipement de terminaison de circuit de données *m*; ~ **collection** *n* COMP collecte de données *f*, regroupement de données *m*, DP collecte de données *f*, regroupement de données *m*, TELECOM collecte de données *f*, rassemblement de données *m*, recueil de données *m*; ~ **collection center** *n* (AmE), ~ **collection centre** *n* (BrE) *(DCC)* TELECOM centre de collecte de données *m*; ~ **collection equipment** *n* TELECOM équipement de collecte *m*; ~ **collection platform** *n* METEO, SPACE *(DCP)* plate-forme de collecte de données *f*; ~ **collection satellite** *n* SPACE satellite de collecte de données *m*; ~ **communication** *n* COMP transmission de données *f*, télé-écriture *f*, télématique *f*, DP transmission de données *f*, télématique *f*; ~ **communication channel** *n (DCC)* TELECOM canal de communication de données *m*, canal de transmission de données *m*, voie de données *f*; ~ **communication network** *n* COMP, DP réseau télématique *m*, TELECOM RCD, réseau de communication de données *m*; ~ **communications equipment** *n (DCE)* TELECOM installation de transmission de données *f*; ~ **communication terminal** *n* COMP, DP terminal de transmission de données *m*; ~ **compaction** *n* COMP, DP compression de données *f*; ~ **compression** *n* COMP, DP compression de données *f*, ELECTRON compression d'information *f*; ~ **concentrator** *n* COMP, DP concentrateur de données *m*; ~ **convention** *n* AERONAUT convention de données *f*; ~ **conversion** *n* ELECTRON conversion d'information *f*, conversion de données *f*, conversion de signaux *f*; ~ **converter** *n* ELECTRON convertisseur d'information *m*, convertisseur de données *m*, convertisseur de signaux *m*;

■ **d** ~ **declaration** *n* COMP déclaration de données *f*; ~ **definition** *n* COMP, DP définition de données *f*; ~ **description** *n* COMP, DP description de données *f*; ~ **description language** *n (DDL)* COMP langage de description de données *m*; ~ **dictionary** *n* COMP, DP dictionnaire de données *m*; ~ **display terminal** *n* TV console de visualisation de données *f*; ~ **division** *n* COMP *COBOL* division de données *f*; ~ **domain** *n* ELECTRON domaine logique *m*;

■ **e** ~ **element** *n* COMP élément d'information *m*, DP élément de donnée *m*, ELECTRON élément d'information *m*; ~ **element separator** *n* TELECOM séparateur d'éléments de données *m*; ~ **encryption** *n* COMP chiffrement de données *m*, DP cryptage de données *m*; ~ **entry** *n* COMP entrée de données *f*, DP, ELECTRON saisie de données *f*; ~ **extraction** *n* ELECTRON extraction d'information *f*;

~ f ~ **field** *n* COMP rubrique *f*, DP champ de données *m*; ~ **file** *n* COMP, DP fichier de données *m*; ~ **flowchart** *n* DP organigramme de données *m*; ~ **form** *n* PROD ENG grille de saisie *f*; ~ **format** *n* DP format de données *m*;

~ g ~ **gathering** *n* COMP, DP collecte de données *f*;

~ h ~ **hierarchy** *n* COMP, DP hiérarchie de données *f*;

~ i ~ **independence** *n* COMP, DP autonomie de données *f*; ~ **integrity** *n* TELECOM intégrité de données *f*; ~ **item** *n* COMP article *m*, donnée élémentaire *f*, DP donnée élémentaire *f*, élément d'information *m*, élément de donnée *m*;

~ l ~ **link** *n* COMP, DP liaison de données *f*, ELECTRON liaison de transmission de données *f*, liaison informatique *f*, SPACE *communications*, TELECOM liaison de données *f*; ~ **link connection** *n (DLC)* TELECOM connexion pour liaison de données *f*; ~ **link connection identifier** *n (DLCI)* TELECOM identificateur de connexion de liaison consolidée *m*; ~ **link control** *n* AERONAUT commande de liaison de données *f*, COMP contrôle de liaison de données *m*, DP, TELECOM *(DLC)* commande de liaison de données *f*; ~ **link control protocol** *n* COMP procédure de liaison *f*, DP protocole de transmission *m*; ~ **link escape** *n (DLE)* COMP, DP échappement en transmission *m*, échappement à la transmission *m*; ~ **link layer** *n* DP couche de liaison de données *f*, TELECOM couche de chaînage de données *f*, couche de liaison de données *f*; ~ **link service** *n (DLS)* TELECOM service de liaison de données *m*; ~ **logger** *n* COMP enregistreur de données *m*, DP enregistreur *m*, INSTRUMENT enregistreur de données *m*; ~ **logging** *n* COMP enregistrement chronologique de données *m*, DP, NUCLEAR enregistrement de données *m*;

~ m ~ **management** *n (DM)* COMP, DP gestion de données *f*, TELECOM gestion de données *f*; ~ **manipulation language** *n (DML)* COMP langage de manipulation de données *m*; ~ **medium** *n* COMP, DP support d'informations *m*, support de données *m*; ~ **memory** *n (DM)* DP mémoire de données *f*; ~ **model** *n* COMP, DP structure de données *f*; ~ **modulation** *n* TELECOM modulation de données *f*; ~ **multiplexer** *n* TELECOM, TRANSP multiplexeur de données *m*; ~ **multiplexing** *n* ELECTRON multiplexage d'informations *m*;

~ n ~ **name** *n* COMP, DP nom de donnée *m*; ~ **network** *n* COMP, DP, TELECOM réseau de données *m*; ~ **network identification code** *n (DNIC)* TELECOM code d'identification de réseau de données *m (CIRD)*;

~ o ~ **origination** *n* COMP création de données *f*, DP création de données *f*, émission de données *f*; ~ **origin authentication** *n* TELECOM authentification de l'origine de données *f*; ~ **output** *n* INSTRUMENT sortie de données *f*;

~ p ~ **packet** *n* TELECOM paquet de données *m*; ~ **path** *n* COMP flux de données *m*, DP, ELECTRON chemin de données *m*; ~ **phase** *n* TELECOM phase de données *f*; ~ **port** *n* TELECOM accès de données numériques *m*; ~ **preparation** *n* COMP, DP préparation de données *f*; ~ **privacy** *n* (BrE) *(cf data security)* COMP, DP confidentialité de données *f*; ~ **private wire** *n* TELECOM liaison spécialisée transmission de données *f*; ~ **processing** *n*

(DP) COMP, DP, ELECTRON, TELECOM traitement de données *m (TD)*; ~ **processing center** *n* (AmE), ~ **processing centre** *n* (BrE) *(DPC)* DP centre de traitement d'informations *m*, centre de traitement de données *m*, centre informatique *m*, TELECOM centre de traitement de données *m*; ~ **processing system** *n* DP système de traitement d'information *m*, système de traitement de données *m*, système informatique *m*, NUCLEAR système de traitement de données *m*; ~ **processing terminal equipment** *n* TELECOM équipement terminal de traitement de données *m*; ~ **protection** *n* COMP, DP protection des données *f*;

~ q ~ **query** *n* COMP, DP consultation de données *f*, interrogation de données *f*;

~ r ~ **rate** *n* COMP vitesse de transmission de données *f*; ~ **record** *n* COMP, DP enregistrement de données *m*; ~ **recorder** *n* COMP, DP, ELEC enregistreur de données *m*; ~ **recording** *n* COMP, DP, TELECOM enregistrement de données *m*; ~ **recording back** *n* PHOTO dos avec enregistrement de données de prise de vue *m*; ~ **recovery system** *n* RAD PHYS système d'acquisition de données *m*; ~ **reduction** *n* COMP, DP réduction de données *f*; ~ **relay satellite** *n (DRS)* SPACE satellite relais de données *m*; ~ **representation** *n* COMP, DP représentation de données *f*; ~ **retrieval** *n* COMP recherche des données *f*, DP extraction des données *f*, recherche d'information *f*;

~ s ~ **security** *n* (AmE) *(cf data privacy)* COMP, DP confidentialité de données *f*; ~ **set** *n* COMP, DP ensemble de données *m*, GAS TECH jeu de données *m*; ~ **set definition** *n* COMP, DP définition de la structure de données *f*; ~ **set identifier** *n (DSI)* TELECOM identificateur de modem *m*; ~ **set ready** *n (DSR)* COMP, TELECOM modem prêt *m*, poste de données prêt *m*; ~ **sheet** *n* VEHICLES fiche *f*; ~ **signaling rate** *n* (AmE), ~ **signalling rate** *n* (BrE) TELECOM débit binaire *m*; ~ **sink** *n* ELEC ENG récepteur d'information *m*, TELECOM collecteur de données *m*; ~ **source** *n* ELEC ENG émetteur d'informations *m*, TELECOM station de données *f*; ~ **station** *n* COMP, DP station de données *f*; ~ **storage** *n* COMP, DP mémorisation de données *f*, stockage de données *m*, ELEC ENG mémorisation d'information *f*, NUCLEAR mise en mémoire de données *f*; ~ **store** *n (DS)* COMP mémoire de données *f*; ~ **stream** *n* COMP, DP flot de données *m*, ELEC ENG flux d'informations *m*, TELECOM flot de données *m*; ~ **structure** *n* COMP, DP structure de données *f*; ~ **switch** *n* TELECOM commutateur de données *m*; ~ **switching** *n* TELECOM commutation de données *f*; ~ **switching exchange** *n (DSE)* COMP, TELECOM centre de commutation de données *m*;

~ t ~ **table** *n* PROD ENG table de données *f*; ~ **table failure** *n* PROD ENG défaut de la table de données *m*; ~ **table section specifier** *n* PROD ENG spécificateur de la section de la table de données *m*; ~ **tablet** *n* COMP, DP tablette Rand *f*, tablette à numériser *f*; ~ **table word address** *n* PROD ENG adresse de mots de la table de données *f*; ~ **terminal** *n* COMP, DP terminal de données *m*, TELECOM terminal de traitement de données *m*; ~ **terminal equipment** *n (DTE)* AERONAUT, COMP, TELECOM équipement terminal de données *m*, équipement terminal de traitement de données *m (ETD)*; ~ **terminal ready** *n* TELECOM terminal de données prêt *m*; ~ **transfer** *n* COMP, DP transfert de données *m*; ~ **transfer rate** *n* COMP débit de transfert de données *m*, vitesse de transfert de données *f*, DP vitesse de transfert de données *f*, TELECOM rapidité de transfert de données *f*;

~ transfer requested n TELECOM transfert de données demandé m; **~ transfer system** n TELECOM système de transmission de données m; **~ transmission** n COMP, DP transmission de données f; **~ transmission balloon** n MILIT, TELECOM ballon de transmission de données m; **~ transmission channel** n COMP, DP voie de transmission de données f; **~ transmission rate switch** n PROD ENG interrupteur de sélection de la vitesse de transmission de données m; **~ transport network** n TELECOM réseau de transport m; **~ type** n COMP, DP type de données m;

▪**V** **~ validation** n COMP, DP validation de données f; **~ vet** n COMP, DP validation de données f;

▪**W** **~ word** n COMP, DP mot de données m

databank n COMP, DP, ELECTRON banque de données f, informathèque f

database n COMP, DP, ELECTRON base de données f, informathèque f, TELECOM base de données f; **~ administrator** n (DBA) COMP, DP administrateur de base de données m; **~ management** n (DBM) COMP, DP gestion de base de données f (GBD); **~ management software** n TELECOM système de gestion de bases de données m; **~ management system** n (DBMS) COMP, DP, TELECOM système de gestion de bases de données m (SGBD); **~ manager** n COMP, DP gestionnaire de base de données m; **~ mapping** n COMP configuration de base de données f; **~ query** n COMP, DP interrogation de base de données f

datagram n COMP, DP, TELECOM packet switching datagramme m

dataphone n (TM) COMP, DP modem m, ELECTRON coupleur téléphonique m

datarom n (TM) OPT Sony datarom m (MD)

date:¹ **out of ~** adj PROP MAT suranné

date² n GEOL âge m, âge absolu m; **~ and time of transmission** n TELECOM date et heure de transmission f; **~ code** n PACKAGING code dateur m; **~ of filling** n PATENTS date de dépôt f; **~ freight inward** n PROD ENG date d'arrivée usine f; **~ of grant** n PATENTS date de délivrance f; **~ line** n NAUT ligne de changement de date f; **~ of manufacture** n PACKAGING date de fabrication f; **~ or time of preparation** n TELECOM date ou heure de préparation f; **~ of registration** n PATENTS date d'enregistrement f

dater n COMP, DP horodateur m

datholite n MINERAL datolite f

dating n GEOL, PHYS datation f; **~ program** n COMP programme horodateur m

datiscin n CHEM datiscine f

dative: **~ bond** n CHEM liaison dative f

datolite n MINERAL datolite f

datum n COMP donnée f, CONST base f, base d'opérations f, ligne d'opérations f, pieu de fondation m, plan de comparaison m, point de repère m, repère m, DP, TESTING donnée f; **~ horizon** n GEOL horizon repère m, niveau repère m; **~ level** n CONST plan de comparaison m; **~ line** n CONST base f, base d'opérations f, ligne d'opérations f, MECH ligne de référence f, MECH ENG axe de référence m, ligne de référence f, SPACE ligne de référence f; **~ plane** n CONST plan de comparaison m, GEOL surface de référence f; **~ point** n CONST point de repère m, repère m

daub vt PROD ENG founding garnir

daubing n PROD ENG founding garnissage m

daughter: **~ board** n ELECTRON carte enfichable f, carte fille f; **~ isotope** n GEOL isotope fille m, isotope radio-

génique m; **~ nuclide** n RAD PHYS noyau du descendant radioactif m; **~ product** n PHYS, RAD PHYS descendant radioactif m

davit n MECH lifting gear bossoir m, NAUT bossoir m, portemanteau m; **~ fall** n NAUT garant de bossoir m

Davy: **~ lamp** n COAL TECH lampe Davy f

davyne n MINERAL davyne f

day n PHYS jour m; **~ boat** n NAUT bateau diurne m; **~ drift** n MINING fendue f, galerie de niveau débouchant au jour f; **~ exterior** n CINEMAT extérieur jour m; **~ for night** n CINEMAT effet de nuit m, nuit américaine f; **~ hole** n MINING due to subsidence fondis à jour m; **~ level** n MINING fendue f, galerie de niveau débouchant au jour f; **~ range** n AERONAUT portée diurne f; **~ tank** n C&G four journalier m, NUCLEAR for oil caisse de service f, réservoir journalier m, réservoir relais m; **~ to busy hour ratio** n TELECOM rapport du trafic journalier au trafic à l'heure chargée m; **~ traffic** n TELECOM trafic journalier m

day-fuel: **~ tank** n NUCLEAR caisse de service f, réservoir journalier m, réservoir relais m

Day-Glo: **~ paint** n (TM) COLOURS peinture luminescente f, P&R peinture lumineuse f

daylight n MECH ENG ouverture du moule f, P&R press ouverture libre f; **~ colliery** n COAL TECH houillère à ciel ouvert f; **~ color film** n (AmE), **~ colour film** n (BrE) PHOTO film couleur lumière du jour m; **~ exposure** n PHOTO prise de vue à la lumière du jour f; **~ film** n CINEMAT pellicule lumière de jour f; **~ lamp** n CINEMAT lampe lumière de jour f; **~ loading** n CINEMAT chargement à la lumière du jour m; **~ loading tank** n PHOTO cuve à chargement en plein jour f; **~ magazine** n CINEMAT magasin plein jour m; **~ mine** n MINING fondrière f, mine à ciel ouvert f, minière à ciel ouvert f; **~ photography** n PHOTO photographie à la lumière du jour f; **~ screen** n CINEMAT écran plein jour m

day-night: **~ mirror** n VEHICLES écran antiéblouissant m

dayworks n pl CONST travaux en régie m pl

dazzle n SAFETY lumière éblouissante f

dB abbr (decibel) ACOUSTICS, PHYS, POLLUTION, RAD PHYS, RECORDING dB (décibel)

DBA abbr (database administrator) COMP, DP administrateur de base de données m

DBM abbr COMP (database management), DP (database management) GBD (gestion de base de données), ELECTRON (double-balanced mixer) mélangeur symétrique double m

DBMS abbr (database management system) COMP, DP, TELECOM SGBD (système de gestion de bases de données)

DBS abbr (direct broadcasting satellite) TELECOM satellite de transmission en direct m

DBST abbr (double bituminous surface treatment) CONST revêtement bicouche m

DC¹ abbr COMP (device control), DP (device control) gestion des périphériques f, ELEC ENG (direct current) CC (courant continu), ELEC ENG (directional coupler) coupleur directif m, ELECTRON (direct current), PROD ENG (direct current), RAIL (direct current), RECORDING (direct current), TELECOM (direct current), TV (direct current) CC (courant continu)

DC:² **~ ammeter** n ELEC ENG ampèremètre continu m, ampèremètre pour courant continu m; **~ amplification** n ELECTRON amplification d'un courant continu f; **~ amplifier** n ELECTRON amplificateur à courant continu m; **~ balancer** n ELEC generator dynamo compensatrice *f*; ~ **bias** *n* RECORDING polarisation en courant continu *f*; ~ **biasing** *n* TV polarisation en courant continu *f*; ~ **boost** *n* PROD ENG amplificateur à courant continu *m*; ~ **bridge** *n* ELEC ENG pont à courant continu *m*; ~ **circuit** *n* ELEC ENG circuit à courant continu *m*; ~ **clamp diode** *n* TV diode de clamp *f*, diode de niveau *f*; ~ **component** *n* TELECOM composante continue *f*; **converter** *n* ELEC convertisseur en courant continu *m*; ~ **current gain** *n* ELECTRON gain en courant continu *m*; ~ **erase head** *n* RECORDING tête d'effacement en courant continu *f*; ~ **generation** *n* ELEC ENG génération continue *f*; ~ **generator** *n* ELEC ENG génératrice à courant continu *f*, ELEC ENG génératrice continue *f*, génératrice à courant continu *f*, PHYS dynamo à courant continu *f*, génératrice à courant continu *f*; ~ **high-tension power transmission** *n* ELEC ENG transport d'énergie haute tension en courant continu *m*; ~ **input** *n* ELEC ENG entrée continue *f*, entrée en courant continu *f*; ~ **insertion** *n* TV insertion de la composante continue *f*; ~ **isolation** *n* ELEC ENG isolement en courant continu *m*; ~ **Josephson effect** *n* ELEC ENG, PHYS effet Josephson continu *m*; ~ **level** *n* TV niveau de la composante continue *m*; ~ **machine** *n* ELEC ENG machine à courant continu *f*; ~ **meter** *n* ELEC appareil de mesure pour courant continu *m*; ~ **motor** *n* ELEC, ELEC ENG, PHYS moteur à courant continu *m*; ~ **network** *n* ELEC ENG réseau à courant continu *m*; ~ **noise** *n* RECORDING bruit de polarisation continue *m*; ~ **output** *n* ELEC ENG sortie continue *f*, sortie en courant continu *f*; ~ **potentiometer** *n* ELEC *relay* potentiomètre à courant continu *m*; ~ **relay** *n* ELEC ENG relais à courant continu *m*; ~ **resistance** *n* ELEC ENG résistance en courant continu *f*; ~ **servomotor** *n* ELEC ENG servomoteur à courant continu *m*; ~ **signaling** *n* (AmE), ~ **signalling** *n* (BrE) ELECTRON transmission par courant continu *f*; ~ **supply** *n* ELEC *network* alimentation continue *f*, ELEC ENG alimentation à courant continu *f*; ~ **switching** *n* ELEC ENG commutation de courant continu *f*; ~ **transducer** *n* ELEC ENG capteur à courant continu *m*; ~ **transformer** *n* ELEC ENG transformateur à courant continu *m*; ~ **voltage** *n* ELEC ENG tension continue *f*; ~ **voltage source** *n* ELEC ENG source de tension continue *f*; ~ **voltmeter** *n* ELEC ENG voltmètre continu *m*, voltmètre à courant continu *m*, voltmètre à tension continue *m*

DC/DC: ~ **converter** *n* SPACE convertisseur continu-continu *m*

DCC *abbr* ELEC *(double-cotton-covered)* guipé au coton double, TELECOM *(data communication channel)* canal de communication de données *m*, canal de transmission de données *m*, voie de données *f*, TELECOM *(data collection centre, data collection center)* centre de collecte de données *m*

DC-coupled: ~ **amplifier** *n* ELECTRON amplificateur à liaison directe *m*

DCD *abbr (data carrier detect)* TELECOM détection de porteuse de données *f*

DCE[1] *abbr* TELECOM *(data circuit terminal equipment)* ETCD *(équipement terminal de circuit de données)*, TELECOM *(data communications equipment)* installation de transmission de données *f*

DCE:[2] ~ **source** *n* TELECOM origine ETCD *f*

D-channel *n* TELECOM *ISDN* canal D *m*; ~ **virtual circuit** *n* TELECOM *ISDN* circuit virtuel sur canal D *m*

DCME[1] *abbr (digital circuit multiplication equipment)* TELECOM EMCN *(équipement de multiplication de circuit numérique)*

DCME:[2] ~ **frame** *n* TELECOM trame EMCN *f*; ~ **function** *n* TELECOM fonction EMCN *f*; ~ **gain** *n* TELECOM gain de l'EMCN *m*; ~ **overload** *n* TELECOM mode de surcharge EMCN *m*, surcharge EMCN *f*

DCMG *abbr (digital circuit multiplication gain)* TELECOM GMCN *(gain de l'équipement de multiplication de circuit numérique)*

DCMS *abbr (digital circuit multiplication system)* TELECOM SMCN *(système de multiplication de circuit numérique)*

DCP *abbr (data collection platform)* SPACE plate-forme de collecte de données *f*

DCS *abbr* TELECOM *(defined context set)* ensemble des contextes définis *m*, TELECOM *(digital command signal)* signal de commande numérique *m*

DC-to-AC: ~ **conversion** *n* ELEC ENG conversion cc-ca *f*, conversion continu-alternatif *f*, conversion de continu en alternatif *f*; ~ **converter** *n* ELEC ENG convertisseur cc-ac *m*, convertisseur continu-alternatif *m*, convertisseur de continu en alternatif *m*

DC-to-DC: ~ **conversion** *n* ELEC ENG conversion continu-continu *f*; ~ **converter** *n* ELEC ENG convertisseur continu-continu *m*

DDC *abbr (direct digital control)* COMP, DP commande numérique directe *f*

DDD *abbr (AmE) (direct distance dialing)* TELECOM interurbain automatique *m*, sélection à distance de l'abonné demandé *f*

DDE *abbr (direct data entry)* COMP, DP entrée directe de données *f*

DDI *abbr* (BrE) *(direct dialling in)* TELECOM accès directe à l'arrivée *f*, selection directe à un poste *f*

DDL *abbr (data description language)* COMP langage de description de données *m*

DDP *abbr (distributed data processing)* COMP informatique distribuée *f*

de: ~ **Broglie waves** *n pl* ELEC ENG, PHYS, RAD PHYS ondes brogliennes *f pl*, ondes de de Broglie *f pl*; ~ **luxe edition** *n* PRINT édition de luxe *f*

deacidification *n* HYDROL élimination de CO_2 *f*

deactivate *vt* COAL TECH désactiver, MECH ENG désexciter, neutraliser

deactivation *n* CHEM désactivation *f*

dead[1] *adj* COAL TECH stérile

dead:[2] ~ **ahead** *adv* NAUT droit devant; ~ **astern** *adv* NAUT droit derrière; ~ **slow ahead** *adv* NAUT *engine* en avant très lente; ~ **slow astern** *adv* NAUT *engine* en arrière très lente

dead:[3] ~ **air** *n* TV coupure d'antenne *f*, temps mort *m*; ~ **anneal** *n* THERMOD *metals* recuit de coalescence *m*; ~ **axle** *n* MECH ENG essieu fixe *m*; ~ **band** *n* ELEC ENG *of regulator* plage d'insensibilité *f*, plage neutre *f*; ~ **bolt** *n* CONST *locksmithing* pêne dormant *m*; ~ **calm** *n* HYDROL *marine*, NAUT *meteorology* calme plat *m*; ~ **center** *n* (AmE), ~ **centre** *n* (BrE) MECH point mort *m*, MECH ENG *of lathe* pointe *f*, VEHICLES *of engine, piston* point mort *m*; ~ **coil** *n* SPRINGS spire morte *f*; ~ **dike** *n* (AmE) *see dead dyke*; ~ **dyeing** *n* COLOURS teinture mate *f*, teinture terne *f*; ~ **dyke** *n* (BrE) FUELLESS digue sans centrale *f*; ~ **end** *n* MECH ENG bout mort *m*, RECORDING *of room* zone morte *f*; ~ **ended feeder** *n* ELEC *supply* feeder final *m*, feeder à impasse *m*, ligne à impasse *f*; ~ **end feeder** *n* ELEC *supply* feeder final *m*, feeder à impasse *m*, ligne à impasse *f*; ~ **end station** *n*

TRANSP gare en cul-de-sac *f*; ~ **end switch** *n* MINING interrupteur de chantier *m*; ~ **end tower** *n* ELEC *supply network* pylone d'étai *m*, pylône d'arrêt *m*, pylône étayé *m*; ~ **end trap** *n* REFRIG piège à l'aspiration *m*; ~ **freight** *n* PETR TECH faux fret *m*, fret sur le vide *m*; ~ **ground** *n* MINING morts-terrains *m pl*; ~ **halt** *n* COMP arrêt immédiat *m*; ~ **line anchor** *n* PETR TECH ancrage du brin mort *m*; ~ **load** *n* CONST poids mort *m*, poids propre *m*; ~ **loss system** *n* PROD ENG système à perte sèche *m*; ~ **man's control** *n* TRANSP dispositif de l'homme mort *m*; ~ **oil** *n* PETR TECH huile morte *f*; ~ **pulley** *n* MECH ENG poulie folle *f*; ~ **reckoning** *n* AERONAUT *navigation*, NAUT *navigation* navigation à l'estime *f*, OCEANOG estime *f*, point estimé *m*; ~ **reckoning position** *n* NAUT, OCEANOG point estimé *m*; ~ **room** *n* ACOUSTICS salle sourde *f*, PHYS *anechoic room* chambre sourde *f*, salle sourde *f*, RECORDING chambre sourde *f*; ~ **sand** *n* PROD ENG *founding* sable brûlé *m*, sable de râperie *m*, sable gris *m*; ~ **sector** *n* RAIL section neutre *f*; ~ **short circuit** *n* ELEC ENG court-circuit franc *m*; ~ **soft anneal** *n* THERMOD *metals* recuit complet *m*, recuit d'adoucissement complet *m*; ~ **spindle** *n* MECH ENG arbre de la poupée mobile *m*, *of lathe* arbre *m*; ~ **spot** *n* CINEMAT point mort *m*; ~ **steam** *n* HYDR EQUIP, THERMOD vapeur d'échappement *f*, vapeur épuisée *f*; ~ **stick landing** *n* AERONAUT atterrissage sans moteur *m*; ~ **tide** *n* OCEANOG étale de courant *m*; ~ **time** *n* COMP, DP temps mort *m*, ELECTRON temps de récupération *m*; ~ **wall** *n* CONST mur orbe *m*; ~ **water** *n* OCEANOG eau morte *f*, remous *m*; ~ **works** *n pl* NAUT *ship design* oeuvres mortes *f pl*; ~ **zone** *n* COMP, DP zone inactive *f*, RECORDING *of room* zone morte *f*

deadbeam: ~ **axle** *n* AUTO faux essieu *m*

deadbeat *n* RECORDING oscillation annulée *f*

dead-burned *adj* THERMOD *ceramics* cuit à mort, surcuit

dead-center: ~ **notch** *n* (AmE), **dead-centre notch** *n* (BrE) MECH ENG *quadrant* cran de point mort *m*

deaden *vt* MECH ENG amortir

deadening *n* CONST *building* amortissement *m*, opération de rendre rugueux *f*

dead-front: ~ **connector** *n* ELEC ENG connecteur à contacts protégés *m*

deadhead *n* MECH ENG *tailstock of lathe* contre-pointe *f*, contre-poupée *f*, poupée courante *f*, poupée mobile *f*, PROD ENG *shrinkage head* masselotte *f*

deading *n* PROD ENG *lagging* enveloppe *f*, garniture *f*

dead-length-type: ~ **chuck** *n* MECH ENG *machine tools* mandrin type sans retrait *m*

deadlight *n* NAUT *shipbuilding* contre-hublot *m*, RAIL panneau à claire-voie *m*

deadline *n* CINEMAT, TV date limite *f*; ~ **conformity** *n* PROD ENG respect des délais *m*

deadlock *n* COMP blocage complet *m*, CONST serrure à pêne dormant *f*, DP blocage *m*

deadly: ~ **embrace** *n* COMP blocage complet *m*

deadman *n* NAUT *deck fittings* bonhomme *m*, PETR point fixe d'amarrage *m*

deadplate *n* C&G plaque de refroidissement *f*, PROD ENG *front support of grate bars* plaque d'avant-foyer *f*, sole *f*

deadrise *n* NAUT *ship design* relevé des varangues *m*

deads *n pl* MINING déblais de mine *m pl*, déchets *m pl*, rebuts *m pl*, stériles *m pl*

dead-smooth: ~ **cut** *n* PROD ENG *of file* coupe très douce *f*

dead-weight *n* MECH poids mort *m*, NAUT *ship design*, PETR TECH port en lourd *m*; ~ **pressure gage** *n* (AmE),

~ **pressure gauge** *n* (BrE) PHYS manomètre à piston *m*; ~ **scale** *n* NAUT *ship design* échelle de charge *f*; ~ **tonnage** *n* PETR TECH port en lourd *m*; ~ **tons** *n* PETR TECH port en lourd utile *m*

deadwood *n* NAUT *boat building* massif *m*

dead-work *n* MINING dispositifs de mines *m pl*, travaux de premier établissement *m pl*, travaux préparatoires *m pl*

dead-workings *n* MINING chantier en mort-terrain *m*

deaerator *n* AERONAUT, PETR TECH désaérateur *m*

deaf-muteness *n* ACOUSTICS surdi-mutité *f*

deafness *n* ACOUSTICS surdité *f*

deal *n* CONST ais *m*, madrier *m*, planche *f*

dealer: ~ **room technology** *n* TELECOM technologie des salles de transaction *f*

dealkalization *n* C&G désalcalinisation *f*

deaminase *n* CHEM déaminase *f*

Dean: ~ **and Stark apparatus** *n* LAB EQUIP *water content* appareil Dean Stark *m*

deanamorphoser *n* CINEMAT désanamorphoseur *m*

deasphalted: ~ **oil** *n* (DAO) PETR TECH huile désasphaltée *f*

debacle *n* OCEANOG débâcle *f*

deballasting: ~ **water** *n* POLLUTION eau de déballastage *f*

debiteuse *n* C&G débiteuse *f*; ~ **bubble** *n* C&G bouillon de débiteuse *m*

debituminization *n* COAL TECH débituminisation *f*

deblock *vt* COMP, DP dégrouper

deblocking *n* COMP, DP dégroupage *m*

debond: ~ **length** *n* PROP MAT longueur de décohésion *f*

debonding *n* PROP MAT décohésion *f*, décollage *m*

debottlenecking *n* PETR TECH dégoulottage *m*

debriefing *n* SPACE débreffage *m*

debris *n* COAL TECH détritus *m*, GEOL déblais *m pl*, débris *m pl*, éboulis *m*, METALL débris *m pl*; ~ **flow** *n* GEOL coulée boueuse *f*; ~ **removal** *n* PETR TECH *on sea bed* nettoyage *m*

debug *vt* COMP, DP déboguer, mettre au point

debugger *n* COMP débogueur *m*, programme de déverminage *m*, programme de mise au point *m*, DP programme de déverminage *m*, programme de mise au point *m*

debugging *n* COMP, DP mise au point *f*

debunching *n* ELECTRON dégroupement *m*

debur *vt* MECH ENG ébavurer

deburred: ~ **end** *n* SPRINGS extrémité ébavurée *f*

deburring *n* C&G débandage *m*, MECH, MECH ENG ébavurage *m*; ~ **machine** *n* MECH ENG *machine tool* machine à ébavurer *f*, SPRINGS ébarbeuse *f*; ~ **tool** *n* MECH ENG fraise conique à ébavurer *f*

Debye: ~ **frequency** *n* PHYS fréquence de Debye *f*; ~ **model** *n* PHYS *solids* modèle de Debye *m*; ~ **temperature** *n* PHYS température de Debye *f*

Debye-Waller: ~ **factor** *n* CRYSTALL facteur de Debye-Waller *m*

deca- *pref (da)* METR déca *(da)*

decade: ~ **attenuator** *n* ELECTRON atténuateur à dix positions *m*; ~ **box** *n* AERONAUT, ELEC ENG boîte à décades *f*; ~ **capacitance box** *n* ELEC ENG boîte de capacités *f*; ~ **inductance box** *n* ELEC ENG boîte d'inductances *f*; ~ **oscillator** *n* ELECTRON oscillateur à décades *m*; ~ **resistance box** *n* ELEC ENG boîte de résistance *f*; ~ **scaler** *n* ELECTRON diviseur par dix *m*, échelle de comptage décimale *f*, échelle de dix *f*, échelle décimale *f*

decaffeinated *adj* FOOD TECH décaféiné

decagon n GEOM décagone m

decagram n (AmE), **decagramme** n (BrE) METR décagramme m

decahedral adj GEOM décaèdre

decahedron n GEOM décaèdre m

decahydronaphthalene n CHEM décahydronaphtalène m, décaline f

decal n (AmE) (cf transfer) C&G décalcomanie f

decalcification n HYDROL décalcification f

decalcify vt CHEM décalcifier

decalin n CHEM décahydronaphtalène m, décaline f

decaliter n (AmE), **decalitre** n (BrE) METR décalitre m

decameter n (AmE), **decametre** n (BrE) METR décamètre m

decametric: ~ **wave** n TELECOM onde décimétrique f

decane n CHEM décane m

decanning n NUCLEAR of fuel element dégainage retraitement m

decanoic adj CHEM décanoïque

decanol n CHEM décanol m

decant vt CHEM, CHEM TECH décanter, transvaser

decantation n CHEM TECH décantage m, décantation f, transvasement m, FOOD TECH, PETR TECH, PROP MAT décantation f; ~ **glass** n CHEM TECH décanteur m, récipient de séparation m; ~ **rate** n CHEM TECH vitesse de décantation f, vitesse de dépôt f, vitesse de sédimentation f; ~ **speed** n CHEM TECH vitesse de décantation f, vitesse de dépôt f, vitesse de sédimentation f; ~ **tank** n CHEM TECH récipient séparateur m; ~ **vessel** n CHEM TECH décanteur m, récipient de séparation m

decanter n CHEM TECH appareil à décanter m, POLLUTION chambre de décantation f

decanting n CHEM décantation f; ~ **glass** n CHEM TECH décanteur m; ~ **machine** n CHEM TECH machine à décanter f

decarb vt (AmE) (cf decarbonize) COAL TECH décarboniser

decarbonate vt CHEM TECH, COAL TECH décarbonater

decarbonation n GEOL décarbonatation f

decarbonization n CHEM décarburation f, COAL TECH décarbonisation f, THERMOD décalaminage m, décarbonisation f

decarbonize vt CHEM décarburer, CHEM TECH, COAL TECH décarboniser, THERMOD décalaminer, décarboniser

decarbonizing n CHEM décalaminage m

decarboxylase n CHEM décarboxylase f

decarboxylation n CHEM décarboxylation f

decarburization n PROP MAT décarburation f

decatize vt TEXTILES décatir

decatizing n TEXTILES décatissage m; ~ **machine** n TEXTILES décatiseur m

decay[1] n ELECTRON évanouissement m, NUCLEAR of atom décroissance f, désintégration f, RAD PHYS radioactive désintégration f, RECORDING affaiblissement m, amortissement m, décroissance f, TV décroissance de luminescence f, désintégration f; ~ **cavity** n NUCLEAR puits de désactivation m; ~ **chain** n PHYS chaîne de désintégration f; ~ **characteristic** n ELEC ENG caractéristique de persistance f; ~ **constant** n GEOL, PHYS, RAD PHYS constante de désintégration f; ~ **curve** n RAD PHYS courbe de désintégration f, RECORDING courbe de décroissance f; ~ **date** n SPACE spacecraft date de retombée f; ~ **factor** n ELEC ENG facteur d'amortissement m, RECORDING facteur de décroissance m; ~

mode n RAD PHYS mode de désintégration m; ~ **particle** n PART PHYS particule de désintégration f; ~ **rate** n ACOUSTICS taux de décroissance m, ELECTRON of cathode ray tube brightness temps de décroissance m, vitesse de décroissance f, RAD PHYS taux de désintégration m, TV ratio de décroissance m, taux de décroissance m, temps de décroissance m; ~ **time** n COMP, DP temps de descente m, ELEC ENG of device dial temps de retour à zéro m, ELECTRON of gas tube temps d'extinction m, of pulse temps de descente m, of storage tube temps de mémorisation m, PETR temps de dégradation m, PHYS of pulse temps de descente m, temps de décroissance m, temps de suppression m

decay[2] vi PHYS nuclear, RAD PHYS radioactivity se désintégrer

decelerate vti MECH, PHYS décélérer, ralentir, retarder

decelerated adj PHYS décéléré, ralenti, retardé

deceleration n MECH, PHYS décélération f, ralentissement m, retardation f, SPACE décélération f; ~ **lane** n TRANSP voie de décélération f, voie de ralentissement f; ~ **parachute** n TRANSP parachute frein m; ~ **time** n COMP, DP temps de décélération m

decelerometer n SPACE décéléromètre m

decentralized[1] adj COMP, DP décentralisé

decentralized:[2] ~ **system** n TELECOM système décentralisé m

deception: ~ **signal** n ELECTRON signal de diversion m

deceptive: ~ **packaging** n PACKAGING emballage trompeur m

dechenite n MINERAL déchénite f

dechlorination n HYDROL déchloration f

deci pref (d) METR déci

decibel n (dB) ACOUSTICS, PHYS, POLLUTION, RAD PHYS, RECORDING décibel m (bel); ~ **scale** n RECORDING échelle en décibels f

deciduous: ~ **wood** n PAPER TECH bois en feuillu m, bois non-résineux m

decigram n (AmE), **decigramme** n (BrE) METR décigramme m

deciliter n (AmE), **decilitre** n (BrE) METR décilitre m

decimal[1] adj DP, MATH décimal

decimal:[2] ~ **candle** n METR bougie décimale f, pyr m; ~ **notation** n COMP, DP numération décimale f, MATH, TELECOM notation décimale f; ~ **point** n COMP, DP, MATH virgule décimale f

decimal-to-binary: ~ **conversion** n ELECTRON conversion décimale-binaire f; ~ **converter** n ELECTRON convertisseur décimal-binaire m

decimeter n (AmE), **decimetre** n (BrE) METR décimètre m

decineper n ACOUSTICS décinéper m

decinormal adj CHEM solution décinormal

decipher vt ELECTRON déchiffrer

deciphering n ELECTRON déchiffrage m

decipherment n TELECOM déchiffrement m

decision n COMP, DP décision f ~ **content** n COMP contenu décisionnel m, DP quantité de décision f; ~ **height** n AERONAUT hauteur de décision f; ~ **speed** n (V1) AERONAUT vitesse de décision f (V1); ~ **table** n DP table de décision f; ~ **theory** n MATH théorie de la décision f; ~ **tree** n DP arbre de décision m

deck n CONST bridge chaussée f, tablier m, DP for magnetic tapes dérouleur de bande magnétique m, of cards jeu de cartes m, MINING of mine, shaft plancher m, of shaft cage étage m, NAUT shipbuilding pont m; ~ **beam** n NAUT shipbuilding barrot de pont m; ~ **bridge** n

CONST pont à tablier supérieur *m*; ~ **cargo** *n* NAUT
pontée *f*; ~ **crane** *n* NAUT grue de bord *f*; ~ **fittings** *n pl*
NAUT accastillage de pont *m*; ~ **girder** *n* NAUT *shipbuilding* hiloire sous barrots *f*; ~ **light** *n* NAUT lentille de
pont *f*, projecteur de pont *m*; ~ **line** *n* NAUT ligne de
pont *f*, livet de pont *m*; ~ **load** *n* NAUT pontée *f*; ~
longitudinal *n* NAUT *shipbuilding* lisse de pont *f*, longitudinal de pont *m*; ~ **officer** *n* NAUT officier de pont *m*;
~ **pillar** *n* NAUT *shipbuilding* épontille *f*; ~ **plan** *n* NAUT
ship design plan des ponts *m*; ~ **plate** *n* NAUT tôle de
pont *f*; ~ **plating** *n* NAUT *shipbuilding* bordé de pont *m*;
~ **sprinkler system** *n* NAUT dispositif à eau diffusée sur
pont *m*; ~ **stringer** *n* NAUT virure de gouttière *f*; ~
structure *n* NAUT *shipbuilding* structure de pont *f*; ~
switch *n* ELEC ENG commutateur à galette *m*; ~ **transverse** *n* NAUT *shipbuilding* barrot transversal *m*,
transversal du pont *m*

decked *adj* NAUT *shipbuilding* ponté

decker *n* PAPER TECH épaississeur *m*

deckhead *n* NAUT plafond *m*; ~ **light** *n* NAUT plafonnier *m*

deck-hull: ~ **bonding** *n* NAUT *shipbuilding* liaison pont-
coque *f*

decking *n* CONST carrelage *m*, parquetage *m*, planchéiage *m*, NAUT *shipbuilding* pontage *m*

deckle *n* PAPER TECH couverte *f*, largeur totale *f*; ~ **board**
n PAPER TECH réglette de bordure *f*; ~ **edge** *n* PAPER
TECH bord à la cuve *m*; ~ **pulley** *n* PAPER TECH tambour
de couverture *m*; ~ **strap** *n* PAPER TECH courroie-
guide *f*

deckled *adj* PACKAGING *paper* frangeux

decladding *n* NUCLEAR dégainage retraitement *m*

declaration *n* COMP, DP déclaration *f*

declarative *n* COMP, DP déclaration *f*, déclarative *f*; ~
statement *n* COMP, DP instruction déclarative *f*

declare *vt* COMP, DP déclarer

declination *n* ASTRON, FUELLESS, NAUT *celestial navigation*, PETR, PHYS déclinaison *f*; ~ **angle** *n* AERONAUT
angle de déclinaison *m*; ~ **axis** *n* ASTRON, INSTRUMENT
axe de déclinaison *m*; ~ **bearing** *n* INSTRUMENT palier
de déclinaison *m*; ~ **circle** *n* INSTRUMENT, PHYS cercle
de déclinaison *m*; ~ **drive** *n* ASTRON moteur horaire *m*;
~ **gear** *n* INSTRUMENT mécanisme de déclinaison *m*

decline *n* HYDROL baisse *f*

declinometer *n* PHYS déclinomètre *m*

declutch *vti* MECH ENG, VEHICLES débrayer

decoction *n* FOOD TECH décoction *f*

decode *vt* COMP, DP, ELECTRON, SPACE *communications*
décoder, TELECOM déchiffrer, décoder, TV décoder

decode-encode *vt* TV décoder-coder

decoder *n* COMP, DP, ELECTRON, TELECOM, TV décodeur *m*

decoding *n* COMP, DP, ELECTRON, SPACE *communications*
décodage *m*, TELECOM déchiffrement *m*, décodage *m*,
TV décodage *m*, décryptage *m*; ~ **device** *n* TRANSP
dispositif de décodage *m*; ~ **matrix** *n* TV matrice de
décodage *f*

decohesion *n* METALL décohésion *f*

decoiler *n* PROD ENG débobinoir *m*

decollate *vt* COMP, DP déliasser

decollator *n* COMP, DP, PRINT déliasseuse *f*

decolorizer *n* (AmE), **decolourizer** *n* (BrE) C&G décolorant *m*

decommissioned *adj* NAUT *ship* désarmé

decommissioning *n* NUCLEAR déclassement *m*

decommutation *n* ELECTRON décommutation *f*

decommutator *n* ELECTRON décommutateur *m*

decompiler *n* COMP décompilateur *m*

decompose *vt* CHEM décomposer

decomposing: ~ **agent** *n* CHEM décomposant *m*

decomposition *n* CHEM, COMP, DP, FOOD TECH, PETR
TECH décomposition *f*, PROP MAT décomposition *f*,
désagrégation *f*; ~ **by heat** *n* THERMOD décomposition
thermique *f*; ~ **temperature** *n* PACKAGING température
de pourriture *f*

decompression *n* OCEANOG, PETR décompression *f*; ~
chamber *n* NAUT, PETR chambre de décompression *f*,
PETR TECH caisson de décompression *m*, chambre de
décompression *f*; ~ **chart** *n* OCEANOG table de plongée
f; ~ **meter** *n* OCEANOG décompressimètre *m*; ~ **sickness**
n OCEANOG maladie de décompression *f*; ~ **stop** *n*
OCEANOG *diving* palier de décompression *m*; ~ **tables** *n*
pl PETR tables de décompression *f pl*; ~ **time** *n* PETR
temps de décompression *m*

deconfining: ~ **momentum** *n* NUCLEAR impulsion d'a-
blation *f*

decontamination *n* CHEM, CHEM TECH, PROP MAT, RAD
PHYS décontamination *f*; ~ **factor** *n* RAD PHYS facteur
de décontamination *m*; ~ **plant** *n* PROP MAT installation de décontamination *f*; ~ **system** *n* NUCLEAR
système de décontamination *m*

deconvolution *n* ELEC, ELECTRON, NUCLEAR, TELECOM
déconvolution *f*

deconvolved *adj* ELECTRON déconvolué

decorating: ~ **kiln** *n* C&G four à décorer *m*; ~ **lehr** *n* C&G
arche à décorer *f*

decoration: ~ **firing** *n* C&G décoration au four *f*

decorative: ~ **cutting** *n* C&G taille *f*; ~ **varnish** *n* P&R
peinture à effet *f*, vernis à effet *m*

decorrelation *n* TELECOM décorrélation *f*

decorticator *n* FOOD TECH décortiqueuse *f*

decoupled *adj* COMP, DP découplé

decoupling *n* CHEM, ELEC *in AC circuit*, ELEC ENG, SPACE
communications, TELECOM découplage *m*; ~ **capacitor**
n ELEC ENG condensateur de découplage *m*; ~ **filter** *n*
ELECTRON filtre de découplage *m*

decoy: ~ **tank** *n* MILIT faux char d'assaut *m*

decrab *vt* AERONAUT décraber

decrease: ~ **in definition** *n* PHOTO diminution de la
netteté *f*

decrement[1] *n* ELECTRON, PHYS décrément *m*; ~ **in reactivity** *n* NUCLEAR baisse de réactivité *f*

decrement[2] *vt* COMP, DP décrémenter, PRINT diminuer
par fractions régulières

decrementer *n* COMP décrémenteur *m*, DP décrémenteur *m*

decrepitation: ~ **test** *n* C&G essai de décrépitation *m*

decrypt *vt* COMP, DP, ELECTRON décrypter

decryption *n* COMP, DP décryptage *m*, TELECOM déchiffrage *m*

decyl *n* CHEM décyle *m*; ~ **alcohol** *n* CHEM alcool décylique *m*; ~ **bromide** *n* CHEM bromure de décylique *m*

dedendum *n* MECH *gears* creux *m*, MECH ENG profondeur
du creux *f*; ~ **circle** *n* MECH ENG cercle d'évidement *m*; ~
line *n* MECH ENG *in straightgearing* droite d'évidement *f*, ligne de racine *f*

dedicated[1] *adj* COMP dédié, spécialisé, DP dédié, spécialisé

dedicated:[2] ~ **channel** *n* TELECOM voie exclusive *f*, TV
chaîne dédiée *f*, chaîne spécialisée *f*; ~ **chip** *n* ELECTRON
puce spécialisée *f*; ~ **computer** *n* COMP, DP ordinateur
spécialisé *m*; ~ **frequency** *n* TELECOM fréquence réser-

vée f; ~ **line** n COMP, DP ligne dédiée f, ligne spécialisée f, TELECOM ligne spécialisée f; ~ **mode** n COMP, DP mode dédié m; ~ **port** n TELECOM accès par liaison spécialisée m; ~ **signaling channel** n (AmE), ~ **signalling channel** n (BrE) TELECOM canal spécialisé pour la signalisation m

dedust vt COAL TECH dépoussiérer

deduster n COAL TECH dépoussiéreur m

dedusting: ~ **unit** n CONST unité de dépoussiérage f

dee n PHYS cyclotron D, dé m

de-emphasis n ACOUSTICS, ELECTRON, RECORDING, SPACE communications, TV désaccentuation f

de-emulsifier n FOOD TECH désémulsionnant m, MAR POLL désémulsifiant m

de-emulsifying: ~ **agent** n FOOD TECH désémulsionnant m

de-energization n ELEC ENG coupure du courant d'excitation f, désexcitation f

de-energize vt ELEC ENG couper le courant d'excitation, désexciter, PHYS désamorcer, PROD ENG isoler

de-energized: ~ **position** n PROD ENG état de repos m

deep[1] adj TEXTILES shade foncé

deep[2] n OCEANOG fosse f, fossé m; ~ **adit** n WATER SUPP galerie d'écoulement f; ~ **borehole** n MINING sondage profond m; ~ **boring** n MINING forage à grande profondeur m, sondage à grande profondeur m; ~ **color tone** n (AmE), ~ **colour tone** n (BrE) P&R paint ton plein m; ~ **cut** n C&G taille profonde f ~ **depletion** n ELEC ENG déplétion profonde f; ~ **depression** n METEO forte dépression f; ~ **drawing** n MECH, SPRINGS emboutissage profond m; ~ **drawing die** n MECH ENG for forming outillage d'emboutissage profond m; ~ **drawing film** n PACKAGING film pour emboutissage profond m; ~ **drawing foil** n PACKAGING aluminium mince pour emboutissage profond m; ~ **drawing machine** n PACKAGING machine pour emboutissage profond f; ~ **drillhole** n MINING sondage profond m; ~ **drilling** n MINING forage à grande profondeur m, sondage à grande profondeur m; ~ **etching** n C&G gravure profonde f; ~ **etching bath** n C&G bain pour gravure profonde m; ~ **etching paste** n C&G pâte pour gravure profonde f; ~ **fading** n ELECTRON signals évanouissement prononcé m; ~ **foundation** n COAL TECH fondation profonde f; ~ **groove ball bearing** n MECH ENG roulement à billes à gorge profonde m; ~ **ground water** n WATER SUPP eau souterraine profonde f; ~ **inelastic collision** n NUCLEAR collision inélastique en profondeur f; ~ **mine** n MINING mine à grande profondeur f; ~ **nut** n CONST écrou haut m; ~ **rejection trap** n ELECTRON filtre coupe-bande à flancs raides m; ~ **scattering layer** n (DSL) OCEANOG couche diffusante profonde f; ~ **shade** n TEXTILES coloris foncé m; ~ **sleek** n C&G filasse taillée f; ~ **space** n SPACE espace lointain m; ~ **space mission** n SPACE mission interplanétaire f, mission spatiale lointaine f; ~ **space probe** n SPACE sonde d'espace lointain f, sonde lointaine f; ~ **space tracing** n ASTRON poursuite dans l'espace lointain f; ~ **space transponder** n SPACE transpondeur pour sonde en espace lointain m, transpondeur pour sonde lointaine m; ~ **stabilization** n COAL TECH stabilisation profonde f; ~ **tank** n TRANSP caisse profonde f; ~ **ultraviolet radiation** n ELEC ENG rayonnement ultraviolet lointain m; ~ **well** n HYDROL puits profond m, WATER SUPP puits creux m, puits profond m; ~ **well thermometer** n (DWT) PETR thermomètre de fond m

deep-drawn: ~ **packaging** n PACKAGING emballage pro-

fondément embouti m

deepening n MINING approfondissement m

deepest: ~ **ballast condition** n NAUT condition de ballastage maximal f; ~ **seagoing draft** n (AmE), ~ **seagoing draught** n (BrE) NAUT ship design tirant d'eau maximal d'exploitation m

deepfreeze n FOOD TECH packaging navire congélateur m, congélateur horizontal m, REFRIG, THERMOD congélateur m; ~ **packaging** n PACKAGING emballage surgelé m; ~ **ship** n OCEANOG congélateur m, navire congélateur m

deep-freeze vt FOOD TECH, THERMOD surgeler

deep-freezing n PACKAGING, REFRIG, THERMOD surgélation f

deep-frozen[1] adj FOOD TECH congelé à basse température, surgelé, PACKAGING, THERMOD surgelé

deep-frozen:[2] ~ **packaging** n PACKAGING emballage surgelé m

deep-fryer n FOOD TECH friteuse f

deep-hole: ~ **boring** n MECH ENG alésage des trous profonds m

deep-mined: ~ **coal** n COAL TECH charbon d'exploitation souterraine m

deep-pattern: ~ **G cramp** n CONST happe à gros ventre f

deep-sea n NAUT haute mer f; ~ **cable** n NAUT câble des grandes profondeurs m; ~ **diver** n NAUT plongeur sous-marin m; ~ **fan** n GEOL cône de mer profonde m, OCEANOG cône sous-marin m, delta abyssal m; ~ **fishery** n OCEANOG gran de pêche f, pêche hauturière f, pêche au large f; ~ **fishing** n NAUT pêche hauturière f, OCEANOG pêche au large f; ~ **floor** n GEOPHYS fond océanique m; ~ **navigation** n NAUT navigation au long cours f, navigation hauturière f; ~ **oasis** n OCEANOG oasis sous-marine f; ~ **pilot** n NAUT pilote hauturier m; ~ **trench** n GEOPHYS fosse sous-marine f; ~ **trough** n OCEANOG sillon sous-marin m

deep-water: ~ **diving** n PETR plongée profonde f; ~ **dock** n CONST bassin en eaux profondes m; ~ **harbor** n (AmE), ~ **harbour** n (BrE) NAUT port de toute marée m, port en eau profonde m; ~ **line** n NAUT loaded ship ligne de flottaison en charge f; ~ **route** n OCEANOG route en eau profonde f; ~ **waves** n pl PHYS ondes de gravité en eau profonde f pl

de-excitation n GEOPHYS désexcitation f

default[1] adj COMP, DP par défaut

default:[2] ~ **value** n TELECOM valeur par défaut f

defecation n CHEM TECH clarification f, défécation f

defect n CHEM, CRYSTALL, ELEC ENG, METALL défaut m, NUCLEAR défaut m, défectuosité f, PAPER TECH, QUALITY défaut m; ~ **analysis** n RAD PHYS analyse de défaut f; ~ **annealing** n ELECTRON élimination de défaut par recuit f; ~ **conduction** n ELEC ENG conduction lacunaire f; ~ **counting** n QUALITY comptage de défaut m; ~ **density** n ELECTRON taux de défaut m; ~ **fracture** n PROP MAT défaut intercristallin m; ~ **in distribution** n C&G défaut de répartition m; ~ **scattering** n NUCLEAR diffusion par défaut f; ~ **structure** n METALL structure de défaut f

defective[1] adj QUALITY défectueux

defective:[2] ~ **fuel rod** n NUCLEAR crayon combustible défectueux m; ~ **scale** n ACOUSTICS gamme défective f

deferred: ~ **addressing** n COMP, DP adressage différé m; ~ **charges** n pl PROD ENG frais payés à l'avance m pl

defiberer n (AmE) see defibrer

defibering n (AmE) see defibring

defibration n PAPER TECH défibrage transversal m

defibrer *n* (BrE) PAPER TECH affûteuse *f*, défibreur en continu *m* ~ **pit** *n* PAPER TECH fosse sous défibreur *f*

defibring *n* (BrE) PAPER TECH défibrage *m*

deficit: ~ **reactivity** *n* NUCLEAR antiréactivité *f*

defile *n* CONST *physical geography* défilé *m*

defined: ~ **context set** *n (DCS)* TELECOM ensemble des contextes définis *m*

definite: ~ **integral** *n* MATH intégrale au sens de Riemann *f*, intégrale définie *f*

definition *n* CINEMAT définition *f*, netteté *f*, COMP, DP *graphics* définition *f*, résolution *f*, ELECTRON, PHOTO définition *f*; ~ **adjustment** *n* CONTROL mise au point du diaphragme *f*; ~ **chart** *n* CINEMAT mire de netteté *f*; ~ **test pattern** *n* TV mire de définition *f*

definitive: ~ **time relay** *n* ELEC relais à action différée *m*

deflagrate *vi* CHEM, MINING déflagrer, SAFETY déflagrer, exploser violemment

deflagrating: ~ **explosive** *n* MINING explosif déflagrant *m*

deflagration *n* MINING déflagration *f*

deflaker *n* PAPER TECH dépastilleur *m*

deflash *vt* P&R débavurer, ébarber, ébavurer

deflate *vt* MECH ENG dégonfler

deflation *n* VEHICLES *tyre* dégonflement *m*

deflect *vt* MECH ENG défléchir, détourner, dévier, RAD PHYS déflecter, TV dévier, WATER SUPP *stream* détourner

deflected: ~ **beam** *n* TV faisceau dévié *m*

deflecting: ~ **coil** *n* NUCLEAR bobine de déflexion *f*, déflecteur *m*, PHYS bobine de déflection *f*; ~ **electrode** *n* NUCLEAR *of mass spectrometer* électrode de déviation *f*; ~ **valve** *n* HYDR EQUIP clapet *m*, soupape de dérivation *f*

deflection *n* AERONAUT débattement *m*, CONST flèche *f*, ELECTRON déflexion *f*, GEOPHYS déviation *f*, MECH flexion *f*, fléchissement *m*, flèche *f*, MECH ENG, METALL déflexion *f*, NUCLEAR *of fuel element* flèche *f*, PHYS déflection *f*, déviation *f*, RAD PHYS déflection *f*, SPACE *spacecraft* déviation *f*, flexion *f*; ~ **amplifier** *n* ELECTRON amplificateur de déviation *m*; ~ **angle** *n* TV angle de déviation *m*; ~ **by electric fields** *n* RAD PHYS déviation par champs électriques *f*; ~ **by magnetic fields** *n* RAD PHYS déviation par champs magnétiques *f*; ~ **coil** *n* ELEC ENG bobine de déviation *f*; ~ **electrode** *n* ELEC ENG électrode de déviation *f*; ~ **factor** *n* ELECTRON facteur de déviation *m*; ~ **magnet** *n* TV aimant de déviation *m*; ~ **magnetometer** *n* RAD PHYS magnétomètre à déviation *m*; ~ **plate** *n* ELECTRON, RAD PHYS plaque de déviation *f*, SPACE *spacecraft* déflecteur *m*, plaque de déflection *f*, TV plaque de déviation *f*; ~ **ratio** *n* SPRINGS degré de flèche *m*, rapport de flèche *m*; ~ **sensitivity** *n* ELECTRON sensibilité de la déviation *f*; ~ **system** *n* TV bloc de déviation *m*; ~ **to solid** *n* SPRINGS flèche à spires jointives *f*; ~ **tube** *n* RAD PHYS tube à déviation *m*; ~ **under load** *n* SPRINGS flèche sous charge *f*; ~ **when assembled** *n* SPRINGS flèche en place *f*; ~ **yoke** *n* ELECTRON bloc de déviation *m*, déviateur *m*; ~ **yoke pullback** *n* TV jeu du bloc de balayage *m*

deflector *n* AERONAUT déflecteur *m*, grille à aube *f*, CHEM TECH, FUELLESS déflecteur *m*, PAPER TECH mur déflecteur *m*, TELECOM déflecteur *m*; ~ **chute** *n* C&G déflecteur *m*; ~ **plate** *n* AERONAUT plaque de déviation *f*, CHEM TECH tôle de transfert *f*

deflocculant *n* CHEM défloculant *m*

defloccating: ~ **agent** *n* P&R *paints* agent défloculant *m*

defloccation *n* CHEM, HYDROL défloculation *f*

defoamer *n* PAPER TECH antimousse *m*

defoaming: ~ **agent** *n* CHEM additif antimoussant *m*, FOOD TECH antimousse *m*, PETR TECH additif *m*, additif antimousse *m*, agent antimousse *m*

defocus:[1] ~ **effect** *n* CINEMAT flou artistique *m*; ~ **transition** *n* CINEMAT enchaîné au flou *m*

defocus[2] *vt* CINEMAT défocaliser, passer au flou, PROP MAT défocaliser

defocusing *n* ELECTRON, PROP MAT défocalisation *f*

defogging: ~ **fan** *n* AERONAUT ventilateur de désembuage *m*

defoliant *n* CHEM défoliant *m*

deform *vt* MECH déformer

deformable: ~ **rear section** *n* TRANSP partie terminale déformable *f*

deformation *n* CHEM *of molecule*, COAL TECH, GEOL déformation *f*, MECH distorsion *f*, déformation *f*, METALL, NUCLEAR *of nucleus*, P&R, PROP MAT, RAD PHYS *of nucleus* déformation *f*; ~ **ellipsoid** *n* GEOL ellipsoïde de déformation *m*; ~ **modulus** *n* COAL TECH module de déformation *m*; ~ **point** *n* C&G température de ramollissement dilatométrique *f*

deformational: ~ **phase** *n* GEOL *of event* phase de déformation *f*

defrost:[1] ~ **cycle** *n* REFRIG cycle de dégivrage *m*

defrost[2] *vt* FOOD TECH décongeler, REFRIG dégivrer

defrost[3] *vi* FOOD TECH, REFRIG se dégivrer

defroster *n* VEHICLES *accessory* dégivreur *m*

defrosting *n* FOOD TECH décongélation *f*, dégivrage *m*, MECH ENG, REFRIG dégivrage *m*; ~ **test** *n* MECH ENG *of refrigerated cabinet* essai de dégivrage *m*

degas *vt* CHEM TECH dégager du gaz, dégazer, ELECTRON *electric valves* dégazer, MINING *workings* assainir; ~ **workings** *vt* MINING assainir un chantier contaminé

degasification *n* HYDROL dégazage *m*

degasifying *n* CHEM TECH dégagement gazeux *m*, dégazage *m*, extraction de gaz *f*

degasser *n* CHEM TECH, GEOL, HEAT ENG dégazeur *m*

degassing *n* CHEM TECH, ELECTRON *of electric valve*, OCEANOG dégazage *m*

degauss *vt* COMP, MECH ENG, PROD ENG, RECORDING, TV démagnétiser

degausser *n* RECORDING démagnétiseur *m*, effaceur magnétique *m*, TV effaceur magnétique *m*

degaussing *n* COMP, TV démagnétisation *f* ~ **coil** *n* TV bobine de démagnétisation *f*

degeneracy *n* ELECTRON, PHYS dégénérescence *f*

degenerate[1] *adj* ELECTRON, METALL, PHYS dégénéré

degenerate:[2] ~ **electron gas** *n* RAD PHYS gaz électronique dégénéré *m*; ~ **matter** *n* ASTRON, CHEM matière dégénérée *f*; ~ **semiconductor** *n* ELECTRON semiconducteur dégénéré *m*

degeneration *n* ELECTRON dégénération *f*, RAD PHYS *of energy level* dégénérescence *f*

degradation *n* COMP fonctionnement en mode dégradé *m*, DP dégradation *f*, MECH ENG dégradation *f*, détérioration *f*, NUCLEAR *of particles* dégradation *f*, perte *f*, P&R *of fault*, PHYS *of energy* dégradation *f*, QUALITY dégradation *f*, perte de qualité *f*, SPACE dégradation *f*, TV dégradation *f*, détérioration *f*, perte de qualité *f*

degraded: ~ **minute** *n (DM)* TELECOM minute dégradée *f*; ~ **operating conditions** *n pl* SPACE fonctionnement en mode dégradé *m*; ~ **signal** *n* TV signal dégradé *m*; ~ **sync** *n* TV synchronisation défectueuse *f*

degrease *vt* ELEC, FOOD TECH, MECH dégraisser

degreaser *n* ELEC, MECH dégraissant *m*

degreasing *n* C&G, CONST, MECH, MECH ENG dégraissage *m*; ~ **agent** *n* ELEC, MECH dégraissant *m*; ~ **compound** *n* PACKAGING composition dégraissante *f*; ~ **tank** *n* FOOD TECH citerne de dégraissage *f*

degree *n* GEOM, METR, PHYS *of freedom* degré *m*; ~ **Celsius** *n* METR degré Celsius *m*; ~ **of coherence** *n* OPT, TELECOM degré de cohérence *m*; ~ **of compaction** *n* COAL TECH, CONST degré de compactage *m*; ~ **of compliance** *n* TRANSP taux d'obéissance *m*; ~ **of consolidation** *n* COAL TECH degré de consolidation *m*; ~ **of crimp** *n* TEXTILES degré de frisure *m*; ~ **of drying** *n* CONST degré de siccité *m*, degré de séchage *m*; ~ **of heat** *n* THERMOD degré de chaleur *m*; ~ **of incombustibility** *n* PAPER TECH degré d'incombustibilité *m*; ~ **Kelvin** *n* METR degré Kelvin *m*; ~ **of non-flammability** *n* PAPER TECH degré d'ininflammabilité *m*; ~ **of pollution** *n* POLLUTION degré de pollution *m*; ~ **of polymerization** *n* P&R degré de polymérisation *m*; ~ **of protection** *n* PROD ENG indice de protection *m*; ~ **of purification** *n* WATER SUPP degré d'épuration *m*; ~ **of saturation** *n* COAL TECH, TRANSP degré de saturation *m*; ~ **of temperature** *n* THERMOD degré de température *m*; ~ **of utilization** *n* TRANSP charge d'utilisation *f*, degré d'utilisation *m*

degum *vt* TEXTILES *silk* décreuser

degumming *n* FOOD TECH dégommage *m*

dehumidification *n* HEATING séchage *m*

dehumidifier *n* HEATING séchoir *m*, NUCLEAR *of evaporator* déshydrateur *m*, REFRIG déshumidificateur *m*

dehumidify *vt* HEATING dessécher, REFRIG assécher

dehydrate *vt* CHEM, GEOL, REFRIG déshydrater

dehydrating: ~ **agent** *n* CHEM TECH agent déshydratant *m*, desséchant *m*, déshydratant *m*

dehydration *n* CHEM anhydrisation *f*, déshydratation *f*, CHEM TECH dessiccation *f*, déshydratation *f*, hydroextraction *f*, GEOL, PETR TECH déshydratation *f*

dehydrator *n* CHEM TECH agent déshydratant *m*, desséchant *m*, déshydratant *m*, REFRIG déshydrateur *m*

dehydrofreezing *n* FOOD TECH déshydratation-congélation *f*, réfrigération par déshydratation *f*, REFRIG déshydratation-congélation *f*

dehydrogenase *n* DETERGENTS déhydrase *f*, déhydrogénase *f*, FOOD TECH déshydrogénase *f*

dehydrogenate *vt* CHEM déshydrogéner

dehydrogenated *adj* CHEM déshydrogéné

dehydrogenation *n* CHEM, PROP MAT déshydrogénation *f*

dehydroluminosterol *n* CHEM déshydroluminostérol *m*

de-ice *vt* AERONAUT, HEATING, SPACE dégivrer

de-icer *n* AERONAUT, HEATING, SPACE dégivreur *m*; ~ **boot** *n* AERONAUT boudin de dégivrage *m*, SPACE dégivreur pneumatique *m*

de-icing *n* AERONAUT, HEATING dégivrage *m*, REFRIG fusion *f*, SPACE dégivrage *m*; ~ **air** *n* AERONAUT air de dégivrage *m*; ~ **air outlet** *n* AERONAUT sortie d'air de dégivrage *f*; ~ **air temperature indicator** *n* AERONAUT indicateur de température de l'air de dégivrage *m*; ~ **duct** *n* AERONAUT gaine de dégivrage *f*; ~ **pump** *n* AERONAUT pompe éthylglycol *f*

deinked: ~ **paper stock** *n* PAPER TECH pâte de vieux papiers désencrés *f*

deinking *n* PAPER TECH désencrage *m*

deinterleave *vt* ELECTRON désentrelacer

deinterleaving *n* ELECTRON désentrelacement *m*

deionized: ~ **water** *n* ELEC eau déionisée *f*

deionizer *n* LAB EQUIP *of water* déminéralisateur *m*

deionizing: ~ **grid** *n* ELECTRON grille de désionisation *f*

de-ironing *n* C&G déferrisation magnétique *f*

DEL *abbr* *(delete character)* COMP, DP caractère de suppression *m*

delaminate *vt* P&R *adhesives* délaminer

delamination *n* C&G décollement *m*, P&R, PROP MAT délaminage *m*

delay:[1] **off** ~ *adv* PROD ENG au repos; **on** ~ *adv* PROD ENG au travail

delay[2] *n* COMP, DP délai *m*, retard *m*, ELEC *in relay, switch* retard *m*, ELEC ENG *in opening or closure of relay contacts* temporisation *f*, ELECTRON délai *m*, retard *m*, NUCLEAR *of appointed time* retard *m*, SPACE retard *m*, *communications* délai *m*, TELECOM, TRANSP retard *m*; ~ **cable** *n* TV câble à retard *m*; ~ **cap** *n* MINING amorce à retard *f*, détonateur à retardement *m*; ~ **circuit** *n* ELEC, ELECTRON circuit à retard *m*, TELECOM ligne à retard *f*, TV circuit à retard *m*; ~ **component** *n* NUCLEAR élément retard *m*; ~ **detonator** *n* MINING amorce à retard *f*, détonateur à retardement *m*; ~ **distortion** *n* ELECTRON distorsion de phase *f*, distorsion du temps de propagation *f*, distorsion du temps de transit de groupe *f*, distorsion non-linéaire *f*, RECORDING distorsion de phase *f*, TV distorsion du temps de propagation *f*, distorsion du temps de transit *f*; ~ **firing** *n* MINING amorçage à retardement *m*; ~ **generator** *n* ELECTRON générateur à retard *m*; ~ **line** *n* COMP, ELECTRON, PHYS, TV ligne à retard *f*; ~ **line storage** *n* NUCLEAR *memory* mémoire à lignes de retard *f*, mémoire à propagation *f*; ~ **lock loop** *n* TELECOM boucle à retard de phase *f*; ~ **mode relay** *n* TELECOM mode d'exploitation avec attente *m*; ~ **multivibrator** *n* ELECTRON multivibrateur à retard *m*; ~ **relay** *n* ELEC relais retardé *m*, relais temporisé *m*, ELEC ENG relais temporisé *m*; ~ **switch** *n* CONTROL, ELEC interrupteur à fonctionnement retardé *m*; ~ **time** *n* ELEC *of switch* durée de retard *f*, TELECOM temporisation *f*, temps de retard *m*, TV retard *m*; ~ **unit** *n* NUCLEAR *element* élément retard *m*

delay[3] *vt* ELEC *relay, switch* retarder, ELEC ENG *opening or closure of relay contacts* temporiser, ELECTRON *execution order* introduire un délai, retarder, temporiser, *pulse transmission* temporiser

delay-action: ~ **detonator** *n* MINING amorce à allumage retardé *f*, amorce à retard *f*, détonateur à retardement *m*

delayed: ~ **automatic gain control** *n* *(delayed AGC)* ELECTRON commande automatique de gain à seuil *f*, RECORDING contrôle de gain automatique retardé *m*; ~ **blanking signal** *n* TV signal de suppression différé *m*; ~ **broadcast** *n* TV transmission différée *f*; ~ **coking** *n* THERMOD cokéfaction différée *f*; ~ **critical reactor** *n* NUCLEAR réacteur critique différé *m*; ~ **explosion** *n* MINING explosion retardée *f*; ~ **fracture** *n* METALL rupture retardée *f*; ~ **hardening** *n* THERMOD *of steel* trempe différée *f*, trempe interrompue *f*, trempe étagée *f*; ~ **modified phase-shift keying** *n* *(delayed MSPK)* ELECTRON modulation par déplacement de phase modifiée avec retard *f*; ~ **MSPK** *n* *(delayed modified phase-shift keying)* ELECTRON modulation par déplacement de phase modifiée avec retard *f*; ~ **neutron** *n* PHYS neutron différé *m*, RAD PHYS neutron retardé *m*; ~ **neutron failed fuel element monitor** *n* NUCLEAR détection de rupture de gaine par neutrons différés *f*; ~**scanning** *n* TV analyse différée *f*; ~ **sweep** *n* ELECTRON balayage dilaté *m*

delayed-action: ~ **circuit-breaking** *n* ELEC ENG déclenchement retardé *m*; **~ fuse** *n* ELEC ENG fusible temporisé *m*; **~ release** *n* PHOTO déclencheur à retardement *m*

delaying: **~ sweep** *n* ELECTRON balayage retardant *m*; **~ time base** *n* ELECTRON base de temps retardante *f*

deleatur *n* PRINT deleatur *m*, signe d'effacement *m*

delessite *n* MINERAL délessite *f*

delete:[1] **~ character** *n* *(DEL)* COMP, DP caractère de suppression *m*, suppression *f*

delete[2] *vt* COMP, DP annuler, effacer, supprimer, éliminer

deletion *n* COMP, DP, TELECOM suppression *f*; **~ record** *n* COMP, DP enregistrement d'annulation *m*

Delezenne: **~ scale** *n* ACOUSTICS gamme de Delezenne *f*

Delf: **~ flask** *n* HYDROL bouteille de Delf *f*

Delft *n* C&G poterie de Delft *f*

delftware *n* C&G poterie de Delft *f*

delimiter *n* COMP, DP, PRINT *computers* délimiteur *m*

deliquesce *vi* CHEM tomber en déliquescence

deliquescence *n* CHEM, FOOD TECH déliquescence *f*

deliquescent *adj* CHEM déliquescent

delivered: **~ site** *n* CONST franco à pied d'oeuvre

deliverer *n* PACKAGING livreur *m*

delivery *n* C&G déflecteur *m*, FOOD TECH *food-processing machinery*, MECH ENG, NUCLEAR, PAPER TECH *of pump* débit *m*, PRINT livraison *f*, recette *f*, sortie *f*, PROD ENG livraison fournisseur *f*, réception fournisseur *f*, *drawtaper* dépouille *f*, *of pattern from mould* sortie *f*, WATER SUPP *pump* refoulement *m*; **~ box** *n* PROD ENG *of pump* chapelle de refoulement *f*; **~ channel** *n* WATER SUPP canal distributeur *m*; **~ cone** *n* PROD ENG *of injector* ajutage divergent *m*, cône divergent *m*, divergent *m*, tuyère divergente *f*; **~ cycle** *n* PROD ENG délai de livraison *m*; **~ date** *n* PACKAGING date de livraison *f*; **~ delay** *n* PACKAGING période de livraison *f*; **~ head** *n* NUCLEAR hauteur de refoulement *f*, hauteur manométrique *f*, WATER SUPP hauteur de refoulement *f*; **~ hose** *n* WATER SUPP tuyau de refoulement *m*; **~ into the mains** *n* (BrE) *(cf delivery into the utility network)* NUCLEAR *of electricity* fourniture au réseau *f*; **~ into the utility network** *n* (AmE) *(cf delivery into the mains)* NUCLEAR *of electricity* fourniture au réseau *f*; **~ lead time** *n* PROD ENG délai de livraison *m*; **~ lift** *n* WATER SUPP hauteur de refoulement *f*; **~ main** *n* WATER SUPP conduite de refoulement *f*; **~ nozzle** *n* PROD ENG *of injector* ajutage divergent *m*, cône divergent *m*, divergent *m*, tuyère divergente *f*; **~ pipe** *n* AUTO conduite d'alimentation *f*, tuyau d'injection *m*, WATER SUPP conduite de refoulement *f*, tubulure de refoulement *f*, tuyau de refoulement *m*; **~ pressure** *n* WATER SUPP pression de refoulement *f*; **~ race** *n* WATER SUPP canal distributeur *m*; **~ schedule** *n* PROD ENG calendrier de livraison *m*, plan de livraison *m*, programme de livraison *m*; **~ sheet** *n* PROD ENG liste de colisage *f*; **~ side** *n* NUCLEAR *of pump, blower* côté du refoulement *m*; **~ tanker** *n* PROD ENG citerne de livraison *f*; **~ ticket** *n* PROD ENG bon de livraison *m*, bordereau de livraison *m*, ticket de réception *m*; **~ time** *n* PROD ENG délai de livraison *m*; **~ tube** *n* PROD ENG tube donneur *m*, *of injector* ajutage divergent *m*, cône divergent *m*, divergent *m*, tuyère divergente *f*; **~ valve** *n* HYDR EQUIP clapet *m*, soupape de refoulement *f*

delocalized: **~ electron** *n* PETR TECH électron délocalisé *m*

delorenzite *n* NUCLEAR delorenzite *f*

DELPHI: **~ detector** *n* PART PHYS détecteur DELPHI *m*

delphinin *n* CHEM delphinine *f*

delphinine *n* CHEM delphinine *f*

delphinite *n* MINERAL delphinite *f*

Delphinus *n* ASTRON Dauphin *m*

delta *n* ELEC ENG, HYDROL, PETR TECH delta *m*; **~ bonding** *n* CHEM liaison delta *f*; **~ connection** *n* ELEC connexion en triangle *f*, couplage en triangle *m*, ELEC ENG montage en triangle *m*, PHYS connexion en triangle *f*; **~ fitting** *n* MECH ENG ferrure en delta *f*; **~ fold** *n* PRINT pli delta *m*; **~ function** *n* PETR fonction delta *f*; **~ modulation** *n* COMP *(DM)*, ELECTRON, SPACE *communications*, TELECOM modulation delta *f*; **~ network** *n* ELEC ENG réseau en delta *m*; **~ plain** *n* GEOL plaine deltaïque *f*; **~ ray** *n* NUCLEAR, RAD PHYS rayon delta *m*; **~ star connection** *n* ELEC connexion triangle-étoile *f*; **~ wing** *n* TRANSP aile en delta *f*

deltaic[1] *adj* GEOL, PETR TECH deltaïque

deltaic:[2] **~ platform** *n* OCEANOG plate-forme deltaïque *f*

delta-to-star: **~ conversion** *n* ELEC *connection* transformation delta-étoile *f*

deluge *n* METEO déluge *m*, pluie diluvienne *f*

deluster *vt* (AmE), **delustre** *vt* (BrE) TEXTILES délustrer

demagnetization *n* ELEC, PHYS, PROP MAT, TV démagnétisation *f*, désaimantation *f* **~ loss** *n* RECORDING perte par démagnétisation *f*

demagnetize *vt* COAL TECH démagnétiser, PHYS, PROP MAT, TV démagnétiser, désaimanter

demagnetizer *n* MECH ENG démagnétisateur *m*

demagnetizing: **~ equipment** *n* PROD ENG appareil à démagnétiser *m*; **~ field** *n* ELEC, PHYS champ démagnétisant *m*

demand: **~ assignment** *n* SPACE *communications* affectation à la demande *f*; **~ management** *n* PROD ENG gestion des besoins *f*, gestion des demandes *f*; **~ meter** *n* ELEC ENG compteur de consommation *m*; **~ paging** *n* COMP, DP pagination sur demande *f*; **~ right of way** *n* TRANSP demande de droit de passage *f*

demand-responsive: **~ system** *n* TRANSP autobus à la demande *m*

demand-scheduled: **~ bus service** *n* TRANSP autobus au cadran *m*

demantoid *n* MINERAL démantoïde *f*

demarcation *n* OCEANOG *of maritime zones* délimitation *f*

demethylate *vt* CHEM déméthyliser

demethylation *n* CHEM déméthylation *f*

demi: **~ circle** *n* CONST *surveying* graphomètre *m*

demijohn *n* C&G dame-jeanne *f*

demineralization *n* HEAT ENG *boiler water treatment* déminéralisation *f*, HYDROL *of sea water* dessalement *m*, déminéralisation *f*

demineralize[1] *vt* CHEM TECH déminéraliser

demineralize[2] *vti* HYDROL déminéraliser

demineralized[1] *adj* HYDROL déminéralisé

demineralized:[2] **~ water** *n* CONST, HYDROL eau déminéralisée *f*

demineralizing *n* CHEM TECH déminéralisation *f*; **~ plant** *n* NUCLEAR déminéraliseur *m*

demister *n* AERONAUT antibuée *m*, dispositif antibuée *m*, AUTO désembueur-dégivreur *m*; **~ system** *n* VEHICLES système de désembuage *m*

demo: **~ reel** *n* CINEMAT bobine de présentation *f*

demodulate *vt* ELECTRON, TV démoduler

demodulated *adj* ELECTRON *signal* démodulé

demodulation *n* COMP, ELECTRON, PHYS, SPACE *communications*, TELECOM, TV démodulation *f* demodulator *n* COMP, ELECTRON démodulateur *m*, PHYS démodulateur *m*, détecteur *m*, SPACE *communications*, TELECOM, TV démodulateur *m*

demold *n* (AmE) *see* demould

demolding *n* (AmE) *see* demoulding

demonstrated: ~ capacity *n* PROD ENG capacité effective *f*, capacité réelle *f*

demould *n* (BrE) C&G démoulage *m*

demoulding *n* (BrE) P&R démoulage *m*

demulsification *n* PROP MAT désémulsification *f*

demulsifying: ~ product *n* POLLUTION produit démulsifiant *m*

demultiplex *vt* ELECTRON démultiplexer

demultiplexer *n* COMP, DP, ELECTRON, TELECOM démultiplexeur *m*

demultiplexing *n* COMP, DP, ELECTRON, TELECOM démultiplexage *m*

demultiplexor *n* COMP, DP, TELECOM démultiplexeur *m*

demurrage *n* PETR TECH surestarie *f*

denatured: ~ alcohol *n* CHEM, FOOD TECH alcool dénaturé *m*

dendrite *n* CRYSTALL, METALL, MINERAL dendrite *f*

dendritic[1] *adj* CHEM, CRYSTALL, METALL dendritique

dendritic:[2] ~ drainage pattern *n* HYDROL tracé dendritique du réseau hydrographique *m*; ~ form *n* GEOL, PROP MAT formation dendritique *f*; ~ structure *n* PROP MAT structure dendritique *f*

denesting: ~ magazine *n* PACKAGING dispositif automatique de désemboîtement *m*

denial *n* TELECOM *of service* déni *m*

denier *n* TEXTILES denier *m*

denitrification *n* HYDROL, POLLUTION dénitrification *f*

denominator *n* MATH dénominateur *m*

dense: ~ core *n* ASTRON noyau compact *m*; ~ crown *n* C&G crown dense *m*; ~ flint *n* C&G flint dense *m*; ~ liquid *n* COAL TECH liquide dense *m*; ~ medium *n* COAL TECH milieu dense *m*

densimeter *n* FOOD TECH, PETR TECH densimètre *m*

densimetry *n* FOOD TECH densimétrie *f*

densitometer *n* ACOUSTICS, CINEMAT, PAPER TECH, PHYS densitomètre *m*

densitometry *n* PHOTO, PHYS densitométrie *f*

density *n* CHEM densité *f*, COAL TECH masse volumique *f*, COMP, CONST, DP, GAS TECH densité *f*, GEOL masse spécifique *f*, masse volumique *f*, MECH densité *f*, P&R densité *f*, densité massique *f*, PETR TECH densité *f*, masse volumique *f*, poids spécifique *m*, PHYS masse volumique *f*, *of states* densité d'états *f*, PROD ENG masse volumique *f*, PROP MAT, TEXTILES densité *f*; ~ bottle *n* LAB EQUIP pycnomètre *m*; ~ current *n* HYDROL courant de densité *m*; ~ curve *n* PRINT courbe des densités *f*; ~ filling machine *n* PACKAGING machine de remplissage volumétrique *f*; ~ log *n* GEOPHYS diagramme de densité *m*, PETR TECH diagraphie de densité *f*; ~ modifier *n* FOOD TECH modificateur de densité *m*; ~ modulation *n* ELECTRON modulation de densité *f*; ~ of pile *n* TEXTILES densité du poil *f*; ~ range *n* PRINT écart des densités *m*; ~ test *n* CONST essai de densité *m*; ~ waves *n pl* ASTRON ondes de densité *f pl*

densometer *n* PAPER TECH porosimètre à cylindre *m*

dent[1] *n* MECH bosselure *f*, MECH ENG bosselure *f*, creux *m*, déformation creuse *f*, empreinte *f*, indentation *f*

dent[2] *vt* MECH, MECH ENG bosseler

dental: ~ ceramic *n* C&G céramique dentaire *f*

dented: ~ knob *n* MECH ENG bouton cranté *m*

denting *n* NUCLEAR constriction *f*

denudation *n* GEOL dénudation *f*, METALL appauvrissement *m*

denuded: ~ zone *n* METALL zone appauvrie *f*

deodorizing *n* HYDROL *of sewage* désodorisation *f*

deoxidation *n* MINING *of the air* désoxydation de l'air *f*, force *f*, PROP MAT désoxydation *f*

deoxidization *n* CHEM désoxydation *f*

deoxidizer *n* CHEM désoxydant *m*

deoxyribonucleic: ~ acid *n (DNA)* CHEM acide désoxyribonucléique *m (ADN)*

depacketizer *n* TELECOM dépaqueteur *m*, désassembleur de paquets *m*

depalletization *n* PACKAGING dépalettisation *f*

depalletizer *n* PACKAGING chariot dépalettisateur *m*

departure: ~ curves *n pl* PETR courbes de correction *f pl*; ~ from nuclear boiling *n* NUCLEAR crise d'ébullition *f*, échauffement critique *m*; ~ terminal *n* TRANSP terminal *m*

dependability *n* MECH ENG pertinence *f*, QUALITY sûreté de fonctionnement *f*

dependent[1] *adj* PROD ENG tributaire

dependent:[2] ~ claim *n* PATENTS revendication dépendante *f*; ~ exchange *n* TELECOM centre satellite *m*, satellite *m*; ~ navigation *n* SPACE navigation dépendante *f*; ~ patent *n* PATENTS brevet dépendant *m*; ~ variable *n* MATH *in a function* variable dépendante *f*

dephased *adj* ELEC *current* déphasé

dephasing: ~ coefficient *n* ACOUSTICS déphasage linéique de propagation acoustique *m*

dephlegmate *vt* CHEM déflegmer

dephlegmator *n* NUCLEAR déflegmateur *m*

dephosphorization *n* CHEM TECH, PROP MAT déphosphoration *f*

deplete *vt* NUCLEAR appauvrir

depleted[1] *adj* NUCLEAR *nuclear fuel* appauvri

depleted:[2] ~ uranium *n* MILIT uranium appauvri *m*, uranium dégradé *m*

depletion *n* CHEM *of mixture* appauvrissement *m*, ELECTRON appauvrissement *m*, déplétion *f*, GEOL appauvrissement *m*, NUCLEAR, WATER SUPP épuisement *m*; ~ layer *n* ELECTRON zone d'appauvrissement *f*, zone de déplétion *f*, PHYS couche d'arrêt *f*, zone de déplétion *f*; ~ layer photodiode *n* ELECTRON photodiode à zone de déplétion *f*; ~ mode *n* ELECTRON mode d'appauvrissement *m*, mode de déplétion *m*; ~ rate *n* PETR TECH taux d'épuisement *m*

depletion-mode: ~ FET *n* ELECTRON transistor à effet de champ à déplétion *m*

deployable: ~ antenna *adj* SPACE *communications* antenne déployable *f*

depocenter *n* (AmE), depocentre *n* (BrE) GEOL foyer de sédimentation maximum *m*, point de sédimentation maximum *m*

de-poisoning *n* NUCLEAR élimination des poisons *f*

depolarization *n* CHEM, ELEC ENG dépolarisation *f*, SPACE *communications* dépolarisation *f*, transpolarisation *f*

depolarize *vt* ELEC ENG dépolariser

depolarizer *n* CHEM dépolarisateur *m*

depolarizing: ~ agent *n* ELEC *of cell* dépolarisant *m*; ~ field *n* PHYS, RECORDING champ dépolarisant *m*

depolluted *adj* POLLUTION *water* dépollué

depolluting: ~ ship *n* MAR POLL, POLLUTION navire dépollueur *m*

depolymerization *n* CHEM, P&R, PACKAGING dépolymérisation *f* deposit *n* CHEM *settlings, as by precipitation* dépôt *m*, sédiment *m*, COAL TECH dépôt *m*, CONST gisement *m*, gîte *m*, GEOL dépôt *m*, PACKAGING consignation *f*, PATENTS, WATER SUPP dépôt *m*; ~ **bottle** *n* PACKAGING bouteille consignée *f*; ~ **copies** *n pl* PRINT exemplaires devant obligatoirement être déposés *m pl*; ~ **of ore** *n* MINING gisement de minerai *m*, gîte métallifère *m*

deposited: ~ **layer** *n* ELECTRON couche déposée *f*; ~ **matter** *n* POLLUTION matière déposée *f*

deposition *n* ELECTRON déposition *f*, dépôt *m*, POLLUTION dépôt *m*, précipitation *f*; ~ **rate** *n* POLLUTION taux de dépôt *m*; ~ **value** *n* POLLUTION valeur des retombées *f*; ~ **velocity** *n* POLLUTION vitesse de dépôt *f*, vitesse de sédimentation *f*

depositional: ~ **fabric** *n* PETR structure sédimentaire *f*; ~ **fault** *n* GEOL faille syngénétique *f*; ~ **sequence** *n* GEOL séquence sédimentaire *f*

depot *n* MINING parc *m*

depreciation *n* PETR TECH dépréciation *f*, PROD ENG dépréciation des capitaux *f*

depress *vt* COAL TECH déprimer

depressed: ~ **cladding** *n* OPT gaine optique déprimée *f*, TELECOM gaine déprimée *f*; ~ **deck car** *n* (AmE) *(cf well wagon)* RAIL *vehicles* wagon kangourou *m*, wagon à évidement central *m*; ~ **thread** *n* C&G filet aminci *m*

depression *n* MECH ENG dépression *f*, dépression motrice *f*, METEO dépression *f*; ~ **bar** *n* C&G dépresseur *m*; ~ **cone** *n* WATER SUPP cône d'appel *m*; ~ **spring** *n* WATER SUPP source de dépression *f*, source de déversement *f*

depressor *n* OCEANOG dépresseur *m*

depressurization *n* PROD ENG, SPACE dépressurisation *f*; ~ **accident** *n* NUCLEAR accident de dépressurisation *m*; ~ **valve** *n* MECH ENG *of water crane* clapet de dépression *m*, robinet de chute de pression *m*, soupape de décompression *f*, vanne de dépressurisation *f*

depressurize[1] *vt* AERONAUT, PROD ENG, SPACE dépressuriser

depressurize[2] *vi* NUCLEAR supprimer la pression

depressurized: ~ **condition** *n* PROD ENG état dépressurisé *m*

depth *n* NAUT *naval architecture* creux *m*, épaisseur *f*, *of water* profondeur *f*; ~ **below pitch line** *n* MECH ENG *gearing* hauteur au-dessous du primitif *f*, profondeur du creux *f*; ~ **charge** *n* MILIT charge sous-marine *f*; ~ **controller** *n* PETR régulateur de profondeur *m*; ~ **curve** *n* OCEANOG isobathe *f*; ~ **of cut** *n* MECH *tools* profondeur de passe *f*, MECH ENG *machine tool work* profondeur de coupe *f*, profondeur de passe *f*, serrage *m*, PROD ENG *of sawing machine* hauteur maximum du trait de scie *f*, hauteur maximum à scier *f*; ~ **dose** *n* RAD PHYS *of ionizing radiation* dose en profondeur *f*; ~ **of the draw bar** *n* C&G enfoncement de la barre d'étirage *m*; ~ **of field** *n* CINEMAT, METALL, PHOTO, PHYS *of field*, TV profondeur de champ *f*; ~ **of field scale** *n* PHOTO échelle de profondeur de champ *f*; ~ **finder** *n* NAUT *navigation* sondeur *m*; ~ **of focus** *n* CINEMAT, GEOPHYS, PHOTO, PHYS profondeur de foyer *f*, TV différence focale *f*; ~ **of focus adjustment** *n* CONTROL mise au point du diaphragme *f*, réglage de la profondeur de champ *m*; ~ **of focus scale** *n* PHOTO échelle de profondeur de foyer *f*; ~ **for freeboard** *n* NAUT *ship design* creux de franc-bord *m*; ~ **of frictional influence** *n* OCEANOG profondeur de frottement *f*; ~ **gage** *n* (AmE), ~ **gauge** *n* (BrE) MECH *tools* jauge de profondeur *f*, METR calibre de profondeur *m*, OCEANOG

profondimètre *m*, PROD ENG *loam moulding* témoin de profondeur *m*; ~ **of immersion** *n* TRANSP profondeur d'immersion *f*; ~ **indicator** *n* MINING indicateur de niveau des cages *m*; ~ **of investigation** *n* GEOPHYS profondeur d'investigation *f*, PETR parée d'une recherche *f*; ~ **meter** *n* OCEANOG profondimètre *m*; ~ **of penetration** *n* NUCLEAR *in welding*, TESTING profondeur de pénétration *f*; ~ **point** *n* PETR point subsurface *m*; ~ **recorder** *n* OCEANOG sondeur *m*; ~ **rudder** *n* OCEANOG barre de plongée *f*; ~ **of shade** *n* TEXTILES intensité du coloris *f*; ~ **sounder** *n* NAUT, OCEANOG sondeur *m*; ~ **of thread** *n* CONST *screws* saillie *f*; ~ **to draught ratio** *n* NAUT *ship design* rapport creux-tirant d'eau *m*; ~ **of water** *n* FUELLESS profondeur d'eau *f*, HYDROL hauteur d'eau *f*, profondeur d'eau *f*

depulping: ~ **screen** *n* COAL TECH tamis déschlammeur *m*

depurination *n* CHEM dépurination *f*

deputy *n* MINING délégué mineur *m*

derail *vt* RAIL *of train* faire dérailler

derailing: ~ **points** *n* (BrE) *(cf derailing switch)* RAIL aiguille de déraillement *f*; ~ **switch** *n* (AmE) *(cf derailing points)* RAIL aiguille de déraillement *f*

derailment *n* RAIL déraillement *m*

derating *n* ELEC ENG dératage *m*

derivative *n* CHEM, ELECTRON dérivé *m*, MATH dérivée *f*; ~ **control** *n* ELEC régulation à dérivation *f*; ~ **control regulator** *n* CONTROL régulateur à dérivation *m*; ~ **control unit** *n* CONTROL régulateur à dérivation *m*

derive *vt* CHEM dériver

derived: ~ **circuit** *n* ELEC, ELEC ENG circuit dérivé *m*, circuit en dérivation *m*; ~ **current** *n* ELEC *branch* courant dérivé *m*; ~ **energy** *n* PETR TECH énergie secondaire *f*, énergie transformée *f*; ~ **fossil** *n* GEOL fossile remanié *m*; ~ **fuel** *n* PETR TECH énergie secondaire *f*, énergie transformée *f*; ~ **gust velocity** *n* AERONAUT amplitude maximum de l'intensité de rafale *f*; ~ **product** *n* CHEM dérivé *m*, produit dérivé *m*; ~ **unit** *n* MECH ENG, PHYS unité dérivée *f*

dernbachite *n* MINERAL dernbachite *f*

deroofing *n* GEOL *of intrusion* mise à nu *f*

derrick *n* AERONAUT *of helicopter* potence de manutention *f*, CONST bigue *f*, chèvre *f*, chèvre verticale *f*, derrick *m*, grue derrick *f*, FUELLESS tour de forage *f*, MECH *lifting gear* bigue *f*, NAUT *of cargo vessel* mât de charge *m*, PETR derrick *m*, PETR TECH derrick *m*, tour de forage *f*; ~ **boom** *n* NAUT *cargo loading* mât de charge *m*, TRANSP flèche *f*; ~ **cellar** *n* PETR TECH avant-puits *m*; ~ **crane** *n* CONST chèvre *f*, chèvre verticale *f*, derrick *m*, grue derrick *f*; ~ **crown** *n* PETR TECH sommet du derrick *m*; ~ **floor** *n* PETR TECH plancher de manoeuvre *m*; ~ **girt** *n* CONST entretoise de derrick *f*; ~ **man** *n* PETR, PETR TECH accrocheur *m*; ~ **mast** *n* TRANSP mât de charge *m*; ~ **monkey** *n* PETR TECH accrocheur *m*; ~ **post** *n* CONST montant de derrick *m*

derricking: ~ **crane** *n* CONST grue à volée basculante *f*, grue à volée variable *f*

derusting *n* MECH ENG dérouillage *m*

desalinate *vti* CHEM TECH, HYDROL dessaler

desalinated *adj* CHEM TECH, HYDROL dessalé

desalination *n* CHEM TECH dessalement *m*, déminéralisation *f*, HYDROL *of sea water*, NAUT, OCEANOG dessalement *m*; ~ **plant** *n* CHEM TECH installation de dessalement *f*, usine de dessalement *f*, CONST unité de dessalage *f*, unité de dessalement *f*, WATER SUPP installation de dessalement *f*; ~ **reactor** *n* NUCLEAR réacteur de dessalement *m*

desalinization *n* CHEM TECH dessalement *m*; ~ **plant** *n* CHEM TECH installation de dessalement *f*, usine de dessalement *f*

desalinize *vt* CHEM TECH dessaler

desalt *vt* CHEM TECH dessaler, déminéraliser

desalting *n* CHEM TECH déminéralisation *f*, PETR TECH dessalage *m*

desander *n* PETR, PETR TECH dessableur *m*

desaturate *vt* TV désaturer

desaturated: ~ **color** *n* (AmE), ~ **colour** *n* (BrE) TV couleur désaturée *f*

desaturation *n* OCEANOG dégazage *m*, désaturation *f*

descale *vt* DETERGENTS décalaminer, détartrer, enlever les dépôts, MECH décalaminer, PROD ENG *boiler* désincruster, détartrer, piquer

descaling *n* DETERGENTS décalaminage *m*, détartrage *m*

descendant *n* COMP *tree*, DP *tree* descendant *m*

descender *n* PRINT descendante *f*, jambage *m*

descending: ~ **node** *n* SPACE noeud descendant *m*

descent *n* SPACE descente *f*; ~ **engine** *n* SPACE moteur de freinage *m*; ~ **orbit** *n* SPACE orbite de descente *f*; ~ **path** *n* SPACE trajectoire de descente *f*; ~ **stage** *n* SPACE module de descente *m*

descloizite *n* MINERAL descloizite *f*

descramble *vt* SPACE *communications*, TELECOM désembrouiller

descrambler *n* SPACE *communications*, TELECOM désembrouilleur *m*

descrambling *n* SPACE *communications*, TELECOM désembrouillage *m*

description *n* PATENTS description *f*, SAFETY *of environmental noise* caractérisation *f*

descriptive *adj* PATENTS descriptif

descriptor *n* COMP, DP descripteur *m*

deseasonalize *vt* PROD ENG désaisonnaliser

desemulsifying: ~ **agent** *n* PROP MAT agent désémulsifiant *m*

desensitization *n* MINING désensibilisation *f*, flegmatisation *f*, PHOTO, TELECOM désensibilisation *f*

desensitize *vt* MINING désensibiliser, flegmatiser

desensitizer *n* MINING flegmatisant *m*, PHOTO désensibilisateur *m*

desensitizing: ~ **bath** *n* PHOTO bain désensibilisateur *m*

desert: ~ **pediment** *n* GEOL glacis désertique *m*

deshielding: ~ **effect** *n* NUCLEAR effet de blindage négatif *m*

deshrinking: ~ **process** *n* CINEMAT traitement antiretrait *m*

de-shunting *n* RAIL déshuntage *m*, raté de shunt *m*

desiccant[1] *adj* HEATING dessiccatif

desiccant[2] *n* CHEM desséchant *m*, déshydratant *m*, FOOD TECH agent dessiccateur *m*, siccatif *m*, PACKAGING *silica gel* desséchant *m*, REFRIG déshydratant *m*, THERMOD desséchant *m*, siccatif *m*; ~ **bag** *n* PACKAGING sachet desséchant *m*

desiccate *vt* CHEM déshydrater, FOOD TECH, HEATING, THERMOD dessécher

desiccated *adj* FOOD TECH déshydraté, séché, THERMOD desséché, déshydraté

desiccation *n* CHEM dessiccation *f*, CHEM TECH assèchement *m*, dessiccation *f*, dessèchement *m*, FOOD TECH dessiccation *f*, séchage *m*, PACKAGING dessèchement *m*, PETR TECH dessèchement *m*, déshydratation *f*, REFRIG, THERMOD dessiccation *f*; ~ **crack** *n* GEOL fente de dessication *f*, fissure de dessication *f*; ~ **ratio** *n* REFRIG

of freeze-dried food taux de dessiccation *m*

desiccative *adj* CHEM TECH dessiccatif, déshydratant, siccatif

desiccator *n* CHEM, CHEM TECH dessiccateur *m*, FOOD TECH *food-processing machinery* dessiccateur *m*, séchoir *m*, HEATING, LAB EQUIP dessiccateur *m*; ~ **screen** *n* CHEM TECH plaque perforée pour dessiccateurs *f*

design[1] *n* COMP conception *f*, étude *f*, CONST conception *f*, projet *m*, étude *f*, DP conception *f*, étude *f*, PATENTS dessin *m*, modèle *m*, PRINT maquette *f*, PROD ENG conception *f*, exécution *f*, étude *f*, SAFETY conception *f*; ~ **aid** *n* COMP, DP aide à la conception *f*; ~ **airspeed** *n* AERONAUT *airworthiness* vitesse de calcul *f*; ~ **automation** *n* COMP conception automatisée *f*, DP automatisation de la conception *f*; ~ **basis case** *n* SPACE *spacecraft* cas dimensionnant *m*; ~ **basis event** *n* NUCLEAR événement de référence *m*; ~ **burn-up** *n* NUCLEAR combustion massique de préférence *f*; ~ **criterion** *n* NUCLEAR, PROD ENG critère de conception *m*; ~ **cruising speed** *n* AERONAUT *airworthiness* vitesse de calcul en croisière *f*; ~ **department** *n* NAUT *ship design* bureau d'études *m*, service d'études *m*, PROD ENG bureau de dessin *m*; ~ **diving speed** *n* AERONAUT vitesse limite de piqué *f*, *airworthiness* vitesse de calcul en piqué *f*; ~ **draftsman** *n* (AmE) *(cf design draughtsman)* MECH ENG dessinateur concepteur *m*, dessinateur-projeteur *m*; ~ **draughtsman** *n* (BrE) *(cf design draftsman)* MECH ENG dessinateur concepteur *m*, dessinateur-projeteur *m*; ~ **flaps extended speed** *n* AERONAUT *airworthiness* vitesse de calcul volets sortis *f*; ~ **flight weight** *n* AERONAUT masse de calcul de l'avion en vol *f*; ~ **flood** *n* HYDROL crue nominale *f*; ~ **flow** *n* HYDROL débit nominal *m*; ~ **irradiation level** *n* NUCLEAR combustion massique de préférence *f*; ~ **landing speed** *n* AERONAUT vitesse de calcul d'atterrissage *f*; ~ **landing weight** *n* AERONAUT masse de calcul à l'atterrissage *f*; ~ **language** *n* COMP langage d'analyse *m*; ~ **load** *n* AERONAUT charge théorique *f*; ~ **office** *n* CONST bureau d'études *m*, charrette *f*, NAUT *naval architecture* bureau d'études *m*; ~ **outside temperature** *n* HEATING température externe de calcul *f*; ~ **pressure** *n* REFRIG pression de service maximale *f*; ~ **rough air speed** *n* AERONAUT *airworthiness* vitesse de calcul en air turbulent *f*, vitesse de calcul en atmosphère agitée *f*; ~ **specification and requirements** *n pl* PROD ENG critères de conception et d'essais *m pl*; ~ **speed** *n* TRANSP vitesse de conception *f*; ~ **speed for maximum gust intensity** *n* AERONAUT *airworthiness* vitesse de calcul pour l'intensité de rafale maximale *f*; ~**storm** *n* HYDROL averse nominale *f*; ~ **takeoff mass** *n* AERONAUT *airworthiness* masse de calcul au décollage *f*, poids de calcul au décollage *m*; ~ **taxi weight** *n* AERONAUT masse de calcul pour le roulement au sol *f*, poids de calcul pour les évolutions au sol *m*, masse de calcul de roulage *f*; ~ **to buckling strength** *n* SPACE *spacecraft* dimensionnement au flambage *m*; ~ **to ultimate strength** *n* SPACE *spacecraft* dimensionnement à la rupture *m*; ~ **to yield point** *n* SPACE *spacecraft* dimensionnement au point du système *m*, dimensionnement à la limite élastique *m*; ~ **volume** *n* TRANSP trafic de projet *m*; ~ **waterline** *n* NAUT *ship design* flottaison de tracé *f*; ~ **waterplane** *n* NAUT *ship design* flottaison de tracé *f*; ~ **weight** *n* AERONAUT masse de calcul *f*; ~ **wheel load** *n* AERONAUT *airworthiness* charge de calcul par roue *f*; ~ **wing area** *n* AERONAUT surface alaire *f*, *airworthiness* surface conventionnelle de la voilure *f*

design[2] *vt* CONST dessiner, projeter, étudier, MECH concevoir, étudier

designate *vt* TELECOM préassigner

designated: ~ **frequency** *n* TELECOM fréquence désignée *f*; ~ **office** *n* PATENTS office désigné *m*

designation *n* ACOUSTICS, PATENTS désignation *f*

designed: ~ **power required output** *n* NUCLEAR puissance exigée *f*

designer *n* PROD ENG *person* dessinateur *m*; ~ **handbook** *n* TELECOM livre du concepteur *m*

design-related: ~ **defect** *n* NUCLEAR *of fuel element* défaut de conception *m*

desilication *n* PROP MAT désiliciage *m*

desiliconization *n* PROP MAT désiliciation *f*

desiliconizing *n* PROP MAT désiliciage *m*

desilter *n* PETR TECH désilteur *m*

desilting: ~ **basin** *n* HYDROL bassin de dessablement *m*, bassin de désiltage *m*

desire: ~ **line** *n* TRANSP ligne de désir *f*

desired: ~ **value** *n* NUCLEAR valeur assignée *f*

desize *vt* TEXTILES désencoller

desizing *n* C&G désensimage *m*, TEXTILES désencollage *m*

deskside: ~ **system** *n* COMP, DP boîtier tour *m*

desktop[1] *adj* COMP, DP desktop

desktop:[2] ~ **computer** *n* COMP, DP ordinateur de bureau *m*; ~ **publishing** *n* *(DTP)* COMP, DP, PRINT publication assistée par ordinateur *f* *(PAO)*

deslime *vt* COAL TECH déschlammer

desliming *n* COAL TECH déschlammage *m*; ~ **screen** *n* COAL TECH crible déschlammeur *m*, tamis déslimeur *m*

deslurry *vt* COAL TECH déschlammer

deslurrying *n* COAL TECH déschlammage *m*

desmine *n* MINERAL desmine *f*

desmotropy *n* CHEM desmotropie *f*

desorb *vt* CHEM désorber

desorption *n* CHEM, COAL TECH, PROP MAT désorption *f*

despiking: ~ **circuit** *n* ELEC ENG suppresseur de transitoires *m*

despin:[1] ~ **system** *n* SPACE *spacecraft* dispositif de contrarotation *m*

despin[2] *vt* SPACE *spacecraft* contregyrer, dégyrer, ralentir

despun *adj* SPACE *spacecraft* contrarotatif

destacking *n* PACKAGING *of pallets* désempilement *m*

destination: ~ **bin** *n* PROD ENG casier destinataire *m*, lieu destinataire *m*; ~ **network** *n* *(DN)* TELECOM réseau de destination *m*

destroy: ~ **by fire** *vt* THERMOD détruire au feu, réduire en cendres

destroyer *n* NAUT *navy* contre-torpilleur *m*, destroyer *m*, grand escorteur *m*

destruction: ~ **process** *n* PACKAGING procédé destructif *m*

destructive: ~ **breakdown** *n* ELEC ENG, ELECTRON claquage destructif *m*; ~ **element** *n* SAFETY élément destructeur *m*; ~ **interference** *n* ELEC ENG, PHYS, WAVE PHYS interférence destructive *f*; ~ **plate-margin** *n* GEOL marge de plaque en subduction *f*; ~ **read** *n* COMP, DP lecture destructive *f*; ~ **test** *n* MECH ENG essai destructif *m*

destructor *n* THERMOD *waste* four à incinération d'ordures ménagères *m*

desulfonation *n* (AmE) *see desulphonation*

desulfuration *n* (AmE) *see desulphuration*

desulfurization *n* (AmE) *see desulphurization*

desulfurize *vt* (AmE) *see desulphurize*

desulfurizing: ~ **furnace** *n* (AmE) *see desulphurizing furnace*

desulphonation *n* (BrE) CHEM désulfonation *f*

desulphuration *n* (BrE) CHEM désoufrage *m*, désulfuration *f*

desulphurization *n* (BrE) CHEM désoufrage *m*, COAL TECH, PETR TECH, POLLUTION, PROP MAT désulfuration *f*

desulphurize *vt* (BrE) CHEM désoufrer, désulfurer

desulphurizing: ~ **furnace** *n* (BrE) PROD ENG four à pyrite *m*

desuperheat *vt* HEAT ENG désurchauffer

desuperheater *n* HEAT ENG désurchauffeur *m*

detachable[1] *adj* MECH ENG amovible, détachable, mobile, rapporté, PHOTO amovible

detachable:[2] ~ **handle** *n* MECH ENG poignée amovible *f*; ~ **jaws** *n* MECH ENG *of vice* mâchoires rapportées *f pl*; ~ **keyboard** *n* DP clavier amovible *m*, PROD ENG clavier détachable *m*, clavier indépendant *m*; ~ **nose cone** *n* AERONAUT cône de nez amovible *m*, cône de nez démontable *m*, pointe avant amovible *f*; ~ **pod** *n* AERONAUT *helicopter* nacelle amovible *f*; ~ **pressure plate** *n* PHOTO presseur démontable *m*; ~ **union** *n* MECH ENG *pipe fitting* raccord de tuyau amovible *m*

detached: ~ **end** *n* SPRINGS bout décollé *m*

detaching: ~ **hook** *n* MINING *overwind gear* crochet de sûreté *m*, déclic d'attelage *m*

detachment *n* GEOL décollement *m*, MECH ENG décrochement *m*, désattelage *m*, dételage *m*; ~ **device** *n* MECH ENG dispositif de désattelage *m*, dispositif de dételage *m*

detack *n* PRINT produit antitirant *m*

detail: ~ **gage** *n* (AmE), ~ **gauge** *n* (BrE) MECH ENG calibre de détail *m*; ~ **log** *n* PETR diagramme détaillé *m*; ~ **rendition** *n* TV rendu des détails *m*

detailed: ~ **billing** *n* TELECOM facturation détaillée *f*; ~ **procedure** *n* *(DP)* TELECOM procédure détaillée *f*; ~ **survey** *n* CONST levé de détail *m*

detect *vt* ELECTRON, PART PHYS détecter

detectability *n* OPT détectivité *f*

detected *adj* ELECTRON *signal* détecté

detection *n* ACOUSTICS, ELECTRON, RAD PHYS *of radioactivity*, SPACE *communications* détection *f*; ~ **loop** *n* TRANSP boucle de détection *f*; ~ **system inside the vehicle** *n* TRANSP système embarqué de détection *m*; ~ **system outside the vehicle** *n* TRANSP système de détection au sol *m*; ~ **threshold** *n* OPT, TELECOM seuil de détection *m*

detectivity *n* TELECOM détectivité *f*

detector *n* ELEC *demodulation*, ELEC ENG, ELECTRON, MECH ENG détecteur *m*, OCEANOG sonde *f*, OPT, PHYS, TELECOM détecteur *m*; ~ **circuit** *n* ELECTRON circuit de détection *m*, montage détecteur *m*; ~ **diode** *n* ELECTRON diode de détection *f*, diode détectrice *f*; ~ **signal** *n* ELECTRON signal du détecteur *m*; ~ **tubes for short-term sampling** *n pl* SAFETY tube détecteur pour échantillonnage rapide *m*

detent *n* MECH ENG chien *m*, cliquet *m*, détente *f*

detention: ~ **basin** *n* WATER SUPP bassin de retenue *m*; ~ **reservoir** *n* HYDROL réservoir de régulation *m*, réservoir à débit non réglable *m*, WATER SUPP réservoir d'écrêtement des crues *m*

detergency *n* CHEM détergence *f*, DETERGENTS pouvoir

détergent *m*

detergent[1] *adj* CHEM TECH lessiviel

detergent[2] *n* CHEM détergent *m*, détersif *m*, CHEM TECH abluant *m*, détergent *m*, détersif *m*, nettoyant *m*, agent de lavage *m*, produit de lavage *m*, DETERGENTS produit lessiviel *m*, *oils* dégraissant *m*, PETR TECH, PROP MAT détergent *m*, TEXTILES détersif *m*; ~ **additive** *n* DETERGENTS additif au détergent *m*; ~ **effect** *n* DETERGENTS effet détergent *m*; ~ **oil** *n* DETERGENTS, VEHICLES *lubrication* huile détergente *f*; ~ **paste** *n* DETERGENTS pâte à détacher *f*; ~ **power** *n* DETERGENTS pouvoir détergent *m*

deteriorate *vt* PACKAGING détériorer

deterioration *n* P&R, PACKAGING détérioration *f*

determinant *n* COMP, DP, MATH déterminant *m*

determination *n* SAFETY *of compounds* dosage *m*, *of gas concentration* détermination *f*, THERMOD *of calorific value* détermination *f*

deterministic *adj* COMP, DP déterministe

detonatable *adj* MINING, THERMOD détonant, explosible

detonate *vt* MINING détoner, faire détoner, THERMOD détoner, exploser, faire détoner, faire exploser, faire sauter

detonating: ~ **cord** *n* MINING cordeau détonant *m*, cordeau détonant de mineur *m*, SPACE cordeau de transmission *m*; ~ **explosive** *n* MINING explosif *m*, explosif détonant *m*; ~ **fuse** *n* MINING cordeau détonant *m*, cordeau détonant de mineur *m*; ~ **point** *n* MINING température de détonation *f*; ~ **relay** *n* MINING microconnecteur *m*, relais de détonation *m*

detonation *n* MINING, SAFETY, THERMOD détonation *f*, explosion *f*, VEHICLES détonation *f*; ~ **pressure** *n* MINING pression de détonation *f*; ~ **temperature** *n* MINING température de détonation *f*; ~ **velocity** *n* MINING vitesse de détonation *f*; ~ **wave** *n* MINING *accidental* onde explosive *f*, *deliberate* onde de détonation *f*

detonator *n* MINING amorce *f*, capsule *f*, détonateur de mine *m*, détonateur *m*, RAIL pétard *m*, SPACE *spacecraft*, THERMOD détonateur *m*; ~ **cap** *n* MINING détonateur *m*

detrital[1] *adj* PETR détritique

detrital:[2] ~ **sediment** *n* OCEANOG sédiment détritique *m*

detune *vt* ELECTRON désaccorder

detuning *n* ELECTRON désaccord *m*, modification de l'accord *f*

deuteric: ~ **alteration** *n* GEOL altération deutérique *f*, altération postmagmatique *f*

deuteride *n* CHEM deutéride *m*, hydrure lourd *m*

deuterium *n* CHEM deutérium *m*, NUCLEAR deutérium *m*, hydrogène lourd *m*, PHYS deutérium *m*

deuteron *n* PART PHYS, PHYS deutéron *m*

deuteroproteose *n* CHEM deutéroprotéose *f*

deuton *n* CHEM, PART PHYS, PHYS deuton *m*, deutéron *m*

develop *vt* CINEMAT développer, CONST développer, mettre au point, GEOM *solid figure, algebraic function* développer, MECH ENG mettre au point, MINING tracer

developed: ~ **image** *n* PHOTO cliché développé *m*; ~ **luminosity** *n* RAD PHYS *radiative experiments* luminosité accrue *f*

developer *n* CINEMAT révélateur *m*, PHOTO développeur *m*, révélateur *m*; ~ **for soft contrast** *n* PHOTO révélateur donnant doux *m*; ~ **streaks** *n pl* CINEMAT marques de développement *f pl*

developing: ~ **bath** *n* CINEMAT bain de développement *m*, PHOTO bain de développement *m*, bain révélateur

m; ~ **clip** *n* PHOTO pince de développement *f*; ~ **drum** *n* CINEMAT, PHOTO tambour de développement *m*; ~ **reel** *n* (AmE) *(cf developing spiral)* PHOTO spire porte-film *f*; ~ **spiral** *n* (BrE) *(cf developing reel, developing spool)* PHOTO spire porte-film *f*; ~ **spool** *n* (AmE) *(cf developing spiral)* PHOTO spire porte-film *f*; ~ **tank** *n* CINEMAT, PHOTO cuve de développement *f*; ~ **tank thermometer** *n* PHOTO thermomètre de développement *m*; ~ **tongs** *n pl* PHOTO pince de développement *f*

development *n* CONST aménagement du terrain *m*, extension *f*, mise au point *f*, MECH ENG développement *m*, perfectionnement *m*, MINING chassage *m*, percement *m*, PETR TECH mise en valeur *f*, THERMOD *of heat* dégagement *m*; ~ **and subsequent manufacture** *n* MECH ENG étude et suivi de fabrication *f*; ~ **by rock chutes** *n* MINING traçage au rocher *m*; ~ **fog** *n* CINEMAT voile de développement *m*; ~ **heading** *n* MINING galerie de traçage *f*, voie de traçage *f*; ~ **phase** *n* PETR TECH phase de développement *f*; ~ **project** *n* PETR TECH projet pilote *m*; ~ **tank** *n* CINEMAT, PHOTO cuve de développement *f*; ~ **test** *n* SPACE essai de mise au point *m*; ~ **time** *n* CINEMAT durée de développement *f*, période d'élaboration *f*; ~ **well** *n* PETR TECH puits de développement *m*; ~ **work** *n* MINING dispositifs de mines *m pl*, travaux de premier établissement *m pl*, travaux préparatoires *m pl*

deviated: ~ **drilling** *n* PETR TECH forage dirigé *m*, forage dévié *m*; ~ **well** *n* PETR TECH puits dévié *m*

deviation *n* MATH dispersion *f*, MECH ENG écart *m*, NAUT *of compass*, PHYS *of light ray* déviation *f*, PROD ENG écart *m*, SPACE divergent *m*, *communications* excursion *f*, TELECOM dérive *f*, TV excursion *f*; ~ **control** *n* CONTROL contrôle de la déviation *m*, régulation d'une déviation *f*; ~ **detector** *n* AERONAUT détecteur d'écart *m*; ~ **from criticality** *n* NUCLEAR écart de la criticité *m*; ~ **indicator** *n* AERONAUT indicateur de déviation *m*; ~ **measurement** *n* TELECOM *technique* écartométrie *f*; ~ **mirror** *n* INSTRUMENT miroir de déviation *m*; ~ **prism** *n* INSTRUMENT, TELECOM prisme de déviation *m*; ~ **ratio** *n* ELECTRON indice de modulation *m*; ~ **signal** *n* AERONAUT signal d'écart *m*; ~ **well** *n* PETR déviation *f*, puits dévié *m*

device *n* COMP DP dispositif *m*, périphérique *m*, MAR POLL dispositif *m*, MECH ENG appareil *m*, dispositif *m*, PAPER TECH dispositif *m*, PROD ENG appareil *m*, dispositif *m*, TELECOM dispositif *m*; ~ **control** *n* *(DC)* COMP, DP gestion des périphériques *f*; ~ **controller** *n* COMP, TELECOM contrôleur de périphériques *m*; ~ **driver** *n* COMP, DP gestionnaire de périphérique *m*, pilote de périphérique *m*; ~ **mark** *n* PATENTS marque figurative *f*; ~ **queue** *n* COMP, DP file d'attente d'un dispositif *f*, file d'attente d'un périphérique *f*; ~ **reserve** *n* COMP, DP réserve de périphérique *f*

devil *n* PROD ENG poêle à flamber *m*

devil's: ~ **claw** *n* CONST béquette *f*, chien *m*, tendeur articulé *m*, tendeur à pouce articulé *m*

devitrification *n* C&G dévitrification *f*; ~ **stone** *n* C&G pierre de dévitrification *f*

devitrify *vi* C&G dévitrifier

Devonian *adj* GEOL dévonien

dew: ~ **cap** *n* INSTRUMENT parasoleil *m*; ~ **indicator** *n* TV indicateur d'humidité *m*; ~ **point** *n* AERONAUT, FOOD TECH point de rosée *m*, HEAT ENG point de rosée *m*, *temperature* température au point de rosée *f*, METEO, PAPER TECH, PETR, PHYS, REFRIG point de rosée *m*; ~ **point depression** *n* REFRIG écart du point de rosée *m*; ~

point hygrometer n REFRIG hygromètre à point de rosée m; ~ **point measurement** n C&G mesure du point de rosée f; ~ **point temperature** n NUCLEAR point de rosée m, THERMOD température au point de rosée f; ~ **retting** n TEXTILES rouissage à terre m

Dewar: ~ **flask** n CHEM TECH, LAB EQUIP, PHYS vase de Dewar m

dewater vt HYDR EQUIP pump désamorcer, MINING a mine assécher, drainer, épuiser, TEXTILES déshydrater

dewatered: ~ **waste** n NUCLEAR liquid, slurry déchets déshydratés m pl

dewaterer n MINING cuve de décantation f

dewatering n CHEM déshydratation f, CONST assèchement m, dénoyage m, exhaure f, vidage m, épuisement m, MINING assèchement m, exhaure f, épuisement m, PETR déballastage m, PETR TECH, TEXTILES déshydratation f; ~ **point** n TEXTILES limite de déshydratation f; ~ **press** n PAPER TECH presse essoreuse f; ~ **pump** n MINING pompe d'épuisement f; ~ **roll** n PAPER TECH rouleau essoreur m; ~ **under load** n TEXTILES foulonnage m

dewdrop: ~ **glass** n C&G verre goutte d'eau m

deweylite n MINERAL deweylite f

dextran n CHEM dextrane f

dextrin n CHEM, FOOD TECH, P&R adhesives, PRINT dextrine f

dextrorotatory adj CHEM compound, FOOD TECH, PHYS dextrogyre

dextrose n CHEM dextrose m

Deybe-Hückel: ~ **theory** n CHEM théorie de Deybe-Hückel f

DF[1] abbr (direction finding) TELECOM goniométrie f, radiogoniométrie f

DF:[2] ~ **receiver** n NAUT radio récepteur gonio m

D-handle n CONST shovel manche m, manche à oeil m

diabase n (AmE) (cf dolerite) GEOL dolérite f, PETR diabase f

diacetic adj CHEM diacétique

diacetyl n CHEM diacétyle m

diacetylacetone n CHEM diacétylacétone f

diacetylene n CHEM diacétylène m

diachronous adj GEOL diachrone

diaclasite n MINERAL diaclasite f

diacritical adj COMP, DP diacritique

diadochite n MINERAL diadochite f

diadochy n GEOL monocristalline f, solution solide f

diaeresis n PRINT tréma m

diagenesis n FUELLESS, GEOL, PETR, PETR TECH diagénèse f

diagenetic adj PETR TECH diagénétique

diagnosis n COMP, DP diagnostic m

diagnostic[1] adj COMP, DP de diagnostic, diagnostique

diagnostic:[2] ~ **aid** n TELECOM outil de diagnostique m; ~ **error message** n COMP, DP message de diagnostique d'erreur m; ~ **program** n COMP, DP programme de diagnostic m; ~ **report** n COMP, DP diagnostic m; ~ **test** n COMP, DP test de diagnostic m

diagnostics n COMP, DP, TELECOM diagnostic m

diagonal[1] adj GEOM diagonal

diagonal[2] n GEOM diagonale f, NUCLEAR brace barre diagonale f, diagonale f; ~ **brace** n WATER SUPP of lock-gate bracon m; ~ **cutters** n pl MECH ENG tool pince coupante diagonale f; ~ **cutting nippers** n pl MECH ENG pinces coupantes diagonales f pl; ~ **joiner** n CINEMAT colleuse en biais f; ~ **lines** n pl NAUT naval architecture lisses planes f pl, sections obliques f pl; ~ **member rod** n

NUCLEAR steel barre diagonale f, diagonale f; ~ **ply tire** n (AmE), ~ **ply tyre** n (BrE) P&R rubber pneu diagonal m, pneumatique diagonal m; ~ **ram longwall face** n MINING taille en dressant au bélier f; ~ **register** n PRINT repérage diagonal m; ~ **scale** n MECH ENG drawing contre-échelle f, échelle transversale f; ~ **splice** n CINEMAT collure en biais f; ~ **stay** n HYDR EQUIP of boiler contreventement diagonal de chaudière m; ~ **strength** n NAUT naval architecture résistance diagonale f; ~ **weir** n HYDROL déversoir en biais m

diagonally adv GEOM diagonalement, en diagonale

diagram n COMP, DP diagramme m, MATH représentation graphique f, PROD ENG dessin schématique m, diagramme m, graphique m, plan graphique m, schéma m, schème m, épure f, for calculation of spiral springs abaque m, TELECOM diagramme m; ~ **of Corliss valve gear** n PROD ENG diagramme de la distribution Corliss m, épure de la distribution Corliss f

dial[1] n ELEC of instrument cadran m, échelle f, INSTRUMENT, MECH ENG faceplate, TELECOM, VEHICLES cadran m; ~ **gage** n (AmE), ~ **gauge** n (BrE) MECH ENG comparateur à cadran m, METEO measuring comparateur mécanique m; ~ **impulse** n (DP) TELECOM impulsion décimale f; ~ **indicating calipers** n pl (AmE), ~ **indicating callipers** n pl (BrE) METR calibres à cadran indicateur m pl; ~ **indicating gage** n (AmE), ~ **indicating gauge** n (BrE) METR calibre à cadran indicateur m; ~ **indicating micrometer** n METR micromètre à tambour m; ~ **plate** n MECH ENG faceplate cadran m; ~ **sight** n MILIT hausse circulaire f; ~ **telephone** n TELECOM téléphone à cadran m; ~ **thermometer** n REFRIG thermomètre à cadran m; ~ **tone delay** n TELECOM durée d'attente de tonalité f

dial[2] vt TELECOM number composer, signaler (Can)

dial[3] vi TELECOM numéroter; ~ **a number** vi TELECOM faire un numéro

dial-a-bus n TRANSP autobus à la demande m

dialing n (AmE) see dialling

dialkene n PETR TECH diène m

diallage n MINERAL diallage m

dialling n (BrE) MINING levé de plan à la boussole m, TELECOM composition f, numérotation f, sélection f ~ **code** n (BrE) TELECOM indicatif m; ~ **error** n (BrE) TELECOM erreur de numérotation f; ~ **period** n (BrE) TELECOM durée de numérotation f

diallogite n MINERAL diallogite f

dialog n (AmE) see dialogue

dialogite n MINERAL dialogite f

dialogue n (BrE) COMP, DP dialogue m ~ **equalizer** n RECORDING compresseur automatique m; ~ **replacement** n CINEMAT doublage en boucle m; ~ **track** n CINEMAT bande son synchrone f, TV piste du dialogue f

dial-type: ~ **metallic pressure gage** n (AmE), ~ **metallic pressure gauge** n (BrE) MECH ENG manomètre métallique indicateur m

dial-up: ~ **port** n TELECOM accès par réseau commuté m

dialuric: ~ **acid** n CHEM tatronylurée f

dialysate n CHEM dialysate m

dialyse vt CHEM dialyser

dialysis n CHEM dialyse f

dialytic adj CHEM dialytique

diamagnetic[1] adj PETR, PHYS, PROP MAT diamagnétique

diamagnetic:[2] ~ **anisotropy** n RAD PHYS anisotropie diamagnétique f; ~ **material** n ELEC substance diamagnétique f; ~ **shielding of the nucleus** n RAD

PHYS écran diamagnétique du noyau *m*; ~ **susceptibility** *n* RAD PHYS susceptibilité diamagnétique *f*

diamagnetics *n* RAD PHYS diamagnétiques *f pl*

diamagnetism *n* CHEM, ELEC, ELEC ENG, PHYS, RAD PHYS diamagnétisme *m*

diameter *n* GEOM *of circle* diamètre *m*; ~ **across flats** *n* MECH ENG diamètre sur plats *m*; ~ **equalization** *n* ACOUSTICS correction de diamètre *f*

diametral: ~ **groove pitch** *n* ACOUSTICS pas de sillonnage *m*

diametric *adj* GEOM diamétral

diametrical[1] *adj* ELEC, GEOM diamétral

diametrical:[2] ~ **winding** *n* ELEC *machine* enroulement diamétral *m*

diametrically: ~ **opposed** *adv* GEOM diamétralement opposé

diamide *n* CHEM diamide *m*

diamine *n* CHEM diamine *f*

diaminodiphenylmethane *n* P&R *curing agent* diaminodiphénylméthane *m*

diamond *n* C&G *to cut glass* diamant *m*, MECH ENG burin en pointe de diamant *m*, MINERAL diamant *m*, PRINT *paper* second choix *m*; ~ **bit** *n* PETR TECH trépan à diamant *m*; ~ **boring crown** *n* MINING *drilling*, PROD ENG couronne à pointes de diamant *f*; ~ **cleaving** *n* PROD ENG clivage de diamant *m*, fendage du diamant *m*, sciage du diamant *m*; ~ **cold chisel** *n* MECH ENG burin en pointe de diamant *m*; ~ **core drill** *n* PETR TECH carottier au diamant *m*, PROD ENG sonde à pointes de diamant et à tube carottier *f*; ~ **crossing** *n* RAIL TO, traversée *f*, traversée oblique *f*; ~ **crown set** *n* MINING couronne à pointes de diamant *f*; ~ **cut pattern** *n* C&G taille en diamants *f*; ~ **cutter** *n* PROD ENG *person* diamantaire *m*; ~ **cutting** *n* PROD ENG tranchant diamanté *m*; ~ **cutting edge** *n* C&G coupe du diamant *f*; ~ **drill** *n* GAS TECH couronne diamantée *f*, PROD ENG foreuse à pointes de diamant *f*, perforateur diamanté *m*, perforatrice diamantée *f*, perforatrice à diamants *f*, perforatrice à pointes de diamant *f*, sonde à pointes de diamant *f*, sondeuse à diamant *f*; ~ **driller** *n* MINING *person* sondeur au diamant *m*; ~ **drilling** *n* MINING forage au diamant *m*, perforation au diamant *f*, sondage au diamant *m*, PETR TECH forage au diamant *m*; ~ **dust** *n* MINING poussière de diamant *f*, égrisé *m*; ~ **field** *n* MINING champ diamantifère *m*; ~ **grinding-wheel** *n* MECH ENG meule diamantée *f*, meule à base de diamant *f*; ~ **held upright** *n* C&G diamant tenu droit *m*; ~ **held with firm grip** *n* C&G diamant tenu piquant *m*; ~ **ink** *n* COLOURS encre pour gravure sur verre *f*; ~ **lattice** *n* METALL réseau du diamant *m*; ~ **matrix** *n* MINING roche mère du diamant *f*; ~ **mine** *n* MINING mine de diamants *f*; ~ **mining** *n* MINING exploitation des mines de diamants *f*; ~ **nose chisel** *n* MECH ENG burin en pointe de diamant *m*; ~ **paste** *n* METALL pâte diamantée *f*; ~ **pencil** *n* C&G diamant pour couper le verre *m*, CONST diamant de vitrier *m*, pointe de diamant *f*; ~ **point** *n* CONST diamant de vitrier *m*, pointe de diamant *f*, MECH ENG *lathe* outil à pointe de diamant *m*, pointe de diamant *f*, SPRINGS bout trapézoïdal *m*; ~ **point chisel** *n* MECH ENG burin en pointe de diamant *m*; ~ **point engraving** *n* C&G gravure au diamant *f*; ~ **point tool** *n* MECH ENG outil à pointe de diamant *m*, pointe de diamant *f*; ~ **powder** *n* MINING poussière de diamant *f*, égrisé *m*; ~ **riffle** *n* WATER SUPP *sluices* riffle en losanges *m*; ~ **ring effect** *n* ASTRON effet d'anneau de diamants *m*; ~ **saw** *n* MECH ENG scie à base de diamant

f; ~ **slitting wheel** *n* C&G scie à diamants *f*; ~ **stylus** *n* RECORDING pointe en diamant *f*; ~ **tool** *n* CONST diamant de vitrier *m*, pointe de diamant *f*, MECH outil diamanté *m*, MECH ENG outil au diamant *m*, outil à pointe de diamant *m*, pointe de diamant *f*; ~ **winding** *n* ELEC *in machine*, ELEC ENG enroulement en losange *m*; ~ **wire lattice** *n* CONST treillage métallique en losange *m*

diamond-bearing *adj* MINING diamantifère

diamond-held: ~ **trailing** *n* C&G diamant tenu traînant *m*

diamondiferous *adj* MINING diamantifère

diamond-tipped: ~ **pen** *n* LAB EQUIP *for marking* stylo à pointe de diamant *m*

diaphanous *adj* PROP MAT diaphane

diaphasic *adj* TRANSP *jet* diaphasique

diaphone *n* NAUT *navigation aid, foghorn* diaphone *m*

diaphorite *n* MINERAL diaphorite *f*

diaphragm *n* CINEMAT diaphragme *m*, iris *m*, MECH diaphragme *m*, MECH ENG *of pump* membrane *f*, PHOTO diaphragme *m*, RECORDING membrane *f*; ~ **cellular cofferdam** *n* HYDROL batardeau cellulaire à cellules gabionnées *m*; ~ **clutch** *n* AUTO embrayage à diaphragme *m*; ~ **compressor** *n* MECH ENG compresseur à membrane *m*; ~ **fuel pump** *n* VEHICLES pompe à essence à membrane *f*; ~ **jig** *n* COAL TECH bac à diaphragme *m*; ~ **meter** *n* GAS TECH appareil à diaphragme *m*, compteur à diaphragme *m*; ~ **presetting** *n* CINEMAT présélection de diaphragme *f*; ~ **pressure vessel** *n* MECH ENG réservoir à pression à membrane *m*; ~ **pump** *n* MAR POLL, WATER SUPP pompe à diaphragme *f*; ~ **valve** *n* MECH ENG vanne à membrane *f*

diaphragm-type: ~ **washbox** *n* COAL TECH bac à diaphragme *m*

diapir *n* GEOL, PETR TECH diapir *m*

diapositive *n* PHOTO diapositive *f*

diaschistic *adj* PETR diaschiste

diaspore *n* MINERAL diaspore *m*

diastase *n* CHEM céréaline *f*, diastase *f*, FOOD TECH diastase *f*

diastem *n* PETR diastème *f*

diastereoisomer *n* CHEM diastéréo-isomère *m*

diathermal *adj* PHYS diathermane, diatherme

diathermanous *adj* THERMOD diathermane

diathermic *adj* THERMOD diathermane

diatom *n* PETR diatomée *f*

diatomaceous: ~ **brick** *n* HEAT ENG *thermal insulation* brique de diatomite *f*; ~ **earth** *n* FOOD TECH terre à diatomées *f*, GEOL diatomite *f*, terre à diatomées *f*, HYDROL, REFRIG terre à diatomées *f*

diatomic[1] *adj* CHEM diatomique

diatomic:[2] ~ **gas** *n* PHYS gaz diatomique *m*; ~ **molecule** *n* RAD PHYS molécule diatomique *f*

diatomite *n* GEOL, HEAT ENG *insulation*, MINERAL diatomite *f*

diatonic[1] *adj* ACOUSTICS *scale* diatonique

diatonic:[2] ~ **semitone** *n* ACOUSTICS demi-ton diatonique *m*; ~ **tetrachord** *n* ACOUSTICS tétracorde diatonique *f*

diatreme *n* GEOL *volcanic pipe* cheminée volcanique diatrème *f*

diazo *n* CHEM *compound* diazo *m*, PRINT diazoïque *m*; ~ **coating** *n* PRINT couche diazoïque *f*; ~ **compound** *n* CHEM diazoïque *m*

diazoacetic *adj* CHEM diazoacétique

diazobenzene *n* CHEM diazobenzène *m*

diazoimide *n* CHEM diazoïmide *m*

diazole *n* CHEM diazole *m*

diazomine n CHEM diazominé m

diazonium n CHEM diazonium m

diazotize vt CHEM diazoter

dibasic adj CHEM bibasique, dibasique

dibenzanthracene n CHEM dibenzanthracène m

dibenzopyrrole n CHEM dibenzopyrrole m

dibenzoyl n CHEM dibenzoyle m

dibenzylamine n CHEM dibenzylamine f

dibromobenzene n CHEM dibromobenzène m

dibromohydrin n CHEM dibromohydrine f

dibromosuccinic adj CHEM dibromosuccinique

dibutyl: ~ **phthalate** n P&R plasticizer phtalate de dibutyle m

dibutyrin n CHEM dibutyrine f

dice vt FOOD TECH couper en dés

dichloracetic adj CHEM dichloracétique

dichloride n CHEM bichlorure m

dichloroacetone n CHEM dichloroacétone f

dichlorobenzene n CHEM dichlorobenzène m

dichloroethane n CHEM dichloroéthane f

dichlorohydrin n CHEM dichlorohydrine f

dichotomizing: ~ **search** n COMP, DP recherche de Fibonacci f, recherche dichotomique f

dichotomy n ASTRON dichotomie f

dichroic[1] adj PHYS dichroïque

dichroic:[2] ~ **filter** n CINEMAT, ELECTRON, OPT, TELECOM filtre dichroïque m; ~ **fog** n CINEMAT, PHOTO voile dichroïque m; ~ **glass** n C&G verre dichroïque m; ~ **LCD** n ELECTRON afficheur LCD dichroïque m, afficheur dichroïque m, afficheur à cristaux liquides dichroïques m; ~ **liquid crystals** n pl ELECTRON cristaux liquides dichroïques m pl; ~ **mirror** n CINEMAT, OPT, TELECOM miroir dichroïque m

dichroism n CHEM, CRYSTALL, PHYS dichroïsme m

dichroïte n MINERAL dichroïte f

dichromate n CHEM bichromate m, dichromate m

dickinsonite n MINERAL dickinsonite f

Dictaphone n (TM) RECORDING Dictaphone m (MD)

dictation: ~ **machine** n RECORDING Dictaphone m (MD)

dictionary n COMP, DP dictionnaire m

DID abbr (AmE) (direct inward dialing) TELECOM accès direct à l'arrivée m, selection directe à un poste f

Didyme: ~ **comma** n ACOUSTICS comma de Didyme m

didymium n CHEM didyme m, didymium m

die[1] n C&G, CINEMAT matrice f, MECH presswork matrice f, threading, wire drawing filière f, MECH ENG moule m, engine link block coulisseau m, for wire, bar and tube drawing filière d'étirage et de tréfilage f, for threading filière de filetage f, in conjunction with punches matrice f, MINING for ore stamps dé m, semelle f, PRINT buse pour envoi sous pression de la solution de couchage f, emporte-pièce m, forme de découpe f, PROD ENG matrice f, matrice à découper f, for wiredrawing filière f, filière à étirer f, for tup of power hammer frappe f, frappe supérieure f, panne du pilon f, for anvil of power hammer tas m, tas inférieur m, of amalgamating pan semelle f, solid die, for engineer's screw stock coussinet-lunette m, lunette f, lunette à fileter f, lunette à tarauder f; ~ **bar** n MECH ENG bouterolle f; ~ **cast** n PROD ENG coulée en matrice f; ~ **cast body** n PROD ENG corps en métal moulé m; ~ **casting** n PROD ENG coulée en matrice f, coulée sous pression f, PROP MAT coulée par injection f; ~ **casting die** n MECH ENG moule pour fonderie sous pression m; ~ **casting machine** n MECH ENG machine à mouler en coquille f; ~ **chuck** n PROD ENG mandrin à coussinets m; ~ **cut** n

PRINT forme de découpe f; ~ **cutting** n PRINT découpe à l'emporte-pièce f; ~ **forging** n PROD ENG matriçage m; ~ **guide** n PROD ENG screw stock guide-coussinets m; ~ **head** n PROD ENG screw-cutting coussinet m, filière f plateau porte-coussinets m, porte-coussinets m, porte-lunette m; ~ **holder** n MECH ENG in press, PROD ENG for punching machine porte-matrice m; ~ **in one piece** n PROD ENG screw stock lunette d'une seule pièce f; ~ **in two halves** n MECH ENG screw stock coussinet en deux pièces m; ~ **nut** n PROD ENG écrou taraudeur m; ~ **plate** n PROD ENG screw-cutting filière f, wiredrawing filière f, filière à étirer f; ~ **set** n MECH ENG for stamping, punching bloc à colonnes m

die:[2] ~ **out** vi GEOL se terminer en biseau

die-cast[1] adj MECH materials coulé sous pression

die-cast[2] vt MECH ENG mouler sous pression

die-cut vt PRINT découper à l'emporte-pièce

dieldrin n CHEM, FOOD TECH dieldrine f

dielectric[1] adj CHEM, ELEC capacitor, PRINT diélectrique

dielectric[2] n ELEC ENG, PHYS, TELECOM diélectrique m; ~ **absorption** n ELEC ENG absorption diélectrique f; ~ **antenna** n SPACE communications antenne cierge f, TELECOM antenne diélectrique f; ~ **breakdown** n ELEC rupture diélectrique f; ~ **charge** n TELECOM charge diélectrique f; ~ **condenser** n ELEC condensateur diélectrique m; ~ **constant** n ELEC ENG, P&R constante diélectrique f, PHYS relative permittivity permittivité relative f; ~ **current** n ELEC ENG courant diélectrique m; ~ **heater** n MECH ENG réchauffeur diélectrique m; ~ **heating** n ELEC, ELEC ENG, HEATING chauffage diélectrique m; ~ **hysteresis** n ELEC, ELEC ENG hystérésis diélectrique f; ~ **isolation** n ELEC ENG isolement diélectrique m; ~ **loss** n ELEC, ELEC ENG, PHYS perte diélectrique f; ~ **loss angle** n ELEC angle de pertes diélectriques m; ~ **material** n ELEC ENG corps diélectrique m; ~ **medium** n ELEC ENG milieu diélectrique m; ~ **polarization** n ELEC ENG polarisation diélectrique f; ~ **property** n ELEC propriété diélectrique f; ~ **resistance** n ELEC of capacitor rigidité diélectrique f, résistance diélectrique f; ~ **resonator** n TELECOM résonateur diélectrique m; ~ **resonator filter** n SPACE communications filtre à résonateur diélectrique m; ~ **rigidity test** n ELEC ENG essai de rigidité diélectrique m; ~ **strength** n ELEC of capacitor rigidité diélectrique f, résistance diélectrique f, ELEC ENG, PHYS, PROP MAT rigidité diélectrique f; ~ **susceptibility** n ELEC susceptibilité diélectrique f; ~ **swelling** n NUCLEAR gonflement diélectrique m; ~ **thawing** n REFRIG décongélation diélectrique f

Diels-Alder: ~ **reaction** n CHEM réaction de Diels-Alder f

diene n CHEM diène m, compound allène m

di-ergol: ~ **technology** n SPACE technologie diergol f

dies n pl MECH ENG for extruding, forming, press tools outillage m; ~ **for metallic powders** n pl MECH ENG outillage pour poudre métallique m; ~ **for motor body panels** n pl MECH ENG press tools outillage pour tôles de carrosserie automobile m; ~ **for pressing** n pl MECH ENG outillage pour presses m; ~ **for punching** n MECH ENG outillage de poinçonnage m; ~ **for stamping** n MECH ENG outillage d'emboutissage m

diesel: ~ **compression tester** n AUTO compressiomètre pour moteur diesel m; ~ **engine** n AUTO, NAUT, PROD ENG, TRANSP, VEHICLES moteur diesel m; ~ **fuel** n AUTO gazole m, PETR TECH diesel oil m, TRANSP gazole m, VEHICLES gas-oil m, gazole m; ~ **gas** n GAS TECH fuel gaz m; ~ **generator standby power plant** n NUCLEAR groupe électrogène de secours m; ~ **generator unit**

service car n (AmE) *(cf diesel generator unit service wagon)* RAIL *vehicles* wagon de service à groupe diesel-électrique m; ~ **generator unit service wagon** n (BrE) *(cf diesel generator unit service car)* RAIL *vehicles* wagon de service à groupe diesel-électrique m; ~ **hammer** n COAL TECH pilon diesel m; ~ **oil** n TRANSP carburant diesel m

diesel-driven: ~ **generating set** n ELEC ENG groupe électrogène diesel m

diesel-electric: ~ **drive** n TRANSP propulseur diesel-électrique m; ~ **engine** n TRANSP moteur diesel-électrique m; ~ **locomotive** n RAIL locomotive diesel-électrique f; ~ **power station** n ELEC ENG centrale diesel f; ~ **railcar** n (AmE) RAIL autorail diesel-électrique m; ~ **shunting motor tractor** n RAIL locotracteur diesel-électrique de manoeuvre m

diesel-hydraulic: ~ **engine** n MECH ENG moteur diesel-hydraulique m; ~ **locomotive** n RAIL, TRANSP locomotive diesel-hydraulique f

diesel-hydromechanical: ~ **locomotive** n RAIL locomotive diesel à transmission hydromécanique f

dieseling n AUTO cognement m

diesel-powered: ~ **compressor** n MECH ENG compresseur entraîné par moteur diesel m

die-sinking n MECH ENG forçage par matrice m; ~ **machine** n MECH ENG machine à fraiser les matrices et les moules f

die-stamping n MECH *presswork* estampage m, matriçage m, PRINT impression en timbrage-relief f; ~ **press** n PAPER TECH presse à découper f

die-stock n PROD ENG filière f, filière à coussinets f, porte-filière m

dietary: ~ **fiber** n (AmE), ~ **fibre** n (BrE) FOOD TECH fibre alimentaire f; ~ **sugar** n FOOD TECH sucre de fermentation m

diethanolamine n CHEM, DETERGENTS diéthanolamine f

die-threading: ~ **machine** n MECH ENG machine à fileter à la filière f

diethyl: ~ **ether** n DETERGENTS éther diéthylique m

diethylene n DETERGENTS diéthylène m

diethylenic adj CHEM diéthylénique

difference n COMP, DP différence f, THERMOD *in temperature* écart m; ~ **amplifier** n ELECTRON amplificateur de différence m; ~ **channel** n RECORDING canal de différence m; ~ **check control** n CONTROL contrôle par différences m; ~ **frequency** n ELECTRON fréquence de différence f, fréquence différentielle f; ~ **limen** n RECORDING seuil différentiel m; ~ **note** n RECORDING note différentielle f; ~ **signal** n ELECTRON signal de différence m

differential[1] adj MATH différentiel

differential[2] n AUTO, C&G *controlling plunger and shear movements in bottle-making* différentiel m, MATH différentielle f, MECH *vehicles*, MECH ENG différentiel m, VEHICLES *transmission* différentiel m, engrenage différentiel m; ~ **ammeter** n ELEC ampèremètre différentiel m; ~ **amplifier** n ELECTRON, PHYS, TELECOM amplificateur différentiel m; ~ **bevel gear** n VEHICLES *transmission* pignon conique de différentiel m; ~ **braking** n AERONAUT freinage différentiel m; ~ **calculus** n MATH calcul différentiel m; ~ **capacitor** n ELEC ENG condensateur variable différentiel m; ~ **carrier** n AUTO carter de différentiel m; ~ **case** n AUTO boîtier de différentiel m; ~ **chain block** n MECH *lifting gear* palan différentiel m, NUCLEAR poulie différentielle f; ~ **coefficient** n MATH coefficient différentiel m; ~ **coil** n ELEC

bobine différentielle f; ~ **comparator** n ELECTRON comparateur différentiel m; ~ **control rod worth** n NUCLEAR efficacité différentielle f; ~ **corrections** n pl NAUT *navigation by satellite* mesures différentielles de correction f pl; ~ **delay** n ELECTRON retard différentiel m; ~ **effect** n AERONAUT effet différentiel m; ~ **equation** n MATH équation différentielle f; ~ **focusing** n CINEMAT mise au point sélective f; ~ **gain** n ELECTRON gain différentiel m, TV amplification différentielle f, gain différentiel m; ~ **galvanometer** n ELEC, ELEC ENG galvanomètre différentiel m; ~ **geometry** n GEOM géométrie différentielle f; ~ **governor** n CONTROL régulateur différentiel m; ~ **GPS data** n pl NAUT *navigation by satellite* données différentielles GPS f pl; ~ **head** n FUELLESS colonne d'eau différentielle f; ~ **input** n ELECTRON entrée différentielle f; ~ **lock** n VEHICLES *transmission* verrouillage de différentiel m; ~ **magnetometer** n ELEC magnétomètre différentiel m; ~ **measuring instrument** n INSTRUMENT instrument de mesure différentiel m; ~ **microphone** n ACOUSTICS, RECORDING microphone différentiel m; ~ **mode** n ELECTRON mode différentiel m; ~ **mode attenuation** n OPT, TELECOM affaiblissement modal différentiel m; ~ **mode delay** n OPT, TELECOM temps de propagation de groupe modal différentiel m; ~ **mode signal** n ELECTRON signal d'entrée différentiel m; ~ **modulation** n ELECTRON modulation différentielle f; ~ **phase** n ELECTRON *(DP)*, TV phase différentielle f; ~ **phase-shift keying** n *(DPSK)* ELECTRON modulation DPSK f, modulation par déplacement de phase différentielle f; ~ **pinion** n AUTO satellite m; ~ **pressure** n PETR TECH pression différentielle f; ~ **pressure controller** n CONTROL régulateur différentiel de pression m; ~ **pressure gage** n (AmE), ~ **pressure gauge** n (BrE) MECH manomètre différentiel m; ~ **protection relay** n ELEC relais différentiel m; ~ **pulley** n PHYS poulie différentielle f; ~ **pulse code modulation** n *(DPCM)* ELECTRON modulation PCM différentielle f, modulation différentielle par impulsions codées f; ~ **quantum efficiency** n OPT, TELECOM rendement quantique différentiel m; ~ **ratio** n AUTO rapport de pont m; ~ **regulator** n CONTROL régulateur à action différentielle m; ~ **relay** n ELEC relais différentiel m, relais à action différée m, ELEC ENG relais différentiel m; ~ **rotation** n ASTRON *of galaxy rotating at different speeds* rotation différentielle f; ~ **scanning calorimetry** n P&R *analysis* calorimétrie par analyse différentielle f, RAD PHYS calorimétrie différentielle à balayage f, THERMOD calorimétrie différentielle programmée f, calorimétrie différentielle à balayage f, calorimétrie par analyse différentielle f; ~ **settlement** n CONST *of foundations* tassement différentiel m; ~ **shrinkage** n TEXTILES retrait différentiel m; ~ **side gear** n AUTO pignon planétaire m; ~ **signal** n ELECTRON signal différentiel m; ~ **signal source** n ELECTRON source de signaux différentiels f; ~ **spider** n VEHICLES *transmission* croisillon de différentiel m; ~ **spider pinion** n VEHICLES *transmission* satellite de différentiel m; ~ **system** n TESTING *coil arrangements* système différentiel m; ~ **temperature** n PETR TECH température différentielle f; ~ **thermal analysis** n *(DTA)* CONST, P&R, POLLUTION, THERMOD analyse thermique différentielle f *(ATD)*; ~ **thermocouple** n THERMOD couple thermoélectrique différentiel m; ~ **thermometer** n THERMOD thermomètre différentiel m; ~ **threshold** n ACOUSTICS seuil différentiel m; ~ **threshold of frequency** n ACOUSTICS seuil différentiel de fréquence *m*; ~ **threshold of sound pressure level** *n* ACOUSTICS seuil différentiel de niveau de pression acoustique *m*; ~ **time** *n* ELECTRON temps différentiel *m*; ~ **topology** *n* GEOM topologie différentielle *f*; ~ **transducer** *n* ELEC ENG capteur différentiel *m*; ~ **transformer** *n* ELEC, ELEC ENG transformateur différentiel *m*; ~ **voltage** *n* ELEC ENG tension différentielle *f*; ~ **voltmeter** *n* ELEC voltmètre différentiel *m*; ~ **winding** *n* ELEC ENG enroulement différentiel *m*

differentially-excited: ~ **compound generator** *n* ELEC dynamo compound à excitation différentielle *f*

differentiated *adj* ELECTRON *signal* différentié, GEOL *igneous rock or suite* différencié, évolué, MATH différentié

differentiating: ~ **circuit** *n* ELECTRON circuit différentiateur *m*, différentiateur *m*

differentiation *n* MATH différentiation *f*, dérivation *f*

difficult: ~ **ground** *n* CONST sol difficile *m*

diffracted: ~ **beam** *n* CRYSTALL faisceau diffracté *m*; ~ **wave** *n* PHYS onde diffractée *f*

diffraction *n* CRYSTALL, ELEC ENG, OPT, PETR, PHOTO, PHYS, TELECOM, WAVE PHYS *of waves* diffraction *f*; ~ **grating** *n* OPT, PHYS, PROP MAT, TELECOM, WAVE PHYS réseau de diffraction *m*; ~ **pattern** *n* CRYSTALL diagramme de diffraction *m*, METALL dessin de diffraction *m*, diagramme de diffraction *m*, PROP MAT image de diffraction *f*; ~ **spectrograph** *n* NUCLEAR spectrographe à réseau *m*; ~ **spectrum** *n* RAD PHYS spectre de diffraction *m*; ~ **spot** *n* CRYSTALL tache de diffraction *f*

diffractometer *n* CRYSTALL, PROP MAT diffractomètre *m*

diffractometry *n* PETR TECH diffractométrie *f*

diffusate *n* PROP MAT diffusat *m*

diffuse[1] *adj* PROP MAT diffus

diffuse:[2] ~ **blue reflectance factor** *n* PAPER TECH facteur de réflectance diffuse dans le bleu *m*; ~ **field** *n* ACOUSTICS champ diffus *m*; ~ **field method** *n* RECORDING méthode en champ diffus *f*; ~ **light density** *n* OPT densité en lumière diffuse *f*; ~ **light recorder** *n* INSTRUMENT enregistreur de lumière dispersée *m*; ~ **nebula** *n* ASTRON, SPACE nébuleuse diffuse *f*; ~ **radiation** *n* FUELLESS, SPACE rayonnement diffus *m*; ~ **reflection** *n* ELEC ENG, RAD PHYS réflexion diffuse *f*; ~ **scattering method** *n* NUCLEAR *in X-ray crystallography* méthode de diffusion diffuse *f*

diffuse[3] *vt* PHOTO diffuser

diffused: ~ **alloy transistor** *n* ELECTRON transistor à jonction par diffusion et alliage *m*; ~ **emitter-collector transistor** *n* ELECTRON transistor à émetteur et collecteur diffusés *m*; ~ **junction** *n* ELECTRON jonction par diffusion *f*; ~ **layer** *n* ELECTRON couche diffusée *f*; ~ **light** *n* CINEMAT lumière diffuse *f*; ~ **photodiode** *n* ELECTRON photodiode à jonction par diffusion *f*

diffuser *n* CHEM TECH diffuseur *m*, CINEMAT écran diffuseur *m*, FUELLESS diffuseur *m*, PHOTO *for incident light measurement* calotte diffusante *f*, REFRIG *in air conditioning system*, TELECOM diffuseur *m*; ~ **blade** *n* CHEM TECH palette de diffuseur *f*; ~ **lens** *n* INSTRUMENT lentille de flou *f*, lentille diffusante *f*; ~ **scrim** *n* CINEMAT écran diffuseur *m*

diffusing[1] *adj* C&G *glass* diffusant

diffusing:[2] ~ **substance** *n* PROP MAT diffusant *m*

diffusiometer *n* OCEANOG diffusiomètre *m*

diffusion *n* CHEM *of fluids*, COAL TECH, CONST, ELECTRON, PHYS, POLLUTION, PROP MAT diffusion *f*; ~ **across the magnetic field** *n* NUCLEAR diffusion à travers le champ

magnétique *f*; ~ **annealing** *n* CHEM TECH homogénéisation *f*; ~ **apparatus** *n* CHEM TECH appareil de diffusion *m*; ~ **area** *n* REFRIG *of air stream in air conditioning* surface couverte *f*; ~ **cell** *n* CHEM TECH cellule de diffusion *f*; ~ **coefficient** *n* ELECTRON, PHYS coefficient de diffusion *m*; ~ **current** *n* ELEC *electrolysis* courant de diffusion *m*; ~ **defect** *n* ELECTRON défaut de diffusion *m*; ~ **doping** *n* ELECTRON dopage par diffusion *m*; ~ **effect filter** *n* CINEMAT bonnette de flou *f*; ~ **hardening** *n* NUCLEAR *of neutron spectrum* durcissement par diffusion *m*; ~ **kernel** *n* NUCLEAR noyau de l'intégrale de diffusion *m*; ~ **length** *n* ELECTRON longueur de diffusion *f*; ~ **mean free path** *n* NUCLEAR libre parcours moyen de diffusion *m*; ~ **oven** *n* CHEM TECH, ELECTRON four à diffusion *m*; ~ **pump** *n* INSTRUMENT pompe *f*, MECH ENG, PHYS pompe à diffusion *f*; ~ **tower** *n* CHEM TECH tour de diffusion *f*

diffusionless: ~ **reaction** *n* METALL réaction sans diffusion *f*

diffusivity *n* FLUID PHYS, PROP MAT diffusivité *f*

digest *vt* RECYCLING digérer

digested: ~ **sludge** *n* HYDROL *sewage* boue digérée *f*

digester *n* HYDROL *sewage* digesteur *m*, PAPER TECH lessiveur *m*, RECYCLING digesteur *m*, THERMOD autoclave *m*; ~ **gas** *n* HYDROL *sewage* gaz de digestion *m*, RECYCLING biogaz *m*, gaz de digestion *m*, THERMOD *sewage treatment* gaz de curage *m*

digestible[1] *adj* RECYCLING assimilable par l'organisme, digestible

digestible:[2] ~ **organic matter** *n (DOM)* RECYCLING matière organique digestible *f (MOD)*

digestion *n* CHEM minéralisation *f*, PAPER TECH lessivage *m*, RECYCLING digestion *f*; ~ **apparatus** *n* LAB EQUIP *analysis* minéralisateur *m*; ~ **tank** *n* HYDROL *sewage* digesteur *m*, THERMOD *sewage treatment* chambre de digestion des boues *f*; ~ **time** *n* HYDROL *sewage* temps de digestion *m*

digestive[1] *adj* RECYCLING digestif

digestive:[2] ~ **enzyme** *n* RECYCLING enzyme digestive *f*; ~ **system** *n* RECYCLING appareil digestif *m*

digger *n* COAL TECH piqueur *m*, MINING *person* chercheur *m*, orpailleur *m*, pailleteur *m*

digging *n* COAL TECH creusement *m*, CONST creusage *m*, creusement *m*, déblayage *m*, excavation *f*, fouille *f*; ~ **bucket** *n* TRANSP godet de la pelle *m*; ~ **bucket teeth** *n* TRANSP dents de fouille de la pelle *f pl*; ~ **face** *n* MINING *dredging* front de dragage *m*; ~ **ladder** *n* MINING *of dredge* élinde *f*; ~ **machine** *n* CONST excavateur *m*, terrasseur *m*; ~ **technique** *n* CONST technique de déblayage *f*, technique de forage *f*

diggings *n pl* MINING exploitation *f*, gisements alluvionnaires *m pl*, minière *f*, placer *m*

digit *n* COMP, DP chiffre *m*

digital:[1] ~ **all** ~ *adj* ELECTRON entièrement numérique CINEMAT, COMP, DP, ELECTRON, PHYS numérique, RECORDING digital, TELECOM numérique

digital:[2] ~ **actuator** *n* ELEC ENG actionneur numérique *m*; ~ **adder** *n* ELECTRON additionneur numérique *m*; ~ **ammeter** *n* ELEC ampèremètre digital *m*, ampèremètre numérique *m*; ~ **attenuator** *n* ELECTRON atténuateur numérique *m*; ~ **audio tape** *n (DAT)* COMP bande audio-numérique *f*, RECORDING cassette numérique *f*; ~ **camera** *n* TV caméra numérique *f*; ~ **carrier module** *n* TELECOM module multiplex numérique *m*; ~ **cassette** *n* COMP cassette numérique *f*; ~ **chip** *n* ELECTRON puce numérique *f*; ~ **circuit** *n* COMP, DP circuit numérique *m*, ELECTRON circuit numérique *m*, montage numérique *m*, TELECOM circuit numérique *m*; ~ **circuit design** *n* ELECTRON conception des circuits numériques *f*; ~ **circuit multiplication equipment** *n* *(DCME)* TELECOM terminal de concentration numérique des conversations *m*, équipement de multiplication de circuit numérique *m*; ~ **circuit multiplication gain** *n* *(DCMG)* TELECOM gain de l'équipement de multiplication de circuit numérique *m* *(GMCN)*; ~ **circuit multiplication system** *n* *(DCMS)* TELECOM système de multiplication de circuit numérique *m* *(SMCN)*; ~ **clock** *n* COMP, DP horloge numérique *f*; ~ **code** *n* ELECTRON code numérique *m*; ~ **coding** *n* ELECTRON codage numérique *m*, TELECOM codage sous forme numérique *m*; ~ **command signal** *n* *(DCS)* TELECOM signal de commande numérique *m*; ~ **communications** *n pl* COMP, DP communications numériques *f pl*, communications numérisées *f pl*; ~ **computer** *n* COMP, DP calculateur numérique *m*, ordinateur numérique *m*; ~ **connection** *n* TELECOM connexion numérique *f*; ~ **control** *n* COMP, CONTROL, DP, ELEC *computer*, MECH ENG, PROD ENG, TELECOM, TV commande numérique *f*; ~ **control box** *n* AUTO boîtier de commande électronique *m*; ~ **control system** *n* CONTROL système de commande numérique *m*; ~ **converter** *n* ELECTRON convertisseur numérique *m*; ~ **cross-connect** *n* *(DXC)* TELECOM brasseur-répartiteur numérique *m*; ~ **cross-connect equipment** *n* TELECOM équipement multiplexeur-aiguilleur numérique *m*; ~ **data** *n* ELECTRON données numériques *f pl*, informations numériques *f pl*; ~ **device** *n* ELECTRON dispositif numérique *m*; ~ **display** *n* ELECTRON, INSTRUMENT affichage numérique *m*; ~ **distribution frame** *n* TELECOM répartiteur numérique *m*; ~ **domain** *n* ELECTRON domaine numérique *m*; ~ **error** *n* TELECOM erreur numérique *f*; ~ **exchange** *n* TELECOM autocommutateur numérique *m*, commutateur numérique *m*; ~ **feedback** *n* TELECOM asservissement numérique *m*; ~ **filling** *n* TELECOM remplissage numérique *m*; ~ **filter** *n* ELECTRON, TELECOM filtre numérique *m*; ~ **filtering** *n* COMP, DP, ELECTRON, TELECOM filtrage numérique *m*; ~ **flight data recorder** *n* AERONAUT enregistreur numérique de données de vol *m*; ~ **framer** *n* TV circuit numérique de synchronisation *m*, synchroniseur numérique *m*; ~ **frame structure** *n* TELECOM structure de la trame numérique *f*; ~ **hierarchy** *n* TELECOM hiérarchie numérique *f*; ~ **identification frame** *n* TELECOM trame d'identification numérique *f*; ~ **image** *n* ELECTRON image numérique *f*; ~ **image processing** *n* ELECTRON traitement numérique des images *m*; ~ **input** *n* ELECTRON entrée numérique *f*; ~ **input signal** *n* ELECTRON signal d'entrée numérique *m*; ~ **instantaneous frequency measurement** *n* ELECTRON mesure numérique de la fréquence instantanée *f*; ~ **instrument** *n* ELEC appareil de mesure numérique *m*; ~ **integrated circuit** *n* ELECTRON circuit intégré numérique *m*; ~ **integration** *n* ELECTRON intégration numérique *f*; ~ **integrator** *n* ELECTRON intégrateur numérique *m*; ~ **interface** *n* TELECOM interface numérique *f*; ~ **interference** *n* TELECOM brouillage numérique *m*; ~ **logic** *n* ELECTRON logique numérique *f*; ~ **loop** *n* TELECOM boucle numérique *f*; ~ **main network switching center** *n* (AmE), ~ **main network switching centre** *n* (BrE) *(DMNSC)* TELECOM centre de commutation numérique du réseau principal *m*; ~ **matched filter** *n* ELECTRON filtre adapté numérique *m*; ~ **modulation** *n* ELECTRON, PHYS, TELECOM modulation

numérique *f*; ~ **modulation link** *n* TELECOM liaison numérique *f*; ~ **modulation system** *n* TELECOM système à modulation numérique *m*; ~ **multimeter** *n* ELEC ENG multimètre numérique *m*; ~ **multiplex** *n* ELECTRON multiplex numérique *m*, multiplexeur numérique *m*; ~ **multiplexer** *n* *(DM)* TELECOM multiplexeur numérique *m*; ~ **multiplexing** *n* ELECTRON, PHYS multiplexage numérique *m*; ~ **multiplication** *n* ELECTRON multiplication numérique *f*; ~ **multiplier** *n* ELECTRON multiplieur numérique *m*; ~ **network** *n* *(DN)* TELECOM réseau numérique *m*; ~ **optical disc** *n* (BrE) OPT DON, disque optique numérique *m*; ~ **optical disk** *n* COMP, DP, OPT (AmE) DON, disque optique numérique *m* ~ **output** *n* ELECTRON sortie numérique *f*; ~ **output signal** *n* ELECTRON signal de sortie numérique *m*; ~ **pad** *n* TELECOM complément de ligne numérique *m*; ~ **phase modulation** *n* TELECOM modulation en phase des signaux numériques *f*; ~ **phase shifting** *n* ELECTRON déphasage numérique *m*; ~ **plotter** *n* COMP, DP traceur numérique *m*; ~ **process computer system** *n* NUCLEAR système de traitement numérique *m*; ~ **processing** *n* ELECTRON, TELECOM traitement numérique *m*; ~ **pseudo-noise sequence** *n* TELECOM séquence numérique de pseudo-bruit *f*; ~ **pulse stream** *n* TELECOM train d'impulsions numériques *m*; ~ **radio system** *n* *(DRS)* SPACE faisceau hertzien numérique *m*; ~ **readout** *n* COMP, DP affichage digital *m*, affichage numérique *m*, ELEC *instrument* affichage digital *m*, lecture digitale *f*, lecture numérique *f*, INSTRUMENT affichage numérique *m*, TELECOM lecture numérique *f*; ~ **readout measuring instrument** *n* METR appareil de mesure à affichage numérique *m*, appareil de mesure numérique *m*; ~ **readout micrometer** *n* METR micromètre à lecture digitale *m*; ~ **recorder** *n* NUCLEAR enregistreur numérique *m*; ~ **recording** *n* RECORDING, TELECOM, TV enregistrement numérique *m*; ~ **regeneration** *n* ELECTRON régénération numérique *f*; ~ **regenerator** *n* ELECTRON répéteur numérique *m*; ~ **representation** *n* COMP, DP, ELECTRON représentation numérique *f*; ~ **satellite concentrator** *n* TELECOM CNS, concentrateur numérique satellite *m*; ~ **section** *n* *(DS)* TELECOM section numérique *f*; ~ **selective calling** *n* *(DSC)* TELECOM appel sélectif numérique *m*; ~ **signal** *n* COMP, DP, ELECTRON, PHYS, TELECOM signal numérique *m*; ~ **signal analysis** *n* ELECTRON analyse numérique des signaux *f*; ~ **signal analyzer** *n* ELECTRON analyseur numérique de signaux *m*; ~ **signal processing** *n* COMP, DP, ELECTRON traitement numérique de signaux *m*; ~ **signature** *n* TELECOM signature numérique *f*; ~ **simulation model** *n* GAS TECH modèle numérique de simulation *m*; ~ **speech** *n* ELECTRON parole numérique *f*; ~ **speech compression** *n* TELECOM CNP, concentration numérique de la parole *f*; ~ **speech interpolation** *n* *(DSI)* TELECOM concentration numérique des conversations *f* *(CNC)*; ~ **speech synthesis** *n* ELECTRON synthèse numérique de la parole *f*; ~ **subscriber access unit** *n* TELECOM terminaison numérique réseau *f*; ~ **subtractor** *n* ELECTRON soustracteur numérique *m*; ~ **switch** *n* TELECOM autocommutateur numérique *m*, commutateur numérique *m*; ~ **switching** *n* TELECOM commutation numérique *f*; ~ **switching center** *n* (AmE), ~ **switching centre** *n* (BrE) TELECOM centre de commutation numérique *m*; ~ **switching element** *n* *(DSE)* TELECOM organe de commutation automatique *m*; ~ **switching equipment** *n* ELEC ENG matériel de commutation numérique *m*; ~ **switching matrix** *n* TE-

LECOM matrice temporelle symétrique *f*; ~ **switching network** *n* TELECOM réseau de connexion numérique *m*; ~ **switching system** *n* TELECOM système de commutation numérique *m*; ~ **technique** *n* PROP MAT technique digitale *f*; ~ **television** *n* TV télévision numérique *f*; ~ **transit command** *n* TELECOM commande d'émission numérique *f*; ~ **transmission** *n* TELECOM transmission numérique *f*; ~ **trunk interface** *n* (*DTI*) TELECOM module multiplex numérique *m*; ~ **tuning** *n* ELECTRON accord numérique *m*; ~ **TV receiver** *n* TV récepteur TV numérique *m*; ~ **videodisc** *n* (BrE) OPT vidéodisque numérique *m*; ~ **videodisk** *n* (AmE) *see digital videodisc*; ~ **video effects** *n pl* (*DVE*) TV effets spéciaux *m pl*, effets spéciaux numériques *m pl*; ~ **videotape recorder** *n* (*DVTR*) TV magnétoscope numérique *m*; ~ **voltmeter** *n* ELEC ENG voltmètre numérique *m*

digital-analog: ~ **conversion** *n* (AmE), **digital-analogue conversion** *n* (BrE) TELECOM conversion numérique-analogique *f*

digitalin *n* CHEM digitaline *f*

digitalis *n* FOOD TECH digitaline *f*

digitalization *n* COMP, DP, PHYS, TELECOM numérisation *f*

digitalized *adj* SPACE *communications* numérisé

digitally-encoded: ~ **videodisc** *n* (BrE) OPT vidéodisque numérique *m*; ~ **videodisk** *n* (AmE) *see digitally-encoded videodisc*

digital-to-analog[1] *adj* (AmE) *see digital-to-analogue*

digital-to-analog[2] *adj* (*D-to-A*) COMP, DP numérique-analogique

digital-to-analog[3] *n* (AmE) *see digital-to-analogue*

digital-to-analogue[1] *adj* (BrE) (*D-to-A*) TV numérique-analogique

digital-to-analogue[2] *n* (BrE) (*D-to-A*) CINEMAT numérique-analogique *m*; ~ **conversion** *n* (BrE) ELECTRON, RECORDING conversion numérique-analogique *f*; ~ **converter** *n* (BrE) ELECTRON, TELECOM, TV convertisseur numérique-analogique *m*

digitization *n* COMP, DP, NUCLEAR *of signal*, PHYS, TELECOM numérisation *f*

digitize *vt* COMP, DP digitaliser, numériser, ELEC chiffrer, ELECTRON convertir en numérique, mettre sous forme numérique, numériser, MECH ENG *model* numériser une maquette, PHYS numériser, PRINT *column of numbers* composer, RECORDING numériser, TV convertir en numérique, numériser

digitized[1] *adj* TELECOM numérisé

digitized[2]: ~ **data** *n* ELECTRON, TELECOM données numérisées *f pl*, informations numérisées *f pl*; ~ **image** *n* ELECTRON image numérisée *f*; ~ **signal** *n* ELECTRON signal numérisé *m*; ~ **speech** *n* TELECOM signal vocal numérisé *m*

digitizer *n* COMP, DP, ELECTRON numériseur *m*

digitizing *n* ELECTRON numérisation *f*; ~ **rate** *n* ELECTRON cadence de numérisation *f*; ~ **tablet** *n* COMP, DP table à numériser *f*, tablette à numériser *f*

diglycidyl: ~ **ether** *n* P&R *epoxy resin* éther glycidique *m*

diguanide *n* CHEM diguanide *m*

dihedral[1] *adj* GEOM dièdre

dihedral[2] *n* AERONAUT dièdre *m*; ~ **angle** *n* GEOM, METALL angle dièdre *m*; ~ **antenna** *n* TELECOM antenne dièdre *f*

dihydroacridine *n* CHEM dihydroacridine *f*

dihydrobenzene *n* CHEM dihydrobenzène *m*

dihydrocarveol *n* CHEM dihydrocarvéol *m*

dihydrocarvone *n* CHEM dihydrocarvone *f*

dihydroergotamine *n* CHEM dihydroergotamine *f*

dihydronaphthalene *n* CHEM dihydronaphtalène *m*

dihydrostreptomycin *n* CHEM dihydrostreptomycine *f*

dihydrotachysterol *n* CHEM dihydrotachystérol *m*

dihydroxyacetone *n* CHEM dihydroxyacétone *f*

dike *n see dyke*

dilatable *adj* COAL TECH dilatable

dilatancy *n* COAL TECH dilatabilité *f*, P&R *viscosity* dilatance *f*

dilatant *adj* COAL TECH *soil* dilatable

dilatation *n* PROP MAT dilatation *f*

dilatational: ~ **wave** *n* GEOL onde P *f*, onde de dilatation *f*

dilation *n* GAS TECH, GEOM dilatation *f*

dilatometer *n* PHYS dilatomètre *m*

dilator *n* GEOM dilatation *f*

diluent *n* CHEM, P&R *coatings, adhesives*, PAPER TECH diluant *m*

dilute[1] *adj* METALL *alloy, solution*, PROP MAT *alloy, solution* dilué

dilute[2] *vt* CHEM TECH diluer, délayer, COAL TECH, P&R *coatings, adhesives*, PAPER TECH diluer

diluting: ~ **agent** *n* CHEM TECH diluant *m*, délayant *m*, PROP MAT diluant *m*

dilution *n* CHEM, CHEM TECH, PETR TECH dilution *f*; ~ **refrigerator** *n* PHYS, REFRIG réfrigérateur à dilution *m*

dim:[1] ~ **letters** *n pl* (BrE) C&G dessin flou *m*

dim[2] *vt* CINEMAT assombrir, PHOTO *light* affaiblir, réduire

dimension[1] *n* COMP, DP, PHYS dimension *f*, PRINT format *m*; ~ **line** *n* MECH ENG *drawings* ligne de cote *f*

dimension[2] *vt* PROD ENG *drawing* coter

dimensional: ~ **check** *n* CONTROL contrôle des mesures *m*, contrôle dimensionnel *m*; ~ **compatibility** *n* TELECOM compatibilité dimensionnelle *f*; ~ **control** *n* PROD ENG *production* commande par autocalibrage *f*; ~ **equation** *n* PHYS équation de dimensions *f*; ~ **inspection** *n* CONTROL contrôle dimensionnel *m*; ~ **measuring instruments** *n pl* METR instruments de mesure dimensionnelle *m pl*; ~ **requirements** *n pl* SAFETY conditions dimensionnelles *f pl*; ~ **stability** *n* CINEMAT, NUCLEAR *of fuel element*, PACKAGING, PAPER TECH, PRINT, TESTING stabilité dimensionnelle *f*

dimensioned: ~ **sketch** *n* PROD ENG croquis coté *m*

dimensioning *n* COMP, DP dimensionnement *m*, MECH ENG *sizes marked*, PROD ENG *marking of drawing with sizes* cotation *f*

dimer *n* CHEM, PROP MAT dimère *m*

dimeric *adj* CHEM dimère

dimethyl *n* CHEM diméthyle *m*; ~ **sulfate** *n* (AmE) *see dimethyl sulphate* ~ **sulfone** *n* (AmE) *see dimethyl sulphone* ~ **sulphate** *n* (BrE) CHEM sulfate de diméthyle *m*; ~ **sulphone** *n* (BrE) CHEM sulfone de diméthyle *f*

dimethylacetic *adj* CHEM diméthylacétique

dimethylamine *n* CHEM diméthylamine *f*

dimethylaniline *n* CHEM diméthylaniline *f*

dimethylarsine *n* CHEM diméthylarsine *f*

dimethylbenzene *n* CHEM diméthylbenzène *m*

dimethylformamide *n* CHEM diméthylformamide *m*

dimethylglyoxime *n* CHEM diméthylglyoxime *f*

diminished: ~ **arch** *n* CONST *architectural structure* voûte surbaissée *f*, *bridge* arche surbaissée *f*, *curve described* arc surbaissé *m*; ~ **interval** *n* ACOUSTICS intervalle diminué *m*

diminishing: ~ **stop bevel** *n* C&G biseau arrêté en arrondi *m*

dimmer *n* CINEMAT gradateur *m*, rhéostat *m*, ELEC atténuateur *m*; ~ **cap** *n* AERONAUT bonnette à trèfle *f*,

cabochon *m*, trèfle occultable *m*; ~ **quadrant** *n* CINE-
MAT manette de commande d'éclairage *f*; ~ **switch** *n*
CONTROL interrupteur de lumière réduite *m*, interrupteur à gradation de lumière rhéostatique *m*, ELEC
commutateur de mise en veilleuse *m*, interrupteur à
gradation de lumière rhéostatique *m*, variateur de
lumière *m*, ELEC ENG interrupteur à graduation de
lumière *m*; ~ **system** *n* AERONAUT système d'atténuation *m*, système de gradation *m*

dimming: ~ **resistance** *n* CONTROL régulateur d'éclairage *m*

dimorphism *n* CHEM *of crystals* dimorphie *f*, dimor-
phisme *m*

dimple *n* C&G fossette *f*, METALL cupule *f*

dimpled: ~ **hole** *n* MECH ENG trou embrevé *m*

dimpling *n* MECH ENG embrèvement *m*

DIN[1] *abbr* (*Deutsche Industrienorm*) MECH ENG DIN
(*Deutsche Industrienorm*)

DIN:[2] ~ **rail** *n* PROD ENG rail DIN *m*; ~ **size** *n* PRINT
international paper size format international *m*; ~
speed *n* PHOTO *German industrial standard* vitesse en
DIN *f*

dinaphthyl *n* CHEM dinaphtyle *m*

dinas: ~ **brick** *n* C&G brique dinas *f*

dinghy *n* NAUT annexe *f*, canot pneumatique *m*, dinghy *m*, dériveur *m*, youyou *m*

dinging: ~ **hammer** *n* MECH ENG marteau à garnir *m*

dinitrobenzene *n* CHEM dinitrobenzène *m*

dinitrocresol *n* CHEM dinitrocrésol *m*

dinitronaphthalene *n* CHEM dinitronaphtalène *m*

dinitrophenol *n* CHEM dinitrophénol *m*

dinitrotoluene *n* CHEM dinitrotoluène *m*

dinky: ~ **reel** *n* PRINT bobineau *m*

dintheader *n* MINING rabaseuse *f*

dinucleotide *n* CHEM dinucléotide *m*

dioctyl: ~ **phthalate** *n* P&R *plasticizer* phtalate de dioc-
tyle *m*

diode *n* COMP, DP, ELEC *rectifier*, ELECTRON diode *f*,
NUCLEAR diode *f*, tube diode *m*, PHYS, TELECOM, VEHI-
CLES *electrical, ignition* diode *f*; ~ **amplifier** *n* ELECTRON
amplificateur paramétrique à diode *m*; ~ **array** *n* TELE-
COM réseau de diodes *m*; ~ **characteristic** *n* ELECTRON
caractéristique de diode *f*; ~ **crosspoint** *n* TELECOM
point de connexion à diode *m*; ~ **frequency multiplier** *n*
ELECTRON multiplicateur de fréquence à diode *m*; ~
gate *n* ELECTRON porte à diode *f*; ~ **laser** *n* ELECTRON
laser à diode *m*, OPT diode laser *f*, laser à injection *m*,
laser à semi-conducteur *m*, PHYS laser à semi-conducteur *m*; ~ **limiter** *n* ELECTRON limiteur d'amplitude à
diode *m*; ~ **logic** *n* ELECTRON logique à diodes *f*; ~ **mixer**
n ELECTRON mélangeur à diode *m*; ~ **modulation** *n*
ELECTRON démodulation par diode *f*; ~ **modulator** *n*
ELECTRON démodulateur à diode *m*, modulateur à
diode *m*; ~ **oscillator** *n* ELECTRON oscillateur à diode
m; ~ **phase shifter** *n* ELECTRON déphaseur à diode *m*; ~
photodetector *n* OPT, TELECOM photodiode *f*; ~ **string** *n*
ELECTRON chaîne de diodes *f*; ~ **suppression** *n* ELEC-
TRON antiparasitage à diode *m*; ~ **suppressor** *n*
ELECTRON diode antiparasite *f*; ~ **switch** *n* TV commu-
tateur à diode *m*; ~ **tube** *n* ELECTRON tube diode *m*,
NUCLEAR diode *f*, tube diode *m*; ~ **voltage** *n* ELECTRON
tension de diode *f*

diode-connected: ~ **transistor** *n* ELECTRON transistor
monté en diode *m*; ~ **tube** *n* ELECTRON tube monté en
diode *m*

diode-transistor: ~ **logic** *n* (*DTL*) COMP, ELECTRON logi-

que à diodes et transistors *f*

diode-type: ~ **dual input** *n* PROD ENG entrée double à
diode *f*

diol *n* CHEM diol *m*

diolefin *n* PETR TECH dioléfine *f*

Dion: ~ **axle** *n* AUTO pont de Dion *m*

diopside *n* MINERAL diopside *m*

dioptase *n* MINERAL dioptase *m*

diopter *n* (AmE), **dioptre** *n* (BrE) PHYS dioptrie *f*, SPACE
dioptre *m* ~ **lens** *n* (BrE) CINEMAT bonnette dioptrique *f*

dioptric: ~ **adjuster** *n* CINEMAT correcteur dioptrique *m*;
~ **system** *n* ASTRON système dioptrique *m*

diorite *n* PETR diorite *f*

dioxide *n* CHEM bioxyde *m*, dioxyde *m*

dioxin *n* CHEM dioxine *f*

dioxytartaric *adj* CHEM dioxytartarique

dip[1] *prep* MINING en inclinaison

dip[2] *n* C&G *of bait in making sheet glass* trempe *f*, CONST
of overhead line flèche *f*, inclination *f*, pente *f*, FUEL-
LESS pente d'inclinaison *f*, GEOL, MINING pendage *m*,
NAUT *of sextant* dépression *f*, PETR inclinaison *f*, PETR
TECH pendage *m*, TEXTILES adhérisation *f*; ~ **angle** *n*
GEOPHYS dépression de l'horizon *f*; ~ **brazing** *n* CONST
brasage fort par trempage *m*, brasage par trempage
m; ~ **circle** *n* GEOPHYS boussole d'inclinaison *f*; ~ **circle**
needle *n* GEOPHYS aiguille d'inclinaison *f*; ~ **coat** *n*
COATINGS revêtement au trempé *m*, revêtement de
contact *m*; ~ **coating** *n* COATINGS revêtement au trempé *m*, revêtement de contact *m*, P&R revêtement par
trempage *m*, PACKAGING revêtement par immersion
m, PAPER TECH couchage par immersion *m*, PROD ENG
revêtement par immersion *m*; ~ **compass** *n* GEOPHYS
boussole d'inclinaison *f*; ~ **dyeing** *n* COLOURS teinture
par immersion *f*; ~ **equator** *n* GEOPHYS équateur magnétique *m*; ~ **fault** *n* GEOL faille oblique *f*, faille
transversale *f*, faille parallèle à la direction du
pendage *f*, PETR faille pentée *f*; ~ **freezing** *n* PACKA-
GING surgelage par immersion *m*; ~ **needle** *n* GEOPHYS
aiguille d'inclinaison *f*, inclinatoire magnétique *m*; ~
net *n* OCEANOG carrelet *m*, haveneau *m*, épuisette *f*; ~
pickup *n* TEXTILES substance retenue après immersion
f; ~ **roller** *n* PRINT rouleau barboteur *m*, rouleau de
bassine *m*, rouleau plongé *m*; ~ **slip** *n* GEOL rejet net *m*,
rejet transversal *m*; ~ **slope** *n* GEOL revers de cuesta *m*;
~ **switch** *n* AUTO interrupteur de lumière réduite *m*,
PROD ENG micro-interrupteur *m*

dip[3] *vt* PACKAGING plonger, PAPER TECH immerger,
tremper, PROD ENG plonger, tremper, TEXTILES adhé-
riser

DIP[1] *abbr* (*dual-in-line package*) COMP, DP, ELEC ENG
boîtier DIP *m*, boîtier à deux rangées de broches *m*

DIP:[2] ~ **battery** *n* ELEC ENG batterie en boîtier DIP *f*; ~
component *n* ELECTRON composant en boîtier DIP *m*;
~ **relay** *n* ELEC ENG relais en boîtier DIP *m*; ~ **switch** *n*
ELEC ENG commutateur en boîtier DIP *m*

dipalmitin *n* CHEM dipalmitine *f*

diparachlorobenzyl *n* CHEM diparachlorobenzyle *m*

dip-coated: ~ **paper** *n* PAPER TECH papier couché au
trempé *m*

diphase *adj* ELEC ENG diphasé

diphead *n* MINING *coal mining* vallée *f*

diphenyl *n* CHEM phénylbenzène *m*

diphenylamine *n* CHEM diphénylamine *f*

diphenylmethane: ~ **diisocyanate** *n* P&R *curing agent*
diisocyanate de diphénylméthane *m*

diphthong *n* PRINT diphtongue *f*
diplacusis *n* ACOUSTICS diplacousie *f*
diplexer *n* TELECOM diplexeur *m*
dipolar *adj* CHEM *molecule* dipolaire
dipole *n* ELEC *of charge, aerial,* ELEC ENG, METALL dipôle *m*; ~ **aerial** *n* NAUT *radio communication,* TV antenne dipôle *f*; ~ **antenna** *n* TELECOM antenne en réseau de doublet *f*; ~ **moment** *n* CHEM *of diatomic molecule* moment dipolaire *m,* ELEC ENG moment dipôle *m*
dipole-dipole: ~ **interaction** *n* RAD PHYS interaction dipolaire *f*
dipped: ~ **headlights** *n pl* (BrE) *(cf low beams)* VEHICLES phares code *m pl*
dipper: ~ **dredger** *n* NAUT drague à pelle *f*
dipping *n* PAPER TECH trempage *m,* PRINT barbotage *m*; ~ **process** *n* PACKAGING procédé d'immersion *m*; ~ **refractometer** *n* INSTRUMENT réfractomètre à immersion *m*; ~ **roller** *n* PRINT barboteur *m,* rouleau de bassine *m*; ~ **varnish** *n* COATINGS vernis au trempé *m,* vernis à immersion *m*
dipstick *n* AUTO jauge d'huile *f,* MECH ENG jaugeur à canne *m,* VEHICLES *lubrication* jauge d'huile *f*
dip-varnish *vt* COATINGS, COLOURS vernir par immersion
dipyre *n* MINERAL dipyre *m*
Dirac: ~ **constant** *n* PHYS *h-bar* constante réduite de Planck *f*; ~ **function** *n* PETR fonction Dirac *f*
direct[1] *adj* COMP, DP direct, TELECOM point-à-point, WATER SUPP direct
direct[2] *adv* COMP, DP, TELECOM direct
direct:[3] ~ **access** *n* COMP, DP accès direct *m*; ~ **access memory** *n* ELEC ENG mémoire à accès direct *f*; ~ **access storage** *n* COMP, DP mémoire à accès direct *f*; ~ **AC converter** *n* ELEC convertisseur direct de courant alternatif *m*; ~ **acting control** *n* CONTROL régulation directe *f,* régulation à action directe *f*; ~ **acting overhead camshaft** *n* AUTO arbre à cames en tête à attaque directe *m*; ~ **acting pump** *n* WATER SUPP pompe à action directe *f*; ~ **action pump** *n* WATER SUPP pompe à action directe *f*; ~ **address** *n* COMP, DP adresse directe *f*; ~ **addressing** *n* COMP, DP adressage direct *m*; ~ **axis subtransient emf** *n* ELEC *machine* force électromotrice subtransitoire longitudinale *f*; ~ **axis transient emf** *n* ELEC *machine* force électromotrice transitoire longitudinale *f*; ~ **breakthrough** *n* NUCLEAR percée directe *f*; ~ **broadcasting by satellite** *n* TV radiodiffusion directe par satellite *f*; ~ **broadcasting satellite** *n* (*DBS*) TELECOM satellite de transmission en direct *m*; ~ **broadcast satellite** *n* SPACE, TV satellite de radiodiffusion directe *m*; ~ **casting** *n* PROD ENG coulée en première fusion *f*; ~ **cell** *n* TRANSP pile directe *f*; ~ **cold hydrogen cell** *n* TRANSP pile froide directe à hydrogène *f*; ~ **component** *n* ELEC *of current* composante directe *f*; ~ **contact condenser** *n* PROD ENG condenseur par mélange *m,* condenseur à mélange *m*; ~ **control** *n* ELEC ENG, MECH ENG commande directe *f*; ~ **conversion** *n* FUELLESS conversion directe *f*; ~ **coupling** *n* ELEC *AC circuits* couplage *m,* ELEC ENG liaison directe *f,* liaison en courant continu *f,* ELECTRON liaison directe *f,* FUELLESS accouplement direct *m,* attaque directe *f*; ~ **current** *n* (*DC*) ELEC, ELEC ENG, ELECTRON, PHYS, PROD ENG, RAIL, RECORDING, TELECOM, TV courant continu *m* (*CC*); ~ **current component** *n* ELEC composante de courant continu *f*; ~ **current converter** *n* TELECOM convertisseur courant continu *m,* convertisseur à courant continu *m*; ~ **current coupler** *n* TELECOM coupleur directif *m*; ~ **current distortion** *n* NUCLEAR

distorsion en courant continu *f*; ~ **current generator** *n* ELEC générateur de courant continu *m,* génératrice à courant continu *f*; ~ **current machine** *n* ELEC ENG machine à courant continu *f*; ~ **current motor** *n* ELEC, ELEC ENG, PHYS moteur à courant continu *m*; ~ **current network** *n* ELEC *supply network* réseau à courant continu *m*; ~ **current output** *n* ELEC ENG sortie continue *f,* sortie en courant continu *f*; ~ **current potentiometer** *n* ELEC potentiomètre à courant continu *m*; ~ **current relay** *n* ELEC relais à courant continu *m*; ~ **current supply** *n* ELEC alimentation continue *f*; ~ **current traction motor** *n* TRANSP moteur de traction à courant continu *m*; ~ **current transformer** *n* ELEC transformateur de tension continue *m*; ~ **current voltage source** *n* ELEC ENG source de tension continue *f*; ~ **cycle boiling reactor** *n* NUCLEAR réacteur bouillant à cycle direct *m*; ~ **data entry** *n* (*DDE*) COMP, DP entrée directe de données *f*; ~ **DC converter** *n* ELEC convertisseur direct de courant continu *m*; ~ **delivery** *n* PROD ENG livraison directe *f*; ~ **dialling in** *n* (BrE) (*DDI*) *(cf direct inward dialing)* TELECOM accès directe à l'arrivée *f,* sélection directe à un poste *f*; ~ **digital control** *n* (*DDC*) DP commande numérique directe *f*; ~ **disc** *n* (BrE) OPT disque à gravure directe *m*; ~ **disk** *n* (AmE) *see direct disc*; ~ **distance dialing** *n* (AmE) (*DDD, subscriber trunk dialling*) TELECOM interurbain automatique *m,* sélection à distance de l'abonné demandé *f*; ~ **distance dialing access code** *n* (AmE) *(cf subscriber trunk dialling access code)* TELECOM préfixe interurbain *m*; ~ **draft boiler** *n* (AmE), ~ **draught boiler** *n* (BrE) PROD ENG chaudière à flamme directe *f*; ~ **drive** *n* MECH ENG engrenage de prise directe *m,* prise directe *f*; ~ **duplicating film** *n* PHOTO pellicule pour l'obtention de contretypes directs *f*; ~ **dye** *n* TEXTILES colorant direct *m*; ~ **electron beam writing** *n* ELECTRON gravure directe par faisceau d'électrons *f*; ~ **emulsion** *n* PRINT émulsion directe *f*; ~ **energy conversion** *n* ELEC ENG conversion directe d'énergie *f*; ~ **expansion** *n* REFRIG détente directe *f*; ~ **expansion refrigeration system** *n* REFRIG refroidissement par détente directe *m*; ~ **file** *n* COMP, DP fichier direct *m*; ~ **fitting shank** *n* MECH ENG *machine tools* emmanchement direct *m*; ~ **flight** *n* AERONAUT vol direct *m*; ~ **force** *n* MECH ENG effort direct *m*; ~ **frequency modulation** *n* ELECTRON modulation de fréquence directe *f*; ~ **frequency synthesis** *n* ELECTRON synthèse de fréquence directe *f*; ~ **frequency synthesizer** *n* ELECTRON synthétiseur de fréquence à synthèse directe *m*; ~ **gravure** *n* PRINT gravure directe *f*; ~ **hydrogen-oxygen cell** *n* TRANSP pile directe à hydrogène-oxygène *f*; ~ **initiation** *n* MINING amorçage antérieur *m*; ~ **injection** *n* AUTO injection directe *f*; ~ **injection engine** *n* TRANSP moteur à injection directe *m*; ~ **input** *n* ELECTRON entrée directe *f*; ~ **interception** *n* POLLUTION interception directe *f*; ~ **inward dialing** *n* (AmE) (*DID*) *(cf direct dialling in)* TELECOM accès direct à l'arrivée *m,* accès direct à un poste *m,* sélection directe à un poste *f*; ~ **inward dialling** *n* (BrE) TELECOM accès direct à un poste *m*; ~ **irrigation** *n* HYDROL irrigation directe *f*; ~ **leaching** *n* GAS TECH lessivage direct *m*; ~ **light** *n* PHOTO lumière directe *f*; ~ **line** *n* (*DL*) TELECOM liaison spécialisée *f,* ligne directe *f,* ligne privée *f*; ~ **link wiring** *n* TEXTILES câblage à liaison directe *m*; ~ **losses** *n pl* HYDROL pertes directes *f pl*; ~ **loudspeaker** *n* ACOUSTICS haut-parleur à rayonnement direct *m*; ~ **maintenance** *n* NUCLEAR *by manual means* entretien direct *m*; ~ **memory access** *n* COMP

(DMA), DP accès direct à la mémoire *m*, directive *f*; ~ **metal mastering** *n (DMM)* PROD ENG, RECORDING gravure directe sur métal *f*; ~ **methanol-air cell** *n* TRANSP pile directe méthanol-air *f*; ~ **modulation** *n* ELECTRON modulation dans l'étage final *f*; ~ **orbit** *n* SPACE orbite directe *f*; ~ **output** *n* ELECTRON sortie directe *f*; ~ **outward dialling** *n (DOD)* TELECOM accès direct au réseau *m*, prise directe du réseau *f*; ~ **overcurrent release** *n* ELEC *tripping device* déclencheur direct à maximum de courant *m*; ~ **pattern generation** *n* ELECTRON gravure sans masque ni réticule *f*; ~ **photonuclear effect** *n* NUCLEAR réaction photonucléaire directe *f*; ~ **piezoelectric effect** *n* ELEC ENG effet piézoélectrique direct *m*; ~ **poisoning** *n* POLLUTION intoxication directe *f*; ~ **positive process** *n* CINEMAT procédé inversible *m*; ~ **pouring gate** *n* PROD ENG *in mould* chenal de coulée en chute directe *m*; ~ **power component** *n* ELEC ENG composant de puissant discret *m*; ~ **print** *n* CINEMAT copie contact *f*; ~ **radiation** *n* FUELLESS rayonnement direct *m*; ~ **rail fastening** *n* RAIL attache de rail direct *f*; ~ **read after write** *n (DRAW)* OPT contrôle en cours d'enregistrement *m*; ~ **reading** *n* MECH ENG lecture directe *f*; ~ **reading instrument** *n* ELEC appareil à lecture directe *m*, INSTRUMENT instrument à lecture directe *m*; ~ **read-out instrument** *n* ELEC appareil à lecture directe *m*; ~ **recording** *n* RECORDING enregistrement direct *m*, enregistrement synchrone *m*; ~ **roving** *n* C&G roving direct *m*; ~ **runoff** *n* HYDROL écoulement direct *m*; ~ **satellite broadcasting** *n* TELECOM radiodiffusion directe par satellite *f*, TV diffusion directe par satellite *f*; ~ **screen** *n* PRINT tramé direct *m*; ~ **sequence** *n (DS)* TELECOM séquence directe *f*; ~ **sound level** *n* RECORDING niveau de son direct *m*; ~ **starting** *n* ELEC *of motor* démarrage sous pleine tension *m*; ~ **strand cable** *n* OPT câble classique à fibres enrobées *m*; ~ **stress** *n* MECH ENG contrainte directe *f*; ~ **suction skimmer** *n* MAR POLL récupérateur à succion directe *m*, écrémeur à succion directe *m*; ~ **viewfinder** *n* CINEMAT viseur sans parallaxe *m*; ~ **view storage tube** *n* ELECTRON tube à mémoire à vision directe *m*; ~ **vision prism** *n* PHYS *Amici prism* prisme d'Amici *m*, prisme en toit *m*, prisme à vision directe *m*; ~ **voltage regulation** *n* ELEC régulation de tension continue *f*; ~ **wave** *n* GEOL onde directe *f*; ~ **write electron beam** *n* ELECTRON faisceau d'électrons à gravure directe *m*; ~ **writing** *n* ELECTRON gravure directe *f*, gravure par faisceau d'électrons dirigé *f*

direct[4] *vt* CINEMAT diriger, mettre en scène, réaliser, TELECOM *traffic* aiguiller

direct-coupled[1] *adj* COMP, DP à couplage direct

direct-coupled:[2] ~ **amplifier** *n* ELECTRON amplificateur à liaison directe *m*

direct-drive: ~ **propeller** *n* AERONAUT hélice sans réducteur *f*, hélice à prise directe sans réducteur *f*, hélice à prise directe *f*

directed: ~ **beam display** *n* ELECTRON visualisation à balayage cavalier *f*; ~ **bond** *n* CRYSTALL liaison dirigée *f*

directing *n* ELECTRON *signals* aiguillage *m*, orientation *f*; ~ **line** *n* MECH ENG directrice *f*

direction: ~ **of coiling** *n* SPRINGS sens d'enroulement *m*; ~ **commutator** *n* ELEC commutateur de direction *m*; ~ **control valve** *n* MECH ENG vanne de commande de sens *f*; ~ **finder** *n* AERONAUT goniomètre *m*; ~ **finder antenna** *n* TRANSP antenne radiogoniométrique *f*; ~ **finding** *n* PHYS *radar* goniométrie *f*, TELECOM *(DF)* goniométrie

f, radiogoniométrie *f*; ~ **finding receiver** *n* NAUT récepteur gonio *m*; ~ **of flow** *n* HYDROL *of river* sens *m*; ~ **indicator** *n* AUTO commutateur des clignotants *m*, VEHICLES clignoteur *m*, indicateur de direction *m*; ~ **of lay** *n* ELEC *of cable component* sens de câblage *m*; ~ **of rolling** *n* SPRINGS sens de laminage *m*; ~ **sign** *n* CONST panneau de signalisation *m*, signal de direction *m*, CONTROL signal de direction *m*; ~ **switch** *n* ELEC *of machine tool* commutateur de direction *m*; ~ **of traffic** *n* RAIL sens de la marche *m*; ~ **of twist** *n* TEXTILES sens de torsion *m*; ~ **of wiredrawing** *n* SPRINGS sens d'étirage *m*

directional: ~ **aerial** *n* TV antenne directionnelle *f*; ~ **aid** *n* TRANSP *traffic* aide directionnelle *f*; ~ **antenna** *n* SPACE *communications*, TELECOM antenne directive *f*, TV antenne directionnelle *f*; ~ **beam** *n* ELECTRON faisceau dirigé *m*, TELECOM faisceau directionnel *m*; ~ **beam transmitter** *n* TV émetteur orienté *m*; ~ **blue reflectance factor** *n* PAPER TECH facteur de réflectance directionnelle dans le bleu *m*; ~ **census** *n* TRANSP comptage directionnel *m*; ~ **characteristic** *n* RECORDING caractéristique directionnelle *f*; ~ **control valve** *n* PROD ENG distributeur *m*; ~ **coupler** *n* ELEC ENG, OPT coupleur directif *m*, PHYS coupleur directionnel *m*, TELECOM coupleur directif *m*; ~ **coupler switch** *n* TELECOM commutateur optique à coupleur directif *m*; ~ **coupling** *n* ELEC ENG couplage directif *m*; ~ **detector** *n* TRANSP détecteur directionnel *m*; ~ **drilling** *n* PETR forage directionnel *m*, forage dirigé *m*, PETR TECH forage dirigé *m*, forage dévié *m*; ~ **fabric** *n* GEOL structure orientée *f*; ~ **filter** *n* ELECTRON filtre de sens de transmission *m*; ~ **gyro** *n* AERONAUT gyro directionnel *m*, TRANSP gyroscope directionnel *m*; ~ **lighting** *n* CINEMAT éclairage dirigé *m*; ~ **microphone** *n* ACOUSTICS, RECORDING microphone directionnel *m*; ~ **optical coupler** *n* OPT coupleur optique directif *m*; ~ **pattern** *n* ACOUSTICS diagramme directionnel *m*; ~ **relay** *n* ELEC, ELEC ENG relais directionnel *m*; ~ **response** *n* ELECTRON réponse directionnelle *f*; ~ **selectivity** *n* TV directivité *f*, sensibilité directionnelle *f*; ~ **stability** *n* SPACE *spacecraft* stabilité directionnelle *f*, stabilité en cap *f*, stabilité en lacet *f*, TRANSP stabilité de route *f*; ~ **structure** *n* GEOL structure orientée *f*; ~ **well** *n* PETR TECH puits dévié *m*

directionality: ~ **factor** *n* FUELLESS facteur de directivité *m*, facteur directionnel *m*

directionally-structured: ~ **raschel goods** *n* TEXTILES tissu rachel *m*

directions *n pl* TEXTILES tendances *f pl*; ~ **for use** *n* PACKAGING mode d'emploi *m*

directive *n* COMP, DP directive *f*

directivity *n* SPACE *communications* directivité *f*; ~ **factor** *n* ACOUSTICS facteur de directivité *m*; ~ **index** *n* ACOUSTICS indice de directivité *m*

directly: ~ **earthed** *adj* (BrE) *(cf directly grounded)* ELEC ENG mis directement à la terre; ~ **grounded** *adj* (AmE) *(cf directly earthed)* ELEC ENG mis directement à la terre

directly-heated: ~ **cathode** *n* ELEC ENG cathode à chauffage direct *f*

director *n* SPACE directeur *m*; ~ **valve** *n* PROD ENG vanne d'aiguillage *f*

director's: ~ **finder** *n* CINEMAT viseur multifocal *m*, viseur à champ variable *m*

directory *n* COMP catalogue *m*, répertoire *m*, DP répertoire *m*; ~ **assistance** *n* TELECOM assistance-annuaire *f*

(Can), service d'assistance annuaire *m*, service des renseignements *m*; ~ **control system** *n* TELECOM système à commande directe *m*; ~ **enquiries** *n* (BrE) *(cf directory information)* TELECOM *service* assistance-annuaire *f* (Can), service d'assistance annuaire *m*, servicedes renseignements *m*; ~ **information** *n* (AmE) *(cf directory enquiries)* TELECOM assistance-annuaire *f* (Can), service d'assistance annuaire *m*, service des renseignements *m*; ~ **information tree** *n (DIT)* TELECOM arbre d'information d'annuaire *m*; ~ **number** *n (DN)* TELECOM numéro d'annuaire *m*, numéro d'appel *m*; ~ **store** *n* TELECOM fichier d'abonnés *m*; ~ **user agent** *n* TELECOM agent d'usager d'annuaire *m*

direct-to-plate: ~ **imaging system** *n* PRINT système de fabrication directe des formes imprimantes *m*

dirt *n* C&G crachat *m*, COAL TECH gangue stérile *f*, QUALITY saleté *f*; ~ **band** *n* COAL TECH banc stérile *m*; ~ **packing machine** *n* MINING machine de remblayage *f*; ~ **trap** *n* MECH ENG *for pipeline, valve, fitting* collecteur de boue *m*

dirty: ~ **shoulder** *n* C&G épaule sale *f*

dirty-water: ~ **pump** *n* NUCLEAR pompe à eau usée *f*

DIS *abbr (draft international standard)* TELECOM projet de norme internationale *m*

disable *vt* COMP, DP désactiver, ELEC ENG mettre hors service

disabling: ~ **signal** *n* CONTROL signal d'interdiction *m*

disaccharide *n* CHEM disaccharide *m*

disappearing: ~ **filament pyrometer** *n* PHYS pyromètre à disparition de filament *m*

disarm[1] *vt* MILIT désarmer

disarm[2] *vti* COMP, DP désarmer

disassemble *vt* MECH ENG désassembler

disassembler *n* COMP désassembleur *m*

disassembly *n* MECH ENG dégroupage *m*, démontage *m*, déshabillage *m*

disc *n* (BrE) COMP, DP *see disk*, MECH ENG plateau *m*, *of eccentric* bossage *m*, disque *m*, estomac *m*, RECORDING, TV disque *m*; ~ **area** *n* (BrE) AERONAUT *of helicopter* surface du disque balayé *f*; ~ **armature** *n* (BrE) ELEC, ELEC ENG induit à disque *m*; ~ **bit** *n* (BrE) PETR TECH trépan à disque *m*; ~ **brake** *n* (BrE) AUTO, MECH, VEHICLES frein à disque *m*; ~ **brake calliper** *n* (BrE) RAIL *vehicles* mâchoire de frein à disque *f*; ~ **brakepad** *n* (BrE) AUTO plaquette de frein à disque *f*; ~ **brake tools** *n pl* (BrE) AUTO outils pour freins à disque *m pl*; ~ **braking system** *n* (BrE) AUTO, CONST système de frein à disque *m*; ~ **capacitor** *n* (BrE) ELEC ENG condensateur bouton *m*; ~ **centre wheel** *n* (BrE) VEHICLES roue pleine *f*, roue à voile plein *f*; ~ **clutch** *n* (BrE) MECH, VEHICLES embrayage à disque *m*; ~ **crank** *n* (BrE) PROD ENG coude circulaire *m*, manivelle à plateau *f*, plateau-manivelle *m*; ~ **filter** *n* (BrE) COAL TECH filtre à disque *m*; ~ **galaxy** *n* (BrE) ASTRON galaxie à disque *f*; ~ **grinder** *n* (BrE) C&G lapidaire *m*, PROD ENG machine à disque émerisé *f*; ~ **grinding** *n* (BrE) C&G douci-rond *m*; ~ **head** *n* (BrE) OPT tête de lecture de disque *f*; ~ **key** *n* (BrE) MECH ENG clavette à disque *f*; ~ **loading** *n* (BrE) AERONAUT charge du disque balayé *f*; ~ **mastering** *n* (BrE) OPT gravure par pressage *f*, pressage industriel *m*; ~ **mill** *n* (BrE) COAL TECH, FOOD TECH broyeur à disque *m*; ~ **piston** *n* (BrE) HYDR EQUIP piston à plateau *m*; ~ **platter** *n* (BrE) OPT support disque *m*; ~ **player** *n* (BrE) OPT lecteur de disque *m*; ~ **polishing** *n* (BrE) C&G poli-rond *m*; ~ **recorder** *n* (BrE) ACOUSTICS machine à graver les disques *f*, RECORDING

enregistreur à disque *m*; ~ **resonator filter** *n* (BrE) ELECTRON filtre à disque résonnant *m*; ~ **sander** *n* (BrE) MECH ENG disqueuse *f*; ~ **sanding machine** *n* (BrE) MECH ENG ponceuse à disque *f*; ~ **sandpapering machine** *n* (BrE) PROD ENG machine à poncer à plateau *f*; ~ **seal tube** *n* (BrE) ELECTRON lampe phare *f*; ~ **shutter** *n* (BrE) CINEMAT obturateur à disque *m*; ~ **signal** *n* (BrE) RAIL disque *m*, signal à cocarde *m*; ~ **skimmer** *n* (BrE) MAR POLL récupérateur à disque *m*, écrémeur à disque *m*, POLLUTION récupérateur à disque *m*; ~ **spring** *n* (BrE) MECH ENG rondelle ressort *f*; ~ **valve** *n* (BrE) HYDR EQUIP soupape à disque *f*; ~ **winding** *n* (BrE) ELEC *of transformer* enroulement en disque *m*

discard[1] *n* MECH chute *f*

discard[2] *vt* MECH ENG, TEXTILES rebuter

discharge[1] *n* COAL TECH, ELEC *of condenser, arc*, ELEC ENG décharge *f*, HYDROL déverser, MAR POLL déversement *m*, rejet *m*, écoulement *m*, évacuation *f*, MECH ENG *of pump* refoulement *m*, NUCLEAR *of pump, compressor, blower*, PAPER TECH débit *m*, PHYS décharge *f*, POLLUTION rejet *m*, RECYCLING décharge *f*, rejet *m*, REFRIG refoulement *m*, WATER SUPP décharge *f*, écoulement *m*, *of stream, weir* débit *m*, portée *f*, *volume flow rate* débit *m*; ~ **at sea** *n* MAR POLL, POLLUTION rejet en mer *m*; ~ **button** *n* MECH ENG bouton de percussion *m*; ~ **canal** *n* WATER SUPP canal d'évacuation *m*; ~ **capacitor** *n* ELEC ENG condensateur à décharge *m*; ~ **channel** *n* HYDROL canal de décharge *m*; ~ **circuit** *n* ELEC ENG circuit de décharge *m*; ~ **coefficient** *n* FUELLESS, SPACE coefficient de débit *m*; ~ **current** *n* ELEC, ELEC ENG courant de décharge *m*; ~ **flume** *n* WATER SUPP canal de jaugeage *m*, rigole d'évacuation *f*; ~ **head** *n* HYDROL *of pump* hauteur géométrique de refoulement *f*, NUCLEAR *of pump* hauteur de refoulement *f*, hauteur manométrique *f*, WATER SUPP *of pump* hauteur de refoulement *f*; ~ **lamp** *n* ELEC tube à décharge lumineuse *m*, ELEC ENG lampe à décharge *f*; ~ **lift** *n* WATER SUPP *of pump* hauteur de refoulement *f*; ~ **mass curve** *n* HYDROL courbe des débits cumulés *f*; ~ **microphone** *n* RECORDING microphone à décharge ionique *m*; ~ **nozzle** *n* NUCLEAR *of pump, fan* pompe *f*, raccord de tuyau *m*; ~ **pipe** *n* RECYCLING canal d'évacuation *m*, canal de déversement *m*, WATER SUPP *of pump* tuyau d'écoulement *m*, tuyau de discharge *m*; ~ **pond** *n* NUCLEAR *for spent fuel elements* bassin de décharge *m*; ~ **pressure** *n* MECH ENG pression de décharge *f*, REFRIG pression de refoulement *f*; ~ **printing** *n* TEXTILES impression au rongeant *f*; ~ **rate** *n* RECYCLING débit *m*; ~ **regulator** *n* FUELLESS régulateur d'écoulement *m*, SPACE *spacecraft* régulateur de charge *m*; ~ **resistor** *n* ELEC résistance de décharge *f*; ~ **sluice** *n* WATER SUPP écluse d'évacuation *f*; ~ **temperature** *n* REFRIG température de refoulement *f*, THERMOD *of compressor* température de décharge *f*; ~ **tube** *n* ELECTRON, PHYS tube à décharge *m*; ~ **valve** *n* HYDR EQUIP, MECH ENG clapet de décharge *m*, REFRIG vanne de refoulement *f*; ~ **welding** *n* PROD ENG soudage à décharge *m*

discharge[2] *vt* MAR POLL rejeter, MILIT *firearm* décharger, NAUT licencier, *cargo, ballast* débarquer, décharger, *ship* délester, *water* décharger, évacuer, POLLUTION rejeter, RECYCLING rejeter, évacuer, TELECOM *battery* décharger

discharge:[3] ~ **into the sea** *vti* HYDROL affluer dans la mer, déboucher dans la mer, tomber dans la mer

discharged *adj* ELEC *battery* déchargé, WATER SUPP *water* évacué

discharging: **~ arch** *n* CONST arc de décharge *m*, arc en décharge *m*; **~ of the cage** *n* MINING décagement *m*, déchargement de la cage *m*

disclination *n* METALL disclinaison *f*

disclosure: **~ of the invention** *n* PATENTS *part of description* exposé de l'invention *m*

discoloration *n* (AmE), **discolouration** *n* (BrE) C&G altération de la couleur *f*, P&R *defect*, PAPER TECH décoloration *f*

disconformity *n* GEOL discordance *f*, discordance de ravinement *f*, lacune *f*

disconnect:[1] **~ relay** *n* ELEC ENG relais de coupure *m*, relais de mise hors circuit *m*; **~ rod** *n* NUCLEAR *of control rod drive mechanism* tige de démontage *f*; **~ switch** *n* PROD ENG sectionneur *m*

disconnect[2] *vt* COMP, DP déconnecter, ELEC ENG débrancher, déconnecter, MECH ENG débrancher, déclencher; **~ from the circuit** *vt* ELEC débrancher

disconnecting *n* SPACE découplage *m*; **~ switch** *n* ELEC sectionneur *m*, ELEC ENG disjoncteur *m*, interrupteur séparateur *m*, sectionneur *m*

disconnection *n* ELEC coupure *f*, déconnexion *f*, ELEC ENG mise hors circuit *f*

disconnector *n* RAIL sectionneur *m*

discontinue *vt* CONTROL interrompre

discontinued: **~ approach** *n* AERONAUT approche interrompue *f*

discontinuity *n* GEOL discontinuité *f*; **~ layer** *n* OCEANOG couche de discontinuité *f*, couche de saut *f*

discontinuous: **~ amplifier** *n* ELECTRON amplificateur par tout ou rien *m*; **~ glide** *n* METALL glissement discontinu *m*; **~ reinforcement** *n* PROP MAT renforcement discontinu *m*; **~ spectrum** *n* RAD PHYS spectre discontinu *m*

discordance *n* ACOUSTICS, GEOL discordance *f*

discovery *n* PETR découverte *f*; **~ shaft** *n* MINING puits de recherche *m*; **~ well** *n* PETR puits de découverte *m*

discrepancy *n* MECH ENG anomalie *f*

discrete[1] *adj* COMP, DP discret

discrete:[2] **~ amplifier** *n* ELECTRON amplificateur discret *m*; **~ bipolar transistor** *n* ELECTRON transistor bipolaire discret *m*; **~ capacitor** *n* ELEC ENG condensateur discret *m*; **~ channel** *n* TELECOM canal discret *m*; **~ component** *n* ELEC ENG, TELECOM composant discret *m*; **~ filter** *n* ELECTRON filtre discret *m*; **~ Fourier transform** *n* ELECTRON transformée de Fourier discrète *f*; **~ frequency** *n* ELECTRON fréquence discrète *f*; **~ input/output** *n* PROD ENG entrée/sortie tout ou rien *f*; **~ manufacturing** *n* PROD ENG production discontinue *f*; **~ resistor** *n* ELEC ENG résistance discrète *f*; **~ sampling** *n* QUALITY échantillonnage simple *m*; **~ semiconductor device** *n* ELECTRON composant à semi-conducteur discret *m*; **~ signal** *n* ELECTRON signal discret *m*

discretionary: **~ wiring** *n* ELECTRON *wafers* interconnexion sélective *f*

discriminant *n* MECH ENG discriminant *m*; **~ function** *n* MATH fonction discriminante *f*

discriminating: **~ circuit breaker** *n* ELEC interrupteur à retour de courant *m*; **~ protective system** *n* ELEC *circuit breaker* interrupteur à retour de courant *m*; **~ relay** *n* ELEC relais directionnel *m*; **~ satellite exchange** *n* TELECOM satellite discriminateur *m*, satellite à autonomie d'acheminement restreinte *m*

discrimination *n* ELECTRON, TESTING discrimination *f*

discriminator *n* ELECTRON, MECH ENG, OPT, TELECOM discriminateur *m*, TV discriminateur de fréquence *m*, détecteur *m*

discussion: **~ tube arrangement** *n* INSTRUMENT pièce de fixation des tubes de discussion *f*

disc-wire-type: **~ mechanical filter** *n* (BrE) RECORDING filtre mécanique à disques et à fils *m*

disembark *vt* NAUT débarquer

disembarkation *n* NAUT débarquement *m*

disengage *vt* MECH déconnecter, dégager, désembrayer, MECH ENG déboîter

disengagement *n* MECH ENG *of tool head* dégagement *m*

disengaging: **~ gear in front** *n* MECH ENG débrayage sur le devant *m*; **~ lever** *n* MECH ENG *machine tool* levier de débrayage *m*

dish[1] *n* C&G *for roller in manufacture of rolled plate* bassin *m*, CHEM capsule *f*, LAB EQUIP coupelle *f*, *evaporation* capsule *f*, cristallisoir *m*, *f* cuvette coupelle *f*, PHOTO cuvette *f*; **~ aerial** *n* TELECOM antenne parabolique *f*; **~ antenna** *n* ASTRON, SPACE *communications* antenne parabolique *f*; **~ heater** *n* PHOTO chauffe-bain *m*, réchauffeur électrique pour cuvette *m*; **~ rocker** *n* PHOTO balance-cuvette *f*; **~ thermometer** *n* PHOTO thermomètre à cuvette *m*

dish[2] *vt* PROD ENG bomber

disharmonic *adj* GEOL disharmonique

dished[1] *adj* MECH embouti

dished:[2] **~ bottom** *n* NUCLEAR *of pressure vessel* fond bombé *m*; **~ head** *n* MECH fond embouti *m*; **~ washer** *n* MECH ENG rondelle bombée *f*; **~ wheel** *n* PROD ENG *emery wheel* meule à cuvette *f*

dish-ended: **~ boiler** *n* HYDR EQUIP chaudière à fonds bombés *f*

dishing: **~ shallow depression** *n* NUCLEAR *fuel pellets* nacelle de pastille *f*, évidement *m*

dishpan *n* TV antenne parabolique *f*, parabole *f*; **~ spacer** *n* MECH ENG entretoise conique *f*

disilane *n* CHEM disilane *m*

disincrustant *n* PROD ENG *for boiler* désincrustant *m*, tartrifuge *m*

disinfect *vt* HYDROL, SAFETY désinfecter

disinfectant *n* SAFETY produit désinfectant *m*

disinfection *n* SAFETY, WATER SUPP désinfection *f*

disinfest *vt* SAFETY désinfester

disintegrate[1] *vt* PACKAGING désintégrer

disintegrate[2] *vi* RAD PHYS se désintégrer

disintegration: **~ energy** *n* RAD PHYS énergie de désintégration radioactive *f*

disintegrator *n* FOOD TECH broyeur *m*, désintégrateur *m*, PAPER TECH, PROD ENG désintégrateur *m*

disjoint[1] *adj* MATH disjoint

disjoint[2] *vt* MECH ENG désassembler

disjointing *n* MECH ENG désassemblage *m*

disjunction *n* COMP, DP, ELECTRON disjonction *f*

disk:[1] **~ resident** *adj* COMP, DP résidant sur disque

disk[2] *n* COMP, DP disque *m*, MECH ENG (AmE) plateau *m*, *of eccentric* bossage *m*, disque *m*, estomac *m*, RECORDING, TV (AmE) disque *m*; **~ antenna** *n* (AmE) TELECOM antenne à disque *f*; **~ area** *n* (AmE) *see disc area*; **~ armature** *n* (AmE) *see disc armature*; **~ bit** *n* (AmE) *see disc bit*; **~ brake** *n* (AmE) *see disc brake*; **~ brake calliper** *n* (AmE) *see disc brake calliper*; **~ brake pad** *n* (AmE) *see disc brake pad*; **~ brake tools** *n pl* (AmE) *see disc brake tools*; **~ braking system** *n* (AmE) *see disc braking system* **~ capacitor** *n* (AmE) *see disc capacitor*; **~ cartridge** *n* COMP, DP cartouche de disque *f*; ~ **center wheel** *n* (AmE) *see disc centre wheel*; ~ **clutch** *n* (AmE) MECH, VEHICLES *see disc clutch*; ~ **controller** *n* COMP, DP contrôleur de disque *m*; ~ **crank** *n* (AmE) *see disc crank*; ~ **drive** *n* COMP, DP unité d'entraînement de disque *f*, unité de disque *f*; ~ **file** *n* COMP, DP fichier sur disque *m*, fichier disque *m*; ~ **filter** *n* (AmE) *see disc filter*; ~ **galaxy** *n* (AmE) *see disc galaxy*; ~ **grinder** *n* (AmE) *see disc grinder*; ~ **grinding** *n* (AmE) *see disc grinding*; ~ **head** *n* (AmE) *see disc head*; ~ **key** *n* (AmE) *see disc key*; ~ **loading** *n* (AmE) *see disc loading*; ~ **mastering** *n* (AmE) *see disc mastering*; ~ **mill** *n* (AmE) *see disc mill*; ~ **operating system** *n* *(DOS)* COMP, DP système d'exploitation à disque *m* *(DOS)*; ~ **pack** *n* COMP, DP chargeur de disques *m*; ~ **piston** *n* (AmE) *see disc piston* ~ **platter** *n* (AmE) *see disc platter*; ~ **player** *n* (AmE) *see disc player*; ~ **polishing** *n* (AmE) *see disc polishing*; ~ **recorder** *n* (AmE) *see disc recorder*; ~ **resonator filter** *n* (AmE) *see disc resonator filter*; ~ **sander** *n* (AmE) *see disc sander*; ~ **sanding machine** *n* (AmE) *see disc sanding machine*; ~ **sandpapering machine** *n* (AmE) *see disc sandpapering machine*; ~ **seal tube** *n* (AmE) ELECTRON *see disc seal tube*; ~ **sector** *n* COMP, DP secteur de disque *m*; ~ **shutter** *n* (AmE) *see disc shutter*; ~ **signal** *n* (AmE) *see disc signal*; ~ **skimmer** *n* (AmE) *see disc skimmer*; ~ **space** *n* COMP, DP espace disque *m*; ~ **spring** *n* (AmE) *see disc spring*; ~ **store** *n* (AmE) TELECOM mémoire à disque *f*; ~ **unit** *n* COMP, DP unité de disque *f*, unité de disque magnétique *f*; ~ **valve** *n* (AmE) *see disc valve*; ~ **winding** *n* (AmE) *see disc winding*

diskette *n* COMP, DP disquette *f* ~ **drive** *n* COMP, DP unité de disquette *f*

disk-wire-type: ~ **mechanical filter** *n* (AmE) *see disc-wire-type mechanical filter*

dislevelment *n* CONST dénivellation *f*, dénivellement *m*

dislocation *n* CRYSTALL dislocation *f*, GEOPHYS dislocation *f*, déplacement *m*, METALL, PROP MAT dislocation *f* ~ **annihilation** *n* METALL élimination des dislocations *f*; ~ **core** *n* METALL coeur de dislocation *m*; ~ **debris** *n* METALL débris de dislocations *m*; ~ **density** *n* METALL densité de dislocations *f*; ~ **image analysis** *n* PROP MAT analyse d'images de dislocations *f*; ~ **junction** *n* METALL jonction de dislocation *f*; ~ **kink** *n* METALL décrochement sur une dislocation *n*, torticolis de dislocation *m*; ~ **line** *n* CRYSTALL, PROP MAT ligne de dislocation *f*; ~ **loop** *n* CRYSTALL boucle de dislocation *f*; ~ **mechanism** *n* CRYSTALL, PROP MAT mécanisme de dislocation *m*; ~ **velocity** *n* METALL vitesse de dislocation *f*; ~ **wall** *n* CRYSTALL paroi de dislocation *f*

dislodge *vt* CONST disloquer, déchausser, décoller, détacher

dismantle *vt* MECH ENG désassembler, *machine* démonter

dismantlement *n* MILIT démantèlement *m*, laying up *m*

dismantling *n* MECH ENG démantèlement *m*, démontage *m*, NUCLEAR *of fuel assembly* désassemblage *m*, *of nuclear installation* démantèlement *m*; ~ **chamber** *n* CONST chambre de décintrage *f*, chambre de démontage *f*

dismast *vt* NAUT démâter

dismasting *n* NAUT démâtage *m*

dismount *vt* MECH ENG *machine* démonter

dismutation *n* CHEM dismutation *f*

disomose *n* MINERAL disomose *m*

disorder *n* METALL désordre *m*

disordered: ~ **chain** *n* CHEM *of polymer* chaîne désordonnée *f*; ~ **solid solution** *n* PROP MAT solution solide désordonnée *f*; ~ **state** *n* PROP MAT état désordonné *m*

disorientation *n* METALL désorientation *f*

disparaging: ~ **statements** *n pl* PATENTS déclarations dénigrantes *f pl*

dispatch *vt* PROD ENG répartir

dispatcher *n* COMP, DP, TRANSP répartiteur *m*

dispatching *n* PROD ENG répartition *f*; ~ **cold store** *n* REFRIG entrepôt frigorifique de distribution *m*

dispenser *n* FOOD TECH, LAB EQUIP *analysis*, PACKAGING distributeur *m*; ~ **cathode** *n* ELEC ENG cathode de réserve *f*

dispensing *n* TEXTILES dosage *m*; ~ **glass** *n* C&G verre à médicaments *m*; ~ **machine** *n* PACKAGING distributrice *f*

dispersant *n* MAR POLL, PETR TECH, POLLUTION dispersant *m*; ~ **spraying** *n* MAR POLL pulvérisation de dispersants *f*, épandage de dispersants *m*

disperse:[1] ~ **dye** *n* TEXTILES colorant dispersé *m*

disperse[2] *vi* MAR POLL, POLLUTION se disperser

dispersed *adj* TELECOM *system* dispersé

dispersing: ~ **agent** *n* COAL TECH dispersant *m*, FOOD TECH, HYDROL agent dispersant *m*, P&R *pigments, polymers* agent dispersant *m*, dispersant *m*, POLLUTION agent dispersant *m*

dispersion *n* CHEM TECH, COAL TECH, COMP *variation*, CRYSTALL, DP *variation*, METALL, OPT, P&R, PHYS, PROP MAT, RAD PHYS, TELECOM dispersion *f*, WAVE PHYS *of colours due to refraction* dispersion des couleurs *f*; ~ **coefficient** *n* CHEM TECH coefficient de fuite *m*; ~ **cone** *n* CHEM TECH cône de dispersion *m*; ~ **equation** *n* PHYS équation de dispersion *f*; ~ **fuel** *n* NUCLEAR combustible en dispersion *m*; ~ **grating** *n* CHEM TECH réseau de dispersion *m*; ~ **hardening** *n* METALL durcissement par dispersion *m*; ~ **kneader** *n* CHEM TECH malaxeur à dispersion *m*, pétrisseur *m*; ~ **paint** *n* COLOURS peinture dispersion *f*; ~ **relation** *n* PHYS relation de dispersion *f*; ~ **spectrum** *n* PROP MAT spectre dispersé *m*; ~ **strengthening** *n* CHEM TECH durcissement par phase dispersée *m*; ~ **test** *n* GAS TECH essai de dispersion *m*; ~ **train** *n* NUCLEAR auréole de dispersion *f*

dispersion-cooled: ~ **reactor** *n* NUCLEAR réacteur refroidi par un écoulement en phase dispersée *m*

dispersive: ~ **delay line** *n* ELECTRON ligne à retard dispersive *f*; ~ **medium** *n* CHEM TECH, PHYS milieu dispersif *m*; ~ **power** *n* PHYS pouvoir dispersif *m*

dispersivity *n* CHEM TECH dispersivité *f*

dispersoid *n* CHEM TECH matière dispersée *f*

displace *vt* ELEC ENG *brush* décaler, NUCLEAR déplacer

displaced[1] *adj* MECH ENG décalé, NUCLEAR *atom* déplacé

displaced:[2] ~ **threshold** *n* AERONAUT *of runway* seuil décalé *m*

displacement *n* ACOUSTICS élongation *f*, AUTO cylindrée *f*, cylindrée totale *f*, COMP *addresses*, DP *addresses*, ELEC ENG, GAS TECH déplacement *m*, GEOL décalage *m*, déplacement *m*, rejet *m*, GEOPHYS dislocation *f*, déplacement *m*, MECH ENG débattement *m*, NAUT *ship design* déplacement *m*, tonnage *m*, PHYS, WATER SUPP déplacement *m*; ~ **current** *n* ELEC courant de déplacement *m*, ELEC ENG courant de déplacement *m*, courant diélectrique *m*, PHYS courant de déplacement *m*; ~ **error** *n* AERONAUT *instrument landing system* erreur d'écart *f*; ~ **fan** *n* PROD ENG ventilateur déplaceur *m*, ventilateur statique *m*, ventilateur volumogène *m*; ~ **of phase** *n* ELEC *alternating current* déphasage *m*; ~ **spike** *n* NUCLEAR *in solid* zone de déplacement *f*; ~ **thickness** *n*

MECH ENG épaisseur de déplacement *f*; ~ **variable** *n* SPACE *spacecraft* inconnue de déplacement *f*

display[1] *n* COMP, DP affichage *m*, visualisation *f*, ELEC affichage *m*, PACKAGING étalage *m*, PRINT affichage *m*, SPACE affichage *m*, présentation *f*, visualisation *f*, écrande visualisation *m*, TELECOM affichage *m*, TEXTILES exposition *f*, TRANSP *in vehicle* tableau *m*; ~ **adaptor** *n* COMP, DP adaptateur d'écran *m*; ~ **box** *n* PACKAGING boîte factice *f*; ~ **brilliance** *n* NAUT *radar* brillance de l'écran *f*; ~ **case** *n* REFRIG vitrine *f*; ~ **console** *n* COMP, DP, TELECOM console de visualisation *f*; ~ **controller** *n* COMP, DP contrôleur d'écran *m*; ~ **device** *n* COMP *of computer* visu *f*, visuel *m*; ~ **driver** *n* COMP, DP gestionnaire d'écran *m*, pilote d'écran *m*; ~ **faces** *n pl* PRINT caractères de fantaisie *m pl*, caractères de titrage *m pl*; ~ **format** *n* NUCLEAR format d'affichage *m*, PROD ENG format graphique *m*; ~ **menu** *n* COMP, DP menu d'écran *m*; ~ **packaging** *n* PACKAGING emballage d'étalage *m*; ~ **processor** *n* COMP, DP processeur d'écran *m*; ~ **retention** *n* ELECTRON conservation de la trace *f*; ~ **screen** *n* ELECTRON, TELECOM écran de visualisation *m*; ~ **setting** *n* COMP, DP format d'écran *m*; ~ **station interface** *n (DSI)* TELECOM interface de poste d'affichage *m*; ~ **storage tube** *n* ELECTRON tube à mémoire à vision directe *m*; ~ **terminal** *n* SPACE *communications* console de visualisation *f*; ~ **tube** *n* ELECTRON tube de présentation *m*; ~ **type** *n* PRINT *in WYSIWYG system* caractères de titrage *m pl*, caractères écran dans les systèmes WYSIWYG *m pl*; ~ **window** *n* C&G vitrine *f*

display[2] *vt* COMP, DP afficher, ELECTRON présenter, visualiser, SPACE afficher, montrer, présenter, visualiser, TELECOM *screen image* afficher, visualiser, TEXTILES exposer

displayed: ~ **speed system** *n* TRANSP système de vitesse affichée *m*; ~ **waveform** *n* ELECTRON *on oscilloscope* signal visualisé *m*

disposable: ~ **protective clothing** *n* SAFETY vêtements de protection à jeter *m pl*; ~ **syringe** *n* LAB EQUIP *analysis* seringue à usage unique *f*

disposal *n* MAR POLL élimination *f*; ~ **by nuclear transmutation** *n* NUCLEAR *of waste* élimination par transmutation nucléaire *f*; ~ **site** *n* CONST site d'évacuation *m*; ~ **tank** *n* SPACE *spacecraft* réservoir *m*, réservoir d'eaux usées *m*

disproportionation *n* CHEM disproportionnement *m*

disruption *n* NUCLEAR *of chain reaction* arrêt *m*; ~ **to service** *n* TELECOM dérangement *m*

disruptive[1] *adj* ELEC ENG disruptif, MINING *blasting* brisant

disruptive:[2] ~ **discharge** *n* ELEC ENG décharge brusque *f*, décharge disruptive *f*; ~ **strength** *n* ELEC ENG, ELECTR rigidité diélectrique *f*; ~ **voltage** *n* ELEC tension disruptive *f*, ELEC ENG tension de rupture *f*, tension disruptive *f*

dissecting: ~ **microscope** *n* INSTRUMENT microscope à dissection *m*; ~ **scissors** *n pl* LAB EQUIP *biology* ciseaux à dissection *m pl*; ~ **tray** *n* LAB EQUIP *biology* cuvette à dissection *f*

dissection *n* GEOM dissection *f*; ~ **needle** *n* LAB EQUIP *biology* aiguille à dissection *f*

dissector: ~ **tube** *n* TV tube dissecteur *m*

dissipate *vt* MECH ENG évacuer

dissipated: ~ **power** *n* ELEC puissance dissipée *f*

dissipation *n* ELEC ENG dissipation *f*, RAD PHYS *thermodynamics* dissipation d'énergie *f*; ~ **coefficient** *n* PHYS

sound coefficient de dissipation *m*; ~ **factor** *n* ELEC, PHYS facteur de dissipation *m*

dissipative: ~ **loss** *n* ELEC ENG pertes dissipatives *f pl*; ~ **medium** *n* PHYS milieu dissipatif *m*

dissociable *adj* CHEM dissociable

dissociate *vi* CHEM se dissocier

dissociated *adj* GAS TECH dissocié

dissociation *n* CHEM, COAL TECH dissociation *f*, CRYSTALL *of crystal defect* décomposition *f*; ~ **constant** *n* CHEM constante de dissociation *f*; ~ **energy** *n* GAS TECH énergie de dissociation *f*

dissolubility *n* CHEM dissolubilité *f*

dissolubleness *n* CHEM dissolubilité *f*

dissolute *adj* CHEM TECH dissous

dissolution *n* CHEM, CHEM TECH, PROP MAT dissolution *f*

dissolve[1] *n* CINEMAT fondu *m*, fondu enchaîné *m*

dissolve[2] *vt* CHEM, CINEMAT, GAS TECH dissoudre

dissolve:[3] ~ **away** *vi* CHEM TECH dissoudre, extraire en dissolvant; ~ **out** *vi* CHEM TECH dissoudre, extraire en dissolvant

dissolved[1] *adj* CHEM dissous

dissolved:[2] ~ **gas** *n* GAS TECH gaz dissous *m*; ~ **inorganic carbon** *n* POLLUTION carbone inorganique dissous *m*; ~ **organic carbon** *n* POLLUTION COD, carbone organique dissous *m*; ~ **organic matter** *n* POLLUTION matière organique dissoute *f*; ~ **oxygen** *n (DO)* POLLUTION oxygène dissous *m (OD)*

dissolvent *n* CHEM TECH dissolvant *m*, solvant *m*, PAPER TECH dissolvant *m*

dissolver *n* CHEM solvant *m*, CHEM TECH dissolvant *m*, solvant *m*

dissolving *n* CHEM, CHEM TECH dissolution *f*; ~ **pulp** *n* PAPER TECH pâte dissolvante *f*, pâte pour transformation chimique *f*; ~ **shutter** *n* CINEMAT obturateur pour fondu *m*; ~ **tank** *n* PAPER TECH bac de dissolution *m*

dissonance *n* ACOUSTICS, WAVE PHYS *of sound* dissonance *f*

dissymmetric *adj* GEOM dissymétrique

dissymmetrical *adj* GEOM dissymétrique

dissymmetry *n* CHEM asymétrie *f*, GEOM dissymétrie *f*, MATH *of mirror images* réflexion *f*

distance *n* PHYS *spatial separation* distance *f*, parcours *m*; ~ **apart** *n* MECH ENG écartement *m*; ~ **bar** *n* MECH ENG pièce d'écartement *f*; ~ **between centers** *n* (AmE) *see distance between centres*; ~ **between centers of gear wheel and pinion** *n* (AmE) *see distance between centres of gear wheel and pinion*; ~ **between centers of journals** *n* (AmE) *see distance between centres of journals*; ~ **between centres** *n* (BrE) MECH ENG distance des centres *f*, entre-axe *m*, *of lathe* distance entre pointes *f*, entre-pointes *m*, longueur entre pointes *f*; ~ **between centres of gear wheel and pinion** *n* (BrE) MECH ENG distance des centres d'une roue d'engrenage et d'un pignon *f*; ~ **between centres of journals** *n* (BrE) MECH ENG entre-axe des fusées *m*; ~ **between rails** *n* RAIL écartement des rails *m*; ~ **between sleepers** *n* RAIL *track* créneau de voie *m*; ~ **of drill from column** *n* MECH ENG écartement du foret à la colonne *m*; ~ **finder** *n* NAUT télémètre *m*; ~ **logged** *n* NAUT distance parcourue *f*; ~ **meter** *n* CINEMAT télémètre *m*; ~ **piece** *n* CONST *between bars of grate* entretoise *f*, pièce d'écartement *f*, MECH ENG pièce d'écartement *f*; ~ **piece spacer** *n* MECH ENG pièce d'écartement *f*; ~ **relay** *n* ELEC relais télécommandé *m*; ~ **run** *n* NAUT *navigation* distance parcourue *f*; ~ **scale** *n* CINEMAT échelle des distances *f*, PHOTO échelle de mise au point *f*; ~ **switch** *n* ELEC interrupteur à distance *m*

distance-measuring: ~ **equipment** *n (DME)* AERONAUT dispositif de mesure de la distance de l'avion à la station *m*, interrogateur de distance *m*, mesureur *m*, équipement de mesure de distance *m*

distant: ~ **caution signal** *n* RAIL signal avancé d'avertissement *m*, signal d'avertissement à distance *m*; ~ **collision** *n* NUCLEAR choc lointain *m*, collision lointaine *f*; ~ **field** *n* TELECOM champ lointain *m*; ~ **source** *n* POLLUTION source éloignée *f*; ~ **water fishing** *n* OCEANOG pêche lointaine *f*; ~ **water supply** *n* WATER SUPP alimentation en eau à distance *f*

distemper[1] *n* COLOURS couleur à détrempe *f*, peinture à la colle *f*, P&R *paint* peinture en détrempe *f*, peinture à la colle *f*, PROD ENG *paint* détrempe *f*

distemper[2] *vt* COLOURS badigeonner, peindre en détrempe

distensional: ~ **fault** *n* GEOL faille de distension *f*

disthene *n* MINERAL disthène *m*

distil[1] *vt* (BrE) CHEM distiller; ~ **off** *vt* (BrE) CHEM TECH distiller, THERMOD *drive off* chasser par distillation

distil[2] *vi* (BrE) CHEM se distiller, THERMOD distiller, extraire par distillation

distill[1] *vt* (AmE) *see* distil

distill[2] *vi* (AmE) *see* distil

distillate *n* CHEM distillation *f*, produit de la distillation *m*, PETR TECH, THERMOD distillat *m*

distillation *n* CHEM distillation *f*, produit de la distillation *m*, *product* distillat *m*, PETR TECH *product*, PROP MAT *product*, THERMOD *product* distillat *m*, distillation *f*, produit de la distillation *m* ~ **apparatus** *n* LAB EQUIP *glassware* appareil de distillation *m*; ~ **by ascent** *n* CHEM TECH, THERMOD distillation droite *f*; ~ **by descent** *n* CHEM TECH, THERMOD distillation vers le bas *f*; ~ **by steam entraining** *n* CHEM TECH distillation par entraînement à la vapeur *f*; ~ **chamber** *n* CHEM TECH chambre de distillation *f*; ~ **column** *n* CHEM TECH colonne de distillation *f*; ~ **drying** *n* PROP MAT séchage par distillation *m*; ~ **flask** *n* CHEM TECH alambic *m*, matras *m*, LAB EQUIP *glassware* ballon à distillation *m*, THERMOD alambic *m*, matras *m*; ~ **gas** *n* CHEM TECH, THERMOD gaz de distillation *m*; ~ **range** *n* THERMOD intervalle de distillation *m*; ~ **retort** *n* THERMOD alambic *m*, matras *m*; ~ **tail** *n* CHEM TECH, THERMOD queue de distillation *f*, résidu de distillation *m*; ~**test** *n* CHEM TECH analyse fractionnée *f*; ~ **tower** *n* CHEM TECH, PETR TECH, THERMOD colonne de distillation *f*

distilled *adj* HYDROL *water*, VEHICLES *water* distillé

distiller *n* CHEM TECH distillateur *m*

distillery *n* CHEM TECH, FOOD TECH distillerie *f*; ~ **residue** *n* FOOD TECH *brewing* vinasse de distillerie *f*

distilling: ~ **apparatus** *n* CHEM TECH appareil de distillation *m*; ~ **flask** *n* CHEM TECH alambic *m*, matras *m*; ~ **tube** *n* CHEM TECH tube de distillation *m*, tube distillateur *m*

distinctiveness *n* PATENTS caractère distinctif *m*

distorted[1] *adj* ELECTRON *signal* déformé

distorted[2] ~ **wave method** *n* NUCLEAR méthode des ondes déformées *f*

distorting *adj* C&G *mirror*, INSTRUMENT *lens* déformant

distortion *n* ACOUSTICS distorsion *f*, CINEMAT déformation *f*, ELEC, ELECTRON distorsion *f*, MECH ENG déformation *f*, P&R, PHYS, PROP MAT distorsion *f*, RAIL gauchissement *m*, RECORDING, TELECOM, TV distorsion *f*; ~ **lens** *n* CINEMAT lentille déformante *f*; ~ **meter** *n* RECORDING mesureur de distorsion *m*

distortion-limited: ~ **operation** *n* TELECOM fonctionnement limité par la distorsion *m*

distortion-measuring: ~ **bridge** *n* RECORDING pont de mesure de distorsion *m*

distress:[1] **in** ~ *adj* NAUT *ship* en détresse, en perdition

distress:[2] ~ **alert** *n* NAUT signal de détresse *m*; ~ **alerting** *n* TELECOM alerte en cas de détresse *f*; ~ **beacon** *n* NAUT *giving automatic location by satellite*, SPACE balise de détresse *f*; ~ **call** *n* AERONAUT *giving automatic location by satellite* appel de détresse *m*;~ **flare** *n* NAUT feu de détresse *m*, fusée de détresse *f*, fusée éclairante *f*; ~ **radiocall system** *n* TELECOM système de détresse radioélectrique *m*; ~ **signal** *n* AERONAUT signal de détresse *m*, CONTROL signal d'alarme *m*, signal de détresse *m*, NAUT signal de détresse *m*

distributed[1] *adj* COMP, DP distribué, réparti, PROD ENG décentralisé, TELECOM distribué

distributed:[2] ~ **architecture** *n* COMP architecture distribuée *f*, architecture répartie *f*, DP architecture répartie *f*; ~ **array processor** *n* COMP, DP multiprocesseur distribué *m*; ~ **capacitance** *n* ELEC ENG capacité répartie *f*; ~ **control system** *n* PROD ENG système d'automatisme réparti *m*, TELECOM système à commande répartie *m*; ~ **database** *n* COMP, DP base de données répartie *f*; ~ **data processing** *n (DDP)* COMP informatique distribuée *f*, informatique répartie *f*; ~ **digital processing** *n* NUCLEAR traitement numérique réparti *m*; ~ **element circuit** *n* ELEC ENG circuit à constantes réparties *m*; ~ **inductance** *n* ELEC ENG inductance répartie *f*; ~ **multi-antenna system** *n* TELECOM système à plusieurs antennes réparties *m*; ~ **network** *n* COMP, DP réseau distribué *m*, réseau décentralisé *m*; ~ **operating system** *n* COMP système d'exploitation distribué *m*; ~ **PBX** *n* TELECOM autocommutateur privé réparti *m*; ~ **processing** *n* COMP, DP traitement distribué *m*, PROD ENG traitement réparti *m*

distributing: ~ **board** *n* ELEC, VEHICLES *ignition* tableau distributeur *m*; ~ **canal** *n* WATER SUPP canal distributeur *m*; ~ **pipe** *n* NUCLEAR conduit principal *m*, WATER SUPP tuyau distributeur *m*

distribution *n* C&G répartition *f*, ELEC *supply*, GAS TECH, HYDR EQUIP *sequence of operations* distribution *f*, MECH ENG diffusion *f*, *of bending stress* répartition *f*, VEHICLES *ignition* distribution *f*; ~ **amplifier** *n* TV amplificateur de distribution *m*; ~ **board** *n* ELEC ENG, TELECOM *power supply* tableau de distribution *m*; ~ **box** *n* ELEC, ELEC ENG boîte de distribution *f*; ~ **bus** *n* ELEC jeu de barres de distribution *m*; ~ **cabinet** *n* ELEC ENG armoire de distribution *f*; ~ **cable** *n* ELEC, ELEC ENG câble de distribution *m*; ~ **center** *n* (AmE), ~ **centre** *n* (BrE) TELECOM centre de distribution *m*; ~ **chain** *n* PACKAGING chaîne de distribution *f*; ~ **chamber** *n* MECH ENG *air conditioning* boîte de répartition *f*; ~ **diagram** *n* HYDROL diagramme de distribution *m*, MECH ENG *of slide valve* diagramme de distribution *m*, épure de régulation *f*; ~ **frame** *n* TELECOM répartiteur *m*; ~ **function** *n* MATH fonction de répartition *f*; ~ **fuse board** *n* ELEC tableau de distribution à fusibles *m*; ~ **network** *n* CONST, ELEC, ELEC ENG réseau de distribution *m*, TELECOM réseau de connexion *m*, *exchange switching* réseau de distribution *m*; ~ **primary link** *n (DPL)* TELECOM liaison primaire pour les services de distribution *f*; ~ **ring** *n* NUCLEAR conduit distributeur d'eau d'alimentation *m*; ~ **stage** *n* TELECOM étage de brassage *m*; ~ **station** *n* ELEC ENG poste de distribution *m*; ~ **steel** *n* CONST *reinforcement* armature transversale *f*, barre de réparation *f*; ~ **substation** *n* ELEC poste de distribution *m*; ~ **system** *n* ELEC *supply network*, ELEC ENG réseau de distribution *m*, système de distribution *m*, GAS TECH chaîne d'approvisionnement *f*, WATER SUPP système de distribution *m*; ~ **technique** *n* PACKAGING technique de distribution *f*; ~ **valve** *n* MECH ENG vanne de répartition *f*

distributive: ~ **fault** *n* GEOL faille en gradins *f*

distributor *n* ELEC conducteur de distribution *m*, MECH, MECH ENG, PACKAGING, PAPER TECH distributeur *m*, répartiteur *m*, VEHICLES *ignition* distributeur *m*; ~ **arm** *n* VEHICLES *ignition* doigt d'allumeur *m*; ~ **cam** *n* VEHICLES *ignition* came de rupture *f*; ~ **cap** *n* AUTO tête d'allumeur *f*, VEHICLES *ignition* chapeau d'allumeur *m*; ~ **clamp bolt** *n* AUTO vis de fixation du distributeur *f*; ~ **drive** *n* VEHICLES *ignition* commande d'allumeur *f*; ~ **finger** *n* AUTO doigt de distribution *m*; ~ **housing** *n* AUTO carter d'allumeur *m*; ~ **injection pump** *n* AUTO pompe rotative à distributeur *f*; ~ **rotor** *n* AUTO doigt de distribution *m*, VEHICLES *ignition* rotor d'allumeur *m*; ~ **shaft** *n* AUTO, VEHICLES *ignition* arbre d'allumeur *m*; ~ **suppressor** *n* VEHICLES *ignition* dispositif d'antiparasitage pour allumeur *m*

district: ~ **heating** *n* HEATING chauffage d'un groupe d'îlots *m*, THERMOD *scheme* chauffage urbain *m*; ~ **heating station** *n* THERMOD centrale de chauffage urbain *f*

disturb *vt* CONST *ground* remuer, retourner

disturbance *n* METEO, PETR perturbation *f*

disturbed: ~ **compass** *n* NAUT compas qui s'affole *m*; ~ **field** *n* (*cf stable field*) METEO champ perturbé *m*

disulfide *n* (AmE), **disulphide** *n* (BrE) CHEM bisulfure *m*, disulfure *m*

disused: ~ **quarry** *n* MINING carrière abandonnée *f*

DIT *abbr* (*directory information tree*) TELECOM arbre d'information d'annuaire *m*

ditch *n* AERONAUT amerrissage forcé *m*, COAL TECH fossé *m*, CONST canal *m*, fossé *m*, rigole *f*, tranchée *f*, HYDROL fossé *m*, PETR tranchée *f*, WATER SUPP fossé *m*, rigole *f*; ~ **canal** *n* WATER SUPP canal à niveau *m*; ~ **drainage** *n* HYDROL *sewage* drainage par fossés *m*; ~ **irrigation** *n* WATER SUPP irrigation à la raie *f*; ~ **line** *n* WATER SUPP canalisation *f*

ditcher *n* CONST *civil engineering* trancheuse *f*

ditching *n* AERONAUT amerrissage forcé *m*

dither *n* ELECTRON activation *f*; ~ **oscillator** *n* ELECTRON oscillateur d'activation *m*

dithering *n* DP *graphics* juxtaposition de points *f*, simulation de nuances *f*

dithiobenzoic *adj* CHEM dithiobenzoïque

dithionate *n* CHEM dithionate *m*

dithionic *adj* CHEM dithionique

diurnal[1] *adj* ASTRON, GEOPHYS, METEO *amplitude* diurne

diurnal:[2] ~ **libration** *n* ASTRON libration diurne *f*; ~ **motion** *n* ASTRON mouvement diurne *m*; ~ **parallax** *n* ASTRON parallaxe diurne *f*; ~ **phase** *n* SPACE phase diurne *f*; ~ **tide** *n* NAUT, OCEANOG marée diurne *f*; ~ **variation** *n* NAUT *in barometric pressure and temperature* variation diurne *f*; ~ **wave** *n* OCEANOG onde diurne *f*

divalence *n* CHEM divalence *f*

divalent *adj* CHEM divalent

dive[1] *n* AERONAUT piqué *m*, piqué en vol *m*, SPACE *spacecraft* piqué *m*

dive[2] *vi* AERONAUT, SPACE *spacecraft* piquer

diver *n* OCEANOG, PETR plongeur *m*, scaphandrier *m*; ~

lockout submersible *n* OCEANOG sous-marin crache-plongeur *m*

diver's: ~ **cramps** *n* OCEANOG colique des scaphandriers *f*; ~ **umbilical** *n* OCEANOG ombilical *m*

divergence *n* NUCLEAR *of reactor, nuclear chain reaction*, PHYS *of vector field* divergence *f*, SPACE divergent *m*

divergent[1] *adj* MATH, OPT divergent

divergent:[2] ~ **lens** *n* INSTRUMENT lentille concave *f*, lentille divergente *f*, lentille à bord épais *f*; ~ **meniscus** *n* PHOTO ménisque divergent *m*; ~ **nozzle** *n* PHYS *of wind tunnel* divergent *m*; ~ **plate boundary** *n* GEOL frontière de plaques divergentes *f*, limite de plaques lithosphériques divergentes *f*

diverging *n* TRANSP divergence *f*; ~ **lens** *n* CINEMAT lentille divergente *f*, INSTRUMENT lentille concave *f*, lentille divergente *f*, lentille à bord épais *f*, PHYS lentille divergente *f*; ~ **volume** *n* TRANSP débit après convergence *m*

diversion *n* TRANSP *of traffic* déviation *f*, WATER SUPP *of river* détournement *m*, *of stream* dérivation *f*; ~ **canal** *n* HYDROL, WATER SUPP canal de dérivation *m*; ~ **channel** *n* HYDROL canal de dérivation *m*; ~ **cut** *n* HYDROL canal de dérivation *m*; ~ **dam** *n* HYDROL barrage de dérivation *m*; ~ **tunnel** *n* HYDROL *dams* galerie de dérivation *f*

diversity *n* TELECOM diversité *f*

divert *vt* CONST détourner, *traffic* dévier

diverter *n* PETR TECH déviateur *m*

diverting *n* WATER SUPP *of river* détournement *m*, *of stream* dérivation *f*

divide *vt* COMP, DP, MATH diviser

divided: ~ **beam** *n* METR réglette *f*; ~ **circle** *n* GEOM cercle gradué *m*, INSTRUMENT cercle gradué *m*, limbe vertical de calage *m*; ~ **dial** *n* MECH ENG cadran divisé *m*, cadran gradué *m*; ~ **highway** *n* (AmE) (*cf dual carriageway*) CONST route à double chaussée *f*, route à terre-plein central *f*, TRANSP créneau de dépassement *m*; ~ **pitch** *n* MECH ENG *of screw* pas apparent *m*

dividend *n* COMP, DP, MATH dividende *m*

divider *n* COMP, DP, ELECTRON diviseur *m*, MECH ENG compas droit *m*, compas droit à pointes *m*, compas à diviser *m*, compas à pointes sèches *m*, intercalaire *m*, PROD ENG compas droit *m*, compas droit à pointes *m*, compas à diviser *m*, compas à pointes sèches *m*, TELECOM diviseur *m*

dividers *n pl* GEOM, METR compas à pointes sèches *m*, MINING *shaft timbering* moises *f pl*, NAUT *navigation* compas à pointes sèches *m*, PROD ENG compas droit *m*, compas droit à pointes *m*, compas à diviser *m*, compas à pointes sèches *m*

dividing: ~ **apparatus** *n* PROD ENG *for hexagonal and octagonal nuts* appareil diviseur *m*; ~ **attachment** *n* MECH ENG *machine tool* appareil diviseur *m*; ~ **box** *n* ELEC boîte de séparation *f*; ~ **circle** *n* MECH ENG *gearing* cercle de contact *m*, cercle de division *m*, cercle primitif *m*, primitif *m*, trait de division *m*; ~ **circuit** *n* ELECTRON circuit diviseur *m*; ~ **heads** *n pl* MECH ENG *for milling machine* appareil diviseur *m*, poupée diviseuse et sa contre-pointe *f*; ~ **multivibrator** *n* ELECTRON multivibrateur monté en diviseur *m*; ~ **wheel** *n* MECH ENG roue de division *f*, roue diviseuse *f*

diving *n* OCEANOG, PETR plongée *f*; ~ **bell** *n* NAUT cloche à plongeur *f*, OCEANOG cloche de plongée *f*, cloche à plongeur *f*, jupe *f*, tourelle de plongée *f*, PETR, PETR TECH cloche de plongée *f*; ~ **brake** *n* AERONAUT frein de piqué *m*; ~ **cylinder** *n* OCEANOG bloc-bouteilles *m*; ~ **depth** *n* OCEANOG fond *m*; ~ **equipment** *n* OCEANOG, PETR équipement de plongée *m*; ~ **gear** *n* OCEANOG, PETR équipement de plongée *m*; ~ **helmet** *n* OCEANOG casque *m*; ~ **hood** *n* OCEANOG cagoule *f*; ~ **mask** *n* OCEANOG masque de plongée *m*; ~ **operation** *n* OCEANOG intervention sous-marine *f*; ~ **plate** *n* OCEANOG barre de plongée *f*; ~ **rudder** *n* NAUT *of submarine* gouvernail de profondeur *m*; ~ **saucer** *n* OCEANOG SP, soucoupe plongeante *f*; ~ **suit** *n* OCEANOG combinaison de plongée *f*, habit de plongée *m*, vêtement de plongée *m*, scaphandre *m*; ~ **supervisor** *n* OCEANOG chef de palanquée *m*, chef de plongée *m*; ~ **support barge** *n* OCEANOG barge de plongée *f*; ~ **tank** *n* OCEANOG bloc-bouteilles *m*

divinyl *n* CHEM divinyle *m*

divisible *adj* MATH divisible

division *n* COMP division *f*, CONST *partition* cloison *f*, division *f*, séparation *f*, DP division *f*, GEOL coupure *f*, MATH division *f*, PHYS *of amplitude* division *f*, *of wavefront* division *f*; ~ **inserting equipment** *n* PACKAGING *for container* équipement pour mettre en place les divisions *m*; ~ **plate** *n* MECH ENG plateau de division *m*, plateau diviseur *m*; ~ **point** *n* MECH ENG point de montage *m*; ~ **wheel** *n* MECH ENG roue de division *f*, roue diviseuse *f*

divisor *n* COMP, DP, MATH diviseur *m*

divorced: ~ **pearlite** *n* METALL perlite divisée *f*

DL *abbr* TELECOM *(data link)* liaison de données *f*, TELECOM *(direct line)* ligne directe *f*, ligne privée *f*

D-layer *n* GEOPHYS, PHYS couche D *f*

DLC *abbr* TELECOM *(data link control)* commande de liaison de données *f*, TELECOM *(data link connection)* connexion pour liaison de données *f*

DLCI *abbr (data link connection identifier)* TELECOM identificateur de connexion de liaison consolidée *m*

DLE *abbr (data link escape)* COMP, DP échappement en transmission *m*, échappement à la transmission *m*

D-link *n* RAIL *vehicles* manille de tendeur *f*

DLS *abbr (data link service)* TELECOM service de liaison de données *m*

DM *abbr* COMP *(data management)* gestion de données *f*, COMP *(delta modulation)* modulation delta *f*, DP *(data memory)* mémoire de données *f*, DP, TELECOM *(data management)* gestion de données *f*, TELECOM *(degraded minute)* minute dégradée *f*, TELECOM *(digital multiplexer)* multiplexeur numérique *m*

DMA *abbr (direct memory access)* COMP accès direct à la mémoire *m*

DME *abbr (distance-measuring equipment)* AERONAUT interrogateur de distance *m*, équipement DME *m*

DML *abbr (data manipulation language)* COMP langage de manipulation de données *m*

DMM *abbr (direct metal mastering)* PROD ENG, RECORDING gravure directe sur métal *f*

DMNSC *abbr (digital main network switching centre)* TELECOM centre de commutation numérique du réseau principal *m*

DMOS: ~ **technology** *n* ELECTRON technique DMOS *f*; ~ **transistor** *n* ELECTRON transistor DMOS *m*

DN *abbr* TELECOM *(directory number)* numéro d'appel *m*, TELECOM *(destination network)* réseau de destination *m*, TELECOM *(digital network)* réseau numérique *m*

DNA *abbr (deoxyribonucleic acid)* CHEM ADN *(acide désoxyribonucléique)*

DNIC *abbr (data network identification code)* TELECOM CIRD *(code d'identification de réseau de données)*

do:[1] ~ **work on contract** *vi* PROD ENG travailler au forfait, travailler en l'entreprise

do:[2] ~ **not drop** *phr* PACKAGING *handling or marking label* ne pas laisser tomber; ~ **not throw** *phr* PACKAGING *handling or marking label* ne pas jeter

DO *abbr (dissolved oxygen)* POLLUTION OD *(oxygène dissous)*

dobby *n* TEXTILES ratière *f*

dobby-weave: ~ **fabric** *n* TEXTILES tissu armuré *m*

dock[1] *n* NAUT bassin *m*, dock *m*, quai *m*; ~ **wall** *n* CONST *building*, NAUT *dry dock* bajoyer *m*; ~ **warehouse** *n* NAUT dock *m*; ~ **work** *n* PROD ENG manutention portuaire *f*

dock[2] *vt* NAUT, SPACE *spacecraft* accoster

dock[3] *vi* NAUT arriver au bassin, arriver aux docks, arriver à quai, faire entrer au bassin, faire entrer au dock, SPACE *spacecraft* s'amarrer

dockage *n* FOOD TECH *milling, baking* impuretés *f pl*, NAUT droits de bassin *m pl*, droits de dock *m pl*

docker *n* (BrE) *(cf longshoreman)* NAUT arrimeur *m*, docker *m*, débardeur *m*

docket *n* PROD ENG bordereau *m*, ticket *m*, étiquette *f*

docking *n* NAUT *of ship* mise au bassin *f*, passage au bassin *m*, SPACE accostage *m*, attelage *m*, collision *f*, amarrage *m*, *of spacecraft* abordage *m*; ~ **adaptor** *n* SPACE adaptateur d'accostage *m*, *of spacecraft* adaptateur d'accostage *m*; ~ **guidance system** *n* AERONAUT système de guidage pour l'accostage *m*; ~ **maneuver** *n* (AmE), ~ **manoeuvre** *n* (BrE) NAUT manoeuvre d'abordage *f*; ~ **piece** *n* SPACE *of spacecraft* pièce d'amarrage *f*; ~ **port** *n* SPACE *of spacecraft* port d'accostage *m*; ~ **probe** *n* SPACE *of spacecraft* sonde d'accostage *f*; ~ **procedure** *n* AERONAUT procédure de stationnement *f*; ~ **tunnel** *n* SPACE *of spacecraft* tunnel d'accostage *m*; ~ **unit** *n* SPACE *of spacecraft* pièce d'amarrage *f*

dockyard *n* NAUT *naval* arsenal maritime *m*, *shipbuilding* chantier de construction navale *m*, chantier naval *m*

doctor *n* P&R *coating* docteur *m*, PAPER TECH racle *f*; ~ **blade** *n* PACKAGING couteau nettoyeur *m*, PAPER TECH lame de racle *f*, racloir *m*, PRINT racle *f*, racle d'essuyage *f*; ~ **roll** *n* PAPER TECH rouleau égaliseur *m*, PRINT rouleau avec racle *m*, rouleau distributeur *m*

docudrama *n* CINEMAT drame vécu *m*

document[1] *n* COMP, DP document *m*; ~ **film** *n* PHOTO pellicule pour la reproduction réduite de documents *f*; ~ **glass** *n* C&G verre inactinique *m*; ~ **reader** *n* COMP, DP lecteur de document *m*; ~ **reading** *n* COMP, DP lecture de documents *f*; ~ **retrieval** *n* COMP, DP recherche documentaire *f*; ~ **sorter** *n* COMP, DP trieuse de documents *f*

document[2] *vt* PROD ENG *data* répertorier

documentary *n* CINEMAT documentaire *m*; ~ **film-maker** *n* CINEMAT documentariste *m*

documentation *n* COMP, DP documentation *f*

DOD *abbr (direct outward dialling)* TELECOM accès direct au réseau *m*, prise directe du réseau *f*

dodecagon *n* GEOM dodécagone *m*

dodecahedral *adj* GEOM dodécaèdre

dodecahedron *n* GEOM dodécaèdre *m*

dodecane *n* CHEM, DETERGENTS dodécane *m*

dodecyl: ~ **benzene** *n* DETERGENTS dodécylbenzène *m*

dodge *vt* PHOTO cacher

dodgers *n pl* PRINT prospectus *m pl*

doeglic *adj* CHEM doéglique

doff *n* C&G levée *f*

doffer: ~ **comb** *n* TEXTILES peigne détacheur *m*

doffing *n* TEXTILES levée *f*; ~ **devices** *n* TEXTILES système de levée des supports de filature *m*

dog *n* MECH doigt d'entraînement *m*, toc *m*, MECH ENG crabot *m*, griffe *f*, *for lathe faceplate* poupée *f*, poupée à pompe *f*, *lathe carrier* doguin *m*, toc *m*, *pawl* chien *m*, cliquet *m*, doigt d'encliquetage *m*, détente *f*, *sling dog* patte d'élingue *f*, MINING *casing dog* arrache-tuyau *m*, *grab iron* accrocheur *m*, *landing dog, kep* clichage *m*, taquet *m*, PROD ENG *for box lugs* agrafe *f*, serre *f*, *of timberclip, log carriage, log-sawing machine* griffe *f*; ~ **bone** *n* AERONAUT barre d'ancrage *f*; ~ **chuck** *n* MECH ENG *of lathe* mandrin à toc *m*, plateau pousse-toc *m*, plateau à toc *m*, plateau-toc *m*; ~ **clutch** *n* AUTO embrayage à griffe *m*, MECH ENG crabotage *m*, VEHICLES *gearbox* embrayage à griffe *m*; ~ **coupling** *n* MECH ENG accouplement à griffe *m*; ~ **hook** *n* MECH ENG *sling dog* patte d'élingue *f*; ~ **hook sling** *n* MECH ENG bréguet *m*, élingue à pattes *f*; ~ **iron** *n* PROD ENG clameau *m*, crampon *m*, crochet d'assemblage *m*, happe *f*; ~ **spike** *n* RAIL *track* crampon *m*; ~ **wheel** *n* MECH ENG *ratchet wheel* roue à chien *f*, roue à cliquet *f*, roue à rochet *f*

doghouse *n* (BrE) C&G niche d'enfournement *f*, PETR TECH abri de sondeur *m*

dogleg *n* PETR patte de chien *f*, PETR TECH patte de chien *f*; ~ **stairs** *n pl* CONST escalier rampe-sur-rampe *m*, escalier à deux volées *m*

DOHC: ~ **engine** *n* AUTO moteur à soupapes symétriques *m*

doldrums *n pl* METEO calmes équatoriaux *m pl*, région des calmes *f*, pot-au-noir *m*, NAUT zone calme *f*, OCEANOG calmes équatoriaux *m pl*

dolerite *n* (*cf diabase*) GEOL, PETR dolérite *f*

dolerophane *n* MINERAL dolérophanite *f*

dolerophanite *n* MINERAL dolérophanite *f*

doline *n* WATER SUPP doline *f*

dolly[1] *n* C&G ferret à mors en terre *m*, CINEMAT chariot de travelling *m*, dolly *m*, MECH chariot de transport *m*, PROD ENG *material handling* diabolo *m*, *riveting* tas *m*, tas à bouteroller *m*; ~ **shot** *n* CINEMAT plan travelling *m*; ~ **track** *n* CINEMAT rail de travelling *m*

dolly[2] *vi* CINEMAT faire un travelling; ~ **back** *vi* CINEMAT faire un travelling arrière; ~ **in** *vi* CINEMAT faire un travelling avant

dolomite *n* C&G, CHEM dolomite *f*, GEOL, MINERAL dolomie *f*, dolomite *f*, PETR, PETR TECH dolomite *f*, PROP MAT dolomie *f*; ~ **brick** *n* CONST brique de dolomie *f*

dolomitic: ~ **limestone** *n* GEOL calcaire dolomitique *m*

dolostone *n* GEOL dolomie *f*

dolphin *n* NAUT *mooring post, beacon* duc d'Albe *m*

DOM *abbr* (*digestible organic matter*) RECYCLING MOD (*matière organique digestible*)

domain *n* ELECTRON, PHYS domaine *m*; ~ **structure** *n* METALL structure en domaines *f*, PHYS structure de domaines *f*

domain-specific: ~ **part** *n* (*DSP*) TELECOM partie spécifique du domaine *f*

dome *n* ASTRON dôme *m*, C&G calotte *f*, CONST *architecture* dôme *m*, *of cock, tap* boisseau *m*, GAS TECH, GEOL dôme *m*, HYDR EQUIP dôme *m*, dôme de prise de vapeur *m*, dôme à vapeur *m*, PROD ENG *of furnace* couronne *f*, dôme *m*, voûte *f*; ~ **cap** *n* PROD ENG couvercle du dôme *m*; ~ **casing** *n* PROD ENG enveloppe du dôme *f*; ~ **cover** *n* PROD ENG enveloppe du dôme *f*; ~

gas *n* GAS TECH gaz de dôme *m*; ~ **head** *n* PROD ENG couvercle du dôme *m*; ~ **nut** *n* MECH ENG écrou de dôme *m*; ~ **pad** *n* MECH ENG embout de levage mâle *m*; ~ **riveter** *n* HYDR EQUIP riveteuse *f*; ~ **roof** *n* CONST comble en dôme *m*, toit en coupole *m*; ~ **shutter** *n* ASTRON trappe *f*

domeless: ~ **telescope** *n* INSTRUMENT télescope à tour *m*

domestic: ~ **appliance** *n* (BrE) (*cf home appliance*) ELEC appareil domestique *m*, appareil ménager *m*; ~ **boiler** *n* MECH ENG chauffe-eau ménager *m*; ~ **coal** *n* COAL TECH charbon domestique *m*; ~ **consumer** *n* ELEC consommateur de courant domestique *m*; ~ **electric installation** *n* (BrE) (*cf home electric installation*) ELEC ENG installation domestique *f*; ~ **electronic equipment** *n* (BrE) (*cf home electronic equipment*) ELEC ENG matériel électronique grand public *m*; ~ **emission** *n* POLLUTION émissions intérieures *f pl*; ~ **flight** *n* AERONAUT vol intérieur *m*; ~ **freezer** *n* REFRIG congélateur domestique *m*, congélateur ménager *m*; ~ **fuel oil** *n* PETR TECH fuel-oil domestique *m*; ~ **gas** *n* GAS TECH gaz domestique *m*; ~ **gas appliance** *n* HEATING appareil ménager à gaz *m*; ~ **refrigerator** *n* MECH ENG, REFRIG réfrigérateur ménager *m*; ~ **service** *n* AERONAUT service intérieur *m*; ~ **sewage** *n* HYDROL eau usée domestique *f*, RECYCLING eau usée domestique *f*, eaux-vannes *f pl*; ~ **waste** *n* WATER SUPP déchets domestiques *m pl*; ~ **waste water** *n* HYDROL, WATER SUPP eau usée domestique *f*; ~ **water** *n* HYDROL eau domestique *f*, WATER SUPP eau de distribution *f*; ~ **water supply** *n* WATER SUPP approvisionnement en eau domestique *m*

domeykite *n* MINERAL domeykite *f*

dominant[1] *adj* ACOUSTICS dominant

dominant:[2] ~ **anion** *n* POLLUTION anion dominant *m*, anion majeur *m*, anion principal *m*; ~ **cation** *n* POLLUTION cation dominant *m*, cation majeur *m*, cation principal *m*; ~ **mode** *n* ELEC ENG *waveguides* mode fondamental *m*, PHYS *waveguides* mode dominant *m*, mode fondamental *m*

done: ~ **bit** *n* PROD ENG bit de fin *m*

donor *n* CHEM *atom*, COMP *chip manufacturing*, ELECTRON donneur *m*; ~ **atom** *n* ELECTRON, PHYS atome donneur *m*; ~ **impurity** *n* ELECTRON impureté donneuse *f*, impureté du type donneur *f*; ~ **level** *n* ELECTRON niveau d'énergie donneur *m*, niveau donneur *m*

do-nothing: ~ **instruction** *n* COMP instruction vide *f*, instruction fictive *f*

doodlebugger *n* PETR TECH prospecteur *m*

door *n* PROD ENG *for observing action of mechanism* porte *f*, regard *m*, VEHICLES *body* porte *f*; ~ **bar** *n* CONST barre de porte *f*; ~ **blocking** *n* RAIL *vehicles* condamnation des portières *f*; ~ **bolt** *n* CONST verrou de porte *m*; ~ **brand** *n* CONST barre de porte *f*; ~ **case** *n* CONST bâti de porte *m*, bâti dormant *m*, dormant de porte *m*; ~ **casing** *n* CONST bâti de porte *m*, bâti dormant *m*, dormant de porte *m*, VEHICLES garniture de porte *f*; ~ **catch** *n* VEHICLES arrêt de porte *m*; ~ **framing** *n* CONST *frame and timbers around* huisserie *f*; ~ **glass** *n* VEHICLES vitre de porte *f*; ~ **handle** *n* CONST poignée *f*, poignée de porte *f*, VEHICLES poignée de porte *f*; ~ **hinge hub** *n* CONST moyeu à charnière *m*; ~ **knob** *n* CONST bouton de porte *m*; ~ **lock** *n* VEHICLES serrure de porte *f*; ~ **locking** *n* RAIL *vehicles* verrouillage des portes *m*; ~ **locking mechanism** *n* VEHICLES verrouillage de porte *m*; ~ **opening** *n* CONST baie de porte *f*, jour de porte *m*; ~ **panel** *n* CONST panneau de porte *m*;

~ pillar *n* VEHICLES montant de porte *m*; **~ post** *n* CONST montant de porte *m*, poteau d'huisserie *m*; **~ rack** *n* REFRIG *in domestic refrigerator* balconnet *m*; **~ sill** *n* CONST *placed between posts at some distance from ground* appui de porte *m*, *resting on ground* seuil de porte *m*

doorframe *n* CONST châssis de porte *m*, encadrement de porte *m*, *case into which door is fitted* bâtide porte *m*, bâti dormant *m*, dormant de porte *m*

door-to-door: ~ delivery *n* RAIL camionnage *m*

doorway *n* CONST *opening* baie de porte *f*

dopamine *n* CHEM dopamine *f*

dopant *n* COMP *chip manufacturing* dopeur *m*, ELECTRON impureté *f*, OPT, PHYS, TELECOM dopant *m*

dope[1] *n* PETR additif *m*, produit d'addition *m*, lubrifiant *m*; **~ mark** *n* C&G tache de graisse *f*; **~ sheet** *n* CINEMAT fiche de rapport de tournage *f*; **~ station** *n* PETR station de revêtement *f*

dope[2] *vt* CHEM *crystal*, OPT, PHYS *semiconductor*, TELECOM doper

doped[1] *adj* COMP *chip manufacturing*, ELECTRON, PHYS dopé

doped:[2] **~ fiber** *n* (AmE), **~ fibre** *n* (BrE) OPT fibre de silice *f*; **~ semiconductor** *n* ELECTRON semi-conducteur dopé *m*; **~ silica fiber** *n* (AmE), **~ silica fibre** *n* (BrE) OPT fibre de silice dopée *f*

doping *n* C&G graissage du moule *m*, ELECTRON, PHYS *semiconductors*, PROP MAT, TELECOM dopage *m*; **~ a-gent** *n* ELECTRON agent de dopage *m*; **~ compensation** *n* ELECTRON compensation par dopage *f*; **~ level** *n* ELECTRON niveau de dopage *m*; **~ profile** *n* ELECTRON profil de dopage *m*

Doppler: ~ bandwidth *n* ELECTRON bande passante Doppler *f*; **~ broadening** *n* PHYS, RAD PHYS *spectral lines* élargissement Doppler *m*; **~ effect** *n* ELECTRON, PETR, PHYS effet Doppler *m*; **~ filter** *n* ELECTRON filtre Doppler *m*; **~ filtering** *n* ELECTRON filtrage Doppler *m*; **~ frequency** *n* ELECTRON fréquence Doppler *f*; **~ inertial loop** *n* SPACE *spacecraft* bouclage inertiel Doppler *m*; **~ modulation** *n* ELECTRON modulation Doppler *f*; **~ navigation** *n* PETR, SPACE *spacecraft* navigation Doppler *f*; **~ shift** *n* ASTRON déplacement Doppler *m*, PETR effet Doppler *m*, RECORDING glissement de fréquence Doppler *m*, SPACE dérive Doppler *f*; **~ width** *n* RAD PHYS largeur Doppler *f*

Doppler-Fizeau: ~ displacement shift *n* ACOUSTICS déplacement Doppler-Fizeau *m*; **~ effect** *n* ACOUSTICS, WAVE PHYS effet Doppler-Fizeau *m*

dopplerite *n* MINERAL dopplérite *f*

Dorado *n* ASTRON Dorade *f*

dormant: ~ lock *n* CONST serrure à pêne dormant *f*; **~ terminal** *n* COMP, DP terminal inactif *m*

dormer *n* CONST *building* lucarne *f*

DOS *abbr* (*disk operating system*) COMP, DP DOS (*système d'exploitation à disque*)

dosage *n* COAL TECH dosage *m*

dose *n* CHEM dose *f*; **~ accumulated by workers** *n* RAD PHYS *radioactivity* dose accumulée par les travailleurs *f*; **~ constant** *n* RAD PHYS constante de dose *f*; **~ equivalent** *n* PHYS équivalent de dose *m*; **~ rate** *n* PHYS, RAD PHYS débit de dose *m*; **~ rate effect** *n* RAD PHYS effet du débit de dose *m*; **~ response** *n* POLLUTION dose effet *f*; **~ response relationship** *n* POLLUTION rapport dose-effet *m*, rapport entre les doses et les effets *m*, rapport entre les doses et les réactions *m*

dosimeter *n* PHYS, RAD PHYS dosimètre *m*; **~ glass** *n* C&G verre pour dosimètre *m*

dosimetry *n* PHYS, RAD PHYS dosimétrie *f*

dosing *n* CHEM dosage *m*; **~ apparatus** *n* PACKAGING dispositif de dosage *m*; **~ feeder** *n* PACKAGING alimentation-dosage *f*; **~ machine** *n* PACKAGING machine pour doser *f*; **~ packing** *n* PACKAGING emballage dosé *m*; **~ pump** *n* PACKAGING pompe à doser *f*

dot *n* PAPER TECH, TEXTILES point *m*; **~ etching** *n* PRINT gravure du point *f*; **~ generator** *n* ELECTRON mire de convergence *f*; **~ grating** *n* TV treillis à pointe *m*; **~ interlace scanning** *n* TV analyse entrelacée point par point *f*; **~ matrix** *n* COMP, DP, ELECTRON matrice de points *f*; **~ printer** *n* COMP, DP, PRINT imprimante matricielle *f*

dot-matrix: ~ printer *n* COMP, DP, PRINT imprimante matricielle *f*

dotted: ~ frame *n* PRINT cadre en pointillé *m*

dot-to-dot *adv* PRINT point-à-point

double:[1] **~ Babcock plan** *n* TELECOM plan en double Babcock *m*; **~ bevel** *n* C&G biseau double *m*; **~ bituminous surface treatment** *n* (*DBST*) CONST revêtement bicouche *m*; **~ blackwall hitch** *n* NAUT gueule-de-loup double *f*; **~ blade cutter** *n* PAPER TECH coupeuse à deux couteaux *f*; **~ bond** *n* CHEM liaison double *f*; **~ bottom** *n* NAUT *shipbuilding* double fond *m*; **~ bottom plan** *n* NAUT *naval architecture* plan du double fond *m*; **~ break** *n* PROD ENG double rupture *f*; **~ break switch** *n* ELEC interrupteur à double rupture *m*; **~ bridge** *n* ELEC pont double *m*; **~ bucket collector** *n* POLLUTION collecteur à deux augets *m*; **~ buffering** *n* COMP double mise en mémoire tampon *f*, double tamponnage *m*; **~ cable release** *n* PHOTO déclencheur souple double *m*; **~ calipers** *n pl* (AmE), **~ callipers** *n pl* (BrE) CONST compas d'épaisseur *m*, compas maître de danse *m*, maître-à-danser *m*; **~ camera extension** *n* PHOTO double tirage de la chambre *m*; **~ casing** *n* MECH ENG double enveloppe *f*; **~ cavity mold** *n* (AmE), **~ cavity mould** *n* (BrE) C&G moule à double cavité *m*; **~ circuit brake** *n* TRANSP double circuit de freinage *m*; **~ claw** *n* CINEMAT double griffe *m*; **~ condenser pole piece** *n* INSTRUMENT bobine déviatrice *f*; **~ conversion** *n* ELECTRON double changement de fréquence *m*; **~ core cable** *n* ELEC câble à deux conducteurs *m*; **~ crew operation** *n* AERONAUT travail en équipage double *m*; **~ crossover** *n* CONST traversée-bretelle *f*, RAIL jonction double *f*; **~ crossover road** *n* CONST traversée-bretelle *f*; **~ crucible technique** *n* OPT, TELECOM procédé du double creuset *m*; **~ cylinder engine** *n* MECH ENG machine bicylindrique *f*, moteur bicylindrique *m*; **~ delta connection** *n* ELEC montage en triangle double *m*; **~ delta wing** *n* AERONAUT voilure en double delta *f*; **~ diamond crossing with slips** *n* RAIL *track configuration* TJD, traversée-jonction double *f*; **~ diffused transistor** *n* ELECTRON transistor à double diffusion *m*; **~ diffusion** *n* ELECTRON double diffusion *f*; **~ disc sandpapering machine** *n* (BrE) PROD ENG machine à poncer à deux plateaux *f*; **~ disc winding** *n* (BrE) ELEC *of transformer* enroulement en disques doubles *m*; **~ disk sandpapering machine** *n* (AmE) *see double disc sandpapering machine*; **~ disk winding** *n* (AmE) *see double disc winding*; **~ drum dryer** *n* FOOD TECH séchoir à deux cylindres *m*; **~ dyeing** *n* TEXTILES double teinture *f*; **~ earth fault** *n* (BrE) (*cf double ground fault*) ELEC défaut de mise à la terre sur deux phases *m*; **~ edge grinder** *n* C&G meuleuse à double arête *f*; **~ 8 film** *n* CINEMAT pellicule double huit *f*; **~ engine** *n* MECH ENG machine bicylindrique *f*, moteur bicylindrique *m*; ~ **entries** *n pl* MINING galeries jumelles doubles *f pl*, voies conjuguées doubles *f pl*; ~ **equal angle cutter** *n* MECH ENG fraise isocèle *f*; ~ **exposure** *n* CINEMAT double exposition *f*, PHOTO double exposition *f*, doublés *m pl*; ~ **flat** *n* ACOUSTICS double bémol *m*; ~ **floor** *n* CONST *with one binder* plancher double *m*, *with more than one binder* plancher sur poutre *m*; ~ **galaxy** *n* ASTRON galaxie double *f*; ~ **gap erase head** *n* RECORDING tête d'effacement à double entrefer *f*; ~ **glazing** *n* CONST, HEAT ENG double vitrage *m*; ~ **glazing unit** *n* C&G vitrage double *m*; ~ **ground fault** *n* (AmE) *(cf double earth fault)* ELEC défaut de mise à la terre sur deux phases *m*; ~ **hairline** *n* PRINT double filet très fin pour délimiter une zone *m*; ~ **half-round file** *n* PROD ENG feuille-de-sauge *f*, lime feuille-de-sauge *f*; ~ **helical gear** *n* MECH ENG engrenage hélicoïdal double *m*, engrenage à chevrons *m*; ~ **housing planing machine** *n* MECH ENG raboteuse à deux montants *f*; ~ **hull** *n* NAUT *shipbuilding* double coque *f*; ~ **inlet fan** *n* MECH ENG, REFRIG ventilateur à deux ouïes *m*; ~ **insulation** *n* ELEC ENG isolation double *f*; ~ **insulator** *n* ELEC ENG isolateur double *m*; ~ **joint** *n* PETR doublage *m*; ~ **Kelvin bridge** *n* ELEC pont double de Kelvin *m*; ~ **ladder** *n* CONST *civil engineering* échelle à coulisse deux plans *f*; ~ **leaf spring** *n* SPRINGS ressort bilame *m*; ~ **legend** *n* PROD ENG désignation double *f*; ~ **letter** *n* PRINT ligature *f*; ~ **loop** *n* SPRINGS anneau double *m*; ~ **moding** *n* ELECTRON *of magnetron* instabilité de mode d'oscillation *f*; ~ **modulation** *n* ELECTRON double modulation *f*; ~ **mortise-and-tenon joint** *n* CONST assemblage à tenon et mortaise doubles *m*; ~ **offset gravure** *n* PRINT gravure double offset *f*, gravure à double transfert *f*; ~ **overhead camshaft** *n* VEHICLES *engine* double arbre à cames en tête *m*; ~ **perforation** *n* CINEMAT double perforation *f*; ~ **perf stock** *n* CINEMAT pellicule à double perforation *f*; ~ **pitch roof** *n* CONST comble à deux rampants *m*, comble à deux pans symétriques *m*, comble à deux pentes *m*, comble à deux versants *m*, comble à deux égouts *m*; ~ **plate dry clutch** *n* AUTO embrayage bidisque à sec *m*; ~ **platform pallet** *n* PACKAGING palette à deux étages *f*; ~ **play tape** *n* RECORDING bande double durée *f*; ~ **precision** *n* COMP, DP double précision *f*; ~ **precision arithmetic** *n* COMP, DP arithmétique en double précision *f*; ~ **pump** *n* PROD ENG double pompe *f*; ~ **rail** *n* ELECTRON *logic circuits* double état *m*; ~ **reduction rear axle** *n* AUTO pont arrière à double démultiplication *m*; ~ **reflector antenna** *n* TELECOM antenne à double réflecteur *f*; ~ **refraction** *n* CRYSTALL biréfringence *f*, RAD PHYS réfraction double *f*; ~ **ridge waveguide** *n* ELEC ENG guide d'ondes à double nervure *m*; ~ **row ball bearing** *n* MECH ENG roulement à deux rangées de billes *m*; ~ **rule** *n* PRINT double filet *m*; ~ **ruling** *n* PRINT filets doubles *m pl*; ~ **seizure** *n* TELECOM prise double *f*; ~ **shackle** *n* SPRINGS jumelle *f*; ~ **sharp** *n* ACOUSTICS double dièse *m*; ~ **sheet detector** *n* PRINT détecteur de double feuille *m*; ~ **sideband modulation** *n* ELECTRON modulation à deux bandes latérales *f*; ~ **sideband modulator** *n* ELECTRON modulateur à deux bandes latérales *m*; ~ **sideband transmission** *n* TV transmission à deux bandes latérales *f*; ~ **16 film** *n* (AmE) *(cf double 16 stock)* CINEMAT pellicule 32 mm *f*; ~ **16 stock** *n* (BrE) *(cf double 16 film)* CINEMAT pellicule 32 mm *f*; ~ **skin** *n* NAUT *ship design* double coque *f*; ~ **speed motor** *n* ELEC moteur à double vitesse *m*; ~ **spread**

PRINT double page *f*; ~ **squirrel cage motor** *n* ELEC moteur à double cage *m*; ~ **squirrel cage winding** *n* ELEC ENG enroulement à cage double *m*; ~ **strap butt joint** *n* MECH ENG noeud de jonction renforcé *m*; ~ **stub** *n* PRINT double talon *m*; ~ **super effect** *n* TV double action hétérodyne *f*; ~ **tackle** *n* NAUT palan à deux brins *m*; ~ **take** *n* CINEMAT tournage à deux caméras *m*; ~ **tenon joint** *n* CONST assemblage à double tenon *m*, assemblage à tenon et mortaise doubles *m*; ~ **Thompson bridge** *n* ELEC pont double de Thompson *m*; ~ **timbering** *n* MINING boisage armé *m*, longrinage *m*; ~ **tone ink** *n* COLOURS encre double-ton *f*; ~ **triode** *n* ELECTRON double triode *f*; ~ **wall corrugated fiberboard** *n* (AmE), ~ **wall corrugated fibreboard** *n* (BrE) PACKAGING carton ondulé à double cannelure *m*; ~ **weight paper** *n* PHOTO papier épais *m*; ~ **wheel lathe** *n* MECH ENG tour double à roues montées *m*, tour à trains montés *m*; ~ **wire system** *n* ELEC *supply network* réseau à deux conducteurs *m*; ~ **wishbone suspension** *n* AUTO suspension par quadrilatères *f*; ~ **word buffering** *n* DP mise en mémoire tampon de deux mots *f*, mise en tampon de deux mots *f*

double² *vt* NAUT *cape, mooring lines* arrondir, doubler, PRINT *word* répéter

double-acting *adj* AUTO *shock absorber*, FUELLESS *servomotor*, MECH, MECH ENG *cylinder*, PROD ENG *cylinder*, REFRIG *compressor* à double effet

double-armature: ~ **relay** *n* ELEC relais à double armature *m*

double-balanced: ~ **mixer** *n* *(DBM)* ELECTRON mélangeur symétrique double *m*

double-band: ~ **projector** *n* (AmE) *(cf double-headed projector)* CINEMAT appareil de projection double bande *m*

double-base: ~ **diode** *n* ELECTRON diode double base *f*

double-battened¹ *adj* PACKAGING *case* à latte double

double-battened:² ~ **case** *n* PACKAGING caisse à latte double *f*

double-bended *adj* C&G *glass* à double bombage

double-beveled: ~ **chisel** *n* (AmE) *see double-bevelled chisel* ~ **turning chisel** *n* (AmE) *see double-bevelled turning chisel*

double-bevelled: ~ **chisel** *n* (BrE) CONST ciseau de deux chanfreins *m*, fermoir *m*; ~ **turning chisel** *n* (BrE) CONST fermoir de tour *m*

double-button *adj* RECORDING *microphone* à double capsule

double-cord: ~ **switchboard** *n* TELECOM commutateur à dicorde *m*

double-cotton-covered *adj* *(DCC)* ELEC *conductor* guipé au coton double, guipé de deux couches coton

double-cut *adj* PROD ENG *file* à double taille, à taille croisée

double-cutting *adj* MECH ENG *planing machine* travaillant dans les deux sens de marche

doubled: ~ **lens** *n* PHOTO objectif dédoublable *m*

double-deck: ~ **crown furnace** *n* C&G four à double voûte *m*

double-decked *adj* PACKAGING *pallet* à étages

double-density¹ *adj* COMP, DP à double densité

double-density:² ~ **recording** *n* COMP, DP enregistrement en double densité *m*

double-ended *n* PROD ENG *wrench* extrémité à double fonction *f*; ~ **handsaw file** *n* PROD ENG tiers-point double *m*; ~ **match plane** *n* CONST rabot à deux rainures *m*; ~ **piston rod cylinder** *n* MECH ENG cylindre à piston effet *m*

double-face: ~ **corrugated board** *n* PACKAGING carton ondulé à double face *m*; ~ **crepe paper** *n* PACKAGING papier crêpé à double face *m*; ~ **wax paper** *n* PACKAGING papier paraffiné à double face *m*

double-faced: ~ **sledgehammer** *n* CONST *uphand sledge* marteau à devant *m*

double-fed *adj* ELEC *motor* à double alimentation

double-flanged: ~ **traveling wheel** *n* (AmE), ~ **travelling wheel** *n* (BrE) PROD ENG *of runner of overhead travelling crane* galet à deux joues *m*

double-gun: ~ **tube** *n* TV *of cathode ray tube* tube cathodique à deux faisceaux *m*

double-headed: ~ **camera** *n* CINEMAT caméra image-son *f*; ~ **projector** *n* (BrE) *(cf double-band projector)* CINEMAT appareil de projection double bande *m*; ~ **rail** *n* RAIL *track* rail à double champignon *m*; ~ **shaping machine** *n* MECH ENG étau-limeur double *m*

double-image *n* CINEMAT image fantôme *f*

double-layer[1] *adj* COATINGS double couche, à deux couches

double-layer[2] *n* COATINGS couche double *f*; ~ **coating** *n* TELECOM revêtement bicouche *m*; ~ **winding** *n* ELEC *of coil* enroulement à deux couches *m*

double-pass: ~ **boiler** *n* HEATING chaudière à deux passes *f*

double-pole: ~ **double-throw** *n* *(DPDT)* ELEC, ELEC ENG bipolaire double course *f*, bipolaire à deux directions *f*; ~ **double-throw knife switch** *n* ELEC commutateur bipolaire à couteaux *m*; ~ **single-throw switch** *n* *(DPST)* ELEC, ELEC ENG contact à deux directions *m*, interrupteur bipolaire à une direction *m*; ~ **snap switch** *n* *(DPSS)* ELEC commutateur bipolaire à bascule *m*; ~ **switch** *n* CINEMAT, ELEC, ELEC ENG interrupteur bipolaire *m*

double-print *vt* CINEMAT *negative* tirer deux fois, PRINT imprimer en deux poses

double-pure-rubber-covered *adj* *(DPRC)* ELEC *conductor* guipé de deux couches caoutchouc

doubler *n* MECH ENG renfort *m*, TELECOM doubleur *m*

double-sided: ~ **disk** *n* COMP disquette double face *f*, DP disque double face *m*; ~ **distribution frame** *n* TELECOM répartiteur à double face *m*; ~ **insert** *n* PRINT encart double-face *m*; ~ **printed circuit** *n* ELECTRON circuit imprimé double face *m*; ~ **printed circuit board** *n* ELECTRON carte à circuit imprimé double face *f*; ~ **substrate** *n* ELECTRON substrat double face *m*; ~ **tape** *n* PACKAGING ruban double face adhésive *m*

double-skinned *adj* MECH ENG *pressure vessel* à double parois

doublet *n* CHEM *spectroscopy*, FUELLESS *geothermal power* doublet *m*, PHOTO objectif dédoublable *m*, PHYS *spectroscopy* doublet *m*, PRINT doublon *m*; ~ **lens** *n* PHOTO objectif dédoublable *m*

double-threaded *adj* CONST *screw* à deux filets

double-throw: ~ **contact** *n* ELEC ENG contact inverseur *m*; ~ **knife switch** *n* ELEC commutateur à couteaux à deux directions *m*, commutateur à manette *m*; ~ **switch** *n* ELEC commutateur à deux directions *m*, ELEC ENG inverseur *m*, PHYS commutateur à deux directions *m*

double-tuned: ~ **amplifier** *n* ELECTRON amplificateur à bande élargie *m*; ~ **cavity** *n* ELECTRON cavité à deux fréquences d'accord *f*; ~ **circuit** *n* ELECTRON circuit à accord décalé *m*; ~ **filter** *n* ELECTRON filtre à circuits couplés *m*

double-twist *adj* GEOM à double torsade

double-winding: ~ **armature** *n* ELEC induit à enroulement double *m*

double-window: ~ **fiber** *n* (AmE), ~ **fibre** *n* (BrE) OPT fibre à deux fenêtres *f*

double-wound: ~ **armature** *n* ELEC induit à enroulement double *m*; ~ **generator** *n* ELEC alternateur à double enroulement *m*; ~ **transformer** *n* ELEC transformateur à double enroulement *m*, ELEC ENG transformateur à point milieu *m*

doubly: ~ **refracting** *adj* CRYSTALL biréfringent

dough *n* P&R pâte *f*; ~ **mixer** *n* P&R mélangeur de pâte *m*; ~ **molding** *n* (AmE), ~ **moulding** *n* (BrE) C&G moulage de prémix *m*

doughnut *n* GEOM beignet *m*

dove: ~ **prism** *n* OPT prisme basculant *m*

dovetail[1] *n* CONST queue-d'aronde *f*, queue-d'hirondelle *f*, INSTRUMENT glissière de fixation *f*, MECH queue d'aronde *f*; ~ **cutter** *n* MECH ENG fraise conique *f*, PROD ENG fraise conique *f*, fraise à tailler les queues-d'aronde *f*; ~ **form tool** *n* MECH ENG outil de profil conique *m*; ~ **halved joint** *n* CONST assemblage à queue d'aronde à mi-bois *m*; ~ **joint** *n* CONST assemblage à queue *m*, assemblage à queue d'aronde *m*, assemblage à queue d'hirondelle *m*, MECH assemblage à queue d'aronde *m*; ~ **lap joint** *n* CONST assemblage à queue d'aronde à recouvrement *m*

dovetail[2] *vt* CONST assembler à queue d'aronde

dowel[1] *n* CONST goujon *m*, goujon prisonnier *m*, tampan *m*, PROD ENG *of core box* goujon *m*; ~ **hole** *n* CONST *of draw-pinned slot mortice and tenon joint* trou de cheville *m*; ~ **pin** *n* CONST goujon *m*, goujon prisonnier *m*, PROD ENG goujon *m*; ~ **pin parallel** *n* MECH ENG pied de positionnement cylindrique *m*; ~ **pin with extracting thread** *n* MECH ENG pied de positionnement cylindrique à trou taraudé *m*

dowel[2] *vt* CONST goujonner, PROD ENG cheviller, joindre par des chevilles

down:[1] ~ **by the stern** *adj* NAUT *ship* sur cul

down:[2] ~ **by the head** *adv* NAUT *ship* sur nez

down:[3] ~ **converter** *n* TELECOM changeur abaisseur de fréquence *m*; ~ **counter** *n* ELECTRON compteur soustractif *m*, PROD ENG décompteur *m*; ~ **counter rung** *n* PROD ENG ligne de décompteur *f*; ~ **dip** *n* PETR TECH aval pendage *m*; ~ **gust** *n* AERONAUT rafale descendante *f*; ~ **line** *n* RAIL *track* voie descendante *f*; ~ **link** *n* SPACE liaison descendante *f*; ~ **link feeder link** *n* TELECOM trajet descendant de la liaison de connexion *m*; ~ **lock** *n* AERONAUT verrouillage position train sorti *m*; ~ **pulse** *n* ELECTRON impulsion de décomptage *f*; ~ **quark** *n* PART PHYS, PHYS quark bas *m*; ~ **runner** *n* PROD ENG *in mould* coulée *f*, jet de coulée *m*, trou de coulée *m*

downbending *n* GEOL flexure *f*

downbuckle *n* GEOL affaissement tectonique *m*, fossé *m*

downcast *n* MINING courant d'air descendant *m*, puits d'appel *m*, puits d'appel d'air *m*, puits d'entrée *m*, puits d'entrée d'air *m*, puits de refoulement d'air *m*, rejet en bas *m*; ~ **shaft** *n* MINING puits d'appel *m*, puits d'appel d'air *m*, puits d'entrée *m*, puits d'entrée d'air *m*, puits de refoulement d'air *m*

downcolor *n* (AmE), **downcolour** *n* (BrE) PRINT encre déposée sur le papier *f*

downcomer *n* NUCLEAR tube de condensation *m*, PETR TECH déversoir *m*, PROD ENG *of blast furnace* prise de gaz latérale *f*

down-cut: ~ **milling** *n* MECH ENG *machine tools* fraisage en opposition *m*

downdip *adv* GEOL en aval pendage

downdraft *n* (AmE), **downdraught** *n* (BrE) AERONAUT courant d'air descendant *m*, courant d'air rabattant *m*, courant descendant *m*, MECH ENG courant d'air descendant *m*; ~ **carburetor** (AmE), ~ **carburettor** *n* (BrE) AUTO carburateur à tirage par bas *m*, VEHICLES carburateur inversé *m*

down-enable: ~ **bit** *n* PROD ENG bit de validation de décompteur *m*

downfaulted: ~ **side** *n* GEOL *of fault* compartiment abaissé d'une faille *m*

downfeed *n* MECH ENG *machine tools* avance descendante *f*

downgrading *n* PROD ENG déclassement *m*

downhaul *n* NAUT *rope* hale-bas *m*

downhill: ~ **slope** *n* CONST déclivité vers le bas *f*

downhole[1] *adj* PETR TECH dans le puits

downhole:[2] ~ **conditions** *n pl* PETR TECH conditions de fond *f pl*; ~ **measurements** *n pl* PETR TECH mesures de fond *f pl*; ~ **safety valve** *n* PETR vanne de sécurité de subsurface *f*, PETR TECH vanne de sécurité de fond *f*

downline *n* RAIL *track* voie impaire *f*

download:[1] ~ **operation** *n* PROD ENG opération de téléchargement *f*

download[2] *vt* COMP, DP, TELECOM télécharger

downloadable *adj* COMP, DP, TELECOM téléchargeable

downloading *n* COMP, DP, TELECOM téléchargement *m*

downrange: ~ **station** *n* SPACE station aval *f*

downspout *n* CONST bec de descente *m*

downstream[1] *adj* (*cf upstream*) FLUID PHYS aval, HYDROL aval, d'aval, NAUT *on river*, PHYS en aval, TEXTILES aval *m*

downstream[2] *adv* (*cf upstream*) CONST en aval, CONST aval, FLUID PHYS, GAS TECH, HYDROL, MECH, NAUT *on river*, SPACE, TRANSP en aval

downstream:[3] ~ **cutwater** *n* WATER SUPP *of bridge pier* arrière-bec *m*; ~ **face** *n* HYDROL *dams* parement aval *m*; ~ **fairing** *n* REFRIG carénage aval *m*; ~ **keyer** *n* TV incrustateur aval *m*; ~ **level** *n* HYDROL niveau d'eau en aval *m*; ~ **process** *n* TEXTILES procédé aval de fabrication *m*

downstroke *n* AUTO, MECH, MECH ENG, VEHICLES *engine* course descendante *f*; ~ **press** *n* P&R presse descendante *f*, presse à mouvement descendant *f*

downtake *n* PROD ENG *of blast furnace* prise de gaz latérale *f*

downtime *n* AERONAUT temps d'immobilisation *m*, temps de panne *m*, COMP temps d'arrêt *m*, DP temps d'immobilisation *m*, MECH ENG temps d'arrêt *m*, NUCLEAR temps d'indisponibilité *m*, PETR TECH temps mort *m*, PROD ENG temps d'arrêt *m*, TELECOM durée d'interruption *f*, TV temps mort *m*; ~ **cost** *n* PACKAGING frais de temps d'arrêt *m*

downward:[1] ~ **compatible** *adj* COMP, DP à compatibilité descendante

downward:[2] ~ **compatibility** *n* COMP, DP compatibilité vers le bas *f*, compatibilité descendante *f*; ~ **gradient** *n* CONST pente *f*; ~ **modulation** *n* ELECTRON modulation par réduction d'amplitude *f*; ~ **motion** *n* PROD ENG mouvement descendant *m*; ~ **stroke** *n* MECH, MECH ENG *machine tool* course descendante *f*

downwarp *n* GEOL fléchissement *m*

downwash *n* AERONAUT déflexion vers le bas *f*

downwind[1] *adj* FUELLESS vent en poupe

downwind[2] *adv* FUELLESS vent arrière, vent en poupe,

METEO dans le sens du vent, sous le vent, NAUT au portant, vent arrière, POLLUTION dans la direction du vent

downwind[3] *n* AERONAUT, FUELLESS vent arrière *m*; ~ **leg** *n* AERONAUT branche vent arrière *f*, branche vent rabattant *f*

downy: ~ **mildew** *n* FOOD TECH *phytopathology* mildiou *m*

dowser *n* CINEMAT volet pare-feu *m*, HYDROL sourcier *m*

DP[1] *abbr* COMP (*data processing*), DP (*data processing*), ELECTRON (*data processing*) TD (*traitement de données*), ELECTRON (*differential phase*) phase différentielle *f*, GEOL (*datum plane*) surface de référence *f*, TELECOM (*data processing*) TD (*traitement de données*), TELECOM (*dial impulse*) impulsion décimale *f*, TELECOM (*detailed procedure*) procédure détaillée *f*

DP:[2] ~ **end of data** *n* DP fin de données *f*

DPC *abbr* (*data processing centre, data processing center*) DP centre de traitement d'informations *m*, centre de traitement de données *m*, centre informatique *m*, TELECOM centre de traitement de données *m*

DPCM *abbr* (*differential pulse code modulation*) ELECTRON modulation PCM différentielle *f*, modulation différentielle par impulsions codées *f*

DPDT[1] *abbr* (*double-pole double-throw*) ELEC, ELEC ENG bipolaire double course *f*, bipolaire à deux directions *f*

DPDT:[2] ~ **relay** *n* ELEC ENG relais DPDT *m*, relais inverseur bipolaire *m*, relais à deux contacts inverseurs *m*, relais à double contact inverseur *m*; ~ **switch** *n* ELEC ENG inverseur bipolaire *m*

DPL *abbr* (*distribution primary link*) TELECOM liaison primaire pour les services de distribution *f*

DPRC *abbr* (*double-pure-rubber-covered*) ELEC guipé deux couches caoutchouc

DPS *abbr* (*double-pole switch*) ELEC interrupteur bipolaire *m*

DPSK *abbr* (*differential phase-shift keying*) ELECTRON modulation DPSK *f*, modulation par déplacement de phase différentielle *f*

DPSS *abbr* (*double-pole snap switch*) ELEC commutateur bipolaire à bascule *m*

DPST[1] *abbr* (*double-pole single-throw switch*) ELEC, ELEC ENG contact à deux directions *m*, interrupteur bipolaire à une direction *m*

DPST:[2] ~ **relay** *n* ELEC, ELEC ENG relais DPST *m*, relais interrupteur bipolaire *m*, relais à deux contacts interrupteurs *m*, relais à double contact interrupteur *m*; ~ **switch** *n* ELEC, ELEC ENG interrupteur bipolaire *m*, interrupteur bipolaire à une direction *m*

Draco *n* ASTRON Dragon *m*

dracone *n* MAR POLL citerne souple flottante *f*, outre flottante *f*, réservoir souple flottant *m*

draft[1] *n* (AmE) *see draught*

draft[2] *vt* TEXTILES étirer

drafting *n* TEXTILES étirage *m*; ~ **system** *n* TEXTILES système d'étirage *m*

draftsman *n* (AmE) *see draughtsman*

drag[1] *n* AERONAUT, FLUID PHYS, FUELLESS *wind power* traînée *f*, MECH résistance au mouvement *f*, traînée *f*, METALL traînage *m*, étrainage *m*, MINING *blasting* curette *f*, *dredge* drague *f*, *of mine* résistance *f*, *safety dog or backstay of mine car* chambrière *f*, reculoire *f*, NAUT *ship design* résistance *f*, traînée *f*, PHYS *aerodynamics* traînée *f*, PRINT ralentissement *m*, PROD ENG dépôt *m*, *founding* corps *m*, dessous *m*, dessous de châssis *m*, SPACE *spacecraft*, TRANSP traînée *f*; **~ angle** *n* AERONAUT angle de traînée *m*; **~ axis** *n* AERONAUT axe de traînée *m*; **~ bit** *n* PETR TECH trépan à lames *m*; **~ brace** *n* AERONAUT bielle de recul *f*, contrefiche de verrouillage du train *f*, genouillère de train avant *f*; **~ brake** *n* TRANSP aérofrein *m*; **~ chute** *n* AERONAUT parachute de queue *m*, SPACE *spacecraft* parachute de freinage *m*; **~ chute cover** *n* AERONAUT gaine de parachute de queue *f*; **~ coefficient** *n* AERONAUT, AUTO, FLUID PHYS, FUELLESS, NAUT *ship design*, PHYS, TRANSP coefficient de traînée *m*, VEHICLES *body* coefficient de pénétration *m*; **~ cup** *n* AERONAUT cloche de mesure *f*, cloche de tachymètre *f*; **~ cup skirt** *n* AERONAUT jupe de cloche *f*; **~ damper** *n* AERONAUT amortisseur de traînée *m*; **~ fold** *n* GEOL crochon de faille *m*; **~ hinge** *n* AERONAUT *of helicopter* axe de traînée *m*; **~ lift** *n* TRANSP téléski *m*; **~ link** *n* AERONAUT barre de rappel *f*, béquille *f*, contrefiche longitudinale *f*, étrésillon *m*, VEHICLES *steering* barre d'accouplement *f*, bielle de connexion *f*; **~ moment** *n* AERONAUT moment de traînée *m*; **~ on a sphere** *n* FLUID PHYS traînée d'une sphère *f*; **~ parachute** *n* TRANSP parachute-frein *m*; **~ roller** *n* CINEMAT galet guide *m*; **~ rudder** *n* AERONAUT gouverne de direction par effet de frein *f*; **~ screw** *n* MECH, MECH ENG vis de rappel *f*; **~ stop** *n* AERONAUT butée de traînée *f*

drag² *vt* DP déplacer

drag³ *vi* NAUT *fishing* pêcher à la drague, *sea bottom* draguer, déraper; **~ anchor** *vi* NAUT chasser sur l'ancre

dragging *n* NAUT *anchor, moored buoy* dérADAGE *m*, dérapage *m*, *of sea bottom* dragage *m*

dragline: **~ excavator** *n* CONST excavateur dragline *m*, grue dragline *f*

dragnet *n* OCEANOG chalut *m*, senne *f*; **~ fishing** *n* OCEANOG pêche à la traîne *f*

dragrope *n* OCEANOG fune *f*

drain¹ *n* COAL TECH drain *m*, CONST drain *m*, *sewer* égout *m*, ELEC ENG, HYDROL drain *m*, NAUT dalot *m*, nable *m*, évacuation *f*, PETR TECH, PHYS *transistor* drain *m*, PROD ENG évacuation *f*, RECYCLING conduite d'évacuation *f*; **~ bias** *n* ELEC ENG polarisation du drain *f*; **~ cock** *n* CONST purgeur *m*, robinet de purge *m*, robinet purgeur *m*, MECH ENG robinet de vidange *m*, PROD ENG robinet de purge *m*, VEHICLES *radiator* robinet de vidange *m*; **~ connector** *n* MECH ENG prise de vidange *f*; **~ contact** *n* ELEC ENG contact de drain *m*; **~ cup** *n* PROD ENG cuvette d'égouttage *f*, poche de vidange *f*; **~ current** *n* ELEC ENG courant de drain *m*; **~ nipple** *n* MECH ENG embout de drain *m*; **~ pan** *n* REFRIG égouttoir *m*; **~ pen** *n* MECH ENG bac de récupération *m*; **~ plug** *n* AUTO, PRODUCTION, VEHICLES *engine, transmission* bouchon de vidange *m*; **~ shaft** *n* MINING puits de drainage *m*; **~ solenoid** *n* MECH ENG solénoïde de vidange *m*; **~ tap** *n* PETR TECH piquage *m*; **~ terminal** *n* ELEC ENG borne du drain *f*; **~ testing and cleaning equipment** *n* CONST *building* appareil à déboucher et à nettoyer les tuyaux *m*; **~ trap** *n* CONST siphon *m*; **~ valve** *n* MECH ENG clapet de vidange *m*, robinet de drainage *m*, soupape de vidange *f*, NAUT soupape de purge *f*, RAIL *vehicles* purgeur *m*; **~ well** *n* MINING puits absorbant *m*; **~ wire** *n* ELEC, PROD ENG fil de blindage *m*

drain² *vt* CHEM *liquid* essorer, CONST *ditch* saigner, *land* assécher, drainer, égoutter, épuiser, HYDROL *land* drainer, *water from ditch by means of channel* évacuer, MECH purger, vidanger, vider, MINING *firedamp* drai-

ner, *methane* drainer, *mine* assécher, drainer, épuiser, PAPER TECH égoutter, PROD ENG *cylinder* purger, RECYCLING assainir, assécher, drainer, vidanger, WATER SUPP drainer, faire écouler, faire égoutter, purger, saigner, égoutter, épuiser, évacuer, *pond* assécher, dessécher, *pump* désamorcer

drain:³ **~ off** *vi* WATER SUPP faire écouler, évacuer les eaux

drainable: **~ unusable fuel** *n* AERONAUT carburant non utilisable récupérable *m*

drainage *n* HYDROL drainage *m*, MECH ENG vidange *f*, MINING exhaure *f*, épuisement *m*, PAPER TECH égouttage *m*, PETR TECH drainage *m*, PROD ENG vidange *f*, RECYCLING assainissement *m*, WATER SUPP assainissement *m*, drainage *m*, assèchement *m*, dessèchement *m*, écoulement *m*, épuisement *m*; **~ area** *n* HYDROL bassin hydrographique *m*, PETR surface de drainage *f*, WATER SUPP bassin hydrologique *m*, bassin versant *m*; **~ basin** *n* HYDROL bassin hydrographique *m*, bassin versant *m*, WATER SUPP bassin hydrologique *m*, bassin versant *m*, versant *m*; **~ channel** *n* OCEANOG émissaire *m*, WATER SUPP canal d'assèchement *m*, canal de dessèchement *m*, chenal de déversement *m*; **~ chest** *n* PAPER TECH caisse d'égouttage *f*; **~ density** *n* HYDROL densité de drainage *f*; **~ ditch** *n* HYDROL fossé de drainage *m*, WATER SUPP canal d'épuisement *m*, rigole d'assèchement *f*, collecteur-fossé *m*, rigole de drainage *f*; **~ gallery** *n* HYDROL *dams* galerie de drainage *f*; **~ level** *n* MINING galerie d'assèchement *f*, galerie d'écoulement *f*, galerie de drainage *f*; **~ pattern** *n* GEOL réseau hydrographique *m*; **~ pump** *n* WATER SUPP pompe d'épuisement *f*; **~ structure** *n* CONST ouvrage d'assainissement *m*; **~ system** *n* NAUT système de vidange *m*, RECYCLING réseau d'assainissement *m*; **~ terrace** *n* AERONAUT terrasse de colature *f*; **~ well** *n* MINING puits de drainage *m*

drainer *n* PAPER TECH caisse d'égouttage *f*

draining *n* MINING assèchement *m*, exhaure *f*, épuisement *m*, WATER SUPP assèchement *m*, dessèchement *m*, drainage *m*, purge *f*, écoulement *m*, épuisement *m*; **~ engine** *n* WATER SUPP machine d'exhaure *f*, machine d'épuisement *f*, moteur d'épuisement *m*; **~ rack** *n* FOOD TECH *food-processing machinery*, LAB EQUIP *cleaning* égouttoir *m*; **~ screen** *n* COAL TECH crible d'égouttage *m*

drain-off: **~ cock** *n* CONST purgeur *m*, robinet de purge *m*, robinet purgeur *m*

drainpipe *n* CONST tuyau de drainage *m*

dram *n* METR drachme *f*

DRAM *abbr* (*dynamic random access memory*) COMP, DP mémoire dynamique *f*

drape¹ *n* TEXTILES drapé *m*; **~ folds** *n pl* GEOL plis de couverture *m pl*, plis de fond *m pl*, plis de revêtement *m pl*

drape² *vt* GEOL coiffer, TEXTILES draper

draping: **~ properties** *n* TEXTILES propriétés de drapage *f pl*

draught *n* (BrE) (*cf draft*) CONST *current of air in chimney* courant *m*, courant d'air *m*, tirage *m*, *ventilation* aérage *m*, HEATING tirage *m*, MECH ENG *current of air entering by aperture, indraught* appel d'air *m*, entrée d'air *f*, venue du vent *f*, *current of air* courant d'air *m*, vent *m*, NAUT *of ship* tirant d'eau *m*, PROD ENG *difference in area between one pass and the next* entrée des cannelures *f*, rentrée des cannelures *f*, *drop of pattern-drawing machine* hauteur de démoulage *f*, *taper given* *to pattern for casting* dépouille *f*, PRODUCTION projet *m*, TRANSP tirant d'eau *m*; ~ **bar** *n* (BrE) RAIL *vehicles* barre de traction *f*; ~ **box** *n* (BrE) HYDR EQUIP *of turbine* chambre d'aspiration *f*; ~ **engine** *n* (BrE) MINING machine d'extraction *f*, moteur d'extraction *m*; ~ **gauge** *n* (BrE) PROD ENG indicateur de tirage *m*; ~ **hole** *n* (BrE) PROD ENG *of furnace* ventouse *f*; ~ **machine** *n* (BrE) PROD ENG *pattern-drawing* machine à démouler *f*; ~ **marks** *n pl* (BrE) NAUT *ship design* échelle de tirant d'eau *f*; ~ **regulator** *n* (BrE) HEATING régulateur de tirage *m*, PROD ENG registre *m*, registre régulateur *m*; ~ **tube** *n* (BrE) FUELLESS aspirateur-diffuseur *m*, HYDR EQUIP *of turbine* chambre d'aspiration *f*; ~ **zones** *n pl* (BrE) TEXTILES zones d'étirage *f pl*

draughtsman *n* (BrE) MECH dessinateur industriel *m*, NAUT *ship design* dessinateur *m*, traceur *m*, PRINT dessinateur *m*, graphiste *m*, illustrateur *m*, PROD ENG dessinateur *m*, traceur *m*

dravite *n* MINERAL dravite *f*

dravos *n* TRANSP conteneur non normalisé *m*

draw[1] *n* PAPER TECH entraînement *m*, tirage *m*, PROD ENG retirure *f*, tassement *m*; ~ **bench** *n* PROD ENG argue *f*, banc d'étirage *m*, banc à tirer *m*, banc à étirer *m*, étireur *m*; ~ **bore** *n* CONST *of tenon* trou de cheville *m*; ~ **bore pin** *n* CONST cheville *f*; ~ **gate** *n* WATER SUPP *sluice gate* vanne d'écluse *f*; ~ **gear spring plate** *n* RAIL *vehicles* plaque d'appui du ressort de traction *f*; ~ **hook** *n* PROD ENG *moulder's tool* aiguille à retirer les pièces battues *f*, RAIL *vehicles* crochet de traction *m*; ~ **hook bar** *n* RAIL *QEK coupling* tige de crochet de traction *f*; ~ **ring** *n* MECH ENG serre-flan *m*; ~ **rod** *n* C&G baguette étirée *f*; ~ **roll** *n* PAPER TECH rouleau entraîneur *m*; ~ **screw** *n* MECH ENG vis de rappel *f*; ~ **spike** *n* PROD ENG *moulder's tool* aiguille à retirer les pièces battues *f*; ~ **stick** *n* PROD ENG *moulder's tool* aiguille à retirer les pièces battues *f*; ~ **taper** *n* PROD ENG *founding* dépouille *f*; ~ **works** *n* PETR, PETR TECH treuil de forage *m*

draw[2] *vt* NAUT *of ship, depth for floating* caler, tirer, tracer, PAPER TECH entraîner, PROD ENG *metal into wire* affiler, arguer, filer, fileter, passer à la filière, tirer, tirer à l'argue, tréfiler, *metal into tubes, bars* étirer, TEXTILES *to stretch, draw out* étirer; ~ **the charge** *vt* PROD ENG défourner; ~ **out of a kiln** *vt* PROD ENG défourner, tirer d'un four

draw[3] *vi* CONST *of chimney, to have draught* tirer; ~ **water** *vi* OCEANOG *of ship* caler

DRAW *abbr (direct read after write)* OPT contrôle en cours d'enregistrement *m*

drawback *n* PROD ENG *founding* pièce battue *f*, pièce de rapport *f*, pièce rapportée *f*, tiroir *m*; ~ **spring** *n* MECH ENG ressort de rappel *m*

drawbar *n* MECH ENG *machine tools* tige de rappel *f*, RAIL tige de traction *f*, *vehicles* barre de traction *f*, VEHICLES *of trailer* barre d'accouplement *f*, barre de remorque *f*, timon *m*; ~ **bolt** *n* VEHICLES *of trailer* boulon d'attelage *m*, boulon de timon *m*; ~ **guide** *n* RAIL *vehicles* guide de crochet de traction *m*

drawbridge *n* CONST *bascule bridge* pont à bascule *m*, *lifting* pont levant *m*, *rolling* pont roulant *m*, *turning* pont tournant *m*

draw-down[1] *n* PETR TECH rabattement *m*, PROD ENG tassement *m*, WATER SUPP rabattement *m*; ~ **of water in aquifer** *n* FUELLESS baisse du niveau aquifère *f*

draw-down[2] *vt* WATER SUPP destocker

drawframe *n* TEXTILES banc d'étirage *m*

drawhole *n* PROD ENG *taphole of furnace* coulée *f*, oeil *m*, trou de coulée *m*, trou de gueuse *m*

draw-in: ~ **chuck** *n* MECH ENG *machine tools* mandrin type rentrant *m*; ~ **spring chuck** *n* MECH ENG mandrin de serrage élastique *m*

drawing *n* C&G séparation magnétique *f*, CONST *of nail* arrachage *m*, extraction *f*, GEOM dessin *m*, MINING *hauling, tramming* herchage *m*, herschage *m*, roulage *m*, *hoisting, winding* extraction *f*, remonte *f*, remontée *f*, NAUT *naval architecture* dessin *m*, plan *m*, P&R *fibres* orientation *f*, tirage *m*, PATENTS dessin *m*, PROD ENG *founding, of pattern* démoulage *m*, *wiredrawing* filetage *m*, tirage *m*, étirage *m*, TEXTILES étirage *m*, WATER SUPP *of water from well* puisage *m*, puisement *m*; ~ **alongside** *n* NAUT *of ship to quay or to another ship* accostage *m*; ~ **bench** *n* PROD ENG *wiredrawing* argue *f*, banc d'étirage *m*, banc à étirer *m*, étireur *m*; ~ **block** *n* PROD ENG *wiredrawing* bobine de tirerie *f*; ~ **board** *n* CONST planche à dessin *f*, table à dessin *f*, MECH, NAUT *naval architecture* planche à dessin *f*; ~ **casting** *n* CONST *well-boring* arrachage du tubage d'isolement *m*; ~ **the charge** *n* PROD ENG défournement *m*; ~ **engine** *n* MINING machine d'extraction *f*, moteur d'extraction *m*; ~ **file** *n* PROD ENG fichier de plans *m*; ~ **ink** *n* COLOURS encre de Chine *f*, PRINT encre de Chine *f*, encre à dessin *f*; ~ **list** *n* PROD ENG liste des pièces *f*; ~ **machine** *n* C&G étireur *m*; ~ **press** *n* MECH ENG *machine tool* presse à emboutir *f*; ~ **print** *n* CONST dessin *m*; ~ **process** *n* TELECOM *fibre optic cable* fibrage *m*; ~ **punch** *n* MECH ENG poinçon d'emboutissage *m*; ~ **tower** *n* C&G gaine d'étirage *f*; ~ **up** *n* PATENTS *of report* établissement *m*

drawknife *n* CONST plane *f*

drawn[1] *adj* C&G *glass* étiré, *stem* tiré, COATINGS *galvanized coating* retréfilé, MECH ENG *wire* tréfilé, PROD ENG *tube* étiré; ~ **from the wood** *adj* FOOD TECH en fût

drawn:[2] ~ **wire** *n* MECH ENG fil tréfilé *m*

draw-off: ~ **tap** *n* MECH ENG robinet de puisage *m*

drawoff *n* WATER SUPP vidange *f*

draw-out: ~ **switchgear** *n* ELEC appareillage débrochable *m*; ~ **unit** *n* ELEC cellule débrochable *f*, tiroir débrochable *m*

drawplate *n* PROD ENG filière *f*, filière à étirer *f*

drawtube *n* INSTRUMENT tube porte-oculaire *m*

dredge[1] *n* CONST drague *f*, MINING drague *f*, machine à draguer *f*, NAUT *machine* drague *f*; ~ **boat** *n* MINING bateau dragueur *m*, bateau-dragueur *m*, bateau-rabot *m*; ~ **bucket** *n* MINING godet de drague *m*, NAUT godet de drague *m*, hotte de drague *f*; ~ **bucket ladder** *n* MINING élinde de drague *f*; ~ **chain** *n* MINING, NAUT chaîne dragueuse *f*; ~ **elevator** *n* MINING élévateur de drague *m*; ~ **ladder** *n* MINING élinde de drague *f*; ~ **mining** *n* MINING exploitation des alluvions au moyen de drague *f*; ~ **net** *n* NAUT *fishing* filet de drague *m*; ~ **plant** *n* MINING outillage de drague *m*; ~ **pump** *n* NAUT pompe de drague *f*

dredge[2] *vt* NAUT *channel* curer, draguer, dévaser

dredger *n* MAR POLL drague *f*, MINING drague *f*, machine à draguer *f*, NAUT *boat* dragueur *m*, *person* ouvrier dragueur *m*, pêcheur à la drague *m*, TRANSP drague *f*; ~ **bucket** *n* TRANSP godet de drague *m*

dredging *n* MINING, NAUT, OCEANOG dragage *m*; ~ **face** *n* MINING front de dragage *m*; ~ **field** *n* MINING champ de dragage *m*; ~ **ground** *n* MINING terrains de dragage *m pl*; ~ **operations** *n* NAUT travaux de dragage *m pl*; ~ **sand** *n* CONST sable de dragage *m*

dredgings *n* HYDROL boues de dragage *f pl*

Dreschel: ~ **bottle** *n* LAB EQUIP *glassware* flacon laveur de Durand *m*

dress:[1] ~ **material** *n* TEXTILES tissu pour robe *m*

dress[2] *vt* NAUT pavoiser, PROD ENG *casting* nettoyer

dress:[3] ~ **ship overall** *vi* NAUT *naval* envoyer le grand pavois, pavoiser

dressed[1] *adj* FOOD TECH apprêté, préparé

dressed:[2] ~ **stone** *n* CONST *for building* pierre parée *f*, pierre taillée *f*; ~ **width of warp** *n* TEXTILES largeur de chaîne *f*

dresser *n* COAL TECH pointerolle *f*, PROD ENG *emery wheel* décrasse-meule *m*, rhabilleur *m*, *founding* dessableur *m*; ~ **cutter** *n* MECH ENG molette à dresser *f*

dressing *n* C&G rhabillage *m*, COAL TECH préparation mécanique *f*, CONST *of stone* dressage *m*, taille *f*, PROD ENG *castings* dessablage *m*, nettoyage *m*, *of emery wheel* rhabillage *m*;~ **shop** *n* PROD ENG *in foundry* atelier de dessablage *m*; ~ **works** *n pl* MINING atelier d'enrichissement *m*, atelier de préparation mécanique *m*

drexon: ~ **card** *n* OPT lasercard drexon *m*

dried[1] *adj* FOOD TECH déshydraté, THERMOD desséché, déshydraté, sec, séché

dried:[2] ~ **brick** *n* CONST brique crue *f*

drift[1] *n* ACOUSTICS, AERONAUT *motion* dérive *f*, CONST *of bore hole* déviation *f*, ELEC dérive *f*, HYDROL *direction of current* direction *f*, sens *m*, MAR POLL dérive *f*, MECH *tools* chasse-goupille *m*, jet *m*, MECH ENG jet d'extraction *m*, *for loosening and removing taper* shank drills from sockets broche de déchassage *f*, keydrift chasse-clavette *m*, chasse-clé *m*, *rivet drift* broche *f*, broche d'assemblage *f*, mandrin *m*, METR *of measuring instrument* dérive *f*, MINING chassage *m*, chassante *f*, costière *f*, galerie chassante *f*, galerie d'allongement *f*, galerie de direction *f*, galerie en direction *f*, galerie *f*, galerie de recherches *f*, *cross drift* recoupe *f*, viaille *f*, volée *f*, NAUT *of current, ship* direction *f*, dérive *f*, PETR décalage *m*, déplacement *m*, dérive *f*, PROD ENG dérive *f*, *casing swedge* emboutissoir *m*, redresse-tubes *m*, redresseur *m*, SPACE, TELECOM dérive *f*; ~ **angle** *n* AERONAUT, TRANSP angle de dérive *m*; ~ **azimuth** *n* PETR azimut *m*; ~ **bolt** *n* PROD ENG chasse-boulon *m*; ~ **current** *n* NAUT courant de surface *m*, OCEANOG courant de dérive *m*; ~ **error** *n* AERONAUT *of altimeter* erreur de dérive *f*; ~ **ice** *n* NAUT glaces flottantes *f pl*; ~ **indicator** *n* AERONAUT cinémodérivomètre *m*, dérivomètre *m*, indicateur de dérive *m*;~ **in flight** *n* AERONAUT dérive en vol *f*; ~ **lock** *n* TV opération à constance du nombre de ligne *f*; ~ **mining** *n* MINING exploitation au fond *f*, mine au fond *f*; ~ **net** *n* NAUT filet dérivant *m*; ~ **orbit** *n* SPACE orbite de dérive *f*; ~ **pin** *n* MECH ENG broche *f*, broche d'assemblage *f*, mandrin *m*, cheville d'assemblage *f*; ~ **plate** *n* MECH ENG plaque d'extracteur *f*; ~ **punch** *n* MECH ENG *tool* chasse-goupilles *m*; ~ **region** *n* ELECTRON zone de migration *f*; ~ **space** *n* ELECTRON espace de regroupement *m*, espace de glissement *m*; ~ **stope** *n* MINING chantier chassant *m*, gradin chassant *m*, taille chassante *f*; ~ **tube** *n* ELECTRON tube de glissement *m*, tube de regroupement *m*, MECH ENG tube d'emmanchement *m*; ~ **tunnel** *n* ELECTRON tunnel *m*; ~ **velocity** *n* METALL vitesse d'entraînement *f*, vitesse de dérive *f*

drift[2] *vt* HYDROL apporter, charrier, dériver, emporter, entraîner

drift[3] *vi* NAUT dépaler, dériver

drifter *n* NAUT *fishing boat* bateau de pêche à filets traînants *m*, OCEANOG dériveur *m*

drifting *n* CONST amoncellement *m*, MECH ENG brochage *m*, mandrinage *m*, MINING chassage *m*, percement *m*, percement de galeries de recherche *m*, percement de galeries en direction *m*; ~ **buoy** *n* NAUT *meteorology* bouée dérivante *f*; ~ **flight** *n* AERONAUT vol en dérapage *m*; ~ **float** *n* OCEANOG flotteur dérivant *m*; ~ **level** *n* MINING chassage *m*, costière *f*, galerie chassante *f*, galerie d'allongement *f*, galerie de chassage *f*, galerie de direction *f*, galerie en direction *f*; ~ **snow** *n* METEO chasse-neige *m*

driftmeter *n* AERONAUT dérivomètre *m*

driftwood *n* NAUT bois flottant *m*

drill[1] *n* COAL TECH engin de forage *m*, CONST fleuret *m*, MECH foret *m*, MECH ENG *bit for drilling mill* foret *m*, mèche *f*, *drill holder or drillstock* drille *f*, porte-foret *m*, porte-mèche *m*, MINING *rock-drilling, earth-boring* burin *m*, fleuret *m*, foreuse *f*, perforateur *m*, perforatrice *f*, pistolet *m*, sondeuse *f*; ~ **barge** *n* PETR TECH barge de forage *f*; ~ **bit** *n* COAL TECH couronne de forage *f*, foret *m*, MINING couronne *f*, taillant *m*, trépan *m*, *of rockdrill, hammerdrill* fleuret *m*, PETR TECH outil de forage *m*, trépan *m*; ~ **bit studs** *n pl* PETR TECH dents de trépan *f pl*; ~ **bushing** *n* MECH canon de perçage *m*, MECH ENG douille à percer *f*; ~ **casing** *n* MINING conducteur tubulaire *m*, tube conducteur *m*, tube guide *m*, tube guidede sondage *m*; ~ **chain** *n* MINING chaîne d'allongement *f*; ~ **chuck** *n* MECH ENG mandrin porte-foret *m*, mandrin porte-mèche *m*; ~ **collar** *n* PETR, PETR TECH masse-tige *f*; ~ **column** *n* PETR train de forage *m*; ~ **core** *n* MINING carotte *f*, carotte-témoin *f*, témoin *m*; ~ **cutting** *n* GAS TECH déblai de forage *m*; ~ **cuttings** *n pl* PETR TECH débris de forage *m pl*; ~ **floor** *n* PETR plancher de forage *m*; ~ **gage** *n* (AmE), ~ **gauge** *n* (BrE) MECH ENG *for measuring angle of twistdrill bevel* calibre d'affûtage *m*, *for measuring size of drill* jauge pour mèche *f*; ~ **grinder** *n* MECH ENG machine à affûter les forets *f*, machine à affûter les mèches *f*; ~ **head** *n* MECH ENG tête porte-foret *f*; ~ **holder** *n* MECH ENG porte-foret *m*, porte-mèche *m*, MINING porte-fleuret *m*; ~ **hole** *n* MINING forage *m*, sondage *m*, trou de sonde *m*, trou *m*; ~ **jar** *n* MINING coulisse *f*; ~ **joint** *n* MINING assemblage de rallonges *m*; ~ **locater** *n* MECH ENG centreur de foret *m*; ~ **pin** *n* CONST *of lock* broche *f*; ~ **pipe** *n* MINING rallonge *f*, tige de sonde *f*, PETR tige de forage *f*, PETR TECH tige de forage *f*, train de forage *m*; ~ **pipe coupling** *n* MINING emmanchement de tige de sonde *m*; ~ **pole joint** *n* MINING assemblage de rallonges *m*; ~ **press** *n* MECH perceuse sensitive *f*, perceuse à colonne *f*, MECH ENG foreuse à colonne *f*, machine à percer montée sur colonne *f*; ~ **rig** *n* MINING appareil de sondage *m*; ~ **rod** *n* MINING barre de sonde *f*, rallonge *f*, tige de sonde *f*, tige de fleuret *f*, tige de forage *f*, PETR tige de forage *f*; ~ **rod coupling** *n* MINING emmanchement de tige de sonde *m*; ~ **rod grab** *n* MINING arrache-sonde *m*, tire-sonde *m*; ~ **rod joint** *n* MINING assemblage de rallonges *m*; ~ **rope** *n* MINING câble de forage *m*, câble de sondage *m*; ~ **sharpener** *n* MECH ENG machine à affûter les forets *f*, machine à affûter les mèches *f*; ~ **ship** *n* NAUT, PETR navire de forage *m*, PETR TECH bateau de forage *m*, navire de forage *m*; ~ **site** *n* MINING emplacement de forage *m*, emplacement de sondage *m*; ~ **socket** *n* MECH ENG boîte à forets *f*, douille pour forets *f*, manchon pour foret *m*; ~ **steel** *n* MECH ENG acier pour forets *m*, acier pour mèches *m*, MINING acier pour fleurets *m*; ~ **stem** *n* PETR train de forage *m*; ~ **stem test** *n* FUELLESS essai aux tiges *m*, PETR TECH essai aux tiges *m*, essai de formation *m*; ~ **string** *n* PETR train de forage *m*, PETR TECH garniture de forage *f*, train de tiges *m*; ~ **string drag** *n* PETR TECH frottement du train de tiges *m*

drill[2] *vt* MECH forer, percer, MECH ENG forer, percer, perforer, MINING forer, percer, PAPER TECH percer

drill[3] *vi* MINING faire des forages, faire des sondages, pratiquer un trou de sonde; ~ **a borehole** *vi* CONST faire des sondages, percer un sondage, pratiquer un trou de sonde; ~ **offshore** *vi* NAUT forer au large

drillability *n* PETR TECH forabilité *f*

drillable *adj* PETR TECH forable

drilled: ~ **fillister head screw** *n* MECH ENG vis à tête cylindrique forcée *f*; ~ **well** *n* HYDROL puits tubé *m*

driller *n* PETR chef sondeur *m*, PETR TECH maître-sondeur *m*

drilling *n* COAL TECH forage *m*, menu de forage *m*, GAS TECH forage *m*, MECH ENG *in metal* forage *m*, percement *m*, perçage *m*, MINING forage *m*, percement *m*, sondage *m*, *in rock or earth* percement *m*, percée *f*, perforage *m*, perforation *f*, PAPER TECH perçage *m*, PROD ENG ajutage *m*; ~ **attachment** *n* MECH ENG *machine tools* dispositif de perçage *m*; ~ **barge** *n* PETR ponton de forage *m*; ~ **bit** *n* MINING *earth-boring* trépan *m*, PETR outil de forage *m*; ~ **break** *n* PETR avancement rapide *m*; ~ **cable** *n* MINING câble de forage *m*, câble de sondage *m*; ~ **conditions** *n pl* PETR TECH paramètres de forage *m pl*; ~ **contractor** *n* PETR entrepreneur de forage *m*; ~ **crew** *n* PETR TECH équipe de forage *f*; ~ **debris** *n* COAL TECH sédiments de forage *m pl*; ~ **engineer** *n* PETR, PETR TECH ingénieur de forage *m*; ~ **equipment** *n* MINING installation de sondage *f*, matériel de forage *m*; ~ **floor** *n* PETR TECH plancher de manoeuvre *m*; ~ **jar** *n* MINING *boring* coulisse *f*; ~ **jig** *n* MECH ENG calibre de forage *m*, gabarit de perçage *m*; ~ **line** *n* PETR, PETR TECH câble de forage *m*; ~ **machine** *n* MECH perceuse *f*, sondeuse *f*, MECH ENG *metal-drilling* foreuse *f*, foreuse mécanique *f*, machine à percer *f*, perceuse *f*, MINING *rock-drilling, earth-boring* foreuse *f*, perforateur mécanique *m*, perforatrice *f*, perforatrice mécanique *f*, sonde *f*; ~ **mast** *n* PETR mât de forage *m*; ~ **mud** *n* PETR boue de forage *f*; ~ **operations** *n* PETR TECH opérations de forage *f pl*; ~ **pillar** *n* MECH ENG forerie à colonne *f*, *machine tool* support de porte-foret *m*; ~ **plant** *n* MINING *boring* installation de sondage *f*, matériel de forage *m*; ~ **platform** *n* NAUT *on drill ship*, PETR, PETR TECH plate-forme de forage *f*; ~ **program** *n* (AmE), ~ **programme** *n* (BrE) PETR TECH programme de forage *m*; ~ **rate** *n* CONST cadence de forage *f*, PETR TECH vitesse d'avancement *f*; ~ **rig** *n* MINING appareil de sondage *m*, PETR TECH appareil de forage *m*, équipement de forage *m*; ~ **site** *n* MINING emplacement de forage *m*, emplacement de sondage *m*, PETR emplacement de sondage *m*; ~ **spindle** *n* MECH ENG arbre porte-foret *m*, bouche porte-mèche *f*; ~ **superintendent** *n* PETR chef de forage *m*; ~ **template** *n* MECH ENG calibre de forage *m*; ~ **tool** *n* CONST *earth-boring* outil de forage *m*, outil de sondage *m*, outil foreur *m*; ~ **winch** *n* MINING treuil de forage *m*, treuil de manoeuvre *m*

drillings *n pl* COAL TECH copeaux de forage *m pl*, MINING farine *f*

drinking: ~ **water** *n* CONST, FOOD TECH, HYDROL, WATER SUPP eau potable *f*; ~ **water cooler** *n* REFRIG fontaine réfrigérée *f*; ~ **water quality** *n* WATER SUPP qualité d'eau potable *f*; ~ **water supply** *n* HYDROL alimentation en eau potable *f*, distribution d'eau potable *f*, WATER SUPP alimentation en eau potable *f*

drip *n* FOOD TECH *butchery* jus de décongélation *m*, REFRIG *liquid produced on thawing* exsudat *m*; ~ **cock** *n* CONST purgeur *m*, robinet purgeur *m*; ~ **cup** *n* CONST cuvette d'égouttage *f*; ~ **pump** *n* WATER SUPP pompe de purge *f*; ~ **tray** *n* PROD ENG récipient d'égouttement *m*, REFRIG *for fluid produced by defrosting* bac de dégivrage *m*

drip-dry *adj* TEXTILES lavé-séché, *printed on label* ne pas repasser

drip-feed: ~ **lubrication** *n* MECH ENG graissage à compte-gouttes *m*; ~ **lubricator** *n* MECH ENG compte-gouttes *m*, graisseur compte-gouttes *m*, graisseur verse-gouttes *m*

drip-proof *adj* MECH ENG abrité; ~ **screen-protected** *adj* MECH ENG abrité-grillagé

drivage *n* MINING chassage *m*, chassante *f*, galerie chassante *f*, galerie d'allongement *f*, galerie de chassage *f*, galerie de direction *f*, galerieen direction *f*

drive[1] *n* COMP, DP unité *f*, MECH entraînement *m*, transmission *f*, MECH ENG commande *f*, transmission *f*, entraînement *m*, MINING chassage *m*, chassante *f*, galerie chassante *f*, galerie d'allongement *f*, galerie de chassage *f*, galerie de direction *f*, galerie en direction *f*, tête motrice *f*, *mine level* galerie *f*, PAPER TECH, TEXTILES *power transmission* commande *f*, VEHICLES *transmission* entraînement *m*, propulsion *f*, traction *f*; ~ **battery** *n* TRANSP batterie de traction *f*; ~ **bit** *n* MECH ENG dé d'entraînement *m*; ~ **block** *n* MINING *boring* bloc de battage *m*; ~ **bolt** *n* PROD ENG chasse-boulon *m*; ~ **chain** *n* VEHICLES *of engine, transmission* chaîne d'entraînement *f*; ~ **coil** *n* ELEC ENG bobine d'excitation *f*; ~ **end** *n* ELEC ENG côté entraînement *m*; ~ **fit** *n* MECH ENG ajustement à force *m*, montage à frottement dur *m*; ~ **head** *n* MINING *boring* bloc de tête de tubage *m*; ~ **knob** *n* INSTRUMENT *horizontal circle* molette d'entraînement *f*; ~ **line** *n* AUTO pignon d'attaque du différentiel *m*; ~ **mechanism** *n* CINEMAT mécanisme d'entraînement *m*; ~ **motor** *n* CINEMAT moteur d'entraînement *m*, moteur de commande *m*, ELEC, PHOTO moteur d'entraînement *m*; ~ **pin** *n* CINEMAT téton d'entraînement *m*, MECH ENG axe d'entraînement *m*, doigt d'entraînement *m*, pion d'entraînement *m*; ~ **pinion** *n* AUTO pignon de démarreur *m*, VEHICLES *of drive shaft* pignon d'attaque *m*, *of gearbox* pignon entraîneur *m*; ~ **pinion shaft** *n* AUTO pignon d'attaque *m*, VEHICLES *drive shaft* arbre d'attaque *m*; ~ **pipe** *n* MINING *boring* tube perforateur *m*; ~ **power** *n* MECH ENG puissance d'entraînement *f*; ~ **pulley** *n* VEHICLES *of alternator* poulie d'entraînement *f*; ~ **sampler** *n* MINING tube perforateur *m*; ~ **shaft** *n* (AmE) *(cf propeller shaft)* AUTO arbre de commande *m*, MECH ENG arbre d'entraînement *m*, VEHICLES arbre de boîte de vitesses *m*, arbre primaire *m*, VEHICLES *transmission* arbre de transmission *m*, cardan de transmission *m*; ~ **shaft tunnel** *n* (AmE) *(cf propeller shaft tunnel)* VEHICLES *transmission* tunnel de l'arbre de transmission *m*; ~ **shoe** *n* MINING sabot coupant *m*, sabot tranchant *m*; ~ **side** *n* PAPER TECH côté transmission *m*, PRINT *(DS)* côté commande *m*; ~ **sprocket** *n* CINEMAT tambour denté d'entraînement *m*, TV tambour d'entraînement *m*, VEHICLES *of chain drive* pignon d'entraînement à chaîne *m*; ~ **system** *n* MECH ENG ensemble de propulsion *m*, TEXTILES système de commande *m*; ~ **train** *n* VEHICLES *transmission* train de roulement *m*, transmission *f*; ~ **tube** *n* MINING tube perforateur *m*; ~ **voltage** *n* TV attaque de grille *f*; ~ **wheel** *n* AUTO roue motrice *f*, VEHICLES *in transmission* roue manante *f*

drive² *vt* CONST *a screw* serrer, visser, MECH attaquer, commander, entraîner, MECH ENG battre, chasser, cogner, enfoncer, ficher, pousser, refouler, PAPER TECH conduire, SPACE *spacecraft* chasser, conduire, entraîner, TEXTILES *of person* actionner, TRANSPORT conduire; ~ **in** *vt* CONST clouer, serrer, visser, MECH ENG battre, chasser, cogner, enfoncer, ficher, pousser, refouler; ~ **into** *vt* MECH ENG chasser, cogner, enfoncer, ficher

driven: ~ **disc** *n* (BrE) MECH ENG disque mené *m*; ~ **disk** *n* (AmE) *see driven disc*; ~ **element** *n* MECH ENG élément mené *m*; ~ **plate** *n* AUTO plateau de pression *m*, VEHICLES *of clutch* disque d'embrayage *m*; ~ **plate assembly** *n* AUTO plateau de friction *m*, plateau de pression *m*; ~ **tool holder** *n* MECH ENG *machine tool* porte-outil entraîné *m*; ~ **wheel** *n* MECH ENG roue menée *f*

driver *n* ACOUSTICS moteur *m*, COMP, DP gestionnaire *m*, pilote *m*, MECH ENG roue menante *f*, roue motrice *f*, *key drift* chasse-clavette *m*, chasse-clé *m*, *lathe dog, carrier* doguin *m*, toc *m*, *rivet drift* broche *f*, broche d'assemblage *f*, mandrin *m*, PROD ENG poinçon *m*, RAIL *personnel* mécanicien *m* (Fra), *train* conducteur *m* (Bel); ~ **card** *n* PROD ENG carte de commande *f*; ~ **chuck** *n* MECH ENG *of lathe* mandrin à toc *m*, plateau pousse-toc *m*, plateau à toc *m*, plateau-toc *m*; ~ **plate** *n* MECH ENG *of lathe* mandrin à toc *m*, plateau pousse-toc *m*, plateau à toc *m*, plateau-toc *m*; ~ **stage** *n* AUTO étage exciteur *m*, SPACE *communications* étage d'excitation *m*

driver's: ~ **cab** *n* (BrE) *(cf engineer's cab)* RAIL *vehicles* abri *m*, abri du mécanicien *m*, cabine *f*, cabine de conduite *f*; ~ **cabin** *n* RAIL *vehicles* cabine *f*, cabine de conduite *f*; ~ **windscreen** *n* (BrE) *(cf driver's windshield)* RAIL *vehicles* pare-brise *m*; ~ **windshield** *n* (AmE) *(cf driver's windscreen)* RAIL *vehicles* pare-brise *m*

driverless *adj* TRANSP *car* sans conducteur, *taxi* sans chauffeur

driving *n* CONST *of screw* serrage *m*, *well-sinking* enfoncement *m*, MECH ENG attaque *f*, commande *f*, transmission *f*, MINING chassage *m*, percement *m*, percement de galeries de recherche *m*, percement de galeries en direction *m*, RAIL *vehicles* conduite *f*; ~ **axle** *n* AUTO, VEHICLES *transmission* essieu moteur *m*, pont moteur *m*; ~ **belt** *n* MECH ENG *by which engine drives machinery* courroie de commande *f*, *for conveying motion* courroie de transmission *f*; ~ **block** *n* CONST *well casing* bloc de battage *m*; ~ **crew** *n* RAIL personnel de conduite *m*; ~ **desk** *n* RAIL *vehicles* pupitre de commande *m*; ~ **disc** *n* (BrE) MECH ENG disque d'entraînement *m*; ~ **disk** *n* (AmE) *see driving disc* ~ **dog** *n* MECH ENG *machine tools* pousse-toc *m*; ~ **drum** *n* TRANSP tambour d'entraînement *m*; ~ **element** *n* MECH ENG élément menant *m*; ~ **end** *n* MECH extrémité motrice *f*; ~ **fit** *n* MECH ENG montage à frottement dur *m*; ~ **force** *n* METALL, TEXTILES force motrice *f*; ~ **gear** *n* MECH ENG commande *f*, organes de commande *m pl*, transmission *f*, engrenage d'attaque *m*, engrenage de commande *m*, engrenage menant *m*, pignon d'attaque *m*; ~ **head** *n* MECH ENG tête d'axe *f*; ~ **in** *n* CONST *of*

nail enfoncement *m*, *of screw* serrage *m*; ~ **level** *n* MINING chassage *m*, chassante *f*, costière *f*, galerie chassante *f*, galerie d'allongement *f*, galerie de chassage *f*, galerie de direction *f*, galerie en direction *f*; ~ **mirror** *n* INSTRUMENT rétroviseur *m*; ~ **motor car** *n* TRANSP automotrice *f*; ~ **out of keys** *n* MECH ENG chassage des clavettes *m*, décalage *m*, décoincement *m*; ~ **out of wedges** *n* MECH ENG chassage des clavettes *m*, décalage *m*, décoincement *m*; ~ **pinion** *n* MECH ENG pignon d'attaque *m*, pignon d'entraînement *m*, pignon de commande *m*; ~ **potential** *n* ELEC ENG potentiel accélérateur *m*; ~ **pressure** *n* MECH ENG pression motrice *f*; ~ **propeller** *n* TRANSP hélice tractive *f*; ~ **pulley** *n* MECH ENG poulie d'entraînement *f*, PROD ENG poulie conductrice *f*, poulie d'attaque *f*, poulie de commande *f*, poulie menante *f*, poulie motrice *f*, poulie de transmission *f*; ~ **pulse** *n* TV impulsion excitatrice *f*; ~ **shaft** *n* MECH ENG arbre d'attaque *m*, arbre de commande *m*, arbre de couche *m*, arbre menant *m*, arbre moteur *m*, NAUT *of engine* arbre moteur *m*; ~ **side** *n* PROD ENG *of belt* brin conducteur *m*, brin menant *m*, brin moteur *m*, brin tendu *m*; ~ **signals** *n pl* TV signaux de synchronisation *m pl*; ~ **tenons** *n pl* MECH ENG *for parallel shank tools* tenons d'entraînement *m pl*; ~ **trailer car** *n* TRANSP automotrice intermédiaire *f*; ~ **unit** *n* TRANSP motrice *f*; ~ **wheel** *n* CINEMAT roue d'entraînement *f*, MECH ENG roue menante *f*, roue motrice *f*, *flywheel* volant *m*, volant d'entraînement *m*, volant de chasse *m*, volant de commande *m*, *wheel communicating motion* roue de transmission *f*, TRANSP roue motrice *f*

drizzle *n* METEO bruine *f*, crachin *m*

drogue *n* NAUT *emergency anchor* ancre de cape *f*, ancre flottante *f*; ~ **chute** *n* SPACE *spacecraft* parachute stabilisateur *m*, parachute-frein *m*

drone *n* SPACE drone *m*; ~ **helicopter** *n* AERONAUT hélicoptère téléguidé *m*

droop *n* ELECTRON affaissement du sommet *m*, chute du sommet *f*, décroissance *f*; ~ **flap** *n* TRANSP volet de bord d'attaque *m*; ~ **nose** *n* AERONAUT nez basculant *m*; ~ **nose aircraft** *n* AERONAUT avion à nez basculant *m*; ~ **rate** *n* ELECTRON taux de décroissance *m*; ~ **restrainer** *n* MECH ENG butée d'affaissement *f*, butée statique *f*; ~ **restraining ring** *n* MECH ENG anneau réciproque *m*, couronne de butée basse *f*; ~ **restraining shaft** *n* MECH ENG doigt de butée d'affaissement *m*

drop¹ *n* C&G pendeloque *f*, CONST *key hole cover* cache-entrée *m*, FOOD TECH, PAPER TECH goutte *f*, PROD ENG *of pattern-withdrawing machine* hauteur de démoulage *f*, REFRIG *air conditioning* retombée *f*, SPACE *spacecraft* largage *m*; ~ **arm** *n* AERONAUT levier de commande *m*, AUTO bielle pendante *f*, VEHICLES *steering* bielle de commande de direction *f*, levier de commande de direction *m*; ~ **arrow** *n* CONST *surveying* fiche plombée *f*; ~ **bed frame** *n* VEHICLES *chassis* cadre surbaissé *m*, châssis surbaissé *m*; ~ **box** *n* WATER SUPP boîte inférieure de décharge *f*; ~ **cable** *n* TV câble d'arrivée *m*; ~ **center rim** *n* (AmE), ~ **centre rim** *n* (BrE) AUTO, VEHICLES jante à base creuse *f*; ~ **counter** *n* PACKAGING compte-gouttes *m*; ~ **forging** *n* MECH pièce estampée *f*, PROD ENG estampage *m*, forgeage mécanique *m*, pilonnage *m*, ébauche matricée *f*; ~ **formation** *n* FLUID PHYS formation de gouttes *f*; ~ **frame indicator** *n* TV indicateur de compensation du temps réel *m*; ~ **frame mode** *n* TV mode de compensation du temps réel *m*; ~ **grate** *n* PROD ENG *of furnace* jette-feu *m*; ~

hammer *n* COAL TECH mouton à déclic *m*, CONST mouton *m*, mouton de battage *m*, MECH ENG marteau à chute libre *m*, PROD ENG marteau-pilon à friction *m*; ~ **height** *n* COAL TECH hauteur de chute *f*; ~ **hole** *n* COAL TECH cheminée à charbon *f*; ~ **keel** *n* NAUT aile de dérive *f*, quille de dérive *f*; ~ **leg** *n* PAPER TECH colonne barométrique *f*; ~ **line** *n* PROD ENG bretelle de raccordement *f*; ~ **line wiring** *n* PROD ENG bretelle de raccordement *f*; ~ **pile hammer** *n* MECH sonnette *f*; ~ **point** *n* FLUID PHYS point de formation de gouttes *m*, REFRIG point de goutte *m*; ~ **point apparatus** *n* LAB EQUIP *lubricating greases* appareil à point de goutte *m*; ~ **runner** *n* PROD ENG chenal de coulée en chute directe *m*; ~ **shadow** *n* CINEMAT ombrage continu *m*; ~ **shipment** *n* PROD ENG livraison directe *f*; ~ **test** *n* PACKAGING essai de chûte *m*, PROP MAT *falling weight test* essai de résistance au choc *m*; ~ **test machine** *n* PROP MAT appareil de choc *m*; ~ **valve** *n* HYDR EQUIP soupape *f*; ~ **valve gear** *n* HYDR EQUIP clapet *m*; ~ **watermark** *n* PAPER TECH tache de goutte d'eau dans la feuille *f*; ~ **wire** *n* TEXTILES cavalier *m*; ~ **zone** *n* MILIT *parachuting* zone de saut *f*, SPACE *spacecraft* zone de largage *f*

drop[2] *vt* PRINT abaisser, SPACE *spacecraft* larguer

drop[3] *vi* NAUT *of wind* s'abattre, PAPER TECH goutter; ~ **anchor** *vi* NAUT mouiller; ~ **the voltage** *vi* ELEC ENG dévolter

drop-down: ~ **menu** *n* COMP, DP menu déroulant *m*

drop-forge *vt* PROD ENG estamper, étamper

drop-forged[1] *adj* PROD ENG matricé

drop-forged:[2] ~ **rivetless chain** *n* MECH ENG chaîne à maillons non-rivés forgés par estampage *f*; ~ **steel dog** *n* PROD ENG *of lathe* toc en acier estampé *m*; ~ **steel spanner** *n* PROD ENG clef en acier estampé *f*

drop-in *n* COMP lecture de parasite *f*, DP, ELEC ENG information parasite *f*; ~ **package** *n* ELEC ENG boîtier enfichable *m*

droplet *n* METEO, POLLUTION gouttelette *f*

drop-out *n* COMP, DP perte d'information par affaiblissement *f*, perte d'information *f*, ELEC ENG *insufficient amplitude* perte de niveau *f*, *of mains* creux detension *m*, *of relay* relâchement *m*, PRINT couleurs illisibles *f pl*, encre illisible *f*, zones imprimantes ne prenant pas l'encre sur la plaque *f pl*, RECORDING *in signal* drop *m*, TV manque de signal *m*, paille *f*, perte de niveau *f*; ~ **compensator** *n* TV compensateur de perte de niveau *m*, correcteur de pailles *m*; ~ **current** *n* ELEC, ELEC ENG courant de relâchement *m*, courant de retombée *m*; ~ **switch signal** *n* TV signal de commutation de pailles *m*; ~ **time** *n* ELEC *of relay* temps de retour *m*, PROD ENG désexcitation *f*; ~ **voltage** *n* ELEC ENG tension de relâchement *f*, tension de retombée *f*

drop-pan *n* MECH ENG réservoir *m*

dropped:[1] ~ **axle** *n* VEHICLES *transmission* essieu coudé *m*, essieu surbaissé *m*; ~ **side** *n* GEOL *of fault* compartiment abaissé d'une faille *m*

dropped:[2] **not to be** ~ *phr* PACKAGING *handling marking, label* ne pas laisser tomber

dropper *n* LAB EQUIP *glassware*, PAPER TECH compte-gouttes *m*

dropping: ~ **bottle** *n* LAB EQUIP *glassware* flacon compte-gouttes *m*; ~ **resistor** *n* ELEC ENG résistance chutrice *f*; ~ **tube** *n* LAB EQUIP compte-gouttes capillaire *m*; ~ **zone** *n* MILIT *parachuting* zone de saut *f*

dross *n* COAL TECH déchets *m pl*; ~ **filter** *n* GAS TECH piège à crasse *m*

drowned: ~ **flow** *n* FLUID PHYS écoulement submergé *m*; ~ **nappe** *n* HYDROL nappe noyée *f*; ~ **river valley** *n* HYDROL aber *m*; ~ **turbine** *n* HYDR EQUIP turbine immergée *f*, turbine noyée *f*; ~ **valley** *n* HYDROL vallée noyée *f*; ~ **weir** *n* HYDROL déversoir noyé *m*, WATER SUPP déversoir noyé *m*, déversoir à nappe noyée *m*

DRS *abbr* SPACE *(digital radio system)* faisceau hertzien numérique *m*, SPACE *(data relay satellite)* satellite relais de données *m*

drum *n* CINEMAT tambour *m*, COAL TECH fût *m*, COMP, DP tambour *m*, HYDR EQUIP *of steam engine indicator* barillet *m*, *of steam turbine* tambour *m*, MAR POLL fût *m*, MECH fût *m*, fût d'huile *m*, tambour *m*, touret *m*, P&R *container* fût *m*, PACKAGING bidon *m*, fût *m*, PAPER TECH tambour *m*, PROD ENG baril *m*, fût *m*, *for mixing, washing* cuve-cylindre *f*, tambour *m*, *for power transmission* tambour *m*, *of capstan* cloche *f*, *winding barrel* cylindre *m*, tambour *m*, TV disque porte-têtes *m*; ~ **altimeter** *n* AERONAUT altimètre à tambour *m*; ~ **armature** *n* ELEC, ELEC ENG induit en tambour *m*; ~ **brake** *n* AUTO frein à tambour *m*; ~ **brake tools** *n pl* AUTO *car maintenance* outils pour freins à tambour *m pl*; ~ **cam** *n* PROD ENG came à cylindre *f*, came à tambour *f*; ~ **cobber** *n* COAL TECH séparateur à tambour *m*; ~ **controller** *n* ELEC *switch* commutateur à cames *m*; ~ **cooler** *n* REFRIG refroidisseur à tambour *m*; ~ **debarker** *n* PAPER TECH tambour écorceur *m*; ~ **development** *n* CINEMAT développement sur tambour *m*; ~ **drive** *n* MECH ENG commande par tambour *f*; ~ **dryer** *n* COAL TECH sécheur à tambour *m*, FOOD TECH séchoir rotatif *m*, séchoir à cylindre *m*, séchoir à tambour *m*, TEXTILES séchoir à tambour *m*, THERMOD sécheur rotatif *m*, tambour sécheur *m*; ~ **dyeing** *n* COLOURS teinture au tonneau *f*; ~ **feeder** *n* TEXTILES prédélivreur à tambour *m*; ~ **filter** *n* COAL TECH filtre à tambour *m*, HYDROL filtre rotatif *m*, filtre à tambour *m*; ~ **freeze dryer** *n* REFRIG lyophilisateur à tambour *m*; ~ **furnace** *n* THERMOD *rotary furnace* four rotatif *m*, four tournant *m*, four à tambour *m*; ~ **gate** *n* FUELLESS *dams* vanne cylindrique *f*; ~ **kiln** *n* THERMOD *cement* four trommel *m*, four à tambour *m*; ~ **lens** *n* INSTRUMENT lentille à échelons *f*; ~ **mix** *n* CONST malaxage à tambour *m*; ~ **plotter** *n* (AmE) *(cf barrel plotter)* COMP, DP traceur à tambour *m*; ~ **printer** *n* (AmE) *(cf barrel printer)* COMP, DP imprimante à tambour *f*; ~ **scanner** *n* PRINT scanner à tambour *m*, TV disque explorateur *m*, tambour d'analyse *m*; ~ **screen** *n* HYDROL tamis rotatif *m*, tamis à tambour *m*; ~ **separator** *n* COAL TECH séparateur à tambour *m*; ~ **shaft** *n* MECH ENG arbre du tambour *m*; ~ **skimmer** *n* MAR POLL récupérateur à tambour *m*, écrémeur à tambour *m*; ~ **starter** *n* ELEC *switch* commutateur à cames *m*; ~ **store** *n* TELECOM mémoire à tambour *f*; ~ **switch** *n* ELEC commutateur cylindrique *m*, commutateur à tambour *m*; ~ **titler** *n* CINEMAT titreuse à tambour *f*; ~ **washer** *n* CONST laveur à tambour *m*, tambour débourbeur *m*, tambour laveur *m*; ~ **winding** *n* ELEC ENG enroulement en tambour *m*

drumhead *n* PROD ENG *of capstan* couronne *f*, couronne à barres *f*, tête *f*

drum-type: ~ **controller** *n* CONTROL contrôleur à cylindre *m*, contrôleur à tambour *m*

druse *n* GEOL géode *f*, vacuole *f*

drusy *adj* GEOL drusique à géodes

dry[1] *adj* TEXTILES sec, THERMOD déshydraté, sec

dry:[2] ~ **acid deposit** *n* POLLUTION dépôt d'acide sec *m*; ~

acidic fallout n POLLUTION dépôt acide sec m, retombées acides sèches f pl; **~ adiabatic lapse rate** n POLLUTION gradient adiabatique sec m; **~ air** n METEO air sec m; **~ back** n PRINT of ink changement d'aspect m, perte de brillant f; **~ battery** n ELEC ENG batterie sèche f; **~ broke** n PAPER TECH cassés secs m pl; **~ bulb temperature** n HEAT ENG température au thermomètre sec f; **~ bulb thermometer** n HEAT ENG, REFRIG thermomètre sec m, THERMOD thermomètre sec m, thermomètre à boule sèche m, thermomètre à réservoir sec m; **~ bulk carrier** n NAUT, TRANSP navire transporteur de vrac sec m, vraquier sec m; **~ bulk container** n TRANSP conteneur à pulvérulents m; **~ cargo ship** n NAUT, TRANSP navire transporteur de vrac sec m; **~ cell** n ELEC, ELEC ENG, PHYS pile sèche f; **~ circuit** n ELEC ENG circuit à très bas niveau m; **~ clutch** n VEHICLES embrayage à sec m; **~ color** n (AmE), **~ colour** n (BrE) COLOURS couleur en poudre f; **~ compression** n REFRIG fonctionnement en régime de surchauffe m, marche en régime de surchauffe f; **~ connection** n ELEC ENG connexion à sec f; **~ connector** n ELEC ENG connecteur sec m; **~ content** n PAPER TECH siccité f; **~ cooling tower** n REFRIG tour de refroidissement sec f; **~ creping** n PAPER TECH crêpage à sec m; **~ crushing** n COAL TECH broyage à sec m; **~ crust** n COAL TECH couche durcie f; **~ density** n COAL TECH masse volumique sèche f, CONST densité sèche f; **~ deposition** n POLLUTION dépôt sec m, retombées sèches f pl; **~ desulfurization process** n (AmE), **~ desulphurization process** n (BrE) POLLUTION processus de désulfuration sec m; **~ distillation** n CHEM distillation sèche f; **~ dock** n CONST cale sec f, dock sec m, NAUT bassin de radoub m, cale sèche f, dock de carénage m, forme de radoub m; **~ down** n PRINT of ink séchage entraînant une perte de brillant m; **~ dust removal** n SAFETY dépoussiérage à fonctionnement sec m; **~ electrolyte** n ELEC ENG électrolyte sec m; **~ engine** n AERONAUT réacteur sec m; **~ expansion evaporator** n REFRIG évaporateur à détente sec m; **~ flashover voltage** n ELEC of arc tension de contournement sec f; **~ freeze** n PACKAGING lyophilisation f; **~ gas** n GAS TECH gaz pauvre m, gaz sec m, PETR gaz sec m; **~ grinding** n SPRINGS meulage sec m; **~ heat** n TEXTILES chaleur sèche f; **~ hole** n MINING trou de sonde pratiqué sec m, trou sec m, PETR, PETR TECH puits sec m; **~ ice** n CHEM neige carbonique f, FOOD TECH carboglace f, glace carbonique f, REFRIG glace carbonique f, glace sèche f; **~ ice bunker** n REFRIG in refrigerated vehicle compartiment à glace carbonique m; **~ joint** n ELEC connection soudure défectueuse f; **~ lamination** n PRINT pelliculage sec m; **~ lens** n (cf immersion lens) LAB EQUIP objectif sec m; **~ mass** n SPACE communications masse sèche f; **~ matter** n HYDROL sewage matière sèche f, résidu sec m; **~ mud** n PETR TECH boue sèche f; **~ natural gas** n PETR TECH gaz pauvre m, gaz sec naturel m; **~ offset** n PRINT offset sec m; **~ offset ink** n PRINT encre pour offset sèche f; **~ offset printing** n PACKAGING imprimerie par offset sèche f; **~ powder fire extinguisher** n SAFETY extincteur d'incendie à poudre m; **~ power** n AERONAUT of engine puissance sans injection d'eau f; **~ precipitation** n POLLUTION précipitations sèches f pl; **~ precision grinding** n MECH ENG machine tools rectification sec f; **~ pulp** n PAPER TECH pâte sèche f; **~ rot** n NAUT in wood pourriture sèche f; **~ run** n COMP, DP passage d'essai m, PROD ENG essai à vide m; **~ season** n METEO saison sèche f; **~ solids content** n PAPER TECH

teneur en matière sèche f; **~ splicer** n CINEMAT colleuse sèche f; **~ spray** n C&G mauvais nappage m; **~ standpipe** n CONST building colonne sèche f; **~ steam** n FUELLESS, HEATING vapeur sèche f; **~ stone wall** n CONST mur en pierres sèches m; **~ sump** n VEHICLES of engine carter sec m; **~ sump lubrication** n AUTO graissage à carter sec m; **~ tapping** n PRINT accrochage sec sur sec m; **~ transfer** n PRINT caractères de transfert sec m pl, lettres de transfert sec f pl; **~ tree** n PETR TECH tête de production au sec f; **~ valley** n HYDROL vallée sèche f; **~ weight** n AERONAUT of aircraft plafond utile m, of engine poids sec m, PACKAGING masse sèche f, poids sec m, poids à vide m, SPACE spacecraft masse sèche f, poids à vide m; **~ well** n PETR TECH puits sec m, WATER SUPP puits d'infiltration m

dry³ vt COAL TECH sécher, PROP MAT of clay dessécher, THERMOD assécher, déshydrater, sécher; **~ by cold air** vt THERMOD sécher par de l'air froid; **~ by heat** vt THERMOD sécher par chauffage, sécher à la chaleur; **~ out** vt THERMOD assécher, dessécher, déshydrater, sécher

dry⁴ vi COAL TECH sécher

dry:⁵ ~ up vti HYDROL tarir

dry-air: ~ filter n HEAT ENG filtre à air sec m

dry-clean vt TEXTILES nettoyer à sec

dry-cleaning n DETERGENTS nettoyage à sec m; **~ agent** n DETERGENTS renforçateur de nettoyage m

dry-dock¹ vt NAUT mettre en cale sèche

dry-dock² vi NAUT entrer en cale sèche

dryer n CHEM séchoir m, COAL TECH sécheur m, MECH ENG dessiccateur m, dessécheur m, sécheur m, séchoir m, P&R siccatif m, PRINT sécheuse f, ink agent séchant m, siccatif m, paper séchoir m, rotating sécheur m, TEXTILES séchoir m, THERMOD dessiccateur m, déshydrateur m, sécheur m, séchoir m; **~ fabric** n TEXTILES toile sécheuse f; **~ felt** n PAPER TECH feutre sécheur m; **~ for grinding wheel** n MECH ENG sécheur pour moule abrasif m; **~ glazer** n PHOTO sécheuse-glaceuse f; **~ mill** n COAL TECH broyeur-sécheur m; **~ section** n PAPER TECH sécherie f

dry-heat-set vt TEXTILES thermofixer à sec

drying n CHEM, COAL TECH, P&R of paint, PAPER TECH séchage m, PETR TECH dessiccation f, séchage m, TEXTILES séchage m, THERMOD assèchement m, dessiccation f, déshydratage f, séchage m; **~ agent** n PACKAGING produit desséchant m, THERMOD siccatif m; **~ air** n COAL TECH air de séchage m; **~ area** n FOOD TECH zone de séchage f; **~ cabinet** n CINEMAT armoire de séchage f, MECH ENG armoire à sécher f, for welding electrodes armoire à sécher f, P&R paint, plastics armoire de séchage f; **~ chamber** n PROD ENG chambre de séchage f, séchoir m, étuve f; **~ column** n LAB EQUIP glassware colonne à dessécher f; **~ cupboard** n FOOD TECH armoire séchoir f, canal-séchoir m, séchoir m, étuve sèche f; **~ cylinder** n DETERGENTS cylindre de séchage m, tambour de séchage m, PAPER TECH cylindre sécheur m, TEXTILES tambour sécheur m; **~ drum** n CONST tambour à sécher m, DETERGENTS cylindre de séchage m, tambour de séchage m; **~ felt** n PRINT feutre de séchage m; **~ floor** n PROD ENG aire de séchage f; **~ frame** n PHOTO cadre de séchage m; **~ furnace** n MECH ENG étuve f, PROD ENG four de séchage m, four sécheur m; **~ house** n PROD ENG chambre de séchage f, séchoir m, étuve f; **~ kiln** n COAL TECH four séchoir m, FOOD TECH séchoir m, touraille f, PROD ENG four de séchage m, four sécheur m; **~ machine** n PACKAGING sécheuse *f*; ~ **mark** *n* CINEMAT marque de séchage *f*; ~ **meter** *n* PAPER TECH siccamètre *m*; ~ **oil** *n* FOOD TECH, P&R *paint binder*, PROD ENG *in paint* huile siccative *f*; ~ **out** *n* THERMOD dessèchement *m*; ~ **oven** *n* COAL TECH étuve *f*, FOOD TECH séchoir *m*, touraille *f*, étuve de dessication *f*, PACKAGING sécheur *m*, PAPER TECH étuve *f*, TEXTILES four de séchage *m*; ~ **room** *n* PROD ENG chambre de séchage *f*, séchoir *m*, étuve *f*; ~ **section** *n* FOOD TECH zone de séchage *f*; ~ **shrinkage** *n* CONST *of concrete* retrait de séchage *m*; ~ **stove** *n* PROD ENG séchoir *m*, étuve de séchage *f*, TEXTILES four séchoir *m*; ~ **system** *n* GAS TECH système de séchage *m*; ~ **tower** *n* FOOD TECH tour de séchage *f*; ~ **tunnel** *n* FOOD TECH *food-processing machinery* séchoir-tunnel *m*, PACKAGING tunnel de séchage *m*; ~ **up** *n* HYDROL *of stream* tarissement *m*; ~ **varnish** *n* COATINGS vernis siccatif *m*

dry-mount *vt* PHOTO coller à sec

dry-mounting: ~ **press** *n* PHOTO presse à coller à sec *f*; ~ **tissue** *n* PHOTO feuille adhésive *f*

dryness *n* COAL TECH, PAPER TECH siccité *f*, TEXTILES siccité *f*, sécheresse *f*; ~ **fraction of steam** *n* HEAT ENG taux de vapeur sèche *m*; ~ **ratio** *n* REFRIG taux de siccité *m*; ~ **test** *n* REFRIG contrôle de siccité *m*

dry-out *n* NUCLEAR assèchement *m*

dry-running: ~ **compressor** *n* MECH ENG compresseur sec *m*, compresseur à marche sèche *m*

dry-storage: ~ **battery** *n* ELEC accumulateur sec *m*

dry-type: ~ **cooler** *n* REFRIG refroidisseur de type sec *m*; ~ **power transformer** *n* ELEC ENG transformateur de puissance type sec *m*; ~ **transformer** *n* ELEC transformateur sec *m*

DS *abbr* COMP *(data store)* mémoire de données *f*, PRINT *(drive side)* côté commande *m*, TELECOM *(digital section)* section numérique *f*, TELECOM *(direct sequence)* séquence directe *f*

DSC *abbr* *(digital selective calling)* TELECOM appel sélectif numérique *m*

DSE *abbr* COMP *(data switching exchange)* centre de commutation de données *m*, TELECOM *(data switching exchange)* centre de commutation de données *m*, commutateur de données *m*, TELECOM *(digital switching element)* organe de commutation automatique *m*

D-shackle *n* NAUT *fittings* manille droite *f*

DSI *abbr* TELECOM *(digital speech interpolation)* CNC *(concentration numérique des conversations)*, TELECOM *(data set identifier)* identificateur de modem *m*, TELECOM *(display station interface)* interface de poste d'affichage *m*

DSL *abbr* *(deep scattering layer)* OCEANOG couche diffusante profonde *f*

DSP *abbr* ELECTRON *(digital signal processing)* traitement numérique de signaux *m*, TELECOM *(domain-specific part)* partie spécifique du domaine *f*

DSR *abbr* *(data set ready)* COMP, TELECOM modem prêt *m*, poste de données prêt *m*

DST *abbr* *(drill stem test)* PETR TECH essai de formation *m*

D-star *n* OPT détectivité normée *f*, détectivité spécifique *f*, TELECOM *normalized detectivity* détectivité normée *f*

DTA *abbr* *(differential thermal analysis)* CONST, P&R, POLLUTION, THERMOD ATD *(analyse thermique différentielle)*

DTE *abbr* *(data terminal equipment)* AERONAUT, COMP, TELECOM ETD, ETTD *(équipement terminal de données)*

DTI *abbr* *(digital trunk interface)* TELECOM module multiplex numérique *m*

DTL *abbr* *(diode-transistor logic)* COMP, ELECTRON logique à diodes et transistors *f*

D-to-A[1] *abbr* *(digital-to-analog, digital-to-analogue)* TV numérique-analogique

D-to-A[2] *adj* *(digital-to-analog, digital-to-analogue)* CINEMAT numérique-analogique

DTP *abbr* *(desktop publishing)* COMP, DP, PRINT PAO *(publication assistée par ordinateur)*

D-type: ~ **flip-flop** *n* ELECTRON bascule D *f*, bascule de type D *f*

dual[1] *adj* GEOM double

dual:[2] ~ **carburetor** *n* (AmE), ~ **carburettor** *n* (BrE) AUTO, MECH carburateur à double corps *m*; ~ **carriageway** *n* (BrE) *(cf divided highway)* CONST route à double chaussée *f*, route à terre-plein central *f*, TRANSP créneau de dépassement *m*; ~ **clevis** *n* MECH ENG double chape *f*; ~ **compressor** *n* MECH ENG compresseur double *m*; ~ **cone loudspeaker** *n* RECORDING haut-parleur à double cône *m*; ~ **control** *n* AERONAUT double commande *f*; ~ **control switch** *n* RAIL aiguillage à deux voies symétriques *m*; ~ **discharge head** *n* MECH ENG tête double de percussion *f*; ~ **flight control system** *n* AERONAUT commandes de vol doubles *f pl*; ~ **fuel** *n* SPACE biergol *m*; ~ **fuel engine** *n* TRANSP moteur à deux combustibles *m*; ~ **fuel pressure gage** *n* (AmE), ~ **fuel pressure gauge** *n* (BrE) AERONAUT manomètre double de pression kérosène *m*; ~ **fuel system** *n* TRANSP moteur hybride *m*; ~ **indicator** *n* MECH ENG indicateur double *m*, récepteur double *m*; ~ **induction log** *n* PETR diagramme double induction *m*; ~ **input** *n* PROD ENG, TV entrée double *f*; ~ **input conversion kit** *n* PROD ENG kit de conversion double entrée *m*; ~ **instruction** *n* AERONAUT vol en double commande *m*; ~ **instruction time** *n* AERONAUT temps d'instruction en double commande *m*; ~ **network** *n* PHYS réseau dual *m*; ~ **platform** *n* AERONAUT centrale bigyroscopique *f*; ~ **point breaker** *n* AUTO rupteur à deux lignes *m*; ~ **power supply** *n* ELEC ENG alimentation double *f*; ~ **pressure controller** *n* REFRIG régulateur combiné haute-basse pression *m*, régulateur haute-basse pression *m*; ~ **pressure valve** *n* PROD ENG double vanne de pression *m*; ~ **rod** *n* AERONAUT bielle double *f*; ~ **slot** *n* PROD ENG module double *m*; ~ **supply voltage** *n* ELEC ENG double tension d'alimentation *f*; ~ **tandem helicopter** *n* TRANSP hélicoptère à rotors en tandem *m*; ~ **tandem wheel undercarriage** *n* AERONAUT train d'atterrissage en tandem de diabolos *m*; ~ **track** *n* ACOUSTICS trace bilatérale *f*; ~ **wheels** *n pl* AERONAUT roues en diabolo *f pl*, roues jumelées *f pl*, *undercarriage* diabolo *m*

dual-beam: ~ **cathode-ray tube** *n* ELECTRON tube cathodique à deux faisceaux *m*, tube cathodique bifaisceau *m*

dual-capacitor: ~ **motor** *n* ELEC moteur à condensateur à deux capacités *m*

dual-carrier: ~ **transmission** *n* TELECOM transmission par double porteuse *f*; ~ **visual direction finding** *n* TELECOM radiogoniométrie visuelle à deux canaux de réception *f*

dual-circuit: ~ **brake** *n* TRANSP double circuit de freinage *m*

dual-coil: ~ **latching relay** *n* ELEC ENG relais à enroulement de maintien *m*

dual-current: ~ **locomotive** *n* RAIL *vehicles* locomotive bicourant *f*

dual-flow: ~ **jet engine** *n* AERONAUT réacteur à double flux *m*

dual-format: ~ **camera** *n* PHOTO caméra biformat *f*

dual-ganged *adj* ELEC *potentiometer* jumelé

dual-in-line: ~ **package** *n* *(DIP)* COMP, DP, ELEC ENG boîtier DIP *m*, boîtier à deux rangées de broches *m*

dual-knife: ~ **cutter** *n* PAPER TECH coupeuse à deux couteaux *f*

dual-level: ~ **plan** *n* TELECOM plan à double niveau *m*

dual-mode: ~ **bus** *n* TRANSP autobus bimodal *m*

dual-port: ~ **memory** *n* COMP, DP mémoire à double accès *f*

dual-position: ~ **button** *n* CONTROL bouton à deux positions *m*

dual-processor: ~ **load-sharing system** *n* TELECOM système à deux calculateurs en partage de trafic *m*; ~ **system** *n* TELECOM système double *m*, système à deux calculateurs *m*

dual-purpose[1] *adj* CONTROL à double usage, à fonction double

dual-purpose:[2] ~ **dredger** *n* NAUT drague mixte *f*; ~ **function** *n* CONTROL fonction double *f*; ~ **vehicle** *n* VEHICLES voiture mixte *f*

dual-rotor: ~ **helicopter** *n* AERONAUT hélicoptère birotor *m*

dual-signaling: ~ **telephone** *n* (AmE), **dual-signalling telephone** *n* (BrE) TELECOM poste à clavier mixte *m*

dual-spin: ~ **satellite** *n* SPACE *spacecraft* satellite à double rotation *m*, satellite à plate-forme contrarotative *m*; ~ **stabilization** *n* SPACE *spacecraft* stabilisation contrarotative *f*, stabilisation double par rotation *f*

dual-standard: ~ **monitor** *n* TV moniteur bistandard *m*

dual-temperature: ~ **refrigerator** *n* REFRIG réfrigérateur-congélateur *m*

dual-window: ~ **fiber** *n* (AmE), ~ **fibre** *n* (BrE) OPT fibre à deux fenêtres *f*

dub[1] *n* TV copie *f*

dub[2] *vt* CINEMAT copier, doubler, postsynchroniser, sonoriser, RECORDING copier, doubler, TV copier, repiquer; ~ **up** *vt* TV transférer de petit format en format professionnel

dubbed: ~ **corner** *n* C&G coin mouché *m*; ~ **version** *n* CINEMAT version doublée *f*

dubbing *n* ACOUSTICS montage *m*, COATINGS enduit des tanneurs *m*, RECORDING réenregistrement *m*, TV doublage *m*; ~ **chart** *n* CINEMAT feuille de mixage *f*; ~ **console** *n* RECORDING console son *f*; ~ **cue sheet** *n* RECORDING feuille de mixage *f*; ~ **room** *n* RECORDING cabine de réenregistrement *f*; ~ **studio** *n* RECORDING studio de mixage *m*; ~ **theater** *n* (AmE), ~ **theatre** *n* (BrE) CINEMAT studio de doublage *m*

duckbill: ~ **pliers** *n pl* (BrE) *(cf needle nose pliers)* MECH ENG *tool* pince plate à bec-de-canard *f*

duct *n* MECH canalisation *f*, tuyauterie *f*, MECH ENG conduite *f*, PROD ENG caniveau *m*, conduit *m*, REFRIG *for air conditioning* conduit *m*, gaine *f*, TELECOM canalisation *f*, conduit *m*; ~ **distribution** *n* REFRIG répartition de gaines d'air *f*; ~ **layout** *n* PROD ENG agencement de goulottes pour fils *m*; ~ **work** *n* PROD ENG goulottes *f pl*, REFRIG réseau de distribution *m*

ducted: ~ **fan** *n* MECH ENG *operating within casing* ventilateur enveloppé *m*, TRANSP soufflante canalisée *f*; ~ **fan engine** *n* AERONAUT moteur à soufflante canalisée *m*, MECH ENG moteur à ventilateur enveloppé *m*; ~ **fan turbo engine** *n* TRANSP turboréacteur à double flux *m*;

~ **propeller** *n* TRANSP hélice carénée *f*

ductile[1] *adj* CRYSTALL, METALL, PROP MAT ductile

ductile:[2] ~ **brittle transition** *n* METALL transition ductile-fragile *f*; ~ **crack** *n* METALL fissure ductile *f*; ~ **fiber** *n* (AmE), ~ **fibre** *n* (BrE) PROP MAT fibre ductile *f*; ~ **fracture** *n* CRYSTALL, METALL rupture ductile *f*; ~ **iron pipe** *n* MECH ENG tuyau en fonte ductile *m*

ductility *n* CRYSTALL, METALL ductilité *f*

ducting *n* MECH ENG conduite *f*

ductor-type: ~ **ink fountain** *n* COLOURS encrier à lame *m*

due: ~ **date** *n* PROD ENG date d'exigibilité *f*

duff *n* COAL TECH charbon pulvérulent *m*

dufrenite *n* MINERAL dufrénite *f*

dufrenoysite *n* MINERAL dufrénoysite *f*

dug-in[1] *adj* MILIT retranché

dug-in[2] *n* MILIT abri de protection *m*

dug-out[1] *adj* MILIT creusé

dug-out[2] *n* MILIT abri de défense *m*, tranchée-abri *f*

dulcin *n* CHEM dulcine *f*

dulcine *n* CHEM dulcine *f*

dull[1] *adj* MECH *tools* émoussé, PROP MAT, TEXTILES terne

dull:[2] ~ **bit** *n* PETR TECH trépan usé *m*; ~ **coal** *n* COAL TECH charbon mat *m*; ~ **finish** *n* COLOURS finition terne *f*, TEXTILES finition mate *f*; ~ **luster** *n* (AmE), ~ **lustre** *n* (BrE) PROP MAT éclat terne *m*; ~ **surface** *n* PROP MAT surface opaque *f*

dulling: ~ **spray** *n* CINEMAT bombe à mater *f*

Dulong: ~ **and Petit's law** *n* PHYS loi de Dulong et Petit *f*

dumb: ~ **barge** *n* NAUT *water transport* chaland sans moteur *m*, TRANSP allège *f*, gabare *f*; ~ **drift** *n* MINING galerie en cul-de-sac *f*; ~ **furnace** *n* MINING foyer d'aérage *m*; ~ **plate** *n* PROD ENG plaque d'avant-foyer *f*, sole *f*; ~ **terminal** *n* COMP, DP terminal muet *m*

dumb-bell *n* METALL interstitiel dissocié *m*

dummy[1] *adj* PACKAGING factice

dummy[2] *n* PRINT maquette en volume *f*, prémaquette *f*; ~ **bearing race** *n* MECH ENG fausse bague de roulement *f*; ~ **cartridge** *n* MINING fausse cartouche *f*, saucisson *m*; ~ **fiber** *n* (AmE), ~ **fibre** *n* (BrE) TELECOM fibre amorce *f*; ~ **grenade** *n* MILIT grenade d'exercice *f*; ~ **instruction** *n* COMP instruction fictive *f*; ~ **part** *n* MECH ENG pièce factice *f*; ~ **stage** *n* SPACE étage incite *m*; ~ **target** *n* MILIT cible-mannequin *f*

dumortierite *n* MINERAL dumortiérite *f*

dump[1] *n* COAL TECH décharge *f*, COMP vidage *m*, CONST *tipping device* basculeur *m*, culbuteur *m*, verseur *m*, CONST *dumping ground* chantier de dépôt *m*, chantier de versage *m*, décharge *f*, dépôt des déblais *m*, DP vidage *m*, MINING chantier de dépôt *m*, chantier de versage *m*, dépôt des déblais *m*, crassier *m*, terril *m*, RECYCLING décharge *f*, dépôt *m* ~ **area** *n* PROD ENG zone de vidage mémoire *f*; ~ **bucket** *n* (AmE) *(cf tipping bucket)* CONST benne basculante *f*, benne à bascule *f*; ~ **car** *n* (AmE) *(cf dump wagon)* TRANSP wagon à benne basculante *m*; ~ **check** *n* COMP contrôle par vidage *m*, DP contrôle de vidage *m*; ~ **cooling** *n* SPACE *spacecraft* refroidissement par fluide perdu *m*; ~ **grate** *n* PROD ENG jette-feu *m*; ~ **heap** *n* MINING halde *f*, halde de déblais *f*, halde de déchets *f*, tas de rejets *m*; ~ **lorry** *n* (BrE) *(cf dump truck)* TRANSPORT chariot à benne basculante *m*; ~ **site** *n* CONST culbuteur des wagons *m*, terril *m*, MINING chantier de dépôt *m*, chantier de versage *m*, dépôt des déblais *m*, terris *m*, RECYCLING site de décharge *m*; ~ **skip** *n* CONST skip à bascule *m*; ~ **trap liquid return** *n* REFRIG retour de liquide à haute pression *m*; ~ **truck** *n* (AmE) *(cf* *tipper*) COAL TECH verseur *m*, CONST *device for tipping trucks* basculeur *m*, culbuteur *m*, verseur *m*, TRANSP culbuteur *m*, TRANSP chariot à benne basculante *m*, TRANSP tombereau *m*; ~ **wagon** *n* (BrE) *(cf dump car)* TRANSP wagon à benne basculante *m*

dump² *vt* MAR POLL rejeter, MINING *ore into chute* bouter, culbuter, PAPER TECH tremper, RECYCLING rejeter

dump:³ ~ **fuel in flight** *vi* SPACE vidanger carburant en vol

dumped *adj* COAL TECH mise en décharge, évacué

dumper *n* CONST dumper *m*, tombereau *m*, *civil engineering* motobasculeur *m*, TRANSP camion benne *m*

dumping *n* *(cf tipping)* AERONAUT largage de carburant *m*, CONST basculement *m*, culbutage *m*, déchargement *m*, déversement *m*, CONST chavirement *m*, culbutement *m*, versage *m*, MINING dépôt *m*, mise à terris *f*, PAPER TECH trempage *m*, POLLUTION décharge *f*, dépôt de déchets *m*, RECYCLING décharge *f*; ~ **bucket** *n* CONST benne basculante *f*, benne à bascule *f*, TRANSP benne basculante *f*; ~ **circuit** *n* TV circuit basculant *m*; ~ **ground** *n* MINING chantier de dépôt *m*, chantier de versage *m*, dépôt des déblais *m*, terris *m*, RECYCLING site de décharge *m*; ~ **mechanism** *n* PACKAGING mécanisme de décharge *m*; ~ **station** *n* CONST station de culbutage *f*

dumpy: ~ **level** *n* CONST niveau à lunette *m*

dune: ~ **buggy** *n* TRANSP auto des sables *f*, voiture des dunes *f*

dunite *n* PETR dunite *f*

duodecimo *n* PRINT in-douze *m*

duotone: ~ **ink** *n* COLOURS encre double-ton *f*

dupe:¹ ~ **negative** *n* CINEMAT contretype négatif *m*; ~ **positive** *n* CINEMAT positif pour contretyper *m*

dupe² *vt* CINEMAT contretyper, tirer

duple: ~ **ink** *n* PRINT encre double-ton *f*

duplex¹ *adj* COMP, DP, ELEC ENG, TELECOM duplex

duplex:² ~ **automatic vacuum brake** *n* MECH ENG frein à vide duplex automatique *m*; ~ **board** *n* PACKAGING *multiple construction board* carton à couches multiples *m*; ~ **boring machine** *n* MECH ENG machine à aléser à deux broches opposées *f*; ~ **burner** *n* TRANSP brûleur à double débit *m*; ~ **cable** *n* ELEC câble à deux âmes torsadées *m*; ~ **chain** *n* AUTO, VEHICLES *transmission* chaîne duplex *f*; ~ **compound winding engine** *n* MECH ENG machine d'extraction compound bicylindrique *f*; ~ **compressor** *n* HYDR EQUIP compresseur à cylindres jumelés *m*; ~ **crank** *n* MECH ENG manivelle double *f*; ~ **cylinder engine** *n* MECH ENG machine bicylindrique *f*, moteur bicylindrique *m*; ~ **engine** *n* MECH ENG machine bicylindrique *f*, moteur bicylindrique *m*; ~ **filter** *n* PROD ENG filtre duplex *m*; ~ **ink** *n* COLOURS encre double-ton *f*; ~ **lap winding** *n* ELEC *machine* enroulement imbriqué parallèle double *m*; ~ **lever punch** *n* MECH ENG poinçonneuse duplex *f*; ~ **metal** *n* PROP MAT métal dumet *m*; ~ **operation** *n* COMP opération en mode duplex *f*, DP fonctionnement en mode duplex *m*; ~ **pump** *n* HYDR EQUIP pompe duplex *f*, pompe à double effet *f*; ~ **punching bear** *n* MECH ENG poinçonneuse duplex *f*; ~ **steel** *n* PROP MAT acier manufacturé en procédé duplex *m*; ~ **waterproof board** *n* PACKAGING carton duplex imperméable *m*

duplexer *n* TELECOM duplexeur *m*

duplicata *n* PRINT deuxième feuille d'une série dans une liasse *f*

duplicate¹ *n* PHOTO contre-type *m*, duplicata *m*, document duplicata *m*, photo contretype *f*, PRINT contre-type *m*; ~ **feeder** *n* ELEC *supply* feeder secondaire *m*; ~ **I/O addressing** *n* PROD ENG adressage par complémentaire des E/S *m*; ~ **standard** *n* SPRINGS étalon *m*; ~ **supply** *n* ELEC réseau double *m*

duplicate² *vt* COMP reproduire, DP dupliquer, reproduire, PHOTO contretyper, TV copier, repiquer

duplicating: ~ **film** *n* PHOTO pellicule pour contretype *f*; ~ **recorder** *n* INSTRUMENT enregistreur-duplicateur *m*; ~ **stencil base paper** *n* PAPER TECH papier support pour stencil *m*

duplication *n* ACOUSTICS duplication *f*; ~ **check** *n* CONTROL contrôle par duplication *m*

durability *n* MECH ENG longévité *f*, METR résistance à l'usure *f*, P&R durabilité *f*, PROP MAT durée de vie *f*, QUALITY durabilité *f*, TEXTILES durée *f*; ~ **test** *n* PACKAGING essai de durabilité *m*, SPRINGS essai d'endurance *m*

durable *adj* QUALITY durable

duralumin *n* MECH *materials* duralumin *m*

durangite *n* MINERAL durangite *f*

duration *n* HYDR EQUIP *of compression of steam* durée *f*; ~ **of expansion of steam** *n* HYDR EQUIP phase de détente de la vapeur *f*; ~ **of totality** *n* ASTRON *of solar eclipse* durée de la totalité *f*

durene *n* CHEM durène *m*

durn *n* MINING *mine-timbering* cadre *m*, châssis *m*, châssis de mine *m*

durometer *n* LAB EQUIP, P&R, PAPER TECH, PRINT duromètre *m*

durum: ~ **wheat** *n* FOOD TECH blé dur *m*, froment vitreux *m*

dust¹ *n* COAL TECH, CONST, POLLUTION, SAFETY poussière *f*; ~ **and spray protective hood** *n* SAFETY bonnet de protection pour travaux au pistolet *m*; ~ **aspirator** *n* PACKAGING aspirateur de poussière *m*; ~ **bag** *n* SAFETY *for vacuum cleaner or fan* sac à poussière *m*; ~ **blouse** *n* SAFETY blouse antipoussière *f*; ~ **boot** *n* VEHICLES *on gearshift lever* pare-poussière *m*; ~ **cap** *n* MECH ENG bouchon antipoussière *m*; ~ **catcher** *n* CHEM TECH capteur de poussière *m*, COAL TECH capteur de poussière *m*, sac à poussière *m*; ~ **chamber** *n* COAL TECH chambre de dépoussiérage *f*; ~ **coal** *n* COAL TECH charbon pulvérulent *m*; ~ **collector** *n* CHEM TECH capteur de poussière *m*, COAL TECH capteur de poussière *m*, collecteur de poussière *m*, P&R dépoussiéreur *m*; ~ **content** *n* POLLUTION teneur en poussière *f*; ~ **control** *n* CHEM TECH captage de poussière *m*; ~ **counter** *n* INSTRUMENT compteur de poussière micrométrique *m*; ~ **cover** *n* MECH ENG, SAFETY cache-poussière *m*; ~ **exhaust fan** *n* COAL TECH aspirateur de poussière *m*, SAFETY aspirateur de poussière *m*, ventilateur de refoulement de poussière *m*; ~ **exhausting device** *n* PACKAGING dispositif-extracteur de poussière *m*; ~ **explosion** *n* COAL TECH coup de poussière *m*; ~ **filter** *n* COAL TECH dépoussiéreur *m*; ~ **guard** *n* COAL TECH pare-poussière *m*, PACKAGING cache-poussière *m*; ~ **hood** *n* SAFETY cagoule antipoussière *f*; ~ **mask** *n* SAFETY masque antipoussière *m*, masque à poussière *m*; ~ **mill** *n* FOOD TECH pulvérisateur *m*; ~ **monitor** *n* NUCLEAR moniteur de contamination par poussière *m*; ~ **particles** *n pl* POLLUTION particules de poussière *f pl*; ~ **photosphere** *n* ASTRON *around protostar* photosphère de poussière *f*; ~ **removal** *n* PROD ENG dépoussiérage *m*; ~ **removal plant** *n* SAFETY *for flue gas* installation de dépoussiérage *f*; ~ **removal system** *n* PACKAGING système dépoussiéreur *m*; ~ **seal** *n* AUTO pare-poussière *m*; ~ **separator** *n* SAFETY *cleaning* *equipment for air* dépoussiéreur *m*; ~ **suppression system** *n* CONST système dépoussiéreur *m*

dust[2] *vt* FOOD TECH saupoudrer

dustbin: ~ **lorry** *n* (BrE) *(cf garbage track)* RECYCLING benne à ordures *f*

duster *n* PETR puits improductif *m*, puits sec *m*, PHOTO blaireau pour dépoussiérage *m*, blaireau pour épousseter *m*

dusting *n* PAPER TECH peluchage *m*, *of coated paper* poudrage *m*; ~ **bag** *n* PROD ENG *founding* sac à poussière *m*; ~ **brush** *n* PHOTO blaireau pour dépoussiérage *m*, blaireau pour épousseter *m*; ~ **unit** *n* PRINT antimaculeur à poudre *m*, poudreuse *f*

dust-laden *adj* COAL TECH chargé de poussière, *atmosphere* poussiéreux, SAFETY *atmosphere* chargé de poussière, poussiéreux

dustproof[1] *adj* ELEC *equipment* étanche aux poussières, MECH ENG protégé contre les poussières, PACKAGING étanche aux poussières, PROD ENG cache-poussière, SAFETY protégé contre les poussières

dustproof:[2] ~ **motor** *n* ELEC moteur étanche aux poussières *m*

dust-tight *adj* PACKAGING étanche aux poussières, PROD ENG protégé contre la poussière

Dutch: ~ **drop** *n* C&G goutte de verre *f*; ~ **roll** *n* AERONAUT *of swept wing aircraft* roulis hollandais *m*; ~ **tile** *n* C&G carreau céramique *m*

duty *n* PROD ENG cycle de service *m*, *of machine* rendement *m*; ~ **cycle** *n* MECH cycle opératoire *m*, PROD ENG coefficient d'utilisation *m*; ~ **pump** *n* PROD ENG pompe de service *f*

D-valve *n* HYDR EQUIP tiroir en D *m*

DVE *abbr (digital video effects)* TV effets spéciaux *m pl*, effets spéciaux numériques *m pl*

DVTR *abbr (digital videotape recorder)* TV magnétoscope numérique *m*

dwarf *n* ASTRON *type of star*, SPACE *type of star* naine *f*, étoile naine *f*; ~ **galaxy** *n* ASTRON galaxie naine *f*; ~ **nova** *n* ASTRON nova naine *f*; ~ **star** *n* ASTRON, SPACE naine *f*, étoile naine *f*

dwell *n* MECH *of cam* arrêt d'excentricité *m*; ~ **angle** *n* AUTO angle de fermeture *m*, VEHICLES *ignition* angle de contact *m*, angle dwell *m*; ~ **setting** *n* PROD ENG réglage de position *m*; ~ **time** *n* C&G temps de séjour *m*, MECH temps d'arrêt *m*, TEXTILES *in stenter* temps de séjour *m*

DWT *abbr (deep well thermometer)* PETR thermomètre de fond *m*

DXC *abbr* TELECOM *(digital cross-connect)* brasseur-répartiteur numérique *m*, TELECOM *(digital cross-connect equipment)* équipement multiplexeur-aiguilleur numérique *m*

DX-stuffing: ~ **signal** *n* TELECOM signal de bourrage DX *m*

dy *n* COAL TECH dy *m*

Dy *(dysprosium)* CHEM Dy *(dysprosium)*

dyadic *adj* DP dyadique

dye[1] *n* CHEM colorant *m*, teint *m*, teinture *f*, PAPER TECH couleur *f*, TEXTILES colorant *m*; ~ **laser** *n* PHYS laser à colorant *m*; ~ **liquor** *n* TEXTILES liqueur de teinture *f*; ~ **penetrant test** *n* MECH essai de ressuage *m*; ~ **room** *n* COLOURS teinturerie *f*; ~ **shop** *n* COLOURS teinturerie *f*; ~ **toning** *n* CINEMAT, PHOTO virage *m*; ~ **transfer process** *n* CINEMAT procédé "dye transfer" *m*, PHOTO procédé par transfert hydrotypique *m*

dye[2] *vt* COLOURS teindre, PAPER TECH colorer, PHOTO teindre, TEXTILES colorer; ~ **fast** *vt* COLOURS teindre en

colorants solides; ~ **in the piece** *vt* TEXTILES teindre en pièce; ~ **turkey red** *vt* COLOURS teindre au rouge turc; ~ **under pressure** *vt* TEXTILES teindre sous pression

dyed[1] *adj* COLOURS teint

dyed:[2] ~ **yarn** *n* TEXTILES fil teint *m*

dyehouse *n* COLOURS teinturerie *f*

dyeing *n* COLOURS coloration *f*, teinture *f*, TEXTILES teinture *f*; ~ **affinity** *n* TEXTILES affinité tinctoriale *f*

dyer *n* COLOURS teinturier *m*

dyestuff *n* TEXTILES colorant *m*

dying *n* MECH ENG matriçage *m*

dyke *n* (BrE) CONST, FUELLESS digue *f*, HYDROL barrage *m*, digue *f*, WATER SUPP digue *f*

dynamic[1] *adj* COMP, DP dynamique

dynamic:[2] ~ **address translation** *n (DAT)* COMP traduction dynamique d'adresse *f*; ~ **allocation** *n* COMP affectation dynamique *f*, attribution dynamique *f*, DP affectation dynamique *f*, allocation dynamique *f*, attribution dynamique *f*; ~ **balance** *n* MECH ENG équilibre dynamique *m*; ~ **balancing** *n* AERONAUT équilibrage dynamique *m*; ~ **brake** *n* RAIL *vehicles* frein rhéostatique *m*; ~ **braking** *n* TRANSP freinage dynamique *m*; ~ **component** *n* AERONAUT élément dynamique *m*; ~ **conditions** *n pl* ELEC ENG régime dynamique *m*; ~ **convergence** *n* TV convergence dynamique *f*; ~ **correction** *n* PETR correction dynamique *f*; ~ **distortion** *n* ACOUSTICS distorsion dynamique *f*; ~ **dump** *n* COMP, DP vidage dynamique *m*; ~ **force calibration** *n* MECH ENG étalonnage dynamique *m*; ~ **friction** *n* PHYS frottement dynamique *m*; ~ **heating** *n* THERMOD chauffage dynamique *m*; ~ **interaction** *n* METALL interaction dynamique *f*; ~ **load control** *n* TELECOM contrôle dynamique de la charge *m*; ~ **loading** *n* CONST chargement dynamique *m*, METALL sollicitation dynamique *f*; ~ **loudspeaker** *n* ACOUSTICS haut-parleur à bobine mobile *m*; ~ **memory** *n* COMP, DP mémoire dynamique *f*; ~ **metamorphism** *n* FUELLESS métamorphisme dynamique *m*, GEOL dynamométamorphisme *m*; ~ **microphone** *n* RECORDING microphone électrodynamique *m*, microphone à bobine mobile *m*; ~ **model** *n* SPACE *spacecraft* modèle dynamique *m*; ~ **movement detector** *n* TRANSP détecteur de passage *m*; ~ **noise suppressor** *n* RECORDING limiteur de bruit dynamique *m*; ~ **overvoltage** *n* ELEC ENG surtension transitoire *f*; ~ **parameter** *n* COMP, DP paramètre dynamique *m*; ~ **positioning** *n* PETR, PETR TECH positionnement dynamique *m*; ~ **power consumption** *n* ELEC ENG consommation dynamique *f*; ~ **presence detector** *n* TRANSP détecteur de présence dynamique *m*; ~ **pressure** *n* AERONAUT, METEO pression dynamique *f*; ~ **programming** *n* COMP programmation dynamique *f*; ~ **property** *n* P&R propriété dynamique *f*; ~ **RAM** *n* COMP, DP RAM dynamique *f*; ~ **random access memory** *n (DRAM)* COMP, DP mémoire dynamique *f*; ~ **range** *n* ACOUSTICS dynamique *f*, PETR amplitude dynamique *f*, RAD PHYS gamme dynamique *f*, RECORDING rapport signal-bruit *m*, échelle de dynamique *f*, TV dynamique *f*, plage de contraste *f*; ~ **resistance** *n* ELEC résistance dynamique *f*; ~ **response** *n* TELECOM réponse dynamique *f*; ~ **similarity** *n* FLUID PHYS similitude dynamique *f*; ~ **sounding** *n* COAL TECH sondage dynamique *m*; ~ **stability** *n* AERONAUT, TELECOM stabilité dynamique *f*; ~ **stress** *n* MECH ENG contrainte dynamique *f*; ~ **test** *n* METALL essai dynamique *m*; ~ **tide** *n* OCEANOG marée dynamique *f*; ~ **toe angle** *n* VEHICLES *steering* angle de pincement dynamique *m*; ~ **trimming** *n* ELEC ENG ajustage dynamique *m*; ~ **viscosity** *n* FLUID PHYS, FUELLESS, P&R, PHYS viscosité dynamique *f*

dynamical *adj* FLUID PHYS *process*, METALL *recovery* dynamique

dynamics *n* MECH, PHYS dynamique *f*

dynamite *n* MINING dynamite *f*; ~ **cartridge** *n* MINING cartouche de dynamite *f*; ~ **store** *n* MINING dynamitière *f*

dynamo *n* ELEC, ELEC ENG, NAUT *electrics*, VEHICLES *electrical system* dynamo *f*; ~ **blaster** *n* MINING exploseur à dynamo *m*; ~ **effect** *n* SPACE effet dynamo *m*; ~ **exploder** *n* MINING exploseur à dynamo *m*

dynamo-electric *adj* ELEC ENG dynamo-électrique

dynamograph *n* MECH dynamographe *m*

dynamometer *n* ELEC, LAB EQUIP *measuring energy*, MECH dynamomètre *m*, OCEANOG tensiomètre *m*; ~ **wattmeter** *n* ELEC wattmètre électrodynamique *m*

dynamometric: ~ **dynamo** *n* ELEC *generator* alternateur

pilote à aimants permanent *m*

dynamotor *n* ELEC dynamoteur *m*, ELEC ENG commutatrice *f*

dyne *n* METR *unit of force in CGS system* dyne *f*

dynode *n* PHYS dynode *f*

dysanalyte *n* MINERAL dysanalyte *f*

dysbaric *adj* OCEANOG *arthropathy* dysbarique, *emphysema* dysbarique

dysbarism *n* OCEANOG dysbarisme *m*

dysclasite *n* MINERAL dysclasite *f*

dyscrasite *n* MINERAL dyscrase *f*, dyscrasite *f*

dysluite *n* MINERAL dysluite *f*

dysodile *n* MINERAL dysodile *f*

dyspnea *n*,

dyspnoea *n* OCEANOG dispnée *f*

dysprosium *n* (*Dy*) CHEM dysprosium *m* (*Dy*)

DZUS: ~ **fastener** *n* SPACE *spacecraft* attache DZUS *f*

E

E [1] *abbr (exa-)* METR E *(exa-)*

E :[2] ~ **and M signaling** *n* (AmE), ~ **and M signalling** *n* TELECOM signalisation TRON et RON *f*

EA *abbr (external access equipment)* TELECOM équipement d'accès externe *m*

EAF [1] *abbr (electric arc furnace)* COAL TECH four à arc électrique *m*

EAF:[2] ~ **dust** *n* COAL TECH poussière provenant de four à arc électrique *f*

ear *n* MECH ENG oreille *f*, *of fan, of centrifugal pump* oeillard *m*, ouïe *f*; ~ **plug** *n* SAFETY bouchon d'oreille *m*; ~ **protection** *n* ACOUSTICS protecteur d'oreilles *m*; ~ **protectors** *n pl* LAB EQUIP *safety* casque antibruit *m*, SAFETY dispositifs de protection des oreilles *m pl*

earlier: ~ **application** *n* PATENTS demande antérieure *f*; ~ **priority** *n* PATENTS priorité antérieure *f*

early [1] *adj* GEOL *age* précoce

early:[2] ~ **admission** *n* PROD ENG *slide valve* admission anticipée *f*, avance à l'admission *f*; ~ **failure** *n* ELEC ENG défaillance prématurée *f*; ~ **failure period** *n* QUALITY période de défaillance précoce *f*, période de défaillance rapide *f*; ~ **finish** *n* TV fin avancée *f*; ~ **finish audio** *n* TV *editing mode* fin son avancée *f*; ~ **finish video** *n* TV *editing mode* fin image avancée *f*; ~ **publication** *n* PATENTS publication précoce *f*; ~ **release** *n* PROD ENG *slide valve* avance à l'émission *f*, échappement anticipé *m*; ~ **start** *n* TV début avancé *m*; ~ **start audio** *n* TV *editing mode* début son avancé *m*; ~ **start video** *n* TV *editing mode* début image avancé *m*; ~ **warning radar** *n* NAUT *navy* radar de veille lointaine *m*

Early: ~ **effect** *n* ELECTRON effet Early *m*

earmuffs *n pl* CONST *civil engineering*, LAB EQUIP *safety* casque antibruit *m*, SAFETY *industrial hearing protectors* casque antibruit *m*, serre-tête *m*

Earnshaw's: ~ **theorem** *n* PHYS théorème d'Earnshaw *m*

earphone *n* ACOUSTICS écouteur *m*

earpiece *n* TELECOM pavillon *m*

earth [1] *adj* SPACE terrien

earth [2] *n* (BrE) *(cf ground)* COAL TECH terre *f*, ELEC *connection*, ELEC ENG masse *f*, terre *f*, PHYS masse *f*, TELECOM terre *f*, VEHICLES *electrical system* masse *f*, terre *f*; ~ **arrester** *n* (BrE) *(cf ground arrester)* GEOPHYS court-circuiteur de mise à la terre *m*; ~ **auger** *n* MINING cuiller *f*, cuillère *f*, tarière à glaise *f*; ~ **bar** *n* (BrE) *(cf ground bar)* ELEC *connection* piquet de terre *m*; ~ **borer** *n* MINING cuiller *f*, cuillère *f*, tarière à glaise *f*; ~ **bus** *n* (BrE) *(cf ground bus)* ELEC *connection* barre omnibus de terre *f*, PRODUCTION barette de masse *f*; ~ **cable** *n* (BrE) *(cf ground cable)* ELEC ENG câble de mise à la masse *m*, câble de terre *m*, VEHICLES *electrical system* câble de mise à la masse *m*; ~ **clamp** *n* (BrE) *(cf ground clamp)* ELEC *connection* borne de terre *f*; ~ **clip** *n* (BrE) *(cf ground clip)* ELEC *connection* collier de mise à la terre *m*; ~ **conductor** *n* (BrE) *(cf ground conductor)* ELEC conducteur de terre *m*, ELEC ENG fil de terre *m*; ~ **connection** *n* (BrE) *(cf ground connection)* AUTO câble de mise à la masse *m*, ELEC prise de terre *f*, ELEC ENG connexion de terre *f*; ~ **connector** *n*

(BrE) *(cf ground connector)* PROD ENG serre-fils de mise à la terre *m*; ~ **core** *n* GEOPHYS barysphère *f*, nifé *m*, noyau terrestre *m*; ~ **current** *n* (BrE) *(cf ground current)* ELEC courant à la terre *m*, GEOPHYS courant tellurique *m*; ~ **dam** *n* HYDROL, WATER SUPP barrage en terre *m*; ~ **detector** *n* (BrE) *(cf ground detector)* ELEC ENG détecteur de terre *m*; ~ **electrode** *n* (BrE) *(cf ground electrode)* AUTO électrode de masse *f*, ELEC électrode de terre *f*, ELEC ENG électrode de mise à la terre *f*; ~ **fall** *n* CONST glissement de terre *m*, éboulement de terres *m*; ~ **fault** *n* (BrE) *(cf ground fault)* ELEC défaut à la terre *m*, PROD ENG défaut de terre *m*; ~ **fault current** *n* (BrE) *(cf ground fault current)* PROD ENG courant de défaut de mise à la terre *m*; ~ **fault protection** *n* (BrE) *(cf ground fault protection)* ELEC protection contre les défauts à la terre *f*; ~ **fault tray** *n* (BrE) *(cf ground fault tray)* PROD ENG relais de défaut à la terre *m*; ~ **grab** *n* COAL TECH cuiller *f*; ~ **indicator** *n* (BrE) *(cf ground indicator)* ELEC ENG indicateur de terre *m*; ~ **inductor** *n* GEOPHYS inducteur terrestre *m*; ~ **lead** *n* (BrE) *(cf ground lead)* ELEC ENG conducteur de masse *m*, conducteur de terre *m*; ~ **leakage** *n* (BrE) *(cf ground leakage)* ELEC perte à la terre *f*, ELEC ENG fuite par la terre *f*; ~ **leakage circuit breaker** *n* (BrE) *(cf ground leakage circuit breaker)* ELEC disjoncteur différentiel *m*; ~ **leakage current** *n* (BrE) *(cf ground leakage current)* ELEC courant de fuite à la terre *m*; ~ **leakage detector** *n* (BrE) *(cf ground leakage detector)* ELEC détecteur de fuite *m*, détecteur à la terre *m*; ~ **leakage meter** *n* (BrE) *(cf ground leakage meter)* ELEC mesureur de terre *m*; ~ **line** *n* (BrE) *(cf ground line)* ELEC ENG ligne de masse *f*, ligne de terre *f*; ~ **loop** *n* (BrE) *(cf ground loop)* PROD ENG boucle de masse *f*; ~ **lug** *n* (BrE) *(cf ground lug)* ELEC, PROD ENG cosse de mise à la terre *f*; ~ **oil** *n* PETR huile de pierre *f*, huile de roche *f*, naphte minéral *m*, naphte natif *m*, pétrole *m*; ~ **pin** *n* (BrE) *(cf ground pin)* PROD ENG lamelle de masse *f*; ~ **plane** *n* (BrE) *(cf ground plane)* PHYS plan de masse *m*; ~ **plate** *n* (BrE) *(cf ground plate)* ELEC ENG prise de terre *f*, GEOPHYS plaque de terre *f*; ~ **potential** *n* (BrE) *(cf ground potential)* ELEC potentiel de la terre *m*; ~ **pressure** *n* COAL TECH pression des terres *m*; ~ **pressure at rest** *n* COAL TECH pression des terres au repos *f*; ~ **pressure coefficient** *n* COAL TECH coefficient de pression des terres *m*; ~ **radiation** *n* GEOPHYS rayonnement terrestre *m*; ~ **rammer** *n* CONST dame *f*, demoiselle *f*, hie *f*, pilon *m*; ~ **reservoir** *n* WATER SUPP réservoir enterré *m*; ~ **resistance** *n* (BrE) *(cf ground resistance)* ELEC résistance de la terre *f*; ~ **resistance meter** *n* (BrE) *(cf ground resistance meter)* ELEC telluromètre *m*; ~ **return** *n* (BrE) *(cf ground return)* ELEC ENG retour par la masse *m*, retour par terre *m*, GEOPHYS retour par terre *m*, PROD ENG retour à la terre *m*, TELECOM retour par terre *m*; ~ **rod** *n* (BrE) *(cf ground rod)* ELEC *connection* piquet de terre *m*, GEOPHYS perche de mise à la terre *f*, piquet de terre *m*; ~ **sensing apparatus** *n* (BrE) *(cf ground sensing apparatus)* PROD ENG appareil détecteur de défaut de masse *m*; ~ **sensor** *n* GEOPHYS détecteur d'orientation terrestre *m*; ~ **spike** *n (cf ground spike)* GEOPHYS perche de mise à la terre *f*, piquet de terre *m*; ~ **station** *n* SPACE *satellite communications*, TELECOM *satellite communications* station terrienne *f*, TV station terrestre *f*, station terrienne *f*; ~ **switch** *n* (BrE) *(cf ground switch)* ELEC interrupteur de mise à la terre *m*; ~ **terminal** *n* (BrE) *(cf ground terminal)* ELEC borne de terre *f*, ELEC ENG borne de masse *f*, borne de terre *f*, prise de terre *f*, PROD ENG *electricity* borne de terre *f*; ~ **terminal arrester** *n* (BrE) *(cf ground terminal arrester)* ELEC *connection* éclateur de mise à la terre *m*; ~ **tide** *n* OCEANOG marée terrestre *f*; ~ **tremor** *n* GEOPHYS tremblement de terre *m*; ~ **wire** *n* (BrE) *(cf ground wire)* ELEC ENG fil de masse *m*, fil de terre *m*, ELECTR prise de terre *f*, PROD ENG conducteur de terre *m*, TV fil de terre *m*

earth[3] *vt* (BrE) *(cf ground)* ELEC *connection*, ELEC ENG, PHYS, TELECOM, VEHICLES *electrical system* mettre à la masse, mettre à la terre

Earth: ~ **capture vehicle** *n* SPACE *spacecraft* véhicule de rentrée en orbite terrestre *m*; ~ **curvature** *n* SPACE courbure de la Terre *f*; ~ **escape stage** *n* SPACE étage destiné à échapper à l'attraction terrestre *m*; ~ **escape velocity** *n* SPACE deuxième vitesse cosmique *f*; ~ **exploration satellite service** *n* SPACE *communications* service d'exploration de la Terre par satellite *m*; ~ **observation satellite** *n* SPACE satellite d'observation de la Terre *m*; ~ **orbit** *n* SPACE orbite terrestre *f*; ~ **orbit rendez-vous** *n* SPACE rendez-vous sur orbite terrestre *m*; ~ **parking orbit** *n* SPACE orbite d'attente à proximité de la Terre *f*; ~ **potential** *n* SPACE potentiel terrestre *m*; ~ **receiver** *n* SPACE *communications* récepteur terrestre *m*; ~ **reentry altitude** *n* SPACE altitude de rentrée *f*; ~ **remote sensing satellite** *n* SPACE satellite de télédétection terrestre *m*; ~ **resources research satellite** *n* SPACE satellite de détection des ressources terrestres *m*; ~ **satellite** *n* SPACE satellite terrestre *m*; ~ **synchronous orbit** *n* SPACE orbite géosynchrone *f*; ~ **synchronous satellite** *n* SPACE satellite géosynchrone *m*

Earth's: ~ **atmosphere** *n* SPACE atmosphère terrestre *f*; ~ **axis** *n* SPACE axe de la Terre *m*; ~ **core** *n* FUELLESS noyau terrestre *m*; ~ **crust** *n* FUELLESS croûte terrestre *f*, GEOL, GEOPHYS écorce terrestre *f*; ~ **magnetic field** *n* ELEC, GEOPHYS, PHYS champ géomagnétique *m*, champ magnétique terrestre *m*

earth-balanced *adj* ELEC ENG équilibré par rapport à la terre

earthdrill *n* COAL TECH cuiller *f*

earthed[1] *adj* (BrE) *(cf grounded)* ELEC, ELEC ENG *connected to frame*, TELECOM mis à la masse, mis à la terre

earthed:[2] ~ **base connection** *n* (BrE) *(cf grounded base connection)* ELEC ENG montage à base commune *m*; ~ **collector connection** *n* (BrE) *(cf grounded collector connection)* ELEC ENG montage à collecteur commun *m*; ~ **emitter connection** *n* (BrE) *(cf grounded emitter connection)* ELEC ENG montage à émetteur commun *m*; ~ **neutral system** *n* (BrE) *(cf grounded neutral system)* ELEC système avec neutre à la terre *m*; ~ **switch** *n* (BrE) *(cf grounded switch)* ELEC commutateur de sécurité *m*; ~ **system** *n* (BrE) *(cf grounded system)* PROD ENG système relié à la terre *m*

earthenware *n* C&G articles en faïence *m pl*, poterie commune *f*; ~ **decorator** *n* C&G peintre sur faïence *m*; ~ **glazing** *n* C&G glaçure de faïence *f*; ~ **jar** *n* C&G récipient en grès *m*; ~ **pipe** *n* C&G tuyau en poterie *m*,

CONST tuyau de terre *m*; ~ **sieve** *n* C&G passoire en grès *f*; ~ **slab** *n* C&G carreau de faïence *m*; ~ **tank** *n* C&G cuve en grès *f*

earthing *n* (BrE) *(cf grounding)* CONST mise en terre *f*, prise de terre *f*, ELEC ENG, RAIL, SPACE mise à la masse *f*, mise à la terre *f*; ~ **bus** *n* (BrE) *(cf grounding bus)* ELEC *connection* barre de terre *f*; ~ **clip** *n* (BrE) *(cf grounding clip)* ELEC *connection* borne de terre *f*; ~ **electrode conductor** *n* (BrE) *(cf grounding electrode conductor)* PROD ENG conducteur de mise à la terre *m*; ~ **electrode system** *n* (BrE) *(cf grounding electrode system)* PROD ENG système de mise à la terre *m*; ~ **paddle** *n* (BrE) *(cf grounding paddle)* RAIL perche de mise à terre *f*; ~ **path** *n* (BrE) *(cf grounding path)* PROD ENG chemin de mise à la terre *m*; ~ **pole** *n* (BrE) *(cf grounding pole)* RAIL perche de mise à terre *f*; ~ **position** *n* (BrE) *(cf grounding position)* ELEC *switch* position de mise à la terre *f*; ~ **reactor** *n* (BrE) *(cf grounding reactor)* ELEC ENG réactance de la prise de terre *f*; ~ **regulation** *n* (BrE) *(cf grounding regulation)* PROD ENG régulation de mise à la terre *f*; ~ **rod** *n* (BrE) *(cf grounding rod)* ELEC *connection* piquet de terre *m*, RAIL perche de mise à terre *f*; ~ **strip** *n* (BrE) *(cf grounding strip)* ELEC ENG bride de terre *f*; ~ **switch** *n* (BrE) *(cf grounding switch)* CONTROL interrupteur de mise à la terre *m*, ELEC commutateur de mise à la terre *m*, sectionneur de terre *m*, ELEC ENG commutateur de mise à la terre *m*

earthmoving *n* CONST terrassement *m*; ~ **machinery** *n* CONST, MECH ENG engins de terrassement *m pl*

Earth-orbiting[1] *adj* SPACE en orbite autour de la Terre

Earth-orbiting:[2] ~ **mission** *n* SPACE mission circumterrestre *f*

earthquake *n* GEOPHYS séisme *m*, tremblement de terre *m*; ~ **focus** *n* GEOPHYS foyer *m*, foyer du séisme *m*, hypocentre *m*; ~ **intensity** *n* GEOPHYS intensité sismique *f*

earthquake-proof: ~ **construction** *n* CONST *building* construction parasismique *f*

earthshine *n* ASTRON, SPACE clair de Terre *m*

Earth-to-orbit: ~ **shuttle** *n* SPACE, TELECOM navette spatiale *f*

earthwork *n* CONST *operation* terrassement *m*, travaux de terrassement *m pl*; ~ **embankment** *n* CONST terrassement en remblai *m*

earthworking: ~ **tools** *n pl* CONST outils de terrassement *m pl*

earthworks: ~ **cubature** *n* CONST *quantities* cubature *f*; ~ **cubing** *n* CONST cubature *f*

ease:[1] ~ **of access** *n* MECH facilité d'accès *f*; ~ **of machining** *n* MECH usinabilité *f*; ~ **of maintenance** *n* MECH maintenabilité *f*; ~ **of operation** *n* MECH facilité d'utilisation *f*, PROP MAT facilité de manipulation *f*

ease:[2] ~ **forward** *vt* AERONAUT *controls* rendre la main

easer *n* MINING trou de dégagement *m*, trou de dégraissage *m*, *blasting* mine de dégraissage *f*; ~ **hole** *n* MINING trou de dégagement *m*, trou de dégraissage *m*

east *adj* NAUT de l'est

easterlies *n pl* METEO vents de l'est *m pl*

easterly *adj* NAUT d'est

easy: ~ **connection** *n* TELECOM connectique facilitée *f*; ~ **fire** *n* C&G flamme molle *f*; ~ **glide** *n* CRYSTALL glissement facile *m*; ~ **glide region** *n* METALL région de glissement facile *f*; ~ **opening tag** *n* PACKAGING languette pour ouverture facile *f*; ~ **payment** *n* TELECOM règlement simplifié *m*; ~ **peel off self-adhesive label** *n*

PACKAGING étiquette autocollante facile à peler *f*

eaves *n pl* CONST larmier *m*, égout *m*; **~ board** *n* CONST chanlate *f*, planche d'égout *f*, volige chanlattée *f*; **~ course** *n* C&G battellement *m*; **~ gutter** *n* CONST gouttière pendante *f*; **~ trough** *n* CONST gouttière pendante *f*

EB *abbr* COMP *(electron beam)*, ELEC *(electron beam)* microscope faisceau électronique *m*, ELECTRON *(electron beam)* faisceau d'électrons *m*, METALL *(electron beam)* faisceau électronique *m*, NUCLEAR *(electron beam)*, PART PHYS *(electron beam)* faisceau d'électrons *m*, TELECOM *(erroneous block)* bloc erroné *m*, TELECOM *(electron beam)*, TV *(electron beam)* faisceau électronique *m*, WAVE PHYS *(electron beam)* faisceau d'électrons *m*

ebb[1] *n* NAUT jusant *m*, OCEANOG déchet de la marée *m*, jusant *m*, reflux *m*; **~ current** *n* FUELLESS marée descendante *f*; **~ generation** *n* FUELLESS génération de reflux *f*; **~ stream** *n* NAUT, OCEANOG courant de jusant *m*; **~ tide** *n* FUELLESS marée descendante *f*, HYDROL jusant *m*, marée descendante *f*, NAUT *navigation tides* marée de jusant *f*, marée descendante *f*, reflux *m*, O-CEANOG descendante *f*, marée descendante *f*

ebb[2] *vi* NAUT *tide* baisse de la marée *f*, descendre, reflux *m*

EBC *abbr (electron beam curing)* PRINT réticulage *m*, séchage de surface par bombardement d'électrons *m*, séchage de surface par faisceau d'électrons *m*

EBCDIC[1] *abbr (extended binary coded decimal interchange code)* COMP, DP, ELECTRON code EBCDIC *m* *(code décimal codé binaire étendu)*

EBCDIC:[2] **~ code** *n* COMP, DP, ELECTRON code EBC-DIC *m*

EBCS[1] *abbr (European barge carrier system)* TRANSP système EBCS *m*

EBCS:[2] **~ lighter** *n* TRANSP barge type EBCS *f*

E-bend *n* ELEC ENG *waveguides* coude en E *m*

ebonite *n* ELEC *insulator* ébonite *f*, P&R *vulcanization* caoutchouc durci *m*, vulcanite *f*, ébonite *f*

EBS *abbr (electron-bombarded semiconductor)* ELEC-TRON triode EBS *f*, triode à cible *f*

ECC *abbr* COMP *(error correcting code)*, DP *(error correcting code)*, ELECTRON *(error correcting code)*, SPACE *(error correcting code) communications* code correcteur d'erreurs *m*, TELECOM *(embedded control channel)* canal de commande intégré *m*, TELECOM *(error correcting code)* code correcteur d'erreurs *m*

eccentric *n* MECH, MECH ENG excentrique *m*, TEXTILES fil ondé *m*; **~ anomaly** *n* ASTRON, SPACE anomalie excentrique *f*; **~ bit** *n* MINING *boring*, PETR TECH *drilling* trépan excentrique *m*; **~ bush** *n* MECH ENG bague excentrique *f*; **~ cam** *n* MECH ENG came désaxée *f*; **~ chisel** *n* MINING trépan excentrique *m*; **~ chuck** *n* MECH ENG *lathe* excentrique *m*, mandrin excentrique *m*; **~ collar** *n* MECH ENG bague d'excentrique *f*, collier d'excentrique *m*; **~ disc** *n* (BrE) MECH ENG bossage de l'excentrique *m*, disque d'excentrique *m*, estomac d'excentrique *m*, poulie excentrique *f*; **~ disk** *n* (AmE) *see eccentric disc* **~ gear** *n* MECH ENG engrenage excentrique *m*, pignon excentrique *m*; **~ hook** *n* MECH ENG bec de cane *m*, pied-de-biche *m*; **~ hoop** *n* MECH ENG bague d'excentrique *f*, collier d'excentrique *m*; **~ loading** *n* CONST chargement excentrique *m*; **~ orbit** *n* ASTRON orbite excentrique *f*; **~ rod** *n* MECH bielle d'excentrique *f*, MECH ENG barre d'excentrique *f*, bielle d'excentrique *f*, tige d'excentrique *f*; **~ shaft** *n*

MECH ENG arbre à excentrique *m*; **~ sheave** *n* MECH ENG bossage de l'excentrique *m*, disque d'excentrique *m*, estomac d'excentrique *m*, poulie excentrique *f*; **~ strap** *n* MECH ENG bague d'excentrique *f*, collier d'excentrique *m*

eccentric-drive: **~ slotting machine** *n* MECH ENG mortaiseuse excentrique *f*

eccentricity *n* ACOUSTICS, ASTRON excentricité *f*, MECH excentricité *f*, faux rond *m*, SPACE excentricité *f*

ECD *abbr* PETR TECH *(equivalent circulating density) drilling* densité équivalente de circulation *f*, TELECOM *(error control device)* dispositif de protection contre les erreurs *m*

ecdysone *n* CHEM ecdysone *f*

ecgonine *n* CHEM ecgonine *f*

echelette: **~ grating** *n* PHYS *optics* réseau en échelette *m*

echelon: **~ grating** *n* PHYS *optics* réseau en échelon *m*; **~ lens** *n* INSTRUMENT lentille Fresnel plane *f*

echinochromes *n pl* CHEM échinochromes *m pl*

echinoderms *n* GEOL échinodermes *m*

echo *n* ACOUSTICS écho simple *m*, COMP, DP écho *m*, ELECTRON signal réfléchi *m*, écho *m*, PHYS, RECORDING, SPACE *communications*, WAVE PHYS écho *m*; **~ cancellation** *n* ELECTRON suppression d'écho *f*; **~ canceller** *n* ELECTRON suppresseur d'écho *m*; **~ chamber** *n* ACOUSTICS chambre sonore *f*, RECORDING chambre d'écho *f*, chambre de réverbération *f*; **~ check** *n* COMP, DP contrôle par écho *m*; **~ detection** *n* OCEANOG détection *f*; **~ distortion** *n* ELECTRON distorsion due à l'écho *f*; **~ image** *n* PRINT image fantôme *f*; **~ integration** *n* OCEANOG échointégration *f*; **~ ranging** *n* OCEANOG détection *f*; **~ signal** *n* ELECTRON signal d'écho *m*; **~ sounder** *n* NAUT *electronic equipment* sondeur par ultrasons *m*, sondeur à écho *m*, échosondeur *m*, OCEA-NOG sondeur multifaisceau *m*, échosondeur *m*, WAVE PHYS échosondage *m*; **~ sounding** *n* NAUT *navigation* sondage par ultrasons *m*, OCEANOG détection *f*, sondage *m*; **~ suppression** *n* ELECTRON suppression d'écho *f*; **~ suppressor** *n* *(ES)* COMP, DP, ELECTRON, SPACE *communications*, TELECOM suppresseur d'écho *m*

echo-cancelling: **~ chip** *n* ELECTRON puce suppresseur d'écho *f*

echograph *n* PHYS échogramme *m*, échographe *m*

echoless: **~ chamber** *n* TELECOM chambre anéchoïque *f*

echolocation *n* ACOUSTICS écholocalisation *f*, OCEANOG détection *f*

echometry *n* GAS TECH échométrie *f*

echoplex *n* COMP, DP échoplex *m*

ECL[1] *abbr (emitter-coupled logic)* COMP, ELECTRON logique ECL *f*, logique à couplage par émetteurs *f*

ECL:[2] **~ gate array** *n* ELECTRON matrice prédiffusée ECL *f*

eclipse *n* ASTRON occultation *f*, éclipse *f*, SPACE éclipse *f*; **~ period** *n* SPACE période d'éclipse *f*; **~ year** *n* ASTRON année dracontique *f*

eclipsing: **~ binaries** *n pl* ASTRON étoiles binaires éclipsantes *f pl*; **~ variable star** *n* ASTRON étoile variable éclipsante *f*

ecliptic *n* ASTRON, SPACE écliptique *m*

eclogite *n* PETR éclogite *f*

ECN *abbr (explicit congestion notification)* TELECOM notification d'encombrement explicite *f*

ecological: **~ damage** *n* MAR POLL, POLLUTION dégradation écologique *f*; **~ disruption** *n* MAR POLL, POLLUTION perturbations écologiques *f pl*; **~ factor** *n* POLLUTION facteur écologique *m*; ~ **pyramid** *n* POLLUTION pyramide alimentaire *f*; ~ **recovery** *n* MAR POLL, POLLUTION assainissement écologique *m*

ecology *n* MAR POLL, POLLUTION écologie *f*; ~ **cullet** *n* C&G, RECYCLING calcin recyclé *m*

economic: ~ **order quantity** *n* PROD ENG lot économique *m*, quantité économique *f*; ~ **project** *n* PETR TECH *commerce, prospecting* projet économique *m*; ~ **quality** *n* QUALITY qualité économique *f*; ~ **risk** *n* QUALITY risque économique *m*

economical: ~ **speed** *n* NAUT vitesse économique *f*

economized: ~ **DC magnet** *n* PROD ENG aimant CC à faible consommation *m*

economizer *n* HEATING, HYDR EQUIP *for boiler feed water* économiseur *m*; ~ **jet** *n* VEHICLES *carburettor* gicleur d'économie *m*

economy: ~ **size pack** *n* PACKAGING emballage économique *m*; ~ **of space** *n* PACKAGING utilisation de l'emplacement *f*

ecosphere *n* ASTRON écosphère *f*

ecosystem *n* POLLUTION écosystème *m*

EDAX *abbr (energy dispersive analysis by X-rays)* CHEM système de microanalyse par dispersion en énergie *m*

eddy[1] *n* FLUID PHYS, HYDROL tourbillon *m*, NAUT, OCEANOG, PHYS remous *m*, tourbillon *m*; ~ **brake** *n* (BrE) ELEC ENG frein à courant de foucault *m*, TV frein magnétique *m*; ~ **current** *n* ELEC, ELEC ENG courant de Foucault *m*, PHYS courant de Foucault *m*, courant parasite *m*, TESTING, TV courant de Foucault *m*; ~ **current brake** *n* ELEC ENG, MECH, RAIL *vehicles* frein à courant de Foucault *m*, TV frein magnétique *m*; ~ **current braking** *n* ELEC *motor*, ELEC ENG freinage à courant de Foucault *m*; ~ **current circuit** *n* ELEC circuit à courant de Foucault *m*; ~ **current flow meter** *n* NUCLEAR débitmètre à courant de Foucault *m*; ~ **current inspection** *n* ELEC ENG contrôle par courant de Foucault *m*, RAIL auscultation par courant de Foucault *f*; ~ **current loss** *n* PHYS, TV perte par courant de Foucault *f*; ~ **diffusion** *n* NUCLEAR *vorticity* diffusion turbulente *f*; ~ **flow** *n* COAL TECH, REFRIG écoulement turbulent *m*; ~ **rail brake** *n* TRANSP *current* frein linéaire à courant de Foucault *m*; ~ **wind** *n* METEO, NAUT revolin *m*, OCEANOG revolin *m*, rivolin *m*

eddy[2] *vi* NAUT tourbillonner

eddying: ~ **current** *n* OCEANOG courant de retour *m*

edenite *n* MINERAL édénite *f*

edestin *n* CHEM édestine *f*

edge[1] *n* CRYSTALL arête *f*, DP *of card* bord *m*, GEOM *of cube* arête *f*, INSTRUMENT pointeur *m*, MECH *welding* arête *f*, chanfrein *m*, tranchant *m*, MECH ENG *of blade* coupant *m*, fil *m*, tranchant *m*, *of slide valve, cylinder port* arête *f*,bord *m*, rebord *m*, PACKAGING bord *m*, PHYS arête *f*, bord *m*, TEXTILES lisière *f*; ~ **as cut** *n* C&G bord brut de coupe *m*; ~ **bowl** *n* C&G coupelle *f*; ~ **box member** *n* AERONAUT caisson de bordure *m*; ~ **coals** *n pl* COAL TECH dressants de houille *m pl*; ~ **coding** *n* CINEMAT numéro de bord *m*; ~ **connector** *n* ELEC ENG connecteur de carte enfichable *m*; ~ **control assembly** *n* NUCLEAR assemblage combustible périphérique *m*; ~ **control element** *n* NUCLEAR élément de commande périphérique *m*; ~ **correction** *n* TV correction de contour *f*; ~ **corrosion** *n* TESTING corrosion de bord *f*; ~ **crack** *n* C&G amorce *f*; ~ **creep** *n* C&G altération de bord *f*; ~ **cushion** *n* PACKAGING amortissement sur le bord *m*; ~ **cutter** *n* PAPER TECH bordeuse *f*, coupe-bordure *m*, coupe-feuilles hydraulique *m*, jet de bordure

m; ~ **damping** *n* RECORDING amortissement périphérique *m*; ~ **dislocation** *n* CRYSTALL dislocation coin *f*, METALL dislocation du bord *f*; ~ **distance** *n* MECH ENG cote de trusquinage *f*; ~ **doctor** *n* PRINT racle latérale *f*; ~ **effect** *n* ELEC ENG effet de bord *m*, PHYS effet d'arête *m*; ~ **enhancement** *n* TV accentuation des contours *f*; ~ **fine grinding** *n* C&G doucissage d'un joint *m*; ~ **flaking** *n* C&G détachement de bord *m*; ~ **flare** *n* CINEMAT voile latéral *m*, voile marginal *m*; ~ **fogging** *n* CINEMAT voile latéral *m*, voile marginal *m*; ~ **fracture** *n* C&G lèvre de fracture *f*; ~ **fusion** *n* C&G rebrûlage *m*; ~ **guide** *n* C&G guide de bord *m*, CINEMAT presseur latéral *m*; ~ **gumming machine** *n* PACKAGING machine à coller les bords *f*; ~ **holder** *n* C&G pince de bord *f*; ~ **latching** *n* ELECTRON verrouillage sur front *m*; ~ **lighting** *n* ELEC ENG éclairage par la tranche *m*; ~ **melting** *n* C&G rebrûlage *m*; ~ **mill** *n* P&R broyeur à meules *m*, mélangeur à meules *m*, PROD ENG broyeur à meules verticales *m*; ~ **notch** *n* CINEMAT encoche *f*, encoche latérale *f*; ~ **number** *n* CINEMAT numéro de bord *m*; ~ **numbering** *n* CINEMAT piétage *m*; ~ **numbering machine** *n* CINEMAT machine à piéter *f*; ~ **peeling** *n* C&G détachement de bord *m*; ~ **plate** *n* CONST *of lock* rebord *m*, têtière *f*; ~ **preparation** *n* MECH *welding* préparation de chanfreins *f*; ~ **protection** *n* PACKAGING protection des bords *f*; ~ **range limit** *n* PROD ENG tolérance sur le bord *f*; ~ **rate** *n* ELECTRON vitesse de montée *f*; ~ **rolls** *n pl* C&G molettes *f pl*; ~ **runner** *n* PAPER TECH meuleton *m*, PROD ENG meule verticale *f*; ~ **runner mill** *n* C&G broyeur à meules verticales *m*; ~ **seam** *n* COAL TECH dressant *m*; ~ **of the sheet** *n* C&G bord de feuille *m*; ~ **shelling** *n* C&G détachement de bord *m*; ~ **socket connector** *n* ELEC ENG connecteur encartable *m*; ~ **spray** *n* PAPER TECH coupe-feuilles hydraulique *m*; ~ **squirt** *n* PAPER TECH coupe-feuilles hydraulique *m*; ~ **steepness** *n* ELECTRON raideur du front *f*; ~ **stripe** *n* CINEMAT piste latérale *f*; ~ **tool making** *n* PROD ENG taillanderie *f*; ~ **tools** *n pl* PROD ENG outils coupants *m pl*, outils tranchants *m pl*, taillanderie *f*; ~ **track** *n* CINEMAT piste latérale *f*; ~ **of track banding** *n* TV effet de bande de bord de piste *m*; ~ **trim** *n* TEXTILES débordure *f*; ~ **trimmer** *n* MECH ENG *tool* coupe-bordure *m*; ~ **water** *n* PETR eau de bordure *f*; ~ **wheel** *n* PROD ENG meule verticale *f*; ~ **wheel grinding machine** *n* PROD ENG machine à meule travaillant sur périphérie *f*; ~ **winding** *n* ELEC *on machine* enroulement en barres posées sur chant *m*

edge:[2] ~ **with a groove** *vt* C&G rainer

edge-emitting: ~ **light-emitting diode** *n* (*ELED*) OPT diode électroluminescente à émission longitudinale *f*, TELECOM diode électroluminescente à émission par la tranche *f*

edger: ~ **block** *n* (AmE) (*cf jamb block*) C&G brique de main *f*

edgestone *n* PROD ENG meule verticale *f*

edge-to-edge *adj* MECH ENG bord à bord

edge-triggered: ~ **flip-flop** *n* ELECTRON bascule déclenchée par front *f*

edgewise: ~ **bend** *n* ELEC ENG coude en H *m*; ~ **growth** *n* METALL allongement du bord *m*

edging *n* C&G débordage *m*, MECH ENG passe-poil *m*, profilé de bordure *m*; ~ **iron** *n* CONST *gardening* coupe-gazon *m*; ~ **machine** *n* INSTRUMENT appareil de façonnage *m*; ~ **panel** *n* AERONAUT panneau de bordure *m*; ~ **paper** *n* PAPER TECH papier à border *m*

EDI[1] *abbr* TELECOM (*electronic document interchange*), *(electronic data interchange)* EDI *(échange de données informatisées)*

EDI:[2] ~ **access unit** *n (EDI-AU)* TELECOM unité d'accès EDI *f*; ~ **forwarding** *n* TELECOM retransmission EDI *f*; ~ **message** *n (EDIM)* TELECOM message EDI *m*; ~ **message store** *n (EDI-MS)* TELECOM mémoire de messages EDI *f*; ~ **messaging** *n (EDIMG)* TELECOM messagerie EDI *f*; ~ **messaging environment** *n (EDIME)* TELECOM environnement de messagerie EDI *m*; ~ **messaging system** *n (EDIMS)* TELECOM système de messagerie EDI *m*; ~ **messaging user** *n* TELECOM utilisateur de la messagerie EDI *m*; ~ **notification** *n (EDIN)* TELECOM notification EDI *f*; ~ **user** *n* TELECOM utilisateur EDI *m*; ~ **user agent** *n (EDI-UA)* TELECOM agent d'usager EDI *m*, agent d'utilisateur EDI *m*

EDI-AU *abbr (EDI access unit)* TELECOM unité d'accès EDI *f*

edible: ~ **acid** *n* FOOD TECH acide comestible *m*

EDIM[1] *abbr (EDI message)* TELECOM message EDI *m*

EDIM:[2] ~ **responsibility** *n* TELECOM responsabilité EDIM *f*

EDIME *abbr (EDI messaging environment)* TELECOM environnement de messagerie EDI *m*

EDIMG[1] *abbr (EDI messaging)* TELECOM messagerie EDI *f*

EDIMG:[2] ~ **user** *n* TELECOM utilisateur de la messagerie EDI *m*

EDI-MS *abbr (EDI message store)* TELECOM mémoire de messages EDI *f*

EDIMS *abbr (EDI messaging system)* TELECOM système de messagerie EDI *m*

EDIN *abbr (EDI notification)* TELECOM notification EDI *f*

edingtonite *n* MINERAL édingtonite *f*

Edison: ~ **cell** *n* ELEC accumulateur fer-nickel *m*

edit[1] *n* COMP, DP édition *f*; ~ **master** *n* CINEMAT copie de montage *f*; ~ **mode** *n* TV mode de montage électronique *m*, mode édition *m*; ~ **pulse** *n* TV impulsion de montage *f*; ~ **sync** *n* TV synchronisme de montage *m*

edit[2] *vt* CINEMAT monter, COMP, DP mettre en forme, éditer, TV monter

edited: ~ **print** *n* CINEMAT copie montée *f*

edit-in *n* TV point d'entrée *m*

editing *n* CINEMAT montage *m*, COMP, DP mise en forme *f*, édition *f*, PRINT mise en forme *f*, montage en page *m*, montage sur film *m*, montage sur écran *m*, RECORDING, TV montage *m*; ~ **block** *n* RECORDING réglette de montage *f*; ~ **machine** *n* CINEMAT table de montage *f*; ~ **on original** *n* TV montage sur original *m*; ~ **rack** *n* CINEMAT chutier *m*; ~ **room** *n* CINEMAT salle de montage *f*; ~ **shot list** *n* CINEMAT découpage définitif *m*

editor *n* CINEMAT monteur *m*, COMP, DP éditeur *m*, TV monteur *m*

editorial: ~ **newsroom** *n* TV salle de rédaction du journal *f*

edit-out *n* TV point de sortie *m*

EDI-UA *abbr (EDI user agent)* TELECOM agent d'usager EDI *m*, agent d'utilisateur EDI *m*

EDM *abbr (electrodischarge machining)* MECH ENG usinage par électro-érosion *m*, PROD ENG électro-érosion *f*

EDP *abbr (electronic data processing)* COMP informatique *f*, traitement électronique de données *m*, DP, ELECTRON informatique *f*

EDTA *abbr (ethylenediamino tetra-acetic acid)* DETER-

GENTS acide éthylène-diamino-tétracétique *m*

EDTV *abbr (extended definition television)* TV télévision à définition améliorée *f*

eduction *n* HEATING *of steam* éduction *f*; ~ **port** *n* HYDR EQUIP *on steam cylinder* orifice d'échappement *m*; ~ **valve** *n* HYDR EQUIP clapet d'échappement *m*, soupape *f*

eductor *n* MECH ENG conduite d'aspiration *f*, conduite de succion *f*

E-E *abbr* TV *(electronic-to-electronic)* direct modulateur-démodulateur, vidéo-sur-vidéo, TV *(electronic editing)* montage électronique *m*

eelworm *n* FOOD TECH anguillule *f*

EEROM *abbr (electrically-erasable ROM)* COMP, DP ROM effaçable électriquement *f*, mémoire morte effaçable électriquement *f*

EFA *abbr (essential fatty acid)* FOOD TECH acide gras essentiel *m*

effect *n* FLUID PHYS effet *m*, MECH action *f*, effet *m*, résultat *m*, TELECOM effet *m*; ~ **filter** *n* CINEMAT filtre à effet *m*; ~ **lighting** *n* CINEMAT éclairage à effet *m*

effective[1] *adj* ACOUSTICS effectif, MECH effectif, efficace, utile

effective:[2] ~ **acoustic center** *n* (AmE), ~ **acoustic centre** *n* (BrE) RECORDING centre acoustique effectif *m*; ~ **address** *n* DP adresse effective *f*; ~ **aperture** *n* CINEMAT ouverture utile *f*, PHOTO diamètre utile du diaphragme *m*; ~ **aperture of a lens** *n* PHOTO ouverture utile d'un objectif *f*; ~ **area** *n* SPACE *communications* surface équivalente *f*; ~ **bandwidth** *n* RECORDING largeur de bande effective *f*; ~ **candle power** *n* PHOTO luminosité réelle *f*; ~ **center of acoustic source** *n* (AmE), ~ **centre of acoustic source** *n* (BrE) ACOUSTICS centre acoustique d'une source *m*; ~ **coil diameter** *n* TESTING diamètre de bobine effectif *m*; ~ **cross-sectional area** *n* MECH section effective *f*, section utile *f*; ~ **current** *n* ELEC ENG intensité efficace *f*; ~ **data transfer rate** *n* COMP cadence utile de transfert de données *f*, DP vitesse réelle de transfert de données *f*; ~ **drop height** *n* COAL TECH hauteur effective de chute *f*; ~ **electromotive force** *n* ELEC force électromotrice effective *f*, force électromotrice efficace *f*; ~ **evaporation** *n* WATER SUPP évaporation efficace *f*; ~ **freezing time** *n* REFRIG temps effectif de congélation *m*; ~ **gap length** *n* ACOUSTICS longueur efficace d'entrefer *f*, RECORDING entrefer effectif *m*, TV longueur efficace d'entrefer *f*; ~ **grain size** *n* COAL TECH taille effective de grain *f*; ~ **head** *n* FUELLESS chute d'eau utile *f*, HYDR EQUIP mesure d'une grandeur dépassant sa valeur de référence *f*; ~ **heating surface** *n* THERMOD *boilers* surface chauffante *f*; ~ **horsepower** *n* MECH ENG cheval effectif *m*, puissance au frein en chevaux *f*, puissance effective en chevaux *f*; ~ **horsepower hour** *n* MECH ENG cheval heure effectif *m*; ~ **image field** *n* PHOTO champ utile *m*; ~ **latent heat of fusion** *n* THERMOD chaleur de fusion *f*; ~ **load** *n* PACKAGING charge efficace *f*; ~ **mass** *n* ACOUSTICS masse efficace *f*; ~ **mode volume** *n* OPT, TELECOM volume optique des modes *m*; ~ **particle density** *n* NUCLEAR masse volumique effective *f*; ~ **permeability** *n* PETR perméabilité relative *f*, perméabilité réelle *f*; ~ **picture signal** *n* TV signal d'image effectif *m*; ~ **pile length** *n* COAL TECH longueur utile de pieu *f*; ~ **pitch** *n* AERONAUT *propeller* avance par tour *f*, pas effectif *m*; ~ **porosity** *n* PETR porosité effective *f*; ~ **power** *n* ELEC puissance effective *f*, MECH ENG puissance au frein *f*, puissance effective *f*, puissance utile *f*; ~ **precipitation**

n METEO pluie effective *f*, pluie efficace *f*, précipitation efficace *f*; ~ **radiated power** *n (ERP)* TELECOM puissance apparente rayonnée *f*; ~ **range** *n* MILIT *of firearm* portée utile *f*; ~ **resistance** *n* ELEC ENG, PHYS résistance effective *f*, TESTING résistance utile *f*; ~ **slit width** *n* TV largeur de fente optimum *f*; ~ **sound pressure** *n* ACOUSTICS pression acoustique efficace *f*, POLLUTION pression acoustique effective *f*; ~ **steam pressure** *n* HYDR EQUIP pression effective de la vapeur *f*, NUCLEAR *above atmosphere* pression effective de la vapeur *f*, surpression de vapeur *f*; ~ **stress** *n* COAL TECH tension efficace *f*, PETR TECH *geology* contrainte effective *f*; ~ **temperature** *n* THERMOD température effective *f*; ~ **temperature range** *n* THERMOD domaine de température effective *m*; ~ **tension** *n* MECH ENG tension effective *f*; ~ **traffic** *n* TELECOM trafic efficace *m*; ~ **value** *n* ELEC ENG valeur effective *f*; ~ **voltage** *n* ELEC ENG tension efficace *f*

effectiveness *n* MAR POLL efficacité *f*

effectivity: ~ **terms** *n pl* PROD ENG conditions de validité *f pl*

effects *n pl* CINEMAT bruitages *m pl*, effets spéciaux *m pl*, trucages *m pl*, TV bruitages *m pl*, TV effets spéciaux *m pl*, trucages *m pl*; ~ **bank** *n* TV banc de trucages *m*, unité de commutation pour effets spéciaux *f*; ~ **box** *n* CINEMAT porte-caches *m*; ~ **bus** *n* TV voie de trucages *f*; ~ **of earthquakes** *n pl* GEOPHYS effet du séisme *m*, macrosismologie *f*; ~ **generator** *n* TV générateur d'effets *m*, générateur de trucages *m*; ~ **loudspeaker** *n* RECORDING haut-parleur d'effets spéciaux *m*

effervescence *n* CHEM effervescence *f*

effervescent *adj* FOOD TECH *of drinks* effervescent, gazeux, pétillant

efficiency *n* ELEC *equipment* rendement *m*, MECH efficacité *f*, rendement *m*, MECH ENG, NUCLEAR rendement *m*, PHYS *heat engines, machines* rendement *m*, *light* efficacité *f*, PROD ENG, RECORDING *of amplifier* rendement *m*, SPACE *communications* efficacité *f*, rendement *m*; ~ **diode** *n* ELECTRON diode d'efficacité *f*; ~ **survey** *n* CONTROL contrôle de rendement *m*

efficient[1] *adj* MECH, PHYS efficace

efficient:[2] ~ **packaging** *n* PACKAGING emballage efficace *m*

effloresce *vi* CHEM effleurir, tomber en efflorescence

efflorescence *n* CHEM efflorescence *f*

efflorescent *adj* CHEM efflorescent

effluent *n* HYDROL émissaire *m*, HYDROL *rivers* eau usée *f*, effluent *m*, NUCLEAR effluent *m*, rejet *m*, PETR TECH *refinery* effluent *m*; ~ **channel** *n* WATER SUPP émissaire d'effluent *m*; ~ **discharge** *n* RECYCLING décharge d'effluent *f*; ~ **monitor** *n* RECYCLING système de contrôle de la radioactivité d'effluent *m*; ~ **purification process** *n* RECYCLING procédé d'épuration d'effluent *m*; ~ **standard** *n* RECYCLING norme de rejet d'effluent *f*; ~ **treatment plant** *n* WATER SUPP installation de traitement des eaux usées *f*; ~ **weir** *n* NUCLEAR *separating waste* déversoir de superficie *m*

effluvium *n* CHEM effluve *m*

efflux *n* WATER SUPP dépense *f*, effluence *f*

effort: ~ **current** *n* ELEC ENG courant watté *m*

effusion *n* NUCLEAR *of gases through holes larger than those applicable to diffusion*, PHYS effusion *f*; ~ **oven** *n* ELECTRON four à effusion *m*

E-field *n (electric field)* PHYS excitation électrique *f*

EFT *abbr (electronic funds transfer)* TELECOM transfert électronique de fonds *m*

EFTPOS *abbr (electronic funds transfer at point of sale)* TELECOM transfert électronique de fonds au point de vente *m*

EFTS *abbr (electronic funds transfer system)* COMP système de télépaiement *m*, virement électronique *m*

EGA *abbr (enhanced graphics adaptor)* COMP *card* EGA *(adapteur graphique couleur)*

egg: ~ **calipers** *n pl* (AmE), ~ **callipers** *n pl* (BrE) MECH ENG compas dit 1/2 8 de chiffre *m*; ~ **yolk index** *n* FOOD TECH index vitellinique *m*, indice de coloration *m*, indice de jaune d'oeuf *m*

egg-shaped[1] *adj* GEOM ovale

egg-shaped:[2] ~ **thimble** *n* PROD ENG *for rope* cosse ovale *f*

eggshell: ~ **finish** *n* COLOURS finition coquille d'oeuf *f*

Ehrenfest's: ~ **equations** *n pl* PHYS relations d'Ehrenfest *f pl*

EHT[1] *abbr (extra high tension)* ELECTRON, TV THT *(très haute tension)*

EHT:[2] ~ **rectifier** *n* TV redresseur THT *m*; ~ **supply** *n* TV alimentation THT *f*

eicosane *n* CHEM eicosane *m*

eicosyl: ~ **alcohol** *n* CHEM alcool eicosylique *m*

eiderdown *n* TEXTILES édredon *m*

eigenfrequency *n* RAD PHYS *of system*, SPACE *spacecraft* fréquence propre *f*

eigenfunction *n* PHYS fonction propre *f*

eigenshadow *n* SPACE *spacecraft* ombre propre *f*

eigenvalue *n* COMP, ELECTRON, PHYS valeur propre *f*

eigenvector *n* COMP, ELECTRON, PHYS vecteur propre *m*

eight-ball: ~ **mike** *n* RECORDING petit micro en forme de bille *m*

eight-bit: ~ **accuracy** *n* ELECTRON précision de huit bits *f*; ~ **byte** *n* ELECTRON octet *m*; ~ **conversion** *n* ELECTRON numérisation sur huit bits *f*; ~ **converter** *n* ELECTRON numériseur à huit bits *m*; ~ **output** *n* ELECTRON sortie sur huit bits *f*

eight-channel: ~ **recorder** *n* INSTRUMENT enregistreur à huit canaux *m*

eighth-order: ~ **Chebyshev filter** *n* ELECTRON filtre de Chebychev du huitième ordre *m*

eight-level: ~ **code** *n* ELECTRON code à huit moments *m*

eight-phase: ~ **shift keying** *n* ELECTRON modulation de phase à huit états *f*

eight-ply: ~ **belting** *n* PROD ENG courroies en huit épaisseurs *f pl*, courroies à huit plis *f pl*

eight-point: ~ **recorder** *n* INSTRUMENT enregistreur à huit courbes *m*

eight-sided: ~ **reamer** *n* MECH ENG équarrissoir à huit pans *m*

eight-station: ~ **machine** *n* SPRINGS machine à huit postes *f*

eight-track: ~ **recorder** *n* RECORDING magnétophone huit pistes *m*

eighty-column: ~ **card** *n* DP carte 80 colonnes *f*

Einstein: ~ **coefficient** *n* RAD PHYS coefficient d'Einstein *m*; ~ **displacement** *n* ASTRON déplacement relativiste vers le rouge *m*; ~ **photoelectric equation** *n* ELEC ENG équation photo-électrique d'Einstein *f*; ~ **temperature** *n* PHYS température d'Einstein *f*

Einstein-de-Haas: ~ **effect** *n* PHYS effet Einstein-de-Haas *m*

einsteinium *n (Es)* CHEM einsteinium *m (Es)*

Einthoven: ~ **galvanometer** *n* ELEC galvanomètre Einthoven *m*

Einzel: ~ **lens** *n* NUCLEAR lentille unipotentielle *f*

EIRP *abbr* *(equivalent isotropically-radiated power)* SPACE *communications* PIRE *(puissance isotrope rayonnée équivalente)*

EIT *abbr* *(encoded information type)* TELECOM type d'informations codées *m*, type de codage *m*

ejecta *n pl* GEOL projections volcaniques *f pl*, éjecta *m pl*

ejectable: ~ **capsule** *n* SPACE *spacecraft* capsule éjectable *f*, module éjectable *m*; ~ **nose cone** *n* SPACE *spacecraft* coiffe éjectable *f*

ejectamenta *n pl* GEOL projections volcaniques *f pl*

ejected: ~ **beam** *n* NUCLEAR *from reactor, accelerator* faisceau d'éjection *m*, faisceau sorti *m*

ejection *n* MECH expulsion *f*, éjection *f*; ~ **force** *n* SPACE *of spacecraft* force d'éjection *f*; ~ **guide bush** *n* MECH ENG *diecasting* bague de guidage *f*; ~ **guide pillar** *n* MECH ENG *diecasting* colonne de guidage *f*; ~ **pin** *n* MECH ENG *diecasting* éjecteur cylindrique *m*; ~ **seat** *n* AERONAUT siège éjectable *m*

ejector *n* MECH, MECH ENG éjecteur *m*, P&R *press* système d'éjection *m*, éjecteur *m*; ~ **condenser** *n* HYDR EQUIP condenseur éjecteur *m*, condenseur à trompe *m*, condenseur à éjection *m*; ~ **cycle refrigeration system** *n* REFRIG système frigorifique à éjection *m*; ~ **pin** *n* MECH ENG tige d'éjection *f*, MECH ENG *die set* extracteur *m*; ~ **plate** *n* MECH ENG *injection mould*, P&R *plastics* plaque d'éjection *f*; ~ **pump** *n* MECH ENG pompe à éjecteur *f*; ~ **retaining plate** *n* MECH ENG *diecasting* contre-plaque d'éjection *f*; ~ **seat** *n* AERONAUT siège éjectable *m*; ~ **sleeve** *n* MECH ENG éjecteur tubulaire *m*; ~ **stop piece** *n* MECH ENG doigt butée *m*; ~ **valve** *n* MECH ENG soupape d'éjection *f*

ejector-type: ~ **trim exhaust system** *n* PACKAGING système avec ventilation pour couper et éjecter les déchets *m*

ekebergite *n* MINERAL ékebergite *f*

Ekman: ~ **flow** *n* HYDROL, OCEANOG écoulement d'Ekman *m*; ~ **forcing** *n* OCEANOG succion d'Ekman *f*; ~ **layer** *n* HYDROL, OCEANOG couche Ekman *f*; ~ **spiral** *n* OCEANOG spirale d'Ekman *f*

EL *abbr* *(elevated line)* TRANSP métro aérien *m*

elaeolite *n* MINERAL élaeolite *f*, éléolite *f*

elaeostearic *adj* CHEM élaeostéarique

elaidic *adj* CHEM élaïdique

elaidin *n* CHEM élaïdine *f*

elapsed: ~ **time** *n* COMP, DP temps écoulé *m*, MECH laps de temps écoulé *m*; ~ **time counter** *n* MECH totalisateur d'heures de marche *m*

elasmose *n* MINERAL élasmose *f*

elasmosine *n* MINERAL élasmose *f*

elastic[1] *adj* MECH *materials*, P&R élastique

elastic:[2] ~ **aftereffects** *n pl* FLUID PHYS *turbulence* répercussions élastiques *f pl*; ~ **bitumen** *n* MINERAL élatérite *f*; ~ **collision** *n* NUCLEAR collision élastique *f*, PHYS choc élastique *m*; ~ **constant** *n* FLUID PHYS, METALL constante élastique *f*; ~ **deformation** *n* PACKAGING, PROP MAT déformation élastique *f*; ~ **elongation** *n* PACKAGING allongement élastique *m*; ~ **impact** *n* NUCLEAR collision élastique *f*; ~ **impedance** *n* PETR impédance acoustique *f*; ~ **instability** *n* AERONAUT tendance au flambage *f*; ~ **limit** *n* CONST limite d'élasticité *f*, limite élastique *f*, MECH *materials* limite élastique *f*, P&R limite d'élasticité *f*, limite élastique *f*, PACKAGING limite d'élasticité *f*, PHYS limite d'élasticité *f*, limite élastique *f*, PROP MAT limite d'élasticité *f*, SPRINGS limite élastique *f*; ~ **mode** *n* SPACE *spacecraft* mode élastique *m*; ~ **modulus** *n* PROP MAT module

d'élasticité *m*; ~ **nut** *n* PROD ENG écrou fendu *m*; ~ **properties** *n pl* FLUID PHYS propriétés élastiques *f pl*; ~ **range** *n* MECH *materials* domaine élastique *m*; ~ **scattering** *n* PART PHYS, PHYS, RAD PHYS diffusion élastique *f*; ~ **stop nut** *n* MECH ENG écrou autofreiné *m*, écrou indesserrable *m*, écrou élastique *m*; ~ **stretch** *n* PACKAGING allongement élastique *m*; ~ **wave** *n* ELEC ENG, PHYS onde élastique *f*; ~ **wheel** *n* TRANSP roue élastique *f*

elasticity *n* MECH *materials*, METALL élasticité *f*, NAUT *wood, metal* flexibilité *f*, élasticité *f*, P&R, PHYS, PROP MAT élasticité *f*

elastomer *n* CHEM, P&R, PETR TECH, REFRIG élastomère *m*; ~ **membrane tank** *n* SPACE *spacecraft* réservoir à membrane élastomère *m*; ~ **seal** *n* PROD ENG joint d'étanchéité en élastomère *m*

elastoplastic[1] *adj* PROP MAT élastoplastique

elastoplastic:[2] ~ **analysis** *n* PROP MAT analyse élastoplastique *f*

elaterite *n* MINERAL élatérite *f*

elbow *n* LAB EQUIP *glassware*, MECH, NUCLEAR *of manipulator* coude *m*; ~ **height handrail** *n* CONST rampe d'escalier *f*; ~ **joint** *n* MECH ENG genou *m*, joint articulé *m*; ~ **pads** *n pl* SAFETY coussinets pour coudes *m pl*, coussinets à coude *m pl*; ~ **tongs** *n pl* PROD ENG badine *f*, tenaille à bec recourbé *f*, tenaille à cornières *f*; ~ **union** *n* CONST raccord coudé *m*, raccord en équerre *m*

elbow-high *adj* CONST à hauteur d'appui

Elcometer: ~ **thickness gage** *n* (AmE), ~ **thickness gauge** *n* (BrE) P&R *instrument* jauge d'épaisseur Elcometer *f*

elderflower *n* FOOD TECH sureau *m*

elected: ~ **office** *n* PATENTS office élu *m*

electret *n* PHYS électrète *m*; ~ **foil microphone** *n* ACOUSTICS microphone à électret *m*, RECORDING microphone électrostatique *m*

electric[1] *adj* ELEC, ELECTRON électrique

electric:[2] ~ **actuator** *n* SPACE *spacecraft* actionneur électrique *m*; ~ **arc** *n* ELEC *lighting*, ELEC ENG, GAS TECH, PHYS arc électrique *m*; ~ **arc cutting** *n* THERMOD coupage à l'arc électrique *m*; ~ **arc furnace** *n* COAL TECH, ELEC *heating* four à arc électrique *m*, MECH ENG four à arc de fusion d'acier *m*, THERMOD four à arc *m*; ~ **arc heater** *n* MECH ENG réchauffeur à arc *m*; ~ **arc welding** *n* PROD ENG, THERMOD soudage à l'arc électrique *m*; ~ **bell** *n* ELEC sonnette électrique *f*; ~ **blanket** *n* HEAT ENG couverture électrique *f*; ~ **blanket heating** *n* HEAT ENG chauffage par jaquette électrique *m*; ~ **blasting** *n* MINING mise à feu électrique *f*, tir électrique *m*; ~ **blasting cap** *n* MINING amorce électrique *f*; ~ **blasting machine** *n* MINING exploseur électrique *m*; ~ **braking** *n* ELEC *motor, generator* freinage électrique *m*; ~ **bus** *n* TRANSP autobus électrique *m*; ~ **cable joint** *n* RAIL point de coupure du câble électrique *m*; ~ **calamine** *n* MINERAL calamine *f*, hémimorphite *f*; ~ **cell** *n* ELEC ENG pile électrique *f*; ~ **circuit** *n* ELEC circuit électrique *m*; ~ **coil** *n* ELEC ENG bobine électrique *f*; ~ **conduction** *n* ELEC ENG conduction électrique *f*; ~ **conduit** *n* ELEC ENG tube protecteur électrique *m*; ~ **constant** *n* ELEC ENG constante électrique *f*, *permittivity* permittivité *f*, permittivité du vide *f*, PHYS constante électrique *f*; ~ **control** *n* ELEC ENG commande électrique *f*; ~ **convector** *n* THERMOD convecteur électrique *m*; ~ **current** *n* ELEC, ELEC ENG, PHYS, TELECOM courant électrique *m*;

~ **current carrier** n RAD PHYS porteur d'électricité m, porteur de charge m; ~ **defrosting** n REFRIG dégivrage électrique m; ~ **delay detonator cap** n MINING détonateur électrique à retardement m; ~ **delay line** n ELECTRON ligne à retard électrique f; ~ **delivery lorry** n (BrE) (cf electric delivery truck) TRANSPORT camionnette électrique f; ~ **delivery truck** n (AmE) (cf electric delivery lorry) TRANSP camionnette électrique f; ~ **detonator** n MINING amorce électrique f, détonateur électrique m; ~ **dipole** n ELEC ENG dipôle électrique m, doublet électrique m, PHYS dipôle électrique m; ~ **dipole moment** n ELEC ENG moment de dipôle électrique m, moment électrique dipolaire m, PHYS moment électrique dipolaire m; ~ **discharge** n ELEC ENG décharge électrique f; ~ **discharge laser** n ELECTRON laser à décharge électrique m; ~ **displacement** n ELEC ENG déplacement électrique m, PHYS *D-field* déplacement électrique m, induction électrique f; ~ **drill** n ELEC, MECH perceuse électrique f; ~ **drive** n PHOTO entraînement électrique m; ~ **dryer** n ELEC, HEATING séchoir électrique m; ~ **efficiency** n ELEC ENG rendement électrique m; ~ **energy** n ELEC, PHYS énergie électrique f; ~ **eye** n ELEC ENG cellule photoélectrique f; ~ **fan** n SAFETY ventilateur électrique m; ~ **field** n ELEC, ELEC ENG champ électrique m, PHYS champ électrique m, excitation électrique f, RECORDING, TELECOM, TV champ électrique m; ~ **field gradient** n ELEC ENG gradient de champ électrique m; ~ **field strength** n ELEC ENG, PHYS intensité du champ électrique f; ~ **filter** n ELECTRON filtre électrique m; ~ **fire** n ELEC *heating* radiateur électrique m; ~ **firing** n MINING allumage électrique m, tir électrique, tir électrique des coups de mine m, mise à feu électrique f; ~ **flux** n ELEC ENG flux de déplacement électrique m, PHYS flux électrique m; ~ **force** n ELEC ENG force électrique f; ~ **fuel pump** n VEHICLES pompe à essence à commande électromagnétique f; ~ **furnace** n COAL TECH, ELEC four électrique m; ~ **generator** n ELEC ENG génératrice électrique m, NUCLEAR génératrice f, TV générateur m; ~ **heater** n ELEC *heating* radiateur électrique m, MECH ENG réchauffeur à arc m, *for water* chaudière électrique f; ~ **heating** n ELEC, HEAT ENG chauffage électrique m; ~ **heating pad** n THERMOD coussin électrique m; ~ **hoist** n MECH *lifting gear* palan électrique m; ~ **hot plate** n THERMOD réchaud électrique f; ~ **hysteresis** n RECORDING hystérésis électrique f; ~ **image** n ELEC ENG image électrique f; ~ **induction check** n CONTROL contrôle par induction électrique m; ~ **induction furnace** n ELEC ENG four électrique à induction m; ~ **interlock** n PROD ENG bloc d'interverrouillage électrique m; ~ **interlocking system** n ELEC *safety* asservissement électrique m; ~ **lighter** n ELEC *gas appliance* allumeur électrique m; ~ **lighting** n ELEC éclairage électrique m; ~ **linkage** n (AmE) (cf electric transmission) ELEC *supply network* transmission électrique f; ~ **locomotive** n RAIL locomotive électrique f; ~ **log** n PETR TECH *drilling, prospecting* diagraphie électrique f; ~ **loss** n ELEC *equipment* perte électrique f; ~ **machine** n ELEC ENG machine électrique f; ~ **magnet** n TELECOM électro-aimant m; ~ **mixer** n FOOD *tech* batteur électrique m, mixer m; ~ **moped** n TRANSP cyclomoteur électrique m; ~ **motor** n ELEC ENG moteur électrique m, électromoteur m, TRANSP moteur électrique m; ~ **noise** n ELECTRON bruit électrique m; ~ **oscillation** n ELECTRON oscillation électrique f; ~ **oven** n THERMOD four électrique m; ~ **penetration** n NUCLEAR traversée électrique f;

~ **pick-up** n TRANSP fourgonnette électrique f; ~ **plug** n ELEC *supply*, LAB EQUIP prise de courant mâle f; ~ **polarization** n ELEC *dielectric*, PHYS polarisation électrique f; ~ **pole** n ELEC ENG pôle électrique m; ~ **potential** n ELEC, ELEC ENG, PHYS potentiel électrique m; ~ **power** n ELEC puissance électrique f, énergie électrique f, ELEC ENG puissance électrique f; ~ **power line** n THERMOD ligne de transport de l'électricité f, ligne électrique f; ~ **power station** n ELEC centrale électrique f, ELEC ENG centrale électrique f, station électrique f, usine électrique f, MINING, TELECOM centrale électrique f; ~ **power substation** n ELEC poste électrique m, sous-station électrique f; ~ **power system** n ELEC ENG réseau de distribution d'énergie m; ~ **power transmission** n ELEC ENG transport d'énergie électrique m; ~ **propulsion lorry** n (BrE) (cf electric propulsion truck) TRANSPORT camion à propulsion électrique m; ~ **propulsion truck** n (AmE) (cf electric propulsion lorry) TRANSP camion à propulsion électrique m; ~ **pulse** n ELEC ENG impulsion électrique f; ~ **quadrupole** n ELEC ENG quadrupôle électrique m; ~ **quadrupole transitions** n pl RAD PHYS transitions quadripôles électriques f pl; ~ **railcar** n ELEC automotrice électrique f; ~ **relay** n ELEC, ELEC ENG relais électrique m; ~ **resistance** n ELEC, ELEC ENG, PHYS résistance électrique f; ~ **resistance furnace** n ELEC ENG four électrique à résistance m; ~ **road vehicle** n TRANSP véhicule électrique routier m; ~ **rocket engine** n MECH ENG moteur électrique de fusée m; ~ **saw** n ELEC scie électrique f; ~ **shock** n ELEC *safety* décharge électrique f, ELEC ENG choc électrique m, SAFETY choc électrique m, secousse électrique f; ~ **shotfirer** n MINING exploseur électrique m; ~ **shotfiring** n MINING mise à feu électrique f, tir électrique m; ~ **signal** n ELEC ENG signal électrique m; ~ **smelting** n ELEC ENG fusion électrique f; ~ **socket** n ELEC *supply*, LAB EQUIP prise de courant femelle f; ~ **spark** n ELEC *discharge* étincelle électrique f; ~ **stapling machine** n PROD ENG agrafeuse électrique f; ~ **starter** n ELEC *automotive* démarreur électrique m; ~ **steam boiler** n MECH ENG chaudière à vapeur électrique f; ~ **storage heater** n THERMOD radiateur électrique à accumulation m; ~ **surface heater** n MECH ENG chauffage électrique de surface m; ~ **susceptibility** n ELEC ENG, PHYS susceptibilité électrique f; ~ **transducer** n ELEC ENG transducteur électrique m; ~ **transmission** n (BrE) (cf electric linkage) ELEC *supply network* transmission électrique f; ~ **transport vehicle** n TRANSP camionnette électrique f; ~ **trolley** n TRANSP chariot électrique m; ~ **tuning** n ELECTRON accord électrique m; ~ **utility** n ELEC ENG usine électrique f; ~ **variable** n ELEC grandeur électrique f; ~ **vehicle** n TRANSP véhicule électrique m; ~ **wave** n ELEC ENG onde électrique f; ~ **welding** n ELEC soudage électrique f; ~ **wire break alarm** n ELEC *safety* appareil de contrôle de rupture de fil m; ~ **wiring** n ELEC ENG circuitage électrique m

electrical[1] *adj* ELEC, ELECTRON électrique

electrical:[2] ~ **accident** n SAFETY accident électrique m; ~ **admittance** n TELECOM admittance électrique f; ~ **appliance** n TEXTILES appareil électrique m; ~ **blasting** n MINING allumage électrique m; ~ **breakdown** n ELEC ENG claquage m, claquage électrique m; ~ **cable** n MECH ENG câble électrique m; ~ **capacitance** n TELECOM capacité électrique f; ~ **characteristic** n ELEC ENG, ELECTRON caractéristique électrique f; ~ **charge** n ELEC, ELEC ENG, PART PHYS, PHYS, TELECOM charge électrique *f*; ~ **circuit** *n* ELECTRON, TELECOM circuit électrique *m*; ~ **component** *n* ELEC ENG composant électrique *m*; ~ **conductance** *n* TELECOM conductance électrique *f*; ~ **conduction** *n* ELEC ENG conduction électrique *f*; ~ **conductivity** *n* ELEC ENG conductibilité électrique *f*; ~ **conductor** *n* ELEC ENG conducteur électrique *m*, PHYS conducteur d'électricité *m*, conducteur électrique *m*; ~ **conductor seal** *n* NUCLEAR joint du conducteur électrique *m*; ~ **connection** *n* ELEC ENG connexion électrique *f*; ~ **connector** *n* ELEC ENG connecteur électrique *m*; ~ **contact** *n* ELEC, ELEC ENG contact électrique *m*; ~ **continuity** *n* ELEC ENG continuité électrique *f*; ~ **control board** *n* NUCLEAR salle de commande électrique *f*, tableau de distribution électrique *m*; ~ **control room** *n* NUCLEAR salle de commande électrique *f*, tableau de distribution électrique *m*; ~ **double layer** *n* CHEM *surface* couche double électrique *f*; ~ **drive** *n* NUCLEAR *of control rod* commande électrique *f*; ~ **dust removal installation** *n* SAFETY installation de dépoussiérage à l'électricité *f*; ~ **earth connector** *n* (BrE) *(cf electrical ground connector)* NAUT prise de masse *f*; ~ **efficiency** *n* ELEC ENG rendement électrique *m*; ~ **energy** *n* ELEC ENG énergie électrique *f*; ~ **engineering** *n* ELEC, ELECTRON électrotechnique *f*; ~ **equipment** *n* ELEC ENG matériel électrique *m*; ~ **fault** *n* QUALITY défaut électrique *m*; ~ **filter** *n* ELECTRON filtre électrique *m*; ~ **fire risk** *n* SAFETY risque d'incendie dû à l'électricité *m*; ~ **ground connector** *n* (AmE) *(cf electrical earth connector)* NAUT prise de masse *f*; ~ **hazard** *n* SAFETY risque lié à l'électricité *m*; ~ **household appliance** *n* ELEC appareil électroménager *m*; ~ **hum** *n* (AmE) *(cf mains hum)* ELEC *supply* bruit de courant alternatif *m*, ELEC ENG ronflement du secteur *m*; ~ **hygrometer** *n* REFRIG hygromètre électrique *m*; ~ **impedance** *n* RECORDING impédance électrique *f*; ~ **input** *n* ELEC ENG, ELECTRON entrée électrique *f*; ~ **installation** *n* ELEC, ELEC ENG, NAUT installation électrique *f*; ~ **installation work** *n* ELEC travaux d'installation *m pl*; ~ **insulating board** *n* PAPER TECH carton diélectrique *m*; ~ **insulating paper** *n* PAPER TECH papier diélectrique *m*; ~ **insulation** *n* ELEC ENG isolement électrique *m*; ~ **kinetic impedance** *n* ACOUSTICS impédance électrique cinétique *f*; ~ **log** *n* PETR diagramme électrique *m*; ~ **machine** *n* ELEC ENG machine électrique *f*; ~ **measuring apparatus** *n* SAFETY appareil de mesure électrique *m*; ~ **network** *n* PHYS réseau électrique *m*; ~ **noise** *n* (AmE) *(cf mains noise)* ELECTRON bruit électrique *m*, RECORDING bruit de secteur *m*; ~ **oscillation** *n* WAVE PHYS oscillation électrique *f*; ~ **oscillator** *n* ELECTRON oscillateur électrique *m*; ~ **outlet** *n* (AmE) *(cf mains socket)* ELEC ENG prise secteur *f*; ~ **output** *n* ELEC ENG, ELECTRON sortie électrique *f*, NUCLEAR *of reactor* puissance électrique *f*; ~ **panel** *n* NAUT tableau électrique *m*; ~ **plug** *n* (AmE) ELEC *connection* prise au secteur *f*, ELEC ENG fiche de prise de courant *f*, ELEC ENG fiche secteur *f*; ~ **potential** *n* ELEC ENG potentiel électrique *m*; ~ **power** *n* ELEC, ELEC ENG, NUCLEAR *of reactor*, TELECOM puissance électrique *f*; ~ **power supply** *n* ELEC ENG alimentation en énergie électrique *f*; ~ **properties** *n pl* CONST propriétés électriques *f pl*; ~ **protection equipment** *n* SAFETY appareillage de protection contre l'électricité *m*; ~ **ratings** *n pl* PROD ENG caractéristiques électriques *f pl*; ~ **relay** *n* ELEC ENG relais électrique *m*; ~ **resistivity** *n* P&R résistivité électrique *f*; ~ **resonator** *n* ELECTRON résonateur électrique *m*; ~ **safety requirements** *n pl*

SAFETY conditions requises de sécurité pour alimentation en électricité *f pl*, prescriptions de sécurité pour l'électricité *f pl*; ~ **sawing** *n* NUCLEAR sciage électrique *m*; ~ **shot-firing** *n* MINING allumage électrique *m*; ~ **signal** *n* ELECTRON signal électrique *m*; ~ **solenoid** *n* PROD ENG électrovanne *f*; ~ **storm** *n* METEO orage électrique *m*; ~ **supply** *n* (BrE) *(cf mains supply)* ELEC *network* alimentation secteur *f*, réseau *m*, PHYS alimentation secteur *f*; ~ **survey** *n* PETR inspections électriques *f pl*, travaux électriques *m pl*; ~ **tape** *n* PROD ENG ruban isolant *m*; ~ **test** *n* ELEC ENG, TESTING essai électrique *m*; ~ **transmission line** *n* ELEC ENG ligne de transmission électrique *f*; ~ **wiring** *n* ELEC ENG, VEHICLES *electrical system* câblage électrique *m*; ~ **wiring diagram** *n* NAUT schéma du circuit électrique *m*; ~ **zero** *n* ELEC *of instrument*, INSTRUMENT zéro électrique *m*; ~ **zero adjuster** *n* ELEC, INSTRUMENT dispositif de remise à zéro électrique *m*

electrically-driven *adj* MECH, PHOTO à entraînement électrique

electrically-erasable: ~ **ROM** *n* *(EEROM)* COMP, DP ROM effaçable électriquement *f*, mémoire morte effaçable électriquement *f*

electrically-held: ~ **crosspoint** *n* TELECOM point de connexion à maintien électrique *m*

electrically-operated[1] *adj* (AmE) *(cf mains-operated)* ELEC *appliance* alimenté du réseau, ELEC ENG alimenté par le secteur

electrically-operated:[2] ~ **valve** *n* PROD ENG électrovanne *f*

electrically-pumped: ~ **laser** *n* ELECTRON laser à pompage électrique *m*

electrically-tuned: ~ **oscillator** *n* ELECTRON oscillateur accordé électriquement *m*, oscillateur à accord électrique *m*

electrical-optical[1] *adj* *(E-O)* TELECOM électrique-optique

electrical-optical:[2] ~ **isolation** *n* PROD ENG isolation opto-électrique *f*

electrician *n* CINEMAT électricien *m*

electricity *n* ELEC ENG, PHYS électricité *f*; ~ **distribution** *n* ELEC distribution d'énergie électrique *f*; ~ **generated** *n* NUCLEAR *of nuclear power station* production d'électricité *f*; ~ **generating station** *n* CONST centrale électrique *f*; ~ **generation** *n* ELEC ENG génération d'électricité *f*; ~ **meter** *n* ELEC, ELEC ENG compteur électrique *m*; ~ **supply** *n* CONST alimentation électrique *f*, ELEC alimentation en électricité *f*; ~ **supply system** *n* ELEC ENG réseau d'alimentation *m*; ~ **transmission** *n* THERMOD transport de l'électricité *m*

electrification *n* ELEC *supply* électrification *f*, PHYS électrisation *f*

electrify *vt* ELEC ENG électrifier, électriser

electroacoustic[1] *adj* RECORDING électroacoustique

electroacoustic:[2] ~ **chain** *n* ACOUSTICS chaîne électroacoustique *f*; ~ **transducer** *n* ACOUSTICS, ELEC ENG transducteur électroacoustique *m*

electroacoustical: ~ **reciprocity coefficient** *n* ACOUSTICS coefficient de réciprocité électroacoustique *m*

electroacoustics *n* ELEC ENG électroacoustique *f*

electroanalysis *n* CHEM analyse électrolytique *f*, électroanalyse *f*

electrobus *n* TRANSP électrobus *m*

electrocapillarity *n* CHEM électrocapillarité *f*

electrocapillary *adj* CHEM électrocapillaire

electrochemical[1] *adj* CHEM électrochimique

electrochemical:[2] ~ **capacitor** n TELECOM condensateur électrochimique m; ~ **energy** n ELEC ENG énergie électrochimique f; ~ **series** n CHEM série électrochimique des tensions f

electrochemistry n CHEM, ELEC électrochimie f

electrocochleography n ACOUSTICS électrocochléographie f

electrode n CHEM, CONST welding, ELEC, ELEC ENG, LAB EQUIP electrochemistry, MECH welding, METALL, PHYS, TV électrode f; ~ **admittance** n ELEC admittance d'électrode f; ~ **bias** n ELEC ENG polarisation d'électrode f; ~ **bias voltage** n ELEC ENG tension de polarisation d'électrode f; ~ **boiler** n HEAT ENG chauffe-eau à électrode m; ~ **carbon** n ELEC ENG charbon d'électrode m; ~ **characteristic** n ELEC ENG caractéristique d'électrode f; ~ **configuration** n TELECOM configuration d'électrode f; ~ **gap** n ELEC ENG espace entre électrodes m; ~ **holder** n CONST welding, ELEC ENG porte-électrode m; ~ **potential** n ELEC, PHYS potentiel d'électrode m; ~ **tip** n ELEC point d'électrode m

electrodeposit n COATINGS couche galvanique f, couche galvanoplastique f, revêtement galvanique m

electrodeposition n CONST paint application électrodéposition f, ELEC ENG galvanoplastie f, électrodéposition f

electrodermal: ~ **effect** n ACOUSTICS effet électrodermal m

electrodialysis n CHEM électrodialyse f

electrodischarge: ~ **machining** n (EDM) MECH ENG usinage par électro-érosion m, PROD ENG électro-érosion f

electrodrilling n COAL TECH forage électro-hydraulique m

electrodynamic: ~ **instrument** n ELEC appareil électrodynamique m; ~ **levitation** n TRANSP sustentation électrodynamique f; ~ **loudspeaker** n ACOUSTICS, RECORDING haut-parleur électrodynamique m; ~ **microphone** n ACOUSTICS, RECORDING microphone électrodynamique m; ~ **relay** n ELEC relais électrodynamique m

electrodynamics n ELEC, PHYS électrodynamique f

electrodynamometer n ELEC, PHYS électrodynamomètre m

electrofluorescence n NUCLEAR électroluminescence f

electroforming n ELEC ENG électroformage m

electrogalvanizing n PROP MAT électrogalvanisation f

electroglow n SPACE électro-incandescence f

electrographic: ~ **analysis** n RAD PHYS analyse électrographique f; ~ **ink** n COLOURS encre conductrice f; ~ **printer** n COMP, DP imprimante électrographique f

electrokinetic[1] adj CHEM électrocinétique

electrokinetic:[2] ~ **energy** n ELEC énergie électrocinétique f

electrokinetics n ELEC ENG, PHYS électrocinétique f

electroluminescence n ELECTRON, NUCLEAR, OPT, PHYS, TELECOM électroluminescence f

electroluminescent: ~ **display** n COMP, DP écran électroluminescent m, ELECTRON affichage par électroluminescence m, afficheur électroluminescent m

electrolysis n CHEM, ELEC, ELEC ENG, PHYS, PRINT, PROP MAT électrolyse f

electrolyte n CHEM, ELEC, ELEC ENG, P&R, PHYS, TELECOM électrolyte m

electrolytic[1] adj CHEM, ELEC electrochemistry, PHYS électrolytique

electrolytic:[2] ~ **bath** n ELEC, ELEC ENG bain électrolytique m; ~ **capacitor** n ELEC, ELEC ENG condensateur électrolytique m, PHYS condensateur électrochimique m, condensateur électrolytique m; ~ **cell** n ELEC ENG cellule d'électrolyse f, cellule électrolytique f, PHYS cellule d'électrolyse f, cellule électrolytique f; ~ **conductivity** n ELEC conductibilité électrolytique f; ~ **display** n ELECTRON affichage électrolytique m; ~ **etching** n NUCLEAR marquage électrolytique m; ~ **galvanizing** n PROP MAT zingage à froid m; ~ **hygrometer** n REFRIG hygromètre électrolytique m; ~ **marking** n MECH ENG on metal conductors marquage électrolytique m; ~ **rectifier** n ELEC, ELEC ENG redresseur électrolytique m; ~ **unit** n ELEC ENG version électrolytique f, PHYS électrolyseur m; ~ **zinc** n PROP MAT zinc électrolytique m

electrolyze vt CHEM, PHYS électrolyser

electrolyzer n CHEM électrolyseur m

electromagnet n CHEM, ELEC, ELEC ENG, PHYS électro-aimant m, TV solénoïde m, électro-aimant m; ~ **loudspeaker** n ACOUSTICS haut-parleur à électro-aimant m

electromagnetic[1] adj CHEM, ELEC, MECH électromagnétique

electromagnetic:[2] ~ **brake** n RAIL, TRANSP frein électromagnétique m; ~ **calorimeter** n PART PHYS, RAD PHYS calorimètre électromagnétique m; ~ **chuck** n MECH ENG mandrin électromagnétique m; ~ **clutch** n MECH, TRANSP embrayage électromagnétique m; ~ **compatibility** n ELEC ENG, SPACE (EMC) compatibilité électromagnétique f; ~ **coupling** n ELEC ENG couplage électromagnétique m, TRANSP embrayage électromagnétique m; ~ **current meter** n OCEANOG courantomètre électromagnétique m; ~ **damper** n GEOPHYS amortisseur électromagnétique m; ~ **damping** n ELEC amortissement électromagnétique m; ~ **deflection** n ELEC ENG déviation électromagnétique f; ~ **disturbance** n TELECOM perturbation électromagnétique f; ~ **energy** n ELEC ENG, PHYS énergie électromagnétique f; ~ **energy pulse** n ELEC ENG impulsion d'énergie électromagnétique f; ~ **environment** n SPACE environnement électromagnétique m; ~ **field** n ELEC, ELEC ENG, PHYS, WAVE PHYS champ électromagnétique m; ~ **fixing device** n MECH ENG dispositif de serrage électromagnétique m; ~ **flowmeter** n ELEC ENG débitmètre électromagnétique m; ~ **focusing** n ELEC ENG focalisation électromagnétique f; ~ **force** n ELEC, ELEC ENG, PART PHYS between particles force électromagnétique f; ~ **ignition** n AUTO allumage électromagnétique m; ~ **induction** n ELEC ENG, PHYS, PROD ENG, TESTING induction électromagnétique f; ~ **interaction** n RAD PHYS interaction électromagnétique f; ~ **interference** n (EMI) COMP interférence électromagnétique f, ELEC ENG, PROD ENG parasites électromagnétiques m pl, SPACE perturbation électromagnétique f; ~ **interference filter** n ELECTRON filtre antiparasite m; ~ **interference filtering** n ELECTRON filtrage des parasites m; ~ **isolation** n ELEC ENG isolement électromagnétique m; ~ **lateral guidance system** n TRANSP guidage magnétique latéral m; ~ **lens** n ELEC ENG lentille électromagnétique f, TV lentille électronique f; ~ **levitation** n TRANSP sustentation électromagnétique f; ~ **loudspeaker** n ACOUSTICS, RECORDING haut-parleur électromagnétique m; ~ **microphone** n ACOUSTICS, RECORDING microphone électromagnétique m; ~ **mode** n OPT mode électromagnétique *m*; ~ **moment** *n* ELEC moment électromagnétique *m*; ~ **momentum** *n* PHYS quantité de mouvement électromagnétique *f*; ~ **pulse** *n* ELEC ENG, TELECOM impulsion électromagnétique *f*; ~ **pump** *n* NUCLEAR *for liquid metals* pompe électromagnétique *f*; ~ **radiation** *n* ELEC, ELEC ENG, METEO, OPT, PHYS, PROD ENG, RAD PHYS, WAVE PHYS rayonnement électromagnétique *m*; ~ **relay** *n* ELEC ENG relais électromagnétique *m*; ~ **resonator** *n* ELECTRON résonateur électromagnétique *m*; ~ **screen** *n* PHYS blindage électromagnétique *m*, écran électromagnétique *m*; ~ **shielding** *n* ELEC écran électromagnétique *m*; ~ **shutter release** *n* PHOTO déclencheur électromagnétique *m*; ~ **spectrum** *n* ELEC ENG, ELECTRON, RAD PHYS spectre électromagnétique *m*; ~ **tuning** *n* ELECTRON accord électromagnétique *m*; ~ **unit** *n* ELEC unité électromagnétique *f*; ~ **vulnerability** *n* ELEC ENG vulnérabilité électromagnétique *f*; ~ **wave** *n* ELEC, ELEC ENG, PHYS onde électromagnétique *f*, RAD PHYS faisceau hertzien *m*, TELECOM, WAVE PHYS onde électromagnétique *f*; ~ **wave equations** *n pl* RAD PHYS équations des faisceaux hertziens *f pl*; ~ **wave polarization** *n* ELEC ENG polarisation d'onde électromagnétique *f*

electromagnetically-operated *adj* ELEC ENG commandé par électro-aimant

electromagnetism *n* CHEM, ELEC, PHYS électromagnétisme *m*

electromechanical: ~ **coupling factor** *n* ACOUSTICS coefficient de couplage électromécanique *m*; ~ **device** *n* ELEC ENG dispositif électromécanique *m*; ~ **exchange** *n* TELECOM autocommutateur électromécanique *m*, central électromécanique *m*; ~ **filter** *n* ELECTRON filtre électromécanique *m*; ~ **recording** *n* RECORDING enregistrement électromécanique *m*; ~ **relay** *n* ELEC ENG relais électromécanique *m*; ~ **switching** *n* TELECOM commutation électromécanique *f*; ~ **switching system** *n* TELECOM système de commutation électromécanique *m*; ~ **switching unit** *n* TELECOM autocommutateur électromécanique *m*; ~ **transducer** *n* ACOUSTICS, ELEC ENG transducteur électromécanique *m*

electromechanics *n* ELEC électromécanique *f*

electromeric: ~ **effect** *n* CHEM effet électromérique *m*

electrometeor *n* GEOPHYS météore radioélectrique *m*

electrometer *n* ELEC, ELEC ENG, GEOPHYS, LAB EQUIP, PHYS électromètre *m*; ~ **amplifier** *n* ELECTRON amplificateur d'électromètre *m*; ~ **tube** *n* ELEC ENG, ELECTRON tube électromètre *m*

electrometric: ~ **titration** *n* CHEM dosage potentiométrique *m*, titrage potentiométrique *m*

electrometry *n* ELEC ENG électrométrie *f*

electromobile *n* TRANSP électromobile *m*

electromotive: ~ **force** *n* *(emf)* ELEC, ELEC ENG, PHYS force électromotrice *f* *(fém)*

electromotor *n* ELEC ENG moteur électrique *m*

electron *n* CHEM, ELEC, ELEC ENG, GAS TECH, PART PHYS, PHYS électron *m*; ~ **accelerator** *n* PART PHYS accélérateur d'électrons *m*; ~ **attachment** *n* NUCLEAR *in forming ions* attachement d'un électron *m*, fixation d'un électron *f*; ~ **beam** *n* *(EB)* COMP, ELEC microscope faisceau électronique *m*, ELECTRON faisceau d'électrons *m*, METALL faisceau électronique *m*, NUCLEAR, PART PHYS faisceau d'électrons *m*, TELECOM, TV faisceau électronique *m*, WAVE PHYS faisceau d'électrons *m*; ~ **beam acceleration** *n* ELECTRON accélération du faisceau d'électrons *f*; ~ **beam alignment method** *n*

ELECTRON méthode d'alignement en gravure par faisceau d'électrons *f*; ~ **beam annealing** *n* ELECTRON recuit par faisceau d'électrons *m*; ~ **beam bombardment furnace** *n* NUCLEAR four à faisceau d'électrons *m*; ~ **beam curing** *n* NUCLEAR *of lacquers, varnishes* cure par faisceau d'électrons *f*, étuvage par faisceau d'électrons *m*, PRINT *(EBC)* réticulage *m*, séchage de surface par bombardement d'électrons *m*, séchage de surface par faisceau d'électrons *m*; ~ **beam cutting** *n* ELECTRON découpage par faisceau d'électrons *m*; ~ **beam direct writing** *n* ELECTRON gravure par faisceau d'électrons dirigé *f*; ~ **beam focusing** *n* ELECTRON concentration du faisceau d'électrons *f*; ~ **beam laser** *n* ELECTRON laser à faisceau d'électrons *m*; ~ **beam lithography** *n* ELECTRON gravure par faisceau d'électrons *f*, gravure électronique *f*; ~ **beam lithography machine** *n* ELECTRON graveur à faisceau d'électrons *m*; ~ **beam machining** *n* ELECTRON usinage par faisceau d'électrons *m*; ~ **beam mask** *n* ELECTRON masque pour gravure par faisceau d'électrons réparti *m*; ~ **beam melting** *n* NUCLEAR fusion par faisceau d'électrons *f*; ~ **beam parametric amplifier** *n* ELECTRON amplificateur paramétrique à faisceau d'électrons *m*; ~ **beam processing** *n* ELECTRON traitement par faisceau d'électrons *m*; ~ **beam projection lithography** *n* ELECTRON gravure par faisceau d'électrons réparti *f*; ~ **beam projection printer** *n* ELECTRON graveur à faisceau d'électrons réparti *m*; ~ **beam pumping** *n* ELECTRON pompage par faisceau d'électrons *m*; ~ **beam resist** *n* ELECTRON résist pour faisceau d'électrons *m*; ~ **beam scanning** *n* ELECTRON balayage par faisceau d'électrons *m*; ~ **beam test** *n* RAD PHYS essai à faisceau d'électrons *m*; ~ **beam tube** *n* ELECTRON tube à faisceau d'électrons *m*; ~ **beam voltage** *n* TV tension du faisceau électronique *f*; ~ **beam welding** *n* CONST, NUCLEAR soudage par faisceau d'électrons *m*; ~ **bombardment** *n* ELECTRON bombardement par électrons *m*, PART PHYS bombardement électronique *m*; ~ **bombardment thruster** *n* SPACE *spacecraft* moteur-fusée électronique *m*; ~ **capture** *n* PHYS capture des électrons *f*, capture électronique *f*, RAD PHYS capture électronique *f*; ~ **capture detector** *n* POLLUTION détecteur à capture d'électrons *m*, détecteur à capture électronique *m*; ~ **cascade** *n* NUCLEAR cascade d'électrons *f*, gerbe électronique *f*; ~ **cloud** *n* CHEM, NUCLEAR *part of atoms* cortège électronique *m*, RAD PHYS, TV nuage électronique *m*; ~ **collision** *n* TELECOM collision d'électrons *f*; ~ **conductivity** *n* RAD PHYS conductivité électronique *f*; ~ **continuum** *n* NUCLEAR spectre continu d'électrons *m*; ~ **cooling** *n* PART PHYS refroidissement électronique *m*; ~ **coupling** *n* ELEC ENG, ELECTRON couplage électronique *m*; ~ **coupling oscillator** *n* ELECTRON oscillateur à couplage électronique *m*; ~ **current** *n* ELEC ENG courant d'électrons *m*, courant électronique *m*; ~ **cyclotron** *n* PART PHYS cyclotron à électrons *m*; ~ **cyclotron frequency** *n* NUCLEAR fréquence gyromagnétique *f*; ~ **density** *n* CHEM densité d'électrons *f*, PHYS densité d'électrons *f*, densité électronique *f*, nombre volumique électronique *m*; ~ **density distribution** *n* CRYSTALL distribution de densité électronique *f*; ~ **detection** *n* PART PHYS détection d'électrons *f*; ~ **device** *n* ELEC ENG dispositif à électrons *m*; ~ **diffraction** *n* CRYSTALL, RAD PHYS diffraction électronique *f*; ~ **diffraction pattern** *n* CRYSTALL diagramme de diffraction électronique *m*; ~ **drift** *n* NUCLEAR *in a plasma* dérive des électrons *f*; ~ **emission** *n* ELECTRON, PART PHYS émission d'électrons *f*; ~ **emitter** *n* ELECTRON émetteur d'électrons *m*; ~ **energy filter** *n* RAD PHYS filtre d'énergie électronique *m*; ~ **energy loss** *n* RAD PHYS perte d'énergie électronique *f*; ~ **energy loss spectroscopy** *n* RAD PHYS spectroscopie de la perte d'énergie électronique *f*; ~ **flood lithography** *n* ELECTRON gravure par flux d'électrons *f*; ~ **gas** *n* PHYS gaz électronique *m*; ~ **gun** *n* ELECTRON canon à électrons *m*, INSTRUMENT canon à électrons *m*, source d'électrons *f*, PHYS, RAD PHYS, TV canon à électrons *m*; ~ **gun current** *n* TV courant global du faisceau *m*; ~ **hole pair** *n* PHYS paire électron-trou *f*; ~ **hole recombination** *n* NUCLEAR recombinaison électron trou *f*; ~ **image** *n* ELECTRON image électronique *f*; ~ **imaging** *n* ELECTRON visualisation par flux d'électrons *f*; ~ **impact ion engine** *n* SPACE *spacecraft* propulseur ionique à choc électronique *m*; ~ **induced activation** *n* RAD PHYS déclenchement induit par électrons *m*; ~ **irradiation** *n* SPACE irradiation en électrons *f*; ~ **lens** *n* ELECTRON, INSTRUMENT, PHYS, TV lentille électronique *f*; ~ **linear accelerator** *n* PART PHYS accélérateur linéaire d'électrons *m*; ~ **mass** *n* CHEM *(em)* masse électronique *f*, PART PHYS masse de l'électron *f*, masse électronique *f*; ~ **micrograph** *n* RAD PHYS micrographe électronique *m*; ~ **microscope** *n* ELECTRON, INSTRUMENT, LAB EQUIP, METALL, PHYS, TELECOM microscope électronique *m*; ~ **microscopy** *n* ELECTRON microscopie électronique *f*; ~ **mirror** *n* ELECTRON miroir à électrons *m*, INSTRUMENT miroir électronique *m*; ~ **multiplier** *n* ELECTRON, RAD PHYS multiplicateur d'électrons *m*; ~ **multiplier phototube** *n* ELECTRON tube photomultiplicateur *m*; ~ **multiplier tube** *n* ELECTRON tube à multiplicateur d'électrons *m*; ~ **neutrino** *n* PHYS neutrino électronique *m*; ~ **optics** *n* PHYS optique électronique *f*; ~ **pair** *n* PART PHYS paire d'électrons *f*; ~ **paramagnetic resonance** *n (EPR)* PHYS résonance paramagnétique électronique *f*; ~ **path** *n* NUCLEAR trajectoire d'électrons *f*, TV trajectoire électronique *f*; ~ **population** *n* SPACE population d'électrons *f*; ~ **positive hole** *n* NUCLEAR trou *m*, trou électronique *m*; ~ **probe** *n* NUCLEAR *narrow beam* sonde électronique *f*; ~ **radiography** *n* NUCLEAR électronographie *f*; ~ **ray** *n* ELECTRON rayon cathodique *m*; ~ **scanning** *n* NUCLEAR balayage électronique *m*; ~ **scanning beam** *n* TV faisceau électronique analyseur *m*; ~ **scavenger** *n* NUCLEAR intercepteur d'électrons *m*; ~ **shell** *n* CHEM, NUCLEAR *of atom*, PART PHYS, PHYS couche électronique *f*; ~ **shower** *n* NUCLEAR cascade d'électrons *f*, gerbe électronique *f*; ~ **sink** *n* NUCLEAR puits d'électrons *m*; ~ **source** *n* ELECTRON source d'électrons *f*; ~ **specific charge** *n* NUCLEAR charge spécifique d'électrons *f*; ~ **spectroscopic diffraction** *n* RAD PHYS diffraction spectroscopique des électrons *f*; ~ **spectroscopic imaging** *n* RAD PHYS projection d'image par spectroscopie électronique *f*; ~ **spectroscopy** *n* PHYS spectroscopie électronique *f*; ~ **spectroscopy for chemical analysis** *n (ESCA)* CHEM spectroscopie électronique pour analyses chimiques *f*; ~ **spin** *n* CHEM spin de l'électron *m*, spin électronique *m*; ~ **spin resonance** *n (ESR)* PART PHYS résonance de spin électronique *f*, PHYS résonance de spin électronique *f*, résonance magnétique électronique *f*; ~ **spin resonance magnetometer** *n* NUCLEAR magnétomètre *m*; ~ **storage ring** *n* PART PHYS anneau de stockage des électrons *m*; ~ **stream** *n* TV flux électronique *m*; ~ **synchrotron** *n* PART PHYS synchrotron à électrons *m*; ~

theory of metals *n* RAD PHYS théorie électronique des métaux *f*; ~ **trajectory** *n* NUCLEAR trajectoire d'électrons *f*; ~ **transfer diode** *n* PHYS diode à transfert d'électrons *f*; ~ **tube** *n* ELECTRON tube électronique *m*; ~ **tube base** *n* ELECTRON culot de tube électronique *m*; ~ **tube envelope** *n* ELECTRON enveloppe de tube électronique *f*; ~ **tube grid** *n* ELECTRON grille de tube électronique *f*; ~ **tube heater** *n* ELECTRON filament de tube électronique *m*; ~ **tube holder** *n* ELECTRON culot de tube électronique *m*; ~ **tube neck** *n* ELECTRON col d'ampoule *m*; ~ **tube oscillator** *n* ELECTRON oscillateur à tube électronique *m*; ~ **wave magnetron** *n* ELECTRON magnétron à ondes électroniques *m*; ~ **wave tube** *n* ELECTRON tube à onde électronique *m*

electron-bombarded: ~ **semiconductor** *n (EBS)* ELECTRON triode EBS *f*, triode à cible *f*

electronegative *adj* CHEM électronégatif

electronic[1] *adj* ELEC, ELECTRON électronique

electronic:[2] ~ **anti-locking device** *n* TRANSP système électronique antiblocage *m*; ~ **anti-skid system** *n* TRANSP système électronique antiblocage des roues *m*; ~ **balance** *n* LAB EQUIP balance électronique *f*; ~ **beam forming** *n* ELECTRON mise en forme électronique du faisceau *f*; ~ **beam steering** *n* ELECTRON balayage électronique du faisceau *m*; ~ **bearing cursor** *n* NAUT *radar* alidade électronique *f*; ~ **bearing line** *n* NAUT *radar* alidade électronique *f*; ~ **bearing marker** *n* NAUT *radar* alidade électronique *f*; ~ **braking control** *n* TRANSP freinage électronique *m*; ~ **calculator** *n* COMP calculateur électronique *m*; ~ **car** *n* TRANSP voiture électronique *f*; ~ **carburetor** *n* (AmE), ~ **carburettor** *n* (BrE) TRANSPORT carburateur électronique *m*; ~ **chart** *n* NAUT *navigation* carte marine électronique *f*; ~ **chart display** *n* NAUT *navigation* visualisation des cartes électriques *f*; ~ **chopper** *n* ELECTRON découpeur à transistor *m*; ~ **circuit** *n* ELECTRON, TELECOM circuit électronique *m*; ~ **circuit integration** *n* ELECTRON intégration des circuits électroniques *f*; ~ **clock** *n* ELECTRON, TELECOM horloge électronique *f*; ~ **commutation** *n* TRANSP commutation électronique *f*; ~ **comparator** *n* MECH ENG *dimensional measurement* comparateur électronique *m*; ~ **component** *n* COMP, DP, ELECTRON, TELECOM composant électronique *m*; ~ **compound** *n* METALL composé électronique *m*; ~ **configuration** *n* PHYS configuration électronique *f*; ~ **control** *n* CONTROL régulation électronique *f*, NAUT *equipment on board*, TRANSP commande électronique *f*; ~ **control system** *n* ELECTRON système de commande électronique *m*; ~ **control unit** *n* AUTO module électronique *m*; ~ **counter** *n* ELECTRON compteur électronique *m*; ~ **countermeasures** *n pl* MILIT contremesures électroniques *f pl*; ~ **counting** *n* ELECTRON comptage électronique *m*; ~ **crosspoint** *n* TELECOM point de connexion électronique *m*; ~ **data interchange** *n (EDI)* TELECOM échange de données informatisées *m*, échange électronique de données *m (EDI)*; ~ **data processing** *n (EDP)* COMP informatique *f*, traitement électronique de données *m*, ELECTRON informatique *f*; ~ **device** *n* ELECTRON dispositif électronique *m*; ~ **digital theodolite** *n* CONST *surveying* théodolite électronique et digital *m*; ~ **direction reverser** *n* TRANSP inverseur de marche électronique *m*; ~ **directory** *n* TELECOM annuaire électronique *m*; ~ **display micrometric head** *n* METR lecteur électronique de mesure micrométrique *m*; ~ **document interchange** *n (EDI)* TELECOM échange de documents informatisés *m (EDI)*; ~ **dot generator** *n* PRINT générateur électronique de points *m*; ~ **editing** *n (E-E)* TV montage électronique *m*; ~ **engineering** *n* ELECTRON ingénierie électronique *f*; ~ **engraving** *n* PRINT gravure électronique *f*; ~ **equipment** *n* ELECTRON matériel électronique *m*; ~ **exchange** *n* TELECOM central électronique *m*, commutateur électronique *m*; ~ **filing** *n* COMP, DP archivage électronique *m*; ~ **frequency control** *n* ELECTRON commande électronique de fréquence *f*; ~ **funds transfer** *n* DP virement électronique *m*, TELECOM télécollecte *f*, télépaiement *m*, TELECOM transfert électronique de fonds *m*; ~ **funds transfer at point of sale** *n (EFTPOS)* TELECOM transfert électronique de fonds au point de vente *m*; ~ **funds transfer system** *n (EFTS)* COMP système de télépaiement *m*, virement électronique *m*; ~ **gage** *n* (AmE) *see electronic gauge*; ~ **gaging probe** *n* (AmE) *see electronic gauging probe*; ~ **gauge** *n* (BrE) METR calibre électronique *m*; ~ **gauging probe** *n* (BrE) MECH ENG palpeur de calibrage électronique *m*; ~ **heat capacity** *n* PHYS capacité thermique électronique *f*; ~ **heat conductivity** *n* NUCLEAR conductibilité thermique électronique *f*; ~ **heating** *n* ELEC ENG chauffage électronique *m*; ~ **ignition** *n* AUTO allumage transistorisé sans rupteur *m*, allumage électronique *m*, TRANSP *vehicles*, VEHICLES allumage électronique *m*; ~ **imaging** *n* ELECTRON imagerie électronique *f*; ~ **injection** *n* AUTO injection électronique *f*; ~ **instrument** *n* ELECTRON appareil électronique *m*; ~ **instrument module** *n* NUCLEAR module d'instrumentation électronique *m*; ~ **integrated circuit** *n* ELECTRON circuit intégré électronique *m*; ~ **intelligence** *n* ELECTRON renseignement électronique *m*; ~ **key system** *n* TELECOM système d'intercommunications électronique *m*; ~ **mail** *n (EM)* COMP, DP, ELECTRON, TELECOM courrier électronique *m*, messagerie électronique *f*; ~ **mailbox** *n* COMP, DP boîte aux lettres électronique *f*, ELECTRON boîte à lettres électronique *f*, TELECOM boîte aux lettres électronique *f*, boîte à lettres électronique *f*; ~ **mail service** *n* COMP service courrier électronique *m*; ~ **matting** *n* TV cache électronique *m*; ~ **memory** *n* ELEC ENG mémoire électronique *f*; ~ **message switch** *n* TELECOM commutateur électronique de messages *m*; ~ **message system** *n (EMS)* TELECOM système de commutation électronique de messages *m*, système de messagerie électronique *m*; ~ **messaging** *n* COMP, DP, ELECTRON messagerie électronique *f*; ~ **metering of fuel injection** *n* TRANSP injecteur d'essence à dosage électronique *m*; ~ **microphone** *n* RECORDING microphone électronique *m*; ~ **module** *n* ELECTRON module électronique *m*; ~ **news gathering** *n (ENG)* TV journalisme électronique *m*, production vidéo en reportage *f*; ~ **office** *n* COMP, DP bureau électronique *m*; ~ **partition function** *n* NUCLEAR somme des états électroniques *f*; ~ **point of sale** *n (EPOS)* COMP point de vente électronique *m*; ~ **polarization** *n* PHYS, RAD PHYS polarisation électronique *f*; ~ **power supply** *n* ELEC ENG alimentation régulée *f*; ~ **publishing** *n* COMP publication assistée par ordinateur *f*, ELECTRON édition électronique *f*; ~ **relay** *n* ELEC relais électronique *m*; ~ **rocket engine** *n* SPACE moteur-fusée électronique *m*; ~ **scanning** *n* PRINT lecture au scanner *f*, scanning *m*; ~ **semiconductor** *n* NUCLEAR *as distinguished from ionic semiconductor* semi-conducteur électronique *m*; ~ **signal processing** *n* ELECTRON traitement électronique des signaux *m*; ~ **signature** *n* COMP signature

électronique *f*; ~ **speech synthesis** *n* ELECTRON synthèse électronique de la parole *f*; ~ **speed control** *n* TRANSP réglage électronique de vitesse *m*; ~ **speed controller** *n* TRANSP variateur électronique de vitesse *m*; ~ **structure** *n* NUCLEAR *of atom, molecule, electron* structure électronique *f*; ~ **subshell** *n* RAD PHYS *atomic structure* sous-couche électronique *f*; ~ **surveillance** *n* TELECOM surveillance électronique *f*; ~ **switch** *n* COMP, DP commutateur électronique *m*; ~ **switching** *n* TELECOM commutation électronique *f*; ~ **switching system** *n (ESS)* TELECOM système de commutation électronique *m*; ~ **test pattern** *n* ELECTRON mire électronique *f*; ~ **timer** *n* ELECTRON, PHOTO minuterie électronique *f*; ~ **traffic aids** *n pl* TRANSP aides électroniques à la circulation routière *f pl*; ~ **tube** *n* ELECTRON tube électronique *m*; ~ **tuning** *n* ELECTRON accord électronique *m*, réglage électronique *m*, TELECOM accord électronique *m*; ~ **tuning range** *n* ELECTRON plage d'accord électronique *f*; ~ **tuning sensitivity** *n* ELECTRON sensibilité de l'accord électronique *f*; ~ **valve** *n* ELECTRON tube électronique *m*; ~ **warfare** *n (EW)* ELECTRON guerre électronique *f*; ~ **weighing scales** *n* PACKAGING balance électronique *f*

electronically-controlled[1] *adj* ELECTRON à commande électronique

electronically-controlled:[2] ~ **valve** *n* CONST électrovanne *f*

electronically-tuned: ~ **filter** *n* ELECTRON filtre à accord électronique *m*; ~ **oscillator** *n* ELECTRON oscillateur à accord électronique *m*

electronics *n* COMP, DP, ELEC ENG, PROD ENG électronique *f*

electronic-to-electronic *adj (E-to-E, E-E)* TV direct modulateur-démodulateur, vidéo-sur-vidéo

electron-impregnated: ~ **migma** *n* NUCLEAR éligma *m*

electronographic: ~ **camera** *n* PART PHYS caméra électronographique *f*

electron-positron: ~ **annihilation** *n* PART PHYS annihilation électron-position *f*; ~ **collider** *n* PART PHYS collisionneur linéaire électron-positron *m*; ~ **encounter** *n* PART PHYS rencontre électron-positron *f*

electron-to-atom: ~ **ratio** *n* NUCLEAR concentration des électrons liants *f*

electronvolt *n (eV)* ELEC ENG, METR, PART PHYS, PHYS électron-volt *m (eV)*

electro-optic[1] *adj* TELECOM électro-optique

electro-optic:[2] ~ **effect** *n* OPT effet électro-optique *m*; ~ **switch** *n* TELECOM commutateur électro-optique *m*

electro-optical[1] *adj* ELECTRON électro-optique

electro-optical:[2] ~ **distance measuring instrument** *n* INSTRUMENT tachéomètre électro-optique *m*; ~ **modulator** *n* ELECTRON modulateur électro-optique *m*; ~ **signal processing** *n* ELECTRON traitement optique des signaux *m*

electro-osmosis *n* CHEM électro-osmose *f*

electro-osmotic *adj* CHEM électro-osmotique

electrophilic *adj* CHEM électrophile, électrophilique

electrophoresis *n* CHEM, ELEC, LAB EQUIP électrophorèse *f*; ~ **cell** *n* LAB EQUIP cuve d'électrophorèse *f*

electrophoretic: ~ **enamelling** *n* COLOURS peinture électrophorétique *f*; ~ **migration** *n* NUCLEAR mouvement électrophorétique *m*

electrophorus *n* ELEC ENG électrophore *m*

electrophotographic: ~ **printer** *n* COMP, DP imprimante électrophotographique *f*

electrophotography *n* PRINT électrophotographie *f*

electroplatable *adj* COATINGS métallisable, métallisable par galvanisation

electroplate[1] *n* COATINGS cliché *m*, galvano *m*

electroplate[2] *vt* COATINGS métalliser par galvanisation, électroplaquer, ELEC *process* galvaniser, ELEC ENG plaquer

electroplated[1] *adj* COATINGS galvanisé, métallisé, ELEC galvanisé; ~ **with tin** *adj* COATINGS étamé par électrolyse

electroplated:[2] ~ **coating** *n* COATINGS dépôt électrolytique *m*; ~ **terne** *n* COATINGS plomb déposé électrolytiquement *m*

electroplating *n* COATINGS couche galvanique *f*, couche galvanoplastique *f*, revêtement galvanique *m*, galvanoplastie *f*, métallisation *f*, électrodéposition *f*, ELEC *process* galvanisation *f*, métallisation électrolytique *f*, ELEC ENG galvanoplastie *f*, électrodéposition *f*, PROP MAT électrodéposition *f*; ~ **bath** *n* COATINGS bain galvanoplastique *m*, bain électrolytique *m*

electropneumatic: ~ **brake** *n* TRANSP frein électropneumatique *m*

electropolishing *n* METALL, SPRINGS polissage électrolytique *m*

electropositive[1] *adj* CHEM *ion*, PROP MAT électropositif

electropositive:[2] ~ **element** *n* RAD PHYS élément électropositif *m*

electroproduction: ~ **at threshold** *n* NUCLEAR électroproduction près du seuil *f*

electroscope *n* ELEC, PHYS électroscope *m*

electrosensitive: ~ **paper** *n* COMP, DP papier électrosensible *m*; ~ **printer** *n* COMP, DP imprimante électrosensible *f*; ~ **safety system** *n* SAFETY *on press brakes* système de sécurité électrosensible *m*

electrosilver *vt* ELEC ENG argenter par galvanoplastie

electrosilvering *n* ELEC ENG argenture galvanique *f*

electroslag: ~ **welding** *n* CONST soudage sous laitier *m*, soudage vertical sous laitier *m*, MECH soudage électrique sous laitier *m*, NUCLEAR soudage sous laitier électroconducteur *m*, PROP MAT soudure à électrolaitier *f*

electrospark: ~ **machining** *n* MECH ENG usinage par étincelage *m*

electrospraying *n* NUCLEAR pulvérisation électrique *f*

electrostatic[1] *adj* ELEC *charge*, TELECOM électrostatique

electrostatic:[2] ~ **air filter** *n* HEAT ENG, SAFETY filtre à air électrostatique *m*; ~ **attraction** *n* ELEC, ELEC ENG attraction électrostatique *f*; ~ **charge** *n* ELEC, PROP MAT charge électrostatique *f*; ~ **coating** *n* PROP MAT enduction électrostatique *f*; ~ **collector** *n* NUCLEAR détection de rupture de gaine à collection électrostatique *f*; ~ **CRT** *n* ELECTRON tube cathodique à déviation électrostatique *m*; ~ **enamelling** *n* COLOURS laquage électrostatique *m*; ~ **energy** *n* PROP MAT énergie électrostatique *f*; ~ **exciter** *n* ACOUSTICS excitateur électrostatique *m*; ~ **field** *n* ELEC, PHYS champ électrostatique *m*; ~ **filter** *n* ELECTRON filtre électrostatique *m*, électrofiltre *m*; ~ **flux** *n* ELEC flux électrostatique *m*; ~ **flux density** *n* ELEC densité de flux électrostatique *f*; ~ **focusing** *n* ELEC concentration électrostatique *f*, focalisation électrostatique *f*; ~ **force** *n* ELEC ENG force électrostatique *f*; ~ **generator** *n* ELEC génération électrostatique *f*, ELEC ENG générateur électrostatique *m*; ~ **induction** *n* ELEC induction électrostatique *f*, PHYS influence électrostatique *f*; ~ **ion oscillation** *n* NUCLEAR *plasma* oscillation ionique électrostatique *f*; ~ **lens** *n* ELEC ENG, PHYS, RAD PHYS lentille électrostatique *f*; ~ **loudspeaker** *n* ACOUSTICS, RECORDING haut-parleur électrostatique *m*; ~ **microphone** *n* ACOUSTICS, RECORDING microphone électrostatique *m*; ~ **plotter** *n* COMP, DP traceur électrostatique *m*; ~ **potential energy** *n* GEOPHYS énergie potentielle électrostatique *f*; ~ **powder coating** *n* COLOURS laquage électrostatique de couleurs en poudre *m*, P&R *paint* enduit électrostatique *m*, peinture électrostatique *f*; ~ **precipitator** *n* (*ESP*) POLLUTION dépoussiéreur électrique *m*, précipitateur électrostatique *m*, séparateur électrique *m*, électrofiltre *m*; ~ **printer** *n* COMP, DP imprimante électrostatique *f*; ~ **relay** *n* ELEC relais électrostatique *m*; ~ **screen** *n* ELECTRON écran électrostatique *m*, PHYS blindage électrostatique *m*, écran électrostatique *m*; ~ **spray painting** *n* COLOURS peinture électrostatique au pistolet *f*

electrostatics *n* ELEC, ELEC ENG, PHYS électrostatique *f*

electrostriction *n* PHYS électrostriction *f*

electrosynthesis *n* CHEM électrosynthèse *f*

electrotechnical: ~ **porcelain** *n* ELEC ENG porcelaine électrotechnique *f*

electrotechnics *n* ELEC électrotechnique *f*

electrotechnology *n* ELEC électrotechnique *f*

electrothermal[1] *adj* ELEC électrothermique

electrothermal:[2] ~ **booster** *n* SPACE propulseur électrothermique *m*; ~ **printer** *n* COMP, DP imprimante électrothermique *f*

electrotype *n* PRINT cliché stéréo *m*, cliché électrotypique *m*

electrovan *n* TRANSP camionnette électrique *f*

electroweak: ~ **theory** *n* PART PHYS, PHYS théorie électrofaible *f*; ~ **unification energy** *n* PART PHYS énergie d'unification électrofaible *f*

electrowinning *n* CHEM extraction électrolytique *f*

ELED *abbr* (*edge-emitting light-emitting diode*) OPT diode électroluminescente à émission longitudinale *f*, TELECOM diode électroluminescente à émission par la tranche *f*

elemack *n* CINEMAT chariot Elemack *m*

element *n* CHEM, COMP, DP, ELEC *circuit*, ELECTRON élément *m*, HYDR EQUIP *of sectional boiler* élément de chaudière modulaire *m*, MATH *set theory*, MECH ENG *fundamental, essential part* élément *m*, OPT jonc *m*, PHYS élément *m*; ~ **specific activity** *n* NUCLEAR activité massique de l'élément *f*

elementary: ~ **charge** *n* PHYS charge élémentaire *f*; ~ **enrichment factor** *n* NUCLEAR facteur d'enrichissement unitaire *m*; ~ **loudspeaker** *n* ACOUSTICS haut-parleur élémentaire *m*; ~ **particle** *n* PART PHYS, PHYS particule élémentaire *f*; ~ **separation effect** *n* NUCLEAR effet simple de séparation *m*; ~ **separative power** *n* NUCLEAR pouvoir séparateur unitaire *m*; ~ **servicing sheet** *n* PROD ENG fiche d'entretien élémentaire *f*

elephant: ~ **boiler** *n* HYDR EQUIP chaudière à bouilleurs *f*

eletromagnetic: ~ **field** *n* TELECOM champ électromagnétique *m*; ~ **radiation** *n* TELECOM rayonnement électromagnétique *m*

elevated: ~ **line** *n* (*EL*) TRANSP métro aérien *m*; ~ **monorail** *n* TRANSP monorail surélevé *m*; ~ **platform** *n* RAIL quai surélevé *m*; ~ **rapid transit system** *n* TRANSP métro aérien *m*; ~ **runway** *n* CONST estacade *f*, voie surélevée *f*; ~ **stress level** *n* PROD ENG niveau de contrainte élevé *m*; ~ **track** *n* RAIL estacade *f*, voie en estacade *f*, TRANSP voie surélevée *f*

elevating: ~ **machinery** *n* MECH ENG machines élévatoires *f pl*; ~ **screw** *n* MECH ENG vis monte-et-baisse *f*; ~ **table** *n* MECH table élévatrice *f*; ~ **wheel** *n* MECH ENG roue élévatoire *f*, MILIT *artillery* volant de pointage en élévation *m*

elevation *n* CONST *altitude* altitude *f*, hauteur *f*, élévation *f*, MECH hauteur *f*, niveau *m*, NAUT *navigation* hauteur *f*, élévation *f*; ~ **above sea level** *n* METEO altitude au-dessus du niveau de la mer *f*, hauteur au-dessus du niveau de la mer *f*; ~ **adjusting screw** *n* INSTRUMENT vis de réglage de hausse *f*; ~ **angle** *n* CONST angle de site *m*, SPACE hauteur *f*, site *m*, TELECOM angle de site *m*; ~ **guidance** *n* AERONAUT guidage vertical *m*; ~ **head** *n* NUCLEAR hauteur géométrique *f*

elevator *n* AERONAUT gouverne de profondeur *f*, CONST ascenseur *m*, *goods* élévateur *m*, MECH ascenseur *m*, monte-charge *m*, PETR TECH *drilling* élévateur *m*, PROD ENG ascenseur *m*, lift *m*, monte-charge *m*, élévateur *m*, TRANSP monte-charge *m*; ~ **bucket** *n* PROD ENG auget d'élévateur *m*, godet d'élévateur *m*; ~ **control** *n* AERONAUT commande de profondeur *f*; ~ **cup** *n* PROD ENG auget d'élévateur *m*, godet d'élévateur *m*; ~ **deflection** *n* AERONAUT braquage de profondeur *m*; ~ **follow-up** *n* AERONAUT transmitteur de profondeur *m*; ~ **hoist** *n* AERONAUT dispositif de hissage des volets de profondeur *m*; ~ **trim** *n* AERONAUT trim de profondeur *m*

elevon *n* TRANSP élevon *m*

eligma *n* NUCLEAR éligma *m*

ellagic *adj* CHEM ellagique

ellagitannin *n* CHEM acide ellagitannique *m*

ellipse *n* GEOM ellipse *f*; ~ **of inertia** *n* MECH ellipse d'inertie *f*

ellipsis *n* PRINT ellipse *f*

ellipsoid[1] *adj* GEOM ellipsoïde

ellipsoid[2] *n* GEOM, PHYS ellipsoïde *m*

ellipsoidal *adj* PROP MAT ellipsoïdal

ellipsometer *n* PHYS ellipsomètre *m*

elliptic[1] *adj* GEOM elliptique

elliptic:[2] ~ **filter** *n* ELECTRON filtre elliptique *m*; ~ **polarization** *n* RAD PHYS polarisation elliptique *f*; ~ **response curve** *n* ELECTRON courbe de réponse d'un filtre elliptique *f*; ~ **spring** *n* MECH ENG pincette *f*, ressort à pincette *m*, SPRINGS ressort elliptique *m*, ressort à pincette *m*

elliptical[1] *adj* GEOM elliptique

elliptical:[2] ~ **arch** *n* CONST arc elliptique *m*, voûte elliptique *f*, *of bridge* arche elliptique *f*; ~ **galaxy** *n* ASTRON galaxie elliptique *f*; ~ **gear** *n* MECH ENG engrenage elliptique *m*; ~ **geometry** *n* GEOM géométrie elliptique *f*; ~ **mirror** *n* INSTRUMENT, PHYS miroir elliptique *m*; ~ **orbit** *n* ASTRON, PHYS orbite elliptique *f*; ~ **polarization** *n* PHYS, SPACE *communications* polarisation elliptique *f*; ~ **space** *n* GEOM espace elliptique *m*; ~ **stern** *n* NAUT arrière rond *m*; ~ **universe** *n* ASTRON univers elliptique *m*

elliptically-polarized: ~ **wave** *n* ACOUSTICS, PHYS onde polarisée elliptiquement *f*

ellipticity *n* SPACE *communications* ellipticité *f*

elliptone *n* CHEM elliptone *f*

ellsworthite *n* NUCLEAR ellsworthite *f*

elongated[1] *adj* MECH allongé, oblong, PRINT *type* allongé

elongated:[2] ~ **grain** *n* METALL grain allongé *m*; ~ **hole** *n* MECH trou oblong *m*, MECH ENG trou ovalisé *m*

elongation *n* ASTRON élongation *f*, MECH ENG ovalisation *f*, METALL *of specimen* allongement *m*, P&R élongation

f, PAPER TECH, PHYS allongement *m*; ~ **at break** *n* P&R allongement à la rupture *m*; ~ **of the cylinder** *n* C&G longeage du cylindre *m*; ~ **east** *n* ASTRON élongation de l'est *f*; ~ **west** *n* ASTRON élongation de l'ouest *f*

ELSBM *abbr (exposed location single-buoy mooring)* PETR TECH amarrage à point unique *m*, bouée d'amarrage à point unique *f*, bouée monoposte *f*

ELT *abbr (emergency locator transmitter)* TELECOM radiobalise de détresse *f*, émetteur de localisation d'urgence *m*

eluate *n* CHEM éluat *m*

eluent *n* CHEM, NUCLEAR *solvent* éluant *m*

elute *vt* CHEM éluer

eluting: ~ **agent** *n* NUCLEAR éluant *m*

elution *n* CHEM, CHEM TECH élution *f*, FOOD TECH élutriation *f*

elutriate *vt* CHEM TECH décanter

elutriating: ~ **funnel** *n* CHEM TECH cône d'élution *m*; ~ **machine** *n* CHEM TECH machine à décanter *f*

elutriation *n* C&G minutage *m*, CHEM élutriation *f*, CHEM TECH débourrage *m*, lavage *m*; ~ **chamber** *n* CHEM TECH chambre d'élutriation *f*; ~ **test** *n* CONST *civil engineering* essai d'entraînement *m*

elvan *n* GEOL *microgranite vein* filon de granite *m*, microgranite *m*, PETR elvan *m*

elvanite *n* PETR elvan *m*

em *n* CHEM *(electron mass)* masse électronique *f*, PRINT *(emquad)* em *m* *(quadratin)*

EM *abbr* COMP *(electronic mail, E-mail)* courrier électronique *m*, messagerie électronique *f*, COMP *(end of medium)* fin de support *f*, DP *(electronic mail, E-mail)*, ELECTRON *(electronic mail, E-mail)*, TELECOM *(electronic mail, E-mail)* courrier électronique *m*, messagerie électronique *f*

E-mail *n (EM)* COMP courrier électronique *m*, messagerie électronique *f*, DP, ELECTRON courrier électronique *m*, TELECOM courrier électronique *m*, messagerie électronique *f*

emanating: ~ **power** *n* RAD PHYS pouvoir émanateur *m*

emanation *n* CHEM, NUCLEAR émanation *f*

embankment *n* MINING remblai *m*, terrassement en remblai *m*, RAIL remblai *m*; ~ **pile** *n* COAL TECH pieu pour remblai *m*; ~ **piling** *n* COAL TECH battage de pieux pour remblai *m*

embed *vt* CONST encastrer

embedded[1] *adj* COMP imbriqué, DP encastré, incorporé, MECH ENG encastré; ~ **in the wall** *adj* CONST encastré dans le mur

embedded:[2] ~ **control channel** *n (ECC)* TELECOM canal de commande intégré *m*; ~ **loop** *n* TRANSP boucle noyée dans la chaussée *f*; ~ **operations channel** *n (EOC)* TELECOM canal d'exploitation intégré *m*

embedding *n* P&R *process* enrobage *m*; ~ **in concrete** *n* NUCLEAR bétonnage *m*

embedment *n* CONST *of beam, column* section d'encastrement *f*

embelin *n* CHEM embeline *m*

embodied *adj* MECH ENG solidaire

embodiment *n* PATENTS *of invention* mode particulier *m*

embolden *vt* PRINT *typestyle* mettre en caractères gras

embolite *n* MINERAL embolite *f*

emboss *vt* PAPER TECH gaufrer

embossed[1] *adj* MECH ENG gaufré

embossed:[2] ~ **calender** *n* PACKAGING calandre gaufrée *f*; ~ **groove recording** *n* RECORDING enregistrement à sillon repoussé *m*; ~ **label** *n* PACKAGING étiquette en relief *f*; ~ **paper** *n* PACKAGING papier en relief *m*, PAPER TECH papier gaufré *m*

embossing *n* C&G gravure à relief prononcé *f*, P&R *process*, PAPER TECH, PRINT gaufrage *m*; ~ **calender** *n* PAPER TECH gaufreuse *f*; ~ **closure** *n* PACKAGING fermeture estampée *f*; ~ **machine** *n* PACKAGING machine pour estamper *f*; ~ **press** *n* PACKAGING estampeuse *f*; ~ **roll** *n* PAPER TECH rouleau gaufreur *m*

embossment *n* MECH ENG gaufrage *m*

embrittled *adj* PROD ENG durci

embrittlement *n* METALL, NUCLEAR, PROP MAT fragilisation *f*

EMC *n* (*electromagnetic compatibility*) SPACE compatibilité électromagnétique *f*

emerald *n* MINERAL émeraude *f*; ~ **copper** *n* MINERAL dioptase *m*

emerged *adj* GEOL émergé

emergence *n* GEOL *of seafloor*, OCEANOG émersion *f*

emergency[1] *adj* MECH, SAFETY d'urgence, de secours, SPACE *spacecraft* d'urgence, de détresse, de secours

emergency[2] *n* SAFETY alerte *f*, cas d'urgence *m*, cas urgent *m*, SPACE *spacecraft* évacuation *f*; ~ **aids** *n* TRANSP aides d'urgence *f pl*; ~ **air lock** *n* NUCLEAR sas de secours *m*; ~ **attention** *n* TELECOM *fault maintenance* relèvement d'urgence *m*; ~ **battery** *n* ELEC, ELEC ENG batterie de secours *f*; ~ **beacon** *n* SPACE *communications* balise de détresse *f*; ~ **brake** *n* AERONAUT frein de détresse *m*, TRANSP frein de secours *m*; ~ **brake system** *n* VEHICLES freinage de secours *m*; ~ **button** *n* CONTROL, ELEC *safety* bouton d'urgence *m*; ~ **cable** *n* TRANSP câble de secours *m*; ~ **call** *n* TELECOM appel d'urgence *m*; ~ **call system** *n* TRANSP système d'appel d'urgence *m*; ~ **capsule** *n* SPACE *spacecraft* capsule d'évacuation *f*; ~ **case** *n* SAFETY urgence *f*; ~ **center** *n* (AmE), ~ **centre** *n* (BrE) SAFETY poste de secours *m*; ~ **condition** *n* NUCLEAR *needing shutdown for repair* situation d'urgence *f*; ~ **control** *n* AERONAUT, SAFETY commande de secours *f*; ~ **core coolant** *n* NUCLEAR caloporteur de secours *m*; ~ **crash barrier** *n* TRANSP barrière d'arrêt *f*; ~ **descent** *n* AERONAUT descente rapide *f*; ~ **diesel generator** *n* NUCLEAR diesel de secours *m*; ~ **door** *n* CONST porte de secours *f*; ~ **door switch** *n* CONTROL contacteur de porte *m*; ~ **drill** *n* NAUT exercice d'évacuation *m*; ~ **equipment** *n* AERONAUT équipement de secours *m*, SAFETY appareillage de secours *m*; ~ **escape** *n* SPACE *spacecraft* évacuation d'urgence *f*; ~ **escape tower** *n* SPACE *spacecraft* tour de sauvetage *f*; ~ **evacuation of buildings** *n* SAFETY évacuation d'urgence des lieux *f*; ~ **exit** *n* AERONAUT issue de secours *f*, CONST, SAFETY sortie de secours *f*; ~ **first aid procedure** *n* SAFETY procédure de premier secours d'urgence *f*; ~ **fishplating** *n* (*cf applying of emergency joint bars*) RAIL éclissage de fortune *m*; ~ **flotation gear** *n* AERONAUT système de flottabilité de secours *m*; ~ **installation** *n* TELECOM installation de secours *f*; ~ **landing** *n* AERONAUT atterrissage d'urgence *m*, SPACE *spacecraft* atterrissage d'urgence *m*, atterrissage forcé *m*; ~ **lighting** *n* ELEC éclairage de sécurité *m*; ~ **location beacon** *n* AERONAUT radiophare de repérage d'urgence *m*; ~ **locator transmitter** *n* NAUT *satellite rescue services* émetteur de localisation d'urgence *m*, TELECOM radiobalise de détresse *f*, émetteur de localisation d'urgence *m*; ~ **maintenance** *n* COMP maintenance d'urgence *f*, maintenance de secours *f*, DP maintenance d'urgence *f*; ~ **measures** *n pl* SAFETY mesures de secours *f pl*; ~ **mode** *n* SPACE *spacecraft* mode de

secours *m*; ~ **position-indicating radio beacon** *n* (*E-PIRB*) NAUT, TELECOM radiobalise de localisation de sinistre *f*; ~ **power generator** *n* MECH groupe de secours *m*; ~ **power supply** *n* ELEC alimentation de secours *f*; ~ **procedure** *n* AERONAUT procédure de secours *f*; ~ **rocket** *n* NAUT fusée de détresse *f*; ~ **service** *n* SAFETY *medical* service des urgences *m*; ~ **services** *n pl* TELECOM services d'urgence *m pl*; ~ **shutdown** *n* COMP, DP, NUCLEAR arrêt d'urgence *m*; ~ **shutdown of the reactor** *n* NUCLEAR arrêt d'urgence du réacteur *m*, assemblage d'arrêt d'urgence *m*; ~ **shutdown rod** *n* NUCLEAR barre d'arrêt d'urgence *f*; ~ **sign** *n* SAFETY signe de secours *m*; ~ **signal** *n* CONTROL signal d'alarme *m*, signal de détresse *m*; ~ **slide** *n* AERONAUT glissière d'évacuation d'urgence *f*, toboggan d'évacuation *m*, toboggan de secours *m*; ~ **spillway** *n* WATER SUPP canal de décharge *m*, évacuateur de secours *m*; ~ **stop** *n* SAFETY arrêt d'urgence *m*; ~ **supply tank** *n* AERONAUT nourrice de secours *f*; ~ **switch** *n* CONTROL interrupteur d'urgence *m*, interrupteur de secours *m*; ~ **system** *n* AERONAUT circuit de secours *m*; ~ **telephone** *n* TELECOM poste de secours *m*, TRANSP poste téléphonique sur autoroute *m*; ~ **treatment** *n* SAFETY traitement de secours *m*; ~ **turn** *n* NAUT *shiphandling* abattée d'urgence *f*

emergency-stopping: ~ **device** *n* SAFETY *of machines* dispositif d'arrêt d'urgence *m*

emergent *adj* GEOL émergent

emerging-foil: ~ **craft** *n* TRANSP hydroptère à ailes émergentes *m*

emerizing *n* TEXTILES émerisage *m*

emersion *n* ASTRON émersion *f*

emery *n* C&G, MECH, PROD ENG émeri *m*; ~ **belt polishing machine** *n* PROD ENG machine à courroie émerisée *f*; ~ **cloth** *n* MECH toile émeri *f*, MECH ENG toile abrasive *f*, PROD ENG toile émeri *f*, toile émerisée *f*; ~ **grinder** *n* PROD ENG machine à meule d'émeri *f*; ~ **grinding machine** *n* PROD ENG machine à meule d'émeri *f*; ~ **machine** *n* PROD ENG machine à meule d'émeri *f*; ~ **paper** *n* MECH papier-émeri *m*, PROD ENG papier émerisé *m*, papier-émeri *m*; ~ **powder** *n* MECH ENG potée d'émeri *f*; ~ **washing** *n* C&G lotionnage d'émeri *m*; ~ **wheel** *n* MECH meule émeri *f*, PROD ENG meule en émeri *f*, meule émeri *f*; ~ **wheel attachment** *n* PROD ENG porte-meule *m*; ~ **wheel dresser** *n* PROD ENG dresse-meule *m*, décrasse-meule *m*, rhabilleur pour meules d'émeri *m*; ~ **wheel spindle** *n* PROD ENG arbre porte-meule *m*

emerylite *n* MINERAL émerylite *f*

emeryllite *n* MINERAL émerylite *f*

emetine *n* CHEM émétine *f*

emf *abbr* (*electromotive force*) ELEC, ELEC ENG, PHYS fém (*force électromotrice*)

EMI *abbr* COMP (*electromagnetic interference*) interférence électromagnétique *f*, PROD ENG (*electromagnetic induction*) induction électromagnétique *f*, SPACE (*electromagnetic interference*) perturbation électromagnétique *f*

emission *n* AERONAUT *engine*, COMP, DP, PART PHYS, POLLUTION émission *f*, RAD PHYS rayonnement *m*, VEHICLES *exhaust* gaz d'échappement *m*, émission *f*; ~ **band** *n* PHYS bande d'émission *f*; ~ **chamber** *n* INSTRUMENT chambre d'émission *f*; ~ **control** *n* CONTROL contrôle d'émission *m*; ~ **data** *n pl* POLLUTION données d'émission *f pl*; ~ **electron microscope** *n* ELECTRON microscope électronique à émission *m*; ~ **inventory** *n* POLLUTION inventaire des émissions *m*; ~ **line** *n* PHYS

raie d'émission *f*; ~ **microscope** *n* INSTRUMENT microscope à émission *m*; ~ **microscopy** *n* METALL
microscopie à émission *f*; ~ **nebula** *n* ASTRON, SPACE
nébuleuse à raies d'émission *f*, nébuleuse à émission *f*;
~ **point** *n* POLLUTION lieu d'émission *m*; ~ **source** *n*
POLLUTION source *f*, source d'émission *f*, source émettrice *f*, émetteur *m*; ~ **spectral analysis** *n* RAD PHYS
analyse par spectroscopie d'émission *f*; ~ **spectrum** *n*
PHYS spectre d'émission *m*, RAD PHYS spectre de
rayonnement *m*, SPACE spectre d'émission *m*; ~ **standard** *n* POLLUTION limite d'émission *f*, norme
d'émission *f*

emissions *n pl* RAD PHYS *radiation monitoring* dégage-
ments *m pl*

emissive: ~ **diode** *n* ELECTRON diode émissive *f*

emissivity *n* HEAT ENG, OPT, PHYS émissivité *f*, RAD PHYS
émettivité *f*, TELECOM émissivité *f*

emit *vt* COMP, DP émettre, RAD PHYS *thermal radiation*
fournir, THERMOD *heat* dégager, *steam* émettre

emittance *n* FUELLESS émittance *f*

emitted: ~ **radiation** *n* RAD PHYS rayonnement émis *m*

emitter *n* COMP, DP, ELEC ENG, PHYS *transistor*, RAD
PHYS, TELECOM émetteur *m*; ~ **base breakdown** *n* ELEC-
TRON claquage de la jonction émetteur-base *m*; ~ **base
junction** *n* ELECTRON jonction émetteur-base *f*; ~
contact *n* ELEC ENG contact d'émetteur *m*; ~ **electrode**
n ELEC ENG électrode émettrice *f*; ~ **follower** *n* ELEC ENG
montage émetteur-suiveur *m*, PHYS montage collecteur commun *m*; ~ **region** *n* ELEC ENG zone de
l'émetteur *f*, zone émettrice *f*

emitter-coupled: ~ **logic** *n* (*ECL*) COMP, ELECTRON logique ECL *f*, logique à couplage par émetteurs *f*; ~ **logic
gate array** *n* ELECTRON matrice prédiffusée ECL *f*

emodic *adj* CHEM émodique

emodin *n* CHEM émodine *f*

empennage *n* AERONAUT empennage *m*

empirical: ~ **formula** *n* CHEM formule empirique *f*; ~
operation factor *n* MECH ENG coefficient numérique
forfaitaire *m*; ~ **temperature** *n* THERMOD température
empirique *f*

emplacement: ~ **age** *n* GEOL âge de mise en place *m*

emplectite *n* MINERAL emplectite *f*

employee *n* PATENTS employé *m*, employée *f*

employer *n* PATENTS employeur *m*, employeuse *f*

empties *n pl* PACKAGING vidanges *f pl*; ~ **siding** *n* RAIL
voie de concentration des vides *f*

empty[1] *adj* COMP, DP vide, PROD ENG à vide

empty:[2] ~ **band** *n* PHYS *solid state* bande vide *f*; ~ **hole** *n*
PETR trou libre *m*; ~ **machine** *n* PROD ENG machine
marchant à blanc *f*, machine marchant à vide *f*; ~
medium *n* COMP, DP support vide *m*; ~ **string** *n* COMP,
DP chaîne vide *f*; ~ **weight** *n* AERONAUT masse à vide *f*

emptying: ~ **plug** *n* PROD ENG tampon de vidange *m*

emquad *n* (*em*) PRINT quadratin *m* (*em*)

EMS *abbr* COMP (*expanded memory specification*)
norme EMS *f* (*spécification de mémoire étendue*),
TELECOM (*electronic message system*) système de
commutation électronique de messages *m*, système de
messagerie électronique *m*

Emsian *adj* GEOL emsien

emulate *vt* COMP, DP, ELECTRON émuler

emulation *n* COMP, DP, ELECTRON émulation *f*

emulator *n* COMP, DP, ELECTRON, TELECOM émulateur *m*

emulsifiability *n* CHEM TECH émulsionnabilité *f*

emulsifiable *adj* CHEM TECH émulsionnable

emulsification *n* CHEM émulsification *f*, émulsionne-

ment *m*, CHEM TECH émulsionnement *m*

emulsified[1] *adj* CHEM TECH émulsionné

emulsified:[2] ~ **fuel** *n* AERONAUT carburant émulsifié *m*,
carburant émulsionné *m*

emulsifier *n* CHEM émulseur *m*, émulsificateur *m*, CHEM
TECH agent émulsifiant *m*, émulsifiant *m*, émulsionnant *m*, FOOD TECH émulsifiant *m*, NUCLEAR
émulsionneuse *f*, P&R *compounding ingredient* émulseur *m*, émulsifiant *m*, émulsionneuse *f*, PAPER TECH
émulgateur *m*

emulsify[1] *vt* CHEM, CHEM TECH, P&R émulsionner, PAPER
TECH émulsifier, PHOTO, POLLUTION émulsionner

emulsify[2] *vi* PRINT provoquer une émulsion, s'émulsionner

emulsifying[1] *adj* CHEM TECH émulsifiant, émulsionnant

emulsifying:[2] ~ **agent** *n* CHEM émulsifiant *m*, CHEM TECH
agent émulsifiant *m*, émulsifiant *m*, émulsionnant *m*,
P&R *compounding ingredient* émulseur *m*, émulsifiant
m, PACKAGING émulsionnant *m*, PROD ENG agent é-
mulseur *m*; ~ **liquid** *n* CHEM TECH liquide émulsionnant
m, SAFETY liquide émulseur *m*; ~ **machine** *n* CHEM TECH
machine à émulsionner *f*, émulsionneuse *f*, NUCLEAR
émulsionneuse *f*

emulsin *n* CHEM TECH émulsine *f*

emulsion *n* CHEM, CINEMAT, P&R *physical state*, PETR
TECH *drilling mud* émulsion *f*, PHOTO couche-image *f*,
surface sensible *f*, émulsion *f*, PHYS émulsion *f*; ~
adhesive *n* PACKAGING colle en émulsion *f*; ~ **batch** *n*
CINEMAT lot de fabrication *m*; ~ **batch number** *n* PHO-
TO numéro de l'émulsion *m*, numéro de lot de
fabrication *m*; ~ **binder** *n* CHEM TECH liant à émulsion
m; ~ **breaker** *n* MAR POLL casseur d'émulsion *m*, désémulsifiant *m*, POLLUTION briseur d'émulsion *m*; ~ **in** *n*
CINEMAT enroulement intérieur *m*; ~ **layer** *n* COATINGS
couche photographique *f*; ~ **mud** *n* PETR boue émulsionnée *f*; ~ **out** *n* CINEMAT enroulement extérieur *m*; ~
paint *n* COLOURS, CONST peinture-émulsion *f*, P&R
peinture d'émulsion *f*, peinture émulsionnée *f*, PROD
ENG peinture-émulsion *f*; ~ **persistence** *n* CHEM TECH
stabilité d'émulsion *f*; ~ **pile-up** *n* CINEMAT dépôt de
pellicule *m*; ~ **polymerization** *n* P&R polymérisation en
émulsion *f*; ~ **position** *n* CINEMAT sens de l'émulsion *m*;
~ **side** *n* CINEMAT côté émulsion *m*; ~ **speed** *n* CINEMAT
sensibilité de l'émulsion *f*; ~ **stripping** *n* PRINT grattage
de l'émulsion *m*; ~ **test** *n* CHEM TECH essai d'émulsion *m*

emulsion-coated[1] *adj* PACKAGING couché à l'émulsion

emulsion-coated:[2] ~ **paper** *n* PAPER TECH papier couché
par émulsion *m*

EMW *abbr* (*Equivalent Mud Weight*) PETR TECH *drilling*
DBE (*densité de boue équivalente*)

en: ~ **echelon folds** *n pl* GEOL plis en relais *m pl*, plis en
échelon *m pl*; ~ **space** *n* PRINT demi-cadratin *m*, largeur moyenne des caractères *f*

enable:[1] ~ **pulse** *n* COMP, DP, ELECTRON impulsion de
validation *f*; ~ **signal** *n* ELECTRON signal de validation *m*

enable[2] *vt* COMP, DP, ELECTRON *logic gate* valider, PROD
ENG *forces* activer

enabled: ~ **gate** *n* ELECTRON porte validée *f*

enabling *n* ELECTRON validation *f*; ~ **signal** *n* COMP signal
de validation *m*, CONTROL signal d'autorisation *m*, signal de validation *m*, DP signal d'autorisation *m*

enamel[1] *n* C&G, COATINGS émail *m*, COLOURS vernis *m*,
CONST peinture vernissante *f*, P&R *paint* peinture *f*,
vernis *m*, émail *m*, PROD ENG émail *m*; ~ **board** *n*

PACKAGING carton glacé *m*; ~ **color** *n* (AmE), ~ **colour** *n* (BrE) C&G couleur émail *f*; ~ **firing** *n* C&G décoration au four *f*; ~ **paint** *n* COATINGS, COLOURS laque-émail *f*, peinture laquée *f*; ~ **varnish** *n* COATINGS laque-émail *f*, COLOURS laque-émail *f*, peinture-émail *f*

enamel[2] *vt* COATINGS engober, laquer au vernis à cuire, plomber, revêtir d'émail, vernir au vernis à cuire, vernisser, émailler, COLOURS vernir au vernis à cuire

enamel:[3] ~ **bake** *vi* COLOURS laquer à la laque à cuire

enamel-covered *adj* COATINGS laqué, verni

enameled[1] *adj*, *n* (AmE) *see* enamelled

enameler *n* (AmE) *see* enameller

enameling *n* (AmE) *see* enamelling

enamelled[1] *adj* (BrE) COATINGS *ceramics, paint* verni, émaillé

enamelled:[2] ~ **copper wire** *n* (BrE) COATINGS fil en cuivre émaillé *m*, ELEC ENG fil émaillé en cuir *m*; ~ **iron** *n* (BrE) PROD ENG tôle émaillée *f*; ~ **paper** *n* (BrE) COATINGS papier satiné *m*; ~ **wire** *n* (BrE) COATINGS fil émaillé *m*, ELEC *conductor*, ELEC ENG fil verni *m*, fil émaillé *m*

enameller *n* (BrE) COATINGS vernisseur à la laque *m*

enamelling *n* (BrE) COATINGS laquage *m*, vernissage au vernis à cuivre *m*, émaillage *m*, émaillure *f*, COLOURS laquage *m*, HEATING émaillage *m*, PACKAGING vernissage *m*, PROD ENG émaillage *m*; ~ **furnace** *n* (BrE) COATINGS four à émailler *m*; ~ **kiln** *n* (BrE) COATINGS four à émailler *m*; ~ **line** *n* (BrE) COATINGS chaîne de vernissage *f*, tapis roulant *m*; ~ **sheet** *n* (BrE) CO-ATINGS tôle à émailler *f*; ~ **stove** *n* (BrE) COATINGS four à cuire la laque *m*, four à cuire la peinture *m*

enantiomer *n* CHEM énantiomère *m*

enantiomorph *n* CRYSTALL énantiomorphe

enantiomorphic *adj* CHEM énantiomorphe, CRYSTALL énantiomorphique

enantiomorphism *n* CHEM énantiomorphie *f*, énantiomorphisme *m*, CRYSTALL énantiomorphisme *m*

enantiomorphous *adj* CHEM énantiomorphe

enantiotropic *adj* CHEM, CRYSTALL énantiotrope

enargite *n* MINERAL énargite *f*

encapsulated: ~ **source** *n* NUCLEAR source scellée *f*; ~ **type** *n* COMP, DP type encapsulé *m*

encapsulating: ~ **glass** *n* C&G enveloppe étanche en verre *f*

encapsulation *n* NUCLEAR enrobage *m*, scellement *m*, P&R *process* enrobage *m*; ~ **mold** *n* (AmE), ~ **mould** *n* (BrE) MECH ENG moule de bouchonnage *m*

encase *vt* CONST enrober, occulter

encased[1] *adj* CONST *engineering* encastré

encased:[2] ~ **beam** *n* CONST poutre encastrée *f*

encaustic: ~ **tile** *n* C&G tuile vernie *f*

encipher *vt* ELECTRON chiffrer

encipherment *n* ELECTRON chiffrage *m*, TELECOM chiffrement *m*

encircling: ~ **coil** *n* TESTING bobine annulaire *f*

enclave *n* PETR enclave de roche éruptive *f*

enclosed[1] *adj* MECH ENG enfermé, PACKAGING inclus

enclosed:[2] ~ **casing** *n* HYDR EQUIP *of turbine* bâche *f*, enveloppe *f*, huche *f*; ~ **fuse** *n* ELEC fusible tubulaire *m*, ELEC ENG fusible enfermé *m*; ~ **gears** *n pl* MECH ENG engrenages enfermés dans des carters *m pl*, engrenages recouverts de gaines protectrices *m pl*; ~ **motor** *n* ELEC moteur blindé *m*, moteur cuirassé *m*, ELEC ENG moteur blindé *m*, moteur fermé *m*; ~ **sea** *n* OCEANOG mer fermée *f*

enclosing: ~ **wall** *n* CONST mur d'enceinte *m*, mur de clôture *m*

enclosure *n* ACOUSTICS enceinte *f*, CONST clôture *f*, enceinte *f*, enclos *m*, NUCLEAR, PHYS *enclosed space* enceinte *f*, PROD ENG armoire *f*, boîtier *m*; ~ **of palisades** *n* CONST enceinte de palissades *f*

encode *vt* COMP, DP coder, encoder, ELECTRON coder, TELECOM chiffrer, coder, TV coder

encoded: ~ **information type** *n* (*EIT*) TELECOM type d'informations codées *m*, type de codage *m*; ~ **pulses** *n pl* TV impulsions codées *f pl*; ~ **signal** *n* ELECTRON signal codé *m*; ~ **stereo** *n* RECORDING stéréophonie codée *f*

encoder *n* COMP encodeur *m*, DP codeur *m*, encodeur *m*, ELECTRON codeur *m*, PROD ENG circuit codeur *m*, TV codeur *m*; ~ **shaft** *n* PROD ENG axe du codeur *m*

encoding *n* COMP, DP codage *m*, encodage *m*, ELECTRON codage *m*, PACKAGING encodage *m*, SPACE *communications*, TELECOM codage *m*; ~ **altimeter** *n* AERONAUT altimètre codeur *m*; ~ **potentiometer** *n* SPACE *communications* potentiomètre de codage *m*

encompass *vt* MECH ENG enclaver

encounter: ~ **rate** *n* MAR POLL taux de rencontre *m*

encrinitic: ~ **limestone** *n* GEOL calcaire à crinoïdes *m*, calcaire à encrines *m*

encrustation *n* GEOL encroûtement *m*

encrypt *vt* ELECTRON crypter

encrypted: ~ **speech** *n* TELECOM signal vocal codé *m*

encryption *n* COMP chiffrage *m*, codage *m*, encryptage *m*, DP encryptage *m*, ELECTRON cryptage *m*, TELECOM chiffrement *m*, TV *of broadcast signal* cryptage *m*; ~ **chip** *n* ELECTRON puce de cryptage *f*

end *n* COMP, DP fin *f*, PROD ENG embout *m*, TEXTILES fil *m*; ~ **of address** *n* COMP, DP fin d'adresse *f*; ~ **address field** *n* PROD ENG adresse de fin de zone *f*; ~ **of block** *n* COMP (*EOB*), DP fin de bloc *f*; ~ **box** *n* WATER SUPP *sluices* boîte de queue *f*; ~ **bracket** *n* MINING *for equipping* chaise en bout *f*, équerre-applique *f*; ~ **bunker refrigerated truck** *n* REFRIG wagon frigorifique à bac d'extrémité *m*; ~ **cap** *n* ELEC ENG *wire* embout *m*; ~ **cleat** *n* COAL TECH limet parallèle à l'inclinaison *m*; ~ **coil** *n* SPRINGS spire d'extrémité *f*, spire terminale *f*; ~ **of communication** *n* (*EOC*) TELECOM fin de communication *m*; ~ **of communication signal** *n* TELECOM signal de fin de communication *m*; ~ **of connecting rod** *n* MECH ENG tête de bielle *f*; ~ **contraction** *n* HYDROL *flow of water over weirs* contraction latérale *f*; ~ **credits** *n pl* CINEMAT génériques de fin *m pl*; ~ **cutting nippers** *n pl* PROD ENG pince coupante en bout *f*; ~ **of data** *n* (*EOD*) COMP, DP fin de données *f*; ~ **deckle** *n* PAPER TECH tiroir *m*; ~ **distortion** *n* ELECTRON décalage des flancs arrières *m*; ~ **door** *n* (BrE) (*cf pit door*) C&G bouclier *m*; ~ **dump** *n* CONST basculeur en bout *m*; ~ **fence** *n* PROD ENG bit de fin *m*; ~ **of file** *n* (*EOF*) COMP, DP fin de fichier *f*; ~ **fitting** *n* NUCLEAR bout *m*, extrémité *f*; ~ **of flight** *n* SPACE *spacecraft* fin de vol *f*; ~ **float** *n* NUCLEAR *between AGR fuel element grids* jeu *m*; ~ **forming** *n* SPRINGS *of spring coil* formation de spires terminales *f*; ~ **frame member** *n* PACKAGING *in container* barre pour cadre d'extrémité *f*; ~ **group** *n* CHEM *organic compound* extrémité d'une chaîne *f*; ~ **of job** *n* (*EOJ*) COMP, DP fin de travail *f*; ~ **leader** *n* CINEMAT amorce de fin *f*, amorce finale *f*; ~ **of lehr** *n* C&G sortie d'arche *f*; ~ **of life cladding rupture** *n* NUCLEAR rupture de gaine en fin de vie *f*; ~ **of line packaging** *n* PACKAGING emballage en fin de chaîne de production *m*; ~ **mark** *n* COMP, DP marque de fin *f*; ~ **measure** *n* METR mesure à bouts *f*; ~ **of medium** *n* COMP (*EM*), DP fin de support *f*; **~ member** *n* GEOL pôle *m*, pôle de mélange *m*; **~ of message** *n (EOM)* COMP, DP, TELE-COM fin de message *f*; **~ mill** *n* MECH ENG fraise de bout *f*, fraise en bout *f*, fraise radiale *f*; **~ mill with indexable inserts** *n* MECH ENG fraise en bout à plaquettes amovibles *f*; **~ nippers** *n pl* MECH ENG *tool* tenailles de mécanicien *f pl*; **~ panel** *n* MECH ENG panneau d'extrémité *m*, PACKAGING panneau final *m*; **~ piece** *n* SPACE, SPRINGS embout *m*; **~ plate** *n* PROD ENG *boiler* plaque d'extrémité *f*, plaque terminale *f*; **~ play** *n* MECH, MECH ENG jeu axial *m*; **~ point** *n* CHEM *of reaction* fin *f*; **~ pointer** *n* PROD ENG pointeur de fin *m*; **~ of reel** *n* COMP, DP fin de bobine *f*; **~ rib** *n* AERONAUT nervure d'extrémité *f*, nervure de rive *f*; **~ rung** *n* PROD ENG ligne de fin *f*; **~ screen** *n* ELECTRON écran d'extrémité *m*; **~ section** *n* NUCLEAR *of fuel element* bout *m*, extrémité *f*; **~ sheet** *n* PRINT feuille de garde *f*; **~ slate** *n* CINEMAT claquette de fin *f*; **~ statement address** *n* PROD ENG adresse de fin *f*; **~ stop** *n* MECH ENG embout arrêtoir *m*; **~ of stroke** *n* MECH ENG *of tool, piston* bout de course *m*; **~ suction centrifugal pump** *n* MECH ENG pompe centrifuge à aspiration en bout *f*; **~ system** *n* TELECOM système d'extrémité *m*; **~ of tape** *n (EOT)* COMP, DP fin de bande *m*; **~ of tape marker** *n* COMP, DP repère de fin de bande *m*; **~ of text** *n (ETX)* COMP, DP fin de texte *f*; **~ thickness** *n* SPRINGS *of spring coil* épaisseur de l'extrémité *f*; **~ thrust bearing** *n* MECH ENG butée à l'arrière *f*; **~ of transaction** *n (EOT)* TELECOM fin de transaction *f*; **~ of transmission** *n (EOT)* COMP, DP fin de transmission *f*; **~ of transmission block** *n (ETB)* COMP, DP fin de bloc de transmission *f*; **~ of travel** *n* MECH ENG *of tool, piston* bout de course *m*; **~ use** *n* TEXTILES emploi final *m*; **~ user** *n* COMP, DP, TELECOM *network* utilisateur final *m*; **~ wall bracket** *n* MINING *for equipping* chaise en bout *f*, équerre-applique *f*; **~ winding spacer** *n* NUCLEAR pièce d'écartement de la tête de bobine *f*

end-and-end: ~ lease *n* TEXTILES envergure *f*

end-around: ~ carry *n* COMP, DP report circulaire *m*; **~ shift** *n* COMP, DP permutation circulaire *f*

endboard *n* CINEMAT claquette de fin *f*, PRINT plaque d'extrémité *f*

endfire: ~ antenna *n* SPACE *communications* antenne à rayonnement longitudinal *f*; **~ array antenna** *n* TELE-COM antenne à rayon longitudinal *f*, antenne à rayonnement longitudinal *f*

endless[1] *adj* PAPER TECH sans fin

endless:[2] **~ belt** *n* VEHICLES *cooling system* courroie sans fin *f*; **~ cable** *n* TRANSP câble sans fin *m*; **~ chain** *n* PAPER TECH, VEHICLES chaîne sans fin *f*; **~ hexagonal belt** *n* MECH ENG courroie hexagonale sans fin *f*; **~ magnetic loop cartridge** *n* ACOUSTICS cartouche pour bande magnétique sans fin *f*; **~ pin chain** *n* TEXTILES chaîne sans fin à picots *f*; **~ printing** *n* PRINT impression en continu *f*; **~ screw** *n* MECH ENG vis sans fin *f*; **V-belt** *n* MECH ENG *antistatic* courroie trapézoïdale sans fin *f*; **~ wide V-belt** *n* MECH ENG courroie trapézoïdale large sans fin *f*

endlink *n* CHEM *of polymer* lien en bout *m*

endoatmospheric *adj* SPACE *spacecraft* endoatmosphérique

endoenzyme *n* CHEM enzyme intracellulaire *f*

endogenetic *adj* PETR endogénétique

endogenic *adj* PETR endogène

endomorph *n* MINERAL endomorphe *m*

endorsing: ~ ink *n* COLOURS encre à tampons *f*, encre à timbres *f*

endoscope *n* NUCLEAR, PHYS, SPACE *spacecraft* endoscope *m*

endoscopy *n* NUCLEAR, PHYS, SPACE endoscopie *f*

endosperm *n* FOOD TECH *of grain* endosperme *m*

endothermic[1] *adj* C&G, CHEM, SPACE *spacecraft* endothermique

endothermic:[2] **~ process** *n* PETR TECH *refining*, PROP MAT processus endothermique *m*; **~ reaction** *n* FUELLESS *solar power*, GAS TECH réaction endothermique *f*

end-to-end[1] *adj* COMP, DP de bout en bout

end-to-end:[2] **~ control** *n* COMP contrôle de bout en bout *m*, DP commande de bout en bout *f*; **~ digital connectivity** *n* TELECOM connexité numérique de bout en bout *f*; **~ encipherment** *n* TELECOM chiffrement de bout en bout *m*; **~ information indicator** *n* TELECOM indicateur d'information de bout en bout *m*; **~ method indicator** *n* TELECOM indicateur de méthode de bout en bout *m*; **~ protocol** *n* COMP, DP protocole de bout en bout *m*

endurance *n* AERONAUT autonomie *f*, autonomie théorique *f*, endurance *f*, PROP MAT endurance *f*, SPACE *spacecraft* autonomie *f*, durée *f*, endurance *f*, TEXTILES durée *f*; **~ limit** *n* CRYSTALL *in fatigue test* limite d'endurance *f*, limite de résistance *f*, METALL limite d'endurance *f*; **~ ratio** *n* NUCLEAR rapport d'endurance *m*; **~ tensile strength** *n* MECH ENG résistance permanente à la traction *f*; **~ test** *n* MECH ENG, METR essai d'endurance *m*, PROD ENG essai d'abrasion *m*, QUALITY essai d'endurance *m*, SPACE *spacecraft* essai d'endurance *m*, *spacecraft* essai de durée *m*, SPRINGS essai d'endurance *m*

energetic: ~ start-up *n* NUCLEAR *of nuclear power plant* démarrage énergétique *m*

energization *n* ELEC ENG, RAD PHYS excitation *f*

energize *vt* ELEC ENG alimenter, mettre sous tension, PROD ENG activer

energized[1] *adj* ELEC, ELEC ENG sous tension, PROD ENG excité

energized:[2] **~ relay** *n* PROD ENG relais en position enclenchée *m*

energizing: ~ circuit *n* ELEC ENG circuit d'excitation *m*; **~ current** *n* ELEC ENG courant d'excitation *m*

energy[1] *adj* PHYS, THERMOD énergétique

energy[2] *n* CHEM, CRYSTALL, ELEC, ELEC ENG, MECH, PHYS, THERMOD énergie *f*; **~ absorption** *n* TELECOM absorption d'énergie *f*; **~ and dissipation spectra in turbulence** *n pl* FLUID PHYS spectres d'énergie et de dissipation de la turbulence *m pl*; **~ availability factor** *n* ELEC ENG *electrical* taux de disponibilité en énergie *m*; **~ balance** *n* GAS TECH, THERMOD bilan énergétique *m*, WATER SUPP bilan d'énergie *m*; **~ balance in turbulence** *n* FLUID PHYS bilan d'énergie en turbulence *m*; **~ balance of the soil** *n* HYDROL bilan radiatif *m*, bilan radiatif du sol *m*, bilan énergétique du sol *m*; **~ band gap** *n* NUCLEAR écart énergétique *m*; **~ budget** *n* POLLUTION bilan énergétique *m*; **~ cascade** *n* FLUID PHYS cascade d'énergie *f*; **~ conservation** *n* THERMOD conservation d'énergie *f*, économie d'énergie *f*; **~ consumption** *n* PHYS consommation d'énergie *f*, THERMOD consommation d'énergie *f*, dépense d'énergie *f*; **~ content** *n* THERMOD contenu énergétique *m*; **~ control** *n* CONTROL régulation d'énergie *f*; **~ conversion** *n* ELEC ENG, THERMOD conversion d'énergie *f*; **~ conversion factor** *n* RAD PHYS facteur de conversion d'énergie *m*; **~ converter** *n* ELEC ENG, TELECOM, THERMOD convertisseur d'énergie *m*; **~ crisis** *n* THERMOD crise d'énergie *f*, crise énergétique *f*; **~ degradation** *n*

NUCLEAR dégradation *f*, perte *f*; **~ demand** *n* THERMOD demande d'énergie *f*, demande énergétique *f*; **~ densities of radiation** *n pl* RAD PHYS densités énergiques de rayonnement *f pl*; **~ dispersal** *n* SPACE *communications* dispersion d'énergie *f*; **~ dispersive analysis by X-rays** *n (EDAX)* CHEM système de microanalyse par dispersion en énergie *m*; **~ dissipator** *n* HYDROL *dams* dissipateur d'énergie *m*; **~ efficiency** *n* THERMOD rendement énergétique *m*; **~ exchange reaction** *n* NUCLEAR réaction d'échange d'énergie *f*; **~ excitance** *n* OPT excitance énergétique *f*; **~ extraction** *n* FUELLESS extraction d'énergie *f*; **~ flow chart** *n* THERMOD diagramme du flux énergétique *m*; **~ fluence** *n* PHYS fluence énergétique *f*; **~ fluence rate** *n* PHYS débit de fluence énergétique *m*; **~ flux** *n* OPT, RAD PHYS flux énergétique *m*; **~ form** *n* GAS TECH source d'énergie *f*; **~ gap** *n* PHYS *semiconductor* écart énergétique *m*; **~ irradiance** *n* OPT éclairement énergétique *m*; **~ level** *n* GEOPHYS, PART PHYS *of atom*, PHYS, RAD PHYS *of atom* niveau d'énergie *m*, niveau énergétique *m*; **~ loss** *n* ELEC, GAS TECH perte d'énergie *f*; **~ meter** *n* ELEC ENG compteur d'énergie *m*; **~ pattern factor** *n* FUELLESS facteur de formation d'énergie *m*; **~ range** *n* RAD PHYS *of emitted particles* gamme d'énergie *f*; **~ recovery** *n* RECYCLING récupération de l'énergie *f*, THERMOD récupération d'énergie *f*; **~ recovery factor** *n* FUELLESS facteur de récupération d'énergie *m*; **~ recuperation** *n* THERMOD récupération d'énergie *f*; **~ regeneration** *n* THERMOD récupération d'énergie *f*; **~ saving** *n* PROD ENG, THERMOD économie d'énergie *f*; **~ selecting electron microscope** *n* INSTRUMENT microscope électronique à filtrage en énergie *m*; **~ source** *n* SPACE *spacecraft* source d'énergie *f*; **~ spectrum** *n* SPACE spectre énergétique *m*; **~ storage** *n* ELEC ENG accumulation d'énergie *f*, THERMOD accumulation d'énergie *f*, emmagasinage d'énergie *m*, stockage d'énergie *m*; **~ storage capacitor** *n* ELEC ENG condensateur accumulateur d'énergie *m*, condensateur pour accumulation d'énergie *m*; **~ storage device** *n* SPACE *spacecraft* dispositif de stockage d'énergie *m*; **~ supply** *n* FUELLESS approvisionnement énergétique *m*, fourniture d'énergie *f*, THERMOD alimentation d'énergie *f*; **~ technology** *n* POLLUTION technologie énergétique *f*; **~ transfer** *n* GEOPHYS, THERMOD transfert d'énergie *m*; **~ transfer coefficient** *n* PHYS *nuclear physics* coefficient de transfert d'énergie *m*; **~ transference by vibration** *n* WAVE PHYS *travelling wave* transfert d'énergie par vibration *m*; **~ transformation** *n* ELEC transformation d'énergie *f*; **~ transmission** *n* THERMOD transport d'énergie *m*; **~ valley** *n* NUCLEAR *in bond energy diagram* vallée d'énergie *f*; **~ waste** *n* GAS TECH gaspillage d'énergie *m*

energy-intensive *adj* THERMOD *equipment, industries* grande consommatrice d'énergie, à grande consommation d'énergie

energy-saving *adj* THERMOD faible consommatrice d'énergie, à faible consommation d'énergie

ENG *abbr (electronic news gathering)* TV journalisme électronique *m*, production vidéo en reportage *f*

engage[1] *vt* MECH embrayer, MECH ENG attaquer, emboîter, enclencher, *clutch, gear* embrayer

engage[2] *vi* MECH ENG mordre, s'engrener, être en prise, s'embrayer

engaged *adj* MECH ENG embrayé, PROD ENG *engine* embrayé, *gear* en prise

engagement *n* MECH ENG enclenchement *m*, engrenage *m*, engrènement *m*, prise *f*, *of clutch* embrayage *m*

engaging *n* MECH ENG embrayage *m*, engrenage *m*, engrènement *m*, prise *f*

engine *n* MECH ENG, NAUT *for ship or boat* machine *f*, moteur *m*, SPACE *spacecraft* propulseur *m*, VEHICLES moteur *m*; **~ air intake** *n* AERONAUT entrée d'air réacteur *f*; **~ air intake extension** *n* AERONAUT raccordement d'entrée d'air réacteur *m*; **~ angle command** *n* SPACE *spacecraft* ordre de braquage de tuyère *m*; **~ anti-icing gate valve** *n* AERONAUT vanne de dégivrage réacteur *f*; **~ bearing** *n* MECH ENG palier de machine *m*, NAUT palier *m*; **~ bed-plate** *n* NAUT bâti d'assise du moteur *m*; **~ block** *n* MECH, MECH ENG bloc-moteur *m*, VEHICLES bloc-cylindres *m*; **~ body** *n* NAUT corps de moteur *m*, SPACE *spacecraft* corps de propulseur *m*; **~ brake** *n* VEHICLES *system* frein moteur *m*; **~ breakdown** *n* VEHICLES panne de moteur *f*; **~ builder** *n* MECH ENG constructeur de machine *m*; **~ bypass air** *n* AERONAUT air de dilution *m*, air de dilution moteur *m*, flux secondaire *m*, flux secondaire réacteur *m*; **~ capacity** *n* VEHICLES cylindre *m*; **~ coasting down time** *n* AERONAUT *jet* durée d'autorotation *f*; **~ combustion chamber** *n* MECH ENG chambre d'explosion du moteur *f*, chambre de combustion dumoteur *f*; **~ compartment** *n* NAUT chambre du moteur *f*, VEHICLES compartiment-moteur *m*; **~ cooling system** *n* NAUT circuit de refroidissement moteur *m*; **~ couple** *n* MECH ENG couple moteur *m*; **~ cradle** *n* AERONAUT berceau moteur *m*, bâti moteur *m*, support de turbine *m*; **~ crank** *n* MECH ENG manivelle de machine *f*; **~ de-icing** *n* AERONAUT dégivrage réacteur *m*; **~ emission control** *n* MECH ENG contrôle d'échappement de moteur *m*; **~ exhaust system** *n* MECH ENG échappement de moteur *m*, NAUT circuit d'échappement moteur *m*; **~ failure** *n* NAUT panne de moteur *f*; **~ fan** *n* AUTO ventilateur *m*; **~ fittings** *n pl* MECH ENG appareillage de moteurs *m*; **~ flameout** *n* AERONAUT extinction du réacteur *f*, SPACE *spacecraft* extinction accidentelle du moteur *f*; **~ flywheel** *n* MECH ENG volant de machine *m*; **~ frame** *n* MECH ENG *stationary engine* bâti de machine *m*, NAUT bâti moteur *m*; **~ fuel supply** *n* NAUT alimentation en combustible moteur *f*; **~ fuel system** *n* MECH ENG système de carburant moteur *m*; **~ hoist** *n* AERONAUT treuil réacteur *m*; **~ hours indicator** *n* NAUT compteur d'heures de marche *m*; **~ house** *n* PROD ENG bâtiment des machines *m*, bâtiment des moteurs *m*, machinerie *f*; **~ instruments** *n pl* AERONAUT instruments moteur *m pl*; **~ jet wash** *n* AERONAUT souffle des réacteurs *m*; **~ maintenance** *n* NAUT entretien du moteur *m*; **~ maker** *n* PROD ENG *person* constructeur de machines *m*; **~ malfunction** *n* NAUT défaut de fonctionnement du moteur *m*; **~ manufacturer** *n* SPACE *propulsion* motoriste *m*; **~ mounting** *n* AUTO tampon *m*; **~ mountings** *n pl* SPACE *spacecraft* fixations du moteur *f pl*; **~ muffler** *n (AmE) (cf engine silencer)* MECH ENG silencieux moteur *m*; **~ nacelle** *n* AERONAUT fuseau réacteur *m*; **~ nacelle stub** *n* AERONAUT mât de liaison *m*, mât réacteur *m*; **~ nozzle cluster** *n* AERONAUT groupe d'injecteurs *m*; **~ oil** *n* MECH ENG huile pour organe de machine *f*, VEHICLES huile pour moteur *f*; **~ operation** *n* NAUT conduite du moteur *f*; **~ overhaul** *n* NAUT révision du moteur *f*; **~ pedestal** *n* MECH socle de machine *m*; **~ pick-up** *n* VEHICLES reprise *f*; **~ pit** *n* PROD ENG fosse à piquer le feu *f*, fosse à visiter *f*; **~ pod** *n* AERONAUT nacelle moteur *f*; **~ pressure ratio** *n* AERONAUT rapport de pressions moteur *m*, rapport manométrique du réacteur *m*; ~ **ratings** *n pl* AERONAUT performances du moteur *f pl*; ~ **relight push button** *n* AERONAUT bouton de rallumage réacteur *m*; ~ **room** *n* NAUT chambre des machines *f*, PROD ENG chambre du moteur *f*, machinerie *f*, salle des machines *f*; ~ **room log** *n* NAUT journal des machines *m*; ~ **room telegraph** *n* NAUT cadran de transmission d'ordres *m*; ~ **run-up** *n* AERONAUT point fixe réacteur *m*; ~ **seating** *n* NAUT carlingage des machines *m*; ~ **shaft bearing** *n* AERONAUT palier réacteur *m*; ~ **shed** *n* RAIL dépôt de locomotives *m*, remise à locomotives *f*, remise à machines *f*; ~ **shop** *n* AUTO *maintenance* station-service moteur *f*; ~ **shutdown in flight** *n* AERONAUT arrêt d'un moteur en vol *m*, coupure d'un moteur en vol *f*; ~ **shut-off stop** *n* AERONAUT butée réacteur éteint *f*; ~ **silencer** *n* (BrE) *(cf engine muffler)* MECH ENG silencieux moteur *m*; ~ **speed** *n* AERONAUT, AUTO régime moteur *m*, VEHICLES régime *m*; ~ **stand** *n* AERONAUT bâti de réception moteur *m*; ~ **starter/crank switch** *n* AERONAUT inverseur démarrage/ventilation *m*; ~ **starting control box** *n* AERONAUT boîte de démarrage réacteur *f*; ~ **support** *n* AUTO berceau moteur *m*, support de moteur *m*; ~ **support arch** *n* AERONAUT arceau support de réacteur *m*; ~ **support plug** *n* AUTO patte d'attache du moteur *f*; ~ **test stand** *n* AERONAUT banc d'essai réacteur *m*, SPACE *spacecraft* banc d'essai moteur *m*; ~ **torque** *n* AERONAUT, AUTO, MECH ENG couple moteur *m*; ~ **trolley** *n* AERONAUT chariot de transport réacteur *m*; ~ **valve** *n* MECH ENG soupape moteur *f*; ~ **ventilation system** *n* NAUT circuit de ventilation moteur *m*; ~ **vibration** *n* AERONAUT vibration moteur *f*; ~ **winding house** *n* MINING bâtiment des machines *m*; ~ **windmilling** *n* AERONAUT *helicopter* autorotation du réacteur *f*, réacteur en autorotation *m*, réacteur en rotation libre *m*

engine-driven[1] *adj* PROD ENG actionné par moteur, commandé par moteur, marchant au moteur

engine-driven:[2] ~ **pump** *n* AERONAUT pompe entraînée par réacteur *f*

engineer *n* MECH ingénieur *m*, mécanicien *m*, NAUT *aboard ship* ingénieur mécanicien *m*, mécanicien *m*, RAIL *personnel* mécanicien *m* (Fra), *vehicles* conducteur *m* (Bel); ~ **officer** *n* NAUT *aboard ship* ingénieur mécanicien *m*

engineer's: ~ **cab** *n* (AmE) *(cf driver's cab)* RAIL abri *m*, abri du mécanicien *m*, cabine *f*, cabine de conduite *f*; ~ **chain** *n* CONST chaîne d'arpentage *f*; ~ **stores** *n pl* PROD ENG fournitures pour usines *f pl*; ~ **surface plate** *n* PROD ENG marbre *m*, marbre d'ajusteur *m*, marbre à dresser *m*

engineered: ~ **barrier** *n* NUCLEAR barrière de confinement *f*, barrière technique *f*

engineering *n* CONST *civil engineering* génie civil *m*, MECH génie *m*, ingénierie *f*, technique *f*, MECH ENG art de l'ingénieur *m*, ingénierie *f*, science de l'ingénieur *f*; ~ **and design department** *n* MECH ENG bureau d'études *m*; ~ **and methods** *n pl* PROD ENG études et méthodes *f pl*; ~ **calculations record** *n* MECH ENG dossier de calcul *m*; ~ **change** *n* PROD ENG modification technique *f*; ~ **data** *n* PROD ENG données techniques *f pl*; ~ **department** *n* MECH, MECH ENG service technique *m*, PROD ENG bureau d'études *m*; ~ **drawing** *n* MECH ENG dessin d'étude *m*, NAUT dessin industriel *m*; ~ **drawing block** *n* MECH ENG cartouche d'un dessin *f*; ~ **facilities** *n pl* MECH moyens industriels *m pl*; ~ **issue level** *n* PROD

ENG niveau technique *m*; ~ **model** *n* SPACE modèle d'étude *m*; ~ **office** *n* MECH bureau d'études *m*; ~ **order wire** *n* (*EOW*) TELECOM ligne d'ordre technique *f*; ~ **standards** *n pl* MECH ENG manuel des études *m*; ~ **work station** *n* COMP poste de travail technique *m*, DP poste de travail d'ingénieur *m*

engines: all ~ operating *phr* AERONAUT tous moteurs en fonctionnement

English: ~ **blue** *n* C&G bleu de faïence *m*; ~ **china** *n* C&G porcelaine tendre anglaise *f*; ~ **finish** *n* PRINT fini à l'anglaise *m*; ~ **mount** *n* ASTRON monture anglaise *f*

English-type: ~ **axis mounting** *n* INSTRUMENT monture anglaise à axe *f*

engobe *n* C&G engobe *m*

engrave *vt* PRINT graver

engraved: ~ **blanket** *n* PRINT blanchet gravé *m*

engraver *n* C&G graveur *m*

engraving *n* ACOUSTICS burin de gravure *m*, C&G gravure à la roue *f*, ELECTRON, PRINT gravure *f*; ~ **depth** *n* PRINT profondeur de gravure *f*; ~ **head** *n* PRINT tête à graver *f*; ~ **in relief** *n* C&G gravure à relief prononcé *f*; ~ **lathe** *n* C&G tour de gravure *m*; ~ **rubber** *n* PRINT caoutchouc à graver *m*

enhance *vt* FOOD TECH mettre en valeur, rehausser le goût, relever, rehausser l'arôme de, PRINT accentuer, mettre en relief, souligner, TEXTILES rehausser

enhanced: ~ **graphics adaptor** *n* (*EGA*) COMP *card* adaptateur graphique couleur *m* (*EGA*); ~ **oil recovery** *n* (*EOR*) PETR TECH récupération assistée du pétrole *f* (*RAP*); ~ **service** *n* TELECOM service amélioré *m*

enhancement *n* TELECOM amélioration *f*; ~ **mode** *n* ELECTRON mode d'enrichissement *m*; ~ **mode FET** *n* ELECTRON TEC à enrichissement *m*

enharmonic: ~ **note** *n* ACOUSTICS note enharmonique *f*

enhydrite *n* MINERAL enhydre *m*

enlarge *vt* PHOTO agrandir

enlarged: ~ **image** *n* PHYS image agrandie *f*; ~ **loop** *n* SPRINGS anneau agrandi *m*, anneau élargi *m*

enlargement *n* INSTRUMENT grossissement *m*, PHOTO *act*, PRINT agrandissement *m*; ~ **print** *n* CINEMAT copie gonflée *f*, PHOTO épreuve par agrandissement *f*

enlarger *n* PHOTO, PRINT agrandisseur *m*; ~ **baseboard** *n* PHOTO table d'agrandisseur *f*; ~ **camera** *n* PHOTO chambre d'agrandissement *f*; ~ **column** *n* PHOTO colonne d'agrandisseur *f*; ~ **support** *n* PHOTO bâti d'agrandisseur *m*

enlarging *n* INSTRUMENT grossissement *m*; ~ **camera** *n* PHOTO chambre d'agrandissement *f*, PRINT agrandisseur *m*; ~ **hole** *n* MINING *blasting* mine de dégraissage *f*; ~ **meter** *n* PHOTO posemètre d'agrandissement *m*

enol *n* CHEM énol *m*

enolase *n* CHEM énolase *f*

enolic *adj* CHEM énolique

enolization *n* CHEM énolisation *f*

ENQ *abbr* (*enquiry character*) COMP caractère d'interrogation *m*

enquiry: ~ **character** *n* (*ENQ*) COMP caractère d'interrogation *m*

enrich *vt* COAL TECH, FOOD TECH enrichir

enriched: ~ **fuel** *n* NUCLEAR combustible enrichi *m*; ~ **material** *n* RAD PHYS *radiochemistry* matière enrichie *f*; ~ **nuclear fuel** *n* NUCLEAR combustible enrichi *m*; ~ **reactor** *n* NUCLEAR réacteur enrichi *m*; ~ **uranium** *n* PHYS uranium enrichi *m*

enrichment *n* CHEM enrichissement *m*, COAL TECH enri-

chissement *m*, valorisation *f*, FOOD TECH, PHYS *of uranium*, PROP MAT enrichissement *m*; ~ **tails** *n* NUCLEAR teneur de rejet *f*
ensemble: ~ **activity** *n* TELECOM activité globale *f*
ensign *n* NAUT *flags* pavillon *m*
enstatite *n* MINERAL enstatite *f*
entablature *n* PROD ENG *of power hammer, forging press, etc* entablement *m*
entangle *vt* TEXTILES emmêler
entanglement *n* SAFETY enchevêtrement *m*, happement *m*, saisie *f*
entangling: ~ **net** *n* OCEANOG folle *f*
enter[1] *vt* DP enregistrer, entrer, ELECTRON *data* saisir
enter[2] *vi* COMP enregistrer, entrer, inscrire
enteramine *n* CHEM sérotonine *f*
entering: ~ **air temperature** *n* REFRIG température d'entrée d'air *f*; ~ **file** *n* PROD ENG lime d'entrée *f*; ~ **tap** *n* PROD ENG premier taraud *m*, taraud conique *m*, taraud ébaucheur *m*; ~ **traffic** *n* TRANSP trafic entrant *m*
enthalpy *n* CHEM, COAL TECH, FUELLESS, GAS TECH, HEAT ENG *latent heat*, MECH *thermodynamics*, PHYS, RAD PHYS *thermodynamic function*, SPACE, THERMOD enthalpie *f*; ~ **of formation** *n* THERMOD enthalpie de formation *f*; ~ **of vaporization** *n* THERMOD enthalpie de vaporisation *f*
entity *n* COMP, DP, QUALITY entité *f*
entrainment *n* CHEM, FLUID PHYS entraînement *m*; ~ **current** *n* OCEANOG courant d'entraînement *m*
entrance: ~ **pupil** *n* PHYS pupille d'entrée *f*
entrap *vt* MAR POLL *oil slick* piéger
entrapped: ~ **air** *n* P&R air occlus *m*, PACKAGING air inclus *m*; ~ **gas** *n* GAS TECH gaz captif *m*
entropic: ~ **flux** *n* THERMOD flux d'entropie *m*
entropy *n* ASTRON, CHEM, COMP, DP, FUELLESS, MECH *thermodynamics*, PHYS, TELECOM, THERMOD entropie *f*; ~ **of fusion** *n* THERMOD entropie de fusion *f*; ~ **of vaporization** *n* THERMOD entropie de vaporisation *f*
entry *n* COAL TECH galerie maîtresse *f*, galerie principale *f*, mère-galerie *f*, voie principale *f*, COMP, DP entrée *f*; ~ **in stock** *n* PROD ENG entrée en stock *f*; ~ **instruction** *n* COMP, DP instruction d'entrée *f*; ~ **into force** *n* PATENTS entrée en vigueur *f*; ~ **into orbit** *n* SPACE *spacecraft* mise sur orbite *f*; ~ **pillar** *n* COAL TECH jambe *f*; ~ **point** *n* COMP, DP point d'entrée *m*; ~ **queue** *n* COMP, DP file d'attente d'entrée *f*; ~ **stump** *n* COAL TECH jambe *f*; ~ **timbering** *n* MINING boisage de voie maîtresse *m*
enumeration *n* COMP, DP, MATH énumération *f*; ~ **type** *n* COMP, DP type énumératif *m*
envelope *n* ELEC ENG enveloppe *f*, ELECTRON *electron tube* ampoule *f*, PACKAGING, TELECOM enveloppe *f*, TV ampoule *f*; ~ **curve** *n* MECH courbe enveloppe *f*; ~ **delay** *n* SPACE *communications* temps de propagation de groupe *m*; ~ **delay distortion** *n* SPACE *communications* distorsion de temps de groupe *f*; ~ **paper** *n* PAPER TECH papier pour enveloppes postales *m*; ~ **switch** *n* TELECOM commutateur d'enveloppes *m*, commutateur par enveloppes *m*; ~ **velocity** *n* TELECOM vitesse de groupe *f*
enveloping: ~ **machine** *n* PACKAGING machine pour envelopper *f*; ~ **tooth wheel** *n* MECH ENG *worm gearing* roue à dents creuses *f*, roue à denture creuse *f*
environment:[1] ~ **friendly** *adj* PACKAGING sans contamination de l'environnement
environment[2] *n* COMP, DP, POLLUTION environnement *m*, PROD ENG ambiance *f*, milieu ambiant *m*, QUALITY environnement *m*, SPACE environnement *m*, milieu *m*; ~ **cooling** *n* REFRIG refroidissement de l'ambiance *m*,

refroidissement de l'environnement *m*; ~ **division** *n* COMP *COBOL* division d'environnement *f*; ~ **survey satellite** *n* SPACE satellite d'étude de l'environnement *m*
environmental[1] *adj* POLLUTION lié à l'environnement, pour l'environnement
environmental:[2] ~ **and safety engineering** *n* SAFETY ingénierie de l'environnement et de la sécurité *f*; ~ **cleanliness** *n* SAFETY propreté de l'environnement *f*; ~ **cleanliness in enclosed spaces** *n* SAFETY propreté de l'environnement dans les espaces clos *f*; ~ **compatibility** *n* POLLUTION compatibilité avec l'environnement *f*; ~ **conditions** *n pl* METR, PROD ENG conditions d'environnement *f pl*; ~ **control** *n* CONTROL contrôle du milieu naturel *m*, contrôle du milieu vital *m*, POLLUTION contrôle de l'environnement *m*; ~ **control system** *n* SPACE *spacecraft* système de climatisation *m*; ~ **hazard** *n* QUALITY danger pour l'environnement *m*; ~ **health** *n* SAFETY santé de l'environnement *f*; ~ **impact** *n* POLLUTION impact sur l'environnement *m*; ~ **impact statement** *n* POLLUTION constat d'impact sur l'environnement *m*; ~ **law** *n* POLLUTION droit de l'environnement *m*; ~ **noise** *n* SAFETY bruit ambiant *m*, bruit de l'environnement *m*; ~ **planning** *n* POLLUTION aménagement de l'environnement *m*; ~ **protection** *n* POLLUTION, PROD ENG, RECYCLING protection de l'environnement *f*; ~ **protection agency** *n* POLLUTION agence pour la protection de l'environnement *f*; ~ **quality standards** *n pl* MAR POLL, POLLUTION normes d'environnement *f pl*; ~ **radioactivity** *n* RAD PHYS radioactivité ambiante *f*; ~ **risk** *n* QUALITY risque pour l'environnement *m*; ~ **stress** *n* SPACE *spacecraft* contraintes dues à l'environnement *f pl*; ~ **test** *n* SPACE essai d'ambiance *m*, essai en environnement *m*; ~ **test chamber** *n* SPACE simulateur d'environnement spatial *m*; ~ **testing** *n* MECH essai climatique *m*, essai d'environnement *m*, QUALITY essai en environnement *m*, essai pour l'environnement *m*; ~ **testing procedure** *n* SAFETY procédure de contrôle de l'environnement *f*; ~ **torque** *n* SPACE couple perturbateur dû à l'environnement *m*
environmentally: ~ **friendly** *adj* PACKAGING sans contamination de l'environnement
enzyme *n* CHEM, DETERGENTS, FOOD TECH enzyme *f*
E-O *abbr* (*electrical-optical*) TELECOM électrique-optique
EOB *abbr* (*end of block*) COMP fin de bloc *f*
EOC *abbr* TELECOM (*embedded operations channel*) canal d'exploitation intégré *m*, TELECOM (*end of communication*) fin de communication *m*
Eocene *adj* GEOL éocène
EOD *abbr* (*end of data*) COMP, DP fin de données *f*
EOF *abbr* (*end of file*) COMP fin de fichier *f*
EOJ *abbr* (*end of job*) COMP fin de travail *f*
EOM *abbr* (*end of message*) COMP, TELECOM fin de message *f*
EOR *n* (*enhanced oil recovery*) PETR TECH RAP (*récupération assistée du pétrole*)
eosin *n* CHEM éosine *f*
EOT[1] *abbr* COMP, DP (*end of tape*) fin de bande *m*, COMP, DP (*end of transmission*) fin de transmission *f*, TELECOM (*end of transaction*) fin de transaction *f*
EOT:[2] ~ **marker** *n* COMP, DP repère de fin de bande *m*
Eötvös: ~ **balance** *n* PHYS balance d'Eötvös *f*
EOW *abbr* (*engineering order wire*) TELECOM ligne d'ordre technique *f*

EP[1] *abbr* GEOPHYS *(equilibrium potential)* potentiel d'équilibre *m*, TELECOM *(erroneous period)* période erronée *f*

EP:[2] ~ **brake** *n* RAIL frein EP *m*

epeiric: ~ **sea** *n* GEOL mer épicontinentale *f*

epeirogenesis *n* GEOL épirogénèse *f*

epeirogenic: ~ **movement** *n* GEOL mouvement épirogénique *m*

ephedrine *n* CHEM éphédrine *f*

ephemerides *n pl* SPACE éphémérides *f pl*

ephemeris *n* ASTRON éphéméride *f*; ~ **time** *n* ASTRON temps des éphémérides *m*

epicenter *n* (AmE) *see* epicentre

epicentral: ~ **area** *n* GEOPHYS zone de l'épicentre *f*

epicentre *n* (BrE) GEOL, GEOPHYS, PHYS épicentre *m*

epichlorhydrin *n* CHEM épichlorhydrine *f*

epicinchonine *n* CHEM épicinchonine *f*

epiclastic *adj* PETR épiclastique

epicontinental[1] *adj* PETR épicontinental

epicontinental:[2] ~ **sea** *n* GEOL mer marginale *f*, mer épicontinentale *f*

epicoprostanol *n* CHEM épicoprostérine *f*

epicycle *n* ASTRON épicycle *m*

epicyclic[1] *adj* MECH *gears* épicyclique, épicycloïdal

epicyclic:[2] ~ **gear** *n* NAUT *engine* réducteur épicyclique *m*, réducteur épicycloïdal *m*; ~ **gear train** *n* MECH *gears* train d'engrenages planétaire *m*, train d'engrenages épicycloïdal *m*, MECH ENG train épicycloïdal *m*; ~ **train** *n* MECH ENG train épicycloïdal *m*

epicycloid *n* GEOM épicycloïde *f*

epicycloidal[1] *adj* MECH *gears*, MECH ENG épicycloïdal

epicycloidal:[2] ~ **gear** *n* MECH ENG engrenage épicycloïdal *m*

epidehydroandrosterone *n* CHEM épidéhydroandrostérone *f*

epidiascope *n* PHOTO épidiascope *m*

epidote *n* MINERAL épidote *f*

epigenic *adj* GEOL épigénique

epimer *n* CHEM épimère *m*

epimerization *n* CHEM épimérisation *f*

EPIRB *abbr* *(emergency position-indicating radio beacon)* NAUT, TELECOM radiobalise de localisation de sinistre *f*

episode *n* POLLUTION épisode *m*

epistilbite *n* MINERAL épistilbite *f*

epitaxial[1] *adj* ELECTRON, PROP MAT épitaxial

epitaxial:[2] ~ **deposition** *n* ELECTRON dépôt épitaxial *m*; ~ **dislocation** *n* METALL dislocation épitaxiale *f*; ~ **growth** *n* ELECTRON croissance d'une couche épitaxiale *f*, croissance épitaxiale *f*, PROP MAT croissance épitaxiale *f*; ~ **layer** *n* CRYSTALL, ELECTRON, PROP MAT, TELECOM couche épitaxiale *f*; ~ **orientation** *n* PROP MAT orientation épitaxiale *f*; ~ **transistor** *n* ELECTRON transistor épitaxial *m*; ~ **wafer** *n* ELECTRON plaquette épitaxiée *f*

epitaxy *n* CRYSTALL, ELECTRON, METALL, PROP MAT, RAD PHYS épitaxie *f*; ~ **reactor** *n* ELECTRON réacteur d'épitaxie *m*

epithermal *adj* GEOL *mineralization* épithermal

epizone *n* GEOL épizone *f*

E-plane *n* ELEC ENG *waveguides* plan E *m*; ~ **bend** *n* ELEC ENG *waveguides* coude plan E *m*

epoch *n* GEOL *time*, PETR *stratigraphy* époque *f*

EPOS *abbr* *(electronic point of sale)* COMP point de vente électronique *m*

epoxide[1] *adj* CHEM époxyde

epoxide[2] *n* CHEM époxyde *m*

epoxidized: ~ **oil** *n* P&R *paint binder* huile époxidique *f*

epoxy[1] *adj* CHEM époxyde

epoxy:[2] ~ **buffer** *n* TELECOM *fibre cable* gaine époxy *f*, revêtement ETFE *m*, revêtement primaire *m*; ~ **matrix** *n* SPACE *spacecraft* matrice époxyde *f*; ~ **resin** *n* CHEM résine époxyde *f*, CONST résine époxidique *f*, ELEC *insulation* résine époxy *f*, résine époxyde *f*, P&R, PACKAGING, PROP MAT résine époxyde *f*

EPR *n* *(electron paramagnetic resonance)* PHYS résonance paramagnétique électronique *f*

EPROM *abbr* *(erasable PROM)* COMP PROM effaçable *f*

epsomite *n* MINERAL epsomite *f*

equa-area: ~ **projection** *n* GEOL projection équivalente *f*

equal: ~ **arm bridge** *n* ELEC *circuit* pont à bras égaux *m*; ~ **loudness contour** *n* ACOUSTICS ligne isosonique *f*; ~ **pressure** *n* OCEANOG équipression *f*; ~ **temperament** *n* ACOUSTICS tempérament égal *m*

equality *n* COMP, DP égalité *f*

equalization *n* ACOUSTICS correction *f*, COMP, DP, ELECTRON compensation *f*, MECH compensation *f*, égalisation *f*, équilibre de pression *m*, RECORDING, TELECOM égalisation *f*; ~ **curve** *n* ELECTRON courbe d'égalisation *f*

equalize *vt* OCEANOG compenser, équilibrer

equalizer *n* COMP, DP égaliseur *m*, égalisateur *m*, ELECTRON égaliseur *m*, RECORDING filtre correcteur *m*, égaliseur *m*, REFRIG égalisateur de pression *m*, TELECOM correcteur *m*, égalisateur *m*, égaliseur *m*, TV circuit correcteur de distorsion *m*, égaliseur *m*; ~ **bar** *n* AUTO régulateur *m*; ~ **circuit** *n* TELECOM réseau correcteur *m*, réseau de correction *m*; ~ **spring** *n* MECH ENG ressort compensateur *m*; ~ **tank** *n* REFRIG réservoir égalisateur *m*

equalizing *n* AERONAUT équilibrage *m*; ~ **amplifier** *n* TV amplificateur correcteur *m*; ~ **damper** *n* REFRIG registre d'égalisation *m*; ~ **feeder** *n* ELEC *supply* feeder égalisateur *m*; ~ **file** *n* PROD ENG lime à égaliser *f*; ~ **gear** *n* MECH ENG différentiel *m*, engrenage différentiel *m*; ~ **pulse** *n* TV impulsion d'égalisation *f*; ~ **tank** *n* WATER SUPP bassin de compensation *m*, bassin de stabilisation *m*

equally: ~ **spaced** *adj* MECH ENG équidistant

equal-sided: ~ **angles** *n pl* CONST *angle iron* cornières à ailes égales *f pl*, cornières à branches égales *f pl*

equal-time: ~ **point** *n* AERONAUT *navigation* point équi-temps *m*

equant *adj* GEOL équidimensionnel

equation *n* CHEM, MATH équation *f*

equator *n* ASTRON, NAUT équateur *m*

equatorial: ~ **bulge** *n* ASTRON renflement équatorial *m*; ~ **calms** *n pl* METEO *doldrums* calmes équatoriaux *m pl*, pot-au-noir *m*, région des calmes équatoriaux *f*, OCEANOG calmes équatoriaux *m pl*; ~ **climate** *n* METEO climat équatorial *m*; ~ **crossing** *n* SPACE intersection avec le plan de l'équateur *f*; ~ **orbit** *n* SPACE orbite équatoriale *f*; ~ **orbiting satellite** *n* SPACE satellite sur orbite équatoriale *m*; ~ **zone** *n* (*cf torrid zone*) METEO zone intertropicale *f*

equiangular[1] *adj* GEOM équiangle

equiangular:[2] ~ **triangle** *n* GEOM triangle équilatéral *m*

equiaxed: ~ **grain** *n* METALL grain équiaxe *m*

equidistant *adj* CONST, GEOM, MECH ENG équidistant

equigranular *adj* GEOL *of minerals* isogranulaire, équigranulaire

equilateral *adj* GEOM équilatéral

equilenin *n* CHEM équilenine *f*

equilibrium:[1] **not in ~** *adj* PHYS hors d'équilibre

equilibrium[2] *n* GEOL, MECH, PETR TECH *state of well during drilling*, PHYS équilibre *m*; **~ constant** *n* CHEM *of reaction* constante d'équilibre *f*; **~ density** *n* PETR TECH *drilling* densité d'équilibre *f*; **~ deviation** *n* PROP MAT écart à l'équilibre *m*; **~ diagram** *n* PROP MAT diagramme d'équilibre *m*; **~ equation** *n* PHYS équation d'équilibre *f*; **~ length** *n* OPT longueur d'équilibre *f*, TELECOM longueur d'équilibrage *f*; **~ mode distribution** *n* OPT, TELECOM répartition des modes à l'équilibre *f*, équilibre des modes *m*; **~ mode distribution length** *n* OPT longueur d'équilibre *f*, TELECOM longueur d'équilibrage *f*; **~ potential** *n* (*EP*) GEOPHYS potentiel d'équilibre *m*; **~ radiation pattern** *n* OPT, TELECOM diagramme de rayonnement à l'équilibre *m*; **~ saturation** *n* PETR saturation d'équilibre *f*; **~ system** *n* GEOPHYS système d'équilibre *m*; **~ tide** *n* FUELLESS marée d'équilibre *f*, OCEANOG marée statique *f*; **~ valve** *n* HYDR EQUIP soupape d'équilibrage *f*, soupape d'équilibrage à manchon *f*

equimolecular *adj* CHEM équimoléculaire

equinoctial: **~ tide** *n* FUELLESS marée d'équinoxe *f*, NAUT grande marée *f*

equinox *n* ASTRON équinoxe *m*

equip *vt* MINING *mine* doter, *shaft* armer, NAUT *ship* armer, PROD ENG *works*, PRODUCTION outiller, TELECOM équiper

equipartition *n* PHYS *energy* équipartition *f*

equiphase: **~ surface** *n* ELEC ENG surface équiphase *f*

equipment *n* CONST matériel *m*, équipage *m*, MECH ENG équipement *m*, PROD ENG capital équipement *m*, matériel *m*; **~ disabled** *n* TELECOM équipement neutralisé *m*; **~ layer** *n* TELECOM couche d'équipement *f*; **~ manufacturer** *n* NAUT fabricant d'équipement *m*; **~ services** *n pl* AERONAUT servitudes avion *f pl*; **~ specification** *n* QUALITY spécification du matériel *f*

equipotential[1] *adj* ELEC, ELEC ENG équipotentiel

equipotential[2] *n* PHYS équipotentiel *m*; **~ connection** *n* ELEC ENG connexion équipotentielle *f*; **~ line** *n* SPACE ligne équipotentielle *f*; **~ surface** *n* ELEC *electrostatics*, ELEC ENG surface équipotentielle *f*, GEOPHYS surface équipotentielle terrestre *f*, PHYS, SPACE surface équipotentielle *f*

equipressure *n* OCEANOG équipression *f*

equivalence *n* COMP, DP équivalence *f*; **~ gate** *n* COMP, DP porte NI exclusif *f*; **~ operation** *n* COMP, DP opération NI exclusif *f*

equivalent *n* PHYS équivalent *m*; **~ absorption area** *n* ACOUSTICS aire d'absorption équivalente *f*; **~ airspeed** *n* AERONAUT vitesse équivalente au sol *f*, équivalent de vitesse *m*; **~ area** *n* SPACE surface équivalente *f*; **~ circuit** *n* ELEC circuit équivalent *m*, ELEC ENG, ELECTRON schéma équivalent *m*, PHYS circuit équivalent *m*; **~ circulating density** *n* (*ECD*) PETR TECH *drilling* densité équivalente de circulation *f*; **~ conductance** *n* PHYS conductance équivalente *f*; **~ density** *n* PETR TECH *drilling* densité de boue équivalente *f*, densité équivalente *f*, densité équivalente de la boue *f*; **~ depth** *n* PETR TECH *drilling* profondeur équivalente *f*; **~ isotropically-radiated power** *n* (*EIRP*) SPACE *communications* puissance isotrope rayonnée équivalente *f* (*PIRE*); **~ neutral density** *n* PRINT densité neutre équivalente *f*; **~ noise temperature** *n* SPACE *communications* température équivalente de bruit *f*; **~ per million** *n* POLLUTION équivalent par million *m*; **~**

proportions *n pl* CHEM proportions réciproques *f pl*; **~ random traffic intensity** *n* TELECOM intensité de trafic équivalent *f*; **~ resistance** *n* ELEC résistance équivalente *f*; **~ shaft horsepower** *n* MECH ENG puissance équivalente sur arbre *f*; **~ standard smoke** *n* POLLUTION FNE, fumée normalisée équivalente *f*; **~ step index** *n* (*ESI*) TELECOM indice à saut équivalent *m*; **~ step index profile** *n* OPT, TELECOM profil d'indice à saut équivalent *m*; **~ thermal conductivity** *n* HEAT ENG conductivité thermique équivalente *f*; **~ thermal network** *n* THERMOD réseau thermique équivalent *m*; **~ vertical gust speed** *n* AERONAUT *airworthiness* équivalent de vitesse de rafale verticale *m*

Equivalent: **~ Mud Weight** *n* (*EMW*) PETR TECH *drilling* densité de boue équivalente *f* (*DBE*)

Equuleus *n* ASTRON Petit Cheval *m*

Er (*erbium*) CHEM Er (*erbium*)

era *n* GEOL ère *f*

erasable: **~ data disc** *n* (BrE) OPT DON effaçable *m*, DON à enregistrement effaçable *m*; **~ data disk** *n* (AmE) *see erasable data disc* **~ disc drive** *n* (BrE) OPT unité de disque effaçable *f*; **~ disk drive** *n* (AmE) *see erasable disc drive* **~ optical disc** *n* (BrE) OPT disque optique effaçable *m*, disque optique réinscriptible *m*, disque optique réutilisable *m*; **~ optical disk** *n* (AmE) *see erasable optical disc* **~ optical drive** *n* OPT unité de disque effaçable *f*; **~ optical memory** *n* OPT mémoire optique effaçable *f*; **~ optical storage** *n* OPT mémoire optique effaçable *f*; **~ PROM** *n* (*EPROM*) COMP PROM effaçable *f*, mémoire effaçable *f*; **~ storage** *n* COMP, DP mémoire effaçable *f*

erase:[1] **~ button** *n* CONTROL bouton à effacer *m*; **~ frequency** *n* RECORDING fréquence d'effacement *f*; **~ head** *n* COMP, DP, RECORDING, TV tête d'effacement *f*

erase[2] *vt* COMP, DP, RECORDING effacer

eraser *n* TV démagnétiseur *m*, effaceur *m*

erasing: **~ current** *n* RECORDING, TV courant d'effacement *m*; **~ head** *n* TV tête d'effacement *f*; **~ magnetic head** *n* ACOUSTICS tête magnétique d'effacement *f*

erasure *n* ACOUSTICS, RECORDING, TV effacement *m*

erathem *n* GEOL érathème *m*

erbium *n* (*Er*) CHEM erbium *m* (*Er*)

erect:[1] **~ image viewfinder** *n* PHOTO viseur donnant une image redressée *n*

erect[2] *vt* MECH monter, PACKAGING *folding boxes* assembler

erecting: **~ lens** *n* INSTRUMENT lentille de redressement *f*; **~ prism telescope** *n* INSTRUMENT lunette à prismes redresseurs *f*; **~ shop** *n* MECH, NAUT *shipbuilding* atelier de montage *m*, PROD ENG atelier de montage *m*, halle de montage *f*

erection *n* CONST *of buildings* construction *f*, érection *f*, *of scaffold* dressage *m*, échafaudage de montage *m*, PAPER TECH, PROD ENG *of machinery* montage *m*; **~ jig** *n* NAUT *shipbuilding* jig de montage *m*; **~ plan** *n* PROD ENG *for machinery* plan de montage *m*

erector *n* MECH monteur *m*, PROD ENG *of machinery* ajusteur-monteur *m*, monteur *m*, RAIL érecteur *m*

erg *n* METR erg *m*

ergmeter *n* METR ergomètre *m*

ergol *n* SPACE, THERMOD ergol *m*

ergonomic[1] *adj* PACKAGING, PROD ENG *design* ergonomique

ergonomic:[2] **~ design principles** *n pl* SAFETY *machines* principes d'étude ergonomique *m pl*

ergonomics *n* COMP, DP, MECH ENG, SAFETY, SPACE ergonomie *f*

ergonomist *n* MECH ENG ergonome *m*

ergonomy *n* PACKAGING, PROD ENG ergonomie *f*

ergot *n* FOOD TECH *phytopathology* ergot *m*; ~ **alkaloids** *n pl* CHEM alcaloïdes de l'ergot *m pl*

ergotinine *n* CHEM ergotinine *f*

Eridanus *n* ASTRON Eridan *m*

erinite *n* MINERAL érinite *f*

Erlenmeyer: ~ **flask** *n* LAB EQUIP *glassware* fiole Erlenmeyer *f*, fiole conique *f*

erode *vt* CONST éroder, HYDROL affouiller, dégrader, éroder, METEO éroder

eroding *n* HYDROL affouillement *m*, dégradation *f*

erosion *n* CHEM, COAL TECH, CONST, FUELLESS, GEOL, HYDROL érosion *f*, RAIL *of embankment* ravinement *m*; ~ **rate** *n* SPACE *spacecraft* taux d'érosion *m*

erosional: ~ **unconformity** *n* GEOL discordance d'érosion *f*, discordance de ravinement *f*

erosive: ~ **burning** *n* SPACE combustion érosive *f*

ERP *abbr (effective radiated power)* TELECOM puissance apparente rayonnée *f*

ERRA *abbr* (BrE) *(European Recycling and Recovery Association)* PACKAGING Association européenne pour le recyclage et la récupération *f*

erratic: ~ **block** *n* GEOL *glacial deposit* bloc erratique *m*

erroneous: ~ **block** *n (EB)* TELECOM bloc erroné *m*; ~ **period** *n (EP)* TELECOM période erronée *f*

error [1] *n* COMP, DP, ELECTRON, PHYS erreur *f*; ~ **analysis** *n* COMP, DP analyse d'erreurs *f*; ~ **burst** *n* COMP rafale d'erreurs *f*, DP paquet d'erreurs *m*, rafale d'erreurs *f*; ~ **check** *n* TELECOM *maritime* contrôle d'erreurs *m*; ~ **check character** *n* TELECOM *maritime* caractère de contrôle d'erreurs *m*; ~ **check signal** *n* TELECOM *maritime* caractère de contrôle d'erreurs *m*; ~ **code** *n* COMP, DP code d'erreur *m*; ~ **control** *n* COMP, DP traitement d'erreurs *m*; ~ **control device** *n (ECD)* TELECOM dispositif de protection contre les erreurs *m*; ~ **correcting code** *n (ECC)* COMP, DP, ELECTRON, SPACE *communications* code correcteur d'erreurs *m*, TELECOM codage pour correction d'erreurs *m*, code correcteur d'erreurs *m*; ~ **correction** *n* COMP, CONTROL, DP, ELECTRON correction d'erreurs *f*, TELECOM correction d'erreurs *f*, correction de distorsion *f*, réduction d'erreurs *f*; ~ **correction signal** *n* CONTROL signal de correction d'erreurs *m*; ~ **density** *n* TELECOM concentration d'erreurs *f*; ~ **detecting code** *n (cf self-checking code)* COMP, DP, ELECTRON code détecteur d'erreurs *m*; ~ **detection** *n* COMP, CONTROL, DP, ELECTRON, TELECOM, TV détection d'erreurs *f*; ~ **detection coding** *n* TELECOM codage de détection d'erreurs *m*; ~ **detector** *n* TELECOM détecteur d'erreurs *m*; ~ **diagnosis** *n* TELECOM diagnostic d'erreurs *m*; ~ **diagnostic** *n* COMP, DP diagnostic d'erreurs *m*; ~ **diagnostics** *n* COMP outils de diagnostique d'erreurs *m pl*; ~ **distribution** *n* MATH répartition d'erreurs *f*; ~ **estimation** *n* MATH estimation de l'ordre de grandeur de l'erreur *f*; ~ **indication** *n* CONTROL signalisation des défauts *f*; ~ **list** *n* COMP, DP liste d'erreurs *f*; ~ **management** *n* COMP, DP gestion d'erreurs *f*; ~ **message** *n* COMP, DP, TELECOM message d'erreurs *m*; ~ **of omission** *n* QUALITY erreur par omission *f*; ~ **pattern** *n* TELECOM configuration d'erreurs *f*; ~ **probability** *n* TELECOM probabilité d'erreurs *f*; ~ **program** *n* COMP programme d'erreurs *m*; ~ **protection** *n* ELECTRON, TELECOM protection contre les erreurs *f*; ~ **protection code** *n* TELECOM code de protection contre les erreurs *m*; ~ **rate** *n* COMP, DP, ELECTRON, TELECOM taux d'erreurs *m*; ~ **rate measurement** *n* TELECOM mesure de taux d'erreurs *f*; ~ **recovery** *n* COMP, DP reprise après erreur *f*, TELECOM retour au fonctionnement normal *m*; ~ **report** *n* COMP liste d'erreurs *f*, rapport d'erreurs *m*, DP rapport d'erreurs *m*; ~ **retrieval** *n* QUALITY recherche d'erreurs *f*; ~ **signal** *n* AERONAUT, CONTROL, ELECTRON signal d'erreur *m*; ~ **susceptibility** *n* TELECOM sensibilité aux erreurs *f*; ~ **trapping** *n* COMP, DP interception d'erreurs *f*

error: [2] ~ **and omissions excepted** *phr* PRINT sauf erreurs ou omissions

errored: ~ **second** *n (ES)* TELECOM seconde avec erreur *f*

erubescite *n* MINERAL érubescite *f*

erucic *adj* CHEM érucique

eruption *n (cf inrush)* FLUID PHYS, GAS TECH éruption *f*; ~ **point** *n* GEOL *volcanic* centre éruptif *m*

eruptive: ~ **star** *n* ASTRON étoile éruptive *f*

erythrin *n* CHEM érythrine *f*

erythrite *n* MINERAL érythrite *f*

erythritol *n* CHEM érythritol *m*

erythropsin *n* CHEM pourpre rétinien *m*

erythrose *n* CHEM érythrose *m*

erythrosine *n* CHEM érythrosine *f*

erythrulose *n* CHEM érythrulose *m*

Es *(einsteinium)* CHEM Es *(einsteinium)*

ES [1] *abbr* COMP *(echo suppressor)*, DP *(echo suppressor)*, ELECTRON *(echo suppressor)*, SPACE *(echo suppressor)* suppresseur d'écho *m*, TELECOM *(errored second)* seconde avec erreur *f*, TELECOM *(echo suppressor)* suppresseur d'écho *m*

ES: [2] ~ **paper** *n* PRINT papier collé à la pâte *m*

ESA *abbr (European Space Agency)* ASTRON, SPACE ASE *(Agence spatiale européenne)*

Esaki: ~ **diode** *n* ELECTRON, PHYS diode Esaki *f*

ESC *abbr (escape, escape key)* COMP, DP ESC *(échappement)*

ESCA *abbr (electron spectroscopy for chemical analysis)* CHEM spectroscopie électronique pour analyses chimiques *f*

escalator *n* CONST escalator *m*, escalier mécanique *m*, escalier à marches mobiles *m*, CONST escalier roulant *m*, escalier à marches mobiles *m*, TRANSP escalier mécanique *m*, escalier roulant *m*

escape *n* COMP *(ESC)*, DP *(ESC)* échappement *m* *(ESC)*, SPACE évacuation *f*; ~ **capsule** *n* PETR TECH *offshore operations* capsule de sauvetage *f*; ~ **character** *n* COMP, DP caractère d'échappement *m*; ~ **chute** *n* AERONAUT manche d'évacuation *f*, manche d'évacuation sur toboggan *f*, rampe d'évacuation *f*, toboggan d'évacuation *m*, toboggan de secours *m*, SPACE manche d'évacuation *f*, rampe d'évacuation *f*; ~ **device** *n* SAFETY dispositif de sortie de secours *m*; ~ **hatch** *n* SPACE écoutille d'évacuation *f*; ~ **key** *n* COMP, DP touche d'échappement *f*; ~ **lane** *n* TRANSP bande d'arrêt d'urgence *f*; ~ **module** *n* SPACE *spacecraft* véhicule de sauvetage *m*; ~ **peak** *n* RAD PHYS *gamma radiation* pic de fuite *m*; ~ **rocket stage** *n* SPACE *spacecraft* étage de libération *m*; ~ **rope** *n* AERONAUT corde d'évacuation *f*; ~ **sequence** *n* COMP, DP séquence ESC *f*, séquence d'échappement *f*; ~ **valve** *n* HYDR EQUIP clapet de décharge *m*, clapet de sûreté *m*, détendeur *m*, soupape de trop-plein *f*; ~ **velocity** *n* ASTRON, PHYS, SPACE vitesse de libération *f*

escapement *n* PRINT approche espace acceptable entre deux caractères *f*; ~ **mechanism** *n* MECH ENG *clo-*

ckwork échappement *m*

escarpment *n* OCEANOG accore *f*, escarpement *m*, talus *m*

eschinite *n* MINERAL aeschynite *f*, eschynite *f*

escort: ~ **ship** *n* NAUT *navy* bâtiment d'escorte *m*, escorteur *m*

esculin *n* CHEM esculine *f*

escutcheon *n* (AmE) *(cf scutcheon)* CONST *locksmithing* entrée de serrure *f*, écusson *m*

eserine *n* CHEM ésérine *f*

ESI[1] *abbr (equivalent step index)* TELECOM indice à saut équivalent *m*

ESI:[2] ~ **profile** *n* OPT, TELECOM profil d'indice à saut équivalent *m*; ~ **refractive index difference** *n* OPT, TELECOM saut d'indice équivalent *m*

ESP *abbr (electrostatic precipitator)* POLLUTION dépoussiéreur électrique *m*, précipitateur électrostatique *m*, séparateur électrique *m*, électrofiltre *m*

esparto: ~ **paper** *n* PRINT papier alfa *m*; ~ **pulp** *n* PAPER TECH pâte d'alfa *f*

ESR *abbr (electron spin resonance)* PART PHYS résonance de spin électronique *f*, PHYS résonance de spin électronique *f*, résonance magnétique électronique *f*

ESS *abbr (electronic switching system)* TELECOM système de commutation électronique *m*

essential: ~ **fatty acid** *n (EFA)* FOOD TECH acide gras essentiel *m*; ~ **feature** *n* PATENTS caractéristique essentielle *f*; ~ **oil** *n* FOOD TECH huile essentielle *f*

essonite *n* MINERAL essonite *f*, hessonite *f*

establishing: ~ **shot** *n* CINEMAT plan d'ensemble *m*, plan général *m*

estar: ~ **base** *n* CINEMAT support estar *m*

estate: ~ **car** *n* (BrE) *(cf station wagon)* TRANSP familiale *f*

ester *n* CHEM, DETERGENTS ester *m*; ~ **gum** *n* P&R gomme ester *f*; ~ **interchange** *n* DETERGENTS double décomposition *f*, transestérification *f*; ~ **number** *n* DETERGENTS indice d'ester *m*; ~ **resin** *n* DETERGENTS résine d'esters *f*; ~ **value** *n* DETERGENTS indice d'ester *m*

esterification *n* FOOD TECH estérification *f*

esterify *vt* CHEM estérifier

estimate *n* PROD ENG devis *m*, devis estimatif *m*, état estimatif *m*

estimated: ~ **elapsed time** *n* AERONAUT durée estimée *f*; ~ **flight time** *n* AERONAUT temps de vol estimé *m*; ~ **normal payload** *n* AERONAUT charge marchande normale estimée *f*; ~ **off-block time** *n* AERONAUT heure estimée de départ du poste de stationnement *f*; ~ **position** *n* NAUT *navigation* point estimé *m*; ~ **reckoning** *n* OCEANOG point observé *m*; ~ **time of arrival** *n (ETA)* AERONAUT, NAUT heure prévue d'arrivée *f (HPA)*; ~ **time of departure** *n* AERONAUT, NAUT heure de départ prévue *f*

estimation *n* MATH estimation *f*

estimator *n* C&G releveur *m*, MATH estimateur *m*

estuarine *adj* GEOL estuarien

estuary *n* FUELLESS, HYDROL, NAUT estuaire *m*

ESV *abbr (experimental safety vehicle)* TRANSP voiture expérimentale de sécurité *f*

ET *abbr (exchange termination)* TELECOM terminaison de commutateur *f*

eta: ~ **factor** *n* PHYS facteur êta *m*, nombre des neutrons produits par neutron absorbé *m*; ~ **meson** *n* PHYS méson êta *m*; ~ **neutral meson** *n* PART PHYS méson êta neutre *m*

ETA *abbr (estimated time of arrival)* AERONAUT, NAUT *navigation* HPA *(heure prévue d'arrivée)*

etalon *n* PHYS étalon *m*

ETB *abbr (end of transmission block)* COMP, DP fin de bloc de transmission *f*

etch:[1] ~ **pit** *n* CRYSTALL point d'attaque *m*

etch[2] *vt* METALL attaquer

etched: ~ **surface printing** *n* PRINT impression d'une surface gravée *f*

etching *n* CHEM attaque acide *f*, décapage *m*, gravure *f*, ELECTRON attaque chimique *f*, PRINT morsure *f*, PROP MAT attaque chimique *f*; ~ **ink** *n* COLOURS encre pour verre *f*; ~ **machine** *n* PRINT machine à graver *f*; ~ **solution** *n* METALL solution d'attaque *f*

ethal *n* CHEM éthal *m*

ethanal *n* CHEM éthanal *m*

ethane *n* CHEM, PETR TECH éthane *m*

ethanethiol *n* CHEM éthanethiol *m*

ethanoic: ~ **acid** *n* CHEM acide éthanoïque *m*, FOOD TECH acide acétique *m*

ethanol *n* CHEM éthanol *m*, FOOD TECH alcool éthylique *m*, éthanol *m*, PETR TECH éthanol *m*

ethanolamine *n* CHEM, DETERGENTS éthanolamine *f*

ethanolysis *n* CHEM éthanolyse *f*

ethene *n* CHEM, PETR TECH éthène *m*

ether *n* CHEM éther *m*; ~ **linkage** *n* DETERGENTS liaison éther *f*; ~ **oxide** *n* DETERGENTS oxyde d'éthylène *m*

ethereal *adj* CHEM *of liquid* volatil, éthéré

etherlene: ~ **linkage** *n* DETERGENTS liaison éther *f*

ethionic *adj* CHEM éthionique

ethoxylation *n* DETERGENTS éthoxylation *f*

ethyl *n* PETR TECH éthyle *m*; ~ **acetate** *n* FOOD TECH, P&R acétate d'éthyle *m*; ~ **alcohol** *n* CHEM, FOOD TECH, PETR TECH, PHOTO alcool éthylique *m*; ~ **cellulose** *n* P&R éthylcellulose *f*; ~ **cinnamate** *n* FOOD TECH cinnamate d'éthyle *m*, cinnamate éthylique *m*; ~ **vanillin** *n* FOOD TECH éthyl-vanilline *f*

ethylamine *n* CHEM éthylamine *f*

ethylaniline *n* CHEM éthylaniline *f*

ethylate[1] *n* CHEM éthylate *m*

ethylate[2] *vt* CHEM éthyler

ethylation *n* CHEM éthylation *f*

ethylene *n* CHEM, DETERGENTS, FOOD TECH éthylène *m*, GAS TECH gaz oléfiant *m*, éthylène *m*, P&R, PETR TECH éthylène *m*; ~ **glycol** *n* DETERGENTS glycol *m*, éthylène glycol *m*; ~ **oxide** *n* DETERGENTS oxyde d'éthylène *m*; ~ **propylene rubber** *n* P&R caoutchouc éthylène propylène *m*; ~ **vinyl acetate** *n (EVA)* P&R éthylène-acétate de vinyle *m*

ethylenediamino: ~ **tetra-acetic acid** *n (EDTA)* DETERGENTS acide éthylène-diamino-tétracétique *m*

ethylenic *adj* CHEM éthylénique

ethylic *adj* CHEM éthylique

ethylidene *n* CHEM éthylidène *m*

ethylmorphine *n* CHEM éthylmorphine *f*

ethylsulfuric *adj* (AmE), **ethylsulphuric** *adj* (BrE) CHEM éthylsulfurique

ethylthioethanol *n* PETR TECH éthylthioéthanol *m*

ethylurethane *n* CHEM éthyluréthanne *m*

ethyne *n* CHEM éthyne *m*

E-to-E *abbr (electronic-to-electronic)* TV direct modulateur-démodulateur, vidéo-sur-vidéo

ETS *abbr (European Telecommunication Standard)* TELECOM Norme de télécommunication européenne *f*

ETSI *abbr (European Telecommunication Standardization Institute)* TELECOM Institut européen de

normalisation des télécommunications *m*
ETX *abbr (end of text)* COMP, DP fin de texte *f*
Eu *(europium)* CHEM Eu *(europium)*
eucairite *n* MINERAL eucaïrite *f*, eukaïrite *f*
eucalyptol *n* CHEM eucalyptol *m*
euchroite *n* MINERAL euchroïte *f*
euclase *n* MINERAL euclase *f*
Euclid's: ~ **parallel postulate** *n* GEOM postulat du parallélisme d'Euclide *m*
euclidean[1] *adj* GEOM euclidien
euclidean:[2] ~ **space** *n* GEOM, PHYS espace euclidien *m*
Euclidean: ~ **geometry** *n* GEOM géométrie euclidienne *f*
eucolite *n* MINERAL eucolite *f*
eudialite *n* MINERAL eudialyte *f*
eudialyte *n* MINERAL eudialyte *f*
eudiometer *n* CHEM eudiomètre *m*
eudiometry *n* CHEM eudiométrie *f*
eudnophite *n* MINERAL eudnophite *f*
eugenol *n* CHEM eugénol *m*
eugeosyncline *n* GEOL eugéosynclinal *m*
euhedral *adj* GEOL *texture* automorphe, idiomorphe
eukairite *n* MINERAL eucaïrite *f*, eukaïrite *f*
Euler: ~ **angles** *n pl* PHYS angles d'Euler *m pl*, angles eulériens *m pl*
Euler's: ~ **formula** *n* GEOM formule d'Euler *f*
eulittoral *n* OCEANOG médiolittoral *m*
eulytine *n* MINERAL eulytine *f*
eulytite *n* MINERAL eulytine *f*
euosmite *n* MINERAL euosmite *f*
European: ~ **Alcohol Brandy and Spirit Union** *n* FOOD TECH Union européenne des alcools d'eaux-de-vie et spiritueux *f*; ~ **barge carrier system** *n (EBCS)* TRANSP système EBCS *m*; ~ **Centre for Nuclear Research** *n* PART PHYS Centre européen pour la recherche nucléaire *m*; ~ **collaboration for muon physics** *n* PART PHYS collaboration européenne pour la physique du muon *f*; ~ **Organization for Nuclear Research** *n (CERN)* PART PHYS Conseil européen pour la recherche nucléaire *m (CERN)*; ~ **patent** *n* PATENTS brevet européen *m*; ~ **patent application** *n* PATENTS demande de brevet européen *f*; ~ **Recycling and Recovery Association** *n (ERRA)* PACKAGING Association européenne pour le recyclage et la récupération *f*; ~ **Space Agency** *n (ESA)* ASTRON, SPACE Agence spatiale européenne *f (ASE)*; ~ **Telecommunication Standard** *n (ETS)* TELECOM Norme de télécommunication européenne *f*; ~ **Telecommunication Standardization Institute** *n (ETSI)* TELECOM Institut européen de normalisation des télécommunications *m*
europic *adj* CHEM europique
europium *n (Eu)* CHEM europium *m (Eu)*
europous *adj* CHEM europeux
euroslot *n* PACKAGING eurofente *f*
eustatic[1] *adj* FUELLESS, GEOL, GEOPHYS eustatique
eustatic:[2] ~ **movement** *n* OCEANOG eustasie *f*
eusynchite *n* MINERAL eusynchite *f*
eutectic *n* C&G, CHEM *alloy* eutectique *m*; ~ **alloy overload relay** *n* PROD ENG relais de protection à alliage eutectique *m*; ~ **point** *n* METALL, PROP MAT point eutectique *m*; ~ **transformation** *n* METALL transformation eutectique *f*
eutectoid *n* METALL eutectoïde *m*
eutetic[1] *adj* CHEM eutétique
eutetic:[2] ~ **reaction** *n* METALL réaction eutétique *f*
eutexia *n* CHEM eutexie *f*

eutrophic[1] *adj* RECYCLING eutrophe
eutrophic:[2] ~ **lake** *n* RECYCLING lac eutrophe *m*
eutrophication *n* DETERGENTS, POLLUTION, RECYCLING eutrophisation *f*
eutrophy[1] *n* RECYCLING eutrophie *f*
eutrophy[2] *vi* RECYCLING présenter un phénomène d'eutrophisation
euxenite *n* MINERAL euxénite *f*
euxinic *adj* GEOL euxinique
eV *abbr (electronvolt)* ELECTRON, METR, PART PHYS, PHYS eV *(électron-volt)*
EVA *abbr (ethylene vinyl acetate)* P&R éthylène-acétate de vinyle *m*
evacuate *vt* ELECTRON vider, *tube* pomper, MECH *vessel*, PHYS faire le vide
evacuated: ~ **system** *n* TRANSP système à atmosphère raréfiée *m*; ~ **tube collector** *n* FUELLESS capteur à tubes évacués *m*
evacuation *n* SAFETY évacuation *f*
evaluate *vt* QUALITY, SAFETY évaluer
evaluation *n* QUALITY, SAFETY évaluation *f*
evanescent: ~ **field** *n* OPT, TELECOM champ évanescent *m*; ~ **wave** *n* PHYS onde évanescente *f*
evaporable *adj* HEATING évaporable
evaporate[1] *vt* CHEM TECH vaporiser, évaporer, HEATING évaporer, PHOTO *in vacuum* sublimer sous vide; ~ **dry** *vt* CHEM TECH évaporer jusqu'à sec, évaporer jusqu'à siccité
evaporate[2] *vi* CHEM s'évaporer, CHEM TECH volatiliser, HEATING s'évaporer
evaporated: ~ **latex** *n* P&R latex évaporé *m*; ~ **layer** *n* ELECTRON couche évaporée *f*; ~ **whole milk** *n* FOOD TECH lait entier concentré *m*
evaporating: ~ **apparatus** *n* CHEM TECH appareil à évaporer *m*, vaporisateur *m*, vaporiseur *m*, évaporateur *m*; ~ **basin** *n* CHEM TECH capsule d'évaporation *f*, cuvette d'évaporation *f*, plat d'évaporation *m*, vase évaporateur *m*, cuvette d'évaporation *f*, LAB EQUIP cristallisoir *m*; ~ **boiler** *n* CHEM TECH bassine *f*; ~ **dish** *n* CHEM TECH capsule d'évaporation *f*, cuvette d'évaporation *f*, cuvette de vaporisation *f*, plat d'évaporation *m*, vase évaporateur *m*; ~ **pan** *n* CHEM TECH capsule d'évaporation *f*, cuvette de vaporisation *f*, plat d'évaporation *m*, vase évaporateur *m*, cuvette d'évaporation *f*; ~ **point** *n* CHEM TECH point de vaporisation *m*; ~ **pump** *n* CHEM TECH pompe à évaporation *f*; ~ **temperature** *n* REFRIG température d'évaporation *f*, température de vaporisation *f*; ~ **vessel** *n* CHEM TECH bassine *f*
evaporation *n* GAS TECH, HEATING, HYDROL, PETR TECH *refining*, PHYS, PRINT évaporation *f*, PROP MAT vaporisation *f*, évaporation *f*, THERMOD évaporation *f*; ~ **cooling** *n* CHEM TECH refroidissement par vaporisation *m*, refroidissement par évaporation *m*; ~ **enthalpy** *n* CHEM TECH enthalpie de vaporisation *f*; ~ **loss** *n* CHEM TECH, WATER SUPP perte par évaporation *f*; ~ **meter** *n* CHEM TECH évaporomètre *m*; ~ **pan** *n* WATER SUPP bac d'évaporation *m*; ~ **product** *n* CHEM TECH produit d'évaporation *m*; ~ **pump** *n* CHEM TECH pompe ionique par vaporisation *f*, pompe à sublimation *f*; ~ **tank** *n* HYDROL bac d'évaporation *m*, bac évaporatoire *m*, bassin d'évaporation *m*
evaporative: ~ **capacity** *n* CHEM TECH puissance évaporatrice *f*; ~ **condenser** *n* REFRIG condenseur à autorefroidissement *m*, condenseur à refroidissement parchaleur latente d'évaporation *m*; ~ **cooling** *n* RE-

FRIG, THERMOD refroidissement par évaporation m; ~ **ice** n CHEM TECH glace d'évaporation f

evaporator n CHEM évaporateur m, CHEM TECH appareil à évaporer m, vaporisateur m, vaporiseur m, évaporateur m, HEATING, LAB EQUIP glassware, REFRIG, VEHICLES air conditioner évaporateur m

evaporimeter n CHEM TECH, HYDROL évaporomètre m

evaporite n FUELLESS évaporite f, GEOL roche saline f, évaporite f, PETR évaporite f

evection n ASTRON évection f

even[1] adj DP pair, GEOL lisse, plan, plat, uniforme, égal, PAPER TECH plan, PROD ENG surface lisse, plan m, uni; **on ~ keel** adj NAUT sans différence; **~ with the ground** adj CONST au ras de terre, au rase terre, à fleur de sol

even:[2] **~ and odd courses** n pl TEXTILES rangées de mailles paires et impaires f pl; **~ ground** n CONST terrain plat m, terrain uni m; **~ harmonic** n ELECTRON, PHYS harmonique pair m; **~ keel** n NAUT bonne assiette f, sans-différence m, TRANSP sans-différence m; **~ page** n PRINT page paire f; **~ parity** n COMP, DP, PHYS parité paire f; **~ pitch** n (cf odd pitch) MECH ENG pas exact m

evener: **~ roll** n PAPER TECH rouleau égalisateur m

even-even: **~ nucleus** n PHYS noyau pair-pair m

even-grained: **~ soil** n COAL TECH sol à granulométrie uniforme m

evening: **~ star** n ASTRON planet étoile du berger f

even-odd: **~ nucleus** n PHYS noyau pair-impair m

even-order: **~ filter** n ELECTRON filtre d'ordre pair m

even-sided: **~ angles** n pl PROD ENG angle iron cornières à ailes égales f pl, cornières à branches égales f pl

event[1] n COMP, DP événement m, GEOL horizon sismique m, événement m, HYDR EQUIP of cycle phase du cycle f, of stroke phase de course f, of slide valve phase de distributeurà tiroir f, MATH événement m, PART PHYS événement m, tracking technology événement m, PHYS relativity événement m; **~ handling** n COMP, DP traitement d'événements m; **~ horizon** n ASTRON horizon des évènements m; **~ presentation restriction indicator** n TELECOM indicateur de restriction de divulgation d'événement m; **~ recorder** n ELEC consignateur d'état m, INSTRUMENT enregistreur d'information m

event:[2] **in the ~ of breakdown** phr SAFETY en cas de panne

event-driven adj PROD ENG déclenché par événement

evidence: **~ of use** n PATENTS preuve de l'utilisation f

evolute n GEOM développée f

evolution n (cf involution) ASTRON galaxies, stars évolution f, CHEM of gas dégagement m, MATH évolution f, PHYS évolution f, emission dégagement m

evolve vt CHEM dégager

EW abbr (electronic warfare) ELECTRON guerre électronique f

E-wave n ELEC ENG onde TM f

ex: **~ works** n PROD ENG sortie d'usine f

EX abbr (extinction ratio) TELECOM taux d'extinction m

exa- pref (E) METR exa-(E)

exactitude n PROD ENG exactitude f, justesse f, précision f

exactness n PROD ENG exactitude f, justesse f, précision f

examination n MECH contrôle m, examen m, inspection f, PATENTS, TESTING examen m

examine-off n PROD ENG test à "O" m; **~ key** n PROD ENG touche de test à "O" f

examine-on n PROD ENG test à "1" m; **~ key** n PROD ENG touche de test à "1" f

examiner n PATENTS examinateur m

excavatability n COAL TECH aptitude à l'enlèvement f

excavated: **~ material** n RAIL déblai m

excavating n CONST creusement m, déblai m, excavation f, fouille f, MINING of shaft excavation f

excavation n COAL TECH excavation f, fouille f, CONST process creusement m, déblai m, excavation f, fouille f, MINING déblai m, excavation f, fouille f, of seam dépècement m, of shaft excavation f

excavator n CONST machine, TRANSP excavateur m

excentering: **~ arm** n PETR bras d'excentrage m

exception n COMP anomalie f, exception f, DP anomalie f, exception f, écart m; **~ handler** n COMP, DP gestionnaire d'anomalies m

excess: **~ attenuation** n TELECOM supplément d'affaiblissement m; **~ current** n ELEC surintensité de courant f; **~ current switch** n ELEC interrupteur de surcharge m; **~ energy** n THERMOD excédent d'énergie m, surplus d'énergie m; **~ energy meter** n ELEC compteur de surplus d'énergie m; **~ function** n METALL fonction d'excès f; **~ of operating overload** n PROD ENG dépassant la surcharge normale de fonctionnement; **~ pressure** n REFRIG surpression f; **~ temperature** n THERMOD température excédentaire f, température supérieure à la normale f; **~ voltage** n ELEC surtension f; **~ voltage protection** n ELEC protection contre les surtensions f; **~ weight** n PACKAGING surpoids m

excessive: **~ heat** n PROD ENG surchauffe f; **~ production** n PETR production excédentaire f

exchange n COMP, DP échange m, MECH ENG remplacement m; **~ clip** n PROD ENG battery pack pince de montage f; **~ energy** n METALL énergie d'échange f; **~ jump** n COMP saut avec permutation m; **~ line** n TELECOM ligne réseau f; **~ switchboard** n TELECOM commutateur manuel m; **~ termination** n (ET) TELECOM terminaison de commutateur f

exchangeable: **~ cation** n POLLUTION cation échangeable m; **~ disk** n COMP, DP disque amovible m

excitance n RAD PHYS émittance f

excitation n ELEC, ELEC ENG, GEOPHYS, PART PHYS, RAD PHYS, TELECOM excitation f **~ anode** n ELEC ENG anode d'entretien f; **~ circuit** n ELEC ENG circuit d'excitation m; **~ current** n ELEC courant d'excitation m; **~ energy** n RAD PHYS énergie d'excitation f; **~ field** n ELEC ENG champ d'excitation m; **~ frequency** n TESTING fréquence d'excitation f; **~ function** n RAD PHYS fonction d'excitation f; **~ source** n RAD PHYS source d'excitation f; **~ winding** n ELEC enroulement excitation m

excited[1] adj RAD PHYS atom, molecule excité

excited:[2] **~ atom** n PART PHYS atome excité m, atome stimulé m; **~ component** n GAS TECH espèce excitée f; **~ field loudspeaker** n RECORDING haut-parleur à excitation m; **~ state** n CHEM of atom, METALL, PHYS état excité m; **~ state deactivation** n RAD PHYS désactivation d'état excité f

exciter n ELEC generator dynamo excitatrice f, ELEC ENG exciting dynamo excitatrice f, static dynamo excitateur m, FUELLESS turbines excitatrice f; **~ lamp** n CINEMAT lampe excitatrice f, lampe phonique f

exciting: **~ dynamo** n ELEC dynamo excitatrice f; **~ field** n TESTING champ électromagnétique du courant d'excitation m

exciton n PHYS exciton m

excitron n ELEC ENG excitron m

exclusion: **~ principle** n CHEM principe d'exclusion m

exclusive: **~ fishing zone** n OCEANOG zone de pêche f; ~

licence *n* (BrE) PATENTS licence exclusive *f*; **~ license** *n* (AmE) *see exclusive licence* **~ NOR circuit** *n* ELECTRON circuit NI exclusif *m*; **~ NOR gate** *n* COMP, DP, ELECTRON porte NI exclusif *f*; **~ NOR operation** *n* COMP, DP opération NI exclusif *f*; **~ OR circuit** *n* ELECTRON circuit OU exclusif *m*; **~ OR gate** *n* COMP, DP, ELECTRON porte OU exclusif *f*; **~ OR operation** *n* COMP, DP opération OU exclusif *f*; **~ right** *n* PATENTS droit exclusif *m*; **~ site** *n* TRANSP site propre *m*

excursion: **~ steamer** *n* TRANSP navire d'excursion *m*

exducer *n* AERONAUT grille directrice de sortie *f*

executable: **~ instruction** *n* COMP, DP instruction exécutable *f*; **~ statement** *n* COMP, DP instruction exécutable *f*

execute:[1] **~ phase** *n* COMP, DP phase d'exécution *f*

execute[2] *vt* COMP, DP exécuter

execution *n* COMP, DP exécution *f*; **~ time** *n* COMP durée d'exécution *f*, DP temps d'exécution *m*

executive *n* COMP *program*, DP *program* superviseur *m*; **~ aircraft** *n* AERONAUT avion d'affaires *m*; **~ helicopter** *n* AERONAUT hélicoptère d'affaires *m*

exercise: **~ area** *n* OCEANOG zone navale d'exercices *f*

exert *vt* PHYS *force* appliquer, exercer

exfoliation *n* GEOL desquamation *f*, exfoliation *f*, écaillage *m*, PHYS exfoliation *f*

exhalation: **~ valve** *n* AERONAUT clapet d'expiration *m*

exhaust *n* AERONAUT *engine* échappement *m*, *jet engine* éjection *f*, HEAT ENG, PAPER TECH, VEHICLES échappement *m*; **~ back pressure** *n* AERONAUT contre-pression à l'échappement *f*; **~ brake** *n* VEHICLES ralentisseur sur échappement *m*; **~ case** *n* AERONAUT carter de sortie *m*; **~ cavity** *n* HYDR EQUIP *slide valve* chambre de décompression d'un distributeur à tiroir *f*; **~ cleaning installation** *n* SAFETY installation de purification d'air évacué *f*, installation pour l'épuration d'air d'échappement *f*; **~ cone** *n* AERONAUT cône d'échappement *m*; **~ cover** *n* HYDR EQUIP *of slide valve* couverture de l'orifice d'échappement *f*; **~ draft** *n* (AmE), **~ draught** *n* (BrE) MECH ENG *ventilation* aérage mécanique par aspiration *m*, aérage négatif *m*; **~ edge** *n* HYDR EQUIP *of slide valve* bord d'attaque *m*, bord intérieur *m*; **~ fan** *n* HEAT ENG, MECH ventilateur aspirant *m*, MECH ENG ventilateur aspirant *m*, ventilateur négatif *m*, PAPER TECH ventilateur aspirant *m*; **~ gas** *n* AUTO gaz brûlé *m*, MECH *vehicles* gaz d'échappement *m*, POLLUTION effluent gazeux *m*, gaz d'échappement *m*; **~ gas cleaning** *n* THERMOD épuration de gaz d'échappement *f*; **~ gas combustion** *n* TRANSP postbrûleur *m*; **~ gas emission** *n* TRANSP émission de gaz d'échappement *f*; **~ gas indicator** *n* AUTO indicateur de température de gaz *m*; **~ gas recirculation** *n* TRANSP recirculation des gaz de carter *m*; **~ gas recirculation with air injection** *n* TRANSP recirculation des gaz de carter accompagnée d'injection d'air *f*; **~ gas temperature** *n* AERONAUT température des gaz d'échappement *f*; **~ gas test** *n* CONTROL contrôle de gaz brulé *m*, contrôle de gaz d'échappement *m*; **~ gas turbine** *n* AUTO turbine à gaz d'échappement *f*; **~ lap** *n* HYDR EQUIP couverture de l'orifice d'échappement *f*; **~ lead** *n* HYDR EQUIP avance linéaire à l'échappement *f*, avance à l'échappement *f*; **~ manifold** *n* AERONAUT, AUTO, MECH collecteur d'échappement *m*, THERMOD collecteur des gaz brûlés *m*, VEHICLES collecteur d'échappement *m*; **~ muffler** *n* (AmE) (*cf exhaust silencer*) AUTO pot d'échappement *m*; **~ nozzle** *n* AERONAUT tuyère d'éjection des gaz *f*; **~ nozzle breech** *n* AERONAUT culotte de tuyère de réac-

teur *f*; **~ passage** *n* AUTO chapelle d'échappement *f*, chapelle de sortie *f*; **~ pipe** *n* AERONAUT, NAUT *engine*, THERMOD tuyau d'échappement *m*; **~ port** *n* AUTO *engine* orifice d'échappement *m*, HYDR EQUIP lumière d'échappement *f*, orifice d'échappement *m*, VEHICLES *engine* lumière d'échappement *f*; **~ recycling** *n* TRANSP recirculation des gaz de carter *f*; **~ silencer** *n* (BrE) (*cf exhaust muffler*) AUTO pot de détente *m*; **~ steam** *n* FOOD TECH, HYDR EQUIP vapeur d'échappement *f*; **~ steam turbine** *n* HEAT ENG turbine à vapeur d'échappement *f*; **~ stroke** *n* AUTO course d'échappement *f*, temps d'échappement *m*, VEHICLES *engine* course d'échappement *f*; **~ system** *n* VEHICLES système d'échappement *m*; **~ trail** *n* AERONAUT traînée d'échappement *f*; **~ turbine** *n* HEAT ENG turbine à vapeur d'échappement *f*; **~ turbocharger** *n* AUTO turbocompresseur à gaz *m*; **~ valve** *n* AUTO soupape d'échappement *f*, HYDR EQUIP clapet d'échappement *m*, clapet de décharge *m*, soupape d'échappement *f*, soupape de décharge *f*, LAB EQUIP soupape d'échappement *f*, PAPER TECH vanne d'échappement *f*, VEHICLES *engine* soupape d'échappement *f*; **~ vent installations** *n pl* SAFETY installations d'aspiration *f pl*

exhausted: **~ developer** *n* PHOTO révélateur épuisé *m*; **~ vein** *n* MINING filon épuisé *m*

exhauster *n* FOOD TECH exhausteur *m*, MECH ENG aspirateur *m*, exhausteur *m*

exhausting *n* MINING *of air* aspiration *f*

exhaustion *n* NUCLEAR épuisement *m*; **~ box** *n* FOOD TECH boîte sous vapeur *f*; **~ creep** *n* METALL fluage par épuisement *m*

exhibition *n* PATENTS exposition *f*

exhumed: **~ anticlinal fold** *n* GEOL boutonnière *f*

existing[1] *adj* CONST existant

existing:[2] **~ light** *n* CINEMAT lumière ambiante *f*; **~ plant** *n* POLLUTION usine en service avant 1975 *f*, usine existante *f*

exit *n* COMP, DP sortie *f*; **~ angle** *n* HYDR EQUIP angle de sortie *m*; **~ cone** *n* PHYS *of nozzle* divergent conique *m*; **~ point** *n* COMP, DP point de sortie *m*; **~ pupil** *n* PHYS pupille de sortie *f*; **~ taxiway** *n* AERONAUT sortie de piste *f*; **~ velocity** *n* HYDR EQUIP vitesse de sortie *f*

exjunction *n* COMP disjonction *f*, disjonction exclusive *f*, DP OU exclusif *m*, disjonction *f*

exoatmospheric *adj* SPACE exoatmosphérique

exobase *n* SPACE exobase *f*

exobiology *n* ASTRON exobiologie *f*

exosphere *n* SPACE exosphère *f*

exothermal *adj* THERMOD exothermique

exothermic[1] *adj* CHEM *reaction*, SPACE *spacecraft*, THERMOD exothermique

exothermic:[2] **~ process** *n* PETR TECH *refining* processus exothermique *m*

exotic: **~ chip** *n* ELECTRON puce spéciale *f*; **~ fauna** *n* GEOL faune exotique *m*, faune introduite *m*; **~ signal** *n* ELECTRON signal truqué *m*

expand *vi* GEOM grossir, HYDR EQUIP *steam* se détendre

expandable[1] *adj* COMP, DP, TELECOM extensif, évolutif

expandable:[2] **~ pallet** *n* PACKAGING palette extensible *f*

expanded[1] *adj* SPACE *spacecraft* détendu

expanded:[2] **~ cellular plastic** *n* REFRIG *insulating* mousse de plastique expansé *f*; **~ cork** *n* REFRIG liège expansé *m*; **~ data table** *n* PROD ENG table de données étendue *f*; **~ memory** *n* COMP, DP mémoire étendue *f*; **~ memory manager** *n* COMP, DP gestionnaire de mémoire étendue *m*; **~ memory specification** *n* COMP, DP spécification de mémoire étendue f; ~ **metal** n MECH métal déployé m; ~ **perlite** n HEAT ENG perlite expansée f; ~ **plastic** n P&R plastique expansé m, plastique mousse m; ~ **polystyrene** n P&R polystyrène expansé m, PACKAGING polystyrène mousse m; ~ **polythene packaging** n PACKAGING emballage en polythène mousse m; ~ **rubber** n P&R caoutchouc expansé m, caoutchouc mousse m; ~ **scale** n METR échelle dilatée f; ~ **sweep** n ELECTRON balayage avec loupe m, balayage dilaté m

expander n PROD ENG, RECORDING expanseur m; ~ **module** n PROD ENG module d'extension m

expanding: ~ **mandrel** n MECH ENG mandrin extensible m

expansibility n THERMOD of gases expansibilité f

expansion n ASTRON of the universe expansion f, CHEM of gas dilation f, ELECTRON augmentation f, expansion f, élargissement n, HYDR EQUIP détente f, expansion f, MATH développement m, MECH dilatation f, détente f, expansion f, P&R, PHYS dilatation f, expansion f, PRINT déformation f, RECORDING expansion f, REFRIG of fluid détente f, SPACE spacecraft détente f, expansion f, extension f, SPRINGS détente f, THERMOD dilatation f, of gases détente f, expansion f; ~ **bellows** n pl MECH soufflet de dilatation m; ~ **bend** n REFRIG lyre de dilatation f; ~ **bit** n PETR TECH trépan réglable m; ~ **board** n COMP, DP carte d'extension f; ~ **bolt** n MECH ENG boulon de dilatation m; ~ **box** n HYDR EQUIP boîte de dilatation f, boîte de détente f; ~ **cable** n PROD ENG câble d'extension m; ~ **cam** n HYDR EQUIP taquet de détente m; ~ **card** n COMP, DP, ELECTRON carte d'extension f; ~ **chamber** n MECH ENG chambre de détente f; ~ **coupling** n HYDR EQUIP manchon de dilatation m; ~ **duration** n HYDR EQUIP of steam période de détente f, temps de détente m; ~ **engine** n MECH ENG machine à détente f, machine à expansion f, moteur à détente m; ~ **of an expression** n MATH développement d'une expression m; ~ **filter** n ELECTRON filtre d'expansion m, filtre élargisseur d'impulsions m; ~ **gear** n MECH ENG détente f; ~ **joint** n CONST, HYDR EQUIP joint de dilatation m; ~ **loop** n REFRIG boucle de dilatation f; ~ **network** n TELECOM réseau d'expansion m; ~ **notch** n HYDR EQUIP cran de détente d'un secteur denté m; ~ **nozzle** n AERONAUT jet engine tuyère f; ~ **period** n HYDR EQUIP période de détente f, temps de détente m; ~ **plate** n HYDR EQUIP plaque de détente f; ~ **point** n HYDR EQUIP point de détente m; ~ **reamer** n PROD ENG alésoir extensible m, alésoir à lames mobiles m, alésoir à lames rapportées m; ~ **ring** n PETR TECH drilling anneau de dilatation m; ~ **slide** n HYDR EQUIP glissière de détente f, opercule de détente m; ~ **slot** n COMP, DP connecteur d'extension m, emplacement libre m, slot d'extension m, ELECTRON emplacement pour carte d'extension m; ~ **space** n C&G chambre d'expansion f; ~ **stage** n TELECOM étage d'expansion m; ~ **storage tube** n ELECTRON tube à mémoire à projection m; ~ **stress** n HYDR EQUIP force de dilatation f; ~ **stroke** n MECH ENG piston course de détente f, THERMOD motor course de détente f, course motrice f; ~ **tank** n AUTO, HEAT ENG, MECH vase d'expansion m; ~ **trap** n HYDR EQUIP trappe de dilatation f; ~ **tube** n LAB EQUIP glassware tube d'élargissement m; ~ **turbine** n AERONAUT, REFRIG turbine de détente f; ~ **valve** n HYDR EQUIP clapet d'expansion m, clapet de détente m, soupape d'expansion f, soupape de détente f, tiroir d'expansion m, tiroir de détente m, MECH ENG soupape de dilatation f, REFRIG détendeur m, soupape de détente f; ~ **vessel** n MECH ENG réservoir de détente m;

~ **wave** n AERONAUT sonic boom onde de détente f

expectation n COMP espérance f

expected: ~ **approach time** n AERONAUT heure d'approche prévue f

expedite vt PROD ENG modifier la priorité

expedition n PROD ENG accélération f, urgence f

expeditor n PROD ENG suiveur des pièces m

expendable[1] adj MECH consommable, jetable, SPACE spacecraft consommable

expendable:[2] ~ **item** n MECH ENG élément consommable m; ~ **pallet** n TRANSP palette perdue f

experience: ~ **curve** n TEXTILES courbe d'expérience f

experiment n CHEM, PHYS, SPACE expérience f; ~ **module** n SPACE module d'expérience m; ~ **package** n SPACE bloc expérimental m

experimental[1] adj CHEM, NUCLEAR, PART PHYS, PHYS, RAD PHYS expérimental

experimental:[2] ~ **basin** n WATER SUPP bassin versant expérimental m; ~ **helicopter** n AERONAUT hélicoptère expérimental m; ~ **model** n MECH maquette f; ~ **physicist** n PART PHYS physicien expérimentateur m; ~ **safety vehicle** n (ESV) TRANSP voiture expérimentale de sécurité f; ~ **section** n CONST planche expérimentale f; ~ **solid disc flywheel** n (BrE) MECH ENG volant à disque plein expérimental m; ~ **solid disk flywheel** n (AmE) see experimental solid disc flywheel ~ **television** n TV télévision expérimentale f

expert: ~ **system** n COMP, DP système expert m

expiration: ~ **of timer** n (AmE) (cf expiry of timer) TELECOM maritime expiration de la temporisation f

expiry: ~ **date** n CINEMAT date d'expiration f; ~ **of timer** n (BrE) (cf expiration of timer) TELECOM maritime expiration de la temporisation f

explicit: ~ **address** n COMP, DP adresse explicite f; ~ **congestion notification** n (ECN) TELECOM notification d'encombrement explicite f

explode[1] vt THERMOD faire détoner, faire éclater

explode[2] vi THERMOD faire explosion, éclater

exploded: ~ **view** n MECH of drawing vue éclatée f, éclaté mécanique m, MECH ENG of drawing vue éclatée f

exploder n MINING amorce f, capsule f, détonateur m, exploseur m

exploding: ~ **of detonator** n RAIL écrasement d'un pétard m

exploitation: ~ **in industry** n PATENTS application industrielle f

exploration n PETR TECH exploration f; ~ **drilling** n PETR TECH forage d'exploration m; ~ **drive** n MINING galerie de recherches f; ~ **level** n MINING galerie de recherches f; ~ **licence** n (BrE) PETR TECH permis d'exploration m; ~ **license** n (AmE) see exploration licence ~ **phase** n PETR TECH phase d'exploration f; ~ **pit** n MINING trou de prospection m; ~ **platform** n SPACE plate-forme d'exploration f; ~ **rig** n PETR TECH plate-forme d'exploration f; ~ **shaft** n MINING puits de recherche m; ~ **trench** n MINING tranchée de prospection f, tranchée de recherches f; ~ **well** n PETR, PETR TECH puits d'exploration m; ~ **work** n MINING travaux d'exploration m pl

exploratory: ~ **drilling** n GAS TECH forage d'exploration m, PETR TECH forage d'exploration m, sondage de recherche m; ~ **well** n PETR puits d'exploration m, puits de recherche m

Explorer: ~ **satellite** n ASTRON satellite Explorer m

exploring: ~ **coil** n ELEC magnetic field bobine exploratrice f

explosimeter *n* LAB EQUIP *inflammable gases* explosimètre *m*

explosion *n* PETR TECH, SAFETY, SPACE explosion *f*; ~ **breccia** *n* GEOL *volcanic* brèche d'explosion volcanique *f*; ~ **dies** *n pl* MECH ENG outillage de formage par explosion *m*; ~ **suppression** *n* SAFETY suppression des explosions *f*; ~ **wave** *n* MINING onde explosive *f*

explosion-proof[1] *adj* AERONAUT, MECH antidéflagrant, MINING antidéflagrant, antigrisouteux, PACKAGING antidéflagrant, PROP MAT inexplosible

explosion-proof:[2] ~ **glazing** *n* C&G vitrage antiexplosion *m*

explosive[1] *adj* THERMOD explosif

explosive[2] *n* CHEM, SAFETY, SPACE explosif *m*, THERMOD matière explosive *f*; ~ **atmosphere** *n* SAFETY atmosphère explosive *f*; ~ **bolt** *n* MECH, SPACE boulon explosif *m*; ~ **combustion** *n* MINING déflagration *f*; ~ **decompression** *n* OCEANOG, THERMOD décompression explosive *f*; ~ **forming** *n* MECH, THERMOD formage par explosion *m*; ~ **mixture** *n* AUTO mélange détonant *m*; ~ **sensitivity** *n* MINING sensibilité *f*

explosives: ~ **magazine** *n* MINING dynamitière *f*, dépôt d'explosifs *m*, poudrière *f*

explosive-type: ~ **rivet** *n* MECH rivet explosif *m*

exponent *n* COMP, DP, MATH exposant *m*

exponential[1] *adj* ELEC, MATH exponentiel

exponential:[2] ~ **amplifier** *n* ELECTRON amplificateur exponentiel *m*; ~ **curve** *n* ELEC, MATH exponentielle *f*; ~ **decay** *n* ELECTRON décroissance exponentielle *f*; ~ **distribution** *n* COMP distribution exponentielle *f*, répartition exponentielle *f*, DP répartition exponentielle *f*; ~ **horn** *n* ACOUSTICS pavillon exponentiel *m*; ~ **tube** *n* ELECTRON tube à pente variable *m*

export: ~ **licence** *n* (BrE) NAUT licence d'exportation *f*; ~ **license** *n* (AmE) *see export licence* ~ **packaging** *n* PACKAGING emballage pour l'exportation *m*

expose *vt* CINEMAT, PHOTO exposer

exposed: ~ **location single-buoy mooring** *n* (*ELSBM*) PETR TECH *distribution, shipping* amarrage à point unique *m*, bouée d'amarrage à point unique *f*, bouée monoposte *f*

exposure *n* PHOTO exposition *f*, *period of time* durée de pose *f*, temps de pose *m*, PHYS exposition *f*, pose *f*, POLLUTION exposition *f*, PRINT exposition *f*, insolation *f*, pause *f*; ~ **at the surface** *n* OCEANOG émersion *f*; ~ **calculating chart** *n* PHOTO tableau calculateur *m*; ~ **calculator** *n* CINEMAT calculateur de temps de pose *m*, guide d'exposition *m*; ~ **control tape** *n* CINEMAT *in printer* bande de réglage *f*; ~ **counter** *n* PHOTO compteur d'images *m*; ~ **dose** *n* RAD PHYS *ionizing radiation* dose d'exposition *f*; ~ **duration** *n* CINEMAT temps de pose *m*; ~ **factor** *n* PHOTO coefficient de pose *m*; ~ **index** *n* PHOTO indice de pose *m*; ~ **latitude** *n* CINEMAT, PHOTO latitude d'exposition *f*, latitude de pose *f*; ~ **limit** *n* SAFETY limite d'exposition *f*; ~ **meter** *n* CINEMAT, PHOTO, PHYS posemètre *m*; ~ **meter needle** *n* PHOTO aiguille de posemètre *f*; ~ **meter using needle-matching system** *n* PHOTO posemètre couplé *m*; ~ **risk** *n* SAFETY *radiation* risque d'exposition *m*; ~ **scale** *n* PHOTO échelle des temps de pose *f*; ~ **test** *n* CINEMAT essai d'exposition *m*, essai de pose *m*; ~ **time** *n* PHOTO durée de pose *f*, temps de pose *m*; ~ **timer** *n* PHOTO posemètre d'agrandissement à minuterie *m*; ~ **to fumes** *n* SAFETY exposition aux vapeurs *f*; ~ **to radiation** *n* P&R exposition aux radiations *f*; ~ **value** *n* CINEMAT indice de lumination *m*

express: ~ **parcel service** *n* RAIL *vehicles* messagerie accélérée *f*; ~ **train** *n* RAIL *vehicles* train express *m*, TRANSP train de grande ligne *m*, train express *m*; ~ **tramway** *n* TRANSP tramway express *m*

expression *n* COMP, DP expression *f*

expulsion *n* PETR TECH expulsion *f*; ~ **fuse** *n* ELEC fusible à expulsion *m*, ELEC ENG coupe-circuit à expulsion dirigée *m*; ~ **rate** *n* PETR TECH vitesse d'expulsion *f*

expulsion-type: ~ **lightning arrester** *n* ELEC ENG parafoudre à expulsion *m*

extend *vt* COMP allonger, étendre, MECH ENG *tool life* prolonger, PRINT *inks* allonger

extended: ~ **addressing** *n* COMP, DP adressage étendu *m*; ~ **application layer structure** *n* (*XALS*) TELECOM structure en couches d'application étendue *f*; ~ **bandwidth system** *n* TELECOM *amateur radio* système à bande élargie *m*; ~ **binary coded decimal interchange code** *n* (*EBCDIC*) COMP, DP, ELECTRON code décimal codé binaire étendu *m* (*code EBCDIC*); ~ **definition television** *n* (*EDTV*) TV télévision à définition améliorée *f*; ~ **inspection** *n* CONTROL contrôle poussé *m*; ~ **interaction oscillator** *n* ELECTRON oscillateur à interaction étendue *m*; ~ **interaction tube** *n* ELECTRON tube à interaction répartie *m*; ~ **length** *n* SPRINGS longueur développée *f*; ~ **node** *n* METALL noeud étendu *m*; ~ **piston rod** *n* MECH ENG contre-tige de piston *f*; ~ **play record** *n* RECORDING enregistrement longue durée *m*; ~ **range loudspeaker** *n* RECORDING haut-parleur à réponse étendue *m*; ~ **runway centerline** *n* (AmE), ~ **runway centreline** *n* (BrE) AERONAUT prolongement de l'axe de piste *m*; ~ **surface heat exchanger** *n* MECH ENG échangeur de chaleur de grande superficie *m*; ~ **type** *n* PRINT caractères large *m*

extender *n* COLOURS matière de charge *f*, P&R *compounding* agent d'étalement *m*, charge *f*, pigment de charge *m*, étalement *m*; ~ **oil** *n* PETR TECH *refining* huile d'extension *f*

extensibility *n* COMP, DP, MECH ENG, P&R, PROP MAT extensibilité *f*

extensible: ~ **addressing** *n* COMP, DP adressage extensible *m*; ~ **language** *n* COMP, DP langage extensible *m*

extension *n* GEOL extension *f*, MECH ENG extension *f*, prolongation *f*, prolongement *m*, PHOTO *of bellows* tirage *m*, PHYS *length* allongement *m*, TELECOM poste supplémentaire *m*; ~ **bell** *n* TELECOM sonnerie de poste *f*; ~ **bellows** *n pl* PHOTO soufflet à tirage variable *m*; ~ **bellows unit** *n* CINEMAT rallonge à soufflet *f*; ~ **bit** *n* MECH ENG mèche extensible *f*; ~ **cable** *n* CINEMAT câble de rallonge *m*, câble prolongateur *m*, rallonge *f*, ELEC ENG cordon prolongateur *m*; ~ **connector plug** *n* MECH ENG *injection mould cooling* rallonge de raccord *f*; ~ **cord** *n* AERONAUT câble prolongateur *m*; ~ **ladder** *n* CONST échelle à coulisse *f*; ~ **lead** *n* CINEMAT baladeuse *f*, rallonge *f*, LAB EQUIP *electric supply* prolongateur *m*; ~ **line** *n* MECH ENG *drawing* ligne de départ de cote *f*; ~ **piece** *n* MECH ENG allonge *f*, barre de rallonge *f*, rallonge *f*, tige de rallonge *f*, *for box spanner* clef de rallonge *f*; ~ **reel** *n* ELEC ENG enrouleur de câble électrique *m*; ~ **ring** *n* PHOTO bague intermédiaire *f*; ~ **shaft** *n* MECH ENG nez d'arbre *m*; ~ **socket** *n* MECH ENG douille allonge *f*; ~ **spring** *n* MECH ENG, SPRINGS ressort de traction *m*; ~ **of time limits** *n* PATENTS prorogation des délais *f*; ~ **tripod** *n* PHOTO pied à trois branches extensibles *m*, trépied extensible *m*; ~ **tube** *n* CINEMAT tube rallonge *m*, LAB EQUIP *glassware* prolongateur *m*, PHOTO tube rallonge *m*; ~ **well** *n* PETR TECH *drilling* puits d'extension *m*

extensive: **~ quantity** *n* PHYS grandeur extensive *f*

extensometer *n* CONST extensomètre *m*, MECH jauge de contrainte *f*, METR, PAPER TECH extensiomètre *m*

extent *n* MINING, PATENTS *of protection* étendue *f*, PRINT *of document* longueur *f*

exterior *n* CINEMAT extérieur *m*, tournage en extérieurs *m*; **~ angle** *n* GEOM angle extérieur *m*; **~ finish** *n* CO-LOURS peinture pour extérieur *f*; **~ packaging machine** *n* PACKAGING suremballeuse *f*; **~ pole generator** *n* ELEC dynamo à pôles extérieurs *f*; **~ surface** *n* PACKAGING surface extérieure *f*

external[1] *adj* POLLUTION allochtone, externe

external:[2] **~ access equipment** *n* (*EA*) TELECOM équipement d'accès externe *m*; **~ blocking** *n* TELECOM blocage externe *m*; **~ caliper gage** *n* (AmE), **~ calliper gauge** *n* (BrE) MECH ENG calibre simple femelle *m*; **~ chamfer** *n* SPRINGS chanfrein extérieur *m*; **~ circuit** *n* ELEC circuit extérieur *m*; **~ combustion engine** *n* MECH ENG moteur à explosion externe *m*, TRANSP moteur à combustion externe *m*; **~ cylindrical gage** *n* (AmE), **~ cylindrical gauge** *n* (BrE) MECH ENG bague *f*, calibre à bague *m*; **~ defrosting** *n* REFRIG dégivrage par l'extérieur *m*; **~ device** *n* COMP, DP dispositif externe *m*; **~ disturbance** *n* ELEC perturbation extérieure *f*; **~ electromagnetic wave** *n* RAD PHYS onde électromagnétique externe *f*; **~ equalizer valve** *n* REFRIG détendeur à égalisation extérieure de pression *m*; **~ force** *n* METALL force extérieure *f*; **~ gas pressure cable** *n* ELEC câble à pression externe de gaz *m*; **~ geomagnetic field** *n* GEOPHYS champ géomagnétique extérieur *m*; **~ graticule** *n* ELECTRON graticule extérieur *m*; **~ inductance** *n* ELEC inductance extérieure *f*; **~ injection** *n* AUTO injection indirecte *f*; **~ input** *n* ELECTRON entrée extérieure *f*, POLLUTION apport allogène *m*; **~ insulation** *n* ELEC isolation externe *f*; **~ interface** *n* SPACE interface externe *f*; **~ interrupt** *n* COMP, DP interruption externe *f*; **~ load carrying** *n* AERONAUT *helicopter* transport de charge par élingue *m*; **~ magnetic field** *n* ELEC champ magnétique extérieur *m*; **~ magnetosphere** *n* GEOPHYS magnétosphère externe *f*; **~ memory** *n* COMP, DP, ELEC ENG mémoire externe *f*; **~ micrometer** *n* MECH ENG palmer d'extérieur *m*; **~ modulation** *n* ELECTRON modulation extérieure *f*; **~ noise** *n* ELECTRON bruit externe *m*; **~ photoelectric effect** *n* OPT effet photoélectrique externe *m*, photoémission *f*, TELECOM effet photoélectrique externe *m*; **~ plasticizer** *n* P&R plastifiant extérieur *m*; **~ pole generator** *n* ELEC dynamo à pôles extérieurs *f*; **~ prestressing** *n* CONST *concrete* précontrainte extérieure *f*; **~ reference** *n* COMP, DP référence externe *f*; **~ resistance** *n* ELEC résistance externe *f*; **~ resistor** *n* ELEC ENG résistance extérieure *f*; **~ screw** *n* PROD ENG vis mâle *f*, vis pleine *f*; **~ screw thread finish** *n* C&G bague à vis *f*; **~ setup** *n* PROD ENG préparation en temps masqué *f*, réglage externe *m*; **~ signal** *n* ELECTRON signal extérieur *m*; **~ signal source** *n* ELECTRON source extérieure de signaux *f*; **~ sort** *n* COMP tri externe *m*, DP tri de fusionnement *m*, tri externe *m*; **~ source** *n* ELECTRON source extérieure *f*; **~ storage** *n* COMP, DP mémoire externe *f*; **~ synchronization** *n* ELECTRON synchronisation extérieure *f*; **~ thread** *n* MECH ENG filet extérieur *m*, filetage extérieur *m*; **~ thread fastener** *n* MECH ENG élément de fixation fileté mâle *m*; **~ torque** *n* MECH ENG moment de torsion externe *m*; **~ traffic** *n* TRANSP trafic en transit *m*; **~ voltage** *n* ELEC ENG tension extérieure *f*; **~ voltage**

source *n* ELEC ENG source de tension extérieure *f*

externides *n pl* GEOL zones externes *f pl*

extinct: **~ volcano** *n* GEOL volcan éteint *m*

extinction *n* ASTRON, CRYSTALL, GAS TECH extinction *f*; **~ of light** *n* RAD PHYS absorption de lumière *f*; **~ potential** *n* ELEC ENG potentiel d'extinction *m*, tension d'extinction *f*; **~ ratio** *n* (*EX*) TELECOM taux d'extinction *m*; **~ zone** *n* GAS TECH zone d'extinction *f*

extinguisher *n* MECH ENG extincteur *m*; **~ percussion** *n* AERONAUT percussion de bouteille *f*; **~ striker** *n* AERONAUT percuteur d'extincteur *m*

extinguishing: **~ foam** *n* THERMOD *fire* mousse carbonique *f*

extra: **~ digit** *n* TELECOM chiffre supplémentaire *m*; **~ high tension** *n* (*EHT*) ELECTRON, TV très haute tension *f* (*THT*); **~ high-voltage cable** *n* ELEC *supply* câble à très haute tension *m*; **~ labor** *n* (AmE), **~ labour** *n* (BrE) PROD ENG rectification *f*, retouche *f*; **~ thin sheet glass** *n* C&G verre extra-mince *m*

extract[1] *n* CHEM, GAS TECH, PAPER TECH extrait *m*; **~ from the register** *n* PATENTS extrait de registre *m*

extract[2] *vt* CHEM extraire, CONST arracher, extraire, GAS TECH, PAPER TECH extraire

extractable: **~ component** *n* TESTING matière extractible *f*; **~ sulfur** *n* (AmE), **~ sulphur** *n* (BrE) P&R soufre extractif *m*

extractant *n* FOOD TECH solvant d'extraction *m*

extraction *n* COAL TECH extraction *f*, CONST *of nail* arrachage *m*, extraction *f*, PETR TECH *drilling, refining, etc* extraction *f*; **~ fan** *n* LAB EQUIP ventilateur *m*; **~ hood** *n* LAB EQUIP hotte *f*; **~ process** *n* PETR TECH *drilling, refining etc* procédé d'extraction *m*; **~ rate** *n* FOOD TECH taux d'extraction *m*, HYDROL taux de soutirage *m*; **~ thimble** *n* FOOD TECH *machinery* enveloppe d'extracteur *f*, LAB EQUIP *Soxhlet apparatus* cartouche à extraction *f*

extractive: **~ distillation** *n* FOOD TECH distillation extractive *f*, distillation par extraction *f*

extractor *n* CHEM TECH colonne d'extraction *f*, CONST extracteur *m*, MECH ENG tire-aiguille *m*, P&R *moulding*, PAPER TECH extracteur *m*; **~ basket** *n* CHEM TECH récipient de la centrifugeuse *m*; **~ fan** *n* CHEM TECH exhausteur *m*, ventilateur extracteur *m*, MECH ENG ventilateur extracteur *m*; **~ fan system** *n* SAFETY système de ventilation par extraction *m*

extrados *n* CONST *of arch* extrados *m*

extradynamite *n* MINING explosif nitraté *m*

extragalactic *adj* ASTRON, SPACE extragalactique

extrahard: **~ paper** *n* PHOTO papier ultradur *m*

extraneous: **~ noise** *n* RECORDING, TELECOM bruit parasite *m*

extraordinary: **~ ray** *n* PHYS rayon extraordinaire *m*

extrapolate *vt* QUALITY extrapoler

extrapolation *n* QUALITY extrapolation *f*

extrasmooth: **~ file** *n* PROD ENG lime très douce *f*

extrasoft: **~ paper** *n* PHOTO papier ultradoux *m*

extraterrestrial[1] *adj* ASTRON extraterrestre, SPACE extraterrestre

extraterrestrial:[2] **~ life** *n* ASTRON, SPACE vie extraterrestre *f*

extra-vehicular: **~ pressure garment** *n* SPACE combinaison spatiale pressurisée *f*

extreme: **~ breadth** *n* NAUT *ship design* largeur hors tout *f*; **~ close-up** *n* CINEMAT très gros plan *m*; **~ coil** *n* SPRINGS spire d'extrémité *f*; **~ depth** *n* NAUT *shipbuilding* profondeur de carène *f*; **~ draft** *n* (AmE), **~**

draught *n* (BrE) NAUT *ship design* tirant d'eau maximal *m*; ~ **overtravel limit switch** *n* PROD ENG interrupteur de position de surcourse extrême *m*, interrupteur de position de sécurité *m*; ~ **pressure additive** *n* PETR TECH additif extrême pression *m*

extremely: ~ **low frequency** *n* ELEC *alternating current* fréquence ultrabasse *f*

extrinsic: ~ **conductivity** *n* ELEC ENG conductibilité extrinsèque *f*; ~ **joint loss** *n* OPT, TELECOM perte extrinsèque de raccordement *f*; ~ **junction loss** *n* OPT perte extrinsèque de raccordement *f*; ~ **photoconductivity** *n* ELEC ENG photoconduction extrinsèque *f*; ~ **semiconductor** *n* COMP, ELECTRON, PHYS semiconducteur extrinsèque *m*

extrudability *n* P&R extrusion *f*

extrude *vi* P&R boudiner, extruder

extruded: ~ **cellular plastic** *n* REFRIG *for insulating* mousse de plastique extrudé *f*; ~ **film** *n* P&R feuille extrudée *f*; ~ **insulation** *n* ELEC *cable* isolation extrudée *f*; ~ **seal** *n* MECH ENG profilé d'étanchéité *m*

extruder *n* P&R boudineuse *f*, extrudeuse *f*, PAPER TECH extrudeuse *f*, PROP MAT presse à filage *f*

extruding: ~ **machine** *n* P&R boudineuse *f*

extrusion *n* FOOD TECH, MECH, MECH ENG extrusion *f*, P&R boudinage *m*, PAPER TECH extraction *f*, extrusion *f*; ~ **blow molding** *n* (AmE), ~ **blow moulding** *n* (BrE) PACKAGING extrusion-soufflage *f*; ~ **coating** *n* PAPER TECH, PRINT couchage par extrusion *m*; ~ **die** *n* MECH ENG *for plastics or metal* outillage d'extrusion *m*, P&R filière de boudinage *f*; ~ **diecasting** *n* MECH ENG formage par fluage *m*; ~ **flange** *n* MECH ENG aile de cornière *f*; ~ **gun** *n* MECH ENG pistolet à extrusion *m*; ~ **head** *n* MECH ENG *machine tools* tête d'extrusion *f*; ~ **machine** *n* P&R boudineuse *f*, extrudeuse *f*, PACKAGING *for tubes* boudineuse *f*

extrusion-coated: ~ **paper** *n* PAPER TECH papier couché par extrusion *m*

extrusive: ~ **rock** *n* FUELLESS roche d'épanchement *f*, GEOL roche effusive *f*, roche volcanique *f*

exudation *n* CHEM, P&R exsudation *f*

exude *vt* CHEM, P&R exsuder

eye *n* C&G *of pot furnace*, MECH ENG *of tool*, METEO *of cyclone*, NAUT *of rope, metal fitting, etc* oeil *m*, PROD ENG *of furnace, cupola* regard *m*, *of needle* chas *m*, oeil *m*; ~ **diagram** *n* TELECOM diagramme de l'oeil *m*, diagramme en oeil *m*; ~ **drop bottle** *n* C&G flacon de collyre *m*; ~ **end** *n* MECH ENG embout à oeil *m*; ~ **face and neck protection** *n* SAFETY protection des yeux du visage et du cou *f*; ~ **filter** *n* SAFETY filtre pour les yeux *m*; ~ **injury** *n* SAFETY blessure aux yeux *f*, blessure à l'oeil *f*; ~ **lens** *n* INSTRUMENT lentille convergente *f*; ~ **protection filter** *n* SAFETY *welding* filtre de protection des yeux *m*; ~ **protection glasses** *n pl* C&G verres protecteurs *m pl*; ~ **protectors** *n pl* INSTRUMENT lunettes de sûreté *f pl*, lunettes protectrices *f pl*, SAFETY lunettes de protection *f pl*; ~ **rinse bottles** *n pl* SAFETY flacons pour douche oculaire *m pl*; ~ **shields** *n pl* INSTRUMENT lunettes de sûreté *f pl*, lunettes protectrices *f pl*; ~ **strain** *n* SAFETY fatigue oculaire *f*; ~ **tube** *n* ASTRON *of telescope* tube porte-oculaire *m*

eyebolt *n* MECH anneau de levage *m*, boulon à oeil *m*, piton *m*, MECH ENG *for lifting* anneau à tige *m*, boulon à oeil *m*, oeil à queue filetée *m*, oreille *f*, NAUT *deck fittings* piton de filière *m*, piton à oeil *m*, PROD ENG, VEHICLES *clutch* boulon à oeil *m*

eyecup *n* CINEMAT, PHOTO oeilleton d'oculaire *m*

eyed: ~ **punch** *n* PROD ENG poinçon à oeil *m*; ~ **rivet snap** *n* PROD ENG bouterolle à oeil *m*; ~ **rod** *n* PROD ENG tige à oeil *f*

eyehandle *n* PROD ENG manche à oeil *m*

eyehook *n* PROD ENG croc *m*; ~ **and thimble** *n* PROD ENG croc à cosse *m*

eyelet *n* PACKAGING, PRINT, PROD ENG oeillet *m*

eyelevel *n* CONST hauteur de l'oeil *f*, hauteur des yeux *f*

eyeloop *n* SPRINGS boucle-oeil *f*

eyepiece *n* ASTRON *of telescope* oculaire *m*, CINEMAT oculaire de visée *m*, oeilleton *m*, INSTRUMENT, LAB EQUIP *microscope* oculaire *m*, PHOTO *of direct-vision viewfinder* lentille dioptrique *f*, oeilleton de visée *m*, PHYS oculaire *m*, PROD ENG *of furnace, cupola* lunette de regard *f*, SPACE oculaire *m*; ~ **focusing knob** *n* INSTRUMENT bouton de mise au point de l'oculaire *m*; ~ **holder** *n* INSTRUMENT tube porte-oculaire *m*; ~ **lens** *n* INSTRUMENT, PHOTO oculaire *m*; ~ **micrometer** *n* MECH ENG micromètre-objectif *m*

eyeplate *n* NAUT anneau *m*

eyeshade *n* SAFETY visière *f*

eyeshape: ~ **pattern** *n* TELECOM diagramme en oeil *m*

eyesplice *n* NAUT *rope* épissure à oeil *f*, épissure à oeillet *f*

eyewash *n* SAFETY collyre *m*

F

f *abbr (femto-)* METR f *(femto-)*

F [1] *abbr (farad)* METR F *(farad)*

F [2] *(fluorine)* CHEM F *(fluor)*

FAA *abbr (facility accepted message)* TELECOM SUAC *(message d'acceptation de service supplémentaire)*

fabric *n* GEOL texture *f*, PAPER TECH toile synthétique *f*, PETR fabrique *f*, structure *f*, SPACE *spacecraft* tissu *m*, étoffe *f*, TEXTILES tissu *m*; ~ **care** *n* TEXTILES entretien de tissu *m*; ~ **construction** *n* TEXTILES contexture d'un tissu *f*; ~ **dust collector** *n* SAFETY dépoussiéreur à tissu *m*; ~ **element** *n* GEOL élément structural *m*; ~ **filter** *n* POLLUTION séparateur à tissu filtrant *m*; ~ **in rope form** *n* TEXTILES tissu en boyau *m*; ~ **sample** *n* TEXTILES échantillon *m*; ~ **softener** *n* DETERGENTS produit assouplissant *m*; ~ **weight** *n* TEXTILES poids du tissu *m*; ~ **width** *n* TEXTILES largeur du tissu *f*

fabricate *vt* MECH réaliser en tôlerie

fabricated: ~ **structure** *n* SPACE *spacecraft* structure manufacturée *f*

fabricating: ~ **shop** *n* MECH atelier de tôlerie *m*

fabrication: ~ **technique** *n* ELECTRON méthode de fabrication *f*; ~ **yield** *n* ELECTRON rendement de fabrication *m*

fabrication-related: ~ **fuel defect** *n* NUCLEAR *of fuel element* défaut de fabrication *m*

fabricator *n* CONST fabricant *m*, fabricateur *m*

Fabry-Pérot: ~ **interferometer** *n* PHYS, SPACE interféromètre de Fabry-Pérot *m*

façade *n* CONST *of building* façade *f*

face [1] *n* COAL TECH taille *f*, CONST *of slope* parement *m*, *of wall* pan *m*, parement *m*, *tunnel works* face de taille *f*, GEOM face *f*, MINING front *m*, front d'abattage *m*, front d'attaque *m*, front de taille *m*, PHYS *of cube* face *m*, PRINT caractère *m*, partie ouverte d'un cahier *f*, PROD ENG *of anvil* aire *f*, table *f*, *of hammer* aire *f*, face *f*, tête *f*; ~ **and support system** *n* MINING soutènement des extrémités de taille *m*; ~ **chuck** *n* MECH ENG *of lathe* plateau *m*; ~ **cleat** *n* COAL TECH limet parallèle à la direction *m*; ~ **cutter** *n* MECH ENG fraise axiale *f*, fraise de face *f*; ~ **dust** *n* PROD ENG *founding* poncif *m*; ~ **flange** *n* PROD ENG *of slide valve* barrette *f*, patin *m*; ~ **gap** *n* NUCLEAR fente frontale *f*; ~ **gear** *n* MECH ENG engrenage conique plat *m*; ~ **grinder** *n* MECH ENG machine à rectifier à meule à 90 *f*; ~ **grinding** *n* PROD ENG rectifiage frontal *m*; ~ **hole** *n* MINING trou de front *m*; ~ **lathe** *n* MECH ENG tour en l'air *m*, tour en l'air à plateau vertical *m*, tour à facer *m*; ~ **milling cutter** *n* MECH ENG fraise à dresser *f*, fraise à surfacer *f*; ~ **milling grinder** *n* MECH ENG fraise à surfacer *f*; ~ **roll** *n* PAPER TECH largeur de rouleau *f*; ~ **shield** *n* PROD ENG masque de soudure *m*, SAFETY écran de protection du visage *m*, *welding* masque *m*; ~ **spanner** *n* MECH ENG clef à griffes sur le côté *f*; ~ **stock** *n* PRINT support d'impression dont les surfaces ont été traitées *m*; ~ **string** *n* CONST *stairbuilding* limon *m*; ~ **visor** *n* SAFETY visière *f*; ~ **wall** *n* CONST mur de revêtement *m*; ~ **wheel** *n* PROD ENG *emery wheel* lapidaire *m*, meule lapidaire *f*, meule travaillant sur face *f*

face [2] *vt* PROD ENG *lathe work* dresser, dresser sur face, TEXTILES revêtir

face-centered: [1] ~ **cubic** *adj* (AmE) *see face-centred cubic*

face-centered: [2] ~ **lattice** *n* (AmE) *see face-centred lattice*

face-centred: [1] ~ **cubic** *adj* (BrE) *(FCC)* CHEM, CRYSTALL cubique à faces centrées *(CFC)*

face-centred: [2] ~ **lattice** *n* (BrE) METALL réseau à faces centrées *m*

faced: [1] ~ **with silk** *adj* TEXTILES à revers de soie

faced: [2] ~ **flange** *n* PROD ENG bride dressée sur face *f*

face-down: ~ **TAB** *n* ELEC ENG connexion inversée sur bande *f*

faceplate *n* ELECTRON *of cathode tube* dalle *f*, MECH ENG *of lathe* plateau *m*, NAUT *shipbuilding* tôle bandeau *f*, TV fenêtre *f*, fond *m*; ~ **chuck** *n* MECH ENG *of lathe* plateau *m*; ~ **coupling** *n* MECH ENG accouplement à plateaux *m*, manchon à plateaux *m*; ~ **dog** *n* MECH ENG *of lathe* poupée à griffes *f*; ~ **jaw** *n* MECH ENG *of lathe* poupée à griffes *f*; ~ **mounting** *n* MECH ENG *of lathe* montage en l'air *m*; ~ **starter** *n* ELEC *of motor* démarreur à plots *m*

faceted [1] *adj* (AmE) *see facetted*

faceted: [2] ~ **bubble** *n* (AmE) *see facetted bubble* ~ **growth** *n* (AmE) *see facetted growth* ~ **ring** *n* (AmE) *see facetted ring*

facetted [1] *adj* (BrE) C&G taille côtes plates

facetted: [2] ~ **bubble** *n* (BrE) NUCLEAR *in fuel pellet* bulle facettée *f*; ~ **growth** *n* (BrE) METALL croissance à facettes *f*; ~ **ring** *n* (BrE) NUCLEAR *of pressure vessel* ceinture facettée *f*

face-up: ~ **TAB** *n* ELEC ENG connexion normale sur bande *f*

facies *n* GEOL *metamorphic and sedimentary*, PETR faciès *m*

facilities *n pl* AERONAUT installations et services *f pl*, TV installations *f pl*, moyens techniques *m pl*

facility *n* PROD ENG unité de production *f*, îlot de fabrication *m*, TELECOM service complémentaire *m*; ~ **accepted message** *n (FAA)* TELECOM message d'acceptation de service supplémentaire *m (SUAC)*; ~ **availability** *n* AERONAUT disponibilité de l'installation *f*; ~ **failure** *n* AERONAUT défaillance d'une installation *f*; ~ **indicator** *n* TELECOM indicateur de service supplémentaire *m*; ~ **rejected message** *n (FRJ)* TELECOM message de refus de service supplémentaire *m (SURF)*; ~ **reliability** *n* AERONAUT fiabilité de l'installation *f*; ~ **request message** *n (FAR)* TELECOM message de demande de service supplémentaire *m (SUDM)*

facing [1] *adj* GEOL dirigé vers

facing [2] *n* CONST parement *m*, revêtement *m*, *of dam* masque *m*, MECH ENG *machine tools* surfaçage *m*, TEXTILES revers *m*; ~ **attachment** *n* MECH ENG *machine tools* dispositif de surfaçage *m*; ~ **block** *n* C&G parement extérieur *m*; ~ **brick** *n* CONST brique de parement *f*; ~ **direction** *n* GEOL direction de vergence *f*, vergence *f*; **~ fabric** *n* TEXTILES tissu apparent *m*; **~ head** *n* MECH ENG *machine tools* plateau porte-chariot à surfacer *m*; **~ matter** *n* PRINT face texte *f*; **~ tool** *n* MECH ENG outil à dresser les faces *m*, *lathe* outil à dresser *m*; **~ tool for roughing** *n* MECH ENG dégrossissage *m*, outil à dresser les faces *m*

FACR *abbr (first article configuration review)* SPACE revue de conformité du premier article *f*

facsimile *n* COMP, DP, PRINT fac-similé *m*, TELECOM *copy* fac-similé *m*, télécopie *f*; **~ compression** *n* TELECOM compression de télécopie *f*; **~ interworking function** *n (FAXFIF)* TELECOM fonction d'interfonctionnement télécopie *f*; **~ machine** *n* COMP, DP, TELECOM télécopieur *m*; **~ message** *n* TELECOM message par télécopieur *m*; **~ telegraphy** *n* TELECOM phototélégraphie *f*, télégraphie fac-similée *f*

factor *n* COMP, DP facteur *m*, PROD ENG coefficient *m*; **~ analysis** *n* MATH analyse factorielle *f*

factorial[1] *adj* MATH factoriel

factorial[2] *n* COMP, MATH *symbol* factorielle *f*; **~ magnification** *n* INSTRUMENT grossissement de loupe *m*

factorization *n* MATH factorisation *f*

factorize *vt* MATH factoriser

factory:[1] **~ adjusted** *adj* MECH réglé en usine; **~ assembled** *adj* PROD ENG assemblé en usine

factory[2] *n* MECH, PROD ENG, SAFETY usine *f*; **~ acceptance** *n* MECH *contracts* recette en usine *f*; **~ assembled system** *n* REFRIG système frigorifique préassemblé *m*; **~ cullet** *n* C&G calcin d'usine *m*; **~ fumes** *n pl* SAFETY fumées d'usine *f pl*; **~ inspection** *n* CONTROL, MECH contrôle en usine *m*; **~ inspector** *n* SAFETY inspecteur du travail *m*; **~ ship** *n* NAUT navire usine *m*, OCEANOG baleinier *m*, bateau usine *m*, navire baleinier *m*, REFRIG navire usine *m*; **~ siding** *n* RAIL *track* voie d'usine *f*; **~ supplies** *n pl* PROD ENG matières consommables *f pl*

Factory: ~ Act *n* (BrE) SAFETY législation industrielle *f*

factotum: ~ initial *n* PRINT lettrine encastrée *f*

facula *n* ASTRON facule *f*

facultative: ~ aerobe *n* FOOD TECH aérobie facultatif *m*

fade[1] *n* ACOUSTICS, CINEMAT fondu *m*; **~ out** *n* CINEMAT fermeture en fondu *f*, fondu au noir *m*; **~ shutter** *n* CINEMAT obturateur pour fondu *m*

fade[2] *vt* CINEMAT fondre, RECORDING varier lentement un niveau; **~ down** *vt* RECORDING diminuer progressivement le niveau, réduire progressivement le volume; **~ in** *vt* RECORDING faire apparaître lentement, monter progressivement; **~ out** *vt* CINEMAT fermer dans un fondu, RECORDING faire disparaître lentement; **~ up** *vt* RECORDING augmenter progressivement

fade[3] *vi* TEXTILES *of fabric* se faner; **~ out** *vi* CINEMAT disparaître en fondu

faded *n* TEXTILES délavé *m*

fade-in *n* CINEMAT ouverture en fondu *f*

fade-proof *adj* PRINT résistant à la lumière

fader *n* ELECTRON atténuateur *m*, RECORDING potentiomètre linéaire *m*, équilibreur *m*

fade-resistant *adj* PRINT résistant à la lumière

fade-to-black *n* CINEMAT fondu au noir *m*

fade-to-white *n* CINEMAT fondu au blanc *m*

fading *n* CINEMAT affaiblissement *m*, ELECTRON affaiblissement *m*, fading *m*, évanescence *f*, évanouissement *m*, PHYS évanouissement *m*, PRINT affaiblissement *m*, SPACE, TELECOM évanouissement *m*; **~ comet** *n* ASTRON faible *f*; **~ regulator** *n* CONTROL régulateur variable d'affaiblissement *m*

faecal[1] *adj* (BrE) HYDROL *sewage*, RECYCLING fécal

faecal:[2] **~ matter** *n* (BrE) HYDROL, RECYCLING matières fécales *f pl*

faeces *n* (BrE) HYDROL *sewage* fèces *f pl*, RECYCLING excreta *m pl*, fèces *f pl*, matières fécales *f pl*

fahl: ~ ore *n* MINERAL fahlerz *m*

fahlerz *n* MINERAL fahlerz *m*

fahlunite *n* MINERAL fahlunite *f*

Fahrenheit: ~ scale *n* PHYS échelle Fahrenheit *f*

fail[1] *vt* CONST défaillir, défaire

fail[2] *vi* MECH casser, tomber en panne, PROD ENG manquer, *injector* se désamorcer

failed: ~ circuit *n* NUCLEAR circuit défectueux *m*; **~ element detection system** *n* NUCLEAR *especially of PWR* système de détection de rupture de gaine *m*; **~ fuel element monitor** *n* NUCLEAR détection de rupture de gaine à collection électrostatique *f*; **~ loop** *n* NUCLEAR circuit défectueux *m*

fail-safe[1] *adj* ELEC à sûreté intégrée, ELEC ENG à sécurité intrinsèque, MECH à sécurité intégrée, SPACE à sécurité intrinsèque, TRANSP à sûreté intégrée

fail-safe:[2] **~ design** *n* NUCLEAR conception sûre en cas de défaillance *f*; **~ device** *n* (BrE) *(cf fail-to-safety device)* SAFETY mécanisme à sûreté intégrée *m*; **~ operation** *n* COMP fonctionnement à sécurité intégrée *m*, DP fonctionnement autoprotégé *m*, fonctionnement à sécurité intégrée *m*; **~ system** *n* CONTROL sécurité intrinsèque *f*, sûreté intégrée *f*; **~ work methods** *n pl* PROD ENG systèmes antierreurs *m pl*

fail-soft *adj* COMP, DP à dégradation contrôlée, SPACE à dégradation restreinte

fail-to-safety: ~ device *n* (AmE) *(cf fail-safe device)* SAFETY mécanisme à sûreté intégrée *m*

failure *n* COMP défaillance *f*, panne *f*, CONST *of bridge* cassure *f*, *of equipment* défaillance *f*, CONTROL interruption *f*, interruption de marche *f*, interruption de service *f*, CRYSTALL *by breaking* rupture *f*, DP défaillance *f*, panne *f*, ELEC *of equipment* défaillance *f*, ELEC ENG *of equipment* défaillance *f*, panne *f*, *of test* échec *m*, GAS TECH *of equipment* défaillance *f*, MECH défaillance *f*, défaut *m*, panne *f*, MECH ENG non-fonctionnement *m*, panne *f*, rupture *f*, METALL faille *f*, ruine *f*, PROD ENG *of injector* désamorçage *m*, PROP MAT faille radiale *f*, rupture *f*, QUALITY défaillance *f*, défaut *m*, panne *f*, SPACE *of equipment* défaillance *f*, panne *f*, TELECOM *of equipment* défaillance *f*; **~ data card** *n* AERONAUT carte d'incident *f*; **~ indicator** *n* CINEMAT avertisseur de panne *m*; **~ load** *n* COAL TECH charge de rupture *f*; **~ logging** *n* COMP, DP consignation des pannes *f*; **~ mechanism** *n* QUALITY mécanisme de défaillance *m*; **~ moment** *n* MECH moment de rupture *m*; **~ rate** *n* COMP, DP, ELEC ENG taux de défaillance *m*, MECH ENG taux de panne *m*, QUALITY taux de défaillance *m*, TELECOM taux de défaillance *m*, taux de panne *m*; **~ recovery** *n* COMP, DP reprise après incident *f*

faired *adj* AERONAUT caréné

fairing *n* AERONAUT capot de carénage *m*, carénage *m*, capotage *m*, profilage *m*, REFRIG *of air conditioning fan* carénage *m*, SPACE carénage *m*, coiffe *f*

fairlead *n* AERONAUT guide-câble *m*, NAUT *deck equipment* chaumard *m*

fairway *n* FUELLESS chenal *m*, NAUT *navigation* chenal *m*, passage *m*, passe *f*, OCEANOG chenal de navigation *m*; **~ navigation** *n* NAUT chenalage *m*

faithful *adj* RECORDING *reproduction* fidèle

fake *n* PROD ENG *cast-iron cement* mastic de fonte *m*

fakes *n pl* COAL TECH havrits *m pl*

fall[1] *n* HYDR EQUIP *difference of level* chute *f*, HYDROL *river level* baisse *f*, décrue *f*, OCEANOG baisse *f*, PHYS *in temperature* baisse *f*, chute *f*, PROD ENG *of drilling spindle, tool holder* course verticale *f*, descente *f*, WATER SUPP *between two water levels* chute *f*, hauteur de chute *f*; ~ **cleanup** *n* MINING déblaiement *m*, relèvement *m*; ~ **of earth** *n* CONST éboulement *m*, éboulement de terre *m*, éboulis *m*; ~ **of ground** *n* CONST éboulement *m*, éboulement de terre *m*, éboulis *m*; ~ **in hydraulic head** *n* HYDROL chute de pression hydraulique *f*; ~ **of rock** *n* CONST éboulement de rocher *m*, éboulis de roches *m*; ~ **of the tide** *n* NAUT baisse de l'eau *f*; ~ **time** *n* ELECTRON temps de descente *m*, PHYS *pulse* temps de descente *m*, temps de décroissance *m*, temps de suppression *m*

fall:[2] ~ **within the scope of** *vt* PATENTS tomber dans le domaine de

fall:[3] ~ **in** *vi* CONST s'ébouler; ~ **off** *vi* NAUT *sailing* abattre sous le vent; ~ **out of order** *vi* PROD ENG se déranger, se fausser; ~ **overboard** *vi* NAUT tomber à la mer

fallback *n* COMP reprise *f*, DP reprise *f*, reprise après incident *f*, NUCLEAR *in cratering explosion* éjecta *m pl*

falling: ~ **edge** *n* ELECTRON flanc arrière *m*; ~ **film** *n* DETERGENTS film ruisselant *m*, film tombant *m*; ~ **gradient** *n* CONST pente *f*; ~ **sluice** *n* HYDROL vanne plongeante *f*; ~ **sphere viscometer** *n* LAB EQUIP viscomètre à chute de bille *m*; ~ **tide** *n* FUELLESS, NAUT marée descendante *f*, OCEANOG descendante *f*, marée descendante *f*, reflux *m*; ~ **water table** *n* (*cf receding water table*) HYDROL baisse de la nappe phréatique *f*

fall-off *n* ELECTRON pente *f*

fallout *n* PHYS retombée *f*, POLLUTION retombée *f*, retombées *f pl*, RAD PHYS retombée *f*; ~ **shelter** *n* NUCLEAR abri antiretombées *m*

fall-safe: ~ **light metal ladder** *n* SAFETY échelle en métal léger garantie contre les chutes *f*

false[1] *adj* COMP, DP faux

false:[2] ~ **alarm** *n* TELECOM fausse alarme *f*; ~ **alarm probability** *n* TELECOM probabilité de fausse alarme *f*; ~ **back** *n* PRINT dos à ressort *m*; ~ **body** *n* C&G couleur trop épaisse *f*, PRINT thixotropie *f*; ~ **bottom** *n* PROD ENG double fond *m*, faux fond *m*; ~ **call** *n* TELECOM appel erroné *m*; ~ **calling rate** *n* TELECOM taux d'appels intempestifs *m*; ~ **ceiling** *n* REFRIG faux plafond *m*; ~ **cleavage** *n* GEOL pseudoclivage *m*; ~ **closure** *n* ELEC ENG fermeture intempestive *f*; ~ **color** *n* (AmE), ~ **colour** *n* (BrE) DP fausse couleur *f*; ~ **core** *n* PROD ENG *founding* pièce battue *f*, pièce de rapport *f*, pièce rapportée *f*, tiroir *m*; ~ **core molding** *n* (AmE), ~ **core moulding** *n* (BrE) PROD ENG moulage en pièces battues *m*; ~ **echo** *n* OCEANOG faux écho *m*; ~ **floor** *n* REFRIG faux plancher *m*; ~ **frame** *n* AERONAUT faux couple *m*; ~ **plain** *n* TEXTILES faux uni *m*; ~ **rib** *n* AERONAUT fausse nervure *f*; ~ **signal** *n* ELECTRON faux signal *m*, signal de diversion *m*; ~ **spar** *n* AERONAUT faux longeron *m*; ~ **switching** *n* ELEC enclenchement intempestif *m*; ~ **topaz** *n* MINERAL citrine *f*; ~ **tripping** *n* ELEC *relay* déclenchement intempestif *m*; ~ **warning** *n* AERONAUT fausse alarme *f*

falsework *n* CONST *of vault* décintrage *m*, décintrement *m*

famatinite *n* MINERAL famatinite *f*

Famennian *adj* GEOL famennien

family: ~ **of elements** *n* RAD PHYS *radioactive series* famille des éléments *f*; ~ **package** *n* PACKAGING emballage familial *m*; ~ **of particles** *n* PART PHYS famille de particules *f*

fan[1] *n* AUTO, CONST, ELEC *of appliance* ventilateur *m*, ELEC ENG *of cable* peigne *m*, MECH, MECH ENG *for moving air, gas with small increase of pressure*, MINING, PAPER TECH, PHYS, PROD ENG *of machine*, REFRIG ventilateur *m*, TRANSP soufflante *f*, ventilateur *m*, *of jet engine* soufflante *f*, VEHICLES soufflante *f*, ventilateur *m*; ~ **beam** *n* ELECTRON faisceau en éventail *m*; ~ **belt** *n* AUTO courroie de ventilateur *f*, courroie de ventilation *f*, MECH, VEHICLES courroie de ventilateur *f*; ~ **blade** *n* AUTO, MECH pale de ventilateur *f*, REFRIG pale d'hélice *f*, VEHICLES *cooling* pale de ventilateur *f*; ~ **blower** *n* MECH ENG ventilateur *m*; ~ **brake** *n* MECH ENG frein à palettes *m*; ~ **coil unit** *n* REFRIG batterie ventilée *f*; ~ **cooling** *n* THERMOD refroidissement par air forcé *m*, refroidissement par ventilateur *m*; ~ **cut** *n* MINING bouchon en éventail *m*; ~ **drift** *n* MINING galerie de ventilateur *f*; ~ **engine** *n* TRANSP réacteur à double flux *m*; ~ **guard** *n* REFRIG grille de protection *f*; ~ **heater** *n* HEATING radiateur soufflant *m*, MECH ENG ventilateur de chauffage *m*, THERMOD radiateur soufflant *m*; ~ **in** *n* COMP, DP, ELEC ENG entrance *f*; ~ **jet** *n* TRANSP réacteur à double flux *m*; ~ **jet engine** *n* THERMOD *bypass, turbofan engine* turboréacteur à double flux *m*; ~ **jet turbine** *n* TRANSP turbine haute pression *f*; ~ **marker beacon** *n* AERONAUT radiobalise en éventail *f*, radioborne en éventail *f*, NAUT radioborne en éventail *f*; ~ **motor** *n* REFRIG moteur de ventilateur *m*; ~ **performance** *n* HEAT ENG puissance de ventilateur *f*; ~ **performance curve** *n* HEAT ENG courbe de puissance de ventilateur *f*; ~ **pulley** *n* AUTO, VEHICLES poulie de ventilateur *f*; ~ **pump** *n* PAPER TECH pompe de mélange *f*; ~ **shroud** *n* AUTO tuyère de ventilateur *f*; ~ **station** *n* CONST *tunnelling* poste de ventilation *m*; ~ **wheel** *n* MECH ENG, SAFETY tourniquet de ventilateur *m*

fan:[2] ~ **cool** *vt* THERMOD refroidir par ventilateur

fan-assisted: ~ **air heater** *n* HEAT ENG générateur pulseur d'air chaud *m*, SAFETY générateur d'air chaud pulsé *m*

fancy: ~ **frame** *n* PRINT cadre de fantaisie *m*; ~ **type** *n* PRINT caractères de fantaisie *m pl*; ~ **woven fabric** *n* TEXTILES tissu fantaisie *m*; ~ **yarn** *n* TEXTILES fil fantaisie *m*

fanfold *n* PRINT pli accordéon *m*, pli paravent *m*, pli zigzag *m*, PROD ENG pliage accordéon *m*; ~ **paper** *n* (BrE) (*cf fanfold stationery*) COMP papier accordéon *m*, papier à pliage accordéon *m*, papier à pliage paravent *m*; ~ **stationery** *n* (BrE) (*cf fanfold paper*) COMP papier accordéon *m*, papier à pliage accordéon *m*, papier à pliage paravent *m*

fang *n* MECH ENG soie *f*; ~ **bolt** *n* CONST boulon de scellement ordinaire *m*

fangs *n pl* MINING clichages *m pl*, taquets *m pl*

fan-in: ~ **factor** *n* ELEC ENG facteur d'entrance *m*

fanned: ~ **cable** *n* ELEC ENG câble à peigne *m*; ~ **circulation** *n* HEATING circulation forcée *f*

fanning: ~ **out** *n* PROD ENG éclatement en éventail *m*

fan-out *n* COMP, DP, ELEC ENG sortance *f*, PRINT phénomène d'élargissement du papier *m*

fan-powered: ~ **burner** *n* MECH ENG brûleur à ventilateur *m*

fantail *n* CONST *carpentry* queue-d'aronde *f*, queue-d'hironde *f*, NAUT *boatbuilding* voûte *f*; ~ **joint** *n* CONST assemblage en queue d'hironde *m*, assemblage à queue *m*, assemblage à queue d'aronde *m*

far: ~ **infrared** *n* PHYS rayonnement infrarouge lointain *m*, RAD PHYS infrarouge lointain *m*; ~ **range** *n* SPACE portée distale *f*; ~ **space** *n* SPACE espace lointain *m*; ~ **ultraviolet** *n* PHYS rayonnement ultraviolet lointain *m*, RAD PHYS ultraviolet lointain *m*

FAR *abbr (facility request message)* TELECOM SUDM *(message de demande de service supplémentaire)*

farad *n* ELEC *unit*, ELEC ENG *unit*, METR, PHYS farad *m*

faraday *n* PHYS faraday *m*

Faraday: ~ **cage** *n* ELEC, ELEC ENG, NUCLEAR, PHYS cage de Faraday *f*; ~ **circulator** *n* ELEC ENG circulateur à effet Faraday *m*; ~ **constant** *n* PHYS constante de Faraday *f*; ~ **cylinder** *n* ELEC, PHYS cylindre de Faraday *m*; ~ **dark space** *n* ELECTRON zone obscure de Faraday *f*, PHYS espace sombre de Faraday *m*; ~ **effect** *n* ELEC ENG, PHYS effet Faraday *m*; ~ **rotation** *n* SPACE effet Faraday *m*, rotation de Faraday *f*; ~ **screen** *n* ELEC ENG écran de Faraday *m*

Faraday's: ~ **disc** *n* (BrE) PHYS disque de Faraday *m*; ~ **disk** *n* (AmE) *see Faraday's disc*; ~ **laws** *n pl* ELEC, PHYS lois de Faraday *f pl*

far-end: ~ **block error** *n (FEBE)* TELECOM erreur de bloc à l'extrémité distante *f*; ~ **receive failure** *n (FERF)* TELECOM défaut en réception à l'extrémité distante *m*, dérangement de réception à l'extrémité *m*

far-field: ~ **analysis** *n* TELECOM analyse du champ lointain *f*; ~ **diffraction pattern** *n* OPT diagramme de diffraction de Fraunhofer *m*, diagramme de diffraction en champ lointain *m*, diagramme de rayonnement en champ lointain *m*, répartition de lumière *f*; ~ **intensity** *n* SPACE *communications* intensité en champ éloigné *f*; ~ **pattern** *n* TELECOM *radiation* diagramme de rayonnement en champ lointain *m*; ~ **radiation pattern** *n* OPT diagramme de rayonnement en champ lointain *m*, répartition de lumière *f*; ~ **region** *n* OPT, TELECOM région de champ lointain *f*

farinaceous *adj* FOOD TECH farinacé, farineux

farinograph *n* FOOD TECH farinographe *m*

Farmer's: ~ **reducer** *n* PHOTO affaiblisseur de Farmer *m*

farming: ~ **out** *n* PETR TECH *commerce, licensing* amodiation *f*

farnesol *n* CHEM farnésol *m*

faröelite *n* MINERAL féroélite *f*

FAS *abbr* TELECOM *(flexible access switch)* commutateur à accès flexible *m*, TELECOM *(frame alignment signal)* signal de verrouillage de trame *m*

fascia *n* CONST chanlate *f*, volige chanlattée *f*; ~ **board** *n* CONST chanlate *f*, volige chanlattée *f*

fashioning: ~ **mechanism** *n* TEXTILES mécanisme d'armure *m*

fassaite *n* MINERAL fassaïte *f*

fast[1] *adj* CHEM *colour* résistant, TEXTILES solide

fast:[2] ~ **and loose pulleys** *n pl* PROD ENG poulies folles et fixes *f pl*; ~ **beam experiment** *n* RAD PHYS expérience à faisceau surgénéré *f*; ~ **breathing** *n* OCEANOG polypnée *f*; ~ **burst** *n* NUCLEAR *of fuel clad* rupture brutale de gaine *f*; ~ **circuit switch** *n* TELECOM commutateur de circuits rapides *m*; ~ **color** *n* (AmE), ~ **colour** *n* (BrE) PRINT couleur résistant à la lumière *f*; ~ **developer** *n* PHOTO révélateur rapide *m*; ~ **feed** *n* MECH ENG *machine tool* avance rapide *f*; ~ **forward** *n* RECORDING, TV avance rapide *f*; ~ **Fourier transform** *n (FFT)* COMP transformation de Fourier rapide *f*, ELECTRON transformation de Fourier rapide *f*, transformée de Fourier rapide *f*; ~ **frequency hopping** *n* ELECTRON sauts de fréquence rapides *m pl*; ~ **frequency-shift**

keying *n* TELECOM manipulation par déplacement de fréquence rapide *f*; ~ **head** *n* PROD ENG *of lathe* poupée fixe *f*; ~ **headstock** *n* PROD ENG poupée fixe *f*; ~ **insertion** *n* NUCLEAR *of control rod* rejet *m*; ~ **logic** *n* ELECTRON logique rapide *f*; ~ **motion** *n* TV mouvement rapide *m*; ~ **neutron** *n* NUCLEAR, PHYS neutron rapide *m*; ~ **packet switch** *n (FPS)* TELECOM commutateur de paquets rapide *m*; ~ **particle** *n* NUCLEAR particule rapide *f*; ~ **playback** *n* TV lecture accélérée *f*; ~ **pull-down** *n* TV escamotage rapide *m*; ~ **pulley** *n* PROD ENG poulie fixe *f*; ~ **reactor** *n* NUCLEAR réacteur à neutrons rapides *m*; ~ **reverse-recovery rectifier** *n* ELEC ENG redresseur à court temps de transition inverse *m*; ~ **rewind** *n* RECORDING retour rapide *m*; ~ **rise pulse** *n* ELECTRON impulsion à court temps de montée *f*; ~ **rise signal** *n* ELECTRON signal à court temps de montée *m*; ~ **slaving** *n* AERONAUT recalage rapide *m*; ~ **slaving relay** *n* AERONAUT relais de recalage rapide *m*; ~ **stock** *n* CINEMAT pellicule sensible *f*; ~ **sweep** *n* ELECTRON balayage rapide *m*; ~ **train** *n* (AmE) *(cf express train)* RAIL *vehicles* train express *m*, TRANSP train de grande ligne *m*, train express *m*; ~ **update** *n* TELECOM mise à jour rapide *f*; ~ **update request** *n* TELECOM demande de rafraîchissement rapide *f*; ~ **wave** *n* ELEC ENG onde normale *f*; ~ **wave tube** *n* ELECTRON tube à onde normale *m*; ~ **wheel** *n* PROD ENG *fixed on axle* roue calée *f*, roue fixe *f*

fast:[3] ~ **forward** *vt* TV avancer rapidement

fast:[4] ~ **fusion-fission assembly at zero thermal power** *phr* NUCLEAR assemblage hybride rapide de puissance nulle *m*

fast-acting[1] *adj* ELEC ENG *fuse* instantané, *relay* rapide

fast-acting:[2] ~ **trip** *n* MECH ENG déclencheur à action instantanée *m*; ~ **trip valve** *n* NUCLEAR soupape d'arrêt d'urgence à action rapide *f*

fast-breeder: ~ **reactor** *n* PHYS surrégénérateur rapide *m*; ~ **reactor technology** *n* NUCLEAR technologie des surgénérateurs *f*

fast-changing *adj* ELECTRON *signal* à variation rapide

fast-curing *adj* P&R *plastics, rubber* cuit-vite

fasten *vt* MECH attacher, fixer, TEXTILES attacher; ~ **with sleeper screws** *vt* (BrE) *(cf fasten with tie screws)* RAIL tirefonner; ~ **with tie screws** *vt* (AmE) *(cf fasten with sleeper screws)* RAIL tirefonner

fastener *n* MECH attache *f*, élément de fixation *m*, MECH ENG élément de fixation *m*, PROD ENG agrafe *f*, fermoir *m*, SPACE attache *f*, élément de fixation *m*

fastening *n* CONST *strap, stirrup* armature *f*, armature de charpente *f*, lien *m*, étrier *m*, MECH fixation *f*, MECH ENG épinglage *m*, épinglage avant rivetage *m*, PROD ENG attache *f*, fermeture *f*, lien *m*

fastenings *n* TEXTILES attaches *f pl*

fast-fission: ~ **factor** *n* PHYS facteur de fission rapide *m*

fastness *n* TEXTILES solidité *f*; ~ **to light** *n* TEXTILES solidité à la lumière *f*; ~ **to perspiration** *n* TEXTILES résistance à la transpiration *f*; ~ **to rubbing** *n* TEXTILES résistance à l'abrasion *f*; ~ **to washing** *n* TEXTILES résistance au lavage *f*

fast-recovery: ~ **diode** *n* ELECTRON diode à court temps de transition *f*

fast-reservation: ~ **protocol** *n (FRP)* TELECOM protocole de réservation rapide *m*

fast-switching: ~ **power rectifier** *n* ELEC ENG redresseur pour commutation rapide *m*; ~ **power transistor** *n* ELECTRON transistor de puissance à commutation rapide *m*

fast-to-light *adj* PRINT solide à la lumière
fast-tuned: ~ **filter** *n* ELECTRON filtre à accord rapide *m*; ~ **oscillator** *n* ELECTRON oscillateur à accord instantané *m*
fat *n* FOOD TECH graisse *f*, lipide *m*, matière grasse *f*, PAPER TECH graisse *f*; ~ **clay** *n* PETR TECH *geology* argile grasse *f*; ~ **coal** *n* COAL TECH charbon gras *m*, houille grasse *f*; ~ **concrete** *n* CONST béton gras *m*, béton riche en ciment *m*; ~ **edge** *n* P&R *paint defect* larme *f*; ~ **lime** *n* PAPER TECH chaux grasse *f*; ~ **mortar** *n* CONST béton gras *m*, béton riche en ciment *m*
fatal: ~ **accident** *n* SAFETY accident mortel *m*; ~ **error** *n* COMP erreur irrécupérable *f*, DP erreur fatale *f*
fate: ~ **of oil** *n* MAR POLL évolution des hydrocarbures *f*
father: ~ **file** *n* COMP, DP fichier générateur *m*
fathom *n* METR fathom *m*, NAUT, OCEANOG brasse *f*
fatigue *n* CRYSTALL, MECH *materials*, P&R fatigue *f*, PROP MAT fatigue de matériel *f*; ~ **crack** *n* METALL, SPACE *spacecraft* fissure de fatigue *f*; ~ **failure** *n* METALL faille par fatigue *f*; ~ **fracture** *n* CRYSTALL cassure de fatigue *f*, rupture par fatigue *f*; ~ **hardening** *n* METALL durcissement par fatigue *m*; ~ **inspection** *n* AERONAUT contrôle de fatigue *m*; ~ **precrack** *n* NUCLEAR amorce de fissure de fatigue *f*, crique initiale *f*; ~ **properties** *n pl* MECH *materials* caractéristiques de fatigue *f pl*; ~ **resistance** *n* SPRINGS tenue à la fatigue *f*; ~ **softening** *n* METALL adoucissement par fatigue *m*; ~ **strength** *n* AERONAUT endurance *f*, résistance à la fatigue *f*, MECH *materials* résistance à la fatigue *f*, METALL charge de rupture en fatigue *f*, SPACE *spacecraft* résistance à la fatigue *f*; ~ **test** *n* AERONAUT, METALL essai de fatigue *m*; ~ **testing machine** *n* SPRINGS machine d'essai de fatigue *f*
fattening: ~ **ground** *n* OCEANOG aire de nutrition *f*
fatty: ~ **acid** *n* CHEM *organic acid*, DETERGENTS acide gras *m*, FOOD TECH acide oléique *m*, PAPER TECH acide gras *m*; ~ **acid glyceride** *n* FOOD TECH acétoglycéride *f*; ~ **alcohol** *n* CHEM *long chain alcohol*, DETERGENTS alcool gras *m*; ~ **amine** *n* DETERGENTS amine grasse *f*; ~ **clay** *n* C&G argile grasse *f*
faucet *n* (AmE) (*cf tap*) CONST *cock* robinet *m*, LAB EQUIP *services* robinet d'eau *m*, MECH robinet *m*; ~ **joint** *n* CONST *in pipes* assemblage à emboîtement *m*, joint à emboîtement *m*; ~ **key** *n* CONST clef de robinet *f*
faujasite *n* MINERAL faujasite *f*
fault *n* COAL TECH faille *f*, COMP, DP défaillance *f*, défaut *m*, ELEC, ELEC ENG défaut *m*, GEOL faille *f*, MECH défaut *m*, MINING, PETR TECH *geology* faille *f*, PROD ENG *flaw in metal* cran *m*, défaut *m*, faille *f*, PRODUCTION paille *f*, TELECOM, TEXTILES défaut *m*; ~ **basin** *n* GEOL, PETR TECH *geology* bassin d'effondrement *m*; ~ **bundle** *n* GEOL faisceau de failles *m*; ~ **clearance** *n* TELECOM relève de dérangement *f*; ~ **code chart** *n* PROD ENG tableau de codes de défauts *m*; ~ **conglomerate** *n* MINING conglomérat de faille *m*; ~ **detection** *n* COMP, DP, GAS TECH détection d'anomalie *f*, TELECOM détection de défauts *f*; ~ **detector** *n* ELEC détecteur de défaut *m*, *cable* localisateur de défaut *m*; ~ **diagnosis** *n* COMP, DP diagnostic de panne *m*; ~ **display** *n* TELECOM visualisation de défaut *f*; ~ **drag** *n* GEOL rebroussement des lèvres d'une faille *m*; ~ **gouge** *n* GEOL mylonite pulvérente *f*; ~ **identification code chart** *n* PROD ENG tableau de codes d'identification de défaut *m*; ~ **indicator** *n* PROD ENG témoin de défaut *m*; ~ **light** *n* PROD ENG voyant de défaut *m*; ~ **maintenance** *n* TELECOM maintenance corrective *f*; ~ **plane** *n* GEOL plan de faille *m*; ~

reception center *n* (AmE), ~ **reception centre** *n* (BrE) (*FRC*) TELECOM service de dépannage *m*; ~ **recovery** *n* PROD ENG élimination d'erreur *f*; ~ **reporting** *n* PROD ENG signalisation d'erreur *f*; ~ **resistance** *n* ELEC ENG résistance de défaut *f*; ~ **spring** *n* WATER SUPP source de faille *f*; ~ **time** *n* COMP temps d'arrêt *m*, DP temps d'arrêt *m*, temps de défaillance *m*; ~ **tolerance** *n* ELEC ENG tolérance à défaut *f*; ~ **trace** *n* GEOL ligne de faille *f*; ~ **trap** *n* PETR TECH *hydrocarbon formation* piège par faille *m*; ~ **tree** *n* CONTROL arbre de défaillance *m*, arbre de défaut *m*; ~ **voltage circuit breaker** *n* ELEC déclencheur par tension de défaut *m*
fault-finding *n* ELEC ENG dépannage *m*; ~ **table** *n* MECH ENG tableau de dépannage *m*
fault-free *adj* TELECOM sans défaillance
faultless *adj* TEXTILES irréprochable
fault-tolerant[1] *adj* COMP insensible aux fautes, à tolérance de pannes, DP tolérant aux fautes, à tolérance de fautes, ELEC ENG tolérant aux défauts
fault-tolerant:[2] ~ **system** *n* COMP système insensible aux défaillances *m*, DP système à tolérance de pannes *m*
faulty[1] *adj* ELEC, MECH, TEXTILES défectueux
faulty:[2] ~ **call** *n* TELECOM communication défectueuse *f*; ~ **connection** *n* SAFETY connexion défectueuse *f*, TELECOM *call* communication défectueuse *f*; ~ **insulation** *n* ELEC isolation défectueuse *f*; ~ **line** *n* ELEC ENG ligne défectueuse *f*; ~ **operation** *n* MECH ENG fonctionnement défectueux *m*, mauvais fonctionnement *m*; ~ **sheet ejection signal** *n* PACKAGING signal d'éjection de feuille défectueuse *m*
faunal: ~ **province** *n* GEOL province faunistique *f*
faunistic: ~ **province** *n* GEOL province faunistique *f*
fauserite *n* MINERAL fausérite *f*
fax[1] *n* (*facsimile, fax machine*) COMP, DP, TELECOM télécopieur *m*; ~ **machine** *n* (*fax*) COMP, DP, TELECOM télécopieur *m*
fax[2] *vt* TELECOM envoyer par télécopieur
FAXFIF *abbr* (*facsimile interworking function*) TELECOM fonction d'interfonctionnement télécopie *f*
fayalite *n* C&G, MINERAL fayalite *f*
FCC[1] *abbr* (*face-centered cubic, face-centred cubic*) CHEM, CRYSTALL CFC (*cubique à faces centrées*)
FCC:[2] ~ **lattice** *n* CHEM, CRYSTALL réseau CFC *m*
FCC-based: ~ **structure** *n* CRYSTALL structure de type CFC *f*
FDAU *abbr* (*flight data acquisition unit*) AERONAUT boîtier d'acquisition de données de vol *m*
FDDI *abbr* (*fiber-distributed data interface, fibre-distributed data interface*) TELECOM interface de données avec distribution par fibre *f*
FDHM *abbr* (*full-duration half-maximum*) OPT *pulse*, TELECOM durée à mi-crête *f*
FDM *abbr* (*frequency-division multiplexing*) COMP MPF (*multiplexage par partage des fréquences*), MRF (*multiplexage par répartition en fréquence*), ELECTRON MRF (*multiplexage par répartition en fréquence*), PHYS MA (*multiplexage analogique*), MPF (*multiplexage par partage des fréquences*), MRF (*multiplexage par répartition en fréquence*), TELECOM MRF (*multiplexage par répartition en fréquence*)
FDMA *abbr* (*frequency-division multiple access*) SPACE, TELECOM AMRF (*accès multiple à répartition en fréquence*)
FDR *abbr* (*final design review*) SPACE RDF (*revue de définition finale*)

FDS: ~ **system** n *(frequency-division switching system)* TELECOM système de commutation en modulation de fréquence m

FDX *abbr (full-duplex)* COMP duplex intégral

Fe *(iron)* CHEM Fe *(fer)*

FE *abbr* TELECOM *(format effector)* caractère de mise en page f, TELECOM *(functional entity)* entité fonctionnelle f

FEA *abbr (functional entity action)* TELECOM action d'entité fonctionnelle f

feasibility n MINING exploitabilité f; ~ **study** n COMP, CONST, DP analyse préalable f, étude de faisabilité f

feather[1] n C&G crachat m, CONST fausse languette f, languette f, languette rapportée f, languette venue de bois f, MECH ENG *shaft key* clavette linguiforme f, languette f; ~ **edge** n CONST bord en biseau m, chape f, bord à angle vif m, feuillure f; ~ **joint** n CONST assemblage à rainure et languette m; ~ **key** n NUCLEAR clavette parallèle f; ~ **ore** n MINERAL jamesonite f; ~ **tongue** n CONST fausse languette f, languette f, languette rapportée f

feather[2] vi PRINT *page* s'élargir entre la première couche

feathered[1] *adj* AERONAUT *propeller* en drapeau

feathered:[2] ~ **pitch** n AERONAUT *of propeller* pas d'hélice en drapeau m

feather-edge: ~ **file** n PROD ENG lime à dossière f, lime à fendre f, lime à losange f

feather-edged: ~ **brick** n CONST brique à couteau f

feathering n AERONAUT *of propeller* mise en drapeau f; ~ **angle** n AERONAUT angle d'attaque de pale m, angle d'incidence de pale m; ~ **effect** n AERONAUT effet drapeau m

feather-necked: ~ **bolt** n PROD ENG boulon à ergot m

feathers n pl PRINT *on adhesive* tracés parasites m pl

featherweight: ~ **paper** n PRINT papier ultraléger m

feature n CINEMAT long métrage m, COMP caractéristique f, DP caractéristique f, fonction f, FLUID PHYS, PATENTS, PROD ENG caractéristique f; ~ **extraction** n COMP, DP extraction de caractéristiques f

FEBE *abbr (far-end block error)* TELECOM erreur de bloc à l'extrémité distante f

FEC *abbr (forward error correction)* COMP correction d'erreurs sans voie de retour f

fecal[1] *adj* (AmE) *see faecal*

fecal:[2] ~ **matter** n (AmE) *see faecal matter*

feces n (AmE) *see faeces*

FECN *abbr (forward explicit congestion notification)* TELECOM notification d'encombrement explicite émise vers l'avant f

fed-in: ~ **winding** n ELEC enroulement à fils semés par l'entaille m

fee n PATENTS taxe f

feed[1] n AUTO, COAL TECH, COMP, DP, ELEC *supply network*, ELEC ENG *power supply* alimentation f, HYDR EQUIP débit m, MECH avance f, P&R *moulding, extruding*, PAPER TECH alimentation f, PETR TECH charge f, PROD ENG alimentation f, amenage m, avancement m, entraînement m, pression f, *lathe* work avance f, TV alimentation f, WATER SUPP paquet d'eau m, éclusée f; ~ **and bleed** n NUCLEAR alimentation et soutirage f; ~ **box** n MECH ENG *machine tools* boîte des avances f, PAPER TECH caisse d'alimentation f, PROD ENG boîte d'alimentation f, régulateur d'alimentation m; ~ **bush** n MECH ENG *injection mould* bague de préinjection f; ~ **cable** n ELEC ENG câble d'alimentation m; ~ **chart** n MECH ENG *machine tool* tableau indicateur des

avances m; ~ **check** n CONTROL contrôle d'avancement m; ~ **circuit** n ELEC circuit d'alimentation m; ~ **claw** n CINEMAT griffe d'entraînement f; ~ **cock** n PROD ENG robinet d'alimentation m, robinet de charge m; ~ **enrichment** n NUCLEAR *of fuel* enrichissement initial m; ~ **gear** n PROD ENG appareil d'alimentation m; ~ **guides** n pl PRINT guides de marge m pl; ~ **head** n PROD ENG *founding* masselotte f; ~ **hole** n COMP, DP perforation d'entraînement f; ~ **hopper** n CONST trémie f, trémie d'alimentation f, MECH *process* trémie d'alimentation f, PACKAGING trémie d'entrée f, PROD ENG trémie d'alimentation f, trémie de chargement f; ~ **hose union** n PETR TECH *mud lines* goulotte f; ~ **limiter** n MECH ENG limiteur d'avance m; ~ **magazine** n CINEMAT boîte-magasin débitrice f, MECH ENG *machine tool* mécanisme d'alimentation m; ~ **motion** n PROD ENG mouvement d'avancement m, mouvement de déplacement m, mouvement de pression m; ~ **pipe** n PROD ENG tuyau d'arrivée m, *for supplying water to boiler* tuyau d'alimentation m, tuyau de prise d'eau m; ~ **plate** n MECH ENG *injection mould* plaque de répartition des canaux d'injection f; ~ **pump** n HEATING, PROD ENG pompe d'alimentation f; ~ **rack** n MECH ENG *machine tools* crémaillère d'avance f, PROD ENG *lubricating rack* rampe de distribution f, rampe de graissage f; ~ **range** n MECH ENG *machine tool* gamme des avances f; ~ **rate** n COAL TECH débit m; ~ **reel** n CINEMAT bobine débitrice f; ~ **regulator** n CONTROL régulateur d'alimentation m, régulateur d'amenée m; FOOD TECH *milling* cylindre d'alimentation m; ~ **roll** n MECH ENG cylindre d'entraînement m, cylindre entraîneur m, rouleau entraîneur m, PAPER TECH rouleau d'alimentation m; ~ **roller** n FOOD TECH *food-processing machinery* rouleau d'alimentation m, MECH ENG cylindre d'entraînement m, cylindre entraîneur m, rouleau entraîneur m; ~ **runner** n P&R *plastics* canal d'alimentation m; ~ **screw** n MECH, MECH ENG *of lathe* vis-mère f; ~ **shaft** n MECH ENG *of lathe* barre de chariotage f, barre de commande de chariotage f; ~ **sleeve** n MECH ENG fourreau d'avance m; ~ **spool** n CINEMAT bobine débitrice f; ~ **sprocket** n CINEMAT tambour débiteur m; ~ **system** n SPACE circuit d'alimentation m; ~ **table** n PRINT margeur m, table d'entrée f; ~ **tank** n PETR TECH *refinery* réservoir d'alimentation m, PROD ENG bâche d'alimentation f; ~ **valve** n PETR TECH *refinery* vanne d'alimentation f; ~ **waveguide** n ELEC ENG guide d'ondes d'alimentation m

feed[2] vt COMP, DP, ELEC ENG *power supply*, MECH alimenter, PROD ENG *founding* pomper, TV alimenter, transmettre; ~ **back** vt CONTROL réappliquer, réinjecter

feedback n COMP réaction f, rétroaction f, CONTROL bouclage m, rétroaction f, DP réaction f, rétroaction f, ELECTRON action de retour f, bouclage m, réaction f, réinjection f, rétroaction f, MECH *controls* contre-réaction f, NUCLEAR rétroaction f, PHYS contre-réaction f, RECORDING contre-réaction f, réaction f, rétroaction f, TELECOM contre-réaction f, TV effet Larsen m, rétroaction f, WAVE PHYS rétroaction f; ~ **admittance** n CONTROL admittance inverse de transfert f, admittance supplémentaire due à la réaction d'anode f; ~ **AGC** n TELECOM CAG à contre-réaction f; ~ **amplifier** n ELECTRON amplificateur à contre-réaction m; ~ **chain** n CONTROL chaîne de réaction f; ~ **channel** n RECORDING canal de retour m; ~ **circuit** n CONTROL circuit de réaction m, RECORDING retour d'écoute m, TV circuit de réaction m, retour de signal m, réaction f; ~ **coil** n ELEC ENG bobine de réaction f; ~ **control** n CONTROL réglage à réaction m, ELEC ENG asservissement m; ~ **control loop** n CONTROL boucle de rétroaction f; ~ **control system** n ELEC ENG système asservi m; ~ **current** n ELECTRON courant de retour m, courant réfléchi m; ~ **encoder** n CONTROL codeur à réinjection m; ~ **factor** n CONTROL taux de réaction m; ~ **loop** n CONTROL boucle de rétroaction f, ELECTRON chaîne de rétroaction f, for closed-loop control system chaîne de retour f, MECH controls boucle de contre-réaction f, PROD ENG boucle de rétroaction f; ~ **oscillation** n RECORDING oscillation de réaction f; ~ **oscillator** n CONTROL oscillateur de rétroaction m, ELECTRON oscillateur de réaction m; ~ **penetration control** n CONTROL réglage de la pénétration par réaction m; ~ **process optimization** n CONTROL optimisation à réaction f; ~ **ratio** n CONTROL taux de réaction m, ELECTRON taux de rétroaction m, of amplifier taux de contre-réaction m, of oscillator taux de réaction m; ~ **resistor** n ELEC ENG résistance de contre-réaction f; ~ **signal** n CONTROL contre-signal m, signal de rétroaction m, ELECTRON signal de retour m, signal de rétroaction m, PROD ENG signal de rétroaction m; ~ **suppressor** n CONTROL suppresseur de rétroaction m; ~ **system** n CONTROL système de réinjection m, système de rétroaction m; ~ **theory** n CONTROL théorie de réinjection f, théorie de rétroaction f; ~ **transfer function** n CONTROL fonction de transfert de réaction f; ~ **value** n CONTROL valeur effective f; ~ **voltage** n ELEC ENG tension de rétroaction f; ~ **winding** n ELEC ENG enroulement de contre-réaction m

feedboard n PRINT margeur m, table de marge f

feeder n C&G distributeur m, ELEC supply network artère f, ligne d'alimentation f, ELEC ENG ligne d'alimentation f, GEOL igneous filon nourricier m, MECH ENG machine tool dispositif d'alimentation m, PACKAGING chargeur m, PRINT margeur m, PROD ENG alimentateur m, shrinkage head masselotte f, SPACE communications ligne d'alimentation f, TEXTILES chute f; ~ **airline** n AERONAUT transport compagnie subsidiaire f, transporteur aérien d'apport m; ~ **bar** n ELEC supply barre d'alimentation f; ~ **cable** n COMP, DP câble d'alimentation m, ELEC supply network artère f, ligne d'alimentation f, TV câble conducteur m, câble d'alimentation m; ~ **gate** n C&G registre m; ~ **header** n NUCLEAR collecteur d'alimentation m; ~ **line** n AERONAUT bretelle f, ligne d'apport intérieur f, RAIL antenne f, ligne affluente d'apport f, ligne affluente de ramassage f; ~ **link** n SPACE communications liaison de connexion f; ~ **lock** n NUCLEAR for spherical fuel elements écluse d'alimentation f; ~ **nose** n C&G cuvette d'avant-corps f; ~ **opening** n C&G entrée du canal de distribution f; ~ **pipe** n NUCLEAR tuyau d'amenée m; ~ **plunger** n C&G poinçon m; ~ **ship** n NAUT, TRANSP navire collecteur m; ~ **tank** n AERONAUT nourrice f; ~ **train** n RAIL vehicles train de ramassage m; ~ **yarn** n TEXTILES fil d'alimentation m

feedforward n PROD ENG décalage en entrée m; ~ **AGC** n TELECOM CAG avec réaction vers l'avant f; ~ **control** n COMP, DP régulation par anticipation f

feeding n PAPER TECH alimentation f, device chargement m, PROD ENG alimentation f, amenage m, avancement m, entraînement m, pression f, TEXTILES alimentation f; ~ **device** n PACKAGING appareil d'alimentation m,

dispositif de remplissage m; ~ **ground** n OCEANOG aire de nutrition f; ~ **process** n (AmE) (cf method of feeding) C&G mode d'alimentation m; ~ **regulator** n CONTROL régulateur d'alimentation m; ~ **roll** n PAPER TECH rouleau d'alimentation m; ~ **system** n PAPER TECH système d'alimentation m; ~ **table** n PACKAGING table d'alimentation f; ~ **transformer** n ELEC transformateur d'alimentation m

feedlays n pl PRINT guides de marge m pl

feedline n NUCLEAR of gas centrifuge conduite d'alimentation f

feed-reversing: ~ **gear** n MECH ENG changement de marche du mouvement de pression m

feedstock n ELEC ENG matière première f, PETR TECH charge f, basic hydrocarbons charge d'alimentation f, produit de base m

feedthrough n ELEC ENG traversée f, MECH traversée de paroi f, PHYS trou de traversée m, SPACE spacecraft traversée f; ~ **capacitor** n ELEC ENG condensateur de traversée m; ~ **insulator** n ELEC ENG traversée isolante f

feedwater n HEAT ENG eau d'alimentation f, HYDROL eau d'alimentation f, boilers eau d'alimentation de chaudière f, MECH process, NAUT engine, PAPER TECH, WATER SUPP eau d'alimentation f; ~ **heater** n HEAT ENG, PROD ENG réchauffeur d'eau d'alimentation m; ~ **inlet nozzle** n NUCLEAR of steam generator tubulure d'entrée de l'eau d'alimentation f; ~ **manifold** n NUCLEAR conduit distributeur d'eau d'alimentation m; ~ **pump** n MECH ENG tuyau d'amenée m; ~ **softening** n HEAT ENG adoucissement de l'eau d'alimentation m; ~ **treatment** n HYDROL traitement des eaux de chaudière m

feel: ~ **mechanism** n SPACE mécanisme de contact m; ~ **plate** n P&R plastics plaque de pré-éjection f; ~ **simulator** n SPACE simulateur de sensation m; ~ **simulator valve** n AERONAUT détendeur de sensation musculaire m

feeler n PRINT jauge d'épaisseur f; ~ **gage** n (AmE), ~ **gauge** n (BrE) METR calibre à lames m, jauge d'épaisseur f, NUCLEAR jauge d'épaisseur f, VEHICLES calibre d'épaisseur m, jauge d'épaisseur f

feet: ~ **per second** n pl CINEMAT pieds par seconde m pl

Fehling's: ~ **solution** n CHEM reagent réactif cupro-alcalin m

feint: ~ **rules** n pl PRINT filets de guidage m pl

feldspar n C&G, CHEM, MINERAL feldspath m

felt n PAPER TECH, TEXTILES feutre m; ~ **and foam joint** n CONST joint feutre et mousse m; ~ **board** n PAPER TECH carton feutre m, carton feutré m; ~ **carrying roll** n PAPER TECH rouleau de feutre m; ~ **conditioner** n PAPER TECH conditionneur de feutre m; ~ **direction mark** n PAPER TECH flèche de direction de marche sur le feutre f; ~ **dryer** n PAPER TECH sécheur de feutre m; ~ **mark** n PAPER TECH marque de feutre f; ~ **polisher** n C&G polissoir en feutre m; ~ **roll** n PAPER TECH rouleau de feutre m; ~ **side** n PAPER TECH côté feutre m; ~ **stretcher** n PAPER TECH tendeur de feutre m; ~ **washer** n MECH ENG rondelle de feutre f; ~ **whipper** n PAPER TECH batteur de feutre m

felting n PAPER TECH feutrage m; ~ **power** n PAPER TECH pouvoir feutrant m

female: ~ **connector** n ELEC fiche femelle f, ELEC ENG connecteur femelle m; ~ **contact** n ELEC ENG contact femelle m; ~ **guide** n TV guide à dépression m; ~ **thread** n MECH ENG filetage femelle m

femto- pref (f) METR femto- (f)

fence:[1] **~ boom** n MAR POLL barrage barrière m; **~ code** n PROD ENG code séparateur m

fence:[2] **~ in** vt CONST clôturer, entourer, isoler

fenchene n CHEM fenchène m

fenchone n CHEM fenchone f

fenchyl n CHEM fenchyle m

fend:[1] **~ off** vt NAUT parer, repousser

fend:[2] **~ off a collision** vi NAUT *shiphandling* parer un abordage

fender n *(cf bumper)* AUTO pare-chocs m, MAR POLL défense f, MECH pare-chocs m, NAUT *deck equipment* défense f, paillet m, pare-battage m, VEHICLES *body* aile f, garde-boue m, VEHICLES *body* pare-chocs m

Fenske: **~ helices** n pl LAB EQUIP *distillation* hélices Fenske f pl

FEP abbr *(front-end processor)* COMP processeur frontal m

FERF abbr *(far-end receive failure)* TELECOM défaut en réception à l'extrémité distante m, dérangement de réception à l'extrémité m

Fermat's: **~ principle** n PHYS principe de Fermat m

ferment vi CHEM *of liquids* fermenter

fermentation n CHEM, FOOD TECH, HYDROL *sewage* fermentation f

fermenter n FOOD TECH cuve de fermentation f, fermenteur m

Fermi: **~ energy** n PHYS énergie de Fermi f; **~ level** n PHYS niveau de Fermi m; **~ sphere** n PHYS sphère de Fermi f; **~ surface** n PHYS surface de Fermi f; **~ wave vector** n PHYS vecteur d'onde de Fermi m

Fermi-Dirac: **~ distribution** n PHYS distribution de Fermi-Dirac f; **~ statistics** n pl PHYS statistiques de Fermi-Dirac f pl

fermion n PART PHYS, PHYS fermion m

fermium n *(Fm)* CHEM fermium m *(Fm)*

ferrate n CHEM ferrate m

ferredoxin n CHEM ferredoxine f

ferric[1] adj CHEM ferrique

ferric:[2] **~ oxide** n RECORDING oxyde ferrique m

ferricyanide n CHEM ferricyanure m

ferricyanogen n CHEM ferricyanogène m

ferrimagnetic adj PHYS ferrimagnétique

ferrimagnetism n PHYS ferrimagnétisme m

ferrioxalic adj CHEM ferrioxalique

ferrite n CHEM, ELEC, ELEC ENG, PHYS ferrite f; **~ core** n COMP tore de ferrite m, DP, ELEC *of transformer, computer* noyau en ferrite m, ELEC ENG *magnetic memory* tore de ferrite m, *of transformer* noyau en ferrite m; **~ head** n RECORDING, TV tête en ferrite f; **~ isolator** n ELEC ENG isolateur à ferrite m; **~ limiter** n ELEC ENG limiteur à ferrite m; **~ phase shifter** n ELEC ENG déphaseur à ferrite m; **~ rod** n ELEC ENG, PHYS bâtonnet de ferrite m; **~ rotator** n ELEC ENG gyrateur à ferrite m

ferritic[1] adj MECH *materials*, METALL ferritique

ferritic:[2] **~ cast iron** n PROP MAT fonte ferritique f; **~ stainless steel** n MECH ENG acier inoxydable ferritique m

ferritin n CHEM ferritine f

ferritizing: **~ annealing** n METALL, PROP MAT *metallurgy* ferritisation f

ferroalloy n PROP MAT ferro-alliage m; **~ briquette** n PROP MAT briquette de ferro-alliage f

ferroan: **~ dolomite** n GEOL *rock* ankérite f, dolomie ferrifère f

ferroconcrete n CONST *boatbuilding* béton armé m

ferrocyanate n CHEM cyanoferrate m

ferrocyanide n CHEM cyanoferrate m

ferrocyanogen n CHEM cyanofer m, ferrocyanogène m

ferrodynamic: **~ wattmeter** n ELEC wattmètre ferrodynamique m

ferroelectric[1] adj PHYS ferroélectrique

ferroelectric:[2] **~ crystal** n ELEC ENG cristal ferroélectrique m

ferroelectricity n ELEC ENG, PHYS ferroélectricité f

ferrogallic: **~ ink** n COLOURS encre à écrire f

ferromagnetic[1] adj PHYS, PROP MAT, TESTING ferromagnétique

ferromagnetic:[2] **~ amplifier** n ELECTRON amplificateur ferromagnétique m; **~ instrument** n INSTRUMENT instrument ferromagnétique m; **~ material** n ELEC substance ferromagnétique f, ELEC ENG corps ferromagnétique m, PETR matériau ferromagnétique m; **~ particles** n pl PROP MAT particules ferromagnétiques f pl

ferromagnetism n ELEC, PHYS, RECORDING ferromagnétisme m

ferromolybdenum n METALL, PROP MAT ferromolybdène m

ferronickel n METALL, PROP MAT ferronickel m; **~ cell** n ELEC ENG accumulateur Edison m, accumulateur nickel-fer m

ferroprussiate n CHEM ferroprussiate m

ferroresonance n ELEC ENG ferrorésonance f; **~ circuit** n ELEC ENG circuit ferrorésonnant m

ferrosoferric adj CHEM ferrosoferrique

ferrous[1] adj CHEM *oxide* ferreux

ferrous:[2] **~ oxide** n C&G oxyde ferreux m; **~ sulfate** n (AmE), **~ sulphate** n (BrE) CHEM vitriol vert m

ferruginous adj GEOL ferrugineux

ferrule n MECH manchon m, virole f, MECH ENG coupelle serre-gaine f, OPT bague f, ferrule f, TELECOM bague f, ferrule f, virole f; **~ resistor** n ELEC ENG résistance à bagues f

ferry n NAUT bac m, malle f, transbordeur m, traversier m (Can); **~ cable** n TRANSP traille f; **~ flight** n AERONAUT convoyage m, vol de convoyage m; **~ landing stage** n TRANSP appontement m, ponton m; **~ service** n NAUT, TRANSP ligne de bac f

ferryboat n NAUT bac m, ferry-boat m, malle f, transbordeur m, traversier m (Can), TRANSP bac m, ferry-boat m, transbordeur m, traversier m (Can)

ferrying n NAUT transport par bac m, transport par ferry m

fertile: **~ isotope** n PHYS isotope fertile m

ferulic adj CHEM férulique

festoon n GEOL feston m, PAPER TECH boucle d'accrocheuse f; **~ cross-bedding** n GEOL stratification en feston f, stratification entrecroisée f

FET[1] abbr *(field-effect transistor)* COMP, ELECTRON, OPT, PHYS TEC *(transistor à effet de champ)*

FET:[2] **~ amplifier** n ELECTRON, SPACE *communications* amplificateur à TEC m; **~ front end** n ELECTRON circuit d'entrée à TEC m; **~ input** n ELECTRON entrée d'un TEC f

fetch[1] n COMP extraction f, DP lecture f; **~ instruction** n COMP instruction d'extraction f, DP instruction de lecture f

fetch[2] vt COMP extraire, prélever, DP extraire, lire, prélever

fetch[3] vi NAUT atteindre, gagner

fettling n C&G *of earthenware* évidage m

Feynman: **~ diagram** n PHYS diagramme de Feynman m

FF[1] *abbr (form feed)* COMP, PRINT alimentation en papier *f*, avance-papier *m*

FF:[2] **~ carbon black** *n (fine furnace carbon black)* P&R *rubber filler* noir FF *m*

FFT *abbr (fast Fourier transform)* COMP, ELECTRON transformation de Fourier rapide *f*

F-head: **~ engine** *n* AUTO moteur à soupapes en tête et latérales *m*

FHP: **~ motor** *n (fractional horsepower motor)* ELEC ENG moteur fractionnaire *m*

fiber *n* (AmE) *see fibre*

fiber-distributed: **~ data interface** *n* (AmE) *see fibre-distributed data interface*

fiberglass *n* (AmE) *see fibreglass*

fiberizer *n* (BrE) PAPER TECH dépastilleur *m*

fiber-like: **~ material** *n* (AmE) *see fibre-like material*

fiberoptic (AmE) *see fibreoptic*

fiber-reinforced: **~ sand** *n* (AmE) *see fibre-reinforced sand*

fiber-type: **~ sling** *n* (AmE) *see fibre-type sling*

Fibonacci: **~ search** *n* COMP, DP recherche de Fibonacci *f*, recherche dichotomique *f*; **~ sequence** *n* MATH suite de Fibonacci *f*

fibre *n* (BrE) C&G, PAPER TECH, TELECOM, TEXTILES fibre *f*; **~ axis** *n* (BrE) OPT, TELECOM axe de la fibre *m*; **~ bonding** *n* (BrE) PROP MAT liaison des fibres *f*; **~ buffer** *n* (BrE) OPT gainage *m*, revêtement secondaire *m*, TELECOM matelas protecteur *m*; **~ bundle** *n* (BrE) C&G botte *f* (Bel), OPT, TELECOM faisceau de fibres *m*; **~ cladding** *n* (BrE) OPT gaine *f*, gaine optique *f*; **~ coating** *n* (BrE) OPT protection *f*, revêtement *m*; **~ coiling plate** *n* (BrE) TELECOM plateau enrouleur de fibre *m*; **~ composition** *n* (BrE) PACKAGING, PAPER TECH, PRINT composition fibreuse *f*; **~ content** *n* (BrE) TEXTILES pourcentage de fibres *m*; **~ core** *n* (BrE) OPT coeur de fibre *m*, TV noyau à fibres *m*; **~ debonding** *n* (BrE) PROP MAT séparation des fibres *f*; **~ drum** *n* (BrE) NUCLEAR *for radioactive wastes* fût allégé *m*, PACKAGING fût contre-plaqué *m*; **~ excess length** *n* (BrE) OPT surlongueur *f*; **~ feeder** *n* (BrE) C&G alimentation en fibres primaires *f*; **~ gasket** *n* (BrE) MECH joint en fibre *m*; **~ helix** *n* (BrE) OPT serpentin *m*; **~ jacket** *n* (BrE) OPT enrobage *m*, revêtement secondaire *m*, TELECOM enrobage *m*; **~ optics** *n* (BrE) C&G optique de fibre *f*, CINEMAT fibre optique *f*, COMP, DP, ELEC ENG optique de fibre *f*, OPT optique de fibres *f*, PHYS optique de fibre *f*; **~ optics equipment** *n* (BrE) LAB EQUIP *lighting* équipement fibre optique *m*; **~ pigtail** *n* (BrE) OPT fibre amorce *f*; **~ puffing** *n* (BrE) PRINT gonflement des fibres *m*; **~ rope** *n* (BrE) MECH ENG corde de fibre *f*; **~ scattering** *n* (BrE) OPT, TELECOM diffusion de fibrage *f*; **~ tear** *n* (BrE) PRINT déchirure des fibres *f*; **~ texture** *n* (BrE) METALL texture fibreuse *f*; **~ to the building** *n* (BrE) *(FTTB)* TELECOM fibre jusqu'à l'immeuble *f*; **~ to the kerb** *n* (BrE) *(FTTC)* TELECOM fibre jusqu'au trottoir *f*; **~ to the home** *n* (BrE) *(FTTH)* TELECOM fibre jusqu'au logement *f*; **~ to the office** *n* (BrE) *(FTTO)* TELECOM fibre jusqu'au bureau *f*

fibre-distributed: **~ data interface** *n* (BrE) *(FDDI)* TELECOM interface de données avec distribution par fibre *f*

fibreglass *n* (BrE) CONST, NAUT *boatbuilding material* fibre de verre *f*, P&R *plastics* fibre de verre *f*, laine de verre *f*, tissu de verre *m*, PROD ENG fibre de verre *f*

fibre-like: **~ material** *n* (BrE) CONST *building* matériau fibreux *m*

fibreoptic: **~ cable** *n* (BrE) COMP, DP, ELEC ENG câble à fibre optique *m*, OPT câble en fibres optiques *m*, câble à fibre optique *m*; **~ cladding** *n* (BrE) TELECOM gaine de fibre optique *f*; **~ connection** *n* (BrE) ELEC ENG connexion à fibre optique *f*; **~ connector** *n* (BrE) ELEC ENG connecteur pour fibre optique *m*; **~ modem** *n* (BrE) ELECTRON modem pour fibre optique *m*; **~ network** *n* (BrE) ELEC ENG réseau à fibre optique *m*; **~ receiver** *n* (BrE) ELEC ENG récepteur à fibre optique *m*, TELECOM module de réception optique *m*; **~ splice** *n* (BrE) TELECOM raccord de fibres optiques *m*; **~ technology** *n* (BrE) ELEC ENG technique à fibre optique *f*; **~ terminal device** *n* (BrE) OPT dispositif d'extrémité de liaison optique *m*, terminal de liaison optique *m*, TELECOM dispositif d'extrémité de fibre optique *m*, terminal de fibre optique *m*; **~ transducer** *n* (BrE) ELEC ENG capteur à fibre optique *m*; **~ transmission** *n* (BrE) OPT, TELECOM transmission par fibres optiques *f*; **~ transmission system** *n* (BrE) ELEC ENG système de transmission à fibre optique *m*; **~ transmitter** *n* (BrE) ELEC ENG émetteur à fibre optique *m*

fibre-reinforced: **~ sand** *n* (BrE) CONST sable armé de fibres *m*

fibre-type: **~ sling** *n* (BrE) SAFETY élingue *f*, élingue du type corde en fibre *f*

fibril *n* ASTRON fibrille *f*

fibrillating *n* PAPER TECH fibrillation *f*

fibrillation *n* PAPER TECH fibrillation *f*

fibrizer *n* (AmE) *see fiberizer*

fibroin *n* CHEM fibroïne *f*

fibroptic: **~ receiver** *n* (BrE) TELECOM récepteur optique *m*

fibrous[1] *adj* PAPER TECH fibreux

fibrous:[2] **~ fracture** *n* METALL rupture fibreuse *f*, rupture à nerfs *f*, NUCLEAR rupture fibreuse *f*; **~ insulation** *n* HEAT ENG isolation fibreuse *f*; **~ layer** *n* PAPER TECH couche fibreuse *f*; **~ microstructure** *n* METALL microstructure fibreuse *f*; **~ peat** *n* COAL TECH tourbe fibreuse *f*; **~ texture** *n* CRYSTALL texture fibreuse *f*; **~ waste** *n* TEXTILES déchets fibreux *m pl*

fiche[1] *n* COMP, DP microfiche *f*

fiche[2] *vt* COMP, DP mettre sur microfiche

ficin *n* CHEM ficine *f*

Fick's: **~ law** *n* PHYS loi de Fick *f*

fictitious: **~ binding energy** *n* NUCLEAR énergie fictive de liaison *f*

fiddle *n* NAUT *retaining bar* barre à roulis *f*; **~ block** *n* NAUT *deck fittings* poulie à violon *f*; **~ drill** *n* MECH ENG foret à archet *m*

fidelity *n* ACOUSTICS fidélité *f*

field *n* ACOUSTICS, CINEMAT, COMP, DP, ELEC *electric, magnetic* champ *m*, ELEC ENG champ *m*, *in a conductor* champ *m*, PETR champ *m*, gisement *m*, PETR TECH *deposit* champ *m*, gisement *m*, TV trame *f*; **~ of action** *n* CINEMAT champ d'action *m*; **~ artillery** *n* MILIT artillerie de campagne *f*; **~ balancing equipment** *n* MECH ENG *vibration test* appareils d'équilibrage sur site *m pl*; **~ battery** *n* MILIT *artillery* batterie de campagne *f*; **~ book** *n* CONST *surveying* livre de topographie *m*; **~ camera** *n* PHOTO chambre portative *f*; **~ centering control** *n* (AmE), **~ centring control** *n* (BrE) TV réglage de centrage de trame *m*; **~ circuit** *n* ELEC *of machine* circuit de champ *m*; **~ coil** *n* ELEC *of machine* bobinage d'excitation *m*, bobinage de champ *m*, bobine de champ *f*, enroulement inducteur *m*, ELEC ENG bobine d'excitation *f*, bobine de champ *f*, enroulement d'excitation *m*, RECORDING bobine de champ *f*; **~**

convergence *n* TV convergence de trame *f*; ~ **current** *n* ELEC *of machine*, ELEC ENG courant d'excitation *m*; ~ **delimiter** *n* COMP, DP délimiteur de champ *m*; ~ **depth** *n* TELECOM profondeur du champ *f*; ~ **desorption mass spectrometer** *n* NUCLEAR spectromètre de masse à désorption par champ électrique *m*; ~ **diaphragm** *n* METALL diaphragme de champ *m*; ~ **direction** *n* ELEC ENG direction de champ *f*; ~ **discharge switch** *n* NUCLEAR interrupteur de champ magnétique *m*; ~ **divider** *n* TV diviseur de fréquence de trame *m*; ~ **effect** *n* ELECTRON, TELECOM effet de champ *m*; ~ **electron microscope** *n* INSTRUMENT microscope électronique à émission de champ *m*; ~ **emission** *n* ELECTRON émission de champ *f*, émission par effet de champ *f*, émission à froid *f*, PHYS émission de champ *f*; ~ **emission microscope** *n* INSTRUMENT microscope électronique à émission de champ *m*, PHYS microscope à émission de champ *m*; ~ **engineer** *n* MECH ingénieur de terrain *m*; ~ **excitation** *n* ELEC *of machine* excitation de champ *f*; ~ **flutter** *n* NUCLEAR flottement magnétique *m*; ~ **flyback** *n* TV retour de trame *m*; ~ **of force** *n* ELEC ENG champ de forces *m*; ~ **free emission current** *n* NUCLEAR *of surface* courant d'émission à champ nul *m*; ~ **frequency** *n* TV fréquence de balayage vertical *f*, fréquence de trame *f*; ~ **gating circuit** *n* TV circuit déclencheur de trame *m*; ~ **glasses** *n pl* INSTRUMENT jumelles *f pl*; ~ **glass magnifier** *n* C&G jumelle-loupe *f*; ~ **illumination** *n* INSTRUMENT lampe d'éclairage du champ de l'objet *f*; ~ **of image** *n* CINEMAT champ d'image *m*; ~ **intensity** *n* ELEC intensité de champ *f*; ~ **investigation** *n* COAL TECH recherche sur place *f*; ~ **ion microscope** *n* INSTRUMENT, PHYS microscope ionique à émission de champ *m*; ~ **joint station** *n* PETR station d'enrobage *f*; ~ **label** *n* COMP, DP étiquette d'un champ *f*; ~ **latex** *n* P&R *rubber* latex plantation *m*; ~ **length** *n* COMP, DP taille d'un champ *f*; ~ **lens** *n* INSTRUMENT diaphragme de champ *m*, lentille antérieure *f*, lentille de champ *f*, lentille frontale *f*, PHOTO lentille de champ *f*; ~ **line** *n* ELEC ENG, PHYS ligne de champ *f*; ~ **magnet** *n* ELEC ENG, RECORDING aimant de champ *m*; ~ **microphone** *n* RECORDING micro de reportage *m*; ~ **monitoring** *n* CONTROL contrôle de trame *m*; ~ **neutralizing magnet** *n* TV aimant de blindage *m*; ~ **of nuclear forces** *n* NUCLEAR champ de forces nucléaires *m*; ~ **oxide** *n* ELECTRON oxyde épais *m*; ~ **pick-up** *n* TV reportage en extérieur *m*; ~ **pole** *n* ELEC ENG pôle de champ *m*; ~ **processing** *n* PETR traitement préliminaire du pétrole *m*; ~ **programmable logic array** *n* (*FPLA*) COMP, DP réseau à logique programmable par l'utilisateur *m*; ~ **rate flicker** *n* TV papillotement de trame *m*; ~ **regulator** *n* ELEC *of motor* rhéostat de champ *m*, ELEC ENG régulateur de champ *m*; ~ **reversal** *n* GEOL inversion de champ magnétique *f*; ~ **reversed mirror reactor** *n* NUCLEAR réacteur à miroirs à champ renversé *m*; ~ **rheostat** *n* ELEC *of machine* rhéostat de champ *m*, ELEC ENG rhéostat d'excitation *m*; ~ **of sharpness** *n* CINEMAT champ de netteté *m*; ~ **shift switch** *n* TV commutateur de trame *m*; ~ **spider** *n* ELEC *of machine* croisillon d'induit *m*; ~ **stop** *n* PHYS diaphragme de champ *m*; ~ **strength** *n* ELEC, ELEC ENG intensité de champ *f*; ~ **strength meter** *n* ELEC intensimètre *m*; ~ **suppressor** *n* ELEC affaiblisseur de champ *m*; ~ **sync** *n* TV synchro trame *f*; ~ **sync alignment** *n* TV alignement des têtes sur la synchronisation de trame *m*; ~ **tilt** *n* TV inclinaison de trame *f*; ~ **trial** *n* MAR POLL essai en pratique *m*, essai sur le terrain *m*, SPACE essai en vraie

grandeur *m*, TELECOM phase pilote *f*; ~ **vector** *n* ELEC ENG vecteur champ *m*; ~ **of view** *n* ASTRON *of instrument* champ optique *m*, CINEMAT champ visuel *m*; ~ **voltage** *n* ELEC *of machine* tension d'excitation *f*; ~ **weld** *n* NUCLEAR soudure sur chantier *f*; ~ **winding** *n* ELEC enroulement inducteur *m*, ELEC ENG enroulement de champ *m*, enroulement inducteur *m*; ~ **wire** *n* ELEC ENG fil de campagne *m*; ~ **wiring** *n* PROD ENG câblage extérieur *m*; ~ **wiring arm** *n* PROD ENG bras de câblage extérieur *m*; ~ **work** *n* MILIT ouvrage de campagne *m*

Field: ~ **tube** *n* NUCLEAR *of steam generator* tube de Field *m*

field-breaking: ~ **switch** *n* NUCLEAR interrupteur de champ magnétique *m*

field-effect: ~ **amplifier** *n* ELECTRON amplificateur à effet de champ *m*; ~ **transistor** *n* COMP, DP, ELECTRON,, OPT, PHYS transistor à effet de champ *m*; ~ **transistor amplifier** *n* SPACE *communications* amplificateur à transistor à effet de champ *m*

field-engraved *adj* PROD ENG gravé par le client

field-expandable *adj* PROD ENG extensible sur le site

field-programmable: ~ **device** *n* COMP, DP dispositif programmable par l'utilisateur *m*

field-tested *adj* MECH éprouvé en clientèle

FIFO *abbr* (*first-in first-out*) COMP, DP PEPS (*premier entré premier sorti*)

fifth *n* ACOUSTICS quinte *f*; ~ **generation** *n* COMP, DP cinquième génération *f*; ~ **wheel** *n* VEHICLES *semitrailer* sellette *f*; ~ **wheel kingpin** *n* VEHICLES *semitrailer* axe d'attelage *m*, pivot d'attelage *m*; ~ **wheel kingpin axis** *n* VEHICLES *semitrailer* axe de la sellette *m*

fifth-generation: ~ **computer** *n* COMP, DP ordinateur de cinquième génération *m*

figurative: ~ **constant** *n* COMP, DP constante figurative *f*; ~ **device** *n* PATENTS marque combinée *f*

figure *n* PATENTS *of drawing* figure *f*, PRINT illustration *f*, silhouette *f*; ~ **of merit** *n* ELECTRON, SPACE facteur de mérite *m*; ~ **shift** *n* TELECOM inversion chiffres *f*; ~ **space** *n* PRINT espacement idéal *m*

figured: ~ **rolled glass** *n* (BrE) C&G verre imprimé *m*

figure-of-eight: ~ **knot** *n* NAUT noeud en forme de huit *m*; ~ **stairs** *n pl* CONST escalier en huit *m*; ~ **stellarator tube** *n* NUCLEAR tube de stellarator en forme de huit *m*

figures: ~ **shift** *n* COMP inversion chiffres *f*, DP décalage de chiffres *m*

figuring *n* C&G chiffrage *m*

filament *n* ASTRON filament *m*, CONST *of light* filament *m*, filament lumineux *m*, ELEC *of light bulb*, ELEC ENG, INSTRUMENT, P&R *of textiles* filament *m*, PHYS *of fluid* filet *m*, *of wire* filament *m*, TEXTILES filament *m*; ~ **current** *n* ELEC *of valve, tube* courant de chauffage *m*, ELEC ENG courant dans le filament *m*, courant de chauffage *m*; ~ **denier** *n* TEXTILES denier du brin *m*; ~ **resistance** *n* ELEC *of valve, tube* résistance de filament *f*; ~ **temperature** *n* ELEC *of valve, tube* température de filament *f*; ~ **transformer** *n* ELEC ENG transformateur de chauffage *m*

file[1] *n* COMP, DP fichier *m*, MECH *tool* lime *f*, PRINT fichier *m*, PROD ENG lime *f*, TELECOM fichier *m*, VEHICLES *tool* lime *f*; ~ **access** *n* COMP, DP accès fichier *m*; ~ **activity ratio** *n* COMP taux de mouvements de fichiers *m*, DP taux de mouvements de fichier *m*; ~ **creation** *n* COMP, DP création de fichier *f*; ~ **description** *n* COMP, DP description de fichier *f*; ~ **directory** *n* COMP, DP répertoire de fichier *m*; ~ **identifier** *n* COMP, DP identificateur de fichier *m*; ~ **label** *n* COMP, DP étiquette de fichier *f*; ~ **maintenance** *n* COMP, DP mise à jour de fichier *f*, tenue de fichier *f*; ~ **management** *n* COMP, DP gestion de fichier *f*; ~ **mark** *n* COMP, DP marque de fichier *f*; ~ **operation** *n* PROD ENG opération sur fichier *f*; ~ **organization** *n* COMP, DP organisation de fichier *f*; ~ **picture** *n* PHOTO cliché d'archives *m*; ~ **preparation** *n* COMP, DP préparation de fichier *f*; ~ **processing** *n* COMP, DP traitement de fichier *m*; ~ **protection** *n* COMP, DP protection de fichier *f*; ~ **recovery** *n* COMP, DP récupération de fichier *f*; ~ **restore** *n* COMP, DP restauration de fichier *f*; ~ **security** *n* COMP, DP sécurité de fichier *f*; ~ **separator** *n* COMP, DP séparateur de fichier *m*; ~ **server** *n* COMP, DP serveur de fichier *m*; ~ **sharing** *n* COMP, DP partage de fichier *m*; ~ **size** *n* COMP, DP taille de fichier *f*; ~ **store** *n* COMP, DP mémoire de masse *f*; ~ **structure** *n* COMP, DP structure de fichier *f*; ~ **transfer** *n* COMP, DP transfert de fichier *m*; ~ **transfer access and manipulation service element** *n* *(FTAMSE)* TELECOM élément de service de l'accès aux transfert et manipulation *m*; ~ **updating** *n* COMP mise à jour du fichier *f*, DP mise à jour de fichier *f*

file:[2] ~ **an application** *vi* PATENTS déposer une demande; ~ **a patent application** *vi* TEXTILES déposer un brevet

filename *n* COMP, DP nom de fichier *m*; ~ **extension** *n* COMP, DP extension de nom de fichier *f*

filicic *adj* CHEM filicique

filigree: ~ **formation** *n* ASTRON structure filamenteuse *f*

filing *n* COMP, DP archivage *m*, PATENTS dépôt *m*, PROD ENG limage *m*

filings *n pl* PROD ENG limaille *f*

fill[1] *n* C&G enfournement *m*, COAL TECH remblai *m*; ~ **and seal machine** *n* PACKAGING machine pour remplir et fermer *f*; ~ **hole** *n* PACKAGING orifice de charge *m*; ~ **level** *n* PACKAGING niveau de remplissage *m*; ~ **raise** *n* MINING descenderie de remblai *f*

fill[2] *vt* C&G enfourner, MINING endiguer, terrasser, remblayer, PRINT *text* garnir, PROD ENG *cistern, lamp, empty cask* emplir, remplir; ~ **up** *vt* CONST *ditch* combler, remblayer, remplir

filled: ~ **binder** *n* CONST liant fillerisé *m*

filler *n* C&G charge *f*, COLOURS bouche-pores *m*, COMP élément de remplissage *m*, CONST *building* fines *f pl*, *civil engineering* farine *f*, DP élément de remplissage *m*, ELEC *cable* bourrage *m*, ELEC ENG *between wires of cable* matelas *m*, NUCLEAR *in painting* matériau d'apport *m*, P&R matière de remplissage *f*, *compounding ingredient* charge *f*, PAPER TECH charge *f*, PROD ENG recharge *f*, PROP MAT matière de remplissage *f*; ~ **alloy** *n* CONST métal d'alliage *m*; ~ **cap** *n* MECH bouchon *m*, VEHICLES *fuel, lubrication, transmission* bouchon de remplissage *m*; ~ **character** *n* COMP, DP caractère de remplissage *m*; ~ **coat** *n* COLOURS bouche-pores *m*; ~ **compartment flap** *n* VEHICLES *fuel* trappe *f*, trappe à essence *f*; ~ **metal** *n* CONST métal d'alliage *m*, métal d'apport *m*, métal d'apport *m*, MECH *welding*, PROD ENG *welding* métal d'apport *m*; ~ **pass** *n* PETR passe de remplissage *f*; ~ **rod** *n* PROD ENG *welding* baguette de métal d'apport *f*, baguette de soudure *f*; ~ **wire** *n* MECH *welding* fil d'apport *m*

fillet *n* AERONAUT congé de raccordement *m*, karman *m*, *of airframe* carénage de raccordement *m*, CONST *feather tongue* fausse languette *f*, languette *f*, languette rapportée *f*, *hollow moulding* congé *m*, congé de raccordement *m*, MECH ENG *of gear* rayon de raccordement *m*, PROD ENG *of screw* filet *m*; ~ **gutter** *n*

CONST *building* solin *m*; ~ **radius** *n* RAIL congé de raccord *m*; ~ **slick** *n* PROD ENG *founding* lissoir à congé *m*; ~ **weld** *n* MECH soudure d'angle *f*

filleted: ~ **joint** *n* CONST *carpentry* assemblage à languette rapportée *m*

filleting: ~ **machine** *n* OCEANOG fileteuse *f*

fill-in: ~ **flash** *n* PHOTO éclair d'appoint *m*; ~ **light** *n* CINEMAT, PHOTO lumière d'appoint *f*; ~ **screen** *n* CINEMAT panneau réflecteur *m*

filling *n* C&G *of furnace, prior to start of melting operation*, COMP remplissage *m*, CONST *masonry work* blocage *m*, remplissage *m*, DP remplissage *m*, FOOD TECH *bottles, jars* ouillage *m*, remplissage *m*, GAS TECH remplissage *m*, MINING *gobbing* remblayage *m*, NUCLEAR *of fuel between fuel and can* remplissage *m*; ~ **and capping machine** *n* PACKAGING machine pour remplir et encapsuler *f*; ~ **and dosing machine** *n* PACKAGING machine pour doser et remplir *f*; ~ **coefficient** *n* TELECOM coefficient de remplissage *m*; ~ **device** *n* PACKAGING dispositif de remplissage *m*; ~ **end** *n* (AmE) *(cf doghouse)* C&G niche d'enfournement *f*; ~ **hole** *n* MECH, SPACE *spacecraft* orifice de remplissage *m*; ~ **line** *n* PACKAGING chaîne de remplissage *f*; ~ **machine** *n* PACKAGING machine de remplissage *f*; ~ **material** *n* NUCLEAR matériau d'apport *m*; ~ **metal** *n* PROD ENG *for autogenous welding* métal d'apport *m*; ~ **nozzle** *n* PACKAGING ajutage de remplissage *m*; ~ **pipe** *n* NAUT tuyau de remplissage *m*; ~ **plate** *n* NAUT *in deck* nable de remplissage *m*; ~ **plug** *n* PROD ENG bouchon de remplissage *m*; ~ **point** *n* C&G remplissage *m*; ~ **raise** *n* MINING descenderie de remblai *f*; ~ **up** *n* PROD ENG colmatage *m*; ~ **valve** *n* SPACE *spacecraft* vanne de remplissage *f*; ~ **vibrator** *n* PACKAGING vibreur de remplissage *m*

fillister *n* CONST feuilleret *m*, *of window sash* feuillure *f*; ~ **head machine screw** *n* MECH ENG, PROD ENG vis à tête cylindrique bombée *f*; ~ **plane** *n* CONST feuilleret *m*

fillistered: ~ **joint** *n* CONST assemblage à feuillure *m*

film[1] *n* CHEM *thin membrane* pellicule *f*, CINEMAT film *m*, pellicule *f*, COATINGS couche mince *f*, feuille mince *f*, film *m*, enduit *m*, HYDR EQUIP *of water between two plates in boiler* couche d'eau *f*, MECH couche mince *f*, feuille mince *f*, pellicule *f*, P&R feuille *f*, PHOTO film *m*, pellicule *f*, PROD ENG *of oil* pellicule *f*; ~ **advance lever** *n* PHOTO levier d'avancement de pellicule *m*; ~ **aperture assembly** *n* CINEMAT platine de fenêtre *f*; ~ **backing** *n* PHOTO *of roll film, 120mm* papier protecteur *m*; ~ **bin** *n* CINEMAT chutier *m*; ~ **blowing** *n* P&R soufflage de feuille *m*; ~ **boiling** *n* NUCLEAR caléfaction *f*, ébullition par film *f*, REFRIG ébullition pelliculaire *f*; ~ **can** *n* CINEMAT boîte de film *f*; ~ **capacitor** *n* ELEC ENG condensateur à bande plastique *m*, condensateur à film *m*; ~ **cartoning** *n* PACKAGING encartonnage final *m*; ~ **cassette** *n* INSTRUMENT magasin de film photographique *m*; ~ **casting** *n* P&R *process* coulage de feuille *m*; ~ **channel** *n* CINEMAT couloir presseur *m*; ~ **checker** *n* CINEMAT vérificateur de film *m*; ~ **clip** *n* PHOTO pince de film *f*; ~ **coating** *n* PACKAGING revêtement de film *m*; ~ **composition** *n* PRINT composition sur film *f*; ~ **cooling** *n* SPACE refroidissement par film *m*, refroidissement pelliculaire *m*, TRANSP refroidissement par film fluide *m*, refroidissement pelliculaire *m*; ~ **cutting** *n* PROD ENG découpe de film *f*; ~ **director** *n* CINEMAT metteur en scène *m*, réalisateur *m*; ~ **dosimeter** *n* RAD PHYS *radiation* dosimètre de film *m*, dosimètre photographique *m*; ~ **drive** *n* CINEMAT entraînement de film *m*; ~ **drum** *n* CINEMAT tambour d'entraînement *m*; ~ **dryer** *n* PHOTO séchoir de film *m*; ~ **drying drum** *n* CINEMAT tambour de séchage *m*; ~ **drying machine** *n* CINEMAT sécheuse de film *f*; ~ **extrusion** *n* P&R *process* extrusion de feuille *f*; ~ **extrusion equipment** *n* PACKAGING équipement pour l'extrusion de films *m*; ~ **fading** *n* CINEMAT affaiblissement d'image *m*; ~ **feeder pin** *n* CINEMAT griffe d'entraînement *f*; ~ **flat** *n* PRINT film monté *m*; ~ **footage counter** *n* CINEMAT compteur en pieds *m*; ~ **gage** *n* (AmE) *see film gauge* ~ **gate** *n* CINEMAT couloir du film *m*; ~ **gauge** *n* (BrE) CINEMAT format de pellicule *m*; ~ **holder** *n* PHOTO porte-film *m*; ~ **horse** *n* CINEMAT râtelier *m*; ~ **lamination** *n* PACKAGING stratification en film *f*; ~ **leader** *n* PHOTO amorce de pellicule *f*; ~ **length** *n* CINEMAT longueur de film *f*, métrage *m*; ~ **pick-up** *n* TV défileur cinéma *m*, télécinéma *m*; ~ **plane** *n* CINEMAT plan de pellicule *m*; ~ **rack** *n* PHOTO cadre pour développement de film *m*; ~ **register punch** *n* PRINT dispositif de perforation pour la mise en repérage des films *m*; ~ **resistor** *n* ELEC ENG résistance à couche *f*; ~ **rewind handle** *n* PHOTO manivelle de réembobinage *f*; ~ **scanner** *n* TV télécinéma *m*; ~ **shrinkage** *n* PHOTO retrait de pellicule *m*; ~ **splitting** *n* PRINT partage du film d'encre *m*, séparation du film d'encre *f*; ~ **spool** *n* PHOTO bobine de pellicule *f*; ~ **thickness** *n* P&R *paint, adhesives* épaisseur de couche *f*; ~ **threading** *n* CINEMAT chargement *m*; ~ **transducer** *n* SPACE capteur pelliculaire *m*; ~ **transfer** *n* TV kinescopage *m*, transfert sur film *m*; ~ **transmitter** *n* TV émetteur de télécinéma *m*; ~ **transport** *n* CINEMAT avancement de pellicule *m*; ~ **transport lever** *n* PHOTO levier d'avancement de film *m*; ~ **transport sprocket** *n* PHOTO pignon d'entraînement de pellicule *m*; ~ **tree** *n* CINEMAT chutier *m*; ~ **type indicator** *n* PHOTO indicateur de film *m*; ~ **winder** *n* PHOTO bouton d'enroulement *m*; ~ **wrap** *n* PACKAGING enveloppement avec film *m*; ~ **wrapping machine** *n* PACKAGING machine pour envelopper avec film *f*; ~ **wrinkling** *n* CINEMAT tuilage *m*

film² *vt* CINEMAT cinématographier, filmer, porter à l'écran, tourner; ~ **shoot** *vt* CINEMAT faire des prises de vues, filmer, tourner

film-applying: ~ **lid and heat-sealing machine** *n* PACKAGING machine pour appliquer un opercule et le sceller à chaud *f*

film-forming *adj* P&R *paint binder* filmogène

filming: ~ **speed** *n* CINEMAT cadence de prise de vue *f*

film-maker *n* CINEMAT cinéaste *m*

filmset *n* (BrE) (*cf photocomposer*) PRINT photocompositeur *m*, photocompositeuse *f*

filmsetter *n* PRINT photocomposeuse *f*

film-to-tape: ~ **transfer** *n* CINEMAT, TV transfert de film sur vidéo *m*

filter¹ *n* ASTRON, CHEM TECH, COAL TECH, COMP, CONST, DP, ELEC *network*, ELECTRON, LAB EQUIP, MECH, PAPER TECH, PETR TECH *geology, seismic survey, refinery*, PHOTO, PHYS, SPACE *spacecraft*, TELECOM, VEHICLES *carburettor, oil* filtre *m*; ~ **aid** *n* CHEM TECH adjuvant de filtrage *m*; ~ **amplifier** *n* ELECTRON amplificateur de filtre actif *m*; ~ **amplitude response** *n* ELECTRON réponse en amplitude de filtre *f*; ~ **attenuation** *n* ELECTRON atténuation de filtre *f*; ~ **attenuation band** *n* RECORDING bande d'atténuation de filtre *f*; ~ **bag** *n* CHEM TECH filtre à manche *m*, filtre à sacs *m*, COAL TECH manche *f*; ~ **bank** *n* ELECTRON banc de filtres *m*; ~ **bank system** *n* TELECOM *maritime satellite* système à

banc de filtres *m*; ~ **basin** *n* RECYCLING bassin de filtrage *m*; ~ **bed** *n* CHEM TECH couche filtrante *f*, lit filtrant *m*, NUCLEAR lit filtrant *m*, RECYCLING lit de filtration *m*, WATER SUPP bassin de filtration *m*; ~ **bowl** *n* VEHICLES *of carburettor* boîtier de filtre *m*; ~ **bypass** *n* PROD ENG dérivation de filtre *f*; ~ **cake** *n* CHEM TECH gâteau de filtre *m*, gâteau de filtre-presse *m*, COAL TECH gâteau *m*, gâteau de filtre *m*, PAPER TECH gâteau de filtre-presse *m*; ~ **capacitor** *n* ELEC ENG condensateur de filtrage *m*; ~ **cartridge** *n* CHEM TECH cartouche filtrante *f*, filtre de rechange *m*, MECH, VEHICLES *oil* cartouche de filtre *f*; ~ **characteristic function** *n* ELECTRON fonction caractéristique de filtre *f*; ~ **choke** *n* ELEC *network* self de filtrage *f*, ELEC ENG bobine de lissage *f*; ~ **cloth** *n* C&G étoffe à filtrer *f*, CHEM TECH tissu filtrant *m*, toile pour filtre-presses *f*, WATER SUPP tissu filtrant *m*, toile de filtre *f*, toile filtrante *f*; ~ **crystal** *n* ELECTRON quartz de filtrage *m*; ~ **cutoff frequency** *n* ELECTRON fréquence de coupure de filtre *f*; ~ **cyclone** *n* CHEM TECH cyclone filtre *m*; ~ **discrimination** *n* ELECTRON pouvoir discriminateur de filtre *m*; ~ **drum** *n* CHEM TECH tambour filtrant *m*; ~ **dryer** *n* CHEM TECH séchoir filtre *m*, REFRIG déshydrateur filtre *m*; ~ **element** *n* PROD ENG élément filtrant *m*; ~ **factor** *n* CINEMAT coefficient de filtre *m*, PHOTO facteur de prolongation de temps de pose *m*; ~ **feeder** *n* RECYCLING organisme filtreur *m*; ~ **feed trough** *n* CHEM TECH, COAL TECH cuve de filtre *f*; ~ **flask** *n* CHEM TECH bouteille à filtre *f*, fiole à filtre *f*; ~ **frame** *n* CHEM TECH cadre filtreur *m*, corps de filtre *m*, disque filtreur *m*; ~ **frequency** *n* ELECTRON fréquence centrale de filtre *f*, RAD PHYS fréquence passante *f*; ~ **frequency response** *n* ELECTRON réponse en fréquence de filtre *f*; ~ **funnel** *n* CHEM *liquid separation* entonnoir *m*, LAB EQUIP entonnoir à filtre *m*, *glassware* entonnoir à filtration *m*; ~ **gallery** *n* WATER SUPP galerie filtrante *f*; ~ **gravel** *n* CHEM TECH gravier de filtrage *m*, gravier filtrant *m*, WATER SUPP gravier filtrant *m*; ~ **holder** *n* CINEMAT, TV porte-filtre *m*; ~ **house** *n* NUCLEAR atelier de filtration *m*; ~ **jig** *n* SPACE gabarit de filtrage *m*, masque de filtrage *m*; ~ **kit** *n* CINEMAT jeu de filtres *m*; ~ **layer** *n* CHEM TECH couche filtrante *f*, CINEMAT couche filtre *f*; ~ **lens** *n* INSTRUMENT lentille filtre *f*; ~ **mask** *n* SPACE *communications* gabarit de filtrage *m*, masque de filtrage *m*; ~ **mass** *n* PAPER TECH masse filtrante *f*; ~ **membrane** *n* LAB EQUIP membrane filtrante *f*; ~ **order** *n* ELECTRON ordre de filtre *m*; ~ **paper** *n* CHEM papier-filtre *m*, CHEM TECH papier joseph *m*, papier-filtre *m*, LAB EQUIP, PAPER TECH papier-filtre *m*; ~ **pass band** *n* ELECTRON bande passante de filtre *f*; ~ **phase response** *n* ELECTRON réponse en phase de filtre *f*; ~ **pick-up** *n* INSTRUMENT logement de filtre *m*; ~ **plant** *n* WATER SUPP installation de filtrage *f*; ~ **plugging value** *n* CHEM TECH indice du bouchage de filtre *m*; ~ **pole** *n* ELECTRON pôle de filtre *m*; ~ **press** *n* C&G, CHEM TECH, COAL TECH filtre presse *m*, FOOD TECH presse à filtrer *f*, LAB EQUIP filtre presse *m*, presse-filtre *m*, PAPER TECH filtre presse *m*; ~ **press cloth** *n* CHEM TECH tissu filtrant *m*, tissu pour filtre *m*; ~ **pulp** *n* CHEM TECH masse filtrante *f*; ~ **pump** *n* LAB EQUIP trompe à eau à vide *f*; ~ **response** *n* ELECTRON réponse de filtre *f*; ~ **run** *n* NUCLEAR durée de service *f*; ~ **screen** *n* P&R *equipment, paint* filtre tressé *m*, PHOTO verre filtre *m*, PROD ENG crible à grille filtrante *m*, écran filtre *m*; ~ **section** *n* ELECTRON cellule de filtre *f*; ~ **set** *n* PHOTO jeu de filtres *m*; ~ **shaping** *n* ELECTRON mise en forme par filtre *f*; ~

siphon n CHEM TECH siphon à filtre m; ~ **slot** n CINEMAT fente pour filtre f; ~ **stuff** n CHEM TECH masse filtrante f; ~ **support** n LAB EQUIP support de filtre m; ~ **synthesis** n ELECTRON synthèse de filtre f; ~ **tank** n WATER SUPP bassin de filtration m; ~ **template** n SPACE gabarit de filtrage m, masque de filtrage m, gabarit de filtre m; ~ **thickener** n COAL TECH filtre épaississeur m; ~ **transmittance** n CHEM TECH transmission au travers de filtre f; ~ **turret** n PRINT disque porte-filtres m, tourelle des filtres f; ~ **well** n WATER SUPP puits filtrant m; ~ **zeros** n pl ELECTRON zéros de filtre m

filter² vt CHEM TECH clarifier, filtrer, passer au filtre, CONST, ELECTRON, PHOTO, RECYCLING filtrer; ~ **by suction** vt CHEM TECH filtrer par aspiration, filtrer à la trompe; ~ **out** vt CHEM TECH séparer par filtration

filterability n COAL TECH filtrabilité f

filter-and-sample: ~ **detector** n TELECOM détecteur à filtre et échantillonnage m

filtered: ~ **QPSK** n TELECOM maritime satellite MDPQ avec filtrage f

filtering n CHEM filtrage m, filtration f, CHEM TECH filtration f, COMP filtrage m, CONST criblage m, tamisage m, DP, ELECTRON, GEOL, TELECOM filtrage m; ~ **candle** n NUCLEAR bougie filtrante f; ~ **charcoal** n CHEM TECH charbon filtrant m, COAL TECH charbon à filtrer m; ~ **cone** n CHEM TECH cône à filtrer m; ~ **cup** n CHEM TECH vase à filtration m; ~ **facepiece for protection against particles** n SAFETY pièce faciale filtrante contre les particules f; ~ **flask** n CHEM TECH flacon à filtrer m; ~ **layer** n CHEM TECH lit filtrant m; ~ **limit** n CHEM TECH limite de filtrabilité f; ~ **plants for dust and fibres** n pl SAFETY textile industry systèmes de filtres pour poussières et fibres m pl; ~ **screen** n CHEM TECH filtre tamis m; ~ **unit** n POLLUTION élément filtrant m; ~ **well** n CHEM TECH puits filtrant m

filters: ~ **for photographic and visual operation** n pl ASTRON filtres pour l'observation visuelle et la photographie m pl

filtrate n CHEM filtrat m, CHEM TECH filtrat m, produit de filtrage m, produit filtré m, produit passé m, COAL TECH, RECYCLING filtrat m; ~ **loss** n PETR filtrat en eau libre m, perte de filtrat f, perte en eau libre f

filtration n CHEM filtrage m, filtration f, CONST filtrage m, filtration f, PAPER TECH, PETR TECH refining, geology, PROD ENG filtration f, RECYCLING filtrage m, filtration f; ~ **flask** n LAB EQUIP vase de filtration m; ~ **plant** n COAL TECH atelier de filtration m; ~ **tester** n PAPER TECH filtramètre m; ~ **vat** n WATER SUPP bac de filtration m, cuve de filtration f, cuve filtrante f

fin n C&G ailette f, MECH ailette f, nervure f, NAUT shipbuilding aileron m, NUCLEAR ailette f, nervure f, PROD ENG founding balcon m, balène f, balètre f, bavure f, ébarbure f, REFRIG ailette f; ~ **cooling** n NUCLEAR refroidissement par ailettes m; ~ **efficiency** n REFRIG rendement d'ailette m; ~ **keel** n NAUT shipbuilding aileron m; ~ **leading edge** n AERONAUT arête de dérive f; ~ **line** n PHYS ligne à ailette f; ~ **slot** n REFRIG rainure de fixation f; ~ **spar box** n AERONAUT caisson de dérive m; ~ **stub frame** n AERONAUT chapelle de structure f; ~ **stub top rib** n AERONAUT nervure de fermeture de chapelle f

final: ~ **amplification** n ELECTRON amplification de puissance f; ~ **amplifier** n ELECTRON amplificateur de puissance m; ~ **anode** n TV anode finale f; ~ **approach** n AERONAUT approche finale f; ~ **approach fix** n AERONAUT point d'approche finale m, repère d'approche

finale m; ~ **approach path** n AERONAUT trajectoire d'approche finale f; ~ **approach point** n AERONAUT point d'approche finale m, repère d'approche finale m; ~ **assembly** n NUCLEAR ensemble terminal m, PROD ENG atelier de montage final m; ~ **blanking** n TV postsuppression f; ~ **blow** n C&G soufflage final m; ~ **coat** n COLOURS couche de finition f, finition f, peinture de finition f; ~ **cut** n CINEMAT montage définitif m; ~ **design review** n (FDR) SPACE revue de définition finale f (RDF); ~ **drive** n AUTO couple final m, réduction finale f; ~ **fuel burn-up** n NUCLEAR combustion massique finale f; ~ **image tube** n INSTRUMENT fenêtre d'observation de l'image finale f, viseur de l'écran fluorescent m; ~ **inspection** n CONTROL, QUALITY contrôle final m; ~ **mix** n CINEMAT, RECORDING mixage définitif m; ~ **modulator** n ELECTRON modulateur final m; ~ **position setting** n NUCLEAR fin de course f, réglage de mise au point m; ~ **proof** n PRINT dernière épreuve f, épreuve tierce f; ~ **settling tank** n WATER SUPP décanteur secondaire m; ~ **shooting script** n CINEMAT découpage technique définitif m; ~ **treatment** n PACKAGING traitement final m; ~ **trial composite** n CINEMAT copie de présentation f; ~ **trial print** n CINEMAT copie standard avec étalonnage définitif f; ~ **trip assembly** n NUCLEAR dispositif terminal de déclenchement m

finally: ~ **galvanized coating** n COATINGS revêtement non retréfilé m, revêtement zingué non retréfilé m

financing n PETR TECH commerce financement m

find: ~ **one's bearings** vi CONST s'orienter

finder n ASTRON auxiliary telescope chercheur m, CINEMAT viseur m, INSTRUMENT chercheur m, PHOTO viewfinder for camera viseur m; ~ **hood** n PHOTO capuchon de visée m; ~ **point punch** n PROD ENG pointeau m, pointeau de mécanicien m

fine¹ adj PROP MAT free from impurity fin

fine:² ~ **on the bow** adv NAUT près de l'avant

fine:³ ~ **adjustment** n ELECTRON réglage fin m, INSTRUMENT bouton de déplacement lent m, bouton de mise au point précise m, vis micrométrique f, NUCLEAR réglage fin m, PROD ENG réglage de précision m, TV réglage fin m; ~ **aggregate** n CONST gravier fin m, gravier à grains fins m; ~ **batt** n TEXTILES nappage fin m; ~ **blanking die** n MECH ENG press tool outillage de découpage fin m; ~ **blanking press** n MECH ENG presse découpage fin f; ~ **castings** n pl (cf heavy castings) PROD ENG petites pièces f pl; ~ **coal** n COAL TECH charbon pulvérulent m; ~ **concentration mill** n PROD ENG ore atelier de travail des fines m; ~ **control** n NUCLEAR of reactor pilotage m, réglage m; ~ **control member** n NUCLEAR élément de contrôle fin m; ~ **control rod** n MECH ENG machine tool barre de pilotage f; ~ **count** n TEXTILES titre fin m; ~ **counts yarns** n pl TEXTILES filés fins m pl; ~ **cracks** n pl MECH ENG craquelures f pl; ~ **crusher** n PROD ENG broyeur des fins m; ~ **crushing** n COAL TECH concassage fin m, PROD ENG broyage fin m; ~ **crushing mill** n CHEM TECH broyeur à cylindres m; ~ **cut** n CINEMAT montage fin m; ~ **emery cloth** n MECH ENG toile émeri fine f; ~ **focus sleeve** n INSTRUMENT bague porte-oculaire f; ~ **furnace carbon black** n (FF carbon black) P&R rubber filler noir FF m; ~ **gage** n (AmE), ~ **gauge** n (BrE) TEXTILES jauge fine f; ~ **grain developer** n CINEMAT, PHOTO révélateur à grain fin m; ~ **gravel** n CONST gravillons m pl, menu gravier m; ~ **grinding** n COAL TECH broyage fin m; ~ **line** n ELECTRON element of *monolithic integrated circuit* trait fin *m*, *printed circuits* ruban étroit *m*, PRINT trait fin *m*; ~ **line printed circuit** *n* ELECTRON circuit imprimé à rubans étroits *m*; ~ **pitch** *n* AERONAUT *of propeller* petit pas *m*; ~ **pitch screw** *n* CONST vis à pas fin *f*; ~ **sand** *n* COAL TECH sable fin *m*, terrain de sable fin *m*, CONST sable fin *m*, sablon *m*, PETR sablon *m*; ~ **screen** *n* PRINT trame fine *f*, trame serrée *f*; ~ **screen halftone** *n* PRINT demi-teinte à trame fine *f*; ~ **silt** *n* GEOL limon fin *m*; ~ **slip** *n* METALL glissement fin *m*; ~ **soil** *n* COAL TECH sol à grains fins *m*; ~ **solder** *n* PROD ENG soudure grasse *f*; ~ **structure** *n* PHYS *spectroscopy*, RAD PHYS *atomic spectroscopy* structure fine *f*; ~ **structure constant** *n* PHYS constante de structure fine *f*; ~ **structure splitting** *n* NUCLEAR dédoublement de structure fine *m*; ~ **trommel** *n* PROD ENG trommel des fins *m*; ~ **tuning** *n* ELECTRON accord fin *m*, TELECOM mise au point *f*; ~ **worm drive** *n* MECH ENG transmission par vis sans fin précise *f*

fine-fluted *adj* MECH ENG *reamer* à fines rainures

fine-grain *n* METALL grain fin *m*; ~ **image** *n* PHOTO image à faible granulation *f*; ~ **master** *n* CINEMAT lavande *f*, marron *m*, positif grain fin pour contretype *m*

fine-grained[1] *adj* CINEMAT à grain fin, GEOL finement grenu, à grain fin, METALL, PROP MAT à grain fin

fine-grained:[2] ~ **wheel** *n* PROD ENG *emery* meule à grain fin *f*

finely-threaded: ~ **micrometer screw** *n* MECH ENG vis à pas couché de haute précision *f*

fineness *n* CONST *of sand*, NAUT *shipbuilding*, PAPER TECH finesse *f*; ~ **ratio** *n* AERONAUT *streamlined body* allongement *m*, rapport de finesse *m*, MECH ENG rapport de finesse *m*

finery *n* PROD ENG *for cast iron* affinerie *f*, mazerie *f*; ~ **furnace** *n* PROD ENG *for cast iron* affinerie *f*, mazerie *f*

fines *n pl* COAL TECH charbonnaille *f*, fins *m pl*, CONST *fine aggregate, sand* fines *f pl*, sable fin pour béton *m*, MINING *ore* fines *f pl*, fins *m pl*, PAPER TECH fines dans la pâte *f pl*

finesse *n* OPT, PHYS finesse *f*

fine-textured *adj* GEOL à grain fin

fine-time: ~ **based instruction** *n* PROD ENG instruction de temporisateur ultrarapide *f*

FINGAL: ~ **process** *n* NUCLEAR *of vitrification* procédé FINGAL *m*

finger *n* AERONAUT jetée *f*, MECH ENG doigt *m*, doigt de retenue *m*; ~ **action tool** *n* NUCLEAR *of manipulator* pince exécutant les actions des doigts *f*; ~ **bar** *n* MECH ENG doigt *m*, doigt de retenue *m*; ~ **grip clip** *n* AERONAUT lyre d'accrochage *f*; ~ **guide plate** *n* MECH ENG *machine tool* plaque de guidage *f*; ~ **nut** *n* CONST papillon *m*; ~ **plate** *n* CONST plaque de propreté *f*; ~ **post** *n* CONST poteau indicateur *m*; ~ **release** *n* PHOTO *of camera shutter* déclenchement au doigt *m*; ~ **stall** *n* SAFETY doigtier *m*

fingering *n* GEOL *of deposit, strata*, PETR digitation *f*

finial *n* CONST *roof ornament* épi *m*

fining: ~ **lap** *n* INSTRUMENT meule de finition *f*; ~ **period** *n* PROD ENG *Bessemer process* période des fumées *f*

finings *n* FOOD TECH colle de poisson *f*

fining-up: ~ **sequence** *n* GEOL séquence positive *f*

finish[1] *n* C&G bague *f*, COLOURS, MECH finition *f*, PAPER TECH apprêt *m*, fini *m*, PRINT fini *m*, PROD ENG fini *m*, finition *f*, TEXTILES *in relation to sizing* apprêt *m*

finish[2] *vt* PROD ENG achever, finir, TEXTILES finir

finished[1] *adj* FOOD TECH *fermentation* prêt au débit

finished:[2] ~ **appearance** *n* TEXTILES apparence soignée *f*;

~ **fabric** *n* TEXTILES tissu apprêté *m*; ~ **goods** *n* TEXTILES produits finis *m pl*; ~ **goods store** *n* PACKAGING magasin pour produits finis *m*; ~ **middlings** *n* COAL TECH mixtes définitifs *m pl*; ~ **product** *n* PROP MAT produit fini *m*; ~ **quartz** *n* ELECTRON lame complète *f*; ~ **width of cloth** *n* TEXTILES largeur finie *f*

finisher *n* CONST *public works* finisseur *m*; ~ **scutcher** *n* TEXTILES batteur finisseur *m*

finishing *n* C&G finissage *m*, PAPER TECH façonnage *m*, finissage *m*, PRINT finition *f*, *bookbinding* façonnage *m*, PROD ENG protection *f*; ~ **agent** *n* TEXTILES produit d'apprêt *m*; ~ **belt** *n* C&G bande finisseuse *f*; ~ **coat** *n* CONST *painting* dernière couche *f*, P&R *paint* peinture de finissage *f*, peinture définitive *f*; ~ **groove** *n* ACOUSTICS sillon final *m*; ~ **reamer** *n* MECH ENG alésoir de finition *m*; ~ **reamer for Morse tapers** *n* MECH ENG alésoir de finition pour cônes Morse *m*; ~ **sander** *n* MECH ENG *tool* ponceuse vibrante *f*; ~ **stage** *n* TEXTILES stade de finition *m*; ~ **techniques** *n* TEXTILES techniques d'ennoblissement *f pl*; ~ **varnish** *n* COATINGS vernis enduit *m*, COLOURS vernis de finition *m*

finite: ~ **and infinite ordinals** *n pl* GEOM nombres ordinaux finis et transfinis *m pl*; ~ **element** *n* MECH ENG élément limité *m*, PROP MAT élément fini *m*; ~ **element calculation method** *n* MECH méthode de calcul par éléments finis *f*; ~ **elements for mechanical engineering** *n pl* MECH ENG éléments finis pour le dessin mécanique *m pl*; ~ **elements methods** *n pl* MECH ENG *structural dynamics* méthodes des éléments finis *f pl*; ~ **element structural model** *n* SPACE *spacecraft* modèle de structure par éléments finis *m*; ~ **impulse response** *n (FIR)* ELECTRON réponse impulsionnelle finie *f*; ~ **impulse response filter** *n* ELECTRON filtre à réponse impulsionnelle finie *m*, TELECOM filtre à réponse impulsionnelle *m*, filtre à réponse infinie à une impulsion *m*; ~ **range interaction** *n* NUCLEAR interaction à portée finie *f*

finned: ~ **can** *n* NUCLEAR *fuel cladding* gaine à ailettes *f*; ~ **cooler** *n* THERMOD réfrigérant à ailettes *m*; ~ **heater** *n* THERMOD convecteur à ailettes *m*; ~ **radiator** *n* AUTO radiateur à ailettes *m*; ~ **surface** *n* HEAT ENG *heat exchangers* surface à lames *f*; ~ **tube** *n* MECH tube à ailettes *m*

fiorite: ~ **terrace** *n* GEOPHYS terrasse de travertin *f*

FIR[1] *abbr (finite impulse response)* ELECTRON réponse impulsionnelle finie *f*

FIR:[2] ~ **filter** *n* TELECOM filtre RIF *m*

fire[1] *n* GAS TECH inflammation *f*, SAFETY incendie *m*, THERMOD *blaze* feu *m*, incendie *m*; ~ **alarm** *n* CONTROL, ELEC, NAUT, SAFETY avertisseur d'incendie *m*, THERMOD alerte *f*; ~ **area** *n* NUCLEAR espace coupe-feu *m*; ~ **blanket** *n* SAFETY couverture d'incendie *f*; ~ **bridge** *n* PROD ENG *of furnace* autel *m*, pont *m*; ~ **bulkhead** *n* NAUT *ship design* cloison coupe-feu *f*, cloison pare-feu *f*, SPACE *spacecraft* cloison pare-feu *f*; ~ **cell** *n* NUCLEAR espace coupe-feu *m*; ~ **chamber** *n* HYDR EQUIP *steam boiler* chambre de combustion *f*, chambre à feu *f*, PROD ENG *of metallurgical furnace* chauffe *f*; ~ **control plan** *n* NAUT plan de lutte contre l'incendie *m*; ~ **correction** *n* MILIT rectification du tir *f*; ~ **curtain** *n* THERMOD rideau coupe-feu *m*; ~ **damage** *n* QUALITY dommage causé par le feu *m*, SAFETY dégâts d'incendie *m pl*; ~ **damper** *n* HEAT ENG *protection* clapet coupe-feu *m*; ~ **detecting wire** *n* AERONAUT faisceau de détection incendie *m*; ~ **detection and alarm system** *n* SAFETY système de détection d'incendie et d'alarme *m*;

~ **detection harness** *n* AERONAUT harnais pyrométrique *m*; ~ **detection loop** *n* SPACE *spacecraft* boucle de détection incendie *f*; ~ **detection system** *n* NAUT circuit de détection d'incendie *m*; ~ **detector** *n* CONTROL, SAFETY détecteur d'incendie *m*; ~ **door** *n* PROD ENG porte coupe-feu *f*, porte de foyer *f*, SAFETY porte anti-incendie *f*, THERMOD porte coupe-feu *f*; ~ **drill** *n* SAFETY exercice de sauvetage anti-incendie *m*, THERMOD exercice d'évacuation *m*; ~ **engine** *n* SAFETY pompe à incendie *f*, THERMOD fourgon-pompe *f*, pompe à feu *f*, pompe à incendie *f*; ~ **escape** *n* CONST appareil de sauvetage *m*, engin de sauvetage *m*, échelle de sauvetage *f*, SAFETY échelle de sauvetage *f*, THERMOD escalier de secours *m*; ~ **exit** *n* THERMOD sortie de secours *f*; ~ **extinguisher** *n* CONST, NAUT extincteur d'incendie *m*, SAFETY bouteille extincteur *f*, extincteur d'incendie *m*, THERMOD extincteur *m*; ~ **extinguisher fillings** *n pl* SAFETY matières de remplissage des extincteurs *f pl*; ~ **finish** *n* C&G poli au feu *m*; ~ **finisher** *n* C&G rebrûleuse *f*; ~ **grate** *n* PROD ENG grille de foyer *f*; ~ **hazard** *n* AERONAUT danger d'incendie *m*, SAFETY, THERMOD danger d'incendie *m*, risque d'incendie *m*; ~ **hole** *n* PROD ENG *of furnace* orifice de chauffe *m*; ~ **hose** *n* CONST, SAFETY tuyau d'incendie *m*, THERMOD tuyau souple d'incendie *m*; ~ **hose coupling** *n* SAFETY manchon pour tuyau d'incendie *m*; ~ **hose nozzle** *n* SAFETY bec de diffuseur anti-incendie *m*, bec de tuyaux d'incendie *m*, lance anti-incendie *f*; ~ **hose reel** *n* SAFETY dévidoir de tuyaux d'incendie *m*; ~ **hydrant** *n* CONST, NAUT, SAFETY bouche d'incendie *f*, THERMOD bouche d'incendie *f*, prise d'eau à incendie *f*; ~ **ladder** *n* CONST échelle de sauvetage *f*, SAFETY échelle de sauvetage *f*, échelle à incendie *f*; ~ **lamp** *n* PROD ENG *for skin-drying* poêle à flamber *m*; ~ **load** *n* THERMOD charge calorifique *f*, charge d'incendie *f*; ~ **lobby** *n* THERMOD sas coupe-feu *m*, sas d'incendie *m*; ~ **marks** *n pl* C&G marques de feu *f pl*; ~ **monitor** *n* MAR POLL lance canon *f*, lance monitor *f*, lance tourelle *f*; ~ **point** *n* REFRIG point d'inflammation *m*, point de feu *m*, SAFETY robinet d'incendie *m*; ~ **polishing** *n* C&G rebrûlage *m*; ~ **post** *n* SAFETY poste d'incendie *m*; ~ **precautions** *n pl* SAFETY précautions contre l'incendie *f pl*; ~ **prevention** *n* SAFETY ignifugation *f*, mesures de sécurité contre l'incendie *f pl*, THERMOD prévention incendie *f*; ~ **protection** *n* SAFETY protection contre l'incendie *f*; ~ **protection door** *n* SAFETY porte ignifugée *f*; ~ **protection gate** *n* SAFETY portail ignifugé *m*; ~ **protection plan** *n* SAFETY plan de protection contre l'incendie *m*; ~ **pump** *n* CONST pompe d'incendie *f*, pompe à feu *f*, SAFETY, THERMOD pompe d'incendie *f*; ~ **regulations** *n pl* SAFETY consignes en cas d'incendie *f pl*; ~ **rescue appliance** *n* SAFETY engin de sauvetage *m*, équipement de sauvetage anti-incendie *m*; ~ **rescue path** *n* AERONAUT *firefighting* trouée d'évacuation *f*; ~ **research** *n* SAFETY étude d'incendie *f*; ~ **resistance** *n* P&R résistance au feu *f*, tenue au feu *f*; ~ **riser** *n* THERMOD conduite ascendante pour les bouches d'incendie *f*; ~ **rising main** *n* THERMOD conduite ascendante pour les bouches d'incendie *f*; ~ **room** *n* PROD ENG *of blast furnace* cuve *f*, vide *m*; ~ **safety** *n* MILIT sûreté du tir *f*, SAFETY *in building* sécurité anti-incendie *f*; ~ **safety signs** *n pl* SAFETY signes de sécurité contre l'incendie *m pl*; ~ **screen** *n* PROD ENG écran *m*, écran ignifuge *m*, SAFETY pare-feu *m*, écran ignifuge *m*; ~ **siren** *n* SAFETY sirène d'incendie *f*; ~ **spread prevention** *n* SAFETY

mesure de sécurité contre la propagation d'incendie *f*; ~ **sprinkler** *n* SAFETY appareil d'arrosage *m*, diffuseur anti-incendie *m*, sprinkler *m*; ~ **stop** *n* THERMOD mur coupe-feu *m*; ~ **test** *n* SAFETY contrôle d'inflammabilité *m*; ~ **tube** *n* NUCLEAR tube de fumée *m*, tube-foyer *m*; ~ **valve** *n* MECH ENG bouche d'incendie *f*; ~ **wall** *n* AERONAUT cloison pare-feu *f*, tôle pare-feu *f*, PETR TECH *safety* mur coupe-feu *m*, SPACE *spacecraft* cloison pare-feu *f*; ~ **wire** *n* AERONAUT cordon détecteur d'incendie *m*, détecteur à fil continu *m*

fire^2 *vt* C&G cuire, FOOD TECH brûler; ~ **over** *vt* C&G chauffer à vide; ~ **up** *vt* THERMOD *boiler* allumer, s'échauffer, *glass* attremper

fire:^{3} ~ **a blank** *vi* MILIT tirer à blanc

fireboat *n* NAUT bateau-pompe *m*

firebox *n* HEATING boîte à feu *f*, RAIL *vehicles* foyer *m*, THERMOD boîte à feu *f*, *locomotive* chambre de combustion *f*, foyer *m*; ~ **tube plate** *n* RAIL *vehicles* plaque tubulaire de foyer *f*

firebreak *n* THERMOD *forestry* pare-feu *m*; ~ **glass** *n* SAFETY verre coupe-feu *m*

firebrick *n* C&G, CONST, HEATING, PROP MAT *construction* brique réfractaire *f*, THERMOD brique de chamotte *f*, brique réfractaire *f*

fireclay *n* C&G, GEOL argile réfractaire *f*, THERMOD argile réfractaire *f*, chamotte *f*; ~ **brick** *n* LAB EQUIP *furnace* brique en argile à feu *f*; ~ **crucible** *n* C&G creuset en terre réfractaire *m*; ~ **mold** *n* (AmE), ~ **mould** *n* (BrE) C&G casette *f*

fired: ~ **clay** *n* C&G argile cuite *f*; ~ **earthenware** *n* C&G terre cuite *f*; ~ **pressure vessel** *n* MECH ENG réservoir à pression cuit *m*; ~ **tube** *n* ELECTRON tube amorcé *m*; **under** ~ **furnace** *n* C&G four à brûleurs dans le siège *m*

firedamp *n* COAL TECH, MINING grisou *m*, THERMOD gaz de mines *m*, grisou *m*, méthane *m*

firedamp-proof: ~ **machine** *n* COAL TECH machine pour atmosphère grisouteuse *f*

firedog *n* HEATING chenet *m*

fired-on *adj* C&G vitrifié

fire-extinguishing: ~ **agent** *n* SAFETY agent extincteur d'incendie *m*

firefighting *n* CONST lutte anti-incendie *f*, SAFETY, THERMOD lutte contre l'incendie *f*; ~ **axe** *n* SAFETY hache pour combattre l'incendie *f*; ~ **equipment** *n* SAFETY équipement de lutte contre l'incendie *m*; ~ **personnel** *n* SAFETY personnel anti-incendie *m*; ~ **team** *n* SAFETY équipe pour combattre l'incendie *f*; ~ **vehicle** *n* SAFETY véhicule pour combattre l'incendie *m*

fireguard *n* THERMOD garde-feu *f*

firelight *n* THERMOD lueur du feu *f*

firelighter *n* HEAT ENG allume-feu *m*

firelock *n* THERMOD sas coupe-feu *m*, sas d'incendie *m*

fire-polished^1 *adj* C&G poli au feu

fire-polished:^{2} ~ **edge** *n* C&G bord rebrûlé *m*

fireproof^1 *adj* AERONAUT antidéflagrant, ELEC *material, equipment* ignifuge, résistant au feu, *safety* antidéflagrant, antigrisouteux, MECH coupe-feu, à l'épreuve du feu, PACKAGING incombustible, PROD ENG ignifuge, incombustible, à l'épreuve du feu, SAFETY antidéflagrant, pare-feu, résistant aux flammes, ignifugé, ininflammable, résistant au feu, à l'épreuve du feu, THERMOD antidéflagrant, incombustible, ininflammable, réfractaire, résistant aux flammes, à l'épreuve du feu

fireproof:^{2} ~ **bulkhead** *n* AERONAUT, SPACE cloison pare-feu *f*; ~ **clothing** *n* SAFETY vêtements antiflamme *m pl*;

~ **coat** *n* COLOURS peinture anti-incendie *f*; ~ **coating** *n* P&R *paint* peinture anti-incendie *f*, peinture ignifuge *f*, peinture incombustible *f*; ~ **color** *n* (AmE), ~ **colour** *n* (BrE) COLOURS couleur résistant au feu *f*; ~ **drilling machine** *n* MINING perforatrice antidéflagrante *f*; ~ **enclosure** *n* SAFETY enceinte pare-feu *f*; ~ **floor** *n* SAFETY plancher incombustible *m*; ~ **glass** *n* C&G verre pare-flamme *m*; ~ **lighting installation** *n* (AmE) *(cf flameproof lighting installation)* ELEC luminaire antidéflagrant *m*; ~ **motor** *n* ELEC ENG moteur antigrisouteux *m*, THERMOD moteur antidéflagrant *m*; ~ **paint** *n* COLOURS peinture anti-incendie *f*; ~ **pottery** *n* C&G objet en terre réfractaire *m*; ~ **stirrer** *n* LAB EQUIP *mixing* agitateur antidéflagrant *m*; ~ **telephone system** *n* CONST réseau téléphonique ignifuge *m*

fireproof[3] *vt* SAFETY ignifuger, THERMOD ignifuger, rendre à l'épreuve de feu

fireproofed *adj* THERMOD ignifugé

fireproofing *n* THERMOD ignifugeage *m*; ~ **paint** *n* COLOURS peinture incombustible *f*

fire-resistant[1] *adj* HEATING réfractaire, PROD ENG ignifuge, ignifugé, SAFETY ignifugé, THERMOD ignifuge, résistant au feu

fire-resistant:[2] ~ **bulkhead** *n* THERMOD cloison coupe-feu *f*, cloison d'incendie *f*; ~ **coating** *n* COATINGS couche coupe-feu *f*, couche résistante au feu *f*, enduit coupe-feu *m*, enduit résistant au feu *m*, THERMOD *for steel beams* enduit pare-feu *m*, revêtement ignifuge *m*, revêtement pare-feu *m*; ~ **door** *n* SAFETY porte coupe-feu *f*; ~ **layer** *n* COATINGS couche ignifuge *f*; ~ **paint** *n* COLOURS peinture anti-incendie *f*, THERMOD peinture anti-incendie *f*, peinture ignifuge *f*, peinture incombustible *f*, peinture pare-feu *f*; ~ **paper** *n* PAPER TECH papier ignifugé *m*

fire-resisting[1] *adj* THERMOD ignifuge, résistant au feu

fire-resisting:[2] ~ **bulkhead** *n* THERMOD cloison coupe-feu *f*, cloison d'incendie *f*; ~ **coating** *n* THERMOD *steel beams* enduit pare-feu *m*, revêtement ignifuge *m*, revêtement pare-feu *m*; ~ **paint** *n* THERMOD peinture anti-incendie *f*, peinture ignifuge *f*, peinture incombustible *f*, peinture pare-feu *f*

fire-retardant[1] *adj* P&R *paint, plastics, rubber* antifeu, ignifuge, PROD ENG ignifuge

fire-retardant:[2] ~ **coat** *n* NUCLEAR *surface layer* revêtement coupe-feu *m*

fire-retarding *adj* THERMOD ignifuge

fireseal *n* AERONAUT joint ignifuge *m*

fireship *n* THERMOD bateau-feu *m*

firestone *n* C&G pierre à feu *f*

firetrap *n* SAFETY souricière en cas d'incendie *f*

fire-tube: ~ **boiler** *n* HEATING *multi-tubular* chaudière à tubes de fumée *f*

firing *n* C&G cuisson *f*, ELEC ENG *drying of hybrid circuit* cuisson *f*, *of gas tube, thyristor, triac* amorçage *m*, *of reactor* basculement *m*, ELECTRON *of magnetron* excitation par une impulsion *f*, *of thick-film hybrid circuits* cuisson *f*, MINING allumage *m*, mise à feu *f*, SPACE mise à feu *f*; ~ **circuit** *n* MINING circuit de tir *m*; ~ **on** *n* C&G cuisson *f*; ~ **order** *n* VEHICLES *of engine* ordre d'allumage *m*; ~ **pin** *n* MILIT *of grenade* percuteur *m*; ~ **pulse** *n* ELEC ENG *of gas tube, thyristor, triac* impulsion d'amorçage *f*; ~ **range** *n* C&G intervalle de cuisson *m*; ~ **temperature** *n* C&G température de cuisson *f*; ~ **test** *n* SPACE essai de mise à fin *m*; ~ **time** *n* ELEC ENG *of gas tube, thyristor, triac* instant d'amorçage *m*; ~ **voltage** *n* ELEC ENG *of gas tube, thyristor, triac* tension d'amor-

çage *f*; ~ **window** *n* SPACE fenêtre de lancement *f*

firkin *n* FOOD TECH demi-petit fût *m*

firm[1] *adj* TEXTILES ferme

firm:[2] ~ **allocation** *n* PROD ENG affectation ferme *f*; ~ **capacity** *n* NUCLEAR puissance garantie *f*; ~ **ground** *n* CONST terrain ferme *m*; ~ **handle** *n* TEXTILES toucher ferme *m*

firmer: ~ **gouge** *n* MECH ENG *tool* gouge de sculpteur *f*

firmly: ~ **set fabric** *n* TEXTILES tissu serré *m*

firm-planned *adj* PROD ENG planifié ferme

firmware *n* COMP micrologiciel *m*, PRINT software spécifique existant sous une forme hardware *m*; ~ **chip set** *n* PROD ENG jeu de microprogrammes *m*

first: ~ **aid** *n* SAFETY premiers secours *m pl*, secours d'urgence *m pl*; ~ **aider** *n* SAFETY *person* secouriste *m*; ~ **anode** *n* ELEC ENG première anode *f*; ~ **answer print** *n* CINEMAT copie "0" *f*, copie zéro *f*; ~ **arrivals** *n pl* GEOL premières arrivées *f pl*; ~ **article configuration review** *n (FACR)* SPACE revue de conformité du premier article *f*; ~ **assembly** *n* CINEMAT montage bout à bout *m*, premier montage *m*; ~ **choice group** *n* TELECOM *circuit* faisceau de premier choix *m*; ~ **coat** *n* COLOURS peinture primaire *f*; ~ **condenser lens** *n* INSTRUMENT lentille de condenseur *f*; ~ **connection to grid** *n* NUCLEAR *mains* premier raccordement au réseau *m*; ~ **critical experiment** *n* NUCLEAR première divergence *f*; ~ **criticality** *n* NUCLEAR criticité initiale *f*; ~ **degree burn** *n* SAFETY brûlure au premier degré *f*; ~ **detector** *n* ELECTRON changeur de fréquence *m*; ~ **divergence** *n* NUCLEAR première divergence *f*; ~ **dogwatch** *n* MILIT premier petit quart *m*; ~ **down ink** *n* PRINT encre du premier groupe *f*, encre qui s'imprime *f*; ~ **dryer** *n* PAPER TECH *dryer felt* embarqueur *m*; ~ **firing** *n* C&G première cuisson *f*; ~ **flight neutron** *n* NUCLEAR neutron vierge *m*; ~ **generation** *n* COMP, DP première génération *f*; ~ **generation computer** *n* COMP, DP ordinateur de première génération *m*; ~ **harmonic** *n* ELECTRON harmonique 1 *m*, premier harmonique *m*; ~ **IF amplifier** *n* ELECTRON amplificateur à première fréquence intermédiaire *m*, premier amplificateur à fréquence intermédiaire *m*; ~ **injection** *n* ELECTRON première injection *f*; ~ **intermediate frequency** *n* ELECTRON première fréquence intermédiaire *f*; ~ **ionization potential** *n* PHYS potentiel de première ionisation *m*; ~ **law** *n* PHYS *of thermodynamics* premier principe de la thermodynamique *m*; ~ **local oscillator** *n* ELECTRON premier oscillateur local *m*; ~ **mate** *n* NAUT *merchant navy* officier en second *m*, second *m*; ~ **mixer** *n* ELECTRON premier changeur de fréquence *m*; ~ **nearest neighbours** *n* METALL premiers voisins *m pl*; ~ **officer** *n* NAUT officier en second *m*, second *m*; ~ **order filter** *n* ELECTRON filtre du premier ordre *m*; ~ **oxidizing print** *n* C&G première cuisson *f*; ~ **pair of rollers** *n* C&G rubicon *m*; ~ **quarter** *n* ASTRON premier quartier *m*; ~ **runnings** *n pl* FOOD TECH *fermentation* produit de tête *m*, têtes *f pl*; ~ **trial composite** *n* CINEMAT première copie standard *f*; ~ **unit** *n* CINEMAT équipe principale *f*; ~ **watch** *n* MILIT premier quart *m*; ~ **window fiber** *n* (AmE), ~ **window fibre** *n* (BrE) *(FWF)* OPT fibre à 0,85mm *f*

first-aid: ~ **box** *n* SAFETY boîte de pansement *f*, trousse de premiers secours *f*; ~ **cabinet** *n* SAFETY armoire de premier secours *f*, armoire sanitaire *f*; ~ **course** *n pl* SAFETY cours de secourisme *m pl*; ~ **kit** *n* SAFETY trousse de premiers secours *f*; ~ **post** *n* NAUT poste de premier secours *m*; ~ **procedure** *n* SAFETY procédure de premier secours *f*, traitement de secours d'urgence *m*; ~ **treatment room** *n* SAFETY poste de premier secours *m*; ~ **work** *n* SAFETY premiers secours *m pl*

first-in: ~ **first-out** *n (FIFO)* COMP, DP *premier entré premier sorti m (PEPS)*

first-order: ~ **quantity** *n* GEOM quantité du premier ordre *f*; ~ **reaction** *n* CHEM, METALL réaction du premier ordre *f*; ~ **transition** *n* PHYS transition du premier ordre *f*

first-stage: ~ **planet gear** *n* AERONAUT *helicopter* planétaire primaire *m*; ~ **sun gear** *n* AERONAUT couronne mobile de réduction *f*

first-time: ~ **inspection** *n* CONTROL contrôle en première inspection *m*

firth *n* NAUT *geography* bras de mer *m*

fisetin *n* CHEM fisétin *m*

fish *n* PETR TECH poisson *m*; ~ **basket** *n* OCEANOG bourriche *f*; ~ **breeding** *n* (AmE) *(cf fish farming)* FOOD TECH, OCEANOG pisciculture *f*; ~ **corral** *n* OCEANOG bordigue *f*; ~ **detector** *n* OCEANOG détecteur *m*; ~ **farmer** *n* OCEANOG alevinier *m*; ~ **farming** *n* (BrE) *(cf fish breeding)* FOOD TECH, OCEANOG pisciculture *f*; ~ **filleting** *n* OCEANOG filetage *m*; ~ **finder** *n* OCEANOG loupe à poisson *f*; ~ **gig** *n* OCEANOG foène *f*; ~ **glue** *n* PRINT colle-émail *f*; ~ **meal** *n* OCEANOG farine de poisson *f*; ~ **meal fishery** *n* OCEANOG pêche minotière *f*; ~ **oil** *n* CHEM huile de poisson *f*; ~ **paper** *n* ELEC ENG fibre vulcanisée *f*; ~ **pass** *n* FUELLESS passe à poisson *f*; ~ **pond** *n* OCEANOG parc *m*; ~ **protein concentrate** *n (FPC)* OCEANOG concentré de protéines de poisson *m (CPP)*; ~ **scope** *n* OCEANOG loupe à poisson *f*; ~ **smoking** *n* OCEANOG fumage de poisson *m*; ~ **stock** *n* OCEANOG stock *m*; ~ **tank** *n* OCEANOG vivier *m*; ~ **trade** *n* NAUT, OCEANOG mareyage *m*

fisher: ~ **boom** *n* CINEMAT perchette *f*; ~ **science** *n* OCEANOG halieutique *f*

fisherman's: ~ **bend** *n* NAUT *knot* noeud d'orin *m*, noeud de pêcheur *m*; ~ **needle** *n* OCEANOG *fishing gear* aiguille à filet *f*, navette *f*

fishery *n* NAUT lieu de pêche *m*, pêcherie *f*, OCEANOG *industry* chasse *f*, pêche *f*, *place* pêcherie *f*; ~ **conservation zone** *n* OCEANOG cantonnement de pêche *m*, conserverie *f*; ~ **protection vessel** *n* NAUT garde-pêche *m*, OCEANOG vedette garde-pêche *f*; ~ **reserve** *n* OCEANOG cantonnement de pêche *m*, conserverie *f*; ~ **science** *n* OCEANOG halieutique *f*

fish-eye: ~ **lens** *n* CINEMAT objectif fish-eye *m*, objectif ultra grand angle *m*, PHOTO objectif fish-eye *m*

fishing *n* OCEANOG chasse *f*, pêche *f*, PETR, PETR TECH *for lost object* repêchage *m*; ~ **boat** *n* NAUT barque de pêcheur *f*, bateau de pêche *m*; ~ **drift** *n* NAUT *net* filet traînant *m*; ~ **drift net** *n* NAUT filet traînant *m*; ~ **efficiency** *n* OCEANOG efficacité de pêche *f*; ~ **effort** *n* OCEANOG effort de pêche *m*; ~ **expert** *n* OCEANOG halieutiste *m*; ~ **fleet** *n* NAUT flottille de pêche *f*; ~ **gear** *n* OCEANOG engin de pêche *m*, train de pêche *m*; ~ **ground** *n* NAUT lieu de pêche *m*, pêcherie *f*; ~ **net** *n* OCEANOG filet *m*, filet de pêche *m*; ~ **patrol boat** *n* OCEANOG vedette garde-pêche *f*; ~ **port** *n* NAUT port de pêche *m*; ~ **power** *n* OCEANOG capacité de pêche *f*, puissance de pêche *f*; ~ **pressure** *n* OCEANOG pression de pêche *f*; ~ **rights** *n pl* NAUT droits de pêche *m pl*; ~ **smack** *n* NAUT barque de pêche *f*, bateau de pêche *m*; ~ **socket** *n* PETR TECH *for retrieving lost objects* souricière *f*; ~ **tool** *n* PETR TECH *for retrieving lost objects* outil de repêchage *m*; ~ **trip** *n* OCEANOG campagne de

pêche *f*; ~ **vessel** *n* NAUT, OCEANOG navire de pêche *m*; ~ **zone** *n* OCEANOG zone de pêche *f*

fishnet *n* TEXTILES filet de pêche *m*

fishplate *n* (BrE) *(cf joint bar)* RAIL éclisse *f*; ~ **block** *n* RAIL *track* entretoise-éclisse *f*

fishplating *n* (BrE) *(cf applying of joint bars)* RAIL éclissage *m*

fishpole: ~ **boom** *n* CINEMAT perchette *f*

fishtail: ~ **bit** *n* PETR TECH trépan en queue de poisson *m*

fissile[1] *adj* PHYS fissile

fissile[2] *n* NUCLEAR fissile *m*; ~ **inventory ratio** *n* NUCLEAR *fissile fuel in core at startup* rapport d'inventaire fissile *m*; ~ **isotope** *n* PHYS isotope fissile *m*; ~ **material** *n* RAD PHYS matière fissile *f*

fission: ~ **cross-section** *n* PHYS section efficace de fission *f*; ~ **fragments** *n pl* PHYS fragments de fission *m pl*; ~ **gas plenum** *n* NUCLEAR *in fuel element* chambre d'accumulation des gaz de fission *f*; ~ **ionization chamber** *n* NUCLEAR *for slow neutrons* chambre d'ionisation à fission *f*; ~ **neutron** *n* RAD PHYS neutron de fission *m*; ~ **recoil** *n* NUCLEAR recul à la fission *m*; ~ **spike** *n* NUCLEAR *radiation damage* pointe de fission *f*; ~ **track dating** *n* GEOL, PHYS datation par traces de fission *f*

fissionable *adj* PHYS fissionnable

fissium *n* NUCLEAR fissium *m*

fissure *n* CONST fissure *f*, GEOPHYS crevasse *f*, fissure *f*, OCEANOG *iceberg* crevasse *f*; ~ **water** *n* COAL TECH eau de fissure *f*

fissured: ~ **acoustic tile** *n* RECORDING panneau acoustique *m*

fist *n* PRINT vignette typographique représentant une main *f*

fit[1] *n* MECH ENG montage *m*, PRINT registre *m*

fit[2] *vt* C&G réunir, CONST *two beams one into the other* enclaver, MECH adapter, ajuster, monter, MECH ENG adapter, agencer, ajuster, monter, *lid to box* ajuster, *nozzle on end of pipe* adapter, *one part into another* emboîter, NAUT *parts on ship or boat* installer, monter; ~ **in** *vt* MECH ENG emboîter, enclaver; ~ **into** *vt* MECH ENG emboîter, enclaver; ~ **out** *vt* MECH ENG outiller, équiper, NAUT *ship* accastiller, armer, PRODUCTION outiller, équiper; ~ **with** *vt* MECH ENG garnir de, munir de, pourvoir de

fit[3] *vi* MECH ENG aller, s'adapter, s'agencer, s'ajuster, se monter; ~ **in** *vi* MECH ENG s'emboîter, s'enclaver; ~ **together** *vi* GEOM s'emboîter

FITE *abbr (forward interworking telephony event)* TELECOM événement téléphonique d'interfonctionnement vers l'avant *m*

fitments *n pl* MECH ENG garniture *f*, garnitures *f pl*

fits: ~ **and clearances** *n pl* MECH ENG jeux de montage *m pl*

fitted: ~ **with** *adj* TELECOM doté de

fitter *n* MECH *person* ajusteur *m*, monteur *m*, MECH ENG *person* ajusteur *m*, ajusteur-monteur *m*, monteur *m*, mécanicien ajusteur *m*, mécanicien constructeur *m*

fitter's: ~ **hammer** *n* MECH ENG marteau d'ajusteur *m*

fitting *n* MECH accessoire *m*, raccord *m*, MECH ENG accessoire *m*, embout *m*, adaptation *f*, agencement *m*, ajustage *m*, montage *m*, monture *f*, *of one piece into another* emboîtement *m*, NAUT *shipbuilding* fixation *f*, montage *m*; ~ **bolt** *n* MECH ENG axe de fixation *m*; ~ **device** *n* MECH ENG appareil d'ajustage *m*, appareil de montage *m*; ~ **dimensions** *n pl* MECH ENG dimensions d'interchangeabilité *f pl*; ~ **shop** *n* MECH ENG atelier d'ajustage *m*; ~ **stand** *n* NUCLEAR support de montage *m*

fitting-out *n* CONST équipement *m*, NAUT *of ship* armement *m*, équipement *m*; ~ **berth** *n* NAUT quai d'armement *m*

fittings *n pl* CONST agencements *m pl*, MECH ENG accessoires *m pl*, appareillage *m*, appareils *m pl*, ferrures *f pl*, garniture *f*, garnitures *f pl*, montures *f pl*, organes accessoires *m pl*, NAUT *of ship* accastillage *m*, PROD ENG raccorderie *f*

five-axis: ~ **numerical control** *n* MECH ENG commande numérique à cinq axes *f*

five-layer: ~ **barrier film laminate** *n* PACKAGING film barrière stratifié en cinq couches *m*

five-legged: ~ **transformer** *n* ELEC transformateur à cinq colonnes *m*

five-sided: ~ **broach** *n* MECH ENG alésoir à cinq pans *m*, équarrissoir à cinq pans *m*

fix[1] *n* NAUT *navigation* point observé *m*, SPACE *spacecraft* point *m*

fix[2] *vt* CONST ancrer, arrêter, assujettir, caler, emmancher, fixer, poser, *beam* assujettir, *floor joist to wall* ancrer, *lock* poser, MECH ENG *piston firmly on rod* emmancher, PAPER TECH fixer

fixed[1] *adj* MECH fixe, stationnaire

fixed:[2] ~ **amplitude** *n* ELECTRON amplitude constante *f*; ~ **angle sounding** *n* OCEANOG sondage par segments capables *m*; ~ **armature** *n* ELEC *generator, motor* induit fixe *m*; ~ **attenuator** *n* ELECTRON atténuateur fixe *m*; ~ **base notation** *n* COMP numération à base fixe *f*, DP notation à base fixe *f*; ~ **beacon** *n* NAUT *navigation mark* balise fixe *f*; ~ **beam** *n* CONST *strength of materials* poutre encastrée *f*; ~ **caliper** *n* (AmE), **calliper** *n* (BrE) AUTO étrier fixe *m*; ~ **capacitor** *n* ELEC ENG, PHYS condensateur fixe *m*; ~ **carbon** *n* CHEM carbone fixe *m*; ~ **coil** *n* ELEC bobine fixe *f*; ~ **command control** *n* CONTROL réglage de valeur fixe *m*, régulation de maintien *f*; ~ **contact** *n* ELEC *relay*, ELEC ENG contact fixe *m*; ~ **data processing terminal equipment** *n* TELECOM ETTD-F, équipement terminal de traitement de données fixe *m*; ~ **delay** *n* ELEC *of relay switch* délai constant *m*; ~ **delivery pump** *n* PROD ENG pompe à débit fixe *f*; ~ **disk** *n* COMP, DP disque fixe *m*; ~ **displacement motor** *n* PROD ENG moteur à cylindrée fixe *m*; ~ **distance lights** *n pl* AERONAUT *airport* feux de distance constante *m pl*; ~ **end moment** *n* CONST moment d'encastrement *m*; ~ **equipment** *n* CONST équipement fixe *m*; ~ **error on radio altimeter** *n* AERONAUT marche altimétrique *f*; ~ **field** *n* COMP, DP champ fixe *m*; ~ **fire extinguisher** *n* SAFETY *built-in* extincteur d'incendie encastré *m*; ~ **focus** *n* PHOTO foyer fixe *m*, mise au point fixe *f*; ~ **focus camera** *n* PHOTO appareil à mise au point fixe *m*; ~ **focus lens** *n* CINEMAT objectif à mise au point fixe *m*, PHOTO objectif à foyer fixe *m*; ~ **format** *n* COMP, DP format fixe *m*; ~ **frequency magnetron** *n* ELECTRON magnétron non accordable *m*, magnétron à fréquence fixe *m*; ~ **frequency oscillator** *n* ELECTRON oscillateur non accordable *m*, oscillateur à fréquence fixe *m*; ~ **frequency synthesizer** *n* ELECTRON synthétiseur à fréquence fixe *m*; ~ **gain filter** *n* ELECTRON filtre à gain fixe *m*; ~ **gain filtering** *n* ELECTRON filtrage par filtre à gain fixe *m*; ~ **generator** *n* SPACE *spacecraft* générateur fixe *m*; ~ **grate** *n* HEATING grille fixe *f*; ~ **guard** *n* SAFETY protection fixe *f*; ~ **head** *n* COMP, DP tête fixe *f*; ~ **length** *n* COMP, DP longueur fixe *f*; ~ **length block** *n* COMP, DP bloc de longueur fixe *m*; ~

length record *n* COMP, DP enregistrement de longueur fixe *m*; ~ **lift** *n* MINING jeu fixe *m*, jeu posé *m*; ~ **light** *n* NAUT *navigation marks* feu fixe *m*; ~ **load** *n* ELEC ENG charge fixe *f*; ~ **loop** *n* SPRINGS oeil fixe *m*; ~ **loss** *n* ELEC *of machine* composante constante de pertes *f*; ~ **oil** *n* CHEM huile fixe *f*; ~ **order quantity** *n* PROD ENG quantité fixe de réapprovisionnement *f*; ~ **pitch propeller** *n* AERONAUT hélice à pas fixe *f*; ~ **plant** *n* PROD ENG matériel fixe *m*; ~ **point** *n* CONST point de repère *m*, point fixe *m*, DP, TELECOM virgule fixe *f*; ~ **point arithmetic** *n* COMP, DP arithmétique en virgule fixe *f*; ~ **point net** *n* NUCLEAR grille de points fixes *f*; ~ **point notation** *n* DP notation en virgule fixe *f*; ~ **point part** *n* DP mantisse *f*; ~ **pole** *n* ELEC *of motor* pôle fixe *m*; ~ **radix notation** *n* DP notation à base fixe *f*; ~ **reflector radio telescope** *n* ASTRON radiotélescope à antenne fixe *m*; ~ **resistor** *n* ELEC, ELEC ENG, PHYS résistance fixe *f*; ~ **ring gear** *n* AERONAUT couronne fixe de réducteur *f*; ~ **roller sluice gate** *n* FUELLESS vanne à roues fixes *f*; ~ **satellite service** *n* (*FSS*) SPACE service fixe par satellite *m*; ~ **sequencer** *n* TELECOM séquenceur fixe *m*; ~ **set** *n* MINING jeu fixe *m*, jeu posé *m*; ~ **sieve jig** *n* PROD ENG bac à piston *m*, crible hydraulique à piston *m*, crible à grille fixe *m*, crible à piston *m*; ~ **spindle circular saw bench** *n* PROD ENG scie circulaire à axe fixe *f*; ~ **stator vane** *n* AERONAUT aube fixe de stator *f*; ~ **steady rest** *n* MECH ENG *of lathe* lunette fixe *f*; ~ **stick stability** *n* AERONAUT stabilité manche bloqué *f*; ~ **stinger** *n* PETR rampe fixée *f*; ~ **stop** *n* MECH ENG butée fixe *f*; ~ **table** *n* C&G *in mirror-making* table fixe *f*; ~ **target experiment** *n* PART PHYS expérience avec cible fixe *f*; ~ **tuned cavity resonator** *n* ELECTRON cavité résonnante à accord fixe *f*; ~ **tuning** *n* ELECTRON accord fixe *m*; ~ **wheel** *n* MECH ENG *fast on axle* roue calée *f*, roue fixe *f*; ~ **wing** *n* AERONAUT voilure fixe *f*; ~ **wing aircraft** *n* AERONAUT avion à voilure fixe *m*; ~ **word length** *n* COMP, DP longueur de mot fixe *f*; ~ **word length computer** *n* COMP, DP ordinateur à mots de longueur fixe *m*

fixer *n* CINEMAT bain de fixage *m*, fixateur *m*

fixing *n* GAS TECH fixation *f*, MECH ENG ancrage *m*, calage *m*, emmanchement *m*, fixage *m*, pose *f*; ~ **agent** *n* PAPER TECH fixatif *m*; ~ **bath** *n* CINEMAT bain de fixage *m*; ~ **screw** *n* CONST, MECH ENG vis de fixation *f*; ~ **thread** *n* PHOTO pas de vis de fixation *m*

fixture *n* MECH ENG *fixed member* pièce fixe *f*, pièce à demeure *f*, *machine tools* montage *m*, METR *for testing and gauging* montage *m*

fixtures *n pl* MECH ENG fixations *f pl*; ~ **and fittings** *n pl* CONST agencements *m pl*

Fizeau: ~ **fringes** *n pl* PHYS franges de Fizeau *f pl*

fjord *n* NAUT, OCEANOG fiord *m*, fjord *m*

flag[1] *n* CINEMAT drapeau *m*, nègre *m*, volet *m*, COMP drapeau *m*, CONST *paving stone* dalle *f*, DP drapeau *m*, GEOL dalle *f*, NAUT drapeau *m*, pavillon *m*, PRINT balise *f*, drapeau code *m*; ~ **bit** *n* COMP, DP bit indicateur *m*, PROD ENG bit interne *m*; ~ **build** *n* C&G anneau de relance *m*; ~ **captain** *n* NAUT *navy* commandant d'un navire amiral *m*; ~ **of convenience** *n* NAUT pavillon de complaisance *m*; ~ **officer** *n* NAUT *navy* officier général *m*; ~ **signal** *n* NAUT *communications* signal à pavillon *m*; ~ **switch** *n* CONTROL interrupteur actionné par tige *m*; ~ **window** *n* AERONAUT fenêtre sur instruments *f*

flag[2] *vt* COMP, DP signaler

flagging *n* CONST dallage *m*, TV distorsion de l'image *f*

flagship *n* NAUT *navy* navire amiral *m*

flagstaff *n* NAUT mât de pavillon *m*

flagstone *n* CONST, GEOL dalle *f*; ~ **pavement** *n* CONST dallage *m*, pavé en dalles *m*

flake[1] *n* GEOL copeau *m*, PRINT flocon *m*, écaille *f*, PROP MAT paillette *f*; ~ **glass** *n* C&G paillette de verre *f*

flake[2] *vt* NAUT *rope* lover

flake[3] *vi* PAPER TECH se diviser en lamelles

flaked: ~ **rail** *n* RAIL rail exfolié *m*

flakiness: ~ **index** *n* CONST coefficient d'écaillement *m*

flaking *n* PAPER TECH arrachage *m*, PRINT arrachage *m*, écaille *f*, PROP MAT *peeling* écaillement *m*

flaky: ~ **arsenic** *n* C&G anhydride arsénieux *m*

flame[1] *n* CHEM, SAFETY, THERMOD flamme *f*; ~ **arc** *n* ELEC ENG arc de flammes *m*; ~ **arrester** *n* CONST *welding* arrêt de flamme *m*, PETR TECH *safety* coupe-flamme *m*, SPACE pare-flamme *m*; ~ **attenuation** *n* C&G étirage par la flamme *m*; ~ **bridge** *n* PROD ENG autel *m*, pont *m*; ~ **cleaning** *n* CONST *of surface* décapage aux gaz *m*, décapage par flamme *m*; ~ **control** *n* HEATING dispositif de contrôle de flamme *m*; ~ **cutter** *n* MECH chalumeau de coupe *m*; ~ **cutting** *n* CONST *welding* coupage à gaz *m*, MECH oxycoupage *m*, THERMOD découpage à la flamme *m*, oxycoupage *m*; ~ **cutting torch** *n* THERMOD *welding* chalumeau *m*; ~ **detector** *n* CONTROL, HEATING détecteur de flamme *m*; ~ **emission spectroscopy** *n* PHYS spectroscopie de flamme en émission *f*; ~ **failure** *n* THERMOD défaut de flamme *m*, extinction de flamme *f*; ~ **gouging** *n* CONST *welding* gougeage *m*; ~ **holder** *n* AERONAUT stabilisateur de flamme *m*; ~ **hydrolysis** *n* OPT hydrolyse à la flamme *f*; ~ **photometer** *n* LAB EQUIP *analysis* photomètre de flamme *m*; ~ **photometric detector** *n* POLLUTION détecteur photométrique à flamme *m*, détecteur à photométrie de flamme *m*; ~ **plate** *n* PROD ENG tôle de coup de feu *f*; ~ **projector** *n* MILIT lance-flammes *m*; ~ **spectroscopy** *n* THERMOD spectroscopie de flamme *f*; ~ **spectrum** *n* PHYS, THERMOD spectre de flamme *m*; ~ **spray coating** *n* COATINGS revêtement au pistolet à flamme *m*; ~ **spraying** *n* NUCLEAR projection à flamme *f*; ~ **thrower** *n* MILIT, THERMOD lance-flammes *m*; ~ **trap** *n* AERONAUT, SAFETY antiretour de flamme *m*, THERMOD dispositif antiretour de flamme *m*, VEHICLES *of engine* pare-étincelles *m*; ~ **tube** *n* NUCLEAR tube de fumée *m*, tube-foyer *m*, PROD ENG *of brazing lamp* tube brûleur *m*; ~ **welding** *n* P&R soudage à flamme *m*

flame:[2] ~ **harden** *vt* THERMOD tremper à flamme

flameout *n* SPACE extinction *f*, extinction accidentelle *f*, *spacecraft* arrêt par extinction *m*, THERMOD *gas turbines, burnout* extinction de flamme *f*

flameproof[1] *adj* AERONAUT antidéflagrant, ELEC *safety* antidéflagrant, antigrisouteux, SAFETY antidéflagrant, pare-feu, résistant aux flammes, THERMOD antidéflagrant, incombustible, ininflammable, réfractaire, résistant aux flammes, à l'épreuve du feu

flameproof:[2] ~ **clothing** *n* SAFETY vêtements antiflamme *m pl*; ~ **coat** *n* COATINGS couche protectrice anti-feu *f*; ~ **drilling machine** *n* MINING perforatrice antidéflagrante *f*; ~ **enclosure** *n* SAFETY enceinte pare-feu *f*; ~ **glass** *n* C&G verre pare-flamme *m*; ~ **lighting installation** *n* (BrE) (*cf fireproof lighting installation*) ELEC luminaire antidéflagrant *m*; ~ **motor** *n* ELEC ENG moteur antigrisouteux *m*, THERMOD moteur antidéflagrant *m*; ~ **stirrer** *n* LAB EQUIP *mixing* agitateur antidéflagrant *m*; ~ **switch** *n* ELEC *safety* interrupteur antidéflagrant *m*, interrupteur antigrisouteux *m*

flame-resistant *adj* AERONAUT ignifuge, incombustible, SAFETY incombustible

flame-retardant *n* P&R *paint, plastics, rubber* ignifuge *m*; ~ **conveyor belt** *n* MECH ENG courroie transporteuse résistant aux flammes *f*

flaming[1] *adj* THERMOD en flammes, enflammé, flambant

flaming:[2] ~ **coal** *n* COAL TECH charbon bitumineux *m*, charbon gras *m*, houille grasse *f*

flammability *n* AERONAUT, P&R, PACKAGING, SAFETY, THERMOD inflammabilité *f*

flammable[1] *adj* P&R, SAFETY, THERMOD *inflammable* inflammable

flammable:[2] ~ **atmosphere** *n* SAFETY atmosphère inflammable *f*; ~ **liquid** *n* SAFETY liquide inflammable *m*; ~ **material** *n* SAFETY matériel inflammable *m*; ~ **vapor** *n* (AmE), ~ **vapour** *n* (BrE) SAFETY vapeur inflammable *f*

flammé: ~ **yarn** *n* TEXTILES fil flammé *m*

flange[1] *n* ACOUSTICS, AUTO flasque *m*, CONST *of built-up girder* chapeau *m*, plate-bande *f*, *of girder* semelle *f*, ELEC *connection*, ELEC ENG bride *f*, LAB EQUIP *opening* rebord *m*, MAR POLL bride d'assemblage *f*, MECH bride *f*, collerette *f*, flasque *m*, MECH ENG boudin *m*, bride *f*, rebord *m*, flasque *m*, *of Archimedean screw* marche *f*, *of* barrel of winch joue *f*, PETR TECH *of pipelines* bride *f*, PROD ENG *of cylinder* bride *f*, *of flanged travelling wheel of runner of overhead* joue *f*, *of grooved pulley* mâchoire *f*, *of tube* bride *f*, collerette *f*, *sheet metal working* collet *m*, rebord *m*, SPACE bride d'assemblage *f*, collerette *f*, flasque *m*, TEXTILES disque *m*, VEHICLES *of wheel* bride *f*; ~ **coupling** *n* MECH ENG accouplement à plateaux *m*, manchon à plateaux *m*; ~ **cutout** *n* PROD ENG découpe de la plage de montage *f*; ~ **face** *n* PROD ENG face jointive *f*; ~ **joint** *n* MECH ENG assemblage à bride *m*, assemblage à bride boulonnée *m*, joint à boudin *m*, joint à bride *m*; ~ **motor** *n* ELEC moteur à bride *m*, MECH moteur électrique à bride *m*; ~ **mounting** *n* PROD ENG assemblage par brides *m*, SPACE montage à bride *m*; ~ **pipe** *n* CONST conduite à bride *f*, tuyau à bride *m*; ~ **plate** *n* CONST plaque à rebord *f*, *of built-up girder* chapeau *m*, plate-bande *f*, *plates of steel suitable for flanging* tôles pour bordages *f pl*, PROD ENG plaque de montage *f*; ~ **pulley** *n* MECH ENG poulie à joue *f*, poulie à rebord *f*; ~ **smoother** *n* PROD ENG *moulder's tool* lissoir à bride *m*; ~ **tile** *n* CONST tuile à rebord *f*; ~ **wheel** *n* MECH ENG roue à boudin *f*, roue à bourrelet *f*, roue à mentonnet *f*

flange[2] *vt* MECH ENG tomber, PROD ENG *plate* border, rabattre le bord de, *tube* rabattre la collerette de

flange:[3] ~ **up** *vi* PETR TECH *on pipeline* poser le dernier raccord

flanged[1] *adj* MECH à collerette

flanged:[2] ~ **ball valve** *n* MECH ENG robinet à tournant sphérique à bride *m*; ~ **bolt** *n* MECH ENG vis à collerette *f*; ~ **bottom** *n* C&G bavure au fond *f*; ~ **cap** *n* PACKAGING capsule bridée *f*; ~ **cast-iron pipe** *n* CONST tuyau de fonte à bride *m*; ~ **edge** *n* MECH ENG bord tombé *m*, PACKAGING bord bridé *m*; ~ **fitting** *n* MECH ENG *pipe fitting* tuyau à bride *m*; ~ **gear** *n* MECH ENG engrenage gardé *m*, engrenage à joues *m*, roue épaulée *f*, engrenage à bride *m*, engrenage à plateau *m*; ~ **guide** *n* MECH ENG palier de guidage *m*; ~ **nut** *n* MECH ENG écrou à collet *m*; ~ **pipeline** *n* MECH ENG *cast-iron pipeline* tuyauterie à bride *f*; ~ **press finish** *n* C&G bavure de bague *f*; ~ **pressure pipe** *n* MECH ENG tuyau de pression à bride *m*; ~ **shaft** *n* MECH ENG arbre bridé *m*, arbre à collerette *m*; ~ **tube radiator** *n* AUTO radiateur tubulaire *m*; ~ **union** *n* MECH ENG raccord à bride *m*

flangeless: ~ **brake block** *n* RAIL *vehicles* semelle de sabot de frein sans flasque *f*

flanger *n* PROD ENG machine à border *f*, presse à border *f*, presse à emboutir *f*

flange-to-rail: ~ **clearance** *n* RAIL jeu de boudins *m*

flanging *n* PROD ENG bordage *m*, façonnage de brides *m*, PROP MAT bordage *m*; ~ **machine** *n* PACKAGING emboutisseuse *f*, PROD ENG presse à border *f*, presse à emboutir *f*, *working by revolving mechanism* machine à border *f*; ~ **press** *n* PROD ENG presse à sertir *f*, *working by pressure* presse à border *f*, presse à emboutir *f*; ~ **test** *n* PROD ENG *for tube* essai de rabattement *m*

flank *n* CONST *of arch* rein *m*, MECH *gears* flanc *m*; ~ **gear** *n* MECH ENG engrenage à flanc *m*; ~ **wall** *n* CONST mur en retour *m*

flap *n* AERONAUT volet de courbure *m*, volet hypersustentateur *m*, *aircraft* volet *m*, CONST abattant *m*, trappe *f*, MECH volet *m*, MECH ENG portillon *m*, NUCLEAR *of valve* clapet de soupape *m*, PACKAGING volet *m*, PAPER TECH *of envelope* patte *f*, SPACE *spacecraft* volet *m*, TEXTILES *covering of seam* bavette *f*, *of pocket* rabat *m*; ~ **attenuator** *n* ELECTRON atténuateur à lame *m*; ~ **door** *n* CONST porte à rabat *f*; ~ **gate** *n* FUELLESS, HYDROL vanne basculante *f*; ~ **hinge** *n* CONST briquet *m*; ~ **jack** *n* AERONAUT vérin à bille des volets *m*; ~ **roller carriage** *n* AERONAUT chariot de guidage volets *m*; ~ **snap** *n* PACKAGING fermeture de volet *f*; ~ **track rib** *n* AERONAUT nervure de glissière *f*, nervure glissière *f*; ~ **valve** *n* HYDR EQUIP clapet *m*, soupape à clapet *f*, MECH ENG clapet *m*; ~ **valve pump** *n* PROD ENG pompe à clapet *f*; ~ **wheel with shaft** *n* MECH ENG *coated with abrasive* roue à lamelles sur tige *f*

flapping *n* AERONAUT *of helicopter* battement *m*, battement vertical *m*; ~ **angle** *n* AERONAUT angle battant *m*, angle de basculement *m*, angle debattement *m*, angle de levée de pale *m*; ~ **hinge** *n* AERONAUT *of helicopter* articulation de battement *f*; ~ **hinge pin** *n* AERONAUT *of helicopter* axe de battement *m*, axe de levée de pale *m*; ~ **moment** *n* AERONAUT *of helicopter* moment de battement *m*; ~ **stress peak** *n* AERONAUT *of helicopter* pointe de contrainte en battement *f*

flare[1] *n* AERONAUT fusée éclairante *f*, ASTRON éclat *m*, CINEMAT lumière parasite *f*, reflet *m*, MILIT fusée éclairante *f*, NAUT *emergency equipment at bow* dévers *m*, fumigène *m*, PETR TECH *of platform, refinery* torche *f*, PROD ENG *flaring enlargement* évasement *m*; ~ **pistol** *n* MILIT pistolet à fusée éclairante *m*; ~ **spot** *n* CINEMAT tache lumineuse *f*; ~ **stack** *n* PETR TECH torchère *f*; ~ **star** *n* ASTRON étoile à sursauts *f*

flare[2] *vt* PROD ENG épanouir, TEXTILES évaser

flare:[3] ~ **up** *vi* THERMOD *blaze up* s'embraser, s'enflammer

flared[1] *adj* MECH, TEXTILES évasé

flared:[2] ~ **end** *n* C&G bord évasé *m*; ~ **landing** *n* AERONAUT atterrissage en arrondi *m*; ~ **neck** *n* C&G évasement du col *m*; ~ **section** *n* SPACE *spacecraft* divergent *m*; ~ **tube** *n* PROD ENG tube épanoui *m*

flare-out *n* AERONAUT arrondi *m*

flaring[1] *adj* PROD ENG *opening outward* évasé

flaring[2] *n* C&G évasement *m*, PETR TECH brûlage à la torchère *m*, PROD ENG *enlargement* évasement *m*

flash[1] *n* C&G couche de doublage *f*, CINEMAT flash *m*, séquence brève *f*, éclair *m*, MINING flash *m*, P&R *moulding* bavure *f*, cordon de bavure *m*, PHOTO flash *m*,

lampe flash *f*, lampe-éclair électronique *f*, PRINT flash *m*, éclair *m*, PROD ENG *formed between two parts of mould* toile *f*; ~ **analog-to-digital conversion** *n* (AmE) *see flash analogue-to-digital conversion* ~ **analog-to-digital converter** *n* (AmE) *see flash analogue-to-digital converter* ~ **analogue-to-digital conversion** *n* (BrE) ELECTRON numérisation parallèle *f*; ~ **analogue-to-digital converter** *n* (BrE) ELECTRON numériseur parallèle *m*; ~ **bar** *n* PHOTO barrette flash *f*; ~ **boiler** *n* HYDR EQUIP chaudière à vaporisation instantanée *f*, THERMOD chaudière à évaporation rapide *f*; ~ **bulb** *n* PHOTO ampoule de flash *f*; ~ **contact** *n* PHOTO prise de flash *f*; ~ **conversion** *n* ELECTRON conversion parallèle *f*; ~ **converter** *n* ELECTRON convertisseur parallèle *m*; ~ **cube** *n* PHOTO cube-flash *m*; ~ **cutting** *n* CINEMAT montage rapide *m*; ~ **distillation** *n* CHEM distillation éclair *f*, FOOD TECH distillation flash *f*, THERMOD distillation flash *f*, distillation à détentes multiples *f*, WATER SUPP distillation instantanée *f*; ~ **drum** *n* MECH *process* ballon de détente *m*; ~ **duration** *n* PHOTO délai médian *m*; ~ **evaporation** *n* FOOD TECH évaporation flash *f*, évaporation instantanée *f*, évaporation éclair *f*, NUCLEAR évaporation par détente *f*, évaporation éclair *f*; ~ **exposure** *n* PRINT exposition au flash *f*, exposition secondaire *f*; ~ **fire** *n* THERMOD incendie instantané *m*; ~ **flood** *n* HYDROL crue subite *f*; ~ **frame** *n* CINEMAT image blanche *f*, première image du plan *f*; ~ **gas** *n* REFRIG vapeur instantanée *f*; ~ **heating** *n* FOOD TECH chauffage rapide *m*; ~ **mold** *n* (AmE), ~ **mould** *n* (BrE) P&R *moulding* moule à échappement *m*; ~ **pan** *n* CINEMAT pano filé *m*; ~ **photolysis** *n* CHEM photolyse flash *f*; ~ **point** *n* AUTO température d'inflammation *f*, CHEM point d'inflammation *m*, point d'éclair *m*, FOOD TECH point d'inflammabilité *m*, HEAT ENG *temperature* point d'inflammation *m*, NAUT *of oil* point d'ignition *m*, point d'inflammabilité *m*, P&R, PETR TECH point d'éclair *m*, PHYS, REFRIG, THERMOD point d'inflammation *m*, point d'éclair *m*; ~ **point apparatus** *n* LAB EQUIP *flammable liquids* appareil de mesure du point d'éclair *m*; ~ **ruby** *n* C&G rubis par réchauffement *m*; ~ **shoe** *n* PHOTO griffe-support pour lampe flash *f*; ~ **socket for F and X contact** *n* PHOTO prise de flash F et X *f*; ~ **subcooling** *n* NUCLEAR surrefroidissement flash *m*; ~ **switch** *n* PHOTO commutateur de flash *m*; ~ **test** *n* ELEC ENG essai de claquage *m*; ~ **tester** *n* MECH ENG boîte de claquage *f*; ~ **tube** *n* ELECTRON tube flash *m*, tube à éclair *m*; ~ **undercooling** *n* NUCLEAR surrefroidissement flash *m*; ~ **welding** *n* CONST soudage par résistance par étincelage *m*, soudage par étincelage *m*, PROD ENG soudage par étincelage *m*

flash:[2] ~ **harden** *vt* THERMOD *metal* tremper sélectivement; ~ **over** *vt* THERMOD *electricity* claquer, cracher

flashback *n* CINEMAT retour en arrière *m*, CONST *welding* retour de flamme *m*, THERMOD *welding* retour de flamme *m*, soudage de flamme *m*; ~ **preventer** *n* SAFETY *valve* fusible sec contre le retour de flamme *m*

flashboard *n* WATER SUPP *of dam or sluice gate* hausse *f*

flashed: ~ **glass** *n* (BrE) *(cf overlay)* C&G verre doublé *m*; ~ **opal** *n* C&G verre doublé à l'opale *m*

flasher *n* ELEC *automotive* lampe clignotante *f*, HYDR EQUIP chaudière à vaporisation instantanée *f*, VEHICLES *accessory* clignotant *m*, clignoteur *m*

flashing *n* (BrE) *(cf overlaying)* C&G doublage *m*, CINEMAT flashage *m*, latensification *f*, postlumination *f*, ELEC ENG formation d'un arc *f*, PHOTO postlumination *f*, prélumination *f*; ~ **knob** *n* C&G ballotte *f*; ~ **light** *n*

NAUT *navigation marks* feu à éclat *m*, SAFETY lampe d'alarme clignotante *f*; ~ **light signal** *n* CONTROL signal à éclat lumineux *m*; ~ **signal** *n* NAUT *light* signal à éclats *m*; ~ **warning light** *n* AUTO lampe-témoin clignotante *f*

flashlight *n* ELEC, ELEC ENG lampe de poche *f*, MECH *tools* lampe-torche *f*, PHOTO lumière-éclair *f*

flash-off *n* PRINT évaporation des solvants à la limite de l'ignition *f*

flashover *n* ELEC *of electrode* contournement *m*, ELEC ENG amorçage *m*, contournement *m*, décharge en surface *f*, THERMOD *electricity* claquage *m*, contournement *m*; ~ **voltage** *n* ELEC ENG tension de contournement *f*

flashstage: ~ **cooler** *n* REFRIG refroidisseur intermédiaire à détente *m*

flask *n* C&G flacon *m*, CHEM ampoule *f*, ampoule de laboratoire *f*, ballon *m*, fiole *f*, flacon *m*, FOOD TECH ballon *m*, flacon *m*, LAB EQUIP *glassware* ballon *m*, *narrow-necked* flacon *m*, *wide mouth* flacon *m*, PROD ENG *moulding* châssis *m*, châssis de fonderie *m*, châssis de moulage *m*; ~ **molding** *n* (AmE), ~ **moulding** *n* (BrE) PROD ENG moulage en châssis *m*; ~ **pin** *n* MECH ENG goujon de châssis *m*; ~ **with molded neck** *n* (AmE), ~ **with moulded neck** *n* (BrE) LAB EQUIP *glassware* flacon à col moulé *m*

flat[1] *adj* CONST méplat, plan, plat

flat[2] *n* ACOUSTICS bémol *m*, CINEMAT manquant de contraste, paroi mobile *f*, MECH méplat *m*, plat *m*, OCEANOG platain *m*, platin *m*, PRINT film monté *m*, plat d'un livre *m*; ~ **amplifier** *n* ELECTRON amplificateur à courbe de réponse plate *m*; ~ **and fitted width** *n* TEXTILES largeur en drap à plat et en contours *f*; ~ **and self-tapping screw** *n* MECH ENG vis taraudeuse à bout plat *f*; ~ **angle** *n* GEOM angle plat *m*; ~ **antenna** *n* TELECOM antenne plane *f*; ~ **arch** *n* CONST plate-bande *f*, voûte plate *f*; ~ **back** *n* PRINT dos carré *m*; ~ **back stoping method** *n* MINING méthode en long *f*; ~ **band-pass filter** *n* ELECTRON filtre à large bande *m*; ~ **battery** *n* TELECOM pile épuisée *f*; ~ **belt drive** *n* MECH ENG transmission à courroie plate *f*; ~ **box** *n* PAPER TECH caisse aspirante *f*; ~ **brush** *n* COLOURS brosse à badigeon *f*, pinceau à badigeon *m*, queue de morue *f*; ~ **cable** *n* ELEC câble plat *m*, méplat *m*, ELEC ENG câble en nappe *m*, câble plat *m*; ~ **canvas hose** *n* SAFETY *firefighting* tuyau d'incendie à toile plate *m*; ~ **car** *n* (AmE) (*cf flat-bed wagon, flat wagon*) RAIL *vehicles* wagon plat *m*, TRANSP *rail* wagon plat *m*, wagon à ranchers *m*; ~ **car with side stakes** *n* (AmE) (*cf flat wagon with side stakes*) TRANSP wagon à ranchers *m*; ~ **chipping chiesel** *n* PRODUCTION burin à froid *m*; ~ **chisel** *n* MECH ENG *engineer's* burin *m*, ciseau à froid *m*, MINING *boring* trépan plat *m*, trépan simple *m*; ~ **cold chisel** *n* MECH ENG, PROD ENG burin à froid *m*, ciseau à froid *m*; ~ **color** *n* (AmE), ~ **colour** *n* (BrE) C&G couleur vitrifiable simple *f*; ~ **countersunk rivet** *n* PROD ENG rivet à tête noyée *m*, rivet à tête perdue *m*; ~ **crush resistance** *n* PRINT résistance à l'écrasement *f*; ~ **curve** *n* GEOM courbe aplatie *f*, courbe à grand rayon *f*; ~ **drill** *n* MECH ENG *arrow-headed* foret à langue d'aspic *m*, mèche plate *f*; ~ **edge** *n* C&G joint plat *m*; ~ **edge and bevel** *n* C&G biseau marbre *m*; ~ **ejector pin** *n* MECH ENG éjecteur lame *m*; ~ **engine** *n* AUTO moteur plat *m*, VEHICLES moteur plat *m*, moteur à cylindres opposés à plat *m*; ~ **etching** *n* PRINT gravure chimique du point *f*; ~ **facet** *n* C&G côte plate *f*; ~ **flame burner** *n* LAB EQUIP

heating bec papillon *m*; ~ **form** *n* PRINT liasse sans papier carbone *f*; ~ **formation** *n* ELEC *cable configuration* disposition en nappe *f*; ~ **frequency response** *n* RECORDING réponse uniforme en fréquence *f*; ~ **gasket** *n* NUCLEAR garniture *f*; ~ **glass** *n* C&G verre plat *m*; ~ **knitting** *n* TEXTILES tricotage rectiligne *m*; ~ **knitting machine** *n* TEXTILES métier rectiligne *m*; ~ **lens** *n* INSTRUMENT verre plat à facettes *m*; ~ **lighting** *n* CINEMAT éclairage plat *m*, éclairage sans relief *m*, éclairage uniforme *m*, PHOTO éclairage plat *m*; ~ **mirror** *n* INSTRUMENT miroir plan *m*; ~ **optical tool** *n* C&G plan *m*; ~ **pack** *n* ELECTRON boîtier plat *m*, PACKAGING emballage plié *m*; ~ **pack form** *n* PRINT liasse pliée en zigzag *f*; ~ **packing gasket** *n* NUCLEAR garniture *f*; ~ **paint** *n* COLOURS peinture mate *f*; ~ **pallet** *n* PACKAGING palette plate *f*; ~ **panel display** *n* ELECTRON affichage par panneau *m*, panneau d'affichage plat *m*; ~ **plate** *n* FLUID PHYS plaque plane *f*; ~ **plate collector** *n* FUELLESS *solar power* panneau capteur plat *m*; ~ **pleat** *n* TEXTILES pli couché *m*; ~ **radiator** *n* HEATING radiateur panneau *m*; ~ **rammer** *n* PROD ENG *founding* batte-plate *f*; ~ **relay** *n* ELEC ENG relais extra-plat *m*; ~ **response** *n* ELECTRON réponse uniforme *f*, RECORDING réponse linéaire *f*, réponse uniforme *f*; ~ **response motor** *n* ELEC moteur à caractéristique shunt *m*; ~ **ring dynamo** *n* ELEC *generator* dynamo à anneau plat *f*; ~ **rod** *n* MECH ENG barre de renvoi *f*, tige de transmission *f*; ~ **running wheel** *n* MECH ENG *of runner of overhead travelling wheel* galet plein *m*; ~ **screen** *n* COMP, DP écran plat *m*, PRINT tamis plat *m*, TELECOM, TV écran plat *m*; ~ **screening** *n* PRINT fond tramé simple sans dégradé *m*; ~ **shelf** *n* OCEANOG banc *m*; ~ **spin** *n* AERONAUT vrille à plat *f*; ~ **spot** *n* PRINT *paper* plat sur la bobine qui la fait tourner faux-rond *m*; ~ **spring** *n* SPRINGS ressort plat *m*; ~ **stern** *n* NAUT *boatbuilding* arrière plat *m*; ~ **surface** *n* INSTRUMENT facette plate *f*; ~ **tile** *n* C&G tuile plate *f*; ~ **tint** *n* PRINT grisé mécanique *m*, à-plat *m*; ~ **tire** *n* (AmE) *see flat tyre*; ~ **top** *n* NAUT porte-avions *m*; ~ **topping** *n* PETR saturation numérique *f*, écrêtage numérique *m*; ~ **trajectory** *n* MILIT *artillery* trajectoire horizontale *f*; ~ **transmission belt** *n* MECH ENG courroie plate de transmission *f*; ~ **turn** *n* AERONAUT virage dérapé *m*, virage à plat *m*; ~ **twin** *n* TRANSP bicylindre à plat *m*; ~ **twin engine** *n* AUTO moteur à deux cylindres opposés à plat *m*; ~ **tyre** *n* (BrE) VEHICLES pneu crevé *m*, pneu à plat *m*, pneumatique crevé *m*, pneumatique à plat *m*; ~ **wagon** *n* (BrE) (*cf flat-bed car, flat car*) RAIL *vehicles* wagon plat *m*, TRANSP *rail* wagon plat *m*, wagon à ranchers *m*; ~ **wagon with side stakes** *n* (BrE) (*cf flat car with side stakes*) TRANSP wagon à ranchers *m*; ~ **washer** *n* MECH ENG rondelle plate *f*; ~ **wire** *n* ELEC fil méplat *m*; ~ **yarn** *n* TEXTILES fil plat *m*

flat-bed: ~ **car** *n* (AmE) (*cf flat-bed wagon, flat wagon*) RAIL *vehicles* wagon plat *m*; ~ **cylinder press** *n* PRINT presse à plat *f*; ~ **editing table** *n* CINEMAT table de montage horizontale *f*; ~ **plotter** *n* COMP, DP traceur à plat *m*; ~ **press** *n* PRINT machine à plat *f*; ~ **proofing press** *n* PRINT presse à épreuve à plat *f*; ~ **scanner** *n* COMP, DP scanner à plat *m*; ~ **wagon** *n* (BrE) (*cf flat-bed car, flat car*) RAIL *vehicles* wagon plat *m*

flat-bottomed[1] *adj* NAUT *boat* à fond plat

flat-bottomed:[2] ~ **etch pit** *n* METALL figure d'attaque à fond plat *f*, point d'émergence tronqué *m*; ~ **flask** *n* LAB EQUIP *glassware* ballon à fond plat *m*; ~ **tappet** *n* AUTO poussoir à plateau *m*

flat-crested: ~ **weir** *n* HYDR EQUIP déversoir sur seuil *m*, déversoir à crête épaisse *m*

flat-end: ~ **sack** *n* PACKAGING sac avec extrémité plate *m*

flat-four: ~ **engine** *n* TRANSP moteur quatre cylindres à plat *m*

flat-grinding: ~ **machine** *n* C&G machine à côtes plates *f*

flat-head: ~ **bolt** *n* MECH ENG boulon à tête plate *m*; ~ **screwdriver** *n* PROD ENG tournevis à tête plate *m*

flatness *n* PAPER TECH *of paper* à plat *m*, PROD ENG planéité *f*; ~ **quality** *n* MECH ENG *of measuring faces* qualité de planéité *f*; ~ **tolerance** *n* MECH ENG tolérance de planéité *f*

flat-nose: ~ **pliers** *n pl* MECH ENG pince plate *f*, PROD ENG bec de cane *m*, pince plate *f*, pinces à becs plats *f pl*

flat-nosed: ~ **pliers** *n pl* MECH ENG pince plate *f*, PROD ENG bec de cane *m*, pince plate *f*, pinces à becs plats *f pl*

flat-rate: ~ **fee** *n* PATENTS taxe forfaitaire *f*; ~ **service** *n* TELECOM service à tarif fixe *m*; ~ **tariff** *n* ELEC *consumption* simple tarif *m*

flats *n pl* C&G méplats *m pl*

flat-sheet: ~ **delivery** *n* PRINT sortie à plat *f*

flatted: ~ **parallel shank tool** *n* MECH ENG outil à queue cylindrique à méplat *m*

flattened: ~ **disc of stars** *n* (BrE) ASTRON disque aplati des étoiles *m*; ~ **disk of stars** *n* (AmE) *see flattened disc of stars*

flattening *n* C&G aplatissage *m*, *of cylinder* étendage *m*, GEOL aplanissement *m*, PROD ENG écrasement *m*, PROP MAT polissage *m*, VEHICLES *tyre* aplatissement *m* ~ **kiln** *n* C&G four à étendre *m*; ~ **table** *n* C&G lagre *m*; ~ **test** *n* PHYS essai d'aplatissement *m*; ~ **tool** *n* C&G polissoir *m*

flatter *n* C&G fletteur *m*, PROD ENG *flatting hammer* aplatissoir *m*

flatting *n* C&G flettage *m*; ~ **mill** *n* PROD ENG aplatisserie *f*, laminerie *f*, *machine* aplatissoir *m*, RAIL laminoir *m*; ~ **pigment** *n* P&R *paint* pigment de lissage *m*; ~ **varnish** *n* COATINGS vernis flatting *m*, vernis à poncer *m*, CO-LOURS vernis à poncer *m*; ~ **works** *n pl* PROD ENG aplatisserie *f*, laminerie *f*

flat-top: ~ **chain** *n* MECH ENG *for conveyor* chaîne charnière *f*; ~ **culvert** *n* CONST dalot *m*

flavan *n* CHEM flavane *m*

flavanone *n* CHEM flavanone *f*

flavin *n* CHEM flavine *f*

flavone *n* CHEM, FOOD TECH flavone *f*

flavonoid *n* FOOD TECH flavonoïde *f*

flavonol *n* CHEM flavonol *m*

flavoprotein *n* FOOD TECH flavoprotéine *f*

flavopurpurin *n* CHEM flavopurpurine *f*

flavor[1] *n* (AmE) *see flavour*

flavor[2] *vt* (AmE) *see flavour*

flavoring *n* (AmE) *see flavouring*

flavour[1] *n* (BrE) FOOD TECH arôme *m*, produit aromatique *m*, saveur *f* ~ **enhancer** *n* (BrE) FOOD TECH rehausseur de saveur *m*, releveur de goût *m*; ~ **potentiator** *n* (BrE) FOOD TECH exhausteur d'arôme *m*; ~ **of quark** *n* PART PHYS saveur de quark *f*

flavour[2] *vt* (BrE) FOOD TECH aromatiser

flavouring *n* (BrE) FOOD TECH arôme *m*, produit aromatique *m*

flaw *n* MECH *materials* défaut *m*, NUCLEAR défaut *m*, défectuosité *f*, *of material* caverne cavité *f*, PAPER TECH défaut du papier *m*, QUALITY défaut *m*

flawless *adj* PAPER TECH sans défaut

F-layer *n* GEOPHYS, PHYS couche F *f*, couche d'Appleton *f*

fleam: ~ **tooth** *n* MECH ENG *of saw* dent droite *f*

fleam-tooth: ~ **saw** *n* MECH ENG dent droite *f*

fleating *n* MAR POLL barrage flottant *m*

fleet *n* NAUT escadre *f*, flotte *f*, RAIL *vehicles* parc voiture *m*, parc wagons *m*, TRANSP parc *m*, *aircraft, ships* flotte *f*; ~ **admiral** *n* NAUT *navy* amiral d'escadre *m*; ~ **weight** *n* AERONAUT masse flotille *f*, masse moyenne *f*

Fleet: ~ **Air Arm** *n* (BrE) *(cf Naval Air Service)* NAUT *Royal Navy* Aéronavale *f*

Fleming's: ~ **rules** *n pl* ELEC *electromagnetism* règles de Fleming *f pl*

flesh: ~ **side** *n (cf grain side)* PROD ENG *of belt* côté chair *m*

fleuron *n* PRINT marque de l'imprimeur *f*, ornement *m*, vignette *f*

flex *n* ELEC ENG fil souple *m*

flexi: ~ **arm** *n* CINEMAT bras articulé *m*

flexibility *n* NAUT flexibilité *f*, élasticité *f*, P&R, TEXTILES flexibilité *f*; ~ **factor** *n* MECH ENG facteur de flexibilité *m*; ~ **strength** *n* TELECOM tenue à la flexion *f*

flexible[1] *adj* TEXTILES flexible

flexible:[2] ~ **access switch** *n (FAS)* TELECOM commutateur à accès flexible *m*; ~ **cable** *n* ELEC câble souple *m*, ELEC ENG câble flexible *m*; ~ **conductor** *n* ELEC *cable* âme souple *f*, ELEC ENG conducteur flexible *m*; ~ **connection** *n* RAIL *vehicles* flexible *m*; ~ **construction** *n* CONST *roads* surfaçage souple *m*; ~ **control** *n* MECH ENG commande flexible *f*, commande téléflex *f*, téléflex *m*; ~ **coupling** *n* MECH ENG accouplement flexible *m*, raccord flexible *m*, accouplement élastique *m*, manchon d'accouplement élastique *m*, manchon élastique *m*; ~ **disk** *n* COMP, DP disque souple *m*; ~ **drive** *n* MECH entraînement par flexible *m*; ~ **drive shaft** *n* MECH ENG flexible d'entraînement *m*; ~ **ducting** *n* CONST gaines souples *f pl*; ~ **gasket** *n* MECH ENG garniture flexible *f*; ~ **hose** *n* CONST tuyau souple *m*, MAR POLL flexible *m*; ~ **hose connection** *n* MINING raccordement du flexible *m*; ~ **hose coupling** *n* MINING raccordement du flexible *m*; ~ **hose union** *n* MINING raccordement du flexible *m*; ~ **joint** *n* MECH ENG joint flexible *m*; ~ **metal conduit** *n* MECH ENG gaine métallique souple *f*; ~ **metallic hose** *n* MECH ENG tuyau métallique flexible *m*; ~ **mounting** *n* MECH ENG silentbloc *m*; ~ **oil storage tank** *n* MILIT réservoir flexible pour carburant *m*; ~ **package** *n* PACKAGING conserve souple *f*; ~ **packaging** *n* PRINT emballage souple *m*; ~ **packaging machine** *n* PACKAGING machine pour emballage flexible *f*; ~ **pipe** *n* MECH ENG conduite souple *f*, tuyauterie souple *f*; ~ **printed circuit** *n* ELECTRON circuit imprimé souple *m*, circuit imprimé à substrat souple *m*, circuit souple *m*; ~ **reflector** *n* SPACE *spacecraft* réflecteur souple *m*; ~ **resistor** *n* ELEC ENG résistance flexible *f*; ~ **rotor balance** *n* MECH ENG équilibrage des rotors flexibles *m*; ~ **shaft** *n* MECH ENG arbre flexible *m*, flexible *m*, transmission flexible *f*; ~ **shaft adaptor** *n* MECH ENG embout de flexible *m*; ~ **shaft coupling** *n* MECH ENG accouplement articulé *m*; ~ **stay bolt** *n* MECH ENG tirant articulé permettant la dilatation de la plaque *m*; ~ **steel piping** *n* MECH ENG tuyau métallique flexible *m*; ~ **tool changing system** *n* MECH ENG *for injection moulding* système flexible de rechange d'outils *m*; ~ **tubing** *n* MECH ENG tuyauterie flexible *f*; ~ **waveguide** *n* ELEC ENG, SPACE *communications* guide d'ondes flexible *m*; ~ **wire** *n* ELEC ENG fil souple *m*; ~ **wire saw** *n* MECH ENG *tool* scie de poche *f*

flexing: ~ **endurance** *n* P&R résistance aux flexions répétées *f*; ~ **resistance** *n* P&R résistance à la flexion *f*

flexion *n* CONST, RAIL flexion *f*; ~ **spring** *n* MECH ENG ressort de flexion *m*

flexo-folder-gluer *n* PACKAGING colleuse-plieuse flexible *f*

flexographic: ~ **ink** *n* PRINT encre flexographique *f*; ~ **printing** *n* P&R, PRINT flexographie *f*

flexography *n* P&R, PRINT flexographie *f*

flexural: ~ **rigidity** *n* PHYS rigidité flexionnelle *f*; ~ **slip folding** *n* GEOL plissement concentrique par flexion *m*; ~ **strength** *n* MECH *materials*, NUCLEAR, P&R, PRINT résistance à la flexion *f*

flexure-mode: ~ **resonator** *n* ELECTRON résonateur à flexion *m*

flick: ~ **pan** *n* CINEMAT pano filé *m*

flicker:[1] ~ **free** *adj* CINEMAT exempt de scintillement, COMP, DP sans scintillement

flicker[2] *n* CINEMAT, COMP, DP scintillement *m*, TV papillotement *m*; ~ **blade** *n* CINEMAT pale de scintillement *f*; ~ **control** *n* CONTROL régulation par plus ou moins *f*, régulation par tout ou rien *f*, régulation à deux positions *f*; ~ **frequency** *n* CINEMAT fréquence de scintillement *f*, TV fréquence de papillotement *f*; ~ **noise** *n* ELECTRON bruit de scintillation *m*, bruit de scintillement *m*; ~ **photometer** *n* PHYS photomètre de papillotement *m*

flicker[3] *vi* CINEMAT scintiller, ELECTRON clignoter

flickering *n* TELECOM papillotement *m*

flier *n* CONST *stair-building* marche carrée *f*, marche droite *f*

fliers *n pl* CONST *straight flight of stairs* escalier droit *m*, escalier à rampe droite *m*

flight *n* AERONAUT vol *m*, CONST volée *f*, PROD ENG *push plate of conveyor* palette *f*, SPACE vol *m*; ~ **attitude** *n* AERONAUT assiette de vol *f*; ~ **clearance** *n* AERONAUT autorisation de vol *f*; ~ **compartment** *n* AERONAUT poste d'équipage *m*, poste de pilotage *m*; ~ **compartment access stairway** *n* AERONAUT échelle accès au poste de pilotage *f*; ~ **compartment lights** *n pl* AERONAUT éclairage du poste de pilotage *m*; ~ **computer** *n* AERONAUT calculateur de vol *m*; ~ **controller** *n* AERONAUT contrôleur de vol *m*; ~ **controls** *n pl* AERONAUT, SPACE commandes de vol *f pl*; ~ **conveyor** *n* PROD ENG convoyeur à palettes *m*, transporteur à palettes *m*, transporteuse à palettes *f*; ~ **crew** *n* AERONAUT personnel navigant *m*, équipage de conduite *m*, équipage de vol *m*, équipage technique *m*; ~ **data** *n* AERONAUT données de vol *f pl*; ~ **data acquisition unit** *n (FDAU)* AERONAUT boîtier d'acquisition de données de vol *m*; ~ **data recorder** *n* AERONAUT enregistreur de données de vol *m*; ~ **data system** *n* SPACE *spacecraft* système de données de vol *m*; ~ **deck** *n* AERONAUT poste d'équipage *m*, poste de pilotage *m*, NAUT *of aircraft carrier* pont d'envol *m*; ~ **director** *n* AERONAUT directeur de vol *m*; ~ **documentation** *n* AERONAUT documentation de vol *f*; ~ **engineer** *n* AERONAUT mécanicien navigant *m*; ~ **engineer's panel** *n* AERONAUT meuble mécanicien *m*, planche de bord mécanicien *f*; ~ **engineer's seat** *n* AERONAUT siège mécanicien *m*; ~ **envelope** *n* AERONAUT diagramme de manoeuvre et de rafales *m*, domaine de vol *m*; ~ **holding pattern** *n* AERONAUT circuit d'attente en vol *m*; ~ **information** *n* AERONAUT information de vol *f*; ~ **information center** *n* (AmE), ~ **information centre** *n* (BrE) AERONAUT centre d'information de vol *m*; ~ **information service** *n* AERONAUT service d'information de vol *m*; ~ **instruments** *n pl* AERONAUT instruments de vol *m pl*; ~ **instrument system** *n* CONTROL contrôleur de vol *m*; ~ **level** *n* AERONAUT niveau de vol *m*, plage de vol *f*; ~ **of locks** *n* HYDROL *on canal* échelle d'écluses *f*, écluses étagées *f pl*; ~ **log** *n* AERONAUT carnet de vol *m*, journal de bord *m*; ~ **maneuver** *n* (AmE), ~ **manoeuvre** *n* (BrE) AERONAUT manoeuvre de vol *f*, manoeuvre en vol *f*; ~ **manual** *n* AERONAUT manuel de vol *m*; ~ **model** *n* SPACE modèle de vol *m*; ~ **occurrence** *n* SPACE *spacecraft* événement de vol *m*; ~ **path** *n* AERONAUT trajectoire de vol *f*; ~ **path recorder** *n* INSTRUMENT enregistreur de trajectoire de vol *m*, enregistreur de vol *m*; ~ **plan** *n* AERONAUT plan de vol *m*; ~ **plan data** *n* AERONAUT données de plan de vol *f pl*; ~ **progress board** *n* AERONAUT tableau de progression de vol *m*; ~ **readiness review** *n (FRR)* SPACE revue d'aptitude au vol *f (RAV)*; ~ **recorder** *n* AERONAUT enregistreur de bord *m*, enregistreur de vol *m*; ~ **refueling probe** *n* (AmE), ~ **refuelling probe** *n* (BrE) TRANSP prise de ravitaillement en vol *f*; ~ **regularity message** *n* AERONAUT message intéressant la régularité des vols *m*; ~ **sequence** *n* SPACE *spacecraft* séquence de vol *f*; ~ **simulator** *n* AERONAUT simulateur de pilotage *m*, simulateur de vol *m*, COMP, DP simulateur de vol *m*; ~ **spectrum** *n* AERONAUT spectre de vol *m*; ~ **of stairs** *n* CONST volée d'escalier *f*; ~ **status** *n* AERONAUT caractère spécial du vol *m*, situation réglementaire du vol *f*; ~ **technical error** *n* AERONAUT erreur technique de vol *f*; ~ **test** *n* AERONAUT, SPACE essai en vol *m*; ~ **test center** *n* (AmE), ~ **test centre** *n* (BrE) AERONAUT centre d'essais en vol *m*; ~ **test recorder** *n* AERONAUT enregistreur pour essais en vol *m*; ~ **transition** *n* AERONAUT *in-flight* transition en vol *f*; ~ **visibility** *n* AERONAUT visibilité en vol *f*

flighted: ~ **departure** *n* RAIL départ en batterie *m*

flint *n* C&G verre extra-blanc *m*, GEOL silex *m*

flinty: ~ **ash** *n* GEOL cinérite *f*; ~ **crush rock** *n* GEOL pseudotachylite *f*

flip: ~ **chip** *n* ELECTRON puce à protubérances *f*; ~ **coil** *n* ELEC ENG bobine exploratrice *f*; ~ **spout closure** *n* PACKAGING capsule à levier *f*

flip-flop *n* COMP, DP, ELECTRON bascule *f*, PHYS bascule bistable *f*

float[1] *n* AUTO, COAL TECH flotteur *m*, CONST taloche *f*, MECH flotteur *m*, MECH ENG lime à simple taille *f*, NAUT, PETR, TRANSP, VEHICLES *carburettor* flotteur *m*, WATER SUPP aileron *m*, alichen *m*, alichon *m*, aube *f*, jantille *f*, palette *f*, volet *m*, flotteur *m*; ~ **altitude** *n* SPACE *spacecraft* plafond *m*; ~ **chamber** *n* AUTO cuve à niveau constant *f*, VEHICLES *carburettor* chambre de flotteur *f*; ~ **glass** *n* C&G verre flotté *m*; ~ **gold** *n* MINING or flottant *m*, paillettes d'or *f pl*; ~ **life** *n* ELEC ENG *of storage battery* durée de vie en tampon *f*; ~ **mineral** *n* MINING paillettes métalliques *f pl*; ~ **needle** *n* AUTO pointeau *m*; ~ **regulator** *n* CONTROL régulateur à flotteur *m*; ~ **seaplane** *n* TRANSP hydravion monomoteur *m*; ~ **switch** *n* ELEC ENG, REFRIG interrupteur à flotteur *m*; ~ **trap** *n* HYDR EQUIP *of steam engine* purgeur à flotteur *m*; ~ **valve** *n* HEAT ENG soupape à flotteur *f*, HYDR EQUIP robinet à flotteur *m*, soupape à flotteur *f*, MECH ENG clapet à flotteur *m*, valve à flotteur *f*, REFRIG soupape à flotteur *f*

float[2] *vt* PHYS faire flotter, mettre à flot; ~ **off** *vt* NAUT *stranded ship* renflouer

float[3] *vi* NAUT flotter, être à flot, PHYS flotter; ~ **off** *vi* NAUT *of stranded ship* se dégager, se déséchouer

float-and-sink: ~ **analysis** *n* COAL TECH analyse densimétrique par liqueurs denses *f*

floatboard *n* WATER SUPP aileron *m*, alichen *m*, alichon *m*, aube *f*, jantille *f*, palette *f*

float-controlled: ~ **alarm whistle** *n* HYDR EQUIP sifflet d'alarme à flotteur *m*

float-cut: ~ **file** *n* MECH ENG lime à simple taille *f*

floater *n* C&G barrage flottant *m* (Fra), flotteur *m* (Bel), PROD ENG flotteur *m*; ~ **lug** *n* (BrE) *(cf floater notcher)* C&G talon de barrage *m*; ~ **notcher** *n* (AmE) *(cf floater lug)* C&G talon de barrage *m*

floating[1] *adj* MECH flottant

floating[2] *n* P&R *paint defect* démêlage vertical *m*; ~ **accent** *n* PRINT accent flottant *m*, accent superposé *m*, accent séparé *m*; ~ **action controller** *n* CONTROL régulateur intégral *m*, régulateur à action intégrale *m*, régulateur à corrélation intégrale *m*; ~ **anchor nut** *n* MECH ENG écrou flottant *m*; ~ **axle** *n* VEHICLES *transmission* essieu flottant *m*, pont flottant *m*; ~ **battery** *n* ELEC ENG batterie-tampon *f*; ~ **beacon** *n* NAUT *navigation mark* balise flottante *f*; ~ **boom** *n* POLLUTION barrage flottant *m*, NAUT pont de bateaux *m*, pont de radeaux *m*; ~ **bush** *n* MECH ENG bras porte-outils oscillant *m*; ~ **caliper** *n* (AmE), ~ **calliper** *n* (BrE) AUTO étrier flottant *m*; ~ **carrier modulation** *n* ELECTRON modulation à taux constant *f*; ~ **charge** *n* ELEC ENG charge d'entretien *f*; ~ **control** *n* CONTROL régulation flottante *f*; ~ **crane** *n* NAUT ponton-grue *m*; ~ **derrick** *n* CONST bigue flottante *f*; ~ **dock** *n* CONST dock flottant *m*, dock à immersion *m*, NAUT dock flottant *m*; ~ **dredge** *n* MINING bateau dragueur *m*, bateau-drague *m*, bateau-rabot *m*; ~ **engine** *n* AUTO moteur flottant *m*; ~ **flexible tank** *n* MAR POLL citerne souple flottante *f*; ~ **gate** *n* ELECTRON grille en l'air *f*, grille à potentiel flottant *f*; ~ **gear** *n* AERONAUT *of helicopter* atterrisseur à flotteurs *m*, montage flottabilité *m*; ~ **gold** *n* MINING or flottant *m*, paillettes d'or *f pl*; ~ **grid** *n* ELEC ENG grille en l'air *f*, grille à potentiel flottant *f*; ~ **hydrographic dredge** *n* OCEANOG drague flottante *f*, drague hydrographique *f*; ~ **input** *n* ELEC ENG entrée flottante *f*; ~ **line** *n* NAUT *for rescue* filin flottant *m*; ~ **output** *n* ELEC ENG sortie flottante *f*; ~ **pick-up** *n* PRINT balise flottante *f*; ~ **pile** *n* COAL TECH pieu flottant *m*; ~ **platen** *n* MECH ENG plateau flottant *m*; ~ **platform** *n* OCEANOG plate-forme flottante *f*; ~ **point** *n* DP, TELECOM virgule flottante *f*; ~ **point arithmetic** *n* COMP, DP arithmétique en virgule flottante *f*; ~ **point notation** *n* DP notation en virgule flottante *f*; ~ **point number** *n* DP nombre en virgule flottante *m*; ~ **point operation** *n* COMP, DP opération en virgule flottante *f*; ~ **point processor** *n* *(FPP)* COMP, DP processeur en virgule flottante *m*; ~ **potential** *n* ELEC ENG potentiel flottant *m*; ~ **rig** *n* PETR TECH *offshore operations* plate-forme flottante *f*; ~ **shaft** *n* MECH ENG arbre flottant *m*; ~ **spindle** *n* MECH ENG arbre flottant *m*; ~ **supply** *n* ELEC *network* alimentation séparée *f*; ~ **switch** *n* PRINT interrupteur à flotteur *m*; ~ **tool-holder** *n* MECH ENG mandrin oscillant *m*; ~ **wire drag** *n* OCEANOG drague flottante *f*, drague hydrographique *f*; ~ **zone melting method** *n* NUCLEAR fusion de zone sans creuset *f*, technique de zone flottante *f*

float-on-float-off: ~ **vessel** *n* NAUT navire porte-barges *m*

floatplane *n* TRANSP hydravion monomoteur *m*

flocculant *n* CHEM TECH, COAL TECH, P&R *rubber* floculant *m*

flocculate[1] *n* CHEM TECH floculat *m*

flocculate[2] *vi* CHEM floconner, floculer, CHEM TECH se séparer en flocons

flocculation *n* CHEM, CHEM TECH, COAL TECH, FOOD TECH, P&R *paint defect*, PETR TECH *of solid in liquid* floculation *f*; ~ **point** *n* CHEM TECH point de floculation *m*; ~ **test** *n* CHEM TECH test de floculation *m*

flocculator *n* CHEM TECH floculant *m*

flocculence *n* CHEM TECH floculation *f*

flocculent[1] *adj* CHEM TECH floculeux

flocculent:[2] ~ **gypsum** *n* HEAT ENG gypse floculeux *m*

flocculus *n* ASTRON plage floculaire *f*

flock *n* P&R *coating* flocon *m*

flocking *n* GAS TECH flockage *m*

floe *n* OCEANOG floe *m*

flong *n* PAPER TECH carton pour flan de clicherie *m*

flood:[1] **in** ~ *adj* HYDROL *river* en crue

flood[2] *n* CINEMAT projecteur d'ambiance *m*, projecteur à lumière unie *m*, HYDROL crue *f*, inondation *f*, NAUT *river, lockers, tide* flot *m*, inondation *f*, PRINT débordement *m*, inondation *f*; ~ **abatement** *n* WATER SUPP diminution de crue *f*; ~ **and doctor techniques** *n pl* PRINT techniques de couchage à la racle *f pl*; ~ **arch** *n* WATER SUPP arche de décharge pour les hautes eaux *f*; ~ **basalt** *n* GEOL basalte de plateau *m*, coulic basaltique *m*; ~ **bed** *n* HYDROL *of river* lit majeur *m*; ~ **cock** *n* WATER SUPP robinet d'arrosage *m*; ~ **control** *n* FUELLESS gestion de crue *f*, HYDROL maîtrise de crue *f*, WATER SUPP lutte contre les inondations *f*; ~ **control measures** *n pl* FUELLESS aménagements de gestion de crue *m pl*, aménagements de lutte des inondations *m pl*, HYDROL aménagements de maîtrise de crue *m pl*; ~ **control works** *n pl* FUELLESS, HYDROL ouvrage de crue *m*, WATER SUPP ouvrage contre les inondations *m*; ~ **deposits** *n pl* HYDROL délaissés de crue *m pl*, laisses de crue *m pl*; ~ **irrigation** *n* HYDROL irrigation par infiltration *f*, WATER SUPP irrigation par submersion *f*; ~ **loss** *n* FUELLESS perte par inondation *f*; ~ **mitigation measures** *n pl* HYDROL aménagements de maîtrise de crue *m pl*; ~ **peak** *n* HYDROL pointe de crue *f*; ~ **plain** *n* GEOL plaine d'inondation *f*, HYDROL lit de hautes eaux *m*, lit majeur *m*, plaine alluviale *f*, plaine alluviale d'inondation *f*, plaine d'inondation *f*, WATER SUPP plaine d'inondation *f*; ~ **prevention** *n* WATER SUPP prévention de crue *f*; ~ **relief measures** *n pl* HYDROL aménagements de maîtrise de crue *m pl*; ~ **spillway** *n* WATER SUPP évacuateur de crue *m*; ~ **stream** *n* NAUT *navigation, tide*, OCEANOG courant de flot *m*; ~ **tide** *n* HYDROL flot *m*, marée montante *f*, NAUT *navigation* flot *m*, flux *m*, marée montante *f*, OCEANOG flot *m*, marée montante *f*, flux *m*; ~ **of water** *n* HYDROL coup d'eau *m*; ~ **wave** *n* HYDROL onde de crue *f*

flood[3] *vt* AUTO, MECH noyer, NAUT *river, lockers, tide* inonder, noyer, VEHICLES *carburettor* titiller

flood[4] *vi* HYDROL *river*, NAUT déborder

flooded[1] *adj* HYDROL envahi par l'eau, envahi par les eaux, inondé, noyé, submergé, NAUT *ship* envahi par l'eau

flooded:[2] ~ **beam** *n* CINEMAT faisceau élargi *m*; ~ **evaporator** *n* REFRIG évaporateur noyé *m*; ~ **jet** *n* AUTO gicleur noyé *m*

floodgate *n* NAUT *of lock* porte d'écluse *f*, porte de bassin de marée *f*, vanne *f*, WATER SUPP vanne plongeante *f*

flooding *n* C&G clotte *f*, ELECTRON arrosage *m*, HYDROL noyage *m*, OCEANOG ennoyage *m*, P&R *paint defect* démêlage horizontal *m*, PRINT *of pigments into paper* dégorgement *m*; ~ **gun** *n* ELECTRON canon d'arrosage *m*, canon de lecture *m*; ~ **pattern** *n* GEOPHYS diagramme d'engorgement *m*

floodlight *n* ELEC, ELEC ENG projecteur *m*

floodlighting *n* ELEC, ELEC ENG éclairage par projection *m*

floods *n pl* HYDROL crues *f pl*

flood-type: ~ **cooling** *n* REFRIG refroidissement par immersion *m*, réfrigération par immersion dans l'eau glacée *f*

floor[1] *n* CINEMAT plateau *m*, COAL TECH *of coal seam* mur *m*, CONST *bridge* chaussée *f*, *of bridge* aire *f*, *of basin, reservoir* aire *f*, plafond *m*, *of building, house, structure* plancher *m*, *storey of building* étage *m*, *top face, made of tile or cement block* carrelage *m*, *top face, tongued and grooved or made of wood block* parquet *m*, *top face, square-joined* plancher *m*, MINING mur *m*, *of mine level* sole *f*, NAUT *shipbuilding* plancher *m*, varangue *f*, PROD ENG *of foundry* chantier *m*, sol *m*, *on which an operation or process takes place* aire *f*, WATER SUPP *of chamber of lock* radier *m*; ~ **and wall self-adhesive PVC tile** *n* P&R *building* dalle PVC autocollante pour sol et mur *f*; ~ **beam** *n* AERONAUT traverse support de plancher *f*; ~ **bedding** *n* PROD ENG *founding* mise en chantier *f*; ~ **contact switch** *n* ELEC interrupteur à commande au pied *m*; ~ **hanger** *n* MINING *of mine level* chaise de sol *f*; ~ **hatch** *n* AERONAUT trappe de plancher *f*; ~ **heating** *n* HEAT ENG chauffage par le sol *m*; ~ **heave** *n* MINING gonflement *m*; ~ **joist** *n* CONST solive de plancher *f*; ~ **pan** *n* VEHICLES *body* plancher *m*; ~ **panel** *n* AERONAUT panneau de plancher *m*; ~ **plate** *n* MECH plaque de parquet *f*, NAUT *shipbuilding* tôle de varangue *f*; ~ **polish** *n* DETERGENTS encaustique *m*, encaustique à parquets *m*; ~ **sand** *n* PROD ENG *founding* sable de chantier *m*, sable de remplissage *m*, sable vieux *m*, vieux sable *m*; ~ **shift** *n* VEHICLES *gearbox* commande au plancher *f*; ~ **shots** *n* COAL TECH mine au sol *f*; ~ **stock** *n* PROD ENG stock atelier *m*; ~ **switch** *n* ELEC *of lift, elevator* commutateur d'étage *m*; ~ **tile** *n* C&G dalle *f*; ~ **varnish** *n* COATINGS vernis pour plancher *m*

floor[2] *vt* CONST *square-joined* planchéier, *with tile or cement block* carreler, *with tongue and groove, or wood block* parqueter

flooring *n* CONST *of bridge* platelage *m*, SAFETY planchéiage *m*; ~ **nail** *n* CONST clou à parquet *m*; ~ **tile** *n* CONST carreau de carrelage *m*

floorman *n* PETR TECH *drilling* ouvrier de plancher *m*

floor-mounting *n* MECH ENG *machine tool* montage au sol *m*

floorspace *n* CONST encombrement *m*, encombrement sur le plancher *m*, espace de la planche *m*, *of building* surface des étages *f*, PACKAGING encombrement *m*; ~ **occupied** *n* CONST encombrement *m*, encombrement sur le plancher *m*

floor-type: ~ **surfacing and boring lathe** *n* MECH ENG tour en l'air sur taque *m*

floor-warming: ~ **cable** *n* MECH ENG câble de chauffage par le plancher *m*

flop *n* P&R *paint* flop *m*

flopover *n* TV inversion gauche-droite *f*; ~ **process** *n* NUCLEAR processus Umklapp *m*

floppy: ~ **disk** *n* COMP, DP, TELECOM disque souple *m*, disquette *f* ~ **disk drive** *n* COMP, DP lecteur de dis-

quettes *m*, unité de disque souple *f*; ~ **disk reader** *n* COMP, DP TELECOM lecteur de disquette *m*

flos: ~ **ferri** *n* MINERAL flos ferri *m*

flotation *n* CHEM *of mineral*, COAL TECH flottation *f*, MINING flottage *m*, NAUT flottaison *f*; ~ **chamber** *n* MAR POLL *of boom* chambre de flottaison *f*; ~ **collar** *n* PETR TECH *offshore operations* flotteur d'embase *m*, SPACE *spacecraft* collier de flottaison *m*; ~ **froth** *n* CHEM TECH écume de flottation *f*; ~ **liquid** *n* CHEM TECH eau chargée de flottation *f*, milieu dense *m*; ~ **method** *n* PETR méthode de flottation *f*; ~ **plant** *n* CHEM TECH atelier de flottation *m*; ~ **process** *n* COAL TECH procédé de flottation *m*, MINING procédé par flottage *m*; ~ **tank** *n* NAUT caisson de flottabilité *m*, réservoir de flottabilité *m*

flotel *n* PETR TECH *accommodation platform* plate-forme d'hébergement *f*

flotilla *n* NAUT escadrille *f*, flotille *f*

flotsam *n* NAUT épaves flottantes *f pl*

flounder: ~ **point** *n* PETR TECH *drilling* embourbement *m*

flow[1] *n* C&G débit du courant *m*, COAL TECH écoulement *m*, COMP flux *m*, DP circulation *f*, flux *m*, FLUID PHYS, FUELLESS écoulement *m*, HYDR EQUIP débit *m*, HYDROL *of river, tide, current* courant *m*, cours *m*, flot *m*, flux *m*, écoulement *m*, *of water above crest of weir* plan d'eau *m*, *of water* ruissellement *m*, MECH *hydraulics*, METALL écoulement *m*, P&R *plastics, coatings* fluage *m*, fluidité *f*, flux *m*, plasticité *f*, écoulement *m*, PACKAGING *of goods* mouvement *m*, PAPER TECH débit *m*, PETR TECH *of oil* écoulement d'huile *m*, PHYS *electrical* circulation *f*, *of fluid* cours *m*, écoulement *m*, PROD ENG *stream of molten matter* coulée *f*, REFRIG *of fluid*, TEXTILES, THERMOD *of gas*, WATER SUPP *motion* écoulement *m*; ~ **alarm** *n* PROD ENG alarme de débit *f*; ~ **banding** *n* GEOL litage de flux *m*; ~ **behavior** *n* (AmE), ~ **behaviour** *n* (BrE) PROP MAT conditions d'écoulement *f pl*; ~ **box** *n* PAPER TECH caisse d'arrivée de pâte *f*; ~ **cleavage** *n* GEOL clivage de flux *m*; ~ **coefficient** *n* FLUID PHYS, FUELLESS coefficient de débit *m*; ~ **control** *n* COMP, DP commande de flux *f*, contrôle de flux *m*, HEATING dispositif de contrôle de débit *m*, PROD ENG régulation d'écoulement *f*, TELECOM commande de flux *f*; ~ **control device** *n* CONTROL contrôleur de débit *m*; ~ **controller** *n* PROD ENG régulateur de débit *m*; ~ **control valve** *n* MECH ENG vanne-limiteur de débit *f*, PROD ENG régulateur de débit *m*; ~ **cup** *n* LAB EQUIP *viscosity of liquid* coupe consistométrique *f*, P&R *paints, instrument* godet *m*; ~ **delta** *n* OCEANOG delta de marée *m*; ~ **direction** *n* COMP, DP sens de circulation *m*, sens de la liaison *m*; ~ **distributor** *n* PAPER TECH distributeur *m*, répartiteur *m*; ~ **divisor** *n* PROD ENG diviseur de débit *m*; ~ **fatigue** *n* MECH ENG fatigue due au débit *f*; ~ **foam wrap** *n* PACKAGING mousse de calage en feuille *f*; ~ **fold** *n* GEOL pli de fluage *m*; ~ **governor** *n* CONTROL régulateur d'écoulement *m*; ~ **of heat** *n* THERMOD flux thermique *m*; ~ **in open channels** *n* FLUID PHYS écoulement dans des canaux découverts *m*, écoulement à surface libre dans les canaux *m*; ~ **instability** *n* FLUID PHYS instabilité des écoulements *f*; ~ **limit** *n* ELEC ENG limite d'écoulement *f*; ~ **line** *n* COMP ligne de liaison *f*, DP ligne de flux *f*, PETR collecte *f*, conduite d'écoulement *f*, ligne de flux *f*, PETR TECH *of wellhead, pipeline* canalisation *f*, conduite d'écoulement *f*, ligne de flux *f*, TELECOM ligne de liaison *f*; ~ **line temperature** *n* PETR TECH *wellhead operations* température à la goulotte *f*; ~ **lobe** *n* GEOL loupe de glissement *f*; ~ **nozzle** *n* MECH

ENG tuyère débit *f*; **~ path** *n* PROD ENG *hydraulic system* voie de passage *f*; **~ pattern** *n* FLUID PHYS configuration d'écoulement *f*, dessin des lignes de courant *m*, REFRIG configuration d'écoulement *f*, WATER SUPP diagramme d'écoulement *m*, image d'écoulement *f*; **~ pipe** *n* HYDR EQUIP tuyau adducteur *m*, tuyau évacuateur *m*; **~ point** *n* C&G température de fluage *f*, FLUID PHYS, PETR TECH *viscosity*, PRINT point d'écoulement *m*; **~ rate** *n* FLUID PHYS, GAS TECH, HYDROL, MECH *hydraulics* débit *m*, PETR TECH *drilling, production* débit d'écoulement *m*, PHYS, WATER SUPP *volume rate* débit *m*; **~ rate controller** *n* CONTROL régulateur de débit *m*, MECH ENG limiteur de débit *m*; **~ regulator** *n* CONTROL régulateur d'écoulement *m*; **~ resistance** *n* ACOUSTICS résistance à l'écoulement *f*; **~ resistance coefficient** *n* HYDROL indice de résistance par friction *m*; **~ resistivity** *n* ACOUSTICS résistance spécifique à l'écoulement *f*; **~ schedule** *n* PETR programme de production *m*; **~ sheet** *n* COAL TECH schéma de traitement *m*, MINING schéma de lavage *m*, PETR TECH *engineering* schéma de principe *m*; **~ shop** *n* PROD ENG fabrication en ligne *f*; **~ speed** *n* FLUID PHYS vitesse d'écoulement *f*; **~ spinning** *n* MECH ENG fluotournage *m*; **~ stress** *n* PHYS contrainte d'écoulement *f*; **~ switch** *n* ELEC commutateur de flux *m*, PROD ENG contacteur de débit *m*; **~ tank** *n* PETR bac tampon *m*, réservoir tampon *m*, stockage tampon *m*, réservoir de stockage *m*; **~ transmitter** *n* PAPER TECH capteur de débit *m*; **~ of water** *n* CONST *through a pump* débit d'eau *m*; **~ wrapping machine** *n* PACKAGING ensacheuse tubulaire *f*

flow² *vt* FUELLESS écouler; **~ along** *vt* HYDROL courir, diriger, suivre la direction de; **~ into** *vt* HYDROL se verser dans

flow³ *vi* COMP, DP circuler, FLUID PHYS couler, HYDROL couler, s'écouler, PHYS circuler, TEXTILES s'écouler

flowable: ~ solids reactor *n (FSR)* NUCLEAR réacteur à suspension solide *m*

flowage *n* GEOL écoulement fluage *m*, écoulement plastique *m*

flowchart *n* DP, PHYS organigramme *m*; **~ block** *n* DP bloc d'organigramme *m*; **~ connector** *n* COMP, DP renvoi d'organigramme *m*; **~ symbol** *n* DP symbole d'organigramme *m*; **~ text** *n* DP légende d'organigramme *f*

flowcharting *n* DP établissement d'organigramme *m*

flower *n* CONST *civil engineering* fleur *f*

flowgraph *n* DP ordinogramme *m*

flow-in: ~ process *n* TEXTILES processus d'écoulement *m*

flowing¹ *adj* HYDROL *stream*, WATER SUPP *water* coulant

flowing:² **~ pressure** *n* PETR pression d'écoulement *f*; **~ tide** *n* FUELLESS marée montante *f*; **~ well** *n* PETR puits éruptif *m*

flowmeter *n* COAL TECH débitmètre *m*, rhéomètre *m*, CONST *welding*, ELEC ENG, HYDROL, LAB EQUIP, PAPER TECH, PETR TECH *in refinery, pipeline*, PHYS débitmètre *m*, THERMOD *gas* compteur à gaz *m*, WATER SUPP débitmètre *m*

flow-regulating: ~ valve *n* WATER SUPP vanne régulatrice de débit *f*

FLS *abbr* TELECOM *(frame loss second)* seconde avec perte de trame *f*, TELECOM *(free line signal)* signal d'inoccupation *m*

fluate *n* CHEM fluate *m*

fluctuate *vi* ELEC varier

fluctuating: ~ error *n* TV erreur de fluctuation de base de temps *f*; **~ noise** *n* ACOUSTICS bruit fluctuant *m*; **~**

stress *n* METALL contrainte variable *f*

fluctuation *n* ELEC variation *f*

flue *n* C&G carneau de cheminée *m*, HEAT ENG carneau *m*, PROD ENG *of boiler* carneau intérieur *m*, foyer intérieur cylindrique *m*, tube-foyer *m*, *of chimney* tuyau *m*, *of furnace* carneau *m*, THERMOD conduit *m*; **~ boiler** *n* PROD ENG chaudière à carneau intérieur *f*, chaudière à foyer intérieur cylindrique *f*, chaudière à tube-foyer *f*; **~ dust** *n* COAL TECH cendre volante *f*, cendres volantes *f pl*, poussière de fumée *f*; **~ gas** *n* GAS TECH gaz de carneau *m*, HEAT ENG gaz de fumée *m*, PHYS gaz de carneau *m*, POLLUTION fumées *f pl*, gaz de combustion *m*, THERMOD gaz brûlé *m*, gaz de combustion *m*, gaz de fumée *m*; **~ gas cleaning installation** *n* SAFETY installation d'épuration de gaz brûlés *f*; **~ gas desulfurization** *n* (AmE), **~ gas desulphurisation** *n* (BrE) POLLUTION désulfuration des effluents gazeux *f*, désulfuration des gaz de combustion *f*; **~ gas scrubber** *n* THERMOD épurateur des gaz de fumée *m*; **~ gas scrubbing** *n* THERMOD lavage des gaz de fumée *m*, épuration des gaz de fumée *f*; **~ lining** *n* HEAT ENG tuyau de cheminée *m*; **~ plate** *n* PROD ENG *of boiler* plaque tubulaire *f*; **~ sheet** *n* PROD ENG *of boiler* plaque tubulaire *f*; **~ tube** *n* NUCLEAR tube de fumée *m*, tube-foyer *m*

flued: ~ heater *n* MECH ENG chauffage à conduit de cheminée *m*

flueless: ~ heater *n* HEAT ENG appareil de chauffage non raccordé *m*, MECH ENG chauffage sans conduit de cheminée *m*

fluellite *n* MINERAL fluellite *f*

fluence *n* PHYS fluence *f*

fluff *n* PAPER TECH bourre *f*

fluffing *n* PAPER TECH peluchage *m*

fluid¹ *adj* FLUID PHYS fluide

fluid² *n* CHEM, FLUID PHYS, PETR, PHYS fluide *m*; **~ bed** *n* CHEM TECH bain fluidisé *m*, couche fluidifiée *f*, couche turbulente *f*, lit fluidifié *m*, lit fluidisé *m*; **~ breathing** *n* OCEANOG respiration liquidienne *f*; **~ cooler** *n* REFRIG aérorefroidisseur *m*, aéroréfrigérant *m*; **~ coupling** *n* PROD ENG *production* coupleur hydraulique *m*, VEHICLES *transmission* embrayage hydraulique *m*; **~ cracking** *n* CHEM TECH craquage catalytique fluide *m*; **~ drive** *n* MECH transmission hydraulique *f*; **~ dynamics** *n* FLUID PHYS dynamique des fluides *f*; **~ engineering** *n* FLUID PHYS génie des écoulements *m*; **~ flow** *n* FLUID PHYS écoulement fluide *m*, PETR TECH écoulement *m*; **~ head** *n* CINEMAT tête fluide *f*; **~ inclusion** *n* GEOL inclusion fluide *f*; **~ inlet** *n* MECH ENG entrée de fluides *f*; **~ logic circuit** *n* MECH ENG logique par les fluides *f*; **~ mechanics** *n* FLUID PHYS mécanique des fluides *f*; **~ particle** *n* FLUID PHYS particule de fluide *f*; **~ permeability** *n* HEAT ENG perméabilité au fluide *f*; **~ physics** *n* PHYS physique des fluides *f*; **~ pipeline** *n* MECH ENG tuyauterie pour fluides *f*; **~ power systems** *n pl* MECH ENG transmissions hydrauliques et pneumatiques *f pl*; **~ pressure** *n* FLUID PHYS pression du fluide *f*; **~ receiver** *n* MECH ENG réservoir de fluide *m*; **~ waves** *n pl* FLUID PHYS ondes dans les fluides *f pl*

fluidal: ~ structure *n* GEOL *of igneous rock* structure fluidale *f*, texture fluidale *f*; **~ texture** *n* GEOL *of igneous rock* structure fluidale *f*, texture fluidale *f*

fluid-bed: ~ furnace *n* NUCLEAR four à lit fluidisé *m*; **~ granulator** *n* CHEM TECH granulateur en lit fluidisé *m*; **~ roasting** *n* CHEM TECH grillage par fluidisation *m*

fluid-catalyst: ~ process *n* CHEM TECH craquage catalytique à lit fluide *m*, procédé au catalyseur fluide *m*

fluid-gate: ~ **printing** *n* CINEMAT tirage humide *m*
fluidic: ~ **device** *n* MECH ENG dispositif fluidique *m*
fluidics *n* FLUID PHYS fluidique *f*
fluidification: ~ **device** *n* PAPER TECH dispositif de fluidification *m*
fluidify *vt* PAPER TECH fluidifier
fluidity *n* FLUID PHYS, PHYS fluidité *f*
fluidization *n* COAL TECH, PETR fluidisation *f*
fluidize *vt* PAPER TECH fluidifier
fluidized: ~ **bed** *n* CHEM TECH bain fluidisé *m*, couche fluidifiée *f*, couche turbulente *f*, lit fluidifié *m*, lit fluidisé *m*, HEATING *combustion*, POLLUTION lit fluidisé *m*; ~ **bed coating** *n* CHEM TECH revêtement en bain fluidisé *m*, COATINGS revêtement en lit fluidisé *m*; ~ **bed combustion** *n* POLLUTION CLF, combustion sur lit fluidisé *f*; ~ **bed dryer** *n* CHEM TECH séchoir en lit fluidisé *m*, FOOD TECH *food-processing machinery* séchoir à lit fluidisé *m*, HEATING *combustion* séchoir en lit fluidisé *m*; ~ **bed freezing** *n* REFRIG congélation sur plaque réfrigérante *f*; ~ **bed gasification** *n* CHEM TECH gazéification en lit fluidisé *f*; ~ **bed kiln** *n* CHEM TECH four à lit fluidisé *m*; ~ **bed reduction** *n* CHEM TECH réduction en lit fluidisé *f*; ~ **bed sintering** *n* CHEM TECH frittage en turbulence *m*, trempage dans la poudre fluidisée *m*; ~ **bed vibro-cooler** *n* CHEM TECH refroidisseur vibrant à tourbillon *m*
fluid-level: ~ **switch** *n* PROD ENG contacteur de niveau de liquide *m*
fluid-power: ~ **cylinder** *n* MECH ENG cylindre de transmission hydraulique *m*
fluid-tight: ~ **packing** *n* PROD ENG garniture étanche *f*
fluke *n* NAUT *of anchor* patte *f*
flume *n* COAL TECH kermet *m*, CONST canal sur appuis *m*, FUELLESS caniveau *m*, PROD ENG *of mill* abée *f*, auge *f*, buse *f*, bée *f*, reillère *f*, WATER SUPP caniveau *m*, rigole *f*, *artificial open channel* canal d'amenée *m*, canal de dérivation *m*, canal de prise *m*, canal en bois *m*, canal en planches *m*, canalisation d'amenée *f*, dérivation *f*, *turbine chamber* chambre d'eau *f*, réservoir *m*
fluoanthene *n* CHEM fluoanthène *m*
fluoanthrene *n* CHEM fluoanthrène *m*
fluocerine *n* MINERAL fluocérine *f*, fluocérite *f*
fluocerite *n* MINERAL fluocérine *f*, fluocérite *f*
Fluon *n* (TM) P&R Fluon *m* (MD), polytétrafluoréthylène *m*
fluorene *n* CHEM fluorène *m*
fluorenone *n* CHEM fluorénone *f*
fluorescein *n* CHEM fluorescéine *f*
fluorescence *n* CHEM, PHYS, RAD PHYS, WAVE PHYS fluorescence *f*; ~ **analysis** *n* RAD PHYS analyse par fluorescence *f*; ~ **excitation spectrum** *n* RAD PHYS spectre d'activation de fluorescence *m*; ~ **microscope** *n* INSTRUMENT microscope à fluorescence *m*
fluorescent[1] *adj* CHEM, COLOURS, PRINT, PROP MAT fluorescent
fluorescent:[2] ~ **discharge tube** *n* RAD PHYS tube fluorescent *m*; ~ **lamp** *n* ELEC ENG lampe fluorescente *f*, PHYS lampe fluorescente *f*, tube fluorescent *m*; ~ **lighting** *n* ELEC, ELEC ENG, GAS TECH éclairage fluorescent *m*; ~ **penetration test** *n* MECH ressuage fluorescent *m*; ~ **screen** *n* ELEC *of oscilloscope*, ELECTRON, INSTRUMENT, PHYS écran fluorescent *m*; ~ **substance** *n* RAD PHYS substance fluorescente *f*; ~ **tube** *n* ELEC *lighting* tube fluorescent *m*; ~ **whitening** *n* PAPER TECH blanchissement par agents fluorescents *m*; ~ **X-ray spectrometer** *n* RAD PHYS spectromètre à fluorescence de rayons

X *m*
fluoridation *n* CHEM fluoration *f*, fluoruration *f*
fluoride *n* CHEM fluorure *m*; ~ **opal glass** *n* C&G verre opale au fluorure *m*
fluorine *n* (F) CHEM fluor *m* (F)
fluorite *n* (BrE) C&G, CHEM spath fluor *m*, MINERAL fluorine *f*, fluorite *f*; ~ **lens** *n* (BrE) INSTRUMENT lentille fluorurée *f*
fluoroborate *n* CHEM fluoroborate *m*
fluoroboric *adj* CHEM fluoroborique
fluorocarbon: ~ **refrigerant** *n* REFRIG frigorigène fluorocarboné *m*; ~ **resin** *n* P&R résine fluorocarbonée *f*
fluoroform *n* CHEM fluoroforme *m*
fluorography *n* PROP MAT, RAD PHYS radiophotographie *f*
fluorophosphate *n* CHEM fluorophosphate *m*
fluoroscopic *adj* PROP MAT *examination* fluoroscopique
fluoroscopy *n* ELEC ENG fluoroscopie *f*
fluorosilicate *n* CHEM fluorosilicate *m*
fluorosilicic *adj* CHEM fluorosilicique
fluorspar *n* (AmE) *see* fluorite
fluosulfonic *adj* (AmE),
fluosulphonic *adj* (BrE) CHEM fluorosulphonique
fluroaluminate *n* CHEM fluroaluminate *m*
flush:[1] ~ **left** *adj* PRINT au fer à gauche; ~ **right** *adj* PRINT au fer à droite
flush:[2] ~ **left** *adv* PRINT au fer à gauche; ~ **right** *adv* PRINT au fer à droite
flush[3] *n* WATER SUPP chasse *f*; ~ **aerial** *n* AERONAUT antenne encastrée *f*, antenne mortaise *f*, antenne noyée *f*; ~ **antenna** *n* TELECOM antenne encastrée *f*, antenne plaquée *f*; ~ **bolt** *n* PROD ENG boulon à tête noyée *m*, boulon à tête perdue *m*; ~ **box** *n* WATER SUPP réservoir de chasse *m*; ~ **cut** *n* PROD ENG coupe à ras *f*; ~ **deck** *n* NAUT *boat building* plat-pont *m*, pont ras *m*; ~ **gate** *n* WATER SUPP vanne de chasse *f*; ~ **head** *n* PROD ENG tête affleurante *f*; ~ **head rivet** *n* MECH ENG rivet à tête affleurée *m*; ~ **joint** *n* PROD ENG joint lisse *m*; ~ **lifting ring** *n* NAUT *deck fitting* anneau sur platine *m*; ~ **lock** *n* CONST *locksmithing* serrure encastrée *f*, serrure entaillée *f*; ~ **mount** *n* PROD ENG montage affleurant *m*; ~ **mounted antenna** *n* SPACE antenne encastrée *f*; ~ **mounted lens** *n* PHOTO objectif rentrant *m*; ~ **mounting** *n* ELEC *of switch* montage encastré *m*; ~ **operated** *n* PROD ENG tête affleurante *f*; ~ **plating** *n* NAUT *boat building* bordé à franc-bord *m*; ~ **pond** *n* WATER SUPP bassin de chasse *m*; ~ **riveting** *n* PROD ENG rivure à bande de recouvrement *f*, rivure à couvre-joint *f*, rivure à franc-bord *f*; ~ **setting** *n* PRINT composition à l'américaine *f*; ~ **switch** *n* ELEC commutateur encastré *m*; ~ **tank** *n* WATER SUPP réservoir de chasse *m*; ~ **wiring** *n* ELEC *supply network* câblage encastré *m*
flush[4] *vt* PROD ENG affleurer; ~ **up** *vt* PROD ENG affleurer
flush[5] *vi* WATER SUPP curer, donner une chasse à; **be ~ with** *vi* PROD ENG s'affleurer avec, être au niveau de, être de niveau avec, être à fleur de
flushboard *n* WATER SUPP *of dam or sluice gate* hausse *f*
flushed: ~ **zone** *n* PETR zone lavée *f*
flushing *n* MAR POLL lessivage rapide *m*, MECH rinçage *m*, MINING *fire extinction* embouage *m*, POLLUTION lessivage rapide *m*, PRINT voile au rouge *f*, PROD ENG rinçage *m*, WATER SUPP *water-flush drilling* curage *m*, injection d'eau *f*; ~ **basin** *n* OCEANOG bassin de chasse *m*; ~ **connector** *n* MECH ENG prise de rinçage *f*; ~ **tools** *n pl* MINING outils de curage *m pl*
flush-type: ~ **push button** *n* CONTROL bouton affleu-

rant *m*, bouton encastré *m*

flute *n* C&G cannelure *f*, côte creuse *f*, CONST *groove* cannelure *f*, rainure *f*, MECH, PAPER TECH cannelure *f*, PRINT *in corrugated card* cannelure *f*, flûte *f*, plissement *m*, SPACE *spacecraft* cannelure *f*; ~ **mark** *n* GEOL flute-mark *m*, marque de courant en forme de flûte *f*

fluted *adj* MECH, PAPER TECH *paper*, PRODUCTION cannelé

fluteless[1] *adj* MECH ENG *small tools* sans rainure

fluteless:[2] ~ **screwing tap** *n* MECH ENG taraud sans rainures *m*

fluter *n* PAPER TECH canneleuse *f*

fluting *n* CONST cannelure *f*, rainurage *m*, évidage *m*; ~ **corrugating medium** *n* PAPER TECH papier à canneler pour carton ondulé *m*; ~ **corrugating paper** *n* PAPER TECH papier à canneler *m*; ~ **medium** *n* PAPER TECH papier à canneler pour carton ondulé *m*; ~ **paper** *n* PAPER TECH papier à canneler *m*

flutter *n* ACOUSTICS scintillement *m*, AERONAUT vibration aéroélastique *f*, *aerodynamics* flottement *m*, flutter *m*, PRINT instabilité *f*, RECORDING battement *m*, flottement *m*, pleurage *m*, scintillement *m*, TELECOM scintillation *f*, TV pleurage *m*, sautillement *m*; ~ **echo** *n* ACOUSTICS écho flottant *m*, TV écho multiple *m*; ~ **effect** *n* TV effet de chevrotement *m*; ~ **factor** *n* ACOUSTICS taux de fluctuation *m*, RECORDING facteur de pleurage *m*; ~ **rate** *n* TV *on sound* taux de pleurage *m*

fluttering: ~ **of brightness level** *n* TV pompage *m*; ~ **seat** *n* HYDR EQUIP *of valve* siège oscillant *m*; ~ **video level** *n* TV niveau vidéo oscillant *m*

fluvial: ~ **alluvium** *n* WATER SUPP alluvions fluviales *f pl*; ~ **hydraulics** *n* WATER SUPP hydraulique fluviale *f*

fluviatile *adj* GEOL fluviatile

fluvio-glacial *adj* GEOL fluvio-glaciaire

fluvio-marine *adj* GEOL fluvio-marin

flux[1] *n* C&G fondant *m*, CONST *welding*, ELEC *magnetism*, ELEC ENG, MECH *welding*, PHYS flux *m*, PROD ENG décapant de soudure *m*, PROP MAT fondant *m*; ~ **density** *n* ELEC *magnetism* induction magnétique *f*, PHYS densité de flux *f*; ~ **gate** *n* (AmE) *(cf flux valve)* AERONAUT détecteur de flux *m*, sonde électromagnétique *f*, vanne de flux *f*; ~ **gate magnetometer** *n* (AmE) *(cf flux valve magnetometer)* ELEC ENG magnétomètre à noyau saturable *m*, PETR magnétomètre à induction *m*; ~ **leakage** *n* ELEC ENG fuites de flux *f pl*; ~ **line** *n* C&G ligne de flottaison *f*, ELEC ENG ligne de flux *f*; ~ **line attack** *n* C&G coup de sabre *m*; ~ **line block** *n* C&G bloc de flottaison *m*; ~ **linkage** *n* ELEC ENG flux embrassé *m*; ~ **powder** *n* COAL TECH fondant *m*; ~ **quantum** *n* PHYS fluxoïde *m*, quantum de flux *m*; ~ **of radiation** *n* RAD PHYS flux de rayonnement *m*; ~ **valve** *n* (BrE) *(cf flux gate)* AERONAUT détecteur de flux *m*, sonde électromagnétique *f*, vanne de flux *f*; ~ **valve magnetometer** *n* (BrE) *(cf flux gate magnetometer)* ELEC ENG magnétomètre à noyau saturable *m*, PETR magnétomètre à induction *m*

flux[2] *vt* PROD ENG rocher, PROP MAT couvrir de fondant

flux-cored: ~ **arc welding** *n* CONST soudage à l'arc avec fil fourré *m*; ~ **arc welding with active-gas shielding** *n* CONST soudage à l'arc sous gaz actif avec fil fourré *m*; ~ **wire** *n* CONST *welding* fil à flux incorporé *m*

fluxing *n* CONST *welding* fluxage *m*; ~ **agent** *n* PROP MAT fondant *m*

fluxmeter *n* ELEC *magnetism*, ELEC ENG, PHYS fluxmètre *m*

fly[1] *n* MECH ENG volant *m*, volant d'entraînement *m*,

volant de chasse *m*, volant de commande *m*, vane, as of radiometer moulinet *m*, PROD ENG *vaned speed-regulating device* volant *m*; ~ **ash** *n* COAL TECH cendre volante *f*, cendres volantes *f pl*, PAPER TECH cendre volatile *f*, cendres volatiles *f pl*, POLLUTION cendre volante *f*, cendres volantes *f pl*; ~ **ball governor** *n* PROD ENG régulateur de Watt *m*, régulateur à boules *m*, régulateur à force centrifuge *m*; ~ **bar with two balls** *n* PROD ENG balancier à boules *m*; ~ **board** *n* PRINT table de recette *f*; ~ **crank** *n* PROD ENG contre-manivelle *f*; ~ **governor** *n* CONTROL régulateur à ailettes *m*, volant à ailettes *m*; ~ **nut** *n* PROD ENG papillon *m*, écrou papillon *m*, écrou à oreilles *m*; ~ **press** *n* PROD ENG balancier *m*, découpoir à la main *m*, presse de découpage volante *f*, presse à balancier *f*; ~ **pulley** *n* MECH ENG poulie-volant *f*; ~ **regulator** *n* CONTROL régulateur à ailettes *m*, volant à ailettes *m*; ~ **roll** *n* PAPER TECH rouleau de renvoi de feuille *m*; ~ **sheet** *n* PAPER TECH feuille volante *f*; ~ **shunting** *n* RAIL méthode tir au but *f*, *vehicles* manoeuvre au lancer *f*; ~ **shuttle loom** *n* TEXTILES métier à navette *m*; ~ **tipping** *n* RECYCLING décharge illégale *f*

fly[2] *vt* NAUT *a flag* battre

fly[3] *vi* PROD ENG *riveting* sauter, se déboutonner; ~ **off** *vi* PROD ENG *riveting* sauter, se déboutonner

flyback *n* ELECTRON retour du faisceau *m*; ~ **blanking** *n* TV suppression du retour *f*; ~ **transformer** *n* TV transformateur de retour de spot *m*

fly-by *n* AERONAUT, SPACE *past planet or satellite* survol *m*; ~ **effect** *n* SPACE *spacecraft* effet d'accélération *m*; ~ **point** *n* SPACE *spacecraft* point de survol *m*

flyer *n* CONST *stair-building* marche carrée *f*, marche droite *f*

flyers *n pl* CONST escalier droit *m*, escalier à rampe droite *m*

flyer-spinning: ~ **frame** *n* TEXTILES métier continu à ailettes *m*

flying: ~ **arch** *n* C&G voûte surbaissée *f*; ~ **boat** *n* AERONAUT hydravion monocoque *m*, hydravion à coque *m*, TRANSP hydravion *m*; ~ **bridge** *n* CONST pont volant *m*, NAUT passerelle haute *f*, passerelle supérieure *f*; ~ **buttress** *n* CONST arc-boutant *m*, pilier d'arc-boutant *m*; ~ **erase head** *n* TV effacement par tête volante *m*; ~ **hours** *n pl* AERONAUT heures de vol *f pl*; ~ **insert** *n* PRINT encart volant *m*; ~ **lead** *n* PROD ENG conducteur volant *m*; ~ **mesh** *n* OCEANOG maille folle *f*; ~ **paster** *n* PRINT collage en marche au dérouleur *m*, dérouleur à collage en marche *m*; ~ **scaffold** *n* CONST échafaud en encorbellement *m*, échafaud à bascule *m*, échafaudage en bascule *m*; ~ **shore** *n* CONST *building* étrésillon *m*; ~ **sparks** *n pl* SAFETY étincelles volantes *f pl*; ~ **spot** *n* TV spot mobile *m*; ~ **squad** *n* CONST équipe volante *f*, *personnel* force mobile *f*; ~ **test bench** *n* AERONAUT banc d'essai volant *m*; ~ **time** *n* AERONAUT nombre d'heures de vol *m*, temps de fonctionnement *m*, temps de vol *m*

Flying: ~ **Horse** *n* *(cf Pegasus)* ASTRON Pégase *m*

flying-spot: ~ **scanner** *n* TV analyseur à spot mobile *m*; ~ **tube scanner** *n* TV tube analyseur à spot mobile *m*

flymesh *n* OCEANOG maille folle *f*

fly-off *n* HYDROL évaporation totale *f*, évapotranspiration *f*

flyover *n* TRANSP passage supérieur *m*; ~ **noise measurement point** *n* AERONAUT *aircraft noise* point de mesure survolé au décollage *m*

flysch *n* GEOL flysch *m*

flyweight n MECH ENG masselotte f

flywheel n AUTO volant moteur m, MECH volant d'inertie m, MECH ENG volant m, volant d'entraînement m, volant de chasse m, volant de commande m, PROD ENG *vaned speed-regulating device*, REFRIG volant m, VEHICLES *of engine* volant moteur m; ~ **housing** n VEHICLES *of engine* carter de volant m; ~ **ring gear** n MECH ENG *machine tool* couronne de lancement f; ~ **starter ring gear** n VEHICLES *engine* couronne du volant f

Fm *(fermium)* CHEM Fm *(fermium)*

FM[1] *abbr (frequency modulation)* COMP, ELEC, ELECTRON, PHYS, RECORDING, TELECOM, TV, WAVE PHYS MF *(modulation de fréquence)*

FM:[2] ~ **carrier** n ELECTRON porteuse FM f, porteuse modulée en fréquence f; ~ **modem** n ELECTRON modem à MF m; ~ **recording** n RECORDING enregistrement à modulation de fréquence m; ~ **signal** n ELECTRON signal FM m, signal modulé en fréquence m; ~ **stereo** n RECORDING émission en stéréophonie et modulation de fréquence f; ~ **transmitting signal** n RAD PHYS signal de transmission FM m

FMBS *abbr (frame-mode bearer service)* TELECOM service support en mode trame m

F-number n PHOTO ouverture du diaphragme f, PHYS ouverture relative f

foam[1] n C&G, CHEM, COAL TECH, DETERGENTS mousse f, FOOD TECH mousse f, écume f, NAUT *on sea*, OCEANOG écume f, P&R *plastic, elastomer*, PAPER TECH, PROP MAT, TEXTILES mousse f, THERMOD *fire extinguisher* extincteur à mousse carbonique m, extincteur à mousse chimique m; ~ **backing** n TEXTILES fonds mousse m pl; ~ **blanket** n AERONAUT tapis de mousse m; ~ **booster** n FOOD TECH exalteur de mousse m; ~ **boosting** n DETERGENTS renforçateur de moussage m, renforçateur de mousse m; ~ **breaker** n CHEM TECH agent antimoussant m, antimousse m; ~ **compound** n AERONAUT agent producteur de mousse m, émulseur m; ~ **dilution** n CHEM TECH délayage des écumes m; ~ **drainage** n CHEM TECH essorage de la mousse m; ~ **extinguisher** n AERONAUT extincteur à mousse m, SAFETY dispositif d'extinction à mousse m, extincteur à mousse m; ~ **fire extinguisher** n SAFETY extincteur d'incendie à mousse m; ~ **glass** n C&G verre cellulaire m; ~ **inhibitor** n CHEM TECH additif antimousse m, PAPER TECH antimousse m; ~ **layer** n TEXTILES couche de mousse f; ~ **layer-forming flame-proofing agent** n SAFETY enduit antiflamme moussant m; ~ **line** n C&G ligne de mousse f; ~ **mat drying** n FOOD TECH séchage de mousse m; ~ **material** n CONST *building* matériau alvéolaire m; ~ **packaging and cushioning** n PACKAGING emballage mousse avec tampon amortisseur m; ~ **persistence** n CHEM TECH stabilité de mousse f; ~ **separation** n CHEM TECH séparation par écumage f; ~ **tank** n PAPER TECH bac à mousse m; ~ **vacuum drying** n FOOD TECH séchage de mousse sous vide m

foam[2] vt CHEM TECH transformer en mousse

foam[3] vti CHEM TECH mousser, écumer, TEXTILES mousser

foamed: ~ **glass** n C&G verre expansé m; ~ **plastic** n P&R plastique mousse m; ~ **polystyrene and polyethylene molder** n (AmE), ~ **polystyrene and polyethylene moulder** n (BrE) PACKAGING machine à mouler le polystyrène et le polyéthylène mousse f; ~ **rubber** n P&R caoutchouc expansé m, caoutchouc mousse m; ~ **slag** n PROP MAT laitier mousseux m; ~ **slag aggregate** n HEAT ENG agrégat de laitier mousseux m

foamer n CHEM TECH, DETERGENTS agent moussant m, moussant m

foaming n C&G moussage m, CHEM TECH moussage m, écumage m, PETR TECH *properties of liquids* moussage m, PRINT mélange encre-eau provoquant de la mousse sur la plaque m, émulsion f, PROD ENG moussage m; ~ **agent** n CHEM TECH agent moussant m, moussant m, FOOD TECH agent moussant m; ~ **test** n AERONAUT essai de moussage m

foamy adj CHEM TECH mousseux, écumeux, TEXTILES mousseux

FOB *abbr (free on board)* NAUT *commerce, shipping* FOB *(franco à bord)*

focal: ~ **depth** n GEOL profondeur de l'hypocentre f, profondeur du foyer f; ~ **length** n ASTRON *of telescope* focale f, longueur focale f, CINEMAT longueur focale f, PHOTO, PHYS distance focale f, RAD PHYS *of electrostatic lens* longueur focale f; ~ **plane** n CINEMAT, ELECTRON plan focal m, PHOTO plan d'image m, PHYS plan focal m; ~ **plane shutter** n PHOTO obturateur de plaque m, obturateur focal m; ~ **point** n CINEMAT, PHOTO foyer m; ~ **range** n CINEMAT gamme des focales f; ~ **spot** n ELECTRON spot lumineux m; ~ **time** n TV distance focale de lentille électronique f

focimeter n INSTRUMENT fronto-focomètre m

focus:[1] **in** ~ adv PHOTO au point

focus[2] n ASTRON *of telescope*, CINEMAT, GEOM foyer m, GEOPHYS *of seism* foyer m, foyer du séisme m, hypocentre m, PHYS *focal point* foyer m; ~ **knob** n INSTRUMENT bouton moleté m, crémaillère de fixation f; ~ **modulation** n TV *of cathode ray tube* modulation de convergence f; ~ **on film** n CINEMAT mise au point sur pellicule f; ~ **pulling** n CINEMAT réglage de mise au point m; ~ **setting** n PHOTO réglage de mise au point m

focus[3] vt CINEMAT faire la mise au point, ELECTRON concentrer, focaliser, PHOTO, PHYS mettre au point, WAVE PHYS focaliser; ~ **for infinity** vt PHOTO mettre au point sur l'infini

focused[1] adj PHYS mis au point

focused:[2] ~ **beam** n WAVE PHYS rayon focalisé m; ~ **ion beam** n RAD PHYS faisceau d'ions mis au point m; ~ **log** n PETR diagramme focalisé m

focusing n ELECTRON *cathode ray tube* concentration f, *of particle beam* focalisation f, PHOTO mise au point f; ~ **aid** n PHOTO dispositif de mise au point m; ~ **anode** n ELEC ENG anode de concentration f, anode de focalisation f; ~ **coil** n ELEC ENG bobine de concentration f, bobine de focalisation f, TV bobine de focalisation f; ~ **control** n TV commande de mise au point f, commande de netteté f, commande de point f; ~ **device** n CONTROL dispositif de mise au point m; ~ **diode** n INSTRUMENT lentille électronique f; ~ **electrode** n ELEC ENG, TV électrode de focalisation f; ~ **knob** n CINEMAT bouton de mise au point m, INSTRUMENT bouton moleté m, crémaillère de fixation f; ~ **lamp** n ELEC projecteur convergent m; ~ **lens** n INSTRUMENT lentille convergente f; ~ **lever** n CINEMAT levier de mise au point m; ~ **magnet** n ELEC ENG, SPACE *communications* aimant de concentration m, TV aimant de focalisation m; ~ **magnifier** n INSTRUMENT loupe de mise au point f; ~ **magnifying glass** n INSTRUMENT loupe de mise au point f; ~ **mount** n CINEMAT rampe hélicoïdale f; ~ **range** n PHOTO latitude de mise au point f; ~ **ring** n CINEMAT bague de mise au point f, INSTRUMENT bague de correction dioptrique f, PHOTO bague de mise au point f; ~ **screen** n CINEMAT verre dépoli m, INSTRU-

MENT écran de mise au point *m*, PHOTO verre dépoli de la mise au point *m*; ~ **screen frame** *n* PHOTO cadre à dépoli *m*; ~ **sleeve** *n* INSTRUMENT bague de mise au point *f*; ~ **stage** *n* PHOTO glissière de réglage *f*

FoE *abbr (Friends of the Earth)* POLLUTION Amis de la Terre *m pl*

foehn *n see föhn*

FOF *abbr (freeze-out fraction)* TELECOM fraction de gel *f*

fog[1] *n* ACOUSTICS, CINEMAT, PHOTO voile *m*, PRINT brouillard *m*, manque de netteté *m*, voile de netteté *f*, REFRIG brouillard *m* ~ **bank** *n* METEO banc de brouillard *m*; ~ **dispersal** *n* AERONAUT dénébulation *f*; ~ **gun** *n* CINEMAT machine à brouillard *f*; ~ **lamp** *n* VEHICLES phare antibrouillard *m*, projecteur antibrouillard *m*; ~ **signal** *n* NAUT signal de brume *m*; ~ **warning** *n* NAUT *meteorology* avertissement de brume *m*

fog[2] *vt* ACOUSTICS, CINEMAT, PHOTO voiler

föhn *n* METEO foehn *m*

foil *n* CRYSTALL *electron microscope specimen* feuille *f*, PAPER TECH racle d'égouttage *f*, PROD ENG clinquant *m*, feuille *f*; ~ **backing machine** *n* PACKAGING machine d'estampage pour feuilles minces *f*; ~ **craft** *n* PAPER TECH papier métallisé *m*; ~ **sampler** *n* COAL TECH carottier à rubans *m*; ~ **sealing** *n* PACKAGING opercule en aluminium mince *m*; ~ **tooling** *n* MECH ENG outillage pour feuilles métalliques *m*

foil-forming: ~ **plant** *n* PROD ENG installation de formage de feuille *f*

fold[1] *n* GEOL, PAPER TECH, PETR pli *m*, TESTING plissement *m*; ~ **axis** *n* GEOL axe d'un pli *m*; ~ **brush setting** *n* PROD ENG réglage brosse plis *m*; ~ **carton** *n* PACKAGING boîte pliante *f*; ~ **limb** *n* GEOL flanc d'un pli *m*; ~ **nappe** *n* GEOL nappe de charriage *f*

fold[2] *vt* PAPER TECH, PRINT plier; ~ **back** *vt* PROD ENG rabattre; ~ **down** *vt* PROD ENG rabattre; ~ **over** *vt* PROD ENG rabattre

foldaway *adj* MECH ENG escamotable

foldback *n* RECORDING retour d'écoute *m*

folded:[1] ~ **and collated** *adj* PRINT plié et assemblé

folded:[2] ~ **bottom box** *n* PACKAGING boîte avec fond plié *f*; ~ **network** *n* TELECOM réseau replié *m*

folder *n* PRINT plieuse *f*; ~ **unit** *n* PRINT plieuse *f*

folder-gluer *n* PACKAGING machine à plier et à coller *f*

folding[1] *adj* MECH ENG rabattable

folding[2] *n* ELECTRON repliement *m*, GEOL plissement *m*, PAPER TECH pliage *m*, PROD ENG pliage *m*, plissement *m*, pliure *f*; ~ **and seaming machine** *n* PACKAGING machine à plier et à agrafer les boîtes *f*; ~ **axis** *n* AERONAUT *of helicopter* axe de repliage *m*; ~ **bicycle** *n* TRANSP bicyclette pliante *f*; ~ **blade** *n* AERONAUT *of helicopter* pale repliable *f*; ~ **box** *n* PACKAGING, PAPER TECH boîte pliante *f*; ~ **boxboard** *n* PAPER TECH boîtes pliantes *f pl*; ~ **box erecting machine** *n* PACKAGING assembleuse de cartons *f*; ~ **box setting machine** *n* PACKAGING assembleuse de cartons *f*; ~ **camera** *n* PHOTO chambre pliante *f*; ~ **carton** *n* PACKAGING boîte pliante *f*; ~ **cylinder** *n* PRINT cylindre plieur *m*; ~ **doors** *n pl* CONST portes battantes *f pl*, portes repliantes *f pl*; ~ **drum** *n* PRINT tambour de pliage *m*; ~ **frequency** *n* PETR fréquence Nyquist *f*; ~ **joint** *n* CONST assemblage à charnière *m*; ~ **lens** *n* INSTRUMENT loupe pliante *f*, loupe à manche pliante *f*; ~ **machine** *n* PAPER TECH plieuse *f*, PROD ENG machine de pliage *f*, machine à plier *f*, plieuse *f*; ~ **machine for cardboard** *n* MECH ENG plieuse à carton *f*; ~ **pocket magnifier** *n* INSTRUMENT loupe pliante *f*, loupe à manche pliante *f*; ~ **propeller** *n*

NAUT *boat building* hélice bec-de-canard *f*; ~ **pylon** *n* AERONAUT *of helicopter* pylône repliable *m*; ~ **roller** *n* PRINT rouleau plieur *m*; ~ **rule** *n* (AmE) *(cf jointed rule)* CONST règle articulée *f*, METEO mètre pliant *m*; ~ **seat** *n* (AmE) *(cf tip-up seat)* VEHICLES strapontin *m*; ~ **sides** *n pl* PACKAGING côtés pliants *m pl*; ~ **sight** *n* CONST *for alidade* pinnule à charnière *f*; ~ **station** *n* PRINT poste de pliage *m*; ~ **strength** *n* PACKAGING résistance au pliage *f*; ~ **test** *n* PACKAGING essai de pliage *m*; ~ **wing aircraft** *n* AERONAUT avion à ailes repliables *m*

foldover *n* PETR pli déversé *m*; ~ **edge** *n* PRINT dépassant *m*, onglet de retour *m*; ~ **leg** *n* PHOTO branche articulée *f*

Foley: ~ **track** *n* RECORDING bande effets sonores *f*

foliar *adj* POLLUTION *surface* foliaire

foliated[1] *adj* GEOL folié, schisteux

foliated:[2] ~ **coal** *n* COAL TECH charbon lamelleux *m*; ~ **crystalline rock** *n* GEOL roche cristallophyllienne *f*, roche foliée *f*; ~ **tellurium** *n* MINERAL tellure auroplombifère *m*

foliation *n* GEOL feuilletage *m*, foliation *m*, schistosité *f*

folic: ~ **acid** *n* FOOD TECH acide folique *m*

folinic *adj* CHEM folinique

folio[1] *n* PRINT folio *m*, numéro *m*, numéro de page *m*, in-folio *m*

folio[2] *vt* PRINT numéroter

follow:[1] ~ **range** *n* ELECTRON plage d'accord automatique *f*; ~ **rest** *n* MECH ENG *of lathe* lunette à suivre *f*; ~ **spot** *n* CINEMAT poursuiteur *m*, projecteur de poursuite *m*

follow:[2] ~ **F-stop** *vt* CINEMAT compenser le diaphragme

follow:[3] ~ **focus** *vi* CINEMAT suivre le point

follower *n* COAL TECH prolongateur de pieu *m*, MECH ENG couvercle du piston *m*, *cam* galet *m*, roulette *f*, *driven pulley* poulie conduite *f*, poulie menée *f*, *gearing* roue conduite *f*, roue menée *f*, *of planing machine* palpeur *m*, PROD ENG *of stuffing box* chapeau *m*; ~ **bush** *n* PROD ENG *of stuffing box* bague du chapeau *f*, grain du chapeau *m*; ~ **controller** *n* CONTROL régulateur en cascade *m*; ~ **roll** *n* PAPER TECH rouleau entraîné *m*

following: ~ **gear** *n* MECH ENG engrenage mené *m*; ~ **wind** *n* NAUT vent arrière *m*

follow-up: ~ **controller** *n* CONTROL régulateur en cascade *m*

font *n* DP fonte *f*, PRINT famille de caractère *f*, fonte de caractères *f*, police *f*, police de caractères *f*; ~ **mold** *n* (AmE), ~ **mould** *n* (BrE) C&G moule à réservoir *m*

food: ~ **additive** *n* FOOD TECH additif alimentaire *m*; ~ **chemistry** *n* FOOD TECH chimie alimentaire *f*; ~ **control** *n* QUALITY contrôle alimentaire *m*; ~ **grade film** *n* PACKAGING film spécial pour l'alimentation *m*; ~ **grade packaging film** *n* PACKAGING film pour emballage alimentaire *m*; ~ **inspection** *n* QUALITY contrôle de nourriture *m*; ~ **irradiation** *n* FOOD TECH irradiation alimentaire *f*; ~ **nutritive requirements** *n* FOOD TECH besoins nutritifs alimentaires *m pl*; ~ **packaging** *n* PACKAGING emballage alimentaire *m*; ~ **poisoning** *n* FOOD TECH intoxication alimentaire *f*; ~ **preservative** *n* FOOD TECH préservatif pour produits alimentaires *m*; ~ **science** *n* FOOD TECH bromatologie *f*, science de l'alimentation *f*, science des aliments *f*; ~ **tray** *n* PACKAGING barquette *f*

food-processing: ~ **plant** *n* FOOD TECH entreprise de transformation des produits alimentaires *f*

foodstuff *n* FOOD TECH denrée alimentaire *f*, produit

alimentaire *m*

food-wrapping: ~ **machinery** *n* PACKAGING machine pour emballage alimentaire *f*

foolscap *n* PRINT foolscap *m*

foot *n* CONST *of anvil* patin *m*, METR *measure* pied *m*, MINING chevet *m*, mur *m*, sol *m*, NAUT *edge of sail* bordure *f*, *measurement* pied *m*, *support* support *m*; ~ **brake** *n* VEHICLES frein à pied *m*; ~ **candle** *n* CINEMAT bougie-pied *f*; ~ **carrier** *n* C&G aidant *m*; ~ **change lever** *n* (BrE) *(cf foot gearshift)* VEHICLES *on motorcycle gearbox* commande des vitesses au pied *f*, sélecteur au pied *m*; ~ **dimmer** *n* (AmE) *(cf foot dip switch)* AUTO *on car* pédale phare code *f*; ~ **dimmer switch** *n* (AmE) *(cf foot dip switch)* AUTO *on car* pédale phare code *f*; ~ **dip switch** *n* (BrE) *(cf foot dimmer switch, foot dimmer)* AUTO *on car* pédale phare code *f*; ~ **gearshift** *n* (AmE) *(cf foot change lever)* VEHICLES *on motorcycle gearbox* commande des vitesses au pied *f*, sélecteur au pied *m*; ~ **lambert** *n* CINEMAT lambert-pied *m*; ~ **pump** *n* AUTO *on car*, MECH ENG pompe à pied *f*; ~ **switch** *n* CONTROL interrupteur à commande au pied *m*, interrupteur à pédale *m*, INSTRUMENT interrupteur à pédale *m*; ~ **valve** *n* MECH ENG clapet de pied *m*, soupape de pied *f*

foot-activated: ~ **starter switch** *n* CONTROL interrupteur de démarrage à pédale *m*

footage *n* CINEMAT longueur *f*, métrage *m*; ~ **counter** *n* CINEMAT compteur en pieds *m*, métreuse *f*

footboard *n* (AmE) *(cf monkey board)* PETR, PETR TECH plate-forme d'accrochage *f*

footboards *n pl* C&G planchettes *f pl*

footbridge *n* CONST passerelle *f*, pont dormant *m*, RAIL passerelle en dessus *f*, TRANSP passerelle *f*

foot-candle *n* METR bougie-pied *f*

foothold *n* CONST assiette pour le pied *f*

footing *n* COAL TECH piédestal *m*, CONST assiette pour le pied *f*, *of building* empattement *m*; ~ **block** *n* CONST *shoring* couchis *m*, patin *m*, plate-forme *f*, semelle *f*, sole *f*

footlights *n pl* CINEMAT rampe *f*

footnote: ~ **call-out** *n* PRINT appel de note *m*, astérisque *f*, puce *f*

foot-operated: ~ **control** *n* MECH ENG commande au pied *f*; ~ **score** *n* C&G croquage à pédale *m*

footprint *n* SPACE *of beam* empreinte *f*, TV *of satellite* empreinte *f*, région couverte *f*

footrest *n* VEHICLES *of motorcycle* repose-pied *m*

footscrew *n* MECH ENG vis arrêtoir *f*, vis calante *f*, vis de bride *f*, vis de calage *f*

footstep *n* MECH ENG crapaudine *f*, palier de pied *m*; ~ **bearing** *n* MECH ENG crapaudine *f*, palier de pied *m*

footstock *n* MECH ENG *of lathe* contre-pointe *f*, contre-poupée *f*, poupée courante *f*, poupée mobile *f*

footwall *n* GEOL *of vein, layer* mur *m*, MINING chevet *m*, mur *m*, sol *m*, *of mine working* aval pendage *m*, aval pendage d'une galerie *m*; ~ **seam** *n* CONST gîte en aval pendage *m*

footway *n* CONST trottoir *m*

footwear: ~ **for protection against burns** *n* SAFETY protection par chaussures contre les brûlures *f*

foraminiferal *adj* GEOL à foraminifère

forbidden: ~ **band** *n* PHYS, RAD PHYS bande interdite *f*; ~ **combination check** *n* CONTROL contrôle par détection de code interdit *m*; ~ **decay mode** *n* RAD PHYS *atomic transition* mode de désintégration interdite *m*; ~ **energy band** *n* NUCLEAR écart énergétique *m*; ~ **transition** *n*

NUCLEAR transition non favorisée *f*, PHYS, RAD PHYS *in atomic nuclei* transition interdite *f*

force[1] *n* HYDROL *of waterfall* force *f*, PHYS force *f*, *of inertia* force d'inertie *f*, *of repulsion* force de répulsion *f*; ~ **of attraction** *n* PHYS force d'attraction *f*; ~ **balance transducer** *n* ELEC ENG transducteur à balance de forces *m*; ~ **disable command** *n* PROD ENG commande d'invalidation de forçage *f*; ~ **enable command** *n* PROD ENG commande de validation de forçage *f*; ~ **fan** *n* PROD ENG ventilateur foulant *m*, ventilateur positif *m*, ventilateur soufflant *m*; ~ **fit** *n* MECH emmanchement à force *m*, MECH ENG ajustement à frottement dur *m*, montage à force *m*; ~ **of friction** *n* MECH ENG force de frottement *f*; ~ **of gravity** *n* ASTRON force de gravité *f*; ~ **line** *n* GEOPHYS, MECH ligne de force *f*; ~ **link** *n* AERONAUT bielle à contact *f*; ~ **majeure** *n* CONST force majeure *f*; ~ **pump** *n* PROD ENG pompe foulante *f*, pompe refoulante *f*, pompe à piston plongeur *f*, pompe à plongeur *f*; ~ **selection** *n* PROD ENG sélection de forçage *f*; ~ **table** *n* PROD ENG table des forçages *f*; ~ **unit** *n* MECH ENG unité de force *f*

force[2] *vt* MINING *the tampling* projeter; ~ **off** *vt* PROD ENG forcer à zéro; ~ **on** *vt* MECH ENG emmancher par effort, PROD ENG forcer à un

forced: ~ **air cooling** *n* MECH ENG refroidissement forcé à l'air *m*; ~ **air furnace** *n* (AmE) *(cf forced draught burner)* GAS TECH brûleur à air soufflé *m*; ~ **circulation boiler** *n* HEATING chaudière à circulation d'eau forcée *f*; ~ **convection** *n* FLUID PHYS, GAS TECH, HEAT ENG, PHYS convection forcée *f*; ~ **convection edge** *n* PRINT séchage par convection forcée *m*; ~ **convection lehr** *n* C&G arche à convection forcée *f*; ~ **cooling** *n* MECH ENG refroidissement forcé *m*; ~ **development** *n* CINEMAT développement poussé *m*; ~ **draft** *n* (AmE) *see forced draught* ~ **draft air-cooled condenser** *n* (AmE) *see forced draught air-cooled condenser* ~ **draft burner** *n* (AmE) *see forced draught burner* ~ **draft cooling** *n* (AmE) *see forced draught cooling* ~ **draft furnace** *n* (AmE) *see forced draught furnace* ~ **draught** *n* (BrE) CONST *in chimney*, HEATING tirage forcé *m*, MECH ENG *blown current of air* air soufflé *m*, courant d'air forcé *m*, vent soufflé *m*, *ventilation* aérage positif *m*, ventilation mécanique par insufflation *f*; ~ **draught air-cooled condenser** *n* (BrE) REFRIG condenseur à air forcé *m*; ~ **draught burner** *n* (BrE) *(cf forced air furnace)* GAS TECH brûleur à air soufflé *m*, MECH ENG brûleur à courant d'air forcé *m*; ~ **draught cooling** *n* (BrE) REFRIG refroidissement à air aspiré *m*, refroidissement à air forcé *m*; ~ **draught furnace** *n* (BrE) PROD ENG four à air forcé *m*, four à air soufflé *m*, four à tuyère et courant d'air forcé *m*; ~ **feed lubrication** *n* AUTO graissage sous pression *m*; ~ **fit bush** *n* MECH ENG coquille à montage forcé *f*; ~ **landing** *n* AERONAUT atterrissage forcé *m*; ~ **lubrification** *n* REFRIG graissage sous pression *m*; ~ **oil cooling** *n* MECH ENG refroidissement forcé à l'huile *m*; ~ **oscillation** *n* ELECTRON, PHYS oscillation forcée *f*; ~ **ventilation** *n* MECH ENG ventilation forcée *f*, PROD ENG forçage *m*; ~ **ventilation motor** *n* ELEC moteur refroidi à l'air forcé *m*; ~ **vibration** *n* ACOUSTICS, PHYS vibration forcée *f*; ~ **warm air** *n* HEATING air chaud forcé *m*; ~ **water cooling** *n* MECH ENG refroidissement forcé à l'eau *m*

force-feed: ~ **lubrication** *n* MECH ENG, PROD ENG graissage sous pression *m*

force-off: ~ **command** *n* PROD ENG commande de forçage à "O" *f*

force-on: ~ **command** *n* PROD ENG commande de forçage à "1" *f*

forcing *n* CONST *of lock* forcement *m*, MINING refoulement *m*; ~ **down** *n* MINING refoulement *m*; ~ **indicator** *n* PROD ENG témoin de forçage *m*; ~ **key** *n* PROD ENG touche de forçage *f*; ~ **open the points** *n* RAIL talonnage d'aiguille *m*

ford[1] *n* CONST gué *m*

ford[2] *vt* HYDROL *river* passer, traverser

fording *n* CONST gué *m*

fore[1] *adj* NAUT avant, de l'avant

fore[2] *adv* NAUT avant; ~ **and aft** *adv* NAUT de l'avant à l'arrière

fore:[3] ~ **deep** *n* GEOL avant-fosse *f*; ~ **edge** *n* PRINT marge extérieure *f*, *of book* tranche extérieure *f*; ~ **observation** *n* CONST *levelling* coup avant *m*; ~ **vacuum** *n* PHYS prévide *m*

fore-and-aft: ~ **cyclic control support** *n* AERONAUT *of helicopter* support profondeur *m*; ~ **cyclic pitch** *n* AERONAUT *of helicopter* pas cyclique longitudinal *m*; ~ **line** *n* NAUT *ship design* axe longitudinal *m*

forebay *n* HYDR EQUIP chambre d'équilibre *f*, chambre à eau *f*, OCEANOG avant-port *m*, WATER SUPP *headrace* bief d'amont *m*, biez d'amont *m*

forecast: ~ **horizon** *n* PROD ENG horizon de planification *m*, horizon de prévision *m*; ~ **interval** *n* PROD ENG maille de prévision *f*; ~ **period** *n* PROD ENG période élémentaire de prévision *f*

forecasting *n* COMP, DP, WATER SUPP prévision *f*

forecastle *n* NAUT *shipbuilding* gaillard d'avant *m*, poste avant *m*

foredeck *n* NAUT pont avant *m*

forefoot *n* NAUT *shipbuilding* brion *m*

foreground[1] *adj* COMP, DP d'avant-plan

foreground:[2] **in the** ~ *adv* PHOTO au premier plan

foreground:[3] *n* CINEMAT avant-plan *m*, premier plan *m*; ~ **job** *n* COMP travail de premier plan *m*, DP tâche de premier plan *f*; ~ **miniature** *n* CINEMAT maquette de premier plan *f*; ~ **processing** *n* COMP, DP traitement de premier plan *m*; ~ **program** *n* COMP programme d'avant-plan *m*

forehearth *n* C&G canal de distribution *m*, PROD ENG *of furnace* avant-creuset *m*; ~ **entrance** *n* C&G boîte aux lettres *f*

foreign: ~ **cullet** *n* C&G calcin étranger *m*; ~ **emissions** *n pl* POLLUTION émissions étrangères *f pl*; ~ **matter** *n* PROD ENG impuretés *f pl*; ~ **source** *n* POLLUTION source externe *f*, source extérieure *f*

foreland *n* GEOL avant-pays *m*, OCEANOG avant-pays marin *m*

forelock *n* MECH ENG clavette *f*; ~ **bolt** *n* MECH ENG boulon à clavette *m*

forelocking *n* MECH ENG clavetage *m*

foreman *n* C&G chef de place *m*, CONST conducteur *m*, contremaître *m*, PROD ENG chef *m*, chef d'équipe *m*, chef de poste *m*, contremaître *m*; ~ **shunter** *n* RAIL brigadier de manoeuvre *m*

foremast *n* NAUT mât de misaine *m*

foremelter *n* C&G filière de préfusion *f*

forepeak *n* NAUT pic avant *m*

forepoling *n* MINING *timber support* enfilage *m*, poussage *m*

fore-runnings *n pl* FOOD TECH *fermentation* produit de tête *m*, têtes *f pl*

foresail *n* NAUT misaine *f*

foreseen *adj* TELECOM interruption prévisible

foreset: ~ **beds** *n pl* GEOL dépôts deltaïques frontaux *m pl*

foreshore *n* GEOL estran *m*, plage *f*, OCEANOG estran *m*

foresight *n* CONST *surveying* coup avant *m*, MILIT *of rifle* guidon *m*, MINING *levelling* coup avant *m*

forestay *n* NAUT étai avant *m*; ~ **pin** *n* NAUT axe d'étai *m*

forestaysail *n* NAUT trinquette *f*

forestry: ~ **research** *n* POLLUTION recherche forestière *f*

forewinning: ~ **heading** *n* MINING galerie de traçage *f*

forge *n* PROD ENG atelier de forge *m*, atelier de forgeron *m*, atelier de maréchal ferrant *m*, forge *f*; ~ **back** *n* PROD ENG plaque de contre-feu *f*; ~ **bellows** *n pl* PROD ENG soufflerie de forge *f*, soufflet de forge *m*; ~ **hammer** *n* PROD ENG marteau de forgeron *m*, marteau à forger *m*, marteau-pilon *m*, pilon *m*; ~ **roll** *n* PROD ENG cylindre forgeur *m*; ~ **scale** *n* PROD ENG battitures *f pl*, martelures *f pl*, paille de fer *f*, scories de forge *f pl*, écailles *f pl*; ~ **welding** *n* CONST, PROD ENG soudage à la forge *m*

forged[1] *adj* MECH *materials*, PROD ENG forgé; ~ **in one piece** *adj* PRODUCTION venu de forge

forged:[2] ~ **end** *n* SPRINGS extrémité forgée *f*; ~ **eye** *n* SPRINGS oeil forgé *m*; ~ **shackle** *n* MECH ENG *for lifting* manille forgée *f*; ~ **steel lifting hook** *n* MECH ENG crochet de levage en acier forgé *m*; ~ **wing attachment** *n* AERONAUT ferrure forgée d'attache voilure-fuselage *f*

forging *n* MECH *materials* forgeage *m*, pièce forgée *f*, PROD ENG *piece of forged work* pièce de forge *f*, pièce forgée *f*, pièce venue de forge *f*; ~ **dies** *n pl* MECH ENG outillage de forgeage *m*; ~ **press** *n* PROD ENG presse à forger *f*

fork[1] *n* C&G fourche *f*, CONST *bifurcation, of road, river, railway* bifurcation *f*, MECH ENG *of clutch* embrayeur *m*, fourchette *f*, *of knuckle joint* chape *f*, VEHICLES *of motorcycle gearbox, clutch* fourche *f*; ~ **arm** *n* MECH ENG fourchette *f*; ~ **bar** *n* MECH ENG barre de débrayage *f*; ~ **center** *n* (AmE), ~ **centre** *n* (BrE) MECH ENG *lathe* pointe à trois dents *f*; ~ **chuck** *n* MECH ENG griffe *f*, mandrin à trois pointes *m*, mandrin à tulipe *m*; ~ **head** *n* MECH ENG tête de bielle à fourche *f*; ~ **leg** *n* VEHICLES *of motorcycle* montant de fourche *m*; ~ **mount** *n* ASTRON monture à fourche *f*; ~ **mounting** *n* INSTRUMENT fourche *f*, monture en fourche *f*; ~ **oscillator** *n* ELECTRON oscillateur à diapason *m*; ~ **push rod** *n* VEHICLES *of clutch* tringle de fourchette *f*; ~ **return spring** *n* VEHICLES *of clutch* ressort de rappel de fourchette *m*; ~ **truck** *n* TRANSP chariot élévateur à fourche *m*; ~ **wrench** *n* MECH ENG clé à fourche *f*

fork:[2] ~ **a belt off** *vt* MECH ENG débrayer une courroie; ~ **a belt on** *vt* MECH ENG embrayer une courroie

forked: ~ **connection** *n* ELEC couplage en zigzag double *m*; ~ **pipe** *n* CONST tuyau bifurqué *m*

fork-end: ~ **connecting rod** *n* MECH ENG bielle avec tête à fourche *f*, bielle à fourche *f*

fork-lever: ~ **roller** *n* PROD ENG levier-fourche à galets *m*

forklift: ~ **truck** *n* CONST, PACKAGING chariot élévateur à fourche *m*, PROD ENG chariot à fourches *m*, TRANSP chariot élévateur à fourche *m*

form[1] *n* COMP imprimé *m*, CONST *physical geography* forme *f*, modelé *m*, relief *m*, DP imprimé *m*, PATENTS *of abstract* forme *f*, *printed* formulaire *m*, PRINT cahier sortant d'une rotative *m*, forme imprimante *f*, PROD ENG *mould for making concrete work* coffrage *m*; ~ **drag** *n* AERONAUT traînée de forme *f*; ~ **error** *n* METR *of workpiece* erreur de forme *f*; ~ **feed** *n* *(FF)* COMP,

PRINT *computer printers* alimentation en papier *f*, avance-papier *m*; ~ **feed character** *n* COMP, DP caractère de changement de page *m*; ~ **fill and seal machine** *n* PACKAGING formeuse-remplisseuse-scelleuse *f*; ~ **grinding** *n* MECH ENG rectification de profilage *f*; ~ **milling** *n* MECH ENG chantournage à la fraise *m*, PROD ENG fraisage de forme *m*; ~ **milling cutter** *n* MECH ENG fraise de forme *f*; ~ **milling cutter with constant profile** *n* MECH ENG fraise de forme à profil constant *f*; ~ **roller** *n* PRINT rouleau toucheur *m*; ~ **shim** *n* MECH ENG cale de forme *f*; ~ **stop** *n* COMP arrêt de fin de papier *m*, DP arrêt pour fin de papier *m*

form:[2] ~ **fill and seal** *vt* PRINT former remplir et sceller

form:[3] ~ **the fiber** *vi* (AmE), ~ **the fibre** *vi* (BrE) TELECOM fibrer

formal[1] *adj* CHEM formel

formal:[2] ~ **language** *n* COMP langage formel *m*; ~ **logic** *n* COMP, DP logique formelle *f*; ~ **parameter** *n* COMP, DP paramètre formel *m*

formaldehyde *n* CHEM, P&R *raw material*, PROP MAT, TEXTILES formaldéhyde *m*; ~ **sulfoxylate** *n* (AmE), ~ **sulphoxylate** *n* (BrE) FOOD TECH formaldéhyde-sulfoxylate *m*

formalin *n* CHEM solution aqueuse de formol *f*

formamide *n* CHEM formamide *m*, formiamide *m*

formant *n* ACOUSTICS zone formante *f*, zone formantique *f*; ~ **vocoder** *n* TELECOM *maritime satellite* codeur à fréquences vocales de formants *m*

format[1] *n* COMP, DP format *m*, PRINT dimension *f*, format *m*, TV format *m*

format[2] *vt* COMP, DP formater, PRINT formater, initialiser

formate *n* CHEM formiate *m*

formation *n* GEOL *mappable lithostratigraphic unit* formation *f*, PAPER TECH texture *f*, *of sheet* formation *f*, structure *f*; ~ **energy** *n* METALL énergie de formation *f*; ~ **evaluation** *n* PETR TECH *petroleum geology* évaluation des formations traversées *f*; ~ **factor** *n* PETR facteur de formation *m*; ~ **flight** *n* AERONAUT vol en formation *m*; ~ **fluid** *n* PETR TECH *geology* fluide de formation *m*; ~ **pressure** *n* GEOL pression de formation *f*, PETR TECH *geology* pression de formation *f*, pression de la roche-magasin *f*; ~ **pressure gradient** *n* GEOL, PETR TECH *geology* gradient de pression de formation *m*; ~ **resistivity** *n* PETR *geology* facteur de formation *m*, résistivité de formation *f*; ~ **test** *n* PETR TECH *geology* essai de formation *m*; ~ **tester** *n* PAPER TECH appareil de mesure de l'épair *m*, PETR testeur de formation *m*; ~ **volume factor** *n* PETR facteur volumétrique de formation *m*; ~ **water** *n* PETR, PETR TECH *geology* eau de formation *f*

formatter *n* COMP formateur *m*, programme de formatage *m*, DP formateur *m*

formatting *n* COMP, DP, TELECOM formatage *m*

formazyl *n* CHEM formazyle *m*

formed: ~ **cutter** *n* MECH ENG fraise de forme *f*; ~ **milling cutter** *n* MECH ENG fraise de forme *f*

former *n* C&G mouleur *m*, ELEC ENG mandrin *m*, INSTRUMENT calibre *m*, MECH ENG cintre *m*, PAPER TECH calibre *m*, formeur *m*, PRINT cône *m*, entonnoir *m*, triangle *m*, PROD ENG *strickle* trousse *f*, *templet* calibre *m*, calibre de forme *m*, calibre reproducteur *m*, gabarit *m*, patron *m*, singe *m*; ~ **folder** *n* PRINT plieuse à triangle *f*; ~ **roller** *n* C&G roulette à gabarit *f*; ~ **winding** *n* C&G enroulement sur gabarit *m*

formic *adj* CHEM formique

forming *n* MECH *materials* façonnage *m*, formage *m*, P&R *process*, PROD ENG formage *m*; ~ **fabric** *n* PAPER TECH toile de formation *f*; ~ **lathe** *n* MECH ENG tour à copier *m*, tour à singer *m*, tour à touche *m*; ~ **roll** *n* PAPER TECH rouleau de formation *m*; ~ **shoe** *n* PAPER TECH sabot de formation *m*; ~ **temperature** *n* PACKAGING température de façonnage *f*; ~ **tool** *n* MECH ENG outil de forme *m*, outil de reproduction *m*, outil à calibrer *m*; ~ **tool holder** *n* MECH ENG *of lathe* porte-outil de reproduction *m*; ~ **tools** *n pl* MECH ENG outillage de formage *m*; ~ **with sheets** *n* C&G moulage à la croûte *m*

formset *n* PRINT document administratif en plusieurs parties *m*, liasse *f*

formula *n* CHEM, PHOTO *developer* formule *f*

formulation *n* P&R *process, recipe* formulation *f*

formwork *n* CONST coffrage *m*, MECH ENG *tool* marteau de coffreur *m*; ~ **oil** *n* CONST huile de coffrage *f*

form-wound: ~ **coil** *n* ELEC bobine formée sur gabarit *f*, enroulement préformé *m*

formyl *n* CHEM formyle *m*

Fornax *n* ASTRON Fourneau *m*

forsterite *n* MINERAL forstérite *f*

fortification *n* FOOD TECH enrichissement *m*

fortified *adj* FOOD TECH enrichi, fortifié

Fortin: ~ **barometer** *n* LAB EQUIP, PHYS baromètre Fortin *m*

forty-five: ~ **rpm record** *n* RECORDING disque 45 tours (quarante-cinq tours) *m*

forward[1] *adj* AERONAUT avant, NAUT avant, de l'avant, sur l'avant

forward[2] *adv* NAUT avant, de l'avant, sur l'avant; ~ **of the beam** *adv* NAUT sur l'avant du travers

forward:[3] ~ **amplifier** *n* ELECTRON amplificateur sans contreréaction *m*; ~ **bias** *n* ELEC ENG, PHYS polarisation directe *f*; ~ **characteristic** *n* ELECTRON caractéristique directe *f*; ~ **combustion** *n* PETR combustion en avance *f*, combustion à co-courant *f*; ~ **conductance** *n* ELEC *of semiconductor* conductance directe *f*, conductance en l'état passant *f*; ~ **contactor** *n* PROD ENG contacteur marche avant *m*; ~ **current** *n* ELEC *of semiconductor*, ELEC ENG courant direct *m*; ~ **error correction** *n* COMP *(FEC)*, TELECOM correction d'erreurs sans voie de retour *f*; ~ **explicit congestion notification** *n* *(FECN)* TELECOM notification d'encombrement explicite émise vers l'avant *f*; ~ **input signal** *n* TELECOM signal d'entrée vers l'avant *m*; ~ **interworking telephony event** *n* *(FITE)* TELECOM événement téléphonique d'interfonctionnement vers l'avant *m*; ~ **link** *n* SPACE *communications* liaison aller *f*; ~ **path** *n* ELEC ENG chaîne d'action *f*, chaîne directe *f*; ~ **perpendicular** *n* NAUT *ship design* perpendiculaire avant *f*; ~ **resistance** *n* ELEC *of semiconductor* résistance directe *f*; ~ **scattering** *n* RECORDING réflexion en direct *f*; ~ **scheduling** *n* PROD ENG chargement au plus tôt *m*, chargement aval *m*, jalonnement au plus tôt *m*, jalonnement aval *m*; ~ **station** *n* PROD ENG poste aval *m*; ~ **stroke interval** *n* TV temps d'aller *m*; ~ **takeoff** *n* AERONAUT *of helicopter* décollage avant *m*; ~ **wave** *n* ELEC ENG onde directe *f*, onde progressive *f*, onde progressive directe *f*

forward[4] *vt* PRINT faire avancer

forward-backward: ~ **counter** *n* TV compteur-décompteur *m*

forwarded: ~ **notification** *n* TELECOM notification retransmise *f*

forwarding: ~ **agent** n (BrE) *(cf freight agent)* NAUT, TRANSP transitaire m; ~ **office** n (BrE) *(cf freight office)* TRANSP bureau des départs m; ~ **roller** n PRINT rouleau d'entraînement m; ~ **sucker** n PRINT sucette f, ventouse d'entraînement f

forward-swept: ~ **wing** n AERONAUT aile en flèche négative f, voilure à flèche inverse f, voilure à flèche négative f

forward-traveling: ~ **wave** n (AmE), **forward-travelling wave** n (BrE) ELEC ENG onde directe f, onde progressive f, onde progressive directe f

fossil n GEOL fossile m; ~ **copal** n MINERAL copal fossile m; ~ **fuel** n POLLUTION, THERMOD combustible fossile m; ~ **imprint** n GEOL empreinte fossile f; ~ **nuclear reactor** n NUCLEAR réacteur nucléaire naturel m; ~ **radiation** n SPACE rayonnement fossile m; ~ **water** n HYDROL eau fossile f, eau primitive f

fossil-bearing adj GEOL fossilifère

fossil-fuel: ~ **power station** n ELEC, THERMOD centrale thermique à combustibles fossiles f

fossiliferous adj GEOL fossilifère

fossilize vt GEOL fossiliser

Foucault: ~ **pendulum** n PHYS pendule de Foucault m

foul:[1] ~ **anchor** n NAUT ancre engagée f, ancre surjalée f, ancre surpattée f; ~ **bottom** n NAUT carène sale f, *bad holding ground* fond de mauvaise tenue m, *dirty ground* fond sale m; ~ **gas** n GAS TECH gaz non purifié m; ~ **ground** n NAUT mauvais fond m; ~ **mine gas** n MINING mofette f; ~ **water** n RECYCLING eau sale f, eau souillée f; ~ **weather gear** n NAUT ciré m; ~ **wind** n NAUT *weather* vent contraire m

foul[2] vt MAR POLL boucher, encrasser, engorger, MECH ENG fausser, NAUT *anchor, rope, ship, engine* engager, entrer en collision avec, se heurter contre, surjaler

fouled[1] adj PROD ENG encrassé

fouled:[2] ~ **anchor** n NAUT ancre engagée f, ancre surjalée f, ancre surpattée f

fouling: ~ **factor** n REFRIG facteur d'encrassement m

foundation n COAL TECH fondation f, travaux de fondation m pl, CONST assiette f, assise f, base f, fondation f, fondement m, semelle f; ~ **block** n CONST massif de fondation m; ~ **bolt** n CONST boulon de fondation m; ~ **plate** n CONST plaque d'assise f, plaque de base f, plaque de fond f, plaque de fondation f, taque d'assise f

founder[1] n PROD ENG *person* fondeur m

founder[2] vi NAUT *of boat* couler, sombrer

founder's: ~ **black** n COATINGS enduit de noir m

founding n PROD ENG *art* fonderie f, *operation of casting* fonte f, moulage m

foundry n COAL TECH, HEATING, PROD ENG fonderie f; ~ **abrasive cutoff and grinding machine** n MECH ENG tronçonneuse à meule et rectifieuse de fonderie f; ~ **blower** n PROD ENG ventilateur de fonderie m; ~ **flask** n PROD ENG châssis de fonderie m, châssis de moulage m; ~ **iron** n PROD ENG fonte de moulage f; ~ **ladle** n PROD ENG poche f, poche de coulée f, poche de fonderie f, poche de fondeur f, poche à fonte f; ~ **riddle** n PROD ENG tamis de mouleur m; ~ **sand** n CONST sable de fonderie m, PROD ENG sable de fonderie m, sable de moulage m; ~ **scrap** n PROD ENG bocage de fonte m, débris de fonte m, déchets de fonderie m pl, scraps de fonderie m pl, vieilles fontes f pl

fount n *see font*

fountain n PRINT bassine f, encrier m ~ **blade** n PRINT lame d'encrier f; ~ **keys** n pl PRINT clés d'encrier f pl; ~ **runner** n PROD ENG *in mould* chenal de coulée en source

m; ~ **screw** n PRINT vis d'encrier f

four: ~ **master** n NAUT quatre-mâts m; ~ **vector** n PHYS quadrivecteur m

four-barrel: ~ **carburetor** n (AmE), ~ **carburettor** n (BrE) AUTO carburateur quadruple m

four-centered: ~ **arch** n (AmE), **four-centred arch** n (BrE) CONST *curve described* arc aplati m, arc à quatre centres m, *structure* voûte aplatie f, voûte à quatre centres f

four-channel: ~ **amplifier** n ELECTRON amplificateur à quatre voies m

four-circle: ~ **diffractometer** n CRYSTALL diffractomètre à quatre cercles m

four-color: ~ **printing** n (AmE) *see four-colour printing*; ~ **process** n (AmE) *see four-colour process*; ~ **process ink** n (AmE) *see four-colour process ink*

four-colour: ~ **printing** n (BrE) PRINT impression en quatre couleurs f, quadrichromie f; ~ **process** n (BrE) PRINT impression en quatre couleurs f, quadrichromie f; ~ **process ink** n (BrE) PRINT encre quadrichromique f

four-column: ~ **forging press** n PROD ENG presse à forger à quatre colonnes f

four-concentric: ~ **circle refractive index template** n TELECOM gabarit d'indice de réfraction à quatre cercles concentriques m

four-concentric-circle: ~ **near-field template** n OPT, TELECOM gabarit à quatre cercles concentriques en champ proche m; ~ **refractive index template** n OPT gabarit d'indice de réfraction à quatre cercles concentriques m

four-cylinder: ~ **motorcycle** n TRANSP moto à quatre cylindres f

Fourdrinier n PAPER TECH table plate de fabrication f; ~ **paper machine** n PAPER TECH machine à papier à table plate f

four-engine: ~ **jet aircraft** n AERONAUT quadriréacteur m

four-flute: ~ **twist hand reamer** n MECH ENG alésoir à main à quatre tranchants en hélice m

fourfold: ~ **rotation axis** n CRYSTALL axe d'ordre quatre m, axe quadratique m; ~ **tripod stand** n PHOTO pied à quatre brisures m

four-high n PROD ENG double duo m, quarto m; ~ **rod mill** n PROD ENG laminoir double duo m

Fourier: ~ **analysis** n ELECTRON analyse de Fourier f, MATH analyse harmonique f, PHYS analyse de Fourier f; ~ **integral** n PHYS intégrale de Fourier f; ~ **series** n CRYSTALL série de Fourier f, MATH suite de Fourier f, PHYS série de Fourier f; ~ **transform** n CRYSTALL, ELECTRON, PHYS transformée de Fourier f; ~ **transformation** n ELECTRON, PHYS transformation de Fourier f; ~ **transform spectroscopy** n PHYS spectroscopie de Fourier f

four-jaw: ~ **independent chuck** n MECH ENG plateau à quatre griffes indépendantes m

four-layer: ~ **diode** n ELECTRON diode à quatre couches f

four-level: ~ **maser** n ELECTRON maser à quatre niveaux m

four-phase adj ELECTRON quadriphase

four-plate n CINEMAT table de montage à quatre plateaux f

four-ply adj PROD ENG *belting* en quatre épaisseurs, à quatre plis

four-polar adj ELEC *generator* quadripolaire, tétrapolaire

four-pole[1] adj ELEC *generator* quadripolaire, tétrapolaire

four-pole:[2] ~ **filter** n ELECTRON filtre à quatre pôles m; ~ **generator** n ELEC dynamo quadripolaire f, dynamo tétrapolaire f

four-port: ~ **directional control valve** n MECH ENG distributeur à quatre orifices m

four-quadrant: ~ **multiplier** n ELECTRON multiplicateur à quatre quadrants m

four-roll: ~ **reverse pan feed** n PRINT gravure à quatre rouleaux inversés f

four-screw: ~ **bell chuck** n MECH ENG mandrin à quatre vis m

four-seat: ~ **aircraft** n AERONAUT quadriplace m

four-sided[1] adj GEOM quadrilatère

four-sided:[2] ~ **sketch** n PACKAGING croquis quadrangulaire m

four-signature: ~ **coding system** n TELECOM système de codage à quatre signatures m

four-solar: ~ **mass limit** n ASTRON limite à quatre masses solaires f

four-spindle: ~ **drilling machine** n PROD ENG machine à percer à quatre forets f

four-star: ~ **petrol** n AUTO essence super f

four-stroke: ~ **cycle** n AUTO cycle à quatre temps m, VEHICLES of engine cycle Beau de Rochas m, cycle à quatre temps m; ~ **engine** n AUTO, MECH, MECH ENG, NAUT diesel, VEHICLES moteur à quatre temps m

four-terminal n ELEC ENG network quadripôle m

fourth n ACOUSTICS quarte f; ~ **generation** n COMP, DP quatrième génération f; ~ **generation computer** n COMP, DP ordinateur de quatrième génération m

fourth-power: ~ **law** n TV loi de correction biquadratique f

four-throw: ~ **geared pump** n PROD ENG pompe à quatre corps et à engrenages f

four-tool: ~ **tool post** n MECH ENG of lathe porte-outil revolver à quatre faces m, porte-outil à tourelle carrée m; ~ **turret** n MECH ENG of lathe porte-outil revolver à quatre faces m, porte-outil à tourelle carrée m

four-track: ~ **recorder** n RECORDING magnétophone quatre pistes m; ~ **recording** n RECORDING enregistrement à quart de piste m

four-way n CINEMAT synchroniseuse à quatre tambours f; ~ **bit** n PETR TECH trépan à quatre lames m; ~ **cock** n WATER SUPP robinet à quatre eaux m, robinet à quatre voies m; ~ **dusting** n PRINT poudrage exécuté sur les quatre côtés m; ~ **extension socket** n ELEC ENG bloc quadriprise m; ~ **pallet** n PACKAGING palette à quatre entrées f; ~ **powdering** n PRINT poudrage exécuté sur les quatre côtés m

four-wheel: ~ **brake system** n VEHICLES système de freinage à quatre roues m; ~ **drive** n AUTO, VEHICLES transmission quatre roues motrices f pl; ~ **drive vehicle** n TRANSP véhicule à quatre roues motrices m

four-wing: ~ **bit** n PETR TECH trépan à deux taillants m

four-wire: ~ **circuit** n COMP, DP circuit quatre fils m; ~ **crosspoint** n TELECOM point de connexion à quatre fils m; ~ **repeater** n ELECTRON répéteur à quatre fils m; ~ **switch** n TELECOM autocommutateur à quatre fils m, commutateur à quatre fils m; ~ **switching system** n TELECOM autocommutateur à quatre fils m, commutateur à quatre fils m; ~ **system** n ELEC ENG système à quatre fils m

fowlerite n MINERAL fowlérite f

FPC abbr (fish protein concentrate) OCEANOG CPP (concentré de protéines de poisson)

FPLA abbr (field programmable logic array) COMP, DP réseau à logique programmable par l'utilisateur m

FPP abbr (floating point processor) COMP, DP processeur en virgule flottante m

FPS abbr (fast packet switch) TELECOM commutateur de paquets rapide m

Fr (francium) CHEM Fr (francium)

fractal n COMP, DP fractale f

fraction n PETR TECH refining, distillation coupe f, fraction f, PRINT fraction f

fractional[1] adj MATH fractionnaire

fractional:[2] ~ **crystallization** n GEOL igneous process cristallisation fractionnée f; ~ **distillation** n CHEM TECH distillation fractionnée f, PETR TECH refining distillation fractionnée f, fractionnement m; ~ **frequency deviation** n ELECTRON dérive de fréquence à long terme f; ~ **horsepower motor** n ELEC moteur de puissance fractionnaire m, ELEC ENG (FHP motor) moteur fractionnaire m; ~ **low-power condensing unit** n REFRIG groupe frigorifique à faible puissance m; ~ **part** n COMP, DP partie fractionnaire f; ~ **pitch** n MECH ENG of screw pas bâtard m; ~ **pitch winding** n ELEC of armature, ELEC ENG enroulement à pas partiel m; ~ **slot winding** n ELEC ENG enroulement à nombre fractionnaire par pôle et par phase m

fractionating: ~ **apparatus** n CHEM TECH appareil de fractionnement m; ~ **column** n CHEM TECH colonne de fractionnement f, tour de fractionnement f, LAB EQUIP distillation, PETR TECH refinery colonne de fractionnement f

fractionation n CHEM of oil, solvent, PROP MAT fractionnement m

fracture[1] n COAL TECH cassure f, CRYSTALL cassure f, rupture f, FUELLESS cassure f, MECH materials cassure f, fracture f, NUCLEAR, PROP MAT, QUALITY rupture f; ~ **behavior** n (AmE), ~ **behaviour** n (BrE) METALL comportement à la rupture m; ~ **cleavage** n GEOL clivage de fracture m; ~ **cone** n C&G cône de fracturation m; ~ **criterion** n METALL critère de rupture m; ~ **gradient** n GEOL gradient de fracturation m, PETR TECH geology gradient de fracturation m, gradient de pression de fracturation m; ~ **log** n PETR diagramme de fracture m, log de fracturation m; ~ **mechanics** n MECH materials, PROP MAT mécanique de fracture f; ~ **mirror** n C&G miroir de fracture m; ~ **pattern** n C&G dessin de fragmentation m; ~ **plane** n GEOPHYS plan de fracture m; ~ **pressure** n GEOL, PETR TECH geology pression de fracturation f; ~ **stress** n PROP MAT charge de rupture rationnelle f; ~ **test** n MECH ENG essai par rupture m; ~ **toughness** n P&R résistance à la rupture f, ténacité de rupture f; ~ **zone** n GEOPHYS zone de fracture f

fracture[2] vt PROP MAT fracturer

fracture[3] vi GEOPHYS, PROP MAT se fracturer

fractured[1] adj PROP MAT crevassé

fractured:[2] ~ **and faulted chalk** n CONST craie fracturée et faillée f

fracturing n GEOL degré de fissures m, fissuration f, formation de fissures f, fracturation f, PETR TECH geology fracturation f

fragile adj PACKAGING handling marking label on package fragile

fragment vt COAL TECH fragmenter

fragmental: ~ **rock** n GEOL roche détritique f

fragmentation n COMP, DP, METALL fragmentation f

fragmented adj COAL TECH rock meuble

fragmenting: ~ **shell** n MILIT cartouche à grenaille f

fragments: ~ **from worn tools** n pl SAFETY fragments d'outils abîmés m pl

frame[1] n COMP cadre m, trame f, CONST *casing of door or window* bâti m, bâti dormant m, dormant m, *for walls or partitions* pan m, *of roof, bridge* charpente f, *outer frame or skeleton* carcasse f, châssis de charpente m, *set of shores* batterie d'étais f, DP cadre m, trame f, ELEC ENG *of device* châssis m, *of motor* carcasse f, ELECTRON trame f, MECH cadre m, charpente f, châssis m, MECH ENG cadre m, charpente f, châssis m, couple m, *of engine, machine tool* bâtim, NAUT *shipbuilding* cadre m, carcasse f, châssis m, membrure f, PACKAGING cadre m, PAPER TECH bâti m, PHOTO *around photograph* cadre m, PHYS *of reference* référentiel m, PRINT cadre m, châssis m, trame f, châssis de montage m, RAIL *vehicles* châssis m, SPACE *communications*, TELECOM trame f, TEXTILES bâti m, TV cadre m, image f, VEHICLES *body* cadre m, WATER SUPP *of sluice gate* tableau m; ~ **adjuster** n CINEMAT dispositif de cadrage m; ~ **alignment** n SPACE *communications*, TELECOM, TV verrouillage de trame m; ~ **alignment signal** n *(FAS)* TELECOM signal de verrouillage de trame m; ~ **angle** n NAUT *shipbuilding* cornière de membrure f; ~ **bridge** n CONST pont en charpente m; ~ **by frame** n CINEMAT, TV image par image f; ~ **cap** n MECH ENG chapeau de couple m; ~ **counter** n CINEMAT compteur d'images m, PHOTO compteur de poses m, compteur de vues m, *camera* compteur d'images m; ~ **crossbeam** n MECH ENG traverse de couple f; ~ **cross member** n MECH ENG contrefiche de couple f; ~ **edging** n MECH ENG bordure d'encadrement f; ~ **efficiency** n SPACE *communications* rendement de trame m; ~ **fixing** n CONST *building* cheville cadre f; ~ **frequency** n TV fréquence image f; ~ **generator** n TELECOM générateur de trame m; ~ **grid** n ELECTRON grille-cadre f; ~ **house** n CONST maison en pans de bois f; ~ **length** n SPACE *communications* longueur de trame f; ~ **line** n CINEMAT ligne de cadrage f, TV barrette f; ~ **line leader** n CINEMAT amorce cadrée f; ~ **loss second** n *(FLS)* TELECOM seconde avec perte de trame f; ~ **monitoring** n CONTROL contrôle de trame m; ~ **plan** n MECH ENG *ship design* plan des couples m, plan des formes m, vertical du plan des formes m; ~ **pulse** n TV impulsion image f; ~ **rate** n CINEMAT fréquence d'images f, TV fréquence image f; ~ **saw** n PROD ENG *handsaw* scie ordinaire f, *power saw* scie à châssis f; ~ **saw file** n MECH ENG barboche f, lime à lanterne f; ~ **slip** n TV décalage vertical m; ~ **spacing** n NAUT *shipbuilding* écartement des membrures m; ~ **store** n TV mémoire d'images f; ~ **synchronization** n SPACE *communications* synchronisation de trame f, TELECOM verrouillage de trame m; ~ **synchronization control** n TV réglage de la stabilité verticale m; ~ **sync pulse** n TV impulsion de synchronisation d'image f

frame[2] vt NAUT *ship, boat* construire la carcasse, PHOTO cadrer

framed: ~ **floor** n CONST plancher sur poutre pan de bois m; ~ **set square** n MECH ENG équerre assemblée à jour f

frame-mode: ~ **bearer service** n *(FMBS)* TELECOM service support en mode trame m

frame-slotted: ~ **system** n TELECOM *land mobile* système crénelé à trame m

framework n CONST ossature f, *of crane* charpente f

framing n CONST charpente f, ossature f, *for walls or partitions* pan m, TV cadrage m, verrouillage de trame m; ~ **chisel** n CONST bec d'âne m, bédane m, bédane de menuisier m; ~ **control** n TV réglage du cadrage m; ~

knob n CINEMAT bouton de cadrage m; ~ **mask** n TV masque du cadrage m; ~ **signal** n CONTROL signal de cadrage m, signal de verrouillage de trame m

Francis: ~ **turbine** n FUELLESS turbine Francis f

francium n *(Fr)* CHEM francium m *(Fr)*

Franck-Hertz: ~ **experiment** n PHYS expérience de Franck et Hertz f

frangulin n CHEM franguline f

Frank-Condon: ~ **principle** n PHYS principe de Frank-Condon m

franklinite n MINERAL franklinite f

Frank-Read: ~ **source** n CRYSTALL source de Frank-Read f

Frasnian adj GEOL frasnien

fraudulent: ~ **use** n TELECOM usage frauduleux m

Fraunhofer: ~ **diffraction** n PHYS diffraction de Fraunhofer f; ~ **diffraction pattern** n OPT, TELECOM diagramme de diffraction de Fraunhofer m; ~ **line** n ASTRON, PHYS raie de Fraunhofer f; ~ **region** n SPACE *communications* région de Fraunhofer f

FRC abbr *(fault reception centre, fault reception center)* TELECOM service de dépannage m

freak n C&G déformé m; ~ **wave** n OCEANOG vague anormale f; ~ **weather** n NAUT temps anormal m

free[1] adj CHEM *uncombined* libre, non-combiné, à l'état libre, PROP MAT débarrassé, non affecté, *exempt or released* exempt; ~ **alongside ship** adj NAUT *shipping* franco long du bord, franco sous palan; ~ **from slag** adj THERMOD *coal* sans scorie; ~ **on board** adj *(FOB)* NAUT *commerce, shipping* franco à bord *(FOB)*

free[2] adv ~ **alongside ship** adv NAUT *shipping* franco long du bord, franco sous palan; ~ **of charge** adv TELECOM à titre gratuit; ~ **on board** adv *(FOB)* NAUT *commerce, shipping* franco à bord *(FOB)*; ~ **on quay** adv NAUT *shipping* franco à quai

free[3] ~ **acidity** n CHEM acidité libre f; ~ **air anomaly** n GEOL, GEOPHYS anomalie à l'air libre f; ~ **air cone resonance** n RECORDING résonance de la membrane à l'air libre f; ~ **air correction** n GEOPHYS correction à l'air libre f; ~ **air crystal oscillator** n ELECTRON oscillateur à quartz non thermostaté m; ~ **air peak overpressure** n AERONAUT *of sonic boom* surpression de crête en air libre f; ~ **air reduction** n GEOPHYS réduction d'altitude f; ~ **area** n REFRIG section libre de passage d'air f; ~ **atmosphere** n METEO atmosphère libre f; ~ **bar filter** n ELECTRON filtre à tige résonnante m; ~ **beam** n CONST *strength of materials* poutre en porte-à-faux f; ~ **charge** n PHYS charge libre f; ~ **convection flow** n FLUID PHYS écoulement convectif libre m, écoulement libre de convection m; ~ **deflection** n SPRINGS flèche libre f; ~ **delivery pump** n PROD ENG pompe à chute libre f; ~ **drop height** n AERONAUT hauteur de chute libre f; ~ **electrical motional impedance** n ACOUSTICS impédance électrique cinétique en vibration libre f; ~ **electrical vibration impedance** n ACOUSTICS impédance électrique en vibration libre f; ~ **electron** n ELEC *charged particle*, PART PHYS électron libre m, PHYS électron de conduction m, électron libre m; ~ **electron density** n RAD PHYS densité d'électrons libres f; ~ **end** n MINING *blasting* surface dégagée f, surface libre f, PROD ENG *of rope, pulley block chain* brin libre m; ~ **energy** n CHEM, METALL, PHYS, THERMOD énergie libre f; ~ **face** n MINING *blasting* surface dégagée f, surface libre f; ~ **fall** n AERONAUT chute libre f, MINING *deep boring* joint à chute libre m, PACKAGING chute libre f; ~ **fall boring** n CONST forage à chute libre *m*, sondage à chute libre *m*; ~ **fall drilling** *n* CONST forage à chute libre *m*, sondage à chute libre *m*; ~ **falling stamp** *n* CONST pilon à chute libre *m*; ~ **fall jump** *n* MILIT *parachuting* saut en chute libre *m*; ~ **fall pump** *n* PROD ENG pompe à chute libre *f*; ~ **field** *n* COMP zone libre *f*, DP champ banalisé *m*; ~ **field conditions** *n pl* RECORDING conditions en champ libre *f pl*; ~ **field response** *n* RECORDING réponse en champ libre *f*; ~ **field tension efficiency** *n* ACOUSTICS efficacité en tension en champ libre *f*; ~ **flight** *n* SPACE vol libre *m*; ~ **flight test** *n* SPACE essai en vol libre *m*; ~ **flow** *n* PROP MAT écoulement libre *m*; ~ **flow air conditioning unit** *n* REFRIG climatiseur à air et ventilation libre *m*, climatiseur à ventilation libre *m*; ~ **flow conditions** *n pl* PROP MAT écoulement libre du matériau *m*; ~ **flow product** *n* PACKAGING produit à écoulement libre *m*; ~ **format** *n* COMP, DP format libre *m*; ~ **grid** *n* ELECTRON grille en l'air *f*; ~ **ground water** *n* WATER SUPP eau souterraine libre *f*, nappe libre *f*; ~ **gyro** *n* AERONAUT gyroscope libre *m*; ~ **gyroscope** *n* AERONAUT gyroscope libre *m*; ~ **heat** *n* THERMOD chaleur sensible *f*; ~ **hydrogen** *n* PROP MAT hydrogène libre *m*; ~ **length** *n* MECH ENG *of spring*, SPRINGS longueur libre *f*; ~ **linear oscillation** *n pl* MECH ENG oscillation linéaire libre *f*; ~ **line signal** *n (FLS)* TELECOM signal d'inoccupation *m*; ~ **list** *n* COMP, DP liste libre *f*; ~ **longitudinal oscillation** *n* MECH ENG oscillation longitudinale libre *f*; ~ **mechanical impedance** *n* ACOUSTICS impédance mécanique libre *f*; ~ **milling ore** *n* MINING minerai contenant du métal à l'état libre *m*, minerai dont le métal est totalement amalgamable *m*; ~ **milling quartz** *n* PROP MAT quartz à or libre *m*; ~ **nappe** *n* HYDROL nappe libre *f*, nappe à surface libre *f*; ~ **oscillation** *n* ELEC *galvanometer*, ELECTRON, PHYS oscillation libre *f*; ~ **oscillation period** *n* GEOPHYS période propre *f*; ~ **overall weir** *n* HYDROL déversoir dénoyé *m*; ~ **piston gas turbine** *n* MECH ENG turbine à gaz à piston libre *f*; ~ **port** *n* NAUT, TRANSP port franc *m*; ~ **pratique** *n* NAUT libre pratique *m*; ~ **radical** *n* CHEM, FOOD TECH radical libre *m*; ~ **radical reaction** *n* P&R *chemical term* réaction des radicaux libres *f*; ~ **roller sluice gate** *n* FUELLESS *of dam* vanne à roues libres *f*; ~ **rotor** *n* AERONAUT *of helicopter* rotor libre *m*; ~ **shaft** *n* MECH ENG arbre flottant *m*; ~ **source** *n* NUCLEAR source non blindée *f*; ~ **space basic loss** *n* TELECOM affaiblissement en espace libre *m*; ~ **space loss** *n* SPACE *communications* affaiblissement d'espace libre *m*; ~ **stock** *n* PAPER TECH pâte maigre *f*; ~ **stream** *n* FLUID PHYS écoulement extérieur *m*; ~ **stream velocity** *n* PHYS vitesse en amont *f*; ~ **sulfur** *n* (AmE), ~ **sulphur** *n* (BrE) P&R *rubber, vulcanization* soufre libre *m*; ~ **surface** *n* NAUT *ship design* carène liquide *f*, PHYS *of liquid* surface libre *f*; ~ **surface effect** *n* NAUT *ship design* effet des carènes liquides *m*; ~ **travel** *n* AUTO course morte *f*; ~ **turbine** *n* AERONAUT turbine libre *f*; ~ **vibration** *n* ACOUSTICS vibration libre *f*, PHYS oscillation libre *f*

free:[4] ~ **from gas** *vt* THERMOD dégazer; ~ **off** *vt* NAUT *sailing* débrider

free[5] *vi* NAUT *of wind* adonner; ~ **off** *vi* NAUT *sailing* adonner

free-blown *adj* C&G soufflé bouche

freeboard *n* NAUT *ship, boat building* franc-bord *m*; ~ **allowances** *n* NAUT *ship design* corrections de franc-bord *f pl*

freeness *n* PAPER TECH raffinage *m*; ~ **recorder** *n* PAPER TECH enregistreur de degré de raffinage *m*; ~ **tester** *n* PAPER TECH égouttamètre *m*; ~ **value** *n* PAPER TECH indice d'égouttage *m*

freephone: ~ **call** *n* (BrE) *(cf toll-free call)* TELECOM appel gratuit *m*, appel sans frais *m* (Can); ~ **number** *n* (BrE) *(cf toll-free number)* TELECOM numéro d'appel sans frais *m* (Can), numéro vert *m*

free-running: ~ **frequency** *n* ELECTRON fréquence d'oscillation libre *f*; ~ **oscillator** *n* ELECTRON oscillateur non piloté *m*; ~ **signal** *n* ELECTRON signal fourni en l'absence du pilotage *m*; ~ **timer** *n* PROD ENG temporisateur non asservi *m*

freestanding[1] *adj* PACKAGING indépendant

freestanding:[2] ~ **insert** *n* PRINT encart libre *m*

freeway[1] *adj* (AmE) *(cf motorway)* CONST autoroutier

freeway[2] *n* (AmE) *(cf motorway)* CONST autoroute *f*, TRANSP autoroute urbaine *f*

freewheel *n* MECH roue libre *f*; ~ **mechanism** *n* MECH mécanisme à roue libre *m*, MECH ENG dispositif de roue libre *m*, mécanisme de roue libre *m*

freewheel-driven: ~ **head** *n* MECH ENG anneau de roue libre *m*

freewheeling: ~ **diode** *n* ELECTRON diode de roue libre *f*, PROD ENG diode de protection *f*

freeze:[1] ~ **concentration** *n* CHEM TECH, REFRIG concentration par congélation *f*

freeze[2] *vt* CINEMAT *picture* figer, FOOD TECH congeler, PAPER TECH geler, PHYS *deep-freeze* surgeler, *food* congeler, REFRIG *food* congeler, *water* geler, THERMOD congeler, geler; ~ **out** *vt* REFRIG séparer par congélation

freeze[3] *vi* METEO, PHYS *become frozen* geler, THERMOD se congeler

freeze-dried[1] *adj* CHEM TECH séché par congélation, FOOD TECH, REFRIG lyophilisé

freeze-dried:[2] ~ **product** *n* PACKAGING produit lyophilisé *m*

freeze-dry[1] *n* FOOD TECH lyophiliser

freeze-dry[2] *vt* THERMOD lyophiliser, réfrigérer sous vide

freeze-dryer *n* CHEM TECH chambre de séchage par congélation *f*, REFRIG lyophilisateur *m*

freeze-drying *n* CHEM TECH dessiccation par congélation *f*, lyophilisation *f*, FOOD TECH cryodessiccation *f*, lyophilisation *f*, PACKAGING, REFRIG, THERMOD lyophilisation *f*

freeze-frame *n* TV arrêt sur image *m*, image fixe *f*

freeze-out *n* TELECOM gel *m*; ~ **fraction** *n* SPACE *communications* taux de mutilation *m*, TELECOM fraction de gel *f*

freeze-picture *n* TELECOM gel de l'image *m*; ~ **request** *n* TELECOM demande de gel de l'image *f*

freezer *n* FOOD TECH *packaging*, MECH ENG congélateur *m*, REFRIG congélateur *m*, conservateur ménager de denrées congelées *m*, THERMOD congélateur *m*, réfrigérateur *m*; ~ **burn** *n* REFRIG brûlure de congélation *f*; ~ **capacity** *n* REFRIG charge d'un congélateur *f*; ~ **compartment** *n* REFRIG caisson congélateur *m*, compartiment congélateur *m*; ~ **trawler** *n* OCEANOG congélateur *m*, congélateur navire *m*; ~ **vessel** *n* OCEANOG congélateur *m*, congélateur navire *m*

freeze-thaw: ~ **resistance** *n* REFRIG résistance à la congélation-décongélation *f*

freeze-up *n* REFRIG bouchage par congélation *m*, THERMOD *meteorology* gel *m*, prise en glace *f*

freezing[1] *adj* PHYS frigorifique

freezing[2] *n* METALL gélation *f*, PAPER TECH gel *m*, PHYS, REFRIG congélation *f*; ~ **capacity** *n* REFRIG capacité de congélation *f*; ~ **liquid** *n* CHEM liquide réfrigérant *m*; ~ **machine** *n* PROD ENG appareil frigorifique *m*, machine frigorifique *f*; ~ **medium** *n* REFRIG milieu de congélation *m*; ~ **mixture** *n* PHYS mélange frigorifique *m*, REFRIG *of salts and crushed ice* mélange congélateur *m*; ~ **plant** *n* REFRIG installation de congélation *f*; ~ **plateau** *n* REFRIG *or thermal arrest* palier de congélation *m*; ~ **point** *n* NAUT point de congélation *m*, PACKAGING point de gel *m*, PHYS point de congélation *m*, température de congélation *f*, REFRIG point de congélation *m*, THERMOD *of water* point de gel *m*; ~ **rate** *n* REFRIG vitesse de congélation *f*; ~ **room** *n* REFRIG chambre de congélation *f*; ~ **section** *n* REFRIG *in food-processing plant* atelier de congélation *m*; ~ **trawler** *n* REFRIG givre *m*; ~ **tube** *n* PROD ENG tube congélateur *m*, tube frigorifique *m*; ~ **tunnel** *n* REFRIG tunnel de congélation *m*

freibergite *n* MINERAL freibergite *f*

freieslebenite *n* MINERAL freieslébenite *f*

freight[1] *n* NAUT, PETR TECH *commerce, shipping* fret *m*; ~ **agent** *n* (AmE) *(cf forwarding agent)* NAUT, TRANSP, transitaire *m*; ~ **barge** *n* TRANSP chaland *m*; ~ **car** *n* (AmE) *(cf goods van, freight wagon)* TRANSP wagon pour les expéditions en détail *m*; ~ **chute** *n* (AmE) *(cf goods chute)* TRANSP toboggan *m*; ~ **container** *n* TRANSP conteneur de transport *m*; ~ **depot** *n* TRANSP gare de marchandises *f*, TRANSP quai de chargement *m*; ~ **house** *n* (AmE) TRANSP halle aux marchandises *f*; ~ **inwards** *n pl* (AmE) *(cf goods inwards)* RAIL arrivages *m pl*; ~ **locomotive** *n* RAIL *vehicles* locomotive à marchandises *f*; ~ **office** *n* (AmE) *(cf forwarding office)* TRANSP bureau des départs *m*; ~ **porter** *n* (AmE) *(cf goods porter)* RAIL agent de manutention *m*; ~ **rate** *n* PACKAGING tarif de transport pour marchandises *m*, PETR TECH *commerce, shipping tariff* fret *m*; ~ **shed** *n* (AmE) *(cf goods shed)* TRANSP halle aux marchandises *f*; ~ **station** *n* (AmE) *(cf goods station)* TRANSP gare de marchandises *f*; ~ **terminal** *n* PACKAGING gare de marchandises *f*; ~ **train** *n* RAIL *vehicles* convoi à marchandises *m*, train de marchandises *m*; ~ **truck** *n* (AmE) *(cf goods van, goods lorry)* TRANSP camion de fret *m*; ~ **van** *n* (AmE) *(cf goods van)* TRANSP wagon couvert *m*, wagon pour les expéditions en détail *m*; ~ **wagon** *n* (BrE) *(cf freight car)* TRANSP wagon pour les expéditions en détail *m*; ~ **yard** *n* (AmE) *(cf goods yard)* RAIL *vehicles* dépôt de marchandises *m*; ~ **yard foreman** *n* (AmE) *(cf goods yard foreman)* RAIL chef de triage *m*

freight[2] *vi* NAUT donner à fret, fréter

freighter *n* NAUT *ship* affréteur *m*, cargo *m*, navire de charge *m*, TRANSP cargo *m*

freightliner: ~ **train** *n* RAIL *vehicles* train-bloc de conteneurs *m*

French:[1] ~ **casement** *n* CONST porte-fenêtre *f*; ~ **doors** *n pl* (AmE) *(cf French windows)* CONST porte-fenêtre *f*; ~ **embossing** *n* C&G gravure nuancée *f*; ~ **fold** *n* PRINT pli français *m*, pli à la française *m*; ~ **folder** *n* PRINT dépliant français *m*, pli français *m*, pli à la française *m*; ~ **National Railways** RAIL SNCF, Société nationale des chemins de fer français *f*; ~ **polish** *n* COATINGS vernis d'ébéniste au shellac *m*; ~ **standard** *n* MECH ENG norme française *f*; ~ **windows** *n pl* (BrE) *(cf French doors)* CONST porte-fenêtre *f*

French:[2] ~ **polish** *vt* COLOURS vernir au tampon

Frenkel: ~ **defect** *n* CRYSTALL défaut de Frenkel *m*

freon *n* CHEM fréon *m*

frequency *n* ACOUSTICS, COMP, DP, ELEC *of wave*, ELEC-TRON, PETR fréquence *f*, PHYS fréquence *f*, *of gyration* gyrofréquence *f*, RECORDING, WAVE PHYS fréquence *f*; ~ **adjustment** *n* ELECTRON réglage de fréquence *m*; ~ **agility** *n* ELECTRON agilité en fréquence *f*; ~ **alignment** *n* TELECOM verrouillage de fréquence *m*; ~ **allocation** *n* RECORDING *of microphone*, TELECOM allocation de fréquence *f*, TV attribution de fréquence *f*; ~ **band** *n* COMP, DP, ELEC *of signal*, ELECTRON, NAUT *radar, radio*, TELECOM bande de fréquence *f*; ~ **calibrator** *n* ELECTRON générateur de fréquences étalons *m*; ~ **change** *n* ELECTRON variation de fréquence *f*; ~ **changer** *n* ELEC *converter* convertisseur de fréquence *m*, ELECTRON changeur de fréquence *m*; ~ **channel** *n* TELE-COM canal de fréquence *m*; ~ **characteristic** *n* TELECOM caractéristique fréquentielle *f*; ~ **compensation** *n* E-LECTRON compensation de fréquence *f*, RECORDING compensation en fréquence *f*; ~ **component** *n* ELEC-TRON composante *f*, composante fréquencielle *f*; ~ **compressive feedback demodulator** *n* SPACE *communications* démodulateur à compression de fréquence *m*; ~ **control** *n* TELECOM commande de fréquence *f*, contrôle de fréquence *m*; ~ **conversion** *n* ELECTRON changement de fréquence *m*, conversion de fréquence *f*, TELECOM conversion de fréquence *f*; ~ **converter** *n* ELEC, ELECTRON convertisseur de fréquence *m*, TELE-COM changeur *m*; ~ **counter** *n* ELECTRON compteur-fréquencemètre *m*, fréquencemètre à comptage d'impulsions *m*; ~ **coverage** *n* ELECTRON gamme de fréquences couvertes *f*; ~ **current converter** *n* ELEC convertisseur fréquence-courant *m*; ~ **curve** *n* MATH courbe de distribution *f*; ~ **cutoff** *n* ELECTRON point de coupure en fréquence *m*; ~ **decoupling** *n* SPACE *spacecraft* découplage en fréquence *m*; ~ **demodulation** *n* ELECTRON, TELECOM démodulation de fréquence *f*; ~ **demodulator** *n* ELECTRON, TELECOM démodulateur de fréquence *m*; ~ **departure** *n* ELEC-TRON glissement de fréquence *m*; ~ **detector** *n* ELECTRON détecteur de fréquence différentielle *m*; ~ **deviation** *n* ELECTRON excursion de fréquence *f*; ~ **displacement** *n* TELECOM déplacement de fréquence *m*; ~ **distortion** *n* PHYS *attenuation distortion* distorsion d'affaiblissement *f*, RECORDING distorsion de fréquence *f*; ~ **distribution** *n* COMP distribution de fréquences *f*, DP attribution de fréquences *f*, distribution de fréquences *f*, MATH densité *f*, distribution *f*, METALL spectre de fréquences *m* ~ **distribution curve** *n* MATH *statistics* courbe de distribution de fréquence *f*; ~ **diversity** *n* TELECOM diversité de fréquence *f*; ~ **divider** *n* ELEC démultiplicateur de fréquence *m*, TELECOM diviseur de fréquence *m*; ~ **domain** *n* ELECTRON domaine fréquenciel *m*; ~ **domain signal processing** *n* ELECTRON traitement fréquenciel *m*; ~ **doubler** *n* ELEC, ELECTRON, PHYS, TELECOM doubleur de fréquence *m*; ~ **drift** *n* ELEC, ELECTRON, TELECOM dérive de fréquence *f*; ~ **encoding** *n* TELECOM codage à fréquence *m*; ~ **fall-off** *n* ELEC chute de fréquence *f*; ~ **flutter** *n* ACOUSTICS effet de flottement *m*; ~ **hopping** *n* ELECTRON fonctionnement en sauts de fréquence *m*, TELECOM *land mobile* sauts de fréquence *m pl*; ~ **interlace** *n* TV entrelacement spectral *m*; ~ **inversion** *n* TELECOM *land mobile* inversion de fréquence *f*; ~ **losses** *n pl* TV atténuation en fréquence *f*; ~ **meter** *n* ELEC ENG, TELECOM fréquence-mètre *m*; ~ **modulation** *n* (FM) COMP, ELEC *alternating current*, ELECTRON, PHYS, RECORDING, TELECOM, TV, WAVE PHYS modulation de fréquence *f* (MF); ~ **modulation modem** *n* ELECTRON modem à modulation de fréquence *m*; ~ **modulation noise** *n* TELECOM bruit à modulation de fréquence *m*; ~ **modulator** *n* ELECTRON, TV modulateur de fréquence *m*; ~ **monitor** *n* CONTROL contrôleur de fréquence *m*; ~ **multiplexing** *n* TELECOM multiplexage en fréquence *m*; ~ **multiplication** *n* ELECTRON multiplication de fréquence *f*; ~ **multiplier** *n* ELECTRON, TELECOM multiplicateur de fréquence *m*; ~ **multiplier klystron** *n* ELECTRON klystron multiplicateur de fréquence *m*; ~ **noise** *n* ELECTRON bruit de fréquence *m*; ~ **offset** *n* ELECTRON écart de fréquence *m*; ~ **overlap** *n* TV bande commune *f*, recouvrement de fréquence *m*; ~ **pulling** *n* ELECTRON entraînement de fréquence *m*, glissement aval *m*, glissement aval de fréquence *m*; ~ **pushing** *n* ELECTRON glissement amont *m*, glissement amont de fréquence *m*, poussée de fréquence *f*; ~ **of radiation** *n* RAD PHYS *emitted by atom* fréquence de rayonnement *f*; ~ **range** *n* ELEC *of alternating current* bande de fréquences *f*, gamme de fréquences *f*, RECORDING gamme de fréquences *f*, étendue de fréquence *f*, TV gamme de fréquences *f*; ~ **record** *n* RECORDING disque de fréquence *m*; ~ **of recurrence** *n* ASTRON fréquence de répétition *f*; ~ **regulation** *n* TELECOM régulation de fréquence *f*; ~ **rejection** *n* ELECTRON élimination de fréquence *f*; ~ **relay** *n* ELEC ENG relais de fréquence *m*; ~ **resolution** *n* ELECTRON définition en fréquence *f*; ~ **response** *n* CINEMAT courbe de fréquence *f*, ELECTRON réponse amplitude-fréquence *f*, réponse en fréquence *f*, OPT, RECORDING réponse en fréquence *f*, TELECOM réponse de fréquence *f*, réponse en fréquence *f*, WAVE PHYS réponse fréquentielle *f*; ~ **response curve** *n* ELECTRON, RECORDING courbe de réponse en fréquence *f*; ~ **retrace** *n* ELECTRON reproductibilité de fréquence *f*; ~ **reuse** *n* SPACE *communications*, TELECOM réutilisation de fréquence *f*; ~ **scale** *n* ELECTRON échelle de fréquence *f*; ~ **scanner** *n* TELECOM balayeur de fréquence *m*; ~ **scanning** *n* RECORDING, TELECOM balayage de fréquence *m*; ~ **selective amplifier** *n* ELECTRON amplificateur sélecteur de fréquence *m*; ~ **selective filter** *n* ELECTRON filtre à bande étroite *m*; ~ **selector** *n* TELECOM sélecteur de fréquence *m*; ~ **separation** *n* ELECTRON séparation des fréquences *f*; ~ **shift** *n* COMP déplacement de fréquence *m*, DP déplacement de fréquence *m*, glissement de fréquence *m*, TELECOM déplacement de fréquence *m*; ~ **shift keying** *n* (*FSK*) COMP, DP, ELECTRON modulation par déplacement de fréquence *f* (*MDF*), TELECOM manipulation par déplacement de fréquence *f*, modulation par déplacement de fréquence *f*, TV modulation par déplacement de fréquence *f* (*MDF*); ~ **source** *n* ELECTRON source de fréquence *f*; ~ **spectrum** *n* COMP, DP, ELECTRON, RECORDING, WAVE PHYS spectre de fréquences *m*; ~ **stabilizer** *n* ELEC stabilisateur de fréquence *m*; ~ **standard** *n* ELECTRON étalon de fréquence *m*; ~ **sweep** *n* ELECTRON balayage en fréquence *m*, TELECOM balayage de fréquence *m*; ~ **synthesis** *n* ELECTRON synthèse de fréquence *f*; ~ **synthesizer** *n* ELECTRON synthétiseur de fréquence *m*; ~ **test** *n* RAD PHYS essai de fréquence *m*; ~ **tracking** *n* SPACE *communications* poursuite en fréquence *f*; ~ **transducer** *n* ELEC ENG changeur de fréquence *m*; ~ **transformer** *n* ELEC transformateur de fréquence *m*; ~ **translation** *n* TV transposition de fréquence *f*; ~ **transposition** *n* RECORDING transposition de fréquence *f*; ~ **tuning** *n* ELECTRON réglage de la fréquence d'accord *m*, TELECOM accord en fréquence *m*; ~ **uncertainty band** *n* TELECOM bande d'incertitude des fréquences *f*

frequency-division: ~ **multiple access** *n* (*FDMA*) SPACE *communications*, TELECOM accès multiple à répartition en fréquence *m* (*AMRF*); ~ **multiplexer** *n* ELECTRON multiplexeur à répartition de fréquence *m*; ~ **multiplexing** *n* (*FDM*) COMP multiplexage par partage des fréquences *m* (*MPF*), multiplexage par répartition en fréquence *m* (*MRF*), ELECTRON multiplexage par répartition en fréquence *m* (*MRF*), PHYS multiplexage analogique (*MA*) *m*, multiplexage par partage des fréquences *m* (*MPF*), multiplexage par répartition en fréquence *m* (*MRF*), TELECOM multiplexage par répartition en fréquence *m* (*MRF*); ~ **switching system** *n* (*FDS system*) TELECOM commutateur en fréquence *m*, système de commutation en modulation de fréquence *m*

frequency-hopping: ~ **oscillator** *n* ELECTRON oscillateur à sauts de fréquence *m*

frequency-modulated *adj* ELECTRON modulé en fréquence

fresh[1] *adj* GEOL frais, non altéré, PROP MAT frais, nouveau, *water* doux

fresh:[2] ~ **fish trade** *n* NAUT, OCEANOG mareyage *m*; ~ **fuel** *n* NUCLEAR combustible neuf *m*, combustible non irradié *m*; ~ **uranium** *n* NUCLEAR uranium frais *m*

freshet *n* HYDROL avalaison *f*, avalasse *f*

freshness *n* HEATING *ventilation* fraîcheur *f*; ~ **seal** *n* PACKAGING opercule fraîcheur *m*

freshwater[1] *adj* GEOL *fauna, sedimentary environment* d'eau douce, dulçaquicole

freshwater[2] *n* GAS TECH, HYDROL, NAUT, PETR, WATER SUPP eau douce *f*; ~ **allowance** *n* NAUT *ship design* correction pour eau douce *f*; ~ **condenser** *n* NAUT distillateur *m*; ~ **drilling mud** *n* PETR boue de forage à l'eau douce *f*; ~ **interface** *n* HYDROL interface eau douce *f*; ~ **mud** *n* PETR TECH *drilling* boue à l'eau douce *f*; ~ **stock** *n* WATER SUPP provision d'eau douce *f*

Fresnel: ~ **biprism** *n* PHYS biprisme de Fresnel *m*; ~ **diffraction** *n* PHYS diffraction de Fresnel *f*; ~ **diffraction pattern** *n* OPT, TELECOM diagramme de diffraction de Fresnel *m*; ~ **lens** *n* CINEMAT lentille de Fresnel *f*, INSTRUMENT lentille cylindrique de Fresnel *f*, PHOTO, PHYS lentille de Fresnel *f*; ~ **mirrors** *n pl* PHYS miroirs de Fresnel *m pl*; ~ **reflection** *n* OPT, TELECOM réflexion de Fresnel *f*; ~ **reflection method** *n* TELECOM méthode de réflexion de Fresnel *f*; ~ **region** *n* DP, TELECOM région de Fresnel *f*; ~ **zone** *n* TELECOM zone de Fresnel *f*; ~ **zone blockage** *n* TELECOM blocage de la zone de Fresnel *m*

Fresnel's: ~ **formulae** *n pl* PHYS formules de Fresnel *f pl*

fret: ~ **cutting** *n* PROD ENG découpage *m*, reperçage *m*; ~ **saw** *n* PROD ENG scie à découper *f*, *frame* bocfil *m*, porte-scie à découper *m*, porte-scie à repercer *m*, *machine* sauteuse *f*, scie à chantourner *f*, scie à découperélectrique *f*; ~ **saw blade** *n* PROD ENG scie à découper *f*; ~ **saw frame** *n* PROD ENG bocfil *m*, porte-scie à découper *m*, porte-scie à repercer *m*; ~ **sawing** *n* PROD ENG découpage *m*, reperçage *m*

fretting *n* MECH érosion *f*, PROD ENG usure par frottement *f*; ~ **corrosion** *n* SPRINGS corrosion par friction *f*; ~ **fatigue** *n* METALL fatigue d'usure *f*

fretwork *n* PROD ENG découpure *f*

friable *adj* P&R friable

friction *n* COAL TECH, MECH, MECH ENG frottement *m*, P&R friction *f*, frottement *m*, PAPER TECH friction *f*, frottement *m*, PHYS friction *f*, frottement *m*, PROD

ENG, TEXTILES, TV *of head wheel on tape* frottement *m*;
~ **ball** *n* MECH ENG rotule de friction *f*; ~ **brake** *n*
VEHICLES frein à friction *m*; ~ **brake hoist** *n* PROD ENG
monte-charge à frein de sûreté à friction *m*; ~ **calender**
n PAPER TECH calandre à friction *f*; ~ **clutch** *n* MECH
ENG embrayage à friction *m*; ~ **cone drive** *n* MECH ENG
commande par cônes à friction *f*; ~ **coupling** *n* MECH
ENG manchon à friction *m*; ~ **course** *n* CONST *of*
runway couche de frottement *f*; ~ **damper** *n* AERONAUT
amortisseur de friction *m*; ~ **disc** *n* (BrE) MECH ENG
plateau de friction *m*; ~ **disk** *n* (AmE) *see friction disc* ~
draft gear *n* (AmE) *see friction draught gear* ~ **drag** *n*
AERONAUT traînée de friction *f*, traînée de frottement
f; ~ **draught gear** *n* (BrE) MECH ENG amortisseur à
friction *m*; ~ **drive** *n* CINEMAT entraînement par friction *m*, MECH ENG transmission par friction *f*; ~ **facing**
n AUTO garniture de friction *f*; ~ **force** *n* METALL force
de frottement *f*; ~ **fuse** *n* MINING amorce à friction *f*,
étoupille à friction *f*; ~ **gear** *n* MECH ENG transmission
par frottement *f*; ~ **gearing** *n* MECH ENG transmission
par frottement *f*; ~ **glazing** *n* PAPER TECH glaçage à la
calandre à friction *m*; ~ **hammer** *n* PROD ENG marteau-
pilon à friction *m*; ~ **headstock** *n* MECH ENG *of lathe*
poupée à friction *f*; ~ **loss** *n* FUELLESS perte par frottement *f*; ~ **pile** *n* COAL TECH pieu en milieu pulvérulent
m, CONST pieu à friction *m*; ~ **plate** *n* PROD ENG plaque
de friction *f*, plaque de frottement *f*; ~ **point** *n* MECH
ENG *machine tools* passage dur *m*, point dur *m*; ~ **reel** *n*
PAPER TECH enrouleuse à entraînement périphérique
f; ~ **ring** *n* MECH ENG rondelle de frottement *f*; ~ **roller** *n*
PAPER TECH enrouleuse à entraînement périphérique
f, PROD ENG galet *m*, galet de friction *m*, rouleau de
friction *m*; ~ **screw** *n* MECH ENG presse à balancier *f*; ~
snap-on cap *n* PACKAGING capsule à encliqueter *f*; ~
spring *n* MECH ENG ressort de friction *m*; ~ **stress** *n* ME-
TALL contrainte de frottement *f*; ~ **welding** *n* CONST
soudage par friction *m*; ~ **wheel** *n* MECH ENG cylindre
de friction *m*, roue de friction *f*, roue de frottement *f*,
volant de serrage *m*

frictional[1] *adj* CONST frictionnel

frictional:[2] ~ **damper** *n* MECH amortisseur à friction *m*; ~
drag *n* MECH résistance de frottement *f*; ~ **electricity** *n*
ELEC *phenomenon* triboélectricité *f*; ~ **flow** *n* NUCLEAR
écoulement visqueux *m*; ~ **force** *n* MECH ENG, PHYS
force de frottement *f*; ~ **ignition** *n* MINING inflammation par frottement *f*; ~ **resistance** *n* NAUT *ship design*
résistance de frottement *f*; ~ **torque** *n* SPACE *spacecraft*
couple de frottement *m*

friction-glazed *adj* PAPER TECH glacé par friction

frictionless *adj* MECH sans frottement, MECH ENG sans
friction

friction-type: ~ **bearing** *n* MECH ENG palier à serrage *m*

fridge *n* THERMOD réfrigérateur *m*; ~ **freezer** *n* THERMOD
réfrigérateur à compartiment congélateur *m*

Friedel-Crafts: ~ **reaction** *n* CHEM réaction de Friedel-
Craft *f*; ~ **synthesis** *n* DETERGENTS synthèse
Friedel-Crafts *f*

friedelite *n* MINERAL friedélite *f*

Friends: ~ **of the Earth** *n pl* (*FoE*) POLLUTION Amis de la
Terre *m pl*

frieseïte *n* MINERAL frieséite *f*

frigate *n* NAUT *navy* escorteur *m*, frégate *f*

frigger *n* C&G bousillé *m* (Bel)

frigorific *adj* REFRIG frigorifique, réfrigérant

frilling *n* CINEMAT réticulation *f*

fringe *n* PHYS frange *f*; ~ **effect** *n* AERONAUT effet pelliculaire *m*, ELEC ENG, TV effet de bord *m*; ~ **separation** *n*
PHYS interfrange *f*

fringes *n pl* PHYS *contour* franges de contour *f pl*, *of*
equal inclination franges d'égale inclinaison *f pl*, WAVE
PHYS *due to interference* franges d'interférence *f pl*

fringing *n* TV déformation de champ *f*; ~ **reef** *n* OCEANOG
récif frangeant *m*

frisket *n* PRINT cache *m*

frit *n* C&G fritte *f*

fritted: ~ **glass** *n* C&G verre fritté *m*; ~ **glaze** *n* C&G
glaçure frittée *f*

fritting *n* C&G *of batch* frittage *m*; ~ **furnace** *n* C&G,
HEATING *glassmaking* four à fritte *m*; ~ **zone** *n* C&G
zone de frittage *f*

FRJ *abbr* (*facility rejected message*) TELECOM SURF
(*message de refus de service supplémentaire*)

frogleg: ~ **winding** *n* ELEC ENG enroulement en pattes de
grenouilles *m*

front *n* CONST avant *m*, devant *m*, devanture *f*, face *f*,
façade *f*, *of edifice* façade *f*, METEO front *m*, PROD ENG
of boiler, furnace devanture *f*, façade *f*; ~ **arch** *n* C&G
voûte plate *f*; ~ **axle** *n* VEHICLES *wheels, transmission*
essieu avant *m*, train avant *m*; ~ **blade** *n* MAR POLL
lame d'attaque *f*; ~ **bumper** *n* AUTO *of car* pare-chocs
avant *m*; ~ **cylinder cover** *n* HYDR EQUIP couvercle
avant de cylindre *m*, plateau avant de cylindre *m*; ~
cylinder head *n* HYDR EQUIP couvercle avant de cylindre *m*, plateau avant de cylindre *m*; ~ **delivery** *n* PRINT
sortie de machine *f*; ~ **diaphragm** *n* PHOTO diaphragme
antérieur *m*; ~ **element** *n* PHOTO *of lens* lentille frontale
f; ~ **elevation** *n* MECH ENG vue de face *f*, élévation *f*; ~
engine *n* AUTO moteur avant *m*; ~ **face** *n* MECH ENG
face avant *f*; ~ **fender** *n* (AmE) (*cf front wing*) AUTO *of*
car aile avant *f*; ~ **flasher** *n* AUTO *of car* clignoteur
avant *m*; ~ **focal plane** *n* PHOTO plan focal antérieur *m*;
~ **frame** *n* PHOTO corps avant *m*; ~ **gap** *n* ACOUSTICS
entrefer avant *m*, RECORDING entrefer frontal *m*; ~
guide *n* PRINT taquet de front *m*; ~ **lay** *n* PRINT guide de
front *m*; ~ **lens** *n* INSTRUMENT lentille antérieure *f*,
lentille de champ *f*, lentille frontale *f*; ~ **lens-filter** *n*
INSTRUMENT filtre additionnel *m*; ~ **lip tile** *n* C&G écran
avant *m*; ~ **of pack labeler** *n* (AmE), ~ **of pack labeller** *n*
(BrE) PACKAGING étiqueteuse pour le devant de l'emballage *f*; ~ **panel** *n* MECH ENG face avant *f*, panneau
avant *m*; ~ **piston** *n* AUTO piston primaire *m*; ~ **porch**
switch *n* TV commutation du palier avant *f*; ~ **projec-**
tion *n* CINEMAT projection de face *f*, projection
frontale *f*; ~ **rake angle** *n* MECH ENG *of tool* pente
d'attaque avant *f*; ~ **ring** *n* INSTRUMENT anneau supérieur *m*; ~ **scanning** *n* TV balayage antérieur *m*; ~ **seat** *n*
AUTO *of car* siège avant *m*; ~ **shock absorber** *n* AUTO *of*
car amortisseur avant *m*; ~ **side** *n* PAPER TECH côté
conducteur *m*; ~ **sight** *n* MILIT *of rifle* bouton de mire
m; ~ **standard adjustment** *n* PHOTO *of bellows unit* noix
de réglage frontale *f*; ~ **stop** *n* PRINT butée de front *f*; ~
suspension *n* AUTO suspension avant *f*; ~ **suspension**
cross-member *n* AUTO *of car* traverse d'essieu *f*; ~
tweel *n* C&G registre régulateur *m*; ~ **wall** *n* C&G paroi
aval *f*; ~ **wheel** *n* TRANSP roue avant *f*; ~ **wing** *n* (BrE)
(*cf front fender*) AUTO *car* aile avant *f*

frontal: ~ **area** *n* MECH ENG surface frontale *f*

front-end[1] *adj* COMP, DP frontal

front-end:[2] ~ **computer** *n* COMP ordinateur frontal *m*; ~
equipment *n* PRINT équipement frontal de saisie *m*; ~
loader *n* MAR POLL chargeur frontal *m*; ~ **processor** *n*
COMP (*FEP*) processeur frontal *m*, DP additionneur

complet *m*, TELECOM frontal *m*, ordinateur frontal *m*

front-facing: ~ **roller** *n* PROD ENG galet orienté vers l'avant *m*

frontispiece *n* PRINT frontispice *m*

front-light *vt* PHOTO éclairer de face

front-mounted: ~ **engine** *n* VEHICLES moteur à l'avant *m*

front-wall: ~ **photovoltaic cell** *n* ELEC ENG cellule photovoltaïque à couche antérieure *f*, cellule photoélectrique antérieure *f*

front-wheel:[1] ~ **drive** *adj* TRANSP à traction avant

front-wheel:[2] ~ **alignment** *n* AUTO géométrie du train avant *f*; ~ **drive** *n* AUTO, TRANSP traction avant *f*

frost *n* CINEMAT diffuseur *m*, écran vitré *m*, METEO gel *m*, gelée *f*, REFRIG givre *m*; ~ **action** *n* GEOL gélivation *f*; ~ **back** *n* REFRIG givrage à l'aspiration *m*; ~ **boil** *n* COAL TECH bosse due au gel *f*; ~ **deposit** *n* REFRIG dépôt de givre *m*; ~ **formation** *n* REFRIG *on refrigeration circuit* givrage *m*; ~ **heave** *n* COAL TECH gonflement dû au gel *m*, METEO foisonnement par le gel *m*, poussée de gel *f*, REFRIG soulèvement par congélation *m*; ~ **heaving** *n* METEO foisonnement dû au gel *m*; ~ **level indicator** *n* REFRIG niveau de givrage *m*; ~ **limit** *n* COAL TECH limite du gel *f*; ~ **penetration depth** *n* COAL TECH pénétration du gel *f*; ~ **point** *n* REFRIG point de gelée blanche *m*, point de givre *m*; ~ **susceptibility** *n* COAL TECH gélivité *f*

frostbite *n* REFRIG gelure *f*

frosted[1] *adj* FOOD TECH givré, glacé, REFRIG givré

frosted:[2] ~ **glass** *n* C&G verre maté au sable *m*; ~ **lacquer** *n* COATINGS vernis cristallisant *m*, vernis givré *m*

frost-free: ~ **level** *n* COAL TECH niveau à l'abri du gel *m*

frosting *n* C&G givrage *m*; ~ **bath** *n* C&G bain de givrage *m*

frost-preventive: ~ **agent** *n* PACKAGING agent résistant au gel *m*

frost-resistant *adj* COAL TECH *soil* résistant au gel

frostwork *n* GEOL gélivation *f*

froth *n* COAL TECH écume *f*; ~ **flotation** *n* CHEM TECH flottation par écumage *f*, flottation à la mousse *f*; ~ **flotation plant** *n* MINING flottations de mousses *f pl*

frothing *n* P&R mousse *f*, écume *f*

Froude: ~ **number** *n* PHYS nombre de Froude *m*

frozen[1] *adj* FOOD TECH surgelé, REFRIG *food* congelé, *water* gelé, THERMOD congelé, gelé; ~ **solid** *adj* THERMOD congelé

frozen:[2] ~ **food** *n* THERMOD aliment congelé *m*; ~ **food storage cabinet** *n* MECH ENG congélateur *m*; ~ **food storage room** *n* REFRIG chambre de stockage de produits congelés *f*; ~ **frame** *n* CINEMAT image arrêtée *f*, image figée *f*, image fixe *f*; ~ **ground** *n* COAL TECH sol gelé *m*; ~ **product** *n* PACKAGING produit surgelé *m*

FRP *abbr (fast-reservation protocol)* TELECOM protocole de réservation rapide *m*

FRR *abbr (flight readiness review)* SPACE RAV *(revue d'aptitude au vol)*

fructan *n* CHEM fructosane *m*

fructosan *n* CHEM fructosane *m*

fructose *n* CHEM fructose *m*, lévulose *m*, FOOD TECH fructose *m*, lévulose *m*, sucre de fruit *m*

fruit: ~ **carrier** *n* NAUT agrumier *m*, fruitier *m*; ~ **sugar** *n* CHEM fructose *m*, lévulose *m*, FOOD TECH fructose *m*, lévulose *m*, sucre de fruit *m*; ~ **wrapper** *n* FOOD TECH *packaging* papillote *f*

frusemide *n* CHEM frusemide *m*

FSK[1] *abbr (frequency shift keying)* COMP, DP, ELECTRON, TELECOM, TV MDF *(modulation par déplacement de fréquence)*

FSK:[2] ~ **modem** *n* ELECTRON modem MDF *m*, modem

pour modulation par déplacement de fréquence *m*

FSR *abbr (flowable solids reactor)* NUCLEAR réacteur à suspension solide *m*

FSS *abbr (fixed satellite service)* SPACE service fixe par satellite *m*

F-star *n* ASTRON étoile F *f*

F-stop *n* CINEMAT, PHOTO ouverture du diaphragme *f*

FTAMSE *abbr (file transfer access and manipulation service element)* TELECOM élément de service de l'accès aux transfert et manipulation *m*

FTTB *abbr (fiber to the building, fibre to the building)* TELECOM fibre jusqu'à l'immeuble *f*

FTTC *abbr (fiber to the kerb, fibre to the curb)* TELECOM fibre jusqu'au trottoir *f*

FTTH *abbr (fiber to the home, fibre to the home)* TELECOM fibre jusqu'au logement *f*

FTTO *abbr (fibre to the office, fiber to the office)* TELECOM fibre jusqu'au bureau *f*

FU *abbr (functional unit)* TELECOM unité fonctionnelle *f*

fuchsin *n* CHEM fuchsine *f*, rubine *f*

fuchsite *n* MINERAL fuchsite *f*

fuchsone *n* CHEM fuchsone *f*

fucose *n* CHEM fucose *m*

fucosterol *n* CHEM fucostérol *m*

fucoxanthin *n* CHEM fucoxanthine *f*

fuel[1] *n* NAUT *engine*, PETR TECH carburant *m*, SPACE carburant *m*, combustible *m*, *spacecraft* ergol *m*, THERMOD carburant *m*, chauffage combustible *m*, combustible *m*, fuel *m*, mazout *m*, spatial ergol *m*, VEHICLES carburant *m*, combustible *m*; ~ **assembly** *n* NUCLEAR, PHYS assemblage combustible *m*; ~ **assembly corner rod** *n* NUCLEAR crayon d'angle *m*; ~ **backup pump** *n* SPACE *spacecraft* pompe auxiliaire *f*; ~ **bunker** *n* PROD ENG soute à combustible *f*; ~ **cell** *n* SPACE *spacecraft* pile à combustible *f*, THERMOD cellule électrochimique *f*, pile à combustible *f*; ~ **charge** *n* NUCLEAR charge totale de combustible *f*; ~ **cladding** *n* NUCLEAR matière de gaine *f*, matériau de gainage *m*; ~ **cock** *n* AERONAUT robinet de carburant *m*; ~ **consumption** *n* THERMOD consommation de carburant *f*; ~ **consumption meter** *n* AERONAUT débitmètre totaliseur *m*; ~ **control** *n* AERONAUT commande de richesse du carburant *f*; ~ **control unit** *n* AERONAUT régulateur de carburant *m*; ~ **coolant heat exchanger** *n* AERONAUT échangeur huile-kérosène *m*; ~ **cooling** *n* THERMOD *gas turbines* refroidissement par combustible *m*; ~ **cross feed valve** *n* AERONAUT clapet d'intercommunication de carburant *m*; ~ **cycle** *n* SPACE cycle de combustible *m*; ~ **dump** *n* MILIT dépôt de carburant *m*; ~ **dumping** *n* SPACE *spacecraft* vidange de combustible *f*; ~ **dumping system** *n* SPACE *spacecraft* circuit de vidange *m*, circuit de vide-vite *m*; ~ **dump valve** *n* AERONAUT, SPACE vide-vite *m*; ~ **economy** *n* THERMOD économie de carburant *f*; ~ **expansion box** *n* AERONAUT boîte d'expansion carburant *f*; ~ **filter** *n* AERONAUT filtre de combustible *m*, AUTO filtre à essence *m*; ~ **gage** *n* (AmE) *see fuel gauge*; ~ **gage indicator** *n* (AmE) *see fuel gauge indicator*; ~ **gage transmitter** *n* (AmE) *see fuel gauge transmitter*; ~ **gas** *n* GAS TECH gaz de chauffage *m*; ~ **gauge** *n* (BrE) AUTO jauge d'essence *f*, jauge de carburant *f*; ~ **gauge indicator** *n* (BrE) AERONAUT indicateur de jaugeur de carburant *m*; ~ **gauge transmitter** *n* (BrE) AERONAUT jaugeur de réservoir de carburant *m*; ~ **grade** *n* AERONAUT indice d'octane *m*, qualité de carburant *f*; ~ **handling plant** *n* HEATING matériel de manutention de combustible *m*; ~ **high-pressure pump** *n* VEHICLES pompe à carburant haute pression *f*; ~ **hopper** *n* HEATING trémie charbon *f*; ~ **hose** *n* P&R tuyau d'essence *m*; ~ **indicator** *n* AUTO indicateur de niveau d'essence *m*; ~ **injection** *n* HEAT ENG *automobiles*, THERMOD *automobiles* injection de carburant *f*, VEHICLES injection de carburant *f*, injection de combustible *f*; ~ **injection pump** *n* AUTO pompe d'injection *f*, VEHICLES pompe d'injection de carburant *f*; ~ **injector** *n* MECH ENG injecteur de carburant *m*; ~ **inlet valve** *n* AUTO pointeau *m*; ~ **jet support cover** *n* AERONAUT couvercle porte-gicleur *m*; ~ **level presetting controls** *n pl* AERONAUT boîtier de préaffichage de carburant *m*; ~ **level selector** *n* AERONAUT sélecteur de niveau de carburant *m*; ~ **level transmitter** *n* AERONAUT transmetteur de jaugeur *m*; ~ **line** *n* AUTO tuyauterie d'alimentation *f*, *of car* canalisation de carburant *f*, VEHICLES canalisation d'essence *f*, canalisation de carburant *f*, tuyère d'essence *f*, tuyère de carburant *f*; ~ **load** *n* AERONAUT carburant embarqué *m*; ~ **man** *n* SPACE *spacecraft* ergolier *m*; ~ **measuring unit** *n* SPACE *spacecraft* jauge d'ergol *f*; ~ **nozzle** *n* AUTO injecteur *m*, MECH ENG buse de carburant *f*; ~ **oil** *n* CHEM, CONST *central heating*, HEATING mazout *m*, PETR TECH fuel *m*, fuel-oil *m*, mazout *m*; ~ **oxidizer mixture ratio** *n* SPACE *spacecraft* rapport de mélange carburant-combinant *m*; ~ **pipe** *n* AUTO *of car*, VEHICLES canalisation de carburant *f*; ~ **pump** *n* AERONAUT pompe à carburant *f*, AUTO pompe à essence *f*, MECH *vehicles* pompe à combustible *f*, MECH ENG pompe d'alimentation *f*, NAUT *engine* pompe à combustible *f*, SPACE *spacecraft* pompe à ergol *f*, VEHICLES pompe à carburant *f*, pompe à essence *f*; ~ **reserve** *n* AERONAUT réserve de combustible *f*; ~ **rod** *n* PHYS barre de combustible *f*; ~ **selector** *n* HEATING sélecteur de combustible *m*; ~ **shut-off cock** *n* AERONAUT robinet coupe-feu *m*; ~ **shut-off cock control link** *n* AERONAUT biellette coupe-feu *f*; ~ **system** *n* AERONAUT circuit carburant *m*; ~ **system diagram** *n* NAUT schéma du circuit de combustible *m*; ~ **tank** *n* AERONAUT réservoir de carburant *m*, AUTO réservoir d'essence *m*, MECH *vehicles* réservoir à combustible *m*, SPACE *spacecraft* réservoir d'ergol *m*, VEHICLES réservoir d'essence *m*, réservoir de carburant *m*; ~ **tanker** *n* TRANSP pétrolier ravitailleur *m*; ~ **tank selector switch** *n* AERONAUT inverseur de sélection réservoir *m*; ~ **temperature probe** *n* AERONAUT sonde de température carburant *f*; ~ **transfer** *n* AERONAUT transfert de carburant *m*; ~ **transfer table** *n* NUCLEAR dispositif de déversement *m*; ~ **ullage box** *n* AERONAUT boîte d'expansion carburant *f*

fuel[2] *vt* THERMOD alimenter en combustible

fuel-air: ~ **mixture** *n* THERMOD mélange d'air et de carburant *m*

fuel-costly *adj* SPACE *spacecraft* coûteux en combustible

fuel-efficient *adj* SPACE *spacecraft*, THERMOD économique en combustible

fueler *n* (AmE) *see fueller*

fueling *n* (AmE) *see fuelling*

fueller *n* (BrE) PETR TECH camion ravitailleur *m*

fuelling *n* (BrE) AERONAUT avitaillement *m*, plein *m*, remplissage de carburant *m*, reprise de carburant *f* ~ **vehicle** *n* (BrE) SPACE avitailleur *m*

fuels *n pl* COAL TECH combustibles *m pl*

fugacity *n* CHEM *of gases*, THERMOD *of gases* fugacité *f*

fugistat *n* FOOD TECH fongistatique *m*

fugitive *adj* POLLUTION *emissions* fugitive

fulcrum *n* PHYS pivot *m*, point d'appui *m*; ~ **pin** *n* MECH ENG axe de pivotement *m*

fulgurite *n* GEOL, PROD ENG *lightning tube* fulgurite *f*

full:[1] ~ **and down** *adj* NAUT chargé en poids et en cubage; ~ **voltage AC/DC** *adj* PROD ENG à tension directe CA/CC

full:[2] ~ **ahead** *adv* NAUT *engine* en avant toute; ~ **and by** *adv* NAUT *sailing* au plus près bon plein; ~ **astern** *adv* NAUT *engine* en arrière toute; **in** ~ **swing** *adv* MECH ENG en pleine activité, en pleine exploitation, en pleine marche; **in** ~ **working order** *adv* MECH ENG en pleine activité, en pleine exploitation, en pleine marche

full:[3] ~ **adder** *n* COMP, DP additionneur complet *m*; ~ **aperture** *n* PHOTO pleine ouverture *f*; ~ **band** *n* PHYS *solid state* bande pleine *f*; ~ **beam headlights** *n pl* (BrE) *(cf high beams)* VEHICLES pleins phares *m pl*; ~ **bridge** *n* ELEC *of instrument* pont intégral *m*; ~ **case black** *n* PRINT film noir imprimant sur toute la surface de l'illustration *m*; ~ **circuit** *n* ELEC circuit total *m*; ~ **coverage beam** *n* SPACE *communications* faisceau à couverture totale *m*; ~ **custom circuit** *n* ELECTRON circuit entièrement personnalisé *m*; ~ **dredging depth** *n* WATER SUPP hauteur totale de dragage *f*; ~ **finish** *n* COATINGS apprêt complet *m*; ~ **frame** *n* CINEMAT plein cadre *m*; ~ **frame print** *n* PHOTO tirage en plein *m*; ~ **gear forward** *n* MECH ENG pleine marche avant *f*; ~ **gloss** *n* PRINT brillant supérieur *m*; ~ **glueing** *n* PACKAGING encollage total *m*; ~ **handle** *n* TEXTILES toucher plein *m*; ~ **hardening** *n* SPRINGS trempage à coeur *m*, trempe à coeur *f*; ~ **hardness** *n* SPRINGS dureté à coeur *f*; ~ **head of water** *n* HYDR EQUIP pleine charge d'eau *f*; ~ **moon** *n* ASTRON pleine lune *f*; ~ **out** *n* PRINT composition sans renfoncement ni à droite à gauche *f*; ~ **pipe** *n* HYDR EQUIP conduite forcée *f*, plein tuyau *m*; ~ **point** *n* PRINT point *m*; ~ **power** *n* NAUT *machinery* puissance maximale *f*; ~ **protection** *n* PATENTS protection pleine et entière *f*; ~ **round edge** *n* C&G joint à dos d'âne *m*; ~ **scale** *n* MECH ENG *drawing* grandeur nature *f*, échelle grandeur *f*; ~ **screen editor** *n* COMP, DP éditeur pleine page *m*; ~ **slipper piston** *n* AUTO piston à fenêtres *m*; ~ **stop** *n* PRINT point *m*; ~ **subtractor** *n* COMP, DP soustracteur complet *m*; ~ **sunlight** *n* SPACE plein soleil *m*; ~ **text** *n* COMP, DP texte intégral *m*; ~ **throttle** *n* AERONAUT régime plein *m*; ~ **thrust** *n* SPACE *spacecraft* pleine poussée *f*, poussée de régime *f*; ~ **track** *n* ACOUSTICS, RECORDING pleine piste *f*; ~ **track recorder** *n* RECORDING magnétophone pleine piste *m*; ~ **track recording** *n* RECORDING enregistrement pleine piste *m*; ~ **voltage** *n* ELEC tension directe *f*, ELEC ENG tension nominale *f*, PROD ENG tension directe *f*

full-bodied *adj* PRINT *ink* à forte viscosité

full-bound *adj* PRINT pleine reliure

full-centered: ~ **loop** *n* (AmE), **full-centred loop** *n* (BrE) SPRINGS anneau anglais *m*, anneau ramené au centre *m*

full-color *adj* (AmE), **full-colour** *adj* (BrE) PRINT pleine couleur

full-duplex *adj (FDX)* COMP, DP duplex intégral

full-duration: ~ **half-maximum** *n (FDHM)* OPT durée à mi-crête *f*, TELECOM durée à mi-crête *f*, largeur à mi-crête *f*

fuller's: ~ **earth** *n* GEOL terre à foulon *f*

Fuller-Bonot: ~ **mill** *n* COAL TECH broyeur à boules Fuller-Bonot *m*

full-face: ~ **mask** *n* SAFETY masque complet *m*; ~ **tunnel**

borer *n* MINING excavateur à section entière *m*; **~ type** *n* PRINT caractères pleins *m pl*

full-fat: **~ cheese** *n* FOOD TECH fromage au lait entier *m*, fromage extra-gras *m*, fromage à 50 % de matière grasse *m*

full-floating: **~ axle** *n* AUTO arbre flottant *m*, arbre non-porteur *m*

full-flow: **~ oil filter** *n* VEHICLES *lubrication* filtre à huile à passage total *m*

full-forward: **~ gear** *n* MECH ENG pleine marche avant *f*

full-hardened *adj* SPRINGS trempé à coeur

fulling *n* TEXTILES foulage *m*

full-injection: **~ turbine** *n* HYDR EQUIP turbine à injection intégrale *f*, turbine à injection totale *f*

full-lead: **~ crystal glass** *n* C&G cristal supérieur *m*

full-length: **~ cloth** *n* TEXTILES pièce entière *f*

full-load *n* AERONAUT, ELEC *of generator* pleine charge *f*; **~ configuration** *n* SPACE *spacecraft* configuration chargée *f*; **~ current** *n* PROD ENG courant pleine charge *m*

full-motion: **~ videoconferencing** *n* TELECOM vidéoconférence à images animées *f*

full-open: **~ throttle** *n* AERONAUT butée plein gaz *f*

full-page: **~ advertisement** *n* PRINT annonce pleine page *f*

full-pitch: **~ coil** *n* ELEC enroulement diamétral *m*, enroulement à pas diamétral *m*; **~ winding** *n* ELEC enroulement diamétral *m*, enroulement à pas diamétral *m*, ELEC ENG enroulement à pas diamétral *m*

full-pressure: **~ suit** *n* SPACE *spacecraft* scaphandre *m*

full-range: **~ loudspeaker** *n* RECORDING haut-parleur à large bande *m*

full-tide: **~ duration** *n* OCEANOG tenue du plein *f*

full-twisted: **~ loop** *n* SPRINGS anneau allemand *m*

full-wave: **~ rectification** *n* ELEC *of rectifier* redressement pleine onde *m*, redressement à deux alternances *m*, ELEC ENG redressement pleine onde *m*; **~ rectified AC voltage** *n* PROD ENG tension CA redressé double alternance *f*; **~ rectifier** *n* ELEC ENG redresseur pleine onde *m*, redresseur à deux alternances *m*, PHYS redresseur pleine onde *m*, redresseur à deux alternances *m*, redresseur à double alternance *m*

full-width: **~ half-maximum** *n* OPT, TELECOM largeur à mi-crête *f*, étendue à mi-crête *f*; **~ sample** *n* TEXTILES échantillon sur toute laize *m*

fully: **~ distributed control system** *n* TELECOM système à structure déconcentrée *m*, système à structure éclatée *m*; **~ drawn yarns** *n pl* TEXTILES fils entièrement étirés *m pl*

fully-automatic[1] *adj* INSTRUMENT, MECH ENG *machine tool* automatique

fully-automatic:[2] **~ diaphragm** *n* PHOTO diaphragme présélectif à fermeture automatique *m*; **~ self-adhesive labeling machine** *n* (AmE), **~ self-adhesive labelling machine** *n* (BrE) PACKAGING étiqueteuse autocollante entièrement automatique *f*; **~ stretch wrapper** *n* PACKAGING machine d'emballage entièrement automatique pour film étirable *f*

fully-bleached: **~ pulp** *n* PAPER TECH pâte hautement blanchie *f*

fully-compressed *adj* PROD ENG à fond de course

fully-steerable: **~ radio telescope** *n* see *steerable radio telescope*

fulminate[1] *n* CHEM fulminate *m*

fulminate[2] *vi* CHEM fulminer

fulmination *n* CHEM fulmination *f*

fulminic *adj* CHEM fulminique

fulvene *n* CHEM fulvène *m*

fumaric *adj* CHEM fumarique

fumarole *n* GEOL fumerolle *f*

fume *n* CHEM fumée *f*, gaz *m*, vapeur *f* **~ cupboard** *n* CHEM TECH capot d'aspiration *m*, hotte d'aspiration *f*, hotte fermée *f*, LAB EQUIP hotte *f*, hotte fermée *f*; **~ extraction** *n* CHEM TECH extraction de fumée *f*; **~ extraction cupola** *n* CHEM TECH fumidôme *m*; **~ hood** *n* CHEM TECH capot d'aspiration *m*, hotte d'aspiration *f*, hotte fermée *f*, LAB EQUIP hotte d'aspiration *f*, sorbonne *f*; **~ incinerator** *n* CHEM TECH incinérateur pour les gaz de fumée *m*

fumes *n pl* HEAT ENG gaz de fumée *m*, POLLUTION, PROP MAT fumées *f pl*, SAFETY fumées *f pl*, vapeurs *f pl*

fumigation *n* POLLUTION enfumage *m*, fumigation *f*

fuming: **~ sulfuric acid** *n* (AmE), **~ sulphuric acid** *n* (BrE) CHEM acide sulfurique fumant *m*

fumivorous *adj* COAL TECH fumivore

function *n* COMP, DP, ELECTRON fonction *f*, MATH fonction *f*, transformation *f*, PHYS *of state* fonction *f*; **~ code** *n* DP code de fonction *m*, code de service *m*; **~ division system** *n* TELECOM système à coeur réparti spécialisé *m*; **~ division system architecture** *n* TELECOM architecture à coeur réparti spécialisé *f*; **~ domain** *n* MATH domaine de définition d'une fonction *m*; **~ generator** *n* ELECTRON générateur de fonctions *m*; **~ key** *n* COMP, DP touche de fonction *f*; **~ selector** *n* ELEC *switch* commutateur de fonctions *m*

functional[1] *adj* COMP, DP fonctionnel

functional:[2] **~ analysis** *n* MATH analyse fonctionnelle *f*; **~ character** *n* PRINT caractère fonctionnel *m*; **~ decomposition** *n* COMP, DP décomposition fonctionnelle *f*; **~ design** *n* COMP conception fonctionnelle *f*, étude fonctionnelle *f*, DP conception fonctionnelle *f*, étude fonctionnelle *f*; **~ diagram** *n* DP schéma fonctionnel *m*, MECH ENG schéma de principe *m*; **~ entity** *n* *(FE)* TELECOM entité fonctionnelle *f*; **~ entity action** *n* *(FEA)* TELECOM action d'entité fonctionnelle *f*; **~ group** *n* CHEM groupe de fonction *m*, groupe fonctionnel *m*; **~ group header** *n* TELECOM en-tête de groupe fonctionnel *m*; **~ language** *n* COMP langage fonctionnel *m*; **~ test** *n* COMP, DP test fonctionnel *m*, TELECOM essai de fonctionnement *m*, essai fonctionnel *m*; **~ unit** *n* COMP, DP, TELECOM unité fonctionnelle *f*

functionally-divided: **~ system** *n* TELECOM système en partage de fonctions *m*

fundamental[1] *adj* PART PHYS *principle* fondamental

fundamental[2] *n* ACOUSTICS composante *f*; **~ chord** *n* ACOUSTICS accord fondamental *m*; **~ component** *n* PHYS *vibrations* composante fondamentale *f*; **~ frequency** *n* ACOUSTICS fréquence fondamentale *f*, ELECTRON fondamentale *f*, fréquence fondamentale *f*, TELECOM fréquence fondamentale *f*; **~ mode** *n* ELEC ENG, OPT mode fondamental *m*, PHYS *vibrations* mode fondamental *m*, *waveguide* mode dominant *m*, mode fondamental *m*, SPACE *spacecraft* mode fondamental *m*, mode propre *m*; **~ programing** *n* (AmE), **~ programming** *n* (BrE) PROD ENG programmation de base *f*; **~ tone** *n* ACOUSTICS son fondamental *m*, WAVE PHYS fondamental *m*; **~ unit** *n* see *derived unit* **~ vibration mode** *n* ACOUSTICS mode fondamental de vibration *m*, SPACE mode propre de vibration *m*

fungicidal: **~ varnish** *n* COATINGS vernis fongicide *m*, COLOURS vernis anticryptogamique *m*, vernis fongicide *m*

fungicide n CHEM, P&R *additive* fongicide m; ~ **paint** n PROD ENG peinture fongicide f

fungistat n FOOD TECH *fermentation* fongistat m

fungus-proof adj PROD ENG protégé contre les moisissures

funicular n TRANSP funiculaire m; ~ **railway** n TRANSP funiculaire m

funnel n C&G cône de télévision m, CHEM *liquid separation* ballon de décantage m, CONST cheminée f, entonnoir m, tuyau m, tuyau de cheminée m, ELECTRON cône m, FOOD TECH *for liquid, powder,* LAB EQUIP *for liquids* entonnoir m, MECH cheminée f, entonnoir m, NAUT *ship* cheminée f, PROD ENG coulée f, jet de coulée m, trou de coulée m; ~ **heater** n LAB EQUIP chauffe-entonnoir m; ~ **stand** n LAB EQUIP *filtration* support pour entonnoir m

fur[1] n PROD ENG calcin m, crasses des chaudières f pl, dépôts m pl, incrustation f, tartre m, TEXTILES fourrure f

fur[2] vt PROD ENG désincruster, détartrer, entartrer, incruster

furfural n P&R *raw material* furfural m

furfuraldehyde n P&R *raw material* furaldéhyde f

furfuryl adj CHEM furfuryle

furile n CHEM furile m

furilic adj CHEM furilique

furl vt NAUT *sail* ferler

Furling: ~ **speed** n FUELLESS *wind power* vitesse Furling f

furlong n METR furlong m

furnace n HEATING fourneau m, LAB EQUIP *heating,* PAPER TECH four m, PROD ENG *for smelting, melting, baking* four m, fourneau m, *for heating steam boiler* foyer m; ~ **bar** n PROD ENG barreau de grille m; ~ **bridge** n PROD ENG autel m, pont m; ~ **charge** n C&G charge du four f; ~ **coke** n COAL TECH coke métallurgique m; ~ **fill** n C&G charge du four f; ~ **gas** n PROD ENG combustible de gueulard m, gaz de chauffage m; ~ **grate** n PROD ENG grille de foyer f; ~ **performance** n C&G rendement d'un four m; ~ **plate** n PROD ENG tôles pour foyers f pl

furnish n PAPER TECH composition de fabrication f; ~ **layer** n COATINGS, PAPER TECH couche fibreuse f

furnishing: ~ **fabric** n TEXTILES tissu d'ameublement m

furnishings n pl CONST aménagement m, aménagements commerciaux m pl, équipement commercial m

furniture: ~ **fixtures and fittings** n pl CONST mobilier et agencement m

furon n CHEM furanne m, furfurane m

furring n CONST *of roof* coyau m, PROP MAT entartrage m; ~ **piece** n CONST coyau m

furrow n GEOL cannelure f, sillon m, fosse f, synéclise f

fuse:[1] ~ **protected** adj ELEC ENG protégé par fusible

fuse[2] n ELEC fusible m, plomb m, ELEC ENG fusible m, MILIT amorce f, fusée de déclenchement f, MINING cordeau m, fusée f, mèche f, étoupille f, TV coupe-circuit m, fusible m; ~ **array** n ELEC ENG batterie de fusibles f; ~ **base** n ELEC ENG culot de fusible m; ~ **blown status indicator** n PROD ENG voyant d'état de fusible coupé m, voyant de fusible claqué m; ~ **board** n

ELEC ENG panneau de fusible m; ~ **box** n ELEC, ELEC ENG boîte à fusible f, VEHICLES *electrical system* boîtier à fusible m; ~ **cap** n MILIT coiffe de fusée f; ~ **carrier** n ELEC ENG porte-fusible m; ~ **clip** n PROD ENG pince de fusible f; ~ **cord** n SPACE *spacecraft* cordeau fusant m; ~ **cover** n ELEC, PROD ENG protège-fusible m; ~ **element** n ELEC ENG élément de fusible m; ~ **holder** n ELEC ENG, TV porte-fusible m; ~ **link** n ELEC fil fusible m, ELEC ENG liaison fusible f; ~ **puller** n PROD ENG extracteur de fusible m; ~ **safety pin** n MILIT goupille de sûreté f; ~ **seal sheet** n PACKAGING feuille fondue de fermeture f; ~ **strip** n ELEC lame fusible f; ~ **wire** n ELEC fil fusible m, ELEC ENG fil à fusible m

fuse[3] vt THERMOD fondre, porter à fusion

fused[1] adj THERMOD fondu

fused:[2] ~ **bifocals** n pl C&G verres bifocaux fusionnés m pl; ~ **bundle** n C&G faisceau à bouts compactés m; ~ **quartz** n OPT, TELECOM quartz fondu m; ~ **silica** n C&G, OPT, TELECOM silice fondue f; ~ **silica window** n SPACE *spacecraft* fenêtre en silice fondue f

fusee: ~ **wheel** n PROD ENG *extraction* tambour conique m

fusel: ~ **oil** n FOOD TECH *fermentation* huile de fusel f

fuselage n TRANSP fuselage m; ~ **box** n AERONAUT caisson de fuselage m; ~ **box beam wall** n AERONAUT âme de poutre de fuselage f; ~ **center box** n (AmE), ~ **centre box** n (BrE) AERONAUT poutre centrale du fuselage f; ~ **datum line** n AERONAUT référence du fuselage f; ~ **dorsal fin** n AERONAUT arête dorsale fuselage f; ~ **ground connection** n AERONAUT prise de coque f

fusible[1] adj PROP MAT, THERMOD fusible

fusible:[2] ~ **clay** n C&G argile fusible f; ~ **plug for steam boiler** n HYDR EQUIP plomb fusible pour chaudière à vapeur m, rondelle fusible pour chaudière f

fusing n C&G soudure f, THERMOD coulée f, fusion f; ~ **oven** n P&R *equipment* four de fusion m; ~ **point** n THERMOD point de fusion m

fusion n CHEM fonte f, fusion f, fusionnement m, GAS TECH, P&R *operation,* PHYS, PROP MAT *metallurgy,* THERMOD fusion f; ~ **casting** n C&G coulage par fusion m; ~ **drilling** n COAL TECH forage thermique m; ~ **splice** n OPT, TELECOM épissure par fusion f, épissure par soudage f; ~ **welding** n CONST, PROD ENG, THERMOD soudage par fusion m

fusion-welded: ~ **butt joint** n MECH ENG joint soudé bout à bout par fusion m; ~ **joint** n MECH ENG joint soudé par fusion m

future: ~ **use** n TELECOM utilisation future f

fuzz n PRINT peluche f, poussière de papier f

fuzzy: ~ **image** n PHOTO image défocalisée f; ~ **logic** n COMP logique floue f; ~ **set** n COMP ensemble flou m; ~ **theory** n COMP théorie floue f

FWF abbr *(first window fibre, first window fiber)* OPT fibre à 0,85mm f

FWHM abbr *(full-width half-maximum)* OPT largeur à mi-crête f, étendue à mi-crête f

FX abbr *(effects)* TV trucages m pl

G

G *abbr (giga-)* METR G *(giga-)*

Ga *(gallium)* CHEM Ga *(gallium)*

GA *abbr (go ahead)* TELECOM invitation à continuer *f*

GaAs: ~ laser *n (gallium arsenide laser)* RAD PHYS laser à l'arsinure de gallium *m*

gab *n* HYDR EQUIP bec de cane *m*, pied-de-biche *m*; ~ hook *n* HYDR EQUIP bec de cane *m*, pied-de-biche *m*

gabion *n* CONST gabion *m*

gable *n* CONST *architecture* pignon *m*; ~ roof *n* CONST comble à pignon *m*; ~ wall *n* C&G paroi amont *f*

Gablonz: ~ glassware *n* C&G bimbeloterie *f*

gad *n* MINING pince *f*, *quarrying* coin *m*

gadget *n* C&G pontil à griffes *m*; ~ bag *n* PHOTO sac accessoire *m*

gadolinite *n* MINERAL gadolinite *f*

gadolinium *n (Gd)* CHEM gadolinium *m (Gd)*

gaff *n* NAUT corne *f*, gaffe *f*

gaffer *n* C&G chef de place *m*; ~ grip *n* CINEMAT pince crocodile *f*; ~ tape *n* CINEMAT chatterton grande largeur *m*

gag *n* NUCLEAR limiteur de débit *m*

gage[1] *n* (AmE) *see gauge*

gage[2] *vt* (AmE) *see gauge*

gaged: ~ orifice *n* (AmE) *see gauged orifice* ~ restriction *n* (AmE) *see gauged restriction*

gagger *n* PROD ENG *founding* clou de mouleur *m*, crochet de fonderie *m*

gaging *n* (AmE) *see gauging*

gain *n* COMP, DP gain *m*, ELEC *signal* amplification *f*, gain *m*, ELECTRON coefficient d'amplification *m*, gain *m*, NAUT *radar, echo sounder, radio receiver* gain *m*, RECORDING amplification *f*, facteur d'amplitude *m*, gain *m*, TELECOM gain *m*, TV amplification de puissance *f*, gain *m* ~ adjustment *n* ELECTRON réglage de gain *m*; ~ change *n* ELECTRON changement de gain *m*, variation de gain *f*; ~ compression *n* ELECTRON compression de gain *f*; ~ control *n* ELECTRON commande de gain *f*, RECORDING réglage de volume *m*; ~ curve *n* ELECTRON courbe de gain *f*; ~ drift *n* ELECTRON dérive de gain *f*; ~ frequency characteristic *n* ELECTRON caractéristique gain-fréquence *f*; ~ function *n* ELECTRON fonction de gain *f*; ~ pumping *n* RECORDING pompage de gain *m*; ~ setting *n* ELECTRON réglage de gain *m*; ~ trace *n* PETR trace de gain *f*; ~ trimming *n* ELECTRON ajustage de gain *m*; ~ weighting factor *n* ELECTRON coefficient de pondération de gain *m*

gaining: ~ stream *n* WATER SUPP rivière absorbante *f*

gain-to-noise: ~ temperature ratio *n (G-T)* SPACE *communications* rapport gain-température de bruit *m (G-T)*

galactic[1] *adj* ASTRON galactique

galactic:[2] ~ cannibalism *n* ASTRON cannibalisme galactique *m*; ~ center *n* (AmE), ~ centre *n* (BrE) ASTRON centre galactique *m*; ~ cloud *n* SPACE nuage galactique *m*; ~ collision *n* galaxie à flambée ~ magnetic field *n* ASTRON champ magnétique galactique *m*; ~ noise *n* ELECTRON bruit d'origine galactique *m*, bruit galactique *m*; ~ rotation *n* ASTRON rotation galactique *f*

galactonic *adj* CHEM galactonique

galactosamine *n* CHEM galactosamine *f*

galactose *n* FOOD TECH *monosaccharide* galactose *m*

galaxy *n* ASTRON galaxie *f*

gale: ~ warning *n* METEO avis de coup de vent *m*, avis de tempête *m*, NAUT *meteorology* avis de coup de vent *m*, avis de forte brise *m*

galena *n* CHEM, MINERAL galène *f*, plomb sulfuré *m*

galenite *n* MINERAL galène *f*, plomb sulfuré *m*

galenobismuthite *n* MINERAL galénobismuthite *f*

galenobismutite *n* MINERAL galénobismuthite *f*

Galerkin: ~ weighting *n* NUCLEAR pondération de Galerkin *f*

Galilean: ~ frame *n* PHYS référentiel galiléen *m*; ~ satellites *n pl* ASTRON satellites galiléens *m pl*; ~ space probe *n* ASTRON *Jupiter* sonde spatiale Galilée *f*; ~ telescope *n* PHYS lunette de Galilée *f*; ~ transformation *n* PHYS transformation de Galilée *f*

gall *n* C&G galle *f*

gallate *n* CHEM gallate *m*

gallein *n* CHEM galléine *f*

gallery *n* MECH passerelle *f*, NUCLEAR galerie d'accès *f*; ~ furnace *n* PROD ENG four de galère *m*; ~ in dead ground *n* MINING bacnure *f*, bouveau *m*, bowette *f*, galerie au rocher *f*

galley *n* AERONAUT aménagement hôtelier de bord *m*, meuble cuisine *m*, meuble cuisine de bord *m*, meuble office de bord *m*, office *m*, NAUT cuisine *f*, PRINT fichier brut non paginé *m*, *steel tray* galée *f*; ~ furnishings *n pl* AERONAUT aménagement office *m*; ~ proof *n* PRINT épreuve en placard *f*, épreuve en première *f*

gallic *adj* CHEM gallique

galling *n* NUCLEAR arrachement *m*, grippage *m*, écaillage *m*

gallium *n (Ga)* CHEM gallium *m (Ga)*; ~ arsenide *n* ELECTRON, OPT, PHYS arséniure de gallium *m*; ~ arsenide chip *n* ELECTRON puce d'arséniure de gallium *f*; ~ arsenide component *n* ELECTRON composant à l'arséniure de gallium *m*; ~ arsenide diode *n* ELECTRON diode à l'arséniure de gallium *f*; ~ arsenide laser *n (GaAs laser)* RAD PHYS laser à l'arsinure de gallium *m*; ~ arsenide logic *n* ELECTRON logique à l'arséniure de gallium *f*; ~ arsenide MOS transistor *n* ELECTRON transistor MOS à l'arséniure de gallium *m*; ~ arsenide parametric amplifier diode *n* ELECTRON diode paramétrique à l'arséniure de gallium *f*; ~ arsenide solar cell *n* ELECTRON cellule solaire à l'arséniure de gallium *f*; ~ arsenide substrate *n* ELECTRON substrat en arséniure de gallium *m*

gallon *n* METR, PETR gallon *m*; ~ jug *n* C&G gallon à anse *m*

gallows: ~ frame *n* MINING belle-fleur *f*, chevalement *m*, chevalet d'extraction *m*, châssis à molettes *m*

galvanic[1] *adj* CHEM, ELEC *metals, cell* galvanique

galvanic:[2] ~ cell *n* CHEM cellule galvanique *f*, ELEC pile galvanique *f*, ELEC ENG pile de Volta *f*, pile galvanique *f*, pile électrique *f*; ~ couple *n* ELEC ENG couple galvanique *m*; ~ current *n* ELEC ENG courant galvanique *m*; ~

deposition *n* COATINGS finition galvanique *f*, finition électrolytique *f*; ~ **isolation** *n* ELEC ENG isolement galvanique *m*; ~ **plating** *n* COATINGS finition galvanique *f*, finition électrolytique *f*

galvanics *n* PRINT galvanoplastie *f*

galvanization *n* PROD ENG galvanisation *f*, zingage *m*

galvanize *vt* PROD ENG galvaniser, zinguer

galvanized[1] *adj* MECH *materials* galvanisé, zingué

galvanized:[2] ~ **protective coating** *n* COATINGS couche protectrice galvanisée *f*

galvanizing *n* PROP MAT galvanisation *f*, zingage *m*

galvanometer *n* CINEMAT, ELEC, ELEC ENG galvanomètre *m*, GEOPHYS galvanomètre enregistreur *m*, LAB EQUIP *electrical measurements*, PETR, PHYS galvanomètre *m*; ~ **shunt** *n* ELEC shunt de galvanomètre *m*, ELEC ENG shunt d'ampèremètre *m*

galvanoplastics *n* COATINGS galvanoplastie *f*, métallisation *f*, électrodéposition *f*, PROD ENG galvanoplastie *f*

galvanostatic: ~ **permeation** *n* PROP MAT imprégnation galvanostatique *f*

galvoplates *n pl* PHYS *laser* lames galvanométriques *f pl*

gambier *n* CHEM gambir *m*

gambrel: ~ **roof** *n* (AmE) *(cf mansard roof)* CONST comble brisé *m*, comble en mansarde *m*, comble à la Mansard *m*

game: ~ **theory** *n* MATH théorie des jeux *f*

gamma *n* CINEMAT facteur de contraste *m*, gamma *m*, PETR, TV gamma *m*; ~ **backscatter method** *n* NUCLEAR méthode de rétrodiffusion gamma *f*; ~ **characteristic** *n* ELECTRON *camera tubes* caractéristique de conversion *f*, courbe de gamma *f*; ~ **correction** *n* CINEMAT correction du gamma *f*; ~ **corrector** *n* TV correcteur de gamma *m*; ~ **emission** *n* RAD PHYS rayonnement gamma *m*; ~ **error** *n* TV distorsion de demi-teintes *f*, erreur de gamma *f*; ~ **film** *n* RAD PHYS *radiation detection* film gamma *m*; ~ **fuel scanning** *n* NUCLEAR scrutation gamma du combustible *f*; ~ **ore pulp content meter** *n* NUCLEAR teneurmètre d'eau schlammeuse de minerais à rayons gamma *m*; ~ **particle** *n* PART PHYS particule gamma *f*; ~ **photon activation** *n* RAD PHYS activation photonucléaire *f*; ~ **quench** *n* NUCLEAR trempe gamma *f*; ~ **radiation** *n* ELEC, PHYS, RAD PHYS *photons* rayonnement gamma *m*; ~ **radiography** *n* RAD PHYS gammagraphie *f*; ~ **ray** *n* ELECTRON, PETR, RAD PHYS, WAVE PHYS rayon gamma *m*; ~ **ray absorption analysis** *n* RAD PHYS analyse par absorption des rayons gamma *f*; ~ **ray activation analysis** *n (cf photoactivation analysis)* RAD PHYS analyse par activation dans les photons gamma *f*; ~ **ray astronomy** *n* ASTRON, SPACE astronomie gamma *f*; ~ **ray beam** *n* PART PHYS faisceau de rayons gamma *m*; ~ **ray conversion** *n* RAD PHYS conversion de rayons gamma *f*; ~ **ray escape peak** *n* RAD PHYS pic de fuite de photons *m*; ~ **ray heating** *n* RAD PHYS chauffage à rayons gamma *m*; ~ **ray log** *n* FUELLESS rapport de rayons gamma *m*, GEOPHYS diagramme de rayons gamma *m*, PETR TECH diagraphie de rayons gamma *f*; ~ **ray quantum** *n* PART PHYS quantum de rayonnement gamma *m*; ~ **rays** *n* PHYS rayon gamma *m*; ~ **ray spectrometer** *n* RAD PHYS, WAVE PHYS spectromètre à rayons gamma *m*; ~ **ray survey** *n* NUCLEAR levé gamma *m*, étude des rayons gamma *f*; ~ **ray well logging** *n* PETR TECH diagraphie par rayons gamma *f*; ~ **strip** *n* CINEMAT coin sensitométrique *m*

gamma-gamma: ~ **log** *n* PETR TECH *drilling, prospecting* diagraphie gamma-gamma *f*

gammametric: ~ **ore assay** *n* NUCLEAR essai gammamétrique *m*

gamma-ray: ~ **photon** *n* PART PHYS, RAD PHYS photon gamma *m*; ~ **spectrum** *n* RAD PHYS spectre de rayons gamma *m*

gammexane *n* CHEM gammexane *m*

gamut *n* ACOUSTICS gamme *f*

gang[1] *n* PROD ENG boîtier standard *m*; ~ **capacitor** *n* ELEC condensateurs jumelés *m pl*, ELEC ENG condensateur accouplé *m*; ~ **channel** *n* MECH ENG bande à écrous prisonniers *f*, plaquette porte-écrou *f*; ~ **drill** *n* PROD ENG machine à percer multiple *f*, perceuse à broches multiples *f*; ~ **machining** *n* PROD ENG usinage en série *m*; ~ **milling** *n* PROD ENG fraisage de pièces en série *m*; ~ **piece** *n* MECH ENG *lathe* pont *m*; ~ **press** *n* MECH ENG presse à poinçons sériés *f*; ~ **printing** *n* PRINT impression groupée *f*; ~ **punch** *n* PROD ENG poinçonneuse multiple *f*; ~ **saw** *n* PROD ENG scie à plusieurs lames *f*; ~ **switch** *n* ELEC ENG commutateur à galette *m*; ~ **tool** *n* MECH ENG outil sérié *m*; ~ **tuning capacitor** *n* ELEC ENG condensateur d'accord à cages *m*; ~ **work** *n* PROD ENG fabrication en série *f*

gang[2] *vt* MECH ENG coupler

ganged: ~ **capacitors** *n pl* ELEC ENG condensateurs jumelés *m pl*; ~ **circuit** *n* ELEC ENG, TV circuit à commande unique *m*; ~ **tuning** *n* ELEC ENG accord par commande unique *m*

ganging *n* ELEC *resistances* accouplement *m*, ELEC ENG jumelage *m*, PRINT groupage des positifs pour les analyser ensemble *m*

gangplank *n* NAUT passerelle *f*, planchon de coupée *m*, traversine *f*

gangue: ~ **mineral** *n* COAL TECH minerai de gangue *m*

gangway *n* COAL TECH galerie principale *f*, NAUT coursive *f*, passerelle d'embarquement *f*, passerelle de débarquement *f*, NUCLEAR galerie d'accès *f*, RAIL *vehicles* intercirculation *f*

gantry *n* CONST charpente en forme de portique *f*, portique *m*, WATER SUPP *of dredge* beffroi *m*; ~ **crane** *n* CONST, NAUT grue à portique *f*, NUCLEAR grue à portique *f*, portique *m*, RAIL grue à chevalet *f*, portique *m*; ~ **lathe** *n* MECH ENG tour à barre prismatique *m*; ~ **with hoist** *n* NUCLEAR semi-portique *m*

Gantt: ~ **chart** *n* PROD ENG diagramme de Gantt *m*, planning d'atelier *m*, planning tableau *m*, tableau de suivi d'atelier *m*

gap *n* C&G lacune granulométrique *f*, COMP intervalle *m*, CONST *between rails* brèche *f*, écartement *m*, DP intervalle *m*, ELEC ENG *magnetic circuits* entrefer *m*, *relays* distance entre contacts *f*, GEOL *erosional or sedimentary break* lacune *f*, MECH chaufrein *m*, intervalle *m*, écartement *m*, MECH ENG brèche *f*, bâillement *m*, intervalle *m*, ouverture *f*, vide *m*, *distance* espace *m*, *magnetism* entrefer *m*, *of joint* coupe *f*, *play* jeu *m*, NUCLEAR veine d'eau *f*, *between fuel and cladding* espace libre *m*, PHYS bande interdite *f*, gap *m*, SPACE fente *f*, SPRINGS bâillement *m*, TRANSP *traffic* créneau *m*, TV entrefer *m*; ~ **azimuth** *n* RECORDING azimut d'entrefer *m*; ~ **bed** *n* MECH ENG *lathe* banc rompu *m*; ~ **bridge** *n* MECH ENG *lathe* pont *m*; ~ **depth** *n* ACOUSTICS profondeur d'entrefer *f*, RECORDING largeur d'entrefer *f*, TV profondeur d'entrefer *f*; ~ **detector** *n* TRANSP détecteur de créneaux *m*; ~ **effect** *n* TV effet d'entrefer *m*; ~ **gage** *n* (AmE), ~ **gauge** *n* (BrE) METR calibre à mâchoires *m*, *adjustable, plain* calibre à mâchoires *m*, *screwthread* calibre à mâchoires *m*; ~ **lathe** *n* MECH ENG tour à banc rompu *m*; ~ **length** *n* ACOUSTICS longueur réelle d'entrefer *f*, ELEC ENG largeur d'entrefer *f*, RECORDING longueur d'entrefer *f*; ~ **loss** *n* ACOUSTICS perte d'entrefer *f*, OPT perte par séparation terminale *f*, RECORDING perte d'entrefer *f*, TELECOM *longitudinal offset loss* perte par séparation terminale *f*, TV perte d'entrefer *f*; ~ **setting** *n* TV équilibrage d'entrefer *m*; ~ **sizing** *n* C&G granulométrie discontinue *f*; ~ **spacer** *n* RECORDING cale d'entrefer *f*, pièce d'espacement d'entrefer *f*; ~ **spanner** *n* (BrE) MECH ENG clé à fourche *f*; ~ **width** *n* TV largeur d'entrefer *f*

gapped: ~ **core** *n* ELEC ENG noyau à entrefer *m*

gapping: ~ **switch** *n* TV commutateur à séquence travail-repos *m*

gap-to-gap: ~ **adjustment** *n* PRINT réglage gorge-à-gorge *m*

garage: ~ **ventilating apparatus** *n* SAFETY appareils de ventilation de garage *m pl*

garbage *n* COMP, DP informations parasites *f pl*, informations éparses *f pl*, PACKAGING (AmE) *(cf rubbish)* détritus *m*, PROD ENG (AmE) *(cf rubbish)* déchets *m pl*, détritus *m*, rebuts *m pl*, RECYCLING (AmE) *(cf rubbish)* déchets *m pl*, détritus *m*; ~ **bag** *n* (AmE) *(cf refuse sack)* PACKAGING sac pour les détritus *m*; ~ **chute** *n* (AmE) *(cf rubbish chute)* RECYCLING vide-ordures *m*; ~ **collection** *n* COMP, DP collecte des positions inutiles *f*, regroupement des informations en mémoire *m*, récupération de place en mémoire *f*, récupération des positions inutilisées *f*; ~ **incinerator** *n* (AmE) PACKAGING incinérateur pour détritus *m*; ~ **truck** *n* (AmE) *(cf dustbin lorry)* RECYCLING benne à ordures *f*

garbage-in/garbage-out *n* *(GIGO)* COMP rebut à l'entrée et à la sortie *m*

garboard *n* NAUT galbord *m*; ~ **strake** *n* NAUT *shipbuilding* virure de galbord *f*

garland: ~ **curb** *n* MINING *in mine shaft* gargouille *f*

garment *n* TEXTILES vêtement *m*

garnet *n* CONST penture à T *f*, MINERAL, PROP MAT grenat *m*; ~ **hinge** *n* CONST penture à T *f*

garnierite *n* MINERAL garniérite *f*

gas:¹ ~ **tight** *adj* PROD ENG étanche

gas² *n* CHEM, HEAT ENG gaz *m*, MINING feu brisou *m*, feu grieux *m*, grisou *m*, mofette inflammable *f*, terrou *m*, PETR (AmE) *(cf petrol)* pétrole *m*, PETR TECH (AmE) *(cf petrol)* essence *f*, PHYS, REFRIG, THERMOD gaz *m*, VEHICLES (AmE) *(cf petrol) fuel* essence *f*;

~ a ~ **absorption** *n* GAS TECH, PETR TECH *refining* absorption de gaz *f*; ~ **alarm system** *n* MINING installation d'alarme pour le grisou *f*; ~ **alert** *n* MILIT alerte aux gaz *f*; ~ **analysis** *n* PETR TECH analyse de gaz *f*; ~ **analyzer** *n* GAS TECH, PETR TECH analyseur de gaz *m*;

~ b ~ **baffle** *n* NUCLEAR déflecteur de gaz *m*; ~ **balance** *n* GAS TECH balance à gaz *f*, bilan gazeux *m*; ~ **band** *n* GAS TECH zone de gaz *f*; ~ **bearing** *n* MECH palier à gaz *m*; ~ **blowpipe** *n* PROD ENG chalumeau à gaz *m*; ~ **boiler** *n* THERMOD chauffe-eau à gaz *m*; ~ **bottle** *n* NUCLEAR bouteille à gaz *f*, PROD ENG bombonne à gaz *f*, bouteille à gaz *f*, THERMOD *camping* bidon de gaz *m*, *cylinder* cylindre à gaz comprimé *m*; ~ **burette** *n* LAB EQUIP *analysis* burette à gaz *f*; ~ **burner** *n* HEAT ENG brûleur à gaz *m*, PROD ENG bec de gaz *m*, bec à gaz *m*, brûleur à gaz *m*, THERMOD bec de gaz *m*;

~ c ~ **cap** *n* MINING *safety lamp* auréole *f*, PETR, PETR TECH *petroleum geology* chapeau de gaz *m*, gas cap *m*; ~ **cap drive** *n* PETR TECH *oil recovery* drainage par

expansion du gaz libre *m*; ~ **carbon** *n* COAL TECH charbon de cornue *m*; ~ **carburizing** *n* THERMOD cémentation gazeuse *f*; ~ **cavity** *n* NUCLEAR *weld defect* inclusion gazeuse *f*; ~ **chromatograph** *n* LAB EQUIP *analysis* chromatographe *m*; ~ **chromatography** *n* CHEM, FOOD TECH, PROP MAT CPG, chromatographie en phase gazeuse *f*, THERMOD chromatographie gazeuse *f*; ~ **circuit** *n* HEATING circuit gaz *m*; ~ **circulation loop** *n* NUCLEAR circuit de circulation du gaz *m*; ~ **cleaner** *n* GAS TECH laveur *m*; ~ **cleaning** *n* GAS TECH purification du gaz *f*, épuration du gaz *f*; ~ **cloud** *n* GAS TECH nuage de gaz *m*; ~ **coal** *n* COAL TECH charbon à gaz *m*, houille grasse *f*, houille à gaz *f*; ~ **cock** *n* PROD ENG robinet de conduite de gaz *m*, robinet à gaz *m*; ~ **coke** *n* COAL TECH coke d'usine à gaz *m*, coke de gaz *m*; ~ **completion unit** *n* GAS TECH gaz complétion *m*; ~ **compressor** *n* PROD ENG compresseur à gaz *m*; ~ **condensate deposit** *n* PROP MAT gisement de gaz à condensat *m*; ~ **constant** *n* PHYS constante de gaz parfait *f*; ~ **content** *n* THERMOD teneur en gaz *f*; ~ **cooler** *n* REFRIG refroidisseur à gaz *m*; ~ **cushion** *n* NUCLEAR matelas de gaz *m*; ~ **cutting** *n* PROD ENG oxycoupage *m*, THERMOD découpage au chalumeau *m*, oxycoupage *m*; ~ **cylinder** *n* MECH ENG *storage*, NUCLEAR, PROD ENG bouteille à gaz *f*;

~ d ~ **desulfurization** *n* (AmE), ~ **desulphurisation** *n* (BrE) POLLUTION désulfuration de gaz *f*; ~ **detector** *n* CONTROL, LAB EQUIP *analysis, safety*, MILIT détecteur de gaz *m*, MINING *fire damp* détecteur de grisou *m*, indicateur de gaz *m*; ~ **diode** *n* ELECTRON diode à gaz *f*; ~ **discharge** *n* ELECTRON décharge dans un gaz *f*; ~ **discharge gap** *n* NUCLEAR lame de gaz *f*; ~ **discharge lamp** *n* ELEC *lighting* lampe luminescente à gaz *f*; ~ **dissociation** *n* GAS TECH dissociation de gaz *f*; ~ **drive** *n* GAS TECH poussée de gaz *f*; ~ **drying plant** *n* GAS TECH système de séchage *m*; ~ **dynamic laser** *n* ELECTRON laser à détente *m*;

~ e ~ **embolism** *n* OCEANOG aéroembolisme *m*; ~ **engine** *n* GAS TECH moteur alimenté en gaz *m*, MECH ENG moteur à gaz *m*, PROD ENG machine à gaz *f*, moteur à gaz *m*, *of blast furnace* moteur à gaz *m*, THERMOD moteur à gaz *m*, VEHICLES (AmE) *(cf petrol engine)* moteur à essence *m*; ~ **enrichment** *n* THERMOD enrichissement en gaz *m*; ~ **equation** *n* PHYS équation des gaz *f*; ~ **exploder** *n* PETR canon à gaz *m*; ~ **explosion** *n* COAL TECH coup de grisou *m*; ~ **expulsion** *n* OCEANOG dégazage *m*; ~ **extraction** *n* OCEANOG dégazage *m*;

~ f ~ **factor** *n* GAS TECH teneur en gaz *f*; ~ **feeder** *n* MINING soufflard de grisou *m*, souffleur *m*; ~ **field** *n* GAS TECH gisement de gaz *m*, PETR TECH champ de gaz naturel *m*, THERMOD gisement de gaz naturel *m*; ~ **filter** *n* (AmE) *(cf petrol filter)* VEHICLES *fuel* filtre à essence *m*; ~ **fire** *n* THERMOD radiateur à gaz *m*; ~ **fissure** *n* MINING soufflard de grisou *m*, souffleur *m*; ~ **fitter** *n* PROD ENG *person* appareilleur à gaz *m*, gazier *m*, installateur de chaufferie à gaz *m*; ~ **fittings** *n pl* PROD ENG appareils de distribution du gaz *m pl*; ~ **flare** *n* THERMOD *oil wells* torche *f*; ~ **flow** *n* FLUID PHYS écoulement de gaz *m*, GAS TECH écoulement gazeux *m*; ~ **flue** *n* PROD ENG carneau à gaz *m*; ~ **focusing** *n* ELECTRON concentration par les gaz résiduels *f*; ~ **formation volume factor** *n* PETR facteur volumétrique de gaz *m*; ~ **furnace** *n* PROD ENG four chauffé au gaz *m*, four à gaz *m*;

~ g ~ **generator** *n* PROD ENG gazofacteur *m*, gazogène *m*, générateur de gaz *m*, SPACE générateur de gaz *m*,

THERMOD gazogène *m*; ~ **geyser** *n* HEATING *bathrooms* chauffe-bain à gaz *m*; ~ **giant** *n* ASTRON planète géante gazeuse *f*; ~ **grid** *n* PETR TECH *distribution system* réseau de gaz *m*, THERMOD réseau de gazoducs *m*;

~ h ~ **heating** *n* PROD ENG, THERMOD chauffage au gaz *m*; ~ **heating system** *n* HEAT ENG chaufferie à gaz *f*; ~ **holder** *n* PROD ENG, THERMOD gazomètre *m* réservoir à gaz *m*; ~ **hose** *n* (AmE) *(cf petrol hose)* VEHICLES *fuel* tuyau flexible à essence *m*; ~ **hydrocarbon** *n* GAS TECH hydrocarbure gazeux *m*;

~ i ~ **injection** *n* PETR TECH *oil recovery* injection de gaz *f*; ~ **in place** *n* PETR gaz en place *m*;

~ j ~ **jet** *n* PROD ENG brûleur à jet de gaz *m*, jet de gaz *m*;

~ k ~ **kinetics** *n* THERMOD cinétique des gaz *f*;

~ l ~ **laser** *n* ELECTRON, RAD PHYS laser à gaz *m*; ~ **leak** *n* GAS TECH dégagement gazeux *m*, THERMOD fuite de gaz *f*; ~ **leak detector** *n* LAB EQUIP, THERMOD détecteur de fuite de gaz *m*; ~ **lift** *n* PETR TECH *oil recovery* allégement à gaz *m*, gas-lift *m*; ~ **lighter** *n* HEAT ENG allume-gaz *m*; ~ **liquid chromatography** *n* POLLUTION, THERMOD CGL, chromatographie gaz-liquide *f*; ~ **lock** *n* NUCLEAR *for fuel assemblies* sas à gaz *m*, REFRIG bouchon de vapeur *m*; ~ **log** *n* PETR diagraphie des gaz *f*; ~ **lubricated bearing** *n* NUCLEAR coussinet gazeux *m*, palier à gaz *m*;

~ m ~ **main** *n* PROD ENG conduite maîtresse de gaz *f*, conduite principale de gaz *f*; ~ **mantle** *n* THERMOD manchon Auer *m*; ~ **maser** *n* ELECTRON maser à gaz *m*; ~ **mask** *n* MILIT masque à gaz *m*; ~ **meter** *n* LAB EQUIP, PROD ENG, THERMOD compteur à gaz *m*; ~ **motor** *n* PROD ENG machine à gaz *f*, moteur à gaz *m*; ~ **multiplication factor** *n* ELECTRON facteur de multiplication de gaz *m*;

~ n ~ **nitriding** *n* THERMOD nitruration en phase gazeuse *f*, nitruration à gaz *f*; ~ **noise** *n* ELECTRON bruit d'ionisation *m*;

~ o ~ **oil** *n* PETR TECH *fuel*, THERMOD gas-oil *m*, gazole *m*; ~ **originally in place** *n* PETR gaz initialement en place *m*; ~ **outlet** *n* TRANSP gazoduc *m*;

~ p ~ **pedal** *n* (AmE) *(cf accelerator)* AUTO pédale d'accélérateur *f*; ~ **permeability** *n* P&R, THERMOD perméabilité au gaz *f*; ~ **phase grafting** *n* NUCLEAR greffe en phase gazeuse *f*; ~ **phototube** *n* ELECTRON phototube à gaz *m*, tube photo-électrique à gaz *m*; ~ **pipe** *n* CONST conduit de gaz *m*, conduite de gaz *f*, tuyau de gaz *m*, THERMOD tuyau d'arrivée du gaz *m*, tuyau à gaz *m*, TRANSP conduite de gaz *f*; ~ **pipeline** *n* CONST canalisation de gaz *f*, GAS TECH, PETR, PETR TECH, THERMOD gazoduc *m*; ~ **pliers** *n pl* CONST pinces à gaz *f pl*; ~ **pocket** *n* GAS TECH soufflure *f*; ~ **poker** *n* MECH ENG tisonnier à gaz *m*; ~ **precipitate** *n* METALL précipité de gaz *m*; ~ **pressure** *n* GAS TECH pression de gaz *f*, PHYS pression de gaz *f*, pression gazeuse *f*; ~ **pressure governor** *n* CONTROL régulateur de pression du gaz *m*; ~ **pressure reducing valve** *n* THERMOD détendeur pour gaz sous pression *m*; ~ **pressure regulator** *n* CONTROL régulateur de pression du gaz *m*, HEATING détendeur *m*; ~ **producer** *n* PROD ENG gazofacteur *m*, gazogène *m*, générateur de gaz *m*; ~ **producer gas** *n* GAS TECH gaz pauvre *m*; ~ **pump** *n* (AmE) *(cf petrol pump)* VEHICLES *fuel* distributeur d'essence *m*, pompe à essence *f*; ~ **purger** *n* REFRIG dégazeur *m*; ~ **purging** *n* REFRIG dégazage *m*; ~ **purifier** *n* PROD ENG épurateur de gaz *m*;

~ q ~ **quench** *n* HEATING four de trempe au gaz *m*;

~ r ~ **ratio** *n* ELECTRON coefficient d'amplification *m*;

~ **recovery** *n* POLLUTION production de gaz naturel *f*; ~ **refrigerator** *n* MECH ENG, REFRIG, THERMOD réfrigérateur à gaz *m*; ~ **regulator** *n* CONTROL régulateur de gaz *m*; ~ **reservoir** *n* PETR réservoir à gaz *m*; ~ **retort** *n* PROD ENG cornue à gaz *f*; ~ **return safety device** *n* SAFETY fusible sec contre le retour de gaz *m*; ~ **ring** *n* THERMOD rampe à gaz annulaire *f*;

~ s ~ **saturation** *n* PETR saturation en gaz *f*; ~ **scrubber** *n* NUCLEAR absorbeur-neutralisateur *m*, laveur de gaz *m*; ~ **scrubbing plant** *n* THERMOD épurateur de gaz *m*; ~ **show** *n* PETR TECH *exploration* indice *m*; ~ **solid chromatography** *n* POLLUTION CGS, chromatographie d'adsorption gaz-solide *f*, chromatographie gaz-solide *f*; ~ **spring** *n* MECH ENG ressort à gaz *m*; ~ **stock** *n* PROD ENG filière à gaz *f*; ~ **storage** *n* FOOD TECH conservation sous gaz *f*; ~ **stripper** *n* NUCLEAR *for water coolant* dégazeur *m*, séparateur à gaz *m*;

~ t ~ **tank** *n* GAS TECH gazomètre *m*, PROD ENG gazomètre *m*, réservoir à gaz *m*, VEHICLES (AmE) *(cf petrol tank) fuel* réservoir d'essence *m*; ~ **tanker** *n* NAUT *type of ship* gazier *m*; ~ **tap** *n* PROD ENG *cock* robinet de conduite de gaz *m*, robinet de gaz *m*, robinet à gaz *m*, *for screwing gas pipes* taraud à gaz *m*; ~ **tar** *n* COAL TECH goudron de gaz *m*, goudron de houille *m*; ~ **tetrode** *n* ELECTRON tétrode à gaz *f*; ~ **thermometer** *n* PHYS thermomètre à dilatation de gaz *m*, REFRIG thermomètre à gaz *m*; ~ **thread** *n* *(cf pipe thread)* PROD ENG pas de gaz *m*; ~ **thread pipe stock** *n* PROD ENG filière pour tubes en fer pas de gaz *f*; ~ **transmission line** *n* GAS TECH gazoduc *m*; ~ **triode** *n* ELECTRON triode à gaz *f*; ~ **tube** *n* ELECTRON tube électronique à gaz *m*, tube à gaz *m*; ~ **turbine** *n* AERONAUT turbomoteur *m*, MECH, NAUT *engine*, PROD ENG turbine à gaz *f*, THERMOD turbine à gaz *f*, turbomachine *f*, turbomoteur *m*, turboréacteur *m*, TRANSP turbine à gaz *f*; ~ **turbine bus** *n* TRANSP autobus à turbine à gaz *m*; ~ **turbine engine** *n* AERONAUT turbine à gaz *f*, turbomachine *f*, turbomoteur *m*; ~ **turbine motorcoach** *n* (BrE) *(cf gas turbine railcar)* TRANSP automotrice à turbine à gaz *f*; ~ **turbine power station** *n* ELEC *supply* centrale alimentée au gaz *f*, centrale à turbine à gaz *f*; ~ **turbine railcar** *n* (AmE) *(cf gas turbine motorcoach)* TRANSP automotrice à turbine à gaz *f*; ~ **turbine ship** *n* NAUT navire à turbines à gaz *m*; ~ **turbine train** *n* *(RTG train)* TRANSP rame à turbine à gaz *f*;

~ v ~ **valve** *n* PROD ENG *blast furnace* robinet de gaz *m*, valve à gaz *f*; ~ **vent** *n* MINING soufflard de grisou *m*, souffleur *m*, NUCLEAR carneau à gaz *m*, évent de gaz *m*;

~ w ~ **washer** *n* NUCLEAR absorbeur-neutralisateur *m*, laveur de gaz *m*; ~ **water heater** *n* THERMOD chauffe-eau à gaz *m*; ~ **welded system** *n* MECH ENG système refroidi à gaz *m*; ~ **welding** *n* MECH soudage autogène *m*, THERMOD soudage oxyacétylénique *m*, soudage à gaz *m*; ~ **well** *n* PETR puits de gaz *m*, puits à gaz *m*; ~ **works** *n* PROD ENG usine à gaz *f*

gas-air: ~ **mixture** *n* THERMOD mélange air-gaz *m*

gas-cooled[1] *adj* THERMOD refroidi par gaz, à refroidissement au gaz

gas-cooled:[2] ~ **breeder reactor** *n* *(GCBR)* NUCLEAR réacteur surrégénérateur refroidi au gaz *m*; ~ **nuclear power plant** *n* NUCLEAR réacteur refroidi au gaz *m*

gaseous[1] *adj* CHEM gazeux, MINING grisouteux, PHYS, THERMOD gazeux

gaseous:[2] ~ **acid air pollution index** *n* SAFETY indice de pollution gazeuse acide de l'air *m*; ~ **active medium** *n*

ELECTRON milieu actif gazeux *m*; ~ **combustion product** *n* POLLUTION gaz de combustion *m*; ~ **core reactor** *n* NUCLEAR réacteur à coeur gazeux *m*; ~ **effluent** *n* GAS TECH effluent gazeux *m*; ~ **fuels** *n pl* PETR TECH combustibles gazeux *m pl*; ~ **haloes** *n pl see halo* ~ **medium** *n* POLLUTION milieu gazeux *m*; ~ **phase** *n* THERMOD phase gazeuse *f*; ~ **phase only** *n* THERMOD phase gazeuse seule *f*; ~ **state** *n* GAS TECH état gazeux *m*; ~ **vein** *n* GAS TECH veine gazeuse *f*; ~ **waste** *n* POLLUTION déchet sous forme gazeuse *m*

gases: ~ **and fumes** *n pl* SAFETY *safety hazard* gaz et vapeurs *m pl*

gas-filled[1] *adj* THERMOD rempli de gaz

gas-filled:[2] ~ **cable** *n* ELEC câble sous pression de gaz *m*; ~ **rectifier** *n* ELEC ENG soupape à gaz *f*, tube redresseur à gaz *m*; ~ **rectifier diode** *n* ELEC diode ionique à gaz *f*; ~ **relay** *n* ELECTRON relais à gaz *m*; ~ **switching tube** *n* ELECTRON tube de commutation à gaz *m*; ~ **tube** *n* ELECTRON tube à gaz *m*; ~ **workings** *n* MINING chantier contaminé *m*

gas-fired[1] *adj* HEAT ENG, PROD ENG chauffé à gaz

gas-fired:[2] ~ **furnace** *n* HEAT ENG four chauffé au gaz *m*, four à gaz *m*, THERMOD four à gaz *m*; ~ **heater** *n* MECH ENG radiateur à gaz *m*

gas-flushed *adj* PACKAGING purgé par gaz

gas-free *adj* THERMOD dégazé

gas-fueled: ~ **bus** *n* (AmE) *see gas-fuelled bus*; ~ **car** *n* (AmE) *see gas-fuelled car*

gas-fuelled: ~ **bus** *n* (BrE) TRANSP autobus à gaz *m*; ~ **car** *n* (BrE) TRANSPORT voiture à gaz *f*

gash *n* MECH ENG goujure *f*

gasification *n* CHEM, PETR TECH *refining*, PHYS, PROP MAT, THERMOD gazéification *f*

gasify *vt* CHEM, GAS TECH, PHYS gazéifier

gas-insulated: ~ **line** *n* ELEC *supply network* ligne à isolation gazeuse *f*

gasket *n* AUTO joint d'étanchéité *m*, MECH joint d'étanchéité *m*, joint plan *m*, MECH ENG joint d'étanchéité *m*, joint de chambre *m*, joint plat *m*, rondelle joint *f*, NAUT garniture *f*, garniture de joint *f*, joint étanche *m*, PROD ENG garnissage *m*, garniture *f*, joint d'étanchéité *m*, *packing of hemp or other fibrous stuff* tresse *f*, VEHICLES joint d'étanchéité *m*

gas-loaded: ~ **accumulator** *n* MECH ENG *hydraulic fluid power* accumulateur hydropneumatique *m*

gas-making: ~ **apparatus** *n* PROD ENG appareil gazifère *m*

gasogene *n* PROD ENG gazogène *m*

gas-oil: ~ **contact** *n* PETR interface gaz-huile *f*, surface de contact huile-gaz *f*, ligne de contact gaz-huile *f*; ~ **mixture** *n* (AmE) *(cf petrol-oil mixture)* VEHICLES *two-stroke engine* mélange huile-essence *m*

gasoline *n* (AmE) *(cf petrol)* AUTO, PETR TECH, THERMOD, VEHICLES *fuel* essence *f*; ~ **and oil resistant hose** *n* (AmE) *(cf petrol and oil resisting hose)* P&R tuyau résistant à l'essence et à l'huile *m*; ~ **consumption** *n* (AmE) *(cf petrol consumption)* VEHICLES *engine* consommation d'essence *f*; ~ **dump** *n* (AmE) *(cf petrol dump)* MILIT dépôt d'essence *m*; ~ **engine** *n* (AmE) *(cf petrol engine)* NAUT, THERMOD, VEHICLES moteur à essence *m*; ~ **engine vehicle** *n* (AmE) *(cf petrol engine vehicle)* POLLUTION véhicule à moteur à essence *m*; ~ **filter** *n* (AmE) *(cf petrol filter)* VEHICLES *fuel* filtre à essence *m*; ~ **hose** *n* (AmE) *(cf petrol hose)* P&R tuyau à essence *m*, VEHICLES *fuel* tuyau flexible à essence *m*; ~ **mixture** *n* (AmE) *(cf petrol mixture)* VEHICLES mé-

lange huile-essence *m*; ~ **pump** *n* (AmE) *(cf petrol pump)* VEHICLES *fuel* distributeur d'essence *m*, pompe à essence *f*; ~ **resistance** *n* (AmE) *(cf petrol resistance)* P&R résistance à l'essence *f*; ~ **station** *n* (AmE) *(cf petrol station)* TRANSP station-service *f*; ~ **tank** *n* (AmE) *(cf petrol tank)* VEHICLES *fuel* réservoir d'essence *m*

gasoline-oil: ~ **mixture** *n* (AmE) *(cf petrol-oil mixture)* VEHICLES *two-stroke engine* mélange huile-essence *m*

gasometer *n* MINING, PROD ENG gazomètre *m*

gasometric *adj* CHEM gazométrique

gasometry *n* THERMOD gazométrie *f*

gas-only: ~ **phase** *n* THERMOD phase gazeuse seule *f*

gas-packed *adj* FOOD TECH conditionné sous gaz

gas-proof *adj* MECH ENG, THERMOD étanche au gaz

gassed: ~ **yarn** *n* TEXTILES fil gazé *m*

gas-shielded: ~ **metal arc welding** *n* CONST soudage à l'arc sous protection gazeuse avec fil électrode *m*

gassing *n* CHEM passage au gaz *m*; ~ **power** *n* FOOD TECH *carbonated beverages* pouvoir de formation de gaz *m*

gassy *adj* MINING grisouteux, THERMOD gazeux, riche en gaz

gastight *adj* MECH, THERMOD étanche au gaz

gas-to-oil: ~ **ratio** *n* (*GOR*) PETR rapport gaz-pétrole *m*, PETR TECH proportion gaz-huile *f*

gastropod *n* GEOL gastéropode *m*

gas-water: ~ **contact** *n* PETR interface gaz-eau *f*, ligne de contact gaz-eau *f*, surface de contact eau-gaz *f*

gate[1] *n* CINEMAT fenêtre d'exposition *f*, fenêtre de projection *f*, COMP porte *f*, CONST barrière *f*, porte *f*, DP porte *f*, ELEC ENG électrode de grille *f*, *electrode of transistor* grille *f*, *electrode of thyristor* gâchette *f*, ELECTRON porte *f*, HYDR EQUIP *turbine*, HYDROL *dam* vanne *f*, P&R *moulding* entrée *f*, PHYS *logic circuit* porte *f*, *thyristor* gâchette *f*, *transistor electrode* grille *f*, PROD ENG amorce de coulée *f*, coulée *f*, jet de coulée *m*, trou de coulée *m*, jet *m*, VEHICLES *automatic gearbox* secteur *m*, WATER SUPP *door, valve* vanne *f*, vannelle *f*, vantelle *f*; ~ **accentuator** *n* MECH ENG engrenages pour portes *m pl*; ~ **amplifier** *n* PROD ENG amplificateur d'impulsions *m*; ~ **array** *n* COMP circuit prédiffusé *m*, DP circuit prédiffusé *m*, matrice de portes *f*, ELECTRON matrice de portes *f*, matrice prédiffusée *f*, TELECOM circuit prédiffusé *m*; ~ **array chip** *n* ELECTRON puce à matrice de portes *f*; ~ **bias** *n* ELEC ENG polarisation de la grille *f*, *thyristors* polarisation de la gâchette *f*; ~ **chamber** *n* HYDROL cage de la vanne *f*, WATER SUPP *of a lock* enclave *f*; ~ **contact** *n* ELEC ENG contact de grille *m*; ~ **cutter** *n* MECH ENG coupe-coulées *m*, machine à couper les coulées *f*, PRODUCTION coupe-coulées *m*; ~ **delay** *n* ELECTRON temps de propagation *m*, temps de propagation par porte *m*; ~ **density** *n* ELECTRON densité de portes *f*; ~ **dielectric** *n* ELEC ENG diélectrique de la grille *m*; ~ **drive board** *n* PROD ENG carte commande gachette *f*; ~ **drive signal** *n* ELECTRON signal d'attaque de la grille *m*; ~ **driving board** *n* PROD ENG carte commande gachette *f*; ~ **end box** *n* MINING coffret de chantier *m*; ~ **gear** *n* HYDR EQUIP mécanisme de commande *m*; ~ **hook** *n* CONST gond *m*, gond de porte *m*; ~ **latch** *n* CONST loquet de porte *m*; ~ **leakage current** *n* ELEC ENG courant de fuite de la grille *m*; ~ **pin** *n* PROD ENG *founding* broche de coulée *f*, coulée *f*, mandrin de coulée *m*; ~ **post** *n* CONST montant de porte *m*; ~ **road** *n* COAL TECH allée de desserte *f*, galerie desservant la taille *f*, voie de taille *f*; ~ **shutter** *n* PROD ENG *founding* écluse *f*; ~ **spool** *n* PROD ENG *founding* monte-coulée *m*;

~ stem *n* HYDR EQUIP queue de vanne *f*, tige de vanne *f*, épée de vanne *f*; **~ stick** *n* PROD ENG *founding* broche de coulée *f*, coulée *f*, mandrin de coulée *m*; **~ switch** *n* ELEC interrupteur de porte *m*; **~ valve** *n* HYDR EQUIP vanne à opercule coulissant *f*, MECH ENG robinet à guillotine *m*, robinet-vanne *m*; **~ voltage** *n* ELEC ENG tension de la grille *f*, tension de la gâchette *f*

gate[2] *vt* HYDR EQUIP vanner

gated:[1] **~ off** *adj* PROD ENG bloqué; **~ on** *adj* PROD ENG passant

gated:[2] **~ beam tube** *n* TV tube de phase *m*; **~ diode** *n* ELECTRON diode débloquée par intervalles *f*, diode à déclenchement périodique *f*; **~ flip-flop** *n* ELECTRON bascule commandée par porte *f*; **~ signal** *n* ELECTRON signal transmis par porte *m*

gate-to-cathode: ~ resistor *n* ELEC ENG résistance gâchette-cathode *f*

gate-to-drain: ~ capacitance *n* ELEC ENG capacité grille-drain *f*

gate-to-source: ~ capacitance *n* ELEC ENG capacité grille-source *f*; **~ voltage** *n* ELEC ENG tension grille-source *f*

gate-to-substrate: ~ capacitance *n* ELEC ENG capacité grille-substrat *f*

gateway *n* COMP, DP passerelle *f*, PROD ENG poste d'entrée *m*, poste de travail initial *m*, premier poste de travail *m*, TELECOM passerelle *f*; **~ computer** *n* COMP ordinateur passerelle *m*, DP ordinateur de communication inter-réseau *m*, ordinateur passerelle *m*; **~ network element** *n* TELECOM élément passerelle de réseau *m*

gather:[1] **~ write** *n* COMP, DP écriture avec regroupement *f*

gather[2] *vt* C&G, PROD ENG cueillir, TEXTILES froncer

gather:[3] **~ way** *vi* NAUT *ship* prendre de l'erre

gathered *adj* TEXTILES froncé

gatherer *n* PRINT assembleuse *f*, machine à assembler *f*

gathering *n* C&G cueillage *m*, PRINT cahier *m*, PROD ENG cueillage *m*, TEXTILES fronces *f pl*; **~ bubble** *n* C&G bouillon de cueillage *m*; **~ cylinder** *n* PRINT cylindre collecteur *m*; **~ end** *n* C&G compartiment de travail *m*; **~ hole** *n* C&G ouvreau de cueillage *m*; **~ iron** *n* C&G ferret *m*; **~ machine** *n* (*cf collating machine*) PRINT assembleuse *f*, machine à assembler *f*; **~ shoe** *n* C&G roulette d'assemblage *f*; **~ temperature** *n* C&G température de cueillage *f*

gating *n* COMP, DP déclenchement *m*, ELECTRON sélection par porte *f*, HYDR EQUIP vannage *m*, TV déclenchement *m*, déclenchement périodique *m*; **~ amplifier** *n* RECORDING amplificateur de sélection *m*; **~ pulse** *n* ELECTRON impulsion d'ouverture de porte *f*, impulsion de déblocage *f*, TV impulsion de déclenchement *f*; **~ signal** *n* ELECTRON signal d'ouverture de porte *m*, signal de déblocage *m*; **~ technique** *n* TESTING impulsion technique *f*; **~ transistor** *n* ELECTRON transistor de déblocage *m*

gauge[1] *n* (BrE) CINEMAT format *m*, CONST *railway* écartement *m*, ELEC *measurement, manufacture* gabarit *m*, LAB EQUIP jauge *f*, MECH calibre *m*, indicateur *m*, jauge *f*, MECH ENG indicateur *m*, *template, pattern* calibre *m*, gabarit *m*, METR *instrument* calibre *m*, jauge *f*, PAPER TECH jauge *f*, PROD ENG jauge *f*, *charge gauge of blast furnace* bécasse *f*, tige de jaugeage *f*, *hydraulic system* plage de mesure *f*, QUALITY calibre *m*, RAIL gabarit *m*, TEXTILES jauge *f*, VEHICLES *tool* gabarit *m*; **~ bar** *n* (BrE) CONST *railway* barre d'écartement *f*; **~ block** *n* (BrE) MECH cale étalon *f*, METR cale étalon *f*, calibre

étalon *m*; **~ brick** *n* (BrE) CONST *feather-edged brick* brique à couteau *f*; **~ clearance** *n* (BrE) RAIL *of loading gauge* profil-limite *m*, *track* jeu de la voie *m*; **~ cock** *n* (BrE) WATER SUPP robinet de hauteur d'eau *m*, robinet de jauge *m*; **~ door** *n* (BrE) MINING porte à guichet *f*; **~ glass** *n* (BrE) C&G verre pour niveau *m*, PETR TECH *refinery* regard *m*, PROD ENG niveau *m*, tube de niveau d'eau *m*, tube indicateur de niveau *m*, REFRIG *on sight glass* niveau visible *m*; **~ invariance** *n* (BrE) PHYS invariance de jauge *f*; **~ isolating valve** *n* (BrE) PROD ENG vanne d'isolement de manomètre *f*; **~ number** *n* (BrE) PROD ENG *wire* numéro de jauge *m*, titre de jauge *m*; **~ plane** *n* (BrE) MECH ENG *of assembly* plan de jauge *m*; **~ pressure** *n* (BrE) REFRIG pression effective *f*; **~ stand** *n* (BrE) METR support de jauge *m*; **~ widening** *n* (BrE) RAIL *vehicles* surécartement *m*

gauge[2] *vt* (BrE) PROD ENG cuber, jauger, *cask* jauger, *iron wire* jauger, *metal plate* calibrer, gabarier, TEXTILES mesurer, WATER SUPP *flow of pump* jauger

gauged: ~ orifice *n* (BrE) PETR TECH *pipelines* orifice calibré *m*; **~ restriction** *n* (BrE) PETR TECH *pipelines* orifice calibré *m*

gauging *n* (BrE) MECH ENG contrôle dimensionnel *m*, METR cubage *m*, gabariage *m*, jaugeage *m*, *of measuring instrument* calibrage *m*, PETR TECH jaugeage *m*, *estimating oil reserves* cubage *m*; **~ plate** *n* (BrE) PROD ENG plaque de mesure *f*; **~ ring** *n* (BrE) SPRINGS anneau de calibrage *m*, bague calibre *f*; **~ station** *n* (BrE) WATER SUPP station de jaugeage *f*; **~ tank** *n* (BrE) PETR TECH bac de jaugeage *m*, bac jaugeur *m*

gault *n* GEOL gault *m*

Gault: ~ clay *n* CONST argile du gault *f*

gauss *n* ELEC *unit*, GEOL, RECORDING gauss *m*

Gauss': ~ law *n* PHYS *electrostatics* théorème de Gauss *m*; **~ theorem** *n* ELEC *electric field*, PHYS *vector fields* théorème de Gauss *m*

gaussian: ~ noise *n* PHYS bruit gaussien *m*

Gaussian[1] *adj* OPT gaussien

Gaussian:[2] **~ beam** *n* TELECOM faisceau gaussien *m*; **~ circuit** *n* TV circuit cloche *m*, circuit gaussien *m*; **~ curvature** *n* GEOM courbure de Gauss *f*; **~ curve** *n* GEOM courbe gaussienne *f*, MATH courbe de Gauss *f*; **~ distribution** *n* COMP, DP distribution gaussienne *f*, répartition gaussienne *f*, PHYS distribution de Gauss *f*, distribution normale *f*, RECORDING distribution de Gauss *f*; **~ noise** *n* COMP, DP, ELECTRON, TELECOM bruit gaussien *m*; **~ pulse** *n* TELECOM impulsion gaussienne *f*; **~ quadrature** *n* COMP, DP quadrature gaussienne *f*

Gaussian-filtered: ~ minimum shift keying *n* (*GMSK*) TELECOM modulation à déplacement minimal à filtre gaussien *f*

gaussmeter *n* ELEC gaussmètre *m*

gauze *n* PROD ENG gaze métallique *f*, tamis *m*, toile métallique *f*; **~ strainer** *n* PROD ENG *for funnel* tamis métallique *m*

Gay-Lussac expansion *n* détente de Gay-Lussac

Gay-Lussac's: ~ law *n* PHYS loi de Gay-Lussac *f*

gaylussite *n* MINERAL gaylussite *f*

gazogene *n* PROD ENG gazogène *m*

GCBR *abbr* (*gas-cooled breeder reactor*) NUCLEAR réacteur surrégénérateur refroidi au gaz *m*

G-clamp *n* MECH ENG bride à capote *f*, happe *f*, presse à coller *f*, presse à vis *f*

GCR *abbr* (*group code recording*) COMP enregistrement par codage de groupe *m*, enregistrement par groupe *m*

G-cramp *n* MECH ENG bride à capote *f*, happe *f*, presse à coller *f*, presse à vis *f*, serre-joints *m*

Gd *(gadolinium)* CHEM Gd *(gadolinium)*

Ge *(germanium)* CHEM Ge *(germanium)*

gear[1] *n* MECH *algorithm* engrenage *m*, mécanisme *m*, timonerie *f*, MECH ENG pignon *m*, rouage *m*, roue d'engrenage *f*, roue dentée *f*, *appliance, mechanism* appareil *m*, appareils *mpl*, armature *f*, engins *m pl*, mécanisme *m*, organes *m pl*, *toothed wheel* engrenage *m*, engrenages *m pl*, harnais d'engrenages *m*, NAUT *engine*, PAPER TECH engrenage *m*; **~ assembly** *n* MECH ENG assemblage d'engrenages *m*; **~ blank** *n* MECH ENG ébauche d'engrenage *f*; **~ change** *n* (BrE) *(cf gear-shift)* MECH ENG, VEHICLES *gearbox* changement de vitesse *m*; **~ change lever** *n* (BrE) *(cf gearshift lever)* AUTO *car*, VEHICLES *gearbox* levier de changement de vitesse *m*, levier de commande de vitesse *m*; **~ cone angle** *n* MECH ENG conicité *f*; **~ cutter** *n* MECH ENG fraise à tailler les engrenages *f*, machine à tailler les engrenages *f*, tailleuse d'engrenages *f*; **~ cutting** *n* MECH ENG *gears* taille des engrenages *f*; **~ drive** *n* MECH transmission par engrenages *f*, MECH ENG commande par engrenages *f*, marche par engrenages *f*, *power transmission* transmissionpar engrenages *f*; **~ head** *n* MECH ENG réducteur *m*; **~ hob** *n* MECH ENG fraise mère *f*; **~ hobbing machine** *n* MECH ENG machine à tailler les engrenages par fraise-mère *f*; **~ measuring cylinder** *n* METR cylindre de mesure d'engrenages *m*; **~ milling machine** *n* MECH ENG machine à tailler les engrenages par fraise-disque *f*; **~ puller** *n* VEHICLES *tool* arrache-pignon *m*; **~ pump** *n* AUTO, P&R *pumping of liquids*, PROD ENG, REFRIG pompe à engrenages *f*; **~ ratio** *n* MECH rapport de transformation *m*, MECH ENG multiplication *f*, raison de l'équipe *f*, rapport d'engrenage *m*, VEHICLES *gearbox* rapport de démultiplication *m*; **~ shaft** *n* MECH ENG arbre de poignon *m*; **~ shaping machine** *n* MECH ENG machine à tailler les engrenages par couteau *f*; **~ shaving machine** *n* MECH ENG machine à raser les engrenages *f*; **~ testing machine** *n* METR machine de contrôle des engrenages *f*; **~ tooth** *n* MECH ENG dent d'engrenage *f*; **~ train** *n* MECH ENG train d'engrenages *m*, équipage d'engrenages *m*, VEHICLES train d'engrenages *m*; **~ wheel** *n* MECH *gears* pignon denté *m*, roue dentée *f*, MECH ENG engrenage *m*, rouage *m*, roue d'engrenage *f*, roue dentée *f*; **~ work** *n* MECH ENG rouage *m*, train d'engrenages *m*, équipage d'engrenages *m*

gear[2] *vt* MECH ENG engrener

gear[3] *vi* MECH ENG engrener, s'engrener

gearbox *n* AUTO, MECH boîte de vitesse *f*, MECH ENG boîte d'engrenage *f*, *change-speed* boîte de changement de vitesse *f*, boîte de vitesse *f*, NAUT *engine* boîte d'engrenage *f*, boîte de transmission *f*, PROD ENG réducteur *m*, VEHICLES *transmission* boîte de vitesse *f*; **~ housing** *n* VEHICLES carter de la boîte de vitesses *m*; **~ input shaft** *n* MECH ENG arbre d'entrée de boîte d'engrenages *m*; **~ selector fork** *n* VEHICLES fourchette de sélection *f*

gear-cutting: **~ machine** *n* MECH ENG machine à tailler les engrenages *f*, tailleuse d'engrenages *f*

geared[1] *adj* MECH, MECH ENG à engrenage

geared:[2] **~ center column** *n* (AmE), **~ centre column** *n* (BrE) CINEMAT pied "boule" *m*, PHOTO train d'engrenages commandé par manivelle *m*; **~ head** *n* CINEMAT tête à manivelle *f*; **~ motor** *n* MECH moteur à engrenages *m*, motoréducteur *m*; **~ turbine** *n* MECH turbine à engrenages *f*

gearing[1] *adj* MECH ENG engrenant

gearing[2] *n* MECH ENG *gear wheels* engrenage *m*, engrenages *m pl*, harnais d'engrenages *m*, rouage *m*

gearless *adj* MECH à entraînement direct, MECH ENG sans engrenage

gears *n pl* PROD ENG engrenages *m pl*

gearshift *n* (AmE) *(cf gear change)* MECH ENG, VEHICLES *gearbox* changement de vitesse *m*; **~ lever** *n* (AmE) *(cf gear change lever)* AUTO *car* levier de changement de vitesse *m*, VEHICLES *gearbox* levier de changement de vitesse *m*, levier de commande de vitesse *m*

gear-type: **~ oil pump** *n* AUTO pompe à huile à engrenages *f*

Gedinnian *adj* GEOL gédinnien

gedrite *n* MINERAL gédrite *f*

gegenschein *n* ASTRON *counterglow* gegenschein *m*

gehlenite *n* MINERAL gehlénite *f*

Geiger: **~ counter** *n* NUCLEAR, PART PHYS, PHYS compteur Geiger *m*, RAD PHYS tube Geiger *m*; **~ tube** *n* RAD PHYS tube Geiger *m*

Geiger-Müller: **~ tube** *n* PHYS tube de Geiger-Müller *m*

Geissler: **~ tube** *n* ELECTRON tube de Geissler *m*

GEK *abbr (geomagnetic electro-kinetograph)* OCEANOG dispositif GEK *m*

gel[1] *n* CHEM colloïde *m*, gel *m*, CINEMAT gélatine *f*, P&R *physical state*, PETR TECH *drilling synon, bentonite, smectite* gel *m*, REFRIG gelée *f*; **~ cell** *n* ELEC ENG accumulateur sec *m*, accumulateur à électrolyte gélifié *m*, batterie sèche *f*; **~ coat** *n* COATINGS couche de gel *f*, gel coat *m*, NAUT *GRP construction* gel coat *m*, P&R *polyesters* couche de gel *f*, gel coat *m*; **~ derived microsphere** *n* NUCLEAR microsphère fabriquée par le procédé sol-gel *f*; **~ permeation chromatography** *n* CHEM chromatographie sur gel perméable *f*, LAB EQUIP *analysis* chromatographie par perméation du gel *f*; **~ time** *n* P&R temps de gélification *m*, PACKAGING temps de gélatinisation *m*

gel[2] *vi* CHEM *of colloid* se coaguler, se gélifier

gelatin *n* CHEM gélatine *f*, MINING dynamite gélatinisée *f*, dynamite gélatinée *f*, PACKAGING gélatine *f*; **~ capsule** *n* PACKAGING capsule gélatineuse *f*; **~ dynamite** *n* MINING dynamite gélatinisée *f*, dynamite gélatinée *f*, gélatine-dynamite *f*

gelatine *n see gelatin*

gelatino-bromide *n* CHEM gélatino-bromure *m* **~ process** *n* PHOTO procédé au gélatinobromure d'argent *m*

gelatino-chloride *n* CHEM gélatino-chlorure *m*

gelation *n* CHEM, CHEM TECH, P&R gélification *f*

gelignite *n* CHEM, MINING gélignite *f*

gelling: **~ agent** *n* FOOD TECH, MAR POLL gélifiant *m*, P&R *additive* agent de gélification *m*

gelose *n* CHEM gélose *f*

gelsemine *n* CHEM gelsémine *f*

gem: **~ magnifier** *n* INSTRUMENT loupe de lapidaire *f*

GEM *abbr (ground effect machine)* TRANSP véhicule à effet de sol *m*

Gemini *n pl* ASTRON Gémeaux *m pl*

Geminids *n pl* ASTRON Géminides *m pl*

general: **~ arrangement** *n* CONST aménagement général *m*, arrangement général *m*, plan d'ensemble *m*; **~ arrangement drawing** *n* MECH plan d'ensemble *m*; **~ arrangement plan** *n* NAUT *shipbuilding* plan des aménagements *m*; **~ assembly** *n* MECH ENG planche d'ambiance *f*; **~ atmospheric circulation** *n* METEO circulation atmosphérique *f*; **~ cargo** *n* PACKAGING cargaison diverse *f*; **~ cargo ship** *n* TRANSP cargo pour marchandises diverses *m*; ~ **drawing** *n* NUCLEAR plan d'ensemble *m*; ~ **equation of the circle** *n* GEOM équation générale du cercle *f*; ~ **layout drawing** *n* MECH ENG planche d'ambiance *f*; ~ **localization** *n* TELECOM localisation sommaire *f*; ~ **maintenance** *n* NUCLEAR entretien général *m*, révision générale *f*; ~ **plan** *n* MECH ENG *technical drawing* vue d'ensemble *f*; ~ **theory of relativity** *n* ASTRON, PHYS théorie de la relativité générale *f*; ~ **tolerance** *n* MECH ENG tolérance sur brut *f*; ~ **warning panel** *n* AERONAUT, SAFETY tableau lumineux des alarmes *m*; ~ **yield load** *n* METALL charge générale d'écoulement *f*

generalized: ~ **coordinates** *n pl* PHYS coordonnées généralisées *f pl*

general-purpose[1] *adj* ELEC ENG universel, MECH *tools* d'usage général, universel

general-purpose[2] *n* DETERGENTS usage général *m*; ~ **board** *n* ELECTRON carte universelle *f*; ~ **chip** *n* ELECTRON puce universelle *f*; ~ **computer** *n* *(GP computer)* COMP, DP calculateur universel *m*; ~ **electric vehicle** *n* TRANSP véhicule utilitaire électrique *m*; ~ **laminate** *n* ELECTRON stratifié ordinaire *m*; ~ **language** *n* COMP langage universel *m*; ~ **machine tool** *n* PROD ENG machine-outil à usage général *f*; ~ **relay** *n* ELEC ENG relais universel *m*; ~ **resistor** *n* ELEC ENG résistance ordinaire *f*; ~ **screw thread** *n* MECH ENG filetage à usage général *m*

generate *vt* GEOM *curve* engendrer, RAD PHYS générer

generated:[1] ~ **on chip** *adj* ELECTRON élaboré sur la puce

generated:[2] ~ **address** *n* COMP, DP adresse calculée *f*

generated:[3] **be** ~ *vi* PROD ENG s'engendrer, se produire, être engendré

generating[1] *adj* ELEC ENG générateur

generating[2] *n* PROD ENG engendrement *m*, production *f*; ~ **capacity** *n* ELEC *supply* capacité de production *f*, puissance de production *f*, puissance installée *f*; ~ **cutter** *n* MECH ENG couteau générateur *m*; ~ **grid** *n* FLUID PHYS *fluid turbulence experiments* grille génératrice *f*; ~ **plant** *n* ELEC ENG station électrique *f*, usine de force motrice *f*, usine génératrice *f*, usine électrique *f*; ~ **program** *n* COMP programme générateur *m*; ~ **set** *n* ELEC *supply* groupe électrogène *m*, ELEC ENG groupe générateur *m*, groupe électrogène *m*

generation *n* COMP, DP, ELEC *supply* génération *f*, PROD ENG engendrement *m*, production *f*; ~ **copy** *n* TV génération *f*; ~ **data set** *n* COMP, DP ensemble de données générées *m*; ~ **end** *n* NUCLEAR côté de la génératrice *m*; ~ **number** *n* COMP, DP nombre générateur *m*

generator *n* CINEMAT groupe électrogène *m*, générateur *m*, génératrice *f*, COMP générateur *m*, CONST groupe électrogène *m*, génératrice *f*, DP, ELEC *supply* générateur *m*, ELEC ENG générateur *m*, génératrice *f*, HYDR EQUIP générateur *m*, NAUT *electrics* dynamo *f*, générateur *m*, NUCLEAR, PHYS génératrice *f*, PROD ENG *gas producer* gazogène *m*, *gas* générateur *m*, TELECOM générateur *m*, VEHICLES *electrical system* alternateur *m*, dynamo *f*, générateur *m*, génératrice *f*; ~ **brush** *n* VEHICLES *electrical system* balai d'alternateur *m*; ~ **coal** *n* COAL TECH charbon pour gazogène *m*; ~ **gas** *n* GAS TECH gaz pauvre *m*, PROD ENG gaz de gazogène *m*, gaz pauvre *m*, gaz pauvre en gazogène *m*; ~ **output** *n* ELEC ENG sortie de la génératrice *f*, sortie de la magnéto *f*, sortie du générateur *f*; ~ **output power** *n* ELEC ENG puissance de sortie du générateur *f*, puissance du générateur *f*, puissance fournie par le générateur *f*; ~ **regulator** *n*

CONTROL *automobile* régulateur *m*, régulateur conjoncteur-disjoncteur *m*; ~ **set** *n* ELEC ENG *electricity* groupe électrogène *m*; ~ **signaling** *n* (AmE), ~ **signalling** *n* (BrE) ELEC ENG appel par magnéto *m*; ~ **speed** *n* FUELLESS vitesse génératrice *f*

generic[1] *adj* COMP, DP générique

generic:[2] ~ **cascade** *n* NUCLEAR cascade générique *f*; ~ **flow control** *n* *(GFC)* TELECOM contrôle de flux générique *m*; ~ **name** *n* COMP, DP nom générique *m*

genetic *adj* RAD PHYS *damage* génétique

genetically: ~ **significant dose** *n* POLLUTION dose génétiquement significative *f*

Geneva: ~ **mechanism** *n* MECH ENG entraînement par croix de Malte *m*; ~ **wheel** *n* MECH ENG croix de Malte *f*

genistein *n* CHEM genistéine *f*

genlock *n* RECORDING, TV verrouilleur de synchronisation *m*

genlocking *n* RECORDING, TV système à générateur synchroniseur *m*, système à générateur verrouillé *m*

genny *n* CINEMAT générateur *m*

genthite *n* MINERAL genthite *f*

gentian: ~ **violet** *n* FLUID PHYS *flow visualization* bleu de méthylène *m*

gentianin *n* CHEM gentianine *f*

gentiobiose *n* CHEM gentiobiose *m*

gentiopicrin *n* CHEM gentiopicrine *f*

gentisate *n* CHEM gentisate *m*

gentisic *adj* CHEM gentisique

gentisin *n* CHEM gentisine *f*

gentle: ~ **breeze** *n* METEO brise légère *f*; ~ **heat** *n* THERMOD chaleur modérée *f*

genus *n* GEOM *of a surface* genre *m*

geobarometer *n* GEOL géobaromètre *m*

geocentric[1] *adj* ASTRON géocentrique

geocentric:[2] ~ **coordinate system** *n* ASTRON système de coordonnés géocentriques *m*; ~ **latitude** *n* ASTRON latitude géocentrique *f*

geochemical: ~ **cycle** *n* GEOL cycle géochimique *m*

geochemistry *n* CHEM, GEOL, PETR TECH géochimie *f*

geochronology *n* GEOL, PETR géochronologie *f*

geodesic *n* GEOM géodésique *f*; ~ **navigation** *n* NAUT navigation géodésique *f*; ~ **station** *n* NAUT point géodésique *m*; ~ **survey** *n* CONST mesure de géodésie *f*

geodesy *n* GEOM géodésie *f*

geodetic *n* CONST géodésique; ~ **survey** *n* CONST mesure de géodésie *f*

geodimeter *n* CONST *surveying* géodimètre *m*

geodynamics *n pl* ASTRON, SPACE géodynamique *f*

geographic: ~ **variation** *n* POLLUTION variation spatiale *f*

geographical: ~ **circulation** *n* PRINT diffusion géographique *f*; ~ **range** *n* NAUT *navigation* portée géographique *f*

geohydrology *n* COAL TECH géohydrologie *f*

geoid *n* GEOL, OCEANOG géoïde *m*

geological: ~ **column** *n* GEOL colonne géologique *f*, colonne stratigraphique *f*, log lithostratigraphique *m*; ~ **environment** *n* GAS TECH milieu géologique *m*; ~ **layer** *n* GAS TECH couche géologique *f*; ~ **section** *n* GEOL coupe géologique *f*; ~ **survey** *n* COAL TECH étude géologique *f*, PETR TECH reconnaissance géologique *f*, étude géologique *f*; ~ **timescale** *n* GEOL échelle chronostratigraphique *f*, échelle des temps géologiques *f*

geology *n* COAL TECH, MINING, PETR TECH géologie *f*

geomagnetic[1] *adj* SPACE géomagnétique

geomagnetic:[2] ~ **cutoff energy** *n* SPACE énergie de coupure géomagnétique *f*; ~ **electro-kinetograph** *n*

(GEK) OCEANOG dispositif GEK *m*; ~ **equator** *n* GEO-
PHYS équateur géomagnétique *m*; ~ **latitude** *n*
GEOPHYS latitude géomagnétique *f*; ~ **meridian** *n* GEO-
PHYS méridien géomagnétique *m*; ~ **pole** *n* GEOPHYS
pôle géomagnétique *m*; ~ **reversal** *n* GEOPHYS inversion champ *f*; ~ **secular variation** *n* GEOPHYS variation
séculaire géomagnétique *f*; ~ **storm** *n* ASTRON tempête
magnétique *f*; ~ **tail** *n* SPACE *geophysics* queue de la
magnétosphère *f*

geomagnetism *n* ASTRON, GEOL, GEOPHYS géomagné-
tisme *m*, magnétisme terrestre *m*

geometer *n* GEOM géomètre *m*

geometric[1] *adj* GEOM géométrique

geometric:[2] ~ **albedo** *n* SPACE *spacecraft* albédo géométrique *m*; ~ **beam resolution** *n* NUCLEAR résolution
géométrique du faisceau *f*; ~ **buckling** *n* NUCLEAR
laplacien géométrique *m*; ~ **calibration** *n* TV étalonnage géométrique *m*; ~ **data** *n* CONST données
géométriques *f pl*; ~ **displacement** *n* MECH ENG *hydraulic fuel power* cylindre géométrique *m*; ~ **distribution** *n*
MATH *statistics* loi géométrique *f*; ~ **error** *n* TV distor-
sions géométriques *f pl*, erreur de géométrie *f*; ~ **factor**
n PETR facteur géométrique *m*; ~ **isomer** *n* CHEM isomère géométrique *m*; ~ **mean** *n* COMP moyenne
géométrique *f*; ~ **optics** *n* OPT optique des rayons *f*,
optique géométrique *f*, PHYS, TELECOM optique géométrique *f*; ~ **pitch** *n* AERONAUT *propeller* pas
géométrique *m*; ~ **properties** *n pl* GEOM propriétés
géométriques *f pl*; ~ **representation** *n* GEOM *of numbers*
représentation géométrique *f*; ~ **resolution length** *n*
NUCLEAR *of a thickness gauge* longueur de résolution
géométrique *f*; ~ **sequence** *n* MATH suite géométrique
f; ~ **surface** *n* GEOM surface géométrique *f*; ~ **tolerancing** *n* MECH ENG tolérancement géométrique *m*

geometrician *n* GEOM géomètre *m*

geometry: ~ **of absorption** *n* RAD PHYS *of ionizing radiation* géométrie de l'absorption *f*; ~ **of glide** *n* METALL
géométrie du glissement *f*; ~ **of irradiation** *n* NUCLEAR
géométrie de l'irradiation *f*

geon *n* GEOPHYS géon *m*

geopetal *adj* PETR géopétale

geophone *n* COAL TECH, GAS TECH, GEOL, GEOPHYS, PETR
TECH *seismic survey* géophone *m*

geophysical: ~ **exploration** *n* GEOPHYS exploration géophysique *f*, reconnaissance géophysique *f*; ~ **log** *n*
GEOL, PETR TECH *drilling, prospecting* diagraphie géophysique *f*; ~ **measurement** *n* GAS TECH mesure
géophysique *f*; ~ **prospecting** *n* GEOPHYS prospection
géophysique *f*; ~ **survey** *n* CONST levé géophysique *m*,
GEOL *geophysics* relevé géophysique *m*, étude géophysique *f*, PETR TECH reconnaissance géophysique *f*,
étude géophysique *f*

geophysics *n* COAL TECH, PETR, PETR TECH, PHYS géophysique *f*

geopotential[1] *adj* GEOPHYS géopotentiel

geopotential[2] *n* GEOPHYS potentiel terrestre *m*; ~ **height** *n*
GEOPHYS altitude géopotentielle *f*; ~ **meter** *n* GEOPHYS
mètre géopotentiel *m*

geopressure *n* PETR TECH *drilling, geology* pression de
formation anormale positive *f*

Georgian: ~ **wired glass** *n* C&G verre armé à mailles
carrées soudées *m*

geostatic: ~ **pressure** *n* PETR TECH *geology* pression
géostatique *f*

geostationary: ~ **orbit** *n* PHYS orbite géostationnaire *f*; ~
satellite *n* NAUT *navigation*, PHYS, SPACE, TELECOM, TV

communication by satellite satellite géostationnaire
m; ~ **satellite orbit** *n* SPACE orbite des satellites géosta-
tionnaires *f*

geostrophic: ~ **current** *n* OCEANOG courant géostrophique *m*; ~ **flow** *n* OCEANOG courant géostrophique *m*; ~
wind *n* GEOPHYS vent géostrophique *m*; ~ **wind level** *n*
GEOPHYS niveau de vent géostrophique *m*

geosynchronous[1] *adj* ASTRON *artificial satellite* géosynchrone

geosynchronous:[2] ~ **orbit** *n* SPACE orbite géosynchrone *f*

geosynclinal *adj* GEOL, GEOPHYS géosynclinal

geosyncline *n* GEOL, GEOPHYS, PETR TECH *geology* géosynclinal *m*

geotechnical: ~ **properties** *n pl* GEOL propriétés géote-
chniques *f pl*, propriétés pétrophysiques *f pl*

geotechnics *n* COAL TECH géotechnique *f*

geotectocline *n* GEOPHYS géotectoclinal *m*

geotectonic[1] *adj* GEOL géotectonique

geotectonic[2] *n* GEOPHYS géotectonique *f*

geothermal[1] *adj* FUELLESS, GEOPHYS géothermique

geothermal:[2] ~ **circuit** *n* FUELLESS circuit géothermique
m; ~ **drilling equipment** *n* FUELLESS appareil de forage
géothermique *m*; ~ **energy** *n* PHYS, POLLUTION énergie
géothermique *f*; ~ **energy exploitation** *n* POLLUTION
exploitation d'énergie géothermique *f*; ~ **field** *n* FUEL-
LESS champ géothermique *m*; ~ **gradient** *n* FUELLESS,
GEOL, GEOPHYS, PETR TECH *geology* gradient géothermique *m*; ~ **log** *n* PETR TECH *drilling, prospecting*
diagraphie géothermique *f*; ~ **plant** *n* ELEC centrale
géothermique *f*, FUELLESS installation géothermique
f; ~ **power** *n* FUELLESS géothermie *f*; ~ **power station** *n*
ELEC ENG centrale géothermique *f*; ~ **resources** *n pl*
FUELLESS ressources géothermiques *f pl*

geothermics *n* GEOL, PETR TECH *geology, formation temperatures* géothermie *f*

geothermometer *n* GEOL, GEOPHYS géothermomètre *m*

geotropic: ~ **filling** *n* GEOL remplissage géotropique *m*

geraniol *n* CHEM géraniol *m*

geranyl *n* CHEM géranyle *m*

germ *n* PROP MAT germe *m*

germanide: ~ **glass** *n* C&G verre de germaniure *m*

germanium *n* *(Ge)* CHEM germanium *m* *(Ge)*; ~ **avalanche photodiode** *n* ELECTRON photodiode à
avalanche au germanium *f*; ~ **diode** *n* ELEC, ELECTRON
diode au germanium *f*; ~ **rectifier** *n* ELEC, ELEC ENG
redresseur au germanium *m*; ~ **transistor** *n* ELECTRON
transistor au germanium *m*

German-type: ~ **mounting** *n* INSTRUMENT monture alle-
mande *f*

gersdorffite *n* MINERAL gersdorffite *f*

get[1] *n* COAL TECH production *f*; ~ **byte** *n* PROD ENG accès
octet *m*

get:[2] ~ **under way** *vi* NAUT *sailing* appareiller; ~ **up steam**
vi PROD ENG mettre en pression, mettre sous pression

getter *n* ELEC getter *m*, ELEC ENG fixateur de gaz *m*,
getter *m*, GEOL dégazeur *m*, MINING ouvrier à la
veine *m*, piqueur à la veine *m*, TELECOM dégazeur *m*

geyser *n* FUELLESS, GEOPHYS geyser *m*, HYDROL fontaine
jaillissante *f*, geyser *m*, puits jaillissant *m*

geyserite *n* MINERAL geysérite *f*

g-factor *n* PHYS facteur g *m*

GFC *abbr* *(generic flow control)* TELECOM contrôle de
flux générique *m*

g-force *n* SPACE *spacecraft* force d'accélération *f*

ghost *n* PHOTO spectre secondaire *m*, tache centrale *f*; ~
echo *n* SPACE échofantôme *m*; ~ **image** *n* CINEMAT

double image *f*, filage *m*, image fantôme *f*, écho *m*, TV filage image *m*, image fantôme *f*

giant *n* ASTRON *large star* géant *m*; **~ planets** *n pl* ASTRON planètes géantes *f pl*; **~ pulse** *n* ELECTRON *lasers* impulsion de très grande amplitude *f*

gib *n* MECH ENG contre-clavette *f*, *machine tools* lardon de guidage *m*; **~ and cotter** *n* MECH ENG clavette et contre-clavette *f*; **~ and key** *n* MECH ENG clavette et contre-clavette *f*; **~ head key** *n* MECH ENG clavette à mantonnet *f*, clavette à talon *f*, clavette à tête *f*; **~ shoe** *n* MECH ENG *piston cross-head* semelle *f*

gibbous: ~ moon *n* ASTRON lune dans le deuxième ou le troisième quartier *f*

Gibbs: ~ free energy *n* PHYS enthalpie libre *f*, fonction de Gibbs *f*, énergie libre de Gibbs *f*; **~ phase rule** *n* NUCLEAR règle des phases de Gibbs *f*

gibbsite *n* MINERAL gibbsite *f*

gieseckite *n* MINERAL gieseckite *f*

gig *n* PROD ENG *founding* trousseau transportable *m*

giga- *pref (G)* METR giga-*(G)*

gigabyte *n* COMP, DP, OPT gigaoctet *m*

gigadisc *n* (BrE), **gigadisk** *n* (AmE) OPT gigadisc *m*

gigantolite *n* MINERAL gigantolite *f*

GIGO *abbr (garbage-in/garbage-out)* COMP rebut à l'entrée et à la sortie *m*

gilbert *n* ELEC ENG gilbert *m*

gilbertite *n* MINERAL gilbertite *f*

gilding *n* C&G, PRINT, PROD ENG dorure *f*

gill *n* METR *liquid measure* gill *m*

gilled: ~ tube *n* PROD ENG tube à ailettes extérieures *m*

gilt: ~ edge *n* PRINT tranche dorée *f*

gilt-edged *n* PRINT *bookbinding* doré sur tranche

gimbal *n* MECH suspension à la cardan *f*; **~ joint** *n* MECH ENG cardan *m*; **~ mounting** *n* NAUT suspension à la cardan *f*; **~ suspension** *n* MECH ENG suspension à la cardan *f*

gimlet *n* CONST avant-clou *m*, laceret à vrille *m*, tarière à vrille *f*, vrille *f*

gimp *n* TEXTILES gros fil pour contours *m*

gin *n* CONST chèvre *f*, hie *f*, sonnette *f*; **~ block** *n* MECH ENG poulie à chape croisée *f*; **~ pulley** *n* PROD ENG poulie de chèvre *f*; **~ tackle** *n* PROD ENG agrès *m pl*, agrès de chèvre *m pl*, palan de chèvre *m*; **~ wheel** *n* CONST palan *m*, poulie *f*, treuil d'extraction *m*, treuil de levage *m*

giobertite *n* MINERAL giobertite *f*

Giorgi: ~ system *n* METR système Giorgi *m*, système MKSA *m*, système mètre-kilogramme-seconde-ampère *m*

Giotto: ~ spacecraft *n* ASTRON sonde spatiale Giotto *f*

girasol *n* MINERAL girasol *m*

girasole *n* MINERAL girasol *m*

girder *n* CONST *large beam* ferme *f*, ferme métallique *f*, *small* poutrelle *f*, soliveau *m*, *trussed* ferme *f*, ferme métallique *f*, MECH poutre *f*, poutrelle *f*, NAUT *ship, boat building* hiloire *f*, poutre *f*, poutre métallique *f*; **~ bridge** *n* CONST pont en poutres *m*, pont à poutres *m*

girder-type: ~ frame *n* PROD ENG *steam engine* bâti-baïonnette *m*

girt *n* CONST entretoise *f*

girth: ~ weld *n* MECH joint circonférentiel *m*, NUCLEAR soudure circulaire *f*

gismondine *n* MINERAL gismondite *f*

gismondite *n* MINERAL gismondite *f*

gist *n* PATENTS essence *f*

git: ~ cutter *n* PROD ENG *founding* machine à couper les coulées *f*

give:[1] **~ the finishing touches to** *vt* PROD ENG mettre la dernière main à; **~ off** *vt* PHYS dégager, répandre, émettre, THERMOD *heat* dégager, *steam, smoke* dégager, jeter; **~ a wide berth to** *vt* NAUT *shiphandling* parer, passer au large de

give:[2] **~ the alarm** *vi* SAFETY donner l'alarme; **~ directions** *vi* TEXTILES donner les tendances; **~ out** *vi* PROD ENG *to fail* faillir, faire défaut, émaner, émettre; **~ way** *vi* CONST céder, s'effondrer, s'écrouler, *bridge* s'écrouler

given: ~ code *n* TELECOM code considéré *m*

Givetian *adj* GEOL givétien

give-way: ~ vessel *n* NAUT navire non prioritaire *m*

glacial:[1] *adj* GEOL glaciaire

glacial:[2] **~ acetic acid** *n* CHEM acide acétique glacial *m*, FOOD TECH acide acétique crystallisable *m*; **~ clay** *n* COAL TECH argile alluviale glaciaire *f*; **~ eustasy** *n* OCEANOG glacio-eustatisme *m*; **~ eustatism** *n* OCEANOG glacio-eustatisme *m*; **~ outburst** *n* OCEANOG débâcle *f*; **~ stage** *n* GEOL époque glaciaire *f*

glaciate *vt* GEOL recouvrir de glace, soumettre à l'action d'un glacier

glacier: ~ lake *n* HYDROL lac de barrage glaciaire *m*, lac de glacier *m*; **~ mud** *n* HYDROL boue glaciaire *f*; **~ silt** *n* HYDROL boue glaciaire *f*; **~ snow** *n* HYDROL névé *m*

glairin *n* CHEM barégine *f*, glairine *f*

glance: ~ coal *n* COAL TECH charbon de terre *m*

glancing: ~ collision *n* NUCLEAR collision rasante *f*

gland *n* MECH presse-étoupe *m*, MECH ENG bague de presse-étoupe *f*, presse-garniture *m*, raccord presse-étoupe *m*, MINING *for guide rope* pince *f*, NUCLEAR bride *f*, collet *m*, couverture de la boîte à étoupe *f*, PETR TECH *pipelines, refinery* presse-étoupe *m*, PROD ENG boîte à bourrage *f*, *of stuffing box* chapeau *m*, SPACE *spacecraft* presse-étoupe *m*; **~ steam system** *n* NUCLEAR système de vapeur d'étanchéité *m*

glanded: ~ pump *n* NUCLEAR pompe à presse-étoupe *f*

glare CINEMAT reflet *m*, PRINT éblouissement *m*, éclat excessif *m*, SAFETY lumière éblouissante *f*; **~ shield** *n* AERONAUT auvent d'éclairage *m*, pare-soleil *m*

glare-free *adj* SAFETY antiéblouissement

glaserite *n* MINERAL glaserite *f*

glass:[1] **~ reinforced** *adj* PROD ENG armé de fibre de verre

glass[2] *n* C&G, CHEM, INSTRUMENT verre *m*; **~ analysis** *n* C&G analyse de verre *f*; **~ bar** *n* CONST petit bois *m*; **~ bead** *n* C&G bille de verre *f*; **~ bit** *n* MECH ENG *tool* mèche à verre *f*; **~ block** *n* NUCLEAR *fission product* bloc de verre *m*; **~ box** *n* COMP, DP boîte en verre *f*; **~ brick** *n* C&G brique simple *f*; **~ cameo** *n* C&G camée en verre *m*; **~ capacitor** *n* ELEC ENG condensateur en verre *m*; **~ ceramic** *n* C&G, NUCLEAR *celsian, fresnoite* vitro-céramique *f*; **~ cladding** *n* ELEC ENG gaine en verre *f*; **~ cloth** *n* NAUT tissu de verre *m*, PROD ENG toile verrée *f*; **~ color** *n* (AmE), **~ colour** *n* (BrE) C&G couleur vitrifiable *f*; **~ concrete panel** *n* C&G dalle en béton translucide *f*; **~ container** *n* PACKAGING récipient en verre *m*; **~ continuous filament yarn** *n* C&G fil de silionne *m*; **~ cutter** *n* C&G *person* coupeur de verre *m*, CONST *person* vitrier *m*, *tool* diamant de vitrier *m*, pointe de diamant *f*; **~ cutter's diamond** *n* CONST diamant de vitrier *m*, pointe de diamant *f*; **~ depth** *n* C&G hauteur de verre *f*; **~ dish** *n* C&G cristallisoir *m*; **~ door** *n* CONST porte vitrée *f*; **~ drill** *n* MECH ENG *tool* mèche à verre *f*; **~ dust** *n* C&G poussière de verre *f*; **~ electrode** *n* LAB EQUIP *analysis* électrode en verre *f*; **~**

epox-printed circuit board *n* ELECTRON carte à circuit imprimé en verre-époxy *f*; ~ **epoxy laminate** *n* ELECTRON stratifié verre-époxy *m*, PRINT complexe Epoxy *m*; ~ **fabric** *n* PACKAGING tissu silionne *m*; ~ **fiber** *n* (AmE) *see glass fibre* ~ **fiber laminate** *n* (AmE) *see glass fibre laminate* ~ **fiber mat** *n* (AmE) *see glass fibre mat* ~ **fiber reinforced plastic** *n* (AmE) *see glass fibre reinforced plastic* ~ **fiber reinforcement** *n* (AmE) *see glass fibre reinforcement* ~ **fibre** *n* (BrE) ELEC ENG fibre de verre *f*, HEAT ENG verre filé *m*, NAUT *boat building material*, OPT, P&R *filler, reinforcement* fibre de verre *f*, PACKAGING fil de verre *m*, REFRIG, TELECOM, TEXTILES fibre de verre *f*; ~ **fibre cable** *n* ELEC ENG câble à fibre optique en verre *m*; ~ **fibre laminate** *n* (BrE) PACKAGING plastique stratifié au verre textile *m*; ~ **fibre mat** *n* (BrE) C&G matelas en fibre de verre *m*; ~ **fibre reinforced plastic** *n pl* (BrE) P&R plastique renforcé à la fibre de verre *m*, PACKAGING plastique chargé verre *m*, SAFETY matières plastiques renforcées aux fibres de verre *f pl*; ~ **fibre reinforcement** *n* (BrE) C&G armature de stratifié verre-résine *f*; ~ **former** *n* C&G vitrifiant *m*; ~ **frit** *n* C&G fritte de verre *f*; ~ **glazing** *n* COATINGS glaçure *f*, glaçure de porcelaine *f*, vernissage *m*; ~ **heating panel** *n* C&G panneau chauffant en verre *m*; ~ **holder** *n* ELEC ENG support de quartz en verre *m*; ~ **insulator** *n* C&G, ELEC isolateur en verre *m*; ~ **jar** *n* PACKAGING vase en verre *m*; ~ **jug** *n* C&G broc en verre *m*; ~ **laser** *n* ELECTRON laser à verre *m*; ~ **level controller** *n* C&G régulateur de niveau de verre *m*; ~ **marble** *n* C&G *for production of glass fibre* bille de verre *f*; ~ **melted from batch only** *n* C&G verre de composition *m* (Fra), verre frais *m* (Bel); ~ **melted from cullet** *n* C&G verre de calcin *m* (Fra), verre de groisil *m* (Bel); ~ **microsphere** *n* C&G microbille de verre *f*; ~ **mosaic** *n* C&G mosaïque de verre *f*; ~ **passivation** *n* ELECTRON passivation au verre *f*, passivation à verre *f*; ~ **paving slab** *n* C&G dalle *f*; ~ **plate** *n* LAB EQUIP plaque en verre *f*; ~ **pocket** *n* C&G fontaine *f*; ~ **polyester enclosure** *n* PROD ENG boîtier en polyester armé de fibre de verre *m*; ~ **pressure plate** *n* PHOTO glace d'appui *f*; ~ **refined plastic** *n (GRP)* NAUT *boat building material* matière plastique armée de fibre de verre *f*; ~ **reinforced concrete** *n* C&G béton armé translucide *m*; ~ **reinforced laminate** *n* NUCLEAR verre filé imprégné *m*; ~ **reinforced polyester** *n (GRP)* MECH *materials* polyester armé *m*; ~ **rod** *n* LAB EQUIP *glassware* baguette en verre *f*; ~ **roll dampener** *n* C&G cylindre de verre d'humecteur *m*; ~ **roof** *n* C&G verrière *f*; ~ **roof tile** *n* C&G tuile de verre *f*; ~ **shot** *n* CINEMAT décor sur verre *m*, scène glace *f*; ~ **slide** *n* INSTRUMENT lame porte-objet *f*; ~ **staple fiber yarn** *n* (AmE), ~ **staple fibre yarn** *n* (BrE) C&G fil de verranne *m*; ~ **stirring rod** *n* LAB EQUIP baguette en verre *f*; ~ **stopper** *n* LAB EQUIP bouchon en verre *m*; ~ **substrate** *n* ELECTRON substrat en verre *m*; ~ **tank** *n* LAB EQUIP cuve en verre *f*; ~ **transition temperature** *n* P&R, PROP MAT température de transition vitreuse *f*; ~ **tube** *n* C&G canne *f*, ELECTRON tube en verre *m*, tube à enveloppe en verre *m*; ~ **tubing** *n* LAB EQUIP tube en verre *m*; ~ **ventilating brick** *n* C&G brique d'aération en verre *f*; ~ **wadding** *n* PACKAGING ouate de verre *f*; ~ **washer** *n* LAB EQUIP *cleaning* lave-verrerie *f*; ~ **wool** *n* HEAT ENG laine de verre *f*, P&R *raw material* fibre de verre *f*, laine de verre *f*, PACKAGING vitrofibre *f*, REFRIG *for insulating* laine de verre *f*; ~ **wool filter** *n* C&G filtre en laine de verre *m*; ~ **yield** *n* C&G rendement en verre *m*

glass-beaded: ~ **screen** *n* CINEMAT écran perlé *m*
glass-blower *n* C&G souffleur au chalumeau *m*
glass-blowing *n* C&G soufflage de verre *m*
glass-bonded: ~ **mica** *n* ELEC ENG *insulator* mica vitrifié *m*
glass-coated: ~ **ceramic capacitor** *n* ELEC ENG condensateur céramique à enrobage verre *m*
glass-cutting: ~ **wheel** *n* C&G molette de découpe *f*
glassine *n* FOOD TECH papier cristal *m*, PAPER TECH cristal *m*
glassivation *n* ELECTRON passivation au verre *f*
glassmaker's: ~ **tools** *n pl* C&G outils de verrier *m pl*
glassmaking: ~ **sand** *n* C&G sable de verrerie *m*
glasspaper *n* PROD ENG papier de verre *m*, papier verré *m*
glass-reinforced: ~ **plastic** *n* PROD ENG plastique armé de verre *m*
glassware *n* LAB EQUIP verrerie *f*
glassy: ~ **feldspar** *n* C&G feldspath vitreux *m*; ~ **state** *n* C&G état vitreux *m*
glauberite *n* MINERAL glaubérite *f*
glaucolite *n* MINERAL glaucolite *f*
glauconite *n* GEOL glauconie *f*, MINERAL glauconite *f*; ~ **marl** *n* CONST tourtia *f*
glauconitic *adj* GEOL glauconieux
glaucony *n* GEOL glauconie *f*
glaucophane *n* MINERAL glaucophane *f*
glaze[1] *n* C&G glaçure *f*, PAPER TECH lustre *m*, REFRIG givre transparent *m*, verglas *m*; ~ **grinder** *n* C&G broyeur d'émail *m*; ~ **kiln** *n* C&G four à glaçure *m*
glaze[2] *vt* C&G vitrifier, *building* vitrer, *substrate* enverrer, COATINGS vitrifier, FOOD TECH, PACKAGING, PHOTO glacer, PROD ENG glacer, lustrer, TEXTILES lustrer, satiner
glaze[3] *vi* PROD ENG se glacer
glazed[1] *adj* C&G *pottery* vernissé, COLOURS vitrifié
glazed:[2] ~ **blanket** *n* PRINT blanchet glacé *m*; ~ **board** *n* PACKAGING carton glacé *m*; ~ **brick** *n* CONST brique vernissée *f*, brique émaillée *f*; ~ **door** *n* CONST porte vitrée *f*; ~ **earthenware** *n* C&G faïence *f*; ~ **frame** *n* CONST *window* châssis vitré *m*; ~ **frost** *n* METEO verglas *m*; ~ **millboard** *n* PAPER TECH carton dur *m*; ~ **paper** *n* COATINGS papier satiné *m*, PACKAGING, PAPER TECH, PRINT papier glacé *m*; ~ **pottery** *n* C&G plommure *f*; ~ **sash** *n* CONST *window* châssis vitré *m*; ~ **tile** *n* CONST tuile glacée *f*, tuile vernissée *f*; ~ **yarn** *n* TEXTILES fil glacé *m*
glazier *n* CONST *person* vitrier *m*
glazier's: ~ **diamond** *n* CONST diamant de vitrier *m*, pointe de diamant *f*; ~ **pliers** *n pl* C&G pince à équarrir *f*
glazing *n* C&G *installing windows* pose de vitres *f*, *windows of a building* vitrage *m*, CONST *setting glass* pose de verres *f*, vitrage *m*, FUELLESS *flat plate collector* vitrage *m*, PAPER TECH glaçage *m*, PRINT glacis *m*, glaçage *m*, vernissage *m*, PROD ENG lustrage *m*, *covering with transparent glass* glaçage *m*, TEXTILES glaçage *m*, lustrage *m*; ~ **bar** *n* CONST petit bois *m*, petit bois en fer *m*; ~ **calender** *n* PACKAGING calandre à satiner *f*; ~ **cylinder** *n* PAPER TECH cylindre frictionneur *m*; ~ **industry** *n* C&G vitrerie *f*; ~ **machine** *n* C&G machine à glacer *f*, PACKAGING machine à satiner *f*, PHOTO glaceuse *f*, machine à glacer *f*; ~ **quality** *n* C&G qualité de vitrage *f*; ~ **sheet** *n* PHOTO plaque polie *f*; ~ **varnish** *n* COATINGS vernis brillant *m*
glebe *n* MINING glèbe *f*
glide *n* CRYSTALL glissement *m*; ~ **aerial** *n* AERONAUT

antenne de pente *f*; **~ antenna** *n* AERONAUT antenne de pente *f*; **~ band** *n* METALL bande de glissement *f*; **~ path** *n* AERONAUT alignement de descente *m*, trajectoire d'atterrissage *f*; **~ path beacon** *n* TRANSP radiophare d'alignement de descente *m*; **~ path beam** *n* AERONAUT faisceau de trajectoire d'atterrissage *m*, TRANSP faisceau de radioalignement de descente *m*; **~ path localizer** *n* AERONAUT indicateur de pente *m*, TRANSP radiophare d'alignement de descente *m*; **~ plane** *n* CRYSTALL *symmetry element* plan de réflexion avec glissement *m*, plan de symétrie avec glissement *m*, NUCLEAR *crystal* plan de glissement *m*; **~ ratio** *n* AERONAUT taux de plané *m*; **~ slope** *n* AERONAUT pente radiogoniométrique *f*; **~ slope antenna** *n* AERONAUT antenne de pente *f*

glider *n* AERONAUT, MILIT planeur *m*; **~ tug** *n* MILIT remorqueur de planeur *m*

gliding *n* CRYSTALL glissement *m*; **~ angle** *n* AERONAUT angle de plané *m*; **~ boat** *n* TRANSP hydroglisseur *m*; **~ distance** *n* AERONAUT distance de plané *f*; **~ flight** *n* AERONAUT vol plané *m*; **~ fracture** *n* NUCLEAR rupture par glissement *f*, rupture à nerfs *f*; **~ plane** *n* PROP MAT surface de translation *f*

glissile: **~ dislocation** *n* METALL dislocation glissile *f*

glitch *n* TV rayure *f*

global[1] *adj* COMP, DP global

global:[2] **~ beam** *n* SPACE *communications* faisceau à couverture totale *m*; **~ call** *n* TELECOM appel global *m*; **~ coverage** *n* TELECOM, TRANSP *navigation, communication by satellite* couverture globale *f*; **~ emissions** *n pl* POLLUTION émissions globales *f pl*; **~ positioning system** *n* NAUT *navigation by satellite* système mondial de localisation *m*; **~ sulfur budget** *n* (AmE), **~ sulphur budget** *n* (BrE) POLLUTION bilan global du soufre *m*; **~ variable** *n* COMP, DP variable globale *f*

Global: **~ Environment Monitoring System** *n* POLLUTION Système mondial de surveillance continue de l'environnement *m*; **~ Marine Distress and Safety System** *n* (*GMDSS*) NAUT *sea rescue* Système mondial de détresse et de sécurité en mer *m* (*SMDSM*); **~ Telecommunications System** *n* TELECOM Système mondial de télécommunications *m*

globe: **~ joint** *n* MECH ENG joint à calotte sphérique *m*, joint à genou *m*, joint à rotule *m*, joint à rotule sphérique *m*, jointure sphérique *f*; **~ tap** *n* MECH ENG *screw down tap* robinet à boulet *m*; **~ valve** *n* HYDR EQUIP clapet à bille *m*, robinet à boisseau sphérique *m*, REFRIG soupape à disque *f*, soupape à siège plan *f*

Globigerina: **~ ooze** *n* GEOL *deep-sea sediment* boue à globigérines *f*

globoid: **~ gear** *n* MECH ENG engrenage globoïde *m*, engrenage à vis globique *m*

globular[1] *adj* METALL globulaire

globular:[2] **~ cluster** *n* ASTRON *stars* amas globulaire *m*; **~ coke** *n* COAL TECH perles de coke *f pl*

globule *n* ASTRON amas globulaire *m*, CHEM globule *m*

glory: **~ hole** *n* C&G ouvreau *m*

gloss *n* P&R brillant *m*, lustre *m*, PACKAGING satiné *m*, PAPER TECH brillant *m*, lustre *m*, PRINT brillant *m*, PROD ENG glacé *m*, lustre *m*, PROP MAT brillant *m*; **~ calender** *n* PAPER TECH calandre de satinage *f*; **~ effect** *n* COLOURS effet d'apprêt glacé *m*; **~ finish** *n* COLOURS finition brillante *f*; **~ ink** *n* COLOURS encre brillante *f*; **~ meter** *n* P&R brillancemètre *m*, réflectomètre *m*, PAPER TECH lustromètre *m*; **~ paint** *n* COLOURS, CONST peinture brillante *f*, peinture vernis *f*

glossecolite *n* MINERAL glossecollite *f*

glossiness *n* PROD ENG brillant *m*, lustre *m*

glossing *n* PROD ENG glaçage *m*, lustrage *m*

glossy[1] *adj* CINEMAT, P&R *paint, property* brillant, PACKAGING *paper* satiné, PRINT brillant, TEXTILES lustré

glossy:[2] **~ print** *n* PHOTO épreuve glacée *f*, PRINT bromure *m*

glove: **~ box** *n* NUCLEAR boîte de protection *f*, boîte à gants *f*, VEHICLES *interior* boîte à gants *f*; **~ port** *n* NUCLEAR rond de gant *m*

glow[1] *n* CHEM incandescence *f*, PROP MAT lueur *f*; **~ discharge** *n* ELEC *gas ionisation* décharge luminescente *f*, ELEC ENG décharge luminescente *f*, décharge à lueur *f*, ELECTRON décharge luminescente *f*, PHYS décharge luminescente *f*, effluve *m*, RAD PHYS décharge de lueur *f*; **~ discharge cathode** *n* ELEC ENG cathode à décharge luminescente *f*; **~ discharge lamp** *n* ELEC tube à décharge *m*; **~ discharge rectifier** *n* ELEC ENG redresseur à décharge luminescente *m*; **~ discharge sputtering** *n* NUCLEAR pulvérisation par décharge luminescente *f*; **~ discharge tube** *n* ELECTRON tube à décharge luminescente *m*; **~ lamp** *n* ELEC ENG lampe incandescente *f*, lampe à incandescence *f*; **~ plug** *n* AUTO, THERMOD bougie de préchauffage *f*; **~ switch** *n* ELEC ENG starter *m*, starter au néon *m*

glow[2] *vi* THERMOD être incandescent, être rouge, être à chaleur rouge; **~ red** *vi* PROP MAT rougeoyer

glowing[1] *adj* CHEM, PROP MAT, THERMOD incandescent

glowing:[2] **~ cloud** *n* GEOL *explosive volcanic eruption* nuée ardente *f*; **~ heat** *n* THERMOD chaleur d'incandescence *f*, chaleur rouge *f*; **~ tungsten filament** *n* RAD PHYS filament luisant de tungstène *m*

glucagon *n* CHEM glucagon *m*

glucamine *n* CHEM glucamine *f*

glucaronic *adj* CHEM glucaronique

glucide *n* CHEM glucide *m*

gluconic[1] *adj* CHEM gluconique

gluconic:[2] **~ acid** *n* DETERGENTS acide gluconique *m*

glucoprotein *n* CHEM glucoprotéine *f*, glycoprotéine *f*

glucopyranose *n* CHEM glucopyrannose *m*

glucosamine *n* CHEM glucosamine *f*, glycosamine *f*

glucosan *n* CHEM glucosane *m*

glucose *n* CHEM glucose *m*, ose *m*, sucre de raisin *m*

glucoside *n* CHEM glucoside *m*

glue[1] *n* CHEM ciment *m*, colle *f*, P&R *adhesive* adhésif *m*, colle *f*, PACKAGING, PAPER TECH colle *f*, PRINT adhésif chimique *m*, colle *f*, colle forte *f*, TEXTILES colle *f*; **~ color** *n* (AmE), **~ colour** *n* (BrE) COLOURS peinture à la colle *f*; **~ etching** *n* C&G givrage à la colle *m*; **~ film** *n* PACKAGING couche mince de colle *f*; **~ gumming machine** *n* PACKAGING machine d'encollage *f*; **~ joint** *n* PACKAGING joint collé *m*; **~ layer** *n* COATINGS couche de colle *f*; **~ line** *n* P&R *adhesive* collure *f*; **~ press** *n* PACKAGING serre-joint à coins *m*; **~ size** *n* COLOURS colle de peau *f*; **~ spreading machine** *n* PACKAGING machine à gommer *f*

glue[2] *vt* PAPER TECH encoller

glued: **~ box** *n* PACKAGING boîte collée *f*; **~ seal** *n* PACKAGING fermeture collée *f*; **~ tab** *n* PACKAGING languette collée *f*

glueing *n* PACKAGING collage *m*, PAPER TECH contrecollage *m*; **~ machine** *n* PACKAGING, PRINT encolleuse *f*

gluer *n* PRINT machine à encoller *f*

gluing *n* PROD ENG collage *m*; **~ device** *n* PACKAGING dispositif d'encollage *m*; **~ up** *n* PRINT passure en colle f

gluon n PHYS gluon m; **~ color** n (AmE), **~ colour** n (BrE) PART PHYS couleur de gluon f

glutaconic adj CHEM glutaconique

glutamate n CHEM glutamate m

glutamic adj CHEM glutamique

glutamine n CHEM glutamine f

glutaraldehyde n CHEM glutaraldéhyde m

glutaric adj CHEM acid glutarique

glutathione n CHEM glutathion m

gluten n FOOD TECH gluten m; **~ extensibility** n FOOD TECH baking extensibilité de gluten f, élasticité de gluten f

gluten-free adj FOOD TECH sans gluten

glyceraldehyde n CHEM glycéraldéhyde m

glyceric adj CHEM glycérique

glyceride n CHEM, FOOD TECH glycéride f

glycerin n CHEM glycérol m

glycerine n CHEM glycérol m

glycerol n CHEM glycérol m

glycerophosphate n CHEM glycérophosphate m

glycerophosphoric adj CHEM glycérophosphorique

glyceryl n CHEM glycéryle m; **~ monacoleate** n FOOD TECH acétine f, **~ tristearate** n CHEM tristéarate de glycéryle m

glycine n CHEM, FOOD TECH glycine f

glycocide n CHEM glycocide f, oside m

glycogen n CHEM, FOOD TECH glycogène m

glycol n CHEM, DETERGENTS, REFRIG glycol m; **~ ether** n DETERGENTS éthylène glycol m; **~ solution** n REFRIG eau glycolée f

glycolic adj CHEM glycollique

glycoline n CHEM glycoline f

glycolipid n CHEM glycolipide m

glycollic adj CHEM glycollique

glycolysis n FOOD TECH glycolyse f

glycoside n FOOD TECH glycoside m

glycuronic adj CHEM glycuronique

glycylglycine n CHEM glycylglycine f

glycyrrhizine n CHEM glycyrrhizine f

glyoxal n CHEM glyoxal m

glyoxalidine n CHEM glyoxalidine f

glyoxaline n CHEM glyoxaline f

glyoxime n CHEM glyoxime f

glyoxylic adj CHEM glyoxylique

glyptal: **~ resin** n P&R paint binder alkyd m; **~ resin lacquer** n COLOURS peinture glycérophtalique f

GMAT abbr (Greenwich Mean Astronomical Time) ASTRON temps sidéral moyen de Greenwich m

GMDSS abbr (Global Marine Distress and Safety System) NAUT sea rescue SMDSM (Système mondial de détresse et de sécurité en mer)

gmelinite n MINERAL gmélinite f

GMSK abbr (Gaussian-filtered minimum shift keying) TELECOM modulation à déplacement minimal à filtre gaussien f

GMT abbr (Greenwich Mean Time) PHYS, SPACE TMG (Temps moyen de Greenwich)

gneiss n CONST, GEOL, PROP MAT gneiss m

gneissic adj GEOL gneissique

gnomon n ASTRON gnomon m

gnomonic: **~ projection** n NAUT navigation projection gnomonique f

go:[1] **~ ahead** n (GA) TELECOM invitation à continuer f; **~ and not go** n MECH ENG limit gauge maximum et minimum m; **~ devil** n PETR TECH pipelines cochonnet m, piston racleur m, racleur m, ramoneur m; **~ gage** n (AmE), **~ gauge** n (BrE) (cf no-go gauge) MECH ENG jauge passe f, tampon passe m; **~ plug** n MECH tampon entre m

go:[2] **~ alongside** vt NAUT aborder, accoster

go:[3] **~ about** vi NAUT sailing virer de bord; **~ aground** vi NAUT échouer; **~ alongside** vi NAUT se mettre côte à côte; **~ astern** vi NAUT faire machine arrière, faire marche arrière; **~ critical** vi NUCLEAR reactor atteindre la criticité, diverger; **~ down** vi NAUT ship couler, faire naufrage, sombrer; **~ down by the bows** vi NAUT ship piquer de l'avant; **~ into circuit** vi TELECOM entrer en ligne; **~ out** vi ELEC ENG of a light s'éteindre; **~ to waste** vi HYDROL water se perdre; **~ upstream** vi HYDROL aller en amont, remonter le courant, remonter le cours; **~ via the circuit** vi TELECOM passer par un opérateur, transiter par les opératrices

goaf n MINING waste arrière-taille f

goal: **~ post** n (AmE) (cf inside jamb block) C&G brique intérieure de goulotte f

gob n C&G goutte f, MINING remblai m, waste arrière-taille f; **~ distributor** n C&G cuiller rotative f; **~ feeding** n C&G alimentation par distributeur f; **~ tail** n C&G queue de paraison f; **~ temperature** n C&G température de goutte f

gobbing n C&G succession de renflements f

goethite n MINERAL goethite f

goggles n pl PROD ENG mechanic's, stone-breaker's lunettes f pl, SAFETY industrial lunettes de protection f pl, lunettes protectrices f pl

going n CONST of a step largeur de giron f, largeur de marche f; **~ in hole** n PETR TECH drilling descente de tiges f, rentrée f; **~ over** n PROD ENG screw-cutting passe f

Golay: **~ cell** n PHYS cellule de Golay f

gold n (Au) CHEM or m (Au); **~ blocking** n PRINT clichés pour dorure m pl; **~ chloride** n CHEM chlorure d'or m; **~ cleanup** n MINING levée de la production f, récolte d'or f; **~ conglomerate** n MINING conglomérat aurifère m; **~ cyanide** n CHEM cyanure d'or m; **~ doping** n ELECTRON dopage à l'or m; **~ epoxy** n ELECTRON colle époxy à l'or f; **~ field** n MINING champ aurifère m, champ d'or m, district aurifère m; **~ flashing** n SPACE spacecraft dorure par projection f; **~ foil** n PRINT feuille d'or f; **~ grade** n MINING titre en or fin m; **~ leaf electroscope** n ELEC ENG, PHYS électroscope à feuilles d'or m; **~ mine** n MINING exploitation aurifère f, mine d'or f; **~ ore** n MINING minerai d'or m; **~ plating** n PROP MAT dorure f, SPACE spacecraft dorure électrolytique f; **~ probe method** n NUCLEAR calibration méthode de la sonde d'or f; **~ reef** n MINING conglomérat aurifère m; **~ tenor** n MINING titre en or fin m; **~ toning** n PHOTO virage à l'or m

gold-bearing adj MINING aurifère

gold-doped: **~ diode** n ELECTRON diode dopée à l'or f

golden: **~ beryl** n MINERAL béryl doré m; **~ section** n GEOM section d'or f

goldenrod n PRINT bande de fixation de film f

gold-mining: **~ industry** n MINING industrie aurifère f, industrie de l'or f

gold-plated adj CHEM specimen plaqué or

goliath: **~ crane** n CONST grue-chevalet f

gondola n SPACE nacelle f, TRANSP cableway cabine f; **~ cableway** n TRANSP télécabine à câble sans fin f; **~ car** n (AmE) (cf open wagon) RAIL low, sloping sides wagon découvert m

Gondwanan adj GEOL gondwanien

goniometer *n* CRYSTALL, GEOM, OCEANOG goniomètre *m*

go-no-go *n* MECH ENG maximum et minimum *m*

Gooch: ~ **crucible** *n* LAB EQUIP *filtration* creuset à filtration Gooch *m*

good: ~ **housekeeping** *n* SAFETY service d'entretien efficace *m*; ~ **inwards test** *n* PROD ENG contrôle d'entrée *m*

goods *n pl* PACKAGING marchandises *f pl*, PATENTS produits *m pl*; ~ **chute** *n* (BrE) *(cf freight chute)* TRANSP toboggan *m*; ~ **depot** *n* (BrE) *(cf freight depot)* TRANSP quai de chargement *m*; ~ **inward** *n* PROD ENG marchandises à la réception *f pl*; ~ **inwards** *n pl* (BrE) *(cf freight inwards)* RAIL arrivages *m pl*; ~ **lift** *n* PROD ENG monte-charge *m*, élévateur de marchandises *m*; ~ **lorry** *n* (BrE) *(cf freight truck)* TRANSP camion de fret *m*; ~ **porter** *n* (BrE) *(cf freight porter)* RAIL agent de manutention *m*; ~ **shed** *n* (BrE) *(cf freight shed)* TRANSP halle aux marchandises *f*; ~ **station** *n* (BrE) *(cf freight station)* TRANSP gare de marchandises *f*; ~ **van** *n* (BrE) *(cf freight truck, freight van, freight car)* TRANSP wagon couvert *m*, wagon pour les expéditions en détail *m*; ~ **yard** *n* (BrE) *(cf freight yard)* RAIL *vehicles* dépôt de marchandises *m*; ~ **yard foreman** *n* (BrE) *(cf freight yard foreman)* RAIL chef de triage *m*

gooseneck *n* CINEMAT support flexible *m*, MECH col de cygne *m*, NAUT *boom fitting* vit de mulet *m*, PROD ENG *blast furnace* coude du porte-vent *m*; ~ **pipe** *n* MECH ENG tuyau en col de cygne *m*; ~ **wrench** *n* MECH ENG *tool* clé à col de cygne *f*

goose-necked: ~ **pot carriage** *n* C&G défourneuse *f*

gopher: ~ **hole** *n* MINING sondage au hasard *m*, sondage exécuté au hasard *m*

GOR *abbr (gas-to-oil ratio)* PETR rapport gaz-pétrole *m*, PETR TECH proportion gaz-huile *f*

goslarite *n* MINERAL goslarite *f*

gossan *n* GEOL chapeau altéré *m*, chapeau ferrugineux *m*

gothic: ~ **face** *n* PRINT *type design* caractères gothiques *m pl*

gouge *n* CONST *wood-working tool* ciseau à gouge *m*, gouge *f*, MINING lisière *f*, salbande *f*, salbande argileuse *f*

gouging *n* PROD ENG *welding* gougeage *m*, goujure d'usure *f*; ~ **blowpipe** *n* CONST *welding* chalumeau goujeur *m*

governing *adj* MECH ENG modérateur

government: no ~ **guarantee** *phr* PATENTS SGDG, sans garantie du gouvernement

governor *n* AUTO régulateur *m*, CINEMAT mécanisme régulateur *m*, régulateur *m*, CONTROL dispositif de maintien *m*, régulateur centrifuge *m*, ELEC ENG, FUELLESS régulateur *m*, MECH régulateur centrifuge *m*, MECH ENG modérateur *m*, régulateur *m*, régulateur de vitesse *m*, NAUT *engine*, VEHICLES *engine speed limiter* régulateur *m*; ~ **control link** *n* AERONAUT biellette de vitesse *f*; ~ **control stop** *n* AERONAUT butée régulateur *f*; ~ **model** *n* NUCLEAR *nuclear model* modèle du régulateur *m*; ~ **rod** *n* MECH ENG tringle du régulateur *f*; ~ **valve** *n* HYDR EQUIP robinet régulateur *m*

GP[1] *abbr (Guinier-Preston zone)* CRYSTALL zone Guinier-Preston *f*

GP:[2] ~ **computer** *n* *(general-purpose computer)* COMP, DP calculateur universel *m*

GPU *abbr (ground power unit)* AERONAUT groupe auxiliaire au sol *m*, groupe de démarrage au sol *m*

grab *n* CONST benne automatique *f*, benne piocheuse *f*, benne preneuse *f*, MINING *boring* accrocheur *m*, NAUT *of dredger* benne *f*, grappin *m*, NUCLEAR *of crane or refuelling machine* grappin *m*, PRINT capacité d'accrochage de la colle *f*; ~ **bucket** *n* CONST benne automatique *f*, benne piocheuse *f*, benne preneuse *f*; ~ **crane** *n* CONST grue à grappin *f*; ~ **dredge** *n* CONST drague à mâchoires *f*; ~ **dredger** *n* CONST drague à mâchoires *f*, NAUT drague à benne piocheuse *f*, drague à benne preneuse *f*

grabbing: ~ **clutch** *n* AUTO broutement de l'embrayage *m*; ~ **tap** *n* MINING *boring* taraud accrocheur *m*

graceful: ~ **degradation** *n* COMP traitement réduit *m*, traitement réduit en cas d'incident grave *m*, DP dégradation harmonieuse *f*, dégradation progressive *f*

grad *n* CINEMAT, PHOTO filtre dégradé *m*

gradation *n* COLOURS *of colour* gradation *f*, PRINT contraste *m*, gradation *f*

grade[1] *n* CONST inclinaison *f*, pente *f*, rampe *f*, GEOM gradient *m*, pente *f*, MINING teneur *f*, titre *m*, PHYS *1/100 right angle* grade *m*, PROD ENG *degree of quality* classe *f*, teneur *f*, titre *m*, *of an emery wheel* degré de dureté *m*, PROP MAT *of steel* qualité *f*, QUALITY *technical excellence* classe *f*; ~ **crossing** *n* (AmE) *(cf level crossing)* CONST passage à niveau *m*, RAIL, TRANSP passage à niveau *m*, traverse *f* (Can); ~ **of service** *n* TELECOM qualité d'écoulement du trafic *f*, qualité de service *f*; ~ **stake** *n* (AmE) *(cf level indicator)* RAIL nivelette *f*

grade[2] *vt* CINEMAT étalonner, CONST aménager la pente de, ménager la pente de, régulariser, régulariser la pente de, *earthworks* araser, FOOD TECH calibrer, classer, trier, GEOL classer, trier, PROD ENG *sort*, QUALITY *sort* classer

graded: ~ **bedding** *n* GEOL granoclassement vertical progressif *m*; ~ **coal** *n* COAL TECH charbon calibré *m*; ~ **index** *n* ELEC ENG, OPT gradient d'indice *m*; ~ **index core** *n* ELEC ENG coeur à gradient d'indice *m*; ~ **index fiber** *n* (AmE), ~ **index fibre** *n* (BrE) OPT, PHYS fibre à gradient d'indice *f*; ~ **index profile** *n* OPT profil d'indice à gradient *m*, profil à gradient d'indice *m*; ~ **profile** *n* GEOL équilibre *m*; ~ **seal** *n* C&G soudure avec verres intermédiaires *f*; ~ **sluice** *n* WATER SUPP sluice à pente ménagée *m*; ~ **soil** *n* COAL TECH sol de granulométrie complexe *m*

graded-index: ~ **multimode-optical fiber** *n* (AmE), ~ **multimode-optical fibre** *n* (BrE) ELEC ENG fibre optique multimode à gradient d'indice *f*

grader *n* CINEMAT étalonneur *m*, CONST *civil engineering* décapeuse *f*, niveleuse *f*, *earthmoving equipment* motorgrader *m*, niveleuse *f*, MAR POLL, TRANSP niveleuse *f*; ~ **leveling blade** *n* (AmE), ~ **levelling blade** *n* (BrE) TRANSP lame niveleuse *f*; ~ **waste pond** *n* (AmE) *(cf silt field)* C&G étang à boues *m*

gradient *n* CONST rampe *f*, *falling, rising gradient* inclinaison *f*, pente *f*, ELEC ENG, FLUID PHYS *temperature, pressure* gradient *m*, GEOM *of a curve, specified at a given point* gradient *m*, *of a straight line* pente *f*, PHYS *vector field* gradient *m*, pente *f*, RAIL déclivité *f*, pente *f*; ~ **current** *n* OCEANOG courant de pente *m*; ~ **microphone** *n* ACOUSTICS microphone à gradient *m*; ~ **post** *n* RAIL poteau indicateur de déclivité *m*, poteau indicateur de pente *m*, poteau indicateur de pentes et rampes *m*; ~ **of Reynolds stress** *n* FLUID PHYS gradient de la contrainte de Reynolds *m*; ~ **speed** *n* CINEMAT seuil de sensibilité *m*; ~ **of x%** *n* CONST rampe de 0,0X *f*, rampe de 0m *f*; ~ **of x in 1000** *n* CONST rampe de 0,0X *f*, rampe de 0m *f*

grading *n* C&G granulométrie *f*, CINEMAT étalonnage *m*, COAL TECH tri *m*, CONST *bringing to level, to regular inclination* aménagement de pente *m*, ménagement de pente *m*, régularisation *f*, régularisation de pente *f*, *civil engineering* décapage *m*, régalage *m*, *earthworks* arasement *m*, composition granulométrique *f*, planage *m*, *sieving* granulométrie *f*, PACKAGING triage *m*, PROD ENG *sorting* classement *m*, QUALITY classement *m*, tri *m*, triage *m*, TELECOM *of circuits* classement *m*, gradation *f*; ~ **analysis** *n* CONST analyse granulométrique *f*; ~ **band** *n* CINEMAT bande d'étalonnage *f*; ~ **copy** *n* CINEMAT copie "0" *f*; ~ **coupling loss cable** *n* TELECOM câble à pertes de couplage *m*; ~ **curve** *n* COAL TECH courbe granulométrique *f*; ~ **envelope** *n* CONST enveloppe granulométrique *f*; ~ **index fiber** *n* (AmE), **index fibre** *n* (BrE) TELECOM fibre à gradient d'indice *f*; ~ **sheet** *n* CINEMAT feuille d'étalonnage *f*

gradiomanometer *n* PETR gradiomanomètre *m*

graduated: ~ **braking** *n* RAIL *vehicles* freinage gradué *m*; ~ **circle** *n* GEOM cercle gradué *m*, INSTRUMENT cercle gradué *m*, limbe vertical de calage *m*; ~ **dial** *n* INSTRUMENT, MECH ENG cadran gradué *m*; ~ **filter** *n* CINEMAT filtre dégradé *m*, PHOTO filtre dégradé *m*, filtre nuancé *m*; ~ **flask** *n* LAB EQUIP fiole jaugée *f*; ~ **pipette** *n* LAB EQUIP *glassware* pipette graduée *f*, pipette jaugée *f*; ~ **pocket dosimeter** *n* RAD PHYS dosimètre de poche gradué *m*

graduating: ~ **engine** *n* MECH ENG machine à diviser *f*

graduation *n* LAB EQUIP graduation *f*, PRINT *of colour tones* gradation *f*; ~ **mark** *n* LAB EQUIP *pipette, burette, flask* trait de jauge *m*

graft: ~ **polymer** *n* P&R polymère greffé *m*, polymère implanté *m*; ~ **polymerization** *n* P&R *process, chemistry* polymérisation implantée *f*, polymérisation par greffage *f*

Graham's: ~ **law** *n* PHYS *of diffusion* loi de Graham *f*

grain[1] *n* ACOUSTICS, CINEMAT, COAL TECH, METR *avoirdupois or troy weight* grain *m*, MINING *quarrying* fil de pierre *m*, NAUT *of wood* fil *m*, grain *m*, PRINT *papermaking* sens des fibres *m*, PROP MAT fil *m*, grain *m*; ~ **alcohol** *n* FOOD TECH alcool éthylique *m*; ~ **boundary** *n* CRYSTALL, METALL joint de grain *m*, NUCLEAR joint *m*, PROP MAT joint de grain *m*; ~ **boundary diffusion** *n* METALL diffusion intergranulaire *f*; ~ **boundary migration** *n* METALL migration des joints de grains *f*; ~ **clumping** *n* PHOTO agglomération de grain *f*; ~ **direction** *n* PRINT sens machine *m*, sens papier *m*; ~ **fraction** *n* COAL TECH fraction granulométrique *f*; ~ **refinement** *n* METALL affinement des grains *m*; ~ **shape** *n* COAL TECH forme de grain *f*; ~ **side** *n* (*of flesh side*) PROD ENG *of belt* côté cuir *m*; ~ **size** *n* COAL TECH dimension des grains *f*, taille de grain *f*, CRYSTALL taille de grain *f*, METALL grosseur du grain *f*, taille de grain *f*, PROP MAT grosseur du grain *f*; ~ **size analysis** *n* MECH ENG *bonded abrasives* granulométrie *f*; ~ **size classification** *n* PROP MAT *metallurgy* classement granulométrique *m*, étude granulométrique *f*; ~ **size distribution** *n* GEOL, SPRINGS granulométrie *f*; ~ **structure** *n* COAL TECH structure des grains *f*, PROP MAT structure granulaire *f*; ~ **test** *n* C&G méthode sur poudre calibrée *f*

grain[2] *vt* PROD ENG grener

grained: ~ **paper** *n* PAPER TECH papier grainé *m*

graininess *n* PRINT grain de la photo *m*

graining *n* PAPER TECH grainage *m*, PHOTO granulation *f*; ~ **machine** *n* PAPER TECH grainoir *m*

grainless *adj* PHOTO *emulsion* sans grains

grain-refining: ~ **anneal** *n* THERMOD *metals* recuit d'affinage *m*

grains: **in** ~ *adj* PROP MAT en grains

grainstone *n* GEOL calcaire à éléments jointifs liés par la sparite *m*

gram *n* (AmE) *see* **gramme**

grammage *n* PAPER TECH grammage *m*

grammar *n* COMP, DP grammaire *f*

grammatite *n* MINERAL grammatite *f*

gramme *n* (BrE) CHEM *mass*, METR, PHYS gramme *m* ~ **calorie** *n* (BrE) METR *heat unit* petite calorie *f*; ~ **centimetre** *n* (BrE) METR *heat unit* petite calorie *f*; ~ **equivalent** *n* (BrE) CHEM *of compound* gramme-équivalent *m*; ~ **in mass** *n* (BrE) METR gramme-masse *m*; ~ **ion** *n* (BrE) METR ion-gramme *m*; ~ **molecule** *n* (BrE) METR mole *f*, molécule-gramme *f*; ~ **per square metre** *n* (BrE) PRINT gramme au mètre carré *m*

Gramme: ~ **ring** *n* ELEC *coil* enroulement en anneau *m*; ~ **winding** *n* ELEC *coil* enroulement en anneau *m*

gramophone *n* RECORDING gramophone *m*

granary *n* FOOD TECH grenier *m*

grand: ~ **slam** *n* PETR grand schelem *m*; ~ **unification energy** *n* PART PHYS, PHYS énergie de grande unification *f*; ~ **unified theory** *n* (*GUT*) PART PHYS, PHYS théorie de grande unification *f*

granite *n* CONST, GEOL, PROP MAT granit *m*, granite *m*; ~ **surface plate** *n* MECH ENG marbre de contrôle en granite *m*

granite-gneiss *n* GEOL orthogneiss *m*

granitell *n* PETR granitelle *m*

granitelle *n* PETR granitelle *m*

granitite *n* PETR granitite *f*

granitization *n* GEOL, PROP MAT granitisation *f*

granitoid *adj* GEOL granitoïde *m*, PROP MAT *texture* granitoïde

granny: ~ **knot** *n* NAUT noeud de vache *m*

granophyre *n* PETR granophyre *m*

grant[1] *n* PATENTS délivrance *f*

grant:[2] ~ **a licence** *vt* PATENTS délivrer un brevet

granular[1] *adj* CONST granulaire, GEOL, PROP MAT grenu

granular:[2] ~ **ash** *n* METALL soude granulaire *f*; ~ **fracture** *n* NUCLEAR rupture granulaire *f*; ~ **material** *n* CONST matériau granulaire *m*, matériau grenu *m*; ~ **noise** *n* TELECOM bruit de grenaille *m*; ~ **structure** *n* PROP MAT structure granulaire *f*

granularity *n* COMP, DP granularité *f*, PHOTO granulation *f*, PROP MAT grenu *m*

granulate *vt* CHEM TECH granuler, grenailler, PACKAGING granuler

granulated[1] *adj* GEOL granuleux

granulated:[2] ~ **cork** *n* REFRIG liège granulé *m*; ~ **glass** *n* C&G verre granulé *m*

granulates *n pl* CHEM TECH granulés *m pl*

granulating: ~ **crusher** *n* CHEM TECH broyeur-granulateur *m*, moulin à granules *m*; ~ **grate** *n* CHEM TECH grille à granuler *f*; ~ **hammer** *n* CHEM TECH marteau à granuler *m*; ~ **machine** *n* CHEM TECH granulatoire *m*, PACKAGING machine à granuler *f*; ~ **roller** *n* CHEM TECH cylindre cannelé *m*, cylindre à granuler *m*

granulation *n* C&G *of the batch*, CHEM TECH, COAL TECH, PROP MAT granulation *f*; ~ **pitch** *n* CHEM TECH point de grainage *m*

granulator *n* CHEM TECH granulateur *m*, sécheur à tambour *m*

granule *n* PACKAGING granule *m*; ~ **material** *n* CHEM

TECH matière granulée *f*; **~ size distribution** *n* C&G analyse granulométrique *f*

granulometric[1] *adj* COAL TECH granulométrique

granulometric:[2] **~ analysis** *n* (BrE) *(cf screen analysis)* C&G analyse granulométrique *f*

granulometry *n* COAL TECH granulométrie *f*

grape: ~ sugar *n* FOOD TECH sucre de raisin *m*

grapeshot *n* MILIT mitraille *f*

grapestone *n* PETR calcaire pisolithique *m*

graph[1] *n* COMP, DP graphe *m*, MATH représentation graphique *f*; **~ paper** *n* PAPER TECH papier quadrillé *m*; **~ plotter** *n* COMP, DP traceur de courbes *m*; **~ of stellar luminosity plotted against temperature** *n* ASTRON diagramme de la luminosité stellaire en fonction de la température *n*; **~ theory** *n* MATH théorie graphique *f*

graph[2] *vt* MATH représenter graphiquement

graphic *n* PRINT graphique *m*; **~ arts** *n* PRINT industries graphiques *f pl*; **~ character** *n* COMP, DP caractère graphique *m*; **~ display adaptor** *n* COMP ,DP adaptateur d'écran graphique *m*, carte graphique *f*; **~ geometry** *n* GEOM géométrie projective *f*; **~ software package** *n* COMP, DP progiciel graphique *m*; **~ tablet** *n* TV palette graphique *f*

graphical: ~ editing *n* COMP, DP édition graphique *f*; **~ representation** *n* COMP, DP représentation graphique *f*; **~ symbol** *n* SAFETY *for fire protection plans* symbole graphique *m*

graphics *n* COMP, DP graphique *m*; **~ coordinated with bottle labels** *n* PACKAGING graphiques coordonnés avec étiquettes pour bouteilles *m pl*; **~ plotter** *n* COMP, DP traceur de courbes *m*; **~ tablet** *n* COMP, DP tablette graphique *f*; **~ work station** *n* COMP, DP poste de travail graphique *m*, poste graphique *m*, station de travail graphique *f*

graphite *n* CHEM graphite *m*, mine de plomb *f*, plombagine *f*, MINERAL graphite *m*; **~ block** *n* NUCLEAR *brick* bloc de graphite *m*; **~ brush** *n* ELEC *electrical machine* balai en graphite *m*; **~ clad fuel element** *n* NUCLEAR élément combustible à gaine en graphite *m*; **~ coating** *n* NUCLEAR *on clad inner can surface* revêtement en graphite *m*; **~ grease** *n* MECH *materials* graisse graphitée *f*; **~ guide tube** *n* NUCLEAR tube guide en graphite *m*; **~ paint** *n* COLOURS peinture à graphite *f*; **~ shielding** *n* NUCLEAR bouclier à graphite *m*; **~ shrinkage** *n* NUCLEAR retrait de graphite *m*; **~ structure** *n* NUCLEAR empilement de graphite *m*

graphitization *n* METALL graphitisation *f*

grapnel *n* MECH ENG, NAUT grappin *m*

grapple *n* NAUT, NUCLEAR, TRANSP grappin *m*

grappling: ~ hook *n* NAUT crochet *m*, grappin *m*

graptolitic: ~ shale *n* GEOL schiste argileux à graptolites *m*

grasping: ~ margin *n* PRINT marge de prise *f*

grass *n* ELECTRON pointes de bruit *f pl*, *background noise* herbe *f*, MINING jour *m*, surface *f*, NUCLEAR *on oscilloscope* herbe *f*

grate *n* HEATING grille *f*, PROD ENG *fire grate* grille *f*, *grid for cores or moulds* armature *f*, *of ore stamp* tamis *m*; **~ area** *n* CONST surface de grille *f*; **~ bar** *n* PROD ENG fer à barreaux de grille *m*, fers à barreaux de grille *m pl*

grate-shaking: ~ rig *n* PROD ENG mécanisme de manoeuvre de la grille *m*

graticule *n* CINEMAT quadrillage *m*, réseau quadrillé *m*, réticule *m*, ELECTRON graticule *m*, INSTRUMENT croisée de fils *f*, repère de visée *m*, TV réticule *m*

grating *n* ELEC ENG *waveguides* sélecteur de mode *m*,

PROD ENG grillage *m*, grille *f*, *for cores or moulds* armature *f*, TV mire de réglage *f*, quadrillage *m*; **~ converter** *n* ELEC ENG convertisseur de mode à réseau *m*; **~ spectrograph** *n* NUCLEAR spectrographe à réseau *m*

gratings *n pl* NAUT *cockpit* caillebotis *m*

graupel *n* METEO *soft hail* grésil *m*

grave *vt* NAUT *ship maintenance* radouber

gravel *n* COAL TECH gravier *m*, terrain graveleux *m*, CONST gravier *m*, graviers *m pl*, GEOL, PETR gravier *m*; **~ pit** *n* CONST carrière de gravier *f*, gravière *f*, WATER SUPP gravière *f*

graveyard: ~ orbit *n* SPACE orbite de rebut *f*

gravimeter *n* GEOPHYS aéromètre *m*, gravimètre *m*, PHYS gravimètre *m*

gravimetric[1] *adj* COAL TECH, GEOPHYS gravimétrique

gravimetric:[2] **~ analysis** *n* PETR TECH *prospecting* analyse gravimétrique *f*; **~ survey** *n* GEOL levé gravimétrique *m*, PETR TECH gravimétrie *f*

gravimetry *n* GEOL, GEOPHYS, PETR TECH, PHYS gravimétrie *f*

graving: ~ dock *n* NAUT cale sèche *f*, forme de radoub *f*

gravitation *n* ASTRON gravitation *f*, PHYS, SPACE attraction *f*, gravitation *f*; **~ collapse** *n* SPACE collapse gravitationnel *m*, effondrement gravitationnel *m*; **~ constant** *n* SPACE constante gravitationnelle *f*

gravitational[1] *adj* ASTRON de gravitation, gravitationnel

gravitational:[2] **~ acceleration** *n* GEOL accélération par la pesanteur *f*; **~ collapse** *n* ASTRON écroulement de gravitation *m*, *of dense clouds of gas* and dust effondrement gravitationnel *m*; **~ constant** *n* ASTRON, GEOPHYS, PHYS constante de gravitation *f*; **~ contraction** *n* ASTRON contraction gravitationnelle *f*; **~ field** *n* ASTRON champ de gravitation *m*, champ gravitationnel *m*, PHYS champ de gravitation *m*, champ gravitationnel *m*, *Earth's* champ de pesanteur *m*; **~ force** *n* POLLUTION force gravitationnelle *f*; **~ lens** *n* ASTRON lentille gravitationnelle *f*; **~ mass** *n* PHYS masse gravitationnelle *f*; **~ potential** *n* PHYS potentiel gravitationnel *m*; **~ water** *n* COAL TECH eau de pénétration *f*; **~ wave** *n* ASTRON onde gravitationnelle *f*, OCEANOG onde de gravité *f*, PHYS onde gravitationnelle *f*; **~ wave aerial** *n* RAD PHYS antenne à ondes gravitationnelles *f*; **~ well** *n* ASTRON *of a black hole* puits de gravitation *m*

gravitational:[3] **under ~ force** *phr* ASTRON sous l'effet de la gravitation

graviton *n* PHYS graviton *m*

gravity *n* ASTRON gravité *f*, MECH, PHYS, SPACE gravité *f*, pesanteur *f*; **~ acceleration** *n* PHYS accélération de la pesanteur *f*, accélération due à la gravité *f*, SPACE accélération de la pesanteur *f*; **~ anomaly** *n* GEOPHYS anomalie de la gravité *f*, anomalie de la pesanteur *f*, anomalie gravimétrique *f*; **~ casting** *n* MECH ENG moulage en coquille *m*; **~ collapse structure** *n* GEOL structure d'affaissement tectonique *f*, structure d'effondrement gravitaire *f*; **~ concentrator** *n* PAPER TECH épaisseur par gravité *f*; **~ dam** *n* HYDROL barrage poids *m*; **~ diecasting die** *n* MECH ENG matrice de moulage en coquille *f*; **~ draining** *n* PETR drainage sous l'action de la pesanteur *m*; **~ drop absorber rod** *n* NUCLEAR absorbeur de chute libre *m*; **~ filler plug** *n* AERONAUT bouchon de remplissage par gravité *m*; **~ filling** *n* SPACE *spacecraft* remplissage par gravité *m*; **~ filling machine** *n* PACKAGING machine de remplissage par gravité *f*; **~ flow** *n* NUCLEAR écoulement gravitaire *m*; **~**

free *n* PHYS agravité *f*; ~ **gliding** *n* GEOL glissement gravitaire *m*, glissement par gravité *m*, tectonique d'entraînement *f*, tectonique d'écoulement *f*; ~ **governor** *n* CONTROL régulateur à poids *m*; ~ **gradient boom** *n* SPACE *spacecraft* bras à gradient de pesanteur *m*; ~ **gradient stabilization** *n* SPACE *spacecraft* stabilisation par gradient de gravité *f*; ~ **gradient torque** *n* SPACE *spacecraft* moment gravitationnel *m*; ~ **incline** *n* CONST plan automoteur *m*, plan incliné automoteur *m*; ~ **meter** *n* GEOPHYS, PHYS gravimètre *m*; ~ **mold for casting** *n* (AmE), ~ **mould for casting** *n* (BrE) MECH ENG moule pour fonderie par gravité *m*; ~ **plane** *n* CONST plan automoteur *m*, plan incliné automoteur *m*; ~ **platform** *n* PETR TECH plate-forme-poids *f*, structure-poids *f*; ~ **refueling** *n* (AmE), ~ **refuelling** *n* (BrE) AERONAUT, SPACE remplissage par gravité *m*; ~ **regulator** *n* CONTROL régulateur à poids *m*; ~ **road** *n* CONST plan automoteur *m*, plan incliné automoteur *m*; ~ **roller** *n* PACKAGING transrouleur *m*; ~ **roller conveyor** *n* PACKAGING transrouleur *m*; ~ **slide** *n* GEOL loupe d'écoulement *f*, éboulis de gravité *m*; ~ **spillway dam** *n* CONST barrage poids déversoir *m*; ~ **stamp** *n* PROD ENG pilon à chute libre *m*; ~ **switch** *n* ELEC ENG berceau commutateur *m*; ~ **unit** *n* PETR unité d'accélération *f*, unité de gravité *f*; ~ **vacuum transit train** *n* (*GVT train*) TRANSP train GVT *m*; ~ **water** *n* HYDROL eau gravitaire *f*; ~ **wave** *n* OCEANOG, PHYS, WAVE PHYS onde de gravité *f*

gravure *n* PRINT héliogravure *f*; ~ **coating** *n* PAPER TECH couchage par gravure *m*; ~ **ink** *n* COLOURS encre hélio *f*, encre hélioliquide *f*, encre pour héliogravure *f*; ~ **printing** *n* PACKAGING impression en taille-douce *f*, PRINT héliogravure *f*, impression en gravure *f*; ~ **printing ink** *n* COLOURS encre hélio *f*, encre hélioliquide *f*, encre pour héliogravure *f*; ~ **roller** *n* PRINT cylindre hélio *m*, rouleau gravé *m*, rouleau de tôle piquée *m*; ~ **tissue** *n* PRINT papier au charbon hélio *m*

gravure-coated: ~ **paper** *n* PAPER TECH papier couché par gravure *m*

gray:[1] **in the ~** *adj* (AmE) *see in the grey*

gray[2] *n see grey*[2]

gray[3] *n* (*Gy*) METR, PHYS, RAD PHYS gray *m* (*Gy*)

Gray: ~ **code** *n* SPACE *communications* code de Gray *m*

graywacke *n* (AmE) *see greywacke*

grazing *n* ACOUSTICS broutement *m* ~ **incidence** *n* PHYS incidence rasante *f*

grease[1] *n* AUTO, MECH, PAPER TECH graisse *f*; ~ **box** *n* PROD ENG boîte d'essieu *f*, boîte de graissage *f*, boîte à huile *f*; ~ **cap** *n* VEHICLES graisseur *m*; ~ **cock** *n* PROD ENG robinet graisseur *m*; ~ **cup** *n* PROD ENG godet graisseur *m*, graisseur *m*; ~ **gun** *n* CONST pistolet graisseur *m*, MECH ENG pompe de graissage *f*, VEHICLES *tool* pompe à graisse *f*; ~ **lubricator** *n* PROD ENG godet graisseur *m*, graisseur *m*; ~ **mark** *n* C&G tache de graisse *f*; ~ **packing gland** *n* MECH ENG boîte à graisse *f*; ~ **pencil** *n* CINEMAT crayon gras *m*; ~ **resistance** *n* P&R résistance aux matières grasses *f*; ~ **retainer** *n* MECH ENG retient-graisse *m*

grease[2] *vt* PROD ENG graisser, lubrifier

greaseproof[1] *adj* PACKAGING étanche à la graisse, PAPER TECH imperméable aux corps gras

greaseproof:[2] ~ **paper** *n* FOOD TECH papier parcheminé *m*, papier-parchemin *m*, PACKAGING papier parcheminé *m*, PAPER TECH papier ingraissable *m*, papier simili-sulfurisé *m*

greaser *n* PROD ENG godet graisseur *m*, graisseur *m*

grease-resistant: ~ **board** *n* PACKAGING, PAPER TECH carton imperméable à la graisse *m*; ~ **paper** *n* PACKAGING papier imperméable à la graisse *m*, PAPER TECH papier imperméable à la graisse *m*, papier ingraissable *m*

greasing *n* PAPER TECH graissage *m*, PROD ENG graissage *m*, lubrification *f*; ~ **agent** *n* FOOD TECH *bakeries* matière grasse *f*

great: ~ **circle** *n* PHYS grand cercle *m*; ~ **circle chart** *n* NAUT *navigation* carte de grande cercle *f*; ~ **circle course** *n* NAUT route du grand cercle *f*, route orthodromique *f*; ~ **circle path** *n* SPACE trajet suivant un grand cercle *m*; ~ **circle route** *n* AERONAUT *navigation* orthodromie *f*, route du grand cercle *f*, route orthodromique *f*; ~ **red spot** *n* ASTRON *Jupiter* tache rouge *f*; ~ **white spot** *n* ASTRON *Saturn* tache blanche *f*

Great: ~ **Bear** *n* ASTRON Grande Ourse *f*

greatest: ~ **common divisor** *n* MATH plus grand commun diviseur *m*

greedy: ~ **of water** *adj* PROP MAT avide d'eau

green:[1] ~ **adder** *n* TV circuit mélangeur pour le vert *m*; ~ **beam** *n* TV faisceau pour le vert *m*; ~ **beam laser** *n* ELECTRON laser à faisceau vert *m*, laser à rayon vert *m*; ~ **black level** *n* TV niveau minimal du signal vert *m*; ~ **compact** *n* NUCLEAR *before sintering* compact vert *m*; ~ **concrete** *n* CONST béton frais *m*; ~ **earth** *n* MINERAL terre verte *f*; ~ **feldspar** *n* MINERAL feldspath vert *m*; ~ **flash** *n* ASTRON éclair vert *m*; ~ **gun** *n* ELECTRON, TV canon du faisceau vert *m*; ~ **hide** *n* PROD ENG peau crue *f*, peau verte *f*; ~ **LED status indicator DC power ON** *n* PROD ENG indicateur d'état à DEL verte pour présence tension CC *m*; ~ **mineral** *n* CHEM vert de cuivre *m*; ~ **patch distortion** *n* C&G bleu *m* (Fra), transparent *m* (Bel); ~ **peak level** *n* TV niveau maximal du signal vert *m*; ~ **pellet** *n* NUCLEAR compact vert *m*; ~ **period** *n* TRANSP *traffic control* temps de passage *m*; ~ **phase** *n* TRANSP *traffic control* temps de vert *m*; ~ **pot** *n* C&G pot cru *m*; ~ **primary** *n* TV vert primaire *m*; ~ **print** *n* CINEMAT copie fraîche *f*; ~ **quark** *n* PHYS quark vert *m*; ~ **screen grid** *n* TV grille-écran verte *f*; ~ **sea** *n* OCEANOG grosse mer *f*, mer houleuse *f*, paquet de mer *m*; ~ **time** *n* TRANSP *traffic control* durée de vert *f*; ~ **vitriol** *n* CHEM vitriol vert *m*

green[2] *vt* COLOURS teindre en vert

greenhouse: ~ **effect** *n* FUELLESS, GEOPHYS, METEO, PHYS, POLLUTION, REFRIG effet de serre *m*

greenockite *n* MINERAL greenockite *f*

greenovite *n* MINERAL greenovite *f*

greensand *n* GEOL sable glauconieux vert *m*, PROD ENG *founding* sable vert *m*

greenschist *n* GEOL schiste vert *m*

green-stained *adj* GEOL *weathered flints* verdi

greenstone *n* CONST *newly quarried* pierre verte *f*, GEOL roche verte *f*; ~ **belt** *n* GEOL ceinture de roches vertes *f*

Greenwich: ~ **Mean Astronomical Time** *n* (*GMAT*) ASTRON temps sidéral moyen de Greenwich *m*; ~ **Mean Time** *n* (*GMT*) PHYS Temps moyen de Greenwich *m*, temps solaire moyen de Greenwich *m*, SPACE Temps moyen de Greenwich *m* (*TMG*)

Gregorian: ~ **reflector antenna** *n* TELECOM antenne à réflecteur grégorien *f*; ~ **telescope** *n* PHYS télescope de Gregory *m*

greisening *n* GEOL formation de greisen *f*

greisenization *n* GEOL formation de greisen *f*

grenade *n* MILIT grenade *f*; ~ **launcher** *n* MILIT lance-grenades *m*

grey:[1] **in the ~** *adj* (BrE) TEXTILES écru

grey:[2] **~ balance** *n* (BrE) PRINT équilibre des gris *m*; **~ blibs** *n* (BrE) C&G bouillon de sel allongé *m*; **~ body** *n* (BrE) TV corps gris *m*; **~ cast iron** *n* (BrE) MECH *materials* fonte grise *f*; **~ component replacement** *n* (BrE) PRINT équilibrage électronique des gris *m*; **~ contents** *n pl* (BrE) PRINT teneur en gris *f*; **~ copper ore** *n* (BrE) MINERAL cuivre gris *m*; **~ cutting** *n* (BrE) C&G taille blanche *f*; **~ glass filter** *n* (BrE) INSTRUMENT filtre optique *m*; **~ iron pipe** *n* (BrE) MECH ENG tuyau en fonte grise *m*; **~ manganese ore** *n* (BrE) MINERAL manganite *f*; **~ scale** *n* (BrE) CINEMAT gamme de gris *f*, échelle de gris *f*, DP échelle de gris *f*, PHOTO gamme de gris *f*, PRINT échelle de gris *f*, TV gamme de gris *f*, mire de gris *f*, échelle de gradations *f*, échelle de gris *f*; **~ scale value** *n* (BrE) TV luminosité équivalente *f*

greywacke *n* (BrE) GEOL *muddy sandstone* grauwacke *f*, PETR grès feldspathique *m*

grid *n* COAL TECH grille *f*, ELEC *electrode* grille *f*, *supply network* réseau *m*, ELEC ENG *electrical distribution system* secteur *m*, ELECTRON *manufacture of printed circuit boards* grille internationale *f*, *tubes* grille *f*, HYDROL claie *f*, NUCLEAR *electrode*, PHYS grille *f*, PROD ENG *for cores, moulds* armature *f*, *grate, grating* grille *f*, TEXTILES grillage *m*; **~ bar** *n* PROD ENG *rolled sections* barreau de grille *m*, fer à barreaux de grille *m*, fers à barreaux degrille *m pl*; **~ bias** *n* ELEC ENG polarisation de la grille *f*; **~ capacitor** *n* ELEC ENG condensateur de fuite de grille *m*; **~ cathode capacitance** *n* ELEC ENG capacité grille-cathode *f*; **~ characteristic** *n* ELECTRON caractéristique de grille *f*; **~ coil** *n* PROD ENG serpentin à grille *m*; **~ current** *n* ELEC ENG courant de grille *m*; **~ driving power** *n* ELEC ENG puissance d'excitation de grille *f*; **~ following behavior** *n* (AmE), **~ following behaviour** *n* (BrE) NUCLEAR suivi du réseau *m*; **~ leak resistor** *n* PHYS résistance de fuite de grille *f*; **~ modulation** *n* ELECTRON modulation par la grille *f*, TV modulation dans la grille *f*; **~ probe** *n* NUCLEAR sonde à grille *f*; **~ sheet** *n* PROD ENG feuille à grille *f*; **~ support plate** *n* NUCLEAR plaque support du sommier *f*; **~ turbulence** *n* FLUID PHYS turbulence au moyen d'une grille *f*, turbulence de grille *f*

grid-controlled: ~ mercury arc rectifier *n* ELEC ENG mutateur *m*; **~ tube** *n* ELECTRON tube à grille de commande *m*

griddle *n* COAL TECH table secoueuse *f*, PROD ENG crible *m*

griddling *n* PROD ENG criblage *m*

gridiron: ~ valve *n* PROD ENG tiroir à grille *m*

grid-spaced: ~ fuel assembly *n* NUCLEAR *element bundle* assemblage combustible à grille d'espacement *m*, grille d'assemblage combustible *f*

grid-type: ~ accumulator *n* PAPER TECH accumulateur à grillage *m*; **~ battery** *n* PAPER TECH accumulateur à grillage *m*

Griffith: ~ flaw *n* C&G faille de Griffith *f*

Griffith's: ~ fracture criterion *n* NUCLEAR critère de Griffith *m*

grillage *n* C&G plancher de sole *m* (Fra), poutrellage de fond *m* (Bel)

grille *n* AUTO *car* grille *f*

grind:[1] **~ and leach process** *n* NUCLEAR *carbide fuels* broyage-dissolution *m*

grind[2] *vt* CHEM, CHEM TECH broyer, triturer, COAL TECH broyer, FOOD TECH concasser, MECH meuler, rectifier, PROD ENG affûter, aiguiser, meuler, émeuler, émou-

dre, broyer, moudre, triturer, rectifier, *cylinder, glass stopper* roder

grindability *n* CHEM TECH aptitude au broyage *f*, broyabilité *f*

grinder *n* C&G *polished plate glass* douci *m*, FOOD TECH broyeur *m*, hachoir à viande *m*, meule *f*, MECH rectifieuse *f*, touret à meuler *m*, MECH ENG machine à rectifier *f*, PAPER TECH affûteuse *f*, défibreur *m*, PROD ENG *person* affûteur *m*, aiguiseur *m*, rémouleur *m*, émouleur *m*; **~ pit** *n* PAPER TECH fosse sous défibreur *f*; **~ spindle** *n* C&G arbre vertical de douci *m*

grinding *n* C&G doucissage *m*, CHEM broyage *m*, trituration *f*, COAL TECH broyage *m*, MECH meulage *m*, rectification *f*, METALL, MINING broyage *m*, P&R *process* meulage *m*, PAPER TECH défibrage *m*, PROD ENG *crushing* broyage *m*, mouture *f*, trituration *f*, *finishing* meulage *m*, émeulage *m*, *lapping* rodage *m*, *sharpening* affûtage *m*, aiguisage *m*, aiguisement *m*; **~ agent** *n* C&G abrasif de doucissage *m*; **~ and polishing** *n* C&G douci-poli *m*; **~ center** *n* (AmE) *see grinding centre*; **~ center with 7 axis** *n* (AmE) *see grinding centre with 7 axis*; **~ centre** *n* (BrE) MECH ENG centre de rectification *m*; **~ centre with 7 axis** *n* (BrE) MECH ENG centre de rectification à 7 axes *m*; **~ cylinder** *n* CHEM TECH cylindre broyeur *m*, cylindre de broyage *m*, moule cylindrique *m*; **~ device** *n* CHEM TECH pulvérisateur *m*; **~ drum** *n* CHEM TECH tambour de broyage *m*; **~ in of a stopper** *n* C&G bouchage *m*; **~ line** *n* PROD ENG *twist drill* trait de centre pour affûtage régulier *m*; **~ machine** *n* MECH ENG *crushing machine* broyeur *m*, machine broyeuse *f*, *fettling, trimming* machine à ébarber *f*, ébarbeuse *f*, *roughing* machine à meuler *f*, *tool, cutter, drill-sharpening* affûteuse *f*, machine à affûter *f*, *truing* machine à rectifier *f*, rectifieuse *f*, PAPER TECH affûteuse *f*, SPRINGS machine à meuler *f*; **~ media** *n* COAL TECH corps broyant *m*; **~ medium** *n* PROP MAT abrasif *m*; **~ mill** *n* CHEM TECH broyeur *m*; **~ pan** *n* PROD ENG cuve d'amalgamation *f*, cuve de broyage *f*, moulin d'amalgamation *m*, pan d'amalgamation *m*; **~ paste** *n* MECH, MECH ENG, PROD ENG pâte à roder *f*; **~ plant** *n* CHEM TECH atelier de broyage *m*; **~ pressure limiter** *n* PAPER TECH limiteur de pression de défibrage *m*; **~ ring** *n* CHEM TECH anneau de broyeur *m*, couronne de concassage *f*; **~ runner** *n* C&G moellon *m*; **~ sand** *n* C&G grès *m*; **~ spindle** *n* MECH ENG arbre porte-meule *m*, axe porte-meule *m*, broche porte-meule *f*; **~ spindle carrier** *n* MECH ENG *machine tools* porte-broche *m*; **~ unit** *n* C&G élément de douci *m*; **~ wheel** *n* C&G, MECH *tools*, MECH ENG meule *f*, PROD ENG meule *f*, meule affûteuse *f*, meule de remouleur *f*, meule à affûter *f*, meule à aiguiser *f*; **~ wheel dressing equipment** *n* MECH ENG matériel de rhabillage de meules *m*

grindstone *n* PAPER TECH meule *f*, PROD ENG meule en grès *f*

grip[1] *n* C&G moletage *m*, CINEMAT machiniste de plateau *m*, COAL TECH preneur *m*, MECH ENG épaisseur de serrage *f*, PROD ENG emprise *f*, *clutching device* griffe *f*, *hold* prise *f*, serrage *m*; **~ hook** *n* NUCLEAR crochet de traction *m*; **~ nut** *n* PROD ENG contre-écrou *m*; **~ pipe wrench** *n* MECH ENG clé en deux pièces pour tubes *f*

grip[2] *vt* PROD ENG agripper, pincer, prendre, saisir, serrer

grip[3] *vi* NAUT *anchor* prendre fond

gripper: ~ pad *n* PRINT blanc de prise *m*; **~ tool** *n* NUCLEAR *of a fuel assembly* appareil de préhension *m*

grippers: ~ and yarn carriers *n* TEXTILES pinces et transporteurs de fil *f pl*

gripping: ~ **dog** *n* PROD ENG *of timber clip, log carriage, log sawing* griffe *f*; ~ **jaws** *n pl* PROD ENG mâchoires de serrage *f pl*; ~ **pad** *n* PROD ENG mordache *f*

grit *n* CONST graviers *m pl*, graviers à grains fins *m pl*, sable *m*, gravillon *m*, MECH abrasif de décapage *m*, PETR grès *m*, PROD ENG *abrasive* grain *m*, grain abrasif *m*, *wheel swarf, from grindstone* boue de meule *f*; ~ **blasting** *n* CONST jet d'abrasif *m*, projection d'abrasif *f*, MECH décapage par projection *m*, sablage *m*; ~ **spreader** *n* TRANSP gravillonneuse *f*; ~ **trap** *n* HYDROL dessableur *m*

gritter *n* TRANSP gravillonneuse *f*

gritting *n* CONST gravillonnage *m*

grizzly *n* COAL TECH crible à barreaux *m*, PROD ENG grille *f*, grille à barreaux *f*, harpe *f*

groin *n see* groyne

groined: ~ **vault** *n* CONST voûte d'arête *f*, voûte en arc de cloître *f*

grommet *n* ELEC ENG passe-fil *m*, MECH ENG *separating part* erse *f*, NAUT *ropes, engine* bague d'étoupe *f*, erse *f*, erseau *m*

groove *n* ACOUSTICS sillon *m*, CONST *to receive cock bead* gueule-de-loup *f*, noix *f*, rainure *f*, MECH gorge *f*, rainure *f*, MECH ENG logement *m*, saignée *f*, *in rolling mill roll* cannelure *f*, *of grooved pulley or sheave* gorge *f*, NUCLEAR *of turbine rotor* rainure *f*, OPT rainure *f*, sillon *m*, PAPER TECH rainure *f*, PROD ENG cannelure *f*, entaille *f*, gorge *f*, rainure *f*, sillon *m*, strie *f*, rainurage *m*, *in boiler plate* sillon *m*, *of screw* creux *m*, vide *m*, écuelle *f*, SPACE cannelure *f*; ~ **angle** *n* RECORDING angle de gravure *m*; ~ **drift** *n* PROD ENG mandrin pour rainures *m*; ~ **guard** *n* ACOUSTICS garde du sillon *f*; ~ **punch** *n* PROD ENG bigorne à gouttière *f*; ~ **shape** *n* ACOUSTICS profil du sillon *m*; ~ **spacing** *n* RECORDING pas des sillons *m*; ~ **speed** *n* ACOUSTICS vitesse de défilement *f*, RECORDING vitesse linéaire du sillon *f*

groove-cutting: ~ **chisel** *n* MECH *tools* bédane *m*

grooved[1] *adj* PAPER TECH rainé, PROD ENG cannelé, entaillé, strié, à gorge, à gorges, à rainure, à rainures

grooved:[2] ~ **and feathered joint** *n* CONST assemblage à fausse languette *m*, assemblage à languette rapportée *m*; ~ **ball bearing** *n* MECH ENG roulement à billes avec gorge *m*; ~ **cable** *n* OPT câble à jonc rainuré *m*, TELECOM câble cylindrique rainuré *m*; ~ **cone** *n* MECH ENG cône à corde *m*; ~ **cylinder cam** *n* MECH ENG came à cylindre à rainure *f*; ~ **pin** *n* MECH ENG goupille cannelée *f*; ~ **press** *n* PAPER TECH presse rainurée *f*; ~ **pulley** *n* MECH ENG poulie à gorge *f*; ~ **rail** *n* RAIL rail encastré *m*, rail à gorges *m*; ~ **roll** *n* MECH ENG cylindre cannelé *m*, cylindre à cannelures *m*, PAPER TECH rouleau rainuré *m*; ~ **roller** *n* MECH ENG *friction roller* molette à gorge *f*, poulie à gorge *f*, roue à gorge *f*; ~ **wheel** *n* MECH ENG *pulley for gut or round band* poulie à corde *f*

grooving *n* MECH ENG sillonnement d'usure *m*, PROD ENG entaillage *m*, rainurage *m*, évidage *m*, évidement *m*; ~ **iron** *n* CONST *matching plane* fer de bouvet simple *m*; ~ **machine** *n* MECH ENG machine à rainer *f*; ~ **plane** *n* CONST *matching-plane* bouvet femelle *m*, bouvet à rainure *m*

groroilite *n* MINERAL groroïlite *f*

gross *n* METR grosse *f*; ~ **area** *n* FUELLESS *of collector* aire brute *f*; ~ **calorific value** *n* GAS TECH, HEAT ENG PCS, pouvoir calorifique supérieur *m*; ~ **flow** *n* NUCLEAR débit brut *m*; ~ **heat loss** *n* HEAT ENG perte de chaleur brute *f*; ~ **horsepower** *n* MECH ENG cheval indiqué *m*,

puissance indiquée en chevaux *f*; ~ **installed capacity** *n* NUCLEAR puissance installée brute *f*; ~ **margin** *n* PROD ENG marge brute *f*; ~ **register** *n* NAUT *tonnage* jauge brute *f*; ~ **requirements** *n pl* PROD ENG besoins bruts *m pl*; ~ **thrust** *n* AERONAUT poussée brute *f*; ~ **ton** *n* METR tonne forte *f*, NAUT tonneau de jauge *m*; ~ **tonnage** *n* NAUT jauge brute *f*, tonnage brut *m*, PETR TECH *shipping* jauge brute *f*; ~ **vehicle weight** *n* (*GVW*) VEHICLES poids maximum en charge *m*, poids total en charge *m* (*PTC*), poids total maximum *m* (*PTM*); ~ **volume** *n* PACKAGING volume brut *m*; ~ **weight** *n* AERONAUT masse brute *f*, masse maximale *f*, METR, PACKAGING, TEXTILES poids brut *m*

grossular *n* MINERAL grossulaire *f*, grossularite *f*

grossularite *n* MINERAL grossulaire *f*, grossularite *f*

ground[1] *adj* SPRINGS meulé, rectifié; ~ **free** *adj* (AmE) ELEC *circuit* non mis à la terre

ground[2] *n* COAL TECH sol *m*, COAL TECH terre *f*, ELEC (AmE) (*cf earth*) connection, ELEC ENG (AmE) (*cf earth*) masse *f*, terre *f*, PHYS masse *f*, PRODUCTION, TELECOM terre *f*, VEHICLES (AmE) (*cf earth*) *electrical system* masse *f*, terre *f*; ~ **address** *n* TELECOM adresse au sol *f*; ~ **angle** *n* AERONAUT angle d'atterrissage *m*; ~ **angle shot** *n* CINEMAT plan en contre plongée *m*; ~ **arrester** *n* (AmE) (*cf earth arrester*) GEOPHYS court-circuiteur de mise à la terre *m*; ~ **bar** *n* (AmE) (*cf earth bar*) ELEC piquet de terre *m*; ~ **base** *n* C&G pontil *m*; ~ **bus** *n* (AmE) (*cf earth bus*) ELEC *connection* barre omnibus de terre *f*, PROD ENG barette de masse *f*; ~ **bus mounting** *n* PROD ENG fixation de la barrette de masse *f*; ~ **cable** *n* (AmE) (*cf earth cable*) ELEC ENG câble de mise à la masse *m*, câble de terre *m*, VEHICLES *electrical system* câble de mise à la masse *m*; ~ **clamp** *n* (AmE) (*cf earth clamp*) ELEC borne de terre *f*; ~ **clearance** *n* VEHICLES *body* garde au sol *f*; ~ **clip** *n* (AmE) (*cf earth clip*) ELEC *connection* collier de mise à la terre *m*; ~ **closed end** *n* SPRINGS *of spring coil* spire terminale fermée et meulée *f*; ~ **cloth** *n* TEXTILES fond d'impression *m*; ~ **coat** *n* COATINGS *enamel* couche de base *f*, enduit de débauche *m*; ~ **color** *n* (AmE), ~ **colour** *n* (BrE) C&G couleur de fond *f*, COLOURS couleur broyée *f*; ~ **conductor** *n* (AmE) (*cf earth conductor*) ELEC conducteur de terre *m*, ELEC ENG fil de terre *m*; ~ **connection** *n* (AmE) (*cf earth connection*) AUTO câble de mise à la masse *m*, ELEC prise de terre *f*, ELEC ENG connexion de terre *f*; ~ **connector** *n* (AmE) (*cf earth connector*) PROD ENG serre-fils de mise à la terre *m*; ~ **current** *n* (AmE) (*cf earth current*) ELEC courant à la terre *m*, GEOPHYS courant tellurique *m*, PROD ENG courant de masse *m*; ~ **detector** *n* (AmE) (*cf earth detector*) ELEC ENG détecteur de terre *m*; ~ **detector light** *n* PROD ENG *electricity* voyant de défaut de masse *m*; ~ **effect** *n* AERONAUT effet au sol *m*; ~ **effect machine** *n* (*GEM*) TRANSP véhicule à effet de sol *m*; ~ **electrode** *n* (AmE) (*cf earth electrode*) AUTO électrode de masse *f*, ELEC électrode de terre *f*, ELEC ENG électrode de mise à la terre *f*; ~ **end** *n* SPRINGS extrémité meulée *f*; ~ **fabric** *n* TEXTILES fond d'impression *m*; ~ **facilities** *n* SPACE infrastructures *f pl*; ~ **fault** *n* (AmE) (*cf earth fault*) ELEC défaut à la terre *m*, PROD ENG défaut de terre *m*; ~ **fault current** *n* (*cf earth fault current*) PROD ENG courant de défaut de mise à la terre *m*; ~ **fault protection** *n* (AmE) (*cf earth fault protection*) ELEC protection contre les défauts à la terre *f*; ~ **fault tray** *n* (AmE) (*cf earth fault tray*) PROD ENG relais de défaut à la terre *m*; ~ **fault trip** *n* PROD ENG défaut dû à un défaut de masse *m*; ~ **frame** *n* RAIL aiguille semi-automatique *f*; ~ **glass** *n* CINEMAT dépoli *m*, verre dépoli *m*; ~ **glass circle** *n* PHOTO anneau dépoli *m*; ~ **glass joint** *n* LAB EQUIP rodage en verre *m*; ~ **glass joint clamp** *n* LAB EQUIP pince à rodage *f*; ~ **glass screen** *n* INSTRUMENT verre dépoli de projection *m*, PHOTO écran en verre dépoli *m*; ~ **glass screen with microprism spot** *n* PHOTO verre dépoli à microprismes *m*; ~ **glass screen with reticule** *n* PHOTO verre dépoli à quadrillage *m*; ~ **glass with Fresnel lens** *n* PHOTO verre dépoli à échelons de Fresnel *m*; ~ **indicator** *n* (AmE) *(cf earth indicator)* ELEC ENG indicateur de terre *m*; ~ **installation** *n* AERONAUT infrastructure *f*; ~ **layer** *n* METEO couche limite de surface *f*; ~ **lead** *n* *(cf earth lead)* ELEC ENG conducteur de masse *m*, conducteur de terre *m*; ~ **leakage** *n* (AmE) *(cf earth leakage)* ELEC perte à la terre *f*, ELEC ENG fuite par la terre *f*; ~ **leakage circuit breaker** *n* (AmE) *(cf earth leakage circuit breaker)* ELEC disjoncteur différentiel *m*; ~ **leakage current** *n* (AmE) *(cf earth leakage current)* ELEC courant de fuite à la terre *m*; ~ **leakage detector** *n* (AmE) *(cf earth leakage detector)* ELEC détecteur de fuite à la terre *m*; ~ **leakage meter** *n* (AmE) *(cf earth leakage meter)* ELEC mesureur de terre *m*; ~ **level** *n* NUCLEAR niveau normal *m*; ~ **level concentration** *n* POLLUTION *of pollutants* concentration au niveau du sol *f*; ~ **lighting** *n* AERONAUT balisage *m*; ~ **line** *n* (AmE) *(cf earth line)* ELEC ENG ligne de masse *f*, ligne de terre *f*; ~ **loop** *n* (AmE) *(cf earth loop)* PROD ENG boucle de masse *f*; ~ **lug** *n* (AmE) *(cf earth lug)* ELEC, PROD ENG cosse de mise à la terre *f*; ~ **movement** *n* GAS TECH mouvement de terrain *m*; ~ **network** *n* TELECOM réseau au sol *m*; ~ **noise** *n* ELECTRON bruit de fond *m*; ~ **operation** *n* AERONAUT manoeuvre au sol *f*, SPACE *spacecraft* mise en oeuvre au sol *f*; ~ **pigtail end** *n* SPRINGS extrémité queue de cochon meulée *f*; ~ **pin** *n* (AmE) *(cf earth pin)* PROD ENG lamelle de masse *f*; ~ **plane** *n* (AmE) *(cf earth plane)* GEOM plan géométrique *m*, PHYS plan de masse *m*; ~ **plate** *n* (AmE) *(cf earth plate)* ELEC ENG prise de terre *f*; ~ **potential** *n* (AmE) *(cf earth potential)* ELEC potentiel de la terre *m*, SPACE potentiel terrestre *m*; ~ **power supply** *n* AERONAUT source d'alimentation extérieure *f*; ~ **power unit** *n* *(GPU)* AERONAUT groupe auxiliaire au sol *m*, groupe de démarrage au sol *m*; ~ **radio station** *n* AERONAUT station radio *f*; ~ **resistance** *n* (AmE) *(cf earth resistance)* ELEC résistance de la terre *f*; ~ **resistance meter** *n* (AmE) *(cf earth resistance meter)* ELEC telluromètre *m*; ~ **resonance** *n* AERONAUT résonance au sol *f*; ~ **return** *n* (AmE) *(cf earth return)* ELEC ENG retour par la masse *m*, retour par terre *m*, PROD ENG retour à la terre *m*, TELECOM retour par terre *m*; ~ **rod** *n* (AmE) *(cf earth rod)* ELEC *connection* piquet de terre *m*, GEOPHYS perche de mise à la terre *f*, piquet de terre *m*; ~ **segment** *n* SPACE *communications* composante terrienne *f*, secteur terrien *m*; ~ **sensing apparatus** *n* (AmE) *(cf earth sensing apparatus)* PROD ENG appareil détecteur de défaut de masse *m*; ~ **service equipment** *n* AERONAUT servitudes au sol *f pl*; ~ **speed** *n* AERONAUT vitesse au sol *f*; ~ **spike** *n* (AmE) *(cf earth spike)* GEOPHYS piquet de terre *m*; ~ **staff** *n* AERONAUT personnel au sol *m*; ~ **state** *n* CHEM *atom* état normal d'énergie *m*, PART PHYS *atom*, PHYS état fondamental *m*; ~ **state frequency** *n* RAD PHYS fréquence fondamentale *f*; ~ **state transition** *n* PART PHYS transition de l'état fondamental *f*; ~ **station** *n* SPACE station au sol *f*; ~ **stopper** *n* LAB EQUIP *glassware* bouchon à rodage *m*, PACKAGING bouchon en verre dépoli *m*; ~ **swell** *n* NAUT lame de fond *f*, OCEANOG lame de fond *f*, onde fondamentale *f*; ~ **switch** *n* (AmE) *(cf earth switch)* ELEC interrupteur de mise à la terre *m*; ~ **tackle** *n* NAUT *mooring* apparaux de mouillage *m pl*; ~ **target** *n* MILIT objectif au sol *m*, objectif terrestre *m*; ~ **terminal** *n* (AmE) *(cf earth terminal)* ELEC *connection* borne de terre *f*, ELEC ENG borne de masse *f*, borne de terre *f*, prise de terre *f*, PROD ENG *electricity* borne de terre *f*; ~ **terminal arrester** *n* (AmE) *(cf earth terminal arrester)* ELEC éclateur de mise à la terre *m*; ~ **test** *n* AERONAUT essai au sol *m*, vérification au sol *f*, SPACE essai au sol *m*; ~ **thread tap** *n* MECH ENG taraud à filets rectifiés *m*; ~ **visibility** *n* AERONAUT visibilité au sol *f*; ~ **water** *n* COAL TECH eau artésienne *f*, nappe d'eau souterraine *f*, HYDROL eau phréatique *f*, eau souterraine *f*, nappe phréatique *f*, WATER SUPP eau souterraine *f*, nappe phréatique *f*; ~ **water basin** *n* WATER SUPP bassin d'eau souterraine *m*; ~ **water catchment** *n* WATER SUPP captage de l'eau souterraine *m*; ~ **water contour** *n* HYDROL hydroisohypse de la nappe phréatique *f*; ~ **water contour map** *n* HYDROL carte des isoplèthes de la nappe phréatique *f*; ~ **water depth** *n* WATER SUPP profondeur de la nappe phréatique *f*; ~ **water inrush** *n* HYDROL venue d'eau souterraine *f*; ~ **water investigation** *n* HYDROL étude hydrogéologique *f*; ~ **water level** *n* CONST nappe phréatique *f*, niveau de l'eau phréatique *m*, HYDROL nappe phréatique *f*, WATER SUPP nappe d'eau souterraine *f*, nappe phréatique *f*, niveau de la nappe aquifère *m*; ~ **water resources** *n* WATER SUPP ressources en eaux souterraines *f pl*; ~ **water supply** *n* COAL TECH source d'eau souterraine *f*, WATER SUPP nappe phréatique *f*; ~ **water table** *n* COAL TECH niveau d'émergence de la nappe d'eau *m*, WATER SUPP surface de la nappe phréatique *f*; ~ **wave** *n* NAUT *oceanography* vague de fond *f*, OCEANOG onde fondamentale *f*, TELECOM onde de sol *f*, onde directe *f*; ~ **wire** *n* (AmE) *(cf earth wire)* ELEC ENG fil de masse *m*, fil de terre *m*, ELECTR prise de terre *f*, PROD ENG conducteur de terre *m*, TV fil de terre *m*

ground³ *vt* AERONAUT immobiliser, ELEC (AmE) *(cf earth)* *connection*, ELEC ENG (AmE) *(cf earth)* mettre à la masse, mettre à la terre, PHYS mettre à la masse, TELECOM mettre à la masse, mettre à la terre, VEHICLES (AmE) *(cf earth)* *electrical system* mettre à la masse, mettre à la terre

ground⁴ *vi* NAUT *of ship* atterrir, mettre au sec, toucher le fond

ground-controlled¹ *adj* SPACE *spacecraft* contrôlé à partir du sol

ground-controlled:² ~ **approach** *n* AERONAUT percée en GCA *f*, système d'approche contrôlée au sol *m*; ~ **approach system** *n* TRANSP système d'approche contrôlée du sol *m*

grounded¹ *adj* (AmE) *(cf earthed)* ELEC mis à la terre, ELEC ENG mis à la masse, mis à la terre, TELECOM mis à la terre

grounded:² ~ **base connection** *n* (AmE) *(cf earthed base connection)* ELEC ENG montage à base commune *m*; ~ **collector connection** *n* (AmE) *(cf earthed collector connection)* ELEC ENG montage à collecteur commun *m*; ~ **emitter connection** *n* (AmE) *(cf earthed emitter connection)* ELEC ENG montage à émetteur commun *m*; ~ **neutral system** *n* (AmE) *(cf earthed neutral* *system)* ELEC système avec neutre à la terre *m*; ~ **switch** *n* (AmE) *(cf earthed switch)* ELEC commutateur de sécurité *m*; ~ **system** *n* (AmE) *(cf earthed system)* PROD ENG système relié à la terre *m*

ground-in: ~ **cutting rake** *n* MECH ENG brise-copeau meulé *m*

grounding *n* AERONAUT *of aircraft* interdiction de vol *f*, CONST mise en terre *f*, prise de terre *f*, ELEC ENG mise à la masse *f*, mise à la terre *f*, MAR POLL *by accident* échouement *m*, *caused by natural conditions* échouage *m*, RAIL, SPACE mise à la masse *f*, mise à la terre *f*; ~ **bar** *n* AERONAUT barre de masse *f*; ~ **bus** *n* (AmE) *(cf earthing bus)* ELEC barre de terre *f*; ~ **clip** *n* (AmE) *(cf earthing clip)* ELEC borne de terre *f*; ~ **electrode conductor** *n* (AmE) *(cf earthing electrode conductor)* PROD ENG conducteur de mise à la terre *m*; ~ **electrode system** *n* (AmE) *(cf earthing electrode system)* PROD ENG système de mise à la terre *m*; ~ **paddle** *n* (AmE) *(cf earthing paddle)* RAIL perche de mise à terre *f*; ~ **path** *n* (AmE) *(cf earthing path)* PROD ENG chemin de mise à la terre *m*; ~ **pole** *n* (AmE) *(cf earthing pole)* RAIL perche de mise à terre *f*; ~ **position** *n* (AmE) *(cf earthing position)* ELEC position de mise à la terre *f*; ~ **reactor** *n* (AmE) *(cf earthing reactor)* ELEC ENG réactance de la prise de terre *f*; ~ **regulation** *n* (AmE) *(cf earthing regulation)* PROD ENG régulation de mise à la terre *f*; ~ **rod** *n* (AmE) *(cf earthing rod)* ELEC piquet de terre *m*, RAIL perche de mise à terre *f*; ~ **strip** *n* (AmE) *(cf earthing strip)* ELEC ENG bride de terre *f*; ~ **switch** *n* (AmE) *(cf earthing switch)* CONTROL interrupteur de mise à la terre *m*, ELEC commutateur de mise à la terre *m*, sectionneur de terre *m*, ELEC ENG commutateur de mise à la terre *m*

groundnut: ~ **oil** *n* (BrE) FOOD TECH huile d'arachide *f*

grounds *n pl* PATENTS *for opposition, revocation* motifs *m pl*

groundsill *n* CONST *of doorframe* seuil *m*, CONST *of timber frame for walls, partitions* sablière basse *f*, MINING *of set of timber* semelle *f*, sole *f*

ground-to-air: ~ **communication** *n* AERONAUT communications dans le sens sol-air *f pl*; ~ **missile** *n* MILIT missile sol-air *m*

ground-to-ground: ~ **missile** *n* MILIT missile sol-sol *m*

groundwave *n* RAD PHYS onde au sol *f*

groundwood *n* PAPER TECH pâte mécanique de meule *f*; ~ **pulp** *n* PAPER TECH pâte mécanique de défibreur *f*

groundwood-free: ~ **paper** *n* PRINT papier sans pâte mécanique *m*

group[1] *n* CHEM groupe *m*, groupement *m*, radical *m*, COMP, DP, MATH groupe *m*, RAIL *of sidings* faisceau *m*, TELECOM faisceau *m*, groupe primaire *m*, groupement *m*; ~ **call identity** *n* TELECOM identité d'appel de groupe *f*; ~ **code recording** *n* COMP enregistrement par codage de groupe *m*, enregistrement par groupe *m*, DP marque de groupe *f*; ~ **collective dose** *n* POLLUTION équivalent de dose pour un groupe *m*; ~ **of commodities** *n* PACKAGING groupe de marchandises *m*; ~ **delay** *n* ELEC ENG délai de groupe *m*, retard de groupe *m*; ~ **delay linear distortion** *n* SPACE *communications* distorsion linéaire de phase *f*; ~ **distribution frame** *n* TELECOM répartiteur de groupe primaire *m*; ~ **index** *n* OPT, TELECOM indice de groupe *m*; ~ **mark** *n* COMP, DP marque de groupe *f*; ~ **occulting light** *n* NAUT *navigation marks* feu à occultation groupée *m*; ~ **separator** *n* (*GS*) COMP séparateur de groupes *m*, DP bande de protection *f*; ~ **switching center** *n* (AmE) *see group*

switching centre; ~ **switching center catchment area** *n* (AmE) *see group switching centre catchment area;* ~ **switching center exchange area** *n* (AmE) *see group switching centre exchange area;* ~ **switching centre** *n* (BrE) (*GSC*) TELECOM centre de transit *m*, commutateur à autonomie d'acheminement *m*; ~ **switching centre catchment area** *n* (BrE) TELECOM ZAA, zone à autonomie d'acheminement *f*; ~ **switching centre exchange area** *n* (BrE) TELECOM ZAA, zone à autonomie d'acheminement *f*; ~ **theory** *n* MATH théorie des groupes *f*; ~ **transmission delay** *n* TELECOM temps de propagation de groupe *m*; ~ **velocity** *n* ACOUSTICS, GEOPHYS, OPT, PHYS, TELECOM, TRANSP vitesse de groupe *f*

group[2] *vt* ELEC ENG grouper

groupage: ~ **car** *n* (AmE) *(cf groupage wagon)* RAIL *vehicles* wagon de groupage *m*; ~ **traffic** *n* RAIL *vehicles* trafic de groupage *m*; ~ **traffic forwarder** *n* RAIL *vehicles* groupeur *m*; ~ **wagon** *n* (BrE) *(cf groupage car)* RAIL *vehicles* wagon de groupage *m*

grouping *n* ELEC ENG *telephone lines* groupement *m*; ~ **switch** *n* ELEC ENG interrupteur de groupe *m*, interrupteur inverseur *m*

grout[1] *n* CONST coulis hydraulique d'injection *m*, mortier d'injection *m*, mortier liquide *m*; ~ **curtain** *n* CONST *dams* rideau d'injection *m*, voile d'étanchéité *f*

grout[2] *vt* CONST couler

grouting *n* COAL TECH injection *f*, CONST coulis *m*, injection de ciment *f*, *process* travaux d'injection *m pl*, NUCLEAR injection de ciment *f*; ~ **equipment** *n* CONST matériel d'injection *m*

growler *n* ELEC appareil d'essai d'induit *m*

grown: ~ **junction** *n* ELECTRON jonction formée au tirage *f*, jonction tirée *f*

grown-in: ~ **dislocation** *n* METALL dislocation originelle *f*

growth *n* FLUID PHYS *of perturbation* croissance *f*, METALL gonflement de la fonte *m*, NUCLEAR augmentation *f*, croissance *f*, PROP MAT gonflement de la fonte *m*; ~ **anticline** *n* GEOL anticlinal de croissance *m*; ~ **fault** *n* (AmE) *(cf synsedimentary fault)* GEOL faille de croissance *f*, faille synsédimentaire *f*; ~ **pattern** *n* METALL figures de croissance *f pl*; ~ **spiral** *n* METALL spirale de croissance *f*; ~ **step** *n* METALL marche de croissance *f*; ~ **twin** *n* METALL macle de croissance *f*

groyne *n* (BrE) NAUT, OCEANOG, WATER SUPP épi *m*

GRP *abbr* MECH *(glass reinforced polyester)* polyester armé *m*, NAUT *(glass refined plastic) boatbuilding material* matière plastique armée de fibre de verre *f*

grub: ~ **screw** *n* MECH ENG vis sans tête *f*, vis sans tête à tige lisse *f*

grünauite *n* MINERAL grunauite *f*

grunerite *n* MINERAL grunérite *f*

Grus *n* ASTRON Grue *f*

GS *abbr (group separator)* COMP séparateur de groupes *m*, DP bande de protection *f*

GSC *abbr (group switching centre, group switching center)* TELECOM centre de transit *m*, commutateur à autonomie d'acheminement *m*

G-star *n* ASTRON étoile G *f*

G-T *abbr (gain-to-noise temperature ratio)* SPACE *quality factor* G-T *(rapport gain-température de bruit)*

guaiac: ~ **gum** *n* FOOD TECH résine de gaïacol *f*

guaiacol *n* CHEM gaïacol *m*

guaiaconic *adj* CHEM gaïaconique

guaiaretic *adj* CHEM gaïarétique

guanidine *n* CHEM guanidine *f*
guanine *n* CHEM guanine *f*
guano *n* CHEM guano *m*
guanosine *n* CHEM guanosine *f*
guanyl *n* CHEM guanyle *m*
guarantee: ~ **cap** *n* PACKAGING capsule de garantie *f*; ~ **closure** *n* PACKAGING fermeture de garantie *f*; ~ **period** *n* SPACE durée de garantie *f*
guaranteed: ~ **draw off** *n* FUELLESS débit garanti *m*; ~ **flight path** *n* AERONAUT trajectoire garantie *f*; ~ **thrust** *n* AERONAUT poussée garantie *f*; ~ **weight** *n* AERONAUT masse garantie *f*
guard[1] *n* ELEC *safety* dispositif de sûreté *m*, MECH capot de protection *m*, MECH ENG carter *m*, carter d'engrenage *m*, couvre-engrenages *m*, gaine protectrice contre les accidents *f*, *machine tools* cache de sécurité *m*, capot *m*, capot de protection *m*, carter de sécurité *m*, *of wheel* couvre-roue *m*, *to prevent bars wrapping round rolling mill rolls* garde *f*, PRINT onglet *m*, PROD ENG *cage* gaine *f*, protecteur *m*, *safety* volet *m*, RAIL *vehicles* chef de train *m*, SAFETY barrière *f*, grille *f*, protection *f*, garde *f*, *cage* gaine *f*, protecteur *m*, *of wheel* couvre-roue *m*, *on machine* carter de protection *m*, dispositif de sûreté *m*; ~ **against debris** *n* MECH ENG grille de protection d'entrée *f*; ~ **band** *n* COMP, DP bande de protection *f*, TV bande de protection *f*, piste de sécurité *f*; ~ **circuit** *n* ELEC ENG circuit de garde *m*; ~ **iron** *n* RAIL *vehicles* chasse-pierres *m*; ~ **log** *n* PETR diagramme gardé *m*; ~ **plate** *n* PROD ENG plaque de protection *f*; ~ **ring** *n* ELEC *electric field*, ELEC ENG, PHYS anneau de garde *m*, PROD ENG manchon de sécurité *m*; ~ **ring capacitor** *n* ELEC ENG condensateur à anneau de garde *m*; ~ **space** *n* TELECOM *land mobile* espacement de garde *m*; ~ **time** *n* SPACE *communications* temps de garde *m*; ~ **track** *n* RECORDING piste de garde *f*; ~ **vessel** *n* NUCLEAR cuve de sécurité *f*; ~ **wire** *n* ELEC *overhead line* fil de garde *m*, ELEC ENG fil protecteur *m*
guard's[2] ~ **against** *vt* SAFETY parer à, protéger contre
guard's: ~ **van** *n* (BrE) *(cf caboose)* RAIL *vehicles* fourgon *m*
guarded[1] *adj* SAFETY *machine* protégé
guarded:[2] ~ **gears** *n pl* MECH ENG engrenages enfermés dans des carters *m pl*, engrenages recouverts de gaines protectrices *m pl*, SAFETY engrenages enfermés dans des carters *m pl*, engrenages protégés sous capot *m pl*, engrenages protégés sous carter *m pl*; ~ **input** *n* ELEC ENG entrée gardée *f*; ~ **output** *n* ELEC ENG sortie gardée *f*
guarding *n* SAFETY protection *f*; ~ **relay** *n* ELEC ENG relais de maintien *m*
guardrail *n* CONST glissière de sécurité *f*, main courante de garde *f*, *handrail* garde-corps *m*, garde-fou *m*, NAUT *deck equipment* filière *f*, garde-corps *m*, rambarde *f*, SAFETY *for enclosure* barrière de sécurité *f*, *handrail* garde-corps *m*, garde-fou *m*, rambarde *f*
gudgeon *n* CONST goujon *m*, goujon prisonnier *m*, MECH ENG *crosshead pin* tourillon de crosse *m*, tourillon de la tête de piston *m*, *of shaft, pin, pivot, journal* goujon *m*, tourillon *m*, MINING *of winding pulley* arbre *m*, PROD ENG *of core barrel, of winch barrel* tourillon *m*; ~ **pin** *n* MECH axe de piston *m*, MECH ENG *crosshead pin* tourillon de crosse *m*, tourillon de la tête de piston *m*, VEHICLES *engine, piston* axe de piston *m*
guidance *n* SPACE *spacecraft* guidage *m*; ~ **antenna** *n* SPACE *spacecraft* antenne de guidage *f*; ~ **by automatic road signs** *n* TRANSP guidage routier automatique *m*;

~ **cushion** *n* TRANSP coussin de guidage *m*; ~ **magnet** *n* TRANSP aimant de guidage *m*; ~ **navigation system** *n* SPACE *spacecraft* système de guidage et de navigation *m*; ~ **receiver** *n* SPACE *spacecraft* récepteur de guidage *m*
guide *n* C&G main de coulée *f*, HYDR EQUIP *of turbine* directrice *f*, MECH ENG galet *m*, galet de renvoi *m*, galet guide *m*, poulie-guide *f*, *for solid die stock* guide *m*, *tool* canon *m*, MINING *mine cage* coulant *m*, guidage *m*, guide *m*, guidonnage *m*, PAPER TECH guide *m*, TEXTILES passette *f*; ~ **bar** *n* MECH ENG *of crosshead* glissière *f*, glissière de crosse *f*, guide *m*, guide de la tête de piston *m*, TEXTILES barre de passettes *f*; ~ **beam** *n* TRANSP poutre conductrice *f*; ~ **bearer** *n* MECH ENG *of crosshead guides* support des glissières *m*; ~ **bearing** *n* INSTRUMENT palier-guide *m*; ~ **blade** *n* HYDR EQUIP *of turbine* aube directrice *f*; ~ **block** *n* MECH ENG *injection mould* glissière *f*, *of crosshead guides* tasseau de fixation des glissières *m*; ~ **bush** *n* MECH ENG bague de guidage *f*, canon de guidage *m*, ogive de guidage *f*, *machine tool* bague cylindrique *f*, bague à collerette *f*; ~ **bushing** *n* NUCLEAR *of control rod* boîte-guide *f*; ~ **clamp** *n* MECH ENG bride de retenue de bague de guidage *f*; ~ **cross tie** *n* MECH ENG *of crosshead guides* support des glissières *m*; ~ **error** *n* TV erreur de base de temps due au guide *f*; ~ **funnel** *n* PETR entonnoir de guidage *m*; ~ **line** *n* PETR ligne de fer *f*, ligne guide *f*, PROD ENG consigne *f*; ~ **line tensioner** *n* PETR dispositif de mise sous tension constante de lignes guides *m*; ~ **mill** *n* PROD ENG *iron and steel manufacture* laminoir à guides *m*; ~ **number** *n* PHOTO nombre guide *m*; ~ **nut** *n* MECH ENG écrou-guide *m*; ~ **pillar** *n* MECH ENG *die set* colonne de guidage *f*, *diecasting die* colonne épaulée *f*, *injection mould* colonnede guidage *f*; ~ **pin** *n* MECH broche de guidage *f*, MECH ENG axe de guidage *m*, pion de centrage *m*; ~ **plate** *n* MECH ENG *die set* plaque de guidage *f*; ~ **plates** *n pl* PROD ENG *of links of roller chain* flasques *m pl*; ~ **pulley** *n* MECH ENG galet *m*, galet de renvoi *m*, galet guide *m*, poulie-guide *f*; ~ **ramp** *n* MECH ENG rampe de guidage *f*; ~ **ring** *n* HYDR EQUIP *of a turbine* couronne directrice *f*, couronne fixe *f*, distributeur de turbine *m*; ~ **roll** *n* PAPER TECH rouleau guide *m*; ~ **roller** *n* CINEMAT galet guide *m*, PROD ENG rouleau de guidage *m*, rouleau guide *m*, TEXTILES rouleau guide *m*; ~ **rope** *n* PROD ENG câble de guidage *m*, câble guide *m*; ~ **screw** *n* MECH ENG *lathe* vis-mère *f*; ~ **shoe** *n* MINING *of mine cage* griffe de guidage *f*, main courante *f*, main de guidage *f*; ~ **stock** *n* PROD ENG filière à guide *f*; ~ **tooth** *n* MECH ENG dent de repère *f*; ~ **track** *n* RECORDING piste de référence *f*, piste témoin *f*; ~ **tube** *n* MECH ENG tube de guidage *m*, MINING *boring* conducteur tubulaire *m*, tube conducteur *m*, tube-guide *m*; ~ **vane** *n* FUELLESS *turbines* aube directrice *f*, HYDR EQUIP, MECH aube directrice *f*, aube fixe *f*, REFRIG *of fan* aube directrice *f*; ~ **vane servomotor** *n* FUELLESS servomoteur de l'aube directrice *m*; ~ **vane vibration** *n* FUELLESS vibration de l'aube directrice *f*; ~ **wavelength** *n* PHYS longueur d'onde dans le guide *f*; ~ **wheel** *n* TRANSP roue directrice *f*; ~ **yoke** *n* MECH ENG *of crosshead guides* support des glissières *m*
guided: ~ **air-cushion vehicle** *n* TRANSP aéroglisseur guidé *m*; ~ **beam diameter** *n* OPT diamètre du faisceau guidé *m*; ~ **light transport system** *n* RAIL système de transport léger et guidé *m*; ~ **long range missile** *n* MILIT missile téléguidé à grand rayon d'action *m*; ~ **missile** *n* MILIT missile téléguidé *m*; ~ **public mass transporta-**

tion system *n* TRANSP système guidé de transport public collectif *m*; ~ **radiation system** *n* TELECOM *land mobile* système à rayonnement guidé *m*; ~ **road** *n* TRANSP route guidée *f*; ~ **subsonic missile** *n* MILIT engin subsonique téléguidé *m*; ~ **wave** *n* OPT, TELECOM onde guidée *f*; ~ **weapon** *n* MILIT engin autoguidé *m*

guidelines *n pl* MECH ENG principes directeurs *m pl*

guidepoles *n pl* CONST *of a pile-driver* jumelles *f pl*

guidepost *n* CONST poteau indicateur *m*, PETR colonne guide *f*, montant de guidage *m*, montant de guide *m*, poteau de guidage *m*

guiderail *n* MECH ENG rail-guide *m*, TRANSP rail de guidage *m*

guides *n pl* MINES coulantage *m*

guideway *n* TRANSP poutre porteuse *f*; ~ **at grade** *n* TRANSP voie à niveau *f*

guiding *n* MECH ENG guidage *m*, guidonnage *m*; ~ **dimension** *n* SPRINGS valeur à titre indicatif *f*; ~ **line** *n* PROD ENG trait de repère *m*; ~ **mark** *n* NAUT *navigation*, PROD ENG repère *m*

guillotine *n* PACKAGING guillotine *f*, PROD ENG, SAFETY cisaille à guillotine *f*; ~ **gate** *n* MINING barrière à guillotine *f*; ~ **shears** *n* MECH, PROD ENG cisaille à guillotine *f*; ~ **shutter** *n* PHOTO obturateur à guillotine *m*; ~ **splicer** *n* CINEMAT colleuse à scotch *f*

guillotining *n* PAPER TECH massicotage *m*, massicotage refente de feuilles *m*

guillotining-trimming *n* PAPER TECH massicotage-rognage *m*

Guinier-Preston: ~ **zone** *n* (GP) CRYSTALL zone Guinier-Preston *f*

gulf *n* NAUT *geography*, OCEANOG golfe *m*

gulleting: ~ **saw file** *n* PROD ENG lime ronde à scies *f*

gulley: ~ **sucker** *n* MAR POLL camion d'assainissement *m*

gulonic *adj* CHEM gulonique

gulose *n* CHEM gulose *m*

gum[1] *n* CHEM, PRINT gomme *f*; ~ **guaiacum** *n* FOOD TECH résine de gaïacol *f*; ~ **lac** *n* COATINGS vernis à résine *m*; ~ **lake** *n* COATINGS vernis à résine *m*; ~ **tragacanth** *n* FOOD TECH gomme adragante *f*

gum[2] *vt* PROD ENG encrasser; ~ **up** *vt* PROD ENG encrasser

gumbo *n* PETR gumbo *m*, PETR TECH *drilling* argile fluante *f*

gummed: ~ **edge** *n* PACKAGING bord gommé *m*; ~ **label** *n* PACKAGING étiquette gommée *f*; ~ **paper** *n* PACKAGING papier gommé *m*; ~ **paper tape** *n* PACKAGING ruban de fixage *m*

gumming *n* PAPER TECH gommage *m*, PROD ENG encrassement *m*; ~ **machine** *n* PACKAGING machine à engommer *f*; ~ **up** *n* PROD ENG encrassement *m*

gummite *n* MINERAL gummite *f*

gun *n* MILIT canon *m*; ~ **barrel** *n* MILIT fût de canon *m*; ~ **carriage** *n* MILIT affût de canon *m*; ~ **efficiency** *n* TV rendement de canon *m*; ~ **perforator** *n* PETR TECH *drilling* perforateur à balles *m*; ~ **pit** *n* MILIT emplacement de canon *m*; ~ **shield** *n* MILIT bouclier fixe de canon *m*; ~ **swab brush** *n* MILIT écouvillon *m*

guncotton *n* MINING coton-poudre *m*, fulmicoton *m*

gunite *n* CONST gunite *f*

guniting *n* C&G, CONST gunitage *m*

gunmetal *n* MECH bronze au zinc *m*, MILIT, PROP MAT bronze à canon *m*; ~ **bearings** *n pl* MECH ENG dés en bronze *m pl*, *of mandrel* coussinets en bronze *m pl*; ~ **bush** *n* MECH ENG buselure en bronze *f*, coquille en bronze *f*; ~ **bushing** *n* MECH ENG buselure en bronze *f*, coquille en bronze *f*

Gunn: ~ **amplifier** *n* ELECTRON amplificateur à diode Gunn *m*; ~ **diode** *n* ELECTRON diode Gunn *f*, diode à effet Gunn *f*, PHYS diode Gunn *f*; ~ **diode effect** *n* PHYS diode Gunn *f*, diode à effet Gunn *f*; ~ **effect** *n* ELECTRON effet Gunn *m*; ~ **effect diode** *n* ELECTRON diode Gunn *f*, diode à effet Gunn *f*

gunnel *n* NAUT lisse de plat-bord *f*

gunning *n* CONST gunitage *m*

gunpod *n* CINEMAT crosse d'épaule *f*

gunpowder *n* MILIT poudre à canon *f*

Gunter's: ~ **chain** *n* CONST chaîne de Gunter *f*

gunwale *n* NAUT lisse de plat-bord *f*

gurry: ~ **bait** *n* OCEANOG boette *f*, bouette *f*

gusset *n* NAUT *shipbuilding* gousset *m*, PRINT angle interne *m*, gousset *m*; ~ **wrinkles** *n pl* PRINT pattes d'oies *f pl*

gusseted: ~ **layflat tubing** *n* PACKAGING tubes aplatis avec gousset *m pl*

gust[1] *n* AERONAUT embardée *f*, rafale *f*, METEO rafale *f*, NAUT *of wind* grain *m*, rafale *f*; ~ **alleviation factor** *n* AERONAUT coefficient d'atténuation de rafale *m*; ~ **envelope** *n* AERONAUT enveloppe de rafale *f*; ~ **formation time** *n* AERONAUT durée de formation d'une rafale *f*; ~ **gradient distance** *n* AERONAUT distance de formation d'une rafale *f*; ~ **intensity** *n* AERONAUT intensité de rafale *f*; ~ **load factor** *n* AERONAUT facteur de charge de rafale *m*; ~ **load limit** *n* AERONAUT charge de rafales limite *f*; ~ **lock** *n* AERONAUT blocage des gouvernes *m*, frein de gouverne *m*; ~ **V-n diagram** *n* AERONAUT diagramme de rafales en V-n *m*

gust[2] *vi* METEO souffler en rafales, souffler fort

gut[1] *n* OCEANOG goulet *m*

gut[2] *vt* OCEANOG étriper

GUT *abbr* (*grand unified theory*) PART PHYS, PHYS théorie de grande unification *f*

Gutenberg: ~ **discontinuity** *n* FUELLESS discontinuité Gutenberg *f*

gutta-percha *n* CHEM, P&R gutta-percha *f*

gutter *n* AERONAUT larmier *m*, CONST caniveau *m*, cunette *f*, rigole *f*, rigole d'assèchement *f*, *for roof* chéneau *m*, gouttière *f*, MECH ENG caniveau *m*, gouttière *f*, rigole *f*, PRINT blanc transversal *m*, gouttière *f*, marge longitudinale en rotative *f*, marge transversale en feuilles *f*; ~ **bracket** *n* CONST crochet de gouttière *m*, *for attaching to rafter* collier *m*, crochet de gouttière *m*, *to drive* crochet de gouttière à queue en pointe *m*; ~ **tile** *n* C&G tuile creuse *f*

guttering *n* AERONAUT ravinement *m*

guy *n* CONST, MECH hauban *m*, NAUT *rope* bras *m*, retenue *f*; ~ **anchor** *n* PETR TECH *derrick* ancrage de haubanage *m*; ~ **insulator** *n* ELEC ENG isolateur d'arrêt *m*; ~ **ring** *n* PETR TECH *derrick* anneau de haubanage *m*; ~ **rope** *n* CONST câble de haubanage *m*; ~ **wire** *n* ELEC ENG hauban *m*

guying *n* CONST haubanage *m*

guyot *n* GEOL guyot *m*, volcan sous-marin *m*, OCEANOG guyot *m*

GVT: ~ **train** *n* (*gravity vacuum transit train*) TRANSPORT train GVT *m*

GVW *abbr* (*gross vehicle weight*) VEHICLES PTC (*poids total en charge*), PTM (*poids total maximum*)

Gy *abbr* (*gray*) METR, PHYS, RAD PHYS Gy (*gray*)

G-Y: ~ **axis** *n* TV *colour difference signal* axe V-Y *m*; ~ **matrix** *n* TV matrice V-Y *f*; ~ **signal** *n* TV signal V-Y *m*

gymnite *n* MINERAL gymnite *f*

gynocardic *adj* CHEM gynocardique

gypseous *adj* CHEM gypseux

gypsiferous[1] *adj* GEOL gypsifère

gypsiferous:[2] ~ **shale** *n* GEOL argile gypsifère *f*

gypsum *n* CHEM gypse *m*, pierre à plâtre *f*, MINERAL, PETR, PETR TECH, PROP MAT gypse *m*; ~ **quarry** *n* MINING carrière de pierre à plâtre *f*, plâtrière *f*

gypsum-bearing *adj* GEOL gypsifère

gypsy *n* NAUT *winch* poupée *f*; ~ **winch** *n* PROD ENG treuil d'applique *m*

gyrating: ~ **mass** *n* MECH *flywheel* masse d'inertie *f*

gyrator *n* PHYS *waveguide* gyrateur *m*

gyratory: ~ **crusher** *n* FOOD TECH *food-processing machinery* broyeur giratoire *m*, concasseur giratoire *m*

gyro: ~ **amplifier** *n* AERONAUT amplificateur de gyro *m*; ~ **caging** *n* AERONAUT blocage des gyros *m*, tulipage *m*; ~ **data switching control** *n* AERONAUT boîte de commutation gyro *f*; ~ **horizon** *n* AERONAUT horizon gyroscopique *m*, SPACE *spacecraft*, TRANSP horizon artificiel *m*; ~ **instruments** *n pl* AERONAUT instruments gyroscopiques *m pl*; ~ **laser** *n* SPACE gyrolaser *m*; ~ **resetting** *n* AERONAUT recalage de gyro *m*; ~ **stabilization** *n* TRANSP stabilisation par gyroscope *f*; ~ **unbalance** *n* AERONAUT désaccord gyro *m*

gyrobus *n* TRANSP gyrobus *m*

gyroclinometer *n* SPACE *spacecraft* gyroclinomètre *m*

gyrocompass *n* AERONAUT, NAUT gyrocompas *m*

gyrodyne[1] *adj* AERONAUT *helicopter* combiné

gyrodyne[2] *n* AERONAUT hélicoptère combiné *m*

gyromagnetic: ~ **effects** *n pl* PHYS effets gyromagnétiques *m pl*; ~ **ratio** *n* PHYS rapport gyromagnétique *m*

gyrometer *n* SPACE gyromètre *m*

gyropilot *n* NAUT *compass* gyropilote *m*

gyroplane *n* AERONAUT, TRANSP autogyre *m*

gyroscope *n* MECH, PHYS, SPACE gyroscope *m*

gyroscopic[1] *adj* AERONAUT, MECH, PHYS, SPACE, TRANSP gyroscopique

gyroscopic:[2] ~ **compass** *n* AERONAUT compas gyroscopique *m*, gyrocompas *m*, NAUT compas gyroscopique *m*; ~ **force** *n* FUELLESS effort gyroscopique *m*; ~ **head** *n* CINEMAT tête gyroscopique *f*; ~ **platform** *n* AERONAUT centrale gyroscopique *f*; ~ **sight** *n* MILIT viseur gyroscopique de tir *m*; ~ **torque** *n* AERONAUT couple gyroscopique *m*; ~ **tripod head** *n* CINEMAT plate-forme gyroscopique *f*

gyro-stabilized: ~ **platform** *n* SPACE plate-forme gyroscopique *f*

gyrostabilizer *n* AERONAUT, CINEMAT stabilisateur gyroscopique *m*

gyrostat *n* CHEM, PHYS gyrostat *m*

gyrostatic *adj* CHEM gyrostatique

gyrosyn: ~ **compass** *n* AERONAUT *helicopter* compas gyrosyn *m*; ~ **compass indicator** *n* AERONAUT indicateur gyro compas *m*

gyrotron *n* TELECOM gyrotron *m*

gyttja *n* COAL TECH gyttja *f*

H

h *abbr (hecto-)* METR h *(hecto-)*
H[1] *abbr (henry)* ELEC, ELEC ENG, METR, PHYS H *(henry)*
H[2] *(hydrogen)* CHEM H *(hydrogène)*
Ha *(hahnium)* CHEM Ha *(hahnium)*
Haber: ~ process *n* CHEM procédé de Haber *m*
habit *n* CRYSTALL faciès *m*, METALL habitus *m*; ~ plane *n* CRYSTALL plan d'accolement *m*, METALL plan d'habitus *m*
habitat *n* PETR habitat *m*, localisation *f*
habitation: ~ module *n* SPACE habitacle *m*
hacking: ~ knife *n* CONST *glazing* couteau à démastiquer *m*; ~ stitch *n* TEXTILES point de bâti *m*
hackle[1] *n* (AmE) *(cf hackle mark)* C&G fracture en lancette *f*; ~ mark *n* (BrE) *(cf hackle)* C&G fracture en lancette *f*
hackle[2] *vt* TEXTILES peigner
hackling *n* TEXTILES peignage à la grande peigneuse *m*
hacksaw *n* MECH *tools* scie à métaux *f*, MECH ENG porte-scie à métaux *m*, scie à métaux *f*, *machine* scie à mouvement alternatif *f*; ~ blade *n* MECH ENG lame de scie à métaux *f*; ~ frame *n* MECH ENG porte-scie à métaux *m*, scie à métaux *f*
hade[1] *n* GEOL angle du plan de pendage avec la verticale *m*
hade[2] *vi* GEOL s'incliner par rapport à la verticale
Ha-Dec: ~ mount *n* ASTRON, SPACE monture Angle Horaire-Déclinaison *f*
hadron *n* PART PHYS, PHYS hadron *m*; ~ detection *n* PART PHYS détection de hadrons *f*
hadronic: ~ calorimeter *n* PART PHYS, RAD PHYS calorimètre hadronique *m*
haematein *n* (BrE) CHEM hématéine *f*
haematic *adj* (BrE) CHEM hématique *f*
haematin *n* (BrE) CHEM hématine *f*
haematite *n* (BrE) CHEM, MINERAL, PROP MAT hématite *f*; ~ pig iron *n* (BrE) PROP MAT hématite *f*
haematolite *n* (BrE) MINERAL hématolite *f*
haematoporphyrin *n* (BrE) CHEM hématoporphyrine *f*
haematoxylin *n* (BrE) CHEM hématoxyline *f*
haemoglobin *n* (BrE) CHEM hémoglobine *f*
haemolysin *n* (BrE) CHEM hémolysine *f*
haemolysis *n* (BrE) CHEM hémolyse *f*.
haemolytic *adj* (BrE) CHEM hémolytique
haemopyrrole *n* (BrE) CHEM hémopyrrol *m*
haemosiderin *n* (BrE) CHEM hémosidérine *f*
haemotoxin *n* (BrE) CHEM hémotoxine *f*
hafnium *n* *(Hf)* CHEM hafnium *m* *(Hf)*
Hager: ~ disc *n* (BrE) C&G assiette *f*
hahnium *n* *(Ha)* CHEM hahnium *m* *(Ha)*
Haidinger: ~ fringes *n pl* PHYS franges de Haidinger *f pl*
hail[1] *n* METEO, NAUT, PHYS grêle *f*
hail[2] *vt* NAUT héler
hail[3] *vi* METEO grêler; ~ from a port *vi* NAUT dépendre d'un port
hailing: ~ distance *n* NAUT portée de voix *f*
hailstone *n* METEO, PHYS grêlon *m*
hailstorm *n* METEO orage de grêle *m*
hair *n* TEXTILES *fibre strand* brin *m*; ~ hygrometer *n* LAB

EQUIP *humidity measurement*, PHYS, REFRIG hygromètre à cheveu *m*; ~ light *n* CINEMAT lumière de décrochement *f*; ~ protectors *n pl* SAFETY protecteurs pour cheveux *m pl*; ~ pyrites *n* MINERAL millérite *f*
haircord: ~ carpet *n* TEXTILES tapis haircord *m*
hairiness *n* TEXTILES chardage *m*
hairline *n* PRINT curseur *m*, délié *m*, fente imperceptible *f*, *relief* trait fin *m*; ~ crack *n* MECH *materials* microfissure *f*, NUCLEAR *in concrete surface* tapure *f*; ~ register *n* PRINT repérage très précis *m*; ~ space *n* PRINT espace d'un point *m*
hairpin: ~ cooler *n* C&G épingle à l'eau *f*; ~ spring *n* MECH ENG ressort en épingle *m*; ~ tube *n* MECH ENG tube en épingle à cheveux *m*
hairspring *n* MECH ENG ressort spirale *m*
hairstroke *n* PRINT terminaison *f*
hairy: ~ roving *n* C&G stratifil poilu *m*
halation *n* ELECTRON *cathode tube* halo *m*, PHOTO halo de réflexion *m*
half:[1] ~ astern *adv* NAUT *engine* en arrière demie
half:[2] ~ adder *n* COMP, DP, ELECTRON demi-additionneur *m*; ~ beam *n* NAUT *shipbuilding* barrotin *m*; ~ belt *n* PRODUCTION courroie tordue d'un demi-tour *f*; ~ bridge *n* ELEC ENG demi-pont *m*; ~ bridge arrangement *n* ELEC ENG montage en demi-pont *m*; ~ bridge piece *n* MECH ENG *lathe* demi-pont *m*; ~ bushing *n* MECH ENG demi-bague *f*; ~ clamp *n* MECH ENG demi-collier *m*; ~ cleat *n* MECH ENG demi-peigne *m*; ~ cup *n* MECH ENG demi-cuvette *f*; ~ cycle *n* ELEC ENG alternance *f*, NUCLEAR *atomic physics* demi-vie *f*; ~ elliptic spring *n* MECH ENG demi-pincette *f*, ressort à demi-pincette *m*; ~ flange *n* MECH ENG demi-collerette *f*; ~ gap bed *n* MECH ENG *lathe* banc demi-rompu *m*; ~ integral spin *n* PHYS spin demi-entier *m*; ~ life *n* CHEM demi-vie *f*, GEOL demi-période *f*, période radioactive *f*, période de décomposition *f*, NUCLEAR demi-période de radioactivité *f*, PART PHYS demi-vie *f*, période *f*, période radioactive *f*; ~ line *n* GEOM demi-droite *f*; ~ mask *n* SAFETY demi-masque *m*; ~ plate camera *n* PHOTO chambre de format moyen *f*; ~ pulse *n* ELECTRON demi-amplitude d'impulsion *f*; ~ round edge *n* C&G joint arête abattue et arête arrondie *m*; ~ section *n* PROD ENG *drawing* demi-coupe *f*; ~ sectional beam *n* TEXTILES *for warp knitting* demi-ensouple sectionnelle *f*; ~ set *n* MINING cadre à un seul montant *m*; ~ sheetwork *n* PRINT imposition en demi-feuille *f*; ~ space *n* CONST *stairbuilding* double quartier tournant *m*, palier de repos *m*; ~ subtractor *n* COMP, DP, ELECTRON demi-soustracteur *m*; ~ thickness *n* PHYS couche de demi-atténuation *f*; ~ thrust washer *n* MECH ENG demi-flasque de butée *f*; ~ tide *n* NAUT mi-marée *f*; ~ tide level *n* OCEANOG niveau de mi-marée *m*; ~ timbering *n* CONST demi-boisage *m*; ~ track recording *n* RECORDING enregistrement à demi-piste *m*; ~ track vehicle *n* MILIT véhicule autochenilles *m*; ~ truss *n* CONST *building* demi-ferme *f*; ~ turn stairs *n* CONST escalier à double quartier tournant *m*; ~ twist *n* PROD ENG demi-tordu *m*; ~ union *n* MECH ENG demi-raccord

m; ~ **value layer** *n (HVL)* NUCLEAR, PHYS couche de demi-atténuation *f (CDA)*; ~ **value thickness** *n* PHYS couche de demi-atténuation *f*; ~ **white glass** *n* C&G verre demi-blanc *m*; ~ **word** *n* COMP, DP demi-mot *m*

half-ahead *adj* NAUT *engine* en avant demie

half-binding *n* PRINT demi-toile avec coins *f*, reliure demi-peau *f*

half-bound *adj* PRINT demi-ton, relié demi-teinte, simili, en demi-reliure

half-breadth: ~ **plan** *n* NAUT *shipbuilding* demi-vue du plan des formes *f*, projection horizontale *f*

half-duplex[1] *adj (HDX)* COMP semi-duplex

half-duplex[2] *n* DP semi-duplex *m*; ~ **operation** *n* COMP opération en mode semi-duplex *f*, DP semi-duplex *m*

half-hard *adj* PROP MAT mi-dur

half-mast *adj* NAUT *flag* en berne

half-moon: ~ **ring spanner** *n* MECH ENG *tool* clé polygonale demie-lune *f*

half-power: ~ **beam width** *n* SPACE *communications* largeur de faisceau à demi-puissance *f*; ~ **width** *n* ELECTRON largeur de faisceau à demi-puissance *f*

halfshaft *n* VEHICLES *transmission* arbre d'essieu *m*, arbre de pont *m*

half-size: ~ **drawing** *n* PROD ENG dessin demi-nature *m*, dessin en demi-grandeur naturelle *m*

half-sized: ~ **board** *n* ELECTRON carte demi-longueur *f*

halftone *n* ACOUSTICS demi-ton tempéré *m*, PRINT demi-teinte *f*, demi-ton *m*, simili *f*; ~ **block** *n* PHOTO cliché simili *m*, similigravure *f*; ~ **dot** *n* PRINT point de trame *m*; ~ **exposure** *n* PRINT insolation des demi-teintes *f*; ~ **ink** *n* PRINT encre demi-teinte *f*; ~ **paper** *n* PRINT papier pour demi-teintes *m*; ~ **process** *n* PRINT similigravure *f*; ~ **reproduction** *n* PRINT reproduction des demi-teintes *f*, similigravure *f*; ~ **selection** *n* PRINT sélection des couleurs *f*

half-wave *n* ELEC *alternating current* demi-onde *f*; ~ **dipole** *n* PHYS dipôle demi-onde *m*; ~ **dipole aerial** *n* RAD PHYS antenne de dipôle à demi-onde *f*; ~ **line** *n* PHYS ligne demi-onde *f*; ~ **plate** *n* PHYS lame demi-onde *f*; ~ **rectification** *n* ELEC redressement demi-onde *m*, ELEC ENG redressement d'une alternance *m*, redressement d'une seule alternance *m*, redressement demi-onde *m*; ~ **rectifier** *n* ELEC redresseur demi-onde *m*, ELEC ENG redresseur demi-onde *m*, redresseur à une alternance *m*, PHYS redresseur demi-onde *m*, redresseur à simple alternance *m*, redresseur à une alternance *m*; ~ **transmission line** *n* ELEC *supply* ligne de transmission demi-onde *f*

half-width *n* PHYS demi-largeur *f*, largeur à mi-hauteur *f*, RAD PHYS *spectrometry* demi-largeur *f*; ~ **printing press** *n* PRINT presse demi-laize *f*

halide *n* CHEM halogénure *m*, halogène *m*, sel *m*, PRINT halogénure *m*

halite *n* MINERAL, PROP MAT halite *f*

Hall: ~ **coefficient** *n* PHYS constante de Hall *f*; ~ **effect** *n* ELEC *electromagnetism*, PHYS, RAD PHYS, SPACE effet Hall *m*; ~ **field** *n* PHYS champ de Hall *m*; ~ **generator** *n* AUTO déclencheur à effet Hall *m*; ~ **integrated circuit** *n* AUTO circuit intégré Hall *m*; ~ **ion-thruster** *n* SPACE *spacecraft* moteur ionique à effet Hall *m*; ~ **magnetometer** *n* PHYS magnétomètre de Hall *m*; ~ **mobility** *n* PHYS mobilité Hall *f*; ~ **probe** *n* PHYS, RAD PHYS sonde de Hall *f*; ~ **resistance** *n* PHYS résistance de Hall *f*; ~ **voltage** *n* PHYS tension de Hall *f*

Halley's: ~ **comet** *n* ASTRON comète de Halley *f*

hallmark *n* PROD ENG poinçon *m*, poinçon de garantie *m*

halloysite *n* MINERAL halloysite *f*

halmyrolysis *n* GEOL altération sous-marine *f*, halmyrolyse *f*

halo *n* ASTRON, ELECTRON, PRINT, SPACE halo *m*; ~ **of dispersion** *n* NUCLEAR auréole de dispersion *f*; ~ **orbit** *n* SPACE orbite en halo *f*

halocarbon: ~ **refrigerant** *n* REFRIG frigorigène hydrocarbure halogéné *m*

halogen *n* CHEM, CINEMAT halogène *m*; ~ **lamp** *n* ELEC lampe à halogène *f*

halogenated: ~ **hydrocarbon solvent** *n* PROD ENG solvant aux halogénures d'hydrocarbones *m*

halogenation *n* CHEM halogénation *f*, haloïdation *f*

halogenous *adj* CHEM halogène

halography *n* CHEM halographie *f*

haloid[1] *adj* CHEM haloïde

haloid[2] *n* CHEM halosel *m*, haloïde *m*

halokinesis *n* GEOL, PETR TECH halocinèse *f*

halon *n* SPACE *spacecraft* halon *m*; ~ **fire extinguisher** *n* SAFETY extincteur d'incendie à halon *m*; ~ **foam and powder firefighting installation** *n* SAFETY installation d'extinction à halon à mousse et à poudre *f*

halotechny *n* CHEM halotechnie *f*

halotrichite *n* MINERAL halotrichite *f*

halt[1] *n* COMP arrêt *m*, DP arrêt *m*, halte *f*; ~ **instruction** *n* COMP instruction d'arrêt *f*, DP instruction d'interruption *f*; ~ **sign** *n* CONST stop *m*

halt[2] *vt* COMP, DP arrêter, interrompre, stopper

halved: ~ **belt** *n* PROD ENG courroie croisée *f*, courroie demi-tordue *f*, courroie tordue d'un demi-tour *f*; ~ **joint** *n* CONST *woodwork* assemblage à mi-bois *m*, coupe à mi-bois *f*, entaille à mi-bois *f*, PROD ENG *cast-iron work* assemblage à mi-fonte *m*, *wrought-iron work* assemblage à mi-fer *m*

halving *n* CONST assemblage à mi-bois *m*, coupe à mi-bois *f*, entaille à mi-bois *f*, PROD ENG *cast-iron work* assemblage à mi-fonte *m*, *wrought-iron work* assemblage à mi-fer *m*

halyard *n* AERONAUT, NAUT *running rigging* drisse *f*

Hamilton's: ~ **equations** *n pl* PHYS équations de Hamilton *f pl*

Hamiltonian *adj* PHYS hamiltonien

Hamilton-Jacobi: ~ **equation** *n* PHYS équation de Hamilton-Jacobi *f*

hammer *n* C&G martelage *m*, COAL TECH, MECH *tools* marteau *m*, PROD ENG *power hammer* marteau *m*, marteau-pilon *m*, pilon *m*, *sledge* marteau *m*, masse *f*, massette *f*, têtu *m*; ~ **crusher** *n* COAL TECH broyeur à marteaux *m*; ~ **die** *n* MECH ENG *for forming* outillage de martelage de formage *m*; ~ **drill** *n* CONST marteau perforateur *m*, perforatrice percutante *f*, perforatrice à percussion *f*, MECH ENG *tool* foret marteau *m*, MINING marteau perforateur *m*; ~ **drive screw** *n* MECH ENG boulon à tête en T *m*; ~ **enamel** *n* COLOURS laque martelée *f*; ~ **finish** *n* P&R *paint, property* effet martelé *m*; ~ **grab** *n* CONST *civil engineering* trépan-benne *m*; ~ **head** *n* PROD ENG *of power hammer* mouton *m*, pilon *m*; ~ **head screw** *n* MECH ENG vis à tête rectangulaire *f*; ~ **mill** *n* FOOD TECH broyeur à marteaux *m*; ~ **pick** *n* PROD ENG pic à tête *m*, pioche à bec pointu et marteau *f*; ~ **plug** *n* CONST *building* cheville clou *f*; ~ **riveting** *n* PROD ENG rivetage au marteau *m*; ~ **scale** *n* PROD ENG battitures *f pl*, martelures *f pl*, paille de fer *f*, scories de forge *f pl*, écailles *f pl*; ~ **slag** *n* PROD ENG battitures *f pl*, martelures *f pl*, paille de fer *f*, scories de forge *f pl*, écailles *f pl*; ~ **tone finish** *n* COLOURS laque martelée *f*

hammered: ~ **glass** n C&G verre martelé m
hammer-hardened adj SPRINGS écroui
hammering n CONST martelage m, NUCLEAR of piping fouettement m, PROD ENG battage m, martelage m, martèlement m, REFRIG in piping coup de bélier m
Hamming: ~ **code** n SPACE communications code de Hamming m; ~ **distance** n TELECOM land mobile distance de Hamming f
hand:[1] **by ~** adv PROD ENG manuellement, à force de bras, à la main; **by ~ power** adv PROD ENG manuellement, à force de bras, à la main
hand[2] n LAB EQUIP pointer aiguille f, SPRINGS sens d'enroulement m; ~ **assembled work** n PACKAGING travail d'assemblage manuel m; ~ **automatic switch** n NUCLEAR commutation manuelle automatique f; ~ **baggage** n AERONAUT bagages à main m pl; ~ **bagging** n PACKAGING mise en sac manuelle f; ~ **baking** n FOOD TECH confection artisanale f; ~ **barrow** n CONST brouette f; ~ **basher** n CINEMAT lampe 800 watts sur batterie f; ~ **bellows** n pl C&G piston robinet m; ~ **binding** n PRINT reliure à la main f; ~ **block printing** n TEXTILES impression manuelle au pochoir f; ~ **brace** n MECH ENG chignole f; ~ **centrifuge** n LAB EQUIP centrifugeur à main m; ~ **chain** n CONST chaîne à main f, PROD ENG of pulley block, hoist chaîne de manoeuvre f; ~ **composition** n PRINT composition à la main f; ~ **control** n CONTROL, ELECTR commande à la main f; ~ **cranked camera** n CINEMAT caméra à manivelle f; ~ **dog** n MINING boring tringle de suspension f; ~ **dosing** n PACKAGING dosage manuel m; ~ **downfeed** n MECH ENG machine tools descente manuelle f; ~ **drill** n MECH tools perceuse à main f; ~ **drive** n CINEMAT entraînement à main m; ~ **expansion valve** n REFRIG détendeur manuel m, soupape de détente manuelle f; ~ **feed** n MECH ENG machine tools avance manuelle f, PACKAGING alimentation manuelle f; ~ **file** n PROD ENG lime plate à main f; ~ **finishing stick** n MECH ENG abrasives bâton d'affûtage à la main m; ~ **flare** n NAUT signal feu à main m; ~ **flywheel pump** n PROD ENG pompe à volant f; ~ **glass** n INSTRUMENT miroir à main m; ~ **grenade** n MILIT grenade à main f; ~ **hammer** n PROD ENG marteau à main m; ~ **hold** n SAFETY prise de main f; ~ **hole** n PROD ENG boiler regard de lavage m, trou de bras m, trou de sel m, trou à main m; ~ **labeler** n (AmE), ~ **labeller** n (BrE) PACKAGING étiqueteuse manuelle f; ~ **lay-up** n C&G moulage au contact m, P&R laminates moulage au contact m, moulage à la main m; ~ **lever** n MECH ENG levier à main m; ~ **lever feed** n MECH ENG pression à la main par levier f; ~ **lift net** n OCEANOG balance f, haveneau m; ~ **mike** n RECORDING micro main m; ~ **mirror** n INSTRUMENT miroir à main m; ~ **nut** n PROD ENG papillon m, écrou papillon m, écrou à oreilles m; ~ **off** n TELECOM transfert m; ~ **packing** n PACKAGING emballage manuel m; ~ **press** n PRINT presse à bras f; ~ **printing** n PRINT impression manuelle f; ~ **pump** n PROD ENG pompe à bras f, pompe à main f, SAFETY firefighting pompe à main f; ~ **railing** n CONST garde-corps m, garde-fou m, lisse f, main courante f, NUCLEAR main courante f; ~ **rammer** n PROD ENG moulding fouloir à main m; ~ **rope** n PROD ENG of pulley block, hoist corde de manoeuvre f; ~ **sampling** n COAL TECH échantillonnage manuel m; ~ **screening** n COAL TECH tamisage à main m; ~ **screen printing** n TEXTILES impression au cadre manuel f; ~ **shears** n pl PROD ENG for metal cisailles à main f pl, hachard m; ~ **shield** n SAFETY écran de protection des

mains m; ~ **signal** n CONTROL signal de main m; ~ **signaling** n (AmE), ~ **signalling** n (BrE) CONTROL pilotage manuel m, signalisation manuelle f; ~ **signals** n pl SAFETY mechanical lifting signaux manuels m pl; ~ **stamp** n PROD ENG metalworking étampeuse à main f; ~ **sucker** n C&G poignée à ventouses f; ~ **tachometer** n PACKAGING compteur de tours manuel m; ~ **tap** n PROD ENG screw cutting taraud à main m; ~ **throttle control** n AUTO commande manuelle des gaz f; ~ **tool** n MECH, PROD ENG lathe outil à main m; ~ **tools** n pl PROD ENG outillage à main m, petit outillage m; ~ **truck** n PROD ENG diable m, diable brouette m; ~ **vice** n (BrE) MECH tools étau à main m, MECH ENG détret m, tenaille à vis f, étau à main m, étau à vis m; ~ **vise** n (AmE) see hand vice ~ **washing** n PROD ENG lavage à la main m; ~ **wheel** n MECH volant de manoeuvre m, MECH ENG for driving volant pour commande à bras m, without handle volant m, volant à main m, with handle volant à manivelle m, volant à poignée m; ~ **winch** n PROD ENG treuil à bras m, treuil à manivelle m; ~ **wire pull** n NUCLEAR tirette à main f; ~ **working** n PROD ENG travail manuel m, travail à la main m
hand-blown: ~ **glass** n C&G verre soufflé bouche m
handbook n MECH ENG, PROD ENG aide-mémoire m, manuel m
handbrake n MECH ENG frein à main m, VEHICLES frein de stationnement m, frein à main m; ~ **cable** n AUTO car câble de frein à main m; ~ **lever** n AUTO levier de frein à main m
handed: ~ **assembly** n MECH ENG ensemble symétrique m
hand-fed adj PRINT alimenté à la main
handgrip n CINEMAT poignée f, MECH ENG corps de poignée m, PHOTO poignée f; ~ **with shutter release** n CINEMAT poignée à déclencheur f
hand-guided: ~ **machine** n SAFETY machine guidée à la main f
hand-held[1] adj SAFETY machine actionné à la main
hand-held:[2] ~ **camera** n CINEMAT caméra de reportage f, caméra à l'épaule f; ~ **electric tool** n SAFETY outil électrique à main m; ~ **machine** n SAFETY machine tenue à main f; ~ **mobile radio** n CONST radio portable f; ~ **portable power tool** n MECH ENG outil à moteur portatif m; ~ **programmer** n PROD ENG terminal de programmation portatif m; ~ **receiver** n TELECOM récepteur portatif m; ~ **terminal** n TELECOM terminal de poche m
handle[1] n CONST of drawer boucle f, MECH tools manche m, manette f, poignée f, MECH ENG manivelle f, of electrical switch or steam throttle manette f, of hand crank maneton m, of pincers, nippers, tongs branche f, MINING, PACKAGING poignée f, PROD ENG manche m, poignée f, of basket or pail anse f, SPACE spacecraft manette f, poignée f, TEXTILES toucher m, VEHICLES manette f; ~ **lever** n MECH ENG levier à poignée m; ~ **plate** n MECH ENG cuvette de poignée f; ~ **switch** n MECH ENG commutateur à manette m, commutateur à manivelle m; ~ **welding machine** n PROD ENG machine à souder les anses f
handle[2] vt MECH manier, manipuler, NAUT sails gouverner, manoeuvrer, PROD ENG emmancher, manipulate manier, manipuler, manutentionner, tool manier, TEXTILES manipuler
handling n MECH ENG manoeuvre f, manutention f, PACKAGING of goods, of returnables manutention f, PAPER TECH manutention f, PROD ENG manipulation maniement m, manipulation f, manutention f, provi-

ding with handle emmanchement *m*, SAFETY *of dangerous materials* manipulation *f*, manutention *f*, SPACE *spacecraft* conduite *f*, maniement *m*, TELECOM traitement *m*, TEXTILES manipulation *f*; ~ **and filling equipment** *n* PACKAGING équipement de manutention et de remplissage *m*; ~ **and installing instructions** *n pl* PACKAGING conseils de montage *m pl*, prescriptions d'utilisation *f pl*; ~ **characteristics** *n pl* SPACE *spacecraft* caractéristiques de pilotage *f pl*; ~ **equipment** *n* PACKAGING équipement de manutention *m*; ~ **lugs** *n pl* (AmE) *(cf lifting lugs)* MECH ENG joue de manutention *f*; ~ **time** *n* TEXTILES temps de manipulation *m*

handmade: ~ **paper** *n* PRINT *papermaking* papier à la cuve *m*

hand-mixed: ~ **concrete** *n* CONST béton malaxé à la main *m*

hand-operated[1] *adj* MECH, SPACE à commande manuelle

hand-operated:[2] ~ **machine** *n* PACKAGING machine fonctionnant manuellement *f*; ~ **power shovel** *n* MECH ENG pelle semi-automatique *f*; ~ **pull** *n* NUCLEAR tirette à main *f*; ~ **switch** *n* ELEC interrupteur manuel *m*, interrupteur à main *m*

handover *n* NUCLEAR *of power plant* remise *f*

hand-pick *vt* COAL TECH scheider

handpower: ~ **hacksaw** *n* PROD ENG scie alternative à main *f*; ~ **warehouse goods lift** *n* PROD ENG monte-charge à bras pour magasin *m*

handpunch *n* COMP, DP perforateur manuel *m*, PROD ENG poinçon à main *m*

handrail *n* CONST garde-corps *m*, garde-fou *m*, lisse *f*, main courante *f*, rampe *f*, MECH garde-corps *m*, main courante *f*, rambarde *f*, NAUT, TRANSP main courante *f*

handrest *n* INSTRUMENT support d'appui *m*; MECH ENG *lathe* support à main *m*, support à éventail *m*, ~ **socket** *n* MECH ENG *lathe* semelle de support à main *f*

handsaw *n* CONST scie égoïne *f*, égoïne *f*, scie à main *f*

handscrew *n* MECH ENG *jackscrew* vérin *m*, vérin à vis *m*

handset *n* PROD ENG, TELECOM combiné *m*; ~ **cord** *n* TELECOM cordon *m*

hands-free *adj* TELECOM mains libres

handshake *n* COMP, DP établissement de connexion *m*, établissement de liaison *m*

handshaking *n* COMP affirmation de connexion *f*, échange de données avec protocole *m*, établissement de communication *m*, établissement de liaison *m*, DP échange de données avec protocole *m*, établissement de communication *m*, établissement de liaison *m*

handsheet *n* PAPER TECH formette *f*; ~ **machine** *n* PRINT formette *f*

hands-off: ~ **operation** *n* COMP, DP opération non assistée *f*

hands-on: ~ **introduction** *n* PROD ENG introduction pratique *f*; ~ **operation** *n* COMP, DP opération assistée *f*

handspike *n* MECH *tools* pince-levier *f*, MECH ENG anspect *m*, levier *m*

hand-transmitted: ~ **vibration** *n* SAFETY vibration transmise par les mains *f*; ~ **vibration hazard** *n* SAFETY *electric drills* risque dû aux vibrations transmises à la main *m*

handwork *n* PRINT travail à la main *m*, PROD ENG travail manuel *m*, travail à la main *m*

handy[1] *adj* MECH *tools* bien en main, pratique

handy:[2] ~ **billy** *n* NAUT *tackle* palan mousse *m*

hang[1] *n* PROD ENG *blast furnace* accrochage *m*; ~ **ratio** *n* OCEANOG coefficient d'armement *m*

hang[2] *vt* OCEANOG *net* armer, PROD ENG pendre, suspendre; ~ **up** *vt* PROD ENG pendre, suspendre

hang[3] *vi* PROD ENG *blast furnace* s'accrocher; ~ **up** *vi* TELECOM raccrocher

hangar *n* AERONAUT hangar *m*

hanger *n* CONST sabot *m*, MECH ENG *shaft* chaise *f*, PROD ENG crochet de suspension *m*; ~ **pipe** *n* MECH support de tuyauterie *m*; ~ **with bearings** *n* MECH ENG chaise palier *f*

hanging *n* OCEANOG *of net* armement *m*, PROD ENG *action* suspension *f*; ~ **bucket** *n* PROD ENG benne suspendue *f*; ~ **indent** *n* PRINT ligne en sommaire *f*; ~ **lamp** *n* ELEC ENG lampe à suspension *f*; ~ **post** *n* CONST *of door or gate* chardonnet *m*, poteau tourillon *m*; ~ **ratio** *n* OCEANOG coefficient d'armement *m*; ~ **rod** *n* MINING tringle de suspension *f*; ~ **scaffold** *n* CONST *building* échafaud volant *m*, échafaudage volant *m*; ~ **stage** *n* CONST *building* échafaud volant *m*, échafaudage volant *m*; ~ **stairs** *n pl* CONST *building* escalier en encorbellement *m*, escalier suspendu *m*; ~ **steps** *n pl* CONST *building* escalier en encorbellement *m*, escalier suspendu *m*; ~ **thread** *n* TEXTILES fil non coupé *m*; ~ **tool** *n* PROD ENG *metal turning* crochet *m*, outil à crochet *m*; ~ **up** *n* PROD ENG suspension *f*; ~ **wall** *n* GEOL lèvre supérieure d'une faille *f*, toit d'une couche *m*

hangover *n* NUCLEAR retard *m*; ~ **time** *n* SPACE *communications*, TELECOM temps de maintien *m*

hangtag *n* PACKAGING étiquette volante *f*

hang-up *n* COMP, DP arrêt imprévu *m*, PROD ENG arrêt machine *m*, arrêt système *m*

hank *n* NAUT *rope* andaillot *m*, TEXTILES écheveau *m*

Hanle: ~ **effect** *n* RAD PHYS effet Hanle *m*

haplite *n* PETR aplite *f*

harbor *n* (AmE), **harbour** *n* (BrE) NAUT port *m* ~ **dues** *n pl* NAUT droits de port *m pl*; ~ **ferry** *n* TRANSP bac *m*; ~ **master** *n* NAUT capitaine de port *m*; ~ **master's office** *n* NAUT capitainerie *f*; ~ **station** *n* NAUT *trade* gare maritime *f*

hard[1] *adj* CINEMAT contrasté, dur, PROP MAT dur; ~ **drawn** *adj* SPRINGS *of steel* tréfilé dur; ~ **faced** *adj* MECH ENG rechargé en dur; ~ **on the helm** *adj* NAUT *ship* ardent; ~ **sized** *adj* PRINT très collé

hard:[2] ~ **bromide paper** *n* PHOTO papier au bromure donnant dur *m*; ~ **chrome finish** *n* MECH ENG finition chromée dure *f*; ~ **chrome plating** *n* COATINGS revêtement en chrome dur *m*, MECH ENG *for tools, gauges* recouvrement de chrome dur *m*; ~ **coal** *n* COAL TECH anthracite *m*, charbon anthraciteux *m*; ~ **contact** *n* ELEC, PROD ENG contact sec *m*; ~ **copy** *n* COMP copie papier *f*, imprimé *m*, DP copie imprimée *f*, copie papier *f*, tirage *m*, épreuve *f*, PRINT sortie sur imprimante *f*, épreuve *f*, SPACE *technology* épreuve *f*; ~ **decision decoding** *n* TELECOM décodage à décision dure *m*; ~ **disc** *n* (BrE) TELECOM disque dur *m*; ~ **disk** *n* (AmE) *see hard disc* ~ **drawn wire** *n* SPRINGS fil tréfilé dur *m*; ~ **error** *n* COMP, DP erreur matérielle *f*; ~ **fired gate drive** *n* PROD ENG système d'amplification d'impulsions *m*; ~ **formation bit** *n* PETR TECH trépan pour formations dures *m*; ~ **glass** *n* C&G verre dur *m*; ~ **grade** *n* PROD ENG *emery wheels* degré de dureté dur *m*; ~ **ground** *n* GEOL fond marin durci *m*; ~ **handle** *n* TEXTILES toucher dur *m*; ~ **landing** *n* AERONAUT atterrissage brutal *m*, atterrissage dur *m*, SPACE amarrage dur *m*, atterrissage dur *m*; ~ **limited signal** *n* ELECTRON signal écrêté à niveau constant *m*; ~ **limiter** *n* ELECTRON écrêteur à niveau constant *m*; ~ **limiting** *n* ELECTRON limitation d'amplitude à niveau constant *f*; ~ **magnetic material** *n* MECH, PHYS matériau magnétique dur *m*; ~ **metal burr** *n* MECH ENG fraise-lime en métal dur *f*; ~ **plating** *n* COATINGS revêtement en chrome dur *m*; ~ **porcelain** *n* C&G porcelaine dure *f*; ~ **processing channel carbon black** *n* P&R *rubber pigment, filler* noir HPC *m*; ~ **pulse** *n* ELECTRON impulsion pointue *f*; ~ **radiation** *n* RAD PHYS rayonnement dur *m*; ~ **sectoring** *n* COMP, DP sectorisation matérielle *f*; ~ **shoulder** *n* CONST accotement stabilisé *m*; ~ **soldering** *n* PROD ENG *brazing* brasage fort *m*, brasure *f*, SPACE brasage fort *m*; ~ **sphere model** *n* CRYSTALL modèle de sphères dures *m*; ~ **tube** *n* ELECTRON tube à vide poussé *m*; ~ **vacuum** *n* ELECTRON vide poussé *m*; ~ **water** *n* WATER SUPP eau dure *f*; ~ **water filter** *n* WATER SUPP filtre anticalcaire *m*; ~ **wheel** *n* PROD ENG meule dure *f*; ~ **X-ray** *n* PHYS, RAD PHYS rayon X dur *m*

hardboard *n* CONST, PACKAGING panneau dur *m*

hard-bound *adj* PRINT relié en dur

hardcore *n* CONST blocage *m*, tessou de briques *m*

hard-edged: ~ **matte** *n* CINEMAT cache à bords francs *m*

harden[1] *vt* PROD ENG durcir, endurcir

harden[2] *vi* PROP MAT s'endurcir

hardenability *n* CRYSTALL trempabilité *f*, METALL durcibilité *f*, SPRINGS trempabilité *f*

hardened: ~ **dowel pin** *n* MECH ENG goupille cylindrique trempée *f*; ~ **oil** *n* PROD ENG huile hydrogénée *f*; ~ **stainless steel** *n* PROD ENG acier inoxydable trempé *m*

hardener *n* CINEMAT bain tannant *m*, P&R *compounding ingredient* durcisseur *m*, PHOTO tannant *m*

hardening *n* COAL TECH, CONST *of concrete*, METALL durcissement *m*, P&R *coatings* cuisson *f*, durcissement *m*, vulcanisation *f*, PROP MAT endurcissement *m*, trempe *f*, REFRIG *of ice cream*, SPACE durcissement *m*; ~ **bath** *n* PRINT bain de durcissement *m*; ~ **on the glazing** *n* C&G cuisson en couverte *f*

hard-face *vt* MECH ENG surfacer dur

hardfacing *n* CONST *welding* couche antiusure *f*, MECH *materials* chargement en métal dur *m*, NUCLEAR rechargement dur *m*, soudage dur *m*

hardness *n* CHEM *of water, substance* dureté *f*, CONST dureté de l'eau *f*, CRYSTALL, MECH *materials*, METALL, P&R, PAPER TECH dureté *f*; ~ **reference standards** *n pl* MECH ENG blocs de référence de duretés *m pl*; ~ **scale** *n* MECH *materials* échelle de dureté *f*; ~ **test** *n* MECH *materials*, PHYS essai de dureté *m*; ~ **tester** *n* LAB EQUIP *instrument*, MECH ENG duromètre *m*, METR appareil pour mesures de dureté *m*, P&R *instrument*, PAPER TECH duromètre *m*; ~ **testing** *n* PROP MAT essai de dureté *m*

hard-over: ~ **signal** *n* ELECTRON signal d'amplitude excessive *m*

hardpan *n* GEOL horizon pédologique induré *m*

hard-sectored *adj* COMP sectorisé matériellement, *disk* à secteurs fixes, DP *disk* à sectorisation matérielle

hardware *n* COMP, DP matériel *m*, MECH quincaillerie *f*, PETR hardware *m*, TELECOM matériel *m*; ~ **acceptance test** *n* CONTROL contrôle du matériel *m*; ~ **check** *n* COMP vérification matérielle *f*, DP vérification de matériel *f*; ~ **configuration** *n* COMP, DP configuration matérielle *f*; ~ **handshaking** *n* PROD ENG échange d'amplification d'impulsions *m*; ~ **maintenance** *n* COMP, DP maintenance de matériel *f*; ~ **reliability** *n* COMP, DP fiabilité du matériel *f*; ~ **resources** *n pl* COMP, DP ressources matérielles *f pl*; ~ **review** *n* PROD ENG rappel sur le matériel *m*; ~ **stack** *n* COMP, DP pile câblée

f; ~ **upgrade** *n* COMP amélioration matérielle *f*, DP extension matérielle *f*, évolution matérielle *f*

hardwire *vt* PROD ENG câbler

hard-wired: ~ **programable switching system** *n* (AmE), ~ **programmable switching system** *n* (BrE) TELECOM système à programme câblé *m*

hardwired[1] *adj* COMP, DP, ELEC ENG câblé

hardwired:[2] ~ **logic** *n* COMP, DP logique câblée *f*

hardwood *n* CONST bois dur *m*, PAPER TECH bois de feuillu *m*; ~ **pulp** *n* PAPER TECH pâte de feuillus *f*

harmaline *n* CHEM harmaline *f*

H-armature *n* ELEC *machine* induit en I *m*, induit en double T *m*

harmful[1] *adj* PETR TECH *substance* nocif, SAFETY nocif, nuisible

harmful:[2] ~ **effect** *n* POLLUTION effet nocif *m*, effet nuisible *m*; ~ **substance** *n* SAFETY substance nocive *f*

harmfulness *n* POLLUTION nocivité *f*

harmine *n* CHEM harmine *f*

harmonic[1] *adj* GEOM harmonique

harmonic[2] *n* ACOUSTICS harmonique *m*, ELECTRON fréquence harmonique *f*, harmonique *m*, signal harmonique *m*, MECH, PHYS *vibrations*, WAVE PHYS harmonique *m*; ~ **analysis** *n* ELECTRON, MECH, PHYS, TELECOM analyse harmonique *f*; ~ **analyzer** *n* ELECTRON analyseur harmonique *m*, PHYS analyseur d'harmoniques *m*; ~ **attenuation** *n* ELECTRON atténuation d'une harmonique *f*; ~ **component** *n* OCEANOG *of tides* onde de marée *f*; ~ **content** *n* ELECTRON contenu en harmoniques *m*; ~ **distortion** *n* ELECTRON, PROP MAT, TELECOM distorsion harmonique *f*; ~ **filter** *n* ELECTRON, SPACE *communications* filtre d'harmonique *m*; ~ **function** *n* ELECTRON fonction harmonique *f*; ~ **generation** *n* ELECTRON génération d'harmoniques *f*; ~ **generator** *n* ELECTRON, PHYS, TELECOM générateur d'harmoniques *m*; ~ **generator varactor** *n* ELECTRON diode varicap pour génération d'harmoniques *f*; ~ **mean** *n* MATH moyenne harmonique *f*; ~ **minor scale** *n* ACOUSTICS gamme mineure dite harmonique *f*; ~ **mixer** *n* ELECTRON mélangeur harmonique *m*; ~ **mode** *n* ELECTRON mode partiel *m*; ~ **order** *n* ELECTRON rang d'un harmonique *m*; ~ **oscillation** *n* PHYS oscillation harmonique *f*; ~ **oscillator** *n* ELECTRON, PHYS oscillateur harmonique *m*; ~ **point** *n* GEOM point harmonique *m*; ~ **ratio** *n* GEOM ratio harmonique *m*; ~ **rejection** *n* ELECTRON atténuation des harmoniques *f*, réjection des harmoniques *f*; ~ **response characteristic** *n* WAVE PHYS caractéristique de réponse harmonique *f*; ~ **series** *n* ACOUSTICS série harmonique *f*; ~ **suppressor** *n* RAD PHYS filtre d'harmonique *m*; ~ **tidal constituent** *n* OCEANOG composante de la marée *f*; ~ **waves** *n pl* WAVE PHYS ondes harmoniques *f pl*

harmonics *n* PROD ENG, WAVE PHYS harmonique *m*

harmony *n* ACOUSTICS harmonie *f*

harmotome *n* MINERAL harmotome *m*

harness *n* MILIT *of parachute* harnais *m*, SPACE *spacecraft* harnais *m*, toron *m*; ~ **cable** *n* ELEC harnais de câbles *m*, MECH *electricity* faisceau de câbles *m*, harnais de câbles *m*

harnessing *n* WATER SUPP *waterfall* aménagement *m*

harper: ~ **machine** *n* PAPER TECH machine à papier à table inversée *f*

harpoon *n* OCEANOG flèche *f*, harpon *m*; ~ **gun** *n* OCEANOG canon lance-harpon *m*

harsh: ~ **handle** *n* TEXTILES toucher rêche *m*

hartine *n* MINERAL hartine *f*

hartite *n* MINERAL hartite *f*

Hartley: ~ **oscillator** *n* ELECTRON oscillateur Hartley *m*

harvest: ~ **moon** *n* ASTRON lune de la moisson *f*, lune de septembre *f*, pleine lune d'automne *f*

HASAWA *abbr* (BrE) *(Health and Safety at Work Act)* SAFETY avis d'interdiction *m*

hash *n* COMP, DP hash *m*, tracé parasite sur un écran cathodique *m*; ~ **function** *n* COMP, DP fonction hash *f*; ~ **table** *n* COMP, DP table de hash-code *f*, table de calcul d'adresses *f*

hashing *n* COMP, DP adressage calculé *m*, hachage *m*

hasp *n* CONST *locksmithing* moraillon *m*

hat: ~ **roller** *n* MINING *wagons* poulie-support *f*

hatch *n* AERONAUT trappe *f*, NAUT capot *m*, descente *f*, écoutille *f*, SPACE *of spacecraft* trappe *f*, écoutille *f*; ~ **coaming** *n* NAUT hiloire d'écoutille *f*; ~ **cover** *n* NAUT *of ship* panneau d'écoutille *m*, panneau de descente *m*

hatchback *n* TRANSP hayon *m*; ~ **automobile** *n* VEHICLES voiture à deux volumes *f*, voiture à hayon arrière *f*; ~ **car** *n* TRANSP voiture à cinq portes *f*, voiture à trois portes *f*, VEHICLES voiture à deux volumes *f*, voiture à hayon arrière *f*

hatchet *n* PROD ENG hache à main *f*, hachette *f*

hatchetine *n* MINERAL hatchettine *f*

hatchettite *n* MINERAL hatchettine *f*

hatching *n* MECH ENG hachure *f*

hatchite *n* NUCLEAR hatchite *f*

hatchway *n* NAUT descente *f*, écoutille *f*

hauerite *n* MINERAL hauérite *f*

haul[1] *n* NAUT prise *f*, pêche *f*, OCEANOG prise *f*

haul:[2] ~ **alongside** *vt* NAUT accoster; ~ **down** *vt* NAUT *flag, sail* affaler; ~ **in** *vt* NAUT *rope* border, embraquer, haler à bord; ~ **on board** *vt* OCEANOG haler à bord; ~ **taut** *vt* NAUT *rope* embraquer, raidir; ~ **up** *vt* NAUT *boat* haler à sec, rentrer

haul[3] *vi* NAUT *rope, boat, net* haler

haulage: ~ **cable** *n* TRANSP câble tracteur *m*; ~ **contractor** *n* TRANSP entreprise de transport *f*; ~ **road** *n* COAL TECH, MINING voie de transport *f*; ~ **way** *n* MINING galerie de roulage *f*, voie de roulage *f*

haulier *n* TRANSP *roads* entreprise de transport *f*

hauling: ~ **and winding engine** *n* MINING moteur de roulage et d'extraction *m*

haunch *n* CONST renfort carré *m*, *bevelled* renfort en chaperon *m*, *carpentry* renfort *m*, *of arch* rein *m*

haunched: ~ **mortise-and-tenon joint** *n* CONST assemblage à tenon avec renfort carré *m*

hausmannite *n* MINERAL hausmannite *f*

Hauterivian *adj* GEOPHYS Hauterivien

hauyne *n* MINERAL haüyne *f*

hauynite *n* MINERAL haüyne *f*

Hawaiian-type: ~ **volcano** *n* GEOL bouclier de lave *m*, volcan de type hawaïen *m*

hawk *n* CONST *plastering* taloche *f*

hawse *n* NAUT écubier *m*; ~ **pipe** *n* NAUT *shipbuilding* manchon d'écubier *m*, écubier *m*

hawser *n* MECH ENG aussière *f*, haussière *f*, NAUT aussière *f*, haussière *f*

hay: ~ **band** *n* PROD ENG *founding* corde en foin *f*, torche de foin *f*; ~ **rope** *n* PROD ENG *founding* corde en foin *f*, torche de foin *f*

hayesine *n* MINERAL hayésine *f*

hazard *n* AERONAUT risque *m*, QUALITY danger *m*, phénomène dangereux *m*, risque *m*, SAFETY danger *m*, péril *m*, risque *m*; ~ **analysis** *n* QUALITY analyse des phénomènes dangereux *f*, analyse du risque *f*; ~ **bea-**

con *n* AERONAUT phare de danger *m*; ~ **prevention** *n* SAFETY *buildings* prévention des risques *f*; ~ **warning lights** *n pl* VEHICLES témoin de signalisation de détresse *m*; ~ **warning system** *n* AUTO feux de détresse *m*, signal de détresse *m*

hazardous: ~ **substance** *n* SAFETY substance dangereuse *f*; ~ **zone** *n* SAFETY zone dangereuse *f*, zone à risque *f*

haze *n* METEO brume *f*, P&R voile *m*, POLLUTION brume *f*; ~ **filter** *n* CINEMAT filtre antibrouillard *m*

hazy *adj* METEO brumeux, épais, TEXTILES *outline* flou

h-bar *n* PHYS *Planck constant* constante réduite de Planck *f*

H-bar *n* CONST fer double T *m*, fer en H *m*, fer à I *m*, fer à double T *m*

H-beam *n* CONST poutre en double T *f*, poutrelle *f*, solive en fer à double T *f*

H-bomb *n* NUCLEAR bombe à hydrogène *f*

HC *abbr* *(high-cube container)* TRANSP HC *(conteneur hors-cotes)*

H-cell *n* ELEC ENG cellule en H *f*

HCF *abbr* *(highest common factor)* MATH PGCD *(plus grand commun diviseur)*

hcp *abbr* *(hexagonal close-packed structure)* CRYSTALL structure hexagonale compacte *f*

HCP: ~ **lattice** *n* NUCLEAR réseau hexagonal compact *m*

HD *abbr* *(heavy-duty oil)* PETR TECH huile à haute tenue *f*

HDB2 *abbr* *(high-density bipolar of order 2 code)* TELECOM code bipolaire à haute densité d'ordre 2 *m*

HDLC *abbr* *(high-level data link control)* COMP, DP, TELECOM commande de liaison de données à haut niveau *m*, procédure HDLC *f*

HDPE *abbr* *(high-density polyethylene)* PACKAGING polyéthylène à haute densité *m*

HDTV *abbr* *(high-definition television)* TELECOM, TV TVHD *(télévision à haute définition)*

HDW: ~ **barge carrier** *n* TRANSP navire porte-chalands HDW *m*

HDX *abbr* *(half-duplex)* COMP semi-duplex

He *(helium)* CHEM He *(hélium)*

HE11: ~ **mode** *n* *(fundamental mode)* OPT mode fondamental *m*

head[1] *n* CINEMAT *of roll of film* début *m*, *of tripod* tête *f*, COMP tête *f*, CONST collecteur *m*, cuvette *f*, hotte *f*, *of pile* tête *f*, *of slate* chef de tête *m*, DP tête *f*, HYDR EQUIP chute *f*, hauteur d'eau *f*, hauteur de chute *f*, hauteur de pompage *f*, LAB EQUIP *of still* chapiteau *m*, MECH ENG tête *f*, *of cylinder* fond *m*, plateau *m*, *of lathe* poupée *f*, poupée fixe *f*, *of piston* corps *m*, *of planing machine* porte-outil *m*, *of wedge, key* tête *f*, MINING avancement *m*, avancée *f*, galerie d'avancement *f*, *of quarry* carreau *m*, NAUT toilette *f*, *of sail* point de drisse *m*, têtière *f*, PETR TECH *of fluid* hauteur manométrique *f*, PRINT blanc de papier *m*, têtière *f*, titre *m*, PROD ENG *dead head* masselotte *f*, *of hammer* corps *m*, tête *f*, *of power hammer* mouton *m*, pilon *m*, *of rivet* rivure *f*, tête *f*, *of stamp* surcharge *f*, tête *f*, *of screw, bolt, nail* tête *f*; ~ **adjustment** *n* TV réglage des têtes *m*, équilibrage de l'entrefer *m*; ~ **alignment** *n* RECORDING, TV alignement des têtes *m*; ~ **amplifier** *n* SPACE *communications* préamplificateur *m*; ~ **assembly** *n* RECORDING bloc de têtes *m*, TV bloc de têtes *m*, porte-têtes *m*; ~ **banding** *n* TV effet de bande *m*; ~ **beam** *n* CONST semelle *f*, solive de tête *f*, traverse *f*; ~ **box** *n* PAPER TECH caisse d'arrivée de pâte *f*, WATER SUPP *sluices* boîte de tête *f*; ~ **cap** *n* PRINT coiffe *f*; ~ **cap**

screw *n* MECH ENG vis à tête cylindrique *f*; ~ **channel** *n* TV voie d'une tête *f*; ~ **clogging** *n* TV colmatage d'une tête *m*; ~ **crash** *n* COMP, DP écrasement de tête *m*; ~ **crown** *n* WATER SUPP bief d'amont *m*, biez d'amont *m*; ~ **driver** *n* RAIL chef de traction *m*; ~ **drum** *n* TV tambour de têtes *m*, tambour à têtes magnétiques *m*; ~ **end process** *n* NUCLEAR *stuffing box* traitement initial *m*; ~ **feed** *n* MECH ENG *machine tools* avance de la tête *f*; ~ **frame** *n* MINING belle-fleur *f*, chevalement *m*, chevalet d'extraction *m*, châssis àmolettes *m*, cadre de superficie *m*, tour d'extraction *f*; ~ **gap** *n* COMP, DP entrefer de tête *m*, TV entrefer *m*; ~ **gasket** *n* VEHICLES joint de culasse *m*; ~ **gate** *n* FUELLESS *of dam* porte d'amont *f*, WATER SUPP *before water wheel* vanne de travail *f*, vanne lançoire *f*, vanne motrice *f*, *of canal lock* porte d'amont *f*; ~ **house** *n* MINING chevalement-abri *m*; ~ **leader** *n* CINEMAT amorce départ *f*, amorce opérateur *f*; ~ **life** *n* TV longévité de la tête magnétique *f*; ~ **limit** *n* HYDR EQUIP hauteur d'eau limite *f*; ~ **line** *n* TEXTILES ligne d'ouverture du filet *f*; ~ **lining** *n* VEHICLES *interior* garnissage de pavillon *m*; ~ **margin** *n* PRINT marge de tête *f*; ~ **metal** *n* PROD ENG *founding* masselotte *f*; ~ **misalignment loss** *n* RECORDING perte par désalignement de la tête *f*; ~ **miter sill** *n* (AmE), ~ **mitre sill** *n* (BrE) WATER SUPP *canal lock* busc d'amont *m*; ~ **out** *n* CINEMAT début de bobine *m*; ~ **pipe** *n* HYDR EQUIP conduite d'amenée *f*, tuyau d'amenée *m*, WATER SUPP *of pump* tubulure de refoulement *f*; ~ **plate** *n (cf groundsill)* CONST *of frame* sablière haute *f*, NAUT *shipbuilding* tôle de tête *f*; ~ **position pulse** *n* TV impulsion de position de tête *f*; ~ **response** *n* TV réponse en fréquence de la tête *f*; ~ **sea** *n* NAUT mer debout *f*; ~ **servo lock** *n* TV asservissement du tambour des têtes *m*; ~ **shot** *n* CINEMAT gros plan de tête *m*; ~ **slate** *n* CINEMAT claquette du début *f*; ~ **sluice** *n* WATER SUPP sluices de tête *m pl*; ~ **space** *n* FOOD TECH espace de tête *m*; ~ **tracking** *n* TV centrage des têtes *m*; ~ **wall** *n* CONST *of culvert* mur de tête *m*; ~ **of water** *n* CONST hauteur de charge *f*, hauteur de chute *m*, FUELLESS colonne d'eau *f*, HYDR EQUIP hauteur d'eau *f*, hauteur de chute *f*, HYDROL colonne d'eau *f*; ~ **of water pressure** *n* HYDR EQUIP charge *f*, hauteur d'eau *f*, pression de l'eau *f*; ~ **wave** *n* NUCLEAR front de Mach *m*; ~ **wear** *n* TV usure de tête *f*; ~ **wheel** *n* TV disque porte-têtes *m*; ~ **winding** *n* TV bobinage d'une tête *m*

head:[2] ~ **for** *vt* NAUT mettre le cap sur

headband *n* PRINT tranchefile *f*, tranchefile supérieure *f*

headbay *n* WATER SUPP bief d'amont *m*, biez d'amont *m*

headboard *n* MINING écoin *m*, NAUT *sailing* planche de tête *f*, têtière *f*

head-down: ~ **display** *n* AERONAUT, SPACE *spacecraft* visualisation tête basse *f*

headed: ~ **guide bush** *n* MECH ENG canon de guidage *m*

head-end[1] *adj* MECH ENG *engine* AR, arrière

head-end[2] *n* TEXTILES tête de pièce *f*; ~ **of cylinder** *n* MECH ENG arrière-cylindre *m*

header *n* COMP en-tête *m*, CONST *masonry* boutisse *f*, brique boutisse *f*, DP en-tête *m*, NUCLEAR collecteur *m*, PAPER TECH fond de bobine *m*, PRINT titre de rubrique *m*, PROD ENG en-tête *m*, *casting* coulée *f*, jet *m*, jet de coulée *m*, *of superheater* collecteur *m*, TELECOM en-tête *m*; ~ **error control** *n (HEC)* TELECOM contrôle d'erreur d'en-tête *m*, contrôle d'erreur sur l'en-tête *m*; ~ **label** *n* COMP, DP étiquette d'en-tête *f*, PACKAGING cavalier *m*; ~ **pipe** *n* MECH collecteur *m*, tuyau collecteur *m*

headgear *n* AERONAUT équipement de tête *m*, MINING machine à molettes *f*

heading *n* AERONAUT cap *m*, orientation *f*, COMP en-tête *m*, titre *m*, CONST *masonry* assise de boutisses *f*, DP en-tête *m*, titre *m*, MECH ENG avancement *m*, avancée *f*, galerie d'avancement *f*, MINING avancement *m*, NAUT *direction* , SPACE *spacecraft* cap *m*; ~ **and vertical reference unit system** *n* SPACE *spacecraft* centrale de référence de direction et d'attitude *f*; ~ **bond** *n* CONST appareil en boutisses *m*; ~ **chisel** *n* CONST bec d'âne *m*, bédane *m*; ~ **course** *n* CONST *masonry* assise de boutisses *f*; ~ **data generator** *n* AERONAUT centrale de cap *f*; ~ **die** *n* MECH ENG matrice de frappe à froid *f*; ~ **error integrator** *n* AERONAUT intégrateur d'erreur de cap *m*; ~ **error synchronizer amplifier** *n* AERONAUT amplificateur de synchro d'erreur de cap *m*; ~ **face** *n* MINING front d'avancement *m*; ~ **hold** *n* AERONAUT tenue de cap *f*; ~ **indicator** *n* SPACE *spacecraft* indicateur de cap *m*, indicateur de direction *m*; ~ **information** *n* AERONAUT information de cap *f*; ~ **joint** *n* CONST *carpentry* assemblage bout à bout *m*, joint de bout *m*; ~ **machine** *n* MINING coupeuse *f*, excavateur *m*; ~ **remote indicator** *n* AERONAUT indicateur de recopie de cap *m*; ~ **repeater** *n* AERONAUT répétiteur de cap *m*; ~ **selector** *n* AERONAUT sélecteur de cap *m*; ~ **synchronizer** *n* AERONAUT synchroniseur de cap *m*; ~ **synchronizer and lateral path integrator** *n* AERONAUT intégrateur *m*

headlamp *n* AUTO phare *m*, VEHICLES feu de route *m*, phare *m*, projecteur *m*; ~ **bulb** *n* AUTO lampe de phare *f*; ~ **flasher** *n* VEHICLES avertisseur lumineux *m*, avertisseur optique *m*; ~ **lens** *n* AUTO glace de phare *f*

headland *n* NAUT cap *m*, promontoire *m*, OCEANOG cap *m*

headless: ~ **guide bush** *n* MECH ENG canon de guidage cylindrique *m*; ~ **screw** *n* MECH vis sans tête *f*

headlight: ~ **switch** *n* AUTO commutateur de phares *m*

headline *n* NAUT *mooring* amarre debout de l'avant *f*, PRINT titre *m*

head-on *adj* SAFETY *collision* de plein fouet, SPACE *spacecraft*, TRANSP *collision* frontal

headphone: ~ **jack** *n* RECORDING prise pour casque *f*

headphones *n pl* RECORDING casque *m*, casque d'écoute *m*, TELECOM écouteur *m*

headpiece *n* MINING chapeau, NUCLEAR *refuelling* pièce de tête *f*

headrace *n n* HYDR EQUIP canal d'amenée *m*, canal de dérivation *m*, canal de prise d'eau *m*, WATER SUPP canal d'amenée *m*, *of water mill* bief d'amont *m*, biez d'amont *m*; ~ **canal** *n* FUELLESS canal d'amont *m*

headrest *n* VEHICLES appui-tête *m*

headroom *n* CONST hauteur d'échappée *f*, hauteur de passage *f*, échappée *f*, NAUT *shipbuilding* hauteur *f*

headset *n* RECORDING microcasque *m*, TELECOM casque téléphonique *m*; ~ **magnifier** *n* INSTRUMENT loupe serre-tête *f*

headstock *n* MECH poupée fixe *f*, MECH ENG contre-pointe *f*, contre-poupée *f*, poupée courante *f*, poupée mobile *f*, poupée *f*, poupée fixe *f*, MINING belle-fleur *f*, chevalet d'extraction *m*, châssis à molettes *m*, chevalement *m*

head-to-tape: ~ **contact** *n* TV contact tête-bande *m*; ~ **speed** *n* TV vitesse relative tête-bande *f*; ~ **velocity** *n* TV rapport vitesse tête-vitesse bande *m*

head-type: ~ **punch blank** *n* MECH ENG poinçon ébauche cylindrique à tête cylindrique *m*

head-up[1] *adj* NAUT *radar* avant du navire en haut

head-up:[2] ~ **display** *n* AERONAUT collimateur de pilotage *m*, visualisation tête haute *f*, INSTRUMENT colli-mateur de pilotage *m*, SPACE *spacecraft* visualisation tête haute *f*

headwater *n* HYDR EQUIP eau d'adduction *f*, eau d'a-mont *f*, HYDROL *of stream* eau d'amont *f*, WATER SUPP remous *m*; ~ **capture** *n* HYDROL *of river* décapitation *f*; ~ **reach** *n* WATER SUPP bief supérieur *m*

headway *n* NAUT erre en avant *f*, TRANSP espacement entre véhicules *m*; ~ **control** *n* TRANSP régulation des espacements entre véhicules *f*; ~ **distribution analysis** *n* TRANSP analyse de la distribution des espacements *f*; ~ **warning device** *n* TRANSP dispositif avertisseur d'espa-cement *m*

headwind *n* AERONAUT, METEO vent debout *m*, NAUT *meteorology* vent contraire *m*, vent debout *m*

headwork *n* FUELLESS *of dam* ouvrage de prise d'eau *m*, MINING engin extérieur *m*

heald *n* TEXTILES liser *f*; ~ **wire** *n* TEXTILES fil de lisse *m*

health:[1] ~ **and safety requirements** *n pl* SAFETY condi-tions requises pour la santé et la sûreté *f pl*, prescriptions pour la santé et la sécurité *f pl*; ~ **food** *n* FOOD TECH aliment diététique *m*; ~ **hazard** *n* SAFETY risque pour la santé *m*

health:[2] ~ **safety and welfare** *phr* SAFETY *of people at work* la santé la sécurité et le bien-être

health-related: ~ **sampling** *n* SAFETY prélèvement d'é-chantillons lié aux problèmes de santé *m*

heap *n* COMP tas *m*, CONST amas *m*, masse *f*, monceau *m*, tas *m*, DP tas *m*; ~ **sand** *n* PROD ENG *founding* sable de chantier *m*, vieux sable *m*

heaped *adj* CONST accumulé, empilé

hearing: ~ **aid** *n* ACOUSTICS appareil de correction audi-tive *m*; ~ **conservation** *n* SAFETY préservation de l'ouïe *f*; ~ **correction** *n* ACOUSTICS correction auditive *f*; ~ **fatigue** *n* ACOUSTICS fatigue auditive *f*; ~ **loss factor index** *n* ACOUSTICS indice de reste d'audition *m*; ~ **protectors** *n pl* SAFETY protecteurs pour oreilles *m pl*; ~ **test** *n* ACOUSTICS épreuve auditive *f*, SAFETY essai de l'ouïe *m*; ~ **threshold difference** *n* ACOUSTICS écart atonal *m*; ~ **threshold level** *n* ACOUSTICS seuil d'audi-tion *m*

hearing-evoked: ~ **potential** *n* ACOUSTICS potentiel évo-qué auditif *m*

heart: ~ **trowel** *n* CONST truelle à coeur *f*

hearth *n* CONST *of fireplace* foyer *m*, âtre *m*, GAS TECH, HEATING *of furnace* creuset *m*, PROD ENG *of blast, furnace* creuset *m*, ouvrage *m*, *of electric furnace* sole *f*

heat[1] *n* CHEM *property* chaleur *f*, COAL TECH coulée *f*, HEATING, PAPER TECH, PHYS *of reaction*, REFRIG cha-leur *f*, SPACE *spacecraft* chaleur *f*, coulée *f*, TEXTILES, THERMOD chaleur *f*;
off ~ *n* THERMOD *foundry* coulée ratée *f*;

~a ~ **absorber** *n* TEXTILES qui absorbe la chaleur; ~ **absorption** *n* THERMOD absorption de chaleur *f*; ~ **of absorption** *n* THERMOD chaleur d'absorption *f*; ~ **accu-mulation** *n* THERMOD accumulation de chaleur *f*; ~ **accumulator** *n* THERMOD accumulateur de chaleur *m*; ~ **of activation** *n* THERMOD chaleur d'activation *f*; ~ **ageing** *n* P&R vieillissement thermique *m*;

~b ~ **balance** *n* HEAT ENG bilan thermique *m*, PAPER TECH bilan calorifique *m*, REFRIG, THERMOD bilan thermique *m*; ~ **balance chart** *n* THERMOD diagramme du flux thermique *m*; ~ **balance diagram** *n* THERMOD diagramme du flux thermique *m*; ~ **barrier** *n* NUCLEAR *of reactor* barrière thermique *f*, THERMOD blocage thermique *m*; ~ **bridge** *n* HEAT ENG, THERMOD pont

thermique *m*; ~ **build-up** *n* THERMOD développement de chaleur *m*, développement thermique *m*;

~c ~ **capacity** *n* PHYS capacité thermique *f*, THER-MOD capacité calorifique *f*; ~ **caused by friction** *n* THERMOD chaleur de friction *f*; ~ **of combination** *n* THERMOD chaleur de combinaison *f*; ~ **of combustion** *n* CHEM *of substance* chaleur de combustion *f*; ~ **of compression** *n* THERMOD chaleur de compression *f*; ~ **of condensation** *n* METEO, THERMOD chaleur de condensation *f*; ~ **conduction** *n* THERMOD conduction de chaleur *f*; ~ **conductivity** *n* THERMOD conductibilité calorifique *f*, thermoconductibilité *f*; ~ **conductivity meter** *n* THERMOD diagomètre *m*; ~ **conductor** *n* PROD ENG conducteur de chaleur *m*; ~ **constant** *n* THERMOD constante calorifique *f*; ~ **consumption** *n* THERMOD besoins en chaleur *m pl*, consommation de chaleur *f*, demande calorifique *f*, dépense de chaleur *f*; ~ **content** *n* THERMOD enthalpie *f*; ~ **control** *n* CONTROL régula-tion de chaleur *f*; ~ **convection** *n* THERMOD transport de chaleur *m*; ~ **cycle** *n* THERMOD cycle de traitement thermique *m*;

~d ~ **dam** *n* AUTO gorge pare-chaleur *f*; ~ **death** *n* PHYS mort thermique *f*, mort énergétique *f*; ~ **of de-composition** *n* CHEM chaleur de décomposition *f*; ~ **demand** *n* HEAT ENG besoins en chaleur *m pl*, THERMOD besoins en chaleur *m pl*, demande calorifique *f*, de-mande de chaleur *f*; ~ **density** *n* THERMOD densité calorifique *f*, densité de chaleur *f*; ~ **detector** *n* THER-MOD détecteur de chaleur *m*; ~ **dilatation** *n* THERMOD expansion *f*; ~ **discharge** *n* RECYCLING rejet de chaleur *m*; ~ **displacement** *n* THERMOD déplacement de cha-leur *m*; ~ **dissipation** *n* THERMOD dispersion de chaleur *f*, dissipation de chaleur *f*, rayonnement de chaleur *m*; ~ **of dissociation** *n* THERMOD chaleur de dissociation *f*; ~ **distortion** *n* THERMOD déformation due à la chaleur *f*; ~ **drop** *n* THERMOD abaissement *m*, chute de poten-tiel thermique *f*, chute de température *f*;

~e ~ **economizer** *n* THERMOD récupérateur de cha-leur *m*; ~ **effect** *n* THERMOD effet calorifique *m*, effet thermique *m*; ~ **efficiency** *n* THERMOD rendement calo-rifique *m*, rendement thermique *m*; ~ **emission** *n* THERMOD débit calorifique *m*, émission de chaleur *f*; ~ **energy** *n* THERMOD énergie calorifique *f*, énergie ther-mique *f*; ~ **engine** *n* MECH, MECH ENG moteur thermique *m*, PHYS moteur thermique *m*, THERMOD machine *f*; ~ **engineering** *n* MECH ENG ingénierie de la chaleur *f*; ~ **equivalent** *n* THERMOD équivalent mécani-que de la chaleur *m*; ~ **exchange** *n* THERMOD échange de chaleur *m*; ~ **exchanger** *n* FOOD TECH *refrigeration*, FUELLESS échangeur de chaleur *m*, HEAT ENG échan-geur thermique *m*, MECH échangeur de chaleur *m*, MECH ENG échangeur thermique *m*, NAUT *engine* é-changeur de chaleur *m*, NUCLEAR refroidisseur *m*, réfrigérant *m*, PAPER TECH, PETR TECH *refinery* échan-geur de chaleur *m*, PROD ENG échangeur thermique *m*, REFRIG échangeur de chaleur *m*, THERMOD réfrigérant *m*, échangeur de chaleur *m*, échangeur thermique *m*; ~ **exchanger suction accumulator** *n* REFRIG bouteille tampon échangeur *f*, tampon d'aspiration d'échan-geur thermique *m*; ~ **exchanger tube** *n* MECH ENG tube pour échangeur thermique *m*; ~ **expansion** *n* THERMOD *heat dilatation* expansion *f*; ~ **of expansion** *n* THERMOD chaleur d'expansion *f*, chaleur de dilatation *f*;

~f ~ **filter** *n* CINEMAT filtre anticalorique *m*; ~ **flow** *n* GEOL flux de chaleur *m*, flux thermique *m*, HEAT ENG flux de chaleur *m*, THERMOD flux de chaleur *m*, écoulement de chaleur *m*; ~ **flow chart** *n* THERMOD graphique du flux thermique *m*; ~ **flow diagram** *n* THERMOD centrale thermique *f*, diagramme du flux thermique *m*, tableau du flux thermique *m*; ~ **flow line** *n* THERMOD ligne de flux thermique *f*, tracé du flux thermique *m*; ~ **flow rate** *n* PHYS flux thermique *m*; ~ **flush** *n* NUCLEAR *stuffing box* choc thermique *m*; ~ **flux** *n* SPACE flux thermique *m*; ~ **of formation** *n* CHEM, THERMOD chaleur de formation *f*; ~ **forming** *n* THERMOD façonnage à chaud *m*, formage à chaud *m*, thermoformage *m*; ~ **of fusion** *n* THERMOD chaleur de fusion *f*, température de fusion *f*;

~ **g** ~ **generation** *n* THERMOD production de chaleur *f*;

~ **h** ~ **hardening** *n* THERMOD thermodurcissement *m*; ~ **haze** *n* METEO, THERMOD brume sèche *f*; ~ **of hydration** *n* CONST *cement* chaleur d'hydration *f*, chaleur de prise *f*, THERMOD chaleur d'hydratation *f*;

~ **i** ~ **image** *n* THERMOD image obtenue par rayonnement thermique *f*; ~ **induction sealing** *n* PACKAGING thermoscellage par induction *m*; ~ **input** *n* THERMOD apport thermique *m*, entrée calorifique *f*; ~ **insulation** *n* MECH, PACKAGING, PETR TECH, PROP MAT, THERMOD calorifuge *m*, calorifugeage *m*, isolement calorifuge *m*; ~ **insulation effectiveness** *n* THERMOD pouvoir calorifuge *m*; ~ **insulation factor** *n* THERMOD coefficient de résistance à la conductibilité de chaleur *m*; ~ **insulation power** *n* THERMOD pouvoir calorifuge *m*;

~ **l** ~ **lamination** *n* PACKAGING thermosoudage *m*; ~ **load** *n* THERMOD charge thermique *f*; ~ **load plan** *n* POLLUTION plan de protection contre la pollution thermique *m*; ~ **loss** *n* ELEC *resistor* perte de chauffage *f*, HEAT ENG perte de chaleur *f*, PHYS déperdition de chaleur *f*, perte de chaleur *f*, REFRIG perte de chaleur *f*, THERMOD perte calorifique *f*;

~ **m** ~ **mirror** *n* FUELLESS héliostat *m*, miroir adiabatique *m*; ~ **of mixing** *n* THERMOD chaleur de mélange *f*;

~ **n** ~ **of neutralization** *n* THERMOD chaleur de neutralisation *f*;

~ **o** ~ **output** *n* THERMOD débit calorifique *m*, rendement calorifique *m*; ~ **output density** *n* NUCLEAR puissance thermique volumique *f*;

~ **p** ~ **penetration time** *n* THERMOD durée de pénétration de la chaleur *f*, temps de pénétration de la chaleur *m*; ~ **physicist** *n* THERMOD thermicien *m*; ~ **pick-up** *n* REFRIG apport de chaleur *m*; ~ **pipe** *n* SPACE *communications*, TRANSP caloduc *m*; ~ **plug** *n* AUTO, THERMOD bougie de préchauffage *f*; ~ **pump** *n* HEAT ENG, MECH *thermodynamics*, MECH ENG, PHYS pompe à chaleur *f*, THERMOD pompe à chaleur *f*, thermopompe *f*;

~ **r** ~ **radiation** *n* PACKAGING rayonnement calorifique *m*, THERMOD rayonnement calorifique *m*, rayonnement thermique *m*; ~ **of radioactivity** *n* RAD PHYS débit de chaleur de la radioactivité *m*; ~ **rate** *n* THERMOD rendement thermique *m*; ~ **rate curve** *n* THERMOD dérivée de la courbe d'analyse thermique à l'échauffement *f*; ~ **ratio** *n* REFRIG coefficient de chaleur *m*; ~ **of reaction** *n* CHEM, THERMOD chaleur de réaction *f*; ~ **reactivation** *n* PRINT réactivation du hot-melt par la chaleur *f*; ~ **recovery** *n* HEAT ENG, RECYCLING, THERMOD récupération de chaleur *f*; ~ **rejection** *n* HEAT ENG rejet de chaleur *m*; ~ **rejection rate** *n* NUCLEAR *of module* taux d'élimination de la chaleur *m*; ~ **release** *n* NUCLEAR *in fuel assembly* libération de chaleur *f*; ~ **release decal** *n* C&G décalcomanie à chaud *f*; ~ **removal loop** *n* NUCLEAR circuit d'évacuation de la chaleur *m*; ~ **removed** *n* REFRIG

chaleur enlevée *f*; ~ **reservoir** *n* PHYS réservoir thermique *m*, REFRIG réservoir de chaleur *m*; ~ **resistance** *n* P&R, THERMOD résistance à la chaleur *f*; ~ **rise** *n* THERMOD montée en température *f*; ~ **riser tube** *n* AUTO réchauffeur de combustible *m*;

~ **s** ~ **screen** *n* SPACE écran thermique *m*; ~ **seal** *n* PRINT operulage *m*, scellage *m*; ~ **seal apparatus** *n* LAB EQUIP thermosoudeur *m*; ~ **seal coating** *n* PACKAGING couche de scellage *f*; ~ **sealing** *n* COATINGS thermocollage *m*, thermoscellage *m*, thermosoudage *m*, P&R scellage à chaud *m*, soudage *m*, PACKAGING thermosoudure *f*, THERMOD thermoscellage *m*, thermosoudage *m*; ~ **seal label** *n* PACKAGING étiquette thermocollante *f*; ~ **seal laminating** *n* COATINGS couchage par thermocollage *m*, couchage par thermosoudage *m*; ~ **seal tape** *n* PACKAGING ruban thermocollant *m*; ~ **seal temperature** *n* PACKAGING température de thermosoudage *f*; ~ **sensitivity** *n* P&R sensibilité à la chaleur *f*; ~ **sensor** *n* PROP MAT sonde de température *f*, THERMOD détecteur de température *m*, sonde de température *f*; ~ **setting** *n* TEXTILES thermofixage *m*, thermofixation *f*; ~ **shield** *n* AERONAUT manchon incombustible *m*, protection thermique *f*, élément pare-feu *m*, THERMOD ecran thermique *m*, écran de chaleur *m*; ~ **shock test** *n* HEAT ENG *printed circuits*, THERMOD essai de choc thermique *m*; ~ **shrink fitting** *n* THERMOD emmanchement à chaud *m*; ~ **shrinking** *n* COATINGS, THERMOD thermorétrécissement *m*; ~ **shrinking foil** *n* COATINGS pellicule rétractable *f*; ~ **shunt** *n* THERMOD shunt thermique *m*; ~ **sink** *n* ELEC *Zener diode* dissipateur de chaleur *m*, radiateur *m*, ELEC ENG puits de chaleur *m*, PHYS transfert de chaleur *m*, PROD ENG radiateur *m*, SPACE puits thermique *m*, THERMOD dissipateur de chaleur *m*; ~ **of solution** *n* THERMOD chaleur de dissolution *f*, chaleur de solution *f*; ~ **source** *n* REFRIG source de chaleur *f*; ~ **spectrum** *n* THERMOD spectre calorifique *m*; ~ **stability** *n* P&R stabilité à la chaleur *f*, PACKAGING, THERMOD stabilité thermique *f*; ~ **supply** *n* THERMOD adduction de chaleur *f*;

~ **t** ~ **throughput** *n* THERMOD débit de chaleur *m*, débit thermique *m*, rendement thermique *m*; ~ **transfer** *n* HEATING, P&R, PHYS transfert de chaleur *m*, REFRIG transfert de chaleur *m*, transmission de chaleur *f*, transport de chaleur *m*; ~ **transfer coefficient** *n* PHYS, THERMOD coefficient de transmission thermique *m*; ~ **transfer engineer** *n* SPACE *spacecraft* thermicien *m*; ~ **transfer engineering** *n* MECH ENG ingénierie de la transmission de chaleur *f*; ~ **transfer label** *n* PACKAGING étiquette imprimée par transfert thermique *f*; ~ **transfer surface** *n* REFRIG surface d'échange *f*, THERMOD *heat exchanger* surface thermoconductrice *f*; ~ **transformation** *n* THERMOD échange de chaleur *m*; ~ **transition** *n* THERMOD passage de chaleur *m*, écoulement thermique *f*; ~ **transmission** *n* HEAT ENG transmission de chaleur *f*, THERMOD transmission de chaleur *f*, transmission thermique *f*; ~ **trap** *n* NUCLEAR piège thermique *m*; ~ **treatment** *n* COAL TECH, METALL, PROP MAT traitement thermique *m*, THERMOD traitement par trempe et revenu *m*, traitement thermique *m*; ~ **treatment crack** *n* THERMOD fissure *f*; ~ **treatment crack sensitivity** *n* THERMOD sensibilité aux criques de trempe *f*, sensibilité aux fissures de trempe *f*; ~ **treatment diagram** *n* THERMOD diagramme de traitement thermique *m*; ~ **treatment range** *n* SPRINGS gamme de traitement de thermique *f*;

~ **turbine** n NUCLEAR turbine à air chaud f;
~ V ~ **valve** n CONTROL thermostat m; ~ **of vaporization** n THERMOD chaleur d'évaporation f;
~ W ~ **welding** n PACKAGING thermosoudure f
heat[2] vt CHEM chauffer, PHYS chauffer, échauffer, TEXTILES chauffer, THERMOD chauffer, échauffer; ~ **cure** vt THERMOD vulcaniser; ~ **harden** vt THERMOD metals thermodurcir; ~ **seal** vt THERMOD thermosceller, thermosouder; ~ **shrink** vt THERMOD thermorétrécir; ~ **treat** vt THERMOD traiter à chaud, metals tremper, steel tremper et faire revenir; ~ **up** vt C&G attremper, CHEM échauffer, THERMOD faire monter la température, mettre en température, porter à température, glass attremper
heat:[3] ~ **up** vi CHEM, THERMOD s'échauffer
heat-absorbing[1] adj THERMOD qui absorbe la chaleur
heat-absorbing:[2] ~ **filter** n PHOTO filtre anticalorifique m; ~ **glass** n C&G verre athermane m; ~ **glazing** n C&G vitrage athermique m; ~ **power** n THERMOD pouvoir absorbant de chaleur m
heat-activated: ~ **label** n PACKAGING étiquette activable à chaleur f
heat-affected: ~ **zone** n MECH, THERMOD welding zone affectée thermiquement f
heat-and-eat: ~ **food** n PACKAGING produit alimentaire préparé à l'avance m
heat-conducting adj THERMOD thermiquement conducteur, thermoconducteur, thermoconductible
heated: ~ **container** n TRANSP conteneur calorifique m; ~ **platten** n P&R press plateau chauffant m; ~ **windshield pane** n P&R glace chauffante f
heater n ELEC ENG filament chauffant m, filament de chauffage m, MECH thermoplongeur m, PROD ENG réchauffeur m, THERMOD appareil de chauffage m, chauffe-eau m, VEHICLES dispositif de chauffage m; ~ **blower** n AERONAUT ventilateur réchauffeur m; ~ **control** n AUTO commande de chauffage f; ~ **element** n PHOTO tige de chauffe-bain électrique f, PROD ENG élément thermique m; ~ **mat** n REFRIG nappe chauffante f; ~ **power supply** n ELEC ENG filaments d'alimentation m pl; ~ **rod** n NUCLEAR of pressurizer tube de chauffage m; ~ **system** n AUTO chauffage m; ~ **voltage** n ELEC ENG tension de chauffage f
heat-exchanging: ~ **medium** n THERMOD agent caloporteur m, caloporteur m
heat-fix: ~ **tape** n PACKAGING ruban collant après chauffage m
heat-form vt THERMOD hot and cold façonner à chaud, former à chaud, thermoformer
heat-formed adj THERMOD cold formé à chaud, thermoformé
heat-fusible adj THERMOD plastics thermofusible, thermosoudant
heat-generating adj THERMOD thermogène
heat-hardened adj THERMOD thermodurci
heating n AERONAUT réchauffage m, GAS TECH, HEAT ENG, MECH chauffage m, PROD ENG chauffage m, échauffement m, TEXTILES chauffage m, THERMOD electrical, gas chauffage m, chauffage au gaz m, chauffage électrique m; ~ **air** n AERONAUT air de réchauffage m; ~ **appliance** n HEAT ENG appareil de chauffage m; ~ **belt** n HEAT ENG ceinture chauffante f; ~ **blowpipe** n CONST welding chalumeau chauffeur m; ~ **body** n HEATING water heater corps de chauffe m; ~ **cable** n ELEC câble chauffant m; ~ **capacity** n HEAT ENG capacité de chauffe f, THERMOD capacité chauffante f,

capacité de chauffe f, puissance calorifique f; ~ **chamber** n THERMOD industry chambre de chauffe f, laboratory étuve f; ~ **channel** n PACKAGING canal de chauffe m; ~ **circuit** n HEATING circuit de chauffage m; ~ **coil** n HEAT ENG serpentin réchauffeur m, REFRIG serpentin de chauffage m, tube chauffant m, THERMOD bobine d'inductance f, bobine thermique f; ~ **current** n THERMOD courant de chauffage m; ~ **curve** n P&R courbe de chauffage f, THERMOD courbe d'échauffement f; ~ **depth** n THERMOD pénétration de la chaleur f; ~ **device** n MECH ENG dispositif de chauffage m; ~ **element** n AERONAUT, ELEC élément chauffant m, HEAT ENG élément de chauffage m; ~ **engineer** n THERMOD chauffagiste m; ~ **furnace** n THERMOD four de chauffage m, four à réchauffer m; ~ **gas** n GAS TECH gaz de chauffage m; ~ **installation** n THERMOD installation de chauffage f; ~ **jacket** n THERMOD chemise de chauffage f; ~ **mantle** n LAB EQUIP chauffe-ballon m; ~ **melter** n CONST civil engineering fondoir-réchauffeur m; ~ **oil** n THERMOD central heating fuel m, mazout m; ~ **panel** n MECH ENG panneau de chauffage m; ~ **pin** n NUCLEAR épingle chauffante f; ~ **plant** n THERMOD système de chauffage m; ~ **power** n THERMOD pouvoir calorifique m, puissance calorifique f; ~ **resistor** n AERONAUT résistance chauffante f, ELEC résistance de chauffage f; ~ **surface** n HEATING surface de chauffe f, THERMOD surface chauffante f, surface de chauffe f; ~ **surface bundle** n NUCLEAR faisceau de surfaces chauffantes m; ~ **surface tube** n NUCLEAR tube d'écran m; ~ **system** n THERMOD système de chauffage m, VEHICLES chauffage m; ~ **tape** n LAB EQUIP ruban chauffant m; ~ **technician** n MECH ENG technicien en matériel thermique m; ~ **temperature curve** n THERMOD courbe de température de chauffage f; ~ **time** n THERMOD durée de mise en température f, temps de mise à température m; ~ **tunnel** n PACKAGING tunnel de chauffe m; ~ **zone** n THERMOD zone de chauffage f
heating-up n C&G attrempage m; ~ **curve** n THERMOD courbe de mise à température f, durée de mise en température f, temps de mise à température m; ~ **time** n PROP MAT temps d'échauffement m, THERMOD durée de mise en température f, temps de mise à température m
heat-insulated[1] adj HEAT ENG, MECH, THERMOD lagged calorifugé
heat-insulated:[2] ~ **container** n THERMOD conteneur frigorifique m; ~ **lorry** n (cf insulated lorry, insulated truck) THERMOD camion isothésure m
heat-insulating[1] adj PHYS athermane, calorifugé, THERMOD calorifuge
heat-insulating:[2] ~ **jacket** n THERMOD matelas de calorifugeage m; ~ **wall** n AERONAUT paroi de calorifugeage f
heat-proof[1] adj PACKAGING résistant à la chaleur, SAFETY calorifuge, THERMOD résistant au chaud, résistant à la chaleur
heat-proof:[2] ~ **protective clothing** n SAFETY vêtements de protection thermique m pl
heat-protective: ~ **clothing** n SAFETY vêtements de protection contre la chaleur m pl; ~ **material** n SAFETY tissu de protection thermique m
heat-resistant[1] adj HEATING, PACKAGING, PHYS réfractaire, PROP MAT résistant à la chaleur, SAFETY calorifugé, réfractaire, SPACE spacecraft réfractaire, résistant à la chaleur, thermorésistant, THERMOD résistant au chaud, résistant à la chaleur
heat-resistant:[2] ~ **coating** n COATINGS couche résistante

à la chaleur *f*, enduit résistant à chaud *m*, enduit résistant à la chaleur *m*; ~ **gloves** *n pl* LAB EQUIP *safety* gants de protection antichaleur *m pl*, SAFETY gants calorifuges *m pl*

heat-resisting[1] *adj* SPACE réfractaire, THERMOD résistant au chaud, résistant à la chaleur

heat-resisting:[2] ~ **glass** *n* C&G verre résistant au choc thermique *m*, THERMOD verre calorifuge *m*

heat-retaining *adj* THERMOD qui conserve la chaleur

heat-sealable[1] *adj* THERMOD thermoscellable, thermosoudable

heat-sealable:[2] ~ **paper** *n* COATINGS, PACKAGING papier thermosoudable *m*

heat-sealed[1] *adj* THERMOD thermoscellé, thermosoudé

heat-sealed:[2] ~ **wrappings** *n* THERMOD emballage thermoscellé *m*

heat-sealing[1] *adj* COATINGS thermosoudable, PAPER TECH thermocollable

heat-sealing:[2] ~ **adhesive** *n* PACKAGING adhésif thermosoudable *m*; ~ **and welding machine** *n* PACKAGING machine de fermeture thermosoudable *f*; ~ **device** *n* PACKAGING dispositif de thermosoudage *m*; ~ **equipment** *n* PACKAGING équipement de thermosoudage *m*; ~ **machine** *n* PACKAGING machine de thermosoudage *f*

heat-seeking *adj* SPACE *spacecraft* guidé par infrarouge, THERMOD *missiles* guidé par infrarouge, thermoguidé

heat-sensitive[1] *adj* P&R, THERMOD thermosensible

heat-sensitive:[2] ~ **material** *n* PACKAGING matériel thermosensible *m*; ~ **paint** *n* THERMOD peinture *f*

heat-set[1] *adj* PRINT qui se fixe à la chaleur

heat-set:[2] ~ **adhesive paper** *n* COATINGS papier thermocollant *m*; ~ **ink** *n* COLOURS encre sensible à la température *f*, encre séchant par la chaleur *f*; ~ **labeling** *n* (AmE), ~ **labelling** *n* (BrE) PRINT étiquetage à chaud *m*

heat-setting *adj* THERMOD prenant à la chaleur, thermodurcissant

heat-shrinkable[1] *adj* THERMOD thermorétractable, thermorétrécissable

heat-shrinkable:[2] ~ **film** *n* (BrE) *(cf heat-shrinkable wrap)* THERMOD pellicule thermorétractable *f*, pellicule thermorétrécissable *f*; ~ **sleeve** *n* COATINGS gaine rétrécissable par la chaleur *f*, gaine thermorétractable *f*; ~ **wrap** *n* (AmE) *(cf heat-shrinkable film)* THERMOD *shrink wrap* pellicule thermorétractable *f*, pellicule thermorétrécissable *f*

heat-shrunk *adj* MECH emmanché à chaud, THERMOD thermorétracté, thermorétréci

heat-stabilized *adj* THERMOD stabilisé par la chaleur, thermostabilisé

heat-stable *adj* THERMOD stable à la chaleur, thermostable

heat-stretched: ~ **fiber** *n* (AmE), ~ **fibre** *n* (BrE) TEXTILES fibre étirée à la chaleur *f*

heat-transmitting: ~ **glass** *n* C&G verre diathermane *m*

heat-treatable *adj* THERMOD *steel* apte à la trempe et au revenu, durcissable par précipitation

heat-treated *adj* THERMOD trempé et revenu, *metals* trempé mûri

heatwave *n* METEO canicule *f*, vague de chaleur *f*, THERMOD vague de chaleur *f*

heave[1] *n* GEOL composante horizontale *f*, OCEANOG, PETR TECH *of rig, drill ship* pilonnement *m*; ~ **compensator** *n* PETR, PETR TECH *offshore* compensateur de pilonnement *m*

heave[2] *vt* NAUT *anchor* lever; ~ **in** *vt* NAUT *mooring lines* rentrer

heave[3] *vi* NAUT *ship* virer; ~ **to** *vi* NAUT caranguer, mettre en panne, se mettre en panne, se mettre à la cape

heavenly: ~ **body** *n* ASTRON, SPACE corps céleste *m*

heaving: ~ **displacement of buoy** *n* FUELLESS déplacement de tangage d'une bouée *m*; ~ **line** *n* NAUT *for towing, mooring* attrape *f*, filin flottant *m*, filin flottant de sauvetage *m*, ligne d'attrape *f*

heavy[1] *adj* C&G *of container* épais, MECH fort, épais; ~ **duty** *adj* MECH ENG de grande puissance, à grand rendement

heavy:[2] ~ **anode** *n* ELEC ENG anode massive *f*; ~ **anti-aircraft gun** *n* MILIT canon lourd contre-avion *m*; ~ **antitank gun** *n* MILIT canon antichar lourd *m*; ~ **armament** *n* MILIT artillerie lourde *f*; ~ **artillery** *n* MILIT artillerie lourde *f*; ~ **breakdown crane** *n* (BrE) RAIL grue de relevage *f*; ~ **castings** *n pl* *(cf fine castings)* PROD ENG grosses pièces *f pl*; ~ **crepe** *n* PAPER TECH crêpe lourd *m*; ~ **crude** *n* PETR TECH brut lourd *m*; ~ **crude oil** *n* PETR TECH pétrole brut lourd *m*; ~ **cut** *n* MECH ENG *machine tools* forte passe *f*; ~ **displacement** *n* NAUT *boat design* déplacement lourd *m*; ~ **duty** *n* PROD ENG service intensif *m*; ~ **ends** *n pl* PETR TECH *refining* fractions lourdes *f pl*; ~ **engineering** *n* CONST industrie lourde *f*; ~ **fractions** *n pl* PETR TECH fractions lourdes *f pl*; ~ **freight vehicle traffic** *n* (AmE) *(cf heavy goods vehicle traffic)* TRANSP circulation des poids lourds *f*; ~ **gage** *n* (AmE), ~ **gauge** *n* (BrE) TEXTILES grosse jauge *f*; ~ **goods vehicle** *n* *(HGV)* TRANSP poids lourd *m*; ~ **goods vehicle traffic** *n* (BrE) *(cf heavy freight vehicle traffic)* TRANSP circulation des poids lourds *f*; ~ **group** *n* NUCLEAR groupe lourd *m*; ~ **hydrocarbon fractions** *n pl* PETR TECH fractions lourdes d'hydrocarbures *f pl*; ~ **hydrogen** *n* CHEM, NUCLEAR, PHYS hydrogène lourd *m*; ~ **ink** *n* PRINT encre tirante *f*; ~ **ironwork** *n* CONST grosse serrurerie *f*; ~ **jet** *n* TRANSP gros porteur *m*; ~ **liquid test** *n* COAL TECH analyse densimétrique par liquides denses *f*, analyse densimétrique par liquides lourds *f*; ~ **lorry** *n* (BrE) *(cf heavy truck)* TRANSP, VEHICLES poids lourd *m*; ~ **metal** *n* COAL TECH métal lourd *m*, POLLUTION métaux lourds *m pl*, RAD PHYS, RECYCLING métal lourd *m*; ~ **metal difference technique** *n* NUCLEAR technique de différence de teneur en métaux lourds *f*; ~ **minerals** *n pl* GEOL minéraux lourds *m pl*; ~ **motor lorry** *n* (BrE) *(cf heavy motor truck)* TRANSP train routier *m*; ~ **motor truck** *n* (AmE) *(cf heavy motor lorry)* TRANSP train routier *m*; ~ **nut** *n* MECH ENG écrou haut *m*; ~ **panels** *n pl* C&G côtes épaisses *f pl*; ~ **particle** *n* GAS TECH particule lourde *f*; ~ **peak** *n* NUCLEAR pic lourd *m*; ~ **sea** *n* OCEANOG paquet de mer *m*; ~ **seas** *n pl* NAUT grosse mer *f*; ~ **seed** *n* C&G fin serré *m*; ~ **spar** *n* MINERAL baryte *f*; ~ **swell** *n* NAUT grosse houle *f*; ~ **tank** *n* MILIT char d'assaut lourd *m*; ~ **truck** *n* (AmE) *(cf heavy lorry)* TRANSP, VEHICLES poids lourd *m*; ~ **vehicle elevator** *n* (AmE) *(cf heavy vehicle lift)* TRANSP monte-charge pour véhicule lourd *m*; ~ **vehicle lift** *n* (BrE) *(cf heavy vehicle elevator* TRANSP, monte-charge pour véhicule lourd *m*; ~ **water** *n* *(cf deuterium oxide)* CHEM, NUCLEAR, PHYS eau lourde *f*; ~ **water degasifier** *n* NUCLEAR dégazeur d'eau lourde *m*; ~ **water plant** *n* NUCLEAR centrale d'eau lourde *f*; ~ **water reactor** *n* NUCLEAR réacteur à eau lourde *m*; ~ **water spray nozzle** *n* NUCLEAR tuyère d'injection de l'eau lourde *f*; ~ **water vapor** *n* (AmE), ~ **water vapour** *n* (BrE) NUCLEAR vapeur d'eau lourde *f*; ~ **weather** *n*

NAUT *meteorology* gros temps *m*

heavy-bodied: ~ **ink** *n* PRINT encre à forte viscosité *f*

heavy-duty[1] *adj* DETERGENTS pour nettoyage des surfaces difficiles, MECH à usage intensif

heavy-duty:[2] ~ **ball bearing** *n* MECH ENG roulement à billes pour forte charge *m*; ~ **contact** *n* ELEC ENG contact à grand pouvoir de coupure *m*; ~ **gear** *n* MECH ENG engrenage de fatigue *m*; ~ **lathe** *n* MECH ENG tour parallèle très renforcé *m*; ~ **lift** *n* CONST grue pour poids lourds *f*, monte-charge *n* MECH ENG rondelle extra-serrante *f*; ~ **oil** *n* (HD) PETR TECH huile à haute tenue *f*; ~ **rectangular magnetic chuck** *n* MECH ENG plateau rectangulaire magnétique type lourd *m*

heavy-ion: ~ **fusion** *n* NUCLEAR fusion d'ions lourds *f*

heavy-lift: ~ **derrick** *n* NAUT *cargo* bigue *f*; ~ **helicopter** *n* AERONAUT hélicoptère de transport lourd *m*; ~ **launch vehicle** *n* (HLLV) SPACE *spacecraft* lanceur lourd *m*; ~ **vehicle** *n* SPACE *spacecraft* cargo spatial *m*

heavy-oil: ~ **engine** *n* AUTO moteur à huile lourde *m*

heavy-section: ~ **rolls** *n pl* MECH ENG train à gros profilés *m*

heavy-type: ~ **plummer block** *n* PROD ENG palier renforcé *m*

heavyweight[1] *adj* PRINT lourd

heavyweight:[2] ~ **motorcycle** *n* TRANSP moto grande routière *f*

hebronite *n* MINERAL hébronite *f*

HEC *abbr (header error control)* TELECOM contrôle d'erreur d'en-tête *m*, contrôle d'erreur sur l'en-tête *m*

hectare *n* METR hectare *m*

hecto- *pref* (*h*) METR hecto-(*h*)

hectogram *n* (AmE), **hectogramme** *n* (BrE) METR hectogramme *m*

hectoliter *n* (AmE), **hectolitre** *n* (BrE) METR hectolitre *m*

hectometer *n* (AmE), **hectometre** *n* (BrE) METR hectomètre *m*

hectowatt *n* ELEC ENG hectowatt *m*

hedenbergite *n* MINERAL hédenbergite *f*

hedge *n* PROD ENG stock stratégique *m*

hedging *n* PROD ENG stock stratégique *m*

hedonic: ~ **scale** *n* FOOD TECH échelle hédonique *f*

hedyphane *n* MINERAL hédyphane *m*

heel[1] *n* C&G talon *m*, MECH ENG *of G cramp* patin *m*, *of tool* talon *m*, NAUT bande *f*, gîte *f*; ~ **block** *n* MECH ENG cale de sécurité *f*; ~ **plate** *n* NAUT *shipbuilding* tôle de pied *f*; ~ **post** *n* WATER SUPP *of lock gate* poteau tourillon *m*

heel[2] *vi* NAUT avoir de la bande, avoir de la gîte, donner de la bande, gîter

heeling: ~ **moment** *n* NAUT *ship design* moment d'inclinaison *m*, moment d'inclinaison transversale *m*, moment du couple inclinant *m*

Hegman: ~ **fineness-of-grind gage** *n* (AmE), ~ **fineness-of-grind gauge** *n* (BrE) P&R *for paint* jauge de broyage Hegman *f*

height *n* COMP, DP, FUELLESS *of wave*, MECH ENG *of working part*, NAUT *of tide* hauteur *f*, PHYS hauteur *f*, *above sea level* altitude *f*, *dimension* cote *f*, élévation *f*, PRINT *of capital letters* hauteur *f*, WAVE PHYS amplitude *f*; ~ **above impost level** *n* CONST *of arch* flèche *f*, hauteur sous clef *f*, montée *f*; ~ **above pinch line** *n* MECH ENG *gearing* hauteur au-dessus du primitif *f*, saillie *f*; ~ **adjustment** *n* CONTROL, INSTRUMENT réglage vertical *m*; ~ **of centers** *n* (AmE), ~ **of centres** *n* (BrE) MECH ENG *lathe* HDP, hauteur des pointes *f*; ~ **correc-**

tion *n* GEOPHYS correction d'altitude *f*; ~ **of fall** *n* PACKAGING hauteur de chute *f*; ~ **gage** *n* (AmE) ~ **gauge** *n* (BrE) GEOPHYS altimètre *m*, METR *micrometer* calibre de hauteur *m*; ~ **hovering** *n* TRANSP hauteur en sustentation *f*; ~ **of instrument** *n* CONST *surveying* hauteur de l'instrument en station *f*; ~ **position** *n* NUCLEAR *of control member* position en hauteur *f*; ~ **of swell** *n* NAUT *sea* amplitude de la houle *f*; ~ **of type** *n* PRINT hauteur du caractère *f*, hauteur typographique *f*

heightening *n* CONST rehaussement *m*, surhaussement *m*, surélévation *f*, surélèvement *m*

height-keeping: ~ **error** *n* AERONAUT erreur de tenue d'altitude *f*

height-off: ~ **cushion** *n* TRANSP hauteur à flot *f*

height-on: ~ **cushion** *n* TRANSP hauteur de vol *f*

height-to-paper *n* PRINT hauteur du caractère *f*, hauteur typographique *f*

Heisenberg: ~ **uncertainty principle** *n* PART PHYS principe d'incertitude de Heisenberg *m*

held-up[1] *adj* PROD ENG suspendu

held-up:[2] ~ **order** *n* PROD ENG ordre de fabrication suspendu *m*

heliacal[1] *adj* ASTRON héliaque

heliacal:[2] ~ **rising** *n* ASTRON lever héliaque *m*; ~ **setting** *n* ASTRON coucher héliaque *m*

helianthin *n* CHEM hélianthine *f*

helianthine *n* CHEM hélianthine *f*

helical[1] *adj* GEOM, MECH ENG, TV en hélice, hélicoïdal, hélicoïde, à hélice

helical:[2] ~ **antenna** *n* TELECOM antenne en hélice *f*, antenne hélicoïdale *f*; ~ **coil-type heat exchanger** *n* NUCLEAR échangeur de chaleur à tubes hélicoïdaux *m*; ~ **dislocation** *n* CRYSTALL dislocation en hélice *f*, METALL dislocation hélicale *f*; ~ **gear** *n* AUTO engrenage à denture hélicoïdale *m*, MECH engrenage hélicoïdal *m*, MECH ENG pignon hélicoïdal *m*, VEHICLES *transmission, differential* engrenage à denture hélicoïdale *m*; ~ **groove** *n* MECH ENG rampe hélicoïdale *f*; ~ **instability** *n* NUCLEAR instabilité en hélice *f*, tire-bouchon *m*; ~ **potentiometer** *n* ELEC *resistance* potentiomètre hélicoïdal *m*; ~ **recording** *n* TV enregistrement hélicoïdal *m*; ~ **scan** *n* COMP, DP balayage hélicoïdal *m*, TV lecture hélicoïdale *f*; ~ **scanner** *n* NAUT antenne en hélice *f*; ~ **scanning** *n* ELECTRON balayage hélicoïdal *m*; ~ **spring** *n* MECH ressort à boudin *m*, PHYS ressort hélicoïdal *m*, ressort à boudin *m*

helical-scan: ~ **videotape recorder** *n* TV magnétoscope à défilement hélicoïdal *m*

helicin *n* CHEM hélicine *f*

helicoid[1] *adj* GEOM, MECH ENG hélicoïdal, hélicoïde

helicoid[2] *n* GEOM hélicoïde *m*

helicoidal[1] *adj* MECH ENG, PROP MAT hélicoïdal, hélicoïde

helicoidal:[2] ~ **machining** *n* MECH ENG usinage hélicoïdal *m*; ~ **motion** *n* NUCLEAR mouvement hélicoïdal *m*

helicopter[1] *n* AERONAUT aérodyne à voilure tournante *m*, hélicoptère *m*, TRANSP héliporter *m*; ~ **avionics package** *n* AERONAUT unité avionique d'hélicoptère *f*; ~ **gunship** *n* MILIT hélicoptère avec armement lourd *m*; ~ **landing deck** *n* TRANSP plate-forme d'atterrissage pour hélicoptère *f*; ~ **landing platform** *n* TRANSP hélisurface *f*; ~ **landing surface** *n* TRANSP hélisurface *f*; ~ **pad** *n* MAR POLL aire d'atterrissage *f*, NAUT plate-forme d'appontage d'hélicoptère *f*; ~ **shuttle service** *n* AERONAUT liaison navette par hélicoptère *f*; ~ **station** *n* TRANSP héligare *f*

helicopter[2] *vt* AERONAUT héliporter

helicopter-lifted *adj* AERONAUT, MAR POLL, TRANSP héliporté

heligyro *n* TRANSP héligyre *m*

heli-lifting *n* AERONAUT levage par hélicoptère *m*

helimagnetism *n* PHYS hélimagnétisme *m*

heliocentric[1] *adj* ASTRON héliocentrique

heliocentric:[2] **~ parallax** *n* ASTRON parallaxe héliocentrique *f*; **~ system** *n* ASTRON système héliocentrique *m*

heliodor *n* MINERAL héliodore *m*

heliometer *n* ASTRON héliomètre *m*

Helios: ~ spacecraft *n* ASTRON vaisseau spatial Hélios *m*; **~ space probe** *n* ASTRON sonde d'espace Hélios *f*, sonde spatiale Hélios *f*

heliostat *n* ASTRON, FUELLESS héliostat *m*

heliothermal: ~ process *n* FUELLESS procédé héliothermique *m*

heliotrope *n* MINERAL héliotrope *m*

heliotropic *adj* FUELLESS héliotropique

heliotropin *n* CHEM héliotropine *f*, pipéronal *m*

heliox *n* OCEANOG héliox *m*

helipad *n* AERONAUT aire d'atterrissage pour hélicoptère *f*, PETR TECH *offshore* hélisurface *f*, TRANSP hélistation *f*

heliport *n* AERONAUT, MAR POLL, PETR TECH *shore installation*, TRANSP héligare *f*, héliport *m*; **~ deck** *n* TRANSP héliport *m*

helipot *n* ELEC *resistance* potentiomètre hélicoïdal *m*

helistop *n* AERONAUT, TRANSP hélistation *f*

helium *n (He)* CHEM hélium *m (He)*; **~ dehydrator unit** *n* NUCLEAR déshydrateur d'hélium *m*; **~ dilution refrigerator** *n* PHYS réfrigérateur à dilution d'hélium *m*; **~ leak detection** *n* NUCLEAR détection de fuites à l'hélium *f*; **~ leak test** *n* NUCLEAR essai d'étanchéité à l'hélium *m*; **~ production** *n* ASTRON production d'hélium *f*; **~ voice** *n* OCEANOG voix de l'hélium *f*

helium-neon: ~ laser *n (He-Ne laser)* RAD PHYS laser à hélium-néon *m*

helix *n* CHEM, GEOM, MECH ENG hélice *f*; **~ antenna** *n* SPACE *communications* antenne hélice *f*; **~ traveling-wave tube** *n* (AmE), **~ travelling-wave tube** *n* (BrE) ELECTRON tube à onde progressive à hélice *m*; **~ waveguide** *n* ELEC ENG guide d'ondes hélicoïdal *m*

helixing *n* ELEC ENG spiralage *m*

helm[1] *n* NAUT *boat* barre *f*; **~ damage** *n* NAUT avarie de barre *f*; **~ indicator** *n* NAUT indicateur d'angle de barre *m*

helm[2] *vt* NAUT barrer

helmet *n* PETR, SAFETY casque de protection *m*; **~ cap lubricator** *n* PROD ENG graisseur à casque *m*, graisseur à chapeau mobile *m*

Helmholtz: ~ coil *n* PHYS bobine de Helmholtz *f*; **~ free energy** *n* PHYS fonction de Helmholtz *f*, énergie libre de Helmholtz *f*; **~ galvanometer** *n* ELEC galvanomètre de Helmholtz *m*; **~ resonator** *n* ACOUSTICS résonateur acoustique de Helmholtz *m*, résonateur de Helmholtz *m*, PHYS résonateur de Helmholtz *m*

helmsman *n* NAUT homme de barre *m*

help: ~ directory *n* PROD ENG répertoire d'aides *m*; **~ message** *n* COMP, DP message d'aide *m*; **~ program** *n* COMP, DP programme d'aide *m*; **~ screen** *n* COMP, DP écran d'aide *m*

helper: ~ spring *n* SPRINGS ressort compensateur *m*

helve *n* PROD ENG manche *m*

helver *n* PROD ENG manche *m*

helvine *n* MINERAL helvine *f*, helvite *f*

helvite *n* MINERAL helvine *f*, helvite *f*

hem *n* TEXTILES ourlet *m*

hematein *n* (AmE) *see haematein*

hematic *adj* (AmE) *see haematic*

hematin *n* (AmE) *see haematin*

hematite *n* (AmE) *see haematite*

hematolite *n* (AmE) *see haematolite*

hematoporphyrin *n* (AmE) *see haematoporphyrin*

hematoxylin *n* (AmE) *see haematoxylin*

hemi-acetal *n* CHEM hémiacétal *m*

hemicellulose *n* CHEM hémicellulose *f*

hemiellipsoidal: ~ bottom *n* NUCLEAR *of pressure vessel* bombé à petit rayon de carré *m*, fond hémi-ellipsoïdal *m*; **~ head** *n* NUCLEAR bombé à petit rayon de carré *m*, fond hémi-ellipsoïdal *m*

hemimetallic *adj* CHEM hémimétallique

hemimorphite *n* MINERAL hémimorphite *f*

hemipinic *adj* CHEM hémipinique

hemisphere *n* GEOM hémisphère *m*

hemispherical: ~ combustion chamber *n* AUTO chambre de combustion hémisphérique *f*; **~ coverage** *n* TELECOM couverture hémisphérique *f*

hemoglobin *n* (AmE) *see haemoglobin*

hemolysin *n* (AmE) *see haemolysin*

hemolysis *n* (AmE) *see haemolysis*

hemolytic *adj* (AmE) *see haemolytic*

hemopyrrole *n* (AmE) *see haemopyrrole*

hemosiderin *n* (AmE) *see haemosiderin*

hemotoxin *n* (AmE) *see haemotoxin*

hemp *n* NAUT chanvre *m*; **~ gasket** *n* PROD ENG tresse en chanvre *f*; **~ packing** *n* PROD ENG garniture de chanvre *f*; **~ rope** *n* PACKAGING cordage de chanvre *m*

He-Ne: ~ laser *n (helium-neon laser)* PHYS laser à hélium-néon *m*

henry *n (H)* ELEC, ELEC ENG, METR, PHYS henry *m (H)*

heparin *n* CHEM héparine *f*

hepatite *n* MINERAL hépatite *f*

heptad *n* CHEM heptade *f*

heptagon *n* GEOM heptagone *m*

heptagonal *adj* GEOM heptagonal

heptahedron *n* GEOM heptaèdre *m*

heptane *n* CHEM, PETR TECH heptane *m*

heptatonic: ~ scale *n* ACOUSTICS gamme heptatonique *f*

heptavalent *adj* CHEM heptavalent

heptene *n* CHEM heptène *m*

heptode *n* ELECTRON heptode *f*

heptose *n* CHEM heptose *m*

heptyl *n* CHEM heptyle *m*

heptylene *n* CHEM heptylène *m*

heptylic *adj* CHEM heptylique

heptyne *n* CHEM heptyne *m*

Hercules *n* ASTRON Hercule *m*

hercynite *n* MINERAL hercynite *f*

herder: ~ effect *n* MAR POLL effet repousseur *m*

herding: ~ agent *n* MAR POLL agent repousseur *m*, repousseur *m*

hermaphroditic: ~ connector *n* ELEC ENG connecteur banalisé *m*; **~ contact** *n* ELEC ENG contact banalisé *m*

hermetic: ~ closure *n* PACKAGING fermeture hermétique *f*; **~ compressor** *n* MECH ENG *for refrigerants* compresseur entièrement hermétique *m*; **~ seal** *n* PACKAGING fermeture totalement étanche *f*; **~ sealing** *n* NUCLEAR joint hermétique *m*, TELECOM scellement hermétique *m*

hermetically-sealed[1] *adj* ELEC ENG en boîtier hermétique, MECH hermétiquement clos

hermetically-sealed:[2] **~ compressor unit** *n* REFRIG motocompresseur hermétique *m*; ~ **unit** *n* ELEC ENG version hermétique *f*

heroin *n* CHEM héroïne *f*

herring: ~ **boat** *n* OCEANOG harenguier *m*; ~ **net** *n* OCEANOG harenguière *f*

herringbone *n* MECH ENG chevron *m*; ~ **bar** *n* PROD ENG *grate bar* barreau à chevrons *m*; ~ **cross lamination** *n* GEOL stratification transverse en chevrons *f*; ~ **distortion** *n* C&G distorsion en arête de hareng *f*; ~ **fin** *n* NUCLEAR ailette *f*; ~ **gear** *n* MECH engrenage à denture en chevrons *m*, MECH ENG double hélical *m*, engrenage hélicoïdal double *m*, engrenage à chevrons *m*, pignon à chevrons *m*; ~ **pattern parquet flooring** *n* CONST parquet en arête de poisson *m*, parquet à point de Hongrie *m*; ~ **teeth** *n pl* MECH ENG *gears* dents chevronnées *f pl*; ~ **timbering** *n* MINING boisage armé *m*, longrinage *m*; ~ **weave** *n* TEXTILES armure chevronnée *f*

herringboning *n* TV perturbation en boucles *f*

hertz *n* (*Hz*) ELEC, ELEC ENG, METR, PETR, PHYS, TV hertz *m* (*Hz*)

Hertzian[1] *adj* ELEC *oscillator* hertzien

Hertzian:[2] ~ **beam** *n* TV faisceau hertzien *m*; ~ **dipole** *n* SPACE *communications* doublet de Hertz *m*; ~ **fracture** *n* C&G cône de Hertz *m*

Hertzsprung-Russell: ~ **diagram** *n* ASTRON diagramme HR *m*, diagramme de Hertzsprung-Russell *m*

hesperidin *n* CHEM, FOOD TECH hespéridine *f*

hesperitin *n* CHEM hespéritine *f*

hessian *n* TEXTILES toile de jute *f*

hessite *n* MINERAL argent telluré *m*, hessite *f*

hessonite *n* MINERAL essonite *f*, hessonite *f*

heteroatom *n* CHEM hétéroatome *m*

heteroatomic *adj* CHEM hétéroatomique

heteroauxin *n* CHEM hétéroauxine *f*

heterocyclic *adj* CHEM hétérocyclique

heterodyne: ~ **conversion** *n* ELEC ENG changement de fréquence hétérodyne *m*; ~ **conversion transducer** *n* ELEC ENG changeur de fréquence hétérodyne *m*; ~ **detection** *n* TELECOM détection hétérodyne *f*; ~ **sound analyzer** *n* RECORDING analyseur de son hétérodyne *m*; ~ **wavemeter** *n* WAVE PHYS ondemètre hétérodyne *m*

heterodyning *n* TV hétérodynation *f*

heterogeneous[1] *adj* METALL hétérogène

heterogeneous:[2] ~ **reactor** *n* NUCLEAR réacteur hétérogène *m*

heterogenite *n* MINERAL hétérogénite *f*

heterojunction *n* ELECTRON, OPT, TELECOM hétérojonction *f*; ~ **FET** *n* ELECTRON TEC à hétérojonction *m*

heterolabeling *n* (AmE), **heterolabelling** *n* (BrE) NUCLEAR hétéromarquage *m*

heterometric *adj* (*cf homometric*) GEOL hétérométrique

heteromorphite *n* MINERAL hétéromorphite *f*

heteropolar *adj* CHEM hétéropolaire

heteroside *n* CHEM hétéroside *m*

heterosite *n* MINERAL hétérosite *f*

heteroxanthine *n* CHEM hétéroxanthine *f*

Hettangian *adj* GEOPHYS Hettangien

heulandite *n* MINERAL heulandite *f*

heuristic *adj* COMP, DP heuristique

hew *vt* COAL TECH piquer

hewer *n* CONST *for stone, wood* tailleur *m*

hex *n* COMP (*hexadecimal*) hexadécimal, NUCLEAR hexafluorure d'uranium *m* ~ **headed bolt** *n* PROD ENG boulon à tête hexagonale *m*; ~ **head wrench** *n* MECH

tools clé six-pans *f*

hexacontane *n* CHEM hexacontane *m*

hexacosane *n* CHEM hexacosane *m*

hexad *n* CHEM atome *m*, hexavalent *m*, ion *m*, radical *m*

hexadecane *n* CHEM hexadécane *m*

hexadecimal *adj* (*hex*) COMP, DP hexadécimal

hexadic *adj* CHEM hexavalent

hexadiene *n* CHEM hexadiène *m*

hexagon *n* GEOM hexagone *m*; ~ **head** *n* MECH tête hexagonale *f*, tête à six pans *f*, MECH ENG tête à six pans *f*; ~ **head bolt and hexagon nut** *n* MECH ENG boulon tête et écrou 6 pans *m*; ~ **head screw** *n* MECH vis à tête hexagonale *f*, PROD ENG vis à tête à six pans *f*; ~ **nut** *n* MECH ENG écrou hexagonal *m*; ~ **socket screw** *n* MECH, MECH ENG vis à six pans creux *f*; ~ **socket screw with flat point** *n* MECH ENG vis sans tête à six pans *f*; ~ **turret lathe** *n* MECH ENG tour à tourelle hexagonale *m*; ~ **voltage** *n* ELEC *six-phase system* tension en hexagone *f*

hexagonal[1] *adj* CRYSTALL, GEOM, PROP MAT hexagonal

hexagonal:[2] ~ **close-packed lattice** *n* NUCLEAR réseau hexagonal compact *m*; ~ **close-packed structure** *n* (*hcp*) CRYSTALL structure hexagonale compacte *f*; ~ **die nut** *n* MECH ENG filière hexagonale pour filetage à la main *f*; ~ **head bolt** *n* MECH ENG boulon à six pans *m*; ~ **key** *n* MECH ENG *tool* clé mâle *f*; ~ **mesh-wired glass** *n* C&G verre armé à mailles hexagonales *m*; ~ **metal** *n* PROP MAT métal hexagonal *m*; ~ **nut** *n* MECH ENG écrou à six pans *m*

hexahedral *adj* GEOM hexaèdre

hexahedron *n* GEOM hexaèdre *m*

hexahydrobenzene *n* CHEM hexahydrobenzène *m*

hexahydrobenzoic *adj* CHEM hexahydrobenzoïque

hexahydrophenol *n* CHEM hexahydrophénol *m*

hexahydropyridine *n* CHEM hexahydropyridine *f*, pipéridine *f*

hexamethylene: ~ **diisocyanate** *n* P&R hexaméthylène tétramine *m*

hexamethyltetramine *n* CHEM urotropine *f*

hexane *n* CHEM, PETR TECH hexane *m*

hexanol *n* CHEM hexanol *m*

hexatonic: ~ **scale** *n* ACOUSTICS gamme hexatonique *f*

hexavalent *adj* CHEM hexavalent, sexvalent

hexene *n* CHEM hexène *m*

hexidecimal: ~ **notation** *n* DP numération hexadécimale *f*

hexode *n* ELECTRON hexode *f*

hexogen *n* CHEM hexogène *m*

hexosan *n* CHEM hexosane *m*

hexose *n* CHEM hexose *m*

hexyl *n* CHEM hexyl *m*; ~ **alcohol** *n* CHEM alcool hexylique *m*

hexylene *n* CHEM hexylène *m*

hexylic *adj* CHEM hexylique

hexyne *n* CHEM hexyne *m*

Hf (*hafnium*) CHEM Hf (*hafnium*)

HF[1] *abbr* (*high-frequency*) AERONAUT, ELEC, ELEC ENG, ELECTRON HF (*haute fréquence*)

HF:[2] ~ **carrier** *n* ELECTRON porteuse HF *f*; ~ **erase head** *n* RECORDING tête d'effacement à haute fréquence *f*; ~ **signal** *n* ELECTRON signal HF *m*, signal à fréquence HF *m*, signal à haute fréquence *m*; ~ **signal generator** *n* ELECTRON générateur de signaux HF *m*; ~ **spectrum** *n* ELECTRON spectre HF *m*; ~ **transformer** *n* ELEC ENG transformateur HF *m*, transformateur à haute fréquence *m*; ~ **transistor** *n* ELECTRON transistor HF *m*, transistor haute fréquence *m*

Hg *(mercury)* CHEM Hg *(mercure)*

HG: ~ **driver** *n* CONST conducteur de poids lourds *m*

H-girder *n* CONST poutre en double T *f*, solive en fer à double T *f*

HGV[1] *abbr (heavy goods vehicle)* TRANSP poids lourd *m*

HGV:[2] ~ **traffic** *n* TRANSP trafic lourd *m*

H-hinge *n* CONST paumelle double *f*

HHSV *abbr (high hypothetical speed vehicle)* TRANSP véhicule à grande vitesse hypothétique *m*

HI: ~ **region** *n* ASTRON région HI *f*

hiatus *n* GEOL *break* lacune *f*, PETR hiatus *m*

hickey *n* (AmE) ELEC *connection* prise mâle et femelle *f*

hidden: ~ **bar code identification** *n* PACKAGING identification avec code à barres masqué *f*, ~ **layer** *n* PETR couche cachée *f*

hiddenite *n* MINERAL hiddénite *f*

hide-faced: ~ **mallet** *n* MECH ENG maillet de cuir *m*

hiding-power *n* P&R *paint* pouvoir couvrant *m*

hierarchical: ~ **model** *n* COMP, DP modèle hiérarchique *m*; ~ **object-oriented design** *n* COMP, DP *(HOOD)* conception hiérarchique orientée objet *f*; ~ **system** *n* TELECOM système hiérarchisé *m*, système à structure hiérarchique *m*

hierarchy *n* COMP, DP hiérarchie *f*

hi-fi: ~ **sound** *n* TV *VHS sound system* système à son hi-fi *m*

Higgs: ~ **boson** *n* PART PHYS boson de Higgs *m*; ~ **particle** *n* PART PHYS particule de Higgs *f*

high[1] *adj* MECH ENG *height* de haut, de hauteur, en hauteur, haut, PAPER TECH haut; ~ **band** *adj* TV high band, à fréquence élevée; ~ **fidelity** *adj* RECORDING haute-fidélité

high[2] *n* GEOL culmination d'un pli *f*, METEO anticyclone *m*, zone de haute pression *f*; ~ **angle dip** *n* GEOL pendage élevé *m*; ~ **angle shot** *n* CINEMAT plan en plongée *m*; ~ **barrier** *n* PACKAGING haute barrière *f*, PRINT haute barrière *m*; ~ **beams** *n pl* (AmE) *(cf full beam headlights)* VEHICLES *headlights* pleins phares *m pl*; ~ **bit-rate ATM network mixer** *n* TELECOM brasseur de réseau à haut débit ATM *m*; ~ **concentration** *n* POLLUTION forte concentration *f*; ~ **contrast film** *n* CINEMAT pellicule à contraste élevé *f*; ~ **degree of protection** *n* PROD ENG indice élevé de protection *m*; ~ **discharge temperature cutout** *n* REFRIG thermostat de sécurité de refoulement *m*; ~ **elongation furnace carbon black** *n* P&R *pigment* noir HEF *m*; ~ **end computer** *n* COMP ordinateur de haute gamme *m*; ~ **end computing** *n* COMP grande informatique *f*; ~ **explosive** *n* MILIT explosif puissant *m*, MINING explosif *m*, explosif brisant *m*, explosif détonant *m*, explosif à grande vitesse de détonation *m*, explosif de grande puissance *m*; ~ **flow rate** *n* PROD ENG débit élevé *m*; ~ **flux reactor** *n* NUCLEAR réacteur à haut flux *m*; ~ **gear** *n* MECH ENG grande multiplication *f*; ~ **gloss** *n* P&R *paint* brillant *m*; ~ **gloss foil** *n* PACKAGING laminage à pellicule brillante *m*; ~ **gloss paper** *n* PACKAGING papier glacé *m*; ~ **gradient** *n* CONST forte pente *f*; ~ **hat** *n* CINEMAT petit pied de caméra *m*; ~ **head** *n* FUELLESS colonne d'eau élevée *f*; ~ **hypothetical speed vehicle** *n* *(HHSV)* TRANSP véhicule à grande vitesse hypothétique *m*; ~ **impedance state** *n* ELEC ENG état à haute fréquence *m*; ~ **key** *n* CINEMAT haute lumière *f*, éclairage intense *m*; ~ **key document** *n* PRINT document sous-développé *m*, document surexposé *m*; ~ **lift devices** *n pl* AERONAUT hypersustentateurs *m pl*; ~ **lift-lock** *n* HYDROL *canals* écluse à grande chute *f*; ~ **logic level** *n* ELECTRON

niveau logique haut *m*; ~ **loss** *n* TELECOM affaiblissement élevé *m*, atténuation forte *f*; ~ **modulus fabric** *n* PROP MAT *glass fibre* tissu haut-module *m*; ~ **modulus furnace carbon black** *n* *(HMF carbon black)* P&R *pigment* noir HMF *m*; ~ **output tape** *n* RECORDING bande magnétique à niveau de sortie élevée *f*; ~ **picture level** *n* TV luminance élevée *f*; ~ **pitch** *n* AERONAUT *helicopter* grand pas *m*; ~ **purity pigment** *n* P&R *paint* pigment à grand teint *m*; ~ **resistance** *n* PHYS résistance élevée *f*, TELECOM *(HR)* haute résistance *f*; ~ **Reynolds number** *n* FLUID PHYS nombre de Reynolds élevé *m*; ~ **seas** *n pl* OCEANOG haute mer *f*; ~ **side lobe** *n* ELECTRON lobe secondaire de grande amplitude *m*; ~ **specific speed wheel** *n* FUELLESS roue à grande vitesse spécifique *f*; ~ **sulfur content** *n* (AmE), ~ **sulphur content** *n* (BrE) CHEM haute teneur en soufre *f*, PETR TECH forte teneur en soufre *f*; ~ **tide** *n* FUELLESS, HYDROL marée haute *f*, NAUT marée haute *f*, pleine mer *f*, OCEANOG pleine mer *f*; ~ **water** *n* HYDROL haute mer *f*, *river* hautes eaux *f pl*, *tidal* haut de l'eau *m*, marée haute *f*, plein de l'eau *m*, NAUT *tides* grandes eaux *f pl*, hautes eaux *f pl*, pleine mer *f*; ~ **water level** *n* CONST plus hautes eaux *f pl*; ~ **water line** *n* HYDROL ligne des hautes eaux *f*; ~ **water mark** *n* HYDROL *sea* laisse de haute mer *f*, limite de la marée *f*, NAUT laisse de pleine mer *f*, OCEANOG laisse de haute mer *f*; ~ **water ordinary spring tide** *n* *(HWOST)* FUELLESS plus hautes eaux des grandes marées ordinaires *f pl*; ~ **water overflow** *n* WATER SUPP évacuateur de crues *m*

high-amplitude: ~ **pulse** *n* ELECTRON impulsion de grande amplitude *f*; ~ **signal** *n* ELECTRON signal de grande amplitude *m*

high-brightness: ~ **screen** *n* ELECTRON écran à haute luminosité *m*

high-bulk: ~ **spun yarn** *n* TEXTILES filé à gonflant élevé *m*

high-conductance: ~ **diode** *n* ELECTRON diode à haute conductance *f*

high-conductivity: ~ **steel** *n* PROP MAT acier à conductivité élevée *m*

high-cube: ~ **container** *n* *(HC)* TRANSP conteneur hors-cotes *m* *(HC)*

high-current: ~ **diode** *n* ELECTRON diode à fort courant *f*; ~ **transistor** *n* ELECTRON transistor pour forts courants *m*

high-definition: ~ **television** *n* *(HDTV)* TELECOM, TV télévision à haute définition *f* *(TVHD)*

high-density[1] *adj* DP compact

high-density:[2] ~ **bipolar of order 2 code** *n* *(HDB2)* TELECOM code bipolaire à haute densité d'ordre 2 *m*; ~ **integrated circuit** *n* ELECTRON circuit intégré à haute densité *m*; ~ **logic** *n* ELECTRON logique à haute densité *f*; ~ **polyethylene** *n* PACKAGING *(HDPE)*, PROP MAT polyéthylène à haute densité *m*

high-dose: ~ **implant** *n* ELECTRON impureté implantée à haute dose *f*

high-energy: ~ **astronomy** *n* ASTRON astronomie des hautes énergies *f*; ~ **astrophysics** *n* ASTRON astrophysique à énergie haute *f*; ~ **beam** *n* ELECTRON faisceau à haute énergie *m*; ~ **beam experiment** *n* RAD PHYS expérience à faisceau de haute énergie *f*; ~ **electron** *n* ELECTRON électron à haute énergie *m*; ~ **electron diffraction** *n* PART PHYS diffraction d'électrons de grande énergie *f*; ~ **electron-positron beams** *n pl* PART PHYS faisceaux d'électrons et de positrons de haute énergie *m pl*; ~ **elementary particle** *n* PART PHYS particule élémentaire de haute énergie *f*; ~ **environment** *n*

GEOL milieu sédimentaire à forte énergie *m*; ~ **fusion** *n* NUCLEAR fusion à haute énergie *f*; ~ **ion** *n* ELECTRON ion à haute énergie *m*; ~ **kaon beams** *n pl* PART PHYS faisceaux de kaons de haute énergie *m pl*; ~ **laser** *n* ELECTRON laser de puissance *m*; ~ **muon beams** *n pl* PART PHYS faisceaux de muons de haute énergie *m pl*; ~ **particle** *n* ELECTRON particule à haute énergie *f*; ~ **physics** *n* PHYS, RAD PHYS physique des hautes énergies *f*; ~ **proton** *n* SPACE proton à haute énergie *m*; ~ **radiation** *n* RAD PHYS rayonnement de grande énergie *m*, rayonnement à haute énergie *m*; ~ **tape** *n* TV bande de haute énergie *f*

higher: ~ **dimensions** *n pl* GEOM dimensions supérieures *f pl*; ~ **high water** *n* OCEANOG pleine mer supérieure *f*

higher-layer: ~ **function** *n* (*HLF*) TELECOM fonction de couche supérieure *f*

higher-level: ~ **service** *n* TELECOM service de niveau élevé *m*

higher-order: ~ **path adaptation** *n* (*HPA*) TELECOM adaptation de conduit d'ordre supérieur *f*; ~ **path connection** *n* (*HPC, lower-order path connection*) TELECOM connexion de conduit d'ordre supérieur *f*; ~ **path termination** *n* (*HPT*) TELECOM terminaison de conduit d'ordre supérieur *f*

highest: ~ **common factor** *n* (*HCF*) MATH plus grand commun diviseur *m* (*PGCD*)

high-fiber *adj* (AmE), **high-fibre** *adj* (BrE) FOOD TECH à haute teneur en cellulose

high-frequency *n* (*HF*) ELEC *supply*, ELECTRON haute fréquence *f* (*HF*) **very** ~ *n* (*VHF*) ELECTRON, SPACE, TELECOM, TV, WAVE PHYS très haute fréquence *f* (*VHF*) (*HF*) AERONAUT, ELEC ENG haute fréquence *f* (*HF*); ~ **amplification** *n* ELECTRON amplification à haute fréquence *f*; ~ **cable** *n* ELEC *alternating current* câble à haute fréquence *m*; ~ **carrier** *n* ELECTRON porteuse à haute fréquence *f*; ~ **compensation** *n* RECORDING compensation des hautes fréquences *f*; ~ **component** *n* ELECTRON composante à fréquence élevée *f*; ~ **current** *n* ELEC *alternating current* courant à haute fréquence *m*; ~ **discharge** *n* GAS TECH décharge haute fréquence *f*; ~ **distribution frame** *n* TELECOM répartiteur de hautes fréquences *m*; ~ **filter** *n* RECORDING filtre pour hautes fréquences *m*; ~ **furnace** *n* ELEC ENG four à haute fréquence *m*; ~ **generator** *n* ELEC générateur à haute fréquence *m*; ~ **heating** *n* ELEC chauffage par haute fréquence *m*, ELEC ENG chauffage HF *m*, chauffage à haute fréquence *m*; ~ **horn loudspeaker** *n* RECORDING haut-parleur à pavillon pour haute fréquence *m*; ~ **induction brazing** *n* CONST brasage par induction à haute fréquence *m*; ~ **line** *n* PHYS ligne en haute fréquence *f*; ~ **network analysis** *n* ELEC ENG analyse des réseaux à haute fréquence *f*; **very** ~ **omnirange** *n* (*VHFO*) TRANSP radiophare omnidirectionnel VHF *m*; ~ **printed circuit** *n* ELECTRON circuit imprimé haute fréquence *m*; ~ **printed circuit board** *n* ELECTRON carte à circuit imprimé haute fréquence *f*; ~ **signal** *n* ELECTRON signal à fréquence élevée *m*; ~ **spectrum** *n* ELECTRON spectre des hautes fréquences *m*; ~ **switching** *n* ELEC ENG commutation à haute fréquence *f*; ~ **thawing** *n* REFRIG dégel par radio fréquence *m*; ~ **transformer** *n* ELEC ENG transformateur à haute fréquence *m*; ~ **transistor** *n* ELECTRON transistor haute fréquence *m*; ~ **welding** *n* PACKAGING soudure à haute fréquence *f*; ~ **welding equipment** *n* PACKAGING équipement de soudure à haute fréquence *m*

high-gain: ~ **amplifier** *n* ELECTRON amplificateur à grand gain *m*; ~ **power amplifier** *n* ELECTRON amplificateur de puissance à grand gain *m*

high-gamma: ~ **camera tube** *n* ELECTRON tube analyseur à grand gamma *m*

high-grade[1] *adj* COAL TECH de haute qualité, à haute teneur, à forte teneur

high-grade[2] *n* CHEM haute teneur *f*; ~ **heat** *n* NUCLEAR chaleur de haute qualité *f*; ~ **metamorphism** *n* GEOL catamétamorphisme *m*; ~ **ore** *n* COAL TECH minerai riche *m*; ~ **steel** *n* PROP MAT acier affiné *m*

high-gravity: ~ **gasoline** *n* (AmE) (*cf high-gravity petrol*) AUTO essence légère *f*; ~ **petrol** *n* (BrE) (*cf high-gravity gasoline*) AUTO essence légère *f*

high-intensity: ~ **discharge lamp** *n* CINEMAT lampe à décharge haute intensité *f*; ~ **electric arc** *n* ELEC arc à haute intensité *m*; ~ **ion beams** *n pl* RAD PHYS faisceaux d'ions à forte intensité *m pl*; ~ **operation** *n* RAD PHYS fonctionnement à forte intensité *m*

high-irradiance: ~ **laser beam** *n* ELECTRON faisceau laser à grande densité de puissance *m*

high-level: ~ **data link control** *n* COMP, DP, TELECOM (*HDLC*) commande de liaison de données à haut niveau *m*, procédure de liaison de données à haut niveau *f*, procédure (*HDLC*); ~ **dosimetry** *n* RAD PHYS dosimétrie de haut niveau *f*; ~ **injection** *n* ELECTRON injection à haut niveau *f*; ~ **language** *n* COMP langage évolué *m*; ~ **logic** *n* ELECTRON logique à haut niveau *f*; ~ **modulation** *n* ELECTRON modulation à haut niveau *f*; ~ **signal** *n* ELECTRON signal à haut niveau *m*; ~ **waste** *n* RECYCLING déchets de forte activité *m pl*

highlight:[1] ~ **tearing** *n* TV déchirure des plages claires *f*

highlight[2] *vt* PRINT mettre en vedette, souligner

highlights *n pl* PHOTO hautes lumières *f pl*, PRINT grandes lumières *f pl*, grands blancs *m pl*, hautes lumières *f pl*

highly-acid: ~ **slag** *n* PROD ENG laitier ultra-acide *m*

highly-auriferous: ~ **gravel** *n* MINING gravier à haute teneur d'or *m*

highly-basic: ~ **slag** *n* PROD ENG laitier ultra-basique *m*

highly-enriched: ~ **uranium** *n* NUCLEAR uranium très enrichi *m*

highly-flammable *adj* SAFETY très inflammable

highly-flexible *adj* PROD ENG hautement polyvalent

highly-inclined: ~ **seam** *n* MINING couche de fort pendage *f*, dressant *m*

highly-loaded *adj* PROD ENG fortement sollicité

highly-plastic: ~ **clay** *n* C&G argile grasse *f*

highly-skilled: ~ **worker** *n* PROD ENG ouvrier professionnel *m*

highly-stable: ~ **oscillator** *n* ELECTRON oscillateur ultra-stable *m*

high-order[1] *adj* COMP, DP de poids fort, de poids le plus fort

high-order:[2] ~ **bit** *n* COMP, DP bit de gauche *m*, bit de poids fort *m*; ~ **cyclic pitch** *n* AERONAUT *helicopter* pas multicyclique *m*; ~ **delay** *n* ELECTRON retard d'ordre élevé *m*; ~ **filter** *n* ELECTRON filtre d'ordre élevé *m*; ~ **harmonic** *n* ELECTRON harmonique de rang élevé *m*; ~ **network** *n* TELECOM réseau d'ordre supérieur *m*

high-pass: ~ **filter** *n* (*cf low-pass filter*) COMP, DP, ELEC, ELECTRON, PHYS, RECORDING, TELECOM, TV filtre passe-haut *m*; ~ **filtering** *n* (*cf low-pass filtering*) ELECTRON filtrage passe-haut *m*

high-performance[1] *adj* PHYS performant

high-performance[2] *n* RECORDING haute performance *f*; ~ **battery** *n* TRANSP accumulateur performant *m*; ~ **fan**

_n_ REFRIG ventilateur à haute technologie _m_; **~ liquid chromatography** _n_ POLLUTION chromatographie liquide à grande vitesse _f_, chromatographie liquide à haute performance _f_; **~ night vision goggles** _n pl_ MILIT lunettes de nuit à hautes performances _f pl_

high-potential: ~ socket _n_ NUCLEAR prise haute tension _f_

high-power: ~ amplifier _n_ SPACE _communications_ amplificateur de puissance _m_; **~ bipolar transistor** _n_ ELECTRON transistor bipolaire de grande puissance _m_; **~ field glasses** _n pl_ INSTRUMENT jumelles à fort grossissement _f pl_; **~ laser** _n_ NUCLEAR laser de puissance _m_, laser multikilowatts _m_; **~ linear motor** _n_ TRANSP moteur linéaire de grande puissance _m_; **~ load** _n_ ELEC ENG charge de grande puissance _f_; **~ microscope** _n_ INSTRUMENT microscope à fort grossissement _m_; **~ rectifier** _n_ ELEC ENG redresseur de grande puissance _m_; **~ SCR** _n_ ELEC ENG thyristor de grande puissance _m_; **~ transformer** _n_ ELEC transformateur de grande puissance _m_; **~ transmission** _n_ TELECOM transmission à grande puissance _f_; **~ tube** _n_ ELECTRON tube de grande puissance _m_

high-pressure[1] _adj_ PHYS à haute pression

high-pressure[2] _n_ GAS TECH haute pression _f_, PHYS haute pression _f_, pression élevée _f_; **~ area** _n_ METEO anticyclone _m_, zone de haute pression _f_; **~ blowpipe** _n_ CONST _welding_ chalumeau à haute pression _m_; **~ compressor** _n_ MECH ENG compresseur haute pression _m_; **~ controller** _n_ REFRIG régulateur de haute pression _m_; **~ float valve** _n_ REFRIG soupape haute pression à flotteur _f_; **~ flushing** _n_ MAR POLL lavage haute pression _m_, lessivage à haute pression _m_; **~ gage** _n_ (AmE), **~ gauge** _n_ (BrE) REFRIG manomètre de refoulement _m_; **~ heating system** _n_ HEATING chauffage à haute pression _m_; **~ hot water system** _n_ HEATING installation de chauffage d'eau à haute pression _f_; **~ liquid chromatography** _n_ (HPLC) CHEM, FOOD TECH, LAB EQUIP, POLLUTION chromatographie liquide à haute pression _f_ (CLHP); **~ mercury lamp** _n_ ELEC lampe à mercure à haute pression _f_; **~ nerve syndrome** _n_ OCEANOG syndrome nerveux des hautes pressions _m_; **~ nervous syndrome** _n_ OCEANOG SNHP, syndrome nerveux des hautes pressions _m_; **~ piston compressor** _n_ MECH ENG compresseur à piston à haute pression _m_; **~ safety cutout** _n_ REFRIG pressostat de sécurité de haute pression _m_; **~ tank** _n_ SPACE _spacecraft_ réservoir haute pression _m_; **~ tire** _n_ (AmE), **~ tyre** _n_ (BrE) TRANSP, VEHICLES pneu haute pression _m_; **~ vacuum pump** _n_ MECH ENG pompe à vide préliminaire _f_; **~ washing** _n_ MAR POLL décapage au jet à haute pression _m_; **~ zone** _n_ METEO anticyclone _m_, zone de haute pression _f_

high-protein _adj_ FOOD TECH riche en protéines

high-resolution _n_ COMP, DP haute définition _f_, haute résolution _f_; **~ graphics** _n pl_ COMP graphiques haute définition _m pl_; **~ scan** _n_ RAD PHYS scanographie à haute résolution _f_; **~ study of line profiles** _n_ RAD PHYS _spectral lines_ étude haute-résolution des profils des raies _f_

high-risk: ~ areas of work _n pl_ SAFETY zones de travail à haute risque _f pl_

high-sensitivity: ~ tachometer _n_ MECH ENG tachymètre de haute précision _m_

high-solid: ~ mud _n_ PETR TECH _drilling_ boue à forte teneur en solides _f_

high-speed[1] _adj_ MECH _materials_ rapide, à grande vitesse

high-speed[2] _n_ MECH ENG allure rapide _f_, grande vitesse _f_, marche rapide _f_; **~ auxiliary jet** _n_ AUTO gicleur auxi-

liaire de puissance _m_; **~ buffeting** _n_ AERONAUT buffeting à grande vitesse _m_, buffêtement à grande vitesse _m_; **~ camera** _n_ CINEMAT caméra grande vitesse _f_; **~ drill** _n_ MECH foret en acier rapide _m_; **~ duplication** _n_ TV copie à grande vitesse _f_, duplication à grande vitesse _f_; **~ engine** _n_ MECH moteur rapide _m_, NAUT diesel rapide _m_; **~ exit taxiway** _n_ AERONAUT voie de sortie rapide _f_; **~ facsimile** _n_ TELECOM télécopie rapide _f_; **~ film** _n_ CINEMAT pellicule rapide _f_, pellicule sensible _f_; **~ film processing** _n_ CINEMAT développement à grande vitesse _m_; **~ gas turbine motor coach** _n_ (BrE) (cf high-speed gas turbine railcar) TRANSP turbotrain à grande vitesse _m_; **~ gas turbine railcar** _n_ (AmE) (cf high-speed gas turbine motor coach) TRANSP turbotrain à grande vitesse _m_; **~ grinding machine** _n_ MECH ENG _for helicoidal machining_ rectifieuse à haute vitesse _f_; **~ ground transportation** _n_ TRANSP transport terrestre à grande vitesse _m_; **~ inspection** _n_ PACKAGING inspection rapide _f_; **~ lens** _n_ PHOTO objectif à grande ouverture _m_; **~ logic** _n_ ELECTRON logique rapide _f_; **~ mesh** _n_ ELECTRON grille rapide _f_; **~ modem** _n_ ELECTRON modem rapide _m_, modem à grande vitesse de transmission _m_; **~ motor** _n_ ELEC _machine_ moteur à grande vitesse _m_; **~ multirack counting system** _n_ PACKAGING système de comptage à haute vitesse sur baies multiples _m_; **~ particle** _n_ NUCLEAR particule rapide _f_; **~ passenger conveyor** _n_ TRANSP tapis roulant rapide _m_; **~ printer** _n_ PRINT imprimante ultrarapide _f_; **~ relay** _n_ ELEC relais à action rapide _m_; **~ rotary tablet compression machine** _n_ PACKAGING pastilleuse rotative à grand rendement _f_; **~ small tools** _n pl_ MECH ENG petit outillage en acier rapide _m_; **~ steel** _n_ MECH _materials_ acier rapide _m_; **~ steel small tools** _n pl_ (HSS small tools) MECH ENG petit outillage en acier rapide _m_; **~ switching diode** _n_ ELECTRON diode de commutation rapide _f_; **~ switching transistor** _n_ ELECTRON transistor de commutation rapide _m_; **~ train** _n_ (HST) RAIL train à grande vitesse _m_ (TGV)

high-stop: ~ filter _n_ (cf low-stop filter) MECH ENG filtre passe-bas _m_

high-tack: ~ pressure-sensitive adhesive _n_ PACKAGING adhésif fort autocollant _m_

high-temperature[1] _adj_ HEAT ENG à température élevée, PHYS à haute température, à température élevée

high-temperature[2] _n_ PHYS haute température _f_, température élevée _f_; **~ alloy** _n_ MECH _materials_ alliage pour hautes températures _m_; **~ creep** _n_ METALL fluage à haute température _m_; **~ fuel cell** _n_ TRANSP pile à haute température _f_; **~ gas radiant panel** _n_ HEATING panneau rayonnant à gaz à température élevée _m_; **~ grease** _n_ MECH _materials_ graisse pour hautes températures _f_; **~ insulation** _n_ ELEC isolation à haute température _f_; **~ molten salts fuel battery** _n_ (AmE) TRANSP accumulateur aux sels fondus à haute température _m_; **~ short time** _n_ (HTST) FOOD TECH pasteurisation HTST _f_; **~ solid electrolyte cell** _n_ TRANSP pile à haute température à électrolyte solide _f_; **~ strength test** _n_ TESTING essai d'endurance haute température _m_; **~ superconductivity** _n_ PHYS supraconductivité à haute température _f_

high-tenacity: ~ fiber _n_ (AmE), **~ fibre** _n_ (BrE) TEXTILES fibre haute ténacité _f_

high-tensile[1] _adj_ MECH _materials_ à haute résistance à la traction, PROP MAT à haute résistance

high-tensile:[2] **~ steel** _n_ MECH _materials_ acier à haute résistance _m_

high-tension n *(HT)* ELEC *supply*, ELEC ENG, PHYS haute tension f *(HT)*; **~ detonator** n MINING détonateur à HI m, détonateur à haute intensité m; **~ power supply** n ELEC ENG centrale à haute tension f, installation à haute tension f, station à haute tension f; **~ terminal** n AUTO borne haute tension f

high-torque[1] adj MECH à couple élevé

high-torque:[2] **~ motor** n MECH moteur à couple élevé m

high-usage: **~ circuit group** n TELECOM faisceau à fort trafic m

high-vacuum[1] adj MECH à vide poussé

high-vacuum[2] n PHYS vide poussé m; **~ cathode ray tube** n TV tube cathodique à vide élevé m; **~ furnace** n MECH ENG four à vide poussé m; **~ tube** n ELECTRON tube à vide poussé m

high-velocity: **~ scanning** n TV analyse par électrons de haute vitesse f; **~ stars** n pl ASTRON étoiles ultra rapides f pl

high-voltage[1] adj PHYS à haute tension

high-voltage[2] n *(HV)* ELEC *supply*, ELECTRON, PHYS haute tension f *(HT)*; **~ bus** n ELEC *distribution* barre à haute tension f; **~ cable** n ELEC *supply*, INSTRUMENT câble à haute tension m; **~ circuit breaker** n ELEC *switch* interrupteur à haute tension m; **~ electron microscope** n INSTRUMENT microscope électronique à haute tension m; **~ equipment** n ELEC équipement à haute tension m; **~ grid** n ELEC *supply* réseau primaire m; **~ impulse generator** n ELEC générateur de choc m, générateur à haute tension m; **~ insulation** n ELEC isolation à haute tension f; **~ motor** n ELEC moteur à haute tension m; **~ porcelain** n ELEC *insulation* porcelaine à haute tension f; **~ power supply** n ELEC ENG alimentation à très haute tension f; **~ rectifier** n ELEC redresseur à haute tension m; **~ switch gear** n ELEC appareillage à haute tension m, installation de distribution à haute tension f; **~ system** n ELEC *supply* réseau primaire m; **~ tester** n ELEC essayeur à haute tension m; **~ transformer** n ELEC transformateur HT m, transformateur à haute tension m; **~ transmission line** n ELEC *distribution* ligne à haute tension f; **~ winding** n ELEC *transformer* enroulement à haute tension m

highway n (BrE) COMP bus m, CONST route f, voie publique f, DP, TELECOM bus m, TRANSP autoroute f; **~ bridge** n CONST pont pour routes m, pont-route m

high-wing: **~ plane** n AERONAUT avion à aile haute m

high-yield n PAPER TECH haut rendement m; **~ pulp** n PAPER TECH pâte à haut rendement f

HII: **~ region** n ASTRON région HII f

HII-type: **~ nebula** n ASTRON, SPACE nébuleuse de type HI f; **~ region** n ASTRON HI type de nébuleuse m

hilt n PROD ENG *of pick* manche m

hindrance n SAFETY empêchement m, entrave f, gêne f, obstacle m

hinge n CONST *of cabinet* fiche f, *of gate* penture f, GEOL, INSTRUMENT, MECH charnière f, MECH ENG articulation f, charnière f, VEHICLES charnière f; **~ and ball joint** n MECH ENG rotule d'articulation f; **~ and pin** n CONST charnière et gond f, charnière et pivot f; **~ cover** n PROD ENG couvercle articulé m; **~ fitting** n MECH ENG embout d'articulation m, ferrure d'articulation f; **~ fork** n AERONAUT fourche d'articulation f; **~ joint** n CONST assemblage à charnière m; **~ moment** n AERONAUT *helicopter* moment de charnière m; **~ pin** n CONST broche de charnière f, cheville f, rivure f, MECH ENG axe d'articulation m, broche de charnière f; **~ post** n CONST barreau de côtière m, montant de côtière

m; **~ shaft** n MECH ENG arbre d'articulation m; **~ spindle** n REFRIG axe de charnière m; **~ with knobbed pin** n CONST fiche à bouton f; **~ yoke** n MECH ENG noix d'articulation f

hinged[1] adj MECH pivotant, sur charnières, MECH ENG rabattable

hinged:[2] **~ body microscope** n INSTRUMENT microscope à genouillère m; **~ bolt fitting** n MECH ENG *pipes* raccord à boulon à charnière m; **~ lid** n PACKAGING couvercle à charnières m; **~ panel** n MECH ENG panneau ouvrant m; **~ plug orifice closure** n PACKAGING capsule autopénétrante à charnière f; **~ suspension** n MECH ENG suspension articulée f

hinging n MECH ENG articulation f; **~ post** n CONST barreau de côtière m, montant de côtière m

hinterland n GEOL arrière-pays m

hip n CONST arête f, arêtier m, chevron arêtier m, *of gable* croupe f; **~ rafter** n CONST arêtier m, chevron arêtier m, chevron de long pan m; **~ roof** n CONST comble en croupe m; **~ roof with ridge** n CONST comble à deux longs pans avec croupes m; **~ tile** n CONST arêtière f, tuile arêtière f

hip-and-ridge: **~ roof** n CONST comble à deux longs pans avec croupes m, toit en croupe et faîte m

hip-and-valley: **~ roof** n CONST combles s'intersectant m pl

hipped: **~ ridge roof** n CONST comble à deux longs pans avec croupes m; **~ roof** n CONST comble en croupe m

H-iron n CONST fer double T m, fer en H m, fer à I m, fer à double T m, poutrelle f

hiss: **~ filter** n RECORDING filtre de sifflement m

histamine n CHEM histamine f

histogram n DP, MATH, PHYS, TELECOM histogramme m

histology: **~ bath** n LAB EQUIP *section mounting* bain pour histologie m

histone n CHEM histone f

historical: **~ data** n pl POLLUTION données antérieures f pl, données historiques f pl

hit[1] n COMP correspondance f, frappe f, coïncidence f, DP correspondance f, coïncidence f, frappe f; **~ and miss damper** n HEAT ENG registre à glissières m; **~ or miss governor** n AERONAUT régulateur par tout ou rien m; **~ or miss selector valve** n MECH ENG sélecteur tout ou rien m

hit[2] vt COMP, DP frapper

hitch[1] n MECH *vehicles* crochet d'attelage m, MINING potelle f, NAUT *ropes* clé f, noeud m, VEHICLES crochet d'attelage m; **~ pin** n PROD ENG cheville d'attache f

hitch[2] vt MECH *vehicles* atteler, MINING *timbering* empoter

hit-on-the-fly: **~ printer** n COMP, DP imprimante à la volée f

Hittorf: **~ dark space** n ELECTRON zone obscure de Crookes f

HI-type: **~ nebula** n ASTRON, SPACE nébuleuse de type HI f

HLF n *(higher-layer function)* TELECOM fonction de couche supérieure f

HLLV abbr *(heavy-lift launch vehicle)* SPACE lanceur lourd m

HMF: **~ carbon black** n *(high modulus furnace carbon black)* P&R *pigment, filler* noir HMF m

HMI: **~ lamp** n CINEMAT lampe HMI f

Ho *(holmium)* CHEM Ho *(holmium)*

hoar: **~ frost** n METEO, REFRIG gelée blanche f

hob n MECH fraise mère f, MECH ENG *for cutting screw-*

chasers fraise pour peigne *f*, *for cutting wormwheels* vis fraise *f*, *gear cutting machine* fraise mère *f*, *mastertap* matrice *f*, taraud matrice *m*, taraud mère *m*; ~ **cutting** *n* MECH ENG taillage par fraise-mère *m*; ~ **tap** *n* MECH ENG *mastertap* matrice *f*, taraud matrice *m*, taraud mère *m*

hobbing *n* MECH ENG fraisage à la vis-mère *m*, PROD ENG forçage *m*

hoe *n* CONST *agriculture* houe *f*

Hoffman: ~ **electrometer** *n* ELEC électromètre de Hoffman *m*

hog[1] *n* PAPER TECH désintégrateur *m*

hog[2] *vi* NAUT s'arquer, *ship* donner de l'arc à, prendre de l'arc

hogback *n* GEOL crête monoclinale symétrique *f*

hog-backed: ~ **bridge** *n* CONST pont en dos d'âne *m*

hogging *n* C&G peau de crapaud *f*

hogging-ejector: ~ **hoist** *n* NUCLEAR mécanisme de levage *m*

hoist[1] *n* MECH *lifting gear* palan *m*, treuil *m*, MINING cordée *f*, trait *m*, *drilling winch* treuil de forage *m*, treuil de manoeuvre *m*, *hoisting engine* machine d'extraction *f*, moteur d'extraction *m*, NAUT guindant *m*, PROD ENG appareil de levage *m*, monte-charge *m*, treuil *m*, SAFETY appareil de levage *m*, cordée *f*, TRANSP treuil *m*; ~ **arm** *n* AERONAUT *helicopter* potence *f*, potence de treuil *f*; ~ **boom** *n* AERONAUT *helicopter* poutre de treuil *f*; ~ **cable cutter** *n* AERONAUT *helicopter* cisaille de câble de treuil *f*; ~ **controller** *n* CONTROL contrôleur de levage *m*; ~ **fitting** *n* AERONAUT *helicopter* ferrure de hissage *f*; ~ **lever** *n* AERONAUT *helicopter* manche treuilliste *m*; ~ **operator** *n* AERONAUT treuilliste *m*; ~ **pump** *n* AERONAUT *helicopter* pompe de treuil *f*; ~ **room** *n* MINING bâtiment des machines *m*, salle de la machine *f*

hoist[2] *vt* AERONAUT hisser, lever, MECH hisser, MINING remonter, PROD ENG enlever, extraire, hisser, lever, monter, remonter; ~ **the colors** *vt* (AmE), ~ **the colours** *vt* (BrE) NAUT *flag* arborer le pavillon, hisser les couleurs; ~ **to the surface** *vt* MINING monter au jour, remonter au jour, remonter à la surface

hoist:[3] ~ **ore** *vi* MINING remonter le minerai au jour, remonter le minerai à la surface

hoisting *n* MINING extraction *f*, remonte *f*, remontée *f*, PROD ENG extraction *f*, hissage *m*, levage *m*, remonte *f*, remontée *f*; ~ **appliances** *n pl* PROD ENG appareils d'extraction *m pl*, appareils de levage *m pl*, engins de levage *m pl*; ~ **block** *n* AERONAUT moufle *m*, PROD ENG moufle mobile *m*, poulie mobile *f*; ~ **bucket** *n* PROD ENG benne d'extraction *f*, cuffat *m*, tonne *f*; ~ **carriage** *n* AERONAUT chariot de hissage *m*; ~ **compartment** *n* CONST *of shaft* cage d'extraction *f*, compartiment d'extraction *m*; ~ **crab** *n* PROD ENG treuil *m*, treuil d'extraction *m*; ~ **dog** *n* MINING *boring* accrocheur *m*; ~ **drum** *n* MINING tambour de machine d'extraction *m*; ~ **engine** *n* MINING machine d'extraction *f*, moteur d'extraction *m*; ~ **eye** *n* AERONAUT oeil de levage *m*; ~ **gear** *n* MECH ENG engins de levage *m pl*, PROD ENG appareils d'extraction *m pl*, appareils de levage *m pl*, engins de levage *m pl*; ~ **jack** *n* PROD ENG cric *m*; ~ **plug** *n* MINING *boring* clef de relevée *f*; ~ **pulley** *n* MINING molette *f*, poulie de chevalement *f*; ~ **reel** *n* MINING *for flat rope* bobine d'extraction *f*; ~ **ring** *n* AERONAUT anneau de hissage *m*, anneau de levage *m*; ~ **rope** *n* MINING câble d'extraction *m*, PROD ENG *of cableway* corde de levage *f*, câble de levage *m*; ~ **shaft** *n* MINING puits d'extrac-

tion *m*; ~ **sling** *n* AERONAUT élingue de hissage *f*, élingue de levage *f*; ~ **system** *n* MINING installation d'extraction par cages *f*, installation d'extraction par cages à berlines *f*; ~ **tackle** *n* PROD ENG agrès *m pl*, appareil de levage *m*, engins de levage *m pl*

hold:[1] **on** ~ *adv* TELECOM en garde

hold[2] *n* AERONAUT *of aircraft* soute *f*, NAUT *of ship*, OCEANOG cale *f*, PROD ENG prise *f*, SPACE, TRANSP soute *f*; ~ **control** *n* TV régleur de synchronisation *m*; ~ **current** *n* ELEC *relay, thyristor* courant de maintien *m*; ~ **time** *n* COMP, DP, SPACE temps de maintien *m*

hold[3] *vt* COMP, DP maintenir, PROD ENG *chuck, cramp* serrer, TELECOM *conversation* échanger; ~ **back** *vt* RAIL *train* décaler; ~ **up** *vt* MECH ENG appuyer, soutenir, supporter, tenir

hold[4] *vi* PROD ENG tenir bon, tenir ferme; ~ **fast** *vi* PROD ENG tenir bon, tenir ferme; ~ **up** *vi* PROD ENG *riveting* tenir le coup

Holden: ~ **effect** *n* NUCLEAR *in reactor* effet Holden *m*

holder *n* ELEC ENG *for lamps* douille *f*, MECH ENG *stand* support *m*, PAPER TECH porte-cylindres *m*

Holder: ~ **comma** *n* ACOUSTICS comma holdérien *m*

holdfast *n* MECH ENG crampon *m*, patte *f*, *for bench* valet d'établi *m*, valet de menuisier *m*, PROD ENG *nail* clou à patte *m*

hold-in: ~ **path** *n* PROD ENG chemin de retenue *m*

holding *n* AERONAUT attente *f*, ELEC ENG entretien *m*, *thyristors* maintien *m*; ~ **anode** *n* ELEC ENG anode d'entretien *f*; ~ **apron** *n* AERONAUT *airport* plate-forme d'attente de circulation *f*; ~ **bay** *n* AERONAUT *airport* plate-forme d'attente de circulation *f*; ~ **beam** *n* ELECTRON faisceau d'entretien *m*, faisceau de régénération *m*; ~ **capacity** *n* MECH ENG *of chuck* diamètre de serrage *m*, PACKAGING capacité *f*, PROD ENG capacité de rétention *f*; ~ **coil** *n* ELEC ENG enroulement de maintien *m*; ~ **collet** *n* MECH ENG *machine tools* pince de serrage *f*; ~ **current** *n* ELEC ENG courant de maintien *m*; ~ **device** *n* MECH ENG dispositif de serrage *m*; ~ **fixture** *n* MECH ENG outillage de fixation *m*; ~ **path** *n* AERONAUT trajectoire d'attente *f*; ~ **pattern** *n* AERONAUT circuit d'attente *m*; ~ **pedestal** *n* NUCLEAR tréteau *m*; ~ **point** *n* AERONAUT point d'attente *m*; ~ **power** *n* PROD ENG puissance de serrage *f*; ~ **procedure** *n* AERONAUT procédure d'attente *f*; ~ **siding** *n* RAIL voie de garage *f*, voie de remisage *f*; ~ **speed** *n* AERONAUT vitesse d'attente *f*; ~ **stack** *n* AERONAUT circuit d'attente *m*, pile d'attente *f*; ~ **time** *n* TELECOM durée d'occupation *f*, temps d'occupation *m*; ~ **up** *n* MECH ENG suspension *f*

holding-down: ~ **bolt** *n* PROD ENG boulon de fixation *m*

hold-out *n* PRINT accrochage normal de l'encre sur papier *m*

hold-over: ~ **coil** *n* REFRIG *of condenser* serpentin accumulateur *m*

hold-short: ~ **line** *n* (AmE) *(cf lead-out line)* AERONAUT ligne de guidage de sortie *f*, AERONAUT *apron marking* ligne de guidage d'entrée *f*

hold-up *n* MECH ENG tenue *f*

hole[1] *n* CONST *bore hole* forage *m*, sondage *m*, trou de sonde *m*, *well* puits *m*, ELEC ENG *electron hole* lacune *f*, trou *m*, MECH ENG *cavity* creux *m*, fosse *f*, orifice *m*, ouverture *f*, *in emery wheel* oeillard *m*, trou *m*, NUCLEAR trou *m*, trou électronique *m*, OCEANOG fosse *f*, trou *m*, PAPER TECH orifice *m*, PETR TECH forage *m*, puits *m*, sondage *m*, trou *m*, PHYS *semiconductors* trou *m*, PROD ENG *pit* fosse *f*, fouille *f*; ~ **conduction** *n* ELEC ENG conduction lacunaire *f*; ~ **saw** *n* MECH ENG *tool* scie trépan *f*; ~ **scraper** *n* MINING *blasting* curette *f*

hole[2] *vt* CONST *pierce* trouer, MINING haver, souchever, sous-caver, souschever

hole[3] *vi* CONST pratiquer un trou, *dig* percer

holed[1] *adj* MINING havé, souchevé, sous-cavé, souschevé

holed:[2] ~ **nut** *n* PROD ENG écrou à trous *m*

holing *n* MINING havage *m*, percement du massif *m*, souchevage *m*, sous-cave *f*; ~ **and shearing machine** *n* COAL TECH haveuse-rouilleuse *f*; ~ **machine** *n* COAL TECH rouilleuse *f*; ~ **prop** *n* MINING cale *f*, tasseau *m*

Hollerith: ~ **card** *n* COMP, DP carte Hollerith *f*; ~ **code** *n* COMP, DP code Hollerith *m*

hollow[1] *n* CONST cavité *f*, creux *m*, entonnoir *m*, fondrière *f*, OCEANOG creux *m*, dépression *f*, TESTING enfoncement *m*; ~ **anode** *n* ELEC *electrode* anode creuse *f*; ~ **bolt** *n* MECH ENG vis creuse *f*; ~ **cathode ion source** *n* NUCLEAR source d'ions à cathode creuse *f*; ~ **circular shaft** *n* MECH ENG arbre creux cylindrique *m*; ~ **conductor** *n* ELEC conducteur creux *m*, âme creuse *f*; ~ **glass block** *n* C&G brique creuse en verre *f*; ~ **gravity dam** *n* HYDROL barrage poids évidé *m*; ~ **neck** *n* C&G col creux *m*; ~ **pin** *n* MECH ENG axe creux *m*; ~ **ram** *n* MECH ENG *tool* vérin creux *m*; ~ **rivet** *n* MECH ENG rivet creux *m*, rivet tubulaire *m*; ~ **shaft** *n* MECH ENG arbre creux *m*; ~ **target** *n* NUCLEAR cible creuse *f*; ~ **tread** *n* RAIL *vehicles* creux du bandage *m*; ~ **ware** *n* C&G verre creux *m*; ~ **ware presser** *n* C&G mouleur en faïence *m*

hollow[2] *vt* CONST *undermine*, MINING caver, PROD ENG *make hollow* creuser, évider; ~ **out** *vt* CONST, MINING caver, PROD ENG creuser, évider

hollowing *n* CONST creusement *m*, évidage *m*, évidement *m*; ~ **out** *n* CONST creusement *m*, évidage *m*, évidement *m*

hollowness *n* CONST cavernosité *f*, creux *m*

hollow-type: ~ **track girder** *n* TRANSP poutre guide creuse *f*

holmium *n (Ho)* CHEM holmium *m (Ho)*

Holocene *n* GEOL *stratigraphy* holocène *m*

hologram *n* PHYS, WAVE PHYS hologramme *m*

holographic: ~ **exchange** *n* TELECOM commutateur holographique *m*; ~ **quality control** *n* CONTROL contrôle holographique de la qualité *m*; ~ **scanner** *n* COMP scanner holographique *m*, DP lecteur holographique *m*

holography *n* COMP, DP, PHYS, RAD PHYS, SPACE *spacecraft*, WAVE PHYS holographie *f*

holohedral: ~ **class** *n* CRYSTALL classe holoédrique *f*

holster *n* PROD ENG *standard of rolling mill* cage *f*, colonne *f*

holy: ~ **roll** *n* PAPER TECH rouleau perforé *m*

home: ~ **appliance** *n* (AmE) *(cf domestic appliance)* ELEC appareil domestique *m*, appareil ménager *m*; ~ **automation** *n* GAS TECH domotique *f*; ~ **computer** *n* COMP ordinateur domestique *m*, DP ordinateur familial *m*; ~ **depot** *n* RAIL établissement d'attache *m*; ~ **electric installation** *n* (AmE) *(cf domestic electric installation)* ELEC installation domestique *f*; ~ **electronic equipment** *n* (AmE) *(cf domestic electronic equipment)* ELEC ENG matériel électronique grand public *m*; ~ **exchange** *n* TELECOM central d'origine *m*; ~ **freight** *n* NAUT fret de retour *m*; ~ **furnishing** *n* TEXTILES tissu d'ameublement *m*; ~ **port** *n* NAUT port d'attache *m*; ~ **ports** *n pl* NAUT ports de la métropole *m pl*; ~ **position** *n* PROD ENG position de repos *f*; ~ **signal** *n* (BrE) *(cf home switch)* RAIL signal d'entrée *m*; ~ **station** *n* RAIL gare d'attache *f*; ~ **switch** *n* (AmE) *(cf*

home signal) RAIL signal d'entrée *m*; ~ **textiles** *n pl* TEXTILES textiles de maison *m pl*; ~ **to work traffic** *n* TRANSP trafic habitation travail *m*; ~ **trade** *n* NAUT cabotage *m*

Home: ~ **Office socket** *n* (BrE) ELEC *connection* prise de sécurité *f*

home-produced: ~ **textiles** *n pl* TEXTILES textiles de production nationale *m pl*

homeward[1] *adv* NAUT de retour, vers la métropole

homeward:[2] ~ **passage** *n* NAUT traversée de retour *f*

homeward-bound *adj* NAUT *ship, cargo* de retour, à destination de son port d'attache

homilite *n* MINERAL homilite *f*

homing *n* AERONAUT radiogoniométrie *f*, ralliement *m*, MILIT radio ralliement *m*, SPACE *spacecraft* autoguidage *m*, radio ralliement *m*; ~ **active guidance** *n* AERONAUT autoguidage actif *m*; ~ **beacon** *n* AERONAUT radiophare de rappel *m*; ~ **device** *n* MILIT autodirecteur *m*, *of missile* tête chercheuse *f*; ~ **head** *n* SPACE *spacecraft* tête autodirectrice *f*; ~ **passive guidance** *n* AERONAUT autoguidage passif *m*; ~ **radar** *n* NAUT radar d'autoguidage *m*; ~ **semi-active guidance** *n* AERONAUT autoguidage semi-actif *m*

homocentric: ~ **beam** *n* PHYS *optics* faisceau isogène *m*

homocline *n* GEOL pli monoclinal *m*

homocyclic *adj* CHEM homocyclique

homodyne: ~ **oscillator** *n* ELECTRON oscillateur de régénération de porteuse *m*

homogeneity *n* PROP MAT homogénéité *f*

homogeneous[1] *adj* CHEM, METALL, PROP MAT homogène

homogeneous:[2] ~ **cladding** *n* OPT gaine optique homogène *f*, TELECOM gaine homogène *f*; ~ **deformation** *n* GEOL déformation homogène *f*; ~ **isotropic turbulence** *n* FLUID PHYS turbulence homogène isotrope *f*; ~ **medium** *n* PHYS milieu homogène *m*; ~ **radiation** *n* PHYS rayonnement monoénergétique *m*; ~ **reactor** *n* TRANSP réacteur homogène *m*; ~ **stimulus** *n* RAD PHYS *activation by light* radiation monochromatique *f*

homogenization *n* METALL, P&R homogénéisation *f*

homogenizer *n* LAB EQUIP homogénéisateur *m*

homogenizing *n* HEATING homogénéisation *f*

homograph *n* GEOM homographie *f*

homographic *adj* GEOM homographique

homojunction *n* ELECTRON, OPT, TELECOM homojonction *f*

homologation *n* VEHICLES *regulations* homologation *f*

homologous[1] *adj* CHEM, METALL, PROP MAT homologue

homologous:[2] ~ **series** *n* PETR TECH *refining*, PROP MAT série homologue *f*

homometric *adj* *(cf heterometric)* GEOL isogranulaire

homopolar: ~ **generator** *n* ELEC génératrice homopolaire *f*, ELEC ENG génératrice homopolaire *f*, machine homopolaire *f*; ~ **machine** *n* ELEC ENG machine homopolaire *f*

homopolymer *n* P&R homopolymère *m*

homopolymerization *n* P&R homopolymérisation *f*

homopyrrole *n* CHEM homopyrrole *m*

homoterephthalic *adj* CHEM homotéréphtalique

homothetical *adj* PRINT homothétique

hone[1] *n* PROD ENG affiloire *f*, pierre à aiguiser *f*

hone[2] *vt* MECH *tools* roder, roder à la pierre

honestone *n* PROD ENG affiloire *f*, pierre à aiguiser *f*

honey: ~ **stone** *n* MINERAL pierre de miel *f*

honeycomb[1] *n* AERONAUT, SPACE *communications* nid d'abeilles *m*, nida *m*; ~ **material** *n* PACKAGING matériel alvéolé *m*; ~ **protection system** *n* PACKAGING système alvéolé de protection *m*; ~ **radiator** *n* AUTO radiateur à nids d'abeille *m*; ~ **structure** *n* AERONAUT construction en nid d'abeilles *f*, structure alvéolaire *f*, structure nida *f*, CONST *weathering* structure alvéolaire *f*, GEOL *weathering* structure alvéolaire *f*, structure en nid d'abeille *f*, PACKAGING construction alvéolée *f*; ~ **texture** *n* GEOL *weathering* structure alvéolaire *f*, structure en nid d'abeille *f*; ~ **winding** *n* ELEC ENG bobinage en nid d'abeilles *m*

honeycomb[2] *vt* CONST cribler

honeycombing *n* CONST *concrete* nid d'abeilles *m*, soufflage de foute *m*

honing *n* MECH ENG *machine tools* polissage *m*, prérodage *m*, rodage *m*; ~ **guide** *n* MECH ENG *tools* guide d'affûtage *m*; ~ **machine** *n* MECH, MECH ENG machine à roder *f*; ~ **stone** *n* MECH *tools* pierre à roder *f*, MECH ENG bâton rodoir *m*, pierre à aiguiser *f*

hood *n* (*cf bonnet*) AUTO capot *m*, CONST *of pile* chapeau *m*, *penthouse, porch roof* auvent *m*, ELEC ENG *of lamp* capot *m*, capuchon *m*, chapeau *m*, MECH ENG capot d'instrument *m*, PAPER TECH hotte *f*, PHOTO *for lens* parasoleil *m*, PROD ENG *of forge, laboratory* hotte *f*, VEHICLES *body* capot-moteur *m*; ~ **catch** *n* (AmE) (*cf bonnet catch*) VEHICLES *body* attache capot *f*; ~ **for emery wheels** *n* PROD ENG capuchon pour meules d'émeri *m*, couvre-meule *m*; ~ **latch** *n* (AmE) (*cf bonnet lock* AUTO dispositif de fermeture du capot *m*; ~ **lock** *n* (AmE) (*cf bonnet lock*) AUTO dispositif de fermeture du capot *m*

HOOD *abbr* (*hierarchical object-oriented design*) COMP, DP conception hiérarchique orientée objet *f*

hoof: ~ **mark** *n* C&G marque en fer à cheval *f*

hook[1] *n* C&G manique *f*, CONST crampon *m*, crochet *m*, *gate hinge* bourdonneau *m*, *of hook and hinge* gond *m*, MECH *lifting gear* crochet *m*, MECH ENG croc *m*, crochet *m*, crochet de suspension *m*, *fastener* agrafe *f*, PETR crochet *m*, SPRINGS boucle *f*, crochet *m*, TEXTILES agrafe *f*, *of needle* crochet *m*; ~ **and eye** *n* MECH ENG agrafe et porte *f*; ~ **and hinge** *n* CONST gond et penture *m*, penture *f*; ~ **and pin wrench** *n* MECH ENG *tools* clé à ergots *f*; ~ **block** *n* MECH ENG boulon à croc *m*, boulon à crochet *m*, poulie à croc *f*; ~ **end** *n* SPRINGS glissoir *m*; ~ **gear** *n* HYDR EQUIP bec de cane *m*, pied-de-biche *m*; ~ **length** *n* SPRINGS longueur de boucle *f*; ~ **load** *n* PETR TECH *drilling* charge au crochet *f*; ~ **mark** *n* C&G marque en fer à cheval *f*; ~ **opening** *n* SPRINGS ouverture de la boucle *f*; ~ **radius** *n* SPRINGS rayon de la boucle *m*; ~ **spanner** *n* (BrE) (*cf hook wrench*) MECH ENG clé à griffe *f*; ~ **tooth** *n* MECH ENG *saw* dent crochue *f*, dent à crochet *f*; ~ **with eye** *n* MECH ENG croc *m*; ~ **wrench** *n* (AmE) (*cf hook spanner*) MECH ENG clé à griffe *f*

hook[2] *vt* MECH ENG agrafer

hookah *n* OCEANOG narguilé *m*

Hooke's: ~ **law** *n* CONST, PHYS loi de Hooke *f*

hooked: ~ **lid** *n* PACKAGING couvercle à crochet *m*; ~ **lock** *n* PACKAGING verrou à crochet *m*; ~ **tooth** *n* MECH ENG *saw* dent crochue *f*, dent à crochet *f*

hookrope *n* OCEANOG vérine *f*

hoop[1] *n* CONST *for pile* frette *f*, MECH cerceau *m*, cercle *m*, frette *f*, MECH ENG, PACKAGING cercle *m*, PROD ENG frette *f*, *of cask* cerceau *m*, cercle *m*; ~ **iron** *n* CONST fer feuillard *m*, feuillard de fer *m*, PACKAGING feuillard pour cercler les emballages *m*

hoop[2] *vt* MECH cercler, fretter

hooped: ~ **concrete** *n* CONST béton fretté *m*

hooping *n* PACKAGING cerclage *m*, PROD ENG cerclage *m*, frettage *m*

hooter *n* PROD ENG sirène *f*, sirène d'alarme *f*, trompe d'alarme *f*

hopcalite *n* CHEM hopcalite *f*

hopeite *n* MINERAL hopéite *f*

hopper *n* MECH trémie *f*, MECH ENG *machine tools* magasin *m*, NAUT chaland à clapets *m*, PAPER TECH trémie *f*, PROD ENG trémie *f*, *blast furnace* cup *m*, TEXTILES trémie d'alimentation *f*; ~ **barge** *n* NAUT chaland à clapets *m*; ~ **car** *n* (AmE) (*cf hopper wagon*) RAIL wagon à déchargement par le fond *m*; ~ **dredger** *n* NAUT drague porteuse *f*; ~ **head** *n* CONST *of downpipe* cuvette *f*, hotte *f*; ~ **wagon** *n* (BrE) (*cf hopper car*) RAIL *vehicles* wagon à déchargement par le fond *m*

hopping: ~ **patch** *n* TV spot lumineux décalant *m*

hordein *n* CHEM hordéine *f*

horizon *n* ASTRON horizon *m*, GEOL horizon *m*, niveau *m*, NAUT, PETR TECH *strata* horizon *m*; ~ **distance** *n* ASTRON distance d'horizon *f*; ~ **glass** *n* INSTRUMENT *of sextant* miroir fixe *m*; ~ **sensor** *n* SPACE *spacecraft* détecteur d'horizon *f*

horizontal[1] *adj* GEOM horizontal

horizontal[2] *n* GEOM horizontale *f*; ~ **amplifier** *n* ELECTRON amplificateur horizontal *m*; ~ **and top loader cartoner** *n* PACKAGING encartonneuse à chargement horizontal et par-dessus *f*; ~ **and vertical bar of flight direction** *n* AERONAUT barre de tendance *f*; ~ **and vertical dimensioning** *n* PROD ENG cotes horizontales et verticales *f pl*; ~ **and vertical wrapping machine** *n* PACKAGING encartonneuse horizontale et verticale *f*; ~ **arm** *n* INSTRUMENT bras de support horizontal *m*; ~ **axis** *n* CONST axe horizontal *m*, MATH axe des abscisses *m*, axe horizontal *m*; ~ **bar** *n* TV barre horizontale *f*; ~ **base** *n* INSTRUMENT bras de support horizontal *m*; ~ **blanking** *n* TV suppression de ligne *f*; ~ **blanking interval** *n* TV intervalle de suppression horizontale *m*; ~ **cartoning machine** *n* PACKAGING encartonneuse horizontale *f*; ~ **case loader** *n* PACKAGING encaisseuse latérale *f*; ~ **centering control** *n* (AmE), ~ **centring control** *n* (BrE) TV dispositif de décentrement *m*; ~ **component** *n* PHYS composante horizontale *f*; ~ **coordinate system** *n* ASTRON système de coordonnées horizontales *m*; ~ **cut longwall face** *n* MINING taille horizontale à havage *f*; ~ **deflecting plates** *n pl* PHYS plaques pour la déviation horizontale *f pl*; ~ **deflection** *n* ELECTRON déviation horizontale *f*; ~ **deflection coil** *n* ELEC ENG bobine de déviation horizontale *f*; ~ **deflection control** *n* TV réglage de la largeur de l'image *m*; ~ **deflection plate** *n* ELECTRON plaque de déviation horizontale *f*, TV électrode de déviation horizontale *f*; ~ **displacement** *n* GEOL rejet horizontal *m*; ~ **drawing process** *n* C&G procédé d'étirage *m*; ~ **dynamic convergence** *n* TV convergence dynamique horizontale *f*; ~ **elevator** *n* TRANSP ascenseur horizontal *m*; ~ **engine** *n* AUTO, VEHICLES moteur horizontal *m*; ~ **grinding disc** *n* C&G plateau de flette *m*; ~ **grinding disk** *n* (AmE) *see horizontal grinding disc*; ~ **hold** *n* TV stabilité horizontale *f*; ~ **hold control** *n* TV réglage de la fréquence de lignes *m*, réglage de la stabilité horizontale *m*; ~ **lock** *n* TV asservissement horizontal *m*; ~ **milling machine** *n* SAFETY machine à fraiser horizontale *f*; ~ **parity** *n* COMP, DP parité longitudinale *f*; ~ **plane** *n* GEOM plan horizontal *m*; ~ **ploughed longwall face** *n* (BrE) MINING taille horizontale à rabot *f*; ~ **plowed longwall face** *n* (AmE) *see horizontal ploughed* *longwall face*; **~ polarization** *n* ELEC ENG, PHYS, TELECOM polarisation horizontale *f*; **~ radius** *n* CONST *roads* rayon horizontal *m*; **~ resolution** *n* TV définition horizontale *f*; **~ scanning** *n* TV balayage horizontal *m*; **~ scanning frequency** *n* TV fréquence d'analyse horizontale *f*; **~ seismograph** *n* GEOPHYS sismographe *m*, sismographe horizontal *m*, sismomètre *m*; **~ separation** *n* GEOL rejet horizontal *m*; **~ shaft Pelton Wheel** *n* FUELLESS roue Pelton à arbre horizontal *f*; **~ situation indicator** *n* AERONAUT indicateur de situation horizontale *m*; **~ spacing** *n* PROD ENG espacement horizontal *m*; **~ stabilizer** *n* AERONAUT empennage horizontal *m*; **~ stack** *n* PETR sommation horizontale *f*; **~ strut** *n* AERONAUT contrefiche horizontale *f*; **~ sweep** *n* TV balayage horizontal *m*; **~ sync** *n* TV synchronisation horizontale *f*; **~ tabulation** *n* COMP, DP *(HT)* tabulation horizontale *f*; **~ tangent screw** *n* INSTRUMENT vis de rappel du mouvement en azimut *f*; **~ travel** *n* PROD ENG débattement horizontal *m*; **~ wind shear** *n* AERONAUT cisaillement horizontal du vent *m*; **~ wrapping** *n* PACKAGING emballage horizontal *m*

horizontal-stabilizer: ~ centre fishplate *n* AERONAUT morue *f*

horn *n* ACOUSTICS pavillon acoustique *m*, AERONAUT corne de gouverne *f*, guignol de gouvernes *m*, AUTO avertisseur *m*, CONTROL bouton-poussoir d'avertisseur *m*, MINING *of reel* bras *m*, NAUT *navigation* nautophone *m*, SPACE *communications* cornet *m*, VEHICLES *safety* avertisseur sonore *m*; **~ antenna** *n* SPACE *communications* antenne cornet *f*; **~ balance** *n* AERONAUT compensateur d'évolution *m*, compensation à corne débordante *f*, corne de compensation *f*; **~ button** *n* CONTROL bouton-poussoir d'avertisseur *m*; **~ gate** *n* PROD ENG *founding* chenal de coulée en source *m*; **~ lead** *n* MINERAL plomb corné *m*; **~ loudspeaker** *n* ACOUSTICS, RECORDING haut-parleur à pavillon *m*; **~ socket** *n* MINING cloche de repêchage *f*, douille de secours *f*

hornbeam *n* PAPER TECH charme *m*
hornblende *n* MINERAL hornblende *f*
hornblendite *n* PETR hornblendite *f*
hornfels *n* GEOL cornéenne *f*
horological: ~ instruments *n pl* INSTRUMENT instruments horaires *m pl*
Horologium *n* ASTRON Horloge *f*
horse *n* C&G chevalet *m*, MINING nerf *m*, PROD ENG *in blast furnace* carcas *m*, cochon *m*, loup *m*, *loam moulding* trousseau à potence murale *m*, *trestle* chevalet *m*, chèvre *f*, tréteau *m*; **~ power** *n* MINES cheval *m*
Horsehead: ~ nebula *n* ASTRON, SPACE nébuleuse Tête de Cheval *f*
horsepower *n* AUTO cheval vapeur *m*, puissance en chevaux *f*, MECH ENG cheval *m*, cheval de force *m*, cheval dynamique *m*, cheval vapeur *m*, puissance en chevaux *f*, METR cheval vapeur *m*; **~ hour** *n* MECH ENG cheval heure *m*
horseshoe: ~ arch *n* CONST *curve* arc en fer à cheval *m*, arc outrepassé *m*, *structure* voûte en fer à cheval *f*, voûte outrepassée *f*; **~ foot** *n* LAB EQUIP *microscope* pied en forme de fer à cheval *m*; **~ lifebuoy** *n* NAUT *safety* bouée en fer à cheval *f*; **~ magnet** *n* ELEC, MECH ENG, PHYS aimant en fer à cheval *m*; **~ main** *n* PROD ENG *blast furnace* conduite circulaire de vent *f*; **~ mount** *n* ASTRON, INSTRUMENT monture en fer à cheval *f*; **~ mounting** *n* INSTRUMENT monture en fer à cheval *f*; **~ sections** *n pl* MECH ENG fers cavaliers *m pl*

horseshoe-fired: ~ furnace *n* C&G four à boucle *m*
horticultural: ~ cast glass *n* C&G verre jardinier translucide imprimé *m*; **~ glass** *n* C&G verre horticole *m*
hose *n* CONST tuyau *m*, LAB EQUIP *connection* tuyau souple *m*, MECH, MINING, PAPER TECH tuyau flexible *m*, PROD ENG boyau *m*, conduite souple *f*, manche *f*, tuyau *m*, tuyau flexible *m*, SPACE *spacecraft* tuyau flexible *m*; **~ clamp** *n* MECH collier de serrage *m*, MECH ENG collier de serrage *m*, collier de serrage pour tuyaux flexibles *m*; **~ clip** *n* MECH ENG bride pour tuyaux flexibles *f*; **~ connection** *n* MECH ENG raccord pour tuyaux flexibles *m*; **~ coupler** *n* CONST collier par tuyau *m*, raccord rapide *m*; **~ coupling** *n* PROD ENG raccord de tuyaux *m*, raccord pour tuyaux *m*; **~ hanger** *n* PROD ENG crochet de suspension des boyaux *m*; **~ knitting** *n* TEXTILES tricotage *m*; **~ nozzle** *n* MECH ENG buse de tuyau flexible *f*; **~ reel** *n* PROD ENG dévidoir à bobine *m*, dévidoir à tuyaux *m*
hosepipe *n* MECH ENG tuyau flexible *m*
hosiery *n* TEXTILES *business* bonneterie *f*
hospital: ~ ship *n* NAUT navire-hôpital *m*
host *n* COMP, DP hôte *m*; **~ computer** *n* COMP, DP ordinateur hôte *m*; **~ exchange** *n* TELECOM commutateur de rattachement *m*; **~ rock** *n* GEOL roche magasin *f*, roche réservoir *f*
hostile: ~ environment *n* RAD PHYS milieu hostile *m*
hot:[1] **~ air blower** *n* LAB EQUIP *heating* soufflerie à air chaud *f*; **~ air duct** *n* AERONAUT tube d'amenée d'air chaud *m*; **~ air engine** *n* TRANSP moteur à air chaud *m*; **~ air finish** *n* COATINGS apprêt à l'air chaud *m*; **~ air gallery** *n* AERONAUT rampe de soufflage *f*; **~ air heater** *n* HEAT ENG calorifère *m*; **~ air impingement dryer** *n* TEXTILES séchoir à soufflage d'air chaud *m*; **~ air radiation heating system** *n* SAFETY chauffage à radiation d'air chaud *m*; **~ air sizing machine** *n* TEXTILES encolleuse à air-chaud *f*; **~ air stream** *n* TEXTILES jet d'air chaud *m*; **~ air valve** *n* AERONAUT vanne d'air chaud *f*; **~ backup** *n* PROD ENG processeur de secours *m*; **~ blade sealing** *n* PACKAGING fermeture avec lame chauffée *f*; **~ blast furnace** *n* PROD ENG four à vent chaud *m*; **~ bonding** *n* THERMOD collage à chaud *m*, fluage à chaud *m*; **~ box** *n* RAIL *vehicles* boîte chaude *f*; **~ box detector** *n* RAIL, TRANSP détecteur de boîte chaude *m*; **~ bright and radiating nebula** *n* ASTRON *type HII*, SPACE *type HII* nébuleuse à raies d'émission lumineuses et chaudes *f*; **~ brines** *n pl* OCEANOG saumure *f*; **~ bulb engine** *n* AUTO moteur à boule chaude *m*; **~ calendering** *n* PAPER TECH calandrage à chaud *m*; **~ camera** *n* TV caméra à l'antenne *f*; **~ carrier diode** *n* ELECTRON diode à porteurs chauds *f*; **~ cathode** *n* ELEC ENG cathode chaude *f*, cathode chauffée *f*, cathode à émission thermoélectronique *f*; **~ cathode gas tube** *n* ELECTRON tube à cathode chaude *m*; **~ cathode tube** *n* ELECTRON tube à cathode chaude *m*, tube à gaz à cathode chaude *m*; **~ clamping** *n* SPRINGS bridage à chaud *m*; **~ covering** *n* COATINGS couverture en zinc *f*; **~ creep** *n* *(cf cold creep)* THERMOD fluage à chaud *m*; **~ curing** *n* THERMOD *thermosetting* thermodurcissement *m*; **~ cyclone** *n* COAL TECH cyclone chaud *m*; **~ dark matter** *n* ASTRON matière noire chaude *f*; **~ dip galvanizing** *n* COATINGS galvanisation à chaud *f*; **~ dip** *n* PRINT immersion à chaud *f*; **~ dip galvinizing** *n* COATINGS galvinisation à chaud *f*; **~ dip galvanised coating** *n* COATINGS revêtement zingué à chaud *m*; **~ dip metal coating** *n* COATINGS revêtement à chaud *m*; **~ dipping** *n* PACKAGING immersion à chaud *f*; **~ drawing** *n* THER-

MOD étirage à chaud *m*; ~ **end coating** *n* C&G traitement de surface à chaud *m*; ~ **filling** *n* PACKAGING remplissage à chaud *m*; ~ **foil** *n* PRINT marquage à chaud *m*; ~ **foil carton coder** *n* PACKAGING encodeur pour cartons recouverts d'aluminium mince *m*; ~ **forging** *n* THERMOD forgeage à chaud *m*; ~ **forging die** *n* MECH ENG outillage de forgeage chaud *m*; ~ **forming** *n* MECH façonnage à chaud *m*, PROD ENG formage à chaud *m*; ~ **gas bypass valve** *n* REFRIG vanne de dérivation des gaz chauds *f*; ~ **gas defrosting** *n* REFRIG dégivrage par gaz chauds *m*; ~ **glass wire** *n* C&G cordeline *f*; ~ **glass wire cutting** *n* C&G découpe au fil de verre chaud *f*; ~ **gluing** *n* PACKAGING collage à chaud *m*; ~ **junction** *n* ELEC *thermocouple* soudure chaude *f*, PROD ENG soudure de thermocouple *f*; ~ **key** *n* COMP touche d'activation *f*, touche directe *f*, DP touche directe *f*; ~ **mix** *n* CONST *bituminous surfacing* enrobage à chaud *m*; ~ **mold** *n* (AmE), ~ **mould** *n* (BrE) C&G moule en plein *m*; ~ **pass** *n* PETR deuxième passe *f*, passe chaude *f*; ~ **presetting** *n* SPRINGS préconformation à chaud *f*; ~ **pressing** *n* METALL pressage à chaud *m*, PACKAGING estampage à chaud *m*, PROP MAT pressage à chaud *m*; ~ **prestressing** *n* SPRINGS précontrainte à chaud *f*; ~ **refueling** *n* (AmE), ~ **refuelling** *n* (BrE) NUCLEAR rechargement sans arrêt *m*; ~ **rolling** *n* THERMOD laminage à chaud *m*; ~ **runner manifold** *n* MECH ENG *injection mould* distributeur de buse chaude *m*; ~ **runner system** *n* MECH ENG *injection mould* système à coulée à chaud *m*; ~ **section** *n* AERONAUT *of engine* partie chaude *f*; ~ **shot wind tunnel** *n* AERONAUT soufflerie à arc bref *f*; ~ **shrink fit** *n* MECH ENG ajustement à chaud *m*; ~ **spark plug** *n* AUTO bougie chaude *f*; ~ **spot** *n* C&G point chaud *m*, PHOTO foyer lumineux *m*; ~ **springs** *n pl* OCEANOG source hydrothermale *f*; ~ **spring water** *n* OCEANOG eau hydrothermale marine *f*; ~ **sprue brushing** *n* MECH ENG buse chauffante *f*; ~ **stand-by** *n* SPACE *spacecraft* attente opérationnelle *f*; ~ **stand-by system** *n* TELECOM système en microsynchronisme *m*; ~ **start** *n* AERONAUT démarrage avec surchauffe *m*; ~ **strength** *n* MECH ENG usinabilité à chaud *f*, THERMOD résistance à chaud *f*; ~ **tear** *n* MECH *materials* fissuration à chaud *f*; ~ **transfer label** *n* PACKAGING étiquette décalquée à chaud *f*; ~ **water boiler** *n* MECH ENG chaudière à eau chaude *f*; ~ **water bottle** *n* HEATING bouillotte *f*; ~ **water heater** *n* MECH ENG radiateur à eau chaude *m*; ~ **water heating system** *n* HEATING chauffage à eau chaude *m*; ~ **water jet** *n* GEOPHYS jet d'eau chaude *m*; ~ **water tank** *n* HEATING réservoir d'eau chaude *m*; ~ **water washing** *n* MAR POLL lavage à l'eau chaude *m*; ~ **wire ammeter** *n* ELEC ampèremètre thermique à fil *m*, ampèremètre à fil chaud *m*; ~ **wire anemometer** *n* PHYS anémomètre à fil chaud *m*, anémomètre à résistance électrique *m*; ~ **wire-drawing die** *n* MECH ENG outillage pour tréfilage de fils à chaud *m*; ~ **wire microphone** *n* ACOUSTICS microphone à fil chaud *m*; ~ **wire relay** *n* ELEC relais thermique *m*; ~ **wire voltmeter** *n* ELEC voltmètre à fil chaud *m*; ~ **wire wattmeter** *n* ELEC wattmètre à fil chaud *m*; ~ **working** *n* C&G, METALL travail à chaud *m*

hot:[2] ~ **rivet** *vt* MECH ENG riveter à chaud; ~ **roll** *vt (cf cold roll)* THERMOD *metals* laminer à chaud

hot:[3] ~ **draw** *vi* THERMOD étirer à chaud

hot-bond *vt* THERMOD coller à chaud

Hotchkiss: ~ **drive** *n* VEHICLES transmission Hotchkiss *f*, transmission par arbre apparent *f*

hot-coating: ~ **shop** *n* COATINGS atelier de galvanisation *m*, atelier de zingage *m*

hot-coiled[1] *adj* SPRINGS enroulé à chaud

hot-coiled:[2] ~ **cylindrical helical spring** *n* SPRINGS ressort hélicoïdal cylindrique enroulé à chaud *m*

hot-cycle: ~ **rotor wing** *n* AERONAUT aile rotor à cycle chaud *f*

hot-dimpling: ~ **process** *n* MECH ENG procédé de soyage à chaud *m*

hot-drawn *adj* THERMOD étiré à chaud

hotel: ~ **glassware** *n* C&G verrerie pour limonadiers *f*; ~ **platform** *n* PETR TECH *offshore operations* plate-forme d'hébergement *f*; ~ **rig** *n* PETR TECH *offshore operations* plate-forme d'hébergement *f*

hot-forge *vt (cf cold forge)* THERMOD forger à chaud

hot-forged *adj* THERMOD forgé à chaud

hot-formed *adj* SPRINGS façonné à chaud, formé à chaud

hot-melt: ~ **adhesive** *n* P&R colle fusible *f*, PACKAGING colle thermofusible *f*, PRINT adhésif thermoplastique *m*, colle à chaud *f*; ~ **coating** *n* PAPER TECH couchage par coulage à chaud *m*, couchage par fusion *m*, PRINT couchage au hot-melt *m*; ~ **glue** *n* PRINT colle hot-melt *f*

hot-melt-coated: ~ **paper** *n* PAPER TECH papier couché par fusion *m*, PRINT papier couché à chaud *m*

hot-melts *n pl* PRINT colles à chaud maintenues à une température de fusion *f pl*

hotplate *n* LAB EQUIP *heating* plaque chauffante *f*

hot-rolled *adj* MECH *materials*, THERMOD laminé à chaud

hot-setting: ~ **adhesive** *n* P&R adhésif durcissant à chaud *m*; ~ **glue** *n* P&R, PACKAGING colle durcissante à chaud *f*

hot-shoe: ~ **flash contact** *n* PHOTO contact central pour flash *m*

hot-smoked *adj* FOOD TECH fumé à chaud

hot-stamp: ~ **imprint** *n* PRINT repiquage par estampage à chaud *m*

hot-stamped *adj* PRINT estampé à chaud

hot-stamping *n* PACKAGING marquage à chaud *m*, PRINT estampage à chaud *m*; ~ **foil** *n* PACKAGING feuillet mince pour estampage à chaud *m*

hotted-up *adj* (BrE) *(cf souped-up)* VEHICLES *engine* gonflé

Houdini: ~ **eye-light** *n* ELEC *lighting* projecteur ponctuel *m*

hounds *n pl* NAUT *mast* capelage *m*, jottereaux *m pl*

hour *n* PHYS heure *f*; ~ **angle** *n* ASTRON angle horaire *m*; ~ **circle** *n* METR cercle horaire *m*; ~ **of green signal indication** *n* TRANSP *traffic control* heure de feu vert *f*; ~ **hand** *n* METR *of clock, watch* petite aiguille *f*

hourglass *n* C&G sablier *m*; ~ **calipers** *n* (AmE), ~ **callipers** *n* (BrE) MECH ENG compas dit huit *m*, compas dit huit de chiffre *m*; ~ **screw** *n* PROD ENG vis globique *f*, vis globoïde *f*, vis à filets convergents *f*; ~ **screw gear** *n* PROD ENG engrenage globoïde *m*, engrenage à vis globique *m*, engrenage à vis sans fin globique *m*; ~ **spring** *n* PROD ENG ressort de sommier *m*

hourly: ~ **output** *n* PACKAGING rendement horaire *m*

house[1] *n* CONST *of crane* cabine *f*, guérite *f*; ~ **builder** *n* CONST constructeur de maisons *m*; ~ **corrections** *n pl* PRINT correction en première *f*; ~ **exchange system** *n* TELECOM système d'intercommunication *m*; ~ **flag** *n* NAUT *merchant navy* pavillon de compagnie *m*; ~ **organ** *n* PRINT journal d'entreprise *m*; ~ **paint** *n* COLOURS peinture bâtiment *f*, peinture pour façades *f*, P&R peinture bâtiment *f*; ~ **style** *n* PRINT style maison *m*; ~ **trailer** *n* (AmE) *(cf caravan)* VEHICLES caravane de camping *f*, remorque de camping *f*; ~ **wiring switch**

n ELEC interrupteur d'installation *m*

house[2] *vt* CONST *carpentry* emboîter, encastrer

houseboat *n* TRANSP coche de plaisance *m*

housed: ~ **joint** *n* CONST assemblage à encastrement *m*; ~ **string** *n* CONST *stair building* limon droit *m*, limon à la française *m*

household: ~ **coal** *n* COAL TECH charbon domestique *m*; ~ **frozen food storage cabinet** *n* REFRIG conservateur ménager de denrées congelées *m*; ~ **fuel** *n* COAL TECH combustible de ménage *m*; ~ **porcelain** *n* C&G porcelaine pour ménage *f*; ~ **refrigerator** *n* REFRIG réfrigérateur ménager *m*; ~ **waste** *n* RECYCLING ordures ménagères *f pl*

housekeeping *n* COMP, DP aménagement *m*, QUALITY télémaintenance *f*, SPACE *spacecraft* service à bord *m*, télémaintenance *f*; ~ **operation** *n* COMP opération de servitude *f*, DP opération de gestion interne *f*; ~ **telemetry** *n* QUALITY télémaintenance *f*, SPACE *spacecraft* télémaintenance *f*, télémesures de maintenance *f pl*

housing *n* CONST emboîtement *m*, encastrement *m*, logement *m*, *putting under cover* mise à l'abri *f*, FUELLESS cadre *m*, MECH ENG *engineering* carter *m*, *for plummer block* niche *f*, *of planing machine* jumelle *f*, *of planing mill* montant *m*, *of rolling mill* cage *f*, colonne *f*, PHOTO *of camera* boîtier *m*, PRINT emboîtage *m*, mise sous emballage *f*; ~ **lock** *n* CINEMAT verrouillage de carter *m*

hover: ~ **control** *n* AERONAUT *helicopter* tenue de stationnaire *f*; ~ **flight coupler** *n* AERONAUT *helicopter* coupleur de vol stationnaire *m*; ~ **pallet** *n* TRANSP palette sur coussin d'air *f*

hovercraft *n* AERONAUT, NAUT, TRANSP aéroglisseur *m*; ~ **train** *n* TRANSP aérotrain *m*

hoverheight *n* TRANSP hauteur de vol *f*

hovering *n* AERONAUT *helicopter* vol stationnaire *m*; ~ **capability** *n* AERONAUT *helicopter* possibilité de vol stationnaire *f*; ~ **craft** *n* TRANSP véhicule sur coussin d'air *m*

hoverport *n* NAUT gare d'aéroglisseur *f*, port d'aéroglisseurs *m*, TRANSP port d'aéroglisseurs *m*

hovertrain *n* TRANSP aérotrain *m*

howitzer *n* MILIT obusier *m*

howler *n* TELECOM hurleur *m*

howling *n* ACOUSTICS son hululé *m*, RECORDING effet Larsen *m*

hp *abbr* (*horsepower*) AUTO cheval vapeur *m*, puissance en chevaux *f*

HP: ~ **shoe** *n* PROD ENG sabot HP *m*

HPA *abbr* (*higher-order path adaptation*) TELECOM adaptation de conduit d'ordre supérieur *f*

HPC[1] *abbr* (*higher-order path connection*) TELECOM connexion de conduit d'ordre supérieur *f*

HPC:[2] ~ **carbon black** *n* P&R *pigment, filler* noir HPC *m*

H-plane *n* ELEC ENG plan H *m*; ~ **bend** *n* ELEC ENG coude en H *m*

HPLC *abbr* (*high-pressure liquid chromatography*) CHEM, FOOD TECH, LAB EQUIP, POLLUTION CLHP (*chromatographie liquide à haute pression*)

HPT *abbr* (*higher-order path termination*) TELECOM terminaison de conduit d'ordre supérieur *f*

HR *abbr* (*high resistance*) TELECOM haute résistance *f*

H-rate *n* PRINT taux de transfert thermique *m*

HSS: ~ **small tools** *n* (*high-speed steel small tools*) MECH ENG petit outillage en acier rapide *m*

HST *abbr* (*high-speed train*) RAIL TGV (*train expérimental à grande vitesse*)

HT[1] *abbr* COMP, DP (*horizontal tabulation*) tabulation horizontale *f*, ELEC (*high-tension*), ELEC ENG (*high-tension*), PHYS (*high-tension*) HT (*haute tension*)

HT:[2] ~ **supply** *n* ELEC alimentation haute tension *f*

HTST *abbr* (*high-temperature short time*) FOOD TECH pasteurisation HTST *f*

hub *n* AERONAUT *helicopter* corps de moyeu *m*, COMP, DP moyeu *m*, MECH *welding* attente *f*, moyeu *m*, MINING *winding* estomac *m*, TELECOM centre de transit privé *m*, TRANSP plaque tournante *f*, TV noyau *m*, VEHICLES *wheel* moyeu *m*; ~ **cap** *n* AUTO enjoliveur de roue *m*, VEHICLES *wheel* cache-moyeu *m*, enjoliveur *m*; ~ **cover plate** *n* AERONAUT chapeau de moyeu *m*; ~ **extractor** *n* MECH ENG arrache-moyeu *m*, pompage *m*; ~ **flange** *n* AUTO flasque de moyeu *m*; ~ **flapping stiffness** *n* AERONAUT *helicopter* rigidité du moyeu de battement *f*; ~ **grip** *n* MECH ENG chape sur moyeu *f*; ~ **polling** *n* COMP scrutation par passage de témoin *f*, DP invitation à émettre de proche en proche *f*; ~ **puller** *n* MECH arrache-moyeu *m*; ~ **spacer** *n* AERONAUT *helicopter* butée de moyeu *f*; ~ **tilt stop** *n* AERONAUT *helicopter* butée d'inclinaison de moyeu *f*

Hubble: ~ **classification** *n* ASTRON *of galaxies* classification de Hubble *f*; ~ **diagram** *n* ASTRON diagramme de Hubble *m*; ~ **parameter** *n* ASTRON paramètre de Hubble *m*; ~ **space telescope** *n* ASTRON télescope spatial Hubble *m*

Hubble's: ~ **constant** *n* ASTRON, SPACE *communications* constante de Hubble *f*; ~ **law** *n* ASTRON Loi de Hubble *f*

hubnerite *n* MINERAL hubnérite *f*

hub-type: ~ **flange** *n* MECH ENG *pipe fitting* bride à moyeu *f*; ~ **spindle** *n* MECH ENG *machine tools* broche type à moyeu *f*

HUD *abbr* (*head-up display*) INSTRUMENT collimateur de pilotage *m*

hudge *n* MINING benne *f*

hue *n* PHOTO ton *m*, PRINT teinte dominante *f*, tonalité *f*, tonalité chromatique *f*; ~ **consistency** *n* PRINT teinte dominante restant égale tout au long du tirage *f*; ~ **control** *n* TV contrôle de tonalité *m*

huge: ~ **star** *n* ASTRON grosse étoile *f*

hulk *n* NAUT carcasse de navire *f*

hull *n* AERONAUT carène *f*, quille *f*, NAUT *shipbuilding*, WATER SUPP *of dredge* coque *f*; ~ **drawings** *n pl* NAUT *shipbuilding* plan des couples *m*; ~ **girder** *n* NAUT *shipbuilding* membrure *f*, poutre-navire *f*; ~ **insurance** *n* NAUT assurance sur corps *f*; ~ **resistance** *n* NAUT *shipbuilding* résistance de la carène *f*; ~ **step** *n* AERONAUT redan *m*

hull-borne *adj* TRANSP suspendu sur coque

hum *n* ACOUSTICS bourdonnement *m*, AERONAUT *engine* ronflement *m*, COLOURS teinte nuageuse *f*, ELEC ENG ronflement *m*; ~ **bar** *n* TV barre de ronflement *f*; ~ **pickup** *n* RECORDING captage de ronflement *m*; ~ **voltage** *n* ELEC ENG tension de ronflement *f*

human: ~ **error** *n* QUALITY, SAFETY erreur humaine *f*, faute humaine *f*; ~ **error probability** *n* QUALITY probabilité d'erreur humaine *f*; ~ **exposure to mechanical vibrations** *n* SAFETY exposition humaine aux vibrations mécaniques *f*; ~ **failure** *n* QUALITY défaillance humaine *f*; ~ **failure cause** *n* QUALITY cause de défaillance humaine *f*; ~ **reliability** *n* QUALITY fiabilité humaine *f*

humble: ~ **hook** *n* MINING *overwind gear* crochet de sûreté *m*, déclic d'attelage *m*

humboldtilite *n* MINERAL humboldtilite *f*

humboldtine *n* MINERAL humboldtine *f*

hum-bucking: ~ **coil** *n* ELEC ENG, RECORDING, TV bobine antironflement *f*

humectant *n* CHEM humectant *m*

humic *adj* CHEM humique

humid[1] *adj* THERMOD humecté, humide, mouillé

humid:[2] ~ **air** *n* METEO air humide *m*; ~ **volume** *n* REFRIG volume massique *m*

humidification *n* THERMOD humidification *f*

humidifier *n* AERONAUT humidificateur *m*, PAPER TECH humecteuse *f*, REFRIG humidificateur *m*, THERMOD humecteur *m*, humidificateur *m*

humidify *vt* PAPER TECH, REFRIG, THERMOD humidifier

humidistat *n* REFRIG humidiostat *m*

humidity *n* HEATING, METEO, PAPER TECH, PHYS, REFRIG, THERMOD humidité *f*; ~ **absorber** *n* PACKAGING absorbeur d'humidité *m*; ~ **of the air** *n* PACKAGING humidité atmosphérique *f*; ~ **index** *n* METEO indice d'humidité *m*; ~ **indicator** *n* PACKAGING indicateur d'humidité *m*; ~ **loss** *n* THERMOD *sublimation, freeze drying* perte d'humidité *f*; ~ **measurement** *n* NAUT hygrométrie *f*

humidity-resistant *adj* THERMOD résistant à l'humidité

humite *n* MINERAL humite *f*

hummocked: ~ **ice** *n* OCEANOG chaos de glace *m*

hummocks *n* OCEANOG torose *f*

hummocky: ~ **ice** *n* OCEANOG torose *f*

hump: ~ **shunting** *n* RAIL *vehicles* manoeuvre par gravité *f*

humulene *n* CHEM humulène *m*

humus *n* CHEM humus *m*, terreau *m*, COAL TECH humus *m*, CONST humus *m*, terre végétale *f*; ~ **tank** *n* WATER SUPP décanteur secondaire *m*

Hund: ~ **rules** *n pl* PHYS règles de Hund *f pl*

hundred: ~ **per cent inspection** *n* CONTROL contrôle cent-pour-cent *m*; ~ **year storm** *n* PETR TECH *offshore* tempête centenaire *f*; ~ **year wave** *n* PETR TECH *offshore* vague centenaire *f*

hungry[1] *adj* MINING stérile

hungry:[2] ~ **surface** *n* PRINT surface très absorbante *f*

hunting *n* AERONAUT *of helicopter rotor blade* mouvement de traînée *m*, ELEC *machines* pompage *m*, ELEC ENG pompage *m*, *measuring device* oscillation *f*, REFRIG *rotating devices, automatic control systems* pompage *m*; ~ **blade** *n* AERONAUT *helicopter* pale traînante *f*

hureaulite *n* MINERAL hureaulite *f*

hurley *n* MINING wagonnet *m*

hurricane *n* METEO cyclone tropical *m*, ouragan *m*; ~ **deck** *n* NAUT pont de manoeuvre *m*; ~ **lamp** *n* CONST, NAUT lampe-tempête *f*

husk *vt* FOOD TECH *grain* décortiquer

husked *adj* FOOD TECH décortiqué, écossé

hutch *n* MINING huche *f*, wagon à minerai *m*

Huygens': ~ **eyepiece** *n* PHYS oculaire de Huygens *m*; ~ **principle** *n* PHYS, RAD PHYS principe de Huygens *m*

HV *abbr* *(high-voltage)* ELEC, ELECTRON, PHYS HT *(haute tension)*

HVL *abbr* *(half value layer)* NUCLEAR, PHYS CDA *(couche de demi-atténuation)*

H-wave *n* ELEC ENG onde TE *f*

HWOST *abbr* *(high water ordinary spring tide)* FUELLESS plus hautes eaux des grandes marées ordinaires *f pl*

hyacinth *n* MINERAL hyacinthe *f*

hyaline *adj* GEOL hyalin, transparent, vitreux

hyalite *n* MINERAL hyalite *f*

hyaloclastic: ~ **rock** *n* GEOL hyaloclastite *f*

hyaloclastite *n* GEOL hyaloclastite *f*, palagonite *f*, roche pyroclastique vitreuse *f*

hyalogen *n* CHEM hyalogène *m*

hyalophane *n* MINERAL hyalophane *f*

hybrid: ~ **bus** *n* TRANSP autobus à traction électrique avec montage hybride *m*; ~ **call processor** *n* TELECOM calculateur hybride *m*; ~ **circuit** *n* ELECTRON, PHYS circuit hybride *m*; ~ **computer** *n* COMP, DP ordinateur hybride *m*; ~ **electromagnetic wave** *n* ELEC motor onde électromagnétique hybride *f*; ~ **engine** *n* TRANSP moteur hybride *m*; ~ **foil craft** *n* TRANSP hydroptère hybride *m*; ~ **integrated circuit** *n* ELECTRON, TELECOM circuit intégré hybride *m*; ~ **junction** *n* ELECTRON jonction hybride *f*; ~ **microcircuit** *n* ELECTRON microcircuit hybride *m*; ~ **mode** *n* OPT, TELECOM mode hybride *m*; ~ **orbital** *n* CHEM *atomic orbitals* orbitale hybride *f*; ~ **parameter** *n* ELECTRON paramètre H *m*, paramètre hybride *m*; ~ **platform** *n* PETR TECH *offshore* plateforme hybride *f*; ~ **propellent** *n* SPACE propergol hybride *m*; ~ **propulsion** *n* TRANSP propulsion hybride *f*; ~ **scale** *n* PETR échelle hybride *f*; ~ **switch** *n* TELECOM commutateur hybride *m*; ~ **system** *n* TELECOM installation mixte *f*, système hybride *m*, TRANSP système hybride *m*; ~ **vehicle** *n* TRANSP véhicule hybride *m*

hybridization *n* CHEM *of atomic orbitals* hybridisation *f*

hydantoic: ~ **acid** *n* CHEM acide hydantoïque *m*

hydantoin *n* CHEM hydantoïne *f*

Hydra *n* ASTRON Hydre *f*

hydracrylic *adj* CHEM *acid* hydracrylique

hydrant *n* WATER SUPP bouche d'eau *f*, bouche hydrante *f*; ~ **system** *n* PETR TECH oléoréseau *m*

hydrargillite *n* MINERAL hydrargillite *f*

hydrastic *adj* CHEM hydrastique

hydrastine *n* CHEM hydrastine *f*

hydrate[1] *n* CHEM hydrate *m*

hydrate[2] *vt* CHEM, GEOL hydrater

hydrated[1] *adj* GEOL hydraté

hydrated:[2] ~ **layer** *n* C&G couche hydratée *f*; ~ **lime** *n* CONST chaux hydratée *f*

hydration *n* CHEM, CONST *of cement*, GEOL hydratation *f*

hydratropic *adj* CHEM hydratropique

hydraulic[1] *adj* MECH, REFRIG hydraulique

hydraulic:[2] ~ **accumulator** *n* AERONAUT, MECH ENG, P&R *press* accumulateur hydraulique *m*; ~ **actuating cylinder** *n* HYDR EQUIP vérin hydraulique *m*; ~ **battery** *n* AERONAUT accumulateur hydraulique *m*; ~ **bottom heave** *n* COAL TECH relevage hydraulique du sol *m*; ~ **brake servo** *n* AUTO servofrein hydraulique *m*; ~ **brake system** *n* MECH ENG système hydraulique de freinage *m*; ~ **bulging dies** *n pl* MECH ENG outillage d'hydro-formage *m*; ~ **circulation system** *n* PETR TECH *drilling* forage à injection *m*; ~ **clamping** *n* MECH ENG pressage hydraulique *m*; ~ **classification** *n* COAL TECH classification hydraulique *f*; ~ **clutch** *n* HYDR EQUIP embrayage hydraulique *m*; ~ **compensator** *n* PETR TECH *offshore platform* compensateur hydraulique de pilonnement *m*; ~ **conductivity** *n* FUELLESS, HYDROL conductivité hydraulique *f*; ~ **control** *n* CONTROL régulation hydraulique *f*; ~ **conveyor ram** *n* MINING pousseur hydraulique pour convoyeurs *m*; ~ **copy mill** *n* MECH ENG machine hydraulique de reproduction *f*; ~ **cylinder** *n* MECH ENG cylindre hydraulique *m*; ~ **detector** *n* TRANSP détecteur hydraulique *m*; ~ **diffusivity** *n* HYDROL diffusivité hydraulique *f*; ~ **discontinuity** *n* HYDROL discontinuité hydraulique *f*; ~ **drive** *n* MECH ENG transmission hydraulique *f*; ~ **efficiency** *n* FUEL-

LESS rendement hydraulique *m*, HYDROL efficacité hydraulique *f*; ~ **equipment** *n* MECH ENG matériel hydraulique *m*; ~ **failure** *n* SAFETY panne hydraulique *f*; ~ **fittings** *n pl* HYDR EQUIP accessoires de circuit hydraulique *m pl*; ~ **fluid** *n* HYDR EQUIP liquide de circuit hydraulique *m*; ~ **fluid power** *n* MECH ENG transmission hydraulique *f*; ~ **fluid reservoir** *n* MECH ENG réservoir de fluide hydraulique *m*; ~ **fracturing** *n* FUELLESS fissuration hydraulique *f*, PETR fracturation hydraulique *f*; ~ **generator** *n* HYDR EQUIP centrale hydraulique *f*, générateur de pression hydraulique *m*, SPACE centrale hydraulique *f*; ~ **grade line** *n* HYDROL ligne d'eau *f*; ~ **gradient** *n* HYDROL gradient hydraulique *m*; ~ **head** *n* HYDR EQUIP charge hydraulique *f*, PETR TECH *fluid flow* niveau hydraulique *m*; ~ **hose** *n* P&R tuyau hydraulique *m*; ~ **impulse test** *n* MECH ENG essai à impulsion hydraulique *m*; ~ **jack** *n* CONST vérin hydraulique *m*, HYDR EQUIP cric hydraulique *m*, vérin hydraulique *m*, MECH vérin hydraulique *m*, MECH ENG cylindre hydraulique *m*; ~ **jet propulsion** *n* TRANSP propulsion par jet hydraulique *f*; ~ **jump** *n* HYDROL ressaut *m*; ~ **linkage** *n* AUTO commande hydraulique *f*, conduite hydraulique *f*; ~ **locking** *n* HYDR EQUIP verrouillage hydraulique *m*; ~ **loss** *n* NUCLEAR perte hydraulique *f*, pertes hydrauliques *f pl*; ~ **machinery** *n* MECH ENG machinerie hydraulique *f*; ~ **motor** *n* MECH ENG moteur hydraulique *m*; ~ **packing seal** *n* MECH ENG garniture d'étanchéité hydraulique *f*; ~ **performance test** *n* MECH ENG essai de fonctionnement hydraulique *m*; ~ **piston discharger** *n* CONST système d'évacuation à piston hydraulique *m*; ~ **power** *n* HYDR EQUIP énergie hydraulique *f*; ~ **power pack** *n* MINING, SPACE *spacecraft* centrale hydraulique *f*; ~ **press** *n* LAB EQUIP, P&R presse hydraulique *f*; ~ **pressure source** *n* HYDR EQUIP générateur *m*, génératrice de pression hydraulique *f*; ~ **pressure supply** *n* HYDR EQUIP source d'énergie hydraulique *f*; ~ **pressure test** *n* CONTROL contrôle de pression hydraulique *m*, PROD ENG contrôle de la pression hydraulique *m*; ~ **proof pressure** *n* REFRIG pression d'essai hydraulique *f*; ~ **prop** *n* MINING étançon hydraulique *m*; ~ **ram** *n* FUELLESS pilon hydraulique *m*, MINING pousseur hydraulique *m*; ~ **reservoir** *n* HYDR EQUIP réservoir de fluide hydraulique *m*; ~ **rotary percussion drill** *n* MINING perforatrice à percussion rotative hydraulique *f*; ~ **sheet cutter** *n* PAPER TECH coupe-feuilles hydraulique *m*; ~ **status** *n* GAS TECH régime hydraulique *m*; ~ **system** *n* AUTO circuit hydraulique *m*, HYDR EQUIP circuit hydraulique *m*, système hydraulique *m*, NAUT hydraulique *f*; ~ **thrust** *n* FUELLESS poussée hydraulique *f*; ~ **transmission system** *n* MECH ENG transmission hydraulique *f*; ~ **valve lifter** *n* AUTO poussoir à commande hydraulique *m*; ~ **winch** *n* MINING treuil hydraulique *m*

hydraulically-operated: ~ **device** *n* MECH ENG dispositif actionné hydrauliquement *m*; ~ **valve** *n* MECH ENG, REFRIG vanne hydraulique *f*

hydraulics *n* HYDR EQUIP, MECH, PETR TECH hydraulique *f*

hydrazide *n* CHEM hydrazide *f*

hydrazine *n* CHEM, SPACE *propulsion* hydrazine *f*; ~ **propulsion** *n* SPACE *spacecraft* propulsion à hydrazine *f*; ~ **propulsion system** *n* SPACE *spacecraft* système de propulsion à hydrazine *m*

hydrazoate *n* CHEM azoture *m*

hydrazoic *adj* CHEM azohydrique, hydrazoïque

hydric *adj* CHEM hydrique

hydride *n* CHEM, METALL hydrure *m*

hydrindene *n* CHEM hydrindène *f*, indane *f*

hydriodic *adj* CHEM hydriodique

hydriodide *n* CHEM iodhydrate *m*

hydro: ~ **cooling** *n* REFRIG refroidissement hydraulique *m*

hydroaromatic *adj* CHEM hydroaromatique

hydrobilirubin *n* CHEM hydrobilirubine *f*

hydrobromic *adj* CHEM bromhydrique

hydrobromide *n* CHEM bromhydrate *m*

hydrocarbon *n* CHEM carbure d'hydrogène *m*, hydrocarbure *m*, GEOL *oil* hydrocarbure *m*, MAR POLL huile *f*, hydrocarbure *m*, pétrole *m*, PETR TECH *petroleum*, POLLUTION, VEHICLES *fuel* hydrocarbure *m*; ~ **aerosol propellant** *n* PETR TECH gaz propulseur *m*; ~ **feedstocks** *n pl* PETR TECH hydrocarbures de base *m pl*; ~ **fire** *n* SAFETY feu d'hydrocarbure *m*; ~ **resin** *n* PROP MAT résine à hydrocarbures *f*; ~ **saturation** *n* PETR saturation d'hydrocarbures *f*; ~ **slick** *n* PETR TECH, POLLUTION nappe d'hydrocarbures *f*; ~ **trap** *n* PETR TECH piège d'hydrocarbures *m*, piège pétrolifère *m*

hydrocarbonate *n* CHEM hydrocarbonate *m*

hydrocarbonic *adj* CHEM hydrocarboné

hydrocellulose *n* CHEM hydrocellulose *f*

hydrochloric[1] *adj* CHEM chlorhydrique

hydrochloric:[2] ~ **acid** *n* CHEM, DETERGENTS acide chlorhydrique *m*

hydrocinnamic *adj* CHEM hydrocinnamique

hydroclone *n* CHEM TECH hydroclone *m*

hydrocortisone *n* CHEM cortisol *m*, hydrocortisone *f*

hydrocotarnine *n* CHEM hydrocotarnine *f*

hydrocracker *n* PETR TECH hydrocraqueur *m*

hydrocracking *n* PETR TECH, PROP MAT hydrocraquage *m*

hydrocyanic *adj* CHEM cyanhydrique

hydrocyanite *n* MINERAL hydrocyanite *f*

hydrocyclone *n* COAL TECH, PETR TECH hydrocyclone *m*

hydrodesulfurization *n* (AmE), **hydrodesulphurization** *n* (BrE) POLLUTION hydrodésulfuration *f*

hydrodolomite *n* MINERAL hydrodolomite *f*

hydrodynamic[1] *adj* CHEM, GEOL, NAUT, PETR TECH, PHYS hydrodynamique

hydrodynamic:[2] ~ **bearing** *n* SPACE *spacecraft* palier hydrodynamique *m*; ~ **damping factor** *n* FUELLESS facteur d'amortissement hydrodynamique *m*; ~ **drag** *n* TRANSP traînée hydrodynamique *f*; ~ **instability** *n* GAS TECH instabilité hydrodynamique *f*; ~ **lift** *n* TRANSP portance hydrodynamique *f*; ~ **load** *n* HYDROL charge hydrodynamique *f*; ~ **model** *n* FUELLESS modèle hydrodynamique *m*; ~ **skimmer** *n* MAR POLL récupérateur dynamique *m*, écrémeur dynamique *m*; ~ **thrust** *n* HYDROL *pressure* poussée hydrodynamique *f*

hydrodynamics *n* FLUID PHYS, NAUT hydrodynamique *f*, PETR TECH hydrodynamisme *m*, PHYS hydrodynamique *f*

hydroelastic: ~ **suspension** *n* AUTO suspension hydrolastique *f*

hydroelectric: ~ **generating station** *n* ELEC ENG aménagement hydro-électrique *m*; ~ **generator** *n* ELEC générateur hydraulique *m*, générateur hydro-électrique *m*, ELEC ENG générateur hydraulique *m*; ~ **power** *n* ELEC *supply* énergie hydraulique *f*, énergie hydro-électrique *f*, FUELLESS houille blanche *f*, énergie hydro-électrique *f*, hydro-électricité *f*; ~ **power plant** *n* ELEC ENG centrale hydro-électrique *f*, station hydroélectrique *f*, usine hydro-électrique *f*, FUELLESS usine hydro-électrique *f*; ~ **power station** *n* ELEC *supply* centrale hydro-électrique *f*, ELEC ENG centrale hydro-électrique *f*, station hydro-électrique *f*, usine hydro-électrique *f*, FUELLESS usine hydro-électrique *f*, HYDROL centrale hydraulique *f*, centrale hydro-électrique *f*; ~ **project** *n* CONST projet hydro-électrique *m*

hydroelectricity *n* ELEC *supply* hydro-électricité *f*

hydroextract *vt* TEXTILES déshydrater

hydroextraction *n* TEXTILES déshydratation *f*

hydroextractor *n* TEXTILES *mangle* essoreuse à rouleaux *f*, *spin-dryer* essoreuse à tambour *f*

hydrofluoric *adj* CHEM fluorhydrique

hydrofluoride *n* CHEM fluorhydrate *m*

hydrofoil *n* AERONAUT hydroptère *m*, NAUT *type of craft* hydrofoil *m*, navire à ailes portantes *m*, TRANSP aile d'hydroptère *f*, hydroptère *m*; ~ **rudder** *n* OCEANOG barre de plongée *f*

hydroforming *n* PROP MAT hydroformage *m*; ~ **plant** *n* PROP MAT unité d'hydroforming *f*

hydroformulation *n* PROP MAT hydroformulation *f*

hydrogen *n* (H) CHEM hydrogène *m* (H); ~ **bond** *n* CHEM, CRYSTALL liaison hydrogène *f*; ~ **gas** *n* CHEM gaz hydrogène *m*; ~ **index** *n* PETR indice d'hydrogène *m*; ~ **ion concentration** *n* CHEM concentration des ions d'hydrogène *f*; ~ **liquid** *n* THERMOD hydrogène liquide *m*; ~ **peroxide** *n* CHEM eau oxygénée *f*, peroxyde d'hydrogène *m*, SPACE peroxyde d'hydrogène *m*; ~ **plasma** *n* GAS TECH plasma d'hydrogène *m*; ~ **spectral line** *n* RAD PHYS raie spectrale d'hydrogène *f*; ~ **sulfide** *n* (AmE), ~ **sulphide** *n* (BrE) CHEM, FOOD TECH hydrogène sulfuré *m*, POLLUTION acide sulphydrique *m*, hydrogène sulfuré *m*, sulfure d'hydrogène *m*; ~ **tank** *n* SPACE *spacecraft* réservoir d'hydrogène *m*; ~ **thyratron** *n* ELECTRON thyratron à l'hydrogène *m*

hydrogenate *vt* CHEM, FOOD TECH hydrogéner

hydrogenated[1] *adj* CHEM, FOOD TECH hydrogéné

hydrogenated:[2] ~ **fat** *n* FOOD TECH graisse hydrogénée *f*

hydrogenation *n* CHEM, DETERGENTS, FOOD TECH, PETR TECH *refining*, PROP MAT hydrogénation *f*

hydrogenator *n* FOOD TECH *processing* appareil d'hydrogénation *m*, hydrogénateur *m*

hydrogenous *adj* GEOL thalassogène

hydrogen-oxygen: ~ **mixture** *n* OCEANOG hydrox *m*

hydrogeochemistry *n* GEOL géochimie de l'eau *f*

hydrogeological: ~ **map** *n* HYDROL carte hydrogéologique *f*

hydrogeology *n* HYDROL, WATER SUPP hydrogéologie *f*

hydrograph *n* WATER SUPP hydrogramme *m*

hydrographic[1] *adj* NAUT hydrographique

hydrographic:[2] ~ **basin** *n* GEOL bassin hydrographique *m*; ~ **chart** *n* HYDROL *marine*, NAUT *navigation* carte hydrographique *f*; ~ **dredging** *n* OCEANOG dragage hydrographique *m*; ~ **office** *n* NAUT bureau des cartes et plans *m*; ~ **signal** *n* OCEANOG signal hydrographique *m*; ~ **survey** *n* OCEANOG levé hydrographique *m*; ~ **survey vessel** *n* NAUT navire hydrographique *m*

hydrographical *adj* NAUT hydrographique

hydrography *n* FUELLESS, HYDROL, NAUT, OCEANOG hydrographie *f*

hydrojet *n* TRANSP hydrojet *m*; ~ **propulsion** *n* TRANSP propulsion par jet d'eau *f*

hydrokinetic: ~ **brake** *n* TRANSP frein hydrocinétique *m*

hydrologic: ~ **balance** *n* HYDROL, WATER SUPP bilan hydrologique *m*; ~ **cycle** *n* GEOL cycle de l'eau *m*, WATER SUPP cycle hydrologique *m*; ~ **investigation** *n*

HYDROL étude hydrologique *f*; ~ **study** *n* CONST étude hydrologique *f*; ~ **year** *n* HYDROL année hydrologique *f*; ~ **yearbook** *n* HYDROL annuaire hydrologique *m*

hydrologist *n* CONST hydrologiste *m*, hydrologue *m*

hydrology *n* COAL TECH, CONST, OCEANOG, WATER SUPP hydrologie *f*

hydrolysis *n* CHEM, FOOD TECH, GEOL, P&R, PROP MAT hydrolyse *f*

hydromagnesite *n* MINERAL hydromagnésite *f*

hydromechanical: ~ **clutch** *n* MECH ENG embrayage hydromécanique *m*; ~ **governor** *n* FUELLESS régulateur hydromécanique *m*

hydromechanics *n* FLUID PHYS hydromécanique *f*

hydrometallurgy *n* COAL TECH hydrométallurgie *f*

hydrometer *n* COAL TECH densimètre *m*, ELEC *accumulator* aréomètre *m*, densimètre *m*, FOOD TECH aréomètre *m*, hydromètre *m*, HYDROL hydromètre *m*, LAB EQUIP *liquids* densimètre *m*, PETR TECH *prospecting, refining* hydromètre *m*, PHYS densimètre *m*, hydromètre *m*, VEHICLES *accumulator* aréomètre *m*

hydrometric: ~ **state** *n* HYDROL degré hydrométrique *m*, état hygrométrique *m*, METEO degré hydrométrique *m*, état hydrométrique *m*

hydrometry *n* CHEM, HYDROL, PHYS, WATER SUPP hydrométrie *f*

hydronomy *n* OCEANOG hydronomie *f*

hydrophane *n* MINERAL hydrophane *f*

hydrophile: ~ **balance** *n* DETERGENTS équilibre hydrophile *m*

hydrophilic *adj* CHEM, COAL TECH hydrophile

hydrophobic *adj* CHEM hydrophobe, hydrophobique, COAL TECH hydrophobe

hydrophone *n* OCEANOG, PETR TECH *seismic survey*, TELECOM hydrophone *m*

hydroplane *n* NAUT hydravion *m*, hydroglisseur *m*, OCEANOG, TRANSP hydroglisseur *m*

hydropneumatic: ~ **accumulator** *n* MECH ENG accumulateur hydraulique *m*; ~ **brake** *n* TRANSP frein hydropneumatique *m*; ~ **chamber** *n* OCEANOG chambre hydropneumatique *f*; ~ **suspension** *n* AUTO suspension oléo-pneumatique *f*, VEHICLES suspension hydropneumatique *f*

hydroquinone *n* CHEM hydroquinone *f*

hydrorefining *n* PROP MAT hydroraffinage *m*

hydroscience *n* WATER SUPP science de l'eau *f*

hydrosilicate *n* CHEM hydrosilicate *m*

hydroskimmer *n* TRANSP hydroglisseur *m*

hydrosol *n* CHEM hydrosol *m*

hydrosopoline *n* CHEM hydrosopoline *f*

hydrosphere *n* HYDROL, OCEANOG, POLLUTION hydrosphère *f*

hydrostatic[1] *adj* MECH, PHYS hydrostatique

hydrostatic:[2] ~ **balance** *n* FLUID PHYS balance hydrostatique *f*, LAB EQUIP *instrument* tensiomètre *m*; ~ **bearing** *n* MECH palier hydrostatique *m*; ~ **curves** *n pl* NAUT *ship design* courbes hydrostatiques *f pl*; ~ **equilibrium** *n* THERMOD équilibre hydrostatique *m*; ~ **equipment** *n* MECH ENG matériel hydrostatique *m*; ~ **head** *n* PETR TECH *drilling* charge hydrostatique *f*; ~ **level** *n* OCEANOG niveau d'équilibre *m*; ~ **load** *n* HYDROL charge hydrostatique *f*; ~ **pressure** *n* COAL TECH, FLUID PHYS, GAS TECH pression hydrostatique *f*, GEOL pression de formation normale *f*, pression hydrostatique *f*, HYDROL, OCEANOG pression hydrostatique *f*, PETR TECH *geology* pression de formation normale *f*, pression hydrostatique *f*, REFRIG pression hydrostatique *f*;

~ stress *n* METALL contrainte hydrostatique *f*; **~ transmission** *n* MECH transmission hydrostatique *f*

hydrostatics *n* CONST, FLUID PHYS hydrostatique *f*, PHYS hydrostatique *f*, statique des fluides *f*, WATER SUPP hydrostatique *f*

hydrosulfide *n* (AmE) *see* hydrosulphide

hydrosulfite *n* (AmE) *see* hydrosulphite

hydrosulfurous: ~ acid *n* (AmE) *see* hydrosulphurous acid

hydrosulphide *n* (BrE) CHEM sulfhydrate *m*

hydrosulphite *n* (BrE) CHEM hydrosulfite *m*

hydrosulphurous: ~ acid *n* (BrE) CHEM acide hydrosulfureux *m*

hydro-test *n* MECH épreuve hydraulique *f*

hydrothermal[1] *adj* GEOL hydrothermal

hydrothermal:[2] **~ deposit** *n* GEOL dépôt hydrothermal *m*, gisement minéral hydrothermal *m*; **~ ecosystem** *n* OCEANOG oasis sous-marine *f*; **~ process** *n* FUELLESS processus hydrothermal *m*; **~ vent** *n* OCEANOG source hydrothermale *f*

hydrous *adj* CHEM aqueux, hydraté, GEOL *of minerals* hydraté

hydrox *n* OCEANOG hydrox *m*

hydroxy-capped *adj* CHEM coiffée par hydroxie

hydroxyethylcellulose *n* CHEM, PETR TECH hydroxyéthylcellulose *f*

hydroxyl *n* CHEM hydroxyle *m*

hydroxylated *adj* CHEM, FOOD TECH hydroxylé

hydroxyl-free: ~ glass *n* C&G verre sans hydroxyles *m*

hydrozincite *n* MINERAL hydrozincite *f*

Hydrus *n* ASTRON Hydre mâle *f*

hygrometer *n* LAB EQUIP, METEO, PETR TECH, PHYS, REFRIG hygromètre *m*

hygrometry *n* METEO, REFRIG, WATER SUPP hygrométrie *f*

hygroscope *n* PHYS hygroscope *m*

hygroscopic[1] *adj* CHEM, CONST, HYDROL, MECH *materials*, PHYS hygroscopique, PROP MAT avide d'eau

hygroscopic:[2] **~ water** *n* HYDROL, WATER SUPP eau hygroscopique *f*

hygrosensibility *n* PAPER TECH sensibilité aux variations hygrométriques *f*

hygrostability *n* PAPER TECH inertie à l'eau *f*

hyocholanic *adj* CHEM hyocholanique

hyoscine *n* CHEM hyoscine *f*, scopolamine *f*

hypabyssal: ~ rock *n* GEOL roche intrusive de semi-profondeur *f*

hypautomorphic *adj* GEOL hypidiomorphe

hyperabrupt: ~ junction *n* ELECTRON jonction hyperabrupte *f*; **~ varactor diode** *n* PHYS diode varactor hyperabrupt *f*

hyperapnea *n* OCEANOG hyperapnée *f*

hyperballistic *adj* SPACE hyperbalistique

hyperballistics *n* SPACE hyperbalistique *f*

hyperbaric: ~ arthralgia *n* OCEANOG dysbarique, syndrome articulaire des hautes pressions *m*; **~ center** *n* (AmE), **~ centre** *n* (BrE) OCEANOG centre hyperbare *m*; **~ chamber** *n* OCEANOG, PETR TECH caisson hyperbare *m*; **~ environment** *n* OCEANOG ambiance hyperbare *f*

hyperbary *n* OCEANOG hyperbarie *f*

hyperbola *n* GEOM hyperbole *f*

hyperbolic[1] *adj* GEOM hyperbolique

hyperbolic:[2] **~ geometry** *n* GEOM géométrie hyperbolique *f*; **~ navigation** *n* NAUT navigation hyperbolique *f*; **~ orbit** *n* SPACE orbite hyperbolique *f*; **~ position-fixing system** *n* NAUT *navigation* système hyperbolique de localisation *m*; **~ space** *n* GEOM espace hyperbolique *m*; **~ universe** *n* ASTRON univers hyperbolique *m*

hyperboloid *n* GEOM hyperboloïde *m*

hypercardioid: ~ microphone *n* ACOUSTICS microphone hypercardioïde *m*

hypercharge *n* PHYS hypercharge *f*

hypereutectic *adj* METALL hypereutectique

hypereutectoid: ~ steel *n* METALL acier hypereutectoïde *m*

hyperfine: ~ structure *n* PHYS, RAD PHYS structure hyperfine *f*

hypergeometric: ~ distribution *n* MATH *statistics* loi hypergéométrique *f*

hypergol *n* SPACE *spacecraft* hypergol *m*

hypergolic[1] *adj* SPACE *spacecraft* hypergolique

hypergolic:[2] **~ ignition** *n* SPACE *spacecraft* allumage spontané *m*; **~ property** *n* SPACE *spacecraft* hypergolicité *f*

hypergroup *n* TELECOM groupe tertiaire *m*

hyperkapnia *n* OCEANOG hypercapnie *f*

hyperon *n* PART PHYS, PHYS hypéron *m*

hyperoxia *n* OCEANOG hypéroxie *f*

hyperoxide *n* CHEM hyperoxyde *m*

hyperoxie *n* OCEANOG hypéroxie *f*

hyperplane *n* GEOM hyperplan *m*

hypersaline: ~ water *n* OCEANOG eau hyperhaline *f*

hypersalinity *n* OCEANOG sursalure *f*

hypersensitize *vt* CINEMAT latensifier

hypersonic[1] *adj* SPACE hypersonique

hypersonic:[2] **~ aircraft** *n* AERONAUT avion hypersonique *m*; **~ flow** *n* FLUID PHYS écoulement hypersonique *m*; **~ speed** *n* PHYS vitesse hypersonique *f*

hypersthene *n* MINERAL hypersthène *m*

hypersurface *n* GEOM hypersurface *f*

hypertext *n* COMP, DP hypertexte *m*

hyperthermal: ~ field *n* FUELLESS champ hyperthermique *m*

hyperventilation *n* OCEANOG hyperventilation *f*

hyphen *n* PRINT tiret *m*; **~ ladders** *n pl* PRINT échelle de tirets *f*

hyphenation: ~ and justification programme *n* PRINT programme de césure et justification *m*

hypidiomorphic *adj* GEOL hypidiomorphe

hypocenter *n* (AmE), **hypocentre** *n* (BrE) GEOL foyer *m*, hypocentre *m*, GEOPHYS foyer du séisme *m*, hypocentre *m*

hypochlorate *n* CHEM hypochlorate *m*

hypochloric *adj* CHEM hypochlorique

hypochlorite *n* CHEM hypochlorite *m*

hypochlorous: ~ acid *n* CHEM acide hypochloreux *m*

hypoeutectic *adj* METALL hypoeutectique

hypoid[1] *adj* MECH *gears* hypoïde

hypoid:[2] **~ bevel gear** *n* MECH roue conique hypoïde *f*; **~ gear** *n* MECH ENG engrenage hypoïde *m*; **~ gearing** *n* AUTO, VEHICLES couple conique à denture hypoïde *m*

hyponeuston *n* OCEANOG hyponeuston *m*

hypophosphate *n* CHEM hypophosphate *m*

hypophosphite *n* CHEM hypophosphite *m*

hypophosphoric *adj* CHEM hypophosphorique

hypophosphorous *adj* CHEM hypophosphoreux

hyposulfite *n* (AmE) *see* hyposulphite

hyposulfurous: ~ acid *n* (AmE) *see* hyposulphurous acid

hyposulphite *n* (BrE) CHEM, CINEMAT hyposulfite *m*

hyposulphurous: ~ acid *n* (BrE) CHEM acide hyposulfureux *m*

hypotenuse *n* GEOM hypoténuse *f*

hypothermal *adj* GEOL *mineralization* hypothermal

hypothermia *n* NAUT hypothermie *f*

hypothermic: ~ **blanket** *n* REFRIG *hibernation* couverture réfrigérante *f*

hypothesis *n* CHEM hypothèse *f*

hypotonic *adj* CHEM hypotonique

hypsographic: ~ **curve** *n* GEOL courbe hypsographique *f*

hypsometer *n* PHYS hypsomètre *m*

hypsometric[1] *adj* PETR hypsométrique

hypsometric:[2] ~ **map** *n* HYDROL carte hypsométrique *f*; ~ **tint** *n* COLOURS encre hypsométrique *f*

hystarazin *n* CHEM hystarazine *f*

hysteresis *n* ELEC *curve*, ELEC ENG, MECH, METALL, P&R, PETR, PHYS, RECORDING hystérésis *f*; ~ **coefficient** *n* ELEC *magnetization* coefficient d'hystérésis *m*; ~ **curve** *n* ELEC courbe d'hystérésis *f*; ~ **error** *n* AERONAUT *altimeter* erreur d'hystérésis *f*; ~ **loop** *n* ELEC boucle d'hystérésis *f*, ELEC ENG cycle d'hystérésis *m*, METALL boule d'hystérésis *f*, cycle d'hystérésis *m*, P&R cycle d'hystérésis *m*, PHYS boucle d'hystérésis *f*, cycle d'hystérésis *m*, TV cycle d'hystérésis *m*; ~ **loss** *n* ELEC ENG, P&R *electrical* , PHYS perte par hystérésis *f*; ~ **motor** *n* ELEC ENG moteur à hystérésis *m*

Hz *abbr (hertz)* ELEC, ELEC ENG, METR, PETR, PHYS, TV Hz *(hertz)*

I

I *(iodine)* CHEM I *(iode)*

I/F *abbr (interface)* TELECOM interface *f*

I/O *abbr (input/output)* COMP, PROD ENG E/S *(entrée/sortie)*

I/O: ~ **adaptor** *n* PROD ENG adapteur des E/S *m;* ~ **channel communication** *n* PROD ENG canal de transmission des E/S *m;* ~ **chassis** *n* PROD ENG châssis d'E/S *m;* ~ **chassis module slot** *n* PROD ENG emplacement de châssis d'E/S *m;* ~ **designation** *n* PROD ENG structure d'E/S *f;* ~ **device status** *n* PROD ENG état des E/S physiques *m;* ~ **hardware** *n* PROD ENG organe d'E/S *m;* ~ **module** *n* PROD ENG module d'E/S *m;* ~ **module group** *n* PROD ENG groupe de modules d'E/S *m;* ~ **module placement** *n* PROD ENG implantation des modules d'E/S *f;* ~ **rack** *n* PROD ENG rack d'E/S *m;* ~ **scanner** *n* PROD ENG scrutateur des E/S *m;* ~ **scan time** *n* PROD ENG temps de scrutation des E/S *m;* ~ **status indicator** *n* PROD ENG voyant d'états des E/S *m;* ~ **terminal location address** *n* PROD ENG adresse d'emplacement de borne d'E/S *f*

IAGC *abbr (instantaneous automatic gain control)* CONTROL régulateur automatique de niveau *m*

IAS *abbr (immediate access store)* COMP mémoire à accès immédiat *f*

IAT *abbr (International Atomic Time)* ASTRON TAI *(Temps Atomique International)*

IAVC *abbr (instantaneous automatic volume control)* CONTROL régulateur automatique de niveau *m*

I-axis *n* TV axe *m*

I-beam *n* CONST poutre en double T *f*, poutrelle *f*, solive en fer à double T *f*

IBG *abbr (interblock gap)* COMP espace entre blocs *m*

IC *abbr (integrated circuit)* COMP, ELEC, ELECTRON, PHYS, TELECOM, TV CI *(circuit intégré)*

ICB *abbr (incoming calls barred)* TELECOM interdiction des appels à l'arrivée *f*

ice:[1] ~ **accretion** *n* WATER SUPP givrage *m;* ~ **bank cooler** *n* REFRIG refroidisseur à accumulation de glace *m;* ~ **bank evaporator** *n* REFRIG évaporateur accumulateur de glace *m;* ~ **bank tank** *n* REFRIG bac à accumulation de glace *m;* ~ **barrier** *n* OCEANOG barrière de glace *f;* ~ **blower** *n* REFRIG lance-glace *m;* ~ **breakup** *n* OCEANOG débâcle *f;* ~ **bunker** *n* REFRIG bac à glace *m;* ~ **cake** *n* REFRIG glaçon stationnaire *m*, pain de glace *m;* ~ **can** *n* REFRIG mouleau à glace *m;* ~ **cap** *n* OCEANOG calotte glaciaire *f;* ~ **cellar** *n* REFRIG glacière *f;* ~ **condenser** *n* NUCLEAR condenseur à glace *m;* ~ **crusher** *n* REFRIG broyeur à glace *m;* ~ **cube tray** *n* REFRIG tiroir à glace *m;* ~ **detector** *n* AERONAUT avertisseur de givrage *m*, avertisseur détecteur *m*, détecteur de givrage *m;* ~ **detector relay** *n* AERONAUT relais avertisseur de givrage *m;* ~ **dump table** *n* REFRIG table de démoulage *f;* ~ **field** *n* NAUT, OCEANOG banquise *f;* ~ **floe** *n* NAUT *meteorology* banquise flottante *f;* ~ **guard** *n* AERONAUT grille antigivre *f;* ~ **island** *n* OCEANOG île de glace *f;* ~ **jam** *n* HYDROL embâclement *m;* ~ **lens** *n* COAL TECH lentille de glace *f;* ~ **maker** *n* REFRIG générateur de glace *m;* ~ **melting equivalent** *n* REFRIG chaleur latente

de la glace *f;* ~ **pack** *n* NAUT, OCEANOG banquise *f;* ~ **point** *n* PHYS point de la glace fondante *m*, température de la glace fondante *f;* ~ **probe** *n* AERONAUT tête d'avertisseur de givrage *f*, tête de détection de givrage *f;* ~ **refrigerator** *n* REFRIG réfrigérateur *m;* ~ **ridge** *n* OCEANOG ondin *m*, ride de glace *f;* ~ **ripple** *n* OCEANOG ride de glace *f;* ~ **sheet** *n* OCEANOG calotte glaciaire *f*, inlandsis *m;* ~ **shelf** *n* OCEANOG plate-forme flottante *f;* ~ **slab** *n* REFRIG plateau de glace *m;* ~ **storage room** *n* REFRIG réserve à glace *f;* ~ **target** *n* NUCLEAR cible en glace *f;* ~ **tip** *n* REFRIG basculeur à mouleaux de glace *m;* ~ **warning sign** *n* TRANSP signal avertisseur de verglas *m;* ~ **water** *n* REFRIG eau de fusion de la glace *f*

ice[2] *vi* REFRIG glacer

icebound *adj* NAUT *port* fermé par les glaces, *ship* bloqué par les glaces, fermé par les glaces, retenu par les glaces

icebreaker *n* MILIT, NAUT *ship* brise-glace *m*

icebreaking: ~ **cargo ship** *n* TRANSP cargo brise-glace *m;* ~ **oil tanker** *n* TRANSP pétrolier brise-glace *m*

ice-cold *adj* THERMOD glacial

iced *adj* REFRIG *water* glacé

ice-free: ~ **water** *n* OCEANOG glace navigable *f*

ice-making: ~ **capacity** *n* REFRIG capacité de production de glace *f;* ~ **compartment** *n* MECH ENG *of refrigerator* compartiment de production de glace *m;* ~ **machine** *n* THERMOD glacière *f;* ~ **plant** *n* THERMOD glacière *f*

ice-patterned: ~ **glass** *n* C&G verre givré à la colle *m*

ice-pushed: ~ **ridge** *n* OCEANOG bourrelet glacial *m*

icing *n* NAUT *on ship* formation de glace *f*, givrage *m*, REFRIG glaçage *m;* ~ **probe** *n* AERONAUT sonde de givrage *f*

icon *n* DP icône *f*

I-connecting: ~ **rod** *n* AUTO bielle en I *f*

iconoscope *n* ELECTRON iconoscope *m*

I-core *n* ELEC ENG noyau droit *m*, noyau magnétique droit *m*

icosahedral *adj* GEOM icosaèdre

icosahedron *n* GEOM icosaèdre *m*

ICRP *n (International Commission on Radiological Protection)* RAD PHYS Commission internationale pour la protection radiologique *f*

icy *adj* THERMOD glacial, glacé

ID *abbr* COMP *(identification)*, DP *(identification)* ID *(identification)*, MECH *(inner diameter, inside diameter)* diamètre intérieur *m*, TELECOM *(identifier)* identificateur *m*

IDD *abbr (International Direct Dialing, International Direct Dialling)* TELECOM Automatique International *m*

IDDD *abbr (International Direct Distance Dialing, International Direct Distance Dialling)* TELECOM Automatique International *m*

ideal: ~ **bunching** *n* ELECTRON groupement parfait *m;* ~ **conditions** *n pl* TRANSP conditions idéales *f pl;* ~ **filter** *n* ELECTRON filtre idéal *m;* ~ **gas** *n* PHYS gaz idéal *m*, gaz parfait *m;* ~ **mixture ratio** *n* AUTO dosage parfait *m;* ~ **rectifier** *n* ELEC ENG redresseur parfait *m;* ~ **transfor-**

mer *n* ELEC ENG transformateur parfait *m*; **~ velocity** *n* FUELLESS vitesse idéale *f*

I-demodulator *n* TV démodulateur I *m*

identification *n* ACOUSTICS, COMP, DP identification *f*, MECH ENG identification *f*, repérage *m*, PART PHYS *of particles*, SAFETY *of hazards* identification *f*; **~ beacon** *n* AERONAUT phare d'identification *m*; **~ character** *n* COMP, DP caractère d'identification *m*; **~ code** *n* COMP, DP, TELECOM code d'identification *m*; **~ code qualifier** *n* TELECOM qualificatif du code d'identification *m*; **~ of contents** *n* SAFETY *industrial gas containers* marquage pour l'identification du contenu *m*; **~ division** *n* COMP *COBOL* division d'identification *f*; **~ light** *n* AERONAUT feu d'identification *m*; **~ signal** *n* TV signal d'identification *m*; **~ sleeve** *n* MECH ENG manchon repère *m*; **~ strip** *n* PROD ENG bague de repérage *f*; **~ tag** *n* SAFETY plaque d'identification *f*

identified: **~ resources** *n pl* FUELLESS ressources identifiées *f pl*

identifier *n* COMP, DP, TELECOM identificateur *m*

identify *vt* CHEM, COMP, DP identifier

identity *n* COMP, DP, MATH *symbol* identité *f*; **~ element** *n* MATH élément neutre *m*

identity-based: **~ security policy** *n* TELECOM politique de sécurité fondée sur l'identité *f*

ideogram *n* DP idéogramme *m*

IDF *abbr (intermediate distribution frame)* TELECOM RI *(répartiteur intermédiaire)*

IDI *abbr (initial domain identifier)* TELECOM IDI *(identificateur du domaine initial)*

idioblastic *adj* GEOL automorphe, à faces bien cristallisées

idiomorphic[1] *adj* PETR idiomorphe

idiomorphic:[2] **~ crystal** *n* METALL cristal idiomorphe *m*

idiomorphous *adj* PETR idiomorphe

iditol *n* CHEM iditol *m*

idle[1] *adj* PROD ENG *machinery, works* en chômage, inactif, inoccupé, TELECOM libre

idle:[2] **~ adjustment screw** *n* AUTO, VEHICLES *carburettor* vis de réglage de ralenti *f*; **~ and low speed circuit** *n* AUTO dispositif du ralenti *m*; **~ character** *n* COMP, DP caractère d'attente *m*; **~ component** *n* ELEC *alternating current* composante déwattée *f*, ELEC ENG composante réactive *f*; **~ current** *n* ELEC *alternating current* courant déwatté *m*, courant à vide *m*; **~ gear** *n* VEHICLES *gearbox* pignon fou *m*; **~ jet** *n* AUTO, VEHICLES *carburettor* gicleur de ralenti *m*; **~ period** *n* ELECTRON période de repos *f*; **~ pulley** *n* MECH ENG poulie folle *f*; **~ return** *n* MECH ENG *machine tool work* retour à blanc *m*, retour à vide *m*; **~ roller** *n* TV galet libre *m*; **~ shipping** *n* NAUT *sea transport* navires désarmés *m pl*, navires inemployés *m pl*, tonnage inemployé *m*; **~ side** *n* PROD ENG *of belt* brin conduit *m*, brin lâche *m*, brin mené *m*, brin mou *m*; **~ state** *n* TELECOM état de disponibilité *m*; **~ stroke** *n* MECH ENG course à blanc *f*, course à vide *f*; **~ throttle stop** *n* AERONAUT butée ralentie *f*; **~ time** *n* COMP temps mort *m*, DP temps d'inactivité *m*; **~ working channel** *n* TELECOM *land mobile* voie de trafic au repos *f*

idle[3] *vi* MECH tourner au ralenti, tourner à vide, VEHICLES *of engine* marcher au ralenti, tourner au ralenti

idler *n* CINEMAT galet fou *m*, galet libre *m*, MECH galet tendeur *m*, MECH ENG roue intermédiaire *f*, roue parasite *f*, *guide pulley* galet *m*, galet de renvoi *m*, galet guide *m*, poulie-guide *f*, *tightening pulley* galet tendeur *m*, poulie de tension *f*, rouleau de tension *m*, RAIL

vehicles essieu porteur d'avant *m*, TV galet libre *m*; **~ arm** *n* AUTO bras de renvoi *m*; **~ frequency** *n* ELECTRON fréquence idler *f*; **~ pulley** *n* MECH ENG poulie folle *f*

idling *n* ELEC *of motor* marche à vide *f*, service à vide *m*, VEHICLES *of engine* marche au ralenti *f*, ralenti *m*; **~ speed** *n* MECH allure de ralenti *f*

IDN *abbr (integrated digital network)* TELECOM RNI *(réseau numérique intégré)*

idocrase *n* MINERAL idocrase *f*

idonic *adj* CHEM idonique

idosaccharic *adj* CHEM idosaccharique

idose *n* CHEM idose *m*

IDP *abbr* DP *(integrated data processing)* traitement intégré de l'information *m*, traitement intégré des données *m*, TELECOM *(initial domain part)* partie du domaine initial *f*

idranal *n* CHEM idranal *m*

idrialite *n* MINERAL idrialite *f*

IDSE *abbr (international data switching exchange)* TELECOM centre international de commutation de données *m*

IDT *abbr (interdigital transducer)* TELECOM transducteur interdigital *m*

IF[1] *abbr (intermediate frequency)* ELECTRON, TELECOM FI *(fréquence intermédiaire)*

IF:[2] **~ amplification** *n* ELECTRON, TELECOM amplification FI *f*; **~ amplifier** *n* ELECTRON, TELECOM amplificateur FI *m*; **~ filter** *n* ELECTRON, TELECOM filtre FI *m*; **~ rejection** *n* ELECTRON, TELECOM atténuation à la fréquence intermédiaire *f*, réjection à la fréquence intermédiaire *f*; **~ signal** *n* ELECTRON, TELECOM signal FI *m*; **~ stage** *n* ELECTRON, TELECOM étage FI *m*

IFM *abbr (instantaneous frequency measurement)* ELECTRON mesure de fréquence instantanée *f*

IFRB *abbr (International Frequency Registration Board)* SPACE *communications* Comité international d'enregistrement des fréquences *m*

IFU *abbr (interworking functional unit)* TELECOM unité fonctionnelle d'interfonctionnement *f*

IG *abbr (interpolation gain)* TELECOM gain de concentration *m*

IGFET *abbr (insulated gate FET)* ELECTRON TEC à grille isolée *m*

I-girder *n* CONST poutre en double T *f*, poutrelle *f*, solive en fer à double T *f*

igloo: **~ container** *n* TRANSP igloo *m*

IGN *abbr (international gateway node)* TELECOM NTI *(noeud de transit international)*

igneous: **~ complex** *n* GEOL complexe magmatique *m*; **~ rock** *n* FUELLESS roche d'épanchement *f*, roche ignée *f*, GEOL roche ignée *f*, roche magmatique *f*, PETR roche ignée *f*; **~ suite** *n* GEOL cortège de roches ignées *m*, série ignée *f*, série magmatique *f*

ignimbrite *n* GEOL dépôt pyroclastique soudé *m*, ignimbrite *f*

ignite *vt* CHEM allumer, NUCLEAR *plasma*, POLLUTION enflammer, SPACE *spacecraft* allumer, mettre à feu

igniter *n* ELEC ENG igniteur *m*, MECH ENG allumeur *m*, rallumeur *m*, SPACE *spacecraft* allumeur *m*

ignition *n* AERONAUT, AUTO allumage *m*, CHEM allumage *m*, ignition *f*, inflammation *f*, CINEMAT *of arc*, ELEC *internal combustion engine* allumage *m*, ELEC ENG *of gas tube* amorçage *m*, MECH *vehicles* allumage *m*, P&R *operation* allumage *m*, ignition *f*, SAFETY ignition *f*, SPACE *spacecraft*, VEHICLES allumage *m*; **~ advance** *n* AERONAUT avance à l'allumage *f*; **~ arch** *n* HEAT ENG voûte d'allumage *f*; ~ **burner** *n* HEAT ENG brûleur d'allumage *m*; ~ **capacitor** *n* AUTO condensateur d'allumage *m*; ~ **circuit** *n* SPACE *spacecraft* circuit d'allumage *m*; ~ **coil** *n* AERONAUT, AUTO, ELEC ENG bobine d'allumage *f*; ~ **device** *n* HEAT ENG dispositif d'allumage *m*; ~ **distributor** *n* AUTO distributeur d'allumage *m*, MECH ENG distributeur *m*; ~ **experiment** *n* NUCLEAR expérience d'ignition *f*; ~ **generator** *n* AERONAUT générateur d'allumage *m*; ~ **harness** *n* AERONAUT rampe d'allumage *f*; ~ **key** *n* AUTO clef de contact *f*; ~ **loss** *n* COAL TECH perte au feu *f*, POLLUTION perte au feu *f*, perte par calcination *f*; ~ **magneto** *n* VEHICLES magnéto d'allumage *f*; ~ **plug** *n* AUTO, MECH *vehicles*, VEHICLES bougie d'allumage *f*; ~ **point** *n* AUTO point d'allumage *m*, MECH *vehicles* vis platinée *f*, PETR TECH point d'inflammation *m*, PHYS point d'éclair *m*; ~ **poker** *n* MECH ENG tisonnier d'allumage *m*; ~ **setting** *n* AUTO calage d'allumage *m*; ~ **starter switch** *n* AUTO interrupteur d'allumage *m*; ~ **switch** *n* CONTROL, VEHICLES interrupteur d'allumage *m*; ~ **system** *n* SPACE *spacecraft* système d'allumage *m*; ~ **timing** *n* AUTO, VEHICLES calage d'allumage *m*; ~ **transformer** *n* ELEC ENG transformateur d'allumage *m*

ignitron *n* ELEC, ELEC ENG ignitron *m*; ~ **locomotive** *n* RAIL *vehicles* locomotive à ignitrons *f*; ~ **rectifier** *n* ELEC ENG redresseur à ignitrons *m*

ignore: ~ **character** *n* COMP, DP caractère d'omission *m*

I-head: ~ **engine** *n* AUTO moteur à soupapes en tête *m*; ~ **valve train** *n* AUTO dispositif de commande des soupapes en tête *m*

IHS *abbr (integrated home system)* COMP domotique *f*

IIR[1] *abbr (infinite impulse response)* ELECTRON réponse impulsionnelle infinie *f*, TELECOM réponse infinie à une impulsion *f*

IIR:[2] ~ **filter** *n* TELECOM filtre à réponse infinie à une impulsion *m*

I²L *abbr (integrated injection logic)* ELECTRON I²L *(logique intégrée à injection)*

ILD *abbr (injection laser diode)* OPT diode laser *f*, laser à injection *m*, laser à semi-conducteur *m*, TELECOM laser à injection *m*

iliac *adj* CHEM *crest* iliaque

illegal: ~ **character** *n* COMP, DP caractère interdit *m*, caractère non valide *m*; ~ **dumping** *n* WATER SUPP déversement illégal *m*; ~ **instruction** *n* COMP, DP instruction illégale *f*; ~ **operation** *n* COMP, DP opération illégale *f*

illegible *adj* PRINT illisible

illite *n* COAL TECH, MINERAL, PETR TECH illite *f*

ill-sorted *adj (cf nongrade)* GEOL mal trié

illuminance *n* PHYS éclairement lumineux *m*

illuminated[1] *adj* TELECOM *fibre optic source* excité

illuminated:[2] ~ **dial** *n* PHOTO cadran lumineux *m*; ~ **dial instrument** *n* INSTRUMENT instrument à éclairage intérieur *m*; ~ **folding lens** *n* INSTRUMENT loupe éclairante de poche *f*; ~ **push button** *n* PROD ENG bouton-poussoir lumineux *m*; ~ **reticle eyepiece** *n* ASTRON oculaire à réticule éclairé *m*; ~ **source** *n* RAD PHYS source illuminée *f*

illuminating: ~ **apparatus** *n* LAB EQUIP *lighting microscopy* appareil d'éclairage *m*; ~ **mirror** *n* INSTRUMENT miroir d'éclairage *m*

illumination *n* CINEMAT éclairage *m*, ELEC ENG *luminous flux intensity* illumination *f*, éclairement *m*, METALL illumination *f*, éclairage *m*, PRINT éclairement *m*; ~ **angle** *n* PRINT angle d'éclairement *m*; ~ **beam path** *n* INSTRUMENT trajet de faisceau lumineux *m*; ~ **efficiency** *n* SPACE *communications* rendement d'illumination *m*; ~ **mirror** *n* INSTRUMENT *for horizontal or vertical scale* miroir d'éclairage *m*; ~ **optics** *n pl* INSTRUMENT lentilles d'éclairage *f pl*, optique d'éclairage *f*; ~ **path** *n* INSTRUMENT trajet de faisceau lumineux *m*

illustrate *vt* PRINT illustrer

illustrated: ~ **lettercard** *n* PAPER TECH carte-lettre illustrée *f*

illustration *n* PRINT illustration *f*

ilmenite *n* MINERAL, PROP MAT ilménite *f*

ILS[1] *abbr (instrument landing system)* AERONAUT système d'atterrissage aux instruments *m*, système d'atterrissage radiogoniométrique *m*, SPACE, TRANSP système d'atterrissage aux instruments *m*

ILS:[2] ~ **beam** *n* SPACE faisceau ILS *m*

ilsemannite *n* MINERAL ilsemannite *f*

ilvaite *n* MINERAL ilvaïte *f*

IM *abbr* TELECOM *(intermodulation product)* produit d'intermodulation *m*, TELECOM *(interface module)* unité de raccordement *f*

IMA *abbr (input message acknowledgment)* TELECOM accusé de réception de message d'entrée *m*

image[1] *n* C&G contre-dessin *m*, CINEMAT cadre *m*, image *f*, COMP, DP image *f*, PHOTO cliché *m*, image *f*, PHYS image *f*, PRINT image *f*, zone imprimante texte et illustrations *f*, zone imprimée avec texte et image *f*, *computer* zone affichée à l'écran *f*; ~ **analysis** *n* TELECOM analyse de l'image *f*; ~ **analyzer** *n* TELECOM analyseur d'image *m*; ~ **and waveform monitor** *n* TV moniteur d'image et de forme d'onde *m*, oscilloscope de profil *m*; ~ **area** *n* CINEMAT surface d'image *f*, PRINT surface de la page *f*, zone imprimante *f*; ~ **attenuation coefficient** *n* ELECTRON affaiblissement sur images *m*; ~ **carrier** *n* TV onde porteuse d'image *f*, porteuse vidéo *f*; ~ **charge** *n* ELEC ENG charge-image *f*, image électrique *f*; ~ **compression** *n* ELECTRON compression d'images *f*; ~ **contraction** *n* TV resserrement de l'image *m*; ~ **control coil** *n* TV bobine de cadrage *f*; ~ **conversion** *n* ELECTRON, TELECOM conversion d'images *f*; ~ **converter** *n* CINEMAT, ELECTRON, INSTRUMENT convertisseur d'images *m*; ~ **converter tube** *n* ELECTRON tube convertisseur d'images *m*; ~ **digitization** *n* ELECTRON numérisation des images *f*; ~ **digitizer** *n* ELECTRON numériseur de signaux vidéo *m*; ~ **dislocation** *n* METALL dislocation image *f*; ~ **dissector** *n* ELECTRON tube dissecteur *m*; ~ **enhancement** *n* ASTRON accentuation des images *f*, amélioration des images *f*, ELECTRON amélioration des images *f*, SPACE accentuation des images *f*, amélioration des images *f*, TV amélioration des images *f*; ~ **enhancer** *n* TV correcteur de détails *m*; ~ **erecting prism** *n* INSTRUMENT prisme à redressement *m*; ~ **field** *n* CINEMAT champ d'image *m*; ~ **file** *n* ELECTRON fichier vidéo *m*; ~ **flicker** *n* TV scintillement *m*; ~ **frequency** *n* ELECTRON fréquence image *f*; ~ **frequency interference** *n* ELECTRON réception de la fréquence-image *f*; ~ **iconoscope** *n* ELECTRON iconoscope-image *m*, supericonoscope *m*; ~ **impedance** *n* ACOUSTICS, ELEC ENG, PHYS impédance image *f*; ~ **intensifier** *n* ASTRON intensificateur d'image *m*, ELECTRON intensificateur d'image *m*, tube intensificateur d'image *m*, INSTRUMENT amplificateur de brillance *m*, intensificateur d'image *m*; ~ **intensifier tube** *n* ELECTRON intensificateur d'image *m*, tube intensificateur d'image *m*, INSTRUMENT intensificateur d'image *m*, TV tube amplificateur de lumière *m*; ~ **lag** *n*

TV rémanence d'image f; ~ **orthicon** n ELECTRON image orthicon f, tube image orthicon m; ~ **phase-change coefficient** n ELECTRON déphasage sur images m; ~ **plane** n CINEMAT plan image m; ~ **processing** n COMP, ELECTRON, TELECOM traitement d'images m; ~ **projection** n ELECTRON *lithography* gravure par projection f; ~ **reactor** n NUCLEAR pile image f; ~ **refreshing** n COMP rafraîchissement d'image m, régénération d'image f, DP rafraîchissement d'image m; ~ **restoration** n COMP, DP restauration d'images f; ~ **retention** n TV rémanence f; ~ **scale** n CINEMAT échelle de l'image f; ~ **scanner** n TV analyseur d'image m; ~ **sensor** n TELECOM détecteur d'image m; ~ **sequence** n TELECOM séquence d'images f; ~ **setter** n PRINT photocomposeuse pleine page f; ~ **signal** n ELECTRON signal image m, signal vidéo m; ~ **steadiness** n CINEMAT stabilité d'image f; ~ **storage** n ELEC ENG, ELECTRON mémorisation d'images f; ~ **storage tube** n ELECTRON tube image à mémoire m; ~ **table** n PROD ENG table des données f, table-image f; ~ **transfer** n TELECOM transfert d'image m; ~ **transfer coefficient** n ELECTRON coefficient de transfert sur images m, exposant de transfert sur images m; ~ **transfer exponent** n ACOUSTICS exposant d'affaiblissement sur images m; ~ **transmission** n TELECOM transmission d'image f

image[2] *vt* COMP, DP projeter, représenter, représenter par une image

imager n COMP, DP imageur m

imaginary: ~ **number** n MATH nombre imaginaire m

imaging n ELECTRON visualisation f, PRINT action de préparer la forme imprimante f; ~ **array** n ELECTRON groupement de photodétecteurs m, matrice de photodétecteurs f; ~ **chip** n ELECTRON puce vidéo f; ~ **mechanism** n OPT système optique m; ~ **system** n OPT système optique m; ~ **systems** n pl PRINT systèmes infographiques m pl, systèmes électroniques de préparation des formes imprimantes m pl

Imax: ~ **process** n CINEMAT procédé Imax m

imbalance n PRINT déséquilibre m

imbibition n HYDROL imbibition f

imbricate *adj* GEOL imbriqué

imbricated[1] *adj* GEOL imbriqué

imbricated:[2] ~ **structure** n GEOL *stacked thrusts, schuppen* structure en écailles f

Imhof: ~ **sedimentation cone** n LAB EQUIP *glassware* cône à sédimentation d'Imhof m

imide n CHEM imide m

imido n CHEM imide m

imidogen n CHEM imidogène m

imine n CHEM, VEHICLES imine f

imitation[1] *adj* PAPER TECH artificiel

imitation:[2] ~ **art paper** n PAPER TECH papier surglacé m; ~ **chromoboard** n PACKAGING carton imitation chromo m

imitative: ~ **deception** n ELECTRON diversion par imitation de signaux f

immature: ~ **sandstone** *adj* GEOL immature

immediate: ~ **access** n COMP, DP accès direct m; ~ **access store** n *(IAS)* COMP mémoire à accès immédiat f; ~ **address** n COMP, DP adresse immédiate f; ~ **addressing** n COMP, DP adressage immédiat m; ~ **data** n COMP, DP données directes f pl; ~ **I/O** n PROD ENG E/S immédiate f; ~ **I/O update instruction** n PROD ENG instruction de rafraîchissement prioritaire des E/S f; ~ **input** n PROD ENG entrée prioritaire f; ~ **input date** n PROD ENG rafraîchissement prioritaire d'entrée m; ~

output n PROD ENG sortie prioritaire f; ~ **output date** n PROD ENG rafraîchissement prioritaire de sortie m; ~ **update** n PROD ENG rafraîchissement prioritaire m

immerse *vt* CHEM, PAPER TECH immerger

immersed *adj* PHYS plongé

immersion n ASTRON, CHEM immersion f, GEOM *of sphere* immersion f, *topology* plongement m, PAPER TECH immersion f; ~ **coating** n PACKAGING trempage m; ~ **cooling** n REFRIG refroidissement par immersion m; ~ **electron lens** n TV lentille électronique à immersion f; ~ **freezing** n PACKAGING, REFRIG congélation par immersion f; ~ **heater** n ELEC, ELEC ENG thermoplongeur m, HEATING réchauffeur à immersion m, LAB EQUIP plongeur chauffant m, MECH, MECH ENG thermoplongeur m; ~ **lens** n INSTRUMENT lentille à immersion f, LAB EQUIP *microscope* objectif à immersion m; ~ **milk cooler** n REFRIG refroidisseur à lait par immersion m; ~ **muffle** n C&G moufle plongeur m; ~ **objective** n INSTRUMENT lentille à immersion f, METALL, PHYS objectif à immersion m; ~ **oil** n METALL huile à immersion f; ~ **painting** n PACKAGING vernissage par immersion m; ~ **plating** n COATINGS revêtement par immersion m; ~ **well** n PROD ENG douille de protection type immersion f

immiscible *adj* CHEM, FOOD TECH, PETR TECH immiscible

immobile: ~ **dislocation** n METALL dislocation immobile f

IMO *abbr* *(International Maritime Organization)* NAUT OMI *(Organisation maritime internationale)*

IMP *abbr* ASTRON *(interplanetary monitoring platform)* plate-forme d'observation interplanétaire f, TELECOM *(interface message processor)* serveur de message m

impact n COAL TECH choc m, CONST, MECH choc m, impact m, PHYS choc m, impact m, percussion f; ~ **avalanche transit-time diode** n *(IMPATT diode)* ELECTRON, PHYS diode à avalanche à temps de propagation f *(diode Impatt)*; ~ **breaker** n COAL TECH concasseur à impact m; ~ **check** n NUCLEAR essai au choc m; ~ **crater** n SPACE cratère d'impact m; ~ **crusher** n COAL TECH broyeur par percussion m, concasseur à mâchoires à cadence rapide m; ~ **energy** n METALL énergie de choc f; ~ **excitation** n *(cf impulse excitation)* RAD PHYS excitation par choc f; ~ **fluorescence** n TV fluorescence par impact f; ~ **fracture** n NUCLEAR rupture f, rupture aux chocs f; ~ **ionization** n *(cf impulse excitation)* RAD PHYS ionisation par choc f; ~ **load** n AERONAUT à-coup m; ~ **microphone** n RECORDING microphone à contact m; ~ **noise analyzer** n RECORDING analyseur de bruit de choc m; ~ **parameter** n PHYS paramètre d'impact m; ~ **plate** n COAL TECH plaque de choc f; ~ **polystyrene** n P&R polystyrène-choc m; ~ **pressure** n AERONAUT pression d'arrêt f, pression dynamique f; ~ **printer** n COMP imprimante à impact f; ~ **resistance** n PACKAGING résistance aux chocs f, TRANSP résistance de rencontre f; ~ **screen** n COAL TECH crible à chocs m, PROD ENG crible à percussion m; ~ **screwdriver** n MECH ENG *tool* tournevis à frapper m; ~ **sound transmission level** n ACOUSTICS niveau de transmission du bruit de choc m; ~ **statement** n POLLUTION constat d'impact m; ~ **strength** n MECH *materials*, NUCLEAR résilience f, P&R résistance aux chocs f, PHYS résilience f; ~ **stress** n PACKAGING contrainte au choc f; ~ **study** n GAS TECH, WATER SUPP étude d'impact f; ~ **test** n METALL essai de résilience m, METR, PACKAGING essai au choc m, PHYS essai de choc m, essai de résilience m, TRANSP essai de choc m; ~

theory of line broadening *n* RAD PHYS *spectral lines* théorie de choc d'élargissement des raies *f*; ~ **toughness** *n* PROP MAT résilience au choc *f*; ~ **velocity** *n* METALL vitesse de choc *f*; ~ **wrench** *n* MECH ENG *tool* clef à chocs *f*

impaction *n* POLLUTION impact *m*

impact-sound: ~ **reducing material** *n* ACOUSTICS matériau insonore *m*

impairment: ~ **of hearing index** *n* ACOUSTICS indice de perte d'audition *m*

impart *vt* MECH ENG *rotary motion* imprimer; ~ **energy to** *vt* PHYS, THERMOD communiquer l'énergie à

IMPATT: ~ **diode** *n* *(impact avalanche transit-time diode)* ELECTRON, PHYS diode Impatt *f* *(diode à avalanche à temps de propagation)*; ~ **oscillator** *n* ELECTRON oscillateur à diode Impatt *m*

impedance *n* ELEC, ELEC ENG, PHYS *of free space*, RECORDING, TELECOM, TESTING impédance *f*; ~ **analysis** *n* TESTING analyse d'impédance *f*; ~ **bond** *n* RAIL connection inductive *f*; ~ **bridge** *n* ELEC ENG pont d'impédance *m*; ~ **characteristic** *n* ELEC ENG caractéristique d'impédance *f*; ~ **coil** *n* ELEC ENG bobine d'arrêt *f*, bobine d'impédance *f*; ~ **compensator** *n* RECORDING compensateur d'impédance *m*; ~ **conversion** *n* ELEC ENG conversion d'impédance *f*; ~ **corrector** *n* ELEC adaptateur d'impédance *m*; ~ **coupling** *n* ELEC ENG liaison par inductance et capacité *f*; ~ **diagram** *n* TESTING schéma d'impédance *m*; ~ **drop** *n* ELEC *of voltage* chute d'impédance *f*; ~ **earthed neutral system** *n* (BrE) *(cf impedance grounded neutral system)* ELEC réseau à neutre non-directement à la terre *m*; ~ **grounded neutral system** *n* (AmE) *(cf impedance earthed neutral system)* ELEC réseau à neutre non-directement à la terre *m*; ~ **matching** *n* ELEC ENG, PHYS, RECORDING adaptation d'impédance *f*; ~ **matching network** *n* ELEC ENG, PHYS réseau d'adaptation d'impédance *m*; ~ **matching transformer** *n* ELEC ENG transformateur d'adaptation d'impédance *m*; ~ **mismatch** *n* ELEC ENG mauvaise adaptation d'impédance *f*; ~ **network** *n* PROD ENG réseau résistif *m*; ~ **ratio** *n* RECORDING rapport d'impédance *m*; ~ **ratio at low temperature** *n* PROD ENG rapport d'impédance à basse température *m*; ~ **recorder** *n* INSTRUMENT enregistreur d'impédance *m*; ~ **relay** *n* ELEC relais d'impédance *m*; ~ **transformer** *n* PHYS convertisseur d'impédance *m*; ~ **voltage** *n* ELEC ENG impédance nominale de court-circuit *f*; ~ **voltage at rated current** *n* ELEC *of transformer* tension nominale de court-circuit *f*

impedor *n* ELEC ENG élément à impédance *m*

impeller *n* AERONAUT roue à aubes *f*, *of turbine engine* rotor de compresseur *m*, AUTO turbine *f*, COAL TECH agitateur *m*, MECH impulseur *m*, NUCLEAR *of blower* roue mobile *f*, PAPER TECH propulseur *m*, PROD ENG *of centrifugal pump* couronne mobile *f*, roue mobile *f*, VEHICLES *of pump* turbine *f*; ~ **backplate** *n* REFRIG *of fan* disque arrière *m*

imperative *adj* COMP, DP impératif

imperfect: ~ **dielectric** *n* ELEC diélectrique imparfait *m*

impermeability *n* CONST, PAPER TECH, PROP MAT, TELECOM imperméabilité *f*

impermeable[1] *adj* CONST, GAS TECH, GEOL, HYDROL imperméable, étanche, PACKAGING imperméable, PETR, WATER SUPP imperméable, étanche

impermeable:[2] ~ **layer** *n* GAS TECH couverture imperméable *f*, couverture étanche *f*

impervious *adj* CONST, HYDROL, PACKAGING, PAPER

TECH, PETR, PROP MAT imperméable, étanche

imperviousness *n* *(cf perviousness)* FUELLESS réluctance *f*, PROD ENG *of joint* herméticité *f*, étanchéité *f*

impetus *n* MECH ENG force d'impulsion *f*, impulsion *f*

impinge: ~ **on** *vt* MECH se heurter à

impingement *n* GEOL poinçonnement *m*, MECH ENG impact *m*, METALL collision *f*, PRINT impact de l'air sur la bande *m*; ~ **drying** *n* CINEMAT séchage par soufflage *m*

impinger *n* CHEM flacon de lavage *m*

impinging: ~ **particle** *n* NUCLEAR particule bombardante *f*, particule incidente *f*

implant[1] *n* ELECTRON implant *m*, implantation *f*; ~ **and anneal** *n* ELECTRON implantation et recuit *f*; ~ **dose** *n* ELECTRON dose d'impuretés implantées *f*

implant[2] *vt* PROD ENG implanter

implantation *n* ELECTRON implantation *f*

implanted *adj* ELECTRON *base, diode, transistor* implanté

implement[1] *n* MECH ENG instrument *m*

implement[2] *vt* MECH ENG mettre en oeuvre, TEXTILES exécuter

implementation *n* COMP, DP réalisation *f*, GEOL, TELECOM mise en oeuvre *f*, TEXTILES exécution *f*

implicit: ~ **differentiation** *n* MATH différentiation implicite *f*; ~ **function** *n* MATH fonction implicite *f*

implied: ~ **addressing** *n* COMP, DP adressage implicite *m*

implode *vi* ELECTRON imploser

implosion *n* CHEM, ELECTRON, NUCLEAR *of black body radiation* implosion *f*, PROD ENG implosion *f*, *of boiler* écrasement *m*; ~ **weapon** *n* MILIT, NUCLEAR arme à implosion *f*

imporosity *n* PROP MAT imporosité *f*

import:[1] ~ **licence** *n* (BrE) NAUT licence d'importation *f*; ~ **license** *n* (AmE) *see import licence*

import[2] *vt* DP *data*, TELECOM *data* importer

importation *n* DP importation *f*

impose *vi* PRINT imposer, procéder à l'imposition de

imposed: ~ **pressure gradients** *n pl* FLUID PHYS gradients de pression imposés *m pl*

imposing: ~ **surface** *n* PRINT surface d'imposition *f*, table d'imposition *f*; ~ **table** *n* PRINT marbre d'imposition *m*

imposition *n* PRINT imposition *f*

impost *n* CONST *architecture* imposte *f*, sommier *m*

impounding: ~ **reservoir** *n* WATER SUPP retenue *f*

impoverishment *n* NUCLEAR *of ores* épuisement *m*

impregnant *n* CHEM agent d'imprégnation *m*

impregnate *vt* CHEM, TEXTILES imprégner

impregnated[1] *adj* PAPER TECH imprégné

impregnated:[2] ~ **cable** *n* ELEC câble imprégné *m*; ~ **cathode** *n* ELEC ENG cathode imprégnée *f*; ~ **coil** *n* ELEC ENG bobine imprégnée *f*; ~ **fabric** *n* PACKAGING tissu imprégné *m*; ~ **paper** *n* PACKAGING, PRINT papier imprégné *m*; ~ **paper insulation** *n* ELEC *cable conductor* isolation au papier préimprégné *f*

impregnating *n* PRINT imprégnation *f*; ~ **agent** *n* PACKAGING imprégnant *m*; ~ **machine** *n* PACKAGING machine à imprégner *f*; ~ **varnish** *n* COATINGS, ELEC *insulation* vernis à imprégnation *m*; ~ **wax** *n* PACKAGING cire à imprégner *f*

impregnation *n* CONST *civil engineering*, P&R *process*, PAPER TECH imprégnation *f*, PROD ENG *of timber* imbibition *f*, imprégnation *f*, injection *f*, TEXTILES imprégnation *f*

impress *vt* TEXTILES imprimer

impressed: ~ **electromotive force** *n* ELEC *voltage* force électromotrice appliquée *f*; ~ **voltage** *n* ELEC tension appliquée f

impression n C&G piquage m, PRINT impression f, PROD ENG empreinte f, impression f, TEXTILES impression f; **~ blanket** n PRINT blanchet m; **~ cylinder** n P&R *equipment* cylindre d'impression m, PRINT cylindre de contre-pression m; **~ pad** n PACKAGING tambour imprimeur m; **~ roller** n P&R *equipment* rouleau d'impression m

imprint[1] n PAPER TECH empreinte f, PRINT colophon m, marque d'éditeur f, marque d'imprimeur f, repiquage m

imprint[2] vt PRINT repiquer

imprinter n PACKAGING imprimante f

imprinting n PRINT repiquage m; **~ unit** n PRINT élément de repiquage m

improper: ~ time n PHYS *relativity* temps impropre m

improved: ~ diesel engine n TRANSP moteur diesel amélioré m; **~ pattern** n PROD ENG modèle perfectionné m; **~ type** n PROD ENG modèle perfectionné m

improvement: ~ notice n SAFETY avis d'amélioration m; **~ patent** n PATENTS brevet de perfectionnement m

improver n FOOD TECH *baking* améliorant m, PETR TECH agent améliorant m

impulse n MECH impulsion f, MECH ENG impulsion f, *of a force* impulsion f, PAPER TECH, PETR, PHYS *product of force and time*, TELECOM impulsion f; **~ counter** n ELEC compteur d'impulsions m; **~ coupling** n MECH ENG accouplement à déclic m; **~ current** n ELEC courant d'impulsion m, courant de choc m; **~ dispersion** n OPT dispersion d'une impulsion f; **~ excitation** n RAD PHYS (*cf impact ionization*), TELECOM excitation par choc f; **~ function** n CONTROL fonction impulsionnelle f, ELECTRON fonction impulsion f; **~ generator** n ELEC *test equipment* générateur d'impulsions m, génératrice d'impulsion f, ELEC ENG générateur de tension de choc m; **~ heat sealer** n PACKAGING soudage par impulsion m; **~ noise** n ACOUSTICS, COMP, DP bruit impulsionnel m, SPACE *communications*, TELECOM bruit impulsif m; **~ regenerator** n RAD PHYS filtre d'impulsions m; **~ relay** n ELEC ENG relais à impulsions m; **~ response** n OPT réponse impulsionnelle f, PETR réponse d'impulsions f, réponse impulsionnelle f, TELECOM réponse impulsionnelle f; **~ test** n ELEC ENG essai sous tension de choc m; **~ turbine** n MECH, MECH ENG turbine à action f, turbine à impulsion f, PROD ENG turbine d'action f, turbine à action f, turbine à impulsion f, turbine à libre déviation f; **~ voltage** n ELEC tension d'impulsion f, tension de choc f, ELEC ENG tension de choc f; **~ wheel** n PROD ENG roue-turbine à impulsion f

impulsion n MECH ENG impulsion f

impulsive[1] adj MECH ENG impulsif, propulsif

impulsive:[2] **~ noise** n ACOUSTICS bruit impulsionnel m

impulsiveness: ~ ratio n TELECOM *air safety* rapport impulsionnel m

impureness n CHEM impureté f

impurity n CHEM impureté f, ELECTRON agent de dopage m, impureté f, dopant m, METALL, QUALITY impureté f; **~ atom** n CRYSTALL impureté f; **~ concentration** n ELECTRON concentration d'impuretés f; **~ concentration profile** n ELECTRON profil de concentration d'impuretés m; **~ diffusion** n ELECTRON diffusion d'impuretés f; **~ level** n ELECTRON niveau d'impuretés m; **~ scattering** n ELECTRON diffusion par les impuretés f

In (*indium*) CHEM In (*indium*)

inaccuracy: ~ of measurement n METR incertitude de mesurage f

inactinic adj C&G *glass* inactinique

inactivation n CHEM inactivation f

inactive[1] adj CHEM inactif, inerte, sans action, COMP, DP, ELECTRON inactif, NAUT *ship* désarmé

inactive:[2] **~ coil** n SPRINGS spire morte f; **~ inventory** n PROD ENG stock dormant m, stock inactif m

in-and-out: ~ bolt n MECH ENG boulon libre m; **~ calipers** n pl (AmE), **~ callipers** n pl (BrE) MECH ENG compas maître de danse m, compas maître-à-danser m, maître-à-danser m

in-band: ~ signaling n (AmE), **~ signalling** n (BrE) SPACE *communications* signalisation intrabande f

in-betweener n CINEMAT intervalliste m

inboard[1] adj AERONAUT intérieur

inboard:[2] **~ binding** n PRINT reliure avec mors et ficelles f

inbound: ~ heading n AERONAUT cap retour m; **~ stock point** n PROD ENG aire de stockage amont f, plot d'entrée m; **~ traffic** n TRANSP trafic entrant m

in-call: ~ modification n TELECOM *ISDN* modification en cours d'appel f

in-camera: ~ effect n CINEMAT trucage à la prise de vue m

in-can: ~ system n PRINT système d'emballage en boîtes de métal m

incandescence n CHEM incandescence f

incandescent[1] adj RAD PHYS *solid* incandescent

incandescent:[2] **~ lamp** n ELEC, ELEC ENG lampe à incandescence f

incendiary adj MILIT *bomb* incendiaire

in-center adj (AmE), **in-centre** adj (BrE) GEOM en-centre

inch n METR pouce m, pouce anglais m **~ screw thread** n MECH ENG filetage en pouces m

inches: ~ per second n pl (*IPS*) DP, RECORDING pouces par seconde m pl (*PPS*)

inching n CINEMAT pas-à-pas m, PROD ENG marche par à-coups f; **~ and plugging service** n PROD ENG marche par à-coups et freinage par contre-courant f; **~ knob** n CINEMAT bouton d'avance à main m

incidence n OPT, PHYS *angle of attack* incidence f; **~ angle** n AERONAUT angle d'incidence m; **~ oscillation** n AERONAUT oscillation d'incidence f; **~ probe** n AERONAUT antenne d'incidence f, détecteur d'incidence m

incident n OPT, TRANSP incident m; **~ beam** n CRYSTALL, PHYS faisceau incident m; **~ data reporting** n AERONAUT compte rendu de données d'incident m; **~ illumination** n INSTRUMENT éclairage incident m; **~ light** n CINEMAT, PHOTO, RAD PHYS lumière incidente f; **~ light attachment** n PHOTO intégrateur m, écran diffuseur m; **~ particle** n NUCLEAR particule bombardante f, particule incidente f; **~ ray** n PHYS rayon incident m, WAVE PHYS rayon d'incidence m; **~ signal** n ELECTRON signal incident m; **~ top lighting** n INSTRUMENT éclairage incident m; **~ warning sign** n TRANSP signal avertisseur d'incident m; **~ wave** n PHYS, WAVE PHYS onde incidente f

incidental: ~ amplitude modulation n ELECTRON modulation d'amplitude parasite f; **~ frequency modulation** n ELECTRON modulation de fréquence parasite f; **~ modulation** n ELECTRON modulation parasite induite f

incinerate vt THERMOD incinérer

incinerated adj THERMOD brûlé, carbonisé, incinéré, réduit en cendres

incinerator n CONST brûleur de déchets m, HEATING, POLLUTION, THERMOD incinérateur m

incipient: ~ crack n AERONAUT amorce de crique f,

NUCLEAR amorce de fissure *f*; ~ **fatigue failure** *n* AERO-
NAUT début de rupture *m*

incised-leaf-type: ~ **camouflage net** *n* MILIT filet de
camouflage avec feuilles découpées *m*

inclination *n* ASTRON inclinaison *f*, CONST *of machine
blade* dévers *m*, perte *f*, GEOM, PHYS inclinaison *f*

incline *n* CONST *falling* pente *f*, *inclined plane* plan *m*,
plan incliné *m*, *rising gradient* rampe *f*, MECH ENG
self-acting plan automoteur *m*, plan incliné automoteur *m*; ~ **hole** *n* MINING trou incliné *m*; ~ **shaft** *n*
MINING puits incliné *m*

inclined[1] *adj* GEOL, GEOM incliné

inclined:[2] ~ **channel** *n* NUCLEAR *in reactor* canal incliné
m; ~ **drive shaft** *n* AERONAUT *of helicopter* transmission
oblique *f*; ~ **fold** *n* GEOL pli oblique *m*; ~ **hole** *n* MINING
trou incliné *m*; ~ **plane** *n* CONST, GEOM, PHYS plan
incliné *m*; ~ **ramp** *n* PETR rampe inclinée *f*; ~ **shaft** *n*
MINING puits incliné *m*

inclining: ~ **test** *n* NAUT *naval architecture* essai d'inclinaison *m*, essai de stabilité *m*

inclinometer *n* COAL TECH clinomètre *m*, GEOPHYS inclinomètre *m*, indicateur de pente *m*, PETR
inclinomètre *m*, PHYS clinomètre *m*

inclusion *n* CRYSTALL, METALL, MINERAL, NUCLEAR,
PETR, QUALITY, TESTING inclusion *f*

inclusive: ~ **AND circuit** *n* ELECTRON circuit ET inclusif
m; ~ **AND gate** *n* ELECTRON porte ET inclusif *f*; ~ **OR
circuit** *n* ELECTRON circuit OU inclusif *m*; ~ **OR gate** *n*
COMP, DP, ELECTRON porte OU inclusif *f*; ~ **OR operation** *n* COMP, DP opération OU inclusif *f*

incoherence *n* OPT, TELECOM incohérence *f*

incoherent[1] *adj* METALL, OPT incohérent

incoherent:[2] ~ **light** *n* TELECOM, WAVE PHYS lumière
incohérente *f*; ~ **radiation** *n* PHYS, TELECOM rayonnement incohérent *m*; ~ **twin** *n* METALL macle non
cohérente *f*

incombustibility *n* PROP MAT incombustibilité *f*

incombustible *adj* PACKAGING, PROP MAT incombustible

incoming[1] *adj* TELECOM entrant

incoming:[2] ~ **call** *n* TELECOM communication d'arrivée *f*,
trafic d'arrivée *m*; ~ **calls barred** *n* (*ICB*) TELECOM
interdiction des appels à l'arrivée *f*; ~ **circuit** *n* TELE-
COM circuit entrant *m*; ~ **feed** *n* TV arrivée *f*, signal
d'entrée *m*; ~ **freight** *n* PROD ENG transport sur achats
m; ~ **group** *n* TELECOM faisceau entrant *m*; ~ **line** *n*
TELECOM ligne entrante *f*; ~ **line fuse** *n* PROD ENG ligne
de fusible entrante *f*; ~ **message** *n* COMP message en
réception *m*, message entrant *m*; ~ **power** *n* CONTROL
puissance reçue *f*; ~ **power terminal** *n* PROD ENG borne
de branchement secteur *f*; ~ **procedure** *n* TELECOM
maritime-mobile procédure d'arrivée *f*; ~ **register** *n*
TELECOM enregistreur d'arrivée *m*; ~ **signal** *n* ELEC-
TRON signal reçu *m*, TELECOM signal d'entrée *m*; ~
traffic *n* TELECOM trafic entrant *m*; ~ **trunk circuit** *n*
TELECOM joncteur d'arrivée *m*, joncteur entrant *m*; ~
voltage monitor *n* PROD ENG dispositif de contrôle de
la tension d'entrée *m*; ~ **web** *n* PRINT bande entrant
dans la machine *f*

incoming-calls-barred: ~ **line** *n* TELECOM ligne spécialisée départ *f*

incommensurable: ~ **with** *adj* MATH sans rapport avec

incompatible: ~ **element** *n* GEOL élément hygromagma-
tophile *m*, élément incompatible *m*

incompetent *adj* GEOL *strata* incompétent, tendre

incomplete: ~ **roof penetration** *n* NUCLEAR *of weld* man-

que de pénétration *m*

incompressibility *n* PROP MAT incompressibilité *f*

incompressibilty *n* FLUID PHYS incompressibilité *f*

incompressible[1] *adj* CHEM incompressible

incompressible:[2] ~ **flow** *n* FLUID PHYS, PHYS écoulement
incompressible *m*

inconclusive: ~ **test** *n* PHYS essai peu concluant *m*

in-connector *n* TELECOM *maritime-mobile* connecteur
d'entrée *m*

in-core: ~ **fuel cycle** *n* NUCLEAR cycle du combustible en
pile *m*; ~ **fuel life** *n* NUCLEAR vie du combustible dans le
coeur *f*; ~ **instrument assembly** *n* NUCLEAR instrumentation interne du coeur *f*; ~ **ionization chamber** *n*
NUCLEAR chambre d'ionisation interne du coeur *f*; ~
power manipulator *n* NUCLEAR robot dans le coeur *m*

incorporate: ~ **into** *vt* HYDROL *to draw into* entraîner
dans

incorrodible *adj* CHEM inattaquable par les acides, PROP
MAT inoxydable

increase: ~ **in contrast** *n* PHOTO augmentation du
contraste *f*

increased: ~ **resistance rotor** *n* ELEC *of generator, motor*
induit à résistance élevée *m*

increasing: ~ **flow** *n* HYDROL *of river* crue *f*

increment[1] *n* ELECTRON incrément *m*, MATH différentielle *f*, TEXTILES augmentation *f*

increment[2] *vt* ELECTRON incrémenter, TEXTILES augmenter

incremental[1] *adj* TEXTILES supplémentaire

incremental:[2] ~ **capacitance** *n* ELEC capacité différentielle *f*; ~ **compiler** *n* COMP compilateur incrémentiel
m; ~ **digital recorder** *n* INSTRUMENT enregistreur numérique incrémentiel *m*; ~ **inductance** *n* ELEC
inductance différentielle *f*; ~ **permeability** *n* TESTING
perméabilité incrémentielle *f*; ~ **plotter** *n* COMP, DP
traceur incrémentiel *m*; ~ **tape recorder** *n* INSTRUMENT
enregistreur sur bande à pas de progressions *m*; ~
tuning *n* ELECTRON accord par paliers *m*

increment-decrement: ~ **counter** *n* ELECTRON compteur-décompteur *m*

incubator *n* HEATING incubateur *m*, LAB EQUIP *microbiology* armoire d'incubation *f*

incunabulum *n* PRINT *book* incunable *m*

Ind *abbr* (*indication*) TELECOM indication *f*

indamine *n* CHEM indamine *f*

indan *n* CHEM hydrindène *f*, indane *f*

indanthrene *n* CHEM indanthrène *m*

indanthrone *n* CHEM indanthrone *m*

indazine *n* CHEM indazine *f*

indazole *n* CHEM indazole *m*

indefinite: ~ **integral** *n* MATH intégrale primitive *f*

indelible: ~ **ink** *n* COLOURS encre indélébile *f*

indene *n* CHEM indène *m*

indent[1] *n* CONST *carpentry* adent *m*, endent *m*, PRINT
marque *f*, renfoncement dans le texte *m*

indent[2] *vt* PRINT emboutir, marquer, rentrer, renfoncer

indentation *n* MECH ENG, METALL empreinte *f*, PROD ENG
dentelure *f*, indentation *f*, indenture *f*, échancrure *f*; ~
hardness *n* P&R dureté par pénétration *f*, dureté à la
pénétration de labille *f*

indented: ~ **bill of material** *n* PROD ENG nomenclature
arborescente *f*, nomenclature multivineuse *f*; ~ **chain**
n MECH ENG chaîne en gerbe *f*; ~ **wheel** *n* MECH ENG
cupped chain sheave poulie à empreintes *f*, roue à
empreintes *f*

indenter: ~ **tectonics** *n* GEOL poinçonnement *m*

independent: ~ **claim** *n* PATENTS revendication indépendante *f*; ~ **control** *n* NUCLEAR régulation autonome *f*; ~ **crane** *n* CONST grue centrale *f*, grue de milieu *f*; ~ **cutoff valve** *n* PROD ENG tiroir d'expansion *m*, tiroir de détente *m*, tiroir à tuile de détente *m*; ~ **excitation** *n* ELEC ENG excitation indépendante *f*, excitation séparée *f*; ~ **feeder** *n* ELEC *supply* feeder final *m*, ligne d'alimentation *f*; ~ **film-maker** *n* CINEMAT cinéaste indépendant *m*, cinéaste pigiste *m*; ~ **front suspension** *n* AUTO, VEHICLES suspension avant à roues indépendantes *f*; ~ **navigation** *n* SPACE navigation indépendante *f*; ~ **particle model** *n* NUCLEAR *of nucleus*, PHYS *nuclear physics* modèle à particules indépendants *m*; ~ **rear suspension** *n* AUTO, VEHICLES suspension arrière à roues indépendantes *f*; ~ **sideband modulation** *n* ELECTRON modulation BLI *f*, modulation à bandes latérales indépendantes *f*

indeterminate: ~ **waste** *n* RECYCLING déchets de faible et moyenne activité *m pl*

index[1] *n* CHEM indice *m*, COMP, DP index *m*, indice *m*, MECH ENG index *m*, repère *m*, répertoire *m*, *pointer* aiguille *f*, langue *f*, languette *f*; ~ **bar** *n* NAUT *of sextant* alidade *f*; ~ **card** *n* PAPER TECH fiche *f*; ~ **centers** *n pl* (AmE), ~ **centres** *n pl* (BrE) MECH ENG *milling machine* appareil diviseur *m*; ~ **contrast** *n* OPT *refractive* contraste d'indice *m*; ~ **dial** *n* MECH ENG *machine tools* plateau de division *m*, plateau diviseur *m*; ~ **dip** *n* OPT, TELECOM creux central d'indice *m*; ~ **error** *n* NAUT *celestial navigation* erreur de collimation *f*, erreur instrumentale *f*; ~ **fossil** *n* GEOL fossile caractéristique *m*; ~ **hole** *n* COMP *of floppy disk* trou d'index *m*, DP *of floppy disk* trou de repérage *m*; ~ **mineral** *n* GEOL *marking metamorphic zone* minéral caractéristique *m*; ~ **mirror** *n* INSTRUMENT *of sextant* miroir mobile *m*; ~ **plate** *n* MECH ENG *machine tools* plateau de division *m*, plateau diviseur *m*; ~ **profile** *n* OPT, TELECOM *refractive* profil d'indice *m*; ~ **of refraction** *n* OPT indice de réfraction *m*; ~ **register** *n* COMP, DP registre d'index *m*; ~ **tab** *n* PRINT onglet *m*, onglet débordant *m*; ~ **table** *n* MECH plateau diviseur *m*; ~ **tube** *n* TV tube à rubans fluorescents *m*; ~ **value** *n* NUCLEAR *of controlled quantity* valeur assignée *f*

index[2] *vt* COMP, DP indexer

indexable: ~ **hard metal insert** *n* MECH ENG *cutting tool* plaquette amovible en métal dur *f*

indexed: ~ **addressing** *n* COMP, DP adressage indexé *m*; ~ **file** *n* COMP, DP fichier indexé *m*; ~ **sequential access** *n* COMP, DP accès séquentiel indexé *m*; ~ **sequential file** *n* COMP, DP fichier séquentiel indexé *m*

indexing *n* COMP indexation *f*, recherche indexée *f*, CRYSTALL indexation *f*, DP indexation *f*, recherche indexée *f*

index-matching: ~ **material** *n* OPT, TELECOM substance adaptatrice d'indice *f*

India: ~ **ink** *n* COLOURS, PRINT encre de Chine *f*, encre à dessin *f*

Indian: ~ **ink** *n* COLOURS, PRINT encre de Chine *f*, encre à dessin *f*

indic *adj* CHEM indique

indican *n* CHEM indican *m*

indicated[1] *adj* MECH ENG nominal

indicated:[2] ~ **air speed** *n* AERONAUT vitesse badin *f* vitesse indiquée *f*; ~ **flight path** *n* AERONAUT trajectoire de vol indiquée *f*; ~ **horsepower** *n* MECH ENG puissance nominale en chevaux *f*; ~ **pitch angle** *n* AERONAUT *of helicopter* valeur de pas indiquée *f*; ~ **value** *n* NUCLEAR

valeur indiquée *f*

indicating *n* MECH ENG signalisation *f*; ~ **instrument** *n* INSTRUMENT instrument à aiguille *m*, instrument à cadran *m*; ~ **lamp** *n* PRINT lampe de signalisation *f*; ~ **stop** *n* MECH ENG butée de signalisation *f*; ~ **thermometer** *n* REFRIG thermomètre à lecture directe *m*

indication *n* (*Ind*) TELECOM indication *f*; ~ **of source** *n* PATENTS indication de provenance *f*

indicator *n* AERONAUT *light signal* clignoteur *m*, COMP, DP indicateur *m*, HYDR EQUIP indicateur *m*, *steam engine* dynamomètre de machine à vapeur *m*, manomètre *m*, MECH ENG *instrument* récepteur *m*, WATER SUPP indicateur *m*; ~ **bay** *n* NUCLEAR *of mass spectrometer* bâti de la partie de mesure *m*; ~ **color** *n* (AmE), ~ **colour** *n* (BrE) COLOURS couleur de marquage *f*; ~ **diagram** *n* PHYS diagramme de l'indicateur *m*; ~ **gate** *n* ELECTRON créneau de sensibilisation *m*; ~ **lamp** *n* ELEC lampe témoin *f*, RAIL *vehicles* avertisseur lumineux *m*, voyant lumineux *m*; ~ **light** *n* AERONAUT voyant lumineux *m*, voyant électrique *m*, PROD ENG voyant lumineux *m*; ~ **needle** *n* PHOTO aiguille de mesure *f*; ~ **paper** *n* PACKAGING, PHOTO papier indicateur *m*; ~ **plant** *n* MECH ENG plante indicatrice *f*; ~ **plate** *n* SAFETY *on firefighting equipment* plaque de signalisation *f*; ~ **species** *n* POLLUTION espèce indicatrice *f*, indicateur écologique *m*; ~ **tube** *n* ELECTRON tube indicateur *m*

indicators *n* VEHICLES *accessories* signalisation *f*

indicatrix *n* CRYSTALL indicatrice *f*

indices *n pl* CRYSTALL indices *m pl*

indicial: ~ **response** *n* CONTROL, ELECTRON réponse indicielle *f*

indicolite *n* MINERAL indicolite *f*, indigolite *f*

indifference *n* CHEM indifférence *f*

indigo *n* CHEM indigo *m*, indigotine *f*

indigolite *n* MINERAL indicolite *f*, indigolite *f*

indirect: ~ **addressing** *n* COMP, DP adressage indirect *m*; ~ **color separation** *n* (AmE), ~ **colour separation** *n* (BrE) PRINT sélection indirecte en deux temps *f*; ~ **control** *n* ELEC ENG commande indirecte *f*; ~ **control system** *n* TELECOM système à commande indirecte *m*; ~ **expansion refrigeration system** *n* REFRIG système indirect de refroidissement *m*; ~ **fire** *n* MILIT tir décalé *m*; ~ **frequency modulation** *n* ELECTRON modulation de fréquence indirecte *f*; ~ **frequency synthesis** *n* ELECTRON synthèse de fréquence indirecte *f*; ~ **frequency synthesizer** *n* ELECTRON synthétiseur de fréquence à synthèse indirecte *m*; ~ **gap semiconductor** *n* ELECTRON semi-conducteur à transitions indirectes *m*; ~ **heater-type cathode** *n* ELEC ENG cathode à chauffage indirect *f*; ~ **illumination** *n* ELEC ENG éclairage indirect *m*; ~ **initiation** *n* MINING amorçage postérieur *m*; ~ **injection diesel engine** *n* TRANSP moteur diesel à préchambre *m*; ~ **leaching** *n* GAS TECH lessivage inverse *m*; ~ **lighting** *n* CINEMAT éclairage indirect *m*; ~ **light reflector** *n* INSTRUMENT réflecteur à éclairage *m*; ~ **man-hour** *n* MECH ENG homme-heure indirect *m*; ~ **overcurrent release** *n* ELEC *circuit breaker* déclencheur indirect à maximum de courant *m*; ~ **overhead camshaft** *n* AUTO arbre à cames en tête à attaque indirecte *m*; ~ **photoconductivity** *n* ELECTRON photoconduction indirecte *f*; ~ **priming** *n* MINING amorçage postérieur *m*; ~ **process** *n* PRINT sélection indirecte *f*; ~ **rectifier** *n* ELEC redresseur indirect *m*

indirectly-heated: ~ **cathode** *n* ELEC ENG cathode équipotentielle *f*, cathode à chauffage indirect *f*

indirubin *n* CHEM indirubine *f*

indirubine *n* CHEM indirubine *f*

indiscriminate: ~ **dumping** *n* RECYCLING décharge non contrôlée *f*

indissoluble *adj* PROP MAT indissoluble

indistinguishability *n* PHYS *of identical particles* indiscernabilité *f*

indium *n* (*In*) CHEM indium *m* (*In*)

individual: ~ **channel flow control** *n* NUCLEAR régulation indépendante du débit dans le canal individuel *f*; ~ **control** *n* TRANSP microrégulation *f*; ~ **drive** *n* MECH ENG *for machine tools* commande individuelle *f*; ~ **dust removal apparatus** *n* SAFETY appareils de dépoussiérage individuels *m pl*, dépoussiéreurs individuels *m pl*; ~ **protection equipment** *n* (*IPE*) MILIT *chemical warfare* équipement de protection individuelle *m*; ~ **risk** *n* QUALITY risque individuel *m*; ~ **store** *n* TELECOM mémoire individuelle *f*; ~ **tool range alarm bit** *n* PROD ENG bit d'alarme pour chaque outil *m*; ~ **water supply** *n* WATER SUPP alimentation en eau individuelle *f*, approvisionnement *m*

indogen *n* CHEM indogène *m*

indogenide *n* CHEM indogénide *m*

indole *n* CHEM indole *m*

indoleacetic *adj* CHEM indoléacétique

indolin *n* CHEM indoline *f*

indoline *n* CHEM indoline *f*

indone *n* CHEM indone *f*, indénone *f*

indoor: ~ **antenna** *n* ELEC ENG antenne intérieure *f*; ~ **cable** *n* ELEC câble pour installation intérieure *m*; ~ **installation** *n* ELEC installation intérieure *f*; ~ **insulation** *n* ELEC isolation d'intérieur *f*; ~ **lighting** *n* ELEC ENG éclairage intérieur *m*; ~ **wiring** *n* ELEC ENG installation intérieure *f*

indophenin *n* CHEM indophénine *f*

indophenol *n* CHEM indophénol *m*

indoxyl *n* CHEM indoxyle *m*

indoxylic *adj* CHEM indoxylique

indoxylsulfuric *adj* (AmE), **indoxylsulphuric** *adj* (BrE) CHEM indoxylesulfurique

indraft *n* (AmE) **indraught** *n* (BrE) MECH ENG appel d'air *m*, entrée d'air *f*, venue du vent *f* ~ **of air** *n* MECH ENG appel d'air *m*, entrée d'air *f*, venue du vent *f*

induce *vt* ELEC, PHYS induire

induced[1] *adj* CHEM, ELEC *current, voltage, charge*, PHYS induit

induced:[2] ~ **air** *n* MECH ENG air forcé *m*; ~ **angle of attack** *n* AERONAUT angle induit *m*; ~ **charge** *n* CHEM, ELEC *electrostatics*, ELEC ENG charge induite *f*; ~ **current** *n* ELEC *electromagnetism*, TELECOM courant induit *m*; ~ **draft** *n* (AmE) *see induced draught*; ~ **draft burner** *n* (AmE) *see induced draught burner*; ~ **draft fan** *n* (AmE) *see induced draught fan*; ~ **drag** *n* AERONAUT traînée induite *f*; ~ **draught** *n* (BrE) HEATING tirage induit *m*, MECH ENG *in chimney* tirage induit *m*, *ventilation* aérage mécanique par aspiration *m*, aérage négatif *m*; ~ **draught burner** *n* (BrE) MECH ENG brûleur à tirage induit *m*; ~ **draught fan** *n* (BrE) MECH ENG ventilateur aspirant *m*, ventilateur négatif *m*; ~ **electromotive force** *n* ELEC, ELEC ENG force électromotrice induite *f*; ~ **emf** *n* PHYS force électromotrice induite *f*; ~ **failure** *n* COMP, DP panne induite *f*; ~ **field** *n* ELEC *electromagnetism* champ induit *m*; ~ **noise current** *n* PROD ENG courant de bruit induit *m*; ~ **nuclear reaction** *n* NUCLEAR réaction nucléaire induite *f*; ~ **overvoltage test** *n* ELEC *transformer* essai à surtension induite *m*; ~ **radioactivity** *n* PART PHYS radioactivité artificielle *f*, radioactivité induite *f*; ~ **voltage** *n* ELEC *electromagnetism*, TELECOM tension induite *f*

inducer *n* AERONAUT grille directrice d'entrée *f*

inducing: ~ **flow** *n* CONST *of well* amorçage de l'écoulement *m*, amorçage du débit *m*; ~ **system** *n* PHYS *emf induction* système inducteur *m*

in-duct: ~ **method** *n* REFRIG essai de conduit *m*

inductance *n* ELEC *electromagnetism*, ELEC ENG, PHYS, RECORDING, TELECOM inductance *f*; ~ **box** *n* ELEC ENG boîte d'inductances *f*; ~ **bridge** *n* ELEC *measurement*, ELEC ENG pont d'inductance *m*; ~ **coil** *n* ELEC *electromagnetism*, ELEC ENG bobine d'inductance *f*; ~ **meter** *n* ELEC henrymètre *m*, selfmètre *m*

inductance-capacitance: ~ **filter** *n* ELECTRON filtre à inductance et capacité *m*

inductility *n* PROP MAT inductilité *f*

induction *n* ELEC, ELEC ENG, MATH, PHYS, TELECOM induction *f*, VEHICLES *in engine, carburation* admission *f*; ~ **accelerator** *n* RAD PHYS accélérateur à induction *m*; ~ **coil** *n* AUTO bobine d'allumage *f*, bobine d'induction *f*, ELEC, ELEC ENG, PHYS, VEHICLES *ignition* bobine d'induction *f*; ~ **current** *n* ELEC ENG courant d'induction *m*, courant induit *m*; ~ **displacement** *n* ELEC *alternating current* déphasage inductif *m*; ~ **field** *n* ELEC ENG, TV champ d'induction *m*; ~ **flux** *n* ELEC ENG flux inducteur *m*; ~ **frequency converter** *n* ELEC convertisseur de fréquence à induction *m*; ~ **furnace** *n* ELEC ENG, PHYS, PROD ENG four à induction *m*; ~ **generator** *n* ELEC alternateur asynchrone *m*, alternateur à fer tournant *m*, ELEC ENG alternateur asynchrone *m*, générateur asynchrone *m*, génératrice asynchrone *f*; ~ **hardening** *n* ELEC ENG, METALL, PROP MAT trempe par induction *f*; ~ **heater** *n* ELEC ENG inducteur de chauffage *m*; ~ **heating** *n* ELEC ENG, MECH, P&R, PROP MAT chauffage par induction *m*; ~ **inner seal** *n* PACKAGING opercule soudé par impulsion *m*; ~ **instrument** *n* ELEC ENG appareil à induction *m*; ~ **log** *n* PETR diagramme d'induction *m*, diagramme par induction *m*, log d'induction *m*; ~ **loop detector** *n* TRANSP détecteur à boucle d'induction *m*; ~ **motor** *n* ELEC moteur asynchrone *m*, ELEC ENG moteur asynchrone *m*, moteur à induction *m*, PHYS moteur à induction *m*, PROD ENG moteur asynchrone *m*, TRANSP moteur à induction *m*; ~ **period** *n* METALL temps d'induction *m*; ~ **pickup** *n* MECH ENG capteur inductif *m*; ~ **pipe** *n* HYDR EQUIP tuyau d'admission *m*; ~ **port** *n* HYDR EQUIP *of steam cylinder* lumière d'admission *f*, lumière d'entrée *f*, orifice d'admission *m*, orifice d'entrée *m*; ~ **pump** *n* ELEC ENG pompe asynchrone *f*, pompe à induction *f*; ~ **regulator** *n* CONTROL, ELEC transformer régulateur à induction *m*; ~ **relay** *n* ELEC, ELEC ENG relais à induction *m*; ~ **sealer** *n* PACKAGING thermoscelleuse par induction *f*; ~ **stroke** *n* VEHICLES *of engine* course d'admission *f*; ~ **valve** *n* AUTO, HYDR EQUIP soupape d'admission *f*; ~ **voltage** *n* ELEC ENG tension d'induction *f*, tension induite *f*; ~ **voltage regulator** *n* ELEC ENG survolteur d'induction *m*; ~ **welding** *n* ELEC ENG soudure par induction *f*, PROD ENG soudage par induction *m*

inductive: ~ **capacitor** *n* ELEC ENG condensateur inductif *m*; ~ **circuit** *n* ELEC circuit inducteur *m*; ~ **coordination** *n* ELEC ENG coordination inductive *f*; ~ **coupling** *n* ELEC *inductor* couplage inductif *m*, ELEC ENG couplage inductif *m*, couplage par induction *m*; ~ **drop** *n* ELEC *of voltage* chute inductive *f*; ~ **feedback** *n* ELEC ENG réaction inductive *f*; ~ **heating** *n* THERMOD chauffage inductif *m*; ~ **load** *n* ELEC *alternating current*, ELEC ENG, TELECOM charge inductive *f*; ~ **plasma** *n* GAS TECH plasma inductif *m*; ~ **potential divider** *n* ELEC *auto-transformer* potentiomètre inductif *m*; ~ **proximity switch** *n* ELEC ENG détecteur de proximité inductif *m*; ~ **reactance** *n* ELEC, ELEC ENG, PHYS réactance inductive *f*; ~ **reaction rail** *n* TRANSP rail de réaction *m*; ~ **resistor** *n* ELEC ENG résistance inductive *f*; ~ **wirewound resistor** *n* ELEC ENG résistance bobinée inductive *f*

inductometer *n* ELEC inductomètre *m*, ELEC ENG variomètre étalonné *m*

inductor *n* ELEC ENG bobine d'inductance *f*, inductance *f*; ~ **alternator** *n* ELEC *generator*, ELEC ENG alternateur à fer tournant *m*; ~ **machine** *n* ELEC ENG machine à fer tournant *f*

indulin *n* CHEM induline *f*

indurate *vt* PROP MAT endurcir

indurated *adj* PROP MAT endurci

induration *n* GEOL durcissement *m*, induration *f*, lithification *f*, PROP MAT durcissement *m*

Indus *n* ASTRON Indien *m*, Oiseau Indien *m*

industrial: ~ **accident** *n* SAFETY accident du travail *m*; ~ **alcohol** *n* FOOD TECH alcool dénaturé *m*; ~ **application** *n* PATENTS application industrielle *f*; ~ **automation** *n* MECH ENG automatisation industrielle *f*; ~ **bulk container system** *n* PACKAGING système de conteneurs industriels pour le transport en vrac *m*; ~ **carrier** *n* TRANSP transporteur pour compte propre *m*; ~ **cleaning material** *n* DETERGENTS produit de nettoyage pour l'industrie *m*; ~ **clothing** *n* SAFETY vêtements pour l'industrie *m pl*; ~ **controller** *n* PROD ENG automate industriel *m*; ~ **diamond** *n* MINING *drilling* carbonado *m*, diamant noir *m*; ~ **discharge** *n* WATER SUPP eau résiduelle industrielle *f*; ~ **dispute** *n* PROD ENG conflit du travail *m*; ~ **effluent** *n* HYDROL, WATER SUPP eau résiduelle industrielle *f*; ~ **electronic equipment** *n* ELEC ENG matériel électronique industriel *m*; ~ **electronics** *n* ELEC ENG électronique industrielle *f*; ~ **electronic tube** *n* ELECTRON tube électronique industriel *m*; ~ **engineering** *n* PROD ENG génie industriel *m*; ~ **eye protectors** *n pl* SAFETY protecteurs industriels pour les yeux *m pl*; ~ **fishery** *n* OCEANOG pêche industrielle *f*; ~ **furnace** *n* GAS TECH four industriel *m*; ~ **gloves** *n pl* SAFETY gants pour l'industrie *m pl*; ~ **hearing protectors** *n* SAFETY protecteurs industriels pour oreilles *m pl*; ~ **hygiene** *n* SAFETY hygiène du travail *f*; ~ **injury** *n* SAFETY accident du travail *m*, blessure industrielle *f*; ~ **injury benefit** *n* SAFETY indemnité d'accident du travail *f*; ~ **insurance** *n* SAFETY assurance contre les accidents du travail *f*; ~ **interference** *n* ELEC ENG parasites industriels *m pl*; ~ **irradiator** *n* NUCLEAR irradiateur industriel *m*; ~ **isotope** *n* NUCLEAR isotope industriel *m*; ~ **magnetron** *n* ELECTRON magnétron industriel *m*; ~ **nuclear power** *n* NUCLEAR énergie nucléaire industrielle *f*; ~ **oven** *n* MECH ENG four industriel *m*, étuve industrielle *f*; ~ **overalls** *n pl* SAFETY salopette pour l'industrie *f*; ~ **packaging** *n* NUCLEAR conditionnement industriel *m*; ~ **packing** *n* PACKAGING emballage industriel *m*; ~ **process** *n* POLLUTION procédé industriel *m*; ~ **process water** *n* HYDROL eau industrielle *f*; ~ **property** *n* PATENTS propriété industrielle *f*; ~ **robot** *n* SAFETY *precaution* robot industriel *m*; ~ **safety** *n* SAFETY sécurité au travail *f*; ~ **safety helmet** *n* SAFETY casque de protection pour l'industrie *m*; ~ **standard** *n* COMP, DP norme industrielle *f*; ~ **truck** *n* SAFETY *code* chariot

automoteur *m*; ~ **valves** *n pl* MECH ENG robinetterie industrielle *f*; ~ **waste** *n* RECYCLING déchets industriels *m pl*, effluent industriel *m*, WATER SUPP déchets industriels *m pl*; ~ **wastewater** *n* HYDROL eau résiduelle industrielle *f*, RECYCLING eau résiduaire *f*; ~ **water** *n* WATER SUPP eau industrielle *f*; ~ **X-ray apparatus** *n* INSTRUMENT dispositif détecteur aux rayons X *m*

inedible *adj* FOOD TECH inconsommable

in-edit *n* TV point d'entrée *m*

ineffective[1] *adj* PROP MAT inefficace

ineffective:[2] ~ **airtime** *n* TELECOM durée des émissions sans effet *f*; ~ **call** *n* TELECOM appel inefficace *m*

ineffectual *adj* PROP MAT inefficace

inefficient *adj* PROP MAT inefficace

inelastic: ~ **collision** *n* PHYS choc inélastique *m*, RAD PHYS collision inélastique *f*; ~ **neutron scattering** *n* PHYS diffusion inélastique des neutrons *f*; ~ **scattering** *n* PHYS diffusion inélastique *f*

inelasticity *n* PROP MAT inélasticité *f*

inequality *n* COMP inégalité *f*

inert[1] *adj* CHEM inactif, indifférent, inerte, PETR TECH, PROP MAT inerte

inert:[2] ~ **gas** *n* GAS TECH gaz inerte *m*, NUCLEAR gaz neutre *m*; ~ **gas blanketing** *n* NUCLEAR couverture avec gaz inerte *f*; ~ **generator** *n* GAS TECH générateur de gaz inerte *m*; ~ **gas welding** *n* MECH ENG soudage en atmosphère inerte *m*, PROD ENG soudage à l'arc en atmosphère inerte *m*

inertia *n* MECH inertie *f*, MECH ENG force d'inertie *f*, inertie *f*, PHYS, POLLUTION inertie *f*; ~ **drive** *n* AUTO lanceur à inertie *m*; ~ **governor** *n* MECH ENG régulateur à volant d'inertie *m*; ~ **reel** *n* MECH ENG tambour à inertie *m*; ~ **switch** *n* CONTROL, ELEC ENG interrupteur à inertie *m*

inertial[1] *adj* MECH, PHYS inertiel

inertial:[2] ~ **accelerometer** *n* SPACE accéléromètre inertiel *m*; ~ **confinement** *n* PHYS confinement inertiel *m*; ~ **current** *n* OCEANOG courant d'inertie *m*; ~ **force** *n* MECH, PHYS force d'inertie *f*; ~ **frame** *n* PHYS repère inertiel *m*, SPACE trièdre de référence d'inertie *m*; ~ **guidance** *n* SPACE *spacecraft* guidage inertiel *m*, guidage par inertie *m*; ~ **mass** *n* PHYS masse d'inertie *f*; ~ **navigation** *n* OCEANOG, SPACE navigation par inertie *f*; ~ **navigation platform** *n* SPACE plate-forme inertielle *f*; ~ **navigation system** *n* AERONAUT (*INS*), NAUT (*cf INS*) système de navigation inertielle *m*, système de navigation par inertie *m*; ~ **oscillation** *n* OCEANOG oscillation d'inertie *f*; ~ **platform** *n* MECH ENG plate-forme à inertie *f*; ~ **reference frame** *n* SPACE référentiel d'inertie *m*; ~ **reference system** *n* SPACE référentiel d'inertie *m*; ~ **sensing system** *n* SPACE *communications* télémétrie inertielle *f*; ~ **sensor** *n* SPACE *spacecraft* détecteur inertiel *m*; ~ **separator** *n* NUCLEAR séparateur centrifuge *m*; ~ **starter** *n* MECH lanceur Bendix *m*; ~ **unit** *n* SPACE *spacecraft* centrale inertielle *f*; ~ **wave** *n* OCEANOG onde d'inertie *f*

Inertial: ~ **Upper Stage** *n* (*IUS*) SPACE étage supérieur inertiel *m*

inerting *n* PETR TECH *production safety* inertage *m*; ~ **system** *n* NUCLEAR couverture avec gaz inerte *f*

inexplosive *adj* PROP MAT inexplosible

inextensible *adj* PROP MAT inextensible

INF *abbr* (*information message*) TELECOM message d'information *m*

infall *n* WATER SUPP *of reservoir* orifice d'arrivée *m*

infeed *n* MECH ENG *machine tools* avance en plongée *f*,

PRINT débiteur *m*, partie du matériel par laquelle pénètre la matière première *f*, PROD ENG avance en plongée *f*; ~ **roller** *n* PRINT rouleau de débiteur *m*

inference *n* COMP, DP inférence *f*; ~ **engine** *n* COMP, DP, ELEC ENG moteur d'inférence *m*

inferior: ~ **characters** *n pl* PRINT caractères en indice *m pl*, chiffre en index *m*, indice *m*; ~ **coal** *n* COAL TECH mixtes de triage *m pl*; ~ **conjunction** *n* ASTRON conjonction inférieure *f*; ~ **figures** *n pl* PRINT caractères en indice *m pl*, chiffre en index *m*, indice *m*; ~ **letters** *n pl* PRINT caractères en indice *m pl*, chiffre en index *m*, indice *m*; ~ **planet** *n* ASTRON planète inférieure *f*

infill: ~ **wall** *n* CONST mur de remplissage *m*

infilling *n* GEOL *of basin, vein* remplissage *m*

infiltrating: ~ **water** *n (cf percolating water)* HYDROL eau d'infiltration *f*, WATER SUPP eau d'infiltration *f*, eau de percolation *f*

infiltration *n* COAL TECH, HYDROL, WATER SUPP infiltration *f*; ~ **basin** *n* HYDROL bassin d'infiltration *m*; ~ **gallery** *n* WATER SUPP galerie filtrante *f*; ~ **rate** *n* HEATING débit d'infiltration *m*; ~ **water** *n* HYDROL eau d'infiltration *f*

infinite: ~ **attenuation** *n* ELECTRON atténuation infinie *f*; ~ **baffle loudspeaker** *n* RECORDING haut-parleur à baffle infini *m*; ~ **impulse response** *n (IIR)* ELECTRON réponse impulsionnelle infinie *f*, TELECOM réponse infinie à une impulsion *f*; ~ **impulse response digital filter** *n* TELECOM filtre à réponse infinie à une impulsion *m*; ~ **impulse response filter** *n* ELECTRON filtre à réponse impulsionnelle infinie *m*; ~ **loop** *n* COMP boucle infinie *f*

infinitely: ~ **thick layer** *n* RAD PHYS couche infiniment épaisse *f*

infinitesimal *adj* GEOM infinitésimal

infix: ~ **notation** *n* COMP, DP notation infixée *f*

inflammability *n* PROP MAT inflammabilité *f*, THERMOD combustibilité *f*, inflammabilité *f*

inflammable[1] *adj* PACKAGING, PROP MAT inflammable, THERMOD combustible, inflammable

inflammable:[2] ~ **materials** *n pl* PROP MAT *avoided in the US; usually flammable* matières inflammables *f pl*

inflatable[1] *adj* MAR POLL gonflable

inflatable:[2] ~ **boat** *n* NAUT bateau pneumatique *m*; ~ **coldroom** *n* REFRIG chambre froide gonflable *f*; ~ **dinghy** *n* AERONAUT, NAUT canot pneumatique *m*; ~ **seal** *n* NUCLEAR joint d'étanchéité gonflable *m*; ~ **slide** *n* AERONAUT toboggan gonflable *m*; ~ **weir** *n* WATER SUPP déversoir gonflable *m*

inflate *vt* PHYS gonfler

inflated: ~ **structure** *n* CONST *building* structure gonflable *f*

inflation *n* MAR POLL gonflage *m*; ~ **cuff** *n* MAR POLL *of boom* manche à gonfler *f*; ~ **pressure** *n* PROD ENG pression de gonflage *f*

inflected: ~ **arch** *n* CONST arc renversé *m*

inflection *n* PROP MAT inflexion *f*

inflexibility *n* PROP MAT inflexibilité *f*

in-flight: ~ **dumping** *n* AERONAUT *of fuel* vidange en vol *f*; ~ **operation** *n* SPACE *spacecraft* mise en oeuvre en vol *f*; ~ **operational planning** *n* AERONAUT *meteorology* planning en vol *m*; ~ **refueling probe** *n* (AmE), ~ **refuelling probe** *n* (BrE) TRANSP prise de ravitaillement en vol *f*; ~ **sequence** *n* SPACE *spacecraft* séquence de vol *f*; ~ **thrust vectoring** *n* SPACE *spacecraft* orientation de la poussée en vol *f*

inflow *n* AERONAUT flux induit *m*, WATER SUPP influx *m*; ~ **angle** *n* AERONAUT angle d'induit *m*, angle entre vitesse d'un point de pale et vitesse relative *m*; ~ **canal** *n* WATER SUPP canal d'amenée *m*; ~ **ratio** *n* AERONAUT paramètre de flux axial *m*; ~ **of water** *n* WATER SUPP influx d'eau *m*

influence *n* CHEM influence *f*; ~ **line** *n* CONST *bridge design* ligne d'influence *f*

influent: ~ **stream** *n* HYDROL cours d'eau émissif *m*; ~ **water** *n* HYDROL eau de pénétration *f*

influx: ~ **of water** *n* WATER SUPP venue d'eau *f*

informatics *n* COMP, DP informatique *f*

information *n* COMP, DP, ELECTRON information *f*, PRINT renseignement *m*; ~ **bit** *n* COMP, DP bit d'information *m*; ~ **content** *n* COMP contenu informationnel *m*, DP quantité d'information *f*; ~ **flow** *n* COMP, DP circulation de l'information *f*; ~ **highway** *n* COMP, TELECOM autoroute d'informations *f*; ~ **message** *n (INF)* TELECOM message d'information *m*; ~ **processing** *n (IP)* COMP, DP, ELECTRON traitement de l'information *m*; ~ **processing system** *n* TELECOM système de traitement de l'information *m*; ~ **product data** *n* PROD ENG fiche technique d'information *f*; ~ **receiver station** *n (IRS)* TELECOM station de réception d'informations *f*; ~ **reference system** *n (IRS)* TELECOM système de référence intermédiaire *m (SRI)*; ~ **request message** *n (INR)* TELECOM message de demande d'information *m (IND)*; ~ **retrieval** *n (IR)* COMP, DP recherche documentaire *f*; ~ **retrieval system** *n* COMP, DP système de recherche documentaire *m*; ~ **sending station** *n* TELECOM station émettrice d'informations *f*; ~ **separator** *n (IS)* COMP séparateur d'informations *m*; ~ **signs** *n* RAIL signalétique *f*; ~ **source** *n* COMP, DP source d'informations *f*; ~ **storage** *n* COMP, DP mémorisation d'information *f*, TV stockage d'information *m*; ~ **storage and retrieval** *n (ISR)* COMP, DP stockage-restitution des données *m*; ~ **system** *n* COMP *(IS)* système informatique *m*, TELECOM système d'information *m*; ~ **technology** *n (IT)* COMP informatique *f*, TELECOM informatique *f*, télématique *f*; ~ **theory** *n* COMP, DP, ELECTRON théorie de l'information *f*; ~ **transfer rate** *n* TELECOM débit de transfert d'informations *m*; ~ **type** *n (IT)* TELECOM type d'information *m*

information-hiding *n* COMP, DP dissimulation d'information *f*, masquage d'information *m*

in-frame: ~ **coding** *n* TELECOM codage intratrame *m*

infraproteins *n pl* CHEM infraprotéines *f pl*

infrared[1] *adj* ASTRON, OPT, P&R *radiation*, PAPER TECH, RAD PHYS infrarouge

infrared[2] *n (IR)* PHYS infrarouge *m (IR)*; ~ **astronomical satellite** *n (IRAS)* ASTRON satellite astronomique infrarouge *m (IRAS)*; ~ **astronomy** *n* ASTRON astronomie infrarouge *f*; ~ **burner** *n* GAS TECH brûleur infrarouge *m*; ~ **cinematography** *n* CINEMAT prise de vues en infrarouge *f*; ~ **cirrus** *n* ASTRON cirrus infrarouge *m*; ~ **detector** *n* TRANSP détecteur à infrarouge *m*; ~ **dryer** *n* PRINT sécheur à infrarouge *m*; ~ **element** *n* HEAT ENG élément infrarouge *m*; ~ **emulsion** *n* PHOTO, RAD PHYS émulsion sensible à l'infrarouge *f*; ~ **exhaust gas analyzer** *n* AUTO analyseur de gaz d'échappement à rayons infrarouges *m*; ~ **film** *n* PHOTO film infrarouge *m*; ~ **filter** *n* RAD PHYS filtre infrarouge *m*; ~ **heating** *n* HEAT ENG chauffage aux rayons infrarouges *m*, RAD PHYS chauffage infrarouge *m*; ~ **image converter** *n* TV tube convertisseur d'image à infrarouge *m*; ~ **laser** *n* ELECTRON laser infrarouge *m*; ~ **LED** *n* ELECTRON diode lumineuse infrarouge *f*; ~ **light** *n* RAD PHYS rayonnement infrarouge *m*; ~ **link** *n* TV liaison par infrarouges *f*; ~ **map** *n* ASTRON carte infrarouge *f*; ~ **microscope** *n* INSTRUMENT microscope infrarouge *m*; ~ **motion alarm** *n* SAFETY avertisseur infrarouge des mouvements *m*, détecteurs de mouvements à infrarouges *m pl*; ~ **movement-sensing alarm** *n* SAFETY avertisseur infrarouge des mouvements *m*; ~ **oven** *n* PROD ENG étuve de séchage à infrarouge *f*; ~ **panel heating** *n* HEATING panneaux radiants à rayons infrarouges *m pl*; ~ **photography** *n* PHOTO prise de vue en infrarouge *f*; ~ **process ink** *n* PRINT encre séchant aux infrarouges *f*; ~ **radiant panel** *n* GAS TECH panneau radiant infrarouge *m*; ~ **radiation** *n* FUELLESS, PHYS, POLLUTION rayonnement infrarouge *m*, RAD PHYS radiation infrarouge *f*, SPACE, WAVE PHYS rayonnement infrarouge *m*; ~ **remote control** *n* MECH ENG télécommande à infrarouge *f*; ~ **satellite** *n* ASTRON satellite infrarouge *m*; ~ **sensor** *n* SPACE détecteur d'infrarouge *m*; ~ **source** *n* ASTRON source infrarouge *f*; ~ **spectrometer** *n* RAD PHYS spectromètre infrarouge *m*; ~ **spectrophotometer** *n* CHEM, LAB EQUIP *analysis* spectrophotomètre à infrarouge *m*; ~ **spectrophotometry** *n* CHEM spectrophotométrie dans l'infrarouge *f*; ~ **spectroscopy** *n* CHEM, PHYS spectroscopie à infrarouge *f*; ~ **spectrum** *n* PHYS, RAD PHYS spectre infrarouge *m*; ~ **telescope** *n* ASTRON télescope infrarouge *m*; ~ **therapy** *n* RAD PHYS thérapie infrarouge *f*

infrared-sensitive[1] *adj* PHOTO, RAD PHYS sensible à l'infrarouge

infrared-sensitive:[2] ~ **emulsion** *n* PHOTO, RAD PHYS émulsion sensible à l'infrarouge *f*

infrasonic: ~ **frequency** *n* ACOUSTICS, PHYS fréquence infrasonore *f*; ~ **speed** *n* PHYS vitesse infrasonique *f*

infrasound *n* ACOUSTICS, PHYS infrason *m*

infrastructure *n* COMP, DP infrastructure *f*

infringement *n* PATENTS contrefaçon *f*

infringer *n* PATENTS contrefacteur *m*

infusibility *n* PROP MAT infusibilité *f*

infusible *adj* PROP MAT infusible

infusion: ~ **bottle** *n* C&G flacon soluté *m*

infusorial: ~ **earth** *n* MINERAL farine fossile *f*

ingate *n* PROD ENG amorce de coulée *f*

ingest *vt* POLLUTION ingérer, intégrer

ingoing: ~ **air current** *n* MINING courant d'air entrant *m*

ingot *n* COAL TECH, MECH *materials* lingot *m*, PROD ENG lingot *m*, saumon *m*; ~ **mold** *n* (AmE), ~ **mould** *n* (BrE) MECH *materials* lingotière *f*, PROD ENG lingotière *f*, moule à lingots *m*

ingredient *n* CHEM principe *m*

ingress *n* CONST entrée *f*, *water* admission *f*; ~ **of water** *n* PROD ENG pénétration d'eau *f*

inhaul *n* OCEANOG hale-à-bord *m*

inhauler *n* OCEANOG hale-à-bord *m*

inherent: ~ **addressing** *n* COMP, DP adressage intrinsèque *m*; ~ **availability** *n* AERONAUT disponibilité intrinsèque *f*; ~ **color** *n* (AmE), ~ **colour** *n* (BrE) COLOURS couleur naturelle *f*; ~ **feedback** *n* ELECTRON régulation naturelle *f*, NUCLEAR rétroaction inhérente *f*; ~ **noise** *n* RECORDING bruit inhérent *m*; ~ **noise pressure** *n* ACOUSTICS *of microphone* pression de bruit *f*; ~ **regulation** *n* ELECTRON régulation naturelle *f*

inherently: ~ **stable reactor** *n* NUCLEAR réacteur à stabilité inhérente *m*

inheritance *n* COMP, DP héritage *m*

inhibit *vt* CHEM empêcher, inhiber, retarder, COMP, DP

inhiber, ELECTRON inhiber, *of logic gate* interdire

inhibiting: ~ **input** *n* ELECTRON entrée du signal d'interdiction *f*; ~ **pulse** *n* ELECTRON impulsion d'interdiction *f*; ~ **signal** *n* CONTROL, ELECTRON signal d'interdiction *m*

inhibition *n* CHEM inhibition *f*, ELECTRON inhibition *f*, *of logic gate* interdiction *f*

inhibitor *n* CHEM *of reaction*, DETERGENTS, FOOD TECH, P&R *compounding ingredient*, PRINT, PROP MAT, WATER SUPP inhibiteur *m*

inhomogeneity *n* C&G, PROP MAT inhomogénéité *f*

in-house: ~ **software** *n* COMP logiciel maison *m*; ~ **standard** *n* NUCLEAR norme de l'installation *f*, norme de l'usine *f*

initial[1] *adj* SPACE initial

initial[2] *n* PRINT initiale *f*, lettrine *f*; ~ **advance** *n* AUTO avance initiale à l'allumage *f*; ~ **approach** *n* AERONAUT approche initiale *f*; ~ **approach fix** *n* AERONAUT repère d'approche initiale *m*; ~ **approach path** *n* AERONAUT trajectoire d'approche initiale *f*; ~ **approach point** *n* AERONAUT repère d'approche initiale *m*; ~ **climb out** *n* AERONAUT montée au décollage *f*, montée initiale *f*; ~ **condition** *n* PROP MAT condition initiale *f*; ~ **connection charge** *n* TELECOM tarif de raccordement *m*; ~ **crack growth** *n* NUCLEAR croissance initiale d'une fissure *f*; ~ **criticality** *n* NUCLEAR criticité initiale *f*; ~ **current** *n* ELEC, ELEC ENG courant initial *m*; ~ **dip** *n* GEOL pendage originel *m*; ~ **domain identifier** *n* (IDI) TELECOM identificateur du domaine initial *m* (IDI); ~ **domain part** *n* (IDP) TELECOM partie du domaine initial *f*; ~ **fissile charge** *n* NUCLEAR première charge fissile *f*; ~ **forming charge** *n* AUTO courant initial de charge *m*; ~ **fusion temperature** *n* REFRIG température de fusion commençante *f*; ~ **gross weight** *n* AERONAUT masse brute initiale *f*; ~ **inspection** *n* CONTROL contrôle en première inspection *m*; ~ **inverse voltage** *n* ELEC tension initiale inverse *f*; ~ **level** *n* POLLUTION *water* niveau initial *m*; ~ **magnetization curve** *n* PHYS courbe de la première aimantation *f*, courbe de la première magnétisation *f*; ~ **program load** *n* (IPL) COMP programme de chargement initial *m*; ~ **ratio** *n* GEOL rapport initial *m*; ~ **reservoir pressure** *n* PETR pression initiale de réservoir *f*; ~ **settlement** *n* COAL TECH tassement initial *m*; ~ **setup procedure** *n* COMP procédure d'initialisation du système *f*; ~ **stability** *n* NAUT *naval architecture* stabilité initiale *f*; ~ **stage** *n* METALL premier stade *m*; ~ **state** *n* COMP, DP état initial *m*; ~ **stress** *n* SPRINGS contrainte initiale *f*; ~ **tension** *n* SPRINGS précharge *f*; ~ **velocity** *n* SPACE vitesse initiale *f*; ~ **verification** *n* METR vérification primitive *f*

initialization *n* COMP, DP entrée *f*, initialisation *f*, mise en oeuvre *f*

initialize *vt* COMP initialiser, mettre à la valeur initiale, ELECTRON initialiser, mettre à l'état initial

initiating: ~ **electrode** *n* ELEC ENG électrode d'amorçage *f*; ~ **explosive** *n* MINING explosif d'amorçage *m*, explosif primaire *m*; ~ **particle** *n* NUCLEAR particule germe *f*; ~ **spark** *n* ELEC ENG étincelle d'amorçage *f*

initiation *n* CHEM initiation *f*, MINING amorçage *m*; ~ **of fracture** *n* NUCLEAR amorçage *m*

initiator *n* CHEM, FOOD TECH initiateur *m*

inject *vt* GAS TECH injecter, PROD ENG injecter, lancer, SPACE injecter, injecter sur orbite

injected: ~ **gas** *n* PETR gaz injecté *m*

injection *n* AUTO injection *f*, ELECTRON injection *f*, *of* *signal input to a circuit* application *f*, GAS TECH, PROD ENG injection *f*, PROP MAT inoculation *f*, SPACE, VEHICLES *of fuel* injection *f*; ~ **blow molding** *n* (AmE) *see injection blow moulding*; ~ **blow molding machine** *n* (AmE) *see injection blow moulding machine*; ~ **blow moulding** *n* (BrE) P&R *process* moulage par injection-gonflage *m*, moulage par injection-soufflage *m*; ~ **blow moulding machine** *n* (BrE) PACKAGING machine de moulage par soufflage *f*; ~ **borehole** *n* NUCLEAR forage d'injection *m*; ~ **cock** *n* HYDR EQUIP prise de vapeur de l'injecteur *f*; ~ **condenser** *n* HYDR EQUIP condenseur par injection *m*, condenseur à injection *m*, condenseur à jet *m*; ~ **filling** *n* PACKAGING remplissage par injection *m*; ~ **gneiss** *n* GEOL gneiss à injection *m*, migmatite *f*; ~ **grid** *n* AERONAUT grille d'attaque *f*, ELECTRON grille de l'oscillateur local *f*; ~ **laser** *n* ELECTRON laser à injection *m*; ~ **laser diode** *n (ILD)* OPT diode laser *f*, laser à injection *m*, TELECOM laser à injection *m*; ~ **level** *n* ELECTRON niveau d'injection *m*; ~ **locking** *n* ELECTRON synchronisation par injection *f*; ~ **logic** *n* ELECTRON logique à injection *f*; ~ **machine** *n* SAFETY presse à injection *f*; ~ **mold** *n* (AmE) *see injection mould*; ~ **mold for rubber** *n* (AmE) *see injection mould for rubber*; ~ **mold for thermoplastics** *n* (AmE) *see injection mould for thermoplastics*; ~ **mold for thermosetting resins** *n* (AmE) *see injection mould for thermosetting resins*; ~ **molding** *n* (AmE) *see injection moulding*; ~ **molding compound** *n* (AmE) *see injection moulding compound*; ~ **molding machine** *n* (AmE) *see injection moulding machine*; ~ **molding press** *n* (AmE) *see injection moulding press*; ~ **molding pressure** *n* (AmE) *see injection moulding pressure*; ~ **mould** *n* (BrE) C&G moule à injection *m*; ~ **mould for rubber** *n* (BrE) MECH ENG moule pour injection de caoutchouc *m*; ~ **mould for thermoplastics** *n* (BrE) MECH ENG moule pour injection de thermoplastique *m*; ~ **mould for thermosetting resins** *n* (BrE) MECH ENG moule pour injection thermodurcissable *m*; ~ **moulding** *n* (BrE) P&R, PACKAGING, PROD ENG, PROP MAT moulage par injection *m*; ~ **moulding compound** *n* (BrE) PACKAGING, PROD ENG matière à mouler par injection *f*; ~ **moulding machine** *n* (BrE) SAFETY presse à injection *f*; ~ **moulding press** *n* (BrE) P&R presse à injection *f*; ~ **moulding pressure** *n* (BrE) PACKAGING pression de moulage par injection *f*; ~ **nozzle** *n* AUTO, VEHICLES *for fuel* injecteur *m*; ~ **nozzle holder** *n* AUTO porte-injecteur *m*; ~ **orbit** *n* SPACE trajectoire d'injection *f*; ~ **pipe** *n* HYDR EQUIP tuyau d'injection *m*; ~ **procedure** *n* NAUT *GRP repair* procédé d'injection *m*; ~ **pump** *n* CONST, MECH ENG, NAUT *of engine* pompe d'injection *f*; ~ **system** *n* PROP MAT système d'injection *m*; ~ **valve** *n* LAB EQUIP *gas chromatography* vanne d'injection *f*; ~ **well** *n* NUCLEAR forage d'injection *m*, PETR, PETR TECH puits d'injection *m*, WATER SUPP puits de drainage *m*

injection-locked: ~ **laser** *n* OPT, TELECOM laser verrouillé par injection *m*; ~ **oscillator** *n* ELECTRON, SPACE *communications* oscillateur synchronisé par injection *m*; ~ **oscillator demodulator** *n* SPACE *communications* démodulateur à oscillateur synchronisé par injection *m*

injector *n* AUTO, ELECTRON, GAS TECH, HYDR EQUIP, MECH, VEHICLES *for fuel* injecteur *m*; ~ **test pump** *n* AUTO *maintenance* , MECH ENG pompe à tarer les injecteurs *f*; ~ **throttle** *n* HYDR EQUIP prise de vapeur de l'injecteur *f*

injure *vt* PROP MAT déformer

injurious *adj* SAFETY nuisible, préjudiciable; ~ **to the**

eyes *adj* SAFETY nuisible aux yeux

injury *n* SAFETY blessure *f*, lésion *f*

ink[1] *n* COLOURS, PAPER TECH encre *f*, PRINT encre *f*, encre d'impression *f*; ~ **blade** *n* PRINT lame d'encrier *f*; ~ **coverage** *n* PRINT *process* couverture en encre *f*; ~ **coverage ratio** *n* PAPER TECH poids d'encre par unité de surface *m*; ~ **deck** *n* PRINT encrage *m*, ensemble des rouleaux d'encrage *m*; ~ **duct** *n* COLOURS encrier *m*; ~ **ductor** *n* PRINT preneur d'encre *m*; ~ **flow** *n* PRINT débit de l'encre *m*; ~ **form roller** *n* PRINT toucheur d'encre *m*; ~ **fountain** *n* COLOURS, PRINT encrier *m*; ~ **fountain roller** *n* PRINT rouleau d'encrier *m*; ~ **gloss** *n* PRINT brillant de l'encre *m*; ~ **jet printer** *n* COMP, PACKAGING, PRINT imprimante à jet d'encre *f*; ~ **jet system** *n* COMP, PACKAGING système à jet d'encre *m*; ~ **knife** *n* PRINT couteau d'encrier *m*, lame d'encrier *f*; ~ **lay-down** *n* PRINT couverture en encre *f*, distribution de l'encre sur la forme imprimante *f*; ~ **maker** *n* PRINT fabricant d'encre *m*, fabricant d'encre d'impression *m*; ~ **mixer** *n* PRINT mélangeur d'encre *m*; ~ **recorder** *n* INSTRUMENT enregistreur à encre *m*, enregistreur à plume *m*; ~ **tank** *n* PRINT réservoir d'encre *m*; ~ **transfer** *n* PRINT transfert d'encre *m*; ~ **writer** *n* INSTRUMENT enregistreur à encre *m*, enregistreur à plume *m*

ink:[2] ~ **the image** *vi* PRINT encrer la plaque, encrer la surface imprimante; ~ **the plate** *vi* PRINT encrer le report

inked: ~ **ribbon** *n* COMP ruban encreur *m*

inking *n* PAPER TECH encrage *m*; ~ **train** *n* PRINT train des rouleaux d'encrage *m*

inkless *adj* PACKAGING *ink jet system* sans encre

inky *n* CINEMAT spot 250 watt *m*

inky-dink *n* CINEMAT spot 250 watt *m*

inland: ~ **call** *n* TELECOM appel intérieur *m*; ~ **haulage** *n* TRANSP acheminement intérieur *m*; ~ **navigation** *n* NAUT batellerie *f*, navigation fluviale *f*, navigation intérieure *f*; ~ **sea** *n* HYDROL mer fermée *f*; ~ **waters** *n* WATER SUPP eaux intérieures *f pl*; ~ **water transport** *n* NAUT batellerie *f*, transport fluvial *m*; ~ **waterway** *n* NAUT réseau navigable *m*

inlandsis *n* OCEANOG inlandsis *m*

inlay *n* TV incrustation *f*

inlet *n* AUTO orifice d'aspiration *m*, HYDROL anse *f*, crique *f*, MECH admission *f*, arrivée *f*, MECH ENG admission *f*, appel d'air *m*, entrée d'air *f*, venue du vent *f*, entrée *f*, MINING admission *f*, NAUT *geography* anse *f*, OCEANOG calanque *f*, grau *m*, PAPER TECH orifice d'admission *m*, PROD ENG arrivée *f*, entrée *f*, orifice d'admission *m*, orifice d'arrivée *m*, orifice d'entrée *m*, *of fan, of centrifugal pump* oeillard *m*, ouïe *f*, TELECOM accès d'arrivée *m*, entrée *f*, point d'entrée *m*, WATER SUPP pertuis d'entrée *m*; ~ **case** *n* MECH ENG carter d'entrée *m*; ~ **connection** *n* PROD ENG raccord d'entrée *m*; ~ **end** *n* NUCLEAR *of turbine* côté d'admission *m*; ~ **jumper** *n* NUCLEAR tuyau d'amenée *m*; ~ **manifold** *n* (BrE) *(cf intake manifold)* AERONAUT *of engine* collecteur d'admission *m*, AUTO tubulure d'admission *f*, MECH ENG collecteur d'entrée *m*, VEHICLES *of engine* collecteur d'admission *m*; ~ **muffler** *n* (AmE) *(cf inlet silencer)* MECH silencieux d'aspiration *m*; ~ **pipe** *n* PROD ENG conduite d'arrivée *f*, tuyau d'arrivée *m*; ~ **port** *n* (BrE) *(cf intake port)* AUTO orifice d'admission *m*, C&G brûleur côté feu *m*, VEHICLES *of engine* lumière d'admission *f*, orifice d'admission *m*; ~ **pressure** *n* COAL TECH pression d'alimentation *f*; ~ **silencer** *n* (BrE) *(cf inlet muffler)* MECH silencieux d'aspiration *m*; ~ **strainer** *n* PROD ENG crépine d'aspiration *f*; ~ **temperature** *n* POLLUTION température d'entrée *f*; ~ **throat** *n* AERONAUT *of engine* col d'admission *m*; ~ **valve** *n* AUTO soupape d'admission *f*, HYDR EQUIP clapet d'admission *m*, soupape d'admission *f*, VEHI-CLES soupape d'admission *f*; ~ **velocity** *n* HYDR EQUIP *of turbines* vitesse d'entrée *f*

inlier *n* GEOL fenêtre *f*
in-line¹ *adj* MECH ENG aligné
in-line² *adv* MECH en ligne, PRINT dans le sens de défilement du papier, en continu, en ligne
in-line:³ ~ **contact coding** *n* PACKAGING code de contact pour chaîne de production *m*; ~ **cylinder engine** *n* MECH ENG moteur à cylindres en ligne *m*; ~ **cylinders** *n pl* AUTO cylindres en ligne *m pl*; ~ **engine** *n* AUTO moteur à cylindres en ligne *m*, MECH ENG, NAUT moteur en ligne *m*; ~ **finishing equipment** *n* PACKAGING équipement de finissage sur chaîne de production *m*; ~ **head** *n* RECORDING tête alignée *f*; ~ **position** *n* PRINT imposition *f*, mise en page en lignes *f*; ~ **pressure connection** *n* PROD ENG raccord de circuit de pression *m*; ~ **processing** *n* COMP traitement direct *m*, DP traitement direct *m*, traitement immédiat *m*; ~ **stereophonic tape** *n* RECORDING bande stéréophonique à enregistrement aligné *f*; ~ **variation** *n* C&G coup de rouleau *m*; ~ **web press** *n* PRINT rotative avec façonnage *f*, rotative en continu *f*
inner: ~ **batter** *n* CONST contre-fruit *m*; ~ **bottom** *n* NAUT *naval architecture* double fond *m*; ~ **bottom longitudinal** *n* NAUT lisse de plafond de double fond *f*; ~ **bottom plating** *n* NAUT plafond de double fond *m*; ~ **conductor** *n* TELECOM conducteur central *m*; ~ **core** *n* GEOL *of the Earth* noyau interne *m*, noyau terrestre *f*; ~ **covering** *n* ELEC *cable insulation* revêtement d'assemblage *m*; ~ **diameter** *n (ID)* MECH diamètre intérieur *m*; ~ **electron** *n* RAD PHYS électron interne *m*; ~ **engine shroud** *n* AERONAUT virole intérieure de réacteur *f*; ~ **form** *n* PRINT forme du second côté *f*, forme intérieure *f*; ~ **harbor** *n* (AmE), ~ **harbour** *n* (BrE) NAUT arrière-port *m*; ~ **lining** *n* NAUT *of hull* contre-moule *m*; ~ **locking button** *n* CONTROL bouton intérieur de condamnation *m*; ~ **margin** *n* PRINT marge de petit fond *f*; ~ **marker** *n* AERONAUT balise intérieure *f*, radioborne intérieure *f*; ~ **orbital complex** *n* RAD PHYS *atomic structure* complexe à orbitales internes *m*; ~ **planet** *n* ASTRON planète intérieure *f*; ~ **planet mission** *n* SPACE mission vers les planètes intérieures *f*; ~ **port** *n* NAUT arrière-port *m*; ~ **skin** *n* NAUT *shipbuilding, boatbuilding* bordé intérieur *m*; ~ **tube** *n* VEHICLES *of tyre* chambre à air *f*; ~ **wall** *n* TELECOM *of glass fibre* paroi interne *f*
innovative: ~ **finishes** *n pl* TEXTILES innovations d'ennoblissement *f pl*
innoxious *adj* PROP MAT inoffensif
inoculation *n* NUCLEAR ensemencement *m*, PROP MAT inoculation *f*
inorganic¹ *adj* CHEM *substance* minéral, PROP MAT inorganique
inorganic:² ~ **chemistry** *n* CHEM chimie minérale *f*; ~ **chromium compound** *n* CHEM composé inorganique de chrome *m*; ~ **liquid laser** *n* ELECTRON laser à liquide inorganique *m*; ~ **zinc paint** *n* COLOURS peinture au zinc *f*
inorganical *adj* PROP MAT inorganique
inosine *n* CHEM, FOOD TECH inosine *f*
inositol *n* CHEM, FOOD TECH inositol *m*
inoxidizable *adj* CHEM, PROP MAT inoxydable

in-package: ~ **desiccation** *n* REFRIG dessiccation dans les paquets *f*
in-phase¹ *adj* ELECTRON, PHYS, TV en phase
in-phase² *adv* WAVE PHYS en phase
in-phase:³ ~ **component** *n* ELECTRON composante en phase *f*; ~ **current** *n* ELEC courant en phase avec la tension *m*; ~ **signal** *n* ELECTRON signal en phase *m*
in-pile: ~ **experiment** *n* NUCLEAR expérience en pile *f*; ~ **loop** *n* NUCLEAR boucle de réacteur *f*, boucle en pile *f*
in-process: ~ **gaging** *n* (AmE), ~ **gauging** *n* (BrE) METR dispositif de calibrage en cours de service *m*; ~ **inspection in manufacturing** *n* QUALITY contrôle en cours de fabrication *m*; ~ **inventory** *n* PROD ENG en-cours de fabrication *m*, en-cours de production *m*, stock atelier *m*, stock en cours *m*
input¹ *n* COMP, DP, ELEC *of current, voltage*, ELECTRON entrée *f*, GEOL apport *m*, HYDR EQUIP admission *f*, PHYS entrée *f*, RAD PHYS énergie d'entrée *f*, TV entrée *f*; ~ **admittance** *n* ELEC ENG admittance d'entrée *f*; ~ **amplifier** *n* ELECTRON amplificateur d'entrée *m*; ~ **area** *n* COMP, DP zone d'entrée *f*; ~ **attenuator** *n* ELECTRON atténuateur d'entrée *m*; ~ **back-off** *n* SPACE *communications of TWT* recul d'entrée *m*; ~ **bevel pinion shaft** *n* AERONAUT *of helicopter* arbre de pignon conique d'attaque *m*, queue de pignon conique d'attaque *f*; ~ **buffer** *n* COMP, DP tampon d'entrée *m*; ~ **buffer amplifier** *n* ELECTRON amplificateur séparateur d'entrée *m*; ~ **capacitance** *n* ELEC ENG capacité d'entrée *f*; ~ **capacitor** *n* ELEC ENG condensateur d'entrée *m*; ~ **cavity** *n* ELECTRON cavité d'entrée *f*; ~ **circuit** *n* ELEC, ELEC ENG circuit d'entrée *m*; ~ **circuit terminal** *n* PROD ENG borne du circuit d'entrée *f*; ~ **connection diagram** *n* PROD ENG schéma de branchement d'entrée *m*; ~ **control** *n* ELECTRON limitation d'entrée *f*; ~ **current** *n* ELEC courant d'entrée *m*; ~ **data** *n* COMP, DP données d'entrée *f pl*; ~ **device** *n* COMP, DP dispositif d'entrée *m*, unité d'entrée *f*, ELEC ENG dispositif d'entrée *m*, organe d'entrée *m*; ~ **electrode** *n* ELEC ENG électrode d'entrée *f*; ~ **file** *n* COMP, DP fichier d'entrée *m*; ~ **filter** *n* ELECTRON, SPACE *communications* filtre d'entrée *m*; ~ **filtering** *n* ELECTRON filtrage à l'entrée *m*; ~ **filter time delay** *n* PROD ENG filtre d'entrée de retardement *m*; ~ **gap** *n* ELECTRON espace de modulation *m*; ~ **gas** *n* GAS TECH gaz injecté *m*, PETR gaz d'injection *m*; ~ **gate** *n* ELECTRON porte logique d'entrée *f*; ~ **image table** *n* PROD ENG table des données d'entrée *f*, table-image d'entrée *f*; ~ **impedance** *n* ELEC ENG, PHYS, TELECOM, TV impédance d'entrée *f*; ~ **lead** *n* ELEC ENG conducteur d'entrée *m*; ~ **level** *n* TELECOM, TV niveau d'entrée *m*; ~ **message acknowledgment** *n (IMA)* TELECOM accusé de réception de message d'entrée *m*; ~ **power** *n* ELEC ENG consommation *f*, puissance absorbée *f*, puissance fournie *f*, PROD ENG, TELECOM, TV puissance d'entrée *f*; ~ **power factor** *n* PROD ENG facteur de charge d'entrée *m*; ~ **power fuse** *n* PROD ENG fusible principal d'alimentation *m*; ~ **processor** *n (IP)* COMP processeur d'entrée *m*; ~ **pulse** *n* ELECTRON impulsion d'entrée *f*; ~ **queue** *n* COMP file d'attente en entrée *f*, DP file d'attente d'entrée *f*; ~ **record** *n* COMP, DP enregistrement d'entrée *m*; ~ **resistance** *n* ELEC ENG résistance d'entrée *f*; ~ **resonator** *n* ELECTRON résonateur d'entrée *m*; ~ **response** *n* ELECTRON réponse au signal d'entrée *f*; ~ **scaling** *n* PROD ENG mise à l'échelle *f*; ~ **section indicator** *n* PROD ENG voyant des entrées *m*; ~ **sensor** *n* PROD ENG capteur d'entrée *m*; ~ **shaft** *n* MECH ENG arbre d'entrée *m*, VEHICLES *of clutch, gearbox*

arbre primaire *m*; ~ **shaft bearing** *n* VEHICLES *of clutch* roulement de l'arbre primaire *m*; ~ **shell** *n* AUTO cloche de liaison *f*; ~ **signal** *n* CONTROL signal d'entrée *m*, ELECTRON signal appliqué à l'entrée *m*, signal d'entrée *m*, TV signal d'entrée *m*; ~ **signal conditioning** *n* ELECTRON mise en forme du signal d'entrée *f*; ~ **signal power** *n* ELECTRON puissance d'entrée *f*, puissance du signal d'entrée *f*; ~ **signal quantization** *n* ELECTRON quantification du signal d'entrée *f*; ~ **signal-to-noise ratio** *n* ELECTRON rapport signal-bruit à l'entrée *m*; ~ **simulator** *n* PROD ENG simulateur d'entrées *m*; ~ **simulator strip** *n* PROD ENG bornier de simulation des entrées *m*; ~ **stage** *n* ELECTRON étage d'entrée *m*; ~ **stage gain** *n* ELECTRON gain de l'étage d'entrée *m*; ~ **tapping** *n* ELEC ENG sélection de la tension *f*; ~ **terminal** *n* ELEC *connection* borne d'entrée *f*, ELEC ENG borne d'arrivée *f*, borne d'entrée *f*; ~ **terminal strip** *n* PROD ENG bornier des entrées *m*; ~ **transaction accepted for delivery** *n* (*ITD*) TELECOM acceptation pour remise *f*; ~ **transaction rejected** *n* (*ITR*) TELECOM rejet de transaction d'entrée *m*; ~ **transductor** *n* ELEC ENG transducteur d'entrée *m*; ~ **transformer** *n* ELEC ENG, PHYS transformateur d'entrée *m*; ~ **transient protection** *n* PROD ENG protection contre les transitoires en entrée *f*; ~ **voltage** *n* ELEC tension d'entrée *f*, ELEC ENG tension appliquée à l'entrée *f*, tension d'entrée *f*, tension à l'entrée *f*, PROD ENG attaque *f*, tension à l'entrée *f*

input[2] *vt* ELECTRON appliquer, entrer, introduire

input/output *n* COMP, DP, ELEC *of voltage, current*, PROD ENG *(I/O)* entrée/sortie *f* (*E/S*); ~ **buffer** *n* COMP, DP tampon d'entrée/sortie *m*; ~ **bus** *n* COMP, DP bus d'entrée/sortie *m*; ~ **channel** *n* COMP, DP canal d'entrée/sortie *m*; ~ **control** *n* COMP, DP commande d'entrée/sortie *f*; ~ **controller** *n* CONTROL contrôleur d'entrée/sortie *m*; ~ **device** *n* COMP, DP dispositif d'entrée/sortie *m*, unité d'entrée/sortie *f*; ~ **file** *n* COMP, DP fichier d'entrée/sortie *m*; ~ **instruction** *n* COMP, DP instruction d'entrée/sortie *f*; ~ **interrupt** *n* COMP, DP interruption d'entrée/sortie *f*; ~ **port** *n* COMP, DP port d'entrée/sortie *m*; ~ **processor** *n* COMP (*IOP*), DP processeur d'entrée/sortie *m*; ~ **register** *n* COMP registre d'entrée/sortie *m*, DP registre d'entrées/sorties *m*; ~ **switching** *n* COMP, DP commutation d'entrées/sorties *f*

input/output-limited *adj* COMP limité par les entrées/sorties

input-limited *adj* COMP limité par la vitesse des périphériques d'entrée

inputting *n* ELECTRON application *f*

inquiry *n* COMP consultation *f*, interrogation *f*, DP consultation *f*, consultation de données *f*, interrogation *f*; ~ **control** *n* COMP gestion des requêtes *f*, DP pilotage des requêtes *m*; ~ **processing** *n* COMP, DP traitement des demandes *m*; ~ **station** *n* COMP, DP poste d'interrogation *m*

INR *abbr* (*information request message*) TELECOM IND (*message de demande d'information*)

in-reactor: ~ **experiment** *n* NUCLEAR expérience en pile *f*

inrush *n* FLUID PHYS irruption *f*, HYDROL *of water* invasion *f*, irruption *f*, venue *f*, MINING *of water* venue *f*; ~ **current** *n* ELEC ENG appel de courant *m*; ~ **current limiter** *n* ELEC ENG limiteur d'appel de courant *m*; ~ **current protection** *n* ELEC ENG protection contre l'appel de courant *f*

INS *n* (*inertial navigation system*), AERONAUT, NAUT système de navigation inertielle *m*, système de naviga-

tion par inertie *m*

inscattering *n* NUCLEAR diffusion au dedans *f*

inscribed: ~ **circle** *n* GEOM cercle inscrit *m*

in-seam: ~ **miner** *n* MINING abatteuse en veine *f*

insect-proof *adj* PACKAGING résistant aux insectes

insert[1] *n* AUTO clavette *f*, COMP, DP insertion *f*, MECH insert *m*, MECH ENG encart *m*, pièce rapportée *f*, P&R *plastics* insert *m*, insertion *f*, PACKAGING pièce rapportée *f*, PRINT encart *m*, PROD ENG pièce rapportée *f*; ~ **bit** *n* PETR TECH trépan à pastilles *m*; ~ **camera** *n* TV caméra titres *f*; ~ **cavity** *n* MECH ENG *die-casting* logement de bloc porte-empreinte *m*; ~ **earphone** *n* ACOUSTICS écouteur à embout *m*; ~ **edit** *n* TV montage d'un enchaînement *m*; ~ **editing** *n* TV montage par insertion *m*; ~ **nut** *n* MECH écrou prisonnier *m*; ~ **production** *n* PRINT fabrication d'encarts *f*; ~ **shot** *n* CINEMAT insert *m*, plan de détail *m*; ~ **spring** *n* AUTO ressort de clavette *m*

insert[2] *vt* CINEMAT, COMP, DP insérer, PROD ENG insérer, intercaler, introduire

insertable: ~ **sack** *n* PACKAGING sac pouvant être inséré *m*

inserted[1] *adj* MECH ENG encastré

inserted:[2] ~ **blade milling cutter** *n* MECH ENG fraise à dents rapportées *f*, fraise à lames rapportées *f*, fraises à lames amovibles *f pl*; ~ **jaws** *n pl* MECH ENG *of vice* mâchoires rapportées *f pl*; ~ **joint** *n* PROD ENG joint à insertion *m*; ~ **joint casing** *n* PROD ENG tubage à joint à insertion *m*; ~ **scram rod** *n* NUCLEAR barre d'arrêt d'urgence injectée *f*; ~ **tooth broach** *n* MECH ENG *of broaching machine* broche à denture rapportée *f*; ~ **tooth milling cutter** *n* MECH ENG fraise à lames amovibles *f*

inserting *n* PAPER TECH *of sheets* encartage *m*

insertion *n* PRINT insertion *f*, PROD ENG insertion *f*, intercalation *f*, introduction *f*; ~ **gain** *n* PHYS gain d'insertion *m*; ~ **loss** *n* OPT *of component* affaiblissement d'insertion *m*, perte d'insertion *f*, PHYS perte d'insertion *f*, TELECOM affaiblissement d'insertion *m*, perte d'insertion *f*; ~ **schedule** *n* PRINT calendrier des insertions *m*

inset *n* PRINT encart volant de petite taille *m*; ~ **joint** *n* MECH ENG *of pliers, scissors* maillure encastrée *f*

inset-insert *n* PRINT encart *m*, insertion *f*

insetting *n* PAPER TECH *bookbinding* encartage *m*

inshore[1] *adj* NAUT côtier

inshore[2] *adv* NAUT près de terre

inshore:[3] ~ **current** *n* OCEANOG courant d'entraînement *m*; ~ **fishery** *n* OCEANOG pêche côtière *f*; ~ **pilot** *n* NAUT lamaneur *m*; ~ **pilotage** *n* NAUT lamanage *m*; ~ **waters** *n pl* (*cf coastal waters*) OCEANOG eaux continentales *f pl*

inside: ~ **amalgamation plate** *n* MECH ENG plaque d'amalgamation intérieure *f*; ~ **back cover** *n* PRINT troisième de couverture *f*; ~ **calipers** *n pl* (AmE), ~ **callipers** *n pl* (BrE) MECH ENG compas d'intérieur *m*; ~ **clearance slide valve** *n* HYDR EQUIP découvert intérieur d'un tiroir *m*; ~ **coil diameter** *n* SPRINGS diamètre intérieur d'enroulement *m*; ~ **corner edge** *n* PACKAGING coin de surface intérieure *m*; ~ **corner tool** *n* MECH ENG outil à dresser *m*; ~ **cover** *n* HYDR EQUIP recouvrement intérieur *m*, recouvrement à l'échappement *m*; ~ **diameter** *n* MECH diamètre intérieur *m*, MECH ENG diamètre dans oeuvre *m*; ~ **form** *n* PRINT forme du second côté *f*, forme intérieure *f*; ~ **gear** *n* MECH ENG engrenage intérieur *m*; ~ **jamb block** *n* (BrE) *(cf goal post)* C&G brique intérieure de goulotte *f*; ~ **lap slide valve** *n* HYDR EQUIP recouvrement intérieur *m*, recouvrement à l'échappement *m*; ~ **lead slide valve** *n* HYDR EQUIP avance linéaire à l'échappement *f*, avance à l'échappement *f*, avance à l'émission *f*; ~ **measuring faces** *n pl* MECH ENG *of calliper* faces de mesure intérieure *f pl*; ~ **screw** *n* MECH ENG vis creuse *f*, vis femelle *f*, PRODUCTION vis creuse *f*; ~ **thread** *n* MECH ENG filet intérieur *m*, pas d'écrou *m*; ~ **threading tool** *n* MECH ENG outil à fileter intérieurement *m*; ~ **tool** *n* MECH *tools* outil à tourner intérieur *m*; ~ **vapor phase oxidation** *n* (AmE), ~ **vapour phase oxidation** *n* (BrE) *(IVPO)* TELECOM dépôt en phase vapeur interne *m*; ~ **welding** *n* MECH soudage intérieur *m*

inside-and-outside: ~ **calipers** *n pl* (AmE), ~ **callipers** *n pl* (BrE) MECH ENG compas maître de danse *m*, compas maître-à-danser *m*, maître-à-danser *f*

inside-fired: ~ **boiler** *n* PROD ENG chaudière à chauffage intérieur *f*, chaudière à foyer intérieur *f*

in:[1] **situ** ~ *adv* CONST, MECH in situ, sur place

in:[2] **situ** ~ **combustion** *n* PETR combustion in situ *f*; **in** ~ **concrete** *n* CONST béton coulé en place *m*, béton coulé sur place *m*; **in** ~ **monitoring** *n* NUCLEAR surveillance sur site *f*; **in** ~ **pile** *n* COAL TECH pieu moulé dans le sol *m*

insolation *n* ASTRON insolation *f*, FUELLESS ensoleillement *m*, GEOPHYS, PHYS *radiation*, PRINT, REFRIG insolation *f*

insolubility *n* PROP MAT, TEXTILES insolubilité *f*

insoluble *adj* PETR TECH, PROP MAT insoluble; ~ **in water** *adj* TEXTILES insoluble à l'eau

insonorous *adj* PROP MAT insonore

inspect *vt* CONTROL contrôler, NAUT arraisonner, SPACE *tests, management* contrôler

inspection *n* C&G choix *m*, MECH contrôle *m*, inspection *f*, PROD ENG contrôle *m*, inspection *f*, reconnaissance *f*, visite *f*, contrôle *m*, QUALITY contrôle *m*, inspection *f*, SAFETY visite *f*, *of workplace* inspection *f*, SPACE contrôle *m*; ~ **by attributes** *n* QUALITY contrôle par attributs *m*; ~ **by variables** *n* QUALITY contrôle par paramètres *m*; ~ **card** *n* PROD ENG fiche de contrôle *f*, QUALITY carte de contrôle *f*; ~ **chamber** *n* CONST regard *m*, trou d'homme *m*, trou de visite *m*; ~ **cover** *n* PROD ENG porte de visite *f*, regard de visite *m*; ~ **cycle** *n* AERONAUT cycle de visites *m*; ~ **door** *n* MECH regard *m*, PROD ENG porte de visite *f*, regard de visite *m*; ~ **equipment** *n* PACKAGING équipement d'inspection *m*, QUALITY matériel de contrôle *m*; ~ **of files** *n* PATENTS *application* inspection du dossier *f*; ~ **fitting** *n* PROD ENG boîte de regard *f*; ~ **gage** *n* (AmE) *see inspection gauge*; ~ **gallery** *n* HYDROL *of dam* mousson *f*; ~ **gauge** *n* (BrE) MECH ENG calibre de contrôle *m*, gabarit de vérification *m*; ~ **hatch** *n* SPACE *spacecraft* porte de visite *f*, regard *m*; ~ **hole** *n* MECH ENG, SPACE regard *m*; ~ **lamp** *n* ELEC ENG baladeuse *f*, lampe baladeuse *f*, lampe de contrôle *f*; ~ **level** *n* QUALITY niveau de contrôle *m*; ~ **lot** *n* QUALITY lot de contrôle *m*; ~ **panel** *n* AERONAUT *of airframe* panneau de visite *m*, porte de visite *f*; ~ **pit** *n* PROD ENG fosse à visiter *f*; ~ **platform** *n* CONST nacelle de visite *f*; ~ **procedure** *n* METR procédure de contrôle *f*; ~ **record** *n* METR registre d'une procédure de contrôle *m*; ~ **specification** *n* QUALITY spécification de contrôle *f*; ~ **stamp** *n* PROD ENG tampon de contrôle *m*; ~ **window** *n* PACKAGING voyant *m*

inspector *n* CONTROL contrôleur *m*, MECH, QUALITY contrôleur *m*, inspecteur *m*

inspirator *n* MECH ENG injecteur aspirant *m*

inspissation *n* CHEM asphaltisation *f*, épaississement *m*

instability *n* CHEM, ELEC ENG, PACKAGING instabilité *f*, RAIL *fixed equipment, of track* danse *f*; ~ **phenomena** *n pl* FLUID PHYS phénomènes d'instabilité *m pl*; ~ **of rotating Couette flow** *n* FLUID PHYS instabilité dans les écoulements tournants de Couette *f*

install *vt* COMP, DP installer, NAUT monter, *locks on canal* écluser, PRINT *printer terminal* installer, PROD ENG monter, *printer* configurer

installation *n* COMP, CONST, DP, PROD ENG, TELECOM installation *f*; ~ **accessories** *n pl* PROD ENG accessoires d'installation *m pl*; ~ **call forwarding** *n* TELECOM *ISDN* renvoi temporaire de l'ITA *m*, renvoi temporaire de l'installation *m*; ~ **error** *n* PROD ENG erreur due à l'installation *f*; ~ **for reducing sulfur emissions** *n* (AmE), ~ **for reducing sulphur emissions** *n* (BrE) SAFETY installation de désulfuration de gaz de fumée *f*; ~ **switch** *n* ELEC interrupteur d'installation *m*

installed: ~ **capacity** *n* ELEC *supply* puissance installée *f*; ~ **power** *n* VEHICLES *of engine* puissance installée *f*

instance *n* COMP, DP réalisation *f*

instant: ~ **flowmeter** *n* WATER SUPP débitmètre instantané *m*; ~ **gamma radiation** *n* RAD PHYS *in activation analysis* rayonnement gamma instantané *m*; ~ **replay** *n* TV reproduction instantanée *f*

instantaneous: ~ **acoustic energy per unit volume** *n* ACOUSTICS énergie volumique acoustique instantanée *f*; ~ **acoustic kinetic energy per unit volume** *n* ACOUSTICS énergie volumique cinétique acoustique instantanée *f*; ~ **acoustic potential energy per unit volume** *n* ACOUSTICS énergie volumique potentielle acoustique instantanée *f*; ~ **automatic gain control** *n* *(IAGC)* CONTROL régulateur automatique de niveau *m*; ~ **automatic volume control** *n* *(IAVC)* CONTROL régulateur automatique de niveau *m*; ~ **concentration** *n* POLLUTION concentration instantanée *f*, niveau instantané de nuisance *m*; ~ **current** *n* ELEC courant instantané *m*, ELEC ENG intensité instantanée du courant *f*; ~ **detonator** *n* MINING détonateur instantané *m*, détonateur électrique instantané *m*; ~ **electric blasting cap** *n* MINING détonateur instantané *m*, détonateur électrique instantané *m*; ~ **electric dipole moment** *n* RAD PHYS moment de dipôle électrique instantané *m*; ~ **exposure** *n* PHOTO instantané *m*, pose instantanée *f*; ~ **failure intensity** *n* QUALITY intensité de rupture instantanée *f*, *of material* intensité d'échec instantanée *f*; ~ **failure rate** *n* QUALITY taux de défaillances instantanées *m*; ~ **firing** *n* MINING tir instantané *m*; ~ **frequency** *n* ELECTRON, SPACE *communications* fréquence instantanée *f*; ~ **frequency estimation demodulator** *n* SPACE *communications* démodulateur à estimation de la fréquence instantanée *m*; ~ **frequency measurement** *n* *(IFM)* ELECTRON mesure de fréquence instantanée *f*; ~ **recording** *n* ACOUSTICS enregistrement direct *m*, RECORDING enregistrement simultané *m*; ~ **relay** *n* ELEC relais à action instantanée *m*, ELEC ENG relais instantané *m*, relais non temporisé *m*; ~ **release** *n* ELEC *switch* déclencheur instantané *m*, MECH ENG débrayage instantané *m*; ~ **sound power** *n* ACOUSTICS puissance acoustique instantanée *f*; ~ **sound power per unit area** *n* ACOUSTICS puissance surfacique acoustique instantanée *f*; ~ **sound pressure** *n* ACOUSTICS pression acoustique instantanée *f*; ~ **speech power** *n* ACOUSTICS puissance vocale instantanée *f*; ~ **tracking error** *n* SPACE *communications* erreur de poursuite instantanée *f*; ~ **value** *n* CONTROL, ELEC *of voltage*, PHYS valeur instantanée *f*; ~ **voltage** *n* ELEC tension instantanée *f*; ~ **water heater** *n* HEATING chauffe-eau instantané *m*

in-step *adj* ELEC ENG en phase, en synchronisme, PRINT en phase, synchrone

instroke *n* HYDR EQUIP *of piston* course de retour *f*, mouvement de recul *m*, retour *m*

instruction *n* COMP, DP instruction *f*; ~ **book** *n* MECH ENG, PROD ENG manuel d'instructions *m*; ~ **code** *n* COMP, DP code d'instructions *m*; ~ **cycle** *n* COMP, DP cycle d'instruction *m*; ~ **decoder** *n* COMP, DP décodeur d'instructions *m*; ~ **execution** *n* COMP, DP exécution d'instruction *f*; ~ **fetching** *n* COMP extraction d'instruction *f*, DP lecture d'instruction *f*; ~ **format** *n* COMP, DP format d'instruction *m*; ~ **length** *n* COMP, DP longueur d'instruction *f*; ~ **manual** *n* PROD ENG manuel d'instructions *m*; ~ **panel** *n* PROD ENG tableau de bord *m*; ~ **plate** *n* PROD ENG plaquette d'instructions *f*; ~ **register** *n* COMP, DP registre d'instruction *m*; ~ **repertoire** *n* COMP, DP répertoire d'instructions *m*; ~ **set** *n* COMP, DP, PROD ENG jeu d'instructions *m*; ~ **stream** *n* COMP, DP flot d'instructions *m*; ~ **syntax** *n* PROD ENG syntaxe des instructions *f*

instructions: ~ **for opening** *n pl* PACKAGING instructions pour ouvrir *f pl*; ~ **for use** *n pl* PACKAGING, PROD ENG mode d'emploi *m*

instrument:[1] ~ **restricted** *adj* AERONAUT réservé aux instruments

instrument[2] *n* AERONAUT, COMP, DP instrument *m*, ELEC *for measurement* appareil de mesure *m*, instrument *m*, mesureur *m*, ELEC ENG appareil *m*, MECH ENG appareil *m*, appareil mécanique *m*, instrument *m*, NAUT instrument *m*; ~ **approach** *n* AERONAUT approche aux instruments *f*; ~ **approach chart** *n* AERONAUT carte d'approche aux instruments *f*; ~ **approach procedure** *n* AERONAUT procédure d'approche aux instruments *f*; ~ **approach runway** *n* AERONAUT piste avec approche aux instruments *f*; ~ **basin** *n* INSTRUMENT plateau d'instruments *m*; ~ **board** *n* INSTRUMENT tableau d'instruments *m*; ~ **cord** *n* TELECOM cordon flexible *m*; ~ **dial** *n* INSTRUMENT échelle graduée *f*; ~ **error** *n* INSTRUMENT erreur instrumentale *f*, MECH ENG erreur due à l'instrument *f*; ~ **flight** *n* TRANSP vol aux instruments *m*; ~ **flight rules** *n pl* AERONAUT règles de vol aux instruments *f pl*; ~ **flying** *n* AERONAUT vol aux instruments *m*; ~ **landing** *n* AERONAUT atterrissage aux instruments *m*; ~ **landing system** *n (ILS)* AERONAUT système d'atterrissage aux instruments *m*, système d'atterrissage radiogoniométrique *m*, SPACE *spacecraft*, TRANSP système d'atterrissage aux instruments *m*; ~ **lighting** *n* INSTRUMENT éclairage des instruments *m*; ~ **maker** *n* INSTRUMENT mécanicien de précision *m*; ~ **mounting plate** *n* INSTRUMENT plaque instrumentale *f*; ~ **panel** *n* AERONAUT, AUTO planche de bord *f*, tableau de bord *m*, NAUT, PROD ENG, VEHICLES *accessories* tableau de bord *m*; ~ **range** *n* INSTRUMENT étendue de mesure *f*; ~ **rating** *n* AERONAUT qualification de vol aux instruments *f*; ~ **shunt** *n* ELEC ENG shunt d'ampèremètre *m*; ~ **switch** *n* ELEC ENG commutateur d'appareil *m*; ~ **transformer** *n* ELEC réducteur de mesure *m*, transformateur de mesure *m*, ELEC ENG transformateur de mesure *m*

instrument[3] *vt* NAUT équiper d'instruments

instrumentation *n* COMP, DP instrumentation *f*, INSTRUMENT équipement d'instruments *m*; ~ **amplifier** *n*

ELECTRON amplificateur de mesure *m*

instruments *n pl* PETR TECH *drilling, refinery* instrumentation *f*

instrument-type: ~ **relay** *n* ELEC ENG relais galvanométrique *m*

insulant *n* REFRIG isolant *m*

insular[1] *adj* OCEANOG *arc* insulaire

insular:[2] ~ **shelf** *n* OCEANOG plate-forme insulaire *f*, socle insulaire *m*

insulate *vt* CONST, ELEC, PHYS, PROP MAT isoler

insulated[1] *adj* CONST, ELEC ENG isolé, REFRIG isolé, isotherme, SAFETY *tools* isolé; ~ **against heat** *adj* PROP MAT calorifuge

insulated:[2] ~ **body** *n* REFRIG *of refrigerated vehicle* caisse isolée *f*, caisse isotherme *f*; ~ **cable** *n* ELEC, ELEC ENG câble isolé *m*; ~ **conductor** *n* ELEC âme *f*, ELEC *of cable*, ELEC ENG conducteur isolé *m*, TELECOM fil isolé *m*; ~ **conduit** *n* ELEC *installation* tube isolant *m*; ~ **container** *n* TRANSP conteneur isotherme *m*; ~ **core** *n* ELEC *cable conductor* conducteur isolé *m*; ~ **gate FET** *n (IGFET)* ELECTRON TEC à grille isolée *m*; ~ **lorry** *n* REFRIG camion isolé *m*, camion isotherme *m*, THERMOD camion frigorifique *m*; ~ **openings** *n pl* REFRIG menuiseries isolantes *f pl*; ~ **rail** *n* RAIL *track* rail isolé *m*; ~ **tooling** *n pl* SAFETY outillage isolé *m pl*; ~ **tools** *n pl* SAFETY outils isolés *m pl*; ~ **truck** REFRIG camion isolé *m*, camion isotherme *m*, *of railway carriage* wagon isolé *m*, wagon isotherme *m*, THERMOD camion frigorifique *m*; ~ **wire** *n* ELEC ENG fil isolé *m*

insulating[1] *adj* ELEC ENG isolant, PROP MAT isolant, isolateur, REFRIG isolant

insulating:[2] ~ **board** *n* ELEC carton comprimé *m*, presspahn *m*, HEAT ENG carton isolant *m*, PACKAGING panneau isolant *m*; ~ **brick** *n* HEAT ENG brique isolante *f*; ~ **cement** *n* REFRIG ciment isolant *m*; ~ **compound** *n* ELEC ENG matière isolante *f*, PACKAGING pâte isolante *f*; ~ **cover** *n* PROD ENG capot isolant *m*; ~ **covering** *n* ELEC ENG enveloppe isolante *f*; ~ **film** *n* COATINGS film isolant *m*, PROP MAT pellicule isolante *f*; ~ **fishplate** *n* (BrE) *(cf insulating joint bar)* RAIL éclisse isolante *f*; ~ **glass for fire protection** *n* SAFETY verre isolant de protection contre le feu *m*; ~ **gloves** *n pl* SAFETY gants isolants *m pl*; ~ **jacketing** *n* PROD ENG enveloppe calorifuge *f*; ~ **joint** *n* ELEC ENG manchon isolant *m*; ~ **joint bar** *n* (AmE) *(cf insulating fishplate)* RAIL éclisse isolante *f*; ~ **lacquer** *n* COATINGS vernis d'émaillage *m*; ~ **lagging** *n* PROD ENG *nonconductive to heat* enveloppe calorifuge *f*; ~ **layer** *n* COATINGS, ELEC ENG, PACKAGING couche isolante *f*; ~ **mastic** *n* REFRIG mastic isolant *m*; ~ **mat** *n* ELEC *insulator* tapis isolant *m*; ~ **material** *n* CONST matériau isolant *m*, *building* isolant thermique *m*, ELEC ENG corps isolant *m*, matière isolante *f*, MECH matériau isolant *m*, PACKAGING matériel isolant *m*; ~ **oil** *n* ELEC, ELEC ENG, PETR TECH huile isolante *f*; ~ **paper** *n* ELEC, PAPER TECH papier isolant *m*; ~ **plate** *n* ELEC ENG plaque isolante *f*; ~ **properties** *n pl* PACKAGING propriétés isolantes *f pl*; ~ **sheath** *n* ELEC ENG gaine isolante *f*; ~ **sheet** *n* PACKAGING feuille isolante *f*; ~ **sleeve** *n* ELEC ENG manchon isolant *m*, PROD ENG gaine isolante *f*; ~ **substrate** *n* ELEC ENG, SPACE *spacecraft* substrat isolant *m*; ~ **tape** *n* ELEC, ELEC ENG ruban isolant *m*; ~ **varnish** *n* COATINGS, ELEC vernis isolant *m*; ~ **wall panel** *n* CONST *building* vêture isolante *f*; ~ **washer** *n* ELEC, ELEC ENG disque isolant *m*; ~ **wax** *n* ELEC ENG cire isolante *f*

insulation *n* C&G isolation *f*, CONST, ELEC *of conductor* isolation *f*, isolement *m*, ELEC ENG *of conductor* isolation *f*, *of conductor* isolement *m*, MECH *materials*, NAUT, P&R *heat, electricity*, PHYS, PROP MAT, REFRIG, SAFETY *against sound, vibration* isolation *f*, TELECOM isolant *m*, isolation *f*, isolement *m*; ~ **against heat and cold** *n* NAUT isolation thermique *f*, SAFETY isolation contre la chaleur et le froid *f*; ~ **against heat gain** *n* THERMOD calorifugeage frigorifique *m*; ~ **against heat loss** *n* THERMOD calorifugeage *m*; ~ **breakdown** *n* ELEC rupture d'isolation *f*, ELEC ENG claquage de l'isolant *m*; ~ **bush** *n* MECH ENG *for welding equipment* bague isolante *f*; ~ **cap** *n* MECH ENG capuchon isolant *m*; ~ **class** *n* ELEC classe d'isolation *f*; ~ **defect** *n* ELEC ENG défaut d'isolement *m*; ~ **distance** *n* ELEC ENG distance d'isolement *f*; ~ **finish** *n* REFRIG enduit pour isolation *m*; ~ **pipe** *n* MECH ENG tuyau isolant *m*; ~ **resistance** *n* ELEC ENG, PHYS résistance d'isolement *f*; ~ **screen** *n* ELEC *of cable conductor* écran sur enveloppe isolante *m*; ~ **tester** *n* CONTROL contrôleur d'isolement *m*, ELEC mesureur d'isolation *m*; ~ **withstand voltage** *n* ELEC, PROD ENG tension d'isolement *f*

insulator *n* CHEM, CONST isolant *m*, ELEC isolant *m*, isolateur *n*, ELEC ENG isolant *m*, *separating two conductors* isolateur *m*, PHYS isolant *m*, PROD ENG *device* isolateur *m*, *material* isolant *m*, TELECOM isolant *m*; ~ **cap** *n* ELEC capot d'isolateur *m*; ~ **clamp** *n* ELEC ENG agrafe d'isolateur *f*; ~ **pin** *n* PROD ENG ferrure d'isolateur *f*

insulin *n* CHEM insuline *f*

insweep *n* C&G jable *m*

intact: ~ **stability** *n* NAUT *ship design* stabilité à l'état intact *f*

intaglio *n* C&G taille-gravure *f*, PRINT taille-douce *f*; ~ **cylinder** *n* PRINT cylindre de taille-douce *m*; ~ **printing** *n* PACKAGING, PRINT impression en taille-douce *f*

intake *n* AERONAUT *of engine* admission *f*, HYDR EQUIP *of steam* prise de vapeur *f*, HYDROL marécage *m*, prise d'eau *f*, MECH orifice d'admission *m*, orifice d'aspiration *m*, MECH ENG admission *f*, appel *m*, prise *f*, aspiration *f*, entrée *f*, *ear of fan, of centrifugal pump* oeillard *m*, ouïe *f*, WATER SUPP canal de prise d'eau *m*; ~ **airway** *n* COAL TECH voie d'entrée d'air *f*; ~ **canal** *n* WATER SUPP canal d'amenée *m*; ~ **chamber** *n* HYDROL bassin de dégrossissage *m*; ~ **guide vane** *n* AERONAUT aube de guidance *f*, aube de prérotation *f*, aube directrice *f*, aube directrice d'entrée *f*; ~ **guide vane ram** *n* AERONAUT vérin des aubes de guidage *m*; ~ **manifold** *n* (AmE) (*cf inlet manifold*) AERONAUT *of engine* collecteur d'admission *m*, AUTO tubulure d'admission *f*, MECH *vehicles* collecteur d'admission *m*, MECH ENG collecteur d'entrée *m*, VEHICLES *of engine* collecteur d'admission *m*; ~ **port** *n* (AmE) (*cf inlet port*) AUTO orifice d'admission *m*, C&G brûleur côté feu *m*, VEHICLES *engine* lumière d'admission *f*, orifice d'admission *m*; ~ **shaft** *n* MINING puits d'appel *m*, puits d'appel d'air *m*, puits d'entrée *m*, puits d'entrée d'air *m*, puits de refoulement d'air *m*; ~ **sluice** *n* WATER SUPP écluse de prise *f*; ~ **structure** *n* WATER SUPP ouvrage de prise d'eau *m*; ~ **system** *n* MECH ENG *for fluid* système d'entrée *m*; ~ **tower** *n* HYDROL *of reservoir* tour de prise d'eau *f*; ~ **valve** *n* HYDR EQUIP soupape d'admission *f*, PRINT soupape d'admission *f*, vanne d'admission *f*

integer *n* DP, MATH entier *m*; ~ **type** *n* COMP, DP type entier *m*

integral[1] *adj* MECH ENG solidaire

integral[2] *n* MATH *of function* intégrale *f*; ~ **action regula-**

tor *n* CONTROL régulateur à action intégrale *m*; ~ **aluminium foil forming plant** *n* (BrE) PROD ENG installation de formage de feuille d'aluminium intégrée *f*; ~ **aluminum foil forming plant** *n* (AmE) *see integral aluminium foil forming plant* ~ **control** *n* CONTROL contrôle intégral *m*; ~ **injection** *n* AUTO injection directe *f*; ~ **power supply** *n* PROD ENG alimentation intégrée *f*; ~ **reinforced handle** *n* PACKAGING poignée renforcée intégrée *f*; ~ **runner** *n* FUELLESS *turbines* roue à auges intégrales *f*; ~ **sampling** *n* TELECOM échantillonnage intégral *m*; ~ **spin** *n* PHYS spin entier *m*; ~ **tank** *n* MECH ENG *aeronautical* réservoir intégré *m*; ~ **tripack** *n* CINEMAT émulsion multicouche *f*; ~ **water management** *n* WATER SUPP gestion intégrale des eaux *f*

integrally: ~ **cast** *adj* MECH *materials* venu de fonderie

integral-way: ~ **columns** *n pl* MECH ENG *machine tools* montants à glissière incorporée *m pl*

integrate *vt* COMP, DP intégrer

integrated[1] *adj* ELECTRON intégré; ~ **safety** *adj* SPACE à sécurité intégrée

integrated:[2] ~ **access** *n* TELECOM accès intégré *m*; ~ **bipolar transistor** *n* ELECTRON transistor bipolaire intégré *m*; ~ **capacitor** *n* ELEC ENG condensateur intégré *m*; ~ **charge** *n* ELEC ENG charge accumulée *f*; ~ **circuit** *n* (*IC*) COMP, ELEC, ELECTRON, PHYS, TELECOM, TV circuit intégré *m* (*CI*); ~ **circuit connection** *n* ELEC ENG connexion de circuit intégré *f*; ~ **circuit design** *n* ELECTRON conception des circuits intégrés *f*; ~ **circuit element** *n* ELECTRON élément de circuit intégré *m*; ~ **circuit fabrication** *n* ELECTRON fabrication de circuits intégrés *f*; ~ **circuit layout** *n* ELECTRON dessin des circuits intégrés *m*; ~ **circuit mask** *n* ELECTRON masque pour circuits intégrés *m*; ~ **circuit package** *n* ELECTRON boîtier de circuit intégré *m*; ~ **circuitry** *n* ELECTRON circuit sous forme intégrée *m*; ~ **circuit substrate** *n* ELECTRON substrat de circuit intégré *m*; ~ **circuit wafer** *n* ELECTRON plaquette de circuits intégrés *f*; ~ **data processing** *n* (*IDP*) DP traitement intégré de l'information *m*, traitement intégré des données *m*; ~ **digital exchange** *n* TELECOM système de commutation MIC intégrée *m*, système de commutation intégrée *m*; ~ **digital network** *n* (*IDN*) TELECOM réseau numérique intégré *m* (*RNI*); ~ **digital services exchange** *n* TELECOM centre RNIS *m*; ~ **filter** *n* ELECTRON filtre intégré *m*; ~ **function** *n* ELECTRON fonction intégrée *f*; ~ **home system** *n* (*IHS*) COMP domotique *f*; ~ **hybrid component** *n* ELECTRON composant hybride intégré *m*; ~ **hybrid resistor** *n* ELEC ENG résistance hybride intégrée *f*; ~ **injection logic** *n* (*IL*) ELECTRON logique intégrée à injection *f* (*IL*); ~ **logic circuit** *n* ELECTRON circuit logique intégré *m*; ~ **logic gate** *n* ELECTRON porte logique intégrée *f*; ~ **modem** *n* COMP modem intégré *m*; ~ **MOS transistor** *n* ELECTRON transistor MOS intégré *m*; ~ **office system** *n* COMP (*IOS*) bureautique intégrée *f*, système BI *m*, TELECOM circuit intégré logique *m*, système bureautique intégré *m*; ~ **optical circuit** *n* (*IOC*) OPT, TELECOM circuit d'optique intégré *m*, circuit intégré optique *m*; ~ **optical switch** *n* TELECOM commutateur optique intégré *m*; ~ **optical switching matrix** *n* TELECOM matrice de commutation optique intégrée *f*; ~ **optoelectronic circuit** *n* TELECOM circuit optoélectronique intégré *m*; ~ **services digital network** *n* (*ISDN*) TELECOM réseau numérique à intégration des services *m* (*RNIS*); ~ **services exchange** *n* TELECOM autocommutateur numérique à intégration de services *m*; ~ **services PABX** *n* TELECOM PABX à intégration de services *m*; ~ **system** *n* TELECOM système intégré *m*; ~ **tank** *n* TRANSP *of methane carrier* cuve intégrée *f*; ~ **transit time** *n (ITT)* PETR TECH *seismic survey* intégration du temps de trajet *f*; ~ **voice-data PABX** *n* TELECOM autocommutateur privé voix-données *m*; ~ **voice-data switch** *n* TELECOM autocommutateur à intégration voix-données *m*; ~ **weapon system** *n* AERONAUT système d'armes intégré *m*

integrating: ~ **capacitor** *n* ELEC ENG condensateur d'intégration *m*, condensateur intégrateur *m*; ~ **circuit** *n* ELEC ENG circuit intégrateur *m*, intégrateur *m*, montage intégrateur *m*; ~ **flowmeter** *n* AERONAUT débitmètre totaliseur *m*; ~ **meter** *n* ELEC ENG compteur d'énergie *m*; ~ **network** *n* AERONAUT réseau d'intégration *m*

integration *n* ELECTRON, MATH, SPACE *of satellite*, TELECOM intégration *f*; ~ **density** *n* ELECTRON densité d'intégration *f*; ~ **gain** *n* ELECTRON gain d'intégration *m*; ~ **model** *n* SPACE *trials* modèle d'intégration *m*; ~ **period** *n* ELEC ENG période d'intégration *f*; ~ **time** *n* ELEC ENG, ELECTRON temps d'intégration *m*

integrator *n* CHEM, ELEC ENG, ELECTRON, TRANSP intégrateur *m*; ~ **amplifier** *n* AERONAUT amplificateur d'intégration *m*

integrity *n* COMP, DP, TELECOM intégrité *f*

intellectual: ~ **property** *n* PATENTS propriété intellectuelle *f*

intelligent[1] *adj* COMP, DP intelligent

intelligent:[2] ~ **labeling machine** *n* (AmE), ~ **labelling machine** *n* (BrE) PACKAGING étiqueteuse intelligente *f*; ~ **terminal** *n* COMP, DP terminal intelligent *m*

intelligibility *n* ACOUSTICS, RECORDING intelligibilité *f*; ~ **index** *n* ACOUSTICS indice d'intelligibilité *m*

Intelsat: ~ **Operations Center** *n (IOS)* SPACE *communications* Centre d'exploitation intelsat *m*

intended: ~ **flight path** *n* AERONAUT trajectoire de vol prévue *f*

intense: ~ **light** *n* WAVE PHYS lumière intense *f*

intensification *n* ELECTRON intensification *f*, PHOTO renforcement *m*, renforçage *m*

intensifier *n* HYDR EQUIP multiplicateur de pression *m*; ~ **electrode** *n* TV électrode postaccélératrice *f*; ~ **ring** *n* TV anneau postaccélérateur *m*; ~ **tube** *n* ELECTRON tube intensificateur *m*; ~ **vidicon** *n* ELECTRON vidicon intensificateur *m*

intensify *vt* ELECTRON intensifier

intensity *n* CHEM, ELEC *of current, electromagnetic field*, ELECTRON, GAS TECH intensité *f*, OPT *equivalent of irradiance* éclairement *m*, *proportional to irradiance* intensité *f*; ~ **distribution** *n* CRYSTALL distribution d'intensité *f*, RAD PHYS *spectrography* répartition d'intensité *f*; ~ **level** *n* ELEC ENG niveau d'intensité *m*; ~ **of light** *n* RAD PHYS intensité de lumière *f*; ~ **modulation** *n* ELECTRON modulation d'intensité *f*; ~ **spectrum level** *n* RECORDING niveau de spectre d'intensité *m*

intensive: ~ **projector** *n* ELEC *lighting* projecteur convergent *m*; ~ **quantity** *n* PHYS grandeur intensive *f*

intentional: ~ **discharge** *n* MAR POLL, POLLUTION rejet intentionnel *m*

interact *vi* CHEM, RAD PHYS interagir

interaction *n* CHEM, COMP, DP interaction *f*, MECH ENG réaction *f*, METALL interaction *f*; ~ **energy** *n* METALL énergie d'interaction *f*; ~ **gap** *n* ELECTRON espace d'interaction *m*; ~ **space** *n* ELECTRON *of crossed field tubes* espace d'interaction *m*

interactive[1] *adj* COMP interactif, DP conversationnel, interactif

interactive:[2] ~ **compact disc** *n* (BrE) OPT disque compact interactif *m*; ~ **compact disk** *n* (AmE) *see interactive compact disc*; ~ **disc** *n* (BrE) OPT disque interactif *m*; ~ **disk** *n* (AmE) *see interactive disc*; ~ **graphics** *n* DP infographie interactive *f*; ~ **media** *n pl* COMP moyens de communication interactifs *m pl*; ~ **mode** *n* COMP, DP mode interactif *m*; ~ **network** *n* TELECOM réseau interactif *m*; ~ **primary link** *n (IPL)* TELECOM liaison primaire pour les services interactifs *f*; ~ **system** *n* TELECOM système interactif *m*; ~ **television** *n* TV télévision interactive *f*; ~ **terminal** *n* TELECOM borne interactive *f*; ~ **videodisc** *n* (BrE) OPT vidéodisque interactif *m*; ~ **videodisk** *n* (AmE) *see interactive videodisc*; ~ **videography** *n* TELECOM *videotext* vidéographie interactive *f*; ~ **videotex** *n* TELECOM vidéotex interactif *m*

interatomic[1] *adj* CRYSTALL *distance* interatomique

interatomic:[2] ~ **forces** *n pl* RAD PHYS forces interatomiques *f pl*

interblock: ~ **gap** *n* COMP espace entre blocs *m*, espace interbloc *m*, DP interconnexion *f*

intercell: ~ **hand-off** *n* TELECOM *land mobile* transfert entre les cellules *m*; ~ **switching** *n* TELECOM *land mobile* commutation des voies entre cellules *f*

intercept *n* GEOM, SPACE interception *f*; ~ **announcer** *n* TELECOM guide parlant *m*; ~ **bearing** *n* AERONAUT gisement d'interception *m*; ~ **point** *n* SPACE point d'interception *m*

interception: ~ **equipment** *n* TELECOM équipement d'interception *m*

interceptor: ~ **sewer** *n* HYDROL égout captant *m*

interchange *n* CONST *roads* raccordement *m*, échangeur *m*, RAIL correspondance *f*; ~ **control reference** *n* TELECOM référence de contrôle de l'échange *f*; ~ **date** *n* TELECOM date d'échange *f*; ~ **header** *n* TELECOM en-tête d'échange *m*; ~ **receiver identification** *n* TELECOM identification du destinataire de l'échange *f*; ~ **recipient** *n* TELECOM destinataire de l'échange *m*; ~ **sender** *n* TELECOM expéditeur de l'échange *m*; ~ **sender identification** *n* TELECOM identification de l'expéditeur de l'échange *f*; ~ **time** *n* TELECOM heure de l'échange *f*; ~ **track** *n* RAIL voie d'échange *f*

interchangeability *n* MECH ENG interchangeabilité *f*

interchangeable[1] *adj* MECH ENG amovible, PHOTO interchangeable

interchangeable:[2] ~ **focusing screen** *n* PHOTO verre de visée interchangeable *m*; ~ **lens** *n* INSTRUMENT, PHOTO objectif interchangeable *m*; ~ **objectives** *n pl* INSTRUMENT objectifs interchangeables *m pl*; ~ **part** *n* MECH ENG pièce permutable *f*; ~ **waist-level finder** *n* PHOTO capuchon de visée interchangeable *m*

interchannel: ~ **interference** *n* ELEC ENG interférence entre fréquences d'émissions *f*; ~ **time difference** *n* RECORDING différence de temps entre canaux *f*

interchip: ~ **signal delay** *n* ELECTRON temps de propagation des signaux entre boîtiers *m*, temps de propagation entre boîtiers *m*

intercircuit: ~ **signal delay** *n* ELECTRON temps de propagation des signaux entre circuits *m*, temps de propagation entre circuits *m*

intercity: ~ **air service** *n* AERONAUT service aérien interurbain *m*; ~ **train** *n* TRANSP train interurbain *m*, train interville *m*; ~ **transport** *n* TRANSP transport interurbain *m*

intercom *n* RECORDING, TELECOM interphone *m*; ~ **microphone** *n* CINEMAT microphone d'ordre *m*

interconnected: ~ **controls** *n pl* AERONAUT commandes conjuguées *f pl*; ~ **network** *n* ELEC réseau interconnecté *m*; ~ **systems** *n pl* ELEC réseau interconnecté *m*

interconnecting: ~ **cable** *n* CONST *electricity* câble de raccordement *m*; ~ **feeder** *n* ELEC *supply* artère d'interconnexion *f*; ~ **line** *n* ELEC *supply* artère d'interconnexion *f*; ~ **pipework** *n* PROD ENG tuyauterie de raccordement *f*

interconnection *n* AERONAUT, COMP, DP, ELEC *systems*, ELEC ENG interconnexion *f*; ~ **cable** *n* ELEC ENG câble d'interconnexion *m*; ~ **layer** *n* ELECTRON couche d'interconnexions *f*; ~ **network** *n* TELECOM RI, réseau d'interconnexion *m*; ~ **topology** *n* COMP topologie des interconnexions *f*, DP topologie d'interconnexion *f*

intercooler *n* PROD ENG *of air compressor* réservoir réfrigérant intermédiaire *m*

intercutting *n* CINEMAT montage alterné *m*

interdiffusion *n* PROP MAT interdiffusion *f*

interdigital: ~ **capacitor** *n* PHYS condensateur interdigital *m*; ~ **line** *n* PHYS ligne interdigitale *f*; ~ **magnetron** *n* ELECTRON magnétron à ligne interdigitée *m*; ~ **transducer** *n (IDT)* TELECOM transducteur interdigital *m*

interdigitation *n* GEOL interdigitation *f*

interdupe *n* CINEMAT contre-type *m*

interelectrode: ~ **capacitance** *n* ELEC ENG capacité entre électrodes *f*

interexchange *adj* (BrE) *(cf interoffice)* TELECOM entre centraux

interface[1] *n* COMP interface *f*, jonction *f*, DP, ELECTRON, MECH ENG, METALL interface *f*, PETR surface de séparation *f*, PROP MAT, TELECOM interface *f*; ~ **boundary** *n* METALL limite interfaciale *f*; ~ **card** *n* ELECTRON carte d'interface *f*; ~ **chip** *n* ELECTRON puce d'interface *f*; ~ **circuit** *n* ELECTRON, TELECOM circuit d'interface *m*; ~ **energy** *n* METALL énergie interfaciale *f*; ~ **level** *n* MECH ENG niveau interfacial *m*; ~ **logic** *n* ELECTRON logique d'interface *f*; ~ **message processor** *n (IMP)* TELECOM serveur de message *m*; ~ **module** *n (IM)* TELECOM unité de raccordement *f*; ~ **requirement** *n* COMP, DP condition de liaison *f*; ~ **suppression** *n* PROD ENG antiparasitage d'interface *m*; ~ **unit** *n* COMP, DP interface *f*

interface[2] *vt* COMP interfacer, PROD ENG mettre en interface, SPACE interfacer

interfacial: ~ **angle** *n* CRYSTALL angle dièdre *m*, angle entre faces *m*; ~ **tension** *n* MAR POLL tension interfaciale *f*

interfacing *n* SPACE interfaçage *m*

interfere *vi* PHYS interférer

interference *n* ACOUSTICS, COMP, DP interférence *f*, ELEC *fault* parasite *m*, ELECTRON interférence *f*, parasites *m pl*, MECH ENG *gearing* arc-boutement *m*, OPT, PHYS, RECORDING interférence *f*, SPACE *communications* brouillage *m*, TELECOM brouillage *m*, interférence *f*, parasitage *m*, TV brouillage *m*, interférence *f*, parasites *m pl*, WAVE PHYS *from two close vibrating sources* interférence *f*; ~ **area** *n* TV zone de brouillage *f*; ~ **bands** *n pl* WAVE PHYS franges d'interférence *f pl*; ~ **color** *n* (AmE), ~ **colour** *n* (BrE) COLOURS couleur irisée *f*; ~ **eliminator** *n* TV filtre antiparasite *m*; ~ **figure** *n* CRYSTALL figure d'interférence *f*; ~ **filter** *n* ELEC *of circuit*, ELECTRON filtre antiparasite *m*, OPT, PHYS filtre interférentiel *m*, RECORDING filtre d'interférence *m*, SPACE *spacecraft*, TELECOM filtre interférentiel *m*, TV

filtre antiparasite *m*; ~ **fit** *n* MECH ENG ajustement avec serrage *m*; ~ **fringes** *n pl* PHYS, WAVE PHYS franges d'interférence *f pl*; ~ **generator** *n* ELECTRON générateur de parasites *m*; ~ **method** *n* MECH ENG *of measurement* méthode interférentielle *f*; ~ **microphone** *n* RECORDING microphone à interférence *m*; ~ **microscope** *n* INSTRUMENT, METALL, PHYS microscope interférentiel *m*; ~ **noise** *n* ELECTRON bruit dû aux parasites *m*, parasites industriels *m pl*, TESTING bruit dû aux brouillages *m*; ~ **pattern** *n* WAVE PHYS *of two waves combining* figure d'interférence *f*; ~ **reduction factor** *n* SPACE *communications* facteur de réduction du brouillage *m*; ~ **rejection** *n* ELECTRON atténuation des parasites *f*, réjection des parasites *f*, NAUT *radio, radar* élimination des interférences *f*; ~ **ripples** *n pl* GEOL rides d'interférence *f pl*; ~ **signal** *n* ELECTRON signal parasite *m*; ~ **suppression** *n* TELECOM antiparasitage *m*

interfering: ~ **signal** *n* ELECTRON signal perturbateur *m*, SPACE signal brouilleur *m*

interferometer *n* METR, OPT, PHYS, TELECOM interféromètre *m*

interfield: ~ **cut** *n* TV raccord pendant la suppression de trame *m*

interfingering *n* GEOL interdigitation *f*

interfoliated *adj* GEOL *metamorphic rocks* intercalé

interformational: ~ **conglomerate** *n* PETR conglomérat polygénique *m*

interframe: ~ **coding** *n* TELECOM codage intertrame *m*

intergalactic: ~ **medium** *n* ASTRON milieu intergalactique *m*

interglacial: ~ **phase** *n* GEOL épisode interglaciaire *m*; ~ **stage** *n* GEOL *interstadial* épisode interglaciaire *m*

intergranular[1] *adj* METALL, PROP MAT intergranulaire

intergranular:[2] ~ **fracture** *n* PROP MAT défaut intercristallin *m*, SPRINGS rupture intergranulaire *f*

intergrowth *n* GEOL *mineral texture* enchevêtrement *m*

interhalogen: ~ **compound** *n* CHEM composé inter-halogène *m*

interim: ~ **injunction** *n* PATENTS injonction provisoire *f*; ~ **orbit** *n* SPACE orbite d'attente *f*

interionic *adj* CHEM *distance* interionique

interior *n* VEHICLES *of car* habitacle *m*; ~ **angles** *n pl* GEOM angles intérieurs *m pl*; ~ **coating** *n* PACKAGING couche intérieure *f*; ~ **lining** *n* PACKAGING revêtement intérieur *m*; ~ **packaging** *n* PACKAGING emballage intérieur *m*; ~ **strengthening bar** *n* PACKAGING barre intérieure de renforcement *f*; ~ **wrapping** *n* PACKAGING enveloppe intérieure *f*

interlace:[1] ~ **sequence** *n* TV ordre d'entrelacement *m*

interlace[2] *vt* COMP, DP, ELECTRON entrelacer, TEXTILES entrecroiser

interlaced: ~ **scanning** *n* ELECTRON balayage entrelacé *m*, TV analyse entrelacée *f*, balayage entrelacé *m*

interlacing *n* TEXTILES entrecroisure *f*; ~ **and crimping** *n* TEXTILES entrecroisure et frisure *f*

interlayer *adj* PETR TECH *petroleum geology* interfoliaire

interleaf *n* PRINT intercalaire *m*

interleave *vt* COMP, DP, ELECTRON imbriquer

interleaved: ~ **transmission signal** *n* TV signal de transmission cocanalisée *m*

interleaving *n* COMP *nesting*, DP *nesting*, ELECTRON imbrication *f*, PAPER TECH *of one sheet between two others* intercalage *m*, TV cocanalisation *f*

interlimb: ~ **angle** *n* GEOL *of angle* angle entre flancs *m*

interline *vt* TEXTILES mettre une doublure intermédiaire à, mettre une doublure à

interlining *n* AERONAUT *air transport* échanges intercompagnies *m pl*, TEXTILES doublure intermédiaire *f*; ~ **material** *n* TEXTILES toile tailleur *f*

interlock[1] *n* AERONAUT verrouillage *m*, CINEMAT couplage *m*, interlock *m*, verrouillage *m*, COMP verrouillage *m*, *of channel* blocage *m*, CONTROL asservissement *m*, DP blocage *m*, verrouillage *m*, ELEC ENG enclenchement *m*, verrouillage *m*, PROD ENG entrebarre *f*, verrouillage *m*, TV asservissement *m*; ~ **circuit** *n* ELEC ENG circuit d'enclenchement *m*; ~ **contact** *n* ELEC ENG contact d'enclenchement *m*; ~ **control** *n* AERONAUT commande d'interdiction *f*; ~ **device** *n* CINEMAT système de verrouillage *m*; ~ **relay** *n* ELEC relais à verrouillage *m*, ELEC ENG relais d'enclenchement *m*; ~ **switch** *n* ELEC ENG commutateur d'enclenchement *m*

interlock[2] *vt* ELEC ENG verrouiller, MECH ENG enclencher

interlock[3] *vi* MECH ENG engrener, mordre, TEXTILES s'imbriquer

interlocked *adj* PROD ENG entrebarré

interlocking *n* AERONAUT enclenchement *m*, MECH verrouillage réciproque *m*, MECH ENG enclenchement *m*; ~ **guard** *n* SAFETY barrière à enclenchement *f*; ~ **milling cutter** *n* MECH ENG fraise composée *f*; ~ **relay** *n* ELEC relais à verrouillage *m*; ~ **system** *n* RECORDING système de verrouillage électrique *m*, SAFETY *mechanical, hydraulic, electric or pneumatic* système d'enclenchement *m*

interlocutory: ~ **injunction** *n* PATENTS injonction provisoire *f*

intermediate *n* PROP MAT produit intermédiaire *m*; ~ **approach** *n* AERONAUT approche intermédiaire *f*; ~ **approach fix** *n* AERONAUT repère d'approche intermédiaire *m*; ~ **approach point** *n* AERONAUT repère d'approche intermédiaire *m*; ~ **bulk container** *n* PACKAGING conteneur intermédiaire à pulvérents *m*; ~ **case** *n* AERONAUT carter intermédiaire *m*; ~ **chemical** *n* PETR TECH *refining* intermédiaire *m*, produit intermédiaire *m*; ~ **coat** *n* COATINGS couche intermédiaire *f*; ~ **design review** *n* SPACE revue de conception intermédiaire *f*; ~ **distribution frame** *n* (IDF) TELECOM répartiteur intermédiaire *m* (RI); ~ **exposure** *n* PRINT exposition intermédiaire *f*; ~ **frame** *n* TEXTILES banc à broches intermédiaires *m*; ~ **frequency** *n* (IF) ELECTRON, TELECOM fréquence intermédiaire *f* (FI); ~ **frequency amplification** *n* ELECTRON, TELECOM amplification à fréquence intermédiaire *f*; ~ **frequency amplifier** *n* ELECTRON amplificateur à fréquence intermédiaire *m*, NAUT *radio, radar* ampli FI *m*, TELECOM amplificateur à fréquence intermédiaire *m*; ~ **frequency filter** *n* ELECTRON, TELECOM filtre à fréquence intermédiaire *m*; ~ **frequency rejection** *n* ELECTRON, TELECOM atténuation à la fréquence intermédiaire *f*, réjection à la fréquence intermédiaire *f*; ~ **frequency signal** *n* ELECTRON, TELECOM, TV signal à fréquence intermédiaire *m*; ~ **frequency stage** *n* ELECTRON, TELECOM étage à fréquence intermédiaire *m*; ~ **gear** *n* MECH ENG engrenage de transmission *m*; ~ **gearbox** *n* AERONAUT *of helicopter* renvoi intermédiaire *m*; ~ **image** *n* PHYS image intermédiaire *f*; ~ **layer** *n* COATINGS couche intermédiaire *f*; ~ **lens** *n* INSTRUMENT lentille de diffraction *f*; ~ **multiple ringing** *n* TV suroscillation *f*; ~ **negative** *n* CINEMAT contretype négatif *m*; ~ **positive** *n* CINEMAT interpositif *m*, positif intermédiaire *m*; ~ **pressure cylinder** *n* HYDR EQUIP cylindre intermédiaire de machine à vapeur *m*, cylindre à moyenne

pression *m*; ~ **reversal negative** *n* CINEMAT internégatif *m*; ~ **rock** *n* GEOL roche de type intermédiaire *f*; ~ **satellite band** *n* TELECOM bande intermédiaire satellite *f*; ~ **sealing glass** *n* (BrE) *(cf solder glass)* C&G verre intermédiaire *m*; ~ **shaft** *n* MECH ENG arbre secondaire *m*, axe secondaire *m*; ~ **steam engine cylinder** *n* HYDR EQUIP cylindre intermédiaire de machine à vapeur *m*, cylindre à moyenne pression *m*; ~ **storage** *n* COMP mémoire intermédiaire *f*; ~ **system** *n* (IS) TELECOM système intermédiaire *m*; ~ **trunk** *n* (IT) TELECOM canal interurbain intermédiaire *m*; ~ **type of soil** *n* COAL TECH sol moyen *m*; ~ **vector boson** *n* PHYS vecteur boson intermédiaire *m*; ~ **voltage winding** *n* ELEC enroulement à tension intermédiaire *m*; ~ **water level** *n* WATER SUPP niveau d'eau intermédiaire *m*; ~ **waters** *n pl* OCEANOG eaux intermédiaires *f pl*; ~ **wheel** *n* MECH ENG *in gearing* roue intermédiaire *f*, roue parasite *f*

intermediate-image: ~ **screen** *n* INSTRUMENT fenêtre d'observation de la première image *f*, viseur de la première image *m*

intermeshed: ~ **loops** *n pl* TEXTILES boucles entrecroisées *f pl*

intermetallic: ~ **composite** *n* PROP MAT composite intermétallique *m*; ~ **compound** *n* METALL, PROP MAT composé intermétallique *m*; ~ **matrix** *n* PROP MAT matrice intermétallique *f*; ~ **phase** *n* PROP MAT phase intermétallique *f*; ~ **precipitate** *n* PROP MAT précipité intermétallique *m*

intermingled: ~ **yarn** *n* TEXTILES fil texturé par assemblage *m*

intermittent: ~ **agitation** *n* PHOTO agitation effectuée par intervalles *f*; ~ **board machine** *n* PAPER TECH enrouleuse pour carton *f*; ~ **claw** *n* CINEMAT griffe d'entraînement *f*; ~ **contact printer** *n* CINEMAT tireuse par contact image par image *f*; ~ **duty** *n* ELEC *of equipment* service intermittent *m*; ~ **fault** *n* ELEC défaut intermittent *m*; ~ **flow** *n* HYDROL écoulement non permanent *m*; ~ **light** *n* CINEMAT lumière pulsée *f*; ~ **load** *n* ELEC *of generator* charge intermittente *f*; ~ **noise** *n* ACOUSTICS bruit intermittent *m*; ~ **prism** *n* CINEMAT prisme rotatif *m*; ~ **production** *n* PROD ENG production discontinue *f*, production par sections homogènes *f*; ~ **signal** *n* CONTROL signal clignotant *m*; ~ **spring** *n* WATER SUPP source intermittente *f*

intermodal: ~ **container** *n* TRANSP conteneur multimodal *m*; ~ **distortion** *n* TELECOM distorsion modale *f*; ~ **traffic** *n* RAIL *vehicles* trafic intermodal *m*; ~ **transport** *n* REFRIG transport combiné *m*

intermodulation *n* ELECTRON, RECORDING, SPACE *communications*, TELECOM intermodulation *f*, TV intermodulation *f*, transmodulation *f*; ~ **distortion** *n* ELECTRON, RECORDING distorsion d'intermodulation *f*; ~ **noise** *n* SPACE *communications* bruit d'intermodulation *m*; ~ **product** *n* ELECTRON, SPACE *communications*, TELECOM produit d'intermodulation *m*

intermolecular[1] *adj* CHEM intermoléculaire

intermolecular:[2] ~ **bond** *n* PROP MAT liaison intermoléculaire *f*

intermount: ~ **basin** *n* GEOL bassin structural *m*, cuvette *f*

internal: ~ **angle** *n* GEOM angle interne *m*; ~ **battery** *n* ELEC ENG pile incorporée *f*; ~ **blocking** *n* TELECOM blocage interne *m*; ~ **breakdown** *n* REFRIG dégradation interne *f*; ~ **burner** *n* C&G brûleur à combustion interne *m*; ~ **caliper gage** *n* (AmE), ~ **calliper gauge** *n* (BrE) MECH

ENG calibre mâle *m*, calibre simple *m*; ~ **chamfer** *n* SPRINGS chanfrein interne *m*; ~ **clock** *n* TELECOM horloge interne *f*; ~ **coil** *n* TESTING bobine encerclée de matériau à essayer *f*; ~ **combustion engine** *n* AUTO, ELEC ENG, MECH moteur à combustion interne *m*, MECH ENG moteur à explosion *m*, PETR TECH, PROD ENG, TRANSP, VEHICLES moteur à combustion interne *m*; ~ **conversion** *n* PHYS *nuclear* conversion interne *f*; ~ **crack** *n* METALL fissure interne *f*; ~ **cylindrical gage** *n* (AmE), ~ **cylindrical gauge** *n* (BrE) MECH ENG bouchon *m*, calibre à bouchon *m*, tampon *m*; ~ **damping** *n* AERONAUT amortissement interne *m*; ~ **defrosting** *n* REFRIG dégivrage par l'intérieur *m*; ~ **delivery slip** *n* PROD ENG bordereau de livraison *m*; ~ **demand** *n* PROD ENG demande interne *f*; ~ **diagnostic test** *n* PROD ENG test de diagnostic interne *m*; ~ **diameter** *n* PROD ENG *of pipe* diamètre intérieur *m*; ~ **energy** *n* PHYS, RAD PHYS *thermodynamics* énergie interne *f*; ~ **erosion** *n* COAL TECH érosion interne *f*; ~ **expanding brake** *n* MECH ENG frein à dilatation interne *m*; ~ **extension** *n* TELECOM poste intérieur *m*; ~ **friction** *n* C&G frottement interne *m*, MECH ENG frottement intérieur *m*, METALL frottement interne *m*, PROP MAT frottement interne *m*, frottement intérieur *m*; ~ **gain** *n* ELECTRON gain interne *m*; ~ **gas pressure cable** *n* ELEC câble à pression interne de gaz *m*; ~ **gear** *n* AUTO denture intérieure *f*, MECH ENG engrenage intérieur *m*; ~ **graticule** *n* ELECTRON graticule intérieur *m*; ~ **grinder** *n* MECH ENG machine à rectifier les surfaces intérieures *f*; ~ **grinding** *n* MECH ENG *machine tools* rectification intérieure *f*; ~ **grinding wheel** *n* PROD ENG meule aléseuse *f*; ~ **input signal** *n* TELECOM signal d'entrée interne *m*; ~ **installation** *n* ELEC ENG montage interne *m*; ~ **lacquering** *n* PACKAGING vernissage intérieur *m*; ~ **logic signal** *n* PROD ENG signal de la logique interne *m*; ~ **magnetosphere** *n* GEOPHYS magnétosphère interne *f*; ~ **memory** *n* COMP, ELEC ENG mémoire interne *f*; ~ **micrometer** *n* MECH ENG calibre à tige coulissante et vis micrométrique *m*, palmer d'intérieur *m*; ~ **mirror lamp** *n* CINEMAT lampe à réflecteur incorporé *f*; ~ **noise** *n* ELECTRON bruit interne *m*, bruit propre *m*; ~ **oxidation** *n* METALL oxydation interne *f*; ~ **photoelectric effect** *n* ELECTRON, OPT, TELECOM effet photoélectrique interne *m*; ~ **plasticizer** *n* P&R *compounding ingredient* plastifiant intérieur *m*; ~ **pole dynamo** *n* ELEC *generator* alternateur à pôles intérieurs *m*; ~ **pole generator** *n* ELEC alternateur à pôles intérieurs *m*; ~ **pressure** *n* WATER SUPP pression intérieure *f*; ~ **priority** *n* PROD ENG priorité interne *f*; ~ **program error flag** *n* (AmE), ~ **programme error flag** *n* (BrE) PROD ENG indicateur d'erreur de programme *m*; ~ **reference point** *n* (IRP) TELECOM point de référence interne *m*; ~ **reflection** *n* RAD PHYS réflexion interne *f*; ~ **resistance** *n* ELEC *cell* résistance interne *f*; ~ **scour** *n* COAL TECH érosion interne *f*; ~ **screw** *n* C&G bague à pas de vis intérieur *f*, PROD ENG vis femelle *f*; ~ **setup** *n* PROD ENG préparation avec immobilisation *f*, préparation interne *f*, réglage avec immobilisation *m*, réglage interne *m*; ~ **shaft** *n* MINING beurtia *m*, bure *m*, puits intérieur *m*; ~ **shield** *n* ELECTRON armature interne *f*, blindage interne *m*, écran interne *m*; ~ **sort** *n* COMP tri interne *m*; ~ **source** *n* POLLUTION source intérieure *f*; ~ **storage** *n* (AmE) *(cf internal store)* COMP, PROD ENG mémoire interne *f*; ~ **store** *n* (BrE) *(cf internal storage)* COMP mémoire interne *f*; ~ **stress** *n* METALL contrainte interne *f*; ~ **structure** *n* PART PHYS *of proton* structure interne *f*; ~ **temperature** *n* PACKAGING température intérieure *f*; ~ **thread fastener** *n* MECH ENG élément de fixation fileté femelle *m*; ~ **timing mechanism** *n* PROD ENG mécanisme de temporisation interne *m*; ~ **traffic** *n* TELECOM trafic interne *m*; ~ **waters** *n* OCEANOG eaux intérieures *f pl*; ~ **wave** *n* OCEANOG onde interne *f*; ~ **wheel case** *n* AERONAUT carter interne *m*; ~ **wiring** *n* TELECOM câblage intérieur *m*

international: ~ **airport** *n* AERONAUT aéroport international *m*; ~ **air route** *n* AERONAUT route aérienne internationale *f*; ~ **application** *n* PATENTS demande internationale *f*; ~ **data switching exchange** *n* (IDSE) TELECOM centre international de commutation de données *m*; ~ **date line** *n* NAUT ligne de changement de date *f*; ~ **gateway exchange** *n* TELECOM commutateur de transit international *m*; ~ **gateway node** *n* (IGN) TELECOM noeud de transit international *m* (NTI); ~ **hydrological program** *n* (AmE), ~ **hydrological programme** *n* (BrE) WATER SUPP programme hydrologique international *m*; ~ **operations service** *n* TELECOM service d'exploitation internationale *m*; ~ **packet-switched data network** *n* TELECOM réseau international de transmission par paquets *m*; ~ **packet-switching gateway exchange** *n* TELECOM noeud de transit international *m*; ~ **referral system** *n* (IRS) POLLUTION système international de référence *m*; ~ **registration** *n* PATENTS enregistrement international *m*; ~ **searching authority** *n* PATENTS administration chargée de la recherche internationale *f*; ~ **signaling control part** *n* (AmE), ~ **signalling control part** *n* (BrE) (ISCP) TELECOM sous-système de contrôle de signalisation *m*; ~ **soundtrack** *n* CINEMAT bande son internationale *f*; ~ **standard** *n* CONST norme internationale *f*; ~ **standard thread** *n* MECH ENG pas système international *m*; ~ **switching center** *n* (AmE), ~ **switching centre** *n* (BrE) (ISC) TELECOM centre de commutation international *m*, centre international automatique *m*; ~ **system of units** *n* (SI) METR système international d'unités *m* (SI); ~ **telegraph alphabet** *n* AERONAUT alphabet télégraphique international *m*; ~ **transit exchange** *n* (INTTR) TELECOM commutateur de transit international *m*; ~ **unit** *n* ELEC unité internationale *f*; ~ **waters** *n pl* NAUT *sea areas* eaux internationales *f pl*

International: ~ **Atomic Time** *n* (IAT) ASTRON Temps Atomique International *m*; ~ **Commission on Illumination** *n* PHYS *CIE* CIE *f*, Commission internationale de l'éclairage *f*; ~ **Commission on Radiological Protection** *n* (ICRP) RAD PHYS Commission internationale pour la protection radiologique *f*; ~ **Direct Dialing** *n* (AmE) (IDD) TELECOM Automatique International *m*; ~ **Direct Distance Dialing** *n* (AmE) (IDDD, *International Subscriber Dialling*) TELECOM Automatique International *m*; ~ **Fisheries Organization** *n* OCEANOG Organisation internationale de pêche *f*; ~ **Frequency Registration Board** *n* (IFRB) SPACE *communications* Comité international d'enregistrement des fréquences *m*; ~ **Maritime Organization** *n* (IMO) NAUT *official body* Organisation maritime internationale *f* (OMI); ~ **Radio Consultative Committee** *n* (CCIR) TELECOM Comité consultatif international des radiocommunications *m* (CCIR); ~ **Register of Potentially Toxic Chemicals** *n* (IRPTC) POLLUTION Registre international des substances potentiellement toxiques *m* (RISCPT); ~ **Sea Bed Area** *n* OCEANOG Zone internationale des fonds marins *f*; ~ **Sea Bed Authority** *n* OCEANOG Autorité internationale des fonds marins *f*; ~ **Standards Organization** *n (ISO)* MECH ENG, TELE-COM Organisation internationale de normalisation *f* *(ISO)*; ~ **Subscriber Dialling** *n* (BrE) *(ISD, International Direct Distance Dialing)* TELECOM Automatique International *m*; ~ **Telecommunication Union** *n* TELECOM *official body* Union internationale des télécommunications *f*; ~ **Telegraph and Telephone Consultative Committee** *n (CCITT)* TELECOM Comité consultatif international télégraphique et téléphonique *m (CCITT)*; ~ **Transit Centre** *n* SPACE *communications* Centre de transit international *m*; ~ **Ultraviolet Explorer Satellite** *n (IUE)* ASTRON Satellite Explorer pour l'étude dans l'ultraviolet *m*, Satellite international ultraviolet Explorer *m*

internegative *n* CINEMAT internégatif *m*, PRINT négatif réalisé par contact *m*

Internet *n* TELECOM Internet *m*

internetting *n* COMP, DP interconnexion de réseaux *f*

internides *n pl* GEOL zones internes *f pl*

interocean: ~ **channel** *n* OCEANOG canal interocéanique *m*, canal maritime *m*

interoffice *adj* (AmE) *(cf interexchange)* TELECOM entre centraux

interoperation: ~ **time** *n* PROD ENG temps interopération *m*

interoperative: ~ **time** *n* PROD ENG temps interopératoire *m*

inter-PABX: ~ **tie circuit** *n* TELECOM ligne de jonction *f* (Can), ligne interautomatique *f*

interparticle: ~ **spacing** *n* METALL distance interparticulaire *f*

interpenetration: ~ **twin** *n* CRYSTALL macle par pénétration *f*

interpersonal: ~ **messaging system** *n* TELECOM système de messagerie interpersonnelle *m*

interphase: ~ **short circuit** *n* ELEC court-circuit entre phases *m*

interpile: ~ **sheeting** *n* COAL TECH blindage entre pieux *m*

interplanetary[1] *adj* SPACE interplanétaire

interplanetary:[2] ~ **dust** *n* ASTRON poussières interplanétaires *f pl*; ~ **flight** *n* SPACE vol interplanétaire *m*; ~ **gas** *n* ASTRON gaz interplanétaire *m*; ~ **medium** *n* ASTRON milieu interplanétaire *m*; ~ **mission** *n* SPACE mission interplanétaire *f*; ~ **monitoring platform** *n (IMP)* AS-TRON plate-forme d'observation interplanétaire *f*; ~ **probe** *n* SPACE sonde interplanétaire *f*; ~ **travel** *n* SPACE voyage interplanétaire *m*

interplant *adj* PROD ENG inter-usines, interateliers

interpolate *vt* PRINT interclasser

interpolating *adj* ELECTRON *filter* interpolateur

interpolation *n* COMP, DP, MATH, TELECOM interpolation *f*; ~ **gain** *n (IG)* TELECOM gain de concentration *m*; ~ **of speech signals** *n* TELECOM concentration des signaux vocaux *f*

interpolator *n* TELECOM interpolateur *m*

interpole *n* ELEC *of DC motor* pôle auxiliaire *m*; ~ **machine** *n* ELEC machine à pôle intermédiaire *f*

interpret *vt* COMP, DP interpréter

interpretation *n* COMP, DP interprétation *f*

interpretative: ~ **language** *n* COMP langage interprétatif *m*

interpreter *n* COMP, DP interpréteur *m*

interprocessor: ~ **link** *n* TELECOM liaison intercalculateur *f*

interrogate *vt* COMP, DP interroger

interrogation *n* COMP, DP consultation de données *f*, interrogation *f*; ~ **mode** *n* ELECTRON mode d'interrogation *m*

interrogator: ~ **transponder** *n* TELECOM interrogateur-répondeur *m*

interrupt[1] *n* COMP, DP interruption *f*; ~ **mask** *n* COMP, DP masque d'interruption *m*; ~ **period** *n* PROD ENG durée d'interruption *f*; ~ **priority** *n* COMP, DP priorité d'interruption *f*; ~ **signal** *n* COMP, DP signal d'interruption *m*; ~ **value** *n* PROD ENG valeur d'interruption *f*; ~ **vector** *n* COMP, DP vecteur d'interruptions *m*

interrupt[2] *vt* COMP, CONTROL, DP interrompre

interrupted: ~ **ageing** *n* (BrE) P&R vieillissement étagé *m*; ~ **aging** *n* (AmE) *see interrupted ageing*; ~ **flow** *n* TRANSP écoulement discontinu *m*; ~ **tooth tap** *n* MECH ENG taraud à denture interrompue *m*

interrupter *n* ELEC *switch* interrupteur *m*, ELEC ENG rupteur *m*, TELECOM interrupteur *m*

interrupting: ~ **voltage** *n* ELEC ENG tension de rupture *f*

interruption *n* ELEC ENG interruption *f*, GAS TECH effacement *m*, TELECOM *by telephone operator* entrée en ligne *f*

intersatellite: ~ **link** *n* SPACE *communications* liaison intersatellite *f*; ~ **link acquisition** *n* SPACE établissement d'une liaison entre satellites *m*; ~ **service** *n* SPACE *communications* service intersatellite *m*

intersect *vt* GEOL entrecouper, intersecter, recouper, GEOM intersecter

intersecting[1] *adj* GEOM intersecté

intersecting:[2] ~ **arcs** *n pl* GEOM arcs intersectés *m pl*; ~ **lines** *n pl* GEOM lignes intersectées *f pl*; ~ **planes** *n pl* GEOM plans intersectés *m pl*; ~ **vein** *n* GEOL filon croiseur *m*

intersection *n* CHEM, COMP, DP, GEOM intersection *f*; ~ **angle** *n* CONST *surveying* angle d'intersection *m*; ~ **point** *n* CONST *surveying* point d'intersection *m*

interstage: ~ **cooler** *n* REFRIG refroidisseur intermédiaire *m*; ~ **transformer** *n* ELEC ENG transformateur intermédiaire *m*

interstellar[1] *adj* ASTRON interstellaire, SPACE intersidéral, interstellaire

interstellar:[2] ~ **absorption line** *n* ASTRON *in spectra of stars* raie d'absorption interstellaire *f*; ~ **cloud** *n* AS-TRON nuage interstellaire *m*; ~ **dust** *n* ASTRON poussières interstellaires *f pl*; ~ **magnetic field** *n* AS-TRON champ magnétique interstellaire *m*; ~ **matter** *n* ASTRON, SPACE matière interstellaire *f*; ~ **medium** *n* ASTRON milieu interstellaire *m*; ~ **molecules** *n pl* AS-TRON molécules interstellaires *f pl*; ~ **space** *n* ASTRON espace interstellaire *m*, SPACE espace intersidéral *m*, espace interstellaire *m*

interstice *n* COAL TECH vide *m*, CONST, HYDROL interstice *m*

interstitial: ~ **atom** *n* CRYSTALL atome interstitiel *m*; ~ **compound** *n* CHEM composé interstitiel *m*; ~ **solid solution** *n* CRYSTALL solution solide interstitielle *f*; ~ **water** *n* COAL TECH, HYDROL, OCEANOG, PETR, PETR TECH *geology*, WATER SUPP eau interstitielle *f*

interswitchboard: ~ **tie-circuit** *n* TELECOM ligne interstandard *f*

intersymbol: ~ **interference** *n* ELECTRON interférence intersymbole *f*, interférence longitudinale *f*, TELECOM brouillage entre symboles *m*, brouillage intersymbole *m*

intertidal: ~ **deposits** *n pl* GEOL dépôts intercotidaux *m* *pl*, dépôts intertidaux *m pl*; ~ **zone** *n* MAR POLL estran *m*, zone intertidale *f*

interturn: ~ **capacitance** *n* ELEC *of coil* capacitance entre spires *f*; ~ **insulation** *n* ELEC *of coil* isolation entre spires *f*

interval *n* ACOUSTICS, GEOL intervalle *m*; ~ **difference** *n* ACOUSTICS différence d'intervalles *f*; ~ **timer** *n* COMP, DP temporisateur *m*; ~ **velocity** *n* PETR TECH *seismic survey* vitesse de tranche *f*

intervention *n* COMP, DP intervention *f*; ~ **signal** *n* CONTROL signal d'intervention *m*

interworking *n* TELECOM interfonctionnement *m*; ~ **functional unit** *n* *(IFU)* TELECOM unité fonctionnelle d'interfonctionnement *f*; ~ **protocol** *n* *(IWP)* TELECOM protocole d'interfonctionnement *m*

interwoven *adj* PROD ENG imbriqué

into: ~ **the wind** *adv* AERONAUT face au vent

intonation *n* ACOUSTICS intonation *f*

intraclast *n* GEOL intraclaste *f*

intracratonic *adj* GEOL *of basin* intracratonique

intrados *n* CONST *of arch* douelle *f*, intrados *m*

intragranular *adj* METALL intragranulaire

intramodal: ~ **distortion** *n* OPT distorsion intramodale *f*, distorsion par dispersion *f*, TELECOM distorsion intramodale *f*

intramolecular *adj* CHEM intramoléculaire

intramontane: ~ **basin** *n* GEOL bassin d'entremont *m*

intraoffice: ~ **junctor circuit** *n* (AmE) TELECOM circuit de connexion local *m*

intraplate[1] *adj* GEOL *tectonic setting* intraplaque

intraplate:[2] ~ **volcanism** *n* GEOL volcanisme intraplaque *m*

intricate *adj* MECH ENG complexe

intrinsic[1] *adj* CHEM intrinsèque

intrinsic:[2] ~ **angular momentum** *n* PART PHYS moment angulaire intrinsèque *m*; ~ **barrier diode** *n* ELECTRON diode à couche intrinsèque *f*; ~ **conductivity** *n* ELEC, ELEC ENG conductibilité intrinsèque *f*; ~ **curvature** *n* GEOM courbure intrinsèque *f*; ~ **distribution** *n* RAD PHYS *of frequencies* répartition intrinsèque *f*; ~ **error** *n* METR *of measuring instrument* erreur intrinsèque *f*; ~ **forecast** *n* PROD ENG prévision intrinsèque *f*; ~ **impedance** *n* ELEC *electromagnetism* impédance intrinsèque *f*; ~ **joint loss** *n* OPT, TELECOM perte intrinsèque de raccordement *f*; ~ **noise** *n* ELECTRON bruit propre *m*; ~ **permeability** *n* ELEC *electromagnetism* perméabilité intrinsèque *f*; ~ **photoconductivity** *n* ELECTRON photoconduction intrinsèque *f*; ~ **semiconductor** *n* COMP, DP, ELECTRON, PHYS semiconducteur intrinsèque *m*; ~ **stability** *n* FLUID PHYS stabilité intrinsèque *f*; ~ **temperature** *n* ELECTRON température intrinsèque *f*; ~ **temperature range** *n* ELECTRON plage de températures intrinsèques *f*; ~ **viscosity** *n* FLUID PHYS viscosité intrinsèque *f*

intrinsically: ~ **safe** *adj* ELEC ENG intrinsèquement sûr, à sécurité intrinsèque, SAFETY *electrical apparatus, circuits* intrinsèquement sûr

introscopy *n* NUCLEAR endoscopie *f*

intruder: ~ **presence detector** *n* TELECOM détecteur d'une présence intruse *m*

intrusion *n* GEOL, PETR intrusion *f*

intrusive[1] *adj* FUELLESS intrusif

intrusive:[2] ~ **sheet** *n* GEOL *igneous body* filon-couche *m*

INTTR *abbr* *(international transit exchange)* TELECOM commutateur de transit international *m*

intumescence: ~ **compound** *n* SAFETY composé ignifuge

moussant *m*

intumescent[1] *adj* P&R *paint* intumescent

intumescent:[2] ~ **paint** *n* COLOURS peinture intumescente *f*

inulin *n* CHEM, FOOD TECH inuline *f*

inundation *n* HYDROL crue *f*, inondation *f*, WATER SUPP submersion *f*

invaded: ~ **zone** *n* PETR zone d'invasion *f*, zone envahie *f*

invalid *adj* TELECOM *message* non valide

invariant[1] *adj* GEOM invariant

invariant[2] *n* GEOM invariant *m*

invasive: ~ **techniques** *n pl* RAD PHYS techniques d'invasion *f pl*

in-vehicle: ~ **aural communication system** *n* TRANSP système de communication auditive embarqué *m*; ~ **visual display** *n* TRANSP système d'affichage embarqué *m*

invention *n* PATENTS invention *f*

inventive: ~ **step** *n* PATENTS activité inventive *f*

inventor *n* PATENTS inventeur *m*

inventory *n* PACKAGING inventaire *m*, PETR TECH valeurs d'exploitation *f pl*, PROD ENG inventaire *m*, stock *m*; ~ **change** *n* PROD ENG variation de stock *f*; ~ **control** *n* PROD ENG gestion des stocks *f*; ~ **profile** *n* PROD ENG profil prévisionnel de stock *m*; ~ **reporting** *n* PROD ENG liste de stock *f*, situation du stock *f*, suivi de stock *m*, édition de l'inventaire *f*; ~ **turnover** *n* PROD ENG rotation des stocks *f*, taux de rotation des stocks *m*; ~ **valuation** *n* PROD ENG valorisation de stock *f*; ~ **wipe-off** *n* PROD ENG dépréciation de stock *f*

inverse[1] *adj* MATH, MECH ENG inverse, réciproque

inverse:[2] **in** ~ **proportion** *adv* MECH ENG en raison inverse de; **in** ~ **ratio** *adv* MECH ENG en raison inverse de

inverse[3] *n* MATH, MECH ENG inverse *m*, réciproque *f*; ~ **Compton effect** *n* PHYS effet Compton inverse *m*; ~ **direction** *n* ELEC ENG sens de non-conduction *m*; ~ **dovetail cutter** *n* MECH ENG fraise conique à cône renversé *f*; ~ **feedback** *n* ELEC ENG, ELECTRON contre-réaction *f*; ~ **feedback filter** *n* ELECTRON filtre de contre-réaction *m*; ~ **gain** *n* ELECTRON gain inverse *m*; ~ **image** *n* MATH antécédent *m*; ~ **induced armature** *n* ELEC *of generator, motor* induit inverse *m*; ~ **initiation** *n* MINING amorçage inverse *m*; ~ **limiter** *n* ELECTRON limiteur à seuil *m*; ~ **modulation** *n* ELECTRON modulation inverse *f*; ~ **photoelectric effect** *n* ELECTRON effet photoélectrique inverse *m*; ~ **piezoelectric effect** *n* ELEC ENG, PHYS effet piézoélectrique inverse *m*; ~ **primary creep** *n* METALL fluage primaire inverse *m*; ~ **ratio** *n* MATH raison inverse *f*, MECH ENG raison inverse *f*, rapport réciproque *m*; ~ **square law** *n* PHYS loi de l'inverse du carré *f*; ~ **time relay** *n* ELEC relais à temps dépendant *m*; ~ **voltage** *n* PROD ENG tension inverse *f*; ~ **voltage rating** *n* PROD ENG valeur nominale de tension inverse *f*

inversely:[1] ~ **as** *adv* MECH ENG en raison inverse de

inversely:[2] ~ **proportional numbers** *n pl* MATH nombres inversement proportionnels *m pl*

inversion *n* ELECTRON, PETR inversion *f*, TV *of image* redressement *m*; ~ **axis** *n* CRYSTALL axe d'inversion *m*; ~ **center** *n* (AmE), ~ **centre** *n* (BrE) CRYSTALL centre d'inversion *m*; ~ **layer** *n* ELECTRON, POLLUTION, TELECOM couche d'inversion *f*; ~ **temperature** *n* ELEC *of thermocouple*, PHYS température d'inversion *f*

invert[1] *n* COAL TECH *inverted arch*, CONST *inverted arch* radier *m*; ~ **glass** *n* C&G verre inverse *m*; ~ **sugar** *n* CHEM, FOOD TECH sucre inverti *m*

invert^2 *vt* COMP, DP inverser, HYDROL faire des méandres
invertase *n* CHEM, FOOD TECH invertase *f*
inverted^1 *adj* CINEMAT inversé
inverted:^{2} ~ **arch** *n* CONST *curve* arc renversé *m*, *structure* radier *m*; ~ **burner** *n* PROD ENG *for gas* bec renversé *m*; ~ **chip** *n* ELECTRON puce à bosses *f*; ~ **commas** *n pl* PRINT guillemets *m pl*; ~ **converter** *n* ELEC convertisseur de courant continu en courant alternatif *m*; ~ **cylinder engine** *n* PROD ENG machine à cylindre renversé *f*; ~ **file** *n* COMP, DP fichier inversé *m*; ~ **fold** *n* GEOL pli renversé *m*; ~ **image** *n* PHOTO image renversée de haut en bas *f*, PHYS image renversée *f*; ~ **microscope** *n* INSTRUMENT microscope inversé *m*; ~ **pattern accumulator** *n* HYDR EQUIP accumulateur de pression hydraulique inversé *m*; ~ **pleat** *n* TEXTILES pli creux *m*; ~ **population** *n* ELECTRON population inversée *f*; ~ **T-shaped track girder** *n* TRANSP poutre en T inversé *f*
inverter *n* CINEMAT convertisseur *m*, COMP, DP inverseur *m*, ELEC *transducer* onduleur *m*, ELEC ENG inverseur *m*, ELECTRON onduleur *m*, PHYS *logic gate* inverseur *m*, TELECOM inverseur *m*, onduleur *m*; ~ **gate** *n* ELECTRON porte inverseuse *f*; ~ **knob** *n* INSTRUMENT commande de rotation du prisme inverseur *f*; ~ **oscillator** *n* ELECTRON oscillateur d'onduleur *m*
inverting: ~ **amplifier** *n* ELECTRON amplificateur inverseur *m*; ~ **input** *n* ELECTRON *of differential amplifier* entrée inverseuse *f*; ~ **mirror** *n* INSTRUMENT miroir d'inversion *m*; ~ **prism** *n* INSTRUMENT prisme à redressement *m*; ~ **transistor** *n* ELECTRON transistor inverseur *m*
investigate *vt* SAFETY *complaint* examiner
investigation *n* MECH ENG enquête *f*; ~ **of brazability** *n* MECH ENG étude de l'aptitude au brasage *f*; ~ **test** *n* SPACE essai d'investigation *m*
investment: ~ **casting die** *n* MECH ENG matrice de moulage à ligne perdue *f*; ~ **mold for casting** *n* (AmE), ~ **mould for casting** *n* (BrE) MECH ENG moule pour fonderie à la cire perdue *m*
inviscid: ~ **flow distribution** *n* FLUID PHYS répartition d'écoulement non-visqueux *f*; ~ **motion** *n* FLUID PHYS mouvement inviscide *m*
invisible: ~ **cursor** *n* PROD ENG curseur virtuel *m*; ~ **ink** *n* COLOURS encre sympathique *f*
invitation: ~ **to send** *n* COMP invitation à émettre *f*, DP invitation à transmettre *f*; ~ **to transmit** *n* TELECOM invitation à émettre *f*
invoice: ~ **mass** *n* TESTING, TEXTILES masse facturée *f*; ~ **weight** *n* TEXTILES poids facturé *m*
invoiced: ~ **mass** *n* PAPER TECH *of pulp* masse facturée *f*
invoking: ~ **CMISE service user** *n* TELECOM utilisateur du service CMISE lanceur *m*
involute^1 *adj* GEOM de développante, de développante de cercle, à développante, à développante de cercle
involute^2 *n* GEOM développante *f*; ~ **arc** *n* GEOM arc de développante *m*; ~ **cam** *n* MECH ENG came à développement *f*, excentrique à développement *m*; ~ **of a circle** *n* GEOM développante de cercle *f*; ~ **gear** *n* MECH ENG engrenage à développante *m*, engrenage à développante de cercle *m*; ~ **gear cutters** *n pl* MECH ENG fraises à tailler les engrenages à développante *f pl*; ~ **gearing** *n* MECH ENG engrenage à développante *m*, engrenage à développante de cercle *m*; ~ **spline** *n* MECH ENG cannelure en développante *f*
involution *n* (*cf evolution*) GEOM, MATH involution *f*
inward:^{1} ~ **bound** *adj* NAUT *ship, port traffic* d'entrée, en retour, entrant

inward:^{2} ~ **flow turbine** *n* PROD ENG turbine centripète *f*; ~ **flux** *n* PHYS flux entrant *m*; ~ **propagating wave** *n* TELECOM onde régressive *f*; ~ **traffic** *n* TRANSP trafic entrant *m*
IOC *abbr* (*integrated optical circuit*) OPT, TELECOM circuit d'optique intégré *m*, circuit intégré optique *m*
iodargyrite *n* MINERAL iodargyrite *f*
iodate *n* CHEM iodate *m*
iodembolite *n* MINERAL iodobromite *f*
iodic *adj* CHEM iodique
iodide *n* CHEM iodure *m*
iodine *n* (*I*) CHEM iode *m* (*I*); ~ **flask** *n* LAB EQUIP *glassware, analysis* fiole à iode *f*; ~ **laser** *n* ELECTRON laser à iode *m*; ~ **number** *n* FOOD TECH indice d'iode *m*, valeur d'iode *f*; ~ **value** *n* FOOD TECH indice d'iode *m*, valeur d'iode *f*, P&R *chemical property* indice d'iode *m*
iodize *vt* CHEM iodurer
iodoaurate *n* CHEM iodo-aurate *m*
iodobenzene *n* CHEM iodobenzène *m*
iodobromite *n* MINERAL iodobromite *f*
iodoform *n* CHEM iodoforme *m*
iodohydrin *n* CHEM iodohydrine *f*
iodomercurate *n* CHEM iodomercurate *m*
iodometric *adj* CHEM iodométrique
iodometry *n* CHEM iodométrie *f*
iodonium *n* CHEM iodonium *m*
iodopsin *n* CHEM iodopsine *f*
iodoso- *pref* CHEM iodosé-
iodosobenzene *n* CHEM iodosobenzène *m*
iodous *adj* CHEM iodeux
iodyrite *n* MINERAL iodargyrite *f*
iolite *n* MINERAL iolite *f*
ion *n* CHEM, ELEC *charged particle*, ELECTRON, GAS TECH, PART PHYS, PETR TECH, PHYS ion *m* ~ **accelerator** *n* PART PHYS accélérateur d'ions *m*; ~ **beam** *n* ELECTRON, RAD PHYS faisceau d'ions *m*; ~ **beam focusing column** *n* RAD PHYS colonne de mise au point des faisceaux d'ions *f*; ~ **beam lithography** *n* ELECTRON gravure par faisceau d'ions *f*; ~ **beam optical system** *n* RAD PHYS système optique à faisceau d'ions *m*; ~ **bombardment** *n* PHYS bombardement ionique *m*; ~ **budget** *n* POLLUTION bilan ionique *m*; ~ **burn** *n* ELECTRON tache ionique *f*; ~ **chromatograph** *n* LAB EQUIP *analysis* chromatographe *m*; ~ **cluster** *n* RAD PHYS amas d'ions *m*, essaim d'ions *m*; ~ **current** *n* RAD PHYS courant ionique *m*; ~ **emission microscope** *n* INSTRUMENT microscope à émission ionique *m*; ~ **engine** *n* SPACE *spacecraft* moteur ionique *m*; ~ **exchange** *n* CHEM échange d'ions *m*; ~ **exchange glass** *n* C&G verre pour échange ionique *m*; ~ **exchange isotherm** *n* RAD PHYS *constant temperature activity* isotherme d'échange *f*; ~ **exchange resin** *n* PROP MAT résine échangeuse d'ions *f*; ~ **exchange technique** *n* OPT, TELECOM procédé par échange d'ions *m*; ~ **exchange water purifier** *n* LAB EQUIP *analysis* appareil de production d'eau pure à échange d'ions *m*; ~ **gun** *n* PROD ENG canon à ions *m*; ~ **implantation** *n* ELECTRON, PART PHYS implantation d'ions *f*; ~ **ion collision** *n* PART PHYS collision ion-ion *f*; ~ **laser** *n* ELECTRON laser ionique *m*, MECH ENG laser à ions *m*; ~ **pair** *n* CHEM *of electrolyte*, RAD PHYS *radiology* paire d'ions *f*; ~ **propulsion** *n* SPACE *spacecraft* propulsion ionique *f*; ~ **pump** *n* MECH ENG pompe d'ions *f*, PHYS pompe ionique *f*; ~ **rocket** *n* SPACE *spacecraft* propulseur ionique *m*; ~ **rocket engine** *n* SPACE *spacecraft* propulseur à fusée à ions *m*; ~ **selective electrode** *n* (*ISE*) LAB EQUIP *electrochemistry* électrode

sélective *f*; ~ **source** *n* PHYS source d'ions *f*; ~ **spectrum** *n* RAD PHYS spectre d'ions *m*; ~ **spot** *n* TV tache ionique *f*; ~ **sputtering** *n* CHEM *of specimen* pulvérisation ionique *f*; ~ **thruster** *n* SPACE *spacecraft* moteur ionique *m*; ~ **trap** *n* ELECTRON piège à ions *m*, TV grille d'arrêt *f*, piège à ions *m*

ionic[1] *adj* HYDROL, RAD PHYS ionique

ionic:[2] ~ **atmosphere** *n* RAD PHYS atmosphère ionique *f*; ~ **bombardment** *n* ELECTRON bombardement ionique *m*; ~ **bond** *n* CHEM liaison ionique *f*, CRYSTALL liaison hétéropolaire *f*, liaison ionique *f*, RAD PHYS liaison ionique *f*; ~ **concentration** *n* GEOPHYS concentration ionique *f*; ~ **conductance** *n* RAD PHYS conductivité ionique équivalente *f*; ~ **loudspeaker** *n* ACOUSTICS, RECORDING haut-parleur ionique *m*; ~ **mobility** *n* RAD PHYS mobilité d'ion *f*; ~ **polarization** *n* PHYS polarisation ionique *f*; ~ **product** *n* CHEM produit ionique *m*; ~ **propulsion** *n* SPACE *spacecraft* propulsion ionique *f*; ~ **radius** *n* CRYSTALL, RAD PHYS rayon ionique *m*; ~ **strength** *n* RAD PHYS force ionique *f*; ~ **yield** *n* RAD PHYS rendement ionique *m*

ionization *n* ASTRON, ELEC *charging of atoms*, ELEC ENG, GAS TECH, GEOPHYS, PART PHYS, PHYS, PROP MAT ionisation *f*; ~ **by collision** *n* PHYS ionisation par choc *f*, ionisation par impact *f*; ~ **chamber** *n* PART PHYS, PHYS chambre d'ionisation *f*; ~ **current** *n* ELECTRON courant d'ionisation *m*; ~ **detector** *n* RAD PHYS détecteur par ionisation *m*; ~ **energy** *n* GAS TECH, PHYS, RAD PHYS énergie d'ionisation *f*; ~ **gage** *n* (AmE), ~ **gauge** *n* (BrE) PHYS jauge à ionisation *f*; ~ **loss** *n* PART PHYS perte d'énergie par ionisation *f*, RAD PHYS perte d'énergie par ion *f*; ~ **potential** *n* PHYS, RAD PHYS potentiel d'ionisation *m*; ~ **rate** *n* PART PHYS taux d'ionisation *m*; ~ **threshold** *n* GAS TECH seuil d'ionisation *m*; ~ **unit** *n* PRINT dispositif d'ionisation *m*; ~ **vacuum gage** *n* (AmE), ~ **vacuum gauge** *n* (BrE) REFRIG jauge à vide *f*, manomètre à chambre d'ionisation *m*, manomètre à vide *m*

ionize *vt* GEOPHYS, PHYS ioniser

ionized[1] *adj* GAS TECH, GEOPHYS, PHYS ionisé

ionized:[2] ~ **argon laser** *n* ELECTRON laser à argon ionisé *m*; ~ **atom** *n* PART PHYS atome ionisé *m*; ~ **environment** *n* SPACE milieu ionisé *m*; ~ **state** *n* PART PHYS état ionisé *m*

ionizing: ~ **layer** *n* ELEC *charge* couche ionisante *f*; ~ **particle** *n* RAD PHYS particule ionisante *f*; ~ **radiation** *n* ELEC, PHYS, POLLUTION, RAD PHYS, WAVE PHYS rayonnement ionisant *m*; ~ **wet washer** *n* SAFETY laveur humide ionisant *m*

ionographic *adj* COMP *printer* ionographique

ionone *n* CHEM ionone *f*

ionosphere *n* ASTRON, GEOPHYS, PHYS, WAVE PHYS ionosphère *f*; ~ **layer** *n* GEOPHYS couche ionosphérique *f*

ionospheric: ~ **recorder** *n* GEOPHYS sondeur ionosphérique *m*; ~ **scintillation** *n* ASTRON scintillation ionosphérique *f*; ~ **substorm** *n* GEOPHYS orage élémentaire *m*, sous-orage ionosphérique *m*

ionotropy *n* CHEM ionotropie *f*

IOP *abbr* (*input/output processor*) COMP processeur d'entrée/sortie *m*

IOS *abbr* COMP (*integrated office system*) bureautique intégrée *f*, système BI *m*, SPACE (*Intelsat Operations Center*) Centre d'exploitation intelsat *m*

IP *abbr* COMP (*input processor*) processeur d'entrée *m*, COMP (*information processing*), DP (*information processing*), ELECTRON (*information processing*)

traitement de l'information *m*

IPA *abbr* DETERGENTS (*isopropyl acid*) alcool isopropylique *m*, isopropanol *m*, PRINT (*isopropylic alcohol*) alcool isopropylique *m*

IPE *n* (*individual protection equipment*) MILIT *chemical warfare* équipement de protection individuelle *m*

ipecac *n* FOOD TECH ipéca *m*, ipécacuana *m*

ipecacuanha *n* FOOD TECH ipéca *m*, ipécacuana *m*

ipecacuanic *adj* CHEM ipécacuanique

IPL *abbr* COMP (*initial program load*) programme de chargement initial *m*, TELECOM (*interactive primary link*) liaison primaire pour les services interactifs *f*

IPS *abbr* (*inches per second*) COMP, RECORDING PPS (*pouces par seconde*)

Ir (*iridium*) CHEM Ir (*iridium*)

IR *abbr* COMP (*information retrieval*), DP (*information retrieval*) recherche documentaire *f*, OPT (*infrared*), PHYS (*infrared*), RAD PHYS (*infrared*) IR (*infrarouge*)

IRAS *abbr* (*infrared astronomical satellite*) ASTRON IRAS (*satellite astronomique infrarouge*)

iraser *n* ELECTRON iraser *m*

IR-drop *n* ELEC *resistance* chute de résistance *f*

iridescence *n* C&G reflet irisé *m*, MAR POLL irisation *f*

iridescent *adj* C&G *glass* irisé

iridic *adj* CHEM iridique

iridite *n* CHEM iridite *f*

iridium *n* (*Ir*) CHEM iridium *m* (*Ir*); ~ **osmine** *n* MINERAL iridosmine *f*

iridizing *n* C&G irisation *f*

iridosmine *n* MINERAL iridosmine *f*

iris *n* CINEMAT, PHYS *waveguide* iris *m*; ~ **control button** *n* TV bouton de commande du diaphragme *m*; ~ **diaphragm** *n* INSTRUMENT diaphragme iris *m*; ~ **fade** *n* CINEMAT fondu au diaphragme *m*

Irish: ~ **moss** *n* FOOD TECH mousse d'Irlande *f*

iris-out *n* CINEMAT fermeture à l'iris *f*

iron[1] *n* CHEM, COAL TECH fer *m*; ~ **alum** *n* CHEM alun de fer *m*; ~ **band cutter** *n* PACKAGING tronçonneuse pour feuillard de cerclage *f*; ~ **black** *n* COATINGS vernis pour les ferrures *m*; ~ **blue pigment** *n* COLOURS pigment bleu de fer *m*; ~ **bridge** *n* CONST pont métallique *m*; ~ **carbonate** *n* CHEM carbonate de fer *m*; ~ **chromate** *n* CHEM chromate de fer *m*; ~ **core** *n* ELEC ENG noyau de fer *m*; ~ **core transformer** *n* ELEC, ELEC ENG transformateur à noyau de fer *m*; ~ **core voltmeter** *n* ELEC voltmètre ferrodynamique *m*; ~ **deposit** *n* MINING gîte de fer *m*; ~ **filings** *n pl* CHEM, PHYS limaille de fer *f*; ~ **founding** *n* PROD ENG fonderie de fer *f*, fonderie de fonte *f*, moulage des pièces en fonte *m*; ~ **foundry** *n* PROD ENG fonderie de fer *f*, fonderie de fonte *f*; ~ **garnet** *n* MINERAL grenat ferreux *m*; ~ **girder** *n* CONST poutre de fer *f*; ~ **loss** *n* ELEC *of transformer*, PHYS perte dans le fer *f*; ~ **meteorite** *n* ASTRON météorite ferreuse *f*; ~ **ore** *n* CHEM mine de fer *f*, minerai de fer *m*; ~ **oxide** *n* CHEM, PROP MAT oxyde de fer *m*; ~ **oxide pigment** *n* COLOURS pigment d'oxyde de fer *m*, pigment à base d'oxyde de fer *m*; ~ **pig** *n* PROD ENG gueuse *f*; ~ **pigment** *n* COLOURS pigment de fer *m*; ~ **pipe** *n* CONST *cast-iron* conduite en fonte *f*, tuyau de fonte *m*, *wrought-iron* conduite de fer *f*, tuyau de fer *m*; ~ **piping** *n* CONST *wrought-iron* conduites de fer *f pl*, conduits de fer *m pl*, tuyautage de fer *m*, tuyaux de fer *m pl*; ~ **plate** *n* PROD ENG *cast* plaque de fonte *f*, *wrought* plaque de fer *f*; ~ **plating** *n* NAUT bordé en fer *m*; ~ **pyrite** *n* MINERAL pyrite *f*, pyrite jaune *f*, pyrite martiale *f*, pyrite de fer *f*; ~ **rod** *n* PROD ENG tige de fer *f*, tringle de fer *f*, verge de

fer *f*; ~ **salt** *n* DETERGENTS sel ferrique *m*; ~ **scale** *n* PROD ENG battitures *f pl*, battitures de fer *f pl*, martelures *f pl*, paille de fer *f*, scories de forge *f pl*, écailles de fer *f pl*; ~ **sheeting** *n* PROD ENG tôle de fer *f*; ~ **slips** *n pl* C&G règles de coulée *f pl*; ~ **wire** *n* PROD ENG fil de fer *m*; ~ **wire gauze** *n* PROD ENG toile en fil de fer *f*; ~ **wire rope** *n* PROD ENG câble en fer *m*, câble en fil de fer *m*

iron[2] *vt* TEXTILES repasser; ~ **out** *vt* TEXTILES faire disparaître au fer

ironbound[1] *adj* PROD ENG cerclé de fer, fretté de fer

ironbound:[2] ~ **mallet** *n* PROD ENG marteau à têtes rapportées *m*

ironclad: ~ **headstock** *n* MECH ENG *all-gear, single-pulley completely enclosed* poupée blindée *f*; ~ **shaft** *n* MINING puits blindé *m*

iron-core: ~ **ammeter** *n* ELEC ampèremètre ferrodynamique *m*

irone *n* CHEM irone *f*

ironing *n* TEXTILES repassage *m*

iron-shod *adj* PROD ENG ferré

ironstone *n* GEOL roche ferrugineuse *f*, MINERAL mine de fer *f*, minerai de fer *m*, minerai ferreux *m*

ironwork *n* CONST charpente en fer *f*, ferrerie *f*, ferrure *f*, ferrures *f pl*, PROD ENG serrurerie *f*

ironworking *n* CONST *heavy* charpenterie en fer *f*, *light* petite charpenterie en fer *f*, serrurerie *f*

ironworks *n* PROD ENG *foundry* fonderie de fer *f*, fonderie de fonte *f*, *metallurgical* usine sidérurgique *f*

IRP *abbr (internal reference point)* TELECOM point de référence interne *m*

IRPTC *abbr (International Register of Potentially Toxic Chemicals)* POLLUTION RISCPT *(Registre international des substances potentiellement toxiques)*

irradiance *n* FUELLESS irradiation *f*, OPT éclairement *m*, PHYS éclairement lumineux *m*, TELECOM *power density* puissance électromagnétique surfacique *f*, quotient éclairement énergétique *m*

irradiated *adj* PHYS irradié

irradiation *n* POLLUTION, RAD PHYS irradiation *f*, SPACE *communications* rayonnement *m*; ~ **chamber** *n* RAD PHYS chambre d'irradiation *f*; ~ **of food** *n* PACKAGING irradiation alimentaire *f*; ~ **hardening** *n* METALL durcissement par irradiation *m*; ~ **loop** *n* RAD PHYS boucle d'irradiation *f*

irrational[1] *adj* MATH irrationnel

irrational:[2] ~ **number** *n* DP nombre irrationnel *m*

irrecoverable[1] *adj* COMP, DP irrécupérable

irrecoverable:[2] ~ **error** *n* COMP, DP erreur irrécupérable *f*

irreducible[1] *adj* COMP *polynomial* irréductible

irreducible:[2] ~ **water saturation** *n* PETR saturation en eau irréductible *f*

irregular: ~ **edge** *n* C&G liséré *m*; ~ **galaxies** *n pl* ASTRON galaxies irrégulières *f pl*; ~ **polyhedron** *n* GEOM polyèdre irrégulier *m*; ~ **variables** *n pl* ASTRON variables irrégulières *f pl*; ~ **yarn** *n* TEXTILES fil irrégulier *m*

irrelevant *adj* PATENTS étranger au sujet

irreversible[1] *adj* PHYS, PROP MAT *trap* irréversible

irreversible:[2] ~ **colloids** *n pl* CHEM colloïdes irréversibles *m pl*

irrigate *vt* HYDROL irriguer

irrigation *n* HYDROL, WATER SUPP irrigation *f*; ~ **by surface flooding** *n* HYDROL, WATER SUPP irrigation par ruissellement *f*; ~ **canal** *n* WATER SUPP canal d'irrigation *m*; ~ **cooler** *n* REFRIG refroidisseur à ruissellement *m*; ~ **project** *n* HYDROL projet d'aménagement par irrigation *m*

irritant[1] *adj* SAFETY irritant

irritant[2] *n* SAFETY irritant *m*; ~ **substance** *n* SAFETY *main hazard* substance irritante *f*

irrotational[1] *adj* FLUID PHYS, PHYS irrotationnel

irrotational:[2] ~ **field** *n* PHYS champ irrotationnel *m*; ~ **flow** *n* FLUID PHYS, PHYS écoulement irrotationnel *m*

irruption *n* WATER SUPP venue *f*, *of water* irruption *f*

IRS *abbr* POLLUTION *(international referral system)* système international de référence *m*, TELECOM *(information reference system)* SRI *(système de référence intermédiaire)*, TELECOM *(information receiver station)* station de réception d'informations *f*

IS[1] *abbr* COMP *(information system)* système informatique *m*, COMP *(information separator)* séparateur *m*, TELECOM *(intermediate system)* système intermédiaire *m*

IS:[2] ~ **machine** *n* C&G machine sectionnelle *f*

ISA: ~ **segment** *n* TELECOM segment ISA *m*

isallobar *n* METEO isallobare *f*

isanomals *n pl* GEOL isanomales *f pl*

isatic *adj* CHEM isatique

isatin *n* CHEM isatine *f*

isatogenic *adj* CHEM isatogénique

isatropic *adj* CHEM isatropique

ISC *abbr (international switching center, international switching centre)* TELECOM centre de commutation international *m*

ISCP[1] *abbr (international signalling control part, international signaling control part)* TELECOM sous-système de contrôle de signalisation *m*

ISCP:[2] ~ **application entity** *n (ISCPAE)* TELECOM entité d'application ISCP *f*

ISCPAE *abbr (ISCP application entity)* TELECOM entité d'application ISCP *f*

ISD *abbr (International Subscriber Dialling)* TELECOM Automatique International *m*

ISDN[1] *abbr (integrated services digital network)* TELECOM RNIS *(réseau numérique à intégration des services)*

ISDN:[2] ~ **access** *n* TELECOM accès au RNIS *m*; ~ **exchange** *n* TELECOM centre RNIS *m*; ~ **primary rate access** *n* TELECOM accès au débit primaire au RNIS *m*; ~ **switch** *n* TELECOM autocommutateur RNIS *m*; ~ **user part** *n* TELECOM SSUR, sous-système usager réseau *m*, sous-système utilisateur pour le RNIS *m*

ISE *abbr (ion selective electrode)* LAB EQUIP *electrochemistry* électrode sélective *f*

isentropic[1] *adj* PHYS isentropique, THERMOD *anisentropic* isentrope, isentropique

isentropic:[2] ~ **compressibility** *n* PHYS compressibilité isentropique *f*

isethionate *n* CHEM iséthionate *m*

isethionic *adj* CHEM iséthionique

isinglass *n* FOOD TECH colle de poisson *f*, ichtyocolle *f*, isinglass *m*, gélatine d'esturgeon *f*, gélatinede poisson *f*

Islamic: ~ **lunar calendar** *n* ASTRON calendrier lunaire musulman *m*

island: ~ **arc** *n* GEOL, OCEANOG arc insulaire *m*; ~ **platform** *n* RAIL quai en îlot *m*

islet *n* HYDROL, NAUT *geography* îlot *m*

ISO[1] *abbr (International Standards Organization)* MECH ENG, TELECOM ISO *(Organisation internationale de normalisation)*

ISO:[2] ~ **metric thread** *n* MECH ENG filetage métrique ISO *m*; ~ **miniature metric thread** *n* MECH ENG filetage miniature métrique ISO *m*; ~ **standard** *n* QUALITY norme ISO *f*

isoallyl *n* CHEM isoallyle *m*, propényle *m*

isoamyl *n* CHEM isoamyle *m*

isoamylic *adj* CHEM isoamylique

isoapiol *n* CHEM isoapiol *m*

isoapiole *n* CHEM isoapiol *m*

isobar *n* METEO isobare *f*, ligne isobare *f*, ligne isobarique *f*, NAUT, PETR *atom*, PHYS *atom* isobare *f*

isobaric: ~ **map** *n* METEO carte isobarique *f*; ~ **spin** *n (cf isospin)* PHYS isospin *m*, spin isobarique *m*, spin isotopique *m*

isobath *n* GEOL, NAUT, OCEANOG, PETR isobathe *f*

isoborneol *n* CHEM isobornéol *m*

isobutane *n* CHEM, PETR TECH isobutane *m*

isobutyl *n* CHEM isobutyle *m*

isobutylene *n* CHEM isobutylène *m*, isobutène *m*

isobutylic *adj* CHEM isobutylique

isobutyric *adj* CHEM isobutyrique

isocheim *n* METEO isochimène *f*; ~ **core** *n* METEO isochore *f*

isochemical: ~ **metamorphism** *n* GEOL métamorphisme isochimique *m*, métamorphisme topochimique *m*

isochime *n* METEO isochimène *f*

isochor *n* PHYS isochore *f*

isochore *n* GEOL *fluid inclusions*, PHYS isochore *f*

isochronal: ~ **annealing** *n* METALL recuit isochrone *m*; ~ **surface** *n* GEOL isochrone *f*; ~ **time line** *n* GEOL isochrone *f*

isochrone *n* GEOL diagramme de Nicolaysen *f*, isochrone *f*; ~ **diagram** *n* GEOL diagramme de Nicolaysen *f*, diagramme isochrone *m*, isochrone *f*

isochronism *n* PETR isochronisme *m*

isochronous[1] *adj* COMP, DP isochrone

isochronous:[2] ~ **transmission** *n* COMP, DP transmission isochrone *f*

isocinchomeronic *adj* CHEM isocinchoméronique

isoclinal[1] *adj* GEOPHYS isoclinal

isoclinal:[2] ~ **fold** *n* PETR pli isoclinal *m*; ~ **line** *n* PHYS isocline *f*

isocline *n* GEOPHYS isoclinal *m*

isoclinic: ~ **line** *n* GEOPHYS ligne isocline *f*

isocracking *n* PETR isocraquage *m*

isocrotonic *adj* CHEM isocrotonique

isocyanate *n* CHEM, P&R *plastics, raw material*, PROP MAT isocyanate *m*; ~ **plastic** *n* PROP MAT plastique isocyanate *m*

isocyanic *adj* CHEM isocyanique

isocyanide *n* CHEM carbylamine *f*, isocyanure *m*

isocyclic *adj* CHEM isocyclique

isodulcital *n* CHEM isodulcite *f*

isodynamic: ~ **flux lines** *n pl* GEOPHYS contour de flux constant *m*; ~ **line** *n* GEOPHYS courbe isodynamique *f*

isoelectric[1] *adj* CHEM *point* isoélectrique

isoelectric:[2] ~ **vehicle** *n* TRANSP automobile isoélectrique *f*

isofacies *n* GEOL courbe d'isofaciès *f*, isofaciès *m*

isofenchol *n* CHEM isofenchol *m*

isoflavone *n* CHEM isoflavone *f*

isoformate *n* CHEM isoformat *m*

isoforming *n* CHEM procédé de reformage catalytique *m*

isogal *n* GEOL isogal *m*

isogam *n* GEOL isogamme *f*

isogonal *adj* GEOM isogone, GEOPHYS isogone *f*

isogonic: ~ **line** *n* GEOPHYS ligne isogone *f*

isograd *n* GEOL *metamorphic* isograde *f*

isogram *n* METEO, PETR isogramme *m*

isohaline *n* GEOL isohaline *f*, ligne d'égale salinité *f*

isohel *n* METEO isohèle *f*

isohypse *n* GEOL isohypse *f*

isokinetic: ~ **sampling** *n* QUALITY échantillonnage isocinétique *m*

isolable *adj* CHEM isolable

isolac *n* COATINGS vernis isolant *m*

isolate *vt* CHEM dégager, isoler, ELEC ENG localiser, mettre hors circuit, *galvanically* isoler, SAFETY isoler

isolated: ~ **danger mark** *n* NAUT *navigation marks* marque de danger isolé *f*; ~ **feed through input** *n* ELEC ENG entrée par traversée isolante *f*; ~ **neutral system** *n* ELEC réseau à neutre isolé *m*; ~ **system** *n* PHYS système isolé *m*

isolating *n* PROD ENG isolement *m*; ~ **switch** *n* CONTROL, ELEC interrupteur séparateur *m*, ELEC ENG sectionneur *m*, sectionneur de protection *m*; ~ **valve** *n* LAB EQUIP vanne de sectionnement *f*, PROD ENG robinet d'isolement *m*

isolation *n* COMP, DP isolation *f*, PROD ENG isolement *m*, SPACE *communications* discrimination *f*, découplage *m*, isolement *m*; ~ **amplifier** *n* ELECTRON amplificateur d'isolement *m*; ~ **diode** *n* ELECTRON diode d'isolement *f*; ~ **transformer** *n* ELEC ENG transformateur d'isolement *m*, PROD ENG transformateur isolant *m*; ~ **valve** *n* PROD ENG, SPACE *spacecraft* vanne d'isolement *f*

isolator *n* OPT isolateur affaiblisseur *m*, PHYS *microwaves* affaiblisseur non-réciproque *m*, atténuateur unidirectionnel *m*, isolateur *m*, TELECOM isolateur *m*

isoleucine *n* CHEM isoleucine *f*

isolog *n* (AmE) *see isologue*

isologous *adj* CHEM isologue

isologue *n* (BrE) CHEM isologue *m*

isomer *n* PHYS *nuclear*, PROP MAT isomère *m*

isomeric[1] *adj* PROP MAT isomère

isomeric:[2] ~ **transition** *n* RAD PHYS transition isomérique *f*

isomeride *n* CHEM isomère *m*

isomerism *n* CHEM isomérie *f*, PHYS isomérie *f*, isomérisme *m*

isomerization *n* CHEM, PETR TECH isomérisation *f*

isomers *n pl* PETR TECH, RAD PHYS isomères *m pl*

isometric *adj* CRYSTALL cubique

isomorphism *n* CHEM, CRYSTALL isomorphisme *m*

isomorphous[1] *adj* GEOL isomorphe

isomorphous:[2] ~ **replacement** *n* CRYSTALL substitution isomorphe *f*; ~ **series** *n* CRYSTALL série isomorphe *f*

isonicotinic *adj* CHEM isonicotinique

isonitrile *n* CHEM isonitrile *m*

isooctane *n* CHEM isooctane *m*

isopach *n* GEOL isopaque *m*; ~ **map** *n* GEOL carte d'isopaques *f*, carte isopache *f*, PETR TECH *geophysical survey* isopaque *m*

isoparaffins *n pl* CHEM isoparaffines *f pl*

isopelletierine *n* CHEM isopellétiérine *f*

isopentane *n* CHEM isopentane *m*

isophorone: ~ **diamine** *n* P&R *curing agent* isophorone diamine *f*

isopleth *n* CHEM, GEOL isoplèthe *f*

isopoly: ~ **acid** *n* CHEM isopolyacide *m*

isoprene *n* CHEM isoprène *m*

isoprenoid *n* CHEM isoprénoïde *m*

isopropanol *n* CHEM isopropanol *m*, DETERGENTS alcool isopropylique *m*, isopropanol *m*

isopropenyl *n* CHEM isopropényle *m*

isopropyl[1] *adj* CHEM isopropylique

isopropyl[2] *n* CHEM isopropyle *m*; ~ **acid** *n* *(IPA)* DETER-GENTS alcool isopropylique *m*, isopropanol *m*; ~ **alcohol** *n* FOOD TECH alcool isopropylique *m*

isopropylbenzene *n* CHEM isopropylbenzène *m*

isopropylcarbinol *n* CHEM alcool isobutylique *m*, isopropylcarbinol *m*

isopropylic: ~ **alcohol** *n* *(IPA)* PRINT alcool isopropylique *m*

isoquinoline *n* CHEM isoquinoléine *f*

isosceles: ~ **triangle** *n* GEOM triangle isocèle *m*

isoseismal *adj* GEOPHYS isosiste

isoseismic: ~ **line** *n* GEOL courbe isosiste *f*

isospin *n* *(cf isobaric spin)* PHYS isospin *m*, spin isobarique *m*, spin isotopique *m*

isostacy *n* FUELLESS, GEOL isostasie *f*

isostasy *n* FUELLESS, GEOL isostasie *f*

isostatic: ~ **adjustment** *n* GEOL compensation isostatique *f*

isosteric *adj* CHEM isostérique, isostère

isosterism *n* CHEM isostérie *f*

isostress *n* AERONAUT isocontrainte *f*

isotactic *adj* CHEM *polymer* isotactique

isotherm *n* AERONAUT, GEOL, METEO, NAUT *meteorology*, PETR, PHYS isotherme *f*

isothermal[1] *adj* MECH *thermodynamics*, PHYS isotherme

isothermal:[2] ~ **annealing** *n* METALL recuit isothermique *m*; ~ **compressibility** *n* PHYS compressibilité isotherme *f*; ~ **crystallization** *n* PROP MAT cristallisation isotherme *f*; ~ **curve** *n* PHYS courbe isotherme *f*; ~ **expansion** *n* PHYS dilatation isotherme *f*; ~ **layer** *n* METEO couche isotherme *f*; ~ **quenching** *n* METALL trempe isothermique *f*; ~ **reaction** *n* METALL réaction isotherme *f*; ~ **test** *n* METALL essai isotherme *m*

isotone *n* PHYS isotone *m*

isotope *n* CHEM *of element*, GEOL, NUCLEAR, PART PHYS, PHYS isotope *m*; ~ **geology** *n* GEOL géochimie isotopique *f*; ~ **measurement** *n* COAL TECH mesure aux radionucléides *f*; ~ **separation** *n* PART PHYS séparation des isotopes *f*, séparation isotopique *f*

isotopic: ~ **abundance** *n* NUCLEAR teneur isotopique *f*, PHYS abondance isotopique *f*; ~ **analysis** *n* RAD PHYS analyse isotopique *f*; ~ **anomaly** *n* PHYS anomalie isotopique *f*; ~ **enrichment** *n* PART PHYS enrichisse-ment isotopique *m*; ~ **generator** *n* SPACE *spacecraft* générateur radio-isotopique *m*; ~ **number** *n* PART PHYS nombre isotopique *m*, PHYS *neutron excess* excès de neutrons *m*; ~ **spin** *n* PHYS isospin *m*, spin isobarique *m*, spin isotopique *m*; ~ **tracer** *n* NUCLEAR indicateur isotopique *m*, traceur *m*

isotopically: ~ **tagged compound** *n* NUCLEAR composé marqué *m*

isotopy *n* CHEM isotopie *f*

isotropic[1] *adj* ASTRON isotropique, CRYSTALL, GEOL *me-dia*, OPT *electromagnetic waves*, SPACE *communications*, TELECOM isotrope

isotropic:[2] ~ **antenna** *n* SPACE *communications* antenne isotrope *f*; ~ **distribution** *n* ASTRON *of galaxies* répartition isotropique *f*; ~ **gain** *n* SPACE *communica-*

tions gain isotrope *m*; ~ **medium** *n* PROP MAT milieu isotrope *m*; ~ **turbulence** *n* FLUID PHYS turbulence isotrope *f*

isotropy *n* CRYSTALL, GEOL isotropie *f*

isovalerone *n* CHEM isovalérone *m*

isovanilline *n* CHEM isovanilline *f*

isoweight: ~ **curve** *n* AERONAUT courbe isopoids *f*

isoxazole *n* CHEM isoxazole *m*

ISR *abbr* *(information storage and retrieval)* COMP, DP stockage-restitution des données *m*

issue *n* NUCLEAR carneau à gaz *m*, évent de gaz *m*

isthmus *n* NAUT *geography* isthme *m*

IT *abbr* COMP *(information technology)* informatique *f*, TELECOM *(intermediate trunk)* canal interurbain intermédiaire *m*, TELECOM *(information technology)* informatique *f*, télématique *f*, TELECOM *(information type)* type d'information *m*

itaconic *adj* CHEM itaconique, *acid* itaconique

italic[1] *adj* PRINT italique

italic:[2] ~ **character** *n* DP caractère italique *m*; ~ **type** *n* PRINT caractères italiques *m pl*

italicize *vt* PRINT italiciser

italics *n pl* PRINT italiques *m pl*

itching *n* OCEANOG puces *f pl*

ITD *abbr* *(input transaction accepted for delivery)* TELE-COM acceptation pour remise *f*

item *n* COMP, DP article *m*, élément *m*, MECH ENG article *m*, QUALITY individu *m*, unité *f*, TEXTILES article *m*; ~ **number** *n* MECH ENG repère *m*

itemize *vt* TEXTILES spécifier

iterate *vt* COMP, DP itérer

iteration *n* COMP, DP itération *f*, POLLUTION processus itératif *m*

iterative[1] *adj* COMP, DP itératif

iterative:[2] ~ **guidance** *n* SPACE *spacecraft* guidage par itération *m*; ~ **impedance** *n* ACOUSTICS, ELEC *of quadri-pole*, ELEC ENG, PHYS impédance itérative *f*; ~ **method** *n* COMP, DP méthode itérative *f*; ~ **process** *n* COMP, DP processus itératif *m*

itinerary *n* NAUT itinéraire *m*

ITR *abbr* *(input transaction rejected)* TELECOM rejet de transaction d'entrée *m*

ITT *abbr* *(integrated transit time)* PETR TECH *seismic survey* intégration du temps de trajet *f*

I-type: ~ **semiconductor** *n* ELECTRON semi-conducteur intrinsèque *m*

IUE *abbr* *(International Ultraviolet Explorer Satellite)* ASTRON Satellite Explorer pour l'étude en ultravio-let *m*

IUS *abbr* *(Inertial Upper Stage)* SPACE étage supérieur inertiel *m*

ivory: ~ **board** *n* PAPER TECH bristol *m*

IVPO *abbr* *(inside vapour phase oxidation, inside vapor phase oxidation)* TELECOM dépôt en phase vapeur interne *m*

IWP *abbr* *(interworking protocol)* TELECOM protocole d'interfonctionnement *m*

J

J *abbr (joule)* ELEC, FOOD TECH, MECH, METR, PHYS, THERMOD J *(joule)*

jacinth *n* MINERAL jacinthe *f*

jack[1] *n* CINEMAT fiche *f*, jack *m*, prise *f*, COMP fiche *f*, CONST *sawhorse* chevalet de scieur *m*, chèvre *f*, CONTROL vérin *m*, ELEC *connection* jack *m*, ELEC ENG jack *m*, prise de jack *f*, *plugboard* plot *m*, LAB EQUIP *support* support élévateur *m*, MECH cric *m*, vérin *m*, MECH ENG *rack-and-pinion type* cric *m*, *screw type* vérin *m*, NAUT pavillon de beaupré *m*, PROD ENG vérin *m*, RECORDING fiche *f*, jack *m*, TELECOM jack *m*, VEHICLES *tool* cric *m*; ~ **arch** *n* C&G voûte plate *f*; ~ **box** *n* MECH ENG boîte à jacks *f*; ~ **bush** *n* ELEC ENG douille de jack *f*; ~ **field** *n* CINEMAT panneau de branchement *m*; ~ **flag** *n* NAUT pavillon de beaupré *m*; ~ **leg** *n* MINING pousseur pneumatique *m*, poussoir pneumatique *m*; ~ **off screw** *n* MECH ENG extracteur à vis *m*; ~ **panel** *n* (BrE) *(cf patch panel)* COMP tableau de connexions *m*, RECORDING patch de raccordement jack *m*; ~ **plane** *n* CONST demi-varlope *f*, mouchette *f*, riflard *m*; ~ **plug** *n* CINEMAT connecteur *m*, fiche *f*, jack *m*, prise *f*, ELEC ENG fiche de jack *f*, *plugboard* cavalier *m*; ~ **rafter** *n* CONST *building* empannon *m*; ~ **rod** *n* PROD ENG tige de vérin *f*; ~ **socket** *n* CINEMAT douille *f*, fiche femelle *f*, prise femelle *f*; ~ **strip** *n* ELEC ENG réglette de jacks *f*; ~ **switch** *n* CONTROL commutateur à fiches *m*; ~ **switchboard** *n* ELEC commutateur à jacks *m*

jack[2] *vt* VEHICLES *body* soulever au cric

jacked:[1] ~ **in** *adj* ELEC ENG connecté par jack

jacked:[2] ~ **pile** *n* COAL TECH pieu poussé *m*

jacket[1] *n* ELEC *cable* gaine *f*, ELEC ENG enveloppe *f*, HEATING *boilers* habillage *m*, LAB EQUIP *glassware* enveloppe *f*, MECH chemise *f*, enveloppe *f*, MECH ENG *insulation* enveloppe *f*, NUCLEAR *for heating, cooling* chemise *f*, PETR TECH jacket *m*, PHYS *cable* gaine *f*, PROD ENG *clothing plate* chemise *f*, enveloppe de tôle *f*, tôle d'enveloppe *f*, *non-conducting material* enveloppe *f*, garniture *f*, SPACE *spacecraft* chemise *f*, enveloppe *f* ~ **brush** *n* PAPER TECH brosse rotative *f*; ~ **coldroom** *n* REFRIG chambre froide à double paroi *f*; ~ **cooling** *n* NUCLEAR refroidissement par chemise *m*; ~ **heating system** *n* NUCLEAR système de chauffage de la chemise *m*; ~ **platform** *n* PETR TECH plate-forme en acier *f*

jacket[2] *vt* PROD ENG envelopper, garnir

jacketed *adj* MECH chemisé

jacketing *n* NUCLEAR chemisage *m*, enrobage *m*, TEXTILES tissu pour veste *m*

jackhammer *n* MINING *drilling, boring* burin *m*, fleuret *m*, foreuse *f*, perforateur *m*, pistolet *m*, sondeuse *f*

jackleg: ~ **drill** *n* MINING marteau perforateur à poussoir pneumatique *m*

jackscrew *n* MECH ENG vérin *m*, vérin de calage *m*; ~ **with self-adjusting head** *n* MECH ENG turc à tête inclinable *m*, vérin de calage avec tête à rotule *m*

jackshaft *n* MECH ENG arbre de renvoi *m*, arbre secondaire *m*, axe secondaire *m*, PROD ENG *stamp mill* arbre de relevage *m*

Jackson: ~ **model** *n* NUCLEAR modèle de Jackson *m*

jackup: ~ **platform** *n* PETR plate-forme auto-élévatrice *f*; ~ **rig** *n* PETR TECH plate-forme auto-élévatrice *f*

jacquard: ~ **board** *n* PACKAGING, PAPER TECH carton jacquard *m*; ~ **fabric** *n* TEXTILES tissu jacquard *m*; ~ **paper** *n* PACKAGING, PAPER TECH papier jacquard *m*

Jacquard: ~ **loom** *n* TEXTILES métier jacquard *m*

jad *n* MINING havage *m*, souchevage *m*, sous-cave *f*, souschevage *m*

jadeite *n* MINERAL jadéite *f*

jag:[1] ~ **bolt** *n* CONST boulon de scellement à crans *m*

jag[2] *vt* PROD ENG *caulking* mater, matir, matter

jagged[1] *adj* MECH *tools* ébréché, SAFETY déchiqueté

jagged:[2] ~ **bolt** *n* CONST boulon de scellement à crans *m*; ~ **edge of a blade** *n* SAFETY lame déchiquetée *f*; ~ **edge trimmer** *n* PHOTO cisaille-déchiqueteuse *f*

jagging *n* PROD ENG *caulking* matage *m*

jalapic *adj* CHEM jalapique

jalapin *n* CHEM jalapine *f*

jalousie *n* C&G jalousie *f* (Fra), louvre *m* (Bel)

jalpaite *n* MINERAL jalpaïte *f*

jam[1] *n* CINEMAT bourrage *m*, MECH ENG coincement *m*, PRINT *machine* bourrage *m*; ~ **cleat** *n* NAUT *deck fittings* taquet coinceur *m*; ~ **nut** *n* MECH ENG contre-écrou *m*

jam[2] *vt* HYDR EQUIP *valve* caler, MECH bloquer, caler, coincer, MECH ENG coincer, MILIT brouiller, NAUT bloquer, TELECOM brouiller

jam[3] *vi* MECH s'enrayer, se bloquer, se coincer

jamb *n* C&G jambage de brûleur *m*, CONST *doorway* jambage *m*, montant de porte *m*, poteau d'huisserie *m*, *fireplace* jambage *m*, *window opening* jambage *m*, montant de fenêtre *m*; ~ **block** *n* (BrE) *(cf edger block)* C&G brique de main *f*; ~ **lining** *n* CONST chambranle *m*, châssis de porte *m*; ~ **post** *n* CONST *doorway* jambage *m*, montant de porte *m*, poteau d'huisserie *m*, *window opening* jambage *m*, montant de fenêtre *m*; ~ **stone** *n* CONST jambage en pierre *m*

jamesonite *n* MINERAL jamesonite *f*

jammed *adj* MECH ENG coincé, SPACE *spacecraft* enrayé

jammer *n* ELECTRON, MILIT brouilleur *m*; ~ **oscillator** *n* ELECTRON oscillateur de brouilleur *m*

jamming *n* AUTO grippage *m*, ELECTRON blocage *m*, bourrage *m*, brouillage *m*, MECH ENG coincement *m*, coinçage *m*, MILIT brouillage *m*, TELECOM brouillage *m*, brouillage intentionnel *m*; ~ **signal** *n* ELECTRON signal de brouillage *m*

japan *n* COLOURS laque du Japon *f*; ~ **work** *n* COLOURS laquage *m*

Japanese: ~ **lacquer** *n* COLOURS laque d'orient *f*

japanic *adj* CHEM japanique

jar *n* FOOD TECH bocal *m*, MINING *boring* coulisse *f*, PACKAGING *for preserves* bocal *m*, PROD ENG battement *m*, choc *m*, secousse *f*

jargon *n* MINERAL jargon *m*

jargoon *n* MINERAL jargon *m*

jarosite *n* MINERAL jarosite *f*

jarring *n* PROD ENG battement *m*, choc *m*, secousse *f*; ~

table n PACKAGING table à secousses f; **~ test** n PACKAGING essai de secousses m

jaspé: ~ yarn n TEXTILES fil jaspé m

jasper n GEOL, MINERAL jaspe m

jasperite n GEOL jaspe m

jaspilite n GEOL chert ferrugineux rubané m, jaspilite f

JATO abbr (jet-assisted takeoff) TRANSP décollage assisté m

javelin-shaped: ~ fuel rod n NUCLEAR crayon combustible en forme de javelot m

javellization n CHEM javellisation f

jaw n COAL TECH mâchoire f, MECH tools bec m, mors m, mâchoire f, MECH ENG bec m, mors m, mâchoire f, of knuckle joint chape f, NUCLEAR of grab, manipulator, PAPER TECH mâchoire f; **~ breaker** n MECH ENG broyeur à mâchoires m, concasseur à mâchoires m, PRODUCTION broyeur à mâchoires m; **~ chuck** n MECH ENG plateau à griffes m, machine tools mandrin à mors m; **~ clutch** n MECH ENG embrayage à mâchoires m; **~ clutching** n AUTO crabotage m; **~ crusher** n COAL TECH, LAB EQUIP preparation concasseur à mâchoires m, MECH ENG, PROD ENG broyeur à mâchoires m, concasseur à mâchoires m; **~ dog** n MECH ENG lathe carrier with two jaws toc à coussinets m; **~ fold** n PRINT pli parallèle m; **~ holder** n MECH ENG porte-mâchoire m; **~ plate** n COAL TECH garniture de mâchoires f; **~ steady rest** n MECH ENG machine tools lunette à coussinets f

JCL abbr (job control language) COMP langage de contrôle des travaux m

JDF abbr (junction distribution frame) TELECOM répartiteur de jonction m

jellification n CHEM TECH gélification f

jelly: ~ gum n PRINT gomme gélifiante f

jemmy n (BrE) MECH tools pince-monseigneur f

jenkinsite n MINERAL jenkinsite f

jenny n CINEMAT groupe électrogène m, PROD ENG chariot de roulement m

jeremejevite n MINERAL jérémiéiewite f

jerk n MECH ENG secousse f, à-coup m, SPACE secousse f

jerky: ~ flow n METALL écoulement discontinu m, écoulement irrégulier m

jeroboam n C&G jeroboam m

jerry: ~ can n MILIT bidon à essence m, jerrican m, TRANSP jerrican m, nourrice f

jervine n CHEM jervine f

jet¹ n AERONAUT carburettor gicleur m, space technology avion à réaction propulseur m, ASTRON jet m, AUTO gicleur m, FLUID PHYS giclée f, jet m, GEOL jais m, METALL jet m, MINERAL jais m, jayet m, NUCLEAR fluid, PETR TECH drill bit jet m, PHYS fluid jet m, veine f, nozzle tuyère f, PROD ENG coulée f, jet de coulée m, trou de coulée m, jet m, SPACE spacecraft jet m, TRANSP avion à réaction m, WATER SUPP emission of fluid jet m, nozzle ajutage m **~ aeroplane** n (BrE) TRANSP avion à réaction m; **~ airplane** n (AmE) see jet aeroplane; **~ bit** n PETR TECH trépan à jet m; **~ bit drilling** n PETR TECH forage au trépan à jet m; **~ body** n SPACE corps de propulseur m; **~ cock** n WATER SUPP robinet d'arrosage m; **~ condenser** n HYDR EQUIP condenseur à injection m, condenseur à jet m; **~ cooling** n REFRIG refroidissement par jet d'air froid m, réfrigération par jet d'air froid f; **~ deflector** n SPACE spacecraft déflecteur de jet m; **~ diameter** n FUELLESS diamètre de jet m; **~ drilling** n COAL TECH forage par jet de flammes m; **~ engine** n AERONAUT moteur à réaction m, réacteur m, MECH, SPACE spacecraft moteur à réaction m, THER-

MOD, TRANSP réacteur m; **~ engine fuel** n AERONAUT carburéacteur m; **~ flapped rotor** n AERONAUT helicopter rotor soufflé m; **~ freezing** n REFRIG congélation par jet d'air f; **~ fuel** n AERONAUT carburéacteur m; **~ helicopter** n AERONAUT hélicoptère à réaction m; **~ instability** n FLUID PHYS instabilité d'un jet f; **~ noise suppressor** n AERONAUT silencieux de piste m; **~ nozzle** n AERONAUT tuyère d'éjection f, SPACE spacecraft tuyère f; **~ piercing** n COAL TECH forage à jet m; **~ pipe** n SPACE tuyère f; **~ pipe temperature** n AERONAUT température de tuyère f; **~ plane** n avion à réaction m; **~ propulsion** n AERONAUT réaction f, MILIT, SPACE spacecraft propulsion à réaction f; **~ pump** n NUCLEAR pompe à jet f, WATER SUPP hydroéjecteur m; **~ sled** n PETR traîneau d'ensouillage par injection m; **~ stream** n AERONAUT jet-stream m, METEO courant-jet m; **~ sulfur burner** n (AmE), **~ sulphur burner** n (BrE) PAPER TECH four à soufre pulvérisé m; **~ turbine** n TRANSP turboréacteur m; **~ turbine engine** n TRANSP turboréacteur m; **~ velocity** n SPACE spacecraft vitesse d'éjection f; **~ wash** n AERONAUT jet des réacteurs m

jet² vt FLUID PHYS liquids faire jaillir, gicler

JET abbr (Joint European Torus) NUCLEAR, RAD PHYS JET (tore européen conjoint); **~ Tokamac** abbr NUCLEAR, RAD PHYS JET Tokamac m

jet-assisted: ~ takeoff n (JATO) TRANSP décollage assisté m

jetfoil n NAUT hydroglisseur m

jetsam n NAUT épaves rejetées f pl, OCEANOG jet à la mer m

jettison¹ n OCEANOG jet à la mer m; **~ valve** n AERONAUT vide-vite m, SPACE spacecraft vanne de vidange f, vide-vite m

jettison² vt AERONAUT délester, larguer, vidanger, éjecter, NAUT délester, jeter par-dessus bord, jeter à la mer, SPACE spacecraft larguer, éjecter

jettisonable¹ adj SPACE spacecraft largable

jettisonable:² ~ window n AERONAUT hublot éjectable m

jetty n CONST, NAUT jetée f, OCEANOG épi m

jetway n AERONAUT passerelle f

jeweled adj (AmE) see jewelled

jeweler's: ~ eyepiece n (AmE) see jeweller's eyepiece

jewelled adj (BrE) MECH monté sur rubis

jeweller's: ~ eyepiece n (BrE) INSTRUMENT loupe de lapidaire f

jib n AERONAUT helicopter bras d'un treuil m, CINEMAT bras d'une grue m, CONST of crane crochet m, flèche f, volée f, NAUT sail foc m, NUCLEAR crane flèche f, porte-à-faux m; **~ boom** n MAR POLL tangon écarteur m; **~ crane** n CONST grue à flèche f, grue à volée f, NUCLEAR grue pivotante f, grue à flèche f; **~ post** n CONST crane arbre m, fût m

jig n COAL TECH bac à piston m, crible hydraulique m, MECH tools montage de fabrication m, outillage m, MECH ENG former or templet calibre m, calibre de forme m, gabarit m, singe m, work-holding device and tool guide gabarit m, METR testing and gauging montage m, MINING plan incliné automoteur à simple effet m, plan à simple effet m, pneumatic or dry type oredressing sasseur m, with fixed sieve bac à pistonnage m, crible hydraulique à piston m, crible à grille fixe m, crible à piston m, with movable sieve crible hydraulique m, crible à grille mobile m, hydrotamis m, jig m, OCEANOG leurre m, SAFETY for use with routers gabarit m; **~ bed** n COAL TECH lit de lavage m; **~ borer** n MECH machine à pointer f; **~ boring** n MECH ENG alésage en coordonnées *m*; **boring machine** *n* MECH ENG machine à pointer et à aléser *f*; ~ **boring vice** *n* (BrE) MECH ENG étau pour aléseuse-pointeuse *m*; ~ **boring vise** *n* (AmE) *see jig boring vice*; ~ **brow** *n* MINING plan incliné automoteur à simple effet *m*, plan à simple effet *m*; ~ **bush** *n* MECH ENG guide de perçage *m*; ~ **dyeing** *n* COLOURS teinture au jigger *f*; ~ **grinding** *n* MECH ENG rectification en coordonnées *f*; ~ **mill** *n* MINING *ore-dressing* atelier de concentration des grenailles et sables *m*; ~ **milling** *n* MECH ENG fraisage d'après calibre *m*; ~ **pit** *n* AERONAUT fosse de bâti *f*; ~ **plane** *n* MINING plan incliné automoteur à simple effet *m*, plan à simple effet *m*; ~ **saw blade** *n* MECH ENG *tool* lame pour scie sauteuse *f*; ~ **sieve** *n* COAL TECH grille de lavage *f*; ~ **table** *n* NUCLEAR crible oscillant *m*

jigger *n* TEXTILES mesure d'une once et demie *f* ~ **screen** *n* MINING crible *m*

jigging *n* COAL TECH pistonnage *m*, MINING *ore-dressing* criblage *m*, lavage au bac à piston *m*, lavage au jig *m*, sassage *m*, sassement *m*

jigsaw[1] *n* CONST sauteuse *f*, scie à chantourner *f*, scie à découper *f*

jigsaw[2] *vt* CONST chantourner

jigsawing *n* CONST chantournement *m*

jim: ~ **crow** *n* CONST *clawbar* pince à pied-de-biche *f*

jimmy *n* (AmE) *see jemmy*

jiningite *n* NUCLEAR *thorium mineral* jiningite *f*

J-integral: ~ **method** *n* NUCLEAR méthode d'intégrale de Rice *f*

JIT *abbr (just-in-time)* PACKAGING, TEXTILES juste à temps *m*

jitter *n* COMP gigue *f*, DP instabilité *f*, ELECTRON gigue *f*, instabilité *f*, TELECOM gigue *f*, TV fluctuation de phase *f*, gigue *f*, sautillement *m*

jitter-free *adj* ELECTRON sans gigue, stable

j-j: ~ **coupling** *n* NUCLEAR, PHYS couplage j-j *m*

job *n* COMP, DP travail *m*; ~ **accounting** *n* COMP, DP comptabilisation des travaux *f*; ~ **batch** *n* COMP, DP lot de travaux *m*; ~ **control** *n* COMP gestion des travaux *f*, DP contrôle des travaux *m*, gestion des travaux *f*; ~ **control language** *n (JCL)* COMP langage de contrôle des travaux *m*; ~ **cycle safety audit** *n* CONST audit de sécurité du cycle de travail *m*; ~ **definition** *n* COMP, DP définition des travaux *f*; ~ **oriented terminal** *n* COMP terminal spécialisé travaux *m*; ~ **processing system** *n* COMP, DP système de traitement de travaux *m*; ~ **request** *n* COMP, DP demande de travail *f*; ~ **scheduler** *n* COMP, DP programmateur de travaux *m*; ~ **sequence list** *n* PROD ENG liste d'activités *f*; ~ **shop** *n* PROD ENG fabrication par lots *f*, fabrication à la commande *f*, production à la commande *f*; ~ **stack** *n* COMP file de travaux *f*, DP file de travaux *f*, flot de travaux *m*; ~ **step** *n* COMP, DP étape de travail *f*; ~ **stream** *n* COMP, DP flot de travaux *m*, flux de travaux *m*; ~ **ticket** *n* PROD ENG bon de production *m*, bon de réalisation *m*, bon de travail *m*

jobber: ~ **drill** *n* MECH ENG foret à queue cylindrique court *m*

jobbing *n* PRINT bilboquets *m pl*, bimbeloterie *f*, travaux de ville *m pl*; ~ **contractor** *n* CONST entrepreneur à la tâche *m*; ~ **face** *n* PRINT caractère travaux de ville *m*; ~ **ink** *n* PRINT encre pour les travaux de ville *f*; ~ **type** *n* PRINT caractères de labeur *m pl*

jockey *n* MECH ENG *tightening pulley* galet tendeur *m*, poulie de tension *f*, rouleau de tension *m*; ~ **pulley** *n* MECH galet de tension *m*, MECH ENG galopin de tension

m, PAPER TECH poulie de tension *f*; ~ **roller** *n* MECH ENG *tightening pulley* galet tendeur *m*, poulie de tension *f*, rouleau de tension *m*, PAPER TECH *printing* poulie de tension *f*; ~ **wheel** *n* MECH ENG *tightening pulley* galet tendeur *m*, poulie de tension *f*, rouleau de tension *m*

Jodel: ~ **detector** *n* NUCLEAR *for measuring voids in sodium* détecteur Jodel *m*

jog[1] *n* CRYSTALL *in a dislocation*, METALL cran *m*

jog[2] *vt* PRINT faire marcher par à-coups, taquer

jogged: ~ **screw dislocation** *n* METALL dislocation vis crantée *f*

joggle[1] *n* CONST embrèvement *m*, *dowel, coak* goujon *m*, goujon prisonnier *m*; ~ **joint** *n* CONST *carpentry* assemblage à embrèvement *m*; ~ **piece** *n* MECH ENG *king post* poinçon *m*; ~ **post** *n* MECH ENG *king post* poinçon *m*

joggle[2] *vt* CONST embrever, goujonner

joggling: ~ **table** *n* MINING *ore-dressing* table à secousses *f*

Johannite *n* MINERAL, NUCLEAR johannite *f*

Johansson: ~ **gage** *n* (AmE), ~ **gauge** *n* (BrE) MECH *tools* cale Johansson *f*

Johnson: ~ **noise** *n* ELECTRON bruit Johnson *m*, PHYS bruit d'agitation thermique *m*

join[1] *n* CINEMAT collure *f*, GEOM ligne *f*

join[2] *vt* CINEMAT coller, CONST assembler, joindre, raccorder, réunir, unir, unir ensemble; ~ **on** *vt* CONST rapporter; ~ **a traffic stream** *vt* TRANSP insérer dans un courant de circulation; ~ **up** *vt* CONST *pipes* aboucher, ajointer

joinable: ~ **container** *n* TRANSP conteneur assemblable *m*

joiner *n* CINEMAT colleuse *f*, presse à coller *f*, CONST *person* menuisier *m*

joiner's: ~ **bench** *n* CONST banc de menuisier *m*, établi de menuisier *m*; ~ **bevel** *n* CONST télégraphe de menuisier *m*; ~ **cramp** *n* CONST *sash cramp* sergent *m*, serre-joint *m*, serre-joints *m*; ~ **gage** *n* (AmE), ~ **gauge** *n* (BrE) CONST trousquin *m*, troussequin *m*, trusquin *m*

joinery *n* CONST menuiserie *f*

joining *n* C&G collage *m*, CONST assemblage *m*, emmanchement *m*, jointure *f*, jonction *f*, réunion *f*, union *f*, NUCLEAR *operation* assemblage *m*; ~ **process** *n* PROD ENG procédé d'assemblage *m*

joint *n* CONST articulation *f*, assemblage *m*, jointure *f*, *hinge* joint *m*, ELEC *connection* raccordement *m*, ELEC ENG connexion *f*, GEOL diaclase *f*, fissure *f*, MECH ENG jonction *f*, NUCLEAR *result of joining* assemblage *m*, joint *m*, OPT raccord *m*, PETR joint *m*, section de tube *f*, élément de tube *m*, PRINT mors *m*, saillie *f*, TELECOM raccord *m*, épissure *f*; ~ **applicant** *n* PATENTS codemandeur *m*; ~ **bar** *n* (AmE) *(cf fishplate)* RAIL éclisse *f*; ~ **box** *n* CONST boîte de joint *f*, ELEC *connection* boîte de jonction *f*; ~ **coating** *n* PETR revêtement de joint *m*; ~ **cramp** *n* CONST clameaux *m pl*, clampe *f*, crochet d'assemblage *m*, happe *f*; ~ **designation** *n* PATENTS désignation conjointe *f*; ~ **efficiency** *n* CONST *welding* coefficient de soudure *m*; ~ **plane** *n* GEOL plan de séparation *m*; ~ **preparation** *n* CONST *welding* préparation de joints *f*; ~ **ring** *n* NUCLEAR anneau joint *m*; ~ **riveting** *n* PROD ENG rivure d'assemblage *f*; ~ **set** *n* GEOL ensemble de joints parallèles *m*; ~ **strength** *n* PACKAGING solidité d'un joint *f*; ~ **user** *n* TELECOM co-usager *m*; ~ **venture** *n* CONST *commerce* co-entreprise *f*, joint venture *m*; ~ **water** *n* COAL TECH eau de fissure *f*

Joint: ~ **European Torus** *n (JET)* NUCLEAR, RAD PHYS tore européen conjoint *m (JET)* jointed: ~ **rule** n (BrE) *(cf folding rule, zigzag rule)* CONST règle articulée *f*; ~ **tool-holder** n MECH ENG porte-outil articulé *m*

jointer n CONST rabot d'établi *m*, varlope *f*, PROD ENG machine à faire les joints *f*, TELECOM soudeur *m*, épisseur *m*

jointing n GEOL diaclasage *m*, fissuration *f*, NUCLEAR fissuration *f*, PROD ENG assemblage *m*, emboîtement *m*, TELECOM joint *m*; ~ **machine** n PROD ENG machine à faire les joints *f*; ~ **plane** n CONST varlope *f*; ~ **yard** n C&G atelier de réparation des joints *m*

joint-twisting: ~ **pliers** n pl PROD ENG pince à torsade *f*

joist n CONST poutrelle *f*, solive *f*, soliveau *m*, PACKAGING solive *f*

joisting n CONST solivage *m*

Jominy: ~ **test** n MECH *materials* essai Jominy *m*, essai de trempabilité *m*

Josephson: ~ **constant** n PHYS constante de Josephson *f*; ~ **effect** n ELECTRON, NUCLEAR, PHYS effet Josephson *m*; ~ **junction** n ELECTRON, NUCLEAR, PHYS jonction de Josephson *f*

Jost: ~ **function** n NUCLEAR fonction de Jost *f*

joule n *(J)* ELEC *unit of energy*, FOOD TECH, MECH, METR, PHYS, THERMOD joule *m(J)*

Joule: ~ **effect** n ELEC *heat, current*, ELEC ENG, PHYS effet Joule *m*; ~ **expansion** n PHYS détente de Gay-Lussac *f*, détente de Joule *f*; ~ **heating** n NUCLEAR chauffage ohmique *m*

Joule's: ~ **equivalent** n ELEC *thermodynamics* équivalent mécanique de la chaleur *m*, MECH, PHYS équivalent mécanique de calorie *m*, THERMOD équivalent mécanique de calorie *m*, équivalent mécanique de la chaleur *m*; ~ **heat loss** n ELEC *resistance* perte par effet Joule *f*; ~ **law** n PHYS loi de Joule *f*

Joule-Kelvin: ~ **expansion** n PHYS détente de Joule-Kelvin *f*, détente de Joule-Thomson *f*

Joule-Thomson: ~ **expansion** n PHYS détente de Joule-Kelvin *f*, détente de Joule-Thomson *f*

journal n AUTO, MECH tourillon *m*, MECH ENG *of rolling mill roll* collet *m*, tourillon *m*, NUCLEAR *of bearing*, VEHICLES tourillon *m*; ~ **bearing** n MECH ENG *bearing block* palier *m*, NUCLEAR palier lisse *m*, palier à coussinet lisse *m*; ~ **box** n MECH ENG *bearing block* palier *m*, *enclosing bearing* boîte des coussinets *f*, RAIL *vehicles* boîte d'essieu *f*; ~ **cross** n MECH croisillon de cardan *m*; ~ **turbine** n HYDR EQUIP turbine axiale *f*, turbine parallèle *f*, turbine à paliers lisses *f*

journey: ~ **logbook** n AERONAUT carnet de bord *m*, carnet de route *m*; ~ **time** n RAIL temps de parcours *m*, TRANSP durée du trajet *f*

Jovian[1] adj ASTRON jovien

Jovian:[2] ~ **atmosphere** n ASTRON atmosphère jovienne *f*; ~ **bands** n pl ASTRON bandes de l'atmosphère jovienne *f pl*

Joy's: ~ **valve-gear** n HYDR EQUIP commande de distributeur Joy *f*, distribution Joy *f*

joystick n CINEMAT manche à balai *m*, manette tous azimuts *f*, COMP, DP manche à balai *m*, manette de jeux *f*, SPACE *spacecraft* levier de commande *m*, manche à balai *m*; ~ **selector** n ELEC *switch* commutateur à tige *m*

J-particle n PHYS particule J *f*

judder n SPACE *spacecraft* secousse *f*, trépidation *f*, ébranlement *m*

jug: ~ **hustler** n PETR TECH *geophysics* dérouleur *m*

juglone n CHEM juglon *m*

juice: ~ **content** n FOOD TECH teneur en jus *f*

jukebox n OPT juke-box *m*; ~ **filing system** n OPT système d'archivage avec juke-box *m*

Julian: ~ **calendar** n ASTRON calendrier julien *m*

jumbo n PROD ENG boîte réfrigérante *f*, manchon de refroidissement *m*; ~ **including boom** n MINING jumbo avec flèche *m*; ~ **jet** n AERONAUT gros porteur *m*, TRANSP avion gros porteur *m*, gros porteur *m*, réacteur gros porteur *m*; ~ **roll** n PAPER TECH bobine non rebobinée *f*

jumbo-size adj PROD ENG géant

jump[1] n COMP branchement *m*, saut *m*, DP *of programme* aiguillage *m*, branchement *m*, saut *m*, METALL saut *m*; ~ **cut** n CINEMAT faux raccord *m*, saut de montage *m*, TV faux raccord *m*; ~ **drilling** n CONST forage à la barre *m*; ~ **instruction** n COMP, DP instruction de saut *f*; ~ **lead** n ELEC *connection* jarretière *f*, VEHICLES *electrical system* câble de connexion d'accumulateurs *m*, jarretière *f*; ~ **rate** n METALL vitesse des sauts *f*; ~ **routine** n PROD ENG séquence de saut *f*; ~ **takeoff** n AERONAUT *helicopter* décollage sauté *m*; ~ **weld** n PROD ENG soudure par encollage *f*, soudure par rapprochement *f*; ~ **welding** n PROD ENG soudure par encollage *f*, soudure par rapprochement *f*

jump[2] vt MINING forer à la barre, PROD ENG *wheel tyre, head of a bolt* refouler

jump[3] vi ELEC *arc* jaillir, PROD ENG *saw* avoyer, donner de la voie à

jumper n ELEC *connection* connexion volante *f*, jarretière *f*, ELEC ENG connexion temporaire *f*, fil de connexion *m*, fil volant *m*, *computer* cavalier *m*, MINING barre de carrière *f*, barre de mineur *f*, barre à mine *f*, PROD ENG cavalier *m*, *sawset* tourne-à-gauche pour donner la voie aux scies *m*, TELECOM jarretière *f*, VEHICLES *electrical system* câble de connexion d'accumulateurs *m*, jarretière *f*; ~ **boring** n COAL TECH forage à percussion *m*; ~ **drill** n MINING barre de mineur *f*, barre à mine *f*; ~ **ring** n TELECOM anneau passe-jarretières *m*; ~ **stay** n NAUT *rigging* maroquin *m*, étai de guignol *m*; ~ **strut** n NAUT *mast* guignol *m*; ~ **wire** n TELECOM fil jarretière *m*

jumping: ~ **bolt heads** n pl PROD ENG refoulement des têtes de boulons *m*; ~ **drill** n MINING barre de mineur *f*, barre à mine *f*; ~ **sheet** n SAFETY *fire rescue* toile de sauvetage *f*

junction n COMP jonction *f*, CONST *roads, rivers* bifurcation *f*, embranchement *m*, jonction *f*, DP, ELEC *connection*, PROD ENG *union*, TELECOM jonction *f*; ~ **box** n ELEC *connection*, ELEC ENG boîte de jonction *f*, SPACE *spacecraft* boîte de jonction *f*, boîtier de raccordement *m*; ~ **cable** n ELEC ENG câble de jonction *m*; ~ **capacitance** n ELEC ENG capacité de jonction *f*; ~ **capacitor** n ELEC ENG condensateur à jonction *m*; ~ **diode** n ELEC *semiconductor*, ELECTRON diode à jonction *f*; ~ **distribution frame** n *(JDF)* TELECOM répartiteur de jonction *m*; ~ **FET** n ELECTRON TEC à jonction *m*; ~ **leakage** n ELEC ENG fuites de la jonction *f pl*; ~ **leakage current** n ELEC ENG courant de fuite dans la jonction *m*; ~ **plate** n ELEC ENG plaque de jonction *f*, PROD ENG couvre-joint *m*; ~ **point** n ELEC ENG point de jonction *m*; ~ **points** n RAIL aiguille de bifurcation *m*; ~ **station** n RAIL gare d'embranchement *f*, gare de bifurcation *f*; ~ **tandem exchange** n TELECOM commutateur de transit urbain *m*; ~ **transistor** n ELECTRON, PHYS transistor à jonction *m*

junctor n TELECOM circuit de connexion *m*, joncteur *m*

junk n MECH ferraille *f*, rebuts *m pl*, PROD ENG étoupe *f*; ~

packing *n* PROD ENG garniture d'étoupe *f*; **~ remover** *n* PAPER TECH extracteur de débris *m*; **~ ring** *n* PROD ENG couvercle du piston *m*

junked *adj* PETR TECH *well* rebouché

Jupiter's: **~ red spot** *n* ASTRON tache rouge de Jupiter *f*

Jurassic[1] *adj* GEOL *stratigraphy* jurassique

Jurassic:[2] **~ period** *n* GEOL, PETR TECH jurassique *m*

jury: **~ rudder** *n* NAUT gouvernail de fortune *m*

just[1] *adj* ACOUSTICS strict

just:[2] **~ stage** *n* SPACE premier étage *m*

justification *n* DP justification *f*, PRINT cadrage de la page sur écran *m*, justification *f*, TELECOM justification *f*; **~ key** *n* PRINT touche de justification *f*

justify *vt* DP justifier

justifying: **~ scale** *n* PRINT largeur de justification *f*

just-in-time *adj (JIT)* PACKAGING, TEXTILES juste à temps *m*

jute *n* TEXTILES jute *m*; **~ covering** *n* ELEC ENG enveloppe en jute *f*; **~ sacking** *n* PACKAGING toile de jute *f*; **~ spinning** *n* TEXTILES filature de jute *f*; **~ yarn** *n* TEXTILES fil de jute *m*

juvenile[1] *adj* GEOL juvénile

juvenile:[2] **~ water** *n* GEOL *magmatic* eau hypogée *f*, eau juvénile *f*, eau tellurique *f*, WATER SUPP eau juvénile *f*

juxtaposition: **~ twin** *n* CRYSTALL macle de contact *f*, macle de juxtaposition *f*

K

k *abbr (kilo-)* METR k *(kilo-)*

K CHEM *(potassium)* K (potassium)

K *abbr (kelvin)* METR, PHYS, THERMOD K *(kelvin)*

K-absorption: ~ edge *n* NUCLEAR discontinuité d'absorption *f*

kaempferide *n* CHEM kempféride *f*

kaempferol *n* CHEM kaempférol *m*

kahlerite *n* NUCLEAR kahlerite *f*

kainite *n* MINERAL kaïnite *f*

KALC: ~ process *n (krypton absorption in liquid carbon dioxide)* NUCLEAR procédé KALC *m*

kali *n* CHEM kali *m*

Kalman: ~ filter *n* ELECTRON filtre de Kalman *m*; ~ filtering *n* ELECTRON filtrage de Kalman *m*

kämmererite *n* MINERAL kammérérite *f*

kangaroo: ~ type wagon *n* RAIL wagon kangourou *m*

Kanne: ~ chamber *n* NUCLEAR *for radioactive gas monitoring* chambre de Kanne *f*

kaolin *n* CHEM, MINERAL, P&R *pigment, filler*, PRINT kaolin *m*

kaolinite *n* COAL TECH, MINERAL, PETR TECH, PROP MAT kaolinite *f*

kaolinization *n* FUELLESS, GEOL kaolinisation *f*

kaon *n* PART PHYS, PHYS kaon *m*

kapnite *n* MINERAL capnite *f*

kapok *n* HEAT ENG kapok *m*; ~ oil *n* CHEM huile de kapok *f*

K-Ar: ~ dating *n* GEOL datation K-Ar *f*, datation par la méthode K-Ar *f*

karaya: ~ gum *n* CHEM, FOOD TECH gomme de karaya *f*

Karnaugh: ~ map *n* DP carte de Karnaugh *f*

karst *n* GEOL *limestone region* karst *m*; ~ hydrology *n* WATER SUPP hydrologie karstique *f*

karstenite *n* MINERAL karsténite *f*

karstic: ~ aquifer *n* HYDROL aquifère karstique *m*; ~ conduit *n* HYDROL conduit karstique *m*; ~ spring *n* WATER SUPP source karstique *f*

karyocerite *n* NUCLEAR *uranium mineral* karyocérite *f*

katabatic: ~ front *n (cf anabatic front)* METEO front katabatique *m*

katathermometer *n* HEAT ENG *air currents* cathathermomètre *m*

kauri-butanol *n* CHEM kauri-butanol *m*

Kazanian *adj* GEOL *stratigraphy* kazanien *m*

kb *abbr (kilobyte)* COMP, DP ko *(kilo-octet)*

Kcal *abbr (kilocalorie)* FOOD TECH Kcal *(kilocalorie)*

K-capture *n* PHYS capture K *f*

kCi *abbr (kilocurie)* CHEM kCi *(kilocurie)*

kedge:[1] ~ anchor *n* NAUT ancre à jet *f*

kedge[2] *vt* NAUT *ship* touer, touer avec ancre

K-edge: ~ gamma densitometry *n* NUCLEAR densitométrie gamma de discontinuité d'absorption K *f*

keel *n* AERONAUT poutre principale *f*, NAUT *shipbuilding* lest *m*, quille *f*; ~ laying *n* NAUT pose de la quille *f*; ~ plate *n* NAUT *shipbuilding* tôle de quille *f*; ~ strake *n* NAUT *shipbuilding* virure de quille *f*

keelson *n* NAUT *shipbuilding* carlingue *f*

keen[1] *adj* PRINT affilé, aigu, dépouillé, net, perçant, pointu

keen:[2] ~ edge *n* (BrE) *(cf cutting edge)* CONST *of tool* fil tranchant *m*

keenness *n* CONST *of cutting edge* acuité *f*, finesse *f*

keep:[1] ~ down *vt* PRINT atténuer; ~ out *vt* PRINT blanchir; ~ up *vt* PRINT composer en capitales; ~ up with *vt* TEXTILES rester à la hauteur de

keep:[2] ~ a lookout *vi* NAUT veiller, être de vigie; ~ watch *vi* NAUT faire le quart;~ the work area tidy *vi* SAFETY maintenir la zone de travail en bon ordre

keep:[3] ~ at open width *phr* TEXTILES *fabric* mettre en large; ~ cool *phr* PACKAGING *handling instructions* garder au frais; ~ dry *phr* PACKAGING *handling instructions* craint l'humidité; ~ upright *phr* PACKAGING *handling instructions* ne pas renverser

keep-alive: ~ electrode *n* ELEC ENG électrode d'entretien *f*; ~ oscillator *n* ELECTRON oscillateur d'activation *m*; ~ voltage *n* ELEC ENG tension d'entretien *f*

keeper *n* CONST *lock staple* gâche *f*, *of gate latch* mentonnet *m*, ELEC *magnet* court-circuit magnétique *m*, MECH ENG *lock nut* contre-écrou *m*, *pawl, click* cliquet *m*, détente *f*, PHYS *magnet* armature *f*

keeping: ~ quality *n* FOOD TECH faculté de conservation *f*, REFRIG *of food* aptitude à la conservation *f*; ~ time *n* REFRIG *of food* durée de conservation *f*

keeve *n* MINING bac *m*, cuve *f*

keg *n* CHEM tonnelet *m*

keilhauite *n* MINERAL keilhauite *f*

kelly *n* PETR tige carrée d'entraînement *f*, PETR TECH *drilling* kelly *m*, tige carrée d'entraînement *f*, tige d'entraînement *f*; ~ bushing *n* PETR TECH carré d'entraînement de la tige carrée *m*

kelp *n* FOOD TECH varech *m*

kelvin *n (K)* METR, PHYS, THERMOD kelvin *m (K)*

Kelvin: ~ balance *n* ELEC *measurement* balance de Kelvin *f*; ~ bridge *n* ELEC, ELEC ENG, PHYS pont de Kelvin *m*; ~ degree *n* PRINT degré Kelvin *m*, degré absolu *m*; ~ effect *n* ELEC *thermoelectrics* effet de Kelvin *m*; ~ scale *n* CINEMAT, CONST échelle Kelvin *f*, SPACE échelle Kelvin *f*, échelle thermodynamique *f*; ~ statement *n* PHYS *of second law of thermodynamics* énoncé de Kelvin du second principe *m*; ~ temperature *n* CINEMAT température de couleur *f*, SPACE température Kelvin *f*, température absolue *f*, THERMOD température Kelvin *f*, température absolue *f*, température thermodynamique *f*

kelvinometer *n* CINEMAT kelvinomètre *m*, thermocolorimètre *m*

K-emitter *n* NUCLEAR émetteur K *m*

kemsolene *n* CHEM kemsolène *m*

kennel: ~ coal *n* COAL TECH charbon mat *m*

Kennelly-Heaviside: ~ layer *n* PHYS *E layer* couche E *f*, couche de Kennelly-Heaviside *f*

kep *n* MINING clichage *m*, taquets *m pl*

Kepler's: ~ equation *n* ASTRON équation de Kepler *f*; ~ law of areas *n* SPACE deuxième loi de Kepler *f*, loi des aires de Kepler *f*; ~ laws *n pl* PHYS lois de Kepler *f pl*; ~ laws of planetary motion *n pl* ASTRON lois de Kepler des mouvements des planètes *f pl*

Keplerian: ~ **orbit** *n* SPACE orbite Keplérienne *f*, orbite non perturbée *f*

kept: to be ~ upright *phr* PACKAGING *handling instructions* ne pas renverser

kerargyrite *n* MINERAL cérargyrite *f*

keratin *n* CHEM kératine *f*

keratinization *n* CHEM kératinisation *f*

keratinous *adj* CHEM kératinique

keratogenous *adj* CHEM kératogène

kerb *n* (BrE) CONST bordure *f*, bordure de trottoir *f*

kerbstone *n* (BrE) CONST bordure *f*, bordure de trottoir *f*

kerf *n* COAL TECH havage *m*

kerma *n* PHYS kerma *m*; ~ **rate** *n* PHYS *nuclear* débit de kerma *m*

kermes: ~ **mineral** *n* MINERAL kermésite *f*, kermès minéral *m*

kermesite *n* MINERAL kermésite *f*, kermès minéral *m*

kern *n* PRINT approches *f pl*, crénage *m*, saillie *f*

kernel *n* COMP, DP noyau *m*, NUCLEAR *of integral equation* noyau intégral *m*

kerogen *n* CHEM, GEOL, PETR, PETR TECH *formation of hydrocarbons* kérogène *m*

kerogenite *n* GEOL *oil shale* schiste bitumineux *m*

kerosene *n* (AmE) (*cf paraffin*) CHEM kérosène *m*, pétrole *m*, PETR kérosène *m*, PETR TECH *refining* kérosène *m*, paraffine *f*, PROP MAT paraffine *f*, THERMOD kérosène *f*, pétrole raffiné d'éclairage *m*, TRANSP kérosène *m*; ~ **coating** *n* (AmE) (*cf paraffin coating*) PACKAGING revêtement de paraffine *m*; ~ **oil** *n* (AmE) (*cf paraffin oil*) CHEM huile paraffinée *f*; ~ **series** *n* (AmE) (*cf paraffin series*); ~ **wax** *n* (AmE) (*cf paraffin wax*) CHEM cire de paraffine *f*, paraffine solide *f*, ELEC cire de paraffine f

kerosene-impregnated: ~ **paper** *n* (AmE) (*cf paraffin-impregnated paper*) PACKAGING papier paraffiné *m*

kerosine *n* CHEM kérosène *m*, pétrole *m*

Kerr: ~ **cell** *n* PHYS cellule de Kerr *f*; ~ **electro-optical effect** *n* PHYS effet électro-optique de Kerr *m*; ~ **magneto-optical effect** *n* PHYS effet magnéto-optique de Kerr *m*

kersantite *n* PETR kersantite *f*

kerving *n* MINING havage *m*, souchevage *m*, sous-cave *f*, souschevage *m*

keryl *n* CHEM kérosène chloré *m*

ketazine *n* CHEM cétazine *f*

ketch *n* NAUT ketch *m*

keten *n* CHEM cétène *m*

ketene *n* CHEM cétène *m*

ketimine *n* CHEM cétimine *f*

keto-acids *n pl* CHEM céto-acides *m pl*

keto-enol: ~ **tautomerism** *n* CHEM tautomérie céto-énolique *f*

keto-form *n* CHEM forme cétonique *f*

ketol *n* CHEM indole *m*

ketone *n* CHEM, FOOD TECH, P&R *chemical compound, group* cétone *f*

ketonic *adj* CHEM cétonique

ketose *n* CHEM cétose *m*

kettle *n* CHEM gros ballon *m*, marmite *f*, PROD ENG *for skin drying* poêle à flamber *m*; ~ **dyeing** *n* COLOURS teinture en autoclave *f*

keV *abbr* (*kilo-electronvolt*) CHEM keV (*kilo-électronvolt*)

Kevlar *n* NAUT *ship parts, equipment* kevlar *m*

key[1] *n* ACOUSTICS clef *f*, clé *f*, ton *m*, tonalité *f*, CINEMAT clavette *f*, clef *f*, clé *f*, touche *f*, *electronic replacement of image* incrustation *f*, COMP clef *f*, clé *f*, clef, touche *f*, CONST clé *f*, *of arch* clef de voûte *f*, voussoir de clé *m*, clef *f*, DP clef *f*, clé *f*, touche *f*, ELEC ENG clef *f*, clé *f*, touche *f*, MECH clavette *f*, MECH ENG *engineering components* clavette *f*, *spanner* cale *f*, clef *f*, clé *f*, OCEANOG caye *f*, PRINT plage de couleur *f*, écart de contraste *m*, touche *f*, TELECOM clef *f*, TV clavette *f*, clef *f*, clé *f*, incrustation *f*, touche *f*; ~ **bed** *n* GEOL couche repère *f*, NUCLEAR logement de clavette *m*; ~ **bit** *n* CONST panneton de clef *m*; ~ **bolt** *n* MECH ENG boulon à clavette *m*, PAPER TECH clavette *f*; ~ **coatings on film** *n pl* PRINT surfaces sensibles sur films *f pl*; ~ **drift** *n* MECH ENG chasse-clavette *m*, chasse-clé *m*; ~ **drop** *n* CONST cache-entrée *m*; ~ **field** *n* DP champ de clé *m*; ~ **file** *n* MECH ENG lime à bouter *f*, lime à garnir *f*; ~ **groove** *n* NUCLEAR logement de clavette *m*; ~ **horizon** *n* GEOL niveau repère *m*; ~ **joint** *n* MECH ENG assemblage à clé *m*; ~ **level** *n* TV niveau d'incrustation *m*; ~ **lighting** *n* CINEMAT éclairage dominant *m*; ~ **management** *n* TELECOM gestion des clés *f*; ~ **on flat** *n* MECH ENG clavette posée à plat *f*, clavette à méplat *f*; ~ **plate** *n* CONST entrée de serrure *f*, écusson *m*; ~ **seating** *n* PETR TECH *drilling problem* coincement *m*, trou de serrure *m*; ~ **signature** *n* ACOUSTICS armure de clef *f*; ~ **station** *n* TV station émettrice *f*; ~ **telephone set** *n* TELECOM poste d'intercommunication *m*, téléphone à poussoirs *m* (Can); ~ **telephone system** *n* TELECOM système d'intercommunication *m*, système téléphonique à touches *m*; ~ **which fits a lock** *n* CONST clef qui s'ajuste à une serrure *f*, clé qui va à une serrure *f*

key[2] *vt* MECH ENG caler, claveter, clavetter, coincer, PRINT *colour coding* indiquer, TV incruster; ~ **in** *vt* CINEMAT incruster TELECOM numéroter

key-and-lamp: ~ **unit** *n* TELECOM module à touches et à voyants *m*

keyboard[1] *n* CINEMAT, COMP, DP, ELEC*control* clavier *m*, NUCLEAR commande à clavier *f*, PHYS, PRINT, TELECOM, TV clavier *m*; ~ **encoder** *n* COMP, DP codeur de clavier *m*; ~ **entry** *n* DP entrée au clavier *f*, entrée par clavier *f*; ~ **lockout** *n* COMP, DP verrouillage de clavier *m*; ~ **mask** *n* COMP housse de protection du clavier *f*, DP masque de clavier *m*; ~ **sender** *n* TELECOM émetteur à clavier *m*; ~ **send-receive** *n* (*KSR*) COMP téléscripteur émetteur-récepteur à clavier *m*, émetteur-récepteur à clavier *m*; ~ **template** *n* DP grille de clavier *f*; ~ **tuning** *n* CONTROL contrôle à claviers *m*

keyboard[2] *vt* DP saisir au clavier, PRINT saisir

keycap *n* PRINT surface touche du clavier *f*

keydrive *n* MECH ENG *milling cutters* entraînement par clavette *m*

key-driven *adj* COMP commandé par touche, DP piloté par touche

keyed *adj* MECH claveté

keyer *n* TV incrustateur *m*

keyhole *n* CONST *locksmithing* entrée de serrure *f*; ~ **guard** *n* CONST cache-entrée *m*; ~ **mask** *n* CINEMAT cache en forme de trou de serrure *m*; ~ **saw** *n* CONST scie à guichet *f*

keying *n* CONST *of arch* clavage *m*, MECH ENG calage *m*, clavetage *m*, coinçage *m*, PROD ENG installation de détrompeurs *f*, TELECOM composition au clavier *f*, numérotation *f*; ~ **band** *n* PROD ENG détrompeur *m*, ergot de détrompage *m*; ~ **error** *n* TELECOM erreur de numérotation *f*; ~ **error rate** *n* DP taux de fautes de frappe *m*; ~ **hammer** *n* PROD ENG *of platelayer* chasse à coins *f*, marteau chasse-coins *m*; ~ **in** *n* CONST *of arch* clavage *m*; ~ **signal** *n* TV signal commutateur *m*, signal de clé *m*, signal déclencheur *m*; ~ **up** *n* CONST *of arch* clavage *m*; ~ **wedge** *n* MECH ENG coin de calage *m*

keylight *n* CINEMAT lumière principale *f*, éclairage de base *m*, PHOTO éclairage principal *m*

key-locked: ~ **starting system** *n* MECH ENG système de démarrage verrouillable *m*

keynote *n* ACOUSTICS tonique *f*

key-opening: ~ **can** *n* PACKAGING boîte avec ouverture par clé *f*; ~ **lid** *n* PACKAGING couvercle avec ouverture par clé *m*

key-operated: ~ **selector switch** *n* PROD ENG sélecteur à clé *m*; ~ **switch** *n* CONTROL interrupteur à clef *m*, ELEC interrupteur à clef amovible *m*

keypad *n* COMP, DP bloc de touches *m*, clavier numérique *m*, PHYS clavier *m*, RECORDING clavier numérique *m*, TELECOM cadran à clavier *m*, clavier *m*, TV clavier numérique *m*

key-per-line: ~ **console** *n* (BrE) *(cf key-per-trunk console)* TELECOM poste d'opérateur de classe A *m*

key-per-trunk: ~ **console** *n* (AmE) *(cf key-per-line console)* TELECOM poste d'opérateur de classe A *m*

keypunch *n* COMP, DP perforatrice *f*

keyseat *n* PAPER TECH logement de clavette *m*

keyshelf *n* TELECOM table horizontale *f*, tablette horizontale *f*

keyslot *n* MECH rainure de clavette *f*, PROD ENG encoche *f*

keystone *n* CONST *of arch* clef de voûte *f*, voussoir de clé *m*; ~ **distortion** *n* CINEMAT distorsion trapézoïdale *f*, ELECTRON distorsion en trapèze *f*, distorsion trapézoïdale *f*

keyswitch *n* ELEC ENG interrupteur à touche *m*

keytop: ~ **overlay** *n* COMP cache-clavier *m*, masque de clavier *m*

keyway *n* MECH rainure de clavette *f*, MECH ENG clavetage *m*, rainure de cale *f*, rainure de clavetage *f*, rainure de clavette *f*, NUCLEAR logement de clavette *m*; ~ **cutting machine** *n* PROD ENG *of milling type* machine à fraiser les rainures de cales *f*, *of slotting type* machine à mortaiser les rainures de cales *f*; ~ **cutting tool** *n* PROD ENG machine à canneler portative *f*, outil à rainer *m*

keyword *n* DP mot-clé *m*; ~ **in context** *n* (*KWIC*) COMP, DP mot-clé en contexte *m*; ~ **out of context** *n* (*KWOC*) COMP, DP mot-clé hors contexte *m*; ~ **parameter** *n* COMP, DP paramètre de mot clé *m*; ~ **retrieval** *n* COMP, DP recherche par mot clé *f*

kg *abbr* (*kilogramme, kilogram*) METR kg (*kilogramme*)

khlopinite *n* NUCLEAR khlopinite *f*

kHz *abbr* (*kilohertz*) ELEC kilohertz *m*

kibble *n* MINING benne *f*, cuffat *m*, tonne *f*, OCEANOG moule *m*

kibbler *n* FOOD TECH *milling, baking* égrugeoir *m*

kick *n* PETR TECH *drilling problem* venue *f*; ~ **copy** *n* PRINT exemplaire forcé hors de l'alignement *m*; ~ **down** *n* AUTO rétrogradation forcée *f*, VEHICLES *automatic gearbox* kick-down *m*, rétrogradation forcée *f*; ~ **down switch** *n* AUTO rétrogradeur *m*; ~ **rocket** *n* SPACE fusée d'appoint *f*; ~ **stage** *n* SPACE étage d'impulsion *m*

kickback *n* ELEC ENG tension de rupture *f*; ~ **power supply** *n* ELEC ENG alimentation à très haute tension *f*

kicker *n* PRINT taqueur *m*; ~ **actuator** *n* MECH ENG *diecas-*

ting butée de came d'éjecteur rapide *f*; ~ **box** *n* MECH ENG came d'éjecteur rapide *f*; ~ **light** *n* CINEMAT projecteur de décrochement *m*

kicking: ~ **strap** *n* NAUT *boom* halebas de bôme *m*

kick-off *n* SPACE séparation *f*; ~ **mechanism** *n* SPACE mécanisme de séparation *m*

kick-starter *n* VEHICLES *motorcycle engine* kick-starter *m*

kidney: ~ **stone** *n* GEOL nodule en forme de rognon *m*

kidney-shaped: ~ **slot** *n* MECH ENG fente en haricot *f*

kier *n* PAPER TECH lessiveur *m*, TEXTILES autoclave à blanchiment *m*

kieselguhr *n* GEOL diatomite *f*, terre à diatomées *f*

kieserite *n* MINERAL kiésérite *f*

kieve *n* MINING bac *m*, cuve *f*

Kikuchi: ~ **line** *n* NUCLEAR *electron diffraction* raie de Kikuchi *f*

kill *vt* CINEMAT *light* couper, éteindre, PETR TECH *well* tuer, PRINT *text* supprimer; ~ **a set** *vt* CINEMAT démonter un décor

killing: ~ **agent** *n* METALL calmant *m*, élément de calmage *m*; ~ **a well** *n* PETR TECH maîtrise d'éruption *f*

kiln:[1] ~ **dried** *adj* PROD ENG, THERMOD séché au four

kiln[2] *n* COAL TECH fourneau *m*, CONST four *m*, étuve *f*, FOOD TECH touraille *f*, HEATING, PAPER TECH, PROD ENG four *m*, THERMOD four *m*, fourneau *m*; ~ **drying** *n* CONST séchage à l'étuve *m*; ~ **malt** *n* FOOD TECH malt touraillé *m*

kiln[3] *vt* PROD ENG cuire; ~ **dry** *vt* THERMOD sécher au four, étuver

kilning *n* C&G cuisson *f*

kilo- *pref* (*k*) METR kilo- (*k*)

kilobyte *n* (*kb*) COMP, DP kilo-octet *m* (*ko*)

kilocalorie *n* (*Kcal*) FOOD TECH kilocalorie *f* (*Kcal*)

kilocurie *n* (*kCi*) CHEM kilocurie *m* (*kCi*)

kilo-electronvolt *n* (*keV*) CHEM kilo-électronvolt *m* (*keV*)

kilogram *n* (AmE), **kilogramme** *n* (BrE) (*kg*) METR kilogramme *m* (*kg*) ~ **meter** *n* (BrE) METR kilogram-mètre *m*

kilohertz *n* (*kHz*) ELEC *unit* kilohertz *m*

kiloline *n* METR kiloline *m*

kilometer *n* (AmE), **kilometre** *n* (BrE) (*km*) METR kilomètre *m* (*km*)

kilonem *n* (*kn*) CHEM kilonème *m* (*kn*)

kiloparsec *n* ASTRON kiloparsec *m*

kilostream: ~ **circuit** *n* (TM) TELECOM circuit moyen débit *m*

kilovolt *n* (*kV*) ELEC ENG kilovolt *m* (*kV*)

kilowatt *n* (*kW*) ELEC, ELEC ENG kilowatt *m* (*kW*)

kilowatt-hour *n* ELEC, ELEC ENG, PHYS kilowatt-heure *m*

kimberlite *n* GEOL, PETR kimberlite *f*

Kimmeridgian[1] *adj* GEOL *stratigraphy* kimméridgien *m*

Kimmeridgian[2] *n* GEOL kimméridgien *m*

kindle *vt* THERMOD allumer, mettre le feu à

kindling: ~ **point** *n* THERMOD point d'inflammation *m*

kinematic: ~ **chain** *n* MECH chaîne cinématique *f*; ~ **diagram** *n* MECH ENG schéma cinématique *m*; ~ **envelope** *n* RAIL *vehicles* enveloppe cinématique *f*; ~ **gage** *n* (AmE), ~ **gauge** *n* (BrE) RAIL *vehicles* gabarit cinématique *m*; ~ **viscosity** *n* FLUID PHYS, FUELLESS, MECH *materials*, PHYS, REFRIG viscosité cinématique *f*

kinematics *n* MECH, PHYS cinématique *f*

kinescope *n* ELECTRON kinescope *m*

kinetic[1] *adj* SPACE cinétique

kinetic:[2] ~ **energy** *n* GEOPHYS force vive *f*, énergie cinétique *f*, MECH, MECH ENG, PHYS, SPACE énergie cinétique *f*; **~ energy density** *n* ACOUSTICS densité d'énergie cinétique *f*; **~ heating** *n* PHYS, SPACE *spacecraft* échauffement cinétique *m*; **~ isotope effect** *n* NUCLEAR effet isotopique *m*; **~ pump** *n* MECH ENG pompe cinétique *f*; **~ separation** *n* NUCLEAR *in flight* séparation cinétique *f*, séparation en vol *f*; **~ spectrophotometry** *n* RAD PHYS spectrophotométrie cinétique *f*; **~ theory of gases** *n* PHYS théorie cinétique des gaz *f*; **~ vacuum pump** *n* MECH pompe à vide cinétique *f*

kinetically-induced: **~ buoyancy** *n* POLLUTION flottation due à l'énergie cinétique *f*

kinetics *n* CHEM, GAS TECH, MECH, METALL, NUCLEAR, PHYS, PROP MAT cinétique *f*

king *n* NAUT bordages *m pl*; **~ journal** *n* NUCLEAR appui à pivot *m*, pivot *m*, tourillon *m*; **~ plank** *n* NAUT *shipbuilding* faux étambrai *m*, virure d'axe *f*; **~ post** *n* NAUT *deck fitting* mâtereau *m*; **~ rod** *n* CONST *of roof truss* aiguille *f*, poinçon *m*; **~ roll** *n* PAPER TECH rouleau inférieur de calandre *m*, rouleau porteur *m*

kingbolt *n* MECH ENG cheville ouvrière *f*, pivot central *m*

kingpin *n* MECH *vehicles* pivot d'essieu avant *m*, MECH ENG cheville ouvrière *f*, pivot central *m*; **~ inclination** *n* AUTO inclinaison du pivot *f*

Kingsbury: **~ bearing** *n* MECH palier Mitchell *m*, palier de butée à patins *m*

kink[1] *n* CRYSTALL *in dislocation* décrochement *m*, METALL bande de pliage *f*, décrochement *m*, NAUT *in rope* coque *f*, PROD ENG tortillement *m*; **~ band** *n* METALL bande de pliage *f*; **~ bands** *n pl* GEOL kink-bands *m pl*, zones de flexure *f pl*; **~ instability** *n* NUCLEAR instabilité à coques *f*; **~ plane** *n* GEOL plan de déformation *m*

kink:[2] **~ out of line** *vt* PROD ENG fausser

kiosk *n* CONST *building* kiosque *m*

Kipp's: **~ apparatus** *n* CHEM, LAB EQUIP appareil de Kipp *m*

Kirchhoff's: **~ laws** *n pl* ELEC, ELEC ENG *networks*, PHYS, RAD PHYS lois de Kirchhoff *f pl*

kirving *n* MINING havage *m*, souchevage *m*, sous-cave *f*

kiss: **~ coating** *n* PRINT couchage par effleurage *m*; **~ roll coating** *n* COATINGS revêtement par rouleau de transfert *m*

kissing: **~ circle** *n* GEOM cercle osculateur *m*; **~ cylinder** *n* PRINT cylindre qui en effleure un autre pratiquement sans pression *m*

kit *n* MECH ENG jeu *m*, prêt-à-monter *m*, NUCLEAR jeu *m*, trousse *f*, PROD ENG kit *m*, trousse *f*, trousseau *m*

kitchen: **~ salt** *n* FOOD TECH gros sel *m*; **~ waste** *n* FOOD TECH déchets *m pl*, ordures ménagères *f pl*

kite *n* AERONAUT cerf-volant *m*, GEOM trapèze *m*

Kjeldahl: **~ digestion apparatus** *n* LAB EQUIP *nitrogen analysis* digesteur Kjeldahl minéralisateur *m*, minéralisateur Kjeldahl *m*; **~ method** *n* CHEM méthode de minéralisation Kjeldahl *f*, NUCLEAR *for nitrogen extraction* méthode de Kjeldahl *f*

K-Jetronic: **~ fuel injection system** *n* AUTO système d'injection K-Jetronic *m*

Klein: **~ bottle** *n* GEOM *topology* bouteille de Klein *f*

Klein-Gordon: **~ equation** *n* PHYS équation de Klein-Gordon *f*

klippe *n* GEOL klippe *f*, lambeau de charriage *m*

klystron *n* ELECTRON, PHYS, RAD PHYS, SPACE, TELECOM klystron *m*; **~ amplifier** *n* ELECTRON klystron amplificateur *m*; **~ frequency multiplier** *n* ELECTRON klystron multiplicateur de fréquence *m*; **~ oscillator** *n* ELECTRON klystron oscillateur *m*

km *abbr (kilometre)* METR km *(kilomètre)*

K-meson *n* PART PHYS méson K *m*

kn *abbr (kilonem)* CHEM kn *(kilonème)*

knacker *n* FOOD TECH équarrisseur *m*

kneader *n* PAPER TECH déchiqueteur *m*; **~ pulper** *n* PAPER TECH broyeur *m*

kneading *n* FOOD TECH *baking* pétrissage *m*, PROD ENG pétrissage *m*, pétrissement *m*

knebelite *n* MINERAL knébélite *f*

knee *n* MECH ENG genou *m*, *of curve* jarret *m*, NAUT *shipbuilding* courbe *f*; **~ bend** *n* MECH tube coudé *m*; **~ bracket** *n* CONST console-équerre *f*; **~ fold** *n* GEOL pli en genou *m*; **~ mounting** *n* INSTRUMENT monture coudée *f*; **~ pads** *n pl* SAFETY coussinets pour genoux *m pl*, genouillères *f pl*

knee-type: **~ milling machine** *n* MECH ENG fraiseuse à console *f*

knickpoint *n* (BrE) GEOL entaille de profil *f*, rupture de profil *f*

knife *n* MECH *tools* couteau *m*, lame *f*, PRINT racle *f*, TEXTILES couteau *m*; **~ coater** *n* PAPER TECH coucheuse à racles *f*; **~ cylinder** *n* PAPER TECH cylindre porte-couteaux *m*; **~ edge** *n* PROD ENG *of balance* couteau *m*; **~ edges** *n pl* METR *of balance beam* couteaux du fléau *m pl*; **~ file** *n* MECH ENG lime à couteau *f*, lime-couteau *f*; **~ grinding machine** *n* PROD ENG machine à affûter les lames de couteaux *f*; **~ holder** *n* PAPER TECH porte-couteaux *m*; **~ pleat** *n* TEXTILES pli cassant *m*; **~ spreading** *n* P&R *coating* enduction au couteau *f*, revêtement au couteau *m*; **~ switch** *n* ELEC interrupteur à couteaux *m*; **~ tool** *n* MECH ENG outil couteau *m*

knife-blade: **~ switch** *n* CONTROL interrupteur à couteaux *m*, interrupteur à lame *m*

knifecut *n* PRINT découpe au couteau *f*, découpe à la lame de scie *f*

knife-edge: **~ file** *n* MECH ENG lime à couteau *f*, lime-couteau *f*; **~ rule** *n* METR règle à couteau *f*; **~ switch** *n* NUCLEAR interrupteur à lame *m*

Knight: **~ shift** *n* NUCLEAR déplacement de Knight *m*

knit *vt* TEXTILES tricoter

knitted: **~ fabric** *n* TEXTILES tissu à mailles *m*; **~ glass fabric** *n* C&G tricot de verre textile *m*

knitting *n* TEXTILES tricotage *m*

knob *n* C&G bouton *m*, CONST bouton *m*, pomme *f*, pommette *f*, CONTROL bouton tournant *m*, ELEC ENG, MECH, MECH ENG bouton *m*; **~ lever operator** *n* PROD ENG tête à crosse *f*; **~ tools** *n pl* C&G fers à boutons *m pl*

knobbly: **~ limestone** *n* GEOL calcaire noduleux *m*

knock[1] *n* PETR TECH *internal combustion engine* cliquetis *m*, détonation *f*

knock:[2] **~ out** *vt* PROD ENG *rivet* chasser

knock[3] *vi* MECH ENG cogner, taper

knocked-on: **~ atom** *n* NUCLEAR atome percuté *m*

knocker-off *n* C&G maillet à déglanter *m*

knocking *n* MECH ENG tapage *m*, *of combustion engines* cognement *m*, VEHICLES *engine preignition* détonation *f*

knock-off: **~ cam** *n* MECH ENG came de butée *f*; **~ link** *n* MECH ENG bague-batoir *f*

knock-on *n* NUCLEAR *electron in atomic shell* impact *m*, percussion *f*

knock-out: **~ rod** *n* MECH ENG tige d'éjection *f*

knoll *n* CONST butte *f*, monticule *m*, tertre *m*

knot[1] *n* C&G larme *f*, FUELLESS *nautical speed*, NAUT, PAPER TECH, TEXTILES noeud *m*; **~ breaker** *n* PAPER TECH broyeur de noeuds *m*; **~ extensibility** *n* TEXTILES allongement au noeud *m*; ~ **strength** *n* TEXTILES ténacité au noeud *f*; ~ **theory** *n* GEOM théorie des noeuds *f*; ~ **varnish** *n* COLOURS vernis isolant pour noeuds *m*, vernis knotting *m*

knot[2] *vt* TEXTILES nouer

knotless[1] *adj* TEXTILES sans noeud

knotless:[2] ~ **yarn length** *n* TEXTILES longueur de fil *f*

knotter: ~ **screen** *n* PAPER TECH trieur de noeuds *m*

knotting *n* TEXTILES nouage *m*

knotty *adj* TEXTILES noueux

know-how *n* CONST, PATENTS savoir-faire *m*

knowledge: ~ **base** *n* COMP, DP base de connaissances *f*; ~ **engineering** *n* COMP cognitique *f*; ~ **representation** *n* COMP, DP représentation de connaissances *f*; ~ **representation language** *n* (*KRL*) COMP langage de représentation des connaissances *m*

known: ~ **coal deposit** *n* COAL TECH charbon reconnu *m*

knuckle *n* AUTO fourche *f*, CONST *of hinge* charnon *m*, noeud *m*, oeil *m*, MECH articulation à genouillère *f*, MECH ENG articulation à genouillère *f*; ~ **bearing** *n* MECH ENG roulement d'articulation *m*; ~ **joint** *n* MECH ENG articulation à genouillère *f*, genouillère *f*

knuckle-jointed: ~ **connecting rod** *n* MECH ENG bielle articulée *f*

Knudsen: ~ **effect** *n* NUCLEAR *thermal molecular flow* effet Knudsen *m*, écoulement thermonucléaire *m*

knurl *n* MECH ENG godronnoir *m*, molette *f*

knurled[1] *adj* MECH moleté

knurled:[2] ~ **head fastener** *n* MECH ENG élément de fixation à tête moletée *m*; ~ **nut** *n* MECH ENG molette *f*, écrou godronné *m*, écrou moleté *m*, écrou à molette *m*; ~ **operating shaft** *n* PROD ENG axe cannelé *m*; ~ **screw** *n* MECH ENG vis moletée *f*

knurling *n* C&G granitage *m*, MECH ENG godronnage *m*, moletage *m*; ~ **tool** *n* MECH outil à moleter *m*, MECH ENG godronnoir *m*, molette *f*

kochubeïte *n* MINERAL kotschubéite *f*

koettigite *n* MINERAL köttigite *f*

kollergang *n* PAPER TECH meuleton *m*

koninckite *n* MINERAL koninckite *f*

konleinite *n* MINERAL konlite *f*, konléinite *f*

könlite *n* MINERAL konlite *f*, konléinite *f*

Kossel: ~ **line** *n* NUCLEAR raie de Kossel *f*

kotschubeite *n* MINERAL kotschubéite *f*

köttigite *n* MINERAL köttigite *f*

Kr (*krypton*) CHEM Kr (*krypton*)

kraft: ~ **board** *n* PACKAGING carton kraft *m*; ~ **face liner** *n* PAPER TECH couverture une face kraft *f*; ~ **liner** *n* PACKAGING papier couverture kraft *m*, PAPER TECH couverture kraft *f*; ~ **paper** *n* PACKAGING, PAPER TECH papier kraft *m*; ~ **pulp** *n* PAPER TECH pâte de sulfate *f*, pâte kraft *f*; ~ **sack paper** *n* PACKAGING papier kraft pour sacs *m*

krarup: ~ **cable** *n* ELEC ENG câble krarupisé *m*; ~ **loading** *n* ELEC ENG krarupisation *f*

kremersite *n* MINERAL krémersite *f*

krennerite *n* MINERAL krennérite *f*

kriging *n* WATER SUPP krigeage *m*

KRL *abbr* (*knowledge representation language*) COMP langage de représentation des connaissances *m*

kröhnkite *n* MINERAL krohnkite *f*

Krook's: ~ **collision operator** *n* NUCLEAR opérateur de collisions de Krook *m*

Kruskal: ~ **limit** *n* NUCLEAR limite de Kruskal *f*

krypton *n* (*Kr*) CHEM krypton *m* (*Kr*); ~ **absorption in liquid carbon dioxide** *n* (*KALC process*) NUCLEAR procédé KALC *m*

kryptonate: ~ **of cadmium amalgam** *n* NUCLEAR kryptonate de l'amalgame de cadmium *m*

K-shell *n* NUCLEAR couche K *f*, couche à deux électrons *f*, PHYS *atom* couche K *f*

KSR *abbr* (*keyboard send-receive*) COMP émetteur-récepteur à clavier *m*

K-star *n* ASTRON étoile K *f*

K-state *n* NUCLEAR état K *m*

Kuhn-Thomas-Reich: ~ **sum rule** *n* NUCLEAR règle des sommes de Kuhn-Thomas-Reich *f*

Kundt's: ~ **tube** *n* PHYS tube de Kundt *m*

kupfernickel *n* MINERAL kupfernickel *m*, nickéline *f*

Kutter's: ~ **formula** *n* HYDROL formule de Kutter *f*

kV *abbr* (*kilovolt*) ELEC ENG kV (*kilovolt*)

kW *abbr* (*kilowatt*) ELEC, ELEC ENG kW (*kilowatt*)

KWIC *abbr* (*keyword in context*) COMP, DP mot-clé en contexte *m*

KWOC *abbr* (*keyword out of context*) COMP, DP mot-clé hors contexte *m*

kyanite *n* MINERAL cyanite *f*, disthène *f*

Kynch's: ~ **separation theory** *n* NUCLEAR théorie de la séparation de Kynch *f*

L

l *abbr (litre, liter)* METR l *(litre)*

La *(lanthanum)* CHEM La *(lanthane)*

lab *n* PHOTO labo *m*; **~ data sheet** *n* CINEMAT fiche de laboratoire *f*; **~ report** *n* CINEMAT rapport labo *m*

label¹ *n* COMP, DP, PACKAGING, TEXTILES étiquette *f*; **~ area** *n* ACOUSTICS glace *f*; **~ coding machine** *n* PACKAGING machine à encoder les étiquettes *f*; **~ dispenser** *n* PACKAGING distributeur d'étiquettes *m*; **~ film** *n* PACKAGING étiquette film *f*; **~overprinting machine** *n* PACKAGING composteuse pour repiquage d'étiquettes *f*; **~ record** *n* COMP enregistrement-label *m*, DP article-label *m*, enregistrement identificateur *m*, label *m*; **~ stamper** *n* PROD ENG étiqueteur *m*; **~ stock** *n* PRINT papier pour étiquettes *m*

label² *vt* COMP, DP, TEXTILES étiqueter

labeled¹ *adj* (AmE) *see* labelled

labeled:² **~ atom** *n* (AmE) *see* labelled atom; **~ compound** *n* (AmE) *see* labelled compound

labeler *n* (AmE) *see* labeller

labeling *n* (AmE) *see* labelling

labelled¹ *adj* (BrE) CHEM marqué

labelled:² **~ atom** *n* (BrE) NUCLEAR traceur *m*; **~ compound** *n* (BrE) NUCLEAR composé marqué *m*

labeller *n* (BrE) PACKAGING pistolet d'étiquetage *m*

labelling *n* (BrE) COMP, DP, PACKAGING étiquetage *m*, PROD ENG *of wiring* repérage *m*, RAD PHYS *of radioactive material*, TEXTILES étiquetage *m*; **~ by chemical exchange** *n* (BrE) NUCLEAR marquage par échange chimique *m*; **~ machine** *n* (BrE) PACKAGING étiqueteuse *f*; **~ technique** *n* (BrE) NUCLEAR technique de marquage *f*

labile *adj* CHEM labile, ELECTRON *oscillator* à fréquence télécommandée, GEOL *behaviour of element* labile, *element* mobile

labor *n* (AmE) *see* labour

laboratory *n* CHEM, CINEMAT, PHOTO, PROD ENG *of reverberatory furnace* laboratoire *m* **~ clothing** *n* SAFETY vêtements de laboratoire *m pl*; **~ coat** *n* LAB EQUIP *safety* blouse de protection *f*; **~ compaction** *n* COAL TECH compactage d'échantillons *m*; **~ frame** *n* PHYS référentiel du laboratoire *m*; **~ microscope** *n* INSTRUMENT microscope de recherche *m*; **~ reactor** *n* NUCLEAR réacteur de laboratoire *m*; **~ standard** *n* NUCLEAR source étalon de laboratoire *f*; **~ stool** *n* LAB EQUIP siège *m*, tabouret de laboratoire *m*

labor-saving: **~ machinery** *n* (AmE) *see* labour-saving machinery

labour *n* (BrE) MINING chantier *m* **~ cost** *n* (BrE) PROD ENG coût de production *m*, coût main-d'oeuvre *m*, coût travail *m*; **~ productivity** *n* (BrE) PROD ENG productivité de la main-d'oeuvre *f*; **~ rate** *n* (BrE) PROD ENG cadence de la main-d'oeuvre *f*

labour-saving: **~ machinery** *n* (BrE) PROD ENG machines économisant la main-d'oeuvre *f pl*

labradorite *n* MINERAL labradorite *f*

labyrinth: **~ packing** *n* PROD ENG *for turbines* garniture à labyrinthe *f*; **~ seal** *n* MECH ENG joint labyrinthe *m*, labyrinthe d'étanchéité *m*, NUCLEAR, PACKAGING joint en labyrinthe *m*

lac *n* PROD ENG gomme laque *f*, laque *f*; **~ dye** *n* COLOURS laque de teinturier *f*; **~ varnish** *n* COLOURS vernis à la gomme-laque *m*

lacca *n* COLOURS gomme laque *f*

laccaic *adj* CHEM laccaïque

laccol *n* CHEM laccol *m*

laccolith *n* GEOL, GEOPHYS, PETR laccolite *m*

lace¹ *n* PROD ENG *for belts* lainière *f*, TEXTILES dentelle *f*; **~ punching** *n* MECH ENG perforation en grille *f*

lace² *vt* OCEANOG *fishing net* mailler, PROD ENG *belt* lacer; **~ up** *vt* CINEMAT charger, RECORDING *recorder* amorcer, charger

laced: **~ cable fan** *n* ELEC ENG peigne *m*

Lacerta *n* ASTRON Lézard *m*

Lacey's: **~ formula** *n* HYDROL formule de Lacey *f*

lachrymator *n* CHEM gaz lacrymogène *m*

lacing *n* C&G taille en dentelle *f*, OCEANOG *sail to yard arm* transfilage *m*, RECORDING amorçage *m*, laçage *m*; **~ cord** *n* AERONAUT fil à ligaturer *m*; **~ path** *n* CINEMAT tracé de chargement *m*

lack: **~ of fuel** *n* THERMOD manque de carburant *m*

lacquer¹ *n* COATINGS vernis *m*, COLOURS, CONST, MECH *materials* laque *f*, PROD ENG laque *f*, vernis *m*; **~ disc** *n* (BrE) ACOUSTICS disque verni *m*; **~ disk** *n* (AmE) *see* lacquer disc; **~ fumes** *n pl* SAFETY vapeurs de laque *f pl*; **~ irradiation facility** *n* NUCLEAR installation d'irradiation des laques *f*; **~ recording** *n* RECORDING enregistrement sur laque *m*; **~ sealing** *n* PACKAGING étanchement avec laque *m*

lacquer² *vt* COLOURS laquer

lacquered¹ *adj* COLOURS, MECH *materials* laqué

lacquered:² **~ work** *n* COLOURS laquage *m*

lacquering *n* CINEMAT *of a print* laquage *m*, vernissage *m*, COLOURS, PROP MAT laquage *m*; **~ machine** *n* PACKAGING machine de laquage *f*

lactam *n* CHEM lactame *f*

lactamide *n* CHEM lactamide *f*

lactate *n* CHEM lactate *m*

lactenin *n* CHEM lacténine *f*

lactic *adj* CHEM caséique, lactique

lactide *n* CHEM lactide *m*

lactobutyrometer *n* FOOD TECH lactobutyromètre *m*

lactometer *n* FOOD TECH galactomètre *m*, lactodensimètre *m*

lactone *n* CHEM lactone *f*

lactonic *adj* CHEM lactonique

lactonitrile *n* CHEM lactonitrile *m*

lactonization *n* CHEM lactonisation *f*

lactose *n* CHEM lactose *m*, sucre de lait *m*

lacustrine *adj* GEOL *facies, environment* lacustre

lacy: **~ fabric** *n* TEXTILES tissu dentelé *m*, tissu qui ressemble à la dentelle *m*

ladder *n* CONST échelle *f*, NAUT *of dredge, on ship* descente *f*, échelle *f*, élinde *f*; **~ adder** *n* ELECTRON convertisseur à résistances pondérées *m*; **~ attenuator** *n* ELECTRON atténuateur en échelle *m*; **~ chain** *n* PROD ENG chaîne de Vaucanson *f*; **~ diagram** *n* PROD ENG schéma à relais *m*; ~ **diagram format** *n* PROD ENG structure du schéma à relais *f*; ~ **diagram rung** *n* PROD ENG ligne de schéma à relais *f*; ~ **dredge** *n* NAUT drague à élinde *f*; ~ **filter** *n* ELECTRON filtre en échelle *m*; ~ **network** *n* ELEC ENG, PHYS réseau en échelle *m*; ~ **polymer** *n* P&R polymère en échelle *m*; ~ **road** *n* MINING compartiment des échelles *m*, puits des échelles *m*; ~ **shaft** *n* MINING compartiment des échelles *m*, puits des échelles *m*; ~ **way** *n* MINING compartiment des échelles *m*, puits des échelles *m*

ladder-diagram: ~ **display** *n* PROD ENG affichage du schéma à relais *m*

ladle[1] *n* C&G poche *f* CONST *spoon* cuiller *f*, cuillère *f*, PROD ENG *pot* poche *f*; ~ **crane** *n* PROD ENG pont de coulée *m*

ladle[2] *vt* C&G pocher

ladler *n* C&G pocheur *m*

ladling *n* C&G pochage *m*

LADR *abbr (linear-accelerator-driven reactor)* NUCLEAR réacteur d'accélérateur linéaire *m*

lady's: ~ **bedstraw** *n* FOOD TECH caille-lait *m*, gaillet *m*, gaillet jaune *m*, gaillet vrai *m*

laevorotatory *adj* CHEM *optically active compound* lévorotatoire, PHYS lévogyre

laevulose *n* (BrE) CHEM, FOOD TECH, lévulose *m*

lag[1] *n* ELEC retard *m*, *alternating current* retard de phase *m*, ELEC ENG décalage *m*, ELECTRON déphasage en arrière *m*, retard de phase *m*, MECH ENG *elastic* déformation momentanée *f*, déformation élastique *f*, PROD ENG retard *m*, TV déphasage *m*, retard *m*, rémanence *f*, traînage *m*, WATER SUPP temps de retardement *m*; ~ **angle** *n* AERONAUT angle de retard *m*, angle de traînée *m*; ~ **deposit** *n* GEOL dépôt clastique résiduel *m*; ~ **fault** *n* GEOL faille de charriage *f*; ~ **screw** *n* CONST vis à bois à tête carrée *f*; ~ **of the tide** *n* OCEANOG perdant *m*; ~ **time** *n* PETR TECH temps de remontée de la boue *m*

lag[2] *vt* PROP MAT *insulation* enrober

lag[3] *vi* PHYS être en quadrature retard

lagged *adj* MECH calorifugé

lagging[1] *adj* ELEC ENG déphasé en arrière, en retard

lagging[2] *n* AERONAUT *of helicopter rotor blade* mouvement de traînée *m*, HYDR EQUIP chemisage *m*, enveloppe *f*, garniture *f*, *of steam engine* enveloppe isolante *f*, garniture isolante *f*, MECH calorifuge *m*, MINING *behind wedging curb* lambourde *f*, *forepoling* enfilage *m*, poussage *m*, *timbering* garnissage *m*, PETR TECH *refinery* calorifugeage *m*, PROD ENG *lathing* lattage *m*, lattis *m*, PROP MAT calorifugeage *m*, THERMOD *of pipes, boilers* calorifugeage *m*, isolation thermique *f*; ~ **chrominance** *n* TV chrominance retardée *f*; ~ **piece** *n* MINING palplanche *f*; ~ **system** *n* AERONAUT retardateur *m*, système retardataire *m*; ~ **of the tide** *n* FUELLESS, OCEANOG retard de la marée *m*

lagoon *n* CONST lagune *f*, GEOL lagon *m*, lagune *f*, lagune côtière *f*, HYDROL lagune *f*, OCEANOG lagon *m*, lagune *f*, WATER SUPP lagune *f*; ~ **channel** *n* OCEANOG grau *m*

lagoonal: ~ **deposits** *n pl* GEOL dépôts de lagon *m pl*

lagooning *n* POLLUTION lagunage *m*

Lagrange's: ~ **equations** *n pl* PHYS équations de Lagrange *f pl*

Lagrangian[1] *adj* PHYS lagrangien

Lagrangian:[2] ~ **drifter** *n* NAUT *oceanographic research* flotteur lagrangien *m*

lahar *n* GEOL *volcanic mudflow* coulée de boue *f*, lahar *m*

laid: ~ **lines** *n pl* PAPER TECH vergeures *f pl*; ~ **paper** *n* PAPER TECH, PRINT papier vergé *m*; ~ **paper with rub-**

ber appearance *n* PACKAGING papier vergé fini caoutchouc *m*

laid-up *adj* NAUT *ship* désarmé

laitance *n* CONST laitance *f*

lake *n* COLOURS laque *f*, HYDROL, WATER SUPP lac *m*; ~ **liming** *n* POLLUTION chaulage de lac *m*; ~ **pigment** *n* COLOURS pigment laque *m*; ~ **water** *n* POLLUTION eau lacustre *f*

Lamb: ~ **shift** *n* PHYS déplacement de Lamb *m*

lambda: ~ **particle** *n* PHYS particule lambda *f*; ~ **point** *n* PHYS *cryogenics* point lambda *m*; ~ **probe** *n* AUTO sonde lambda *f*

lambert *n* METR lambert *m*

Lambert's: ~ **cosine law** *n* OPT loi de Lambert *f*, loi du cosinus de Lambert *f*; ~ **law** *n* PHYS loi de Lambert *f*

lambertian: ~ **radiator** *n* OPT, TELECOM source lambertienne *f*; ~ **reflector** *n* OPT réflecteur lambertien *m*; ~ **source** *n* OPT, TELECOM source lambertienne *f*

lamella *n* METALL lamelle *f*

lamellar[1] *adj* GEOL, MECH *materials*, METALL lamellaire

lamellar:[2] ~ **graphite cast iron** *n* MECH *materials* fonte à graphite lamellaire *f*; ~ **pearlite** *n* METALL perlite lamellaire *f*; ~ **structure** *n* METALL structure lamellaire *f*

lamina *n* CHEM feuillet *m*, lame *f*, lamelle *f*, GEOL lamelle *f*, lamine *m*

laminar[1] *adj* CHEM, FLUID PHYS, PROP MAT laminaire

laminar:[2] ~ **flow** *n* AERONAUT, FLUID PHYS, MECH *hydraulics*, PHYS, REFRIG écoulement laminaire *m*; ~ **flow theory** *n* FLUID PHYS théorie des écoulements laminaires *f*; ~ **pipe flow** *n* FLUID PHYS écoulement laminaire *m*, écoulement laminaire dans une conduite *m*; ~ **separation** *n* FLUID PHYS décollement laminaire *m*; ~ **structure** *n* GEOL *igneous texture* structure fluidale *f*; ~ **transistor** *n* ELECTRON transistor laminé *m*

laminarin *n* CHEM polysaccharide du genre laminaria *m*

laminate[1] *n* ELECTRON, MECH *materials* stratifié *m*, P&R, PRINT *plastics* laminé *m*, stratifié *m*, PROP MAT stratifié *m*

laminate[2] *vt* PRINT pelliculer, PROD ENG laminer

laminated[1] *adj* ELEC *capacitor* laminé, GEOL feuilleté, laminé, rubané, NAUT contré, laminé, stratifié, P&R *plastics* laminé, stratifié, PAPER TECH laminé, PROD ENG feuilleté, laminé, à lames

laminated:[2] ~ **armature** *n* ELEC *motor* armature feuilletée *f*, induit feuilleté *m*; ~ **brush** *n* ELEC *machine* balai à lames *m*, ELEC ENG balai multilame *m*; ~ **core** *n* ELEC *of generator, motor, transformer* noyau feuilleté *m*, ELEC ENG noyau feuilleté *m*, noyau magnétique feuilleté *m*; ~ **glass** *n* C&G, TRANSP verre feuilleté *m*; ~ **magnet** *n* ELEC aimant feuilleté *m*, aimant à lames *m*; ~ **materials** *n pl* PROP MAT matériaux feuilletés *m pl*; ~ **pack** *n* PACKAGING emballage laminé *m*; ~ **plastic** *n* ELEC *insulator*, NAUT plastique stratifié *m*, P&R stratifié *m*; ~ **record** *n* RECORDING matériel d'enregistrement feuilleté *m*; ~ **safety glass** *n* C&G verre de sécurité feuilleté armé *m*; ~ **section** *n* P&R profilé stratifié *m*; ~ **sheet** *n* CONST, P&R plaque stratifiée *f*; ~ **strip** *n* P&R bande stratifiée *f*; ~ **structure** *n* PROP MAT structure feuilletée *f*; ~ **torsion bar** *n* AERONAUT faisceau de lames constituant la barre de torsion *m*; ~ **tube** *n* PACKAGING tube enroulé *m*; ~ **windscreen** *n* (BrE) *(cf laminated windshield)* VEHICLES *body* pare-brise en verre feuilleté *m*; ~ **windshield** *n* (AmE) *(cf laminated windscreen)* VEHICLES *body* pare-brise en verre feuilleté *m*

laminating n C&G collage m, PACKAGING, PAPER TECH stratification f; ~ **machine** n PACKAGING machine à contrecoller f; ~ **resistance** n TEXTILES résistance au laminage f; ~ **strength** n PACKAGING résistance de lamination f

lamination n ELEC ENG tôle f, tôle magnétique f, GEOL laminage m, lamination f, P&R plastics laminage m, lamination f, stratification f, PACKAGING structure lamifiée f, PRINT pelliculage m, PROD ENG laminage m; ~ **mold** n (AmE), ~ **mould** n (BrE) MECH ENG, P&R moule stratifié m; ~ **sheet** n COATINGS feuille laminée f, tôle laminée f

laminator n PRINT machine à pelliculer f

lamp n CINEMAT ampoule f, lampe f, ELEC ENG, PHOTO lampe f, PROD ENG drying kettle poêle à flamber m, VEHICLES lighting, warning lights feu m, lampe f, lanterne f; ~ **base** n CINEMAT culot de lampe m; ~ **bulb** n C&G ampoule pour lampe à incandescence f; ~ **cap** n ELEC ENG culot m; ~ **holder** n CINEMAT douille f, ELEC ENG socket douille f, support porte-lampe m; ~ **oil** n PETR TECH kérosène m; ~ **replacement** n PHOTO rechange de lampe f; ~ **room** n MINING lampisterie f; ~ **socket** n PHOTO douille de lampe f

lampadite n MINERAL lampadite f

lampara n OCEANOG senne de plage f; ~ **net** n OCEANOG lampara m

Lampard: ~ **and Thomson capacitor** n PHYS condensateur de Lampard et Thomson m

lamphouse n CINEMAT lanterne f, INSTRUMENT boîte à lumière f, module d'éclairage m

lamphousing n PHOTO boîte à lumière f, tête d'éclairement f

lamprophyre n PETR lamprophyre m

LAN abbr (local area network) COMP, DP, TELECOM RLE (réseau local d'entreprise)

lanarkite n MINERAL lanarkite f

land[1] adj SPACE terrestre

land[2] n MECH ENG of drill saillie f, NAUT terre f, P&R press surface d'appui f, RECORDING of an LP espace intersillon m; ~ **accretion** n WATER SUPP accrétion des terrains f; ~ **air-cushion vehicle** n TRANSP aéroglisseur terrestre m; ~ **breeze** n METEO, NAUT brise de terre f; ~ **cable** n TELECOM câble terrestre m; ~ **container** n TRANSP conteneur terrestre m; ~ **degradation** n POLLUTION dégradation des sols f, dévastation du sol f; ~ **disturbance** n POLLUTION dévastation du sol f; ~ **line** n TELECOM ligne terrestre f; ~ **measure** n CONST mesure agraire f; ~ **measuring** n CONST arpentage m; ~ **measuring chain** n CONST chaîne d'arpentage f; ~ **mobile station** n (LMS) TELECOM station mobile terrestre f; ~ **pollution** n POLLUTION pollution des sols f; ~ **reclamation** n WATER SUPP bonification f; ~ **survey** n CONST arpentage m, levé de terrains m; ~ **surveying** n CONST arpentage m, levé de terrains m; ~ **vehicle** n SPACE spacecraft véhicule terrestre m

land[3] vt NAUT cargo débarquer, décharger, passengers débarquer

land[4] vi AERONAUT, MINING atterrir, NAUT débarquer, on deck apponter, SPACE spacecraft atterrir

Landé: ~ **factor** n PHYS facteur de Landé m

landed: ~ **price** n PETR TECH commerce prix rendu m

lander n SPACE spacecraft module d'atterrissage m; ~ **stage** n SPACE spacecraft module d'atterrissage m

landfall n NAUT navigation atterrissage m

landfill n COAL TECH décharge f, matériau de remblai m, RECYCLING site de décharge m; ~ **site** n MAR POLL décharge f

landfilling n MAR POLL mise en décharge f, RECYCLING décharge contrôlée f

landing n AERONAUT atterrissage m, COAL TECH fixation f, CONST of stairs carré m, palier m, palier de repos m, repos m, MINING atterrissage m, réception f, NAUT accostage m, appontage m, atterrissage m, PROD ENG of furnace plate-forme f, pont de chargement m, SPACE atterrissage m, TRANSP atterrissage m, débarquement m; ~ **approach speed** n AERONAUT, SPACE vitesse d'approche à l'atterrissage f; ~ **area** n AERONAUT, SPACE spacecraft, TRANSP aire d'atterrissage f; ~ **barge** n MILIT chaland de débarquement m; ~ **capsule** n SPACE spacecraft capsule d'atterrissage f; ~ **charge** n (BrE) (cf landing fee) AERONAUT air transport redevance d'atterrissages f; ~ **charges** n pl NAUT frais de débarquement m pl, frais de mise à terre m pl; ~ **chart** n AERONAUT, NAUT navigation carte d'atterrissage f; ~ **craft** n MILIT embarcation de débarquement f, péniche de débarquement f, NAUT, TRANSP péniche de débarquement f; ~ **deck** n TRANSP pont d'envol m; ~ **direction indicator** n AERONAUT indicateur de direction d'atterrissage m; ~ **distance** n AERONAUT distance d'atterrissage f; ~ **distance available** n AERONAUT distance utilisable à l'atterrissage f; ~ **fee** n (AmE) (cf landing charge) AERONAUT air transport redevance d'atterrissages f; ~ **flap** n TRANSP volet d'atterrissage m; ~ **gear** n AERONAUT atterrisseur m, train d'atterrissage m, SPACE train d'atterrissage m, TRANSP train d'atterrissage m, for semitrailer béquille f; ~ **gear bay** n AERONAUT logement du train m; ~ **gear boot retainer** n AERONAUT porte-protecteur de train m; ~ **gear bracing installation** n AERONAUT triangulation du train f; ~ **gear bumper** n AERONAUT butée élastique du train f; ~ **gear compensation rod** n AERONAUT bielle de compensation f; ~ **gear control unit** n AERONAUT boîte de commande train f; ~ **gear diagonal truss** n AERONAUT bielle diagonale f, contrefiche diagonale de train f; ~ **gear door latch** n AERONAUT accrochage des trappes de train m; ~ **gear door unlatching** n AERONAUT décrochage des trappes de train m; ~ **gear door uplock** n AERONAUT boîtier d'accrochage trappes de train m; ~ **gear downlock** n AERONAUT accrochage train bas m; ~ **gear downlock visual check installation** n AERONAUT dispositif de contrôle optique du train m; ~ **gear drop test** n AERONAUT essai de chute limite de train m; ~ **gear extension** n AERONAUT descente du train f, sortie du train d'atterrissage f; ~ **gear fork rod** n AERONAUT biellette double f; ~ **gear hinge beam** n AERONAUT chapiteau m; ~ **gear hinge beam fitting** n AERONAUT candélabre m; ~ **gear leg** n AERONAUT fût de l'atterrisseur m, jambe de atterrissage f; ~ **gear leg support** n AERONAUT support de jambe du train m; ~ **gear lock pin** n AERONAUT broche à ergot de train f; ~ **gear main shock strut** n AERONAUT amortisseur principal m; ~ **gear manual release** n AERONAUT décrochage manuel du train m; ~ **gear master brake cylinder** n AERONAUT distributeur quadruple de freins m; ~ **gear optical inspection system** n AERONAUT indicateur optique d'arrêt du train d'atterrissage m; ~ **gear position indicator** n AERONAUT indicateur de position du train m; ~ **gear retraction lock** n AERONAUT verrou de train rentré m; ~ **gear safety lock** n AERONAUT verrou d'interdiction de levage m; ~ **gear safety override** n AERONAUT effacement de la sécurité de train m; ~ **gear shaft** n AERONAUT axe d'articulation de train principal *m*; ~ **gear shock strut compression** *n* AERONAUT enfoncement du train *m*; ~ **gear sliding valve** *n* AERONAUT coiffe mobile de train *f*; ~ **gear track** *n* AERONAUT voie du train d'atterrissage *f*; ~ **gear unlocking** *n* AERONAUT décrochage du train *m*; ~ **gear uplock** *n* AERONAUT accrochage train rentré *m*, verrou de train rentré *m*; ~ **gear uplock box** *n* AERONAUT boîtier d'accrochage train rentré *m*; ~ **gear well** *n* AERONAUT logement du train *m*; ~ **gear wheel rim fusible plug** *n* AERONAUT fusible d'éclatement sur roue de train *m*; ~ **lane** *n* AERONAUT voie d'approche *f*; ~ **light** *n* AERONAUT phare d'atterrissage *m*; ~ **on water** *n* AERONAUT amerrissage *m*; ~ **path** *n* TRANSP piste d'atterrissage *f*; ~ **pattern turn** *n* AERONAUT virage de procédure *m*; ~ **pier** *n* NAUT embarcadère *m*; ~ **pontoon** *n* TRANSP ponton d'accostage *m*; ~ **procedure** *n* AERONAUT procédure d'approche finale *f*; ~ **riser** *n* CONST *of stairs* contremarche palière *f*; ~ **run** *n* AERONAUT course à l'atterrissage *f*, longueur de roulement à l'atterrissage *f*, parcours à l'atterrissage *m*, roulement à l'atterrissage *m*; ~ **sequence** *n* AERONAUT ordre d'atterrissage *m*, séquence d'atterrissage *f*; ~ **skids** *n* TRANSP patins d'atterrissage *m pl*; ~ **speed** *n* AERONAUT, TRANSP vitesse d'atterrissage *f*; ~ **stage** *n* MINING accrochage *m*, chambre d'accrochage *f*, chambre d'envoyage *f*, envoyage *m*, recette *f*, NAUT *mooring* embarcadère *m*, SPACE module d'atterrissage *m*, TRANSP ponton d'accostage *m*; ~ **station** *n* MINING accrochage *m*, chambre d'accrochage *f*, chambre d'envoyage *f*, envoyage *m*, recette *f*; ~ **step** *n* CONST *of stairs* marche palière *f*, marche-palier *m*; ~ **strip** *n* AERONAUT bande d'atterrissage *f*, piste *f*, piste d'atterrissage *f*; ~ **strip marker** *n* AERONAUT *radio* balise d'entrée de piste *f*; ~ **switch** *n* ELEC *of lift* commutateur d'étage *m*; ~ **system** *n* TRANSP système d'atterrissage *m*, système d'échouage *m*; ~ **trimmer** *n* CONST *of stairs* chevêtre sous la marche palière *m*, solive d'enchevêtrure *f*; ~ **vehicle** *n* SPACE *of spacecraft* véhicule d'atterrissage *m*; ~ **weight** *n* AERONAUT masse à l'atterrissage *f*

landings *n pl* OCEANOG capture *f*

landmark *n* AERONAUT point de repère *m*, CONST borne *f*, point de repère *m*, MILIT point de repère *m*, NAUT *navigation* amer *m*, point de repère *m*, OCEANOG amer *m*

landscape: ~ **format** *n* DP format paysage *m*, format à l'italienne *m*; ~ **photographer** *n* PHOTO paysagiste *m*; ~ **size** *n* PRINT format oblong *m*, format à l'italienne *m*

landscaping *n* CONST travaux paysagers *m pl*

landslide *n* CONST glissement de terre *m*, éboulement de terres *m*, GEOL glissement de terrain *m*, éboulement *m*, RAIL éboulement *m*, éboulement de terrain *m*; ~ **block** *n* GEOL paquet glissé *m*

landslip *n* GEOL glissement de terrain *m*, éboulement *m*, RAIL éboulement *m*, éboulement de terrain *m*

landward *adv* GEOL vers la terre, vers le continent

lane *n* TRANSP couloir *m*, file *f*; ~ **switching** *n* TRANSP déboîtement *m*

Langelier's: ~ **index** *n* HYDROL indice de saturation Langelier *m*

langite *n* MINERAL langite *f*

Langmuir: ~ **effect** *n* METEO effet Langmuir *m*

language *n* COMP langage *m*; ~ **construct** *n* COMP structure de langage *f*; ~ **statement** *n* COMP instruction *f*; ~ **translator** *n* COMP traducteur *m*

lanolin *n* CHEM graisse de laine *f*, lanoline *f*, lanoléine *f*

lanoline *n* CHEM graisse de laine *f*, lanoline *f*, lanoléine *f*

lanosterol *n* CHEM lanostérine *f*

lantern *n* PROD ENG *core barrel* lanterne *f*, *drying kettle* poêle à flamber *m*; ~ **gear** *n* MECH ENG engrenage à fuseaux *m*, engrenage à lanterne *m*; ~ **gearing** *n* MECH ENG engrenage à fuseaux *m*, engrenage à lanterne *m*; ~ **slide** *n* CINEMAT cliché de projection *m*

lanthanide *n* CHEM lanthane *m*, lanthanide *m*; ~ **contraction** *n* CHEM *atomic, ionic radii* contraction lanthanide *f*

lanthanite *n* MINERAL lanthanite *f*

lanthanum *n (La)* CHEM lanthane *m (La)*

lanyard *n* NAUT aiguillette *f*, amarrage *m*, ride *f*

lap[1] *n* C&G polissoir *m*, CONST *roofing* recouvrement *m*, HYDR EQUIP recouvrement de tiroir *m*, *of slide valve* recouvrement *m*, PROD ENG *lapping tool* rodoir *m*, SPRINGS repli de laminage *m*, TEXTILES nappe *f*; ~ **and lead lever** *n* HYDR EQUIP *Walchaerts valve gear* levier d'avance et de retard *m*; ~ **blisters** *n pl* C&G plis avec bouillons *m pl*; ~ **dissolve** *n* CINEMAT fondu enchaîné *m*; ~ **joint** *n* CONST assemblage à clin *m*, assemblage à recouvrement *m*, joint à recouvrement *m*, *halved joint* assemblage à mi-bois *m*, coupe à mi-bois *f*, entaille à mi-bois *f*, MECH *welding* assemblage à recouvrement *m*; ~ **mark** *n* C&G pli de coulée *m*; ~ **riveting** *n* PACKAGING rivure à recouvrement *f*, PROD ENG rivetage à clin *m*, rivure à recouvrement *f*; ~ **valve** *n* HYDR EQUIP tiroir à recouvrement *m*; ~ **weld** *n* NUCLEAR, PACKAGING soudure par recouvrement *f*, PROD ENG soudure par amorces *f*, soudure à chaude portée *f*, soudure à recouvrement *f*; ~ **welding** *n* PROD ENG soudure par amorces *f*, soudure à chaude portée *f*, soudure à recouvrement *f*; ~ **winding** *n* ELEC *machine*, ELEC ENG enroulement imbriqué *m*

lap[2] *vt* MECH, PROD ENG roder

LAP *abbr (line access protocol)* TELECOM protocole d'accès de ligne *m*

lapel: ~ **microphone** *n* ACOUSTICS microphone personnel *m*, RECORDING micro cravate *m*

lapilli *n pl* GEOL lapilli *m pl*

Laplace: ~ **transform** *n* MATH transformée de Laplace *f*, PHYS transformation de Laplace *f*; ~ **transformation** *n* ELECTRON, PHYS transformation de Laplace *f*

Laplace's: ~ **equation** *n* PHYS équation de Laplace *f*

laplacian *n* NUCLEAR, PHYS laplacien *m*

lapless: ~ **valve** *n* HYDR EQUIP tiroir sans recouvrement *m*

lappaconitine *n* CHEM lappaconitine *f*

lapped: ~ **insulation** *n* ELEC *cable conductor* isolation rubanée *f*; ~ **scarf** *n* CONST enture en paume *f*, enture à mi-bois avec abouts carrés *f*

lapping *n* PROD ENG rodage *m*, PROP MAT *engineering* polissage *m*; ~ **compound** *n* PROD ENG pâte de rodage *f*, pâte à roder *f*; ~ **fixture** *n* MECH ENG *machine tools* montage de rodage *m*; ~ **machine** *n* MECH lapidaire *m*, PROD ENG machine à roder *f*; ~ **rib** *n* C&G nervure d'enroulement *f*; ~ **tool** *n* PROD ENG rodoir *m*; ~ **with silicon carbide and diamond slurries** *n* MECH ENG rodage aux boues de carbure de silicium et de diamant *m*

laps *n pl* C&G faux plis *m pl*

laptop: ~ **computer** *n* COMP, DP ordinateur portable *m*, ordinateur portable autonome *m*

lardite *n* MINERAL lardite *f*

large: ~ **angle scattering** *n* NUCLEAR diffusion aux grands angles *f*; ~ **area radiation standard** *n* NUCLEAR étalon de rayonnement à large surface m; ~ **body** n MINING *of ore* massif m; ~ **capacity motorcycle** n TRANSP moto grosse cylindrée f; ~ **capacity truck** n TRANSP truc m; ~ **core glass fiber** n (AmE), ~ **core glass fibre** n (BrE) ELEC ENG fibre de verre à coeur de grand diamètre f; **very ~ crude carrier** n *(VLCC)* PETR TECH très gros transporteur de brut m *(TGTB)*; ~ **eddies** n pl FLUID PHYS grands tourbillons m pl, gros tourbillons m pl; ~ **electron-positron collider** n *(LEP)* PART PHYS grand collisionneur électron-positron m *(LEP)*; ~ **end of connecting rod** n MECH ENG grosse tête de bielle f, tête de bielle f; ~ **format camera** n INSTRUMENT appareil photo grand format m; ~ **format folding camera** n PHOTO chambre grand format à soufflet f; ~ **hadron collider** n *(LHC)* PART PHYS grand collisionneur de hadrons m; ~ **hole-cut** n MINING bouchon à gros trous m; ~ **inflow of water** n HYDROL venue d'eau importante f; ~ **orifice** n HYDROL orifice de grandes dimensions m; ~ **paper** n PRINT papier grand format m; ~ **plate mold** n (AmE), ~ **plate mould** n (BrE) MECH ENG *production of rubber seals, gaskets* moule en grand plateau m; ~ **signal** n ELECTRON grand signal m, signal de grande amplitude m; ~ **size container** n PACKAGING conteneur de grande capacité m

Large: ~ **Magellanic Cloud** n ASTRON Grand nuage de Magellan m

large-aperture: ~ **lens** n PHOTO objectif à grande ouverture m

large-case: ~ **erector** n PACKAGING assembleuse de grandes caisses f

large-hole: ~ **boring** n COAL TECH forage de trou à grand diamètre m

large-scale[1] adj GEOL, GEOPHYSICS *chart* à grande échelle

large-scale:[2] ~ **integrated circuit** n PHYS circuit intégré à grande échelle m; **very ~ integrated circuit** n PHYS *VLSI circuit* circuit intégré à très grande échelle m; ~ **integration** n *(LSI)* COMP, DP, ELECTRON, NAUT *computers on board ship* intégration à grande échelle f *(LSI)*, PHYS intégration à forte densité f, intégration à grande échelle f *(LSI)*, TELECOM intégration à grande échelle f *(LSI)*; **very ~ integration** n *(VLSI)* COMP, DP, ELECTRON, TELECOM intégration à très grande échelle f; ~ **integration circuit** n TELECOM circuit LSI m, circuit intégré à grande échelle m; **very ~ integration circuit** n TELECOM circuit VLSI m, circuit à très grande intégration m, onde myriamétrique f

large-signal: ~ **bandwidth** n ELECTRON bande passante en grands signaux f; ~ **conditions** n pl ELECTRON régime de grands signaux m; ~ **operation** n ELECTRON fonctionnement en grands signaux m

large-value: ~ **capacitor** n ELEC ENG condensateur de forte valeur m; ~ **resistor** n ELEC ENG résistance de forte valeur f

Larmor: ~ **frequency** n PHYS fréquence de Larmor f; ~ **precession** n PHYS précession de Larmor f

larry n MINING chariot de chargement m, wagon de chargement m; ~ **car** n MINING chariot de chargement m, wagon de chargement m

Larsen: ~ **effect** n ACOUSTICS feedback m, CINEMAT effet Larsen m, feedback m, TV feedback m

laser n COMP, DP, ELECTRON, OPT, PHYS, PRINT, PROP MAT, WAVE PHYS laser m; ~ **action** n ELECTRON effet laser m; ~ **alignment** n MECH ENG alignement par laser m; ~ **annealing** n ELECTRON recuit au laser m; ~

bandwidth n ELECTRON largeur de bande d'un rayonnement laser f; ~ **beam** n ELECTRON, NUCLEAR, TELECOM faisceau laser m, WAVE PHYS; ~ **beam emission** n ELECTRON émission d'un faisceau laser f; **beam energy** n ELECTRON énergie d'un faisceau laser f; ~ **beam modulation** n ELECTRON modulation d'un faisceau laser f; ~ **beam recording** n COMP, DP enregistrement par faisceau laser m, TV enregistrement au laser m; ~ **beam welding** n CONST soudage par faisceau laser m; ~ **burst** n ELECTRON salve laser f; ~ **cavity** n ELECTRON cavité laser f, cavité résonante de laser f; ~ **code** n ELECTRON code laser m; ~ **communications** n pl ELECTRON télécommunications par faisceau laser f pl; ~ **cutting** n CONST coupage laser m, ELECTRON découpage au laser m, découpage laser m; ~ **designation** n ELECTRON marquage laser m; ~ **diode** n ELECTRON, OPT diode laser f, PHYS laser à semi-conducteur m, TELECOM diode laser f ~ **disc** n (BrE) OPT disque laser m, disque à lecture laser m, TV disque optique vidéo m, laser disc m; ~ **disk** n (AmE) *see laser disc*; ~ **drill** n ELECTRON perceuse laser f; ~ **drilling** n PROP MAT perçage des matériaux à l'aide d'un laser m; ~ **effect threshold** n OPT seuil d'effet laser m; ~ **emission** n ELECTRON émission laser f; ~ **excitation** n RAD PHYS excitation laser f; ~ **fusion** n NUCLEAR fusion par laser f; ~ **glass** n C&G verre pour laser m; ~ **grading system** n CONST système de réglage des surfaces par rayon laser m; ~ **guidance** n ELECTRON guidage laser m; ~ **gyro** n SPACE *spacecraft* gyrolaser m; ~ **head** n OPT tête optique à laser f; ~ **illumination** n ELECTRON illumination laser f; ~ **impact surface ionization** n NUCLEAR *mass spectrometry* ionisation superficielle par impact laser f; ~ **interferometer** n ELECTRON, MECH ENG interféromètre à laser m; ~ **light beam** n RAD PHYS faisceau de lumière laser m; ~ **machining** n MECH usinage au laser m; ~ **material** n PROP MAT milieu amplifiant m; ~ **measuring instrument** n METR machine de mesure au laser f; ~ **medium** n OPT milieu laser m, TELECOM milieu actif laser m, milieu laser m; ~ **melting** n ELECTRON fusion au laser f; ~ **monitoring systems** n pl RAD PHYS systèmes laser de surveillance m pl; ~ **optical recorder** n ELECTRON enregistreur optique à laser m; ~ **optic disc** n (BrE) OPT disque optique vidéo m; ~ **optic disk** n (AmE) *see laser optic disc*; ~ **pick-up head** n OPT tête optique à laser f; ~ **population mechanism** n RAD PHYS mécanisme de population laser m; ~ **printer** n COMP, OPT, PRINT *computer* imprimante à laser f; ~ **printer-copier** n OPT imprimante-copieur à laser f; ~ **printing** n OPT impression au laser f; ~ **probe mass spectrography** n NUCLEAR spectrographie de masse à sonde laser f; ~ **propulsion** n SPACE *spacecraft* propulsion par laser f; ~ **pulse** n ELECTRON impulsion laser f; ~ **radiation** n ELECTRON, RAD PHYS rayonnement laser m; ~ **radiation hazards** n pl SAFETY dangers des rayons laser m pl; ~ **rangefinder** n ELECTRON télémètre laser m; ~ **retroflector experiment** n RAD PHYS expérience de rétroflecteur laser f; ~ **scriber** n ELECTRON rayeuse laser f; ~ **scribing** n ELECTRON découpe au laser f; ~ **sensor** n ELECTRON capteur laser m; ~ **spectral line** n RAD PHYS raie spectrale laser f; ~ **spectroscopy** n RAD PHYS spectroscopie laser f; ~ **target marker** n MILIT indicateur d'objectif à laser m; ~ **telemetry** n TELECOM télémétrie laser f; ~ **tracker** n ELECTRON laser de poursuite m; ~ **tracking** n ELECTRON poursuite laser f; ~ **transition** n RAD PHYS transition laser f; ~ **trimming** n ELECTRON ajustage au laser *m*, ajustage laser *m*; ~ **vaporization** *n* RAD PHYS vaporisation par laser *f*; ~ **videodisc** *n* (BrE) OPT vidéodisque laser *m*; ~ **videodisk** *n* (AmE) *see laser videodisc*; ~ **vision** *n (LV)* OPT laservision *f*; ~ **warning receiver** *n* ELECTRON détecteur de lasers *m*; ~ **weapon** *n* ELECTRON arme laser *f*; ~ **welding** *n* CONST, ELEC-TRON, PROD ENG, PROP MAT soudage au laser *m*

LASER *abbr (light amplification by stimulated emission of radiation)* RAD PHYS amplification de la lumière par rayonnement stimulé *f*

lasercard *n* OPT lasercard *m*

laser-controlled: ~ **machine** *n* CONST machine asservie au laser *f*

laser-driven: ~ **fusion** *n* NUCLEAR fusion par laser *f*

laser-guided *adj* ELECTRON guidé par laser

Laserjet *n* (TM) OPT laserjet *m* (MD)

laser-optic: ~ **memory** *n (L-OM)* OPT mémoire à lecture par laser *f*; ~ **recording** *n* OPT enregistrement optique au laser *m*; ~ **tape** *n* OPT bande optique laser *f*

laser-produced: ~ **printing plates** *n pl* PRINT plaques imprimantes produites par laser *f pl*

laservision: ~ **disc** *n* (BrE) OPT disque laservision *m*; ~ **disk** *n* (AmE) *see laservision disc*; ~ **player** *n* OPT lecteur laservision *m*; ~ **videodisc** *n* (BrE) OPT disque laservision *m*; ~ **videodisk** *n* (AmE) *see laservision videodisc*

lash[1] *n* MECH ENG jeu *m*

lash[2] *vt* NAUT amarrer, saisir, *ropework* frapper ~ **the helm** *vt* NAUT amarrer la barre

LASH: ~ **carrier** *n (lighter aboard ship carrier)* TRANSP navire porte-barges du type LASH *m*; ~ **lighter** *n* TRANSP barge LASH *f*

lashing *n* MINING *of rods in borehole* fouettement *m*, NAUT *stowage* amarrage *m*, liure *f*, saisissage *m*, OCEA-NOG rousture *f*, PROD ENG *of wires, cables* ligature *f*; ~ **plan** *n* NAUT *stowage* plan d'élingage *m*

lasing *n* ELECTRON émission d'un faisceau laser *f*, émission laser *f*; ~ **medium** *n* ELECTRON milieu actif *m*; ~ **threshold** *n* TELECOM seuil d'effet laser *m*

last: ~ **emergency action** *n* AERONAUT détresse *f*; ~ **feedback** *n* PROD ENG dernier renseignement *m*; ~ **feedback rate** *n* PROD ENG date de dernier retour *f*; ~ **number recall** *n* TELECOM rappel du dernier numéro *m*; ~ **number redial** *n* TELECOM rappel du dernier numéro *m*, répétition du dernier numéro *f*; ~ **quarter** *n* ASTRON dernier quartier *m*; ~ **state** *n* PROD ENG *of output* dernier état *m*

last-choice: ~ **circuit group** *n* TELECOM faisceau de dernier choix *m*; ~ **group** *n* TELECOM faisceau de dernier choix *m*

last-in: ~ **first-out** *n (LIFO)* COMP, DP, PROD ENG dernier entré premier sorti *m*

lasting: ~ **color** *n* (AmE), ~ **colour** *n* (BrE) P&R *paint raw material* grand teint *m*; ~ **pigment** *n* P&R *paint raw material* grand teint *m*

latch[1] *n* COMP bascule *f*, CONST *for gate* loquet *m*, *pawl, bolt* cliquet *m*, verrou *m*, DP bascule *f*, MECH ENG loqueteau *m*, tourniquet *m*, pistolet *m*, verrou à ressort *m*, *of turntable* main d'arrêt *f*, valet d'arrêt *m*, NUCLEAR *control rod drive* cliquet *m*, PACKAGING verrou *m*, TEXTILES palette *f*; ~ **address** *n* PROD ENG adresse de bit de verrouillage *f*; ~ **bit** *n* PROD ENG bit de verrouillage *m*; ~ **bolt** *n* CONST demi-tour *m*, pêne à demi-tour *m*, pêne à ressort *m*; ~ **catch** *n* CONST mentonnet *m*; ~ **circuit** *n* PROD ENG circuit de verrouillage *m*; ~ **instruction** *n* PROD ENG instruction de

verrouillage *f*; ~ **key** *n* PROD ENG touche de verrouillage *f*; ~ **lock** *n* CONST serrure à demi-tour *f*, serrure à ressort *f*; ~ **needle** *n* TEXTILES aiguille à clapet *f*; ~ **pin** *n* CONST mentonnet *m*; ~ **rung** *n* PROD ENG ligne de sortie verrouillée *f*

latch[2] *vt* COMP, DP verrouiller, MECH enclencher, verrouiller, PETR TECH *drilling* accrocher

latched: ~ **bit** *n* PROD ENG bit verrouillé *m*; ~ **lever** *n* MECH ENG levier à poussoir *m*

latching *n* ELEC ENG *relay*, SAFETY verrouillage *m*; ~ **current** *n* ELEC ENG courant d'accrochage *m*; ~ **electro-magnet** *n* ELEC électro-aimant de verrouillage *m*; ~ **position** *n* PROD ENG position de verrouillage *f*; ~ **relay** *n* ELEC relais de verrouillage *m*, relais encliqueté *m*, relais latching *m*, ELEC ENG relais à verrouillage *m*; ~ **transistor** *n* ELECTRON transistor de verrouillage *m*

latch-up *n* SPACE verrouillage anormal *m*

late[1] *adj* GEOL récent, tardif, terminal

late:[2] ~ **admission slide valve** *n* HYDR EQUIP tiroir à admission retardée *m*; ~ **break contact** *n* PROD ENG contact à ouverture retardée *m*; ~ **release slide valve** *n* HYDR EQUIP tiroir à échappement retardé *m*

latency *n* COMP, DP latence *f*, temps de latence *m*

latensification *n* CINEMAT latensification *f*, PHOTO renforcement latent *m*

latent: ~ **evaporation** *n* HYDROL évaporation latente *f*; ~ **heat** *n* CONST, HEAT ENG, MECH *thermodynamics*, METEO, PETR TECH *refining*, PHYS, REFRIG, THERMOD chaleur latente *f*; ~ **heat of compression** *n* THERMOD chaleur latente de compression *f*; ~ **heat of evaporation** *n* THERMOD chaleur latente d'évaporation *f*, froid dû à l'évaporation *m*; ~ **heat of expansion** *n* THERMOD chaleur latente d'expansion *f*; ~ **heat of fusion** *n* PHYS, THERMOD chaleur latente de fusion *f*; ~ **heat of solidification** *n* THERMOD chaleur latente de cristallisation *f*; ~ **heat of transformation** *n* THERMOD chaleur latente de transformation *f*; ~ **heat of vaporization** *n* PHYS, THERMOD chaleur latente de vaporisation *f*; ~ **image** *n* CINEMAT, OPT, PHOTO, PHYS, PRINT image latente *f*; ~ **modulus** *n* METALL modulus latent *m*

lateral *n* MINING galerie en direction *f*, PETR latérale *f*; ~ **accelerometer** *n* AERONAUT accéléromètre transversal *m*, ensemble accéléromètre latéral *m*, ensemble accéléromètre transversal *m*; ~ **area** *n* GEOM aire latérale *f*; ~ **axis** *n* AERONAUT axe latéral *m*, axe transversal *m*; ~ **beam coupler** *n* AERONAUT coupleur de faisceau latéral *m*; ~ **buckling** *n* SPRINGS flambage *m*; ~ **clearance** *n* TRANSP espacement latéral *m*; ~ **contraction** *n* METALL contraction latérale *f*; ~ **crater** *n* GEOL *volcanic feature* cratère adventif *m*; ~ **cyclic control support** *n* AERONAUT *helicopter* support de gauchissement *m*; ~ **cyclic pitch** *n* AERONAUT *helicopter* pas cyclique latéral *m*; ~ **diffusion** *n* ELECTRON diffusion latérale *f*; ~ **divergence** *n* AERONAUT engagement en roulis *m*; ~ **drift landing** *n* AERONAUT atterrissage ripé *m*; ~ **force** *n* TRANSP force latérale *f*; ~ **force coefficient** *n* AERONAUT coefficient de force latérale *m*; ~ **guidance** *n* TRANSP guidage latéral *m*; ~ **inversion** *n* TV inversion latérale *f*; ~ **magnification** *n* INSTRUMENT grossissement latéral *m*, PHYS grandissement latéral *m*; ~ **noise measurement point** *n* AERONAUT point de mesure du bruit latéral *m*; ~ **offset loss** *n* OPT perte par décentrement transversal *f*, TELECOM perte par décalage latéral *f*, perte par décentrement transversal *f*; ~ **path integrator** *n* AERONAUT intégrateur de trajectoire transversale *m*; ~ **planation** *n* GEOL aplanissement des interfluves *m*; ~ **plasma deposition** *n* TELECOM déposition latérale *f*; ~ **recording** *n* ACOUSTICS, RECORDING enregistrement latéral *m*; ~ **separation** *n* GEOL distance des faces d'une faille *f*; ~ **shift** *n* GEOL décalage *m*, décrochement *m*; ~ **stability** *n* SPRINGS, TRANSP stabilité latérale *f*; ~ **stapling** *n* PACKAGING agrafage latéral *m*; ~ **stiffness** *n* SPRINGS rigidité latérale *f*; ~ **structure** *n* ELECTRON structure horizontale *f*; ~ **system** *n* NAUT *navigation marks* système latéral *m*; ~ **tracking angle error** *n* ACOUSTICS erreur de piste latérale *f*; ~ **transistor** *n* ELECTRON transistor horizontal *m*, transistor latéral *m*; ~ **trim** *n* AERONAUT compensation de gauchissement *f*, régulateur de roulis *m*; ~ **variation** *n* GEOL *of facies* variation latérale *f*; ~ **view** *n* INSTRUMENT cliché latéral *m*; ~ **yielding** *n* NUCLEAR *pipes* affaissement latéral *m*

laterally: ~ **inverted image** *n* CINEMAT image inverse latérale *f*

laterite *n* CONST *geology* latérite *f*

latest *adv* PROD ENG au plus tard

late-stage *adj* GEOL récent, tardif, terminal; ~ **magmatic** *adj* GEOL tardimagmatique

latex *n* P&R *rubber, latices*, TEXTILES latex *m*; ~ **backing** *n* TEXTILES dossier latex *m*; ~ **foam** *n* P&R *rubber, foamed rubber* mousse de latex *f*; ~ **paint** *n* COLOURS peinture au latex *f*

lath *n* CONST *plaster* latte *f*, *slate* latte volige *f*, latte volisse *f*, latte à ardoises *f*, volice *f*, volige *f*, GEOL cristal allongé et mince *m*, cristal en forme de lattes *m*; ~ **nail** *n* CONST clou à latter *m*; ~ **wood** *n* CONST bois de refend *m*

lathe *n* MECH, PROD ENG tour *m*; ~ **bed** *n* MECH banc de tour *m*, MECH ENG *machine tools* glissières de tour *f pl*; ~ **bed braced by cross-girths** *n* MECH ENG banc de tour renforcé par des nervures d'entretoisage *m*; ~ **carrier** *n* MECH ENG doguin *m*, toc de tour *m*; ~ **center** *n* (AmE), ~ **centre** *n* (BrE) MECH ENG pointe de tour *f*; ~ **chuck** *n* MECH mandrin de tour *m*; ~ **dog** *n* MECH ENG doguin *m*, toc de tour *m*; ~ **head** *n* MECH ENG poupée de tour *f*; ~ **headstock** *n* MECH ENG poupée de tour *f*; ~ **operator** *n* MECH tourneur *m*; ~ **saddle** *n* MECH chariot de tour *m*; ~ **slide** *n* MECH chariot de tour *m*; ~ **tool post** *n* MECH ENG support d'outils pour tours *m*; ~ **tools** *n pl* MECH ENG outils de tours *m pl*, outils pour tours *m pl*; ~ **work** *n* PROD ENG travail au tour *m*, travail de tour *m*

lather: ~ **booster** *n* FOOD TECH exalteur de mousse *m*

lathing *n* CONST lattage *m*, lattis *m*, voligeage *m*

latitude *n* NAUT *geography, navigation* latitude *f*; ~ **coarse motion clamp** *n* INSTRUMENT vis de blocage du mouvement approximatif de latitude *f*

lattice *n* CHEM réseau *m*, treillis *m*, CONST treillage *m*, treillis *m*, *frame* poutre en treillis *f*, poutre évidée *f*, poutre à jour *f*, poutrelle à croisillons *f*, ELECTRON *crystals* réseau cristallin *m*, MATH treillis *m*, NUCLEAR *atomic pile* réseau *m*, SPACE *spacecraft* réseau *m*, treillis *m*; ~ **beam** *n* CONST *frame* poutre en treillis *f*, poutre évidée *f*, poutre à jour *f*, poutrelle à croisillons *f*; ~ **bracing** *n* CONST charpente à croisillons *f*; ~ **bridge** *n* CONST pont en treillis *m*; ~ **constant** *n* METALL paramètre de réseau *m*; ~ **correspondence** *n* METALL correspondance des réseaux *f*; ~ **defect** *n* ELECTRON *semiconductors* défaut du réseau *m*, METALL défaut réticulaire *m*; ~ **deformation** *n* METALL déformation réticulaire *f*; ~ **filter** *n* ELECTRON filtre en treillis *m*; ~ **girder** *n* CONST *frame* poutre en treillis *f*, poutre évidée *f*, poutre à jour *f*, poutrelle à croisillons *f*, MECH

poutre en treillis *f*; ~ **girder arch** *n* CONST poutrelle métallique de treillis et arceau *f*, poutrelle métallique en arceau *f*; ~ **network** *n* ELEC ENG réseau en treillis *m*, réseau électrique en treillis *m*; ~ **parameters** *n pl* CRYSTALL paramètres de réseau *m pl*; ~ **pitch** *n* NUCLEAR pas de la maille *m*, pas du réseau *m*; ~ **pitch spacing** *n* NUCLEAR pas de la maille *m*, pas du réseau *m*; ~ **plan** *n* TELECOM *land mobile* plan maillé *m*; ~ **plane** *n* CRYSTALL plan réticulaire *m*; ~ **point** *n* CRYSTALL noeud de réseau *m*, point du réseau *m*, METALL pointe réticulaire *f*; ~ **rib** *n* AERONAUT nervure en treillis *f*; ~ **row** *n* CRYSTALL rangée réticulaire *f*; ~ **spacing** *n* METALL espacement réticulaire *m*; ~ **tower** *n* CONST porteau en treillis *m*, pylône *m*, ELEC *overhead supply line* pylône en treillis *m*; ~ **truss** *n* CONST *frame* poutre en treillis *f*, poutre évidée *f*, poutre à jour *f*, poutrelle à croisillons *f*; ~ **work** *n* CONST treillage *m*, treillis *m*

lattice-sided: ~ **container** *n* TRANSP conteneur à claire-voie *m*

lattice-wound: ~ **coil** *n* ELEC ENG bobinage en nid d'abeilles *m*

laudanine *n* CHEM laudanine *f*

laudanosine *n* CHEM laudanosine *f*

Laue: ~ **diagram** *n* RAD PHYS diagramme de Laue *m*; ~ **method** *n* CRYSTALL méthode de Laue *f*

laumonite *n* MINERAL laumonite *f*, laumontite *f*

laumontite *n* MINERAL laumonite *f*, laumontite *f*

launch[1] *n* MECH ENG *promotion* lancement *m*, NAUT embarcation *f*, vedette *f*, SPACE lancement *m*; ~ **area** *n* SPACE aire de lancement *f*; ~ **azimuth** *n* SPACE azimut de lancement *m*; ~ **environment** *n* SPACE environnement de lancement *m*; ~ **escape motor** *n* SPACE moteur d'éjection de secours *m*; ~ **escape system** *n* SPACE système d'éjection de secours *m*, tour d'éjection de secours *f*; ~ **numerical aperture** *n* OPT, TELECOM *(LNA)* ouverture numérique d'injection *f*; ~ **pad** *n* SPACE aire de lancement *f*; ~ **platform** *n* SPACE *vehicles* plate-forme de lancement *f*; ~ **ramp** *n* SPACE *vehicles* rampe de lancement *f*; ~ **ramp shelter** *n* SPACE *vehicles* abri de rampe *m*; ~ **readiness review** *n* SPACE revue d'aptitude au lancement *f*; ~ **site** *n* SPACE ensemble de lancement *m*; ~ **station** *n* MILIT *of rocket* table de lancement *f*; ~ **success probability** *n* SPACE *spacecraft* probabilité de lancement réussi *f*; ~ **tower** *n* SPACE tour de lancement *f*; ~ **vehicle** *n* MILIT, SPACE lanceur *m*; ~ **window** *n* SPACE fenêtre de lancement *f*

launch[2] *vt* NAUT lancer, mettre à flot, mettre à l'eau, mettre à la mer

launched: ~ **missile** *n* MILIT engin lancé d'une rampe *m*

launcher *n* SPACE lanceur *m*, table de lancement *f*; ~ **release gear** *n* SPACE dispositif de libération du lanceur *m*

launching *n* NAUT *of boat* lancement *m*, mise à l'eau *f*, TELECOM lancement *m*; ~ **aircraft** *n* SPACE avion porteur *m*; ~ **base** *n* SPACE base de lancement *f*; ~ **complex** *n* SPACE ensemble de lancement *m*; ~ **configuration** *n* SPACE configuration de lancement *f*; ~ **fiber** *n* (AmE), ~ **fibre** *n* (BrE) OPT amorce *f*, fibre amorce *f*, fibre d'injection *f*, TELECOM fibre d'injection *f*; ~ **gantry** *n* CONST cintre de lancement *m*, portail *m*; ~ **ramp** *n* SPACE rampe de lancement *f*; ~ **ramp for guided missiles** *n* MILIT rampe de lancement pour engins téléguidés *f*; ~ **site** *n* SPACE ensemble de lancement *m*; ~ **tower** *n* SPACE tour de lancement *f*; ~ **trap** *n* PETR gare racleur *f*

launder *vt* TEXTILES blanchir

laundering *n* TEXTILES blanchissage *m*

lauric *adj* CHEM laurique

laurionite *n* MINERAL laurionite *f*

lauryl[1] *adj* CHEM laurylique

lauryl:[2] **~ alcohol** *n* DETERGENTS alcool laurique *m*

lava: ~ flow *n* GEOL *volcanic feature*, PETR coulée de lave *f*; **~ plateau** *n* GEOL champ de lave *m*, nappe de lave *f*, plaine de lave *f*, PETR champ de lave *m*; **~ shield** *n* GEOL bouclier de lave *m*; **~ stream** *n* GEOL, PETR coulée de lave *f*

Lavalier: ~ microphone *n* RECORDING microphone en cravate *m*

lava-like *adj* GEOL *texture* lavique

lavender *n* CINEMAT lavande *f*, marron *m*; **~ print** *n* PHOTO matrice positive *f*

law: ~ of corresponding states *n* PHYS loi des états correspondants *f*; **~ of mass action** *n* PHYS loi d'action de masse *f*; **~ of radioactive decay** *n* RAD PHYS loi de décroissance radioactive *f*

LAW *abbr* (*light anti-armour weapon*) MILIT lance portable antichar *f*

lawn: ~ mower *n* CONST *gardening* tondeuse *f*; **~ rake kit** *n* CONST *gardening* scarificateur *m*

lawrencium *n* (*Lr*) CHEM lawrencium *m* (*Lr*)

laws: ~ of reflection *n pl* PHYS lois de la réflexion *f pl*; **~ of refraction** *n pl* PHYS lois de la réfraction *f pl*; **~ of thermodynamics** *n pl* THERMOD lois de la thermodynamique *f pl*; **~ of vibration of a fixed string** *n pl* WAVE PHYS lois de vibration d'une corde fixe *f pl*

lawsone *n* CHEM lawsone *f*

lawsonite *n* MINERAL lawsonite *f*

laxmannite *n* MINERAL laxmannite *f*

lay[1] *n* CONST *of the land* configuration *f*, ELEC *cable component* assemblage *m*, ELEC ENG pas de torsade *m*, MECH ENG direction des traces d'usinage *f*, PRINT position *f*, repère *m*; **~ barge** *n* PETR ponton à pipeline *m*, *subsea pipelines* barge de pose *f*, PETR TECH *subsea pipelines* barge de pose *f*; **~ day** *n* PETR TECH *commerce, shipping* estarie *f*, jour de planche *m*; **~ edge** *n* PRINT bord marge *m*, guide latéral *m*; **~ flat tubing** *n* PACKAGING tube aplati *m*; **~ marks** *n pl* PRINT marques de repérage *f pl*; **~ ratio** *n* ELEC *cable component* rapport de pas *m*; **~ shaft** *n* MECH ENG arbre intermédiaire *m*, arbre secondaire *m*

lay[2] *vt* CONST mettre en place, *pipes* poser, mettre en place, NAUT *rope, cable* commettre, poser, OCEANOG *net* caler, TELECOM poser; **~ aback** *vt* NAUT *sails* masquer; **~ down** *vt* GEOL déposer, OCEANOG *oyster bed* parquer; **~ off** *vt* PROD ENG *belt* débrayer; **~ on** *vt* PROD ENG *belt* embrayer une courroie; **~ up** *vt* NAUT *boat* désarmer, mettre en rade

lay[3] **~ down the lines** *vi* NAUT *naval architecture* tracer les formes; **~ the dust** *vi* MINING abattre la poussière; **~ the foundations** *vi* CONST jeter les fondations, poser les fondements; **~ out a mine** *vi* MINING aménager un puits, aménager une mine; **~ out a shaft** *vt* MINING aménager un puits, aménager une mine; **~ tracks** *vi* RECORDING coucher les sons sur des pistes

lay-by *n* CONST zone de stationnement *f*

layer *n* COAL TECH couche *f*, CONST lit *m*, *road* couche *f*, DP, ELECTRON, GAS TECH couche *f*, GEOL couche *f*, niveau *m*, strate *f*, METALL, NAUT, P&R *of paint, adhesive, plastic*, SPACE couche *f*, TEXTILES couche *f*, *scrim* canevas *m*, WATER SUPP couche *f*; **under ~** *n* TEXTILES canevas inférieur *m*; **~ deposition** *n* ELECTRON dépôt

d'une couche *m*, formation d'une couche *f*; **~ insulation** *n* ELEC isolation entre couches *f*; **~ line** *n* CRYSTALL strate *f*; **~ management entity** *n* (*LME*) TELECOM entité de gestion de couche *f*; **~ sequence** *n* COAL TECH succession des couches *f*; **~ structure** *n* CRYSTALL structure en couches *f*; **~ thickness gaging** *n* (AmE), **~ thickness gauging** *n* (BrE) NUCLEAR mesure de l'épaisseur des couches *f*; **~ winding** *n* ELEC ENG enroulement à spires jointives *m*

layered: ~ igneous rock *n* GEOL roche intrusive stratifiée *f*; **~ structure** *n* GEOPHYS structure litée *f*

layering *n* GEOL litage *m*, stratification *f*

lay-flat: ~ film bag *n* PACKAGING sac en matériel mince aplati *m*

laying *n* C&G levée *f*, CONST posage *m*, pose *f*, établissement *m*, *piping* mise en place *f*, TELECOM *of loss* pose *f*; **~ barge** *n* PETR barge de pose *f*; **~ on cloth** *n* C&G scellage sur toile *m*; **~ on plaster** *n* C&G plâtrage *m* (Bel), scellage sur plâtre *m* (Fra); **~ of piping** *n* CONST pose de la canalisation *f*; **~ up** *n* C&G scellage *m*; **~ yard** *n* C&G *laying up* scellage *m*

lay-on: ~ roller *n* PRINT rouleau d'enduction *m*, rouleau de distribution *m*

layout *n* COMP *configuration* arrangement *m*, *scheme* disposition *f*, DP *configuration* arrangement *m*, *memory* implantation *f*, *of circuit board* tracé *m*, *scheme* disposition *f*, ELEC *circuit* disposition *f*, MECH implantation *f*, MECH ENG agencement *m*, dispositif *m*, implantation *f*, plan *m*, présentation *f*, PACKAGING tracé *m*, PRINT maquette *f*, mise en page *f*, tracé *m*, PROD ENG configuration *f*, *design* tracé *m*; **~ character** *n* DP caractère de présentation *m*; **~ drawing** *n* MECH plan d'implantation *m*; **~ dye** *n* PROD ENG vernis à tracer *m*

lazarette *n* NAUT coqueron arrière *m*

lazulite *n* MINERAL lazulite *f*

lazurite *n* MINERAL lazurite *f*

lazy: ~ coil *n* ELEC *motor* enroulement progressif *m*

L-band *n* ELECTRON, SPACE *communications* bande L *f*; **~ frequency** *n* NAUT *satellite communications* bande-L de fréquences *f*

L-block *n* C&G bloc L *m*

LC: ~ filter *n* ELECTRON filtre LC *m*

LCA *abbr* TELECOM (*loopback command "audio loop request"*) commande de boucle "demande de boucle audio" *f*, TELECOM (*local calling area*) zone locale *f*

LCD[1] *abbr* (*liquid crystal display*) COMP, DP, ELEC, ELECTRON affichage à cristaux liquides *m*, écran à cristaux liquides *m*, MATH (*least common denominator, lowest common denominator*) PPCMD (*plus petit commun multiple des dénominateurs*), PHYS (*liquid crystal display*) affichage à cristaux liquides *m*, écran à cristaux liquides *m*, TELECOM (*loopback command "digital loop request"*) commande de boucle "demande de boucle numérique" *f*, TV (*liquid crystal display*) affichage à cristaux liquides *m*, écran à cristaux liquides *m*

LCD:[2] **~ module** *n* ELECTRON module d'affichage à cristaux liquides *m*; **~ panel** *n* (*liquid crystal display panel*) ELECTRON panneau à cristaux liquides *m*

LCM *abbr* (*least common multiple, lowest common multiple*) COMP, MATH PPCM (*plus petit commun multiple*)

LCO *abbr* (*loopback command off*) TELECOM commande d'ouverture de boucle *f*

LCV *abbr* (*loopback command "video loop request"*) TELECOM commande de boucle "demande de boucle vidéo" *f*

L-D: ~ **ratio** *n (lift-drag ratio)* AERONAUT finesse *f*, rapport de la portance à la traînée *m*

LD[1] *abbr (lethal dose)* PHYS, POLLUTION DL *(dose létale)*

LD:[2] ~ **process** *n* PROP MAT procédé LD *m*

LD50 *abbr (median lethal dose)* NUCLEAR, POLLUTION, RAD PHYS, SAFETY DL50 *(dose létale médiane)*

LDF *abbr (light distillate feedstock)* PETR TECH distillat de tête *m*

LE *abbr (local exchange)* TELECOM commutateur local *m*

leach[1] *n* HYDROL discontinuité hydraulique *f*; ~ **liquor** *n* CHEM TECH solution de lixiviation *f*

leach[2] *vt* CHEM *lixiviate* lessiver, *percolate* filtrer, GEOL lessiver, lixivier, MAR POLL filtrer, lessiver, lixivier

leach[3] *vti* HYDROL lessiver

leachability *n* COAL TECH lixiviation *f*

leachant *n* NUCLEAR agent lixiviant *m*

leaching *n* C&G lixiviation *f*, CHEM *lixiviation* lessivage *m*, lixiviation *f*, *percolation* filtration *f*, COAL TECH lixiviation *f*, FOOD TECH, GAS TECH, HYDROL lessivage *m*, POLLUTION, PROP MAT lixiviation *f*; ~ **agent** *n* NUCLEAR agent lixiviant *m*; ~ **coefficient** *n* NUCLEAR coefficient de lixiviation *m*; ~ **plant** *n* COAL TECH installation de lixiviation *f*; ~ **time** *n* COAL TECH durée d'attaque *f*; ~ **trench** *n* WATER SUPP fossé d'infiltration *m*

lead[1] *n (Pb)* CHEM plomb *m (Pb)*, ELEC ENG fil d'amenée *m*, *current supply wire* fil conducteur *m*, *of brushes* calage *m*, *supply wire* artère *f*, *wire attached to device* sortie *f*, ELECTRON déphasage en avant *m*, *phase* avance *f*, HYDR EQUIP *slide valve* avance tiroir *f*, MECH ENG *of ignition* avance *f*, *of screw* hauteur du pas *f*, MINING *lode* filon *m*, PRINT chemin du papier *m*, interlignage *m*; ~ **accumulator** *n* PHYS accumulateur au plomb *m*; ~ **additive** *n* POLLUTION additif au plomb *m*; ~ **block** *n* NAUT *deck fittings* poulie de retour *f*; ~ **button** *n* CHEM culot de plomb *m*; ~ **chrome green pigment** *n* COLOURS pigment au chromate de plomb *m*; ~ **chrome-phthalocyanine blue pigment** *n* COLOURS pigment à base de chromate de plomb et bleu de phthalocyanine *m*; ~ **control at work** *n* SAFETY plomb contrôle au travail *m*; ~ **controller** *n* CONTROL régulateur à action différentielle *m*; ~ **crystal glass** *n* C&G cristal au plomb *m*; ~ **deposit** *n* MINING gîte de plomb *m*; ~ **dresser** *n* PROD ENG batte de plombier *f*, batteplate *f*, boursault *m*, bourseau *m*, rabattoir *m*; ~ **filter** *n* TRANSP filtre à plomb *m*; ~ **frame** *n* ELEC ENG grille de connexion *f*; ~ **frame tooling** *n* MECH ENG outillage pour cadre de plomb *m*; ~ **glance** *n* MINERAL plomb sulfuré *m*; ~ **glazing** *n* COATINGS vernis au plomb *m*; ~ **joint** *n* CONST joint de plomb *m*; ~ **lap** *n* PROD ENG rodoir en plomb *m*; ~ **line** *n* NAUT ligne de sonde *f*; ~ **matte** *n* PROD ENG matte de plomb *f*, matte plombeuse *f*; ~ **naphthenate** *n* P&R *paints, polyesters* naphténate de plomb *m*; ~ **ore** *n* MINING minerai de plomb *m*; ~ **paint** *n* COLOURS, CONST peinture à base de plomb *f*; ~ **piping** *n* CONST tuyau en plomb *m*; ~ **refining** *n* PROD ENG raffinage du plomb *m*; ~ **roll** *n* PRINT galet du passage papier *m*, rouleau du passage-papier *m*; ~ **screw** *n* MECH, MECH ENG, *lathe* vis mère *f*, PROD ENG vis mère *f*; ~ **seal** *n* PACKAGING plombage *m*; ~ **sealing pliers** *n pl* PACKAGING pince de plombage *f*; ~ **seal wire** *n* PROD ENG fil plombé *m*; ~ **sheath** *n* ELEC *cable* gaine de plomb *f*, ELEC ENG enveloppe en plomb *f*,

gaine de plomb *f*; ~ **shot** *n* PROD ENG grenaille de plomb *f*; ~ **silicate** *n* C&G métasilicate de plomb *m*; ~ **sulfate** *n* (AmE) *see lead sulphate*; ~ **sulfide** *n* (AmE) *see lead sulphide*; ~ **sulphate** *n* (BrE) CHEM sulfate de plomb *m*; ~ **sulphide** *n* (BrE) CHEM sulfure de plomb *m*; ~ **tetraethyl** *n* CHEM plomb tétraéthyle *m*; ~ **time** *n* ELECTRON temps d'avance *m*, MECH ENG délai *m*, PRINT temps de précalage *m*, PROD ENG délai d'obtention *m*, délai de réalisation *m*, délai de réapprovisionnement *m*, temps d'obtention *m*, temps de cycle *m*, TEXTILES temps de réaction *m*; ~ **time deviation** *n* PROD ENG écart sur délai *m*; ~ **tree** *n* CHEM arbre de Saturne *m*; ~ **zinc** *n* PROP MAT zinc plombifère *m*; ~ **zinc oxide** *n* PROP MAT oxyde de zinc plombifère *m*

lead[2] *vt* CONST plomber

lead:[3] ~ **in phase by half pi** *vi* PHYS être en quadrature avance

lead[4] *vti* PRINT blanchir, interligner

lead-acid: ~ **accumulator** *n* ELEC accumulateur au plomb *m*; ~ **battery** *n* ELEC ENG batterie au plomb *f*, batterie d'accumulateurs au plomb *f*, PHYS batterie au plomb *f*, TRANSP accumulateur au plomb *m*, VEHICLES batterie au plomb *f*, accumulateur au plomb *m*; ~ **cell** *n* ELEC ENG accumulateur au plomb *m*

lead-bearing *adj* MINING plombifère

lead-covered: ~ **cable** *n* ELEC, ELEC ENG câble sous plomb *m*

leaded: ~ **light** *n* C&G vitrail au plomb *m*

leader *n* ACOUSTICS, CINEMAT amorce *f*, CONST *downpipe* descente *f*, descente d'eau *f*, tuyau de descente *m*, tuyau de descente des eaux pluviales *m*, DP *tape* amorce *f*, MECH ENG *master wheel* roue maîtresse *f*, NUCLEAR *spark discharge* leader *m*, PAPER TECH pointe pour engager la feuille *f*, TV amorce *f*; ~ **cloth** *n* TEXTILES tissu entraîneur *m*; ~ **dots** *n pl* PRINT points de conduite *m pl*; ~ **line** *n* MECH ENG ligne de rappel de cote *f*; ~ **tape** *n* RECORDING bande amorce *f*

leaders *n pl* PRINT lignes pointillées *f pl*, pointillés *m pl*, points de conduite *m pl*

lead-free: ~ **gasoline** *n* (AmE) *(cf lead-free petrol)* PETR TECH, POLLUTION essence sans plomb *f*; ~ **paint** *n* COLOURS peinture sans plomb *f*; ~ **petrol** *n* (BrE) *(cf lead-free gasoline)* PETR TECH, POLLUTION essence sans plomb *f*

leadhillite *n* MINERAL leadhillite *f*

lead-in: ~ **cable** *n* ELEC câble d'entrée *m*; ~ **groove** *n* ACOUSTICS spire de départ du sillon *f*, RECORDING sillon d'amorçage *m*; ~ **line** *n* (BrE) *(cf hold-short line)* AERONAUT *apron marking* ligne de guidage d'entrée *f*; ~ **wire** *n* ELEC ENG fil d'amenée *m*

leading *n* DP *printing*, PRINT interlignage *m*, PROD ENG plombage *m*; ~ **block** *n* NAUT *fittings* poulie de retour *f*; ~ **chamfer** *n* MECH ENG chanfrein d'entrée *m*; ~ **edge** *n* AERONAUT bec d'attaque *m*, bord d'attaque *m*, CINEMAT bord de guidage *m*, ELECTRON flanc avant *m*, front *m*, PHYS bord d'attaque *m*, TELECOM front d'onde *m*; ~ **edge flap** *n* TRANSP volet de bord d'attaque *m*; ~ **edge glove** *n* AERONAUT brisure de bord d'attaque *f*, coiffe du bord d'attaque *f*; ~ **edge rib** *n* AERONAUT bec de nervure *m*; ~ **edge slat** *n* AERONAUT bec de bord d'attaque *m*; ~ **light** *n* NAUT *navigation* feu d'alignement *m*; ~ **line** *n* NAUT *navigation* alignement *m*, PATENTS *for reference sign* ligne directrice *f*; ~ **mark** *n* NAUT *navigation* marque d'alignement *f*, point d'alignement *m*; ~ **matter** *n* PRINT interlignage *m*, lingots d'interlignage *m pl*; ~ **note** *n* ACOUSTICS note sensible *f*; **~ roll** *n* PAPER TECH rouleau guide *m*; **~ screw** *n* MECH ENG *lathe* vis-mère *f*; **~ wire** *n* MINING ligne de tir *f*; **~ zero** *n* PROD ENG zéro en tête *m*

leading-edge[1] *adj* PROD ENG sur front de montée

leading-edge:[2] **~ one shot** *n* PROD ENG programmation d'impulsion sur front de montée *f*; **~ one-shot programing** *n* (AmE), **~ one-shot programming** *n* (BrE) PROD ENG programmation d'impulsion sur front de montée *f*; **~ pulse time** *n* TV temps de montée du front d'impulsion *m*

leading-in: ~ roll *n* PAPER TECH rouleau embarqueur *m*; **~ roller** *n* PRINT rouleau d'engagement de la bande *m*; **~ tape** *n* PRINT cordon d'engagement de la bande *m*

leading-on: ~ pulley *n* MECH ENG galet *m*, galet de renvoi *m*, galet guide *m*, poulie-guide *f*

leading-out: ~ line *n* ELEC *circuit* circuit de départ *m*

leadless: ~ chip carrier *n* ELEC ENG porte-puce non enfichable *m*, porte-puce à souder *m*

lead-out: ~ groove *n* ACOUSTICS spire de sortie du sillon *f*, RECORDING sillon de fin d'enregistrement *m*; **~ line** *n* (BrE) (*cf hold-short line*) AERONAUT *apron marking* ligne de guidage de sortie *f*

lead-over: ~ groove *n* ACOUSTICS sillon interplage *m*

lead-sheathed: ~ cable *n* ELEC, ELEC ENG câble sous plomb *m*

lead-smelting: ~ works *n* PROD ENG fonderie de plomb *f*

lead-tin: ~ alloy *n* MECH ENG alliage moulé de plomb et d'étain *m*

lead-wire *n* ELEC ENG fil de traversée *m*

leaf *n* COMP feuille *f*, CONST *of T hinge, strap hinge* branche *f*, *of door* battant *m*, vantail *m*, DP feuille *f*, PRINT feuillet *m*, PROD ENG *moulder's tool* truelle à feuille de laurier *f*, SPRINGS *of leaf spring* lame *f*; **~ area index** *n* POLLUTION indice foliaire *m*; **~ chain** *n* MECH ENG chaîne de levage à mailles jointives *f*; **~ shutter** *n* PHOTO obturateur central à lamelles *m*; **~ spring** *n* MECH ENG ressort de voiture *m*, ressort à lames *m*, ressort à lames superposées *m*, ressort à lames étagées *m*, VEHICLES *suspension* ressort à lames *m*; **~ valve** *n* HYDR EQUIP clapet à charnière *m*, soupape à charnière *f*

leaflet: ~ insertor *n* PACKAGING dispositif d'insertion de dépliants *m*

leaf-shaped: ~ trowel *n* PROD ENG *moulder's tool* truelle à feuille de laurier *f*

leak[1] *n* C&G coulée au four *f*, CONST *crack in receptacle or pipe* voie d'eau *f*, *leakage* coulage *m*, perte *f*, échappement *m*, ELEC *of current, charge* dispersion *f*, fuite *f*, GAS TECH, PHYS fuite *f*, SAFETY fuite *f*, perte *f*; **~ detection** *n* GAS TECH détection de fuite *f*; **~ detector** *n* HEATING détecteur de fuites *m*, PACKAGING indicateur de fuite *m*; **~ light** *n* CINEMAT lumière parasite *f*; **~ rate** *n* NUCLEAR taux de fuite *m*; **~ test** *n* NUCLEAR essai d'étanchéité *m*, REFRIG contrôle d'étanchéité *m*; **~ testing** *n* CONST essai d'étanchéité *m*; **~ tightness** *n* NUCLEAR étanchéité aux fuites *f*; **~ water** *n* WATER SUPP eau de fuite *f*

leak[2] *vt* CONST perdre

leak[3] *vi* CONST *allow to escape* couler, fuir, *allow to enter* faire eau, NAUT faire eau

leakage *n* CONST coulage *m*, ELEC *of current, charge* dispersion *f*, fuite *f*, ELEC ENG *of electricity* fuite *f*, perte *f*, FUELLESS fuite *f*, GAS TECH étanchéité *f*, MAR POLL fuite *f*, perte *f*, écoulement *m*, PHYS, TELECOM fuite *f*, WATER SUPP coulage *m*, fuite *f*, perte *f*, échappement *m*; **~ current** *n* ELEC, ELEC ENG, TELECOM courant de fuite *m*; **~ detection** *n* PACKAGING détec-

tion de fuites *f*; **~ field** *n* TELECOM champ de fuite *m*; **~ flux** *n* ELEC ENG, PHYS flux de fuite *m*; **~ hardening** *n* NUCLEAR *neutron spectrum* durcissement *m*; **~ indicator** *n* ELEC ENG indicateur de terre *m*; **~ indicator system** *n* SAFETY système indicateur de fuite *m*; **~ interception vessel** *n* NUCLEAR cuve de sécurité *f*; **~ loss** *n* ELEC *current* pertes par courant *f pl*; **~ meter** *n* ELEC appareil de mesure de fuite *m*; **~ path** *n* ELEC, ELEC ENG ligne de fuite *f*; **~ radiation** *n* ELEC ENG rayonnement de fuites *m*; **~ resistance** *n* PHYS résistance de fuite *f*; **~ test** *n* PACKAGING essai d'étanchéité *m*; **~ warning** *n* SAFETY avertisseur de fuite *m*; **~ water pump** *n* NUCLEAR pompe de puisard des eaux de fuite *f*

leak-free[1] *adj* REFRIG étanche

leak-free:[2] **~ product** *n* PROD ENG produit sans fuite *m*

leaking: ~ fuel assembly *n* NUCLEAR assemblage combustible inétanche *m*, fuite de l'assemblage combustible *f*

leak-off: ~ pressure *n* PETR TECH *drilling* pression d'injectivité *f*; **~ test** *n* (*LOT*) PETR TECH *drilling* essai de pression *m*, test d'injectivité *m*

leak-tight *adj* MECH étanche aux fuites

leaky: ~ capacitor *n* ELEC ENG condensateur à fortes fuites *m*; **~ mode** *n* OPT, TELECOM mode de fuite *m*; **~ ray** *n* OPT rayon de fuite *m*, rayon tunnel *m*, TELECOM rayon de fuite *m*

lean: ~ coal *n* COAL TECH charbon anthraciteux *m*, charbon maigre *m*, THERMOD charbon anthraciteux *m*; **~ concrete** *n* CONST béton de propreté *m*, béton maigre *m*, forme en béton *f*; **~ die out** *n* AERONAUT extinction par excès d'air *f*; **~ gas** *n* GAS TECH, PETR gaz pauvre *m*; **~ mixture** *n* AERONAUT *engine*, VEHICLES *carburation* mélange pauvre *m*

lean-burn[1] *adj* AUTO, THERMOD à gaz pauvre, à mélange pauvre

lean-burn:[2] **~ engine** *n* THERMOD moteur à combustion pauvre *m*

leaner *n* C&G bouteille penchée *f*

leaning *adj* CONST penchant

lean-plasticity: ~ clay *n* C&G argile maigre *f*

lean-to *n* CONST appentis *m*, panne d'appentis *f*; **~ roof** *n* CONST comble en appentis *m*, toiture à scimple *f*

leap *n* CRYSTALL *in a dislocation* cran *m*, MINING accident *m*, coufflée *f*, crain *m*, cran *m*, rejet *m*

leapfrog: ~ test *n* COMP, DP test saute-mouton *m*

leaping: ~ weir *n* NUCLEAR déversoir de superficie *m*

LEAR *abbr* (*low-energy antiproton ring*) PART PHYS LEAR (*anneau d'antiprotons de basse énergie*)

learning: ~ machine *n* ELECTRON machine auto-adaptative *f*; **~ phase** *n* ELECTRON phase d'apprentissage *f*

lease: ~ band *n* TEXTILES cordon *m*; **~ rod** *n* TEXTILES traverse d'envergure *f*

leased: ~ line *n* COMP ligne louée *f*, DP ligne louée *f*, ligne spécialisée *f*, TELECOM liaison spécialisée *f*; **~ line network** *n* COMP, DP réseau de lignes spécialisées *m*

leasing: ~ reed *n* TEXTILES peigne d'envergure *m*

least:[1] **~ significant** *adj* COMP, DP de poids le plus faible

least:[2] **~ common denominator** *n* (*LCD*) MATH plus petit commun multiple des dénominateurs *m* (*PPCMD*); **~ common multiple** *n* (*LCM*) COMP, MATH plus petit commun multiple *m* (*PPCM*); **~ significant bit** *n* (*LSB*) COMP, PROD ENG bit de poids le plus faible *m*; **~ significant digit** *n* (*LSD*) COMP, PROD ENG chiffre de poids le plus faible *m*; **~ squares method** *n* CRYSTALL, MATH, PHYS méthode des moindres carrés f

leat n PROD ENG *flume, feeder* canal d'amenée m, canal de dérivation m, canal de prise m, dérivation f, *mill flume* abée f, auge f, buse f, bée f, reillère f, WATER SUPP canal d'amenée m

leather: ~ **apron** n SAFETY tablier en cuir m; ~ **bellows** n pl PHOTO soufflet de peau m; ~ **belt** n PROD ENG courroie de cuir f, courroie en cuir f; ~ **belting** n PROD ENG courroies de transmission en cuir f pl; ~ **case** n PHOTO étui de cuir m; ~ **cutting** n PROD ENG découpage du cuir m; ~ **gasket** n PROD ENG garniture en cuir f; ~ **gauntlets** n pl SAFETY gants à crispin en cuir m pl; ~ **packer** n PROD ENG garniture en cuir f; ~ **pulp** n PAPER TECH pâte de cuir f

leatherette n P&R similicuir m

leatherfiber: ~ **board** n (AmE), **leatherfibre board** n (BrE) PAPER TECH synderme m

leather-link: ~ **belting** n PROD ENG courroies en cuir articulé f pl

leave: ~ **open** vt COMP *file* laisser ouvert

leaven n FOOD TECH *milling and baking* levain m

leaving: ~ **a line of traffic** n TRANSP déboîtement m

leavings n pl MINING stériles m pl

Leblanc: ~ **connection** n ELEC montage Leblanc m; ~ **process** n DETERGENTS procédé de Leblanc m

lecithin n FOOD TECH lécithine f

Leclanché: ~ **cell** n ELEC ENG, LAB EQUIP *electricity* pile Leclanché f

LED abbr (*light-emitting diode*) COMP, DP, ELEC, ELECTRON, OPT, PHYS, RAD PHYS, TELECOM, TV DEL (*diode électroluminescente*)

ledeburite n METALL lédéburite f

ledge n CONST *projection* corniche f, rebord m, saillie f, MECH ENG arêtier m, rebord m, ridelle f

ledger n CONST *scaffolding* filière f, moise f, MINING *of lode* mur m, sol m; ~ **wall** n MINING *of lode* mur m, sol m

lee n NAUT abri m, abri contre le vent m, côté sous le vent m; ~ **canvas** n NAUT *accommodation* toile anti-roulis f; ~ **depression** n METEO dépression orographique f, dépression sous le vent f; ~ **lurch** n NAUT *sailing* abattée f; ~ **shore** n NAUT *sailing* terre sous le vent f

leeboard n NAUT *boat building* aile de dérive f, planche de roulis f

leech n NAUT *of sail* chute f

leeward[1] adj NAUT *navigation* sous le vent

leeward[2] adv METEO dans le sens du vent, sous le vent, NAUT *navigation* sous le vent

leeward:[3] ~ **side** n METEO côté sous le vent m

leeway n NAUT *sailing* dérive f; ~ **track** n NAUT *navigation* route surface f

left:[1] ~ **justification** n DP justification à gauche f; ~ **margin** n PRINT marge de gauche f; ~ **shift** n COMP, DP décalage à gauche m; ~ **stereo channel** n RECORDING canal stéréophonique de gauche m; ~ **turning traffic** n TRANSP courant tourne-à-gauche m; ~ **turn phase** n TRANSP *traffic control* phase spéciale pour tourner à gauche f

left:[2] ~ **justify** vt DP justifier à gauche

left-hand: ~ **circular polarization** n (*LHCP*) SPACE *communications* polarisation circulaire gauche f; ~ **coiling** n SPRINGS sens d'enroulement gauche m; ~ **page** n PRINT page de gauche f; ~ **rule** n ELEC *electromagnetism*, PHYS règle de la main gauche f; ~ **side** n PHYS *of equation* premier membre d'une équation m

left-handed adj PHYS *coordinate system* à gauche

leg n INSTRUMENT *tripot* pied m, MECH ENG jambe f, NAUT *tack* bordée f, béquille f, NUCLEAR *of pipe* branche f, TELECOM conducteur m, fil m; ~ **vice** n (BrE) PROD ENG étau à pied m; ~ **vise** n (AmE) *see leg vice*; ~ **wire** n MINING fil de détonateur m

legal: ~ **predecessor** n PATENTS prédécesseur en droit m; ~ **unit of length** n METR unité légale de longueur f

Legendre: ~ **polynomials** n pl PHYS polynômes de Legendre m pl

legroom n VEHICLES emplacement pour les jambes m

lehr: ~ **assistant** n C&G videur d'arche m; ~ **attendant** n C&G conducteur d'arche m; ~ **belt** n C&G tapis m

Leitz: ~ **system** n INSTRUMENT système optique Leitz m

lemon: ~ **chrome** n COLOURS couleur citron f; ~ **color** n (AmE), ~ **colour** n (BrE) COLOURS couleur citron f

length n COMP, DP, PAPER TECH *of reel or roll*, PHYS longueur f, TELECOM *cable* tronçon m; ~ **adjustment** n CONTROL réglage en longueur m; ~ **bar** n METR règle étalon f; ~ **between perpendiculars** n NAUT *ship design* longueur entre perpendiculaires f; ~ **of bore** n MILIT *of gun* longueur de l'âme f; ~ **of channel** n FUELLESS longueur de chenal f; ~ **of a chord** n GEOM *subtending arc* amplitude d'une corde f; ~ **contraction** n PHYS *relativity* contraction des longueurs f; ~ **gage** n (AmE), ~ **gauge** n (BrE) METR calibre de longueur m; ~**indicator** n (*LI*) TELECOM indicateur de longueur m; ~ **inside supports** n SPRINGS *of leaf spring* corde entre appuis f; ~ **of the interval** n METR *between inspections* longueur de l'échelon f; ~ **of lay** n ELEC *cable component* pas d'assemblage m; ~ **margin** n MECH ENG tolérance sur la longueur f; ~ **measuring instrument** n MECH ENG instrument de mesurage de longueur m; ~ **meter** n METR compteur métreur m; ~ **overall** n MECH ENG *of screw, bolt* longueur tête comprise f, NAUT *boat building* longueur hors-tout f; ~ **of page** n PRINT longueur de page f; ~ **of piston stroke** n CONST course du piston f, jeu du piston m, longueur de course du piston f; ~ **of step** n CONST *stair building* emmarchement m, largeur de l'escalier f, longueur d'emmarchement f; ~ **of stroke** n MECH ENG *of tool* course f, course de l'outil f, NUCLEAR course f, levée f; ~ **under head to point** n MECH ENG *of screw, bolt* longueur sous tête f, longueur tête non comprise f

lengthening: ~ **bar** n MECH ENG *for box spanner* clé de rallonge f; ~ **piece** n MECH ENG allonge f, barre de rallonge f, rallonge f, tige de rallonge f; ~ **rod** n MECH ENG allonge f, barre de rallonge f, rallonge f, tige de rallonge f; ~ **tube** n MECH ENG allonge f

lengthways adv MECH ENG de long, en long, en longueur

lengthwise adv MECH ENG de long, en long, en longueur

lens n ASTRON téléobjectif m, CINEMAT lentille f, objectif m, optique f, HYDROL lentille f, INSTRUMENT lentille f, verre m, verre optique m, LAB EQUIP *optics* lentille f, PHOTO lentille f, objectif m, PHYS lentille f, ménisque m, objectif m, PROD ENG *cap of switch* cabochon m, objectif m, SPACE *communications* lentille f; ~ **antenna** n SPACE *communications*, TELECOM antenne à lentille f; ~ **aperture** n PHOTO ouverture de lentille f; ~ **barrel** n CINEMAT barillet m, PHOTO barillet d'objectif m; ~ **cap** n CINEMAT, PHOTO bouchon d'objectif m; ~ **case** n PHOTO étui d'objectif m; ~ **coating** n PHOTO bleutage m, fluoration f; ~ **coverage** n CINEMAT champ visuel m; ~ **cover slide** n PHOTO *of camera* volet de protection de l'objectif m; ~ **flange** n PHOTO rondelle d'objectif f; ~ **flare** n CINEMAT reflet interne m, PHOTO réflection interne *f*; **~ holder** *n* C&G cotret *m*; **~ hood** *n* CINEMAT parasoleil *m*, PHOTO parasoleil d'objectif *m*, parasoleil pour objectif *m*; **~ hood bellows** *n* CINEMAT soufflet de parasoleil *m*; **~ magnification** *n* INSTRUMENT grossissement de loupe *m*; **~ mount** *n* PHOTO monture d'objectif *f*; **~ mounting plate** *n* PHOTO platine d'objectif *f*; **~ movement** *n* PHOTO décentrement *m*; **~ panel** *n* INSTRUMENT module porte-objectifs *m*, PHOTO planchette d'objectif *f*; **~ shutter** *n* PHOTO obturateur d'objectif *m*; **~ squeeze ratio** *n* CINEMAT rapport d'anamorphose *m*; **~ stop** *n* CINEMAT diaphragme *m*, PHOTO ouverture du diaphragme *f*; **~ turret** *n* CINEMAT, OPT, PRINT tourelle d'objectifs *f*; **~ vertex** *n* PHOTO pôle de la lentille *m*; **~ with aperture preselector** *n* PHOTO objectif à présélecteur *m*

lensing *n* GEOL stratification lenticulaire *f*

lens-shaped *adj* PHOTO lenticulé

lenticular[1] *adj* GEOL lenticulaire

lenticular:[2] **~ twin** *n* METALL macle lenticulaire *f*

Lenz's: ~ law *n* ELEC *induction*, PHYS loi de Lenz *f*

lenzinite *n* MINERAL lenzinite *f*

Leo *n* ASTRON Lion *m*, Petit Lion *m*

leonhardite *n* NUCLEAR léonhardite *f*

Leonids *n pl* ASTRON Léonides *m pl*

LEP[1] *abbr (large electron-positron collider)* PART PHYS LEP *(grand collisionneur électron-positron)*

LEP:[2] **~ detector** *n* PART PHYS détecteur de LEP *m*

lepidolite *n* MINERAL lépidolite *f*

lepidomelane *n* MINERAL lépidomélane *m*

leptochlorite *n* MINERAL leptochlorite *f*

lepton *n* PART PHYS, PHYS lepton *m*; **~ number** *n* PHYS nombre leptonique *m*

Lepus *n* ASTRON Lièvre *m*

less-than-carload: ~ freight *n* RAIL *vehicles* marchandises de détail *f pl*; **~ freight shipment** *n* RAIL *vehicles* envoi de marchandises de détail *m pl*

let-down *n* AERONAUT descente *f*, percée *f*

lethal: ~ concentration *n* POLLUTION concentration létale *f*; **~ dose** *n (LD)* PHYS *of radioactivity*, POLLUTION dose létale *f (DL)*; **~ effect** *n* POLLUTION effet létal *m*

lethargy *n* RAD PHYS léthargie *f*

let-off: ~ motion *n* TEXTILES mécanisme de déroulement *m*, mécanisme de détente *m*

letter *n* DP, PRINT lettre *f*; **~ quality** *n (LQ)* COMP, PRINT qualité courrier *f*; **~ sag** *n* C&G glissement *m*; **~ shift** *n* TELECOM *telegraphy* inversion de lettres *f*; **~ slip** *n* C&G glissement *m*; **~ spacing** *n* PRINT approches *f pl*, espacement entre les lettres *m*

lettercard *n* PAPER TECH carte-lettre *f*

letterhead *n* PRINT tête de lettre *f*

lettering *n* PRINT lettrage *m*; **~ on bottom** *n* C&G marque sur fond *f*

letterpress[1] *adj* PRINT typographique

letterpress[2] *n* PRINT typographie *f*; **~ printing** *n* PACKAGING typographie *f*; **~ printing machine** *n* PRINT presse typographique *f*, typographique *f*

letters: ~ shift *n* COMP, DP inversion de lettres *f*

lettsomite *n* MINERAL lettsomite *f*

leuchtenbergite *n* MINERAL leuchtenbergite *f*

leucite *n* MINERAL leucite *f*

leuco: ~ compound *n* CHEM *of dye* leucobase *f*

leucocratic *adj* GEOL leucocrate

leucophane *n* MINERAL leucophane *m*

leucophanite *n* MINERAL leucophane *m*

leucopyrite *n* MINERAL leucopyrite *f*

leucosome *n* GEOL leucosome *m*

leucoxene *n* MINERAL leucoxène *m*

levan *n* CHEM lévane *m*

level:[1] **~ with the ground** *adj* CONST au ras de terre, au rase terre, à fleur de sol

level[2] *n* CINEMAT, COMP niveau *m*, CONST niveau *m*, niveau à bulle d'air *m*, palier *m*, DP, ELECTRON, MECH *tools* niveau *m*, METR *bubble* niveau à bulle *m*, electronic niveau *m*, MINING chassage *m*, chassante *f*, costière *f*, galerie *f*, galerie d'allongement *f*, galerie de direction *f*, galerie en direction *f*, galerie de niveau *f*, voie *f*, voie de niveau *f*, niveau *m*, étage *m*, PACKAGING *of filling* niveau *m*, POLLUTION niveau *m*, RAD PHYS, RECORDING niveau *m*, TRANSP *of congestion* degré *m*, *of service* niveau *m*, WATER SUPP bief *m*, biez *m*; **~ above threshold** *n* ACOUSTICS niveau d'audition *m*; **~ adjustment** *n* ELECTRON réglage de niveau *m*; **~ book** *n* CONST *surveying* cahier de nivellement *m*; **~ control** *n* CONTROL contrôle de niveau *m*, PACKAGING réglage du niveau *m*; **~ crossing** *n* (BrE) *(cf grade crossing)* CONST passage à niveau *m*, RAIL, TRANSP passage à niveau *m*, traverse *f* (Can); **~ cruise** *n* AERONAUT croisière en palier *f*; **~ detector** *n* COAL TECH détecteur de niveau *m*; **~ difference** *n* ACOUSTICS isolement acoustique brut *m*; **~ displacement** *n* NUCLEAR déplacement de niveau *m*; **~ drop** *n* MECH ENG baisse de niveau *f*; **~ dyeing** *n* COLOURS teinture uniforme *f*, TEXTILES teinture à l'unisson *f*; **~ flight** *n* AERONAUT vol en palier *m*, vol horizontal *m*; **~ gage** *n* (AmE), **~ gauge** *n* (BrE) HYDROL limnimètre *m*; **~ holding** *n* NUCLEAR maintien de niveau *m*; **~ indicator** *n* MECH ENG indicateur de niveau *m*, NUCLEAR indicateur de niveau *m*, limnimètre *m*, PAPER TECH flotteur d'alarme *m*, RAIL nivelette *f*, RECORDING indicateur de niveau *m*; **~ in the seam** *n* MINING galerie en couche *f*; **~ of intensity** *n* RAD PHYS niveau d'intensité *m*; **~ keel** *n* NAUT bonne assiette *f*; **~ magnetic tape** *n* ACOUSTICS bande magnétique de niveau *f*; **~ meter** *n* CINEMAT indicateur de niveau *m*, NUCLEAR *for liquids only* indicateur de niveau *m*, limnimètre *m*; **~ recorder** *n* RECORDING enregistreur de niveau *m*; **~ recorder controller** *n* CONTROL régulateur de niveau enregistrant *m*, régulateur enregistreur *m*; **~ road** *n* MINING galerie principale *f*, voie maîtresse *f*; **~ running along the strike** *n* MINING chassage *m*, chassante *f*, costière *f*, galerie chassante *f*, galerie d'allongement *f*, galerie de chassage *f*, galerie de direction *f*, galerie en direction *f*; **~ sensor** *n* SPACE canne de niveau *f*; **~ shift** *n* NUCLEAR déplacement de niveau *m*; **~ shifting** *n* ELECTRON décalage de niveau *m*; **~ small caps** *n pl* PRINT petites capitales *f pl*; **~ switch** *n* PROD ENG contacteur de switch *m*

level[3] *vt* CINEMAT mettre de niveau, CONST mettre à niveau, *surveying* niveler, MECH mettre à niveau, PROD ENG aplanir, niveler, unir, égaliser; **~ out** *vt* AERONAUT mettre en palier

leveled *adj* (AmE) *see levelled*

leveling *n* (AmE) *see levelling*

levelled *adj* (BrE) CONST mise à niveau

levelling *n* (BrE) CONST aplanissement *m*, *public works* régalage *m*, *surveying* nivellement *m*, ELECTRON régulation du niveau *f*, MECH mise à niveau *f*, PROD ENG lissage *m*, nivellement *m* **~ agent** *n* (BrE) TEXTILES produit d'unisson *m*; **~ alidade** *n* (BrE) CONST alidade nivelatrice *f*; **~ amplifier** *n* (BrE) ELECTRON amplificateur régulateur de niveau *m*; **~ compass** *n* (BrE)

CONST boussole nivelante *f*; ~instrument *n* (BrE) CONST niveau à lunette *m*; ~ **machine** *n* (BrE) CONST *public works* niveleuse *f*; ~ **mark** *n* (BrE) AERONAUT repère de niveau horizontal *m*; ~ **motor** *n* (BrE) CONST moteur d'érection *m*; ~ **point** *n* (BrE) CONST point de mire *m*; ~ **pole** *n* (BrE) CONST *surveying* mire *f*; ~ **rod** *n* (BrE) CONST *surveying* mire *f*; ~ **screw** *n* (BrE) INSTRU-MENT vis calante *f*, MECH ENG vis arrêtoir *f*, vis calante *f*, vis de bride *f*, vis de calage *f*; ~ **staff** *n* (BrE) CONST *surveying* mire *f*; ~ **unit** *n* (BrE) AERONAUT détecteur gravimétrique *m*

levelness *n* PROD ENG mise à niveau *f*

lever[1] *n* AERONAUT *helicopter* guignol droit *m*, ELEC ENG manette *f*, MECH ENG levier *m*, renvoi *m*, PHYS *handle* manette *f*, *simple machine* levier *m*, VEHICLES manette *f*; ~ **arm** *n* CONST, MECH ENG bras de levier *m*; ~ **balance** *n* MECH ENG peson à contrepoids *m*; ~ **brake** *n* MECH ENG frein à levier *m*; ~ **commutator switch** *n* ELEC commutateur à manette *m*; ~ **draft machine** *n* (AmE), ~ **draught machine** *n* (BrE) PROD ENG *founding* machine à démouler à levier *f*; ~ **escapement** *n* MECH ENG *ratchet mechanism* échappement à manette *m*; ~ **feed** *n* MECH ENG pression à levier *f*; ~ **of the first kind** *n* MECH ENG levier du premier genre *m*, levier interappui *m*; ~ **grip tongs** *n pl* PROD ENG louve à genouillère *f*, louve à pince *f*, pince à genouillère *f*, pinces articulées pour monter les pierres de taille *f pl*, écrevisse *f*; ~ **handle** *n* CONST *of shop door latch* bec de cane *m*; ~ **jack** *n* PROD ENG cric à levier *m*; ~ **lid** *n* PACKAGING couvercle rentrant *m*; ~ **on-off switch** *n* ELEC interrupteur à levier *m*; ~ **press** *n* MECH ENG presse à levier *f*; ~ **punching-and-shearing machine** *n* PROD ENG poinçonneuse-cisaille à levier *f*; ~ **punching machine** *n* PROD ENG poinçonneuse à levier *f*; ~ **ratchet motion** *n* MECH ENG encliquetage à levier *m*; ~ **ring** *n* PACKAGING anneau d'ouverture de boîte *m*; ~ **scales** *n pl* MECH ENG balance romaine *f*, romaine *f*; ~ **of the second kind** *n* MECH ENG levier du deuxième genre *m*, levier interrésistant *m*; ~ **shearing machine with counterweight** *n* PROD ENG cisailles à levier à contrepoids *f pl*; ~ **switch** *n* CONTROL interrupteur à levier *m*, ELEC ENG commutateur à levier *m*, interrupteur à levier *m*, inverseur à levier *m*, NUCLEAR interrupteur à levier *m*; ~ **of the third kind** *n* MECH ENG levier du troisième genre *m*, levier interpuissant *m*; ~ **valve** *n* HYDR EQUIP clapet à levier *m*; ~ **weir** *n* WATER SUPP déversoir à hausses *m*

lever[2] *vt* MECH ENG soulever au moyen d'un levier, soulever avec la pince; ~ **up** *vt* MECH ENG soulever au moyen d'un levier, soulever avec la pince

leverage *n* MECH ENG force de levier *f*; ~ **of a force** *n* MECH ENG bras de levier *m*

lever-feed: ~ **drilling machine** *n* MECH ENG machine à percer avec pression du porte-foret à la main par levier *f*

levigation *n* PROD ENG lévigation *f*

levitation *n* PHYS, SPACE lévitation *f*; ~ **by permanent magnets** *n* TRANSP sustentation magnétique par aimants permanents *f*

levorotatory *adj* CHEM lévorotatoire

levulin *n* CHEM lévuline *f*

levulinic *adj* CHEM lévulique

levulose *n* (AmE) *see laevulose*

levyne *n* MINERAL lévyne *f*

levynite *n* MINERAL lévyne *f*

Lewis: ~ **peak** *n* NUCLEAR pic de Lewis *m*

lexical: ~ **access** *n* TELECOM accès au lexique *m*; ~ **analysis** *n* COMP, DP analyse lexicale *f*

lexicographic: ~ **order** *n* DP ordre lexicographique *m*

Leyden: ~ **jar** *n* ELEC ENG bouteille de Leyde *f*

LF *abbr* COMP *(line feed)*, DP *(line feed)* changement de ligne *m*, saut de ligne *m*, ELEC *(low-frequency)* wave, ELEC ENG *(low-frequency)*, ELECTRON *(low-frequency)* BF *(basse fréquence)*, PRINT *(line feed)* changement de ligne *m*, saut de ligne *m*, RAD PHYS *(low-frequency)*, TELECOM *(low-frequency)* BF *(basse fréquence)*, TELECOM *(line finder)* chercheur de ligne *m*, TELECOM *(line feed)* telegraphy changement de ligne *m*, saut de ligne *m*

LFA *abbr* *(loss of frame alignment)* TELECOM PVT *(perte de verrouillage de trame)*

LFC *abbr* *(local function capabilities)* TELECOM capacité fonctionnelle locale *f*

LHC *abbr* *(large hadron collider)* PART PHYS *being developed at CERN* grand collisionneur de hadrons *m*

LHCP *abbr* *(left-hand circular polarization)* SPACE polarisation circulaire gauche *f*

L-head: ~ **engine** *n* AUTO moteur à soupapes latérales *m*

Li *(lithium)* CHEM Li *(lithium)*

LI *abbr* *(length indicator)* TELECOM indicateur de longueur *m*

liability *n* MAR POLL responsabilité *f*

liberate *vt* PHYS *gas* dégager, libérer

liberation *n* CHEM dégagement *m*

libethenite *n* MINERAL libéthénite *f*

Libra *n* ASTRON Balance *f*

librarian: ~ **program** *n* COMP programme de gestion de bibliothèque *m*

library *n* COMP, DP bibliothèque *f*; ~ **automation** *n* COMP, DP automatisation de bibliothèque *f*; ~ **program** *n* COMP programme de bibliothèque *m*

libration *n* ASTRON libration *f*

licareol *n* CHEM licaréol *m*, linalol *m*

licence *n* (BrE) PATENTS licence *f*, PETR TECH *for prospecting, operating* permis *m*, QUALITY licence *f*; ~ **block** *n* (BrE) PETR TECH *for prospecting, operating* bloc *m*

license *n* (AmE) *see licence*

licenser *n* PATENTS donneur d'une licence *m*

Lichtenberg: ~ **figure** *n* PHYS image de Lichtenberg *f*

licker *n* MECH ENG *lubrication* lécheur *m*

lick-up *n* PAPER TECH prise automatique *f*; ~ **overfelt** *n* PAPER TECH feutre preneur pour prise automatique *m*

lid *n* LAB EQUIP *of container*, MECH couvercle *m*, MINING *timbering mine roadways* écoin *m*, PACKAGING, POLLUTION couvercle *m*

lidar *n* SPACE lidar *m*

lid-sealing: ~ **compound** *n* PACKAGING composition pour fermeture de couvercle *f*

lie[1] *n* CONST *of the land* configuration *f*

lie:[2] ~ **at anchor** *vi* NAUT être à l'ancre; ~ **idle** *vi* MECH ENG être dans l'inaction

liebenerite *n* MINERAL liebénérite *f*

lievrite *n* MINERAL liévrite *f*

life *n* MECH ENG endurance *f*, MINING *of mine* durée *f*, longévité *f*, vie *f*, QUALITY durée de vie *f*, vie *f*; ~ **expectancy** *n* CONST espérance de vie *f*, TELECOM durée de vie *f*; ~ **jacket** *n* AERONAUT gilet de sauvetage *m*, NAUT brassière de sauvetage *f*; ~ **preserver** *n* AERONAUT gilet de sauvetage *m*, CONST *derrick* pieu de sécurité *m*; ~ **raft** *n* NAUT, SAFETY radeau de sauvetage *m*; ~ **support system** *n* OCEANOG logistique vitale *f*,

SPACE équipement de vie *m*; ~ **support technician** *n* OCEANOG ATS, agent technique de saturation *m*; ~ **table** *n* MATH table de vie *f*; ~ **test** *n* ELEC ENG essai d'endurance *m*

lifebelt *n* NAUT ceinture de sauvetage *f*

lifeboat *n* NAUT canot de sauvetage *m*, embarcation de sauvetage *f*; ~ **station** *n* NAUT poste de sauvetage *m*, station de sauvetage *f*

lifeboatman *n* NAUT sauveteur *m*

lifebuoy *n* NAUT bouée couronne *f*

life-cycle: ~ **cost** *n* QUALITY frais d'exploitation et de maintenance *m pl*

lifeline *n* NAUT *safety equipment* filière *f*, garde-corps *m*, ligne de sauvetage *f*

life-load: ~ **curve** *n* PROD ENG courbe durée de charge *f*, courbe durée de vie *f*

life-saving: ~ **apparatus** *n* NAUT, SAFETY appareil de sauvetage *m*

lifetime *n* ELEC ENG durée de vie *f*, MINING *of mine* durée *f*, longévité *f*, vie *f*, PHYS durée de vie *f*, vie moyenne *f*, PROP MAT, SPACE *spacecraft*, TELECOM durée de vie *f*; ~ **expectancy** *n* TELECOM durée de vie *f*

LIFO *abbr (last-in first-out)* COMP, DP, PROD ENG dernier entré premier sorti *m*

lift[1] *n* AERONAUT portance *f*, sustentation *f*, CONST *civil engineering* porte à lever *f*, *goods* élévateur *m*, *of crane* hauteur de levage *f*, *of gate latch* battant *m*, *piling block* course *f*, levée *f*, FUELLESS portance *f*, HYDR EQUIP *of clack valve* levée *f*, HYDROL *canal locks* chute *f*, MECH ENG *of cone, cone pulley* gradin *m*, étage *m*, MINING cordée *f*, trait *m*, foncée *f*, gradin *m*, hauteur verticale *f*, jet *m*, travée *f*, jeu *m*, niveau *m*, étage *m*, NUCLEAR *valve, control rod* course *f*, levée *f*, PHYS portance *f*, WATER SUPP hauteur *f*, hauteur d'élévation *f*, hauteur manométrique *f*, *difference in water level* chute *f*; ~ **bridge** *n* TRANSP pont levant *m*; ~ **center** *n* (AmE), ~ **centre** *n* (BrE) AERONAUT centre de sustentation *m*; ~ **coefficient** *n* AERONAUT, FUELLESS, PHYS coefficient de portance *m*, TRANSP coefficient de sustentation *m*; ~ **component** *n* AERONAUT composante de portance *f*; ~ **curve slope** *n* AERONAUT pente de la courbe de portance *f*; ~ **drive** *n* (BrE) MECH ENG commande pour ascenseurs *f*; ~ **effect** *n* NAUT *naval architecture* effet de portance *m*; ~ **fan** *n* TRANSP soufflante de sustentation *f*; ~ **gate** *n* AUTO hayon *m*, CONST barrière oscillante *f*, barrière à bascule *f*; ~ **magnet** *n* TRANSP aimant de levage *m*; ~ **net** *n* OCEANOG carrelet *m*; ~ **on-off ship** *n* TRANSP navire à chargement vertical *m*; ~ **on-off system** *n* TRANSP manutention verticale *f*; ~ **pipe** *n* CONST tuyau élévatoire *m*; ~ **piston** *n* PROD ENG piston de levage *m*; ~ **pull and push jack and cramp** *n* MECH ENG vérin multiple *m*; ~ **pump** *n* WATER SUPP pompe soulevante *f*, pompe élévatoire *f*; ~ **shaft** *n* (BrE) AERONAUT cage d'ascenseur *f*; ~ **truck** *n* MECH, PACKAGING chariot élévateur *m*; ~ **wall** *n* WATER SUPP *of canal lock* mur de chute *m*

lift[2] *vt* MECH lever, soulever; ~ **incorrectly** *vt* SAFETY soulever incorrectement

lift[3] *vi* TELECOM *handset* décrocher

lift:[4] ~ **here** *phr* PACKAGING soulever ici

lift-and-force: ~ **pump** *n* WATER SUPP pompe aspirante et foulante *f*, pompe aspirante et refoulante *f*

lift-drag: ~ **ratio** *n* AERONAUT *aircraft efficiency* finesse *f*, rapport de la portance à la traînée *m*, NAUT *naval architecture* rapport de la traînée à la poussée *m*, PHYS finesse *f*

lifted: ~ **load** *n* AERONAUT charge soulevée *f*; ~ **throat** *n* C&G gorge au-dessus du niveau de la sole *f*

lifter *n* CONST ascenseur *m*, monte-charge *m*, élévateur *m*, MECH ENG came *f*, virgule *f*, MINING mine de relevage *f*, trou de relevage *m*, PROD ENG clou de mouleur *m*, crochet de fonderie *m*, crochet à ramasser *m*; ~ **hole** *n* MINING trou de relevage *m*

lifting[1] *n* MECH ENG levage *m*, relevage *m*, remonte *f*, remontée *f*, soulèvement *m*, élévation *f*, MINING *of pavement* rebanchage *m*, SAFETY *by hand or arm* soulèvement *m*, *by machine* levage *m*, TRANSP remodelage *m*, restylage *m*; ~ **accidents** *n pl* SAFETY accidents de levage *m pl*; ~ **apparatus** *n* MECH ENG appareil de levage *m*; ~ **appliance** *n* SAFETY appareil de levage *m*; ~ **bag** *n* AERONAUT ballon de levage *m*; ~ **beam** *n* PROD ENG *founding* balancier *m*; ~ **bow** *n* CONST *of hoisting bucket* anse *f*; ~ **bridge** *n* CONST pont levant *m*, NAUT *locks, inland waterways* pont basculant *m*; ~ **capacity with hook** *n* NUCLEAR *of manipulator* capacité de levage *f*; ~ **chain** *n* CONST *of pulley block or hoist* chaîne de charge *f*, chaîne de levage *f*, MECH ENG, PROD ENG, SAFETY chaîne de levage *f*; ~ **dog** *n* MINING *boring* pied-de-boeuf *m*; ~ **equipment** *n* MECH ENG *with 10 tonne capacity* dispositif de levage *m*; ~ **eye** *n* NAUT *deck fittings* ferrure d'élingage *f*; ~ **eyebolt** *n* MECH ENG *machine tool* anneau de levage *m*; ~ **force** *n* PHYS force de lévitation *f*, force portante *f*; ~ **gear** *n* CONST engin de levage *m*, treuil à noix *m*, MECH ENG matériel de levage *m*, MECH ENG appareil de levage *m*, engin de levage *m*, RAIL engin de levage *m*, SAFETY appareil de levage *m*; ~ **hook** *n* CONST crochet *m*, MECH ENG crochet de levage *m*; ~ **injector** *n* MECH ENG injecteur aspirant *m*; ~ **jack** *n* MECH ENG *for replacing bogies* chèvre à véhicule *f*, *lever jack* cric à levier *m*, *rack type* cric *m*, *screw type* vérin *m*, vérin à vis *m*; ~ **lugs** *n pl* (BrE) *(cf handling lugs)* MECH ENG joue de manutention *f*; ~ **machinery** *n* MECH ENG appareils de levage *m pl*, machines acrobatiques *f pl*, machines élévatoires *f pl*; ~ **magnet** *n* ELEC aimant de levage *m*, MECH ENG électro-aimant de levage *m*, électro-aimant porteur *m*; ~ **piston** *n* PROD ENG piston de levage *m*; ~ **platform** *n* AERONAUT plate-forme de levage *f*; ~ **point** *n* MINING *pithead pulley* enlevage *m*; ~ **power** *n* MECH ENG force de levage *f*, force élévatoire *f*, puissance de levage *f*, TRANSP puissance de sustentation *f*; ~ **pressure** *n* TRANSP pression de sustentation *f*; ~ **rod** *n* HYDR EQUIP *of Corliss valve gear* sabre *m*, tige de manoeuvre *f*; ~ **rotor** *n* AERONAUT *of helicopter* rotor sustentateur *m*; ~ **screw** *n* MECH ENG vérin *m*, vérin à vis *m*; ~ **shaft** *n* MECH ENG *link gear* arbre de changement de marche *m*, arbre de relevage *m*; ~ **table** *n* PROD ENG *of rolling mill* tablier releveur *m*; ~ **tackle** *n* MECH ENG appareil de levage *m*, engins de levage *m pl*, NAUT, SAFETY appareil de levage *m*; ~ **valve** *n* HYDR EQUIP clapet de levage *m*; ~ **vehicle** *n* PACKAGING camion élévateur *m*; ~ **wheel** *n* MECH ENG roue élévatoire *f*

lifting:[2] ~ **and moving heavy loads** *phr* SAFETY levage et déplacement des charges lourdes

lifting-body: ~ **aircraft** *n* AERONAUT avion à fuselage portant *m*

lift-latch *n* CONST loquet à bouton *m*, loquet à bouton simple *m*

lift-lock *n* WATER SUPP écluse double *f*, écluse à sas *f*

liftoff *n* SPACE décollage *m*, lancement *m*; ~ **speed** *n* AERONAUT vitesse d'envol *f*; ~ **weight** *n* SPACE poids au décollage *m*

lift-on-lift-off: ~ **vessel** *n* NAUT navire à manutention verticale *m*

lift-to-drag: ~ **ratio** *n* FUELLESS coefficient de glissement *m*, TRANSP coefficient de glissement *m*, rapport sustentation-résistance à l'avancement *m*

lift-type: ~ **device** *n* FUELLESS dispositif à levée verticale *m*

lift-up: ~ **furnace** *n* HEATING four élévateur *m*; ~ **table** *n* MECH ENG table à bascule *f*

ligand *n* CHEM coordinat *m*, ligand *m*, METALL, PROP MAT ligand *m*; ~ **field theory** *n* CHEM *of compounds* théorie du champ ligand *f*

ligature *n* PRINT ligature *f*

light[1] *adj* MECH ENG à vide

light[2] *n* OPT lumière *f*, rayonnement visible *m*, PHOTO, PHYS lumière *f*, VEHICLES feu *m*, feu d'éclairage *m*; ~ **air defence gun** *n* MILIT canon léger contre-avion *m*; ~ **airs** *n pl* NAUT *meteorology* presque calme *m*; ~ **alloy** *n* MECH *materials* alliage léger *m*; ~ **amplification by stimulated emission of radiation** *n (LASER)* RAD PHYS amplification de la lumière par rayonnement stimulé *f*; ~ **amplifier** *n* ELECTRON amplificateur de lumière *m*; ~ **anti-armour weapon** *n (LAW)* MILIT lance portable antichar *f*; ~ **antitank gun** *n* MILIT canon antichar léger *m*; ~ **armament** *n* MILIT armement léger *m*; ~ **artillery** *n* MILIT artillerie légère *f*; ~ **beam** *n* CINEMAT faisceau lumineux *m*, OPT pinceau lumineux *m*, rayon lumineux *m*, PHOTO faisceau lumineux *m*, PHYS faisceau de lumière *m*, TELECOM faisceau optique *m*; ~ **beam galvanometer** *n* RAD PHYS galvanomètre à faisceau de lumière *m*; ~ **beam pickup** *n* RECORDING lecteur à faisceau lumineux *m*; ~ **box** *n* CINEMAT boîte à lumière *f*, négatoscope *m*, PHOTO boîte à lumière *f*; ~ **breeze** *n* METEO brise légère *f*; ~ **buoy** *n* NAUT *navigation marks* bouée lumineuse *f*; ~ **cable** *n* ELEC ENG câble à fibre optique *m*; ~ **center** *n* (AmE), ~ **centre** *n* (BrE) CINEMAT foyer lumineux *m*; ~ **chopper** *n* ELECTRON découpeur optique *m*; ~ **control** *n* CONTROL contrôle d'éclairage *m*; ~ **crown** *n* C&G crown léger *m*; ~ **crude** *n* PETR TECH brut léger *m*; ~ **crude oil** *n* PETR TECH pétrole brut léger *m*; ~ **current** *n* OPT photocourant *m*, TELECOM courant photoélectrique *m*; ~ **detector** *n* RAD PHYS détecteur de lumière *m*, TELECOM photodétecteur *m*, photorécepteur *m*; ~ **displacement** *n* NAUT *of ship* déplacement à vide *m*, *yacht* déplacement léger *m*; ~ **distillate feedstock** *n (LDF)* PETR TECH distillat de tête *m*; ~ **distillates** *n pl* PETR TECH distillats légers *m pl*; ~ **dues** *n pl* NAUT *navigation* droits de phare *m pl*; ~ **energy** *n* RAD PHYS énergie lumineuse *f*; ~ **engine** *n* RAIL *vehicles* locomotive haut-le-pied *f*; ~ **engineering** *n* MECH ENG petite mécanique *f*; ~ **exposure** *n* PHYS exposition lumineuse *f*; ~ **face** *n* DP, PRINT caractères maigres *m pl*; ~ **fastness** *n* P&R résistance à la lumière *f*; ~ **filter** *n* INSTRUMENT filtre coloré *m*, PRINT filtre *m*; ~ **fishing** *n* OCEANOG pêche au feu *f*, pêche au lamparo *f*; ~ **fitting** *n* ELEC ENG appareil d'éclairage *m*, luminaire *m*; ~ **flint** *n* C&G flint léger *m*; ~ **fractions** *n pl* PETR TECH distillats légers *m pl*, fractions légères *f pl*; ~ **gasoline** *n* (AmE) *(cf light petrol)* AUTO essence légère *f*; ~ **guide** *n* PHYS guide de lumière *m*; ~ **gun** *n* COMP, DP crayon optique *m*; ~ **hydrocarbon fractions** *n pl* PETR TECH fractions légères d'hydrocarbures *f pl*; ~ **loading** *n* ELEC ENG faible charge *f*; ~ **locomotive** *n* RAIL *vehicles* locomotive haut-le-pied *f*; ~ **lorry** *n* (BrE) *(cf light truck)*

TRANSPORT camionnette *f*; ~ **meson spectrum** *n* RAD PHYS spectre des mésons légers *m*; ~ **meter** *n* CINEMAT photomètre *m*, PHOTO, PHYS posemètre *m*; ~ **meter cell** *n* PHOTO cellule de posemètre *f*; ~ **meter probe** *n* PHOTO sonde de posemètre *f*; ~ **meter scale** *n* PHOTO calculateur de posemètre *m*; ~ **microscopy** *n* METALL microscopie optique *f*; ~ **modulation** *n* ELECTRON modulation de lumière *f*; ~ **modulator** *n* ACOUSTICS modulateur de lumière *m*; ~ **motorcycle with kickstarter** *n* TRANSP vélomoteur *m*; ~ **multi-role helicopter** *n* TRANSP hélicoptère léger *m*; ~ **observation helicopter** *n* AERONAUT hélicoptère léger d'observation *m*; ~ **output** *n* PHOTO rendement lumineux *m*; ~ **panels** *n pl* C&G côtes minces *f pl*; ~ **peak** *n* NUCLEAR pic léger *m*; ~ **pen** *n* COMP, DP photostyle *m*, PHYS crayon lumineux *m*, photostyle *m*, TV crayon optique *m*; ~ **pen detection** *n* COMP, DP détection par photostyle *f*; ~ **petrol** *n* (BrE) *(cf light gasoline)* AUTO essence légère *f*; ~ **pipe** *n* ELEC ENG conduit de lumière *m*; ~ **pulse** *n* ELECTRON impulsion de lumière *f*; ~ **radiation** *n* NUCLEAR rayonnement de lumière *m*; ~ **rail motor tractor** *n* RAIL *vehicles* locotracteur *m*; ~ **railroad** *n* (AmE) *(cf light railway)* RAIL chemin de fer à voie étroite *m*; ~ **rail transit** *n* (AmE) *(cf light rail transport)* RAIL *vehicles* métro léger *m*; ~ **rail transport** *n* (BrE) *(LRT, light rail transit)* RAIL *vehicles* métro léger *m*; ~ **railway** *n* (BrE) *(cf light railroad)* RAIL réseau à voie étroite *m*; ~ **ray** *n* CINEMAT rayon de lumière *m*, OPT rayon lumineux *m*, rayon optique *m*, PHYS rayon lumineux *m*; ~ **scale switch** *n* PHOTO commutateur de sensibilité *m*; ~ **second** *n* ASTRON seconde-lumière *f*; ~ **section microscope** *n* INSTRUMENT microscope à coupe optique *m*; ~ **section tube** *n* INSTRUMENT tube à coupes optiques *m*; ~ **sensor** *n* ELECTRON capteur de lumière *m*, PROD ENG cellule photoélectrique *f*; ~ **setting** *n* PRINT photocomposition *f*; ~ **shade** *n* TEXTILES coloris clair *m*; ~ **signal** *n* CONTROL artifice *m*, signal lumineux *m*, ELECTRON signal lumineux *m*, RAIL panneau lumineux *m*; ~ **softener** *n* CINEMAT diffuseur *m*; ~ **source** *n* ELECTRON source de lumière *f*, LAB EQUIP luminaire *m*, OPT, PHOTO, PHYS source lumineuse *f*; ~ **spectrum** *n* WAVE PHYS spectre de la lumière *m*; ~ **spot** *n* ELECTRON point lumineux *m*; ~ **spot galvanometer** *n* ELEC galvanomètre à index lumineux *m*, galvanomètre à spot lumineux *m*; ~ **switch** *n* ELEC commutateur d'éclairage *m*; ~ **table** *n* CINEMAT négatoscope *m*; ~ **time** *n* ASTRON temps d'aberration *m*; ~ **tone** *n* COLOURS teinte claire *f*; ~ **trap** *n* CINEMAT chicane *f*, porte à tambour *f*, sas *m*; ~ **truck** *n* (AmE) *(cf light lorry)* TRANSP camionnette *f*; ~ **value** *n* PHOTO indice de lumination *m*, luminombre *m*; ~ **value setting ring** *n* PHOTO bague des indices de lumination *f*; ~ **valve** *n* CINEMAT modulateur de lumière *m*, relais optique *m*; ~ **vessel** *n* NAUT bateau-feu *m*, bateau-phare *m*, navire marchand à vide *m*, TRANSP bateau-feu *m*; ~ **wall socket** *n* ELEC *lighting* prise d'éclairage *f*; ~ **water hybrid reactor** *n (LWHR)* NUCLEAR réacteur hybride à eau légère *m*; ~ **waterline** *n* NAUT flottaison lège *f*; ~ **wave** *n* ELECTRON, WAVE PHYS onde lumineuse *f*; ~ **weather** *n* NAUT *meteorology* petit temps *m*; ~ **weld** *n* NUCLEAR soudure concave *f*; ~ **year** *n* ASTRON, PHYS année-lumière *f*

light-activated: ~ **silicon controlled rectifier** *n* ELEC ENG photothyristor *m*

light-balancing: ~ **filter** *n* CINEMAT filtre correcteur *m*

light-bodied: ~ **ink** *n* PRINT encre manquant de corps *f*

light-colored adj (AmE), **light-coloured** adj (BrE) GEOL clair, leucocrate

light-directing: ~ **block** n C&G brique fonctionnelle f

light-duty adj DETERGENTS pour nettoyages faciles

light-emitting: ~ **diode** n (LED) COMP, DP, ELEC display diode électroluminescente f (DEL), ELECTRON diode luminescente f, diode lumineuse f, diode électroluminescente f, diode émettrice f, diode émissive f, OPT, PHYS diode électroluminescente f (DEL), RAD PHYS diode électroluminescente (DEL) f, diode à rayonnement lumineux f, TELECOM, TV diode électroluminescente f (DEL)

lightening n MAR POLL allégement m; ~ **hole** n AERONAUT, MECH trou d'allégement m

lighter n HEAT ENG briquet m, NAUT type of boat allège f, chaland m, gabare f; ~ **aboard ship carrier** n (LASH carrier) TRANSP navire porte barges de type LASH m, porte-barges LASH m; ~ **carrier** n TRANSP porte-barges m

lighterage n NAUT water transport batelage m, batellerie f; ~ **charges** n pl NAUT water transport frais de batelage m pl

lighterer n MAR POLL navire allégeur m

lightering n MAR POLL allégement m; ~ **vessel** n MAR POLL navire allégeur m

lighterman n NAUT batelier de chaland m

light-fast adj COLOURS résistant à la lumière, solide à la lumière

lighthouse n NAUT phare m; ~ **keeper** n NAUT gardien de phare m

lighting n CINEMAT éclairage m; ~ **and vision control room** n TV régie image-lumière f; ~ **cable** n ELECTRON câble pour l'éclairage m; ~ **cameraman** n CINEMAT directeur de photographie m; ~ **circuit** n ELEC circuit d'éclairage m; ~ **console** n CINEMAT pupitre d'éclairage m; ~ **contrast** n CINEMAT contraste lumineux m; ~ **control** n CONTROL contrôle d'éclairage m; ~ **effect** n CINEMAT effet lumineux m, jeu de lumière m; ~ **efficiency** n AERONAUT helicopter rendement de sustentation m; ~ **engineer** n CINEMAT ingénieur éclairagiste m; ~ **equipment** n PHOTO matériel d'éclairage m; ~ **glass** n C&G verre d'éclairage m; ~ **ratio** n CINEMAT contraste m; ~ **stand** n PHOTO pied d'éclairage m; ~ **system** n ELEC ENG réseau d'éclairage m, SPACE système d'allumage m

lightly: ~ **doped semiconductor** n ELECTRON semi-conducteur faiblement dopé m

light-negative adj PHOTO photorésistant

lightness n PRINT clarté f, légèreté f, PROP MAT légèreté f

lightning n ELEC, ELEC ENG foudre f, éclair m, METEO éclair m; ~ **arrester** n ELEC safety parafoudre m, paratonnerre m, ELEC ENG parafoudre m, GEOPHYS parafoudre m, éclateur m, NAUT deck fitting fusible parafoudre m, SPACE parafoudre m; ~ **arresters for high voltage** n pl SAFETY parafoudres à haute tension m pl; ~ **brace** n MECH ENG drille f; ~ **conductor** n ELEC ENG, GEOPHYS, SAFETY paratonnerre m; ~ **conductor material** n SAFETY matériel de parafoudre m; ~ **current** n ELEC ENG courant de foudre m; ~ **discharge** n ELEC coup de foudre m, éclair m, ELEC ENG décharge fulgurante f; ~ **flash counter** n GEOPHYS compteur d'éclairs m; ~ **path** n ELEC conductor trajectoire de l'éclair f; ~ **proof transformer** n ELEC transformateur résistant à la foudre m; ~ **protection** n ELEC ENG, GEOPHYS protection contre la foudre f; ~ **protection and earthing installation** n (BrE) (cf lightning protection and groun-

ding installation) SAFETY installation de protection contre la foudre et mise à la terre f; ~ **protection and grounding installation** n (AmE) (cf lightning protection and earthing installation) SAFETY installation de protection contre la foudre et mise à la terre f; ~ **protection fuse** n GEOPHYS parafoudre m; ~ **protector** n SAFETY parafoudre m; ~ **rod** n ELEC safety parafoudre m, paratonnerre m, ELEC ENG tige collectrice f, tige de captage f, tige de paratonnerre f, GEOPHYS tige de paratonnerre f, SAFETY paratonnerre m ~ **strike** n METEO coup de foudre m; ~ **stroke** n ELEC phenomenon coup de foudre m; ~ **surge** n ELEC conductor, equipment surtension de foudre f, GEOPHYS surtension f, surtension atmosphérique f; ~ **surge arrester** n GEOPHYS parafoudre pour surtensions m

lightning-resistant[1] adj ELEC ENG résistant à la tenue à la foudre

lightning-resistant:[2] ~ **power line** n ELEC supply ligne de transport d'énergie résistant à la tenue à la foudre f

light-positive adj PHOTO photoconducteur

lightproof adj PACKAGING étanche à la lumière

light-running adj MECH ENG à vide

light-sensitive[1] adj CINEMAT, ELECTRON photosensible, sensible à la lumière, PHOTO sensible à la lumière, PRINT photosensible, sensible à la lumière

light-sensitive:[2] ~ **plate** n PRINT plaque sensible à la lumière f

lightship n NAUT navigation marks bateau-feu m, bateau-phare m, TRANSP bateau feu m

light-struck adj CINEMAT voilé

light-tight adj CINEMAT étanche à la lumière

light-water-cooled: ~ **reactor** n NUCLEAR réacteur refroidi à l'eau m

lightweight[1] adj MECH léger

lightweight:[2] ~ **apparel fabric** n TEXTILES tissu léger pour habillement m; ~ **concrete** n CONST béton léger m; ~ **furnishing fabric** n TEXTILES tissu léger pour ameublement m; ~ **honeycomb structure** n PACKAGING structure légère alvéolée f; ~ **paper** n PAPER TECH papier mince m

lightweight-coated adj PRINT couché léger

lignan n CHEM lignane f

ligneous adj PAPER TECH ligneux

lignin n CHEM, P&R lignine f

lignite n COAL TECH, MINERAL, THERMOD lignite m

lignum: ~ **vitae** n MECH materials bois de gaïac m, NAUT gaïac m

ligroin n CHEM ligroïne f

ligurite n MINERAL ligurite f

like: ~ **charge** n ELEC charge de même signe f; ~ **poles** n pl ELEC magnetism, PHYS pôles de même nom m pl

likelihood n COMP, MATH statistics vraisemblance f

limb n ASTRON limbe m, GEOL flanc m, MATH of instrument bras m; ~ **brightening** n ASTRON éclat de limbe m; ~ **darkening** n ASTRON assombrissement du bord m; ~ **top** n INSTRUMENT porte-tube m

limber: ~ **hole** n NAUT shipbuilding anguiller m

lime n CHEM, COAL TECH, CONST, FOOD TECH mineral chaux f; ~ **burning** n PROD ENG chaufournerie f, cuisson de la chaux f; ~ **burning industry** n PROD ENG cuisson de la chaux f; ~ **defecation** n FOOD TECH défécation au lait de chaux f; ~ **kiln** n HEATING four à chaux m, PROD ENG chaufour m, four à chaux m; ~ **mortar** n PROD ENG mortier de chaux m; ~ **mud** n PETR TECH drilling boue carbonatée f; ~ **mudrock** n GEOL calcilutite f; ~ **paint** n COATINGS enduit à la chaux m; ~

pigment *n* COLOURS pigment à la chaux *m*; ~ **pit** *n* MINING carrière de pierre calcaire *f*, carrière de pierre à chaux *f*, PROD ENG chaufour *m*, four à chaux *m*; ~ **rock** *n* CHEM calcaire *m*; ~ **sandrock** *n* GEOL calcarénite *f*; ~ **scale** *n* FOOD TECH *processing machinery* tartre *m*; ~ **slurry** *n* C&G boue de chaux *f*; ~ **spar** *n* GEOL spath calcaire *m*; ~ **stabilization** *n* CONST stabilisation à la chaux *f*; ~ **water** *n* CHEM eau de chaux *f*; ~ **work** *n* COATINGS enduit à la chaux *m*

limeburning: ~ **kiln** *n* PROP MAT four à chaux *m*

limen *n* TV valeur de seuil *f*

lime-secreting: ~ **algae** *n pl* GEOL algues calcaires *f pl*

limestone *n* C&G calcaire *m*, CHEM pierre calcaire *f*, pierre à chaux *f*, CONST, GEOL, PETR calcaire *m*; ~ **quarry** *n* MINING carrière de pierre calcaire *f*, carrière de pierre à chaux *f*

lime-treated: ~ **mud** *n* PETR TECH *drilling* boue à base de chaux *f*, boue à la chaux *f*

limewash *n* COLOURS peinture à la chaux *f*, CONST blanc de chaux *m*, lait de chaux *m*

limewashing *n* CONST blanchiment à la chaux *m*, échaudage *m*

liming *n* CONST chaulage *m*

limit[1] *n* MATH limite *f*, MECH ENG limite *f*, tolérance *f*, TRANSP *of visibility* seuil critique *m*; ~ **of consistency** *n* COAL TECH limite de consistance *f*; ~ **of error** *n* METR *of measuring instrument* erreur maximale tolérée *f*; ~ **external gage** *n* (BrE), ~ **external gauge** *n* (BrE) MECH ENG bague à tolérance *f*; ~ **gage** *n* (AmE), ~ **gauge** *n* (BrE) MECH ENG calibre de tolérance *m*, calibre à limites *m*, METR calibre de tolérance *m*; ~ **internal gage** *n* (AmE), ~ **internal gauge** *n* (BrE) MECH ENG bouchon à tolérance *m*, tampon à tolérance *m*; ~ **load** *n* AERONAUT *of blade*, ELEC *device* charge limite *f*; ~ **load factor** *n* AERONAUT facteur de charge limite *m*; ~ **rate of descent at touchdown** *n* AERONAUT vitesse limite d'impact *f*; ~ **setting** *n* NUCLEAR fin de course *f*, réglage de mise au point *m*; ~ **size** *n* MECH cote limite *f*; ~ **strip** *n* MECH ENG butée de fin de course *f*, déclencheur de fin de course *m*; ~ **switch** *n* CONTROL interrupteur limiteur *m*, ELEC commutateur de fin de course *m*, interrupteur de fin de course *m*, interrupteur limiteur *m*, ELEC ENG, MECH interrupteur de fin de course *m*, PROD ENG détecteur de position *m*; ~ **test** *n* PROD ENG test sur limites *m*; ~ **of tolerance** *n* METR *mechanical* limite de tolérance *f*; ~ **turbine** *n* HYDR EQUIP turbine limite *f*, turbine à aubes garnies *f*, turbine à réaction nulle *f*, turbine à veine moulée *f*

limit[2] *vt* ELECTRON limiter, écrêter

limited: ~ **authority autopilot** *n* AERONAUT pilotage automatique transparent *m*; ~ **presence detector** *n* TRANSP détecteur de présence limitée *m*; ~ **progressive system** *n* TRANSP système alterné *m*; ~ **signal** *n* ELECTRON signal écrêté *m*; ~ **slip differential** *n* AUTO différentiel à glissement limité *m*, VEHICLES *transmission* différentiel autobloquant *m*; ~ **tightness** *n* MECH ENG *pipework* étanchéité limitée *f*; ~ **train** *n* (AmE) RAIL train à desserte limitée *m*; ~ **waiting queue** *n* TELECOM file d'attente limitée *f*

limiter *n* ELEC ENG limiteur *m*, ELECTRON limiteur *m*, écrêteur *m*, MECH ENG *machine tools*, RECORDING, SPACE *communications*, TELECOM, TV limiteur *m*; ~ **amplifier** *n* RECORDING amplificateur limiteur *m*; ~ **diode** *n* ELECTRON diode de limitation d'amplitude *f*, diode limiteuse *f*, diode écrêteuse *f*, TV diode limitatrice *f*

limiting *n* ELECTRON limitation d'amplitude *f*, écrêtage *m*, RECORDING limitation *f*; ~ **amplifier** *n* ELECTRON amplificateur limiteur *m*; ~ **current** *n* ELEC courant limite *m*; ~ **fuel assembly** *n* NUCLEAR assemblage combustible limiteur *m*; ~ **overload current** *n* ELEC *transformer* courant limite *m*; ~ **resistor** *n* ELEC résistance de limitation du courant *f*; ~ **value** *n* TELECOM valeur limite *f*; ~ **viscosity number** *n* FLUID PHYS indice de viscosité limite *m*

limma *n* ACOUSTICS limma *m*

limnimeter *n* HYDROL limnimètre *m*

limonite *n* MINERAL limonite *f*

limp: ~ **binding** *n* PRINT reliure flexible *f*, reliure souple *f*

limpbound *adj* PRINT à couverture souple

limpet: ~ **mount** *n* CINEMAT monture à ventouse *f*

limy *adj* GEOL *rock* calcaire, carbonaté

linalool *n* CHEM linalol *m*

linarite *n* MINERAL linarite *f*

lindane *n* CHEM lindane *m*

line[1] *n* C&G peignage *m*, COMP ligne *f*, CONST corde *f*, cordeau *m*, ligne *f*, CRYSTALL rangée *f*, *of spectrum, diffraction pattern* raie *f*, DP, ELEC *supply network* ligne *f*, ELEC ENG ligne *f*, ruban *m*, ELECTRON *of resistance* trait *m*, *of spectrum* raie *f*, GEOM, MECH ENG ligne *f*, NAUT corde *f*, *rope, Equator* amarre *f*, cordage *m*, ligne *f*, NUCLEAR ligne *f*, maximum *m*, pic *m*, PRINT filet *m*, ligne *f*, trait *m*, PROD ENG canalisation *f*, RAD PHYS *spectral* raie *f*, RECORDING, TELECOM ligne *f*, THERMOD canalisation *f*, TV ligne *f*, ligne active *f*; ~ **access protocol** *n* (*LAP*) TELECOM protocole d'accès de ligne *m*; ~ **of action** *n* MECH *gearing* ligne de poussée *f*, ligne de pression *f*, normale commune des profils *f*, normale de contact *f*; ~ **adaptor** *n* COMP adaptateur de lignes *m*; ~ **amplifier** *n* ELECTRON, RECORDING amplificateur de ligne *m*; ~ **amplitude control** *n* TV contrôle de la largeur de ligne *m*; ~ **of apsides** *n* SPACE ligne des apsides *f*; ~ **of bearing** *n* GEOL azimut *m*; ~ **blanking** *n* TV suppression de ligne *f*; ~ **blanking level** *n* TV niveau de suppression de ligne *m*; ~ **block** *n* PRINT cliché au trait *m*; ~ **breadth** *n* CRYSTALL largeur de raie *f*; ~ **break** *n* ELEC *supply network* coupure de ligne *f*; ~ **breaker** *n* ELEC *switch* interrupteur principal *m*; ~ **broadening** *n* CRYSTALL élargissement des raies *m*; ~ **of buckets** *n* CONST *elevator, conveyor* chapelet de godets *m*; ~ **of cars** *n* (AmE) (*cf traffic queue*) TRANSP *traffic* file d'attente *f*;~ **of centers** *n* (AmE), ~ **of centres** *n* (BrE) MECH ENG ligne des centres *f*; ~ **choking coil** *n* ELEC ENG piège *m*; ~ **circuit** *n* TELECOM circuit de ligne *m*; ~ **clear signal** *n* RAIL signal à voie libre *m*; ~ **code** *n* PACKAGING code linéaire *m*, TELECOM code en ligne *m*; ~ **commutator** *n* ELEC *switch* commutateur de ligne *m*; ~ **concentrator** *n* TELECOM concentrateur d'abonnés *m*, concentrateur de lignes *m*; ~ **configuration** *n* ELEC ENG configuration de la ligne *f*; ~ **connection** *n* ELEC *consumer supply* branchement *m*; ~ **connection unit** *n* TELECOM unité de raccordement *f*; ~ **of contact** *n* MECH ENG ligne d'action *f*, PRINT ligne de contact *f*; ~ **controller** *n* ELEC ENG régisseur de ligne *m*; ~ **copy** *n* PRINT document au trait *m*; ~ **coupling** *n* ELEC ENG couplage de ligne *m*; ~ **coupling transformer** *n* ELEC ENG transformateur d'alimentation *m*; ~ **crawl** *n* TV déformation de la structure de ligne *f*; ~ **current** *n* ELEC ENG courant de secteur *m*; ~ **of cusps** *n* ASTRON droite des cornes *f*; ~ **cut** *n* PRINT cliché au trait *m*; ~ **diffusion** *n* TV estompage de ligne *m*; ~ **of dip** *n* GEOL direction de pendage *f*; ~ **divider** *n* TV diviseur de fréquence de lignes *m*; ~ **drawing** *n* GEOM, PRINT dessin au trait *m*; ~ **drive connector** *n* PROD ENG connecteur d'amplificateur de ligne *m*; ~ **driver** *n* COMP amplificateur de ligne *m*, excitateur de ligne *m*, DP attaqueur de ligne *m*, circuit d'attaque de ligne *m*, excitateur de ligne *m*, module de commande de ligne *m*; ~ **driver output** *n* PROD ENG sortie amplificateur de ligne *f*; ~ **drive signal** *n* TV signal de déclenchement de ligne *m*; ~ **drop** *n* ELEC *voltage*, ELEC ENG *voltage* chute en ligne *f*; ~ **engraving** *n* PRINT gravure à l'outil *f*; ~ **fault** *n* ELEC ENG défaut en ligne *m*, TELECOM dérangement d'une ligne *m*; ~ **feed** *n* (*LF*) COMP, DP, PRINT, TELECOM *telegraphy* changement de ligne *m*, saut de ligne *m*; ~ **feeding equipment** *n* PACKAGING équipement d'alimentation de chaîne defabrication *m*; ~ **filter** *n* ELECTRON filtre antiparasite *m*; ~ **finder** *n* (*LF*) TELECOM chercheur de ligne *m*; ~ **flax** *n* TEXTILES lin teillé *m*; ~ **of flux** *n* ELEC ENG ligne de flux *f*; ~ **flyback** *n* TV retour du spot de ligne *m*; ~ **focus** *n* TV foyer linéaire *m*; ~ **of force** *n* ELEC *magnetism*, ELEC ENG, PHYS ligne de force *f*; ~ **frequency** *n* TV fréquence de balayage *f*, fréquence de ligne *f*; ~ **graph** *n* DP courbe *f*, graphique linéaire *m*; ~ **group** *n* TELECOM faisceau de lignes *m*; ~ **impedance** *n* ELEC ENG impédance de la ligne *f*; ~ **of impression** *n* PRINT ligne d'impression *f*; ~ **in** *n* RECORDING, TV entrée ligne *f*; ~ **input power** *n* PROD ENG alimentation secteur *f*; ~ **in service** *n* RAIL ligne exploitée *f*; ~ **insulator** *n* ELEC ENG isolateur de ligne *m*; ~ **integral** *n* PHYS intégrale curviligne *f*, intégrale de ligne *f*; ~ **interface** *n* ELEC ENG interface de transmission *f*; ~ **interface module** *n* TELECOM unité de raccordement d'abonnés *f*; ~ **interfacing** *n* ELEC ENG raccordement d'une ligne de transmission *m*; ~ **isolating switch** *n* ELEC *supply network* sectionneur de ligne *m*; ~ **level** *n* RECORDING, TV niveau ligne *m*; ~ **of level** *n* CONST ligne de niveau *f*; ~ **linearity control** *n* TV réglage de la linéarité horizontale *m*; ~ **load control** *n* (*LLC*) TELECOM contrôle de charge de ligne *m* (*CCL*); ~ **losses** *n pl* ELEC *supply network* pertes dans la ligne *f pl*; ~ **module** *n* TELECOM unité de raccordement d'abonnés *f*; ~ **module equipment** *n* (*LME*) TELECOM matériel de modules de lignes *m*; ~ **monitor** *n* TV moniteur de sortie *m*, retour antenne *m*, témoin d'antenne *m*; ~ **of nodes** *n* SPACE *communications* ligne de noeuds *f*; ~ **noise** *n* ELEC ENG, ELECTRON bruit de la ligne *m*; ~ **number** *n* COMP, DP numéro de ligne *m*; ~ **occupied** *n* RAIL voie occupée *f*; ~ **operation** *n* ELEC ENG alimentation par le secteur *f*; ~ **out** *n* RECORDING, TV sortie ligne *f*; ~ **output** *n* TV base de temps de ligne *f*, sortie ligne *f*; ~ **pad** *n* ELEC ENG réseau isolateur *m*; ~ **pin** *n* CONST fiche à barrages *f*; ~ **plate** *n* PRINT cliché au trait *m*; ~ **printer** *n* COMP imprimante ligne par ligne *f*; ~ **profile measurements** *n pl* RAD PHYS *of spectral lines* mesures de profil des raies *f pl*; ~ **protection** *n* ELEC *supply network* protection de ligne *f*; ~ **protector** *n* GEOPHYS protecteur de ligne *m*; ~ **protector cutout** *n* GEOPHYS coupe-circuit protecteur de ligne *m*; ~ **rate** *n* PRINT prix à la ligne *m*; ~ **recorder** *n* INSTRUMENT enregistreur à trace continue *m*; ~ **regulation** *n* ELEC ENG régulation secteur *f*; ~ **relay** *n* ELEC relais d'annonciateur *m*; ~ **rental** *n* TELECOM *of telephone* abonnement *m*; ~ **repeater** *n* TELECOM répéteur de ligne *m*; ~ **replaceable unit** *n* (*LRU*) ELEC ENG unité remplaçable en ligne *f*; ~ **reversal** *n* TELECOM inversion de batterie *f*, inversion de charge en ligne *f*; ~ **scan-**

ning *n* COMP balayage de ligne *m*, ELECTRON balayage ligne à ligne *m*, PRINT balayage ligne par ligne *m*, TELECOM *radar* balayage en ligne *m*; ~ **of section** *n* GEOL trait de coupe *m*; ~ **segment** *n* GEOM segment de droite *m*; ~ **seizure button** *n* TELECOM touche prise de ligne *f*; ~ **serving a siding** *n* RAIL *track* voie de desserte *f*; ~ **shaft** *n* MECH ENG arbre de ligne *m*; ~ **of shafting** *n* MECH ENG ligne d'arbres *f*, ligne de transmission *f*; ~ **of sight** *n* ASTRON ligne de visée *f*, TELECOM en visibilité; ~ **signal** *n* ELECTRON signal transmis par la ligne *m*; ~ **signaling equipment** *n* (AmE), ~ **signalling equipment** (BrE) *n* TELECOM équipement de signalisation de ligne *m*; ~ **slip** *n* TV glissement horizontal *m*; ~ **source** *n* POLLUTION source linéaire *f*, sources alignées *f pl*; ~ **space** *n* PRINT interlignage *m*; ~ **spacing** *n* PRINT interlignage *m*; ~ **spectrum** *n* ACOUSTICS, OPT, PHYS, RAD PHYS, TELECOM spectre de raies *m*; ~ **speed** *n* PACKAGING vitesse de la chaîne de fabrication *f*; ~ **starter** *n* (AmE) (*cf starter*) ELEC *switch* interrupteur de démarrage *m*, starter *m*; ~ **stretcher** *n* PHYS *waveguide* extenseur de ligne *m*; ~ **of strike** *n* GEOL ligne de direction *f*, MINING *of lode* alignement de la direction *m*, ligne de direction *f*; ~ **style** *n* COMP, DP type de ligne *m*; ~ **sweep** *n* TV balayage de ligne *m*; ~ **switching** *n* COMP, DP commutation de lignes *f*; ~ **system** *n* TELECOM groupe quaternaire *m*; ~ **tear** *n* TV déchirement horizontal *m*; ~ **tension** *n* METALL tension de ligne *f*; ~ **terminal** *n* ELEC *connection* borne de ligne *f*, PROD ENG borne côté secteur *f*, borne d'alimentation *f*, borne d'entrée *f*, TELECOM terminal de ligne *m*; ~ **terminated by an impedance** *n* PHYS ligne terminée par une impédance *f*; ~ **termination** *n* (*LT*) PRINT, TELECOM terminaison de ligne *f*; ~ **termination equipment** *n* COMP (*LTE*) équipement de terminaison de ligne *m*, DP algèbre linéaire *f*; ~ **tester** *n* CONTROL contrôleur de circuit *m*, PAPER TECH, PRINT compte-fils *m*; ~ **thrower** *n* NAUT lance-amarre *m*; ~ **tilt** *n* TV inclinaison de ligne *f*; ~ **of traffic** *n* (AmE) (*cf traffic queue*) TRANSP file d'attente *f*; ~ **transient** *n* ELEC onde mobile *f*; ~ **voltage** *n* ELEC *supply network* tension de ligne *f*, ELEC ENG tension du réseau *f*, tension du secteur *f*; ~ **voltage in** *n* PROD ENG entrée d'alimentation *f*; ~ **voltage selector** *n* ELEC ENG sélecteur de tension *m*; ~ **width** *n* RAD PHYS *spectral* largeur de raie *f*; ~ **wiring** *n* PROD ENG câblage des circuits de commande *m*; ~ **work** *n* PRINT illustration au trait *f*, trait *m*, travail de trait *m*

line[2] *vt* COATINGS doubler, plaquer, revêtir, CONST *well* cuveler, tuber, MINING, PRINT *shaft* revêtir, PROD ENG *bearing block with antifriction metal* garnir, recouvrir, *furnace* revêtir; ~ **out** *vt* CONST tracer la coupe de; ~ **up** *vt* CINEMAT aligner, repérer, PRINT mettre en repérage, parangonner; ~ **with metal** *vt* MINING *shaft* blinder; ~ **with tin** *vt* PROD ENG *box* doubler de fer-blanc

line:[3] ~ **clear** *phr* RAIL voie libre *f*
lineals *n pl* PRINT linéales *f pl*
lineament *n* GEOL alignement structural *m*, linéament *m*
linear[1] *adj* PAPER TECH, PHYS linéaire
linear:[2] ~ **absorption coefficient** *n* PHYS coefficient d'absorption linéique *m*; ~ **accelerator** *n* ELEC ENG, PART PHYS, PHYS accélérateur linéaire *m*; ~ **activity** *n* NUCLEAR *of line source* activité linéique *f*; ~ **algebra** *n* COMP, DP algèbre linéaire *f*; ~ **amplification** *n* ELECTRON amplification linéaire *f*; ~ **amplifier** *n* ELECTRON, TELECOM amplificateur linéaire *m*; ~ **approximation** *n* TELECOM approximation linéaire *f*; ~ **array** *n* ELEC-

TRON *of photodetectors, LEDS* barrette *f*; ~ **attenuation coefficient** *n* PHYS *nuclear* coefficient d'atténuation linéique *m*, *telecommunications* coefficient d'affaiblissement linéique *m*; ~ **beam amplifier** *n* ELECTRON amplificateur à faisceau droit *m*; ~ **beam backward wave oscillator** *n* ELECTRON oscillateur à onde régressive à faisceau droit *m*; ~ **beam tube** *n* ELECTRON tube à faisceau droit *m*; ~ **bearings** *n pl* HEAT ENG roulement linéaire *m*; ~ **behavior** *n* (AmE), ~ **behaviour** *n* (BrE) ELECTRON comportement linéaire *m*; ~ **channel** *n* TELECOM canal linéaire *m*; ~ **characteristic** *n* ELECTRON caractéristique rectiligne *f*; ~ **charge density** *n* PHYS densité linéique de charge *f*; ~ **circuit** *n* ELEC circuit linéaire *m*, ELECTRON circuit analogique *m*, circuit linéaire *m*, TELECOM circuit linéaire *m*; ~ **circuit element** *n* ELECTRON élément de circuit linéaire *m*; ~ **code** *n* TELECOM code linéaire *m*; ~ **coefficient** *n* PHYS affaiblissement linéaire *m*, coefficient d'affaiblissement *m*, coefficient d'atténuation *m*; ~ **conditions** *n pl* ELEC ENG régime linéaire *m*; ~ **control** *n* CONTROL, ELEC régulation linéaire *f*; ~ **current network** *n* ELEC *supply* réseau de courant linéaire *m*; ~ **defect** *n* METALL défaut linéaire *m*; ~ **detection** *n* ELECTRON détection linéaire *f*; ~ **detector** *n* ELECTRON détecteur linéaire *m*; ~ **digital voice scrambler** *n* TELECOM brouilleur numérique linéaire de la voix *m*; ~ **disc** *n* (BrE) OPT disque linéaire *m*; ~ **disk** *n* (AmE) *see linear disc*; ~ **dispersion** *n* RAD PHYS *of spectrograph* dispersion linéaire *f*; ~ **distortion** *n* CINEMAT, RECORDING, TELECOM distorsion linéaire *f*; ~ **electric motor** *n* ELEC ENG moteur asynchrone linéaire *m*, moteur linéaire *m*, moteur électrique linéaire *m*; ~ **energy transfer** *n* PHYS *nuclear*, RAD PHYS transfert linéique d'énergie *m*; ~ **expansion coefficient** *n* PHYS coefficient de dilatation linéique *m*; ~ **feedback control system** *n* ELEC ENG système asservi linéaire *m*; ~ **filter** *n* TELECOM filtre linéaire *m*; ~ **filtering** *n* TELECOM filtrage linéaire *m*; ~ **four-terminal network** *n* ELEC quadripôle linéaire *m*; ~ **gray scale** *n* (AmE), ~ **grey scale** *n* (BrE) CINEMAT échelle linéaire des gris *f*; ~ **induction motor** *n* ELEC moteur électrique linéaire *m*, TRANSP moteur linéaire à inducteur *m*; ~ **integrated circuit** *n* ELECTRON circuit intégré analogique *m*; ~ **interpolation** *n* TELECOM interpolation linéaire *f*; ~ **ionization** *n* PHYS ionisation linéique *f*; ~ **kinetic energy** *n* MECH ENG énergie cinétique linéaire *f*; ~ **list** *n* COMP liste séquentielle *f*, DP liste linéaire *f*, liste séquentielle *f*; ~ **magnification** *n* PHYS grandissement linéaire *m*; ~ **matrix** *n* TV matrice linéaire *f*; ~ **modulation** *n* ELECTRON modulation linéaire *f*; ~ **modulator** *n* ELECTRON modulateur linéaire *m*; ~ **motor** *n* TRANSP moteur linéaire *m*; ~ **network** *n* ELEC ENG réseau linéaire *m*, réseau linéaire *m*, PHYS réseau linéaire *m*; ~ **operation** *n* ELEC ENG fonctionnement linéaire *m*; ~ **oscillation** *n* MECH ENG, TELECOM oscillation linéaire *f*; ~ **polarization** *n* ELEC ENG polarisation rectiligne *f*, TELECOM polarisation linéaire *f*, polarisation rectiligne *f*; ~ **polymer** *n* P&R polymère linéaire *m*; ~ **potentiometer** *n* ELEC ENG potentiomètre linéaire *m*; ~ **power amplifier** *n* ELECTRON, TELECOM amplificateur de puissance linéaire *m*; ~ **power supply** *n* ELEC ENG alimentation série *f*, alimentation série à incorporer *f*; ~ **predicting coding** *n* (*LPC*) TELECOM codage prédictif linéaire *m*; ~ **predicting coding vocoder** *n* TELECOM codeur à fréquences vocales *m*; ~ **predictive coding** *n* ELECTRON codage prédictif linéaire *m*; ~ **pressure** *n* PAPER TECH

pression linéaire *f*; ~ **programing** *n* (AmE), ~ **programming** *n* COMP, ELECTRON programmation linéaire *f*; ~ **pulse amplifier** *n* ELECTRON amplificateur d'impulsions linéaire *m*; ~ **register** *n* PRINT repérage linéaire *m*; ~ **regulation** *n* ELEC ENG régulation série *f*; ~ **resistor** *n* ELEC, ELEC ENG, PHYS *ohmic* résistance linéaire *f*; ~ **scale** *n* ELEC *of instrument*, ELECTRON, METR échelle linéaire *f*; ~ **scaling calculation** *n* TELECOM calcul d'extrapolation linéaire *m*; ~ **scan** *n* ELECTRON balayage rectiligne *m*; ~ **Stark effect** *n* PHYS effet Stark linéaire *m*; ~ **thermodynamics** *n* THERMOD thermodynamique linéaire *f*; ~ **time base** *n* ELECTRON base de temps linéaire *f*; ~ **timed acceleration** *n* PROD ENG accélération linéaire temporisée *f*; ~ **transducer** *n* ACOUSTICS transducteur linéaire *m*, ELEC ENG capteur linéaire *m*, transducteur linéaire *m*; ~ **tube** *n* ELECTRON tube à faisceau droit *m*; ~ **turbine** *n* TRANSP turbine linéaire *f*; ~ **variable differential transformer** *n* ELEC ENG transformateur différentiel à translation *m*; ~ **voltage** *n* ELEC ENG tension linéaire *f*; ~ **work hardening** *n* METALL durcissement de travail linéaire *m*

linear-accelerator-driven: ~ **reactor** *n* (*LADR*) NUCLEAR réacteur d'accélérateur linéaire *m*

linear-divided: ~ **machine tool scale** *n* MECH ENG échelle divisée linéaire pour machines-outils *f*

linearity *n* ELEC, ELECTRON, RECORDING, TELECOM linéarité *f*; ~ **control** *n* TV réglage de la linéarité *m*; ~ **error** *n* TV distorsion de linéarité *f*, linéarité défectueuse *f*

linearization: ~ **function** *n* PROD ENG fonction de linéarisation *f*

linearize *vt* CHEM linéariser

linearizer *n* SPACE *communications* linéarisateur *m*

linearly: ~ **polarized mode** *n* (*LP mode*) OPT, TELECOM mode à polarisation rectiligne *m* (*mode LP*); ~ **polarized wave** *n* ACOUSTICS onde polarisée linéairement *f*, ELEC ENG onde à polarisation rectiligne *f*, PHYS onde polarisée rectilignement *f*

lineation *n* GEOL linéation *f*

lined: ~ **bag** *n* PACKAGING sac doublé *m*; ~ **chipboard** *n* PACKAGING panneau d'aggloméré avec doublure *m*, PAPER TECH carton gris mixte *m*; ~ **clamp** *n* MECH ENG collier à garniture de protection *m*; ~ **paper** *n* GEOM papier réglé *m*

line-graduated: ~ **master scales** *n pl* METR règles étalons graduées *f pl*

line-interlaced: ~ **scanning** *n* TV analyse entrelacée *f*

lineman *n* RAIL surveillant de la voie *m*

linen *n* PRINT toile *f*, TEXTILES toile de lin *f*;

line-of-sight: ~ **signal** *n* ELECTRON signal à portée optique *m*

line-operated *adj* ELEC ENG alimenté par le secteur

liner *n* AERONAUT fourrure *f*, tube à flamme *m*, isolant *m*, COAL TECH blindage *m*, MECH chemise *f*, doublure *f*, MECH ENG chemise *f*, NAUT paquebot *m*, NUCLEAR *of pinch device* peau d'étanchéité *f*, PACKAGING doublure *f*, PAPER TECH couverture *f*, PETR colonne perdue *f*, liner *m*, PETR TECH *well* colonne perdue *f*, PRINT doublure de boîtes de carton *f*, doublure de couverture *f*, REFRIG *of refrigerator* cuve interne *f*, TRANSP paquebot *m*; ~ **bag** *n* PACKAGING sac poubelle *m*; ~ **hanger** *n* PETR dispositif de suspension de liner *m*, dispositif de suspension pour tubage perdu *m*, dispositif pour colonne de tubage perdue *m*; ~ **paper** *n* PAPER TECH papier à doubler *m*

lines: ~ **drawing** *n* MECH ENG *ship design* plan des formes *m*, vertical du plan des formes *m*; ~ **of force** *n pl*

GEOPHYS lignes de force *f pl*; ~ **per minute** *n pl* COMP,
DP lignes par minute *f pl*, PRINT lignes à la minute *f pl*;
~ **plan** *n* MECH ENG *naval architecture* plan des
formes *m*, vertical du plan des formes *m*

line-stabilized: ~ **oscillator** *n* ELECTRON oscillateur piloté
par ligne de transmission *m*

line-terminating: ~ **equipment** *n* TELECOM équipement de
terminaison de ligne *m*

line-to-earth: ~ **voltage** *n* (BrE) *(cf line-to-ground voltage)* ELEC *supply network* tension phase-terre *f*

line-to-ground: ~ **voltage** *n* (AmE) *(cf line-to-earth voltage)* ELEC *supply network* tension phase-terre *f*

line-to-line: ~ **voltage** *n* (AmE) *(cf phase-to-phase voltage)* ELEC *three-phase supply* tension composée *f*

line-to-neutral: ~ **voltage** *n* (AmE) *(cf phase-to-neutral voltage)* ELEC *supply network* tension phase-neutre *f*

line-up *n* GEOL *of in-phase arrivals* mise en phase *f*, PETR
alignement *m*, mise en ligne *f*; ~ **clamp** *n* PETR collier
positionneur *m*; ~ **slide** *n* CINEMAT diapositive de
réglage *f*; ~ **tape** *n* TV bande d'alignement *f*, bande de
réglage *f*; ~ **tone** *n* RECORDING tonalité d'étalonnage *f*

lingoid *adj* GEOL en forme de langue

linguiform *adj* GEOL en forme de langue

lining *n* AUTO garniture *f*, COATINGS, CONST revêtement
m, MECH garnissage *m*, revêtement *m*, MINING *of shaft*
revêtement *m*, PAPER TECH doublure *f*, PRINT couche
de protection *f*, doublure *f*, garniture *f*, habillage *m*,
PROD ENG *covering* chemise *f*, doublage *m*, garnissage
m, garniture *f*, revêtement *m*, VEHICLES *of brake or
clutch* garniture *f*, WATER SUPP *of pump* chemise *f*; ~
compound *n* PACKAGING composition de garnissage
f; ~ **fabric** *n* TEXTILES tissu de doublure *m*; ~ **paper** *n*
PACKAGING doublure *f*, PRINT papier de doublure *m*,
préprint *m*; ~ **plate** *n* PROD ENG plaque de revêtement
f; ~ **segment** *n* CONST *tunnelling* voussoir *m*; ~ **sight** *n*
MINING viseur de mine *m*; ~ **tube** *n* MINING tube de
revêtement *m*

lining-up *n* PRINT *bookbinding* contrecollage *m*

link[1] *n* COMP, DP liaison *f*, lien *m*, ELEC *in system* liaison *f*,
MECH articulation *f*, maillon de chaîne *m*, MECH ENG
bielle *f*, biellette *f*, biellette de liaison *f*, lien *m*, étrier
m, *of chain* anneau *m*, chaînon *m*, maillon *m*, *of cable
chain* chaînon *m*, maille *f*, maillon *m*, *of motion*
coulisse *f*, NAUT *of chain* maille *f*, TELECOM liaison *f*,
lien *m*, maillon *m*; ~ **bearing** *n* MECH ENG tourillon de
suspension de la coulisse *m*; ~ **belting** *n* P&R *of machine* courroies en cuir articulé *f pl*; ~ **block** *n* MECH
ENG coulisseau *m*; ~ **block guide** *n* RAIL guide de
coulisseau *m*; ~ **block pin** *n* MECH ENG axe du coulisseau *m*; ~ **budget** *n* SPACE *communications* bilan de
liaison *m*; ~ **chain** *n* MECH ENG, PAPER TECH chaîne à
maillons *f*, PROD ENG chaîne ouverte *f*, chaîne à
maillons *f*, chaîne à maillons ouverts *f*; ~ **coupling** *n*
ELEC ENG liaison par double transformateur *f*; ~ **editing** *n* COMP édition de liens *f*; ~ **editor** *n* COMP, DP
éditeur de liens *m*; ~ **fuse** *n* ELEC coupe-circuit à lame
m, lame fusible *f*, ELEC ENG fusible de liaison *m*; ~
gear *n* MECH ENG coulisse *f*, distribution *f*, distribution à coulisse *f*, détente *f*; ~ **grinder** *n* PROD ENG
machine à rectifier les coulisses de changement de
marche *f*; ~ **hanger** *n* MECH ENG bielle de suspension de
la coulisse *f*; ~ **loader** *n* COMP chargeur-éditeur de liens
m; ~ **margins** *n pl* TELECOM marges applicables à une
liaison *f pl*; ~ **mechanism** *n* MECH ENG embiellage *m*; ~
motion *n* MECH ENG coulisse *f*, distribution *f*, distribution à coulisse *f*, détente *f*; ~ **motion with crossed rods**

n MECH ENG coulisse à barres croisées *f*, coulisse à
barres fermées *f*; ~ **motion with open rods** *n* MECH ENG
coulisse à barres droites *f*, coulisse à barres ouvertes
f; ~ **plate** *n* MECH ENG flasque de coulisse *m*; ~ **power
budget** *n* TELECOM bilan de puissance d'une liaison *m*;
~ **protocol** *n* COMP procédure de commande de liaison
f, DP protocole de liaison *m*; ~ **relay** *n* ELEC ENG relais
hertzien *m*; ~ **rod** *n* MECH ENG bielle de liaison *f*; ~ **support** *n* MECH ENG bielle de suspension de la coulisse *f*; ~
system *n* TELECOM système à mailles *m*; ~ **trainer** *n*
AERONAUT maquette d'entraînement au sol *f*, simulateur de pilotage *m*; ~ **valve motion** *n* MECH ENG coulisse *f*, distribution *f*, distribution à coulisse *f*,
détente *f*

link[2] *vt* ELEC ENG relier; ~ **up** *vt* TELECOM relier

linkage *n* CHEM *atoms* , COMP, DP liaison *f*, MECH liaison
f, tringlerie *f*, MECH ENG embiellage *m*, tringlerie *f*,
NUCLEAR *mechanism* tiges *f pl*, P&R liant *m*, VEHICLES
steering, clutch, brakes timonerie *f*, tringlerie *f*; ~
editor *n* COMP, DP éditeur de liens *m*; ~ **path** *n* COMP
voie de chaînage *f*, DP voie d'enchaînement *f*; ~ **power
steering system** *n* AUTO servodirection timonerie *f*

link-by-link: ~ **encipherment** *n* TELECOM chiffrement de
liaison *m*, chiffrement de liaison par liaison *m*; ~
traffic routing *n* TELECOM acheminement section par
section *m*

linked[1] *adj* MECH couplé; ~ **together** *adj* TELECOM maillé

linked:[2] ~ **circuit** *n* ELEC circuit enchaîné *m*; ~ **traffic
signal control** *n* TRANSP signalisation coordonnée *f*

linking *n* CHEM enchaînement *m*, liaison *f*, TELECOM
maillage *m*

linnaeite *n* MINERAL linnéite *f*

linocut *n* PRINT gravure linoléum *f*

linoleate *n* CHEM linoléate *m*

linoleic[1] *adj* CHEM linoléique

linoleic:[2] ~ **acid** *n* FOOD TECH, P&R *raw material* acide
linoléique *m*

linoleine *n* CHEM linoléine *f*

linolenate *n* CHEM linolénate *m*

linolenic *adj* CHEM linolénique

Linotype *n* (TM) PRINT linotype *f* (MD); **setting** (TM)
PRINT linotypie *f* (MD)

linseed: ~ **oil** *n* CHEM huile de graine de lin *f*, huile de lin
f, CONST *ship maintenance* huile de lin *f*; ~ **oil
lacquer** *n* COATINGS vernis à l'huile de lin *m*

lint *n* OCEANOG alèze *f*, PRINT peluche *f*, poussière de
papier *f*

lintel *n* CONST linteau *m*, sommier de porte *m*, traverse *f*

lint-free: ~ **cloth** *n* MECH chiffon non-pelucheux *m*

linting *n* PAPER TECH peluchage *m*

lion's: ~ **claw** *n* CONST pince chien *m*, tendeur articulé *m*,
tendeur à pouce articulé *m*

lip *n* C&G buvant *m*, CONST *of bucket* lèvre *f*, LAB EQUIP
of beaker bec *m*, MECH ENG *of drill* lèvre *f*, PROD ENG *of
crucible* coulée *f*, *of furnace* rive *f*; ~ **bolt** *n* PROD ENG
boulon à ergot *m*; ~ **joint pliers** *n pl* MECH ENG pinces
réglables à deux positions *f pl*; ~ **microphone** *n* ACOUSTICS microphone labial *m*; ~ **reading** *n* ACOUSTICS
lecture labiale *f*; ~ **seal** *n* MECH joint à lèvres *f*, MECH
ENG bague d'étanchéité à lèvres *f*, joint à lèvres *m*; ~
sync *n* CINEMAT postsynchronisation *f*, synchronisation labiale *f*, RECORDING synchronisme des lèvres *m*

lipase *n* CHEM lipase *f*, saponase *f*

lipid *n* CHEM lipide *m*

lipoid *adj* CHEM lipoïde

lipophile *n* CHEM lipophile *m*

lipophilic *adj* CHEM lipophile *m*

lipopolysaccharide *n* CHEM lipopolysaccharide *m*

lipositol *n* CHEM liposite *f*

liposoluble *adj* CHEM liposoluble

lipped: ~ cover tile *n* (BrE) *(cf seal block)* C&G brique couvre-goulotte avec bec *f*; ~ table scarf with key *n* CONST enture à mi-bois avec tenons d'about et clef *f*

lip-type: ~ seal *n* MECH ENG bague d'étanchéité à lèvres *f*

liquation *n* CHEM liquation *f*

liquefaction *n* CHEM, GAS TECH, PHYS *of gases* liquéfaction *f*,   THERMOD fluidification *f*, fusion *f*, liquéfaction *f*

liquefied: ~ gas *n* GAS TECH gaz liquéfié *m*; ~ natural gas *n (LNG)* GAS TECH, PETR TECH gaz naturel liquéfié *m (GNL)*; ~ natural gas and liquefied petroleum gas carrier *n* THERMOD *shipping* méthanier *m*; ~ petroleum gas *n (LPG)* GAS TECH, HEAT ENG, PETR TECH gaz de pétrole liquéfié *m (GPL)*

liquefier *n* REFRIG liquéfacteur *m*

liquefy *vt* CHEM liquéfier, THERMOD fluidifier, liquéfier

liquescence *n* CHEM liquescence *f*

liquescent *adj* CHEM liquescent

liquid[1] *adj* CHEM, THERMOD liquide

liquid[2] *n* PHYS, REFRIG, THERMOD liquide *m*; ~ air *n* THERMOD air liquide *m*; ~ ammonia *n* THERMOD ammoniaque liquide *f*; ~ bipropellant propulsion *n* SPACE *spacecraft* propulsion biliquide *f*; ~ breathing *n* OCEANOG respiration liquidienne *f*; ~ charge *n* PROP MAT, REFRIG *in thermostat* charge liquide *f*; ~ chiller *n* REFRIG congélateur à liquide *m*; ~ chlorine *n* THERMOD chlore liquide *m*; ~ chromatography *n* POLLUTION chromatographie en phase liquide *f*, chromatographie liquéfiée *f*; ~ compass *n* NAUT compas liquide *m*; ~ controller *n* ELEC ENG rhéostat à liquide *m*; ~ coolant *n* THERMOD liquide de refroidissement *m*; ~ cooler *n* MECH ENG réfrigérateur à liquide *m*; ~ cooling *n* THERMOD refroidissement par liquide *m*; ~ crystal *n* CRYSTALL, NUCLEAR, TELECOM cristal liquide *m*; ~ crystal display *n (LCD)* COMP, DP, ELEC affichage à cristaux liquides *m*, écran à cristaux liquides *m*, ELECTRON affichage à cristaux liquides *m*, afficheur à cristaux liquides *m*, écran à cristaux liquides *m*, PHYS, TV affichage à cristaux liquides *m*, écran à cristaux liquides *m*; ~ crystal display module *n* ELECTRON module d'affichage à cristaux liquides *m*; ~ crystal display panel *n (LCD panel)* ELECTRON panneau à cristaux liquides *m*; ~ crystals *n pl* ELECTRON, PETR TECH cristaux liquides *m pl*; ~ detergent *n* DETERGENTS détergent liquide *m*; ~ droplets *n pl* POLLUTION gouttelettes liquides *f pl*; ~ drop model *n* PHYS *atomic nucleus* modèle de la goutte liquide *m*; ~ effluent *n* GAS TECH effluent liquide *m*; ~ flow *n* FLUID PHYS, NUCLEAR écoulement liquide *m*; ~ flow indicator *n* REFRIG indicateur de passage de liquide *m*; ~ fuel *n* THERMOD propergol liquide *m*, *fuse* combustible liquide *m*; ~ fuel engine *n* THERMOD moteur à combustible liquide *m*; ~ fuel rocket *n* THERMOD fusée à propergol liquide *f*; ~ gas *n* GAS TECH gaz liquéfié *m*; ~ gas engine *n* TRANSP moteur à gaz liquéfié *m*; ~ gases *n* THERMOD gaz liquides *m pl*; ~ gate *n* CINEMAT fenêtre à tirage humide *f*; ~ gate printing *n* CINEMAT tirage humide *m*, tirage par immersion *m*; ~ gold *n* C&G or liquide *m*; ~ helium *n* THERMOD hélium liquide *m*; ~ hydrocarbon *n* GAS TECH hydrocarbure liquide *m*; ~ hydrogen *n* SPACE hydrogène liquide *m*; ~ injection valve *n* REFRIG vanne d'injection de liquide *f*; ~ kerosene (AmE) *(cf*

liquid paraffin) CHEM, THERMOD huile de paraffine *f*, paraffine liquide *f*; ~ laser *n* ELECTRON laser à liquide *m*; ~ lasing medium *n* ELECTRON milieu actif liquide *m*; ~ level *n* PACKAGING niveau du liquide *m*, PETR TECH niveau liquide *m*; ~ level control *n* PACKAGING contrôle du niveau d'un liquide *m*; ~ level indicator *n* PACKAGING indicateur du niveau d'un liquide *m*; ~ limit *n* COAL TECH, CONST limite de liquidité *f*; ~ limit device *n* COAL TECH appareil de limite de liquidité *m*; ~ measure *n* METR mesure de capacité pour les liquides *f*; ~ metal *n* COAL TECH, PROP MAT métal liquide *m*; ~ metal heat exchanger *n* THERMOD échangeur thermique à métal liquide *m*; ~ metal ion source *n* RAD PHYS source d'ions à métal liquide *f*; ~ monopropellant *n* THERMOD *rockets* monergol liquide *m*; ~ natural gas *n (LNG)* THERMOD gaz naturel liquéfié *m (GNL)*; ~ natural gas bus *n* TRANSP autobus à gaz naturel liquéfié *m*; ~ natural gas carrier *n* TRANSP méthanier *m*; ~ nitrogen *n* SPACE azote liquide *m*; ~ oxygen *n* SPACE, THERMOD oxygène liquide *m*; ~ oxygen explosive *n* MINING explosif à l'oxygène liquide *m*, oxylignite *m*; ~ paraffin *n* (BrE) *(cf liquid kerosene)* CHEM, THERMOD huile de paraffine *f*, paraffine liquide *f*; ~ petroleum gas bus *n* TRANSP autobus à gaz liquéfié *m*; ~ petroleum gas engine *n* AUTO moteur à gaz de pétrole liquéfié *m*; ~ phase epitaxy *n* ELECTRON épitaxie en phase liquide *f*; ~ propellant *n* SPACE, THERMOD *rockets* propergol liquide *m*; ~ propellant rocket *n* SPACE fusée à propergol liquide *f*; ~ propellant system *n* SPACE *spacecraft* filière à propulseurs liquides *f*; ~ receiver *n* REFRIG *of condenser* réservoir de liquide *m*, vase *f*; ~ rheostat *n* ELEC *resistance* rhéostat liquide *m*; ~ sloshing *n* SPACE *spacecraft* ballottement de liquide *m*; ~ slug *n* REFRIG poche de liquide *f*; ~ antistain spray *n* PRINT antimaculateur liquide *m*; ~ starter *n* ELEC ENG rhéostat à liquide *m*; ~ starter resistance *n* ELEC *resistor* rhéostat de démarrage à liquide *m*; ~ starting resistance *n* ELEC *resistor* rhéostat de démarrage à liquide *m*; ~ steel *n* PROP MAT acier liquide *m*; ~ suction heat exchanger *n* REFRIG échangeur thermique à liquide-vapeur *m*; ~ thermometer *n* THERMOD thermomètre à liquide *m*; ~ tripropellant *n* THERMOD *rockets* liquide triergol *m*; ~ vapor equilibrium diagram *n* (AmE), ~ vapour equilibrium diagram *n* (BrE) THERMOD courbe des points d'ébullition *f*; ~ waste *n* RECYCLING effluent liquide *m*

liquid-cooled[1] *adj* THERMOD refroidi par liquide

liquid-cooled:[2] ~ engine *n* AUTO moteur à refroidissement par eau *m*

liquidity: ~ index *n* COAL TECH indice de liquidité *m*

liquid-metal-cooled *adj* THERMOD refroidi par du métal liquide

liquid-only: ~ phase *n* THERMOD phase liquide seule *f*

liquid-packaging: ~ line *n* PACKAGING chaîne d'emballage pour liquides *f*

liquid-proof[1] *adj* PACKAGING résistant aux liquides

liquid-proof:[2] ~ carton *n* PACKAGING carton résistant aux liquides *m*

liquidus *n* CHEM *phase diagram* liquidus *m*; ~ line *n* METALL ligne liquidus *f*

liquified[1] *adj* THERMOD liquéfié

liquified:[2] ~ petroleum gas *n* AUTO, TRANSP *(LPG)* gaz de pétrole liquéfié *m (GPL)*

liquor *n* CHEM liqueur *f*, solution *f*

liquor-to-goods: ~ ratio *n* TEXTILES rapport liqueur-poids de tissu *m*

l
iroconite *n* MINERAL liroconite *f*

L-iron *n* CONST cornière *f*, fer cornière *m*, fer d'angle *m*, fer en L *m*, fer en équerre *m*, équerre *f*

LISP *abbr (list processing language)* COMP langage de traitement de listes *m*

Lissajous: ~ **figures** *n pl* PHYS courbes de Lissajous *f pl*

list[1] *n* COMP, DP liste *f*, NAUT bande *f*; ~ **of lights** *n* NAUT livre des phares *m*; ~ **processing** *n* COMP, DP traitement de liste *m*; ~ **processing language** *n (LISP)* COMP langage de traitement de listes *m*; ~ **structure** *n* COMP, DP structure de liste *f*

list[2] *vt* COMP, DP lister

list[3] *vi* NAUT avoir de la bande, pencher sur le côté

listed: not ~ *adj* PROD ENG non répertorié

listening-in *n* TELECOM écoute silencieuse *f*

listing *n* COMP, DP listage *m*

listric: ~ **fault** *n* GEOL faille courbe *f*, faille listrique *f*

liter *n* (AmE) *see* litre

literal *n* DP littéral *m* ~ **error** *n* PRINT coquille *f*

litharge *n* CHEM, P&R litharge *f*

lithergol *n* SPACE lithergol *m*, propergol hybride *m*, THERMOD *rockets* lithergol *m*, propergol liquide *m*

lithic[1] *adj* GEOL lithique

lithic:[2] ~ **tuff** *n* GEOL conglomérat *m*, tuf volcanique *m*

lithification *n* GEOL lithification *f*

lithionite *n* MINERAL lithionite *f*

lithium *n (Li)* CHEM lithium *m (Li)*; ~ **battery** *n* ELEC ENG pile au lithium *f*; ~ **production** *n* ASTRON production de lithium *f*

lithium-chlorine: ~ **storage battery** *n* TRANSP accumulateur lithium-chlore *m*

lithoclast *n* GEOL débris carbonaté remanié *m*

lithofacies *n* GEOL lithofaciès *m*

lithogenous *adj* GEOL lithogénétique

lithograph *n* PRINT image lithographie *f*

lithographic: ~ **color** *n* (AmE), ~ **colour** *n* (BrE) COLOURS couleur lithographique *f*; ~ **mask** *n* ELECTRON masque de gravure *m*, RAD PHYS *production of integrated circuits* masque lithographique *m*; ~ **oil** *n* COATINGS vernis lithographique *m*; ~ **print** *n* PRINT gravure lithographique *f*; ~ **process** *n* ELECTRON procédé lithographique *m*; ~ **slate** *n* CHEM pierre lithographique *f*; ~ **stone** *n* CHEM pierre lithographique *f*; ~ **varnish** *n* COATINGS vernis lithographique *m*

lithography *n* ELECTRON gravure *f*, PRINT lithographie *f*, procédé lithographique *m*, lithographie offset *f*

lithologic *adj* GEOL lithologique

lithological *adj* GEOL lithologique

lithomarge *n* MINERAL lithomarge *f*

lithophile: ~ **element** *n* GEOL lithophile *f*, élément à forte affinité pour l'oxygène *m*

lithoplate *n* PRINT plaque lithographique *f*

lithopone *n* CHEM *mineral* lithopone *m*

lithosphere *n* FUELLESS lithosphère *f*, écorce terrestre *f*, GEOL, GEOPHYS, POLLUTION lithosphère *f*

lithostatic: ~ **pressure** *n* GEOL pression géostatique *f*, pression lithostatique *f*

lithostratigraphic: ~ **unit** *n* GEOL unité lithostratigraphique *f*

lithothamnion: ~ **ridge** *n* OCEANOG trottoir *m*

litmus *n* CHEM tournesol *m*; ~ **paper** *n* CHEM papier de tournesol *m*

litre *n* (BrE) METR, PHYS litre *m*

Little: ~ **Bear** *n* ASTRON Petite Ourse *f*

Littleton: ~ **softening point** *n* C&G température de Littleton *f*

littoral[1] *adj* OCEANOG littoral

littoral:[2] ~ **current** *n* OCEANOG dérive littorale *f*; ~ **drift** *n* HYDROL cheminement littoral *m*; ~ **retreat** *n* OCEANOG *beach* démaigrissement *m*, démaigrissement littoral *m*; ~ **zone** *n* GEOL *of sedimentation* domaine côtier *m*, zone littorale *f*

live[1] *adj* ELEC, ELEC ENG sous tension, PHYS branché, sous tension, TV en direct

live[2] ~ **action** *n* CINEMAT scène en direct *f*; ~ **axle** *n* MECH ENG essieu tournant *m*, VEHICLES *transmission* essieu moteur *m*; ~ **bait** *n* OCEANOG boette *f*, bouette *f*; ~ **bait fishing** *n* OCEANOG pêche au vif *f*; ~ **broadcast** *n* TV émission en direct *f*; ~ **camera** *n* TV caméra à l'antenne *f*; ~ **center** *n* (AmE), ~ **centre** *n* (BrE) MECH ENG *of lathe* pointe de la poupée fixe *f*; ~ **circuit** *n* ELEC ENG circuit sous tension *m*; ~ **coal** *n* COAL TECH charbon ardent *m*; ~ **coverage** *n* TV reportage en direct *m*; ~ **end** *n* RECORDING *of room* zone active *f*; ~ **grenade** *n* MILIT grenade active *f*; ~ **head** *n* MECH ENG *of lathe* poupée fixe *f*; ~ **line** *n* ELEC *supply* ligne sous tension *f*; ~ **line indicator** *n* ELEC *safety, overhead line* indicateur de ligne sous tension *m*; ~ **load** *n* CONST charge d'exploitation *f*, poids roulant *m*; ~ **microphone** *n* RECORDING micro branché *m*, micro ouvert *m*; ~ **oil** *n* THERMOD pétrole brut qui contient ses gaz d'origine *m*; ~ **rail** *n* TRANSP rail conducteur *m*; ~ **round** *n* MILIT balle vive *f*; ~ **shell** *n* MILIT obus chargé *m*; ~ **sound** *n* RECORDING son direct *m*; ~ **spindle** *n* MECH ENG *of lathe* arbre de la poupée fixe *m*, arbre mandrin *m*, mandrin principal *m*; ~ **steam** *n* HYDR EQUIP vapeur fraîche *f*, vapeur vive *f*, NUCLEAR *of turbine* vapeur fraîche *f*, vapeur principale *f*, vapeur vive *f*, THERMOD vapeur fraîche *f*; ~ **steam injector** *n* HYDR EQUIP injecteur de vapeur vive *m*; ~ **storage** *n* WATER SUPP emmagasinement vidangeable *m*; ~ **studio** *n* RECORDING studio actif *m*, studio réverbérant *m*; ~ **wire** *n* ELEC ENG fil sous tension *m*

live-end: ~ **dead-end studio** *n* RECORDING studio à zone active et à zone morte *m*

lively: ~ **handle** *n* TEXTILES toucher nerveux *m*

living: ~ **community** *n* POLLUTION communauté vivante *f*

lixiviation *n* CHEM lessivage *m*, lixiviation *f*, POLLUTION lixiviation *f*

LLC *abbr* TELECOM *(line load control)* CCL *(contrôle de charge de ligne)*, TELECOM *(logical link control)* commande de liaison logique *f*

Lloyd's: ~ **mirror** *n* PHYS miroir de Lloyd *m*

LLV *abbr (lunar logistics vehicle)* SPACE véhicule logistique lunaire *m*

lm *abbr (lumen)* METR lm *(lumen)*

LME *abbr* TELECOM *(layer management entity)* entité de gestion de couche *f*, TELECOM *(line module equipment)* matériel de modules de lignes *m*

LMS *abbr (land mobile station)* TELECOM station mobile terrestre *f*

LNA *abbr* ELECTRON *(low-noise amplifier)*, SPACE *(low-noise amplifier)* communications, TELECOM *(low-noise amplifier)* amplificateur à faible bruit *m*, TELECOM *(launch numerical aperture)* ouverture numérique d'injection *f*

L-network *n* ELEC ENG réseau en L *m*

LNG[1] *abbr* GAS TECH *(liquefied natural gas)*, PETR TECH *(liquefied natural gas)*, THERMOD *(liquid natural gas)* GNL *(gaz naturel liquéfié)*

LNG:[2] ~ **bus** *n* TRANSP autobus à gaz naturel liquéfié *m*; ~ **carrier** *n* TRANSP méthanier *m*; ~ **tanker** *n* NAUT transporteur de gaz naturel liquéfié *m*

LNG-LPG: ~ **carrier** *n* THERMOD *shipping* méthanier *m*

LO *abbr (local oscillator)* TELECOM oscillateur local *m*

load:[1] **under ~** *adj* VEHICLES en charge

load[2] *n* COAL TECH, COMP, CONST, ELEC *supply*, ELEC ENG, HYDROL, MECH charge *f*, MECH ENG effort *m*, METALL charge *f*, sollicitation *f*, NAUT charge *f*, chargement *m*, PAPER TECH charge *f*, PHYS charge *f*, effort *m*, force *f*, PROD ENG charge *f*, charge de travail *f*, REFRIG, TELECOM charge *f*; ~ **and trim sheet** *n* AERONAUT *aircraft* devis de poids et de centrage *m*; ~ **angle** *n* ELEC *machine* angle de charge *m*; ~ **application** *n* AERONAUT application des charges *f*; ~ **at break** *n* P&R charge à la rupture *f*; ~ **at length** *n* SPRINGS charge à la longueur *f*; ~ **capacitance** *n* ELEC ENG capacité de la charge *f*; ~ **capacity** *n* AERONAUT *of circuit breaker* capacité limite *f*; ~ **cast** *n* GEOL figure de charge *f*, marque de charge *f*; ~ **chain** *n* MECH ENG *of pulley block, hoist* chaîne de charge *f*, chaîne de levage *f*, PROD ENG, SAFETY *of hoist* chaîne de charge *f*; ~ **characteristic** *n* AERONAUT caractéristique en charge *f*, ELEC ENG caractéristique de la charge *f*; ~ **circuit** *n* ELEC circuit d'utilisation *m*, circuit utilisateur *m*, TELECOM circuit de charge *m*; ~ **commutated converter** *n* ELEC convertisseur à commutation par la charge *m*; ~ **conveyor** *n* MINING transporteur de chargement *m*; ~ **curve** *n* ELEC *supply network*, ELEC ENG courbe de charge *f*; ~ **diagram** *n* MECH diagramme de charge *m*; ~ **dispatcher** *n* ELEC *supply network* répartiteur de charge *m*; ~ **displacement** *n* NAUT *ship design* déplacement en charge *m*; ~ **distribution** *n* AERONAUT, CONST répartition de charges *f*; ~ **duration curve** *n* ELEC *supply network* diagramme de charges classées *m*; ~ **factor** *n* AERONAUT coefficient de charge *m*, facteur de charge *m*, ELEC ENG facteur d'utilisation *m*, facteur de charge *m*, MECH facteur de charge *m*, PETR TECH taux de charge *m*, REFRIG facteur de charge *m*, TRANSP *traffic* facteur de saturation *m*; ~ **fluctuation** *n* ELEC fluctuation de charge *f*; ~ **fluctuation pattern** *n* SPACE *spacecraft* gabarit de fluctuation des charges *m*; ~ **frequency control** *n* ELEC *machine* réglage fréquence-puissance *m*; ~ **governor** *n* PAPER TECH régulateur de pression hydraulique *m*; ~ **hook-up** *n* AERONAUT *helicopter* accrochage de la charge *m*; ~ **impedance** *n* ELEC ENG, PHYS, TELECOM impédance de charge *f*; ~ **inductance** *n* ELEC ENG inductance de la charge *f*; ~ **in suspension** *n* HYDROL charge en suspension *f*; ~ **leads** *n pl* ELEC ENG conducteur de la charge *m*; ~ **limiting** *n* ELEC ENG limitation de la charge *f*; ~ **line** *n* AERONAUT ligne de charge *f*, ELEC ENG droite de charge *f*, NAUT flottaison en charge *f*, ligne de charge *f*; ~ **loss** *n* ELEC pertes dues à la charge *f pl*; ~ **metamorphism** *n* GEOL métamorphisme général *m*; ~ **on top** *n* MINING chargement par-dessus *m*; ~ **on top process** *n* POLLUTION chargement sur résidus *m*, procédé de chargement sur résidus *m*; ~ **peak** *n* ELEC *supply network* pointe de charge *f*; ~ **point** *n* COMP, DP point de charge *m*; ~ **regulation** *n* ELEC ENG régulation par rapport à la charge *f*; ~ **release** *n* AERONAUT largage de la charge *m*; ~ **resistance** *n* ELEC ENG, PHYS résistance de la charge *f*; ~ **resistor** *n* ELEC résistance ballast *f*, ELEC ENG résistance de charge *f*; ~ **rope** *n* MINING *hoisting* câble d'équilibre *m*, câble de contrepoids *m*; ~ **sharing system** *n* TELECOM système en partage de charge *m*; ~ **shedding** *n* ELEC *supply* délestage de consommation *m*, ELEC ENG délestage *m*; ~ **switch** *n* ELEC sectionneur

à coupure en charge *m*; ~ **tap changer** *n* ELEC changeur de prises en charge *m*; ~ **terminal** *n* PROD ENG borne côté charge *f*, borne de sortie *f*; ~ **test** *n* ELEC essai de charge *m*; ~ **tester** *n* ELEC ENG contrôleur de batteries "entre bornes" *m*; ~ **transfer** *n* ELEC *supply* report de charge *m*, TELECOM transfert de charge *m*; ~ **value** *n* TRANSP *traffic* taux de saturation *m*; ~ **waterline** *n* NAUT *boatbuilding* flottaison en charge *f*

load[3] *vt* CINEMAT, COMP, CONST, DP, ELEC ENG, MECH, NAUT, PRINT, RECORDING charger

load:[4] ~ **a ship** *vi* NAUT faire la cargaison

load-bearing: ~ **capacity** *n* COAL TECH force portante *f*; ~ **wall** *n* CONST mur portant *m*, mur porteur *m*, mur porté *m*

load-carrying: ~ **balloon system** *n* MILIT système de ballon porteur de charge *m*

loaded[1] *adj* NAUT *cargo ship* en charge

loaded:[2] ~ **cable** *n* ELEC ENG câble chargé *m*, TELECOM câble chargé *m*, câble pupinisé *m*; ~ **capacity** *n* COAL TECH capacité de fixation *f*; ~ **displacement** *n* NAUT *of ship* déplacement en charge *m*; ~ **governor** *n* MECH ENG régulateur à masse centrale *m*; ~ **impedance** *n* ACOUSTICS impédance en charge normale *f*; ~ **line** *n* ELEC ENG ligne chargée *f*; ~ **spring** *n* SPRINGS ressort chargé *m*; ~ **wheel** *n* PROD ENG meule encrassée *f*

loader *n* COMP chargeur *m*, programme de chargement *m*, PROD ENG *machine* chargeuse *f*, TRANSP chargeuse *f*, *attached to network* chargeur *m*

load-indicating: ~ **bolt** *n* MECH ENG boulon avec indication de charge *m*

loading *n* COMP *file, program*, DP *file, program* chargement *m*, ELEC ENG application d'une charge *f*, HYDROL *sewage* mise en charge *f*, MINING, NAUT, PAPER TECH, PHYS, PROD ENG chargement *m*, RECORDING *of loudspeaker* impédance de charge *f*, SPACE *spacecraft* chargement *m*, sollicitation *f*, TRANSP chargement *m*; ~ **area** *n* AERONAUT *of airport* aire de chargement *f*; ~ **belt** *n* MINING sauterelle *f*; ~ **block** *n* SPRINGS bloc standard *m*; ~ **boom** *n* NAUT *fishing* corne de charge *f*; ~ **bridge** *n* TRANSP pont de transbordement *m*, portique de chargement *m*; ~ **capacity** *n* TRANSP charge limite *f*; ~ **chute** *n* MINING couloir de chargement *m*; ~ **coil** *n* ELEC bobine de pupinisation *f*, ELEC ENG bobine de charge *f*, PHYS *communication cables* bobine de pupinisation *f*; ~ **conveyor** *n* TRANSP bande de chargement *f*; ~ **crane** *n* RAIL grue de chargement *f*; ~ **density** *n* MINING densité de chargement *f*; ~ **dock** *n* TRANSP quai de chargement *m*; ~ **door** *n* AERONAUT porte cargo *f*; ~ **factor** *n* AERONAUT coefficient d'occupation *m*, SPACE *communications* facteur de charge *m*; ~ **function** *n* METALL fonction de charge *f*; ~ **gage** *n* (AmE), ~ **gauge** *n* (BrE) RAIL *vehicles* gabarit de charge *m*; ~ **platform** *n* CONST plate-forme de chargement *f*, RAIL *vehicles* trottoir de chargement *m*, TRANSP plate-forme de chargement *f*; ~ **pocket** *n* MINING poche doseuse *f*; ~ **ramp** *n* AERONAUT rampe de chargement *f*; ~ **room** *n* CINEMAT chambre noire *f*; ~ **shovel** *n* CONST *civil engineering* pelleteuse-chargeuse *f*; ~ **siding** *n* TRANSP voie de chargement *f*; ~ **slot** *n* TV *of cassette recorder* fente de chargement *f*; ~ **spool** *n* CINEMAT bobine à joues *f*; ~ **stick** *n* MINING bourroir *m*; ~ **system** *n* MINING installation de chargement *f*; ~ **test** *n* CONST épreuve de charge *f*

load-no: ~ **charge ratio** *n* TRANSP rapport poids en charge-poids à vide *m*

load-sensitive: ~ **braking** *n* TRANSP freinage auto-variable *m*

loam *n* CONST *building* pisé *m*, *soil* terre forte *f*, terre grasse *f*, GEOL glaise végétale *f*, terre végétale *f*, PROD ENG potée *f*, terre *f*, WATER SUPP glaise *f*; ~ **board** *n* PROD ENG *founding* planche à trousser *f*; ~ **cake** *n* PROD ENG *founding* motte de recouvrement *f*; ~ **core** *n* PROD ENG *founding* noyau en terre *m*; ~ **mold** *n* (AmE), ~ **mould** *n* (BrE) PROD ENG *founding* moule de terre *m*; ~ **plate** *n* PROD ENG *founding* armature du dessous *f*, plaque de fond *f*

lob *n* MINING filon en gradins *m*

lobe *n* MECH *of cam* bossage *m*, SPACE lobe radioélectrique *m*, *communications* lobe *m*

lobelia: ~ **alkaloid** *n* CHEM alcaloïde de lobélie *m*

lobeline *n* CHEM lobéline *f*

lobinine *n* CHEM lobinine *f*

local[1] *adj* COMP, DP local

local:[2] ~ **alignment** *n* ELECTRON alignement local *m*; ~ **area network** *n* *(LAN)* COMP, DP réseau local d'entreprise *m* *(RLE)*, TELECOM réseau de zone locale *m*, réseau intra-ZAA *m*, réseau local d'entreprise *m* *(RLE)*; ~ **battery** *n* ELEC ENG batterie locale *f*; ~ **call** *n* TELECOM appel local *m*, communication locale *f*, communication urbaine *f*; ~ **calling area** *n* *(LCA)* TELECOM zone locale *f*; ~ **capacity** *n* TRANSP capacité locale *f*; ~ **charge rate call** *n* TELECOM appel à prix partagé *m*; ~ **charge rate trunk call** *n* TELECOM appel à prix partagé *m*; ~ **communications network** *n* TELECOM RCL, réseau de communication local *m*; ~ **control** *n* MECH commande locale *f*; ~ **controller** *n* TRANSP régulateur de carrefour *m*; ~ **copy** *n* TELECOM copie locale *f*; ~ **distribution cable** *n* TELECOM câble de raccordement *m*; ~ **distribution network** *n* TELECOM réseau local de raccordement *m*; ~ **emission** *n* POLLUTION émission locale *f*; ~ **emission source** *n* POLLUTION source locale *f*; ~ **exchange** *n* TELECOM centre de rattachement *m*, commutateur d'abonnés *m*, TELECOM commutateur local *m*; ~ **exchange area** *n* TELECOM circonscription *f*, zone à autonomie d'acheminement *f*; ~ **function capabilities** *n pl* *(LFC)* TELECOM capacité fonctionnelle locale *f*; ~ **I/O PC** *n* PROD ENG automate programmable à E/S locales *m*; ~ **intersection controller** *n* TRANSP régulateur de carrefour *m*; ~ **junction** *n* TELECOM jonction urbaine *f*; ~ **line concentrator** *n* TELECOM concentrateur d'abonnés *m*; ~ **maintenance** *n* TELECOM maintenance locale *f*; ~ **mean time** *n* NAUT *astronomical navigation* temps moyen local *m*; ~ **network** *n* TELECOM réseau local *m*; ~ **operation** *n* TELECOM exploitation locale *f*; ~ **oscillator** *n* ELECTRON, PHYS, SPACE *communications*, TELECOM oscillateur local *m*; ~ **oscillator frequency** *n* ELECTRON fréquence de l'oscillateur local *f*; ~ **oscillator signal** *n* ELECTRON signal de l'oscillateur local *m*; ~ **oscillator tube** *n* ELECTRON tube de l'oscillateur local *m*; ~ **oxidation** *n* ELECTRON oxydation sélective *f*; ~ **program** *n* (AmE), ~ **programme** *n* (BrE) TRANSP microprogramme de régulation *m*; ~ **reference** *n* TELECOM référence locale *f*; ~ **standards and code of practice** *n pl* PROD ENG normes et codes locaux appropriés *m pl*; ~ **stress** *n* METALL contrainte locale *f*; ~ **switch** *n* TELECOM commutateur local *m*; ~ **traffic** *n* CONST circulation locale *f*, TRANSP trafic local *m*; ~ **traffic information** *n* TRANSP information routière locale *f*; ~ **train** *n* (AmE) *(cf slow train)* RAIL *vehicles* omnibus *m*, train omnibus *m*; ~ **user terminal** *n* NAUT *satellite location* station utilisatrice locale *f*, TELECOM

station terminale d'usager local *f*; ~ **variable** *n* COMP, DP variable locale *f*; ~ **yielding** *n* METALL cédation locale *f*

local: ~ **group** *n* ASTRON *of galaxies* groupe local *m*; ~ **sidereal time** *n* ASTRON temps sidéral local *m*

localize *vt* COMP, DP localiser

localized: ~ **disturbance** *n* FLUID PHYS agitation localisée *f*; ~ **dyeing** *n* COLOURS teinture partielle *f*; ~ **fringes** *n pl* PHYS franges localisées *f pl*

localizer *n* TRANSP radiophare d'alignement de piste *m*; ~ **beam** *n* AERONAUT faisceau de radiophare de balisage *m*; ~ **beam heading** *n* AERONAUT cap d'une piste *m*

locally: ~ **high vorticity** *n* FLUID PHYS tourbillon élevé localement *m*; ~ **homogeneous geometry** *n* GEOM géométrie localement homogène *f*; ~ **oxided junction** *n* ELECTRON jonction à oxydation sélective *f*

locate *vt* ELEC ENG localiser, *telegraph, telephone* rechercher, NAUT *ship, mark, man overboard* repérer, PROD ENG délimiter, localiser

locating *n* CONST emplacement *m*, localisation *f*, TELECOM repérage *m*; ~ **arbor** *n* MECH ENG arbre de repérage *m*; ~ **device** *n* MECH ENG dispositif de repérage *m*; ~ **disc** *n* (BrE) MECH ENG pastille de positionnement *f*; ~ **disk** *n* (AmE) *see locating disc*; ~ **hole** *n* MECH ENG piétage femelle *m*, trou de piétage *m*; ~ **key** *n* MECH clavette d'assemblage *f*; ~ **pin** *n* MECH téton d'assemblage *m*, MECH ENG détrompeur *m*, goujon repère *m*, *die set* ergot de positionnement *m*, PHOTO goupille d'arrêt *f*; ~ **rib** *n* PROD ENG nervure de positionnement *f*; ~ **screw** *n* MECH ENG vis d'épinglage *f*; ~ **spigot** *n* MECH ENG téton de centrage *m*; ~ **stud** *n* MECH ENG piétage mâle *m*

location *n* CINEMAT extérieur *m*, COMP emplacement *m*, CONST *act* emplacement *m*, localisation *f*, *position* assiette *f*, emplacement *m*, situation *f*, DP emplacement *m*, MECH ENG implantation *f*, lieu *m*, position *f*, positionnement *m*, PETR emplacement *m*; ~ **address** *n* PROD ENG adresse d'emplacement *f*; ~ **management** *n* PROD ENG gestion des emplacements *f*; ~ **shooting** *n* CINEMAT tournage en extérieurs *m*; ~ **spigot** *n* MECH ENG rondelle de centrage *f*, *injection mould* couronne de centrage *f*; ~ **unit** *n* CINEMAT deuxième équipe *f*

locator *n* MECH ENG pied de positionnement *m*

lock[1] *n* COMP verrou *m*, CONST loqueteau de fermeture *m*, rayon de braquage *m*, verrou *m*, serrure *f*, serrure encloisonnée *f*, *of river, canal* écluse *f*, DP verrou *m*, ELECTRON *oscillator* synchronisation *f*, HYDROL *canal* écluse *f*, NAUT *inland waterways, harbours* fermeture *f*, sas *m*, écluse *f*, PRINT verrouillage *m*, SAFETY *device* serrure *f*, VEHICLES *body* serrure *f*, verrouillage *m*, WATER SUPP *canal* écluse *f*; ~ **and block** *n* RAIL block à circulation intéressée *m*; ~ **and block system** *n* RAIL block à circulation intéressée *m*; ~ **and inland lake canal** *n* WATER SUPP canal à écluses et à lac intérieur *m*; ~ **bolt** *n* CONST crémone *f*, pêne de serrure *m*; ~ **bush** *n* CONST bobine de verrou *f*, douille de verrou *f*; ~ **casing** *n* CONST boîtier de verrou *m*; ~ **chamber** *n* NAUT *canal, harbour* sas *m*, WATER SUPP chambre d'écluse *f*, chambre des portes *f*, coffre d'écluse *m*, sas d'écluse *m*; ~ **cup** *n* CONST cuvette de verrou *f*; ~ **dues** *n pl* NAUT *inland waterways* droits d'écluse *m pl*, droits de sas *m pl*; ~ **fitting** *n* CONST ferrure de verrouillage *f*; ~ **gate** *n* HYDROL *of canal*, NAUT *of canal, harbour* porte d'écluse *f*, WATER SUPP porte d'écluse *f*, écluse *f*; ~ **grip pliers** *n pl* (BrE) *(cf locking pliers, vise grips)* MECH

ENG pince-étau f; **~ grip wrench** n MECH ENG clé-étau f;
~ groove n AUTO logement de clavette m; **~ house** n
WATER SUPP maison éclusière f; **~ keeper** n NAUT
gardien d'écluse m, éclusier m; **~ key** n CONST clé de
serrure f; **~ rail** n CONST of door traverse du milieu f; **~
ring for ball bearings** n MECH ENG anneau d'arrêt de la
cage à bille m; **~ saw** n CONST scie à guichet f; **~ screw** n
MECH ENG vis de blocage f; **~ sill** n WATER SUPP busc m,
seuil d'écluse m; **~ staple** n CONST gâche f; **~ stop** n
MECH ENG butée d'accrochage f; **~ washer** n MECH
rondelle d'arrêt f, MECH ENG rondelle Grower f, ron-
delle-frein f, rondelle-éventail f; **~ wire** n MECH ENG fil
à freiner m; **~ wire twist** n MECH ENG ligature de
fil-frein f

lock² vt CINEMAT caler, verrouiller, COMP verrouiller,
CONST fermer à clef, DP, MECH verrouiller, MECH ENG
clamp bloquer, PRINT, RAIL switch verrouiller, WATER
SUPP boat écluser; **~ off** vt CINEMAT bloquer; **~ out
power sources** vt PROD ENG isoler les sources d'alimentation

lock³ vi MECH ENG se bloquer

lockable: ~ connector n ELEC ENG connecteur verrouillable m

lockage n WATER SUPP of boat éclusage m

lock-down: ~ switch n ELEC commutateur à tourner-
pousser m

locked:¹ ~ down adj PROD ENG retenu en position verrouillée; **~ in phase quadrature** adj ELECTRON asservi à
rester en quadrature

locked:² ~ canal n WATER SUPP canal éclusé m; **~ loop** n
TELECOM boucle à verrouillage f; **~ oscillator** n ELEC-
TRON oscillateur asservi m; **~ rotor current** n ELEC
asynchronous machine courant à rotor bloqué m; **~
rotor impedance characteristic** n ELEC asynchronous
machine caractéristique à rotor bloqué f; **~ rotor
torque** n ELEC machine torque à rotor bloqué f

locker n NAUT shipbuilding, boatbuilding, interior caisson m, coffre m, placard m, soute m, équipet m

lock-in: ~ amplifier n ELECTRON amplificateur synchrone m; **~ range** n ELECTRON oscillator demi-plage
de synchronisation f

locking n CONST fermeture f, fermeture à la clef f,
verrouillage m, MECH ENG clamping, METALL blocage
m, TV synchronisation f, WATER SUPP of boat éclusage
m; **~ attachment** n PROD ENG dispositif de verrouillage
m; **~ bar** n RAIL pédale de calage f, pédale de verrouillage f, pédale de verrouillage mécanique de signal f,
pédale mécanique d'aiguille f; **~ bolt** n CONST verrou
de fermeture m; **~ cam** n MECH ENG came de blocage f;
~ cover n PROD ENG capot de verrouillage m; **~ device**
n ELEC safety dispositif de verrouillage m, MECH ENG
dispositif de blocage m, dispositif de verrouillage m;
~ device for fire-resisting doors n SAFETY dispositif de
verrouillage pour portes coupe-feu m; **~ handle** n
CONST poignée de verrouillage f; **~ knob** n INSTRU-
MENT bouton de blocage m; **~ lab** n PROD ENG clapet de
verrouillage m, patte de verrouillage f; **~ latch** n PROD
ENG loquet de verrouillage m; **~ mechanism** n CINE-
MAT mécanisme de blocage m, MECH ENG blocage m; **~
notch** n RAIL vehicles encoche de verrou f; **~ pin** n
MECH ENG broche de verrouillage f, doigt de verrouillage m, goupille-frein f, pion de verrouillage m; **~
plate** n MECH ENG plaque-frein f; **~ pliers** n pl (AmE)
(cf lock grip pliers) MECH ENG pince-étau f; **~ plunger**
n MECH ENG gearbox bonhomme de verrouillage m; **~
push button** n CONTROL bouton-poussoir à verrouil-

lage m; **~ ring** n CINEMAT bague de blocage f; **~ stud** n
MECH ENG téton de blocage m; **~ washer** n MECH ENG
rondelle de blocage f; **~ of wheels** n RAIL enrayage m
lock-knit n TEXTILES charmeuse f
lock-mortise: ~ chisel n CONST empenoir m
locknut n MECH contre-écrou m, MECH ENG contre-écrou m, écrou indesserrable m, écrou-frein m, PROD
ENG contre-écrou m
lock-on n AERONAUT accrochage m
lockout n COMP blocage m; **~ coil** n PROD ENG bobine
d'arrêt f; **~ solenoid** n PROD ENG solénoïde d'arrêt m; **~
valve** n AERONAUT speed brake clapet commandé m
lockpin n MECH ENG épingle de freinage f
lockplate n MECH ENG frein plat m, plaquette d'arrêt f,
plaquette-frein f, platine f, rondelle rectangulaire f,
retient m
locksmith n CONST serrurier m
locksmithery n CONST serrurerie f
locksmithing n CONST serrurerie f
lock-up: ~ relay n ELEC ENG relais à verrouillage électrique m
lockwire: ~ pliers n pl MECH ENG pince à freiner f
lockwork n CONST serrurerie f
locomotive n RAIL vehicles locomotive f; **~ boiler** n
HEATING chaudière de locomotive f; **~ depot** n RAIL
vehicles remise à locomotives f; **~ shed** n RAIL dépôt
de locomotives m; **~ with AC/DC motor converter set** n
RAIL vehicles locomotive monocontinue f, locomotive à groupe monocontinu f
locomotive-holding: ~ siding n RAIL faisceau d'attente m
loctal: ~ base n ELECTRON culot loctal m; **~ tube** n
ELECTRON tube à culot loctal m
locus n GEOM of moving point lieu géométrique m
lode n MINING filon m, gîte filonien m, veine f; **~ channel**
n MINING chenal filonien m; **~ drive** n MINING galerie
de taille f; **~ filling** n MINING remplissage filonien m; **~
mining** n MINING abattage en filon m, exploitation des
filons f, exploitation filonienne f; **~ tin** n MINING étain
de roche m
lodestone n MINERAL pierre d'aimant f
lodge n MINING accrochage m, chambre d'accrochage f,
chambre d'envoyage f, envoyage m, recette f, albra-
que f, pahage m; **~ room** n MINING recette à eau f
loeweite n MINERAL lœwéite f
LOF abbr (loss of frame) TELECOM perte de trame f
lofting n NAUT shipbuilding traçage m
loftsman n NAUT shipbuilding traceur m
log¹ n COMP, DP journal m, GEOL colonne stratigraphique f, MATH (logarithm) log m (logarithme), PAPER
TECH rondin m, PETR diagramme m, PETR TECH prospecting document diagraphie f, TELECOM journal de
bord m; **~ band mill** n PROD ENG scie à ruban pour le
débit des bois en grume f; **~ conveyor** n PROD ENG
convoyeur de grumes m; **~ crosscutting machine** n
PROD ENG scie alternative à tronçonner f; **~ frame** n
PROD ENG scie verticale alternative à plusieurs lames
f; **~ line** n NAUT ligne de loch f; **~ normal distribution** n
MATH loi log-normale f; **~ normal shadowing** n TELE-
COM occultation lognormale f, évanouissement
lent m
log² vt COMP, DP consigner, NAUT enregistrer, inscrire au
journal de bord, porter au journal de bord
log³ ~ in vi COMP entrer dans le système, DP entrer dans
le système, entrer en communication, ouvrir une session, CINEMAT faire le rapport de scripte; PROD ENG
entrer en session; **~ off** vi COMP sortir du système, DP

se déconnecter du système; **~ on** *vi* COMP entrer dans le système, DP entrer dans le système, ouvrir une session, se connecter au système; **~ out** *vi* COMP, DP sortir du système

logarithm *n* COMP, MATH logarithme *m*

logarithmic[1] *adj* MATH logarithmique

logarithmic:[2] **~ amplifier** *n* ELECTRON amplificateur logarithmique *m*; **~ characteristic** *n* ELECTRON caractéristique logarithmique *f*; **~ creep** *n* METALL fluage logarithmique *m*; **~ decrement** *n* ELECTRON, PHYS décrément logarithmique *m*; **~ potentiometer** *n* ELEC ENG potentiomètre logarithmique *m*; **~ scale** *n* ELEC *measurement*, ELECTRON échelle logarithmique *f*; **~ sweep** *n* ELECTRON balayage logarithmique *m*; **~ video amplifier** *n* ELECTRON amplificateur vidéo logarithmique *m*

logatom *n* ACOUSTICS logatome *f*; **~ articulation** *n* TELECOM indice de netteté des logatomes *m*

logbook *n* TRANSP journal de bord *m*

logger *n* ELEC *measurements* enregistreur *m*, INSTRUMENT enregistreur automatique *m*, enregistreur chronologique automatique *m*

loggia *n* CONST *building* loggia *f*

logging *n* PETR TECH *prospecting action* diagraphie *f*, PROD ENG exploitation des bois *f*; **~ head** *n* MECH ENG balancier *m*

logic *n* COMP, DP, ELECTRON logique *f*; **~ addition** *n* ELECTRON addition logique *f*; **~ algebra** *n* ELECTRON algèbre logique *f*; **~ analysis** *n* COMP, DP, ELECTRON analyse logique *f*; **~ analyzer** *n* COMP, ELECTRON analyseur logique *m*; **~ array** *n* ELECTRON matrice logique *f*; **~ card** *n* COMP, DP, ELECTRON carte logique *f*; **~ circuit** *n* COMP, DP, ELECTRON, TELECOM circuit logique *m*; **~ component** *n* ELECTRON composant logique *m*; **~ design** *n* COMP, DP conception logique *f*, étude logique *f*, ELECTRON conception logique *f*; **~ device** *n* COMP, DP, ELECTRON dispositif logique *m*; **~ diagram** *n* DP, ELECTRON, PROD ENG schéma logique *m*; **~ element** *n* COMP, DP, ELECTRON élément logique *m*; **~ family** *n* COMP, DP, ELECTRON famille logique *f*; **~ gate** *n* COMP, DP, ELECTRON, PHYS porte logique *f*; **~ high** *n* ELECTRON haut logique *m*; **~ input signal** *n* ELECTRON signal d'entrée logique *m*; **~ instruction** *n* COMP, DP instruction logique *f*; **~ integrated circuit** *n* ELECTRON circuit intégré logique *m*; **~ level** *n* COMP, DP, ELECTRON niveau logique *m*; **~ level signal** *n* PROD ENG signal à niveau logique *m*; **~ level voltage** *n* PROD ENG tension à niveau logique *f*; **~ low** *n* ELECTRON bas logique *m*; **~ microcircuit** *n* ELECTRON microcircuit logique *m*; **~ operation** *n* DP, ELECTRON opération logique *f*; **~ operator** *n* COMP, DP, ELECTRON opérateur logique *m*; **~ output signal** *n* ELECTRON signal de sortie logique *m*; **~ pattern** *n* ELECTRON combinaison logique *f*; **~ reed block** *n* PROD ENG bloc à lames souples *m*; **~ reed contact** *n* PROD ENG contact à lames souples *m*; **~ signal** *n* ELECTRON signal logique *m*; **~ signal converter** *n* NUCLEAR ensemble terminal *m*; **~ simulation** *n* ELECTRON simulation logique *f*; **~ simulator** *n* ELECTRON simulateur logique *m*; **~ state** *n* ELECTRON état logique *m*; **~ state analysis** *n* ELECTRON analyse d'états logiques *f*; **~ state and timing analyzer** *n* ELECTRON analyseur logique mixte *m*; **~ symbol** *n* COMP, DP symbole logique *m*; **~ test** *n* ELECTRON contrôle logique *m*; **~ tester** *n* ELECTRON contrôleur logique *m*; **~ timing** *n* ELECTRON chronologie *f*; **~ timing analysis** *n* ELECTRON analyse de chronologie *f*; **~ unit** *n* ELEC

control ensemble logique *m*

logical[1] *adj* COMP, DP logique

logical:[2] **~ addressing** *n* COMP, DP adressage logique *m*; **~ block** *n* COMP, DP bloc logique *m*; **~ fault indication** *n* PROD ENG signalisation logique de défauts *f*; **~ file** *n* COMP, DP fichier logique *m*; **~ link control** *n (LLC)* TELECOM commande de liaison logique *f*; **~ operation** *n* COMP, DP opération logique *f*; **~ operator** *n* COMP, DP opérateur logique *m*; **~ page length** *n* PRINT longueur de page logique *f*; **~ record** *n* COMP, DP enregistrement logique *m*; **~ sensor** *n* DP détecteur logique *m*; **~ shift** *n* COMP, DP décalage logique *m*; **~ type** *n* COMP, DP type logique *m*; **~ value** *n* COMP, DP valeur logique *f*; **~ variable** *n* COMP, DP variable logique *f*

log-in *n* COMP ouverture de session *f*, DP début de session *m*, TELECOM nom d'un point d'entrée *m*

logistic: **~ support** *n* AERONAUT soutien logistique *m*

logistics *n* COMP, DP logistique *f*

logo *n* CONST logo *m*, logo type *m*

log-off *n* COMP fin de session *f*, DP fermeture de session *f*, fin de connexion *f*, fin de session *f*

log-on *n* COMP ouverture de session *f*, DP début de session *m*

log-out *n* COMP fin de session *f*

löllingite *n* MINERAL löllingite *f*

L-OM *abbr (laser-optic memory)* OPT mémoire à lecture par laser *f*

LOM *abbr (loss of multiframe)* TELECOM perte de multitrame *f*

lone: **~ pair** *n* CHEM *of electrons* doublet libre *m*

long: **~ acceleration** *n* PROD ENG accélération lente *f*; **~ address acceptance** *n* TELECOM acceptation d'adresses étendues *f*; **~ bed** *n* SPRINGS *of test bench* banc long *m*; **~ blast** *n* NAUT *sound signals* coup long *m*; **~ compass** *n* CONST déclinateur *m*, déclinatoire *m*; **~ descender** *n* PRINT lettre longue *f*; **~ hole blasting** *n* MINING abattage par longs trous *m*, abattage par mines longues *m*, abattage par trous profonds *m*; **~ life** *n* PROD ENG longue-durée de service *f*; **~ line** *n* OCEANOG palangre *f*; **~ loop** *n* TRANSP boucle à longue distance *f*; **~ measure** *n* METR mesure de longueur *f*, mesure linéaire *f*; **~ mission** *n* SPACE *spacecraft* mission de longue durée *f*; **~ normal** *n* GEOPHYS grande normale *f*; **~ oil alkyd** *n* P&R *paint resin* alkyd long en huile *m*; **~ oil varnish** *n* COATINGS vernis fort *m*, vernis gras *m*, vernis long en huile *m*, vernis épargne *m*, COLOURS vernis corsé *m*, vernis long en huile *m*; **~ period** *n* OCEANOG *wave* longue-période *f*; **~ period structure** *n* CRYSTALL structure à longue période *f*; **~ pitch** *n* CINEMAT *of perforation* pas long *m*; **~ pitch screw** *n* CONST vis de pas allongé *f*, MECH ENG vis de pas allongé *f*, vis à pas rapide *f*; **~ pitch winding** *n* ELEC *coil*, ELEC ENG enroulement à pas allongé *m*; **~ pulse** *n* NAUT *radar* impulsion longue *f*; **~ radius curve** *n* GEOM courbe à grand rayon *f*; **~ saw** *n* PROD ENG *pit saw* scie de long *f*; **~ screw** *n* MECH ENG *pipe fitting* longue-vis *f*; **~ shot** *n* CINEMAT plan d'ensemble *m*, plan général *m*, prise de vue éloignée *f*; **~ splice** *n* NAUT *ropework* épissure longue *f*; **~ take** *n* CINEMAT plan séquence *m*; **~ ton** *n* ꞁ TR tonne forte *f*; **~ wave** *n* ELEC, WAVE PHYS *radiation* grande onde *f*; **~ welded rail** *n* (BrE) *(cf ribbon rail)* RAIL long rail soudé *m*

longboat *n* NAUT chaloupe *f*

long-distance: **~ aircraft** *n* AERONAUT avion long-courrier *m*; **~ bus** *n* TRANSP autocar *m*; **~ cable** *n* ELEC ENG câble interurbain *m*, câble à grande distance *m*; **~**

flight *n* TRANSP vol de longue distance *m*; ~ **freight traffic** *n* (AmE) *(cf long-distance goods traffic)* TRANSP trafic de marchandises à longue distance *m*; ~ **gas transport** *n* TRANSP transport de gaz par canalisation *m*; ~ **goods traffic** *n* (BrE) *(cf long-distance freight traffic)* TRANSP trafic de marchandises à longue distance *m*; ~ **line** *n* ELEC ENG ligne interurbaine *f*, ligne à grande distance *f*, TELECOM ligne interurbaine *f*, ligne à grande distance *f*; ~ **road train** *n* TRANSP train routier à longue distance *m*

longevity *n* PROP MAT longévité *f*

long-fluted: ~ **machine reamer** *n* MECH ENG alésoir pour machine à goujures longues *m*

long-focus: ~ **lens** *n* CINEMAT objectif à longue focale *m*, téléobjectif *m*, PHOTO objectif de longue focale *m*

long-haul: ~ **airliner** *n* AERONAUT avion long-courrier *m*; ~ **carriage** *n* TRANSP transport à longue distance *m*; ~ **service** *n* AERONAUT service long-courrier *m*; ~ **truck driver** *n* TRANSP routier *m*

longifolene *n* CHEM longifolène *m*

longitude *n* NAUT *geography, navigation*, SPACE longitude *f*

longitudinal[1] *adj* ELECTRON *device, filter* longitudinal, NAUT *ship design* lisse, longitudinal

longitudinal:[2] ~ **arch kiln** *n* HEATING four à galeries parallèles *m*; ~ **axis** *n* AERONAUT *of aircraft*, MECH ENG axe longitudinal *m*, SPACE *spacecraft* axe de roulis *m*, axe longitudinal *m*; ~ **beam coupler** *n* AERONAUT coupleur de faisceau longitudinal *m*; ~ **chromatic aberration** *n* PHYS aberration chromatique longitudinale *f*; ~ **component** *n* PHYS composante longitudinale *f*; ~ **current** *n* C&G courant longitudinal *m*; ~ **cyclic stick load** *n* AERONAUT *helicopter* effort longitudinal au manche cyclique *m*; ~ **divergence** *n* AERONAUT engagement longitudinal *m*; ~ **filter** *n* ELECTRON filtre longitudinal *m*; ~ **framing** *n* NAUT *shipbuilding* lisse longitudinale *f*; ~ **gap loss** *n* OPT perte par espacement longitudinal *f*; ~ **grinding** *n* PAPER TECH défibrage longitudinal *m*; ~ **magnetic recording** *n* ACOUSTICS enregistrement magnétique longitudinal *m*; ~ **magnification** *n* INSTRUMENT grossissement longitudinal *m*, PHYS grandissement longitudinal *m*; ~ **member** *n* AERONAUT élément longitudinal *m*; ~ **metacenter** *n* (AmE), ~ **metacentre** *n* (BrE) NAUT *naval architecture* métacentre longitudinal *m*; ~ **offset loss** *n* OPT perte par espacement longitudinal *f*, perte par séparation longitudinale *f*, TELECOM perte par espacement longitudinal *f*; ~ **recording** *n* RECORDING, TV enregistrement longitudinal *m*; ~ **redundancy check** *n* *(LRC)* COMP contrôle par redondance longitudinale *m*; ~ **reinforcement** *n* CONST armature dans le sens longitudinal *f*, armature longitudinale *f*, ferraillage longitudinal *m*; ~ **scratch** *n* CINEMAT rayure longitudinale *f*; ~ **section** *n* CONST *roads*, RAIL profil en long *m*; ~ **slot** *n* TELECOM fente longitudinale *f*; ~ **stability** *n* TRANSP stabilité longitudinale *f*; ~ **stress** *n* METALL contrainte longitudinale *f*; ~ **traction test** *n* MECH ENG essai de traction longitudinale *m*; ~ **wave** *n* ACOUSTICS, PHYS, WAVE PHYS onde longitudinale *f*; ~ **wind component** *n* AERONAUT composante longitudinale du vent *f*

long-life[1] *adj* FOOD TECH longue-conservation

long-life:[2] ~ **battery** *n* ELEC ENG batterie de longue durée *f*

long-line: ~ **effect** *n* ELECTRON effet de longue ligne *m*; ~ **relay set** *n* TELECOM unité de raccordement d'abonnés distants *f*

long-lived: ~ **radioisotope** *n* RAD PHYS radio-isotope de période longue *m*

long-necked: ~ **flask** *n* LAB EQUIP *glassware* ballon à col long *m*

long-nose: ~ **pliers** *n pl* MECH pince à becs longs *f*

long-nosed: ~ **pliers** *n pl* PROD ENG pinces longues *f pl*

long-persistence: ~ **screen** *n* TV écran rémanent *m*, écran à longue persistance *m*

long-play: ~ **tape** *n* RECORDING bande longue durée *f*

long-playing: ~ **record** *n* RECORDING disque longue durée *m*, disque microsillon *m*, microsillon *m*

long-range[1] *adj* MILIT à longue portée

long-range:[2] ~ **order** *n* CRYSTALL ordre à grande distance *m*; ~ **radar** *n* MILIT radar à longue portée *m*; ~ **transport** *n* POLLUTION TGD, transport à grande distance *m*; ~ **transport of airborne pollutants** *n* POLLUTION TGDPA, transport à grande distance des polluants aéroportés *m*; ~ **transport of air pollutants** *n* POLLUTION TGDPA, transport à grande distance des polluants aéroportés *m*; ~ **weapon** *n* MILIT canon à longue portée *m*

long-shank: ~ **top** *n* MECH ENG taraud pour machine à queue longue *m*

longshore: ~ **bar** *n* GEOL cordon littoral sableux *m*; ~ **current** *n* OCEANOG dérive littorale *f*

longshoreman *n* (AmE) *(cf docker)* NAUT docker *m*, débardeur *m*

long-tail: ~ **pair** *n* ELECTRON *transistors* paire différentielle *f*

long-term: ~ **stability** *n* ELECTRON stabilité à long terme *f*; ~ **stress behavior** *n* (AmE), ~ **stress behaviour** *n* (BrE) PROP MAT comportement aux efforts de longue durée *m*

longtime: ~ **constant** *n* ELECTRON *transistors* grande constante de temps *f*

longwall: ~ **extraction** *n* MINING longue-taille *f*; ~ **face** *n* MINING longue-taille *f*; ~ **stoping** *n* MINING méthode en long *f*; ~ **system** *n* COAL TECH méthode de longwall *f*

long-way: ~ **signal** *n* ELECTRON signal indirect *m*

look *n* PROP MAT apparence *f*, TEXTILES aspect *m*

look-ahead *n* COMP, DP report parallèle *m*

look-down *n* PAPER TECH aspect *m*

looking: ~ **glass** *n* INSTRUMENT miroir *m*

lookout *n* NAUT *navigation* veille *f*, vigie *f*

look-through *n* PAPER TECH, PRINT épair *m*, épaisseur *f*

look-up *n* COMP consultation de données *f*, DP consultation *f*, consultation de données *f*; ~ **table** *n* COMP, DP table à consulter *f*

loom *n* NAUT *of light* lueur *f*, TEXTILES métier *m*; ~ **speed** *n* TEXTILES vitesse du métier *f*; ~ **state** *n* TEXTILES tombé de métier *m*; ~ **state weft** *n* TEXTILES trame écrue *f*

loop *n* ACOUSTICS boucle *f*, ventre *m*, C&G boucle *f*, CINEMAT boucle *f*, film sans fin *m*, COMP, DP, ELEC *circuit*, ELEC ENG, ELECTRON boucle *f*, GEOM *topology* lacet *m*, HYDROL *river* boucle *f*, NAUT *of rope* anse *f*, boucle *f*, nœud coulant *m*, œil *m*, PAPER TECH boucle d'accrocheuse *f*, PETR, PROD ENG *of controllers*, TELECOM, TEXTILES boucle *f*; ~ **aerial** *n* TELECOM antenne cadre *f*, cadre *m*; ~ **antenna** *n* TELECOM antenne cadre *f*; ~ **coil** *n* ELEC bobine à boucles *f*; ~ **coupling** *n* ELEC ENG couplage par boucle *m*; ~ **fault** *n* PROD ENG défaut de boucle *m*; ~ **feedback signal** *n* ELECTRON signal de rétroaction *m*; ~ **former** *n* CINEMAT boucleur *m*; ~ **gain**

n ELECTRON gain de la boucle *m*; ~ **galvanometer** *n* ELEC galvanomètre à corde *m*, ELEC ENG galvanomètre à cadre *m*; ~ **lever** *n* PROD ENG levier à boucle *m*; ~ **line** *n* RAIL voie en raquette *f*, *track* voie de contournement *f*; ~ **lock** *n* ELECTRON asservissement *m*; ~ **network** *n* COMP, DP réseau en boucle *m*; ~ **printing** *n* CINEMAT tirage en boucle *m*; ~ **statement** *n* COMP instruction de boucle *f*, DP instruction de bouclage *f*; ~ **test** *n* ELEC essai de boucle *m*

loopback *n* TELECOM boucle *f*; ~ **command** *n* TELECOM perte de pointeur *f*; ~ **command "audio loop request"** *n (LCA)* TELECOM commande de boucle "demande de boucle audio" *f*; ~ **command "digital loop request"** *n (LCD)* TELECOM commande de boucle "demande de boucle numérique" *f*; ~ **command "video loop request"** *n (LCV)* TELECOM commande de boucle "demande de boucle vidéo" *f*; ~ **command off** *n (LCO)* TELECOM commande d'ouverture de boucle *f*; ~ **connector** *n* PROD ENG connecteur de boucle *m*

looped[1] *adj* ELEC *circuit*, TELECOM bouclé

looped:[2] ~ **rod** *n* PROD ENG tige bouclée *f*; ~ **signal** *n* TELECOM signal transmis en retour *m*; ~ **yarn** *n* TEXTILES fil bouclé *m*

looping *n* SPRINGS opération à plier les anneaux *f*; ~ **mill** *n* PROD ENG train de machine *m*, train de serpentage *m*, train à serpenter *m*

loop-pile: ~ **carpet** *n* TEXTILES tapis bouclé *m*

loop-through: ~ **operation** *n* PROD ENG fonctionnement avec bouclage *m*

loose[1] *adj* COAL TECH *rock* meuble, ELEC *terminal* desserré, MECH ENG *pulley, reel, sleeve, wheel* fou, PAPER TECH lâche, PROD ENG *wheel* fou, PROD ENG *nut* desserré

loose:[2] ~ **accent** *n* (BrE) *(cf piece accent)* PRINT accent superposé *m*, accent séparé *m*; ~ **ballasting** *n* RAIL ballastage en vrac *m*; ~ **buffer** *n* OPT gainage lâche *m*; ~ **buffering** *n* OPT gainage lâche *m*; ~ **cable** *n* PROD ENG câble mal serti *m*; ~ **construction cable** *n* OPT câble à structure libre *m*; ~ **coupling** *n* COMP, DP, ELEC ENG, PHYS couplage lâche *m*; ~ **dyeing** *n* COLOURS teinture en bourre *f*; ~ **fit** *n* MECH ENG ajustement libre *m*; ~ **freezing** *n* REFRIG congélation en masse divisée *f*; ~ **glass** *n* C&G poussières de verre *f pl*; ~ **head** *n* MECH ENG *of lathe, of horizontal miller* contre-pointe *f*, contre-poupée *f*, poupée courante *f*, poupée mobile *f*; ~ **headstock** *n* MECH ENG *of lathe, of horizontal miller* contre-pointe *f*, contre-poupée *f*, poupée courante *f*, poupée mobile *f*; ~ **pick** *n* TEXTILES duite lâche *f*; ~ **piece** *n* PROD ENG pièce de rapport *f*, pièce rapportée *f*; ~ **pin hinge** *n* CONST fiche à noeud *f*; ~ **plant** *n* MECH ENG matériel mobile *m*, outillage mobile *m*; ~ **ribbon cable** *n* OPT câble ruban à fibres libres *m*, câble à rubans à fibres libres *m*; ~ **seat** *n* HYDR EQUIP *of valve* siège oscillant *m*; ~ **sleeve** *n* MECH ENG manchon fou *m*; ~ **smut** *n* FOOD TECH *phytopathology* charbon nu *m*; ~ **structure cable** *n* OPT, TELECOM câble à fibres libres *m*, câble à structure lâche *m*; ~ **tongue** *n* CONST *carpentry* fausse languette *f*, languette *f*, languette rapportée *f*; ~ **tube cable** *n* OPT, TELECOM câble classique à fibres libres *m*, câble à tubes assemblés *m*; ~ **wheel** *n* MECH ENG *on axle* roue folle *f*; ~ **wool** *n* C&G fibre courte en vrac *f*

loose-leaf *adj* PAPER TECH, PRINT feuillet mobile

loosely-wound: ~ **turn** *n* ELEC ENG spire non jointive *f*

loosen *vt* MECH desserrer, NAUT *rope* donner du jeu, donner du mou, lâcher, PROD ENG *nut* desserrer

looseness *n* PROD ENG *of nut* desserrage *m*

loosening *n* RAIL *of coupling* desserrage *m*; ~ **bar** *n* PROD ENG *founding* barre d'ébranlage *f*; ~ **wedge** *n* MECH ENG coin de desserrage *m*

loose-tongue: ~ **joint** *n* CONST assemblage à fausse languette *m*, assemblage à languette rapportée *m*

LOP *abbr (loss of pointer)* TELECOM perte de pointeur *f*

lophine *n* CHEM lophine *m*

lopolith *n* GEOL lopolite *m*

Loran: ~ **chain** *n* AERONAUT *navigation* chaîne Loran *f*

Lorentz: ~ **constant** *n* PHYS constante de Lorenz *f*; ~ **force** *n* ELEC ENG, PHYS force de Lorentz *f*; ~ **gage** *n* (AmE), ~ **gauge** *n* (BrE) PHYS *electrodynamics* jauge de Lorentz *f*; ~ **transformation** *n* PHYS transformation de Lorentz *f*

Lorentz-Fitzgerald: ~ **contraction** *n* PHYS contraction de Fitzgerald et Lorentz *f*

Lorentz-Lorenz: ~ **formula** *n* PHYS formule de Lorentz-Lorenz *f*

lorried: ~ **troops** *n* MILIT troupes portées *f pl*

lorry *n* AUTO, TRANSP, VEHICLES camion *m*

Los: ~ **Angeles abrasion test** *n* CONST essai Los Angeles d'abrasion *m*, épreuve d'abrasion *f*

LOS *abbr (loss of signal)* TELECOM perte de signal *f*

losing: ~ **stream** *n* HYDROL cours d'eau émissif *m*

loss *n* ELEC *of synchronism* décrochage *m*, ELEC ENG, FUELLESS *of heat*, HYDR EQUIP *of heat* perte *f*, MECH ENG travail nuisible *m*, OPT affaiblissement *m*, atténuation *f*, perte *f*, PATENTS *of priority* perte *f*, TELECOM atténuation *f*, perte *f*, *of transmission* affaiblissement *m*; ~ **angle** *n* ELEC *capacitor* PHYS angle de pertes *m*; ~ **around a corner** *n* TELECOM perte en courbe *f*; ~ **caused by fire** *n* SAFETY dégâts occasionnés par un incendie *m pl*; ~ **of color** *n* (AmE), ~ **of colour** *n* (BrE) C&G changement de teinte *m*; ~ **due to friction** *n* MECH ENG travail des résistances passives *m*; ~ **factor** *n* ELEC energy loss facteur de perte *m*; ~ **of frame** *n (LOF)* TELECOM perte de trame *f*; ~ **of frame alignment** *n (LFA)* TELECOM perte de verrouillage de trame *f (PVT)*; ~ **of load** *n* SPRINGS perte de charge *f*, perte de force *f*; ~ **of multiframe** *n (LOM)* TELECOM perte de multitrame *f*; ~ **of picture lock** *n* TV décrochage vertical de l'image *m*; ~ **of pointer** *n (LOP)* TELECOM perte de pointeur *f*; ~ **of power** *n* MECH ENG perte d'énergie *f*, perte de puissance *f*, perte de travail utile *f*; ~ **of pressure** *n* HYDR EQUIP perte de charge *f*; ~ **prevention** *n* QUALITY antivol *m*, prévention des pertes *f*; ~ **of returns** *n* PETR TECH *drilling* circulation perdue *f*, perte de circulation *f*; ~ **of sheet** *n* C&G perte de feuille *f*; ~ **of signal** *n (LOS)* TELECOM perte de signal *f*; ~ **of track compactness** *n* RAIL déconsolidation de la voie *f*

losses *n pl* PETR TECH *drilling* mud perte *f*

lossfree *adj* ELEC *dielectric* sans pertes

lossless *adj* ELEC ENG sans pertes

loss-mode: ~ **working** *n* TELECOM mode d'exploitation avec perte *m*

lossy: ~ **dielectric** *n* ELEC diélectrique à pertes *m*; ~ **line** *n* ELEC ENG ligne à pertes *f*, PHYS ligne avec pertes *f*; ~ **material** *n* ELEC *dielectric, line* matière imparfaite *f*

lost: ~ **bullet** *n* MILIT balle perdue *f*; ~ **circulation** *n* PETR circulation perdue *f*, PETR TECH *drilling* circulation perdue *f*, perte de circulation *f*; ~ **ends** *n* TEXTILES fils perdus *m pl*; ~ **hole** *n* PETR TECH *drilling* trou perdu *m*; ~ **time** *n* PETR TECH *drilling* temps morts *m pl*; ~ **traffic** *n* TELECOM trafic perdu *m*; ~ **wax** *n* C&G cire perdue *f*; ~ **wax casting** *n* PROD ENG coulée à la cire perdue *f*; ~

wax mold for casting n (AmE), ~ **wax mould for casting** n (BrE) MECH ENG moule pour fonderie à la cire perdue m

lot n CINEMAT *studio complex* complexe de studios m, terrain de studio m; ~ **size** n PROD ENG lot technique m, taille de lot f; ~ **sizing** n PROD ENG lotissement m, quantification des lots f, quantification des ordres f; ~ **splitting** n PROD ENG fractionnement des lots m

LOT abbr (leak-off test) PETR TECH essai de pression m, test d'injectivité m

loudness n ACOUSTICS, PHYS *quantity* sonie f, RECORDING intensité acoustique f; ~ **control** n RECORDING contrôle de sensation d'intensité m; ~ **function** n RECORDING expression de la sensation d'intensité f; ~ **level** n ACOUSTICS niveau d'insonie m, PHYS niveau d'isosonie m, RECORDING niveau de sensation d'intensité m; ~ **pattern** n RECORDING diagramme de sensation d'intensité m; ~ **volume equivalent** n RECORDING volume équivalent de sensation d'intensité m

loudspeaker n ACOUSTICS, ELEC *radio*, PHYS haut-parleur m, RECORDING enceinte f, haut-parleur m, TELECOM haut-parleur m; ~ **damping** n RECORDING amortissement de haut-parleur m; ~ **enclosure** n RECORDING enceinte de haut-parleur f; ~ **housing** n RECORDING enceinte de haut-parleur f; ~ **impedance** n RECORDING impédance de haut-parleur f; ~ **system** n ACOUSTICS, RECORDING système de haut-parleur m

louver n (AmE), **louvre** n (BrE) AUTO persienne f, C&G jalousie f (Fra), louvre m (Bel), CONST persienne f, MECH jalousie f, volet d'aération m, RECORDING *of loudspeaker* persienne f, VEHICLES *body* ouïes de capot f pl

low n GEOL ensellement m, METEO zone de basse pression f ~ **A to B** n TELECOM basse résistance pointe/nuque f; ~ **A to B to earth** n TELECOM basse résistance pointe/nuque/terre f; ~ **A to earth** n TELECOM A-leg basse résistance pointe/terre f; ~ **beams** n pl (AmE) (cf dipped headlights) VEHICLES phares code m pl; ~ **bed trailer** n (BrE) (cf low boy trailer) CONST remorque à fond plat f; ~ **boy trailer** n (AmE) (cf low bed trailer) CONST remorque à fond plat f; ~ **B to earth** n TELECOM B-leg basse résistance nuque/terre f; ~ **capacitance** n ELEC ENG faible capacité f; ~ **coiling index** n SPRINGS indice d'enroulement faible m; ~ **concentration** n ELECTRON faible concentration f; ~ **contrast original** n CINEMAT original bas contraste m; ~ **cost automation technique** n MECH ENG technique d'automatisme à coût réduit f; ~ **cost conversion** n RAD PHYS *solar* conversion à bas coût f; ~ **density** n PROP MAT faible densité f; ~ **density xenon in the Earth's atmosphere** n ASTRON faible densité de xénon dans l'atmosphère terrestre f; ~ **depression** n METEO faible dépression f; ~ **explosive** n MINING explosif lent m, explosif à basse vitesse de détonation m; ~ **gear** n MECH ENG petite multiplication f; ~ **grade** n MINING *of ore* basse teneur f, faible teneur f, pauvreté f, PROP MAT bas titre m; ~ **gradient** n CONST pente faible f; ~ **gravity gasoline** n (AmE) (cf low gravity petrol) AUTO essence lourde f; ~ **gravity petrol** n (BrE) (cf low gravity gasoline) AUTO essence lourde f; ~ **head** n FUELLESS colonne d'eau peu élevée f; ~ **insulation loss** n TELECOM perte d'isolement f; ~ **key** n CINEMAT éclairage faible m; ~ **kiln** n COAL TECH bas fourneau m; ~ **lead gasoline** n (AmE) (cf low lead petrol) AUTO essence à faible teneur en plomb f; ~ **lead petrol** n (BrE) (cf low lead gasoline) AUTO essence à faible

teneur en plomb f; ~ **level of twist** n TEXTILES faible torsion f; ~ **logic level** n ELECTRON niveau logique bas m; ~ **loss** n TELECOM affaiblissement réduit m, atténuation faible f; ~ **pressure** n GAS TECH, PHYS basse pression f; ~ **rate encoding** n (LRE) TELECOM codage à débit réduit m, codage à faible débit m; ~ **reset** n PROD ENG point de réarmement bas m; ~ **resistance** n PHYS résistance faible f, TELECOM faible résistance f; ~ **Reynolds number** n FLUID PHYS nombre de Reynolds faible m; ~ **ring to ground** n TELECOM basse résistance nuque/terre f; ~ **shot** n CINEMAT plan en contre plongée m; ~ **signal level** n ELECTRON bas niveau de signal m; ~ **sulfur content** n (AmE), ~ **sulphur content** n (BrE) PETR TECH *of crude* faible teneur en soufre f; ~ **superheat** n REFRIG faible surchauffe f; ~ **temperature** n REFRIG *below 0c* basse température f; ~ **tenor of ore** n MINING basse teneur de minerai f; ~ **tension** n ELEC *voltage*, ELEC ENG basse tension f; ~ **test gasoline** n (AmE) (cf low test petrol) AUTO essence lourde f; ~ **test petrol** n (BrE) (cf low test gasoline) AUTO essence lourde f; ~ **tide** n FUELLESS, HYDROL marée basse f, NAUT basse mer f, marée basse f, OCEANOG basse mer f; ~ **tip to ground** n TELECOM basse résistance pointe/terre f; ~ **tip to ring** n TELECOM basse résistance pointe/nuque f; ~ **traffic road** n CONST voie à faible circulation f; ~ **vacuum** n PHYS vide bas m, vide peu poussé m, vide primaire m; ~ **visibility landing** n AERONAUT atterrissage par mauvaise visibilité m; ~ **voltage** n (LV) ELEC, ELEC ENG, TELECOM basse tension f; ~ **water** n HYDROL *in river, lake* basses eaux f pl, étiage m, *tide* basse mer f, basses eaux f pl, marée basse f, NAUT *tide* basse mer f, basses eaux f pl, marée basse f, OCEANOG basse mer f

low-alloy: ~ **steel** n METALL acier faiblement allié m

low-altitude: ~ **bombing** n (LAB) AERONAUT bombardement à basse altitude m; ~ **orbit** n SPACE orbite basse f

low-amplitude: ~ **signal** n ELECTRON signal à faible amplitude m

low-angle: ~ **shot** n PHOTO prise de vue en contre-plongée f

low-band: ~ **recording** n TV enregistrement low-band m; ~ **standard** n TV norme à fréquences basses f

low-calorie adj FOOD TECH hypocalorique

low-carbon: ~ **steel** n MECH ENG acier bas carbone m, acier doux m

low-cycle: ~ **fatigue** n CRYSTALL, METALL fatigue oligocyclique f

low-distortion: ~ **modulation** n ELECTRON modulation à faible distorsion f

low-drift: ~ **oscillator** n ELECTRON oscillateur à faible dérive m

Lowell: ~ **light** n CINEMAT lampe Lowell f

low-energy: ~ **antiproton ring** n (LEAR) PART PHYS anneau d'antiprotons de basse énergie m (LEAR); ~ **beam** n ELECTRON faisceau à faible énergie m; ~ **environment** n GEOL milieu sédimentaire à faible énergie m; ~ **focused ion beam** n RAD PHYS faisceau d'ions mis au point de faible énergie m; ~ **laser** n ELECTRON laser à faible énergie m; ~ **nuclear physics** n PART PHYS physique nucléaire à basse énergie f; ~ **radiation** n RAD PHYS rayonnement de faible énergie m; ~ **single-frequency laser** n RAD PHYS laser monofréquence de faible énergie m; ~ **transverse jet** n RAD PHYS *particle research* jet de faible énergie transversal m

lower[1] adj GEOL inférieur

lower:[2] **~ annealing temperature** n C&G température inférieure de recuit f; **~ bainite** n METALL bainite inférieure f; **~ case** n PRINT bas-de-casse m; **~ control limit** n QUALITY limite inférieure de contrôle f; **~ culmination** n ASTRON culmination inférieure f; **~ deck** n NAUT pont inférieur m; **~ harmonic** n ELECTRON harmonique inférieur m, sous-harmonique inférieur m; **~ highwater** n OCEANOG pleine mer inférieure f; **~ limit** n TELECOM limite inférieure f; **~ limit of detectability** n POLLUTION limite de détection f, limite inférieure de détection f, quantité minimale détectable f, sensibilité-limite de détection f; **~ link of rotor shaft** n AERONAUT helicopter branche de compas mâle f; **~ loop** n CINEMAT boucle inférieure f; **~ nibble** n PROD ENG quartet inférieur m; **~ pantograph final warning sign** n RAIL signal de fin de parcours m; **~ ply** n COATINGS couche inférieure f; **~ printing** n PRINT impression située au verso f, impression située en dessous f; **~ quality of service** n TELECOM qualité dégradée f; **~ roll** n MECH ENG rolling mill cylindre femelle m; **~ shaft** n AUTO demi-arbre inférieur m; **~ shroud** n NAUT rigging bas hauban m; **~ side** n PRINT côté inférieur m, verso m; **~ sideband** n (LSB) ELECTRON, TELECOM bande latérale inférieure f; **~ sideband filter** n ELECTRON filtre de bande latérale inférieure m; **~ spool** n CINEMAT bobine réceptrice f; **~ storage basin** n FUELLESS réservoir de stockage inférieur m; **~ subfield** n TELECOM sous-champ inférieur m; **~ surface** n AERONAUT, PHYS of wing intrados m; **~ tank** n AUTO réservoir inférieur m; **~ track** n HYDROL of river tracé inférieur m; **~ workings** n pl MINING chantier inférieur m; **~ yield point** n METALL limite élastique inférieure f

lower[3] vt CONST water table abaisser, ELEC ENG voltage dévolter, NAUT boats amener, mettre à la mer, sails affaler, amener, SAFETY load abaisser, descendre

lowering n PHYS of temperature abaissement m; **~ cradle** n PAPER TECH abaisse-bobines m; **~ table** n PAPER TECH abaisse-bobines m

lower-level: ~ service n TELECOM service de bas niveau m

lower-order: ~ path adaptation n (LPA) TELECOM adaptation de conduit d'ordre inférieur f; **~ path connection** n (LPC, higher-order path connection) TELECOM connexion de conduit d'ordre inférieur f; **~ path termination** n (LPT) TELECOM terminaison de conduit d'ordre inférieur f

lowest: ~ achievable emission rate n POLLUTION taux d'émission le plus bas possible m; **~ common denominator** n (LCD) MATH plus petit commun multiple des dénominateurs m (PPCMD); **~ common multiple** n (LCM) COMP, MATH plus petit commun multiple m (PPCM); **~ hourly traffic** n TRANSP heure creuse f; **~ usable frequency** n (LUF) SPACE fréquence minimale utilisable f

low-fat adj FOOD TECH à faible teneur en matière grasse

low-freezing: ~ dynamite n MINING dynamite antigel f

low-frequency n (LF) ELEC wave, ELEC ENG, ELECTRON, RAD PHYS, TELECOM basse fréquence f (BF); **~ amplification** n ELECTRON amplification BF f, amplification basse fréquence f; **~ amplifier** n ELECTRON amplificateur basse fréquence m; **~ compensation** n ELECTRON correction des basses fréquences f; **~ cut-off** n RECORDING coupure en basse fréquence f; **~ filter** n ELECTRON, RECORDING filtre BF m, filtre basse fréquence m; **~ furnace** n ELEC ENG four BF m, four à basse fréquence m; **~ generator** n ELEC, ELECTRON générateur à basse fréquence m; **~ horn loudspeaker** n

RECORDING haut-parleur à pavillon pour basse fréquence m; **~ image** n SPACE image de basse fréquence f; **~ induction heater** n ELEC ENG inducteur à basse fréquence m; **~ induction heating** n ELEC ENG chauffage BF m, chauffage à basse fréquence m; **~ oscillator** n ELECTRON oscillateur basse fréquence m; **~ response** n ELECTRON réponse aux basses fréquences f; **~ signal** n ELECTRON signal BF m, signal à basse fréquence m

low-gain: ~ amplifier n ELECTRON amplificateur à faible gain m

low-grade: ~ metamorphism n GEOL under low temperatures and pressures épimétamorphisme m

low-high-low: ~ doping profile n ELECTRON profil de dopage en cloche m

low-insertion: ~ force connector n ELEC ENG connecteur à faible effort m; **~ loss** n TELECOM perte d'insertion f

low-leakage: ~ diode n ELECTRON diode à faibles fuites f

low-level: ~ amplification n ELECTRON amplification à bas niveau f; **~ amplifier** n ELECTRON amplificateur de signaux à bas niveau m; **~ DC I-O line** n PROD ENG ligne d'E-S à tension continue bas niveau f; **~ DC out** n PROD ENG tension de sortie continue bas niveau f; **~ DC voltage** n ELEC, PROD ENG tension continue bas niveau f; **~ device** n ELECTRON dispositif à bas niveau m; **~ fault** n PROD ENG défaut de bas niveau m; **~ injection** n ELECTRON injection à bas niveau f; **~ language** n COMP langage bas de gamme m, langage orienté machine m; **~ modulation** n ELECTRON modulation à bas niveau f; **~ signal** n ELECTRON signal à bas niveau m, PROD ENG signal de bas niveau m; **~ transistor** n ELECTRON transistor pour signaux à bas niveau m; **~ video** n TV niveau vidéo faible m; **~ warning light** n MECH ENG voyant de baisse de niveau m; **~ waste** n RECYCLING déchets de faible activité m pl

low-loss: ~ cable n ELEC supply câble à faibles pertes m; **~ dielectric** n ELEC diélectrique à faible pertes m; **~ fiber** n (AmE), **~ fibre** n (BrE) OPT fibre de faible atténuation f, fibre à faible perte f; **~ glass** n C&G verre à faibles pertes diélectriques m; **~ insulator** n ELEC ENG isolant à faibles pertes m

low-manganese: ~ steel n PROP MAT acier à faible teneur de manganèse m

low-noise: ~ amplification n ELECTRON amplification à faible bruit f; **~ amplifier** n (LNA) ELECTRON, SPACE communications, TELECOM amplificateur à faible bruit m; **~ engineering** n MECH ENG étude du travail avec bruit réduit f; **~ preamplifier** n ELECTRON préamplificateur à faible bruit m, RAD PHYS amplificateur à faible bruit m

low-order[1] adj DP de droite, de poids faible

low-order:[2] **~ bit** n COMP bit de droite m; **~ filter** n ELECTRON filtre d'ordre peu élevé m; **~ harmonic** n ELECTRON harmonique de rang peu élevé m; **~ position** n COMP, DP position de droite f

low-pass n AERONAUT passe-bas m; **~ band** n TELECOM bande basse f; **~ filter** n (cf high-pass filter) COMP, DP, ELEC, ELECTRON, PHYS, RECORDING, TELECOM, TV filtre passe-bas m; **~ filtering** n (cf high-pass filtering) ELECTRON filtrage passe-bas m; **~ response** n ELECTRON réponse en passe-bas f; **~ sampled data filter** n ELECTRON filtre passe-bas pour signaux échantillonnés m; **~ section** n ELECTRON cellule passe-bas f

low-plasticity: ~ clay n C&G argile maigre f

low-power[1] adj ELEC ENG de faible puissance

low-power:[2] **~ diode** n ELECTRON diode pour signaux à bas niveau f; **~ distress transmitter** n (LPDT) TELE-

COM émetteur de détresse de faible puissance *m*; ~ **laser diode** *n* TELECOM diode laser à faible puissance *f*

low-pressure ~ **alarm** *n* PROD ENG alarme de basse pression *f*; ~ **area** *n* METEO zone de basse pression *f*; ~ **blowpipe** *n* CONST *welding* chalumeau à basse pression *m*; ~ **compressor** *n* MECH ENG compresseur axial *m*; ~ **controller** *n* REFRIG régulateur basse pression *m*; ~ **filter** *n* PROD ENG filtre basse pression *m*; ~ **float valve** *n* REFRIG soupape basse pression à flotteur *f*; ~ **flushing** *n* MAR POLL lavage basse pression *m*, lessivage à basse pression *m*; ~ **fuel filter** *n* AERONAUT filtre carburant basse pression *m*; ~ **gas burner** *n* HEAT ENG brûleur de gaz à basse pression *m*; ~ **heating** *n* HEAT ENG chauffage à basse pression *m*; ~ **hot water boiler** *n* HEATING chaudière à basse pression *f*; ~ **hot water system** *n* HEATING installation de chauffage d'eau à basse pression *f*; ~ **mercury lamp** *n* ELEC lampe à vapeur de mercure à basse pression *f*; ~ **piston compressor** *n* MECH ENG compresseur à piston à basse pression *m*; ~ **safety cutout** *n* REFRIG pressostat de sécurité de basse pression *m*; ~ **vacuum pump** *n* MECH ENG pompe à vide élevé *f*; ~ **zone** *n* METEO zone de basse pression *f*

low-profile: ~ **bezel** *n* PROD ENG collerette bas profil *f*; ~ **open-end wrench** *n* MECH ENG clé à fourche extra-plate *f*

low-rank: ~ **graywacke** *n* (AmE), ~ **greywacke** *n* (BrE) GEOL grauwacke sans feldspath *f*

low-shaft: ~ **furnace** *n* COAL TECH four de type bas *m*

low-shrink: ~ **base** *n* CINEMAT support à faible retrait *m*

low-slip: ~ **film** *n* PRINT film non glissant *m*

low-solid: ~ **mud** *n* PETR TECH *drilling* boue à faible teneur en solides *f*

low-speed *n* MECH ENG allure lente *f*, faible vitesse *f*, petite vitesse *f*, TELECOM vitesse faible *f*; ~ **camera** *n* CINEMAT caméra avec intervallomètre *f*; ~ **diesel engine** *n* NAUT moteur diesel lent *m*; ~ **electric motor** *n* ELEC ENG moteur électrique à faible vitesse *m*; ~ **engine** *n* NAUT diesel lent *m*; ~ **modem** *n* ELECTRON modem lent *m*, modem à faible vitesse de transmission *m*; ~ **photography** *n* CINEMAT prise de vue au ralenti *f*

low-stop: ~ **filter** *n* *(cf high-stop filter)* MECH ENG filtre passe-haut *m*

low-temperature: ~ **compartment** *n* REFRIG compartiment à basse température *m*; ~ **cooling installation** *n* MECH ENG *for ships and transporters* installation frigorifique à basse température *f*; ~ **display case** *n* REFRIG vitrine à basse température *f*; ~ **insulation** *n* THERMOD calorifugeage frigorifique *m*; ~ **resistance** *n* P&R résistance à température basse *f*; ~ **sinking** *n* THERMOD fonçage par congélation *m*; ~ **techniques** *n pl* THERMOD techniques cryogéniques *f pl*; ~ **thermometer** *n* THERMOD cryomètre *f*

low-tensile: ~ **carbon steel tube** *n* HEATING tube d'acier au carbone à basse tension *m*

low-tension: ~ **detonator** *n* MINING détonateur BI *m*, détonateur à BI *m*, détonateur à basse intensité *m*

low-thrust: ~ **motor** *n* SPACE *spacecraft* moteur à faible poussée *m*

low-to-high: ~ **transition** *n* ELECTRON transition montante *f*

low-torque[1] *adj* PROD ENG à couple bas

low-torque:[2] ~ **operation** *n* PROD ENG fonctionnement à couple bas *m*

low-velocity: ~ **layer** *n* PETR zone altérée *f*

low-volatile: ~ **coal** *n* COAL TECH charbon maigre *m*

low-voltage: ~ **cable** *n* ELEC *supply* câble à basse tension *m*; ~ **electrostatic loudspeaker** *n* RECORDING haut-parleur électrostatique à basse tension *m*; ~ **installation** *n* ELEC ENG installation à basse tension *m*; ~ **network** *n* ELEC *supply* réseau basse tension *m*; ~ **winding** *n* ELEC enroulement à basse tension *m*

low-water: ~ **discharge** *n* WATER SUPP débit d'étiage *m*; ~ **level** *n* WATER SUPP niveau d'étiage *m*; ~ **mark** *n* CONST marque des basses eaux *f*, plus basses eaux *f pl*, HYDROL *of river* étiage *m*, NAUT *tide*, OCEANOG laisse de basse mer *f*

low-wing: ~ **plane** *n* AERONAUT avion à aile basse *m*

low-yield: ~ **clay** *n* PETR argile à faible rendement *f*; ~ **region** *n* ELECTRON partie à faible rendement *f*

lox *n* SPACE oxygène liquide *m*

loxygen *n* CHEM oxygène liquide *m*

LP: ~ **mode** *n* *(linearly polarized mode)* OPT, TELECOM mode LP *m* *(mode à polarisation rectiligne)*

LPA *abbr* *(lower-order path adaptation)* TELECOM adaptation de conduit d'ordre inférieur *f*

LPC *abbr* TELECOM *(linear predicting coding)* codage prédictif linéaire *m*, TELECOM *(lower-order path connection)* connexion de conduit d'ordre inférieur *f*

LPDT *abbr* *(low-power distress transmitter)* TELECOM émetteur de détresse de faible puissance *m*

LPG[1] *abbr* GAS TECH *(liquefied petroleum gas)*, HEAT ENG *(liquefied petroleum gas)*, PETR TECH *(liquefied petroleum gas)*, THERMOD *(liquid petroleum gas)*, TRANSP *(liquified petroleum gas)* GPL *(gaz de pétrole liquéfié)*

LPG:[2] ~ **engine** *n* AUTO moteur à gaz de pétrole liquéfié *m*; ~ **tanker** *n* NAUT transporteur de gaz de pétrole liquéfié *m*

LPM *abbr* *(lines per minute)* COMP, DP LPM *(lignes par minute)*

LPT *abbr* *(lower-order path termination)* TELECOM terminaison de conduit d'ordre inférieur *f*

LQ *abbr* *(letter quality)* COMP, PRINT qualité courrier *f*

Lr *(lawrencium)* CHEM Lr *(lawrencium)*

LRC *abbr* *(longitudinal redundancy check)* COMP contrôle par redondance longitudinale *m*

LRE *abbr* *(low rate encoding)* TELECOM codage à débit réduit *m*, codage à faible débit *m*

LRT *abbr* *(light rail transport)* RAIL *vehicles* métro léger *m*

LRU *abbr* *(line replaceable unit)* ELEC ENG unité remplaçable en ligne *f*

LSB *abbr* COMP *(least significant bit)* bit de plus faible poids *m*, bit de poids faible *m*, ELECTRON *(lower sideband)* bande latérale inférieure *f*, PROD ENG *(least significant bit)* bit de poids le plus faible *m*, TELECOM *(lower sideband)* bande latérale inférieure *f*

LSD *abbr* *(least significant digit)* COMP, DP chiffre de poids le plus faible *m*, PRODUCTION chiffre de poids faible *m*

L-section *n* ELECTRON cellule en L *f*

L-shell *n* PHYS *atom* couche L *f*

LSI[1] *abbr* *(large-scale integration)* COMP, DP, ELECTRON, NAUT, PHYS, TELECOM LSI *(intégration à grande échelle)*

LSI:[2] ~ **circuit** *n* PHYS, TELECOM circuit LSI *m*

L-split: ~ **system** *n* AUTO circuit de freinage double circuit *m*

LT *abbr* *(line termination)* PRINT, TELECOM terminaison de ligne *f*

LTE *abbr (line termination equipment)* COMP équipement de terminaison de ligne *m*

Lu *(lutetium, lutecium)* CHEM Lu *(lutétium)*

lubber: **~ line** *n* AERONAUT *of compass*, NAUT, OCEANOG, SPACE ligne de foi *f*

lubricant *n* AUTO, C&G, CONST, MECH *materials*, P&R *substance*, PETR TECH lubrifiant *m*, PROD ENG huile de graissage *f*, lubrifiant *m*, TEXTILES lubrifiant *m*

lubricate *vt* MECH lubrifier, PROD ENG graisser, lubrifier, huiler, TEXTILES lubrifier

lubricated[1] *adj* GAS TECH lubrifié

lubricated:[2] **~ tape** *n* RECORDING bande lubrifié *f*; **~ thread torque** *n* MECH ENG couple de serrage avec lubrifiant *m*

lubricating *n* PROD ENG graissage *m*, lubrification *f*; **~ nipple** *n* MECH graisseur *m*; **~ oil** *n* AUTO huile de graissage *f*, PROD ENG huile de graissage *f*, huile à graisser *f*, VEHICLES huile lubrifiante *f*; **~ pump** *n* MECH pompe à huile *f*; **~ pump and pipe connections** *n* PROD ENG *lathe* pompe de lubrification et sa tuyauterie *f*; **~ rack** *n* PROD ENG rampe de distribution *f*, rampe de graissage *f*; **~ system** *n* AUTO système de graissage *m*, MECH ENG circuit de graissage *m*; **~ unit** *n* CONST unité de lubrification *f*

lubrication *n* AUTO, PAPER TECH graissage *m*; **~ chart** *n* MECH tableau de graissage *m*; **~ fitting** *n* MECH ENG raccord de graissage *m*; **~ oil** *n* PROD ENG huile de graissage *f*; **~ system** *n* PROD ENG système de graissage *m*

lubricator *n* PROD ENG graisseur *m*

lubrifaction *n* PROD ENG lubrification *f*

lubrification *n* PROD ENG, PROP MAT, REFRIG, VEHICLES graissage *m*, lubrification *f*

Lucite *n* (TM) P&R *plastic* plexiglas *m* (MD), plastique acrylique *m*

LUF *abbr (lowest usable frequency)* SPACE fréquence minimale utilisable *f*

luff[1] *n* NAUT *sail* envergure *f*, guindant *m*; **~ tackle** *n* CONST palan simple *m*

luff[2] *vti* NAUT lofer

luffing: **~ crane** *n* CONST grue à volée basculante *f*, grue à volée variable *f*

lug *n* C&G repère de centrage *m*, MECH oreille *f*, patte *f*, MECH ENG ergot *m*, oreille *f*, NAUT *shipbuilding* taquet *m*, PROD ENG cosse *f*, patte *f*, *of foundry flask* oreille *f*; **~ kit** *n* PROD ENG kit de cosses *m*; **~ nut** *n* (AmE) *(cf wheel nut)* AUTO car écrou de roue *m*

luggage: **~ compartment** *n* (BrE) *(cf baggage compartment)* TRANSP compartiment à bagages *m*, VEHICLES *body* coffre à bagages *m*; **~ trolley** *n* (BrE) TRANSP tracteur à bagages *m*; **~ van** *n* (BrE) *(cf baggage car)* RAIL *vehicles*, TRANSP fourgon à bagages *m*

lull *n* NAUT *in storm* accalmie *f*

lumberback: **~ checks** *n* TEXTILES carreaux quadrillés *m pl*

lumen *n* METR, PHYS lumen *m*

lumenized: **~ lens** *n* INSTRUMENT lentille antireflet *f*, lentille à couche antireflet *f*

lumenizing *n* COATINGS revêtement par couches antiréfléchissantes *m*

lumenmeter *n* PHYS lumenmètre *m*

luminaire *n* ELEC *lighting* luminaire *m*

luminance *n* ELEC ENG *density* densité de flux lumineux émis *f*, luminance *f*, ELECTRON, PHYS luminance *f*, PRINT niveau de luminosité *m*, SPACE *communications*, TELECOM, TV luminance *f*; **~ amplifier** *n* ELECTRON

amplificateur de luminance *m*; **~ carrier output** *n* TV niveau de sortie de luminance *m*; **~ delay** *n* TV retard de luminance *m*; **~ difference signal** *n* TV signal de différence de luminance *m*; **~ ratio** *n* RAD PHYS rapport des luminances *m*; **~ signal** *n* SPACE *communications*, TV signal de luminance *m*

luminescence *n* CHEM *process*, ELEC ENG, PHYS, RAD PHYS, TV luminescence *f*; **~ quantum yield** *n* RAD PHYS rendement quantique de la luminescence *m*; **~ threshold** *n* TV seuil de luminescence *m*

luminescent[1] *adj* CHEM *substance*, ELEC ENG luminescent

luminescent:[2] **~ diode** *n* ELECTRON diode luminescente *f*; **~ discharge** *n* GAS TECH décharge luminescente *f*; **~ glass** *n* C&G verre luminescent *m*; **~ paint** *n* COLOURS peinture luminescente *f*; **~ pigment** *n* COLOURS pigment luminescent *m*

luminosity *n* ASTRON, PART PHYS, PHYS luminosité *f*; **~ coefficient** *n* RAD PHYS facteur d'efficacité lumineuse *m*; **~ factor** *n* RAD PHYS facteur de luminosité *m*; **~ lifetime** *n* RAD PHYS durée de vie lumineuse *f*

luminous: **~ and colored protective clothing** *n* (AmE), **~ and coloured protective clothing** *n* (BrE) SAFETY vêtements de signalisation *m pl*; **~ clothing** *n* SAFETY vêtements lumineux *m pl*; **~ cloud** *n* METEO nuage lumineux *m*, nuage noctilumineux *m*, nuage nocturne lumineux *m*; **~ efficacy** *n* PHYS efficacité lumineuse *f*; **~ energy** *n* WAVE PHYS énergie lumineuse *f*; **~ exitance** *n* PHYS exitance *f*, lumineuse *f*; **~ flux** *n* ELEC ENG, PHYS flux lumineux *m*; **~ intensity** *n* ELEC ENG, PHYS, RAD PHYS intensité lumineuse *f*; **~ paint** *n* COLOURS peinture luminescente *f*; **~ source** *n* RAD PHYS source lumineuse *f*

Lummer-Brodhun: **~ photometer** *n* PHYS photomètre de Lummer et Brodhun *m*

lumnite *n* CHEM ciment fondu *m*

lump *n* CONST bloc *m*, gros morceau *m*, masse *f*, motte *f*, PAPER TECH maton *m*; **~ breaker** *n* PAPER TECH rouleau presseur *m*; **~ coal** *n* COAL TECH charbon en gros morceaux *m*, criblés 80 *m*; **~ glass** *n* C&G bloc *m*; **~ limestone** *n* GEOL calcaire graveleux *m*; **~ ore** *n* MINING gros *m pl*; **~ sugar** *n* FOOD TECH sucre en morceaux *m*; **~ sum freight** *n* PETR TECH *commerce, shipping* affrètement en travers *m*, affrètement à forfait *m*

lumped[1] *adj* PHYS *circuit element* concentré, localisé

lumped:[2] **~ capacitance** *n* ELEC *capacitor* capacité concentrée *f*, ELEC ENG capacité localisée *f*; **~ capacitor** *n* ELEC ENG condensateur localisé *m*; **~ element** *n* ELEC ENG constante localisée *f*; **~ element circuit** *n* ELEC ENG circuit à constantes localisées *m*

lumpless: **~ small coal** *n* COAL TECH menu sortant *m*

lumpy: **~ demand** *n* PROD ENG besoins en dents de scie *m pl*, demande discontinue *f*, demande en dents de scie *f*, demande intermittente *f*

lunar[1] *adj* ASTRON lunaire

lunar:[2] **~ anomalistic month** *n* ASTRON mois anomalistique lunaire *m*; **~ core** *n* ASTRON noyau lunaire *m*; **~ craters** *n pl* ASTRON cratères de la lune *m pl*; **~ eclipse** *n* ASTRON éclipse de la Lune *f*; **~ highlands** *n pl* ASTRON montagnes lunaires *f pl*; **~ logistics vehicle** *n* (LLV) SPACE *spacecraft* véhicule logistique lunaire *m*; **~ maria** *n pl* ASTRON mers lunaires *f pl*; **~ orbit** *n* SPACE orbite lunaire *f*; **~ probe** *n* SPACE sonde lunaire *f*; **~ seismic activity** *n* ASTRON activité sismique lunaire *f*; **~ wave** *n* OCEANOG onde lunaire *f*

lunation *n* ASTRON lunaison *f*

lunisolar: ~ **potential** n SPACE potentiel lunisolaire m; ~ **wave** n OCEANOG onde lunisolaire f

lunnite n MINERAL lunnite f

lupuline n CHEM lupuline f

Lupus n ASTRON Loup m

lurch[1] n NAUT *motion of ship* coup de roulis m, embardée f

lurch[2] vi NAUT *ship* faire une embardée

lure n OCEANOG leurre m

lussatite n MINERAL lussatite f

luster n (AmE) *see lustre*

lusterless adj (AmE) *see lustreless*

lustre n (BrE) C&G reflet métallique m, MINERAL éclat m, TEXTILES brillance f, éclat m ~ **finish** n (BrE) COATINGS apprêt à l'eau m

lustreless adj (BrE) PROP MAT, TEXTILES terne

lustrometer n PAPER TECH lustromètre m

lustrous[1] adj PROP MAT lustré, TEXTILES chatoyant

lustrous:[2] ~ **schists** n pl GEOL schistes lustrés m pl

LUT abbr *(local user terminal)* TELECOM station terminale d'usager local f

lutation n PROD ENG lutation f

lute n PROD ENG lut m

lutecium n *(Lu)* CHEM lutétium m *(Lu)*

lutein n CHEM lutéine f

luteocobaltic adj CHEM lutéocobaltique

luteol n CHEM lutéol m

luteolin n CHEM lutéoline f

luteoline n CHEM lutéoline f

lutetium n *(Lu)* CHEM lutétium m *(Lu)*

lutidine n CHEM lutidine f

lutidinic adj CHEM lutidinique

lutidone n CHEM lutidone f

lutite n GEOL lutite f

lux n METR lux m, PHOTO bougie-mètre f, lux m, PHYS lux m; ~ **value** n PHOTO valeur de lux f

LV[1] abbr ELEC *(low voltage)*, ELEC ENG *(low voltage)* basse tension f, OPT *(laser vision)* laservision f, TELECOM *(low voltage)* basse tension f

LV:[2] ~ **disc** n (BrE) OPT disque laservision m; ~ **disk** n (AmE) *see LV disc* ~ **player** n OPT lecteur laservision m

LWHR abbr *(light water hybrid reactor)* NUCLEAR réacteur hybride à eau légère m

lx abbr *(lux)* METR lx *(lux)*

lye n CHEM lessive f

lying: ~ **shaft** n MECH ENG arbre de transmission horizontal m

Lyman: ~ **series** n PHYS, RAD PHYS série de Lyman f

Lynx n ASTRON *constellation* Lynx m

lyogel n CHEM lyogel m

lyophilic adj CHEM lyophile

lyophilizate n REFRIG lyophilisat m

lyophilization n CHEM TECH dessiccation par congélation f, lyophilisation f; ~ **flask** n C&G flacon pour lyophilisation m

lyophily n CHEM lyophillie f

lyophobic adj CHEM insoluble, lyophobe

lyosol n CHEM lyosol m

Lyra n ASTRON Lyre f

lyre-shaped: ~ **bellcrank** n AERONAUT *flight controls* lyre f

lysergic adj CHEM *acid* lysergique

lysine n CHEM lysine f

lysolecithin n CHEM lyosolécithine f

lysophosphatide n CHEM lysophosphatide m

lyxonic adj CHEM lyxonique

lyxose n CHEM lyxose m

M

m *abbr* (milli-) METR m *(milli-)*

M[1] *abbr* (mega-) METR M *(méga-)*

M:[2] ~ **and E track** *n* (*Music and Effects track*) CINEMAT bande son internationale *f*, piste son internationale *f*

mA *abbr* (milliampere) ELEC, ELEC ENG mA *(milliampère)*

MA *abbr* (medium adaptator) TELECOM adaptateur de support *m*

maar *n* GEOL *volcanic explosion crater* maar *m*

MAC *abbr* AERONAUT (*mean aerodynamic chord*) CAM (*corde aérodynamique moyenne*), POLLUTION (*maximum allowable concentration*) concentration maximale admissible *f*, TELECOM (*medium access control*) commande d'accès au support *f*, contrôle d'accès au média *m*

macadam *n* CONST macadam *m*; ~ **spreader** *n* TRANSP épandeur-régleur-dameur *m*

macadamization *n* CONST macadamisage *m*, macadamisation *f*

mace: ~ **oil** *n* FOOD TECH huile de macis *f*, huile de muscade *f*

macerate *vt* CHEM, FOOD TECH macérer

maceration *n* CHEM macération *f*

macerator *n* CHEM macérateur *m*

Mach: ~ **compensator** *n* AERONAUT correcteur de Mach *m*; ~ **number** *n* AERONAUT, PHYS nombre de Mach *m*

Mach's: ~ **principle** *n* PHYS principe de Mach *m*

machinability *n* MECH ENG, PROP MAT usinabilité *f*

machine[1] *n* AUTO, COMP, DP, ELEC ENG, MECH ENG, PAPER TECH, PROD ENG machine *f*; ~ **bolt** *n* MECH ENG boulon mécanicien *m*, boulon rectifié *m*, boulon mécanique *m*;~ **cage** *n* SAFETY *guard* enceinte de protection de machine *f*, protecteur de machine *m*; ~ **center** *n* (AmE), ~ **centre** *n* (BrE) MECH ENG centre d'usinage *m*; ~ **check** *n* COMP erreur machine *f*, DP contrôle automatique *m*, erreur machine *f*; ~ **chest** *n* PAPER TECH cuvier de machine *m*, cuvier de tête *m*, PRINT *papermaking* cuvier de tête *m*; ~ **coal mining** *n* COAL TECH abattage mécanique du charbon *m*; off~ **coater** *n* PAPER TECH coucheuse hors machine *f*; ~ **code** *n* COMP, DP code machine *m*; ~ **cutting** *n* MECH ENG découpage mécanique *m*; ~ **cycle** *n* COMP, DP cycle machine *m*; ~ **deckle** *n* PAPER TECH largeur de toile utilisée *f*; ~ **die plate** *n* MECH ENG filière à la machine *f*; ~ **direction** *n* PAPER TECH largeur de toile utilisée *f*, sens machine *m*, PRINT sens machine *m*; ~ **drilling** *n* MINING forage mécanique *m*, perforation mécanique *f*; ~ **error** *n* COMP, DP erreur machine *f*; ~ **fence** *n* SAFETY *guard* barrière protectrice pour machine *f*, clôture de machine *f*; ~ **fill** *n* PAPER TECH *of paper machine* largeur utile *f*; ~ **finishing** *n* MECH ENG finissage mécanique *m*; ~ **for fine ceramics** *n* C&G machine pour la fabrication de céramique fine *f*; ~ **for making handles** *n* C&G machine à faire des poignées *f*; ~ **for potentially explosive atmosphere** *n* COAL TECH machine pour atmosphère grisouteuse *f*; ~ **guard** *n* SAFETY couvre-roue *m*, gardes de machine *f pl*, protection de machine *f*; ~ **gun** *n* MILIT mitrailleuse *f*; ~ **instruction** *n* COMP, DP instruc-

tion machine *f*; ~ **instruction code** *n* COMP, DP code d'instructions machine *m*; ~ **language** *n* COMP langage machine *m*; ~ **leader** *n* CINEMAT amorce de chargement *f*; ~ **learning** *n* COMP apprentissage automatique *m*, apprentissage d'une machine *m*; ~ **lying idle** *n* MECH ENG machine dans l'inaction *f*; ~ **motion** *n* PROD ENG mouvement de machine *m*; ~ **oil** *n* MECH ENG huile pour mouvement *f*, huile pour mécanisme *f*; ~ **operation** *n* COMP, DP opération machine *f*; ~ **processor** *n* PHOTO développeuse automatique à rouleau *f*; ~ **punch** *n* MECH ENG poinçon à la machine *m*; ~ **room** *n* RECORDING salle des défileurs *f*, salle des machines *f*; ~ **run** *n* MECH ENG passage machine *m*; ~ **running empty** *n* PROD ENG machine marchant à blanc *f*, machine marchant à vide *f*; ~ **running light** *n* MECH ENG machine marchant à blanc *f*, machine marchant à vide *f*; ~ **running on no load** *n* MECH ENG machine marchant à blanc *f*, machine marchant à vide *f*; ~ **running under load** *n* MECH ENG machine marchant chargée *f*; ~ **screw** *n* MECH ENG, PROD ENG vis mécanique *f*, vis à métaux *f*; ~ **shutdown** *n* PROD ENG arrêt de machine *m*; ~ **shutdown circuit** *n* PROD ENG circuit d'arrêt de la machine *m*; ~ **speed** *n* C&G cadence de distribution *f*; ~ **splicer** *n* CINEMAT colleuse à pédale *f*; ~ **start-up** *n* C&G trempe *f*; ~ **status** *n* MECH ENG état de la machine *m*; ~ **stop** *n* C&G arrêt de machine *m*; ~ **system shutdown** *n* PROD ENG arrêt du système de la machine *m*; ~ **tap** *n* MECH ENG taraud pour machines *m*; ~ **time** *n* COMP, DP temps machine *m*; ~ **tool** *n* MECH, MECH ENG machine-outil *f*; ~ **tool brake** *n* MECH ENG frein de machine-outil *m*; ~ **tool design** *n* MECH ENG *ergonomics* étude des machines-outils *f*; ~ **tool scales** *n pl* MECH ENG *circular, divided* échelle divisée ronde pour machine-outils *f*; ~ **tool spindle** *n* MECH ENG broche de machine-outil *f*; ~ **tray** *n* C&G utile de la machine *f*; ~ **utilization degree** *n* PROD ENG taux d'utilisation machine *m*; ~ **vice** *n* (BrE) MECH ENG *working in parallel slides* étau-tiroir *m*; ~ **vise** *n* (AmE) *see machine vice*; ~ **vision verification** *n* PACKAGING *of production quality* vérification visuelle *f*; ~ **width** *n* PRINT largeur de machine *f*; ~ **with closed-circuit ventilation** *n* MECH ENG machine ventilée en circuit fermé *f*; ~ **with open-circuit ventilation** *n* MECH ENG machine ventilée en circuit ouvert *f*; ~ **work** *n* MECH ENG travail mécanique *m*

machine[2] *vt* MECH usiner, PROD ENG travailler, usiner, *casting* usiner

machine-coated[1] *adj* PACKAGING couché machine

machine-coated:[2] ~ **paper** *n* PACKAGING papier couché machine *m*

machined[1] *adj* MECH usiné

machined:[2] ~ **circular plate** *n* MECH ENG galet usiné *m*; ~ **rectangular plate** *n* MECH ENG plaque usinée *f*; ~ **surface** *n* MECH surface usinée *f*

machined-all-over *adj* MECH usiné partout

machine-dependent *adj* COMP, DP dépendant de la machine

machine-divided: ~ **machine tool scale** *n* MECH ENG échelle pour machine-outil divisée par machine *f*

machine-finished [1] *adj* PRINT fini machine

machine-finished: [2] **~ paper** *n* PACKAGING papier fini machine *m*, PRINT papier apprêté *m*; **~ paperboard** *n* (*MF paperboard*) PAPER TECH papier carton apprêté *m*

machine-flush *vt* MECH ENG araser

machine-glazed: **~ board** *n* (*MG board*) PAPER TECH carton frictionné *m*; **~ cylinder** *n* (*MG cylinder*) PAPER TECH frictionneur *m*, frictionneur sécheur *m*; **~ paper** *n* (*MG paper*) PACKAGING, PAPER TECH, PRINT papier frictionné *m*

machine-independent *adj* COMP, DP indépendant de la machine

machine-made: **~ board** *n* PACKAGING carton mécanique *m*; **~ nut** *n pl* MECH ENG écrou décolleté *m*

machine-oriented *adj* COMP, DP orienté machine

machine-readable [1] *adj* COMP, DP lisible par machine

machine-readable: [2] **~ data** *n pl* COMP, DP données lisibles par ordinateur *f pl*

machinery *n* MECH ENG machinerie *f*, machines *f pl*, outillage *m*, pièces *f pl*; **~ hazards** *n pl* SAFETY dangers des machines *m pl*, dangers dûs aux machines *m pl*

machining *n* MECH, MECH ENG, PROD ENG usinage *m*; **~ allowance** *n* PROD ENG *founding* surépaisseur pour usinage *f*; **~ center** *n* (AmE), **~ centre** *n* (BrE) MECH centre d'usinage *m*

machinist *n* PROD ENG *person* machiniste *m*

machmeter *n* AERONAUT machmètre *m*

macle *n* MINERAL macle *f*

maclurin *n* CHEM maclurine *f*

MacPherson: **~ strut** *n* AUTO jambe de suspension *f*, suspension MacPherson *f*, VEHICLES jambe de force *f*, jambe de suspension *f*; **~ strut front suspension** *n* AUTO suspension avant du type MacPherson *f*

macro *n* COMP, DP macro *m*; **~ control** *n* TRANSP macro-régulation *f*; **~ hardness** *n* MECH ENG macrodureté *f*; **~ lens** *n* CINEMAT objectif avec mise au point très rapprochée *m*, objectif macro *m*

macro-assembler *n* COMP, DP macroassembleur *m*

macrobend *n* ELEC ENG macrocourbure *f*; **~ loss** *n* OPT, TELECOM affaiblissement par macrocourbures *m*

macrobending *n* OPT, TELECOM macrocourbures *f pl*

macroclimate *n* METEO macroclimat *m*

macrocomponent *n* PROP MAT *gravimetric analysis* macroconstituant *m*

macrocyclic *adj* CHEM macrocyclique

macro-instruction *n* (*macro*) COMP, DP macroinstruction *f*

macromodular: **~ steam generator** *n* NUCLEAR générateur de vapeur macromodulaire *m*

macromolecular [1] *adj* CHEM macromoléculaire

macromolecular: [2] **~ dispersion** *n* FOOD TECH dispersion colloïdale *f*, dispersion macromoléculaire *f*

macromolecule *n* CHEM, P&R macromolécule *f*

macropolymer *n* CHEM macropolymère *m*

macroprocessor *n* COMP, DP macroprocesseur *m*

macroradiography *n* NUCLEAR macroradiographie *f*

macroscopic: **~ cross section** *n* NUCLEAR section macroscopique efficace *f*; **~ flux variation** *n* NUCLEAR variation de flux macroscopique *f*; **~ variables** *n pl* PHYS variables macroscopiques *f pl*

macroseismic *adj* GEOPHYS *vibration* macrosismique

macrostructural *adj* CHEM macrostructural

macrostructure *n* CHEM macrostructure *f*

macrowaste *n* POLLUTION macrodéchet *m*

macula *n* ASTRON macule *f*

made: [1] **~ by hand** *adj* PROD ENG fait à la main; **~ by machine** *adj* PROD ENG fait mécaniquement; **~ by machinery** *adj* PROD ENG fait mécaniquement; **~ in sections** *adj* PROD ENG démontable

made: [2] **~ block** *n see mortise block*

MAF *abbr* (*management applications function*) TELECOM fonction d'application de gestion *f*

mafic *adj* GEOL mafique

mag: **~ card** *n* PRINT carte magnétique *f*

MAG: **~ welding** *n* (*metal active gas welding*) CONST, THERMOD soudage MAG *m*

magamp *n* (*magnetic amplifier*) ELEC ENG amplificateur magnétique *m*

magazine *n* CINEMAT, MECH ENG chargeur *m*, magasin *m*, MINING dépôt *m*, poudrière *f*; **~ back** *n* PHOTO dos magasin *m*; **~ camera** *n* CINEMAT caméra à chargeur *f*; **~ creel** *n* TEXTILES cantre magasin *m*

mag-dyno *n* ELEC *automotive* dynamo-magnéto *f*

Magellan: **~ spacecraft** *n* ASTRON *orbiting Venus* sonde de Magellan *f*

Magellanic: **~ Clouds** *n pl* ASTRON nuages de Magellan *m pl*; **~ stream** *n* ASTRON courant magellanique *m*

magenta *n* PRINT magenta *m*

magic: **~ eye** *n* ELECTRON oeil magique *m*; **~ number** *n* PHYS nombre magique *m*

magmatic: **~ differentiation** *n* GEOL différenciation magmatique *f*; **~ stoping** *n* GEOL assimilation des roches encaissantes *f*

magnesia *n* CHEM, HEAT ENG magnésie *f*

magnesian [1] *adj* CHEM, GEOL magnésien

magnesian: [2] **~ concrete** *n* CONST béton de magnésium *m*; **~ limestone** *n* GEOL calcaire magnésien *m*

magnesic *adj* CHEM magnésique

magnesioferrite *n* MINERAL magnésioferrite *f*

magnesite *n* CHEM *mineral* giobertite *f*, magnésite *f*, MINERAL, P&R *paint, raw material* magnésite *f*; **~ brick** *n* CONST brique de magnésite *f*; **~ chrome refractory** *n* C&G réfractaire de magnésie-chrome *m*

magnesium *n* (*Mg*) CHEM magnésium *m* (*Mg*); **~ alloy** *n* PROP MAT alliage de magnésium *n*; **~ carbonate** *n* HEAT ENG carbonate de magnésie *m*; **~ concrete** *n* CONST béton de magnésium *m*; **~ silver chloride cell** *n* ELEC ENG pile au chlorure d'argent-magnésium *f*; **~ sulfate** *n* (AmE), **~ sulphate** *n* (BrE) DETERGENTS sulfate de magnésium *m*

magnesol *n* CHEM magnésol *m*

magnet *n* ELEC, ELEC ENG, LAB EQUIP, PART PHYS, PHYS, RECORDING, TELECOM aimant *m*; **~ coil** *n* ELEC ENG bobine d'électro-aimant *f*; **~ core** *n* ELEC ENG noyau d'électro-aimant *m*; **~ crane** *n* PROD ENG pont roulant à électro-aimant de levage *m*, pont roulant à électro-aimant porteur *m*; **~ spheric cavity** *n* SPACE *geophysics* cavité aimant sphérique *f*

magnetic [1] *adj* ELEC, NAUT *compass bearing*, PHYS, RECORDING, SPACE magnétique

magnetic: [2]

~ a **~ adjustable link** *n* MECH ENG éclisse magnétique réglable *f*; **~ alignment** *n* RECORDING alignement magnétique *m*; **~ amplifier** *n* ELEC ENG amplificateur magnétique *m*, PHYS *saturable reactor* amplificateur magnétique *m*, inductance saturable *f*, transducteur *m*, SPACE *spacecraft* amplificateur magnétique *m*; **~ anomaly** *n* GEOL, GEOPHYS anomalie magnétique *f*; **~ arc blowout contact** *n* MECH ENG contact à soufflage magnétique *m*; **~ armature loudspeaker** *n* RECORDING haut-parleur à armature magnétique *m*; **~ attraction** *n*

ELEC attraction magnétique *f*; ~ **axis** *n* ASTRON, GEO-PHYS, SPACE axe magnétique *m*; ~ **azimuth** *n* GEOPHYS azimut magnétique *m*;

▪ **b** ~ **balance** *n* GEOPHYS balance magnétique *f*; ~ **balance track** *n* CINEMAT piste magnétique de compensation *f*; ~ **bay** *n* GEOPHYS baie magnétique *f*; ~ **beam compressing** *n* PART PHYS concentration magnétique du faisceau *f*; ~ **bearing** *n* AERONAUT, GEOPHYS relèvement magnétique *m*, MECH, SPACE *spacecraft* palier magnétique *m*; ~ **bearing momentum wheel** *n* SPACE *spacecraft* volant d'inertie sur paliers magnétiques *m*; ~ **bias** *n* ELEC ENG polarisation magnétique *f*, RECORDING, TV polarisation *f*, prémagnétisation *f*; ~ **blowout** *n* ELEC ENG soufflage magnétique *m*; ~ **blowout circuit breaker** *n* ELEC disjoncteur à soufflage magnétique *m*; ~ **blowout contacts** *n pl* MECH ENG plots à soufflage magnétique *m pl*; ~ **bottle** *n* PHYS bouteille magnétique *f*; ~ **bubble memory** *n* COMP mémoire à bulles *f*, mémoire à bulles magnétiques *f*, ELEC ENG mémoire à bulles magnétiques *f*;

▪ **c** ~ **card** *n* COMP, DP carte magnétique *f*; ~ **card reader** *n* COMP, DP lecteur de cartes magnétiques *m*; ~ **cell** *n* COMP, DP cellule magnétique *f*; ~ **centering ring** *n* (AmE) *see magnetic centring ring*; ~ **center track** *n* (AmE), ~ **centre track** *n* (BrE) CINEMAT piste magnétique centrale *f*; ~ **centring ring** *n* (BrE) SPACE *spacecraft* anneau de centrage magnétique *m*; ~ **circuit** *n* ELEC, ELEC ENG, PHYS, SPACE *spacecraft* circuit magnétique *m*; ~ **clutch** *n* ELEC *of vehicle* embrayage magnétique *m*, ELEC ENG embrayage électrique *m*, MECH ENG embrayage magnétique *m*; ~ **coating** *n* CINEMAT enduit magnétique *m*, RECORDING revêtement magnétique *m*, TV dépôt magnétique *m*, enduit magnétique *m*; ~ **compass** *n* AERONAUT compas magnétique *m*, INSTRU-MENT boussole magnétique *f*; ~ **confinement** *n* PHYS confinement magnétique *m*; ~ **constant** *n* ELEC ENG, PHYS constante magnétique *f*; ~ **cooling** *n* REFRIG refroidissement magnétique *m*; ~ **core** *n* COMP tore magnétique *m*, DP noyau magnétique *m*, ELEC ENG *of circuit* noyau *m*, noyau magnétique *m*, *of memory* tore *m*, tore magnétique *m*; ~ **core memory** *n* ELEC ENG mémoire à tores *f*; ~ **coupling** *n* ELEC *transformer* couplage magnétique *m*; ~ **coupling coefficient** *n* ELEC *transformer* coefficient de couplage magnétique *m*; ~ **course** *n* NAUT *navigation* cap magnétique *m*; ~ **crack detector** *n* MECH ENG métalloscope *m*; ~ **cushion** *n* TRANSP coussin magnétique *m*; ~ **cushion train** *n* TRANSP coussin magnétique *m*, train à coussin magnétique *m*; ~ **cycle** *n* ASTRON *of sun*, GEOPHYS cycle magnétique *m*;

▪ **d** ~ **daily variation** *n* GEOPHYS variation magnétique diurne *f*; ~ **damping** *n* ELEC ENG amortissement par courants de Foucault *m*, GEOPHYS amortissement magnétique *m*; ~ **declination** *n* GEOPHYS déclinaison magnétique *f*, variation magnétique *f*, naut *navigation*, PHYS déclinaison magnétique *f*; ~ **deflection** *n* GEO-PHYS, NUCLEAR déviation magnétique *f*, PART PHYS déflexion magnétique *f*; ~ **depolarization of resonance radiation** *n* RAD PHYS dépolarisation magnétique de la radiation de résonance *f*; ~ **detector** *n* TRANSP détecteur magnétique *m*; ~ **deviation** *n* GEOPHYS déviation magnétique *f*; ~ **dip** *n* GEOPHYS, PETR inclinaison magnétique *f*; ~ **dipole** *n* PHYS dipôle magnétique *m*; ~ **dipole moment** *n* PHYS moment magnétique dipolaire *m*; ~ **dipole transitions** *n pl* RAD PHYS transitions

dipôles magnétiques *f pl*; ~ **disc** *n* (BrE) ELEC, ELEC ENG, RECORDING disque magnétique *m*; ~ **discontinuity** *n* GEOPHYS discontinuité magnétique *f*; ~ **disk** *n* (AmE) *see magnetic disc*; ~ **domain** *n* ELEC ENG domaine de Weiss *m*, domaine magnétique *m*; ~ **doorstop** *n* CONST arrêtoir-butoir magnétique *m*; ~ **drag** *n* TRANSP traînée magnétique *f*; ~ **drain plug** *n* MECH ENG bouchon magnétique *m*; ~ **drum** *n* DP, ELEC ENG tambour magnétique *m*; ~ **drum memory** *n* ELEC ENG mémoire à tambour magnétique *f*;

▪ **e** ~ **echo** *n* RECORDING écho magnétique *m*; ~ **energy** *n* ELEC, ELEC ENG, PHYS énergie magnétique *f*; ~ **epitaxial layer** *n* ELECTRON couche épitaxiale magnétique *f*; ~ **equator** *n* GEOPHYS, PHYS équateur magnétique *m*; ~ **erasing head** *n* TV tête magnétique d'effacement *f*;

▪ **f** ~ **face** *n* MECH ENG face magnétique *f*; ~ **field** *n* ELEC, ELEC ENG, GEOL, PHYS, RECORDING, TELECOM, TESTING, TV champ magnétique *m*; ~ **field antenna** *n* GEOPHYS antenne à champ magnétique *f*; ~ **field configuration** *n* NUCLEAR, RAD PHYS configuration du champ magnétique *f*; ~ **field gradient** *n* ELEC ENG gradient de champ magnétique *m*; ~ **field intensity** *n* ELEC intensité du champ magnétique *f*; ~ **field lines** *n pl* RAD PHYS lignes des champs magnétiques *f pl*; ~ **field strength** *n* ELEC, ELEC ENG intensité du champ magnétique *f*, PETR force magnétique *f*, intensité magnétique *f*, PHYS *H-field* intensité du champ magnétique *f*; ~ **film** *n* CINEMAT bande magnétique *f*, pellicule magnétique *f*, COATINGS enduit magnétique *m*; ~ **film projector** *n* CINEMAT projecteur avec son magnétique *m*; ~ **filter** *n* MECH ENG filtre magnétique *m*; ~ **fishing tool** *n* PETR TECH outil de repêchage magnétique *m*; ~ **flux** *n* ELEC flux magnétique *m*, ELEC ENG, PHYS flux d'induction magnétique *m*, flux magnétique *m*, RAD PHYS flux d'induction magnétique *m*, RECORDING, TESTING, TV flux magnétique *m*; ~ **flux density** *n* ELEC induction magnétique *f*, PHYS *B-field* densité de flux magnétique *f*, induction magnétique *f*, TESTING densité du flux magnétique *f*; ~ **flux density meter** *n* GEOPHYS fluxmètre *m*, gaussmètre *m*; ~ **flux linkage** *n* FUELLESS couplage de flux magnétique *m*; ~ **flux surface** *n* NUCLEAR surface magnétique *f*; ~ **flywheel** *n* ELEC ENG volant magnétique *m*; ~ **focusing** *n* ELEC ENG concentration magnétique *f*, focalisation magnétique *f*; ~ **force** *n* ELEC, GEOPHYS, PETR force magnétique *f*; ~ **force welding** *n* NUCLEAR soudage par force magnétique *m*;

▪ **h** ~ **head** *n* ACOUSTICS, COMP, DP, RECORDING, TV tête magnétique *f*; ~ **head core** *n* TV noyau de tête magnétique *m*; ~ **head gap** *n* TV entrefer d'une tête magnétique *m*; ~ **heading** *n* AERONAUT cap magnétique *m*, route magnétique *f*; ~ **holdfast** *n* MECH ENG plot magnétique avec extracteur *m*; ~ **holding** *n* MECH ENG bridage magnétique *m*; ~ **hysteresis** *n* ELEC, ELEC ENG hystérésis magnétique *f*; ~ **hysteresis loop** *n* ELEC boucle d'hystérésis magnétique *f*;

▪ **i** ~ **inclination** *n* GEOPHYS inclinaison magnétique *f*; ~ **inclinometer** *n* GEOPHYS aiguille d'inclinaison *f*, inclinatoire magnétique *m*; ~ **indicator** *n* MECH ENG indicateur magnétique *m*, voyant magnétique *m*; ~ **induction** *n* ELEC ENG *density* densité de flux magnétique *f*, induction magnétique *f*, PETR induction magnétique *f*, PHYS *B-field* densité de flux magnétique *f*, induction magnétique *f*, RECORDING, TELECOM induction magnétique *f*; ~ **induction current loop** *n*

TELECOM boucle d'induction magnétique *f*; ~ **induction density** *n* ELEC densité de flux magnétique *f*; ~ **induction flux** *n* ELEC ENG flux d'induction magnétique *m*; ~ **ink** *n* COMP, DP, PRINT encre magnétique *f*; ~ **ink character recognition** *n* (*MICR*) COMP, DP reconnaissance magnétique de caractères *f* (*RMC*); ~ **intensity** *n* GEOPHYS intensité magnétique *f*, RAD PHYS force magnétique *f*, intensité magnétique *f*; ~ **interference** *n* GEOPHYS interférence magnétique *f*, parasites magnétiques *m pl*; ~ **interference field** *n* GEOPHYS champ magnétique parasite *m*; ~ **interval** *n* GEOL période de polarité géomagnétique *f*; ~ **isotope separation** *n* NUCLEAR séparation des isotopes magnétiques *f*;

■**l** ~ **lag** *n* MECH ENG hystérésis *f*; ~ **latching relay** *n* ELEC ENG relais à verrouillage électrique *m*; ~ **latitude** *n* GEOPHYS inclinaison magnétique *f*, PHYS latitude magnétique *f*; ~ **latitude effect** *n* GEOPHYS effet d'inclinaison magnétique *m*; ~ **leakage** *n* ELEC ENG fuites magnétiques *f pl*; ~ **lens** *n* ELEC ENG, INSTRUMENT, PHYS, RAD PHYS *to focus electron beams* lentille magnétique *f*; ~ **levitation** *n* PHYS lévitation magnétique *f*, TRANSP sustentation magnétique *f*; ~ **line of force** *n* ELEC ENG ligne de force magnétique *f*; ~ **loop detector** *n* TRANSP détecteur à boucle magnétique *m*; ~ **lunar daily variation** *n* GEOPHYS variation magnétique diurne lunaire *f*;

■**m** ~ **map** *n* GEOPHYS carte magnétique *f*; ~ **master** *n* CINEMAT mixage magnétique original *m*; ~ **material** *n* ELEC ENG corps magnétique *m*; ~ **measurements** *n pl* ASTRON mesures magnétiques *f pl*; ~ **media** *n pl* COMP support d'enregistrement magnétique *m*, DP support magnétique *m*; ~ **medium** *n* ACOUSTICS, ELEC ENG support magnétique *m*; ~ **meridian** *n* GEOPHYS, PHYS méridien magnétique *m*; ~ **method** *n* GEOPHYS méthode d'exploration magnétique *f*; ~ **mine** *n* MILIT mine magnétique *f*; ~ **mirror** *n* PHYS miroir magnétique *m*; ~ **moment** *n* ELEC, PART PHYS *spin of electron, proton,* PHYS moment magnétique *m*; ~ **monopole** *n* PHYS monopôle magnétique *m*;

■**n** ~ **needle** *n* GEOPHYS aiguille aimantée *f*, MECH ENG *for instrument* aimant de signalisation *m*; ~ **north** *n* GEOPHYS nord magnétique *m*; ~ **north pole** *n* PHYS pôle nord magnétique *m*;

■**o** ~ **objective** *n* INSTRUMENT lentille magnétique *f*; ~ **order** *n* METALL ordre magnétique *m*; ~ **overload relay** *n* ELEC relais magnétique de surcharge *m*;

■**p** ~ **particle** *n* TV particule magnétique *f*; ~ **particle examination** *n* MECH magnétoscopie *f*; ~ **particle inspection** *n* MECH ENG contrôle magnétoscopique *m*; ~ **particle orientation** *n* TV orientation des particules magnétiques *f*; ~ **permeability** *n* ELEC, ELEC ENG, PETR perméabilité magnétique *f*; ~ **pick-up** *n* RECORDING lecteur magnétique *m*; ~ **polarization** *n* ACOUSTICS, ELEC ENG polarisation magnétique *f*; ~ **pole** *n* ELEC, GEOPHYS, PHYS pôle magnétique *m*; ~ **pole strength** *n* GEOPHYS intensité du pôle magnétique *f*; ~ **potential** *n* ELEC ENG potentiel magnétique *m*; ~ **printing echo** *n* RECORDING diaphonie magnétique *f*, effet d'écho magnétique *m*, écho magnétique *m*; ~ **printing effect** *n* ACOUSTICS effet d'empreinte magnétique *m*; ~ **print-through** *n* RECORDING effet de copie magnétique *m*, TV effet d'empreinte magnétique *m*, effet d'écho *m*, écho magnétique *m*; ~ **probe** *n* NUCLEAR sonde magnétique *f*; ~ **prospecting** *n* GEOPHYS recherche minière magnétique *f*; ~ **pyrites** *n* MINERAL pyrrhotite *f*;

■**q** ~ **quantum number** *n* PHYS nombre quantique

magnétique *m*;

■**r** ~ **rack** *n* MECH ENG règle-support magnétique *f*; ~ **recorder** *n* ACOUSTICS enregistreur magnétique *m*; ~ **recording** *n* ACOUSTICS, COMP, DP, RECORDING, TELECOM, TV enregistrement magnétique *m*; ~ **recording film** *n* RECORDING pellicule à enregistrement magnétique *f*; ~ **recording medium** *n* TV support pour enregistrement magnétique *m*; ~ **recording standard** *n* RECORDING norme d'enregistrement magnétique *f*; ~ **reproducer** *n* TV lecteur magnétique *m*; ~ **repulsion** *n* ELEC ENG répulsion magnétique *f*; ~ **resistance** *n* ELEC ENG résistance magnétique *f*; ~ **resonance** *n* ELEC ENG, PHYS résonance magnétique *f*; ~ **resonance spectroscopy** *n* RAD PHYS spectroscopie à résonance magnétique *f*; ~ **reversal** *n* GEOL inversion magnétique *f*;

■**s** ~ **saturation** *n* ELEC *of ferromagnetic material*, ELEC ENG saturation magnétique *f*; ~ **saturation AC** *n* TESTING saturation magnétique ca *f*; ~ **saturation DC** *n* TESTING saturation magnétique cc *f*; ~ **scalar potential** *n* PHYS potentiel scalaire magnétique *m*; ~ **screening** *n* ELEC *magnetic field* blindage antimagnétique *m*; ~ **separator** *n* COAL TECH séparateur magnétique *m*, séparateur magnétique à rubans *m*, MINING *ore dressing* séparateur magnétique *m*, trieur magnétique *m*, trieur électromagnétique *m*, électrotrieuse *f*, NUCLEAR trieur magnétique *m*, PROD ENG séparateur magnétique *m*; ~ **shell** *n* PHYS feuillet magnétique *m*; ~ **shielding** *n* ELEC ENG blindage magnétique *m*; ~ **solar quiet day variation** *n* GEOPHYS variation magnétique diurne des jours calmes *f*; ~ **sound stripe** *n* CINEMAT piste magnétique couchée *f*; ~ **soundtrack** *n* CINEMAT piste sonore magnétique *f*, RECORDING piste de son magnétique *f*; ~ **south** *n* GEOPHYS sud magnétique *m*; ~ **south pole** *n* PHYS pôle sud magnétique *m*; ~ **spectrograph** *n* GEOPHYS spectrographe magnétique *m*; ~ **starter** *n* ELEC *of motor* démarreur magnétique *m*, PROD ENG démarreur à base d'électro-aimant *m*; ~ **stirrer** *n* LAB EQUIP *mixing* agitateur magnétique *m*; ~ **stock** *n* CINEMAT pellicule magnétique *f*; ~ **storage medium** *n* ELEC ENG support magnétique d'information *m*; ~ **storm** *n* ASTRON tempête magnétique *f*, GEOPHYS, SPACE orage magnétique *m*; ~ **stripe** *n* GEOL bande d'aimantation *f*, RECORDING piste magnétique couchée *f*; ~ **striped film** *n* CINEMAT pellicule avec piste couchée *f*; ~ **stripe sound head** *n* CINEMAT lecteur pour piste magnétique couchée *m*; ~ **striping** *n* CINEMAT pistage *m*, RECORDING pistage magnétique *m*; ~ **substance** *n* PROP MAT substance magnétique *f*; ~ **survey** *n* GEOPHYS prospection magnétique *f*; ~ **susceptibility** *n* ELEC, PETR, PHYS susceptibilité magnétique *f*; ~ **suspension** *n* TRANSP sustentation magnétique *f*;

■**t** ~ **tape** *n* ACOUSTICS, COMP, DP, ELEC, GEOPHYS, PRINT, RECORDING, TELECOM bande magnétique *f*, TV bande magnétique *f*, ruban magnétique *m*, bande magnétique *f*; ~ **tape cartridge** *n* COMP, DP cartouche de bande magnétique *f*; ~ **tape noise** *n* RECORDING bruit de bande magnétique *m*; ~ **tape recorder** *n* RECORDING enregistreur sur bande magnétique *m*, enregistreur à bande magnétique *m*, magnétophone *m*; ~ **tape unit** *n* COMP, DP unité à bande magnétique *f*; ~ **thermometer** *n* REFRIG thermomètre magnétique *m*; ~ **thickness gage** *n* (AmE), ~ **thickness gauge** *n* (BrE) LAB EQUIP *for paints* jauge magnétique d'épaisseur *f*; ~ **thin film** *n* ELECTRON couche mince magnétique *f*; ~ **tool rack** *n* CONST râtelier magnétique *m*; ~ **transfer** *n*

CINEMAT repiquage magnétique *m*; ~ **transition** *n* ME-TALL transition magnétique *f*;

~ v ~ variation *n* GEOPHYS déclinaison magnétique *f*, variation magnétique *f*, NAUT *navigation* déclinaison magnétique *f*; ~ **variometer** *n* GEOPHYS variomètre magnétique *m*; ~ **vector potential** *n* PHYS potentiel vecteur magnétique *m*;

~ w ~ wave *n* ELEC ENG onde magnétique *f*; ~ **wire** *n* ACOUSTICS fil magnétique *m*

magnetically-latched: ~ **crosspoint** *n* TELECOM point de connexion à maintien magnétique *m*

magnetism *n* ELEC, PHYS magnétisme *m*

magnetite *n* MINERAL, NUCLEAR *heavy concrete aggregate*, PROP MAT magnétite *f*

magnetization *n* ELEC, ELEC ENG, GEOL, PETR, PHYS, RECORDING, TELECOM, TV aimantation *f*, magnétisation *f*; ~ **curve** *n* ELEC ENG courbe d'aimantation *f*

magnetize *vt* ELEC ENG aimanter, magnétiser, PHYS aimanter

magnetized [1] *adj* ELEC aimanté

magnetized:[2] ~ **head** *n* RECORDING tête magnétisée *f*; ~ **plasma** *n* NUCLEAR magnétoplasma *m*

magnetizing: ~ **coil** *n* ELEC bobine magnétisante *f*, ELEC ENG bobine de magnétisation *f*; ~ **current** *n* ELEC ENG courant magnétisant *m*; ~ **field** *n* ELEC ENG champ magnétisant *m*; ~ **force** *n* ELEC champ d'aimantation *m*

magneto *n* ELEC *automotive*, ELEC ENG, NAUT *electrics*, VEHICLES *ignition* magnéto *f*; ~ **bearing** *n* MECH ENG roulement de magnéto *m*; ~ **ignition** *n* AUTO allumage par magnéto *m*; ~ **switchboard** *n* TELECOM standard à magnéto *m*

magnetoconductivity *n* TELECOM magnétoconductivité *f*

magnetodiode *n* ELECTRON magnétodiode *f*

magnetoelectric: ~ **generator** *n* ELEC ENG générateur magnéto-électrique *m*

magnetoelectricity *n* ELEC ENG magnéto-électricité *f*

magnetogasdynamics *n* (*MGD*) NUCLEAR magnétodynamique des gaz *f*

magnetogram *n* GEOPHYS magnétogramme *m*

magnetograph *n* GEOPHYS magnétographe *m*

magnetographic: ~ **printer** *n* COMP imprimante magnétographique *f*

magnetohydrodynamic [1] *adj* (*MHD*) ELEC ENG, GEOPHYS, SPACE magnétohydrodynamique (*MHD*)

magnetohydrodynamic:[2] ~ **conversion** *n* ELEC ENG, GEOPHYS conversion magnétohydrodynamique *f*; ~ **converter** *n* ELEC ENG, NUCLEAR, SPACE convertisseur magnétohydrodynamique *m*; ~ **generation** *n* ELEC ENG génération magnétohydrodynamique *f*; ~ **generator** *n* ELEC ENG générateur magnéto-hydrodynamique *m*; ~ **instability** *n* GEOPHYS instabilité magnétohydrodynamique *f*; ~ **pump** *n* ELEC ENG pompe magnétohydrodynamique *f*; ~ **wave** *n* GEOPHYS onde magnétohydrodynamique *f*

magnetohydrodynamics *n* FLUID PHYS, GEOPHYS, PHYS magnétohydrodynamique *f*

magnetometer *n* AERONAUT, ELEC, GEOPHYS, PETR, PHYS magnétomètre *m*; ~ **boom** *n* SPACE *craft* perche de magnétomètre *f*; ~ **survey** *n* PETR TECH magnétométrie *f*

magnetometry *n* PETR TECH magnétométrie *f*

magnetomotive: ~ **force** *n* (*mmf*) ELEC, PHYS force magnétomotrice *f* (*fmm*)

magneton *n* PHYS magnéton *m*

magneto-optic: ~ **memory** *n* OPT mémoire magnéto-op-

tique *f*

magneto-optical: ~ **disc** *n* (BrE) OPT (*m-o disc*), RECORDING disque magnéto-optique *m*, disque magnétoscopique *m*; ~ **disk** *n* (AmE) *see magneto-optical disc*; ~ **effect** *n* OPT effet magnéto-optique *m*

magnetophone *n* GEOPHYS magnétophone *m*

magnetoplasma *n* NUCLEAR magnétoplasma *m*

magnetoresistance *n* PHYS magnétorésistance *f*

magnetoresistor: ~ **potentiometer** *n* ELEC potentiomètre de magnétorésistance *m*

magnetoscope *n* GEOPHYS, TELECOM magnétoscope *m*

magnetosphere *n* ASTRON, GEOPHYS, SPACE magnétosphère *f*; ~ **bow shock** *n* SPACE onde de choc géomagnétique *f*

magnetostatic *adj* NUCLEAR, PHYS magnétostatique

magnetostriction *n* ELEC ENG, PHYS magnétostriction *f*; ~ **loudspeaker** *n* ACOUSTICS haut-parleur à magnétostriction *m*; ~ **microphone** *n* ACOUSTICS microphone à magnétostriction *m*

magnetostrictive: ~ **material** *n* ELEC ENG corps magnétostrictif *m*; ~ **transductor** *n* ELEC ENG transducteur magnétostrictif *m*, transducteur à magnétostriction *m*

magnetotail *n* SPACE queue de la magnétosphère *f*

magneto-telluric: ~ **prospecting** *n* GEOPHYS prospection magnéto-tellurique *f*

magnetron *n* ELECTRON, MECH ENG, PHYS magnétron *m*; ~ **amplifier** *n* ELECTRON magnétron amplificateur *m*; ~ **arcing** *n* ELEC ENG claquage d'un magnétron *m*; ~ **oscillator** *n* ELECTRON magnétron oscillateur *m*

magnetting *n* C&G déferrisation magnétique *f*

magnification *n* INSTRUMENT grossissement *m*, PHYS grandissement *m*; ~ **changer** *n* INSTRUMENT changeur de grossissement *m*; ~ **effectiveness** *n* INSTRUMENT *of magnifier* grossissement utile *m*; ~ **factor** *n* CINEMAT rapport d'agrandissement *m*, INSTRUMENT coefficient de qualité *m*; ~ **scale** *n* INSTRUMENT grandissement *m*

magnified: ~ **viewfinder image** *n* PHOTO image de viseur grossie *f*

magnifier *n* INSTRUMENT loupe *f*; ~ **enlargement** *n* INSTRUMENT grossissement de loupe *m*

magnify *vt* PHYS grossir

magnifying [1] *adj* INSTRUMENT grossissant

magnifying [2] *n* INSTRUMENT grossissement *m*; ~ **glass** *n* INSTRUMENT, LAB EQUIP *optics*, MECH *tools*, PHYS loupe *f*, PRINT compte-fils *m*, loupe *f*; ~ **lens** *n* INSTRUMENT lentille grossissante *f*, PRINT compte-fils *m*, loupe *f*; ~ **picture viewer** *n* INSTRUMENT loupe photoscopique *f*; ~ **power** *n* PHYS grossissement *m*; ~ **sight** *n* ASTRON lunette de visée *f*

magnitude *n* ASTRON magnitude *f*, PHYS *of quantity* grandeur *f*, *of star* magnitude *f*; ~ **class** *n* ASTRON *star* magnitude stellaire *f*

magnitude-frequency: ~ **curve** *n* ACOUSTICS courbe d'amplitude-fréquence *f*

magnon *n* PHYS magnon *m*

magnox: ~ **reactor** *n* NUCLEAR réacteur Magnox *m*

Magnus: ~ **effect** *n* PHYS effet Magnus *m*

mag-optical: ~ **print** *n* CINEMAT copie sons magnétique et optique *f*

maiden: ~ **flight** *n* AERONAUT premier vol *m*; ~ **nut** *n* MECH ENG écrou de serrage *m*; ~ **voyage** *n* NAUT *of ship*, SPACE voyage inaugural *m*

mail: ~ **and cargo terminal** *n* TRANSP bâtiment de fret et de poste *m*; ~ **server** *n* TELECOM serveur de messagerie *m*; ~ **train** *n* RAIL train postal *m*, train-poste *m*; ~ **van** *n*

TRANSP voiture postale *f*

mailing *n* COMP, DP publipostage *m*; ~ **sleeve** *n* PACKA-
GING manchon pour expédition postale *m*; ~ **tube** *n*
(AmE) *(cf postal tube)* PACKAGING tube pour expédi-
tion postale *m*, tube pour transmission postale *m*

mailmerge *n* COMP, DP publipostage *m*

mail-order: ~ **packed** *adj* FOOD TECH conditionné pour
expédition postale

main *n* (BrE) CONST *conduit pipe* canalisation principale
f, collecteur *m*, conduite *f*, conduite maîtresse *f*,
conduite principale *f*; ~ **air supply hose** *n* (AmE) *(cf
main air supply pipe)* RAIL *for pneumatically-operated
equipment* conduite principale *f*; ~ **air supply pipe** *n*
(BrE) *(cf main air supply hose)* RAIL *for pneumatically-operated equipment* conduite principale *f*; ~ **anode**
n ELEC ENG anode principale *f*; ~ **bar** *n* ELEC ENG barre
principale *f*; ~ **battery** *n* AERONAUT *of aircraft* batterie
de bord *f*; ~ **beam** *n* CONST longeron *m*, maîtresse
poutre *f*, NAUT maître bau *m*, SPACE *communications*
faisceau principal *m*; ~ **bearing** *n* AUTO palier *m*, CONST
palier principal *m*, roulement principal *m*, NAUT *of
engine*, VEHICLES *of engine* palier principal *m*; ~ **bearing bushing** *n* AUTO coussinet de palier *m*; ~ **brake
hose** *n* (AmE) *(cf main brake pipe)* RAIL *electropneumatic* conduite générale *f*; ~ **brake pipe** *n* (BrE) *(cf
main brake hose)* RAIL *electropneumatic* conduite générale *f*; ~ **burner** *n* HEAT ENG brûleur principal *m*; ~
busbar *n* TELECOM barre omnibus principale *f*; ~ **casting** *n* PROD ENG *centre casting, centre plate*
crapaudine *f*; ~ **chute** *n* MINING maître couloir *m*; ~
circuit *n* ELEC *of network* circuit principal *m*; ~
conductor *n* ELEC ENG conducteur principal *m*, ligne
principale *f*; ~ **contacts** *n pl* ELEC contacts principaux
m pl; ~ **crack** *n* METALL fissure principale *f*; ~ **deck** *n*
NAUT pont principal *m*; ~ **distribution frame** *n (MDF)*
TELECOM répartiteur d'entrée *m*; ~ **drain** *n* CONST drain
collecteur *m*, maître drain *m*; ~ **drive** *n* MECH ENG
transmission principale *f*; ~ **drive gear** *n* AUTO pignon
entraîneur *m*; ~ **drive shaft** *n* AERONAUT *of helicopter*
arbre de transmission principale *m*, transmission au
rotor principal *f*; ~ **drive unit** *n* INSTRUMENT mécanisme de commande principal *m*; ~ **exchange** *n*
TELECOM commutateur de rattachement *m*, commutateur principal *m*; ~ **exposure** *n* PRINT exposition
principale *f*; ~ **feed motion** *n* MECH ENG mouvement
d'avance principal *m*; ~ **gap** *n* ELEC ENG voie de décharge principale *f*; ~ **gate** *n* COAL TECH voie
principale *f*, PROD ENG *in mould* chenal de coulée *m*; ~
gear axle beam *n* AERONAUT basculeur de train principal *m*; ~ **gearbox** *n* AERONAUT *of helicopter* boîte de
transmission principale *f*; ~ **gearbox support** *n* AERO-
NAUT *of helicopter* bâti mécanique *m*; ~ **gear sliding
door** *n* AERONAUT trappe sous train *f*; ~ **girder** *n* CONST
longeron *m*, maîtresse poutre *f*; ~ **intake airway** *n*
MINING voie principale d'entrée d'air *f*; ~ **international
switching center** *n* (AmE), ~ **international switching
centre** *n* (BrE) TELECOM centre international de transit
principal *m*; ~ **international trunk switching center** *n*
(AmE), ~ **international trunk switching centre** *n* (BrE)
TELECOM centre international de transit principal *m*; ~
intervals on the diatonic scale *n* ACOUSTICS principaux
intervalles de la gamme diatonique *m pl*; ~ **isolating
valve** *n* NUCLEAR vanne d'isolement principal *f*; ~ **jet** *n*
AUTO, VEHICLES *in carburettor* gicleur principal *m*;
landing gear *n* AERONAUT *of helicopter* atterrisseur
principal *m*, train principal *m*; ~ **landing gear brace-**

strut *n* AERONAUT contrefiche de train principal *f*; ~
landing gear door *n* AERONAUT porte du train principal *f*; ~ **leaf** *n* SPRINGS *of leaf spring* lame maîtresse *f*; ~
leg *n* NUCLEAR branche principale *f*; ~ **line** *n* CONST
railway voie principale *f*, RAIL ligne d'artère *f*, voie
principale *f*, grande ligne *f*, TELECOM ligne téléphonique principale *f*; ~ **line railroad** *n* (AmE) *(cf main line
railway)* TRANSP ligne principale de chemin de fer *f*; ~
line railway *n* (BrE) *(cf main line railroad)* TRANSP
ligne principale de chemin de fer *f*; ~ **load** *n* CONST
charge principale *f*; ~ **lode** *n* MINING filon mère *m*, filon
principal *m*, veine centrale *f*; ~ **memory** *n* COMP mémoire principale *f*; ~ **mirror** *n* INSTRUMENT miroir
primaire parabolique *m*, miroir principal *m*; ~ **pin** *n*
MECH ENG *kingbolt* cheville ouvrière *f*, pivot central *m*;
~ **pole** *n* ELEC *terminal* pôle principal *m*; ~ **power
disconnect** *n* PROD ENG sectionneur d'alimentation
secteur *m*; ~ **press** *n* PAPER TECH presse principale *f*; ~
quantum number *n* AERONAUT nombre quantique
principal *m*; ~ **reflector** *n* SPACE *communications* réflecteur principal *m*; ~ **regulator valve** *n* AUTO soupape
régulatrice *f*; ~ **reinforcement** *n* CONST armature principale *f*; ~ **repeater distribution frame** *n* TELECOM répartiteur principal de station de répéteurs *m*; ~ **return
airway** *n* MINING voie principale de retour d'air *f*; ~ **rib**
n AERONAUT nervure forte *f*; ~ **road** *n* CONST *highway*
grande route *f*, route principale *f*, TRANSP route principale *f*; ~ **roadway** *n* COAL TECH galerie principale *f*; ~
rod *n* MECH ENG *main connecting rod* bielle motrice *f*; ~
rotor *n* AERONAUT *of helicopter* rotor principal *m*; ~
rotor blade *n* AERONAUT *of helicopter* pale principale
de rotor *f*; ~ **rotor head** *n* AERONAUT *of helicopter* tête
de rotor principal *f*; ~ **rotor shaft** *n* AERONAUT *of
helicopter* arbre de rotor *m*, mât rotor *m*; ~ **runner** *n*
PROD ENG *in mould* chenal de coulée *m*; ~ **scope tube** *n*
INSTRUMENT tube *m*; ~ **sewer** *n* CONST égout collecteur
m, HYDROL collecteur principal *m*, égout principal *m*,
RECYCLING collecteur principal *m*; ~ **shaft** *n* AERO-
NAUT arbre porte-galet *m*, arbre primaire *m*, arbre
principal *m*, maître couple *m*, AUTO, MECH arbre principal *m*, MECH ENG arbre principal *m*, axe principal *m*,
transmission principale *f*, MINING puits central *m*,
puits principal *m*, VEHICLES *of gearbox* arbre principal
m; ~ **shaft bearing** *n* NAUT *shipbuilding* bague de sortie
d'étambot *f*; ~ **sheet track** *n* NAUT *deck fittings* barre
d'écoute de grande voile *f*; ~ **shroud** *n* NAUT *rigging*
galhauban *m*; ~ **solar generator** *n* SPACE générateur
solaire principal *m*; ~ **spillway** *n* HYDROL déversoir
principal *m*; ~ **spring** *n* MECH ENG grand ressort *m*,
MILIT *of firing mechanism* ressort principal *m*; ~ **station** *n (MS)* ELECTRON poste principal *m (PP)*; ~
steam *n* NUCLEAR *of turbine* vapeur fraîche *f*, vapeur
principale *f*, vapeur vive *f*; ~ **steam pipe** *n* HYDR EQUIP
conduite maîtresse de vapeur *f*, tuyau principal de
vapeur *m*; ~ **storage** *n* (AmE) *(cf main store)* COMP
mémoire principale *f*; ~ **store** *n* (BrE) *(cf main storage)* COMP mémoire principale *f*; ~ **switch** *n* CONTROL
interrupteur général *m*, interrupteur principal *m*, ELEC
interrupteur principal *m*, ELEC ENG interrupteur général *m*; ~ **switching contacts** *n pl* ELEC contacts
principaux de coupure *m pl*; ~ **tap** *n* MECH ENG robinet-
coffret *m*; ~ **terminal** *n* AUTO borne centrale *f*; ~ **track** *n*
CONST *railway*, RAIL voie principale *f*; ~ **trading route** *n*
NAUT *shipping* route commerciale *f*; ~ **trunk exchange
area** *n* TELECOM zone de transit principale *f*; ~ **trunk
switching center** *n* (AmE), ~ **trunk switching centre** *n*

(BrE) TELECOM centre de transit principal *m*; ~ **unit** *n*
MECH ENG élément principal *m*; ~ **valve** *n* HEATING
vanne principale *f*; ~ **walls** *n pl* CONST *of building* gros
murs *m pl*

mainbrace *n* NAUT *rigging* grand bras de vergue *m*

mainframe *n* COMP gros ordinateur *m*

mainmast *n* NAUT grand mât *m*

mainplane *n* AERONAUT *of aircraft* plan principal *m*

mains *n* (BrE) *(cf supply network)* ELEC, ELEC ENG
alimentation secteur *f*, réseau *m*, TV alimentation
secteur *f*, WATER SUPP réseau de distribution *m*; ~
adaptor *n* (BrE) *(cf current adaptor)* ELEC ENG adaptateur secteur *m*; ~ **cable** *n* (BrE) *(cf supply cable)*
ELEC ENG câble secteur *m*; ~ **current** *n* (BrE) *(cf supply
current)* ELEC ENG courant secteur *m*; ~ **frequency** *n*
(BrE) *(cf current frequency)* ELEC, ELEC ENG fréquence de réseau *f*; ~ **hum** *n* (BrE) *(cf electrical hum)*
ELEC bruit de courant alternatif *m*, ELEC ENG ronflement du secteur *m*; ~ **lead** *n* (BrE) *(cf supply lead)*
ELEC ENG conduite d'amenée de secteur *f*; ~ **noise** *n*
(BrE) *(cf electrical noise)* ELECTRON bruit électrique
m, RECORDING bruit de courant *m*, bruit de secteur *m*;
~ **plug** *n* (BrE) *(cf electrical plug)* ELEC *connection*
prise au secteur *f*, ELEC ENG fiche secteur *f*; ~ **rectifier** *n*
(BrE) *(cf current rectifier)* ELEC redresseur de secteur
m; ~ **socket** *n* (BrE) *(cf electrical outlet)* ELEC ENG
prise secteur *f*; ~ **supply** *n* (BrE) *(cf electrical supply)*
ELEC *network* alimentation secteur *f*, réseau *m*, PHYS
alimentation secteur *f*; ~ **switch** *n* (BrE) *(cf current
switch)* CONTROL interrupteur d'alimentation *m*, ELEC
commutateur de secteur *m*, interrupteur d'alimentation *m*, ELEC ENG interrupteur d'alimentation *m*; ~
transformer *n* (BrE) *(cf current transformer)* ELEC
transformateur d'alimentation *m*, transformateur de
courant *m*, ELEC ENG transformateur secteur *m*, ELEC-
TRON transformateur d'alimentation *m*; ~ **voltage** *n*
(BrE) *(cf supply voltage)* ELEC tension du réseau *f*,
ELEC ENG, TV tension du secteur *f*; ~ **water** *n* (BrE) *(cf
city water)* HYDROL eau de ville *f*

mainsail *n* NAUT grand-voile *f*

mainsheet *n* NAUT écoute de grand-voile *f*, *for sail*
grande écoute *f*

mains-operated *adj* (BrE) *(cf electrically-operated)*
ELEC *appliance* alimenté du réseau, ELEC ENG alimenté
par le secteur

mainstay *n* NAUT *rigging* étai de grand mât *m*

maintain [1] *vt* MECH entretenir, maintenir, PHYS *current*
entretenir

maintain: [2] ~ **aseptic area conditions** *vi* SAFETY conserver
les conditions des locaux aseptisées, maintenir les
locaux dans des conditions aseptiques; ~ **course and
speed** *vi* NAUT maintenir route et vitesse

maintainability *n* PROD ENG facilité d'entretien *f*, maintenabilité *f*, QUALITY, SPACE maintenabilité *f*

maintained: ~ **contact push button** *n* PROD ENG bouton-
poussoir à accrochage *m*; ~ **oscillation** *n* PHYS
oscillation entretenue *f*

maintainer *n* CONST *civil engineering* entreteneur *m*

maintenance *n* COMP, DP maintenance *f*, MECH entretien
m, maintenance *f*, PAPER TECH entretien *m*, PROD ENG
entretien *m*, maintien *m*, SAFETY entretien *m*, SPACE,
TV entretien *m*, maintenance *f*; ~ **cell description** *n*
(MCD) TELECOM description de cellule de maintenance *f*; ~ **cost** *n* QUALITY coût de maintenance *m*; ~
current *n* ELEC *of relay, thyristor* courant de maintien
m; ~ **data card** *n* PROD ENG carte d'entretien *f*; ~

function *n* TELECOM fonction de maintenance *f*; ~ **level**
n RAIL niveau d'intervention *m*; ~ **manual** *n* AERO-
NAUT, PROD ENG manuel d'entretien *m*; ~ **period** *n*
CONST délai de garantie *m*; ~ **processor** *n* TELECOM
calculateur d'exploitation et de maintenance *m*; ~
recorder *n* AERONAUT enregistreur de maintenance *m*;
~ **service provider** *n* *(MSP)* TELECOM prestataire de
service de maintenance *m*; ~ **shop** *n* CONST atelier
d'entretien *m*

mainway *n* MINING galerie maîtresse *f*, galerie principale *f*, mère-galerie *f*, voie maîtresse *f*, voie
principale *f*

maisonette *n* CONST *building* duplex *m*

majolica *n* C&G majolique *f*; ~ **colors** *n pl* (AmE), ~
colours *n pl* (BrE) C&G couleurs pour majolique *f pl*; ~
painter *n* C&G peintre en majolique *m*; ~ **tile** *n* C&G
carreau de majolique *m*; ~ **ware** *n* C&G articles de
majolique *m pl*

major: ~ **account holder** *n* TELECOM client grand compte
m; ~ **alarm** *n* TELECOM alarme majeure *f*; ~ **arc** *n* GEOM
of circle arc majeur *m*; ~ **axis** *n* GEOM *of an ellipse* grand
axe *m*; ~ **common chord** *n* ACOUSTICS accord parfait
majeur *m*; ~ **control** *n* CONTROL contrôle majeur *m*,
contrôle principal *m*, contrôle à l'étage supérieur *m*; ~
fault bit *n* PROD ENG bit de défaut majeur *m*; ~ **hazard** *n*
QUALITY danger majeur *m*, risque *m*; ~ **inspection** *n*
AERONAUT grande visite *f*; ~ **overhaul** *n* NUCLEAR entretien général *m*, révision générale *f*; ~ **railroad
junction** *n* (AmE) *(cf major railway junction)* RAIL
noeud ferroviaire *m*; ~ **railway junction** *n* (BrE) *(cf
major railroad junction)* RAIL noeud ferroviaire *m*; ~
road *n* CONST route principale *f*; ~ **scale** *n* ACOUSTICS
gamme majeure *f*; ~ **scale of equal temperament** *n*
ACOUSTICS gamme de Rameau-Bach *f*, gamme tempérée *f*, gamme à tempérament égal *f*; ~ **second** *n*
ACOUSTICS seconde majeure *f*; ~ **seventh** *n* ACOUSTICS
septième majeure *f*; ~ **sixth** *n* ACOUSTICS sixte majeure
stricte *f*; ~ **source** *n* POLLUTION source majeure *f*; ~
third *n* ACOUSTICS tierce majeure *f*; ~ **whole tone** *n*
ACOUSTICS ton majeur *m*

Majorana: ~ **force** *n* NUCLEAR force d'échange de position opérateur *f*, force de Majorana *f*

majority: ~ **carrier** *n* ELECTRON, PHYS porteur majoritaire *m*; ~ **carrier diode** *n* ELECTRON diode à porteurs
majoritaires *f*; ~ **carrier transistor** *n* ELECTRON transistor unipolaire *m*; ~ **gate** *n* ELECTRON porte logique
majoritaire *f*, porte majoritaire *f*; ~ **logic** *n* ELECTRON
logique majoritaire *f*

make [1] *n* ELEC ENG *in circuit*, MECH ENG *contact* fermeture *f*, PROD ENG travail *m*, *manufacture* fabrication *f*;
~ **contact** *n* ELEC *relay* contact normalement ouvert *m*,
contact à fermeture *m*, ELEC ENG contact travail *m*; ~
current *n* ELEC ENG courant à la fermeture *m*; ~ **pulse** *n*
ELEC ENG impulsion de fermeture *f*; ~ **relay** *n* ELEC
relais à fermeture *m*; ~ **time** *n* ELEC *relay* durée d'établissement *f*

make [2] *vt* ELEC ENG *circuit* fermer, NAUT *a port* arriver à,
PATENTS *invention* réaliser, PROD ENG *tool* confection-
ner; ~ **allowance for** *vt* METR tenir compte de; ~ **a call to**
vt TELECOM appeler, effectuer un appel à, téléphoner
à; ~ **a collect call to** *vt* (AmE) *(cf make a reverse charge
call to)* TELECOM appeler en PCV; ~ **fast** *vt* NAUT *boom*
capeler, *line, boat* amarrer, *load* brêler; ~ **flush** *vt* MECH
ENG affleurer; ~ **good** *vt* PROD ENG *wear and tear*
remédier à, réparer; ~ **impermeable** *vt* CONST imperméabiliser; ~ **ready** *vt* PRINT *press* caler; ~ **a reverse**

charge call to vt (BrE) *(cf make a collect call to)* TELECOM appeler en PCV; ~ up vt PRINT mettre en page; ~ a valuation of vt SAFETY faire l'estimation de

make:[3] ~ a cable with fibers vi (AmE), ~ a cable with fibres vi (BrE) OPT câbler en fibres; ~ heavy weather vi NAUT *of ship* bourlinguer; ~ a joint vi CONST faire un joint; ~ a round trip vi PETR TECH faire un aller-retour, faire une manoeuvre; ~ sail vi NAUT *ship* faire voile; ~ a survey vi CONST faire un levé, faire un levé de plans; ~ a tack vi NAUT *sailing* tirer un bord; ~ a tight joint vi PROD ENG faire joint étanche; ~ a turn round winch with line vi NAUT faire un tour mort; ~ water vi NAUT faire eau

make-and-break n ELEC ENG établissement-coupure m; ~ coil n ELEC bobine à trembleur f; ~ contact n ELEC ENG contact repos-travail m; ~ device n ELEC *switch* interrupteur m; ~ ignition n AUTO allumage par rupteur m

make-break: ~ time n ELEC *of relay* durée de rétablissement de coupure f

make-make: ~ contact n ELEC *relay* relais double travail m

maker n PROD ENG constructeur m, *manufacturer* fabricant m

maker's: ~ mark n PROD ENG *of essayer* poinçon m, poinçon de garantie m

make-ready n PRINT calage m, précalage m, préparation f; ~ sheet n PRINT feuille de mise en train f; ~ time n PRINT temps de précalage m

makeshift[1] adj SPACE de fortune

makeshift[2] n PROD ENG dispositif de circonstance m, dispositif de fortune m, moyen de fortune m, pis- aller m

make-up n PRINT mise en page f, montage m, WATER SUPP eau d'appoint f; ~ fuel n NUCLEAR combustible d'appoint m; ~ gas n GAS TECH gaz d'appoint m; ~ hydrogen n CHEM hydrogène d'appoint m; ~ mirror n INSTRUMENT miroir de courtoisie m; ~ rate n MECH ENG taux d'appoint m; ~ water n FOOD TECH eau d'appoint f, HYDROL eau de compensation f, REFRIG eau d'appoint f

making n CONST *of road, of reinforced concrete* confection f, PAPER TECH opération de fabrication f; ~ capacity n ELEC *of relay*, ELEC ENG pouvoir de fermeture m; ~ a connection n PETR TECH ajout de tige m; ~ of cores n PROD ENG *founding* noyauterie f; ~ on blowpipe n C&G travail sur mors battu m; ~ on a post n C&G travail sur poste soufflé m; ~ up n PROD ENG *of joint*, TEXTILES confection f

making-up n C&G lutage m, PHOTO *of baths* préparation f

malachite n MINERAL malachite f

malacolite n MINERAL malacolite f

malacon n MINERAL malacon m, malakon m, NUCLEAR malacon m

malakon n MINERAL malacon m, malakon m

malate n CHEM malate m

malaxage n MECH ENG malaxage m

malaxator n MECH ENG malaxeur m

maldonite n MINERAL maldonite f

male: ~ caliper gage n (AmE), ~ calliper gauge n (BrE) MECH ENG calibre simple mâle m; ~ cone n MECH ENG cône mâle m; ~ connector n ELEC ENG connecteur mâle m; ~ plug n TELECOM fiche mâle f; ~ screw n MECH ENG vis mâle f, vis pleine f; ~ thread n MECH ENG *tooling* filet extérieur m, filetage mâle m

maleic: ~ acid n CHEM acide maléique m; ~ ester n DETERGENTS ester maléique m

maleimide n CHEM maléimide m

malfunction n COMP, DP, METR défaillance f, SPACE *spacecraft* mauvais fonctionnement m; ~ detection n CONTROL contrôle d'avaries m, contrôle de dérangements m; ~ indication n CONTROL signalisation des défauts f; ~ signal n CONTROL signal d'incident m, signal de dérangement m

malfunctioning n MECH ENG mauvais fonctionnement m

malic[1] adj CHEM malique

malic:[2] ~ acid n FOOD TECH acide malique m

malicious: ~ call n TELECOM appel malveillant m; ~ call tracing n TELECOM identification d'appels malveillants f

mallardite n MINERAL mallardite f

malleability n METALL, PROP MAT malléabilité f

malleable[1] adj MECH *materials* malléable

malleable:[2] ~ cast iron n MECH *materials*, PROP MAT fonte malléable f

malleablizing n HEATING malléabilisation f

malleation n PROD ENG martelage m

mallet n C&G gland m, MECH *tools* maillet m, PROD ENG batte f, maillet m, mailloche f

malonamide n CHEM malonamide m

malonate n CHEM malonate m

malonic adj CHEM malonique

malonitrile n CHEM malonitrile m

malt[1] n CHEM, FOOD TECH malt m; ~ house n (AmE) *(cf maltings)* FOOD TECH malterie f

malt[2] vt FOOD TECH malter

maltase n CHEM, FOOD TECH maltase f

Maltese: ~ cross n MECH croix de Malte f; ~ cross assembly n CINEMAT bloc de croix m; ~ cross mechanism n MECH ENG entraînement par croix de Malte m; ~ cross movement n CINEMAT entraînement par croix de Malte m

maltha n MINERAL malthe m

malthacite n MINERAL malthacite f

malting: ~ barley n FOOD TECH *fermentation, milling* orge de brasserie f, orge germé f, orge à malter f

maltings n pl (BrE) *(cf malt house)* FOOD TECH malterie f

maltose n CHEM maltose m

Malus: ~ law n PHYS loi de Malus f

mammillated adj GEOL mamelonné

mammoth: ~ tanker n TRANSP superpétrolier m

man vt NAUT *boat* équiper, *ship* armer

MAN abbr *(metropolitan area network)* TELECOM réseau de zone urbaine m

managed: ~ object n *(MO)* TELECOM objet géré m; ~ object class n *(MOC)* TELECOM classe d'objet géré f

management: ~ applications function n *(MAF)* TELECOM fonction d'application de gestion f; ~ center n (AmE), ~ centre n (BrE) TELECOM centre de gestion m; ~ chart n PROD ENG tableau de bord m; ~ domain n *(MD)* TELECOM domaine de gestion m; ~ information n TELECOM information de gestion f; ~ information base n *(MIB)* TELECOM base d'informations de gestion f, base de données de gestion f; ~ information system n *(MIS)* COMP, DP système intégré de gestion m *(SIG)*; ~ report n PROD ENG tableau de bord m; ~ unit n TELECOM organe de gestion m

mandatory: ~ sign n SAFETY signe obligatoire m; ~ standard n CONST norme obligatoire f

man-day n PROD ENG capacité journalière par employé f, homme-jour m

mandelic *adj* CHEM mandélique

mandrel *n* C&G mandrin *m*, COAL TECH pic à deux pointes *m*, MECH ENG mandrin *m*, *spindle* arbre *m*, MINING pic à deux pointes *m*, P&R *of extrusion press* mandrin *m*, torpille *f*;~ **nose** *n* MECH ENG *of lathe* nez du mandrin *m*; ~ **running in bearings** *n* MECH ENG mandrin tournant dans des coussinets *m*

mandril *n see* mandrel

maneuver [1] *n* (AmE) *see* manoeuvre[1]

maneuver [2] *vt* (AmE) *see* manoeuvre[2]

maneuverability *n* (AmE) *see* manoeuvrability

maneuverable *adj* (AmE) *see* manoeuvrable

maneuvering: ~ **load** *n* (AmE) *see* manoeuvring load

manganate *n* CHEM manganate *m*

manganese *n* *(Mn)* CHEM manganèse *m (Mn)* ~ **bronze** *n* CHEM bronze au manganèse *m*; ~ **dioxide** *n* ELEC ENG *in batteries* dioxyde de manganèse *m*; ~ **nodule** *n* GEOL nodule de manganèse *m*, nodule polymétallique *m*; ~ **steel** *n* MECH *materials* acier au manganèse *m*,PROP MAT acier contenant du manganèse *m*

manganic *adj* CHEM manganique

manganiferous *adj* GEOL manganésifère

manganite *n* CHEM manganite *f*, MINERAL acerdèse *f*, manganite *f*

manganocalcite *n* MINERAL manganocalcite *f*

manganous [1] *adj* CHEM manganeux

manganous:[2] ~ **sulfate bath method** *n* (AmE), ~ **sulphate bath method** *n* (BrE) NUCLEAR méthode du bain de sulfate de manganèse *f*

manhole *n* CONST *of aqueduct, sewer* regard *m*, trou d'accès *m*, *shelter* abri *m*, caponnière *f*, niche *f*, niche de refuge *f*, refuge *m*, retraite *f*, trou d'accès *m*, trou d'homme *m*, trou de visite *m*, ELEC *supply* puits à câbles *m*, trou d'homme *m*, HYDROL regard de service *m*, regard de visite *m*, MECH ouverture de visite *f*, trou d'homme *m*, MECH ENG trou d'homme *m*, MINING passage *m*, NUCLEAR trou d'homme *m*, SPACE trou d'homme *m*, trou de visite *m*; ~ **cover** *n* MECH tape de trou d'homme *f*; ~ **door** *n* CONST plaque de trou d'homme *f*; ~ **gasket** *n* MECH joint de trou d'homme *m*; ~ **plate** *n* CONST plaque de trou d'homme *f*

man-hour *n* CONST homme-heure *m*, PROD ENG capacité horaire par employé *f*, homme-heure *m*

manifold [1] *adj* GEOM *topology* divers

manifold [2] *n* AERONAUT galerie *f*, rampe de distribution *f*, GEOM *topology* variété *f*, LAB EQUIP *glassware*, MECH, MECH ENG *of superheater* collecteur *m*, NUCLEAR collecteur *m*, conduit principal *m*, PETR TECH claviature *f*, PRINT rampe de distribution de la couche *f*, PROD ENG collecteur *m*; ~ **drying apparatus** *n* REFRIG hérisson *m*; ~ **pressure** *n* AERONAUT pression d'admission *f*; ~ **system** *n* MAR POLL collecteur *m*, système collecteur *m*

manipulating *n* PROD ENG manipulation *f*, manoeuvre *f*; ~ **device** *n* MECH ENG *for technical components* dispositif de manoeuvre *m*; ~ **industrial robot** *n* MECH ENG, PROD ENG robot manipulateur industriel *m*

manipulation *n* PROD ENG manipulation *f*, manoeuvre *f*; ~ **detection** *n* TELECOM détection de modification *f*

man-machine: ~ **interaction** *n* COMP, DP dialogue homme-machine *m*; ~ **interface** *n* *(MMI)* COMP, DP, SPACE *spacecraft* interface homme-machine *f*; ~ **ratio** *n* PROD ENG ratio homme-machine *m*; ~ **relationship** *n* TELECOM RHM, relation homme-machine *f*

man-made: ~ **earthquake** *n* POLLUTION séisme anthropogénique *m*; ~ **fiber** *n* (AmE), ~ **fibre** *n* (BrE) HEAT ENG fibre chimique *f*, PACKAGING fibre synthétique *f*;

~ **noise** *n* SPACE bruit artificiel *m*

manned: ~ **flight** *n* SPACE vol habité *m*; ~ **helicopter** *n* AERONAUT hélicoptère piloté *m*; ~ **maneuvring unit** *n* (AmE), ~ **manoeuvring unit** *n* (BrE) SPACE fauteuil volant *m*; ~ **module** *n* SPACE habitacle *m*; ~ **orbiting laboratory** *n* *(MOL)* SPACE laboratoire orbital habité *m*; ~ **space research** *n* SPACE recherche spatiale au moyen de vols habités *f*; ~ **workshop** *n* SPACE atelier spatial *m*

mannide *n* CHEM mannide *m*

manning *n* NAUT *of ship* armement *m*, armement en personnel *m*, dotation de personnel *f*

Manning's: ~ **formula** *n* HYDROL formule de Manning *f*

mannitan *n* CHEM mannitane *m*

mannite *n* CHEM mannite *f*

mannitol *n* CHEM mannitol *m*

mannonic *adj* CHEM mannonique

mannose *n* CHEM mannose *m*

manoeuvrability *n* (BrE) AERONAUT manoeuvrabilité *f*, MECH ENG maniabilité *f*, NAUT *of ship* capacité de manoeuvre *f*, manoeuvrabilité *f*, NUCLEAR *of power level* manoeuvrabilité *f*, TRANSP maniabilité *f*

manoeuvrable *adj* (BrE) NAUT manoeuvrable

manoeuvre [1] *n* (BrE) MECH ENG, NAUT manoeuvre *f*

manoeuvre [2] *vt* (BrE) NAUT manoeuvrer

manoeuvring: ~ **load** *n* (BrE) AERONAUT *airworthiness* charge de manoeuvre *f*

man-of-war *n* MILIT navire de guerre *m*, NAUT navire de guerre *m*, vaisseau de guerre *m*

manometer *n* LAB EQUIP *pressure*, PAPER TECH, PETR TECH, PHYS manomètre *m*

manometric: ~ **pressure governor** *n* CONTROL régulateur manométrique de pression *m*; ~ **pressure regulator** *n* CONTROL régulateur manométrique de pression *m*; ~ **switch** *n* CONTROL interrupteur manométrique *m*, interrupteur à pression *m*, ELEC commutateur actionné par la pression *m*

manpack: ~ **radio** *n* MILIT radio portative *f*

manpower *n* PROD ENG capital travail *m*, main-d'oeuvre *f*, personnel *m*

manrider *n* CONST *tunnelling* draisine *f*

manriding: ~ **car** *n* MINING wagon pour le personnel *m*

mansard: ~ **roof** *n* (BrE) *(cf gambrel roof)* CONST comble brisé *m*, comble en mansarde *m*, comble à la Mansard *m*

mantissa *n* COMP, DP, MATH mantisse *f*

mantle *n* COAL TECH cône d'usure *m*, GEOL, GEOPHYS enveloppe *f*, manteau *m*, manteau terrestre *m*, PROD ENG *of blast furnace* chemise extérieure *f*, enveloppe extérieure *f*; ~ **block** *n* C&G linteau de niche d'enfournement *m*; ~ **plume** *n* GEOL panache mantellique *m*

manual [1] *adj* MECH manuel

manual [2] *n* PROD ENG *handbook* aide-mémoire *m*, manuel *m*; ~ **adjustment** *n* CONTROL réglage à la main *m*; ~ **arc welding** *n* CONST soudage à l'arc manuel *m*, MECH soudage manuel à l'arc *m*; ~ **attempt** *n* TELECOM tentative manuelle *f*; ~ **blowpipe** *n* MECH ENG *for cutting, welding* chalumeau manuel *m*; ~ **board** *n* TELECOM meuble manuel *m*; ~ **bypass** *n* PROD ENG déblocage manuel *m*; ~ **choke control** *n* AUTO tirette de volet de départ *f*; ~ **cocking** *n* PHOTO *of shutter* armement manuel *m*; ~ **control** *n* AERONAUT commande manuelle *f*, CONST commande manuelle *f*, contrôle manuel *m*, système de commande manuelle *m*, CONTROL commande manuelle *f*, commande à la main *f*, contrôle manuel *m*, ELEC commande manuelle *f*, commande à la main *f*, MECH commande manuelle *f*; ~ **control indicator** *n* PHOTO indicateur de commande manuelle *m*; ~ **damper** *n* HEAT ENG registre manuel *m*; ~ **defrost** *n* REFRIG dégivrage manuel *m*; ~ **dimmer** *n* CINEMAT rhéostat à commande manuelle *m*; ~ **disarming** *n* SPACE *spacecraft* désarmement manuel *m*; ~ **editing** *n* TV montage manuel *m*; ~ **exchange** *n* TELECOM central manuel *m*; ~ **gain control** *n* ELECTRON réglage manuel du gain *m*; ~ **gearbox** *n* VEHICLES boîte de vitesses à commande manuelle *f*, boîte à commandemanuelle *f*; ~ **handling** *n* NUCLEAR manuelle *f*, manutention manuelle *f*; ~ **input** *n* COMP, DP entrée manuelle *f*; ~ **labor** *n* (AmE), ~ **labour** *n* (BrE) PROD ENG main-d'oeuvre *f*, travail manuel *m*, travail à la main *m*; ~ **lifting techniques** *n pl* SAFETY *methods of working* techniques de soulèvement manuel *f pl*; ~ **lift truck** *n* PACKAGING chariot de levage à commande manuelle *m*; ~ **metal arc welding** *n* MECH ENG soudage manuel à l'arc *m*; ~ **operation** *n* COMP, DP opération manuelle *f*; ~ **override** *n* PROD ENG possibilité de commande manuelle *f*; ~ **regulator** *n* CONTROL régulateur à main *m*; ~ **remote control** *n* AERONAUT commande manuelle à distance *f*; ~ **reset** *n* ELEC *controls* retour manuel *m*; ~ **shutdown** *n* NUCLEAR arrêt manuel *m*; ~ **switching** *n* ELEC ENG commutation manuelle *f*; ~ **system** *n* TELECOM système manuel *m*; ~ **threading** *n* CINEMAT chargement manuel *m*; ~ **transmission** *n* AUTO boîte mécanique *f*; ~ **working** *n* TELECOM commutation manuelle *f*

manual-lubricating: ~ **equipment** *n* MECH ENG matériel de graissage à main *m*

manually-controlled *adj* CONTROL commandé à la main, à commande manuelle, ELEC ENG à commande manuelle

manufacture *n* PROD ENG fabrication *f*; ~ **of forging dies and punches** *n* MECH ENG fabrication de matrices et poinçons en forgeage à froid *f*; ~ **of small bottles** *n* C&G flaconnage *m*

manufactured [1] *adj (mfd)* PROP MAT manufacturé

manufactured: [2] ~ **edible fat** *n* FOOD TECH graisse comestible artificielle *f*; ~ **gas** *n* GAS TECH gaz de ville *m*, gaz manufacturé *m*

manufacturer's: ~ **discretion** *n* MECH ENG choix du fabricant *m*, initiative du fabricant *f*

manufacturing *n* PROD ENG fabrication *f*, façonnage *m*; ~ **bill of material** *n* PROD ENG nomenclature de fabrication *f*; ~ **control** *n* CONTROL contrôle de fabrication *m*; ~ **cycle** *n* PROD ENG cycle de fabrication *m*, cycle de production *m*, délai de fabrication *m*, délai de production *m*; ~ **documents** *n pl* PROD ENG dossier de fabrication *m*; ~ **follow-up** *n* PROD ENG suivi d'atelier *m*, suivi de fabrication *m*, suivi de production *m*; ~ **lead time** *n* PROD ENG cycle de fabrication *m*, cycle de production *m*, délai defabrication *m*, délai de production *m*; ~ **location** *n* PROD ENG cellule de fabrication *f*, cellule de production *f*; ~ **papers** *n pl* PRODeng dossier atelier *m*; ~ **resource planning** *n* PROD ENG gestion de la production assistée par ordinateur *f*, planification des ressources de l'entreprise *f*; ~ **tolerances** *n pl* SPRINGS tolérances de fabrication *f pl*

manuscript *n* PRINT copie *f*, manuscrit *m*

manway *n* MINING compartiment des échelles *m*, galerie de circulation *f*, passage *m*, PETR TECH trou d'homme *m*

man-week *n* PROD ENG capacité hebdomadaire par semaine *f*, homme-semaine *m*

many-body: ~ **problem** *n* SPACE problème à n corps *m*

man-year *n* PROD ENG capacité hebdomadaire *f*, homme-an *m*

many-nuclear: ~ **transfer reaction** *n* NUCLEAR réaction de transfert de nombreux nucléons *f*

map: ~ **paper** *n* PAPER TECH papier pour cartes géographiques *m*

MAP *abbr (modified atmosphere packaging)* PRINT emballage en atmosphère modifiée *m*

mapper *n* CONST cartographe *m*

mapping *n* CONST cartographie *f*

maraging: ~ **steel** *n* METALL acier maraging *m*

marble [1] *n* GEOL marbre *m*; ~ **bushing** *n* C&G filière à billes *f*; ~ **furnace** *n* C&G four à billes *m*; ~ **quarry** *n* MINING carrière de marbre *f*, marbrière *f*

marble [2] *vt* PAPER TECH jasper

marbling *n* PAPER TECH jaspage *m*, PRINT jaspage des tranches *m*

marcasite *n* MINERAL marcassite *f*

mare *n* ASTRON mare *f*

margarate *n* CHEM margarate *m*

margaric *adj* CHEM margarique

margarine *n* CHEM glycéryle margarate *m*, margarine *f*

margarite *n* MINERAL margarite *f*

margarodite *n* MINERAL margarodite *f*

margin *n* COMP marge *f*, CONST pureau *m*, DP marge *f*, GEOL limite *f*, marge *f*, zone bordière *f*, HYDROL bord *m*, limite *f*, lisière *f*, marge *f*, rive *f*, MECH ENG *tolerance, limit* limite *f*, tolérance *f*, PATENTS, PRINT marge *f*; ~ **gluer** *n* PACKAGING encolleuse sur marge *f*; ~ **over** *n* MECH ENG tolérance en plus *f*; ~ **under** *n* MECH ENG tolérance en moins *f*

marginal: ~ **check** *n* COMP, DP contrôle des tolérances *m*; ~ **field** *n* PETR TECH gisement marginal *m*; ~ **plateau** *n* OCEANOG plateau marginal *m*; ~ **relay** *n* ELEC relais à action différée *m*; ~ **sea** *n* GEOL, OCEANOG mer marginale *f*; ~ **test** *n* COMP, DP contrôle des tolérances *m*; ~ **testing** *n* CONTROL contrôle marginal *m*; ~ **trench** *n* GEOL fosse océanique *f*

marialite *n* MINERAL marialite *f*

marigram *n* FUELLESS marégramme *m*

marigraph *n* OCEANOG marégraphe *m*

marina *n* NAUT marina *m*, port de plaisance *m*

marinade *n* OCEANOG marinade *f*

marine [1] *adj* GEOL marin, NAUT marin, maritime

marine: [2] ~ **acoustics** *n pl* OCEANOG acoustique sous-marine *f*; ~ **aggregates** *n pl* OCEANOG granulats marins *m pl*; ~ **air-cushion vehicle** *n* TRANSP aéroglisseur marin *m*; ~ **aquaculture** *n* OCEANOG mariculture *f*; ~ **architect** *n* NAUT architecte naval *m*, ingénieur en construction navale *m*; ~ **band** *n* GEOL intercalation marine *f*; ~ **boiler** *n* HEATING chaudière marine *f*; ~ **diesel oil** *n* NAUT huile diesel pour les machines marines *f*; ~ **disposal** *n* RECYCLING évacuation dans la mer *f*; ~ **drilling rig** *n* CONST plate-forme de forage en mer *f*; ~ **engineer** *n* NAUT ingénieur mécanicien *m*; ~ **engineering** *n* NAUT mécanique navale *f*; ~ **environment** *n* POLLUTION milieu marin *m*; ~ **farm** *n* OCEANOG ferme marine *f*; ~ **fish farming** *n* OCEANOG mariculture *f*; ~ **grazing** *n* OCEANOG pacage en mer *m*, pacage marin *m*; ~ **hovercraft** *n* TRANSP aéroglisseur marin *m*; ~ **insurance** *n* NAUT assurance maritime *f*; ~ **laboratory** *n* OCEANOG laboratoire marin *m*, laboratoire maritime *m*, laboratoire océanographique *m*; ~ **loss** *n* NAUT perte maritime *f*; ~ **propeller** *n* TRANSP hélice marine *f*; ~ **radar band** *n* NAUT bande radar maritime *f*; ~ **radar**

frequency *n* NAUT bande radar maritime *f*; ~ **radiant boiler** *n* HEATING chaudière marine à rayonnement *f*; ~ **radiant reheat boiler** *n* HEATING chaudière marine à réchauffer à rayonnement *f*; ~ **refrigeration plant** *n* REFRIG installation frigorifique marine *f*; ~ **riser** *n* PETR TECH tube prolongateur *m*; ~ **safety** *n* SAFETY sûreté du transport maritime *f*; ~ **sediment** *n* OCEANOG sédiment marin *m*

Mariner: ~ **space probe** *n* ASTRON sonde spatiale Mariner *f*

mariner's: ~ **compass** *n* NAUT compas de mer *m*; ~ **needle** *n* GEOPHYS aiguille aimantée *f*

maritime[1] *adj* NAUT de la mer, maritime

maritime:[2] ~ **air** *n* METEO air maritime *m*; ~ **climate** *n* METEO climat maritime *m*; ~ **community** *n* NAUT communauté maritime *f*; ~ **equatorial air** *n* METEO *monsoon* air équatorial maritime *m*, mousson *f*; ~ **industry** *n* NAUT secteur des transports maritimes *m*, secteur maritime *m*; ~ **law** *n* NAUT droit de la mer *m*, droit maritime *m*; ~ **mobile satellite service** *n* NAUT service mobile maritime par satellite *m*; ~ **peril** *n* NAUT fortune de mer *f*; ~ **radio beacon** *n* NAUT radiobalise maritime *f*, radiophare *m*; ~ **safety** *n* NAUT sécurité maritime *f*; ~ **satellite** *n* SPACE *communications* satellite de télécommunications maritimes *m*; ~ **switching center** *n* (AmE), ~ **switching centre** *n* (BrE) *(MSC)* TELECOM centre de commutation maritime *m*; ~ **terminal** *n* TRANSP gare maritime *f*

mark[1] *n* COMP, DP marque *f*, NAUT amer *m*, marque *f*, PATENTS marque *f*, PROD ENG *line, scratch* marque *f*, repère *m*, trace *f*, *of assayer* poinçon *m*, poinçon de garantie *m*; ~ **point** *n* CONST point de repère *m*; ~ **reader** *n* COMP, DP lecteur de marques *m*; ~ **reading** *n* COMP, DP lecture de marques *f*; ~ **scanning** *n* COMP, DP lecture de marques *f*, lecture optique de marques *f*; ~ **sensing** *n* COMP, DP lecture de marques *f*, lecture optique de marques *f*; ~ **with high reputation** *n* PATENTS marque de haute renommée *f*

mark[2] *vt* MAR POLL baliser; ~ **out** *vt* CONST *route* tracer

mark[3] *vti* PROD ENG *with marking or scribing gauge* trusquiner

marked: ~ **idle channel** *n* *(MIC)* TELECOM repérage des voies au repos *m*; ~ **yarn** *n* TEXTILES fil chiné *m*

marker *n* C&G témoin *m*, COMP, DP marqueur *m*, GEOL horizon sismique *m*, marqueur *m*, MECH ENG index d'instrument *m*, TELECOM marqueur *m*, TRANSP balise *f*, marqueur *m*; ~ **beacon** *n* AERONAUT radioborne *f*; ~ **bed** *n* GEOL horizon repère *m*; ~ **buoy** *n* NAUT bouée de balisage *f*; ~ **control system** *n* TELECOM système à marquage centralisé *m*; ~ **lamp** *n* VEHICLES *lighting* feu d'encombrement *m*; ~ **light** *n* CINEMAT lampe de marquage *f*; ~ **pulse** *n* ELECTRON impulsion de marquage *f*, marqueur *m*; ~ **system** *n* TELECOM système à marquage centralisé *m*

market: ~ **closeness** *n* TEXTILES proximité des marchés *f*; ~ **price** *n* TEXTILES prix courant *m*; ~ **research** *n* TEXTILES étude de marché *f*

marketability *n* TEXTILES possibilité de commercialisation *f*

marketable: ~ **gas** *n* GAS TECH gaz marchand *m*

marking *n* CONST *levelling operations* repérage *m*, PAPER TECH marquage *m*, PROD ENG gravure *f*, inscription *f*, marquage *m*, TELECOM, TESTING *of samples*, TEXTILES marquage *m*; ~ **awl** *n* PROD ENG tracelet *m*, traceret *m*, traçoir *m*; ~ **equipment** *n* PACKAGING machine à marquer *f*; ~ **felt** *n* PAPER TECH feutre marqueur *m*; ~ **gage**

n (AmE), ~ **gauge** *n* (BrE) MECH ENG trusquin à tracer *m*, PROD ENG trusquin *m*, trusquin à pointe *m*; ~ **ink** *n* COLOURS encre à marquer *f*, encre à marquer le linge *f*; ~ **label** *n* PACKAGING étiquette de repérage *f*; ~ **machine** *n* PACKAGING machine à marquer *f*; ~ **out** *n* C&G traçage *m*; ~ **press** *n* PAPER TECH presse à molette *f*; ~ **sequence** *n* TELECOM séquence de marquage *f*

mark-space: ~ **ratio** *n* PHYS rapport cyclique *m*

marl *n* WATER SUPP marne *f*

marlaceous *adj* GEOL marneux

marlinspike *n* NAUT *ropework* épissoir *m*

marly[1] *adj* GEOL marneux

marly:[2] ~ **clay** *n* WATER SUPP argile marneuse *f*; ~ **loam** *n* GEOL fausse glaise *f*

marmolite *n* MINERAL marmolite *f*

marquenched: ~ **wire** *n* SPRINGS fil trempé en étages *m*

marquenching *n* SPRINGS trempe étagée *f*

marquetry *n* C&G marqueterie en verre *f*

marriage: ~ **roll** *n* P&R *carpet coating* rouleau marieur *m*

married: ~ **print** *n* CINEMAT copie standard *f*; ~ **sound** *n* CINEMAT son associé à l'image *m*

marring *n* PRINT *of impression* décharge *f*, maculage *m*

marry: ~ **up** *vt* CINEMAT combiner, tirer standard

Mars ~ **segment** *n* SPACE *communications* composante martienne *f*

marsh *n* WATER SUPP marais *m*, marécage *m*; ~ **gas** *n* MINING brisou *m*, grisou *m*; ~ **island** *n* OCEANOG hallig *m*

marshaling *n* (AmE) *see marshalling*

Marshall: ~ **test** *n* CONST *asphalting* essai Marshall *m*

marshalling *n* (BrE) RAIL classement *m*; ~ **area** *n* (BrE) TRANSP *for containers* aire de manutention de conteneurs *f*; ~ **track** *n* (BrE) *(cf switching track)* RAIL *vehicles* voie de classement *f*; ~ **yard** *n* (BrE) *(cf switching yard)* RAIL chantier de triage *m*, gare de triage *f*

marshy[1] *adj* GEOL palustre, HYDROL marécageux

marshy:[2] ~ **environment** *n* GEOL milieu marécageux *m*, milieu palustre *m*

Martens: ~ **test** *n* P&R essai de Martens *m*

martensite *n* CRYSTALL, PROP MAT martensite *f*

martensitic[1] *adj* METALL, PROP MAT martensitique

martensitic:[2] ~ **transformation** *n* CRYSTALL, PROP MAT transformation martensitique *f*

Martian[1] *adj* ASTRON martien

Martian:[2] ~ **year** *n* ASTRON année martienne *f*

martite *n* MINERAL martite *f*

marver *n* C&G marbre *m*; ~ **mark** *n* C&G marbre *m*

marvering *n* C&G marbrage *m*

Marx: ~ **generator** *n* NUCLEAR générateur de Marx *m*

maser *n* ELECTRON, PHYS, TELECOM maser *m*

mash *n* FOOD TECH trempe *f*; ~ **liquor** *n* FOOD TECH eau d'empâtage *f*; ~ **tun** *n* FOOD TECH *fermentation* cuve de fermentation *f*

masher *n* FOOD TECH *fermentation* hydrateur *m*

mashing *n* FOOD TECH brassage *m*

mask *n* CINEMAT cache *m*, masque *m*, vignette *f*, COMP, DP, ELECTRON masque *m*, PHOTO cache *m*, SAFETY *protective clothing* masque *m*; ~ **alignment** *n* ELECTRON alignement du masque *m*; ~ **attachment** *n* CINEMAT porte-cache *m*; ~ **carrier** *n* ELECTRON porte-masque *m*; ~ **data** *n* PROD ENG données de masque *f pl*; ~ **generation** *n* ELECTRON fabrication de masques *f*; ~ **microphone** *n* ACOUSTICS microphone de masque *m*; ~ **run-out** *n* ELECTRON dilatation du masque *f*; ~ **set** *n* ELECTRON jeu de masques *m*; ~ **shot** *n* CINEMAT plan avec cache *m*

masked: ~ **lithography** *n* ELECTRON gravure avec masque *f*

masking *n* COMP, DP, ELECTRON, PRINT, RECORDING *of sound* masquage *m*; ~ **effect** *n* ACOUSTICS effet de masque *m*; ~ **frame** *n* PHOTO châssis-presse à margeur mobile *m*, margeur *m*; ~ **lacquer** *n* COLOURS laque pour cache *f*; ~ **level audiogram** *n* ACOUSTICS audiogramme d'un effet de masque *m*; ~ **paint** *n* COLOURS peinture couvrante *f*, peinture opaque *f*; ~ **paste** *n* COLOURS encre de masquage *f*; ~ **tape** *n* CINEMAT bande cache *f*, ruban cache *m*, PACKAGING cache ruban *m*

maskless: ~ **lithography** *n* ELECTRON gravure sans masque *f*

mask-programmable [1] *adj* COMP, DP programmable par masque

mask-programmable: [2] ~ **array** *n* ELECTRON matrice de portes programmable par masquage *f*; ~ **filter** *n* ELECTRON filtre programmé par masquage *m*

mason *n* CONST maçon *m*

masonite *n* MINERAL masonite *f*

masonry *n* C&G maçonnerie *f*, CONST maçonnage *m*, maçonnerie *f*; ~ **dam** *n* HYDROL barrage en maçonnerie *m*; ~ **drill** *n* MECH ENG foret pour bâtiment *m*; ~ **earth dam** *n* HYDROL barrage en maçonnerie et terre *m*; ~ **nail** *n* CONST *building* clou maçonnerie *m*; ~ **work** *n* CONST maçonnage *m*, maçonnerie *f*, ouvrage en maçonnerie *m*

masquerade *n* TELECOM usurpation d'identité *f*

mass *n* CHEM masse *f*, GEOPHYS masse *f*, masse du mobile *f*, PHYS masse *f*; ~ **absorption coefficient** *n* PHYS coefficient d'absorption massique *m*; ~ **accretion rate** *n* ASTRON taux d'accrétion de la masse *m*; ~ **action law** *n* CHEM loi d'action de masse *f*; ~ **airflow** *n* AERONAUT débit masse *m*; ~ **assignment** *n* NUCLEAR détermination du nombre de masse *f*; ~ **balance** *n* NUCLEAR bilan massique *m*; ~ **budget** *n* SPACE *communications* bilan de masse *m*; ~ **concentration** *n* SAFETY concentration en masse *f*; ~ **concrete** *n* CONST béton de masse *m*, gros béton *m*; ~ **defect** *n* PHYS défaut de masse *m*; ~ **effect** *n* NUCLEAR effet de masse *m*; ~ **energy equivalence** *n* PHYS équivalence masse-énergie *f*; ~ **energy transfer coefficient** *n* PHYS coefficient de transfert d'énergie massique *m*; ~ **excess** *n* PHYS excès de masse *m*; ~ **flow** *n* AERONAUT débit massique *m*, GEOL écoulement en masse *m*, NUCLEAR débit massique *m*; ~ **flow rate** *n* REFRIG débit masse *m*; ~ **flux** *n* FLUID PHYS *through pipe* flux massique *m*; ~ **fraction** *n* NUCLEAR fraction massique *f*, teneur en masse *f*; ~ **fuel rate of flow** *n* AERONAUT débit de carburant *m*; ~ **number** *n* PART PHYS, PHYS nombre de masse *m*; ~ **on a vertical spring** *n* MECH ENG masse tenue par un ressort vertical *f*; ~ **per unit length** *n* PHYS masse linéique *f*; ~ **per unit volume** *n* PHYS masse volumique *f*; ~ **production** *n* NAUT *shipbuilding* construction en série *f*, PROD ENG fabrication en série *f*, production de masse *f*, production à la chaîne *f*; ~ **rate** *n* PHYS *of flow* débit massique *m*; ~ **resistivity** *n* ELEC résistivité de masse *f*; ~ **spectrograph** *n* PHYS, RAD PHYS spectrographe de masse *m*; ~ **spectrometer** *n* LAB EQUIP *analysis*, PHYS, PROP MAT spectromètre de masse *m*; ~ **spectrometer-type leak detector** *n* MECH ENG *vacuum technology* détecteur de fuites à spectromètre de masse *m*; ~ **spectrometry** *n* CHEM *analysis*, PHYS, PROP MAT spectrométrie de masse *f*; ~ **spectrum** *n* PHYS, RAD PHYS spectre de masse *m*; ~ **spectrum**

analysis *n* RAD PHYS analyse par spectroscopie de masse *f*; ~ **storage** *n* COMP mémoire de grande capacité *f*, mémoire de masse *f*; ~ **sulfur dioxide concentration** *n* (AmE), ~ **sulphur dioxide concentration** *n* (BrE) SAFETY *in ambient air* concentration en masse de dioxyde de soufre *f*; ~ **termination** *n* ELEC ENG multiconnexion *f*; ~ **transfer** *n* ASTRON *in close binary stars* transfert de masse *m*

massicot *n* CHEM, MINERAL massicot *m*

massive [1] *adj* GEOL *texture* homogène, massif, sans structure définie

massive: [2] ~ **reaction** *n* METALL transformation massive *f*; ~ **star** *n* ASTRON étoile massive *f*

mass-luminosity: ~ **relationship** *n* ASTRON *of main sequence stars* rapport masse-luminosité *m*

mass-terminated: ~ **cable** *n* ELEC ENG câble plat *m*

mast *n* CONST *of derrick crane* anche *f*, NAUT, PETR mât *m*; ~ **crane** *n* NAUT *cargo loading* bigue *f*; ~ **foot** *n* NAUT pied de mât *m*; ~ **foot safety rail** *n* NAUT *boat building, deck fittings* balconnet de pied de mât *m*; ~ **rake** *n* NAUT inclinaison du mât *f*; ~ **step** *n* NAUT emplanture de mât *f*; ~ **tabernacle** *n* NAUT embase de mât *f*

master [1] *n* ACOUSTICS père *m*, COMP, DP maître *m*, RECORDING original *m*, *of disc recording* matrice *f*, TV bande de première génération *f*, enregistrement original *m*, original *m*; ~ **alloy** *n* PROP MAT alliage-mère *m*; ~ **card** *n* COMP, DP carte maîtresse *f*; ~ **change** *n* (MC) TRANSP spécification de changement notifié *f*; ~ **clock** *n* COMP, DP horloge mère *f*, horloge principale *f*, TELECOM horloge mère *f*, horloge pilote *f*; ~ **console** *n* COMP, DP console principale *f*; ~ **control** *n* TV régie finale *f*; ~ **control desk** *n* PRINT pupitre principal de commande *m*; ~ **control fader** *n* TV potentiomètre général *m*; ~ **controller** *n* TRANSP poste central *m*; ~ **control panel** *n* TV pupitre de régie finale *m*; ~ **control relay** *n* PROD ENG relais principal de commande *m*, relais-maître *m*; ~ **control reset** *n* (MCR) PROD ENG contrôle relaismaître *m*; ~ **control room** *n* (MCR) TV régie centrale *f*; ~ **cylinder** *n* AERONAUT *of brake* distributeur quadruple de freins *m*, maître-cylindre *m*, émetteur de freinage *m*, AUTO, VEHICLES *of brake, clutch* maître-cylindre *m*; ~ **disc** *n* (BrE) OPT disque matrice *m*, master disque *m*, matrice de fabrication *f*; ~ **disk** *n* DP *in CD ROM mastering* disque original *m*, OPT *see master disc*; ~ **engine** *n* AERONAUT réacteur pilote *m*; ~ **file** *n* COMP fichier principal *m*, DP fichier maître *m*; ~ **frequency** *n* ELECTRON fréquence pilote *f*; ~ **fuse** *n* MINING cordeau-maître *m*; ~ **gage** *n* (AmE) *see master gauge*; ~ **gain control** *n* ELECTRON commande générale de gain *f*, RECORDING potentiomètre principal de gain *m*; ~ **gauge** *n* (BrE) MECH ENG calibre d'ensemble *m*, calibre mère *m*; ~ **group** *n* TELECOM groupe tertiaire *m*; ~ **help directory** *n* PROD ENG répertoire d'aide principale *m*; ~ **indicator** *n* MECH ENG indicateur principal *m*; ~ **key** *n* CONST, PROD ENG passe-partout *m*; ~ **leaf** *n* AUTO *of suspension* lame maîtresse *f*; ~ **lode** *n* MINING filon mère *m*, filon principal *m*; ~ **mariner** *n* NAUT *merchant navy* capitaine marchand *m*; ~ **mask** *n* ELECTRON masque primaire *m*; ~ **monitor** *n* TV moniteur d'émission *m*, récepteur de contrôle final *m*; ~ **negative** *n* CINEMAT négatif original *m*; ~ **oscillator** *n* ELECTRON maître oscillateur *m*, oscillateur pilote *m*, PHYS maître oscillateur *m*, oscillateur maître *m*, oscillateur pilote *m*; ~ **pattern** *n* ELECTRON motif primaire *m*; ~ **positive** *n* CINEMAT positif pour contretype *m*; ~ **processor** *n* TELECOM processeur maître *m*; ~ **production schedule** *n* PROD ENG plan directeur du plan *m*; ~ **program** *n* (AmE), ~ **programme** *n* (BrE) TRANSP macroprogramme de régulation *m*; ~ **pulse** *n* ELECTRON impulsion pilote *f*; ~ **record** *n* COMP enregistrement principal *m*; ~ **scheduler** *n* PROD ENG directeur du plan *m*, responsable du plan *m*; ~ **spline** *n* MECH ENG dent mère *f*; ~ **station** *n* COMP, DP station principale *f*; ~ **switch** *n* CONTROL, ELEC interrupteur général *m*, interrupteur principal *m*, ELEC ENG commutateur principal *m*, interrupteur général *m*, TV interrupteur général *m*; ~ **tap** *n* MECH ENG matrice *f*, taraud matrice *m*, taraud mère *m*; ~ **tape** *n* DP bande de départ *f*, bande de référence *f*, bande maîtresse *f*, bande originale *f*, RECORDING bande maîtresse *f*, TV bande mère *f*, bande originale *f*; ~ **wheel** *n* MECH ENG roue maîtresse *f*

master[2] *vt* RECORDING faire la copie originale de

master's: ~ **certificate** *n* NAUT brevet de capitaine *m*

mastering *n* OPT gravure par pressage *f*, pressage industriel *m*

master-slave: ~ **flip-flop** *n* ELECTRON bascule maître-esclave *f*; ~ **system** *n* COMP, DP système maître-esclave *m*

masthead *n* NAUT tête de mât *f*; ~ **light** *n* NAUT *navigation* feu de tête de mât *m*

mastic *n* CONST, NAUT, PETR mastic *m*

mastication *n* P&R *operation, rubber* mastication *f*

mat[1] *adj* PROP MAT, TEXTILES mat

mat[2] *n* COAL TECH radier *m*, PAPER TECH matelas de fibres *m*, PRINT flan *m*, matrice *f*, PROP MAT mat *m*; ~ **enameling** *n* (AmE), ~ **enamelling** *n* (BrE) COATINGS vernissage mat *m*; ~ **formation** *n* C&G formation du matelas de verre *f*; ~ **ink** *n* COLOURS encre mate *f*; ~ **lacquer** *n* COATINGS vernis mat *m*; ~ **reinforcement** *n* CONST treillis d'armature *m*; ~ **surface paper** *n* PRINT papier mat *m*

mat[3] *vt* TEXTILES emmêler; ~ **down** *vt* CINEMAT mater

match:[1] ~ **cut** *n* TV coupure non-sensible *f*; ~ **dissolve** *n* TV fondu analogique *m*; ~ **hooks** *n pl* CONST croc à ciseaux *m*; ~ **plate** *n* PROD ENG plaque porte-modèle *f*, plaque-modèle *f*; ~ **truck** *n* RAIL *vehicles* wagon raccord *m*

match[2] *vt* CINEMAT conformer, CONST *joinery* bouveter, PROD ENG apparier, assortir, faire coïncider, TV conformer

matchboard *n* CONST *carpentry* planche bouvetée *f*, PROD ENG *founding* plaque-modèle en bois *f*

matched[1] *adj* PHYS adapté

matched:[2] ~ **cladding** *n* OPT gaine optique compensée *f*, TELECOM gaine adaptée *f*; ~ **conics technique** *n* SPACE méthode des sphères d'action d'influence *f*; ~ **diodes** *n pl* ELECTRON diodes appariées *f pl*; ~ **filter** *n* ELECTRON filtre adapté *m*; ~ **filtering** *n* ELECTRON filtrage adapté *m*; ~ **impedance** *n* ELEC ENG impédance adaptée *f*; ~ **load** *n* ELEC ENG, PHYS charge adaptée *f*; ~ **resistors** *n pl* ELEC ENG résistances appariées *f pl*; ~ **transistors** *n pl* ELECTRON transistors appariés *m pl*; ~ **tubes** *n pl* ELECTRON tubes appariés *m pl*; ~ **waveguide** *n* ELEC ENG guide d'ondes adapté *m*

matching: ~ **amplifier** *n* ELECTRON amplificateur d'adaptation *m*; ~ **attenuation** *n* ELECTRON affaiblissement d'adaptation *m*; ~ **machine** *n* CONST *joinery* machine à bouveter *f*; ~ **plane** *n* CONST bouvet à joindre *m*; ~ **planes** *n pl* CONST *pair* bouvet en deux morceaux *m*; ~ **transformer** *n* ELEC, ELEC ENG transformateur d'adaptation *m*

mate *n* NAUT *merchant navy* second capitaine *m*

mate's: ~ **receipt** *n* NAUT *merchant navy* reçu de bord *m*

mated: ~ **contacts** *n pl* ELEC ENG contacts en contact *m pl*, contacts mis en contact *m pl*

material *n* CHEM matière *f*, CONST matériau *m*, MECH ENG matière *f*; ~ **buckling** *n* NUCLEAR laplacien matière *m*; ~ **damping** *n* PROP MAT amortissement des matériaux *m*; ~ **defects** *n pl* MECH ENG défauts de matière *m pl*; ~ **dispersion** *n* OPT, TELECOM dispersion de matériaux *f*; ~ **dispersion coefficient** *n* OPT coefficient de dispersion du matériau *m*; ~ **dispersion parameter** *n* TELECOM coefficient de dispersion du matériau *m*; ~ **flow** *n* PACKAGING circulation de matériel *f*; ~ **handling crane** *n* PACKAGING grue de manutention de matériaux *f*; ~ **issue** *n* PROD ENG retrait de stock *m*, sortie de matière *f*, sortie de stock *f*; ~ **issue note** *n* PROD ENG bon de sortie matière *m*; ~ **item file** *n* PROD ENG fichier article *m*; ~ **pollution** *n* POLLUTION pollution solide *f*; ~ **quantity per unit** *n* PROD ENG coefficient d'utilisation *m*; ~ **requirement planning** *n* PROD ENG planification des besoins en matières *f*; ~ **scattering** *n* OPT, TELECOM diffusion de matériaux *f*; ~ **testing** *n* MECH ENG essai des matériaux *m*

materials *n pl* CONST, SAFETY, TEXTILES matériaux *m pl*; ~ **handling** *n* NUCLEAR manutention de matériaux *f*; ~ **reclamation** *n* RECYCLING récupération des matériaux *f*; ~ **specification** *n* QUALITY spécification des matériaux *f*; ~ **testing reactor** *n (MTR)* NUCLEAR réacteur d'essais de matériaux *m*; ~ **testing system** *n* TEXTILES système pour tester les matériaux *m*

mathematical: ~ **chance** *n* MATH probabilité mathématique *f*; ~ **induction** *n* COMP, DP raisonnement par récurrence *m*; ~ **model** *n* COMP, DP, ELECTRON modèle mathématique *m*, GAS TECH modèle de calcul *m*; ~ **particle** *n* NUCLEAR particule nue *f*; ~ **physics** *n* PHYS physique mathématique *f*; ~ **probability** *n* MATH probabilité mathématique *f*; ~ **programming** *n* COMP programmation mathématique *f*

mathematics *n* COMP, DP mathématiques *f pl*

mating *n* MECH raccordement *m*; ~ **connector** *n* PROD ENG connecteur d'accouplement *m*; ~ **flange** *n* MECH, NUCLEAR contre-bride *f*; ~ **surfaces** *n pl* MECH ENG plan de joint *m*

matlockite *n* MINERAL matlockite *f*

matrass *n* (AmE) *(cf bolthead flask)* LAB EQUIP *glassware* ballon à col court *m*

matrix *n* COMP matrice *f*, CONST *civil engineering* agglomérant *m*, DP matrice *f*, GEOL matrice *f*, matrice des roches *f*, MATH, METALL matrice *f*, PROD ENG moule *m*, TV matrice *f*; ~ **circuit** *n* TELECOM circuit matriciel *m*; ~ **configuration** *n* TELECOM interconnexion en matrice *f*; ~ **display** *n* TELECOM affichage matriciel *m*; ~ **failure** *n* PROP MAT rupture de matrice *f*; ~ **fiber interface** *n* (AmE), ~ **fibre interface** *n* (BrE) PROP MAT interface matrice-fibre *f*; ~ **fuel** *n* NUCLEAR combustible de matrice *m*; ~ **hairline** *n* PRINT espace fin *m*; ~ **mechanics** *n* PHYS mécanique des matrices *f*; ~ **printer** *n* COMP, PRINT imprimante matricielle *f*; ~ **signalization** *n* TRANSP signalisation à matrice lumineuse *f*

matrixing *n* TV matriçage *m*

matt[1] *adj* PROP MAT, TEXTILES mat

matt[2] *n* CINEMAT cache *m*; ~ **box** *n* CINEMAT parasoleil avec porte-filtre et porte-cache *m*; ~ **cutting** *n* C&G taille non polie *f*; ~ **finish** *n* COLOURS finition mate *f*; ~ **glaze** *n* C&G glaçure mate *f*; ~ **paper** *n* PHOTO, PRINT papier mat *m*; ~ **screen** *n* INSTRUMENT verre dépoli de projection *m*; ~ **vitrifiable color** *n* (AmE), ~ **vitrifiable**

colour *n* (BrE) C&G couleur vitrifiable mate *f*

matte [1] *n* CINEMAT cache *m*, GAS TECH, METALL, PROP MAT matte *f*; ~ **and counter-matte** *n* CINEMAT cache et contrecache *m*; ~ **box** *n* CINEMAT, PHOTO porte-cache *m*; ~ **shot** *n* CINEMAT plan cache-contrecache *m*

matte: [2] ~ **out** *vt* CINEMAT éliminer par cache

matted *adj* PRINT maté

matter *n* PRINT copie *f*, manuscrit *m*

matt-etching: ~ **paste** *n* C&G pâte pour gravure mate *f*; ~ **salt** *n* C&G sel à mater *m*

matting *n* P&R *paint* mattage *m*; ~ **amplifier** *n* TV incrusteur *m*, truqueur électronique *m*

mattock *n* CONST *grubbing* pioche à défricher *f*, pioche à défricher à hache *f*, pioche-hache *f*,pick décintroir de talus *m*, décintroir à talus *m*

mattress *n* HEAT ENG *thermal insulation*, TEXTILES matelas *m*; ~ **cover** *n* TEXTILES protège-matelas *m*; ~ **ticking** *n* TEXTILES toile à matelas *f*

maturation *n* PETR TECH maturation *f*; ~ **pond** *n* WATER SUPP bassin de maturation *m*

mature: ~ **river** *n* HYDROL cours d'eau au stade de maturité *m*

maturing *n* PAPER TECH maturation *f*, stabilisation *f*; ~ **temperature** *n* C&G température de vitrification *f*

matzo *n* FOOD TECH pain azyme *m*

maul *n* CONST *quarrying* maillet *m*, mailloche *f*

mauveine *n* CHEM mauvéine *f*

maximal: ~ **stress** *n* PRINT contrainte maximale *f*, effort maximal *m*; ~ **sustainable yield** *n* OCEANOG production maximale équilibrée *f*

maximization *n* TELECOM maximisation *f*

maximum *n* NUCLEAR ligne *f*, maximum *m*, pic *m*; ~ **admissible power** *n* TELECOM puissance maximale admissible *f*; ~ **allowable belt stress** *n* MECH ENG contrainte maximum admissible de la courroie *f*; ~ **allowable concentration** *n* (*MAC*) POLLUTION concentration maximale admissible *f*; ~ **allowable pressure** *n* PROD ENG pression maximale admissible *f*; ~ **axial thrust** *n* FUELLESS poussée axiale maximale *f*; ~ **beam** *n* NAUT *boatbuilding* largeur hors tout *f*; ~ **bending moment** *n* SPACE *spacecraft* instant d'inclinaison maximale *m*, instant de courbure maximale *m*; ~ **capacity** *n* NUCLEAR *of nuclear power plant* puissance électrique maximale possible *f*, PAPER TECH capacité de pointe maximum *f*; ~ **consumption** *n* HYDROL *of water* consommation de pointe *f*; ~ **continuous power** *n* AERONAUT puissance maximale continue *f*; ~ **current** *n* ELEC courant maximal *m*; ~ **current rating** *n* ELEC ENG intensité maximale admissible *f*; ~ **cutout** *n* ELEC ENG disjoncteur à maximum *m*; ~ **daily runoff** *n* HYDROL débit de pointe journalier *m*; ~ **deckle** *n* PAPER TECH largeur de toile utile *f*; ~ **demand** *n* ELEC *supply* demande maximale *f*, ELEC ENG demande maximum *f*; ~ **depth** *n* OCEANOG profondeur de destruction *f*; ~ **design speed** *n* VEHICLES vitesse maximum de conception *f*; ~ **dressed width of warp** *n* TEXTILES largeur de chaîne maximum *f*; ~ **elevation figure** *n* PRINT *mapmaking* indication d'élévation maximale *f*; ~ **emission concentration** *n* POLLUTION CMI, concentration maximale d'immixtion *f*, teneur maximale des émissions *f*; ~ **engine overspeed** *n* AERONAUT survitesse maximale du moteur *f*; ~ **entropy principle** *n* RAD PHYS principe d'entropie maximale *m*; ~ **except takeoff power** *n* (*METO power*) AERONAUT puissance METO *f*; ~ **exposure limit** *n* SAFETY limite maximale d'exposition *f*; ~ **flap extended speed** *n* AERONAUT

vitesse maximale volets sortis *f*; ~ **flood level** *n* HYDROL niveau maximum de crue *m*; ~ **flux heat** *n* NUCLEAR flux de chaleur maximum *m*; ~ **fuel central temperature** *n* NUCLEAR température centrale maximale combustible *f*; ~ **hourly runoff** *n* HYDROL débit de pointe horaire *m*; ~ **hourly volume** *n* TRANSP débit horaire maximal *m*; ~ **instantaneous power** *n* SPACE puissance instantanée maximale *f*; ~ **landing gear extended speed** *n* AERONAUT vitesse maximale du train d'atterrissage sorti *f*; ~ **landing gear operating speed** *n* AERONAUT vitesse maximale de sortie du train d'atterrissage *f*; ~ **lift** *n* AERONAUT portance maximum *f*; ~ **likelihood** *n* MATH maximum de vraisemblance *m*; ~ **load** *n* AERONAUT, NAUT *cargo* charge limite *f*; ~ **melting rate** *n* C&G capacité de fusion *f*; ~ **numerical aperture** *n* OPT ouverture numérique maximale *f*; ~ **operating altitude** *n* AERONAUT altitude maximum en exploitation *f*; ~ **output** *n* ELEC *of generator* puissance utile maximale *f*; ~ **output mixture ratio** *n* AUTO dosage de puissance maximum *m*; ~ **payload** *n* AERONAUT charge marchande maximum *f*; ~ **permissible deviation** *n* MECH ENG écart maximal toléré *m*; ~ **permissible dose** *n* RAD PHYS dose maximale admissible *f*; ~ **permissible error** *n* METR erreur maximale tolérée *f*; ~ **permissible flatness error** *n* MECH ENG écart maximal admis de planéité *m*; ~ **permissible Mach number** *n* AERONAUT nombre de Mach maximal admissible *m*; ~ **permissible occupational whole-body dose** *n* RAD PHYS dose maximale d'activité professionnelle *f*; ~ **permissible operating speed** *n* AERONAUT vitesse maximale en exploitation *f*; ~ **power** *n* ELEC *supply* puissance maximale *f*; ~ **power at rated wind speed** *n* FUELLESS puissance maximale à la vitesse nominale du vent *f*; ~ **power input** *n* ELEC ENG puissance absorbée maximale *f*; ~ **power requirement** *n* PROD ENG puissance maximum absorbée *f*; ~ **power transmission** *n* ELEC ENG transmission du maximum d'énergie *f*; ~ **rated step voltage** *n* ELEC *tap changer* tension d'échelon assignée maximale *f*; ~ **rated through- current** *n* ELEC courant traversant assigné maximal *m*; ~ **relative time interval error** *n* (*MRTIE*) TELECOM erreur relative maximum d'intervalle de temps *f*; ~ **ripple current** *n* PROD ENG ondulation efficace maximale *f*; ~ **rotor speed** *n* AERONAUT régime maximum rotor *m*; ~ **shaft speed** *n* FUELLESS *wind power* vitesse maximale de l'arbre *f*; ~ **signal** *n* ELECTRON signal maximal *m*; ~ **signal amplitude** *n* ELECTRON amplitude maximale du signal *f*; ~ **sound pressure** *n* ACOUSTICS pression acoustique maximale *f*; ~ **speed** *n* AERONAUT *of aircraft*, NAUT *of ship* vitesse maximale *f*; ~ **speed in level flight with rated power** *n* AERONAUT vitesse maximale en palier au régime moteur nominal *f*; ~ **spring back load** *n* AERONAUT charge maximum de réaction élastique *f*; ~ **theoretical numerical aperture** *n* TELECOM ouverture numérique théorique maximale *f*; ~ **threshold speed** *n* AERONAUT vitesse maximale au seuil *f*; ~ **time interval error** *n* (*MTIE*) TELECOM *erreur maximum d'intervalle de temps f*; ~ **total load** *n* CONST charge totale maximale *f*; ~ **total weight** *n* VEHICLES poids maximum en charge *m*, poids total maximum *m*; ~ **trimmed machine width** *n* PACKAGING largeur maximum de coupe d'une machine *f*, PAPER TECH largeur rognée maximale de la machine *f*; ~ **usable frequency** *n* (*MUF*) ELEC ENG fréquence maximale utilisable *f*; ~ **voltage** *n* ELEC tension maximale *f*; ~ **voltage relay** *n* ELEC relais à maximum de tension *m*; ~

weight *n* PACKAGING poids maximum *m*; ~ **welding current** *n* CONST courant de soudage maximal *m*; ~ **wheel vertical load** *n* AERONAUT charge verticale maximum sur roues *f*

maximum-minimum: ~ **thermometer** *n* HEAT ENG thermomètre à maximums et minimums *m*, LAB EQUIP thermomètre à maxima et minima *m*, PHYS thermomètre à maximums et minimums *m*, THERMOD thermomètre à maxima et minima *m*

maxite *n* MINERAL maxite *f*

maxwell *n* (*Mx*) ELEC *magnetic flux*, ELEC ENG *magnetic flux* maxwell *m* (*Mx*)

Maxwell: ~ **distribution** *n* PHYS distribution de Maxwell *f*

Maxwell's: ~ **equations** *n pl* PHYS équations de Maxwell *f pl*

Mayday *n* AERONAUT, NAUT *radio distress signal* mayday *m*

Mb *abbr* (*megabyte*) COMP, DP Mo (*méga-octet*)

M-bit *n* TELECOM bit M *m*, bit de continuation *m*

MC *abbr* (*master change*) TRANSP spécification de changement notifié *f*

MCA *abbr* (*multipoint command assign token*) TELECOM commande multipoint d'assignation de jeton *f*

MCC *abbr* (*multipoint command conference*) TELECOM commande multipoint de conférence *f*

MCD *abbr* (*maintenance cell description*) TELECOM description de cellule de maintenance *f*

MCF *abbr* (*message communication function*) TELECOM fonction de communication de messages *f*

MCFD *abbr* (*millions of cubic feet per day*) PETR TECH *unit of volume in prospecting, production* millions de pieds cubes par jour *m pl*

MCN *abbr* (*multipoint command negating MCS*) TELECOM commande multipoint de neutralisation de MCS *f*

MCR *abbr* PROD ENG (*master control reset*) contrôle relais maître *m*, TELECOM (*multipoint command release token*) commande multipoint de libération de jeton *f*, TV (*master control room*) régie centrale *f*

MCS *abbr* (*multipoint command symmetrical data transmission*) TELECOM commande multipoint de transmission symétrique des données *f*

MCT *abbr* (*multipoint command token claim*) TELECOM commande multipoint de demande de jeton *f*

MCV *abbr* (*multipoint command visualization forcing*) TELECOM commande multipoint d'imposition de visualisation *f*

Md (*mendelevium*) CHEM Md (*mendélévium*)

MD *abbr* TELECOM (*mediation device*) dispositif de médiation *m*, équipement de médiation *m*, TELECOM (*management domain*) domaine de gestion *m*

MDF *abbr* (*main distribution frame*) TELECOM répartiteur d'entrée *m*

MDI *abbr* (*diphenylmethane diisocyanate*) P&R *curing agent* diisocyante de diphénylméthane *m*

MDR *abbr* (*memory data register*) COMP, DP registre mémoire de données *m*

meadow: ~ **ore** *n* MINING fer des marais *m*, minerai de fer des marais *m*, minerai de tourbières *m*

meager: ~ **clay** *n* (AmE), **meagre clay** *n* (BrE) C&G argile maigre *f*

mean *n* COMP, DP, MATH moyenne *f*; ~ **absolute deviation** *n* PROD ENG écart absolu moyen *m*; ~ **aerodynamic chord** *n* (*MAC*) AERONAUT corde aérodynamique moyenne *f* (*CAM*); ~ **annual variation** *n* NAUT *of tide* amplitude moyenne annuelle *f*; ~ **anomaly** *n* ASTRON,

SPACE anomalie moyenne *f*; ~ **bond energy** *n* NUCLEAR énergie moyenne de liaison *f*; ~ **busy hour** *n* TELECOM heure chargée moyenne *f*; ~ **chord of the control surface** *n* AERONAUT corde moyenne de la gouverne *f*; ~ **daily flow** *n* WATER SUPP débit journalier moyen *m*; ~ **density of matter** *n* ASTRON densité moyenne de la matière *f*; ~ **deviation** *n* ELEC, MATH écart moyen *m*; ~ **draft** *n* (AmE), ~ **draught** *n* (BrE) NAUT *ship design* tirant d'eau moyen *m*; ~ **error** *n* ELEC erreur moyenne *f*; ~ **free path** *n* ACOUSTICS libre parcours moyen *m*, METALL parcours libre moyen *m*, PHYS libre parcours moyen *m*; ~ **geometric chord** *n* GEOM corde géométrique moyenne *f*; ~ **glide path error** *n* AERONAUT erreur moyenne d'alignement de descente *f*; ~ **hourly runoff** *n* HYDROL débit moyen horaire *m*; ~ **lethal dose** *n* (*MLD*) NUCLEAR, POLLUTION, RAD PHYS, SAFETY dose létale moyenne *f* (*DLM*); ~ **life** *n* PHYS vie moyenne *f*, QUALITY durée de vie moyenne *f*; ~ **lifetime** *n* PHYS durée de vie moyenne *f*; ~ **opinion score** *n* (*MOS*) TELECOM note moyenne d'opinion *f*; ~ **pitch angle** *n* AERONAUT pas moyen *m*; ~ **sea level** *n* NAUT *navigation* niveau moyen de la mer *m*, OCEANOG niveau d'équilibre *m*, niveau hydrostatique *m*, niveau moyen de la mer *m*; ~ **sidereal day** *n* ASTRON jour sidéral moyen *m*; ~ **solar time** *n* SPACE temps solaire moyen *m*; ~ **speed** *n* TRANSP vitesse moyenne *f*; ~ **square error** *n* (*MSE*) COMP, DP, MATH erreur quadratique moyenne *f*; ~ **square value** *n* ELEC valeur moyenne quadratique *f*; ~ **square velocity** *n* PHYS vitesse quadratique moyenne *f*; ~ **stress** *n* METALL contrainte moyenne *f*; ~ **sun** *n* ASTRON soleil moyen *m*; ~ **temperature difference** *n* HEATING différence moyenne de température *f*, REFRIG écart moyen de température *m*; ~ **tidal range** *n* FUELLESS marnage moyen *m*; ~ **time between failures** *n* (*MTBF*) COMP, DP moyenne de temps de bon fonctionnement *f* (*MTBF*), temps moyen entre pannes *m*, ELEC ENG moyenne de temps entre pannes *f*, temps moyen entre pannes *m*, MECH, QUALITY, SPACE moyenne de temps de bon fonctionnement *f* (*MTBF*), temps moyen de bon fonctionnement *m*; ~ **time between removals** *n* (*MTBR*) SPACE temps moyen entre réparations *m*; ~ **time to failure** *n* (*MTTF*) QUALITY durée moyenne avant défaillance *f*; ~ **time to repair** *n* (*MTTR*) COMP, DP, ELEC ENG temps moyen de réparation *m*, MECH, SPACE durée moyenne de réparation *f*; ~ **trajectory** *n* MILIT *artillery* trajectoire moyenne *f*; ~ **value** *n* ELEC, PHYS valeur moyenne *f*; ~ **value recorder** *n* INSTRUMENT enregistreur de valeurs moyennes *m*; ~ **wind speed** *n* FUELLESS vitesse moyenne du vent *f*

meander [1] *n* HYDROL méandre *m*

meander [2] *vi* HYDROL serpenter

meandering *n* CONST *surveying* cheminement *m*

meaningless: ~ **data** *n* COMP informations parasites *f pl*

means: ~ **of escape** *n pl* SAFETY moyens d'évacuation *m pl*, *from fire in buildings* moyens de fuite *m pl*

measurable: ~ **quantity** *n* METR erreur maximale tolérée *f*

measurand *n* ELECTRON grandeur mesurée *f*, METR mesurande *f*

measure [1] *n* CHEM *proportion, percentage* dose *f*, COMP, DP mesure *f*, METR décamètre à ruban *m*, mesure à ruban *f*, mètre à ruban *m*, ruban *m*, mesure *f*, mètre *m*, *in circular case* roulette *f*, PRINT justification *f*

measure [2] *vt* CHEM doser, mesurer, MECH ENG *to calibrate* tarer, METR mesurer au mètre, métrer, *land* arpenter, mesurer, *solids* cuber

measured: ~ **current** n ELEC courant à mesurer m; ~ **quantity** n ELECTRON grandeur mesurée f; ~ **ton** n NAUT tonneau d'encombrement m; ~ **voltage** n ELEC *current* tension à mesurer f

measurement n CHEM dosage m, mesure f, ELECTRON mesure f, METR *action* mesurage m, mesure f, *in metres* métrage m, *of land* arpentage m, mesurage m, *of solids* cubage m, *size, number* dimension f, RAD PHYS *of atomic density*, SAFETY *of environmental noise*, WAVE PHYS *of wavelength* mesure f; ~ **and evaluation of vibration severity** n SAFETY mesurage et évaluation de l'intensité vibratoire m; ~ **chamber** n INSTRUMENT chambre de mesure f; ~ **control** n CONTROL contrôle des mesures m; ~ **process** n METR processus de mesure m; ~ **of quantities** n CONST métrage m, métré m; ~ **range selector** n INSTRUMENT sélecteur des plages d'étude m, sélecteur des zones de mesure m; ~ **standard** n METR *for comparison of other measuring instruments* étalon m; ~ **of the vibration produced by portable machines** n SAFETY mesurage des vibrations émises par les machines portatives m

measurements: ~ **reactor** n NUCLEAR réacteur de mesure m; ~ **while drilling** n pl (MWD) PETR TECH mesures en cours de forage f pl

measuring n CHEM dosage m, mesure f, METR *in metres* métrage m, *of land* arpentage m, mesurage m, *of solids* cubage m, PRINT, SAFETY mesurage m; ~ **amplifier** n ELECTRON amplificateur de mesure m; ~ **apparatus** n CONST appareil de mesure m, appareillage de mesure m, INSTRUMENT instruments de métrologie m pl; ~ **block** n MECH ENG *tool-setting gauge* calibre prismatique m; ~ **bridge** n MECH ENG pont de mesure m; ~ **chain** n CONST chaîne d'arpentage f, chaîne d'arpenteur f; ~ **cylinder** n LAB EQUIP *glassware, analysis* éprouvette graduée f, PHOTO *for processing chemicals* gobelet gradué m, éprouvette graduée f; ~ **desk** n NUCLEAR poste de mesure m; ~ **device** n INSTRUMENT, METR dispositif de mesure m; ~ **equipment** n ELEC appareil de mesure m; ~ **error** n METR erreur de mesurage f; ~ **instrument** n ELEC appareil de mesure m, METR appareil de mesure m, instrument de mesure m; ~ **machine** n METR machine de mesure f; ~ **microscope** n INSTRUMENT loupe de lecture f, microscope de lecture m, microscope de mesure m; ~ **oscilloscope** n ELEC oscilloscope mesureur m; ~ **relay** n ELEC ENG relais de mesure m; ~ **rod** n METR pige rigide f; ~ **spark gap** n ELEC ENG éclateur de mesure m; ~ **system** n ELEC système de mesure m; ~ **tape** n METR décamètre à ruban m, mesure à ruban f, mètre à ruban m, *in circular case* roulette f, ruban m; ~ **transducer** n METR transducteur de mesure m; ~ **tube** n CHEM tube pour dosage m; ~ **weir** n HYDROL, WATER SUPP déversoir de mesure m

meat: ~ **hook** n FOOD TECH croc de boucherie m, esse f

mechanic n PROD ENG *person* mécanicien m, ouvrier mécanicien m, serrurier mécanicien m

mechanical: ~ **admittance** n ACOUSTICS admittance mécanique f; ~ **air filter** n HEAT ENG filtre à air mécanique m; ~ **behavior of materials** n (AmE) *see mechanical behaviour of materials*; ~ **behavior test** n (AmE) *see mechanical behaviour test*; ~ **behaviour of materials** n (BrE) TESTING comportement mécanique de matériaux m; ~ **behaviour test** n (BrE) GAS TECH essai de comportement mécanique m; ~ **bond** n NUCLEAR *of fuel and can* liaison mécanique f; ~ **boy** n C&G machine à mouiller f; ~ **broom** n CONST balayeuse mécanique f,

déblayeur mécanique m, pelle mécanique f; ~ **chopper** n NUCLEAR hacheur de faisceau m, système de pulsationde faisceau m; ~ **classifier** n COAL TECH classeur mécanique m; ~ **collector** n POLLUTION dépoussiéreur mécanique m; ~ **components** n pl MECH ENG éléments de machines m pl; ~ **concentration** n PROD ENG concentration mécanique f; ~ **contactor** n ELEC *of relay* contacteur mécanique m; ~ **cutter** n PETR excavatrice f; ~ **decanning** n NUCLEAR dégainage mécanique m; ~ **decladding** n NUCLEAR dégainage mécanique m; ~ **dividing head** n MECH ENG poupée diviseuse à commande mécanique f; ~ **draftsman** n (AmE), ~ **draughtsman** n (BrE) PROD ENG traceur mécanicien m; ~ **drawing** n PROD ENG dessin géométrique m; ~ **drive** n MECH ENG entraînement mécanique m; ~ **editing** n TV montage physique m; ~ **efficiency** n FUELLESS, MECH ENG rendement mécanique m; ~ **end stop** n ELEC *tap changer* fin de course mécanique f; ~ **endurance** n PROD ENG durée de vie f; ~ **energy** n MECH ENG travail moteur m, travail mécanique m, énergie mécanique f; ~ **engineer** n PROD ENG ingénieur mécanicien m; ~ **engineering** n PROD ENG construction mécanique f; ~ **equivalent of heat** n MECH équivalent mécanique de calorie m, THERMOD équivalent calorifique m, équivalent mécanique de la chaleur m; ~ **error** n TV erreur due au mécanisme f; ~ **exhaust air installations** n pl SAFETY installations d'épuration d'air d'échappement f pl; ~ **filter** n ELECTRON filtre mécanique m; ~ **firing** n MECH ENG *stoking* chauffage mécanique m; ~ **fuel pump** n AUTO pompe à essence mécanique f, VEHICLES *supply* pompe à essence à commande mécanique f; ~ **grab** n CONST benne preneuse f, excavateur m, pelle mécanique f; ~ **handling equipment** n MECH ENG engins de manutention m pl; ~ **hazards** n pl SAFETY dangers dûs aux dispositifs mécaniques m pl; ~ **impedance** n ACOUSTICS, ELEC ENG impédance mécanique f; ~ **instability** n METALL instabilité mécanique f; ~ **interlock** n PROD ENG bloc d'interverrouillage mécanique m; ~ **isolation** n SAFETY *against vibration* isolation mécanique f; ~ **latch** n PROD ENG bloc d'accrochage mécanique m; ~ **life** n ELEC ENG, PROD ENG durée de vie mécanique f; ~ **locking** n MECH ENG verrouillage mécanique m; ~ **modulation** n ELECTRON modulation mécanique f; ~ **operation** n MECH ENG *of valve* commande mécanique f; ~ **optical switch** n TELECOM commutateur optomécanique m; ~ **oscillation** n ACOUSTICS oscillation mécanique f; ~ **overlay** n PRINT calque de travail m; ~ **piping** n HYDROL renard m; ~ **polishing** n MECH ENG, METALL polissage mécanique m; ~ **properties** n pl CONST, FLUID PHYS *of fluids* propriétés mécaniques f pl, MECH ENG propriétés mécaniques f pl, *of fasteners* caractéristiques mécaniques f pl, P&R propriétés mécaniques f pl; ~ **pulp** n PAPER TECH pâte mécanique f; ~ **pulp board** n PACKAGING carton de pâte mécanique m, PAPER TECH carton bois m, carton de pâte mécanique m; ~ **reactance** n ACOUSTICS réactance mécanique f; ~ **recorder** n ACOUSTICS enregistreur mécanique m; ~ **recording** n ACOUSTICS, RECORDING enregistrement mécanique m; ~ **refrigeration** n MECH ENG réfrigération mécanique f; ~ **resistance** n ACOUSTICS résistance mécanique f; ~ **resonance** n PHYS résonance mécanique f; ~ **sampler** n COAL TECH échantillonneur mécanique m; ~ **servo-link device** n CONTROL élément mécanique d'asservissement m; ~ **setting** n PRINT composition mécanique f; ~ **shock test** n METR essai de choc mécanique m; ~ **splice** *n* OPT, TELECOM épissure mécanique *f*, TV collage physique *m*; ~ **stability** *n* P&R stabilité mécanique *f*; ~ **stage** *n* INSTRUMENT chariot *m*, platine à chariot *f*, PHOTO platine à coordonnées *f*; ~ **stage control** *n* INSTRUMENT bouton de commande du chariot *m*; ~ **stoker** *n* HEATING *furnace* appareil d'alimentation *m*; ~ **stop unit** *n* MECH ENG butée mécanique *f*; ~ **strength** *n* PROP MAT résistance mécanique *f*; ~ **system** *n* ACOUSTICS, MECH ENG *cooling, lubricating, power transmission* système mécanique *m*; ~ **testing** *n* MECH ENG essai mécanique *m*; ~ **tint** *n* PRINT *engraving* fond tramé *m*; ~ **transmission** *n* FUELLESS transmission mécanique *f*; ~ **transmission system** *n* MECH ENG système de transmission mécanique *m*; ~ **trencher** *n* PETR excavatrice *f*; ~ **tripping device** *n* ELEC *circuit breaker* déclencheur mécanique *m*; ~ **vibration** *n* ACOUSTICS vibration mécanique *f*; ~ **wave** *n* ELEC ENG onde mécanique *f*; ~ **wear** *n* CONST, PROD ENG usure mécanique *f*; ~ **weathering** *n* GEOL *of rocks* désagrégation physique *f*, érosion mécanique *f*, PETR altération mécanique *f*; ~ **woodpulp** *n* PACKAGING, PAPER TECH pâte mécanique *f*; ~ **woodpulp board** *n* PAPER TECH carton de pâte mécanique *m*; ~ **woodpulp paper** *n* PAPER TECH papier de pâte mécanique *m*; ~ **zero adjustment** *n* ELEC *of instrument* ajustement de zéro mécanique *m*

mechanically-blocked: ~ **electrical impedance** *n* ACOUSTICS impédance électrique en blocage mécanique *f*

mechanically-tuned: ~ **magnetron** *n* ELECTRON magnétron à accord mécanique *m*; ~ **oscillator** *n* ELECTRON oscillateur à accord mécanique *m*

mechanicals *n pl* PRINT maquette *f*, montage papier *m*

mechanics *n* MECH ENG, PHYS mécanique *f*

mechanism *n* MECH ENG mécanique *f*, mécanisme *m*, organes *m pl*

mechanized: ~ **coal-winning** *n* COAL TECH abattage mécanique du charbon *m*

mechanothermal: ~ **effect** *n* THERMOD effet mécanothermique *m*

meconate *n* CHEM méconate *m*

meconic *adj* CHEM méconique *m*

meconin *n* CHEM méconine *f*

media *n* TV média *m*

mediamarimeter *n* OCEANOG médimaremètre *m*

median *n* COMP, DP, GEOM, MATH *statistics* médiane *f*; ~ **lethal concentration** *n* POLLUTION CL50, concentration létale à 50% *f*; ~ **lethal dose** *n* (*LD50*) NUCLEAR, POLLUTION, RAD PHYS *ionizing radiation*, SAFETY dose létale à 50% *f*, dose létale médiane *f* (*DL50*); ~ **line** *n* PETR TECH ligne médiane *f*; ~ **valley** *n* GEOL vallée axiale *f*, vallée centrale de la dorsale médio-océanique *f*

mediant *n* ACOUSTICS médiante *f*

mediation: ~ **device** *n* (*MD*) TELECOM dispositif de médiation *m*, équipement de médiation *m*; ~ **function** *n* (*MF*) TELECOM fonction de médiation *f*

mediator *n* PART PHYS *of electromagnetic force* médiatrice *f*

medicinal *adj* CHEM *oil* médicamenteux, médicinal

mediterranean: ~ **climate** *n* METEO climat de type méditerranéen *m*, climat méditerranéen *m*

medium *n* COMP, DP support *m*, PHYS milieu *m*, PRINT liant véhicule *m*, médium *m*, WATER SUPP milieu *m*; ~ **access control** *n* (*MAC*) TELECOM commande d'accès au support *f*, contrôle d'accès au média *m*; ~ **adaptor** *n* (*MA*) TELECOM adaptateur de support *m*; ~ **close-up** *n* CINEMAT plan mi-moyen *m*; ~ **distillates** *n pl* PETR

TECH distillats moyens *m pl*; ~ **frequency** *n* (*MF*) ELEC ENG moyenne fréquence *f*; ~ **grade** *n* MINING *of ore* teneur moyenne *f*, PROD ENG *of emery wheel* degré de dureté moyen *m*; ~ **grinding** *n* PROD ENG *between coarse and fine* broyage moyen *m*; ~ **head** *n* FUELLESS colonne d'eau moyenne *f*, colonne moyenne d'eau *f*; ~ **rate** *n* TELECOM *call charge* tarif blanc *m*; ~ **shot** *n* CINEMAT plan moyen *m*; ~ **thermal carbon black** *n* (*MT carbon black*) P&R *rubber pigment, filler* noir MT *m*; ~ **voltage** *n* ELEC ENG tension moyenne *f*; ~ **wave** *n* (*MW*) ELEC, WAVE PHYS *radio* onde moyenne *f*; ~ **wave band** *n* NAUT bande hectométrique *f*

medium-angle: ~ **lens** *n* PHOTO objectif normal *m*, objectif à angle moyen *m*

medium-energy: ~ **nuclear physics** *n* NUCLEAR physique nucléaire des énergies moyennes *f*

medium-frequency: ~ **furnace** *n* ELEC ENG four MF *m*, four à moyenne fréquence *m*; ~ **heating** *n* ELEC ENG chauffage MF *m*, chauffage à moyenne fréquence *m*

medium-grade: ~ **metamorphism** *n* GEOL mésométamorphisme *m*

medium-graded *adj* COAL TECH *soil* à coefficient d'uniformité moyen

medium-grained *adj* GEOL à grain moyen

medium-hard *adj* PROP MAT mi-dur

medium-power: ~ **amplifier** *n* ELECTRON amplificateur de moyenne puissance *m*

medium-processing: ~ **channel carbon black** *n* (*MPC carbon black*) P&R *rubber pigment, filler* noir MPC *m*

medium-range: ~ **aircraft** *n* AERONAUT moyen-courrier *m*; ~ **airliner** *n* AERONAUT moyen-courrier *m*

medium-scale: ~ **integration** *n* (*MSI*) COMP, DP, ELECTRON, TELECOM intégration à moyenne échelle *f*

medium-sized *adj* PRINT *papermaking* mi-collé

medium-soft: ~ **grade** *n* PROD ENG *of emery wheel* degré de dureté tendre moyen *m*

medium-speed: ~ **engine** *n* NAUT diesel semi-rapide *m*

medium-type: ~ **ball bearings** *n* PROD ENG roulement à billes pour charge moyenne *m*

medium-volatile: ~ **coal** *n* COAL TECH charbon gras *m*

medium-voltage: ~ **system** *n* ELEC ENG réseau de moyenne tension *m*; ~ **vacuum contactor** *n* PROD ENG contacteur moyenne tension à coupure sous vide *m*

meerschaum *n* MINERAL écume de mer *f*

meet [1] *vt* SAFETY *requirements* satisfaire à

meet [2] *vi* WATER SUPP confluer, se rencontrer

meeting *n* CONST rencontre *f*; ~ **post** *n* WATER SUPP *of lock gate* montant de busc *m*, poteau battant *m*, poteau busqué *m*

meet-me: ~ **bridge** *n* TELECOM dispositif de téléréunion *m*; ~ **conference call** *n* TELECOM conférence rendez-vous *f*, téléréunion *f*

MEFP *abbr* (*minimum error-free pad*) TELECOM période minimale sans erreur *f*

mega- *pref* (*M*) METR méga-(*M*)

megabyte *n* (*Mb*) COMP, DP méga-octet *m* (*Mo*)

megachip *n* ELECTRON mégapuce *f*

megacycle *n* ELEC *frequency* mégacycle *m*

megadoc *n* OPT *Phillips* mégadoc *m*

megadyne *n* METR mégadyne *f*

megahertz *n* ELEC *frequency* mégacycle *m*, mégahertz *m*, PETR, TV mégahertz *m*

megaparsec *n* ASTRON mégaparsec *m*

megascale *adj* GEOL à grande échelle

megastream: ~ **circuit** *n* TELECOM circuit à haut débit *m*

megawatt *n* (*MW*) ELEC *power* mégawatt *m* (*MW*)

Megger *n* (TM) ELEC mégohmmètre *m*, ohmmètre à magnéto *m*, ELEC ENG mégohmmètre *m*, GEOPHYS megger *m* (MD)

megohm *n* ELEC *unit of resistance*, ELEC ENG mégohm *m*

meionite *n* MINERAL mionite *f*, méionite *f*

Meissner: ~ **effect** *n* ELECTRON *superconductors*, PHYS effet Meissner *m*

Meker: ~ **burner** *n* LAB EQUIP *heating* bec Meker *m*

mel *n* ACOUSTICS, RECORDING mel *m*

melaconite *n* MINERAL mélaconite *f*

melamine *n* CHEM, TEXTILES mélamine *f*; ~ **formaldehyde resin** *n* P&R résine de mélamine *f*; ~ **resin** *n* ELEC *insulation* résine de mélamine *f*

melampyrite *n* CHEM dulcitol *m*, mélampyrite *f*

melanin *n* CHEM mélanine *f*

melanite *n* MINERAL mélanite *f*

melanocratic *adj* GEOL mélanocrate

melanosome *n* GEOL mélanosome *m*

melanterite *n* MINERAL mélantérite *f*

Melde's: ~ **experiment** *n* PHYS expérience de Melde *f*

melding *n* PRINT incorporation *f*, mélange *m*

melibiose *n* CHEM mélibiose *m*

melilite *n* MINERAL mélilite *f*

melinite *n* MINERAL mélinite *f*

meliphane *n* MINERAL mélinophane *f*, méliphanite *f*

meliphanite *n* MINERAL mélinophane *f*, méliphanite *f*

mellite *n* MINERAL mellite *m*

mellitic *adj* CHEM mellitique

mellitose *n* CHEM mélitose *m*, raffinose *m*

mellon *n* CHEM mellon *m*

melt [1] *n* PROD ENG fonte *f*; ~ **flow rate** *n* FLUID PHYS débit de matière fondue *m*

melt [2] *vt* CHEM faire fondre, PAPER TECH fondre, PROD ENG faire fondre, fondre, TEXTILES fondre, THERMOD dissoudre, faire fondre, fondre, fuser, porter à fusion; ~ **down** *vt* THERMOD faire fondre, fondre, liquéfier

melt [3] *vti* METEO *snow, ice* fondre

meltable *adj* PROP MAT, THERMOD fusible

meltdown *n* NUCLEAR fusion *f*

melted *adj* METEO fondu, THERMOD fondu, fusé

melter *n* PROD ENG *crucible* creuset *m*, pot *m*

melting [1] *adj* METEO en fusion, fondant

melting [2] *n* PAPER TECH, PHYS fusion *f*, PROD ENG fonte *f*, fusion *f*, PROP MAT, TEXTILES fusion *f*, THERMOD coulée *f*, fusion *f*; ~ **bath** *n* THERMOD bain de fusion *m*; ~ **core catcher** *n* NUCLEAR cendrier *m*, récupérateur du coeur *m*; ~ **crucible** *n* THERMOD coupelle *f*, creuset *m*, têt *m*; ~ **furnace** *n* COAL TECH, THERMOD four de fusion *m*; ~ **heat** *n* THERMOD chaleur de fusion *f*; ~ **point** *n* CHEM, METEO, P&R, PAPER TECH point de fusion *m*, PHYS point de fusion *m*, température de fusion *f*, PROP MAT, REFRIG, TEXTILES point de fusion *m*, THERMOD point de fluage *m*, point de fusion *m*; ~ **point curve** *n* THERMOD courbe de fusion *f*; ~ **pot** *n* CHEM creuset *m*, PROD ENG *crucible* creuset *m*, pot *m*, THERMOD *crucible* coupelle *f*, creuset *m*; ~ **range** *n* THERMOD domaine de fusion *m*, plage de fusion *f*, régime de fusion *m*; ~ **test** *n* THERMOD essai de fusion *m*; ~ **time** *n* THERMOD *period* durée de fusion *f*

member *n* COMP, DP, GEOL membre *m*, MATH *of equation* membre *m*, *of set* élément *m*, MECH ENG membre *m*, membrure *f*

members *n pl* CONST *of frame* parties *f pl*, pièces *f pl*

membership *n* COMP, DP appartenance *f*

membrane *n* SPACE *spacecraft* membrane *f*; ~ **filter** *n* (AmE), ~ **filtre** *n* (BrE) CHEM TECH filtre microporeux *m*, filtre moléculaire *m*, filtre à diaphragme *m*, LAB EQUIP membrane filtrante *f*; ~ **keyboard** *n* ELEC ENG, PROD ENG clavier à membrane *m*; ~ **keyswitch** *n* ELEC ENG interrupteur de clavier à membrane *m*; ~ **loudspeaker** *n* ACOUSTICS haut-parleur à membrane *m*

memory *n* COMP, ELEC ENG mémoire *f*; ~ **access** *n* COMP, DP accès mémoire *m*, ELEC ENG accès à la mémoire *m*; ~ **backup** *n* PROD ENG mémoire de sauvegarde *f*; ~ **bank** *n* COMP bloc de mémoire *m*; ~ **bit location** *n* PROD ENG emplacement de bit de mémoire *m*; ~ **capacity** *n* COMP, DP, ELEC ENG capacité de mémoire *f*; ~ **card** *n* COMP, DP carte de mémoire *f*; ~ **cartridge** *n* PROD ENG module mémoire *m*; ~ **chip** *n* COMP, DP puce de mémoire *f*; ~ **circuit** *n* TELECOM circuit de mémoire *m*; ~ **colors** *n pl* (AmE), ~ **colours** *n pl* (BrE) PRINT couleurs de référence *f pl*, couleurs-mémoire *f pl*; ~ **compaction** *n* COMP, DP compaction de mémoire *f*, compression de mémoire *f*; ~ **compression** *n* COMP, DP compaction de mémoire *f*, compression de mémoire *f*; ~ **controller** *n* ELEC ENG régisseur de mémoire *m*; ~ **cycle** *n* COMP, DP cycle de mémoire *m*; ~ **data register** *n* (*MDR*) COMP, DP registre mémoire de données *m*; ~ **dump** *n* COMP, DP vidage mémoire *m*; ~ **hierarchy** *n* COMP, DP hiérarchie de mémoire *f*; ~ **location** *n* COMP adresse mémoire *f*, DP position de mémoire *f*; ~ **management** *n* COMP, DP gestion de mémoire *f*; ~ **map** *n* COMP, DP carte de mémoire *f*, topogramme mémoire *m*, topographie mémoire *f*, PROD ENG configuration mémoire *f*; ~ **module** *n* COMP, DP module de mémoire *m*; ~ **module socket** *n* PROD ENG connecteur du module mémoire *m*; ~ **parity error** *n* PROD ENG erreur de parité en mémoire *f*; ~ **protection** *n* COMP, DP protection mémoire *f*; ~ **protect keyswitch** *n* PROD ENG commutateur à clef de protection de mémoire *m*; ~ **random access** *n* COMP accès aléatoire à la mémoire *m*, accès sélectif à la mémoire *m*, DP accès aléatoire à la mémoire *m*; ~ **store** *n* TV mémoire de stockage *f*; ~ **store switch** *n* PROD ENG commutateur de mémoire *m*; ~ **system** *n* TV système à mémoire *m*; ~ **tracking** *n* PROD ENG recherche d'erreurs dans la mémoire *f*; ~ **transistor** *n* ELECTRON transistor de mémorisation *m*; ~ **tube** *n* ELECTRON tube à mémoire *m*

memory-resident *adj* COMP, DP résidant en mémoire

mend *vt* TEXTILES raccommoder

mendelevium *n* (*Md*) CHEM mendélévium *m* (*Md*)

mending *n* PROD ENG raccommodage *m*, réparation *f*, TEXTILES raccommodage *m*; ~ **link** *n* MECH ENG fausse maille *f*

mendipite *n* MINERAL mendipite *f*

mendozite *n* MINERAL mendozite *f*

menilite *n* MINERAL ménilite *f*

meniscus *n* CONST, GEOM, PHYS ménisque *m*, THERMOD *foundry* surface du bain *f*; ~ **lens** *n* INSTRUMENT lentille ménisque *f*, PHOTO objectif ménisque *m*, PHYS lentille ménisquée *f*

Mensa *n* ASTRON Table *f*

mensuration *n* GEOM mesurage *m*

menthane *n* CHEM menthane *m*

menthanediamine *n* CHEM menthanédiamine *f*

menthanol *n* CHEM menthanol *m*

menthanone *n* CHEM menthanone *f*

menthene *n* CHEM menthène *m*

menthenol *n* CHEM menthénol *m*

menthenone *n* CHEM menthénone *f*

menthofuran *n* CHEM menthofurane *m*

menthol *n* CHEM menthol *m*

menthone *n* CHEM menthone *f*

menthyl *n* CHEM menthyle *m*

menu *n* COMP, DP menu *m*; ~ **screen** *n* COMP, DP affichage menu *m*, écran de menu *m*

menu-driven [1] *adj* COMP guidé par menu, mode menu, piloté par menu, DP guidé par menu, piloté par menu

menu-driven: [2] ~ **application** *n* COMP programme piloté par menu *m*

mepacrine *n* CHEM mépacrine *f*

meprobamate *n* CHEM méprobamate *m*

merbromin *n* CHEM merbromine *f*

mercantile: ~ **marine** *n* NAUT marine marchande *f*

mercaptal *n* CHEM mercaptal *m*

mercaptan *n* CHEM, P&R *rubber additive* mercaptan *m*, PETR TECH mercaptan *m*, thioalcool *m*, thiol *m*, POLLUTION mercaptan *m*

mercaptide *n* CHEM mercaptide *m*

mercaptoacetic *adj* CHEM mercaptoacétique

mercaptol: ~ **process** *n* CHEM procédé de désulfuration *m*

mercaptomerin *n* CHEM mercaptomérine *f*

Mercator: ~ **chart** *n* NAUT *navigation* carte Mercator *f*; ~ **plotting chart** *n* OCEANOG gabarit de Mercator *m*; ~ **projection** *n* NAUT *navigation* projection de Mercator *f*, système Mercator *m*, SPACE projection de Mercator *f*

Mercator-Holder: ~ **scale** *n* ACOUSTICS gamme de Mercator-Holder *f*

mercerization *n* CHEM mercerisation *f*

merchant: ~ **fleet** *n* NAUT flotte de commerce *f*, flotte marchande *f*; ~ **haulage** *n* TRANSP acheminement par le chargeur *m*; ~ **marine** *n* NAUT marine marchande *f*; ~ **navy** *n* NAUT marine marchande *f*; ~ **ship** *n* NAUT navire de commerce *m*, navire marchand *m*

merchantman *n* NAUT navire marchand *m*

mercuration *n* CHEM mercuration *f*

mercurial *adj* CHEM *ointment* mercuriel

mercuric *adj* CHEM mercurique

mercurification *n* CHEM extraction du mercure *f*, mercurification *f*

mercury *n* (*Hg*) CHEM mercure *m* (*Hg*); ~ **arc** *n* ELEC ENG arc au mercure *m*; ~ **arc converter** *n* ELEC *alternating current* convertisseur à arc de mercure *m*; ~ **arc lamp** *n* ELEC *lighting* lampe à mercure *f*, RAD PHYS lampe à arc à mercure *f*; ~ **arc rectifier** *n* ELEC ENG redresseur à vapeur de mercure *m*; ~ **barometer** *n* LAB EQUIP, METEO, METR, PHYS baromètre à mercure *m*; ~ **battery** *n* ELEC ENG pile au mercure *f*; ~ **bromide laser** *n* ELECTRON laser à bromure de mercure *m*; ~ **cell** *n* ELEC ENG pile au mercure *f*; ~ **circuit breaker** *n* CONTROL interrupteur de Foucault *m*, interrupteur à mercure *m*; ~ **delay line** *n* ELECTRON ligne à retard au mercure *f*; ~ **fulminate** *n* CHEM fulminate de mercure *m*; ~ **intensification** *n* PHOTO renforcement au mercure *m*; ~ **interrupter** *n* (AmE), ~ **interruptor** *n* (BrE) ELEC eng interrupteur à mercure *m*; ~ **laser** *n* ELECTRON laser à mercure *m*; ~ **ore** *n* MINING cinabre *m*, minerai de mercure *m*; ~ **pool cathode** *n* ELEC ENG cathode à bain de mercure *f*, cathode à mercure *f*; ~ **pool tube** *n* ELEC ENG tube à cathode liquide *m*, ELECTRON tube à cathode de mercure *m*; ~ **rectifier** *n* ELEC ENG redresseur à vapeur de mercure *m*; ~ **relay** *n* ELEC relais à mercure *m*; ~ **switch** *n* CONTROL contact basculant à mercure *m*, interrupteur basculant à mercure *m*, ELEC interrupteur basculant à mercure *m*, interrupteur de Foucault *m*, ELEC ENG interrupteur à mercure *m*, inverseur à

mercure *m*; ~ **thermometer** *n* PHYS, REFRIG thermomètre à mercure *m*; ~ **vapor** *n* (AmE) *see mercury* vapour; ~ **vapor lamp** *n* (AmE) *see mercury vapour lamp*; ~ **vapor rectifier** *n* (AmE) *see mercury vapour rectifier*; ~ **vapor turbine** *n* (AmE) *see mercury vapour turbine*; ~ **vapour** *n* (BrE) CHEM, CONST vapeur de mercure *f*; ~ **vapour lamp** *n* (BrE) ELEC ENG lampe à vapeur de mercure *f*; ~ **vapour rectifier** *n* (BrE) ELEC ENG redresseur à vapeur de mercure *m*; ~ **vapour turbine** *n* (BrE) MECH ENG turbine à vapeur de mercure *f*

mercury-wetted: ~ **contact** *n* ELEC ENG contact mouillés au mercure *m*; ~ **reed relay** *n* ELEC ENG relais à tiges à contacts mouillés au mercure *m*

merge [1] *n* COMP, DP fusion *f*; ~ **volume** *n* TRANSP débit après convergence *m*

merge [2] *vti* COMP, DP fusionner

merged: ~ **bipolar technology** *n* ELECTRON technique bipolaire fusionnée *f*; ~ **transistor logic** *n* (*MTL*) ELECTRON logique à transistors fusionnés *f*

merging *n* COMP fusion *f*, TRANSP convergence *f*; ~ **control** *n* TRANSP régulation de la convergence *f*

meridian *n* ASTRON *observatory* méridien *m*, *of planet* méridien *m*, SPACE méridien *m*; ~ **circle** *n* INSTRUMENT *telescope* cercle méridien *m*; ~ **gyro** *n* SPACE *spacecraft* gyroscope méridien *m*; ~ **ray** *n* OPT rayon méridien *m*; ~ **telescope** *n* INSTRUMENT lunette méridienne *f*; ~ **transit** *n* SPACE passage au méridien *m*

meridional *adj* SPACE, TELECOM *ray* méridien

merogenesis *n* GAS TECH segmentation *f*

meroxene *n* MINERAL méroxène *m*

mesa: ~ **diode** *n* ELECTRON diode mésa *f*; ~ **process** *n* ELECTRON procédé mesa *m*; ~ **transistor** *n* ELECTRON transistor mésa *m*

mesaconic *adj* CHEM mésaconique

MESFET *abbr* (*metal semiconductor field effect transistor*) ELECTRON transistor MESFET *m*

mesh [1] *n* COAL TECH maille *f*, ouverture de maille *f*, ELEC *of system*, ELEC ENG *of network* maille *f*, ELECTRON *of storage tube* grille *f*, FOOD TECH *machinery* maille *f*, MECH ENG *engagement, gearing* engrenage *m*, engrènement *m*, prise *f*, OCEANOG, PAPER TECH, PHYS *of electric circuit*, PROD ENG, SPACE *spacecraft*, TEXTILES, WATER SUPP maille *f*; ~ **connection** *n* ELEC connexion en triangle *f*, connexion polygonale *f*, ELEC ENG *of storage tube terminals* montage en triangle *m*, PHYS connexion en triangle *f*; ~ **current** *n* ELEC ENG courant entre les phases *m*; ~ **network** *n* ELEC *supply* réseau interconnecté *m*, réseau maillé *m*, SPACE *communications* réseau en étoile *m*; ~ **pin** *n* OCEANOG *of net* moule *m*; ~ **sandwich** *n* SPACE sandwich treillis *m*; ~ **size** *n* COAL TECH ouverture *f*, MECH ouverture de maille *f*, OCEANOG maillage *m*; ~ **storage tube** *n* ELECTRON tube à mémoire à grille *m*

mesh [2] *vt* MECH ENG engrener

mesh [3] *vi* MECH ENG engrener, s'engrener, être en prise

meshed: ~ **loops** *n* TEXTILES boucles liées par tricotage *f pl*; ~ **network** *n* COMP, DP réseau maillé *m*, ELEC *supply* réseau interconnecté *m*, réseau maillé *m*; ~ **stitches** *n pl* TEXTILES points entremêlés *m pl*

meshing *n* MECH *gears* engrènement *m*, MECH ENG *coming into gear* engrenage *m*, engrènement *m*, prise *f*

mesidine *n* CHEM mésidine *f*

mesitylene *n* CHEM mésitylène *m*

mesitylenic *adj* CHEM mésitylénique

mesolite *n* MINERAL mésolite *f*

mesolittoral *n* OCEANOG médiolittoral *m*

mesomeric *adj* CHEM mésomérique, mésomère
mesomerism *n* CHEM mésomérie *f*
mesomorphic: ~ **phase** *n* CRYSTALL phase mésomorphe *f*
meson *n* CHEM méson *m*, particule mésique *f*, PART PHYS, PHYS méson *m*
mesophase *n* CRYSTALL *liquid crystals* phase mésomorphe *f*
mesorcinol *n* CHEM mésorcine *f*
mesosphere *n* ASTRON, GEOPHYS, SPACE mésosphère *f*
mesostructure *n* CRYSTALL, PROP MAT *polycrystalline materials* mésostructure *f*
mesotartaric *adj* CHEM mésotartrique
mesothorium *n* CHEM mésothorium *m*
mesotype *n* MINERAL mésotype *m*
mesoxalic *adj* CHEM mésoxalique
mesozoic *n* PETR TECH mésozoïque *m*, ère secondaire *f*
mess *n* NAUT *sailors'* réfectoire *m*; ~ **deck** *n* NAUT *on ship* poste d'équipage *m*, poste des matelots *m*
message *n* COMP, DP, TELECOM message *m*; ~ **communication function** *n (MCF)* TELECOM fonction de communication de messages *f*; ~ **handling** *n (MH)* TELECOM messagerie *f*; ~ **handling system** *n (MHS)* TELECOM messagerie *f*, système de messagerie *m*; ~ **header** *n* COMP, DP, TELECOM en-tête de message *m*; ~ **pager** *n* TELECOM récepteur de radiomessagerie *m*; ~ **processing equipment** *n* NAUT *satellite communications* équipement de traitement de messages *m*; ~ **register** *n* TELECOM compteur de taxes *m*; ~ **retrieval** *n* COMP, DP extraction de message *f*, TELECOM consultation des messages *f*; ~ **routing** *n* COMP, DP acheminement des messages *m*; ~ **signal unit** *n (MSU)* TELECOM trame sémaphore de message *f*; ~ **sink** *n* COMP, DP collecteur de messages *m*; ~ **slip** *n* PROD ENG formulaire de message *m*; ~ **source** *n* COMP, DP source de messages *f*; ~ **store** *n (MS)* TELECOM mémoire de messages *f*; ~ **store area** *n* PROD ENG zone de mémorisation des messages *f*; ~ **storing** *n* TELECOM archivage des messages *m*; ~ **switch** *n* TELECOM commutateur de messages *m*; ~ **switching** *n* COMP, DP, TELECOM commutation de messages *f*; ~ **switching center** *n* (AmE), ~ **switching centre** *n* (BrE) TELECOM centre de commutation de messages *m*; ~ **switching network** *n* TELECOM réseau à commutation de messages *m*; ~ **switching processor** *n* TELECOM processeur de commutation de messages *m*; ~ **switching system** *n* TELECOM système de commutation de messages *m*; ~ **text** *n* COMP, DP texte de message *m*; ~ **transfer** *n* COMP, DP, TELECOM transfert de messages *m*; ~ **transfer agent** *n (MTA)* TELECOM agent de transfert de messages *m*; ~ **transfer part** *n* TELECOM SSTM, sous-système de transport de messages *m*; ~ **transfer system** *n (MTS)* TELECOM système de transfert de messages *m*
Message-master *n* (TM) TELECOM *British Telecom* récepteur de radiomessagerie *m*
message-oriented: ~ **text interchange system** *n (MOTIS)* TELECOM système d'échange de textes en mode message *m*
message-switched: ~ **network** *n* COMP, DP réseau à commutation de messages *m*
messaging *n* COMP, DP messagerie *f*
messenger *n* NAUT touline de passage *f*; ~ **line** *n* NAUT touline de passage *f*
Messier: ~ **catalogue** *n* ASTRON catalogue de Messier *m*; ~ **number** *n* ASTRON numéro de Messier *m*
metabasic: ~ **rock** *n* GEOL métabasite *f*

metabasite *n* GEOL métabasite *f*
metabisulfite *n* (AmE), **metabisulphite** *n* (BrE) CHEM métabisulfite *m*
metaborate *n* CHEM métaborate *m*
metaboric *adj* CHEM métaborique
metacenter *n* (AmE), **metacentre** *n* (BrE) NAUT *naval architecture*, PHYS métacentre *m*
metacentric: ~ **height** *n* NAUT *naval architecture* distance métacentrique *f*, hauteur métacentrique *f*
metachlorite *n* MINERAL métachlorite *f*
metachlorotoluene *n* CHEM métachlorotoluène *m*
metachrome: ~ **dyeing** *n* COLOURS teinture au métachrome *f*
metacinnabarite *n* MINERAL sulfure mercurique noir *m*
metacresol *n* CHEM métacrésol *m*
metacrylic *adj* CHEM métacrylique
metadyne *n* ELECTRON métadyne *f*
metal [1] *n* C&G verre fondu *m*, CONST *for road* matériaux d'empierrement *m pl*, MINING *ore* minerai *m*, pierre de mine *f*, PROD ENG *cast iron* fonte *f*, métal *m*; ~ **active gas welding** *n (MAG welding)* CONST, THERMOD soudage MAG *m*; ~ **alloy** *n* PROP MAT alliage métallique *m*; ~ **arc welding** *n* THERMOD soudage à l'arc *m*; ~ **beam foil** *n* RAD PHYS feuille de métal à faisceau *f*; ~ **bonding** *n* PROP MAT soudage de métaux *m*; ~ **box** *n* (BrE) *(cf metal can)* PACKAGING boîte métallique *f*; ~ **can** *n* (AmE) *(cf metal box)* PACKAGING boîte métallique *f*; ~ **cavity fixing umbrella** *n* CONST *building* cheville métallique corps creux *f*; ~ **coat** *n* COATINGS plaqué en métal *m*, revêtement métallique *m*; ~ **coating** *n* COATINGS métallisation *f*, plaqué en métal *m*, revêtement métallique *m*, schoopage *m*, MECH ENG métallisation *f*, PACKAGING revêtement métallique *m*, PROD ENG métallisation *f*, TV revêtement métallique *m*; ~ **coating of reflectors** *n* COATINGS dépôt de couches réfléchissantes *m*; ~ **conductor cable** *n* TELECOM câble métallique *m*; ~ **cone tube** *n* ELECTRON tube à cône métallique *m*; ~ **dark slide** *n* PHOTO châssis en métal *m*; ~ **decorating machine** *n* PRINT machine à impression sur métal *f*; ~ **depth** *n* C&G hauteur de verre *f*; ~ **detector** *n* CONST *for walls* détecteur électrique de métaux *m*, PACKAGING détecteur de métaux *m*; ~ **drift** *n* COAL TECH galerie au rocher *f*; ~ **drum** *n* PACKAGING fût métallique *m*; ~ **edging case** *n* PACKAGING boîte avec bord métallique *f*; ~ **enameling works** *n* (AmE), ~ **enamelling works** *n* (BrE) COATINGS émaillerie *f*, émaillerie industrielle *f*; ~ **eyelet** *n* PROD ENG oeillet de métal *m*; ~ **fatigue** *n* PROP MAT fatigue des métaux *f*; ~ **filament** *n* ELEC ENG filament métallique *m*; ~ **film** *n* ELECTRON couche métallique *f*; ~ **film resistor** *n* ELEC ENG résistance à couche métallique *f*; ~ **foil** *n* PACKAGING feuille métallique mince *f*; ~ **founding** *n* PROD ENG moulage des métaux *m*; ~ **gate** *n* ELECTRON grille métallique *f*; ~ **gate CMOS integrated circuit** *n* ELECTRON circuit intégré CMOS à grilles métalliques *m*; ~ **glaze** *n* ELECTRON couche résistive vitrifiée *f*; ~ **glaze film** *n* COATINGS couche de métal lustré *f*; ~ **glaze resistor** *n* ELEC ENG résistance à couche épaisse *f*; ~ **inert gas welding** *n (MIG welding)* CONST, THERMOD soudage MIG *m*; ~ **master** *n* RECORDING disque mère métallique *m*; ~ **matrix composite** *n* PROP MAT composite à matrice métallique *m*; ~ **mining** *n* MINING exploitation des mines des métaux *f*, exploitation minièrede métaux *f*; ~ **oxide** *n* PROP MAT oxyde métallique *m*; ~ **particles** *n pl* PROD ENG limaille *f*; ~ **pick-up** *n* PROD ENG arrachement de métal *m*; ~ **plating** *n*

COATINGS plaqué en métal *m*, revêtement métallique *m*;~ **position switch** *n* PROD ENG interrupteur de position avec boîtier métallique *m*; ~ **powder** *n* METALL poudre de métal *f*; ~ **recovery** *n* COAL TECH récupération de métal *f*; ~ **rectifier** *n* ELEC redresseur métal *m*; ~ **refinery** *n* PROD ENG usine d'affinage de métaux *f*, usine métallurgique d'affinage *f*; ~ **reflector** *n* INSTRUMENT réflecteur métallique *m*; ~ **removal** *n* MECH ENG enlèvement de matière sur la pièce *m*; ~ **saw** *n* PROD ENG scie à métaux *f*; ~ **scrap** *n* PROP MAT déchets métalliques *m pl*; ~ **semiconductor field effect transistor** *n* (*MESFET*) ELECTRON transistor MESFET *m*; ~ **shears** *n pl* PROD ENG cisailles à métaux *f pl*; ~ **sheath** *n* ELEC ENG enveloppe métallique *f*, gaine métallique *f*; ~ **slitting saw** *n* MECH ENG fraise-scie *f*; ~ **slitting saw with fine teeth** *n* MECH ENG fraise-scie à denture fine *f*; ~ **strip closure** *n* PACKAGING fermeture avec bande métallique *f*; ~ **tube** *n* ELECTRON tube métallique *m*; ~ **vapor laser** *n* (AmE), ~ **vapour laser** *n* (BrE) ELECTRON laser à vapeur métallique *m*

metal [2] *vt* CONST *road* empierrer, ferrer

metal-air: ~ **battery** *n* TRANSP accumulateur métal-air *m*

metalanguage *n* COMP métalangage *m*

metalation *n* (AmE) *see metallation*

metal-bound: ~ **mallet** *n* PROD ENG marteau à têtes rapportées *m*

metal-ceramic: ~ **bond** *n* PROP MAT liaison métal-céramique *f*

metal-clad [1] *adj* MECH blindé, cuirassé

metal-clad:[2] ~ **conductor** *n* ELEC *cable* âme armée de métal *f*, âme plaquée *f*; ~ **substrate** *n* ELECTRON substrat plaqué *m*

metal-coat *vt* COATINGS appliquer une couche réfléchissante à, métalliser, plaquer

metal-coated [1] *adj* PROD ENG métallisé

metal-coated:[2] ~ **conductor** *n* ELEC *of cable* âme revêtue d'une couche métallique *f*; ~ **thread** *n* COATINGS fil guipé de métal *m*, fil métallisé *m*

metal-cutting: ~ **band-saw blade** *n* MECH ENG lame de scie à ruban à métaux *f*; ~ **saw blade** *n* MECH ENG lame de scie à métaux *f*

metaldehyde *n* CHEM métaldéhyde *m*

metal-faced *adj* COATINGS métallisé

metal-grinding: ~ **regulations** *n pl* SAFETY *dry and wet* règlements relatifs au meulage des métaux *m pl*

metaliferous *adj* (AmE) *see metalliferous*

metaline *adj* (AmE) *see metalline*

metaling *n* (AmE) *see metalling*

metalization *n* (AmE) *see metallization*

metalized: ~ **film** *n* (AmE) *see metallized film*; ~ **film capacitor** *n* (AmE) *see metallized film capacitor*; ~ **hole** *n* (AmE) *see metallized hole*; ~ **mica capacitor** *n* (AmE) *see metallized mica capacitor*; ~ **paint** *n* (AmE) *see metallized paint*; ~ **paper** *n* (AmE) *see metallized paper*; ~ **paper capacitor** *n* (AmE) *see metallized paper capacitor*; ~ **screen** *n* (AmE) *see metallized screen*

metalizing *n* (AmE) *see metallizing*

metallation *n* (BrE) CHEM métallation *f*

metalled: ~ **road** *n* (BrE) (*cf paved road*) CONST chaussée empierrée *f*, route empierrée *f*, route ferrée *f*

metallic: ~ **bond** *n* METALL liaison métallique *f*; ~ **circuit** *n* ELEC ENG circuit métallique *m*; ~ **coating** *n* MECH ENG, PACKAGING, TELECOM revêtement métallique *m*; ~ **conductor** *n* ELEC ENG conducteur métallique *m*; ~ **conductor cable** *n* TELECOM câble à conducteurs métalliques *m*; ~ **core** *n* ASTRON *of a planet* noyau

métallique *m*; ~ **crosspoint** *n* TELECOM point de connexion métallique *m*; ~ **glass** *n* PROP MAT verre métallique *m*; ~ **ink** *n* COLOURS encre métallisée *f*; ~ **luster** *n* (AmE), ~ **lustre** *n* (BrE) CHEM *property* éclat métallique *m*; ~ **mirror** *n* INSTRUMENT miroir métallique *m*; ~ **paper** *n* PACKAGING papier doublé métal *m*; ~ **pigment paint** *n* COLOURS peinture métallisée *f*, peinture à pigment métallique *f*; ~ **rectifier** *n* ELEC ENG redresseur métal-semiconducteur *m*, redresseur sec *m*; ~ **resistor** *n* ELEC résistance métallique *f*; ~ **sheath** *n* ELEC *cable conductor* gaine métallique *f*; ~ **stop foil** *n* RECORDING feuille d'arrêt métallique *f*; ~ **structure** *n* CONST structure métallique *f*

metalliferous *adj* (BrE) CHEM métallifère

metalline *adj* (BrE) CHEM métallin

metal-lined: ~ **shaft** *n* MINING puits blindé *m*

metalling *n* (BrE) (*cf paving*) CONST *civil engineering* empierrement *m*

metallization *n* (BrE) CONST, ELECTRON, PHYS métallisation *f*, PROD ENG métallisage *m*, métallisation *f*, PROP MAT, SPACE *craft* métallisation *f*; ~ **layer** *n* (BrE) ELECTRON couche de métallisation *f*; ~ **mask** *n* (BrE) ELECTRON masque de métallisation *m*

metallized: ~ **film** *n* (BrE) PACKAGING film métallisé *m*; ~ **film capacitor** *n* (BrE) ELEC ENG condensateur métallisé *m*, condensateur à diélectrique métallisé *m*; ~ **hole** *n* (BrE) ELEC *printed circuit board* trou métallisé *m*; ~ **mica capacitor** *n* (BrE) ELEC ENG condensateur au mica métallisé *m*; ~ **paint** *n* (BrE) COLOURS, P&R peinture métallisée *f*; ~ **paper** *n* (BrE) PACKAGING papier métallisé *m*; ~ **paper capacitor** *n* (BrE) ELEC condensateur au papier métallisé *m*; ~ **screen** *n* (BrE) ELECTRON écran métallisé *m*

metallizing *n* (BrE) C&G métallisation *f*

metallogenetic [1] *adj* (BrE) PROP MAT métallogénétique

metallogenetic:[2] ~ **province** *n* (BrE) GEOL province métallogénique *f*

metallographic: ~ **microscope** *n* (BrE) LAB EQUIP microscope métallographique *m*

metallography *n* (BrE) METALL métallographie *f*

metalloid *n* (BrE) CHEM métalloïde *m*

metalloidal *adj* (BrE) CHEM métalloïdique

metallo-organic: ~ **pigment** *n* (BrE) COLOURS pigment organométallique *m*

metallurgic: ~ **coke** *n* COAL TECH coke métallurgique *m*

metallurgical: ~ **furnace** *n* MECH ENG four métallurgique *m*; ~ **waste** *n* COAL TECH déchet métallurgique *m*

metalogenetic [1] *adj* (AmE) *see metallogenetic*

metalogenetic:[2] ~ **province** *n* (AmE) *see metallogenetic province*

metalographic: ~ **microscope** *n* (AmE) *see metallographic microscope*

metalography *n* (AmE) *see metallography*

metaloid *n* (AmE) *see metalloid*

metaloidal *adj* (AmE) *see metalloidal*

metalo-organic: ~ **pigment** *n* (AmE) *see metallo-organic pigment*

metal-oxide: ~ **semiconductor** *n* (*MOS*) COMP semiconducteur à oxyde métallique *m* (*MOS*); ~ **semiconductor capacitor** *n* ELEC ENG condensateur MOS *m*; ~ **semi-conductor delay line** *n* ELECTRON ligne à retard MOS *f*; ~ **semiconductor driver** *n* ELECTRON attaqueur MOS *m*; ~ **semiconductor gate** *n* ELECTRON porte MOS *f*; ~ **semiconductor logic circuit** *n* ELECTRON circuit logique MOS *m*; ~ **semiconductor power transistor** *n* ELECTRON transistor de puissance MOS *m*; ~ **semiconductor technology** *n* ELECTRON technique MOS *f*; ~ **semiconductor transistor** *n* ELECTRON transistor MOS *m*

metal-sawing: ~ **machine** *n* PROD ENG machine à scier les métaux *f*

metal-semiconductor: ~ **junction** *n* ELECTRON jonction métal-semi-conducteur *f*

metal-sheathed: ~ **cable** *n* ELEC ENG câble à fils armés *m*; ~ **conductor** *n* ELEC ENG conducteur à fils armés *m*

metal-to-metal: ~ **clutch** *n* MECH ENG embrayage métallique *m*

metalwork *n* PROD ENG serrurerie *f*

metalworker *n* PROD ENG ouvrier serrurier *m*, serrurier *m*

metalworking *n* PROD ENG serrurerie *f*, travail des métaux *m*

metamer *n* CHEM composé métamère *m*

metameric [1] *adj* CHEM métamère

metameric: [2] ~ **colors** *n pl* (AmE), ~ **colours** *n pl* (BrE) PRINT couleurs métamériques *f pl*

metamerism *n* CHEM métamérie *f*

metamict *adj* GEOL métamicte

metamorphic: ~ **differentiation** *n* GEOL différenciation métamorphique *f*; ~ **facies** *n* GEOL faciès de métamorphisme *m*, faciès métamorphique *m*; ~ **grade** *n* GEOL degré de métamorphisme *m*; ~ **rock** *n* FUELLESS roche métamorphique *f*; ~ **zone** *n* GEOL zone de métamorphisme *f*, zone métamorphique *f*

metanil *n* CHEM jaune de métanile *m*

metanilic *adj* CHEM métanilique

metaphosphate *n* CHEM métaphosphate *m*

metaphosphoric *adj* CHEM métaphosphorique

metarsenious *adj* CHEM métarsénieux

metasediment *n* GEOL métasédiment *m*, roche sédimentaire métamorphisée *f*

metasilicate *n* CHEM silicate double *m*

metasilicic *adj* CHEM métasilicique

metasomatism *n* GEOL métasomatose *f*

metastability *n* PROP MAT métastabilité *f*

metastable [1] *adj* RAD PHYS métastable

metastable: [2] ~ **atom** *n* RAD PHYS atome métastable *m*; ~ **equilibrium** *n* PHYS équilibre métastable *m*; ~ **loss rate** *n* RAD PHYS taux de perte métastable *m*; ~ **state** *n* METALL, PHYS état métastable *m*

metastannic *adj* CHEM métastannique

metathesis *n* CHEM substitution *f*

metavolcanic *n* GEOL roche métavolcanique *f*, roche volcanique métamorphisée *f*

metaxite *n* MINERAL métaxite *f*

meteor *n* ASTRON, METEO, SPACE météore *m*; ~ **burst communication** *n* SPACE *communications* communication au moyen d'essaims de météores *f*; ~ **burstlink** *n* SPACE *communications* liaison par rafales météoriques *f*; ~ **crater** *n* ASTRON cratère météorique *m*; ~ **dust** *n* ASTRON, SPACE poussière cosmique *f*; ~ **echo** *n* SPACE *craft* écho de météores *m*, écho de météorites *m*; ~ **shower** *n* ASTRON flux de météore *m*; ~ **storm** *n* ASTRON grêle de météore *f*, pluie de météore *f*; ~ **swarm** *n* ASTRON essaim de météore *m*, grêle de météore *f*

meteoric: ~ **water** *n* HYDROL eau météorique *f*

meteorite *n* ASTRON, SPACE météorite *f*; ~ **influx** *n* SPACE arrivée de météorites *f*

meteoroid *n* ASTRON, SPACE météoroïde *m*

meteorological: ~ **conditions** *n pl* METEO conditions météorologiques *f pl*; ~ **data** *n pl* POLLUTION données météorologiques *f pl*; ~ **inversion** *n* POLLUTION inver-

sion météorologique *f*; ~ **satellite** *n* SPACE satellite météorologique *m*; ~ **satellite service** *n* SPACE service de météorologie par satellite *m*; ~ **sensor** *n* NAUT capteur météorologique *m*; ~ **station** *n* METEO poste météorologique *m*, station météorologique d'observation *f*; ~ **tide** *n* OCEANOG marée météorologique *f*

meteorology *n* AERONAUT, NAUT météorologie *f*

meter *n* (AmE) METR *see* metre

metering *n* GAS TECH comptage *m*, PRINT distribution de l'encre par des rouleaux distributeurs *f*, distribution de l'encre par la racle *f*, TELECOM comptage *m* ~ **equipment** *n* PACKAGING équipement mesureur *m*; ~ **friction** *n* PRINT friction liée à la distribution de la couche *f*; ~ **hole** *n* MECH ENG orifice calibré *m*; ~ **jet** *n* MECH ENG gicleur calibré *m*; ~ **land** *n* PROD ENG épaulement de mesure *m*; ~ **pump** *n* LAB EQUIP *fluid handling* pompe doseuse *f*; ~ **rate** *n* TELECOM palier de comptage *m*; ~ **roller** *n* PRINT rouleau distributeur *m*, rouleau débiteur *m*; ~ **valve** *n* AUTO limiteur de freinage *m*, MECH ENG soupape de dosage *f*

meter-type: ~ **relay** *n* ELEC ENG relais galvanométrique *m*

methacrylate *n* P&R méthacrylate *m*

methacrylic *adj* CHEM méthacrylique

methadone *n* CHEM méthadone *f*

methanal *n* CHEM formaldéhyde *m*, méthanal *m*

methanation *n* GAS TECH méthanation *f*

methane *n* CHEM, GAS TECH, METEO, PETR TECH, SAFETY méthane *m*; ~ **bacterium** *n* CHEM bactérie de méthane *f*, bactérie méthanophile *f*; ~ **borehole rig** *n* PETR TECH foreuse pour dégazage *f*; ~ **carrier** *n* NAUT *type of ship*, TRANSP méthanier *m*; ~ **carrier with self-supporting tank** *n* TRANSP méthanier à cuve autoporteuse *m*; ~ **detector** *n* MINING *fire damp* détecteur de grisou *m*, grisoumètre *m*; ~ **draining boring** *n* COAL TECH forage pour le captage du grisou *m*; ~ **fermentation** *n* HYDROL *sewage*, METEO fermentation méthanique *f*; ~ **gas** *n* CHEM méthane *m*; ~ **indicator** *n* MINING *fire damp* détecteur de grisou *m*, grisoumètre *m*; ~ **series** *n* GAS TECH carbures saturés *m pl*; ~ **tanker** *n* PETR TECH méthanier *m*

methanoic *adj* CHEM formique

methanol *n* CHEM alcool méthylique *m*, méthanol *m*, GAS TECH méthanol *m*; ~ **cell** *n* TRANSP pile au méthanol *f*

methanolic *adj* CHEM dans le méthanol

methanometer *n* MINING *fire damp* détecteur de grisou *m*, indicateur de gaz *m*

methenamine *n* CHEM méthénamine *f*

methimazol *n* CHEM méthimazole *m*

methionic *adj* CHEM méthionique

method *n* CHEM méthode *f*, voie *f*, PHYS méthode *f*, procédé *m*, PRINT méthode *f*; ~ **of costing** *n* MECH ENG méthode d'estimation du prix de revient *f*; ~ **of feeding** *n* (BrE) *(cf feeding process)* C&G mode d'alimentation *m*; ~ **of measurement** *n* CONST mode de métré *m*, méthode de métrage *f*; ~ **of routing** *n* RAIL méthode d'acheminement *f*

methods: ~ **engineer** *n* MECH ENG technicien méthodes *m*; ~ **manager** *n* MECH ENG responsable des méthodes *m*

methol *n* CHEM méthol *m*

methoxybenzene *n* CHEM anisol *m*

methoxyethanol *n* CHEM méthylcellosolve *m*

methoxyl *n* CHEM méthoxyle *m*

methuselah *n* C&G mathusalem *m*

methyl *n* CHEM méthyle *m*; ~ **acetate** *n* CHEM, DETER-

GENTS acétate de méthyle *m*; ~ **alcohol** *n* CHEM, P&R alcool méthylique *m*; ~ **bromide** *n* CHEM bromure de méthyle *m*; ~ **chloride** *n* CHEM chlorure de méthyle *m*; ~ **ester** *n* DETERGENTS ester méthylique *m*; ~ **ethyl ketone** *n* CHEM méthyléthylcétone *m*; ~ **ethyl ketoxime** *n* P&R *paint additive* méthyléthylcétoxime *m*; ~ **iodide** *n* CHEM iodure de méthyle *m*; ~ **tertiary-butyl ether** *n* PETR TECH éther méthyltributylique *m*

methylal *n* CHEM méthylal *m*

methylamine *n* CHEM méthylamine *f*

methylaniline *n* CHEM méthylaniline *f*

methylate¹ *n* CHEM méthylate *m*

methylate² *vt* CHEM méthyler

methylated: ~ **spirit** *n* CHEM alcool dénaturé *m*, alcool à brûler *m*; ~ **spirits** *n pl* CHEM mélange de méthanol *m*, COLOURS alcool dénaturé *m*, alcool ordinaire *m*, alcool ordinaire dénaturé par méthylation *m*

methylation *n* CHEM méthylation *f*

methylene: ~ **iodide** *n* CHEM iodure de méthylène *m*

methylic *adj* CHEM méthylique

methylnaphthalene *n* CHEM méthylnaphtalène *m*

methylpentose *n* CHEM méthylpentose *m*

methylpropane *n* CHEM méthylpropane *m*

meticulous: ~ **inspection** *n* CONST inspection minutieuse *f*

METO: ~ **power** *n* (*maximum except takeoff power*) AERONAUT puissance METO *f*

metol *n* CHEM métol *m*

Metonic: ~ **cycle** *n* ASTRON cycle de Meton *m*

metre *n* (BrE) METR mètre *m*; ~ **gauge** *n* (BrE) RAIL *track* voie d'un mètre *f*; ~ **kilogramme-second-ampere-system** *n* (BrE) (*MKSA system*) METR système mètre-kilogramme-seconde-ampère *m* (*système MKSA*)

metric¹ *adj* COMP, DP, METR métrique

metric:² ~ **carat** *n* METR *precious stones* carat métrique *m*; ~ **centner** *n* METR quintal métrique *m*; ~ **fine-pitch thread** *n* MECH ENG filetage métrique à pas fin *m*; ~ **horsepower** *n* METR cheval *m*; ~ **key** *n* NUCLEAR clé dynamométrique *f*; ~ **quintal** *n* METR quintal métrique *m*; ~ **system** *n* METR système métrique *m*; ~ **ton** *n* METR tonne *f*, tonne métrique *f*, PETR TECH tonne *f*;~ **tonne** *n* METR tonne *f*; ~ **trapezoidal screw thread** *n* MECH ENG filetage métrique trapézoïdal *m*; ~ **wave** *n* TELECOM onde métrique *f*

metrical¹ *adj* METR métrique

metrical:² ~ **geometry** *n* GEOM géométrie métrique *f*

metrology *n* TESTING métrologie *f*

metropolitan: ~ **area network** *n* (*MAN*) TELECOM réseau de zone urbaine *m*; ~ **network** *n* TELECOM réseau métropolitain *m*; ~ **railroad** *n* (AmE) (*cf metropolitan railway*) TRANSP métropolitain *m*; ~ **railway** *n* (BrE) (*cf metropolitan railroad*) TRANSP métropolitain *m*; ~ **switch** *n* TELECOM commutateur urbain *m*

Meyer: ~ **bar** *n* PRINT barre Meyer *f*

MF¹ *abbr* ELEC (*modulation frequency*) *alternating current* fréquence de modulation *f*, ELEC ENG (*medium frequency*) moyenne fréquence *f*, ELECTRON (*modulation frequency*) fréquence de modulation *f*, TELECOM (*mediation function*) fonction de médiation *f*, TELECOM (*multiple frequency*) fréquence multiple *f*

MF:² ~ **generator** *n* TELECOM générateur de signalisation multifréquence *m*, générateur multifréquence *m*; ~ **paperboard** *n* (*machine-finished paperboard*) PAPER TECH papier carton apprêté *m*; ~ **sender-receiver** *n* TELECOM signaleur multifréquence *m*; ~ **telephone** *n* TELECOM poste à fréquences vocales *m*, poste à touches musicales *m*

MFA *abbr* (*multiframe alignment*) TELECOM verrouillage de multitrame *m*

mfd *abbr* (*manufactured*) PROP MAT manufacturé

MFM: ~ **modulation** *n* (*modified frequency modulation*) ELECTRON modulation MFM *f*, modulation de fréquence modifiée *f* (*modulation MFM*)

mg *abbr* (*milligram, milligramme*) METR mg (*milligramme*)

Mg (*magnesium*) CHEM Mg (*magnésium*)

MG: ~ **board** *n* (*machine-glazed board*) PAPER TECH carton frictionné *m*; ~ **cylinder** *n* (*machine-glazed cylinder*) PAPER TECH frictionneur *m*, frictionneur sécheur *m*; ~ **machine** *n* PAPER TECH machine frictionneuse *f*; ~ **paper** *n* (*machine-glazed paper*) PACKAGING, PAPER TECH, PRINT papier frictionné *m*

MGD *abbr* (*magnetogasdynamics*) NUCLEAR magnétodynamique des gaz *f*

MH *abbr* (*message handling*) TELECOM messagerie *f*

MHD¹ *abbr* (*magnetohydrodynamic*) ELEC ENG, GEOPHYS, SPACE MHD (*magnétohydrodynamique*)

MHD:² ~ **conversion** *n* ELEC ENG, GEOPHYS conversion MHD *f*; ~ **converter** *n* ELEC ENG, NUCLEAR, SPACE convertisseur MHD *m*; ~ **generation** *n* ELEC ENG génération MHD *f*; ~ **generator** *n* ELEC ENG générateur MHD *m*; ~ **instability** *n* GEOPHYS instabilité MHD *f*; ~ **pump** *n* ELEC ENG pompe MHD *f*; ~ **wave** *n* GEOPHYS onde MHD *f*

MHS *abbr* (*message handling system*) TELECOM messagerie *f*, système de messagerie *m*

miargyrite *n* MINERAL miargyrite *f*

MIB *abbr* (*management information base*) TELECOM base d'informations de gestion *f*, base de données de gestion *f*

MIC *abbr* ELECTRON (*microwave integrated circuit*) circuit hybride hyperfréquence *m*, PHYS (*microwave integrated circuit*) circuit intégré micro-onde *m*, TELECOM(*marked idle channel*) repérage des voies au repos *m*

mica *n* C&G, CHEM *mineral*, ELEC *dielectric, insulator*, ELEC ENG, MINERAL, P&R *raw material*, PETR, PROP MAT mica *m*; ~ **capacitor** *n* ELEC ENG condensateur au mica *m*; ~ **dielectric capacitor** *n* ELEC condensateur au mica *m*

micaceous¹ *adj* GEOL micacé

micaceous:² ~ **iron ore** *n* MINERAL fer micacé *m*; ~ **iron oxide** *n* P&R *paint pigment* oxyde de fer micacé *m*

micaschist *n* GEOL micaschiste *m*

micelle *n* CHEM *of colloid*, P&R *chemical term* micelle *f*

Michelson: ~ **interferometer** *n* PHYS interféromètre de Michelson *m*

Michelson-Morley: ~ **experiment** *n* PHYS expérience de Michelson *f*

micoquille *n* C&G semi-coquille lunetterie *f*

MICR *abbr* (*magnetic ink character recognition*) COMP, DP RMC (*reconnaissance magnétique de caractères*)

micrite *n* GEOL *microcrystalline calcite matrix* micrite *f*

micro *n* COMP, DP micro *m*

micro- *pref* METR micro-

microammeter *n* ELEC ENG micro-ampèremètre *m*

microampere *n* ELEC micro-ampère *m*

microanalysis *n* CHEM, PROP MAT micro-analyse *f*

microanalytic *adj* CHEM micro-analytique

microanalytical *adj* CHEM micro-analytique

microbend *n* ELEC ENG microcourbure *f*, microréflexion *f*; ~ **loss** *n* OPT, TELECOM affaiblissement par micro-courbures *m*

microbending *n* OPT, TELECOM microcourbure *f*

microbiological: ~ **hazard** *n* SAFETY risque de la micro-biologie *m*

microbubble *n* OPT microbulle *f*

microburette *n* CHEM microburette *f*

microcellular: ~ **rubber** *n* P&R caoutchouc microcellulaire *m*

microchannel *n* ELECTRON microcanal *m*; ~ **image intensifier** *n* ELECTRON tube intensificateur d'images à microcanaux *m*; ~ **plate** *n* ELECTRON galette de microcanaux *f*

microchemistry *n* CHEM microchimie *f*

microchip *n* ELECTRON micropuce *f*, RAD PHYS puce électronique *f*

microcircuit *n* COMP, DP, ELECTRON microcircuit *m*

microclimate *n* METEO microclimat *m*

microcline *n* MINERAL microcline *m*

microcode *n* COMP, DP microcode *m*

microcomponent *n* PROP MAT élément microcircuit *m*

microcomputer *n* COMP, DP micro-ordinateur *m*

microcontrol *n* TRANSP microrégulation *f*

microcontroller *n* COMP, DP microcontrôleur *m*

microcosmic *adj* CHEM *salt* microcosmique

microcrack *n* OPT microfracture *f*

microcreep *n* METALL microfluage *m*

microcrêping *n* PAPER TECH microcrêpage *m*

microcrystalline [1] *adj* CHEM microcristallin

microcrystalline: [2] ~ **limestone** *n* GEOL calcaire microcristallin *m*; ~ **wax** *n* PETR TECH *petrol* cire microcristalline *f*

microdevitrification *n* OPT microdévitrification *f*

microdistillation *n* CHEM microdistillation *f*

microelectronics *n* COMP, DP, ELECTRON micro-électronique *f*

microelement *n* CHEM micro-élément *m*, oligo-élément *m*

microencapsulated: ~ **coating** *n* PRINT couche autocopiante *f*, couche à microcapsules *f*

microfarad *n* ELEC, ELEC ENG microfarad *m*

microfiche *n* COMP, DP, PRINT microfiche *f*; ~ **reader** *n* COMP, DP, PRINT lecteur de microfiche *m*

microfilm *n* COMP, DP, PHOTO, PRINT microfilm *m*; ~ **reader** *n* COMP, DP lecteur de microfilm *m*; ~ **recorder** *n* COMP, DP enregistreur sur microfilm *m*

microfilter *n* WATER SUPP microfiltre *m*

microfloppy: ~ **disk** *n* COMP, DP microdisquette *f*

microfold *n* GEOL crénulation *f*, micropli *m*

microfossil *n* GEOL microfossile *m*

microgranite *n* PETR microgranite *m*

microgranular *adj* GEOL microgrenu

micrograph *n* CRYSTALL micrographie *f*

micrographic: ~ **method** *n* MECH ENG méthode micrographique *f*; ~ **microscope** *n* INSTRUMENT microscope métallographique *m*

microgravity *n* ASTRON, SPACE microgravité *f*, micropesanteur *f*

microgroove *n* ACOUSTICS microsillon *m*; ~ **record** *n* RECORDING disque microsillon *m*; ~ **recording** *n* RECORDING enregistrement à microsillon *m*

microhardness *n* METALL, P&R microdureté *f*

microhenry *n* ELEC microhenry *m*

microhm *n* ELEC ENG microhm *m*

microinstruction *n* COMP, DP micro-instruction *f*

microlite *n* MINERAL microlite *f*

microlog *n* PETR microlog *m*

micromachining *n* RAD PHYS micro-usinage *m*

micrometeorite *n* ASTRON micrométéorite *f*

micrometer *n* LAB EQUIP *measuring thickness*, MECH *tools* palmer *m*, MECH ENG calibre à vis micrométrique *m*, micromètre *m*, palmer *m*, METR palmer *m*, *depth* micromètre de profondeur *m*, *external, internal, stick, height* micromètre *m*, PAPER TECH micromètre d'épaisseur *m*, PHYS palmer *m* ~ **calipers** *n pl* (AmE), ~ **callipers** *n pl* (BrE) MECH ENG calibre à vis micrométrique *m*, micromètre *m*, palmer *m*; ~ **screw** *n* INSTRUMENT bouton de réglage du micromètre *m*, MECH ENG vis micrométrique *f*

micrometre *n* (BrE) METR micron *m*

micrometric [1] *adj* METR micrométrique

micrometric: [2] ~ **spark discharger** *n* ELEC éclateur à intervalle micrométrique *m*

micrometry *n* MECH ENG micrométrie *f*

micromicron *n* METR micro-micron *m*

micromil *n* METR micromillimètre *m*, micron *m*

micromillimeter *n* (AmE), **micromillimetre** *n* (BrE) METR micromillimètre *m*, micron *m*

microminiaturization *n* ELECTRON microminiaturisation *f*

micron *n* METR micromillimètre *m*, micron *m* ~ **barrier** *n* ELECTRON barrière du micron *f*, mur du micron *m*; ~ **circuit** *n* ELECTRON circuit micronique *m*

micronic *adj* MECH ENG *filter* micronique

micronize *vt* CHEM microniser

micronized *adj* P&R *pigments, fillers* micronisé

micronutrient *n* HYDROL oligo-élément *m*, élément oligodynamique *m*

microorganism *n* HYDROL, POLLUTION micro-organisme *m*

microperthite *n* MINERAL microperthite *f*

microphone *n* ACOUSTICS, ELEC *transmission*, PHYS, RECORDING microphone *m*; ~ **amplifier** *n* RECORDING amplificateur de microphone *m*; ~ **blanket** *n* RECORDING écran de microphone *m*; ~ **boom** *n* RECORDING perche de microphone *f*; ~ **cable** *n* RECORDING câble de microphone *m*; ~ **diaphragm** *n* RECORDING diaphragme de microphone *m*; ~ **power supply** *n* RECORDING alimentation de microphone *f*; ~ **shield** *n* RECORDING blindage de microphone *m*; ~ **stand** *n* RECORDING support de microphone *m*; ~ **transformer** *n* RECORDING transformateur de microphone *m*

microphonic *adj* RECORDING microphonique

microphotography *n* CINEMAT microphotographie *f*

microphotometer *n* RAD PHYS microphotomètre *m*

micropipette *n* LAB EQUIP *glassware, analysis* micropipette *f*

micropit *n* OPT microcuvette *f*

microprobe *n* RAD PHYS microsonde *f*

microprocessor *n* COMP, DP, ELEC, ELECTRON, MECH ENG, PRINT, SPACE *communications* microprocesseur *m*; ~ **chip** *n* ELECTRON puce microprocesseur *f*; ~ **control** *n* ELECTRON commande à microprocesseur *f*, TELECOM commande par microprocesseurs *f*

microprogram *n* COMP, DP microprogramme *m*

microprogramming *n* COMP, DP microprogrammation *f*

micropump *n* MECH ENG micropompe *f*

microresistivity: ~ **log** *n* GEOPHYS diagramme de micro-résistivité *m*

microrheology *n* METALL microrhéologie *f*

microribbon *adj* TELECOM microruban

microrocket *n* SPACE *spacecraft* micropropulseur *m*

microscope n INSTRUMENT, LAB EQUIP *instrument* microscope m, METR *for toolmaker* microscope m, *measuring* microscope de mesure m, PHYS microscope m; **~ adaptor** n PHOTO adaptateur pour photomicrographie m, dispositif de microphotographie m, adaptateur pour photomicrographie m; **~ body** n INSTRUMENT tube électronique m; **~ camera** n INSTRUMENT appareil photo de microscope m; **~ condenser** n LAB EQUIP condenseur pour microscope m; **~ eyepiece** n INSTRUMENT oculaire du microscope de lecture m; **~ slide** n C&G verre couvre-objet m, LAB EQUIP lame pour microscope f; **~ slide cover slip** n LAB EQUIP lamelle pour microscope f; **~ stage** n INSTRUMENT platine f, porte-objet m; **~ tube** n INSTRUMENT tube électronique m

microscopic: **~ dust** n SAFETY *in workshop air* poussières microscopiques f pl; **~ photometer** n INSTRUMENT microscope à photomètre m; **~ stage** n INSTRUMENT platine f, porte-objet m; **~ state** n RAD PHYS état microscopique m

Microscopium n ASTRON Microscope m

microscopy n CHEM microscopie f

microsecond n COMP, DP microseconde f

microsegregation n METALL microségrégation f

microslot adj TELECOM à microfente

microspheres n pl P&R *pigments* microsphères f pl

microstrain n METALL microdéformation f

microstrainer n WATER SUPP microtamis m

microstrip n ELECTRON ligne microruban f, PHYS microbande f, microruban m

microstructure n COAL TECH, CRYSTALL, GEOL microstructure f

microswitch n ELEC disjoncteur miniature m, ELEC ENG microrupteur m; **~ box** n AERONAUT boîtier de minirupteurs m

microsyringe n LAB EQUIP *gas chromatography* microseringue f

microthruster n SPACE *spacecraft* micropropulseur m

microtome n LAB EQUIP *microscopy* microtome m

microtwin n METALL micromacle f

microvolt n ELEC, ELEC ENG microvolt m

microwavable: **~ packaging** n PACKAGING emballage convenant aux fours à hyperfréquence m

microwave n ELEC, ELECTRON, PHYS, TELECOM, WAVE PHYS micro-onde f, onde hyperfréquence f, onde ultracourte f; **~ absorption** n TELECOM absorption hyperfréquence f; **~ aerial** n TELECOM antenne à hyperfréquences f; **~ amplification** n ELECTRON amplification hyperfréquence f; **~ amplification by stimulated emission of radiation** n SPACE *communications* effet maser m; **~ amplifier** n ELECTRON, PHYS amplificateur hyperfréquence m, TELECOM amplificateur à hyperfréquences m; **~ amplifier tube** n ELECTRON tube amplificateur hyperfréquence m; **~ antenna** n TELECOM antenne à hyperfréquences f; **~ attenuation** n ELECTRON atténuation en hyperfréquence f; **~ attenuator** n ELECTRON atténuateur hyperfréquence variable m, TELECOM atténuateur hyperfréquence m; **~ background radiation** n ASTRON rayonnement micro-onde de corps noir m, PHYS rayonnement cosmologique m, rayonnement universel m; **~ band-pass filter** n ELECTRON filtre passe-bande hyperfréquence m; **~ band-stop filter** n ELECTRON filtre coupe-bande hyperfréquence m; **~ beam** n TELECOM faisceau hertzien m; **~ cavity** n ELECTRON cavité hyperfréquence f; **~ circuit** n ELECTRON circuit

hyperfréquence m; **~ circulator** n TELECOM circulateur à hyperfréquences m; **~ delay line** n ELECTRON ligne à retard hyperfréquence f; **~ diode** n ELECTRON diode hyperfréquence f; **~ discharge** n GAS TECH décharge micro-onde f; **~ filter** n ELECTRON filtre hyperfréquence m; **~ frequency** n ELECTRON, PHYS, RECORDING, TV, TELECOM hyperfréquence f; **~ generator** n ELECTRON générateur hyperfréquence m; **~ integrated circuit** n *(MIC)* ELECTRON circuit hybride hyperfréquence m, PHYS circuit intégré micro-onde m; **~ inversion** n RAD PHYS inversion de micro-onde f; **~ landing system** n *(MLS)* AERONAUT système d'atterrissage hyperfréquence m; **~ limiter** n ELECTRON limiteur hyperfréquence m; **~ link** n PHYS liaison hertzienne f, TELECOM, TV relais hertzien m; **~ low-pass filter** n ELECTRON filtre passe-bas hyperfréquence m; **~ mixer** n ELECTRON mélangeur hyperfréquence m; **~ modulator** n TELECOM modulateur hyperfréquence m; **~ module** n ELECTRON module hyperfréquence m; **~ oscillator** n ELECTRON oscillateur hyperfréquence m; **~ oscillator tube** n ELECTRON tube oscillateur hyperfréquence m; **~ oven** n ELEC ENG, FOOD TECH four à micro-ondes m; **~ phase changer** n TELECOM déphaseur hyperfréquence m; **~ power** n ELEC ENG puissance hyperfréquence f; **~ power amplification** n ELECTRON amplification de puissance hyperfréquence f; **~ power amplifier** n ELECTRON amplificateur de puissance hyperfréquence m; **~ power transistor** n ELECTRON transistor de puissance hyperfréquence m; **~ printed circuit** n ELECTRON circuit imprimé hyperfréquence m; **~ resonator** n ELECTRON, TELECOM résonateur à hyperfréquences m; **~ signal** n ELECTRON signal hyperfréquence m; **~ signal generator** n ELECTRON générateur de signaux hyperfréquence m, générateur hyperfréquence m; **~ signal source** n ELECTRON source d'hyperfréquences f, source de signaux hyperfréquence f; **~ spectroscopy** n PHYS spectroscopie à hyperfréquences f, RAD PHYS spectroscopie de micro-ondes f; **~ spectrum** n RAD PHYS spectre de micro-ondes m; **~ substrate** n ELECTRON substrat pour hyperfréquences m; **~ synthesizer** n ELECTRON synthétiseur hyperfréquence m; **~ system** n TELECOM système hertzien m; **~ systems** n pl TELECOM faisceaux hertziens m pl; **~ technology** n SPACE *craft* technologie des hyperfréquences f; **~ thawing** n REFRIG dégel par micro-ondes m, dégivrage par micro-ondes m; **~ tower** n TELECOM pylône hertzien m, tour hertzienne f; **~ transistor** n ELECTRON transistor hyperfréquence m; **~ transistor amplifier** n ELECTRON amplificateur à transistor hyperfréquence m; **~ transmission line** n ELEC ENG ligne de transmission hyperfréquence f, ligne hyperfréquence f; **~ tube** n ELECTRON tube hyperfréquence m, tube à onde lente m, MECH ENG tube hyperfréquence m, tube micro-ondes m; **~ tunable filter** n ELECTRON filtre accordable hyperfréquence m

midband: **~ frequency** n ELECTRON fréquence à mibande f; **~ gain** n ELECTRON gain à mi-bande m

middle [1] adj GEOL moyen, PAPER TECH *of board* intérieur

middle [2] n PROD ENG *cheek of three-part foundry flask* chape f, chape de châssis f; **~ cut** n PROD ENG *files, rasps* taille moyenne f; **~ distillate** n PETR TECH *petrol* distillat moyen m; **~ ground** n NAUT *geography* banc de milieu m, banc médian m; **~ infrared** n RAD PHYS infrarouge moyen m; **~ knife-edge** n MECH ENG *of balance* couteau central m, couteau du fléau m; **~ layer** n TEXTILES canevas intermédiaire m; **~ marker** n AERO-

NAUT *of instrument landing system* radiobalise moyenne *f*, radiobalise médiane *f*, radioborne intermédiaire *f*; ~ **part** *n* PROD ENG *cheek of three-part foundry flask* chape *f*; ~ **pile segment** *n* COAL TECH pieu intermédiaire *m*; ~ **rail** *n* CONST *of door* traverse du milieu *f*

middles *n pl* MINING mixtes *m pl*

middletones *n pl* PRINT demi-teintes *f pl*, demi-tons *m pl*

middlings *n pl* COAL TECH mixtes *m pl*, FOOD TECH *milling, baking* issues de blé *f pl*, recoupe de blé *f*, MINING mixtes *m pl*; ~ **bran** *n* FOOD TECH *milling, baking* recoupettes *f pl*

mid-engine *n* AUTO moteur au centre *m*

midfeather *n* C&G cloison médiane de brûleur *f*

midocean: ~ **ridge** *n* GEOL dorsale médio-océanique *f*

midpoint: ~ **anchor** *n* RAIL point d'anticheminement *m*; ~ **earthing** *n* (BrE) *(cf midpoint grounding)* ELEC *of connection* prise de terre symétrique *f*; ~ **grounding** *n* (AmE) *(cf midpoint earthing)* ELEC *of connection* prise de terre symétrique *f*

midrange: ~ **loudspeaker** *n* RECORDING haut-parleur pour fréquences moyennes *m*

midrib *n* METALL arête centrale *f*

midship [1] *adj* NAUT au centre du navire

midship: [2] ~ **beam** *n* NAUT *naval architecture* maître bau *m*; ~ **body** *n* NAUT *naval architecture* partie centrale de la coque *f*; ~ **frame** *n* NAUT *naval architecture* maître couple *m*; ~ **section** *n* NAUT *naval architecture* coupe au maître *f*, maîtresse partie *f*, section transversale *f*

midshipman *n* NAUT *navy* aspirant *m*

midships *adv* NAUT au milieu du navire

mid-shot *n* CINEMAT plan moyen *m*

midstream *n* HYDROL milieu du courant *m*

midtravel *n* MECH ENG mi-course *f*

midwall *n* MINING cloison médiane *f*

mid-wing *n* AERONAUT aile médiane *f*; ~ **plane** *n* AERONAUT avion à aile demi-surélevée *m*

MIG: ~ **welding** *n* *(metal inert gas welding)* CONST, THERMOD soudage MIG *m*

migmatization *n* GEOL migmatisation *f*

migrate *vi* CHEM *of ions*, PETR migrer

migration *n* CHEM *of ions*, P&R *of plasticizer*, PETR TECH *of hydrocarbons* migration *f*

mike: ~ **tap** *n* CINEMAT clap micro *m*, microphotographie *f*

MIL *abbr* *(multipoint indication loop)* TELECOM indication multipoint de boucle *f*

milarite *n* MINERAL milarite *f*

mild: ~ **steel** *n* MECH ENG acier doux *m*

mildew *n* FOOD TECH mildiou *m*

mildewproofing *n* COATINGS apprêt antimoissisure *m*

mile *n* METR, TRANSP mille anglais *m*

mileage *n* TRANSP kilométrage *m*; ~ **recorder** *n* (BrE) AUTO compteur kilométrique *m*

milepost *n* RAIL poteau kilométrique *m*

miles: ~ **per gallon** *n pl* *(mpg)* TRANSP milles par gallon *m pl*

milestone *n* MECH *of project* étape *f*, TRANSP borne kilométrique *f*

military: ~ **observation satellite** *n* SPACE satellite d'observation militaire *m*

milk: ~ **cooler** *n* REFRIG refroidisseur à lait *m*; ~ **fat** *n* FOOD TECH matière grasse de lait *f*; ~ **glass** *n* C&G verre laiteux *m*; ~ **powder** *n* FOOD TECH poudre de lait *f*; ~ **protein** *n* FOOD TECH protéine du lait *f*; ~ **tanker** *n* TRANSP camion laitier *m*

milkiness *n* C&G voile *m*

Milky: ~ **Way** *n* ASTRON Voie Lactée *f*

mill [1] *n* COAL TECH bocard *m*, MINING cheminée *f*, cheminée à minerai *f*, P&R *equipment*, PAPER TECH *grinding device* moulin *m*, PROD ENG *crushing, grinding machine* broyeur *m*, moulin *m*, *for reducing ores by a process other than melting* atelier *m*, atelier de préparation mécanique *m*, *rolling mill* laminoir *m*, train *m*, équipage *m*, *stamp-milling machine* bocard *m*, moulin *m*; ~ **course** *n* WATER SUPP bief de moulin *m*, biez de moulin *m*; ~ **gearing** *n* MECH ENG rouage *m*; ~ **hole** *n* MINING cheminée *f*, cheminée à minerai *f*; ~ **race** *n* WATER SUPP bief de moulin *m*, biez de moulin *m*; ~ **result** *n* PROD ENG rendement du bocard *m*; ~ **run** *n* PROD ENG campagne *f*; ~ **scale** *n* PROD ENG scories de laminoir *f pl*; ~ **tail** *n* WATER SUPP bief d'aval *m*, biez de fuite *m*

mill [2] *vt* COAL TECH comminuer, traiter, FOOD TECH broyer, MECH fraiser, PROD ENG *to form, slot in milling machine* fraiser, *to knurl* godronner, moleter, *to stamp, to crush, to grind* bocarder, broyer, moudre

mill: [3] ~ **between centers** *vi* (AmE), ~ **between centres** *vi* (BrE) PROD ENG fraiser entre pointes

millboard *n* PACKAGING carton gris *m*, PAPER TECH, PRINT carton à l'enrouleuse *m*

milled [1] *adj* MECH ENG moleté

milled: [2] ~ **head** *n* MECH ENG bouton moleté *m*; ~ **knob** *n* MECH ENG bouton moleté *m*; ~ **nut** *n* MECH ENG molette *f*, écrou godronné *m*, écrou moleté *m*, écrou à molette *m*; ~ **ore** *n* MINING minerai bocardé *m*, minerai broyé *m*

miller *n* PROD ENG fraiseuse *f*, machine à fraiser *f*

Miller: ~ **bridge** *n* ELEC *of circuit* pont de Miller *m*; ~ **indices** *n pl* CRYSTALL, METALL indices de Miller *m pl*

millerayes *n* TEXTILES tissu mille-raies *m*

millerite *n* MINERAL millérite *f*

mill-finished: ~ **paper** *n* PRINT papier fini en machine *m*

milli- *pref* *(m)* METR milli- *(m)*

milliammeter *n* ELEC, ELEC ENG milliampèremètre *m*

milliampere *n* *(mA)* ELEC, ELEC ENG milliampère *m* *(mA)*

millibar *n* METR millibar *m*

millicron *n* METR micromillimètre *m*, millicron *m*

milligram *n* (AmE), **milligramme** *n* (BrE) *(mg)* METR milligramme *m* *(mg)*

Millikan: ~ **conductor** *n* ELEC *cable* âme segmentée *f*

Millikan's: ~ **experiment** *n* PHYS expérience de Millikan *f*

millimeter *n* (AmE), **millimetre** *n* (BrE) *(mm)* METR millimètre *m* *(mm)* ~ **astronomy** *n* ASTRON astronomie millimétrique *f*; ~ **wave amplification** *n* ELECTRON amplification des ondes millimétriques *f*; ~ **wave amplifier** *n* ELECTRON amplificateur en ondes millimétriques *m*; ~wave astronomy *n* ASTRON astronomie onde-millimétrique *f*; ~ **wavelength emission** *n* RAD PHYS rayonnement à longueur d'ondes *m*; ~ **wave magnetron** *n* ELECTRON magnétron à ondes millimétriques *m*; ~ **waves** *n pl* PHYS ondes millimétriques *f pl*; ~ **wave source** *n* ELECTRON source d'ondes millimétriques *f*, source millimétrique *f*; ~ **wave travelling-wave tube** *n* ELECTRON TOP en ondes millimétriques *m*, TOP millimétrique *m*, tube à onde progressive millimétrique *m*; ~ **wave tube** *n* ELECTRON tube en ondes millimétriques *m*, tube millimétrique *m*

millimetric *adj* ELECTRON *wave* millimétrique

milling *n* CHEM TECH broyage *m*, comminution *f*, fragmentation *f*, COAL TECH broyage *m*, FOOD TECH industrie meunière *f*, meunerie *f*, minoterie *f*, MINING bocardage *m*, broyage *m*, PAPER TECH broyage *m*, PROD ENG *forming with milling machine* fraisage *m*, fraisement *m*, *knurling* godronnage *m*, moletage *m*, TEXTILES foulage *m*; **~ attachment** *n* MECH ENG *machine tools* dispositif de fraisage *m*; **~ cutter** *n* MECH ENG fraise *f*; **~ cutter sharpening machine** *n* PROD ENG machine à affûter les fraises *f*; **~ cutter with inserted teeth** *n* MECH ENG fraise à dents rapportées *f*, fraise à lames amovibles *f*, fraise à lames rapportées *f*; **~ cutter with spiral teeth** *n* MECH ENG fraise à denture hélicoïdale *f*; **~ cutter with straight teeth** *n* MECH ENG fraise à denture droite *f*; **~ cutting arbor** *n* MECH ENG mandrin porte-fraise *m*; **~ file** *n* PROD ENG lime-fraiseuse à main *f*; **~ head** *n* MECH ENG tête porte-fraise *f*, *machine tools* plateau porte-chariot à fraiser *m*; **~ industry** *n* FOOD TECH industrie meunière *f*, meunerie *f*, minoterie *f*; **~ jig** *n* MECH ENG calibre de fraisage *m*, singe *m*, touche *f*, gabarit de fraisage *m*; **~ liquid** *n* CHEM TECH liquide de broyage *m*; **~ machine** *n* MECH fraiseuse *f*, PROD ENG fraiseuse *f*, machine à fraiser *f*, SAFETY fraiseuse *f*; **~ machine arbor** *n* MECHeng arbre porte-fraise *m*, broche porte-fraise *f*, mandrin porte-fraise *m*, PROD ENG arbre porte-fraise *m*, broche porte-fraise *f*; **~ machine cutter arbor** *n* PROD ENG arbre porte-fraise *m*, broche porte-fraise *f*, mandrin porte-fraise *m*; **~ process** *n* FOOD TECH mouture *f*, procédé de mouture *m*; **~ tool** *n* PROD ENG *knurling* godronnoir *m*, molette *f*

millions: **~ of cubic feet per day** *n pl* *(MCFD)* PETR TECH millions de pieds cubes par jour *m pl*; **~ of instructions per second** *n pl* *(MIPS)* COMP, DP, PRINT millions d'instructions par seconde *m pl* *(MIPS)*

millisecond *n (ms)* COMP, DP milliseconde *f (ms)*; **~ delay cap** *n* MINING amorce à microretard *f*, détonateur à microretard *m*; **~ delay detonator** *n* MINING amorce à microretard *f*, détonateur à microretard *m*

millivolt *n (mV)* ELEC, ELEC ENG millivolt *m (mV)*

millivoltmeter *n* ELEC millivoltmètre *m*

milliwatt *n (mW)* ELEC ENG milliwatt *m (mW)*

milliwattmeter *n* ELEC milliwattmètre *m*

millstone *n* FOOD TECH meule *f*; **~ grit** *n* GEOL grès meulière *m*, PROD ENG grès meulier *m*, grès molaire *m*, meulière *f*, millstonegrit *m*, molarite *f*, pierre de meule *f*, pierre meulière *f*, silex meulier *m*

millwright *n* MECH ajusteur-monteur *m*

MIMD *abbr (multiple-instruction multiple-data)* COMP, DP MIMD *(multiflux d'instruction-multiflux de données)*

mimetene *n* MINERAL mimétite *f*

mimetite *n* MINERAL mimétite *f*

mimic: **~ board** *n* ELEC tableau synoptique *m*

mincer *n* FOOD TECH hachoir *m*

mine [1] *n* MILIT mine *f*, MINING exploitation *f*, mine *f*; **~ access** *n* CONST *tunnels, dams* descenderie *f*, galerie d'accès *f*; **~ car** *n* MINING berlaine *f*, berline *f*, TRANSP berline *f*; **~ chamber** *n* MINING chambre de mine *f*, fourneau de mine *m*, mine *f*, trou de mine *m*; **~ detector** *n* MILIT détecteur de mines *m*; **~ development** *n* MINING traçage *m*; **~ entrance** *n* MINING entrée de galerie *f*; **~ fan** *n* MINING ventilateur *m*, ventilateur de puits *m*; **~ hoist** *n* MINING machine d'extraction *f*, moteur d'extraction *m*; **~ level** *n* MINING galerie de mine *f*, galerie de niveau de mine *f*; **~ opening** *n* MINING chambre de mine *f*; **~ pumping** *n* MINING exhaure *f*, épuisement *m*; **~ railroad** *n (AmE)*, **~ railway** *n (BrE)* TRANSP chemin de fer minier *m*; **~ resistance** *n* MINING résistance de la mine *f*; **~ run** *n* MINING tout-venant *m*;

~ shaft *n* MINING puits de mine *m*; **~ stone** *n* MINING minerai *m*, pierre de mine *f*; **~ timber** *n* MINING bois de mine *m*; **~ tin** *n* MINING étain de roche *m*; **~ yield** *n* COAL TECH extraction d'une mine *f*

mine [2] *vt* MINING abattre, exploiter, fouiller, fouiller la terre

mine [3] *vi* MINING faire des travaux miniers

mineability *n* MINING exploitabilité *f*

mineable *adj* MINING exploitable

mined *adj* MILIT *area* miné

mined-out: **~ area** *n* MINING chantier abandonné *m*

minefield *n* MILIT champ de mines *m*

minelayer *n* MILIT, NAUT *naval* mouilleur de mines *m*

minelaying *n* NAUT *naval* mouillage de mines *m*; **~ ship** *n* NAUT mouilleur de mines *m*

miner *n* COAL TECH mineur *m*

mineral [1] *adj* COAL TECH, MINERAL minéral

mineral [2] *n* COAL TECH charbon *m*, minéral *m*, MINERAL minéral *m*; **~ analysis** *n* CHEM analyse minérale *f*; **~ assemblage** *n* GEOL paragénèse *f*; **~ caoutchouc** *n* MINERAL caoutchouc minéral *m*; **~ chemistry** *n* CHEM *inorganic* chimie inorganique *f*, chimie minérale *f*; **~ coal** *n* COAL TECH charbon minéral *m*; **~ color** *n (AmE)*, **~ colour** *n (BrE)* COLOURS couleur minérale *f*, pigment minéral *m*; **~ deposit** *n* MINING gisement de minerai *m*, gîte métallifère *m*, gisement minier *m*, gisement minéral *m*, gîte minéral *m*; **~ fiber** *n (AmE)*, **~ fibre** *n (BrE)* HEAT ENG fibre minérale *f*; **~ insulation** *n* ELEC *of cable conductor* isolation minérale *f*; **~ isochrone** *n* GEOL isochrone sur minéraux *f*; **~ naphtha** *n* COAL TECH naphta minéral *m*; **~ oil** *n* AUTO huile minérale *f*, COAL TECH pétrole *m*, P&R *raw material* huile minérale *f*; **~ pigment** *n* COLOURS pigment minéral *m*; **~ pitch** *n* CONST asphalte *m*, bitume minéral *m*; **~ processing** *n* COAL TECH minéralurgie *f*; **~ rights** *n pl* PETR TECH droits miniers *m pl*; **~ soil** *n* COAL TECH terre minérale *f*; **~ spring** *n* WATER SUPP source minérale *f*; **~ tallow** *n* MINERAL suif minéral *m*; **~ tar** *n* CONST goudron minéral *m*, MINERAL bitume glutineux *m*; **~ water** *n* HYDROL eau minérale *f*, eau minérale naturelle *f*; **~ wool** *n* HEAT ENG coton minéral *m*, REFRIG *for insulating* laine de roche *f*

mineral-insulated: **~ cable** *n* ELEC, ELEC ENG câble à isolation minérale *m*

mineralization *n* CHEM, GEOL minéralisation *f*

mineralizer *n* CHEM minéralisateur *m*

mineralizing *adj* CHEM minéralisateur

mineral-matter-free *adj* POLLUTION matières minérales exclues *f pl*

mineralogic *adj (AmE)*, **mineralogical** *adj (BrE)* GEOL minéralogique

mineralogist *n* MINERAL minéralogiste *m*

mineralogy *n* GEOL, PETR TECH minéralogie *f*

minerogenic *adj* COAL TECH minérogène

minerogenous *adj* COAL TECH minérogène

miners': **~ bar** *n* MINING barre de mineur *f*, barre à mine *f*

minestuff *n* MINING minerai *m*, pierre de mine *f*

minesweeper *n* MILIT, NAUT *naval* dragueur de mines *m*

minesweeping *n* NAUT *naval* dragage de mines *m*

mini *n* COMP, DP mini *m*; **~ pusher tug** *n* TRANSP mini-pousseur *m*

miniature *n* CINEMAT maquette *f*, modèle réduit *m*; **~ aircraft index** *n* AERONAUT maquette fixe sur instruments *f*; **~ ball bearing** *n* MECH ENG roulement à billes miniatures *m*; **~ binoculars** *n pl* INSTRUMENT jumelles de poche *f pl*; **~ bottle** *n* C&G mignonnette *f*; **camera** *n*

INSTRUMENT appareil photo petit format *m*, PHOTO appareil photographique petit format *m*; ~ **chemical agent**detector *n* MILIT *chemical warfare* détecteur de contamination chimique miniature *m*; ~ **circuit breaker** *n* ELEC, ELEC ENG disjoncteur miniature *m*; ~ **film** *n* PHOTO film de petit format *m*; ~ **film cassette** *n* INSTRUMENT magasin petit format *m*; ~ **magnetron** *n* ELECTRON magnétron miniature *m*; ~ **maker** *n* CINEMAT modéliste *m*; ~ **relay** *n* ELEC ENG relais miniature *m*; ~ **screw thread** *n* MECH ENG filetage miniature *m*; ~ **traveling-wave tube** *n* (AmE), ~ **travelling-wave tube** *n* (BrE) ELECTRON mini-TOP *m*

miniaturization *n* COMP miniaturisation *f*, DP miniaturisation *f*, programmation à temps d'accès minimal *f*

mini-bundle: ~ **cable** *n* OPT câble mini-bundle *m*

minicam *n* TV caméra miniature *f*

minicassette *n* RECORDING minicassette *f*

minicomputer *n* COMP, DP mini-ordinateur *m*

minigroove: ~ **recording** *n* RECORDING enregistrement à minisillon *m*

minimal: ~ **submanifolds** *n pl* GEOM sous-variétés à surface minimale *f pl*; ~ **surface** *n* GEOM surface minimale *f*

minima-maxima: ~ **check** *n* CONTROL contrôle minimums-maximums *m*

minimum: ~ **calibrated speed** *n* AERONAUT *in flight during normal stall* vitesse corrigée en vol *f*; ~ **charge** *n* TELECOM tarif minimum *m*; ~ **circuit breaker** *n* ELEC ENG interrupteur à minimum *m*; ~ **consumption** *n* HYDROL *of water* consommation minimale *f*; ~ **control speed during landing approach** *n* AERONAUT vitesse minimale de contrôle à l'approche *f*; ~ **control speed in the air** *n* AERONAUT vitesse minimale de contrôle en air libre *f*; ~ **control speed on the ground** *n* AERONAUT vitesse minimale de contrôle au sol *f*; ~ **current relay** *n* ELEC relais à minimum de courant *m*; ~ **daily runoff** *n* HYDROL débit minimal journalier *m*; ~ **demonstrated threshold speed** *n* AERONAUT vitesse minimale de démonstration au seuil *f*; ~ **descent altitude** *n* AERONAUT altitude minimale de descente *f*; ~ **descent height** *n* AERONAUT hauteur minimale de descente *f*; ~ **detectable signal** *n* ELECTRON signal minimal détectable *m*; ~ **deviation** *n* PHYS minimum de déviation *m*; ~ **error-free pad** *n* (*MEFP*) TELECOM période minimale sans erreur *f*; ~ **glide path** *n* AERONAUT alignement de descente minimal *m*; ~ **hourly runoff** *n* HYDROL débit minimal horaire *m*; ~ **irradiation** *n* RAD PHYS *of sample* irradiation minimale *f*; ~ **lethal dose** *n* POLLUTION dose létale minimale *f*; ~ **low water** *n* WATER SUPP étiage *m*; ~ **payable** *n* TELECOM minimum de perception *m*; ~ **power relay** *n* ELEC relais à minimum de puissance *m*; ~ **safe altitude** *n* AERONAUT altitude minimale de sécurité *f*; ~ **signal** *n* ELECTRON signal minimal *m*; ~ **stress** *n* METALL contrainte minimale *f*; ~ **takeoff**safety speed *n* AERONAUT vitesse minimale de sécurité au décollage *f*; ~ **theoretical thickness** *n* NAUT *of hull* épaisseur théorique minimale *f*; ~ **unstick speed** *n* AERONAUT vitesse minimale de déjaugeage *f*; ~ **voltage** *n* ELEC tension minimale *f*; ~ **weather conditions** *n pl* AERONAUT minimum d'atterrissage *m*; ~ **weight** *n* PACKAGING poids minimum *m*; ~ **welding current** *n* CONST courant de soudage minimal *m*

minimum-access: ~ **programming** *n* COMP, DP programmation à temps d'accès minimal *f*

minimum-dressed: ~ **width of warp** *n* TEXTILES largeur de chaîne minimum *f*

minimum-focusing: ~ **distance** *n* CINEMAT distance de mise au point minimum *f*

minimum-shift: ~ **keying** *n* (*MSK*) ELECTRON modulation à déplacement minimal *f*, TELECOM manipulation par déplacement minimal *f*

mining *n* COAL TECH abattage *m*, exploitation *f*, exploitation de mines *f*, exploitation minière *f*, travaux d'exploitation *m pl*, travaux de mines *m pl*, travaux miniers *m pl*, HYDROL *of groundwater* exploitation *f*; ~ **appliances** *n pl* MINING engins de mines *m pl*, matériel de mines *m*, outillage de mines *m*; ~ **area** *n* MINING domaine minier *m*; ~ **bucket** *n* MINING benne d'extraction *f*; ~ **claim** *n* MINING claim minier *m*, concession de mines *f*, concession minière *f*; ~ **of coal** *n* COAL TECH charbonnage *m*; ~ **concession** *n* MINING claim minier *m*, concession de mines *f*, concession minière *f*; ~ **cradle** *n* MINING *ore dressing* berceau *m*, cradle *m*; ~ **engineer** *n* MINING ingénieur civil des mines *m*, ingénieur des mines *m*; ~ **engineering** *n* MINING art des mines *m*, technique minière *f*; ~ **hole** *n* MINING chambre de mine *f*, fourneau de mine *m*, mine *f*, trou de mine *m*; ~ **machine** *n* MINING déhouilleuse *f*; ~ **timber** *n* MINING bois de mine *m*

minirail *n* TRANSP minirail *m*

minisubmersible *n* OCEANOG scooter sous-marin *m*

minium *n* CHEM, MINERAL minium *m*

minivan *n* TRANSP monospace *m*

Minkowski: ~ **space** *n* PHYS espace de Minkowski *m*

minor: ~ **alarm** *n* TELECOM alarme mineure *f*; ~ **and major servicing operations** *n pl* AERONAUT opérations d'entretien mineures et majeures *f pl*; ~ **arc** *n* GEOM *of circle* arc mineur *m*; ~ **axis** *n* GEOM *of an ellipse* petit axe *m*; ~ **base check** *n* AERONAUT petite visite *f*; ~ **check** *n* AERONAUT petite visite *f*; ~ **control** *n* CONTROL contrôle annexe *m*, contrôle au niveau inférieur *m*, contrôle secondaire *m*, contrôle mineur *m*; ~ **diameter** *n* MECH ENG diamètre de fond de filet *m*; ~ **diameter error** *n* METR erreur de diamètre de fond de filet *f*; ~ **planet** *n* ASTRON astéroïde *m*, petite planète *f*, SPACE planétoïde *m*; ~ **repairs** *n pl* PROD ENG petites réparations *f pl*, réparations peu importantes *f pl*, RAIL RA, réparations accidentelles *f pl*; ~ **road** *n* CONST route secondaire *f*, voie à faible circulation *f*; ~ **second** *n* ACOUSTICS seconde mineure *f*; ~ **semitone** *n* ACOUSTICS demi-ton mineur *m*; ~ **seventh** *n* ACOUSTICS septième mineure *f*; ~ **sixth** *n* ACOUSTICS sixte mineure *f*; ~ **third** *n* ACOUSTICS tierce mineure *f*; ~ **whole tone** *n* ACOUSTICS ton mineur *m*

minority: ~ **carrier** *n* ELECTRON, PHYS porteur minoritaire *m*

minus: ~ **acceleration** *n* MECH ENG accélération négative *f*; ~ **amount** *n* GEOM quantité négative *f*; ~ **correction** *n* PRINT correction minime *f*; ~ **sight** *n* CONST *surveying* coup avant *m*; ~ **tapping** *n* ELEC prise soustractive *f*

minute [1] *adj* CHEM *very small* minime, minuscule, *very exact* minutieux

minute [2] *n* CONST *surveying* minute d'angle *f*, METR, PHYS *of time* minute *f*; ~ **examination** *n* PROD ENG inspection minutieuse *f*; ~ **hand** *n* METR *of clock, of watch* grande aiguille *f*

minutely *adv* CHEM minutieusement

miogeosyncline *n* GEOL miogéosynclinal *m*

mionite *n* MINERAL mionite *f*, méionite *f*

MIPS *abbr* (*millions of instructions per second*) COMP, DP, PRINT MIPS (*millions d'instructions par seconde*)

mirabilite *n* MINERAL mirabilite *f*

mirbane n CHEM mirbane f

mirror n PHYS miroir m, VEHICLES accessory rétroviseur m; ~ **condenser lamp** n CINEMAT lampe à miroir incorporé f; ~ **electron microscope** n INSTRUMENT microscope électronique à miroir m; ~ **finish** n MECH poli miroir m, MECH ENG polissage à reflets m, PROD ENG super-polissage m; ~ **galvanometer** n ELEC galvanomètre à miroir m; ~ **image** n CHEM of molecule image inversée f, CINEMAT image réfléchie f; ~ **lens** n PHOTO objectif à miroir m; ~ **nucleus** n PHYS noyau image m, noyau miroir m; ~ **nuclides** n pl PHYS nucléides images m pl, nucléides miroirs m pl; ~ **plane** n CRYSTALL plane of symmetry plande réflexion m, plan de symétrie m, plan miroir m; ~ **shot** n CINEMAT plan miroir m; ~ **shutter** n CINEMAT obturateur reflex m

mirror-coated: ~ **lamp** n PHOTO lampe à ampoule métallisée f

mirror-making n C&G miroiterie f

mirror-plating n C&G métallisation spéculaire f

MIS [1] abbr COMP (management information system), DP (management information system) SIG (système intégré de gestion), TELECOM (multipoint indication secondary status) indication multipoint d'état secondaire f

MIS: [2] ~ **transistor** n ELECTRON transistor MIS m

misalignment n MECH ENG défaut d'alignement m, PRINT désalignement m, mauvais alignement m; ~ **loss** n OPT, TELECOM perte extrinsèque de raccordement f

miscibility: ~ **gap** n METALL lacune de miscibilité f

miscible [1] adj CHEM, PETR TECH miscible

miscible: [2] ~ **slug flooding** n PETR déplacement en phases miscibles m; ~ **substance** n POLLUTION substance miscible f

MISD abbr (multiple-instruction single-data) COMP, DP MISD (multiflux d'instruction-monoflux de donnés)

misfire n ELEC ENG défaut d'amorçage m, raté d'amorçage m, MINING raté m, raté d'allumage m

misfit n METALL lattice désaccord de réseau m

misleading adj PATENTS trompeur

mismatch n ELEC ENG défaut d'adaptation m, désadaptation f, mauvaise adaptation f, MECH ENG déport m, faux alignement m; ~ **factor** n ELEC ENG coefficient de désadaptation m

mismatched [1] adj ELEC, PHYS désadapté

mismatched: [2] ~ **camera** n TV caméra mal équilibrée f; ~ **seams** n pl TEXTILES coutures inégales f pl

misorientation n PROP MAT erreur d'orientation f

mispickel n MINERAL mispickel m

misplaced: ~ **size** n COAL TECH déclassé m

misprint n PRINT coquille f, erreur typographique f

misregister n PRINT repérage défectueux m

misregistration n PRINT repérage défectueux m, mauvais repérage m, TV défaut de calage m

missed-approach: ~ **procedure** n AERONAUT procédure d'approche interrompue f

missile n MILIT missile m, projectile m; ~ **cradle** n MILIT berceau pour missile m; ~ **warhead** n MILIT charge militaire f, SPACE charge de missile f, ogive f

missing: ~ **cap detector** n PACKAGING dispositif pour déceler les capsules manquantes m; ~ **mass** n ASTRON masse cachée f, masse manquante f; ~ **pill equipment** n PACKAGING équipement pour déceler les pilules manquantes m

missorting n MECH ENG erreur de tri f

mist n METEO brume f, buée f, PETR TECH brouillard m, POLLUTION brouillard m, brume f, panache m, REFRIG buée f

misting n PRINT brouillard d'encre m, brume f, voltige f

miter n (AmE) see mitre

mitigation n MAR POLL atténuation f, diminution f, réduction f

mitre n (BrE) C&G biseau m, CONST onglet m, PRINT biseau m, onglet m ~ **bevel** n (BrE) C&G chanfrein plat m; ~ **bevel both sides** n (BrE) C&G double chanfrein m; ~ **board** n (BrE) CONST boîte d'onglet f, boîte à onglets f; ~ **box** n (BrE) CONST boîte d'onglet f, boîte à onglets f; ~ **cutting machine** n (BrE) CONST machine à couper d'onglet f; ~ **fence** n (BrE) CONST of saw bench guide d'onglet m; ~ **gear** n (BrE) CONST engrenage à onglet m, engrenage à quarante cinq degrés m; ~ **grinding machine** n (BrE) C&G machine à biseaux f; ~ **joint** n (BrE) CONST assemblage en onglet m, assemblage à onglet m, onglet d'encadrement m; ~ **machine** n (BrE) CONST machine à couper d'onglet f; ~ **post** n (BrE) WATER SUPP of lock gate montant de busc m, poteau battant m, poteau busqué m; ~ **return** n (BrE) C&G chanfrein d'ajustage m; ~ **sill** n (BrE) WATER SUPP busc m, seuil d'écluse m; ~ **square** n (BrE) CONST équerre à onglet f

MIV abbr (multipoint indication visualization) TELECOM indication multipoint de visualisation f

mix [1] n C&G composition f, FOOD TECH mélange m, préparation f, P&R mélange m; ~ **and dispense storage system** n PACKAGING sy⬥ème de magasinage mélangeur distributeur m; ~ **design** n CONST of concrete étude de composition f; ~ **dissolve** n TV fondu enchaîné m; ~ **proportions** n pl CONST dosage du mélange m

mix [2] vt CHEM substances mélanger, CONST mortar gâcher, malaxer, mélanger, PAPER TECH mélanger, RECORDING mixer, mélanger, TV faire un mixage de, mixer; ~ **down** vt RECORDING mixer

mixdown n RECORDING mixage m

mixed [1] adj CHEM mixte

mixed: [2] ~ **adhesive** n PACKAGING colle de mélange f; ~ **average sample** n HYDROL échantillon moyen m; ~ **batch store** n C&G réserve de composition f; ~ **cargo ship** n NAUT navire mixte m; ~ **dislocation** n CRYSTALL, METALL dislocation mixte f; ~ **flow fan** n REFRIG ventilateur hélico-centrifuge m; ~ **flow pump** n MECH ENG pompe hélico-centrifuge f, MINING pompe à flux mélangé f; ~ **gage track** n (AmE) see mixed gauge track; ~ **gas** n GAS TECH gaz mixte m; ~ **gauge track** n (BrE) RAIL voie à double écartement f; ~ **levitation** n TRANSP sustentation mixte f; ~ **light** n PHOTO éclairage mixte m; ~ **liquor** n WATER SUPP liqueur mixte f; ~ **path** n SPACE trajet mixte m; ~ **power supply** n TRANSP alimentation mixte f; ~ **process** n ELECTRON procédé mixte m; ~ **radiation** n RAD PHYS rayonnement mixte m; ~ **refrigerant cascade** n REFRIG cascade incorporée f; ~ **sewage and waste water treatment** n WATER SUPP épuration en mélange des eaux usées f; ~ **strawboard** n PAPER TECH carton de paille mixte m; ~ **strawpaper** n PAPER TECH papier de paille mixte m; ~ **syncs** n pl TV signaux de synchronisation mixtes m pl; ~ **technology** n ELECTRON technique mixte f; ~ **terrain** n TELECOM surface aléatoire f; ~ **tide** n OCEANOG marée mixte f; ~ **ware** n C&G assortiment m

mixed-base: ~ **notation** n COMP numération à base mixte f, DP notation à base multiple f

mixed-logic: ~ **board** n ELECTRON carte mixte f, carte à logique mixte f

mixed-radix: ~ **notation** n COMP numération à base

mixte *f*, DP notation à base multiple *f*

mixer *n* C&G *batch plant operator* composeur *m*, CHEM TECH appareil à mélanger *m*, mélangeur *m*, mélangeuse *f*, COAL TECH agitateur *m*, CONST malaxeur *m*, *of gases for welding* dispositif mélangeur *m*, ELECTRON *microwaves* mélangeur *m*, *of radio, television receiver* changeur de fréquence *m*, MECH ENG malaxeur *m*, mélangeur *m*, P&R *equipment*, PAPER TECH, PHYS mélangeur *m*, RECORDING mixeur *m*, mélangeur *m*, SPACE *communications* mélangeur *m*, TV mixeur *m*; ~ **amplifier** *n* TV amplificateur de mélange *m*; ~ **bellcrank** *n* AERONAUT *of helicopter* renvoi de combinateur *m*; ~ **diode** *n* ELECTRON diode mélangeuse *f*; ~ **preamplifier** *n* ELECTRON mélangeur-préamplificateur *m*; ~ **rod** *n* AERONAUT *of helicopter* bielle de combinateur *f*, béquille de combinateur *f*; ~ **stage** *n* ELECTRON étage changeur de fréquence *m*, étage mélangeur *m*; ~ **truck** *n* CONST *for ready mixed cement* camion avec malaxeur *m*, camion bétonnière *m*; ~ **tube** *n* ELECTRON tube changeur de fréquence *m*

mixing [1] *adj* CHEM TECH mélangeur

mixing [2] *n* ACOUSTICS mixage *m*, mélange *m*, CONST malaxage *m*, PAPER TECH mélange *m*, PETR TECH *of mud* malaxage *m*, PROD ENG malaxage *m*, malaxation *f*, mélange *m*, mixage *m*; ~ **amplifier** *n* ELECTRON amplificateur mélangeur *m*; ~ **and blending equipment** *n* PACKAGING équipement de mélange et de dosage *m*; ~ **basin** *n* HYDROL bassin mélangeur *m*, WATER SUPP bassin d'homogénéisation *m*; ~ **booth** *n* RECORDING cabine de mixage *f*; ~ **box** *n* C&G maie *f*, PAPER TECH caisse de mélange *f*; ~ **chamber** *n* AUTO chambre de carburation *f*, GAS TECH chambre de mélange *f*, VEHICLES *of carburettor* chambre de carburation *f*; ~ **chest** *n* PAPER TECH caisse de mélange *f*; ~ **cylinder** *n* PROD ENG cylindre malaxeur *m*; ~ **desk** *n* RECORDING console de mixage *f*, pupitre de mixage *m*, table de mixage *f*, TV console de mixage *f*; ~ **mill** *n* CHEM TECH moulin mélangeur *m*, PROD ENG broyeur-malaxeur *m*, broyeur-mélangeur *m*; ~ **mortar** *n* CHEM TECH mortier de gâchage *m*; ~ **pan mill** *n* CHEM TECH broyeur-mélangeur à meules *m*, mélangeur à meules verticales *m*; ~ **plant** *n* PROD ENG mélangeur *m*; ~ **propeller** *n* CHEM TECH agitateur à hélice *m*; ~ **pump** *n* PAPER TECH pompe de mélange *f*; ~ **rate** *n* CONST taux de mélange *m*; ~ **room** *n* C&G atelier de composition *m*, RECORDING cabine de mixage *f*; ~ **sheet** *n* RECORDING feuille de mixage *f*; ~ **sieve** *n* CHEM TECH tamis à tambour *m*; ~ **tank** *n* CHEM TECH cuve-mélangeur *f*, CINEMAT cuve de préparation des bains *f*; ~ **technique** *n* CHEM TECH mélange *m*, technique de mélange *f*; ~ **time** *n* CONST durée de gâchage *f*, PETR TECH temps de mixage *m*; ~ **transistor** *n* ELECTRON transistor mélangeur *m*; ~ **trough** *n* C&G maie *f*; ~ **unit** *n* AERONAUT *of helicopter* combinateur de pas *m*; ~ **valve** *n* MECH ENG soupape mélangeuse *f*; ~ **vessel** *n* CHEM TECH réservoir de mélange *m*

mix-in-place *n* CONST *civil engineering* mélangeage sur le chantier *m*, mélangeage sur place *m*

mixture *n* CHEM mixtion *f*, mélange *m*, FOOD TECH mélange *m*, préparation *f*, PETR TECH mélange *m*; ~ **composition** *n* SPACE richesse de mélange *f*; ~ **control** *n* AERONAUT commande de richesse du carburant *f*, *of engine* commande de mélange *f*, commande de richesse *f*, commande de richesse du mélange *f*; ~ **ratio** *n* AUTO dosage du mélange *m*

MIZ *abbr* (*multipoint indication zero communication*)

TELECOM indication multipoint de non-communication *f*

mizzen *n* NAUT *sail* voile d'artimon *f*; ~ **mast** *n* NAUT mât d'artimon *m*

mizzonite *n* MINERAL mizzonite *f*

MKSA: ~ **system** *n* (*meter kilogram-second-ampere-system, metre kilogramme-second-ampere-system*) METR système MKSA *m* (*système mètre-kilogramme-seconde-ampère*)

MLD *abbr* (*mean lethal dose*) NUCLEAR, POLLUTION, RAD PHYS, SAFETY DLM (*dose létale moyenne*)

MLM *abbr* (*multilongitudinal modes*) TELECOM MLM (*modes longitudinaux multiples*)

MLS *abbr* (*microwave landing system*) AERONAUT système d'atterrissage hyperfréquences *m*

mm *abbr* (*millimeter, millimetre*) METR mm (*millimètre*)

mmf *abbr* (*magnetomotive force*) ELEC, PHYS fmm (*force magnétomotrice*)

MMI *abbr* (*man-machine interface*) COMP, DP, SPACE *spacecraft* interface homme-machine *f*

MMIC *abbr* (*monolithic microwave integrated circuit*) PHYS circuit intégré monolithique micro-ondes *m*

Mn (*manganese*) CHEM Mn (*manganèse*)

mnemonic *adj* DP *code* mnémonique

m-o: ~ **disc** *n* (BrE) (*magneto-optical disc*) OPT disque magnéto-optique *m*, disque magnétoscopique *m*; ~ **disk** *n* (AmE) *see m-o disc*

Mo (*molybdenum*) CHEM Mo (*molybdène*)

MO *abbr* (*managed object*) TELECOM objet géré *m*

mobile: ~ **aeronautical station** *n* SPACE station mobile aéronautique *f*; ~ **belt** *n* GEOL zone mobile *f*, zone orogénique *f*; ~ **camera** *n* TV caméra autonome *f*; ~ **component** *n* POLLUTION élément mobile *m*; ~ **control unit** *n* TV régie mobile *f*; ~ **crane** *n* CONST grue camion *f*, grue mobile *f*; ~ **crusher** *n* COAL TECH concasseur mobile *m*; ~ **data processing terminal equipment** *n* TELECOM ETTD-MT, équipement terminal mobile terrestre de traitement de données *m*; ~ **fire-extinguisher** *n* SAFETY extincteur mobile *m*; ~ **hose reel** *n* SAFETY *firefighting equipment* dévidoir mobile *m*; ~ **installation** *n* TELECOM installation mobile *f*; ~ **land station** *n* SPACE station mobile terrestre *f*; ~ **location registration** *n* TELECOM enregistrement de la position de la station mobile *m*; ~ **logging unit** *n* GAS TECH unité mobile de mesure *f*; ~ **maritime station** *n* SPACE station mobile maritime *f*; ~ **mounting** *n* INSTRUMENT support mobile *m*; ~ **radio station** *n* TELECOM mobile *m*; ~ **satellite communications** *n* NAUT communications mobiles par satellite *f pl*; ~ **satellite service** *n* SPACE *communications* service mobile par satellite *m*; ~ **station** *n* (*MS*) PRINT, SPACE, TELECOM station mobile *f*; ~ **switching center** *n* (AmE), ~ **switching centre** *n* (BrE) (*MSC*) TELECOM centre de commutation mobile *m*; ~ **telephone service** *n* (*MTS*) TELECOM service radiotéléphonique mobile *m* (*SRM*); ~ **unit** *n* CINEMAT car de reportage *m*

mobile-to-base: ~ **relay** *n* TELECOM relais nominal *m*

mobility *n* CHEM *ionic*, PETR, PHYS, PROP MAT *of metal* mobilité *f*; ~ **ratio** *n* PETR coefficient de mobilité *m*

Möbius: ~ **strip** *n* GEOM *topology* ruban de Möbius *m*

MOC *abbr* (*managed object class*) TELECOM classe d'objet géré *f*

mock *n* TEXTILES teinture *f*; ~ **cake** *n* TEXTILES gâteau pour teinture *m*

mock-up *n* NAUT *ship, boat design* maquette *f*, modèle *m*, PRINT *of finished book* , PROD ENG, SPACE maquette *f*

modacrylic *n* TEXTILES modacrylique *m*

modal: ~ **dispersion** *n* OPT dispersion modale *f*, distorsion modale *f*; ~ **distortion** *n* TELECOM distorsion modale *f*; ~ **noise** *n* OPT, TELECOM bruit modal *m*; ~ **note** *n* ACOUSTICS note modale *f*

mode *n* ACOUSTICS, COMP, DP, ELECTRON mode *m*, GEOL *of rock* composition minéralogique *f*, mode *m*, PRINT mode *m*, PROD ENG mode *m*, méthode *f*; ~ **change** *n* COMP, DP changement de mode *m*; ~ **control** *n* CONTROL régulateur de mode *m*; ~ **coupling** *n* OPT, TELECOM couplage des modes *m*; ~ **distortion** *n* TELECOM distorsion modale *f*; ~ **field diameter** *n* OPT diamètre du champ de mode *m*, TELECOM diamètre du champ de mode *m*, diamètre du faisceau guidé *m*; ~ **filter** *n* ELECTRON, OPT, TELECOM filtre de mode *m*; ~ **hopping** *n* OPT, TELECOM saut de mode *m*; ~ **jump** *n* ELECTRON changement de mode *m*; ~ **jumping** *n* OPT, TELECOM saut de mode *m*; ~ **locking** *n* ELECTRON synchronisation des modes *f*; ~ **mixer** *n* OPT brasseur de modes *m*, brouilleur de modes *m*, embrouilleur de mode *m*, TELECOM brasseur de modes *m*, mélangeurde modes *m*; ~ **of operation** *n* TELECOM mode de fonctionnement *m*, mode opératoire *m*; ~ **scrambler** *n* OPT, TELECOM embrouilleur de mode *m*; ~ **selector switch** *n* AERONAUT sélecteur de vol *m*; ~ **separation** *n* ELECTRON séparation des modes *f*; ~ **stripper** *n* TELECOM extracteur de modes de gaine *m*; ~ **volume** *n* OPT, TELECOM volume des modes *m*

model *n* COMP, DP modèle *m*, NAUT *naval architecture*, SPACE maquette *f*, modèle *m*, TELECOM modèle *m*; ~ **builder** *n* CINEMAT constructeur de modèle réduit *m*, modéliste *m*; ~ **calibration** *n* POLLUTION calibrage de modèle *m*, étalonnage de modèle *m*; ~ **railroad** *n* (AmE) *(cf model railway)* RAIL chemin de fer miniature *m*, chemin de fer modèle réduit *m*; ~ **railway** *n* (BrE) *(cf model railroad)* RAIL chemin de fer miniature *m*, chemin de fer modèle réduit *m*; ~ **shot** *n* CINEMAT plan de maquette *m*; ~ **test** *n* NAUT *naval architecture* essai sur modèle réduit *m*

modeling *n* (AmE), **modelling** *n* (BrE) COMP, DP, ELECTRON, GEOL modélisation *f*, PROD ENG modelage *m*, QUALITY modélisation *f* ~ **clay** *n* PROD ENG argile à modeler *f*; ~ **light** *n* CINEMAT éclairage de relief *m*

mode-locked: ~ **laser** *n* ELECTRON laser à modes synchronisés *m*

modem *n* COMP adaptateur de lignes *m*, modem *m*, modulateur-démodulateur *m*, DP modem *m*, modulateur-démodulateur *m*, ELECTRON coupleur téléphonique *m*, modem *m*, PRINT modem *m*, modulateur-démodulateur *m*, TELECOM modem *m*; ~ **board** *n* ELECTRON carte modem *f*; ~ **interchange** *n* COMP, DP échange par modem *m*; ~ **interface** *n* COMP, DP, ELECTRON interface modem *f*; ~ **interfacing** *n* ELECTRON raccordement par modem *m*; ~ **link** *n* PROD ENG liaison modulateur-démodulateur *f*; ~ **receiver** *n* ELECTRON récepteur de modem *m*; ~ **transmitter** *n* ELECTRON transmetteur de modem *m*

moderate: ~ **gale** *n* METEO grand frais *m*; ~ **weather** *n* NAUT temps maniable *m*

moderator *n* ELECTRON modérateur *m*, PHYS *nuclear* modérateur *m*, ralentisseur *m*, RAD PHYS *atomic energy* ralentisseur *m*

modern: ~ **construction** *n* CONST construction moderne *f*; ~ **face** *n* PRINT caractère de face Didot *m*; ~ **figures** *n*

pl PRINT chiffres arabes *m pl*

mode-setting: ~ **knob** *n* PROD ENG bouton de sélection de mode *m*

modification: ~ **indicator** *n* TELECOM indicateur de modification *m*; ~ **kit** *n* PROD ENG jeu de modification *m*, lot de modification *m*; ~ **proposal** *n* PROD ENG avis de modification *m*

modified: ~ **atmosphere packaging** *n* *(MAP)* PRINT emballage en atmosphère modifiée *m*; ~ **cotton system** *n* TEXTILES système de coton modifié *m*; ~ **frequency modulation** *n* *(MFM modulation)* ELECTRON modulation de fréquence modifiée *f* *(modulation MFM)*; ~ **starch** *n* FOOD TECH amidon modifié *m*; ~ **system** *n* TEXTILES système de coton modifié *m*

modifier *n* COAL TECH modificateur *m*

modify *vt* COMP, DP, ELECTRON modifier, GEOM affecter

moding *n* ELECTRON instabilité de mode *f*

modular[1] *adj* COMP, DP modulaire

modular:[2] ~ **arithmetic** *n* COMP, DP, MATH arithmétique modulaire *f*; ~ **gaging system** *n* (AmE), ~ **gauging system** *n* (BrE) METR système d'étalonnage modulaire *m*; ~ **labeling system** *n* (AmE), ~ **labelling system** *n* (BrE) PACKAGING système d'étiquetage modulaire *m*; ~ **programming** *n* COMP programmation modulaire *f*; ~ **surface cleaner** *n* PACKAGING nettoyeur de surface modulaire *m*; ~ **unit** *n* MECH ENG élément standard *m*; ~ **units for machine-tool construction** *n pl* MECH ENG éléments standard pour la construction des machines-outils *m pl*

modularity *n* COMP, DP, QUALITY modularité *f*

modulate *vt* ELECTRON, PHYS, RECORDING, TELECOM, TV moduler

modulated: ~ **beam** *n* ELECTRON faisceau modulé *m*; ~ **carrier** *n* ELECTRON, TV porteuse modulée *f*; ~ **continuous wave** *n* TV onde entretenue modulée *f*; ~ **groove** *n* ACOUSTICS sillon modulé *m*; ~ **oscillator** *n* ELECTRON oscillateur modulé *m*; ~ **signal** *n* TELECOM signal modulé *m*; ~ **space** *n* ACOUSTICS plage de modulation *f*; ~ **structure** *n* METALL structure modulée *f*; ~ **wave** *n* ELECTRON, RECORDING onde modulée *f*

modulating: ~ **signal** *n* ELECTRON signal de modulation *m*, signal modulant *m*, RECORDING signal modulant *m*; ~ **wave** *n* ELECTRON onde de modulation *f*, onde modulante *f*, TV onde modulante *f*

modulation *n* ACOUSTICS, COMP, DP, ELEC *of wave*, ELECTRON, PHYS, RECORDING, SPACE *communications*, TELECOM, WAVE PHYS modulation *f*; ~ **amplifier** *n* ELECTRON amplificateur de modulation *m*; ~ **analysis** *n pl* TESTING analyse de modulation *f*; ~ **angle** *n* ACOUSTICS angle de modulation *m*; ~ **band** *n* ELECTRON bande de modulation *f*; ~ **depth** *n* ELECTRON profondeur de modulation *f*, PHYS profondeur de modulation *f*, taux de modulation *m*; ~ **electrode** *n* TV électrode de commande *f*; ~ **envelope** *n* RECORDING enveloppe de modulation *f*; ~ **factor** *n* ELECTRON facteur de modulation *m*, PHYS profondeur de modulation *f*, taux de modulation *m*; ~ **frequency** *n* *(MF)* ELEC *alternating current*, ELECTRON fréquence de modulation *f*; ~ **grid** *n* TV grille de modulation *f*; ~ **index** *n* ELECTRON indice de modulation *m*; ~ **level** *n* WAVE PHYS niveau de modulation *m*; ~ **monitor** *n* CONTROL contrôleur de modulation *m*; ~ **noise** *n* ACOUSTICS, ELECTRON, RECORDING, TELECOM, TV bruit de modulation *m*; ~ **transfer function** *n* ELECTRON fonction de transfert de modulation *f*

modulator *n* COMP, DP, ELECTRON, TELECOM modulateur *m*, TV modulateur *m*, étage modulateur *m*; ~ **diode** *n* ELECTRON diode modulatrice *f*; ~ **driver** *n* ELECTRON étage d'attaque du modulateur *m*; ~ **logic board** *n* PROD ENG carte logique de modulation *f*

modulator-demodulator *n* COMP, DP, TELECOM modulateur-démodulateur *m*

module *n* COMP, DP, ELEC *equipment*, ELECTRON, HYDR EQUIP, MECH ENG *gearing*, PETR TECH module *m*, SPACE bloc de puissance *m*; ~ **extraction pad** *n* PROD ENG patte d'extraction de module *f*; ~ **group** *n* PROD ENG ensemble de modules *m*; ~ **set** *n* ELECTRON jeu de modules *m*

modulus *n* MATH *for congruences* module *m*, *of complex number* coefficient *m*, PETR module *m*, PHYS *of vector* module *m*, norme *f*, valeur absolue *f*; ~ **of compression** *n* NAUT *GRP construction* coefficient d'écrasement *m*; ~ **of elasticity** *n* AERONAUT module d'élasticité *m*, module d'élasticité apparent *m*, module de Colomb *m*, module de Young *m*, COAL TECH, CONST, MECH ENG, METALL module d'élasticité *m*, NAUT *GRP construction* coefficient d'élasticité *m*, P&R, PHYS module d'élasticité *m*; ~ **of elongation** *n* P&R module d'allongement *m*; ~ **of rigidity** *n* PHYS coefficient de cisaillement *m*, module de cisaillement *m*

modus: ~ **operandi** *n* PROD ENG mode d'opérer *m*

mofette *n* FUELLESS *hot spring* mofette *f*

Moho: ~ **discontinuity** *n* GEOL discontinuité de Mohorovicic *f*

Mohorovicic: ~ **discontinuity** *n* GEOL discontinuité de Mohorovicic *f*

Mohr's: ~ **clip** *n* LAB EQUIP *rubber tubing* pince de Mohr *f*

moiety *n* CHEM *of molecule* fraction *f*, morceau *m*, partie *f*

moil *n* C&G calotte *f*

moiré *n* TV moiré *m*; ~ **effect** *n* TV moiré *m*; ~ **fringes** *n pl* PHYS franges moirées *f pl*; ~ **pattern** *n* ACOUSTICS moirage *m*

moist *adj* PAPER TECH humide, THERMOD humecté, humide

moisten *vt* FOOD TECH humecter, THERMOD humecter, humidifier, mouiller

moistener *n* PAPER TECH humecteuse *f*

moistening *n* CHEM humidification *f*, mouillage *m*; ~ **device** *n* PACKAGING dispositif humectant *m*; ~ **equipment** *n* PACKAGING humidificateur *m*

moistness *n* CHEM humidité *f*

moisture *n* CHEM humidité *f*; ~ **absorber** *n* CONST *building* absorbeur d'humidité *m*; ~ **and temperature detector** *n* TRANSP détecteur de température et d'humidité *m*; ~ **content** *n* CHEM teneur en eau *f*, COAL TECH teneur en humidité *f*, CONST teneur en eau *f*, FOOD TECH teneur en eau *f*, PACKAGING teneur en eau *f*, PAPER TECH humidité *f*, teneur en eau *f*, REFRIG, TESTING *textiles* teneur en eau *f*, TEXTILES teneur en humidité *f*, WATER SUPP taux d'humidité *m*, teneur en eau *f*; ~ **determination** *n* PACKAGING détermination de l'humidité *f*; ~ **expansion** *n* PAPER TECH traînée humide *f*; ~ **index** *n* METEO indice d'humidité *m*; ~ **regain** *n* PAPER TECH, TESTING *textiles*, TEXTILES reprise d'humidité *f*; ~ **regain in the standard atmosphere** *n* TESTING *textiles* reprise d'humidité dans l'atmosphère normale *f*; ~ **test** *n* PACKAGING test d'humidité *m*; ~ **transfer** *n* REFRIG, TEXTILES transfert d'humidité *m*

moisture-absorbent: ~ **bag** *n* PACKAGING sachet dessiccant *m*

moisture-proof *adj* PACKAGING à l'épreuve de l'humidité, PROP MAT protégé contre l'humidité

moisture-repellent *adj* PACKAGING humidifuge

moisture-resistant *adj* PACKAGING résistant à l'humidité

moisture-set: ~ **ink** *n* COLOURS encre séchant en milieu humide *f*

mol *abbr (mole)* CHEM, METR, PHYS mol *(môle)*

MOL *abbr (manned orbiting laboratory)* SPACE laboratoire orbital habité *m*

molale *adj* CHEM molal

molality *n* CHEM *of solution* molalité *f*

molar[1] *adj* CHEM molaire, qui se rapporte à la masse

molar:[2] ~ **gas constant** *n* PHYS constante molaire des gaz *f*; ~ **heat capacity** *n* PHYS capacité thermique molaire *f*; ~ **internal energy** *n* PHYS énergie interne molaire *f*; ~ **volume** *n* PHYS volume molaire *m*

molarity *n* CHEM molarité *f*

mold[1] *n* (AmE) *see* mould

mold[2] *vt* (AmE) *see* mould

molded[1] *adj* (AmE) *see* moulded

molded:[2] ~ **board** *n* (AmE) *see* moulded board; ~ **breadth** *n* (AmE) *see* moulded breadth; ~ **casting** *n* (AmE) *see* moulded casting; ~ **contact block** *n* (AmE) *see* moulded contact block; ~ **depth** *n* (AmE) *see* moulded depth; ~ **displacement** *n* (AmE) *see* moulded displacement; ~ **draft** *n* (AmE) *see* moulded draught; ~ **hose** *n* (AmE) *see* moulded hose; ~ **plastics** *n pl* (AmE) *see* moulded plastics; ~ **printing plate** *n* (AmE) *see* moulded printing plate; ~ **pulp products** *n pl* (AmE) *see* moulded pulp products

molder *n* (AmE) *see* moulder

molding *n* (AmE) *see* moulding

mold-resistant *adj* (AmE) *see* mould-resistant (mol)

mole *n* CHEM *(mol) of element, compound* môle *f (mol)*, CONST *civil engineering* tunnelier *m*, METR *(mol)* môle *f (mol)*, NAUT brise-lames *m*, môle *m*, OCEANOG môle *m*, PHYS *(mol)* môle *f (mol)*, WATER SUPP môle *m* ~ **drainage** *n* CONST drainage à la charrue taupe *m*; ~ **fraction** *n* METALL, REFRIG fraction molaire *f*; ~ **head** *n* OCEANOG musoir *m*; ~ **titer** *n* (AmE), ~ **titre** *n* (BrE) REFRIG titre molaire *m*

molecular: ~ **beam epitaxy** *n* ELECTRON épitaxie par faisceaux moléculaires *f*; ~ **cloud** *n* ASTRON nuage moléculaire *m*; ~ **conductivity** *n* THERMOD conductivité moléculaire *f*; ~ **depression of freezing point** *n* THERMOD dépression moléculaire du point de congélation *f*; ~ **electronics** *n* ELECTRON électronique moléculaire *f*; ~ **elevation of boiling point** *n* THERMOD élévation moléculaire du point d'ébullition *f*; ~ **field** *n* PHYS champ moléculaire *m*; ~ **gas laser** *n* ELECTRON laser à gaz moléculaire *m*; ~ **heat** *n* THERMOD chaleur moléculaire *f*; ~ **hydrogen cloud** *n* ASTRON nuage d'hydrogène moléculaire *m*; ~ **laser** *n* ELECTRON laser moléculaire *m*; ~ **orbital** *n* CHEM *of atoms in molecule* orbite moléculaire *f*, PHYS orbitale moléculaire *f*; ~ **pump** *n* PHYS pompe moléculaire *f*; ~ **radiation** *n* ASTRON rayonnement moléculaire *m*; ~ **refractivity** *n* PHYS réfractivité moléculaire *f*; ~ **sieve** *n* CHEM *device* tamis moléculaire *m*; ~ **spectroanalysis** *n* RAD PHYS spectranalyse moléculaire *f*; ~ **spectrum** *n* PHYS spectre moléculaire *m*; ~ **vibrational energy level** *n* RAD PHYS niveau énergétique de vibration de la molécule *m*; ~ **weight** *n* PETR TECH poids moléculaire *m*

molecule *n* PETR TECH, PHYS molécule *f*; ~ **beam** *n*

TELECOM faisceau moléculaire *m*

molleton *n* TEXTILES molleton *m*

mollusc: ~ **detacher** *n* OCEANOG détroqueuse *f*; ~ **detaching** *n* OCEANOG détroquage *m*; ~ **harvesting** *n* OCEANOG détroquage *m*

molten[1] *adj* THERMOD en fusion, fondu

molten:[2] ~ **core** *n* SPACE noyau en fusion *m*; ~ **glass** *n* C&G verre fondu *m*; ~ **materials** *n pl* SAFETY matériaux en fusion *m pl*; ~ **metal** *n* PROP MAT métal fondu *m*, SAFETY métal en fusion *m*; ~ **metal splash** *n* SAFETY *protective clothing* projection de métal fondu *f*; ~ **pool** *n* PROD ENG *welding* bain de fusion *m*

molybdate *n* CHEM molybdate *m*

molybdenite *n* MINERAL molybdénite *f*

molybdenum *n* (*Mo*) CHEM molybdène *m* (*Mo*)

molybdic: ~ **ocher** *n* (AmE), ~ **ochre** *n* (BrE) MINERAL molybdine *f*, molybdite *f*, molybdénocre *f*

molybdite *n* MINERAL molybdite *f*, molybdénocre *f*

molysite *n* MINERAL molysite *f*

moment *n* CONST, MECH, MECH ENG, PHYS *of force* moment *m*; ~ **about an axis** *n* PHYS moment par rapport à un axe *m*; ~ **arm** *n* MECH ENG bras de levier *m*; ~ **coefficient** *n* MECH ENG coefficient de moment *m*; ~ **of couple** *n* MECH moment d'un couple *m*; ~ **of inertia** *n* CONST *design*, NAUT *naval architecture*, PHYS moment d'inertie *m*

momentaneous: ~ **capacity** *n* TRANSP capacité momentanée *f*

momentary: ~ **action** *n* ELEC ENG action momentanée *f*; ~ **action switch** *n* ELEC ENG interrupteur monostable *m*, interrupteur à action momentanée *m*; ~ **close push button** *n* PROD ENG bouton-poussoir à fermeture momentanée *m*; ~ **contact push button** *n* PROD ENG bouton-poussoir à impulsions *m*; ~ **contact switch** *n* PROD ENG bouton-poussoir à contact momentané *m*; ~ **overload protection** *n* ELEC, PROD ENG protection contre les surcharges momentanées *f*; ~ **push key** *n* PROD ENG touche à impulsion *f*

momentum *n* MECH quantité de mouvement *f*, MECH ENG force vive *f*, moment *m*, quantité de mouvement *f*, PHYS quantité de mouvement *f*; ~ **wheel** *n* SPACE *spacecraft* roue cinétique *f*, volant d'inertie *m*

monacid *n* CHEM monacide *m*

monadic[1] *adj* CHEM monoatomique, univalent, COMP, DP monadique

monadic:[2] ~ **operation** *n* COMP, DP opération monadique *f*

monatomic[1] *adj* CHEM monoatomique

monatomic:[2] ~ **gas** *n* PHYS gaz monoatomique *m*

monaural[1] *adj* ACOUSTICS, RECORDING monaural

monaural:[2] ~ **record** *n* RECORDING disque monoral *m*

monazite *n* MINERAL, PROP MAT monazite *f*

monheimite *n* MINERAL monheimite *f*

monitor[1] *n* COMP, DP moniteur *m*, ELEC appareil de surveillance *m*, moniteur *m*, INSTRUMENT instrument de vérification *m*, moniteur *m*, PROD ENG *capstan head* porte-outil revolver *m*, revolver *m*, tourelle *f*, tourelle revolver *f*, RAD PHYS moniteur *m*, RECORDING appareil de contrôle *m*, TELECOM moniteur *m*, TESTING dispositif de surveillance *m*, TV moniteur *m*, RECORDING appareil témoin *m*; ~ **head** *n* RECORDING tête de contrôle *f*; ~ **lathe** *n* PROD ENG tour avec porte-outil revolver *m*, tour avec tourelle revolver *m*, tour à revolver *m*, tour-revolver *m*; ~ **record** *n* PETR film de contrôle *m*; ~ **unit** *n* TELECOM unité de surveillance *f*

monitor[2] *vt* CINEMAT contrôler, COMP contrôler, surveil-

ler, CONTROL contrôler, DP analyser, contrôler, surveiller, MAR POLL contrôler, PROD ENG contrôler, surveiller, RECORDING contrôler, piloter, surveiller, TEXTILES contrôler

monitoring *n* PROD ENG surveillance *f*, RECORDING contrôle *m*, écoute *f*, SPACE, TELECOM, TEXTILES surveillance *f*, TV contrôle *m*, visionnage *m*; ~ **amplifier** *n* RECORDING amplificateur de contrôle *m*; ~ **and maintenance** *n* TELECOM surveillance et maintenance *f*; ~ **controller** *n* PROD ENG contrôleur de surveillance *m*; ~ **loudspeaker** *n* CINEMAT haut-parleur de cabine *m*, RECORDING haut-parleur de contrôle *m*, haut-parleur témoin *m*; ~ **satellite** *n* SPACE satellite de surveillance *m*; ~ **system** *n* RAD PHYS système de monitorage *m*

monkey *n* CONST *pile hammer, drop hammer* mouton *m*, mouton de battage *m*; ~ **block** *n* PROD ENG retour de palan *m*; ~ **board** *n* (BrE)(*cf footboard*) PETR, PETR TECH plate-forme d'accrochage *f*; ~ **carriage** *n* PROD ENG *of overhead travelling crane* chariot de roulement *m*; ~ **pot** *n* C&G potelet *m*; ~ **wrench** *n* MECH ENG clef anglaise *f*, clef universelle *f*, clef à crémaillère *f*, clef à molette *f*, clef à mâchoires mobiles *f*

mono: ~ **amplifier** *n* RECORDING amplificateur monocanal *m*; ~ **key** *n* TV incrustation noir et blanc *f*

mono-accelerator: ~ **CRT** *n* ELECTRON tube cathodique sans postaccélération *m*

monoacetin *n* CHEM monoacétine *f*

monoacid *n* CHEM monoacide *m*

monoacidic *adj* CHEM monoacide

monoalcoholic *adj* CHEM monoalcoolique

monoamide *n* CHEM monoamide *m*

monoamine *n* CHEM monoamine *f*

monoamino *adj* CHEM monoaminé

monoatomic[1] *adj* CHEM monoatomique

monoatomic:[2] ~ **fluid** *n* GAS TECH fluide monoatomique *m*

monobasic *adj* CHEM monobasique

monobath *n* CINEMAT bain unique *m*

monobeam: ~ **system** *n* TRANSP système monopoutre *m*

monobloc: ~ **concrete sleeper** *n* (BrE) *(cf monobloc concrete tie)* RAIL traverse monobloc en béton *f*; ~ **concrete tie** *n* (AmE) *(cf monobloc concrete sleeper)* RAIL traverse monobloc en béton *f*

Monoceros *n* ASTRON Licorne *f*

monochord *adj* ACOUSTICS monocorde

monochromatic[1] *adj* OPT, PHYS monochromatique, PRINT monochromatique, monochrome

monochromatic:[2] ~ **lens** *n* INSTRUMENT lentille monochromatique *f*; ~ **light** *n* METALL lumière monochromatique *f*, WAVE PHYS lumière monochrome *f*; ~ **radiation** *n* OPT rayonnement monochromatique *m*, RAD PHYS radiation monochromatique *f*, TELECOM rayonnement monochromatique *m*

monochromator *n* OPT, PHYS, TELECOM monochromateur *m*

monochrome[1] *adj* COMP, DP, PRINT monochrome

monochrome[2] *n* CINEMAT monochrome *m*, noir et blanc *m*; ~ **dyeing** *n* COLOURS teinture au métachrome *f*; ~ **receiver** *n* TV récepteur monochrome *m*, récepteur noir et blanc *m*; ~ **signal** *n* SPACE *communications* signal monochrome *m*

monocline *n* GEOL monoclinal *m*; ~ **fold** *n* PETR pli monoclinal *m*

monoclinic[1] *adj* CHEM *crystal*, CRYSTALL monoclinique

monoclinic:[2] ~ **system** *n* METALL système monoclinique *m*

monocoque[1] *adj* SPACE monocoque

monocoque:[2] ~ **structure** *n* SPACE *spacecraft* structure monocoque *f*

mono-crystalline: ~ **silicon** *n* SPACE *spacecraft* silicium monocristallin *m*

monocular: ~ **telescope** *n* INSTRUMENT longue-vue *f*, télescope monoculaire *m*

monoenergetic *adj* PHYS monocinétique, monoénergétique

monoethylenic *adj* CHEM monoéthylénique

monofilament *n* P&R monofilament *m*; ~ **yarn** *n* TEXTILES fil monobrin *m*

monogenetic *adj* GEOL *conglomerate* monogénique

monohalogen *adj* CHEM monohalogéné

monohydrate *n* CHEM monohydrate *m*

monohydrated *adj* CHEM monohydraté

monohydric *adj* CHEM monohydrique

monolayer *n* CHEM monocouche *f*

monoleaf: ~ **spring** *n* SPRINGS ressort monolame *m*

monolithic: ~ **amplifier** *n* ELECTRON amplificateur monolithique *m*; ~ **array** *n* ELECTRON groupement monolithique *m*, matrice monolithique *f*; ~ **filter** *n* ELECTRON, TELECOM filtre monolithique *m*; ~ **integrated circuit** *n* ELECTRON circuit intégré monolithique *m*, circuit monolithique *m*, TELECOM circuit intégré monolithique à semi-conducteurs *m*, fibre monomode *f*; ~ **microwave integrated circuit** *n (MMIC)* PHYS circuit intégré monolithique micro-ondes *m*

monomer *n* CHEM, P&R, PETR TECH, PRINT, PROP MAT monomère *m*

monomeric *adj* CHEM, P&R monomère

monomial *n* MATH monôme *m*

monomict *adj* GEOL *conglomerate* monogénique

monomineralic *adj* GEOL monominéral

monomode: ~ **fiber** *n* (AmE), ~ **fibre** *n* OPT, PHYS fibre monomode *f*

monomolecular: ~ **layer** *n* CHEM couche monomoléculaire *f*; ~ **reaction** *n* CHEM réaction monomoléculaire *f*

monomotor: ~ **bogie** *n* (BrE) *(cf monomotor truck)* TRANSP bogie monomoteur *m*; ~ **truck** *n* (AmE) *(cf monomotor bogie)* TRANSP bogie monomoteur *m*

monophase[1] *adj* ELEC *supply* monophasé

monophase:[2] ~ **reaction** *n* METALL réaction monophasée *f*

monophonic: ~ **pick-up** *n* ACOUSTICS tête de lecture monophonique *f*; ~ **recording** *n* ACOUSTICS, RECORDING enregistrement monophonique *m*; ~ **sound system** *n* RECORDING équipement sonore monophonique *m*

monopolar[1] *adj* ELEC *supply* monopolaire, unipolaire

monopolar:[2] ~ **line** *n* ELEC *supply* ligne monopolaire *f*

monopole: ~ **antenna** *n* TELECOM antenne unipolaire *f*

monopropellant *n* CHEM monergol *m*; ~ **thruster** *n* SPACE *spacecraft* propulseur monergol *m*

monorail *n* CONST monorail *m*, MINING monorail *m*, monorail suspendu *m*, RAIL monorail *m*, rail central *m*, TRANSP monorail *m*; ~ **conveyor** *n* MINING convoyeur monorail *m*, TRANSP monorail suspendu *m*; ~ **grab trolley** *n* TRANSP chariot monorail à grappin *m*

monosaccharide *n* CHEM monosaccharide *m*

monosaccharoses *n pl* CHEM monosaccharoses *m pl*

monosodium: ~ **glutamate** *n (MSG)* FOOD TECH glutamate de sodium *m*, glutamate monosodique *m*

monostable[1] *adj* COMP, DP, ELECTRON monostable

monostable[2] *n* PHYS monostable *m*; ~ **multivibrator** *n* ELECTRON multivibrateur monostable *m*

monostearin *n* CHEM monostéarine *f*

monosubstituted *adj* CHEM monosubstitué

monotron *n* ELECTRON monotron *m*

monotropic *adj* METALL *reaction* monotropique

monovalence *n* CHEM monovalence *f*, univalence *f*

monovalency *n* CHEM monovalence *f*, univalence *f*

monovalent *adj* CHEM monovalent, univalent

monoxide *n* CHEM oxyde de carbone *m*, protoxyde *m*

monsoon *n* METEO mousson *f*; ~ **climate** *n* METEO climat de moussons *m*; ~ **rain** *n* METEO pluie de mousson *f*

Monte: ~ **Carlo method** *n* COMP méthode de Monte-Carlo *f*

montebrasite *n* MINERAL montebrasite *f*

monticellite *n* MINERAL monticellite *f*

montmorillonite *n* COAL TECH, MINERAL, PETR TECH montmorillonite *f*

monument *n* CONST *surveying* borne-signal *f*

monumenting *n* CONST *surveying* pose de bornes-signaux *f*

monzonite *n* PETR monzonite *f*

mood: ~ **lighting** *n* CINEMAT éclairage d'ambiance *m*

moon *n* ASTRON lune *f*; ~ **pool** *n* PETR moon-pool *m*, PETR TECH puits central *m*; ~ **segment** *n* SPACE *communications* composante lunaire *f*

moon's: ~ **rotation** *n* ASTRON rotation de la lune *f*

Mooney: ~ **scorch** *n* P&R *rubber* grillage Mooney *m*; ~ **viscosity** *n* P&R plasticité Mooney *f*, viscosité Mooney *f*

moonlight *n* ASTRON clair de lune *m*

moonrise *n* ASTRON lever de lune *m*

moonset *n* ASTRON coucher de lune *m*

moonstone *n* MINERAL pierre de lune *f*

moor *vt* MAR POLL amarrer, NAUT amarrer, mouiller

moored: ~ **buoy** *n* NAUT bouée ancrée *f*

mooring *n* MAR POLL amarrage *m*, amarre *f*, poste d'amarrage *m*, NAUT *action* amarrage *m*, mouillage *m*, *equipment, line, rope* amarre *f*; ~ **berth** *n* NAUT poste d'amarrage *m*; ~ **bitt** *n* NAUT bitte d'amarrage *f*; ~ **bollard** *n* TRANSPORT borne d'amarrage à terre *f*; ~ **bracket** *n* MAR POLL bitte d'amarrage *f*; ~ **buoy** *n* MAR POLL coffre d'amarrage *m*, NAUT bouée de corps mort *f*, *navigation* bouée d'amarrage *f*, coffre d'amarrage *m*, corps mort *m*, PETR bouée de mouillage *f*; ~ **chain** *n* MAR POLL chaîne d'amarrage *f*, chaîne de mouillage *f*; ~ **cleat** *n* NAUT *boatbuilding, deck fittings* taquet d'amarre *m*; ~ **gear** *n* NAUT *of ship* apparaux d'amarrage *m pl*; ~ **harness** *n* AERONAUT filet d'amarrage *m*; ~ **line** *n* NAUT amarre *f*; ~ **pile** *n* NAUT borne d'amarrage *f*, pieu d'amarrage *m*; ~ **post** *n* NAUT borne d'amarrage *f*, pieu d'amarrage *m*; ~ **ring** *n* AERONAUT anneau d'amarrage au sol *m*, tirant d'amarrage *m*

mopboard *n* (AmE) *(cf skirting board)* CONST plinthe *f*, CONST filet d'embase *m*, plinthe *f*

moped *n* TRANSP cyclomoteur *m*

mop-end: ~ **brush** *n* PROD ENG *for polishing* brosse dite moignon *f*, moignon *m*

moraine *n* COAL TECH moraine *f*

mordant *n* CHEM mordant *m*; ~ **dyeing** *n* PHOTO teinture sur mordançage *f*

more: ~ **bit** *n* TELECOM bit de continuation *m*

morenosite *n* MINERAL morénosite *f*

morin *n* CHEM morin *m*

morindin *n* CHEM morindine *f*

morion *n* MINERAL morion *m*

morning: ~ **star** n ASTRON étoile du matin f

morphine n CHEM morphine f

morpholine n CHEM, DETERGENTS morpholine f

morphology n PROP MAT morphologie f

morphometric adj GEOL analysis morphoscopique

morphotropic adj CHEM morphotropique

morphotropism n CHEM morphotropie f

morphotropy n CHEM morphotropie f

morrhuol n CHEM morruol m

Morse: ~ **taper** n MECH ENG cône Morse m; ~ **taper center** n (AmE), ~ **taper centre** n (BrE) MECH ENG of lathe pointe à cône Morse f; ~ **taper pin** n MECH ENG goupille au cône Morse f; ~ **taper shank** n MECH ENG queue cône Morse f; ~ **taper shank drill** n MECH ENG queue de foret avec cônes f; ~ **taper shank twist drill** n MECH ENG foret hélicoïdal à queue conique au cône Morse m

mortar n CHEM, CINEMAT mortier m, CONST gâchis m, mortier m, LAB EQUIP, MILIT, PROD ENG of stamp mill mortier m; ~ **bed** n CONST, PROD ENG of stamp mill fondation du mortier f; ~ **block** n PROD ENG of stamp mill bloc de fondation du mortier m; ~ **box** n PROD ENG of stamp mill mortier m; ~ **mill** n PROD ENG broyeur à mortier m; ~ **mixer** n CONST malaxeur à mortier m, tonneau à malaxer le mortier m, tonneau à mortier m

mortise n CONST, PROD ENG of tackle block mortaise f; ~ **block** n MECH ENG, PROD ENG poulie à mortaise f; ~ **boring bit** n CONST amorçoir à mortaises m, dégorgeoir à mortaises m, ébauchoir à mortaises m; ~ **chisel** n CONST bec d'âne m, bédane m, ciseau bédane m; ~ **gage** n (AmE), ~ **gauge** n (BrE) CONST trusquin m, trusquin à double traçoir m; ~ **joint** n CONST assemblage à tenon et à mortaise m; ~ **lock** n CONST serrure à larder f, serrure à mortaiser f; ~ **wheel** n PROD ENG inserted wooden cogs rouet m

mortise-and-tenon: ~ **heel joint** n CONST assemblage oblique à tenon et mortaise avec embrèvement m; ~ **joint** n CONST assemblage à tenon et à mortaise m

mortising n CONST mortaisage m; ~ **and boring machine** n PROD ENG machine à mortaiser et percer f; ~ **machine** n CONST dispositif mortaiseuse m, mortaiseuse f, PROD ENG machine mortaiseuse f, machine à mortaiser f, mortaiseuse f; ~ **machine with oscillating tool action** n MECH ENG mortaiseuse à outil oscillant f

morvenite n MINERAL morvénite f

morvin n CHEM malléine f

MOS [1] abbr COMP (metal-oxide semiconductor) MOS (semi-conducteur à oxyde métallique), TELECOM (mean opinion score) note moyenne d'opinion f

MOS: [2] ~ **capacitor** n ELEC ENG condensateur MOS m; ~ **delay line** n ELECTRON ligne à retard MOS f; ~ **driver** n ELECTRON attaqueur MOS m; ~ **gate** n ELECTRON porte MOS f; ~ **logic circuit** n ELECTRON circuit logique MOS m; ~ **power transistor** n ELECTRON transistor de puissance MOS m; ~ **technology** n ELECTRON technique MOS f; ~ **transistor** n ELECTRON transistor MOS m

mosaic n ELECTRON, FOOD TECH phytopathology mosaïque f

mosandrite n MINERAL mosandrite f

Moseley's: ~ **law** n PHYS loi de Moseley f

mosquitocide n CHEM culicide m

moss: ~ **agate** n MINERAL agate mousse f

Mössbauer: ~ **effect** n PHYS effet Mössbauer m

most: [1] ~ **significant** adj COMP de poids fort, de poids le plus fort, DP de poids fort

most: [2] ~ **significant bit** n (MSB) COMP, DP bit de poids fort m, bit le plus significatif m, PROD ENG, TELECOM bit de poids fort m; ~ **significant character** n COMP, DP caractère le plus significatif m; ~ **significant digit** n (MSD) COMP, DP chiffre de poids fort m, chiffre le plus significatif m, PROD ENG chiffre de poids fort m

mother n ACOUSTICS mère f; ~ **crystal** n ELECTRON bloc primaire m, quartz naturel m; ~ **liquor** n FOOD TECH eau-mère f; ~ **lode** n MINING filon mère m, filon principal m; ~ **ship** n NAUT navire-mère m, SPACE vaisseau-mère m, TRANSP navire-mère m

Mother: ~ **Hubbard bit** n PETR TECH trépan Mère Hubbard m

motherboard n COMP, DP, ELECTRON carte mère f, fond de panier m

mother-of-pearl: ~ **bead** n C&G perle nacrée f

motion n MECH, PHYS of particle mouvement m; ~ **analysis** n CINEMAT chronophotographie f; ~ **analysis camera** n CINEMAT caméra pour analyse de mouvement f; ~ **blur** n PHOTO flou de bougé m; ~ **detector** n TRANSP détecteur de passage m; ~ **indicator** n MECH ENG indicateur de vitesse m, tachymètre m; ~ **in a straight line** n MECH, PHYS mouvement rectiligne m; ~ **picture** n CINEMAT film m; ~ **picture camera** n CINEMAT appareil de prises de vue cinématographique m; ~ **picture speed** n CINEMAT fréquence d'images f; ~ **plate** n MECH ENG support des glissières m; ~ **unsharpness** n CINEMAT flou de mouvement m

motional adj ACOUSTICS impedance motionnel

MOTIS abbr (message-oriented text interchange system) TELECOM système d'échange de textes en mode message m

motive: ~ **force** n NAUT ship design force motrice f

motor n AUTO, ELEC, ELEC ENG moteur m, MECH ENG machine f, mobile m, moteur m, moteur m, SPACE moteur m; ~ **armature** n ELEC induit moteur m; ~ **bogie** n (BrE) (cf motor truck) RAIL vehicles bogie moteur m; ~ **branch circuit** n PROD ENG circuit de dérivation de moteur m; ~ **brush** n PRINT balai de moteur m, charbon m; ~ **case** n SPACE corps de propulseur m; ~ **control** n TV asservissement de moteur m; ~ **controller** n PROD ENG contrôleur moteur m; ~ **converter** n ELEC ENG convertisseur à cascade m; ~ **cruiser** n TRANSP vedette rapide f; ~ **drive** n ELEC ENG commande par moteur f, entraînement par moteur m, PHOTO entraînement par moteur m, RECORDING moteur d'entraînement m; ~ **ferry** n TRANSP bac à moteur m; ~ **generator** n ELEC ENG moteur générateur m; ~ **grader** n CONST niveleuse f, TRANSP niveleuse à lame f; ~ **home** n TRANSP autocaravane f; ~ **nameplate** n PROD ENG plaque signalétique du moteur f; ~ **phase current** n PROD ENG courant de phase moteur m; ~ **power loss** n PROD ENG perte d'énergie au moteur f; ~ **pump** n MAR POLL motopompe f; ~ **rating** n PROD ENG puissance de moteur f; ~ **rewind** n CINEMAT réenroulement au moteur m; ~ **sailer** n NAUT bateau mixte m, motor-sailer m; ~ **scooter** n TRANSP scooter m; ~ **shaft** n MECH ENG of machine tool arbre moteur m; ~ **ship** n NAUT navire à moteur m; ~ **spirit** n PETR TECH carburant auto m, essence f; ~ **starter** n ELEC ENG démarreur de moteur m; ~ **switching** n PROD ENG valeur nominale de commutation des moteurs f; ~ **truck** n (AmE) (cf motor bogie) RAIL vehicles bogie moteur m; ~ **vessel** n NAUT navire à moteur m; ~ **winding** n PROD ENG bobinage de moteur m

motorail n RAIL TAC, train autos-couchettes m

motor-assisted: ~ **bicycle** n TRANSP cyclomoteur m

motorboat *n* NAUT bateau à moteur *m*, vedette *f*, vedette automobile *f*, TRANSP canot à moteur *m*

motorboating *n* ELECTRON amorçage basse fréquence *m*, bruit de moteur de bateau *m*, motorboating *m*

motorcar *n* TRANSP automobile *f*; **~ parts** *n pl* VEHICLES pièces d'automobile *f pl*

motorcoach *n* TRANSP autocar *m*, automotrice *f*

motor-drive: **~ mechanism** *n* ELEC mécanisme d'entraînement à moteur *m*

motor-driven [1] *adj* ELEC ENG entraîné par un moteur, à moteur, MECH motorisé

motor-driven: [2] **~ conveyor** *n* PROD ENG convoyeur actionné par moteur *m*; **~ level** *n* INSTRUMENT niveau à moteur *m*; **~ system** *n* TELECOM système à entraînement mécanique *m*

motor-generator: **~ set** *n* ELEC ENG, MECH ENG groupe moteur-générateur *m*

motorized: **~ driving pulley** *n* MECH ENG tambour moteur *m*; **~ zoom lens** *n* CINEMAT zoom à commande électrique *m*

motorman *n* PETR TECH homme de cabestan *m*

motor-propelled: **~ patrol boat** *n* MILIT patrouilleur motopropulsé *m*

motorway [1] *adj* (BrE) *(cf freeway)* CONST autoroutier

motorway [2] *n* (BrE) *(cf freeway)* CONST, TRANSP autoroute *f*

mottled *adj* GEOL bariolé, bigarré, moucheté, PACKAGING moucheté, PRINT grumeleux, marbré, moutonneux

mottramite *n* MINERAL mottramite *f*

mould [1] *n* (BrE) FOOD TECH moule *m*, NAUT gabarit *m*, *shipbuilding-GRP, wood, steel* moule *m*, P&R *press* moule *m*, PAPER TECH forme *f*, PROD ENG *founding* creux *m*, moule *m*, PROP MAT moule *m*; **~ blowing** *n* (BrE) C&G moulage par soufflage *m*, soufflage au moule *m* (Bel); **~ coating** *n* (BrE) C&G laquage de moule *m*; **~ dryer** *n* (BrE) PROD ENG *founding* four de séchage des moules *m*; **~ emptier** *n* (BrE) C&G videur de moule *m*; **~ engraving** *n* (BrE) MECH ENG gravure des moules *f*; **~ for casting** *n* (BrE) MECH ENG moule de fonderie *m*; **~ for food products** *n* (BrE) MECH ENG moule pour produits alimentaires *m*; **~ for glass-reinforced polyester** *n* (BrE) *(mould for GRP)* MECH ENG moule pour polyester chargé de verre *m*; **~ for glassware** *n* (BrE) MECH ENG moule pour la verrerie *m*; **~ for GRP** *n* (BrE) *(mould for glass-reinforced polyester)* MECH ENG moule pour polyester chargé de verre *m*; **~ for mineral materials** *n* (BrE) MECH ENG *glass, ceramics, concrete* moule pour matières minérales *m*; **~ for plastics** *n* (BrE) MECH ENG moule pour plastiques *m*; **~ for rubber** *n* (BrE) MECH ENG moule pour caoutchouc *m*; **~ for structural foam** *n* (BrE) MECH ENG moule pour mousse à peau intégrée *m*; **~ for thermoplastics** *n* (BrE) MECH ENG moule pour thermoplastiques *m*; **~ for thermoset plastics** *n* (BrE) MECH ENG moule pour plastiques thermodurcis *m*; **~ holder** *n* (BrE) C&G charnière porte-moule *f*; **~ insert** *n* (BrE) P&R *equipment* insert de moule *m*; **~ loft** *n* (BrE) NAUT *shipbuilding* salle des gabarits *f*, salle à tracer *f*; **~ maker** *n* (BrE) C&G ouvrier mouleur *m*; **~ mark** *n* (BrE) C&G couture *f*, marque de moule *f*; **~ oil** *n* (BrE) CONST huile de coffrage *f*; **~ paper** *n* (BrE) PRINT papier à la forme *m*; **~ plates** *n pl* (BrE) MECH ENG plaques de moules *f pl*; **~ printing** *n* (BrE) PAPER TECH empreinte *f*; **~ shrinkage** *n* (BrE) P&R retrait au moulage *m*; **~ texturing** *n* (BrE) MECH ENG texturage des moules *m*

mould [2] *vt* (BrE) C&G mouler

moulded [1] *adj* (BrE) PAPER TECH moulé; **not ~** *adj* (BrE) C&G dessin flou

moulded: [2] **~ board** *n* (BrE) PACKAGING carton d'emboutissage *m*, PAPER TECH carton moulé *m*; **~ breadth** *n* (BrE) NAUT *ship design* largeur hors membres *f*; **~ casting** *n* (BrE) PROD ENG pièce moulée *f*; **~ contact block** *n* (BrE) PROD ENG bloc de contacts moulé *m*; **~ depth** *n* (BrE) NAUT *naval architecture* creux sur quille *m*; **~ displacement** *n* (BrE) NAUT *ship design* déplacement hors membres *m*; **~ draught** *n* (BrE) NAUT *ship design* profondeur de carène *f*, tirant d'eau sur quille *m*; **~ hose** *n* (BrE) P&R tuyau moulé *m*; **~ plastics** *n pl* (BrE) P&R matières plastiques moulées *f pl*; **~ printing plate** *n* (BrE) PRINT plaque imprimante moulée *f*; **~ pulp products** *n pl* (BrE) PAPER TECH produits en cellulose moulée *m pl*

moulder *n* (BrE) PROD ENG *person* mouleur *m*, ouvrier mouleur *m*

moulding *n* (BrE) ACOUSTICS moulage *m*, pressage *m*, CONST *ornamental strip* moulure *f*, ELEC ENG, GAS TECH moulage *m*, NAUT *shipbuilding* gabariage *m*, moulage *m*, P&R *process* moulage *m*, PROD ENG *founding* moulage *m*, *ornamental strip* baguette de moulure *f*, PROP MAT moulage *m*; **~ bench** *n* (BrE) PROD ENG banc de moulage *m*; **~ box** *n* (BrE) PROD ENG châssis *m*, châssis de fonderie *m*, châssis de moulage *m*; **~ cycle** *n* (BrE) P&R cycle de moulage *m*; **~ flask** *n* (BrE) PROD ENG châssis *m*, châssis de fonderie *m*, châssis de moulage *m*; **~ floor** *n* (BrE) PROD ENG chantier de moulage *m*, moulerie *f*; **~ hole** *n* (BrE) PROD ENG fosse de moulage *f*; **~ machine** *n* (BrE) CONST *woodworking* machine à faire les moulures *f*, machine à moulurer *f*, moulurière *f*, PROD ENG *founding* machine à mouler *f*; **~ powder** *n* (BrE) P&R *plastics* poudre à mouler *f*; **~ sand** *n* (BrE) PROD ENG sable *m*, sable de fonderie *m*, sable de moulage *m*; **~ shop** *n* (BrE) PROD ENG atelier de moulage *m*; **~ with clay batts** *n* (BrE) C&G moulage à la croûte *m*; **~ with clay sheets** *n* (BrE) C&G moulage à la croûte *m*

mould-resistant *adj* (BrE) PACKAGING résistant au moisi

mount [1] *n* ASTRON *of telescope*, CINEMAT *of lens* monture *f*, MECH ENG bâti *m*, PHOTO monture *f* **~ of front element** *n* PHOTO barillet de la lentille frontale *m*; **~ hope roller** *n* PACKAGING, PRINT rouleau déplisseur *m*

mount [2] *vt* COMP, DP, ELECTRON monter, PROD ENG emmancher, enchâsser, monter; **~ flush** *vt* PROD ENG encastrer

mountain: **~ breeze** *n* METEO brise de montagne *f*; **~ chain** *n* GEOL chaîne de montagne *f*; **~ climate** *n* METEO climat de montagne *m*; **~ cork** *n* MINERAL liège de fossile *m*, liège de montagne *m*; **~ flesh** *n* MINERAL chair fossile *f*, chair minérale *f*; **~ leather** *n* MINERAL cuir de montagne *m*; **~ mass** *n* COAL TECH pression de la roche *f*; **~ paper** *n* MINERAL carton de montagne *m*, carton fossile *m*, carton minéral *m*, papier de montagne *m*; **~ railroad** *n* (AmE) *(cf mountain railway)* RAIL, TRANSP chemin de fer de montagne *m*; **~ railway** *n* (BrE) *(cf mountain railroad)* RAIL, TRANSP chemin de fer de montagne *m*; **~ road** *n* CONST route de montagne *f*; **~ soap** *n* MINERAL savon de montagne *m*; **~ tallow** *n* MINERAL suif minéral *m*; **~ wood** *n* MINERAL bois de montagne *m*

mounted: [1] **~ on frictionless bearings** *adj* MECH ENG emmanché sur roulements sans friction

mounted:[2] ~ **artillery** n MILIT artillerie portée f; ~ **filter** n PHOTO filtre serti m

mounter-proofer n PRINT machine à monter les plaques et tirer les épreuves f

mounting n ELECTRON montage m, MECH ENG *machine tool* châssis-support m, PHOTO *of camera, light* fixation f, *slides, transparencies* montage m, PROD ENG ferrures f pl, garniture f, monture f; ~ **base** n MECH ENG socle de fixation m; ~ **bath** n LAB EQUIP *section mounting* bain pour histologie m; ~ **bezel** n PROD ENG cadre de montage m; ~ **bolt** n MECH ENG boulon de montage m; ~ **bracket** n PHOTO barrette de fixation f, PROD ENG support de montage m; ~ **foot** n PHOTO sabot de fixation m; ~ **hardware set** n PROD ENG jeu d'éléments de montage m; ~ **layout** n PROD ENG schéma de montage m; ~ **pad** n MECH ENG bossage de montage m; ~ **polarization** n ELEC ENG détrompage m, polarisation mécanique f; ~ **rail** n PROD ENG rail de montage m

mouse n COMP, DP souris f; ~ **hole** n FUELLESS *geothermal drilling equipment*, PETR trou de souris m, PETR TECH trou de rat m, trou de souris m; ~ **software** n COMP logiciel souris m

mouth n ACOUSTICS bouche f, CONST *of plane* lumière f, mortaise f, *of rock breaker* embouchure f, gueule f, HYDROL *of river* bouche f, embouchure f, embouchure f, MINING *of drift* amorce f, entrée f, *of mine* bouche f, orifice m, pit carreau m, NAUT *of river, strait* bouche f, embouchure f, PROD ENG *of blast furnace* gueulard m, *of furnace, converter* bouche f, gueule f, taphole of furnace coulée f, oeil m, troude coulée m, trou de gueuse m, WATER SUPP *of river* embouchure f; ~ **blowing** n C&G soufflage à la bouche m; ~ **tools** n pl C&G fers à goulot m pl

mouth-blown: ~ **glass** n C&G verre soufflé bouche m

mouthpiece n TELECOM embouchure f

movable: ~ **bridge** n NAUT *locks, inland waterways* pont mobile m; ~ **contact** n ELEC, PROD ENG contact mobile m; ~ **contact crossbar** n PROD ENG *electricity* support des contacts mobiles m; ~ **core** n ELEC *of transformer* noyau mobile m; ~ **rotor blade** n AERONAUT *of helicopter* aube mobile de rotor f; ~ **stop** n MECH ENG butée mobile f

move:[1] ~ **time** n PROD ENG délai d'acheminement m, temps d'acheminement m, temps de déplacement m, temps de manutention m, temps de transfert m, temps de transport m

move:[2] ~ **the center line** vi (AmE), ~ **the centre line** vi (BrE) CONST décaler l'axe

movement n GAS TECH hétérogénéité f, MECH ENG déplacement m, marche f, mouvement m; ~ **file** n COMP fichier des mouvements m

move-out: ~ **correction** n GEOL correction dynamique f

mover n MECH ENG *moving power* force motrice f, mobile m, moteur m

movie n CINEMAT film m; ~ **projector** n (AmE) *(cf cinema projector)* ELEC projecteur ciné m

moving: ~ **armature** n ACOUSTICS équipage mobile m; ~ **background** n CINEMAT fond mobile m; ~ **belt flat box** n PAPER TECH caisse aspirante à courroies mobiles f; ~ **carpet** n TRANSP tapis roulant m; ~ **charge** n ELEC ENG charge mobile f; ~ **coil** n ELEC bobine mobile f, ELEC ENG bobine mobile f, *of galvanometer* cadre mobile m; ~ **coil ammeter** n ELEC ampèremètre magnéto-électrique m; ~ **coil galvanometer** n ELEC galvanomètre à cadre mobile m, ELEC ENG galvanomètre magnéto-électrique m, galvanomètre à cadre mobile m, PHYS galvanomètreà cadre mobile m; ~ **coil loudspeaker** n RECORDING haut-parleur à bobine mobile m; ~ **coil meter** n ELEC ENG appareil à cadre mobile m; ~ **coil microphone** n ACOUSTICS microphone à bobine mobile m, PHYS microphone électrodynamique m, RECORDING microphone à bobine mobile m; ~ **coil pick-up** n RECORDING lecteur à bobine mobile m; ~ **coil relay** n ELEC relais magnéto-électrique m; ~ **coil voltmeter** n ELEC voltmètre magnéto-électrique m; ~ **contact** n ELEC ENG contact mobile m; ~ **fiber switch** n (AmE), ~ **fibre switch** n (BrE) TELECOM commutateur à déplacement de fibre m; ~ **floor** n TRANSP tapis roulant m; ~ **formwork** n CONST coffrage glissant m, coffrage mobile m; ~ **grate** n HEATING grille mobile f; ~ **iron instrument** n ELEC, ELEC ENG, INSTRUMENT instrument ferromagnétique m, instrument à fer mobile m; ~ **iron meter** n ELEC, INSTRUMENT instrument ferromagnétique m, instrument à fer mobile m; ~ **load** n CONST *live* poids roulant m; ~ **magnet cartridge** n RECORDING cartouche à aimant mobile f; ~ **magnet galvanometer** n ELEC galvanomètre à aiguille mobile m, ELEC ENG galvanomètre à aimant mobile m; ~ **magnet instrument** n INSTRUMENT instrument à aimant mobile m, instrument à aimant tournant m; ~ **magnet medium** n ELEC ENG support magnétique à défilement m; ~ **pavement** n (BrE) *(cf moving sidewalk)* TRANSP trottoir roulant m; ~ **platform** n (BrE) *(cf moving sidewalk)* CONST trottoir roulant m; ~ **saw** n SAFETY scie mobile f; ~ **sidewalk** n (AmE) *(cf moving platform)* AERONAUT *at airport*, CONST, TRANSP trottoir roulant m; ~ **staircase** n (BrE) *(cf escalator)* CONST escalier roulant m, escalier à marches mobiles m; ~ **stairway** n (BrE) *(cf escalator)* CONST escalier roulant m, escalier à marches mobiles m; ~ **table** n C&G table mobile f; ~ **traffic** n TRANSP circulation en mouvement f

Moy: ~ **head** n CINEMAT tête panoramique Moy f

MPC: ~ **carbon black** n *(medium-processing channel carbon black)* P&R *rubber pigment, filler* noir MPC m

mpg abbr *(miles per gallon)* TRANSP milles par gallon m pl

MRTIE abbr *(maximum relative time interval error)* TELECOM erreur relative maximum d'intervalle de temps f

ms abbr *(millisecond)* COMP, DP ms *(milliseconde)*

MS abbr ELECTRON *(main station)* PP *(poste principal)*, PRINT *(mobile station)*, SPACE *(mobile station)* station mobile f, TELECOM *(message store)* mémoire de messages f, TELECOM *(multiplex section)* section de multiplexage f, TELECOM *(mobile station)* station mobile f

MSB abbr *(most significant bit)* COMP, PROD ENG, TELECOM bit de poids fort m

MSC abbr TELECOM *(maritime switching centre, maritime switching center)* centre de commutation maritime m, TELECOM *(mobile switching centre, mobile switching center)* centre de commutation mobile m

MSD abbr *(most significant digit)* COMP, DP, PROD ENG chiffre de poids fort m, chiffre le plus significatif m

MSE abbr *(mean square error)* COMP, DP, MATH erreur quadratique moyenne f

MSG abbr *(monosodium glutamate)* FOOD TECH glutamate de sodium m, glutamate monosodique m

M-shell n PHYS *atom* couche M f

MSI [1] abbr *(medium-scale integration)* COMP, DP, ELECTRON, TELECOM intégration à moyenne échelle f

MSI:[2] ~ **circuit** *n* TELECOM circuit MSI *m*, circuit à intégration à échelle moyenne *m*

MSK *abbr (minimum-shift keying)* ELECTRON modulation à déplacement minimal *f*, TELECOM manipulation par déplacement minimal *f*

MSN *abbr (multiple-subscriber number)* TELECOM numéro d'abonné multiple *m*

MSP *abbr* TELECOM *(maintenance service provider)* prestataire de service de maintenance *m*, TELECOM *(multiplex section protection)* protection de section de multiplexage *f*

MST *abbr (multiplex section termination)* TELECOM terminaison de section de multiplexage *f*

M-star *n* ASTRON étoile M *f*

MSU *abbr (message signal unit)* TELECOM trame sémaphore de message *f*

mSv-year *n* RAD PHYS mSv-year *m*

MT [1] *abbr (message transfer)* TELECOM transfert de messages *m*

MT:[2] ~ **carbon black** *n (medium thermal carbon black)* P&R *rubber pigment, filler* noir MT *m*

MTA *abbr (message transfer agent)* TELECOM agent de transfert de messages *m*

MTBF *abbr (mean time between failures)* COMP, DP, MECH, QUALITY, SPACE MTBF *(moyenne de temps de bon fonctionnement)*

MTBR *abbr (mean time between removals)* SPACE temps moyen entre réparations *m*

MTIE *abbr (maximum time interval error)* TELECOM erreur maximum d'intervalle de temps *f*

MTL *abbr (merged transistor logic)* ELECTRON logique à transistors fusionnés *f*

MTPI *abbr (multiplexer timing physical interface)* TELECOM interface physique de rythme de multiplexeur *f*

MTR *abbr (materials testing reactor)* NUCLEAR réacteur d'essais de matériaux *m*

MTS *abbr* TELECOM *(mobile telephone service)* SRM *(service radiotéléphonique mobile)*, TELECOM *(multiplexer timing source)* source de rythme de multiplexeur *f*, TELECOM *(message transfer system)* système de transfert de messages *m*

MTTF *abbr (mean time to failure)* QUALITY durée moyenne avant défaillance *f*

MTTR *abbr (mean time to repair)* COMP, DP, ELEC ENG temps moyen de réparation *m*, MECH, SPACE durée moyenne de réparation *f*

M-type: ~ **microwave tube** *n* ELECTRON tube de type M *m*, tube hyperfréquence de type M *m*; ~ **tube** *n* ELECTRON tube de type M *m*

mucic *adj* CHEM mucique

muciferous *adj* CHEM mucipare

muciform *adj* CHEM muciforme

mucilaginous *adj* CHEM mucilagineux

mucin *n* CHEM mucine *f*

mucipheric *adj* CHEM mucipare

mucoitin-sulfuric *adj* (AmE), **mucoitin-sulphuric** *adj* (BrE) CHEM mucoïtine-sulfurique

muconic *adj* CHEM muconique

mucoprotein *n* CHEM mucoprotéine *f*

mud *n* MINING boue *f*, bourbe *f*, limon *m*, vase *f*, OCEANOG boue *f* ~ **analysis log** *n* PETR TECH diagraphie d'analyse des boues *f*; ~ **bit** *n* MINING *boring* cuiller *f*, tarière à glaise *f*, PETR TECH trépan à boue *m*; ~ **bottom** *n* MINING fond de boue *m*; ~ **box** *n* PETR, PETR TECH boîte à boue *f*, PROD ENG *sluices* boîte à débourbage *f*; ~ **cake** *n* PETR cake *m*; ~ **circulation** *n* PETR circulation

de boue *f*; ~ **coal** *n* COAL TECH charbon limoneux *m*; ~ **cock** *n* PROD ENG *of boiler* robinet de vidange *m*; ~ **column** *n* PETR TECH colonne de boue *f*; ~ **content** *n* WATER SUPP teneur en boue *f*; ~ **crack** *n* GEOL fente de retrait *f*; ~ **density** *n* PETR densité de boue *f*; ~ **door** *n* PROD ENG *of boiler* regard de lavage *m*, trou de bras *m*, trou de sel *m*, trou à main *m*; ~ **engineer** *n* PETR TECH ingénieur des boues *m*; ~ **filtrate** *n* PETR filtrat de boue *m*; ~ **flap** *n* VEHICLES pare-boue *m*; ~ **flow** *n* GEOL coulée boueuse *f*; ~ **fluid** *n* PETR TECH boue d'injection *f*; ~ **hose** *n* PETR flexible à boue *m*; ~ **line** *n* PETR TECH *drilling* conduite de boue *f*, *sea bed* fond de mer *m*, sol marin *m*; ~ **log** *n* GEOPHYS diagramme des boues *m*, PETR log de chantier *m*, PETR TECH diagraphie d'analyse des boues *f*, diagraphie de boue de forage *f*; ~ **logging** *n* PETR détection des indices dans la boue *f*; ~ **losses** *n pl* PETR TECH perte *f*, pertes *f pl*; ~ **pit** *n* PETR TECH bourbier *m*; ~ **plug** *n* PROD ENG *of boiler* porte de vidange *f*; ~ **pump** *n* MINING, PETR pompe à boue *f*, PETR TECH pompe de circulation *f*, pompe à boue *f*; ~ **pump valve** *n* PETR TECH clapet de pompe à boue *m*; ~ **return line** *n* PETR TECH goulotte à boue *f*; ~ **ring** *n* PETR TECH anneau de boue *m*; ~ **system** *n* PETR TECH circuit des boues *m*; ~ **tank** *n* PETR TECH bac à boue *m*, bassin à boue *m*; ~ **volcano** *n* FUELLESS salse *f*, PETR TECH volcan de boue *m*; ~ **weight** *n* PETR densité de boue *f*, PETR TECH densité de boue *f*, poids des boues *m*

mudflap *n* VEHICLES *accessory* bavette garde-boue *f*

mudflat *n* HYDROL *geography* vasière *f*

mudguard *n* (BrE) *(cf fender)* VEHICLES *body* aile *f*, garde-boue *m*, pare-boue *m*

mudsill *n* CONST seuil *m*, sole gravière *f*, traverse de fondation *f*

mudstone *n* GEOL argilite *f*, pélite *f*

MUF *abbr (maximum usable frequency)* ELEC ENG fréquence maximale utilisable *f*

muff *n* MECH ENG manchon *m*; ~ **coupling** *n* MECH ENG accouplement à manchon *m*, manchon cylindrique *m*

muffle *n* C&G, HEATING, PROD ENG *pulley block* moufle *m*; ~ **furnace** *n* HEATING, LAB EQUIP *heating*, PROD ENG four à moufle *m*; ~ **lehr** *n* C&G arche mouflée *f*; ~ **support** *n* C&G support de moufle *m*

muffler *n* (AmE) *(cf silencer)* AUTO silencieux *m*, MECH pot d'échappement *m*, silencieux *m*, VEHICLES *exhaust system* amortisseur de bruit *m*, pot d'échappement *m*, silencieux *m*; ~ **jacket** *n* AUTO enveloppe de silencieux *f*; ~ **shell** *n* AUTO enveloppe de silencieux *f*

mull *n* CHEM dispersion *f*, pâte *f*

Müllen: ~ **tester** *n* PAPER TECH éclatomètre *m*

muller *n* PROD ENG *of amalgamating pan* patin *m*

Mullin's: ~ **effect** *n* P&R *rubber* effet Mullin *m*

mullion *n* C&G meneau *m*; ~ **structure** *n* GEOL structures orientées parallèles aux linéations tectoniques *f pl*

mullite *n* MINERAL mullite *f*

mullock *n* MINING stériles *m pl*

mullocking *n* MINING travaux au rocher *m pl*

multiaccess: ~ **system** *n* COMP, DP système multiaccès *m*

multi-address: ~ **instruction** *n* COMP, DP instruction multi-adresse *f*

multi-addressing *n* TELECOM multi-adressage *m*

multiagent: ~ **munitions** *n pl* MILIT *chemical warfare* munitions à agents multiples *f pl*

multianode: ~ **rectifier** *n* ELEC ENG mutateur polyanodique *m*, redresseur polyanodique *m*, soupape rectifier *f*

multiaxle: ~ **heavy freight vehicle** *n* (AmE) *(cf multiaxle*

heavy goods vehicle) TRANSP camion 'mille pattes' *m*;
~ **heavy goods vehicle** *n* (BrE) *(cf multiaxle heavy freight vehicle)* TRANSP camion 'mille pattes' *m*

multiband: ~ **antenna** *n* PHYS antenne multibande *f*; ~ **filter** *n* TELECOM filtre multibande *m*

multibeam [1] *adj* SPACE *communications* multifaisceau

multibeam: [2] ~ **antenna** *n* SPACE *communications* antenne multifaisceau *f*; ~ **cathode ray tube** *n* *(multibeam CRT)* ELECTRON tube cathodique multifaisceau *m*; ~ **CRT** *n* *(multibeam cathode ray tube)* ELECTRON tube cathodique multifaisceau *m*; ~ **echo sounder** *n* OCEANOG multifaisceau *m*, sondeur multifaisceau *m*; ~ **sounder** *n* OCEANOG multifaisceau *m*, sondeur multifaisceau *m*

multibearer: ~ **service** *n* TELECOM *ISDN* service à supports multiples *m*

multibreak: ~ **circuit breaker** *n* ELEC disjoncteur à coupure multiple *m*

multibroad *n* CINEMAT projecteur focalisable *m*

multiburst *n* TV salve multiple *f*

multicavity: ~ **klystron** *n* ELECTRON, PHYS klystron multicavité *m*; ~ **magnetron** *n* ELECTRON magnétron à cavités *m*

multicellular *adj* ACOUSTICS *loudspeaker* multicellulaire

multichannel [1] *adj* NAUT *radio, satellite communications* multivoies

multichannel: [2] ~ **amplifier** *n* ELECTRON amplificateur multivoie *m*; ~ **analyzer** *n* PHYS analyseur multicanaux *m*; ~ **carrier** *n* SPACE *communications* porteuse multivoie *f*; ~ **elementary loudspeaker** *n* ACOUSTICS haut-parleur élémentaire à voies multiples *m*; ~ **filter** *n* TELECOM filtre multivoie *m*; ~ **loudspeaker** *n* RECORDING haut-parleur multicanal *m*; ~ **monitoring** *n* NAUT *radio* contrôle multivoies *m*; ~ **protocol** *n* COMP, DP protocole multivoie *m*; ~ **selector** *n* TV sélecteur de canal *m*

multiclique: ~ **mode** *n* TELECOM mode multiclique *m*

multicollector: ~ **transistor** *n* ELECTRON transistor multicollecteur *m*

multicolor: ~ **printing** *n* (AmE) *see multicolour printing*; ~ **rotary printing machine** *n* (AmE) *see multicolour rotary printing machine*

multicolored *adj* (AmE) *see multicoloured*

multicolour: ~ **printing** *n* (BrE) PACKAGING, PRINT impression en plusieurs couleurs *f*, impression polychrome *f*; ~ **rotary printing machine** *n* (BrE) PRINT rotative pour la couleur *f*

multicoloured *adj* (BrE) COLOURS de couleurs diverses

multicomponent [1] *adj* CHEM à plusieurs constituants

multicomponent: [2] ~ **glass fiber** *n* (AmE), ~ **glass fibre** *n* (BrE) OPT fibre de verre à composants multiples *f*, fibre multicomposant *f*

multiconductor: ~ **cable** *n* ELEC câble multiconducteur *m*, câble multipolaire *m*, ELEC ENG câble multiconducteur *m*; ~ **locking plug** *n* ELEC *connection* prise DIN *f*

multicopy: ~ **business forms** *n pl* PAPER TECH formulaires à copies multiples *m pl*

multicore: ~ **cable** *n* ELEC câble multiple *m*, ELEC ENG connecteur multicontact *m*, câble multiconducteur *m*, câble multiple *m*, TV câble multifibres *m*, câble multipaires *m*

multicylinder: ~ **dryer section** *n* PAPER TECH sécherie multicylindrique *f*; ~ **engine** *n* AUTO moteur polycylindrique *m*; ~ **injection pump** *n* AUTO pompe en ligne *f*

multidecking: ~ **system** *n* TRANSP système à ponts multiples *m*

multidentate *adj* CHEM *ligand* multidenté

multidestination: ~ **carrier** *n* SPACE *communications* porteuse multidestination *f*; ~ **mode** *n* TELECOM mode multidestination *m*

multidimensional: ~ **filtering** *n* TELECOM filtrage multidimensionnel *m*; ~ **modelling** *n* COMP modélisation multidimensionnelle *f*

multidrill: ~ **head** *n* MECH ENG tête de perçage multiple *f*

multidrop: ~ **link** *n* COMP, DP liaison multipoint *f*

multielectrode: ~ **tube** *n* ELECTRON tube multi-électrode *m*

multiemitter: ~ **transistor** *n* ELECTRON transistor multiémetteur *m*

multiengine: ~ **helicopter** *n* AERONAUT hélicoptère multimoteur *m*

multifiber: ~ **cable** *n* (AmE) *see multifibre cable*; ~ **joint** *n* (AmE) *see multifibre joint*

multifibre: ~ **cable** *n* (BrE) ELEC ENG, OPT, TELECOM câble multifibre *m*; ~ **joint** *n* (BrE) OPT connexion globale *f*, raccordement collectif *m*, raccordement global *m*, TELECOM raccord multifibre *m*

multifilament: ~ **machine** *n* TEXTILES multifilament traité en long *m*; ~ **yarn** *n* TEXTILES fil multifilament *m*

multifocal: ~ **finder** *n* CINEMAT viseur multifocal *m*, viseur à champ variable *m*; ~ **glasses** *n pl* INSTRUMENT lentilles multifocales *f pl*, lentilles à foyer progressif *f pl*

multiframe: ~ **alignment** *n* *(MFA)* TELECOM verrouillage de multitrame *m*

multifrequency: ~ **antenna** *n* TELECOM antenne multibande *f*; ~ **generator** *n* TELECOM générateur de signalisation multifréquence *m*, générateur multifréquence *m*; ~ **receiver** *n* TELECOM récepteur de signalisation MF *m*, récepteur de signalisation multifréquence *m*; ~ **sender-receiver** *n* TELECOM signaleur multifréquence *m*

multifuel: ~ **engine** *n* AUTO, THERMOD, TRANSP moteur polycarburant *m*; ~ **heater** *n* MECH ENG réchauffeur à multicombustibles *m*

multifunction: ~ **tester** *n* ELEC ENG contrôleur multifonction *m*

multigage: ~ **isolator** *n* (AmE) *see multigauge isolator*; ~ **projector** *n* (AmE) *see multigauge projector*

multigauge: ~ **isolator** *n* (BrE) PROD ENG isolateur multiple *m*; ~ **projector** *n* (BrE) CINEMAT appareil de projection multiformat *m*

multigrade: ~ **oil** *n* AUTO, VEHICLES *lubrication* huile multigrade *f*

multigraded: ~ **soil** *n* COAL TECH sol à coefficient d'uniformité élevé *m*

multigrid: ~ **tube** *n* ELECTRON tube multigrille *m*, tube à plusieurs grilles *m*

multigrip: ~ **pliers** *n pl* MECH ENG pince multiprise *f*, pince réglable *f*

multigun: ~ **tube** *n* ELECTRON tube multicanon *m*

multihead *adj* TEXTILES à têtes multiples

multihull *n* NAUT *type of boat* multicoque *f*

multihulled: ~ **ship** *n* TRANSP navire multicoque *m*

multi-image: ~ **lens** *n* CINEMAT objectif multi-images *m*

multi-impression: ~ **hot runner mold** *n* (AmE), ~ **hot runner mould** *n* (BrE) MECH ENG moule pour coulée à chaud à empreintes multiples *m*; ~ **mold** *n* (AmE), ~ **mould** *n* (BrE) MECH ENG *plastic moulding*, P&R moule à empreintes multiples *m*; ~ **unscrewing tools** *n pl* MECH ENG outils de dévissage à empreintes multiples *m pl*

multilane: ~ **labeling system** *n* (AmE), ~ **labelling system** *n* (BrE) PACKAGING système d'étiquetage à voies multiples *m*; ~ **machine** *n* PACKAGING machine à voies multiples *f*

multilayer[1] *adj* SPACE *spacecraft* multicouche

multilayer:[2] *n* CHEM multicouche *f*; ~ **aquifer** *n* HYDROL aquifère multicouche *m*; ~ **board** *n* PAPER TECH carton multicouche *m*; ~ **coil** *n* ELEC bobine à plusieurs couches *f*; ~ **color film** *n* (AmE), ~ **colour film** *n* (BrE) CINEMAT pellicule couleur multicouches *f*; ~ **filtration** *n* WATER SUPP filtration sur couches multiples *f*; ~ **headbox** *n* PAPER TECH caisse d'arrivée multijet *f*; ~ **paper** *n* PAPER TECH papier multicouches *m*; ~ **printed circuit** *n* ELECTRON, TELECOM circuit imprimé multicouche *m*; ~ **resist** *n* ELECTRON résist multicouche *m*; ~ **thick film** *n* ELECTRON couche épaisse en multicouche *f*; ~ **thin film** *n* ELECTRON couche mince en multicouche *f*

multileaf: ~ **damper** *n* REFRIG registre à persiennes *m*

multilevel: ~ **bill of material** *n* PROD ENG nomenclature arborescente *f*, nomenclature multiniveau *f*; ~ **modulation** *n* ELECTRON modulation multiniveau *f*; ~ **system** *n* TELECOM système à niveaux multiples *m*

multilongitudinal: ~ **modes** *n pl (MLM)* TELECOM modes longitudinaux multiples *m pl (MLM)*

multimaterial: ~ **recycling** *n* PACKAGING récupérage de matériaux mélangés *m*

multimedia[1] *adj* COMP multimédia

multimedia:[2] ~ **filter** *n* HYDROL filtre multicouche *m*

multimetal: ~ **plate** *n* PRINT plaque multimétallique *f*

multimeter *n* CONTROL contrôleur universel *m*, ELEC ENG, TV multimètre *m*

multimicroprocessor: ~ **system** *n* TELECOM système à structure multimicro *m*

multimirror: ~ **telescope** *n* ASTRON télescope multimiroirs *m*

multimodal: ~ **traffic** *n* RAIL *vehicles* trafic multimodal *m*

multimode: ~ **distortion** *n* OPT dispersion multimode *f*, TELECOM distorsion modale *f*; ~ **fiber** *n* (AmE), ~ **fibre** *n* (BrE) OPT, PHYS fibre multimode *f*; ~ **group delay** *n* OPT, TELECOM temps de propagation de groupe modal différentiel *m*; ~ **laser** *n* OPT, TELECOM laser multimodal *m*; ~ **optical fiber** *n* (AmE), ~ **optical fibre** *n* (BrE) ELEC ENG fibre optique multimode *f*

multinomial *n* MATH polynôme *m*

multioctave: ~ **tunable filter** *n* ELECTRON filtre accordable multioctave *m*; ~ **tunable oscillator** *n* ELECTRON oscillateur accordable multioctave *m*; ~ **tuning** *n* ELECTRON accord multioctave *m*, accord sur plusieurs octaves *m*

multipack *n* PACKAGING emballage à usages multiples *m*

multipath: ~ **fading** *n* TELECOM évanouissement dû à la propagation par trajets multiples *m*; ~ **propagation** *n* TELECOM propagation par trajets multiples *f*; ~ **reflections** *n pl* TELECOM réflexions par trajets multiples *f pl*; ~ **signals** *n pl* TV signaux à plusieurs voies *m pl*

multiphase[1] *adj* ELEC *motor* multiphasé, ELECTRON, GEOL *metamorphism, deformation* polyphasé

multiphase:[2] ~ **controller** *n* TRANSP régulateur multiphase *m*; ~ **digital model** *n* GASTECH modèle numérique maillé *m*

multipin *adj* ELEC ENG multibroche

multiplane: ~ **animation** *n* CINEMAT animation sur plusieurs plans *f*

multiplate: ~ **clutch** *n* MECH ENG embrayage à disques *m*

multiplay *n* ACOUSTICS enregistrement fractionnel *m*

multiple[1] *adj* CHEM multiple

multiple[2] *n* METR *of unit, measurement*, PETR multiple *m*; ~ **access** *n* SPACE *communications*, TELECOM accès multiple *m*; ~ **band-pass filter** *n* RECORDING filtre multiple passe-bande *m*; ~ **barge convoy set** *n* TRANSP convoi poussé *m*; ~ **beam** *n* TELECOM faisceau multiple *m*; ~ **beam antenna** *n* PHYS, TELECOM antenne multifaisceau *f*; ~ **beam interference** *n* PHYS interférence à ondes multiples *f*; ~**beam slashing** *n* TEXTILES encollage multi-ensouple *m*; ~ **blade spring** *n* MECH ENG ressort à lames multiples *m*; ~ **board** *n* PACKAGING carton multiple *m*; ~ **cone loudspeaker** *n* RECORDING haut-parleur à membrane multiple *m*; ~ **contact switch** *n* ELEC commutateur à gradins *m*, ELEC ENG interrupteur à plusieurs contacts *m*; ~ **control** *n* CONTROL contrôle multiple *m*; ~ **current generator** *n* ELEC ENG génératrice polymorphique *f*; ~ **daylight press** *n* P&R presse à plusieurs étages *f*; ~ **development** *n* FUELLESS aménagement multiple *m*; ~ **diffraction** *n* TELECOM diffraction multiple *f*; ~ **disc clutch** *n* (BrE) AUTO embrayage multidisque *m*, MECH ENG embrayage à disques *m*; ~ **disk clutch** *n* (AmE) *see multiple disc clutch*; ~ **drilling machine** *n* MECH perceuse multibroche *f*, PROD ENG perceuse à broches multiples *f*; ~ **earthing connection** *n* (BrE) *(cf multiple grounding connection)* PROD ENG connexion à plusieurs masses *f*; ~ **echo** *n* ACOUSTICS, OCEANOG, RECORDING écho multiple *m*; ~ **expansion engine** *n* PROD ENG machine à multiple expansion *f*; ~ **exposure** *n* CINEMAT exposition multiple *f*, surimpression *f*, PHOTO surimpressions multiples *f pl*; ~ **feeder** *n* ELEC *supply* feeder multiple *m*; ~ **feed rack** *n* PROD ENG rampe de graissage à départs multiples *f*; ~ **frame printing** *n* CINEMAT tirage répété de la même image *m*; ~ **frequency** *n* *(MF)* TELECOM fréquence multiple *f*; ~ **of gearing** *n* MECH ENG train d'engrenages *m*, équipage d'engrenage *m*; ~ **glazing unit** *n* C&G vitrage multiple *m*; ~ **grounding connection** *n* (AmE) *(cf multiple earthing connection)* PROD ENG connexion à plusieurs masses *f*; ~ **hearth furnace** *n* HEATING four à sole multiple *m*; ~ **layer color film** *n* (AmE), ~ **layer colour film** *n* (BrE) PRINT film couleur à couches multiples *m*; ~ **leaf damper** *n* MECH ENG registre à organes mobiles multiples *m*; ~ **machining** *n* PROD ENG usinage en série *m*; ~ **microphone** *n* ACOUSTICS, RECORDING microphone multiple *m*; ~ **milling** *n* PROD ENG fraisage de pièces en série *m*; ~ **mode transportation system** *n* TRANSP système multimodal *m*;~ **modulation** *n* ELECTRON modulation multiple *f*; ~ **operator welding set** *n* PROD ENG groupe de soudage à postes multiples *m*; ~ **order filter** *n* ELECTRON filtre d'ordre multiple *m*; ~ **path** *n* SPACE trajet multiple *m*; ~ **pile-up** *n* TRANSP carambolage *m*, collision en chaîne *f*; ~ **plate capacitor** *n* ELEC condensateur à lames multiples *m*; ~ **plate clutch** *n* MECH ENG embrayage à plateaux multiples *m*; ~ **proportions** *n* CHEM *law of* proportions multiples *f pl*; ~ **row blasting** *n* MINING tir en plusieurs rangées *m*; ~ **sampling** *n* TELECOM échantillonnage multiple *m*; ~ **seizure** *n* TELECOM prise multiple *f*; ~ **socket** *n* ELEC *connection* prise multiple *f*; ~ **soundtrack** *n* RECORDING piste sonore multiple *f*; ~ **special electrical logging** *n* PETR TECH diagraphie électrique à espacements *f*; ~ **speed camera** *n* CINEMAT caméra à vitesse variable *f*; ~ **splitting** *n* NUCLEAR dédoublement de structure fine *m*; ~ **star** *n* ASTRON étoile multiple *f*; ~ **switch** *n* ELEC commutateur en parallèle *m*; ~ **switchboard** *n* TELECOM commutateur multiplex *m*, multiple *m*; ~ **twin quad** *n* ELEC ENG quarte à paires combinables *f*; ~ **V-belt drive** *n* MECH ENG transmission à courroie trapézoïdale multiple *f*; ~ **wedge** *n* MINING coin multiple *m*; ~ **winding** *n* ELEC *of transformer*, ELEC ENG enroulement multiple *m*

multiple-instruction: ~ **multiple-data** *adj (MIMD)* COMP, DP multiflux d'instruction-multiflux de données *m (MIMD)*; ~ **single-data** *adj (MISD)* COMP, DP multiflux d'instruction-monoflux de donnés *m (MISD)*

multiple-outlet: ~ **plug** *n* TV prise multiple *f*

multiple-punching: ~ **machine** *n* PROD ENG poinçonneuse multiple *f*

multiple-ram: ~ **broaching machine** *n* MECH ENG machine à brocher à plusieurs coulisseaux *f*

multiple-reflector: ~ **antenna** *n* TELECOM antenne à réflecteurs multiples *f*

multiple-rung: ~ **display** *n* PROD ENG affichage à plusieurs lignes *m*

multiple-server: ~ **queue** *n* TELECOM file d'attente à serveurs multiples *f*

multiple-skirt: ~ **system** *n* TRANSP système de sustentation multijupe *m*

multiple-skirted: ~ **plenum chamber** *n* TRANSP coussin d'air multiple à jupes souples *m*

multiple-spindle: ~ **drill** *n* PROD ENG machine à percer multiple *f*, perceuse à broches multiples *f*; ~ **drilling head** *n* MECH ENG tête de perçage multiple *f*

multiple-step: ~ **control** *n* CONTROL régulation à positions multiples *f*; ~ **regulation** *n* CONTROL régulation à positions multiples *f*, régulation à échelons multiples *f*

multiple-stranded: ~ **conductor** *n* ELEC *cable* âme en torons *f*

multiple-subscriber: ~ **number** *n (MSN)* TELECOM numéro d'abonné multiple *m*

multiplet *n* PHYS *spectroscopy*, RAD PHYS multiplet *m*

multiple-threaded: ~ **screw** *n* PROD ENG vis à plusieurs filets *f*

multiple-tool: ~ **lathe** *n* MECH ENG tour à outils multiples *m*

multiple-unit: ~ **train** *n* TRANSP rame automotrice *f*; ~ **tube** *n* ELECTRON tube multiple *m*

multiple-use: ~ **carbonizing base paper** *n* PAPER TECH papier pour support carbone multifois *m*

multiple-wire: ~ **system** *n* ELEC système à plusieurs conducteurs *m*

multiplex [1] *n* COMP, DP multiplexeur *m*, ELECTRON multiplexeur *m*, signal multiplex *m*, TV multiplexeur *m*; ~ **channel** *n* ELECTRON voie d'un multiplex *f*; ~ **circuit** *n* PROD ENG circuit de multiplexage *m*; ~ **lap winding** *n* ELEC *of electrical machine* enroulement imbriqué parallèle multiple *m*; ~ **operation** *n* ELECTRON exploitation en multiplex *f*; ~ **section** *n (MS)* TELECOM section de multiplexage *f*; ~ **section alarm indication signal** *n* TELECOM SM-SIA, signal d'indication d'alarme de section de multiplexage *m*; ~ **section overhead** *n* TELECOM SDSM, surdébit de section de multiplexage *m*; ~ **section protection** *n (MSP)* TELECOM protection de section de multiplexage *f*; ~ **section termination** *n (MST)* TELECOM terminaison de section de multiplexage *f*; ~ **space switch** *n* TELECOM commutateur spatial multiplex *m*; ~ **timing generator** *n* TELECOM générateur de rythme de multiplexeur *m*; ~ **transmission** *n* TV transmission en multiplex *f*

multiplex [2] *vt* COMP, DP multiplexer, ELECTRON grouper,

multiplexer, TELECOM multiplexer

multiplexer *n* COMP, DP, ELECTRON, TELECOM, TV multiplexeur *m*; ~ **channel** *n* COMP, DP canal multiplexeur *m*; ~ **timing physical interface** *n (MTPI)* TELECOM interface physique de rythme de multiplexeur *f*; ~ **timing source** *n (MTS)* TELECOM source de rythme de multiplexeur *f*

multiplexing *n* COMP, DP, SPACE *communications*, TELECOM multiplexage *m*; ~ **frequency** *n* ELECTRON fréquence de multiplexage *f*; ~ **identification** *n* TELECOM identification de multiplexage *f*

multiplicand *n* COMP, DP, MATH multiplicande *m*

multiplication *n* COMP, DP, MATH multiplication *f*

multiplicative *adj* MATH multiplicatif

multiplicator *n* TELECOM multiplicateur *m*

multiplicity *n* PHYS multiplicité *f*

multiplier *n* COMP, DP multiplicateur *m*, ELECTRON multiplicateur *m*, multiplieur *m*, TELECOM multiplicateur *m*; ~ **phototube** *n* INSTRUMENT cellule à multiplication des électrons *f*, photomultiplicateur *m*

multiplug: ~ **adaptor** *n* ELEC ENG fiche à prises multiples *f*

multiply [1] *adj* PACKAGING à plusieurs épaisseurs

multiply: [2] ~ **board** *n* PACKAGING carton multijet *m*; ~ **sack** *n* PACKAGING sac à plusieurs épaisseurs *m*

multiply [3] *vt* COMP, DP multiplier; ~ **by** *vt* MATH multiplier par

multiplying: ~ **gear** *n* MECH ENG engrenage multiplicateur *m*; ~ **gearing** *n* MECH ENG engrenage multiplicateur *m*; ~ **glass** *n* INSTRUMENT loupe *f*; ~ **wheel** *n* MECH ENG engrenage multiplicateur *m*

multipoint: ~ **command assign token** *n (MCA)* TELECOM commande multipoint d'assignation de jeton *f*; ~ **command conference** *n (MCC)* TELECOM commande multipoint de conférence *f*; ~ **command negating MCS** *n (MCN)* TELECOM commande multipoint de neutralisation de MCS *f*; ~ **command release token** *n (MCR)* TELECOM commande multipoint de libération de jeton *f*; ~ **command symmetrical data transmission** *n (MCS)* TELECOM commande multipoint de transmission symétrique des données *f*; ~ **command token claim** *n (MCT)* TELECOM commande multipoint de demande de jeton *f*; ~ **command visualization forcing** *n (MCV)* TELECOM commande multipoint d'imposition de visualisation *f*; ~ **gluing machine** *n* PACKAGING machine d'encollage à points multiples *f*; ~ **indication loop** *n (MIL)* TELECOM indication multipoint de boucle *f*; ~ **indication secondary status** *n (MIS)* TELECOM indication multipoint d'état secondaire *f*; ~ **indication secondary status transistor** *n* ELECTRON transistor multipoint d'état secondaire *m*; ~ **indication visualization** *n (MIV)* TELECOM indication multipoint de visualisation *f*; ~ **indication zero communication** *n (MIZ)* TELECOM indication multipoint de non-communication *f*; ~ **link** *n* COMP, DP liaison multipoint *f*; ~ **modem link** *n* PROD ENG liaison à modulateur-démodulateur multipoint *f*; ~ **recorder** *n* INSTRUMENT enregistreur multicourbe *m*

multipolar [1] *adj* ELEC *machine* multipolaire

multipolar: [2] ~ **armature** *n* ELEC *of generator, motor* induit multipolaire *m*

multipole *n* PHYS multipôle *m*; ~ **filter** *n* ELECTRON filtre multipôle *m*

multipolling *n* TELECOM multirelève *f*

multiport *adj* COMP, DP multiport

multiported: ~ **valve** *n* PROD ENG tiroir à orifices multiples *m*

multiposition: ~ **relay** *n* ELEC relais à plusieurs positions *m*; ~ **switch** *n* ELEC ENG commutateur *m*

multiprocessing *n* COMP, DP multitraitement *m*; ~ **system** *n* COMP, DP système de multitraitement *m*

multiprocessor *n* COMP, DP multiprocesseur *m*; ~ **control** *n* CONTROL contrôle par multiprocesseur *m*; ~ **system** *n* TELECOM système multiprocesseur *m*

multiprogramming *n* COMP, DP multiprogrammation *f*; ~ **system** *n* COMP, DP système de multiprogrammation *m*

multipurpose [1] *adj* CONTROL à fonction multiple; ~ **function** *adj* CONTROL à fonction multiple

multipurpose: [2] ~ **carrier** *n* TRANSP cargo polyvalent *m*; ~ **cold store** *n* REFRIG entrepôt frigorifique polyvalent *m*; ~ **helicopter** *n* AERONAUT hélicoptère polyvalent *m*, hélicoptère à missions multiples *m*; ~ **material pipeline** *n* TRANSP système de voie intégrale *m*; ~ **ship** *n* NAUT *merchant navy* cargo polyvalent *m*; ~ **vessel** *n* PETR TECH navire support multitâche *m*

multirange [1] *adj* ELEC à plusieurs gammes

multirange: [2] ~ **meter** *n* ELEC appareil de mesure à calibres multiples *m*, appareil de mesure à plusieurs gammes *m*

multirate: ~ **switching system** *n* TELECOM système de commutation multidébit *m*

multiscreen *n* TV polyécran *m*, écrans multiples *m pl*

multisection: ~ **filter** *n* ELECTRON filtre à plusieurs cellules *m*; ~ **prefilter** *n* ELECTRON préfiltre à plusieurs cellules *m*

multisegment: ~ **magnetron** *n* ELECTRON magnétron à anode à segments multiples *m*

multisensor: ~ **image** *n* SPACE image multicapteur *f*

multiservice-switching: ~ **system** *n* TELECOM autocommutateur multiservice *m*

multiskirt: ~ **system** *n* TRANSP système de sustentation multijupe *m*

multisnack: ~ **bagging** *n* PACKAGING emballage multicasse-croûte *m*

multispiral: ~ **scanning disc** *n* (BrE) TV disque d'analyse à hélices multiples *m*; ~ **scanning disk** *n* (AmE) *see multispiral scanning disc*

multistage: ~ **amplifier** *n* ELECTRON amplificateur à plusieurs étages *m*; ~ **circuit** *n* TELECOM circuit multiétage *m*; ~ **compression** *n* REFRIG compression à plusieurs étages *f*; ~ **compressor** *n* MECH ENG compresseur à plusieurs étages *m*; ~ **network** *n* TELECOM réseau à étages *m*, réseau à étages multiples *m*; ~ **progression tooling** *n* MECH ENG outillage de progression en étapes multiples *m*; ~ **pumping** *n* MINING épuisement en répétitions *m*; ~ **refrigerating plant** *n* REFRIG installation frigorifique étagée *f*; ~ **rocket** *n* SPACE *spacecraft* fusée multiétage *f*

multistandard *adj* TV multistandard

multistock: ~ **headbox** *n* PAPER TECH caisse d'arrivée multijet *f*

multistrand *n* NAUT *rope* multitoron *m*

multistringer *n* MECH ENG multilisse *m*

multitasking *n* COMP, DP exploitation en multitâche *f*, traitement multitâche *m*

multithreading *n* COMP, DP multichaînage *m*, multiprogrammation *f*

multithroat: ~ **vane** *n* AERONAUT aube à cols multiples *f*

multitool: ~ **lathe** *n* MECH ENG tour à outils multiples *m*

multitrack: ~ **recorder** *n* INSTRUMENT enregistreur à pistes multiples *m*; ~ **recording** *n* ACOUSTICS enregistrement multiple *m*; ~ **recording system** *n* RECORDING

système d'enregistrement multipiste *m*

multitube: ~ **heat exchanger** *n* HEAT ENG échangeur multitubulaire *m*; ~ **nozzle** *n* AERONAUT tuyère multilobe *f*, tuyère multitube *f*

multiturn: ~ **encoder** *n* PROD ENG codeur multitours *m*; ~ **potentiometer** *n* ELEC potentiomètre hélicoïdal *m*, ELEC ENG potentiomètre multitour *m*; ~ **valve actuator** *n* MECH ENG servomoteur multitour pour robinetterie *m*

multiunit: ~ **container** *n* PACKAGING récipient à unités multiples *m*; ~ **developing tank** *n* PHOTO cuve à développement multiple *f*; ~ **tank spiral** *n* PHOTO spire multiple *f*

multiuser: ~ **system** *n* COMP, DP système multiutilisateur *m*

multivalence *n* CHEM polyvalence *f*

multivariable: ~ **recorder** *n* INSTRUMENT enregistreur à plusieurs voies *m*

multivat: ~ **board machine** *n* PAPER TECH machine à carton multiforme *f*

multi-V-belt *n* MECH ENG transmission à courroie trapézoïdale multiple *f*

multivibrator *n* ELECTRON, PHYS, TELECOM multivibrateur *m*

multiwall: ~ **corrugated board** *n* PRINT carton ondulé à plusieurs épaisseurs de cannelures *m*; ~ **sack** *n* PACKAGING sac à plusieurs épaisseurs *m*

multiwinding: ~ **transformer** *n* ELEC transformateur à plusieurs enroulements *m*

multiwire *adj* MECH ENG multifilaire

mu-metal *n* PHYS mumétal *m*

municipal: ~ **dump** *n* RECYCLING décharge municipale *f*; ~ **waste** *n* WATER SUPP déchets urbains *m pl*; ~ **water** *n* HYDROL eau de ville *f*, eau municipale *f*

munjistin *n* CHEM munjeestine *f*, munjistine *f*

muon *n* PART PHYS, PHYS muon *m*; ~ **decay track** *n* RAD PHYS voie de désintégration muonique *f*; ~ **magnetic moment** *n* RAD PHYS moment magnétique du muon *m*; ~ **neutrino** *n* PART PHYS neutrino muonique *m*, neutrino *m*, PHYS neutrino muon *m*, neutrino muonique *m*

murchisonite *n* MINERAL murchisonite *f*

murexide *n* CHEM murexide *f*

muriated *adj* CHEM chlorhydraté

Musca *n* ASTRON Mouche *f*

muscarine *n* CHEM muscarine *f*

muscovite *n* MINERAL muscovite *f*

mush: ~ **winding** *n* ELEC *of small alternating current machine* enroulement en vrac *m*, enroulement à fils jetés *m*

mushroom: ~ **anchor** *n* NAUT ancre champignon *f*; ~ **head** *n* PROD ENG *operator* tête coup-de-poing *f*; ~ **head bolt** *n* MECH ENG boulon à tête en goutte-de-suif *m*; ~ **insulator** *n* ELEC ENG isolateur en champignon *m*; ~ **stopper** *n* C&G bouchon casquette *m*; ~ **valve** *n* AUTO soupape-champignon *f*; ~ **ventilator** *n* NAUT *deck fittings* champignon d'aération *m*

music: ~ **power rating** *n* RECORDING données en puissance musicale *f pl*

Music: ~ **and Effects track** *n* *(M and E track)* CINEMAT bande son internationale *f*, piste son internationale *f*

musical: ~ **interval** *n* WAVE PHYS intervalle musical *m*; ~ **scale** *n* ACOUSTICS échelle musicale *f*

music-power-handling: ~ **capacity** *n* RECORDING capacité de puissance musicale soutenue *f*

mussel: ~ **bed** *n* OCEANOG moulière *f*; ~ **breeding** *n* OCEANOG mytiliculture *f*; ~ **culture** *n* OCEANOG mytiliculture *f*

mustard: ~ **gas** *n* CHEM gaz moutarde *m*; ~ **oil** *n* FOOD TECH essence de moutarde *f*, sénévol *m*

mustard-seed: ~ **oil** *n* FOOD TECH huile de moutarde *f*

mutarotation *n* CHEM mutarotation *f*

mute [1] *adj* PRINT muet, silencieux

mute: [2] ~ **film** *n* CINEMAT copie image *f*; ~ **shot** *n* CINEMAT plan muet *m*

muteness *n* ACOUSTICS mutité *f*

mutilated: ~ **gear** *n* MECH ENG engrenage partiellement denté *m*; ~ **wheel** *n* MECH ENG roue dentée en partie *f*

muting *n* PETR atténuation *f*, muting *m*; ~ **device** *n* TELECOM dispositif silencieux *m*

mutual: ~ **coupling** *n* TELECOM couplage mutuel *m*; ~ **impedance** *n* TELECOM impédance mutuelle *f*; ~ **inductance** *n* ELEC inductance mutuelle *f*, ELEC ENG facteur d'induction mutuelle *m*, inductance mutuelle *f*, PHYS inductance mutuelle *f*; ~ **inductance coupling** *n* ELEC ENG couplage par inductance mutuelle *m*; ~ **induction** *n* ELEC, ELEC ENG, PHYS induction mutuelle *f*; ~ **inductor** *n* ELEC bobine de couplage *f*, inducteur auxiliaire *m*; ~ **synchronization** *n* TELECOM synchronisation mutuelle *f*

mux *n* (*multiplexer*) COMP, DP, ELECTRON, TELECOM, TV multiplexeur *m*

muzzle *n* MILIT bouche *f*

mV *abbr* (*millivolt*) ELEC, ELEC ENG mV (*millivolt*)

mW *abbr* (*milliwatt*) ELEC mW (*milliwatt*)

MW [1] *abbr* ELEC (*megawatt*) MW (*mégawatt*), ELEC (*medium wave*), WAVE PHYS (*medium wave*) onde moyenne *f*

MW: [2] ~ **band** *n* NAUT *radio* bande hectométrique *f*

MWD *abbr* (*measurements while drilling*) PETR TECH mesures en cours de forage *f pl*

M-wrap *n* TV enroulement M *m*

Mx *abbr* (*maxwell*) ELEC ENG Mx (*maxwell*)

mycoprotein *n* FOOD TECH mycoprotéine *f*

mycotoxin *n* FOOD TECH *phytopathology* mycotoxine *f*

mylar: ~ **base** *n* TV support mylar *m*

mylonite *n* GEOL mylonite *f*

myocin *n* CHEM myocine *f*

myrcene *n* CHEM myrcène *m*

myria- *pref* METR myria-

myriagram *n* (AmE), **myriagramme** *n* (BrE) METR myriagramme *m*

myristic [1] *adj* CHEM myristique

myristic: [2] ~ **alcohol** *n* DETERGENTS alcool myristique *m*

myristin *n* CHEM myristine *f*

myristyl *adj* CHEM myristyle

myronic *adj* CHEM myronique

myrosin *n* CHEM myrosine *f*

mysorin *n* MINERAL mysorine *f*

mytilotoxine *n* CHEM mytilotoxine *f*

N

n *abbr* (*nano-*) METR n (*nano-*)

N[1] *abbr* (*newton*) ELEC, METR, PHYS N (*newton*)

N[2] (*nitrogen*) CHEM N (*azote*)

n⁺-type: ~ **semiconductor** *n* ELECTRON semi-conducteur de type N fortement dopé *m*, semi-conducteur de type N⁺ *m*

Na (*sodium*) CHEM Na (*sodium*)

NA *abbr* (*numerical aperture*) OPT ouverture numérique *f*

nacelle *n* AERONAUT nacelle *f*; ~ **intake ring** *n* AERONAUT entrée d'air fuseau réacteur *f*

nacreous: ~ **pigment** *n* P&R pigment nacré *m*

nacrite *n* MINERAL nacrite *f*

NAD *abbr* (*noise amplitude distribution*) TELECOM distribution d'amplitude de bruit *f*

nadir *n* ASTRON nadir *m*

nagatelite *n* NUCLEAR nagatélite *f*

nagyagite *n* MINERAL nagyagite *f*

nail[1] *n* CONST clou *m*, pointe *f*, MECH clou *m*, MINING aiguille *f*, épinglette *f*; ~ **claw** *n* CONST pied-de-biche *m*, pied-de-chèvre *m*, pince *f*; ~ **extractor** *n* CONST arrache-clou *m*, tire-clou *m*; ~ **puller** *n* PACKAGING tire-clou *m*; ~ **punch** *n* CONST chasse-clou *m*, chasse-pointe *m*; ~ **set** *n* CONST chasse-clou *m*, chasse-pointe *m*, pousse-pointe *m*

nail[2] *vt* CONST clouer

nailing *n* CONST clouage *m*, clouement *m*, clouure *f*; ~ **machine** *n* PACKAGING machine chasse-clou *f*

nailmaking *n* PROD ENG clouterie *f*

NAK *abbr* (*negative acknowledgement*) COMP, DP accusé de réception négatif *m*

name *n* COMP, DP nom *m*; ~ **plate** *n* ELEC *of appliance* plaque de constructeur *f*, plaque de fabricant *f*, plaque signalétique *f*, MECH plaque de constructeur *f*, MECH ENG plaque d'identification *f*, plaque signalétique *f*, plaquette d'identification *f*; ~ **plate source strength** *n* NUCLEAR débit de la source sur la plaque *m*; ~ **server** *n* TELECOM serveur de noms *m*

names: ~ **of parts** *n pl* PROD ENG dénomination des pièces *f*, nomenclature des pièces *f*

NAND: ~ **circuit** *n* ELECTRON circuit NON-ET *m*; ~ **gate** *n* COMP, DP, ELECTRON, PHYS porte NON-ET *f*; ~ **operation** *n* COMP, DP opération NON-ET *f*

nannofossil *n* GEOL nannofossile *m*

nano- *pref* (*n*) METR nano-(*n*)

nanosecond *n* COMP, DP, METR, PHYS, TV nanoseconde *f*

nantokite *n* MINERAL nantokite *f*

nap[1] *n* TEXTILES poil *m*

nap[2] *vt* TEXTILES gratter

napalm *n* CHEM, MILIT, THERMOD napalm *m*; ~ **bomb** *n* MILIT *chemical warfare* bombe napalm *f*

Naperian: ~ **logarithm** *n* MATH logarithme naturel *m*, logarithme népérien *m*

naphtha *n* CHEM, PETR TECH, THERMOD naphta *m*, naphte *m*

naphthacene *n* CHEM naphtacène *m*

naphthalene *n* CHEM naphtaline *f*, naphtalène *m*, DETERGENTS naphtaline *f*

naphthalenedisulfonic *adj* (AmE), **naphthalenedisulphonic** *adj* (BrE) CHEM naphtalino-disulfoné, naphtaléno-disulfonique

naphthalenic *adj* CHEM naphtalénique

naphthane *n* CHEM décaline *f*

naphthenate *n* CHEM naphténate *m*

naphthene *n* CHEM naphtène *m*

naphthenic *adj* CHEM naphténique

naphthionic *adj* CHEM naphtionique

naphthoic *adj* CHEM naphtoïque

naphthol *n* CHEM naphtol *m* ~ **dyeing** *n* COLOURS teinture au naphtol *f*

naphtholate *n* CHEM naphtolate *m*

naphtholsulfonic *adj* (AmE), **naphtholsulphonic** *adj* (BrE) CHEM naphtol-sulfonique

naphthoquinone *n* CHEM naphtoquinone *f*

naphthoyl *n* CHEM naphtoyle *m*

naphthyl *n* CHEM naphtyle *m*

naphthylamine *n* CHEM naphtylamine *f*

naphthylene *n* CHEM naphtylène *m*

naphthylic *adj* CHEM naphtylique

nappe *n* GEOM *of cone*, HYDR EQUIP, HYDROL nappe *f*

napping *n* TEXTILES grattage *m*

naptha *n* THERMOD kérosène *f*

narangin *n* FOOD TECH narangine *f*

narceine *n* CHEM narcéine *f*

narcotic *adj* CHEM, OCEANOG narcotique

narcotine *n* CHEM narcotine *f*

narghile *n* OCEANOG narguilé *m*

naringenin *n* CHEM naringénine *f*

naringin *n* CHEM naringine *f*

narration: ~ **track** *n* CINEMAT, RECORDING bande commentaire *f*

narrative *n* COMP, DP commentaire *m*

narrow: ~ **angle lens** *n* PHOTO objectif petit angulaire *m*, objectif petit champ *m*; ~ **band amplifier** *n* ELECTRON amplificateur à bande étroite *m*; ~ **band circuit** *n* ELECTRON circuit à bande étroite *m*; ~ **band demodulation** *n* ELECTRON démodulation à bande étroite *f*; ~ **band filter** *n* ELECTRON filtre accordé *m*, filtre à bande étroite *m*, PRINT filtre à bande étroite *m*; ~ **band filtering** *n* ELECTRON filtrage à bande étroite *m*; ~ **band frequency modulation** *n* (*NBFM*) ELECTRON, TELECOM modulation de fréquence à bande étroite *f*; ~ **band interference** *n* ELECTRON parasites à bande étroite *m pl*; ~ **band low-pass filter** *n* ELECTRON filtre passe-bande à bande étroite *m*; ~ **band low-pass filtering** *n* ELECTRON filtrage par filtre passe-bas à bande étroite *m*; ~ **band noise** *n* ELECTRON, TELECOM bruit à bande étroite *m*; ~ **band phase shift keying** *n* (*NBPSK*) TELECOM manipulation par déplacement de phase à bande étroite *f*; ~ **band receiver** *n* TELECOM récepteur à bande étroite *m*; ~ **band rejection filter** *n* ELECTRON filtre coupe-bande à bande étroite *m*; ~ **band response spectrum** *n* NUCLEAR spectre de réponse à bande étroite *m*; ~ **bandsaw hazard** *n* SAFETY risque dû à la scie à ruban étroit *m*; ~ **band signal** *n* ELECTRON, TELECOM signal à bande étroite *m*; ~ **band**

switch *n* TELECOM commutateur à bande étroite *m*; ~ **band switching network** *n* TELECOM réseau de connexion à bande étroite *m*; ~ **band tube** *n* ELECTRON tube à bande étroite *m*; ~ **band voice modulation** *n* *(NBVM)* TELECOM modulation vocale à bande étroite *f*; ~ **belt sanding machine** *n* MECH ENG ponceuse à bande étroite *f*; ~ **bore tube** *n* LAB EQUIP *glassware* tube de faible section *m*; ~ **fabric** *n* TEXTILES ruban *m*; ~ **gage diesel locomotive** *n* (AmE) *see narrow gauge diesel locomotive*; ~ **gage film** *n* (AmE) *see narrow gauge film*; ~ **gage lighting system** *n* (AmE) *see narrow gauge lighting system*; ~ **gage railroad** *n* (AmE) *(see narrow gauge railway)*; ~ **gage track system** *n* (AmE) *see narrow gauge track system*; ~ **gauge diesel locomotive** *n* (BrE) TRANSP locomotive diesel à voie étroite *f*; ~ **gauge film** *n* (BrE) CINEMAT film format réduit *m*; ~ **gauge lighting system** *n* (BrE) AERONAUT *runway* dispositif lumineux à voie étroite *m*; ~ **gauge railway** *n* (BrE) RAIL chemin de fer à voie étroite *m*; ~ **gauge track system** *n* (BrE) TRANSP chemin de fer à voie étroite *m*; ~ **pulse** *n* ELECTRON impulsion étroite *f*; ~ **web** *n* PRINT bande étroite *f*, demi-bande *f*, ruban *m*

narrowcasting *n* TV diffusion pour public ciblé *f*

narrow-neck: ~ **container** *n* C&G verrerie d'emballage à col étroit *f*

narrow-necked: ~ **bottle** *n* LAB EQUIP flacon à col étroit *m*; ~ **flask** *n* LAB EQUIP flacon à col étroit *m*

narrows *n* NAUT *of river* goulet *m*, passe étroite *f*, pertuis *m*, OCEANOG goulet *m*

NASA *abbr (National Aeronautics and Space Administration)* SPACE NASA *(Agence nationale de l'aéronautique et de l'espace)*

nascent: ~ **neutron** *n* NUCLEAR neutron apparaissant au moment de l'émission *m*

national: ~ **code** *n* TELECOM indicatif du pays *m*; ~ **destination code** *n* *(NDC)* TELECOM code national de destination *m*, indicatif national de destination *m*; ~ **grid** *n* NUCLEAR réseau national d'interconnexion *m*; ~ **identification digit** *n* *(NID)* TELECOM chiffre d'identification de nationalité *m*; ~ **navy** *n* NAUT marine de guerre *f*, marine nationale *f*; ~ **number** *n* *(NN)* TELECOM numéro national *m*; ~ **patent** *n* PATENTS brevet national *m*; ~ **significant number** *n* *(NSN)* TELECOM numéro national significatif *m*; ~ **use** *n* *(NU)* TELECOM usage national *m*

National: ~ **Aeronautics and Space Administration** *n* *(NASA)* SPACE Agence nationale de l'aéronautique et de l'espace *f (NASA)*; ~ **Pipe Taper** *n* *(NPT)* MECH ENG filetage NPT *m*; ~ **Television Standards Committee** *n* (AmE) *(NTSC system)* TV American broadcast standard système NTSC *m*

native[1] *adj* MINERAL natif, à l'état natif

native:[2] ~ **mode** *n* COMP, DP mode natif *m*

NATM *abbr (New Austrian Tunnelling Method)* CONST nouvelle méthode autrichienne de percement des tunnels *f*

natrolite *n* MINERAL natrolite *f*

natron *n* CHEM soude carbonatée *f*, MINERAL natron *m*

natronitre *n* C&G nitrate de sodium *m*

natural *n* ACOUSTICS bécarre *m*; ~ **acidification** *n* POLLUTION acidification naturelle *f*; ~ **adhesive** *n* SAFETY colle naturelle *f*; ~ **ageing** *n* (BrE) METALL, P&R *of plastics, coatings* vieillissement naturel *m*, THERMOD *metals* mise en solution *f*, précipitation *f*; ~ **aging** *n* (AmE) *see natural ageing* ~ **air-cooled condenser** *n* REFRIG condenseur à air par convection *m*; ~ **circula-**

tion boiling water reactor *n* NUCLEAR réacteur à eau bouillante à circulation naturelle *m*; ~ **color** *n* (AmE), ~ **colour** *n* (BrE) COLOURS couleur naturelle *f*, TEXTILES coloris naturel *m*; ~ **convection** *n* FLUID PHYS, GAS TECH, HEAT ENG, PHYS convection naturelle *f*; ~ **convection cooling** *n* NUCLEAR refroidissement à convection naturelle *m*, REFRIG refroidissement par convection naturelle *m*; ~ **cooling** *n* THERMOD refroidissement naturel *m*; ~ **draft** *n* (AmE) *see natural draught*; ~ **draft cooling** *n* (AmE) *see natural draught cooling*; ~ **drainage** *n* WATER SUPP déversement naturel *m*; ~ **draught** *n* (BrE) HEATING tirage naturel *m*; ~ **draught cooling** *n* (BrE) THERMOD refroidissement à tirage naturel *m*; ~ **dry gas** *n* GAS TECH gaz sec naturel *m*; ~ **environment** *n* POLLUTION, WATER SUPP milieu naturel *m*; ~ **fiber** *n* (AmE), ~ **fibre** *n* (BrE) TEXTILES fibre naturelle *f*; ~ **frequency** *n* ACOUSTICS, ELEC *of oscillation* fréquence propre *f*, ELECTRON fréquence naturelle *f*, fréquence propre *f*, MECH ENG *of vibration* fréquence naturelle *f*, PETR, PHYS, SPACE, SPRINGS fréquence propre *f*, WAVE PHYS *of vibration* fréquence naturelle *f*; ~ **frequency oscillation** *n* ELECTRON oscillation à la fréquence propre *f*; ~ **gas** *n* GAS TECH, HEAT ENG, PETR TECH, POLLUTION, THERMOD gaz naturel *m*; ~ **gas deposit** *n* GAS TECH gisement naturel de gaz *m*; ~ **gas engine** *n* TRANSP moteur à gaz naturel *m*; ~ **gas liquid** *n* *(NGL)* GAS TECH, PETR TECH liquide de gaz naturel *m (LGN)*; ~ **gas liquids tanker** *n* *(NGL tanker)* PETR TECH méthanier *m*; ~ **groundwater recharge** *n* WATER SUPP réalimentation naturelle d'eau souterraine *f*; ~ **harbor** *n* (AmE), ~ **harbour** *n* (BrE) NAUT port naturel *m*; ~ **harmonics** *n pl* WAVE PHYS harmoniques naturels *m pl*; ~ **language** *n* COMP, DP langage naturel *m*; ~ **light** *n* CINEMAT lumière du jour *f*; ~ **line width** *n* RAD PHYS largeur propre de raie spectrale *f*; ~ **logarithm** *n* MATH logarithme naturel *m*, logarithme népérien *m*; ~ **mode of vibration** *n* ACOUSTICS mode normal de vibration *m*, SPACE mode naturel de vibration *m*, mode normal de vibration *m*; ~ **nuclear reactor** *n* NUCLEAR réacteur nucléaire naturel *m*; ~ **number** *n* DP entier naturel *m*, MATH naturel *m*, nombre naturel *m*; ~ **oscillation** *n* MECH ENG oscillation propre *f*; ~ **period** *n* ELECTRON période propre *f*; ~ **person** *n* PATENTS personne physique *f*; ~ **radioactivity** *n* PHYS, RAD PHYS radioactivité naturelle *f*; ~ **radionuclide** *n* PHYS, RAD PHYS radionucléide naturel *m*; ~ **rubber** *n* P&R caoutchouc naturel *m*; ~ **satellite** *n* ASTRON satellite naturel *m*; ~ **shade** *n* TEXTILES coloris naturel *m*; ~ **sine** *n* GEOM *of an angle* sinus naturel *m*; ~ **uranium fuel** *n* NUCLEAR combustible d'uranium naturel *m*; ~ **uranium slug** *n* NUCLEAR barreau en uranium naturel *m*; ~ **ventilation** *n* NUCLEAR ventilation naturelle *f*; ~ **void** *n* GAS TECH vide naturel *m*; ~ **whole number** *n* GEOM nombre entier naturel *m*; ~ **width** *n* NUCLEAR *of energy level* largeur naturelle *f*

naturally: ~ **acid lake** *n* POLLUTION lac acide naturel *m*

naturally-occurring: ~ **element** *n* NUCLEAR élément naturel *m*

nature-identical *adj* FOOD TECH identique au produit naturel, nature-identique

naumannite *n* MINERAL naumannite *f*

nautical[1] *adj* NAUT marin, nautique

nautical:[2] ~ **almanac** *n* NAUT éphémérides nautiques *f pl*; ~ **celestial globe** *n* OCEANOG navisphère *f*; ~ **mile** *n* METEO mille nautique *m*, NAUT mille marin *m*, OCEANOG mille nautique *m*

naval[1] *adj* NAUT naval

naval:[2] ~ **architect** *n* NAUT architecte naval *m*, ingénieur en construction navale *m*; ~ **architecture** *n* NAUT architecture navale *f*, génie maritime *m*; ~ **base** *n* NAUT base navale *f*; ~ **brass** *n* MECH *materials* laiton qualité marine *m*; ~ **dockyard** *n* NAUT arsenal maritime *m*; ~ **engineer** *n* NAUT mécanicien de la marine *m*; ~ **forces** *n pl* NAUT armée de mer *f*, marine de guerre *f*; ~ **maneuvers zone** *n* (AmE), ~ **manoeuvres zone** *n* (BrE) OCEANOG zone navale d'exercices *f*

Naval: ~ **Air Service** *n* (AmE) *(cf Fleet Air Arm)* NAUT *forces* Aéronavale *f*

Navier-Stokes: ~ **equation** *n* PHYS équation de Navier-Stokes *f*

navigability *n* NAUT navigabilité *f*

navigable[1] *adj* NAUT navigable; **in ~ condition** *adj* NAUT *ship* en état de prendre la mer

navigable:[2] ~ **channel** *n* HYDROL passe *f*; ~ **river** *n* HYDROL rivière franchissable *f*

navigate[1] *vt* NAUT commander, gouverner

navigate[2] *vi* NAUT naviguer

navigating: ~ **bridge** *n* NAUT passerelle de navigation *f*

navigation *n* NAUT, TRANSP navigation *f*, WATER SUPP *waterway* canal de navigation *m*; ~ **afloat** *n* TRANSP navigation sur coque *f*; ~ **by dead reckoning** *n* OCEANOG navigation à l'estime *f*; ~ **by sounding** *n* NAUT navigation à la sonde *f*; ~ **channel** *n* HYDROL, TRANSP chenal de navigation *m*; ~ **light** *n* AERONAUT feu de bord *m*, feu de navigation *m*, feu de position *m*, NAUT feu de navigation *m*, feu de position *m*, feu de route *m*; ~ **lock** *n* HYDROL écluse *f*; ~ **officer** *n* NAUT officier navigateur *m*; ~ **radar** *n* NAUT radar de navigation *m*; ~ **warning signal** *n* TELECOM signal d'avis aux navigateurs *m*; ~ **zone** *n* OCEANOG zone de navigation *f*

navigational[1] *adj* NAUT de navigation

navigational:[2] ~ **instruments** *n pl* NAUT aides à la navigation *f pl*

naviplane *n* TRANSP naviplane *m*

navy *n* NAUT marine *f*, marine de guerre *f*, marine militaire *f*

Nb *(niobium)* CHEM Nb *(niobium)*

NB *abbr (nominal bore)* NUCLEAR *of pipe or tube* diamètre nominal *m*, section nominale de passage *f*

NBFM *abbr (narrow band frequency modulation)* ELECTRON, TELECOM modulation de fréquence à bande étroite *f*

NBPSK *abbr (narrow band phase shift keying)* TELECOM manipulation par déplacement de phase à bande étroite *f*

NBVM *abbr (narrow band voice modulation)* TELECOM modulation vocale à bande étroite *f*

NC[1] *abbr* (numerical control) CONTROL, MECH ENG, PROD ENG CN (commande numérique)

NC:[2] ~ **contact** *n* PROD ENG contact "O" *m*, contact "O" à ouverture *m*; ~ **jig borer** *n* MECH ENG aléseur en coordonnées à commande numérique *m*; ~ **machine** *n* MECH ENG machine à CN *f*; ~ **machine tool** *n* MECH ENG machine à CN *f*

NCC *abbr (network control centre, network control center)* TELECOM centre de gestion *m*, centre de gestion de réseau *m*

n-channel *n* ELECTRON canal N *m*; ~ **device** *n* ELECTRON dispositif à canal N *m*; ~ **discrete FET** *n* ELECTRON TEC discret à canal N *m*; ~ **integrated MOS transistor** *n* ELECTRON transistor MOS canal N intégré *m*, transistor MOS intégré à canal N *m*; ~ **pulldown transistor** *n* ELECTRON transistor d'excursion basse à canal N *m*; ~ **silicon gate MOS process** *n* ELECTRON procédé MOS canal n à grille silicium *m*; ~ **technology** *n* ELECTRON technique du canal N *f*

N-connection *n* TELECOM connexion N *f*

n-core: ~ **cable** *n* ELEC ENG câble à n conducteur *m*

NCR *abbr (network control room)* TV régie de continuité *f*, régie finale *f*

NCS *abbr (network coordination station)* SPACE station de coordination du réseau *f*

Nd *(neodymium)* CHEM Nd *(néodyme)*

NDC *abbr (national destination code)* TELECOM code national de destination *m*, indicatif national de destination *m*

NDF *abbr (new data flag)* TELECOM fanion de nouvelles données *m*, indicateur de nouvelles données *m*

NDM *abbr (normal disconnected mode)* TELECOM mode normal déconnecté *m*

NDN *abbr (nondelivery notification)* TELECOM notification de non-remise *f*

NDR *abbr (normalized drilling rate)* PETR TECH vitesse d'avancement normalisée *f*

NDT *abbr (nondestructive testing)* SPACE essai non destructif *m*

Ne *(neon)* CHEM Ne *(néon)*

NE *abbr (network element)* TELECOM élément de réseau *m*

neap: ~ **tide** *n* *(cf spring tide)* FUELLESS marée de morteeau *f*, HYDROL marée de morte-eau *f*, marée de quadrature *f*, OCEANOG marée de morte-eau *f*

near: ~ **barrier fission** *n* NUCLEAR fission tout près de la barrière *f*; ~ **collision** *n* AERONAUT quasi-abordage *m*, quasi-collision *f*; ~ **critical reactor** *n* NUCLEAR réacteur presque critique *m*; ~ **end crosstalk** *n* ELEC ENG paradiaphonie *f*; ~ **field** *n* TELECOM champ proche *m*; ~ **field analysis** *n* TELECOM analyse du champ proche *f*; ~ **field diffraction pattern** *n* OPT diagramme de diffraction en champ proche *m*, diagramme de rayonnement en champ proche *m*, TELECOM diagramme de diffraction en champ proche *m*; ~ **field intensity** *n* SPACE *communications* intensité en champ proche *f*; ~ **field pattern** *n* TELECOM diagramme de rayonnement en champ proche *m*; ~ **field radiation pattern** *n* TELECOM diagramme de rayonnement en champ proche *m*; ~ **field region** *n* OPT, TELECOM région de champ proche *f*; ~ **field scanning technique** *n* OPT exploration en champ proche *f*, TELECOM exploration du champ proche *f*; ~ **infra red** *n* PHYS *radiation* rayonnement infrarouge proche *m*; ~ **infrared** *n* RAD PHYS infrarouge proche *m*; ~ **letter quality** *n* *(NLQ)* COMP, DP qualité pseudo-courrier *f*; ~ **mesh** *n* COAL TECH grain limite *m*; ~ **miss** *n* AERONAUT, SPACE quasi-abordage *m*, quasi-collision *f*; ~ **parabolic orbit** *n* SPACE orbite quasi-parabolique *f*; ~ **range** *n* SPACE portée proximale *f*; ~ **ultraviolet** *n* PHYS *radiation* rayonnement ultraviolet proche *m*, RAD PHYS ultraviolet proche *m*

nearest: ~ **neighbor** *n* (AmE) *see nearest neighbour*; ~ **neighbor coupling** *n* (AmE) *see nearest neighbour coupling*; ~ **neighbor interaction** *n* (AmE) *see nearest neighbour interaction*; ~ **neighbour** *n* (BrE) CRYSTALL premier voisin *m*; ~ **neighbour coupling** *n* (BrE) NUCLEAR *X-ray crystallography* couplage des voisins les plus proches *m*; ~ **neighbour interaction** *n* (BrE) CRYSTALL interaction de premiers voisins *f*

nearing-up: ~ **pulley** *n* MECH ENG *endless rope haulage* poulie motrice *f*

nearly: **~ perfect crystal** n METALL cristal presque parfait m

nearshore adj GEOL côtier, littoral

neat adj MAR POLL pur

neat's-foot: **~ oil** n FOOD TECH huile de pied de boeuf f

nebula n ASTRON, SPACE nébuleuse f

nebulium n CHEM nébulium m

nebulizer n CHEM nébuliseur m

nebulosity n ASTRON nébulosité f

necessary: **~ assistance and appliances for handling machinery** n MECH ENG aides et engins nécessaires à la manoeuvre des pièces f pl

neck n AUTO goulot de remplissage m, C&G col m, CONST of chisel collet m, ELECTRON of cathode ray tube col m, LAB EQUIP of flask col m, of retort col m, MECH col m, METALL striction f, PAPER TECH gorge f, PROD ENG of metallurgical furnace rampant m, of rolling mill roll collet m, tourillon m; **~ flange** n MECH ENG pipe fitting bride à collet f; **~ mold** n (AmE) see neck mould; **~ molding** n (AmE) see neck moulding; **~ molding plane** n (AmE) see neck moulding plane; **~ mould** n (BrE) CONST congé m; **~ moulding** n (BrE) CONST congé m; **~ moulding plane** n (BrE) CONST congé m; **~ ring** n C&G moule de bague m; **~ ring holder** n C&G porte-moule de bague m; **~ shield** n SAFETY col protecteur m

necking n MECH ENG rétreint m, METALL striction de diamètre f, étranglement m, PHYS, PROP MAT striction f; **~ region** n PROP MAT région de striction f

needle n CONST cale f, faux entrait m, LAB EQUIP pointeau m, pointer aiguille f, MINING blasting, PAPER TECH, RECORDING, TEXTILES, VEHICLES carburettor aiguille f; **~ bar** n TEXTILES barre d'aiguilles f; **~ bearing** n MECH ENG, PRINT roulement à aiguilles m; **~ bed** n TEXTILES fonture f; **~ dam** n WATER SUPP barrage à aiguilles m, barrage à fermettes m; **~ dial** n LAB EQUIP of instrument cadran à aiguille m; **~ drag** n RECORDING résistance d'aiguille f; **~ etching** n C&G guillochage m; **~ file** n MECH ENG lime à aiguille f; **~ follower** n MECH ENG surface texture examination palpeur aiguille m; **~ galvanometer** n ELEC galvanomètre à aiguille mobile m; **~ holder** n RECORDING porte-aiguille m; **~ jet** n VEHICLES carburettor gicleur à aiguille m; **~ lubricator** n PROD ENG godet en verre à tige m, graisseur à tige m, graisseur à épinglette m; **~ noise** n RECORDING bruit d'aiguille m; **~ nose pliers** n pl (AmE) (cf duckbill pliers) MECH ENG tool pince plate à bec-de-canard f; **~ roller bearings** n pl MECH ENG paliers à aiguilles m pl; **~ valve** n AUTO pointeau m, CHEM robinet à pointeau m, vanne à aiguille f, FUELLESS soupape à pointeau f, LAB EQUIP gas control robinet à pointeau m, MECH ENG pointeau m, robinet à pointeau m, valve à pointeau f, NUCLEAR soupape à aiguille f, REFRIG vanne à pointeau f; **~ valve guide** n AUTO guide du pointeau m

needled: **~ felt** n PAPER TECH feutre aiguilleté m

needle-nose: **~ pliers** n MECH ENG pinces à mâchoires pointues f pl

needle-shaped[1] adj METALL aciculaire

needle-shaped:[2] **~ particle** n METALL particule aciculaire f

needling n TEXTILES aiguilletage m; **~ code** n TEXTILES formule d'aiguilletage f; **~ penetration** n TEXTILES pénétration de l'aiguille f, table d'aiguilletage accrue f

needloom: **~ carpet** n TEXTILES tapis aiguilleté m

Néel: **~ point** n PHYS température de Néel f, REFRIG point de Néel m; **~ temperature** n ELEC température de Néel f

NEF abbr (network element function) TELECOM fonction d'élément de réseau f

negation n COMP, DP négation f

negative[1] adj ELEC electrode négatif

negative[2] n ASTRON cliché m, CINEMAT négatif m, PHOTO cliché m, négatif m, épreuve négative f, PHYS photography cliché m, négatif m; **~ acknowledgement** n (NAK) COMP, DP accusé de réception négatif m; **~ air cushion** n TRANSP coussin d'air négatif m; **~ angle** n GEOM angle négatif m; **~ bank** n AUTO série de plaques négatives f; **~ battery** n TELECOM accumulateur négatif m; **~ bias** n ELEC ENG polarisation négative f; **~ booster** n ELEC ENG dévolteur m; **~ carrier** n PHOTO passe-film m, porte-négatif m; **~ charge** n ELEC electrostatics, ELEC ENG, PHYS charge négative f; **~ cold chamber** n REFRIG armoire réfrigérée négative f; **~ conductance** n ELEC semiconductor conductance négative f; **~ conductor** n ELEC ENG conducteur négatif m; **~ copying process** n PRINT procédé de copie négative m; **~ curvature** n GEOM courbure négative f; **~ cutter** n CINEMAT monteur de négatif m; **~ cutting** n CINEMAT montage du négatif m; **~ echo** n TV image fantôme négative f; **~ electrode** n ELEC, ELEC ENG électrode négative f; **~ feedback** n ELECTRON contre-réaction f, réaction négative f, RECORDING réaction négative f, WAVE PHYS contre-réaction f; **~ feeder** n ELEC supply artère de retour f, feeder de retour m; **~ flux image reactor** n NUCLEAR réacteur négatif m; **~ Gauss curvature** n GEOM courbure de Gauss négative f; **~ glow** n PHYS lumière négative f; **~ grounded terminal** n AUTO borne négative à la masse f; **~ image** n PHOTO image négative f; **~ impedance** n ELEC ENG impédance négative f; **~ impedance converter** n ELEC ENG convertisseur d'impédance négative m; **~ integer** n MATH entier négatif m; **~ ion** n ELEC charged particle, PART PHYS ion négatif m, PHYS anion m, ion négatif m; **~ lens** n INSTRUMENT lentille concave f, lentille divergente f, lentille à bord épais f; **~ lens surface** n INSTRUMENT verre négatif m; **~ logic** n ELECTRON logique négative f; **~ magnetostriction** n ELEC ENG magnétostriction négative f; **~ meniscus lens** n INSTRUMENT lentille ménisque divergent f; **~ meson** n PART PHYS méson négatif m; **~ modulation** n ELECTRON modulation négative f; **~ notification** n (NN) TELECOM notification négative f; **~ number** n CINEMAT numéro de bord m; **~ perforation** n CINEMAT perforation arrondie f, perforation négative f; **~ photoresist** n ELECTRON photorésist négatif m, résist optique négatif m; **~ picture phase** n TV polarité négative du signal image f; **~ plate** n AUTO, PRINT plaque négative f; **~ pole** n ELEC terminal, ELEC ENG pôle négatif m; **~ power supply** n ELEC ENG alimentation négative f; **~ pressure** n MECH ENG dépression f; **~ pressure signs** n pl SAFETY plaques estampées à vide f pl; **~ print** n PHOTO copie négative f; **~ rake** n MECH ENG coupe négative f, of cutting tool angle négatif de dépouille m; **~ reactance** n ELEC ENG réactance négative f; **~ reactivity** n NUCLEAR antiréactivité f; **~ reactor** n NUCLEAR réacteur négatif m; **~ resist** n ELECTRON résist négatif m; **~ resistance** n ELEC, ELEC ENG résistance négative f; **~ resistance amplifier** n ELECTRON amplificateur à résistance négative m; **~ resistance diode** n ELECTRON diode à résistance négative f; **~ resistance oscillator** n ELECTRON, PHYS oscillateur à résistance négative m; **~ scanning** n TV analyse d'image négative f; **~ skin friction** n COAL TECH frottement latéral négatif m; **~ sleeve** n PHOTO pochette pour négatif *f*; ~ **terminal** *n* AUTO, ELEC, ELEC ENG, VEHICLES *electrical system* borne négative *f*; ~ **track** *n* CINEMAT négatif son *m*; ~ **video signal** *n* TV polarité négative du signal image *f*; ~ **viewer** *n* PHOTO négatoscope *m*; ~ **voltage** *n* ELEC ENG tension négative *f*; ~ **voltage supply** *n* ELEC ENG alimentation en tension négative *f*; ~ **working plate** *n* PRINT plaque négative *f*

negatively:[1] ~ **skewed** *adj* GEOM de travers à gauche

negatively:[2] ~ **doped region** *n* PHYS région dopée négativement *f*

negator *n* COMP complémenteur *m*, DP complémenteur *m*, inverseur *m*

negatron *n* ELECTRON, PART PHYS négaton *m*

negotiate: ~ **a curve** *vi* RAIL *vehicles* franchir une courbe, s'inscrire en courbe

nematic: ~ **liquid crystals** *n pl* ELECTRON cristaux liquides nématiques *m pl*; ~ **phase** *n* CRYSTALL phase nématique *f*

N-entity *n* TELECOM entité N *f*

neoabietic *adj* CHEM néoabiétique

neoclassical: ~ **pinch effect** *n* NUCLEAR effet de striction néoclassique *m*

neodymium *n (Nd)* CHEM néodyme *m (Nd)*; ~ **laser** *n* ELECTRON laser au néodyme *m*

neoergosterol *n* CHEM néoergostérol *m*

neon *n (Ne)* CHEM néon *m (Ne)*; ~ **fluorescent tube** *n* RAD PHYS tube fluorescent au néon *m*; ~ **glow lamp** *n* ELEC indicateur au néon *m*, témoin au néon *m*; ~ **indicator** *n* ELEC ENG indicateur au néon *m*; ~ **lamp** *n* ELEC ENG lampe au néon *f*; ~ **tube** *n* ELEC *lighting*, ELEC ENG, PHYS tube au néon *m*

neo-pilot: ~ **tone** *n* RECORDING tonalité pilote *f*

neoprene *n* CHEM, CONST néoprène *m*, P&R néoprène *m*, polychloroprène *m*, PACKAGING néoprène *m*; ~ **molded seal** *n* (AmE), ~ **moulded seal** *n* (BrE) P&R *synthetic rubber* joint moulé en néoprène *m*

neotectonic *adj* GEOL néotectonique

neovolcanic *adj* GEOL néovolcanique

NEP *abbr (noise equivalent power)* OPT, TELECOM PEB *(puissance équivalente de bruit)*

neper *n* ACOUSTICS, ELECTRON, PHYS néper *m*

nepheline *n* MINERAL néphéline *f*; ~ **syenite** *n* C&G néphéline syénite *f*

nephelinite *n* PETR néphélinite *f*

nephelinyte *n* PETR néphélinite *f*

nephelite *n* MINERAL néphéline *f*

nephelometer *n* LAB EQUIP *for analysis of turbidity* néphélomètre *m*

nephelometry *n* CHEM néphélémétrie *f*

nephrite *n* MINERAL néphrite *f*

neptunium *n (Np)* CHEM neptunium *m (Np)*

neritic: ~ **water** *n* OCEANOG eau néritique *f*; ~ **zone** *n* GEOL zone néritique *f*

Nernst: ~ **bridge** *n* ELEC ENG pont de Nernst *m*

nerol *n* CHEM nérol *m*

nerve *n* P&R *of rubber* nerf *m*

nest[1] *n* MECH ENG *of gear wheels* équipage *m*, *of springs* faisceau *m*, MINING *of ore* nid *m*, PRINT imposition des formes *f*, positionnement des formes *f*

nest[2] *vt* COMP, DP emboîter

nested[1] *adj* COMP emboîté, DP emboîté, imbriqué, MATH emboîté

nested:[2] ~ **intervals** *n pl* MATH famille de segments emboîtés *f*, suite de segments emboîtés *f*; ~ **loop** *n* DP boucle emboîtée *f*

nesting *n* COMP emboîtement *m*, DP emboîtement *m*, imbrication *f*; ~ **box** *n* PACKAGING boîte pour emboîtement *f*; ~ **magazine** *n* PACKAGING magasin d'emboîtement *m*

net *n* NAUT, OCEANOG filet *m*, PETR TECH *tonnage* jauge nette *f*; ~ **area** *n* FUELLESS *of collector* aire nette *f*; ~ **breeding rate** *n* NUCLEAR rapport de surrégénération *m*; ~ **calorific value** *n* HEAT ENG pouvoir calorifique inférieur *m*; ~ **charge** *n* ELEC ENG charge résultante *f*; ~ **control station** *n* ELEC poste de commande du réseau *m*; ~ **depth** *n* OCEANOG chute d'un filet *f*; ~ **donator** *n* POLLUTION exportateur net *m*; ~ **drum** *n* OCEANOG tambour *m*; ~ **frame** *n* OCEANOG monture *f*; ~ **heat loss** *n* HEAT ENG perte de chaleur nette *f*; ~ **income** *n* PETR TECH revenu net *m*; ~ **making** *n* OCEANOG filetage *m*; ~ **mender** *n* OCEANOG ramendeur *m*; ~ **mending** *n* OCEANOG ramendage *m*; ~ **mouth** *n* OCEANOG gueule *f*; ~ **output** *n* GEOPHYS production nette *f*, rayonnement nocturne *m*; ~ **pay zone** *n* PETR zone productive effective *f*; ~ **positive suction head** *n* NUCLEAR *of pump* hauteur d'alimentation requise *f*; ~ **receiver** *n* POLLUTION importateur net *m*; ~ **refrigeration effect** *n* REFRIG puissance frigorifique nette *f*; ~ **register** *n* NAUT jauge nette *f*; ~ **repairer** *n* OCEANOG ramendeur *m*; ~ **roller** *n* OCEANOG tambour *m*; ~ **sling** *n* NAUT *for loading cargo* filet de chargement *m*; ~ **time interval** *n* TRANSP intervalle de temps net entre véhicules *m*; ~ **ton** *n* METR tonne courte *f*; ~ **tonnage** *n* NAUT tonnage net *m*, PETR TECH jauge nette *f*; ~ **weight** *n* TEXTILES poids net *m*; ~ **wing area** *n* AERONAUT surface nette de l'aile *f*

netsonde *n* OCEANOG sondeur de filet *m*

netting *n* CONST grillage *m*, treillage *m*, treillis *m*, OCEANOG alèze *f*, nappe *f*; ~ **frame** *n* OCEANOG métier à filet *m*; ~ **needle** *n* OCEANOG aiguille à filet *f*, navette *f*

network *n* COMP réseau *m*, CONST grillage *m*, réseau *m*, treillage *m*, treillis *m*, DP, ELEC *supply* réseau *m*, ELEC ENG *of circuit elements, telecommunications, stations* réseau *m*, *transmitters, television* chaîne *f*, ELECTR quadripôle *m*, P&R réseau *m*, PHYS *electronic circuit* réseau *m*, PROD ENG lacis *m*, réseau *m*, *system of cross-lines* lacis *m*, réseau *m*, SPACE *communications*, TRANSP réseau *m*, TV chaîne *f*, réseau *m*; ~ **access control** *n* COMP, DP contrôle d'accès au réseau *m*; ~ **analysis** *n* ELEC *supply*, ELEC ENG analyse des réseaux *f*; ~ **analyzer** *n* COMP, DP, ELEC *supply*, ELEC ENG, TELECOM analyseur de réseaux *m*; ~ **architecture** *n* COMP, DP architecture de réseau *f*; ~ **breakdown** *n* TELECOM panne de réseau *f*; ~ **broadcast repeater station** *n* TV émetteur relais *m*; ~ **cable** *n* TELECOM câble de réseau *m*; ~ **card** *n* COMP carte réseau *f*; ~ **constant** *n* ELEC ENG constante du réseau *f*; ~ **control center** *n* (AmE), ~ **control centre** *n* (BrE) *(NCC)* TELECOM centre de gestion *m*, centre de gestion de réseau *m*; ~ **control channel** *n* COMP, DP voie de contrôle de réseau *f*; ~ **controller** *n* COMP, DP contrôleur de réseau *m*; ~ **control room** *n (NCR)* TV régie de continuité *f*, régie finale *f*; ~ **coordination station** *n (NCS)* SPACE *communications* station de coordination du réseau *f*; ~ **coverage** *n* TV couverture d'un réseau *f*; ~ **cue** *n* TV indicatif de décrochage *m*, top de réseau *m*; ~ **database** *n* COMP, DP base de données en réseau *f*; ~ **delay** *n* COMP, DP délai de réseau *m*; ~ **discard indicator** *n* TELECOM indicateur de rejet par le réseau *m*; ~ **element** *n (NE)* TELECOM élément de réseau *m*; ~ **element function** *n (NEF)* TELECOM fonction d'élément de réseau *f*; ~ **former** *n* C&G formateur de réseau *m*; ~ **gateway** *n* TELECOM passerelle de réseau *f*; ~ **identifica-**

tion *n* TV indicatif réseau *m*; ~ **interconnection** *n* COMP, DP interconnexion de réseaux *f*; ~ **interface card** *n* COMP, DP carte d'interface réseau *f*; ~ **layer** *n* COMP, DP couche de réseau *f*; ~ **layer relay** *n (NLR)* TELECOM relais de couche réseau *m*; ~ **load analysis** *n* COMP, DP étude de la charge de réseau *f*; ~ **management** *n* COMP, DP gestion de réseaux *f*; ~ **management application service element** *n (NM-ASE)* TELECOM élément de service d'application pour la gestion de réseau *m*; ~ **management center** *n* (AmE), ~ **management centre** *n* (BrE) *(NMC)* TELECOM centre de gestion de réseau *m*; ~ **manager** *n* COMP, DP administrateur de réseau *m*; ~ **map** *n* TELECOM *exchange data store* image de réseau *f*; ~ **model** *n* COMP, DP modèle de réseau *m*; ~ **modifier** *n* C&G modificateur de réseau *m*; ~ **node interface** *n (NNI)* TELECOM interface de noeuds de réseau *f*; ~ **operating system** *n (NOS)* COMP système d'exploitation de réseau *m*; ~ **operators maintenance channel** *n (NOMC)* TELECOM canal de maintenance des exploitants de réseau *m*; ~ **parameters** *n pl* PHYS constantes de réseau *f pl*; ~ **performance** *n (NP)* TELECOM performance du réseau *f*; ~ **protection** *n* ELEC *supply* protection de réseau *f*; ~ **protocol data unit** *n (NPDU)* TELECOM unité de données du protocole de réseau *f*; ~ **regulator** *n* CONTROL régulateur de réseau *m*; ~ **service** *n (NS)* TELECOM service de réseau *m*; ~ **service access point** *n (NSAP)* TELECOM point d'accès au service de réseau *m*; ~ **simulator** *n* COMP, DP simulateur de réseau *m*; ~ **software** *n* COMP logiciel de réseau *m*; ~ **specialist** *n* COMP expert en réseaux informatiques *m*; ~ **spur** *n* ELEC ENG extrémité du réseau *f*; ~ **station** *n* COMP, DP station de réseau *f*; ~ **supervision and management** *n* TELECOM surveillance et gestion des réseaux *f*; ~ **supervisor** *n* TELECOM superviseur *m*; ~ **synthesis** *n* ELEC, ELEC ENG synthèse des réseaux *f*; ~ **terminal equipment** *n (NTE)* TELECOM équipement terminal de réseau *m*; ~ **termination** *n (NT)* TELECOM terminaison de réseau *f*; ~ **theory** *n* ELEC ENG théorie des réseaux *f*; ~ **topology** *n* COMP, DP topologie de réseau *f*; ~ **virtual terminal** *n (NVT)* COMP, DP terminal virtuel de réseau *m*

networked *adj* TELECOM communicant, communiquant, coopérant, en réseau

networking *n* COMP, DP connexion en réseau *f*

network-like *adj* AERONAUT réticulaire

neural: ~ **network** *n* COMP, DP réseau neuronal *m*

neuraminic *adj* CHEM neuraminique

neurodine *n* CHEM neurodine *f*

neuron *n* COMP, DP neurone *m*

neutral[1] *adj* CHEM indifférent, neutre, ELEC, PHYS neutre

neutral[2] *n* MECH, VEHICLES *gearbox* point mort *m*; ~ **amber glass** *n* C&G verre neutre brun type I *m*; ~ **armature** *n* ELEC *relay* relais indifférent *m*; ~ **atom** *n* PART PHYS atome neutre *m*; ~ **atom beam injection** *n* NUCLEAR injection de faisceau d'atomes neutres *f*; ~ **axis** *n* CONST *design*, SPRINGS axe neutre *m*; ~ **burnout** *n* NUCLEAR épuisement des neutres *m*; ~ **compensator** *n* ELEC ENG transformateur d'amortissement *m*; ~ **conductor** *n* ELEC ENG *multiple-wire distributing system* conducteur neutre *m*, fil neutre *m*; ~ **current** *n* PHYS courant neutre *m*; ~ **density** *n* PRINT densité neutre *f*; ~ **density filter** *n* CINEMAT filtre gris neutre *m*, écran gris neutre *m*, PHOTO filtre neutre *m*, écran gris neutre *m*; ~ **flame** *n* CONST *welding* flamme normale *f*; ~ **gas** *n* SPACE gaz neutre *m*; ~ **glass** *n* C&G verre neutre *m*; ~ **gray** *n* (AmE), ~ **grey** *n* (BrE) PRINT gris neutre *m*; ~ **particle** *n* PHYS particule neutre *f*; ~ **particle detector**

n NUCLEAR détecteur de particules neutres *m*; ~ **point** *n* PHYS point neutre *m*; ~ **point displacement voltage** *n* ELEC *supply network* tension de déplacement du point neutre *f*; ~ **polar relay** *n* ELEC ENG relais non polarisé *m*; ~ **relay** *n* ELEC relais non polarisé *m*, ELEC ENG relais à position neutre *m*; ~ **section** *n* RAIL *contact line* section neutre *f*; ~ **shade** *n* TEXTILES coloris neutre *m*; ~ **state** *n* PART PHYS neutralité *f*, état neutre *m*; ~ **sulfite** *n* (AmE) *see neutral sulphite*; ~ **sulfite pulp** *n see neutral sulphite pulp*; ~ **sulphite** *n* (BrE) PAPER TECH sulfite neutre *m*; ~ **sulphite pulp** *n* (BrE) PAPER TECH pâte au sulfite neutre *f*; ~ **terminal** *n* ELEC *connection* borne neutre *f*; ~ **test card** *n* CINEMAT gamme de gris *f*; ~ **tint** *n* COLOURS teinte neutre *f*; ~ **tinted glass** *n* C&G verre gris *m*; ~ **transmission** *n* DP transmission à signal unipolaire *f*; ~ **wedge** *n* CINEMAT coin gris neutre *m*; ~ **white glass** *n* C&G verre neutre blanc type I *m*; ~ **wire** *n* ELEC *circuit* fil neutre *m*; ~ **zone** *n* ELEC ENG plage neutre *f*

neutrality *n* CHEM neutralité *f*

neutralization *n* CHEM neutralisation *f*, tamponnage *m*, tamponnement *m*, COAL TECH, DETERGENTS, ELEC *of charge*, ELEC ENG, HYDROL *of detergents*, P&R *chemistry* neutralisation *f*; ~ **pond** *n* NUCLEAR bassin de neutralisation *m*

neutralized: ~ **amplifier** *n* ELECTRON amplificateur neutrodyné *m*

neutralizer *n* CHEM neutralisant *m*, SPACE neutraliseur *m*

neutralizing[1] *adj* CHEM neutralisant

neutralizing[2] *n* CHEM neutralisation *f*; ~ **agent** *n* SAFETY agent neutralisant *m*

neutrino *n* PART PHYS, PHYS neutrino *m*

neutron *n* ELEC *neutral particle*, PART PHYS, PETR, PHYS, RAD PHYS neutron *m*; ~ **absorber** *n* NUCLEAR absorbant de neutrons *m*; ~ **activation logging** *n* NUCLEAR diagraphie à activation neutronique *f*; ~ **beam** *n* PART PHYS faisceau de neutrons *m*; ~ **burst** *n* NUCLEAR bouffée de neutrons *f*, salve de neutrons *f*; ~ **capture** *n* PHYS capture des neutrons *f*; ~ **converter doughnut** *n* NUCLEAR *slow to fast* convertisseur de neutrons *m*; ~ **counter tube** *n* NUCLEAR tube compteur de neutrons *m*; ~ **diffraction** *n* CRYSTALL diffraction de neutrons *f*; ~ **excess** *n* PHYS *isotopic number* excès de neutrons *m*; ~ **log** *n* FUELLESS rapport neutronique *m*, PETR diagramme neutron *m*, PETR TECH diagraphie neutron *f*; ~ **logging** *n* GAS TECH diagraphie neutron *f*, PETR TECH diagraphie de neutron *f*; ~ **mass** *n* RAD PHYS masse du neutron *f*; ~ **number** *n* PHYS nombre de neutrons *m*; ~ **radiative capture** *n* RAD PHYS capture radiative du neutron *f*; ~ **scattering** *n* PART PHYS diffusion des neutrons *f*; ~ **source reactor** *n* NUCLEAR réacteur source *m*; ~ **star** *n* ASTRON étoile de neutrons *f*; ~ **thermalization** *n* RAD PHYS thermalisation des neutrons *f*; ~ **yield** *n* PART PHYS rendement des neutrons *m*, taux de neutrons *m*, PHYS *per fission or v-factor* facteur nu *m*, nombre de neutrons produits par fission *m*, *per absorption* facteur êta *m*, nombre de neutrons produits par neutron absorbé *m*

neutron-absorbing: ~ **reaction** *n* NUCLEAR réaction absorbante de neutrons *f*

neutron-gamma: ~ **log** *n* PETR TECH *prospecting* diagraphie neutron-gamma *f*

neutron-neutron: ~ **log** *n* PETR TECH diagraphie neutron-neutron *f*

never: ~ **exceed Mach number** *n* AERONAUT Mach à ne jamais dépasser *m*

nevyanskite *n* MINERAL névianskite *f*

new[1] *adj* CHEM *silver* nouveau

new:[2] ~ **data flag** *n (NDF)* TELECOM fanion de nouvelles données *m*, indicateur de nouvelles données *m*; ~ **element storage drum** *n* NUCLEAR barillet de stockage *m*; ~ **fuel** *n* NUCLEAR combustible neuf *m*, combustible non irradié *m*; ~ **fuel element** *n* NUCLEAR élément combustible neuf *m*; ~ **moon** *n* ASTRON nouvelle lune *f*; ~ **plant** *n* POLLUTION centrale construite après 1975 *f*; ~ **products** *n* MECH ENG produits nouveaux *m pl*

New: ~ **Austrian Tunnelling Method** *n (NATM)* CONST nouvelle méthode autrichienne de percement des tunnels *f*

newel *n* CONST *at top of stairs* pilastre *m*, *of winding stair* noyau *m*, MECH ENG *of Archimedean screw*, PROD ENG *core* noyau *m*; ~ **post** *n* CONST pilastre *m*

news: ~ **network** *n* TV chaîne d'informations *f*, réseau de télécommunication *m*

newscast *n* TV journal télévisé *m*

newshole *n* PRINT colonne réservée aux dernières nouvelles *f*

newspaper: ~ **rotary press** *n* PRINT rotative de presse *f*, rotative à journal *f*

newsprint *n* PAPER TECH, PRINT papier journal *m*

newsreel: ~ **camera** *n* CINEMAT caméra sonore *f*; ~ **cameraman** *n* CINEMAT opérateur d'actualités *m*

newsroom *n* TV salle de rédaction *f*

newton *n (N)* ELEC, METR, PHYS newton *m (N)*

Newton's: ~ **law of cooling** *n* PHYS loi de Newton de refroidissement *f*; ~ **laws of motion** *n pl* ASTRON lois de Newton des mouvements des planètes *f pl*; ~ **rings** *n pl* CINEMAT, PHOTO, PHYS anneaux de Newton *m pl*

Newtonian[1] *adj* ASTRON, PHYS newtonien

Newtonian:[2] ~ **aberration** *n* PHYS aberration de réfraction *f*; ~ **mechanics** *n pl* ASTRON, PHYS mécanique de Newton *f*, mécanique newtonienne *f*; ~ **telescope** *n* ASTRON, PHYS télescope de Newton *m*

next: ~ **nearest neighbors** *n* (AmE), ~ **nearest neighbours** *n* (BrE) METALL seconds voisins *m pl*

N-facility *n* TELECOM facilité N *f*

NGL[1] *abbr (natural gas liquid)* GAS TECH, PETR TECH LGN *(liquide de gaz naturel)*

NGL:[2] ~ **tanker** *n (natural gas liquids tanker)* PETR TECH méthanier *m*

Ni *(nickel)* CHEM Ni *(nickel)*

niacinamide *n* CHEM acide nicotinique *m*, nicotinamide *f*

nialamide *n* CHEM nialamide *m*

nibble *n* COMP, DP quartet *m*

nibbler *n* MECH ENG *tool* cisailles grignotantes *f pl*

nibbling: ~ **machine** *n* (AmE) *(cf power nibbler)* MECH ENG *tool* grignoteuse *f*

Nicad: ~ **battery** *n* PHOTO accumulateur à plaques de nickel et de cadmium *m*

niccolite *n* MINERAL anicolite *f*, niccolite *f*

niccolum *n* CHEM nickel *m*

nick[1] *n* PROD ENG *in screw head* fente *f*, *notch* encoche *f*, entaille *f*, saignée *f*

nick[2] *vt* PROD ENG encocher, entailler

nicked: ~ **tooth milling cutter** *n* MECH ENG fraise à denture interrompue *f*, fraise à denture recoupée *f*

nickel *n (Ni)* CHEM nickel *m (Ni)*; ~ **arsenide** *n* CHEM arséniure de nickel *m*; ~ **bloom** *n* MINERAL annabergite *f*; ~ **cadmium** *n* PROP MAT nickel-cadmium *m*; ~ **cadmium battery** *n* CINEMAT accumulateur au cadmium nickel *m*, ELEC ENG batterie cadmium-nickel *f*, SPACE *craft* batterie d'accumulateurs au nickel-cadmium *f*, TRANSP accumulateur nickel-cadmium *m*; ~ **hydro-**

xide *n* SPACE hydroxyde de nickel *m*; ~ **iron battery** *n* ELEC ENG batterie fer-nickel *f*, SPACE *craft* batterie d'accumulateurs au nickel-fer *f*; ~ **iron storage battery** *n* TRANSP accumulateur nickel-fer *m*; ~ **ocher** *n* (AmE), ~ **ochre** *n* (BrE) MINERAL annabergite *f*; ~ **plating** *n* ELEC *process*, PROD ENG, PROP MAT nickelage *m*; ~ **silver** *n* ELEC ENG maillechort *m*; ~ **zinc storage battery** *n* TRANSP accumulateur nickel-zinc *m*

nickelage *n* PROD ENG nickelage *m*

nickelic *adj* CHEM nickélique

nickeline *n* MINERAL niccolite *f*

nickeling *n* (AmE), **nickelling** *n* (BrE) PROD ENG nickelage *m*

nickelocene *n* CHEM nickelocène *m*

nickelous *adj* CHEM nickéleux

nickel-plate *vt* COATINGS revêtir d'étain-nickel

nickelure *n* PROD ENG nickelure *f*

nicker *n* MECH ENG *of centre bit* traçoir *m*

nicking *n* PROD ENG encochement *m*, entaillage *m*, fendage *m* ~ **machine** *n* COAL TECH rouilleuse *f*

nickpoint *n* (AmE) *see knickpoint*

Nicol: ~ **prism** *n* PHYS nicol *m*, prisme de Nicol *m*

nicopyrite *n* MINERAL pentlandite *f*

nicotine *n* CHEM nicotine *f*

nicotinic *adj* CHEM nicotinique

nicotyrine *n* CHEM nicotyrine *f*

NID *abbr (national identification digit)* TELECOM chiffre d'identification de nationalité *m*

nigger *n* CINEMAT drapeau *m*, nègre *m*, volet *m*, écran opaque *m*

niggles *n* OCEANOG puces *f pl*

night: ~ **effect** *n* CINEMAT effet de nuit *m*; ~ **flight** *n* AERONAUT vol de nuit *m*; ~ **for day** *n* CINEMAT nuit américaine *f*; ~ **range** *n* AERONAUT portée nocturne *f*; ~ **service** *n* TELECOM service de nuit *m*, service hors vacation *m*, service simplifié *m*; ~**sight** *n* MILIT mire pour usage nocturne *f*; ~ **soil** *n* HYDROL matières de vidange *f pl*, RECYCLING fumier humain *m*; ~ **tariff** *n* ELEC *supply* tarif de nuit *m*; ~ **telescope** *n* INSTRUMENT lunette de nuit *f*; ~ **vision goggles** *n* MILIT lunettes de nuit *f pl*; ~ **watch** *n* MILIT *naval duty* quart de nuit *m*; ~ **wave** *n* AERONAUT onde de nuit *f*, onde nocturne *f*; ~ **work** *n* SAFETY travail de nuit *m*

nightglow *n* ASTRON lueur nocturne *f*

nill *n* PROD ENG *forge scale* battitures *f pl*, martelures *f pl*, paille de fer *f*, scories de forge *f pl*, écailles *f pl*

nimbostratus *n (Ns)* METEO nimbo-stratus *m (Ns)*

nine: ~ **digit counter** *n* PACKAGING compteur à neuf chiffres *m*

nine's: ~ **complement** *n* COMP, DP complément à neuf *m*

niobite *n* CHEM, MINERAL niobite *f*

niobium *n (Nb)* CHEM niobium *m (Nb)*

nip *n* MINING *vein, lode* resserrement *m*, serrement *m*, serrée *f*, étranglement *m*, étranglement de terre *m*, étreinte *f*, OCEANOG microfalaise *f*, PAPER TECH zone de contact entre deux rouleaux *f*, PRINT ligne de contact entre deux rouleaux *f*, ligne de tangence *f*, SPRINGS bande *f*; ~ **and tuck folder** *n* PRINT plieuse à lames prenantes et engageantes *f*; ~ **pressure** *n* PAPER TECH *of machine, rollers* pression linéaire *f*, PRINT pression de la ligne de tangence entre les rouleaux *f*

nippers *n pl* PROD ENG pinces *f pl*, pinces de serrage *f pl*, tenailles *f pl*

nipping: ~ **roller** *n* PRINT rouleau pinceur *m*

nipple *n* CONST *plumbing* mamelon *m*, MECH ENG embout de tuyauterie *m*, gland *m*, *plumbing* mamelon *m*, PA-

PER TECH manchon fileté *m*

nit *n* METR nit *m*

niter *n* (AmE) *see* nitre

niter-blued: ~ steel *n* (AmE) *see nitre-blued steel*

nitramine *n* CHEM nitramine *f*

nitrate[1] *n* CHEM azotate *m*, nitrate *m*, POLLUTION nitrate *m* ~ base *n* CINEMAT support de nitrate *m*, support flam *m*, PHOTO support de nitrate *m*; ~ film *n* CINEMAT pellicule nitrate *f*; ~ paper *n* PAPER TECH papier antiasthmatique *m*

nitrate[2] *vt* CHEM nitrer, traiter à l'acide nitrique

nitrate-based: ~ explosive *n* MINING explosif nitraté *m*

nitrated *adj* CHEM nitré

nitratine *n* CHEM matronite *f*, nitratine *f*, MINERAL nitratite *f*

nitration *n* CHEM nitratage *m*, nitration *f*

nitratite *n* MINERAL nitratite *f*

nitrazine *n* CHEM nitrazine *f*

nitre *n* (BrE) CHEM nitre *m*, salpêtre *m*

nitre-blued: ~ steel *n* (BrE) MECH ENG acier bleu en bain de salpêtre *m*

nitric[1] *adj* CHEM azotique, nitrique

nitric:[2] ~ acid *n* CHEM acide azotique *m*, acide nitrique *m*, POLLUTION acide nitrique *m*; ~ oxide *n* POLLUTION monoxyde d'azote *m*, oxyde azotique *m*, oxyde nitrique *m*

nitridation *n* CHEM, PROP MAT nitruration *f*

nitride[1] *n* CHEM nitrure *m*; ~ hardening *n* PROD ENG nitruration *f*

nitride[2] *vt* CHEM nitrurer

nitrided: ~ steel *n* PROD ENG acier nitruré *m*

nitride-fueled: ~ reactor *n* (AmE), nitride-fuelled reactor *n* (BrE) NUCLEAR réacteur à combustible nitrure *m*

nitriding *n* CHEM, MECH ENG, PROP MAT nitruration *f*

nitrification *n* CHEM, HYDROL nitrification *f*

nitrify[1] *vt* CHEM nitrifier

nitrify[2] *vi* CHEM se nitrifier

nitrifying *adj* CHEM nitrifiant

nitrile *n* CHEM nitrile *m*; ~ rubber *n* P&R *synthetic* caoutchouc nitrile *m*; ~ seal *n* PROD ENG joint de protection au nitrile *m*

nitrin *n* CHEM nitrine *f*

nitrite *n* CHEM nitrite *m*

nitritoid *adj* CHEM nitritoïde

nitroamine *n* CHEM nitramine *f*

nitroaniline *n* CHEM nitraniline *f*

nitrobenzene *n* CHEM nitrobenzène *m*

nitrocellulose *n* CHEM nitrocellulose *f*; ~ lacquer *n* COLOURS laque cellulosique *f*, CONST laque nitrocellulosique *f*

nitrocellulosic *adj* CHEM nitrocellulosique

nitrochloroform *n* CHEM chloropicrine *f*, nitrochloroforme *m*

nitro-compound *n* CHEM composé nitré *m*

nitrocotton: ~ explosive *n* MINING explosif au coton nitré *m*, explosif à base de coton nitré *m*

nitroethane *n* CHEM nitro-éthane *m*, nitréthane *m*

nitroform *n* CHEM nitroforme *m*

nitrogelatine *n* MINING gélatine-dynamite *f*

nitrogen *n* (*N*) CHEM azote *m* (*N*); ~ cover gas *n* NUCLEAR couverture d'azote *f*, matelas d'azote *m*; ~ dioxide *n* CHEM bioxyde d'azote *m*, POLLUTION, SAFETY *workplace air* dioxyde d'azote *m*; ~ gas *n* CHEM gaz azote *m*; ~ narcosis *n* OCEANOG narcose à l'azote *f*; ~ oxide *n* POLLUTION oxyde d'azote *m*; ~ pentoxide *n* POLLUTION anhydride nitrique *m*, anhydrite d'azote *f*,

pentoxyde de diazote *m*; ~ peroxide *n* POLLUTION peroxyde d'azote *m*; ~ purging *n* SPACE *of tank on spacecraft* remplissage à l'azote *m*

nitrogen-cooled: ~ reactor *n* NUCLEAR réacteur refroidi par azote *m*

nitrogenous *adj* CHEM azoté

nitroglucose *n* CHEM nitroglucose *f*

nitroglycerine *n* CHEM, MILIT, MINING nitroglycérine *f*

nitroindole *n* CHEM nitroindole *m*

nitromannite *n* CHEM nitromannitol *m*

nitrometer *n* CHEM nitromètre *m*

nitromethane *n* CHEM nitrométhane *m*

nitron *n* CHEM nitron *m*

nitronaphthalene *n* CHEM nitronaphtaline *f*

nitronium *n* CHEM nitronium *m*

nitroparaffin *n* CHEM nitroparaffine *f*

nitrophenol *n* CHEM nitrophénol *m*

nitrosate *n* CHEM nitrosate *m*

nitrosation *n* CHEM nitrosation *f*

nitrosifying *adj* CHEM nitrifiant

nitrosite *n* CHEM nitrosite *f*

nitrosochloride *n* CHEM nitrosochlorure *m*

nitrosubstituted *adj* CHEM nitrosubstitué

nitrosulfuric *adj* (AmE), nitrosulphuric *adj* (BrE) CHEM nitrosulfurique

nitrosyl *n* CHEM nitrosyle *m*

nitrotartaric *adj* CHEM nitrotartarique

nitrotoluene *n* CHEM nitrotoluène *m*

nitrous[1] *adj* CHEM azoteux, nitreux

nitrous:[2] ~ oxide *n* CHEM oxyde nitreux *m*, POLLUTION anhydride hypo-azoteux *m*, hémioxyde d'azote *m*, monoxyde de diazote *m*, oxyde azoteux *m*, oxyde nitreux *m*

nitrox *n* OCEANOG nitrox *m*

nitroxyl *n* CHEM nitryle *m*

nitryl *n* CHEM nitryle *m*

nivation *n* CHEM nivation *f*

nivenite *n* NUCLEAR nivénite *f*

Nixie: ~ tube *n* ELECTRON tube Nixie *m*

N-layer *n* TELECOM couche N *f*

NLQ *abbr (near letter quality)* COMP, DP qualité pseudo-courrier *f*

NLR *abbr (network layer relay)* TELECOM relais de couche réseau *m*

NM-ASE *abbr (network management application service element)* TELECOM élément de service d'application pour la gestion de réseau *m*

NMC *abbr (network management center, network management centre)* TELECOM centre de gestion de réseau *m*

NML *abbr (nuclear magnetic logging)* PETR diagraphie de résonance magnétique nucléaire *m*

NMOS: ~ chip *n* ELECTRON puce NMOS *f*; ~ component *n* ELECTRON composant NMOS *m*; ~ integrated circuit *n* ELECTRON circuit intégré NMOS *m*; ~ logic *n* ELECTRON logique NMOS *f*; ~ transistor *n* ELECTRON transistor NMOS *m*

NMR[1] *abbr (nuclear magnetic resonance)* CHEM, PETR TECH, PHYS, RAD PHYS RMN *(résonance magnétique nucléaire)*

NMR:[2] ~ log *n (nuclear magnetic resonance log)* PETR TECH diagraphie RMN *f*

NN *abbr* TELECOM *(negative notification)* notification négative *f*, TELECOM *(national number)* numéro national *m*

NNE *abbr (non-SDH network element)* TELECOM élément de réseau non SDH *m*

NNI *abbr (network node interface)* TELECOM interface de noeuds de réseau *f*

No *(nobelium)* CHEM No *(nobélium)*

NO: ~ **contact** *n* PROD ENG contact "F" *m*, contact "F" à fermeture *m*; ~ **early make contact** *n* PROD ENG contact "F" à fermeture avancée *m*; ~ **late break contact** *n* PROD ENG contact "O" à ouverture retardée *m*

nobelium *n (No)* CHEM nobélium *m (No)*

noble[1] *adj* CHEM *gas* rare, *metal, gas* noble

noble:[2] ~ **metal** *n* METALL, POLLUTION métal noble *m*

no-break: ~ **power supply** *n* SPACE alimentation sans coupure *f*

noctilucent[1] *adj* ASTRON nocturne lumineux

noctilucent:[2] ~ **cloud** *n* METEO nuage nocturne lumineux *m*, nuage phosphorescent *m*

nocturnal[1] *adj* ASTRON nocturne

nocturnal:[2] ~ **phase** *n* SPACE phase nocturne *f*

nodal: ~ **current** *n* ELEC courant de noeud *m*; ~ **expansion method** *n* NUCLEAR méthode de développement nodal *f*; ~ **head** *n* CINEMAT tête nodale *f*; ~ **line** *n* ACOUSTICS ligne nodale *f*, RECORDING ligne *f*; ~ **plane** *n* PHOTO, PHYS plan nodal *m*; ~ **points** *n pl* PHYS points nodaux *m pl*; ~ **voltage** *n* ELEC *of circuit* tension de noeud *f*

node *n* ACOUSTICS noeud *m*, surface nodale *f*, ASTRON, COMP, CRYSTALL, DP, ELEC *of circuit*, ELEC ENG noeud *m*, ELECTRON point logique *m*, GEOM, METALL, PHYS, TELECOM, WAVE PHYS noeud *m*; ~ **processor** *n* COMP processeur nodal *m*, DP processeur de noeud *m*

nodular: ~ **corrosion** *n* NUCLEAR *fuel element failure* corrosion noduleuse *f*; ~ **limestone** *n* GEOL calcaire noduleux *m*; ~ **marl** *n* GEOL *flinty* marne à rognons *f*

nodule *n* C&G *nodulated blowing wool*, CHEM, COAL TECH nodule *m*, GEOL concrétion *f*, nodule *m*

no-fines: ~ **concrete** *n* CONST béton poreux *m*

nog: ~ **plate** *n* C&G ferrasse *f*; ~ **plate with chevron runner bars** *n* C&G ferrasse à chevrons *f*; ~ **plate with spiral runner bars** *n* C&G ferrasse à aubes *f*

noggin *n* (BrE) CONST *stud partition horizontal member* entretoise *f*

nogging *n* (AmE) *see noggin*

no-go: ~ **gage** *n* (AmE), ~ **gauge** *n* (BrE) *(cf go gauge)* MECH ENG calibre passe pas *m*, jauge passe pas *f*, tampon passe pas *m*

noise *n* ACOUSTICS, COMP, DP, ELECTRON, PHYS, RECORDING *system* , SAFETY, TELECOM bruit *m*, TV brouillage *m*, neige *f*, parasites *m pl*, WAVE PHYS bruit *m*, *radio* parasites *m pl*; ~ **abatement** *n* PRINT atténuation du bruit *f*, SAFETY lutte antibruit *f*; ~ **abatement door** *n* SAFETY *sheet steel* porte de protection contre les bruits *f*; ~ **absorption device** *n* MECH ENG dispositif d'absorption du bruit *m*; ~ **amplitude distribution** *n (NAD)* TELECOM distribution d'amplitude de bruit *f*; ~ **analysis** *n* PETR analyse de bruit *f*, tir de bruit *m*; ~ **and vibration measuring equipment** *n* SAFETY appareils de mesure du bruit et des vibrations *m pl*; ~ **and vibration protection** *n* SAFETY *mechanical engineering* protection contre le bruit et les secousses *f*; ~ **barrier** *n* CONST barrière antibruit *f*, protection antibruit *f*; ~ **bund** *n* CONST digue anti-bruit *f*; ~ **control** *n* SAFETY *acoustics* contrôle du niveau de bruit *m*; ~ **diode** *n* ELECTRON diode à bruit *f*; ~ **dose** *n* SAFETY dose sonore *f*; ~ **emission value** *n* MECH ENG *of machinery* valeurs d'émission acoustique *f pl*; ~ **equivalent power** *n (NEP)* OPT *of photodetector*, TELECOM puissance équivalente de bruit *f (PEB)*; ~ **factor** *n* ELECTRON, PHYS facteur

de bruit *m*, PRINT facteur bruit *m*, facteur de bruit *m*, SPACE facteur de bruit *m*; ~ **field** *n* TELECOM champ de bruit *m*, TV champ perturbateur *m*; ~ **figure** *n* ELECTRON facteur de bruit *m*; ~ **filter** *n* RECORDING filtre de bruit *m*; ~ **floor** *n* RECORDING seuil de bruit *m*; ~ **generator** *n* ELECTRON, TELECOM générateur de bruit *m*; ~ **immunity** *n* COMP, DP immunité aux bruits *f*; ~ **labeling** *n* (AmE), ~ **labelling** *n* (BrE) MECH ENG *acoustics of machinery* repérage du bruit des machines *m*; ~ **level** *n* PRINT niveau sonore *m*, RECORDING niveau de bruit *m*, SAFETY niveau sonore *m*, TELECOM, WAVE PHYS niveau de bruit *m*; ~ **limiter** *n* RECORDING limiteur de bruit *m*; ~ **masking** *n* TELECOM masquage par le bruit *m*; ~ **modulation** *n* RECORDING modulation en bruit *f*, TV modulation par signal de bruit *f*; ~ **nuisance** *n* ACOUSTICS nuisance d'un bruit *f*; ~ **pollution** *n* POLLUTION nuisances acoustiques *f pl*, SAFETY nuisances sonores *f pl*; ~ **power** *n* ELECTRON, NUCLEAR *of reactor* puissance de bruit *f*; ~ **protection** *n* SAFETY insonorisation *f*; ~ **protection booth** *n* SAFETY cabine insonorisante *f*; ~ **protective capsule** *n* SAFETY capsule pour la protection de l'ouïe *f*; ~ **protective hood** *n* SAFETY capot insonorisant *m*; ~ **protective insulating glass** *n* SAFETY verre isolant insonorisant *m*; ~ **protective plug** *n* SAFETY bouchon pour la protection de l'ouïe *m*; ~ **reducer** *n* RECORDING, TELECOM réducteur de bruit *m*; ~ **reduction** *n* PRINT réduction du niveau sonore *f*, RECORDING réduction de bruit *f*, SAFETY *for oscillating conveyors* revêtement antibruit *m*; ~ **reduction slit** *n* RECORDING fente de réduction de bruit *f*; ~ **shield** *n* RECORDING protection contre le bruit *f*; ~ **signal** *n* TV signal de bruit *m*; ~ **source** *n* ELECTRON, POLLUTION source de bruit *f*; ~ **suppression** *n* ELEC ENG suppression des bruits *f*; ~ **suppressor** *n* RECORDING suppresseur de bruit *m*; ~ **temperature** *n* ELEC ENG, SPACE *communications* température de bruit *f*; ~ **voltage** *n* ELEC ENG tension de bruit *f*

noise-abating: ~ **foam panel** *n* SAFETY panneau antibruit en mousse *m*; ~ **wall** *n pl* SAFETY mur antibruit *m*, paroi antibruit *f*

noise-induced: ~ **hearing impairment** *n* SAFETY dommage auditif induit par le bruit *m*

noise-insulating: ~ **equipment** *n* SAFETY matériel de protection contre le bruit *m*

noiseless[1] *adj* PROP MAT, SAFETY silencieux

noiseless:[2] ~ **recording system** *n* RECORDING procédé d'enregistrement "noiseless" *m*; ~ **running** *n* AUTO *of engine* fonctionnement silencieux *m*, marche silencieuse *f*

noiseless-timing: ~ **chain** *n* AUTO chaîne de distribution silencieuse *f*

noisemeter *n* PRINT décibelomètre *m*

noisy: ~ **blacks** *n pl* TV noir perturbé *m*

no-knock: ~ **mixture** *n* AUTO indétonant *m*

no-load[1] *adj* AERONAUT à vide

no-load:[2] ~ **characteristic** *n* AERONAUT caractéristique à vide *f*; ~ **current** *n* ELEC courant à vide *m*; ~ **direct voltage** *n* ELEC tension continue à vide *f*; ~ **force** *n* NUCLEAR *of manipulator* force à vide *f*; ~ **heat consumption** *n* C&G consommation du four à vide *f*; ~ **loss** *n* ELEC pertes à vide *f pl*; ~ **operation** *n* AERONAUT marche à vide *f*, ELEC ENG fonctionnement à vide *m*; ~ **start** *n* ELEC *of motor* démarrage à vide *m*; ~ **test** *n* ELEC essai à vide *m*

NOMC *abbr (network operators maintenance channel)* TELECOM canal de maintenance des exploitants de réseau *m*

nomenclature *n* ASTRON, CHEM, COMP, GEOL, PHYS, PROD ENG nomenclature *f*

nominal: ~ **bore** *n* (*NB*) NUCLEAR *of pipe or tube* diamètre nominal *m*, section nominale de passage *f*; ~ **capacitance** *n* PROD ENG plage de capacité *f*; ~ **capacity** *n* C&G capacité nominale *f*; ~ **concentration** *n* PROP MAT concentration nominale *f*; ~ **content** *n* PACKAGING contenu nominal *m*, PRINT contenu nominal *m*, teneur nominale *f*; ~ **diameter** *n* MECH ENG diamètre nominal *m*; ~ **freezing time** *n* REFRIG temps nominal de congélation *m*; ~ **gust velocity** *n* AERONAUT vitesse nominale de rafale *f*; ~ **operating conditions** *n pl* SPACE *of spacecraft* fonctionnement nominal *m*; ~ **size** *n* MECH ENG cote nominale *f*, PACKAGING dimension nominale *f*; ~ **stress** *n* METALL contrainte nominale *f*; ~ **thickness** *n* QUALITY, TESTING épaisseur nominale *f*; ~ **thrust** *n* SPACE *in vacuum, of spacecraft* poussée nominale *f*; ~ **value** *n* ELEC valeur assignée *f*; ~ **voltage** *n* ELEC *of system* tension nominale d'un système *f*

no-mixing: ~ **cascade** *n* NUCLEAR cascade sans mélange *f*

nomograph *n* PHYS abaque *m*

nonabsorbable *adj* CHEM irrésorbable

nonacceptance *n* QUALITY rebut *m*, refus *m*, rejet *m*

nonacidic: ~ **lake** *n* POLLUTION lac non acide *m*, lac non acidifié *m*

nonacosane *n* CHEM nonacosane *m*

nonamphibious: ~ **hovercraft** *n* TRANSP aéroglisseur non amphibie *m*

nonane *n* CHEM nonane *m*

nonapproved *adj* TELECOM *apparatus* non agréé

nonaqueous[1] *adj* CHEM non aqueux

nonaqueous:[2] ~ **electrolyte battery** *n* TRANSP accumulateur à électrolyte non aqueux *m*

nonarcing *adj* ELEC ENG antiarc

nonassociated: ~ **gas** *n* PETR TECH *exploration* gaz non associé *m*

nonautomatic: ~ **loom** *n* TEXTILES métier non automatique *m*

nonbinary: ~ **code** *n* TELECOM code non binaire *m*

nonbituminous: ~ **coal** *n* COAL TECH charbon maigre *m*

nonblocking: ~ **concentrator** *n* ELEC ENG condensateur sans blocage *m*; ~ **network** *n* ELEC ENG réseau de connexion sans blocage *m*, TELECOM réseau non bloquant *m*; ~ **switch** *n* ELEC ENG commutateur sans blocage *m*

nonbonding: ~ **electron** *n* NUCLEAR électron non-liant *m*

nonboosted: ~ **antenna repeater system** *n* TELECOM système à antennes-relais sans amplification *m*

nonbridging: ~ **contact** *n* ELEC ENG contact sans chevauchement *m*, contact sans court-circuit *m*

nonbroadcast: ~ **rights** *n pl* TV droits d'utilisation hors antenne *m pl*

noncaking[1] *adj* COAL TECH non-collant

noncaking:[2] ~ **coal** *n* COAL TECH charbon non-collant *m*

noncapacitive *adj* ELEC *load* anticapacitif, ELEC ENG *load* non capacitif

noncarbonate: ~ **hardness** *n* HYDROL dureté non carbonatée *f*

noncircularity *n* TELECOM *of cladding, core* non-circularité *f*

noncoherent: ~ **swept tone modulation** *n* TELECOM modulation à balayage de tonalité sans cohérence *f*

noncohesive: ~ **soil** *n* COAL TECH sol pulvérulent *m*

noncoking *adj* COAL TECH non cokéfiant

noncombustibility: ~ **test** *n* SAFETY essai de non-combustibilité *m*

noncompensated: ~ **motor** *n* ELEC ENG moteur incompensé *m*

nonconcentrator: ~ **solar cell** *n* ELEC ENG cellule solaire sans concentrateur *f*

noncondensed: ~ **discharge** *n* ELEC ENG décharge non condensée *f*

nonconductor *n* ELEC *insulator* non-conducteur *m*, PROP MAT non-conducteur *m*, *of heat* calorifuge *m*

nonconfirmed: ~ **service** *n* TELECOM service non confirmé *m*, service sans confirmation *m*

nonconflicting: ~ **traffic flows** *n pl* TRANSP courants de circulation non conflictuels *m pl*

nonconformance *n* PROD ENG non-conformité *f*

nonconformities: ~ **per hundred items** *n pl* QUALITY non-conformités pour cent individus *f pl*, non-conformités pour cent unités *f pl*; ~ **per item** *n pl* QUALITY non-conformités par individu *f pl*, non-conformités par unité *f pl*

nonconformity *n* GEOL discordance *f*, QUALITY non-conformité *f*

nonconjugated *adj* CHEM *bond, compound* non conjugué

nonconservation: ~ **of parity** *n* PHYS non-conservation de la parité *f*, violation de la parité *f*

nonconsumable: ~ **electrode** *n* CONST *welding* électrode réfractaire *f*

noncontact: ~ **suspension** *n* TRANSP suspension sans contact *f*

noncorrodible *adj* PROP MAT inoxydable

noncorrosive *adj* PROP MAT non corrosif

noncrystalline *adj* GEOL non cristallin

noncutting: ~ **return** *n* MECH ENG *of machine tool* retour à blanc *m*, retour à vide *m*; ~ **stroke** *n* MECH ENG *of machine tool* course à blanc *f*, course à vide *f*

nondairy[1] *adj* FOOD TECH non lacté

nondairy:[2] ~ **creamer** *n* FOOD TECH succédané de lait *m*

nondedicated: ~ **signalling channel** *n* TELECOM voie de signalisation non spécialisée *f*

nondegradable *adj* RECYCLING non biodégradable

nondelivery: ~ **notification** *n* (*NDN*) TELECOM notification de non-remise *f*

nondepositional: ~ **gap** *n* GEOL lacune de sédimentation *f*

nondestructive: ~ **materials testing** *n* NUCLEAR contrôle non destructif des matériaux *m*; ~ **read** *n* COMP, DP lecture non destructive *f*; ~ **test** *n* MECH ENG, PHYS essai non destructif *m*; ~ **testing** *n* (*NDT*) SPACE *of spacecraft* essai non destructif *m*; ~ **testing system** *n* MECH ENG système d'essai non destructif *m*; ~ **ultrasonic testing** *n* MECH ENG détection par la méthode ultrasonique *f*

nondimensional: ~ **diameter** *n* FUELLESS diamètre sans dimension *m*

nondispersive: ~ **medium** *n* PHYS milieu non dispersif *m*

nondroppable: ~ **blocks** *n pl* TELECOM blocs non supprimables *m pl*

nonelution *adj* CHEM *chromatography* sans élution

nonencapsulated: ~ **winding dry-type reactor** *n* ELEC bobine d'inductance de type sec à enroulement non encapsulé *f*; ~ **winding dry-type transformer** *n* ELEC transformateur de type sec à enroulement non encapsulés *m*

nonequilibrium: ~ **mode distribution** *n* OPT, TELECOM répartition des modes hors équilibre *f*

nonequivalence: ~ **operation** *n* COMP opération OU

exclusif *f*, DP disjonction *f*, opération OU exclusif *f*

nonerasable: **~ data disc** *n* (BrE) OPT disque optique numérique non effaçable *m*; **~ data disk** *n* (AmE) *see nonerasable data disc* **~ storage** *n* COMP mémoire ineffaçable *f*

non-Euclidean: **~ geometry** *n* GEOM géométrie non euclidienne *f*

nonexpansion: **~ engine** *n* MECH ENG machine sans détente *f*, moteur sans détente *m*

nonexplosive *adj* PROP MAT inexplosible

nonfading: **~ color** *n* (AmE), **~ colour** *n* (BrE) COLOURS couleur résistante *f*, couleur solide à la lumière *f*

nonfat *adj* FOOD TECH dégraissé, non gras, sans gras, sans matière grasse

nonferrous *adj* CHEM non ferreux

nonfiery *adj* MINING non grisouteux

non-flam: **~ film** *n* CINEMAT pellicule non flam *f*

nonflammability *n* PROP MAT incombustibilité *f*, TESTING ininflammabilité *f*

nonflammable[1] *adj* CHEM, SAFETY ininflammable

nonflammable:[2] **~ liquid extinguisher** *n* SAFETY extincteur à liquide dit "ignifuge" *m*

nonfood: **~ packaging** *n* PACKAGING emballage non alimentaire *m*; **~ product** *n* PACKAGING produit non alimentaire *m*

nonfreeze: **~ liquid** *n* REFRIG liquide incongelable *m*

nonfrost-susceptible: **~ soil** *n* COAL TECH sol passif au gel *m*

non-Gaussian: **~ noise** *n* TELECOM bruit non gaussien *m*

nonhalation *n* PRINT antihalo *m*

nonhierarchical: **~ system** *n* TELECOM système à structure démocratique *m*

nonimpact: **~ printer** *n* COMP imprimante sans impact *f*

noninductive[1] *adj* ELEC *load* anti-inductif

noninductive:[2] **~ circuit** *n* ELEC circuit non inductif *m*; **~ load** *n* ELEC *alternating current* charge non inductive *f*; **~ resistor** *n* CONST résistance bobinée non inductive *f*, ELEC résistance non inductive *f*

noninflammable *adj* PACKAGING non inflammable

noninstrument: **~ runway** *n* AERONAUT piste à vue *f*

noninverting: **~ input** *n* CONST entrée non inverseuse *f*

nonionic *adj* DETERGENTS non ionique

nonionizing: **~ radiation** *n* RAD PHYS radiation non ionisante *f*

noniron[1] *adj* TEXTILES repassage superflu

noniron:[2] **~ finish** *n* COATINGS apprêt éliminant le repassage *m*

nonisotropic: **~ materials** *n pl* MECH ENG matériaux non isotropes *m pl*

nonkinking: **~ rope** *n* NAUT cordage qui ne fait pas de coque *m*

nonlamellar: **~ pearlite** *n* METALL perlite non lamellaire *f*

nonlinear[1] *adj* ELEC non linéaire

nonlinear:[2] **~ amplification** *n* TELECOM amplification non linéaire *f*; **~ amplifier** *n* ELECTRON amplificateur non linéaire *m*; **~ circuit** *n* TELECOM circuit non linéaire *m*; **~ condition** *n* CONST régime non linéaire *m*; **~ digital speech** *n* TELECOM signaux vocaux numériques non linéaires *m pl*; **~ distortion** *n* ELECTRON, RECORDING, TELECOM distorsion non linéaire *f*; **~ element** *n* CONST élément non linéaire *m*; **~ filtering** *n* TELECOM filtrage non linéaire *m*; **~ interpolation** *n* TELECOM interpolation non linéaire *f*; **~ network** *n* CONST réseau non linéaire *m*; **~ oscillation** *n* TELECOM oscillation non linéaire *f*; **~ potentiometer** *n* CONST potentiomètre non linéaire *m*; **~ programming** *n* COMP, DP programma-

tion non linéaire *f*; **~ resistance** *n* TELECOM résistance non linéaire *f*; **~ resistor** *n* ELEC résistance non linéaire *f*; **~ scale** *n* CONST, METR échelle non linéaire *f*; **~ scattering** *n* OPT, TELECOM diffusion non linéaire *f*; **~ Stark effect** *n* PHYS effet Stark non linéaire *m*

nonlocalized: **~ fringes** *n pl* PHYS franges non localisées *f pl*

nonlocking *adj* COMP *character* sans maintien, DP sans verrouillage

nonmagnetic *adj* CHEM amagnétique, ELEC amagnétique, antimagnétique, PHYS *steel* non magnétique, PROP MAT amagnétique, non magnétique

nonmandatory *adj* TELECOM facultatif

nonmechanical: **~ hazards** *n pl* SAFETY *dust, electrical accidents, etc* dangers non mécaniques *m pl*

nonmeridian: **~ ray** *n* OPT rayon non méridien *m*

nonmetal *n* CHEM non-métal *m*

nonmetalized: **~ parabolic mirror** *n* (AmE) *see nonmetallized parabolic mirror*

nonmetallic: **~ coating** *n* COATINGS revêtement non métallique *m*; **~ inclusion** *n* METALL, QUALITY inclusion non métallique *f*

nonmetallized: **~ parabolic mirror** *n* (BrE) ASTRON miroir parabolique non aluminé *m*

nonmigratory: **~ plasticizer** *n* P&R *plastics, coatings* plastifiant non migratoire *m*

nonoccluded: **~ front** *n* METEO front non occlus *m*

nononic *adj* CHEM nononic

nonoperating *adj* PROD ENG au repos

nonose *n* CHEM nonose *f*

nonoxidizing *adj* CHEM inoxydant

nonplastic *adj* CONST non plastique

non-plug-in: **~ position switch** *n* PROD ENG interrupteur de position non embrochable *m*; **~ switch** *n* PROD ENG interrupteur non embrochable *m*

nonpolar[1] *adj* CHEM *bond, molecule* non polaire

nonpolar:[2] **~ dielectric** *n* PHYS diélectrique non polaire *m*; **~ solvent** *n* P&R solvant non polaire *m*

nonpolarized: **~ electrolytic capacitor** *n* CONST condensateur électrolytique non polarisé *m*; **~ plug** *n* ELEC *connection* prise de courant irréversible *f*; **~ relay** *n* CONST relais non polarisé *m*, ELEC relais indifférent *m*, relais non polarisé *m*

nonporous *adj* GAS TECH non poreux

nonpressure: **~ pipeline** *n* MECH ENG canalisation sans pression *f*

nonpressurized: **~ refiner** *n* PAPER TECH raffineur atmosphérique *m*; **~ section** *n* AERONAUT *fuselage* partie non étanche *f*

nonprocedural: **~ language** *n* COMP langage non algorithmique *m*

nonreactive[1] *adj* CHEM non réactif, sans réaction

nonreactive:[2] **~ load** *n* ELEC *alternating current* charge non inductive *f*

nonreciprocal: **~ circuit** *n* TELECOM circuit non réciproque *m*; **~ wave guide** *n* TELECOM guide d'ondes non réciproque *m*

nonrecurrent: **~ pulse** *n* ELECTRON impulsion isolée *f*, impulsion non récurrente *f*

nonrecursive: **~ filter** *n* TELECOM filtre non récursif *m*; **~ pulse** *n* ELECTRON filtre non récursif *m*

nonreflecting: **~ glass** *n* C&G verre antiréfléchissant *m*

nonrefractory: **~ material** *n* PHYS matière non réfractaire *f*

nonregenerative: **~ repeater** *n* ELECTRON répéteur analogique *m*, répéteur non régénérateur *m*

nonrelativist *adj* ASTRON non relativiste

nonrenewable: ~ **fuse** *n* ELEC fusible non renouvable *m*

nonrepeatable: ~ **measurement** *n* METR mesurage non répétable *m*

nonreproductible *adj* PACKAGING non reproductible

nonreserved: ~ **space** *n* TRANSP *in traffic lanes* site banal *m*

nonresonant: ~ **line** *n* ELECTRON ligne non résonnante *f*

nonrestricted: ~ **valve** *n* CONST robinet à passage intégral *m*

nonretentive: ~ **latch** *n* PROD ENG verrouillage sans mémoire *m*; ~ **output** *n* PROD ENG sortie non mémorisée *f*; ~ **timer** *n* PROD ENG temporisateur sans mémoire *m*

nonreturn:[1] ~ **to zero** *adj (NRZ)* TELECOM non-retour à zéro; ~ **to zero inverted** *adj (NRZI)* TELECOM non-retour à zéro inversé

nonreturn:[2] ~ **modulation** *n* TELECOM modulation sans retour *f*; ~ **to zero recording** *n* COMP, DP enregistrement sans retour à zéro *m*; ~ **valve** *n* CONST clapet de retenue *m*, vanne antiretour *f*, FUELLESS clapet de non-retour *m*, HYDR EQUIP clapet antiretour *m*, clapet de retenue *m*, MECH ENG soupape de retenue *f*, PROD ENG clapet de non-retour *m*

nonreturnable[1] *adj* FOOD TECH *packaging* perdu

nonreturnable:[2] ~ **bottle** *n* PACKAGING verre perdu *m*; ~ **pallet** *n* PACKAGING palette perdue *f*

nonreusable[1] *adj* COMP, DP non-réutilisable

nonreusable:[2] ~ **pallet** *n* PACKAGING palette perdue *f*

nonreversible[1] *adj* CHEM irréversible

nonreversible:[2] ~ **motor** *n* ELEC moteur non réversible *m*; ~ **plug** *n* ELEC *connection* prise de courant irréversible *f*

nonrotating: ~ **black hole** *n* ASTRON trou noir sans rotation *m*; ~ **star** *n* AERONAUT *helicopter* plateau cyclique fixe *m*

nonrust: ~ **paper** *n* PAPER TECH papier non oxydant *m*

nonsalient: ~ **pole** *n* ELEC pôle lisse *m*

nonsaturated: ~ **logic** *n* ELECTRON logique non saturée *f*

nonsaturation *n* CHEM insaturation *f*

non-SDH: ~ **network element** *n (NNE)* TELECOM élément de réseau non SDH *m*

non-self-sustained: ~ **discharge** *n* CONST décharge non autonome *f*

nonsequence *n* GEOL lacune de sédimentation *f*

nonshorting: ~ **switch** *n* CONST commutateur à contacts sans court-circuit *m*

nonshrink[1] *adj* PAPER TECH irrétrécissable

nonshrink:[2] ~ **treatment** *n* TEXTILES traitement irrétrécissable *m*

nonsimple: ~ **closed curve** *n* GEOM courbe fermée non simple *f*

nonskid: ~ **coating** *n* COATINGS couche antidérapante *f*

nonslip[1] *adj* NAUT *deck surface* antidérapant

nonslip:[2] ~ **deck paint** *n* NAUT *boat building* peinture antidérapante *f*; ~ **differential** *n* AUTO différentiel à blocage automatique *m*; ~ **sole** *n* SAFETY semelle antidérapante *f*

non-soapy: ~ **detergent** *n* DETERGENTS détergent synthétique *m*

nonspill: ~ **battery** *n* (BrE) *(cf sealed battery)* VEHICLES *electrical system* accumulateur inversible *m*

nonstaining *adj* P&R non tachant

nonstandard: ~ **control track** *n* TV piste pilote hors norme *f*; ~ **diamond crossing** *n* RAIL traversée combinée *f*

nonstick *adj* PAPER TECH antiadhérent

nonstoichiometric *adj* CHEM *proportions*, PROP MAT *proportions* non stoechiométrique

nonstop: ~ **flight** *n* AERONAUT vol sans escale *m*; ~ **rapid transit system** *n* TRANSP transport urbain continu *m*; ~ **urban transportation** *n* TRANSP transport urbain continu *m*

nonswiveling *adj* (AmE), **nonswivelling** *adj* (BrE) MECH ENG type non pivotant

nonsync *adj* CINEMAT asynchrone, TV asynchrone, non synchrone

nonsynchronous: ~ **satellite** *n* SPACE satellite à défilement *m*

nontarnish: ~ **paper** *n* PAPER TECH papier non ternissant *m*

nonterminating: ~ **decimal** *n* MATH fraction périodique *f*

nontransparent: ~ **bearer service** *n* TELECOM service support non transparent *m*

nontronite *n* MINERAL nontronite *f*

nonuniform: ~ **motion** *n* PHYS mouvement non uniforme *m*; ~ **source of radiation** *n* RAD PHYS source de radiation non constante *f*

nonvolatile[1] *adj* COMP non volatil, DP non rémanent, non volatil

nonvolatile:[2] ~ **content** *n* P&R extrait-sec *m*; ~ **memory** *n* COMP mémoire rémanente *f*, CONST mémoire non volatile *f*

nonwarp: ~ **glue** *n* PRINT colle flexible qui ne craquèle pas en séchant *f*

nonwirewound: ~ **potentiometer** *n* ELEC potentiomètre à couche *m*; ~ **resistor** *n* CONST résistance non bobinée *f*

nonwound: ~ **rotor** *n* CONST rotor non bobiné *m*

nonwoven[1] *adj* PRINT, TEXTILES non tissé

nonwoven:[2] ~ **carpet** *n* TEXTILES tapis non tissé *m*; ~ **fabric** *n* TEXTILES tissu non tissé *m*; ~ **mat** *n* P&R *glass fibre* mat non tissé *m*; ~ **scrim** *n* C&G grille non tissée *f*

nonyellowing: ~ **paint** *n* P&R peinture non jaunissante *f*

nonyl *n* CHEM nonyle *m*; ~ **alcohol** *n* DETERGENTS alcool nonylique *m*

nonylene *n* CHEM nonylène *m*

nonylic *adj* CHEM nonylique

noon: ~ **sight** *n* NAUT *celestial navigation* méridienne *f*

no-op *n (no-operation no-instruction)* COMP, DP instruction ineffective *f*

no-operation: ~ **no-instruction** *n (no-op)* COMP, DP instruction ineffective *f*

NOR: ~ **circuit** *n* ELECTRON circuit NI *m*; ~ **gate** *n* COMP, DP, ELECTRON porte NI *f*, PHYS porte NI *f*, porte NON-OU *f*; ~ **operation** *n* COMP, DP opération NI *f*

nor'easter *n* NAUT *wind* nord-est *m*

nor'wester *n* NAUT *wind* nord-ouest *m*

noradrenalin *n* CHEM noradrénaline *f*

norator *n* PHYS norateur *m*

norbergite *n* MINERAL norbergite *f*

norbornadiene *n* CHEM norbornadiène *f*

norbornane *n* CHEM norbornane *f*

norbornylene *n* CHEM norbornylène *f*

no-reflow *n* CHEM non-réperfusion *f*

norephedrine *n* CHEM noréphédrine *f*

no-return: ~ **bottle** *n* PACKAGING bouteille non consignée *f*, verre perdu *m*

norite *n* PETR norite *m*

norm *n* GEOL norme *f*

Norma *n* ASTRON Règle *f*

normal[1] *adj* PHYS *at right angles* normal

normal[2] *n* GEOM, PETR normale *f*; ~ **auditory sensation area** *n* ACOUSTICS aire normale d'audition *f*; ~ **axis** *n*

AERONAUT axe normal *m*; ~ **bed** *n* HYDROL *of river* lit mineur *m*; ~ **brake application** *n* RAIL dépression de régime *f*; ~ **conditions** *n pl* MECH ENG régime *m*; ~ **coordinates** *n pl* PHYS coordonnées normales *f pl*; ~ **coupling** *n* NUCLEAR couplage faible *m*, couplage normal *m*; ~ **cubic meter** *n* (AmE), ~ **cubic metre** *n* (BrE) PETR mètre cube normal *m*; ~ **curve** *n* MATH courbe de Gauss *f*, courbe en forme de cloche *f*, courbe gaussienne *f*; ~ **descent angle** *n* AERONAUT pente normale *f*; ~ **disconnected mode** *n* (*NDM*) TELECOM mode normal déconnecté *m*; ~ **distribution** *n* COMP distribution normale *f*, DP répartition normale *f*, PHYS distribution de Gauss *f*, distribution normale *f*; ~ **distribution curve** *n* MATH courbe normale de répartition *f*; ~ **energy level** *n* NUCLEAR *of atom, nucleus, or molecule* niveau normal *m*; ~ **fault** *n* GEOL faille normale *f*; ~ **flow** *n* TRANSP *of traffic* écoulement normal *m*; ~ **form** *n* COMP, DP forme normale *f*; ~ **formation pressure** *n* PETR pression normale de formation *f*, pression normale de gisement *f*; ~ **hearing threshold** *n* ACOUSTICS seuil normal d'audition *m*; ~ **horizontal separation** *n* GEOL composante horizontale du rejet *f*; ~ **inspection** *n* QUALITY contrôle normal *m*; ~ **level** *n* NUCLEAR niveau normal *m*; ~ **listener** *n* ACOUSTICS auditeur normal *m*; ~ **mode** *n* PHYS mode normal *m*; ~ **mode acquisition** *n* SPACE *spacecraft* acquisition du mode normal *f*; ~ **move-out correction** *n* PETR TECH *drilling, prospecting* correction dynamique *f*; ~ **pressure** *n* GEOL, PETR TECH pression de formation normale *f*; ~ **reaction** *n* PHYS *force* réaction normale *f*; ~ **response mode** *n* (*NRM*) TELECOM mode normal de réponse *m*; ~ **reverse switch** *n* TV commutateur inverseur *m*; ~ **rupture** *n* METALL rupture plate *f*; ~ **salt** *n* CHEM sel neutre *m*; ~ **sea water** *n* OCEANOG eau normale *f*; ~ **situation class** *n* TELECOM classe situation normale *f*; ~ **solution** *n* CHEM solution normale *f*; ~ **stress** *n* COAL TECH tension normale *f*; ~ **threshold of painful hearing** *n* ACOUSTICS seuil normal d'audition douloureuse *m*; ~ **throw** *n* GEOL projection verticale du rejet *f*; ~ **traffic** *n* TRANSP trafic normal *m*; ~ **trend** *n* GEOL courbe de compaction normale *f*, tendance normale *f*, PETR TECH courbe de compaction normale *f*, droite de compaction normale *f*, tendance normale *f*; ~ **vacuum** *n* RAIL vide normal *m*; ~ **voltage** *n* CONST tension en régime *f*; ~ **water** *n* NUCLEAR eau ordinaire *f*; ~ **working conditions** *n pl* MECH ENG régime *m*; ~ **Zeeman effect** *n* PHYS effet Zeeman normal *m*

normal:[3] **under** ~ **conditions of use** *phr* PROD ENG dans les conditions usuelles d'utilisation

normality *n* CHEM, QUALITY normalité *f*

normalization *n* COMP, DP, METALL normalisation *f*

normalize *vt* MECH *materials* normaliser

normalized: ~ **detectivity** *n* OPT détectivité normée *f*, détectivité spécifique *f*; ~ **drilling rate** *n* (*NDR*) PETR TECH vitesse d'avancement normalisée *f*; ~ **frequency** *n* OPT fréquence normée *f*, TELECOM fréquence normalisée *f*; ~ **impact sound level** *n* ACOUSTICS niveau normalisé du bruit de choc *m*

normalizing *n* HEATING *furnace process* traitement de normalisation *m*

normally: ~ **closed contact** *n* ELEC *relay* contact de repos *m*, contact de rupture *m*, PROD ENG contact "O" *m*, contact à ouverture *m*; ~ **open contact** *n* CONST, ELEC *relay* contact de travail *m*

normanite *n* MINING normanite *f*

normative: ~ **mineral** *n* GEOL minéral normatif *m*

normorphine *n* CHEM normorphine *f*

nornarceine *n* CHEM nornarcéine *f*

nornicotine *n* CHEM nornicotine *f*

noropianic *adj* CHEM noropianique

north[1] *adj* NAUT du nord

north:[2] ~ **by east** *adv* NAUT *compass point* nord-quart-nord-est; ~ **by west** *adv* NAUT *compass point* nord-quart-nord-ouest

north:[3] ~ **galactic pole** *n* ASTRON pôle Nord galactique *m*; ~ **pole** *n* PHYS pôle Nord *m*; ~ **wind** *n* NAUT vent du nord *m*

North: ~ **Atlantic Current** *n* OCEANOG dérive nord-atlantique *f*; ~ **Atlantic Drift** *n* OCEANOG dérive nord-atlantique *f*; ~ **magnetic pole** *n* GEOPHYS pôle géomagnétique Nord *m*; ~ **Pacific Current** *n* OCEANOG dérive nord-pacifique *f*; ~ **Pacific Drift** *n* OCEANOG dérive nord-pacifique *f*; ~ **Star** *n* ASTRON étoile polaire *f*

northeast[1] *adj* NAUT nord-est

northeast:[2] ~ **by east** *adv* NAUT nord-est-quart-est; ~ **by north** *adv* NAUT nord-est-quart-nord

northeast[3] *n* NAUT nord-est *m*, nordé *m*; ~ **wind** *n* NAUT vent du nord-est *m*

northeaster *n* NAUT *wind* nord-est *m*

northeasterly *adj* NAUT *wind* du nord-est

northeastwards *adv* NAUT vers le nord-est

northerly *adj* NAUT du nord

northern: ~ **latitude** *n* NAUT *navigation* latitude boréale *f*; ~ **lights** *n pl* NAUT aurore boréale *f*

Northern: ~ **Cross** *n* ASTRON croix du Nord *f*

north-northeast *n* NAUT nord-nord-est *m*

north-northwest *n* NAUT nord-nord-ouest *m*

north-up *adj* NAUT *radar* nord en haut

northwards *adj* NAUT vers le nord

northwest[1] *adj* NAUT nord-ouest

northwest:[2] ~ **by north** *adv* NAUT nord-ouest-quart-nord; ~ **by west** *adv* NAUT nord-ouest-quart-ouest *m*

northwest[3] *n* NAUT *wind* nord-ouest *m*; ~ **wind** *n* NAUT vent du nord-ouest *m*

northwester *n* NAUT *wind* nord-ouest *m*

northwesterly *adj* NAUT *wind* du nord-ouest

northwestwards *adv* NAUT vers le nord-ouest

Norton's: ~ **theorem** *n* PHYS théorème de Norton *m*

norvaline *n* CHEM norvaline *f*

Norwegian: ~ **trench** *n* PETR TECH *geology* fossé norvégien *m*

NOS *abbr* (*network operating system*) COMP système d'exploitation de réseau *m*

nose *n* C&G *of blowpipe* mors *m*, MECH ENG *of mandrel, drilling spindle* nez *m*, *of tool* bec *m*, nez *m*, MILIT *of torpedo* cône *m*, PROD ENG ajutage *m*, bec *m*, *of bellows* buse *f*, tuyère *f*, *of the blowpipe of a tuyère* buse *f*, busillon *m*; ~ **cone** *n* AERONAUT cône de nez *m*, pointe avant du fuselage *f*, RECORDING *of microphone* pointe conique *f*, SPACE cône érodable *m*, pointe de fusée-sonde *f*, *of spacecraft* coiffe *f*; ~ **gear** *n* AERONAUT train avant *m*; ~ **gear door** *n* AERONAUT porte du train avant *f*; ~ **gear leg** *n* AERONAUT jambe du train avant *f*; ~ **gear saddle** *n* AERONAUT support du train avant *m*; ~ **gear steering** *n* AERONAUT braquage du train avant *m*; ~ **gear steering base post** *n* AERONAUT palonnier orientation train avant *m*; ~ **gear steer lock** *n* AERONAUT dispositif de verrouillage de diabolo train avant *m*; ~ **gear wheel** *n* AERONAUT roue avant *f*, roulette de nez *f*; ~ **heaviness** *n* AERONAUT tendance à piquer *f*; ~ **key** *n* MECH ENG contre-clavette *f*; ~ **sill** *n* PROD ENG traverse de nez *f*; **~ wheel** *n* AERONAUT train avant *m*; **~ wheel steering** *n* AERONAUT orientation train avant *f*; **~ wheel steering bar** *n* AERONAUT fourche de direction *f*

nosean *n* MINERAL noséane *f*, noséite *f*, nosélite *f*

noseband *n* NAUT *deck equipment* défense d'étrave *f*

nose-in: **~ positioning** *n* AERONAUT, TRANSP *airports* positionnement avant *m*

noselite *n* MINERAL noséane *f*, noséite *f*, nosélite *f*

nose-out: **~ positioning** *n* AERONAUT, TRANSP *airports* positionnement arrière *m*

nosepiece *n* CONST *stud union for pipes* bec d'une tuyère *m*, nez de raccord *m*, PROD ENG *of bellows or similar* buse *f*, tuyère *f*, *of pipe or similar* ajutage *m*, bec *m*

nose-up: **in a ~ attitude** *adj* AERONAUT en cabré

nosing *n* CONST *latch catch, keeper of gate latch* mentonnet *m*, *lock staple, keeper of door bolt* gâche *f*, *of step, stair-building* nez *m*; **~ line** *n* CONST *stair-building* ligne du nez de marche *f*; **~ plane** *n* CONST nez de marche *m*

no-slip: **~ condition** *n* FLUID PHYS *next to channel walls* condition de non-glissement *f*

no-step *phr* AERONAUT à ne pas marcher

NOT: **~ circuit** *n* ELECTRON circuit NON *m*; **~ gate** *n* COMP, DP, ELECTRON, PHYS porte NON *f*; **~ operation** *n* COMP, DP opération NON *f*

notarisation *n* TELECOM notarisation *f*

notation *n* DP, TELECOM notation *f*; **~ convention** *n* PRINT, PROD ENG convention typographique *f*

notch[1] *n* C&G, CINEMAT encoche *f*, CONST *in lock bolt* barbe *f*, MECH *materials* entaille *f*, MECH ENG cran *m*, METALL entaille *f*, PROD ENG cran *m*, encoche *f*, entaille *f*, échancrure *f*, WATER SUPP déversoir en mince paroi *m*, *over weirs* orifice ouvert à sapartie supérieure *m*, échancrure *f*; **~ angle** *n* METALL angle de l'entaille *m*; **~ bending test** *n* MECH ENG essai à la flexion sur éprouvette entaillée *m*; **~ effect** *n* MECH ENG effet d'entaille *m*; **~ filter** *n* ELECTRON filtre coupe-bande à bande étroite *m*, GEOPHYS filtre réjecteur *m*, TELECOM filtre coupe-fréquences *m*, filtre réjecteur *m*, filtre à coupure brusque *m*, filtre à encoches *m*; **~ gaging** *n* (AmE), **~ gauging** *n* (BrE) HYDR EQUIP jaugeage en déversoir *m*; **~ impact test** *n* NUCLEAR essai au choc *m*, essai de résilience *m*; **~ joint** *n* CONST *double* assemblage à double-entaille *m*, *single* assemblage à entaille *m*; **~ toughness** *n* NUCLEAR résilience *f*

notch[2] *vt* CINEMAT encocher, MECH ENG cranter

notched[1] *adj* MECH ENG cranté

notched:[2] **~ band** *n* MECH ENG bande crantée *f*; **~ bar impact test** *n* MECH *materials* essai de résilience sur éprouvette entaillée *m*; **~ belt** *n* VEHICLES *timing* courroie crantée *f*; **~ belt timing** *n* AUTO distribution par courroie crantée *f*; **~ hole** *n* MECH ENG *of screw plate* trou échancré *m*; **~ nozzle** *n* AERONAUT tuyère à lobes *f*; **~ nut** *n* MECH ENG écrou à dents *m*, écrou à entailles *m*, écrou à rainures *m*; **~ stem** *n* MECH ENG tige crantée *f*; **~ weir** *n* HYDROL déversoir de mesure *m*, déversoir à échancrure *m*

notcher *n* CINEMAT encocheuse *f*

notching *n* PROD ENG encochement *m*, entaillage *m*; **~ die** *n* MECH ENG *press tool* outillage d'encochage pour presse *m*; **~ process** *n* PROD ENG procédé d'ajourage *m*

note *n* ACOUSTICS note *f*

notebook *n* COMP, DP notebook *m*

notice: **~ of appeal** *n* PATENTS acte de recours *m*; **~ of opposition** *n* PATENTS acte d'invention *m*

notifiable: **~ accident** *n pl* SAFETY accident à déclarer obligatoirement *m*

notification *n* MAR POLL notification *f*, PATENTS signification *f*

not-under-command: **~ lights** *n pl* NAUT *navigation* feux d'impossibilité de manoeuvre *m pl*

no-twist: **~ roving** *n* C&G stratifil de verre textile torsion zéro *m*

noumeaite *n*,

noumeite *n* MINERAL nouméite *f*

nova *n* ASTRON nova *f*

novelty *n* PATENTS nouveauté *f*

novocaine *n* CHEM novocaïne *f*

novolac *n* P&R novolaque *f*

no-volt: **~ release** *n* ELEC ENG déclenchement à tension nulle *m*

no-voltage: **~ release relay** *n* ELEC relais d'absence de courant *m*

nowel *n* PROD ENG *bottom of foundry flask* corps *m*, dessous *m*, dessous de châssis *m*

noxious *adj* CHEM nocif

nozzle *n* AUTO gicleur *m*, C&G téton *m*, COAL TECH tuyère *f*, CONST *of welding gun* buse *f*, FUELLESS buse *f*, injecteur *m*, tubulure *f*, tuyère *f*, GAS TECH tuyère *f*, LAB EQUIP *glassware* buse *f*, MECH embout *m*, MECH ENG trompe *f*, *nosepiece* ajutage *m*, bec *m*, jet *m*, P&R *extruder*, PAPER TECH buse *f*, PHYS tuyère *f*, PROD ENG tuyère *f*, *branch pipe* lance *f*, lance à eau *f*, *of bellows* buse *f*, tuyère *f*, *of injector* tuyère *f*, *snout at end of blowpipe of tuyère* busillon *m*, SPACE *craft* embout *m*, tuyère *f*; **~ adaptor** *n* MECH ENG adaptateur de tuyère *m*; **~ area** *n* SPACE *of spacecraft* section de tuyère *f*; **~ cowl** *n* AERONAUT capot de buse réacteur *m*; **~ efficiency** *n* SPACE *of spacecraft* indice de qualité d'une tuyère *m*, rendement de tuyère *m*; **~ exit** *n* PHYS sortie de tuyère *f*; **~ expansion area ratio** *n* SPACE rapport des sections *m*; **~ holder** *n* AUTO porte-injecteur *m*; **~ holder spindle** *n* AUTO tige d'injecteur *f*, tige-poussoir *f*; **~ temperature indicator** *n* AERONAUT indicateur de température de tuyère *m*; **~ throat** *n* SPACE *of spacecraft* col de tuyère *m*; **~ tip** *n* PROD ENG bec de tuyère *m*; **~ velocity coefficient** *n* FUELLESS coefficient de vitesse au pointeau *m*

Np *(neptunium)* CHEM Np *(neptunium)*

NP *abbr (network performance)* TELECOM performance du réseau *f*

NPDU *abbr (network protocol data unit)* TELECOM unité de données du protocole de réseau *f*

NPI *abbr* TELECOM *(numbering plan identification)* identification du plan de numérotage *f*, TELECOM *(null pointer indication)* indication de pointeur zéro *f*

NPN: **~ transistor** *n* ELECTRON transistor NPN *m*

n-position: **~ switch** *n* ELEC ENG commutateur à n positions *m*

N-protocol *n* TELECOM protocole N *m*; **~ data unit** *n* TELECOM unité de données du protocole N *f*

NPT[1] *abbr (National Pipe Taper)* MECH ENG filetage NPT *m*

NPT:[2] **~ screwthread** *n* MECH ENG filetage conique NPT *m*

N-relay *n* TELECOM relais N *m*

NRM *abbr (normal response mode)* TELECOM mode normal de réponse *m*

NRZ[1] *abbr (nonreturn to zero)* TELECOM non retour à zéro

NRZ:[2] **~ recording** *n* COMP, DP enregistrement sans retour à zéro *m*

NRZI *abbr (nonreturn to zero inverted)* TELECOM non retour à zéro inversé

Ns *abbr (nimbostratus)* METEO Ns *(nimbo-stratus)*

NS *abbr (network service)* TELECOM service de réseau *m*

NSAP *abbr (network service access point)* TELECOM point d'accès au service de réseau *m*

N-service *n* TELECOM service N *m*; ~ **data unit** *n* TELECOM unité de données de service N *f*

NSN *abbr (national significant number)* TELECOM numéro national significatif *m*

n-step: ~ **starter** *n* ELEC démarreur à n étages *m*

NT *abbr (network termination)* TELECOM terminaison de réseau *f*

NT1-LB *abbr (B-ISDN network termination 1)* TELECOM terminaison de réseau 1 pour le RNIS-LB *f*

NT2-LB *abbr (B-ISDN network termination 2)* TELECOM terminaison de réseau 2 pour le RNIS-LB *f*

NTE *abbr (network terminal equipment)* TELECOM équipement terminal de réseau *m*

nth: ~ **choice group** *n* TELECOM faisceau de l'énième choix *m*; ~ **degree equation** *n* MATH équation du énième degré *f*; ~ **order filter** *n* ELECTRON filtre d'ordre n *m*, filtre d'énième ordre *m*

NT-LB *abbr (B-ISDN network termination)* TELECOM terminaison de réseau pour le RNIS-LB *f*

NTSC: ~ **system** *n* (AmE) *(National Television Standards Committee)* TV système NTSC *m*

n-type *n* ELECTRON type N *m*; ~ **component** *n* ELECTRON composant de type N *m*; ~ **epitaxial layer** *n* ELECTRON couche épitaxiale de type N *f*; ~ **impurity** *n* ELECTRON impureté de type N *f*; ~ **semiconductor** *n* ELECTRON semi-conducteur de type N *m*, semi-conducteur de type N faiblement dopé *m*, PHYS semi-conducteur de type N *m*; ~ **silicon** *n* ELECTRON silicium de type N *m*, silicium dopé N *m*; ~ **substrate** *n* ELECTRON substrat N *m*, substrat de type N *m*, substrat dopé N *m*

NU *abbr (national use)* TELECOM usage national *m*

NUC *abbr (not under command)* NAUT *shiphandling* pas maître de sa commande, pas maître de sa manoeuvre

nuclear[1] *adj* ELEC, MILIT, NUCLEAR, PHYS nucléaire

nuclear:[2] ~ **abundance** *n* PHYS abondance nucléaire *f*; ~ **activity** *n* RAD PHYS activité nucléaire *f*; ~ **battery** *n* CONST batterie nucléaire *f*; ~ **cell** *n* CONST pile nucléaire *f*; ~ **cement log** *n* PETR diagramme nucléaire de cimentation *m*, log nucléaire de cimentation *m*; ~ **charge** *n* PART PHYS charge nucléaire *f*; ~ **cooling** *n* REFRIG désactivation nucléaire *f*; ~ **deformation** *n* NUCLEAR déformation nucléaire *f*; ~ **detection satellite** *n* SPACE satellite de détection d'explosions nucléaires *m*; ~ **energy** *n* ELEC, PHYS énergie nucléaire *f*; ~ **energy control** *n* CONTROL contrôle de l'énergie atomique *m*; ~ **equation of state** *n* RAD PHYS équation nucléaire d'état *f*; ~ **explosion** *n* MILIT explosion nucléaire *f*; ~ **fission** *n* PART PHYS, PHYS fission nucléaire *f*; ~ **fuel** *n* MILIT combustible nucléaire *m*; ~ **fusion** *n* ASTRON, PART PHYS, PHYS fusion nucléaire *f*; ~ **isomerism** *n* PHYS isomérie nucléaire *f*; ~ **log** *n* PETR TECH *prospecting* diagraphie nucléaire *f*; ~ **magnetic log** *n* PETR diagramme nucléaire magnétique *m*; ~ **magnetic logging** *n* *(NML)* PETR diagraphie de résonance magnétique nucléaire *m*; ~ **magnetic resonance** *n* *(NMR)* CHEM *analysis*, PETR TECH, PHYS, RAD PHYS résonance magnétique nucléaire *f (RMN)*; ~ **magnetic resonance log** *n* *(NMR log)* PETR TECH *prospecting* diagraphie par résonance magnétique nucléaire *f*; ~

model *n* PHYS modèle nucléaire *m*; ~ **physicist** *n* PART PHYS physicien de l'atome *m*; ~ **physics** *n* NUCLEAR, PHYS physique nucléaire *f*; ~ **potential** *n* RAD PHYS potentiel nucléaire *m*; ~ **power** *n* PHYS puissance nucléaire *f*; ~ **power plant** *n* CONST centrale atomique *f*, centrale nucléaire *f*, station d'énergie nucléaire *f*, PHYS centrale nucléaire *f*; ~ **power station** *n* CONST centrale atomique *f*, centrale nucléaire *f*, station d'énergie nucléaire *f*, ELEC *generator*, PHYS centrale nucléaire *f*; ~ **power supply** *n* SPACE *of spacecraft* source d'énergie nucléaire *f*; ~ **propulsion** *n* SPACE *of spacecraft* propulsion nucléaire *f*; ~ **quadrupole moment** *n* PHYS moment quadripolaire nucléaire *m*; ~ **radiation** *n* RAD PHYS rayonnement nucléaire *m*; ~ **radiation spectrum** *n* RAD PHYS spectre du rayonnement nucléaire *m*; ~ **reaction** *n* ASTRON *inside active stars*, CHEM, PHYS, RAD PHYS réaction nucléaire *f*; ~ **reaction channel** *n* RAD PHYS canal de réaction nucléaire *m*; ~ **reactor** *n* CONST réacteur nucléaire de puissance *m*, ELEC réacteur nucléaire *m*, NUCLEAR pile atomique *f*, pile nucléaire *f*, réacteur *m*, réacteur nucléaire *m*, PHYS réacteur nucléaire *m*; ~ **reactor poison removal** *n* NUCLEAR élimination du réacteur des poisons nucléaires *f*; ~ **research** *n* RAD PHYS recherche nucléaire *f*; ~ **safety** *n* SAFETY sécurité nucléaire *f*; ~ **shell** *n* MILIT obus à charge nucléaire *m*; ~ **shock waves** *n pl* RAD PHYS ondes de choc nucléaires *f pl*; ~ **spin** *n* PHYS, RAD PHYS spin nucléaire *m*; ~ **symmetry energy** *n* RAD PHYS énergie de symétrie nucléaire *f*; ~ **test** *n* MILIT, TESTING essai nucléaire *m*; ~ **track** *n* NUCLEAR trace nucléaire *f*; ~ **tranche** *n* ELEC *unit of nuclear power* tranche nucléaire *f*; ~ **waste** *n* POLLUTION, RECYCLING déchets nucléaires *m pl*

nuclear-free: ~ **zone** *n* MILIT zone dénucléarisée *f*

nuclear-powered *adj* NAUT *of ship*, TRANSP à propulsion nucléaire

nucleate: ~ **boiling** *n* REFRIG ébullition nucléée *f*

nucleation *n* CRYSTALL *growth* germination *f*, METALL, METEO nucléation *f*, NUCLEAR *of fracture* amorçage *m*, PROP MAT formation de germes cristallins *f*, germination *f*, nucléation *f*; ~ **rate** *n* METALL vitesse de nucléation *f*

nucleic *adj* CHEM nucléique

nuclein *n* CHEM nucléine *f*

nucleohistone *n* CHEM nucléohistone *f*

nucleolin *n* CHEM nucléoline *f*

nucleon *n* NUCLEAR *proton, neutron*, PHYS *proton, neutron* nucléon *m*; ~ **number** *n* PHYS nombre de masse *m*, nombre de nucléons *m*

nucleonics *n* NUCLEAR physique nucléaire *f*, PHYS nucléonique *f*

nucleophilic *adj* CHEM nucléophile

nucleophilicity *n* CHEM nucléophilie *f*

nucleus *n* ASTRON *of galaxy* noyau *m*, C&G germe *m*, COMP, DP, PART PHYS, PHYS noyau *m*, PROD ENG noyau *m*, nucléus *m*, PROP MAT noyau *m*

nuclide *n* PHYS nucléide *m*

nudging *n* SPACE *of spacecraft* à-coups *m pl*

nugget *n* MINING nugget *m*, pépite *f*

NUL *abbr (null character)* COMP, DP caractère nul *m*, nul *m*

null[1] *adj* CHEM *point* nul

null:[2] ~ **character** *n* *(NUL)* COMP, DP caractère nul *m*, nul *m*; ~ **flux suspension** *n* TRANSP *vehicle levitation* sustentation électrodynamique à flux nul *f*; ~ **galvanometer** *n* ELEC, INSTRUMENT zéromètre *m*; ~

instruction n COMP, DP instruction nulle f; ~ **method** n ELEC of measurement méthode de mesure par zéro f, PHYS méthode de compensation f, méthode de réduction au zéro f; ~ **pointer indication** n (NPI) TELECOM indication de pointeur zéro f; ~ **string** n COMP, DP chaîne vide f; ~ **voltage** n ELEC tension nulle f, ELEC ENG potentiel zéro m, tension nulle f

nullator n PHYS nullateur m

number[1] n CHEM nombre m, DP nombre m, numéro m; ~ **of passes** n CONST of road compaction HEATING of passes in a boiler nombre de passes m; ~ **per sample** n TESTING of specimens nombre par échantillon m; ~ **plate** n MECH ENG plaque de numéro f; ~ **of repeats** n TEXTILES nombre de rapports m; ~ **representation** n DP numération f; ~ **of splits** n PROD ENG nombre de fractionnements m, nombre de lots fractionnés m; ~ **system** n DP système de numération m; ~ **theory** n MATH théorie des nombres f

number[2] vt PROD ENG to place number on coter, numéroter; ~ **consecutively** vt PATENTS numéroter consécutivement, numéroter de façon continue

numbered: ~ **copy** n PRINT exemplaire numéroté m

numbering n PHOTO numérotage m, PRINT numérotation f; ~ **apparatus** n PACKAGING numéroteur m; ~ **machine** n PRINT machine à numéroter f; ~ **plan identification** n (NPI) TELECOM identification du plan de numérotage f; ~ **plan indicator** n TELECOM indicateur du plan de numérotage m

numberplate n (BrE) (cf license plate) AUTO, VEHICLES plaque d'immatriculation f

numeral n PRINT chiffre m

numeration n DP numération f

numerator n MATH numérateur m

numeric: ~ **keypad** n COMP, DP bloc numérique m, pavé numérique m; ~ **literal** n DP constante numérique f; ~ **representation** n COMP, DP représentation numérique f

numerical[1] adj MATH numérique

numerical:[2] ~ **analysis** n COMP, DP analyse numérique f; ~ **aperture** n CONST optical fibre, OPT, PHYS, TELECOM ouverture numérique f; ~ **code** n COMP, DP code numérique m; ~ **control** n (NC) COMP, CONTROL, DP, ELEC computer, MECH ENG, PROD ENG, TELECOM, TV commande numérique f (CN); ~ **control machine** n MECH ENG machine à commande numérique f; ~ **control machine tool** n MECH ENG machine à commande numérique f; ~ **control system** n CONTROL système de commande numérique m; ~ **value** n METR valeur numérique f

numerically-controlled adj CONTROL, MECH ENG à commande numérique

numerics n pl PRINT caractères digitaux m pl, chiffres et signes digitaux m pl

nummulitic: ~ **limestone** n GEOL calcaire à nummulites m, pierre à liards f

nurl n MECH ENG godronnoir m, molette f

nurled: ~ **nut** n MECH ENG molette f, écrou godronné m, écrou moleté m, écrou à molette m

nurling n MECH ENG godronnage m, moletage m; ~ **tool** n PROD ENG godronnoir m, molette f

nursery: ~ **cold store** n REFRIG for plants chambre froide à plantes f; ~ **refrigerator** n REFRIG réfrigérateur à biberons m

N-user: ~ **data** n TELECOM données utilisateur-N f pl

nut n MECH, MECH ENG, VEHICLES écrou m; ~ **and bolt works** n pl CONST boulonnerie f, visserie f; ~ **cage** n MECH ENG cage d'écrou f; ~ **lock** n MECH ENG frein d'écrou m; ~ **sizing screen** n COAL TECH crible de reclassement m; ~ **spinner** n MECH ENG tool clé emmanchée f; ~ **splitter** n MECH ENG tool casse-écrous m

nutation n ASTRON, PHYS, SPACE nutation f; ~ **damper** n SPACE of spacecraft amortisseur de nutation m

nutrient n FOOD TECH aliment m, nutritif m, substance nutritive f, MAR POLL nutriment m; ~ **content** n FOOD TECH teneur en substances nutritives f; ~ **loss** n FOOD TECH perte en matières nutritives f; ~ **removal** n HYDROL from water élimination de sels nutritifs f; ~ **requirements** n FOOD TECH besoins en substances nutritives m; ~ **salts** n HYDROL sels nutritifs m pl

nutrition n FOOD TECH alimentation f, nutrition f

nutritional: ~ **supplement** n FOOD TECH complément nutritionnel m

nutritious adj FOOD TECH nourrissant, nutritif

nutritive adj FOOD TECH nourrissant, nutritif

nuts: ~ **and bolts** n pl CONST visserie f, écrous et boulons m pl

nutty: ~ **slack** n COAL TECH déclassés des gros m pl

nux: ~ **vomica** n CHEM noix vomique f, nux vomica f

NVT abbr (network virtual terminal) COMP, DP terminal virtuel de réseau m

n-way: ~ **switch** n ELEC commutateur à n directions m

nydrazid n CHEM nydrazide m

nylon n CHEM, P&R, PRINT nylon m; ~ **bush** n P&R canon nylon m; ~ **line** n NAUT cordage en nylon m; ~ **rope** n MECH ENG corde nylon f; ~ **thread** n P&R textiles fil de nylon m

nylon-reinforced adj PACKAGING renforcé nylon

nylstop: ~ **self-locking nut** n MECH ENG écrou nylstop m

Nyquist: ~ **demodulator** n TV démodulateur à talon m; ~ **frequency** n PETR fréquence Nyquist f

nystatin n CHEM nystatine f

O

O *(oxygen)* CHEM O *(oxygène)*

OA *abbr* COMP *(office automation)* bureautique *f*, TELECOM *(overflow accept)* acceptation de débordement *f*

oakum *n* NAUT *ropes* étoupe *f*

OAM *abbr (operations and maintenance)* TELECOM exploitation et maintenance *f*

OAMC *abbr (operation administration and maintenance centre, operation administration and maintance center)* TELECOM centre de gestion d'exploitation et de maintenance *m*

OAMP *abbr (operation, administration, maintenance and provisioning)* TELECOM exploitation administration maintenance et mise en service *f*

oar *n* NAUT aviron *m*, rame *f*

oarlock *n* NAUT *boat fitting* dame de nage *f*

oasis *n* HYDROL oasis *f*

OB[1] *abbr (outside broadcast)* TV émission transmise de l'extérieur *f*

OB:[2] ~ **unit** *n* TV unité vidéo mobile *f*; ~ **van** *n* TV car régie *m*, car vidéo *m*; ~ **vehicle** *n* TV car régie *m*

obduction *n* GEOL obduction *f*

obedience: ~ **level** *n* TRANSP *traffic control* taux d'obéissance *m*

obelisk *n* GEOM obélisque *f*

object *n* COMP, DP, PHYS, PROD ENG objet *m*; ~ **code** *n* COMP, DP code objet *m*; ~ **in space** *n* SPACE objet spatial *m*; ~ **language** *n* COMP, DP langage résultant *m*; ~ **machine** *n* COMP, DP machine d'exécution *f*; ~ **module** *n* COMP, DP module objet *m*; ~ **program** *n* COMP, DP programme objet *m*; ~ **stage** *n* INSTRUMENT platine *f*, porte-objet *m*

objective *n* ASTRON *of optical instrument*, INSTRUMENT, PHYS *optics* objectif *m*; ~ **aperture** *n* INSTRUMENT ouverture de l'objectif *f*; ~ **detector** *n* TRANSP *traffic* détecteur à capacité *m*; ~ **lens** *n* INSTRUMENT lentille convergente *f*, lentille d'objectif *f*, lentille objective *f*, LAB EQUIP lentille d'objectif *f*, lentille objective *f*, METALL lentille objective *f*; ~ **mirror** *n* ASTRON miroir objectif *m*; ~ **nosepiece** *n* INSTRUMENT porte-objectifs *m*, revolver à objectifs *m*, tourelle porte-objectifs *f*; ~ **pole piece** *n* INSTRUMENT bobine d'objectif *f*; ~ **prism** *n* ASTRON prisme objectif *m*; ~ **turret** *n* INSTRUMENT porte-objectifs *m*, revolver à objectifs *m*, tourelle porte-objectifs *f*

object-oriented: ~ **architecture** *n* COMP, DP architecture orientée objet *f*; ~ **design** *n (OOD)* COMP, DP conception orientée objet *f (COO)*; ~ **programming system** *n* COMP, DP système de programmation orienté objet *m*

oblate[1] *adj* GEOM aplati

oblate:[2] ~ **ellipsoid** *n* GEOM, PHYS ellipsoïde aplati *m*; ~ **nucleus** *n* NUCLEAR noyau aplati *m*; ~ **spheroid** *n* GEOM sphéroïde aplati *m*; ~ **spheromak** *n* NUCLEAR oblimak *m*, sphéromak aplati *m*

oblateness *n* ASTRON aplatissement *m*

obligate: ~ **aerobe** *n* FOOD TECH aérobie strict *m*

obligatory: ~ **well** *n* PETR TECH *contracts, licensing* puits d'obligation *m*

oblimak *n* NUCLEAR oblimak *m*, sphéromak aplati *m*

oblique[1] *adj* GEOM oblique

oblique:[2] ~ **angle** *n* GEOM angle oblique *m*; ~ **arch** *n* CONST *architecture* voûte biaise *f*, *of bridge* arche biaise *f*; ~ **axes** *n pl* MATH axes obliques *m*; ~ **bridge** *n* CONST pont biais *m*; ~ **cone** *n* GEOM cône oblique *m*; ~ **illumination** *n* METALL éclairage oblique *m*; ~ **lighting** *n* PRINT éclairage oblique *m*; ~ **serif** *n* PRINT empattement oblique *m*; ~ **stroke** *n* GEOM *between figures* oblique *f*; ~ **triangle** *n* GEOM triangle oblique *m*

obliquity *n* ASTRON obliquité *f*; ~ **of the eclipse** *n* ASTRON obliquité de l'éclipse *f*

oblong[1] *adj* GEOM oblong

oblong[2] *n* GEOM rectangle *m*; ~ **hole** *n* SPRINGS *on leaf spring* lunette *f*; ~ **page** *n* PRINT page à l'italienne *f*; ~ **size** *n* PRINT format atlas *m*

OBO[1] *abbr (ore-bulk-oil)* PETR TECH minerai-vrac-pétrole *m*

OBO:[2] ~ **carrier** *n (oil-bulk-ore carrier)* TRANSP pétrolier-vracquier-minéralier *m*, transporteur combiné minerai-vrac-pétrole *m*

observable: ~ **universe** *n* ASTRON univers visible *m*

observation *n* CONST *sight* coup *m*, coup de lunette *m*, observation *f*, visée *f*, *with levelling instrument* nivelée *f*, NAUT *celestial navigation* observation *f*; ~ **chamber** *n* OCEANOG lunette de calfat *f*, PETR TECH *diving* caisson d'observation *m*; ~ **grid** *n* NUCLEAR grille de points fixes *f*; ~ **hole** *n* C&G regard *m*; ~ **mirror** *n* INSTRUMENT miroir d'observation *m*; ~ **satellite** *n* SPACE satellite d'observation *m*; ~ **service** *n* TELECOM service de surveillance *m*; ~ **telephone** *n* TELECOM poste de surveillance *m*; ~ **tower** *n* MILIT tour d'observation *f*; ~ **well** *n* GAS TECH puits de contrôle *m*, WATER SUPP puits d'observation *m*

observatory *n* ASTRON observatoire *m*

observed: ~ **altitude** *n* NAUT *sextant* hauteur observée *f*; ~ **position** *n* NAUT *navigation*, OCEANOG point observé *m*; ~ **threshold** *n* NUCLEAR *of reaction* seuil observé *m*

observer *n* AERONAUT observateur *m*

obsidian *n* C&G obsidienne *f*

obsolescence *n* PROD ENG obsolescence *f*, péremption *f*

obsolete *adj* PROD ENG obsolète, périmé

obstacle *n* METALL obstacle *m*; ~ **gain** *n* ELECTRON gain d'obstacle *m*; ~ **hardening** *n* METALL durcissement par obstacles *m*; ~ **in rotating fluid** *n* FLUID PHYS obstacle dans un fluide tournant *m*; ~ **in stratified fluid** *n* FLUID PHYS obstacle dans un fluide stratifié *m*

obstruction *n* CONST bouchage *m*, *in pipe* engorgement *m*, obstruction *f*

obtain *vt* TELECOM *subscriber* joindre

obturating: ~ **plug** *n* MECH ENG tampon obturateur *m*

obturator *n* HEATING, MECH ENG obturateur *m*

obtuse[1] *adj* GEOM obtus

obtuse:[2] ~ **angle** *n* GEOM angle obtus *m*; ~ **triangle** *n* GEOM triangle obtus *m*

obtuse-angled *adj* GEOM obtusangle

obtuse-angular *adj* GEOM obtusangle

obtuseness *n* GEOM *of an angle* obtusité *f*

OCB *abbr (outgoing calls barred)* TELECOM interdiction

des appels au départ *f*

occlude *vt* CHEM *metal* absorber, condenser, retenir

occluded[1] *adj* CHEM occlus

occluded:[2] ~ **front** *n* METEO front occlus *m*

occlusion *n* CHEM, METEO occlusion *f*

occultation *n* ASTRON occultation *f*; ~ **cone for corono-graph** *n* ASTRON cône d'occultation du coronographe *m*

occulting: ~ **light** *n* NAUT *navigation marks* feu à occultation *m*

occupancy: ~ **detector** *n* TRANSP *traffic* détecteur d'occupation *m*; ~ **rate** *n* CONST taux d'occupation *m*, TRANSP *traffic* densité d'occupation *f*

occupational: ~ **hazard** *n* SAFETY risque du métier *m*; ~ **MAC** *n (occupational maximum allowable concentration)* POLLUTION concentration maximale admissible *f*; ~ **maximum allowable concentration** *n (occupational MAC)* POLLUTION concentration maximale admissible *f*; ~ **noise exposure** *n* SAFETY exposition au bruit durant le travail *f*; ~ **safety** *n* SAFETY sécurité au travail *f*; ~ **safety cream** *n* SAFETY crème de protection pour le travail *f*; ~ **threshold limit value** *n (occupational TLV)* POLLUTION concentration maximale admissible *f*; ~ **TLV** *n (occupational threshold limit value)* POLLUTION concentration maximale admissible *f*

occupied: ~ **track** *n* RAIL voie occupée *f*

ocean: ~ **basin** *n* OCEANOG bassin océanique *m*; ~ **bottom** *n* GEOPHYS fond océanique *m*; ~ **crust** *n* GEOL, OCEANOG croûte océanique *f*; ~ **current** *n* NAUT courant océanique *m*; ~ **deeps** *n pl* NAUT *geography* grands fonds *m pl*; ~ **depths** *n pl* NAUT *geography* grands fonds *m pl*; ~ **dynamics** *n* NAUT dynamique des océans *f*; ~ **floor** *n* OCEANOG fond océanique *m*; ~ **floor spreading** *n* GEOL, OCEANOG expansion des fonds océaniques *f*; ~ **going ship** *n* NAUT long-courrier *m*, navire de mer *m*; ~ **liner** *n* NAUT atlantique *m*, paquebot atlantique *m*, TRANSP transatlantique *m*; ~ **navigation** *n* NAUT navigation au long cours *f*, navigation hauturière *f*; ~ **survey vessel** *n* NAUT *type of ship* navire hydrographique *m*; ~ **thermal conversion** *n* FUELLESS conversion thermodynamique de l'océan *f*; ~ **thermal energy** *n* OCEANOG énergie thermique des océans *f*; ~ **trench** *n* GEOL fosse océanique *f*

Ocean: ~ **Data Acquisition System** *n (ODAS)* OCEANOG Système d'acquisition de données océaniques *m (SADO)*

oceanic[1] *adj* METEO océanique

oceanic:[2] ~ **basin** *n* HYDROL, OCEANOG bassin océanique *m*; ~ **crust** *n* GEOL, OCEANOG croûte océanique *f*; ~ **current** *n* METEO courant océanique *m*; ~ **ridge** *n* OCEANOG *mid-ocean* dorsale océanique *f*; ~ **routing chart** *n* NAUT *navigation* grand routier transocéanique *m*

Oceanic: ~ **Data Acquisition System** *n (ODAS)* OCEANOG Système d'acquisition de données océaniques *m (SADO)*

oceanographer *n* METEO, OCEANOG océanographe *m*

oceanographic: ~ **buoy** *n* OCEANOG bouée océanographique *f*; ~ **dredge** *n* OCEANOG drague océanographique *f*; ~ **laboratory** *n* OCEANOG laboratoire maritime *m*; ~ **research ship** *n* NAUT navire de recherche océanographique *m*, OCEANOG navire océanographique *m*

oceanographical *adj* METEO océanographique

oceanography *n* METEO, NAUT, PETR TECH océanographie *f*

oceanology *n* OCEANOG océanologie *f*

ochery: ~ **clay** *n* (AmE), **ochry clay** *n* (BrE) C&G argile ocreuse *f*

OCO: ~ **carrier** *n (oil-coal-ore carrier)* TRANSP navire OCO *m*

OCR[1] *abbr* COMP *(optical character recognition)* ROC *(reconnaissance optique des caractères)*, COMP *(optical character reader)* lecteur optique de caractères *m*, DP *(optical character recognition)* ROC *(reconnaissance optique des caractères)*, DP *(optical character reader)* lecteur optique de caractères *m*, PRINT *(optical character recognition)* ROC *(reconnaissance optique des caractères)*, PRINT *(optical character reader)* lecteur optique de caractères *m*

OCR:[2] ~ **system** *n* PACKAGING système optique d'identification de caractères *m*

o-cresol *n* CHEM crésol *m*

octacosane *n* CHEM octacosane *m*

octad *n* CHEM corps octavalent *m*, radical octavalent *m*

octadecane *n* CHEM octadécane *m*

octadecyl *n* CHEM octadécylène *m*, octodécylène *m*

octagon *n* GEOM octogone *m*

octagonal[1] *adj* GEOM octogonal

octagonal:[2] ~ **nut** *n* MECH ENG écrou à huit pans *m*; ~ **nut angle gage** *n* (AmE), ~ **nut angle gauge** *n* (BrE) MECH ENG équerre à huit pans *f*; ~ **reamer** *n* MECH ENG équarrissoir à huit pans *m*

octahedral *adj* CHEM octaédrique, octaèdre, CRYSTALL, GEOM octaédrique

octahedrite *n* MINERAL octaédrite *f*

octahedron *n* CRYSTALL, GEOM octaèdre *m*

octal[1] *adj* DP octal

octal:[2] ~ **base** *n* MECH ENG culot octal *m*; ~ **notation** *n* DP notation octale *f*; ~ **tube** *n* ELECTRON tube octal *m*

octamer *n* CHEM octamère *m*

octanal *n* CHEM octanal *m*

octane *n* CHEM octane *m*; ~ **index** *n* VEHICLES *petrol* indice d'octane *m*; ~ **number** *n* (ON) PETR TECH, VEHICLES indice d'octane *m*; ~ **number rating** *n (ONR)* AUTO indice d'octane *m*; ~ **rating** *n* VEHICLES indice d'octane *m*

Octans *n* ASTRON Octant *m*

octant: ~ **mirror** *n* INSTRUMENT miroir d'octant *m*

octavalent *adj* CHEM octovalent

octave *n* ACOUSTICS, ELECTRON, PHYS octave *f*; ~ **band** *n* ELECTRON bande d'un octave *f*; ~ **band filter** *n* ELECTRON filtre à bande d'un octave *m*; ~ **band oscillator** *n* ELECTRON oscillateur accordable sur un octave *m*; ~ **filter** *n* RECORDING filtre à octave *m*; ~ **filter set** *n* RECORDING jeu de filtres à octave *m*

octavo *n* PRINT in-octavo *m*

octene *n* CHEM octylène *m*, octène *m*

octet *n* CHEM, COMP, DP octet *m*

octode *n* ELECTRON octode *f*

octose *n* CHEM octose *f*

octovalent *adj* CHEM octovalent

octupole *n* CONST octupôle *m*

octyl *n* CHEM octyle *m*

octyne *n* CHEM octyne *m*

OD *abbr* HYDROL *(oxygen deficit)* déficet d'oxygène *m*, MECH *(outside diameter)*, MECH ENG *(outside diameter)* diamètre extérieur *m*

O-D: ~ **equation** *n (origin and destination equation)* TRANSP *traffic* relation origine-destination *f*; ~ **survey** *n (origin and destination survey)* TRANSP *traffic* étude origine-destination *f*

ODAS *abbr (Ocean Data Acquisition System, Oceanic Data Acquisition System)* OCEANOG SADO *(Système d'acquisition de données océaniques)*

odd[1] *adj* PAPER TECH impair

odd:[2] ~ **container** *n* TRANSP conteneur non normalisé *m*; ~ **harmonic** *n* ELECTRON, PHYS *vibrations* harmonique impair *m*; ~ **page** *n* PRINT page impaire *f*; ~ **parity** *n* COMP imparité *f*, parité impaire *f*, DP imparité *f*, parité impaire *f*, PHYS *wave function* parité impaire *f*; ~ **parity check** *n* CONTROL contrôle d'imparité *m*; ~ **pitch** *n (cf even pitch)* MECH ENG *screw pitch* pas bâtard *m*

odd-even: ~ **check** *n* COMP, DP contrôle de parité *m*; ~ **nucleus** *n* PHYS, RAD PHYS noyau impair-pair *m*

oddments *n pl* PRINT pages liminaires *f pl*

odd-odd: ~ **nucleus** *n* PHYS noyau impair-impair *m*; ~ **spin** *n* NUCLEAR spin impair-impair *m*

odd-order: ~ **filter** *n* ELECTRON filtre d'ordre impair *m*

odds *n pl* MATH chance *f*

odometer *n (cf trip counter)* AUTO compteur kilométrique *m*, CONST odomètre *m*, VEHICLES *instrument* totalisateur partiel *m*

odontograph *n* MECH ENG *for gear teeth* odontographe *m*

odontolite *n* MINERAL fausse turquoise *f*, odontolite *f*

odor *n* (AmE) *see odour*

odorant *n* PETR TECH *gas detection* odorisant *m*

odoriferous *adj* CHEM odorifique

odoriphore *n* CHEM matière odorante *f*

odorization *n* GAS TECH odorisation *f*

odorizer *n* CHEM TECH substance odorante *f*

odorless *adj* (AmE) *see odourless*

odorous *adj* CHEM TECH, POLLUTION odorant

odor-proof *adj* (AmE) *see odour-proof*

odour *n* (BrE) CHEM odeur *f* ~ **control** *n* (BrE) CHEM TECH neutralisation d'odeur *f*, POLLUTION lutte contre les odeurs *f*; ~ **threshold** *n* (BrE) HYDROL *sewage* seuil d'olfaction *m*

odourless *adj* (BrE) CHEM inodore, CHEM TECH inodore, sans odeur, PACKAGING inodore, PROP MAT sans odeur

odour-proof *adj* (BrE) PACKAGING résistant aux odeurs

ODP *abbr (open distribution processing)* TELECOM traitement à distribution ouverte *m*

O-E *abbr (optical-electrical)* TELECOM optique-électrique

oellacherite *n* MINERAL oellacherite *f*

oenanthal *n* CHEM oenanthal *m*

oenanthic *adj* CHEM oenanthique

oenanthin *n* CHEM oenanthine *f*

oenanthol *n* CHEM oenanthol *m*

oenanthylate *n* CHEM oenanthylate *m*

oenanthylic *adj* CHEM oenanthylique

oersted *n* CONST oersted *m*

oestradiol *n* CHEM oestradiol *m*

oestriol *n* CHEM oestriol *m*

oestrone *n* CHEM oestrone *f*

off[1] *adj* CONST arrêté, *transistor* bloqué, ELEC ENG *circuit* coupé, *electricity* fermé

off[2] *n* MECH ENG arrêt *m*

OFF *abbr (optical flexibility frame)* TELECOM répartiteur optique *m*

off-air[1] *adj* TELECOM hors émission, TV retour antenne

off-air:[2] ~ **call setup** *n* TELECOM établissement d'une connexion sans émission *m*; ~ **monitor** *n* TV récepteur d'antenne *m*, récepteur retour antenne *m*; ~ **period** *n* CONST période sans émission *f*; ~ **pick-up** *n* TV récep-

tion directe *f*; ~ **recording** *n* TV enregistrement en direct *m*, simultané antenne *m*

offal *n* FOOD TECH abats *m pl*, issues *f pl*

off-camera *adj* CINEMAT hors champ

off-center *adj* (AmE), **off-centre** *adj* (BrE) MECH ENG décentré, désaxé, PAPER TECH excentré, SPACE décentré, excentré

off-color: ~ **shade** *n* (AmE), **off-colour shade** *n* (BrE) COLOURS teinte défectueuse *f*

off-content *n* C&G mauvaise contenance *f*

off-course *adj* SPACE dévié, dévié de sa route

offcut *n* CINEMAT chute *f*, PACKAGING rognures *f pl*, PAPER TECH à-côté de coupe *m*, PRINT chute de papier *f*

off-cycle: ~ **defrosting** *n* REFRIG dégivrage naturel cyclique *m*

off-delay: ~ **relay** *n* ELEC ENG relais temporisé à l'ouverture *m*

offer *n* TELECOM offre *m*

off-flavor *n* (AmE), **off-flavour** *n* (BrE) FOOD TECH goût défectueux *m*, mauvais goût *m*

off-gas *n* CHEM gaz d'échappement *m*, gaz résiduel *m*, GAS TECH gaz d'évacuation *m*, gaz de dégagement *m*, NUCLEAR *released though the stack* gaz d'échappement *m*, gaz rejeté *m* ~ **condenser** *n* NUCLEAR condenseur des buées *m*

offhand: ~ **working** *n* C&G soufflage bouche *m*

off-hook *adj* TELECOM décroché

office: ~ **automation** *n* COMP *(OA)*, PROD ENG bureautique *f*; ~ **printing machine** *n* PRINT machine de bureau pour l'impression *f*

Office: ~ **for Research and Experiments** *n* RAIL Office de recherches et d'essais *m*

offing:[1] **in the** ~ *adj* NAUT au large

offing[2] *n* NAUT large *m*

offlap *n* GEOL superposition de strates en progradation *f*

off-line[1] *adj* COMP, DP autonome, hors ligne, TELECOM autonome, hors ligne

off-line[2] *adv* COMP, DP, TELECOM en différé

off-line:[3] ~ **computer** *n* NUCLEAR *information system* système informatique hors ligne *m*; ~ **docking** station *n* TRANSP station en dérivation *f*; ~ **editing** *n* TV montage off-line *m*; ~ **processing** *n* COMP traitement autonome *m*, DP traitement en différé *m*; ~ **working** *n* TELECOM exploitation en autonome *f*

off-load *n* PROD ENG déchargement *m*, extraction *f*; ~ **charging** *n* NUCLEAR *fuel loading* chargement avec arrêt *m*, chargement à froid *m*

off-machine: ~ **coating** *n* PAPER TECH couchage hors machine *m*; ~ **creping** *n* PAPER TECH crêpage hors machine *m*

off-mike *adj* RECORDING hors micro

off-peak: ~ **energy storage** *n* NUCLEAR stockage de l'énergie pendant les heures creuses *m*; ~ **load** *n* ELEC ENG charge normale *f*; ~ **period** *n* ELEC *supply* période de faible charge *f*; ~ **power** *n* NUCLEAR puissance en heures creuses *f*

off-period *n* ELEC ENG *of moving contact* position d'ouverture *f*, *of switch* position arrêt *f*

off-position *n* MECH ENG position de repos *f*

off-prints *n pl* PRINT tirés-à-part *m pl*

off-quality *adj* TEXTILES déclassé

off-screen *n* CINEMAT hors champ

offset[1] *adj* MECH ENG décalé, déporté, excentré, PRINT décalqué, décalé, VEHICLES *engine* décalé, désaxé

offset[2] *n* CINEMAT décalage *m*, CONST *projection* décalé *m*, ressaut *m*, saillie *f*, GEOL composante horizontale de déplacement *f*, décalage *m*, décrochement *m*, GEO-PHYS déport horizontal *m*, MECH décalage *m*, défaut d'alignement *m*, MECH ENG brisure *f*, MINING galerie d'écoulement *f*, galerie d'évacuation d'eau *f*, voie d'écoulement *f*, recoupe *f*, vieille *f*, volée *f*, naut *naval architecture* devis de tracé *m*, PRINT décalé *m*, offset *m*, TRANSP décalage *m*, WATER SUPP enclave *f*; ~ **antenna** *n* SPACE *communications* antenne à source décalée *f*; ~ **blade** *n* AERONAUT *helicopter* pale décalée *f*; ~ **carrier system** *n* TV système à porteuses décalées *m*; ~ **coater** *n* PAPER TECH coucheuse à rouleau gravé *f*; ~ **connecting rod** *n* AUTO bielle déportée *f*; ~ **deep printing** *n* PRINT offset en creux *m*; ~ **drive** *n* MINING recoupe *f*, vieille *f*, volée *f*; ~ **flapping hinge** *n* AERONAUT *helicopter* articulation de battement excentrée *f*; ~ **gravure coating** *n* PRINT couchage par gravure offset *m*, couchage par gravure transfert *m*; ~ **lens** *n* CINEMAT objectif à décentrement *m*; ~ **paper** *n* PAPER TECH, PRINT macule *f*; ~ **press** *n* PACKAGING presse offset *f*; ~ **printing** *n* PACKAGING impression offset *f*, PAPER TECH impression offset *f*, impression planographique *f*; ~ **printing press** *n* PRINT presse offset *f*; ~ **reflector** *n* SPACE *communications* réflecteur décalé *m*; ~ **ring spanner** *n* (BrE) MECH ENG *tool* clé polygonale contre-coudée *f*; ~ **ring wrench** *n* MECH ENG *tool* clé polygonale contre-coudée *f*; ~ **roller** *n* PROD ENG galet décalé *m*; ~ **rotary press** *n* PACKAGING presse rotative offset *f*; ~ **signal method** *n* TV système à signal décalé *m*; ~ **temperature** *n* THERMOD *thermostatic switching* température compensée *f*; ~ **viewfinder** *n* CINEMAT viseur latéral *m*; ~ **wrench** *n* MECH ENG clé coudée *f*

offset³ *vt* PRINT décaler, décalquer, perturber

offsetting *n* MECH ENG excentrage *m*, PROD ENG décalage *m*

off-shade *n* PAPER TECH écart de couleur *m*; ~ **dyeing** *n* COLOURS teinture hors-ton *f*

offshore¹ *adj* NAUT au large, PETR TECH au large, marin

offshore² *adv* GEOL vers le large, NAUT au large, PETR TECH au large, en mer, marin

offshore³ *n* OCEANOG large *m*; ~ **bar** *n* GEOL, OCEANOG cordon littoral *m*; ~ **dock** *n* TRANSP dock en mer *m*; ~ **drilling** *n* PETR TECH forage en mer *m*; ~ **drilling rig supply vessel** *n* TRANSP ravitailleur de forage en mer *m*; ~ **field** *n* PETR TECH gisement marin *m*; ~ **fishery** *n* OCEANOG gran de pêche *f*, pêche au large *f*; ~ **fishing** *n* OCEANOG pêche au large *f*; ~ **floating terminal** *n* TRANSP installation de transbordement en mer *f*; ~ **oil industry** *n* PETR TECH offshore *m*; ~ **platform** *n* PETR TECH plate-forme en mer *f*; ~ **port** *n* TRANSP port pétrolier en mer *m*; ~ **terminal** *n* TRANSP port d'éclatement *m*; ~ **trough** *n* OCEANOG sillon prélittoral *m*; ~ **well** *n* POLLUTION puits en mer *m*; ~ **wind** *n* NAUT vent au large *m*, vent de terre *m*

offtake *n* MINING galerie d'écoulement *f*, galerie d'évacuation d'eau *f*, voie d'écoulement *f*, WATER SUPP prise d'eau *f*

off-the-shelf: ~ **information** *n* PACKAGING information disponible immédiatement *f*

off-tune: ~ **frequency** *n* ELECTRON fréquence en dehors de l'accord *f*, fréquence hors accord *f*

OFS *abbr* (*out-of-frame second*) TELECOM seconde de perte du verrouillage de trame *f*

ogee *n* CONST doucine *f*, talon *m*; ~ **plane** *n* CONST doucine *f*

OHA *abbr* (*overhead access*) TELECOM accès au surdébit *m*, accès aux octets de surdébit *m*

OHC *abbr* (*overhead camshaft*) AUTO, MECH, VEHICLES arbre à cames en tête *m*

ohm *n* ELEC, ELEC ENG, METR, PHYS ohm *m*

Ohm's: ~ **law** *n* ELEC loi d'Ohm *f*, ELEC ENG loi de terre *f*, PHYS loi d'Ohm *f*

ohmic¹ *adj* ELEC *resistance*, ELEC ENG ohmique

ohmic:² ~ **conductor** *n* PHYS conducteur linéaire *m*, conducteur ohmique *m*; ~ **contact** *n* ELEC ENG contact ohmique *m*, FUELLESS connexion conductrice *f*, PHYS contact ohmique *m*; ~ **drop** *n* ELEC *resistance* chute de résistance *f*; ~ **loss** *n* ELEC ENG pertes ohmiques *f pl*, pertes par effet Joule *f pl*, PHYS perte ohmique *f*; ~ **losses** *n pl* ELEC *heating* pertes ohmiques *f pl*; ~ **resistance** *n* ELEC résistance ohmique *f*, ELEC ENG résistance en courant continu *f*, résistance ohmique *f*; ~ **value** *n* ELEC ENG valeur ohmique *f*

ohmmeter *n* ELEC, ELEC ENG, MINING, PHYS, TELECOM ohmmètre *m*

OHV: ~ **engine** *n* (*overhead valve engine*) AUTO moteur à soupapes en tête *m*

oil¹ *n* MAR POLL hydrocarbure *m*, PAPER TECH huile *f*, PETR pétrole *m*, PETR TECH *crude* pétrole *m*, *lubricant, fuel* huile *f*, REFRIG huile *f*; ~ **absorption** *n* P&R pigment prise d'huile *f*; ~ **baffle** *n* NUCLEAR chicane pour retenue de l'huile *f*; ~ **basin** *n* PETR TECH *geology* bassin pétrolifère *m*; ~ **bath** *n* LAB EQUIP *heating* bain d'huile *m*; ~ **bath air cleaner** *n* AUTO filtre à air à bain d'huile *m*; ~ **bath air filter** *n* AUTO filtre à air à bain d'huile *m*; ~ **box** *n* PROD ENG boîte d'essieu *f*, boîte de graissage *f*; ~ **break switch** *n* PROD ENG interrupteur à huile *m*; ~ **burner** *n* MECH ENG, THERMOD brûleur à mazout *m*; ~ **burner motor** *n* MECH ENG moteur pour brûleur à mazout *m*; ~ **change** *n* VEHICLES *lubrication* vidange d'huile *f*; ~ **change shop** *n* AUTO *maintenance* station-service vidange *f*; ~ **channel** *n* AUTO canalisation de graissage *f*, MECH ENG *drilling machine table* chenal à huile *m*, rigole pour recevoir l'huile *f*;~ **circuit breaker** *n* ELEC disjoncteur à l'huile *m*, ELEC ENG interrupteur à huile *m*; ~ **clearance vessel** *n* MAR POLL, POLLUTION navire dépollueur *m*; ~ **cock** *n* MECH ENG robinet graisseur *m*; ~ **conservator** *n* ELEC ENG conservateur d'huile *m*; ~ **control ring** *n* AUTO, VEHICLES *piston* segment racleur *m*; ~ **cooler** *n* ELEC *transformer* refroidisseur d'huile *m*, REFRIG, THERMOD refroidisseur à huile *m*, VEHICLES *lubrication* radiateur à l'huile *m*; ~ **cooling** *n* ELEC *transformer* refroidissement à huile *m*, MECH ENG refroidissement par l'huile *m*; ~ **cup** *n* MECH ENG collecteur d'huile *m*, godet graisseur *m*, godet à huile *m*; ~ **dashpot** *n* MECH ENG frein à huile *m*; ~ **dipstick** *n* AUTO jauge d'huile *f*; ~ **discovery** *n* PETR TECH découverte de pétrole *f*; ~ **distributor** *n* MECH ENG rampe de distribution *f*, rampe de graissage *f*; ~ **drain** *n* REFRIG purgeur d'huile *m*; ~ **drain hole** *n* AUTO orifice de vidange d'huile *m*; ~ **drain plug** *n* AUTO, MECH, VEHICLES *lubrication* bouchon de vidange d'huile *m*; ~ **drop** *n* PHYS gouttelette d'huile *f*; ~ **expander ring** *n* AUTO segment racleur à expansion *m*; ~ **exploration** *n* PETR TECH exploration pétrolière *f*; ~ **feed** *n* VEHICLES *lubrication* alimentation en huile *f*; ~ **filler pipe** *n* AUTO tuyau de remplissage d'huile *m*; ~ **filter** *n* AUTO, MECH, MECH ENG, VEHICLES *lubrication* filtre à huile *m*; ~ **filter cap** *n* AUTO bouchon de remplissage d'huile *m*; ~ **firing** *n* CONST chauffage au mazout *m*; ~ **flow** *n* PROD ENG débit d'huile *m*; ~ **formation volume factor** *n* PETR facteur volumétrique d'huile *m*; ~ **gage** *n* (AmE) *see oil gauge*; ~ **gallery** *n* AUTO canalisation de graissage *f*;

~ **gasification** *n* PETR TECH *refinery process* gazéification du pétrole *f*; ~ **gauge** *n* (BrE) MECH ENG jaugeur d'huile *m*, PROD ENG oléomètre *m*; ~ **groove** *n* MECH ENG *in bearings* canal de graissage *m*, pattes d'araignées *f pl*, rainure de graissage *f*; ~ **heating** *n* HEATING chauffage au mazout *m*; ~ **hole** *n* MECH ENG lumière *f*, trou de graissage *m*, trou graisseur *m*; ~ **hydraulic starter** *n* ELEC démarreur à l'huile *m*; ~ **immersion lens** *n* LAB EQUIP objectif à immersion à huile *m*, *microscope* objectif à immersion à l'huile *m*; ~ **inlet** *n* AUTO orifice de remplissage d'huile *m*; ~ **in place** *n* PETR huile en place *f*, PETR TECH *estimating reserves* pétrole en place *m*; ~ **insulator** *n* ELEC ENG isolateur à l'huile *m*; ~ **interrupter** *n* PROD ENG interrupteur à huile *m*; ~ **length** *n* P&R *alkyd resin, varnish* taux d'huile *m*; ~ **level mark** *n* VEHICLES *lubrication* repère du niveau d'huile *m*; ~ **level stick** *n* AUTO jauge d'huile *f*; ~ **line** *n* AUTO canalisation de graissage *f*; ~ **mist** *n* PRINT brouillard d'huile *m*, nébulisation *f*; ~ **mop** *n* MAR POLL cordon oléophile *m*; ~ **packing paper** *n* PACKAGING papier d'emballage paraffiné *m*; ~ **paint** *n* COLOURS peinture à l'huile *f*; ~ **palm** *n* FOOD TECH palmier à huile de Guinée *m*, éléis de Guinée *f*; ~ **pan** *n* AUTO carter *m*, demi-carter inférieur *m*, MECH carter d'huile *m*; ~ **pan gasket** *n* AUTO joint de carter *m*; ~ **paper capacitor** *n* ELEC ENG condensateur au papier imprégné d'huile *m*; ~ **pier** *n* TRANSP quai pétrolier *m*; ~ **pipe** *n* PROD ENG *lubrication* tuyau de graissage *m*; ~ **pipeline** *n* PETR, PETR TECH, TRANSP oléoduc *m*; ~ **pressostat** *n* REFRIG pressostat d'huile *m*; ~ **pressure controller** *n* CONTROL contrôleur de pression d'huile *m*; ~ **pressure gage** *n* (AmE), ~ **pressure gauge** *n* (BrE) AUTO manomètre à huile *m*, CONTROL contrôleur de pression d'huile *m*, indicateur de pression d'huile *m*, VEHICLES *lubrication* manomètre à huile *m*; ~ **pressure safety cutout** *n* REFRIG pressostat de sécurité d'huile *m*; ~ **pressure switch** *n* AERONAUT manocontact *m*, CONTROL interrupteur à pression d'huile *m*; ~ **pressure warning light** *n* AUTO témoin de pression d'huile *m*; ~ **pump** *n* AUTO, CONST, REFRIG, VEHICLES *lubrication* pompe à huile *f*; ~ **pump and pipe connections** *n pl* MECH ENG *for machine tools* pompe de lubrification et sa tuyauterie *f*; ~ **pump gasket** *n* REFRIG joint de pompe à l'huile *m*; ~ **pump spindle** *n* AUTO arbre de commande de la pompe à huile *m*; ~ **quench** *n* HEATING four de trempe à mazout *m*; ~ **quenching** *n* THERMOD trempe à l'huile *f*; ~ **reclaiming** *n* MECH ENG régénération d'huile *f*; ~ **recovery skimmer** *n* POLLUTION récupérateur mécanique *m*; ~ **recovery vessel** *n* MAR POLL, POLLUTION navire dépollueur *m*; ~ **regeneration plant** *n* RECYCLING usine de régénération des huiles usées *f*; ~ **relief valve plunger** *n* AUTO soupape de décharge *f*; ~ **removing system** *n* GAS TECH système de déshuilage *m*; ~ **reservoir** *n* MINING réservoir d'huile *m*, PETR réservoir d'huile *m*, réservoir de pétrole *m*, réservoir de pétrole brut *m*; ~ **ring** *n* MECH ENG rondelle autolubrifiante *f*, PROD ENG anneau de graissage *m*, bague de graissage *f*; ~ **sands** *n pl* PETR sables pétrolifères *m pl*; ~ **saturation** *n* PETR saturation en huile *f*, saturation en pétrole *f*; ~ **scraper** *n* NUCLEAR dispositif racleur d'huile *m*; ~ **scrubbing** *n* PETR TECH *refinery process* épuration de l'huile *f*; ~ **seal** *n* MECH joint étanche à l'huile *m*, MECH ENG joint d'huile *m*, retient-graisse *m*; ~ **seed** *n* FOOD TECH graine oléagineuse *f*; ~ **self-sufficiency** *n* PETR TECH autonomie pétrolière *f*, indépendance pétrolière *f*; ~ **separator** *n* HYDROL déshuileur *m*, séparateur d'huile

m, PAPER TECH déshuileur *m*, REFRIG séparateur d'huile *m*; ~ **shale** *n* PETR schiste bitumineux *m*; ~ **show** *n* PETR TECH *prospecting* indice *m*; ~ **show analyzer** *n* PETR TECH *prospecting* analyseur d'indices *m*; ~ **sight glass** *n* REFRIG voyant d'huile *m*; ~ **sight O-ring** *n* REFRIG joint torique à voyant d'huile *m*; ~ **slick** *n* PETR TECH nappe de pétrole *f*, POLLUTION marée noire *f*, nappe de pétrole *f*; ~ **slick sinking** *n* POLLUTION coulage des nappes *m*; ~ **slinger** *n* MECH ENG bague de protection *f*, déflecteur d'huile *m*; ~ **still** *n* REFRIG rectificateur d'huile *m*; ~ **stimulation** *n* PETR stimulation de gisements d'hydrocarbures liquides *f*; ~ **strainer** *n* AUTO crépine *f*; ~ **sump** *n* AERONAUT puisard d'huile *m*; ~ **switch** *n* ELEC interrupteur à huile *m*, ELEC ENG disjoncteur à l'huile *m*, PROD ENG commutateur à bain d'huile *m*; ~ **tank** *n* CONST réservoir d'huile *m*, ELEC ENG cuve à huile *f*, réservoir d'huile *m*; ~ **tanker** *n* NAUT *type of ship* navire pétrolier *m*, pétrolier *m*, PETR TECH *shipping*, TRANSP pétrolier *m*; ~ **temperature cutout** *n* REFRIG thermostat de sécurité d'huile *m*; ~ **temperature indicator** *n* AERONAUT indicateur de température d'huile *m*; ~ **temperature probe** *n* AERONAUT sonde de température d'huile *f*; ~ **tracing paper** *n* PAPER TECH papier pour calque *m*; ~ **transformer** *n* ELEC ENG transformateur dans l'huile *m*; ~ **trap** *n* HYDROL déshuileur *m*, séparateur d'huile *m*, PETR TECH *geology* piège d'hydrocarbures *m*, piège pétrolifère *m*, WATER SUPP déshuileur *m*; ~ **tube twist drill** *n* MECH ENG mèche hélicoïdale à tube d'huile *f*; ~ **of vitriol** *n* CHEM acide sulfurique *m*, acide vitriolique *m*, huile de vitriol *f*, vitriol *m*; ~ **waste** *n* POLLUTION déchets huileux *m pl*; ~ **well** *n* PETR puits de pétrole *m*; ~ **wiper** *n* NUCLEAR dispositif racleur d'huile *m*

oil[2] *vt* PROD ENG graisser, graisser à l'huile, huiler; ~ **quench** *vt* THERMOD tremper à l'huile

oil-base: ~ **mud** *n* PETR, PETR TECH *drilling* boue à base d'huile *f*

oil-based: ~ **ink** *n* PRINT encre à base d'huile *f*

oil-bearing *adj* PETR, PETR TECH pétrolifère

oil-bound: ~ **distemper** *n* COLOURS couleur à détrempe à base d'huile *f*; ~ **paint** *n* COLOURS peinture à l'huile *f*; ~ **water paint** *n* COLOURS peinture-émulsion *f*

oil-bulk-ore: ~ **carrier** *n* TRANSP transporteur combiné minerai-vrac-pétrole *m*, TRANSP pétrolier-vracquier-minéralier *m*

oil-burning *adj* THERMOD à combustion d'huile

oilcan *n* PROD ENG burette *f*, burette de graissage *f*, burette à huile *f*

oil-carbon: ~ **deposit** *n* AUTO calamine *f*

oilcloth *n* P&R *textiles* toile cirée *f*, PACKAGING tissu huilé *m*, TEXTILES toile cirée *f*

oil-coal-ore: ~ **carrier** *n* (*OCO carrier*) TRANSP navire OCO *m*

oil-concentrating: ~ **agent** *n* POLLUTION agent repousseur *m*

oil-cooled[1] *adj* THERMOD refroidi par de l'huile

oil-cooled:[2] ~ **transformer** *n* ELEC transformateur refroidi par huile *m*, transformateur à refroidissement par huile *m*, ELEC ENG transformateur à huile *m*, transformateur à refroidissement par huile *m*

oil-drenched: ~ **paper** *n* PACKAGING papier imprégné d'huile *m*

oil-eating: ~ **bacterium** *n* RECYCLING bactérie mangeuse de pétrole *f*

oiled: ~ **bearings** *n pl* MECH ENG palier graisseur à bagues *m*, palier à graissage automatique par bagues *m*; ~

canvas *n* PACKAGING canevas huilé *m*

oiler *n* MINING graisseur *m*, PROD ENG *can* burette *f*, burette de graissage *f*, burette à huile *f*, *cup* godet graisseur *m*, godet à huile *m*, *person* graisseur *m*, TEXTILES *person* graisseur *m*

oilfield *n* PETR champ de pétrole *m*, PETR TECH *geology* champ de pétrole *m*, champ pétrolifère *m*, gisement de pétrole *m*

oil-filled: ~ **cable** *n* ELEC câble OF *m*, câble à huile *m*, ELEC ENG câble sous huile *m*, câble à remplissage d'huile *m*; ~ **pipe-type cable** *n* ELEC câble oléostatique *m*, câble à huile en tuyau *m*

oil-fired[1] *adj* THERMOD à combustion de mazout

oil-fired:[2] ~ **boiler** *n* HEAT ENG, HEATING chaudière à mazout *f*; ~ **central heating system** *n* HEAT ENG chauffage central au mazout *m*; ~ **furnace** *n* HEAT ENG foyer à mazout *m*; ~ **installation** *n* MECH ENG foyer à mazout *m*; ~ **power plant** *n* NUCLEAR centrale au fuel *f*; ~ **power station** *n* ELEC *supply* centrale électrique au mazout *f*, HEAT ENG usine électrique à mazout *f*, THERMOD centrale électrique à mazout *f*; ~ **rotary dryer** *n* HEATING *asphalt plant* sécheur rotatif à mazout *m*

oil-forming *adj* CHEM oléfiant

oil-free: ~ **compressor** *n* REFRIG compresseur sans huile *m*

oil-hardened *adj* THERMOD trempé à l'huile

oil-immersed: ~ **capacitor** *n* ELEC condensateur dans l'huile *m*; ~ **transformer** *n* ELEC transformateur immergé dans l'huile *m*

oiling *n* PROD ENG graissage *m*, graissage à l'huile *m*, huilage *m*, huilement *m*, TEXTILES ensimage *m*

oilless: ~ **bearing** *n* MECH ENG coussinet autolubrifiant *m*

oil-moistened: ~ **air filter cartridge** *n* AUTO filtre humide *m*

oilometer *n* MECH ENG, PROD ENG oléomètre *m*

oil-ore: ~ **carrier** *n* *(OO)* NAUT, TRANSP minéralier-pétrolier *m*

oil-painted *adj* COLOURS peint à l'huile

oilproof: ~ **protective gloves** *n pl* SAFETY gants de travail résistants à l'huile *m pl*

oil-quenched *adj* THERMOD trempé à l'huile

oil-resistant *adj* P&R résistant à l'huile

oil-resisting: ~ **hose** *n* P&R tuyau résistant à l'huile *m*

oilskin *n* NAUT *sailing clothes* ciré *m*, P&R *textiles*, TEXTILES toile vernie *f*

oil-softened: ~ **rubber** *n* P&R caoutchouc plastifié à l'huile *m*

oil-soluble *adj* CHEM soluble dans l'huile, P&R *paint* oléosoluble

oilspill *n* MAR POLL déversement d'hydrocarbures *m*, déversement en mer *m*, POLLUTION déversement de pétrole *m*; ~ **response** *n* MAR POLL capacité de réponse à une pollution par les hydrocarbures *f*, intervention en cas de déversement *f*

oilstone *n* MECH ENG *abrasives* pierre à huile *f*, PROD ENG affiloire *f*, pierre à aiguiser *f*, pierre à huile *f*, pierre à morfiler *f*

oil-tempered: ~ **needle** *n* PAPER TECH aiguille à acier huilé *f*

oiltight *adj* PROD ENG étanche à l'huile

oil-water: ~ **contact** *n* PETR ligne de contact huile-eau *f*, surface de contact huile-eau *f*; ~ **interface** *n* MAR POLL plan de séparation eau-huile *m*

ointment *n* CHEM onguent *m*

okenite *n* MINERAL okénite *f*

OK-signal *n* TELECOM signal OK *m*

old: ~ **ground level** *n* CONST niveau ancien des sols *m*, niveau original des sols *m*; ~ **number** *n* TELECOM numéro désaffecté *m*

Oldham: ~ **coupling** *n* MECH accouplement Oldham *m*

oleandrin *n* CHEM oléandrine *f*

oleate *n* CHEM oléate *m*

olefin *n*,

olefine *n* CHEM, DETERGENTS, PETR TECH *chemistry, refining* oléfine *f*

olefinic[1] *adj* CHEM oléfinique

olefinic:[2] ~ **content** *n* CHEM teneur oléfinique *f*

olefins *n pl* PETR oléfines *f pl*

oleic[1] *adj* CHEM oléique

oleic:[2] ~ **acid** *n* FOOD TECH acide oléique *m*; ~ **ink** *n* COLOURS encre oléique *f*

olein *n* CHEM huile absolue *f*, huile de suif *f*, oléine *f*

oleo: ~ **oil** *n* CHEM huile de suif *f*

oleometer *n* CHEM oléomètre *m*

oleophilic[1] *adj* CHEM, MAR POLL oléophile

oleophilic:[2] ~ **belt** *n* MAR POLL courroie oléophile *f*, courroie à hydrocarbures *f*; ~ **belt skimmer** *n* MAR POLL récupérateur à courroie oléophile *m*, écrémeur à courroie oléophile *m*

oleophosphoric *adj* CHEM oléophosphorique

oleoresin *n* CHEM oléorésine *f*

oleoresinous[1] *adj* CHEM oléorésineux

oleoresinous:[2] ~ **paint** *n* CONST peinture oléorésineuse *f*; ~ **varnish** *n* COATINGS vernis oléorésineux *m*, vernis à l'huile *m*

oleovitamin *n* CHEM oléovitamine *f*

oleum *n* CHEM oléum *m*, DETERGENTS acide sulfurique fumant *m*, oléum *m*; ~ **sulfuric acid** *n* (AmE), ~ **sulphuric acid** *n* (BrE) CHEM acide sulfurique fumant *m*

oligoclase *n* MINERAL oligoclase *f*

oligomer *n* CHEM, P&R oligomère *m*

oligomeric *adj* CHEM oligomère

oligomerization *n* P&R *process*, PROP MAT oligomérisation *f*

oligomycyn *n* CHEM oligomycine *f*

oligon: ~ **spar** *n* MINERAL oligonite *f*

oligonite *n* MINERAL oligonite *f*

olistolith *n* GEOL olistolithe *m*

olivenite *n* MINERAL olivénite *f*

olivine *n* MINERAL olivine *f*

OLRT *abbr* (*on-line real-time*) COMP, DP temps réel en ligne

omega: ~ **loop** *n* TV boucle oméga *f*; ~ **minus particle** *n* PHYS particule oméga moins *f*; ~ **wrap** *n* TV enroulement oméga *m*

omnibearing: ~ **indicator** *n* AERONAUT indicateur de relèvement *m*; ~ **selector** *n* AERONAUT sélecteur omnidirectionnel *m*

omnidirectional: ~ **antenna** *n* SPACE *communications* antenne isotrope *f*, antenne équidirective *f*, TELECOM antenne équidirective *f*; ~ **dipole** *n* NAUT *antenna* dipôle omnidirectionnel *m*; ~ **microphone** *n* ACOUSTICS microphone omnidirectionnel *m*; ~ **radiorange** *n* AERONAUT radiophare omnidirectionnel VHF *m*

omnirange: ~ **indicator** *n* AERONAUT indicateur omnidirectionnel *m*

omphacite *n* MINERAL omphacite *f*

OMR *abbr* (*optical mark reading*) COMP, DP lecture optique de marques *f*

OMS *abbr* (*orbital maneuvring system, orbital manoeuvring system*) SPACE système de manoeuvre en orbite *m*

on *adj* ELEC ENG *motor, engine* allumé, en marche, en service, *transistor* débloqué, MECH ENG marche

ON *abbr (octane number)* PETR TECH indice d'octane *m*

on/off[1] *adj* MECH ENG marche/arrêt

on/off[2] *n* CINEMAT marche/arrêt *f*; **~ control** *n* ELEC commande à double position *f*, SPACE commande tout-ou-rien *f*; **~ pilot light** *n* CINEMAT voyant de mise en service *m*; **~ service indicator** *n* PROD ENG indicateur d'état en/hors service *m*; **~ signal** *n* CONTROL signal tout-ou-rien *m*; **~ switch** *n* CINEMAT, ELEC interrupteur *m*, ELEC ENG interrupteur général *m*, MECH ENG sélecteur marche/arrêt *m*, PHOTO interrupteur *m*, PHYS commutateur MA *m*, commutateur marche/arrêt *m*; **~ switch indicator** *n* PROD ENG indicateur d'état en/hors service *m*

on-air: **~ period** *n* ELEC ENG période d'émission *f*; **~ time** *n* TELECOM temps d'émission *m*, TV temps d'antenne *m*, temps de prise d'antenne *m*

on-board[1] *adj* ELECTRON incorporé à la carte, MILIT embarqué, SPACE *craft* embarqué à bord

on-board:[2] **~ circuitry** *n* ELECTRON circuit réalisé sur la carte *m*; **~ communication station** *n* TELECOM station de communication *f*; **~ computer** *n* SPACE *craft* calculateur de bord *m*; **~ equipment** *n* SPACE matériel de bord *m*, matériel embarqué *m*; **~ processing** *n* SPACE *communications* traitement à bord *m*; **~ subscriber** *n* TELECOM abonné à bord *m*; **~ switching** *n* SPACE *communications* commutation à bord *f*; **~ system** *n* SPACE *craft* équipement de bord *m*, équipement embarqué *m*

on-call: **~ bus system** *n* TRANSP autobus à la demande *m*

once-through: **~ boiler** *n* HEATING chaudière à passage unique *f*; **~ charge** *n* NUCLEAR charge à passage unique *f*; **~ cycle** *n* NUCLEAR cycle ouvert *m*; **~ steam generator** *n (OTSG)* NUCLEAR *cycle* générateur de vapeur à passage unique *m*

once-through-then-out *n (OTTO)* NUCLEAR cycle à sortir après passage unique *m*

on-chip: **~ amplification** *n* ELECTRON amplification incorporée *f*, amplification sur la puce *f*; **~ amplifier** *n* ELECTRON amplificateur incorporé *m*; **~ analog-to-digital conversion** *n* (AmE), **~ analogue-to-digital conversion** *n* (BrE) ELECTRON numérisation sur la puce *f*; **~ capacitor** *n* ELEC ENG condensateur intégré *m*; **~ circuit** *n* ELECTRON circuit incorporé *m*, circuit réalisé sur la puce *m*; **~ filter** *n* ELECTRON filtre incorporé *m*; **~ processing** *n* ELECTRON traitement sur la puce *m*; **~ transistor** *n* ELECTRON transistor intégré *m*, transistor réalisé sur la puce *m*

oncolith *n* GEOL oncolithe *m*

on-delay: **~ relay** *n* ELEC ENG relais temporisé à la fermeture *m*

one:[1] **all in ~ piece** *adj* MECH ENG tout d'une pièce; **in ~ piece** *adj* PROD ENG tout d'une pièce

one:[2] **~ second theodolite** *n* INSTRUMENT théodolite universel *m*

one:[3] **~ engine inoperative** *phr* AERONAUT un moteur hors de fonctionnement

ONE: **~ state** *n* ELECTRON état UN *m*, état haut *m*

one's: **~ complement** *n* COMP, DP complément à un *m*

one-address: **~ instruction** *n* COMP, DP instruction à une adresse *f*

one-and-one: **~ lease** *n* TEXTILES enverjure simple *f*

one-bath: **~ development** *n* PRINT développement en un seul bain *m*

one-coil: **~ transformer** *n* ELEC autotransformateur *m*

one-cycle: **~ reactor** *n* NUCLEAR réacteur travaillant à une seule pression *m*

one-cylinder: **~ engine** *n* AUTO moteur monocylindrique *m*, MECH ENG machine à cylindre unique *f*, moteur monocylindrique *m*, moteur à un seul cylindre *m*

one-digit: **~ adder** *n* ELECTRON demi-additionneur *m*; **~ subtractor** *n* ELECTRON demi-soustracteur *m*

one-dimensional *adj* PHYS unidimensionnel

one-element: **~ cell** *n* ELEC ENG pile à un élément *f*

one-light: **~ print** *n* CINEMAT copie à lumière unique *f*

one-off: **~ tooling** *n* MECH ENG outillage d'une seule commande *m*

one-part: **~ die** *n* MECH ENG coussinet d'une seule pièce *m*, coussinet en une pièce *m*; **~ screw plate** *n* MECH ENG filière simple *f*

one-phase[1] *adj* ELEC ENG monophasé

one-phase:[2] **~ controller** *n* TRANSP régulateur monophase *m*

one-piece: **~ base** *n* PROD ENG base monobloc *f*; **~ connector** *n* ELEC ENG connecteur en une partie *m*

one-plus-one: **~ address instruction** *n* DP instruction à une adresse plus une *f*; **~ carrier system** *n* TELECOM système d'abonné à courant porteur *m*

one-point letter spaced *adj* PRINT espacé d'un point

one-pole *adj* ELECTRON unipolaire

one-shot: **~ circuit** *n* ELECTRON circuit monostable *m*; **~ multivibrator** *n* ELECTRON multivibrateur monostable *m*; **~ programing** *n* (AmE), **~ programming** *n* (BrE) PROD ENG programmation d'impulsion *f*; **~ signal** *n* ELECTRON signal non récurrent *m*

one-side: **~ art paper** *n* PRINT papier couché une face *m*; **~ coated board** *n* PACKAGING carton vernis d'un côté *m*; **~ coated paper** *n* PRINT papier couché une face *m*; **~ colored board** *n* (AmE) *see one-side coloured board*; **~ colored paper** *n* (AmE) *see one-side coloured paper*; **~ coloured board** *n* (BrE) PAPER TECH carton coloré une face *m*; **~ coloured paper** *n* (BrE) PAPER TECH papier coloré une face *m*

one-stop: **~ shopping** *n* TELECOM guichet unique *m*

one-time-carbonizing: **~ base paper** *n* PAPER TECH papier pour support carbone une fois *m*

one-to-one: **~ printing** *n* CINEMAT tirage optique normal *m*

one-track: **~ recording** *n* ACOUSTICS enregistrement monotrace *m*

one-up *n* PRINT pose d'origine *f*, sortie de livres un par un *f*

one-way: **~ bottle** *n* PACKAGING bouteille à jeter *f*; **~ container** *n* PACKAGING conteneur non retour *m*; **~ pack** *n* PACKAGING emballage à jeter *m*; **~ pallet** *n* PACKAGING palette à jeter *f*, TRANSP palette perdue *f*; **~ repeater** *n* ELECTRON répéteur unidirectionnel *m*; **~ road** *n* CONST route à sens unique *f*; **~ roller** *n* PROD ENG galet unidirectionnel *m*

ongoing: **~ qualification test** *n* NUCLEAR essai de qualification en fonctionnement *m*

on-hook: **~ condition** *n* TELECOM état de raccrochage *m*; **~ dialing** *n* (AmE), **~ dialling** *n* (BrE) TELECOM numérotation sans décrocher *f*

onion *n* C&G oignon *m*

onionskin: **~ paper** *n* (AmE) *(cf banknote paper)* PAPER TECH papier pour billet de banque *m*

onium: **~ salt** *n* CHEM sel d'onium *m*

onlap *n* GEOL superposition de strates en transgression *f*

on-line[1] *adj* COMP, DP connecté, en ligne, interactif, PRINT, TELECOM en direct; **~ real-time** *adj (OLRT)*

COMP, DP temps réel en ligne

on-line[2] *adv* COMP, DP, TELECOM en direct, en ligne

on-line:[3] ~ **database** *n* COMP, DP base de données en ligne *f*; ~ **gaging** *n* (AmE), ~ **gauging** *n* (BrE) SPRINGS calibrage en ligne *m*; ~ **measurement** *n* NUCLEAR mesure en liaison directe *f*; ~ **processing** *n* COMP, DP traitement en direct *m*; ~ **programing** *n* (AmE), ~ **programming** *n* (BrE) PROD ENG programmation en cours d'exécution *f*, programmation en cours de fonctionnement *f*; ~ **quality monitoring** *n* TEXTILES surveillance de la qualité en production *f*

on-load: ~ **charging** *n* NUCLEAR chargement sans arrêt *m*; ~ **current** *n* ELEC ENG courant en charge *m*, intensité en charge *f*; ~ **fueling** *n* (AmE), ~ **fuelling** *n* (BrE) NUCLEAR chargement sans arrêt *m*; ~ **refueling** *n* (AmE), ~ **refuelling** *n* (BrE) NUCLEAR rechargement sans arrêt *m*; ~ **tap changer** *n* ELEC changeur de prises en charge *m*; ~ **tap changing** *n* ELEC changement de prises en charge *m*; ~ **voltage** *n* ELEC tension en circuit fermé *f*, ELEC ENG tension en charge *f*

on-machine: ~ **coating** *n* PAPER TECH couchage sur machine *m*; ~ **creping** *n* PAPER TECH crêpage sur machine *m*

ONP *abbr (open network provision)* TELECOM provision de réseau ouvert *f*

on-peak: ~ **conditions** *n pl* ELEC *supply* régime à charge maximale *m*

on-position *n* ELEC ENG position de fermeture *f*, position marche *f*

ONR *abbr (octane number rating)* AUTO indice d'octane *m*

on-scene: ~ **commander** *n (OSC)* MAR POLL *OSC* commandant des opérations sur le terrain *m*; ~ **communications** *n pl (OSC)* TELECOM communications sur place *f pl*

onset *n* CHEM départ *m*; ~ **of magnetic field** *n* RAD PHYS *particle decay experiments* déclenchement du champ magnétique *m*

onsetter *n* (BrE) *(cf platman)* MINING accrocheur *m*, clicheur *m*, ouvrier d'accrochage *m*

onsetting *n* MINING accrochage *m*, chambre d'accrochage *f*, chambre d'envoyage *f*, envoyage *m*, recette *f*

on-shift: ~ **operator** *n* NUCLEAR opérateur de quart *m*

onshore[1] *adj* NAUT à terre, PETR TECH côtier, à terre

onshore[2] *adv* NAUT à terre

onshore:[3] ~ **base** *n* PETR TECH *operations* base côtière *f*; ~ **wind** *n* NAUT vent du large *m*

onsite: ~ **maintenance tools** *n pl* CONST outillage pour chantier de maintenance *m*; ~ **waste disposal** *n* NUCLEAR entreposage des déchets sur le site *m*

on-state: ~ **conductivity** *n* ELEC ENG conductibilité à l'état passant *f*; ~ **current** *n* ELEC ENG courant à l'état passant *m*

onyx *n* MINERAL onyx *m*

OO *abbr (oil-ore carrier)* NAUT, TRANSP minéralier-pétrolier *m*

OOD *abbr (object-oriented design)* COMP, DP COO *(conception orientée objet)*

oolitic: ~ **limestone** *n* GEOL calcaire oolithique *m*

Oort: ~ **cloud** *n* ASTRON nuage d'Oort *m*

ooze *n* HYDROL infiltration *f*, suintement *m*, limon *m*, vase *f*, OCEANOG boue *f*

oozing *n* HYDROL infiltration *f*, suintement *m*

op: ~ **amp** *n (operational amplifier)* COMP, DP, ELECTRON, PHYS, TELECOM amplificateur opérationnel *m*; ~ **code** *n (operation code)* COMP, DP, PROD ENG code

op *m (code d'opération)*

opacified *n* REFRIG aérosilicagel opacifié *m*, gel aérobie de silice opacifié *m*

opacifier *n* C&G opacifiant *m* (Fra), opalisant *m* (Bel)

opacifying[1] *adj* CHEM *agent* opacifiant

opacifying:[2] ~ **agent** *n* DETERGENTS agent opacifiant *m*

opacimeter *n* CHEM, PAPER TECH opacimètre *m*

opacity *n* CHEM, PAPER TECH, PHYS, PRINT, PROP MAT, WAVE PHYS opacité *f*; ~ **paper backing** *n* PAPER TECH opacité sur fond papier *f*; ~ **tester** *n* PAPER TECH opacimètre *m*; ~ **white backing** *n* PAPER TECH opacité sur fond blanc *f*

opal *n* MINERAL opale *f*, PRINT opale *f*, épreuve hélio *f*; ~ **glass** *n* C&G verre opale *m*; ~ **printing** *n* CINEMAT tirage en lumière diffuse *m*

OPAL: ~ **detector** *n* PART PHYS détecteur OPAL *m*

opalescence *n* HYDROL *of water* opalescence *f*

opalescent: ~ **glass** *n* C&G verre opalescent *m*

opaline *n* C&G opaline *f*

opaque[1] *adj* PRINT opaque

opaque[2] *n* COATINGS vernis à masquer *m*; ~ **color** *n* (AmE), ~ **colour** *n* (BrE) COLOURS couleur non transparente *f*, couleur opaque *f*; ~ **glass** *n* C&G verre opaque *m*; ~ **leader** *n* CINEMAT amorce opaque *f*; ~ **medium** *n* PHYS milieu opaque *m*; ~ **pigment** *n* COLOURS pigment opacifiant *m*; ~ **substance** *n* RAD PHYS substance opaque *f*

opaqueness *n* PROP MAT opacité *f*

opaquing *n* CINEMAT gouachage *m*

OPC *abbr (originating point code)* TELECOM code du point d'origine *m*

OPEC *abbr (Organization of Petroleum Exporting Countries)* PETR TECH OPEP *(Organisation des pays exportateurs de pétrole)*

open[1] *adj* COMP, DP ouvert, NAUT *boat* non-ponté; ~ **cast** *adj* MINING à ciel ouvert; ~ **circuit** *adj* PHYS en circuit ouvert

open:[2] ~ **air** *n* CONST air libre *m*, grand air *m*; ~ **angle** *n* GEOM angle ouvert *m*; ~ **arc** *n* ELEC ENG arc en air libre *m*; ~ **arc ion source** *n* NUCLEAR source d'ions à arc à flamme découverte *f*; ~ **assembly time** *n* P&R *adhesives* temps d'exposition avant assemblage *m*; ~ **belt** *n* PAPER TECH courroie droite *f*, PROD ENG courroie ouverte *f*; ~ **cell foamed plastic** *n* REFRIG *insulating* mousse de plastique à alvéoles ouvertes *f*; ~ **chain** *n* CHEM chaîne ouverte *f*; ~ **channel** *n* HYDR EQUIP canal découvert *m*; ~ **channel flow** *n* FLUID PHYS écoulements à surface libre *m pl*; ~ **circuit** *n* COAL TECH, ELEC, ELEC ENG, PHYS, PROD ENG circuit ouvert *m*; ~ **circuit characteristics** *n pl* ELEC *equipment* caractéristiques à circuit ouvert *f pl*; ~ **circuit crushing** *n* COAL TECH concassage en circuit ouvert *m*; ~ **circuit current** *n* ELEC courant à vide *m*; ~ **circuit impedance** *n* ELEC, ELEC ENG impédance en circuit ouvert *f*; ~ **circuit operation** *n* ELEC *equipment* fonctionnement à vide *m*; ~ **circuit test** *n* ELEC essai à circuit ouvert *m*; ~ **circuit voltage** *n* ELEC tension de la source *f*, tension en circuit ouvert *f*, ELEC ENG tension en circuit ouvert *f*, tension à vide *f*, FUELLESS tension de repos *f*; ~ **circuit winding** *n* ELEC *transformer* enroulement ouvert *m*; ~ **cluster** *n* ASTRON amas ouvert *m*; ~ **coil armature** *n* ELEC *machine* induit à circuit ouvert *m*; ~ **coil spring** *n* MECH ENG ressort de compression *m*; ~ **conductor** *n* ELEC ENG conducteur coupé *m*; ~ **contact** *n* ELEC *relay* contact de repos *m*; ~ **core transformer** *n* ELEC transformateur à noyau ouvert *m*; ~ **cycle gas turbine** *n*

TRANSP turbine à gaz à circuit ouvert *f*; ~ **delta connection** *n* ELEC connexion en triangle ouvert *f*; ~ **die forging** *n* MECH ENG pièce forgée pour matrice à ouverture *f*; ~ **diggings** *n pl* MINING minière à ciel ouvert *f*; ~ **distribution processing** *n (ODP)* TELECOM traitement à distribution ouverte *m*; ~ **drain** *n* WATER SUPP fossé de drainage *m*; ~ **dump** *n* RECYCLING décharge brute *f*; ~ **end** *n* SPRINGS extrémité non rapprochée *f*, *of spring coil* spire terminale ouverte *f*; ~ **end wrench** *n* MECH ENG clé à fourche *f*, MECH ENG clé à ergots *f*, clé à fourche *f*; ~ **flume** *n* PROD ENG *turbine chamber* chambre d'eau ouverte *f*; ~ **fold** *n* PETR pli ouvert *m*; ~ **front** *n* HYDR EQUIP gueule-bée *f*; ~ **front bin** *n* PROD ENG *storing* bac à bec *m*; ~ **front mechanical power press** *n* MECH ENG presse mécanique à bâti en col de cygne *f*; ~ **fuel cycle** *n* NUCLEAR cycle ouvert *m*; ~ **fuse** *n* ELEC fusible non protégé *m*; ~ **headbox** *n* PAPER TECH caisse d'arrivée ouverte *f*; ~ **heap** *n* PROD ENG *copper smelting* tas de grillage *m*; ~ **hearth furnace** *n* COAL TECH four Martin *m*, four d'aciérie *m*, HEATING fourneau à réverbère *m*, PROD ENG four Martin *m*, four Martin-Siemens *m*, four à creuset *m*, four à sole *m*; ~ **hole** *n* PETR forage à découvert *m*, trou non tubé *m*; ~ **hole completion** *n* PETR complétion en trou ouvert *f*; ~ **hole drilling** *n* PETR TECH forage à découvert *m*; ~ **hood** *n* PAPER TECH hotte ouverte *f*; ~ **loop** *n* AERONAUT boucle ouverte *f*, ELEC *circuit* boucle ouverte *f*, circuit ouvert *m*; ~ **loop oscillator** *n* ELECTRON oscillateur non asservi en phase *m*; ~ **loop transfer function** *n* NUCLEAR fonction de transfert en boucle ouverte *f*; ~ **mill** *n* P&R *equipment, rubber* malaxeur *m*, mélangeur ouvert *m*, mélangeur à cylindres *m*; ~ **network provision** *n (ONP)* TELECOM provision de réseau ouverte *f*; ~ **newel stair** *n* CONST escalier à noyau creux *m*; ~ **order** *n* PROD ENG ordre de fabrication lancé *m*, ordre en fabrication en cours *m*; ~ **pass** *n* PROD ENG *rolling mill* cannelure ouverte *f*, cannelure roulante *f*; ~ **pit** *n* MINING fosse à ciel ouvert *f*, fouille à ciel ouvert *f*; ~ **pit mine** *n* MINING carrière en exploitation à ciel ouvert *f*; ~ **pit mining** *n* NUCLEAR exploitation à ciel ouvert *f*; ~ **position** *n* ELEC *relay* position ouverte *f*; ~ **propeller** *n* TRANSP hélice libre *f*; ~ **quarry** *n* MINING carrière à ciel ouvert *f*; ~ **resonator** *n* ELECTRON cavité résonnante ouverte *f*; ~ **roadstead** *n* NAUT, OCEANOG rade foraine *f*; ~ **sea** *n* NAUT large *m*, OCEANOG large *m*, pleine eau *f*, pleine mer *f*; ~ **seas** *n pl* OCEANOG pleine eau *f*; ~ **slot armature** *n* ELEC *generator, motor* induit à canaux ouverts *m*; ~ **socket ratchet** *n* MECH ENG *tool* cliquet à douilles débouchées *m*; ~ **spiral spring** *n* MECH ENG ressort de compression *m*; ~ **string** *n* CONST *stair building* crémaillère *f*, limon à crémaillère *m*, limon à gradin *m*, limon à l'anglaise *m*; ~ **system** *n* COMP, DP, THERMOD système ouvert *m*; ~ **systems architecture** *n (OSA)* TELECOM architecture de systèmes ouverts *f*; ~ **systems interconnection** *n (OSI)* COMP, DP, TELECOM interconnexion de systèmes ouverts *f (ISO)*; ~ **systems interconnection layers** *n pl (OSI layers)* TELECOM couches OSI *f pl*; ~ **systems interconnection resource** *n (OSI resource)* TELECOM ressource OSI *f*; ~ **turbine chamber** *n* HYDR EQUIP, WATER SUPP chambre d'eau de turbine *f*, réservoir de turbine *m*; ~ **turbine pit** *n* HYDR EQUIP chambre d'eau de turbine *f*, réservoir de turbine *m*; ~ **universe** *n* ASTRON univers ouvert *m*; ~ **wafer rotary switch** *n* ELEC ENG commutateur à galette non fermé *m*; ~ **wagon** *n* (BrE) *(cf gondola car)* RAIL wagon découvert *m*; ~ **wall container** *n* TRANSP conteneur avec porte latérale *m*, conteneur à paroi ouverte *m*; ~ **wall string** *n* CONST *stairbuilding* fausse crémaillère *f*; ~ **water** *n* NAUT mer libre *f*, OCEANOG glace navigable *f*; ~ **windings** *n pl* ELEC *transformer, reactor* enroulements de phase indépendants *m pl*; ~ **wire** *n* PROD ENG câble déconnecté *m*; ~ **wire feeder** *n* ELEC ENG ligne d'alimentation en fils nus *f*; ~ **wire line** *n* ELEC ENG ligne en fils nus *f*; ~ **wire transmission line** *n* ELEC ENG ligne de transmission en fils nus *f*

open:[3] ~ **up** *vt* MINING *quarry* éventer

open:[4] ~ **diaphragm** *vi* PHOTO ouvrir le diaphragme; ~ **fiber** *vi* (AmE), ~ **fibre** *vi* (BrE) TEXTILES ouvrir la fibre; ~ **up** *vi* CINEMAT ouvrir le diaphragme

open:[5] ~ **here** *phr* PACKAGING *handling instructions* ouvrir ici; ~ **this end** *phr* PACKAGING *handling instructions* ouvrir de ce côté

open-and-ground: ~ **end** *n* SPRINGS *of coil* spire terminale ouverte et meulée *f*

opencast: ~ **mine** *n* COAL TECH houillère à ciel ouvert *f*; ~ **mining** *n* MINING exploitation au jour *f*, exploitation à ciel ouvert *f*; ~ **cell** *n* P&R cellule ouverte *f*

open-cell: ~ **cellular plastic** *n* P&R caoutchoucs expansés à cellules ouvertes *m pl*, caoutchoucs mousses à cellules ouvertes *m pl*, plastique alvéolaire à cellules ouvertes *m*

open-cut: ~ **mining** *n* MINING exploitation au jour *f*, exploitation à ciel ouvert *f*

opened: ~ **loop** *n* SPRINGS anneau ouvert *m*

open-ended *adj* TEXTILES non circulaire

opener *n* TEXTILES ouvreuse *f*

open-face: ~ **spotlight** *n* CINEMAT projecteur sans lentille *m*

open-frame: ~ **linear power supply** *n* ELEC ENG alimentation série nue *f*; ~ **power supply** *n* ELEC ENG alimentation nue *f*, alimentation sans coffret *f*; ~ **super calender** *n* PAPER TECH calandre à bâti ouvert *f*; ~ **switching power supply** *n* ELEC ENG alimentation à découpage nue *f*

opening *n* C&G *of cylinder* développement *m*, CONST baie *f*, ouverture *f*, trémie *f*, *aperture* orifice *m*, percée *f*, ELEC ENG *circuit* ouverture *f*, MECH ENG embouchure *f*, lumière *f*, MINING *of quarry* cloche *f*, ouverture *f*, PAPER TECH ouverture *f*; ~ **bit** *n* MECH ENG alésoir *m*, équarrissoir *m*; ~ **instructions** *n pl* PACKAGING instructions pour ouvrir *f pl*; ~ **in thick wall** *n* HYDR EQUIP ajutage cylindrique *m*, gueule-bée *f*, plein tuyau *m*; ~ **in thin partition** *n* HYDR EQUIP orifice en paroi mince *m*; ~ **in thin plate** *n* HYDR EQUIP orifice percé en plaque mince *m*; ~ **mechanism** *n* PACKAGING mécanisme d'ouverture *m*; ~ **shot** *n* CINEMAT premier plan du film *m*, MINING tir avec bouchon *m*; ~ **stock** *n* PROD ENG stock en début de période *m*; ~ **time** *n* ELEC *relay* durée d'ouverture *f*, ELEC ENG *of circuit* temps d'ouverture *m*; ~ **travel** *n* PROD ENG course d'ouverture *f*; ~ **up** *n* MINING *seam* traçage *m*

open-jet: ~ **wind tunnel** *n* PHYS soufflerie libre *f*

open-jointed: ~ **clayware pipe** *n* CONST tuyau d'argile à joint ouvert *m*; ~ **porous pipe** *n* CONST tuyau poreux à joint ouvert *m*

open-sand: ~ **molding** *n* (AmE), ~ **moulding** *n* (BrE) PROD ENG moulage à découvert *m*

open-side: ~ **planing machine** *n* MECH ENG raboteuse à un montant *f*, PROD ENG machine à raboter ouverte sur le côté *f*

open-sight: ~ **alidade** *n* INSTRUMENT alidade à pinnules *f*

open-top: ~ **container** n TRANSP conteneur ouvert m
open-type[1] adj MECH ENG machine specification ouvert
open-type:[2] ~ **compressor unit** n REFRIG motocompresseur ouvert m
open-web: ~ **girder** n CONST poutre en treillis f, poutre évidée f, poutre à jour f, poutrelle àcroisillons f
openwork n MINING chantier à ciel ouvert m, exploitation au jour f, exploitation à ciel ouvert f
operand n COMP, DP opérande m
operate:[1] ~ **current** n ELEC ENG intensité du courant d'appel f; ~ **lag** n ELEC ENG retard à l'appel m; ~ **relay** n ELEC ENG relais au travail m, relais excité m; ~ **time** n ELEC ENG temps de réponse à l'appel m; ~ **voltage** n ELEC ENG tension d'appel f
operate[2] vt MINING exploiter, NUCLEAR power plant conduire, exploiter, PROD ENG actionner, exploiter, manoeuvrer, opérer
operate[3] vi MECH ENG fonctionner
operating[1] adj MECH ENG en marche
operating[2] n PAPER TECH fonctionnement m; ~ **altitude** n SPACE altitude d'exploitation f; ~ **and maintenance application part** n TELECOM SSEM, sous-système pour l'exploitation la maintenance et la gestion m; ~ **condition** n METR of machine état de fonctionnement m; ~ **conditions** n pl ELEC equipment conditions de fonctionnement f pl, conditions de service f pl, ELEC ENG conditions de fonctionnement f pl, régime m; ~ **console** n TELECOM console d'exploitation f; ~ **cost** n QUALITY coût de fonctionnement m; ~ **current** n ELEC courant de fonctionnement m, courant de service m, ELEC ENG courant de fonctionnement m; ~ **cycle** n TRANSP cycle de fonctionnement m; ~ **depth** n OCEANOG profondeur de service f; ~ **error** n COAL TECH erreur opératoire f; ~ **force** n PROD ENG force d'action f; ~ **frequency** n MECH ENG, SPRINGS fréquence de travail f; ~ **fuel cycle** n NUCLEAR campagne de combustion de réacteur f; ~ **hand wheel** n MECH ENG volant de manoeuvre m; ~ **head** n PROD ENG tête d'actionnement f; ~ **hours** n pl PROD ENG heures de fonctionnement f pl, heures opératoires f pl; ~ **hours indicator** n NAUT of engine compteur d'heures de marche m; ~ **instructions** n pl MECH ENG manuel d'instructions m; ~ **lever** n MECH ENG levier de manoeuvre m; ~ **life** n ELEC ENG durée de vie en fonctionnement f; ~ **lifetime** n NUCLEAR of power plant durée de vie f; ~ **limitations** n pl PROD ENG limite d'utilisation f; ~ **magnet** n PROD ENG aimant d'actionnement m; ~ **manual** n MECH ENG manuel d'instructions m; ~ **method** n TEXTILES mode opératoire m; ~ **mode** n ELEC ENG mode de fonctionnement m; ~ **overload** n PROD ENG surcharge normale de fonctionnement f; ~ **permit** n AERONAUT autorisation d'exploitation f, licence d'exploitation f; ~ **point** n ELEC ENG point de fonctionnement m; ~ **position** n TELECOM position f; ~ **pressure** n REFRIG pression de service f, SPACE spacecraft pression de fonctionnement f; ~ **procedure** n PROD ENG consigne d'utilisation f; ~ **radius** n PROD ENG rayon d'actionnement m; ~ **range** n AERONAUT, MILIT of missile rayon d'action m; ~ **shaft** n PROD ENG tige d'actionnement f; ~ **side** n PAPER TECH côté conducteur m; ~ **speed** n TRANSP vitesse de régime f, vitesse maximale réalisable f; ~ **switch** n ELEC interrupteur de service m; ~ **system** n (OS) COMP, TELECOM système d'exploitation m; ~ **system function** n (OSF) TELECOM fonction de système d'exploitation f; ~ **system kernel** n COMP noyau de système d'exploitation m; ~ **temperature** n AERONAUT, REFRIG, SPACE température de fonctionnement f; ~ **time** n PROD ENG durée d'utilisation f, temps de fonctionnement m; ~ **voltage** n ELEC of system, ELEC ENG tension de fonctionnement f, tension de service f, PROD ENG tension d'utilisation f; ~ **weight** n SPACE poids en ordre de marche m; ~ **well** n GAS TECH puits d'exploitation m; ~ **wells** n pl GAS TECH puits en opération m pl

operation n COMP, DP opération f, ELEC ENG of machine fonctionnement m, MATH opération f, MECH ENG manoeuvre f, opération f, stage passe f, SPACE communications, TELECOM exploitation f; ~, **administration, maintenance and provisioning** n (OAMP) TELECOM exploitation administration maintenance et mise en service f; ~ **administration and maintenance center** n (AmE), ~ **administration and maintenance centre** n (BrE) (OAMC) TELECOM centre de gestion d'exploitation et de maintenance m; ~ **analysis** n PROD ENG étude d'exploitation f; ~ **area** n NUCLEAR of hot cell champ d'action m, zone de travail f; ~ **center** n (AmE), ~ **centre** n (BrE) SPACE centre d'opérations m; ~ **code** n (op code) COMP, DP, PROD ENG code d'opération m (code op); ~ **counter** n ELEC tap changer compteur de manoeuvres m; ~ **number** n PROD ENG code d'opération m, numéro d'opération m, numéro de phase m; ~ **register** n COMP, DP registre d'opération m; ~ **table** n COMP, DP table d'opérations f; ~ **temperature** n PROD ENG température de service f; ~ **ticket** n PROD ENG bon de production m, bon de réalisation m, bon de travail m

operational: ~ **amplifier** n (op amp) COMP, DP, ELECTRON, PHYS, TELECOM amplificateur opérationnel m; ~ **amplifier chip** n ELECTRON puce d'amplificateur opérationnel f; ~ **amplifier comparator** n ELECTRON comparateur à amplificateur opérationnel m; ~ **availability** n PROD ENG disponibilité opérationnelle f; ~ **ceiling** n AERONAUT plafond opérationnel m; ~ **current** n PROD ENG courant d'emploi m; ~ **delay** n TRANSP retard conjoncturel m; ~ **depth** n OCEANOG profondeur de service f; ~ **error** n POLLUTION fausse manoeuvre f; ~ **mine** n MINING mine en activité f; ~ **range** n PROD ENG plage d'utilisation f, zone d'utilisation f; ~ **research** n (OR, operations research), COMP, DP recherche opérationnelle f (RO); ~ **test** n METR, PROD ENG essai de fonctionnement m

operations: ~ **and maintenance** n (OAM) TELECOM exploitation et maintenance f; ~ **center** n (AmE), ~ **centre** n (BrE) TELECOM centre d'exploitation m; ~ **manual** n AERONAUT manuel d'exploitation m; ~ **research** n (OR, operational research), COMP, DP recherche opérationnelle f (RO); ~ **room** n TELECOM salle d'exploitation f; ~ **sequence** n PROD ENG séquence des opérations f

operations-related: ~ **defect** n NUCLEAR of fuel element défaut en exploitation m

operative: ~ **contacts** n pl PROD ENG position de travail f; ~ **management** n NUCLEAR of plant gestion opérative f

operator[1] n COMP opérateur m, CONST of equipment conducteur m, DP opérateur m, MINING exploitant m, PETR TECH, PRINT opérateur m, TELECOM opérateur m, opératrice f, téléphoniste m, private exchange standardiste m; ~ **center** n (AmE), ~ **centre** n (BrE) TELECOM centre d'opérateurs m; ~ **command** n COMP, DP, TELECOM commande opérateur f; ~ **console** n COMP, DP console opérateur f; ~ **control** n CONTROL contrôle par l'opérateur m; ~ **message** n COMP, DP message opérateur *m*; ~ **position** *n* TELECOM position d'opératrice *f*, poste d'opérateur *m*; ~ **precedence** *n* COMP, DP priorité des opérateurs *f*; ~ **system** *n* TELECOM système de positions automatisées de téléphonistes *m*, système de positions d'opératrices *m*, système de positions de téléphonistes *m*

operator:[2] **no** ~ **available** *phr* TELECOM pas d'opérateur *m*; ~ **temporarily unavailable** *phr* TELECOM opérateur provisoirement absent

operator's: ~ **console** *n* TELECOM console d'exploitation *f*; ~ **side** *n* PRINT côté fonction *m*; ~ **telephone** *n* TELECOM poste d'opérateur *m*

operator-controlled *adj* CONTROL contrôlé par l'opérateur

ophiolite: ~ **suite** *n* GEOL cortège ophiolitique *m*

Ophiuchus *n* ASTRON Ophiuchus *m*

ophtalmic: ~ **test stand** *n* INSTRUMENT équipement ophtalmologique *m*

ophtalmometer *n* INSTRUMENT ophtalmomètre *m*

opianic *adj* CHEM opianique

opianine *n* CHEM noscapine *f*, pianine *f*

opianyl *n* CHEM opianyle *m*

opiate *n* CHEM narcotique *m*, opiacé *m*, opium *m*

opposed: ~ **cylinders** *n pl* AUTO cylindres opposés *m pl*; ~ **piston engine** *n* MECH ENG moteur à pistons opposés *m*

opposing: ~ **field** *n* ELEC *electromagnetism* champ opposé *m*; ~ **green** *n* TRANSP *traffic control* verts simultanés *m pl*

opposite[1] *adj* GEOM opposé

opposite:[2] ~ **charge** *n* CHEM charge opposée *f*, ELEC charge de signes contraire *f*, charge de signes opposés *f*; ~ **phase** *n* ELEC *alternating current* phase opposée *f*; ~ **sides** *n pl* GEOM *of square* côtés opposés *m pl*; ~ **text** *n* PRINT face texte *f*

opposition *n* ASTRON, PATENTS opposition *f*; ~ **proceedings** *n pl* PATENTS procédure d'opposition *f*

optic: ~ **axis** *n* CRYSTALL, OPT, PHYS, TELECOM axe optique *m*; ~ **storage** *n* OPT archivage optique *m*

optical *n* CINEMAT trucage *m*;

~ a ~ **aberration** *n* TELECOM aberration optique *f*; ~ **absorption** *n* RAD PHYS absorption optique *f*; ~ **activity** *n* CHEM *of compound*, PHYS activité optique *f*; ~ **amplifier** *n* ELECTRON, TELECOM amplificateur optique *m*; ~ **astronomy** *n* ASTRON astronomie optique *f*; ~ **attenuator** *n* TELECOM atténuateur optique *m*; ~ **axis** *n* OPT axe de la fibre optique *m*, PHOTO axe optique *m*, TELECOM axe de la fibre *m*;

~ b ~ **balance** *n* PRINT équilibre optique *m*, équilibre visuel *m*; ~ **bench** *n* CINEMAT, METR banc optique *m*, PHOTO banc optique *m*, support universel *m*, PHYS, PRINT banc optique *m*; ~ **bistability** *n* TELECOM bistabilité optique *f*; ~ **bleaching** *n* DETERGENTS blanchissage optique *m*; ~ **branch** *n* PHYS *solid state theory* branche optique *f*; ~ **brightener** *n* DETERGENTS azurant optique *m*, P&R *paint* agent d'azurage *m*;

~ c ~ **cable** *n* OPT, TELECOM, TV câble optique *m*; ~ **cable assembly** *n* TELECOM câble assemblé *m*; ~ **carrier** *n* ELECTRON porteuse optique *f*; ~ **cavity** *n* OPT cavité optique *f*, RAD PHYS cavité optique *f*, *laser production* cavité optique *f*, TELECOM cavité optique *f*; ~ **center** *n* (AmE), ~ **centre** *n* (BrE) PHYS centre optique *m*, TELECOM point de connexion optique *m*; ~ **characteristic** *n* TELECOM caractéristique optique *f*; ~ **character reader** *n* (OCR) COMP, DP, PRINT lecteur optique de caractères *m*; ~ **character reading system** *n* PACKAGING système de lecture optique de caractères

m, système optique d'identificationde caractères *m*; ~ **character recognition** *n* (OCR) COMP, DP reconnaissance optique des caractères *f* (ROC), PRINT lecture optique *f*, reconnaissance optique des caractères *f* (ROC); ~ **circulator** *n* TELECOM circulateur optique *m*; ~ **coherence** *n* TELECOM cohérence optique *f*; ~ **combiner** *n* OPT, TELECOM combinateur optique *m*; ~ **communications** *n* TELECOM télécommunications optique *f pl*; ~ **comparator** *n* METR comparateur optique *m*; ~ **condenser** *n* CINEMAT condensateur optique *m*; ~ **connector** *n* TELECOM connecteur optique *m*; ~ **correlator** *n* ELECTRON corrélateur optique *m*; ~ **counterpart** *n* ASTRON *of powerful radio sources* contrepartie optique *f*; ~ **coupler** *n* ELEC ENG, OPT, TELECOM coupleur optique *m*; ~ **coupling** *n* ELEC ENG couplage optique *m*;

~ d ~ **database** *n* OPT base de données sur disque optique *f*; ~ **data bus** *n* OPT, TELECOM bus optique *m*; ~ **data disc** *n* (BrE) OPT disque optique numérique *m*; ~ **data disc document filing system** *n* (BrE) OPT système d'archivage sur disque optique numérique *m*, système d'archivage à don *m*;~ **data disk** *n* (AmE) *see optical data disc*; ~ **data disk document filing system** *n* (AmE) OPT système d'archivage sur disque optique numérique *m*, système d'archivage à don *m*; ~ **density** *n* OPT densité optique *f*; ~ **depth** *n* OCEANOG profondeur optique *f*, SPACE épaisseur optique *f*; ~ **detection** *n* ELECTRON détection optique *f*; ~ **detector** *n* ELECTRON, OPT détecteur optique *m*, TELECOM détecteur optique *m*, photodétecteur *m*, récepteur photoélectrique *m*; ~ **digital data disc** *n* (BrE) OPT disque optique numérique *m*; ~ **digital data disk** *n* (AmE) *see optical digital data disc* ~ **disc** *n* (BrE) OPT, RECORDING disque optique *m*; ~ **disc cassette** *n* (BrE) OPT enveloppe de protection *f*; ~ **disc drive** *n* (BrE) OPT lecteur de disque optique *m*, unité d'entraînement de disque optique *f*, unité de disque optique *f*, unité optique *f*; ~ **disc exchanger** *n* (BrE) OPT changeur automatique de disques *m*; ~ **disc filing system** *n* (BrE) OPT système d'archivage sur disque optique numérique *m*, système d'archivage à don *m*; ~ **disc library** *n* (BrE) OPT juke-box *m*; ~ **disc player** *n* (BrE) OPT lecteur de disque optique *m*; ~ **disc reader** *n* (BrE) OPT lecteur de disque optique *m*; ~ **disk** *n* (AmE) *see optical disc*; ~ **disk cassette** *n* (AmE) *see optical disc cassette*; ~ **disk drive** *n* (AmE) *see optical disc drive*; ~ **disk exchanger** *n* (AmE) *see optical disc exchanger*; ~ **disk filing system** *n* (AmE) *see optical disc filing system*; ~ **disk library** *n* (AmE) *see optical disc library*; ~ **disk player** *n* (AmE) *see optical disc player*; ~ **disk reader** *n* (AmE) *see optical disc reader*; ~ **distortion** *n* C&G distorsion optique *f*; ~ **double star** *n* ASTRON étoile double optique *f*; ~ **drive** *n* OPT unité d'entraînement de disque optique *f*, unité de disque optique *f*, unité optique *f*;

~ e ~ **electron** *n* RAD PHYS électron optique *m*; ~ **emitter** *n* OPT émetteur optique *m*; ~ **encoder** *n* SPACE *communications* codeur optique *m*; ~ **enlargement** *n* CINEMAT agrandissement *m*, gonflage *m*; ~ **exchange** *n* TELECOM commutateur optique *m*;

~ f ~ **fiber** *n* (AmE) *see optical fibre*; ~ **fiber cable** *n* (AmE) *see optical fibre cable*; ~ **fiber connector** *n* (AmE) *see optical fibre connector*; ~ **fiber coupler** *n* (AmE) *see optical fibre coupler*; ~ **fiber gyrometer** *n* (AmE) *see optical fibre gyrometer*; ~ **fiber link** *n* (AmE) *see optical fibre link*; ~ **fiber pigtail** *n* (AmE) *see optical fibre pigtail*; ~ **fiber splice** *n* (AmE) *see optical fibre splice*; ~ **fiber transmission** *n* (AmE) *see optical* *fibre transmission*; ~ **fiber transmission system** *n* (AmE) *see optical fibre transmission system*; ~ **fibre** *n* (BrE) C&G, COMP, DP, ELEC ENG, OPT, PHYS, SPACE *craft* fibre optique *f*; ~ **fibre cable** *n* (BrE) OPT câble optique *m*, câble à fibre optique *m*, TELECOM câble à fibres optiques *m*; ~ **fibre connector** *n* (BrE) OPT connecteur de fibres optiques *m*, TELECOM connecteur optique *m*; ~ **fibre coupler** *n* (BrE) OPT, TELECOM coupleur optique *m*; ~ **fibre gyrometer** *n* (BrE) SPACE *craft* gyromètre à fibre optique *m*; ~ **fibre link** *n* (BrE) OPT liaison optique *f*, liaison par fibre optique *f*, TELECOM liaison par fibre optique *f*; ~ **fibre pigtail** *n* (BrE) OPT amorce *f*, fibre d'injection *f*, TELECOM amorce *f*; ~ **fibre splice** *n* (BrE) OPT, TELECOM épissure optique *f*; ~ **fibre transmission** *n* (BrE) OPT, TELECOM transmission par fibres optiques *f*; ~ **fibre transmission system** *n* (BrE) OPT système de transmission sur fibre optique *m*; ~ **filter** *n* ELECTRON, OPT, PRINT, TELECOM filtre optique *m*; ~ **fine grain** *n* CINEMAT marron pour trucages *m*; ~ **flat** *n* CINEMAT lame à faces parallèles *f*, METR verre plan *m*; ~ **flat filter** *n* CINEMAT filtre optique *m*; ~ **flexibility frame** *n* *(OFF)* TELECOM répartiteur optique *m*; ~ **flint** *n* C&G verre d'optique flint *m*; ~ **flux** *n* OPT flux énergétique *m*; ~ **frequency** *n* ELECTRON fréquence optique *f*;

~ **g** ~ **gain** *n* ELECTRON gain optique *m*; ~ **glass** *n* INSTRUMENT, PHOTO verre optique *m*; ~ **graticule** *n* METR réticule d'optique *m*; ~ **guided wave** *n* ELEC ENG onde guidée optique *f*, onde optique guidée *f*;

~ **h** ~ **head** *n* OPT poutre optique *f*, tête optique *f*; ~ **house** *n* CINEMAT laboratoire de trucages *m*; ~ **hybrid circuit** *n* ELECTRON circuit hybride optique *m*;

~ **i** ~ **image** *n* ELECTRON image optique *f*; ~ **input** *n* ELEC ENG entrée optique *f*; ~ **input power** *n* ELEC ENG puissance optique d'entrée *f*; ~ **instrument** *n* INSTRUMENT, PHYS instrument d'optique *m*; ~ **instruments for dimensional measurement** *n pl* METR instruments optiques pour mesure dimensionnelle *m pl*; ~ **integrated circuit** *n* ELECTRON circuit intégré optique *m*, circuit optique *m*, circuit optoélectronique *m*; ~ **interference** *n* TELECOM interférence optique *f*; ~ **isolation** *n* ELEC ENG isolation optique *f*, isolement optique *m*; ~ **isolator** *n* TELECOM isolateur optique *m*; ~ **isomer** *n* CHEM *of compound* isomère optique *m*;

~ **l** ~ **link** *n* OPT liaison optique *f*; ~ **lithography** *n* ELECTRON gravure optique *f*; ~ **logic circuit** *n* ELECTRON circuit logique optique *m*; ~ **logic gate** *n* ELECTRON porte logique optique *f*, porte optique *f*;

~ **m** ~ **mark reader** *n* COMP, DP lecteur optique de marques *m*; ~ **mark reading** *n* *(OMR)* COMP, DP lecture optique de marques *f*; ~ **maser** *n* ELECTRON maser optique *m*; ~ **mask** *n* ELECTRON masque optique *m*; ~ **measuring projector** *n* MECH ENG projecteur de mesure optique *m*; ~ **medium** *n* COMP, DP, OPT support optique *m*; ~ **memory** *n* ELEC ENG, OPT mémoire optique *f*; ~ **memory card** *n* OPT carte à mémoire optique *f*; ~ **modulation** *n* ELECTRON modulation optique *f*; ~ **modulator** *n* ELECTRON, TELECOM modulateur optique *m*; ~ **multiplex** *n* ELECTRON multiplex optique *m*; ~ **multiplexer** *n* ELECTRON, TV multiplexeur optique *m*; ~ **multiplexing** *n* ELECTRON multiplexage optique *m*;

~ **n** ~ **negative** *n* CINEMAT négatif avec trucages *m*;

~ **o** ~ **oscillator** *n* ELECTRON oscillateur optique *m*; ~ **output** *n* ELEC ENG sortie optique *f*; ~ **output power** *n* ELEC ENG puissance de sortie optique *f*;

~ **p** ~ **parametric oscillator** *n* TELECOM oscillateur

paramétrique optique *m*; ~ **path** *n* OPT chemin optique *m*, PHYS marche optique *f*, trajet optique *m*, TELECOM chemin optique *m*; ~ **path length** *n* OPT, TELECOM chemin optique *m*; ~ **pattern** *n* ELECTRON motif optique *m*; ~ **plummet** *n* INSTRUMENT plomb optique *m*; ~ **polarization** *n* TELECOM polarisation optique *f*; ~ **power** *n* ELEC ENG puissance optique *f*, OPT puissance optique *f*, puissance rayonnante *f*, TELECOM puissance optique *f*; ~ **power output** *n* TELECOM puissance optique de sortie *f*; ~ **power source** *n* ELEC ENG rayonnement optique *m*; ~ **print** *n* CINEMAT copie faite sur tireuse optique *f*; ~ **printer** *n* CINEMAT tireuse optique *f*; ~ **printing** *n* PRINT contretypage *m*, impression optique *f*; ~ **processing** *n* TELECOM traitement optique *m*; ~ **profile grinder** *n* MECH ENG rectifieuse de profil optique *f*; ~ **properties** *n pl* PROP MAT caractéristiques optiques *f pl*; ~ **publishing** *n* OPT édition optique *f*; ~ **pulsar** *n* ASTRON pulsar optique *m*; ~ **pulse** *n* ELECTRON impulsion optique *f*; ~ **pumping** *n* ELECTRON, NUCLEAR, PHYS *laser*, RAD PHYS *laser* pompage optique *m*; ~ **pyrometer** *n* PHYS, RAD PHYS pyromètre optique *m*;

~ **r** ~ **radiation** *n* OPT, TELECOM rayonnement optique *m*; ~ **rangefinder** *n* PHOTO télémètre optique *m*; ~ **ray** *n* OPT rayon optique *m*; ~ **reader** *n* METR *machine tools* lecteur optique *m*; ~ **read-only memory** *n* *(OROM)* OPT mémoire morte optique *f*; ~ **receiver** *n* OPT récepteur optique *m*, TELECOM module de réception optique *m*, récepteur optique *m*; ~ **recording** *n* ACOUSTICS, RECORDING, TELECOM enregistrement optique *m*; ~ **refraction** *n* TELECOM réfraction optique *f*; ~ **regenerative receiver** *n* OPT récepteur régénérateur optique *m*; ~ **regenerative repeater** *n* TELECOM répéteur régénérateur optique *m*; ~ **relay** *n* ELEC ENG relais optique *m*; ~ **repeater** *n* OPT, TELECOM répéteur optique *m*; ~ **resist** *n* ELECTRON résist optique *m*; ~ **resonance** *n* ELECTRON résonance optique *f*; ~ **resonator** *n* RAD PHYS *laser production*, TELECOM résonateur optique *m*; ~ **return loss** *n* *(ORL)* TELECOM affaiblissement d'adaptation optique *m*; ~ **ROM** *n* COMP, DP ROM optique *f*;

~ **s** ~ **scanner** *n* COMP scanner optique *m*, DP lecteur optique *m*; ~ **scanning device** *n* *(OSD)* TV analyseur optique *m*; ~ **sensing** *n* ELECTRON détection optique *f*; ~ **sensor** *n* ELECTRON capteur optique *m*, SPACE détecteur optique *m*; ~ **servo** *n* ELEC ENG servomécanisme optique *m*; ~ **sight** *n* SPACE visée optique *f*; ~ **signal** *n* ELECTRON, TELECOM signal optique *m*; ~ **signal conversion** *n* ELEC ENG conversion des signaux optiques *f*; ~ **signal processing** *n* ELECTRON traitement optique des signaux *m*, RAD PHYS processus de signal optique *m*; ~ **solar reflector** *n* *(OSR)* SPACE *craft* réflecteur solaire optique *m*; ~ **sound** *n* CINEMAT son optique *m*, son photographique *m*; ~ **sound camera** *n* CINEMAT caméra son optique *f*; ~ **sound head** *n* CINEMAT lecteur de son optique *m*, tête de lecture de son optique *f*, RECORDING tête de reproduction sonore optique *f*; ~ **sound negative** *n* CINEMAT négatif son optique *m*; ~ **sound positive** *n* CINEMAT copie son optique *f*, positif son optique *m*; ~ **sound recorder** *n* RECORDING enregistreur sonore optique *m*; ~ **sound recording** *n* CINEMAT enregistrement son optique *m*; ~ **sound reproducer** *n* CINEMAT défileur son optique *m*, RECORDING reproducteur sonore optique *m*; ~ **soundtrack** *n* RECORDING piste sonore optique *f*; ~ **spectral analysis** *n* ELECTRON analyse optique spectrale *f*; ~ **spectral analyzer** *n*

ELECTRON analyseur optique spectral *m*; ~ **spectrum** *n* ELECTRON, OPT, RAD PHYS, TELECOM spectre optique *m*; ~ **speed trap detector** *n* TRANSP détecteur optique de vitesse *m*; ~ **splice** *n* OPT TELECOM épissure optique *f*; ~ **stepper** *n* ELECTRON répétiteur optique *m*; ~ **storage** *n* COMP mémoire optique *f*, OPT archivage optique *m*, stockage optique *m*; ~ **storage medium** *n* OPT mémoire optique d'archivage *f*; ~ **switch** *n* ELEC ENG interrupteur optique *m*, TELECOM commutateur optique *m*; ~ **switching** *n* COMP, DP, ELEC ENG, TELECOM commutation optique *f*; ~ **switching crosspoint** *n* TELECOM point de connexion optique *m*; ~ **switching matrix** *n* TELECOM matrice de commutation optique *f*, matrice optique *f*; ~ **switching network** *n* (*OSN*) TELECOM réseau de connexion optique *m*; ~ **switching system** *n* TELECOM système de commutation optique *m*; ~ **system** *n* ELECTRON système optique *m*;

~ **t** ~ **telescope** *n* ASTRON, SPACE télescope optique *m*; ~ **thickness** *n* SPACE, TELECOM épaisseur optique *f*; ~ **time domain reflectometry** *n* (*OTDR*) OPT réflectométrie optique dans le domaine temporel *f*, technique de rétrodiffusion *f*, TELECOM réflectométrie optique dans le domaine temporel *f*; ~ **tool** *n* C&G outil à surfacer *m*; ~ **track** *n* CINEMAT piste son optique *f*; ~ **transfer** *n* CINEMAT repiquage en son optique *m*; ~ **transition** *n* RAD PHYS transition optique *f*; ~ **transmission** *n* COMP transmission par système optoélectronique *f*; ~ **transmission line** *n* ELEC ENG ligne de transmission optique *f*, ligne optique *f*; ~ **transmission system** *n* OPT système de transmission optique *m*; ~ **tuning** *n* TELECOM accord optique *m*;

~ **v** ~ **videodisc** *n* (BrE) OPT disque optique vidéo *m*, vidéodisque optique *m*; ~ **videodisk** *n* (AmE) *see optical videodisc*; ~ **viewfinder** *n* PRINT viseur optique *m*;

~ **w** ~ **wave** *n* ELEC ENG onde optique *f*; ~ **waveguide** *n* ELEC ENG guide d'ondes optiques *m*, guide optique *m*, OPT, TELECOM guide d'ondes optiques *m*; ~ **window** *n* OPT fenêtre spectrale *f*;

~ **z** ~ **zoom** *n* CINEMAT travelling réalisé à la trucage *m*

optical-electrical *adj* (*O-E*) TELECOM optique-électrique

optically:[1] ~ **flat** *adj* PHOTO surfacé; ~ **letter-spaced** *adj* PRINT rectifié visuellement

optically:[2] ~ **active material** *n* OPT, TELECOM substance optiquement active *f*

optically-coupled: ~ **solid-state relay** *n* ELEC ENG relais à semi-conducteur à commande optique *m*

optically-pumped: ~ **laser** *n* ELECTRON laser à pompage optique *m*

optically-smooth: ~ **surface** *n* PHYS poli *m*

optimal: ~ **bias** *n* RECORDING polarisation optimum *f*; ~ **control** *n* TELECOM commande optimale *f*; ~ **controller** *n* NUCLEAR régulateur optimal *m*; ~ **crushing size** *n* COAL TECH maille optimale de libération *f*; ~ **operating method** *n* GAS TECH fonctionnement optimal *m*; ~ **path** *n* TELECOM chemin optimal *m*; ~ **sampling** *n* TELECOM échantillonnage optimal *m*

optimization *n* COMP, DP optimisation *f*

optimize *vt* COMP, DP optimiser

optimum: ~ **bunching** *n* ELECTRON groupement optimal *m*; ~ **burn-up** *n* NUCLEAR combustion optimale *f*; ~ **damping** *n* ELEC ENG amortissement optimal *m*; ~ **grind** *n* COAL TECH maille optimale de libération *f*; ~ **moisture content** *n* CONST teneur optimale de l'eau *f*, teneur optimum en eau *f*; ~ **object illumination** *n* RAD

PHYS éclairage optimal d'un objet *m*; ~ **re-entry corridor** *n* SPACE couloir optimal de rentrée *m*

option *n* PETR TECH *contracts, licensing* option *f*, PROD ENG accessoire *m*, option *f*, variante *f*; ~ **code** *n* COMP code d'option *m*, DP code optionnel *m*

optional[1] *adj* TELECOM facultatif

optional:[2] ~ **equipment** *n* MECH ENG équipement facultatif *m*; ~ **hardware** *n* PROD ENG options matérielles *f pl*; ~ **word** *n* COMP *COBOL*, DP *COBOL* mot facultatif *m*

optionally: ~ **droppable blocks** *n pl* TELECOM blocs éventuellement supprimables *m pl*

optocoupler *n* ELEC ENG coupleur optique *m*, photocoupleur *m*, TELECOM optocoupleur *m*

optoelectronic[1] *adj* OPT optoélectronique, électro-optique, TELECOM optoélectronique

optoelectronic:[2] ~ **amplifier** *n* ELECTRON amplificateur optoélectronique *m*; ~ **chip** *n* ELECTRON puce optoélectronique *f*; ~ **coupler** *n* ELEC ENG composant optoélectronique *m*; ~ **crosspoint** *n* TELECOM point de connexion optoélectronique *m*; ~ **device** *n* ELEC ENG, OPT dispositif optoélectronique *m*; ~ **pickup** *n* MECH ENG capteur optoélectronique *m*; ~ **receiver** *n* TELECOM récepteur optoélectronique *m*; ~ **switch** *n* ELEC ENG interrupteur optoélectronique *m*; ~ **switching matrix** *n* TELECOM matrice de commutation optoélectronique *f*; ~ **transducer** *n* ELEC ENG transducteur optoélectronique *m*

optoelectronics *n* COMP, DP, ELEC ENG, PHYS, TELECOM optoélectronique *f*

optometer *n* INSTRUMENT réfractomètre *m*

optronics *n* ELECTRON optoélectronique *f*

OR[1] *abbr* (*operational research, operations research*) COMP, DP RO (*recherche opérationnelle*)

OR:[2] ~ **circuit** *n* ELECTRON circuit OU *m*; ~ **gate** *n* COMP, DP, ELECTRON, PHYS porte OU *f*; ~ **operation** *n* COMP, DP opération OU *f*

oral: ~ **proceedings** *n pl* PATENTS procédure orale *f*

orange: ~ **peel** *n* C&G chair *f*, P&R *paint defect* peau d'orange *f*

orangite *n* MINERAL orangite *f*

orbit[1] *n* ASTRON, PHYS, SPACE orbite *f*; ~ **control** *n* SPACE contrôle en orbite *m*; ~ **correction** *n* SPACE correction d'orbite *f*; ~ **counter** *n* SPACE compteur d'orbites *m*; ~ **determination** *n* SPACE calcul d'orbite *m*, détermination de l'orbite *f*; ~ **inclination** *n* SPACE inclinaison d'orbite *f*; ~ **modification** *n* SPACE modification de l'orbite *f*; ~ **prediction** *n* SPACE détermination de l'orbite *f*; ~ **support** *n* SPACE maintien en orbite *m*; ~ **tracking** *n* SPACE orbitographie *f*; ~ **trimming** *n* SPACE correction d'orbite *f*

orbit[2] *vt* SPACE graviter, graviter autour de, orbiter

orbital[1] *adj* RAD PHYS, SPACE orbital

orbital[2] *n* CHEM *of electron* orbite *f*, RAD PHYS *atomic electron state* orbitale *f*; ~ **angular momentum** *n* PHYS moment cinétique orbital *m*, RAD PHYS *wave function* moment angulaire orbital *m*; ~ **angular momentum quantum number** *n* PHYS nombre quantique du moment cinétique orbital *m*, nombre quantique orbital *m*; ~ **catch-up** *n* SPACE rattrapage sur orbite *m*; ~ **decay** *n* SPACE dégradation de l'orbite *f*; ~ **electron** *n* RAD PHYS électron orbital *m*; ~ **elements** *n pl* ASTRON *of motion of celestial body* éléments orbitaux *m pl*; ~ **flight** *n* SPACE vol orbital *m*; ~ **glider** *n* SPACE, TRANSP planeur orbital *m*; ~ **injection** *n* SPACE injection sur orbite *f*, mise sur orbite *f*; ~ **maneuvering system** *n* (AmE), ~ **manoeuvring system** *n* (BrE) (*OMS*) SPACE système de manoeuvre en orbite *m*; ~ **moment** *n* RAD PHYS *of atom* moment orbital *m*; ~ **period** *n* SPACE période de révolution *f*; ~ **quantum number** *n* PHYS nombre quantique du moment cinétique orbital *m*, nombre quantique orbital *m*, RAD PHYS nombre quantique azimutal *m*; ~ **rocket** *n* SPACE fusée orbitale *f*; ~ **sander** *n* MECH ENG *tool* ponceuse orbitale *f*; ~ **station** *n* SPACE station orbitale *f*; ~ **transfer vehicle** *n* *(OTV)* SPACE véhicule de transfert interorbital *m*, véhicule de transfert orbital *m*; ~ **vehicle** *n* SPACE véhicule orbital *m*; ~ **velocity** *n* ASTRON vitesse orbitale *f*, PHYS vitesse de révolution orbitale *f*; ~ **workshop** *n* SPACE atelier orbital *m*

orbiter *n* SPACE orbiteur *m*, sonde orbitale *f*; ~ **stage** *n* SPACE module orbital *m*, étage orbital *m*

orbiting *n* SPACE mise sur orbite *f*; ~ **astronomical observatory** *n* ASTRON observatoire astronomique en orbite *m*, observatoire astronomique sur orbite *m*, SPACE observatoire astronomique orbital *m*; ~ **laboratory** *n* SPACE laboratoire en orbite *m*, laboratoire orbital *m*; ~ **object** *n* SPACE objet spatial *m*; ~ **satellite** *n* SPACE satellite en orbite *m*; ~ **solar observatory** *n* ASTRON observatoire solaire en orbite *m*, observatoire solaire sur orbite *m*; ~ **space probe** *n* ASTRON sonde spatiale en orbite *f*

orcein *n* CHEM orcéine *f*

order[1] *n* ACOUSTICS *of a harmonic*, CHEM *of reaction* ordre *m*, COMP, DP ordre *m*, rangement *m*; ~ **hardening** *n* METALL durcissement par ordination *m*; ~ **of interference** *n* PHYS ordre d'interférence *m*; ~ **of magnitude** *n* COMP, DP, PHYS ordre de grandeur *m*; ~ **point** *n* PROD ENG point de commande *m*, seuil de réapprovisionnement *m*; ~ **of precedence** *n* COMP, DP ordre de priorité *m*; ~ **of reaction** *n* METALL ordre de réaction *m*; ~ **shop** *n* PROD ENG fabrication à la commande *f*, production à la commande *f*

order[2] *vt* COMP, DP ordonner, ranger

order:[3] **in the ~ specified** *phr* PATENTS suivant l'ordre indiqué

order-disorder *n* METALL ordre-désordre *m*; ~ **interface** *n* PROP MAT interface ordre-désordre *f*; ~ **model** *n* NUCLEAR modèle ordre-désordre *m*; ~ **transformation** *n* CRYSTALL transformation ordre-désordre *f*

ordered: ~ **alloy** *n* METALL alliage ordonné *m*; ~ **chain** *n* CHEM *of polymer* chaîne ordonnée *f*; ~ **pair** *n* MATH couple *m*; ~ **solid solution** *n* METALL solution solide ordonnée *f*; ~ **tree** *n* COMP, DP arbre ordonné *m*

ordering: ~ **bias** *n* COMP, DP écart d'ordre *m*; ~ **policy** *n* PROD ENG règles d'approvisionnement *f pl*; ~ **rules** *n pl* PROD ENG règles d'approvisionnement *f pl*; ~ **unit** *n* PROD ENG unité de commande *f*

ordinal *n* GEOM nombre ordinal *m*; ~ **number** *n* MATH ordinal *m*

ordinary: ~ **bothway line** *n* TELECOM ligne mixte ordinaire *f*; ~ **ceramic** *n* C&G grosse céramique *f*; ~ **detonator** *n* MINING détonateur ordinaire *m*, détonateur à mèche *m*; ~ **fuse** *n* MINING cordeau ordinaire *m*, mèche ordinaire *f*, fusée de sûreté *f*, mèche de sûreté *f*, mèche ordinaire *f*, étoupille de sûreté *f*; ~ **hexagonal nut** *n* MECH ENG écrou normal *m*; ~ **line** *n* TELECOM ligne mixte ordinaire *f*; ~ **network** *n* TELECOM réseau classique *m*; ~ **points** *n pl* (BrE) *(cf ordinary switch)* RAIL *rolling stock* aiguillage simple *m*; ~ **Portland cement** *n* CONST ciment Portland ordinaire *m*; ~ **ray** *n* PHYS rayon ordinaire *m*; ~ **switch** *n* (AmE) *(cf ordinary points)* RAIL *rolling stock* aiguillage simple *m*; ~ **tap**

water *n* HYDROL eau de conduite ordinaire *f*, eau de robinet ordinaire *f*; ~ **timber set** *n* MINING cadre ordinaire *m*; ~ **water** *n* NUCLEAR *light* eau ordinaire *f*

ordinate *n* COMP, DP ordonnée *f*, MATH axe des ordonnées *m*, axe des y *m*

ordinates *n pl* NAUT *naval architecture* couples de tracé *m pl*, sections transversales *f pl*

ordnance: ~ **gun** *n* MILIT pièce d'artillerie *f*; ~ **material** *n* MILIT matériel de guerre *m*; ~ **survey map** *n* MILIT carte d'état-major *f*; ~ **surveyor** *n* CONST arpenteur du cadastre *m*, géomètre du cadastre *m*

ore[1] *n* COAL TECH minerai *m*; ~ **assaying** *n* NUCLEAR analyse des minerais *f*, essai des minerais *m*; ~ **at grass** *n* MINING minerai à la surface *m*; ~ **bin** *n* MINING caisson *m*, case *f*, coffre *m*, réservoir *m*, caisson à minerai *m*, case à minerai *f*, coffre à minerai *m*, réservoir de minerai *m*, trémie à minerai *f*; ~ **carrier** *n* NAUT *type of ship* minéralier *m*; ~ **contents** *n pl* MINING teneur en minerai *f*; ~ **crusher** *n* MINING broyeur pour minerai *m*, concasseur à minerai *m*; ~ **deposit** *n* MINING gisement *m*, gisement de minerai *m*, gîte métallifère *m*, NUCLEAR gisement de minerai *m*; ~ **dressing** *n* MINING préparation mécanique du minerai *f*; ~ **dump** *n* MINING halde de minerai *f*; ~ **enrichment plant** *n* NUCLEAR usine d'enrichissement du minerai *f*; ~ **extraction** *n* MINING abattage *m*; ~ **feeder** *n* MINING alimentateur de minerai *m*; ~ **formation** *n* MINING formation métallifère *f*; ~ **hopper** *n* MINING trémie à minerai *f*; ~ **mining** *n* MINING exploitation des minerais *f*; ~ **pass** *n* MINING cheminée à minerai *f*; ~ **process** *n* PROD ENG méthode par dilution *f*, *steel manufacture* méthode d'oxydation par le minerai *f*; ~ **sampling** *n* MINING échantillonnage du minerai *m*; ~ **separator** *n* MINING séparateur *m*, trieur *m*, séparateur à minerai *m*; ~ **stamp** *n* MINING bocard à minerai *m*; ~ **testing** *n* NUCLEAR analyse des minerais *f*, essai des minerais *m*; ~ **treatment** *n* MINING traitement du minerai *m*; ~ **washer** *n* MINING laveur à minerai *m*

ore:[2] **to be in ~** *vi* MINING être dans le filon

ore-bearing *adj* MINING métallifère

ore-bulk-oil *n* *(OBO)* PETR TECH minerai-vrac-pétrole *m*

ore-slurry-oil: ~ **tanker** *n* *(OSO tanker)* TRANSP transporteur de minerai sous forme liquide *m*

organ: ~ **stop** *n* C&G jeux d'orgues *m pl*

organic[1] *adj* CHEM organique, FOOD TECH biologique

organic:[2] ~ **acid** *n* CHEM acide organique *m*; ~ **base** *n* CHEM base organique *f*; ~ **chemist** *n* CHEM organicien *m*; ~ **chemistry** *n* CHEM chimie organique *f*; ~ **coating** *n* COATINGS revêtement organique *m*; ~ **compound** *n* CHEM composé organique *m*; ~ **dye laser** *n* RAD PHYS laser à teinture organique *m*; ~ **fluid engine** *n* TRANSP moteur à fluide organique *m*; ~ **glass** *n* C&G vitrorésine *f*; ~ **hygrometer** *n* REFRIG hygromètre organique *m*; ~ **liquid laser** *n* ELECTRON laser à liquide organique *m*; ~ **matter** *n* GEOL *in sediments*, HYDROL *sewage*, PETR TECH *in sediments* matière organique *f*, POLLUTION matières organiques *f pl*; ~ **matter content** *n* HYDROL *sewage* teneur en matière organique *f*; ~ **moderator** *n* NUCLEAR modérateur organique *m*; ~ **pigment** *n* COLOURS pigment organique *m*; ~ **refrigerant** *n* MECH ENG fluide frigorigène organique *m*; ~ **resistor** *n* ELEC ENG résistance au carbone *f*; ~ **soil** *n* COAL TECH terre organique *f*

organization: ~ **and maintenance** *n* TELECOM exploitation et maintenance *f*

Organization: ~ **of Petroleum Exporting Countries** *n*
(OPEC) PETR TECH Organisation des pays exportateurs de pétrole *f (OPEP)*

organochlorines *n pl* RECYCLING composés organochlo-
rés *m pl*

organogenous *adj* COAL TECH organogène

organomagnesium *n* CHEM organomagnésien *m*; ~ **compound** *n* CHEM composé orgomagnésien *m*

organometallic *adj* CHEM organométallique

organosol *n* CHEM organosol *m*

organzine *n* TEXTILES organsin *m*

orient[1] *vt* CONST *surveying* orienter

orient:[2] ~ **an instrument horizontally** *vi* CONST *surveying*
aligner un instrument en plan horizontale, caler un
appareil planimétriquement; ~ **an instrument vertical-
ly** *vi* CONST *surveying* aligner un instrument en plan
verticalement, caler un appareil altimétriquement

orientable: ~ **viewfinder** *n* CINEMAT viseur orientable *m*

oriental: ~ **alabaster** *n* MINERAL albâtre onychite *m*; ~
turquoise *n* MINERAL turquoise orientale *f*

orientated: ~ **polypropylene film** *n* PACKAGING film en
polyprène étiré *m*; ~ **polypropylene label** *n* PACKAGING
étiquette en polyprène étiré *f*

orientation *n* CONST, PRINT orientation *f*; ~ **coherence
function** *n* PROP MAT fonction d'orientation de cohérence *f*; ~ **control** *n* TELECOM commande d'orientation
f; ~ **factor** *n* METALL facteur d'orientation *m*

orientational: ~ **polarization** *n* PHYS polarisation d'o-
rientation *f*, polarisation dipolaire *f*

oriented: ~ **core** *n* PETR carotte orientée *f*; ~ **growth** *n*
METALL croissance orientée *f*; ~ **nucleation** *n* METALL
nucléation orientée *f*

orifice *n* C&G orifice d'écoulement *m*, HYDR EQUIP *under
water* orifice immergé *m*, orifice noyé *m*, MECH ENG
embouchure *f*, orifice *m*, ouverture *f*, PETR TECH *of
pipelines* dispositif déprimogène *m*, orifice *m*, orifice
calibré *m*; ~ **plate** *n* REFRIG diaphragme de mesure *m*; ~
ring *n* C&G cuvette d'écoulement de distributeur *f*

origin: ~ **and destination equation** *n (O-D equation)*
TRANSP relation origine-destination *f*; ~ **and destination survey** *n* *(O-D survey)* TRANSP étude
origine-destination *f*

original *n* CINEMAT négatif original *m*, original inversible *m*, pellicule exposée par la caméra *f*, PRINT
original *m*, TV bande de première génération *f*, enregistrement original *m*, original *m*; ~ **called number** *n*
TELECOM numéro demandé initial *m*; ~ **disc** *n* (BrE)
ACOUSTICS disque original *m*; ~ **disk** *n* (AmE) *see
original disc*; ~ **edition** *n* PRINT livre princeps *m*; ~
inspection *n* QUALITY contrôle en première présentation *m*; ~ **language print** *n* CINEMAT copie en version
originale *f*; ~ **redirection reason** *n* TELECOM indicateur
de raison du renvoi initial *m*; ~ **uncut negative** *n*
CINEMAT négatif original non monté *m*

originating: ~ **exchange** *n* TELECOM central de départ *m*;
~ **junctor** *n* TELECOM joncteur de départ *m*; ~ **point
code** *n (OPC)* TELECOM code du point d'origine *m*; ~
register *n* TELECOM enregistreur de départ *m*; ~ **traffic** *n*
TELECOM trafic de départ *m*, TRANSP trafic interne-ex-
terne *m*

originator *n* TELECOM expéditeur *m*

O-ring *n* MECH, MECH ENG *seal*, P&R joint torique *m*,
VEHICLES *lubrication* anneau torique *m*

Orion *n* ASTRON Orion *f*; ~ **Nebula** *n* ASTRON, SPACE
nébuleuse Orion *f*

Orion's: ~ **belt** *n* ASTRON ceinture d' Orion *f*; ~ **sword** *n*

ASTRON épée d'Orion *f*

ORL *abbr (optical return loss)* TELECOM affaiblissement
d'adaptation optique *m*

orlon *n* CHEM orlon *m*

orlop: ~ **deck** *n* NAUT *ship design* faux pont *m*, faux pont
inférieur *m*

ornamental: ~ **border** *n* PRINT bordure *f*; ~ **rule** *n* PRINT
filet orné *m*

ornithuric *adj* CHEM ornithurique

orogen *n* GEOL orogène *m*

orogene *adj* GEOL orogène

orogenic: ~ **belt** *n* GEOL ceinture orogénique *f*; ~ **cycle** *n*
GEOL cycle orogénique *m*; ~ **phase** *n* GEOL cycle orogénique *m*; ~ **zone** *n* GEOL zone orogénique *f*

orogeny *n* GEOL orogenèse *f*

orotron *n* ELECTRON orotron *m*

orphan *n* PRINT orphelin *m*

orpiment *n* MINERAL orpiment *m*

orrery *n* ASTRON planétarium *m*

orsellic *adj* CHEM orsellique

orsellinic *adj* CHEM orsellinique

orthicon *n* ELECTRON orthicon *m*

orthite *n* MINERAL, NUCLEAR *thorium mineral* orthite *f*

orthobasic *adj* CHEM orthobasique

orthocarbonic *adj* CHEM orthocarbonique

orthocenter *n* (AmE), **orthocentre** *n* (BrE) GEOM orthocentre *m*

orthochemical: ~ **limestone** *n* GEOL calcaire de précipitation chimique *m*

orthochlorite *n* MINERAL orthochlorite *f*

orthochlorotoluene *n* CHEM orthochlorotoluène *m*

orthochromatic: ~ **emulsion** *n* CINEMAT, PHOTO émulsion orthochromatique *f*

orthochromatism *n* CINEMAT orthochromatisme *m*

orthochromatization *n* CINEMAT orthochromatisation *f*

orthoclase *n* MINERAL orthose *m*

orthodromic: ~ **projection** *n* SPACE projection orthodromique *f*

orthodromy *n* NAUT orthodromie *f*

orthoformic *adj* CHEM orthoformique

orthoforming *n* CHEM procédé de craquage catalytique
fluide *m*

orthogonal[1] *adj* GEOM orthogonal

orthogonal:[2] ~ **polarization** *n* TELECOM polarisation orthogonale *f*; ~ **projection** *n* GEOM projection
orthogonale *f*; ~ **scanning** *n* TV analyse orthogonale *f*;
~ **signal** *n* TELECOM signal orthogonal *m*

orthohydrogen *n* CHEM orthohydrogène *m*

ortho-para: ~ **conversion** *n* NUCLEAR transformation
ortho-para *f*

orthophosphate *n* CHEM orthophosphate *m*

orthophosphoric[1] *adj* CHEM orthophosphorique

orthophosphoric:[2] ~ **acid** *n* DETERGENTS acide orthophosphorique *m*

orthoquartzite *n* GEOL grès pur *m*, quartzite sédimentaire *f*

orthorhombic *adj* CRYSTALL orthorhombique

orthoscopic[1] *adj* PHYS orthoscopique

orthoscopic:[2] ~ **eyepiece** *n* ASTRON oculaire orthoscopique *m*

orthosilicate *n* CHEM orthosilicate *m*

orthosilicic *adj* CHEM orthosilicique

orthotropic: ~ **materials** *n pl* MECH ENG matériaux ortho-
tropiques *m pl*

orthovanadic *adj* CHEM orthovanadique

orthoxylene *n* PETR TECH *chemistry, refining* orthoxylène *m*

Os *(osmium)* CHEM Os *(osmium)*

OS *abbr (operating system)* COMP, TELECOM système d'exploitation *m*

OSA *abbr (open systems architecture)* TELECOM architecture de systèmes ouverts *f*

osazone *n* CHEM osazone *f*

OSC *abbr* MAR POLL *(on-scene commander)* commandant des opérations sur le terrain *m*, TELECOM *(on-scene communications)* communications sur place *f pl*

oscillate *vi* ELECTRON, PAPER TECH, WAVE PHYS osciller

oscillating[1] *adj* ELEC oscillant, oscillatoire, ELECTRON *current* périodique, *system* oscillant, *tube* oscillateur, PAPER TECH oscillant

oscillating:[2] ~ **capacitor** *n* ELEC condensateur oscillant *m*; ~ **circuit** *n* ELEC, TV circuit oscillant *m*; ~ **conveyor** *n* MECH ENG transporteur par inertie *m*, transporteur par secousses *m*, SAFETY convoyeur vibrant *m*; ~ **crystal method** *n* RAD PHYS *X-ray diffraction* méthode d'oscillation du cristal *f*; ~ **damper** *n* ELEC *alternating current, galvanometer* amortisseur d'oscillations *m*; ~ **doctor** *n* PAPER TECH docteur oscillant *m*; ~ **electron** *n* NUCLEAR électron oscillant *m*; ~ **quantity** *n* ELECTRON grandeur oscillante *f*; ~ **shower** *n* PAPER TECH rinceur oscillant *m*; ~ **stress** *n* SPRINGS contrainte oscillante *f*; ~ **table** *n* COAL TECH table à secousses *f*; ~ **universe** *n* ASTRON univers oscillant *m*

oscillation *n* ELEC *alternating current*, ELECTRON oscillation *f*, MECH ENG oscillation *f*, va-et-vient *m*, PHYS oscillation *f*, vibration *f*, PRINT mouvement *m*, TELECOM, WAVE PHYS oscillation *f*; ~ **camera** *n* CRYSTALL chambre à oscillation *f*; ~ **frequency** *n* ELECTRON, TELECOM fréquence d'oscillation *f*; ~ **mode** *n* ELECTRON mode d'oscillation *m*; ~ **of a pendulum** *n* MECH ENG oscillation d'un pendule *f*, va-et-vient d'un pendule *m*; ~ **period** *n* ELECTRON période d'oscillation *f*; ~ **of a spring** *n* MECH ENG oscillation d'un ressort *f*

oscillations: ~ **of level** *n pl* CONST dénivellation *f*, dénivellement *m*

oscillator *n* CINEMAT, ELEC, ELECTRON, PHYS oscillateur *m*, PRINT table d'encrage *f*, table de mouillage *f*, SPACE *communications*, TELECOM, WAVE PHYS oscillateur *m*; ~ **bank** *n* ELECTRON batterie d'oscillateurs *f*; ~ **circuit** *n* ELECTRON montage oscillateur *m*; ~ **coil** *n* CINEMAT bobine oscillatrice *f*, ELEC ENG bobine de réaction *f*; ~ **crystal** *n* ELECTRON quartz d'oscillateur *m*, quartz pilote *m*; ~ **drift** *n* ELECTRON dérive de l'oscillateur *f*

oscillatory[1] *adj* TELECOM oscillatoire

oscillatory:[2] ~ **scanning** *n* TV analyse oscillante *f*; ~ **system** *n* ELECTRON système oscillant *m*

oscillogram *n* TV oscillogramme *m*

oscillograph *n* CHEM, ELECTRON, WAVE PHYS oscillographe *m*

oscilloscope *n* COMP, DP, ELEC, ELECTRON, PHYS, TV, WAVE PHYS oscilloscope *m*; ~ **trace** *n* ELECTRON trace d'oscilloscope *f*; ~ **tube** *n* ELECTRON tube d'oscilloscope *m*

osculating: ~ **curves** *n pl* GEOM courbes osculatrices *f pl*

osculatory *adj* GEOM osculateur

OSD *abbr (optical scanning device)* TV analyseur optique *m*

OSF *abbr (operating system function)* TELECOM fonction de système d'exploitation *f*

OSI[1] *abbr (open systems interconnection)* COMP, DP, TELECOM ISO *(interconnexion de systèmes ouverts)*

OSI:[2] ~ **layers** *n pl (open systems interconnection layers)* TELECOM couches OSI *f pl*; ~ **resource** *n (open systems interconnection resource)* TELECOM ressource OSI *f*

osmate *n* CHEM osmiate *m*

osmiate *n* CHEM osmiate *m*

osmic *adj* CHEM osmique

osmious *adj* CHEM osmieux

osmiridium *n* MINERAL osmiridium *m*

osmium *n (Os)* CHEM osmium *m (Os)*

osmol *n* CHEM osmole *f*

osmolarity *n* CHEM osmolarité *f*

osmole *n* CHEM osmole *f*

osmophore *n* CHEM osmophore *m*

osmophoric *adj* CHEM osmophorique

osmosis *n* CHEM *process*, CHEM TECH, HYDROL, PETR TECH, PHYS osmose *f*; ~ **process** *n* CHEM TECH procédé par osmose *m*

osmotic[1] *adj* PHYS osmotique

osmotic:[2] ~ **pressure** *n* GEOPHYS, PETR TECH *geophysics*, PHYS, REFRIG pression osmotique *f*

osmyl *n* CHEM osmyl *f*

OSN *abbr (optical switching network)* TELECOM réseau de connexion optique *m*

OSO: ~ **tanker** *n (ore-slurry-oil tanker)* TRANSP transporteur de minerai sous forme liquide *m*

osone *n* CHEM osone *f*

osotetrazine *n* CHEM osotétrazine *f*

osotriazole *n* CHEM osotriazol *m*

OSR *abbr (optical solar reflector)* SPACE *spacecraft* réflecteur solaire optique *m*

ossein *n* CHEM osséine *f*, ostéine *f*

O-star *n* ASTRON étoile O *f*

ostein *n* CHEM osséine *f*, ostéine *f*

osteolite *n* MINERAL ostéolite *f*

Ostwald: ~ **viscometer** *n* LAB EQUIP viscosimètre type Ostwald *m*

Ostwald's: ~ **dilution law** *n* CHEM *electrolyte* loi de dilution d'Ostwald *f*

OTDR *abbr (optical time domain reflectometry)* OPT réflectométrie optique dans le domaine temporel *f*, technique de rétrodiffusion *f*, TELECOM réflectométrie optique dans le domaine temporel *f*

OTSG *abbr (once-through steam generator)* NUCLEAR générateur de vapeur à passage unique *m*

otter: ~ **board** *n* OCEANOG panneau de chalut *m*

Otto: ~ **cycle** *n* AUTO cycle à quatre temps *m*, VEHICLES *engine* cycle Beau de Rochas *m*

OTTO *abbr (once-through-then-out)* NUCLEAR cycle à sortir après passage unique *m*

ottrelite *n* MINERAL ottrélite *f*

OTV *abbr (orbital transfer vehicle)* SPACE véhicule de transfert interorbital *m*, véhicule de transfert orbital *m*

O-type: ~ **carcinotron** *n* ELECTRON carcinotron de type O *m*; ~ **microwave tube** *n* ELECTRON tube de type O *m*; ~ **tube** *n* ELECTRON tube de type O *m*

ounce *n* METR once *f*, once troy *f*, once avoirdupoids *f*; ~ **avoirdupois** *n* METR once *f*, once avoirdupoids *f*; ~ **troy** *n* METR once *f*, once troy *f*

out *n* PRINT bourdon *m*

outage: ~ **time** *n* NUCLEAR temps d'indisponibilité *m*

outboard[1] *adj* MECH ENG extérieur NAUT *rigging, engine* extérieur, hors-bord

outboard[2] ~ **engine** *n* NAUT moteur hors-bord *m*; ~ **inflatable** *n* TRANSP dinghy à moteur hors-bord *m*; ~ **motorboat** *n* TRANSP canot hors-bord *m*; ~ **speedboat**

n TRANSP canot hors-bord *m*

outbound: ~ **beam** *n* AERONAUT *navigation* faisceau d'é-loignement *m*; ~ **heading** *n* AERONAUT *navigation* cap d'éloignement *m*; ~ **traffic** *n* TRANSP trafic sortant *m*

outbreak *n* THERMOD *of fire* début *m*

outbuildings *n pl* CONST dépendances *f pl*

outcoming: ~ **particle** *n* NUCLEAR particule émise *f*

out-connector *n* COMP, DP connecteur de sortie *m*

outcrop *n* GEOL, MINING affleurement *m*

outdated: ~ **film** *n* CINEMAT pellicule périmée *f*

outdoor: ~ **cable** *n* ELEC câble pour l'extérieur *m*; ~ **electrical installation** *n* ELEC *equipment* poste électrique extérieur *m*; ~ **paint** *n* COLOURS peinture pour l'extérieur *f*; ~ **switchgear** *n* ELEC poste de commutation extérieure *m*

out-edit *n* TV point de sortie *m*

outer[1] *adj* MECH ENG extrême

outer:[2] ~ **axis gimbal** *n* AERONAUT anneau d'azimut *m*; ~ **case** *n* PACKAGING carton extérieur *m*; ~ **conductor** *n* TELECOM conducteur extérieur *m*; ~ **distant signal** *n* RAIL préavertissement *m*, signal de préannonce *m*; ~ **end paper** *n* PRINT feuille de garde *f*; ~ **flap** *n* PACKAGING volet extérieur *m*; ~ **form** (AmE), ~ **forme** *n* (BrE) PRINT forme du premier côté *f*; ~ **fueled zone** *n* (AmE), ~ **fuelled zone** *n* (BrE) NUCLEAR zone chargée de combustible extérieur *f*; ~ **harbor** *n* (AmE), ~ **harbour** *n* (BrE) NAUT, OCEANOG avant-port *m*; ~ **hull** *n* NAUT *ship, boat building* bordé extérieur *m*, coque extérieure *f*; ~ **insulation** *n* ELEC isolation externe *f*; ~ **marker** *n* AERONAUT *of runway* balise extérieure *f*, radioborne extérieure *f*; ~ **orbital complex** *n* RAD PHYS complexe à orbitales externes *m*; ~ **planet** *n* ASTRON planète extérieure *f*, planète supérieure *f*; ~ **planet mission** *n* SPACE mission vers les planètes supérieures *f*; ~ **port** *n* OCEANOG avant-port *m*; ~ **race** *n* MECH ENG bague extérieure de roulement *f*; ~ **side** *n* PRINT côté de première *m*; ~ **skin** *n* NAUT *ship, boat building* bordé extérieur *m*, coque extérieure *f*; ~ **space** *n* SPACE espace extra-atmosphérique *m*

outerwear *n* TEXTILES survêtement *m*

outfall[1] *n* HYDROL *sewage* exutoire *m*, émissaire *m*, RECYCLING déversoir d'égout *m*, WATER SUPP sortie *f*; ~ **pipe** *n* RECYCLING déversoir d'égout *m*; ~ **sewer** *n* RECYCLING déversoir d'égout *m*

outfall:[2] ~ **to sea** *vi* HYDROL *rivers* affluer dans la mer, déboucher dans la mer, tomber dans la mer

outfit *n* MECH ENG ensemble *m*, matériel *m*, nécessaire *m*, outillage *m*, trousse *f*, trousseau *m*, équipage *m*, équipement *m*, PHOTO *equipment* appareillage *m*

outflow *n* PROD ENG écoulement *m*, WATER SUPP débit *m*, décharge *f*, effluence *f*, sortie *f*, écoulement *m*

outgas *vt* CHEM dégazer

outgassing: ~ **index** *n* C&G indice de bullage *m*

outgoing[1] *adj* TELECOM sortant

outgoing:[2] ~ **air current** *n* MINING courant d'air sortant *m*; ~ **call** *n* TELECOM communication de départ *f*; ~ **calls** *n pl* TELECOM appels de départ *m pl*; ~ **calls barred** *n* (*OCB*) TELECOM interdiction des appels au départ *f*; ~ **calls barred line** *n* TELECOM ligne spécialisée arrivée *f*; ~ **channel** *n* TV voie de sortie *f*; ~ **circuit** *n* ELEC circuit de départ *m*, TELECOM circuit sortant *m*; ~ **conveyor belt** *n* PROD ENG bande de convoyeur de sortie *f*; ~ **feed** *n* TV signal de sortie *m*; ~ **group** *n* TELECOM faisceau sortant *m*; ~ **line** *n* TELECOM, TV ligne de sortie *f*; ~ **procedure** *n* TELECOM procédure de départ *f*; ~ **traffic** *n* TELECOM trafic sortant *m*; ~ **trunk circuit** *n* TELECOM

joncteur de départ *m*, joncteur sortant *m*; ~ **web** *n* PRINT bande sortant de la machine *f*

outhaul *n* NAUT *boom fitting* amarrage du point d'écoute *m*, hale-dehors *m*

outlet *n* AUTO orifice de refoulement *m*, ELEC ENG prise de courant *f*, socle de prise de courant *m*, HYDROL *outfall* déversoir *m*, exutoire *m*, MECH ENG sortie *f*, OCEANOG émissaire *m*, PAPER TECH orifice d'évacuation *m*, PROD ENG débouché *m*, issue *f*, orifice de décharge *m*, orifice de sortie *m*, sortie *f*, TELECOM accès de départ *m*, point de sortie *m*, sortie *f*, prise *f*, WATER SUPP dégorgeoir *m*, exutoire *m*, émissaire *m*; ~ **box** *n* ELEC *connection* boîte de distribution *f*, prise femelle *f*; ~ **channel** *n* WATER SUPP rigole de vidange *f*; ~ **connection** *n* PROD ENG raccord de sortie *m*; ~ **edge** *n* NUCLEAR *of turbine* arête de sortie *f*; ~ **flow control** *n* WATER SUPP régulation du débit *f*; ~ **pipe** *n* WATER SUPP tuyau de vidange *m*; ~ **side** *n* NUCLEAR côté du refoulement *m*; ~ **temperature** *n* POLLUTION température de sortie *f*; ~ **valve** *n* AUTO clapet de refoulement *m*, HYDR EQUIP clapet de décharge *m*, soupape d'échappement *f*

outline[1] *n* CINEMAT sommaire *m*, synopsis *m*, MECH ENG configuration *f*, contour *m*, profil *m*, *sketch* dessin au trait *m*, PRINT esquisse *f*; ~ **drawing** *n* MECH ENG plan de forme *m*; ~ **lighting** *n* CINEMAT éclairage de décrochement *m*

outline[2] *vt* PRINT détourer, souligner, mettre en valeur

out-milling *n* MECH ENG fraisage en roulant *m*

out-of-action *adj* MECH ENG hors d'usage, hors service

out-of-balance[1] *adj* MECH ENG, METR comportant un balourd

out-of-balance:[2] ~ **forces** *n pl* MECH ENG force à balourd *f*

out-of-band: ~ **filtering** *n* ELECTRON filtrage des fréquences hors bande *m*; ~ **signaling** *n* (AmE), ~ **signalling** *n* (BrE) SPACE *communications* signalisation hors-bande *f*

out-of-control *adj* CONTROL non maîtrisable

out-of-course: ~ **running** *n* RAIL désheurement *m*

out-of-focus[1] *adj* CINEMAT flou, PHOTO défocalisé

out-of-focus:[2] ~ **image** *n* CINEMAT APHY image floue *f*, PHOTO image défocalisée *f*

out-of-frame[1] *adj* PRINT décadré, décentré

out-of-frame[2] *n* TELECOM DVT, défaut de verrouillage trame *m*; ~ **second** *n* (*OFS*) TELECOM seconde de perte du verrouillage de trame *f*

out-of-gear *adj* MECH ENG désengrené

out-of-jig: ~ **cradle** *n* MECH ENG bâti de reprise *m*

out-of-order *adj* ELEC en panne, MECH ENG dérangé, déréglé, TELECOM en dérangement

out-of-parallelism *n* MECH ENG faux parallélisme *m*

out-of-phase *adj* ELEC *alternating current* déphasé, ELECTRON déphasé, pas en phase, TV déphasé

out-of-pitch[1] *adj* AERONAUT *helicopter* déréglage en pas

out-of-pitch:[2] ~ **blade** *n* AERONAUT *helicopter* décalage de pale *m*

out-of-plumb *adj* CONST hors d'aplomb, MECH ENG dévers, hors d'aplomb

out-of-range *adj* MILIT *artillery* hors de portée

out-of-repair *adj* MECH ENG en mauvais état

out-of-round[1] *adj* AUTO ovalisé, MECH ENG faux rond *m*, PRINT tournant faux-rond

out-of-round:[2] ~ **finish** *n* C&G bague ovalisée *f*; ~ **wear** *n* AUTO ovalisation *f*

out-of-roundness *n* PETR ovalisation *f*; ~ **tolerance** *n*

SPRINGS tolérance de cylindricité f

out-of-sequence: ~ **activity** n PROD ENG activité déclassée f, activité hors séquence f; ~ **operation** n PROD ENG activité déclassée f, opération déclassée f, opération hors séquence f

out-of-service: ~ **time** n TELECOM temps d'intervention m; ~ **track** n RAIL voie impraticable f

out-of-shape adj C&G déformé

out-of-square adj MECH ENG faux équerrage, hors d'équerre, PRINT hors d'équerre, mal équerré

out-of-stock: ~ **situation** n PROD ENG manquant m, rupture de stock f, stock en rupture m

out-of-sync[1] adj TV désynchronisé, non synchrone

out-of-sync:[2] ~ **error** n TELECOM décalage m

out-of-synchronization: ~ **error** n TELECOM décalage m

out-of-tolerance adj MECH ENG hors tolérance

out-of-track adj AERONAUT helicopter déréglage des pales en rotation m

out-of-trim[1] adj AERONAUT hors trim

out-of-trim[2] n AERONAUT aircraft déréglage de la compensation m

out-of-true adj MECH ENG dévers, dévié, faussé, gauchi, ovalisé, voilé, PRINT déformé, faux rond, nonconforme à l'original

out-of-use adj MECH ENG hors d'usage, hors service

outpiece n SPRINGS pièce découpée f

out-point n TV point de sortie m

outport n OCEANOG avant-port m

outpouring n CONST épanchement m

output n COAL TECH production f, COMP, DP, ELEC, ELEC ENG sortie f, GAS TECH, MECH ENG rendement m, MINING production f, rendement m, NUCLEAR fourniture au réseau f, PAPER TECH débit m, PRINT sortie f, PROD ENG débit m, production f, rendement m, TV sortie f; ~ **admittance** n ELEC ENG admittance de sortie f; ~ **amplifier** n ELECTRON, TV amplificateur de sortie m; ~ **angle** n OPT, TELECOM angle de sortie m; ~ **area** n COMP, DP zone de sortie f; ~ **attenuation** n ELECTRON atténuation de sortie f; ~ **attenuator** n ELECTRON atténuateur de sortie m; ~ **back-off** n SPACE communications recul de sortie m; ~ **biasing** n PROD ENG décalage en sortie m; ~ **buffer** n COMP, DP tampon de sortie m; ~ **capacitance** n ELEC ENG capacité de sortie f; ~ **capacitor** n ELEC ENG condensateur de sortie m; ~ **cavity** n ELECTRON cavité de sortie f; ~ **charge** n ELEC ENG charge à la sortie f; ~ **circuit** n ELEC ENG, TELECOM circuit de sortie m; ~ **control** n TV contrôle de sortie m, réglage de modulation m; ~ **current** n ELEC courant de sortie m; ~ **data** n COMP, DP données de sortie f pl; ~ **device** n COMP, DP, PRINT dispositif de sortie m, PROD ENG actionneur m, dispositif de sortie m; ~ **diagram** n PROD ENG diagramme de production m, graphique de production m; ~ **divergence** n TELECOM divergence de sortie f; ~ **earth short** n (BrE) (cf output ground short) PROD ENG sortie à la masse f; ~ **electrode** n ELEC ENG électrode de sortie f; ~ **file** n COMP, DP, PRINT fichier de sortie m; ~ **ground short** n (AmE) (cf output earth short) PROD ENG sortie à la masse f; ~ **image table** n PROD ENG table-image des sorties f; ~ **image table location** n PROD ENG emplacement de la table-image des sorties m; ~ **impedance** n ELEC, ELEC ENG, PHYS, TELECOM, TV impédance de sortie f; ~ **level** n RECORDING, TELECOM, TV niveau de sortie m; ~ **mirror** n INSTRUMENT miroir de sortie m; ~ **monitor** n TV moniteur de sortie m; ~ **override** n PROD ENG asservissement des sorties m; ~ **override instruction** n PROD ENG instruction d'asser-

vissement de sortie f; ~ **phase-to-phase short circuit** n ELEC, PROD ENG court-circuit entre phases en sortie m; ~ **port** n TELECOM sortie f; ~ **power** n ELEC, ELEC ENG, TELECOM puissance de sortie f; ~ **quantity** n ELEC ENG grandeur de sortie f; ~ **queue** n COMP file d'attente en sortie f, DP file d'attente de sortie f; ~ **ramp control** n PROD ENG commande de la rampe de sortie f; ~ **record** n COMP, DP enregistrement de sortie m; ~ **recorder** n INSTRUMENT enregistreur de puissance m; ~ **regulator** n CONTROL régulateur de rendement m; ~ **shaft** n AUTO arbre de sortie m, VEHICLES gearbox arbre secondaire m; ~ **signal** n CONTROL signal de sortie m, ELEC ENG signal de sortie m, signal émis m, TELECOM, TV signal de sortie m; ~ **terminal** n ELEC borne de sortie f, ELEC ENG borne de départ f, borne de sortie f, PROD ENG module de sortie m; ~ **transducer** n ELEC ENG transducteur de sortie m; ~ **transformer** n ELEC, ELEC ENG, PHYS, RECORDING transformateur de sortie m; ~ **voltage** n ELEC, ELEC ENG, TELECOM, TV tension de sortie f; ~ **winding** n ELEC transformer enroulement de sortie m

output-limited[1] adj COMP limité par la vitesse des périphériques de sortie, DP tributaire de la vitesse de sortie

output-limited:[2] ~ **process** n COMP processus limité par la vitesse des périphériques en sortie m, DP processus limité par la sortie m

outrigger n AERONAUT balancine f

outside: ~ **air temperature indicator** n AERONAUT indicateur de température extérieure m; ~ **air temperature probe** n AERONAUT sonde de température extérieure f; ~ **broadcast** n (OB) TV émission transmise de l'extérieur f; ~ **broadcast unit** n TV unité vidéo mobile f; ~ **calipers** n pl (AmE), ~ **callipers** n pl (BrE) MECH ENG compas d'extérieur m, compas d'épaisseur m; ~ **circle** n MECH ENG gearing cercle d'échanfreinement m, cercle de couronne m, cerclede tête m, cercle extérieur m; ~ **clearance** n HYDR EQUIP dégagement extérieur m, interférence extérieure négative f; ~ **coil diameter** n SPRINGS diamètre extérieur d'enroulement m; ~ **diameter** n (OD) MECH, MECH ENG diamètre extérieur m; ~ **dimensions** n pl PACKAGING dimensions extérieures f pl; ~ **gear** n MECH ENG engrenage extérieur m; ~ **guide** n SPRINGS guidage extérieur m; ~ **lab** n CINEMAT laboratoire indépendant m; ~ **lap** n HYDR EQUIP slide valve recouvrement extérieur m, recouvrement à l'admission m; ~ **lead** n HYDR EQUIP slide valve avance linéaire à l'admission f, avance à l'admission f; ~ **measuring faces** n pl MECH ENG caliper faces de mesure extérieure f pl; ~ **paint** n COLOURS peinture pour extérieur f; ~ **pipe** n GAS TECH tube externe m; ~ **plant cable** n TV câble de branchement m, câble de réseau m; ~ **screw** n MECH ENG vis mâle f, vis pleine f; ~ **string** n CONST stairbuilding limon m; ~ **thread** n MECH ENG filet extérieur m

outside-and-inside: ~ **calipers** n pl (AmE), ~ **callipers** n pl (BrE) MECH ENG maître-à-danser m

outside-fired: ~ **boiler** n PROD ENG chaudière à chauffage extérieur f, chaudière à foyer extérieur f

outside-threading: ~ **tool** n MECH ENG outil à fileter extérieurement m

outsize n COAL TECH déclassé m

outstanding adj PROD ENG en instance, en suspens

outstep: ~ **well** n PETR TECH oil exploration puits d'extension m

outstroke n HYDR EQUIP of piston course aller f, course avant f, course directe f

outturn: ~ **sheet** n PAPER TECH feuille échantillon type f

outward:[1] **~ bound** *adj* NAUT *ship* en partance, sortant
outward:[2] **~ angle** *n* GEOM angle externe *m*; **~ flow turbine** *n* HYDR EQUIP turbine centrifuge *f*; **~ flux** *n* PHYS flux sortant *m*; **~ passage** *n* NAUT traversée d'aller *f*; **~ propagating wave** *n* TELECOM onde progressive *f*; **~ traffic** *n* TRANSP trafic sortant *m*
oval[1] *adj* GEOM ovale
oval[2] *n* GEOM ovale *m*; **~ burrs** *n pl* MECH ENG fraises-limes ovales *f pl*; **~ compass** *n* MECH ENG compas d'ellipse *m*, compas elliptique *m*; **~ countersunk rivet** *n* MECH ENG rivet à tête fraisée et goutte de suif *m*; **~ file** *n* MECH ENG lime olive *f*, lime queue-de-rat ovale *f*; **~ head fastener** *n* MECH ENG élément de fixation à tête fraisée bombée *m*; **~ head screw** *n* MECH ENG vis à tête fraisée bombée *f*; **~ knob** *n* CONST *locksmithing* bouton ovale *m*, bouton à olive *m*, olive *f*; **~ pulley** *n* MECH ENG poulie ovale *f*; **~ punt** *n* C&G olive *f*
ovality *n* SPRINGS ovalisation *f*
ovalization *n* PETR TECH *drilling problem* ovalisation *f*
oval-shaped *adj* GEOM en ovale
oven *n* HEATING four *m*, LAB EQUIP étuve *f*, PAPER TECH four *m*, PROD ENG four *m*, étuve *f*, TEXTILES four *m*, étuve *f*, THERMOD four *m*; **~ ageing** *n* (BrE) P&R *process* vieillissement en étuve *m*; **~ aging** *n* (AmE) *see oven ageing*; **~ coke** *n* COAL TECH coke métallurgique *m*; **~ dehydration** *n* REFRIG étuvage *m*; **~ gloves** *n pl* SAFETY gants thermo-isolants *m pl*; **~ with forced convection** *n* LAB EQUIP étuve à convection forcée *f*; **~ with natural convection** *n* LAB EQUIP *heating* étuve à convection naturelle *f*
oven-dried *adj* THERMOD séché au four, étuvé
oven-dry[1] *adj* PAPER TECH sec absolu
oven-dry:[2] **~ tensile strength** *n* TEXTILES résistance anhydre à la traction *f*
ovenproof: ~ glass *n* THERMOD verre culinaire *m*, verre à feu *m*
overageing *n* (BrE) METALL durcissement dépassé *m*
overaging *n* (AmE) *see overageing*
overall[1] *adj* CONST *dimensions*, MECH ENG hors tout
overall[2] *n* TEXTILES combinaison de travail *f* **~ dimensions** *n pl* MECH ENG cotes d'encombrement *f pl*, dimensions hors-tout *f pl*, PACKAGING dimensions totales *f pl*; **~ efficiency** *n* FUELLESS rendement global *m*; **~ internal height** *n* MECH ENG encombrement intérieur en hauteur *m*; **~ length** *n* MECH ENG longueur hors tout *f*, METR longueur totale *f*, TEXTILES longueur hors tout *f*; **~ protective suits** *n pl* SAFETY vêtements à protection intégrale *m pl*; **~ refrigerating effect** *n* REFRIG puissance frigorifique globale *f*; **~ response curve** *n* ACOUSTICS courbe de réponse totale *f*; **~ shade** *n* TEXTILES coloris foncé *m*; **~ time interval** *n* TRANSP *traffic control* intervalle de temps entre véhicules *m*; **~ travel speed** *n* TRANSP vitesse de parcours *f*; **~ travel time** *n* TRANSP temps de parcours *m*; **~ width** *n* MECH ENG largeur hors tout *f*
overalls *n pl* SAFETY bleu de travail *m*, salopette *f*
over-and-under: ~ current relay *n* ELEC relais à maximum et minimum *m*
overarm: ~ machine *n* MECH ENG *milling* bras support *m*
overbalance *vi* SAFETY perdre l'équilibre
overbend *n* PETR convexité *f*
overbias *n* RECORDING overbias *f*
overboard *adv* NAUT par-dessus bord
overbreak *n* MINING *of injector* hors-profil *m*
overbridge *n* CONST pont à tablier inférieur *m*
overbunching *n* ELECTRON groupement excessif *m*

overburden *n* COAL TECH détritus *m*, MINING massif de minerai *m*, morts-terrains *m*, recouvrement *m*, morts-terrains *m*, PETR TECH *geology* charge géostatique *f*; **~ drill** *n* COAL TECH cuiller *f*; **~ effect** *n* PETR effet géostatique *m*; **~ gradient** *n* GEOL, PETR TECH *geology* gradient géostatique *m*; **~ pressure** *n* COAL TECH pression de couverture *f*, PETR TECH *geology* pression géostatique *f*
overcapacity *n* AERONAUT *transport* surcapacité *f*
overcast[1] *adj* METEO couvert
overcast[2] *n* METEO assombrissement atmosphérique *m*
overcharge *n* ELEC *of accumulator* surcharge *f*, REFRIG *of refrigerant* excès de fluide *m*
overcompounding *n* ELEC ENG surcompoundage *m*
overcrank *vt* CINEMAT tourner à une vitesse supérieure à la normale
overcure *n* P&R *fault* surcuisson *f*, survulcanisation *f*
overcurrent *n* ELEC surintensité de courant *f*, ELEC ENG surintensité *f*; **~ blocking device** *n* ELEC *motor drive* dispositif de bloc par surintensité *m*; **~ circuit breaker** *n* ELEC déclencheur à maxima *m*, ELEC ENG disjoncteur de sortie *m*, déclencheur à surintensité *m*; **~ protection** *n* ELEC *safety* protection contre la surintensité de courant *f*, protection à maximum de courant *f*, ELEC ENG protection contre les surintensités *f*; **~ relay** *n* ELEC relais ampèremétrique *m*, relais à maximum *m*; **~ switch** *n* ELEC interrupteur de surcharge *m*; **~ trip** *n* ELEC ENG disjoncteur de surintensité *m*, déclencheur à surintensité *m*
overcutting *n* ACOUSTICS chevauchement *m*
overdamping *n* PHYS suramortissement *m*
overdevelop *vt* PHOTO surdévelopper
overdevelopment *n* CINEMAT surdéveloppement *m*
overdeviation *n* SPACE *communications* surexcursion *f*
overdischarging *n* ELEC ENG décharge excessive *f*
overdosage *n* CHEM surdosage *m*
overdrive[1] *n* AUTO surmultiplicateur *m*, surmultipliée *f*, MECH surmultiplication *f*, VEHICLES *gearbox* surmultiplicateur *m*
overdrive[2] *vt* PROD ENG surmoduler
overdry *vt* PAPER TECH sursécher
overdub *vt* RECORDING ajouter
overdye *vt* TEXTILES surteindre
overexpose *vt* CINEMAT, PHOTO surexposer
overexposed: ~ film *n* PHOTO film surexposé *m*; **~ picture** *n* PHOTO cliché surexposé *m*
overexposure *n* PHOTO excès de pose *m*, pose exagérée *f*, surexposition *f*, RAD PHYS surexposition *f*
overextraction *n* HYDROL *groundwater* surexploitation *f*
overfall-type: ~ fish pass *n* FUELLESS passe à poisson de type à débordement *f*
overfeed *n* MECH ENG, TEXTILES suralimentation *f*; **~ stoker** *n* MECH ENG chargeur mécanique à alimentation par le dessus *m*, foyer mécanique à alimentation par le dessus *m*
overfeeding *n* MECH ENG, REFRIG *of refrigerant to evaporator* suralimentation *f*
overfishing *n* OCEANOG surexploitation *f*, surpêche *f*
overflow[1] *n* CHEM débordement *m*, excédent *m*, COAL TECH surverse *f*, COMP débordement *m*, dépassement *m*, saturation *f*, DP saturation *f*, HYDROL déversoir *m*, trop-plein *m*, lame déversante *f*, MECH trop-plein *m*, MECH ENG débordement *m*, *of injector* trop-plein *m*, WATER SUPP *pipe* trop-plein *m*, tuyau d'écoulement du trop-plein *m*, tuyau de trop-plein *m*; **~ accept** *n* (OA) TELECOM acceptation de débordement *f*; **~ area**

n COMP, DP zone de dépassement de capacité *f*; ~ **dam** *n* HYDROL, WATER SUPP barrage déversoir *m*, digue déversoir *f*; ~ **hole** *n* AUTO orifice de trop-plein *m*; ~ **pipe** *n* AUTO conduite de trop-plein *f*, VEHICLES *cooling system* tuyau de trop-plein *m*, WATER SUPP trop-plein *m*, tuyau d'écoulement du trop-plein *m*, tuyau de trop-plein *m*; ~ **process** *n* C&G procédé d'alimentation par débordement *m*; ~ **traffic** *n* TELECOM trafic de débordement *m*; ~ **valve** *n* HYDR EQUIP clapet de trop-plein *m*, soupape de trop-plein *f*, vanne de trop-plein *f*, RAIL trop-plein *m*

overflow[2] *vt* HYDROL déborder, déverser

overflow:[3] ~ **its banks** *vi* HYDROL *of river* déborder, passer par-dessus ses berges

overfold *n* GEOL pli déversé *m*

overgage: ~ **hole** *n* (AmE), **overgauge hole** *n* (BrE) PETR trou hors calibre *m*

overglazing *n* C&G survitrage *m*

overgrinding *n* COAL TECH surbroyage *m*

overground *adj* COAL TECH surbroyé

overhand: ~ **knot** *n* NAUT demi-noeud *m*; ~ **stope** *n* MINING gradins renversés *m pl*, maintenage *m*; ~ **stoping** *n* MINING abattage en gradins renversés *m*, abattage montant *m*, exploitation en gradins renversés *f*

overhang *n* CONST porte-à-faux *m*, surplomb *m*, VEHICLES *body* porte-à-faux *m*; ~ **spacer** *n* NUCLEAR pièce d'écartement de la tête de bobine *f*

overhanging *n* CONST surplombement *m*; ~ **arm** *n* PROD ENG *of milling machine* support porte-fraise *m*; ~ **crank** *n* MECH ENG manivelle en porte-à-faux *f*; ~ **face** *n* MINING front de taille en porte-à-faux *m*, front de taille en surplomb *m*; ~ **wall** *n* CONST mur déversé *m*, mur en encorbellement *m*, mur en surplomb *m*, mur forjeté *m*, mur suspendu *m*

overhaul[1] *n* AERONAUT *of equipment* révision *f*

overhaul[2] *vt* NAUT *another vessel* dépasser, rattraper, *maintenance* repasser, réviser, PAPER TECH *maintenance* réviser

overhead *n* TELECOM *data transmission* surdébit *m*; ~ **access** *n* (*OHA*) TELECOM accès au surdébit *m*, accès aux octets de surdébit *m*; ~ **bank** *n* CINEMAT batterie de projecteurs au plafond *f*; ~ **bits** *n pl* TELECOM bits d'en-tête *m pl*; ~ **bunker refrigerated truck** *n* REFRIG wagon réfrigéré à bac plafonnier *m*; ~ **cable** *n* ELEC *supply network*, ELEC ENG câble aérien *m*; ~ **camshaft** *n* (*OHC*) AUTO, MECH, VEHICLES arbre à cames en tête *m*; ~ **cone** *n* MECH ENG contre-cône *m*, cône de renvoi *m*; ~ **cone pulley** *n* MECH ENG contre-cône *m*, cône de renvoi *m*; ~ **conveyor** *n* PACKAGING transporteur suspendu *m*; ~ **crane** *n* CINEMAT pont roulant *m*, CONST grue-tour *f*, pont roulant *m*, MECH pont roulant *m*, PROD ENG grue roulante aérienne *f*, pont roulant *m*; ~ **crossover** *n* RAIL caténaire *f*, diagonale *f*; ~ **drum car** *n* (AmE) (*cf overhead drum wagon*) RAIL wagon dérouleur *m*; ~ **drum wagon** *n* (BrE) (*cf overhead drum car*) RAIL wagon dérouleur *m*; ~ **electrical monorail conveyor** *n* MECH ENG monorail à chariots électrifiés *m*; ~ **engine** *n* PROD ENG *steam* machine-pilon *f*; ~ **guard** *n* SAFETY *for high lift rider truck* protège-conducteur *m*; ~ **light** *n* AERONAUT plafonnier *m*; ~ **line** *n* CONST *electricity* câble aérien *m*, ligne aérienne *f*, ELEC *supply network*, ELEC ENG, TELECOM ligne aérienne *f*; ~ **line knuckle** *n* RAIL *tram, catenary* aiguillage tangentiel *m*; ~ **motion** *n* MECH ENG *countershaft* renvoi de mouvement se fixant au plafond *m*,

transmission secondaire à placer en l'air *f*; ~ **network** *n* TELECOM réseau aérien *m*; ~ **panel** *n* AERONAUT panneau de plafond *m*, panneau sur plafond *m*; ~ **pilot bar** *n* MECH ENG *of lathe* barre de guidage en l'air *f*; ~ **power line** *n* ELEC ENG ligne aérienne à courant *f*; ~ **power line fittings** *n pl* ELEC ENG matériel pour lignes aériennes *m*; ~ **railway** *n* TRANSP chemin de fer suspendu *m*, métro aérien *m*; ~ **runway** *n* PROD ENG chemin de fer suspendu *m*, monorail aérien *m*, monorail transporteur *m*, voie ferrée aérienne *f*; ~ **system** *n* ELEC ENG réseau aérien *m*; ~ **track** *n* PROD ENG chemin de fer suspendu *m*, monorail aérien *m*, monorail transporteur *m*, voie ferrée aérienne *f*; ~ **traveling crane** *n* (AmE), ~ **travelling crane** *n* (BrE) PACKAGING grue à pont roulant *f*; ~ **valve** *n* VEHICLES *engine* soupape en tête *f*; ~ **valve engine** *n* (*OHV engine*) AUTO moteur à soupapes en tête *m*

overheat:[1] ~ **thermoresistor** *n* AERONAUT sonde de surchauffe *f*

overheat[2] *vt* THERMOD surchauffer

overheat[3] *vi* THERMOD s'échauffer

overheating *n* ELEC ENG surchauffage *m*, MECH ENG échauffement *m*, PROD ENG surchauffage *m*, surchauffe *f*, PROP MAT surchauffage *m*, SAFETY surchauffe *f*, THERMOD, surchauffage *m*, surchauffe *f*, VEHICLES *of engine* surchauffe *f*

overlap *n* COMP chevauchement *m*, CONST chevauchement *m*, recouvrement *m*, DP chevauchement *m*, GEOL chevauchement *m*, recouvrement *m*, PRINT dépassant *m*, rabat *m*, recouvrement *m*, TV *of heads* recouvrement *m*; ~ **contact** *n* PROD ENG contact chevauchant *m*; ~ **joint** *n* CONST assemblage à recouvrement *m*, joint chevauché *m*, joint à recouvrement *m*; ~ **section** *n* RAIL section tampon *f*

overlapping *n* CONST chevauchement *m*, recouvrement *m*, ELEC ENG chevauchement *m*, METALL superposition *f*, PHYS *of spectra* empiètement *m*, PROP MAT recouvrement *m*; ~ **flaps** *n pl* PACKAGING volets à recouvrement *m pl*

overlay[1] *n* C&G verre doublé *m*, COMP recouvrement *m*, CONST revêtement *m*, DP recouvrement *m*, PRINT calque de préparation *m*, surimpression *f*, TV incrustation *f*, surimpression *f*, transparence électronique *f*; ~ **cladding** *n* MECH *welding* dépôt de revêtement par soudage *m*; ~ **mat** *n* C&G mat overlay *m*

overlay[2] *vt* TV incruster

overlaying *n* (AmE) (*cf flashing*) C&G doublage *m*

overleap: ~ **joint** *n* CONST *halved joint of wood* assemblage à mi-bois *m*, coupe à mi-bois *f*, entaillé à mi-bois *f*

overload[1] *n* COMP surcharge *f*, CONST charge excessive *f*, surcharge *f*, DP, ELEC *current*, ELEC ENG, GAS TECH, PACKAGING, PHYS, PRODeng, RECORDING, SPACE, TELECOM surcharge *f*; ~ **channel** *n* TELECOM canal de surcharge *m*; ~ **current** *n* ELEC *supply, equipment*, ELEC ENG courant de surcharge *m*; ~ **cutout** *n* CONTROL disjoncteur par surintensité de courant *m*, disjoncteur à maxima *m*, interrupteur de surcharge *m*; ~ **factor** *n* ELEC *supply* facteur de surcharge *m*; ~ **fracture** *n* SPRINGS rupture par surcharge *f*; ~ **indicator** *n* ELEC *supply, equipment* avertisseur de surcharge *m*; ~ **level** *n* ELEC ENG, RECORDING niveau de surcharge *m*; ~ **protection** *n* ELEC *circuit, equipment*, ELEC ENG protection contre les surcharges *f*; ~ **protection device** *n* ELEC ENG dispositif de protection contre les surcharges *m*; ~

relay n ELEC relais ampèremétrique m, relais à maximum m, ELEC ENG relais à maximum d'intensité m, PROD ENG relais d'intensité m, relais thermique m; ~ **running** n PROD ENG marche en surcharge f; ~ **switch** n CONTROL interrupteur à maximum de courant m; ~ **test** n ELEC essai de surcharge m; ~ **voltage** n ELEC circuit, equipment tension de surcharge f

overload[2] vt CONST, ELEC circuit, component, ELEC ENG, TELECOM, TV surcharger

overloaded adj PHYS, TELECOM surchargé

overloading n PROD ENG surcharge f, TRANSP traffic degré de congestion m

overlock vt TEXTILES coudre à points de surjet

overlook vt PROD ENG, SAFETY négliger

overmodulation n RECORDING surmodulation f

overoxidize vt CHEM suroxyder

overpass n RAIL passage en dessus m, passage supérieur m, pont par-dessus m

overplacement n MINING terrains de couverture m pl, terrains de recouvrement m pl

overpotential: ~ **protection** n ELEC ENG limiteur de tension m

overpower vt WATER SUPP maîtriser

overpressure n AERONAUT surpression f, PETR pression de formation anormale positive f, surpression f, PROD ENG excès de pression m, surtension f; ~ **test** n PROD ENG essai de surtension m

overprint[1] n CINEMAT surimpression f; ~ **colors** n pl (AmE) ~ **colours** n pl (BrE) PRINT couleurs imprimées en complément sur les autres f pl; ~ **lacquer** n PRINT vernis de surimpression m; ~ **varnish** n PRINT vernis de surimpression m

overprint[2] vt PRINT repiquer, surcharger, surimprimer

overprinting n GEOL geochronology rajeunissement des âges m, remise à zéro f, MECH ENG remise à zéro f, PACKAGING surimpression f, PRINT repiquage m, surimpression f, PROD ENG remise à zéro f

overproduction n PROD ENG surproduction f

overrange n PROD ENG dépassement supérieur m

overrefining n PROD ENG suraffinage m

override:[1] ~ **control** n AERONAUT commande transparente f; ~ **switch** n CONTROL, ELEC interrupteur de dérivation m

override[2] vt PROD ENG neutraliser

overrider n VEHICLES body butoir de pare-chocs m, garde de pare-chocs f

overriding[1] adj MECH prioritaire

overriding[2] n PROD ENG chevauchement m, RAIL of buffers enchevêtrement m

overrun[1] n AERONAUT dépassement de course m, PRINT excédentaire m, exemplaires en supplément de la commande m pl, passe f, VEHICLES engine roulement de poussée m, régime de frein moteur m

overrun[2] vt RAIL station, stop signal brûler

overrun[3] vi TV excéder le temps prévu

overrunning: ~ **clutch** n AERONAUT embrayage à roue libre m

overs n pl PRINT exemplaires imprimés en excès m pl, passe f

oversaturated adj GEOL hypersaturé

oversaturation n TV sursaturation f

overscan n TV surbalayage m

overscore vt PRINT surligner

overseas[1] adj NAUT commerce d'outre-mer

overseas:[2] ~ **container** n TRANSP conteneur pour trafic d'outre-mer m; ~ **packaging** n PACKAGING emballage pour transport maritime m

oversewing n TEXTILES point de surjet m

oversheath n ELEC of cable gaine externe f

overshipment n PROD ENG livraison excédentaire f

overshoot[1] n AERONAUT atterrissage trop long m, ELEC ENG, METALL dépassement m; ~ **distortion** n TV distorsion de suroscillation f

overshoot[2] vt AERONAUT runway effacer, MECH dépasser, RAIL station, stop signal brûler

overshooting n AERONAUT dépassement m

overshot n PETR TECH fishing tool sourcière f; ~ **water wheel** n WATER SUPP roue en dessus f, roue à augets en dessus f; ~ **wheel** n WATER SUPP roue en dessus f, roue à augets en dessus f

oversize[1] adj MECH ENG surdimensionné

oversize[2] n COAL TECH déclassé supérieur m, MECH surépaisseur f, MINING broken ore matières refusées f pl, refus m

oversizing n MECH ENG surdiamétrage m

overspeed n MECH survitesse f, MECH ENG emballement m, survitesse f; ~ **brake** n MECH ENG frein modérable m; ~ **braking at end of hoist** n MINING freinage modéré en fin de cordée m; ~ **control** n FUELLESS contrôle de survitesse m; ~ **gear** n MECH ENG modérateur de vitesse m; ~ **protection** n MECH ENG protection contre la survitesse f; ~ **test** n ELEC machine essai d'emballement m

overspeeder n MECH ENG modérateur de vitesse m

oversquare: ~ **engine** n AUTO moteur super carré m

oversteer[1] n AUTO, VEHICLES survirage m

oversteer[2] vi AUTO survirer, survireur

overstowage n NAUT surarrimage m

overstress n PROD ENG surcharge f

overstressing n METALL surchargement m, PROD ENG surcharge f

overstrike n PRINT substitution f

overstriking n C&G surdéveloppement m

overtaking: ~ **lane** n CONST voie de dépassement f

over-the-road: ~ **system** n REFRIG système de refroidissement en route m

overthrust n GEOL charriage m, chevauchement m, PETR TECH chevauchement m; ~ **block** n GEOL nappe de charriage f; ~ **fold** n GEOL pli-faille couché m; ~ **sheet** n GEOL nappe de charriage f

overtone n ELECTRON harmonique supérieur m

overtop[1] vt HYDROL sea wall déverser, écrêter

overtop:[2] ~ **its banks** vi HYDROL river déborder, passer par-dessus ses berges

overtravel n PROD ENG surcourse f; ~ **detection** n PROD ENG détection de surcourse f

overturn vti MECH ENG basculer

overturned: ~ **fold** n GEOL pli renversé m; ~ **limb** n GEOL flanc inverse m

overturning n SAFETY ayant pour action de renverser, TRANSP capotage m; ~ **moment** n CONST moment de renversement m

overvoltage n CHEM survoltage m, ELEC, ELEC ENG, PHYS surtension f; ~ **breakdown** n ELEC ENG claquage par surtension m; ~ **protection** n ELEC safety protection contre les surtensions f, ELEC ENG coupe-circuit de surtension m, protection contre les surtensions f; ~ **protection device** n ELEC ENG dispositif de protection contre les surtensions m; ~ **relay** n ELEC protection, ELEC ENG relais à maximum de tension m; ~ **release** n ELEC circuit breaker déclencheur de tension m

overweight[1] adj PACKAGING surchargé

overweight[2] *n* METR poids fort *m*

overwind *n* MINING envoi aux molettes *m*, mise aux molettes *f*; ~ **gear** *n* MINING évite-molettes *m*

overwinder *n* MINING évite-molettes *m*; ~ **and overspeeder** *n* MINING évite-molettes modérateur de vitesse *m*

overwinding *n* MINING envoi aux molettes *m*, mise aux molettes *f*; ~ **allowance** *n* MINING hauteur de sécurité *f*; ~ **gear** *n* MINING évite-molettes *m*

overworking *n* PROD ENG surcharge *f*, surmenage *m*

overwrap *n* PACKAGING emballage extérieur *m*

overwrapping: ~ **machinery** *n* PACKAGING machine pour emballage extérieur *f*

overwrite *vt* DP *data* superposer, PRINT mémoriser par dessus, substituer

overwriting *n* COMP *of data*, DP *of data* superposition *f*, superposition d'instructions *f*, écrasement *m*

ovoglobulin *n* CHEM ovoglobuline *f*

ovoid *n* COAL TECH boulet *m*

ovolo *n* CONST boudin *m*, quart-de-rond *m*; ~ **plane** *n* CONST boudin *m*

Owen: ~ **bridge** *n* ELEC *circuit* pont d'Owen *m*

own: ~ **coding** *n* COMP séquence de l'utilisateur *f*, DP séquence utilisateur *f*

owner *n* COMP, DP propriétaire *m*, PATENTS titulaire *m*

own-exchange: ~ **supervisory circuit** *n* TELECOM circuit de connexion local *m*

oxalate *n* CHEM oxalate *m*

oxalated *adj* CHEM oxalaté

oxalic[1] *adj* CHEM oxalique

oxalic:[2] ~ **acid** *n* PHOTO acide oxalique *m*

oxaloacetic *adj* CHEM oxalacétique

oxaluric *adj* CHEM oxalurique

oxalyl *n* CHEM oxalyle *m*

oxalylurea *n* CHEM acide parabanique *m*, oxalylurée *f*, oxalyluréide *f*

oxamic *adj* CHEM oxamique

oxamide *n* CHEM oxamide *m*

oxanilic *adj* CHEM oxanilique

oxanilide *n* CHEM oxanilide *m*

oxazine *n* CHEM oxazine *f*

oxazole *n* CHEM oxazole *m*

Oxberry: ~ **optical printer** *n* CINEMAT tireuse optique Oxberry *f*

oxbow *n* HYDROL bras mort *m*

oxetone *n* CHEM oxétone *f*

Oxford: ~ **gray** *n* (AmE) ~ **grey** *n* (BrE) COLOURS couleur marengo *f*

oxidability *n* CHEM oxydabilité *f*

oxidable *adj* CHEM, PROP MAT oxydable

oxidant *n* CHEM oxydant *m*, THERMOD agent d'oxydation *m*, comburant *m*, oxydant *m*

oxidation *n* CHEM, CINEMAT, ELEC *metals*, HYDROL, POLLUTION, PRINT oxydation *f*; ~ **ditch** *n* HYDROL *sewage* fossé d'oxydation *m*; ~ **ditches** *n pl* WATER SUPP fossé d'oxydation *m*; ~ **ponds** *n pl* WATER SUPP étang d'oxydation *m*; ~ **reduction cell** *n* LAB EQUIP *analysis, electrochemistry* pile à oxydoréduction *f*; ~ **reduction potential** *n* POLLUTION potentiel redox *m*

oxidative: ~ **coupling** *n* GAS TECH couplage oxydant *m*

oxide *n* CHEM, RECORDING, TV oxyde *m*; ~ **build-up** *n* CINEMAT perte d'oxyde *f*, poudrage *m*, RECORDING, TV dépôt d'oxyde *m*; ~ **ceramic lathe tools** *n pl* MECH ENG outils à tourner en céramique d'oxyde *m pl*; ~ **film** *n* COATINGS couche d'oxyde *f*; ~ **layer** *n* COMP couche d'oxyde *f*; ~ **ore** *n* CHEM minerai oxydé *m*; ~ **shedding** *n* TV perte d'oxyde *f*, poudrage *m*; ~ **side** *n* CINEMAT côté

enregistrement *m*, TV *of magnetic tape* côté enregistrement *m*, côté oxyde *m*

oxide-coated: ~ **cathode** *n* ELEC ENG cathode à oxydes *f*

oxidic: ~ **waste** *n* COAL TECH déchet oxydé *m*

oxidizability *n* CHEM oxydabilité *f*

oxidizable *adj* CHEM, PROP MAT oxydable

oxidization *n* CHEM oxydation *f*

oxidize[1] *vt* CHEM oxyder

oxidize[2] *vi* CHEM s'oxyder

oxidizer *n* AERONAUT comburant *m*, CHEM oxydant *m*, SPACE *spacecraft* comburant *m*, oxydant *m*

oxidizing[1] *adj* CHEM, GEOL, SAFETY oxydant

oxidizing:[2] ~ **agent** *n* CHEM, POLLUTION oxydant *m*; ~ **flame** *n* CHEM flamme oxydante *f*, CONST *welding* flamme d'oxydation *f*, flamme oxydante *f*; ~ **substance** *n* SAFETY substance oxydante *f*

oxidoreduction *n* CHEM oxydoréduction *f*

oximation *n* CHEM oximation *f*

oxime *n* CHEM oxime *f*

oximeter *n* CHEM oxymètre *m*

oximetric *adj* CHEM oxymétrique

oximetry *n* CHEM oxymétrie *f*

oxo: ~ **acid** *n* CHEM oxacide *m*, oxyacide *m*; ~ **alcohol** *n* DETERGENTS alcool oxo *m*; ~ **process** *n* DETERGENTS synthèse oxo *f*; ~ **synthesis** *n* DETERGENTS synthèse oxo *f*

oxonium *n* CHEM oxonium *m*

oxozone *n* CHEM oxozone *m*

oxyacetylene: ~ **blowpipe** *n* CONST *welding*, MECH *tools*, PROD ENG chalumeau oxyacétylénique *m*; ~ **welding** *n* CONST soudage oxyacétylénique *m*, MECH soudage au chalumeau *m*, PROD ENG soudage oxyacétylénique *m*, soudure oxyacétylénique *f*, THERMOD soudage au chalumeau *m*, soudage oxyacétylénique *m*; ~ **welding equipment** *n* PROD ENG poste de soudage oxyacétylénique *m*

oxyacid *n* CHEM oxacide *m*, oxyacide *m*

oxycellulose *n* CHEM oxycellulose *f*

oxychloride *n* CHEM oxychlorure *m*

oxycutting *n* MECH *process* oxycoupage *m*

oxycyanide *n* CHEM oxycyanure *m*

oxyfluoride *n* CHEM oxyfluorure *m*

oxygen *n* (O) CHEM oxygène *m* (O); ~ **arc cutting** *n* CONST oxycoupage à l'arc *m*, *welding* coupage à l'arc avec oxygène *m*, découpage à l'arc avec oxygène *m*, PROD ENG oxycoupage *m*; ~ **boosting** *n* C&G suroxygénation *f*; ~ **bottom blowing** *n* METALL, PROP MAT procédé de soufflage d'oxygène par le fond *m*; ~ **breathing apparatus** *n* SAFETY appareil de respiration à oxygène *m*, inhalateur d'oxygène *m*, masque à oxygène *m*, appareil respiratoire à oxygène *m*; ~ **consumption** *n* HYDROL consommation d'oxygène *f*; ~ **cylinder** *n* PROD ENG, SPACE *spacecraft* bouteille d'oxygène *f*; ~ **deficit** *n* (*OD*) HYDROL déficit d'oxygène *m*; ~ **depletion of air** *n* MINING désoxydation de l'air *f*, force *f*; ~ **enrichment** *n* C&G suroxygénation *f*; ~ **furnace** *n* COAL TECH four Martin *m*; ~ **generator** *n* CONST *welding* générateur d'oxygène *m*; ~ **index** *n* AERONAUT indice d'oxygène *m*; ~ **lancing** *n* CONST forage à la lance *m*, lance à oxygène *f*, *welding* forage thermique *m*, PROD ENG *welding* perçage à la lance *m*; ~ **mask** *n* SAFETY, SPACE *spacecraft* masque à oxygène *m*; ~ **outlet** *n* PROD ENG bouche de sortie d'oxygène *f*; ~ **poisoning** *n* OCEANOG hyperventilation *f*; ~ **regulator** *n* SPACE *spacecraft* régulateur d'oxygène *m*; ~ **respirator** *n* SPACE *spacecraft* inhalateur d'oxygène *m*; ~ **self-res-**

cue apparatus n SAFETY appareils d'autosauvetage à oxygène m pl; ~ **self-rescuers** n pl SAFETY appareils d'autosauvetage à oxygène m pl; ~ **supply** n SAFETY for fire or explosion réserve d'oxygène f, SPACE spacecraft alimentation en oxygène f

oxygenase n CHEM oxygénase f

oxygenate vt CHEM, HYDROL oxygéner

oxygenated[1] adj CHEM, HYDROL oxygéné

oxygenated:[2] ~ **water** n HYDROL eau oxygénée f

oxygenation n CHEM, HYDROL oxygénation f; ~ **capacity** n HYDROL capacité d'oxygénation f

oxygen-helium: ~ **mixture** n OCEANOG héliox m

oxygenic adj CHEM oxygéné

oxygenizable adj CHEM oxygénable

oxygen-salinity: ~ **diagram** n OCEANOG diagramme oxygène-salinité m

oxyhaemography n (BrE) CHEM oxyhémographie f

oxyhemography n (AmE) see oxyhaemography

oxyhydric adj CHEM oxhydrique

oxyhydrogen adj CHEM oxhydrique

o-xylene n CHEM orthoxylène m

oxyphilic adj CHEM acidophile

oxyphilous adj CHEM acidophile

oxyphosphate n CHEM oxyphosphate m

oxysalt n CHEM oxysel m

oxysulfide n (AmE), **oxysulphide** n (BrE) CHEM oxysulfure m

oxytetracycline n CHEM oxytétracycline f

oxytoxic adj CHEM ocytoxique

oyster: ~ **bed** n OCEANOG claire f, huîtrière f; ~ **culture** n OCEANOG ostréiculture f; ~ **dredger** n NAUT dragueur d'huîtres m; ~ **farm** n OCEANOG huîtrière f; ~ **farmer** n OCEANOG ostréiculteur m; ~ **fattening pond** n OCEANOG claire f

ozalid n PRINT bleu d'épreuves m, ozalid m; ~ **paper** n PRINT papier ozalid m; ~ **process** n PRINT procédé ozalid m

ozocerite n MINERAL ozocérite f, ozokérite f

ozone n CHEM, METEO, SPACE ozone m; ~ **absorption** n RAD PHYS absorption par ozone f; ~ **concentration** n POLLUTION concentration en ozone f; ~ **layer** n METEO ozonosphère f, POLLUTION couche d'ozone f, SPACE ozonosphère f; ~ **resistance** n P&R résistance à l'ozone f

ozonide n CHEM ozonide m

ozonization n METEO ozonation f, ozonisation f; ~ **plant** n HYDROL installation d'ozonation f

ozonize vti CHEM, METEO ozoner, ozoniser

ozonized adj CHEM ozonisé, HYDROL water ozonisé, ozoné

ozonizer n CHEM ozoniseur m

ozonolysis n CHEM ozonolyse f

ozonoscope n CHEM ozonoscope m

ozonoscopic adj CHEM ozonoscopique

ozonosphere n SPACE couche d'ozone f, ozonosphère f

P

p *abbr* METR *(peta-)* **p** *(peta-)* METR *(pico-)* **p** *(pico-)*

P *(phosphorus)* CHEM P *(phosphore)*

p⁺-region *n* ELECTRON zone P fortement dopée *f*, zone de type P^+ *f*

p⁺-semiconductor *n* ELECTRON semi-conducteur de type P fortement dopé *m*, semi-conducteur de type P^+ *m*

Pa¹ *abbr (pascal)* METR, PETR TECH, PHYS Pa *(pascal)*

Pa² *(protactinium)* CHEM Pa *(protactinium)*

PA¹ *abbr (power amplifier)* TELECOM amplificateur de puissance *m*

PA:² ~ **amplifier** *n (public address amplifier)* RECORDING amplificateur de sonorisation *m*; ~ **container** *n* TRANSP conteneur à porteur aménagé *m*

PABX *abbr (private automatic branch exchange)* TELECOM autocommutateur privé *m*

pace *n* CINEMAT débit *m*, rythme *m*

pachnolite *n* MINERAL pachnolite *f*

pack¹ *n* MINING muretin en pierres sèches *m*, remblai *m*, PACKAGING sachet *m*, PHOTO *of photographic paper* pochette *f*; ~ **handling equipment** *n* PACKAGING équipement de manutention des emballages *m*; ~ **ice** *n* NAUT glace de banquise *f*; ~ **system** *n* MINING étançon hydraulique simple *m*; ~ **wall** *n* MINING mur de remblai *m*, muretin en pierres sèches *m*

pack² *vt* COMP, DP condenser, MECH *with grease* bourrer, garnir, MINING endiguer, remblayer, terrasser, PAPER TECH emballer

package *n* COMP progiciel *m*, ELEC ENG boîtier *m*, PACKAGING emballage *m*, SPACE *spacecraft* bloc de puissance *m*, TEXTILES paquet *m*; ~ **dyeing** *n* COLOURS teinture pour emballages *f*, teinture sur bobines *f*; ~ **for standardization** *n* PACKAGING emballage pour normalisation *m*; ~ **freight** *n* TRANSP marchandises de groupage *f pl*; ~ **lacquer** *n* COATINGS vernis d'emballage déchirable *m*; ~ **reactor** *n* NUCLEAR réacteur préfabriqué *m*, réacteur transportable *m*; ~ **sleeve** *n* TEXTILES support de fil *m*; ~ **test** *n* PACKAGING essai d'emballage *m*

packaged: ~ **boiler** *n* HEAT ENG chaudière monobloc *f*

packaging *n* FOOD TECH conditionnement *m*, emballage *m*, PAPER TECH emballage *m*, PRINT conditionnement *m*, PROD ENG conditionnement *m*, emballage *m*, TEXTILES conditionnement *m*; ~ **area** *n* PROD ENG zone de conditionnement *f*; ~ **line** *n* PACKAGING chaîne d'emballage *f*; ~ **profiles** *n pl* PACKAGING profils d'emballage *m pl*

packed: ~ **bed scrubber** *n* POLLUTION séparateur laveur à garnissage *m*; ~ **column** *n* CHEM *chromatography* colonne à garnissage *f*, CHEM TECH colonne garnie *f*, colonne à corps de remplissage *f*, colonne à garnissage *f*, PETR TECH colonne à garnissage *f*; ~ **decimal** *n* DP décimal condensé *m*; ~ **tower** *n* CHEM TECH colonne garnie *f*, colonne à corps de remplissage *f*, colonne à garnissage *f*

packer *n* MECH ENG garniture étanche *f*, PACKAGING emballeur *m*, PETR packer *m*, TEXTILES emballeur *m*

packer's: ~ **bay** *n* C&G baie d'emballeur *f* (Bel), loge d'emballeur *f* (Fra)

packet *n* COMP DP paquet *m*, paquet de données *m*, PACKAGING emballage *m*, PROD ENG caisse *f*, TELECOM, TEXTILES paquet *m*; ~ **assembler-disassembler** *n (PAD)* COMP, DP, TELECOM assembleur-désassembleur de paquets *m*; ~ **broadcasting** *n* TELECOM télédiffusion de paquets *f*; ~ **data transmission network** *n* TELECOM TRANSPAC, réseau de transmission de données par paquets *m*; ~ **delay** *n* COMP, DP, TELECOM délai de transmission de paquets *m*; ~ **mode bearer service** *n* TELECOM service support en mode paquet *m*; ~ **mode terminal** *n* COMP, DP terminal en mode paquet *m*; ~ **port** *n* TELECOM accès en mode paquet *m*; ~ **radio** *n* TELECOM radiocommunication par paquets *f*; ~ **sequencing** *n* COMP, DP ordonnancement de paquets *m*; ~ **switch** *n (PS)* ELEC, TELECOM commutateur de paquets *m*; ~ **switching** *n* COMP, DP, ELEC ENG communication par paquets *f*, commutation de paquets *f*, TELECOM commutation de paquets *f*; ~ **switching exchange** *n (PSE)* TELECOM centre de commutation de paquets *m*; ~ **switching network** *n* TELECOM réseau à commutation de paquets *m*; ~ **switching node** *n (PSN)* TELECOM noeud à commutation de paquets *m*; ~ **switching processor** *n* TELECOM processeur de commutation de paquets *m*; ~ **transmission** *n* DP transmission de paquets *f*, TELECOM transmission par paquets *f*

packetizer-depacketizer *n* TELECOM assembleur-désassembleur de paquets *m*

packet-switched: ~ **bearer service** *n* TELECOM service support en mode paquet *m*; ~ **network** *n (PSN)* COMP, DP réseau de commutation par paquets *m*

packing *n* MECH garniture d'étanchéité *f*, MECH ENG *act* bourrage *m*, garnissage *m*, *material* garnissage *m*, garniture *f*, MINING remblai *m*, remblayage *m*, OCEANOG rousture *f*, PROD ENG *of sand of a mould* serrage *m*, TEXTILES emballage *m*; ~ **bush** *n* NUCLEAR coquille de garniture *f*; ~ **case** *n* TEXTILES caisse d'emballage *f*; ~ **density** *n* COMP densité d'enregistrement *f*, CRYSTALL densité d'empilement *f*, DP compacité *f*, densité d'enregistrement *f*, ELECTRON densité d'intégration *f*, P&R densité de tassement *f*, TEXTILES densité d'implantation *f*, TV densité d'enregistrement *f*; ~ **effect** *n* NUCLEAR effet de masse *m*; ~ **fraction** *n* OPT *fibre bundle* facteur de remplissage *m*, PHYS défaut de masse relatif *m*, facteur de tassement *m*, rapport du défaut de masse *m*, TELECOM facteur de remplissage *m*; ~ **gland** *n* MECH ENG, PROD ENG, SPACE presse-étoupe *m*; ~ **piece** *n* C&G cuirasse *f*, MECH ENG cale *f*, cale d'appui *f*, selle d'arrêt *f*, semelle *f*; ~ **retainer** *n* MECH ENG porte-garniture *m*; ~ **rings** *n pl* MECH ENG *of piston* segments *m pl*; ~ **seal** *n* NUCLEAR *of a stuffing box* garniture *f*, joint *m*, étoupage *m*; ~ **slip** *n* PROD ENG bon de livraison fournisseur *m*; ~ **station** *n* PACKAGING poste d'emballage *m*; ~ **stick** *n* C&G bourroir *m*; ~ **type** *n* PROD ENG type de conditionnement *m*; ~ **with siccative** *n* PACKAGING emballage avec siccatif inclus *m*

packstone *n* GEOL calcaire avec grains jointifs liés par la micrite *m*, packstone *m*

pad¹ *n* AUTO coussin *m*, C&G tôle *f*, ELEC ENG plage de connexion *f*, ELECTRON *attenuator* réseau atténuateur *m*, MECH patin *m*, MILIT *of tracked vehicle* patin de chenille *m*, OCEANOG bourriche *f*, PRINT habillage *m*, zone d'encollage lié à un schéma *f*, zone de perforation lié à un schéma *f*, SPACE aire *f*, TELECOM atténuateur *m*, TEXTILES coussinet *m*, VEHICLES *disc brake* plaquette de frein *f*, sabot de frein *m*; ~ **break** *n* C&G casse mécanique *f*; ~ **dyeing** *n* COLOURS teinture par foulardage *f*, TEXTILES teinture au foulard *f*; ~ **foundation** *n* COAL TECH semelle élargie *f*; ~ **inside rubber boot** *n* CONST *railway* semelle dans le chausson en caoutchouc *f*; ~ **mangle** *n* TEXTILES foulard *m*; ~ **roller** *n* CINEMAT galet presseur *m*

pad² *vt* COMP, DP remplir, PRINT mettre en tablette, TEXTILES rembourrer

PAD *abbr (packet assembler-disassembler)* COMP, DP, TELECOM assembleur-désassembleur de paquets *m*

padded¹ *adj* MECH rembourré

padded:² ~ **bridge** *n* INSTRUMENT plaquette *f*; ~ **clothing** *n* SAFETY vêtements matelassés *m pl*; ~ **headband** *n* RECORDING *of headphones* étrier capitonné *m*

padding *n* COMP garnissage *m*, remplissage *m*, DP remplissage *m*, MECH ENG rembourrage *m*, rembourrement *m*, PACKAGING rembourrage *m*, PAPER TECH coloration par immersion *f*, TEXTILES ouatinage *m*; ~ **emulsion** *n* PRINT colle servant à la fabrication de blocs papetiers *f*, émulsion servant àl a fabrication de blocs papetiers *f*; ~ **press** *n* PRINT machine à façonner des blocs *f*

paddle *n* C&G spatule *f*, CINEMAT agitateur *m*, HYDR EQUIP pale *f*, pelle *f*, vannelle *f*, vantelle *f*, MECH ENG *of fan, of water wheel* aileron *m*, alichen *m*, alichon *m*, aube *f*, jantille *f*, palette *f*, volet *m*; ~ **board** *n* MECH ENG *of fan, of water wheel* aileron *m*, alichen *m*, alichon *m*, aube *f*, jantille *f*, palette *f*, volet *m*; ~ **boat** *n* NAUT bateau à aubes *m*; ~ **mixer** *n* MINING mélangeur à palettes *m*; ~ **wheel** *n* NAUT, WATER SUPP roue à aubes *f*, roue à palettes *f*

padlock *n* CONST cadenas *m*

Pag: ~ **belt** *n* CINEMAT batterie de ceinture *f*

page¹ *n* COMP, DP, PRINT page *f*; ~ **bearer** *n* PRINT porte-copie *m*, porte-page *m*; ~ **bursting** *n* PRINT flashage de page *m*; ~ **depth** *n* PRINT hauteur de page *f*, justification verticale *f*; ~ **frame** *n* COMP, DP cadre de page *m*; ~ **number** *n* PRINT folio *m*, numéro *m*, numéro de page *m*; ~ **printer** *n* COMP imprimante page par page *f*; ~ **proof** *n* PRINT épreuve en page *f*; ~ **shoe** *n* PRINT porte-page *m*; ~ **table** *n* COMP, DP table de pages *f*

page² *vt* COMP, DP paginer

pager *n* TELECOM récepteur *m*, récepteur d'appel *m*

pages *n (pp)* PRINT pages *f pl*; ~ **per minute** *n (PPM)* COMP, DP pages par minute *f pl*

paginate *vt* COMP, DP paginer, PRINT folioter, paginer

pagination *n* PRINT foliotage *m*, imposition *f*, pagination *f*

paging *n* COMP *display*, DP *display* pagination *f*, TELECOM appel de personnes *m*, téléappel *m*; ~ **channel** *n* TELECOM voie d'appel unilatéral *f*; ~ **service** *n* TELECOM recherche de personnes *f*, service de téléappel *m*

paint *n* CONST, VEHICLES *body* peinture *f*; ~ **fumes** *n pl* SAFETY vapeurs de peinture *f pl*; ~ **mill** *n* C&G broyeur à peinture *m*; ~ **remover** *n* COLOURS décapant pour peintures *m*, décapant solvant *m*; ~ **spray** *n* MECH ENG *tool* pistolet à peinture *m*; ~ **stripper** *n* CONST décapant

m; ~ **thinner** *n* COLOURS diluant *m*

paintbox *n* COMP, DP, TV *electronic graphic system* palette graphique *f*

paintbrush *n* P&R pinceau *m*

paint-burning: ~ **lamp** *n* CONST lampe de peintre en bâtiment *f*

painted: ~ **matte** *n* CINEMAT cache peint *m*

painter *n* NAUT *mooring* amarre *f*, bosse *f*

painting *n* COMP, DP coloriage *m*; ~ **on glass** *n* C&G peinture vitrifiable sur verre *f*; ~ **on porcelain** *n* C&G peinture sur porcelaine *f*; ~ **varnish** *n* COATINGS vernis au pinceau *m*

paint-spraying: ~ **apparatus ventilation system** *n* SAFETY système de ventilation des appareils de peinture au pistolet *m*

paintwork *n* CONST peinturage *m*

pair *n* ELEC ENG *cables* paire *f*; ~ **annihilation** *n* NUCLEAR *particle-antiparticle pairs* annihilation de paires *f*; ~ **of binoculars** *n pl* INSTRUMENT paire de jumelles *f*; ~ **of dividers** *n* MECH ENG compas droit *m*, compas droit à pointes *m*, compas à diviser *m*, compas à pointes sèches *m*, NAUT compas à pointes sèches *m*, PROD ENG compas droit *m*, compas droit à pointes *m*, compas à diviser *m*, compas à pointes sèches *m*; ~ **peaks** *n pl* RAD PHYS *in positron annihilation* pics de paires *m pl*

paired¹ *adj* CHEM *electrons* apparié

paired:² ~ **cable** *n* ELEC, ELEC ENG, TV câble à paires *m*; ~ **electrons** *n pl* RAD PHYS électrons appariés *m pl*, électrons couplés *m pl*

pairing *n* ELEC *cable* câblage en paires *m*, TV appairage *m*

pairs: ~ **of high-mass jets** *n pl* RAD PHYS *particle research* paires de jets de masse élevée *f pl*

PAL¹ *abbr* COMP *(programmable array logic)*, DP *(programmable array logic)* circuit logique programmable *m*, TV *(phase alternation line)* ligne d'alternance de phase *f*, système PAL *m*

PAL:² ~ **color system** *n* (AmE), ~ **colour system** *n* (BrE) TV système couleur PAL *m*

palaeocurrent: ~ **direction** *n* (BrE) GEOL direction de courant ancien *f*, direction de paléocourant *f*

palaeogeographic: ~ **province** *n* (BrE) GEOL domaine paléogéographique *m*

palaeomagnetism *n* (BrE) GEOL, PHYS paléomagnétisme *m*

palaeo-oceanography *n* (BrE) OCEANOG paléocéanographie *f*

palaeopressure *n* (BrE) PETR TECH paléopression *f*

palaeoslope *n* (BrE) GEOL paléopente *f*, pente d'un fond de mer *f*, pente d'une ancienne surface continentale *f*

Palaeozoic *n* (BrE) GEOL *era* paléozoïque *f*, ère primaire *f*

palagonite *n* PETR palagonite *f*

pale *n* CONST *paling, stake* palis *m*, tige *f*

paleocurrent: ~ **direction** *n* (AmE) *see palaeocurrent direction*

paleogeographic: ~ **province** *n* (AmE) *see palaeogeographic province*

paleomagnetism *n* (AmE) *see palaeomagnetism*

paleo-oceanography *n* (AmE) *see palaeo-oceanography*

paleopressure *n* (AmE) *see palaeopressure*

paleoslope *n* (AmE) *see palaeoslope*

Paleozoic *n* (AmE) *see Palaeozoic*

paling *n* CONST *fence* claire-voie *f*, *pale, picket* palis *m*

palisade *n* CONST palissade *f*

palladic *adj* CHEM palladique

palladious *adj* CHEM palladeux

palladium *n (Pd)* CHEM palladium *m (Pd)*

pallasites *n pl* ASTRON pallasites *m pl*

pallet *n* AERONAUT *air transport* palette *f*, palette de chargement *f*, C&G spatule *f*, *for glass containers* palette *f*, *in ceramic industry* tour de potier *m*, TRANSP palette *f* ~ **collar** *n* TRANSP rehausse pour palette *f*; ~ **container** *n* TRANSP conteneur palette *m*; ~ **for anvil** *n* PROD ENG *power hammer* tas *m*, tas inférieur *m*; ~ **for tup** *n* PROD ENG *power hammer* frappe *f*, frappe supérieure *f*, panne du pilon *f*; ~ **hood** *n* PACKAGING capot pour palette *m*; ~ **knife** *n* LAB EQUIP *paints* couteau à palette *m*, MECH ENG couteau de peintre à enduire *m* ~ **load** *n* PACKAGING chargement de palette *m*; ~ **loader** *n* PACKAGING chargeur de palettes *m*; ~ **ship** *n* TRANSP navire porte-palettes *m*; ~ **shrink-wrapping** *n* PACKAGING enveloppe thermorétractable pour palette *f*; ~ **strapping-material** *n* PACKAGING matériel pour le cerclage de palettes *m*; ~ **stretch-wrapping machine** *n* PACKAGING machine pour l'emballage de palettes sous tension *f*; ~ **with loose partition** *n* TRANSP palette à côté démontable *f*; ~ **wrapper** *n* PACKAGING enveloppe pour palette *f*

palleting *n* C&G pelotage *m*

palletizable *adj* PACKAGING, TRANSP palettisable

palletization *n* PACKAGING, TRANSP palettisation *f*

palletize *vt* PACKAGING, TRANSP palettiser

palletized: ~ **board** *n* PACKAGING carton palettisé *m*; ~ **cargo carrier** *n* TRANSP navire pour charges palettisées *m*

palletizing *n* TRANSP palettisation *f*; ~ **adhesive** *n* PACKAGING adhésif pour palettisation *m*; ~ **machine** *n* PACKAGING machine pour palettiser *f*

palm: ~ **kernel oil** *n* FOOD TECH huile de palmiste *f*; ~ **nut oil** *n* CHEM huile de palmiste *f*; ~ **oil** *n* CHEM huile de palme *f*

palmic *adj* CHEM palmique

palmin *n* CHEM palmitine *f*

palmitate *n* CHEM palmitate *m*

palmitic *adj* CHEM palmitique

palmitin *n* CHEM palmitine *f*

palmitone *n* CHEM palmitone *f*

paludal: ~ **environment** *n* GEOL milieu marécageux *m*, milieu palustre *m*

PAM[1] *abbr* COMP, DP, ELECTRON, SPACE, TELECOM *(pulse amplitude modulation)* MIA *(modulation d'impulsions en amplitude)*, TELECOM *(pass-along message)* message à faire passer *m*

PAM:[2] ~ **network** *n* TELECOM réseau MIA *m*

pamphlet: ~ **stitching** *n* PRINT couture au fil textile *f*, couture à cheval *f*

pan[1] *n* C&G ferrasse *f*, CINEMAT panoramique *m*, COAL TECH bassin *m*, LAB EQUIP *balance* plateau *m*, MECH ENG bac *m*, MINING *separating dish* batée *f*, gamelle *f*, sébile *f*, écuelle *f*, PRINT bassine *f*, PROD ENG *amalgamation pan, grinder* cuve d'amalgamation *f*, cuve de broyage *f*, moulin d'amalgamation *m*, pan d'amalgamation *m*; ~ **amalgamator** *n* PROD ENG amalgamateur à cuve *m*; ~ **and scan** *n* TV *of film image* recadrage *m*; ~ **and tilt handle** *n* CINEMAT levier de manoeuvre *m*; ~ **and tilt head** *n* CINEMAT tête panoramique *f*, PHOTO tête basculante *f*; ~ **filter** *n* COAL TECH filtre statique *m*, INSTRUMENT filtre panchromatique *m*; ~ **glass** *n* CINEMAT verre panchro *m*; ~ **handle** *n* CINEMAT manche pour tête panoramique *m*; ~ **head** *n* MECH ENG *rivet* tête plate trapézoïdale *f*; ~ **head rivet** *n* CONST rivet à tête cylindrique *m*, MECH ENG rivet à tête tronconique

m; ~ **head screw** *n* CONST vis à tête cylindrique *f*, MECH ENG vis à tête cylindrique bombée large *f*, PROD ENG vis à tête plate *f*; ~ **head tripod** *n* PHOTO pied à tête panoramique graduée *m*; ~ **lehr** *n* C&G arche à tirer *f*; ~ **mill** *n* PROD ENG *amalgamation pan, grinder* cuve d'amalgamation *f*, cuve de broyage *f*, moulin d'amalgamation *m*, pan d'amalgamation *m*; ~ **pot** *n* RECORDING potentiomètre de panoramique *m*; ~ **roller** *n* PRINT rouleau barboteur *m*, rouleau de bassine *m*; ~ **scales** *n pl* LAB EQUIP *balance* trébuchet à plateaux *m*

pan:[2] ~ **down** *vt* TV faire un panoramique vers le bas

pan[3] *vi* CINEMAT panoramiquer; ~ **down** *vi* CINEMAT faire un panoramique vers le bas

PAN *abbr (peroxoacetylnitrate)* POLLUTION PAN *(peroxoacétylnitrate)*

panabase *n* MINERAL panabase *f*

panaglide *n* CINEMAT système stabilisateur portable *m*

panary: ~ **fermentation** *n* FOOD TECH *baking* fermentation panaire *f*

panavision: ~ **system** *n* CINEMAT procédé panavision *m*

pancake: ~ **coil** *n* ELEC bobine plate *f*, galette *f*, ELEC ENG bobinage extra-plat *m*, TESTING bobine plate *f*, galette *f*; ~ **ice** *n* OCEANOG crêpe de glace *f*; ~ **motor** *n* ELEC ENG moteur plat *m*

pancake-shaped: ~ **annular chamber** *n* NUCLEAR chambre annulaire en forme de beignet *f*

panchromatic[1] *adj* CHEM, CINEMAT, PHOTO, PRINT panchromatique

panchromatic:[2] ~ **emulsion** *n* PHOTO émulsion panchromatique *f*; ~ **film** *n* CINEMAT pellicule panchromatique *f*

pancreatin *n* CHEM pancréatine *f*

pandermite *n* MINERAL pandermite *f*

pane *n* CONST *of glass* carreau *m*, MECH ENG *face or side* pan *m*, PROD ENG *of hammer* panne *f*

panel *n* COAL TECH chambre isolée *f*, panneau *m*, CONST *of door*, ELEC *control*, GAS TECH, MINING, REFRIG, TEXTILES panneau *m*; ~ **button** *n* CONTROL bouton de porte *m*; ~ **cooler** *n* REFRIG panneau refroidisseur *m*; ~ **fabric** *n* TEXTILES tissu pour panneau amovible *m*; ~ **heater** *n* THERMOD panneau chauffant *m*; ~ **heating** *n* THERMOD chauffage mural *m*; ~ **knob** *n* CONTROL bouton de porte *m*; ~ **mounting** *n* ELEC, PROD ENG montage sur panneau *m*; ~ **shears** *n pl* MECH ENG *tool* cisailles passe-franc *f pl*; ~ **system** *n* TELECOM système panel *m*

panflavine *n* CHEM panflavine *f*

panic: ~ **bolt** *n* SAFETY crémone de sûreté *f*

panne *n* TEXTILES velours panne *m*

panning *n* CHEM lavage *m*, COMP, DP translation panoramique *f*

panorama: ~ **periscope** *n* NUCLEAR périscope panoramique *m*

panoramic: ~ **camera** *n* PHOTO appareil panoramique *f*; ~ **lens** *n* PHOTO objectif panoramique *m*; ~ **photograph** *n* PHOTO vue panoramique *f*; ~ **sight** *n* INSTRUMENT lunette de visée *f*; ~ **telescope** *n* INSTRUMENT lunette panoramique *f*, télescope panoramique *m*

pantellerite *n* PETR pantellérite *f*

pantile *n* CONST tuile en S *f*

panting *n* OCEANOG hyperapnée *f*

pantograph *n* ELEC *railway*, MECH ENG *drawing*, RAIL pantographe *m*; ~ **contact strip** *n* RAIL bande d'usure *f*, bande d'usure pantographe *f*; ~ **dresser** *n* MECH ENG *grinding wheels* rhabilleur pantographe *m*; ~ **slippage** *n* RAIL décollement du pantographe *m*; ~ **slipper** *n* RAIL frotteur de pantographe *m*; ~ **tie bar** *n* RAIL entretoise de pantographe *f*

pantograph-wearing: **~ strip** *n* RAIL bande d'usure *f*,
bande d'usure pantographe *f*, bande de frottement *f*

pantonal: **~ scale** *n* ACOUSTICS gamme pantonale *f*

Pantone: **~ process** *n* PRINT procédé Pantone *m*

pantothenate *n* CHEM pantothénate *m*

papain *n* CHEM, FOOD TECH papaïne *f*

papaveraldine *n* CHEM papavéraldine *f*

papaverine *n* CHEM papavérine *f*

paper *n* PAPER TECH papier *m*; **~ bag** *n* PACKAGING sac en
papier *m*, sachet *m*; **~ bag and sack closure** *n* PACKA-
GING fermeture pour sachets et sacs en papier *f*; **~
banding machine** *n* PACKAGING machine pour bander
avec du papier *f*; **~ board in the flat** *n* PAPER TECH
papier carton à plat *m*; **~ capacitor** *n* ELEC, ELEC ENG
cables condensateur au papier *m*; **~ chips** *n pl* PACKA-
GING rognures de papier *f pl*; **~ chromatography** *n*
CHEM chromatographie sur papier *f*; **~ chromatography apparatus** *n* LAB EQUIP *analysis* appareil pour
chromatographie sur papier *m*; **~ chromatography
tank** *n* LAB EQUIP *analysis* cuve pour chromatographie
sur papier *f*; **~ coal** *n* COAL TECH charbon lamelleux *m*;
~ collars *n pl* TEXTILES collerettes *f pl*; **~ conditioning** *n*
PAPER TECH conditionnement du papier *m*; **~ covering**
n COATINGS revêtement extérieur en papier *m*; **~ cutter**
n PRINT massicot *m*; **~ draw** *n* PAPER TECH papier *m*,
tirage du papier *m*; **~ fiber** *n* (AmE), **~ fibre** *n* (BrE)
PACKAGING fibre de papier *f*; **~ flat** *n* PRINT montage-
papier *m*; **~ for conductor insulation** *n* PAPER TECH
papier pour câbles électriques *m*; **~ for laminated
insulators** *n* PAPER TECH papier pour isolants stratifiés
m; **~ for long storage documents** *n* PAPER TECH papier
pour documents de longue conservation *m*; **~ for
punched cards** *n* PAPER TECH papier pour cartes perforées *m*; **~ for textile paper tubes** *n* PAPER TECH papier
pour tubes de filature *m*; **~ gasket** *n* MECH ENG joint
papier *m*; **~ grade** *n* PACKAGING qualité de papier *f*,
PHOTO grade de papier *m*; **~ grain** *n* PAPER TECH grain
d'un papier *m*; **~ hum** *n* (AmE) *see paper stain*; **~
insulation** *n* ELEC isolation au papier *f*; **~ laminate** *n*
PACKAGING papier laminé *m*; **~ liner** *n* PACKAGING
revêtement intérieur en papier *m*; **~ lining** *n* COATINGS
revêtement intérieur en papier *m*; **~ low** *n* COMP approche de fin de papier *f*, DP approche de fin de papier
f, fin de papier imminente *f*; **~ machine** *n* PAPER TECH,
PRINT machine à papier *f*; **~ machine drive** *n* PAPER
TECH commande de machine à papier *f*; **~ making** *n*
PAPER TECH fabrication de papier *f*; **~ making pulp** *n*
PAPER TECH pâte à papier *f*; **~ mill** *n* PAPER TECH
papeterie *f*, RECYCLING papeterie *f*, usine de papeterie
f; **~ negative** *n* PHOTO négatif sur papier *m*; **~ plate** *n*
PRINT plaque offset en papier *f*; **~ polisher** *n* C&G
polissoir en papier *m*; **~ pulp** *n* PRINT pâte de bois *f*,
RECYCLING pâte à papier *f*; **~ roll** *n* PAPER TECH rouleau
de feuille *m*; **~ sack** *n* PACKAGING sac en papier *m*; **~
size** *n* PRINT format de papier *m*; **~ skip** *n* COMP, DP
saut de papier *m*; **~ stain** *n* (BrE) C&G impression de
papier *f*; **~ substance** *n* PRINT grammage *m*, main du
papier *f*, tenue du papier *f*; **~ swelling** *n* PAPER TECH
papier bouffant *m*; **~ tape** *n* DP bande de papier *f*, ELEC
insulation bande en papier *f*; **~ tape loop** *n* DP boucle
de bande de papier *f*; **~ tape punch** *n* DP perforateur de
bande de papier *m*; **~ tape reader** *n* DP lecteur de
bande perforée *m*; **~ throw** *n* (BrE) DP saut de papier
m; **~ wallcovering** *n* COATINGS papier peint *m*; **~ weight**
n PRINT grammage *m*; **~ without finish** *n* PAPER TECH,

PRINT papier non apprêté *m*; **~ wrapping** *n* PACKAGING
emballage en papier *m*

paperback *n* PRINT livre broché *m*

paperboard *n* PACKAGING carton *m*

paper-converting: **~ industry** *n* PACKAGING industrie de
la transformation du papier *f*

paper-insulated: **~ cable** *n* ELEC ENG câble sous papier *m*

papyraceous: **~ lignite** *n* COAL TECH charbon lamelleux *m*

para-autochthonous: **~ unit** *n* GEOL *transported over
short distance* roche subautochtone *f*, unité para-
autochtone *f*

parabanic[1] *adj* CHEM parabanique

parabanic[2]: **~ acid** *n* CHEM acide parabanique *m*, oxalylurée *f*

parabenzene *n* CHEM parabenzène *m*

parabola *n* GEOM parabole *f*

parabole *vt* GEOM parabole *f*

parabolic: **~ antenna** *n* SPACE *communications* antenne
parabolique *f*; **~ creep** *n* METALL fluage parabolique
m; **~ index fiber** *n* (AmE), **~ index fibre** *n* (BrE) OPT
fibre à gradient d'indice *f*, fibre à gradient parabolique *f*, fibreà profil parabolique *f*, PHYS *optical* fibre à
gradient parabolique *f*, fibre à loi parabolique *f*, fibre
à profil parabolique *f*; **~ mesh antenna** *n* SPACE *communications* antenne parabolique à mailles *f*; **~ mirror**
n PHYS miroir parabolique *m*; **~ mirror telescope** *n*
ASTRON télescope à miroir parabolique *m*; **~ profile** *n*
OPT profil parabolique *m*, TELECOM profil d'indice
parabolique *m*, profil parabolique *m*; **~ profile index** *n*
OPT profil d'indice parabolique *m*; **~ reflector** *n* CINE-
MAT, MILIT *radar*, PHOTO réflecteur parabolique *m*; **~
reflector antenna** *n* TELECOM antenne parabolique *f*; **~
reflector microphone** *n* RECORDING microphone à réflecteur parabolique *m*; **~ shading** *n* TV irrégularité
parabolique *f*; **~ spring** *n* SPRINGS ressort parabolique
m; **~ trough conveyor** *n (PTC)* INSTRUMENT miroir
cylindro-parabolique avec foyer tubulaire *m*; **~ velocity** *n* ASTRON, SPACE vitesse parabolique *f*

paraboloidal: **~ antenna** *n* SPACE *communications* antenne parabolique *f*

parabrake *n* SPACE *spacecraft* parachute de freinage *m*

parachor *n* CHEM parachor *m*

parachute *n* AERONAUT voilure de parachutage *f*, voilure de parachute *f*, SPACE *spacecraft* parachute *m*; **~
cluster** *n* MILIT grappe de parachutes *f*; **~ drop** *n* MILIT
descente en parachute *f*; **~ flare** *n* MILIT fusée éclairante avec parachute *f*, NAUT *pyrotechnics, distress
signal* fusée éclairante à parachute *f*; **~ landing** *n* MILIT
atterrissage par parachute *m*; **~ pack** *n* MILIT sac de
parachute *m*; **~ release handle** *n* AERONAUT poignée de
largage de parachute *f*; **~ with pilot** *n* MILIT parachute
avec pilote *m*

parachutist *n* MILIT parachutiste *m*

parachymosin *n* CHEM parachymosine *f*

paracresol *n* CHEM paracrésol *m*

paracusis *n* ACOUSTICS paracousie *f*

paracyanogen *n* CHEM paracyanogène *m*

paradichlorobenzene *n* CHEM paradichlorobenzène *m*

paradigm *n* COMP, DP paradigme *m*

paradoxical: **~ darkness of the night sky** *n* ASTRON paradoxe de l'obscurité du ciel nocturne *m*

paraffin *n* (BrE) *(cf kerosene)* CHEM *alkane* paraffine *f*,
PETR kérosène *m*, PETR TECH kérosène *m*, paraffine *f*,
PROP MAT paraffine *f*, THERMOD kérosène *f*, pétrole
raffiné d'éclairage *m*, TRANSP kérosène *m*; **~ coating** *n*

(BrE) *(cf kerosene coating)* PACKAGING revêtement de paraffine *m*; ~ **oil** *n* (BrE) *(cf kerosene oil)* CHEM huile paraffinée *f*; ~ **series** *n* (BrE) *(cf kerosene series)* PETR TECH série paraffinique *f*; ~ **wax** *n* (BrE) *(cf kerosene wax)* CHEM cire de paraffine *f*, paraffine solide *f*, ELEC cire de paraffine *f*

paraffinic *adj* CHEM paraffinique

paraffin-impregnated: ~ **paper** *n* (BrE) *(cf kerosene-impregnated paper)* PACKAGING papier paraffiné *m*

parafoil *n* SPACE *spacecraft* parachute *m*

paragenesis *n* GEOL paragénèse *f*

paragonite *n* MINERAL paragonite *f*

paragraph *n* COMP, DP paragraphe *m*

parahydrogen *n* CHEM parahydrogène *m*

paraisomer *n* CHEM paraisomère *m*

paraldehyde *n* CHEM paraldéhyde *m*

paralic *adj* GEOL *transitional continental, marine environment* paralique

parallactic[1] *adj* ASTRON parallactique

parallactic:[2] ~ **angle** *n* ASTRON angle parallactique *m*; ~ **ellipse** *n* ASTRON ellipse parallactique *f*; ~ **trigonometry** *n* ASTRON trigonométrie parallactique *f*

parallax *n* ASTRON, CINEMAT, MECH ENG, PHOTO, PHYS parallaxe *f*; ~ **correction** *n* CINEMAT correction de parallaxe *f*

parallax-free: ~ **viewfinder** *n* CINEMAT viseur sans parallaxe *m*

parallel:[1] **in** ~ *adj* PHYS en parallèle COMP, DP, ELEC *circuit*, GEOM, TEXTILES parallèle

parallel[2] *adv* GEOM parallèlement à

parallel:[3] ~ **absorbent baffle** *n* RECORDING baffle à absorption parallèle *m*; ~ **access** *n* COMP, DP accès parallèle *m*; ~ **adder** *n* COMP, DP, ELECTRON additionneur parallèle *m*; ~ **algorithm** *n* COMP algorithme parallèle *m*; ~ **arithmetic** *n* COMP, DP arithmétique parallèle *f*; ~ **arm-type suspension** *n* AUTO suspension à deux bras transversaux *f*; ~ **arrangement** *n* ELEC ENG branchement en parallèle *m*, montage en parallèle *m*; ~ **band** *n* RAD PHYS *vibration spectra* bande de type parallèle *f*; ~ **beam** *n* ELECTRON faisceau de rayons parallèles *m*, PHYS faisceau parallèle *m*; ~ **circuit** *n* ELEC circuit parallèle *m*, MINING circuit en parallèle *m*, TELECOM circuit en parallèle *m*, circuit parallèle *m*; ~ **computer** *n* COMP, DP ordinateur parallèle *m*; ~ **condition** *n* PROD ENG condition en parallèle *f*; ~ **connection** *n* ELEC *circuit* montage en parallèle *m*, ELEC ENG couplage en parallèle *m*, montage en parallèle *m*, MINING couplage en parallèle *m*, couplage parallèle *m*, PHYS montage en parallèle *m*; ~ **control device** *n* ELEC *tap changer* dispositif de commande de marche en parallèle *m*; ~ **conversion** *n* ELECTRON conversion parallèle *f*; ~ **converter** *n* ELECTRON convertisseur parallèle *m*; ~ **cut** *n* MINING bouchon canadien *m*, bouchon parallèle *m*, bouchon à mines parallèles *m*, bouchon à trous parallèles *m*; ~ **digital signal** *n* ELECTRON signal numérique parallèle *m*; ~ **dowel pin** *n* MECH ENG goupille cylindrique *f*; ~ **feeder** *n* ELEC *supply* artère parallèle *f*; ~ **fence** *n* PROD ENG *of saw bench* guide rectiligne *m*; ~ **file** *n* MECH ENG lime parallèle *f*; ~ **flow heat exchanger** *n* HEAT ENG échangeur à courant parallèle *m*, NUCLEAR échangeur de chaleur à courant parallèle *m*, REFRIG échangeur thermique à équicourant *m*; ~ **flow turbine** *n* HYDR EQUIP turbine hélicoïde *f*, turbine à débit axial *f*, turbine à débit parallèle *f*; ~ **fold** *n* GEOL *in which beds maintain the same thickness* pli concentrique *m*, pli formé de couches ayant gardé la même épaisseur *m*,

pli isopaque *m*, pli parallèle *m*; ~ **form** *n* ELEC ENG forme parallèle *f*, mode parallèle *m*; ~ **glueing** *n* PACKAGING collage parallèle *m*; ~ **gutter** *n* CONST *building* chéneau encaissé *m*; ~ **input/output** *n* DP entrée/sortie parallèle *f*; ~ **interface** *n* PRINT *computers* interface parallèle *f*; ~ **involute gear** *n* MECH ENG engrenage parallèle à développante *m*; ~ **jaw capacity** *n* MECH ENG *tool* capacité en becs parallèles *f*; ~ **lay** *n* ELEC ENG disposition parallèle *f*; ~ **lines** *n pl* GEOM lignes parallèles *f pl*; ~ **magazine camera** *n* CINEMAT caméra à chargeurs parallèles *f*; ~ **mark** *n* PRINT signe de parallélisme *m*; ~ **milling cutter** *n* MECH ENG fraise cylindrique *f*; ~ **mounting** *n* ELEC *circuit* montage en parallèle *m*; ~ **mouse** *n* COMP, DP souris à connexion parallèle *f*; ~ **mouse adaptor** *n* COMP, DP interface de souris parallèle *f*; ~ **multiplier** *n* ELECTRON multiplieur parallèle *m*; ~ **operation** *n* PRINT fonctionnement en parallèle *m*; ~ **pin with internal thread** *n* MECH ENG goupille cylindrique à trou taraudé *f*; ~ **pipe thread** *n* MECH ENG filetage cylindrique de tuyauterie *m*; ~ **plate capacitor** *n* ELEC ENG condensateur plan *m*, PHYS condensateur à plaques parallèles *m*; ~ **port** *n* COMP, DP port parallèle *m*; ~ **positioning** *n* AERONAUT, TRANSP *airports* positionnement parallèle *m*; ~ **processing** *n* DP, ELECTRON, TELECOM traitement en parallèle *m*; ~ **resistance** *n* ELEC ENG résistance en parallèle *f*; ~ **resonance** *n* ELECTRON antirésonance *f*, résonance parallèle *f*, PHYS résonance parallèle *f*; ~ **resonant circuit** *n* ELECTRON circuit oscillant parallèle *m*, circuit résonnant parallèle *m*; ~ **rule** *n* MECH ENG règle à tracer des parallèles *f*; ~ **ruler** *n* MECH ENG règle à tracer des parallèles *f*, NAUT *navigation* règles parallèles *f pl*; ~ **search storage** *n* (AmE), ~ **search store** *n* (BrE) COMP mémoire associative *f*; ~ **shank tool** *n* MECH ENG outil à queue cylindrique *m*; ~ **shank twist drill** *n* MECH ENG foret hélicoïdal à queue cylindrique *m*; ~ **spark gap** *n* ELEC éclateur parallèle *m*; ~ **storage** *n* ELEC ENG mémorisation en parallèle *f*; ~ **synchronous system** *n* TELECOM système en réplique synchrone *m*; ~ **transfer** *n* COMP, DP transfert en parallèle *m*; ~ **transmission** *n* COMP, DP, TELECOM transmission en parallèle *f*; ~ **vane attenuator** *n* ELECTRON atténuateur à lame parallèle *m*; ~ **vice** *n* (BrE) MECH ENG étau parallèle *m*; ~ **vise** *n* (AmE) *see parallel vice*; ~ **wire line** *n* ELEC ENG ligne à fils parallèles *f*

parallel-connected[1] *adj* ELEC ENG, PHYS monté en parallèle

parallel-connected:[2] ~ **resistance** *n* ELEC résistance en parallèle *f*

parallel-fed *adj* AERONAUT alimenté en parallèle

parallelism *n* GEOM, MECH ENG, PRINT, TEXTILES parallélisme *m*; ~ **tolerance** *n* SPRINGS tolérance de parallélisme *f*

parallelization: ~ **of fibers** *n* (AmE), ~ **of fibres** *n* (BrE) TEXTILES parallélisation des fibres *f*

parallel-jaw: ~ **tong** *n* NUCLEAR *of manipulator* pince à becs parallèles *f*

parallelogram *n* GEOM, MECH parallélogramme *m*; ~ **of forces** *n* GEOM, PHYS parallélogramme des forces *m*; ~ **of velocities** *n* PHYS parallélogramme des vitesses *m*

parallel-to-serial: ~ **conversion** *n* ELEC ENG conversion de parallèle en série *f*, conversion parallèle-série *f*; ~ **converter** *n* ELEC ENG convertisseur parallèle-série *m*

parallel-wound: ~ **yarn** *n* TEXTILES fil assemblé sans torsion *m*

paramagnetic[1] *adj* ELEC *material*, PHYS paramagnétique

paramagnetic:[2] ~ **amplifier** n ELECTRON amplificateur paramagnétique m; ~ **Curie point** n RAD PHYS point de Curie paramagnétique m; ~ **material** n PETR matériau paramagnétique m; ~ **rail** n TRANSP rail paramagnétique m; ~ **resonance** n ELEC, ELECTRON résonance paramagnétique f, PHYS electron-spin résonance paramagnétique électronique f

paramagnetism n ELEC, PHYS paramagnétisme m

parameter n COMP, DP, ELECTRON, PHYS paramètre m; ~ **out-of-range class** n TELECOM valeur de paramètre erronée f; ~ **passing** n COMP, DP passage de paramètres m; ~ **profile** n TELECOM profil de paramètre m; ~ **substitution** n COMP, DP substitution de paramètres f; ~ **value** n (PV) TELECOM valeur de paramètre f

parameterization n COMP, DP paramétrage m

parametric[1] adj COMP, DP paramétrique

parametric:[2] ~ **amplification** n ELECTRON amplification paramétrique f; ~ **amplifier** n ELECTRON, PHYS, SPACE communications, TELECOM amplificateur paramétrique m; ~ **amplifier diode** n ELECTRON diode pour amplificateur paramétrique f; ~ **analysis** n ELECTRON, PROP MAT analyse paramétrique f; ~ **coordinates** n pl GEOM coordonnées paramétriques f pl; ~ **laser** n ELECTRON laser paramétrique m; ~ **oscillator** n TELECOM oscillateur paramétrique m; ~ **test** n TELECOM test paramétrique m

paramp n ELECTRON amplificateur paramétrique m

paranthine n MINERAL paranthine f

parapet n CONST parapet m; ~ **gutter** n CONST chéneau à l'anglaise m, gouttière en dessus f

paraphase: ~ **amplifier** n ELECTRON montage déphaseur m, TV amplificateur déphaseur m, amplificateur en contrephase m

pararosaniline n CHEM pararosaniline f

parasite n MINERAL parasite m

parasitic[1] adj ELECTRON parasite

parasitic:[2] ~ **aerial** n PHYS passive élément passif m, élément secondaire m; ~ **capacitance** n ELEC ENG capacité parasite f; ~ **capture** n NUCLEAR of neutrons capture parasite f; ~ **component** n ELEC ENG composant parasite m; ~ **coupling** n ELEC ENG, TELECOM couplage parasite m; ~ **crater** n GEOL volcanic feature cratère adventif m; ~ **current** n ELEC ENG courant parasite m; ~ **diode** n ELECTRON diode parasite f; ~ **drag** n AERONAUT traînée parasite f; ~ **element** n PHYS aerial élément non alimenté m; ~ **inductance** n ELEC ENG inductance parasite f; ~ **oscillation** n PHYS, TELECOM oscillation parasite f; ~ **radiation** n TV rayonnement parasite m; ~ **suppressor** n ELECTRON filtre antiparasite m; ~ **transistor** n ELECTRON transistor parasite m

paratartaric adj CHEM paratartarique

paratypical adj CHEM atypique, irrégulier

paraxial: ~ **ray** n OPT, PHYS, TELECOM rayon paraxial m

paraxylene n CHEM, PETR TECH paraxylène m

parboil vt FOOD TECH faire bouillir, faire cuire à demi

parcel n PAPER TECH, TRANSP paquet m; ~ **of ore** n MINING lot de minerai m; ~ **registration card** n TRANSP bulletin d'expédition m

parcelled: ~ **goods** n PACKAGING marchandises empaquetées f pl

parcelling: ~ **machine** n PACKAGING machine pour faire les paquets f

parcels: ~ **chute** n TRANSP toboggan m; ~ **counter** n TRANSP guichet des colis m; ~ **depot** n TRANSP gare de messagerie f; ~ **office** n TRANSP service des colis m

parchment: ~ **paper** n FOOD TECH papier parcheminé m, PACKAGING papier-parchemin végétal m

pare vt PRINT finir, parer, ébarber

parent n COMP node, DP parent m; ~ **acid** n CHEM acide de la même famille m; ~ **fraction** n NUCLEAR fraction mère f; ~ **glass** n C&G verre de base m; ~ **mass peak** n NUCLEAR ligne mère f, pic père m; ~ **nuclide** n NUCLEAR précurseur m, père nucléaire m, RAD PHYS nucléide père m, père nucléaire m; ~ **peak** n NUCLEAR ligne mère f, pic père m; ~ **phase** n METALL phase parente f; ~ **roll** n CINEMAT bobine mère f

parenthesis n PRINT parenthèse f

parenthesis-free: ~ **notation** n DP notation sans parenthèses f

pargasite n MINERAL pargasite f

paring: ~ **chisel** n CONST ciseau long m; ~ **machine** n CONST wood trimmer machine à trancher et dresser les bois en bout f, trancheuse pour le bois de bout f

parison n C&G paraison f; ~ **check** n C&G pli crevé m; ~ **crack** n C&G pli crevé m; ~ **gatherer** n C&G cueilleur de paraison m; ~ **mold** n (AmE), ~ **mould** n (BrE) C&G moule ébaucheur m

parity n COMP, DP, PHYS, RAD PHYS parité f; ~ **bit** n COMP, DP bit de parité m; ~ **check** n COMP, CONTROL, DP, TELECOM contrôle de parité m; ~ **conservation law** n RAD PHYS in quantum interactions loi de conservation de la parité f; ~ **error** n COMP, DP erreur de parité f

park:[1] ~ **orbit** n MILIT of satellite orbite d'attente f

park[2] vt TV of VTR garder en attente

parked[1] adj TELECOM mis en garde

parked:[2] ~ **line** n TELECOM ligne en faux appel f

parking: ~ **area** n AERONAUT aire de stationnement f, CONST parc automobile m, parking m, parc de stationnement m; ~ **brake** n AERONAUT frein de parc m, AUTO, MECH vehicles frein de stationnement m, RAIL freinage d'immobilisation m, VEHICLES frein de stationnement m; ~ **brake lever** n VEHICLES levier du frein de stationnement m; ~ **gear** n AUTO roue de verrouillage f; ~ **lock gear** n AUTO roue de verrouillage f; ~ **meter** n TRANSP horodateur m, parcmètre m, parcomètre m; ~ **orbit** n SPACE orbite d'attente f; ~ **pawl** n AUTO cliquet de stationnement m

parrot-nose: ~ **pipe wrench** n CONST clef à fer creux articulée f

parse vt COMP, DP analyser

parsec n PHYS parsec m

parser n COMP, DP analyseur syntaxique m

parsing n COMP, DP analyse syntaxique f

part[1] n COMP, DP partie f, MECH ENG article m, élément m, élément simple m, PROD ENG of mould coquille f, TEXTILES pièce f, VEHICLES organe m, pièce f, partie f; ~ **load** n AUTO, TRANSP charge partielle f; ~ **loads** n pl TRANSP marchandises de groupage f pl; ~ **number** n PACKAGING référence de pièce f; ~ **owner** n NAUT of ship coarmateur m; ~ **winding starting** n ELEC motor démarrage sur fraction d'enroulement m

part[2] vi MECH ENG come off, come away se décoller

partial[1] adj ACOUSTICS partiel

partial[2] n ACOUSTICS son partiel m; ~ **carry** n COMP, DP report partiel m; ~ **coating** n COATINGS revêtement partiel m; ~ **coherence** n OPT, TELECOM cohérence partielle f; ~ **crystallization** n PROP MAT cristallisation partielle f; ~ **dial** n TELECOM numérotation incomplète f; ~ **discharge** n ELEC condenser décharge partielle f; ~ **discharge inception test** n ELEC essai de seuil de décharge partielle m; ~ **dislocation** n CRYSTALL, METALL dislocation partielle f; ~ **eclipse** n ASTRON éclipse partielle f; ~ **exposure** n PRINT exposition partielle f; ~ **node** n ACOUSTICS noeud imparfait m, ELEC ENG noeud partiel m; ~ **plating** n COATINGS revêtement galvanoplastique partiel m, revêtement partiel m; ~ **pressure** n CHEM *vapour*, PHYS pression partielle f; ~ **recovery refrigeration system** n REFRIG réfrigération à récupération partielle de frigorigène f; ~ **reflection** n WAVE PHYS *of light waves* réflexion partielle f; ~ **response code** n TELECOM code à réponse partielle m; ~ **time to date** n PROD ENG temps partiel réalisé à ce jour m; ~ **trip** n NUCLEAR arrêt d'urgence partiel m; ~ **voltage starting** n ELEC *motor* démarrage sous tension réduite m

particle n ACOUSTICS, COAL TECH, ELECTRON, PART PHYS, PHYS, SAFETY, TEXTILES particule f; ~ **acceleration** n ACOUSTICS accélération d'une particule f; ~ **accelerator** n PART PHYS, PHYS accélérateur de particules m; ~ **beam** n ELECTRON faisceau de particules m; ~ **beam technology** n PART PHYS technologie des faisceaux de particules f, théorie électrofaible f; ~ **board** n MECH *materials* panneau de particules m; ~ **classification** n CHEM TECH classement granulométrique m; ~ **collision** n PART PHYS collision de particules f; ~ **dynamics** n NUCLEAR dynamique du mouvement des particules f; ~ **fluence** n PHYS fluence de particules f; ~ **fluence rate** n PHYS débit de fluence de particules m; ~ **form factor** n CHEM TECH facteur de forme de particules m; ~ **leakage** n NUCLEAR fuite de particules f; ~ **number** n METALL nombre des particules m; ~ **number conservation law** n NUCLEAR loi de la conservation du nombre des particules f; ~ **physics** n PHYS physique des particules f; ~ **reinforcement** n METALL durcissement par particules m; ~ **separation** n PART PHYS séparation des particules f; ~ **size** n CHEM *of substance* grosseur de grain f, CHEM TECH calibre m, METALL, NUCLEAR *of powders* taille des particules f, P&R *of pigment, of filler* granulométrie f, grosseur de particules f; ~ **size analysis** n CHEM TECH analyse granulométrique f, granulométrie f, PROP MAT granulométrie f; ~ **size analyzer** n CHEM TECH analyseur de dimensions des particules m, NUCLEAR granulomètre m; ~ **size curve** n C&G courbe granulométrique f; ~ **size distribution** n CHEM *of powder* granulométrie f, répartition granulométrique f, CONST distribution granulométrique f; ~ **size measurement** n P&R *of fillers, of pigments* mesure de la grosseur des particules f; ~ **size reduction** n CHEM TECH comminution des particules f, COAL TECH réduction granulométrique f; ~ **sizing** n CHEM TECH classement granulométrique m; ~ **spiraling** n (AmE), ~ **spiralling** n (BrE) NUCLEAR mouvement des particules en spirale m; ~ **storage** n PART PHYS stockage des particules m; ~ **trajectories buffeted by turbulent molecules** n pl RAD PHYS *Brownian movement* trajets des particules ballottées par des molécules turbulentes m pl; ~ **velocity** n ACOUSTICS vitesse d'une particule f

particle-like *adj* PART PHYS particulaire

particle-operated: ~ **fluidized bed** n CHEM TECH lit fluidifié à grains m

particles: ~ **which escape without interacting** n pl RAD PHYS particules qui s'échappent sans interagir f pl

particulate n CHEM TECH, PROP MAT matière particulaire f; ~ **air pollution** n POLLUTION pollution atmosphérique par des particules en suspension f; ~ **fluidized bed** n CHEM TECH lit fluidifié homogène m; ~ **materials** n pl POLLUTION matières particulaires f pl, poussières f pl;

~ **matter** n POLLUTION matières particulaires f pl, particules solides f pl

parting n CHEM départ m, MECH ENG décollage m, décollement m, entre-deux m, PROD ENG *of mould* joint m; ~ **blade** n MECH ENG outil à saigner m; ~ **dust** n PROD ENG poussier de sable brûlé m, poussier isolant m; ~ **line** n PROD ENG *foundry* plan de joint m; ~ **pulley** n MECH ENG poulie démontable f, poulie en deux pièces f; ~ **sand** n PROD ENG poussier de sable brûlé m, poussier isolant m; ~ **tool** n MECH ENG outil à tronçonner m, *of lathe* outil à saigner m; ~ **of the waters** n HYDROL partage des eaux m

parting-off: ~ **blade** n MECH ENG *for tool holder* outil à tronçonner m

partition[1] n COMP partition f, CONST cloison f, mur de séparation m, paroi de séparation f, séparation f, cloison de séparation f, dp partition f, NUCLEAR *in extraction cycle* paroi de séparation f; ~ **chromatography** n CHEM chromatographie par partition f; ~ **coefficient** n CHEM *between phases* coefficient de partage m, METALL coefficient de répartition m; ~ **density** n COAL TECH densité de partage f; ~ **function** n PHYS fonction de partition f; ~ **gate** n ELEC ENG grille de partage f; ~ **noise** n ELECTRON bruit de partage m, bruit de répartition m; ~ **size** n COAL TECH dimension de séparation f, maille de partage f; ~ **wall** n CONST mur de cloison m, PACKAGING partition f

partition[2] *vt* COMP découper en partitions, segmenter, DP partitionner

partitioned[1] *adj* COMP cloisonné, segmenté, DP cloisonné, partitionné

partitioned:[2] ~ **charge** n ELEC ENG charge partagée f

partitioning n CHEM partage m, COMP découpage en partitions m, CONST *placing partitions* cloisonnage m, compartimentage m, compartimentation f, *walls* cloisonnement m, DP partitionnement m, ELEC ENG partage m; ~ **insert** n PACKAGING pièce pour partitionner f

part-load: ~ **consignment** n TRANSP envoi de détail m; ~ **efficiency** n MECH ENG rendement à charge partielle m; ~ **freight** n (AmE) *(cf part-load goods, part-load traffic)* TRANSP marchandises de détail f pl; ~ **goods** n pl (BrE) *(cf part-load freight)* TRANSP marchandises de détail f pl; ~ **traffic** n (BrE) *(cf part-load freight)* RAIL marchandises de détail f pl

parton n PHYS parton m

parts: ~ **of a machine** n pl MECH ENG éléments d'une machine m pl; ~ **requisition** n PROD ENG fiche de prélèvement f, fiche de prélèvement de stock f, fiche de ramassage f

parts-per-million n pl (PPM) CHEM parties par million f pl

part-turn: ~ **actuator attachment** n MECH ENG raccordement de servomoteur à fraction de tour m

party: ~ **address** n TELECOM adresse du correspondant f; ~ **wall** n CONST mur de démarcation m, mur mitoyen m

parvoline n CHEM parvoline f

pascal n (Pa) METR, PETR TECH *unit of pressure*, PHYS pascal m (Pa)

Pascal's: ~ **principle** n PHYS *hydrostatics* principe de Pascal m, théorème de Pascal m

Paschen: ~ **series** n PHYS série de Paschen f; ~ **series lines** n pl RAD PHYS *atomic spectrum* lignes de série Paschen f pl

Paschen's: ~ **law** n PHYS loi de Paschen f

Paschen-Back: ~ **effect** n PHYS effet de Paschen-Back m

pass[1] *n* COMP, DP passe *f*, MINING cheminée *f*, NAUT *geography* passe *f*, PROD ENG cannelure *f*, creux *m*, passage *m*, passe *f*; ~ **band** *n* COMP, DP, ELECTRON, MECH ENG, PHYS bande passante *f*, RECORDING passe-bande *m*, TELECOM bande passante *f*; ~ **band attenuation** *n* ELECTRON atténuation dans la bande passante *f*; ~ **band response** *n* ELECTRON réponse dans la bande passante *f*; ~ **transistor** *n* ELECTRON transistor ballast *m*

pass[2] *vt* RAIL *danger signal, stop signal* franchir

pass[3] ~ **for press** *vi* PRINT donner le bon à tirer; ~ **through** *vi* TELECOM transiter; ~ **through a lock** *vi* NAUT écluser

passage *n* AUTO canalisation *f*, NAUT *navigation* traversée *f*, PROD ENG passage *m*, tubulure *f*; ~ **beds** *n pl* GEOL couches de transition *f pl*; ~ **of criticality** *n* NUCLEAR passage de criticité *m*; ~ **detector** *n* TRANSP *traffic* détecteur de passage *m*

passageway *n* MINING galerie *f*, passage *m*

pass-along: ~ **message** *n (PAM)* TELECOM message à faire passer *m*

passenger[1] *adj* SPACE passager

passenger[2] *n* AERONAUT passager *m*, passagère *f*, TRANSP voyageur *m*; ~ **automobile** *n* VEHICLES voiture particulière *f*; ~ **bridge** *n* AERONAUT passerelle télescopique *f*; ~ **cabin** *n* TRANSP cabine des passagers *f*; ~ **car** *n* TRANSP voiture particulière *f*, voiture à passagers *f*, VEHICLES voiture particulière *f*; ~ **car equivalent** *n* TRANSP coefficient d'équivalence en UVP *m*; ~ **car unit** *n (PCU)* TRANSP unité de voiture particulière *f (UVP)*; ~ **coach** *n* TRANSP voiture à passagers *f*; ~ **compartment** *n* TRANSP compartiment des voyageurs *m*; ~ **conveyor** *n (cf moving sidewalk)* AERONAUT *at airport* trottoir roulant *m*, TRANSP bande transporteuse pour piétons *f*; ~ **elevator** *n* (AmE) *(cf passenger lift)* TRANSP ascenseur personnes *m*; ~ **ferry** *n* TRANSP bac à passagers *m*; ~ **flight** *n* TRANSP vol accompagné *m*; ~ **hall** *n* TRANSP *rail* hall de gare *m*; ~ **information center** *n* (AmE), ~ **information centre** *n* (BrE) RAIL gare centre d'informations *f*; ~ **kilometer** *n* (AmE), ~ **kilometre** *n* (BrE) TRANSP voyageur-kilomètre *m*; ~ **lift** *n* (BrE) *(cf passenger elevator)* TRANSP ascenseur personnes *m*; ~ **plane** *n* AERONAUT avion de ligne *m*; ~ **reservation system** *n* TRANSP système de réservation de places *m*; ~ **road train** *n* TRANSP train routier à passagers *m*; ~ **ropeway** *n* TRANSP télécabine *f*, téléphérique pour passagers *m*; ~ **seat** *n* AERONAUT, TRANSP siège passager *m*; ~ **service** *n* TRANSP transport de voyageurs *m*; ~ **ship** *n* NAUT paquebot *m*, TRANSP navire à passagers *m*, paquebot *m*; ~ **terminal** *n* TRANSP terminal voyageurs *m*; ~ **train** *n* TRANSP train voyageurs *m*; ~ **transport** *n* TRANSP trafic voyageurs *m*

passenger-cargo: ~ **ship** *n* TRANSP cargo mixte *m*

passing: ~ **aids** *n* TRANSP *traffic* aides de dépassement *f pl*; ~ **lane** *n* CONST voie de dépassement *f*; ~ **light** *n* VEHICLES feu de croisement *m*; ~ **point** *n* RAIL point d'évitement *m*; ~ **sight distance** *n* TRANSP *traffic* visibilité de dépassement *f*; ~ **track** *n* RAIL voie d'évitement *f*

passivate[1] *vt* SPACE *spacecraft* neutraliser, rendre inerte

passivate[2] *vi* CHEM, ELECTRON, PHYS passiver

passivated[1] *adj* PHYS passivé

passivated[2] ~ **transistor** *n* ELECTRON transistor passivé *m*

passivation *n* CHEM, ELECTRON, PHYS passivation *f*; ~ **glass** *n* C&G verre de passivation *m*; ~ **layer** *n* ELEC-TRON couche de passivation *f*

passive[1] *adj* COMP, DP, ELECTRON passif

passive[2] ~ **aerial** *n* PHYS *parasitic* élément passif *m*, élément secondaire *m*; ~ **air defence** *n* MILIT défense aérienne passive *f*; ~ **alerting** *n* TELECOM alerte passive *f*; ~ **band pass filter** *n* ELECTRON filtre passe-bande passif *m*; ~ **band stop filter** *n* ELECTRON filtre coupe-bande passif *m*; ~ **circuit** *n* PHYS, TELECOM circuit passif *m*; ~ **component** *n* ELECTRON, NUCLEAR *of nuclear power plant*, PHYS *electronic*, TELECOM composant passif *m*; ~ **control** *n* SPACE *spacecraft* contrôle passif *m*; ~ **dipole** *n* ELEC ENG dipôle passif *m*; ~ **earth pressure** *n* COAL TECH butée des terres *f*, CONST poussée de terre passive *f*; ~ **electrodynamic damper** *n* SPACE *spacecraft* amortisseur électrodynamique passif *m*; ~ **element** *n* ELECTRON élément passif *m*; ~ **filter** *n* ELECTRON, TELECOM filtre passif *m*; ~ **filtering** *n* ELECTRON filtrage passif *m*; ~ **flat car** *n* TRANSP voiture plate-forme passive *f*; ~ **infrared detector** *n* TRANSP détecteur à infrarouge *m*; ~ **load** *n* ELEC ENG charge passive *f*; ~ **mode** *n* ELECTRON mode passif *m*; ~ **motor vehicle safety** *n* TRANSP sécurité passive des véhicules automobiles *f*; ~ **network** *n* ELEC, ELEC ENG réseau passif *m*; ~ **occupant restraint system** *n* TRANSP système de sécurité automatique *m*; ~ **optical network** *n (PON)* TELECOM réseau optique passif *m*; ~ **quadripole** *n* ELEC ENG quadripôle passif *m*; ~ **satellite** *n* SPACE satellite réflecteur *m*, TV satellite passif *m*; ~ **seat belt system** *n* TRANSP système passif des ceintures de sécurité *m*; ~ **sensor** *n* SPACE capteur passif *m*; ~ **solar system** *n* CONST *building* système solaire passif *m*; ~ **star** *n* COMP *network topology*, DP étoile passive *f*; ~ **substrate** *n* ELECTRON substrat passif *m*; ~ **system** *n* ACOUSTICS, FUELLESS système passif *m*; ~ **thermal control** *n (PTC)* SPACE régulation thermique passive *f*; ~ **threat** *n* TELECOM menace passive *f*; ~ **transducer** *n* ELEC ENG transducteur passif *m*; ~ **transport unit** *n* TRANSP unité de transport passive *f*

password *n* COMP, DP, TELECOM mot de passe *m*; ~ **protection** *n* COMP, DP protection par mot de passe *f*

paste[1] *n* SPACE *spacecraft* pâte *f*; ~ **fuel** *n* NUCLEAR pâte combustible *f*; ~ **ink** *n* COLOURS encre en pâte *f*; ~ **mold** *n* (AmE) *see paste mould*; ~ **mold press-and-blow process** *n* (AmE) *see paste mould press and blow process*; ~ **mold blowing** *n* (AmE) *see paste mould blowing*; ~ **mould** *n* (BrE) C&G moule enduit *m* (Bel), moule à moulé-tourné *m* (Fra); ~ **mould blowing** *n* (BrE) C&G procédé moulé-tourné *m*, procédé soufflé-tourné *m*; ~ **mould press-and-blow process** *n* (BrE) C&G procédé pressé-soufflé-tourné *m*

paste[2] *vt* PAPER TECH encoller; ~ **up** *vt* PRINT faire un montage papier

pasteboard *n* PRINT carton contrecollé *m*

pasted[1] *adj* PRINT doublé

pasted[2] ~ **board** *n* PAPER TECH carton contrecollé *m*; ~ **ivory board** *n* PAPER TECH carte ivoire contrecollée *f*, carton affiché *m*, carton recouvert par entrecollage *m*; ~ **lined board** *n* PAPER TECH carton affiché *m*, carton recouvert par entrecollage *m*; ~ **paper** *n* PAPER TECH papier contrecollé *m*

paster *n* PAPER TECH collure *f*

paste-up *n* PRINT montage papier *m*

Pasteur: ~ **pipette** *n* LAB EQUIP *glassware* pipette Pasteur *f*

pasteurization *n* CHEM TECH, FOOD TECH, THERMOD pasteurisation *f*

pasteurize *vt* CHEM TECH, FOOD TECH, THERMOD pasteuriser

pasteurized *adj* THERMOD pasteurisé

pasting *n* DP insertion *f*, PAPER TECH collage *m*, contre-collage *m*; ~ **machine** *n* PAPER TECH colleuse *f*

patch[1] *n* DP modification *f*, ELEC ENG *using patch cord* connexion *f*, MAR POLL flaque *f*, MINING *of ore* paquet *m*, PRINT connexion provisoire *f*; ~ **bay** *n* CINEMAT panneau de raccordement *m*, tableau de raccordement *m*; ~ **block** *n* C&G bloc de placage *m* (Fra), placard *m* (Bel); ~ **board** *n* COMP, DP tableau de connexions *m*, TV panneau de brassage *m*, tableau de brassage *m*, tableau de raccordement *m*; ~ **cord** *n* COMP cordon de connexion *m*, DP cordon de connexion *m*, cordon de jonction enfichable *m*, ELEC ENG dicorde *m*; ~ **field** *n* CINEMAT panneau de raccordement *m*, tableau de raccordement *m*; ~ **panel** *n* (AmE) *(cf jack panel)* COMP tableau de connexions *m*, TV panneau de brassage *m*, panneau de raccordement *m*;~ **pocket form** *n* PRINT formulaire à plusieurs formes encollées pour constituer des poches *m*; ~ **splice** *n* CINEMAT collure *f*

patch[2] *vt* CINEMAT brancher, raccorder, COMP corriger, modifier, DP modifier, rapiécer, ELEC ENG connecter, *using patch cord* relier, PRINT raccorder, TV brancher, brasser, raccorder

patching *n* C&G placage *m*, ELEC ENG connexion par dicorde *f*, PROD ENG rapiéçage *m*, rapiècement *m*; ~ **up** *n* PROD ENG rapiéçage *m*, rapiècement *m*

patchwork *n* PROD ENG rapiéçage *m*, rapiècement *m*

patent[1] *n* MECH ENG, PATENTS brevet *m*, brevet d'invention *m*; ~ **agent** *n* MECH ENG agent de brevets *m*, agent de brevets d'invention *m*; ~ **application** *n* PATENTS demande de brevet *f*; ~ **certificate** *n* PATENTS certificat de brevet *m*; ~ **flour** *n* FOOD TECH farine de première qualité *f*, farine de qualité *f*, fleur de farine *f*; ~ **of improvement** *n* MECH ENG brevet de perfectionnement *m*; ~ **log** *n* NAUT loch à hélice *m*; ~ **proprietor** *n* PATENTS titulaire du brevet *m*; ~ **specification** *n* PATENTS *printed* fascicule de brevet *m*

patent[2] *vt* PATENTS faire breveter

patentability *n* PATENTS brevetabilité *f*

patentable: ~ **invention** *n* PATENTS invention brevetable *f*

patented *adj* MECH ENG breveté

patenting *n* HEATING *rod, wire production* patentage *m*

patents: ~ **applied for** *phr* TEXTILES demande de brevet déposée *f*

paternoster: ~ **pump** *n* WATER SUPP chapelet hydraulique *m*, pompe à chapelet *f*, pompe à godets *f*

path *n* AERONAUT trajectoire *f*, COMP chemin *m*, filière *f*, CONST sentier *m*, trottoir *m*, DP chemin *m*, ELEC ENG *of electric current* trajet *m*, GEOM chemin *m*, NAUT *of ship* trajectoire *f*, PHYS *in a medium* chemin *m*, *of particle* trajectoire *f*, *route* trajet *m*, SPACE trajectoire *f*, trajet *m*, TELECOM voie *f* ~ **attenuation** *n* TV affaiblissement de propagation *m*; ~ **correction** *n* MILIT *of rocket* correction de trajet *f*, SPACE *of spacecraft* guidage par itération *m*; ~ **difference** *n* PHYS différence de marche *f*; ~ **of a flame** *n* PROD ENG *in boiler* courant de flamme *m*; ~ **length** *n* NUCLEAR *of single charged particle* longueur de trajectoire *f*; ~ **memory** *n* TELECOM mémoire des itinéraires *f*; ~ **overhead** *n* (*POH*) TELECOM préfixe de conduit *m*, résidu de trajet *m*; ~ **of totality** *n* ASTRON *of solar eclipse* zone de totalité *f*

pathfinder *n* MILIT *parachuting* orientateur-marqueur *m*

pathogenic[1] *adj* HYDROL pathogène

pathogenic:[2] ~ **hazard** *n* SAFETY risque pathogène *m*

pathological: ~ **waste** *n* RECYCLING déchets contaminés *m pl*, déchets pathogènes *m pl*

patina *n* CHEM, PROP MAT patine *f*

patio: ~ **door** *n* C&G porte-fenêtre *f*

patouillet *n* MECH ENG *washer* barboteur *m*, patouille *f*, patouillet *m*

patrimonial: ~ **sea** *n* OCEANOG mer patrimoniale *f*

patrol: ~ **boat** *n* MAR POLL patrouilleur *m*, MILIT patrouilleur *m*, vedette de surveillance *f*, vedette de surveillance côtière *f*, NAUT patrouilleur *m*, vedette de surveillance *f*, vedette de surveillance côtière *f*; ~ **craft** *n* MILIT patrouilleur *m*; ~ **inspection** *n* QUALITY inspection volante *f*

patron *n* PROD ENG *template* calibre *m*, gabarit *m*, patron *m*

pattern[1] *n* COMP, DP forme *f*, ELECTRON configuration *f*, forme *f*, mire *f*, modèle *m*, motif *m*, réseau *m*, schéma *m*, tracé *m*, PROD ENG façon *f*, modèle *m*, forme *f*, *template* calibre *m*, gabarit *m*, patron *m*, SPACE *communications* configuration *f*, diagramme *m*, schéma *m*, TEXTILES *sewing* patron *m*, *weave* armure *f*; ~ **correspondence index** *n* (*PCI*) TELECOM indice de correspondance spectrale *m*; ~ **generation** *n* ELECTRON *lithography* tracé des motifs *m*; ~ **generator** *n* TV générateur de mire *m*; ~ **maker** *n* PROD ENG *person* modeleur *m*, ouvrier modeleur *m*; ~ **making** *n* PROD ENG modelage *m*; ~ **matching** *n* PROD ENG appairement des formes *m*; ~ **molder** *n* (AmE), ~ **moulder** *n* (BrE) PROD ENG *person* mouleur *m*; ~ **plate** *n* PROD ENG *founding* plaque porte-modèles *f*, plaque-modèle *f*; ~ **plating** *n* COATINGS revêtement sélectif *m*; ~ **projector** *n* CINEMAT projecteur de motifs *m*, projecteur de silhouettes *m*; ~ **recognition** *n* COMP, DP, ELECTRON, TELECOM reconnaissance des formes *f*; ~ **registration** *n* ELECTRON *lithography* alignement du motif *m*; ~ **shop** *n* PROD ENG *founding* atelier de modelage *m*

pattern[2] *vt* TEXTILES modeler

patterned: ~ **glass** *n* C&G verre imprimé *m*; ~ **marble** *n* GEOL cipolin *m*

patterning *n* ELECTRON *lithography* formation de motifs *f*, TEXTILES armurage *m*, TV surimposition de fond faux *f*; ~ **capacities** *n pl* TEXTILES possibilités d'armurage *f pl*

Pauli: ~ **exclusion principle** *n* PART PHYS, PHYS principe d'exclusion de Pauli *m*; ~ **principle** *n* CHEM *electrons* principe de Pauli *m*

pause *n* TV arrêt sur image *m*; ~ **control** *n* RECORDING commande de pause *f*, TV commande d'arrêt *f*

paved: ~ **road** *n* (AmE) *(cf metalled road)* CONST chaussée empierrée *f*, route empierrée *f*, route ferrée *f*

pavement *n* (BrE) *(cf sidewalk)* COAL TECH mur *m*, CONST *concrete* chaussée *f*, pavage bétonné *m*, *road surface, stone walks* dallage *m*, pavage *m*, pavement *m*, pavé *m*, trottoir *m*, CONST trottoir *m*, MINING *of mine level* sole *f*; ~ **design** *n* CONST dimensionnement de chaussées *m*, étude de pavé *f*; ~ **light** *n* C&G pavé *m*; ~ **quality concrete** *n* (*PQC*) CONST béton de qualité à paver *m*; ~ **surface evenness** *n* CONST aplatissement de pavement *m*, aplatissement de surface de pavé *m*, uni de pavement *m*

pavement-spreading: ~ **machine** *n* (AmE) *(cf road metal-spreading machine)* TRANSP épandeur-régleur-dameur *m*

paving *n* (AmE) *(cf metalling)* CONST dallage *m*, pavage *m*, pavement *m*, pavé *m*, CONST *civil engineering* empierrement *m*; ~ **block** *n* C&G bloc de pavage *m*; ~ **material** *n* (AmE) *(cf road metal)* CONST matériaux d'empierrement pour route *m pl*; ~ **stone** *n* CONST grès à pavés *m*, pierre de pavage *f*, *single stone* pavé *m*

pavior *n* (AmE) **paviour** *n* (BrE) CONST dalleur *m*, paveur *m*

paviour's: ~ **hammer** *n* CONST marteau de paveur *m*

Pavo *n* ASTRON *Peacock* Paon *m*

pawl *n* MECH cliquet *m*, MECH ENG chien *m*, doigt d'encliquetage *m*, détente *f*, linguet *m*, *of winch* cliquet *m*, cliquet d'arrêt *m*; ~ **bitt** *n* MECH ENG *of capstan* saucier *m*; ~ **coupling** *n* MECH ENG accouplement à cliquet *m*; ~ **head** *n* MECH ENG *of capstan* buttoir *m*; ~ **rim** *n* MECH ENG *of capstan* couronne des linguets *f*; ~ **ring** *n* MECH ENG *of capstan* couronne des linguets *f*

pawl-and-ratchet: ~ **motion** *n* MECH ENG encliquetage à rochet *m*

PAX *abbr (private automatic exchange)* TELECOM central automatique privé *m*

pay:[1] ~ **cable** *n* TV télévision à péage par câble *f*; ~ **dirt** *n* MINING *placer mining* alluvion aurifère *f*, graviers aurifères *m pl*, terre aurifère *f*, terre d'alluvions aurifères *f*; ~television *n* TELECOM télévision à péage *f*; ~ **television network** *n* TELECOM chaîne de TV à péage *f*; ~ **TV** *n* TV télévision à péage *f*; ~ **zone** *n* PETR zone productive *f*, PETR TECH zone productrice *f*

pay[2] *vt* PATENTS *fee* acquitter; ~ **off** *vt* NAUT *sailors, sail* abattre, débarquer; ~ **out** *vt* NAUT *cable* filer

pay-by-use: ~ **basis** *n* TELECOM base de payer-par-utilisation *f*

paying: ~ **off** *n* NAUT *of crew* débarquement *m*

payload *n* AERONAUT charge marchande *f*, charge payante *f*, charge utile *f*, MAR POLL charge *f*, charge utile *f*, SPACE charge utile *f*, TELECOM capacité utile *f*, charge utile *f*, VEHICLES charge utile *f*; ~ **bay** *n* SPACE *spacecraft* soute *f*

payoff *n* SPACE compte rendu *m*, rapport *m*, rendement *m*, retour *m*

payphone *n* TELECOM publiphone *m*

Pb *abbr (lead)* CHEM Pb *(plomb)*

PBX[1] *abbr (private branch exchange)* TELECOM autocommutateur privé *m*, commutateur téléphonique privé *m*

PBX:[2] ~ **switchboard** *n* TELECOM standard privé *m*

PBXIS-LB *abbr* TELECOM autocommutateur privé pour le RNIS-LB *m*

PC[1] *abbr* COMP *(printed circuit)* CI *(circuit imprimé)*, COMP *(personal computer)* OP *(ordinateur personnel)*, DP *(printed circuit)* CI *(circuit imprimé)*, DP *(personal computer)* OP *(ordinateur personnel)*, E-LECTRON *(printed circuit)*, PHYS *(printed circuit)*, TELECOM *(printed circuit)*, TV *(printed circuit)* CI *(circuit imprimé)*

PC:[2] ~ **board** *n* ELECTRON carte à circuit imprimé *f*; ~ **control sequence** *n* PROD ENG séquence de fonctionnement de l'automate programmable *f*

PCB *abbr (printed circuit board)* COMP, DP, ELEC, ELECTRON, TELECOM carte de circuit imprimé *f*

p-channel *n* ELECTRON canal P *m*; ~ **depletion mode MOS transistor** *n* ELECTRON transistor MOS canal P à déplétion *m*; ~ **device** *n* ELECTRON dispositif à canal P *m*; ~ **enhancement mode MOS transistor** *n* ELECTRON transistor MOS canal P à enrichissement *m*; ~ **FET** *n* ELECTRON TEC à canal P *m*; ~ **integrated FET** *n* ELEC-TRON TEC intégré à canal P *m*; ~ **integrated junction**

PET *n* ELECTRON TEC à jonction intégré à canal P *m*

PCI *abbr (pattern correspondence index)* TELECOM indice de correspondence spectrale *f*

PCM[1] *abbr (pulse code modulation)* COMP, DP, ELEC-TRON, PHYS, RAD PHYS, SPACE, TV MIC *(modulation par impulsion codée)*

PCM:[2] ~ **filter** *n* ELECTRON filtre MIC *m*; ~ **multiplexer** *n* ELECTRON multiplexeur MIC *m*; ~ **multiplexing** *n* E-LECTRON multiplexage MIC *m*; ~ **switching system** *n* TELECOM système de commutation MIC *m*; ~ **system** *n* TELECOM système de commutation MIC *m*

PCM-FM: ~ **modulation** *n* ELECTRON modulation MIC-FM *f*

P-controller *n (proportional controller)* CONTROL régulateur proportionnel *m*

p-cresol *n* CHEM paracrésol *m*

PCS *abbr (plastic-clad silica)* OPT, TELECOM silice gratinée de plastique *f*

PCS-fiber *n* (AmE), **PCS-fibre** *n* (BrE) OPT, TELECOM fibre de silice gainée de plastique *f*, fibre silice-plastique *f*

PCT *abbr (peak cladding temperature)* NUCLEAR température maximale de la gaine *f*

PCU *abbr (passenger car unit)* TRANSP UVP *(unité de voiture particulière)*

PCV *abbr (positive crankcase ventilation)* AUTO recyclage des gaz de carter *m*

PCVD *abbr (plasma-activated chemical vapor deposition, plasma-activated chemical vapour deposition)* ELECTRON procédé de dépôt chimique en phase vapeur activé au plasma *m*

pd *abbr (potential difference)* PHYS ddp *(différence de potentiel)*

Pd *(palladium)* CHEM Pd *(palladium)*

PD *abbr* TELECOM *(protocol discriminator)* DP *(discriminateur de protocole)*, TELECOM *(physical delivery)* remise physique *f*

PDAU *abbr (physical delivery access unit)* TELECOM unité d'accès au service de remise physique *f*

PDF *abbr (probability density function)* MATH fonction de densité de probabilité *f*

PDH *abbr (plesiochronous digital hierarchy)* TELECOM hiérarchie numérique plésiochrone *f*

PDM *abbr (pulse duration modulation)* ELECTRON, SPACE MID *(modulation par impulsions de durée)*

PDN *abbr (public data network)* COMP, DP réseau public de données *m*, réseau public de transmission de données *m*

PDR *abbr* ELEC *(power directional relay)* relais directionnel de puissance *m*, SPACE *(preliminary design review)* revue de définition préliminaire *f*

PDS *abbr (physical delivery system)* TELECOM système de remise physique *m*

PDU *abbr (protocol data unit)* TELECOM unité de données du protocole *f*

PE *abbr* COMP *(phase encoding)*, DP *(phase encoding)* enregistrement en modulation de phase *m*, TELECOM *(protocol emulator)* émulateur de protocol *m*

pea: ~ **coal** *n* COAL TECH charbon menu *m*

peak *n* CHEM *in spectrum* pic *m*, NAUT *of sail, anchor* bec *m*, coqueron *m*, pic *m*, NUCLEAR *in energy spectrum* ligne *f*, maximum *m*, pic *m*, PAPER TECH sommet *m*, TV crête de niveau *f*; ~ **amplitude** *n* ELECTRON amplitude de crête *f*, amplitude maximale *f*, RECORDING amplitude de pointe *f*; ~ **arc voltage** *n* ELEC tension d'arc *f*; ~ **brightness** *n* TV hyperluminosité d'aire réduite *f*; ~

busy hour *n* TELECOM heure de pointe *f*; **~ capacity** *n* CONST *electricity* capacité de pointe *f*; **~ cladding temperature** *n (PCT)* NUCLEAR température maximale de la gaine *f*; **~ clipping** *n* ELECTRON écrêtage *m*; **~ concentration** *n* POLLUTION concentration de pointe *f*; **~ current** *n* ELEC *of supply network*, ELEC ENG, PHYS courant de crête *m*; **~ demand** *n* GAS TECH pointe de demande *f*, WATER SUPP consommation de pointe *f*; **~ distortion** *n* TV distorsion de crête *f*; **~ engine speed** *n* VEHICLES régime de pointe *m*; **~ envelope power** *n* TELECOM puissance en crête *f*; **~ factor** *n* ELECTRON, SPACE *communications* facteur de crête *m*; **~ flow** *n* HYDROL débit de pointe *m*; **~ frequency deviation** *n* SPACE *communications* excursion de fréquence crête *f*, TELECOM excursion de fréquence maximale *f*; **~ heat flux** *n* NUCLEAR flux de chaleur maximum *m*; **~ hour** *n* RAIL, TRANSP *traffic* heure de pointe *f*; **~ hour factor** *n (PHF)* TRANSP *traffic* facteur de pointe *m*; **~ hour traffic** *n* RAIL trafic de pointe *m*, TRANSP trafic d'heure de pointe *m*; **~ indicator** *n* ELECTRON indicateur de crête *m*; **~ intensity wavelength** *n* OPT, TELECOM longueur d'onde du maximum d'intensité de rayonnement *f*; **~ inverse voltage** *n* ELEC tension de pointe inverse *f*; **~ level** *n* RECORDING niveau de pointe *m*; **~ limitation** *n* RECORDING limitation de pointe *f*; **~ limiter** *n* CINEMAT limiteur d'amplitude *m*, TV limitateur de crêtes *m*, écrêteur *m*; **~ load** *n* ELEC *of supply network* pointe de charge *f*, ELEC ENG, PAPER TECH charge maximale *f*; **~ load nuclear power plant** *n* NUCLEAR centrale nucléaire de pointe *f*; **~ load power plant** *n* ELEC *supply network* centrale de pointe *f*; **~ load traffic** *n* TRANSP trafic d'heure de pointe *m*, trafic de pointe *m*; **~ luminosity** *n* RAD PHYS luminosité de crête *f*; **~ meter** *n* TV crêtemètre *m*, indicateur de crête *m*; **~ period traffic** *n* TRANSP trafic d'heure de pointe *m*, trafic de pointe *m*; **~ power** *n* ELEC ENG puissance de crête *f*, TV puissance de crête *f*; **~ power output** *n* RECORDING puissance de pointe de sortie *f*; **~ programme meter** *n* RECORDING indicateur de pointe de programme *m*, TV voltmètre de crête *m*; **~ pulse amplitude** *n* ELECTRON amplitude crête d'une impulsion *f*; **~ rate** *n* HYDROL débit de pointe *m*, TELECOM tarif rouge *m* (Fra); **~ recording level** *n* RECORDING niveau de pointe d'enregistrement *m*; **~ revs** *n* VEHICLES *of engine* régime de pointe *m*; **~ signal** *n* TV niveau de crête de signal *m*; **~ signal amplitude** *n* ELECTRON amplitude maximale du signal *f*; **~ sound pressure** *n* ACOUSTICS pression acoustique de crête *f*; **~ speech power** *n* ACOUSTICS puissance vocale de crête *f*; **~ time** *n* TV heures de grande écoute *f pl*; **~ traffic volume** *n* TRANSP débit de pointe *m*; **~ value** *n* ELEC *of current, voltage* tension de crête *f*, ELECTRON valeur crête *f*, valeur de crête *f*, valeur maximale *f*, PHYS, TELECOM valeur de crête *f*; **~ velocity** *n* WATER SUPP vitesse de crête *f*; **~ voltage** *n* ELEC ENG, PHYS, TV tension de crête *f*; **~ voltmeter** *n* ELEC voltmètre de crête *m*; **~ volume velocity** *n* RECORDING vitesse de pointe de volume *f*; **~ water flow** *n* WATER SUPP débit de pointe *m*; **~ white** *n* TV blanc maximal *m*, crête du blanc *f*

peaking *n* ELECTRON correction des fréquences élevées *f*, relèvement des fréquences élevées *m*; **~ capacity** *n* ELEC *of supply network* puissance de crête *f*; **~ circuit** *n* ELECTRON circuit de correction *m*, TV circuit d'augmentation de la pente *m*; **~ control** *n* TV commande de compensation *f*, commande de correction *f*; **~ net-**

work *n* TV circuit de différentiation *m*; **~ transformer** *n* ELEC transformateur de crête *m*

peak-to-average: **~ power ratio** *n* NUCLEAR rapport de puissance crête à la puissance moyenne *m*

peak-to-peak[1] *adv* TV crête à crête

peak-to-peak:[2] **~ amplitude** *n* ELECTRON amplitude de crête à crête *f*, RECORDING amplitude de pointe à pointe *f*; **~ signal amplitude** *n* TV amplitude crête-à-crête du signal *f*; **~ value** *n* ACOUSTICS amplitude crête-à-crête *f*, PHYS valeur crête-à-crête *f*

pean: **~ hammer** *n* PROD ENG marteau à panne *m*

peanut: **~ oil** *n* CHEM huile d'arachide *f*

pearl: **~ ash** *n* DETERGENTS carbonate de potassium *m*; **~ screen** *n* CINEMAT écran perlé *m*

pearlite *n* PROP MAT perlite *f*

pearlstone *n* PETR perlite *f*

pear-shaped: **~ vessel** *n* LAB EQUIP *glassware* récipient en forme de poire *m*

peat *n* CHEM, COAL TECH tourbe *f*; **~ coal** *n* COAL TECH charbon de tourbe *m*

pebble *n* PETR galet *m*; **~ bed** *n* NUCLEAR *reactor* lit de boulets *m*; **~ mill** *n* COAL TECH broyeur à galets *m*, PROD ENG broyeur à galets *m*, tube broyeur à galets *m*, tube broyeur à galets en silex *m*, tube finisseur à galets *m*; **~ paving** *n* CONST cailloutage *m*, pavage en cailloux *m*

PEC *abbr (photoelectric cell)* PHYS, RAD PHYS, SPACE, TV cellule photoélectrique *f*

peck *n* METR peck *m*

pectase *n* CHEM pectase *f*

pectate *n* CHEM pectate *m*

pectic *adj* CHEM pectique

pectin *n* CHEM, FOOD TECH pectine *f*; **~ jelly** *n* FOOD TECH *commercial confectionery* gelée de pectine *f*, pâte de fruits à pectine *f*

pectinose *n* CHEM arabinose *m*

pectizable *adj* CHEM pectisable

pectization *n* CHEM pectisation *f*

pectize *vt* CHEM pectiser

pectolite *n* MINERAL pectolite *f*

pectose *n* CHEM pectose *m*

pectous *adj* CHEM pecteux

pedal *n* VEHICLES *brake, clutch* pédale *f*; **~ adjuster** *n* VEHICLES *brake, clutch* régleur de pédale *m*; **~ damper assembly** *n* AERONAUT amortisseur de palonnier *m*; **~ switch** *n* CONTROL interrupteur à commande au pied *m*, interrupteur à pédale *m*

pedal-operated: **~ control** *n* MECH ENG commande au pied *f*

pedestal *n* MECH socle *m*, MECH ENG *plummer block, bearing* palier *m*, support *m*, *upright standard* socle *m*, NUCLEAR tréteau *m*, PROD ENG *to support barrel of boiler* chandelier *m*, TRANSP *road, rail* support de la voie *m*, TV niveau de noir *m*, palier du noir *m*; **~ adjustment** *n* TV ajustage du palier du noir *m*; **~ base** *n* INSTRUMENT socle-support *m*, structure de support *f*; **~ box** *n* MECH ENG *box enclosing bearing* boîte des coussinets *f*; **~ cover** *n* MECH ENG *of a bearing block* chapeau *m*; **~ level control** *n* TV réglage du niveau du noir *m*

pedestrian: **~ area** *n* TRANSP zone piétonne *f*, zone piétons *f*, zone réservée aux piétons *f*; **~ control** *n* CONTROL commande au pied *f*; **~ control system** *n* CONTROL système de commande piéton *m*; **~ conveyor** *n* TRANSP bande transporteuse *f*; **~ crossing** *n* CONTROL passage clouté *m*, passage pour piétons *m*; **~ phase** *n* TRANSP *traffic control* phase piétons *f*; **~ push**

button n TRANSP *traffic control* bouton-poussoir piétons m; **~ subway** n CONST passage piétons m, passage souterrain m; **~ zone** n TRANSP zone piétonne f, zone piétons f, zone réservée aux piétons f

pedestrian-actuated: ~ signal n TRANSP feu commandé par les piétons m

pedestrian-controlled[1] adj CONTROL commandé par piétons, à commande au pied, à commande pédestre

pedestrian-controlled:[2] **~ crossing** n CONTROL passage commandé par piétons m, passage à commande des piétons m

pedestrian-only: ~ crossing zone n TRANSP zone piétonne f, zone piétons f, zone réservée aux piétons f

pedology n OAL TECH pédologie f

pedometer n PHYS compte-pas m, podomètre m

peel:[1] **~ shim** n MECH ENG cale lamellée f; **~ strength test** n TESTING essai de force d'arrachement m

peel[2] vt FOOD TECH peler, éplucher; **~ off** vt PROD ENG *welding* déboutonner

peel:[3] **~ the lamination off a shim washer** vi MECH ENG peler une rondelle; **~ off in flakes** vi CHEM s'écailler

peelable: ~ protective coating n PACKAGING revêtement de protection pelable m; **~ system** n PACKAGING système détachable m

peeler n PAPER TECH écorceuse f

peeling n ACOUSTICS pelure f, PAPER TECH écorçage m, PROP MAT écaillage m, TEXTILES arrachage de fibre m; **~ off** n CHEM écaillage m, écaillement m; **~ test** n PROD ENG essai d'arrachement m

peel-off: ~ wrapping n PACKAGING emballage pelable m

peen n PROD ENG *of hammer* panne f; **~ hammer** n PROD ENG marteau à panne m

peening n PROD ENG martelage m, matage m

peep: ~ hole n PROD ENG *of furnace* regard m, SPACE *of spacecraft* trou de regard m

peer: ~ entities n pl TELECOM entités homologues f pl; **~ entity authentication** n TELECOM authentification de l'entité homologue f

peer-to-peer[1] adj COMP, DP égal à égal

peer-to-peer:[2] **~ master** n PROD ENG maître d'égal à égal m; **~ slave** n PROD ENG esclave d'égal à égal m

peg[1] n CONST cheville f, *setting out* fiche f, piquet m, MECH cheville f; **~ animation** n CINEMAT animation par cellulose f; **~ bar** n CINEMAT règle à ergots f; **~ board** n CINEMAT grille de commutation à chevilles f, table d'animation f; **~ tooth** n MECH ENG *of saw* dent droite f

peg[2] vt CONST cheviller

Pegasus n ASTRON Pégase m

pegged: ~ tenon joint n CONST assemblage à tenon passant avec clef m

pegging n PROD ENG identification des besoins f; **~ peen** n PROD ENG *founding* pellon m; **~ rammer** n PROD ENG *founding* pellon m

pegmatite n PROP MAT pegmatite f

pelagic: ~ ooze n GEOL boue pélagique f, vase pélagique f; **~ waters** n pl OCEANOG eaux pélagiques f pl

pelargonate n CHEM pélargonate m

pelargonic adj CHEM pélargonique f

pelite n GEOL pélite f

pelitic adj GEOL pélitique

pellet n COAL TECH boulette f, P&R granulé m, pastille f, PROP MAT pastille f; **~ limestone** n GEOL calcaire graveleux m; **~ stack** n NUCLEAR colonne de combustible f

pellet-clad: ~ chemical interaction n NUCLEAR interaction chimique pastille-gaine f; **~ mechanical interaction** n NUCLEAR interaction mécanique gaine-pastille f

pelletierine n CHEM pelletiérine f

pelletizing n P&R agglomération f, PROP MAT pastillage m

pellicular: ~ water n COAL TECH eau pelliculaire f

pelorus n NAUT *navigation* taximètre m

Peltier: ~ coefficient n PHYS coefficient de Peltier m; **~ effect** n ELEC *thermoelectric*, PHYS effet Peltier m

Pelton: ~ turbine n FUELLESS turbine Pelton f; **~ wheel** n FUELLESS roue Pelton f

pen n GEOPHYS stylet d'enregistreur m; **~ light** n ELEC ENG lampe stylo f; **~ plotter** n (AmE) *(cf pen recorder)* COMP, DP traceur à plume m, ELEC enregistreur à plume m, INSTRUMENT enregistreur à encre m, LAB EQUIP enregistreur à plume m; **~ recorder** n (BrE) *(cf pen plotter)* COMP traceur à plume m, DP, ELEC enregistreur à plume m, INSTRUMENT enregistreur à encre m, enregistreur à plume m, LAB EQUIP enregistreur à plume m; **~ ruling machine** n PRINT traceur m

pencil: ~ beam n ELECTRON faisceau très étroit m, RAD PHYS *of light* faisceau étroit m; **~ edging** n C&G façonnage des joints m; **~ glide** n METALL glissement en barreaux m; **~ test** n CINEMAT essai de traçage m

pendant: ~ bracket n MINING chaise pendante f; **~ group** n CHEM *in polymer* groupe pendant m; **~ switch control** n SAFETY contrôle de levage par interrupteur pendant m, contrôle par interrupteur pendant m

pending adj PROD ENG en instance

pendular adj MECH pendulaire

pendulum n GEOPHYS, MECH, PHYS pendule m; **~ bob** n PHYS lentille de pendule f; **~ circuit breaker** n CONTROL interrupteur de contact à pendule m; **~ floater** n C&G sonde pendulaire f; **~ governor** n CONTROL régulateur à boules m; **~ hardness** n P&R *test, coatings* dureté pendulaire f; **~ motion** n MECH ENG oscillation f; **~ regulator** n CONTROL régulateur à boules m; **~ suspension** n TRANSP suspension pendulaire f, *of car* suspension pendulaire de la caisse f; **~ suspension spring** n GEOPHYS suspension élastique du pendule f; **~ vehicle suspension** n TRANSP *monorail* suspension pendulaire f

penecontemporaneous adj GEOL pénécontemporain

penetrating: ~ paint n COLOURS peinture d'imprégnation f; **~ power** n RAD PHYS *of particle radiation* puissance de pénétration f

penetration n COMP, DP, ELECTRON pénétration f, MECH traversée f; **~ CRT** n ELECTRON tube cathodique à pénétration m; **~ depth** n CONST, ELECTRON profondeur de pénétration f; **~ grade** n CONST qualité de pénétration f; **~ method** n NUCLEAR *of materials testing* méthode d'essai à pénétration f; **~ screen** n ELECTRON écran à pénétration m; **~ sleeve** n NUCLEAR fourreau de traversée m, manchette de traversée f; **~ test** n COAL TECH essai de pénétration m; **~ tester** n P&R instrument pénétromètre m; **~ unit** n NUCLEAR *of cables, pipes* passage traversée m

penetrometer n CONST, LAB EQUIP pénétromètre m

peninsula n HYDROL presqu'île f, NAUT *geography* presqu'île f, péninsule f

pennant n NAUT fanion m, flamme f, pavillon m; **~ line** n PETR orin m

pennine n MINERAL pennine f, penninite f

penninite n MINERAL pennine f, penninite f

penny-shaped: ~ crack n METALL fissure circulaire f, NUCLEAR fissure lenticulaire f

pennyweight n METR pennyweight m

penstock *n* FUELLESS *dams*, HYDROL *hydroelectric dams*, NUCLEAR *intake structure* conduite forcée *f*, WATER SUPP canal d'amenée *m*, canal de prise *m*, dérivation *f*, vanne *f*

pent: ~ **roof** *n* CONST comble en appentis *m*

pentachloride *n* CHEM pentachlorure *m*

pentad *n* CHEM corps pentavalent *m*

pentagon *n* GEOM pentagone *m*

pentagonal *adj* GEOM pentagonal

pentagrid: ~ **converter** *n* ELEC ENG changeur penta-grille *m*

pentaguine *n* CHEM pentaguine *f*

pentahedral *adj* GEOM pentaèdre

pentahedron *n* GEOM pentaèdre *m*

pentamethylene *n* CHEM pentaméthylène *m*

pentamethylenediamine *n* CHEM pentaméthylènedia-mine *f*

pentane *n* CHEM, PETR TECH pentane *m*

pentanoic *adj* CHEM pentanoïque

pentanol *n* CHEM alcool amylique *m*, pentanol *m*

pentanone *n* CHEM pentanone *f*

pentaprism *n* PHOTO pentaprisme *m*, prisme en toit *m*

pentasulfide *n* (AmE), **pentasulphide** *n* (BrE) CHEM pentasulfure *m*

pentathionate *n* CHEM pentathionate *m*

pentathionic *adj* CHEM pentathionique

pentatomic *adj* CHEM pentatomique

pentatonic: ~ **scale** *n* ACOUSTICS gamme pentatonique *f*

pentavalence *n* CHEM pentavalence *f*

pentavalent *adj* CHEM pentavalent

pentene *n* CHEM pentène *m*

penthiophene *n* CHEM penthiofène *m*, penthiophène *m*

pentite *n* CHEM pentalcool *m*, pentite *f*, pentitol *m*

pentitol *n* CHEM pentalcool *m*, pentite *f*, pentitol *m*

pentlandite *n* MINERAL pentlandite *f*

pentode *n* ELECTRON, PHYS pentode *f*

pentosan *n* CHEM pentosane *m*

pentosazon *n* CHEM pentosazone *f*

pentose *n* CHEM pentose *m*

pentosid *n* CHEM pentoside *m*

pentoside *n* CHEM pentoside *m*

pentosuric *adj* CHEM pentosurique

pentothal *n* CHEM penthotal *m*, pentoxyde *m*

pentrough *n* WATER SUPP canal d'amenée *m*, canal de prise *m*, dérivation *f*

pentyl *n* CHEM pentyle *m*

pentylenetetrazol *n* CHEM pentétrazol *m*

penumbra *n* ASTRON, PHYS pénombre *f*

penumbral: ~ **eclipse** *n* ASTRON éclipse de pénombre *f*

peonin *n* CHEM péonine *f*

pepper: ~ **alkaloid** *n* CHEM alcaloïde de poivre *m*

peppered: ~ **sandblast** *n* C&G sablé moucheté *m*

pepsin *n* CHEM pepsinase *f*, pepsine *f*, FOOD TECH pep-sine *f*

pepsinogen *n* CHEM pepsinogène *m*

pepsinum *n* CHEM pepsinase *f*, pepsine *f*

peptide: ~ **link** *n* CHEM *in compound* lien peptidique *m*

peptizable *adj* CHEM peptisable

peptizate *vt* CHEM peptiser

peptization *n* CHEM peptisation *f*, DETERGENTS peptisa-tion *f*, transformation gel-sol *f*, FOOD TECH peptisation *f*

peptize *vt* CHEM, DETERGENTS peptiser

peptizer *n* DETERGENTS agent dispersant *m*, peptisant *m*, P&R peptisant *m*

peptolysis *n* CHEM peptolyse *f*

peptonizable *adj* CHEM peptonisable

per:[1] ~ **unit area** *adj* PHYS surfacique; ~ **unit length** *adj* PHYS linéique; ~ **unit mass** *adj* PHYS massique, spécifi-que; ~ **unit volume** *adj* PHYS volumique

per:[2] ~ **capita consumption** *n* WATER SUPP consomma-tion par habitant *f*

peracetic *adj* CHEM peracétique

peracid *n* CHEM peracide *m*

peralkaline *adj* GEOL hyperalcalin

peraluminous *adj* GEOL hyperalumineux

perborate *n* CHEM, DETERGENTS perborate *m*

perbromide *n* CHEM perbromure *m*

percarbonate *n* CHEM percarbonate *m*

perceived: ~ **color** *n* (AmE), ~ **colour** *n* (BrE) COLOURS couleur propre *f*

percentage *n* TEXTILES pourcentage *m*; ~ **awaiting repair** *n* RAIL *vehicles* pourcentage d'immobilisation *m*; ~ **composition** *n* C&G *of glass* formule *f*; ~ **modulation** *n* ELECTRON taux de modulation *m*; ~ **of non-confor-ming items** *n* QUALITY pourcentage d'individus non conformes *m*, pourcentage d'unités non conformes *m*; ~ **synchronization** *n* TV pourcentage de synchroni-sation *m*; ~ **tilt** *n* TV pourcentage de déclivité *m*

perception-reaction: ~ **time** *n* TRANSP *traffic* temps de perception-réaction *m*

perch *n* METR, NAUT *navigation marks* perche *f*

perched: ~ **water** *n* WATER SUPP eau perchée *f*; ~ **water-course** *n* HYDROL cours d'eau perché *m*; ~ **water table** *n* HYDROL surface de nappe suspendue *f*

perchlorate *n* CHEM perchlorate *m*; ~ **explosive** *n* MINING explosif au perchlorate *m*, sevranite *f*

perchloric *adj* CHEM perchlorique

perchloride *n* CHEM perchlorure *m*

perchlorinated *adj* CHEM perchloré

perchromate *n* CHEM perchromate *m*

perchromic *adj* CHEM perchromique

percolate:[1] ~ **through** *vt* HYDROL passer à travers, péné-trer, s'infiltrer dans

percolate[2] *vi* HYDROL s'infiltrer

percolating: ~ **water** *n* HYDROL eau de percolation *f*, WATER SUPP eau d'infiltration *f*, eau de percolation *f*

percolation *n* CHEM infiltration *f*, FOOD TECH *machinery* percolation *f*, suintement *m*, HYDROL filtration *f*, in-filtration *f*, HYDROL percolation *f*

percussion: ~ **cap** *n* MILIT capsule fulminante *f*; ~ **drill** *n* MECH ENG *hammer drill* marteau perforateur *m*, perfo-ratrice percutante *f*, mining *boring* sonde percutante *f*; ~ **drilling** *n* COAL TECH forage à percussion *m*, PETR TECH forage par battage *m*; ~ **fuse** *n* MILIT amorce à percussion *f*, fusée percutante *f*, MINING fusée percu-tante *f*, étoupille à percussion *f*; ~ **mortar** *n* LAB EQUIP *grinding* broyeur à percussion *m*; ~ **needle** *n* MILIT percuteur *m*; ~ **plate** *n* MECH ENG *die set* plaque de choc *f*; ~ **pressure** *n* MILIT force de pénétration *f*; ~ **rig** *n* MINING *boring* appareil de battage *m*; ~ **rivet** *n* MECH ENG riveuse à martelage *f*; ~ **sieve** *n* PROD ENG crible à percussion *m*

percussive: ~ **drilling** *n* COAL TECH forage à percussion *m*; ~ **force** *n* MECH ENG force de percussion *f*, force percutante *f*; ~ **rope boring** *n* COAL TECH forage à percussion *m*; ~ **rope drilling** *n* COAL TECH forage à percussion *m*

percylite *n* MINERAL percylite *f*

pereirine *n* CHEM péreirine *f*

perennial: ~ **spring** *n* HYDROL source intarissable *f*, source permanente *f*, source pérenne *f*

perfect:[1] ~ **binder** *n* PRINT brocheuse automatique sans couture *f*; ~ **binding** *n* PRINT reliure sans couture *f*; ~ **crystal** *n* METALL cristal parfait *m*; ~ **dielectric** *n* ELEC *capacitor* diélectrique parfait *m*; ~ **dislocation** *n* CRYS-TALL dislocation parfaite *f*; ~ **fifth** *n* ACOUSTICS quinte juste *f*; ~ **fluid** *n* PHYS fluide parfait *m*; ~ **fourth** *n* ACOUSTICS quarte juste *f*; ~ **gas** *n* PHYS gaz idéal *m*, gaz parfait *m*, THERMOD gaz parfait *m*; ~ **gas scale** *n* PHYS *of temperature* échelle des gaz parfaits *f*; ~ **mixture ratio** *n* AUTO dosage parfait *m*; ~ **printing** *n* PRINT impression recto-verso *f*, retiration *f*; ~ **reflecting diffuser** *n* PAPER TECH diffuseur parfait par réflexion *m*; ~ **square** *n* MATH carré parfait *m*

perfect[2] *vt* PRINT imprimer au verso

perfect-bound *adj* PRINT *bookbinding* relié sans couture

perfecting *n* PRINT impression recto-verso *f*, retiration *f*; ~ **unit** *n* PRINT groupe imprimant en retiration *m*

perfectly:[1] ~ **bonded** *adj* PROP MAT parfaitement lié

perfectly:[2] ~ **set page** *n* PRINT page sans faute *f*

perforated[1] *adj* DP perforé; ~ **on the reel** *adj* PACKAGING perforé sur rouleau

perforated:[2] ~ **absorbent tile** *n* RECORDING panneau absorbant perforé *m*; ~ **angle** *n* MECH *materials* cornière perforée *f*; ~ **bags on a roll** *n* PACKAGING sacs perforés en rouleau *m pl*; ~ **brick** *n* CONST brique creuse *f*; ~ **casing** *n* PETR colonne d'exploitation *f*, perforation de tubage *f*, tubage perforé *m*; ~ **disc anode** *n* (BrE) TV anode à disque perforé *f*; ~ **disk anode** *n* (AmE) *see perforated disc anode*; ~ **line** *n* PRINT ligne perforée *f*; ~ **overlap** *n* PACKAGING recouvrement perforé *m*; ~ **pipe** *n* PETR tube perforé *m*; ~ **plate** *n* NUCLEAR tôle perforée *f*, *in fuel assembly* plaque perforée *f*; ~ **tape** *n* DP, RECORDING bande perforée *f*, TELECOM ruban perforé *m*

perforating *n* PROD ENG percement *m*, perforage *m*, perforation *f*; ~ **ejector punch** *n* MECH ENG poinçon à collerette avec éjecteur *m*; ~ **gun** *n* PETR TECH perforateur à balles *m*; ~ **machine** *n* CINEMAT perforatrice *f*, PACKAGING perforeuse *f*, PRINT machine à perforer *f*

perforation *n* C&G découpe pointillée *f*, DP, PHOTO *of film* perforation *f*, PROD ENG percement *m*, perforage *m*, perforation *f*; ~ **blade** *n* PRINT lame de perforation *f*; ~ **pitch** *n* CINEMAT pas de perforations *m*; ~ **wheel** *n* PRINT molette de perforation *f*

perforator *n* COMP, DP perforateur *m*, PROD ENG perforatrice *m*, perforatrice *f*

perform[1] *vt* MECH ENG *operation* assurer

perform[2] *vi* TELECOM avérer

performance *n* COMP performance *f*, qualité de fonctionnement *f*, DP performance *f*, MECH ENG rendement *m*, QUALITY exécution *f*; ~ **data** *n* TELECOM informations de fonctionnement *f pl*; ~ **efficiency** *n* PROD ENG taux d'efficacité *m*; ~ **index** *n* CHEM index d'efficacité *m*; ~ **properties** *n pl* MECH ENG caractéristiques de fonctionnement *f pl*; ~ **specification** *n* MECH ENG protocole d'exploitation *m*; ~ **test** *n* ELEC essai de fonctionnement *m*; ~ **testing** *n* QUALITY essai de fonctionnement *m*

performing: ~ **CMISE service user** *n* TELECOM utilisateur du service CMISE exécuteur *m*

perhydride *n* CHEM perhydrure *m*

perhydrol *n* CHEM perhydrol *m*

periapsis *n* ASTRON périapside *m*, SPACE périastre *m*

periastron *n* SPACE périastre *m*

periclase *n* CHEM, MINERAL périclase *f*

periclasite *n* MINERAL périclase *f*

pericline *n* GEOL périclinal *m*, MINERAL péricline *f*

peridot *n* MINERAL péridot *m*

peridotite *n* PETR péridotite *f*

perigee *n* ASTRON, PHYS, SPACE périgée *m*; ~ **kick motor** *n* SPACE moteur de périgée *m*; ~ **stage** *n* SPACE étage de périgée *m*

perihelion *n* ASTRON, FUELLESS, PHYS périhélie *m*

perilla: ~ **seed oil** *n* CHEM huile de perilla *f*

perimeter *n* CONST, GEOM périmètre *m*; ~ **blasting** *n* MINING tir périmétrique *m*; ~ **frame** *n* AUTO cadre périmétrique *m*; ~ **track** *n* AERONAUT piste périphérique *f*

period: ACOUSTICS, ELECTRON, GEOL, PETR, PHYS période *f*; **off** ~ *n* ELEC ENG *circuit* période de coupure *f*, *device* période d'arrêt *f*, période de blocage *f*; **on** ~ *n* ELEC ENG *circuit* période de fonctionnement *f*, *transistor* période de déblocage *f*; ~ **of grace** *n* PATENTS délai supplémentaire *m*; ~ **of lowest flow** *n* HYDROL étiage *m*; ~ **measuring channel** *n* NUCLEAR chaîne de mesure de la constante de temps *f*; ~ **of oscillation** *n* ELEC *alternating current* période d'oscillation *f*; ~ **pulse** *n* ELECTRON impulsion périodique *f*, impulsion récurrente *f*; ~ **range** *n* NUCLEAR domaine de divergence *m*

periodate *n* CHEM périodate *m*

periodic[1] *adj* ELEC périodique, ELECTRON, PHYS périodique

periodic:[2] ~ **acid** *n* CHEM acide périodique *m*; ~ **comet** *n* ASTRON comète périodique *f*; ~ **damping** *n* ELEC ENG amortissement périodique *m*; ~ **function** *n* ELECTRON fonction périodique *f*; ~ **inspection** *n* MECH ENG inspection périodique *f*; ~ **instability** *n* PROP MAT instabilité périodique *f*; ~ **polarity inversion** *n* TV inversion périodique de polarité *f*; ~ **pulse** *n* ELECTRON impulsion récurrente *f*; ~ **quantity** *n* ACOUSTICS, ELECTRON grandeur périodique *f*; ~ **refresh** *n* ELECTRON rafraîchissement périodique *m*; ~ **shutdown** *n* NUCLEAR arrêt périodique *m*; ~ **signal** *n* ELECTRON, TELECOM signal périodique *m*; ~ **sound wave** *n* WAVE PHYS onde sonore périodique *f*; ~ **table** *n* CHEM *of elements* tableau périodique *m*; ~ **time** *n* ELECTRON durée d'une période *f*; ~ **tone** *n* ACOUSTICS son périodique *m*; ~ **variation** *n* GEOPHYS variation périodique *f*; ~ **wave** *n* ELEC ENG onde périodique *f*

periodical: ~ **winds** *n pl* METEO vents périodiques *m pl*

periodicity *n* CRYSTALL, ELECTRON périodicité *f*

periodide *n* CHEM periodure *m*

period-luminosity: ~ **relation** *n* ASTRON relation période-luminosité *f*

peripheral *n* COMP, DP, TELECOM périphérique *m*; ~ **control element** *n* NUCLEAR élément de commande périphérique *m*; ~ **device** *n* COMP, DP périphérique *m*, ELEC ENG périphérique *m*, unité périphérique *f*, TELECOM organe périphérique *m*; ~ **driver** *n* DP pilote de périphérique *m*; ~ **fuel assembly** *n* NUCLEAR assemblage combustible périphérique *m*; ~ **gas** *n* NUCLEAR gaz périphérique *m*; ~ **hem** *n* MILIT *of parachute* bord d'attaque *m*; ~ **interface adaptor** *n* COMP, DP adaptateur d'interface périphérique *m*; ~ **jet air cushion** *n* TRANSP coussin d'air à jet périphérique *m*; ~ **length checking** *n* MECH ENG contrôle de la longueur développée *m*; ~ **management** *n* TELECOM gestion périphérique *f*; ~ **module** *n* TELECOM unité périphérique *f*; ~ **nucleon** *n* NUCLEAR nucléon périphérique *m*; ~ **port** *n* PROD ENG sortie pour périphérique *f*; ~ **processor** *n* COMP, DP processeur périphérique *m*, TELECOM calculateur périphérique *m*; ~ **skirt** *n* TRANSP jupe périphérique *f*; ~ **transfer** *n* COMP, DP transfert périphérique *m*; ~ **unit** *n* COMP, DP unité périphérique *f*; ~ **velocity** *n* FUELLESS vitesse périphérique *f*; ~ **wheel speed** *n* MECH ENG *machine tool* vitesse de meule périphérique *f*

peripheral-limited *adj* COMP limité par le périphérique, DP limité par la vitesse du périphérique

periphery *n* CONST pourtour *m*, périphérie *f*

periscope *n* CINEMAT périscope *m*, snorkel *m*, NAUT *of submarine*, PHYS, SPACE *of spacecraft* périscope *m*; ~ **aerial** *n* PHYS antenne périscopique *f*

periscopic: ~ **lens** *n* PHOTO objectif périscopique *m*; ~ **sextant** *n* SPACE *spacecraft* sextant périscopique *m*

peristaltic: ~ **pump** *n* LAB EQUIP *liquid handling* pompe péristaltique *f*

peritectic: ~ **reaction** *n* METALL réaction péritectique *f*; ~ **transformation** *n* PROP MAT transformation péritectique *f*

peritectoid *n* METALL péritectoïde *m*

perlite *n* PETR perlite *f*; ~ **plaster** *n* HEAT ENG plâtre de perlite *m*

perlon *n* CHEM perlon *m*

permafrost *n* COAL TECH pergélisol *m*, PETR TECH pergélisol *m*, permagel *m*, permafrost *m*

permalloy *n* ELEC *magnetism*, PHYS permalloy *m*

permanence: ~ **of irrotational motion** *n* FLUID PHYS caractère permanent du mouvement irrotationnel *m*

permanent: ~ **anticyclone** *n* METEO anticyclone permanent *m*; ~ **color** *n* (AmE), ~ **colour** *n* (BrE) COLOURS couleur solide *f*, couleur stable *f*; ~ **concrete shuttering** *n* CONST agglo *m*, aggloméré *m*, agglomérés banchés *m pl*, coffrage permanent du béton *m*, coffrage perdu *m*; ~ **current** *n* OCEANOG courant établi *m*; ~ **deformation** *n* METALL déformation permanente *f*; ~ **disability** *n* SAFETY incapacité permanente *f*; ~ **echo** *n* SPACE *spacecraft* écho fixe *m*; ~ **error** *n* COMP, DP erreur persistante *f*; ~ **flow** *n* HYDROL écoulement permanent *m*; ~ **guide base** *n* PETR structure-guide *f*; ~ **guide structure** *n* PETR structure-guide *f*; ~ **ink** *n* COLOURS encre indélébile *f*; ~ **load** *n* COAL TECH charge permanente *f*; ~ **magnet** *n* ELEC, ELEC ENG, MECH ENG, PHYS, TELECOM, TRANSP aimant permanent *m*; ~ **magnet centering** *n* (AmE), ~ **magnet centring** *n* (BrE) TV centrage de l'image par aimants permanents *m*; ~ **magnet electron microscope** *n* INSTRUMENT microscope électronique à lentilles magnétiques *m*; ~ **magnet erasing** *n* RECORDING effacement à aimant permanent *m*; ~ **magnet flowmeter** *n* NUCLEAR débitmètre à aimant permanent *m*; ~ **magnet focusing** *n* ELEC ENG focalisation par aimant permanent *m*; ~ **magnet generator** *n* ELEC ENG, FUELLESS génératrice à aimants permanents *f*; ~ **magnet loudspeaker** *n* ACOUSTICS haut-parleur à aimant permanent *m*; ~ **magnet relay** *n* ELEC relais magnéto-électrique *m*; ~ **magnet split capacitor motor** *n* ELEC ENG moteur à condensateur permanent *m*; ~ **magnet stepper motor** *n* ELEC ENG moteur pas-à-pas à aimant permanent *m*; ~ **magnet synchronous motor** *n* ELEC ENG moteur synchrone à aimants permanents *m*; ~ **memory** *n* COMP, ELEC ENG mémoire permanente *f*; ~ **set** *n* MECH ENG, SPRINGS déformation permanente *f*; ~ **sheen finish** *n* COATINGS apprêt de brillant permanent *m*; ~ **stress** *n* C&G contrainte permanente *f*; ~ **structure** *n* CONST ouvrage d'art *m*, travail d'art *m*; ~ **threshold shift** *n* ACOUSTICS déplacement permanent de seuil *m*; ~ **virtual circuit** *n* (*PVC*) COMP, DP, TELECOM circuit

virtuel permanent *m*; ~ **way installation** *n* RAIL équipement d'une ligne *m*; ~ **work** *n* CONST ouvrage d'art *m*, travail d'art *m*

permanently: ~ **pleated** *adj* TEXTILES indéplissable

permanganate *n* CHEM, HYDROL permanganate *m*

permanganic *adj* CHEM permanganique

permeability *n* CHEM, COAL TECH, CONST, ELEC *magnetism*, FUELLESS, GAS TECH, HYDROL, P&R, PETR, PETR TECH, PHYS, PROP MAT, TESTING, TEXTILES perméabilité *f*; ~ **of air** *n* ELEC ENG perméabilité de l'air *f*; ~ **of free space** *n* ELEC ENG perméabilité absolue *f*, perméabilité du vide *f*, PHYS perméabilité du vide *f*; ~ **logging** *n* PETR TECH diagraphie de perméabilité *f*; ~ **to grease** *n* PACKAGING perméabilité à la graisse *f*

permeable[1] *adj* CHEM, CONST, HYDROL, PETR perméable

permeable:[2] ~ **layer** *n* GAS TECH couche perméable *f*, couche poreuse *f*; ~ **primer** *n* P&R *paint* primaire respirant *m*

permeameter *n* COAL TECH perméamètre *m*

permeance *n* ELEC *magnetism*, ELEC ENG, PAPER TECH, PHYS *magnetism* perméance *f*

Permian: ~ **period** *n* PETR TECH permien *m*

permissible: ~ **current** *n* ELEC ENG intensité admissible *f*; ~ **explosive** *n* (AmE) (*cf permitted explosive*) MINING explosif SGP *m* (Bel), explosif agréé *m*, explosif antigrisouteux *m*, explosif de sécurité *m*, explosif de sécurité grisou poussière *m* (Bel); ~ **level** of interference *n* SPACE *communications* puissance de brouillage admissible *f*; ~ **load** *n* COAL TECH charge admissible *f*; ~ **residual unbalance** *n* MECH ENG *of stiff shafts* balourd résiduel admissible *m*; ~ **voltage** *n* ELEC ENG tension admissible *f*

permissive: ~ **block** *n* RAIL block d'assentiment *m*

permitted: ~ **explosive** *n* (BrE) (*cf permissible explosive*) MINING explosif SGP *m* (Bel), explosif agréé *m*, explosif antigrisouteux *m*, explosif de sécurité *m*, explosif de sécurité grisou poussière *m* (Bel)

permittivity *n* ELEC *capacitor*, ELEC ENG, PHYS, SPACE, TELECOM permittivité *f*; ~ **of air** *n* ELEC ENG permittivité de l'air *f*; ~ **of free space** *n* ELEC ENG permittivité absolue *f*, permittivité du vide *f*

permonosulfuric *adj* (AmE), **permonosulphuric** *adj* (BrE) CHEM permonosulfurique

permutation *n* COMP, DP, MATH permutation *f*

pernitrate *n* CHEM perazotate *m*

pernitric *adj* CHEM perazotique

peroxidation *n* CHEM peroxydation *f*, suroxydation *f*

peroxide *n* CHEM peroxyde *m*, suroxyde *m*

peroxidize *vt* CHEM peroxyder

peroxoacetylnitrate *n* (*PAN*) POLLUTION nitrate de péroxoacétyle *m*, peroxoacétylnitrate *m*

peroxophosphate *n* CHEM peroxophosphate *m*

peroxy: ~ **acid** *n* CHEM peroxyacide *m*

peroxydisulfuric *adj* (AmE), **peroxydisulphuric** *adj* (BrE) CHEM perdisulfurique

perpend *n* CONST *masonry* parpaing *m* ~ **stone** *n* CONST parpaing *m*

perpendicular[1] *adj* GEOM perpendiculaire; ~ **to each other** *adj* METR *coordinate measuring axes* perpendiculaires entre eux

perpendicular:[2] ~ **to** *prep* GEOM perpendiculaire à

perpendicular[3] *n* GEOM normale *f*; ~ **amidships** *n* NAUT *ship design* perpendiculaire milieu *f*; ~ **lines** *n pl* GEOM lignes perpendiculaires *f pl*; ~ **magnetic recording** *n* ACOUSTICS enregistrement magnétique perpendiculaire *m*; ~ **magnetization** *n* TV enregistrement

magnétique perpendiculaire *m*; ~ **recording** *n* RECORDING enregistrement perpendiculaire *m*
perpetual: ~ **inventory** *n* PROD ENG inventaire permanent *m*; ~ **screw** *n* MECH ENG vis sans fin *f*
perrhenate *n* CHEM perrhénate *m*
perrhenic *adj* CHEM perrhénique
persalt *n* CHEM persel *m*
Perseids *n pl* ASTRON Perséides *m pl*
perseulose *n* CHEM perseulose *m*
Perseus *n* ASTRON Persée *m*; ~ **cluster of galaxies** *n* ASTRON amas de galaxies Persée *m*
persistence *n* ELEC *cathode ray tube*, ELECTRON persistance *f*; ~ **characteristic** *n* ELECTRON caractéristique de persistance *f*; ~ **of vision** *n* CINEMAT persistance rétinienne *f*
personal: ~ **call** *n* TELECOM appel avec préavis *m*; ~ **computer** *n (PC)* COMP, DP ordinateur personnel *m (OP)*; ~ **dosimetry** *n* RAD PHYS *radiation measurement* dosimétrie individuelle *f*; ~ **eye protectors** *n pl* SAFETY protecteurs individuels pour les yeux *m pl*; ~ **location beacon** *n* NAUT *shipping* radiobalise individuelle de repérage *f*; ~ **locator beacon** *n* NAUT *satellite location and rescue* balise de localisation portable *f*; ~ **protection** *n* SAFETY protection individuelle *f*; ~ **rapid transport** *n (PRT)* TRANSP transport en commun personnalisé *m*; ~ **sound exposure meter** *n* SAFETY sonomètre de poche *m*
Perspex *n* (TM) NAUT, P&R plexiglas *m* (MD)
persulfate *n* (AmE), **persulphate** *n* (BrE) CHEM persulfate *m*
PERT[1] *abbr (program evaluation and review technique)* CONTROL, PROD ENG méthode du planning PERT *f*
PERT:[2] ~ **chart** *n* DP graphique PERT *m*
perthite *n* MINERAL perthite *f*
perturbation *n* FLUID PHYS, SPACE perturbation *f*; ~ **of orbit** *n* SPACE perturbation d'orbite *f*
perturbed: ~ **frequency** *n* RAD PHYS *spectral energy* fréquence perturbée *f*
perveance *n* ELEC ENG, TELECOM pervéance *f*
perviousness *n (cf imperviousness)* FUELLESS perméance *f*
perylene *n* CHEM pérylène *m*
pesticide *n* CHEM pesticide *m*
pestle *n* CHEM, CHEM TECH, LAB EQUIP *grinding* pilon *m*
PET: ~ **bottle** *n* PACKAGING bouteille en polyéthylène *f*; ~ **film** *n* PACKAGING film de polyéthylène *m*
peta- *pref (p)* METR peta-*(p)*
petalite *n* MINERAL pétalite *f*
Petri: ~ **dish** *n* LAB EQUIP *glassware, microbiology* boîte de Pétri *f*; ~ **net** *n* COMP, DP réseau de Pétri *m*
petridish *n* LAB EQUIP *bacteriology* plaque pour culture *f*
petrochemical[1] *adj* PETR TECH pétrochimique
petrochemical:[2] ~ **plant** *n* PETR TECH usine pétrochimique *f*
petrochemicals *n pl* PETR TECH produits pétrochimiques *m pl*
petrofabric: ~ **analysis** *n* GEOL pétrographie structurale *f*
petrogenetic: ~ **grid** *n* GEOL *metamorphic petrology* diagramme pression-température d'équilibre de phases minérales *m*
petrol *n* (BrE) AUTO *f*, PETR, PETR TECH, THERMOD, VEHICLES *fuel* essence *f*; ~ **and oil resisting hose** *n* (BrE) *(cf gasoline and oil resistant hose)* P&R tuyau résistant à l'essence et à l'huile *m*; ~ **consumption** *n* (BrE) *(cf gasoline consumption)* VEHICLES *of engine* consommation d'essence *f*; ~ **dump** *n* (BrE) *(cf gasoline dump)* MILIT dépôt d'essence *m*; ~ **engine** *n* (BrE) *(cf gasoline engine)* NAUT, THERMOD, VEHICLES moteur à essence *m*; ~ **engine vehicle** *n* (BrE) *(cf gasoline engine vehicle)* POLLUTION véhicule à moteur à essence *m*; ~ **filter** *n* (BrE) *(cf gasoline filter, gas filter)* VEHICLES *fuel* filtre à essence *m*; ~ **hose** *n* (BrE) *(cf gasoline hose)* P&R tuyau à essence *m*, VEHICLES *fuel* tuyau flexible à essence *m*; ~ **mixture** *n* (BrE) *(cf gasoline mixture)* VEHICLES *of two-stroke engine* mélange huile-essence *m*; ~ **pump** *n* (BrE) *(cf gasoline pump, gas pump)* VEHICLES *fuel* distributeur d'essence *m*, pompe à essence *f*; ~ **resistance** *n* (BrE) *(cf gasoline resistance)* P&R résistance à l'essence *f*; ~ **station** *n* (BrE) *(cf gasoline station, road gasoline station)* TRANSP station d'essence *f*, station-service *f*; ~ **tank** *n* (BrE) *(cf gasoline tank)* VEHICLES *fuel* réservoir d'essence *m*
petrolatum *n* CHEM *jelly* vaseline industrielle *f*
petrolene *n* CHEM pétroléine *f*
petroleum *n* PETR, PETR TECH pétrole *m*; ~ **basin** *n* PETR TECH bassin pétrolifère *m*; ~ **company** *n* PROD ENG société pétrolière *f*; ~ **engineer** *n* PETR TECH ingénieur pétrolier *m*; ~ **field** *n* PETR champ pétrolifère *m*; ~ **gas** *n* PETR gaz de pétrole *m*; ~ **geology** *n* PETR TECH géologie du pétrole *f*, géologie pétrolière *f*; ~ **jelly** *n* CHEM sel de pétrole *m*; ~ **naphtha** *n* PETR naphte de pétrole *m*; ~ **product** *n* POLLUTION, PROP MAT produit pétrolier *m*; ~ **province** *n* PETR TECH province pétrolière *f*; ~ **wax** *n* PETR TECH *refining* cire de pétrole *f*
petrolic *adj* CHEM *ether* de pétrole
petrology *n* COAL TECH, PETR TECH pétrologie *f*
petrol-oil: ~ **mixture** *n* (BrE) *(cf gasoline-oil mixture, gas-oil mixture)* VEHICLES mélange huile-essence *m*
petrosilex *n* PETR pétrosilex *m*
petrosulfur: ~ **compounds** *n* (AmE), **petrosulphur compounds** *n pl* (BrE) PETR TECH composés soufrés *m pl*
petticoat: ~ **insulator** *n* ELEC ENG isolateur à cloche *m*
petty: ~ **officer** *n* NAUT *navy* officier marinier *m*, second maître *m*
pet-valve *n* HYDR EQUIP soupape de purge *f*, évent *m*
petzite *n* MINERAL petzite *f*
Petzval: ~ **lens** *n* CINEMAT objectif de Petzval *m*
PFM *abbr (pulse frequency modulation)* COMP, DP, ELECTRON modulation de fréquence d'impulsion *f*
PFR *abbr (power fail restart)* COMP, DP redémarrage automatique *m*
Pfund: ~ **series** *n* PHYS série de Pfund *f*
ph *adj* TELECOM physique
pH[1] *abbr (potential of hydrogen)* CHEM pH *(potentiel hydrogène)*
pH:[2] ~ **control** *n* COAL TECH réglage du pH *m*; ~ **controller** *n* COAL TECH régulateur du pH *m*; ~ **depression** *n* POLLUTION abaissement du pH *m*, baisse du pH *f*, dépression du pH *f*, réduction du pH *f*; ~ **drop** *n* POLLUTION chute du pH *f*; ~ **meter** *n* COAL TECH, LAB EQUIP, METR pH mètre *m*; ~ **number** *n* HYDROL valeur du pH *f*; ~ **value** *n* HYDROL valeur du pH *f*
phacolite *n* GEOL, MINERAL phacolite *f*
Phanerozoic *adj* GEOL phanérozoïque
phanite *n* PETR phtanite *f*, silex noir *m*
phantom: ~ **circuit** *n* ELEC ENG, TELECOM circuit fantôme *m*; ~ **coil** *n* ELEC ENG bobine fantôme *f*; ~ **horizon** *n* GEOPHYS horizon fantôme *m*
phantom-center-channel: ~ **loudspeaker** *n* (AmE), **phantom-centre-channel loudspeaker** *n* (BrE) RECORDING haut-parleur fantôme de canal central *m*
pharmacolite *n* MINERAL pharmacolite *f*

pharmacosiderite *n* MINERAL pharmacosidérite *f*

phase:[1] **in ~ opposition** *adj* ELECTRON, PHYS en opposition de phase; **~ shifted** *adj* ELECTRON déphasé

phase[2] *n* ACOUSTICS *of acoustical vibration* phase d'une vibration acoustique *f, of sinusoidal quantity* phase d'une grandeur sinusoïdale *f,* CHEM *of system,* COMP, DP, ELEC, ELECTRON, METALL, PETR, PHYS, TESTING, THERMOD, TRANSP *traffic control* phase *f;* **~ adaptor** *n* ELEC *alternating current* adaptateur de phase *m;* **~ adjustment** *n* TV mise en phase *f,* réglage de phase *m;* **~ advancer** *n* ELEC *motor* compensateur de phase *m;* **~ alignment** *n* TELECOM, TV verrouillage de phase *m;* **~ alternation line** *n (PAL)* TV ligne d'alternance de phase *f;* **~ ambiguity resolution** *n* SPACE *communications* levée d'ambiguïté sur la phase *f;* **~ angle** *n* AERONAUT, ELEC *alternating current,* ELECTRON, FUELLESS, PHYS, TESTING, WAVE PHYS *of oscillation* angle de phase *m;* **~ boundary** *n* METALL joint d'interphase *m,* limite de phase *f;* **~ changer** *n* ELEC *alternating current* changeur de phase *m,* ELECTRON changeur de phase *m,* déphaseur *m,* TELECOM déphaseur *m;* **~ change velocity** *n* TELECOM vitesse de variation de phase *f;* **~ coefficient** *n* TELECOM déphasage linéique *m;* **~ comparator** *n* ELECTRON, TV comparateur de phase *m;* **~ compensation** *n* ELEC *alternating current,* TELECOM compensation de phase *f;* **~ constant** *n* ACOUSTICS, ELECTRON constante de phase *f,* OPT constante de phase *f,* déphasage linéique *m,* PHYS constante de phase *f,* TELECOM déphasage linéique *m,* TV constante de phase *f;* **~ contrast microscope** *n* LAB EQUIP, PHYS microscope à contraste de phase *m;* **~ control** *n* ELECTRON, TELECOM commande de phase *f,* TV contrôle de tonalité *m,* mise en phase *f;* **~ converter** *n* ELEC *alternating current,* ELECTRON convertisseur de phase *m,* TV déphaseur *m;* **~ current** *n* ELEC *system,* ELEC ENG courant de phase *m;* **~ delay** *n* TV temps de propagation de phase *m;* **~ delay keying** *n* ELECTRON modulation par retard de phase *f;* **~ demodulation** *n* ELECTRON, TELECOM démodulation de phase *f;* **~ demodulator** *n* ELECTRON démodulateur de phase *m;* **~ detector** *n* ELECTRON comparateur de phase *m,* détecteur de phase *m,* TELECOM détecteur de phase *m,* TV discriminateur de phase *m;* **~ diagram** *n* CHEM *of system* diagramme de constitution *m,* diagramme de phase *m,* METALL diagramme d'équilibre *m,* NUCLEAR, TRANSP *traffic control* diagramme de phases *m;* **~ difference** *n* ELEC *transformer* déphasage *m,* ELECTRON différence de phase *f,* écart de phase *m,* PETR différence de phase *f,* PHYS différence de phase *f,* déphasage *m,* RECORDING différence de phase *f,* TELECOM déphasage *m,* TESTING différence de phase *f,* TV déphasage *m,* WAVE PHYS différence de phase *f;* **~ discrimination technique** *n* TESTING technique de discrimination de phase *f;* **~ discriminator** *n* ELECTRON discriminateur de phase *m;* **~ displacement** *n* ELEC *alternating current* déphasage *m;* **~ displacement induction loop**detector *n* TRANSP *traffic control* détecteur à boucle à induction à déphasage *m;* **~ distortion** *n* ELECTRON, PHYS, TELECOM, TV distorsion de phase *f;* **~ distribution** *n* METALL distribution des phases *f;* **~ encoding** *n (PE)* COMP, DP enregistrement en modulation de phase *m;* **~ equalizer** *n* ELEC *alternating current* correcteur de phases *m;* **~ equilibrium** *n* THERMOD équilibre de phase *m;* **~ error** *n* ELECTRON, TV erreur de phase *f;* **~ failure** *n* TV manque de phase *m;* **~ failure protection** *n* PROD ENG protection contre les pannes de phase *f;* **~ generator** *n* ELECTRON générateur de phases *m;* **~ grid** *n* ELEC *alternating current* réseau de phase *m;* **~ insulation** *n* ELEC *alternating current* isolation entre phases *f;* **~ integral** *n* SPACE facteur de phase *m;* **~ inversion** *n* COAL TECH inversion de phase *f,* PETR inversion de phase *f,* opposition de phase *f,* RECORDING inversion de phase *f;* **~ inverter** *n* ELEC *AC/DC circuit* circuit inverseur de phase *m;* **~ jitter** *n* SPACE *communications* fluctuation de phase *f,* gigue de phase *f;* **~ lag** *n* ELEC *alternating current* retard de phase *m,* ELECTRON déphasage en arrière *m,* retard de phase *m,* OCEANOG situation de la marée *f,* PHYS déphasage en arrière *m,* retard de phase *m;* **~ lead** *n* ELEC *alternating current* avance de phase *f,* ELECTRON, PHYS avance de phase *f,* déphasage en avant *m;* **~ lock** *n* TV blocage de phase *m;* **~ locking** *n* ELECTRON asservissement de phase *m,* TELECOM verrouillage de phase *m,* TV accrochage de phase *m,* verrouillage de phase *m;* **~ loss** *n* PROD ENG perte de phase *f;* **~ margin** *n* ELECTRON marge de phase *f;* **~ modulation** *n (PM)* COMP, DP, ELECTRON, PHYS, RECORDING, TELECOM, TV modulation de phase *f (MP);* **~ modulator** *n* ELECTRON, TELECOM modulateur de phase *m;* **~ monitoring** *n* CONTROL contrôle des phases *m;* **~ non-linear distortion** *n* SPACE *communications* distorsion non-linéaire de phase *f;* **~ opposition** *n* ELECTRON opposition de phase *f;* **~ quadrature** *n* ELECTRON quadrature de phase *f;* **~ reference** *n* TV référence de phase *f;* **~ regulation** *n* TELECOM régulation de phase *f;* **~ response** *n* CONTROL, ELECTRON réponse en phase *f;* **~ reversal** *n* ELEC *alternating current* inversion de phase *f,* PETR inversion de phase *f,* opposition de phase *f,* PROD ENG, TV inversion de phase *f;* **~ reversal switch** *n* ELEC ENG inverseur de phase *m;* **~ rule** *n* CHEM *for system* règle des phases *f,* NUCLEAR règle des phases de Gibbs *f;* **~ sequence** *n* ELEC *three-phase system,* ELECTRON ordre de phases *m;* **~ sequence rectifier** *n* ELEC *three-phase system* redresseur à ordre de phases *m;* **~ shift** *n* ELEC *alternating current* déphasage *m,* ELECTRON changement de phase *m,* déphasage *m,* rotation de phase *f,* NUCLEAR *in scattering theory* différence de phase *f,* déphasage *m,* PHYS décalage de phase *m,* déphasage *m,* SPACE *communications,* TRANSP *traffic control* déphasage *m,* TV décalage de phase *m;* **~ shifter** *n* ELEC *alternating current,* ELECTRON, TELECOM déphaseur *m;* **~ shift keying** *n (PSK)* COMP, DP modulation par déplacement de phase *f (MDP),* ELECTRON modulation PSK *f,* modulation par déplacement de phase *f,* SPACE *communications,* TELECOM modulation par déplacement de phase *f (MDP);* **~ shift microphone** *n* ACOUSTICS microphone à déphasage *m,* RECORDING microphone à rotation de phase *m;* **~ shift oscillator** *n* ELECTRON oscillateur à déphasage *m;* **~ skipping** *n* TRANSP *traffic control* escamotage de phase *m;* **~ space** *n* PHYS espace des phases *m;* **~ splitter** *n* ELEC *alternating current* diviseur de phase *m,* RECORDING déphaseur *m;* **~ splitter amplifier** *n* ELECTRON amplificateur déphaseur *m;* **~ splitting** *n* ELEC *alternating current,* ELECTRON division de phase *f;* **~ stability** *n* ELEC *alternating current* stabilité en phase *f,* TELECOM stabilité de phase *f;* **~ terminal** *n* ELEC *connection* borne de phase *f;* **~ to ground** *n* PROD ENG phase à la terre *f;* **~ transformations** *n pl* THERMOD transformations de phase *f pl;* **~ tuning** *n* TELECOM accord en phase *m;* **~ unbalance** *n* PROD ENG déséquilibre de phase *m;* **~ variation** *n* ELEC *alternating current* variation de phase *f;* **~ velocity** *n* PETR, PHYS vitesse de phase *f;* **~ voltage** *n*

ELEC *system* tension de phase *f*; ~ **winding** *n* ELEC enroulement de phase *m*

phase:[3] ~ **shift** *vt* ELECTRON déphaser

phase:[4] ~ **shift** *vti* ELECTRON changer la phase, opérer une rotation de phase

phase-amplitude: ~ **characteristic** *n* TELECOM caractéristique phase-amplitude *f*

phase-balance: ~ **relay** *n* ELEC relais polyphasé *m*

phased[1] *adj* TV en phase

phased:[2] ~ **array antenna** *n* SPACE *communications* antenne réseau à commande de phase *f*; ~ **ignition** *n* SPACE *spacecraft* allumage séquentiel *m*

phase-frequency: ~ **response curve** *n* ACOUSTICS courbe de réponse phase-fréquence *f*

phase-locked: ~ **demodulator** *n* SPACE *communications* démodulateur à verrouillage de phase *m*; ~ **loop** *n* (*PLL*) ELECTRON boucle à blocage de phase *f*, boucle à phase asservie *f*, SPACE *spacecraft*, TELECOM, TV boucle à verrouillage de phase *f*; ~ **oscillator** *n* (*PLO*) ELECTRON oscillateur asservi en phase *m*

phaseolin *n* CHEM phaséoline *f*

phaseolunatin *n* CHEM phaséolunatine *f*

phase-out *n* WAVE PHYS suppression progressive *f*

phaser *n* TV cadreur *m*

phase-reversed: ~ **secondaries** *n pl* ELEC ENG enroulements secondaires montés en opposition *m pl*

phases: ~ **of the moon** *n pl* ASTRON phases de la Lune *f pl*

phase-shaped: ~ **QPSK** *n* TELECOM MDPQ avec mise en forme de phase *f*

phase-shifting: ~ **capacitor** *n* ELEC condensateur déphaseur *m*; ~ **element** *n* ELECTRON élément déphaseur *m*; ~ **network** *n* ELEC *alternating current*, PHYS réseau déphaseur *m*; ~ **transformer** *n* ELEC transformateur déphaseur *m*

phase-to-earth: ~ **fault** *n* (BrE) (*cf phase-to-ground fault*) ELEC *alternating current* défaut monophasé à la terre *m*

phase-to-ground: ~ **fault** *n* (AmE) (*cf phase-to-earth fault*) ELEC *alternating current* défaut monophasé à la terre *m*

phase-to-neutral: ~ **voltage** *n* (BrE) (*cf line-to-neutral voltage*) ELEC *system* tension phase-neutre *f*

phase-to-phase: ~ **voltage** *n* ELEC tension entre phases *f*, *three-phase system* tension composée *f*

phase-wound: ~ **rotor motor** *n* ELEC moteur à rotor bobiné *m*

phasing *n* ELEC *alternating current* calage *m*, ELECTRON, RECORDING *of loudspeakers* mise en phase *f*; ~ **diagram** *n* TRANSP *traffic control* diagramme des signaux lumineux *m*; ~ **plug** *n* RECORDING dispositif de mise en phase *m*; ~ **signal** *n* ELECTRON signal de mise en phase *m*, TV signal de cadrage *m*; ~ **switch** *n* RECORDING commutateur de mise en phase *m*; ~ **unit** *n* AERONAUT *helicopter* déphaseur *m*

phasor *n* ELEC *waveform* phaseur *m*, TESTING vecteur tournant *m*; ~ **representation** *n* ELEC ENG diagramme de Fresnel *m*

PhC *abbr* (*physical connection*) TELECOM connexion physique *f*

pheelgite *n* MINERAL phengite *f*

phellandrene *n* CHEM phellandrène *m*

phenacetin *n* CHEM phénacétine *f*

phenaceturic *adj* CHEM phénacéturique

phenacite *n* MINERAL phénacite *f*

phenacyl *n* CHEM phénacyle *m*

phenadone *n* CHEM méthadone *f*

phenakite *n* MINERAL phénacite *f*

phenanthraquinone *n* CHEM phénanthraquinone *f*

phenanthrazine *n* CHEM phénanthrazine *f*

phenanthridine *n* CHEM phénanthridine *f*

phenanthridone *n* CHEM phénanthridone *f*

phenanthrol *n* CHEM phénanthrol *m*

phenanthroline *n* CHEM phénanthroline *f*

phenate *n* CHEM phénate *m*

phenazine *n* CHEM phénazine *f*

phenazocine *n* CHEM phénazocine *f*

phenazone *n* CHEM phénazone *f*

phenetidine *n* CHEM phénétidine *f*

phenetole *n* CHEM phénétole *m*

pheniramine *n* CHEM phéniramine *f*

phenoclast[1] *adj* PETR phénoclaste

phenoclast[2] *n* GEOL grand fragment détritique *m*, phénoclaste *m*, PETR grand fragment détritique *m*

phenocryst[1] *adj* GEOL, PETR phénocristal, phénocryste

phenocryst[2] *n* GEOL *igneous petrology*, PETR *igneous petrology* phénoblaste *f*, phénocristal *m*

phenol *n* HYDROL phénol *m*

phenolate *n* CHEM phénate *m*, phénolate *m*

phenolic[1] *adj* CHEM phénolique

phenolic:[2] ~ **plastic** *n* P&R phénoplaste *m*, plastique phénolique *m*, PROP MAT phénoplaste *m*; ~ **resin** *n* ELEC *insulation*, P&R résine phénolique *f*

phenolphthalein *n* CHEM phénolphtaléine *f*

phenolsulfonic *adj* (AmE), **phenolsulphonic** *adj* (BrE) CHEM phénolsulfonique

phenomenal: ~ **wave** *n* OCEANOG vague anormale *f*

phenosafranine *n* CHEM phénosafranine *f*

phenothiazine *n* CHEM phénothiazine *f*, thiodiphénylamine *f*

phenoxazine *n* CHEM phénoxazine *f*

phenoxide *n* CHEM phénolate *m*

phenoxybenzene *n* CHEM oxyde de phényle *m*

phenyl *n* CHEM phényle *m*

phenylacetamide *n* CHEM phénylacétamide *m*

phenylacetic *adj* CHEM phénylacétique

phenylalanine *n* CHEM phénylalanine *f*

phenylamine *n* CHEM aniline *f*, phénylamine *f*, PRINT phénylamine *f*

phenylated *adj* CHEM phénylé

phenylenediamine *n* CHEM phénylènediamine *f*

phenylethylamine *n* CHEM phényléthylamine *f*

phenylethylene *n* CHEM phényléthylène *m*

phenylglycine *n* CHEM phénylglycocolle *m*

phenylglycol *n* CHEM phénylglycol *m*

phenylglycolic *adj* CHEM phénylglycolique

phenylhydrazine *n* CHEM phénylhydrazine *f*

phenylhydrazone *n* CHEM phénylhydrazone *f*

phenylhydroxyacetic *adj* CHEM phénylhydroxyacétique

phenylhydroxylamine *n* CHEM phénylhydroxylamine *f*

phenylic *adj* CHEM phénylique

phenylmethane *n* CHEM phénylméthane *m*

phenylpropiolic *adj* CHEM phénylpropiolique

phenylpyrazole *n* CHEM phénylpyrazol *m*

phenylurea *n* CHEM phénylurée *f*

PHF *abbr* (*peak hour factor*) TRANSP *traffic control* facteur de pointe *m*

phial *n* C&G fiole *f*, CHEM fiole *f*, flacon *m*, LAB EQUIP *glassware* fiole *f*

Phillips: ~ **screw** (TM) *n* MECH ENG vis à empreinte Phillips *f* (MD)

phillipsite *n* MINERAL phillipsite *f*

phlegmatize *vt* MINING désensibiliser, flegmatiser

phlobaphene *n* CHEM phlobaphène *m*
phlogopite *n* MINERAL phlogopite *f*
phloretic *adj* CHEM phlorétique
phloretin *n* CHEM phlorétine *f*
phlorhizin *n* CHEM phloridzine *f*
phloridzin *n* CHEM phloridzine *f*
phlorol *n* CHEM phlorol *m*
phlorrhizin *n* CHEM phloridzine *f*
phoenicite *n* MINERAL phoenicite *f*, phoenicochroïte *f*
phoenicochroite *n* MINERAL phoenicite *f*, phoenico-chroïte *f*
Phoenix *n* ASTRON Phénix *m*
phon *n* ACOUSTICS, PHYS phone *m*
phonation *n* ACOUSTICS phonation *f*
phonecard *n* TELECOM télécarte *f*
phonetic: ~ **power** *n* ACOUSTICS puissance phonétique *f*
phono: ~ **adaptor** *n* RECORDING adaptateur de phonographe *m*; ~ **plug** *n* RECORDING connecteur phonographique *m*, fiche CINCH *m*, fiche RCA *f* (MD)
phonolite *n* PETR phonolite *f*
phonolyte *n* PETR phonolite *f*
phonon *n* PHYS phonon *m*; ~ **gas model** *n* PHYS modèle du gaz de phonons *m*
phonovision *n* OPT phonovision *f*
phorone *n* CHEM phorone *f*
phosgene *n* CHEM oxychlorure de carbone *m*, phosgène *m*, MILIT *chemical warfare* phosgène *m*
phosgenite *n* MINERAL phosgénite *f*
phospham *n* CHEM phospham *m*
phosphatase *n* CHEM phosphatase *f*
phosphate *n* CHEM, DETERGENTS, HYDROL phosphate *m*; ~ **coating** *n* COATINGS couche de phosphate insoluble *f*; ~ **ester** *n* DETERGENTS ester phosphorique *m*, phosphate ester *m*; ~ **of lime** *n* CHEM phosphate de chaux *m*; ~ **opal glass** *n* C&G verre opale au phosphate *m*; ~ **rock** *n* PETR roche phosphatée *f*
phosphated *adj* CHEM phosphaté
phosphatic[1] *adj* CHEM phosphatique, phosphaté
phosphatic:[2] ~ **deposits** *n pl* GEOL dépôts phosphatés *m pl*, dépôts phosphorites *m pl*
phosphation *n* CHEM TECH, DETERGENTS phosphatation *f*
phosphatization *n* CHEM TECH, DETERGENTS phosphatation *f*
phosphide *n* CHEM phosphure *m*
phosphine *n* CHEM phosphine *f*
phosphite *n* CHEM phosphite *m*
phosphocatalysis *n* CHEM phosphocatalyse *f*
phosphochalcite *n* MINERAL phosphorocalcite *f*
phosphoglyceric *adj* CHEM phosphoglycérique
phospholipid *n* FOOD TECH phospholipide *m*
phosphomolybdic *adj* CHEM phosphomolybdique
phosphonium *n* CHEM phosphonium *m*
phosphor *n* CHEM phosphore *m*, ELECTRON luminophore *m*, PHYS substance luminescente *f*; ~ **bronze** *n* CHEM, ELEC, ELEC ENG *in switches* bronze phosphoreux *m*; ~ **dot faceplate** *n* TV écran luminescent à points *m*; ~ **screen** *n* TV écran luminescent *m*; ~ **strip** *n* TV ruban luminescent *m*
phosphorated *adj* CHEM phosphoré
phosphorescence *n* ELECTRON, NAUT *in sea*, PHYS, RAD PHYS phosphorescence *f*, SPACE traînée lumineuse *f*
phosphorescent: ~ **material** *n* ELECTRON substance luminescente *f*, substance phosphorescente *f*; ~ **safety signs** *n pl* SAFETY panonceaux phosphorescents de sûreté *m pl*

phosphoric[1] *adj* CHEM phosphorique
phosphoric:[2] ~ **acid** *n* CHEM acide phosphorique *m*
phosphorite *n* MINERAL phosphorite *f*
phosphorize *vt* CHEM phosphoriser
phosphorized *adj* CHEM phosphoré
phosphorochalcite *n* MINERAL phosphorocalcite *f*
phosphorogenic *adj* CHEM phosphorogène
phosphorus *n* (P) CHEM phosphore *m* (P); ~ **doping** *n* ELECTRON dopage au phosphore *m*
phosphoryl *n* CHEM phosphoryle *m*
phosphorylase *n* CHEM phosphorylase *f*
phosphorylated *adj* CHEM phosphorylé
phosphotungstate *n* CHEM phosphotungstate *m*
phot *n* METR phot *m*
photicon *n* ELECTRON photicon *m*
photo: ~ **chamber** *n* INSTRUMENT chambre photographique *f*; ~ **page** *n* PRINT page d'illustrations *f*
photoactivation: ~ **analysis** *n* RAD PHYS analyse par activation dans les photons gamma *f*
photoactive: ~ **transducer** *n* ELEC ENG transducteur photoactif *m*
photocathode *n* ELEC ENG cathode photoémissive *f*, photocathode *f*, PHYS, TV photocathode *f*
photocell *n* CHEM photocellule *f*, CINEMAT cellule photoélectrique *f*, ELEC cellule photoélectrique *f*, photopile *f*, ELECTRON cellule photoélectrique *f*, PHYS cellule photoélectrique *f*, photopile *f*, PRINT cellule photoélectrique *f*
photochemical[1] *adj* POLLUTION photochimique
photochemical:[2] ~ **decomposition** *n* PROP MAT dégradation photochimique *f*; ~ **effect** *n* FUELLESS effet photochimique *m*; ~ **smog** *n* POLLUTION brouillard photochimique oxydant *m*, smog oxydant *m*, smog photochimique *m*, smog photochimique oxydant *m*
photochemistry *n* CHEM, PHOTO photochimie *f*
photoclinometer *n* PETR photoclinomètre *m*
photocomposer *n* (AmE) *(cf filmset)* PRINT photocompositeur *m*, photocompositeuse *f*
photoconducting: ~ **drum** *n* OPT tambour photoconducteur *m*; ~ **layer** *n* OPT couche photoconductrice *f*
photoconductive[1] *adj* ELECTRON, PHOTO photoconducteur
photoconductive:[2] ~ **cell** *n* ELECTRON cellule photoconductrice *f*, dispositif à photoconduction *m*, PHYS cellule photorésistante *f*; ~ **gain** *n* ELECTRON gain de photoconduction *m*
photoconductivity *n* ELECTRON photoconduction *f*, OPT photoconductivité *f*, PHYS photoconduction *f*, photoconductivité *f*, TELECOM photoconductivité *f*
photo-coupled: ~ **solid-state relay** *n* ELEC ENG relais à couplage optique *m*
photocurrent *n* OPT, TELECOM photocourant *m*
photodecomposition *n* PROP MAT décomposition photochimique *f*
photodetachment *n* NUCLEAR *of electron from negative ion* photodétachement *m*
photodetection *n* ELECTRON photodétection *f*
photodetector *n* ELECTRON détecteur photosensible *m*, photodétecteur *m*, OPT détecteur *m*, photodétecteur *m*
photodiode *n* ELECTRON, OPT, PHOTO, PHYS, TELECOM photodiode *f*; ~ **array** *n* ELECTRON groupement de photodiodes *m*, matrice de photodiodes *f*
photodisintegration *n* PHYS photodésintégration *f*
photodissociation *n* CHEM photodissociation *f*
photoelectric[1] *adj* ELEC photoélectrique

photoelectric:[2] ~ **amplifier** *n* ELECTRON amplificateur photoélectrique *m*; ~ **cell** *n* ELEC cellule photoélectrique *f*, photopile *f*, ELECTRON cellule photoélectrique *f*, PHOTO photocellule *f*, PHYS *(PEC)* cellule photoélectrique *f*, photopile *f*, RAD PHYS *(PEC)*, SPACE *(PEC)*, TV *(PEC)* cellule photoélectrique *f*; ~ **current** *n* ELEC, OPT, TELECOM courant photoélectrique *m*; ~ **detector** *n* TRANSP *traffic control* détecteur photoélectrique *m*; ~ **device** *n* ELECTRON dispositif photoélectrique *m*; ~ **effect** *n* ELECTRON, OPT effet photoélectrique *m*, PHYS effet photoélectrique *m*, effet photoélectronique *m*, RAD PHYS, TELECOM effet photoélectrique *m*; ~ **emission** *n* ELECTRON photoémission *f*, émission photoélectrique *f*; ~ **flame-failure detector** *n* CONTROL contrôleur photoélectrique de flammes *m*; ~ **guard** *n* SAFETY barrière photoélectrique *f*; ~ **layer** *n* COATINGS couche photoélectrique *f*; ~ **light barriers and scanners** *n pl* PACKAGING relais et détecteurs photoélectriques *m pl*; ~ **microscope** *n* INSTRUMENT microscope photoélectrique *m*; ~ **pick-up** *n* RECORDING lecteur phonographique photoélectrique *m*; ~ **receiver** *n* OPT récepteur photoélectrique *m*; ~ **register control** *n* PACKAGING repérage photoélectrique *m*; ~ **relay** *n* ELEC, ELEC ENG relais photoélectrique *m*; ~ **threshold** *n* PHYS seuil photoélectrique *m*; ~ **transducer** *n* ELEC ENG transducteur photoélectrique *m*; ~ **tube** *n* ELECTRON tube photoélectrique *m*

photoelectrically-operated: ~ **relay** *n* ELEC ENG relais à commande photoélectrique *m*

photoelectron *n* ELECTRON photoélectron *m*; ~ **spectroscopy** *n* PROP MAT spectroscopie photoélectronique *f*

photoemission *n* ELECTRON photoémission *f*, TV émission photoélectrique *f*; ~ **electron microscope** *n* INSTRUMENT microscope à émission photo-ionique *m*

photoemissive[1] *adj* PHOTO photoémissif

photoemissive:[2] ~ **effect** *n* OPT photoémission *f*, RAD PHYS effet de rayonnement de photons *m*, TELECOM photoémission *f*; ~ **layer** *n* ELECTRON couche photoémissive *f*

photoengrave *vt* ELECTRON photograver

photoengraving *n* ELECTRON, PRINT photogravure *f*

photoflood *n* CINEMAT lampe survoltée *f*; ~ **bulb** *n* PHOTO lampe à incandescence *f*

photofluorography *n* RAD PHYS, SPACE *nuclear technology* radiophotographie *f*

photogalvanic: ~ **cell** *n* FUELLESS cellule photogalvanique *f*

photogenerator *n* ELEC ENG générateur photoélectrique *m*

photogrammetric: ~ **camera** *n* INSTRUMENT appareil de photogrammétrie *m*

photogrammetry *n* CONST *surveying*, SPACE *spacecraft* photogrammétrie *f*

photograph[1] *n* PHOTO cliché *m*, photo *f*, photographie *f*, PHYS photo *f*, photographie *f*

photograph:[2] ~ **with a tripod** *vt* PHOTO photographier sur pied

photographer *n* PHOTO photographe *m*

photographic: ~ **apparatus** *n* PHOTO matériel photographique *m*; ~ **base paper** *n* PAPER TECH papier support photographique *m*; ~ **equipment** *n* PROP MAT matériel photographique *m*; ~ **exposure** *n* ACOUSTICS lumination *f*; ~ **grain** *n* PRINT grain *m*; ~ **negative** *n* ASTRON *of celestial body* cliché *m*; ~ **plate** *n* INSTRUMENT, PHOTO plaque photographique *f*, PRINT planche photographique *f*; ~ **print** *n* PRINT photographie *f*; ~ **proof** *n*

PRINT épreuve photographique *f*

photogravure: ~ **ink** *n* COLOURS encre pour gravure sur cuivre *f*, encre taille-douce *f*

photohalides *n pl* PHOTO halogénures d'argent *m pl*

photoinitiator *n* P&R photoamorceur *m*

photoionization *n* PHYS photoionisation *f*

photolithography *n* ELECTRON photogravure *f*

photoluminescence *n* RAD PHYS photoluminescence *f*

photolysis *n* CHEM *reaction*, FUELLESS photolyse *f*

photolytic *adj* CHEM *reaction* photolytique

photomask *n* ELECTRON masque de photogravure *m*

photomechanical[1] *adj* PRINT photomécanique

photomechanical:[2] ~ **transfer** *n* PRINT reproduction photomécanique *f*

photometer *n* ASTRON, P&R, PHOTO, PHYS, PROP MAT photomètre *m*

photometric: ~ **binary star** *n* ASTRON étoile binaire photométrique *f*; ~ **brightness** *n* RAD PHYS éclat photométrique *m*; ~ **light source** *n* INSTRUMENT source lumineuse du photomètre *f*

photometry *n* PHYS, PROP MAT photométrie *f*

photomicrogram *n* METALL microphotogramme *m*

photomicrograph *n* METALL micrographie *f*

photomicroscope *n* INSTRUMENT microscope de microphotographie *m*

photomultiplier *n* ELECTRON photomultiplicateur *m*, tube photomultiplicateur *m*, INSTRUMENT cellule à multiplication des électrons *f*, photomultiplicateur *m*, PHYS, RAD PHYS photomultiplicateur *m*

photon *n* OPT, PART PHYS, PHYS, RAD PHYS photon *m*; ~ **amplification** *n* PART PHYS amplification du flux de photons *f*, RAD PHYS amplification des photons *f*; ~ **at 21 cm wavelength** *n* ASTRON photon à la longueur d'ondes de 21 cm *m*; ~ **detector** *n* PART PHYS détecteur de photons *m*; ~ **energy** *n* PART PHYS énergie du photon *f*; ~ **energy classification** *n* ASTRON classification en énergie des photons *f*; ~ **log** *n* PETR diamétreur électronique *m*; ~ **noise** *n* OPT, TELECOM bruit photonique *m*

photon-counting: ~ **camera** *n* PART PHYS caméra à compteur de photons *f*

photon-photon: ~ **absorption** *n* PART PHYS absorption photon-photon *f*

photoplotter *n* COMP, DP phototraceur *m*

photopolymer *n* PRINT photopolymère *m*; ~ **coating** *n* PRINT couche photopolymère *f*

photopolymerization *n* CHEM photopolymérisation *f*

photoreaction *n* CHEM photoréaction *f*

photoresist *n* COLOURS laque photosensible *f*, ELECTRON agent photorésistant *m*, photorésist *m*, résist photosensible *m*; ~ **coating** *n* ELECTRON couche de photorésist *f*

photoresistor *n* RAD PHYS photorésistor *m*

photosensitive[1] *adj* CINEMAT sensible à la lumière, PHOTO, PHYS photosensible

photosensitive:[2] ~ **glass** *n* C&G verre photosensible *m*; ~ **resist** *n* COLOURS laque photosensible *f*; ~ **tube** *n* ELECTRON tube photosensible *m*

photosensitivity *n* ELECTRON, PHYS photosensibilité *f*

photosensor *n* ELECTRON photodétecteur *m*

photosphere *n* ASTRON, SPACE photosphère *f*

photospheric: ~ **absorption** *n* RAD PHYS *solar photosphere* absorption photosphérique *f*

photosynthesis *n* CHEM *reaction*, FUELLESS, HYDROL photosynthèse *f*

photosynthetic: ~ **layer** *n* OCEANOG couche de photosynthèse *f*, zone photosynthétique *f*

phototelegraphy *n* TELECOM phototélécopie *f*

phototheodolite *n* INSTRUMENT chambre métrique universelle de photogrammétrie *f*

phototransistor *n* COMP, DP, ELECTRON, RAD PHYS phototransistor *m*

phototube *n* ELECTRON phototube *m*, tube photoélectrique *m*; **~ relay** *n* ELEC ENG relais photoélectrique à tube *m*

phototypesetting *n* PRINT photocomposition *f*

photovaristor *n* ELEC ENG photorésistance *f*

photovoltaic[1] *adj* SPACE photovoltaïque

photovoltaic:[2] **~ cell** *n* ELEC ENG, FUELLESS photopile *f*, PHYS cellule photovoltaïque *f*, SPACE *spacecraft* cellule photovoltaïque *f*, cellule solaire *f*; **~ current** *n* ELEC ENG courant photovoltaïque *m*; **~ effect** *n* ELEC ENG, FUELLESS, OPT, PHYS, SPACE *spacecraft*, TELECOM effet photovoltaïque *m*; **~ generator** *n* ELEC ENG générateur photovoltaïque *m*; **~ solar power plant** *n* ELEC ENG centrale solaire photovoltaïque *f*

phreatic: **~ level** *n* WATER SUPP niveau de la nappe phréatique *m*

PhS *abbr (physical service)* TELECOM service physique *m*

phthalamide *n* CHEM phtalamide *m*

phthalate *n* CHEM phtalate *m*

phthalein *n* CHEM phtaléine *f*

phthalic[1] *adj* CHEM phtalique

phthalic:[2] **~ anhydride** *n* P&R *raw material* acide phtalique *m*

phthalide *n* CHEM phtalide *m*

phthalin *n* CHEM phtaline *f*

phthalocyanine *n* P&R *pigment* phtalocyanine *f*

phugoid *n* AERONAUT phugoïde *m*; **~ effect** *n* AERONAUT effet phugoïde *m*; **~ oscillation** *n* AERONAUT oscillation longitudinale de longue période *f*, oscillation phugoïde *f*

phycology *n* OCEANOG phycologie *f*

phyllite *n* GEOL phyllade *m*, phyllite *f*, PETR phyllite *f*

phyllitic: **~ marble** *n* GEOL marbre phylliteux *m*

phyllonite *n* GEOL mylonite recristallisée *f*

phyric *adj* GEOL *igneous petrology* phyrique

physalite *n* MINERAL physalite *f*

physical[1] *adj* COMP, DP, TELECOM physique

physical:[2] **~ agent** *n* POLLUTION agent physique *m*; **~ balance** *n* LAB EQUIP trébuchet *m*; **~ circuit** *n* ELEC ENG circuit physique *m*; **~ connection** *n* (*PhC*) TELECOM connexion physique *f*; **~ delivery** *n* (*PD*) TELECOM remise physique *f*; **~ delivery access unit** *n* (*PDAU*) TELECOM unité d'accès au service de remise physique *f*, unité d'accès de remise physique *f*; **~ delivery system** *n* (*PDS*) TELECOM système de remise physique *m*; **~ file** *n* COMP, DP fichier physique *m*; **~ helical editing** *n* TV montage manuel pour magnétoscope hélicoïdal *m*; **~ interface** *n* (*PI*) TELECOM interface physique *f*; **~ layer** *n* DP *open systems interconnection*, TELECOM couche physique *f*; **~ layer operations and maintenance** *n* (*PL-OAM*) TELECOM *cell* cellule OAM de la couche physique *f*, cellule OAM de la physique *f*; **~ layer protocol** *n* COMP, DP protocole de la couche physique *m*; **~ layer service** *n* (*PLS*) TELECOM service de la couche physique *m*; **~ medium** *n* TELECOM média physique *m*; **~ medium sublayer** *n* TELECOM sous-couche de support physique *f*, support physique *m*; **~ memory** *n* ELEC ENG mémoire physique *f*; **~ optics** *n* OPT optique ondulatoire *f*, optique physique *f*, PHYS, TELECOM

optique physique *f*; **~ properties** *n pl* PHYS propriétés physiques *f pl*; **~ quadruplex editing** *n* TV montage manuel pour magnétoscope à quatre têtes *m*; **~ record** *n* COMP, DP enregistrement physique *m*; **~ security** *n* TELECOM sécurité physique *f*; **~ service** *n* (*PhS*) TELECOM service physique *m*; **~ vapor deposition** *n* (AmE), **~ vapour deposition** *n* (BrE) PROP MAT *coating technology* dépôt en phase gazeuse par procédé physique *m*; **~ water treatment** *n* WATER SUPP traitement physique de l'eau *m*

physicochemical: **~ environment** *n* POLLUTION environnement physiochimique *m*

physiochemistry *n* CHEM chimie physiologique *f*

physiological: **~ effects** *n pl* SAFETY *human body, occupational hazards* effets physiologiques *m pl*; **~ noise** *n* ACOUSTICS bruit physiologique *m*

physostigmine *n* CHEM physostigmine *f*

phytase *n* FOOD TECH *milling and baking* phytase *f*

phytic: **~ acid** *n* FOOD TECH *milling and baking* acide phytique *m*

phytin *n* FOOD TECH *baking* phytine *f*

phytocidal *adj* CHEM phytocide

phytoplankton: **~ bloom** *n* OCEANOG poussée phytoplanctonique *f*

phytotoxic *adj* CHEM phytotoxique

pi: **~ bond** *n* CHEM *covalent* liaison pi *f*; **~ characters** *n pl* PRINT caractères casseaux *m pl*, caractères inhabituels *m pl*; **~ network** *n* ELEC ENG, PHYS réseau pi *m*; **~ types** *n pl* PRINT caractères inhabituels *m pl*, caractères personnalisés *m pl*; **~ winding** *n* ELEC ENG enroulement en épingle à cheveux *m*

PI *abbr* TELECOM (*presentation indicator*) indicateur de présentation *m*, TELECOM (*physical interface*) interface physique *f*

piano: **~ wire** *n* MECH ENG corde de piano *f*

piazetta *n* CONST *planning* placette *f*

pica *n* PRINT *type size* pica *m*

piccolo: **~ burner** *n* C&G brûleur de pied de feuille *m*

pick[1] *n* C&G débouchoir *m*, MINING *of coal-cutting machine* fleuret *m*, PROD ENG pic *m*, pioche *f*, TEXTILES duite *f*; **~ breaker** *n* COAL TECH concasseur à pointes *m*; **~ hammer** *n* PROD ENG marteau piqueur *m*, marteau à pioche *m*; **~ handle** *n* CONST bois d'une pioche *m*, PROD ENG manche de pic *m*; **~ list** *n* PROD ENG bordereau d'approvisionnement *m*, liste à servir *f*; **~ mattock** *n* PROD ENG décintroir à talus *m*; **~ rate** *n* TEXTILES taux de l'insertion de la trame *m*; **~ resistance** *n* PAPER TECH résistance à l'arrachage *f*

pick[2] *vt* CONST piocher, *lock* crocheter, PAPER TECH arracher; **~ up** *vt* TELECOM capter

pick:[3] **~ up a mooring** *vi* NAUT saisir la bouée

pick-and-claw: **~ crowbar** *n* CONST levier à pied-de-biche et à pointe *m*

pickax *n* (AmE), **pickaxe** *n* (BrE) CONST pioche *f*, PROD ENG pioche de terrassier *f*, pioche ordinaire *f*, pioche à bec plat et pointu *f*

picked: **~ ore** *n* MINING klaubés *m pl*

picker *n* MINING aiguille *f*, épinglette *f*, *ore-dressing, person* klaubeur *m*

picket *n* CONST *surveying* jalon *m*, piquet *m*

picking *n* CONST piochage *m*, piochement *m*, PAPER TECH, PRINT arrachage *m*, TEXTILES arrachage de fibre *m*; **~ of arrivals** *n* GEOL pointé des arrivées *m*; **~ belt** *n* MINING toile de triage *f*; **~ down** *n* C&G débouchage et réamorçage *m*; **~ list** *n* PROD ENG bordereau d'approvisionnement *m*, liste à servir *f*; **~ resistance** *n* PAPER

TECH arrachage *m*; ~ **stock** *n* PROD ENG stock disponible *m*; ~ **table** *n* MINING table de triage *f*

pickle *n* OCEANOG saumure *f*

pickling *n* CHEM décapage *m*, décapage à l'acide *m*, CONST *surface preparation* décapage chimique *m*, NAUT *ship maintenance* décapage *m*; ~ **brine** *n* OCEANOG saumure *f*

picks: ~ **per inch** *n* TEXTILES duites par pouce *f pl*

pick-up *n* AUTO reprise *f*, ELEC *measurement* capteur *m*, MECH ENG fixation *f*, reprise *f*, NUCLEAR capteur *m*, PAPER TECH feutre preneur *m*, prise automatique *f*, RECORDING lecteur *m*, pick-up *m*, TRANSP *electrically-powered transport systems* captation de courant *f*; ~ **angle** *n* MECH ENG cornière de reprise *f*, PRINT angle d'incidence *m*, angle de visualisation *m*; ~ **arm** *n* ACOUSTICS bras de lecture *m*, RECORDING bras de pickup *m*; ~ **fitting** *n* MECH ENG ferrure de reprise *f*; ~ **for contact meter** *n* MECH ENG capteur des profilomètres d'état de surface de contact *m*; ~ **freight train** *n* (AmE) *(cf pick-up goods train)* RAIL *vehicles* train collecteur *m*; ~ **gear** *n* MECH ENG pignon à ergot *m*; ~ **goods train** *n* (BrE) *(cf pick-up freight train, way freight train)* RAIL *vehicles* train collecteur *m*; ~ **head** *n* ACOUSTICS tête de lecture *f*; ~ **roll** *n* PAPER TECH feutre preneur *m*, rouleau leveur aspirant *m*, PRINT rouleau d'alimentation *m*, rouleau preneur *m*, rouleau ramasse-pétouilles *m*; ~ **transmitter** *n* TV émetteur lié à la caméra *m*; ~ **truck** *n* (AmE) *(cf pick-up van)* TRANSP camion plate-forme *m*; ~ **tube** *n* ELECTRON tube analyseur *m*, TV tube analyseur *m*, tube de caméra *m*; ~ **van** *n* (BrE) *(cf pick-up truck)* TRANSPORT camion plate-forme *m*; ~ **voltage** *n* ELEC ENG tension d'appel *f*

pico- *pref (p)* METR pico-*(p)*

picoline *n* CHEM picoline *f*

picosecond *n* COMP, DP picoseconde *f*; ~ **pulse** *n* PART PHYS impulsion d'une durée de l'ordre de la picoseconde *f*

picotite *n* MINERAL picotite *f*

picrate *n* CHEM picrate *m*

picric *adj* CHEM picrique *n*

picrite *n* PETR picrite *f*

picrol *n* CHEM picrol *m*

picrolite *n* MINERAL picrolite *f*

picromerite *n* MINERAL picromérite *f*

picrotin *n* CHEM picrotine *f*

picryl *n* CHEM picryle *m*

PICS *abbr (protocol implementation conformance statement)* TELECOM déclaration de conformité de mise en oeuvre du protocole *f*

pictograph *n* PRINT pictographe *m*

Pictor *n* ASTRON Chevalet du Peintre *m*

pictorial: ~ **symbols** *n pl* SAFETY *hazardous substances* symboles en images *m pl*

picture *n* COMP, DP image *f*, PHOTO cliché *m*, image *f*, TV image *f*; ~ **book** *n* PRINT livre d'images *m*; ~ **breakup** *n* TV cassure d'image *f*; ~ **carrier** *n* ELECTRON porteuse image *f*, porteuse vidéo *f*; ~ **clap** *n* CINEMAT claquette image *f*; ~ **compression** *n* TV compression d'image *f*; ~ **definition** *n* TELECOM définition d'image *f*; ~ **dot** *n* PRINT point de trame *m*; ~ **drift** *n* TV oscillation d'image *f*; ~ **fading** *n* CINEMAT affaiblissement d'image *m*; ~ **failure** *n* TV perte d'image *f*; ~ **flutter** *n* TV pompage *m*; ~ **frame** *n* TV trame d'image *f*; ~ **framing** *n* P&R *paint defect* moirure *f*; ~ **gate** *n* CINEMAT fenêtre d'image *f*; ~ **glass** *n* C&G verre pour encadrement *m*; ~ **head** *n* CINEMAT bloc optique *m*; ~ **library** *n* PHOTO archives

photographiques *f pl*; ~ **lock** *n* TV asservissement automatique *m*; ~ **match** *n* TV équilibrage des caméras *m*; ~ **monitor** *n* TV moniteur *m*, écran témoin *m*; ~ **processing** *n* COMP, DP traitement d'images *m*; ~ **ratio** *n* CINEMAT format de l'image *m*, rapport des dimensions de l'image *m*; ~ **reel** *n* CINEMAT bobine image *f*; ~ **safety area** *n* CINEMAT cadrage visible à l'écran *m*; ~ **shift** *n* TV déplacement de l'image *m*; ~ **signal** *n* ELECTRON signal image *m*, signal vidéo *m*, TELECOM signal vidéo *m*; ~ **size** *n* PHOTO format de l'image *m*; ~ **slip** *n* CINEMAT décrochage d'image *m*, désynchronisation *f*; ~ **strip** *n* PRINT ligne d'analyse *f*, ligne de balayage *f*; ~ **synchronizer** *n* CINEMAT synchroniseuse d'images *f*; ~ **tube** *n* ELECTRON tube image *m*

picture-cueing: ~ **mark** *n* CINEMAT marque de mixage sur copie *f*

pie: ~ **chart** *n* DP camembert *m*, graphique circulaire *m*, graphique à secteurs *m*, diagramme à secteurs *m*, MATH graphique circulaire *m*; ~ **section** *n* ELEC ENG galette élémentaire *f*; ~ **winding** *n* ELEC ENG bobinage en plusieurs galettes *m*

piece: ~ **accent** *n* (AmE) *(cf loose accent)* PRINT accent superposé *m*, accent séparé *m*; ~ **goods** *n* TEXTILES tissu en pièce *m*

piece-dyed *adj* TEXTILES teint en pièce

piedmontite *n* MINERAL piémontite *f*

pier *n* CONST *masonry support of arch* pied-droit *m*, *of bridge, stone* masse *f*, masse de port *f*, pile de port *f*, *of bridge, timber* palée de port *f*, NAUT *jetty, breakwater* jetée *f*, quai *m*; ~ **head** *n* NAUT, OCEANOG musoir *m*

pierce *vt* PROD ENG *mould* épingler, *vent holes* tirer

Pierce: ~ **oscillator** *n* ELECTRON oscillateur Pierce *m*

piercer *n* MECH ENG *bow drill* boîte à forets *f*, foret à arçon *m*, touret *m*, PROD ENG *vent wire* aiguille à trous d'air *f*

piercing *n* PROD ENG *venting* épinglage *m*; ~ **die** *n* MECH ENG *press tools* outil de perçage pour presse *m*, outillage d'ajourage pour presse *m*

piezoelectric[1] *adj* CRYSTALL, ELEC ENG piézoélectrique

piezoelectric:[2] ~ **crystal** *n* ELEC ENG, PROP MAT, TELECOM cristal piézoélectrique *m*; ~ **crystal filter** *n* RAD PHYS filtre piézoélectrique *m*; ~ **detector** *n* TRANSP *traffic control* détecteur piézoélectrique *m*; ~ **effect** *n* ELEC ENG, PHYS, PROP MAT effet piézoélectrique *m*; ~ **element** *n* ELEC ENG élément piézoélectrique *m*; ~ **loudspeaker** *n* RECORDING haut-parleur piézoélectrique *m*; ~ **microphone** *n* ACOUSTICS, RECORDING microphone piézoélectrique *m*; ~ **oscillator** *n* ELEC, ELEC ENG, PHYS oscillateur piézoélectrique *m*; ~ **pick-up** *n* MECH ENG capteur piézoélectrique *m*; ~ **properties** *n pl* ELEC ENG propriétés piézoélectriques *f pl*; ~ **resonator** *n* ELEC ENG résonateur piézoélectrique *m*; ~ **sensor** *n* OPT capteur piézosensible *m*; ~ **substrate** *n* ELEC ENG substrat piézoélectrique *m*; ~ **transducer** *n* ELEC ENG transducteur piézoélectrique *m*

piezoelectricity *n* CRYSTALL, ELEC ENG piézoélectricité *f*

piezoelectric-tuned: ~ **magnetron** *n* ELEC ENG magnétron à accord piézoélectrique *m*

piezometer *n* COAL TECH, CONST piézomètre *m*

piezometric: ~ **head** *n* PETR TECH niveau piézométrique *m*; ~ **map** *n* PETR TECH carte piézométrique *f*; ~ **pressure curve** *n* HYDR EQUIP courbe piézométrique *f*

piezomicrophone *n* ACOUSTICS microphone piézoélectrique *m*

pig *n* PETR piston racleur *m*, racleur *m*, scraper *m*, PETR TECH cochonnet *m*, piston racleur *m*, racleur *m*, ramoneur *m*, PROD ENG fonte *f*, fonte en gueuse *f*, fonte en saumon *f*, gueuse de fonte *f*, *founding* gueuse *f*, saumon *m*; ~ **bed** *n* PROD ENG aire de coulée *f*, lit de gueuse *m*; ~ **boiling** *n* PROD ENG puddlage bouillant *m*, puddlage chaud *m*, puddlage gras *m*, puddlage par bouillonnement *m*; ~ **iron** *n* PROD ENG fonte *f*, fonte en gueuse *f*, fonte en saumon *f*, gueuse de fonte *f*; ~ **of iron** *n* PROD ENG saumon de fonte *m*; ~ **iron breaker** *n* PROD ENG casse-gueuse *m*; ~ **iron yard** *n* PROD ENG *foundry* parc à fonte *m*; ~ **lead** *n* PROD ENG plomb en saumon *m*; ~ **of lead** *n* PROD ENG *founding* saumon de plomb *m*; ~ **metal** *n* PROD ENG métal en gueuse *m*, métal en saumon *m*; ~ **mold** *n* (AmE), ~ **mould** *n* (BrE) PROD ENG gueuse *f*, lit de coulée *m*, lit de gueuse *m*, moule de gueuses *m*, moule à saumons *m*; ~ **yard** *n* PROD ENG *foundry* parc à fonte *m*

pig-and-ore: ~ **process** *n* PROD ENG procédé à la fonte et au minerai *m*

pigeon: ~ **hole** *n* C&G regard de visite latéral *m*

pigeonite *n* MINERAL pigeonite *f*

piggyback *n* TRANSP ferroutage *m*; ~ **satellite** *n* SPACE *craft* satellite additionnel *m*; ~ **traffic** *n* RAIL, TRANSP ferroutage *m*; ~ **transport** *n* TRANSP ferroutage *m*

pigment[1] *n* C&G, CHEM, COLOURS, P&R *paint*, TEXTILES pigment *m*; ~ **dyeing** *n* COLOURS teinture pigmentaire *f*

pigment[2] *vt* TEXTILES pigmenter

pigmentation *n* TEXTILES pigmentation *f*

pigmented *adj* COLOURS pigmenté

pigskin *n* PRINT peau de porc *f*

pigtail *n* ELEC ENG queue de cochon *f*, NUCLEAR tuyau d'amenée *m*; ~ **hook** *n* PROD ENG crochet en queue de cochon *m*

pile[1] *n* COAL TECH pieu *m*, CONST *heap* amas *m*, monceau *m*, pile *f*, tas *m*, *pointed timber* pieu *m*, pilot *m*, ELEC ENG pile *f*, NUCLEAR pile nucléaire *f*, réacteur *m*, réacteur nucléaire *m*, PRINT pile *f*, PROD ENG *fagot* paquet *m*, TEXTILES poil *m*; ~ **block** *n* COAL TECH rallonge de pieu *f*; ~ **board** *n* PRINT plateau *m*, porte-piles *m*; ~ **cap** *n* COAL TECH, CONST chapeau de pieu *m*; ~ **cutoff level** *n* COAL TECH niveau d'arasement de pieu *m*, CONST niveau de recépage de pieux *m*; ~ **drawer** *n* CONST arrache-pieux *m*; ~ **driver** *n* CONST hie *f*, mouton *m*, mouton comprimé *m*, sonneur *m*, sonnettef; ~ **driving** *n* COAL TECH battage de pieux *m*, CONST battage de pieux *m*, battage de pilots *m*, enfoncement de pilots *m*, moutonnage *m*, pilotage *m*; ~ **extractor** *n* CONST arrache-pieux *m*, extracteur des pieux *m*; ~ **ferrule** *n* CONST frette de pieu *f*; ~ **footing** *n* COAL TECH semelle de pieu *f*; ~ **groin** *n* (AmE) *(cf pile groyne)* WATER SUPP épi en pieux *m*; ~ **group** *n* COAL TECH faisceau de pieux *m*, groupe de pieux *m*; ~ **groyne** *n* (BrE) *(cf pile groin)* WATER SUPP épi en pieux *m*; ~ **hammer** *n* (AmE) *(cf piling hammer)* COAL TECH dame *f*, mouton *m*, CONST mouton *m*, mouton de battage *m*; ~ **head** *n* COAL TECH tête de pieu *f*; ~ **height** *n* TEXTILES hauteur de poil *f*; ~ **hoop** *n* CONST frette de pieu *f*; ~ **joint** *n* COAL TECH joint de pieu *m*; ~ **length** *n* COAL TECH longueur de pieu *f*; ~ **plank** *n* CONST palplanche *f*; ~ **point** *n* COAL TECH pointe de pieu *f*; ~ **ram** *n* COAL TECH mouton *m*; ~ **scanner** *n* PRINT détecteur électronique de hauteur de pile *m*; ~ **segment** *n* COAL TECH élément de pieu *m*; ~ **shoe** *n* COAL TECH sabot *m*, CONST sabot de pieu *m*; ~ **situation plan** *n* COAL TECH plan de disposition des pieux *m*; ~ **splice** *n* COAL TECH joint de pieu *m*; ~ **tip** *n* COAL TECH pointe de pieu *f*; ~ **weight** *n* TEXTILES poids de poil *m*; ~ **work** *n* CONST pilotage *m*

pile[2] *vt* CONST *drive piles into* piloter, PROD ENG *fagot* paqueter; ~ **up** *vt* PAPER TECH empiler

pile-driver *n* COAL TECH sonnette *f*

pile-driving: ~ **formula** *n* COAL TECH formule de battage *f*; ~ **record** *n* COAL TECH rapport de battage de pieux *m*

piles *n pl* NAUT *mooring* poteaux *m pl*

pile-up *n* ELEC ENG bloc de contacts *m*

pile-wound: ~ **coil** *n* ELEC enroulement en disque *m*

pilferproof *n* PACKAGING fermeture antivol *f*; ~ **seal** *n* PACKAGING garniture antivol *f*

piling *n* COAL TECH mise en place de pieux *f*, CONST *driving piles* pilotage *m*, *of piles collectively* pieux *m pl*, pilots *m pl*, *stacking* empilage *m*, empilement *m*, PETR TECH pieux en acier *m pl*, PRINT glaçage *m*, PROD ENG empilage *m*, entassement *m*, empilement *m*, *fagotting* paquetage *m*; ~ **frame** *n* CONST sonnette *f*; ~ **hammer** *n* *(cf drop hammer, pile hammer)* CONST marteau de battage *m*, mouton *m*, mouton de battage *m*; ~ **up** *n* CONST empilage *m*, empilement *m*, CRYSTALL empilement *m*, PAPER TECH empilage *m*

pill *vt* TEXTILES boullocher

pillar *n* C&G pilier *m*, CONST colonne *f*, pilier *m*, *pier of arch* pied-droit *m*, GEOPHYS pilier *m*, MINING *coal, ore, barren rock* lopin *m*, massif *m*, pilier *m*, NAUT *shipbuilding* épontille *f*, TELECOM point de distribution secondaire *m*, TRANSP *road, rail* support de la voie *m*; ~ **arch** *n* C&G arcade *f*; ~ **balance** *n* CONST balance à colonne *f*; ~ **buoy** *n* NAUT *navigation mark* bouée à fuseau *f*; ~ **drawing** *n* COAL TECH enlèvement des piliers *m*; ~ **drill** *n* MECH ENG machine à percer montée sur colonne *f*; ~ **drilling machine** *n* MECH ENG machine à percer montée sur colonne *f*; ~ **extraction** *n* COAL TECH dépilage des piliers *m*; ~ **fire hydrant** *n* SAFETY borne d'incendie *f*; ~ **hand rest** *n* CONST *wood-turning lathe* support à main *m*; ~ **hydrant** *n* MECH ENG colonne d'incendie *f*; ~ **scales** *n pl* LAB EQUIP *balance* balance à colonne *f*; ~ **stand** *n* INSTRUMENT potence à colonne *f*, statif à colonne *m*, support à colonne *m*; ~ **working** *n* COAL TECH déhouillement des piliers *m*, enlèvement des piliers *m*

pillbox *n* MILIT fortin *m*

pilling *n* TEXTILES boullochage *m*

pillion *n* VEHICLES *motorcycle* siège arrière *m*

pillow *n* MECH ENG palier *m*, support *m*, *of bearing brush* coussinet *m*, dé *m*, *of pillow block, plummer block* corps *m*; ~ **block** *n* MECH ENG palier *m*, support *m*; ~ **distortion** *n* CINEMAT distorsion en coussinet *f*; ~ **lava** *n* GEOL lave en coussins *f*

pilocarpidine *n* CHEM pilocarpidine *f*

pilocarpine *n* CHEM pilocarpine *f*

pilot[1] *n* AERONAUT *aviation, marine* commandant de bord *m*, pilote *m*, CONTROL pilote de commande *m*, pilote de régulation *m*, NAUT *navigation* pilote *m*, RAIL *vehicles* chasse-bestiaux *m*, TELECOM pilote *m*, TV programme pilote *m*; ~ **balloon** *n* AERONAUT ballon pilote *m*, ballon-sonde *m*; ~ **bearing** *n* AUTO roulement pilote *m*, roulement-guide *m*; ~ **bit** *n* PETR TECH trépan pilote *m*; ~ **boat** *n* NAUT bateau-pilote *m*; ~ **bushing** *n* AUTO bague-guide *f*; ~ **carrier** *n* TELECOM porteuse pilote *f*; ~ **chart** *n* NAUT *navigation* carte de route *f*; ~ **claw** *n* CINEMAT contre-griffe *f*; ~ **cutter** *n* NAUT bateau-pilote *m*; ~ **flag** *n* NAUT pavillon de pilote *m*; ~ **flame** *n* MECH ENG brûleur d'allumage *m*, pilote d'allumage *m*; ~ **frequency** *n* CINEMAT fréquence pilote *f*; ~ **hole** *n* MECH ENG avant-trou *m*, trou pilote *m*, PETR avant-trou *m*; ~ **lamp** *n* (AmE) *(cf pilot light)* CINEMAT lampe témoin *f*, voyant *m*, ELEC ENG lampe témoin *f*, GAS TECH veilleuse *f*, VEHICLES *accessory* lampe témoin *f*, témoin *m*; ~ **light** *n* (BrE) *(cf pilot lamp)* CINEMAT lampe témoin *f*, ELEC ENG lampe témoin *f*, GAS TECH veilleuse *f*, VEHICLES *accessory* lampe témoin *f*, témoin *m*; ~ **network** *n* ELEC *supply* réseau pilote *m*; ~ **plant** *n* COAL TECH usine pilote *f*; ~ **pressure chamber** *n* AERONAUT chambre d'asservissement *f*; ~ **project** *n* PETR TECH projet pilote *m*; ~ **signal** *n* TV signal de commande *m*; ~ **switch** *n* ELEC interrupteur terminal *m*; ~ **system** *n* RECORDING système pilote *m*; ~ **test** *n* COAL TECH essai pilote *m*; ~ **tone** *n* RECORDING tonalité pilote *f*, TV fréquence pilote *f*; ~ **tone cable** *n* CINEMAT câble de fréquence pilote *m*; ~ **tone generator** *n* CINEMAT générateur de fréquence pilote *m*; ~ **tone sound** *n* CINEMAT son piloté *m*; ~ **valve** *n* MECH ENG clapet pilote *m*; ~ **waters** *n* NAUT zone de pilotage *f*; ~ **wheel** *n* MECH ENG *hand wheel with radial handles, as on lathe* volant à poignées radiales *m*; ~ **wire** *n* ELEC ENG fil pilote *m*

pilot[2] *vt* AERONAUT, NAUT piloter

pilot's: ~ **console** *n* AERONAUT banquette de poste de pilotage *f*

pilotage *n* NAUT navigation côtière *f*, pilotage *m*, OCEA-NOG navigation côtière *f*; ~ **waters** *n pl* OCEANOG zone de pilotage *f*; ~ **zone** *n* OCEANOG zone de pilotage *f*

pilotless: ~ **target aircraft** *n* MILIT avion-cible *m*; ~ **target plane** *n* MILIT avion-cible *m*

pilotone *n* CINEMAT fréquence pilote *f*

pilot-operated: ~ **check valve** *n* PROD ENG clapet anti-retour piloté *m*

pimaric *adj* CHEM pimarique

pimelic *adj* CHEM pimélique

pimelite *n* MINERAL pimélite *f*

pi-meson *n* (*pion*) PART PHYS méson pi *m* (*pion*)

p-i-n: ~ **diode** *n* PHYS diode PIN *f*

pin *n* CINEMAT griffe *f*, CONST *of hinge* broche *f*, cheville *f*, goujon *m*, lacet *m*, rivure *f*, tourillon *m*, ELEC ENG patte *f*, picot *m*, *electronic tubes* broche *f*, *of cap of bayonet lamp* ergot *m*, *of plug* fiche *f*, MECH broche *f*, goupille *f*, MECH ENG boulon *m*, cheville *f*, clavette *f*, goupille *f*, *of pivot* pivot *m*, PAPER TECH clavette *f*, PROD ENG broche *f*, douille *f*, *of foundry flask* goujon *m*; ~ **assignment** *n* PROD ENG affectation des broches *f*; ~ **chain** *n* CONST chaîne à fuseau *f*; ~ **connector** *n* CINEMAT connecteur à broches *m*; ~ **coupling** *n* MECH ENG manchon à toc *m*; *of cross-head* *n* HYDR EQUIP *steam engine* tourillon de crosse *m*; ~ **drift** *n* MECH ENG chasse-goupille *m*; ~ **drill** *n* MECH ENG foret à téton cylindrique *m*; ~ **driver** *n* MECH *tools* chasse-goupille *m*; ~ **extractor** *n* MECH ENG *split pins* retire-goupille *m*, tire-goupille *m*; ~ **frame** *n* TEXTILES rame à picots *f*; ~ **insulator** *n* ELEC isolateur tige *m*, ELEC ENG isolateur rigide *m*, isolateur support *m*; ~ **movement** *n* CINEMAT système à griffe *m*; ~ **punch** *n* CONST chasse-goupille *m*, repoussoir *m*; ~ **rack** *n* CINEMAT râtelier *m*; ~ **register** *n* PRINT repérage à tétons *m*; ~ **registration** *n* CINEMAT alignement par griffe *m*; ~ **screen animation** *n* CINEMAT animation sur écran d'épingles *f*; ~ **shears** *n pl* CONST cisailles à goupilles *f pl*; ~ **spanner** *n* (BrE) *(cf pin wrench)* CONST clef à encoches *f*, clef à griffes *f*, MECH ENG clé à ergot *f*; ~ **stenter** *n* TEXTILES rame à picots *f*; ~ **termination** *n* PROD ENG terminaison à broches *f*; ~ **valve** *n* CONST pointeau *m*; ~ **vice** *n* (BrE) CONST étau à main *m*, étau à queue *f*; ~ **vise** *n* (AmE) *see pin vice* ~ **weir** *n* WATER SUPP barrage à aiguilles *m*; ~ **wrench** *n* (AmE) *(cf pin spanner)* CONST clef à

encoches *f*, clef à griffes *f*, MECH ENG clé à ergot *f*

PIN: ~ **attenuator diode** *n* ELECTRON diode atténuatrice PIN *f*; ~ **diode** *n* ELECTRON diode PIN *f*; ~ **diode attenuator** *n* ELECTRON atténuateur à diode PIN *m*; ~ **diode modulation** *n* ELECTRON modulation par diode PIN *f*; ~ **photodiode** *n* ELECTRON, OPT, TELECOM photodiode PIN *f*

pinacol *n* CHEM pinacol *m*

pinacolic *adj* CHEM pinacolique

pinacoline *n* CHEM pinacoline *f*

pinacolone *n* CHEM pinacoline *f*

pinacone *n* CHEM pinacol *m*

pinboard *n* ELEC ENG matrice de programmation *f*

pincers *n pl* CONST tenaille *f*, tenailles *f pl*, tricoises *f pl*

pinch *n* MINING *vein, lode* resserrement *m*, serrement *m*, serrée *f*, étranglement *m*, étranglement de terre *m*, étreinte *f*; ~ **and swell** *n* GEOL boudinage *m*; ~ **cock** *n* CHEM pince d'arrêt *f*, CONST pince *f*, pince universelle *f*; ~ **effect** *n* ACOUSTICS effet de pince *m*, PHYS effet de pincement *m*, effet de striction *m*; ~ **nut** *n* MECH ENG contre-écrou *m*; ~ **point** *n* MECH ENG *handling equipment* point de coincement *m*; ~ **roller** *n* CINEMAT galet presseur *m*, rouleau presseur *m*, PRINT pinceurs *m pl*, rouleau *m*, rouleau premier pli *m*

pinched: ~ **resistor** *n* ELEC ENG résistance à base pincée *f*; ~ **thread** *n* C&G filet rentré *m*

pinchers *n pl* C&G pinces à bec *f pl*

pinching: ~ **bar** *n* CONST pince à talon *f*; ~ **tools** *n pl* C&G fers à étrangler *m pl*

pinch-off: ~ **effect** *n* ELECTRON effet de pincement *m*

pinch-out: ~ **trap** *n* PETR TECH biseautage *m*

pincushion: ~ **distortion** *n* CINEMAT, PHOTO distorsion en coussinet *f*, PHYS distorsion en coussin *f*, TV distorsion en coussinet *f*

PIN-diode: ~ **phase shifter** *n* ELECTRON déphaseur à diode PIN *m*

pine: ~ **oil** *n* DETERGENTS essence de pin *f*

pinene *n* CHEM pinène *m*

PIN-FET: ~ **integrated receiver** *n* OPT, TELECOM récepteur intégré PIN-TEC *m*

pinger *n* OCEANOG générateur d'impulsions sous-marines *m*

pinging *n* (AmE) *cf pinking* AUTO cliquetis *m*, VEHICLES *engine* cliquetage *m*, cliquetis *m*

pinhole *n* CINEMAT trou d'épingle *m*, P&R *paint defect* piqûre d'épingle *f*, PAPER TECH clavette *f*, presse lisse *f*, trou d'épingle *m*, PHOTO, PHYS *optics* sténopé *m*; ~ **camera** *n* PHOTO chambre à sténopé *f*; ~ **photography** *n* PHOTO photographie sténopéique *f*

pinic *adj* CHEM pinique

pinion *n* AUTO pignon *m*, MECH ENG engrenage *m*, pignon *m*, VEHICLES *gearbox* pignon *m*; ~ **gear** *n* AUTO pignon d'attaque *m*, VEHICLES *differential* satellite *m*; ~ **knob** *n* GEOPHYS bouton de mise au point *m*; ~ **shaft flange** *n* AUTO flasque d'arbre du pignon *m*, VEHICLES *transmission* flasque d'arbre d'attaque *m*; ~ **web** *n* MECH ENG toile d'araignée *f*; ~ **wheel** *n* MECH ENG roue à pignon *f*

pinion-cutting: ~ **machine** *n* MECH ENG machine à tailler les pignons *f*

pinite *n* MINERAL pinite *f*

pink:[1] ~ **coloration** *n* COLOURS teinture rose *f*; ~ **glass** *n* C&G rosaline *f*; ~ **noise** *n* ACOUSTICS, PHYS, RECORDING bruit rose *m*; ~ **salt** *n* CHEM sel rose *m*; ~ **topaz** *n* MINERAL topaze rose *f*

pink[2] *vt* MECH ENG croquer

pinked: ~ **edge** n MECH ENG bord croqué m

pinking n (BrE) ~ **shears** n MECH ENG tool ciseaux à cranter m

pinned: ~ **key** n CONST locksmithing clef bénarde f; ~ **key lock** n CONST bénarde f, serrure bénarde f; ~ **tenon joint** n CONST assemblage à tenon avec cheville m, assemblage à tenon passant avec clef m

pinning n CRYSTALL of dislocation ancrage m, blocage m, METALL ancrage m

pinning-up: ~ **device** n TEXTILES dispositif d'accrochage sur picots m

pinonic adj CHEM pinonique

pinpoint[1] n AERONAUT point identifié m, position identifiée f, TRANSP traffic control position identifiée f; ~ **acoustic source** n ACOUSTICS source acoustique ponctuelle f

pinpoint[2] vt MECH ENG localiser

pins n PRINT pointures f pl

pint n METR British, US imperial liquid measure pinte f

pintle n CONST of gate lock tête f, of lock broche f, MECH ENG king pin cheville ouvrière f, pivot central m, NAUT of rudder aiguillot m; ~ **chain** n MECH ENG chaîne avec axes sans douilles f, chaîne en mailles d'acier moulé à goujons f, chaîne à articulations f; ~ **injection nozzle** n AUTO injecteur à jeton m

pin-to-pin: ~ **breakdown** n ELEC ENG claquage entre broches m; ~ **capacitance** n ELEC ENG capacité entre broches f

pion n (pi-meson) PART PHYS, PHYS pion m

Pioneer: ~ **spacecraft** n ASTRON sonde spatiale Pioneer f

pip n C&G repère de centrage m, TELECOM bip sonore m; ~ **under finish** n C&G picot sous la bague m

pipage n CONST carriage through pipes transport par canalisation m, system of pipes canalisation f

pipe[1] n CONST canal m, conduit m, conduite f, tuyau m, of concrete buse f, of key canon m, entrée de clé f, of lock canon m, FLUID PHYS conduit m, tuyau m, MECH tuyau m, PETR TECH tube m, tuyau m; ~ **anchor** n MECH ENG ancrage tubulaire m; ~ **bend** n MECH ENG courbe f; ~ **bender** n CONST cintreur à tubes m, machine à cintrer les tuyaux f; ~ **bends screwed and socketed** n pl MECH ENG courbes filetées avec manchon f pl; ~ **box** n PROD ENG founding châssis à tuyaux m; ~ **cap** n MECH ENG obturateur de tube m; ~ **casing** n COAL TECH tubage m, tube de revêtement m; ~ **clamp** n MINING for lowering wheel casing collier de retenue m, frein de retenue m; ~ **clay** n C&G argile plastique f, CONST argile de pipe f, terre de pipe f; ~ **clay triangle** n LAB EQUIP support for crucible triangle pour creusets m; ~ **clip** n MECH ENG collier de serrage pour tubes m; ~ **components** n pl MECH ENG éléments de tuyauterie m pl; ~ **connection** n CONST lunette f, manchon pour tuyau m, raccord de tuyaux m, MECH ENG raccordement pour tubes m; ~ **connections** n pl CONST tuyauterie f; ~ **cot** n NAUT cadre m; ~ **coupling** n CONST lunette f, manchon pour tuyau m, raccord de tuyaux m, MECH ENG raccord pour tubes m; ~ **cross** n MECH ENG traverse pour tubes f; ~ **cutter** n CONST coupe-tubes m, coupe-tuyaux m; ~ **deck** n PETR aire de stockage f; ~ **diffusion** n METALL diffusion le long des lignes de dislocations f; ~ **fitter** n CONST person tuyauteur m; ~ **fitting** n MECH ENG raccord pour tubes m; ~ **flow** n FLUID PHYS écoulement dans les conduites m; ~ **grab** n CONST accroche-tube m; ~ **hook** n CONST crochet pour tuyaux m, PETR TECH crochet pour tiges m; ~ **joint** n CONST assemblage de tuyauterie m, MECH ENG joint pour tube m, MINING

assemblage de rallonges m; ~ **junction** n MECH ENG jonction de tuyaux f; ~ **key** n (cf barrel key) CONST locksmithing clef forée f; ~ **layer** n CONST civil engineering, MECH ENG pose-tubes m; ~ **laying** n CONST posage de tuyaux m, pose de tuyaux f; ~ **laying barge** n PETR TECH barge de pose f; ~ **manifold** n PETR TECH claviature f, collecteur m; ~ **plug** n MECH ENG bouchon de tube m; ~ **rack** n PETR TECH parc à tiges m; ~ **reducer** n CONST réducteur de tuyau m; ~ **screwing** n CONST filetage de tuyau m, taraudage des tuyaux m; ~ **slick** n PROD ENG lissoir à tuyau m; ~ **smoother** n PROD ENG lissoir à tuyau m; ~ **spanner** n (BrE) CONST clé à tubes f, MECH ENG clé serre-tubes f, clé à tuyauter f; ~ **string** n PETR configuration de pose f; ~ **support** n MECH ENG support de tuyaux m; ~ **tap** n CONST taraud pour tuyauteries m; ~ **thread** n (cf gas thread) MECH ENG filetage de tuyauterie m; ~ **threader** n CONST machine à tarauder les tuyaux f; ~ **threading** n CONST filetage de tuyau m, taraudage des tuyaux m; ~ **tongs** n pl CONST pinces à tuyaux f pl, PETR TECH clé à tiges f; ~ **twister** n CONST clef pour tuyaux f, clef à tubes f; ~ **union** n CONST raccord de tuyaux m, MECH ENG embase de raccord f; ~ **vice** n (BrE) CONST étau de tuyauteur m, étau à tubes m; ~ **vise** n (AmE) see pipe vice; ~ **wrench** n CONST clef pour tubes f, clef pour tuyaux f, clef à fer creux f, clé à tubes f, serre-tubes m, MECH ENG clé serre-tubes f, clé à tuyauter f

pipe[2] vt CONST to convey canaliser, envoyer par canalisation, transporter au moyen d'une canalisation, TV transmettre par ligne

pipe[3] vi CONST to furnish or equip with pipes établir une canalisation dans

pipe-clamping: ~ **element** n MECH ENG élément de serrage pour tube m

pipecoline n CHEM pipécoline f

pipe-collar n CONST collier de tuyau m

pipe-coning: ~ **tool** n CONST fraise ébarbeuse f

pipe-cooling: ~ **grids** n REFRIG of ice skating rink réseau de tubes réfrigérants m

piped: ~ **key** n CONST locksmithing clef forée f; ~ **key lock** n CONST serrure à broche f; ~ **television** n TV télédistribution f

pipeline n COMP pipe-line m, CONST canalisation f, conduite f, pipe-line m, DP pipe-line m, FUELLESS canalisation f, conduite f, GAS TECH canalisation f, MECH ENG pipe-line m, tuyauterie f, NAUT oil oléoduc m, PETR TECH canalisation f, pipe-line m, POLLUTION, TRANSP pipe-line m, WATER SUPP system of pipes canalisation f; ~ **processor** n COMP, DP processeur pipeline m; ~ **system** n TELECOM système en pipeline m; ~ **transportation** n TRANSP transport par conduite m

pipeliner n TRANSP pipe-linier m

pipelining n COMP fonction pipeline f, DP traitement pipeline m, ELECTRON chevauchement m, traitement pipeline m

piperazine n CHEM pipérazine f

piperic adj CHEM pipérique

piperideine n CHEM pipéridéine f

piperidine n CHEM pipéridine f

piperonal n CHEM héliotropine f, pipéronal m

piperylene n CHEM pipérylène m

pipes: ~ **and fittings** n pl CONST tuyauterie f

pipestrap n CONST patte à crochet f

pipette n LAB EQUIP glassware, analysis pipette f; ~ **stand** n LAB EQUIP support, analysis support pour pipettes m

pipetting: ~ **bulb** n LAB EQUIP analysis poire à pipetter f

pipe-type: ~ **cable** *n* ELEC câble en tuyau *m*

pipework *n* MECH tuyauterie *f*; ~ **system** *n* MECH ENG *valves, fittings* système de tuyauterie *m*

pipeworks *n pl* CONST tuyauterie *f*

piping *n* COAL TECH renard *m*, CONST canalisation *f*, conduites *f pl*, conduits *m pl*, tuyautage *m*, tuyauterie *f*, tuyaux *m pl*, HYDROL renard *m*, PAPER TECH cordon *m*, PETR TECH tuyauterie *f*; ~ **network** *n* CONST réseau de canalisations *m*, réseau de conduits *m*; ~ **plan** *n* NAUT *shipbuilding* plan de tuyautage *m*; ~ **seepage** *n* WATER SUPP érosion par suintement *f*

Pirani: ~ **gage** *n* (AmE), ~ **gauge** *n* (BrE) PHYS *vacuum* jauge de Pirani *f*; ~ **vacuum gage** *n* (AmE), ~ **vacuum gauge** *n* (BrE) LAB EQUIP jauge de vide Pirani *f*

pirate: ~ **recording** *n* TV enregistrement pirate *m*

pirn *n* C&G, TEXTILES canette *f*

pirn-winding: ~ **machine** *n* TEXTILES cannetière *f*

Pisces *n* ASTRON Poissons *m pl*

pisciculture *n* OCEANOG pisciculture *f*

Piscis: ~ **Austrinus** *n* ASTRON Poisson austral *m*

pisolite: ~ **limestone** *n* GEOL calcaire pisolithique *m*, calcaire pisolitique *m*

pisolitic: ~ **limestone** *n* GEOL calcaire pisolithique *m*, calcaire pisolitique *m*

pistol: ~ **grip with shutter release** *n* PHOTO poignée-déclencheur *f*; ~ **light** *n* ELEC *lighting* projecteur à main *m*

piston *n* AUTO, HYDR EQUIP, MECH, MECH ENG, MINING, NAUT *engine* piston *m*, PETR TECH cliquetis *m*, PHYS, VEHICLES *engine* piston *m*; ~ **area** *n* MECH ENG surface de piston *f*; ~ **attenuator** *n* ELECTRON atténuateur à piston *m*, PHYS *waveguide* affaiblisseur à piston *m*, atténuateur à piston *m*; ~ **back stroke** *n* HYDR EQUIP course de retour du piston *f*, recul du piston *m*; ~ **blower** *n* MECH ENG machine soufflante *f*, soufflante *f*, soufflet *m*; ~ **body** *n* AUTO corps de piston *m*; ~ **boss** *n* AUTO bossage de piston *m*; ~ **boss bushing** *n* AUTO bague de bossage de piston *f*; ~ **clearance** *n* AUTO jeu du piston *m*, MECH ENG espace libre *m*, espace mort *m*, espace neutre *m*, espace nuisible *m*, VEHICLES *engine* jeu du piston *m*; ~ **compressor** *n* GAS TECH, MECH ENG compresseur à piston *m*; ~ **crown** *n* VEHICLES *engine* tête de piston *f*; ~ **engine** *n* AERONAUT moteur alternatif *m*, moteur à mouvement alternatif *m*, AUTO, MECH ENG moteur à piston *m*; ~ **freezing** *n* AUTO grippage du piston *m*; ~ **head** *n* AUTO tête de piston *f*, MECH ENG corps de piston *m*; ~ **jig** *n* COAL TECH bac à piston *m*; ~ **knock** *n* AUTO cliquetis *m*; ~ **locked to connecting rod** *n* AUTO axe solidaire de la bielle *m*; ~ **packing** *n* MECH ENG *hemp, rubber, leather* bourrage de piston *m*, garniture de piston *f*; ~ **phone** *n* ACOUSTICS pistonphone *m*; ~ **pin** *n* VEHICLES *engine* axe de piston *m*; ~ **pin bushing** *n* AUTO coussinet d'axe de piston *m*; ~ **pin locked to piston** *n* AUTO axe solidaire de piston *m*; ~ **pump** *n* PROD ENG, WATER SUPP pompe à piston *f*; ~ **relief duct** *n* CONST *railway tunnelling* déchargeur de piston *m*, rameau de pistonnement *m*; ~ **ring** *n* AUTO, MECH segment de piston *m*, MECH ENG bague de piston *f*, garniture de piston *f*, segment de piston *m*, VEHICLES *engine* segment de piston *m*; ~ **ring clamp** *n* VEHICLES *tool* tendeur de segments de piston *m*; ~ **ring compressor** *n* AUTO *car maintenance* collier à segments *m*; ~ **ring groove** *n* VEHICLES *engine* gorge de segment de piston *f*; ~ **ring pliers** *n pl* MECH ENG *tool* pince à segments *f*; ~ **rod** *n* AUTO tige de piston *f*, MECH ENG tige de piston *f*, verge de piston *f*, PROD ENG, RAIL *vehicles* tige de piston *f*; ~ **sampler** *n* COAL TECH carottier à piston

m; ~ **seal housings** *n pl* MECH ENG logement de joints de piston *m*; ~ **skirt** *n* AUTO, VEHICLES *engine* jupe du piston *f*; ~ **slap** *n* AUTO, VEHICLES *engine* claquement du piston *m*; ~ **stroke** *n* MECH ENG battement de piston *m*, coup de piston *m*, *length of stroke* course du piston *f*, jeu du piston *f*, levée du piston *f*; ~ **surface** *n* MECH ENG surface de piston *f*; ~ **top** *n* AUTO fond de piston *m*; ~ **valve** *n* MECH ENG tiroir cylindrique *m*, tiroir rond *m*, tiroir à piston *m*; ~ **with clack-valve** *n* MECH ENG piston à clapet *m*; ~ **with extended rod** *n* MECH ENG piston à contre-tige *m*; ~ **with tailrod** *n* MECH ENG piston à contre-tige *m*

piston-type: ~ **preforming unit** *n* MECH ENG *machine tool* préformeuse à piston *f*

pit *n* C&G piqûre *f*, COAL TECH fosse *f*, puits *m*, CONST excavation *f*, fosse *f*, fouille *f*, MAR POLL bac *m*, fosse *f*, soute *f*, MECH ENG *for turntable* fouille *f*, MINING carreau de mine *m*, charbonnage *m*, houillère *f*, mine *f*, mine de charbon *f*, mine de houille *f*, *quarry* carrière *f*, PETR TECH bassin *m*, WATER SUPP fosse *f*, puits *m*, regard *m*; ~ **bank** *n* MINING carreau de mine *m*; ~ **bottom** *n* COAL TECH fixation *f*, MINING fond du puits *m*; ~ **coal** *n* COAL TECH charbon de mine *m*, charbon tout-venant *m*; ~ **door** *n* (AmE) *(cf end door)* C&G bouclier *m*; ~ **eye** *n* MINING fond du puits *m*; ~ **gas** *n* MINING feu brisou *m*, feu grieux *m*, feu terrou *m*, grisou *m*, mofette inflammable *f*, terrou *m*; ~ **gas indicator** *n* MINING *fire damp* détecteur de grisou *m*, grisoumètre *m*; ~ **guides** *n pl* MINING coulantage *m*, coulants *m pl*, guidage *m*, guides *m pl*, guidonnage *m*; ~ **heap** *n* MINING halde *f*, halde de déblais *f*, halde de déchets *f*; ~ **landing** *n* MINING accrochage *m*, chambre d'accrochage *f*, chambre d'envoyage *f*, envoyage *m*, recette de puits *f*; ~ **lever** *n* PETR TECH niveau des bacs *m*; ~ **mouth** *n* MINING bouche de puits *f*, orifice de la fosse *m*; ~ **prop** *n* MINING étai de mine *m*; ~ **sand** *n* MINING sable de carrière *m*, sable terrain *m*; ~ **wood** *n* MINING bois de mine *m*

PIT *abbr (programable interval timer, programmable interval timer)* ELECTRON temporisateur programmable *m*

pitch[1] *n* ACOUSTICS hauteur *f*, tonie *f*, *scale* degré *m*, AERONAUT inclinaison longitudinale *f*, pente longitudinale *f*, tangage *m*, C&G poix *f*, CINEMAT *spacing of perforations* pas *m*, écartement des perforations *m*, COMP pas *m*, CONST *from coal tar* brai *m*, brai de pétrole *m*, *inclination or slope* inclinaison *f*, pente *f*, *natural bitumen* bitume *m*, poix *f*, DP, ELEC *coil*, ELEC ENG *of wires* pas *m*, GEOL *of folds* plongement *m*, MECH *of thread* pas *m*, MECH ENG *of gear, chain* pas *m*, *of rivet centres* écartement *m*, *of screw* filetage *m*, NAUT *motion of ship, propeller* pas *m*, tangage *m*, OPT pas *m*, PAPER TECH poix *f*, PHOTO pas *m*, écartement des perforations *m*, PHYS *attitude of aircraft, boat* tangage *m*, *of sound* hauteur *f*, *spacing* pas *m*, REFRIG inclinaison *f*, SPACE *spacecraft* tangage *m*, WAVE PHYS *of sound wave* hauteur *f*, hauteur du son *f*; ~ **angle** *n* AERONAUT angle d'inclinaison longitudinale *m*, angle de tangage *m*, *helicopter* angle de pas *m*, FUELLESS *airscrew, orbit* angle d'attaque *m*; ~ **arc** *n* MECH ENG arc d'engrènement *m*, arc de prise *m*; ~ **attitude** *n* AERONAUT assiette autour de l'axe longitudinal *f*, assiette longitudinale *f*, SPACE *spacecraft* attitude longitudinale *f*; ~ **axis** *n* AERONAUT axe de profondeur *m*, axe de tangage *m*, SPACE *spacecraft* axe de tangage *m*, axe latéral *m*; ~ **center diameter** *n* (AmE), ~ **centre**

diameter *n* (BrE) AERONAUT diamètre de perçage *m*; ~
chain *n* MECH ENG chaîne calibrée *f*; ~ change axis *n*
AERONAUT *helicopter* axe d'incidence *m*; ~ change
beam *n* AERONAUT *helicopter* té de commande de pas
m; ~ change rod *n* AERONAUT *helicopter* axe de changement de pas *m*; ~ change spider *n* AERONAUT
helicopter araignée de changement de pas *f*, croisillon
de changement de pas *m*, plateau de commande du
rotor arrière *m*; ~ channel *n* AERONAUT chaîne de
tangage *f*; ~ circle *n* MECH ENG cercle de contact *m*,
cercle de division *m*, cercleprimitif *m*, primitif *m*, trait
de division *m*; ~ circle diameter *n* AERONAUT diamètre
de cercle primitif *m*; ~ circumference *n* MECH ENG
gearing circonférence primitive *f*; ~ coal *n* COAL TECH
charbon piciforme *m*; ~ compensation *n* AERONAUT
helicopter compensation de pas *f*; ~ cone *n* MECH ENG
gearing cône de division *m*, cône primitif *m*; ~ control
n AERONAUT réglage de vitesse *m*, *helicopter* commande de pas *f*, commande de profondeur *f*; ~ control
arm *n* AERONAUT *helicopter* bras de commande de pas
m; ~ control lever *n* AERONAUT *helicopter* levier de
commande de pas *m*; ~ control load *n* AERONAUT
helicopter effort de commande de pas *m*; ~ control rod
angle *n* AERONAUT angle de biellette de pas *m*; ~
damper *n* AERONAUT amortisseur de tangage *m*; ~
detector synchro *n* AERONAUT synchro détecteur de
tangage *m*; ~ diameter *n* AERONAUT diamètre primitif
m, diamètre sur flancs de filets *m*, MECH ENG *gearing*
diamètre primitif *m*; ~ diameter error *n* METR *screw
thread gauging* erreur de diamètre sur flancs de filets *f*;
~ diameter ratio *n* AERONAUT *propeller* pas géométrique relatif *m*; ~ gyro *n* SPACE *spacecraft* gyromètre de
tangage *m*; ~ increase *n* AERONAUT *helicopter* augmentation de pas *f*, remise de pas *f*; ~ information *n*
AERONAUT information de tangage *f*; ~ of lead screw *n*
MECH ENG pas de la vis mère *m*; ~ line *n* MECH ENG
cercle de contact *m*, cercle de division *m*, cercle primitif *m*, primitif *m*, trait de division *m*, ligne d'engrènement *f*, *gearing* droite primitive *f*, ligne de division *f*,
ligne primitive *f*, trait de division *m*; ~ pine *n* NAUT
timber pitchpin *m*; ~ point *n* MECH ENG *gearing* point
de contact *m*; ~ polisher *n* C&G polissoir à la poix *m*; ~
radius *n* AERONAUT rayon du cercle primitif *m*, MECH
ENG *gearing* rayon primitif *m*; ~ rate gyro *n* AERONAUT
gyromètre de tangage *m*, gyromètre longitudinal *m*;~
reversing *n* AERONAUT *of propeller*, TRANSP inversion
de pas *f*; ~ roll and yaw axes *n pl* AERONAUT trièdre de
référence *m*, SPACE trièdre de référence d'inertie *m*; ~
of roof *n* CONST *architecture* chute de comble *f*, inclinaison de comble *f*, pente de comble *f*, rampe de
chevrons *f*; ~ roof *n* CONST comble à deux longs pans
m, comble à deux pentes *m*, comble à deux versants *m*,
comble à deux égouts *m*; ~ setting *n* AERONAUT *propeller* calage de pas *m*, réglage de pas *m*; ~ stop *n*
AERONAUT *helicopter* butée de pas *f*; ~ surface *n* MECH
ENG *gearing* surface primitive *f*; ~ synchro *n* AERO-
NAUT synchroniseur de tangage *m*; ~ throttle
synchronizer *n* AERONAUT levier pas-gaz *m*; ~ to be cut
n MECH ENG *screw-cutting* pas à fileter *m*; ~ trim *n* AE-
RONAUT compensation de profondeur *f*; ~ wheel *n*
MECH ENG roue d'engrenage *f*; ~ zone location *n* MECH
ENG *V-belts* emplacement de la zone primitive *m*
pitch[2] *vi* GEOL s'ennoyer, MECH ENG *gear wheels* engre-
ner, s'engrener, NAUT tanguer
pitchblende *n* CHEM pechblende *f*, péchurane *m*, MINE-
RAL pechblende *f*

pitch-correcting: ~ unit *n* AERONAUT *flight controls* correcteur d'effort *m*, vérin correcteur d'effort *m*, vérin
de décrochage *m*
pitched: ~ chain *n* MECH ENG chaîne calibrée *f*
pitch-excited: ~ vocoder *n* TELECOM codeur à fréquences
vocales activé par la hauteur du son *m*
pitching *n* AERONAUT engagement longitudinal *m*, MECH
ENG *gearing* engrenage *m*, engrènement *m*, prise *f*,
NAUT, PHYS *movement* tangage *m*; ~ moment *n* FUEL-
LESS moment de tangage *m*
pitch-locking: ~ system *n* AERONAUT *helicopter* dispositif de verrouillage de pas *m*
pitchstone *n* MINERAL rétinite *f*
pitch-thruster *n* SPACE *spacecraft* moteur antitangage *m*
pitch-up *n* AERONAUT autocabrage *m*
pithead *n* MINING bouche de puits *f*, orifice de la fosse *m*,
carreau de la mine *m*; ~ building *n* MINING bâtiment de
fosse *m*, bâtiment de puits *m*; ~ frame *n* MINING belle-
fleur *f*, chevalement *m*, chevalet d'extraction *m*,
châssis à molettes *m*,tour d'extraction *f*; ~ gear *n* MI-
NING chevalement *m*, machine à molettes *f*, machine à
molettes *f*; ~ pulley *n* MINING molette *f*, poulie de
chevalement *f*; ~ works *n pl* MINING plâtre du puits *m*
pitman *n* MECH ENG bielle *f*; ~ arm *n* AUTO bielle pendante
f, VEHICLES *steering* bielle de commande de direction
f; ~ head *n* MECH ENG tête de bielle *f*
Pitot: ~ tube *n* PHYS tube de Pitot *m*
pitticite *n* MINERAL pitticite *f*, pittizite *f*
pitting *n* C&G criblage *m*, érosion remontante *f*
pittizite *n* MINERAL pitticite *f*, pittizite *f*
pivalic *adj* CHEM pivalique
pivot *n* INSTRUMENT, MECH, MECH ENG pivot *m*, NUCLEAR
appui à pivot *m*, pivot *m*, tourillon *m*; ~ axle *n* VEHI-
CLES *of trailer* essieu balancier *m*; ~ bearing *n* RAIL
crapaudine *f*; ~ bridge *n* CONST pont tournant *m*; ~ pin
n VEHICLES *of trailer* axe de fusée *m*, pivot de fusée *m*; ~
ring *n* AUTO bague d'articulation *f*
pivoted[1] *adj* MECH pivotant
pivoted:[2] ~ armature *n* ELEC ENG armature montée sur
pivots *f*; ~ lever *n* MECH ENG levier pivotant *m*
pivot-hung: ~ sash *n* CONST *window* châssis à pivot *m*; ~
window *n* CONST fenêtre basculante *f*, fenêtre à bascule *f*, *vertical* fenêtre pivotante *f*, fenêtre à pivot *f*
pixel *n* COMP, DP pixel *m*, élément d'image *m*, PRINT pixel
m; ~ carrier *n* PRINT onde porteuse d'image *f*
pixels: ~ per inch *n* COMP, DP pixels par pouce *m pl*
pixlock *n* TV synchronisation *f*
PJC *abbr* (*pointer justification count*) TELECOM compte
de justification de pointeur *m*
PJE *abbr* (*pointer justification event*) TELECOM événement de justification de pointeur *m*
PL *abbr* (*primary link*) TELECOM liaison primaire *f*
PLA *abbr* COMP (*programable logic array, programmable logic array*) réseau logique programmable *m*,
COMP (*programmed logic array*) réseau à logique
programmée *m*, DP (*programable logic array, programmable logic array*) réseau logique
programmable *m*, DP (*programmed logic array*) réseau à logique programmée *m*
placard *n* MECH ENG plaquette sur panneau *f*, étiquette
sur panneau *f*
placer *n* MINING gisement alluvionnaire *m*, minière *f*,
placer *m*; ~ deposit *n* GEOL gîte alluvionnaire *m*,
MINING gisement alluvionnaire *m*; ~ dirt *n* MINING
alluvion aurifère *f*, graviers aurifères *m pl*; ~ gold *n*
MINING or alluvionnien *m*, or de lavage *m*; ~ ground *n*

MINING terrain d'alluvions *m*; ~ **mine** *n* MINING exploitation de placers *f*, exploitation placérienne *f*; ~ **workings** *n pl* MINING exploitation de placers *f*, exploitation placérienne *f*

plage *n* ASTRON plage *f*

plagioclase *n* MINERAL plagioclase *m*

plain[1] *adj* TEXTILES uni

plain:[2] ~ **bearing** *n* MECH ENG palier lisse *m*, palier à coussinets lisses *m*, VEHICLES coussinet lisse *m*, palier lisse *m*; ~ **bearing made from sintered material** *n* MECH ENG palier lisse avec coussinets frittés *m*; ~ **bed lathe** *n* MECH ENG tour à banc droit *m*; ~ **bit** *n* MINING *boring* trépan plat *m*, trépan simple *m*; ~ **color** *n* (AmE), ~ **colour** *n* (BrE) COLOURS teinte unie *f*; ~ **column** *n* CONST *architecture* colonne lisse *f*; ~ **conductor** *n* ELEC *cable* âme nue *f*; ~ **cylindrical boiler** *n* HYDR EQUIP chaudière cylindrique simple *f*; ~ **dyeing** *n* COLOURS teinture uniforme *f*; ~ **fabric** *n* TEXTILES tissu uni *m*; ~ **fitting** *n* MECH ENG ajustement lisse *m*; ~ **gage** *n* (AmE) *see plain gauge*; ~ **gage for pipe threads** *n* (AmE) *see plain gauge for pipe threads*; ~ **gauge** *n* (BrE) MECH ENG vérificateur lisse *m*; ~ **gauge for pipe threads** *n* (BrE) MECH ENG vérificateur lisse de filetage pour tuyauterie *m*; ~ **grinder** *n* MECH ENG machine à rectifier les surfaces cylindriques extérieures *f*; ~ **hub flange** *n* MECH ENG bride à moyeu lisse *f*; ~ **lathe** *n* MECH ENG bidet *m*, tour simple *m*; ~ **length** *n* MECH ENG *of screw* partie lisse *f*; ~ **milling cutter** *n* MECH ENG fraise à rouler *f*; ~ **press roll** *n* PAPER TECH rouleau de presse lisse *m*; ~ **roll** *n* PROD ENG cylindre lisse *m*; ~ **rolled glass** *n* C&G verre de toiture *m*; ~ **sandblast** *n* C&G sablé uni *m*; ~ **slide valve** *n* HYDR EQUIP tiroir simple *m*; ~ **socket** *n* MECH ENG emboîtement lisse *m*; ~ **surface** *n* MECH ENG surface lisse *f*, surface plane *f*, surface unie *f*; ~ **thrust bearing** *n* MECH ENG palier lisse de butée *m*; ~ **tile** *n* CONST tuile plate *f*; ~ **traveling wheel** *n* (AmE), ~ **travelling wheel** *n* (BrE) MECH ENG galet plein *m*; ~ **tread tire** *n* (AmE), ~ **tread tyre** *n* (BrE) VEHICLES pneumatique lisse *m*, pneumatique sans sculpture *m*; ~ **tube** *n* CONST tube lisse *m*; ~ **turning lathe** *n* MECH ENG tour à cylindrer *m*; ~ **ungeared lathe** *n* MECH ENG bidet *m*, tour simple *m*; ~ **washer** *n* MECH ENG rondelle plate *f*, VEHICLES rondelle plane *f*; ~ **washer for metric bolts screws and nuts** *n* MECH ENG rondelle plate pour boulonnerie métrique *f*; ~ **weave** *n* PAPER TECH toile unie *f*, TEXTILES armure unie *f*

plan[1] *n* NAUT *architecture, navigation* carte de détail *f*, carte particulière *f*, plan *m*, projet *m*; ~ **drawing** *n* MECH ENG vue en plan *f*; ~ **position indicator** *n* PHYS *radar* indicateur panoramique *m*; ~ **view** *n* MECH ENG vue en plan *f*

plan[2] *vt* TELECOM planifier, projeter

planar[1] *adj* GEOL plan, plat, GEOM d'un plan

planar:[2] ~ **bipolar transistor** *n* ELECTRON transistor planar bipolaire *m*; ~ **diffusion** *n* ELECTRON diffusion planar *f*; ~ **diode** *n* ELECTRON diode de type planar *f*, diode planar *f*; ~ **epitaxial diode** *n* ELECTRON diode planar épitaxiale *f*; ~ **integrated circuit** *n* ELECTRON circuit intégré de type planar *m*, circuit intégré planar *m*; ~ **line** *n* ELECTRON ligne triplaque *f*; ~ **process** *n* ELECTRON procédé planar *m*, méthode planar *f*; ~ **reflector** *n* INSTRUMENT réflecteur plan *m*; ~ **triode** *n* ELECTRON triode à électrodes planes *f*; ~ **waveguide** *n* ELEC ENG guide d'ondes planes *m*

Planck: ~ **time** *n* ASTRON temps de Planck *m*

Planck's: ~ **constant** *n* PHYS, RAD PHYS constante de Planck *f*; ~ **formula** *n* PHYS formule de Planck *f*, loi de Planck *f*; ~ **law** *n* PHYS relation de Planck *f*, relation de Planck-Einstein *f*, RAD PHYS *radiation, distribution law* loi de Planck *f*, loi de Stefan *f*; ~ **radiation formula** *n* RAD PHYS *energy of black body* formule de radiation de Planck *f*

plane[1] *n* AERONAUT avion *m*, CONST *joiner's tool* rabot *m*, GEOM plan *m*, MECH ENG *engineer's surface plate* marbre *m*, marbre d'ajusteur *m*, marbre à dresser *m*, PHYS *of polarization* plan *m*, TRANSPORT avion *m*; ~ **angle** *n* GEOM angle plan *m*, angle rectiligne *m*; ~ **bit** *n* CONST fer de rabot *m*, fer à raboter *m*, lame de rabot *f*; ~ **figures** *n pl* GEOM *triangles, circles, squares* figures planes *f pl*; ~ **geometry** *n* GEOM géométrie plane *f*; ~ **of incidence** *n* PHYS plan d'incidence *m*; ~ **iron** *n* CONST fer de rabot *m*, fer à raboter *m*, MECH ENG *of machine* lame de raboteuse *f*; ~ **milling** *n* MECH ENG fraisage en plan *m*; ~ **milling machine** *n* MECH ENG fraiseuse à surface longitudinale *f*, machine à fraiser à portique *f*; ~ **mirror** *n* INSTRUMENT, PHYS miroir plan *m*; ~ **parallel waves** *n pl* WAVE PHYS *from distant source* ondes planes parallèles *f pl*; ~ **of polarization** *n* OPT plane de polarisation *m*; ~ **polygon** *n* GEOM polygone plan *m*; ~ **of shear** *n* METALL plan de cisaillement *m*; ~ **stock** *n* CONST fût de rabot *m*; ~ **surface** *n* PROP MAT surface plane *f*; ~ **of symmetry** *n* MECH ENG, METALL plan de symétrie *m*; ~ **table** *n* CONST *surveying* planchette *f*, MINING accrochage *m*, chambre d'accrochage *f*, chambre d'envoyage *f*, envoyage *m*, recette *f*, *ore-dressing* table inclinée à aire plane *f*; ~ **triangle** *n* GEOM triangle rectiligne *m*; ~ **trigonometry** *n* GEOM trigonométrie plane *f*; ~ **wave** *n* ACOUSTICS, ELEC ENG, OPT, PHYS, SPACE, TELECOM onde plane *f*

plane[2] *vt* MECH dresser, planer, raboter

plane-polarized: ~ **wave** *n* PHYS onde polarisée rectilignement *f*, WAVE PHYS onde plane polarisée *f*

planer *n* (AmE) *(cf planing machine)* CONST machine à raboter *f*, raboteuse *f*, MECH raboteuse *f*

planet *n* ASTRON planète *f*; ~ **carrier** *n* AUTO porte-satellite *m*; ~ **gear** *n* AUTO satellite *m*, MECH ENG pignon satellite *m*, satellite *m*, roue planétaire *f*, *sun-and-planet motion* engrenage planétaire *m*, mouche *f*, mouvement planétaire *m*; ~ **gearing** *n* MECH ENG *sun-and-planet motion* engrenage planétaire *m*, mouche *f*, mouvement planétaire *m*; ~ **pinion cage** *n* AERONAUT *helicopter* porte-satellite *m*; ~ **spindle** *n* MECH ENG arbre à mouvement planétaire *m*; ~ **wheel** *n* MECH ENG, VEHICLES roue planétaire *f*

planet-action: ~ **spindle** *n* MECH ENG arbre à mouvement planétaire *m*

planetarium *n* ASTRON planétarium *m*

planetary[1] *adj* ASTRON, MECH *gears* planétaire

planetary:[2] ~ **boundary layer** *n* METEO couche limite planétaire *f*; ~ **gear differential** *n* AUTO différentiel à train planétaire *m*; ~ **gears** *n* AUTO train planétaire *m*; ~ **gear set** *n* AUTO train épicycloïdal *m*; ~ **gear system** *n* AUTO train planétaire *m*; ~ **gear train** *n* MECH ENG train planétaire *m*; ~ **interior** *n* ASTRON structure interne d'une planète *f*; ~ **mill** *n* LAB EQUIP *grinding* broyeur planétaire *m*; ~ **nebula** *n* ASTRON, SPACE nébuleuse planétaire *f*; ~ **paths** *n pl* ASTRON *around the sun* trajectoires planétaires autour du soleil *f pl*; ~ **pinion** *n* AUTO satellite *m*, MECH ENG roue planétaire *f*; ~ **probe** *n* SPACE sonde planétaire *f*; ~ **satellites** *n pl* ASTRON satellites planétaires *m pl*; ~ **volcanism** *n* ASTRON volcanisme planétaire *m*

planetesimals *n pl* ASTRON astéroïdes *m pl*

planetoid *n* ASTRON planétoïde *m*, SPACE petite planète *f*, planétoïde *m*

planimeter *n* CONST *surveying*, GEOM planimètre *m*

planimetry *n* GEOM planimétrie *f*

planing *n* C&G affinage *m*, CONST planage *m*, rabotage *m*; ~ **and thicknessing machine** *n* CONST machine à raboter tirant des bois d'épaisseur *f*; ~ **hull-type ship** *n* TRANSP navire du type TRISEC *m*; ~ **machine** *n* (BrE) (*cf planer*) CONST machine à raboter *f*, raboteuse *f*; ~ **tools** *n pl* CONST outils à raboter *m pl*

planisher *n* MECH ENG *machine* machine à planer *f*, *person* aplaneur *m*, planeur *m*, *tool* outil à planer *m*, plane *f*

planishing *n* MECH ENG planage *m*; ~ **roll** *n* MECH ENG cylindre espatard *m*, cylindre polisseur *m*, espatard *m*; ~ **stake** *n* MECH ENG tas à planer *m*; ~ **tool** *n* MECH ENG outil à planer *m*, plane *f*

planisphere *n* ASTRON planisphère *m*

plank *n* CONST madrier *m*, NAUT *shipbuilding* bordage *m*, planche *f*; ~ **partition** *n* CONST cloison en madriers *f*

planking *n* COAL TECH, CONST madriers *m pl*

plankton: ~ **microscope** *n* INSTRUMENT microscope à plancton *m*

planned: ~ **environment** *n* POLLUTION milieu aménagé *m*; ~ **maintenance** *n* QUALITY maintenance programmée *f*; ~ **projected available stock** *n* PROD ENG stock disponible prévisionnel *m*; ~ **stock movements** *n pl* PROD ENG mouvements de stock prévus *m pl*; ~ **year** *n* PROD ENG année prévisionnelle *f*

planner *n* PROD ENG agent de planning *m*

planning *n* TELECOM planification *f*; ~ **bill of material** *n* PROD ENG macronomenclature *f*; ~ **board** *n* PROD ENG tableau de planning *m*; ~ **horizon** *n* PROD ENG horizon de planification *m*; ~ **interval** *n* PROD ENG fréquence de planification *f*; ~ **permission** *n* CONST permis d'urbanisation *m*, permis de construire *m*; ~ **products** *n pl* PRINT produits de préparation de montage *m pl*

planoconcave: ~ **lens** *n* INSTRUMENT verre plan-concave *m*, PHYS lentille plan-concave *f*

planoconvex: ~ **lens** *n* INSTRUMENT, PHYS lentille plan-convexe *f*

planomiller *n* MECH ENG fraise genre raboteuse *f*

plant *n* CONST engin *m*, équipage *m*, matériel *m*, PROD ENG usine *f*, *equipment* appareils *m pl*, installation *f*, matériel *m*, outillage *m*, REFRIG installation *f*; ~ **pigment** *n* COLOURS pigment végétal *m*

planting *n* PROD ENG *bedding in* mise en chantier *f*

plasma *n* ELECTRON, GAS TECH, MINERAL, PART PHYS, PHYS, SPACE plasma *m*; ~ **arc cutting** *n* CONST coupage plasma *m*; ~ **arc power collector** *n* TRANSP capteur de courant par arc *m*; ~ **cloud** *n* GEOPHYS nuage de plasma *m*; ~ **cutting** *n* CONST coupage plasma *m*; ~ **display** *n* COMP, DP écran à plasma *m*; ~ **engine** *n* SPACE *spacecraft* moteur à propulsion MHD *m*, moteur à propulsion plasmique *m*; ~ **environment** *n* SPACE milieu ionisé *m*; ~ **etching** *n* ELECTRON attaque au plasma *f*; ~ **particle** *n* GEOPHYS particule de plasma *f*; ~ **radiation** *n* GAS TECH rayonnement de plasma *m*; ~ **thruster** *n* SPACE *spacecraft* moteur à propulsion MHD *m*, moteur à propulsion plasmique *m*

plasma-activated: ~ **chemical vapor deposition** *n* (AmE), ~ **chemical vapour deposition** *n* (BrE) (*PCVD*) ELECTRON *process* procédé de CVD activé au plasma *m*, procédé de dépôt chimique en phase vapeur activé au plasma *m*, procédé verneuil au plas-

ma *m*

plasma-developed: ~ **resist** *n* ELECTRON résist développé au plasma *m*

plasmagene: ~ **gas** *n* GAS TECH gaz plasmagène *m*

plasmatron *n* GAS TECH plasmatron *m*

plast: ~ **spraying** *n* COATINGS injection à la flamme *f*, pistolage à la flamme *m*, plastification à chaud *f*

plaster[1] *n* CONST plâtre *m*; ~ **coating** *n* COATINGS plâtrage *m*; ~ **of Paris** *n* CONST plâtre de moulage *m*; ~ **rock** *n* CONST gypse *m*, pierre à plâtre *f*; ~ **stone** *n* CONST gypse *m*, pierre à plâtre *f*

plaster[2] *vt* CONST plâtrer

plastering *n* CONST plâtrage *m*, plâtrerie *f*; ~ **trowel** *n* CONST truelle à plâtre *f*, MECH ENG *tool* plâtroir *m*

plasterwork *n* CONST plâtrage *m*, plâtrerie *f*

plastic *n* P&R, PETR TECH matière plastique *f*, plastique *m*, REFRIG plastique *m*; ~ **blunting** *n* METALL émoussement plastique *m*; ~ **bottle** *n* PHOTO bocal en matière plastique *m*; ~ **capacitor** *n* ELEC ENG condensateur en plastique *m*; ~ **cladding** *n* ELEC ENG gaine en plastique *f*; ~ **clay** *n* GEOL argile plastique *f*; ~ **coating** *n* COATINGS enduction par matière plastique *f*, revêtement plastique *m*, TELECOM revêtement plastique *m*; ~ **covering** *n* COATINGS plastification *f*; ~ **deformation** *n* CONST, CRYSTALL, METALL, P&R, PHYS déformation plastique *f*; ~ **developing tank** *n* PHOTO cuve en matière plastique *f*; ~ **dish** *n* PHOTO cuvette en matière plastique *f*; ~ **explosive** *n* MINING dynamite plastique *f*, plastic *m*, plastique *m*; ~ **fiber** *n* (AmE) *see plastic fibre*; ~ **fiber cable** *n* (AmE) *see plastic fibre cable*; ~ **fibre** *n* (BrE) ELEC ENG, OPT fibre plastique *f*; ~ **fibre cable** *n* (BrE) ELEC ENG câble à fibre en plastique *m*; ~ **film capacitor** *n* ELEC ENG condensateur à film plastique *m*; ~ **flow** *n* METALL, P&R écoulement plastique *m*; ~ **flow properties** *n* P&R adaptation plastique *f*; ~ **foam packaging** *n* PACKAGING emballage en plastique mousse *m*; ~ **foil tooling** *n* MECH ENG outillage pour feuilles plastiques *m*; ~ **instability** *n* METALL instabilité plastique *f*; ~ **laminate covering** *n* COATINGS revêtement aux résines synthétiques *m*; ~ **limit** *n* COAL TECH limite de plasticité *f*, CONST limite plastique *f*; ~ **liner** *n* PACKAGING doublure plastique *f*; ~ **materials** *n pl* SAFETY matériaux plastiques *m pl*; ~ **mount** *n* PHOTO cadre en matière plastique *m*; ~ **pipeline** *n* MECH ENG tuyauterie plastique *f*; ~ **plug** *n* PACKAGING bouchon plastique *m*; ~ **properties** *n pl* FLUID PHYS propriétés plastiques *f pl*; ~ **protective elements** *n pl* SAFETY éléments de protection en matière plastique *m pl*; ~ **sheeting** *n* PACKAGING feuille de plastique *f*; ~ **welding** *n* MECH ENG soudage des plastiques *m*; ~ **welding machine** *n* MECH ENG machine pour le soudage des plastiques *f*; ~ **yield** *n* NUCLEAR fluage *m*, fluage plastique *m*, P&R déformation non élastique *f*

plastic-clad: ~ **silica** *n* (*PCS*) OPT, TELECOM silice gratinée de plastique *f*; ~ **silica fiber** *n* (AmE), ~ **silica fibre** *n* (BrE) OPT fibre de silice gainée de plastique *f*, fibre silice-plastique *f*, TELECOM fibre de silice gainée de plastique *f*

plastic-coated *adj* COATINGS plastifié, revêtu de matière plastique, *on inside* doublé de matière plastique

plastic-insulated: ~ **cable** *n* ELEC ENG, TELECOM câble isolé au plastique *m*

plasticity *n* C&G ouvrabilité *f*, COAL TECH, METALL, P&R, PROP MAT plasticité *f*; ~ **index** *n* COAL TECH, CONST indice de plasticité *m*

plasticize *vt* P&R *coatings, adhesives* plastifier

plasticizer n CHEM plastifiant m, CONST concrete fluidifiant m, plastifiant m, P&R coatings, adhesives plastifiant m, PROP MAT fluidifiant m; ~ **admixture** n CONST concrete fluidifiant m, plastifiant m; ~ **migration** n P&R plastics, coatings migration de plastifiant f

plastic-molded: ~ **footwear** n (AmE), **plastic-moulded footwear** n (BrE) SAFETY chaussures en plastique moulé f pl

plastics n pl CHEM matières plastiques f pl

plastic-sealing: ~ **LCD** n ELECTRON afficheur à cristaux liquides à joint plastique m

plastid n CHEM plaste m, plastide m

plastifying: ~ **admixture** n CONST concrete fluidifiant m, plastifiant m

plastimeter n P&R instrument plastimètre m

plastin n CHEM plastine f

plastisol n P&R plastisol m

plastomer n CHEM, PETR TECH plastomère m

plastometer n PRINT duromètre m

plat n MINING carreau de mine m, plan de la surface m, plan des travaux souterrains m, shaft station chambre d'accrochage f, chambre d'envoyage f, envoyage m, recette f

platband n CONST flat arch plate-bande f, voûte plate f

plate[1] n CHEM of distillation column plateau m, CONST head plate of frame sablière haute f, of lock fond m, palastre m, palâtre m, platine f, wall plate plate-forme f, poutre sablière f, sablière f, sablière de comble f, semelle f, ELEC capacitor lame f, cell plaque f, ELEC ENG plaque f, MECH plaque f, tôle f, MECH ENG galette f, plaque f, plateau m, of machine tool plateau m, table f, of press plateau m, semelle f, METALL plaque f, NAUT shipbuilding tôle f, PRINT illustration plaque f, PROD ENG tôle f, of cast iron plaque f, taque f, PROP MAT tôle f; ~ **amalgamation** n COAL TECH amalgamation à plaques f; ~ **anemometer** n METEO anémomètre à plaque m; ~ **backing** n PRINT feuille d'habillage f; ~ **bending rollers** n pl MECH ENG machine à cintrer les tôles f; ~ **bending rolls** n pl MECH ENG machine à cintrer les tôles f; ~ **block** n C&G pièce à nez f; ~ **boundary** n GEOL frontière d'une plaque f, limite d'une plaque f; ~ **camera** n PHOTO chambre f; ~ **capacitor** n ELEC condensateur à lames m; ~ **changeover** n PRINT changement de plaque m; ~ **circuit** n ELEC ENG circuit anodique m; ~ **clutch** n MECH ENG embrayage à disque m, embrayage à plateau m; ~ **column** n PETR TECH colonne à plateaux f; ~ **column scrubber** n POLLUTION séparateur laveur à plateaux m; ~ **coupling** n MECH ENG accouplement à plateaux m, manchon à plateaux m; ~ **cylinder** n PRINT cylindre-plaque m; ~ **edge planing machine** n MECH ENG chanfreineuse f, machine à chanfreiner f; ~ **flattening and bending machine** n MECH ENG machine à rouler et à cintrer les tôles f; ~ **folding and bending machine** n MECH ENG machine à plier et à couder les tôles f; ~ **freezer** n REFRIG congélateur à plaque m; ~ **gage** n (AmE), ~ **gauge** n (BrE) MECH ENG jauge pour tôle f, jauge pour tôle forte f, METR calibre d'épaisseur m; ~ **girder** n CONST poutre en tôle f; ~ **glass** n C&G polished, flat glace f, verre à glace m, CONST glace de vitrage f; ~ **glazing** n PAPER TECH glaçage au laminoir à plaque m; ~ **glazing calender** n PAPER TECH laminoir à plaque m; ~ **hoist** n PROD ENG lève-tôles m; ~ **holder** n PHOTO châssis porte-plaque m; ~ **ice** n REFRIG glace en plaque f; ~ **iron** n PROD ENG tôle f, tôle de fer f; ~ **iron girder** n CONST poutre en tôle f; ~ **laying** n RAIL vehicles pose de la voie f; ~ **level** n

INSTRUMENT niveau d'alidade m; ~ **link** n MECH ENG gear coulisse à flasques f; ~ **lockup system** n PRINT système d'accrochage de la plaque m; ~ **making** n PRINT fabrication de plaques f; ~ **margin** n GEOL marge d'une plaque f; ~ **mill** n MECH ENG train de tôlerie m; ~ **molding** n (AmE), ~ **moulding** n (BrE) PROD ENG founding moulage sur plaque-modèle m; ~ **printing** n PRINT impression en creux f; ~ **printing machine** n PRINT machine à imprimer en creux f; ~ **processing** n PRINT développement de la plaque m, développement du cliché m, traitement de la plaque m; ~ **processor** n PRINT machine à développer les plaques f; ~ **roll** n MECH ENG cylindre à tôles m; ~ **saw** n MECH ENG scie à tôles f; ~ **shears** n pl MECH ENG cisailles à tôles f pl; ~ **spring** n MECH ENG leaf spring ressort à lames étagées m; ~ **strap** n AUTO barrette f; ~ **tectonics** n GEOL tectonique des plaques f; ~ **web** n NAUT shipbuilding âme en tôle f; ~ **web girder** n CONST poutre à âme pleine f

plate[2] vt ELEC ENG electroplating plaquer, MECH métalliser, plaquer, NAUT shipbuilding border

plateau n PETR TECH plateau m; ~ **level** n PETR TECH palier m, palier de production m

plated-through: ~ **hole** n ELECTRON trou métallisé m

plate-glazed adj PAPER TECH board laminé à la plaque

platelet n P&R pigment paillette f; ~ **structure** n METALL structure de plaquettes f

platen n CINEMAT plateau presseur m, verre presseur m, COMP, DP cylindre m, MECH ENG of machine tool, moulding machine plateau m

plater n PROD ENG person plaqueur m

plater's: ~ **shop** n NAUT atelier des tôles m

plate-straightening: ~ **machine** n RAIL dresseuse de tôles f

plateworks n PROD ENG tôlerie f

platform n COMP plate-forme f, CONST quai m, DP, MECH ENG, PETR TECH plate-forme f, PROD ENG of furnace plate-forme f, pont de chargement m, RAIL quai m; ~ **awning** n RAIL marquise f; ~ **equipment** n PETR TECH oeuvres mortes f pl; ~ **lift** n PROD ENG plate-forme élévatrice f; ~ **truck** n TRANSP camionnette plateau f

platforming n PETR TECH plate-formeur m

plating n ELEC ENG placage m, NAUT boat building bordé m, PROD ENG manufacture of iron plates tôlerie f, overlaying mechanically with more precious metal placage m

plating-out: ~ **test** n PROD ENG épreuve par rabattement f

platinic adj CHEM platinique

platiniridium n CHEM platiniridium m

platinochloride n CHEM platinochlorure m

platinoid adj PROP MAT platinoïde

platinotron n PHYS platinotron m

platinum n (Pt) CHEM platine m (Pt); ~ **crucible** n LAB EQUIP container creuset en platine m; ~ **resistance thermometer** n PHYS thermomètre à résistance de platine m; ~ **sponge** n CHEM mousse de platine f; ~ **wire** n LAB EQUIP analysis fil de platine m

platinum-iridium n CHEM platiniridium m

platman n (AmE) (cf onsetter) MINING accrocheur m, clicheur m, ouvrier d'accrochage m

platoon n TRANSP traffic peloton m; ~ **dispersion** n TRANSP traffic control dispersion d'un peloton f

platt n MINING accrochage m, envoyage m, recette f

platten n P&R platine f; ~ **press** n P&R presse à plusieurs étages f

platter *n* COMP, DP plateau *m*

plattnerite *n* MINERAL plattnérite *f*

play[1] *n* CINEMAT *machinery*, MECH jeu *m*, MECH ENG jeu d'usure *m*, *length of stroke* jeu *m*, levée *f*, *room to move* jeu *m*

play[2] *vt* TV mettre en marche; **~ in** *vt* TV insérer

playback *n* ACOUSTICS surjeu *m*, RECORDING présonorisation *f*, reproduction *f*, reproduction différée *f*, TV lecture *f*, reproduction *f*; **~ amplifier** *n* RECORDING amplificateur de lecture *m*; **~ characteristic** *n* RECORDING caractéristique de lecture *f*, caractéristique de reproduction *f*; TV caractéristique de reproduction *f*; **~ control** *n* RECORDING commande de lecture *f*; **~ head** *n* CINEMAT tête de lecture *f*, tête de reproduction *f*, TV tête de reproduction *f*; **~ level** *n* RECORDING niveau de lecture *m*; **~ loss** *n* RECORDING perte de reproduction *f*, TV pertes de reproduction *f pl*; **~ speed** *n* RECORDING vitesse de lecture *f*; **~ system** *n* RECORDING chaîne de lecture *f*; **~ videotape recorder** *n* TV magnétoscope de lecture *m*

playing: **~ time** *n* CINEMAT durée de projection *f*, RECORDING durée de reproduction *f*

play-only: **~ recorder** *n* RECORDING magnétophone de lecture *m*

pleat[1] *n* TEXTILES pli *m*

pleat[2] *vt* TEXTILES faire des plis

pleated *adj* TEXTILES plissé

pleater *n* TEXTILES plisseur *m*

pleating *n* TEXTILES plissage *m*; **~ machine** *n* TEXTILES machine à plisser *f*

Pleiades *n* ASTRON Pléiades *f pl*

plenum: **~ chamber** *n* AERONAUT chambre de tranquillisation *f*, pot d'équilibrage *m*, AUTO boîte de collecteur d'air *f*, boîte de répartition d'air *f*; **~ chamber** air cushion system *n* TRANSP coussin d'air à cloche *m*; **~ fan** *n* MECH ENG ventilateur foulant *m*, ventilateur positif *m*, ventilateur soufflant *m*; **~ ventilator** *n* MECH ENG ventilateur foulant *m*, ventilateur positif *m*, ventilateur soufflant *m*

plesiochronous: **~ digital hierarchy** *n* (*PDH*) TELECOM hiérarchie numérique plésiochrone *f*

plesiosynchronous: **~ line terminal** *n* TELECOM terminal de ligne plésiochrone *m*; **~ transmission equipment** *n* TELECOM équipement de transmission plésiochrone *m*

Plexiglass: **~ fairing** *n* (TM) AERONAUT plexiglas de saumon d'aile *m* (MD)

pliability *n* PROP MAT liant *m*

pliableness *n* PROP MAT liant *m*

pliancy *n* PROP MAT liant *m*

plied: **~ yarn** *n* TEXTILES fil retors *m*

plier: **~ saw set** *n* CONST pince à donner la voie aux scies *f*

pliers *n pl* ELEC pince *f*, pinces *f pl*, MECH ENG pince *f*, pinces *f pl*, VEHICLES pince *f*

plimsoll: **~ line** *n* NAUT marque de franc-bord *f*

pliofilm *n* CHEM pliofilm *m*

pliolit *n* CHEM pliolite *f*

PLL *abbr* (*phase-locked loop*) ELECTRON boucle à blocage de phase *f*, boucle à phase asservie *f*, SPACE, TELECOM, TV boucle à verrouillage de phase *f*

PLO *abbr* (*phase-locked oscillator*) ELECTRON oscillateur asservi en phase *m*

PL-OAM *abbr* (*physical layer operations and maintenance*) telecom cellule OAM de la couche physique *f*, cellule OAM de la physique *f*

plot[1] *n* AERONAUT *navigation* relevé *m*, COMP, DP tracé *m*, NAUT *navigation* point *m*, tracé *m*

plot[2] *vt* CONST faire le relevé de, lever, rapporter, relever, tracer, GEOM, MATH *graph*, NAUT *course* tracer

plot:[3] **~ a bearing** *vi* NAUT *navigation* porter un relèvement; **~ the position** *vi* NAUT *navigation* déterminer un point, faire le point, relever un pointé

plotter *n* COMP, DP table traçante *f*, traceur *m*

plotting *n* COMP, DP traçage *m*, MILIT *radar* pointage *m*, *topography* tracé *m*, NAUT *navigation* pointage *m*, tracé *m*, tracé de la route *m*; **~ board** *n* COMP, DP table traçante *f*; **~ chart** *n* NAUT *navigation* carte de tracé de navigation *f*; **~ ground** *n* CONST *surveying* relevé du terrain *m*; **~ paper** *n* CONST papier quadrillé *m*; **~ sheet** *n* NAUT *navigation* carte de pointage *f*; **~ table** *n* NAUT *navigation* table traçante *f*

plough *n* (BrE) CONST *joinery* bouvet de deux pièces *m*, bouvet à approfondir *m*, PRINT charrue *f*, soc *m*; **~ anchor** *n* (BrE) NAUT ancre charrue *f*, ancre à soc de charrue *f*; **~ belt** *n* (BrE) MECH ENG boulon de soc *m*; **~ folder** *n* (BrE) PRINT préplieuse *f*; **~ plane** *n* (BrE) CONST *joinery* bouvet de deux pièces *m*, bouvet à approfondir *m*

Plough *n* ASTRON Grand Chariot *m*

ploughed: **~ and feathered joint** *n* (BrE) CONST assemblage à fausse languette *m*; **~ and tongued joint** *n* (BrE) CONST assemblage à fausse languette *m*, assemblage à languette rapportée *m*, assemblage à rainure et languette *m*

ploughshare *n* (BrE) NAUT *anchor* ancre CQR *f*

plow *n* (AmE) *see plough*

plowed: **~ and feathered joint** *n* (AmE) *see ploughed and feathered joint* **~ and tongued joint** *n* (AmE) *see ploughed and tongued joint*

plowshare *n* (AmE) *see ploughshare*

PLS *abbr* (*physical layer service*) TELECOM service de la couche physique *m*

pluck[1] *n* C&G collage *m*

pluck[2] *vt* FOOD TECH plumer

plucking *n* (*cf picking*) TEXTILES arrachage de fibre *m*

plug:[1] **~ compatible** *adj* ELEC ENG totalement compatible

plug[2] *n* C&G mandrin *m*, CINEMAT fiche *f*, prise *f*, CONST bouchon *m*, calibre à bouchon *m*, tampon *m*, coin demi-rond *m*, plat-coin *m*, *of cock* clef *f*, noix *f*, *quarrying and stone-working* coin *m*, coin à pierre *m*, quille *f*, *stopper* bonde *f*, ELEC *connection* fiche *f*, prise mâle *f*, prise mâle de courant *f*, ELEC ENG fiche *f*, fiche de prise de courant *f*, HYDR EQUIP bouchon *m*, MECH bonde *f*, bouchon *m*, NAUT *shipbuilding* bouchon *m*, matrice *f*, PETR TECH bouchon obturateur *m*, PHYS *electronic* fiche *f*, PRINT bouchon utile *m*, prise de courant *f*, PROD ENG bouchon *m*, bouchon d'obturation de trou de coulée *m*, tampon *m*, *at bottom of reservoir* bonde *f*, crapaudine *f*, TELECOM fiche *f*, TV fiche *f*, prise *f*, VEHICLES *drain plug* bouchon *m*, *ignition* bougie *f*, WATER SUPP *hydrant* bouche *f*, bouche d'eau *f*, hydrante *m*; **~ adaptor** *n* ELEC ENG adaptateur *m*, adaptateur de prise de courant *m*, adaptateur de fiche *m*; **~ and cord switchboard** *n* TELECOM commutateur manuel à fiches et jacks *m*, commutateur à fiches et jacks *m*; **~ and socket** *n* PROD ENG connecteur mâle-femelle *m*, TELECOM prise téléphonique *f*; **~ box** *n* ELEC ENG prise de courant *f*; **~ center bit** *n* (AmE), **~ centre bit** *n* (BrE) MECH ENG foret à téton cylindrique *m*; **~ cock** *n* CONST robinet à boisseau conique et à clef *m*, robinet à clef *m*; **~ compatibility** *n* ELEC ENG compatibilité totale *f*; **~ connection** *n* ELEC ENG raccordement à fiches *m*; **~ connector** *n* ELEC ENG contact à fiches *m*;

~ door *n* PROD ENG porte vissée *f*; **~ drill** *n* MECH ENG perforatrice percutante à main *f*; **~ gage** *n* (AmE) CONST calibre à bouchon *m*, tampon *m*, CONST bouchon *m*, MECH ENG bouchon à tolérance *m*, tampon à tolérance *m*, tampon-jauge *m*, METR calibre tampon *m* **~ gauge** *n* (BrE) CONST bouchon *m*, calibre à bouchon *m*, tampon *m*, MECH ENG bouchon à tolérance *m*, tampon à tolérance *m*, tampon-jauge *m*, METR calibre tampon *m*; **~ hole** *n* CONST *of cock* trou de clef *m*; **~ pin** *n* ELEC *connection* pointe de contact *f*; **~ receptacle** *n* ELEC *connection* prise femelle *f*; **~ seat** *n* MECH ENG siège de bonde *m*; **~ socket** *n* CINEMAT fiche femelle *f*, VEHICLES *electrical* prise de courant *f*, *ignition* embout de bougie *m*;**~ switch** *n* CONTROL interrupteur enfichable *m*, ELEC ENG commutateur à fiche *m*; **~ tap** *n* MECH ENG *bottoming* taraud cylindrique *m*, taraud finisseur *m*, troisième taraud *m*, *second* second taraud *m*, taraud demi-conique *m*, taraud intermédiaire *m*; **~ timer** *n* ELEC ENG prise programmable *f*; **~ wire** *n* ELEC ENG fil de connexion *m*

plug[3] *vt* ELEC ENG enficher, NAUT *shipbuilding* boucher, PRINT faire de la publicité; **~ in** *vt* CINEMAT brancher, ELEC *connection* embrocher, enficher, ELEC ENG enficher, raccorder, TV brancher, raccorder

plug:[4] **~ in** *vi* TELECOM enficher, s'enficher

plugboard *n* COMP, DP, ELEC ENG tableau de connexions *m*

pluggable *adj* ELEC ENG enfichable

plugged: ~ mirror *n* NUCLEAR trigma *m*

plugger *n* MECH ENG perforatrice percutante *f*

plugging *n* CONST *of wall* tamponnage *m*, ELEC ENG enfichage *m*, MECH ENG bouchage *m*, tamponnement *m*, MINING *quarrying* enferrure *f*, PETR TECH rebouchage *m*, PRINT bouchage par gain du point *m*, graissage *m*, TEXTILES colmatage *m*; **~ bar** *n* MECH ENG chasse-tampon *m*

plug-in[1] *adj* PROD ENG embrochable

plug-in:[2] **~ coil** *n* ELEC ENG bobine interchangeable *f*; **~ component** *n* ELEC ENG composant enfichable *m*; **~ module** *n* ELEC ENG module enfichable *m*; **~ relay** *n* ELEC ENG relais enfichable *m*; **~ switch** *n* PROD ENG interrupteur embrochable *m*; **~ termination** *n* ELEC *cable accessory* extrémité embrochable *f*, extrémité enfichable *f*, prise embrochable *f*, prise enfichable *f*; **~ unit** *n* ELEC tiroir *m*, unité enfichable *f*, ELEC ENG dispositif enfichable *m*

plug-tenon: ~ joint *n* CONST enture à goujon *f*, enture à simple tenon *f*

plug-type: ~ connection *n* ELEC prise embrochable *f*; **~ connector** *n* TELECOM connecteur enfichable *m*; **~ outlet** *n* ELEC *connection* prise embrochable *f*

plumb:[1] **off ~** *adj* CONST hors d'aplomb CONST droit

plumb[2] *adv* CONST d'aplomb, à plomb

plumb[3] *n* CONST *vertical* aplomb *m*; **~ bob** *n* CONST plomb *m*; **~ line** *n* CONST fil à plomb *m*, plomb *m*

plumb[4] *vt* CONST plomber

plumbago *n* CHEM graphite *m*, plombagine *f*; **~ crucible** *n* PROD ENG creuset en graphite *m*, creuset en mine de plomb *m*, creuset en plombagine *m*

plumbate *n* CHEM plombate *m*

plumber *n* CONST *person* plombier *m*

plumber's: ~ joints *n pl* CONST assemblages de plomberie *m pl*; **~ solder** *n* CONST soudure des plombiers *f*

plumbic *adj* CHEM plombique

plumbicon *n* ELECTRON plumbicon *m*

plumbing *n* CONST plombage *m*, plomberie *f*

plumbite *n* CHEM plumbate *m*

plumbous *adj* CHEM plombeux

plume *n* FLUID PHYS *thermal flows*, OCEANOG *river discharge*, POLLUTION panache *m*; **~ opacity** *n* C&G opacité du panache *f*; **~ rise** *n* POLLUTION ascension de panaches *f*

plummer: ~ block *n* MECH ENG roulement de palier *m*, PROD ENG chaise palier *f*, palier *m*; **~ block bearing** *n* MECH ENG roulement de palier *m*

plummet *n* CONST fil à plomb *m*

plump: ~ gate *n* PROD ENG *founding* chenal de coulée en chute directe *m*

plunge[1] *n* GEOL *of folds* plongement *m*

plunge[2] *vi* GEOL *structural* s'ennoyer

plunger *n* C&G poinçon *m*, ELEC ENG *of incandescent electric lamp holder* piston *m*, *of relay* noyau plongeur *m*, MECH piston plongeur *m*, MECH ENG piston *m*, piston plein *m*, piston plongeur *m*, plongeur *m*, PROD ENG poussoir *m*, VEHICLES *brake, clutch cylinder* plongeur *m*; **~ assist mechanism** *n* C&G couplage came-poinçon *m*; **~ elevator** *n* CONST ascenseur à piston plongeur *m*; **~ fuel pump** *n* AUTO pompe à essence à piston *f*; **~ jig** *n* PROD ENG crible hydraulique à piston *m*, crible à piston *m*; **~ lift** *n* MINING jeu foulant *m*; **~ piston** *n* MECH ENG piston *m*, piston plein *m*, piston plongeur *m*, plongeur *m*; **~ pump** *n* WATER SUPP pompe foulante *f*, pompe refoulante *f*, pompe à piston plongeur *f*, pompe à plongeur *f*; **~ relay** *n* ELEC ENG *of relay* relais à noyau plongeur *m*; **~ ring** *n* C&G cercle *m*; **~ set** *n* MINING jeu foulant *m*; **~ spike** *n* (AmE) *(cf plunger sticking)* C&G collage de poinçon *m*; **~ sticking** *n* (BrE) *(cf plunger spike)* C&G collage de poinçon *m*

plunger-type: ~ jig *n* COAL TECH bac à piston mécanique *m*

plunging *n* CONST *telescope of theodolite* plongée *f*

plurivalent *adj* CHEM plurivalent

plus: ~ diopter *n* (AmE), **~ dioptre** *n* (BrE) CINEMAT bonnette *f*, lentille dioptrique *f*; **~ sign** *n* CONST *surveying* coup arrière *m*; **~ tapping** *n* ELEC prise additive *f*

pluton *n* GEOL *igneous intrusion* corps intrusif igné *m*, pluton *m*

plutonic: ~ magma *n* PETR hypomagma *m*, magma des profondeurs *m*; **~ rock** *n* GEOPHYS roche plutonienne *f*

plutonium *n (Pu)* CHEM plutonium *m (Pu)*

ply *n* AUTO pli *m*, MECH ENG pli *m*, épaisseur *f*, SPACE *spacecraft* couche *f*, nappe *f*, pli *m*, TEXTILES bout *m*, VEHICLES *tyre* pli *m*; **~ glass** *n* C&G *of flat glass* verre feuilleté avec couche intermédiaire en fibres de verre *m*, *of hollow glass* verre creux doublé à l'opale *m*; **~ separation** *n* P&R *tyre* séparation entre plis *f*

plybond: ~ strength *n* P&R *plywood, laminates, rubber* adhérence des couches *f*, adhésion entre les couches *f*

plywood *n* CONST bois composite *m*, bois contreplaqué *m*, bois de contreplacage *m*, contreplaqué *m*, *article* contreplaqué *m*, PACKAGING contreplaqué *m*; **~ adhesive** *n* PACKAGING adhésif pour contreplaqué *m*; **~ case** *n* PACKAGING caisse en contreplaqué *f*; **~ drum** *n* PACKAGING fût en contre-plaqué *m*

Pm *(promethium)* CHEM Pm *(prométhéum)*

PM *abbr (phase modulation)* COMP, DP, ELECTRON, PHYS, RECORDING, TELECOM, TV MP *(modulation de phase)*

PMBX *abbr (private manual branch exchange)* TELECOM commutateur privé manuel *m*

p-n: ~ homojunction diode *n* ELECTRON diode à homojonction PN *f*; **~ junction** *n* ELECTRON, PHYS jonction

PN *f*; ~ **junction diode** *n* ELEC diode à jonction PN *f*,
ELECTRON diode à jonction PN *f*; ~ **rectifier** *n* ELEC ENG
redresseur à jonction PN *m*
PN *abbr (positive notification)* TELECOM notification
positive *f*
pneumatic[1] *adj* MECH ENG, PHYS, VEHICLES pneumatique
pneumatic:[2] ~ **assembly tool** *n* MECH ENG outil pneumatique pour l'assemblage *m*; ~ **brake** *n* VEHICLES frein
pneumatique *m*, frein à air comprimé *m*; ~ **brake
system** *n* MECH ENG système pneumatique de freinage
m; ~ **cell** *n* COAL TECH cellule pneumatique *f*; ~ **clutch** *n*
MECH ENG embrayage pneumatique *m*; ~ **conveying of
bulk materials** *n* MECH ENG transport pneumatique de
matériaux en vrac *m*; ~ **coupling** *n* MECH ENG *power
transmission* accouplement pneumatique *m*; ~ **cylinder** *n* AERONAUT *helicopter* compensateur
pneumatique *m*, MECH ENG cylindre pneumatique *m*;
~ **detector** *n* TRANSP *traffic control* détecteur pneumatique *m*; ~ **drill** *n* CONST *rock drill* perforateur à air
comprimé *m*, perforatrice pneumatique *f*; ~ **equipment** *n* MECH ENG matériel pneumatique *m*; ~ **fluid
power** *n* MECH ENG transmission pneumatique *f*; ~
gage *n* (AmE), ~ **gauge** *n* METR calibre de préréglage
m; ~ **governor** *n* CONTROL régulateur pneumatique *m*;
~ **hammer** *n* MINING marteau pneumatique *m*; ~ **hammer drill** *n* CONST marteau perforateur pneumatique
m; ~ **handling** *n* COAL TECH traitement pneumatique
m; ~ **impact wrench** *n* MECH ENG *tool* clé à chocs
pneumatique *f*; ~ **jig** *n* COAL TECH jig pneumatique *m*,
MECH ENG jig pneumatique *m*, jig à air *m*; ~ **loudspeaker** *n* ACOUSTICS haut-parleur pneumatique *m*; ~
motor *n* MECH ENG machine pneumatique *f*, moteur
pneumatique *m*; ~ **pick** *n* MINING marteau-piqueur *m*;
~ **pipe conveyor** *n* TRANSP convoyeur pneumatique *m*;
~ **power hammer** *n* CONST marteau-pilon atmosphérique *m*; ~ **pump** *n* MECH ENG machine pneumatique *f*; ~
ram *n* COAL TECH mouton pneumatique *m*; ~ **rammer** *n*
PROD ENG *founding* fouloir pneumatique *m*, fouloir à
air comprimé *m*; ~ **release** *n* PHOTO déclencheur pneumatique *m*; ~ **riveter** *n* PROD ENG rivoir pneumatique
m; ~ **sensor** *n* PRINT capteur pneumatique *m*, détecteur pneumatique *m*; ~ **suspension** *n* TRANSP *monorail*
suspension pneumatique *f*; ~ **switch** *n* CONTROL interrupteur pneumatique *m*; ~ **table** *n* COAL TECH table
pneumatique *f*; ~ **tire** *n* (AmE) *see pneumatic tyre*; ~
tool *n* MECH ENG outil pneumatique *m*; ~ **transmission
system** *n* MECH ENG *power transmission* système de
transmission pneumatique *m*; ~ **treatment** *n* COAL
TECH traitement pneumatique *m*; ~ **tyre** *n* (BrE)
TRANSP pneumatique *m*, VEHICLES bandage pneumatique *m*, pneumatique *m*; ~ **valve** *n* MECHeng   valve
pneumatique *f*
pneumatically-operated: ~ **switch** *n* ELEC interrupteur
pneumatique *m*; ~ **valve** *n* MECH ENG vanne de régulation pneumatique *f*
pneumaticity *n* PROP MAT pneumaticité *f*
pneumatics *n* PHYS pneumatique *f*
pneumatic-tired: ~ **metropolitan railroad** *n* (AmE) *(cf
pneumatic-tyred metropolitan railway)* TRANSP métropolitain sur pneumatiques *m*; ~ **roller** *n* (AmE) *see
pneumatic tyred roller*
pneumatic-tyred: ~ **metropolitan railway** *n* (BrE) *(cf
pneumatic-tired metropolitan railroad)* TRANSP métropolitain sur pneumatiques *m* ~ **roller** *n* (BrE) CONST
rouleau à pneus *m*
pneumatolysis *n* GEOL pneumatolyse *f*

PNP[1] *abbr (private numbering plan)* TELECOM PNP
(plan de numérotage privé)
PNP:[2] ~ **transistor** *n* ELECTRON, PHYS transistor PNP *m*
p-n-p-n: ~ **component** *n* ELECTRON composant à quatre
couches *m*; ~ **device** *n* ELECTRON composant à quatre
couches *m*, dispositif à quatre couches *m*
PNX *abbr (private network exchange)* TELECOM commutateur de réseau privé *m*
Po *(polonium)* CHEM Po *(polonium)*
pocket *n* COAL TECH poche *f*, MINING fosse de remplissage *f*, *of ore* poche de minerai *f*, paper tech chambre
de pression *f*; ~ **book** *n* PRINT livre de poche *m*; ~
calculator *n* COMP, DP calculatrice de poche *f*, TELE-
COM calculette *f*; ~ **compass** *n* MILIT boussole de poche
f; ~ **folding machine** *n* PRINT plieuse à poches *f*; ~
grinder *n* PAPER TECH défibreur multipresse *m*; ~ **lamp**
n ELEC *illumination* lampe de poche *f*; ~ **terminal** *n*
TELECOM terminal de poche *m*; ~ **ventilation roll** *n*
PAPER TECH rouleau de ventilation de poche d'air *m*
pocket-ventilating: ~ **duct** *n* PAPER TECH conduit de
ventilation de poche d'air *m*
pocking *n* C&G tavelure *f*
pockmarks *n pl* C&G peau rugueuse *f*
pod *n* SPACE *spacecraft* nacelle *f*
podocarpic *adj* CHEM podocarpique
podophyllin *n* CHEM podophylline *f*
POGO: ~ **effect** *n* SPACE *spacecraft* effet POGO *m*, excitation du satellite par le lanceur *f*
Pogson: ~ **scale of magnitude** *n* ASTRON échelle de
magnitude de Pogson *f*
POH *abbr (path overhead)* TELECOM préfixe de
conduit *m*, résidu de trajet *m*
point[1] *adj* PHYS ponctuel
point:[2] **in** ~ *n* TV point d'entrée *m* ~ **charge** *n* ELEC
electrostatics, PHYS charge ponctuelle *f*; ~ **chuck** *n*
MECH ENG mandrin à toc *m*, plateau pousse-toc *m*,
plateau à toc *m*, plateau-toc *m*; ~ **circle** *n* MECH ENG
gearing cercle d'échanfreinement *m*, cercle de couronne *m*, cercle de tête *m*, cercle extérieur *m*; ~ **code** *n*
TELECOM code de point *m*; ~ **of concurrence** *n* GEOM
point concourant *m*; ~ **of conflict** *n* TRANSP *traffic
control* point de conflit *m*; ~ **of contact** *n* PHYS point de
contact *m*; ~ **contact** *n* ELEC ENG contact ponctuel *m*; ~
contact detector diode *n* ELECTRON diode de détection
à pointe *f*; ~ **contact diode** *n* ELECTRON diode à pointe
f; ~ **contact mixer diode** *n* ELECTRON diode mélangeuse
à pointe *f*; ~ **contact silicon diode** *n* ELECTRON diode à
pointe au silicium *f*; ~ **contact transistor** *n* ELECTRON
transistor à pointes *m*; ~ **defect** *n* CRYSTALL, METALL
défaut ponctuel *m*; ~ **group** *n* CRYSTALL groupe ponctuel *m*; ~ **group symmetry** *n* CRYSTALL symétrie de
groupe ponctuel *f*; ~ **of intersection** *n* GEOM point
d'intersection *m*; ~ **lock plunger** *n* RAIL plongeur *m*; ~
of no return *n* AERONAUT PNR, point de non-retour *m*,
point milieu *m*; ~ **of osculation** *n* GEOM *osculating
curves* point d'osculation *m*; ~ **plate rectifier** *n* ELEC
redresseur point-plaque *m*; ~ **recorder** *n* INSTRUMENT
enregistreur par points *m*; ~ **resistance** *n* COAL TECH
résistance à la pointe *f*; ~ **of sale** *n* *(POS)* COMP, DP
point de vente *m*; ~ **of sale display** *n* PACKAGING
étalage au point de vente *m*; ~ **of sale terminal** *n*
PACKAGING tête de raccordement au point de vente *f*;
~ **set geometry** *n* GEOM géométrie des points d'ensemble *f*; ~ **source** *n* CINEMAT, PHOTO, PHYS source
ponctuelle *f*, POLLUTION lieu d'émission *m*, source
ponctuelle *f*; ~ **source light** *n* PHOTO lumière d'une

source ponctuelle *f*; ~ **source radio transmitter** *n* TRANSP émetteur radio à source ponctuelle *m*; ~ **of support** *n* MECH ENG point d'appui *m*; ~ **switch** *n* RAIL aiguille *f*; ~ **system** *n* PRINT système des points typographiques *m*; ~ **of tangency** *n* GEOM point de tangence *m*; ~ **tool** *n* MECH ENG *lathe* outil à pointe *m*; ~ **vacuum cleaning system** *n* SAFETY installation d'aspiration concentrée *f*

point[3] *vt* CONST *to furnish with point* appointer, appointir, empointer, tailler en pointe

pointable: ~ **generator** *n* SPACE *spacecraft* générateur orientable *m*

pointed: ~ **square head coach screw** *n* CONST vis à bois pointé à tête carrée *f*

pointer *n* COMP *graphics* pointeur *m*, DP *graphics* dispositif de pointage *m*, pointeur *m*, ELEC, ELEC ENG *on instrument dial* aiguille *f*, LAB EQUIP *instrument* aiguille *f*, pointeau *m*, MECH ENG *of meter* aiguille *f*, PRINT curseur *m*, index *m*, RAIL levier de manoeuvre des aiguilles *m*, TELECOM pointeur *m*; ~ **chain** *n* COMP, DP chaîne de pointeurs *f*; ~ **instrument** *n* INSTRUMENT instrument à aiguille *m*, instrument à cadran *m*; ~ **jack** *n* MECH ENG arrache-aiguille *m*; ~ **justification count** *n* *(PJC)* TELECOM compte de justification de pointeur *m*; ~ **justification event** *n* *(PJE)* TELECOM événement de justification de pointeur *m*; ~ **knob** *n* MECH ENG bouton à index *m*, bouton-flèche *m*

Pointers *n pl* ASTRON Gardes *m pl*

pointing *n* CONST appointage *m*, appointissage *m*, *brickwork* jointoiement *m*, jointoyage *m*, SPACE *spacecraft* pointage *m*; ~ **accuracy** *n* SPACE *spacecraft* précision de pointage *f*; ~ **error** *n* SPACE *spacecraft* erreur de pointage *f*; ~ **loss** *n* SPACE *communications* perte par dépointage *f*, TELECOM perte due au pointage *f*

pointless: ~ **ignition** *n* (AmE) AUTO allumage transistorisé sans rupteur *m*

pointolite *n* CHEM lampe à pointe de tungstène *f*

point-operating: ~ **stretcher** *n* RAIL tringle de manoeuvre d'aiguille *f*

points *n* (*cf contact breaker point*) AUTO vis platinée *f*, RAIL (BrE) aiguille *f*, changement de voie *m*; ~ **and crossing** *n* RAIL appareil de voie *m*; ~ **of the compass** *n* *pl* NAUT aires de vent *f pl*; ~ **heating** *n* RAIL réchauffage d'aiguilles *m*; ~ **rod** *n* RAIL tige de manoeuvre d'aiguille *f*; ~ **switching** *n* RAIL aiguillage *m*

point-to-point[1] *adj* COMP, DP point à point

point-to-point:[2] ~ **communication** *n* PROD ENG transmission poste à poste *f*; ~ **line** *n* COMP, DP ligne point à point *f*; ~ **link** *n* ELEC ENG liaison de point à point *f*; ~ **transport** *n* TRANSP transport de point à point *m*; ~ **wiring** *n* ELEC *supply* câblage point par point *m*, ELEC ENG câblage direct *m*

poise *n* METR poise *m*

Poiseuille: ~ **flow** *n* FLUID PHYS écoulement de Poiseuille *m*

Poiseuille's: ~ **law** *n* PHYS loi de Poiseuille *f*

poison *n* SAFETY poison *m*, toxique *m*

poisoning *n* CHEM *of catalyst* empoisonnement *m*, POLLUTION intoxication *f*

poisons: ~ **cupboard** *n* LAB EQUIP *furniture, safety* armoire à poisons *f*

Poisson: ~ **distribution** *n* COMP, DP distribution de Poisson *f*, MATH loi de Poisson *f*, PHYS distribution de Poisson *f*; ~ **traffic** *n* TELECOM trafic poissonnien *m*

Poisson's: ~ **equation** *n* PHYS équation de Poisson *f*; ~

law *n* SPACE loi de Poisson *f*; ~ **ratio** *n* COAL TECH nombre de Poisson *m*, CONST, MECH *materials* coefficient de Poisson *m*, PETR formule de Poisson *f*, PHYS coefficient de Poisson *m*

poker *n* GAS TECH décrasseur *m*, PROD ENG attisoir *m*, cure-feu *m*, fourgon *m*, pique-feu *m*, tisonnier *m*; ~ **vibrator** *n* CONST *concreting* aiguille vibrante *f*, vibrateur à béton *m*

poking *n* PROD ENG attisage *m*, attisement *m*

polar[1] *adj* CHEM *compound* polaire

polar[2] *n* ASTRON, GEOM polaire *f*; ~ **air** *n* METEO air polaire *m*; ~ **Aurora** *n* METEO aurore polaire *f*; ~ **axis** *n* ASTRON axe polaire *m*, INSTRUMENT axe du monde *m*, axe horaire *m*; ~ **axis circle** *n* INSTRUMENT cercle de calage horaire *m*; ~ **cap** *n* ASTRON calotte polaire *f*; ~ **climate** *n* METEO climat polaire *m*; ~ **coordinates** *n pl* ELECTRON, PHYS coordonnées polaires *f pl*; ~ **diagram** *n* PHYS diagramme polaire *m*; ~ **dielectric** *n* PHYS diélectrique polaire *m*; ~ **front** *n* METEO front polaire *m*; ~ **molecule** *n* CHEM, P&R molécule polaire *f*; ~ **orbit** *n* SPACE orbite polaire *f*; ~ **tip** *n* ASTRON calotte polaire *f*; ~ **triangle** *n* GEOM triangle polaire *m*

polarimeter *n* CHEM, LAB EQUIP *analysis*, PHYS, RAD PHYS polarimètre *m*

polarimetric *adj* CHEM polarimétrique

polarimetry *n* CHEM polarimétrie *f*

Polaris *n see North Star*

polariscope *n* PHYS polariscope *m*

polarity *n* CHEM, ELEC, ELEC ENG, PHYS, TV polarité *f*; ~ **control** *n* TV réglage de la polarité *m*; ~ **epoch** *n* GEOL période de polarité géomagnétique *f*; ~ **reversal** *n* ELEC *machine*, ELEC ENG, SPACE *spacecraft* inversion de polarité *f*; ~ **reverser** *n* ELEC *switch* inverseur de polarité *m*; ~ **sign** *n* ELEC *cell* signe de polarité *m*; ~ **tester** *n* ELEC *connections* cherche-pôles *m*, chercheur de pôle *m*

polarity-reversing: ~ **switch** *n* ELEC ENG inverseur de polarité *m*

polarizability *n* CHEM, PHYS polarisabilité *f*

polarizable *adj* CHEM polarisable

polarization *n* ELEC *cell*, ELEC ENG, PHOTO, PHYS, RAD PHYS, SPACE, TELECOM polarisation *f*; ~ **angle** *n* OPT angle de polarisation *m*; ~ **charges** *n* PHYS charge de polarisation *f*; ~ **coupling loss** *n* TELECOM affaiblissement par couplage de polarisation *m*; ~ **current** *n* PHYS courant de polarisation *m*; ~ **duplexer** *n* SPACE *communications* duplexeur de polarisation *m*; ~ **filter** *n* CINEMAT filtre polarisant *m*; ~ **grid** *n* SPACE *communications* grille de polarisation *f*; ~ **isolation** *n* SPACE *communications* découplage de polarisation *m*; ~ **microscope** *n* LAB EQUIP microscope polarisant *m*; ~ **purity** *n* SPACE *communications* pureté de polarisation *f*

polarize *vt* OPT polariser

polarized: ~ **capacitor** *n* ELEC ENG condensateur polarisé *m*; ~ **connector** *n* ELEC ENG connecteur polarisé *m*; ~ **electrolytic capacitor** *n* ELEC ENG condensateur électrolytique polarisé *m*; ~ **light** *n* CINEMAT, PHOTO, PHYS, RAD PHYS, WAVE PHYS lumière polarisée *f*; ~ **plug** *n* ELEC ENG fiche polarisée *f*; ~ **relay** *n* ELEC, ELEC ENG relais polarisé *m*; ~ **waves** *n pl* WAVE PHYS ondes polarisées *f pl*

polarizer[1] *adj* OPT polarisant, polariseur *m*

polarizer[2] *n* LAB EQUIP *microscope*, METALL, PHYS, SPACE *communications*, TELECOM polariseur *m*

polarizing: ~ **angle** *n* OPT angle de polarisation *m*; ~ **filter**

n INSTRUMENT filtre polarisant *m*, module d'observa-tion *m*, PHOTO polariseur *m*; **~ microscope** *n* C&G polariscope *m*, CRYSTALL, INSTRUMENT, LAB EQUIP, PHYS microscope polarisant *m*; **~ prism** *n* INSTRUMENT prisme polariseur *m*; **~ spectacles** *n pl* PHOTO *for stereo viewing* lunettes à verres polarisés *f pl*; **~ sun prism** *n* INSTRUMENT prisme solaire polariseur *m*

polarogram *n* CHEM polarogramme *m*

polarographic *adj* CHEM polarographique

polarography *n* CHEM polarographie *f*

Polaroid *n* (TM) PHYS, RAD PHYS polaroïd *m* (MD); **~ fade** *n* CINEMAT fondu avec filtre polarisant *m*

polaron *n* PHYS polaron *m*

polar-orbiting *adj* SPACE en orbite polaire

pole *n* CONST *post, mast* appui *m*, mât *m*, perche *f*, poteau *m*, *surveyor's levelling pole* mire *f*, ELEC *switch, magnet, machine*, ELEC ENG, GEOM, METR *linear measure* pôle *m*, PAPER TECH perche *f*, PHYS pôle *m*; **~ arrangement** *n* PROD ENG configuration des pôles *f*; **~ box** *n* MINING *boring* boîte de sonde *f*; **~ changer switch** *n* ELEC inverseur de courant *m*; **~ face** *n* TV face polaire *f*; **~ figure** *n* CRYSTALL *X-ray pattern* figure de pôle *f*; **~ hook** *n* MINING *boring* caracole *f*; **~ lathe** *n* MECH ENG tour à pointes *m*; **~ mounting** *n* PROD ENG montage sur poteau *m*; **~ piece** *n* ELEC ENG pièce polaire *f*, MECH ENG masse polaire *f*, PHYS, RECORDING pièce polaire *f*; **~ plate** *n* CONST *building* plate-forme *f*, sablière *f*, sablière de comble *f*; **~ route** *n* TELECOM ligne aérienne *f*; **~ shading** *n* ELEC *generator, motor* déphasage par bague *m*; **~ shoe** *n* ELEC ENG pièce polaire *f*, TV masse polaire *f*; **~ slip** *n* ELEC *machine* glissement de pôle *m*; **~ strength** *n* PHYS intensité de pôle *f*; **~ tip** *n* TV pièce polaire *f*, pointe polaire *f*

Pole: ~ Star *n* ASTRON étoile polaire *f*

polecat *n* CINEMAT barre de soutien extensible *f*, co-lonne télescopique *f*, polecat *m*

pole-changing: ~ starter *n* ELEC *motor* démarreur par changement du nombre de pôles *m*

poleman *n* CINEMAT perchiste *m*

pole-mounted: ~ transformer *n* ELEC *overhead line* trans-formateur sur poteaux *m*, transformateur à poteaux *m*

pole-type: ~ transformer *n* ELEC transformateur sur poteaux *m*, transformateur à poteaux *m*

polianite *n* MINERAL polianite *f*

poling *n* MINING enfilage *m*, poussage *m*

polish[1] *n* COATINGS vernis d'ébéniste *m*, PAPER TECH lustre *m*

polish[2] *vt* C&G éclaircir, MECH polir; **~ till dry** *vt* C&G faire une séchée

Polish: ~ notation *n* DP notation polonaise *f*, notation préfixée *f*

polishable *adj* PROP MAT polissable

polished: ~ edge *n* C&G joint poli *m*; **~ rod** *n* FUELLESS *windmill pump* tige polie *f*; **~ stone value** *n* CONST coefficient de gravier poli *m*; **~ wired glass** *n* C&G glace armée *f*

polisher *n* C&G polisseur *m*, polissoir *m*, PROD ENG *person* polisseur *m*

polishing *n* METALL, P&R *operation* polissage *m*, PROD ENG poli *m*, polissage *m*; **~ agent** *n* C&G agent de polissage *m*; **~ apparatus** *n* PROP MAT polisseuse *f*; **~ head** *n* MECH ENG polissoir *m*, touret pour polisseurs *m*; **~ lathe** *n* MECH ENG polissoir *m*, touret de pousseur *m*; **~ machine** *n* PROD ENG machine à polir *f*; **~ paper** *n* C&G papier berzélius *m*; **~ runner** *n* C&G plateau porte-

feutres *m*; **~ shop** *n* C&G atelier de polissage *m*; **~ unit** *n* C&G élément de poli *m*; **~ wheel** *n* C&G meule de polissage *f*, MECH ENG disque à polir *m*, METALL disque de polissage *m*, disque à polir *m*, PROD ENG meule à polir *f*

poll:[1] **~ adze** *n* CONST herminette à tête *f*; **~ bit** *n* TELECOM bit d'interrogation *m*; **~ pick** *n* CONST pic à tête *m*, pioche à bec pointu et tête *f*

poll[2] *vt* COMP appeler, DP appeler, interroger

polling *n* COMP appel *m*, appel sélectif *m*, appel à émettre *m*, invitation à émettre *f*, interrogation *f*, DP appel sélectif *m*, interrogation *f*, invitation à émettre *f*, TELECOM interrogation préalable *f*, invitation à émet-tre *f*; **~ key** *n* TELECOM clef d'interrogation *f*; **~ selection** *n* COMP, DP interrogation-sélection *f*; **~ system** *n* TELECOM système d'interrogation séquentiel *m*

pollucite *n* MINERAL pollucite *f*

pollutant *n* MAR POLL, POLLUTION polluant *m*, SAFETY pollueur *m*; **~ deposition** *n* POLLUTION retombées des polluants *f pl*

pollute *vt* POLLUTION, QUALITY, SAFETY polluer

polluted[1] *adj* POLLUTION pollué

polluted:[2] **~ rainwater** *n* POLLUTION eaux de pluies pol-luées *f pl*; **~ water** *n* WATER SUPP eau polluée *f*

polluter: ~ pays principle *n* POLLUTION principe pol-lueur-payeur *m*

polluting: ~ agent *n* SAFETY produit polluant *m*

pollution *n* CHEM, QUALITY pollution *f*, SAFETY contami-nation *f*, pollution *f*, SPACE contamination *f*; **~ control** *n* POLLUTION contrôle de l'environnement *m*, lutte contre la pollution *f*; **~ emitter** *n* POLLUTION source de pollution *f*; **~ measurement** *n* SAFETY mesurage de la pollution *m*; **~ research** *n* POLLUTION étude sur la pollution *f*; **~ source** *n* POLLUTION source de pollu-tion *f*

polonium *n (Po)* CHEM polonium *m (Po)*

polyacrylamide *n* PETR TECH polyacrylamide *m*

polyacrylate *n* CHEM, P&R polyacrylate *m*

polyacrylonitrile *n* CHEM polyacrylonitrile *m*

polyamide *n* CHEM, P&R, PROP MAT, TEXTILES polya-mide *m*

polyamine *n* P&R *curing agent* polyamine *f*

polyatomic *adj* CHEM, GAS TECH polyatomique

polybasite *n* MINERAL polybasite *f*

polybutadiene *n* SPACE *spacecraft* polybutadiène *m*

polybutylene *n* P&R polybutylène *m*

polycarbonate *n* ELEC *dielectric*, P&R, PROP MAT polycar-bonate *m*

polychromatic *adj* C&G *glass* polychromatique

polychrome *adj* PRINT polychrome

polycondensation *n* CHEM polycondensation *f*

polycrase *n* MINERAL polycrase *f*

polycrystal *n* PROP MAT polycristal *m*

polycrystalline[1] *adj* PROP MAT polycristallin

polycrystalline:[2] **~ semiconductor** *n* ELECTRON semi-conducteur polycristallin *m*; **~ silicon** *n* ELECTRON silicium polycristallin *m*; **~ solid** *n* CRYSTALL solide polycristallin *m*

polycyclic[1] *adj* CHEM polycyclique

polycyclic:[2] **~ aromatic hydrocarbon** *n* POLLUTION hydrocarbure polycyclique aromatique *m*, hydrocar-bure polynucléaire aromatique *m*

polydentate *adj* CHEM polydenté

polydimethylsiloxane *n* CHEM polydiméthylsiloxane *m*

polyene *n* CHEM polyène *m*

polyenic *adj* CHEM polyénique

polyester *n* CHEM résine de polyester *f*, NAUT *boat building material*, P&R, PROP MAT, TEXTILES polyester *m*; ~ **base** *n* CINEMAT support polyester *m*; ~ **foam** *n* P&R *rubber* mousse de polyester *f*; ~ **paint** *n* CONST peinture de polyester *f*; ~ **resin** *n* CHEM résine de polyester *f*; ~ **tape** *n* RECORDING bande de dorsale polyester *f*
polyesterification *n* CHEM polyestérification *f*
polyether: ~ **foam** *n* P&R mousse de polyéther *f*
polyethylene *n* CHEM polythène *m*, polyéthylène *m*, ELEC *insulator*, NAUT, P&R, PACKAGING, PETR TECH, PROP MAT, TEXTILES polyéthylène *m* ~ **bags on the roll** *n* PACKAGING rouleau de sacs détachables en polythène *m*; ~ **container** *n* PACKAGING récipient en polythène *m*; ~ **glycol** *n* DETERGENTS polyéthylène-glycol *m*; ~ **pallet covers and liners** *n* PACKAGING emballage et doublure en polythène pour palettes *m*; ~ **self-adhesive tape** *n* PACKAGING ruban autocollant en polyéthylène *m*; ~ **terephthalate** *n* ELEC *dielectric*, P&R polyéthylène-téréphtalate *m*
polyfunctional *adj* CHEM polyfonctionnel
polygenetic: ~ **conglomerate** *n* GEOL conglomérat polygénique *m*
polygon *n* GEOM polygone *m*; PHYS ~ **of forces** polygone des forces *m*; ~ **connection** *n* ELEC connexion en polygone *f*
polygonal[1] *adj* GEOM polygonal
polygonal:[2] ~ **delay line** *n* ELECTRON ligne à retard polygonale *f*; ~ **dislocation** *n* METALL dislocation polygonale *f*; ~ **mirror** *n* INSTRUMENT, OPT miroir polygonal *m*
polygonization *n* METALL polygonisation *f*
polygorskite *n* PETR TECH attapulgite *f*
polyhalite *n* MINERAL polyhalite *f*
polyhedral[1] *adj* GEOM polyèdre
polyhedral:[2] ~ **angle** *n* GEOM angle polyèdre *m*
polyhedron *n* CRYSTALL, GEOM, METALL polyèdre *m*
polyhexylmethacrylate *n* P&R polyméthacrylate d'hexyle *m*
polyimide *n* ELECTRON, P&R polyimide *m*; ~ **printed circuit** *n* ELECTRON circuit imprimé au polyimide *m*
polyisoprene *n* CHEM, P&R *synthetic rubber* polyisoprène *m*
polymer *n* CHEM, P&R, PETR TECH, PROD ENG polymère *m*, PROP MAT produit polymérisé *m*, TEXTILES polymère *m*; ~ **fiber** *n* (AmE), ~ **fibre** *n* (BrE) PROP MAT fibre polymère *f*
polymeria *n* CHEM polymérie *f*
polymeric[1] *adj* CHEM polymère
polymeric:[2] ~ **material** *n* PROP MAT matériau polymère *m*
polymerism *n* CHEM polymérie *f*
polymerization *n* CHEM, NAUT *glass-refined plastic construction*, P&R, petr tech, PROP MAT polymérisation *f*
polymerize *vt* CHEM, P&R, PAPER TECH, TEXTILES polymériser
polymerized: ~ **enamel** *n* MECH ENG *production* laque polymérisée *f*
polymerizer *n* TEXTILES *curing oven* polymériseuse *f*
polymetallic: ~ **deposit** *n* PROP MAT gisement polymétallique *m*
polymethacrylate *n* P&R polyméthacrylate *m*
polymethyl: ~ **methacrylate** *n* P&R polyméthacrylate de méthyle *m*
polymethylene *n* CHEM polyméthylène *m*
polymictic: ~ **conglomerate** *n* GEOL conglomérat polygénique *m*

polymignite *n* MINERAL polymignite *f*
polymorphic: ~ **transformation** *n* CRYSTALL transformation polymorphe *f*
polymorphism *n* METALL polymorphisme *m*
polynomial *n* COMP, DP, MATH, PHYS polynôme *m*; ~ **filter** *n* ELECTRON filtre polynomial *m*
polynucleotide *n* CHEM polynucléotide *m*
polyol *n* CHEM, P&R polyol *m*
polyolefin *n* P&R, PROP MAT, TEXTILES polyoléfine *f*; ~ **barrier film** *n* PACKAGING film barrière en polyoléfine *m*; ~ **container** *n* PACKAGING récipient en polyoléfine *m*
polyoxyethylene *n* CHEM polyoxyéthylène *m*
polyoxymethylene *n* CHEM, P&R polyoxyméthylène *m*
polypeptide *n* CHEM polypeptide *m*
polyphase[1] *adj* ELEC *AC network motor* multiphasé, ELEC ENG, GEOL *metamorphism, deformation* polyphasé
polyphase:[2] ~ **circuit** *n* ELEC circuit polyphasé *m*; ~ **current** *n* ELEC courant polyphasé *m*; ~ **generator** *n* ELEC ENG alternateur polyphasé *m*; ~ **induction motor** *n* ELEC ENG moteur asynchrone polyphasé *m*; ~ **motor** *n* ELEC, ELEC ENG moteur polyphasé *m*; ~ **network** *n* ELEC *supply* réseau polyphasé *m*; ~ **synchronous motor** *n* ELEC ENG moteur synchrone polyphasé *m*; ~ **transformer** *n* ELEC, ELEC ENG transformateur polyphasé *m*
polyphenol *n* CHEM polyphénol *m*
polyphosphoric: ~ **acid** *n* DETERGENTS acide polyphosphorique *m*
polypnea *n* OCEANOG polypnée *f*
polypropylene *n* CHEM, ELEC *insulator*, NAUT, P&R, PETR TECH, PROP MAT, TEXTILES polypropylène *m*; ~ **closure** *n* PACKAGING fermeture en polypropylène *f*; ~ **strap** *n* PACKAGING cerclage en polypropylène *m*
polysilicon *n* ELECTRON polysilicium *m*; ~ **gate** *n* ELECTRON grille en polysilicium *f*; ~ **layer** *n* ELECTRON couche de polysilicium *f*
polysiloxane *n* P&R polysiloxane *m*
polystyrene *n* CHEM, P&R, PROP MAT polystyrène *m*; ~ **injection in-mold label** *n* (AmE), ~ **injection in-mould label** *n* (BrE) PACKAGING étiquette moulée en polystyrène *f*
polysulfide *n* (AmE) *see* polysulphide
polysulfone *n* (AmE) *see* polysulphone
polysulphide *n* (BrE) CHEM, P&R *rubber* polysulfure *m*
polysulphone *n* (BrE) CHEM, PROP MAT polysulfone *f*
polytene *n* CHEM polytène *m*
polyterpene *n* CHEM polyterpène *m*
polytetrafluoroethylene *n* P&R polytétrafluoréthylène *m*
polythene *n* CHEM polythène *m*, polyéthylène *m*, NAUT *ship parts, equipment*, PETR TECH polyéthylène *m*
polythermal: ~ **cargo ship** *n* TRANSP cargo polytherme *m*
polyunsaturated *adj* CHEM, FOOD TECH polyinsaturé
polyurethane[1] *adj* P&R polyuréthanique
polyurethane[2] *n* P&R, PROP MAT, TEXTILES polyuréthane *m*; ~ **foam** *n* NAUT *void filler in boat building* mousse de polyuréthane *f*, P&R *synthetic rubber* mousse de polyuréthane *f*, polyuréthane cellulaire *m*, PROP MAT mousse de polyuréthane *f*; ~ **resin** *n* CONST résine polyuréthane *f*
polyvalence *n* CHEM polyvalence *f*
polyvalency *n* CHEM polyvalence *f*
polyvalent *adj* CHEM plurivalent, polyvalent
polyvinyl *n* CHEM, TEXTILES polyvinyle *m*; ~ **acetal** *n* P&R polyvinylacétal *m*; ~ **acetate** *n* P&R polyvinylacétate

m; ~ **alcohol** *n* P&R, PRINT alcool polyvinylique *m*; ~ **alcohol size** *n* TEXTILES colle à l'alcool polyvinyle *f*; ~ **butyral** *n* P&R butyral de polyvinyle *m*; ~ **chloride** *n* (*PVC*) CONST, ELEC ENG, P&R, PROP MAT chlorure de polyvinyle *m*, polychlorure de vinyle *m*, polyvinylchlorure *m*; ~ **ether** *n* P&R polyvinyléther *m*; ~ **fluoride** *n* P&R fluorure de polyvinyle *m*; ~ **process** *n* PRINT procédé à la colle synthétique *m*

polyvinylbenzene *n* CHEM polystyrène *m*

polyvinylidene: ~ **chloride** *n* P&R chlorure de polyvinylidène *m*

polyvinylpyrrolidone *n* (*PVP*) DETERGENTS polyvinylpyrrolidone *m*

POM *abbr* (*polyoxymethylene*) P&R polyoxyméthylène *m*

pomace *n* FOOD TECH *fermentation* drèche *f*

pomaceous: ~ **fruit** *n* FOOD TECH fruits à pépins *m pl*

pome: ~ **fruit** *n* FOOD TECH fruits à pépins *m pl*

PON *abbr* (*passive optical network*) TELECOM réseau optique passif *m*

pond *n* COAL TECH bassin *m*, PAPER TECH cuve *f*, WATER SUPP bief *m*, biez *m*; ~ **depth** *n* PAPER TECH hauteur de la solution de couchage sur le papier *f*

pondage *n* FUELLESS retenue d'eau *f*, stockage d'eau *m*

pontoon *n* CONST, NAUT ponton *m*, PETR ponton *m*, rampe *f*, TRANSP ponton *m*; ~ **bridge** *n* MILIT, TRANSP pont de bateaux *m*; ~ **crane** *n* NAUT grue flottante *f*; ~ **dock** *n* TRANSP dock flottant *m*

pool *n* GAS TECH nappe *f*, PETR zone de production *f*; ~ **block** *n* (BrE) (*cf pool tablet*) C&G masse-tampon *f*; ~ **boiling** *n* REFRIG ébullition libre *f*; ~ **cathode** *n* ELEC ENG cathode liquide *f*; ~ **tablet** *n* (AmE) (*cf pool block*) C&G masse-tampon *f*

pooling: ~ **car** *n* (AmE) TRANSP *railways* wagon de groupage *m*

poop: ~ **deck** *n* NAUT *boat building* pont dunette *m*

poor: ~ **conductor** *n* ELEC ENG mauvais conducteur *m*; ~ **gas** *n* GAS TECH gaz pauvre *m*; ~ **grade** *n* MINING *of ore* basse teneur *f*, faible teneur *f*, pauvreté *f*; ~ **insulant** *n* ELEC ENG mauvais isolant *m*; ~ **insulation** *n* ELEC ENG mauvais isolement *m*; ~ **mixture** *n* AUTO mélange pauvre *m*; ~ **reception area** *n* TV zone d'ombre *f*; ~ **resolution** *n* CINEMAT manque de définition *m*

pop:[1] ~ **gate** *n* PROD ENG *founding* chenal de coulée en chute directe *m*; ~ **rivet** *n* PROD ENG rivet explosif *m*; ~ **stranding** *n* TV décalage transversal des spires *m*

pop[2] *vt* COMP dépiler, DP désempiler

pope: ~ **reel** *n* PAPER TECH enrouleuse pope *f*

pop-in *n* NUCLEAR croissance initiale d'une fissure *f*

poplar *n* PAPER TECH peuplier *m*

poplin *n* TEXTILES popeline *f*

poppet *n* PROD ENG clapet *m*; ~ **head** *n* MECH ENG *lathe* poupée *f*; ~ **holes** *n* MECH ENG *capstan* logements des barres *m pl*; ~ **valve** *n* AUTO soupape-champignon *f*, soupape-clapet *f*, HYDR EQUIP *distribution of steam* clapet à opercule soulevé *m*, PROD ENG soupape à tulipe *f*; ~ **valve gear** *n* HYDR EQUIP distribution par soupapes *f*, distribution à soupape *f*

population: ~ **density of excited atoms** *n* RAD PHYS densité de population des atomes excités *f*; ~ **dose** *n* POLLUTION dose totale pour une population *f*; ~ **equivalent** *n* WATER SUPP équivalent-habitant *m*; ~ **inversion** *n* ELECTRON, PHYS, RAD PHYS *of laser* inversion de population *f*; ~ **inversion mechanism** *n* RAD PHYS *in gas lasers* mécanisme d'inversion de population *m*

populin *n* CHEM populine *f*

pop-up:[1] ~ **type** *adj* PROD ENG de type soulevant

pop-up:[2] ~ **menu** *n* COMP menu en cascade *m*, DP menu en mode fenêtre *m*; ~ **window** *n* COMP fenêtre en cascade *f*, DP mode fenêtre *m*

porcelain *n* C&G, TEXTILES porcelaine *f*; ~ **borer** *n* C&G perceur de porcelaine *m*; ~ **button** *n* C&G bouton de porcelaine *m*; ~ **calcining furnace** *n* C&G four à cuire la porcelaine *m*; ~ **caster** *n* C&G mouleur en porcelaine *m*; ~ **cell** *n* C&G cuve en porcelaine *f*; ~ **clay** *n* C&G terre à porcelaine *f*; ~ **color** *n* (AmE), ~ **colour** *n* (BrE) C&G couleur pour porcelaine *f*; ~ **conduit box** *n* C&G boîte de dérivation en porcelaine *f*; ~ **crucible** *n* C&G, LAB EQUIP *container* creuset en porcelaine *m*; ~ **cup** *n* C&G cloche en porcelaine *f*; ~ **decoration** *n* C&G décoration de la porcelaine *f*; ~ **driller** *n* C&G perceur de porcelaine *m*; ~ **evaporating basin** *n* C&G cuvette d'évaporation en porcelaine *f*; ~ **filter plate** *n* C&G plaque à filtrer en porcelaine *f*; ~ **funnel** *n* C&G entonnoir-filtre *m*; ~ **gilder** *n* C&G doreur sur porcelaine *m*; ~ **goods** *n pl* C&G articles en porcelaine *m pl*; ~ **industry** *n* C&G industrie de la porcelaine *f*; ~ **insulation** *n* ELEC ENG isolation en porcelaine *f*; ~ **insulator** *n* C&G, ELEC, ELEC ENG isolateur en porcelaine *m*; ~ **jasper** *n* C&G jaspe porcelaine *m*; ~ **junction box** *n* C&G boîte de dérivation en porcelaine *f*; ~ **maker** *n* C&G ouvrier porcelainier *m*; ~ **piercer** *n* C&G perceur de porcelaine *m*; ~ **plate** *n* C&G plaque en porcelaine *f*; ~ **polisher** *n* C&G useur sur porcelaine *m*; ~ **reject** *n* C&G porcelaine de rebut *f*; ~ **thread guide** *n* C&G guide-fil en porcelaine *m*; ~ **thrower** *n* C&G tourneur de porcelaine *m*; ~ **tooth** *n* C&G dent en porcelaine *f*; ~ **tube** *n* C&G tube en porcelaine *m*; ~ **utensil** *n* C&G ustensile en porcelaine *m*; ~ **varnish** *n* C&G vernis à porcelaine *m*

porch *n* TV palier *m*; ~ **roof** *n* CONST *penthouse* auvent *m*

pore *n* COAL TECH, GAS TECH pore *m*; ~ **gas pressure** *n* COAL TECH pression du gaz interstitiel *f*; ~ **overpressure** *n* COAL TECH surpression interstitielle *f*; ~ **pressure** *n* COAL TECH pression interstitielle *f*, PETR TECH pression de pore *f*, pression interstitielle *f*; ~ **space** *n* GEOL porosité *f*, volume des pores *m*; ~ **volume** *n* COAL TECH, PETR volume des pores *m*; ~ **water** *n* COAL TECH, OCEANOG eau interstitielle *f*; ~ **water pressure** *n* COAL TECH pression de l'eau interstitielle *f*

poromeric-coated: ~ **fabric** *n* P&R *article* tissu à revêtement poromère *m*

porometer *n* CHEM TECH évaporomètre *m*

porosimeter *n* PAPER TECH porosimètre *m*

porosity *n* ACOUSTICS, CHEM, COAL TECH, CONST, FUELLESS, GAS TECH porosité *f*, HYDROL, METALL, P&R, PAPER TECH, PETR, PETR TECH, PROP MAT, WATER SUPP porosité *f*; ~ **log** *n* PETR TECH diagraphie de porosité *f*; ~ **tester** *n* PAPER TECH porosimètre *m*

porous[1] *adj* FUELLESS, PROP MAT poreux

porous:[2] ~ **absorber** *n* ACOUSTICS absorbant poreux *m*; ~ **layer** *n* GAS TECH couche perméable *f*, couche poreuse *f*; ~ **medium** *n* GAS TECH milieu poreux *m*; ~ **plug** *n* PROP MAT bouchon poreux *m*

porpezite *n* MINERAL porpézite *f*

porphin *n* CHEM porphine *f*

porphyritic *adj* GEOL *igneous texture* porphyrique, porphyroïde

porphyroblastic *adj* GEOL *metamorphic texture* porphyroblastique

porphyroclast *n* GEOL grand fragment dans une mylonite *m*

porphyropsin *n* CHEM porphyropsine *f*

Porro: ~ **prism** *n* INSTRUMENT prisme de Porro *m*

port *n* AERONAUT *navigation* gauche *f*, C&G brûleur *m*, COMP port *m*, porte *f*, DP port *m*, ELEC ENG *waveguides* ouverture *f*, HYDR EQUIP *of steam cylinder* lumière de cylindre à vapeur *f*, orifice *m*, orifice de distribution *m*, MECH, MECH ENG orifice *m*, NAUT bâbord *m*, hublot *m*, port *m*, PHYS point d'accès électronique *m*, PRINT port *m*, SPACE *spacecraft* bâbord *m*, TELECOM point d'accès *m*, TRANSP port *m*, VEHICLES *engine* lumière *f*, orifice *m*; ~ **administration offices** *n* TRANSP bureaux du port *m pl*; ~ **apron** *n* C&G seuil de brûleur *m*; ~ **authorities** *n pl* NAUT autorités portuaires *f pl*; ~ **back wall** *n* (BrE) *(cf port endwall)* C&G pignon de brûleur *m*; ~ **of call** *n* NAUT escale *f*, port d'escale *m*; ~ **charges** *n pl* NAUT droits de port *m pl*; ~ **cold store** *n* REFRIG entrepôt frigorifique portuaire *m*; ~ **of commissioning** *n* NAUT port d'armement *m*; ~ **crown** *n* (BrE) *(cf uptake crown)* C&G voûte de brûleur *f*; ~ **custom house** *n* TRANSP bureau des douanes *m*; ~ **of documentation** *n* (AmE) *(cf port of registry)* NAUT port d'armement *m*; ~ **door** *n* REFRIG porte d'accostage *f*; ~ **endwall** *n* (AmE) *(cf port back wall)* C&G pignon de brûleur *m*; ~ **facilities** *n pl* NAUT infrastructure portuaire *f*, installations portuaires *f pl*; ~ **mouth** *n* C&G collier de brûleur *m*; ~ **neck** *n* C&G gorge de brûleur *f*; ~ **opening** *n* HYDR EQUIP ouverture de la lumière *f*; ~ **of registration** *n* NAUT port d'attache *m*; ~ **of registry** *n* (BrE) *(cf port of documentation)* NAUT *sea transport* port d'attache *m*, port d'immatriculation *m*, NAUT port d'armement *m*; ~ **side wall** *n* C&G flanc de brûleur *m*; ~ **sill** *n* C&G banquette de brûleur *f*; ~ **to throat area ratio** *n* SPACE facteur d'autoserrage *m*; ~ **of transit** *n* NAUT port de transit *m*; ~ **uptake** *n* C&G montée de brûleur *f*; ~ **watch** *n* NAUT *personnel* babordais *m*; ~ **width** *n* MECH ENG *cylinder* largeur de lumière *f*

portable[1] *adj* COMP portable, transportable, DP portable

portable:[2] ~ **appliance** *n* ELEC appareil portatif *m*; ~ **cassette recorder** *n* RECORDING magnétophone à cassette portatif *m*; ~ **coldroom** *n* REFRIG chambre froide démontable *f*; ~ **crane** *n* CONST potence de hissage *f*; ~ **drilling machine** *n* MECH ENG machine à percer portative *f*; ~ **fan** *n* MECH ENG ventilateur portatif *m*; ~ **fire extinguisher** *n* SAFETY bouteille extincteur portative *f*, extincteur portatif *m*; ~ **forge** *n* PROD ENG forge portative *f*, petite forge *f*; ~ **hoisting platform** *n* CONST plate-forme roulante élévatrice *f*; ~ **ladder** *n* SAFETY échelle portative *f*; ~ **lamp** *n* ELEC, ELEC ENG baladeuse *f*; ~ **light** *n* CONST phare portatif *m*; ~ **machine** *n* SAFETY machine portative *f*; ~ **mold** *n* (AmE), ~ **mould** *n* (BrE) P&R *equipment* moule portatif *m*; ~ **pack** *n* TV vidéo portative *f*; ~ **plant** *n* MECH ENG matériel mobile *m*, outillage mobile *m*; ~ **pump** *n* LAB EQUIP *sampling* pompe autonome portative *f*; ~ **receiver** *n* TELECOM récepteur portable *m*; ~ **relay** *n* TV relais mobile *m*; ~ **socket outlet** *n* ELEC *connection* prise femelle de prolongation *f*; ~ **terminal** *n* NAUT *satellite communications, computers* terminal portatif *m*; ~ **transmitter** *n* TV émetteur portatif *m*; ~ **vice bench** *n* (BrE) CONST établi roulant pour étaux *m*, étau roulant *m*; ~ **vice stand** *n* (BrE) CONST établi roulant pour étaux *m*, étau roulant *m*; ~ **vice stand with leg vice** *n* (BrE) CONST étau à pied roulant *m*; ~ **vise bench** *n* (AmE) *see portable vice bench*; ~ **vise stand** *n* (AmE) *see portable vice stand*; ~ **vise stand with leg vise** *n* (AmE) *see portable vice stand with leg vice*; ~ **water storage tank** *n* MILIT réservoir d'eau portatif *m*

portal *n* CONST *of tunnel* entrée *f*; ~ **crane** *n* CONST grue à portique *f*; ~ **mast** *n* NAUT *derrick* mât portique *m*

portface *n* HYDR EQUIP table des lumières *f*

porthole *n* C&G hublot *m*, MECH ENG lumière *f*, orifice *m*, NAUT *equipment* hublot *m*; ~ **fan** *n* MECH ENG ventilateur aspirateur mural *m*

portion: ~ **pack** *n* PACKAGING emballage en portions *m*

portioning: ~ **machine** *n* PACKAGING machine à faire des portions *f*

Portland: ~ **sulfate-resisting cement** *n* (AmE), ~ **sulphate-resisting cement** *n* (BrE) CONST ciment Portland artificiel à haute résistance aux sulfates *m*

portrait *n* PRINT format à la française *m*; ~ **attachment** *n* CINEMAT bonnette d'approche *f*, PHOTO bonnette à portrait *f*; ~ **format** *n* DP format portrait *m*, format à la française *m*; ~ **lens** *n* INSTRUMENT lentille d'approche *f*

POS *abbr (point of sale)* COMP, DP point de vente *m*

Posidriv: ~ **screw** *n* (TM) MECH ENG vis à empreinte Posidriv *f* (MD)

position[1] *n* CINEMAT *of lens* créneau *m*, NAUT *navigation* point *m*, position *f*; ~ **angle** *n* ASTRON angle de position *m*; ~ **by astrocalculation** *n* ASTRON point observé *m*; ~ **exchange force** *n* NUCLEAR force d'échange de position opérateur *f*, force de Majorana *f*; ~ **finder** *n* OCEANOG gonio *m*, goniomètre *m*; ~ **finding** *n* MILIT repérage *m*; ~ **fixing** *n* MILIT localisation *f*; ~ **indicator** *n* PROD ENG indicateur de position *m*; ~ **lever** *n* CONTROL levier de pose *m*; ~ **light** *n* NAUT *navigation*, SPACE, VEHICLES feu de position *m*; ~ **reference system** *n* PETR système de localisation *m*; ~ **switch** *n* CONTROL interrupteur de position *m*, ELEC commutateur de position *m*, ELEC ENG, PROD ENG interrupteur de position *m*; ~ **vector** *n* GEOM, PHYS vecteur de position *m*

position[2] *vt* MECH ENG orienter, positionner, présenter

positional: ~ **crosstalk** *n* TV intermodulation de positionnement *f*

positioner *n* CINEMAT levier de positionnement *m*, MECH ENG positionneur *m*

positioning *n* MECH ENG *drill* mise au point *f*, NAUT localisation *f*; ~ **block** *n* MECH ENG cale de centrage *f*; ~ **control** *n* CONTROL contrôle de positionnement *m*, régulation de position *f*; ~ **repeatability** *n* MECH ENG *machine tool* répétitivité du positionnement *f*; ~ **screw jack** *n* MECH ENG chandelle *f*

positive[1] *adj* ELEC *electrode* positif

positive[2] *n* PHOTO *print* tirage *m*, PRINT positif *m*; ~ **abnormal pressure** *n* PETR TECH pression de formation anormale positive *f*; ~ **acknowledgement** *n* COMP, DP accusé de réception positif *m*; ~ **angle** *n* GEOM angle positif *m*; ~ **bank** *n* AUTO série de plaques positives *f*; ~ **battery** *n* TELECOM accumulateur positif *m*; ~ **bias** *n* ELEC ENG polarisation positive *f*; ~ **charge** *n* ELEC *electrostatics*, ELEC ENG, PHYS charge positive *f*; ~ **cold chamber** *n* REFRIG armoire réfrigérée positive *f*; ~ **column** *n* ELECTRON, PHYS colonne positive *f*; ~ **crankcase ventilation** *n* AUTO, VEHICLES *engine* recyclage des gaz de carter *m*; ~ **curvature** *n* GEOM courbure positive *f*; ~ **displacement compressor** *n* MECH ENG compresseur volumétrique *m*; ~ **displacement pump** *n* HYDR EQUIP, MECH ENG, PROD ENG pompe volumétrique *f*; ~ **displacement vacuum pump** *n* MECH ENG pompe volumétrique à vide *f*; ~ **distortion** *n* CINEMAT distorsion en barillet *f*; ~ **drive** *n* AUTO lanceur à pignon poussé *m*; ~ **drive of Morse tapers** *n* MECH ENG entraînement positif du cône Morse *m*; **~ earthed terminal** *n* (BrE) *(cf positive grounded terminal)* AUTO borne positive à la masse *f*; **~ feedback** *n* CONTROL réaction positive *f*, réinjection positive *f*, rétroaction positive *f*, RAD PHYS, RECORDING réaction positive *f*; **~ film** *n* CINEMAT pellicule positive *f*; **~ Gauss curvature** *n* GEOM courbure de Gauss positive *f*; **~ grounded terminal** *n* (AmE) *(cf positive earthed terminal)* AUTO borne positive à la masse *f*; **~ image** *n* PHOTO image positive *f*; **~ impalement** *n* PRINT engagement positif des pointures *m*; **~ ion** *n* ELEC, PART PHYS, PHYS ion positif *m*; **~ lens** *n* INSTRUMENT lentille convergente *f*, lentille convexe *f*, lentille à bord mince *f*; **~ lens surface** *n* INSTRUMENT verre positif *m*; **~ logic** *n* ELECTRON logique positive *f*; **~ magnetostriction** *n* ELEC ENG magnétostriction positive *f*; **~ meniscus lens** *n* INSTRUMENT lentille ménisque convergente *f*; **~ meson** *n* PART PHYS méson positif *m*; **~ modulation** *n* ELECTRON modulation positive *f*; **~ mold** *n* (AmE) **~ mould** *n* (BrE) P&R *press* moule mâle *m*, moule positif *m*; **~ notification** *n* *(PN)* TELECOM notification positive *f*; **~ perforation** *n* CINEMAT perforation positive *f*, perforation rectangulaire *f*; **~ phase sequence** *n* ELEC *AC generator* ordre de phases positif *m*; **~ phase sequence reactance** *n* ELEC réactance directe *f*, réactance à ordre de phases positif *f*; **~ phase sequence resistance** *n* ELEC résistance directe *f*, résistance à ordre des phases positives *f*; **~ photoresist** *n* ELECTRON photorésist positif *m*; **~ picture phase** *n* TV polarité positive du signal image *f*; **~ pitch** *n* CINEMAT pas positif *m*; **~ plate** *n* AUTO plaque positive *f*; **~ pole** *n* ELEC *connection* pôle positif *m*; **~ power supply** *n* ELEC ENG alimentation positive *f*; **~ ray** *n* ELECTRON rayon positif *m*; **~ release printer** *n* CINEMAT tireuse pour copies standard *f*; **~ resist** *n* ELECTRON résist positif *m*; **~ rewinder** *n* CINEMAT enrouleuse à grande vitesse *f*; **~ separation** *n* CINEMAT extraction positive monochrome *f*; **~ sequence** *n* ELEC *AC* ordre positif *m*, séquence positive *f*; **~ stress** *n* MECH ENG effort de compression *m*, travail à l'écrasement *m*; **~ terminal** *n* AUTO, ELEC *connection*, VEHICLES *accumulator* borne positive *f*

positively:[1] **~ skewed** *adj* GEOM de travers à droite

positively:[2] **~ skewed doped region** *n* PHYS région dopée positivement *f*

positive-type: ~ valve rotator *n* AUTO rotateur mécanique *m*

positon *n* PHYS positon *m*, positron *m*

positron *n* PHYS positon *m*, positron *m*

possession *n* RAIL blanc travaux *m*, intervalle *m*, intervalle travaux *m*

possible: ~ capacity *n* TRANSP capacité possible *f*; **~ reserves** *n pl* PETR TECH réserves possibles *f pl*

post[1] *n* AUTO borne *f*, CONST *of crane* arbre *m*, fût *m*, *of door* montant *m*, poteau d'huisserie *m*, *upright* montant *m*, pieu *m*, poteau *m*, MECH ENG *column for mine drill* affût-colonne *m*, MINING butte *f*, chandelle *f*, montant *m*, pied-droit *m*, étai *m*, NAUT *mooring, marker* poteau *m*, *place of duty* poste *m*; **~ bracket** *n* RAIL potence *f*; **~ insulator** *n* ELEC ENG isolateur de soutien *m*, isolateur support *m*, support isolant *m*; **~ pallet** *n* TRANSP palette à montants *f*

post:[2] **~ hours** *vt* PROD ENG imputer des heures; **~ to stock** *vt* PROD ENG comptabiliser en stock

postaccelerator: ~ CRT *n* ELECTRON tube cathodique à postaccélération *m*

postal: ~ tube *n* (BrE) *(cf mailing tube)* PACKAGING tube pour expédition postale *m*, tube pour transmission postale *m*

postamble *n* COMP position de synchronisation finale *f*, DP synchroniseur final *m*

postcombustion: ~ chamber *n* COAL TECH chambre de postcombustion *f*

postcrane *n* CONST grue à colonne *f*

postdialing: ~ delay *n* (AmE), **postdialling delay** *n* (BrE) TELECOM attente après numérotation *f*

postdriver *n* CONST hie *f*, sonnette *f*

posted: be ~ to a ship *vi* NAUT être affecté à un navire

postemphasis *n* RECORDING, TV postaccentuation *f*

postequalization *n* RECORDING postcompensation *f*, postégalisation *f*

poster: ~ paper *n* PAPER TECH papier pour affiches *m*

postfix: ~ notation *n* DP notation suffixée *f*

postflying: ~ check *n* AERONAUT visite après-vol *f*

postforming *adj* P&R *plastics* postformable

postglacial: ~ clay *n* COAL TECH argile alluviale postglaciaire *f*

postheating[1] *adj* PROD ENG postchauffage

postheating[2] *n* PROP MAT réchauffage *m*

posting *n* PROD ENG imputation *f*

postkinematic *adj* GEOL *metamorphism* post-tectonique

postmortem: ~ program *n* COMP, DP programme d'autopsie *m*

postprocessing *n* ELECTRON post-traitement *m*, traitement ultérieur *m*

postprocessor *n* COMP, DP postprocesseur *m*

postscoring *n* ACOUSTICS postsonorisation *f*

poststaff *n* CONST ogive de montant *f*

postsync: ~ field-blanking interval *n* TV intervalle de suppression de trame après synchronisation *m*

postsynchronization *n* RECORDING postsynchronisation *f*

postsynchronize *vt* CINEMAT doubler, postsynchroniser

postulate *n* MATH axiome *m*, postulat *m*

pot[1] *n* OCEANOG caseyeur *m*, PRINT creuset *m*, pot *m*, RECORDING potentiomètre *m*; **~ arch** *n* C&G arche à pots *f*; **~ arching** *n* C&G attrempage des pots *m*; **~ carriage** *n* C&G diable à pots *m*; **~ clay** *n* C&G argile à pot *f*; **~ cooling** *n* C&G refroidissement dans le pot *m*; **~ furnace** *n* THERMOD four à creuset *m*, fourneau à creuset *m*; **~ insulator** *n* ELEC isolateur en pot *m*; **~ life** *n* P&R *adhesives* vie en pot *f*; **~ mouth** *n* C&G gueule du pot *f*; **~ opal** *n* C&G opale au pot *f*; **~ room** *n* C&G poterie *f*; **~ ruby** *n* C&G rubis direct *m*; **~ scrap** *n* PROD ENG bocage de poterie *m*, débris de fonte de poterie *m*, vieilles fontes de poterie *f pl*; **~ setting** *n* C&G mise de pot *f*; **~ sherds** *n pl* C&G écailles de pots *f pl*; **~ spout** *n* C&G déversoir *m*

pot:[2] **~ anneal** *vt* THERMOD recuire en pot

potable *adj* FOOD TECH potable, WATER SUPP buvable, potable

potash *n* C&G, CHEM potasse *f*; **~ bulb** *n* LAB EQUIP *glassware* tube à potasse *m*; **~ glass** *n* C&G verre potassique *m*

potash-alum *n* CHEM alun de potasse *m*

potassic *adj* GEOL potassique

potassium *n (K)* CHEM potassium *m (K)*; **~ carbonate** *n* DETERGENTS carbonate de potassium *m*; **~ chlorate** *n* CHEM chlorate de potasse *m*, chlorate de potassium *m*; **~ chloride** *n* CHEM chlorure de potassium *m*; **~ cyanide** *n* CHEM cyanure de potassium *m*; **~ hydroxide** *n* CHEM hydroxyde de potassium *m*, potasse caustique *f*; **~**

nitrate *n* CHEM azotate de potassium *m*, nitrate de potassium *m*, nitre *m*, salpêtre *m*, FOOD TECH nitrate de potassium *m*; ~ **permanganate** *n* CHEM permanganate de potasse *m*, permanganate de potassium *m*; ~ **sulfate** *n* (AmE), ~ **sulphate** *n* (BrE) DETERGENTS sulfate de potassium *m*

potato: ~ **blight** *n* FOOD TECH *phytopathology* mildiou de la pomme de terre *m*

potential *n* ELEC, ELEC ENG potentiel *m*, PETR capacité de production *f*, PHYS, SPACE *communications* potentiel *m*; ~ **accident** *n* SAFETY accident potentiel *m*; ~ **barrier** *n* ELEC ENG, PHYS barrière de potentiel *f*; ~ **difference** *n* ELEC, ELEC ENG, PHYS différence de potentiel *f*; ~ **divider** *n* PHYS diviseur de tension *m*; ~ **drop** *n* ELEC chute de tension *f*, ELEC ENG, PHYS chute de potentiel *f*; ~ **energy** *n* PHYS énergie potentielle *f*; ~ **evapotranspiration** *n* WATER SUPP évapotranspiration potentielle *f*; ~ **function** *n* PHYS *fluid mechanics* fonction du potentiel *f*; ~ **geodesic head** *n* NUCLEAR hauteur géométrique *f*; ~ **gradient** *n* ELEC, PHYS gradient de potentiel *m*; ~ **hazard** *n* SAFETY risque potentiel *m*; ~ **of hydrogen** *n* (pH) CHEM potentiel hydrogène *m* (pH); ~ **loop** *n* ELEC *voltage* amplitude maximale de tension *f*; ~ **temperature-salinity diagram** *n* OCEANOG diagramme température potentielle-salinité *m*; ~ **transformer** *n* ELEC, ELEC ENG transformateur de tension *m*; ~ **well** *n* PHYS puits de potentiel *m*

potentiometer *n* CINEMAT, CONST, ELEC *resistor*, ELEC ENG, LAB EQUIP *electrochemistry*, PAPER TECH, PHYS, PROP MAT, RECORDING potentiomètre *m*; ~ **controller** *n* CONTROL régulateur potentiométrique *m*; ~ **rheostat** *n* ELEC *resistor* rhéostat en pont *m*; ~ **slider** *n* ELEC *resistor* curseur de potentiomètre *m*

potentiometric: ~ **head** *n* PETR TECH niveau potentiométrique *m*; ~ **level** *n* PETR TECH niveau potentiométrique *m*; ~ **map** *n* PETR TECH carte potentiométrique *f*; ~ **recorder** *n* INSTRUMENT enregistreur potentiométrique *m*

pothole *n* CONST cloche *f*, *in road* nid de poule *m*, HYDROL marmite *f*, marmite torrentielle *f*, VEHICLES *road* nid de poule *m*

potter's: ~ **beetle** *n* C&G batte *f*; ~ **clay extraction** *n* C&G extraction de terre à poterie *f*; ~ **earth** *n* C&G argile *f*; ~ **ore** *n* C&G alquifoux *m*; ~ **wheel** *n* C&G roue de potier *f*, tour de potier *m*

pottery *n* C&G, PROD ENG poterie *f*; ~ **clay** *n* CONST argile de potier *f*, argile à poterie *f*; ~ **decorator** *n* C&G peintre sur poterie *m*; ~ **kiln** *n* C&G, THERMOD four pour céramique *m*; ~ **maker** *n* C&G faïencier *m*

potting *n* P&R *process* enrobage *m*, PROD ENG encourbage par coulée *m*, SPACE *spacecraft* enrobage *m*, moulage *m*; ~ **compound** *n* SPACE *spacecraft* produit de surmoulage *m*

pot-type: ~ **field rheostat** *n* ELEC *resistance* potentiomètre du réglage de champ *m*

pouch *n* PACKAGING sachet *m*

pouch-making: ~ **machine** *n* PACKAGING machine pour faire les sachets *f*

pound[1] *n* METR livre *f*, livre averdepois *f*, livre avoirdupois *f*; ~ **avoirdupois** *n* METR livre *f*, livre averdepois *f*, livre avoirdupois *f*; ~ **force** *n* METR livre poids *f*; ~ **net** *n* OCEANOG paradière *f*

pound[2] *vt* FOOD TECH broyer, pilonner, égruger, PROD ENG piler

poundal *n* METR poundal *m*

pounder *n* PROD ENG pilon *m*

pounds: ~ **per hour** *n pl* METR livres par heure *f pl*; ~ **per square inch** *n pl* (psi) METR, PETR TECH livres par pouce carré *f pl*

pour:[1] ~ **point** *n* FLUID PHYS point de congélation *m*, point de liquéfaction *m*, PETR TECH, REFRIG point d'écoulement *m*, VEHICLES *oil* point de congélation *m*; ~ **spout** *n* PACKAGING bec pour verser *m*; ~ **spout closure** *n* PACKAGING fermeture avec bec verseur *f*; ~ **spout seal** *n* PACKAGING fermeture avec bec pour verser *f*

pour[2] *vt* CONST *concrete* couler, mettre en place, poser, PAPER TECH déverser

pourable: ~ **slurry** *n* MINING bouillie pompable *f*

pourer *n* PROD ENG *person* couleur *m*

pouring *n* C&G coulée *f*, PRINT faire couler du texte, PROD ENG *founding* coulage *m*, coulée *f*, jet *m*, SAFETY *founding* coulée *f*; ~ **gate** *n* PROD ENG *in mould* coulée *f*, jet de coulée *m*, trou de coulée *m*; ~ **hole** *n* PROD ENG *in mould* coulée *f*, jet de coulée *m*, trou de coulée *m*; ~ **of molten metal** *n* SAFETY coulée du métal en fusion *f*; ~ **sleeve** *n* MECH ENG *diecasting die* conteneur buse *m*

powder:[1] ~ **filled** *adj* ELEC ENG à poudre, à remplissage pulvérulent; ~ **form** *adj* COAL TECH pulvérulent

powder[2] *n* CHEM, P&R *fillers, pigments*, PAPER TECH poudre *f*; ~ **camera** *n* CRYSTALL chambre de poudre *f*; ~ **coating** *n* COATINGS revêtement par poudre *m*, COLOURS revêtement en poudre *m*, P&R enduction de poudre *f*, revêtement en poudre *m*; ~ **diffractometer** *n* CRYSTALL diffractomètre de poudre *m*; ~ **explosive** *n* MINING dynamite pulvérulente *f*, explosif pulvérulent *m*; ~ **metal die** *n* MECH ENG outillage pour métal pulvérisé *m*; ~ **mill** *n* PROD ENG moulin à poudre *m*, poudrerie *f*; ~ **pattern** *n* CRYSTALL diagramme de poudre *m*; ~ **photograph** *n* CRYSTALL cliché de poudre *m*; ~ **store** *n* MINING dépôt d'explosifs *m*, poudrière *f*; ~ **works** *n* PROD ENG poudrerie *f*

powder[3] *vt* PAPER TECH *solid* pulvériser

powdered[1] *adj* C&G *gold* en poudre, P&R *pigments, fillers, plastics* pulvérisé

powdered:[2] ~ **color** *n* (AmE), ~ **colour** *n* (BrE) COLOURS couleur en poudre *f*; ~ **dye** *n* COLOURS colorant en poudre *m*; ~ **egg** *n* FOOD TECH oeuf en poudre *m*; ~ **glass** *n* C&G verre en poudre *m*; ~ **insulant** *n* REFRIG isolant en poudre *m*; ~ **iron core** *n* ELEC ENG noyau de fer divisé *m*

powderiness *n* PROP MAT pulvérulence *f*

powdering *n* PAPER TECH *of coated paper* poudrage *m*; ~ **ink** *n* COLOURS encre en poudre *f*, encre à saupoudrer *f*

powdery[1] *adj* GEOL, PROP MAT pulvérulent

powdery:[2] ~ **mildew** *n* FOOD TECH *phytopathology* oïdium *m*

power[1] *n* AUTO, ELEC puissance *f*, ELEC ENG puissance *f*, tension *f*, énergie *f*, MATH, MECH *physics* puissance *f*, MECH ENG force *f*, force motrice *f*, pouvoir *m*, puissance *f*, énergie *f*, *lever* puissance *f*, *useful energy* travail utile *m*, OPT *optical signal, lens* puissance optique *f*, PAPER TECH force motrice *f*, PHYS *of lens* vergence *f*, *rate of working, capability* pouvoir *m*, puissance *f*, SPACE *spacecraft*, TELECOM puissance *f*; ~ **adaptor** *n* CINEMAT alimentation secteur *f*; ~ **amplification** *n* ELECTRON amplification de puissance *f*; ~ **amplifier** *n* ELEC ENG, ELECTRON, PHYS, RECORDING amplificateur de puissance *m*, SPACE amplificateur d'impulsions *m*, amplificateur de puissance *m*, TELECOM amplificateur de puissance *m*; ~ **amplifier transistor** *n* ELECTRON transistor amplificateur de puissance *m*, transistor de puissance *m*; ~ **amplifier tube** *n* ELECTRON tube amplificateur de puissance *m*, tube de puissance *m*; ~ **and interlock relay box** *n* AERONAUT boîte de relais d'alimentation et d'interdiction de pilote *f*; ~ **bandwidth** *n* ELECTRON bande passante en puissance *f*; ~ **belt** *n* CINEMAT batterie de ceinture *f*; ~ **booster** *n* AUTO servofrein *m*; ~ **brake** *n* AUTO frein assisté *m*, TRANSP servofrein *m*; ~ **bus** *n* SPACE *spacecraft* barre d'alimentation *f*; ~ **cable** *n* ELEC *supply network* câble d'énergie *m*, câble de puissance *m*, ELEC ENG câble d'énergie *m*; ~ **capacitor** *n* ELEC, ELEC ENG condensateur de puissance *m*; ~ **car** *n* RAIL *vehicles* motrice *f*, TRANSP automotrice *f*; ~ **circuit** *n* ELEC circuit de puissance *m*; ~ **coefficient** *n* FUELLESS *wind power* coefficient de puissance *m*; ~ **collection system** *n* TRANSP captation de courant *f*; ~ **conditioning unit** *n* SPACE *spacecraft* unité de conditionnement d'énergie *f*; ~ **consumption** *n* ELEC *supply network* consommation d'énergie *f*, ELEC ENG consommation *f*, puissance absorbée *f*, puissance consommée *f*; ~ **converter** *n* ELEC ENG convertisseur de courant *m*, SPACE *spacecraft* convertisseur d'alimentation *m*; ~ **curves** *n pl* FUELLESS graphes de puissance *m pl*; ~ **cylinder** *n* AUTO vérin *m*; ~ **density** *n* FUELLESS puissance volumique *f*, TELECOM densité de puissance *f*; ~ **diode** *n* ELECTRON diode de puissance *f*; ~ **directional relay** *n* *(PDR)* ELEC relais directionnel de puissance *m*; ~ **dissipation** *n* PROD ENG dissipation de puissance *f*; ~ **distribution** *n* PROD ENG distribution de l'alimentation *f*; ~ **distribution network** *n* SPACE *spacecraft* réseau d'alimentation en énergie *m*, réseau d'énergie *m*; ~ **divider** *n* ELEC *supply*, ELEC ENG, TELECOM diviseur de puissance *m*; ~ **down** *n* ELEC ENG mise hors circuit *f*, mise hors tension *f*, *semiconductor memory* veilleuse *f*, PROD ENG coupure d'alimentation *f*, mise hors tension *f*; ~ **down feature** *n* ELEC ENG *semiconductor memory* mise en veilleuse *f*; ~ **drill** *n* CONST *rock drill* perforatrice mécanique *f*; ~ **drop** *n* CINEMAT chute de tension *f*; ~ **efficiency** *n* RECORDING *of amplifier* rendement en puissance *m*; ~ **fabric** *n* PAPER TECH toile de traction *f*; ~ **factor** *n* ELEC, ELEC ENG, P&R facteur de puissance *m*, PHYS cos *m*, cos phi *m*, cosinus *m*, facteur de puissance *m*, PROD ENG facteur de charge *m*; ~ **factor correction** *n* ELEC ENG correction du facteur de puissance *f*; ~ **fail restart** *n* *(PFR)* COMP, DP redémarrage automatique *m*; ~ **failure** *n* CINEMAT coupure de courant *f*, panne d'électricité *f*, panne de secteur *f*, ELEC ENG coupure de courant *f*, panne de courant *f*, panne de réseau *f*, panne de secteur *f*, *device* panne d'alimentation *f*; ~ **fan** *n* AUTO ventilateur débrayable *m*; ~ **feed** *n* MECH ENG *machine tool* avance automatique *f*, TELECOM alimentation *f*; ~ **feeding** *n* TELECOM alimentation *f*; ~ **flux density** *n* OPT densité surfacique de puissance *f*, SPACE *spacecraft* densité surfacique de puissance *f*, puissance surfacique *f*; ~ **frequency** *n* ELEC *supply network* fréquence industrielle *f*, ELEC ENG fréquence du secteur *f*, fréquence industrielle *f*; ~ **frequency heating** *n* HEATING chauffage à haute fréquence *m*; ~ **gain** *n* ELECTRON, PHYS, RECORDING gain en puissance *m*; ~ **gas** *n* GAS TECH gaz carburant *m*, gaz combustible *m*, gaz de gazogène *m*; ~ **generation** *n* ELEC ENG production d'énergie *f*; ~ **grid** *n* ELEC ENG réseau *m*, réseau de distribution d'énergie *m*, secteur *m*, ELECTR réseau *m*; ~ **hacksaw** *n* MECH ENG machine à scier alternative *f*; ~ **hammer** *n* MECH ENG martinet *m*, PROD ENG mar-

teau à forger *m*, marteau-pilon *m*, pilon *m*; ~ **handling capacity** *n* RECORDING capacité de puissance soutenue *f*; ~ **indicator** *n* PROD ENG témoin de mise sous tension *m*; ~ **inductor** *n* ELEC ENG bobine d'inductance de puissance *f*, inductance de puissance *f*; ~ **input** *n* ELEC ENG puissance absorbée *f*; ~ **interlock bar** *n* PROD ENG barre de verrouillage de l'alimentation *f*; ~ **interlock relay** *n* PROD ENG relais de verrouillage de l'alimentation *m*; ~ **law and index profile** *n* OPT, TELECOM profil d'indice à loi en puissance *m*, profil à loi en puissance *m*; ~ **law index fiber** *n* (AmE), ~ **law index fibre** *n* (BrE) OPT, PHYS fibre à gradient exponentiel *f*; ~ **lead** *n* ELEC, PROD ENG fil de puissance *m*; ~ **limiter** *n* MECH ENG limiteur de puissance *m*; ~ **line** *n* ELEC ENG ligne de transport d'énergie *f*, PROD ENG ligne secteur *f*; ~ **loader** *n* CONST *civil engineering* chargeuse mécanique *f*; ~ **loading** *n* METR charge au cheval *f*, masse au cheval *f*; ~ **loss** *n* ELEC ENG pertes d'énergie *f pl*; ~ **loss ride-through** *n* ELEC, PROD ENG protection contre les microcoupures *f*; ~ **module** *n* ELEC ENG bloc de puissance *m*, PROD ENG module puissance *m*, SPACE bloc *m*; ~ **nibbler** *n* (BrE) *(cf nibbling machine)* MECH ENG *tool* grignoteuse *f*; ~ **oscillator** *n* ELECTRON oscillateur de puissance *m*; ~ **outage** *n* PROD ENG panne d'alimentation *f*; ~ **outlet** *n* ELEC *connection* prise de courant *f*; ~ **output** *n* ELEC ENG puissance de sortie *f*, puissance fournie *f*, FUELLESS, GAS TECH puissance utile *f*; ~ **pack** *n* CINEMAT bloc d'alimentation *m*, ELEC ENG batterie cartouche *f*, bloc d'alimentation *m*, MAR POLL groupe de puissance *m*; ~ **package** *n* SPACE bloc *m*; ~ **per unit area** *n* SPACE *spacecraft* puissance surfacique *f*; ~ **plant** *n* AERONAUT groupe turbo-réacteur *m*, groupe-moteur *m*, ELEC *supply* centrale électrique *f*, ELEC ENG centrale génératrice *f*, centrale électrique *f*, station électrique *f*, usine génératrice *f*, usine électrique *f*, NAUT *engines* groupe propulseur *m*, installation motrice *f*, machines de propulsion *f pl*, SPACE propulseur *m*, TELECOM centrale d'énergie *f*, station d'énergie *f*; ~ **plug** *n* ELEC ENG fiche secteur *f*; ~ **press** *n* SAFETY presse hydraulique *f*; ~ **producer** *n* MECH ENG source d'énergie *f*; ~ **rapid traverse** *n* MECH ENG *machine tools* amenage rapide automatique *m*; ~ **rating** *n* ELEC ENG puissance nominale *f*, RECORDING puissance donnée en puissance *f*; ~ **rectifier** *n* ELEC redresseur de puissance *m*; ~ **reflection coefficient** *n* OPT facteur de réflexion énergétique *m*; ~ **relay** *n* ELEC ENG, PROD ENG relais de puissance *m*; ~ **resistor** *n* ELEC ENG résistance de précision *f*, résistance de puissance *f*; ~ **rewinder** *n* CINEMAT enrouleuse électrique *f*; ~ **saw** *n* MECH ENG scie mécanique *f*; ~ **shovel** *n* CONST *civil engineering* excavateur *m*, pelleteuse *f*; ~ **source** *n* ELEC ENG source d'énergie *f*; ~ **spectral density** *n* SPACE *communications* densité spectrale de puissance *f*; ~ **spectrum** *n* ELEC ENG spectre de puissances *m*; ~ **station** *n* ELECTRON usine à force motrice *f*, MECH ENG bâtiment des moteurs *m*, station de force motrice *f*, station génératrice d'énergie *f*, usine génératrice *f*, PHYS centrale *f*; ~ **steering** *n* AUTO servodirection *f*; ~ **steering pump** *n* AUTO pompe de servodirection *f*; ~ **stroke** *n* AUTO course de combustion *f*; ~ **subsystem** *n* SPACE *spacecraft* sous-système d'alimentation en énergie *m*; ~ **supply** *n* CINEMAT alimentation en courant *f*, alimentation électrique *f*, ELEC *network* alimentation en énergie *f*, distribution d'électricité *f*, ELEC ENG alimentation *f*, alimentation en secteur *f*, alimentation secteur *f*, PHYS, RAIL *vehicles, fixed equipment*, RECORDING, TELECOM alimentation *f*, TV alimentation en courant *f*; ~ **supply circuit** *n* ELEC ENG circuit d'alimentation *m*; ~ **supply duct** *n* RAIL traversée *f*; ~ **supply filter** *n* ELECTRON filtre d'alimentation *m*; ~ **supply input fuse** *n* PROD ENG fusible d'alimentation *m*; ~ **supply interrupt** *n* COMP, DP coupure d'alimentation *f*; ~ **supply unit** *n* ELEC ENG bloc d'alimentation *m*, PROD ENG alimentation *f*; ~ **surge** *n* ELEC ENG pointe de puissance *f*; ~ **switch** *n* ELEC commutateur de précision *m*, PROD ENG interrupteur général *m*; ~ **switching transistor** *n* ELECTRON transistor de commutation de puissance *m*; ~ **system** *n* ELEC ENG réseau d'alimentation *m*, REFRIG *of thermostat* train thermostat *m*; ~ **takeoff** *n* AERONAUT prise de mouvement *f*; ~ **terminal bloc** *n* PROD ENG bornier *m*; ~ **thyristor** *n* TELECOM thyristor de puissance *m*; ~ **tool** *n* MECH outil motorisé *m*; ~ **torquing** *n* PROD ENG serrage de puissance *m*; ~ **tower** *n* FUELLESS *solar* tour de puissance *f*; ~ **train** *n* AERONAUT chaîne dynamique *f*, AUTO chaîne cinématique *f*, transmission *f*; ~ **transformer** *n* ELEC ENG transformateur d'alimentation *m*, PROD ENG transformateur de puissance *m*; ~ **transistor** *n* ELECTRON transistor de puissance *m*; ~ **transmission** *n* ELEC ENG transmission d'énergie *f*; ~ **transmission by belt drive** *n* MECH ENG transmission d'énergie à commande par courroie *f*; ~ **transmission line** *n* ELEC ENG ligne de transport d'énergie électrique *f*, ligne de transport de courant *f*, ligne de transport de courant HT *f*; ~ **transmission network** *n* ELEC ENG réseau de transport d'énergie *m*; ~ **transmission system** *n* MECH ENG système de transmission d'énergie *m*; ~ **tube** *n* ELECTRON tube de puissance *m*; ~ **unit** *n* MECH ENG unité de puissance *f*, PROD ENG groupe moteur *m*, VEHICLES *engine* groupe motopropulseur *m*; ~ **up** *n* ELEC ENG mise sous tension *f*; ~ **wire-wound resistor** *n* ELEC ENG résistance bobinée de puissance *f*; ~ **wiring** *n* PROD ENG câblage de puissance *m*, câblage des lignes de puissance *m*; ~ **wiring kit** *n* PROD ENG jeu de connexions puissance *m*

power:[2] ~ **down** *vt* ELEC ENG mettre hors circuit, mettre hors tension, *semiconductor memory* mettre en veilleuse; ~ **up** *vt* ELEC ENG mettre sous tension

power-assisted: ~ **brake** *n* VEHICLES *braking system* frein assisté *m*, servofrein *m*; ~ **steering** *n* AUTO, TRANSP direction assistée *f*, VEHICLES direction assistée *f*, servodirection *f*

powerhouse *n* FUELLESS centrale électrique *f*

power-operated: ~ **lathe chuck** *n* MECH ENG mandrin à serrage mécanique pour tour *m*

powerpack: ~ **unit** *n* PHOTO accumulateur *m*

power-weight: ~ **ratio** *n* AERONAUT, MECH ENG puissance massique *f*

Poynting's: ~ **theorem** *n* PHYS théorème de Poynting *m*; ~ **vector** *n* PHYS vecteur de Poynting *m*

pozzolanic: ~ **cement** *n* CONST ciment à la pouzzolane *m*

pp *abbr (pages)* PRINT pages *f pl*

PP *abbr (peripheral processor)* TELECOM calculateur périphérique *m*

PPDU *abbr (presentation protocol data unit)* TELECOM unité de données du protocole de présentation *f*

PPM *abbr* CHEM *(parts-per-million)* parties par million *f pl*, COMP *(pages per minute)*, DP *(pages per minute)* pages par minute *f pl*, ELECTRON *(pulse position modulation)* modulation de position d'impulsion *f*, SPACE *(pulse position modulation)* modulation d'impulsion en position *f*

pps *abbr (pulses per second)* TELECOM impulsions par seconde *f pl*

PQC *abbr (pavement quality concrete)* CONST béton de qualité à paver *m*

Pr *(praseodymium)* CHEM Pr *(praséodyme)*

PRA *abbr (primary rate access)* TELECOM accès au débit primaire *m*

practical: ~ **capacity** *n* TRANSP capacité pratique *f*; ~ **capacity under rural conditions** *n* TRANSP capacité pratique rurale *f*; ~ **capacity under urban conditions** *n* TRANSP capacité pratique urbaine *f*; ~ **test method** *n* OPT *optical fibres*, TELECOM méthode de mesure de remplacement *f*; ~ **unit** *n* MECH ENG unité pratique *f*

practician *n* PROD ENG *person* praticien *m*

pragma *n* COMP, DP pragma *m*

pragmatics *n* COMP, DP pragmatique *f*

prase *n* MINERAL prase *m*

praseodymium *n (Pr)* CHEM praséodyme *m (Pr)*

praseolite *n* MINERAL praséolite *f*

pratique *n* NAUT libre-pratique *m*

PRBS *abbr (pseudorandom binary sequence)* TELECOM séquence binaire pseudoaléatoire *f*

preacidification: ~ **alkalinity** *n* POLLUTION alcalinité antérieure *f*, alcalinité initiale *f*, alcalinité originelle *f*

preadmission *n* HYDR EQUIP admission anticipée *f*, avance à l'admission *f*

preaeration *n* HYDROL *sewage* préaération *f*

preageing *n* TELECOM vieillissement préalable *m*

preamble *n* COMP position de synchronisation initiale *f*, DP synchroniseur initial *m*, PATENTS, SPACE *communications* préambule *m*

preamp *n* ELECTRON préamplificateur *m*

preamplification *n* ELECTRON, PETR, PHYS, RECORDING, SPACE, TELECOM préamplification *f*

preamplifier *n* ELECTRON, PETR, PHYS, RECORDING, SPACE, TELECOM préamplificateur *m*

preblowing *n* C&G perçage *m*

prebored: ~ **pile** *n* COAL TECH pieu moulé dans un avant-puits *m*

Precambrian *adj* GEOL précambrien

Precambrian *n* GEOL précambrien *m*

precast[1] *adj* CONST préfabriqué

precast:[2] ~ **concrete** *n* CONST béton préfabriqué *m*; ~ **unit** *n* CONST élément préfabriqué *m*

precast[3] *vt* CONST mouler d'avance, préfabriquer

precasting: ~ **works** *n* CONST chantier de préfabrication *m*, usine de préfabrication *f*

precautionary: ~ **measure** *n* SAFETY mesure de précaution *f*

precautions: ~ **against dust** *n pl* SAFETY précautions contre les poussières *f pl*; ~ **to be taken** *n pl* SAFETY précautions à prendre *f pl*

precedence *n* COMP, DP priorité *f*

precession *n* ASTRON, PHYS, SPACE précession *f*; ~ **camera** *n* CRYSTALL rétigraphe *f*; ~ **of the equinoxes** *n* ASTRON précession des équinoxes *f*; ~ **rate** *n* SPACE vitesse de précession *f*

prechamber *n* VEHICLES *diesel engine* préchambre *f*

precharacterizing: ~ **portion** *n* PATENTS préambule *m*

precharge: ~ **contactor** *n* PROD ENG contacteur de pré-alimentation *m*

precipitability *n* CHEM précipitabilité *f*

precipitable: ~ **water** *n* METEO eau précipitable *f*

precipitant *n* CHEM précipitant *m*

precipitate[1] *n* CHEM précipité *m*, CHEM TECH précipité *m*, sédiment *m*, METALL, PETR TECH précipité *m*

precipitate[2] *vi* CHEM TECH se déposer, se précipiter, se séparer par précipitation

precipitated[1] *adj* CHEM précipité

precipitated:[2] ~ **silica** *n* P&R *filler, pigment* silice précipitée *f*

precipitating: ~ **agent** *n* CHEM TECH précipitant *m*; ~ **tank** *n* CHEM TECH bassin de décantation *m*, vase clarificateur *m*, vase à clarifier *m*

precipitation[1] *n* CHEM, CONST, METALL, METEO, PROP MAT précipitation *f*; ~ **analysis** *n* CHEM TECH analyse par précipitation *f*; ~ **anneal** *n* THERMOD *light metals* recuit de précipitation *m*; ~ **annealing** *n* CHEM TECH recuit de précipitation *m*; ~ **area** *n* CHEM TECH, METEO zone de précipitations *f*, WATER SUPP impluvium *m*; ~ **collector** *n* POLLUTION collecteur de précipitation *m*; ~ **event** *n* POLLUTION événement de précipitation *m*; ~ **gage** *n* (AmE), ~ **gauge** *n* (BrE) WATER SUPP pluviomètre *m*; ~ **hardening** *n* CRYSTALL, METALL durcissement par précipitation *m*, PROD ENG durcissement par précipitation *m*, trempe structurale *f*, THERMOD *atmospheric* maturation *f*; ~ **heat treatment** *n* PROD ENG traitement thermique de précipitation *m*; ~ **tank** *n* CHEM TECH bassin de décantation *m*, vase clarificateur *m*, vase à clarifier *m*; ~ **vessel** *n* CHEM TECH décanteur *m*

precipitation:[2] ~ **harden** *vt* THERMOD *light metals* durcir par précipitation

precipitation-free *adj* PROP MAT exempt de précipités

precipitator *n* CHEM bac *m*, cuve de précipitation *f*, précipitant *m*, précipitateur *m*

precision *n* COMP, DP, PHYS précision *f*; ~ **approach** *n* AERONAUT approche sur radar de précision *f*; ~ **approach procedure** *n* AERONAUT procédure d'approche de précision *f*; ~ **approach radar rating** *n* AERONAUT qualification radar d'approche de précision *f*; ~ **engineering** *n* MECH ENG fabrication de précision *f*; ~ **grinding** *n* PROD ENG *machine tools* rectification de précision *f*; ~ **instrument** *n* INSTRUMENT instrument de mesure de précision *m*, instrument de précision *m*, PHYS instrument de précision *m*; ~ **machine tools** *n pl* MECH ENG machines-outils de précision *f pl*; ~ **machining** *n* MECH ENG usinage de précision *m*; ~ **micrometer** *n* MECH ENG micromètre de précision *m*; ~ **milling** *n* MECH ENG fraisage de précision *m*; ~ **regulator** *n* CONTROL régulateur précis *m*; ~ **roller chain and chain wheel** *n* MECH ENG chaîne de précision à rouleaux et roue dentée *f*; ~ **setting** *n* MECH ENG réglage de précision *m*; ~ **shim** *n* MECH ENG cale de précision *f*; ~ **slide** *n* MECH ENG *for machine tool* chariot de précision *m*; ~ **tachometer** *n* MECH ENG tachymètre de haute précision *m*; ~ **wire-wound resistor** *n* ELEC ENG résistance bobinée de précision *f*

precision-machined: ~ **steel** *n* PROP MAT acier usiné avec précision *m*

precoating *n* COAL TECH précouche *f*, PAPER TECH première couche d'un couchage *f*

precoded: ~ **tag survey** *n* TRANSP *traffic* enquête par papillons *f*

precombustion *n* THERMOD précombustion *f*; ~ **chamber** *n* AUTO *diesel engine*, THERMOD *diesel engine*, VEHICLES *diesel engine* chambre de précombustion *f*

precommissioning: ~ **checks** *n pl* NUCLEAR course d'essai *f*, marche d'essai *f*

preconcentrate *n* COAL TECH préconcentré *m*

preconsolidation: ~ **pressure** *n* COAL TECH tension de préconsolidation *f*

precooked *adj* FOOD TECH cuit à l'avance, précuisiné,

précuit

precooled *adj* FOOD TECH préréfrigéré

precooler *n* REFRIG prérefroidisseur *m*

precooling *n* RAIL préclimatisation *f*

precrushing *n* COAL TECH débitage *m*

precursor: ~ **pollutant** *n* POLLUTION polluant précurseur *m*, précurseur *m*

predecessor: ~ **in title** *n* PATENTS prédécesseur en droit *m*

predelivery: ~ **reminder** *n* PROD ENG relance préventive *f*

predelta: ~ **slope** *n* OCEANOG pente prodeltaïque *f*

predicate *n* COMP, DP prédicat *m*

predicted: ~ **reliability** *n* SPACE *spacecraft* fiabilité prévisionnelle *f*

predictive: ~ **capability** *n* POLLUTION pouvoir de prédiction *m*; ~ **coding** *n* TELECOM codage prédictif *m*

predistortion *n* ACOUSTICS précorrection *f*; ~ **technique** *n* TELECOM technique de distorsion préalable *f*

predryer *n* PAPER TECH présécheur *m*

predub *vt* CINEMAT prémixer

pre-edit *vt* CINEMAT prémonter

pre-emphasis *n* ACOUSTICS, PHYS, RECORDING, SPACE *communications*, TV préaccentuation *f*; ~ **improvement factor** *n* SPACE *communications* facteur d'amélioration par préaccentuation *m*

pre-employment: ~ **health screening** *n* SAFETY examen médical avant embauche *m*

pre-equalization *n* RECORDING précompensation *f*

pre-expediting *n* PROD ENG relance préventive *f*

prefabricated: ~ **package** *n* PACKAGING emballage préfabriqué *m*; ~ **panel** *n* REFRIG panneau préfabriqué *m*

prefabrication *n* NAUT *shipbuilding* préfabrication *f*

preferred: ~ **orientation** *n* CRYSTALL, GEOL orientation préférentielle *f*

prefilter *n* ELECTRON filtre préalable *m*, préfiltre *m*

prefiltering *n* ELECTRON filtrage préalable *m*, préfiltrage *m*

prefiring *adv* SPACE avant-lancement *m*

prefix *n* COMP, DP, TELECOM préfixe *m*; ~ **notation** *n* DP notation préfixée *f*

preflash *vt* CINEMAT prévoiler

preflashing *n* CHEM prévaporisation *f*

preflight: ~ **information** *n* AERONAUT information avant le vol *f*; ~ **planning** *n* AERONAUT planning avant le vol *m*

prefocusing *n* CINEMAT mise au point préalable *f*

prefog *vt* CINEMAT prévoiler

preform *n* C&G, OPT préforme *f*, P&R préforme *f*, ébauche *f*, TELECOM préforme *f*

preformed: ~ **fiber** *n* (AmE), ~ **fibre** *n* (BrE) TELECOM baguette *f*; ~ **spray scrubber** *n* POLLUTION séparateur à pulvérisation *m*

preforming *n* P&R *process* préformage *m*; ~ **press** *n* P&R presse à pastilles *f*

p⁻-region *n* ELECTRON zone P faiblement dopée *f*, zone de type P-*f*

pregnane *n* CHEM prégnane *m*

prehardened *adj* SPRINGS prétrempé

prehardener *n* CINEMAT prétannage *m*

preheat *vt* CONST, HEATING, REFRIG préchauffer, THERMOD préchauffer, échauffer

preheater *n* HEATING, PETR TECH, VEHICLES *diesel engine* préchauffeur *m*

preheating *n* CONST, HEATING, METALL, P&R *plastics, rubber*, PROP MAT préchauffage *m*, RAIL chauffage préalable *m*, préchauffage *m*; ~ **oven** *n* P&R *plastics* étuve de préchauffage *f*

preheptatonic: ~ **scale** *n* ACOUSTICS gamme préheptatonique *f*

prehnite *n* CHEM, MINERAL préhnite *f*

prehnitene *n* CHEM, MINERAL préhnitène *m*

prehnitic *adj* CHEM, MINERAL préhnitique

preignition *n* VEHICLES allumage anticipé *m*

preimpregnation *n* C&G préimprégnation *f*

preionization *n* RAD PHYS préionisation *f*

preleaching *n* COAL TECH préattaque *f*

preliminary: ~ **bath** *n* PHOTO bain préliminaire *m*; ~ **cost estimate** *n* CONST avant-métré *m*, devis préliminaire *m*, détail estimatif préliminaire *m*; ~ **design** *n* CONST avant-projet *m*, avant-étude *f*; ~ **design review** *n (PDR)* SPACE revue de définition préliminaire *f*; ~ **examination** *n* PATENTS examen préliminaire *m*; ~ **examining authority** *n* PATENTS administration chargée de l'examen préliminaire *f*; ~ **seating** *n* MECH ENG prérodage *m*; ~ **sedimentation** *n* HYDROL *sewage* décantation primaire *f*; ~ **treatment** *n* WATER SUPP épuration primaire *f*

preload *n* MECH ENG charge d'étalonnage *f*

premachined: ~ **condition** *n* MECH ENG état de préusinage *m*

premagnetization *n* RECORDING prémagnétisation *f*

pre-main: ~ **sequence star** *n* ASTRON étoile préséquence dominante *f*

premature: ~ **ignition** *n* AUTO allumage prématuré *m*

premetalized: ~ **dye** *n* (AmE), **premetallised dye** *n* (BrE) TEXTILES colorant prémétallisé *m*

premetered: ~ **techniques** *n pl* PRINT techniques de couchage préréglé *f pl*

premium: ~ **fuel** *n* (BrE) *(cf premium gasoline)* AUTO, PETR TECH supercarburant *m*; ~ **gas** *n* (AmE) *(cf premium grade gas)* PETR TECH supercarburant *m*; ~ **gasoline** *n* (AmE) *(cf premium fuel)* AUTO, PETR TECH supercarburant *m*; ~ **grade gas** *n* (AmE) *(cf premium grade petrol, premium gas)* VEHICLES supercarburant *m*; ~ **grade gasoline** *n* (AmE) *(cf premium grade petrol)* VEHICLES supercarburant *m*; ~ **grade petrol** *n* (BrE) *(cf premium grade gas)* PETR TECH, VEHICLES *fuel* supercarburant *m*

premuffler *n* AUTO pot primaire *m*

prepared *adj* FOOD TECH apprêté, préparé

prepegging *n* C&G préimprégnation *f*

preplasticizing *n* P&R préplastification *f*

prepower: ~ **check** *n* PROD ENG vérification avant la mise sous tension *f*

prepreg *n* P&R *laminate* préimprégné *m*

pre-press *n* PRINT mise en train *f*

prepress: ~ **proof** *n* PRINT épreuve de style Cromalin *f*

prepricing *n* PACKAGING mise de prix préalable *f*

preprint *n* PRINT préprint *m*

preprinted[1] *adj* PACKAGING préimprimé

preprinted:[2] ~ **label** *n* PACKAGING étiquette préimprimée *f*

preprocessed *adj* ELECTRON prétraité

preprocessing *n* ELECTRON prétraitement *m*, traitement préalable *m*

preprocessor *n* COMP, DP préprocesseur *m*

preproduction *n* PROD ENG présérie *f*; ~ **aircraft** *n* AERONAUT avion de présérie *m*; ~ **tooling** *n* MECH ENG outillage pour prototypes *m*; ~ **train** *n* RAIL *vehicles* train de présérie *m*

preprogrammed *adj* COMP, DP préprogrammé

prerecord *vt* RECORDING, TV préenregistrer

prerecorded[1] *adj* COMP, DP, TELECOM préenregistré

prerecorded:[2] ~ **magnetic tape** *n* RECORDING bande magnétique préenregistré *f*, bande préenregistrée *f*; ~ **message** *n* TELECOM message préenregistré *m*

preroll *n* TV temps de démarrage *m*; ~ **time** *n* TV intervalle de garde *m*, temps de démarrage *m*

presbyacusis *n* (BrE) ACOUSTICS presbyacousie *f*

presbycusis *n* (AmE) *see presbyacusis*

prescreening *n* COAL TECH précriblage *m*

preseizure: ~ **dialing** *n* (AmE), ~ **dialling** *n* (BrE) TELECOM numérotation sans décrocher *f*

preselection: ~ **gear change** *n* VEHICLES commande de vitesse à présélection *f*, commande à présélection *f*

preselector *n* ELECTRON amplificateur haute fréquence *m*, présélecteur *m*, HEATING présélecteur *m*, VEHICLES *gearbox* présélecteur *m*, présélecteur de vitesse *m*

presence: ~ **equalizer** *n* RECORDING compensateur de présence *m*; ~ **loop** *n* RECORDING boucle d'ambiance *f*, TRANSP *traffic* boucle de présence *f*

presentation: ~ **graphics** *n* COMP, DP graphique de présentation *m*; ~ **indicator** *n (PI)* TELECOM indicateur de présentation *m*; ~ **layer** *n* DP *OSI* couche de présentation *f*; ~ **protocol data unit** *n (PPDU)* TELECOM unité de données du protocole de présentation *f*

preservative *n* PACKAGING agent préservatif *m*, PROD ENG agent de préservation *m*

preserve[1] *n* FOOD TECH conserve *f*

preserve[2] *vt* FOOD TECH conserver, mettre en conserve

preserved: ~ **latex** *n* P&R *rubber* latex préservé *m*

preserving: ~ **jar** *n* (BrE) *(cf canning jar)* C&G bocal à conserves *m*

preset:[1] ~ **frequency** *n* ELECTRON fréquence préréglée *f*; ~ **height** *n* SPRINGS hauteur de préconformation *f*; ~ **length** *n* SPRINGS longueur préréglée *f*; ~ **pot** *n* ELEC *resistance* potentiomètre de réglage *m*; ~ **shutter** *n* PHOTO obturateur à armement préalable *m*; ~ **value** *n* PROD ENG valeur de présélection *f*

preset[2] *vt* COMP, DP prédéfinir, RECORDING prérégler, SPRINGS préconformer

presetting *n* ELECTRON préaffichage *m*, SPRINGS préconformation *f*; ~ **of channels** *n* TV présélection des canaux *f*; ~ **controls** *n pl* AERONAUT boîtier de préaffichage *m*; ~ **gage** *n* (AmE), ~ **gauge** *n* (BrE) METR calibre de préréglage *m*

presignaling: ~ **distance** *n* (AmE), **presignalling distance** *n* (BrE) RAIL distance d'avertissement *f*

presplit: ~ **basting** *n* MINING prédécoupage *m*

presplitting *n* MINING prédécoupage *m*

press[1] *n* PAPER TECH presse *f*, PROD ENG machine à compression *f*, TEXTILES presse *f*; ~ **button** *n* CONTROL bouton pression *m*, bouton à pression *m*, bouton-poussoir *m*; ~ **camera** *n* PHOTO appareil de reportage grand format *m*; ~ **cutting** *n* PROD ENG découpage à la presse *m*; ~ **fabric** *n* PAPER TECH presse à toile synthétique *f*; ~ **felt** *n* PAPER TECH presse à toile synthétique *f*; ~ **fit** *n* PROD ENG ajustement à la presse *m*; ~ **nut** *n* MECH ENG écrou pression *m*, écrou à patte de scellement *m*, écrou à river *m*; ~ **proof** *n* PRINT épreuve conventionnelle sur machine *f*, épreuve sur machine *f*; ~ **roll** *n* PAPER TECH rouleau de presse coucheuse *m*, PRINT rouleau de couchage *m*; ~ **stack** *n* PAPER TECH presses étagées *f pl*; ~ **stud** *n* TEXTILES bouton pression *m*; ~ **switch** *n* CONTROL interrupteur à poussoir *m*

press[2] *vt* PAPER TECH presser, PROD ENG comprimer; ~ **down** *vt* PACKAGING affaisser

pressboard *n* ELEC *insulation* carton comprimé *m*, presspahn *m*, PAPER TECH pressboard *m*

press-button *n* TELECOM bouton-poussoir *m*; ~ **switch** *n* CONTROL interrupteur à bouton-poussoir *m*

pressed: ~ **bimetallic half-thrust washers** *n pl* MECH ENG demi-flasques de butée bimétalliques découpées à la presse *f pl*; ~ **glass** *n* (BrE) *(cf pressware)* C&G verre pressé *m*

pressed-steel: ~ **bucket** *n* PROD ENG godet en tôle d'acier emboutie *m*

presser *n* C&G presseur *m*; ~ **bar** *n* TEXTILES presse *f*

press-finishing: ~ **machine** *n* TEXTILES presse *f*

pressing *n* C&G *article* objet pressé *m*, *operation* pressage *m*, RECORDING *of record* pressage *m*, TEXTILES repassage *m*

pressiometer *n* COAL TECH pressiomètre *m*

pressostat *n* REFRIG *pressure switch* pressostat *m*

presspahn-transformer: ~ **board** *n* PAPER TECH presspahn *m*

presspaper *n* PAPER TECH papier comprimé *m*

press-through: ~ **packaging sheet** *n* PACKAGING feuille d'emballage à enfoncer *f*

press-type: ~ **vertical broaching machine** *n* MECH ENG machine à brocher verticale type presse *f*

pressure *n* AERONAUT, CONST, ELEC ENG, GAS TECH pression *f*, HYDR EQUIP charge *f*, poussée *f*, pression *f*, tension *f*, *of steam* pression de vapeur *f*, tension de vapeur *f*, MECH *mechanics, physics*, PAPER TECH, PHYS, PROP MAT, REFRIG, SPACE pression *f*; ~ **accumulator** *n* PAPER TECH accumulateur de pression *m*; ~ **air system** *n* AERONAUT circuit d'air comprimé *m*; ~ **alarm** *n* PROD ENG alarme de pression *f*; ~ **altimeter** *n* AERONAUT altimètre barométrique *m*; ~ **altitude** *n* AERONAUT altitude-pression *f*; ~ **amplitude** *n* ACOUSTICS pression acoustique maximale *f*; ~ **anemometer** *n* METEO anémomètre de pression *m*; ~ **angle** *n* MECH ENG *gearing* angle de pression *m*; ~ **bomb** *n* PETR enregistreur de pression de fond *m*; ~ **boost valve** *n* AUTO soupape de surpression du convertisseur *f*; ~ **box** *n* PROD ENG boîte de pression *f*; ~ **broadening** *n* PHYS, RAD PHYS *of spectral lines* élargissement par pression *m*; ~ **build-up** *n* AERONAUT établissement de la pression *m*; ~ **bulkhead** *n* AERONAUT *aircraft* cloison pressurisée *f*, cloison étanche *f*, MECH ENG couple étanche *m*; ~ **cable** *n* ELEC câble à pression *m*; ~ **cap** *n* AUTO bouchon de radiateur *m*; ~ **cell** *n* COAL TECH capsule de pression *f*; ~ **change** *n* GAS TECH évolution de pression *f*; ~ **characteristic** *n* METEO caractéristique de pression *f*; ~ **check** *n* C&G glaçure de soufflage *f*; ~ **cloth** *n* PHOTO toile de tension *f*; ~ **coefficient** *n* FUELLESS coefficient d'augmentation de pression *m*, PHYS coefficient de pression *m*; ~ **control** *n* HEATING dispositif de contrôle de pression *m*; ~ **control emergency** *n* PROD ENG régulation de pression en marche de secours *f*; ~ **controller** *n* PAPER TECH pressostat *m*, REFRIG régulateur de pression *m*; ~ **control normal** *n* PROD ENG régulation de pression en marche normale *f*; ~ **cooker** *n* FOOD TECH autocuiseur *m*, cocotte minute *f*, MECH ENG autocuiseur *m*; ~ **cooling** *n* REFRIG refroidissement par pression d'air *m*, refroidissement par pression gazeuse *m*; ~ **curve** *n* HYDR EQUIP courbe de pression *f*, courbe isobare météorologique *f*, courbe manométrique *f*; ~ **delivery** *n* HYDR EQUIP débit sous pression *m*; ~ **detector** *n* GAS TECH capteur de pression *m*; ~ **diecasting die** *n* MECH ENG matrice de moulage sous pression *f*; ~ **difference** *n* HYDR EQUIP différence de pression *f*; ~

differential cutout *n* REFRIG pressostat différentiel *m*; ~ **differential switch** *n* CONTROL interrupteur à pression différentielle *m*; ~ **differential warning valve** *n* AUTO indicateur de chute de pression *m*; ~ **draft** *n* (AmE) *see pressure draught*; ~ **drag** *n* AERONAUT traînée de pression *f*; ~ **draught** *n* (BrE) MECH ENG *ventilation* aérage positif *m*, ventilation mécanique par insufflation *f*; ~ **drop** *n* FUELLESS chute de pression *f*, HEATING perte de charge *f*, HYDR EQUIP baisse de pression *f*, chute de pression *f*, perte de pression *f*, PAPER TECH chute de pression *f*, PETR TECH perte de charge *f*, PROD ENG chute de pression *f*; ~ **dyeing** *n* COLOURS teinture en cuve autoclave *f*; ~ **equalization** *n* OCEANOG équilibrage *m*; ~ **equipment** *n* MECH ENG équipement fonctionnant sous pression *m*, PETR TECH récipient sous pression *m*; ~ **feed** *n* AUTO graissage sous pression *m*; ~ **filling** *n* PACKAGING remplissage sous pression *m*; ~ **filter** *n* CHEM TECH, COAL TECH, WATER SUPP filtre sous pression *m*; ~ **forming** *n* P&R *operation* estampage à pression *m*, formage à pression *m*, gaufrage à pression *m*; ~ **front** *n* MILIT *of explosion* front de choc *m*; ~ **gage** *n* (AmE) *see pressure gauge*; ~ **gate** *n* CINEMAT cadre presseur *m*, cadre à pression *m*, PHOTO cadre presseur *m*; ~ **gauge** *n* (BrE) COAL TECH manomètre *m*, CONST indicateur de pression *m*, jauge de pression *f*, manomètre *m*, CONTROL contrôleur de gonflage *m*, manomètre *m*, HYDR EQUIP, LAB EQUIP *gas*, MECH ENG, PAPER TECH, PETR TECH, PHYS, PROD ENG manomètre *m*, RAIL, REFRIG jauge de pression *f*, manomètre *m*; ~ **governor** *n* CONTROL régulateur manométrique de pression *m*; ~ **gradient** *n* FLUID PHYS, PETR TECH gradient de pression *m*; ~ **graph** *n* INSTRUMENT courbe de tension *f*; ~ **guide** *n* CINEMAT presseur-guide *m*; ~ **hank dyeing** *n* COLOURS teinture en écheveaux sous pression *f*; ~ **head** *n* COAL TECH différence de pression *f*, HYDR EQUIP hauteur manométrique *f*, hauteur piézométrique *f*; ~ **height** *n* AERONAUT altitude de pression *f*; ~ **inlet** *n* AERONAUT *air conditioning* prise de pression *f*; ~ **intensification** *n* PROD ENG multiplication de la pression *f*; ~ **jet** *n* HEAT ENG jet sous pression *m*; ~ **limiting station** *n* CONTROL station de limitation de pression *f*; ~ **loss** *n* HYDR EQUIP chute de pression *f*, perte de charge *f*; ~ **lubrication** *n* AUTO graissage sous pression *m*; ~ **main lines** *n pl* MECH ENG canalisations sous pression *f pl*; ~ **maintenance** *n* PETR maintien de pression *m*; ~ **measurement** *n* SPACE *spacecraft* mesure de pression *f*; ~ **microphone** *n* ACOUSTICS microphone à pression *m*; ~ **mold for casting** *n* (AmE), ~ **mould for casting** *n* (BrE) MECH ENG moule pour fonderie sous pression *m*; ~ **pad** *n* AUTO patin de pression *m*, CINEMAT, PHOTO patin presseur *m*, RECORDING patin presseur *m*, tampon de pression *m*; ~ **pin** *n* MECH ENG *die set* chandelle de pression *f*; ~ **pipe** *n* MECH ENG tube sous pression *m*; ~ **plate** *n* AUTO plateau de pression *m*, CINEMAT presseur *m*, PHOTO presseur *m*, *camera* presse-film *m*, VEHICLES *clutch* plateau de pression *m*; ~ **plate drive strap** *n* AUTO languette d'entraînement du plateau de pression *f*; ~ **plate release lever** *n* AUTO, VEHICLES *clutch* levier de débrayage *m*; ~ **plate spring** *n* VEHICLES *clutch* ressort de pression *m*; ~ **pocket** *n* PAPER TECH chambre de pression *f*; ~ **pump** *n* COAL TECH pompe refoulante *f*, HYDR EQUIP pompe de refoulement *f*, WATER SUPP pompe de pression *f*; ~ **rate-of-change regulating** *n* AERONAUT régulation variométrique *f*; ~ **rate-of-change switch** *n* AERONAUT contacteur variométrique *m*; ~ **ratio** *n* SPACE rapport de détente *m*; ~ **reducer** *n* AERONAUT décompresseur *m*, détendeur *m*, réducteur de pression *m*, SPACE *spacecraft* détendeur *m*; ~ **reduction** *n* PHYS détente *f*; ~ **reflection coefficient** *n* ACOUSTICS facteur de réflexion en pression *m*; ~ **regulating valve** *n* CONTROL régulateur de pression *m*, soupape régulatrice de pression *f*; ~ **regulator** *n* CONST détendeur *m*, CONTROL régulateur de pression *m*, régulateur manométrique de pression *m*, ELEC ENG, HYDR EQUIP régulateur de pression *m*; ~ **relief duct** *n* RAIL rameau de pistonnement *m*; ~ **relief station** *n* CONTROL station de décompression *f*; ~ **relief valve** *n* HYDR EQUIP clapet de surpression *m*, soupape de décharge *f*, MECH ENG soupape *f*, PROD ENG limiteur de pression *m*; ~ **ridge** *n* OCEANOG crête de pression *f*; ~ **roller** *n* ACOUSTICS galet presseur *m*, C&G rouleau presseur *m*, CINEMAT galet presseur *m*, tambour presseur *m*, MECH ENG, RECORDING galet presseur *m*; ~ **screw** *n* MECH ENG vis de pression *f*; ~ **seal** *n* HYDR EQUIP garniture d'étanchéité sous pression *f*, joint étanche sous pression *m*; ~ **set ink** *n* COLOURS encre pressure-set *f*, encre à absorption *f*; ~ **setting** *n* PROD ENG tarage *m*; ~ **shadow** *n* GEOL trace de pression tectonique *f*; ~ **side** *n* HYDR EQUIP côté du refoulement *m*; ~ **sleeve** *n* MECH ENG douille de pression *f*; ~ **stage** *n* HYDR EQUIP *turbine* étage de pression *m*; ~ **surge** *n* HYDR EQUIP coup de bélier *m*, pointe de pression *f*; ~ **switch** *n* ELEC ENG manocontact *m*, HYDR EQUIP contacteur barométrique *m*, contacteur manométrique *m*, PROD ENG pressostat *m*; ~ **system** *n* AERONAUT système barrique *m*; ~ **tendency** *n* METEO tendance de pression *f*; ~ **test** *n* HYDR EQUIP essai sous pression *m*; ~ **transducer** *n* PROD ENG transducteur de pression *m*; ~ **transmitter** *n* HYDR EQUIP transmetteur de pression *m*; ~ **tube** *n* AUTO conduite de pression *f*; ~ **tunnel** *n* FUELLESS *hydroelectric power* galerie en pression *f*; ~ **turbine** *n* HYDR EQUIP turbine à pression *f*, turbine à réaction *f*; ~ **variation** *n* GAS TECH, WAVE PHYS *in stationary wave* variation de pression *f*; ~ **vessel** *n* CONST *grouting* pot à pression *m*, MECH appareil à pression *m*, MECH ENG réservoir à pression *m*, REFRIG récipient sous pression *m*; ~ **wave** *n* TELECOM onde de pression *f*; ~ **welding** *n* CONST, PROD ENG, THERMOD *cold welding* soudage par pression *m*; ~ **well** *n* WATER SUPP puits d'injection *m*

pressure-controlled: ~ **valve** *n* REFRIG vanne pressostatique *f*

pressure-forming: ~ **machine** *n* PACKAGING machine pour former sous pression *f*

pressuremeter: ~ **modulus** *n* COAL TECH module de pressiomètre *m*

pressure-reducing: ~ **valve** *n* CONST *gas* appareil de détente *m*, HYDR EQUIP clapet réducteur de pression *m*, détendeur *m*, manodétendeur *m*, MECH ENG, PROD ENG réducteur de pression *m*, REFRIG vanne réductrice de pression *f*

pressure-sealed: ~ **car** *n* (AmE) *(cf pressure-sealed wagon)* RAIL wagon étanche *m*; ~ **wagon** *n* (BrE) *(cf pressure-sealed car)* RAIL wagon étanche *m*

pressure-sensitive[1] *adj* PRINT sensible à la pression

pressure-sensitive:[2] ~ **adhesive** *n* PRINT ruban adhésif repositionnable *m*; ~ **detector** *n* (AmE) TRANSP *traffic* détecteur à pression *m*; ~ **hot-melt adhesive** *n* PACKAGING colle thermofusible autoadhésive *f*; ~ **labeler** *n* (AmE), ~ **labeller** *n* (BrE) PACKAGING étiqueteuse autocollante *f*; ~ **manometric switch** *n* CONTROL interrupteur manométrique à membrane *m*; ~ **paper** *n* PACKAGING papier autocollant *m*; ~ **tape** *n* PACKAGING ruban autocollant *m*

pressurestat *n* CHEM pressostat *m*

pressure-tight: ~ **joint** *n* MECH ENG *pipe-threading* raccordement avec étanchéité *m*

pressure-welded: ~ **safety grating** *n* SAFETY grille de sécurité soudée à pression *f*

pressurization *n* AERONAUT pressurisation *f*, TRANSP mise en pression *f*

pressurize *vt* REFRIG mettre sous pression

pressurized[1] *adj* MECH pressurisé

pressurized:[2] ~ **connection** *n* ELEC ENG connexion par pression *f*; ~ **floor** *n* AERONAUT plancher pressurisé *m*; ~ **glue feed** *n* PACKAGING alimentation de colle sous pression *f*; ~ **hot water tank** *n* HEATING réservoir à eau chaude sous pression *m*; ~ **natural gas** *n* TRANSP gaz naturel comprimé *m*; ~ **natural gas bus** *n* TRANSP autobus à gaz naturel comprimé *m*

pressurized-water: ~ **reactor** *n* *(PWR)* NUCLEAR réacteur à eau sous pression *m*

pressurizing: ~ **gas** *n* SPACE *spacecraft* gaz de chasse *m*, gaz de pressurisation *m*; ~ **gas tank** *n* SPACE *spacecraft* réservoir de gaz de pressurisation *m*; ~ **manifold** *n* AERONAUT collecteur de pressurisation *m*; ~ **valve** *n* AERONAUT clapet de pressurisation *m*, valve de mise en pression *f*

pressware *n* (AmE) *(cf pressed glass)* C&G verre pressé *m*

prestart: ~ **warning** *n* MECH ENG avertisseur avant la mise en route *m*

prestore *vt* COMP préaffecter, préenregistrer, préstocker, DP préenregistrer, préstocker

prestrain *n* METALL prédéformation *f*

prestressed: ~ **concrete** *n* CONST béton précontraint *m*

prestressing *n* SPRINGS précontrainte *f*, stabilisation *f*

prestriped: ~ **film** *n* CINEMAT pellicule prépistée *f*

prestriping *n* CINEMAT prépistage *m*

pretimed: ~ **signal** *n* TRANSP *traffic control* feu à cycle fixe *m*

pretravel *n* ELEC ENG course morte *f*

pretreated *adj* CHEM, PROP MAT prétraité

pretreating *n* CHEM, PROP MAT prétraitement *m*

pretreatment *n* COAL TECH prétraitement *m*, PROP MAT prétraitement *m*, traitement préalable *m*

pretwist *n* SPRINGS prétorsion *f*

pretzel *n* GEOM *topology* bretzel *m*

prevailing: ~ **torque-type hexagon nut** *n* MECH ENG écrou hexagonal à freinage interne avec couple préalable *m*; ~ **wind** *n* METEO vent dominant *m*, vent régnant *m*

prevent *vt* SAFETY *accidents* prévenir, éviter

prevention: ~ **of atmospheric pollution** *n* POLLUTION lutte contre la pollution atmosphérique *f*; ~ **cost** *n* QUALITY coût de prévention *m*; ~ **of noise pollution** *n* POLLUTION lutte contre le bruit *f*; ~ **of water pollution** *n* POLLUTION lutte contre la pollution des eaux *f*

preventive: ~ **action** *n* QUALITY action préventive *f*; ~ **fire protection** *n* SAFETY ignifugation préventive *f*; ~ **maintenance** *n* COMP maintenance préventive *f*, CONST entretien préventif *m*, DP, TELECOM maintenance préventive *f*

preview[1] *n* TV précontrôle *m*; ~ **monitor** *n* TV écran de contrôle *m*

preview[2] *vt* TV précontrôler, visionner

prevulcanized: ~ **latex** *n* P&R latex prévulcanisé *m*

PRF *abbr* *(pulse repetition frequency)* COMP, DP fréquence de répétition des impulsions *f*, ELECTRON fréquence de récurrence des impulsions *f*, fréquence de répétition des impulsions *f*, TELECOM fréquence de répétition des impulsions *f*

price: ~ **marking** *n* PACKAGING marquage de prix *m*; ~ **tag** *n* PACKAGING étiquette avec prix *f*

priceite *n* MINERAL picéite *f*

prick: ~ **bar** *n* PROD ENG *furnace poker* attisoir *m*, attisonnoir *m*, cure-feu *m*, fourgon *m*, lance *f*, pique-feu *m*, ringard *m*, ringard à lance *m*; ~ **punch** *n* MECH ENG pointeau *m*, pointeau de mécanicien *m*

pricker *n* MINING *blasting* aiguille *f*, épinglette *f*, *boring* lance de sonde *f*, PROD ENG *furnace poker* attisoir *m*, attisonnoir *m*, cure-feu *m*, fourgon *m*, lance *f*, pique-feu *m*, ringard *m*, ringard à lance *m*, *of loam plate, loam mould* broche *f*, *vent wire* aiguille à trous d'air *f*

pricking *n* PROD ENG décrassage *m*

prills-and-oil *n* MINING nitrate d'ammonium et fuel-oil *m*, nitrate-fioul *m*, nitrate-fuel *m*, nitrate-huile *m*

primacord: ~ **fuse** *n* SPACE *spacecraft* cordeau fusant *m*

Primacord *n* MINING cordeau détonant *m*

primary *n* ELEC ENG primaire *m*; ~ **access** *n* TELECOM accès primaire *m*; ~ **armature** *n* ELEC *generator-motor* induit de primaire *m*; ~ **barrel** *n* AUTO corps primaire *m*; ~ **battery** *n* ELEC pile *f*; ~ **blasting** *n* MINING tir primaire *m*; ~ **carbide** *n* METALL carbure primaire *m*; ~ **cell** *n* ELEC ENG pile électrique *f*, élément de pile électrique *m*; ~ **chaincase** *n* VEHICLES *motorcycle transmission* carter de la chaîne primaire *m*; ~ **circuit** *n* ELEC circuit inducteur *m*, circuit primaire *m*; ~ **clarification** *n* WATER SUPP décantation primaire *f*; ~ **coating** *n* OPT, TELECOM revêtement primaire *m*; ~ **coil** *n* TESTING bobine primaire *f*; ~ **collision** *n* TRANSP *traffic* collision primaire *f*; ~ **color** *n* (AmE) *see primary colour*; ~ **colors** *n pl* (AmE) *see primary colours*; ~ **colour** *n* (BrE) COLOURS couleur de base *f*, couleur primaire *f*; ~ **colours** *n pl* (BrE) CINEMAT, PHYS, RAD PHYS *of white light spectrum* couleurs primaires *f pl*; ~ **creep** *n* METALL fluage primaire *m*; ~ **crusher** *n* COAL TECH concasseur dégrossisseur *m*, concasseur primaire *m*, débiteur *m*, MINING broyeur des gros *m*; ~ **crushing** *n* MINING broyage grossier *m*; ~ **cup** *n* AUTO coupelle principale *f*; ~ **current** *n* ELEC *transformer*, ELEC ENG courant primaire *m*; ~ **cyclic variation** *n* AERONAUT *helicopter* variation cyclique principale *f*; ~ **emission** *n* ELECTRON émission primaire *f*; ~ **explosive** *n* MINING explosif d'amorçage *m*, explosif primaire *m*; ~ **extinction** *n* CRYSTALL extinction primaire *f*; ~ **fiber** *n* (AmE), ~ **fibre** *n* (BrE) C&G fibre primaire *f*; ~ **filter** *n* WATER SUPP préfiltre *m*; ~ **focus** *n* ASTRON *of telescope* foyer primaire *m*; ~ **fuel cell** *n* TRANSP pile directe *f*; ~ **grinding** *n* COAL TECH broyage grossier *m*; ~ **headbox** *n* PAPER TECH caisse d'arrivée primaire *f*; ~ **heat exchanger** *n* AERONAUT échangeur primaire *m*; ~ **index** *n* COMP, DP index primaire *m*; ~ **inductance** *n* ELEC *transformer* inductance primaire *f*; ~ **insulation** *n* PROP MAT isolation primaire *f*; ~ **interference** *n* RAD PHYS *in activation analysis* réaction interférence du premier ordre *f*; ~ **ionization** *n* RAD PHYS ionisation primaire *f*; ~ **link** *n* (*PL*) TELECOM liaison primaire *f*; ~ **memory** *n* COMP mémoire principale *f*; ~ **mirror** *n* ASTRON *of telescope* miroir primaire *m*, INSTRUMENT miroir principal *m*; ~ **piston** *n* AUTO piston primaire *m*; ~ **precipitation** *n* HYDROL précipitation primaire *f*; ~ **processor chassis** *n* PROD ENG châssis processeur primaire *m*; ~ **rate access** *n* (*PRA*) TELECOM accès au

débit primaire *m*; ~ **recovery** *n* PETR, PETR TECH récupération primaire *f*; ~ **refrigerant** *n* REFRIG frigorigène primaire *m*; ~ **runway** *n* AERONAUT piste principale *f*; ~ **sample** *n* COAL TECH échantillon primaire *m*; ~ **settlement** *n* COAL TECH tassement primaire *m*; ~ **shaft** *n* AUTO arbre primaire *m*; ~ **shoe** *n* AUTO segment primaire *m*; ~ **standard** *n* PHYS étalon primaire *m*; ~ **storage** *n* (AmE) (*cf primary store*) COMP mémoire principale *f*; ~ **store** *n* (BrE) (*cf primary storage*) COMP mémoire principale *f*; ~ **structure** *n* AERONAUT structure résistante *f*; ~ **tap** *n* ELEC ENG prise au primaire *f*; ~ **treatment** *n* HYDROL *sewage* prétraitement *m*, épuration primaire *f*; ~ **voltage** *n* ELEC *transformer*, ELEC ENG tension primaire *f*; ~ **winding** *n* AUTO bobinage primaire *m*, ELEC *transformer* enroulement de circuit *m*, enroulement primaire *m*, ELEC ENG, PHYS enroulement primaire *m*, TRANSP inducteur *m*

prime:[1] ~ **coat** *n* CONST *roads* couche de fond *f*, imprégnation *f*; ~ **factor** *n* MATH facteur premier *m*; ~ **focus** *n* ASTRON foyer primaire *m*; ~ **lens** *n* CINEMAT objectif primaire *m*, objectif à focale fixe *m*; ~ **meridian** *n* ASTRON méridien origine *m*; ~ **mover** *n* MECH ENG mobile *m*, moteur *m*; ~ **number** *n* MATH nombre premier *m*; ~ **time slot** *n* TV créneau de pointe *m*, début de soirée *m*

prime[2] *vt* HYDR EQUIP *pump* amorcer, *steam boiler* primer, MINING *cartridge* amorcer, PROD ENG *painting* imprimer, WATER SUPP *pump* abreuver, amorcer

prime[3] *vi* COLOURS donner la couche d'impression

primer *n* CHEM allumeur *m*, COATINGS apprêt *m*, enduit de débauche *m*, primaire *m*, COLOURS peinture d'apprêt *f*, CONST *painting* apprêt *m*, MILIT *for detonating* charge amorce *f*, MINING *blasting* cartouche-amorce *f*, P&R *paint* peinture d'apprêt *f*, *rubber, adhesives, paint* couche primaire *f*, primaire *m*, PRINT couche primaire *f*, PROD ENG *paint* apprêt *m*, primaire *m*; ~ **cartridge** *n* MINING cartouche-amorce *f*; ~ **charge** *n* SPACE *spacecraft* charge primaire *f*; ~ **pump** *n* AERONAUT pompe d'amorçage *f*

primeval: ~ **fireball** *n* ASTRON boule de feu primordiale *f*

priming *n* AERONAUT amorçage *m*, dégommage *m*, injection *f*, HYDR EQUIP amorçage *m*, primage *m*, MILIT, MINING *blasting* amorçage *m*, OCEANOG *of tide* avance *f*, revif *m*, PROD ENG *painting* impression *f*, imprimure *f*, WATER SUPP amorce *f*; ~ **charge** *n* MINING charge d'amorçage *f*, SPACE *spacecraft* charge d'amorçage *f*, charge primaire *f*; ~ **coat** *n* PROD ENG *painting* couche d'accrochage *f*, couche d'apprêt *f*, couche d'impression *f*; ~ **cock** *n* WATER SUPP amorceur *m*, robinet d'amorçage *m*; ~ **explosive** *n* MINING explosif d'amorce *m*; ~ **paint** *n* COLOURS peinture d'apprêt *f*; ~ **pipe** *n* WATER SUPP *of pump* fourreau *m*

primitive *n* COMP, DP primitive *f*

primordial: ~ **black hole** *n* ASTRON trou noir primordial *m*

primuline *n* CHEM primuline *f*

Prince: ~ **Rupert drop** *n* C&G larme batavique *f*

principal *n* CONST *frame, roof* arbalétrier *m*, chevron principal *m*; ~ **axis** *n* CRYSTALL axe principal *m*; ~ **axis** *n* PHYS *of solid body* axe principal d'inertie *m*; ~ **color** *n* (AmE), ~ **colour** *n* (BrE) COLOURS couleur élémentaire *f*; ~ **component** *n* MATH composante principale *f*; ~ **curvature** *n* C&G galbe *m*; ~ **maxima** *n pl* PHYS *optics* maxima principaux *m pl*; ~ **member** *n* CONST *of frame* maîtresse pièce *f*; ~ **photography** *n* CINEMAT images première équipe *f pl*; ~ **planes** *n pl* PHYS *optics* plans principaux *m pl*; ~ **points** *n pl* PHYS *optics* points principaux *m pl*; ~ **quantum number** *n* PHYS nombre quantique principal *m*; ~ **rafter** *n* CONST arbalétrier *m*, chevron principal *m*; ~ **ray** *n* PHYS rayon principal *m*; ~ **tapping** *n* ELEC *connection* prise principale *f*

principle *n* PHYS ~ **of complementarity** *n* principe de complémentarité *m*; ~ **of correspondence** *n* principe de correspondance *m*; ~ **of equivalence** *n* principe d'équivalence *m*; ~ **of least action** *n* principe de l'action minimale *m*, principe de moindre action *m*; ~ **of maximum entropy** *n* RAD PHYS principe d'entropie maximale *m*; ~ **of superposition** *n* principe de superposition *m*; ~ **of virtual work** *n* principe des travaux virtuels *m*

print¹ *n* CINEMAT copie *f*, COMP, DP impression *f*, PHOTO copie *f*, tirage *m*, épreuve *f*, PROD ENG empreinte *f*, *projection on core* porte-noyau *m*, portée *f*, portée de noyau *f*, portée de remmoulage *f*; ~ **buffer** *n* PRINT *computers* tampon *m*; ~ **cutter** *n* PRINT graveur sur bois *m*; ~ **drum** *n* COMP, DP tambour d'impression *m*; ~ **dryer** *n* PHOTO sécheuse *f*; ~ **files** *n pl* PRINT papier pour imprimante *m*; ~ **film** *n* CINEMAT pellicule de tirage *f*; ~ **format** *n* COMP, DP format d'impression *m*; ~ **grader** *n* CINEMAT étalonneur *m*; ~ **head** *n* COMP, DP tête d'impression *f*; ~ **maker** *n* PRINT appareil d'impression *m*; ~ **pitch** *n* CINEMAT pas positif *m*; ~ **position** *n* COMP, DP position d'impression *f*; ~ **run** *n* PRINT tirage *m*; ~ **server** *n* COMP, DP serveur d'impression *m*; ~ **shop** *n* PRINT atelier d'imprimerie *m*; ~ **speed** *n* COMP, DP vitesse d'impression *f*; ~ **tongs** *n pl* PHOTO pince de tirage *f*, pince à papier *f*; ~ **viewer** *n* CINEMAT visionneuse *f*, vérificateur de copie *m*; ~ **wheel** *n* COMP marguerite *f*, roue d'impression *f*, DP roue d'impression *f*

print² *vt* CINEMAT tirer, COMP, DP, PAPER TECH imprimer, PHOTO, PRINT tirer, TEXTILES imprimer; ~ **up** *vt* CINEMAT gonfler

printability *n* PAPER TECH aptitude à l'impression *f*, PRINT imprimabilité *f*

print-and-apply: ~ **labeling machine** *n* (AmE), ~ **labelling machine** *n* (BrE) PACKAGING machine pour imprimer et coller les étiquettes *f*

printed ¹ *adj* PATENTS imprimé

printed:² ~ **book** *n* PRINT livre imprimé *m*; ~ **circuit** *n* (*PC*) COMP, DP, ELECTRON, PHYS, TELECOM, TV circuit imprimé *m* (*CI*); ~ **circuit board** *n* (*PCB*) COMP, DP, ELEC, ELECTRON, TELECOM carte de circuit imprimé *f*; ~ **circuit connector** *n* ELEC ENG connecteur de circuit imprimé *m*; ~ **circuit laminate** *n* ELECTRON stratifié pour circuits imprimés *m*; ~ **circuit substrate** *n* ELECTRON substrat de circuit imprimé *m*; ~ **dirt** *n* CINEMAT poussière de tirage *f*, saleté de tirage *f*; ~ **fabric** *n* TEXTILES tissu imprimé *m*; ~ **folding carton** *n* PACKAGING carton imprimé pliant *m*; ~ **matter** *n* PRINT imprimé *m*; ~ **sheet** *n* PRINT feuille imprimée *f*; ~ **wiring** *n* ELECTRON circuit imprimé *m*; ~ **wiring board** *n* ELECTRON carte à circuit imprimé *f*

printer *n* CINEMAT tireuse *f*, COMP imprimante *f*, PHOTO tireuse *f*, PRINT imprimeur *m*, *computer* imprimante *f*, TELECOM *peripheral device* imprimante *f*; ~ **aperture** *n* CINEMAT fenêtre de tirage *f*; ~ **applicator** *n* PACKAGING imprimeur-applicateur *m*; ~ **command** *n* PRINT commande imprimante *f*; ~ **designed for narrow fabric** *n* TEXTILES machine à imprimer conçue pour tissu a-droit *f*; ~ **directory** *n* PRINT répertoire imprimante *m*; ~ **light** *n* CINEMAT lumière de tirage *f*; ~ **machine** *n* PRINT

mécanisme d'impression *m*; ~ **output** *n* PRINT sortie imprimante *f*; ~ **point** *n* CINEMAT point de lumière *m*; ~ **port** *n* PRINT port imprimante *m*; ~ **scale** *n* CINEMAT gamme des lumières *f*; ~ **slotter for corrugated board** *n* PACKAGING imprimeuse et fendeuse pour carton ondulé *f*; ~ **start mark** *n* CINEMAT repère de départ *m*; ~ **sync** *n* CINEMAT synchronisme de tirage *m*

printer's: ~ **black** *n* COLOURS encre d'imprimerie *f*, encre grasse *f*; ~ **color** *n* (AmE), ~ **colour** *n* (BrE) COLOURS colorant pour encre d'imprimerie *m*; ~ **ink** *n* PRINT encre d'impression *f*; ~ **machine** *n* PRINT machine pour l'art graphique *f*; ~ **mark** *n* PRINT marque d'imprimeur *f*; ~ **supply** *n* PRINT ustensile d'imprimerie *m*

printing *n* C&G, COMP, DP, PAPER TECH impression *f*, PHOTO tirage *m*, PRINT, TEXTILES impression *f*; ~ **apparatus** *n* PRINT appareil à imprimer *m*; ~ **area** *n* PRINT région imprimante *f*; ~ **black** *n* COLOURS encre d'imprimerie *f*, encre grasse *f*; ~ **by machine** *n* PRINT impression à la machine *f*; ~ **cam** *n* PRINT came d'impression *f*; ~ **color** *n* (AmE), ~ **colour** *n* (BrE) COLOURS colorant pour encre d'imprimerie *m*; ~ **cylinder** *n* PAPER TECH, PRINT cylindre à imprimer *m*; ~ **disc** *n* (BrE) PRINT disque imprimant *m*, (AmE) *see printing disc*; ~ **down** *n* CINEMAT tirage avec moins de lumière *m*, tirage plus sombre *m*; ~ **echo** *n* TV écho magnétique *m*; ~ **fly press** *n* PRINT presse d'imprimerie rapide *f*; ~ **form** *n* PRINT forme d'impression *f*, forme imprimante *f*; ~ **frame** *n* PRINT châssis *m*; ~ **gate** *n* CINEMAT fenêtre d'impression *f*, fenêtre de tirage *f*; ~ **head** *n* PAPER TECH, PRINT tête d'impression *f*; ~ **implements** *n pl* PRINT ustensiles d'imprimerie *m pl*; ~ **in** *n* PHOTO tirage à travers le dos du papier *m*; ~ **in black** *n* PRINT impression en noir *f*; ~ **ink** *n* P&R, PAPER TECH encre d'imprimerie *f*, PRINT encre d'impression *f*; ~ **lab** *n* CINEMAT laboratoire de tirage *m*; ~ **lake** *n* COLOURS laque d'impression *f*; ~ **loss** *n* CINEMAT pertes au tirage *f pl*; ~ **machine** *n* PRINT machine à impression *f*, TEXTILES machine à imprimer *f*; ~ **mask** *n* PHOTO cache *m*, cadre margeur *m*; ~ **off-line** *n* PACKAGING impression hors chaîne *f*; ~ **on-line** *n* PACKAGING impression sur chaîne *f*; ~ **onsite** *n* PACKAGING impression sur place *f*; ~ **opacity** *n* PAPER TECH opacité d'impression *f*; ~ **paper** *n* PHOTO papier d'agrandissement *m*, PRINT papier d'impression *m*; ~ **press** *n* PRINT presse à imprimer *f*; ~ **pressure** *n* PRINT pression d'impression *f*; ~ **process** *n* PRINT procédé d'impression *m*; ~ **roll** *n* P&R *equipment* cylindre d'imprimerie *m*, rouleau d'imprimerie *m*; ~ **roller** *n* PRINT rouleau *m*; ~ **sheet** *n* PRINT feuille d'impression *f*; ~ **stage** *n* PHOTO porte-négatif *m*; ~ **stock** *n* CINEMAT pellicule de tirage *f*; ~ **technique** *n* PHOTO technique de tirage *f*; ~ **through the base** *n* CINEMAT tirage à travers le support *m*; ~ **time** *n* PHOTO durée de pose *f*; ~ **trade** *n* PRINT industrie graphique *f*; ~ **trade worker** *n* PRINT ouvrier imprimeur *m*; ~ **types** *n pl* PRINT caractères d'imprimerie *m pl*; ~ **varnish** *n* COLOURS laque d'impression *f*, PRINT vernis d'impression *m*; ~ **with four colors** *n* (AmE), ~ **with four colours** *n* (BrE) PRINT impression en quatre couleurs *f*; ~ **works** *n* PRINT imprimerie *f*

printing-out: ~ **emulsion** *n* PHOTO émulsion noircissement direct *f*; ~ **paper** *n* PRINT papier pour sortie d'ordinateur *m*

printings *n* PACKAGING qualité de papier utilisée pour imprimer *f*

printout *n* COMP imprimé *m*, listage *m*, DP sortie imprimée *f*, TELECOM sortie sur imprimante *f*; ~ **paper** *n*

PRINT papier pour imprimante *m*, papier pour sortie d'ordinateur *m*

print-through: ~ **level** *n* TV niveau d'empreinte magnétique *m*

prior: ~ **art** *n* PATENTS état de la technique *m*; ~ **patent** *n* PATENTS brevet antérieur *m*; ~ **use** *n* PATENTS usage antérieur *m*

priority *n* COMP, DP, PATENTS priorité *f*; ~ **interrupt** *n* COMP, DP interruption prioritaire *f*; ~ **order** *n* PROD ENG ordre prioritaire *m*; ~ **processing** *n* COMP traitement par priorités *m*, DP traitement prioritaire *m*; ~ **queue** *n* COMP file d'attente par priorités *f*, DP file d'attente prioritaire *f*; ~ **right** *n* PATENTS droit de priorité *m*; ~ **sequencing** *n* COMP, DP attribution des priorités *f*; ~ **valve** *n* HYDR EQUIP clapet prioritaire *m*, clapet préférentiel *m*

prism *n* C&G, GEOM, LAB EQUIP *optics*, OPT, PHYS, TELECOM prisme *m*; ~ **beam splitter** *n* CINEMAT prisme diviseur de rayons *m*; ~ **binoculars** *n pl* INSTRUMENT jumelles à prismes *f pl*

prismatic: ~ **binoculars** *n pl* INSTRUMENT jumelles à prismes *f pl*; ~ **glass** *n* C&G verre prismatique *m*; ~ **jointing** *n* GEOL prismation *f*, prismation basaltique *f*; ~ **slip** *n* CRYSTALL, PROP MAT glissement de décrochage *m*; ~ **spectrograph** *n* RAD PHYS spectrographe prismatique *m*; ~ **spectrum** *n* RAD PHYS spectre prismatique *m*

pristine: ~ **fiber** *n* (AmE), ~ **fibre** *n* (BrE) C&G fibre vierge *f*; ~ **glass** *n* C&G verre vierge *m*

privacy *n* COMP, DP confidentialité *f*, TELECOM respect de la vie privée *m*

private: ~ **automatic branch exchange** *n* (*PABX*) TELECOM autocommutateur privé *m*; ~ **automatic exchange** *n* (*PAX*) TELECOM central automatique privé *m*; ~ **branch exchange** *n* (*PBX*) TELECOM autocommutateur privé *m*, commutateur téléphonique privé *m*; ~ **car** *n* (AmE) (*cf private wagon*) RAIL *vehicles* wagon de particulier *m*; ~ **dial-up port** *n* TELECOM accès privé par réseau commuté *m*; ~ **management domain** *n* (*PRMD*) TELECOM domaine de gestion privé *m*; ~ **manual branch exchange** *n* (*PMBX*) TELECOM commutateur privé manuel *m*; ~ **manual exchange** *n* TELECOM central manuel privé *m*; ~ **network** *n* TELECOM réseau privé *m*; ~ **network exchange** *n* (*PNX*) TELECOM commutateur de réseau privé *m*; ~ **numbering plan** *n* (*PNP*) TELECOM plan de numérotage privé *m* (*PNP*); ~ **telephone network** *n* TELECOM réseau téléphonique privé *m*; ~ **type** *n* COMP *ADA*, DP *ADA* type privé *m*; ~ **vehicle** *n* VEHICLES voiture particulière *f*; ~ **wagon** *n* (BrE) (*cf private car*) RAIL wagon de particulier *m*; ~ **wire** *n* (*PW*) TELECOM liaison spécialisée *f*

privileged: ~ **instruction** *n* COMP, DP instruction privilégiée *f*; ~ **operation** *n* COMP, DP opération privilégiée *f*

PRM *abbr* (*protocol reference model*) TELECOM modèle de référence de protocole *m*

PRMD *abbr* (*private management domain*) TELECOM domaine de gestion privé *m*

probability *n* COMP, DP, MATH probabilité *f*; ~ **curve** *n* MATH courbe des probabilités *f*; ~ **density** *n* PHYS densité de probabilité *f*; ~ **density function** *n* (*PDF*) MATH fonction de densité de probabilité *f*; ~ **distribution** *n* COMP répartition statistique *f*, DP loi des probabilités *f*, répartition statistique *f*; ~ **of excess delay** *n* TELECOM probabilité de dépassement d'un temps d'attente *f*; ~ **theory** *n* MATH théorie des probabilités *f*

probable: ~ **reserves** *n pl* PETR, PETR TECH réserves probables *f pl*

probe *n* COAL TECH, ELEC *measurement*, GAS TECH sonde *f*, MINING *boring* lance de sonde *f*, OCEANOG sonde *f*, PHYS capteur *m*, sonde *f*, PROP MAT tête de mesure *f*, REFRIG sonde de régulation *f*, SPACE sonde *f*; ~ **microphone** *n* ACOUSTICS microphone sonde *m*, sonde microphonique *f*, RECORDING sonde microphonique *f*

problem *n* PATENTS problème *m*; ~ **definition** *n* COMP, DP définition du problème *f*; ~ **description** *n* COMP, DP description du problème *f*

problem-oriented: ~ **language** *n* COMP langage orienté problème *m*; ~ **software** *n* COMP logiciel de problématique *m*

procaine *n* CHEM procaïne *f*

procedural: ~ **language** *n* COMP langage algorithmique *m*

procedure *n* COMP, DP procédure *f*, MECH ENG marche des opérations *f*, marche à suivre *f*, PROD ENG marche à suivre *f*, mode opératoire *m*, méthode *f*, QUALITY procédure *f*; ~ **division** *n* COMP *COBOL* division d'algorithmes *f*, division de traitement *f*, DP *COBOL* division procédure *f*; ~ **library** *n* COMP bibliothèque de procédures *f*; ~ **name** *n* COMP *COBOL*, DP nom de procédure *m*

procedure-oriented: ~ **language** *n* COMP langage orienté vers le traitement *m*

proceedings *n pl* PATENTS *before the EPO* procédure *f*

process[1] *n* CHEM voie *f*, COAL TECH processus *m*, procédé *m*, COMP, DP processus *m*, PAPER TECH procédé *m*, PROD ENG traitement *m*, procédé *m*, QUALITY processus *m*, procédé *m*, TEXTILES procédé *m*; ~ **automation** *n* COMP automatisme industriel *m*, DP automatisation industrielle *f*, automatisme industriel *m*; ~ **camera** *n* CINEMAT caméra pour effets spéciaux *f*, caméra pour trucages *f*; ~ **chart** *n* PROD ENG enchaînement des opérations *m*, enchaînement opératoire *m*, séquence des opérations *f*; ~ **colors** *n pl* (AmE), ~ **colours** *n pl* (BrE) PRINT couleurs primaires de la quadrichromie *f pl*; ~ **control** *n* CONTROL contrôle d'opération *m*, ELEC ENG commande de processus *f*, QUALITY maîtrise des processus *f*, TELECOM contrôle de processus industriel *m*; ~ **controller** *n* ELEC ENG automate programmable *m*, régisseur de processus *m*; ~ **control system** *n* COMP système de conduite de processus industriel *m*, DP système de commande de processus *m*, système de contrôle de processus *m*; ~ **engineering** *n* PETR TECH ingénierie des procédés *f*; ~ **engraver** *n* PRINT photograveur *m*; ~ **gas** *n* COAL TECH gaz de process *m*; ~ **industry** *n* PROD ENG industrie de transformation *f*; ~ **ink** *n* PRINT encre primaire d'imprimerie *f*; ~ **monitoring** *n* CONTROL contrôle d'opération *m*; ~ **printing** *n* PRINT impression en quadrichromie *f*, impression en quatre couleurs *f*; ~ **quality control** *n* QUALITY maîtrise de la qualité en cours de fabrication *f*; ~ **shot** *n* CINEMAT plan avec transparence *m*; ~ **specification** *n* QUALITY spécification du procédé *f*; ~ **state** *n* COMP, DP état de processus *m*; ~ **suspension** *n* COMP, DP interruption de processus *f*; ~ **water** *n* HYDROL eau de procédé *f*, eau industrielle *f*, WATER SUPP eau industrielle *f*

process[2] *vt* CINEMAT, COMP, DP traiter, FOOD TECH traiter, transformer

processed: ~ **data** *n* COMP donnée élaborée *f*; ~ **disc** *n* (BrE) ACOUSTICS disque moulé *m*; ~ **disk** *n* (AmE) *see* *processed disc*; ~ **ice** *n* REFRIG glace fractionnée *f*

processing *n* COAL TECH, COMP, DP traitement *m*, PAPER TECH mode de fabrication *m*, PATENTS *of application* procédure *f*, PETR TECH façonnage *m*, traitement *m*, triage *m*, PHOTO développement *m*, TELECOM traitement *m*; ~ **card** *n* TELECOM carte de traitement *f*; ~ **drum** *n* PHOTO tambour de développement *m*; ~ **equipment** *n* CINEMAT matériel de laboratoire *m*; ~ **error** *n* PRINT erreur de développement *f*; ~ **facility** *n* GAS TECH installation de traitement *f*; ~ **installation** *n* GAS TECH installation de traitement *f*; ~ **laboratory** *n* CINEMAT laboratoire de tirage *m*; ~ **load** *n* COMP, DP charge de traitement *f*; ~ **machine** *n* PHOTO, PRINT machine à développer *f*; ~ **marks** *n pl* CINEMAT traces de développement *f pl*; ~ **mode** *n* COMP, DP mode de traitement *m*; ~ **plant** *n* MINING atelier de préparation *m*; ~ **power** *n* TELECOM puissance de calcul *f*; ~ **priority code** *n* TELECOM code de priorité de traitement *m*; ~ **time** *n* COMP, DP temps de traitement *m*

processor *n* COMP, DP processeur *m*, PRINT machine à développer *f*, TELECOM processeur *m*; ~ **chassis** *n* PROD ENG châssis processeur *m*; ~ **control** *n* CONTROL contrôle par processeur *m*; ~ **hardware fault** *n* PROD ENG défaut affectant le système processeur *m*; ~ **status word** *n* COMP, DP mot d'état du processeur *m*

processor-limited *adj* COMP, DP limité par le processeur

Proctor: ~ **compaction test** *n* COAL TECH essai de compactage de Proctor *m*; ~ **test** *n* CONST essai Proctor *m*

procurement *n* PROD ENG approvisionnement *m*, obtention *f*; ~ **lead time** *n* PROD ENG cycle d'approvisionnement *m*, délai d'approvisionnement *m*, temps d'obtention total *m*; ~ **request** *n* PROD ENG demande d'achat *f*; ~ **requisition** *n* PROD ENG demande d'achat *f*

prod *n* MECH ENG pointe de contact *f*, PROD ENG *of loam plate, loam mould* broche *f*

prodelta: ~ **clays** *n pl* GEOL argiles de delta *f pl*, sédiments argileux déposés en avant d'un delta *m pl*, sédiments de prodelta *m pl*

prodigiosin *n* CHEM prodigiosus *m*

produce *vt* TV réaliser

producer *n* GAS TECH gazogène *m*, producteur *m*; ~ **coal** *n* COAL TECH charbon pour gazogène *m*; ~ **gas** *n* GAS TECH gaz pauvre *m*, gaz à l'air *m*

producing: ~ **horizon** *n* PETR TECH horizon producteur *m*, horizon productif *m*

product *n* COMP, DP, QUALITY produit *m*; ~ **accounting** *n* PROD ENG comptabilité des produits *f*; ~ **cost** *n* PROD ENG prix de revient unitaire *m*; ~ **family** *n* PROD ENG famille de produits *f*; ~ **feature** *n* PROD ENG caractéristique d'un produit *f*; ~ **group** *n* PROD ENG catégorie produit *f*; ~ **liability** *n* QUALITY responsabilité du fait du produit *f*; ~ **load** *n* REFRIG charge calorifique du produit *f*; ~ **range** *n* PROD ENG gamme de produits *f*, portefeuille de produits *m*; ~ **specification** *n* PROD ENG, QUALITY spécification du produit *f*; ~ **test** *n* QUALITY essai sur produit *m*; ~ **tree** *n* PROD ENG arbre de décomposition *m*, arbre de nomenclature *m*; ~ **type** *n* QUALITY type de produit *m*; ~ **variant** *n* PROD ENG nomenclature des variantes produit *f*; ~ **variant option descriptions** *n pl* PROD ENG désignation de la variante produit *f*

production *n* COAL TECH production *f*, MINING production *f*, rendement *m*, TEXTILES production *f*; ~ **aircraft** *n* AERONAUT avion de série *m*; ~ **batch** *n* QUALITY lot de production *m*; ~ **code** *n* CINEMAT code de production

m; ~ **console** *n* TV pupitre de régie *m*; ~ **control** *n* CONTROL contrôle en cours de fabrication *m*, gestion de la production *f*, PRODeng gestion de la production *f*; ~ **control room** *n* TV régie de production *f*; ~ **date** *n* PROD ENG date de production *f*; ~ **day** *n* PROD ENG jour de production *m*; ~ **drawing** *n* PROD ENG dessin de fabrication *m*; ~ **drilling** *n* PETR TECH forage de production *m*; ~ **expenses** *n pl* CINEMAT frais de production *m pl*; ~ **facilities** *n pl* PETR TECH installation de production *f*, PROD ENG moyens de production *m pl*, TV moyens techniques *m pl*; ~ **flow** *n* TEXTILES flux de production *m*; ~ **layer** *n* PETR TECH couche productrice *f*; ~ **licence** *n* (BrE) PETR TECH permis d'exploitation *m*; ~ **license** *n* (AmE) *see production licence*; ~ **line** *n* MECH ENG ligne de fabrication *f*, NAUT *shipbuilding* chaîne de production *f*, ligne de production *f*, PACKAGING chaîne de production *f*; ~ **mode** *n* GAS TECH phase de production *f*; ~ **order** *n* PROD ENG ordre de fabrication *m*; ~ **order issue** *n* PROD ENG émission d'un ordre de fabrication *f*; ~ **overhead** *n* CINEMAT frais généraux de production *m pl*; ~ **per unit area** *n* C&G production spécifique *f*; ~ **phase** *n* PETR TECH phase de production *f*; ~ **plan** *n* PROD ENG plan directeur de production *m*; ~ **planning** *n* PROD ENG planning de production *m*, QUALITY planification de la production *f*; ~ **platform** *n* PETR, PETR TECH plate-forme de production *f*; ~ **recorder** *n* INSTRUMENT enregistreur de productivité *m*; ~ **rule** *n* COMP, DP règle de production *f*; ~ **schedule** *n* CINEMAT calendrier de production *m*, PROD ENG programme de fabrication *m*; ~ **scheduling** *n* PROD ENG ordonnancement d'atelier *m*; ~ **scheduling and control** *n* PROD ENG gestion d'atelier *f*; ~ **smoothing** *n* PROD ENG lissage de charge *m*, nivellement de charges *m*, régulation de la capacité *f*; ~ **start date** *n* PROD ENG date de début de fabrication *f*; ~ **still** *n* CINEMAT photo de tournage *f*; ~ **string** *n* PETR colonne d'exploitation *f*, colonne de production *f*, PETR TECH colonne de production *f*, tubing de production *m*; ~ **strip board** *n* CINEMAT tableau de répartition du travail de la production *m*; ~ **test** *n* PETR essai de production *m*; ~ **time** *n* PROD ENG délai de fabrication *m*; ~ **tubing** *n* PETR colonne de production *f*, PETR TECH colonne de production *f*, tubing de production *m*; ~ **unit of measure** *n* PROD ENG unité d'oeuvre *f*, unité d'utilisation *f*; ~ **well** *n* GAS TECH puits de production *m*, PETR puits de production *m*, puits productif *m*, PETR TECH puits de production *m*

productive: ~ **time** *n* COMP temps d'exploitation *m*, DP temps productif *m*

productiveness *n* PROD ENG productivité *f*

productivity *n* PROD ENG productivité *f*; ~ **index** *n* PETR indice de productivité *m*

professional: ~ **deafness** *n* ACOUSTICS surdité professionnelle *f*

profile *n* COMP, DP profil *m*, NAUT *ship design* coupe longitudinale *f*, profil *m*, élévation *f*, PHYS profil *m*; ~ **dispersion** *n* OPT, TELECOM dispersion de profil *f*; ~ **dispersion factor** *n* OPT facteur de dispersion de profil *m*; ~ **dispersion parameter** *n* TELECOM facteur de dispersion de profil *m*; ~ **drag** *n* AERONAUT traînée de profil *f*; ~ **grinder** *n* MECH ENG machine à rectifier les surfaces profilées *f*; ~ **grinding** *n* MECH ENG rectification des profils *f*; ~ **parameter** *n* OPT paramètre de profil *m*; ~ **projector** *n* METR projecteur de profil *m*

profiling *n* MECH ENG profilage *m*; ~ **roller** *n* MECH ENG *of milling machine* touche *f*

progesterone n CHEM progestérone f
progradation n OCEANOG accrétion littorale f, progradation f
prograde:[1] ~ **metamorphism** n GEOL métamorphisme prograde m
prograde[2] vi GEOL s'avancer vers le large
program[1] n (AmE) see programme
program[2] vt COMP, DP programmer
programable adj (AmE) see programmable
programed adj (AmE) see programmed
programer n COMP, DP programmeur m, console de programmation f; ~ **unit** n COMP, DP programmateur m
programing n (AmE) see programming
programmable: ~ **array logic** n (BrE) (PAL) COMP, DP circuit logique programmable m; ~ **box** n (BrE) CONST equipment computerization boîtier programmable m; ~ **control** n (BrE) TELECOM commande programmable f; ~ **controller** n PROD ENG automate programmable m; ~ **controller system** n (BrE) PROD ENG système d'automatisme m; ~ **controls** n pl (BrE) PROD ENG automatismes programmables m pl; ~ **device** n COMP, DP dispositif programmable m, TELECOM appareil programmable m; ~ **encoder position switch** n (BrE) PROD ENG interrupteur de position à base de codeur programmable m; ~ **interval timer** n (BrE) (PIT) ELECTRON temporisateur programmable m; ~ **logic array** n (BrE) (PLA) COMP, DP réseau logique programmable m; ~ **logic circuit** n (BrE) TELECOM circuit logique programmable m; ~ **logic controller** n (BrE) PROD ENG automate programmable m; ~ **motor protector** n (BrE) PROD ENG système programmable pour la protection de moteurs m; ~ **oscillator** n (BrE) ELECTRON oscillateur programmable m; ~ **read-only memory** n (BrE) (PROM) COMP, DP ROM programmable f (PROM); ~ **regulation** n (BrE) CONTROL régulation à programme f; ~ **sequencer** n (BrE) TELECOM séquenceur programmable m; ~ **signal generator** n (BrE) ELECTRON source de signaux programmable f; ~ **unijunction transistor** n (BrE) ELECTRON transistor unijonction programmable m
programme[1] n (BrE) TELECOM programme m, TV émission f; ~ **audio track** n (BrE) TV piste sonore de programme 1 f; ~ **cost** n (BrE) TV prix de revient total m; ~ **error flag** n (BrE) PRODUCTION indicateur de défaut du programme m; ~ **identification signal** n (BrE) TV signal d'identification d'émission m; ~ **interrupt** n (BrE) CONTROL interruption de programme f; ~ **repeater** n (BrE) TV relais de programme m, répéteur de programme m; ~ **rung** n (BrE) PRODUCTION ligne de programme f; ~ **scanning** n (BrE) PROD ENG scrutation de programme f; ~ **scan time** n (BrE) PROD ENG temps de scrutation de programme m; ~ **selection button** n (BrE) CONTROL bouton de sélection de programme m; ~ **selector** n (BrE) TELECOM sélecteur de programmes m; ~ **timer** n (BrE) LAB EQUIP programmateur horaire m
programme[2] vt TV programmer
programmed[1] adj CONTROL, ELECTRON programmé
programmed:[2] ~ **check** n (BrE) CONTROL contrôle programmé m; ~ **control** n (BrE) TV commande asservie f; ~ **logic array** n (PLA) COMP, DP réseau à logique programmée m, réseau logique programmable m; ~ **servosystem** n (BrE) SPACE communications asservissement programmé m
programming n COMP, DP programmation f; ~ **language**

n COMP, DP langage de programmation m; ~ **logic** n PROD ENG logique de programmation f; ~ **unit** n COMP, DP programmateur de mémoire morte m
progress n PROD ENG état d'avancement m; ~ **check** n CONTROL contrôle d'avancement m; ~ **control** n CONTROL contrôle d'avancement m, PROD ENG contrôle de l'état d'avancement m
progressive n PRINT gamme d'épreuves progressives f ~ **ageing** n (BrE) P&R of materials vieillissement progressif m; ~ **aging** n (AmE) see progressive ageing; ~ **failure** n COAL TECH rupture progressive f; ~ **interlace** n TV analyse entrelacée progressive f; ~ **proof** n PRINT épreuve progressive f; ~ **rate spring** n SPRINGS ressort progressif m; ~ **switching magazine** n TELECOM système pas à pas m; ~ **system** n TRANSP système de régulation progressive m; ~ **transition** n TELECOM transition progressive f; ~ **waves** n pl WAVE PHYS ondes progressives f pl
prohibited: ~ **area** n NAUT navigation zone interdite f
prohibition: ~ **notice** n SAFETY avis d'interdiction m; ~ **right** n PATENTS droit d'interdire m; ~ **sign** n SAFETY signe d'interdiction m
project[1] n COMP, DP projet m; ~ **controller** n SPACE spacecraft contrôleur de projet m; ~ **design manager** n MECH ENG dessinateur-projeteur m; ~ **manager** n CONST maître d'oeuvre m, PROD ENG directeur de projet m; ~ **monitoring** n CONST suivi de projet m; ~ **production** n PROD ENG gestion par projets f, production par projets f
project[2] vt CINEMAT projeter, visionner, GEOM projeter
projected: ~ **area** n CONST surface projetée f; ~ **available stock** n PROD ENG stock projeté m, stock prévisionnel m; ~ **background** n CINEMAT fond projeté m
projectile n MILIT projectile m; ~ **energy** n MILIT force d'un projectile f
projecting: ~ **end** n SPRINGS of spring coil spire terminale saillante f; ~ **hairs** n TEXTILES brins cassés m pl
projection n CONST avant-corps m, portée f, projection f, ressaut m, saillie f, forme en saillie f, of stone, gutter beyond wall portée f, ressaut m, saillie f, CRYSTALL, GEOM, PHOTO of an image, PHYS of vector, PRINT projection f; ~ **along the c-axis** n CRYSTALL projection le long de l'axe c f; ~ **axis** n CINEMAT axe de projection m; ~ **box** n CINEMAT cabine de projection f; ~ **electron beam lithography** n ELECTRON gravure par faisceau d'électrons réparti f, gravure électronique répartie f; ~ **head** n CINEMAT bloc optique m; ~ **lamp** n CINEMAT lampe de projection f; ~ **length** n CONST longueur dépassante f; ~ **lens** n INSTRUMENT lentille de projection f, PHOTO objectif de projection m; ~ **lithography** n ELECTRON gravure par projection f; ~ **microscope** n INSTRUMENT microscope à projection m; ~ **port** n CINEMAT fenêtre de projection f, hublot de projection m; ~ **printer** n CINEMAT tireuse optique f; ~ **screen** n INSTRUMENT verre dépoli de projection m; ~ **speed** n CINEMAT vitesse de projection f; ~ **television** n TV télévision projetée f, télévision sur grand écran f; ~ **welding** n CONST soudage de saillies m, soudage par bossages m, PROD ENG soudage par projection m
projectionist n CINEMAT opérateur de projection m, projectionniste m
projective: ~ **geometry** n GEOM géométrie projective f
projector n CINEMAT appareil de projection m, projecteur m, PHOTO projecteur m; ~ **attachment** n INSTRUMENT accessoire de projection m; ~ **compass** n NAUT compas à répétition optique m; ~ **lamp** n PHOTO

lampe pour projecteur *f*; ~ **lens** *n* INSTRUMENT lentille de projection *f*; ~ **lens pole piece** *n* INSTRUMENT bobine de concentration *f*

prolate[1] *adj see* oblate

prolate:[2] ~ **ellipsoid** *n* PHYS ellipsoïde prolongé *m*; ~ **spheroid** *n* GEOM sphéroïde allongé *m*

PROM[1] *abbr (programable, programmable read-only memory)* COMP, DP PROM *(ROM programmable)*

PROM:[2] ~ **programmer** *n* COMP, DP programmateur de PROM *m*

promenade: ~ **deck** *n* NAUT pont promenade *m*

promethium *n (Pm)* CHEM prométhéum *m (Pm)*

prominence *n* ASTRON, SPACE protubérance *f*

prominent: ~ **joint** *n* C&G couture en saillie *f*

promontory *n* NAUT promontoire *m*

promoter *n* CHEM activateur *m*, promoteur *m*

promoting *n* CHEM amorçage *m*

prompt[1] *n* COMP, DP guide opérateur *m*, PROD ENG *computers* invite *f*; ~ **neutron** *n* PHYS neutron instantané *m*, neutron prompt *m*, RAD PHYS *fission neutrons* neutron immédiat *m*

prompt[2] *vt* COMP, DP guider

prompter *n* TV projecteur de texte *m*, prompteur *m*, télésouffleur *m*

prong *n* CONST fourchon *m*, MECH ENG branche *f*, dent *f*; ~ **center** *n* (AmE), ~ **centre** *n* (BrE) MECH ENG *lathe* pointe à trois dents *f*; ~ **chuck** *n* MECH ENG griffe *f*, mandrin à trois pointes *m*, mandrin à tulipe *m*

pronged: ~ **shovel** *n* CONST pelle à grille *f*

prontosil *n* CHEM prontosil *m*

Prony: ~ **brake** *n* AUTO frein de Prony *m*

proof *n* PHOTO, PRINT épreuve *f*, PROD ENG *trial* essai *m*, épreuve *f*; ~ **correction marks** *n* PRINT signes de correction *m pl*; ~ **load** *n* AERONAUT *airworthiness*, MECH ENG *of fasteners* charge d'épreuve *f*; ~ **marks** *n pl* PRINT marques de correction de copie *f pl*; ~ **pressure** *n* MECH ENG pression d'épreuve *f*; ~ **test** *n* ELEC essai de surcharge *m*

proofing: ~ **system** *n* PRINT système d'épreuves *m*

proofreading *n* PRINT correction de la copie *f*

prop *n* COAL TECH étai *m*, CONST chandelle *f*, étai *m*, étançon *m*, MECH ENG appui vertical *m*, MINING butte *f*, chandelle *f*, montant *m*, pied-droit *m*, étai *m*, *landing dog, kep* clichage *m*, taquet *m*; ~ **drawing** *n* MINING déboisage *m*

propadiene *n* CHEM propadiène *m*

propaedeutics *n* CHEM propédeutique *f*

propagate[1] *vt* WAVE PHYS propager

propagate[2] *vi* OPT se propager

propagating: ~ **buckle** *n* PETR TECH boucle de propagation *f*

propagation *n* COMP, DP, TELECOM propagation *f*; ~ **coefficient** *n* ACOUSTICS, TELECOM exposant linéique de propagation *m*; ~ **constant** *n* OPT constante de propagation *f*, exposant linéique de propagation *m*, PHYS constante de propagation *f*, TELECOM exposant linéique de propagation *m*; ~ **delay** *n* COMP, DP délai de propagation *m*, SPACE *communications* temps de propagation *m*; ~ **equation** *n* PHYS équation de propagation *f*; ~ **loss** *n* PHYS affaiblissement de propagation *m*, perte de propagation *f*; ~ **medium** *n* ELEC ENG milieu de propagation *m*; ~ **mode** *n* OPT mode de propagation *m*; ~ **path** *n* ELEC ENG trajet de propagation *m*; ~ **sensitivity** *n* MINING sensibilité à l'onde explosive *f*; ~ **velocity** *n* TELECOM, WAVE PHYS vitesse de propagation *f*; ~ **of waves** *n* WAVE PHYS propagation des ondes *f*

propane *n* CHEM, PETR TECH propane *m*; ~ **tanker** *n* PETR TECH propanier *m*

propanoic *adj* CHEM propanoïque

propanol *n* CHEM alcool propylique *m*, propanol *m*

propanone *n* CHEM propanone *f*

propargyl *n* CHEM propargyle *m*

propellant *n* CHEM ergol *m*, propergol *m*, propulsant *m*, POLLUTION propulseur *m*; ~ **force** *n* MILIT *of rocket* force de propulsion *f*; ~ **fuel** *n* SPACE *spacecraft* combustible *m*, propergol *m*; ~ **grain** *n* SPACE *spacecraft* bloc de poudre *m*; ~ **mass** *n* SPACE *spacecraft* masse éjectable *f*

propelled: ~ **charge** *n* MILIT propergol *m*

propeller *n* AERONAUT, MAR POLL hélice *f*, MECH ENG *screw propeller* hélice *f*, propulseur *m*, NAUT *boat building* hélice *f*, PAPER TECH propulseur *m*, TRANSP hélice *f*; ~ **boss** *n* NAUT moyeu d'hélice *m*; ~ **bracket** *n* NAUT chaise d'hélice *f*; ~ **drive** *n* TRANSP propulsion par hélice *f*; ~ **fan** *n* HEAT ENG, MECH ENG ventilateur à hélice *m*, REFRIG soufflerie à hélice *f*, ventilateur hélicoïde *m*, ventilateur à hélice *m*; ~ **governor** *n* AERONAUT régulateur d'hélice *m*; ~ **hub** *n* AERONAUT, NAUT moyeu d'hélice *m*; ~ **pitch** *n* AERONAUT pas de l'hélice *m*; ~ **relay unit** *n* AERONAUT boîtier relais d'hélice *m*; ~ **shaft** *n* (BrE) AERONAUT arbre porte-hélice *m*, AUTO arbre de commande *m*, MECH ENG arbre à came *m*, NAUT *boat building* arbre d'hélice *m*, arbre port-hélice *m*, VEHICLES *transmission* arbre de transmission *m*, cardan de transmission *m*; ~ **shaft tunnel** *n* (BrE) *(cf drive shaft tunnel)* VEHICLES *transmission* tunnel de l'arbre de transmission *m*; ~ **thrust** *n* TRANSP traction d'hélice *f*; ~ **thrust coefficient** *n* TRANSP coefficient de traction d'hélice *m*; ~ **torque** *n* AERONAUT couple d'hélice *m*; ~ **turbine** *n* FUELLESS turbine à hélice *f*; ~ **turbine plane** *n* TRANSP biturbopropulseur *m*; ~ **wash** *n* AERONAUT *slipstream* remous d'hélice *m*

propelling: ~ **charge** *n* MILIT charge propulsive *f*; ~ **force** *n* MECH ENG force propulsive *f*; ~ **gear** *n* MECH ENG appareil de propulsion *m*; ~ **nozzle** *n* AERONAUT tuyère propulsive *f*

propene *n* CHEM, PETR TECH propène *m*

propenoic *adj* CHEM propénoïque

propenyl *n* CHEM propényle *m*

propenylic *adj* CHEM propénylique

proper: ~ **motion** *n* ASTRON mouvement propre *m*; ~ **shutdown** *n* NUCLEAR déclassement *m*; ~ **subset** *n* COMP, DP partie propre *f*; ~ **time** *n* PHYS *relativity* temps propre *m*

properties *n pl* GEOM, TEXTILES propriétés *f pl*

property *n* CHEM *characteristic* caractéristique *f*, propriété *f*, GAS TECH, GEOM, PROP MAT propriété *f*

propfan *n* AERONAUT *propeller* hélice transsonique *f*

propjet: ~ **engine** *n* TRANSP turbopropulseur *m*

proportion *n* CHEM dose *f*, proportion *f*; ~ **of nonconforming items** *n* QUALITY proportion d'individus non conformes *f*, proportion d'unités non conformes *f*

proportional: ~ **action controller** *n* CONTROL régulateur proportionnel *m*; ~ **controller** *n* *(P-controller)* CONTROL régulateur proportionnel *m*; ~ **control unit** *n* CONTROL régulateur proportionnel *m*; ~ **control valve** *n* PROD ENG régulateur proportionnel de débit *m*; ~ **counter** *n* PHYS compteur proportionnel *m*; ~ **pressure controller** *n* CONTROL régulateur proportionnel de pression *m*; ~ **pressure reducing valve** *n* PROD ENG réducteur de pression proportionnel *m*; ~ **reducer** *n* PHOTO affaiblisseur proportionnel *m*; ~ **sampling** *n*

QUALITY échantillonnage proportionnel *m*; ~ **valve** *n* PROD ENG vanne proportionnelle *f*; ~ **weir** *n* HYDROL déversoir à équation linéaire *m*; ~ **widths** *n pl* PRINT chasses proportionnelles *f pl*

proportionate: ~ **arm** *n* ELEC *bridge* résistance proportionnée *f*

proportioner *n* PAPER TECH doseur *m*

proportioning *n* CHEM dosage *m*; ~ **valve** *n* AUTO compensateur de freinage *m*

propping *n* CONST soutènement *m*, étançonnement *m*, étayage *m*, étayement *m*; ~ **agent** *n* PETR matière solide *f*

proprietary: ~ **information** *n* PROD ENG droits de propriété intellectuelle *m pl*

proprietor *n* PATENTS titulaire *m*

propulsion *n* CHEM propulsion *f*, MECH ENG impulsion *f*, propulsion *f*, NAUT, SPACE propulsion *f*; ~ **by air pressure** *n* TRANSP propulsion par pression d'air *f*; ~ **by reaction** *n* SPACE propulsion à réaction *f*; ~ **by spiral drive with varying pitch** *n* TRANSP propulsion par vis d'Archimède à pas variable *f*; ~ **by stationary drive wheels** *n* TRANSP propulsion par galets installés sur la voie *f*; ~ **engine** *n* NAUT moteur de propulsion *m*; ~ **magnet** *n* TRANSP aimant de traction *m*; ~ **system** *n* SPACE système de propulsion *m*, système propulsif *m*; ~ **unit** *n* SPACE bloc de propulsion *m*, ensemble de propulsion *m*

propulsive: ~ **force** *n* MECH ENG force propulsive *f*

propwood *n* CONST bois d'étais *m*, bois de soutènement *m*

propyl *n* CHEM propyle *m*

propylamine *n* CHEM propylamine *f*

propylene *n* CHEM propylène *m*, propène *m*, PETR TECH, PROP MAT propylène *m*; ~ **oxide** *n* DETERGENTS oxyde de propylène *m*

propylic *adj* CHEM propylique

propyne *n* CHEM propyne *m*

propynoic *adj* CHEM propynoïque

prosecute *vt* PATENTS *application* poursuivre

prosopite *n* MINERAL prosopite *f*

prospect: ~ **hole** *n* MINING trou de prospection *m*; ~ **tunnel** *n* MINING tunnel de prospection *m*, tunnel de recherches *m*

prospecting *n* MINING prospection *f*, recherche *f*, PETR TECH exploration *f*, prospection *f*; ~ **dredge** *n* MINING drague de prospection *f*; ~ **level** *n* MINING galerie de prospection *f*, galerie de recherches *f*

prospection *n* MINING prospection *f*, recherche *f*

protactinium *n* (*Pa*) CHEM protactinium *m* (*Pa*)

protagon *n* CHEM protagon *m*

protease *n* CHEM protéase *f*

protect *vt* COMP, DP protéger; ~ **against** *vt* SAFETY protéger contre

protected: ~ **field** *n* COMP, DP champ protégé *m*; ~ **location** *n* COMP, DP emplacement protégé *m*; ~ **screw** *n* MECH ENG *of vice* vis cachée *f*

protecting:[1] ~ **against fire** *adj* THERMOD antifeu

protecting:[2] ~ **chamfer** *n* MECH ENG chanfrein de protection *m*; ~ **the hearing** *n* SAFETY préservation de l'ouïe *f*; ~ **lacquer** *n* COATINGS vernis protecteur *m*

protection *n* COMP, DP, ELEC ENG, SAFETY, SPACE protection *f*; ~ **against dripping water** *n* PROD ENG protection contre l'égouttement d'eau *f*; ~ **against exposure at work** *n* SAFETY protection contre l'exposition au travail *f*; ~ **against gas** *n* MILIT *chemical warfare* protection antigaz *f*; ~ **against heavy seas** *n* NAUT

protection contre les paquets de mer *f*; ~ **against radiation** *n* MILIT *nuclear warfare* protection contre les rayonnements *f*; ~ **cage** *n* OCEANOG cage de tourelle *f*; ~ **capacitor** *n* ELEC ENG condensateur de protection *m*; ~ **circuit** *n* ELEC ENG, TELECOM circuit de protection *m*; ~ **coating** *n* PROD ENG protection *f*; ~ **copy** *n* CINEMAT copie de secours *f*; ~ **diode** *n* ELECTRON diode de protection *f*; ~ **master** *n* CINEMAT marron de sécurité *m*; ~ **of pinch points on idlers** *n* MECH ENG protection des points de coincements sur les rouleaux *f*; ~ **resistor** *n* ELEC ENG résistance de protection *f*; ~ **sleeve** *n* MECH ENG manchon de protection *m*; ~ **time** *n* PROD ENG marge de sécurité *f*, temps de sécurité *m*

Protection: ~ **and Indemnity Association** *n* MAR POLL Mutuelle de protection et d'indemnisation *f*

protective[1] *adj* SAFETY de protection, protecteur

protective:[2] ~ **agent** *n* PACKAGING agent protecteur *m*; ~ **apron** *n* SAFETY tablier de protection *m*; ~ **armour** *n* MILIT blindage de protection *m*; ~ **bonnet** *n* COATINGS recouvrement de protection *m*, revêtement protecteur *m*; ~ **cap** *n* MECH ENG coupelle de protection *f*; ~ **circuit** *n* ELEC circuit protecteur *m*; ~ **clothing** *n* MILIT, SAFETY vêtements de protection *m pl*; ~ **clothing against heat and fire** *n* SAFETY vêtements de protection contre la chaleur et le feu *m pl*; ~ **clothing for rescue services** *n* SAFETY vêtements de protection pour services de sauvetage *m pl*; ~ **coating** *n* COATINGS couche de protection *f*, couche protectrice *f*, enduit protecteur *m*, peinture protectrice *f*, OPT, P&R peinture anticorrosive *f*, PACKAGING couche de protection *f*, PAPER TECH couchage de protection *m*, PHYS *optical fibre* protection *f*, revêtement *m* ~ **coating of paint** *n* COATINGS couche anticorrosive *f*, couche protectrice de peinture *f*; ~ **coat of paint** *n* COATINGS couche anticorrosive *f*, couche protectrice de peinture *f*; ~ **colloid** *n* CHEM colloïde protecteur *m*; ~ **conductor** *n* ELEC ENG fil neutre *m*, terre *f*; ~ **cover** *n* COATINGS recouvrement de protection *m*, revêtement protecteur *m*, PACKAGING enveloppe protectrice *f*; ~ **covering** *n* COATINGS recouvrement de protection *m*, revêtement protecteur *m*; ~ **cream** *n* SAFETY crème protectrice *f*; ~ **film** *n* COATINGS film pelable *m*, pellicule pelable *f*, vernis pelable *m*, vernis pelable de protection *m*, PACKAGING film protecteur *m*; ~ **finish** *n* COATINGS couche de protection *f*, enduit protecteur *m*, peinture protectrice *f*; ~ **footwear** *n* SAFETY chaussures de protection *f pl*; ~ **gaiters** *n* SAFETY guêtres de protection *f pl*; ~ **gas welding machine** *n* SAFETY machine de soudage en atmosphère inerte *f*; ~ **glass** *n* SAFETY verre de protection *m*; ~ **glasses** *n* LAB EQUIP lunettes de protection *f pl*; ~ **glass for welder's goggles** *n* SAFETY verre de protection pour lunettes de soudeur *m*; ~ **gloves** *n pl* SAFETY gants de protection *m pl*; ~ **goggles** *n pl* SAFETY lunettes de protection *f pl*; ~ **goggles for occupational safety** *n pl* SAFETY lunettes de protection pour le travail *f pl*; ~ **gown** *n* SAFETY sarrau de protection *m*; ~ **helmet** *n* PETR, SAFETY casque de protection *m*; ~ **hood** *n* INSTRUMENT capuchon de protection *m*, MILIT *chemical warfare* capuchon protecteur *m*, SAFETY bonnet de protection *m*, cagoule de protection *f*; ~ **layer** *n* COATINGS couche de protection *f*, couche protectrice *f*, PACKAGING couche de protection *f*; ~ **multiple earthing** *n* (BrE) ELEC *installation* mise à la terre de protection multiple *f*; ~ **multiple grounding** *n* (AmE) *see protective multiple earthing*; ~ **oxide coat** *n* COATINGS couche d'oxyde protectrice *f*; ~

paint n C&G vernis de miroiterie m; ~ **relay** n ELEC ENG relais de protection m; ~ **restraint system** n SAFETY système préventif m; ~ **screen** n SAFETY *for cathode ray tubes* écran de protection m; ~ **sheathing** n COATINGS recouvrement de protection m, revêtement protecteur m; ~ **spark gap** n ELEC éclateur de protection m, éclateur de sûreté m; ~ **spectacles** n LAB EQUIP lunettes de protection f pl; ~ **strip** n PROD ENG languette de protection f; ~ **suit** n SAFETY combinaison de protection f; ~ **wrapper** n PACKAGING emballage de protection m

protein n CHEM *compound* protéine f; ~ **fibers** n (AmE), ~ **fibres** n (BrE) TEXTILES fibres protéiques f pl; ~ **size** n TEXTILES colle protéique f

proteinic adj CHEM protéique

proterozoic n GEOL *stratigraphy* protérozoïque m

protid n CHEM *compound* protide m

protide n CHEM *compound* protide m

protobastite n MINERAL protobastite f

protocol n CHEM, COMP, DP, PRINT, SPACE, TELECOM *land mobile* protocole m; ~ **class** n TELECOM classe de protocole f; ~ **control indicator** n TELECOM indicateur de commande de protocole m; ~ **converter** n COMP, DP, TELECOM convertisseur de protocole m; ~ **data unit** n *(PDU)* TELECOM unité de données du protocole f; ~ **discriminator** n *(PD)* TELECOM discriminateur de protocole m *(DP)*; ~ **emulator** n *(PE)* TELECOM émulateur de protocol m; ~ **error class** n TELECOM classe erreur de protocole f; ~ **implementation conformance statement** n *(PICS)* TELECOM déclaration de conformité de mise en oeuvre du protocole f; ~ **reference model** n *(PRM)* TELECOM modèle de référence de protocole m; ~ **unit** n *(PU)* TELECOM unité de protocole f

protolith n GEOL protolithe m

protolysis n CHEM protolyse f

proton n CHEM, ELEC ENG, PART PHYS, PHYS, RAD PHYS proton m; ~ **absorptive capacity** n POLLUTION capacité de fixation des protons f, RAD PHYS CAP, capacité d'absorption des protons f; ~ **beam** n PART PHYS faisceau de protons m; ~ **irradiation** n SPACE irradiation en protons f; ~ **microscope** n INSTRUMENT microscope protonique m; ~ **number** n *(Z)* PART PHYS nombre de protons m *(Z)*; ~ **resonance magnetometer** n PETR magnétomètre à protons m; ~ **supersynchrotron** n PART PHYS supersynchrotron à protons m; ~ **synchrotron** n PART PHYS synchrotron à protons m; ~ **telescope** n INSTRUMENT télescope protonique m

proton-antiproton: ~ **collider** n PART PHYS collisionneur proton-antiproton m; ~ **collision** n PART PHYS collision proton-antiproton f

proton-proton: ~ **collision** n PART PHYS collision proton-proton f

protoplanet n ASTRON protoplanète f

protostar n ASTRON protoétoile f

prototype n COMP, DP, NAUT *naval architecture* prototype m; ~ **stage** n RAD PHYS stade du prototype m; ~ **tooling** n MECH ENG outillage pour prototypes m

protoxide n CHEM protoxyde m

protractor n GEOM rapporteur m, METR *mechanical* rapporteur m, *optical* rapporteur m, NAUT *navigation* rapporteur m

proustite n MINERAL, PROP MAT *mineralogy* proustite f

prove vt MINING reconnaître

proven: ~ **area** n PETR TECH gisement prouvé m, zone prouvée f; ~ **reserves** n PETR réserves sûres f pl, PETR TECH réserves prouvées f pl

provide:[1] ~ **with** vt PROD ENG fournir de, pourvoir de

provide:[2] ~ **an oxygen supply** vi SPACE fournir une réserve d'oxygène; ~ **power** vi PROD ENG rétablir l'alimentation

proving: ~ **cabinet** n FOOD TECH *baking* étuve à fermentation f; ~ **flight** n AERONAUT vol d'épreuve m; ~ **run** n NUCLEAR course d'essai f, marche d'essai f; ~ **trial** n NUCLEAR essai m

provision[1] n TELECOM *of services* fourniture f

provision[2] vt NAUT *ship* approvisionner, ravitailler

provisional: ~ **protection** n PATENTS protection provisoire f

prow n NAUT proue f

proxar n CINEMAT bonnette d'approche f

proximate: ~ **analysis** n CHEM analyse immédiate f

proximity: ~ **effect** n ELEC ENG effet de proximité m; ~ **lithography** n ELECTRON gravure à proximité f; ~ **log** n PETR diagramme de proximité m, log de proximité m, PETR TECH diagramme de proximité f; ~ **mask** n ELECTRON masque de proximité m; ~ **switch** n ELEC interrupteur électrosensible m, ELEC ENG, PROD ENG interrupteur de proximité m; ~ **warning indicator** n AERONAUT avertisseur de proximité m, dispositif avertisseur de proximité m

PRR n PHYS taux de répétition des impulsions m

PRT abbr *(personal rapid transport)* TRANSP transport en commun personnalisé m

prulaurasin n CHEM prulaurasine f

pruner n MECH ENG *tool* émondoir m

pruning: ~ **saw** n MECH ENG *tool* scie à élaguer f

prunt n C&G application à chaud f

Prussian: ~ **blue** n CHEM bleu de Prusse m

prussiate n CHEM prussiate m

prussic: ~ **acid** n CHEM acide prussique m

pry-off: ~ **finish** n C&G bague pour bouchage à levier f

PS abbr *(packet switch)* ELEC, TELECOM commutateur de paquets m

PSA abbr *(particle size analyzer)* NUCLEAR granulomètre m

psaturose n MINERAL stéphanite f

PSE abbr *(packet switching exchange)* TELECOM centre de commutation de paquets m

p-semiconductor n ELECTRON semi-conducteur de type P m

p⁻-semiconductor n ELECTRON semi-conducteur de type P faiblement dopé m

pseudo: ~ **ionone** n CHEM pseudoionone f; ~ **item** n PROD ENG article fantôme m, article fictif m; ~ **random number** n COMP, DP nombre pseudo-aléatoire m

pseudoacid n CHEM pseudacide m

pseudocode n COMP, DP pseudocode m

pseudoelliptic: ~ **filter** n SPACE *communications* filtre pseudo-elliptique m

pseudoinstruction n COMP, DP pseudoinstruction f

pseudolanguage n COMP, DP pseudolangage m

pseudolock n TV pseudoenclenchement m

pseudomalachite n MINERAL pseudomalachite f

pseudomer n CHEM pseudomère m

pseudomeric adj CHEM pseudomérique

pseudomerism n CHEM pseudomérie f

pseudomorph n GEOL *metamorphism* pseudomorphe m

pseudonitrole n CHEM pseudonitrol m

pseudonoise n TELECOM bruit pseudoaléatoire m; ~ **sequence** n NAUT *satellite communications* séquence de bruit pseudoaléatoire *f*

pseudoplastic *n* CHEM pseudoplastique *m*

pseudopotentiometric: ~ **head** *n* PETR TECH niveau pseudopotentiométrique *m*

pseudorandom[1] *adj* TELECOM pseudoaléatoire

pseudorandom:[2] ~ **binary sequence** *n* (*PRBS*) TELECOM séquence binaire pseudoaléatoire *f*; ~ **noise** *n* TELECOM bruit pseudoaléatoire *m*; ~ **noise code** *n* TELECOM code de bruit pseudoaléatoire *m*; ~ **signal** *n* TELECOM signal pseudoaléatoire *m*

pseudosonic: ~ **log** *n* PETR TECH diagraphie pseudosonique *f*; ~ **profile** *n* PETR TECH profil pseudosonique *m*

pseudosphere *n* GEOM pseudosphère *f*

pseudostereophony *n* RECORDING pseudostéréophonie *f*

psi *abbr* (*pounds per square inch*) METR, PETR TECH livres par pouce carré *f pl*

psilomelane *n* MINERAL psilomélane *f*

PSK *abbr* (*phase shift keying*) COMP, DP, ELECTRON, SPACE MDP (*modulation par déplacement de phase*)

PSN *abbr* COMP (*packet-switched network*), DP (*packet-switched network*) réseau de commutation par paquets *m*, TELECOM (*packet-switched network*) réseau de commutation par paquets *m*, TELECOM (*packet switching node*) noeud à commutation de paquets *m*, TELECOM (*public switched network*) réseau public commuté *m*

psophometric: ~ **weighting factor** *n* SPACE *communications* facteur de pondération psophométrique *m*

PSTN *abbr* (*public switched telephone network*) TELECOM réseau téléphonique public commuté *m*

PSW *abbr* (*program status word*) COMP, DP mot d'état du programme *m*

psychotrine *n* CHEM psychotrine *f*

psychrometer *n* LAB EQUIP *humidity*, PAPER TECH, PHYS, REFRIG psychromètre *m*

psychrometry *n* PHYS psychrométrie *f*

Pt (*platinum*) CHEM Pt (*platine*)

PTC *abbr* INSTRUMENT (*parabolic trough conveyor*) miroir cylindro-parabolique avec foyer tubulaire *m*, SPACE (*passive thermal control*) régulation thermique passive *f*

pterin *n* CHEM ptéridine *f*, ptérine *f*

ptomaine *n* CHEM ptomaïne *f*

ptygmatic: ~ **fold** *n* GEOL pli ptygmatique *m*

p-type: ~ **base** *n* ELECTRON base P *f*, base de type P *f*, base dopée P *f*; ~ **collector** *n* ELECTRON collecteur de type P *m*; ~ **conductivity** *n* ELEC ENG conduction par trous *f*; ~ **diffusion** *n* ELECTRON diffusion de type P *f*; ~ **epitaxial layer** *n* ELECTRON couche épitaxiale de type P *f*; ~ **implanted layer** *n* ELECTRON couche implantée de type P *f*; ~ **impurity** *n* ELECTRON impureté de type P *f*; ~ **semiconductor** *n* ELECTRON, PHYS semi-conducteur de type P *m*; ~ **silicon** *n* ELECTRON silicium de type P *m*; ~ **silicon substrate** *n* ELECTRON substrat de silicium de type P *m*

Pu (*plutonium*) CHEM Pu (*plutonium*)

PU *abbr* (*protocol unit*) TELECOM unité de protocole *f*

public: ~ **address amplifier** *n* (*PA amplifier*) RECORDING amplificateur de sonorisation *m*; ~ **address system** *n* AERONAUT *PA system* système de sonorisation cabine *m*; ~ **automobile** *n* TRANSP voiture à jetons *f*; ~ **data network** *n* (*PDN*) COMP, DP réseau public de données *m*, réseau public de transmission de données *m*; ~ **dial-up port** *n* TELECOM point d'accès public *m*; ~ **health** *n* WATER SUPP hygiène publique *f*; ~ **mobile** **network** *n* TELECOM réseau mobile terrestre public *m*; ~ **network** *n* TELECOM réseau public *m*; ~ **road** *n* CONST voie publique *f*; ~ **switched network** *n* (*PSN*) TELECOM réseau public commuté *m*; ~ **switched telephone network** *n* (*PSTN*) TELECOM réseau téléphonique commuté *m*, réseau téléphonique public commuté *m*; ~ **telephone** *n* TELECOM publiphone *m*; ~ **telephone exchange** *n* (BrE) TELECOM commutateur public *m*; ~ **telephone network** *n* TELECOM réseau téléphonique public *m*; ~ **use** *n* PATENTS usage public *m*; ~ **utilities** *n* WATER SUPP services publics *m pl*; ~ **water supply** *n* WATER SUPP approvisionnement en eau public *m*; ~ **works** *n pl* CONST, WATER SUPP travaux publics *m pl*

publish *vt* PATENTS, PRINT publier

pucella *n* C&G pince à ouvrir *f*

puck *n* PRINT galet *m*, palet *m*, souris *f*

puddle *n* HYDROL, WATER SUPP flaque *f*; ~ **ball** *n* PROD ENG balle de puddlage *f*, boule de puddlage *f*, loupe de puddlage *f*; ~ **bar** *n* PROD ENG fer brut *m*, fer ébauché *m*, ébauché de puddlage *m*; ~ **bar train** *n* PROD ENG laminoir de puddlage *m*, laminoir ébaucheur *m*, train de puddlage *m*, train ébaucheur *m*, équipage dégrossisseur *m*; ~ **roll** *n* PROD ENG cylindre dégrossisseur *m*, cylindre ébaucheur *m*, dégrossisseur *m*, ébaucheur *m*; ~ **rolls** *n pl* PROD ENG laminoir de puddlage *m*, laminoir ébaucheur *m*, train de puddlage *m*, train ébaucheur *m*, équipage dégrossisseur *m*; ~ **train** *n* PROD ENG laminoir de puddlage *m*, laminoir ébaucheur *m*, train de puddlage *m*, train ébaucheur *m*, équipage dégrossisseur *m*

puddling: ~ **trough** *n* MINING langelotte *m*

puff[1] *n* C&G coup de souffle *m*

puff[2] *vt* FOOD TECH faire gonfler

pug *n* HYDR EQUIP glaise *f*, MINING argile malaxée *f*, *clay* lisière *f*, salbande *f*, salbande argileuse *f*; ~ **mill** *n* HYDR EQUIP malaxeur à glaise *m*

pulegone *n* CHEM pulégone *f*

Pulfrich: ~ **refractometer** *n* PHYS réfractomètre de Pulfrich *m*

pull[1] *n* C&G production du four *f*, MECH ENG *tractive effort* effort de traction *m*, PAPER TECH étirage *m*, PRINT bonne feuille *f*, feuilles sortant de la machine *f pl*, épreuve *f*, SPACE gravitation *f*; ~ **box** *n* ELEC *installation* boîte tirage *f*; ~ **current** *n* (BrE) (*cf withdrawal current*) C&G courant de tirée *m*; ~ **down** *n* CINEMAT *of film in projector, camera or printer* entraînement intermittent *m*; ~ **down claw** *n* CINEMAT griffe d'entraînement *f*; ~ **down test** *n* REFRIG essai de mise en régime *m*; ~ **ring** *n* PACKAGING anneau de préhension *m*; ~ **rod** *n* MECH ENG tringle de tirage *f*; ~ **roll** *n* C&G tire-fil *m*; ~ **roller** *n* PRINT rouleau d'appel *m*; ~ **switch** *n* ELEC interrupteur à cordon *m*

pull[2] *vt* PAPER TECH étirer, PRINT tirer; ~ **out** *vt* CONST *nail*, MECH ENG *nail* arracher, extraire

pull:[3] ~ **back** *vi* CINEMAT faire un travelling arrière; ~ **focus** *vi* CINEMAT faire la mise au point, suivre le point

pull-apart: ~ **basin** *n* GEOL bassin de transtension *m*, bassin en pull-apart *m*

pull-cord: ~ **switch** *n* CONTROL interrupteur à cordon *m*

pulldown: ~ **menu** *n* COMP, DP, PRINT menu déroulant *m*

pulled: ~ **sugar** *n* FOOD TECH sucre filé *m*, sucre tiré *m*

pulled-in: ~ **selvage** *n* TEXTILES lisière rentrée *f*; ~ **selvedge** *n* TEXTILES lisière rentrée *f*

pulley *n* MECH ENG poulie *f*, poulie de moufle *f*, rouet *m*, réa *f*, MINING molette *f*, poulie *f*, poulie de chevalement *f*, NAUT, PHYS poulie *f*; ~ **block** *n* MECH ENG *shell* with *sheave, sheaves* moufle *m*, poulie *f*, NAUT *purchases* moufle *m*; ~ **block hook** *n* MECH ENG crochet de palan *m*; ~ **coupling** *n* MECH ENG manchon à plateaux à boulons noyés *m*; ~ **for gut band** *n* MECH ENG poulie à corde *f*, touret *m*; ~ **key-seating machine** *n* MECH ENG machine à rainurer les poulies *f*; ~ **lathe** *n* MECH ENG tour à poulies *m*; ~ **sheave** *n* MECH ENG poulie *f*, poulie de moufle *f*, rouet *m*, réa *f*; ~ **shell** *n* MECH ENG chape de poulie *f*; ~ **wheel** *n* MECH ENG poulie *f*, poulie de moufle *f*, rouet *m*, réa *f*

pulleying *n* MINING envoi aux molettes *m*, mise aux molettes *f*

pulley-turning: ~ **lathe** *n* MECH ENG tour à poulies *m*

pull-in: ~ **wheel** *n* PRINT boule *f*, galet d'entraînement *m*

pulling *n* MECH ENG traction *f*, TV décalage de ligne *m*; ~ **casing** *n* WATER SUPP *well-boring* arrachage du tubage d'isolement *m*; ~ **in** *n* TELECOM *cable* tirage en conduite *m*; ~ **out** *n* CONST *nail* extraction *f*, MECH ENG *nail* arrachage *m*, extraction *f*; ~ **rope** *n* MECH ENG câble de tirage *m*, câble de traction *m*, câble tracteur *m*

pull-off: ~ **closure** *n* PACKAGING fermeture à traction *f*; ~ **coupling** *n* ELEC *connection* accouplement à déconnexion par traction *m*

pullout: ~ **length** *n* PROP MAT *debonding* longueur retirée *f*; ~ **resistance** *n* PROP MAT résistance à l'arrachement *f*; ~ **test** *n* PROP MAT essai d'arrachement *m*

pullquotes *n pl* PRINT guillemets *m pl*

pull-through: ~ **winding** *n* ELEC enroulement à fils tirés *m*

pulp *n* COAL TECH pulpe *f*, PAPER TECH, PRINT pâte *f*, PROD ENG pulpe *f*, WATER SUPP pâte à papier *f*; ~ **and paper contraries** *n pl* PAPER TECH impuretés dans la pâte et le papier *f pl*; ~ **board** *n* PRINT carton bois *m*; ~ **charge** *n* PAPER TECH chasse-pâte *f*; ~ **machine** *n* PAPER TECH presse-pâte *m*; ~ **molding system** *n* (AmE), ~ **moulding system** *n* (BrE) PACKAGING système de moulage de pâte *m*; ~ **saver** *n* PAPER TECH presse-pâte *m*, ramasse-pâte *m*

pulper *n* PAPER TECH désintégrateur *m*, triturateur *m*

pulping *n* PAPER TECH mise en pâte *f*

pulpit *n* NAUT *deck equipment* balcon avant *m*

pulpwood *n* PAPER TECH bois à pâte *m*

pulsar *n* ASTRON pulsar *m*; ~ **glitches** *n pl* ASTRON glitches de pulsar *m pl*

pulsatance *n* PHYS pulsation *f*

pulsating: ~ **current** *n* ELEC, ELEC ENG courant pulsé *m*; ~ **flow** *n* FLUID PHYS écoulement pulsant *m*, REFRIG écoulement pulsatoire *m*; ~ **jet engine** *n* AERONAUT pulsoréacteur *m*; ~ **pressure** *n* PROD ENG pression pulsée *f*; ~ **stars** *n pl* ASTRON étoiles vibrantes *f pl*

pulsation *n* ELEC ENG pulsation *f*

pulsator: ~ **jig** *n* COAL TECH bac antisuccion *m*

pulsatory: ~ **current** *n* ELEC ENG courant pulsatoire *m*

pulse[1] *n* COMP, DP, ELEC *voltage*, ELECTRON, OPT, PHYS, RECORDING, SPACE *communications* impulsion *f*, WAVE PHYS pulsation *f*, *radar* impulsion *f*; ~ **accelerator** *n* RAD PHYS accélérateur à impulsion *m*; ~ **amplification** *n* ELECTRON amplification d'impulsion *f*; ~ **amplifier** *n* ELECTRON amplificateur d'impulsion *m*; ~ **amplitude** *n* ELECTRON, RECORDING amplitude d'impulsion *f*; ~ **amplitude modulation** *n* (*PAM*) COMP, DP, ELECTRON, SPACE, TELECOM modulation d'impulsions en amplitude *f* (*MIA*); ~ **amplitude modulation network** *n* TELECOM réseau de modulation par impulsions d'amplitude *m*; ~ **broadening** *n* OPT, TELECOM élargissement d'impulsion *m*, étalement d'impulsion *m*; ~ **capacitor** *n* ELEC condensateur d'impulsion *m*; ~ **carrier** *n* ELEC-

TRON porteuse d'impulsion *f*, TV train porteur *m*; ~ **characteristics** *n pl* ELECTRON caractéristiques des impulsions *f pl*; ~ **circuit** *n* ELEC ENG, ELECTRON circuit à impulsion *m*; ~ **clipper** *n* TV écrêteur d'impulsion *m*; ~ **code** *n* ELECTRON code d'impulsion *m*; ~ **code modulation** *n* COMP (*PCM*) modulation par impulsion et codage *f* (*MIC*), DP (*PCM*), ELECTRON (*PCM*) modulation par impulsion codée *f* (*MIC*), PHYS (*PCM*) modulation par impulsion codée *f*, modulation par impulsion et codage *f* (*MIC*), RAD PHYS (*PCM*) modulation par impulsion codée *f* (*MIC*), RECORDING modulation en impulsion codée *f*, SPACE (*PCM*) modulation par impulsion et codage *f* (*MIC*), TV (*PCM*) modulation par impulsion codée *f*, modulation par impulsion et codage *f* (*MIC*); ~ **coder** *n* ELECTRON codeur d'impulsions *m*, RAD PHYS générateur d'impulsions codées *m*; ~ **compression** *n* TELECOM compression d'impulsion *f*; ~ **counter** *n* ELECTRON compteur d'impulsions *m*; ~ **decay time** *n* RECORDING, TELECOM temps de descente d'impulsion *m*; ~ **dispersion** *n* OPT, TELECOM élargissement d'impulsion *m*, étalement d'impulsion *m*; ~ **duration** *n* ELECTRON durée d'impulsion *f*; ~ **duration modulation** *n* (*PDM*) ELECTRON, SPACE modulation par impulsions de durée *f* (*MID*); ~ **frequency** *n* ELECTRON fréquence d'impulsion *f*; ~ **frequency modulation** *n* (*PFM*) COMP, DP, ELECTRON modulation de fréquence d'impulsion *f*; ~ **function** *n* CONTROL fonction impulsionnelle *f*; ~ **generation** *n* ELECTRON génération d'impulsion *f*; ~ **generator** *n* COMP, DP, ELEC, ELECTRON, PHYS générateur d'impulsions *m*, RAD PHYS filtre d'impulsions *m*, TELECOM générateur d'impulsions *m*; ~ **height** *n* COMP, DP, ELECTRON amplitude d'impulsion *f*; ~ **interval** *n* ELECTRON intervalle entre impulsions *m*; ~ **interval modulation** *n* TV modulation d'intervalle entre impulsions *f*; ~ **jet** *n* AERONAUT pulsoréacteur *m*; ~ **leading edge** *n* TELECOM front avant d'impulsion *m*; ~ **length** *n* ELECTRON, TELECOM durée d'impulsion *f*; ~ **modulation** *n* ELEC *regulation* modulation d'impulsion *f*, ELECTRON modulation par impulsions *f*, *pulse used as carrier* modulation d'impulsion *f*; ~ **modulator** *n* ELECTRON *pulse used as carrier* modulateur d'impulsions *m*, modulateur à impulsions *m*; ~ **phase** *n* ELECTRON phase des impulsions *f*; ~ **phase modulation** *n* ELECTRON modulation de position d'impulsion *f*; ~ **phasing** *n* TV mise en phase d'impulsion *f*; ~ **polarity** *n* ELECTRON polarité d'impulsion *f*; ~ **position** *n* ELECTRON position d'impulsion *f*; ~ **position modulation** *n* (*PPM*) ELECTRON modulation de position d'impulsion *f*, SPACE modulation d'impulsion en position *f*; ~ **profile** *n* TELECOM profil d'impulsion *m*; ~ **rate** *n* ELECTRON fréquence de récurrence *f*, fréquence de récurrence des impulsions *f*; ~ **rate factor** *n* TV taux d'impulsion *m*; ~ **regeneration** *n* ELECTRON, PHYS régénération d'impulsion *f*, TV remise en forme d'impulsion *f*; ~ **regenerator** *n* ELECTRON régénérateur d'impulsion *m*; ~ **relay** *n* ELEC relais d'impulsion *m*; ~ **repetition frequency** *n* (*PRF*) COMP, DP fréquence de répétition des impulsions *f*, ELECTRON fréquence de récurrence des impulsions *f*, fréquence de répétition des impulsions *f*, PHYS, TELECOM fréquence de répétition des impulsions *f*; ~ **repetition interval** *n* ELECTRON période de récurrence *f*; ~ **repetition period** *n* ELECTRON période de récurrence *f*; ~ **repetition rate** *n* PHYS taux de répétition des impulsions *m*; ~ **restoration** *n* TV régénération d'impulsion *f*; ~ **separation** *n* ELECTRON intervalle de séparation entre impulsions *m*; ~ **separator** *n* TV séparateur d'impulsions *m*; ~ **sequence** *n* ELECTRON suite d'impulsions *f*; ~ **shape** *n* ELECTRON forme d'impulsion *f*; ~ **shaping** *n* COMP conformation d'impulsion *f*, DP mise en forme d'impulsion *f*; ~ **signal** *n* ELECTRON signal impulsionnel *m*; ~ **spacing** *n* ELECTRON intervalle entre impulsions *m*; ~ **spike** *n* ELEC *voltage* impulsion parasite *f*; ~ **spreading** *n* TELECOM élargissement d'impulsion *m*, étalement d'impulsion *m*; ~ **sync** *n* TV synchronisation par impulsion *f*; ~ **synthesizer** *n* ELECTRON synthétiseur d'impulsion *m*; ~ **technique** *n* TESTING technique d'impulsion *f*; ~ **tilt** *n* ELECTRON inclinaison du sommet *f*, inclinaison du sommet d'impulsion *f*; ~ **time** *n* ELECTRON instant d'impulsion *m*; ~ **time modulation** *n* ELECTRON modulation de temps d'impulsion *f*; ~ **trailing edge** *n* TELECOM front arrière d'impulsion *m*; ~ **train** *n* COMP, DP, ELECTRON train d'impulsion *m*; ~ **transformer** *n* ELEC ENG, PHYS transformateur d'impulsion *m*; ~ **triggering** *n* TV déclenchement par impulsion *m*; ~ **widening** *n* TELECOM élargissement d'impulsion *m*; ~ **width** *n* COMP, DP, ELECTRON largeur d'impulsion *f*, PHYS durée d'impulsion *f*, largeur d'impulsion *f*, TELECOM largeur d'impulsion *f*, TV durée d'impulsion *f*, largeur d'impulsion *f*; ~ **width modulation** *n* ELECTRON modulation de largeur d'impulsion *f*, SPACE modulation d'impulsions en largeur *f*

pulse:[2] ~ **off** *vi* PROD ENG être temporisé à O; ~ **on** *vi* PROD ENG être temporisé à 1

pulse-controlled *adj* CONTROL contrôlé par impulsions

pulse-counting: ~ **technique** *n* TELECOM technique de comptage par impulsions *f*

pulsed: ~ **afterglow technique** *n* RAD PHYS technique des dernières lueurs pulsées *f*; ~ **current** *n* ELEC courant pulsé *m*; ~ **electron gun** *n* RAD PHYS canon à électrons à pulsation *m*; ~ **lamp** *n* CINEMAT lampe pulsée *f*; ~ **laser** *n* ELECTRON laser pulsé *m*, laser à faisceau pulsé *m*, laser à émission par impulsion *m*, RAD PHYS laser pulsé *m*; ~ **magnetron** *n* ELECTRON magnétron à impulsion *m*; ~ **maser** *n* ELECTRON maser à impulsion *m*; ~ **mode** *n* ELEC ENG régime d'impulsions *m*, ELECTRON régime d'impulsion *m*; ~ **neutron log** *n* PETR TECH diagraphie par impulsion de neutron *f*, diagraphie par neutron pulsé *f*; ~ **operation** *n* ELECTRON fonctionnement en impulsion *m*, fonctionnement en régime d'impulsion *m*; ~ **oscillator** *n* ELECTRON oscillateur à impulsion *m*; ~ **radar detector** *n* TRANSP *traffic control* radar routier à pulsation *m*; ~ **ultrasonic detector** *n* TRANSP détecteur à ultrason à pulsation *m*

pulse-modulated *adj* ELECTRON modulé par impulsion

pulser *n* ELECTRON synchronisateur *m*

pulses: ~ **per second** *n pl (pps)* TELECOM impulsions par seconde *f pl*

pulsojet *n* TRANSP pulsoréacteur *m*

pulverization *n* CHEM, COAL TECH pulvérisation *f*; ~ **burner** *n* MECH ENG brûleur de pulvérisation *m*

pulverize *vt* CHEM pulvériser, CHEM TECH pulvériser, triturer, COAL TECH, CONST pulvériser

pulverized[1] *adj* CHEM TECH en poudre, pulvérisé, trituré

pulverized:[2] ~ **charcoal** *n* COAL TECH charbon pulvérisé *m*; ~ **coal** *n* COAL TECH charbon pulvérisé *m*; ~ **coal firing** *n* HEATING chauffage au charbon pulvérisé *m*

pulverizer *n* CHEM TECH, CONST, PAPER TECH pulvérisateur *m*, WATER SUPP appareil à pulvérisation d'eau *m*, pulvérisateur *m*, vaporisateur *m*, vaporisateur

d'eau *m*

pulverizing: ~ **chamber** *n* CHEM TECH chambre de pulvérisation *f*; ~ **equipment** *n* CHEM TECH installation de pulvérisation *f*, pulvérulence *f*

pulverulent *adj* CHEM TECH pulvérulent

pulvimixer *n* PROD ENG, TRANSP pulvérisateur-mélangeur *m*

pumice *n* C&G pierre ponce *f*, GEOL pierre ponce *f*, ponce *f*; ~ **soap** *n* DETERGENTS savon ponce *m*; ~ **stone** *n* MINERAL pierre ponce *f*, ponce *f*

pumicing *n* PROD ENG ponçage *m*

pump[1] *n* MAR POLL, MINING, NAUT, PHYS, REFRIG, WATER SUPP pompe *f*; ~ **and connections** *n* MECH ENG pompe de lubrification et sa tuyauterie *f*; ~ **barrel** *n* WATER SUPP barillet *m*, corps de pompe *m*, cylindre de pompe *m*; ~ **box** *n* PAPER TECH caisse aspirante *f*; ~ **compartment** *n* WATER SUPP *of shaft* compartiment de l'exhaure *m*, compartiment des pompes *m*; ~ **connection** *n* WATER SUPP raccord de pompe *m*; ~ **cylinder** *n* WATER SUPP barillet *m*, corps de pompe *m*, cylindre de pompe *m*; ~ **dispenser system** *n* PACKAGING système de distribution avec pompe *m*; ~ **dredge** *n* CONST drague pompe *f*, pompe dragueuse *f*; ~ **dredger** *n* CONST drague pompe *f*, pompe dragueuse *f*, NAUT drague aspirante *f*, drague suceuse *f*, drague à succion *f*, extracteur de dévasement *m*; ~ **frequency** *n* SPACE *communications* fréquence instantanée *f*; ~ **gear** *n* PROD ENG, WATER SUPP armature de pompe *f*; ~ **head** *n* HEATING hauteur d'aspiration *f*; ~ **house** *n* WATER SUPP bâtiment de pompe *m*; ~ **housing** *n* AUTO carter de pompe *m*; ~ **pressure** *n* PETR TECH pression d'injection *f*; ~ **rod** *n* WATER SUPP tige de pompe *f*; ~ **room** *n* WATER SUPP chambre de pompe *f*; ~ **shaft** *n* WATER SUPP puits de pompe *m*; ~ **spring bow** *n* MECH ENG compas à pompe *m*, compas-balustre à pompe *m*; ~ **station** *n* WATER SUPP station d'épuisement *f*, station de pompe *f*; ~ **sump** *n* (BrE) WATER SUPP puisard *m*; ~ **turbine** *n* FUELLESS pompe turbine *f*; ~ **valve** *n* PETR TECH clapet de pompe *m*; ~ **water** *n* WATER SUPP eau de puits *f*

pump[2] *vt* WATER SUPP assécher, pomper, puiser avec des pompes, épuiser; ~ **out** *vt* NAUT assécher, WATER SUPP assécher, pomper, puiser avec des pompes, épuiser

pump[3] *vti* NAUT pomper

pumpdown *n* REFRIG *of refrigerant into system* évacuation de frigorigène *f*

pumped: ~ **storage scheme** *n* FUELLESS *hydroelectric power* installation de stockage par pompage *f*

pump-fed: ~ **evaporator** *n* REFRIG évaporateur alimenté par pompe *m*

pumping *n* MINING *founding* pompage *m*, WATER SUPP assèchement *m*, exhaure *f*, pompage *m*, épuisement *m*; ~ **engine** *n* WATER SUPP machine d'exhaure *f*, machine d'épuisement *f*, moteur d'épuisement *m*, moteur à pompes *m*; ~ **equipment** *n* WATER SUPP matériel d'exhaure *m*, matériel d'épuisement *m*, pompes d'épuisement *f pl*; ~ **light** *n* ELECTRON lumière de pompage *f*; ~ **out** *n* WATER SUPP assèchement *m*, exhaure *f*, pompage *m*, épuisement *m*; ~ **photons** *n pl* ELECTRON photons de pompage *m pl*; ~ **pit** *n* COAL TECH puits de pompage *m*; ~ **plant** *n* WATER SUPP matériel d'exhaure *m*, matériel d'épuisement *m*, pompes d'épuisement *f pl*; ~ **schedule** *n* PETR programme de pompage *m*; ~ **shaft** *n* WATER SUPP puits d'exhaure *m*, puits d'épuisement *m*; ~ **sleeper** *n* (BrE) *(cf dancing tie)* RAIL traverse danseuse *f*; ~ **station** *n*

CONST station d'exhaure *f*, station de pompage *f*, NAUT *drydock*, PETR, WATER SUPP station de pompage *f*; ~ **test** *n* COAL TECH essai de pompage *m*, HYDR EQUIP *hydraulics* pompage d'essai *m*, WATER SUPP essai de pompage *m*; ~ **unit** *n* MAR POLL dispositif de pompage *m*, installation de pompage *f*; ~ **well** *n* COAL TECH puits de pompage *m*

punch[1] *n* CINEMAT encocheuse *f*, poinçonneuse *f*, COMP perforateur *m*, CONST *block placed on upper end of pile* avant-pieu *m*, DP perforateur *m*, MECH *tools* poinçon *m*, MECH ENG *centre punch* pointeau *m*, pointeau de mécanicien *m*, *hollow punch* découpoir *m*, emporte-pièce *m*, PAPER TECH emporte-pièce *m*; ~ **card** *n* COMP, DP carte à perforer *f*; ~ **holder** *n* MECH ENG *in press* porte-poinçon *m*; ~ **mark** *n* MECH ENG coup de pointeau *m*; ~ **plate** *n* MECH ENG *die set* plaque porte-poinçon *f*; ~ **prop** *n* MINING *timbering* cale *f*, tasseau *m*; ~ **shank** *n* MECH ENG nez cylindrique fileté *m*; ~ **tape** *n* COMP, DP bande à perforer *f*; ~ **tape reader** *n* COMP, DP lecteur de bande perforée ~ **tape reproducer** *n* COMP reproducteur de bandes perforées

punch[2] *vt* MECH poinçonner, PROD ENG *with hollow punch* découper, découper à l'emporte-pièce, *with solid punch* poinçonner ~ **out** *vt* MECH découper, PROD ENG *with hollow punch* découpage à l'emporte-pièce *m*, découper

punched: ~ **card** *n* COMP, DP carte perforée *f*; ~ **card reader** *n* COMP, DP lecteur de cartes *m*, lecteur de cartes perforées *m*; ~ **card reproducer** *n* COMP, DP reproducteur de cartes perforées *m*; ~ **plate** *n* COAL TECH, CONST tôle perforée *f*; ~ **plate screen** *n* CONST crible en tôle perforée *m*; ~ **tape** *n* COMP, DP bande perforée *f*, TELECOM ruban perforé *m*; ~ **tape producer** *n* DP reproducteur de bandes perforées *m*; ~ **tape reader** *n* COMP, DP lecteur de bande perforée *m*; ~ **tape reproducer** *n* COMP reproducteur de bandes perforées *m*

punching *n* COMP, DP perforation *f*, PROD ENG *disc of metal removed by punch* débouchure *f*, *with hollow punch* découpage *m*, découpage à l'emporte-pièce *m*, *with solid punch* poinçonnage *m*, poinçonnement *m*; ~ **and shearing machine** *n* MECH ENG machine à poinçonner et à cisailler *f*, poinçonneuse-cisaille *f*; ~ **machine** *n* MECH ENG *hollow punch type* découpeuse *f*, *solid-type machine* machine à poinçonner *f*, poinçonneuse *f*; ~ **out** *n* PROD ENG *with hollow punch* découpage *m*, découpage à l'emporte-pièce *m*; ~ **press** *n* PAPER TECH presse à découper *f*; ~ **track** *n* DP piste de perforation *f*

punch-through *n* ELECTRON claquage *m*

punctuation: ~ **mark** *n* PRINT signe de ponctuation *m*

puncture *n* ELECTRON claquage *m*, percement *m*, PAPER TECH perforation *f*; ~ **head** *n* PAPER TECH tête perforante *f*; ~ **test** *n* ELEC *high-voltage equipment* essai de perforation *m*; ~ **tester** *n* PAPER TECH perforamètre *m*

punnet: ~ **tray** *n* (BrE) PACKAGING barquette *f*

punt *n* C&G fond *m*

punty *n* (BrE) *(cf sticking-up iron)* C&G pontil *m*

puntying *n* C&G dépontillage *m*

pup *n* CINEMAT projecteur de 500 watts focalisable *m*

Puppis *n* ASTRON Poupe *f*

purchase *n* MECH ENG *tackle employing ropes and pulleys*, NAUT *lifting gear, running rigging* palan *m*; ~ **block** *n* MECH ENG moufle à estrope double *m*; ~ **fall** *n* MECH ENG courant de palan *m*

purchaser *n* QUALITY acheteur *m*

pure: ~ **car and truck carrier** *n* TRANSP transporteur

d'automobiles et de camions *m*; ~ **car carrier** *n* TRANSP transporteur d'automobiles *m*; ~ **chance traffic** *n* TELECOM trafic de pur hasard *m*; ~ **coal** *n* COAL TECH charbon pur *m*; ~ **resistance** *n* ELEC ENG résistance ohmique *f*, résistance pure *f*; ~ **spectrum** *n* RAD PHYS spectre pur *m*; ~ **tone audiogram** *n* ACOUSTICS audiogramme tonal *m*; ~ **water** *n* HYDROL, WATER SUPP eau pure *f*

purge: ~ **cock** *n* WATER SUPP robinet de vidange *m*; ~ **recovery system** *n* REFRIG groupe de purge *m*; ~ **valve** *n* FUELLESS *geothermal drilling equipment* vanne de purge *f*

purging *n* COMP, DP, PETR TECH purge *f*; ~ **cock** *n* WATER SUPP robinet de vidange *m*

purification *n* CHEM TECH clarification *f*, décantation *f*, épuration *f*, GAS TECH épuration de gaz *f*, PETR TECH épuration *f*; ~ **plant** *n* HYDROL, RECYCLING, WATER SUPP station d'épuration *f*

purified: ~ **gas** *n* GAS TECH gaz épuré *m*; ~ **water** *n* HYDROL eau épurée *f*; ~ **water reservoir** *n* HYDROL réservoir d'eau filtrée *m*; ~ **water tank** *n* HYDROL réservoir d'eau filtrée *m*

purifier *n* CHEM purificateur *m*, épurateur *m*, CHEM TECH nettoyeur *m*, purificateur *m*

purify *vt* CHEM purifier, épurer, CHEM TECH dépurer, laver, épurer, HYDROL, PAPER TECH, PETR TECH, THERMOD épurer

purifying: ~ **agent** *n* CHEM TECH produit à épurer *m*; ~ **apparatus** *n* CHEM TECH appareil de purification *m*

purine *n* CHEM purine *f*

purity *n* GAS TECH pureté *f*

purlin *n* CONST filière *f*, panne *f*, panne filière *f*; ~ **post** *n* CONST jambette *f*

purple:[1] ~ **plague** *n* ELEC ENG peste rouge *f*

purple[2] *vt* COLOURS teindre en pourpre

purpose-designed *adj* PACKAGING fait sur demande

purpose-formulated: ~ **adhesive** *n* PACKAGING colle faite sur demande *f*

purpurin *n* CHEM purpurine *f*

purpuroxanthin *n* CHEM purpuroxanthine *f*

purse: ~ **line** *n* OCEANOG coulisse *f*; ~ **seine** *n* OCEANOG bolinche *f*, cerco *m*, senne coulissante *f*

purser *n* NAUT commis aux vivres *m*, commissaire *m*

pursing *n* OCEANOG boursage *m*

pursuit: ~ **plane** *n* MILIT avion de chasse *m*; ~ **radar** *n* MILIT radar de poursuite *m*

push:[1] ~ **and turn-switch** *n* CONTROL bouton pousser-tourner *m*; ~ **back** *n* AERONAUT, TRANSP *airport* refoulement *m*; ~ **button** *n* CHEM *oiler* bouton-poussoir *m*, CONTROL bouton pression *m*, bouton à pression *m*, bouton-poussoir *m*, ELEC *control*, ELEC ENG, RECORDING, TELECOM bouton-poussoir *m*; ~ **fit** *n* MECH ENG montage à frottement doux *m*; ~ **net** *n* OCEANOG haveneau *m*, trouble *m*; ~ **rod** *n* AUTO poussoir de soupape *m*, MECH poussoir *m*, MECH ENG *machine tool* tige de poussée *f*; ~ **rod switch** *n* PROD ENG interrupteur à poussoir *m*; ~ **screen** *n* PROD ENG crible à secousse *m*; ~ **stick** *n* SAFETY tige-poussoir *f*; ~ **switch** *n* CONTROL interrupteur à poussoir *m*; ~ **through pill pack** *n* PACKAGING emballage pour pousser les pastilles à travers *m*; ~ **tow** *n* TRANSP pousseur *m*; ~ **towing** *n* TRANSP poussage *m*; ~ **tug** *n* TRANSP pousseur *m*

push[2] *vt* CINEMAT *in developer*, PHOTO pousser; ~ **back** *vt* TRANSP *airport* refouler

push[3] *vti* COMP, DP pousser

push-button[1] *adj* MECH ENG à commande automatique

push-button:[2] **~ control panel** *n* ELEC tableau de commande à bouton-poussoir *m*; **~ dial** *n* TELECOM clavier *m*; **~ faucet** *n* (AmE) *(cf push-button tap)* CONST robinet à repoussoir *m*; **~ machine** *n* MECH ENG machine à commande automatique *f*; **~ operation** *n* PHOTO commande par touches *f*; **~ starter** *n* ELEC *motor* démarreur à bouton-poussoir *m*; **~ switch** *n* ELEC ENG interrupteur à bouton-poussoir *m*, PROD ENG commutateur par bouton-poussoir *m*; **~ tap** *n* (BrE) *(cf push-button faucet)* CONST robinet à repoussoir *m*; **~ telephone** *n* TELECOM poste à clavier *m*, téléphone à clavier *m*, téléphone à touches *m*; **~ tuning** *n* CONTROL syntonisation par bouton-poussoir *f*

push-down: **~ blasting machine** *n* MINING exploseur à poignée *m*; **~ list** *n* COMP liste refoulée *f*, DP liste inversée *f*; **~ stack** *n* COMP, DP pile inversée *f*

pushed: **~ punt** *n* C&G fond piqué *m*

pusher: **~ furnace** *n* HEATING four passant *m*; **~ locomotive** *n* (AmE) *(cf banking locomotive)* RAIL locomotive de pousse *f*, locomotive de renfort en queue *f*; **~ operation** *n* (AmE) *(cf banking)* RAIL *vehicles* marche en pousse *f*; **~ propeller** *n* AERONAUT hélice propulsive *f*; **~ tug** *n* NAUT, TRANSP pousseur *m*

push-fit: **~ mount** *n* CINEMAT monture à emboîtement *f*

pushing: **~ down the cullet** *n* C&G enfoncement de calcin *m*; **~ jack** *n* PROD ENG pousseur *m*

push-off: **~ wipe** *n* CINEMAT volet latéral *m*

push-on: **~ mount** *n* PHOTO monture à emboîtement *f*; **~ push-off operation** *n* PROD ENG actionnement par bouton-poussoir à deux positions *m*

pushpit *n* NAUT *deck equipment* balcon arrière *m*

push-plate: **~ conveyor** *n* PROD ENG convoyeur à palettes *m*, transporteur à palettes *m*, transporteuse à palettes *f*

push-pull[1] *adj* TRANSP à moteurs en tandem

push-pull:[2] **~ amplifier** *n* ELECTRON amplificateur push-pull *m*, amplificateur symétrique *m*; **~ circuit** *n* RECORDING circuit push-pull *m*; **~ scanning** *n* OPT lecture différentielle *f*; **~ switch** *n* CONTROL, ELEC interrupteur va-et-vient *m*; **~ train** *n* TRANSP rame réversible *f*

push-through: **~ winding** *n* ELEC *coil* enroulement à bobines en U *m*

push-to-talk[1] *adj* TELECOM appuyer pour parler, presser pour parler

push-to-talk:[2] **~ switch** *n* RECORDING commutateur d'ordre *m*

push-to-test: **~ indicating light** *n* PROD ENG voyant lumineux pousser-test *m*; **~ pilot light** *n* PROD ENG voyant lumineux pousser-test *m*

push-up *n* C&G poussoir de démoulage *m*; **~ list** *n* COMP, DP liste directe *f*; **~ stack** *n* COMP, DP pile directe *f*

put:[1] **~ on file** *adj* TELECOM *telex* archivé

put:[2] **~ byte** *n* PROD ENG transfert par octet *m*

put:[3] **~ into commission** *vt* NAUT *a ship* armer; **~ into operation** *vt* PROD ENG mettre en opération; **~ on board** *vt* NAUT mettre à bord; **~ on hold** *vt* TELECOM mettre en attente, *telephone call* mettre en garde; **~ on standby** *vt* MAR POLL *vessel* mettre en alerte; **~ out** *vt* SAFETY *fire* éteindre; **~ through** *vt* TELECOM mettre en communication; **~ under cover** *vt* CONST mettre à l'abri; **~ up** *vt* CONST construire, élever, ériger

put:[4] **~ ashore** *vi* NAUT mettre à terre; **~ down a borehole** *vi* MINING opérer un sondage, pratiquer un trou de sonde; **~ down in color work** *vi* (AmE), **~ down in**

colour work *vi* (BrE) C&G contrôler au calibre; **~ in electricity** *vi* ELEC *installation* installer l'électricité; **~ on the punty** *vi* C&G empontiller; **~ a ship into commission** *vi* NAUT armer un navire; **~ to sea** *vi* NAUT prendre la mer

putlock *n* CONST boulin *m*

putlog *n* CONST *scaffolding* boulin *m*

putrefy *vi* FOOD TECH pourrir, se putréfier

putrescent *adj* FOOD TECH en putréfaction, putrescent

putrid *adj* FOOD TECH en putréfaction, pourri

putty[1] *n* C&G potée d'étain *f*, CONST mastic *m*, potée d'étain *f*, *glaziers'* mastic de vitrier *m*; **~ joint** *n* CONST joint au minium *m*; **~ knife** *n* CONST couteau à démastiquer *m*, couteau à mastiquer *m*, couteau à parer *m*; **~ powder** *n* CONST potée d'étain *f*

putty[2] *vt* CONST mastiquer

puttying *n* CONST masticage *m*

puzzle: **~ lock** *n* CONST serrure à combinaisons *f*

PV *abbr* *(parameter value)* TELECOM valeur de paramètre *f*

PVC[1] *abbr* COMP *(permanent virtual circuit)* circuit virtuel permanent *m*, CONST *(polyvinyl chloride)* PVC *(polyvinylchlorure)*, DP *(permanent virtual circuit)* circuit virtuel permanent *m*, ELEC ENG *(polyvinyl chloride)*, P&R *(polyvinyl chloride)*, PROP MAT *(polyvinyl chloride)* PVC *(polyvinylchlorure)*, TELECOM *(permanent virtual circuit)* circuit virtuel permanent *m*

PVC:[2] **~ bottle** *n* PACKAGING bouteille en polyvinyle chloride *f*; **~ insert fitment** *n* PACKAGING pièce rapportée en PVC *f*; **~ insulation** *n* ELEC isolation PVC *f*; **~ pressure-sensitive tape** *n* PACKAGING ruban autocollant en polyvinyle chloride *m*; **~ sheath** *n* ELEC ENG gaine en PVC *f*; **~ sleeve** *n* PROD ENG gaine de PCV *f*; **~ tape** *n* RECORDING bande à dorsale PVC *f*

PVC-coated: **~ web** *n* PRINT bande couchée PVC *f*

PVP *abbr* *(polyvinylpyrrolidone)* DETERGENTS polyvinylpyrrolidone *m*

PVT: **~ analysis** *n* PETR analyse PVT *f*

PW *abbr* *(private wire)* TELECOM liaison spécialisée *f*

P-wave *n* GEOL onde P *f*, onde de compression *f*, onde longitudinale *f*, PHYS onde P *f*

PWM *abbr* *(pulse width modulation)* SPACE modulation d'impulsions en largeur *f*

PWR *n* *(pressurized-water reactor)* NUCLEAR réacteur à eau sous pression *m*

p-xylene *n* CHEM paraxylène *m*

pycnite *n* MINERAL pycnite *f*

pycnometer *n* LAB EQUIP *density*, PETR TECH, PHYS pycnomètre *m*

pyelogram: **~ cassette** *n* INSTRUMENT cassette pour urographie *f*

pyelography *n* INSTRUMENT urographie *f*

pyknometer *n* LAB EQUIP *density*, PHYS pycnomètre *m*

pylon *n* AERONAUT pylône *m*, *rigid structure to carry engine* mât *m*, CONST pylône *m*, ELEC *supply network* mât *m*, pylône *m*, ELEC ENG mât *m*, poteau *m*, pylône *m*

pyramid *n* GEOM pyramide *f*; **~ cut** *n* MINING bouchon en pyramide *m*, bouchon pyramidal *m*

pyramidal: **~ plane** *n* METALL plan pyramidal *m*; **~ slip** *n* METALL glissement pyramidal *m*

pyran *n* CHEM pyran *m*, pyranne *m*

pyranometer *n* FUELLESS pyranomètre *m*

pyranose *n* CHEM pyrannose *m*

pyrargyrite *n* MINERAL pyrargyrite *f*

pyrazine *n* CHEM pyrazine *f*

pyrazole *n* CHEM pyrazol *m*
pyrazoline *n* CHEM pyrazoline *f*
pyrazolone *n* CHEM pyrazolone *f*
pyrene *n* CHEM pyrène *m*
pyrgom *n* MINERAL fassaïte *f*
pyrheliometer *n* FUELLESS pyrhéliomètre *m*
pyridazin *n* CHEM pyridazine *f*
pyridine *n* CHEM pyridine *f*
pyridone *n* CHEM pyridone *f*
pyrimidine *n* CHEM *compound* pyrimidine *f*
pyrite *n* MINERAL pyrite *f*, pyrite jaune *f*, pyrite martiale *f*, pyrite de fer *f*, MINING pyrite *f*, pyrite de fer *f*, pyrite jaune *f*
pyrites *n pl* MINERAL pyrites *f pl*
pyritic *adj* MINERAL, PROP MAT pyritique
pyroacetic *adj* CHEM pyroacétique
pyroarsenate *n* CHEM pyroarséniate *m*
pyroboric *adj* CHEM pyroborique
pyrocatechin *n* CHEM pyrocatéchine *f*
pyrochlore *n* MINERAL pyrochlore *m*
pyrochroite *n* MINERAL pyrochroïte *f*
pyroclastic: ~ **rock** *n* GEOL roche pyroclastique *f*
pyroelectric *adj* CRYSTALL pyroélectrique
pyroelectricity *n* CRYSTALL pyroélectricité *f*
pyrogallic *adj* CHEM *acid* pyrogallique, pyrogallol
pyrogallol *n* CHEM pyrogallol *m*
pyrogenic[1] *adj* THERMOD pyrogène
pyrogenic:[2] ~ **reaction** *n* THERMOD pyrogénation *f*
pyrolusite *n* MINERAL pyrolusite *f*
pyrolysis *n* CHEM, FOOD TECH, GAS TECH, PROP MAT pyrolyse *f*
pyrolytic[1] *adj* CHEM pyrolytique
pyrolytic:[2] ~ **coating** *n* C&G dépôt par pyrolyse *m*
pyromeconic *adj* CHEM pyroméconique
pyromellitic *adj* CHEM pyromellique
pyrometer *n* COAL TECH, ELEC, LAB EQUIP *temperature measurement*, PHYS, RAD PHYS, THERMOD pyromètre *m*; ~ **probe** *n* ELEC canne pyrométrique *f*; ~ **protection tube** *n* SAFETY tube protecteur pour pyromètre *m*
pyrometric *adj* THERMOD pyrométrique
pyrometry *n* PHYS, THERMOD pyrométrie *f*
pyromorphite *n* MINERAL pyromorphite *f*
pyromucic *adj* CHEM pyromucique

pyrone *n* CHEM pyrone *f*
pyrope *n* MINERAL pyrope *m*
pyrophoric *adj* CHEM *metal, alloy* pyrophorique
pyrophosphate *n* CHEM pyrophosphate *m*
pyrophosphoric[1] *adj* CHEM pyrophosphorique
pyrophosphoric:[2] ~ **acid** *n* DETERGENTS acide pyrophosphorique *m*
pyrophosphorous *adj* CHEM pyrophosphoreux
pyrophyllite *n* MINERAL, PETR TECH pyrophyllite *f*
pyrorthite *n* MINERAL pyrorthite *f*
pyrosclerite *n* MINERAL pyrosclérite *f*
pyroscope *n* PHYS pyroscope *m*
pyrostat *n* PHYS pyrostat *m*
pyrostibite *n* MINERAL pyrostibite *f*
pyrosulfate *n* (AmE) *see* pyrosulphate
pyrosulfite *n* (AmE) *see* pyrosulphite
pyrosulfuric *adj* (AmE) *see* pyrosulphuric
pyrosulfuryl *adj* (AmE) *see* pyrosulphuryl
pyrosulphate *n* (BrE) CHEM pyrosulfate *m*
pyrosulphite *n* (BrE) CHEM pyrosulfite *m*
pyrosulphuric *adj* (BrE) CHEM pyrosulfurique
pyrosulphuryl *n* (BrE) CHEM pyrosulfuryle
pyrotechnic: ~ **shock** *n* SPACE *spacecraft* choc pyrotechnique *m*; ~ **valve** *n* SPACE *spacecraft* vanne pyrotechnique *f*
pyrotechnics *n* SPACE pyrotechnie *f*
pyroxene *n* MINERAL pyroxène *m*
pyroxyline: ~ **lacquer** *n* COLOURS laque cellulosique *f*
pyrrhotine *n* MINERAL pyrrhotine *f*
pyrrhotite *n* MINERAL pyrrhotine *f*
pyrrole *n* CHEM pyrrol *m*, pyrrole *m*
pyrrolidine *n* CHEM pyrrolidine *f*
pyrrolidone *n* CHEM *compound* pyrrolidone *f*
pyrroline *n* CHEM pyrroline *f*
pyruvate *n* CHEM pyruvate *m*
pyruvic *adj* CHEM pyruvique
Pythagoras': ~ **theorem** *n* GEOM théorème de Pythagore *m*
Pythagorean: ~ **comma** *n* ACOUSTICS comma de Pythagore *m*; ~ **scale** *n* ACOUSTICS gamme de Pythagore *f*
Pyxis *n* ASTRON Boussole *f*

Q

QA *abbr (quality assurance)* MECH assurance de la qualité *f*

QAM *abbr (quadrature amplitude modulation)* COMP, DP, ELECTRON, TELECOM MAQ *(modulation d'amplitude en quadrature)*

QC *abbr (quality control)* QUALITY maîtrise de la qualité *f*

Q-channel *n* ELECTRON voie Q *f*

Q-demodulator *n* ELECTRON démodulateur Q *m*, démodulateur de la voie Q *m*

Q-device *n* NUCLEAR dispositif Q *m*

Q-electron *n* NUCLEAR électron de la couche-Q *m*, électron-Q *m*

Q-factor *n* PHYS facteur Q *m*, facteur de qualité *m*, facteur de surtension *m*, TESTING facteur Q *m*

Q-flag *n* NAUT pavillon Q *m*

q-gas *n* THERMOD gaz q *m*

QL *abbr (query language)* COMP, DP langage d'interrogation *m*

Q-meter *n* PHYS Q mètre *m*

QOS *abbr (quality of service)* TELECOM qualité de service *f*

QP: ~ **device** *n* NUCLEAR dispositif QP *m*

Q-percentile: ~ **life** *n* NUCLEAR percentile d'ordre Q de la durée de vie *m*

QPSK *abbr (quadriphase shift keying, quaternary phase-shift keying)* ELECTRON, TELECOM MDPQ *(modulation par déplacement de phase quadrivalente)*

QSG *abbr (quasi-stellar galaxy)* SPACE galaxie quasi-stellaire *f*

Q-shell *n* NUCLEAR couche Q *f*; ~ **electron** *n* NUCLEAR électron de la couche-Q *m*, électron-Q *m*

Q-signal *n* ELECTRON *(quadrature signal)* signal en Q *m (signal en quadrature)*, TV *in NTSC system* signal Q *m*

QSO *abbr (quasi-stellar object)* ASTRON, SPACE objet quasi-stellaire *m*

QSS *abbr (quasi-stellar radio source)* SPACE quasar *m*

QSTOL: ~ **aircraft** *n (quiet short takeoff and landing aircraft)* AERONAUT avion à décollage et atterrissage courts et silencieux *m*

Q-switched: ~ **laser** *n* ELECTRON laser déclenché *m*, NUCLEAR laser à commutation-Q *m*

Q-switching *n* ELECTRON fonctionnement en mode déclenché *m*, *inhibition of lasers* commutation de Q *f*

QTOL: ~ **aircraft** *n (quiet takeoff and landing aircraft)* AERONAUT ADAS *(avion à décollage et atterrissage silencieux)*

quad *n* ELEC ENG *four conductors*, PHYS *cable* quarte *f*, PRINT cadrat *m*; ~**carburetor** *n* (AmE), ~ **carburettor** *n* (BrE) AUTO carburateur quadruple *m*; ~ **operational amplifier** *n* ELECTRON amplificateur opérationnel quadruple *m*

quadded: ~ **cable** *n* ELEC ENG câble à quartes *m*

quadding *n* ELEC ENG groupement en quarte *m*

quad-in-line: ~ **package** *n (QUIP)* ELECTRON boîtier à quatre rangées de broches *m*

quadrac *n* ELEC ENG quadrac *m*

quadrangle *n* GEOM quadrilatère *m*

quadrangular *adj* GEOM quadrangulaire

quadrant *n* ASTRON quadrant *m*, GEOM quadrant *m*, quart de cercle *m*, MECH ENG *of compass, calipers* quart de cercle *m*, *of screw-cutting lathe* lyre *f*, tête de cheval *f*, *of steam engine* secteur de changement de marche *m*, secteur denté de l'appareil de mise en marche *m*, *sector gear* secteur crénelé *m*, secteur denté *m*, MINING *of pump* balancier d'équerre *m*, varlet *m*; ~ **electrometer** *n* ELEC, ELEC ENG électromètre à quadrants *m*; ~ **plate** *n* MECH ENG *of screw-cutting lathe* lyre *f*, tête de cheval *f*

quadrantal: ~ **error** *n* AERONAUT erreur quadrantale *f*; ~ **height rule** *n* AERONAUT *specified height levels* règle des altitudes quadrantales *f*

quadraphony *n* ACOUSTICS tétraphonie *f*

quadratic[1] *adj* MATH quadratique

quadratic:[2] ~ **profile** *n* OPT profil d'indice parabolique *m*, profil parabolique *m*

quadrature:[1] **in** ~ *adj* ELECTRON, PHYS en quadrature

quadrature[2] *n* ASTRON, COMP, DP quadrature *f*, ELEC *phase* quadrature de phase *f*, ELECTRON, FUELLESS quadrature *f*, GEOM quadrature du cercle *f*, PHYS, TV quadrature *f*; ~ **amplitude modulation** *n* COMP *(QAM)*, DP *(QAM)* modulation d'amplitude en quadrature *f (MAQ)*, ELECTRON modulation en quadrature de phase *f*, ELECTRON *(QAM)*, TELECOM *(QAM)* modulation d'amplitude en quadrature *f (MAQ)*; ~ **amplitude modulator** *n* ELECTRON modulateur d'amplitude à quadrature *m*, modulateur à quadrature *m*; ~ **axis** *n* ELEC *machine* axe de quadrature *m*; ~ **axis component** *n* ELEC *alternating current reactive component* composante transversale *f*; ~ **component** *n* ELEC *alternating current reactive component* composante transversale *f*, ELECTRON composante en quadrature *f*; ~ **control** *n* ELEC *alternating current* réglage en phase *m*; ~ **demodulator** *n* ELECTRON démodulateur de la composante en quadrature *m*; ~ **displacement** *n* TV décalage à angle droit *m*; ~ **error** *n* TV erreur de quadrature *f*; ~ **mirror filter** *n* TELECOM filtre miroir en quadrature *m*; ~ **phase** *n* ELECTRON phase en quadrature *f*; ~ **phase subcarrier signal** *n* TV signal de sous-porteuse en phase orthogonale *m*; ~ **power** *n* ELEC *alternating current circuit* puissance de quadrature *f*; ~ **signal** *n (Q-signal)* ELECTRON signal en quadrature *m (signal en Q)*; ~ **voltage** *n* ELEC *alternating current circuit* tension de quadrature *f*

quadribasic *adj* CHEM quadribasique

quadricone: ~ **bit** *n* PETR TECH trépan quadricône *m*

quadricycle *n* CHEM quadricycle *m*

quadrilateral *adj* GEOM quadrilatère

quadriphase: ~ **shift keying** *n (QPSK)* ELECTRON, TELECOM modulation par déplacement de phase quadrivalente *f (MDPQ)*

quadripole *n* ELEC *supply network*, ELEC ENG, PHYS quadripôle *m*

quadrivalence *n* CHEM tétravalence *f*

quadrivalent *adj* CHEM tétravalent

quadroxide *n* CHEM quadroxyde *m*

quadruple: **~ pair cable** *n* ELEC ENG câble à quatre paires *m*; **~ scanning** *n* TV entrelacement quadruple *m*

quadruplex[1] *adj* TV *recording head configuration* à quatre têtes

quadruplex:[2] **~ videotape recorder** *n* TV magnétoscope à pistes transversales *m*, magnétoscope à quatre têtes *m*

quadrupolar: **~ configuration** *n* NUCLEAR configuration quadripolaire *f*

quadrupole *n* ELEC ENG, PHYS quadrupôle *m*; **~ electric moment** *n* RAD PHYS moment électrique quadripolaire *m*; **~ field** *n* NUCLEAR champ quadripolaire *m*; **~ moment** *n* PHYS moment quadripolaire *m*; **~ potential** *n* NUCLEAR potentiel quadripolaire *m*; **~ resonance** *n* NUCLEAR résonance quadripolaire *f*

qualification: **~ approval** *n* QUALITY homologation de qualification *f*; **~ model** *n* SPACE modèle de qualification *m*; **~ test** *n* NUCLEAR *of instrument*, QUALITY, SPACE essai de qualification *m*; **~ test review** *n* SPACE revue de prononcé de qualification *f*, revue de qualification *f*

qualified: **~ name** *n* COMP, DP nom qualifié *m*

qualitative[1] *adj* CHEM qualitatif

qualitative:[2] **~ analysis** *n* WATER SUPP analyse qualitative *f*; **~ autoradiography** *n* NUCLEAR autoradiographie qualitative *f*; **~ characteristics** *n pl* QUALITY caractéristiques qualitatives *f pl*, caractères qualitatifs *m pl*

quality *n* PROD ENG qualité *f*; **~ acceptance criteria** *n pl* MECH ENG critères de qualité *m pl*; **~ of aggregate** *n* CONST qualité des agrégats *f*; **~ assessment** *n* METR *of manufacturing or inspection process* évaluation de qualité *f*; **~ assurance** *n* CONST, MECH, MECH ENG, NUCLEAR, PROD ENG, QUALITY, SPACE assurance de la qualité *f*; **~ assurance certificate** *n* MECH ENG certificat d'assurance de la qualité *m*; **~ assurance control** *n* CONTROL contrôle pour l'assurance de qualité *m*; **~ assurance examination** *n* NUCLEAR examen de l'assurance de la qualité *m*; **~ assurance in final inspection and test** *n* QUALITY assurance de la qualité en contrôle et essais finals *f*; **~ assurance procedure to BS 5750** *n pl* MECH ENG procédés d'assurance de la qualité selon la norme BS 5750 *m pl*; **~ audit** *n* QUALITY audit qualité *m*; **~ auditor** *n* QUALITY auditeur qualité *m*; **~ control** *n* CONST contrôle de qualité *m*, CONTROL, MECH maîtrise de la qualité *f*, METR *of manufactured goods*, NUCLEAR contrôle de qualité *m*, maîtrise de la qualité *f*, PACKAGING contrôle de qualité *m*, PRINT contrôle de qualité *m*, maîtrise de la qualité *f*, PROD ENG contrôle de qualité *m*, QUALITY, TESTING maîtrise de la qualité *f*; **~ cost** *n* QUALITY coût de la qualité *m*; **~ degradation** *n* TV détérioration de la qualité *f*; **~ economics** *n pl* QUALITY économie de la qualité *f*; **~ engineering** *n* QUALITY technique de gestion de la qualité *f*; **~ factor** *n* PHYS facteur Q *m*, facteur de qualité *m*, facteur de surtension *m*, POLLUTION facteur de qualité *m*; **~ guarantee** *n* PACKAGING garantie de qualité *f*; **~ improvement** *n* QUALITY amélioration de la qualité *f*; **~ inspection** *n* CONTROL contrôle par bon ou mauvais *m*; **~ label** *n* PACKAGING étiquette de qualité *f*; **~ loop** *n* QUALITY boucle de la qualité *f*; **~ losses** *n pl* QUALITY pertes relatives à la qualité *f pl*; **~ management** *n* CONST gestion de la qualité *f*, QUALITY management de la qualité *m*; **~ manual** *n* QUALITY, SPACE manuel de qualité *m*; **~ mark** *n* PACKAGING sigle de qualité *m*; **~ monitoring of ambient air** *n* SAFETY contrôle de la qualité de l'air ambiant *m*; **~ plan** *n* QUALITY plan

qualité *m*; **~ planning** *n* QUALITY planification de la qualité *f*; **~ policy** *n* QUALITY politique de qualité *f*; **~ record** *n* QUALITY enregistrement qualité *m*; **~ of reproduction** *n* CINEMAT qualité d'écoute *f*; **~ of service** *n* (*QOS*) TELECOM qualité de service *f*; **~ spiral** *n* QUALITY spirale de la qualité *f*; **~ surveillance** *n* QUALITY surveillance de la qualité *f*; **~ system** *n* QUALITY système qualité *m*; **~ through design** *n* MECH ENG qualité par dessin *f*; **~ of water** *n* WATER SUPP qualité de l'eau *f*

quality-related: **~ cost** *n* QUALITY frais relatifs à la qualité *m pl*

quantifier *n* MATH prédicat *m*, quantificateur *m*

quantify *vt* CONST quantifier

quantitative[1] *adj* CHEM quantitatif

quantitative:[2] **~ analysis** *n* PROP MAT, WATER SUPP analyse quantitative *f*; **~ characteristics** *n pl* QUALITY caractéristiques quantitatives *f pl*, caractères quantitatifs *m pl*; **~ determination** *n* PROP MAT détermination quantitative *f*

quantity *n* ELECTRON grandeur *f*, nombre *m*, quantité *f*; **~ backorder** *n* PROD ENG reste à livrer *m*; **~ completed** *n* PROD ENG quantité réalisée *f*; **~ declared unfit** *n* PROD ENG quantité rejetée *f*; **~ fuse** *n* MINING amorce de quantité *f*, amorce à fil *f*; **~ governor** *n* CONTROL régulateur de quantité *m*; **~ of heat** *n* PHYS quantité de chaleur *f*; **~ of light** *n* PHYS quantité de lumière *f*; **~ packing** *n* PROD ENG nombre de colis *m*; **~ recorder** *n* INSTRUMENT enregistreur de quantités *m*; **~ surveyor** *n* CONST métreur *m*

quantization *n* COMP, DP, ELECTRON, PHYS quantification *f*; **~ distortion** *n* ELECTRON distorsion de quantification *f*; **~ error** *n* ELECTRON, TELECOM erreur de quantification *f*; **~ level** *n* COMP, DP niveau de quantification *m*, ELECTRON niveau de quantification *m*, échelon de quantification *m*; **~ noise** *n* COMP, DP, SPACE *communications*, TELECOM bruit de quantification *m*; **~ pulse modulation** *n* TELECOM modulation delta *f*

quantize *vt* COMP, DP, ELECTRON quantifier

quantized: **~ delay line** *n* TV ligne à retard quantifié *f*; **~ gate** *n* TV porte quantifiée *f*; **~ pulse modulation** *n* ELECTRON modulation d'impulsions échantillonnées *f*; **~ quantity** *n* ELECTRON grandeur quantifiée *f*; **~ signal** *n* ELECTRON signal quantifié *m*

quantizer *n* COMP, DP quantificateur *m*, ELECTRON circuit de quantification *m*, quantificateur *m*, TELECOM quantificateur *m*

quantum[1] *adj* PHYS quantique

quantum[2] *n* COMP, DP, PART PHYS, PHYS quantum *m*; **~ of action** *n* PHYS quantum d'action *m*; **~ chromodynamics** *n* PART PHYS, PHYS chromodynamique quantique *f*; **~ efficiency** *n* OPT, PHYS, RAD PHYS *of laser*, TELECOM rendement quantique *m*; **~ electrodynamics** *n* PART PHYS, PHYS électrodynamique quantique *f*; **~ field theory** *n* PHYS théorie quantique de champ *f*; **~ Hall effect** *n* PHYS effet Hall quantique *m*; **~ leap** *n* PART PHYS saut quantique *m*, transition quantique *f*; **~ mechanical line shape** *n* RAD PHYS *spectral lines* profil à mécanique quantique *m*; **~ mechanics** *n* PART PHYS, PHYS mécanique quantique *f*; **~ noise** *n* ELECTRON, OPT, TELECOM bruit quantique *m*; **~ number** *n* CHEM *of electron*, NUCLEAR, PART PHYS, PHYS nombre quantique *m*; **~ physics** *n pl* PART PHYS, PHYS physique quantique *f*; **~ state** *n* PART PHYS, SPACE état quantique *m*; **~ statistics** *n pl* PHYS statistiques quantiques *f pl*; **~ theory** *n* CHEM théorie des quanta *f*, théorie quantique *f*, NUCLEAR *from Planck's law* théorie des quanta *f*, PART PHYS théorie des quanta *f*, théorie quantique *f*, SPACE théorie des quanta *f*; ~ **theory of radiation** *n* RAD PHYS théorie quantique de rayonnement *f*; ~ **transistor** *n* ELECTRON transistor quantique *m*; ~ **well** *n* RAD PHYS puits quantique *m*; ~ **yield** *n* PHYS rendement quantique *m*

quantum-limited: ~ **operation** *n* OPT, TELECOM fonctionnement limité par le bruit quantique *m*

quantum-noise-limited: ~ **operation** *n* OPT, TELECOM fonctionnement limité par le bruit quantique *m*

quarantine[1] *n* TRANSP quarantaine *f*; ~ **flag** *n* NAUT pavillon de quarantaine *m*

quarantine[2] *vt* TRANSP mettre en quarantaine

quark *n see* top quark

quark-gluon: ~ **plasma** *n* PART PHYS plasma quark-gluon *m*

quark-lepton: ~ **scheme** *n* PART PHYS schéma des quarks et des leptons *m*

quarried *adj* GEOL exploité, extrait d'une carrière

quarry *n* CONST ballastière *f*, carrière *f*, MINING carrière *f*, mine *f*; ~ **bar** *n* MINING barre de carrière *f*; ~ **face** *n* MINING lit de carrière *m*; ~ **head** *n* MINING carreau de carrière *m*; ~ **stripping** *n* MINING enlèvement des cosses *m*

quarrying *n* MINING abattage en carrière *m*, exploitation de carrière *f*, extraction d'une carrière *f*, tirage *m*; ~ **machine** *n* MINING trancheuse *f*

quarryman *n* MINING carrier *m*, ouvrier carrier *m*

quart *n* METR *British and US liquid measure* quart *m*

quarter *n* METR *avoirdupois weight*, *measure of capacity*, quarter *m* NAUT *ship design* hanche *f*; ~ **belt** *n* (AmE) *see* quartered belt; ~ **berth** *n* NAUT couchette de quart *f*; ~ **elliptic spring** *n* SPRINGS demi-ressort *m*; ~ **fold** *n* PRINT pli d'équerre *m*; ~ **light** *n* (BrE) *(cf quarter window)* AERONAUT *car* déflecteur de porte avant *m*; ~ **mask** *n* SAFETY quart de masque *m*; ~ **platform** *n* PETR plate-forme de quartier *f*; ~ **round** *n* CONST *plane* boudin *m*, quart-de-rond *m*; ~ **round milling cutter** *n* MECH ENG fraise à quart de rond *f*; ~ **space** *n* CONST *stair building* quartier tournant *m*; ~ **tone** *n* PRINT quart de ton *m*, trame à 25% *f*; ~ **track recording** *n* RECORDING enregistrement à quart de piste *m*; ~ **turn belt** *n* PROD ENG courroie semi-croisée *f*, courroie tordue d'un quart *f*; ~ **twist belt** *n* PROD ENG courroie semi-croisée *f*, courroie tordue d'un quart *f*; ~ **wavelength** *n* ELECTRON quart de longueur d'onde *m*; ~ **wave line** *n* PHYS ligne en quart d'onde *f*; ~ **wave plate** *n* PHYS lame quart d'onde *f*; ~ **wave whip antenna** *n* TELECOM antenne fouet quart d'onde *f*; ~ **wind** *n* NAUT vent grand large *m*; ~ **window** *n* (AmE) *(cf quarter light)* AERONAUT *car* déflecteur de porte avant *m*

quarter-binding *n* PRINT demi-reliure *f*

quarter-bound *adj* PRINT relié en demi-cuir

quartered: ~ **belt** *n* (BrE) PROD ENG courroie semi-croisée *f*, courroie tordue d'un quart *f*

quartermaster *n* NAUT quartier-maître *m*

quartet *n* PHYS *spectroscopy* quadruplet *m*; ~ **model** *n* NUCLEAR *structure of nucleus* modèle du quartet *m*

quarto *n* PRINT in-quarto *m*

quartz *n* ELECTRON, MINERAL, PHYS, PROP MAT quartz *m*; ~ **crystal** *n* CINEMAT quartz *m*, COMP, DP, ELEC *clock*, ELECTRON cristal de quartz *m*; ~ **crystal clock** *n* ELEC horloge à quartz *f*; ~ **crystal filter** *n* ELECTRON filtre à quartz *m*; ~ **crystal oscillator** *n* CINEMAT oscillateur piloté par quartz *m*, ELECTRON oscillateur à quartz *m*,

PHYS oscillateur à cristal *m*, oscillateur à quartz *m*; ~ **delay line** *n* ELECTRON, TV ligne à retard à quartz *f*; ~ **frequency source** *n* ELECTRON source de fréquence à quartz *f*, source à quartz *f*; ~ **halogen lamp** *n* CINEMAT lampe à quartz *f*; ~ **iodine** *n* CINEMAT quartz-iode *m*; ~ **iodine lamp** *n* CINEMAT lampe halogène *f*; ~ **light** *n* CINEMAT lumière halogène *f*, lumière quartz *f*; ~ **monochromator** *n* NUCLEAR monochrome à quartz *m*; ~ **oscillator** *n* ELEC *piezoelectric effect*, ELECTRON, TELECOM oscillateur à quartz *m*; ~ **resonator** *n* ELECTRON résonateur à quartz *m*; ~ **sandstone** *n* MINERAL, PROP MAT grès quartzeux *m*; ~ **vein** *n* GEOL filon de quartz *m*; ~ **wedge** *n* CRYSTALL coin en quartz *m*

quartzarenite *n* GEOL arénite quartzique *f*, quartzite sédimentaire *f*

quartzite *n* CONST, GEOL, PROP MAT quartzite *f*

quartzitic: ~ **sandstone** *n* GEOL grès quartzite *m*

quartzose *adj* GEOL quartzeux

quasar *n* ASTRON quasar *m*; ~ **group** *n* ASTRON groupes de quasars *m*

quasiadiabatic: ~ **calorimeter** *n* NUCLEAR calorimètre quasiadiabatique *m*

quasi-albedo: ~ **approach** *n* NUCLEAR méthode quasi albédo *f*

quasi-breeder: ~ **reactor** *n* NUCLEAR réacteur presque régénérateur *m*

quasi-chemical: ~ **approximation** *n* METALL approximation quasi-chimique *f*

quasi-constant: ~ **slip** *n* NUCLEAR glissement quasi-constant *m*

quasi-particle *n* PHYS quasi-particule *f*

quasi-peak: ~ **voltage** *n* TELECOM *air mobile* tension de quasi-crête *f*

quasi-statical[1] *adj* SPACE *spacecraft* quasi-statique

quasi-statical:[2] ~ **loading** *n* SPACE *spacecraft* chargement quasi-statique *m*

quasi-steady: ~ **state** *n* PHYS régime quasi-permanent *m*, régime quasi-stationnaire *m*; ~ **state distribution** *n* METALL distribution quasi-état-fermé *f*

quasi-stellar: ~ **decoupling** *n* SPACE *spacecraft* découplage dynamique *m*; ~ **galaxy** *n* *(QSG)* SPACE *astronomy* galaxie quasi-stellaire *f*; ~ **object** *n* *(QSO)* ASTRON, SPACE objet quasi-stellaire *m*; ~ **radio source** *n* *(QSS)* SPACE quasar *m*; ~ **source** *n* ASTRON *with radio emission* source quasi-stellaire *f*

quassin *n* CHEM quassine *f*

quaternary[1] *adj* CHEM quaternaire

quaternary:[2] ~ **fission** *n* NUCLEAR fission quaternaire *f*; ~ **phase-shift keying** *n* *(QPSK)* ELECTRON, TELECOM modulation par déplacement de phase quadrivalente *f (MDPQ)*

Quaternary *n* GEOL ère quaternaire *f*; ~ **era** *n* GEOL ère quaternaire *f*

quaternion *n* MATH quaternion *m*

quay *n* NAUT, TRANSP quai *m*; ~ **crane** *n* TRANSP grue de quai *f*

quayside: ~ **conveyor** *n* TRANSP convoyeur de quai *m*; ~ **railway** *n* TRANSP convoyeur de quai *m*; ~ **roadway** *n* TRANSP convoyeur de quai *m*

quench[1] *n* METALL trempe *f*; ~ **ageing** *n* (BrE) METALL, NUCLEAR vieillissement après trempe *m*; ~ **aging** *n* (AmE) *see* quench ageing; ~ **hardening** *n* METALL durcissement par trempe *m*, NUCLEAR trempe *f*

quench[2] *vt* CHEM refroidir rapidement, éteindre, MECH *materials*, METALL tremper, THERMOD tremper, éteindre, étouffer

quenched[1] *adj* CRYSTALL trempé

quenched:[2] ~ **cullet** *n* (BrE) *(cf shredded cullet)* C&G calcin tiré à l'eau *m* (Fra), calcinures *f pl* (Bel)

quenching *n* C&G refroidissement rapide *m*, METALL, PROP MAT trempe *f*; ~ **and tempering** *n* SPRINGS opération de trempe et revenu *f*; ~ **bath** *n* METALL bain de trempe *m*; ~ **of luminescence** *n* RAD PHYS extinction de luminescence *f*

quercetin *n* CHEM quercétine *f*

quercitannic *adj* CHEM quercitannique

quercite *n* CHEM quercite *f*, quercitol *m*

quercitin *n* CHEM quercétine *f*

query[1] *n* COMP consultation *f*, interrogation *f*, DP consultation *f*, interrogation *f*; ~ **language** *n* *(QL)* COMP, DP langage d'interrogation *m*; ~ **processing** *n* COMP, DP traitement des demandes *m*

query[2] *vt* COMP, DP consulter

quetch: ~ **rollers** *n* TEXTILES cylindre de pression *m*

quetsh: ~ **unit** *n* TEXTILES ensemble du bain et des rouleaux d'encollage *m*

queue *n* COMP, DP, TELECOM file d'attente *f*; ~ **control** *n* TELECOM mise en file d'attente *f*; ~ **detector** *n* TRANSP *traffic* détecteur de file d'attente *m*; ~ **management** *n* COMP, DP gestion de file d'attente *f*; ~ **warning sign** *n* TRANSP *traffic* signal avertisseur de bouchon *m*

queued: ~ **access** *n* COMP, DP accès par file d'attente *m*; ~ **access method** *n* DP méthode d'accès avec file d'attente *f*

queueing *n* TELECOM formation de files d'attente *f*; ~ **device** *n* TELECOM dispositif de mise en attente *m*; ~ **network** *n* TELECOM réseau de files d'attente *m*; ~ **theory** *n* COMP, DP théorie des files d'attente *f*; ~ **time** *n* TELECOM, TV temps d'attente *m*, temps de mise en attente *m*

quick: ~ **action chuck** *n* MECH ENG mandrin à serrage rapide *m*; ~ **break switch** *n* ELEC interrupteur à action rapide *m*, ELEC ENG interrupteur à rupture brusque *m*; ~ **change aircraft** *n* AERONAUT *passenger, freight* avion rapidement convertible *m*, avion à conversion rapide *m*, avion à transformation rapide *m*; ~ **change drill chuck** *n* MECH ENG porte-mèche à changement rapide *f*; ~ **charge** *n* TRANSP charge rapide *f*; ~ **chill** *n* REFRIG réfrigération rapide *f*; ~ **clay** *n* COAL TECH argile fluide *f*; ~ **closing valve** *n* WATER SUPP vanne à fermeture instantanée *f*; ~ **coupler** *n* SPACE *spacecraft* connecteur rapide *m*; ~ **disconnect** *n* AERONAUT *hydraulics* déconnexion rapide *f*; ~ **freezer** *n* THERMOD congélateur *m*; ~ **switch** *n* CONTROL interrupteur instantané *m*, interrupteur à rupture brusque *m*; ~ **throwover switch** *n* ELEC commutateur rapide *m*

quick-acting: ~ **fuse** *n* MILIT fusée-détonateur à fusion rapide *f*; ~ **regulator** *n* CONTROL régulateur rapide *m*

quick-donning: ~ **oxygen mask** *n* AERONAUT inhalateur d'oxygène d'application rapide *m*

quick-drying *adj* PACKAGING, TEXTILES à séchage rapide

quick-flashing: ~ **light** *n* NAUT feu scintillant *m*

quick-freeze *vt* REFRIG surgeler

quick-freezing[1] *adj* FOOD TECH à congélation rapide

quick-freezing[2] *n* REFRIG congélation rapide *f*, THERMOD surgélation *f*; ~ **installation** *n* MECH ENG installation de congélation rapide *f*; ~ **plant** *n* REFRIG installation de congélation rapide *f*

quick-frozen *adj* REFRIG, THERMOD surgelé

quicklime *n* C&G chaux vive *f*, CHEM chaux anhydre *f*, chaux vive *f*, CONST, MAR POLL chaux vive *f*

quick-release[1] *adj* PRINT à dépouille rapide

quick-release[2] *n* SPACE *spacecraft* déblocage instantané *m*; ~ **clamping system** *n* MECH ENG système de serrage à ouverture rapide *m*; ~ **coupling** *n* PROD ENG raccord rapide *m*; ~ **die** *n* MECH ENG matrice à démontage rapide *f*; ~ **fastener** *n* MECH ENG élément de fixation rapide *m*; ~ **pipe coupling** *n* MECH ENG raccord rapide *m*

quicksand *n* COAL TECH sable boulant *m*, sable flottant *m*, HYDROL lise *f*, sable bouillant *m*, sable boulant *m*, sable mouvant *m*, OCEANOG sable mouvant *m*

quick-setting: ~ **cement** *n* CONST ciment à durcissement rapide *m*, ciment à prise rapide *m*

quicksilver *n* CHEM mercure *m*, vif-argent *m*

quicksilvering *n* PROD ENG *amalgam for mirrors* tain *m*

quickworks *n* NAUT *ship design* oeuvres vives *f pl*

quiesce *vi* COMP, DP s'arrêter doucement, s'arrêter progressivement

quiescent *adj* CHEM quiescent, COMP, DP, ELEC ENG au repos, à l'état de repos

quiescing *adj* COMP, DP mise au repos

quiet: ~ **mode** *n* PRINT mode silencieux *m*; ~ **running** *n* MECH ENG *of engine or machine* marche silencieuse *f*; ~ **short takeoff and landing aircraft** *n* *(QSTOL aircraft)* AERONAUT avion à décollage et atterrissage courts et silencieux *m*; ~ **sun** *n* ASTRON soleil calme *m*; ~ **takeoff and landing aircraft** *n* *(QTOL aircraft)* AERONAUT avion à décollage et atterrissage silencieux *m* *(ADAS)*; ~ **water** *n* WATER SUPP eau calme *f*

quilt[1] *n* TEXTILES couverture piquée *f*

quilt[2] *vt* TEXTILES matelasser

quilter *n* TEXTILES machine à matelasser *f*

quinacrine *n* CHEM mépacrine *f*

quinaldic *adj* CHEM quinaldinique

quinaldine *n* CHEM quinaldine *f*, quinophtalone *f*

quinaldinic *adj* CHEM quinaldinique

quinalizarin *n* CHEM quinalizarine *f*

quinamine *n* CHEM quinamine *f*

quincite *n* MINERAL quincite *f*

quinhydrone *n* CHEM quinhydrone *f*

quinic *adj* CHEM cinchonique, quinique

quinicine *n* CHEM quinicine *f*

quinidine *n* CHEM quinidine *f*

quinine *n* CHEM quinine *f*

quininic *adj* CHEM quinique

quinite *n* CHEM quinite *f*

quinitol *n* CHEM quinite *f*

quinoa *n* CHEM quinoa *m*

quinoid *adj* CHEM quinoïde

quinol *n* CHEM hydroquinone *f*

quinoline *n* CHEM quinoléine *f*

quinolinic *adj* CHEM quinoléique

quinone *n* CHEM quinone *f*

quinonoid *adj* CHEM quinoïde

quinovin *n* CHEM quinovine *f*

quinoxaline *n* CHEM quinoxaline *f*

quinoyle *n* CHEM quinoyle *m*

quinquefid *adj* CHEM quinquefide

quinquevalence *n* CHEM pentavalence *f*

quinquevalent *adj* CHEM pentavalent

quintal *n* METR *metric* quintal métrique *m*

quintet *n* PHYS *spectroscopy* quintet *m*

QUIP *abbr* *(quad-in-line package)* ELECTRON boîtier à quatre rangées de broches *m*

quire *n* PAPER TECH, PRINT main *f*, main du papier *f*, main de papier *f*

quired: ~ **paper** *n* PRINT papier conditionné *m*
quirk *n* CONST *joinery* carré *m*
quoin *n* CONST *brickwork*, MECH ENG *wedge* coin *m*, PROD
  ENG *voussoir* claveau *m*, vousseau *m*, voussoir *m*; ~
  post *n* WATER SUPP *of lock gate* poteau tourillon *m*
quotation *n* PRINT citation *f*; ~ **request** *n* PROD ENG

consultation des fournisseurs *f*
quotes *n pl* PRINT guillemets *m pl*
quotient *n* COMP, DP quotient *m*
Q-value *n* PHYS *nuclear heat of reaction* valeur Q *f*
QWERTY: ~ **keyboard** *n* COMP, DP clavier QWERTY *m*

R

R *abbr (roentgen)* RAD PHYS roentgen *m*

Ra *(radium)* CHEM Ra *(radium)*

rabbet *n* CONST feuillure *f*, guillaume *m*; **~ draft** *n* (AmE), **~ draught** *n* (BrE) NAUT *ship design* profondeur de carène *f*; **~ iron** *n* CONST fer de guillaume *m*; **~ plane** *n* CONST feuilleret *m*, guillaume en navette *m*, guillaume *m*

rabbeted: ~ joint *n* CONST assemblage à feuillure *m*

rabbit: ~ fraction *n* NUCLEAR fraction de recyclage *f*

rabbittite *n* NUCLEAR *uranium mineral* rabbittite *f*

rabbling *n* PROD ENG brassage *m*

Racah: ~ coupling *n* NUCLEAR couplage de Racah *m*

race *n* HYDR EQUIP *water channel* canal *m*, rigole *f*, MECH chemin de roulement *m*, MECH ENG *for balls* chemin de roulement *m*, voie de roulement *f*, NAUT *sea* fort courant *m*, raz *m*, OCEANOG *tide* raz *m*, WATER SUPP *mill race* bief *m*, biez *m*

racemate *n* CHEM racémate *m*

racemic *adj* CHEM racémique

racemization *n* CHEM racémisation *f*

racemize *vt* CHEM racémiser

racemizing *adj* CHEM racémisant

racetrack: ~ holding pattern *n* AERONAUT circuit d'attente en hippodrome *m*

raceway *n* ELEC ENG passage de câbles *m*, HYDR EQUIP canal *m*, rigole *f*, NUCLEAR caniveau *m*, PROD ENG canalisation *f*, WATER SUPP *mill race* bief *m*, biez *m*

racing *n* MECH ENG emballement *m*

rack[1] *n* CINEMAT bâti *m*, châssis *m*, porte-film *m*, ELEC ENG bâti *m*, LAB EQUIP *for test tubes* support *m*, MECH bâti *m*, crémaillère *f*, MECH ENG *unscrewing device* crémaillère *f*, MILIT *for weapons* râtelier d'armes *m*, PAPER TECH crémaillère *f*, PRINT rangement pour les cartes électroniques *m*, PROD ENG crémaillère *f*, TELECOM bâti *m*, TRANSP *rail, vehicles steering* crémaillère *f*; **~ body truck** *n* TRANSP camion plateau *m*; **~ engine** *n* TRANSP locomotive à crémaillère *f*; **~ feed** *n* MECH ENG amenage par crémaillère *m*; **~ gearing** *n* TRANSP engrenage à crémaillère *m*; **~ line** *n* CINEMAT espace inter image *m*; **~ locomotive** *n* TRANSP locomotive à crémaillère *f*; **~ mark** *n* C&G baguette *f*; **~ mount** *n* PACKAGING montage en baie *m*; **~ mountain railroad** *n* (AmE), **~ mountain railway** *n* (BrE) TRANSP chemin de fer de montagne à crémaillère *m*; **~ rail** *n* RAIL crémaillère *f*, rail crémaillère *m*, rail denté *m*, TRANSP crémaillère *f*; **~ railroad** *n* (AmE) *(cf rack railway)* TRANSP chemin de fer à crémaillère *m*; **~ railroad trailer** *n* (AmE) *(cf rack railway trailer)* TRANSP voiture de chemin de fer à crémaillère *f*; **~ railway** *n* (BrE) *(cf rack railroad)* TRANSP chemin de fer à crémaillère *m*; **~ railway trailer** *n* (BrE) *(cf rack railroad trailer)* TRANSP voiture de chemin de fer à crémaillère *f*; **~ track** *n* TRANSP crémaillère *f*; **~ wheel** *n* MECH ENG roue dentée *f*, roue à dents *f*; **~ which engages with a pinion** *n* MECH ENG crémaillère qui engrène avec un pignon *m*; **~ wiring** *n* ELEC ENG câblage du bâti *m*

rack[2] *vt* CINEMAT *lens turret* tourner

rack:[3] **~ focus** *vi* CINEMAT faire la mise au point, suivre le point

rack-and-pin: ~ processing *n* CINEMAT développement au cadre *m*

rack-and-pinion[1] *adj* MECH à crémaillère

rack-and-pinion[2] *n* INSTRUMENT, MECH crémaillère *f*, MECH ENG crémaillère et pignon *f*, pignon et crémaillère *f*, PROD ENG crémaillère *f*; **~ drive gear** *n* NUCLEAR mécanisme de commande à crémaillère *m*; **~ gear** *n* MECH ENG engrenage à crémaillère *m*; **~ jack** *n* MECH ENG cric à crémaillère *m*; **~ railroad** *n* (AmE) *(cf rack-and-pinion railway)* TRANSP chemin de fer à crémaillère *m*; **~ railway** *n* (BrE) *(cf rack-and-pinion railroad)* TRANSP chemin de fer à crémaillère *m*; **~ steering** *n* VEHICLES direction à crémaillère et pignon *f*

racking *n* FOOD TECH soutirage *m*; **~ the carriage of a traveling crane** *n* (AmE), **~ the carriage of a travelling crane** *n* (BrE) MECH ENG translation du chariot d'un pont roulant *f*; **~ pipe** *n* PETR TECH gerbage *m*

rack-mounted *adj* CINEMAT, ELEC ENG monté en bâti

rackover *n* CINEMAT crémaillère *f*

rack-rail: ~ locomotive *n* RAIL *vehicles* locomotive à adhérence mixte *f*

racon *n* NAUT racon *m*

rad *n* RAD PHYS *symbol* rad *m*

radar *n* AERONAUT, ASTRON, MILIT, NAUT, PHYS, RAD PHYS, TELECOM radar *m*; **~ aerial** *n* TELECOM antenne radar *f*; **~ air traffic control** *n* TRANSP sécurité de la navigation aérienne par radar *f*; **~ altimeter** *n* TRANSP sonde altimétrique *f*; **~ altimetry** *n* ASTRON altimétrie radar *f*; **~ antenna** *n* TELECOM, TRANSP antenne radar *f*; **~ approach** *n* AERONAUT, TRANSP approche au radar *f*; **~ approach control center** *n* (AmE), **~ approach control centre** *n* (BrE) TRANSP centre de contrôle radar d'approche *m*; **~ astronomy** *n* ASTRON astronomie radar *f*; **~ beacon** *n* AERONAUT, NAUT, RAD PHYS, TELECOM balise radar *f*, TRANSP radiophare pour radar *m*; **~ beam** *n* NAUT faisceau radar *m*; **~ bearing** *n* NAUT relèvement au radar *m*; **~ blip** *n* AERONAUT plot radar *m*, NAUT spot radar *m*, écho radar *m*; **~ calibration** *n* WAVE PHYS calibrage par radar *m*; **~ coast image** *n* TRANSP image côtière par radar *f*; **~ contact** *n* TRANSP détection par radar *f*; **~ control** *n* AERONAUT, CONTROL, TRANSP contrôle radar *m*; **~ controller** *n* AERONAUT contrôleur radar *m*; **~ detection** *n* NAUT détection au radar *f*; **~ dish** *n* AERONAUT réflecteur parabolique radar *m*; **~ display** *n* AERONAUT visualisation radar *f*, MILIT écran de radar *m*, TRANSP affichage radar *m*; **~ dome** *n* NAUT dôme de radar *m*; **~ echo** *n* AERONAUT écho radar *m*; **~ equipment** *n* MILIT équipement radar *m*, TRANSP matériel de radar *m*; **~ heading** *n* AERONAUT cap radar *m*; **~ homing** *n* TRANSP ralliement par radar *m*; **~ identification** *n* AERONAUT identification radar *f*, TRANSP identification par radar *f*; **~ image** *n* SPACE radargraphie *f*; **~ imager** *n* NAUT appareillage de radiodétection *m*; **~ interference** *n* NAUT brouillage radar *m*; **~ marker beacon** *n* NAUT balise émettrice radar *f*; **~ marker float** *n* TRANSP bouée radar *f*; **~ mast** *n* TRANSP mât radar *m*; **~ monitoring** *n*

AERONAUT surveillance radar *f*, TRANSP surveillance par radar *f*; ~ **navigation** *n* AERONAUT, TRANSP navigation par radar *f*; ~ **operator** *n* MILIT opérateur de radar *m*, NAUT opérateur de radar *m*, radariste *m*; ~ **picket station** *n* TRANSP station piquet radar *f*; ~ **plotting** *n* MILIT *aviation* traçage par radar de la trajectoire de vol *m*, NAUT pointage radar *m*, TRANSP traçage par radar de la trajectoire de vol *m*; ~ **range** *n* MILIT portée radar *f*, TRANSP couverture par radar *f*; ~ **rating** *n* AERONAUT qualification radar *f*; ~ **reflector** *n* NAUT réflecteur radar *m*; ~ **reflector buoy** *n* TRANSP bouée à réflexion de radar *f*; ~ **relay station** *n* TRANSP relais radar *m*; ~ **response** *n* AERONAUT réponse radar *f*; ~ **scan** *n* TRANSP balayage radar *m*; ~ **scanner** *n* MILIT sondeur de radar *m*, NAUT antenne radar *f*, RAD PHYS déchiffreur de radar *m*, scanner à balayage *m*, TRANSP antenne radar *f*, balayeur radar *m*, explorateur radar *m*; ~ **scan pattern** *n* TRANSP schéma de balayage de radar *m*; ~ **scope** *n* TRANSP écran de radar *m*; ~ **screen** *n* AERONAUT, NAUT, TRANSP écran de radar *m*; ~ **sensor** *n* RAD PHYS détecteur radar *m*; ~ **speed meter** *n* TRANSP radiotachymètre *m*; ~ **station** *n* MILIT centre de radar *m*, NAUT station radar *f*; ~ **surveillance** *n* MILIT, TRANSP surveillance par radar *f*; ~ **surveillance system** *n* MILIT système de surveillance radar *m*; ~ **telemeter** *n* MILIT télémètre radar *m*; ~ **tracking** *n* AERONAUT, MILIT poursuite par radar *f*, TRANSP localisation par radar *f*; ~ **tracking station** *n* MILIT station de poursuite radar *f*, TRANSP poste de poursuite par radar *m*; ~ **transponder beacon** *n* AERONAUT, NAUT balise répondeuse radar *f*; ~ **tube** *n* ELECTRON tube radar *m*; ~ **unit** *n* AERONAUT section radar *f*; ~ **vectoring** *n* AERONAUT, TRANSP guidage par radar *m*; ~ **waves** *n pl* RAD PHYS ondes radar *f pl*; ~ **with coherent pulse** *n* RAD PHYS radar à impulsions synchronisées *m*

radar-controlled *adj* TRANSP commandé par radar

radarsonde: ~ **observation** *n* AERONAUT observation de radarsonde *f*

radial[1] *adj* MECH radial

radial:[2] ~ **and axial turbocompressor** *n* MECH ENG turbocompresseur de construction radiale et axiale *m*; ~ **bearing** *n* PAPER TECH palier transversal *m*; ~ **chart recorder** *n* INSTRUMENT enregistreur à diagramme polaire *m*; ~ **component** *n* PHYS composante radiale *f*; ~ **control** *n* OPT asservissement radial *m*; ~ **cylindrical roller bearing** *n* MECH ENG roulement radial à rouleaux cylindriques *m*; ~ **deflecting electrode** *n* TV électrode à déviation radiale *f*; ~ **deviation** *n* PROP MAT excentricité *f*; ~ **diehead** *n* MECH ENG cage de filière radiale *f*; ~ **distribution function** *n* RAD PHYS fonction radiale de distribution *f*; ~ **drilling machine** *n* MECH perceuse radiale *f*; ~ **electrical fields** *n pl* RAD PHYS champ électrique radial *m*; ~ **fault** *n* PROP MAT faille radiale *f*; ~ **feeder** *n* ELEC *supply* artère finale *f*, feeder final *m*, ligne en antenne *f*; ~ **flow fan** *n* HEAT ENG ventilateur centrifuge *m*, ventilateur à courant transversal *m*; ~ **flow tank** *n* HYDROL *sewage* bassin à circulation radiale *m*; ~ **gate** *n* FUELLESS *dams* vanne à secteur *f*; ~ **internal clearance** *n* MECH ENG *roller bearings* jeu interne radial *m*; ~ **lead** *n* ELEC ENG sortie radiale *f*; ~ **lead capacitor** *n* ELEC ENG condensateur à sorties radiales *m*; ~ **lead resistor** *n* ELEC ENG résistance à sorties radiales *f*; ~ **load** *n* PROP MAT charge radiale *f*; ~ **neutron flux** *n* NUCLEAR flux neutronique radial *m*; ~ **part of the wave function** *n* RAD PHYS partie radiale de la fonction d'onde *f*; ~ **ply tire** *n* (AmE), ~ **ply tyre** *n*

(BrE) P&R *rubber* pneu radial *m*, pneu à carcasse radiale *m*, pneumatique radial *m*, pneumatique à carcasse radiale *m*, VEHICLES pneumatique à carcasse radicale *m*; ~ **positioning time** *n* OPT temps de positionnement *m*; ~ **power distribution** *n* NUCLEAR *reactor core* distribution radiale de puissance *f*; ~ **shift** *n* NUCLEAR réarrangement radial *m*; ~ **shuffling** *n* NUCLEAR *fuel assemblies* réarrangement radial *m*; ~ **sludge tank** *n* HYDROL *sewage* scraper à bras radial *m*; ~ **system** *n* ELEC réseau radial *m*; ~ **threading die** *n* MECH ENG coussinet de filière radial *m*; ~ **tire** *n* (AmE), ~ **tyre** *n* (BrE) VEHICLES pneu radial *m*, pneu à carcasse radiale *m*, pneumatique radial *m*; ~ **velocity** *n* ASTRON, FUELLESS vitesse radiale *f*; ~ **width** *n* SPRINGS largeur radiale *f*

radian *n* ELEC, ELECTRON, GEOM, PHYS radian *m*

radiance *n* OPT brillance *f*, luminance *f*, luminance énergétique *f*, PHYS luminance énergétique *f*, radiance *f*, RAD PHYS éclat *m*, SPACE luminance énergétique *f*, TELECOM luminance *f*, luminance énergétique *f*, TV luminance énergétique *f*

radiant[1] *adj* PHYS, THERMOD radiant, rayonnant

radiant[2] *n* ASTRON point radiant *m*; ~ **boiler** *n* HEATING chaudière à rayonnement *f*; ~ **cooler** *n* THERMOD refroidisseur à rayonnement *m*; ~ **cooling** *n* THERMOD refroidissement par radiation *m*; ~ **dryer** *n* PAPER TECH séchoir par rayonnement *m*; ~ **efficiency** *n* PHYS efficacité énergétique relative *f*; ~ **emittance** *n* OPT, TELECOM excitance *f*, excitance énergétique *f*; ~ **energy** *n* PHYS énergie rayonnante *f*, RAD PHYS énergie radiante *f*, TELECOM énergie rayonnante *f*; ~ **energy density** *n* PHYS énergie rayonnante volumique *f*; ~ **energy fluence rate** *n* PHYS *radiant flux density* densité de flux énergétique *f*, débit de fluence énergétique *m*; ~ **excitance** *n* OPT excitance *f*, excitance énergétique *f*, PHYS excitance énergétique *f*, RAD PHYS excitance radiante *f*, excitance énergétique *f*, TELECOM excitance *f*, excitance énergétique *f*; ~ **exposure** *n* PHYS exposition énergétique *f*; ~ **flux** *n* OPT puissance optique *f*, puissance rayonnante *f*, PHYS *radiant power* flux énergétique *m*, puissance rayonnante *f*, RAD PHYS flux de radiation *m*, flux énergétique *m*, TELECOM flux énergétique *m*; ~ **flux density** *n see power flux density* ~ **heat** *n* RAD PHYS *infrared rays*, THERMOD chaleur rayonnante *f*; ~ **heater** *n* HEAT ENG radiateur chauffant *m*, MECH ENG réchauffeur radiant *m*, RAD PHYS radiateur à foyer rayonnant *m*, THERMOD radiateur chauffant *m*, radiateur à rayonnement *m*; ~ **heating** *n* HEATING chauffage à rayonnement *m*, THERMOD chauffage par radiation *m*; ~ **intensity** *n* OPT, PHYS, RAD PHYS, TELECOM intensité de rayonnement *f*, intensité énergétique *f*; ~ **power** *n* OPT flux énergétique *m*, puissance optique *f*, puissance rayonnante *f*, PHYS flux énergétique *m*, puissance rayonnante *f*, TELECOM puissance rayonnante *f*; ~ **quantity** *n* NUCLEAR *optical radiation* quantité photométrique énergétique *f*; ~ **superheater** *n* HEATING surchauffeur à rayonnement *m*

radiate[1] *vt* RAD PHYS rayonner, THERMOD irradier, rayonner, TV rayonner

radiate[2] *vi* GAS TECH émettre un rayonnement, RAD PHYS rayonner

radiated: ~ **energy** *n* RAD PHYS énergie rayonnée *f*; ~ **interference** *n* ELEC ENG parasites rayonnés *m pl*; ~ **output** *n* RAD PHYS énergie rayonnée *f*; ~ **power** *n* TELECOM puissance rayonnée *f*, puissance émise *f*, TV puissance de rayonnement *f*, puissance émise *f*

radiating[1] *adj* RAD PHYS rayonnant

radiating:[2] ~ **cable communication system** *n* TELECOM système de communication par câble rayonnant *m*; ~ **circuit** *n* TV circuit de rayonnement *m*; ~ **particle** *n* PART PHYS particule rayonnante *f*

radiation *n* ELECTRON, METEO, NUCLEAR, OPT, PHYS, POLLUTION, RAD PHYS, SPACE, TELECOM, THERMOD, TV radiation *f*, rayonnement *m*; ~ **absorption analysis** *n* NUCLEAR analyse par absorption *f*; ~ **angle** *n* OPT, TELECOM angle de rayonnement *m*; ~ **belt** *n* RAD PHYS couche de radiation *f*, SPACE ceinture de rayonnements *f*; ~ **burn** *n* RAD PHYS brûlure de radiation *f*; ~ **catalysis** *n* RAD PHYS catalyse sous irradiation *f*; ~ **channel** *n* NUCLEAR chaîne de contrôle d'un rayonnement *f*; ~ **chemistry** *n* NUCLEAR chimie sous rayonnement *f*; ~ **constant** *n* HEAT ENG constante de rayonnement *f*; ~ **counter** *n* RAD PHYS, WAVE PHYS compteur de radiation *m*; ~ **counter tube** *n* ELECTRON tube compteur de radiation *m*; ~ **cross linking** *n* P&R réticulation sous rayonnement *f*; ~ **damage** *n* RAD PHYS dégât par rayonnement *m*, radioendommagement *m*; ~ **degradation** *n* RAD PHYS dégradation par radiation *f*; ~ **detector** *n* LAB EQUIP, RAD PHYS détecteur de radiation *m*; ~ **dose** *n* POLLUTION, RAD PHYS dose de rayonnement *f*, SPACE dose d'irradiation *f*; ~ **dosimetry** *n* RAD PHYS dosimétrie de radiation *f*; ~ **effects reactor** *n* NUCLEAR réacteur pour l'étude des effets de rayonnement *m*; ~ **era** *n* ASTRON époque de rayonnement *f*; ~ **excitation** *n* ELECTRON excitation par rayonnement *f*; ~ **field** *n* RAD PHYS champ de rayonnement *m*; ~ **flux density** *n* NUCLEAR densité de flux énergétique *f*; ~ **frequency** *n* RAD PHYS fréquence de rayonnement *f*; ~ **hardening** *n* ELEC ENG renforcement à radiation *m*, NUCLEAR durcissement par rayonnement *m*; ~ **hardness** *n* ELEC ENG radiorésistance *f*, résistance à radiation *f*, TELECOM tenue à radiation *f*; ~ **hazards** *n pl* SAFETY dangers du rayonnement *m pl*; ~ **heating** *n* RAD PHYS chauffage par radiation *m*; ~ **heat transfer coefficient** *n* HEAT ENG coefficient de rayonnement *m*; ~ **intensity** *n* SPACE *communications* intensité de rayonnement *f*; ~ **ionization** *n* GEOPHYS ionisation par rayonnement *f*; ~ **laws** *n pl* RAD PHYS lois de la radiation *f pl*; ~ **loss** *n* PART PHYS perte d'énergie par rayonnement *f*; ~ **measurement** *n* RAD PHYS mesure de rayonnement *f*; ~ **meter** *n* MILIT *nuclear warfare* contaminamètre *m*; ~ **mode** *n* OPT, TELECOM mode rayonnant *m*; ~ **monitor** *n* RAD PHYS compteur de radiation *m*; ~ **monitoring** *n* CONTROL contrôle du niveau de rayonnement *m*, RAD PHYS surveillance de la radiation *f*, SPACE surveillance de rayonnement *f*; ~ **pattern** *n* OPT *optical fibre*, PHYS, SPACE *communications*, TELECOM diagramme de rayonnement *m*; ~ **physics** *n* NUCLEAR, PHYS physique des rayonnements *f*; ~ **pressure** *n* ACOUSTICS, ASTRON, PART PHYS, PHYS, RAD PHYS pression de rayonnement *f*, pression de radiation *f*; ~ **processing** *n* NUCLEAR traitement par rayonnement *m*; ~ **protection** *n* ELEC ENG protection contre les radiations *f*, POLLUTION protection contre les rayonnements *f*, RAD PHYS protection contre les radiations *f*, SAFETY protection contre les rayonnements *f*; ~ **pyrometer** *n* GEOPHYS, LAB EQUIP, PHYS pyromètre à rayonnement *m*; ~ **reaction force** *n* RAD PHYS force de réaction de radiation *f*; ~ **resistance** *n* NUCLEAR radiorésistance *f*, PHYS résistance de rayonnement *f*; ~ **shield** *n* SAFETY écran

contre le rayonnement *m*; ~ **shielding** *n* RAD PHYS blindage de radiation *m*; ~ **shielding glass** *n* C&G verre absorbant *m*; ~ **sickness** *n* SAFETY mal des rayons *m*; ~ **source** *n* ELECTRON, NUCLEAR source de rayonnement *f*, RAD PHYS source de la radiation *f*; ~ **spectrum** *n* GEOPHYS spectre de rayonnement *m*; ~ **test** *n* CONTROL contrôle radiographique *m*; ~ **treatment** *n* RAD PHYS radiothérapie *f*; ~ **unit** *n* RAD PHYS unité de rayonnement *f*

radiation-induced: ~ **activation** *n* RAD PHYS activation par radiation *f*; ~ **mutation** *n* RAD PHYS mutation radioinduite *f*; ~ **reaction** *n* RAD PHYS réaction chimique des radiations *f*

radiationless: ~ **transition** *n* RAD PHYS transition non-radiative *f*

radiation-proof *adj* RAD PHYS à l'épreuve de la radiation

radiative[1] *adj* RAD PHYS radiatif, rayonnant, THERMOD radiatif

radiative:[2] ~ **capture** *n* PHYS capture radiative *f*; ~ **cascade** *n* RAD PHYS cascade radiative *f*; ~ **collision** *n* RAD PHYS collision radiative *f*; ~ **decay rate** *n* RAD PHYS taux de désintégration radiative *m*; ~ **diffusion** *n* ASTRON diffusion radiative *f*; ~ **experiment** *n* RAD PHYS expérience radiative *f*; ~ **heat transfer** *n* SPACE *spacecraft* échange radiatif *m*; ~ **lifetime** *n see radioactive half life* ~ **recombination** *n* ELECTRON recombinaison radiative *f*; ~ **transfer** *n* ASTRON, RAD PHYS transfert radiatif *m*; ~ **transfer equation** *n* RAD PHYS équation de transfert radiatif *f*; ~ **transition** *n* RAD PHYS transition radiative *f*

radiator *n* AUTO, MECH, THERMOD *for cooling*, VEHICLES *cooling system* radiateur *m*; ~ **blind** *n* VEHICLES *cooling system* rideau de radiateur *m*; ~ **cap** *n* VEHICLES *cooling system* bouchon de radiateur *m*; ~ **core** *n* AUTO, VEHICLES faisceau de radiateur *m*; ~ **drain cock** *n* AUTO robinet de vidange du radiateur *m*; ~ **draining** *n* AUTO vidange du radiateur *f*; ~ **drain tap** *n* VEHICLES robinet de vidange du radiateur *m*; ~ **element** *n* AUTO élément de radiateur *m*; ~ **filler cap** *n* AUTO bouchon de radiateur *m*; ~ **filler neck** *n* AUTO tubulure de remplissage *f*; ~ **fin** *n* AUTO, VEHICLES *cooling system* ailette de radiateur *f*; ~ **flange** *n* AUTO bride de fixation du radiateur *f*; ~ **frame** *n* AUTO cadre de radiateur *m*; ~ **grille** *n* VEHICLES calandre de radiateur *f*; ~ **header** *n* AUTO collecteur de tête *m*, collecteur du radiateur *m*, réservoir supérieur *m*; ~ **hose** *n* AERONAUT tubulure *f*, AUTO, VEHICLES durite de radiateur *f*; ~ **pressure cap** *n* AUTO bouchon de radiateur *m*; ~ **support** *n* AUTO support de radiateur *m*; ~ **thermostat** *n* CONTROL thermostat de radiateur *m*; ~ **vent hose** *n* VEHICLES tuyau flexible de ventilation *m*

radical *n* CHEM *group*, GAS TECH, MATH radical *m*, P&R *group of atoms* espèce *f*, radical *m*; ~ **process** *n* P&R procédé radicalaire *m*

radio[1] *adj* PHYS radioélectrique; ~ **frequency** *adj* ELECTRON à fréquence radioélectrique, à haute fréquence

radio:[2] ~ **aerial** *n* VEHICLES antenne *f*; ~ **altimeter** *n* AERONAUT radioaltimètre *m*; ~ **amateur** *n* TELECOM radioamateur *m*; ~ **antenna** *n* TRANSP antenne radio *f*, VEHICLES antenne *f*; ~ **approach aids** *n* AERONAUT aides d'approche par radio *f pl*; ~ **astrometry** *n* ASTRON, PHYS, SPACE radioastrométrie *f*; ~ **astronomy** *n* ASTRON, PHYS, SPACE radioastronomie *f*; ~ **beacon** *n* AERONAUT phare de radiocompas *m*, radio de ralliement *f*, radiocompas *m*, radiobalise *f*, radioborne *f*, radiophare circulaire *m*, radiophare à rayonnement circulaire *m*, émetteur de la radionavigation *m*, radiophare *m*, NAUT balise radio *f*, RAD PHYS, TRANSP radiophare *m*; ~ **beam** *n* RAD PHYS faisceau radio *m*; ~ **bearing** *n* AERONAUT, NAUT relèvement radiogoniométrique *m*; ~ **broadcasting** *n* TELECOM radiodiffusion *f*; ~ **broadcast satellite** *n* SPACE *communications* satellite de radiodiffusion *m*; ~ **channel** *n* AERONAUT canal radio *m*; ~ **code message** *n* MILIT radiogramme chiffré *m*; ~ **compass** *n* AERONAUT radiocompas *m*, NAUT radiogoniomètre automatique *m*, TRANSP radiocompas *m*; ~ **control system** *n* TELECOM installation de commande par radio *f*; ~ **determination satellite system** *n* NAUT système de radiorepérage par satellite *m*; ~ **direction finder** *n* (*RDF*) AERONAUT radiogoniomètre *m*, NAUT *navigation* radiogonio *m*, radiogoniomètre *m*; ~ **direction finder antenna** *n* TRANSP antenne radiogoniométrique *f*; ~ **direction finding** *n* PHYS, TELECOM radiogoniométrie *f*, TRANSP radio repérage *m*; ~ **direction finding station** *n* AERONAUT station radiogoniométrique *f*; ~ **engineer** *n* NAUT ingénieur radio *m*; ~ **equipment** *n* TRANSP radio de bord *f*; ~ **facility** *n* AERONAUT installation radio *f*; ~ **fix** *n* AERONAUT point observé par radio *m*, point radio *m*, relèvement radio *m*, repère radio *m*, NAUT *navigation* repérage radio *m*; ~ **frequency** *n* (*RF*) ELEC ENG, ELECTRON, RECORDING, TELECOM, TRANSP, TV fréquence radio *f*, radiofréquence *f*; ~ **frequency microphone** *n* RECORDING micro HF *m*, micro haute fréquence *m*; ~ **heliograph** *n* ASTRON héliographe radio *m*; ~ **homing** *n* TELECOM radio ralliement *m*, TRANSP approche radioguidée *f*; ~ **homing beacon** *n* TRANSP balise de radio ralliement *f*; ~ **interference** *n* ELECTRON parasites radioélectriques *m pl*, parasites à haute fréquence *m pl*, WAVE PHYS interférences radio *f pl*; ~ **interferometer** *n* GEOPHYS radio-interféromètre *m*; ~ **labeling** *n* (AmE), ~ **labelling** *n* (BrE) CHEM *of compound, group, atom* marquage radioactif *m*; ~ **link** *n* AERONAUT, NAUT liaison radio *f*, TV faisceau hertzien *m*, liaison hertzienne *f*; ~ **map** *n* ASTRON carte du radio *f*; ~ **marker** *n* TRANSP radiophare d'approche *m*; ~ **monitoring** *n* CONTROL contrôle radio *m*; ~ **navigation** *n* AERONAUT radionavigation *f*, NAUT navigation radioélectrique *f*, radionavigation *f*, TRANSP radionavigation *f*; ~ **noise** *n* ELECTRON bruit radioélectrique *m*; ~ **officer** *n* NAUT officier radio *m*, radionavigant *m*; ~ **operator** *n* NAUT radio navigant *m*; ~ **paging** *n* TELECOM radiomessagerie *f*; ~ **patrol car** *n* TRANSP voiture radio *f*; ~ **position fixing** *n* TRANSP radiogoniométrie *f*; ~ **range** *n* AERONAUT radiophare d'alignement *m*, radiophare à axes *m*, TRANSP radiophare d'alignement *m*; ~ **receiver** *n* PHYS radiorécepteur *m*; ~ **relay** *n* ELEC ENG relais hertzien *m*; ~ **remote control** *n* TRANSP téléguidage électrique *m*; ~ **room** *n* NAUT poste radio de bord *m*; ~ **sensitivity** *n* RAD PHYS radiosensibilité *f*; ~ **signal** *n* ELEC ENG, ELECTRON signal radio *m*, signal radioélectrique *m*; ~ **sonobuoy** *n* NAUT bouée radiosonore *f*; ~ **source** *n* ASTRON radiosource *f*, source chaude *f*, source radioactive *f*, RAD PHYS, SPACE radiosource *f*; ~ **spectrum** *n* ELECTRON spectre des fréquences radioélectriques *m*, spectre radioélectrique *m*, RAD PHYS spectre radio *m*; ~ **star** *n* ASTRON, SPACE *communications* radiosource *f*; ~ **steering** *n* TRANSP commande à distance par radio *f*; ~ **subsystem** *n* TELECOM sous-système radio *m*; ~ **taxicab** *n* TRANSP radio taxi *m*; ~ **telecontrol** *n* TRANSP radio télécommande *f*; ~ **teles-**

cope *n* ASTRON, INSTRUMENT, PHYS radiotélescope *m* ~ **tracking** *n* MILIT localisation par radio *f*; ~ **transmitter** *n* PHYS radioémetteur *m*, émetteur radioélectrique *m*; ~ **wave** *n* ELEC onde radioélectrique *f*, ELEC ENG onde hertzienne *f*, onde radioélectrique *f*, ELECTRON onde hertzienne *f*, onde radio *f*, onde radioélectrique *f*, GEOPHYS onde radioélectrique *f*, PHYS onde hertzienne *f*, onde radioélectrique *f*, TELECOM onde radioélectrique *f*, WAVE PHYS onde hertzienne *f*; ~ **wave hazards** *n pl* SAFETY dangers des ondes radio *m pl*; ~ **wave propagation** *n* RAD PHYS propagation des ondes *f*; ~ **window** *n* PHYS fenêtre radioélectrique *f*

radioactinium *n* CHEM, RAD PHYS radioactinium *m*

radioactivation: ~ **analysis** *n* RAD PHYS analyse par radioactivité *f*

radioactive[1] *adj* PART PHYS, PHYS, RAD PHYS, SAFETY radioactif

radioactive:[2] ~ **body** *n* RAD PHYS corps radioactif *m*; ~ **contamination** *n* PHYS, RAD PHYS contamination radioactive *f*; ~ **dating** *n* PHYS datation par radioactivité *f*, RAD PHYS détermination de l'âge radioactif *f*; ~ **decay** *n* PART PHYS désintégration radioactive *f*, PHYS décroissance radioactive *f*; ~ **decay rate** *n* RAD PHYS taux de désintégration radioactive *m*; ~ **decay series** *n* RAD PHYS série de désintégration radioactive *f*; ~ **disintegration** *n* PHYS désintégration radioactive *f*; ~ **dust** *n* MILIT poussière radioactive *f*; ~ **element** *n* RAD PHYS radioélément *m*; ~ **emanation** *n* RAD PHYS émanation radioactive *f*; ~ **equilibrium** *n* PHYS, RAD PHYS équilibre radioactif *m*; ~ **fallout** *n* NUCLEAR retombée radioactive *f*, retombées nucléaires *f pl*, PHYS, POLLUTION retombée radioactive *f*, retombées radioactives *f pl*; ~ **half life** *n* NUCLEAR période d'un nucléide radioactif *f*; ~ **ion implantation** *n* PART PHYS implantation d'ions radioactifs *f*; ~ **isotope** *n* PART PHYS, PHYS, RAD PHYS isotope radioactif *m*; ~ **log** *n* PETR TECH diagraphie nucléaire *f*; ~ **pollution** *n* POLLUTION pollution radioactive *f*, SAFETY contamination radioactive *f*; ~ **purity** *n* RAD PHYS pureté radioactive *f*; ~ **series** *n* PHYS chaîne radioactive *f*, famille radioactive *f*, RAD PHYS série radioactive *f*; ~ **standard** *n* RAD PHYS étalon radioactif *m*; ~ **substance** *n* POLLUTION, SAFETY substance radioactive *f*; ~ **tracer** *n* PHYS, RAD PHYS traceur radioactif *m*; ~ **transformation** *n* RAD PHYS changement radioactif *m*; ~ **transmutation** *n see* transmutation ~ **waste** *n* NUCLEAR, RAD PHYS déchets radioactifs *m pl*; ~ **waste evaporator** *n* NUCLEAR évaporateur des déchets liquides *m*

radioactivity *n* CHEM, MILIT *nuclear warfare*, NUCLEAR, PART PHYS, PHYS, RAD PHYS radioactivité *f*; ~ **meter** *n* RAD PHYS radioactivimètre *m*

radioanalysis *n* RAD PHYS radioanalyse *f*

radioastronomical: ~ **antenna** *n* TELECOM antenne radioastronomique *f*

radiocaesium *n* (BrE) RAD PHYS radiocésium *m*

radiocarbon *n* PHYS, RAD PHYS radiocarbone *m*; ~ **dating** *n* PHYS datation au radiocarbone *f*

radiocassette *n* RECORDING radiocassette *f*; ~ **deck** *n* VEHICLES *accessory* radiolecteur de cassettes *m*

radiocesium *n* (AmE) *see* radiocaesium

radiochemical *adj* CHEM radiochimique

radiochemistry *n* CHEM chimie radioactive *f*, radiochimie *f*, RAD PHYS chimie radioactive *f*

radiochromatography *n* RAD PHYS radiochromatographie *f*

radiocobalt *n* CHEM, RAD PHYS radiocobalt *m*

radiocommunication *n* NAUT contact par radio *m*, radiocommunication *f*, TELECOM, TRANSP radiocommunication *f*

radio-controlled *adj* TRANSP télécommandé

radiodiagnosis *n* RAD PHYS radiodiagnostic *m*

radiogenic[1] *adj* PHYS radiogénique, radiogène

radiogenic:[2] ~ **isotope** *n* GEOL isotope radiogénique *m*

radiogoniometer *n* OCEANOG, PHYS, RAD PHYS radiogoniomètre *m*

radiogoniometry *n* PHYS, RAD PHYS radiogoniométrie *f*

radiograph[1] *n* INSTRUMENT radiographe *m*

radiograph[2] *vt* INSTRUMENT radiographier

radiographer *n* INSTRUMENT assistant radiographe *m*

radiographic: ~ **examination** *n* MECH ENG, TESTING examen radiographique *m*

radiography *n* INSTRUMENT, PHYS, RAD PHYS radiographie *f*

radioguidance *n* TELECOM radioguidage *m*

radioguide *vt* TRANSP radioguider

radio-guided: ~ **flight** *n* MILIT vol radio guidé *m*

radioiodine *n* CHEM iode radioactif *m*, radio-iode *m*, RAD PHYS radio-iodine *m*

radioisomer *n* CHEM radio-isomère *m*

radioisotope *n* CHEM isotope radioactif *m*, radio-isotope *m*, PART PHYS, PHYS, RAD PHYS radio-isotope *m*; ~ **power generator** *n* SPACE *spacecraft* générateur radio-isotopique *m*

radiolarian: ~ **chert** *n* GEOL radiolarite *f*

radiolite *n* MINERAL radiolite *f*

radiolocation *n* MILIT *radar* radiolocalisation *f*, RAD PHYS radiogoniométrie *f*

radiology *n* RAD PHYS radiologie *f*

radioluminescence *n* RAD PHYS radioluminescence *f*

radiolysis *n* CHEM radiolyse *f*, RAD PHYS radioanalyse *f*, radiolyse *f*

radiomechanic *n* MILIT radiotechnicien *m*

radiometer *n* FUELLESS, GEOPHYS, PHYS radiomètre *m*

radiometric[1] *adj* GEOPHYS radiométrique

radiometric:[2] ~ **age determination** *n* GEOL datation radiométrique *f*; ~ **analysis** *n* RAD PHYS analyse radiométrique *f*; ~ **log** *n* PETR diagramme radiométrique *m*

radiometry *n* CHEM, GEOPHYS radiométrie *f*

radiomicrometer *n* MECH ENG radiomicromètre *m*

radiomimetic *adj* CHEM radiomimétique

radionuclide *n* PHYS, RAD PHYS radionucléide *m*

radio-opaque *adj* RAD PHYS radio-opaque

radiopaging: ~ **system** *n* TELECOM système radioélectrique d'appel *m*

radiophone[1] *n* TRANSP radiotéléphone *m*

radiophone[2] *vt* TRANSP radiotéléphoner

radiorecorder *n* RECORDING radiocassette *f*

radiosonde *n* GEOPHYS, TELECOM radiosonde *f*

radiostrontium *n* CHEM strontium radioactif *m*, RAD PHYS radiostrontium *m*

radiotelephone *n* CONST radiotéléphone *m*; ~ **link** *n* NAUT liaison radiotéléphone *f*

radiotherapy *n* RAD PHYS radiothérapie *f*

radiotoxicity *n* RAD PHYS radiotoxicité *f*

radium *n* (*Ra*) CHEM radium *m* (*Ra*); ~ **emanation** *n* RAD PHYS émanation du radium *f*

radius *n* CONST *of crane* portée *f*, GEOM rayon *m*, MECH ENG *under the head of bolts, screws* rayon d'arrondi sous la tête *m*, OPT, PHYS rayon *m*; ~ **arm** *n* VEHICLES *suspension* barre de force *f*, bielle de force *f*; ~ **of curvature** *n* GEOM rayon de courbure *m*; ~ **of gyration** *n* CONST, MECH ENG rayon de giration *m*

radix *n* COMP, DP base *f*, complément à la base *m*; ~ **complement** *n* COMP, DP complément à la base *m*; ~ **notation** *n* COMP, DP numération à base *f*

radix-minus-one: ~ **complement** *n* COMP, DP complément restreint *m*

radome *n* AERONAUT, NAUT *radar*, SPACE, TELECOM, TRANSP radome *m*

radon *n* (*Rn*) CHEM radon *m* (*Rn*)

raffinose *n* CHEM raffinose *m*

raft *n* COAL TECH radier *m*, NAUT train de bois *m*, *flat craft* radeau *m*

rafter *n* CONST chevron *m*

rag *n* PAPER TECH chiffon *m*; ~ **bolt** *n* CONST boulon de scellement à crans *m*; ~ **breaker** *n* PAPER TECH défileuse à chiffons *f*; ~ **cutter** *n* PAPER TECH couteau à délisser *m*; ~ **duster** *n* PAPER TECH batteur de chiffons *m*; ~ **paper** *n* PAPER TECH, PRINT papier de chiffons *m*; ~ **pulp** *n* PAPER TECH pâte de chiffon *f*; ~ **shredder** *n* PAPER TECH délisseuse *f*; ~ **sorter** *n* PAPER TECH trieuse de chiffons *f*; ~ **thrasher** *n* PAPER TECH batteur de chiffons *m*; ~ **wheel** *n* MECH ENG *sprocket wheel* bouc *m*, hérisson *m*, pignon de Galle *m*, pignon de chaîne *m*, poulie à chicane *f*, PROD ENG *calico mop* disque en drap *m*

ragged:[1] ~ **left** *adj* (BrE) (*cf rag-left*) PRINT *setting* au fer à droite, en drapeau à gauche; ~ **right** *adj* (BrE) (*cf rag-right*) PRINT *setting* au fer à gauche, en drapeau à droite

ragged:[2] ~ **fire** *n* MILIT *artillery* tir dispersé *m*; ~ **setting** *n* PRINT composition en drapeau *f*

ragging *n* MINING scheidage d'épuration *m*, scheidage préalable *m*, scheidage préliminaire *m*

rag-left *adj* (AmE) (*cf ragged left*) PRINT *setting* au fer à droite, en drapeau à gauche

rag-right *adj* (AmE) (*cf ragged right*) PRINT *setting* au fer à gauche, en drapeau à droite

RAI *abbr* (*remote alarm indication*) TELECOM indication d'alarme distante *f*

rail:[1] ~ **mounted** *adj* TRANSP sur rails

rail[2] *n* CONST *bar* barre *f*, barreau *m*, *carpentry* traverse *f*, *of fence or other structure* lierne *f*, *railing* garde-corps *m*, ELEC ENG pôle *m*, NAUT *ship building* lisse *f*, liston *m*, RAIL crémaillère *f*, rail *m*, TRANSP rail *m*; ~ **base** *n* RAIL patin de rail *m*; ~ **brake** *n* TRANSP frein de voie *m*; ~ **break** *n* TRANSP rupture des rails *f*; ~ **clip** *n* RAIL attache-rail *m*, crapaud *m*, *track* crapaud *m*; ~ **coach** *n* TRANSP autorail *m*; ~ **crane** *n* TRANSP grue sur voie ferrée *f*; ~ **crossover** *n* RAIL communication de voies *f*; ~ **ferry** *n* TRANSP train-ferry *m*; ~ **flange** *n* RAIL patin de rail *m*; ~ **foot** *n* RAIL patin de rail *m*; ~ **gage** *n* (AmE), ~ **gauge** *n* (BrE) RAIL gabarit d'écartement *m*, gabarit d'écartement de voie *m*, écartement de la voie *m*, écartement des rails *m pl*, TRANSP écartement des rails *m*; ~ **inspection** *n* RAIL auscultation des rails *f*; ~ **joint** *n* RAIL joint de rail *m*; ~ **junction** *n* RAIL embranchement *m*, jonction *f*, jonction de voies *f*, liaison *f*, liaison de voies *f*, *track* bifurcation de rails *f*; ~ **laying** *n* RAIL pose de rails *f*; ~ **lifter** *n* RAIL soulève-rails *m*; ~ **mill** *n* RAIL usine à rails *f*; ~ **motor car** *n* TRANSP motrice *f*; ~ **motor coach** *n* TRANSP rame automotrice *f*; ~ **motor tractor** *n* TRANSP locotracteur *m*; ~ **motor unit** *n* TRANSP élément automoteur *m*; ~ **profile** *n* RAIL *vehicles* profil du rail *m*; ~ **safety** *n* SAFETY sûreté des transports par voie ferrée *f*; ~ **section** *n* RAIL *vehicles* profil du rail *m*; ~ **shoulder** *n* RAIL congé de raccord de la table de roulement *m*; ~ **splice** *n* RAIL éclisse *f*; ~ **stress** *n* RAIL contrainte dans le rail *f*; ~ **tank car** *n* (AmE) *(cf rail tank wagon)* TRANSP wagon citerne *m*; ~ **tank wagon** *n* (BrE) *(cf rail tank car)* TRANSP wagon citerne *m*; ~ **tongs** *n* RAIL pince à rails *f*, tenaille à rails *f*; ~ **track** *n* MINING voie ferrée *f*; ~ **transport** *n* TRANSP transport par voie ferrée *m*; ~ **transport of road trailers** *n* TRANSP ferroutage *m*; ~ **vehicle** *n* TRANSP véhicule sur rails *m*; ~ **wear tolerance** *n* RAIL tolérance d'usure *f*; ~ **web** *n* RAIL âme de rail *f*; ~ **wheel** *n* MECH ENG *of runner of overhead travelling crane* galet de roulement *m*, roue de translation *f*

railbed *n* RAIL assiette de rails *f*

rail-bending: ~ **device** *n* RAIL appareil à cintrer les rails *m*, cintreuse *f*; ~ **machine** *n* RAIL appareil à cintrer les rails *m*, cintreuse *f*

railbond *n* RAIL connexion de rail *f*, connexion longitudinale de rail *f*, éclisse électrique *f*

railbus *n* TRANSP autobus guidé *m*

railcar *n* RAIL *vehicles* automotrice diesel *f*, TRANSP rame automotrice *f*

rail-carrying: ~ **car** *n* (AmE) *(cf rail-carrying wagon)* RAIL wagon porte-rails *m*; ~ **wagon** *n* (BrE) *(cf rail-carrying car)* RAIL wagon porte-rails *m*

rail-cutting: ~ **machine** *n* RAIL coupeuse de rails *f*

rail-drilling: ~ **machine** *n* RAIL perceuse de rails *f*

rail-grinding: ~ **train** *n* RAIL *vehicles* train de meulage des rails *m*

railhead *n* CONST tête de ligne ferroviaire *f*, RAIL gare centre *f*, *vehicles* champignon du rail *m*

railing *n* CONST barreau de grille *m*, garde-corps *m*, garde-fou *m*, grille *f*, rampe *f*

rail-planing: ~ **machine** *n* RAIL machine à raboter *f*, raboteuse de rails *f*

railroad *n* (AmE) *(cf railway)* TRANSP chemin de fer *m*, rail-route *m*; ~ **arch** *n* (AmE) *(cf railway arch)* CONST arche de pont ferroviaire *f*; ~ **bridge** *n* (AmE) *(cf railway bridge)* CONST pont ferroviaire *m*, TRANSP pont-rail *m*; ~ **carriage** *n* (AmE) *(cf railway carriage)* TRANSP voiture à voyageurs *f*; ~ **center** *n* (AmE) *(cf railway centre)* RAIL noeud ferroviaire *m*; ~ **container** *n* (AmE) *(cf railway container)* TRANSP conteneur ferroviaire *m*; ~ **cutting** *n* (AmE) *(cf railway cutting)* RAIL *fixed works* chemin en déblai *m*, déblai *m*, tranchée *f*; ~ **depot** *n* (AmE) *(cf station)* TRANSP station *f*; ~ **embankment** *n* (AmE) *(cf railway embankment)* RAIL *fixed works* remblai *m*, voie en remblai *f*; ~ **freight car** *n* (AmE) *(cf railway freight coach)* TRANSP wagon à marchandises *m*; ~ **freight terminal** *n* (AmE) *(cf railway freight terminal)* TRANSP gare kangourou *f*; ~ **gate** *n* (AmE) *(cf railway gate)* TRANSP barrière *f*; ~ **inspection trolley** *n* (AmE) *(cf railway inspection trolley)* CONST draisine *f*; ~ **junction** *n* (AmE) *(cf railway junction)* RAIL communication *f*, communication de voies *f*, TRANSP noeud ferroviaire *m*; ~ **line** *n* (AmE) *(cf railway line)* TRANSP section de chemin de fer *f*, voie ferrée *f*; ~ **map** *n* (AmE) *(cf railway map)* RAIL, TRANSP plan du réseau ferroviaire *m*; ~ **material** *n* (AmE) *(cf railway material)* TRANSP matériel ferroviaire *m*; ~ **network** *n* (AmE) *(cf railway network)* TRANSP réseau ferroviaire *m*; ~ **operation** *n* (AmE) *(cf railway operation)* TRANSP exploitation d'un chemin de fer *f*; ~ **overbridge** *n* (AmE) *(cf railway overbridge)* TRANSP passage supérieur *m*; ~ **regulations** *n* (AmE) *(cf railway regulations)* RAIL règlements de chemin de fer *m pl*; ~ **semitrailer** *n* (AmE) *(cf railway semitrailer)*

TRANSP semi-remorque rail-route *f*; ~ **station** *n* (AmE) *(cf railway station)* TRANSP gare *f*; ~ **stock** *n* (AmE) *(cf railway stock)* TRANSP matériel ferroviaire *m*; ~ **terminus** *n* (AmE) *(cf railway terminus)* TRANSP gare tête de ligne *f*; ~ **tie-adzing machine** *n* (AmE) *(cf railway tie-adzing machine)* RAIL saboteuse de traverses *f*; ~ **tie screw** *n* (AmE) *(cf railway sleeper screw)* RAIL tirefond *m*; ~ **tie screwdriver** *n* (AmE) *(cf railway sleeper screwdriver)* RAIL tirefonneuse *f*; ~ **track** *n* (AmE) *(cf railway track)* TRANSP voie ferrée *f*; ~ **transport** *n* (AmE) *(cf railway transport)* TRANSP ferroutage *m*, transport par voie ferrée *m*; ~ **tunnel** *n* (AmE) *(cf railway tunnel)* CONST tunnel ferroviaire *m*; ~ **underbridge** *n* (AmE) *(cf railway underbridge)* TRANSP passage inférieur *m*; ~ **vehicles** *n pl* (AmE) *(cf railway vehicles)* TRANSP matériel roulant *m*

railway *n* (BrE) *(cf railroad)* TRANSP chemin de fer *m*, rail-route *m*; ~ **arch** *n* (BrE) *(cf railroad arch)* CONST arche de pont ferroviaire *f*; ~ **bridge** *n* (BrE) *(cf railroad bridge)* CONST pont ferroviaire *m*, TRANSP pont-rail *m*; ~ **carriage** *n* (BrE) *(cf railroad carriage)* TRANSP voiture à voyageurs *f*; ~ **centre** *n* (BrE) *(cf railroad center)* RAIL noeud ferroviaire *m*; ~ **container** *n* (BrE) *(cf railroad container)* TRANSP conteneur ferroviaire *m*; ~ **cutting** *n* (BrE) *(cf railroad cutting)* RAIL *fixed works* chemin en déblai *m*, déblai *m*, tranchée *f*; ~ **embankment** *n* (BrE) *(cf railroad embankment)* RAIL *fixed works* remblai *m*, voie en remblai *f*; ~ **freight coach** *n* (BrE) *(cf railroad freight car)* TRANSP wagon à marchandises *m*; ~ **freight terminal** *n* (BrE) *(cf railroad freight terminal)* TRANSP gare kangourou *f*; ~ **gate** *n* (BrE) *(cf railroad gate)* TRANSP barrière *f*; ~ **inspection trolley** *n* (BrE) *(cf railroad inspection trolley)* CONST draisine *f*; ~ **junction** *n* (BrE) *(cf railroad junction)* RAIL communication *f*, communication de voies *f*, TRANSP noeud ferroviaire *m*; ~ **line** *n* (BrE) *(cf railroad line)* TRANSP section de chemin de fer *f*, voie ferrée *f*; ~ **map** *n* (BrE) *(cf railroad map)* RAIL, TRANSP plan du réseau ferroviaire *m*; ~ **material** *n* (BrE) *(cf railroad material)* TRANSP matériel ferroviaire *m*; ~ **network** *n* (BrE) *(cf railroad network)* TRANSP réseau ferroviaire *m*; ~ **operation** *n* (BrE) *(cf railroad operation)* TRANSP exploitation d'un chemin de fer *f*; ~ **overbridge** *n* (BrE) *(cf railroad overbridge)* TRANSP passage supérieur *m*; ~ **regulations** *n* (BrE) *(cf railroad regulations)* RAIL règlements de chemin de fer *m pl*; ~ **semitrailer** *n* (BrE) *(cf railroad semitrailer)* TRANSP semi-remorque rail-route *f*; ~ **sleeper screw** *n* (BrE) *(cf railroad tie screw)* RAIL tirefond *m*; ~ **sleeper screwdriver** *n* (BrE) *(cf railroad tie screwdriver)* RAIL tirefonneuse *f*; ~ **station** *n* (BrE) *(cf railroad station)* TRANSP gare *f*; ~ **stock** *n* (BrE) *(cf railroad stock)* TRANSP matériel ferroviaire *m*; ~ **terminus** *n* (BrE) *(cf railroad terminus)* TRANSP gare tête de ligne *f*; ~ **tie-adzing machine** *n* (BrE) *(cf railroad tie-adzing machine)* RAIL saboteuse de traverses *f*; ~ **track** *n* (BrE) *(cf railroad track)* TRANSP voie ferrée *f*; ~ **transport** *n* (BrE) *(cf railroad transport)* TRANSP ferroutage *m*, transport par voie ferrée *m*; ~ **tunnel** *n* (BrE) *(cf railroad tunnel)* CONST tunnel ferroviaire *m*; ~ **underbridge** *n* (BrE) *(cf railroad underbridge)* TRANSP passage inférieur *m*; ~ **vehicles** *n pl* (BrE) *(cf railroad vehicles)* TRANSP matériel roulant *m*

rain: ~ **area** *n* WATER SUPP impluvium *m*; ~ **attenuation** *n* SPACE *communications* atténuation par la pluie *f*; ~ **clutter** *n* NAUT *radar* retour de pluie *m*; ~ **erosion** *n*

METEO érosion par la pluie *f*, érosion pluviale *f*; **~ gage** *n* (AmE), **~ gauge** *n* (BrE) CONST, FUELLESS, LAB EQUIP, METEO, WATER SUPP pluviomètre *m*; **~ scatter** *n* SPACE *communications* diffusion par la pluie *f*

rain-eroded *adj* METEO érodé par la pluie

rainfall *n* METEO précipitations *f pl*; **~ area** *n* WATER SUPP aire de pluie *f*; **~ intensity** *n* METEO intensité de la pluie *f*

rain-free: **~ period** *n* POLLUTION période sèche *f*

rainout *n* POLLUTION lavage *m*, piégeage *m*

rainwater *n* METEO eau de précipitation *f*, eau précipitée *f*; **~ catchment** *n* WATER SUPP recueil des eaux de pluie *m*; **~ downpipe** *n* (BrE) *(cf rainwater downspout)* CONST descente d'eau *f*, tuyau de descente *m*, tuyau de descente des eaux pluviales *m*; **~ downspout** *n* (AmE) CONST tuyau de descente *m*, descente d'eau *f*, tuyau de descente des eaux pluviales *m*; **~ head** *n* CONST coffre de gouttière *m*, cuvette de gouttière *f*, hotte *f*; **~ pipe** *n* CONST descente fluviale *f*; **~ reservoir** *n* HYDROL réservoir des eaux pluviales *m*

rainy: **~ season** *n* METEO hivernage *m*, saison des pluies *f*

raise¹ *n* MINING montage *m*; **~ stope** *n* MINING chantier en remonte *m*, taille montante *f*

raise² *vt* MINING remonter, TEXTILES charder; **~ to a power** *vt* MATH élever à une puissance

raise:³ **~ ore** *vi* MINING remonter le minerai au jour; **~ steam** *vi* PROD ENG produire de la vapeur

raised: **~ beach** *n* GEOPHYS plage en terrasse *f*; **~ countersunk rivet** *n* MECH ENG rivet à tête fraisée et goutte de suif *m*; **~ deck** *n* NAUT *ship* pont surélevé *m*; **~ edge** *n* TEXTILES pliure *f*; **~ head** *n* MECH ENG rivure saillante *f*, *of rivet* tête saillante *f*; **~ head screw** *n* MECH ENG vis à tête en goutte-de-suif *f*, vis à tête saillante *f*; **~ loop** *n* SPRINGS anneau relevé *m*

raised-roof: **~ van** *n* VEHICLES fourgon surélevé *m*

raising *n* CONST *stones by crane* montage *m*, *wall* exhaussement *m*, rehaussement *m*, relèvement *m*, surhaussement *m*, élévation *f*, élèvement *m*, MINING extraction *f*, hissage *m*, remonte *f*, remontée *f*, élévation *f*, remontage *m*, TEXTILES chardage *m*; **~ agent** *n* FOOD TECH *baking* levure *f*, poudre à lever *f*; **~ of the bed level** *n* HYDROL *river* exhaussement *m*; **~ machine** *n* TEXTILES machine à gratter *f*; **~ power** *n* FOOD TECH *baking and fermentation* levée *f*, pousse *f*, pousse des pâtons *f*; **~ steam** *n* PROD ENG production de la vapeur *f*; **~ table** *n* MECH ENG *machine tool* table ascendante *f*

rake *n* ACOUSTICS *of stylus* inclinaison longitudinale *f*, CINEMAT inclinaison *f*, pente *f*, CONST *implement* râteau *m*, NAUT *of mast* inclinaison *f*, quête *f*, PROD ENG crochet à feu *m*, ringard à crochet *m*, roable *m*, roatle *m*, râble *m*, tire-braise *m*; **~ of hutches** *n* MINING convoi de wagons *m*, rame de wagons *f*, train de wagons *m*

raker *n* CONST arc-boutant *m*, contrefiche *f*, étai incliné *m*

raking: **~ fire** *n* MILIT tir en enfilade *m*; **~ shore** *n* CONST arc-boutant *m*, contrefiche *f*, étai incliné *m*; **~ stem** *n* NAUT *shipbuilding* étrave élancée *f*

ralstonite *n* MINERAL ralstonite *f*

ram¹ *n* COAL TECH pilon *m*, CONST bélier *m*, sonnette *f*, vérin *m*, *of clay* bourre *f*, *of pile driver* mouton *m*, *of power hammer* mouton *m*, pilon *m*, MECH vérin *m*, MECH ENG *of shaper* chariot porte-outil *m*, trompette *f*, *plunger* piston *m*, piston plein *m*, piston plongeur *m*, plongeur *m*, NAUT *hydraulics, collision* bélier hydraulique *m*, P&R *press* piston plongeur *m*, PHYS *impact test* mouton *m*; **~ air** *n* MECH ENG air forcé *m*, REFRIG air

dynamique *m*; **~ bow** *n* TRANSP bulbe d'étrave *m*; **~ drag** *n* TRANSP traînée de captation *f*, traînée de prise d'air *f*; **~ effect** *n* AERONAUT *aerodynamics* effet de pression dynamique *m*; **~ penetration test** *n* COAL TECH sondage au pilon *m*; **~ pump** *n* HYDR EQUIP *hydraulic ram* bélier hydraulique *m*, WATER SUPP *force pump* pompe foulante *f*, pompe refoulante *f*, pompe à piston plongeur *f*, pompe à plongeur *f*; **~ recovery** *n* AERONAUT effet de manche *m*, récupération d'air dynamique *f*

ram² *vt* CONST *to drive or tamp* damer, pilonner, MINING bourrer, NAUT *hydraulics, collision* aborder, entrer en collision avec, PROD ENG *founding* battre, fouler, *to compact by pounding* bourrer; **~ home a charge** *vt* MINING bourrer une charge de mine

RAM *abbr (random access memory)* COMP, DP, ELECTRON MEV *(mémoire vive)*

Raman: **~ effect** *n* PHYS, RAD PHYS effet Raman *m*; **~ scattering** *n* PHYS, RAD PHYS diffusion Raman *f*; **~ spectroscopy** *n* PHYS, RAD PHYS spectroscopie Raman *f*

ramark *n* TRANSP *radar* balise ramark *f*, balise émettrice radar *f*

Rameau-Bach: **~ scale** *n* ACOUSTICS gamme de Rameau-Bach *f*

ramjet *n* AERONAUT statoréacteur *m*; **~ engine** *n* AERONAUT, THERMOD, TRANSP statoréacteur *m*

rammed: **~ area** *n* NUCLEAR *for storage* aire damée *f*

rammer *n* CONST *for hammering paving slabs* hie *f*, *paviors' beetle* dame *f*, demoiselle *f*, hie *f*, pilon *m*, *ramming* bourroir *m*, pilon *m*, MILIT *artillery* refouloir *m*, PROD ENG batte *f*, batte de mouleur *f*, fouloir *m*

ramming *n* CONST *tamping*, MINING bourrage *m*, PROD ENG *founding* battage *m*, foulement *m*; **~ bar** *n* MINING bourroir *m*

ramp¹ *n* AERONAUT, ELEC ENG, GEOPHYS, MINING, PAPER TECH, PETR rampe *f*; **~ change of load** *n* NUCLEAR rampe de charge *f*; **~ closure sign** *n* TRANSP signal de fermeture de rampe *m*; **~ generator** *n* ELEC ENG générateur de rampe *m*; **~ metering** *n* TRANSP comptage des accès *m*; **~ services** *n pl* AERONAUT entretien de rampe *m*, servitudes rampe *f pl*; **~ status** *n* AERONAUT situation à la rampe *f*; **~ voltage** *n* ELEC ENG tension en dents de scie *f*; **~ waveform** *n* ELEC ENG signal en dents de scie *m*; **~ weight** *n* AERONAUT masse au parking *f*, masse au stationnement *f*

ramp² *vt* ELEC ENG intégrer

rampant *adj* CONST *architecture* rampant

ramp-to-ramp: **~ time** *n* AERONAUT temps bloc *m*

Ramsden: **~ eyepiece** *n* PHYS oculaire de Ramsden *m*

Ramsden's: **~ chain** *n* CONST chaîne de Ramsden *f*

Rand: **~ tablet** *n* COMP, DP tablette Rand *f*

random¹ *adj* CHEM *copolymer* aléatoire, sans ordre, METR au hasard, par hasard

random:² **~ access** *n* COMP, DP accès aléatoire *m*, accès direct *m*, accès instantané *m*, accès sélectif *m*, PRINT *composing frame*, SPACE *communications* accès aléatoire *m*; **~ access device** *n* COMP dispositif à accès sélectif *m*, DP dispositif à accès direct *m*; **~ access file** *n* COMP, DP fichier à accès direct *m*; **~ access memory** *n* *(RAM)* COMP, DP, ELECTRON mémoire vive *f (MEV)*, mémoire à accès aléatoire *f*, mémoire à accès sélectif *f*; **~ arrangement** *n* METALL arrangement au hasard *m*; **~ distribution** *n* METALL distribution au hasard *f*; **~ error** *n* COAL TECH, METR, PHYS, TELECOM erreur aléatoire *f*; **~ event** *n* ELECTRON événement aléatoire *m*; **~ excita-**

tion *n* TELECOM excitation aléatoire *f*; ~ **failure** *n* ELEC ENG défaillance accidentelle *f*; ~ **field** *n* TELECOM champ aléatoire *m*; ~ **file** *n* COMP, DP fichier à accès sélectif *m*; ~ **loading** *n* METALL sollicitation au hasard *f*; ~ **logic** *n* ELECTRON logique programmable *f*; ~ **logic chip** *n* ELECTRON puce logique programmable *f*; ~ **multiple access** *n* TELECOM accès multiple aléatoire *m*; ~ **noise** *n* ELECTRON bruit aléatoire *m*, GEOPHYS aléatoire complexe *f*, bruit inorganisé *m*, PHYS bruit aléatoire *m*, RECORDING bruit diffus *m*, SPACE, TELECOM bruit aléatoire *m*; ~ **noise generator** *n* ELECTRON générateur de bruit aléatoire *m*, RECORDING générateur de bruit diffus *m*; ~ **noise signal** *n* ELECTRON signal de bruit aléatoire *m*; ~ **noise source** *n* ELECTRON source de bruit aléatoire *f*; ~ **number** *n* COMP, DP, MATH nombre aléatoire *m*; ~ **number generation** *n* TELECOM génération de nombres aléatoires *f*; ~ **number generator** *n* COMP, DP générateur de nombres aléatoires *m*; ~ **phase error** *n* TV erreur de phase aléatoire *f*; ~ **pulse** *n* ELECTRON, TELECOM impulsion aléatoire *f*; ~ **sample** *n* COAL TECH, FOOD TECH *food-processing machinery* échantillon au hasard *m*, MATH échantillon tiré au hasard *m*; ~ **sample reading** *n* PRINT lecture densitométrique d'une zone de document au hasard *f*; ~ **sampling** *n* COAL TECH échantillonnage au hasard *m*, TELECOM échantillonnage aléatoire *m*, TESTING échantillonnage au hasard *m*; ~ **scan** *n* COMP balayage cavalier *m*, balayage omnidirectionnel *m*; ~ **scan device** *n* COMP dispositif à balayage omnidirectionnel *m*, DP dispositif à balayage cavalier *m*; ~ **scattering** *n* NUCLEAR diffusion aléatoire *f*; ~ **signal** *n* ELECTRON signal aléatoire *m*, NAUT *radar* écho aléatoire *m*, TELECOM signal aléatoire *m*; ~ **solution** *n* METALL solution désordonnée *f*; ~ **thermal motion** *n* RAD PHYS *of emitting atoms* mouvement thermique au hasard *m*; ~ **variable** *n* COMP, DP, ELECTRON, MATH variable aléatoire *f*; ~ **voltage** *n* ELEC ENG tension de bruit *f*; ~ **walk** *n* COMP, DP cheminement aléatoire *m*; ~ **winding** *n* ELEC *small AC machines* enroulement en vrac *m*, enroulement à fils jetés *m*, ELEC ENG enroulement à spires non jointives *m*

range[1] *n* AERONAUT *aircraft performance* distance franchissable *f*, *of aircraft* rayon d'action *m*, COMP, DP gamme *f*, ELECTRON distance *f*, *of emitter* portée *f*, *of frequencies* gamme *f*, GAS TECH palette *f*, MILIT distance *f*, portée *f*, *of projectile* portée *f*, NAUT *of cable, navigation, tide, electron equipment* bitture *f*, distance *f*, marnage *m*, portée *f*, PHYS portée *f*, SPACE base de lancement *f*, portée *f*, rayon d'action *m*, TELECOM portée *f*, TEXTILES ligne de produits *f*, TV gamme *f*, portée *f*; ~ **of action per charge** *n* TRANSP rayon d'autonomie par charge *m*; ~ **adjustment** *n* PROD ENG réglage des plages *m*; ~ **of audibility** *n* RECORDING étendue de sensibilité auditive *f*; ~ **card** *n* MILIT *artillery* planchette de tir *f*; ~ **collision** *n* NUCLEAR *between particles* choc lointain *m*, collision lointaine *f*; ~ **dial** *n* MILIT *artillery* échelle de distances *f*; ~ **finding** *n* ELECTRON télémétrie *f*, SPACE mesure de distance *f*, télémétrie *f*; ~ **of half life** *n* RAD PHYS gamme de la demi-vie *f*; ~ **indicator** *n* VEHICLES *automatic gearbox controls* grille *f*; ~ **of movement** *n* NUCLEAR *of control rod* domaine de mouvement *m*; ~ **of points** *n* GEOM écarts *m pl*; ~ **pole** *n* CONST *surveying* jalon *m*; ~ **resolution** *n* SPACE limite de résolution en portée *f*; ~ **of speeds** *n* MECH ENG gamme de vitesses *f*; ~ **switch** *n* ELEC commutateur des zones de mesure *m*, commuta-

teur du champ de mesure *m*; ~ **table** *n* MILIT table de tir *f*; ~ **of transducers** *n* MECH ENG gamme de capteurs *f*; ~ **of vision** *n* MILIT portée visuelle *f*

range[2] *vt* MILIT *gun* pointer; ~ **from** *vt* TELECOM aller de

range[3] *vi* MILIT régler le tir

rangefinder *n* CINEMAT, ELECTRON, MILIT, NAUT, PHOTO télémètre *m*; ~ **window** *n* PHOTO fenêtre de télémètre *f*

ranging *n* SPACE mesure de distance *f*; ~ **fire** *n* MILIT *artillery* tir de réglage *m*; ~ **magnifier** *n* INSTRUMENT loupe de visée *f*; ~ **pole** *n* CONST *surveying* jalon *m*; ~ **rod** *n* CONST *surveying* jalon *m*

rank *n* MATH rang *m*

Rankine: ~ **cycle** *n* HEATING *thermodynamics*, THERMOD cycle de Clausius-Rankine *m*; ~ **cycle engine** *n* TRANSP moteur à circuit Rankine *m*

rap *vt* PROD ENG *founding* ballotter, ébranler

rapeseed: ~ **oil** *vt* FOOD TECH huile de colza *f*

rapid *n* HYDROL rapide *m*; ~ **air cooling** *n* THERMOD refroidissement par air forcé *m*; ~ **annealing** *n* C&G recuit rapide *m*; ~ **automatic transport** *n* TRANSP transport automatique rapide *m*; ~ **change tool holder** *n* MECH ENG porte-outil à serrage rapide *m*; ~ **chill** *n* REFRIG réfrigération rapide *f*; ~ **cooling** *n* THERMOD refroidissement rapide *m*, réfrigération rapide *f*; ~ **exit taxiway** *n* AERONAUT *airport* voie de sortie rapide *f*; ~ **fatigue test** *n* METALL essai rapide de fatigue *m*; ~ **film-advance lever** *n* PHOTO levier-gachette *m*; ~ **filter plant** *n* HYDROL station de filtration rapide *f*; ~ **fire** *n* MILIT tir d'emblée *m*; ~ **fire gun** *n* MILIT *artillery* canon à tir rapide *m*; ~ **heat-up cathode** *n* TV cathode à chauffage direct *f*; ~ **loading system** *n* PHOTO système de chargement rapide *m*; ~ **response** *n* CONTROL réponse rapide *f*; ~ **transit railroad** *n* (AmE) *(cf rapid transit railway)* TRANSP métro urbain et régional *m*; ~ **transit railway** *n* (BrE) *(cf rapid transit railroad)* TRANSP métro urbain et régional *m*; ~ **transit system** *n* *(RTS)* RAIL système de transport rapide *m*

rapid-hardening: ~ **cement** *n* CONST ciment à durcissement rapide *m*, ciment à prise rapide *m*

rapping *n* POLLUTION *of electrodes* frappage *m*, PROD ENG *founding* ballottement *m*, ébranlage *m*

rare[1] *adj* CHEM *gas* rare

rare:[2] ~ **earth glass** *n* C&G verre aux terres rares *m*; ~ **earths** *n pl* CHEM *gas* aux terres rares *m*; ~ **gas tube** *n* ELECTRON tube à gaz inerte *m*

rarefaction *n* PHYS, WAVE PHYS raréfaction *f*

Raschel: ~ **knitting machine** *n* TEXTILES métier Raschel *m*

rasp *n* CONST râpe *f*; ~ **cut** *n* CONST taille en râpe *f*

rasping *n* CONST râpage *m*

raster *n* COMP, DP grille *f*, trame *f*, ELECTRON trame de balayage *f*, PRINT *data processing* quadrillage de l'écran cathodique *m*, PROD ENG trame *f*, TV plage balayée *f*, quadrillage *m*, réseau *m*, trame *f*; ~ **display** *n* COMP image ligne par ligne *f*, DP affichage récurrent *m*, affichage tramé *m*; ~ **generator** *n* TV générateur de trame *m*; ~ **graphics** *n pl* COMP, DP graphique tramé *m*; ~ **pitch** *n* TV espacement des lignes *m*; ~ **scan cathode ray tube** *n* ELECTRON tube cathodique à balayage récurrent *m*; ~ **scan device** *n* COMP, DP dispositif à balayage récurrent *m*; ~ **scan electron beam lithography** *n* ELECTRON gravure par faisceau d'électrons à balayage tramé *f*, gravure à balayage tramé *f*; ~ **scanned beam** *n* ELECTRON faisceau à balayage tramé *m*; ~ **scanning** *n* COMP, DP balayage ligne à ligne *m*, balayage récurrent *m*, balayage télévision *m*, ELECTRON balayage ligne à ligne *m*, balayage tramé *m*, balayage télévision *m*, TV balayage ligne à ligne *m*, balayage télévision *m*

rat: ~ **hole** *n* PETR, PETR TECH trou de rat *m*

ratch[1] *n* MECH ENG roue à chien *f*, roue à cliquet *f*, roue à rochet *f*

ratch[2] *vt* MECH ENG *cut gear teeth on* créneler, denter, endenter, *turn round by a ratchet and pawl* encliqueter

ratchet *n* CONST *carpenter's* vilebrequin à cliquet *m*, MECH ENG cliquet *m*, MECH ENG encliquetage *m*, roue à chien *f*, roue à cliquet *f*, roueà rochet *f*, *engineer's* cliquet *m*, cliquetà canon *m*, raccagnac *m*, *pawl, click, detent* chien *m*, doigt d'encliquetage *m*; ~ **brace** *n* CONST *carpenter's* vilebrequin à cliquet *m*, MECH ENG *engineer's* cliquet *m*, cliquet à canon *m*, raccagnac *m*; ~ **flare nut wrench** *n* MECH ENG *tool* clé à tuyauterie à cliquet *f*; ~ **lever** *n* MECH ENG levier à cliquet *m*; ~ **motion** *n* MECH ENG encliquetage *m*; ~ **screwing stock** *n* MECH ENG filière à cliquet *f*; ~ **spanner** *n* (BrE) *(cf ratchet wrench)* MECH ENG cliquet *m*, cliquet simple *m*, clé à cliquet *f*, clé à rochet *f*; ~ **stop** *n* MECH ENG *of micrometer* bouton à friction *m*, tête à friction *f*; ~ **wheel** *n* MECH ENG roue à chien *f*, roue à cliquet *f*, roue à rochet *f*; ~ **wrench** *n* (AmE) *(cf ratchet spanner)* MECH ENG cliquet *m*, cliquet simple *m*, clé à cliquet *f*, clé à rochet *f*

ratchet-and-pawl: ~ **motion** *n* MECH ENG encliquetage à rochet *m*

ratchetting *n* NUCLEAR *of fuel elements due to thermal cycling* rochetage *m*

rate *n* COMP, DP débit *m*, METR taux *m*, SPRINGS raideur *f*, rigidité *f*; ~ **of absorption** *n* WATER SUPP vitesse d'absorption *f*; ~ **of air change** *n* HEATING taux de changement d'air *m*; ~ **of climb** *n* AERONAUT taux de montée *m*, vitesse ascensionnelle *f*, vitesse de montée *f*, SPACE *(RC)* vitesse ascensionnelle *f*; ~ **of combustion** *n* THERMOD vitesse de combustion *f*; ~ **constant** *n* METALL constante de vitesse *f*; ~ **control** *n* CONTROL contrôle du débit *m*; ~ **of cooling** *n* REFRIG, THERMOD vitesse de refroidissement *f*; ~ **of cure** *n* P&R vitesse de durcissement *f*, *rubber, vulcanization* vitesse de vulcanisation *f*; ~ **of curing** *n* CONST taux de cure *m*, vitesse de maturation *f*; ~ **of current rise** *n* ELEC ENG vitesse d'accroissement du courant *f*; ~ **of descent** *n* AERONAUT vitesse descensionnelle *f*, vitesse verticale de descente *f*; ~ **of drying** *n* THERMOD vitesse de séchage *f*; ~ **of evaporation** *n* COATINGS degré d'évaporation *m*; ~ **of fire** *n* MILIT cadence de tir *f*; ~ **of flow** *n* P&R vitesse de fluage *f*, PHYS, REFRIG, WATER SUPP débit *m*; ~ **gyro** *n* PHYS gyromètre *m*; ~ **of heating** *n* THERMOD vitesse de réchauffement *f*; ~ **of heat release** *n* THERMOD débit calorifique *m*; ~ **of heat transfer** *n* HEATING taux de transfert de chaleur *m*; ~ **of loading** *n* METALL vitesse de montée de la charge *f*; ~ **one half convolutional coding** *n* TELECOM codage par convolution à débit moitié *m*; ~ **of penetration** *n* *(ROP)* PETR TECH taux de pénétration *m*, vitesse d'avancement *f*; ~ **of progress** *n* CONST taux d'avancement *m*; ~ **of rise** *n* ELEC ENG vitesse de montée *f*; ~ **of rise detector** *n* THERMOD détecteur thermovélocimétrique *m*; ~ **of sailing** *n* NAUT allure *f*; ~ **of shear** *n* P&R vitesse de cisaillement *f*; ~ **of spread** *n* CONST taux d'application *m*, THERMOD *of flame* vitesse de propagation *f*; ~ **of travel** *n* NUCLEAR *of control rod* vitesse de déplacement *f*; ~ **of turn** *n* AERONAUT cadence *f*, taux de virage *m*, vitesse angulaire de virage *f*, vitesse de virage *f*; ~ **of voltage**

rise *n* ELEC ENG vitesse d'accroissement de la tension *f*

rated: ~ **altitude** *n* AERONAUT altitude nominale *f*; ~ **capacity** *n* COAL TECH, WATER SUPP capacité nominale *f*; ~ **conditions** *n pl* ELEC ENG conditions nominales *f pl*; ~ **current** *n* ELEC courant assigné *m*, courant nominal *m*, ELEC ENG intensité nominale *f*; ~ **frequency** *n* ELEC fréquence assignée *f*, fréquence nominale *f*; ~ **insulation level** *n* ELEC *test voltages* niveau d'isolement assigné *m*, niveau d'isolement nominal *m*; ~ **insulation voltage** *n* ELEC, PROD ENG tension d'isolement nominale *f*; ~ **load** *n* ELEC ENG charge nominale *f*; ~ **operational current** *n* PROD ENG courant nominal d'emploi *m*; ~ **output** *n* COMP, DP sortie nominale *f*; ~ **power** *n* ELEC puissance assignée *f*, puissance nominale *f*; ~ **power capacity** *n* NUCLEAR *of reactor* puissance nominale *f*; ~ **range** *n* NUCLEAR *of measuring instrument* domaine nominal *m*; ~ **sensing distance** *n* PROD ENG distance nominale de détection *f*; ~ **short-time current** *n* ELEC courant de courte durée assigné *m*, courant de courte durée nominal *m*; ~ **step voltage** *n* ELEC *transformer* tension d'échelon assignée *f*, tension d'échelon nominale *f*; ~ **stop** *n* PROD ENG arrêt par rampe *m*; ~ **thermal current** *n* PROD ENG courant thermique nominal *m*; ~ **through-current** *n* ELEC *tap changer* courant traversant assigné *m*, courant traversant nominale *m*; ~ **value** *n* ELEC *appliance* valeur assignée *f*, valeur nominale *f*; ~ **voltage** *n* ELEC tension assignée *f*, tension nominale *f*, ELEC ENG tension nominale *f*, PROD ENG plage de tension *f*; ~ **voltage ratio** *n* ELEC *transformer* rapport de transformation assigné *m*, rapport de transformation nominal *m*; ~ **voltage of a winding** *n* ELEC tension assignée d'un enroulement *f*; ~ **welding current** *n* CONST courant de soudage nominal *m*; ~ **wind speed** *n* FUELLESS vitesse nominale du vent *f*

rate-of-climb: ~ **indicator** *n* AERONAUT indicateur de vitesse ascensionnelle *m*, variomètre *m*

ratile *n* CHEM ratile *f*, titane oxydé *m*

rating *n* ELEC *appliance* valeur assignée *f*, valeur nominale *f*, ELEC ENG caractéristique *f*, MECH tarage *m*, valeur nominale *f*, PHYS calibre *m*, classement *m*, pouvoir *m*, régime caractéristique *m*, PROD ENG *of relay contacts* puissance de coupure *f*, TV indice de popularité *m*, taux d'audience *m*, taux d'écoute *m*; ~ **pressure** *n* HYDR EQUIP *hydraulics* pression d'étalonnage *f*

ratio *n* MATH proportion *f*, raison *f*, rapport *m*, PHYS rapport *m*, *of specific heats* rapport des chaleurs massiques *m*, REFRIG taux *m*; ~ **arm** *n* ELEC *bridge* résistance proportionnée *f*

ratioed: ~ **capacitors** *n pl* ELEC ENG condensateurs à rapport de capacité *m pl*

rational: ~ **fishery management** *n* OCEANOG gestion rationnelle des stocks *f*; ~ **fish-stock management** *n* OCEANOG gestion rationnelle des stocks *f*; ~ **mechanics** *n pl* MECH ENG mécanique rationnelle *f*; ~ **number** *n* DP, MATH nombre rationnel *m*

rat-tail: ~ **file** *n* MECH ENG lime queue-de-rat *f*, queue-de-rat *f*, lime queue-de-rat ovale *f*

rattle *vt* PROD ENG *founding* dessabler au tonneau

rattler *n* PROD ENG tambour dessableur *m*, tonneau dessableur *m*, tonneau à dessabler *m*

rattling *n* PROD ENG ballottement *m*, claquement *m*, *founding* dessablage au tonneau *m*; ~ **barrel** *n* PROD ENG tambour dessableur *m*, tonneau dessableur *m*, tonneau à dessabler *m*

RAU *abbr (remote acquisition unit)* CONTROL unité d'acquisition décentralisée *f*

raw[1] *adj* COAL TECH, HYDROL *water* brut, PROP MAT cru

raw:[2] ~ **coal** *n* COAL TECH charbon brut *m*; ~ **coal bunker** *n* MINING trémie à tout-venant *f*; ~ **coal screen** *n* COAL TECH crible à tout-venant *m*; ~ **data** *n pl* COMP, DP données brutes *f pl*, ELECTRON données brutes *f pl*, informations brutes *f pl*; ~ **film** *n* CINEMAT pellicule vierge *f*; ~ **gas** *n* GAS TECH gaz brut *m*; ~ **magnetic tape** *n* TV bande magnétique vierge *f*; ~ **material** *n* C&G matière première *f*, COAL TECH matière première *f*, tout-venant *m*, P&R, PAPER TECH, PETR TECH, PROD ENG, TEXTILES matière première *f*; ~ **rubber** *n* P&R caoutchouc brut *m*; ~ **sewage** *n* HYDROL boue fraîche *f*, effluent brut *m*, RECYCLING eau d'égout brute *f*, eau d'égout non traitée *f*, WATER SUPP eau usée brute *f*; ~ **sludge** *n* RECYCLING boue brute *f*, WATER SUPP boue fraîche *f*; ~ **stock** *n* CINEMAT pellicule vierge *f*; ~ **stock dyeing** *n* COLOURS teinture sur fil *f*; ~ **water** *n* WATER SUPP eau brute *f*, eau crue *f*

ray *n* ELECTRON, OPT, TELECOM rayon *m*; ~ **optics** *n pl* OPT optique des rayons *f*, optique géométrique *f*, TELECOM optique des rayons *f*; ~ **path** *n* GEOL trajectoire d'un rayon *f*, PETR TECH lumineux rectiligne *m*, trajectoire d'un rayon *f*; ~ **tracing** *n* TV lancer de rayons *m*

Rayleigh: ~ **criterion** *n* PHYS critère de Rayleigh *m*; ~ **disc** *n* (BrE) ACOUSTICS disque de Rayleigh *m*; ~ **disk** *n* (AmE) *see* Rayleigh disc; ~ **fading** *n* TELECOM évanouissement de Rayleigh *m*; ~ **interferometer** *n* PHYS interféromètre de Rayleigh *m*; ~ **refractometer** *n* PHYS réfractomètre de Rayleigh *m*; ~ **scattering** *n* OPT, PHYS, RAD PHYS, TELECOM diffusion de Rayleigh *f*; ~ **wave** *n* PHYS onde de Rayleigh *f*

Rayleigh-Jeans: ~ **formula** *n* PHYS formule de Rayleigh et Jeans *f*

rayon *n* P&R, TEXTILES rayonne *f*

razor: ~ **wire** *n* MILIT fil de fer barbelé coupant *m*

Rb *(rubidium)* CHEM Rb *(rubidium)*

RBT *abbr (remote batch terminal)* COMP, DP terminal de télétraitement *m*

RC[1] *abbr* ELEC ENG *(resistance-capacitance)*, ELECTRON *(resistance-capacitance)* RC *(résistance-capacité)*, SPACE *(rate of climb)* vitesse ascensionnelle *f*

RC:[2] ~ **coupling** *n* ELEC ENG liaison par résistance et capacitance *f*, ELECTRON couplage RC *m*; ~ **filter-circuit** *n* ELECTRON circuit de filtrage RC *m*; ~ **ladder filter** *n* ELECTRON filtre à cellules RC *m*; ~ **oscillator** *n* ELEC ENG, ELECTRON oscillateur RC *m*

RCTL: ~ **logic** *n* ELECTRON logique RCTL *f*

RCU *abbr (remote concentration unit)* TELECOM concentrateur satellite numérique *m*

RDB *abbr (relational database)* COMP, DP, TELECOM BDR *(base de données relationnelles)*

RDF[1] *abbr (radio direction finder)* AERONAUT radiogoniomètre *m*, NAUT *navigation* radiogonio *m*, radiogoniomètre *m*

RDF:[2] ~ **antenna** *n* TRANSP antenne radiogoniométrique *f*

RDR *abbr (reflection density reference)* PRINT densité de référence d'un document opaque *f*

Re *(rhenium)* CHEM Re *(rhénium)*

Re *abbr (Reynolds number)* RAD PHYS Re *(nombre de Reynolds)*

reach[1] *n* HYDROL *section of river or channel* bief *m*, MECH ENG *of hand* portée *f*, WATER SUPP bief *m*, *of river* section *f*

reach[2] *vt* TELECOM *subscriber* joindre

reacquisition: ~ **mode** *n* SPACE *spacecraft* mode de réacquisition *m*

reactance *n* ELEC, ELEC ENG, PHYS, RECORDING, TESTING réactance *f*; ~ **attenuator** *n* ELECTRON atténuateur réactif *m*; ~ **bond** *n* RAIL connexion réactive *f*; ~ **circuit** *n* ELEC circuit de réactance *m*; ~ **coil** *n* ELEC ENG bobine d'inductance *f*, bobine de réactance *f*; ~ **drop** *n* ELEC chute inductive de tension *f*, ELEC ENG chute réactive *f*; ~ **relay** *n* ELEC ENG relais à impédance *m*

reactance-frequency: ~ **multiplier** *n* ELECTRON multiplicateur de fréquence à réactance *m*

reactant *n* CHEM réactant *m*

reaction *n* CHEM réaction *f*, CONTROL réaction *f*, réponse *f*, PHYS réaction *f*; ~ **and impulse turbine** *n* HYDR EQUIP turbine à action-réaction *f*; ~ **bomb** *n* LAB EQUIP bombe d'attaque *f*; ~ **jet propulsion** *n* AERONAUT propulsion à réaction *f*; ~ **kinetics** *n pl* PROP MAT cinétique de réaction *f*; ~ **molding** *n* (AmE) *see* reaction moulding; ~ **motor** *n* ELEC moteur à réaction *m*; ~ **moulding** *n* (BrE) PROP MAT moulage par réaction *m*; ~ **primer** *n* COATINGS couche de fond au phosphate *f*, couche passivante à phosphate *f*; ~ **rail** *n* RAIL rail de réaction *m*; ~ **rate** *n* CHEM, METALL vitesse de réaction *f*; ~ **sintering process** *n* NUCLEAR *in U-Pu carbide production* procédé de frittage par réaction *m*; ~ **spectroscopy** *n* NUCLEAR spectroscopie des réactions nucléaires *f*; ~ **time** *n* TRANSP *road safety* temps de perception-réaction *m*; ~ **turbine** *n* FUELLESS turbine à réaction *f*, HYDR EQUIP turbine à pression *f*, turbine à réaction *f*, MECH turbine à réaction *f*; ~ **water wheel** *n* WATER SUPP roue à réaction *f*, roue à tuyaux *f*; ~ **wheel** *n* SPACE *spacecraft* roue de réaction *f*, WATER SUPP roue à réaction *f*, roue à tuyaux *f*; ~ **zone** *n* COAL TECH zone de réaction *f*

reactivate *vt* CHEM réactiver

reactivation *n* CHEM, COAL TECH réactivation *f*, GEOL rajeunissement *m*, rejeu *m*

reactive: ~ **circuit** *n* ELEC ENG circuit réactif *m*, circuit à réactance *m*; ~ **component** *n* ELEC ENG composante en quadrature *f*, composante réactive *f*; ~ **current** *n* ELEC *AC circuit* courant déwatté *m*, ELEC ENG courant réactif *m*; ~ **dye** *n* TEXTILES colorant réactif *m*; ~ **element** *n* ELEC ENG élément réactif *m*, élément à réaction *m*; ~ **energy** *n* ELEC *AC system* énergie réactive *f*; ~ **load** *n* ELEC ENG, PHYS, TELECOM charge réactive *f*; ~ **plasma etching** *n* ELECTRON attaque au plasma *f*; ~ **power** *n* ELEC *AC circuit*, ELEC ENG, PHYS puissance réactive *f*; ~ **site** *n* CHEM *in molecule* site réactif *m*; ~ **voltage** *n* ELEC *AC circuit*, PHYS tension réactive *f*

reactivity *n* NUCLEAR, PHYS réactivité *f*; ~ **feed back** *n* NUCLEAR effet rétroactif sur la radioactivité *m*; ~ **surge** *n* NUCLEAR à-coup de réactivité *m*

reactor *n* AUTO, CHEM réacteur *m*, ELEC *coil* bobine de réactance *f*, ELEC ENG bobine de réactance *f*, réacteur *m*, NUCLEAR pile nucléaire *f*, réacteur *m*, réacteur nucléaire *m*; ~ **art** *n* NUCLEAR construction des réacteurs nucléaires *f*; ~ **behavior** *n* (AmE), ~ **behaviour** *n* (BrE) NUCLEAR comportement du réacteur *m*; ~ **charging face** *n* NUCLEAR aire de chargement *f*; ~ **component** *n* NUCLEAR composant d'un réacteur *m*; ~ **control** *n* AERONAUT, CONTROL commande du réacteur *f*; ~ **control board** *n* NUCLEAR pupitre de commande du réacteur *m*; ~ **coolant drain tank** *n* NUCLEAR réservoir des drains du circuit primaire *m*; ~ **coolant inlet nozzle**

n NUCLEAR *of steam generator* tubulure d'entrée du caloporteur primaire *f*; ~ **design** *n* NUCLEAR conception des réacteurs *f*; ~ **engineering** *n* NUCLEAR technique des réacteurs *f*; ~ **hall** *n* NUCLEAR hall du réacteur *m*; ~ **loop** *n* NUCLEAR boucle de réacteur *f*; ~ **tank** *n* NUCLEAR caisson de réacteur *m*, cuve de réacteur *f*; ~ **trip** *n* NUCLEAR arrêt d'urgence du réacteur *m*, déclenchement du réacteur *m*; ~ **vessel** *n* NUCLEAR *nonpressurized*, PHYS caisson de réacteur *m*, cuve de réacteur *f*

read:[1] ~ **only** *adj* COMP, DP à lecture seule

read[2] *n* COMP, DP lecture *f*; ~ **after write** *n* COMP, DP lecture après écriture *f*; ~ **amplifier** *n* ELECTRON amplificateur de lecture *m*; ~ **beam** *n* OPT pinceau de lecture *m*; ~ **error** *n* COMP, DP erreur de lecture *f*; ~ **head** *n* COMP, DP, OPT tête de lecture *f*; ~ **laser** *n* ELECTRON, OPT laser de lecture *m*; ~ **time** *n* COMP, DP temps de lecture *m*, PRINT *computer* temps d'accès *m*; ~ **transistor** *n* ELECTRON transistor de lecture *m*; ~ **while write** *n* COMP, DP lecture et écriture simultanées

read[3] *vt* COMP, DP lire; ~ **out** *vt* COMP, DP extraire, lire

read:[4] ~ **a volume** *vi* PROD ENG relever un volume

reader *n* COMP, DP lecteur *m*, PRINT correcteur *m*

reading *n* CHEM lecture *f*, relevé *m*, valeur *f*, CONST *that which is indicated* cote *f*, lecture *f*, TESTING cote *f*; ~ **beam** *n* ELECTRON faisceau de lecture *m*; ~ **gun** *n* ELECTRON canon de lecture *m*; ~ **microscope** *n* INSTRUMENT loupe de lecture *f*, microscope de lecture *m*, microscope de mesure *m*; ~ **rate** *n* COMP, DP vitesse de lecture *f*

read-mostly: ~ **memory** *n* COMP mémoire à lecture majoritaire *f*

read-only: ~ **disc** *n* (BrE) OPT disque non inscriptible *m*; ~ **disk** *n* COMP, OPT (AmE) disque non inscriptible *m* ~ **medium** *n* OPT support non inscriptible *m*; ~ **memory** *n* (*ROM*) COMP, DP, ELEC ENG, ELECTRON ROM, mémoire fixe *f*, mémoire morte *f*

read-out *n* CHEM lecture *f*, COMP, DP affichage *m*, extraction *f*, lecture *f*, *sample* échantillon *m*, ELEC affichage *m*, TELECOM affichage *m*, sortie *f*; ~ **potentiometer** *n* ELEC potentiomètre d'affichage *m*; ~ **system** *n* MECH ENG système d'affichage *m*, système de lecture *m*

read-write *n* COMP, DP lecture-écriture *f*; ~ **channel** *n* COMP, DP canal de lecture-écriture *m*; ~ **drive** *n* COMP, OPT enregistreur-lecteur *m*; ~ **head** *n* COMP, DP, OPT tête de lecture-écriture *f*; ~ **memory** *n* COMP mémoire de lecture-écriture *f*; ~ **optical drive** *n* OPT unité optique de lecture-écriture *f*

ready[1] *adj* COMP, DP prêt

ready:[2] ~ **meal** *n* FOOD TECH plat cuisiné *m*

ready-for-sending *adj* TELECOM prêt à émettre

ready-made *adj* PHOTO *of solution* prêt à l'emploi

ready-mixed: ~ **concrete** *n* CONST béton industriel *m*, béton prêt à l'emploi *m*, béton à la toupie *m*

ready-to-activate *adj* TELECOM *symbol* prêt à être activé

ready-to-send *adj* COMP prêt à émettre, DP prêt à transmettre

reaeration *n* WATER SUPP réoxygénation *f*

reagency *n* CHEM pouvoir réactif *m*, réaction *f*

reagent *n* CHEM, COAL TECH réactif *m*, P&R agent chimique *m*, PHOTO réactif *m*; ~ **bottle** *n* LAB EQUIP bouteille *f*, *container* flacon *m*

real[1] *adj* COMP, DP réel

real:[2] ~ **address** *n* COMP, DP adresse réelle *f*; ~ **component** *n* ELEC ENG composante active *f*, composante wattée *f*; ~ **gap length** *n* TV longueur réelle d'entrefer *f*;

~ **image** *n* PHYS image réelle *f*; ~ **memory** *n* COMP mémoire réelle *f*; ~ **minor scale** *n* ACOUSTICS gamme mineure réelle *f*; ~ **number** *n* DP, MATH nombre réel *m*; ~ **power** *n* ELEC ENG puissance active *f*; ~ **sound source** *n* ACOUSTICS source sonore réelle *f*; ~ **type** *n* COMP, DP type réel *m*

realgar *n* MINERAL réalgar *m*

realized: ~ **production time** *n* PROD ENG heures effectives de production *f pl*

real-time[1] *adj* ELECTRON en temps réel

real-time[2] *adv* ELECTRON en temps réel

real-time[3] *n* CINEMAT, COMP, DP temps réel *m*; ~ **analysis** *n* ELECTRON analyse en temps réel *f*; ~ **analyzer** *n* ACOUSTICS analyseur en temps réel *m*; ~ **clock** *n* COMP, DP horloge temps réel *f*; ~ **control** *n* TRANSP commande en temps réel *f*; ~ **conversion facility** *n* TELECOM unité de conversion en temps réel *f*; ~ **data** *n pl* COMP données en temps réel *f pl*; ~ **input** *n* COMP, DP entrée en temps réel *f*; ~ **language** *n* COMP langage temps réel *m*; ~ **output** *n* COMP, DP sortie en temps réel *f*; ~ **processing** *n* COMP, DP traitement en temps réel *m*; ~ **repeater satellite** *n* TV satellite de transmission directe *m*; ~ **signal** *n* CONTROL signal en temps réel *m*; ~ **signal processing** *n* ELECTRON traitement de signaux en temps réel *m*; ~ **simulation** *n* ELECTRON simulation en temps réel *f*; ~ **simulator** *n* ELECTRON simulateur en temps réel *m*; ~ **spectral analysis** *n* ELECTRON analyse spectrale en temps réel *f*; ~ **spectral analyzer** *n* ELECTRON analyseur spectral en temps réel *m*; ~ **system** *n* COMP, DP système en temps réel *m*

ream[1] *n* C&G onde *f*, PACKAGING *paper*, PAPER TECH rame de papier *f*, PRINT rame *f*

ream[2] *vt* MECH *tools*, PETR aléser

reamer *n* C&G cône *m*, MECH *tool* alésoir *m*, MECH ENG, MINING *boring* alésoir *m*, équarrissoir *m*, PETR TECH trépan aléseur *m*, PROD ENG, VEHICLES *tool* alésoir *m*; ~ **cutter** *n* MECH ENG fraise pour alésoir *f*; ~ **tap** *n* MECH ENG taraud aléseur *m*; ~ **with spiral flutes** *n* MECH ENG alésoir à cannelures torses *m*, alésoir à rainures torses *m*

reaming *n* MECH ENG alésage *m*, équarrissage *m*, équarrissement *m*; ~ **bit** *n* PETR TECH trépan aléseur *m*; ~ **iron** *n* CONST coin de calfat *m*; ~ **out** *n* MECH ENG alésage *m*, équarrissage *m*, équarrissement *m*; ~ **tool** *n* C&G pince à ouvrir *f*

rear *n* PAPER TECH arrière *m*, TRANSP *of railcar* queue *f*; ~ **axle** *n* MECH *vehicles* essieu arrière *m*, VEHICLES *transmission* essieu arrière *m*, train arrière *m*; ~ **axle assembly** *n* AUTO, VEHICLES *transmission* pont arrière *m*; ~ **axle drive shaft** *n* VEHICLES *transmission* arbre de l'essieu arrière *m*, arbre du pont arrière *m*; ~ **axle flared tube** *n* AUTO trompette de pont arrière *f*; ~ **axle housing** *n* VEHICLES *transmission* carter d'essieu arrière *m*, carter du pont arrière *m*; ~ **axle housing assembly** *n* AUTO pont arrière *m*; ~ **axle shaft** *n* AUTO arbre de différentiel *m*, arbre de roue *m*, demi-arbre *m*; ~ **brake van** *n* RAIL *vehicles* fourgon de queue *m*; ~ **bumper** *n* (BrE) *(cf rear fender)* AUTO pare-chocs arrière *m*; ~ **door** *n* AUTO porte arrière *f*, TRANSP hayon *m*; ~ **dump car** *n* (AmE) *(cf back-discharge wagon)* RAIL *vehicles* wagon à déversement arrière *m*, VEHICLES custode *f*; ~ **end** *n* VEHICLES custode *f*; ~ **end collision** *n* TRANSP collision par l'arrière *f*; ~ **end torque** *n* AUTO couple de réaction *m*; ~ **engine** *n* AUTO moteur à l'arrière *m*, VEHICLES moteur arrière *m*; ~ **engine rear wheel drive** *n* AUTO véhicule à moteur et à propulsion arrière *m*; ~ **fender** *n*

(AmE) AUTO *(cf rear bumper)* pare-chocs arrière *m*, AUTO *(cf rear wing)* aile arrière *f*; ~ **focal plane** *n* PHOTO plan focal postérieur *m*; ~ **focus** *n* PHOTO foyer postérieur *m*; ~ **lamp** *n* VEHICLES feu arrière *m*; ~ **license plate lamp** *n* (AmE) *(cf rear number plate lamp)* AUTO car éclairage de la plaque d'immatriculation *m*; ~ **light** *n* CONST *of vehicle* feu arrière *m*; ~ **lip tile** *n* C&G écran arrière *m*; ~ **marker plate lamp** *n* (AmE) *(cf rear number plate lamp)* AUTO éclairage de la plaque d'immatriculation *m*; ~ **number plate lamp** *n* (BrE) *(cf rear license plate lamp, rear marker plate lamp)* AUTO éclairage de la plaque d'immatriculation *m*; ~ **pillar** *n* MECH ENG bloc à colonnes arrière *m*; ~ **projection** *n* CINEMAT projection par transparence *f*, rétroprojection *f*; ~ **projection screen** *n* CINEMAT écran translucide *m*; ~ **propeller** *n* TRANSP hélice en arrière *f*; ~ **reflector** *n* TRANSP catadioptre *m*; ~ **shutter** *n* CINEMAT obturateur arrière *m*; ~ **spring** *n* MILIT *of firearm* ressort de gâchette *m*; ~ **suspension** *n* AUTO suspension arrière *f*; ~ **tipping trailer** *n* TRANSP remorque basculant en arrière *f*; ~ **window** *n* VEHICLES lunette arrière *f*, vitre arrière *f*, lunette de custode *f*; ~ **wing** *n* (BrE) *(cf rear fender)* AUTO aile arrière *f*

rearer *n* MINING dressant *m*

rear-facing: ~ **roller** *n* PROD ENG galet orienté vers l'arrière *m*

rear-mounted: ~ **engine** *n* AUTO, VEHICLES moteur à l'arrière *m*; ~ **ripper** *n* TRANSP défonceuse portée à l'arrière *f*

rearrangeable: ~ **non-blocking network** *n* TELECOM réseau réarrangeable *m*

rearrangement *n* CHEM *molecular* réarrangement *m*; ~ **collision** *n* NUCLEAR collision avec réarrangement *f*

rear-view: ~ **mirror** *n* AUTO, INSTRUMENT, VEHICLES rétroviseur *m*; ~ **system** *n* TRANSP *traffic* système de rétrovision *m*

rearward: ~ **takeoff** *n* AERONAUT *helicopter* décollage arrière *m*

rear-wheel *n* TRANSP roue arrière *f*; ~ **drive** *n* AUTO traction arrière *f*, TRANSP propulsion arrière *f*, traction arrière *f*, VEHICLES propulsion arrière *f*

reason: ~ **for hold** *n* PROD ENG cause de suspension *f*

reassemble *vt* CONST remonter

reattachment *n* FLUID PHYS *of eddies* recollement *m*

rebate *n* MECH ENG feuillure *f*; ~ **plane** *n* CONST guillaume *m*, rabot à rainurer *m*

rebated: ~ **joint** *n* CONST assemblage à feuillure *m*

reblow *vt* METALL recycler

reboil *n* C&G rebullage *m*; ~ **bubble** *n* C&G bulle de rebullage *f*

reboiler *n* PETR TECH rebouilleur *m*

reboot *vt* COMP, DP relancer

rebore *vt* AUTO, MECH ENG, VEHICLES *motor, cylinder* réaléser

reboring *n* AUTO réalésage *m*

rebound[1] *n* P&R rebondissement *m*; ~ **clip** *n* *(cf brake caliper, caliper)* AUTO étrier *m*

rebound[2] *vi* MILIT rebondir

rebroadcast *vt* TV rediffuser, réémettre

rebuild *vt* CONST rebâtir, reconstruire

rebuilding *n* CONST reconstruction *f*

recalescence *n* PHYS récalescence *f*

recalibrated *adj* RAD PHYS réétalonné

recalibration *n* NUCLEAR réétalonnage *m*, RAD PHYS réétalonnement *m*

recall *n* TELECOM rappel *m*, rétroappel *m*

recasing *n* CONST recuvelage *m*

recast *vt* PROD ENG refondre, remouler

recede *vi* HYDROL *water* baisser, se retirer

receding: ~ **flood** *n* HYDROL décrue *f*; ~ **water table** *n* *(cf falling water table)* HYDROL baisse de la nappe phréatique *f*

receipt *n* COMP, DP réception *f*; ~ **for documents** *n* PATENTS récépissé de documents *m*; ~ **for goods** *n* QUALITY accusé de réception des produits *m*; ~ **of goods** *n* QUALITY réception des produits *f*; ~ **ticket** *n* PROD ENG bordereau de réception *m*

receive:[1] ~ **only** *adj* COMP *teletype*, DP *teletype* à réception seule

receive:[2] ~ **antenna** *n* TELECOM antenne réceptrice *f*; ~ **channel** *n* TELECOM canal de réception *m*; ~ **crystal** *n* ELECTRON quartz d'oscillateur local *m*; ~ **fiber optic terminal device** *n* (AmE), ~ **fibre optic terminal device** *n* (BrE) TELECOM récepteur optique *m*; ~ **filter** *n* ELECTRON filtre de réception *m*; ~ **machine** *n* TELECOM machine réceptrice *f*; ~ **only** *n* COMP réception seule *f*, DP réception seule *f*, à réception seule *f*

receive[3] *vt* COMP, DP recevoir

received: ~ **data** *n pl* TELECOM réception des données *f*; ~ **power** *n* CONTROL puissance reçue *f*; ~ **signal** *n* ELECTRON signal reçu *m*

receiver *n* CHEM récipient *m*, ELECTRON récepteur *m*, LAB EQUIP *glassware* récipient *m*, MECH ENG *of air compressor* réservoir *m*, *of expansion engine* réservoir intermédiaire *m*, PETR TECH bac de recette *m*, récepteur *m*, PHYS récepteur *m*, PROD ENG agent de réception *m*, *of cupola with receiver* avant-creuset *m*, SPACE *communications* récepteur *m*, TELECOM combiné *m*, récepteur *m*, écouteur *m*, TRANSP *radio, radar, satellite*, TV récepteur *m*; ~ **band pass** *n* TV filtre passe-bande de récepteur *m*; ~ **board** *n* ELECTRON carte de réception *f*, carte récepteur *f*, carte réceptrice *f*; ~ **dehydrator** *n* AUTO réservoir déshydrateur *m*; ~ **diode** *n* ELECTRON diode réceptrice *f*; ~ **dryer** *n* AUTO réservoir déshydrateur *m*; ~ **gage** *n* (AmE) *see receiver gauge*; ~ **gain** *n* ELECTRON gain du récepteur *m*; ~ **gauge** *n* (BrE) METR jauge à réservoir *f*; ~ **inset** *n* TELECOM capsule réceptrice *f*; ~ **space** *n* MECH ENG *expansion engine* espace intermédiaire *m*

receiving: ~ **address** *n* PROD ENG adresse de livraison *f*; ~ **aerial** *n* TV antenne réceptrice *f*; ~ **aerial** *n* PHYS antenne réceptrice *f*; ~ **antenna** *n* TV antenne réceptrice *f*; ~ **assembly** *n* NUCLEAR *of radioisotope gauge* bloc récepteur *m*, ensemble récepteur *m*; ~ **department** *n* PROD ENG service réception *m*; ~ **dish aerial** *n* TV antenne parabolique réceptrice *f*; ~ **dish antenna** *n* TV antenne parabolique réceptrice *f*; ~ **drum** *n* PETR TECH bac de recette *m*; ~ **Earth station** *n* TV station de réception terrestre *f*; ~ **inspection** *n* PROD ENG, QUALITY contrôle de réception *m*; ~ **office** *n* PATENTS office récepteur *m*; ~ **range** *n* TV gamme de réception *f*; ~ **trap** *n* PETR gare racleur *f*; ~ **trunk** *n* TRANSP chariot récepteur *m*; ~ **tube** *n* ELECTRON tube de réception *m*; ~ **water** *n* WATER SUPP eau réceptrice *f*

receptacle *n* CHEM récipient *m*, PROD ENG logement *m*

reception *n* COMP, DP réception *f*, PROD ENG livraison fournisseur *f*; ~ **department** *n* PROD ENG service réception *m*; ~ **frequency** *n* ELECTRON fréquence de réception *f*; ~ **level** *n* ELECTRON niveau de réception *m*

receptor *n* POLLUTION récepteur *m*; ~ **region** *n* POLLUTION région collectrice *f*, région réceptrice *f*

recess[1] *n* CONST défoncement *m*, embrasure *f*, enfoncement *m*, recoin *m*, refouillement *m*, retrait *m*, retraite *f*, embrèvement *m*

recess[2] *vt* CONST défoncer, enfoncer, refouiller

recessed: ~ **flange coupling** *n* MECH ENG manchon à plateaux à boulons noyés *m*; ~ **head fastener** *n* MECH ENG élément à fixation à tête noyée *m*; ~ **switch** *n* ELEC commutateur encastré *m*

recessing *n* CONST défoncement *m*, enfoncement *m*; ~ **machine** *n* CONST défonceuse *f*, machine à défoncer *f*; ~ **siding** *n* RAIL voie d'écart *f*

recession *n* HYDROL *of flood* retrait *m*, retraite *f*; ~ **curve** *n* WATER SUPP courbe de décrue *f*, courbe de tarissement *f*; ~ **of the galaxies** *n* ASTRON fuite des galaxies *f*, éloignement des galaxies *m*; ~ **velocity** *n* ASTRON vitesse de fuite *f*, vitesse de récession *f*

recharge[1] *n* HYDROL *catchment area* recharge *f*; ~ **time** *n* PHOTO durée de recharge *f*; ~ **well** *n* WATER SUPP puits de recharge *m*

recharge[2] *vt* ELEC ENG recharger

rechargeable[1] *adj* PHOTO rechargeable

rechargeable:[2] ~ **battery** *n* CINEMAT accumulateur rechargeable *m*, ELEC ENG accumulateur rechargeable *m*, pile rechargeable *f*, TV accumulateur rechargeable *m*; ~ **cell** *n* PHYS pile rechargeable *f*

recharging *n* ELEC ENG recharge *f*; ~ **batteries** *n* CONST recharge des batteries *f*, rechargement des batteries *m*

recheck *vt* METR contrôler de nouveau

recifal: ~ **slope** *n* OCEANOG pente récifale *f*

recipient *n* CHEM récipient *m*, TELECOM destinataire *m*; ~ **identification code** *n* TELECOM code d'identification du destinataire *m*; ~ **reference** *n* TELECOM référence du destinataire *f*; ~ **reference qualifier** *n* TELECOM qualificatif de référence du destinataire *m*

reciprocal[1] *adj* PETR TECH alternatif

reciprocal[2] *n* COMP, DP, GEOM réciproque *f*, MATH inverse *m*, réciproque *f*; ~ **bearing** *n* AERONAUT *navigation* relèvement inverse *m*; ~ **circuit** *n* TELECOM circuit réciproque *m*; ~ **course** *n* NAUT *navigation* route inverse *f*; ~ **gear** *n* MECH ENG engrenage réciproque *m*, engrenage à tour *m*; ~ **lattice** *n* CRYSTALL réseau réciproque *m*; ~ **leg** *n* AERONAUT parcours d'éloignement *m*; ~ **movement** *n* PETR TECH mouvement alternatif *m*; ~ **period** *n* NUCLEAR *of reactor* constante de temps inverse *f*; ~ **probe** *n* PETR sonde réciprocale *f*; ~ **ratio** *n* MECH ENG raison inverse *f*, rapport réciproque *m*; ~ **space** *n* CRYSTALL espace réciproque *m*; ~ **spiral** *n* MECH ENG spirale hyperbolique *f*; ~ **transducer** *n* ACOUSTICS transducteur réciproque *m*

reciprocating[1] *adj* MECH alternatif, MECH ENG alternatif, va-et-vient, à mouvement alternatif

reciprocating:[2] ~ **blade** *n* PRINT racle alternative *f*; ~ **charger** *n* C&G enfourneuse à va-et-vient *f*; ~ **compressor** *n* REFRIG compresseur alternatif *m*; ~ **engine** *n* AERONAUT moteur alternatif *m*, moteur à mouvement alternatif *m*, MECH ENG moteur alternatif *m*, moteur à mouvement alternatif *m*, NAUT machine alternative *f*, VEHICLES moteur à pistons à mouvement alternatif *m*; ~ **internal combustion engine** *n* TRANSP moteur alternatif à combustion interne *m*, moteur à piston à mouvement alternatif *m*; ~ **mill** *n* PROD ENG *rolling* laminoir à mouvement alternatif *m*; ~ **motion** *n* MECH ENG mouvement alternatif *m*, mouvement de va-et-vient *m*, va-et-vient *m*; ~ **parts** *n pl* MECH ENG éléments à mouvement alternatif *m pl*; ~ **piston engine** *n* AERONAUT moteur à pistons *m*; ~ **pump** *n* WATER SUPP

pompe à mouvement alternatif *f*; ~ **saw** *n* PROD ENG scie alternative *f*; ~ **saw blade** *n* MECH ENG lame de scie sabre *f*; ~ **shaft seal** *n* MECH ENG joint d'étanchéité pour arbres à mouvement alternatif *m*

reciprocation *n* GEOM alternance *f*

reciprocity: ~ **effect** *n* CINEMAT effet de réciprocité *m*; ~ **failure** *n* PHOTO écarts de réciprocité *m pl*; ~ **law** *n* CINEMAT loi de réciprocité *f*; ~ **law failure** *n* CINEMAT effet Schwarzschild *m*; ~ **theorem** *n* ELEC ENG, PHYS théorème de réciprocité *m*

recirculate *vt* COAL TECH recycler

recirculating: ~ **ball steering gear** *n* AUTO direction à circulation de billes *f*; ~ **water economy** *n* WATER SUPP déchets *m pl*, ordures ménagères *f pl*

recirculation *n* C&G *of currents in glass tank furnace* courroie *f*; ~ **of fission products** *n* NUCLEAR recirculation des produits de fission *f*

reclaimed: ~ **area** *n* POLLUTION terrain remis en valeur *m*, terrain réhabilité *m*; ~ **rubber** *n* P&R caoutchouc régénéré *m*

reclaiming *n* PETR TECH récupération *f*, régénération *f*

reclamation *n* POLLUTION *of land or water* remise en valeur *f*, RECYCLING récupération *f*

reclean *vt* COAL TECH retraiter

reclining: ~ **seat** *n* VEHICLES siège couchette *m*

reclosable: ~ **pack** *n* PACKAGING emballage pouvant être refermé *m*

recognition *n* ACOUSTICS, COMP, DP reconnaissance *f*

recognized: ~ **private operating agency** *n* TELECOM EPR, exploitation privée reconnue *f*

recoil *n* MECH choc en retour *m*, recul *m*, MECH ENG contrecoup *m*, recul *m*, MILIT *of fire arm, of cannon* recul *m*; ~ **brake** *n* MILIT ensemble récupérateur *m*, frein de recul *m*; ~ **break** *n* MILIT arrêt d'une manoeuvre retardatrice *m*; ~ **electron** *n* PHYS *Compton effect* électron de recul *m*; ~ **energy** *n* MILIT force de recul *f*; ~ **nucleus** *n* PHYS noyau de recul *m*; ~ **slide** *n* MILIT glissière de recul *f*; ~ **spring** *n* MILIT ressort de retour *m*

recoilless[1] *adj* MILIT sans recul

recoilless:[2] ~ **gun** *n* MILIT canon sans recul *m*

recombination *n* ELECTRON, PHYS recombinaison *f*; ~ **base current** *n* ELECTRON courant de recombinaison dans la base *m*; ~ **coefficient** *n* PHYS coefficient de recombinaison *m*; ~ **era** *n* ASTRON époque de recombinaison *f*; ~ **process** *n* ELECTRON processus de recombinaison *m*; ~ **rate** *n* ELECTRON vitesse de recombinaison *f*, PHYS taux de recombinaison *m*

recommendation *n* SPACE *of CCITT or CCIR* recommandation *f*; ~ **indicator** *n* TELECOM indicateur de recommandation *m*

recommended: ~ **production order** *n* PROD ENG ordre de fabrication suggéré *m*; ~ **purchase order** *n* PROD ENG ordre d'achat suggéré *m*; ~ **speed** *n* TRANSP vitesse recommandée *f*

recompile *vi* COMP effectuer une nouvelle compilation

recompression *n* OCEANOG recompression *f*

recondition *vt* PROD ENG reconditionner, remettre à neuf

reconditioning *n* MECH ENG, PROD ENG reconditionnement *m*

reconfigurable *adj* COMP, DP reconfigurable

reconfiguration *n* COMP, DP reconfiguration *f*

reconfigure *vt* COMP, DP reconfigurer

reconnaissance *n* TV repérage *m*; ~ **vehicle** *n* MILIT voiture de reconnaissance *f*

reconnect *vt* ELEC ENG rebrancher, reconnecter

reconnection *n* ELEC ENG rebranchement *m*, reconnexion *f*, TELECOM *of non-payers* relance *f*

reconstruct *vt* COMP, DP reconstruire

reconstruction *n* CONST reconstruction *f*

reconverter *n* ELECTRON dénumériseur *m*

record[1] *n* ACOUSTICS disque *m*, CHEM donnée *f*, COMP enregistrement *m*, *data element* article *m*, DP article *m*, enregistrement *m*, *data element* bilan *m*, PETR film *m*, PHYS enregistrement *m*, RECORDING disque *m*; ~ **amplifier** *n* RECORDING amplificateur d'enregistrement *m*; ~ **book** *n* PROD ENG cahier de suivis *m*; ~ **button** *n* RECORDING bouton d'enregistrement *m*, TV bouton d'enregistrement *m*, touche d'enregistrement *f*; ~ **changer** *n* ACOUSTICS, RECORDING changeur de disques *m*; ~ **class** *n* COMP, DP type d'enregistrement *m*; ~ **creation** *n* COMP, DP création d'enregistrement *f*; ~ **crosstalk** *n* RECORDING intermodulation d'enregistrement *f*; ~ **current** *n* TV courant d'enregistrement *m*; ~ **current optimizer** *n* TV dispositif d'optimisation de courant d'enregistrement *m*; ~ **defeat tab** *n* RECORDING *of cassette*, TV languette empêchant l'enregistrement *f*; ~ **driver** *n* TV amplificateur d'enregistrement *m*; ~ **format** *n* COMP, DP format d'enregistrement *m*; ~ **head** *n* COMP, DP tête d'enregistrement *f*; ~ **ink** *n* COLOURS encre indélébile *f*; ~ **length** *n* COMP, DP longueur d'enregistrement *f*; ~ **library** *n* RECORDING discothèque *f*; ~ **player** *n* ACOUSTICS tourne-disque *m*, RECORDING tourne-disque *m*, électrophone *m*; ~ **separator** *n* *(RS)* COMP séparateur d'articles *m*, séparateur d'enregistrements *m*; ~ **time** *n* PETR temps section *m*; ~ **updating** *n* COMP mise à jour d'articles *f*, mise à jour d'enregistrements *f*, DP mise à jour d'enregistrements *f*

record[2] *vt* COMP, DP enregistrer, GEOPHYS tracer, PHYS enregistrer, relever, PRINT enregistrer, sauvegarder, RECORDING enregistrer, *grooves on disc* graver, TV enregistrer; ~ **in the register** *vt* PATENTS inscrire au registre

recordable: ~ **optical disc** *n* (BrE) OPT disque optique inscriptible *m*; ~ **optical disk** *n* (AmE) *see recordable optical disc*

recorded: ~ **announcement machine** *n* TELECOM appareil à annonce enregistrée *m*, machine parlante *f*; ~ **dose** *n* RAD PHYS dose enregistrée *f*; ~ **public information service** *n* TELECOM service public d'informations enregistrées *m*; ~ **velocity** *n* ACOUSTICS vitesse de signal enregistré *f*; ~ **wavelength** *n* ACOUSTICS longueur d'onde enregistrée *f*

recorder *n* ACOUSTICS, COMP, DP, ELEC, INSTRUMENT, MECH ENG *self-registering apparatus*, RECORDING, TELECOM enregistreur *m*

recorder-player *n* RECORDING enregistreur-lecteur *m*

recording *n* ACOUSTICS, COMP, DP, GEOL, GEOPHYS, TELECOM, TESTING enregistrement *m*, TV bande enregistrée *f*, enregistrement magnétique *m*; ~ **audio-frequency current** *n* RECORDING courant d'enregistrement audiofréquence *m*; ~ **barometer** *n* PHYS barographe *m*, baromètre enregistreur *m*; ~ **booth** *n* RECORDING cabine d'enregistrement *f*; ~ **chain** *n* TV chaîne d'enregistrement *f*; ~ **channel** *n* RECORDING canal d'enregistrement *m*, voie d'enregistrement *f*; ~ **characteristic** *n* ACOUSTICS, RECORDING, TV caractéristique d'enregistrement *f*; ~ **density** *n* COMP, DP densité d'enregistrement *f*; ~ **device** *n* INSTRUMENT enregistreur *m*; ~ **disc** *n* (BrE) RECORDING disque d'enregistrement *m*; ~ **disk** *n* (AmE) *see recording disc*; ~ **drum** *n* RECORDING tambour d'enregistrement *m*; ~ **head** *n* COMP, DP, RECORDING, TV tête d'enregistrement *f*; ~ **level** *n* RECORDING niveau d'enregistrement *m*; ~ **loss** *n* RECORDING pertes d'enregistrement *f pl*; ~ **magnetic head** *n* ACOUSTICS tête magnétique d'enregistrement *f*; ~ **medium** *n* COMP, DP, RECORDING support d'enregistrement *m*; ~ **noise** *n* RECORDING bruit d'enregistrement *m*; ~ **oscillograph** *n* ACOUSTICS oscillographe d'enregistrement *m*; ~ **paper** *n* INSTRUMENT papier d'enregistrement *m*; ~ **process** *n* RECORDING procédé d'enregistrement *m*; ~ **room** *n* RECORDING salle d'enregistrement *f*; ~ **session** *n* RECORDING séance d'enregistrement *f*; ~ **slit** *n* RECORDING fente d'enregistrement *f*; ~ **stage** *n* RECORDING plateau d'enregistrement *m*; ~ **storage tube** *n* ELECTRON tube à mémoire enregistreur *m*; ~ **studio** *n* RECORDING studio d'enregistrement *m*; ~ **stylus** *n* RECORDING burin de gravure *m*; ~ **surface** *n* COMP surface d'écriture *f*, DP surface d'enregistrement *f*; ~ **tape deck** *n* RECORDING platine d'enregistreur sur bande *f*; ~ **thermometer** *n* THERMOD thermomètre enregistreur *m*; ~ **tide gage** *n* (AmE), ~ **tide gauge** *n* (BrE) GEOPHYS marégraphe *m*, marémètre *m*, maréomètre *m*; ~ **track** *n* ACOUSTICS, COMP, DP piste d'enregistrement *f*

recording-reproducing: ~ **electroacoustical frequency response** *n* RECORDING courbe de réponse électroacoustique enregistrement lecture *f*; ~ **harmonic distortion** *n* RECORDING distorsion harmonique en enregistrement-lecture *f*; ~ **magnetic head** *n* ACOUSTICS tête magnétique mixte *f*

record-playback: ~ **head** *n* RECORDING tête d'enregistrement et de lecture *f*, tête d'enregistrement et de reproduction différée *f*

recover *vt* COAL TECH récupérer, POLLUTION, PRINT, RECYCLING recycler, récupérer, TELECOM récupérer

recoverable: ~ **error** *n* COMP, DP erreur récupérable *f*; ~ **orbiter** *n* SPACE orbiteur récupérable *m*; ~ **reserves** *n pl* PETR TECH réserves récupérables *f pl*; ~ **thruster** *n* SPACE propulseur récupérable *m*

recovered: ~ **charge** *n* ELEC ENG charge recouvrée *f*

recovery *n* AERONAUT rétablissement *m*, COAL TECH, COMP, DP, MAR POLL récupération *f*, METALL restauration *f*, NAUT *of person, item at sea*, OCEANOG récupération *f*, P&R récupération *f*, *plasticity test* reprise élastique *f*, PETR, POLLUTION, RECYCLING récupération *f*, SPACE *spacecraft* repêchage *m*, récupération *f*, TEXTILES récupération *f*; ~ **creep** *n* METALL fluage par restauration *m*; ~ **device** *n* MAR POLL appareil de récupération *m*, dispositif de récupération *m*, engin de récupération *m*, récupérateur *m*, POLLUTION récupérateur *m*; ~ **factor** *n* PETR facteur de récupération *m*, PETR TECH coefficient de production *m*, facteur de récupération *m*; ~ **from dynamic loads** *n* ELEC ENG récupération après surcharge *f*; ~ **package** *n* SPACE *spacecraft* ensemble de récupération *m*; ~ **process** *n* PETR TECH procédé de récupération *m*; ~ **rate** *n* METALL vitesse de restauration *f*; ~ **system** *n* MAR POLL système de récupération *m*, NUCLEAR dispositif de récupération *m*; ~ **voltage** *n* ELEC *switch* tension de rétablissement *f*

recrystallization *n* CHEM, CRYSTALL, METALL recristallisation *f*

rectangle *n* GEOM rectangle *m*; ~ **die set** *n* MECH ENG bloc à colonnes rectangulaires *m*; ~ **head fastener** *n* MECH ENG élément à fixation à tête rectangulaire *m*

rectangular[1] *adj* GEOM rectangulaire

rectangular:[2] ~ **cross section** *n* CONST section rectangulaire *f*; ~ **hysteresis loop** *n* ELEC ENG cycle d'hystérésis rectangulaire *m*; ~ **parallel keys** *n pl* MECH ENG clavettes parallèles rectangulaires *f pl*; ~ **pulse** *n* ELECTRON impulsion rectangulaire *f*; ~ **wave** *n* ELEC ENG onde rectangulaire *f*; ~ **waveguide** *n* ELEC ENG guide d'ondes rectangulaire *m*, guide rectangulaire *m*, PHYS guide rectangulaire *m*; ~ **wiring** *n* ELEC ENG armement Lorrain *m*

rectangularity *n* GEOM rectangularité *f*

rectangular-to-circular: ~ **transition** *n* ELEC ENG transition rectangulaire-circulaire *f*

rectification *n* CHEM rectification *f*, ELEC, ELEC ENG redressement *m*, MECH ENG rectification *f*, redressement *m*; ~ **efficiency** *n* ELEC ENG rendement de redressement *m*; ~ **lens** *n* INSTRUMENT lentille de redressement *f*

rectified[1] *adj* CHEM rectifié, redressé

rectified:[2] ~ **alternating current** *n* ELEC ENG courant alternatif redressé *m*; ~ **current** *n* ELEC ENG courant redressé *m*; ~ **output** *n* ELEC ENG sortie redressée *f*; ~ **voltage** *n* ELEC ENG tension redressée *f*

rectifier *n* AUTO redresseur *m*, CHEM rectificateur *m*, CINEMAT, ELEC *AC and DC current*, ELEC ENG, PHYS, RECORDING, TELECOM *power plant*, VEHICLES *electrical system* redresseur *m*; ~ **anode** *n* ELEC ENG plaque de redresseur *f*; ~ **bridge** *n* ELEC ENG pont de redresseurs *m*; ~ **cell** *n* ELEC ENG cellule de redresseur *f*; ~ **diode** *n* ELECTRON diode de redressement *f*; ~ **filter** *n* RECORDING filtre de redressement *m*; ~ **locomotive** *n* RAIL locomotive à redresseurs *f*; ~ **roll** *n* PAPER TECH rouleau perforé *m*; ~ **substation** *n* ELEC ENG sous-station à redresseurs *f*; ~ **transformer** *n* ELEC ENG transformateur de redresseur *m*; ~ **tube** *n* ELEC ENG tube redresseur *m*; ~ **unit** *n* TELECOM redresseur *m*

rectify *vt* ELEC *AC current*, ELEC ENG, PROD ENG redresser

rectifying: ~ **circuit** *n* ELEC ENG circuit de redressement *m*, montage redresseur *m*; ~ **junction** *n* ELEC ENG jonction redresseuse *f*

rectilineal[1] *adj* MECH rectiligne

rectilineal:[2] ~ **motion** *n* MECH, PHYS mouvement rectiligne *m*

rectilinear[1] *adj* MECH ENG rectiligne

rectilinear:[2] ~ **antenna** *n* TELECOM antenne rectiligne *f*; ~ **combing machine** *n* TEXTILES peigneuse rectiligne *f*; ~ **motion** *n* MECH, PHYS mouvement rectiligne *m*; ~ **propagation** *n* PHYS, TV, WAVE PHYS *of light waves* propagation rectiligne *f*; ~ **scanning** *n* TV analyse par lignes *f*

recto *n* PAPER TECH recto *m*

recultivation *n* POLLUTION *of land or water* remise en culture *f*

recumbent: ~ **fold** *n* GEOL pli couché *m*

recuperation *n* CHEM récupération *f*

recuperative: ~ **furnace** *n* C&G four à récupération *m*

recuperator *n* C&G, HEATING récupérateur *m*, PROD ENG récupérateur *m*, régénérateur *m*

recurrent: ~ **pulses** *n pl* ELECTRON impulsions récurrentes *f pl*

recurring[1] *adj* MATH *decimal* périodique

recurring:[2] ~ **decimal** *n* MATH fraction périodique *f*; ~ **unit** *n* CHEM *in polymer* unité récurrente *f*

recursion *n* COMP, DP récurrence *f*

recursive[1] *adj* COMP récurrent, récursif, DP récurrent, récursif

recursive:[2] ~ **filter** *n* ELECTRON, TELECOM filtre récursif

m; ~ **filtering** *n* ELECTRON filtrage récursif *m*; ~ **function** *n* COMP, DP fonction récurrente *f*

recyclable *adj* RECYCLING recyclable

recycle[1] *n* TELECOM recyclage *m*; ~ **time** *n* PHOTO durée de recharge *f*

recycle[2] *vt* CONST, POLLUTION, PROD ENG, RECYCLING recycler

recycled: ~ **bottle** *n* PACKAGING bouteille recyclée *f*; ~ **material** *n* CONST matériau recyclé *m*; ~ **paper** *n* PACKAGING, RECYCLING papier recyclé *m*

recycling *n* C&G, CHEM, COAL TECH, CONST, POLLUTION, PROD ENG, PROP MAT recyclage *m*; ~ **method** *n* RECYCLING méthode de recyclage *f*; ~ **of paper cartons** *n* PACKAGING recyclage des cartonnages *m*; ~ **time** *n* PHOTO temps de recyclage *m*

red: ~ **adder** *n* TV circuit mélangeur pour le rouge *m*; ~ **arsenic** *n* CHEM arsenic sulfuré rouge *m*, MINERAL réalgar *m*; ~ **beam** *n* ELECTRON faisceau rouge *m*, faisceau à lumière rouge *m*, TV faisceau pour le rouge *m*; ~ **beam magnet** *n* TV aimant du faisceau rouge *m*; ~ **beds** *n pl* GEOL formations rouges *f pl*; ~ **black level** *n* TV niveau minimal du signal rouge *m*; ~ **clay** *n* PETR argile rouge *f*; ~ **cobalt** *n* MINERAL cobalt arséniaté *m*; ~ **copper ore** *n* MINERAL cuivre vitreux rouge *m*, MINERAL cuprite *f*; ~ **dwarf** *n* ASTRON naine rouge *f*; ~ **edge** *n* C&G bord rouge *m*; ~ **ensign** *n* NAUT *flags* pavillon marchand *m*; ~ **giant** *n* ASTRON géant rouge *m*; ~ **green blue** *n* (*RGB*) COMP, DP, TV rouge vert bleu *m* (*RVB*); ~ **iron vitriol** *n* MINERAL fer sulfaté rouge *m*; ~ **laser** *n* ELECTRON laser à lumière rouge *m*; ~ **lead** *n* C&G minium de plomb *m*, CHEM minium *m*, P&R minium de plomb *m*; ~ **lead ore** *n* MINERAL plomb rouge *m*; ~ **light** *n* CONTROL feu rouge *m*; ~ **litmus paper** *n* CHEM papier de tournesol rouge *m*; ~ **peak level** *n* TV niveau maximal du signal rouge *m*; ~ **phase** *n* TRANSP *traffic light control* phase de rouge *f*; ~ **primary** *n* TV couleur primaire rouge *f*; ~ **quark** *n* PHYS quark rouge *m*; ~ **rod** *n* FUELLESS *windmill pump* tige rouge *f*; ~ **schorl** *n* MINERAL schorl rouge *m*; ~ **screen grid** *n* TV grille-écran rouge *f*; ~ **signal** *n* ELECTRON signal rouge *m*; ~ **supergiant** *n* ASTRON étoile supergéante rouge *f*; ~ **tide** *n* OCEANOG eaux rouges *f pl*, marée rouge *f*, poussée phytoplanctonique *f*; ~ **tube** *n* ELECTRON tube rouge *m*; ~ **waters** *n pl* OCEANOG eaux rouges *f pl*

red-abstracting: ~ **filter** *n* INSTRUMENT filtre absorbant le rouge *m*

redevelopment *n* CINEMAT redéveloppement *m*, second développement *m*

redhead *n* CINEMAT mandarine *f*, projecteur 800 watts à quartz *m*

red-hot *adj* THERMOD chauffé au rouge, porté au rouge

redirect *vt* TELECOM réacheminer

redirecting: ~ **counter** *n* TELECOM compteur de renvois *m*; ~ **indicator** *n* TELECOM indicateur de renvoi *m*; ~ **number** *n* TELECOM numéro renvoyant l'appel *m*; ~ **reason** *n* TELECOM raison du renvoi *f*

redirection: ~ **number** *n* TELECOM numéro de renvoi *m*

redistil *vt* CHEM cohober, rectifier

redistillation *n* CHEM cohobation *f*, rectification *f*

redistribution *n* ELEC ENG redistribution *f*

redock *vt* SPACE *spacecraft* accoster à nouveau, réaccoster, s'amarrer à nouveau

redose: ~ **cell** *n* LAB EQUIP *analysis, electrochemistry* pile à oxydoréduction *f*

redox *n* CHEM redox *m*; ~ **cell** *n* TRANSP pile redox *f*

redriving *n* COAL TECH creusement *m*, fraçage supplé-

mentaire *f*
redshift *n* ASTRON décalage spectral vers le rouge *m*
reduce[1] *vt* CHEM *oxide* réduire, CONST *board* alléger, amaigrir, amenuiser, amincir, PHOTO affaiblir, atténuer, PROD ENG *plate by passing it through rolls* amincir; ~ **to ashes** *vt* CHEM réduire en cendres; ~ **to its lowest terms** *vt* MATH *fraction* mettre sous forme irréductible; ~ **to powder** *vt* CHEM réduire en poudre; ~ **to width** *vt* CONST *board* tirer de largeur
reduce[2] *vi* COAL TECH réduire; ~ **speed** *vi* MECH ENG ralentir l'allure, réduire la vitesse
reduced: ~ **coordinates** *n pl* PHYS coordonnées réduites *f pl*; ~ **fraction** *n* MATH fraction irréductible *f*; ~ **inspection** *n* QUALITY contrôle réduit *m*; ~ **instruction set computer** *n (RISC)* COMP ordinateur RISC *m*, ordinateur à jeu d'instructions réduit *m*, DP ordinateur à jeu d'instructions réduit *m*; ~ **load configuration** *n* SPACE *spacecraft* configuration déchargée *f*; ~ **mass** *n* PHYS masse réduite *f*; ~ **model** *n* TELECOM modèle réduit *m*; ~ **power tapping** *n* ELEC prise à puissance réduite *f*; ~ **rate** *n* TELECOM tarif réduit *m*; ~ **salt food** *n* FOOD TECH aliment à teneur réduit en sel *m*, produit à teneur réduit en sodium *m*; ~ **sodium** *n* FOOD TECH produit à teneur réduit en sodium *m*; ~ **takeoff and landing aircraft** *n (RTOL aircraft)* AERONAUT avion à décollage et atterrissage réduits *m (ADAR)*
reducer *n* CHEM réducteur *m*, CINEMAT agent réducteur *m*, réducteur *m*, CONST *pipe* réducteur *m*, PHOTO affaiblisseur *m*, faiblisseur *m*
reducible: ~ **polynomial** *n* COMP, DP polynôme réductible *m*
reducing *n* CONST amaigrissement *m*, amenuisement *m*, amincissement *m*, PRINT affaiblissement *m*; ~ **agent** *n* CHEM agent réducteur *m*, réducteur *m*, COAL TECH agent réducteur *m*; ~ **flame** *n* THERMOD flamme réductrice *f*; ~ **furnace** *n* PROD ENG four à réduction *m*; ~ **gas** *n* THERMOD gaz réducteur *m*; ~ **gear** *n* MECH ENG engrenage de réduction de vitesse *m*, engrenage démultiplicateur *m*, engrenage retardateur *m*, engrenage réducteur *m*; ~ **pipe fitting** *n* CONST réducteur *m*; ~ **product** *n* POLLUTION produit de réduction *m*; ~ **valve** *n* LAB EQUIP *gas control* manodétendeur pour gaz *m*, MECH ENG valve de réduction *f*; ~ **wheel** *n* PROD ENG meule à user *f*
reductant *n* CHEM réducteur *m*
reduction *n* CHEM désoxydation *f*, réduction *f*, COAL TECH réduction *f*; ~ **compass** *n* MECH ENG compas de réduction *m*; ~ **crucible** *n* PROD ENG creuset réducteur *m*; ~ **furnace** *n* THERMOD four à réduction *m*; ~ **gear** *n* VEHICLES démultiplicateur *m*; ~ **mask** *n* PHOTO cache réducteur *m*; ~ **print** *n* CINEMAT copie par réduction *f*, PHOTO tirage par réduction *m*; ~ **ratio** *n* COAL TECH rapport de réduction *m*; ~ **room** *n* RECORDING cabine de réduction *f*; ~ **sleeve** *n* MECH ENG douille de réduction *f*; ~ **tube** *n* LAB EQUIP *glassware* tube de réduction *m*
reductive *adj* CHEM réductif
reductor: ~ **cell** *n* CONTROL élément de réduction *m*
redundancy *n* COMP, DP, TELECOM redondance *f*; ~ **check** *n* COMP, CONTROL, DP contrôle par redondance *m*
redundant[1] *adj* COMP, DP redondant
redundant:[2] ~ **code** *n* COMP, DP code redondant *m*
reed *n* CONST *joinery* baguette *f*, NAUT *navigation aid* trompette *f*, TELECOM contact scellé *m*, TEXTILES peigneuse *f*; ~ **contact** *n* PROD ENG, TELECOM contact à lames souples *m*; ~ **contact relay** *n* ELEC relais à lames

souples *m*, relais à lames vibrantes *m*; ~ **relay** *n* ELEC ENG relais à lames souples *m*, relais à tige *m*, TELECOM relais à tige *m*; ~ **relay crosspoint** *n* TELECOM point de connexion à contacts scellés *m*; ~ **relay electronic exchange** *n* TELECOM autocommutateur à relais à tige *m*; ~ **relay switch** *n* ELEC ENG autocommutateur à relais à tiges *m*; ~ **relay switching** *n* ELEC ENG *telephony* commutation par relais à tiges *f*; ~ **relay switching network** *n* ELEC ENG *telephony* réseau de connexion à relais à tiges *m*, réseau à relais à tiges *m*; ~ **relay system** *n* TELECOM système électronique à relais à tige *m*; ~ **switch** *n* ELEC ENG interrupteur à tiges *m*, PHYS interrupteur à lames souples *m*
reeded: ~ **glass** *n* C&G verre cannelé *m* (Fra), verre flûté *m* (Bel)
re-edit *vt* CINEMAT, TV remonter
reedlyte: ~ **glass** *n* C&G verre maté à cannelures *m*
reef[1] *n* MINING reef *m*, NAUT *part of sail* brisant *m*, ris *m*, récif *m*, OCEANOG ris *m*, récif *m*, écueil *m*; ~ **band** *n* OCEANOG bande de ris *f*; ~ **cringle** *n* NAUT patte *f*, *shortening sail* patte de ris *f*; ~ **drive** *n* MINING galerie de taille *f*; ~ **effect** *n* PETR TECH effet de récif *m*; ~ **flat** *n* OCEANOG platier *m*; ~ **front** *n* OCEANOG front récifal *m*; ~ **furrow** *n* OCEANOG sillon récifal *m*; ~ **glacis** *n* OCEANOG glacis récifal *m*; ~ **knoll** *n* OCEANOG bioherme *m*; ~ **knot** *n* NAUT noeud plat *m*; ~ **pediment** *n* OCEANOG glacis récifal *m*; ~ **slope** *n* OCEANOG pente récifale *f*; ~ **spur** *n* OCEANOG éperon corallien *m*
reef[2] *vi* NAUT *part of sail* prendre un ris
reefer: ~ **ship** *n* NAUT cargo frigorifique *m*, navire polytherme *m*
reefing: ~ **pennant** *n* NAUT garcette de ris *f*, itague *f*
reel[1] *n* CINEMAT, COMP, CONST *welding*, DP, ELEC ENG bobine *f*, MAR POLL dérouleur *m*, dévidoir *m*, OCEANOG moulinet *m*, tambour *m*, touret *m*, PAPER TECH enrouleuse *f*, PETR *cable* bobine *f*, PETR dévidoir de câble *m*, touret pour flexibles *m*, PRINT, RECORDING, TV bobine *f*; ~ **capacity** *n* CINEMAT capacité d'une bobine *f*; ~ **drum** *n* PAPER TECH tambour enrouleur *m*; ~ **end** *n* CINEMAT fin de bobine *f*; ~ **feed bags** *n pl* PACKAGING alimentation des sacs sur bobine *f*; ~ **insulator** *n* ELEC ENG poulie isolante *f*; ~ **lifter** *n* PACKAGING dispositif de levage des bobines *m*; ~ **overwrapper** *n* PACKAGING emballage extérieur sur bobine *m*; ~ **of paper** *n* PAPER TECH bobine de papier *f*; ~ **sample** *n* PAPER TECH échantillon pris sur bobine à la machine *m*; ~ **specimen** *n* PAPER TECH échantillon pris sur bobine à la machine *m*; ~ **spindle** *n* CINEMAT, RECORDING axe de bobine *m*; ~ **spool** *n* PAPER TECH mandrin de bobine mère *m*; ~ **wrapping and handling equipment** *n* PACKAGING équipement de manutention des emballages sur bobine *m*
reel[2] *vt* ELEC ENG, PAPER TECH enrouler; ~ **in** *vt* MAR POLL enrouler; ~ **out** *vt* MAR POLL dérouler, dévider
reelage *n* CINEMAT nombre de bobines *m*
reelcore *n* PRINT mandrin de bobine *m*
reeled: ~ **capacitor** *n* ELEC ENG condensateur en bande *m*; ~ **contact** *n* ELEC ENG contact de connexion en bande *m*, contact en bande *m*; ~ **resistor** *n* ELEC ENG résistance en bande *f*
reel-fed: ~ **press** *n* PRINT rotative *f*
reeling *n* ELEC ENG bobinage *m*, enroulement *m*, PAPER TECH bobinage *m*, enroulage *m*; ~ **end** *n* PAPER TECH poste d'enroulage *m*; ~ **machine** *n* P&R dérouleur *m*, dévidoir *m*; ~ **off** *n* PAPER TECH débobinage *m*
reel-to-reel[1] *adj* CINEMAT, RECORDING de bobine à bo-

bine

reel-to-reel:[2] **~ player** *n* RECORDING machine de lecture à bobines *f*; **~ tape recorder** *n* RECORDING magnétophone à bobines *m*

re-embark *vi* NAUT *passengers* rembarquer, se rembarquer

re-entrant[1] *adj* COMP, DP, GEOM rentrant

re-entrant:[2] **~ beam tube** *n* ELECTRON tube à faisceau rentrant *m*

re-entry: ~ vehicle *n* SPACE *spacecraft* véhicule de rentrée *m*

re-etching *n* PRINT regravage du point *m*

reeve *vt* NAUT *rope through block* passer

re-extraction *n* COAL TECH réextraction *f*

reference *n* COMP, DP renvoi *m*, référence *f*; **~ atmosphere** *n* SPACE atmosphère de référence *f*; **~ audio level** *n* RECORDING niveau de référence audio *m*, niveau sonore de référence *m*, TV niveau de référence audio *m*; **~ axis** *n* ACOUSTICS axe de référence *m*; **~ black** *n* TV noir de référence *m*; **~ burst** *n* SPACE *communications* paquet de référence *m*; **~ capacitor** *n* ELEC condensateur étalon *m*; **~ clock** *n* TELECOM horloge de référence *f*; **~ conditions** *n pl* METR conditions de référence *f pl*; **~ coupling** *n* ELEC ENG couplage de référence *m*; **~ edge** *n* TV *of tape* bord de référence *m*; **~ electrode** *n* LAB EQUIP électrode de référence *f*; **~ energy** *n* ACOUSTICS énergie de référence *f*; **~ frequency** *n* TELECOM fréquence de référence *f*; **~ friction condition** *n* AERONAUT *runway* condition de freinage de référence *f*; **~ fuel** *n* PETR TECH combustible de référence *m*; **~ gage** *n* (AmE), **~ gauge** *n* (BrE) MECH ENG calibre de référence *m*, calibre étalon *m*; **~ landing approach speed** *n* AERONAUT vitesse d'approche de référence *f*; **~ level** *n* ELECTRON niveau de référence *m*; **~ line** *n* GEOM ligne de référence *f*, PATENTS ligne directrice *f*; **~ mark** *n* CONST *surveying* repère *m*; **~ noise** *n* ELECTRON bruit de référence *m*; **~ noise source** *n* RECORDING source de bruit de référence *f*; **~ phase** *n* TV phase de référence *f*; **~ piece** *n* TESTING échantillon témoin *m*; **~ point** *n* ACOUSTICS, GEOM point de référence *m*; **~ print** *n* CINEMAT copie de référence *f*; **~ sensibility** *n* TELECOM sensibilité de référence *f*; **~ sensor** *n* AUTO capteur de repère *m*; **~ sign** *n* PATENTS signe de référence *m*; **~ signal** *n* CONTROL, ELECTRON signal de référence *m*; **~ signal input** *n* ELECTRON entrée du signal de référence *f*; **~ signal phase** *n* ELECTRON phase du signal de référence *f*; **~ sound acceleration** *n* ACOUSTICS accélération acoustique de référence *f*; **~ sound intensity** *n* ACOUSTICS intensité acoustique de référence *f*; **~ sound power** *n* ACOUSTICS puissance acoustique de référence *f*; **~ sound pressure** *n* ACOUSTICS, POLLUTION pression acoustique de référence *f*; **~ sound velocity** *n* ACOUSTICS vitesse acoustique de référence *f*; **~ standard** *n* METR étalon de référence *m*; **~ star** *n* ASTRON étoile de référence *f*; **~ station** *n* SPACE *communications* station de référence *f*; **~ strip** *n* CINEMAT bande étalon *f*; **~ surface** *n* TELECOM surface de référence *f*; **~ surface diameter** *n* OPT diamètre de la surface de référence *m*; **~ surface tolerance field** *n* OPT domaine de tolérance de la surface de référence *m*; **~ tape** *n* ACOUSTICS bande de référence *f*, TV bande étalon *f*; **~ temperature** *n* METR température de référence *f*; **~ test method** *n* (*RTM*) OPT méthode de mesure de remplacement *f*, méthode de mesure de référence *f*, TELECOM méthode de mesure de référence *f*; **~ value** *n* SPRINGS valeur à titre indicatif *f*; **~ voltage** *n* ELEC ENG tension de référence *f*; **~ volume** *n* ACOUSTICS volume de référence *m*, RECORDING amplitude de référence *f*, niveau de référence *m*; **~ white** *n* TV blanc de référence *m*

refill *vt* FOOD TECH ouiller, PAPER TECH regarnir

refilling: ~ the brake *vt* RAIL *vehicles* réalimentation du frein *f*

refine *vt* PAPER TECH raffiner

refined[1] *adj* MAR POLL, PAPER TECH raffiné

refined:[2] **~ product** *n* MAR POLL produit raffiné *m*

refinement *n* CHEM affinage *m*, affinement *m*, *petrol*, *sugars* raffinage *m*, COMP raffinement *m*, CRYSTALL *of atomic parameters* affinement *m*, raffinement *m*, DP raffinement *m*

refiner *n* PAPER TECH pile raffineuse *f*, raffineur *m*; **~ bar** *n* PAPER TECH lame de pile *f*

refinery *n* PETR TECH raffinerie *f*, PROD ENG *iron furnace* mazerie *f*, raffinerie *f*, usine de raffinage *f*; **~ gas** *n* PETR TECH, THERMOD gaz de raffinerie *m*

refining *n* (*cf planing*) C&G affinage *m*, PAPER TECH, PETR TECH raffinage *m*, PROP MAT affinage *m*; **~ characteristics** *n pl* PAPER TECH aptitude au raffinage *f*; **~ furnace** *n* HEATING, PROD ENG, THERMOD four d'affinage *m*; **~ glass** *n* CHEM TECH récipient de séparation *m*; **~ plant** *n* PAPER TECH installation de raffinage *f*; **~ zone** *n* C&G zone d'affinage *f*

refinishing *n* P&R *paint* retouche *f*

refit[1] *n* NAUT *of ship* remise en état *f*, réparation *f*

refit[2] *vt* NAUT *of ship* radouber, remettre en état, réarmer

refitting *n* MECH ENG rajustement *m*, regarnissage *m*, NAUT *of ship* radoub *m*, remise en état *f*, réparation *f*

reflect *vt* PHYS refléter, réfléchir

reflectance *n* ASTRON réflectance *f*, ELEC ENG pouvoir réflecteur *m*, réflectance *f*, FUELLESS, OPT réflectance *f*, PHYS facteur de réflexion *m*, réflectance *f*, PRINT pouvoir réfléchissant du papier *m*, SPACE réflectance *f*, TELECOM facteur de réflexion *m*; **~ density** *n* OPT densité optique par transmission *f*; **~ energy factor** *n* OPT facteur de réflexion *m*, facteur de réflexion énergétique *m*; **~ factor** *n* PAPER TECH facteur de réflectance *m*, PHYS, RAD PHYS facteur de réflexion *m*; **~ meter** *n* PAPER TECH réflectomètre *m*

reflected: ~ beam *n* PHYS faisceau réfléchi *m*; **~ beam photo-electric detector** *n* TRANSP détecteur photoélectrique *m*; **~ heat** *n* THERMOD chaleur reflétée *f*; **~ impedance** *n* ELEC ENG impédance ramenée à l'entrée *f*, impédance vue de l'entrée *f*; **~ light** *n* PHOTO lumière réfléchie *f*; **~ light microscope** *n* INSTRUMENT microscope par réflexion *m*, microscope à lumière réfléchie *m*, microscope à éclairage incident *m*; **~ light mirror** *n* INSTRUMENT miroir réfléchissant *m*; **~ light reading** *n* CINEMAT mesure de lumière réfléchie *f*; **~ power** *n* ELEC ENG énergie réfléchie *f*; **~ ray** *n* PHYS, WAVE PHYS rayon réfléchi *m*; **~ resistance** *n* ELEC ENG résistance ramenée au primaire *f*; **~ signal** *n* ELECTRON signal réfléchi *m*; **~ voltage** *n* ELEC ENG tension réfléchie *f*; **~ wave** *n* ELEC ENG, OCEANOG, PHYS, WAVE PHYS onde réfléchie *f*

reflecting: ~ antenna *n* TELECOM antenne à réflecteur *f*; **~ electrode** *n* ELEC ENG électrode réflectrice *f*; **~ goniometer** *n* GEOM goniomètre à réflexion *m*; **~ instrument** *n* INSTRUMENT instrument à miroir *m*; **~ microscope** *n* INSTRUMENT microscope à réflecteur *m*; **~ mirror galvanometer** *n* ELEC galvanomètre à miroir *m*; **~ prism** *n* INSTRUMENT prisme réflecteur *m*, prisme à réflexion totale *m*, OPT prisme réfléchissant *m*; **~ satellite** *n* SPACE *spacecraft* satellite réflecteur *m*; **~ screen** *n* CINEMAT panneau réflecteur *m*, écran réflecteur *m*,

PHOTO écran réflecteur *m*; ~ **stud** *n* CONST clou réflectorisé *m*; ~ **telescope** *n* ASTRON télescope à réflecteur *m*, INSTRUMENT télescope à miroir *m*, télescope à réflecteur *m*, télescope à réflexion *m*, PHYS télescope à réflecteur *m*; ~ **viewfinder** *n* PHOTO viseur obscur *m*, viseur à chambre noire *m*

reflection *n* ACOUSTICS, CRYSTALL réflexion *f*, ELECTRON réflexion *f*, réinjection *f*, GEOM, OPT, PHYS, SPACE *communications*, TELECOM réflexion *f*, WAVE PHYS réflexion *f*, *in mirror* reflet *m*; ~ **coefficient** *n* ELECTRON coefficient de réflexion *m*, OPT coefficient de réflexion *m*, facteur de réflexion *m*, PHYS coefficient de réflexion *m*; ~ **density reference** *n* (*RDR*) PRINT densité de référence d'un document opaque *f*; ~ **electron microscope** *n* ELECTRON microscope électronique à réflexion *m*; ~ **factor** *n* ELECTRON facteur de réflexion *m*, PHYS *reflectance* facteur de réflexion *m*, réflectance *f*; ~ **from ionosphere** *n* WAVE PHYS réflexion par l'ionosphère *f*; ~ **grating** *n* PHYS réseau par réflexion *m*, WAVE PHYS réseau à réflexion *m*; ~ **loss** *n* ELECTRON, RECORDING perte par réflexion *f*; ~ **method** *n* NUCLEAR méthode de rétrodiffusion gamma *f*; ~ **peak** *n* PETR réflexion de pointe *f*; ~ **print** *n* PRINT tirage photo opaque à analyser par réflexion *m*; ~ **shooting** *n* GEOPHYS réflexion sismique *f*; ~ **wave** *n* GEOPHYS onde de réflexion *f*, réflexion *f*

reflective: ~ **coat** *n* COATINGS film de peinture rétroréfléchissant *m*; ~ **disc** *n* (BrE) OPT disque réflecteur *m*; ~ **disk** *n* (AmE) *see reflective disc*; ~ **insulant** *n* REFRIG isolant réfléchissant *m*; ~ **insulation** *n* HEAT ENG isolation réflective *f*; ~ **LCD** *n* ELECTRON afficheur à cristaux liquides à réflexion *m*

reflectivity *n* FUELLESS, HEAT ENG réflectivité *f*, SPACE réflectivité *f*, réflectivité spéculaire *f*; ~ **coefficient** *n* SPACE *communications* coefficient de réflectivité *m*

reflectometer *n* P&R, PAPER TECH réflectomètre *m*

reflector *n* AUTO catadioptre *m*, CINEMAT panneau réflecteur *m*, écran réflecteur *m*, ELECTRON, INSTRUMENT réflecteur *m*, MECH ENG regarnissage *m*, réflecteur *m*, réverbère *m*, PHOTO, PHYS *telescope*, SPACE *communications*, TRANSP réflecteur *m*; ~ **antenna** *n* SPACE *communications* antenne à réflecteur *f*; ~ **electrode** *n* ELEC ENG réflecteur *m*, électrode réflectrice *f*, TV électrode de réflexion *f*; ~ **lamp** *n* CINEMAT lampe à miroir incorporé *f*; ~ **space** *n* ELECTRON *klystrons* espace cavité-réflecteur *m*; ~ **stand** *n* PHOTO pied d'éclairage *m*; ~ **telescope** *n* INSTRUMENT télescope *m*, télescope à miroir *m*, télescope à réflecteur *m*, télescope à réflexion *m*

reflectorized: ~ **board** *n* RAIL signal réflectorisé *m*

reflex[1] *adj* GEOM *angles* rentrant

reflex:[2] ~ **angle** *n* GEOM angle rentrant *m*; ~ **baffle** *n* ACOUSTICS enceinte réflexe *f*; ~ **bunching** *n* ELECTRON groupement après réflexion *m*; ~ **camera** *n* CINEMAT caméra reflex *f*, caméra à visée reflex *f*; ~ **housing** *n* PHOTO système de visée reflex *m*; ~ **klystron** *n* ELECTRON, PHYS klystron reflex *m*; ~ **mirror** *n* PHOTO miroir réflex *m*; ~ **printing method** *n* PHOTO Playertypie *f*, réflectographie *f*; ~ **projection** *n* CINEMAT projection frontale *f*; ~ **reflector** *n* VEHICLES catadioptre *m*, cataphote *m* (MD); ~ **shutter** *n* CINEMAT obturateur à miroir *m*; ~ **viewfinder** *n* PHOTO viseur reflex *m*

refloat *vt* NAUT *ship* déséchouer, remettre à flot, renflouer

reflow: ~ **soldering** *n* ELEC ENG soudage par refusion *m*

reflux *n* CHEM, CHEM TECH, PETR TECH reflux *m*; ~ **boiling** *n* CHEM TECH ébullition au reflux *f*; ~ **condenser** *n* LAB EQUIP *glassware* réfrigérant à reflux *m*, NUCLEAR déflegmateur *m*; ~ **valve** *n* HYDR EQUIP soupape de reflux *f*

refluxer *n* NUCLEAR condensateur à refluement *m*, déflegmateur *m*

refolding *n* GEOL plissement secondaire *m*

reformatting *n* COMP, DP reformatage *m*

reforming *n* PETR TECH reformage *m*

refract *vt* PHYS réfracter

refracted: ~ **near-end method** *n* TELECOM méthode d'exploration du champ réfracté proche *f*, méthode du champ réfracté proche *f*; ~ **near-field method** *n* OPT méthode d'exploration du champ réfracté proche *f*, méthode du champ réfracté proche *f*; ~ **ray** *n* OPT, PHYS, TELECOM rayon réfracté *m*; ~ **ray method** *n* TELECOM méthode d'exploration du champ réfracté proche *f*, méthode du champ réfracté proche *f*

refracting: ~ **prism** *n* OPT prisme réfringent *m*; ~ **telescope** *n* ASTRON lunette d'approche *f*, INSTRUMENT lunette astronomique *f*, télescope à lentilles *m*, PHYS lunette astronomique *f*

refraction *n* NAUT *sextant*, OPT, PHYS, WAVE PHYS réfraction *f*; ~ **grating** *n* LAB EQUIP, OPT grille de réfraction *f*; ~ **loss** *n* RECORDING perte par réfraction *f*; ~ **shooting** *n* GEOPHYS réfraction sismique *f*; ~ **wave** *n* GEOPHYS onde de réfraction *f*, réfraction *f*, PETR onde de réfraction *f*

refractive: ~ **index** *n* CINEMAT, OPT, PHOTO, PHYS, SPACE *communications*, TELECOM, WAVE PHYS indice de réfraction *m*; ~ **index contrast** *n* TELECOM contraste d'indice de réfraction *m*; ~ **index profile** *n* OPT profil d'indice *m*, profil d'indice de réfraction *m*; ~ **power** *n* PHOTO *of lens* pouvoir convergent *m*, pouvoir réfringent *m*

refractivity *n* PHYS, SPACE *communications* réfringence spécifique *f*

refractometer *n* INSTRUMENT, LAB EQUIP, PHYS, RAD PHYS réfractomètre *m*

refractor *n* GEOPHYS réfracteur *m*, INSTRUMENT lunette astronomique *f*, télescope à lentilles *m*, PHYS *telescope* lunette astromique *f*, télescope à lentilles *m*; ~ **telescope** *n* INSTRUMENT lunette astronomique *f*, télescope à lentilles *m*

refractory[1] *adj* CHEM *substance*, HEATING, PROP MAT réfractaire, THERMOD ignifuge, réfractaire, résistant au feu

refractory[2] *n* C&G, PROD ENG réfractaire *m*, THERMOD matériau réfractaire *m*; ~ **brick** *n* HEATING, LAB EQUIP brique réfractaire *f*; ~ **coating** *n* COATINGS enduit réfractaire *m*, revêtement réfractaire de surface *m*; ~ **lining** *n* COATINGS, HEATING revêtement réfractaire *m*, PROP MAT garnissage réfractaire *m*; ~ **material** *n* COAL TECH, GAS TECH matériau réfractaire *m*; ~ **metal** *n* METALL métal réfractaire *m*; ~ **quality** *n* PROP MAT réfractarité *f*; ~ **tube** *n* HEATING tube réfractaire *m*; ~ **wash** *n* COATINGS enduit réfractaire *m*, revêtement réfractaire de surface *m*

reframe *vt* CINEMAT recadrer

refreeze *vt* REFRIG recongeler

refresh[1] *n* COMP, DP, ELECTRON rafraîchissement *m*; ~ **cycle** *n* (AmE) (*cf refresh rate*) COMP, DP cycle de rafraîchissement *m*, vitesse de rafraîchissement; ~ **mode** *n* ELECTRON mode de rafraîchissement *m*; ~ **rate** *n* (BrE) (*cf refresh cycle*) COMP, DP cycle de rafraîchissement *m*, vitesse de rafraîchissement *f*; ~ **signal** *n* ELECTRON signal de rafraîchissement *m*

refresh² vt COMP, DP, ELECTRON rafraîchir
refreshed: ~ image n ELECTRON image rafraîchie f
refrigerant¹ adj CHEM réfrigérant
refrigerant² n AUTO fluide frigorifique m, POLLUTION réfrigérant m, REFRIG fluide frigorigène m, frigorigène m, THERMOD agent réfrigérant m, réfrigérant, VEHICLES cooling system fluide frigorigène m; ~ capacity n REFRIG puissance frigorifique f; ~ charge n REFRIG charge de frigorigène f; ~ circuit n REFRIG circuit du réfrigérant m; ~ compressor n MECH ENG compresseur de réfrigération m, compresseur pour fluides frigorigènes m; ~ connection n REFRIG raccordement frigorifique m; ~ distributor n REFRIG distributeur de frigorigène m, porte f; ~ liquifying set n MECH ENG groupe de liquéfaction pour réfrigérant m; ~ metering device n REFRIG appareil de réglage de débit de fluide m
refrigerant-cooled: ~ compressor n REFRIG compresseur refroidi par gaz réfrigérant m
refrigerate vt REFRIG, THERMOD frigorifier, réfrigérer; ~ by compression vt MECH ENG réfrigérer par compression
refrigerated¹ adj REFRIG frigorifique, réfrigéré
refrigerated:² ~ bakery slab n REFRIG tour de pâtisserie m; ~ car n (AmE) (cf refrigerated wagon) RAIL vehicles, TRANSP wagon frigorifique m; ~ cargo n TRANSP cargaison réfrigérée f; ~ cargo ship n NAUT, TRANSP cargo frigorifique m; ~ cargo vessel n REFRIG navire frigorifique m; ~ container n TRANSP conteneur frigorifique m; ~ counter n REFRIG comptoir frigorifique m; ~ display cabinet n REFRIG vitrine frigorifique f; ~ display case n REFRIG présentoir frigorifique m; ~ farm tank n REFRIG bac de refroidissement à la ferme m; ~ incubator n LAB EQUIP étuve réfrigérée f; ~ lorry n (BrE) REFRIG, THERMOD camion frigorifique m, TRANSP camion isotherme m; ~ showcase n REFRIG vitrine frigorifique f; ~ trailer n REFRIG remorque à fourgon frigorifique f; ~ transport n FOOD TECH transport frigorifique m, REFRIG transport sous froid m, TRANSP transport frigorifique m; ~ truck n REFRIG camion frigorifique m, wagon frigorifique m, THERMOD camion frigorifique m, TRANSP camion isotherme m; ~ vehicle n MECH ENG, REFRIG véhicule frigorifique m; ~ wagon n (BrE) (cf refrigerated car) RAIL vehicles, TRANSP wagon frigorifique m; ~ warehouse n REFRIG entrepôt frigorifique m; ~ window n REFRIG devanture frigorifique f
refrigerating¹ adj MECH ENG frigorifique, REFRIG frigorifique, réfrigérant
refrigerating² n REFRIG refroidissement m, réfrigération f; ~ capacity n REFRIG puissance frigorifique f; ~ circuit n REFRIG circuit de réfrigération m; ~ compressor n REFRIG compresseur frigorifique m; ~ engineer n THERMOD frigoriste m; ~ hold n TRANSP cale froide f; ~ machine n REFRIG machine frigorifique f; ~ plant n MECH ENG, REFRIG, THERMOD installation frigorifique f; ~ system n MECH ENG appareil frigorifique m, machine frigorifique f; ~ unit n REFRIG factory assembled groupe frigorifique m
refrigeration n FOOD TECH réfrigération f, THERMOD réfrigération f, industrial froid industriel m; ~ cabinet n REFRIG meuble réfrigéré m; ~ contractor n REFRIG installateur frigoriste m; ~ cycle n REFRIG cycle de réfrigération m; ~ engineer n REFRIG ingénieur frigoriste m; ~ engineering n FOOD TECH technique du froid f; ~ machine n PACKAGING réfrigérateur m, REFRIG

machine frigorifique f; ~ output n REFRIG production frigorifique f; ~ service engineer n REFRIG dépanneur frigoriste m; ~ ship n TRANSP navire frigorifique m; ~ system n REFRIG système frigorifique m; ~ test n REFRIG essai frigorifique m
refrigerator n MECH ENG household réfrigérateur ménager m, PHYS, REFRIG réfrigérateur m, THERMOD réfrigérant m, réfrigérateur m
refuel vt TRANSP aviation ravitailler en combustible
refueler n (AmE) see refueller
refueling n (AmE) see refuelling
refueller n (BrE) TRANSP tanker m
refuelling n (BrE) AERONAUT, MAR POLL ravitaillement en carburant m, MECH ENG ravitaillement m, TRANSP motor vehicles ravitaillement en essence m ~ aircraft n (BrE) MILIT avion ravitailleur m; ~ boom n (BrE) TRANSP perche de ravitaillement f; ~ craft n (BrE) TRANSP avion-citerne m; ~ in flight n (BrE) TRANSP ravitaillement en vol m; ~ in-flight system n (BrE) TRANSP perche de ravitaillement en vol f; ~ tanker n (BrE) TRANSP camion citerne de ravitaillement m
refuge: ~ hole n CONST abri m, caponnière f, lieu de refuge m, niche f, niche de refuge f, refuge m, retraite f
refund n PATENTS remboursement m
refusal n PATENTS refus m, rejet m
refuse n COAL TECH déchets m pl, rejet m, PAPER TECH déchets m pl, PROD ENG déchets m pl, rebut m, RECYCLING déchets m pl, WATER SUPP déchets m pl, ordures ménagères f pl; ~ collection n RECYCLING collecte f, ramassage m; ~ collection lorry n (BrE) (cf refuse collection truck) TRANSP camion de collecte m; ~ collection truck n (AmE) (cf refuse collection lorry) TRANSP camion de collecte m; ~ collection vehicle n RECYCLING benne à ordures f; ~ dump n RECYCLING décharge f, dépôt m, dépôt de résidus m, WATER SUPP dépotoir m; ~ dumping n (AmE) (cf refuse tipping) WATER SUPP décharge publique f; ~ sack n (BrE) (cf garbage bag) PACKAGING sac pour les détritus m; ~ tipping n (BrE) (cf refuse dumping) WATER SUPP décharge publique f
regasification n GAS TECH regazéification f
regel vi REFRIG regeler
regelation n PHYS regel m, regélation f
regenerate vt COMP, DP régénérer
regenerated: ~ cellulose n PROP MAT cellulose régénérée f; ~ pulse n ELECTRON impulsion régénérée f; ~ rubber n P&R caoutchouc régénéré m
regeneration n CHEM régénération f, épuration f, CINEMAT restauration f, régénération f, COMP, DP, ELECTRON, SPACE communications, TELECOM, WATER SUPP régénération f; ~ mode n GAS TECH phase de régénération f
regenerative¹ adj SPACE communications régénérateur
regenerative:² ~ airheater n SAFETY réchauffeur d'air à régénération m; ~ amplification n ELECTRON amplification avec réaction f; ~ amplifier n ELECTRON amplificateur à réaction m; ~ braking n RAIL vehicles, TRANSP freinage par récupération m; ~ cell n TRANSP pile régénérable f; ~ circuit n ELECTRON montage à réaction m; ~ cooling n REFRIG, THERMOD refroidissement par récupération m; ~ feedback n ELECTRON réaction positive f; ~ furnace n C&G four à régénération m; ~ heating n REFRIG chauffage à récupération de chaleur m; ~ repeater n ELECTRON répéteur régénérateur m
regenerator n ELECTRON, SPACE communications, TELE-

COM régénérateur m; ~ **section** n *(RS)* TELECOM section de régénération f; ~ **section overhead** n TELECOM SDSR, surdébit de section de régénération m; ~ **section termination** n *(RST)* TELECOM terminaison de section de régénération f; ~ **timing generator** n *(RTG)* TELECOM générateur de rythme de régénérateur m

regime n HYDROL *river* régime m

region n ASTRON, GEOM, GEOPHYSICS région f

regional: ~ **airport** n AERONAUT aéroport régional m; ~ **carrier** n AERONAUT transporteur régional m; ~ **express railroad** n (AmE) *(cf regional express railway)* RAIL RER, réseau express régional m; ~ **express railway** n (BrE) *(cf regional express railroad)* RAIL RER, réseau express régional m; ~ **metamorphism** n FUEL-LESS métamorphisme régional m; ~ **patent** n PATENTS brevet régional m; ~ **processor** n *(RP)* TELECOM processeur régional m; ~ **radio warning system** n TRANSP réseau régional de radioguidage m; ~ **railroad traffic** n (AmE) *(cf regional railway traffic)* TRANSP transport par chemin de fer à courte distance m; ~ **railway traffic** n (BrE) *(cf regional railroad traffic)* TRANSP transport par chemin de fer à courte distance m

register[1] n COMP registre m, DP correspondance f, registre m, ELEC ENG registre m, MECH ENG engoujonnage m, PATENTS registre m, PRINT repérage m, repérage point sur point m, PROD ENG *of furnace*, TELECOM registre m; ~ **bar** n CINEMAT ergot de fixation m; ~ **length** n COMP, DP longueur de registre f; ~ **mount** n CINEMAT cadre de positionnement m; ~ **peg** n CINEMAT ergot de positionnement m; ~ **pin** n CINEMAT griffe de fixité f, grille de stabilisation f; ~ **print** n CINEMAT copie à grande fixité f; ~ **ton** n NAUT tonneau de jauge m; ~ **tonnage** n NAUT tonnage net m; ~ **translator** n TELECOM enregistreur-traducteur m

register[2] vt COMP, DP cadrer, MECH ENG engoujonner, MILIT *artillery* installer un tir, PHOTO faire correspondre à

register-controlled: ~ **system** n TELECOM système à enregistreurs m

registered: ~ **depth** n NAUT *ship design* creux de cale m; ~ **mark** n PATENTS marque déposée f; ~ **user** n PATENTS usager inscrit sur le registre m, utilisateur inscrit au registre m

registration n AERONAUT immatriculation f, CINEMAT alignement m, positionnement m, COMP enregistrement m, DP alignement m, cadrage m, PATENTS enregistrement m, inscription f, TV alignement m, calage m; ~ **accuracy** n TV précision d'alignement f; ~ **of artwork** n CINEMAT alignement des cellulos m; ~ **control** n TV contrôle d'alignement m; ~ **drift** n TV dérive d'alignement f; ~ **fire** n MILIT *artillery* réglage du tir m; ~ **holes** n pl CINEMAT trous de positionnement m pl

regolith n ASTRON, GEOL *fragmental surface layer* régolithe m

regression n COMP, DP, GEOL *marine*, MATH régression f

regressive: ~ **overlap** n GEOL superposition des dépôts par progradation f

regrind vt COAL TECH rebroyer

regrinding n PROD ENG rebroyage m

regular[1] adj PRINT régulier

regular:[2] ~ **gas** n (AmE) *(cf regular petrol)* AUTO, VEHI-CLES *fuel* essence ordinaire f; ~ **gasoline** n (AmE) *(cf regular petrol)* AUTO, VEHICLES *fuel* essence ordinaire f; ~ **part load car** n (AmE) *(cf regular part load wagon)* RAIL *vehicles* wagon de course m; ~ **part load wagon** n

(BrE) *(cf regular part load car)* RAIL *vehicles* wagon de course m; ~ **petrol** n (BrE) *(cf regular gas, regular gasoline)* AUTO, VEHICLES *fuel* essence ordinaire f; ~ **polygon** n GEOM polygone régulier m; ~ **tetrahedron** n GEOM tétraèdre régulier m

regularization n WATER SUPP régularisation f

regulate: ~ **the draft** vi (AmE), ~ **the draught** vi (BrE) PROD ENG *of blower* régler la venue du vent

regulated: ~ **bus system** n SPACE *spacecraft* système à barre régulée m; ~ **deposition** n POLLUTION dépôt réglementé m; ~ **output current** n ELEC ENG courant de sortie régulé m; ~ **output voltage** n ELEC ENG tension de sortie régulée f; ~ **power supply** n ELEC ENG alimentation régulée f; ~ **variable** n CONTROL variable commandée f; ~ **voltage** n ELEC ENG tension régulée f

regulating[1] adj CONTROL réglant, f

regulating[2] n CONTROL mise au point f, réglage m, MECH ENG *act of adjusting* réglage m, NUCLEAR pilotage m, réglage m; ~ **amplifier** n CONTROL amplificateur de réglage m; ~ **choke coil** n CONTROL inductance de réglage f; ~ **device** n CONTROL appareil de mise au point m, appareil de réglage m, dispositif régulateur m; ~ **distance** n CONTROL parcours de réglage m; ~ **door** n MINING porte à guichet f; ~ **dynamo** n ELEC *generator* dynamo tampon f; ~ **feed valve** n CONTROL soupape d'alimentation automatique f; ~ **grid** n CONTROL grille régulatrice f; ~ **lever** n CONTROL levier de pose m; ~ **limits** n pl CONTROL zone de réglage f; ~ **motor** n CONTROL servomoteur m; ~ **nut** n MECH ENG écrou de réglage m; ~ **pilot** n CONTROL pilote de commande m, pilote de régulation m; ~ **point** n CONTROL point d'action du réglage m; ~ **power** n CONTROL puissance de régulation f; ~ **range** n CONTROL domaine de réglage m, zone de réglage f; ~ **resistance** n ELEC ENG résistance de réglage f; ~ **screw** n CONTROL vis de réglage f, vis régulatrice f, MECH ENG vis de réglage f; ~ **speed** n CONTROL vitesse de réglage f; ~ **starter** n ELEC démarreur régulateur m; ~ **step** n CONTROL degré de marche m; ~ **switch** n CONTROL réducteur de charge m, réducteur de décharge m; ~ **transformer** n CONTROL transformateur de réglage m, transformateur réglable m, transformateur variable m, LAB EQUIP transformateur variable m; ~ **valve** n LAB EQUIP *fluid control* vanne de réglage f; ~ **variable** n CONTROL variable commandée f

regulation n CHEM réglage m, CONTROL réglage m, régulation f, régulation de maintien f, ELEC ENG régulation f, MECH ENG *act of adjusting* réglage m, SAFETY règlement m, TELECOM régulation f; ~ **loop** n CONTROL, PROD ENG boucle de régulation f; ~ **range** n ELEC ENG plage de régulation f; ~ **ratio** n CONTROL taux de régulation m; ~ **strategy** n TRANSP stratégie de régulation f; ~ **system** n CONTROL système de régulation m; ~ **transformer** n ELEC ENG transformateur régulateur m

regulator n CONTROL appareil de commande m, régulateur m, vérin m, régulateur conjoncteur-disjoncteur m, ELEC ENG régulateur m, système de régulation m, LAB EQUIP, MECH ENG régulateur m, PAPER TECH régleur m, TELECOM régulateur m; ~ **breaker** n CONTROL commutateur de charge m, conjoncteur-disjoncteur m; ~ **cell** n CONTROL élément de réduction m, élément de régulation m; ~ **circuit** n CONTROL circuit de mise au point m, circuit de réglage m; ~ **cutout** n CONTROL commutateur de charge m, conjoncteur-disjoncteur m, ELEC *automotive* commutateur de charge m; ~ **door** n COAL TECH porte régulatrice d'air f; ~ **gate** n HYDR

EQUIP vanne régulatrice *f*

regulatory: ~ **agency** *n* NAUT organisme de contrôle *m*

regulus *n* METALL régule *m*

rehabilitation *n* POLLUTION *of land, water* remise en valeur *f*

reheat[1] *n* C&G réchauffage *m*, HEAT ENG resurchauffe *f*, TRANSP postcombustion *f*, réchauffe *f*

reheat[2] *vt* HEAT ENG resurchauffer, REFRIG réchauffer

reheater *n* HEAT ENG resurchauffeur *m*

reheating *n* C&G, PROP MAT réchauffage *m*

reignition *n* SPACE *spacecraft* réallumage *m*; ~ **voltage** *n* ELEC ENG tension de réamorçage *f*

reimbursement *n* PATENTS remboursement *m*

reinforced[1] *adj see glass fibre reinforced*

reinforced:[2] ~ **board** *n* PAPER TECH carton renforcé *m*; ~ **composite** *n* PROP MAT composite renforcé *m*; ~ **concrete** *n* CONST béton armé *m*, ciment armé *m*, MILIT béton armé *m*; ~ **concrete rounds** *n* CONST ronds lisses *m pl*, ronds à béton *m pl*; ~ **paper** *n* PACKAGING papier renforcé *m*, PAPER TECH papier entoilé *m*, PROP MAT papier armé *m*; ~ **plastic** *n* C&G, P&R, PACKAGING, PROP MAT plastique renforcé *m*; ~ **plastic packaging material** *n* PACKAGING matériel d'emballage en plastique renforcé *m*; ~ **rim** *n* (BrE) *(cf turned rim)* C&G bord de carafe *m*; ~ **timbering** *n* MINING boisage armé *m*, longrinage *m*; ~ **union paper** *n* PAPER TECH papier goudronné renforcé *m*

reinforcement *n* CONST ferraillage *m*, fers d'armature *m pl*, *act* armature *f*, fernure *f*, renforcement *m*, ELEC *cable* frettage *m*, PROP MAT renforcement *m*

reinforcing *n* CONST armature *f*, renforcement *m*; ~ **agent** *n* P&R agent renforçant *m*; ~ **filler** *n* P&R *raw material* charge active *f*, charge renforçante *f*

reinjection *n* PETR TECH réinjection *f*

reintegration *n* CHEM réintégration *f*

reject[1] *n* CINEMAT chute *f*, déchets de film *m pl*, TEXTILES rebuts *m pl*; ~ **disposal** *n* COAL TECH évacuation des résidus *f*; ~ **gate** *n* PAPER TECH écluse *f*

reject[2] *vt* QUALITY rebuter, rejeter, TEXTILES rebuter

rejected: ~ **frequency** *n* ELECTRON fréquence éliminée *f*; ~ **quantity** *n* PROD ENG quantité rebutée *f*

rejection *n* COMP, DP rebut *m*, ELECTRON atténuation *f*, élimination *f*, PATENTS rejet *m*, QUALITY rebut *m*, rejet *m*; ~ **band** *n* ELECTRON bande coupée *f*; ~ **filter** *n* ELECTRON filtre coupe-bande *m*; ~ **note** *n* PROD ENG bon de rejet *m*

rejector *n* ELECTRON réjecteur *m*

rejects *n pl* PROD ENG marchandises rejetées *f pl*, rebuts *m pl*

rejuvenation *n* GEOL rajeunissement *m*, rejeu *m*, PETR TECH rajeunissement *m*

REL *abbr (release message)* TELECOM LIB *(message de libération)*

relation *n* COMP, DP relation *f*

relational[1] *adj* COMP, DP relationnel

relational:[2] ~ **database** *n* (RDB) COMP, DP, TELECOM base de données relationnelles *f* (BDR); ~ **editing** *n* CINEMAT montage par association *m*; ~ **model** *n* COMP, DP modèle relationnel *m*; ~ **operator** *n* COMP, DP opérateur relationnel *m*; ~ **processor** *n* COMP, DP processeur relationnel *m*

relative: ~ **abundance** *n* PHYS abondance relative *f*; ~ **addressing** *n* COMP, DP adressage relatif *m*; ~ **altitude** *n* AERONAUT altitude relative *f*; ~ **angular deviation gain** *n* ACOUSTICS gain relatif de déviation angulaire *m*; ~ **angular deviation loss** *n* ACOUSTICS perte relative de

déviation angulaire *f*; ~ **aperture** *n* PHYS ouverture relative *f*; ~ **atomic mass** *n* PHYS masse atomique relative *f*; ~ **bearing** *n* AERONAUT, OCEANOG gisement *m*; ~ **density** *n* COAL TECH indice de densité *m*, PHYS *specific gravity* densité *f*; ~ **differential threshold** *n* ACOUSTICS seuil différentiel relatif *m*; ~ **dryness** *n* HYDR EQUIP *of wet stream* titre de la vapeur *m*; ~ **efficiency** *n* ACOUSTICS *of transducer* efficacité relative *f*; ~ **error** *n* COMP, DP erreur relative *f*; ~ **evaporation** *n* HYDROL évaporation relative *f*; ~ **evapotranspiration** *n* HYDROL évapotranspiration relative *f*; ~ **frequency** *n* COMP, DP fréquence relative *f*; ~ **grain area** *n* COAL TECH rapport du surface *m*; ~ **harmonic content** *n* ELECTRON taux d'harmoniques *m*; ~ **humidity** *n* HEAT ENG, HEATING, P&R humidité relative *f*, PAPER TECH degré hygrométrique *m*, PHYS, PROP MAT humidité relative *f*, REFRIG degré hygrométrique *m*, humidité relative *f*, TEXTILES, WATER SUPP humidité relative *f*; ~ **humidity of the air** *n* METEO Ha, humidité relative de l'air *f*; ~ **humidity of the ground** *n* HYDROL humidité relative du sol *f*; ~ **linear stopping power** *n* PHYS pouvoir d'arrêt linéique relatif *m*; ~ **luminous efficiency** *n* *(cf luminous efficacy)* PHYS efficacité lumineuse relative *f*; ~ **mass stopping power** *n* PHYS pouvoir d'arrêt massique relatif *m*; ~ **molecular mass** *n* PHYS masse moléculaire relative *f*; ~ **motion** *n* PHYS mouvement relatif *m*; ~ **permeability** *n* ELEC *electromagnetism*, ELEC ENG, PHYS, TESTING perméabilité relative *f*; ~ **permittivity** *n* ELEC *electromagnetism* permittivité relative *f*, ELEC ENG constante diélectrique *f*, permittivité relative *f*, PHYS permittivité relative *f*; ~ **power** *n* ELEC ENG puissance relative *f*; ~ **pressure coefficient** *n* PHYS coefficient relatif de pression *m*; ~ **risk** *n* MATH risque relatif *m*; ~ **signal amplitude** *n* ELECTRON amplitude relative du signal *f*; ~ **slip** *n* ELEC *machinery* glissement relatif *m*; ~ **tone** *n* ACOUSTICS ton relatif *m*; ~ **velocity** *n* MECH ENG, PHYS vitesse relative *f*; ~ **viscosity** *n* FLUID PHYS viscosité relative *f*; ~ **volatility** *n* PROP MAT volatilité relative *f*; ~ **water velocity** *n* FUELLESS vitesse d'eau relative *f*, vitesse relative d'eau *f*

relatively: ~ **negative voltage** *n* ELEC ENG tension négative en valeur relative *f*; ~ **positive voltage** *n* ELEC ENG tension positive en valeur relative *f*

relativistic[1] *adj* PHYS relativiste

relativistic:[2] ~ **mechanics** *n* PHYS, SPACE mécanique relativiste *f*; ~ **particle** *n* SPACE particule relativiste *f*

relativity *n* PHYS relativité *f*; ~ **effect** *n* SPACE phénomène relativiste *m*

relax[1] *vt* MECH, TEXTILES détendre

relax[2] *vi* MECH, SPRINGS relâcher

relaxation *n* ELEC *oscillation*, METALL, P&R relaxation *f*, SPRINGS relaxation *f*, relâchement *m*; ~ **center** (AmE), ~ **centre** *n* (BrE) METALL centre de relaxation *m*; ~ **oscillation** *n* ELECTRON, PHYS oscillation de relaxation *f*; ~ **oscillator** *n* ELECTRON oscillateur à relaxation *m*; ~ **time** *n* ELEC *dielectric* temps de relaxation *m*, temps de relâchement *m*, METALL temps de relaxation *m*

relaxed[1] *adj* SPRINGS, TEXTILES détendu

relaxed:[2] ~ **fiber** *n* (AmE), ~ **fibre** *n* (BrE) TEXTILES fibre détendue *f*

relaxing *n* SPRINGS écrouissage *m*

relay *n* CINEMAT, COMP, DP, ELEC *switch*, ELEC ENG, LAB EQUIP *electricity* relais *m*, MECH ENG moteur asservi *m*, relais-moteur *m*, servomoteur *m*, PHYS, TELECOM, VE-

HICLES *electrical system* relais *m*; ~ **armature** *n* ELEC ENG armature de relais *f*; ~ **coil** *n* ELEC ENG, PROD ENG bobine de relais *f*; ~ **contact** *n* ELEC, ELEC ENG, PROD ENG contact de relais *m*; ~ **control system** *n* CONTROL régulateur à bascule autonome *m*; ~ **core** *n* ELEC ENG noyau de relais *m*; ~ **hum** *n* ELEC ENG ronflement de relais *m*; ~ **interruptor** *n* ELEC *switch* interrupteur de relais *m*; ~ **ladder rung** *n* PROD ENG ligne de schéma à relais *f*; ~ **logic** *n* PROD ENG logique à relais *f*; ~ **magnet** *n* ELEC ENG électro-aimant de relais *m*; ~ **rod** *n* AUTO barre d'accouplement *f*; ~ **satellite** *n* SPACE *communications*, TV satellite relais *m*; ~ **set** *n* TELECOM jeu de relais *m*; ~ **station** *n* TV station relais *f*; ~ **switch** *n* CINEMAT commutateur à relais *m*; ~ **switching system** *n* ELEC ENG système de commutation à relais *m*, système à relais *m*; ~ **system** *n* TELECOM commutateur tout à relais *m*, système tout à relais *m*; ~ **transmitter** *n* TV émetteur relais *m*; ~ **winding** *n* ELEC enroulement de relais *m*

relaying: ~ **and routing function** *n* TELECOM fonction de relais et de routage *f*

release[1] *n* CHEM dégagement *m*, mise en liberté, émission *f*, COMP, DP libération *f*, version *f*, ELEC ENG *electromagnet* déclencheur *m*, *of armature* relâchement *m*, *of link* libération *f*, HYDR EQUIP échappement *m*, émission *f*, MECH ENG *by cam* débrayage *m*, *tripping device* déclenche *f*, déclenchement *m*, déclic *m*, PAPER TECH desserrage *m*, TELECOM libération *f*; ~ **agent** *n* P&R *moulding* agent de démoulage *m*; ~ **bearing** *n* AUTO butée de débrayage *f*; ~ **bearing hub** *n* AUTO support de butée de débrayage *m*; ~ **bearing sleeve** *n* AUTO butée de débrayage *f*; ~ **button** *n* CINEMAT, CONTROL, TV bouton de déclenchement *m*, déclencheur *m*; ~ **current** *n* ELEC ENG *of relay, electromagnet* intensité du relâchement *f*, *of switch* intensité de déclenchement *f*; ~ **of the feed motion** *n* MECH ENG déclenchement du mouvement de pression *m*; ~ **horizon** *n* PROD ENG horizon de lancement *m*; ~ **indicator** *n* TELECOM indicateur de libération *m*; ~ **lag** *n* ELEC ENG retard au relâchement *m*, retard à la retombée *m*; ~ **level** *n* COMP niveau de mise à jour *m*, DP niveau de version *m*; ~ **lever pin** *n* AUTO axe du levier de débrayage *m*; ~ **lever spring** *n* AUTO ressort du levier de débrayage *m*; ~ **mesh** *n* COAL TECH maille de libération *f*; ~ **message** *n (REL)* TELECOM message de libération *m (LIB)*; ~ **negative** *n* CINEMAT contre-type *m*; ~ **period** *n* HYDR EQUIP période d'échappement de la vapeur *f*; ~ **point** *n* HYDR EQUIP commencement de l'échappement *m*; ~ **positive** *n* CINEMAT copie d'exploitation *f*, copie de série *f*, copie standard *f*; ~ **printing** *n* CINEMAT tirage de copies en série *m*; ~ **relay** *n* ELEC relais déclencheur *m*; ~ **rod** *n* AUTO tringle de fourchette *f*; ~ **switch** *n* ELEC commutateur de desserrage *m*; ~ **time** *n* AERONAUT *air traffic* heure de déblocage *f*, ELEC ENG temps de relâchement *m*, RECORDING temps de retour *m*; ~ **valve** *n* HYDR EQUIP soupape de sûreté *f*

release[2] *vt* CHEM dégager, laisser échapper, CINEMAT *film* distribuer, lancer, sortir, GAS TECH relâcher, MECH desserrer, débloquer, libérer, PROD ENG débloquer, relâcher, VEHICLES *brake* desserrer; ~ **for manufacturing** *vt* PROD ENG lancer en fabrication

release-coated: ~ **paper** *n* PAPER TECH desserrage *m*, papier couché anti-adhésif *m*

released[1] *adj* PHYS *energy* dégagé

released:[2] ~ **order** *n* PROD ENG ordre de fabrication lancé *m*

releasing *n* RAIL *vehicles* desserrage *m*; ~ **hook** *n* CONST *of pile driver* déclic *m*

releveling *n* (AmE), **relevelling** *n* (BrE) CONST renivellement *m*

reliability *n* COMP, DP fiabilité *f*, ELEC ENG fiabilité *f*, sûreté de fonctionnement *f*, MECH ENG fiabilité *f*, *of machines* sécurité de fonctionnement *f*, sûreté de fonctionnement *f*, METR fiabilité *f*, PROD ENG fiabilité *f*, sûreté de fonctionnement *f*, PROP MAT, QUALITY, TELECOM fiabilité *f* ~ **analysis** *n* SPACE *spacecraft* étude de fiabilité *f*; ~ **index** *n* CRYSTALL facteur R *m*, facteur de confiance *m*, indice de confiance *m*; ~ **parameter** *n* PROP MAT caractéristique de fiabilité *f*; ~ **test** *n* ELEC ENG essai de fiabilité *m*; ~ **testing** *n* ELEC ENG essai de fiabilité *m*

reliable: ~ **transfer server** *n (RTS)* TELECOM serveur de transfert fiable *m*

relic *adj* GEOL *of mineral or structure* relique, résiduel

relict: ~ **radiation** *n* ASTRON, SPACE rayonnement fossile *m*

relictual *adj* GEOL *of mineral or structure* relique, résiduel

relief *n* MECH décharge *f*, MECH ENG *clearance, backing off* dégagement *m*, dépouille *f*, *machine tool* angle d'incidence *m*; ~ **angle** *n* MECH ENG angle d'incidence *m*; ~ **crew** *n* AERONAUT équipage de relève *m*; ~ **gap** *n* ELEC *spark* éclateur de protection *m*; ~ **hole** *n* MINING trou de dégagement *m*, trou de dégraissage *m*; ~ **printing** *n* PRINT impression en relief *f*; ~ **track** *n* RAIL voie de dédoublement *f*, *in marshalling yard* voie de report *f*; ~ **train** *n* RAIL train complémentaire *m*; ~ **valve** *n* AUTO clapet de décharge *m*, CONTROL soupape de décompression *f*, FUELLESS soupape de sûreté *f*, HYDR EQUIP clapet d'admission *m*, clapet d'appel d'air *m*, clapet de décharge *m*, clapet de surpression *m*, détendeur *m*, soupape de sûreté *f*, *for steam* soupape de détente *f*, MECH soupape de décharge *f*, PETR TECH soupape de détente *f*, PROD ENG clapet de décharge *m*, REFRIG soupape de sûreté *f*, VEHICLES *lubrication* clapet de décharge *m*, soupape de décharge *f*; ~ **weaves** *n pl* TEXTILES armures en relief *f pl*; ~ **well** *n* PETR puits d'intervention *m*, puits de secours *m*, WATER SUPP puits de décharge *m*, puits de décompression *m*

relieve *vt* HYDR EQUIP *valve* décharger, MECH ENG dégager, dépouiller

relieved: ~ **milling cutter** *n* MECH ENG fraise à dents dégagées *f*, fraise à denture à dépouille *f*; ~ **teeth** *n pl* MECH ENG dents dégagées *f pl*, denture à dépouille *f*

reliever *n* MINING trou de dégagement *m*, trou de dégraissage *m*; ~ **hole** *n* MINING trou de dégagement *m*, trou de dégraissage *m*

relieving: ~ **lathe** *n* MECH ENG tour à dégager *m*, tour à dépouiller *m*

reline *vt* VEHICLES *brakes* regarnir

relining *n* PROD ENG redoublement *m*

relinquishment: ~ **requirement** *n* PETR TECH clause de rétrocession *f*

reload *vt* CINEMAT, COMP, DP, PHOTO recharger

reloading *n* PROD ENG rechargement *m*

relocatable[1] *adj* COMP, DP translatable

relocatable:[2] ~ **program** *n* COMP, DP programme translatable *m*

relocate *vt* COMP, DP translater

relocation *n* COMP, DP translation *f*

reluctance *n* ELEC *magnetism*, ELEC ENG, PHYS réluctance *f*; ~ **motor** *n* ELEC, ELEC ENG, TRANSP moteur à réluctance *m*

reluctivity *n* ELEC *magnetism*, PHYS réluctivité *f*

rem *n (roentgen equivalent man)* RAD PHYS rem *m*, équivalent en roentgen pour l'homme *m*; ~ **jet backing** *n* CINEMAT couche antihalo *f*

remainder *n* COMP, DP, MATH reste *m*

remaking *n* PROD ENG *joints* réfection *f*

remanence *n* ELEC *magnetism*, ELEC ENG, PETR, PHYS *retentivity*, RECORDING rémanence *f*

remanent: ~ **charge** *n* ELEC ENG charge rémanente *f*; ~ **flux density** *n* ELEC *magnetization* induction rémanente *f*; ~ **induction** *n* ELEC ENG induction rémanente *f*; ~ **magnetization** *n* PETR magnétisation rémanente *f*, PHYS aimantation rémanente *f*

remedial: ~ **maintenance** *n* COMP, DP maintenance corrective *f*

remelting: ~ **machine** *n* (AmE) *(cf burning-off and edge-melting machine)* C&G coupeuse-rebrûleuse *f*

remetalling *n* (BrE) *(cf repaving, resurfacing)* CONST *roads* rechargement *m*

reminder: ~ **alarm service** *n* TELECOM téléalerte *f*; ~ **call** *n* TELECOM appel de rendez-vous *m*, mémo rappel *m*

remodulation *n* ELECTRON transfert de modulation *m*

remoistenable *adj* PRINT réhumectable

remolded: ~ **sample** *n* (AmE) *see remoulded sample*

remolding *n* (AmE) *see remoulding*

remote[1] *adj* COMP distant, éloigné, à distance, DP éloigné

remote:[2] ~ **access** *n* COMP, DP accès à distance *m*; ~ **acquisition unit** *n (RAU)* CONTROL unité d'acquisition décentralisée *f*; ~ **actuation** *n* CONTROL actionnement à distance *m*, manoeuvre à distance *f*; ~ **alarm** *n* CONTROL téléalarme *f*; ~ **alarm indication** *n (RAI)* TELECOM indication d'alarme distante *f*; ~ **amplifier** *n* ELECTRON amplificateur de reportage *m*; ~ **arming and safety unit** *n* SPACE *spacecraft* dispositif de sécurité et d'armement à distance *m*, dispositif de sécurité et de téléarmement *m*; ~ **batch control** *n* CONTROL télétraitement par lots *m*; ~ **batch processing** *n* COMP, DP télétraitement par lots *m*; ~ **batch terminal** *n (RBT)* COMP, DP terminal de télétraitement *m*; ~ **bridge control** *n* CONTROL télécommande à passerelle *f*; ~ **broadcast** *n* TV émission en extérieur *f*; ~ **bulb thermostat** *n* REFRIG thermostat à bulbe *m*; ~ **channel** *n* PROD ENG canal décentralisé *m*; ~ **concentration unit** *n (RCU)* TELECOM concentrateur satellite numérique *m*; ~ **concentrator** *n* TELECOM concentrateur distant *m*; ~ **control** *n* CINEMAT déclencheur à distance *m*, télécommande *f*, CONST télécommande *f*, CONTROL commande à distance *f*, télécommande *f*, télécouplage *m*, télésurveillance *f*, contrôle à distance *m*, ELEC commande à distance *f*, télécommande *f*, MECH télécommande *f*, PHOTO commande à distance *f*, télécommande *f*, SPACE commande à distance *f*, TELECOM commande à distance *f*, VEHICLES commande à distance *f*; ~ **control by television camera** *n* TRANSP commande à distance par caméra *f*; ~ **control center** *n* (AmE), ~ **control centre** *n* (BrE) CONTROL central de télécommande *m*; ~ **control device** *n* RECORDING dispositif de télécommande *m*; ~ **control focusing** *n* TV mise au point à distance *f*; ~ **control office** *n* CONTROL central de télécommande *m*; ~ **control operation** *n* CONTROL entraînement à distance *m*; ~ **control sign** *n* TRANSP signal actionné par télécommande *m*; ~ **control switch** *n* CONTROL interrupteur à commande à distance *m*; ~

control system *n* CONTROL système de commande à distance *m*, SAFETY système de télécommande *m*; ~ **control technique** *n* CONTROL technique de commandes à distance *f*, technique de télécommande *f*; ~ **control unit** *n* CONTROL régulateur à distance *m*; ~ **data processing** *n* CONTROL téléinformatique *f*, télétraitement de données *m*, TELECOM téléinformatique *f*; ~ **data transmission** *n* CONTROL télétransmission de données *f*; ~ **detection** *n* CONTROL, TELECOM télédétection *f*; ~ **electronics** *n pl* INSTRUMENT bloc électronique *m*; ~ **handling device** *n* SAFETY manipulation par commande à distance *f*; ~ **job entry** *n (RJE)* COMP, DP soumission des travaux à distance *f*; ~ **line concentrator** *n* TELECOM concentrateur d'abonnés distant *m*; ~ **loading** *n* COMP, DP, TELECOM téléchargement *m*; ~ **maintenance** *n* TELECOM télémaintenance *f*; ~ **management** *n* TELECOM télégestion *f*; ~ **manipulator** *n* OCEANOG télémanipulateur *m*; ~ **manipulator arm** *n* SPACE bras télémanipulateur *m*; ~ **metering** *n* NUCLEAR télémesure *f*; ~ **mode** *n* PROD ENG mode déporté *m*; ~ **mode selection** *n* PROD ENG sélection de mode déporté *f*; ~ **monitoring** *n* CONTROL contrôle à distance *m*, TELECOM, TV télésurveillance *f*; ~ **operating terminal** *n* TELECOM poste d'exploitation déporté *m*, terminal d'exploitation éloigné *m*; ~ **operation** *n* TELECOM exploitation à distance *f*; ~ **operations** *n pl (RO)* TELECOM opérations distantes *f pl*; ~ **operation service element** *n (ROSE)* TELECOM élément de service d'opération distante *m*; ~ **operator** *n* OCEANOG télémanipulateur *m*; ~ **pickup point** *n* TV point de captation éloigné *m*; ~ **piloted vehicle** *n* MILIT véhicule commandé à distance *m*; ~ **power supply** *n* ELEC ENG téléalimentation *f*; ~ **program mode** *n* PROD ENG mode de programmation déportée *m*; ~ **reading thermometer** *n* REFRIG thermomètre à lecture à distance *m*; ~ **reset** *n* PROD ENG réarmement à distance *m*; ~ **RTD module** *n* PROD ENG module d'interface déporté pour thermistances PTC *m*; ~ **sensing** *n* COMP, GEOL télédétection *f*, MAR POLL détection à distance *f*, télédétection *f*, SPACE télédétection *f*; ~ **sensing satellite** *n* SPACE *spacecraft* satellite de télédétection *m*; ~ **sensor** *n* CONST capteur à distance *m*; ~ **shutdown circuit** *n* PROD ENG circuit d'arrêt à distance *m*; ~ **switching** *n* TV télécommutation *f*; ~ **switching stage** *n* TELECOM étage de commutation distante *m*; ~ **switching system** *n* TELECOM satellite *m*; ~ **switching unit** *n (RSU)* TELECOM centre satellite *m*; ~ **temperature gage** *n* (AmE), ~ **temperature gauge** *n* (BrE) THERMOD thermomètre à distance *m*, téléthermomètre *m*; ~ **temperature monitoring** *n* THERMOD téléthermométrie *f*; ~ **terminal** *n* COMP, DP terminal éloigné *m*; ~ **test** *n* COMP, DP essai à distance *m*, PROD ENG test déporté *m*; ~ **test mode** *n* PROD ENG mode de test déporté *m*; ~ **transmission technique** *n* CONTROL technique de télétransmission *f*; ~ **unit** *n (RU)* TELECOM unité distante *f*, unité déportée *f*

remote:[3] ~ **control** *vt* CONTROL téléguider

remote-adjusting: ~ **device** *n* CONTROL dispositif de réglage à distance *m*

remote-controlled[1] *adj* CONTROL commandé à distance, télécommandé, télérégulé, TV télécommandé

remote-controlled:[2] ~ **camera** *n* TV caméra télécommandée *f*; ~ **flight** *n* MILIT vol contrôlé à distance *m*, vol téléguidé *m*; ~ **pneumatic valve** *n* MECH ENG soupape pneumatique avec commande à distance *f*; ~ **switch** *n* CONTROL contrôleur à distance *m*, interrupteur à distance *m*, télérupteur *m*; ~ **switching** *n* CONTROL télécouplage *m*

remoulded: ~ **sample** *n* (BrE) COAL TECH échantillon remanié *m*

remoulding *n* (BrE) PROD ENG remoulage *m*

removable[1] *adj* MECH ENG amovible, démontable, mobile, OPT amovible, PROD ENG déposable

removable:[2] ~ **back** *n* PHOTO dos amovible *m*; ~ **coupling link** *n* RAIL *vehicles* manille mobile *f*; ~ **disk** *n* COMP, DP disque amovible *m*; ~ **insert** *n* MECH ENG *tooling*, PROD ENG noyau rapporté *m*; ~ **part** *n* ELEC *circuit* élément démontable *m*

removables *n pl* AERONAUT amovibles *m pl*

removal *n* CONST *of blasted rock* marinage *m*, MAR POLL *of oil* enlèvement *m*, MECH ENG *of machinery* déplacement *m*, MINING *of mineral deposit* enlèvement d'un gîte métallifère *m*, NAUT *from mould of cast* démoulage *m*, POLLUTION *of oil by separators, of organic matter, of suspended solids by sedimentation* épuration *f*; ~ **of iron** *n* C&G déferrisation magnétique *f*; ~ **of locomotive rods** *n* RAIL *vehicles* désembiellage *m*; ~ **of timbering** *n* MINING déboisage *m*, enlèvement du boisage *m*; ~ **van** *n* TRANSP camion de déménagement *m*

remove[1] *vt* HYDROL emporter, enlever, entraîner, MECH ENG *machinery* déplacer, *wire edge from edge of knife* morfiler, NAUT *cast from mould* démouler, PROD ENG *burr from casting* ébarber, SAFETY *dust* dépoussiérer

remove:[2] ~ **an overburden** *vi* MINING décapeler le gîte, enlever les terrains de couverture, pratiquer la découverte, pratiquer le découvert

removing *n* CONST *landmarks* déplacement *m*, PROD ENG *incrustation in boilers* désincrustation *f*; ~ **dust** *n* PROD ENG dépoussiérage *m*, enlèvement des poussières *m*; ~ **an overburden** *n* CONST décapage *m*, découverture *f*, enlèvement des terrains de couverture *m*, enlèvement des terrains stériles superposés *m*

remreed: ~ **crosspoint** *n* TELECOM point de connexion remreed *m*

rendered: ~ **fat** *n* FOOD TECH graisse fondue *f*

rendering *n* CONST revêtement en plâtre *m*

rendezvous: ~ **maneuver** *n* (AmE), ~ **manoeuvre** *n* (BrE) TRANSP technique de rendez-vous *f*; ~ **procedure** *n* SPACE procédure de rendez-vous *f*; ~ **radar** *n* SPACE radar de rendez-vous *m*; ~ **trajectory** *n* SPACE trajectoire de rendez-vous *f*

renewable: ~ **source of energy** *n* FUELLESS, PHYS source d'énergie renouvelable *f*

renewal *n* PATENTS renouvellement *m*; ~ **fee** *n* PATENTS taxe annuelle *f*; ~ **parts list** *n* PROD ENG liste des pièces de rechange *f*

rennet *n* FOOD TECH présure *f*; ~ **casein** *n* FOOD TECH *curdling* caséine de présure *f*

rennin *n* FOOD TECH chymosine *f*, présure *f*, rénine *f*

renovation *n* PROD ENG renouvellement *m*

reorder: ~ **period** *n* PROD ENG période de réapprovisionnement *f*; ~ **point** *n* PROD ENG point de réapprovisionnement *m*; ~ **quantity** *n* PROD ENG quantité de réapprovisionnement *f*

reoxidation *n* POLLUTION réoxygénation *f*

repack *vt* MECH ENG *piston* regarnir

repair:[1] **under** ~ *adv* MECH ENG en réparation, NAUT *of ship* en radoub

repair[2] *n* NAUT *ship* réparation *f*, PROD ENG raccommodage *m*, réfection *f*, réparation *f*; ~ **dock** *n* NAUT bassin de radoub *m*; ~ **link** *n* MECH ENG fausse maille *f*; ~ **outfit** *n* PROD ENG boîte à réparations *f*, nécessaire à répara-

tions *m*, trousse à réparations *f*; ~ **shop** *n* PROD ENG atelier de réparations *m*; ~ **time** *n* COMP, DP durée de réparation *f*, temps de réparation *m*; ~ **track** *n* (BrE) *(cf rip track)* RAIL voie de réparations *f*

repair[3] *vt* ELECTRON réparer, NAUT *ship* radouber, réparer, PROD ENG raccommoder, rajuster, refaire, remettre en état, réparer

repair[4] *vti* NAUT caréner

repairing *n* PROD ENG raccommodage *m*, rajustement *m*, remise en état *f*, réfection *f*, réparation *f*

repaving *n* (AmE) *(cf remetalling)* CONST *roads* rechargement *m*

repeat *n* PRINT pose sur la forme imprimante *f*, report *m*, TV rediffusion *f*; ~ **key** *n* TV touche répétition *f*

repeatability *n* METR *of measurements* répétabilité *f*

repeatable: ~ **measurement** *n* METR mesurage répétable *m*

repeated: ~ **call attempt** *n* TELECOM tentative d'appel répétée *f*; ~ **loading** *n* METALL sollicitation répétée *f*; ~ **signal** *n* ELECTRON signal transmis par un répéteur *m*; ~ **yield point** *n* METALL crochet de traction répété *m*

repeater *n* COMP répéteur *m*, DP relais *m*, répéteur *m*, ELECTRON, PHYS répéteur *m*, SPACE répéteur *m*, répétiteur *m*, TELECOM répéteur *m*; ~ **compass** *n* NAUT, SPACE *spacecraft* compas répétiteur *m*; ~ **deck** *n* TELECOM pont des répéteurs *m*; ~ **satellite** *n* SPACE satellite répéteur *m*; ~ **signal** *n* NAUT *electronic equipment* signal répétiteur *m*

repeating: ~ **coil** *n* CONST translateur *m*; ~ **decimal** *n* MATH fraction périodique *f*; ~ **signal** *n* RAIL signal répétiteur *m*

repeller *n* ELEC ENG réflecteur *m*, électrode réflectrice *f*

repercussion *n* SAFETY contrecoup *m*

repertoire *n* COMP, DP répertoire *m*

repetition:[1] ~ **rate** *n* ELECTRON fréquence de récurrence *f*

repetition:[2] ~ **fire** *vt* MILIT tir coup par coup *m*

repetitive: ~ **flight plan** *n* AERONAUT plan de vol répétitif *m*; ~ **signal** *n* ELECTRON signal récurrent *m*; ~ **sweep** *n* ELECTRON balayage récurrent *m*; ~ **work** *n* PROD ENG fabrication en série *f*

replaceable: ~ **element oil filter** *n* AUTO filtre à huile à cartouche jetable *m*

replacement: ~ **battery assembly** *n* PROD ENG ensemble pile de secours *m*; ~ **cost valuation** *n* PROD ENG valeur de remplacement *f*; ~ **price** *n* PROD ENG prix de renouvellement *m*; ~ **programmer interconnect cable** *n* PROD ENG câble de rechange pour interconnexion de terminal de programmation *m*

replay[1] *n* RECORDING reproduction *f*, TV lecture *f*, reproduction *f*; ~ **characteristic** *n* TV caractéristique de reproduction *f*; ~ **head** *n* RECORDING tête de lecture *f*

replay[2] *vt* RECORDING reproduire

replenisher *n* CINEMAT régénérateur *m*, PHOTO *of developer* solution régénératrice *f*

replenishing: ~ **ship** *n* TRANSP pétrolier ravitailleur *m*; ~ **solution** *n* CINEMAT solution d'entretien *f*

replenishment *n* CINEMAT renouvellement *m*; ~ **lead time** *n* PROD ENG cycle d'approvisionnement *m*, délai d'approvisionnement *m*, temps d'obtention total *m*; ~ **order** *n* PROD ENG commande de réapprovisionnement *f*

replicated: ~ **pattern** *n* ELECTRON motif reproduit *m*

reply *n* ELECTRON réponse *f*

repoint *vt* CONST *brickwork, masonry* rejointoyer

report[1] *n* COMP, DP état *m*, MINING détonation *f*, explosion *f*, SPACE débreffage *m*; ~ **for landing** *n* AERONAUT *meteorology* compte rendu pour l'atterrissage *m*; ~ **for**

takeoff *n* AERONAUT compte rendu pour le décollage *m*; ~ **generation** *n* COMP, DP génération d'états *f*; ~ **program generator** *n* COMP, DP générateur de programme d'états *m*; ~ **sheet** *n* CINEMAT fiche de rapport de tournage *f*

report[2] *vt* SAFETY *accident* signaler

report:[3] ~ **to the port authorities** *vi* NAUT se déclarer aux autorités du port

reportable: ~ **accident** *n* SAFETY accident à déclarer obligatoirement *m*

repository *n* COMP archives *f pl*, référentiel *m*, DP magasin *m*, référentiel *m*, POLLUTION dépôt *m*

representation *n* COMP, DP représentation *f*

representative *n* PATENTS mandataire *f*

reprint *vt* CINEMAT retirer

repro: ~ **proof** *n* PRINT épreuve de photograveur *f*, épreuve de qualité *f*, épreuve pour bon-à-tirer *f*

reprocess *vt* RECYCLING retraiter

reprocessing *n* PROD ENG, RECYCLING retraitement *m*; ~ **plant** *n* RECYCLING usine de retraitement *f*

reproduce *vt* RECORDING reproduire

reproducibility *n* METR *of measurements* reproductibilité *f*

reproducing *n* ACOUSTICS lecture *f*, reproduction *f*; ~ **chain** *n* TV chaîne de reproduction *f*; ~ **characteristic** *n* ACOUSTICS caractéristique de lecture *f*; ~ **head** *n* TV tête de lecture *f*; ~ **loss** *n* ACOUSTICS perte de lecture *f*; ~ **magnetic head** *n* ACOUSTICS tête magnétique de lecture *f*

reproducing-recording: ~ **characteristic** *n* ACOUSTICS caractéristique d'enregistrement-lecture *f*

reproduction *n* ACOUSTICS, RECORDING reproduction *f*; ~ **camera** *n* PRINT banc de reproduction *m*; ~ **characteristics** *n pl* TV caractéristique de reproduction *f*; ~ **level** *n* CINEMAT niveau d'écoute *m*; ~ **loss** *n* TV perte de lecture *f*; ~ **of tonal values** *n* PHOTO rendu des valeurs *m*

reprofiling *n* CONST *roadworks* reprofilage *m*

reprographics *n* COMP, DP reprographie *f*

repudiation *n* TELECOM répudiation *f*

repulping: ~ **equipment** *n* PACKAGING équipement de désintégration *m*

repulsion *n* ELEC ENG, PHYS répulsion *f*; ~ **motor** *n* ELEC, ELEC ENG moteur à répulsion *m*

repulsion-induction: ~ **motor** *n* ELEC ENG moteur à répulsion-induction *m*

repulsive: ~ **force** *n* ELEC *electrostatics, magnetism*, ELEC ENG, PHYS force de répulsion *f*; ~ **junction** *n* METALL jonction répulsive *f*

req *n* (*request*) TELECOM demande *f*

request[1] *n* COMP, DP demande *f*, requête *f*, PATENTS requête *f*, TELECOM demande *f*; ~ **channel** *n* SPACE *communications* canal d'interrogation *m*; ~ **for quotation** *n* PROD ENG consultation des fournisseurs *f*; ~ **for service** *n* TELECOM demande de prestation *f*; ~ **stack** *n* COMP, DP pile de requêtes *f*; ~ **to send** *n* TELECOM demande pour émettre *f*

request[2] *vt* COMP, DP demander

required: ~ **flight path** *n* AERONAUT trajectoire de vol exigée *f*; ~ **frequency** *n* FUELLESS fréquence requise *f*

requirement *n* SAFETY *condition* condition requise *f*, exigence *f*, prescription *f*, TESTING exigence *f*; ~ **explosion** *n* PROD ENG éclatement des besoins *m*

rerecording *n* ACOUSTICS réenregistrement *m*, *multiplayback* surimpression *f*, RECORDING repiquage *m*, réenregistrement *m*; ~ **machine** *n* RECORDING appareil de réenregistrement *m*; ~ **session** *n* RECORDING séance de mixage *f*

reroute *vt* NAUT *shipping* dérouter

rerouting *n* NAUT *shipping* déroutement *m*, TELECOM réacheminement *m*

rerun[1] *n* CHEM recyclage *m*, redistillation *f*, COMP reprise *f*

rerun[2] *vt* COMP, DP repasser, réexécuter

RES *abbr* (*reserved field*) TELECOM champ réservé *m*

resazurin *n* CHEM résazurine *f*

rescheduling *n* PROD ENG rejalonnement *m*

rescue[1] *n* NAUT sauvetage *m*, SAFETY *help* secours *m*, *saving* sauvetage *m*; ~ **and firefighting service** *n* AERONAUT service de sauvetage et de lutte contre l'incendie *m*; ~ **apparatus** *n* NAUT appareil de sauvetage *m*, engins de sauvetage *m pl*, matériel de sauvetage *m*; ~ **blanket** *n* SAFETY *first aid* couverture de sauvetage *f*, couverture de survie *f*, drap de sauvetage *m*; ~ **boat** *n* AERONAUT vedette de sauvetage *f*, NAUT bateau de sauvetage *m*; ~ **chute** *n* SAFETY glissière de sauvetage *f*; ~ **coordination center** *n* (AmE), ~ **coordination centre** *n* (BrE) AERONAUT, NAUT centre de coordination de sauvetage *m*; ~ **dump** *n* COMP, DP vidage de secours *m*; ~ **equipment** *n* AERONAUT équipement de sauvetage *m*, SAFETY matériel de sauvetage *m*, matériel de secours *m*; ~ **helicopter** *n* MILIT, TRANSP hélicoptère de sauvetage *m*; ~ **operation** *n* SAFETY opération de sauvetage *f*; ~ **party** *n* SAFETY équipe de sauvetage *f*; ~ **services** *n pl* SAFETY services de sauvetage *m pl*; ~ **ship** *n* NAUT navire de secours *m*; ~ **station** *n* SAFETY poste de sauvetage *m*; ~ **strap** *n* AERONAUT *shipping* sangle de sauvetage *f*; ~ **vehicle** *n* AERONAUT, SPACE *spacecraft* véhicule de sauvetage *m*; ~ **work** *n* SAFETY travaux de sauvetage *m pl*

rescue[2] *vt* NAUT *man overboard* repêcher, SAFETY sauver, secourir

research: ~ **centre** *n* TELECOM centre de recherche *m*; ~ **development engineer** *n* MECH ENG ingénieur en recherche-développement *m*; ~ **with colliders** *n* PART PHYS recherche auprès de collisionneurs *f*

reseat *vt* VEHICLES *engine valves* rectifier

reserpine *n* CHEM réserpine *f*

reserve: ~ **battery** *n* ELEC ENG pile amorçable *f*; ~ **buoyancy** *n* NAUT *ship design* réserve de flottabilité *f*, TRANSP réserve de flottaison *f*; ~ **capacity** *n* TRANSP coefficient de réserve de capacité *m*

reserved:[1] ~ **for special use** *adj* PROD ENG réservé à un emploi spécifique

reserved:[2] ~ **field** *n* (*RES*) TELECOM champ réservé *m*; ~ **word** *n* COMP, DP mot réservé *m*

reserves *n pl* AERONAUT réserves *f pl*

reservoir *n* FLUID PHYS réservoir *m*, HYDROL bassin *m*, réservoir *m*, réservoir de retenue d'eau *m*, PETR réservoir *m*, PETR TECH roche magasin *f*, réservoir *m*, VEHICLES *oil, fuel, fluid*, WATER SUPP réservoir *m*; ~ **basin** *n* WATER SUPP cuvette de retenue *f*; ~ **capacitor** *n* ELEC ENG condensateur de charge *m*; ~ **conditions** *n pl* PETR conditions de réservoir *f pl*, état de réservoir *m*; ~ **energy** *n* PETR pression de gisement *f*; ~ **lining** *n* WATER SUPP revêtement de retenue *m*; ~ **pressure** *n* PETR, PETR TECH pression de réservoir *f*; ~ **rock** *n* GAS TECH, GEOL, PETR TECH roche réservoir *f*

reset[1] *n* COMP, DP remise à l'état initial *f*, restauration *f*; ~ **button** *n* COMP bouton de restauration *m*, CONTROL bouton-poussoir de réenclenchement *m*, touche de rappel *f*, DP bouton de remise à zéro *m*, bouton de restauration *m*; ~ **knob** *n* CINEMAT, TV bouton de remise à zéro *m*; ~ **push** *n* PROD ENG poussoir à réarmement *m*; ~ **push button** *n* PROD ENG bouton-poussoir de réarmement *m*; ~ **rung** *n* PROD ENG ligne de remise à zéro *f*

reset[2] *vt* CINEMAT remettre au point de départ, remettre à zéro, réenclencher, COMP, DP remettre à zéro, *counter* remettre à l'état initial, MECH recaler, remettre à zéro, MECH ENG remonter, PROD ENG désactiver, mettre à zéro, retomber; ~ **to zero** *vt* MECH ENG *instrument* ramener à zéro, remettre à zéro

reset-set: ~ **flip-flop** *n* (*RS flip-flop*) ELEC bascule RS *f*

reset-set-toggle: ~ **flip-flop** *n* (*RST flip-flop*) ELEC bascule RST *f*

resetting *n* GEOL *geochronology* rajeunissement des âges *m*, remise à zéro *f*, MECH ENG, PROD ENG remise à zéro *f*

resharpening *n* MECH ENG raffûtage *m*

reshipment *n* NAUT réembarquement *m*, réexpédition *f*

reshipping *n* NAUT réembarquement *m*

reshoot *vt* CINEMAT refilmer

reside *vi* COMP, DP résider

resident[1] *adj* COMP, DP résidant

resident:[2] ~ **program** *n* COMP programme résident *m*

residual[1] *adj* COMP, DP résiduel

residual:[2] ~ **austenite** *n* METALL austénite restante *f*, austénite résiduelle *f*; ~ **capacitance** *n* ELEC ENG capacité résiduelle *f*; ~ **charge** *n* ELEC *electrostatics*, ELEC ENG, TV charge résiduelle *f*; ~ **current** *n* ELEC, ELEC ENG courant résiduel *m*; ~ **discharge** *n* ELEC ENG décharge secondaire *f*; ~ **energy** *n* HEATING énergie résiduelle *f*; ~ **flux density** *n* ELEC *magnetization* induction rémanente *f*; ~ **frequency modulation** *n* ELECTRON modulation de fréquence résiduelle *f*; ~ **fuel oil** *n* PETR TECH fuel résiduel *m*; ~ **gap** *n* ELEC ENG entrefer résiduel *m*; ~ **gas** *n* ELECTRON gaz résiduel *m*, POLLUTION gaz résiduaire *m*, gaz résiduel *m*; ~ **magnetism** *n* ELEC, PROD ENG rémanence magnétique *f*; ~ **magnetization** *n* RAD PHYS aimantation rémanente *f*; ~ **moisture** *n* PACKAGING, REFRIG *freeze-dried foods* humidité résiduelle *f*; ~ **noise** *n* COMP, DP bruit résiduel *m*; ~ **oil saturation** *n* (*ROS*) PETR saturation en huile résiduelle *f*; ~ **radioactivity** *n* RAD PHYS radioactivité résiduelle *f*; ~ **range** *n* SPRINGS écartement minime d'exercice *m*; ~ **relay** *n* ELEC relais à point nul *m*; ~ **resistance** *n* ELEC ENG résistance résiduelle *f*; ~ **set** *n* P&R déformation résiduelle *f*; ~ **shrinkage** *n* TEXTILES retrait résiduel *m*; ~ **sideband** *n* TELECOM bande latérale résiduelle *f*; ~ **silver** *n* PHOTO résidu d'argent *m*; ~ **strength** *n* COAL TECH résistance résiduelle *f*; ~ **stress** *n* C&G contrainte résiduelle *f*, CONST contrainte résiduelle *f*, tension résiduelle *f*, PROP MAT, SPRINGS contrainte résiduelle *f*; ~ **water content** *n* OPT teneur en eau résiduelle *f*; ~ **water saturation** *n* PETR saturation résiduelle en eau *f*

residuary *adj* CHEM résiduaire, résiduel

residue *n* CHEM reliquat *m*, résidu *m*, FOOD TECH, MAR POLL, PETR TECH, POLLUTION, WATER SUPP résidu *m*; ~ **arithmetic** *n* COMP, DP arithmétique modulaire *f*; ~ **refining process** *n* PETR TECH raffinage des résidus *m*

resilience *n* COMP, DP résilience *f*, MECH ENG résilience *f*, résistance vive *f*, P&R résilience *f*, PAPER TECH papier couché anti-adhésif *m*, résilience *f*, TEXTILES résilience *f*

resilient[1] *adj* PROP MAT résilient

resilient:[2] ~ **covered roller** *n* PRINT rouleau garni *m*; ~

isolator *n* SAFETY *against vibration* isolateur élastique *m*; ~ **rail** *n* TRANSP voie élastique *f*; ~ **shaft coupling** *n* MECH ENG accouplement élastique pour arbre de transmission *m*

resin *n* CHEM résine *f*, NAUT mastic *m*, résine *f*, P&R *plastics, polymers*, PROP MAT, TEXTILES résine *f*; ~ **oil varnish** *n* COATINGS vernis de résinyle *m*; ~ **roof-bolting system** *n* MINING système d'injection de résine pour boulons de toit *m*

resin-bonded: ~ **plywood** *n* P&R contreplaqué à la résine *m*; ~ **wheel** *n* MECH ENG meule avec liant de résine synthétique *f*

resin-coated: ~ **paper** *n* PRINT bromure *m*, papier RC photographique *m*

resist *n* C&G enduit protecteur *m*, COATINGS vernis à masquer *m*, ELECTRON résist *m*, PRINT réserve *f*; ~ **coating** *n* P&R *paint* vernis à couvrir *m*

resistance ELEC, ELEC ENG, MECH ENG, MINING *of mine*, P&R *physical, electrical property*, PETR, PHYS, PROP MAT, TELECOM, TEXTILES résistance *f*; ~ **box** *n* ELEC ENG boîte de résistance *f*; ~ **butt welding** *n* CONST soudage en bout par résistance pure *m*; ~ **coil** *n* ELEC ENG bobine à résistance *f*; ~ **drop** *n* ELEC chute de résistance *f*; ~ **furnace** *n* ELEC ENG four à résistance *m*; ~ **heating** *n* ELEC chauffage ohmique *m*, THERMOD chauffage ohmique *m*, chauffage par effet joule *m*; ~ **material** *n* ELEC ENG matière pour résistance *f*; ~ **meter** *n* ELEC mesureur de résistance *m*; ~ **on** *n* ELEC ENG résistance à l'état passant *f*; ~ **per unit length** *n* PHYS résistance linéique *f*; ~ **seam welding** *n* CONST soudage à la molette *m*; ~ **spot welding** *n* ELEC, MECH ENG soudage par points *m*; ~ **thermometer** *n* PHYS, REFRIG thermomètre à résistance électrique *m*; ~ **to bending** *n* MECH ENG résistance à la flexion *f*; ~ **to buckling** *n* MECH ENG résistance au flambage *f*; ~ **to crushing** *n* MECH ENG résistance à l'écrasement *f*; ~ **to flow** *n* FLUID PHYS résistance à l'écoulement *f*; ~ **to forward motion** *n* TRANSP traînée *f*; ~ **to heat** *n* THERMOD résistance à la chaleur *f*; ~ **to impact** *n* MECH ENG résistance aux chocs *f*; ~ **to motion** *n* MECH ENG résistance passive *f*; ~ **to shattering** *n* PACKAGING résistance à l'éclatement *f*; ~ **to shearing** *n* MECH ENG résistance au cisaillement *f*; ~ **to shock** *n* MECH ENG résistance aux chocs *f*; ~ **to sliding** *n* MECH ENG résistance au glissement *f*; ~ **to soiling** *n* TEXTILES résistance à la salissure *f*; ~ **to tearing** *n* MAR POLL résistance au déchirement *f*, MECH ENG résistance au déchirement *f*, résistance à l'arrachement *f*; ~ **to tension** *n* MECH ENG résistance à la traction *f*; ~ **to thermal shock** *n* THERMOD résistance aux chocs thermiques *f*; ~ **to twisting** *n* MECH ENG résistance à la torsion *f*; ~ **welding** *n* CONST, ELEC, THERMOD soudage par résistance *m*; ~ **welding equipment** *n* MECH ENG matériel de soudage par résistance *m*; ~ **wire** *n* ELEC fil résistant *m*, ELEC ENG fil résistant *m*, fil à résistances *m*, METALL fil résistant *m*

resistance-capacitance *n* (*RC*) ELEC ENG, ELECTRON résistance-capacité *f* (*RC*); ~ **coupling** *n* ELEC ENG liaison par résistance et capacitance *f*

resistant *adj* P&R résistant; ~ **to impact** *adj* METR résistant aux chocs

resist-coated: ~ **wafer** *n* ELECTRON plaquette enduite de résist *f*

resisting: ~ **torque** *n* AUTO couple résistant *m*

resistive[1] *adj* ELEC ENG résistif

resistive:[2] ~ **attenuator** *n* TELECOM affaiblisseur résistif *m*, atténuateur résistif *m* (Can); ~ **circuit** *n* ELEC ENG,

TELECOM circuit résistif *m*; **~ coupling** *n* ELEC ENG couplage par résistance *m*; **~ element** *n* ELEC ENG élément résistif *m*; **~ load** *n* ELEC *machine* charge active *f*, ELEC ENG, TELECOM charge résistive *f*; **~ thin film** *n* ELECTRON couche mince résistive *f*; **~ voltage divider** *n* ELEC diviseur de tension par résistance *m*

resistivity *n* COAL TECH, ELEC résistivité *f*, ELEC ENG résistivité spécifique *f*, HEAT ENG, P&R, PETR, PETR TECH, PHYS, PROP MAT résistivité *f*; **~ index** *n* PETR indice de résistivité *m*; **~ log** *n* FUELLESS rapport de résistivité *m*, GEOPHYS diagramme de résistivité *m*, PETR TECH diagraphie de résistivité *f*; **~ logging** *n* PETR diagraphie de résistivité *f*; **~ meter** *n* GEOPHYS résistivi-mètre *m*

resistojet *n* SPACE *spacecraft* propulseur électrothermi-que *m*

resistor *n* AUTO résistance *f*, ELEC résistance *f*, résisteur *m*, ELEC ENG, PHYS résistance *f*; **~ core** *n* ELEC ENG support de résistance *m*; **~ ink** *n* COLOURS encre à résistance électrique *f*; **~ ladder** *n* ELEC ENG échelle de résistance *f*; **~ network** *n* ELEC ENG réseau de résistances *m*; **~ string** *n* ELEC ENG chaîne de résistances *f*; **~ trimming** *n* ELEC ENG ajustage de résistance *m*, ajustement de résistance *m*; **~ voltage divider** *n* ELEC ENG diviseur de tension à résistances *m*

resistor-type: ~ spark plug *n* AUTO bougie antiparasite *f*

resite *n* P&R résite *f*

resol *n* P&R résol *m*

resoldering *n* PROD ENG ressoudage *m*, ressoudure *f*

resolution *n* ACOUSTICS résolution *f*, CINEMAT définition *f*, résolution *f*, COMP, DP résolution *f*, ELECTRON définition *f*, TESTING résolution *f*, TV définition *f*, résolution *f*; **~ chart** *n* CINEMAT mire de définition *f*

resolved: ~ shear stress *n* METALL cission réduite *f*, cission résolue *f*, PROP MAT contrainte de cisaillement réduite *f*

resolving: ~ power *n* ASTRON *of telescope* puissance de résolution *f*, CINEMAT, ELECTRON pouvoir sépara-teur *m*, METALL pouvoir de résolution *m*, PHOTO pouvoir de définition *m*, pouvoir séparateur *m*, PHYS pouvoir de résolution *m*, pouvoir séparateur *m*

resonance *n* CHEM *structure, form*, ELEC *alternating current circuit*, ELECTRON, PHYS, RECORDING, TELE-COM, WAVE PHYS résonance *f*; **~ bridge** *n* ELEC *measurement* pont à résonance *m*; **~ broadening** *n* RAD PHYS *spectral lines* élargissement de résonance *m*; **~ curve** *n* TV courbe de résonance *f*; **~ damper** *n* AUTO absorbeur de résonance *m*; **~ filter** *n* RAD PHYS, RECOR-DING filtre résonnant *m*; **~ frequency** *n* RAD PHYS fréquence de résonance *f*; **~ line** *n* RAD PHYS raie de résonance *f*; **~ neutron detector** *n* RAD PHYS détecteur de neutrons à résonance *m*; **~ peak** *n* RAD PHYS pic de résonance *m*, RECORDING pointe de résonance *f*; **~ radiation** *n* RAD PHYS radiation de résonance *f*; **~ screen** *n* COAL TECH crible à résonance *m*; **~ silencer** *n* SAFETY *noise insulation* amortisseur de bruits à réso-nance *m*; **~ spectrum** *n* WAVE PHYS spectre de résonance *m*

resonant[1] *adj* PHYS résonnant

resonant:[2] **~ absorption** *n* TELECOM absorption réson-nante *f*; **~ burning** *n* THERMOD combustion pulsatoire *f*; **~ cavity** *n* ELECTRON, OPT, PHYS, TELECOM cavité résonnante *f*; **~ circuit** *n* ELECTRON circuit oscillant *m*, circuit résonnant *m*, PHYS, TELECOM circuit résonnant *m*; **~ circuit induction loop detector** *n* TRANSP *traffic* détecteur à boucle à induction à circuit résonnant *m*;

~ earthed neutral system *n* (BrE) *(cf resonant groun-ded neutral system)* ELEC réseau compensé par bobine d'extinction *m*; **~ energy transfer** *n* RAD PHYS *between atoms* transfert d'énergie résonnante *m*; **~ frequency** *n* ACOUSTICS, ELECTRON, PHYS, TELECOM, WAVE PHYS fréquence de résonance *f*; **~ grounded neutral system** *n* (AmE) *(cf resonant earthed neutral system)* ELEC réseau compensé par bobine d'extinction *m*; **~ line** *n* ELECTRON ligne accordée *f*, ligne de transmission ac-cordée *f*; **~ line oscillator** *n* ELECTRON oscillateur à ligne accordée *m*; **~ modes** *n pl* RAD PHYS *of optical cavities, gas lasers* modes résonnants *m pl*; **~ optical cavity** *n* OPT cavité optique résonnante *f*; **~ reed relay** *n* ELEC ENG relais à tiges accordées *m*

resonator *n* ELECTRON, TELECOM résonateur *m*; **~ grid** *n* ELECTRON grille de couplage *f*, lèvre de cisaillement *f*

resorcinol *n* CHEM résorcine *f*, résorcinol *m*; **~ resin** *n* P&R résine de résorcine *f*

resorcylic *adj* CHEM résorcylique

resorufine *n* CHEM résorufine *f*

resource *n* COMP, DP, MAR POLL ressource *f*, PROD ENG moyen de production *m*, ressource *f*; **~ allocation** *n* COMP, DP affectation des ressources *f*; **~ sharing** *n* COMP, DP partage de ressources *m*; **~ unavailable class** *n* TELECOM classe ressource indisponible *f*; **~ unit** *n* PROD ENG unité de capacité *f*

resource-sharing: ~ network *n* COMP, DP réseau à par-tage de ressources *m*

respirator *n* OCEANOG appareil respiratoire *m*, SAFETY respirateur *m*; **~ self-rescue apparatus** *n* SAFETY *with carbon monoxide filter* respirateur *m*

respiratory[1] *adj* SAFETY respiratoire

respiratory:[2] **~ filter** *n* SAFETY filtre respiratoire *m*; **~ protection workshop** *n* SAFETY atelier pour la protec-tion de la respiration *m*; **~ protective equipment** *n* SAFETY appareils de protection respiratoire *m pl*

responder *n* AERONAUT *communications* répondeur *m*; **~ beacon** *n* AERONAUT radiophare répondeur *m*

response *n* ACOUSTICS, COMP réponse *f*, CONTROL réac-tion *f*, réponse *f*, DP, ELECTRON, RECORDING réponse *f*, TELECOM réponse *f*, résultat *m*; **~ characteristic** *n* TV courbe de réponse *f*; **~ curve** *n* ELECTRON caractéristi-que *f*, courbe de réponse *f*, RECORDING courbe de réponse *f*; **~ time** *n* COMP temps de réponse *m*, CONTROL temps de manoeuvre *m*, DP, ELECTRON, METR, TELECOM temps de réponse *m*, TESTING durée de réponse *f*; **~ to current** *n* ACOUSTICS réponse au cou-rant *f*; **~ to power** *n* ACOUSTICS réponse à la puissance *f*; **~ to voltage** *n* ACOUSTICS réponse à la tension *f*

responsivity *n* TELECOM sensibilité *f*, sensibilité énergi-que *f*

rest *n* ACOUSTICS silence *m*, MECH ENG support *m*, MI-NING clichage *m*, taquet *m*; **~ mass** *n* PART PHYS *of atom*, PHYS masse au repos *f*; **~ period** *n* AERONAUT période de repos *f*; **~ skids** *n pl* TRANSP patins de repos *m pl*

restackability *n* PACKAGING réempilage *m*

restart[1] *n* AERONAUT *engine* remise en marche *f*, COMP, DP redémarrage *m*, reprise *f*; **~ point** *n* COMP, DP point de reprise *m*

restart[2] *vt* AERONAUT *engine* remettre en marche, COMP redémarrer, reprendre, relancer, DP relancer, repren-dre, MECH ENG *injector* réamorcer, *machinery* remettre, TELECOM *system* redémarrer

restarting: ~ injector *n* MECH ENG injecteur à mise en marche automatique *m*

resting: ~ **contact** *n* ELEC *relay* contact de repos *m*

restitution *n* COMP, DP restitution *f*; ~ **coefficient** *n* PHYS coefficient de restitution *m*

restocking *n* PROD ENG réapprovisionnement *m*

restoration *n* PETR TECH *sea bed* remise en état *f*, PROD ENG réfection *f*; ~ **mode** *n* SPACE *spacecraft* mode de réparation *m*

restore[1] *n* COMP, DP restauration *f*

restore[2] *vt* COMP, DP restaurer, récupérer

restoring: ~ **force** *n* MECH, PHYS force de rappel *f*; ~ **moment** *n* AERONAUT *aerodynamics* moment redresseur *m*, moment stabilisateur *m*; ~ **torque** *n* MECH couple de rappel *m*

restrainer *n* CINEMAT modérateur *m*, retardateur *m*, PHOTO bain retardateur *m*

restricted: ~ **information transfer service** *n* TELECOM *ISDN* service de transfert avec restriction *m*; ~ **service** *n* TELECOM service restreint *m*; ~ **solubility** *n* METALL solubilité limitée *f*

restrictor *n* PROD ENG restricteur *m*, TELECOM discriminateur *m*; ~ **valve** *n* REFRIG vanne restricto-changeuse *f*

restyle *vt* TRANSP remodeler, restyler

restyling *n* TRANSP remodelage *m*, restylage *m*

result *n* METR *of inspection* résultat *m*

resultant *n* MATH, MECH ENG, PHYS résultante *f*

resurfacing *n* (AmE) *(cf remetalling)* CONST *roads* rechargement *m*

resurgence *n* HYDROL *underground river* résurgence *f*

resurgent *adj* WATER SUPP résurgent

resurvey *n* CONST réarpentage *m*

resuscitation: ~ **equipment** *n* SAFETY équipement de réanimation *m*

resuscitator *n* SAFETY réanimateur *m*

resynchronize *vt* TELECOM résynchroniser

retail: ~ **package** *n* PACKAGING emballage de détail *m*

retailer *n* PROD ENG détaillant *m*

retainer *n* MINING système de fixation *m*

retaining: ~ **dam** *n* WATER SUPP barrage de retenue *m*; ~ **plate** *n* MECH ENG *injection mould* plaque dévêtisseuse *f*; ~ **ring** *n* MECH bague d'arrêt *f*, bague de retenue *f*, jonc *m*, PHOTO bague de fixation *f*; ~ **spring** *n* MINING ressort de retenue *m*; ~ **structure** *n* WATER SUPP ouvrage de soutènement *m*; ~ **valve** *n* HYDR EQUIP clapet de freinage *m*, clapet de retenue *m*; ~ **wall** *n* CONST mur de revêtement *m*, mur de soutènement *m*, mur de terrasse *m*, *water* mur de retenue *m*

retake *n* CINEMAT nouvelle prise *f*, plan refait *m*

retard:[1] ~ **and impact fuse** *n* MILIT amorce fonctionnant avec retardement ou par choc *f*

retard[2] *vt* CHEM inhiber, ralentir, SPACE *spacecraft* dégyrer, freiner, retarder

retardation *n* MECH ENG accélération négative *f*; ~ **coil** *n* ELEC bobine d'arrêt *f*; ~ **of moon** *n* ASTRON retard de la lune *m*; ~ **rocket** *n* TRANSP rétrofusée *f*

retarded: ~ **acceleration** *n* MECH ENG accélération négative *f*; ~ **admission** *n* HYDR EQUIP admission différée *f*; ~ **flow** *n* HYDROL écoulement retardé *m*; ~ **motion** *n* MECH ENG mouvement retardé *m*; ~ **potential** *n* PHYS potentiel retardé *m*; ~ **release** *n* HYDR EQUIP échappement différé *m*; ~ **velocity** *n* MECH ENG vitesse retardée *f*

retarder *n* P&R *raw material, vulcanization* retardateur *m*, PAPER TECH retardeur *m*, TRANSP *lorries* ralentisseur *m*; ~ **parachute** *n* MILIT parachute retardateur *m*

retarding: ~ **agent** *n* CONST *concrete* agent de retard de la

prise *m*, retardateur *m*, TEXTILES retardateur *m*

retene *n* CHEM rétène *m*

retention *n* CHEM fixation *f*, rétention *f*, ELEC ENG conservation *f*, HYDROL, WATER SUPP rétention *f*; ~ **of rights** *n* PETR TECH reconduction de droits *f*; ~ **time** *n* ELEC ENG temps de conservation *m*; ~ **valve** *n* MECH ENG soupape à niveau *f*

retentive: ~ **capacity** *n* HYDROL *soil* capacité de rétention *f*; ~ **timer-off day** *n* PROD ENG temporisateur à mémoire au repos *m*; ~ **timer-on** *n* PROD ENG instruction de temporisation à mémoire *f*, temporisateur à mémoire au travail *m*; ~ **timer-on delay** *n* PROD ENG temporisateur à mémoire au travail *m*

retentivity *n* PHYS rémanence *f*, PROP MAT coercivité *f*, TV induction rémanente après induction *f*, persistance *f*

rethreading: ~ **file** *n* MECH ENG *tool* outil à restaurer les filetages *m*

reticle *n* ASTRON *in telescope eyepiece*, CINEMAT, ELECTRON, INSTRUMENT réticule *m*; ~ **eyepiece** *n* ASTRON oculaire à réticule *m*; ~ **illumination knob** *n* INSTRUMENT commande d'éclairage de réticule *f*

reticulated: ~ **mirror** *n* SPACE *spacecraft* miroir réticulé *m*

reticulation *n* CINEMAT, PHOTO *of emulsion*, PRINT réticulation *f*

Reticulum *n* ASTRON Réticule *m*

retinalite *n* MINERAL rétinalite *f*

retinasphalt *n* MINERAL rétinasphalte *m*

retinellite *n* MINERAL rétinellite *f*

retinite *n* MINERAL rétinite *f*

retinning *n* PROD ENG rétamage *m*

retonation: ~ **wave** *n* MINING onde rétrograde *f*

retort *n* CHEM clos *m*, cornue *f*, retorte *m*, vase *m*, CHEM TECH vase clos *m*, HEATING cornue *f*, LAB EQUIP retorte *m*, *glassware* cornue *f*, PETR TECH cornue *f*, PHYS vase *m*; ~ **clamp** *n* LAB EQUIP *support* pince à mâchoires *f*; ~ **coal** *n* COAL TECH charbon de cornue *m*; ~ **stand** *n* LAB EQUIP statif *m*

retouch *vt* PHOTO repiquer, retoucher

retouching *n* C&G, PHOTO, PRINT retouche *f*; ~ **ink** *n* COLOURS encre pour retouche *f*

retrace *n* ELECTRON retour de balayage *m*, retour du faisceau *m*

retractable[1] *adj* MECH escamotable

retractable:[2] ~ **aerial** *n* TV antenne escamotable *f*; ~ **antenna** *n* TV antenne escamotable *f*; ~ **blade knife** *n* MECH ENG couteau à lame rétractable *m*; ~ **filter** *n* PHOTO filtre escamotable *m*; ~ **plane mirror** *n* ASTRON miroir plan escamotable *m*; ~ **wheel** *n* VEHICLES roue relevable *f*

retracting: ~ **spring** *n* AUTO ressort de rappel *m*

retransfer *n* PRINT double décalque *m*

retransmit *vt* TELECOM réémettre

retreaded: ~ **tire** *n* (AmE), ~ **tyre** *n* (BrE) VEHICLES pneu rechapé *m*, pneumatique rechapé *m*

retreat[1] *n* CONST retrait *m*; ~ **mining** *n* MINING exploitation en retour *f*

retreat[2] *vt* COAL TECH, PROD ENG retraiter

retreating: ~ **blade** *n* AERONAUT *helicopter* pale reculante *f*; ~ **blade stall** *n* AERONAUT *helicopter* décrochage à pale reculante *m*

retrieval *n* COMP, DP extraction *f*, recherche *f*, TEXTILES extraction *f*, récupération *f*

retrieve *vt* COMP, DP, TEXTILES *extract* extraire

retroactive: ~ **tenacity** *n* MECH ENG résistance à l'écrasement *f*, résistance à la compression *f*

retrofit[1] *n* COMP, DP mise à niveau *f*, PROD ENG *by manu-*

facturer mise à niveau a posteriori *f,* modification a posteriori *f,* rétrofit *m*

retrofit[2] *vt* FUELLESS ajouter des améliorations

retrofocus: ~ **lens** *n* CINEMAT téléobjectif inversé *m*

retrogradation *n* FOOD TECH rassissement *f*

retrograde[1] *adj* SPACE rétrograde

retrograde:[2] ~ **metamorphism** *n* FUELLESS métamorphisme rétrograde *m,* GEOL diaphtorèse *f,* rétromorphose *f;* ~ **motion** *n* ASTRON mouvement rétrograde *m;* ~ **orbit** *n* ASTRON, SPACE orbite rétrograde *f*

retrogressive: ~ **metamorphism** *n* GEOL rétromorphose *f*

retropack *n* SPACE *spacecraft* faisceau de rétrofusées *m,* module de rétrofusées *m*

retroreflection *n* RAD PHYS rétroflexion *f*

retroreflective: ~ **marker** *n* AERONAUT *airport* balise rétroréfléchissante *f*

retrorocket *n* SPACE *spacecraft,* TRANSP rétrofusée *f;* ~ **sequence** *n* SPACE séquence de freinage par rétrofusées *f*

retrorsine *n* CHEM rétrorsine *f*

retrosequence *n* SPACE *spacecraft* séquence de freinage *f*

retry *n* COMP relance *f,* répétition *f,* DP relance *f,* répétition *f*

retting *n* TEXTILES rouissage *m*

return[1] *n* COMP, DP retour *m;* ~ **address** *n* COMP, DP adresse de retour *f;* ~ **airway** *n* MINING galerie d'évacuation d'air *f,* galerie de retour d'air *f,* voie de retour d'air *f;* ~ **block** *n* MECH ENG galoche *f,* poulie coupée *f;* ~ **cargo** *n* NAUT fret de retour *m;* ~ **channel** *n* COMP, DP voie de retour *f,* RECORDING canal de retour *m,* voie de retour *f;* ~ **circuit** *n* ELEC ENG circuit de retour *m;* ~ **code** *n* COMP, DP code retour *m;* ~ **conductor** *n* ELEC *circuit* circuit de retour *m;* ~ **current** *n* ELEC ENG courant de retour *m,* courant opposé *m,* HYDROL courant de retour *m,* courant rétrograde *m;* ~ **current coefficient** *n* ELEC ENG coefficient d'équilibrage *m;* ~ **of empties** *n* PROD ENG consignation emballage *f,* consigne emballage *f,* emballage consigné *m;* ~ **factor** *n* SPACE facteur de retour *m;* ~ **filter** *n* PROD ENG filtre de retour *m;* ~ **flow compressor** *n* REFRIG compresseur à contre-courant *m,* compresseur à flux inversé *m;* ~ **flue** *n* PROD ENG tube de retour de fumée *m;* ~ **flue boiler** *n* PROD ENG chaudière tubulaire à retour de flamme *f,* chaudière à retour de flamme *f;* ~ **instruction** *n* COMP, DP instruction de retour *f;* ~ **interval** *n* TV durée de retour du spot *f;* ~ **label** *n* PACKAGING étiquette pour le renvoi *f;* ~ **line filtration** *n* PROD ENG filtration dans la canalisation de retour *f;* ~ **path** *n* TELECOM voie de retour *f;* ~ **pulley** *n* MECH ENG poulie de renvoi *f,* poulie de retour *f;* ~ **roller** *n* MECH ENG rouleau de renvoi *m;* ~ **rope** *n* MECH ENG câble de renvoi *m;* ~ **spring** *n* AUTO, PROD ENG ressort de rappel *m;* ~ **stroke** *n* MECH ENG *of piston* course arrière *f,* course de retour *f,* course rétrograde *f,* PHYS choc en retour *m;* ~ **to service** *n* TELECOM retour à l'exploitation *m;* ~ **tube** *n* PROD ENG tube de retour de fumée *m;* ~ **tube boiler** *n* PROD ENG chaudière tubulaire à retour de flamme *f,* chaudière à retour de flamme *f;* ~ **tubular boiler** *n* PROD ENG chaudière tubulaire à retour de flamme *f,* chaudière à retour de flamme *f;* ~ **valve** *n* MECH ENG clapet de non-retour *m;* ~ **wall** *n* CONST mur en aile *m,* mur en retour *m;* ~ **wheel** *n* MECH ENG poulie de renvoi *f,* poulie de retour *f;* ~ **wire** *n* ELEC *circuit* circuit de retour *m,* ELEC ENG fil de retour *m*

return[2] *vt* COMP, DP renvoyer, retourner, PROD ENG *to yield* donner, rendre

return:[3] ~ **to surface** *vi* NAUT *submarine* revenir en surface

returnable: ~ **bottle** *n* PACKAGING bouteille consignée *f;* ~ **container** *n* PACKAGING récipient consigné *m;* ~ **packaging** *n* PACKAGING emballage consigné *m*

returns *n pl* PROD ENG *home scrap* jets et débris provenant de la coulée *m pl;* ~ **and allowances** *n pl* PROD ENG rendus et rabais *m pl*

return-scanning: ~ **beam** *n* TV faisceau analyseur reconduit à la cathode *m*

reusable[1] *adj* COMP, DP réutilisable

reusable:[2] ~ **box** *n* PACKAGING boîte récupérable *f;* ~ **optical disc** *n* (BrE) OPT disque optique réutilisable *m;* ~ **optical disk** *n* (AmE) *see reusable optical disc;* ~ **packaging** *n* PACKAGING emballage récupérable *m*

reuse[1] *n* RECYCLING remploi *m*

reuse[2] *vt* RECYCLING remployer

rev:[1] ~ **counter** *n* (BrE) *(cf tachometer)* VEHICLES *engine, accessory* compte-tours *m*

rev:[2] ~ **up** *vi* VEHICLES *engine* emballer le moteur

revamping *n* PETR TECH remodelage *m*

reveal *n* CONST *architecture* embrasement *m,* embrasement du mur *m,* jouée *f*

revealed: ~ **failure** *n* QUALITY défaillance révélée *f*

revenue: ~ **cutter** *n* NAUT *customs* vedette de la douane *f*

revenue-earning: ~ **train** *n* RAIL *vehicles* train commercial *m*

reverb *n* RECORDING chambre d'écho *f,* chambre de réverbération *f*

reverberant: ~ **field** *n* ACOUSTICS champ réverbéré *m;* ~ **room** *n* RECORDING chambre de réverbération *f*

reverberation *n* ACOUSTICS réverbération *f,* GEOPHYS pédalage *m,* renvoi *m,* réfléchissement *m,* RECORDING réverbération *f;* ~ **chamber** *n* RECORDING, SPACE *spacecraft* chambre de réverbération *f;* ~ **plate** *n* RECORDING plaque de réverbération *f;* ~ **room** *n* ACOUSTICS salle réverbérante *f;* ~ **time** *n* ACOUSTICS durée de réverbération *f,* RECORDING temps de réverbération *m;* ~ **unit** *n* RECORDING chambre d'écho *f,* chambre de réverbération *f*

reverberatory *n* PROD ENG four à réverbère *m;* ~ **chamber** *n* PROD ENG *of furnace* laboratoire *m;* ~ **flame** *n* PROD ENG feu de réverbère *m;* ~ **furnace** *n* PROD ENG four à réverbère *m*

reversal *n* CINEMAT inversible *m,* PRINT inversion *f,* TELECOM *answer signal* inversion de batterie *f,* inversion de charge en ligne *f,* TRANSP *of propeller pitch* inversion *f;* ~ **control channel** *n* TELECOM voie de mobile *f;* ~ **development** *n* CINEMAT développement par inversion *m;* ~ **dupe** *n* CINEMAT copie inversible *f;* ~ **film** *n* CINEMAT pellicule inversible *f;* ~ **finder** *n* CINEMAT viseur inversé *m,* viseur redresseur *m,* PHOTO viseur à image redressée *m;* ~ **master print** *n* CINEMAT contre-dupli *m;* ~ **print** *n* CINEMAT copie inversible *f,* duplicata *m;* ~ **process** *n* CINEMAT procédé inversible *m,* PRINT développement par inversion *m;* ~ **processing** *n* PHOTO développement par inversion *m;* ~ **of the sphere** *n* GEOM retournement de la sphère *m*

reversal-type: ~ **color film** *n* (AmE), ~ **colour film** *n* (BrE) PHOTO film en couleur inversible *m*

reverse[1] *n* CINEMAT marche arrière *f,* MECH, VEHICLES inversion de marche *f,* marche arrière *f;* ~ **action** *n* CINEMAT marche arrière *f,* mouvement inversé *m,* TV marche arrière *f;* ~ **angle** *n* CINEMAT contre-champ *m;*

~ **authentication** *n* COMP, DP authentification inverse *f*; ~ **bias** *n* ELEC ENG, PHYS polarisation inverse *f*; ~ **braking** *n* TRANSP freinage à contre-courant *m*; ~ **channel** *n* COMP, DP voie de retour *f*; ~ **charge call** *n* (BrE) *(cf collect call)* TELECOM appel en PCV *m*, appel à frais virés *m* (Can); ~ **clipping** *n* COMP, DP masquage *m*; ~ **combustion** *n* PETR combustion inversée *f*, combustion à contre-courant *f*; ~ **compatibility** *n* TV rétrocompatibilité *f*; ~ **contact** *n* ELEC ENG contact inverseur *m*; ~ **contactor** *n* PROD ENG contacteur marche arrière *m*; ~ **current** *n* ELEC ENG courant inverse *m*, *in current generator* retour de courant *m*; ~ **current circuit breaking** *n* ELEC *switch* interrupteur à retour de courant *m*; ~ **current relay** *n* ELEC relais directionnel *m*; ~ **cycle defrosting** *n* REFRIG dégivrage par cycle inversé *m*; ~ **deflection** *n* SPRINGS *leaf spring* contre-flèche *f*; ~ **direction** *n* ELEC ENG sens inverse *m*; ~ **direction flow** *n* COMP, DP déroulement en sens inverse *m*; ~ **emission** *n* ELECTRON émission d'électrons par l'anode *f*; ~ **fault** *n* GEOL faille inverse *f*; ~ **flow turbine** *n* FUELLESS turbine à écoulement inversé *f*; ~ **gear** *n* AUTO, VEHICLES pignon de marche arrière *m*; ~ **idler gear** *n* AUTO, VEHICLES pignon inverseur *m*; ~ **idler shaft** *n* AUTO, VEHICLES arbre de marche arrière *m*; ~ **image switch** *n* TV inverseur de polarité *m*; ~ **light** *n* (AmE) *(cf reversing light)* VEHICLES feu de marche arrière *m*, feu de recul *m*; ~ **mask** *n* CINEMAT contre-cache *m*; ~ **motion** *n* TV marche arrière *f*; ~ **osmosis** *n* CHEM TECH osmose de renversement *f*, osmose inverse *f*, CONST *water softening*, HYDROL osmose inverse *f*; ~ **phase relay** *n* ELEC relais à inversion de phase *m*; ~ **pitch** *n* AERONAUT *propeller* pas inverse *m*, pas négatif *m*; ~ **Polish notation** *n* DP notation polonaise inversée *f*, notation suffixée *f*; ~ **press felt** *n* PAPER TECH feutre montant *m*; ~ **printing** *n* CINEMAT tirage inversé *m*, PHOTO tirage à travers le support *m*; ~ **reaction** *n* NUCLEAR réaction inverse *f*; ~ **recovery time** *n* ELECTRON temps de recouvrement inverse *m*; ~ **roll coater** *n* PAPER TECH coucheuse à rouleaux tournant en sens inverse *f*; ~ **roll coating** *n* COATINGS, P&R *process* revêtement par rouleau inverse *m*; ~ **routing** *n* TELECOM acheminement retour *m*; ~ **routing address** *n* TELECOM adresse d'acheminement retour *f*; ~ **scan** *n* TV balayage inversé *m*; ~ **side printing** *n* PACKAGING impression au verso *f*; ~ **thrust** *n* AERONAUT poussée inverse *f*; ~ **traveling wave** *n* (AmE), ~ **travelling wave** *n* (BrE) ELEC ENG onde inverse *f*, onde régressive *f*; ~ **video** *n* COMP, DP vidéo inverse *f*; ~ **voltage** *n* ELEC, ELEC ENG tension inverse *f*; ~ **voltage protection** *n* ELEC ENG protection contre les inversions de polarité *f*; ~ **wipe** *n* PRINT essuyage inversé *m*

reverse[2] *vt* ELECTRON inverser, MECH ENG renverser

reverse:[3] ~ **the motion** *vi* MECH ENG renverser la marche; ~ **the steam** *vi* HYDROL renverser la vapeur

reverse[4] *vti* MECH ENG changer le sens de la marche

reversed: ~ **arch** *n* CONST *architecture* voûte renversée *f*, HYDR EQUIP radier *m*, sole *f*; ~ **controls** *n pl* AERONAUT commandes inversées *f pl*; ~ **image** *n* CINEMAT image inversée *f*; ~ **ogee** *n* CONST doucine renversée *f*; ~ **press** *n* PAPER TECH presse montante *f*; ~ **profile** *n* GEOPHYS profil inversé *m*; ~ **steam** *n* HYDR EQUIP contre-vapeur *f*

reverser *n* ELECTRON inverseur *m*

reversibility *n* CHEM, PHYS, PROP MAT, TRANSP réversibilité *f*

reversible[1] *adj* CHEM, PHYS réversible

reversible:[2] ~ **booster** *n* ELEC ENG survolteur-dévolteur *m*; ~ **gear** *n* MECH ENG engrenage réciproque *m*, engrenage à retour *m*; ~ **motor** *n* ELEC ENG, TRANSP moteur réversible *m*; ~ **pallet** *n* TRANSP palette réversible *f*; ~ **pitch propeller** *n* AERONAUT, NAUT, TRANSP hélice à pas réversible *f*; ~ **ratchet** *n* MECH ENG *tool* cliquet universel *m*; ~ **switch** *n* CONTROL interrupteur inverseur *m*, ELEC ENG commutateur à bascule *m*; ~ **transducer** *n* ACOUSTICS, ELEC ENG transducteur réversible *m*; ~ **trap** *n* PROP MAT *crystallography* piège réversible *m*

reversing *n* ELECTRON inversion *f*, MECH ENG inversion *f*, *motion* changement *m*, inversion *f*, renversement *m*, *the direction of rotation* inversion *f*, MINING *air current* renversement *m*, RAIL *vehicles* marche arrière *f*; ~ **bath** *n* PHOTO bain inverseur *m*; ~ **braking switchgroup** *n* TRANSP combinateur d'inversion et de freinage *m*; ~ **current** *n* OCEANOG courant alternant *m*; ~ **drum switch** *n* ELEC commutateur à inversion *m*; ~ **frame** *n* OCEANOG cadre à renversement *m*; ~ **gear** *n* CINEMAT inverseur de marche *m*, MECH ENG appareil de changement de marche *m*, organes de changement de marche *m pl*, *of lathe* changement de marche *m*, inverseur *m*; ~ **lever** *n* MECH ENG levier de changement de marche *m*, levier inverseur *m*, renvoi *m*; ~ **lever rod** *n* MECH ENG *valve gear* barre de relevage *f*; ~ **light** *n* (BrE) *(cf reverse light)* VEHICLES feu de marche arrière *m*, feu de recul *m*; ~ **link** *n* MECH ENG *link motion* coulisse de changement de marche *f*; ~ **mill** *n* PROD ENG laminoir réversible *m*, train réversible *m*; ~ **motion** *n* MECH ENG *of lathe* changement de marche *m*; ~ **motor** *n* ELEC moteur inversible *m*; ~ **ring** *n* PHOTO bague d'inversion *f*; ~ **rod** *n* MECH ENG *valve gear* barre de relevage *f*, RAIL *steam traction* bielle de changement de marche *f*, *vehicles* bielle de relevage *f*; ~ **screw** *n* MECH ENG vis de changement de marche *f*; ~ **sequencer step operation** *n* PROD ENG inversion de déroulement des pas du séquenceur *f*; ~ **shaft** *n* MECH ENG *valve gear* arbre de changement de marche *m*, arbre de relevage *m*; ~ **steam** *n* HYDR EQUIP renversement de la vapeur *m*; ~ **switch** *n* ELEC ENG inverseur *m*; ~ **valve** *n* HYDR EQUIP soupape d'inversion *f*, soupape de renversement *f*

revertive: ~ **control system** *n* TELECOM système à commande par impulsions inverses *m*, système à impulsions inverses *m*

revetment *n* CONST revêtement *m*

review *n* PRINT revue *f*

revise *vt* PRINT réviser

revised: ~ **edition** *n* PRINT édition révisée *f*

revocation *n* PATENTS nullité *f*

revoke *vt* PATENTS déclarer nul

revolution *n* GEOM *of solid* révolution *f*, MECH ENG révolution *f*, tour *m*, PAPER TECH rotation *f*, SPACE révolution *f*; ~ **counter** *n* MECH ENG compte-tours *m*, compteur de tours *m*; ~ **indication** *n* MECH ENG indicateur de vitesse *m*, tachymètre *m*

revolutions: ~ **per minute** *n pl* AUTO, CINEMAT, PHYS tours par minute *m pl*

revolving: ~ **armature** *n* ELEC ENG induit mobile *m*; ~ **back** *n* PHOTO *camera* dos pivotant *m*; ~ **cutter** *n* MECH ENG molette *f*, molette coupante *f*; ~ **cylinder engine** *n* TRANSP moteur rotatif *m*; ~ **die head** *n* MECH ENG porte-lunette revolver *m*; ~ **head punch** *n* MECH ENG pinces à emporte-pièce à revolver *f pl*; ~ **nosepiece** *n* INSTRUMENT revolver porte-objectifs *m*, LAB EQUIP *microscope* revolver *m*; ~ **punch pliers** *n pl* MECH ENG pince emporte-pièce à tourniquet *f*; ~ **screen** *n* COAL TECH, MINING *ore-dressing* trommel *m*; ~ **shutter** *n* CINEMAT obturateur rotatif *m*; ~ **stage** *n* LAB EQUIP *microscope* platine tournante *f*; ~ **table** *n* MECH ENG table rotative *f*, table tournante *f*; ~ **tool holder** *n* MECH ENG porte-outil revolver *m*

revs *n* VEHICLES régime *m*, vitesse de rotation *f*

rewind[1] *n* PAPER TECH rebobiner; ~ **handle** *n* PHOTO manivelle de réembobinage *f*; ~ **speed** *n* COMP vitesse de rebobinage *f*, DP vitesse de réembobinage *f*; ~ **tension** *n* CINEMAT, RECORDING tension de rebobinage *f*

rewind[2] *vt* CINEMAT réembobiner, réenrouler, COMP, DP, RECORDING, TEXTILES rebobiner

rewinder *n* CINEMAT réembobineuse *f*, réenrouleuse *f*, PAPER TECH rebobineuse *f*, PHOTO réembobineuse *f*

rewinding *n* ELEC *generator, motor*, TEXTILES rebobinage *m*, TV réembobinage *m*

rewiring *n* ELEC *supply* remplacement de câblage *m*

rework: ~ **center** *n* (AmE), ~ **centre** *n* (BrE) PROD ENG section retouches *f*; ~ **routing** *n* PROD ENG gamme de retouche *f*

rewrite[1] *n* COMP, DP réécriture *f*

rewrite[2] *vt* COMP, DP réécrire

Reynolds: ~ **number** *n* AERONAUT *aerodynamics*, FLUID PHYS *(Re) speed of flow, degree of turbulence*, FUEL-LESS, PHYS nombre de Reynolds *m*; ~ **stress** *n* FLUID PHYS contrainte de Reynolds *f*

RF[1] *abbr (radio frequency)* ELEC ENG, ELECTRON, RECORDING, TELECOM, TRANSP, TV RF *(radiofréquence)*

RF:[2] ~ **alternator** *n* ELEC ENG alternateur de fréquences radio *m*; ~ **amplification** *n* ELECTRON amplification de fréquences radioélectriques *f*; ~ **amplifier** *n* ELECTRON amplificateur de fréquences radioélectriques *m*, TELE-COM amplificateur à radiofréquence *m*; ~ **coil** *n* ELEC ENG bobinage haute fréquence *m*; ~ **current** *n* ELEC ENG courant HF *m*, courant à haute fréquence *m*; ~ **current source** *n* ELEC ENG source de courant à haute fréquence *f*; ~ **dub** *n* TV copie en radiofréquence *f*; ~ **generator** *n* ELEC ENG générateur HF *m*; ~ **heating** *n* P&R *process* échauffement par pertes diélectriques *m*; ~ **interference** *n* TV brouillage RF *m*; ~ **microphone** *n* RECORDING micro HF *m*, micro haute fréquence *m*; ~ **oscillator** *n* ELECTRON oscillateur HF *m*, oscillateur haute fréquence *m*; ~ **pulse** *n* TV impulsion de radio-fréquence *f*; ~ **section** *n* ELECTRON partie HF *f*, partie haute fréquence *f*, signal à haute fréquence *m*; ~ **section generator** *n* ELECTRON générateur de signaux HF *m*, générateur de signaux à haute fréquence *m*; ~ **sensor** *n* SPACE *communications* détecteur RF *m*, détecteur d'écart radioélectrique *m*, détecteur d'écartométrie *m*; ~ **shielding** *n* RECORDING, TV anti-parasitage *m*; ~ **stage** *n* ELECTRON étage HF *m*, étage haute fréquence *m*

R-factor *n* CRYSTALL facteur R *m*, facteur de confiance *m*, indice de confiance *m*

RGB[1] *abbr (red green blue)* COMP, DP, TV RVB *(rouge vert bleu)*

RGB:[2] ~ **input** *n* TV entrée RVB *f*; ~ **monitor** *n* COMP, DP moniteur RVB *m*, TV écran de contrôle couleur *m*

Rh *(rhodium)* CHEM Rh *(rhodium)*

rhaetizite *n* MINERAL rhaetizite *f*

rhamnetin *n* CHEM rhamnétine *f*

rhamnitol *n* CHEM rhamnite *m*, rhamnitol *m*

rhamnose *n* CHEM rhamnose *f*

rhenic *adj* CHEM rhénique

rhenium *n (Re)* CHEM rhénium *m (Re)*

rheological: ~ **properties** *n pl* FLUID PHYS propriétés rhéologiques *f pl*; ~ **variable** *n* METALL variable rhéologique *f*

rheology *n* COAL TECH, FLUID PHYS, GAS TECH, P&R, PHYS rhéologie *f*

rheostat *n* AUTO, ELEC *resistance*, ELEC ENG, LAB EQUIP, PHYS rhéostat *m*; ~ **control** *n* CONTROL régulation rhéostatique *f*; ~ **slider** *n* ELEC *resistance* curseur de rhéostat *m*; ~ **sliding contact** *n* AUTO curseur *m*; ~ **starter** *n* ELEC ENG démarreur au rhéostat *m*

rheostatic: ~ **brake** *n* TRANSP frein rhéostatique *m*; ~ **braking** *n* RAIL *vehicles* freinage rhéostatique *m*

rhodite *n* MINERAL rhodite *f*

rhodium *n (Rh)* CHEM rhodium *m (Rh)*; ~ **gold** *n* MINE-RAL rhodite *f*

rhodizite *n* MINERAL rhodizite *f*

rhodochrosite *n* MINERAL rhodochrosite *f*

rhodonite *n* MINERAL rhodonite *f*

rhomb *n* GEOM rhombe *m*

rhombique *n* MINERAL whitneyite *f*

rhombohedral *adj* CRYSTALL rhomboédrique

rhomboid[1] *adj* GEOM rhomboïdal

rhomboid[2] *n* GEOM rhomboïde *m*

rhombus *n* GEOM rhombe *m*

rhumb: ~ **line** *n* NAUT *navigation* loxodromie *f*; ~ **line navigation** *n* NAUT navigation loxodromique *f*

rhumbatron *n* ELECTRON rhumbatron *m*

rhyolite *n* PETR rhyolite *f*

rhyolyte *n* PETR rhyolite *f*

rhythm *n* ACOUSTICS rythme *m*

rhythmic: ~ **beds** *n pl* GEOL série rythmique *f*

rib *n* AERONAUT *aircraft* nervure *f*, COAL TECH planche *f*, MECH nervure *f*, NAUT *shipbuilding* membre *m*, membrure *f*, NUCLEAR ailette *f*, nervure *f*, PAPER TECH, PRINT, PROD ENG, SPACE *spacecraft* nervure *f*, TEXTILES côte *f*; ~ **cooling** *n* NUCLEAR refroidissement par ailettes *m*; ~ **hole** *n* MINING trou de côté *m*; ~ **mark** *n* C&G ligne en crosse *f*

ribband *n* NAUT *of hull* lisse *f*

ribbed[1] *adj* MECH nervuré, TEXTILES côtelé

ribbed:[2] ~ **frame** *n* CONST bâti nervuré *m*; ~ **G cramp** *n* MECH ENG happe à nervure *f*; ~ **piston** *n* AUTO piston nervuré *m*; ~ **radiator** *n* HEATING élément de chauffage à ailettes *m*; ~ **stitch** *n* TEXTILES point de côte *m*; ~ **V-belt** *n* MECH ENG courroie trapézoïdale striée *f*

ribbing *n* PAPER TECH cordon *m*, TEXTILES bord côte *m*; ~ **felt** *n* PAPER TECH feutre marqueur *m*

ribbon *n* C&G feuille *f*, COMP, DP ruban *m*, METR roulette *f*, ruban *m*, PRINT demi-bande *f*, ruban *m*; ~ **brake** *n* MECH ENG frein à bande *m*, frein à ruban *m*, frein à sangle *m*; ~ **cable** *n* ELEC câble plat *m*, câble à ruban *m*, OPT câble à ruban *m*, câble à structure ruban *m*, PROD ENG câble plat *m*, TELECOM câble à ruban *m*, câble à structure ruban *m*; ~ **cellular radiator** *n* AUTO radiateur à nids d'abeille *m*; ~ **guide** *n* RECORDING, TV galet guide *m*; ~ **ice** *n* REFRIG glace en ruban *f*; ~ **loudspeaker** *n* ACOUSTICS, RECORDING haut-parleur à ruban *m*; ~ **machine** *n* C&G machine-ruban *f*; ~ **microphone** *n* ACOUSTICS, RECORDING microphone à ruban *m*; ~ **rail** *n* (AmE) *(cf long welded rail)* RAIL long rail soudé *m*

riboflavin *n* CHEM *compound* riboflavine *f*

ribonucleic *adj* CHEM *acid* ribonucléique

rice: ~ **mill** *n* FOOD TECH rizerie *f*

Rice: ~ **integral method** *n* NUCLEAR méthode d'intégrale de Rice *f*

rich: ~ **clay** *n* C&G argile grasse *f*; ~ **coal** COAL TECH charbon agglutiné *m*, charbon à coke boursouflé *m*; ~ **gas** *n* GAS TECH, PETR gaz riche *m*; ~ **mixture** *n* AUTO, VEHICLES *carburation* mélange riche *m*

Richter: ~ **scale** *n* CONST *earthquake* échelle de Richter *f*

ricinoleic *adj* CHEM *acid* ricinoléique

ricochet *n* MILIT ricochet *m*

riddle *n* COAL TECH crible à grosses mailles *m*, table secoueuse *f*, PROD ENG *screen* crible *m*

riddler *n* PROD ENG cribleuse *f*

riddling *n* PROD ENG criblage *m*

riddlings *n pl* PROD ENG matières refusées *f pl*, refus du crible *m*

ride[1] *n* CONST *of hook and ride* penture *f*

ride:[2] ~ **at anchor** *vi* NAUT être à l'ancre

rideability *n* CONST voitureabilité *f*

rider *n* LAB EQUIP *balance* cavalier *m*; ~ **arch** *n* C&G voussette *f* (Bel), voûtain de chambre *m* (Fra); ~ **plate** *n* NAUT *shipbuilding* tôle supérieure *f*; ~ **roll** *n* PAPER TECH rouleau presseur *m*

ridge[1] *n* CONST arête *f*, crête *f*, faîtage *m*, faîte *m*, NAUT *barometric pressure* crête *f*, OCEANOG dorsale océanique *f*, PROD ENG trace saillante *f*; ~ **beam** *n* CONST *building* faîtage *m*, faîte *m*, faîtière *f*, panne faîtière *f*; ~ **capping** *n* CONST *lead, tile* faîtage *m*; ~ **line** *n* CONST *of roof* ligne de couronnement *f*, ligne de faîte *f*; ~ **piece** *n* CONST *ridge-tree* faîtage *m*, faîte *m*, faîtière *f*, panne faîtière *f*; ~ **plate** *n* CONST faîtage *m*, faîte *m*, faîtière *f*, panne faîtière *f*; ~ **roof** *n* CONST comble à deux longs pans *m*, comble à deux pentes *m*, comble à deux rampes *m*, comble à deux versants *m*, comble à deux égouts *m*; ~ **tile** *n* C&G tuile faîtière *f*, CONST faîtage *m*, faîtière *f*; ~ **waveguide** *n* ELEC ENG guide d'ondes nervuré *m*

ridge[2] *vt* CONST *roof* couronner

ridged: ~ **roof** *n* CONST comble à deux longs pans *m*, comble à deux pentes *m*, comble à deux rampes *m*, comble à deux versants *m*, comble à deux égouts *m*

riding: ~ **cutoff valve** *n* HYDR EQUIP tiroir d'expansion *m*, tiroir de détente *m*; ~ **light** *n* NAUT *navigation* feu de mouillage *m*

riebeckite *n* MINERAL riébeckite *f*

Rieke: ~ **diagram** *n* ELECTRON diagramme d'impédance de charge *m*, diagramme de Rieke *m*

Riemann: ~ **integral** *n* MATH intégrale au sens de Riemann *f*, intégrale définie *f*

Riemannian: ~ **geometry** *n* GEOM géométrie riemannienne *f*

riffle: ~ **sampler** *n* COAL TECH échantillonneur à riffles *m*

riffler *n* MECH ENG *file* rifloir *m*, PAPER TECH sablier *m*

rifle[1] *n* MILIT carabine *f*, fusil *m*; ~ **barrel** *n* MILIT canon de fusil rayé *m*; ~ **bullet** *n* MILIT balle de fusil *f*; ~ **butt** *n* MILIT fût de fusil *m*; ~ **grenade** *n* MILIT grenade à fusil *f*; ~ **grip** *n* CINEMAT crosse *f*, PHOTO poignée crosse *f*; ~ **microphone** *n* RECORDING micro canon *m*; ~ **range** *n* MILIT champ de tir au fusil *m*; ~ **stock** *n* MILIT fût de fusil *m*; ~ **telescope** *n* INSTRUMENT lunette de pointage *f*, MILIT lunette de visée d'un fusil *f*

rifle[2] *vi* MILIT rayer l'âme

rifled: ~ **gun** *n* MILIT *firearms* fusil à canon rayé *m*

rifling *n* MILIT rayure *f*

rift: ~ **tectonics** *n* GEOL formation de rifts *f*, taphrogenèse *f*, tectonique de rifts *f*; ~ **valley** *n* GEOL *intracratonic, mid-ocean ridge* graben intracratonique *m*, graben médio-océanique *m*, vallée axiale *f*

rig[1] *n* MECH ENG *working mechanism* mécanisme de manoeuvre *m*, NAUT, OCEANOG gréement *m*, PETR TECH appareil de forage *m*, plate-forme *f*, PROD ENG *for loam work* appareil à trousser *m*, trousseau *m*, *outfit* équipage *m*; ~ **floor** *n* PETR TECH plancher de manoeuvre *m*

rig[2] *vt* NAUT *ship, mast* gréer, PROD ENG installer, monter, équiper, *with pulley blocks* moufler; ~ **out** *vt* PROD ENG équiper; ~ **up** *vt* PETR monter, PROD ENG installer, équiper, monter

rigger *n* NAUT gréeur *m*

rigging *n* MECH ENG *working mechanism* mécanisme de manoeuvre *m*, NAUT gréage *m*, gréement *m*, OCEANOG gréement *m*; ~ **drawing** *n* NAUT plan de mâture *m*; ~ **position** *n* AERONAUT *aircraft* position de réglage *f*; ~ **screw** *n* NAUT *boat building* ridoir *m*; ~ **up** *n* PETR TECH gréement *m*

right *n* NAUT *direction*, PATENTS droit *m*; ~ **angle** *n* GEOM angle droit *m*; ~ **angle finder** *n* PHOTO viseur à renvoi d'angle *m*; ~ **angle triangle** *n* GEOM triangle rectangle *m*; ~ **ascension** *n* ASTRON, SPACE ascension droite *f*; ~ **circular cone** *n* GEOM cône circulaire droit *m*; ~ **circular cylinder** *n* GEOM cylindre circulaire droit *m*; ~ **justification** *n* COMP, DP justification à droite *f*; ~ **margin** *n* PRINT marge de droite *f*; ~ **shift** *n* COMP, DP décalage à droite *m*; ~ **stereo channel** *n* RECORDING canal stéréo de droite *m*; ~ **to a patent** *n* PATENTS droit au brevet *m*; ~ **turning traffic** *n* TRANSP courant tourne-à-droite *m*; ~ **of way** *n* CONST droit de passage *m*, emprise *f*, NAUT *navigation*, TRANSP droit de passage *m*

right-and-left: ~ **coupling** *n* MECH ENG turnbuckle lanterne *f*, lanterne de serrage *f*; ~ **screw** *n* MECH ENG vis à filet droite et gauche *f*, vis à pas contraires *f*; ~ **screw link** *n* MECH ENG turnbuckle lanterne *f*, lanterne de serrage *f*

right-angled[1] *adj* GEOM perpendiculaire

right-angled:[2] ~ **bend** *n* MECH ENG coude d'équerre *m*; ~ **bend coupling** *n* MECH ENG raccord à coude d'équerre *m*

right-hand[1] *adj* MECH à droite

right-hand:[2] ~ **circular polarization** *n* SPACE *communications* polarisation circulaire droite *f*; ~ **coiling** *n* SPRINGS sens d'enroulement droit *m*; ~ **knife tool** *n* MECH ENG *lathe* outil à couteau à droite *m*; ~ **lock** *n* CONST serrure à droite *f*; ~ **milling cutter** *n* MECH ENG fraise avec denture à droite *f*; ~ **page** *n* PRINT belle page *f*, page de droite *f*; ~ **rule** *n* ELEC *electromagnetism* règle de la main droite *f*, ELEC ENG règle des trois doigts de la main droite *f*, PHYS règle de la main droite *f*; ~ **screw** *n* MECH ENG vis à droite *f*; ~ **side** *n* MATH, PHYS *of equation* second membre *m*; ~ **tap** *n* MECH ENG taraud à droite *m*; ~ **thread** *n* MECH ENG filet à droite *m*, pas à droite *m*; ~ **turnoff** *n* RAIL changement simple *m*

right-handed[1] *adj* PHYS *coordinate system* de sens direct

right-handed:[2] ~ **screw** *n* MECH ENG vis à droite *f*; ~ **spiral** *n* MECH ENG hélice à droite *f*

righting: ~ **lever** *n* NAUT *naval architecture* bras de levier de redressement *m*; ~ **lever arm** *n* NAUT *naval architecture* bras de levier de redressement *m*; ~ **moment** *n* NAUT *naval architecture* couple de rappel *m*, moment de redressement *m*, moment du couple de redressement *m*

right-justified *adj* PRINT au fer à droite

right-justify *vt* COMP, DP justifier à droite

right-of-way *n* AERONAUT *air traffic* priorité de passage *f*, *airport* priorité de passage *f*, servitude de passage *f*

rights: ~ **afforded by** *phr* PATENTS droits conférés par

rigid: ~ **and folding cartons** *n* PACKAGING carton rigide pliant *m*; ~ **automatic coupling** *n* TRANSP attelage automatique rigide *m*; ~ **axle** *n* AUTO, VEHICLES *suspension* essieu rigide *m*; ~ **body** *n* PHYS *analytical mechanics* solide invariable *m*; ~ **box** *n* PACKAGING boîte rigide *f*; ~ **coaxial line** *n* ELEC ENG ligne coaxiale rigide *f*, ligne rigide *f*; ~ **construction** *n* CONST *roads* construction rigide *f*, surfaçage rigide *m*; ~ **coupling** *n* MECH ENG *gear drive* accouplement rigide *m*; ~ **leg** *n* PHOTO *of tripod* branche droite *f*; ~ **pipe** *n* MECH ENG tube rigide *m*; ~ **plastic** *n* P&R plastique rigide *m*; ~ **PVC** *n* PACKAGING polyvinyle chloride rigide *m*; ~ **reflector** *n* SPACE *spacecraft* réflecteur rigide *m*; ~ **rotor** *n* AERONAUT *helicopter*, MECH ENG rotor rigide *m*; ~ **sidewall air cushion** *n* TRANSP coussin d'air à jupes rigides *m*; ~ **sidewall hovercraft** *n* TRANSP aéroglisseur à jupes rigides *m*; ~ **skirt** *n* TRANSP jupe rigide *f*; ~ **skirt hovercraft** *n* TRANSP aéroglisseur à jupes rigides *m*; ~ **stinger** *n* PETR rampe rigide *f*

rigidity *n* PAPER TECH rigidité *f*, PHYS raideur *f*, rigidité *f*; ~ **modulus** *n* COAL TECH module de cisaillement *m*, PHYS coefficient de cisaillement *m*, module de cisaillement *m*, module de rigidité *m*

rill *n* HYDROL ruisselet *m*

rille *n* ASTRON fissure *f*

rim *n* VEHICLES *headlamp* collerette *f*, *wheel* jante *f*; ~ **capacitor** *n* ELEC condensateur à rebord *m*; ~ **flange** *n* VEHICLES *wheel* joue de jante *f*; ~ **syncline** *n* GEOL synclinal bordier *m*

rime *n* REFRIG givre blanc *m*

Rinco: ~ **process** *n* PRINT bobine de carton *f*

ring[1] *n* AUTO segment *m*, C&G anneau de cueillage *m*, CHEM anneau *m*, chaîne fermée *f*, COMP, DP anneau *m*, HYDR EQUIP *of piston* garniture d'étanchéité de piston *f*, segment de piston *m*, MECH anneau *m*, bague *f*, couronne *f*, PHOTO *for carrying strap* oeillet *m*, SPRINGS *loop, hook on end of spring* anneau *m*, TELECOM *wire* conducteur de nuque *m*, fil de nuque *m*, TEXTILES anneau *m*, VEHICLES *piston* segment *m*; ~ **and pinion** *n* AUTO couple conique *m*; ~ **and pinion gearing** *n* AUTO, VEHICLES *differential* renvoi d'angle *m*; ~ **armature** *n* ELEC *generator, motor* induit en anneau *m*; ~ **bolt** *n* NAUT *deck fittings* boucle d'amarrage *f*, piton *m*; ~ **burner** *n* CONST brûleur à couronne *m*; ~ **circuit** *n* (AmE) *(cf ring main)* ELEC, ELEC ENG circuit bouclé *m*; ~ **configuration** *n* TELECOM configuration en anneau *f*, interconnexion en boucle *f*; ~ **core** *n* NUCLEAR noyau toroïdal *m*; ~ **counter** *n* TV compteur en anneau *m*; ~ **end** *n* AUTO bec de segment *m*; ~ **feeder** *n* ELEC *supply network* boucle *f*; ~ **of flame** *n* GAS TECH corolle de flammes *f*; ~ **flash** *n* PHOTO flash annulaire *m*; ~ **frame** *n* AERONAUT *aircraft* couple *m*; ~ **fuselage** *n* AERONAUT couple fuselage *m*; ~ **gage** *n* (AmE) *see ring gauge*; ~ **galaxy** *n* ASTRON galaxie annuaire *f*; ~ **gap** *n* AUTO coupe de segment *f*; ~ **gauge** *n* (BrE) C&G, METR calibre de bague *m*; ~ **gear** *n* AUTO couronne dentée *f*, grande couronne *f*, VEHICLES *differential* couronne *f*; ~ **head** *n* RECORDING tête en anneau *f*, TV tête magnétique annulaire *f*; ~ **joint** *n* AUTO section de segment *f*; ~ **laser** *n* PHYS laser en anneau *m*; ~ **magnet** *n* TV bague-aimant circulaire *f*; ~ **main** *n* (BrE) *(cf ring circuit)* ELEC *circuit*, ELEC ENG circuit bouclé *m*; ~ **main system** *n* ELEC *supply network* réseau bouclé *m*, réseau en boucle *m*; ~ **modulator** *n* RECORDING modulateur en anneau *m*; ~ **network** *n* COMP réseau en anneau *m*, DP réseau en anneau *m*, réseau en boucle *m*, TELECOM réseau en anneau *m*; ~ **pliers** *n pl* MECH ENG *tool* pince à anneaux *f*; ~ **roll crusher** *n* COAL TECH broyeur à anneau cylindrique *m*; ~ **seal** *n* GAS TECH obturateur annulaire *m*; ~ **shears** *n pl* MECH ENG *tool* cisailles à anneaux *f pl*; ~ **spanner** *n* (BrE) *(cf ring wrench)* VEHICLES clef polygonale *f*, clé polygonale *f*; ~ **spinning** *n* TEXTILES filature à anneaux *f*; ~ **spring** *n* SPRINGS ressort à bague *m*; ~ **topology** *n* COMP, DP topologie en anneau *f*; ~ **translator** *n* TELECOM traducteur toroïdal *m*; ~ **tube** *n* TEXTILES tube de filature *m*; ~ **weld** *n* NUCLEAR soudure circulaire *f*; ~ **winding** *n* ELEC *coil* enroulement en anneau *m*; ~ **wrench** *n* (AmE) *(cf ring spanner)* MECH ENG *tool*, VEHICLES clé polygonale *f*

ring[2] *vt* TEXTILES entourer

ring[3] *vi* TELECOM sonner

Ring: ~ **Nebula** *n* ASTRON, SPACE nébuleuse anneau *f*

ringer *n* TELECOM générateur de courant de sonnerie *m*

ringing *n* CONST ondulation *f*, ondulation en bande passante *f*, oscillation *f*, oscillation de dépassement *f*, ELEC ENG *telephone bell* appel par sonnerie *m*, RECORDING *of loudspeaker* oscillation *f*, TELECOM sonnerie *f*; ~ **current** *n* TELECOM courant d'appel *m*; ~ **duration** *n* TELECOM durée de la sonnerie *f*; ~ **machine** *n* TELECOM générateur de courant de sonnerie *m*; ~ **period** *n* TELECOM temps de sonnerie *m*; ~ **test** *n* ELEC contrôle par sonnage *m*

ring-shaped *adj* GEOM annulaire

ring-spinning: ~ **frame** *n* TEXTILES métier continu à anneaux *m*

ring-spun: ~ **yarn** *n* TEXTILES fil de chaîne du continu *m*

ring-type: ~ **thrust washer** *n* MECH ENG rondelle de butée *f*

rink: ~ **floor** *n* REFRIG soubassement de patinoire *m*

rip:[1] ~ **cord** *n* MILIT *parachute* câble de déclenchement *m*; ~ **current** *n* OCEANOG courant d'arrachement *m*, courant sagittal *m*, courant à clapotage *m*, courant de retour *m*; ~ **in** *n* C&G déchirures de bords *f pl*; ~ **pin** *n* MILIT *parachute* broche de câble de déclenchement *f*; ~ **tide** *n* NAUT courant de retour *m*; ~ **track** *n* (AmE) *(cf repair track)* RAIL voie de réparations *f*

rip[2] *vt* CONST défricher, refendre

riparian *adj* HYDROL, WATER SUPP riverain

ripening *n* PHOTO *of emulsion* maturation chimique *f*, PRINT maturation *f*, stabilisation de la taille et de l'organisation des grains *f*

ripidolite *n* MINERAL ripidolite *f*

ripper *n* CONST charrue défonceuse *f*, ripper *m*, défonceuse portée *f*, rippeur *m*, MINING machine de traçage *f*

ripping *n* CONST refente *f*

ripple *n* ACOUSTICS ondulation *f*, CONST ondulation *f*, ondulation résiduelle *f*, HYDROL ride *f*, OCEANOG clapotis *m*, SPACE *communications* roulis *m*; ~ **attenuation** *n* CONST atténuation de l'ondulation résiduelle *f*; ~ **carry adder** *n* COMP, DP additionneur avec report *m*, additionneur en cascade *m*, additionneur simultané *m*; ~ **factor** *n* CONST taux d'ondulation *m*; ~ **filter** *n* CONST filtre d'alimentation *m*, filtre de lissage *m*, filtre de sortie *m*, filtre de sortie d'alimentation *m*, RAD PHYS filtre d'ondulation *m*; ~ **frequency** *n* CONST fréquence d'ondulation *f*, fréquence d'ondulation résiduelle *f*, RAD PHYS fréquence d'ondulation *f*; ~ **mark** *n* GEOL ripple-mark *f*, *sedimentology* filon superficiel *m*, ride de courant *f*, HYDROL ripple-mark *f*,

OCEANOG, PETR ride de plage *f*; ~ **tank** *n* WAVE PHYS *for wave experiment* cuve à rides *f*; ~ **voltage** *n* CONST ondulation de la tension *f*, tension ondulée *f*, ELECTRON tension d'ondulation *f*

riprap *n* CONST enrochement *m*, perré en moellons *m*

RISC *abbr (reduced instruction set computer)* COMP, DP ordinateur RISC *m*, ordinateur à jeu d'instructions réduit *m*

rise[1] *n* CONST *height of step* contremarche *f*, hauteur de marche *f*, *of arch* flèche *f*, hauteur sous clef *f*, montée *f*, HYDROL montée *f*, NAUT *of tide* flux *m*, montée *f*, OCEANOG dorsale océanique *f*; ~ **face** *n* COAL TECH taille montante *f*; ~ **of floor** *n* NAUT *ship design* relevé de formes *m*, relevé de varangue *m*; ~ **time** *n* AERONAUT *sonic boom*, COMP, CONST, DP temps de montée *m*, PETR temps d'élévation *m*, PHYS, RECORDING *of pulse* temps de montée *m*; ~ **workings** *n* COAL TECH taille montante *f*

rise[2] *vt* MINING monter, remonter

rise[3] *vi* HYDROL *of waters* grossir, hausser, monter, *source* prendre sa source, MINES percer en montant, NAUT monter

riser *n* C&G puits *m*, CONST colonne montante *f*, tube montant *m*, tuyau montant *m*, *vertical part of step* contremarche *f*, devant de la marche *m*, ELEC *supply*, PETR colonne montante *f*, PETR TECH colonne montante *f*, tube prolongateur *m*, PROD ENG trou d'évent *m*, évent *m*; ~ **pin** *n* PROD ENG *founding* broche d'évent *f*, mandrin d'évent *m*, évent *m*; ~ **pipe** *n* CONST, PETR colonne montante *f*; ~ **pipeline** *n* PETR TECH tube prolongateur *m*; ~ **stick** *n* PROD ENG *founding* broche d'évent *f*, mandrin d'évent *m*; ~ **tensioner** *n* PETR dispositif de mise sous tension constante d'une colonne montante *m*

rising *n* MINING remontage *m*; ~ **arch** *n* CONST *curve described* arc rampant *m*, *structure* voûte rampante *f*; ~ **gradient** *n* CONST pente montante *f*; ~ **main** *n* CONST *building*, ELEC *supply* colonne montante *f*; ~ **sun magnetron** *n* CONST magnétron à cavités alternées *m*; ~ **tide** *n* FUELLESS, NAUT marée montante *f*, OCEANOG flot *m*, flux *m*

risk *n* QUALITY, SAFETY risque *m*; ~ **assessment** *n* MAR POLL évaluation du risque *f*, QUALITY estimation du risque *f*; ~ **criteria** *n pl* QUALITY critères de risque *m pl*; ~ **evaluation** *n* QUALITY évaluation du risque *f*; ~ **of exposure** *n* RAD PHYS *radiation*, SAFETY *radiation* risque d'exposition *m*; ~ **management** *n* QUALITY gestion des risques *f*, gestion du risque *f*; ~ **quantification** *n* QUALITY quantification du risque *f*; ~ **of suffocation** *n* SAFETY risque d'asphyxie *m*

Ritz: ~ **combination principle** *n* PHYS principe de combinaison de Ritz *m*

river *n* HYDROL rivière *f*, *discharging into sea* fleuve *m*, NAUT *geography* fleuve *m*, rivière *f*, WATER SUPP rivière *f*; ~ **authority** *n* WATER SUPP autorités du bassin fluvial *f pl*; ~ **bank** *n* CONST berge de fleuve *f*, bord de fleuve *f*, bord de rivière *m*; ~ **bar** *n* HYDROL barre de rivière *f*; ~ **basin** *n* FUELLESS, HYDROL, WATER SUPP bassin fluvial *m*; ~ **bed** *n* HYDROL lit de rivière *m*, WATER SUPP lit *m*, lit de rivière *m*; ~ **boat** *n* NAUT bateau fluvial *m*; ~ **bus** *n* TRANSP bus d'eau *m*; ~ **capture** *n* HYDROL captage de rivière *m*; ~ **channel** *n* HYDROL chenal de rivière *m*; ~ **dam** *n* WATER SUPP digue fluviale *f*; ~ **dredge** *n* WATER SUPP drague fluviale *f*; ~ **erosion** *n* HYDROL érosion fluviale *f*, érosion fluviatile *f*; ~ **ferry** *n* NAUT transbordeur fluvial *m*; ~

fleet *n* NAUT *inland water transport* batellerie *f*; ~ **mouth** *n* HYDROL aber *m*, bouche de fleuve *f*, embouchure de fleuve *f*; ~ **navigation** *n* TRANSP navigation fluviale *f*; ~ **port** *n* NAUT port fluvial *m*; ~ **safety** *n* NAUT sécurité de la navigation fluviale *f*; ~ **traffic** *n* NAUT batellerie *f*, trafic fluvial *m*, TRANSP trafic fluvial *m*; ~ **training** *n* HYDROL régularisation d'un cours d'eau *f*, WATER SUPP régularisation *f*; ~ **tug** *n* TRANSP remorqueur de rivière *m*; ~ **user** *n* NAUT utilisateur des rivières *m*; ~ **wall** *n* WATER SUPP bajoyer *m*; ~ **water** *n* HYDROL eau de rivière *f*, eau fluviale *f*; ~ **works** *n* WATER SUPP aménagement des cours d'eau *m*

riverside[1] *adj* HYDROL riverain

riverside[2] *n* HYDROL bord de rivière *m*

rivet *n* CONST clou *m*, clou à river *m*, rivet *m*, MECH, MECH ENG, PROD ENG rivet *m*; ~ **cold press** *n* MECH ENG presse à froid pour rivets *f*; ~ **dolly** *n* CONST tas à bouteroller *m*; ~ **joint** *n* CONST assemblage par rivets *m*; ~ **knocking-off hammer** *n* MECH ENG marteau à découper les rivets *m*; ~ **set** *n* CONST bouterolle *f*, chasse-rivet *m*; ~ **shank diameter** *n* MECH ENG diamètre de tige de rivet *m*; ~ **snap** *n* CONST bouterolle *f*, chasse-rivet *m*

riveted: ~ **lap joint** *n* MECH ENG joint à recouvrement rivé *m*; ~ **plate** *n* CONST tôle rivée *f*; ~ **seam** *n* PACKAGING couture rivetée *f*

riveter *n* CONST *machine* machine à river *f*, machine à riveter *f*, riveuse *f*, rivoir *m*

rivet-heating: ~ **furnace** *n* CONST fourneau à chauffer les rivets *m*

riveting *n* CONST rivetage *m*, rivure *f*, MECH, MECH ENG rivetage *m*, rivure *f*, PROD ENG rivetage *m*; ~ **hammer** *n* CONST marteau à river *m*, marteau-rivoir *m*, rivoir *m*; ~ **machine** *n* CONST machine à river *f*, machine à riveter *f*, riveuse *f*, rivoir *m*; ~ **set** *n* CONST bouterolle *f*, chasse-rivet *m*

riving: ~ **knife** *n* SAFETY couteau à fendre *m*

rivulet *n* HYDROL ru *m*, ruisseau *m*, ruisselet *m*

RJE *abbr (remote job entry)* COMP, DP soumission des travaux à distance *f*

RMS[1] *abbr (root mean square)* CONST, ELECTRON, MATH, TELECOM valeur quadratique moyenne *f*

RMS:[2] ~ **current** *n* ELEC ENG intensité efficace *f*; ~ **frequency deviation** *n* SPACE *communications* excursion de fréquence efficace *f*; ~ **value** *n* RECORDING valeur efficace *f*

Rn *(radon)* CHEM Rn *(radon)*

RO *abbr (remote operations)* TELECOM opérations distantes *f pl*

road *n* CONST *highway* chemin *m*, route *f*, voie *f*, TRANSP route *f*, VEHICLES chaussée *f*, chemin *m*, route *f*; ~ **bead** *n* C&G bille routière *f*; ~ **bed** *n* RAIL plate-forme *f*, plate-forme de la voie *f*; ~ **bridge** *n* CONST pont pour routes *m*, pont-route *m*, TRANSP pont-route *m*; ~ **building** *n* TRANSP construction routière *f*; ~ **building machinery** *n* TRANSP engins de construction routière *m pl*; ~ **camber** *n* VEHICLES *surface* bombement d'une chaussée *m*; ~ **clearance** *n* AUTO, VEHICLES *body* garde au sol *f*; ~ **finishing machine** *n* TRANSP finisseur *m*; ~ **gasoline station** *n* (AmE) *(cf petrol station)* TRANSP station d'essence *f*; ~ **grader** *n* TRANSP niveleuse *f*; ~ **haulage** *n* TRANSP transports routiers *m pl*; ~ **hauler** *n* (AmE), ~ **haulier** *n* (BrE) TRANSP transporteur routier *m*; ~ **head** *n* COAL TECH front d'avancement *m*; ~ **identification sign** *n* TRANSP borne routière *f*; ~ **jam** *n* TRANSP embouteillage *m*; ~ **junction** *n* TRANSP bifurcation *f*; ~ **locomotive** *n* TRANSP locomotive de route *f*; ~ **making** *n* CONST confection de routes *f*, construction de routes *f*, TRANSP construction routière *f*; ~ **map** *n* AUTO carte routière *f*; ~ **marker cone** *n* TRANSP balise de circulation *f*; ~ **message** *n* TRANSP message routier *m*; ~ **metal** *n* (BrE) *(cf paving material)* CONST matériaux d'empierrement pour route *m pl*; ~ **metal-spreading machine** *n* (BrE) *(cf asphalt-spreading machine, pavement-spreading machine)* TRANSP épandeur-régleur-dameur *m*; ~ **news** *n* TRANSP bulletin des routes *m*; ~ **over railway** *n* TRANSP passage supérieur de la route *m*; ~ **painting** *n* CONST peinture routière *f*; ~ **plough** *n* (BrE) TRANSP scarificateur *m*; ~ **plow** *n* (AmE) *see road plough*; ~ **rail** *n* TRANSP rail-route *m*; ~ **rail bus** *n* TRANSP autobus bimodal *m*; ~ **resistance** *n* VEHICLES *tyre* résistance à roulement *f*; ~ **ripper** *n* TRANSP scarificateur *m*; ~ **roller** *n* TRANSP rouleau compresseur *m*; ~ **safety** *n* CONST sécurité routière *f*, SAFETY sécurité des routes *f*, TRANSP sécurité routière *f*; ~ **safety device** *n* SAFETY dispositif de sécurité routière *m*; ~ **safety program** *n* (AmE), ~ **safety programme** *n* (BrE) TRANSP programme de sécurité routière *m*; ~ **sign** *n* CONST panneau de signalisation *m*, VEHICLES panneau de signalisation routière *m*; ~ **signs** *n pl* CONST signalisation *f*; ~ **system** *n* TRANSP réseau routier *m*; ~ **tank car** *n (RTC)* TRANSP camion citerne *m*; ~ **tanker** *n* MAR POLL camion citerne *m*; ~ **tarring machine** *n* TRANSP répandeuse de goudron *f*; ~ **tractor** *n* TRANSP tracteur routier *m*; ~ **traffic** *n* TRANSP circulation routière *f*; ~ **traffic radar** *n* TRANSP cinémomètre radar *m*; ~ **train** *n* TRANSP train routier *m*; ~ **transport** *n* CONST, TRANSP transport routier *m*; ~ **user** *n* TRANSP usager de la route *m*; ~ **vehicle weighing machine** *n* TRANSP pont-bascule pour véhicules routiers *m*; ~ **works** *n* TRANSP travaux routiers *m pl*

road-based: ~ **transmitter** *n* TRANSP émetteur à couverture locale *m*

road-bound *adj* TRANSP routier

road-coated: ~ **paper** *n* PAPER TECH papier couché à la barre filetée *m*

roadheader *n* MINING machine à travers les voies *f*

roads *n pl* NAUT, OCEANOG rade *f*; ~ **which cross** *n pl* CONST arrisement *m*, carrefour *m*

roadside: ~ **radio transmitter** *n* TRANSP émetteur au sol *m*

roadstead *n* NAUT, OCEANOG rade *f*

roadster *n* TRANSP roadster *m*

roadstones *n pl* CONST cailloutis *m*

roadway *n* CONST chaussée *f*, passage carrossable *m*, MINING galerie *f*, voie *f*, TRANSP autoroute *f*, chaussée *f*

roadworthy *adj* TRANSP apte à la mise en circulation

roaming: ~ **capability** *n* TELECOM possibilité de se déplacer *f*; ~ **subscriber** *n* TELECOM abonné itinérant *m*

roaring: ~ **forties** *n pl* NAUT, OCEANOG quarantièmes rugissants *m pl*

roaster *n* PROD ENG four de grillage *m*, four à griller *m*

roasting *n* COAL TECH grillage *m*, FOOD TECH torréfaction *f*, PROD ENG calcination *f*, frittage *m*, grillage *m*, torréfaction *f*; ~ **furnace** *n* PROD ENG four de grillage *m*, four à griller *m*; ~ **kiln** *n* PROD ENG four de grillage *m*, four à griller *m*; ~ **oven** *n* PROD ENG four de grillage *m*, four à griller *m*

robot *n* COMP, DP robot *m*; ~ **gripping device** *n* MECH ENG appareil de serrage et de desserrage de robot *m*

robotic: ~ **arm** *n* PROD ENG bras robotisé *m*; ~ **palletizing**

and stretch system *n* PACKAGING système robotique pour palettiser et mettre sous film étirable *m*

robotics *n* COMP, DP robotique *f*

robustness *n* COMP, DP, TESTING robustesse *f*

Roche: ~ **limit** *n* ASTRON limite de Roche *f*

Rochelle: ~ **salt** *n* CHEM *sodium potassium tartrate*, ELEC ENG *piezoelectric material*, FOOD TECH sel de Seignette *m*

rock *n* COAL TECH roc *m*, roche *f*, GEOL, NAUT roche *f*, rocher *m*; ~ **and roll equipment** *n* RECORDING matériel avec marche avant-arrière *m*; ~ **and roll mixing** *n* CINEMAT, RECORDING mixage en marche avant-arrière *m*; ~ **and roll recording** *n* RECORDING enregistrement avec marche avant-arrière *m*; ~ **bit** *n* PETR TECH trépan pour roches *m*, trépan à molettes *m*; ~ **borer** *n* CONST *machine* foreuse *f*, perforatrice au rocher *f*; ~ **breaker** *n* CONST brise-roche *m*, broyeur de rocher *m*, casse-pierre *m*, concasseur *m*; ~ **capping** *n* MINING chapeau de filon *m*, chef du gisement *m*, tête du gisement *f*; ~ **channeler** *n* (AmE), ~ **channeller** *n* (BrE) CONST, MINING *machine* trancheuse *f*; ~ **dowel** *n* COAL TECH clou à roc *m*, CONST boulon d'ancrage *m*, mèche pour rocher *f*; ~ **drift** *n* MINING bouveau *m*, bovette *f*, bowette *f*, galerie au rocher *f*; ~ **drill** *n* COAL TECH fleuret *m*, foret à roche *m*, CONST fleuret *m*, foreuse *f*, perforatrice *f*, MINING foreuse *f*, perforateur mécanique *m*, perforatrice *f*, perforatrice mécanique *f*, sonde *f*, *rock drilling, earth boring* burin *m*, fleuret *m*, foreuse *f*, perforateur *m*, pistolet *m*, sondeuse *f*; ~ **fill** *n* CONST enrochement *m*, remblai rocheux *m*, WATER SUPP enrochement *m*; ~ **fracture** *n* GEOL lithoclase *f*; ~ **gas** *n* GAS TECH gaz naturel *m*; ~ **layer** *n* WATER SUPP couche rocheuse *f*; ~ **lever** *n* CONST *equalizing bar* balancier de répartition *m*, balancier de suspension *m*; ~ **meal** *n* MINERAL farine fossile *f*; ~ **mechanics** *n* COAL TECH mécanique des roches *f*; ~ **milk** *n* MINERAL lait de roche *m*; ~ **oil** *n* COAL TECH huile de roche *f*, PETR huile de roche *f*, pétrole *m*; ~ **pressure** *n* COAL TECH pression dans le roc *f*, pression de la roche *f*; ~ **rubble** *n* HYDR EQUIP *for hydraulic work* caillasse *f*, moellon *m*; ~ **salt** *n* CHEM halite *f*, sel gemme *m*, FOOD TECH, GAS TECH, MINERAL sel gemme *m*; ~ **shoe** *n* COAL TECH sabot à roc *m*; ~ **slip** *n* GEOL glissement de terrain *m*, éboulement *m*; ~ **sounding** *n* COAL TECH sondage de roc *m*; ~ **tar** *n* PETR pétrole brut *m*; ~ **tip** *n* COAL TECH clou à roc *m*; ~ **type** *n* COAL TECH, PETR type de roche *m*; ~ **wool** *n* HEAT ENG laine de roche *f*; ~ **work** *n* MINING travaux en roche *m pl*; ~ **work explosive** *n* MINING explosif roche *m*, explosif rocher *m*

rockbolt *n* CONST boulon d'ancrage *m*

rock-cutting: ~ **dredger** *n* NAUT drague dérocheuse *f*

rocker *n* C&G fond retombé *m*, MECH culbuteur *m*, MINING *ore dressing* berceau *m*, cradle *m*; ~ **arm** *n* AUTO, VEHICLES *engine, valves* culbuteur *m*; ~ **arm assembly** *n* AUTO rampe de culbuteurs *f*; ~ **arm shaft** *n* AUTO axe de culbuteur *m*; ~ **arm support** *n* AUTO support de culbuteur *m*; ~ **bearing** *n* MECH ENG coussinet de balancier de renvoi *m*; ~ **box** *n* VEHICLES *engine, valves* porte-culbuteurs *m*; ~ **cover** *n* AUTO cache-culbuteurs *m*; ~ **shaft** *n* AUTO *car* axe de culbuteur *m*; ~ **switch** *n* CINEMAT commutateur à bascule *m*, ELEC commutateur à bascule *m*, commutateur à poussoir *m*, interrupteur profilé *m*, ELEC ENG interrupteur basculant *m*

rocket *n* MILIT roquette *f*, NAUT, SPACE fusée *f*; ~ **engine** *n* MECH ENG, SPACE moteur-fusée *m*; ~ **igniter** *n* MILIT allumeur de fusée *m*; ~ **launcher** *n* MILIT lance-fusées *m*, lance-roquettes *m*; ~ **launching site** *n* MILIT aire de lancement *f*; ~ **motor** *n* MILIT moteur-fusée *m*; ~ **pistol** *n* MILIT pistolet lance-fusée *m*; ~ **plane** *n* AERONAUT avion fusée *m*; ~ **plume** *n* MILIT flamme de tuyère *f*; ~ **propellant** *n* MILIT propulsant *m*; ~ **propulsion** *n* SPACE *spacecraft* propulsion par fusée *f*, propulsion à réaction *f*; ~ **signal** *n* MILIT fusée de signaux *f*

rocket-assisted: ~ **projectile** *n* MILIT projectile à décollage assisté *m*

rocketry *n* MILIT technique des fusées *f*

rocking *n* RECORDING recherche du son en marche avant-arrière *f*; ~ **table** *n* C&G table basculante *f*

rockslide *n* GEOL glissement de terrain *m*, éboulement *m*

Rockwell: ~ **hardness test** *n* MECH ENG essai de dureté Rockwell *m*; ~ **hardness testing machine** *n* MECH ENG machine d'essai de dureté Rockwell *f*

rod *n* C&G *optical blank* canon *m*, CONST *surveyors' level staff* mire *f*, *welding* baguette *f*, HYDR EQUIP *of slide valve* bielle de tiroir *f*, *of valve* queue de soupape *f*, tige de soupape *f*, LAB EQUIP tige *f*, MECH barre *f*, bielle *f*, tige *f*, MECH ENG tige *f*, tringle *f*, MINING rallonge *f*, tige *f*, WATER SUPP *of pump* tige *f*; ~ **actuator** *n* PROD ENG actionneur à tige *m*; ~ **coating kiss applicator** *n* PAPER TECH couchage à la barre filetée *m*; ~ **coupling** *n* MINING emmanchement de tiges *m*; ~ **guide** *n* PROD ENG guide de tige *m*; ~ **lever** *n* PROD ENG levier à tige rigide *m*; ~ **linkage** *n* MECH ENG attache de bielle *f*; ~ **mill** *n* COAL TECH broyeur à barre *m*, PROD ENG train de machine *m*, train de serpentage *m*, train à serpenter *m*; ~ **operated disconnect switch** *n* PROD ENG sectionneur à actionneur rotatif *m*; ~ **proof** *n* C&G cordeline *f* (Fra), piqûre *f* (Bel); ~ **seal** *n* MECH ENG joint de tige *m*; ~ **seal housing** *n* MECH ENG logement de joint de tige *m*; ~ **support** *n* MINING *boring* clef de retenue *f*, tourne-à-gauche de support *m*

rodding *n* MINING réparation *f*

rod-end: ~ **plain eye** *n* MECH ENG tenon simple d'extrémité de tige de piston *m*; ~ **spherical eyes** *n pl* MECH ENG tenons à rotule d'extrémité de tige de piston *m pl*

rod-in-tube: ~ **technique** *n* OPT, TELECOM procédé de la tige dans le tube *m*

rods *n pl* MINING corps de sonde *m*, tige de sonde *f*

rod-turning: ~ **tool** *n* MINING *boring* manche de manoeuvre *m*, manivelle *f*, tourne-à-gauche *m*, tourne-à-gauche de manoeuvre *m*

roentgen *n* PHYS, RAD PHYS roentgen *m*; ~ **equivalent man** *n (rem)* RAD PHYS équivalent en roentgen pour l'homme *m*

roentgenoluminescence *n* NUCLEAR luminescence aux rayons X *f*

roentgenometallography *n* NUCLEAR métallographie par rayons X *f*

roll[1] *n* AERONAUT *aerobatic flight* tonneau *m*, CINEMAT bobine *f*, galette *f*, rouleau *m*, MECH ENG cylindre *m*, PAPER TECH rouleau *m*, rouleau presseur *m*, PHYS, SPACE roulis *m*, TEXTILES rouleau *m*; ~ **attitude** *n* SPACE *spacecraft* attitude latérale *f*; ~ **bar** *n* VEHICLES *body* arceau de sécurité *m*; ~ **boiling** *n* TEXTILES décatissage au bouillon *m*; ~ **call polling** *n* COMP scrutation par appel de terminaux *f*, DP scrutation par appel *f*; ~ **channel** *n* AERONAUT *automatic pilot* chaîne de roulis *f*; ~ **coating** *n* COATINGS, P&R *process* revêtement au rouleau *m*; ~ **crimper** *n* PAPER TECH plieuse *f*; ~ **cue** *n* CINEMAT indication de départ *f*; ~ **diameter** *n* TEXTILES diamètre du cylindre *m*; ~ **end** *n* PAPER TECH fond de

bobine *m*; ~ **film** *n* CINEMAT pellicule en bobine *f*, PHOTO pellicule en bobine *f*, pellicule en rouleau *f*, PRINT film en rouleau *m*; ~ **forming equipment** *n* PROD ENG matériel de profilage de feuillard *m*; ~ **head** *n* PAPER TECH fond de bobine *m*; ~ **headbox** *n* PAPER TECH caisse d'arrivée à rouleaux *f*; ~ **in** *n* COMP, DP rappel *m*, transfert en mémoire centrale *m*; ~ **in-roll out** *n* COMP rappel-transfert *m*; ~ **label printing** *n* PACKAGING impression sur étiquettes en rouleau *f*; ~ **length** *n* TEXTILES longueur de tissu sur rouleau *f*; ~ **mark** *n* (AmE) *(cf roller mark)* C&G marque de rouleau *f*; ~ **marking** *n* MECH ENG marquage par roulement *m*; ~ **number** *n* CINEMAT numéro de bobine *m*; ~ **off** *n* RECORDING affaiblissement *m*; ~ **out** *n* COMP retrait *m*, transférer en mémoire auxiliaire, DP retrait *m*; ~ **paper** *n* PRINT papier en bobine *m*; ~ **pocket** *n* PAPER TECH alvéole entre lames de cylindre de pile *f*; ~ **rate gyro** *n* SPACE *spacecraft* gyromètre de roulis *m*; ~ **scale** *n* PROD ENG scories de laminoir *f pl*, écailles de laminage *f pl*; ~ **screen** *n* COAL TECH crible à rouleaux *m*; ~ **shell** *n* PROD ENG *of crushing rolls* anneau de cylindre *m*, bague de cylindre *f*, bandage de cylindre *m*; ~ **sulfur** *n* (AmE), ~ **sulphur** *n* (BrE) CHEM soufre en canon *m*; ~ **test** *n* NAUT *ship design* essai de roulis *m*; ~ **train** *n* PROD ENG train de laminoir *m*, équipage de laminoir *m*; ~ **wringer** *n* TEXTILES essoreuse à rouleaux *f*

roll:[2] ~ **back** *vt* CINEMAT repasser, reprojeter; ~ **in** *vt* COMP, DP rappeler, reloger; ~ **ink on** *vt* COLOURS encrer par rouleaux; ~ **out** *vt* COMP retirer, DP retirer, transférer en mémoire auxiliaire

roll-coated: ~ **paper** *n* PAPER TECH papier couché au rouleau *m*

rolled[1] *adj* PAPER TECH laminé

rolled:[2] ~ **glass** *n* C&G verre laminé *m*; ~ **section** *n* NAUT *shipbuilding* profilé laminé *m*; ~ **steel** *n* PROP MAT acier laminé *m*

roller *n* C&G rouleau de guide *m*, CINEMAT galet *m*, tambour *m*, CONST *person* cylindreur *m*, *road roller* cylindre compresseur *m*, rouleau compresseur *m*, *used with capstan* tourniquet de cabestan *m*, MECH galet *m*, rouleau *m*, roulette *f*, NAUT *sea* lame de houle *f*, rouleau *m*, P&R *equipment* cylindre *m*, rouleau *m*, PAPER TECH porte-cylindres *m*, PRINT rouleau *m*, rouleau en cuir grainé *m*, PROD ENG cylindre *m*, cylindre lamineur *m*, TRANSP galet *m*; ~ **and rotary cutting press** *n* PACKAGING rouleau et presse rotative coupante *m*; ~ **bearing** *n* MECH ENG, VEHICLES roulement à rouleaux *m*; ~ **bit** *n* PETR TECH trépan à molettes *m*; ~ **blind dark slide** *n* PHOTO châssis à rideau *m*; ~ **blind shutter** *n* PHOTO obturateur à rideau *m*, rideau flexible *m*; ~ **boom** *n* NAUT bôme à rouleau *f*; ~ **bridge** *n* CONST pont roulant *m*; ~ **bump** *n* C&G ondulation de rouleau *f*; ~ **caption** *n* CINEMAT déroulant *m*; ~ **chain** *n* MECH ENG chaîne à rouleaux *f*; ~ **clutch** *n* AUTO embrayage à roue libre *m*; ~ **coating** *n* PAPER TECH couchage par rouleaux *m*; ~ **conveyor** *n* MECH ENG train de rouleaux transporteur *m*; ~ **crusher** *n* COAL TECH broyeur à anneau de mouture *m*; ~ **dryer** *n* PRINT sécheur à rouleaux *m*; ~ **dust collector** *n* ELEC ENG aspirateur mobile *m*; ~ **fairlead** *n* NAUT *deck fittings* chaumard à rouleau *m*; ~ **gage** *n* (AmE) *see roller gauge*; ~ **gate** *n* HYDROL *dams* vanne à chenille *f*; ~ **gauge** *n* (BrE) C&G galet de calibrage *m*; ~ **lever** *n* PROD ENG levier à galet *m*; ~ **mark** *n* (BrE) *(cf roll mark)* C&G marque de rouleau *f*; ~ **mill** *n* CHEM TECH, FOOD TECH *milling*, *machinery* moulin à cylindres *m*, PROD ENG broyeur à meules horizontales *m*; ~ **paint** *n* COLOURS peinture au rouleau *f*; ~ **painting** *n* CONST peinture au rouleau *f*; ~ **pallet** *n* TRANSP palette à roulettes *f*; ~ **pin** *n* PROD ENG goupille de galet *f*; ~ **printing** *n* PRINT, TEXTILES impression au rouleau *f*; ~ **setting** *n* TEXTILES réglage de cylindre *m*; ~ **shaft** *n* AUTO arbre porte-galet *m*; ~ **shoe** *n* PROD ENG sabot de rouleau *m*; ~ **tappet** *n* AUTO poussoir à galet *m*; ~ **timing chain** *n* AUTO chaîne de distribution à rouleaux *f*; ~ **titles** *n pl* CINEMAT titres déroulants *m pl*; ~ **tool chest** *n* MECH ENG servante d'outillage *f*; ~ **top of former** *n* PRINT rouleau d'appel avant le triangle *m*, rouleau placé au dessus de la plieuse *m*; ~ **transport** *n* CINEMAT entraînement par friction *m*; ~ **tray** *n* C&G utile à rouleaux *m*; ~ **weir** *n* WATER SUPP déversoir circulaire *m*

roller-type: ~ **governor** *n* CONTROL régulateur coulissant *m*; ~ **regulator** *n* CONTROL régulateur coulissant *m*

roll-in: ~ **refrigerator** *n* REFRIG armoire frigorifique à chariots *f*

roll-in/roll-out *n* DP transfert en mémoire centrale/sur mémoire auxiliaire *m*

rolling *n* CONST *of metalled roads* cylindrage *m*, NAUT *of ship* roulis *m*, PAPER TECH laminage *m*, PROD ENG *of metal* cylindrage *m*, laminage *m*; ~ **bearing** *n* MECH ENG *antifriction* palier de roulement *m*; ~ **bridge** *n* CONST pont roulant *m*; ~ **circle** *n* GEOM roulante *f*; ~ **code band splitting** *n* TELECOM découpage de la bande selon un code de brassage *m*; ~ **door** *n* CONST porte roulante *f*; ~ **friction** *n* PHYS frottement de roulement *m*; ~ **friction coefficient** *n* PHYS coefficient de frottement de roulement *m*; ~ **furnace** *n* PROD ENG four oscillant *m*; ~ **hitch** *n* NAUT *knots* amarrage à fouet *m*; ~ **load** *n* CONST *live load* poids roulant *m*; ~ **loop film transport** *n* CINEMAT entraînement de film à boucle roulant *m*; ~ **mill** *n* MECH ENG laminoir *m*, PROD ENG *establishment* laminerie *f*, *for metal* laminoir *m*, RAIL laminoir *m*, laminoir à rails *m*; ~ **mill roll** *n* PROD ENG cylindre de laminoir *m*, cylindre lamineur *m*, train de laminoir *m*, équipage de laminoir *m*; ~ **mill scale** *n* PROP MAT battitures *f pl*; ~ **mill train** *n* PROD ENG train de laminoir *m*, équipage de laminoir *m*; ~ **moment** *n* AERONAUT *aircraft* moment de roulis *m*; ~ **over** *n* PROD ENG *founding* renversement *m*; ~ **press** *n* PROD ENG presse à cylindre *f*; ~ **process** *n* C&G calandrage *m*; ~ **resistance** *n* VEHICLES résistance à roulement *f*; ~ **shutter** *n* CONST *store door* volet mécanique *m*, volet roulant *m*, volet à rideau *m*; ~ **stability** *n* AERONAUT *aircraft* stabilité en roulis *f*, stabilité transversale *f*; ~ **stock** *n* CONST matériel de chemin de fer *m*, matériel roulant *m*, RAIL *vehicles* matériel roulant *m*; ~ **stock label** *n* RAIL *vehicles* panneau d'identification *m*; ~ **takeoff** *n* AERONAUT décollage avec vitesse initiale *m*

roll-on/roll-off *n* (*ro-ro*) TRANSP roulage *m*, roulier *m*; ~ **port** *n* NAUT port à roulage direct *m*; ~ **ship** *n* TRANSP cargo à roulage direct *m*; ~ **system** *n* TRANSP manutention horizontale *f*; ~ **vessel** *n* NAUT *ferry, cargo boat* cargo à manutention horizontale *m*, navire du type roll-on/roll-off *m*, roulier *m*, TRANSP roulier *m*

roll-out: ~ **Fourdrinier** *n* PAPER TECH table plate sortante *f*

roll-over *n* TRANSP *capsizing, overturning* capotage *m*; ~ **anticline** *n* GEOL *dip reversal structure* anticlinal de compensation *m*; ~ **bar** *n* VEHICLES *body* arceau de sécurité *m*; ~ **draft machine** *n* (AmE), ~ **draught machine** *n* (BrE) PROD ENG *founding* machine à démouler

à renversement *f*; ~ **drop machine** *n* PROD ENG machine à démouler à renversement *f*; ~ **table** *n* PROD ENG *of roll-over machine* table de renversement *f*

rolls *n pl* PROD ENG *crushing* moulin à cylindres *m*, *rolling mill* laminoir *m*, train *m*, équipage *m*

roll-up: ~ **door** *n* VEHICLES *body* porte-rideau *m*

rolo: ~ **ship** *n* TRANSP navire à chargement horizontal et vertical *m*

ROM *abbr* (*read-only memory*) COMP, DP, ELEC ENG, ELECTRON ROM, mémoire fixe *f*, mémoire morte *f*

Roman: ~ **arch** *n* CONST arc plein cintre *m*, arc romain *m*; ~ **numeral** *n* MATH, PRINT chiffre romain *m*; ~ **type** *n* PRINT romain *m*

romeite *n* MINERAL roméite *f*

röntgen *n see roentgen*

rood *n* METR rood *m*

roof *n* CONST couverture *f*, toit *m*, toiture *f*, *of tunnel, cave* voûte *f*, *top of building* comble *m*, MINING toit de la couche *m*, *of mine, lode* ciel *m*, plafond *m*, toit *m*, PROD ENG *of firebox* ciel *m*, RAIL *vehicles* pavillon *m*, VEHICLES pavillon *m*, toit *m* ~ **bolting drilling machine** *n* MINING machine à boulonner au toit *f*; ~ **frame** *n* CONST charpente de comble *f*; ~ **light** *n* C&G dôme *m*; ~ **pitch** *n* CONST chute de comble *f*, inclinaison de comble *f*, pente de comble *f*, rampe de chevrons *f*; ~ **plate** *n* CONST *wall plate* plate-forme *f*, poutre sablière *f*, sablière *f*, sablière de comble *f*, semelle *f*; ~ **prism** *n* PHYS prisme d'Amici *m*, prisme en toit *m*, prisme à vision directe *m*; ~ **rack** *n* VEHICLES galerie de toit *f*; ~ **shielding plate** *n* NUCLEAR dalle de couverture *f*, plaque supérieure *f*, toit-dalle *m*; ~ **truss** *n* CONST ferme de comble *f*

roofer *n* CONST *person* couvreur *m*

roofer's: ~ **hammer** *n* CONST asseau *m*, assette *f*, marteau de couvreur *m*, tille de couvreur *f*

roofing *n* CONST couverture *f*, toiture *f*; ~ **felt** *n* CONST carton bitumé *m*, feutre pour toiture *m*

rooftop: ~ **air conditioning unit** *n* REFRIG climatiseur de toiture *m*; ~ **heliport** *n* AERONAUT héligare sur immeuble *f*, héliport sur immeuble *m*, hélistation sur immeuble *f*

room *n* COAL TECH chambre isolée *f*, CONST chambre *f*, local *m*, salle *f*, MINING chambre *f*, taille *f*; ~ **air conditioning unit** *n* REFRIG climatiseur mobile *m*, conditionneur à air de pièce *m*; ~ **temperature** *n* PHYS température ambiante *f*, température de la pièce *f*, THERMOD température ambiante *f*; ~ **thermostat** *n* CONTROL thermostat d'ambiance *m*, thermostat local *m*, REFRIG thermostat d'ambiance *m*, THERMOD thermostat local *m*

root *n* C&G pied de bord *m*, COMP, DP racine *f*, MECH *welding* talon *m*; ~ **bead** *n* PETR passe de fond *f*; ~ **file system** *n* PROD ENG système de fichiers de base *m*; ~ **mean square deviation** *n* ELEC écart moyen quadratique *m*; ~ **mean square** *n* (*RMS*) CONST valeur quadratique moyenne *f*, ELECTRON valeur efficace *f*, ELECTRON, MATH valeur quadratique moyenne *f*, OPT, PHYS, RECORDING, TELECOM valeur efficace *f*, TELECOM valeur quadratique moyenne *f*; ~ **mean square water level** *n* FUELLESS hauteur d'eau moyenne quadratique *f*; ~ **pass** *n* MECH *welding*, PETR passe de fond *f*; ~ **of weld** *n* CONST racine de la soudure *f*; ~ **zone** *n* GEOL zone d'enracinement *f*

ROP *abbr* (*rate of penetration*) PETR TECH taux de pénétration *m*

rope *n* MECH câble *m*, NAUT corde *f*, câble *m*, *for rigging* cordage *m*, PAPER TECH cordage *m*, câble *m*, SAFETY, TEXTILES cordage *m*; ~ **carrier** *n* PAPER TECH câble d'embarquement *m*; ~ **dyeing** *n* COLOURS teinture en boyau *f*; ~ **hauling** *n* COAL TECH extraction par câble *f*; ~ **marking** *n* TEXTILES casse de teinture *f*; ~ **skimmer** *n* MAR POLL récupérateur à corde flottante *m*, écrémeur à corde flottante *m*; ~ **yarn** *n* TEXTILES fil de caret *m*

ropeless: ~ **hoisting apparatus** *n* MINING appareil d'extraction sans câble *m*

rope-type: ~ **sling** *n* SAFETY élingue *f*, élingue du type câble *f*, élingue du type câble métallique *f*

ropiness *n* FOOD TECH *baking and food processing* caractère visqueux *m*, viscosité *f*

ro-ro *n* *(roll-on/roll-off)* TRANSP roulier *m*; ~ **depot** *n* TRANSP installation de manutention horizontale *f*; ~ **system** *n* TRANSP manutention horizontale *f*

ROS *abbr (residual oil saturation)* PETR saturation en huile résiduelle *f*

rose *n* ELEC ENG rosace *f*, WATER SUPP aspirant *m*, crépine *f*, crépine d'aspiration *f*, grenouillère *f*, lanterne *f*, reniflard *m*, écumoire *f*; ~ **burner** *n* CONST *gas* brûleur à couronne *m*

ROSE *abbr (remote operation service element)* TELECOM élément de service d'opération distante *m*

rosette *n* C&G rosace *f*, PRINT tracé généré par des points correctement imprimés *m*

rosin *n* P&R *raw material* colophane *f*

rostrum: ~ **camera** *n* CINEMAT caméra banc titre *f*, caméra d'animation *f*; ~ **camera operator** *n* CINEMAT opérateur banc-titre *m*

rot[1] *n* NAUT *in wood* pourriture *f*

rot[2] *vt* CONST carier, pourrir

rotameter *n* LAB EQUIP *fluid flow rate* débitmètre à flotteur *m*, PAPER TECH rotamètre *m*, PETR TECH débitmètre à flotteur *m*, PHYS rotamètre *m*

rotary *n* (AmE) CONST *(cf roundabout)* carrefour giratoire *m*, rond-point *m*; ~ **air heater** *n* HEATING réchauffeur d'air rotatif *m*; ~ **amplifier** *n* ELEC ENG amplificateur tournant *m*, dynamo amplificatrice *f*, machine tournante amplificatrice *f*; ~ **bit** *n* PETR TECH trépan pour forage rotary *m*; ~ **brush** *n* PAPER TECH brosse rotative *f*; ~ **capacitor** *n* ELEC condensateur rotatif *m*; ~ **compressor** *n* REFRIG compresseur rotatif *m*; ~ **continuous-core drill** *n* MINING sondeuse rotative à carottage continu *f*; ~ **converter** *n* ELEC commutatrice *f*, convertisseur rotatif *m*, ELEC ENG commutatrice *f*, convertisseur rotatif à induit unique *m*; ~ **crane** *n* CONST grue pivotante *f*, grue tournante *f*; ~ **current** *n* OCEANOG courant giratoire *m*; ~ **current armature** *n* ELEC *generator, motor* induit à courant triphasé *m*; ~ **cutter** *n* PRINT coupeuse rotative *f*; ~ **cutting tool** *n* MECH ENG outil tournant *m*; ~ **discharge** *n* ELEC *spark* éclateur rotatif *m*; ~ **disc valve** *n* (BrE) VEHICLES *two-stroke engine* distributeur rotatif *m*, tiroir rotatif *m*; ~ **disk valve** *n* (AmE) *see rotary disc valve*; ~ **dividing table** *n* MECH ENG plateau diviseur rotatif *m*; ~ **drill** *n* CONST *rock drill* perforatrice rotative *f*; ~ **drilling** *n* COAL TECH forage rotary *m*, MINING forage par rodage *m*, sondage par rodage *m*, PETR, PETR TECH forage rotary *m*; ~ **drum feeder** *n* MECH ENG distributeur à tambour cylindrique *m*; ~ **dryer** *n* PROD ENG séchoir rotatif *m*; ~ **engine** *n* AUTO moteur rotatif *m*, VEHICLES *Wankel engine* moteur à pistons rotatifs *m*; ~ **evaporator** *n* LAB EQUIP *glassware* évaporateur rotatif *m*; ~ **exchange** *n* TELECOM central à sélecteurs rotatifs *m*; ~ **feeder** *n* MECH ENG distributeur rotatif *m*;

~ **feeder and collecting table** *n* PACKAGING alimentateur rotatif et table de collection *m*; ~ **field** *n* ELEC ENG champ tournant *m*; ~ **field converter** *n* ELEC convertisseur à champ magnétique rotatif *m*; ~ **filling** *n* PACKAGING remplissage rotatif *m*; ~ **filter** *n* COAL TECH, WATER SUPP filtre rotatif *m*, filtre à tambour *m*; ~ **frequency converter** *n* ELEC convertisseur de fréquence rotatif *m*; ~ **furnace** *n* PROD ENG four rotatif *m*, four rotatoire *m*, four tournant *m*; ~ **grate** *n* PROD ENG grille rotative *f*; ~ **heading machine** *n* COAL TECH coupeuse rotative *f*; ~ **hearth kiln** *n* HEATING four annulaire à sole tournante *m*; ~ **hose** *n* PETR TECH flexible de rotary *m*; ~ **joint** *n* ELEC ENG joint tournant *m*; ~ **kiln** *n* C&G four circulaire *m*, COAL TECH, HEATING four rotatif *m*; ~ **kiln for cement manufacture** *n* HEATING four rotatif à ciment *m*; ~ **knob** *n* ELEC ENG bouton rotatif *m*; ~ **light switch** *n* CONTROL interrupteur à garrot *m*; ~ **magazine** *n* PHOTO *of slide projector* carrousel *m*; ~ **molding of fiber and rollercoat varnishing** *n* (AmE), ~ **moulding of fibre and rollercoat varnishing** *n* (BrE) PACKAGING moulage et revêtement rotatifs de fibre avec du vernis *m*; ~ **movement** *n* CINEMAT mouvement rotatif *m*; ~ **orbital sander** *n* MECH ENG *tool* ponceuse orbitale rotative *f*; ~ **percussive masonry drill** *n* MECH ENG foret pour bâtiment à rotation et percussion *m*; ~ **piston engine** *n* AUTO moteur rotatif *m*, TRANSP moteur à pistons rotatifs *m*; ~ **piston meter** *n* GAS TECH compteur à piston rotatif *m*; ~ **pneumatic engine** *n* MECH ENG machine rotative pneumatique *f*; ~ **potentiometer** *n* ELEC, ELEC ENG potentiomètre rotatif *m*; ~ **printer** *n* PRINT conducteur *m*; ~ **printing** *n* PRINT impression sur rotative *f*; ~ **printing machine** *n* PRINT presse rotative *f*; ~ **printing press** *n* PACKAGING machine à imprimer à rouleaux *f*, PRINT presse à imprimer rotative *f*; ~ **pump** *n* PHYS, WATER SUPP pompe rotative *f*; ~ **screen** *n* CONST tamis rotatif *m*, trommel *m*, PROD ENG crible rotatif *m*; ~ **screen printing** *n* PRINT impression sérigraphique sur rotative *f*; ~ **screw compressor** *n* PROD ENG compresseur rotatif à vis *m*; ~ **shaft lip-type seal** *n* MECH ENG bague d'étanchéité à lèvres *f*; ~ **shaft seal** *n* MECH ENG joint d'étanchéité pour arbres tournants *m*; ~ **shear blade** *n* MECH ENG lame à cisailles à rouleaux *f*; ~ **single shaft stationary compressor** *n* MECH ENG compresseur rotatif stationnaire à un arbre *m*; ~ **switch** *n* CINEMAT sélecteur rotatif *m*, CONTROL bouton commutateur tournant *m*, commutateur rotatif *m*, interrupteur rotatif *m*, ELEC, ELEC ENG commutateur rotatif *m*, interrupteur rotatif *m*; ~ **system** *n* TELECOM rotary *m*, système rotatif *m*, système rotatif à commande indirecte *m*; ~ **table** *n* MECH ENG plateau tournant porte-pièces *m*, METR *indexing, measuring and setting* platine rotative *f*, PETR, PETR TECH table de rotation *f*; ~ **table sandblast machine** *n* PROD ENG *founding* machine à dessabler à table rotative *f*; ~ **tidal current** *n* OCEANOG courant giratoire *m*; ~ **transformer** *n* ELEC ENG transformateur rotatif *m*; ~ **unit** *n* PRINT joint rotatif *m*; ~ **valve** *n* FUELLESS vanne rotative *f*, HYDR EQUIP distributeur à boisseau *m*; ~ **vane feeder** *n* MECH ENG *handling equipment* écluse rotative *f*; ~ **video head** *n* TV tête vidéo rotative *f*; ~ **wafer switch** *n* ELEC ENG commutateur rotatif à plots *m*; ~ **wall crane** *n* CONST grue pivotante murale *f*; ~ **washer** *n* PROD ENG laveur rotatif *m*; ~ **washing machine** *n* PROD ENG laveur rotatif *m*; ~ **wing aircraft** *n* AERONAUT, TRANSP aéronef à voilure tournante *m*; ~ **wire brush** *n* PAPER TECH brosse d'acier rotative *f*

rotatable: **~ antenna** *n* TELECOM antenne orientable *f*; **~ arm** *n* MAR POLL bras rotatif *m*; **~ nozzle** *n* SPACE *spacecraft* tuyère orientable *f*; **~ water-jet** *n* TRANSP propulseur à jet d'eau rotatif *m*

rotate *vt* COMP, DP faire pivoter, pivoter

rotating: **~ annulus** *n* FLUID PHYS anneau tournant *m*; **~ annulus convection** *n* FLUID PHYS convection dans un anneau tournant *f*; **~ anode tube** *n* CONST tube à anode tournante *m*; **~ armature** *n* ELEC *generator, motor* induit rotatif *m*; **~ beacon** *n* AERONAUT phare rotatif *m*; **~ bending test** *n* METALL essai de flexion rotative *m*; **~ bowl** *n* C&G cuvette tournante *f*; **~ Couette flow** *n* FLUID PHYS écoulement tournant de Couette *m*; **~ crystal method** *n* RAD PHYS méthode du cristal rotatif *f*; **~ drum** *n* GEOPHYS cylindre enregistreur *m*; **~ drum streak camera** *n* CINEMAT caméra à fente à tambour tournant *f*; **~ electrical machine** *n* ELEC ENG machine électrique tournante *f*; **~ field** *n* ELEC *electromagnetism*, TELECOM champ tournant *m*; **~ field instrument** *n* INSTRUMENT instrument à champ magnétique rotatif *m*; **~ fluids** *n pl* FLUID PHYS fluides tournants *m pl*; **~ machine** *n* C&G machine carrousel *f*; **~ mirror** *n* INSTRUMENT, PHYS miroir tournant *m*; **~ mirror streak camera** *n* CINEMAT caméra à fente et miroir tournant *f*; **~ parts** *n pl* MECH ENG *components* éléments tournants *m pl*; **~ piston engine** *n* TRANSP moteur rotatif *m*; **~ prism** *n* OPT prisme tournant *m*; **~ shower** *n* PAPER TECH rinceur rotatif *m*; **~ shutter** *n* CINEMAT obturateur rotatif *m*, obturateur à secteurs *m*; **~ speed** *n* FUELLESS, PETR TECH vitesse de rotation *f*; **~ sprayer** *n* WATER SUPP *sewage* arroseur rotatif *m*; **~ wing aircraft** *n* TRANSP aéronef à voilure tournante *m*

rotation *n* CHEM *optical*, COMP, DP, GEOM, PHYS, SPACE rotation *f*; **~ axis** *n* CRYSTALL axe de rotation *m*; **~ of coordinate axes** *n* GEOM rotation des axes de coordonnées *f*; **~ curve** *n* ASTRON *of galaxy* courbe de rotation *f*; **~ firing** *n* MINING tir à départs successifs *m*; **~ photography** *n* CRYSTALL photographie de cristal tournant *f*; **~ position sensing** *n* COMP, DP détection de position angulaire *f*; **~ spectrum** *n* RAD PHYS spectre de rotation *m*; **~ speed** *n* AERONAUT vitesse de cabrage *f*, vitesse de rotation *f*, FUELLESS, MECH ENG, PETR TECH vitesse de rotation *f*

rotational[1] *adj* GEOM rotatif, rotatoire

rotational:[2] **~ compass** *n* MECH ENG compas à pompe *m*, compas-balustre à pompe *m*; **~ delay** *n* COMP, DP délai d'attente *m*, OPT délai rotationnel *m*; **~ elasticity** *n* MECH ENG élasticité de torsion *f*; **~ energy** *n* PROD ENG énergie rotative *f*; **~ inertia** *n* MECH ENG moment d'inertie *m*; **~ mold** *n* (AmE), **~ mould** *n* (BrE) MECH ENG moule pour moulage rotatif *m*; **~ quantum number** *n* PHYS nombre quantique rotatoire *m*; **~ spectrum** *n* PHYS spectre de rotation *m*; **~ speed** *n* FUELLESS vitesse de rotation *f*; **~ symmetry** *n* GEOM symétrie rotatoire *f*; **~ wave** *n* ACOUSTICS onde tourbillonnaire *f*

rotative: **~ seal** *n* REFRIG garniture rotative *f*

rotatory: **~ power** *n* PHYS pouvoir rotatoire *m*

rotenone *n* CHEM roténone *f*

rothoffite *n* MINERAL rothoffite *f*

rotogravure: **~ printing** *n* P&R héliogravure *f*

rotor *n* AERONAUT *helicopter*, AUTO, COAL TECH, ELEC *generator*, ELEC ENG, PHYS, TRANSP, VEHICLES *ignition, generator* rotor *m*; **~ aircraft** *n* TRANSP giravion *m*; **~ arm** *n* AUTO rotor de distribution *m*, VEHICLES *ignition* doigt d'allumeur *m*, doigt de distributeur *m*; **~ blade** *n*

AERONAUT *helicopter* pale de rotor *f*; **~ diameter** *n* FUELLESS diamètre de rotor *m*; **~ disc** *n* (BrE) AERONAUT disque rotor *m*; **~ disk** *n* (AmE) *see rotor disc*; **~ efficiency** *n* AERONAUT *helicopter* rendement du rotor *m*; **~ field** *n* ELEC *generator* champ d'induit *m*; **~ head** *n* AERONAUT *helicopter* tête de rotor *f*; **~ hub** *n* AERONAUT *helicopter* moyeu de rotor *m*; **~ inflow** *n* AERONAUT *helicopter* flux à travers un rotor *m*; **~ lamination** *n* ELEC ENG tôle du rotor *f*; **~ mast** *n* AERONAUT *helicopter* mât rotor *m*; **~ overspeed** *n* AERONAUT *helicopter* emballement du rotor *m*; **~ plate** *n* ELEC ENG lame de rotor *f*, lame mobile *f*, TRANSP plaque d'induit *f*; **~ radius** *n* AERONAUT *helicopter* rayon du rotor *m*; **~ shaft** *n* ELEC *generator* arbre d'induit *m*; **~ speed** *n* AERONAUT *helicopter* régime rotor *m*; **~ starter** *n* ELEC démarreur de rotor *m*, démarreur rotorique *m*; **~ stream** *n* AERONAUT *helicopter* souffle du rotor *m*; **~ thrust** *n* AERONAUT *helicopter* poussée du rotor *f*; **~ tip velocity** *n* AERONAUT *helicopter* vitesse circonférentielle du rotor *f*; **~ torque** *n* AERONAUT *helicopter* couple rotor *m*; **~ weight** *n* FUELLESS poids du rotor *m*; **~ winding** *n* ELEC ENG bobinage du rotor *m*, bobinage rotorique *m*, enroulement rotorique *m*

rotoscope *vt* CINEMAT projection image par image d'un décor réel *f*

rot-proof *adj* PAPER TECH imputrescible

rotting *n* C&G gravure profonde *f*, CONST *of timber* carie *f*, pourriture *f*, PAPER TECH pourrissage des fibres *m*

rouge *n* C&G potée *f*, PROD ENG rouge d'Angleterre *m*, rouge à polir *m*

rough[1] *adj* PAPER TECH rugueux, PROP MAT rude, *to touch* rude; **~ forged** *adj* PROD ENG brut de forge; **~ rolled** *adj* PROD ENG brut de laminage; **~ stamped** *adj* PROD ENG brut d'estampage

rough:[2] **~ anode** *n* ELEC ENG anode rugueuse *f*; **~ capacity load table** *n* PROD ENG tableau de répartition brute des ressources *m*; **~ coal** *n* COAL TECH charbon tout-venant *m*; **~ cut** *n* CINEMAT premier montage *m*, MECH ENG *files* taille grosse *f*, taille rude *f*; **~ cutting** *n* C&G ébauchage *m*; **~ dressing** *n* CONST *of building stone* taille brute *f*; **~ edge** *n* C&G bord brut de coupe *m*; **~ file** *n* MECH ENG lime bâtarde *f*, lime grosse *f*; **~ grinding** *n* C&G dégrossissage *m*; **~ grinding-wheel** *n* MECH ENG meule à dégrossir *f*; **~ landing** *n* AERONAUT atterrissage brutal *m*, atterrissage dur *m*; **~ mix** *n* RECORDING mise à plat *f*; **~ pea coal** *n* COAL TECH menu brut *m*; **~ road** *n* CONST chemin anfractueux *m*, chemin rude *m*, route rugueuse *f*; **~ rolled glazing** *n* C&G glaçure brute *f*; **~ sea** *n* NAUT mer agitée *f*, mer creuse *f*, mer grosse *f*; **~ surface** *n* MECH ENG, SPRINGS surface rugueuse *f*; **~ vacuum** *n* PHYS vide grossier *m*, vide peu poussé *m*, vide primaire *m*; **~ weather** *n* NAUT temps rude *m*; **~ wood** *n* CONST bois raboteux *m*

rough[3] *vt* COAL TECH dégrossir; **~ down** *vt* CONST *timber* dégrossir, ébaucher

roughcast *n* CONST *plastering* crépi *m*, enduit fouetté *m*, revêtement de cailloutage *m*; **~ gears** *n pl* PROD ENG engrenages bruts de fonte *m pl*; **~ glass** *n* C&G verre brut coulé *m*; **~ plate** *n* C&G glace brute coulée *f*

roughcasting *n* CONST ébauche coulée *f*, PROD ENG pièce brute de fonderie *f*

rough-cut: **~ capacity planning** *n* PROD ENG calcul des charges globales *m*; **~ planning** *n* PROD ENG planification globale *f*

roughed: **~ forging** *n* PROD ENG pièce de forge dégrossie *f*

rougher *n* COAL TECH ébaucheuse *f*

rough-grained *adj* CONST à grain gros, à grain grossier, à gros grain

rough-hewn[1] *adj* CONST dégrossi, ébauché

rough-hewn[2] *adv* CONST grossier

roughing *n* COAL TECH dégrossissage *m*, PROD ENG dégrossissage *m*, dégrossissement *m*, ébauchage *m*; ~ **pass** *n* PROD ENG cannelure ébaucheuse *f*, passe de dégrossissage *f*; ~ **roll** *n* PROD ENG cylindre de dégrossissement *m*, cylindre dégrossisseur *m*, cylindre ébaucheur *m*, dégrossisseur *m*, ébaucheur *m*; ~ **rolls** *n pl* PROD ENG laminoir ébaucheur *m*, train ébaucheur *m*, équipage dégrossisseur *m*; ~ **slot mill** *n* MECH ENG milling cutter fraise à dégrossir les rainures *f*; ~ **tank** *n* WATER SUPP dégrossisseur *m*; ~ **tool** *n* MECH ENG *lathe* outil à charioter *m*, outil à dégrossir *m*; ~ **wheel** *n* INSTRUMENT *for preliminary surfacing* meule de dégrossissage *f*, PROD ENG meule à dégrossir *f*

roughing-down *n* PROD ENG *work* dégrossissage *m*, dégrossissement *m*, ébauchage *m*; ~ **roll** *n* PROD ENG cylindre de dégrossissement *m*, cylindre dégrossisseur *m*, cylindre ébaucheur *m*, dégrossisseur *m*, ébaucheur *m*

rough-machined *adj* MECH ébauché

roughness *n* MECH, PAPER TECH rugosité *f*, PROP MAT anfractuosités *f pl*; ~ **profile** *n* MECH ENG profil de rugosité *m*

roulette *n* MATH roulette *f*

round[1] *n* CONST *of ladder* barreau *m*, échelon *m*, MILIT salve *f*, *when firing gun* coup *m*, MINING volée *f*, NAUT *of beam* bouge *f*; ~ **of ammunition** *n* MILIT coup complet *m*; ~ **arch** *n* CONST *curve described* arc plein cintre *m*, arc romain *m*, *for bridge* arche plein cintre *f*, *structure itself* voûte de plein cintre *f*, voûte en plein cintre *f*; ~ **bar** *n* PROP MAT barre ronde *f*; ~ **bar spring** *n* SPRINGS ressort à barre *m*; ~ **cell** *n* PRINT alvéole ronde *f*; ~ **distance piece** *n* MECH ENG rondelle de compensation *f*; ~ **edge corner smoother** *n* PROD ENG *moulder's tool* lissoir équerre à congé *m*; ~ **ended pouch** *n* PACKAGING *for vacuum packing* sachet à extrémités arrondies *m*; ~ **file** *n* MECH ENG lime ronde *f*; ~ **hole perforating** *n* PRINT perforation à trous ronds *f*; ~ **nut** *n* MECH ENG écrou cylindrique *m*; ~ **pinch plate** *n* PROD ENG plaque porte-poinçon ronde *f*; ~ **punch with conical head** *n* MECH ENG poinçon cylindrique à tête conique *m*; ~ **section coil spring** *n* MECH ENG *die set* ressort hélicoïdal à fil rond *m*; ~ **tone** *n* RECORDING son plein *m*; ~ **trip** *n* PETR aller-retour *m*, PETR TECH aller-retour *m*, manœuvre *f*, SPACE *spacecraft* voyage aller-retour *m*; ~ **turn and two half hitches** *n* NAUT *knot* tour mort et deux demi-clefs *m*

round[2] *vt* COMP, DP arrondir, NAUT *cape* arrondir, doubler, PROD ENG arrondir, *to make cylindrical* cylindrer; ~ **down** *vt* COMP, DP, MATH, PROD ENG arrondir par défaut; ~ **off** *vt* COMP arrondir, DP arrondir au plus près; ~ **up** *vt* COMP, DP arrondir par excès, MATH arrondir au chifre supérieur, PROD ENG arrondir au chiffre supérieur

roundabout *n* (BrE) (*cf traffic circle, rotary*) CONST carrefour giratoire *m*, rond-point *m*

round-bottomed: ~ **flask** *n* LAB EQUIP *glassware* vase à fond rond *m*

rounded: ~ **approach orifice** *n* HYDR EQUIP orifice évasé *m*; ~ **back** *n* PRINT dos arrondi *m*; ~ **edge** *n* C&G joint quart-de-rond *m*

round-edge: ~ **file** *n* MECH ENG lime à bords arrondis *f*,

lime à champs ronds *f*; ~ **milling cutter** *n* MECH ENG fraise à champ rond *f*

round-faced: ~ **pulley** *n* MECH ENG poulie bombée *f*, poulie en dos d'âne *f*

round-head: ~ **bolt** *n* MECH ENG boulon à tête hémisphérique *m*, boulon à tête ronde *m*

round-headed: ~ **bolt** *n* MECH ENG boulon à tête hémisphérique *m*, boulon à tête ronde *m*; ~ **screw** *n* MECH ENG vis à tête ronde *f*

roundhouse *n* RAIL *vehicles* remise à locomotives *f*

rounding *n* COMP, DP arrondi *m*, MATH *numbers* arrondissage *m*, PRINT arrondissure *f*; ~ **code** *n* PROD ENG code arrondi *m*; ~ **error** *n* COMP, DP erreur d'arrondi *f*, MATH erreur d'approximation *f*; ~ **machine** *n* PROD ENG tour pour bâtons ronds *m*; ~ **pulley** *n* MECH ENG poulie bombée *f*; ~ **of rim** *n* C&G arrondissage *m*; ~ **wooden rollers** *n pl* PROD ENG *lathe* cylindrage des rouleaux en bois *m*

roundness *n* GEOL degré d'arrondi *m*, degré d'émoussage *m*

roundness-measuring: ~ **instrument** *n* METR instrument de mesure de la rondeur *m*

round-nose: ~ **pliers** *n pl* MECH ENG pince ronde *f*, pinces à becs ronds *f pl*; ~ **tool** *n* MECH ENG *lathe* grain d'orge *m*, outil à grain-d'orge *m*

round-nosed: ~ **chisel** *n* MECH ENG *engineer's* burin grain-d'orge *m*, dégorgeoir *m*, gouge pleine *f*, grain d'orge *m*; ~ **cold chisel** *n* MECH ENG *engineer's* burin grain-d'orge *m*, dégorgeoir *m*, gouge pleine *f*, grain d'orge *m*

roustabout *n* PETR TECH contremaître de production *m*

route *n* AERONAUT itinéraire *m*, parcours *m*, route *f*, COMP acheminement *m*, itinéraire *m*, route *f*, DP acheminement *m*, route *f*, NAUT itinéraire *m*, route *f*, RAIL itinéraire *m*, *of railway line* tracé *m*, TELECOM faisceau de circuits *m*, voie d'acheminement *f*, TRANSP itinéraire *m*, route *f*; ~ **description** *n* AERONAUT *air traffic* description de route *f*; ~ **familiarization flight** *n* AERONAUT vol de reconnaissance de route *m*; ~ **guidance by radio** *n* TRANSP radioguidage routier *m*; ~ **licence** *n* (BrE) AERONAUT autorisation d'exploitation de route *f*; ~ **licencing** *n* (BrE) AERONAUT autorisation d'exploitation de route *f*; ~ **license** *n* (AmE) *see route licence*; ~ **licensing** *n* (AmE) *see route licencing*; ~ **locking** *n* RAIL enclenchement de transit *m*; ~ **sheet** *n* PROD ENG fiche d'opérations *f*, gamme de fabrication *f*, gamme opératoire *f*

router *n* COMP, DP routeur *m*, MECH ENG *of centre bit* couteau *m*

routine *n* COMP sous-programme *m*; ~ **analysis** *n* QUALITY *of quantitative data* analyse de routine *f*; ~ **inspection** *n* AERONAUT vérification périodique *f*, vérification systématique *f*

routing *n* COMP, DP acheminement *m*, routage *m*, PROD ENG gamme de fabrication *f*, gamme opératoire *f*, TELECOM routage *m*, *traffic* acheminement *m*; ~ **address** *n* TELECOM adresse d'acheminement *f*; ~ **block** *n* PRINT pavé de distribution *m*; ~ **chart** *n* NAUT *navigation* carte routière *f*; ~ **code for part-load traffic** *n* RAIL *vehicles* indice de wagonnage *m*; ~ **control** *n* TELECOM contrôle de routage *m*; ~ **indicator** *n* COMP, DP indicateur de routage *m*; ~ **information** *n* COMP, DP information d'acheminement *f*; ~ **list** *n* PROD ENG *operations* liste de phases opératoires *f*; ~ **machine** *n* MECH ENG machine à défoncer *f*; ~ **system** *n* NAUT système d'organisation du trafic *m*

rove *n* TEXTILES mèche *f*

rover *n* SPACE *spacecraft* astromobile *m*

roving *n* C&G stratifil de verre textile *m*, P&R *glass fibre* stratifil *m*, TEXTILES mèche de banc à broches *f*; ~ **dyeing** *n* TEXTILES teinture sur mèche de banc *f*; ~ **frame** *n* TEXTILES banc à broches *m*; ~ **mike** *n* RECORDING microphone baladeur *m*; ~ **winder** *n* C&G bobinoir roving *m*

row[1] *n* COMP, DP ligne *f*, rang *m*, rangée *f*; ~ **of piles** *n* COAL TECH palée *f*, rangée de pieux *f*; ~ **pitch** *n* COMP espacement des caractères *m*, pas d'écriture *m*, pas longitudinal *m*, DP espacement des caractères *m*, pas longitudinal *m*

row[2] *vi* NAUT ramer

Rowland: ~ **circle** *n* PHYS cercle de Rowland *m*; ~ **experiment** *n* PHYS expérience de Rowland *f*; ~ **mounting** *n* PHYS montage de Rowland *m*

rowlock *n* NAUT *boat fitting* dame de nage *f*

royalty *n* PATENTS, PETR TECH redevance *f*

RP *abbr (regional processor)* TELECOM processeur régional *m*

RR: ~ **Lyrae stars** *n pl* ASTRON étoiles RR Lyrae *f pl*

R-S: ~ **coupling** *n* PHYS couplage R-S *m*, couplage Russell-Saunders *m*

RS[1] *abbr* COMP, DP *(record separator)* séparateur d'articles *m*, séparateur d'enregistrements *m*, TELECOM *(regenerator section)* section de régénération *f*

RS:[2] ~ **flip-flop** *n (reset-set flip-flop)* ELEC bascule RS *f*

RST[1] *abbr (regenerator section termination)* TELECOM terminaison de section de régénération *f*

RST:[2] ~ **flip-flop** *n (reset-set-toggle flip-flop)* ELEC bascule RST *f*

R-star *n* ASTRON étoile R *f*

RSU *abbr (remote switching unit)* TELECOM centre satellite *m*

RT *abbr (radar tracking)* TRANSP localisation par radar *f*

RTC *abbr (road tank car)* TRANSP camion citerne *m*

RTD: ~ **input terminal** *n* PROD ENG borne d'entrée PTC *f*; ~ **output terminal** *n* PROD ENG borne de sortie PTC *f*

RTG[1] *abbr (regenerator timing generator)* TELECOM générateur de rythme de régénérateur *m*

RTG:[2] ~ **train** *n (gas turbine train)* TRANSP rame à turbine à gaz *f*

RTM *abbr (reference test method)* OPT méthode de mesure de remplacement *f*, TELECOM méthode de mesure de référence *f*

RTOL: ~ **aircraft** *n (reduced takeoff and landing aircraft)* AERONAUT ADAR *(avion à décollage et atterrissage réduits)*

RTS *abbr* RAIL *(rapid transit system)* système de transport rapide *m*, TELECOM *(reliable transfer server)* serveur de transfert fiable *m*

Ru *(ruthenium)* CHEM Ru *(ruthénium)*

RU *abbr (remote unit)* TELECOM unité distante *f*

rub[1] *n* (AmE) *(cf scrub mark)* C&G écrasure *f*

rub:[2] ~ **down** *vt* PROD ENG *surface with emery cloth* adoucir; ~ **rust off** *vt* PROD ENG dérouiller

rubber *n* CHEM caoutchouc *m*, gomme *f*, ELEC ENG, P&R, PAPER TECH, PRINT caoutchouc *m*; ~ **belting** *n* MECH ENG courroies de transmission en caoutchouc *f pl*; ~ **blanket** *n* PRINT blanchet de caoutchouc *m*; ~ **boat** *n* NAUT bateau pneumatique *m*; ~ **buffer** *n* MECH ENG *die set* ressort caoutchouc *m*; ~ **bulb** *n* LAB EQUIP *pipette* poire en caoutchouc *f*; ~ **cable** *n* ELEC ENG câble sous caoutchouc *m*; ~ **coating** *n* COATINGS caoutchoutage

m, couverture en caoutchouc *f*, enduit de caoutchouc *m*, gommage *m*, revêtement en caoutchouc *m*;~ **dinghy** *n* MILIT embarcation pneumatique *f*, NAUT canot pneumatique *m*; ~ **engine mounting** *n* AUTO suspension du moteur sur tampons de caoutchouc *f*; ~ **extruder** *n* MECH ENG *machine tool* extrudeuse pour caoutchouc *f*; ~ **hose** *n* P&R tuyau en caoutchouc *m*; ~ **hose for steam** *n* MECH ENG tuyau en caoutchouc pour la vapeur *m*; ~ **insulation** *n* COATINGS isolation au caoutchouc *f*; ~ **latex** *n* P&R latex de caoutchouc *m*; ~ **mark** *n* PAPER TECH marquage à la molette *m*; ~ **mold** *n* (AmE), ~ **mould** *n* (BrE) MECH ENG moule pour caoutchouc *m*; ~ **mounting** *n* VEHICLES *engine* support en caoutchouc *m*; ~ **number** *n* CINEMAT numéro de bord imprimé *m*; ~ **pad** *n* AUTO tampon de caoutchouc *m*; ~ **squeegee** *n* CINEMAT rouleau essoreur en caoutchouc *m*; ~ **stopper** *n* LAB EQUIP bouchon en caoutchouc *m*; ~ **suction hose** *n* WATER SUPP tuyau d'aspiration en caoutchouc *m*; ~ **tip** *n* PHOTO *of tripod* embout en caoutchouc *m*; ~ **tired roller** *n* (AmE) *see rubber tyred roller*; ~ **tubing** *n* LAB EQUIP tuyau en caoutchouc *m*; ~ **tyred roller** *n* (BrE) CONST compacteur à pneus *m*; ~ **varnish** *n* COATINGS gomme laque *f*; ~ **weather seal** *n* VEHICLES *body* bourrelet en caoutchouc *m*, joint d'étanchéité en caoutchouc *m*

rubber-coated *adj* COATINGS caoutchouté, gommé

rubber-covered *adj* COATINGS caoutchouté, gommé

rubber-insulated[1] *adj* COATINGS isolé au caoutchouc

rubber-insulated:[2] ~ **cable** *n* ELEC ENG câble sous caoutchouc *m*

rubberize *vt* COATINGS caoutchouter

rubberized[1] *adj* ELEC *insulation*, P&R caoutchouté

rubberized:[2] ~ **cloth** *n* COATINGS toile caoutchoutée *f*, toile frictionnée *f*

rubber-lined *adj* COATINGS garni de caoutchouc

rubbery *adj* CHEM élastique

rubbing: ~ **off rust** *n* PROD ENG dérouillement *m*; ~ **strake** *n* NAUT bourrelet de défense *m*, liston *m*; ~ **surface** *n* PROD ENG surface de frottement *f*, surface frottante *f*

rubbish *n (cf garbage)* PACKAGING détritus *m*, PROD ENG déchets *m pl*, détritus *m*, rebuts *m pl*, RECYCLING déchets *m pl*, détritus *m*; ~ **chute** *n* (BrE) *(cf garbage chute)* RECYCLING vide-ordures *m*

rubble *n* CONST *for building* blocage *m*, blocaille *f*, détritus *m*, moellon *m*, GEOL, PETR éboulis *m*; ~ **masonry** *n* CONST maçonnerie en moellons *f*; ~ **stone** *n* CONST *for building* blocage *m*, blocaille *f*, moellon *m*

rubbly *adj* CONST blocageux, blocailleux

rubellite *n* MINERAL rubellite *f*

ruberythric *adj* CHEM rubérythrique

rubicelle *n* MINERAL rubicelle *f*

rubidium *n (Rb)* CHEM rubidium *m (Rb)*

rubijervine *n* CHEM rubijervine *f*

rubin *n* CHEM fuchsine *f*, rubine *f*

rub-up *n* P&R *paint colour defect* gommage *m*

ruby *n* CONST, GEOL, MINERAL rubis *m*; ~ **crystal laser** *n* ELECTRON, RAD PHYS laser à cristal de rubis *m*

rudaceous: ~ **rocks** *n pl* GEOL rudites *f pl*

rudder *n* AERONAUT gouverne de direction *f*, NAUT *boat building* gouvernail *m*, PHYS gouvernail de direction *m*, gouverne de direction *f*; ~ **angle indicator** *n* NAUT indicateur d'angle de barre *m*; ~ **bar** *n* AERONAUT palonnier *m*; ~ **blade** *n* NAUT *shipbuilding* safran *m*, safran de gouvernail *m*; ~ **brace** *n* NAUT ferrure de gouvernail *f*; ~ **cable** *n* NAUT *boat building* drosse *f*; ~ **control** *n* AERONAUT commande de direction *f*; ~ **pedal**

n AERONAUT palonnier *m*; ~ **port** *n* NAUT *on ship* trou de jaumière *m*; ~ **post** *n* AERONAUT longeron de gouverne de direction *m*, NAUT étambot *m*; ~ **power unit** *n* AERONAUT servocommande direction *f*; ~ **quadrant** *n* NAUT secteur du gouvernail *m*; ~ **stock** *n* NAUT mèche de gouvernail *f*; ~ **travel** *n* AERONAUT course de gouverne de direction *f*, débattement de gouverne de direction *m*; ~ **trim** *n* AERONAUT compensateur de direction *m*, compensation de direction *f*; ~ **trim light** *n* AERONAUT voyant zéro direction *m*; ~ **trunk** *n* NAUT *shipbuilding* jaumière *f*

rudites *n pl* GEOL rudites *f pl*
ruffle *n* TEXTILES collier de frein *m*
rugosity *n* PETR rugosité *f*
rule[1] *n* COMP, DP, MECH ENG *instrument*, PATENTS règle *f*, PRINT filet *m*; ~ **base** *n* COMP, DP base de règles *f*
rule[2] *vt* PRINT régler
ruler *n* CONST, GEOM *measuring* règle *f*
rules: ~ of the air *n pl* AERONAUT règles de l'air *f pl*
ruling *n* MECH ENG réglage *m*
rumble *n* (BrE) ACOUSTICS, AUTO *car* ronronnement *m*; ~ **filter** *n* RECORDING filtre de roulement *m*; ~ **level** *n* RECORDING niveau de ronronnement *m*; ~ **seat** *n* (AmE) *(cf rumble)* AUTO *car* ronronnement *m*
rumbler *n* PROD ENG *founding* tambour dessableur *m*, tonneau dessableur *m*, tonneau à dessabler *m*
rumblings *n pl* MINING *subterranean* grondements *m pl*
rumple *vt* PAPER TECH froisser
rumpling *n* PAPER TECH froissement *m*
run[1] *n* COMP, DP exécution *f*, passage de programme *m*, HYDROL *streamlet* ruisselet *m*, MECH ENG marche *f*, MINING *of lode* cours *m*, direction *f*, OCEANOG coulée-arrière *f*, PROD ENG *of blast furnace* campagne *f*, roulement *m*; ~ **bearing** *n* AUTO bielle coulée *f*; ~ **current limit** *n* PROD ENG courant limite de fonctionnement *m*; ~ **of ground** *n* MINING coulée de terres *f*, éboulement de terrain *m*; ~ **indicator** *n* PROD ENG voyant marche *m*; ~ **mode** *n* PROD ENG mode d'exécution *m*; ~ **number** *n* TEXTILES numéro de code *m*; ~ **out leader** *n* CINEMAT amorce de fin de bobine *f*; ~ **out signal** *n* CINEMAT signal de fin de bobine *m*; ~ **of sluices** *n* WATER SUPP cours des sluices *m*
run[2] *vt* CINEMAT *camera, projector* faire marcher, CONST flotter, *moulding, bead on joint* pousser, ELEC *solder* couler, MECH ENG actionner, faire fonctionner, faire travailler, *engine* faire travailler, PROD ENG couler, jeter; ~ **alongside** *vt* HYDROL longer; ~ **down** *vt* NAUT *ship* aborder; ~ **dry** *vt* WATER SUPP tarir; ~ **in** *vt* VEHICLES *engine* roder; ~ **off** *vt* PROD ENG *metal from furnace* couler; ~ **out of true** *vt* MECH ENG dévier; ~ **through** *vt* HYDROL couler à travers, passer au travers de, traverser
run[3] *vi* CHEM couler, HYDROL *into sea* affluer, couler, déboucher, MECH ENG fonctionner, marcher, rouler, travailler, tourner, MINING *of ground* couler, NAUT *of ship* courir, faire route, filer, PROD ENG couler; ~ **aground** *vi* NAUT *of ship* échouer; ~ **ashore** *vi* NAUT *of ship* atterrir; ~ **away** *vi* RAIL *vehicles* partir à la dérive; ~ **before the wind** *vi* NAUT *of ship* courir vent arrière; ~ **down** *vi* HYDROL *water* ruisseler; ~ **a drill by compressed air** *vi* MECH ENG actionner une perforatrice par air comprimé; ~ **dry** *vi* HYDROL s'assécher, tarir; ~ **hot** *vi* MECH ENG chauffer; ~ **light** *vi* MECH ENG marcher à blanc, marcher à vide; ~ **off** *vi* HYDROL ruisseler, WATER SUPP *water from tank* couler, vider; ~ **on** *vi* PRINT suivre sans alinéa; ~ **on no load** *vi* MECH ENG

marcher à blanc, marcher à vide; ~ **on overload** *vi* MECH ENG marcher en surcharge; ~ **out** *vi* WATER SUPP découler, s'écouler; ~ **out of the vertical** *vi* MECH ENG dévier de la ligne verticale, s'écarter de la verticale; ~ **over** *vi* WATER SUPP déborder, se déborder; ~ **to waste** *vi* HYDROL *water* se perdre; ~ **under load** *vi see run light, run on no load*
runaway[1] *adj* RAIL *vehicles* à la dérive
runaway[2] *adv* RAIL à la dérive
runaway:[3] ~ **car** *n* (AmE) *(cf runaway wagon)* RAIL *vehicles* wagon à la dérive *m*; ~ **speed** *n* FUELLESS *turbines* vitesse d'emballement *f*; ~ **wagon** *n* (BrE) *(cf runaway car)* RAIL *vehicles* wagon à la dérive *m*
rung *n* CONST *of ladder* barreau *m*, *of ladder* échelon *m*, PROD ENG ligne *f*
runnability *n* PRINT *of paper* comportement *m*
runner *n* FUELLESS *turbine* roue à auges *f*, MECH patin *m*, MECH ENG chariot de roulement *m*, chariot roulant *m*, trolley *m*, galet *m*, galet de roulement *m*, roue de translation *f*, poulie fixe *f*, roue intermédiaire *f*, roue parasite *f*, *guide pulley* galet de renvoi *m*, galet guide *m*, poulie-guide *f*, *movable block of tackle* moufle mobile *m*, poulie mobile *f*, *of turbine, centrifugal pump* couronne mobile *f*, roue mobile *f*, NAUT *running rigging* bastague *f*, itague *f*, PROD ENG chenal de coulée *m*, coulée *f*, jet de coulée *m*, trou de coulée *m*, jet *m*, madrier *m*, PROP MAT barre d'alimentation *f*; ~ **back** *n* C&G plateau porte-ferrasse *m*; ~ **bar** *n* C&G barreau de ferrasse *m*; ~ **basin** *n* PROD ENG *founding* bassin de coulée *m*; ~ **blade** *n* FUELLESS *turbines* aube *f*, HYDR EQUIP aube *f*, pale mobile *f*; ~ **cut** *n* C&G ligne de ferrasse *f*; ~ **pin** *n* PROD ENG broche de coulée *f*, coulée *f*, mandrin de coulée *m*; ~ **stick** *n* PROD ENG broche de coulée *f*, coulée *f*, mandrin de coulée *m*; ~ **vane** *n* HYDR EQUIP *of turbine* aube *f*, pale réceptrice *f*
runnerless: ~ mold plate *n* (AmE), ~ **mould plate** *n* (BrE) MECH ENG plaque de moule sans coulée *f*
running[1] *adj* WATER SUPP coulant; ~ **before wind** *adj* NAUT *in bad weather* en fuite; ~ **light** *adj* RAIL *vehicles* haut le pied, hlp
running[2] *n* COMP déroulement *m*, exécution *f*, passage *m*, CONST *line* tracé *m*, DP déroulement *m*, exécution *f*, passage *m*, HYDROL coulant, MECH ENG *of machinery* fonctionnement *m*, marche *f*, roulement *m*, P&R *paint defect* dégorgement *m*, PAPER TECH *of machinery*, TEXTILES *of machinery* fonctionnement *m*, marche *f*; ~ **accidents** *n pl* SAFETY accidents de fonctionnement *m pl*; ~ **block** *n* MECH ENG moufle mobile *m*, poulie mobile *f*; ~ **bridge** *n* CONST pont roulant *m*; ~ **costs** *n pl* TEXTILES coûts d'exploitation *m pl*, frais d'exploitation *m pl*; ~ **down cutter** *n* MECH ENG *hollow milling cutter* fraise creuse *f*; ~ **end** *n* MECH ENG *of tackle* garant *m*; ~ **fit** *n* MECH ENG montage à glissement *m*; ~ **fix** *n* NAUT *navigation* point par relèvements successifs *m*; ~ **foot** *n* METR pied courant *m*, pied linéaire *m*; ~ **gate** *n* PROD ENG *founding* coulée *f*, jet de coulée *m*, trou de coulée *m*; ~ **gear** *n* MECH ENG organes de roulement *m pl*, roulement *m*, NAUT *engine* attelage *m*; ~ **ground** *n* COAL TECH terre mobile *f*; ~ **head** *n* PRINT titre courant *m*; ~ **in** *n* (BrE) *(cf breaking in)* MECH ENG rodage *m*; ~ **jig** *n* COAL TECH cayat *m*; ~ **light** *n* MECH ENG marche à blanc *f*, marche à vide *f*; ~ **molds** *n pl* (AmE), ~ **moulds** *n pl* (BrE) PROD ENG *pouring* coulée des moules *f*, jet des moules *m*; ~ **off over the surface** *n* HYDROL ruissellement *m*; ~ **on no load** *n* MECH ENG marche à blanc *f*, marche à vide *f*; ~ **on wrong line** *n*

RAIL circulation à contre-voie *f*; ~ **out pit** *n* C&G fosse de coulée *f*; ~ **an overload** *n* MECH ENG marche en surcharge *f*; ~ **rail** *n* MECH ENG *for overhead travelling crane* rail de transaction *m*, RAIL rail de roulement *m*; ~ **rigging** *n* NAUT gréement courant *m*, manoeuvres courantes *f pl*; ~ **soil** *n* COAL TECH terre mobile *f*; ~ **speed** *n* RECORDING vitesse de défilement *f*, TRANSP vitesse de marche *f*; ~ **surface** *n* RAIL plan de roulement *m*, *track* table de roulement *f*; ~ **test** *n* MECH ENG essai de fonctionnement *m*; ~ **time** *n* C&G temps de bobinage *m*, CINEMAT durée de projection *f*, TRANSP durée de marche *f*, temps de marche *m*; ~ **title** *n* PRINT titre courant *m*; ~ **torque** *n* PROD ENG couple de service *m*; ~ **trap** *n* CONST *plumbing* siphon horizontal *m*; ~ **under load** *n* MECH ENG marche en charge *f*; ~ **water** *n* HYDROL eau courante *f*, eau vive *f*, WATER SUPP eau courante *f*; ~ **wheel** *n* MECH ENG *for overhead travelling crane* galet de roulement *m*, roue de translation *f*

runoff *n* AERONAUT sortie latérale de piste *f*, CONST, FUELLESS ruissellement *m*, HYDROL ruissellement *m*, écoulement *m*, MAR POLL eau de ruissellement *f*, POLLUTION eau de ruissellement *f*, ruissellement *m*, écoulement *m*, WATER SUPP ruissellement *m*, écoulement *m*; ~ **coefficient** *n* CONST coefficient de ruissellement *m*, WATER SUPP coefficient d'écoulement *m*

run-of-mine *n* MINING charbon tout-venant *m*, houille tout-venant *f*, tout-venant *m*; ~ **coal** *n* COAL TECH charbon tout-venant *m*, MINING charbon tout-venant *m*, houille tout-venant *f*, tout-venant *m*

run-of-river: ~ **scheme** *n* FUELLESS *hydroelectric power* installation au fil de l'eau *f*; ~ **station** *n* FUELLESS *hydroelectric power* usine au fil de l'eau *f*

runout *n* PROD ENG coulage *m*, coulure *f*, manquant *m*, rupture de stock *f*, stock en rupture *m*

run-time *n* COMP, DP durée d'exécution *f*, PROD ENG délai de production *m*, temps d'exécution *m*, temps machine *m*, temps opératoire *m*; ~ **error** *n* PROD ENG défaut de temps d'exécution *m*, erreur de temps d'exécution *f*; ~ **output** *n* COMP sortie pendant l'exécution du programme *f*, sortie pendant le déroulement du programme *f*; ~ **system** *n* COMP, DP programme superviseur *m*

run-up[1] *n* AERONAUT *engine* point fixe *m*; ~ **area** *n* AERONAUT *airport* aire de point fixe *f*, zone de point fixe *f*; ~ **time** *n* RECORDING temps de lancement *m*

run-up[2] *vi* AERONAUT *engine* faire le point fixe

runway *n* AERONAUT piste *f*, MECH ENG chemin de fer suspendu *m*, monorail aérien *m*, monorail transporteur *m*, voie ferrée aérienne *f*, chemin de roulement *m*, piste de roulement *f*, voie de roulement *f*, voie de translation *f*; ~ **alignment** *n* AERONAUT alignement de piste *m*; ~ **alignment indicator** *n* AERONAUT indicateur d'alignement de piste *m*; ~ **basic length** *n* AERONAUT longueur de base d'une piste *f*; ~ **centerline** *n* (AmE) *see runway centre line*; ~ **centerline light** *n* (AmE) *see runway centreline light*; ~ **centerline marking** *n* (AmE) *see runway centreline marking*; ~ **centreline** *n* (BrE) AERONAUT axe de piste *m*; ~ **centreline light** *n* (BrE) AERONAUT feu d'axe de piste *m*; ~ **centreline marking** *n* (BrE) AERONAUT marque d'axe de piste *f*; ~ **controller**

n CONTROL contrôleur de piste *m*; ~ **crossing light** *n* AERONAUT feu de traversée de piste *m*; ~ **designator** *n* AERONAUT indicatif de piste *m*; ~ **end light** *n* AERONAUT feu d'extrémité de piste *m*; ~ **end safety area** *n* AERONAUT aire de sécurité d'extrémité de piste *f*; ~ **gradient** *n* AERONAUT pente de la piste *f*; ~ **in use** *n* (BrE) *(cf active runway)* AERONAUT piste en service *f*; ~ **number** *n* AERONAUT numéro de la piste *m*; ~ **threshold** *n* AERONAUT entrée de piste *f*, seuil de piste *m*; ~ **threshold marking** *n* AERONAUT marque de seuil de piste *f*; ~ **touchdown zone light** *n* AERONAUT feu de zone de toucher des roues *m*; ~ **visual range** *n* AERONAUT portée visuelle de piste *f*

rupture[1] *n* CHEM *of bond*, CRYSTALL, METALL rupture *f*; ~ **member** *n* REFRIG dispositif de rupture *m*; ~ **strength** *n* METALL résistance à force de rupture *f*

rupture[2] *vt* CHEM *bond* rompre

rupture[3] *vi* CHEM *bond* se rompre

rural: ~ **automatic exchange** *n* TELECOM central automatique rural *m*; ~ **district** *n* ELEC ENG réseau rural *m*; ~ **exchange** *n* TELECOM commutateur rural *m*; ~ **network** *n* TELECOM réseau rural *m*; ~ **switch** *n* TELECOM commutateur rural *m*; ~ **water supply** *n* WATER SUPP approvisionnement en eaux rurales *m*

rush *n* CONST jonc *m*; ~ **of air** *n* MINING chasse d'air *f*, coup d'air *m*; ~ **hour** *n* RAIL, TRANSP *traffic* heure de pointe *f*; ~ **hour factor** *n* TRANSP *traffic* facteur de pointe *m*; ~ **hour traffic** *n* TRANSP trafic d'heure de pointe *m*; ~ **order** *n* PRINT coup de feu *m*

rushes *n pl* CINEMAT production journalière *f*, rushes *m pl*

Russell-Saunders: ~ **coupling** *n* PHYS couplage R-S *m*, couplage Russell-Saunders *m*

rust *n* CHEM, FOOD TECH *phytopathology*, MECH, PAPER TECH rouille *f*, PROP MAT rouillage *m*, rouille *f*, VEHICLES *body* rouille *f*; ~ **film** *n* COATINGS couche mince de rouille *f*, film de rouille *m*; ~ **inhibitor** *n* NAUT antirouille *m*, PAPER TECH antioxydant *m*; ~ **preventive** *n* PACKAGING antirouille *m*; ~ **preventive packaging** *n* PACKAGING emballage antirouille *m*; ~ **protection** *n* PACKAGING protection contre la rouille *f*; ~ **protective paint** *n* COLOURS peinture antirouille *f*; ~ **remover** *n* MECH ENG dérouillant *m*

rustiness *n* CHEM rouillure *f*

rustless *adj* PROP MAT inoxydable

rustproof *adj* PROD ENG inoxydable

rust-proofing *n* MECH ENG traitement antirouille *m*; ~ **paint** *n* COATINGS peinture antirouille *f*

rut *n* CONST ornière *f*

ruthenic *adj* CHEM ruthénique

ruthenium *n* (*Ru*) CHEM ruthénium *m* (*Ru*)

Rutherford: ~ **scattering** *n* PHYS diffusion de Rutherford *f*

rutherfordium *n* CHEM rutherfordium *m*

rutile *n* CHEM, MINERAL rutile *m*

R-wire *n* TELECOM fil-R *m*

R-Y: ~ **axis** *n* TV axe R-Y *m*; ~ **matrix** *n* TV matrice R-Y *f*; ~ **signal** *n* TV signal R-Y *m*

Rydberg: ~ **constant** *n* PHYS constante de Rydberg *f*; ~ **energy** *n* PHYS énergie de Rydberg *f*

S

s *abbr (second)* METR s *(seconde)*
S [1] *abbr (siemens)* METR S *(siemens)*
S [2] *(sulphur, sulfur)* CHEM S *(soufre)*
SA *abbr (section adaptation)* TELECOM adaptation de
section *f*
Sabattier: ~ effect *n* CINEMAT effet Sabattier *m*
Sabine: ~ coefficient *n* ACOUSTICS facteur de Sabine *m*
saccharase *n* FOOD TECH invertase *f*, sucrase *f*
saccharate *n* CHEM saccharate *m*
saccharic *adj* CHEM saccharique
saccharide *n* CHEM saccharide *m*
saccharimeter *n* PHYS saccharimètre *m*
saccharin *n* CHEM saccharine *f*
saccoblast *n* CHEM saccoblaste *m*
sachet *n* (BrE) *(cf pack)* PACKAGING sachet *m*
sack *n* PACKAGING sac *m*; ~ barrow *n* PACKAGING diable
m; ~ filling line *n* PACKAGING chaîne de remplissage de
sacs *f*; ~ filling machine *n* PACKAGING remplisseuse de
sacs *f*; ~ knife *n* PACKAGING couteau pour sacs *m*; ~
scales *n pl* PACKAGING balance d'ensachage *f*; ~ sealer
n PACKAGING machine pour fermer les sacs *f*; ~ sewing
machine *n* PACKAGING machine pour coudre les sacs *f*
sack-closing: ~ machine *n* PACKAGING machine pour
fermer les sacs *f*
sacrificial: ~ anode *n* PETR, PETR TECH anode sacrifi-
cielle *f*
sadden *vt* COLOURS teindre en nuances foncées
saddle *n* MECH ENG *machine tool* cuirasse *f*, traînard *m*,
SPRINGS *of leaf spring* selle *f*; ~ clamp terminal *n* PROD
ENG borne avec serre-fils *f*; ~ feed rate *n* MECH ENG
machine tools vitesse d'avance du chariot porte-outil
f; ~ key *n* MECH ENG clavette creuse *f*, clavette évidée *f*,
clavette à friction *f*; ~ mount combination *n* TRANSP
camion emportant autres camions semi-portés *m*; ~
point *n* METALL point de selle *m*; ~ stitching *n* PRINT
piqûre à cheval *f*; ~ tile *n* CONST tuile en dos d'âne *f*; ~
unit *n* REFRIG groupe frigorifique cavalier *m*
saddlebag: ~ monorail *n* TRANSP monorail à cheval sur
poutre porteuse *f*
saddle-bottomed: ~ car *n* TRANSP fond en dos d'âne *m*; ~
self-discharging car *n* TRANSP fond en dos d'âne pour
autodéchargeur *m*
saddled: ~ finish *n* C&G bague déformée *f*
safe [1] *adj* SAFETY en sécurité, sauf, sûr
safe [2] *n* PROD ENG lisse, SAFETY coffre-fort *m*; ~ action
area *n* CINEMAT zone de sécurité de cadrage *f*, TV
cadrage télévision *m*; ~ area generator *n* TV générateur
de cadre *m*; ~ concentration *n* NUCLEAR concentration
sûre *f*; ~ edge file *n* MECH ENG lime à côté lisse *f*; ~
ground *n* NAUT *mooring* fond de bonne tenue *m*; ~
headway *n* TRANSP *traffic* distance de sécurité *f*; ~
ironing temperature *n* TEXTILES température de repassage *f*; ~ keeping *n* POLLUTION sauvegarde *f*; ~ limit *n*
SAFETY limite de sécurité *f*; ~ load *n* COAL TECH charge
admissible *f*, MECH ENG charge de sécurité *f*; ~ load
indicator *n* SAFETY indicateur de charge admissible *m*;
~ methods of working *n pl* SAFETY méthodes de travail
sûres *f pl*; ~ shutdown earthquake *n* NUCLEAR arrêt sûr

en cas de séisme *m*; ~ storage of flammable liquids *n*
SAFETY entreposage sûr des liquides inflammables *m*;
~ stress under bending *n* MECH ENG charge de sécurité
par flexion *f*; ~ use *n* SAFETY *of explosives* utilisation
sans risques *f*, *of grinding wheels, ladders, hand-held
electrically-operated tools* usage sans risques *m*; ~
water *n* NAUT eau saine *f*; ~ water mark *n* NAUT
navigation marque d'eau saine *f*; ~ working load *n*
SAFETY charge admissible de fonctionnement *f*; ~
working practices *n pl* SAFETY méthodes de travail
sûres *f pl*
safeguarding *n* SAFETY *of buildings* protection *f*
safelight *n* CINEMAT lumière inactinique *f*, PHOTO
darkroom lampe de laboratoire *f*, écran de sûreté *m*; ~
filter *n* PHOTO écran de sûreté *m*
safety [1] *n* MECH, QUALITY sécurité *f*, sûreté *f*, SAFETY
sécurité *f*, sûreté *f*, *of hand-operated machines* usage
sans risques *m*; ~ advisor *n* CONST conseiller de sécurité *m*; ~ apparatus *n* MECH ENG appareil de sûreté *m*,
MINING appareil de sûreté *m*, engin de sûreté *m*, SAFE-
TY appareil de sûreté *m*; ~ appliance *n* MECH ENG engin
de sûreté *m*, MINING appareil de sûreté *m*, engin de
sûreté *m*, SAFETY engin de sûreté *m*, équipement pour
la sécurité *m*; ~ arch *n* CONST arc de décharge *m*, arc en
décharge *m*; ~ at work *n* SAFETY sécurité au travail *f*; ~
barrier *n* SAFETY barrière de sûreté *f*; ~ base *n* CINEMAT
support non flam *m*; ~ belt *n* PETR TECH harnais de
sécurité *m*, SAFETY, TRANSP, VEHICLES ceinture de sécurité *f*; ~ belt anchorage *n* VEHICLES ancrage de la
ceinture de sécurité *m*; ~ boiler *n* PROD ENG chaudière
inexplosible *f*, chaudière multitubulaire *f*; ~ bolt *n*
MECH ENG *of wall plug* cheville de sécurité *f*; ~ bonnet *n*
(BrE) *(cf safety hood)* TRANSP *lorries* arceau de sécurité *m*; ~ catch *n* AUTO crochet de sécurité *m*, MECH ENG
cran de repos *m*, cran de sûreté *m*, MILIT cran de sûreté
m, VEHICLES crochet de sûreté *m*; ~ chain *n* MECH ENG
chaîne de sûreté *f*, SAFETY chaîne de sécurité *f*; ~
clamps *n pl* SAFETY *for tins, cans, buckets* pinces de
sûreté *f pl*; ~ closure *n* PACKAGING fermeture de sécurité *f*; ~ cock *n* MECH ENG robinet de sûreté *m*; ~ code *n*
MECH ENG *for screw conveyors*, SAFETY code de sécurité
m; ~ colors *n pl* (AmE), ~ colours *n pl* (BrE) SAFETY
couleurs des règlements de sécurité *f pl*; ~ committee *n*
SAFETY commission chargée des questions de sécurité
f; ~ container *n* LAB EQUIP récipient de sécurité *m*; ~
cover *n* PROD ENG capot de sécurité *m*; ~ curtain *n*
SAFETY rideau de fer *m*; ~ cutout *n* REFRIG interrupteur
de sécurité *m*, *pressure cutout* pressostat de sécurité *m*;
~ device *n* MECH ENG dispositif de sécurité *m*, dispositif
de sûreté *m*, SAFETY dispositif de sécurité *m*; ~ door *n*
CONST porte de sécurité *f*; ~ drag bar *n* MINING chambrière *f*, reculoire *f*; ~ earth *n* (BrE) *(cf safety ground)*
ELEC prise de terre de sécurité *f*; ~ earth symbol *n* (BrE)
(cf safety ground symbol) PROD ENG *electricity* symbole de terre de sécurité *m*; ~ education *n* SAFETY
formation sur la sécurité *f*; ~ engineering *n* TESTING
ingénierie de la sécurité *f*; ~ equipment *n* SAFETY
équipement de sécurité *m*; ~ explosive *n* MINING explo-

sif de sûreté *m*; ~ **facility** *n* SAFETY *for buildings* installations de sécurité *f pl*, équipement de sécurité *m*; ~ **factor** *n* COAL TECH, CONST coefficient de sécurité *m*, ELEC coefficient de sécurité *m*, facteur de sécurité *m*, NAUT coefficient de sécurité *m*, SAFETY coefficient de sécurité *m*, facteur de sécurité *m*; ~ **film** *n* PHOTO, PRINT film de sûreté *m*; ~ **first campaign** *n* SAFETY campagne contre les accidents *f*; ~ **first training** *n* SAFETY instruction de sécurité *f*; ~ **fittings** *n pl* SAFETY *for buildings* aménagements de sécurité *m pl*, installationsde sécurité *f pl, for hot-water systems* robinetterie de sûreté *f*; ~ **funnel** *n* LAB EQUIP *glassware* tube de sûreté *m*; ~ **fuse** *n* MINING cordeau Bickford *m*, mèche ordinaire *f*, étoupille de sûreté *f*, mèche de mineur *f*, mèche de sûreté *f*, mèche lente *f*; ~ **fuse initiation** *n* MINING allumage par mèche de sûreté *m*; ~ **gasoline tank** *n* (AmE) *(cf safety petrol tank)* TRANSP réservoir de sécurité *m*; ~ **gas tank** *n* (AmE) *(cf safety petrol tank)* TRANSP réservoir de sécurité *m*; ~ **glass** *n* C&G, CONST verre de sécurité *m*, SAFETY glace Sécurit *f*, TRANSP verre de sécurité *m*; ~ **glasses** *n pl* INSTRUMENT lunettes de sûreté *f pl*, lunettes protectrices *f pl*, lunettes à coques latérales *f pl*, LAB EQUIP lunettes de protection *f pl*; ~ **goggles** *n pl* INSTRUMENT lunettes à coques latérales *f pl*, SAFETY lunettes de protection *f pl*; ~ **ground** *n* (AmE) *(cf safety earth)* ELEC prise de terre de sécurité *f*; ~ **ground symbol** *n* (AmE) *(cf safety earth symbol)* PROD ENG *electricity* symbole de terre de sécurité *m*; ~ **guard plate** *n* PROD ENG plaque de sécurité *f*; ~ **handles** *n pl* SAFETY *for chisels* manches de sécurité *m pl*; ~ **harness** *n* AERONAUT, CINEMAT, NAUT, SAFETY harnais de sécurité *m*; ~ **hazard** *n* SAFETY risque pour la sécurité *m*; ~ **headway** *n* TRANSP *traffic* distance de sécurité *f*; ~ **helmet** *n* SAFETY casque de sécurité *m*, TRANSP casque de protection *m*; ~ **hood** *n* (AmE) *(cf safety bonnet)* TRANSP *trucks* arceau de sécurité *m*; ~ **hook** *n* MECH ENG crochet de sûreté *m*, mousqueton *m*; ~ **instructions** *n pl* SAFETY directives de sécurité *f pl*; ~ **interlock** *n* MECH ENG *machine tools* interverrouillage de sécurité *m*; ~ **in working** *n* SAFETY sécurité en usinage *f*; ~ **island** *n* TRANSP refuge pour piétons *m*; ~ **jack** *n* CINEMAT vérin d'immobilisation *m*; ~ **ladder** *n* SAFETY échelle de sécurité *f*; ~ **leaf** *n* SPRINGS lame de sécurité *f*; ~ **lock** *n* CONST serrure de sécurité *f, buildings* verrou de sûreté *m*; ~ **management** *n* QUALITY gestion de la sécurité *f*; ~ **margin** *n* SAFETY marge de sécurité *f*; ~ **measures** *n pl* CONTROL, QUALITY, SAFETY mesures de sécurité *f pl*; ~ **mixing tap** *n* MECH ENG robinet mélangeur de sécurité *m*; ~ **net** *n* SAFETY filet de sécurité *m*; ~ **nut** *n* MECH ENG contre-écrou *m*, écrou de sûreté *m*; ~ **officer** *n* SAFETY responsable de la sécurité *m*; ~ **paper** *n* PAPER TECH papier infalsifiable *m*, PRINT papier de sécurité *m*, papier spécial *m*; ~ **petrol tank** *n* (BrE) *(cf safety gas tank, safety gasoline tank)* TRANSP réservoir de sécurité *m*; ~ **pin** *n* CINEMAT, NAUT *of shackle* goupille de sécurité *f*; ~ **placard** *n* LAB EQUIP panneau de sécurité *m*; ~ **plug** *n* HYDR EQUIP fusible *m*, plomb de sécurité *m*, rondelle fusible *f*; ~ **precaution** *n* SAFETY précautions de sécurité *f*; ~ **pulley block** *n* SAFETY moufle de sécurité *m*; ~ **rail** *n* TRANSP rail de sûreté *m*; ~ **recommendation** *n* AERONAUT recommandation de sécurité *f*; ~ **record** *n* CONST feuille de sécurité *f*, registre de sécurité *m*, taux de sécurité *m*; ~ **regulations** *n pl* SAFETY règlements de sécurité *m pl*; ~ **representative** *n* SAFETY agent de la sécurité *m*, représentant de la

sécurité *m*; ~ **requirement** *n* SAFETY condition de sécurité requise *f*, norme de sécurité *f*, prescription *f*; ~ **requirements and supervision** *n pl* SAFETY conditions requises de sécurité et surveillance *f pl*, prescriptions de sécurité et de surveillance *f pl*; ~ **risk** *n* SAFETY risque pour la sécurité *m*; ~ **rules** *n pl* SAFETY règles de sécurité *f pl*; ~ **screen** *n* LAB EQUIP écran de protection *m*; ~ **sign** *n* LAB EQUIP panneau de sécurité *m*, SAFETY signal de sécurité *m*; ~ **specifications** *n pl* TRANSP prescriptions de sécurité *f pl*; ~ **spectacles** *n pl* SAFETY lunettes de protection *f pl*; ~ **speed** *n* AERONAUT, TRANSP vitesse de sécurité *f*; ~ **spring** *n* MILIT ressort de sûreté *m*; ~ **stock** *n* PROD ENG stock de sécurité *m*; ~ **stop cable** *n* TRANSP câble de retenue *m*; ~ **storage tank** *n* SAFETY réservoir de stockage de sécurité *m*; ~ **switch** *n* ELEC, ELEC ENG interrupteur de sécurité *m*; ~ **time** *n* PROD ENG délai de sécurité *m*; ~ **tube** *n* LAB EQUIP *glassware* tube de sûreté *m*; ~ **unit** *n* SPACE *spacecraft* tête de sécurité *f*; ~ **valve** *n* GAS TECH, HEATING vanne de sécurité *f*, HYDR EQUIP, MECH soupape de sûreté *f*, MECH ENG soupape de dilatation *f*, PROD ENG, SAFETY soupape de sûreté *f*; ~ **valves and fittings** *n pl* SAFETY robinetterie de sûreté *f*; ~ **vessel** *n* SAFETY *for storing flammable liquids* récipient de sécurité *m*; ~ **visor** *n* SAFETY visière de protection *f*; ~ **warning** *n* PROD ENG consigne de sécurité *f*

safety:[2] **be a ~ risk** *vi* SAFETY présenter des risques pour la sécurité

safflorite *n* MINERAL safflorite *f*

safflower: ~ **oil** *n* FOOD TECH huile de carthame *f*

saffron *n* FOOD TECH safran *m*

safranin *n* CHEM safranine *f*

safranine *n* CHEM safranine *f*

safrol *n* CHEM safrol *m*, safrole *m*

safrole *n* CHEM safrol *m*, safrole *m*

sag[1] *n* C&G gauchissement *m*, NUCLEAR flèche *f*; ~ **bend** *n* PETR concavité *f*, coude vertical supérieur *m*; ~ **point** *n* C&G température de fléchissement *f*

sag[2] *vi* NAUT *ship* avoir du contre-arc

sagenite *n* MINERAL sagénite *f*

saggar *n* C&G cassette *f*; ~ **clay** *n* C&G terre à cassettes *f*

sagging *n* C&G ramollissage *m*, NAUT *shipbuilding* contre-arc *m*, P&R *paints* coulure *f*, RAIL flexion *f*

Sagitta *n* ASTRON Flèche *f*

sagittal: ~ **focal line** *n* PHYS focale sagittale *f*

Sagittarius *n* ASTRON Sagittaire *m*; ~ **arm** *n* ASTRON *of Galaxy* bras spiral dans le Sagittaire *m*

sahlite *n* MINERAL salite *f*

sail[1] *n* NAUT voile *f*; ~ **area** *n* NAUT surface de voilure *f*; ~ **locker** *n* NAUT soute à voiles *f*; ~ **loft** *n* NAUT voilerie *f*; ~ **plan** *n* NAUT plan de voilure *m*

sail[2] *vt* NAUT commander, manoeuvrer, piloter, *reciprocal track* suivre

sail[3] ~ **away** *vi* NAUT prendre le large, quitter un port; ~ **over the seas** *vi* NAUT parcourir les mers

sailboard *n* NAUT planche à voile *f*

sailboat *n* (AmE) *(cf sailing boat)* NAUT bateau à voiles *m*, canot à voiles *m*, voilier *m*, TRANSP voilier *m*

sailcloth *n* NAUT laize *f*, toile à voiles *f*

sailing *n* NAUT navigation *f*, navigation à la voile *f*; ~ **boat** *n* (BrE) *(cf sailboat)* NAUT bateau à voiles *m*, canot à voiles *m*, voilier *m*, TRANSP voilier *m*; ~ **dinghy** *n* NAUT dinghy à voile *m*; ~ **directions** *n pl* NAUT *navigation* instructions nautiques *f pl*; ~ **ship** *n* NAUT navire à voiles *m*

sailmaker *n* NAUT *person* voilier *m*

sal: ~ **ammoniac** *n* CHEM sel ammoniac *m*

salacetol *n* CHEM salacétol *m*

saleable: ~ **coal** *n* COAL TECH charbon marchand *m*; ~ **mass** *n* PAPER TECH *of pulp* masse marchande *f*

sales: ~ **engineer** *n* PROD ENG ingénieur commercial *m*; ~ **yarn spinning** *n* TEXTILES filature commerciale *f*

salicin *n* CHEM salicine *f*

salicyl *n* CHEM salicyle *m*

salicylaldehyde *n* CHEM aldéhyde salicylique *m*

salicylate *n* CHEM salicylate *m*

salicylated *adj* CHEM salicylé

salicylic *adj* CHEM salicylique

salient: ~ **pole** *n* ELEC *machines*, ELEC ENG pôle saillant *m*; ~ **pole generator** *n* ELEC *machines* alternateur à pôles saillants *m*, génératrice à pôles saillants *f*; ~ **pole rotor** *n* ELEC ENG rotor à pôles saillants *m*; ~ **pole stator** *n* ELEC ENG stator à pôles saillants *m*

saliferous: ~ **clay** *n* C&G argile salifère *f*

salifiable *adj* CHEM salifiable

saligenin *n* CHEM saligénine *f*

saline[1] *adj* HYDROL salin, saumâtre, WATER SUPP salin

saline:[2] ~ **solution** *n* NUCLEAR saumure *f*, solution saline *f*; ~ **spring** *n* HYDROL source saline *f*, source salée *f*, source saumâtre *f*, WATER SUPP source salée *f*; ~ **water** *n* HYDROL eau saline *f*, WATER SUPP eau salée *f*; ~ **water conversion** *n* WATER SUPP dessalement *m*

salinity *n* CHEM, FUELLESS, HYDROL, NAUT, PETR, PETR TECH, WATER SUPP salinité *f*

salinization *n* HYDROL salinisation *f*

salinometer *n* COAL TECH, OCEANOG salinomètre *m*

salite *n* MINERAL salite *f*

salle *n* PACKAGING *paper mill* salle de finissage *f*

salmanazar *n* C&G salmanazar *m*

salmon: ~ **breeder** *n* OCEANOG salmoniculteur *m*; ~ **culture** *n* OCEANOG salmoniculture *f*; ~ **farmer** *n* OCEANOG salmoniculteur *m*

salmonella *n* FOOD TECH salmonelle *f*, salmonellose *f*

salol *n* CHEM salicylate de phényle *m*, salol *m*

saloon *n* (BrE) NAUT cabine *f*, carré *m*, TRANSP *motor vehicles* berline *f*; ~ **coach** *n* TRANSP voiture non compartimentée *f*; ~ **deck** *n* NAUT pont des emménagements *m*, pont des premières *m*

Salpeter: ~ **process** *n* NUCLEAR réaction de Salpeter *f*

salt[1] *n* CHEM, PETR TECH sel *m*; ~ **balance** *n* OCEANOG bilan ionique *m*, bilan salin *m*; ~ **bath brazing** *n* CONST brasage au bain de sel *m*, brasage au bain salin *m*; ~ **bath furnace** *n* HEATING four à bain de sel *m*; ~ **bubble** *n* C&G bouillon de sel *m*; ~ **cake** *n* C&G sulfate de soude *m*, FOOD TECH sulfate de sodium commercial *m*; ~ **cavity** *n* GAS TECH cavité saline *f*; ~ **column** *n* PETR TECH colonne de sel *f*, doigt de gant *m*; ~ **content** *n* GAS TECH salinité *f*, OCEANOG contenu salin *m*, teneur en sel *f*; ~ **curing** *n* OCEANOG salage *m*; ~ **deposit** *n* GAS TECH massif salifère *m*; ~ **diapirism** *n* GEOL, PETR TECH halocinèse *f*; ~ **dome** *n* GEOL dôme de sel *m*, PETR TECH diapir *m*, dôme de sel *m*; ~ **glaze** *n* COATINGS vernis au sel *m*; ~ **liquor** *n* NUCLEAR saumure *f*, solution saline *f*; ~ **marsh** *n* OCEANOG marais salant *m*; ~ **mist** *n* TESTING *corrosion test* brouillard salin *m*; ~ **pillow** *n* PETR TECH dôme de sel *m*; ~ **refinery** *n* PROD ENG raffinerie de sel *f*, saunerie *f*; ~ **rock** *n* GEOL halite *f*, sel gemme *m*; ~ **spray** *n* COLOURS *paint test* brouillard salin *m*; ~ **spray test** *n* C&G résistance au brouillard salin *f*; ~ **substitute** *n* FOOD TECH substitut de sel *m*; ~ **swamp** *n* WATER SUPP marais salant *m*; ~ **tectonics** *n* GEOL halocinèse *f*, tectonique du sel *f*, PETR TECH halocinèse *f*; ~ **works** *n*

pl PROD ENG raffinerie de sel *f*, saunerie *f*

salt:[2] ~ **out** *vt* CHEM *soap* relarger

saltation *n* HYDROL saltation *f*

salt-bath-hardened: ~ **steel** *n* SPRINGS acier trempé en bain de sels *m*

salt-bearing *adj* GEOL salifère

saltbed *n* HYDROL source saline *f*, source salée *f*, source saumâtre *f*

salted: ~ **atmosphere** *n* REFRIG air salin *m*

saltern *n* FOOD TECH marais salant *m*, saunerie *f*, OCEANOG marais maritime *m*

salt-glazed *adj* COATINGS, COLOURS verni par salage

saltiness *n* HYDROL salinité *f*

salting *n* FOOD TECH salage *m*, salaison *f*; ~ **agent** *n* NUCLEAR agent salin *m*

saltpeter *n* (AmE), **saltpetre** *n* (BrE) C&G salpêtre *m*, CHEM nitre *m*, salpêtre *m*, FOOD TECH salpêtre *m*

saltwater *n* HYDROL eau saline *f*, eau salée *f*, WATER SUPP eau de mer *f* ~ **drilling mud** *n* PETR boue de forage à l'eau salée *f*; ~ **infiltration** *n* HYDROL invasion d'eau salée *f*; ~ **invasion** *n* HYDROL invasion d'eau salée *f*; ~ **mud** *n* PETR TECH boue à l'eau salée *f*; ~ **plant** *n* WATER SUPP halophyte *f*; ~ **wedge** *n* OCEANOG coin salé *m*

salty *adj* HYDROL saumâtre

salvage[1] *n* AERONAUT renflouage *m*, récupération *f*, NAUT matériel récupéré *m*, sauvetage *m*, *payment* indemnité de remorquage *f*, *shipping* renflouage *m*, récupération *f*; ~ **award** *n* NAUT droit de sauvetage *m*, indemnité de sauvetage *f*, prime de sauvetage *f*; ~ **car** *n* (AmE) *(cf salvage lorry)* TRANSP camion dépanneur *m*; ~ **crane** *n* TRANSP grue dépanneuse *f*; ~ **lorry** *n* (BrE) *(cf salvage car, salvage truck)* TRANSP camion dépanneur *m*; ~ **truck** *n* (AmE) *(cf salvage lorry)* TRANSP camion dépanneur *m*; ~ **tug** *n* NAUT remorqueur d'assistance *m*, remorqueur de sauvetage *m*, remorqueur de hautemer *m*, TRANSP remorqueur de haute mer *m*, remorqueur de sauvetage *m*; ~ **vessel** *n* NAUT navire de relevage *m*, navire sauveteur *m*

salvage[2] *vt* NAUT sauver, RECYCLING récupérer

salvaged: ~ **material** *n* RECYCLING matériel récupéré *m*, matériel sauvé *m*

salvaging *n* RECYCLING récupération *f*, TRANSP renflouage *m*

salvarsan *n* CHEM salvarsan 606 *m*

salvo *n* MILIT *gun* salve *f*

SAM *abbr (surface-to-air missile)* MILIT engin sol-air *m*

samarium *n* (*Sm*) CHEM samarium *m* (*Sm*); ~ **effect** *n* NUCLEAR effet samarium *m*

samarskite *n* MINERAL samarskite *f*

sample[1] *n* CHEM prise *f*, échantillon *m*, *for analysis* prise d'essai *f*, COAL TECH, COMP, DP, ELECTRON, MATH *statistics* échantillon *m*, METALL échantillon *m*, éprouvette *f*, P&R, PAPER TECH échantillon *m*, PHYS prélèvement *m*, échantillon *m*, QUALITY, SPACE *communications*, TELECOM, WATER SUPP échantillon *m*; ~ **admission vessel** *n* NUCLEAR *of mass spectrometer* réservoir d'échantillonnage *m*; ~ **captor** *n* QUALITY *water* capteur d'échantillonnage *m*; ~ **changer** *n* NUCLEAR passeur d'échantillons *m*; ~ **divider** *n* LAB EQUIP tamiseur *m*; ~ **holder** *n* NUCLEAR porte-échantillons *m*, porte-éprouvette *m*; ~ **period** *n* PETR intervalle d'échantillon *m*, période d'échantillonnage *f*; ~ **rate** *n* PETR période d'échantillonnage *f*; ~ **size** *n* ELECTRON taille de l'échantillon *f*, METR effectif de l'échantillon *m*; ~ **stabilization** *n* QUALITY stabilisation de l'échantillon *f*; ~ **strip** *n* *(pattern length)* TEXTILES bande échantillon *f*; ~ **surveillance** *n* QUALITY surveillance des échantillons *f*; ~ **swivel arm** *n* NUCLEAR bras pivotant pour les échantillons *m*; ~ **time** *n* PROD ENG période d'échantillonnage *f*

sample[2] *vt* COMP, DP, ELECTRON échantillonner, PHYS prélever, échantillonner, QUALITY, SPACE *communications*, TELECOM échantillonner

sample-and-hold: ~ **circuit** *n* ELEC ENG circuit échantillonneur *m*, échantillonneur *m*

sampled: ~ **data filtering** *n* ELECTRON filtrage de signaux échantillonnés *m*; ~ **data size filter** *n* ELECTRON filtre pour signaux échantillonnés *m*, taille des signaux échantillonnés *f*; ~ **output** *n* CONTROL signal de sortie échantillonné *m*; ~ **output signal** *n* CONTROL signal de sortie échantillonné *m*; ~ **signal** *n* ELECTRON, TELECOM signal échantillonné *m*; ~ **value** *n* ELECTRON valeur échantillonnée *f*, échantillon *m*

sampler *n* COAL TECH échantillonneur *m*, PROD ENG *machine* échantillonneuse *f*, *person* échantillonneur *m*, TELECOM échantillonneur *m*

sampling *n* COMP, DP, ELECTRON, FOOD TECH, PETR, PETR TECH, PHYS échantillonnage *m*, PROD ENG prélèvement d'échantillons *m*, échantillonnage *m*, RECORDING, SPACE *communications*, TELECOM échantillonnage *m*, TESTING prélèvement d'échantillons *m*, WATER SUPP prélèvement *m*, échantillonnage *m*; ~ **amplifier** *n* ELECTRON amplificateur à échantillonnage *m*; ~ **device** *n* LAB EQUIP préleveur *m*, échantillonneur *m*; ~ **equipment** *n* TESTING appareillage de prélèvement *m*; ~ **frequency** *n* TELECOM fréquence d'échantillonnage *f*; ~ **inspection** *n* QUALITY contrôle par échantillonnage *m*; ~ **line** *n* QUALITY *water* conduite d'échantillonnage *f*, ligne d'échantillonnage *f*; ~ **methods** *n pl* QUALITY méthodes d'échantillonnage *f pl*; ~ **network** *n* QUALITY réseau d'échantillonnage *m*; ~ **plan** *n* METR plan d'échantillonnage *m*; ~ **point** *n* COAL TECH point de prélèvement *m*, QUALITY point d'échantillonnage *m*, point de prélèvement *m*; ~ **probe** *n* QUALITY *water* sonde d'échantillonnage *f*; ~ **pump** *n* LAB EQUIP pompe d'échantillonnage *f*; ~ **rate** *n* COMP, DP, ELECTRON cadence d'échantillonnage *f*; ~ **spectrum analyzer** *n* ELECTRON analyseur de spectres à échantillonnage *m*; ~ **theorem** *n* PETR théorème d'échantillonnage *m*; ~ **tube** *n* LAB EQUIP éprouvette *f*; ~ **vertical amplifier** *n* ELECTRON amplificateur vertical à échantillonnage *m*

SAMSARS *abbr (satellite-aided maritime search and rescue system)* TELECOM système de recherche et de sauvetage maritimes par satellite *m*

samson: ~ **post** *n* NAUT *shipbuilding* bitte d'amarrage *f*, épontille *f*

sand[1] *n* COAL TECH terrain sablonneux *m*, PETR arène *f*, sable *m*, PROD ENG sable *m*; ~ **and gravel trap** *n* HYDROL dessableur-dégraveur *m*; ~ **bar** *n* GEOL cordon littoral sableux *m*, OCEANOG barre *f*; ~ **bath** *n* LAB EQUIP *heating* bain de sable *m*; ~ **casting** *n* PROD ENG pièce fondue au sable *f*; ~ **equivalent** *n* CONST équivalent de sable *m*; ~ **filter** *n* COAL TECH filtre à sable *m*; ~ **floor** *n* PROD ENG *foundry* chantier de moulage en sable *m*; ~ **hole** *n* PROD ENG *in casting* trou de sable *m*; ~ **jet** *n* PROD ENG jet de sable *m*, machine au jet de sable *f*; ~ **line** *n* PETR câble de curage *m*, ligne de sable *f*; ~ **mill** *n* P&R *paint* broyeur à sable *m*; ~ **mold** *n* (AmE), ~ **mould** *n* (BrE) PROD ENG moule de sable *m*; ~ **ribbon** *n* OCEANOG ruban de sable *m*; ~ **riddler** *n* PROD ENG *founding* cribleuse *f*; ~ **ripple** *n* OCEANOG ride de plage *f*; ~ **seal** *n*

CONST *roads* scellement à sable *m*; ~ **shop** *n* PROD ENG *foundry* sablerie *f*; ~ **sifter** *n* PROD ENG cribleuse *f*; ~ **trap** *n* HYDROL *sewage* dessableur *m*, PETR TECH piège à sable *m*, WATER SUPP dessableur *m*; ~ **vent** *n* PROD ENG *of mould* trou d'air *m*; ~ **wave** *n* OCEANOG mégaride *f*

sand[2] *vt* PROD ENG sabler

sandbag *n* SAFETY sac de sable *m*

sandbank *n* HYDROL haut-fond sableux *m*, OCEANOG basse *f*, caye *f*

sandbergerite *n* MINERAL sandbergérite *f*

sandblast[1] *n* PROD ENG jet de sable *m*, machine au jet de sable *f*; ~ **apparatus** *n* C&G sableuse *f*; ~ **cleaning room** *n* PROD ENG chambre de dessablage au jet de sable *f*; ~ **machine** *n* PROD ENG sableuse *f*; ~ **obscuring** *n* C&G matage *m*

sandblast[2] *vt* CONST décaper, MECH sabler

sandblasting *n* C&G gravure au jet de sable *f*, CONST jet de sable *m*, sablage *m*, MAR POLL décapage à la sableuse *m*, MECH sablage *m*, NAUT *ship maintenance* décapage *m*, sablage *m*, PROD ENG projection de sable *f*, PROP MAT sablage *m*; ~ **nozzle** *n* C&G buse de sablage *f*

sander *n* PAPER TECH machine à roder *f*

sanding *n* C&G ponçage *m*, CONST *civil engineering* gravillonnage *m*, P&R *finishing* ponçage *m*, PROD ENG sablage *m*

sandow *n* TRANSP câble élastique *m*, élément de suspension élastique *m*

sandpaper[1] *n* MECH papier de verre *m*, PRINT papier-émeri *m*, PROD ENG papier de verre *m*, papier verré *m*

sandpaper[2] *vt* PROD ENG poncer

sandpapering *n* PROD ENG ponçage *m*; ~ **machine** *n* PROD ENG machine à poncer *f*

sand-shale: ~ **ratio** *n* PETR TECH rapport sable-argile *m*

sandstone *n* CONST, GEOL grès *m*, OCEANOG grès de plage *m*, PETR TECH grès *m*

sandtable *n* PAPER TECH sablier *m*

sand-washing *n* PETR TECH curage *m*

sandwich: ~ **panel insulation** *n* REFRIG isolation par panneau sandwich *f*, isolation par panneau stratifié isolant *f*; ~ **windings** *n pl* ELEC enroulements alternés *m pl*, enroulements en disque *m pl*

sandwich-paned: ~ **insulating panel** *n* REFRIG double vitrage *m*, panneau isolant à double vitrage *m*

sandy[1] *adj* GEOL arénacé, sableux

sandy:[2] ~ **bottom** *n* NAUT *of sea* fond de sable *m*; ~ **chalk** *n* GEOL craie sableuse *f*, tuffeau *m*; ~ **clay** *n* CONST, GEOL argile sableuse *f*; ~ **ground** *n* COAL TECH terrain sablonneux *m*; ~ **limestone** *n* GEOL calcaire gréseux *m*, calcaire sableux *m*; ~ **loam** *n* CONST terreau sableux *m*, GEOL limon sableux *m*

sandy-bedded *adj* HYDROL à fond sableux

sanidine *n* MINERAL sanidine *f*

sanitary: ~ **engineering** *n* WATER SUPP technique sanitaire *f*; ~ **paint** *n* COLOURS peinture sanitaire *f*; ~ **ware** *n* C&G poterie de santé *f*; ~ **waste water** *n* WATER SUPP eau usée sanitaire *f*

sanitation *n* WATER SUPP assainissement *m*

sanitization *n* COMP, DP assainissement *m*

sanserif *n* PRINT sans empattement *m*; ~ **face** *n* PRINT caractères antiques *m pl*

santonic *adj* CHEM santonique

santonin *n* CHEM santonine *f*

SAP *abbr (service access point)* TELECOM point d'accès au service *m*

sapele *n* NAUT *boat building* sapelli *m*
SAPI *abbr (service access point identifier)* TELECOM identificateur de point d'accès au réseau *m*
sapogenin *n* CHEM sapogénine *f*
saponification *n* CHEM saponification *f*; ~ **number** *n* FOOD TECH valeur de saponification *f*
saponifier *n* CHEM saponifiant *m*
saponify[1] *vt* CHEM saponifier
saponify[2] *vi* CHEM se saponifier
saponifying *adj* CHEM saponifiant
saponin *n* CHEM saponine *f*
saponite *n* MINERAL saponite *f*
sapphire *n* ELECTRON, MINERAL saphir *m*; ~ **quartz** *n* MINERAL pseudosaphir *m*, quartz bleu *m*; ~ **substrate** *n* ELECTRON substrat en saphir *m*
sapphirine *n* MINERAL saphirine *f*
sapping *n* MINING sapement *m*
sapropel *n* OCEANOG sapropèle *m*; ~ **deposit** *n* GEOL dépôt sapropélitique *m*, sapropèle *m*
sapropelic: ~ **deposit** *n* GEOL dépôt sapropélitique *m*, sapropèle *m*
SAR *abbr (segmentation and reassembly)* TELECOM segmentation et réassemblage *f*
sarcine *n* CHEM sarcine *f*
sarcolactic *adj* CHEM sarcolactique
sarcolite *n* MINERAL sarcolite *f*
sarcosin *n* CHEM sarcosine *f*
sarcosine *n* CHEM sarcosine *f*
sard *n* MINERAL sarde *m*
sardine: ~ **boat** *n* OCEANOG sardinier *m*; ~ **net** *n* OCEANOG sardinal *m*, sardineau *m*
sardonyx *n* MINERAL sardoine *f*
sarkinite *n* MINERAL sarkinite *f*
saros *n* ASTRON saros *f*
sartorite *n* MINERAL sartorite *f*
sash *n* CONST châssis *m*, châssis de fenêtre *m*, châssis mobile *m*; ~ **bar** *n* CONST iron petit bois en fer *m*, *rolled sections*fer à vitrage *m*, *wood* petit bois *m*; ~ **bar iron** *n* CONST *rolled sections* fer à vitrage *m*; ~ **clamp** *n* CONST sergent *m*, serre-joint *m*; ~ **cramp** *n* CONST sergent *m*, serre-joint *m*; ~ **fastener** *n* CONST crampon de fermeture *m*, fermeture simple *f*; ~ **gate** *n* WATER SUPP vanne à coulisse *f*; ~ **iron** *n* CONST fer à vitrage *m*; ~ **window** *n* CONST fenêtre à coulisses *f*, fenêtre à guillotine *f*
sassoline *n* MINERAL sassoline *f*
sassolite *n* MINERAL sassolite *f*
satcom *n (satellite communications)* NAUT satcom *m (communications par satellite)*
satellite *n* AERONAUT *aerodrome*, ASTRON, PHYS satellite *m*, PRINT ordinateur secondaire intégré à un système *m*, satellite *m*, SPACE *communications*, TRANSP satellite *m*; ~ **apogee motor combination** *n* SPACE *spacecraft* composite satellite-moteur d'apogée *m*; ~ **astronomy** *n* ASTRON astronomie par satellite *f*; ~ **channel** *n* TV canal satellite *m*, voie de transmission par satellite *f*; ~ **communications** *n pl* NAUT *(satcom)* communications par satellite *f pl (satcom)*, TELECOM télécommunications par satellite *f pl*; ~ **computer** *n* COMP, DP ordinateur satellite *m*; ~ **coverage area** *n* TV zone de couverture d'un satellite *f*; ~ **design** *n* SPACE *spacecraft* conception de satellite *f*; ~ **dish** *n* TV antenne parabolique *f*; ~ **emergency position indicating radio beacon** *n (satellite EPIRB)* TELECOM RLS par satellite *m*; ~ **EPIRB** *n (satellite emergency position indicating radio beacon)* TELECOM RLS par satellite *m*; ~ **exchange** *n* TELECOM commutateur satellite *m*, satel-

lite central *m*; ~ **link** *n* SPACE *communications* liaison par satellite *f*, TV liaison par satellite *f*, liaison spatiale *f*; ~ **meteorology** *n* SPACE *spacecraft* météorologie spatiale *f*; ~ **navigator** *n (satnav)* NAUT appareil de navigation par satellites *m (satnav)*; ~ **switching** *n* SPACE *communications* commutation à bord du satellite *f*; ~ **telecast** *n* TV émission transmise par satellite *f*; ~ **track** *n* SPACE trace de satellite *f*; ~ **transmission** *n* TELECOM transmission par satellite *f*; ~ **well** *n* PETR puits satellite *m*
Satellite: ~ **System Operation Guide** *n (SSOG)* SPACE *communications* guide d'exploitation des liaisons par satellite *m*
satellite-aided: ~ **maritime search and rescue system** *n (SAMSARS)* TELECOM système de recherche et de sauvetage maritimes par satellite *m*
satin *n* TEXTILES satin *m*; ~ **etch** *n* C&G satiné *m*; ~ **finish** *n* COLOURS finition satinée *f*, PROP MAT fini satiné *m*; ~ **finish glass** *n* C&G verre satiné *m*; ~ **finishing wheel** *n* MECH ENG meule à satiner *f*; ~ **spar** *n* MINERAL spath satiné *m*
satnav *n (satellite navigator)* NAUT satnav *m (appareil de navigation par satellites)*
Satstream: ~ **circuit** *n* TELECOM circuit à haut débit par satellite *m*
saturable: ~ **reactor** *n* ELEC ENG inductance saturable *f*, PHYS amplificateur magnétique *m*, inductance saturable *f*, transducteur *m*; ~ **transformer** *n* ELEC ENG transformateur saturable *m*, transformateur à fer saturé *m*
saturant *n* CHEM produit imprégnant *m*
saturate *adj* CHEM saturé
saturated[1] *adj* CHEM *solution, compound*, CINEMAT saturé, PAPER TECH saturé d'eau, REFRIG saturé
saturated:[2] ~ **air** *n* METEO, REFRIG air saturé *m*; ~ **boiling** *n* NUCLEAR ébullition saturée *f*, ébullition nucléée saturée *f*; ~ **core** *n* ELEC ENG noyau saturé *m*; ~ **diving** *n* PETR plongée à saturation *f*; ~ **hydrocarbon** *n* PETR TECH hydrocarbure saturé *m*; ~ **layer** *n* METEO couche saturée *f*; ~ **logic** *n* ELECTRON logique saturée *f*; ~ **mode** *n* ELECTRON mode saturé *m*; ~ **polyester** *n* P&R polyester saturé *m*; ~ **soil** *n* COAL TECH sol saturé d'eau *m*; ~ **solution** *n* PETR solution saturée *f*; ~ **steam** *n* HEAT ENG vapeur saturée *f*, HEATING vapeur humide *f*, THERMOD vapeur saturée *f*; ~ **steam-cooled heater** *n* NUCLEAR réacteur refroidi à vapeur saturée *m*; ~ **toroidal transformer** *n* ELEC ENG transformateur toroïdal à fer saturé *m*; ~ **transformer** *n* ELEC ENG transformateur saturé *m*; ~ **transistor** *n* ELECTRON transistor saturé *m*; ~ **vapor** *n* (AmE) *see saturated vapour*; ~ **vapor pressure** *n* (AmE) *see saturated vapour pressure*; ~ **vapour** *n* (BrE) PHYS vapeur saturée *f*; ~ **vapour pressure** *n* (BrE) PHYS pression de la vapeur saturante *f*
saturating: ~ **signal** *n* ELECTRON signal saturant *m*
saturation *n* CHEM, COMP *transistor*, DP, ELEC *magnetism*, ELEC ENG, ELECTRON, METEO, NUCLEAR *of irradiated element* saturation *f*, PAPER TECH imprégnation *f*, PHYS, REFRIG, TV saturation *f*; ~ **back-scattering correction** *n* NUCLEAR correction pour la rétrodiffusion saturée *f*; ~ **banding** *n* TV bandes de saturation *f pl*, saturation striée *f*; ~ **characteristics** *n pl* RAD PHYS *in laser cavity* caractéristiques de saturation *f pl*; ~ **conditions** *n pl* ELEC ENG régime de saturation *m*; ~ **current** *n* ELECTRON, PHYS courant de saturation *m*; ~ **deficit** *n* METEO déficit à saturation *m*; ~ **dive** *n* OCEANOG plongée à saturation *f*; ~ **diver** *n* PETR

TECH plongeur à saturation *m*; ~ **diving** *n* OCEANOG, PETR TECH plongée à saturation *f*; ~ **hardening** *n* METALL durcissement par saturation *m*; ~ **induction** *n* ELEC ENG induction à saturation *f*; ~ **level** *n* RECORDING niveau de saturation *m*; ~ **magnetization** *n* ELEC ENG aimantation à saturation *f*; ~ **output power** *n* ELECTRON puissance de sortie à la saturation *f*; ~ **output state** *n* ELECTRON état de sortie à la saturation *m*; ~ **point** *n* SPACE *communications* point de saturation *m*; ~ **region** *n* ELECTRON domaine de saturation *m*; ~ **temperature** *n* REFRIG température de saturation *f*; ~ **voltage** *n* ELEC ENG tension de saturation *f*

Saturn's: ~ **rings** *n pl* ASTRON anneaux de Saturne *m pl*; ~ **shepherd satellites** *n pl* ASTRON satellites bergers de Saturne *m pl*

saucer: ~ **head screw** *n* MECH ENG vis à tête bombée *f*

saussurite *n* PETR jade de Saussure *m*, saussurite *f*

save[1] *n* COMP, DP sauvegarde *f*

save[2] *vt* COMP sauvegarder, sauver, DP sauvegarder, PAPER TECH récupérer

save-all *n* PAPER TECH ramasse-pâte *m*; ~ **tray** *n* PAPER TECH bacholle *f*

saw[1] *n* MECH *tools*, MECH ENG scie *f*; ~ **arbor** *n* (AmE), ~ **arbour** *n* (BrE) MECH ENG arbre porte-scie *m*; ~ **bench** *n* CONST établi à scier *m*; ~ **blade** *n* MECH ENG feuille de scie *f*, lame de scie *f*; ~ **clamp** *n* MECH ENG entaille à affûter les scies *f*, mâchoire à ressort *f*; ~ **cut** *n* CONST trait de scie *m*; ~ **file** *n* MECH ENG lime d'affûtage des scies *f*, lime à scies *f*; ~ **fly** *n* FOOD TECH *phytopathology* mouche à scie *f*, tenthrède *f*; ~ **frame** *n* MECH ENG porte-scie *m*; ~ **guide** *n* MECH ENG guide-lame *m*; ~ **kerf** *n* MECH ENG trait de scie *m*; ~ **log** *n* CONST bille *f*; ~ **pulley** *n* MECH ENG *of band sawing machine* poulie porte-lame *f*, volant porte-lame *m*; ~ **set** *n* MECH ENG tourne-à-gauche pour donner la voie aux scies *m*; ~ **timber** *n* CONST bois de sciage *m*, sciage *m*; ~ **with teeth** *n* MECH ENG scie à dents *f*

saw[2] *vt* MECH scier

SAW[1] *abbr (surface acoustic wave)* ELECTRON, TELECOM onde acoustique de surface *f*

SAW:[2] ~ **compression filter** *n* ELECTRON filtre compresseur d'impulsions à ondes accoustiques de surface *m*; ~ **delay line** *n* ELECTRON ligne à retard à ondes accoustiques de surface *f*; ~ **device** *n* ELECTRON, TELECOM dispositif à ondes acoustiques de surface *m*; ~ **expansion filter** *n* ELECTRON filtre élargisseur d'impulsions à ondes acoustiques de surface *m*; ~ **filter** *n* ELECTRON filtre à ondes acoustiques de surface *m*; ~ **filtering** *n* ELECTRON filtrage par filtre à ondes acoustiques de surface *m*

sawbuck *n* CONST chevalet de scieur *m*, chèvre *f*

sawdust *n* CONST bran de scie *m*, sciure *f*, sciure de bois *f*

sawhorse *n* CONST chevalet de scieur *m*, chèvre *f*

sawing *n* CONST débitage *m*, sciage *m*; ~ **list** *n* PROD ENG liste de découpe *f*, liste de sciage *f*; ~ **machine** *n* CONST machine à scier *f*, MECH ENG machine à scier *f*, scie mécanique *f*; ~ **out** *n* C&G sciage *m*

sawmill *n* CONST moulin à scie *m*, scierie *f*, MINING scierie *f*

sawn-in: ~ **back** *n* PRINT dos cousu *m*

saw-sharpening: ~ **machine** *n* MECH ENG machine à affûter *f*

sawtooth: ~ **current** *n* TV courant en dents de scie *m*; ~ **generator** *n* TV générateur de dents de scie *m*; ~ **oscillation** *n* ELEC oscillation en dent de scie *f*; ~ **oscillator** *n* RECORDING oscillateur en dent de scie *m*; ~ **roof** *n*

CONST comble en dent de scie *m*, comble-shed *m*, shed *m*; ~ **signals** *n pl* RAD PHYS *electronic* signaux en dents de scie *m pl*; ~ **voltage** *n* ELEC ENG, PHYS tension en dents de scie *f*; ~ **waveform** *n* ELEC ENG signal en dents de scie *m*

Sb *(stibium)* CHEM Sb *(antimoine)*

SBA *abbr (slurry-blasting agent)* MINING bouillie explosive *f*, explosif de chargement *m*, explosif en bouillie *m*

S-band *n* ELECTRON bande S *f*; ~ **diode** *n* ELECTRON diode en bande S *f*

SBM *abbr (single buoy mooring)* PETR TECH amarrage à point unique *m*

SBST *abbr (single bituminous surface treatment)* CONST revêtement monocouche *m*

Sc *(scandium)* CHEM Sc *(scandium)*

SC: ~ **paper** *n* PRINT papier satiné *m*

scab *n* FOOD TECH *phytopathology* tavelure *f*, PROD ENG *founding* balèvre *f*, dartre *f*

scabbard *n* MILIT fourreau *m*

scaffold *n* CONST échafaud *m*, échafaudage *m*; ~ **board** *n* CONST planche d'échafaud *f*, plat-bord *m*, plateau *m*; ~ **pole** *n* CONST baliveau *m*, perche *f*, échasse d'échafaud *f*, écoperche *f*

scaffolding *n* CONST, SAFETY échafaudage *m*; ~ **protective nets** *n pl* SAFETY filets de protection d'échafaudage *m pl*

scalar[1] *adj* COMP, DP, MATH scalaire

scalar[2] *n* MATH, PHYS scalaire *m*; ~ **measurement** *n* ELEC ENG mesure scalaire *f*; ~ **network analysis** *n* ELEC ENG analyse scalaire des réseaux *f*; ~ **network analyzer** *n* ELEC ENG analyseur de réseaux scalaire *m*, analyseur scalaire *m*; ~ **potential** *n* ELEC ENG, PHYS potentiel scalaire *m*; ~ **product** *n* PHYS produit scalaire *m*; ~ **resistor** *n* ELEC ENG résistance de mise à l'échelle *f*; ~ **type** *n* COMP, DP type scalaire *m*

scald[1] *n* FOOD TECH, THERMOD échaudure *f*; ~ **mark**[1] FOOD TECH brunissure *f*

scald[2] *vt* FOOD TECH échauder, THERMOD ébouillanter, échauder

scald[3] *vi* SAFETY s'ébouillanter

scalded *adj* THERMOD échaudé

scalding *adj* THERMOD bouillant, brûlant

scale[1] *n* ACOUSTICS *of frequencies* gamme *f*, COMP, CONST *of drawing, plan,* DP échelle *f*, DETERGENTS tartre *m*, ELEC cadran *m*, échelle *f*, GEOM *ruler* graduation *f*, échelle *f*, MECH *materials* calamine *f*, MECH ENG *for weighing, measuring* bassin *m*, plat *m*, plateau de balance *m*, METR échelle *f*, *for weighing* balance *f*, *weighing machine* bascule *f*, PRINT échelle *f*, PROD ENG *flake, exfoliation* écaille *f*, *in boilers* calcin *m*, crasses des chaudières *f pl*, dépôts *m pl*, incrustation *f*, tartre *m*, *iron oxide coating* battitures *f pl*, martelures *f pl*, paille *f*, scories de forge *f pl*, *on castings* balèvre *f*, barbure *f*; ~ **beam** *n* MECH ENG fléau de balance *m*, verge de balance *f*; ~ **of charges** *n* CONST barème *m*; ~ **dial** *n* CINEMAT cadran gradué *m*; ~ **division** *n* ELEC trait du cadran *m*; ~ **drawing** *n* GEOM dessin à l'échelle *m*; ~ **factor** *n* COMP facteur de cadrage *m*, DP facteur d'échelle *m*, échelle *f*; ~ **formation** *n* WATER SUPP entartrage *m*; ~ **illumination** *n* NAUT *radar* éclairage de l'échelle *m*; ~ **of image** *n* PHOTO échelle de l'image *f*; ~ **inhibitor** *n* REFRIG *condensers, cooling towers* antitartrage *m*; ~ **interval** *n* METR valeur d'une division échelon *f*; ~ **length** *n* METR longueur d'échelle *f*; ~ **mark** *n* METR *numbered* graduation chiffrée *f*, *unnumbered* repère *m*; ~ **model** *n* CINEMAT maquette à l'échelle *f*, modèle réduit *m*, GEOM modèle réduit *m*, NAUT *of ship, boat* maquette *f*, modèle réduit *m*; ~ **numbering** *n* METR chiffraison d'une échelle *f*; ~ **pan** *n* MECH ENG bassin *m*, plat *m*, plateau de balance *m*; ~ **paper** *n* PAPER TECH papier quadrillé *m*; ~ **of radial wavefunctions** *n* RAD PHYS échelle des fonctions d'ondes radiales *f*; ~ **range** *n* METR étendue d'échelle *f*; ~ **solvent** *n* HEATING, RAIL désincrustant *m*; ~ **spacing** *n* METR longueur d'une division *f*; ~ **switch** *n* ELEC commutateur des zones de mesure *m*, commutateur du champ de mesure *m*; ~ **trap** *n* REFRIG séparateur d'impuretés *m*

scale² *vt* COMP, DP mettre à l'échelle, MECH ENG *spring* faire la tare d'un ressort, tarer, PROD ENG entartrer, incruster

scale³ *vti* DP changer d'échelle

scalene: ~ **cone** *n* GEOM cône scalène *m*; ~ **triangle** *n* GEOM triangle scalène *m*

scaler *n* ELECTRON circuit diviseur *m*, échelle de comptage *f*

scales *n pl* LAB EQUIP *balance* trébuchet ordinaire *m*, MECH ENG *balance* balance *f*, *weighing machine* bascule *f*

Scales *n pl* ASTRON *constellation* Balance *f*

scaling *n* COMP, DP mise à l'échelle *f*, CONST *closing* bouchage *m*, obturation *f*, scellage *m*, écaillage *m*, PROD ENG étalonnage *m*, *boilers* désincrustation *f*, piquage *m*, *flaking* écaillage *m*, écaillement *m*, PROP MAT écaillage *m*; ~ **bar** *n* MINING barre de mineur *f*, barre à mine *f*; ~ **circuit** *n* ELECTRON circuit diviseur *m*; ~ **factor** *n* ELECTRON facteur d'échelle *m*; ~ **hammer** *n* PROD ENG marteau de piquage *m*, marteau pour piquer les chaudières *m*, marteau à piquer *m*; ~ **a spring** *n* METR tarage d'un ressort *m*; ~ **value** *n* PROD ENG valeur d'étalonnage *f*

scallop *n* TV feston *m*; ~ **culture** *n* OCEANOG pectiniculture *f*

scalloped: ~ **bevel** *n* C&G biseau écailles *m*; ~ **rail** *n* RAIL rail échancré *m*

scalloping *n* TV festonnage *m*

scalpel *n* LAB EQUIP bistouri *m*; ~ **blade** *n* LAB EQUIP lame de bistouri *f*

scalping *n* COAL TECH précriblage *m*; ~ **screen** *n* COAL TECH crible scalpeur *m*

scan¹ *n* AERONAUT balayage *m*, COMP balayage *m*, numérisation *f*, DP balayage *m*, PETR examen périodique *m*, TV analyse *f*, exploration *f*, WAVE PHYS *medical* échographie *f*; ~ **burn** *n* TV brûlure de balayage *f*; ~ **converter** *n* ELECTRON convertisseur de balayage *m*; ~ **platform** *n* SPACE *spacecraft* plate-forme d'exploration *f*; ~ **rate** *n* COMP vitesse de numérisation *f*; ~ **registration** *n* TV alignement des signaux chromatiques *m*; ~ **rings** *n pl* TV suroscillation en début de ligne *f*; ~ **time** *n* PROD ENG temps de scrutation *m*

scan² *vt* COMP balayer, numériser, DP balayer, scannériser, PRINT balayer, PROD ENG scruter, TRANSP *radar* balayer, TV analyser, balayer, explorer, WAVE PHYS *radar* balayer

scandium *n (Sc)* CHEM scandium *m (Sc)*

scanner *n* COMP numériseur *m*, scanner *m*, DP numériseur *m*, scanner *m*, scanneur *m*, ELEC *switch* commutateur du point de mesure *m*, ELECTRON dispositif de balayage *m*, PRINT, RAD PHYS scanner *m*, TELECOM analyseur *m*, TV analyseur *m*, dispositif d'analyse *m*, dispositif d'exploration *m*, dispositif de balayage *m*, scanneur *m*, WAVE PHYS *medical* tomo-

densitomètre *m*; ~ **distributor** *n* TELECOM distributeur analyseur *m*; ~ **printer** *n* INSTRUMENT enregistreur analyseur *m*

scanning *n* AERONAUT balayage *m*, COMP balayage *m*, exploration *f*, numérisation *f*, DP balayage *m*, exploration *f*, ELECTRON, NAUT *radar*, PETR TECH, PHYS balayage *m*, RAD PHYS balayage *m*, scanographie *f*, SPACE balayage *m*, scannage *m*, TELECOM balayage *m*, TV analyse *f*, balayage *m*; ~ **area** *n* TV zone balayée *f*, zone d'analyse *f*; ~ **Auger microscopy** *n* NUCLEAR microscopie à balayage d'Auger *f*; ~ **beam** *n* ELECTRON faisceau de balayage *m*, TV faisceau analyseur *m*, faisceau explorateur *m*; ~ **coil** *n* TV bobine de balayage *f*; ~ **cycle** *n* TV cycle d'analyse *m*; ~ **device** *n* TV dispositif de balayage *m*; ~ **drum** *n* TV tambour de lecture *m*; ~ **electron beam** *n* ELECTRON faisceau d'électrons de balayage *m*; ~ **electron beam lithography** *n* ELECTRON gravure par faisceau d'électrons à balayage *f*; ~ **electron beam system** *n* ELECTRON graveur à faisceau dirigé *m*; ~ **electron microscope** *n* ELEC, ELECTRON, INSTRUMENT, LAB EQUIP, PHYS, RAD PHYS microscope électronique à balayage *m*; ~ **error** *n* TV balayage défectueux *m*; ~ **field** *n* TV champ d'analyse *m*; ~ **gap** *n* TV fente de lecture *f*; ~ **gate** *n* TV fente de lecture *f*; ~ **head** *n* PRINT tête de lecture *f*, TV tête chercheuse *f*; ~ **ion microscopy** *n* RAD PHYS scanographie microscopique aux ions *f*; ~ **laser beam** *n* OPT faisceau de lecture *m*; ~ **light beam** *n* RECORDING *for optical recording on film* faisceau lumineux *m*; ~ **line** *n* ELECTRON, SPACE ligne de balayage *f*, TV ligne active *f*; ~ **mirror electron microscope** *n* INSTRUMENT microscope électronique à balayage avec réflecteur *m*; ~ **printing** *n* CINEMAT tirage optique désanamorphosé recadré *m*; ~ **process** *n* TV procédé d'analyse *m*; ~ **rate** *n* AERONAUT *radar* cadence de balayage *f*, vitesse de balayage *f*, COMP, DP vitesse de balayage *f*; ~ **sequence** *n* PROD ENG séquence de scrutation *f*; ~ **slit** *n* RECORDING *for optical sound track on film* fenêtre d'exposition *f*; ~ **sonar** *n* OCEANOG sonar panoramique *m*, sonar à balayage *m*; ~ **spectrometer** *n* RAD PHYS spectromètre scanographique *m*; ~ **speed** *n* AERONAUT *radar* vitesse d'exploration *f*, vitesse de balayage *f*, COMP, DP, TV vitesse de balayage *f*; ~ **spot control** *n* TV réglage du spot lumineux *m*; ~ **standard** *n* TV norme de balayage *f*; ~ **switch** *n* ELEC ENG commutateur cyclique mécanique *m*, scrutateur mécanique *m*; ~ **yoke** *n* TV culasse de balayage *f*

scantling *n* CONST *dimensions* équarrissage *m*

scantlings *n pl* NAUT *boatbuilding* échantillonnage *m*

scapolite *n* MINERAL scapolite *f*

scar *n* GEOL niche d'arrachement *f*

scarf *n* CONST *carpentry* assemblage à enture *m*, enture *f*, PROD ENG *welding* amorce *f*; ~ **joint** *n* CONST *carpentry* assemblage à enture *m*, enture *f*; ~ **jointing** *n* CONST assemblage à enture *m*, enture *f*; ~ **weld** *n* PROD ENG soudure par amorces *f*, soudure à chaude portée *f*, soudure à recouvrement *f*; ~ **welding** *n* PROD ENG soudure par amorces *f*, soudure à chaude portée *f*, soudure à recouvrement *f*

scarfing *n* C&G embavurage *m*, PROD ENG *welding* amorçage *m*

scarification *n* CONST *public works* scarification *f*

scarifier *n* CONST, TRANSP scarificateur *m*

scarify *vt* CONST décaper, scarifier

scarlet: ~ **lake** *n* COLOURS laque écarlate *f*

scarp *n* OCEANOG talus *m*

scatter n SPACE communications diffusion f; ~ **load** n COMP affectation diffuse de la mémoire f, DP affectation aléatoire de la mémoire f; ~ **proof** n PRINT épreuve couleur progressive f; ~ **read** n COMP, DP lecture avec éclatement f

scatterable: ~ **mines** n pl MILIT mines à éparpiller f pl

scattered: ~ **light** n PRINT lumière spéculaire f, RAD PHYS lumière diffusée f; ~ **neutron** n NUCLEAR neutron diffusé m; ~ **radiation** n RAD PHYS rayonnement diffusé m

scattering n ACOUSTICS diffraction f, CINEMAT diffusion f, dispersion f, CRYSTALL, ELECTRON diffusion f, FUELLESS dispersion f, GEOPHYS diffusion f, dispersion f, METALL dispersion f, NUCLEAR, OPT diffusion f, PETR diffraction f, diffusion f, dispersion f, RAD PHYS, SPACE, TELECOM diffusion f; ~ **angle** n PHYS angle de diffusion m; ~ **coefficient** n TELECOM coefficient de diffusion m; ~ **cross-section** n PHYS section efficace de diffusion f; ~ **factor** n CRYSTALL atomic facteur de diffusion m; ~ **foil** n NUCLEAR feuille de diffusion f; ~ **in** n NUCLEAR diffusion au dedans f; ~ **medium** n NUCLEAR substance diffusante f; ~ **meter** n OCEANOG diffusiomètre m

scatterometer n OCEANOG diffusiomètre m

scaur n GEOPHYS niche d'arrachement f

scavenge: ~ **pump** n PROD ENG pompe de balayage f; ~ **system** n PROD ENG système de balayage m

scavenger: ~ **cell** n COAL TECH cellule d'épuisement f

scavenging n CHEM épuration f, MECH, NAUT engine balayage m, NUCLEAR balayage m, entraînement m, interception f, PETR TECH, WATER SUPP balayage m

scaw n GEOPHYS niche d'arrachement f

SCC abbr (single-cotton-covered) ELEC guipé d'une couche coton

SCCP: ~ **method indicator** n TELECOM indicateur de méthode SSCS m

scenario n CINEMAT continuité dialoguée f, découpage technique m, scénario m, PROD ENG simulated planning scénario m, simulation f

scenery: ~ **lamp** n ELEC lighting projecteur pour les décors m

scene-to-scene: ~ **color grading** n (AmE), ~ **colour grading** n (BrE) CINEMAT étalonnage couleur plan par plan m

scent n CHEM odeur f, parfum m

schedule[1] n CINEMAT plan de tournage m, PROD ENG calendrier m, plan m, échéancier m, SPACE calendrier m, TV grille f; ~ **of machinery** n PROD ENG inventaire des machines m; ~ **speed** n TRANSP vitesse commerciale f

schedule[2] vt PROD ENG jalonner, ordonnancer, planifier, échéancer, TELECOM programmer

scheduled: ~ **flight** n AERONAUT vol régulier m; ~ **maintenance** n COMP maintenance périodique f, DP maintenance systématique f, NUCLEAR maintenance programmée f; ~ **operating time** n TELECOM durée de fonctionnement prévue f; ~ **receipt** n PROD ENG commande attendue f; ~ **reporting signal** n TELECOM signal de compte rendu attendu m; ~ **service** n CONST machinery entretien périodique m, TRANSP service régulier m

scheduler n COMP jobs programmateur m, programs ordonnanceur m, ordonnanceur de programmes m, DP jobs programmateur m, programmateur des travaux m, programs planificateur des programmes m

scheduling n TV programmation f, ~ **algorithm** n COMP, DP algorithme d'ordonnancement m; ~ **option** n PROD

ENG option de jalonnement f

scheelite n MINERAL scheelite f

scheelitine n MINERAL scheelitine f

scheererite n MINERAL scheererérite f

schefferite n MINERAL schefférite f

Schellbach: ~ **tubing** n C&G verre à graduations Schellbach m

schema n COMP schéma m, DP forme f

schematic: ~ **wiring diagram** n NUCLEAR plan de câblage m, schéma des circuits m

scheme n MECH ENG diagram dessin schématique m, schéma m; ~ **arch** n CONST curve arc surbaissé m, structure voûte surbaissée f

Schering: ~ **bridge** n ELEC ENG, PHYS pont Schering m

schiller: ~ **spar** n MINERAL bastite f

schistose adj GEOL schisteux

schistosity n GEOL schistosité f

schistous: ~ **clay** n C&G argile schisteuse f; ~ **coal** n COAL TECH charbon schisteux m

Schlieren: ~ **photography** n PHYS strioscopie f

Schlueter: ~ **motion equation** n NUCLEAR équation de mouvement de Schlueter f

Schmidt: ~ **number** n PHYS nombre de Schmidt m; ~ **system** n INSTRUMENT lentilles de Schmidt f pl; ~ **telescope** n ASTRON télescope de Schmidt m

Schmitt: ~ **trigger** n PHYS trigger de Schmitt m

Schnabel: ~ **car** n (AmE) (cf Schnabel wagon) RAIL vehicles wagon Schnabel m; ~ **wagon** n (BrE) (cf Schnabel car) RAIL wagon Schnabel m

school n OCEANOG banc m

schooner n NAUT goélette f

schorl n MINERAL schorl m

Schottel: ~ **propeller** n TRANSP hélice carénée f

Schottky: ~ **barrier** n ELECTRON, PHYS barrière de Schottky f; ~ **barrier detector diode** n ELECTRON diode de détection à barrière de Schottky f; ~ **barrier diode** n ELECTRON diode à barrière de Schottky f; ~ **barrier FET** n ELECTRON transistor à effet de champ à accès Schottky m; ~ **barrier mixer diode** n ELECTRON diode mélangeuse Schottky f; ~ **barrier rectifier diode** n ELECTRON diode de redressement Schottky f; ~ **bipolar integrated circuit** n ELECTRON circuit intégré bipolaire Schottky m; ~ **clamped transistor** n ELECTRON transistor Schottky m; ~ **clamping diode** n ELECTRON diode de limitation Schottky f; ~ **defect** n CRYSTALL défaut de Schottky m; ~ **device** n ELECTRON composant Schottky m; ~ **diode** n ELECTRON, PHYS diode Schottky f; ~ **effect** n ELECTRON effet Schottky m; ~ **noise** n PHYS bruit de grenaille m, effet de bruit Schottky m; ~ **TTL** n ELECTRON logique TTL Schottky f

schreibersite n MINERAL schreibersite f

Schrödinger: ~ **equation** n PHYS équation de Schrödinger f

Schüfftan: ~ **process** n CINEMAT procédé Schüfftan m

schuilingite n NUCLEAR schuilingite f

schwartzembergite n MINERAL schwarzembergite f

Schwarzschild: ~ **radius** n PHYS rayon de Schwarzschild m

schwatzite n MINERAL schwatzite f

science: ~ **of heat** n THERMOD thermique f

scientific[1] adj CHEM scientifique

scientific:[2] ~ **language** n COMP langage scientifique m; ~ **notation** n MATH notation en puissance dix f

scintillation n ASTRON, PHYS, SPACE communications, TELECOM scintillation f, TEXTILES point de couleur m; ~ **coincidence spectrometer** n NUCLEAR spectromètre à coïncidence à scintillation *m*; ~ **counter** *n* ASTRON, PHYS, RAD PHYS compteur à scintillation *m*; ~ **noise** *n* SPACE communications bruit de scintillation *m*; ~ **spectrometer** *n* RAD PHYS spectromètre à scintillation *m*

scintillator *n* ASTRON, RAD PHYS scintillateur *m*

scissor: ~ **crossing** *n* RAIL bretelle *f*, traversée diagonale *f*; ~ **joint** *n* MECH ENG tools maillure superposée *f*

scissoring *n* COMP découpage *m*, DP détourage *m*

scissors *n pl* MECH ENG ciseaux *m pl*

scleroclase *n* MINERAL scléroclase *f*

sclerometer *n* PHYS scléromètre *m*

scleroprotein *n* FOOD TECH scléroprotéine *f*

SCN abbr (specification change notice) TRANSP spécification de changement notifié *f*

scolecite *n* MINERAL scolécite *f*

scoop *n* CINEMAT projecteur d'ambiance *m*, LAB EQUIP pelle *f*, MAR POLL écope *f*, POLLUTION benne de ramassage *f*; ~ **dump car** *n* (AmE) (cf scoop dump wagon) TRANSP wagon basculant avec bec *m*; ~ **dump wagon** *n* (BrE) (cf scoop dump car) TRANSP wagon basculant avec bec *m*; ~ **net** *n* OCEANOG balance *f*, haveneau *m*, épuisette *f*; ~ **tipper** *n* RAIL, TRANSP *l* wagon basculant avec bec *m*; ~ **water-wheel** *n* WATER SUPP tympan *m*; ~ **wheel** *n* WATER SUPP tympan *m*; ~ **wheel elevator** *n* TRANSP roue élévatrice à godets *f*; ~ **wheel feeder** *n* TRANSP roue élévatrice à godets *f*

scooter *n* TRANSP scooter *m*

scope *n* COMP, DP portée *f*, MECH ENG of standard domaine d'application *m*, PATENTS étendue *f*, of claim portée *f*, PROD ENG of warranty modalités *f pl*, TEXTILES possibilités d'armurage *f pl*, TV sujet *m*

scorch[1] *n* P&R vulcanization fixation *f*, grillage *m*, vulcanisation *f*

scorch[2] *vt* THERMOD dessécher

scorched *adj* THERMOD desséché

scorching: ~ **tendency** *n* P&R vulcanization tendance au grillage *f*

scorchy *adj* P&R vulcanization précoce

score[1] *n* PRINT rainer *m*, RECORDING music partition *f*

score[2] *vt* PRINT tracer, tracer au couteau

score:[3] ~ **a hit** *vi* MILIT on target toucher le but

scored[1] *adj* PAPER TECH rainé

scored:[2] ~ **pulley** *n* MECH ENG poulie à gorge *f*

scoria *n* GEOL scorie *f*

scoring *n* C&G rayage *m*, PRINT marquage *m*, rainage *m*; ~ **session** *n* RECORDING séance d'enregistrement de musique *f*

scorodite *n* MINERAL scorodite *f*

scorpion: ~ **dolly** *n* CINEMAT chariot de travelling à écartement variable *m*

Scorpion: the ~ *n* ASTRON Scorpion *m*

Scorpius *n* ASTRON Scorpion *m*

scotch *n* MECH ENG stopping block cale *f*

scotching *n* MECH ENG calage *m*

scotchlight: ~ **signal** *n* RAIL signal réflectorisé *m*

Scott: ~ **connection** *n* ELEC transformer montage Scott *m*

scour[1] *n* FUELLESS dams, HYDROL wash of water affouillement *m*, WATER SUPP chasse *f*, chasse d'eau *f*

scour[2] *vt* DETERGENTS décrasser, lessiver, récurer, FUELLESS, HYDROL affouiller, PROD ENG clean décaper, dégraisser, WATER SUPP rincer

scour-and-fill *n* GEOL ravinement et remblayage *m*

scouring *n* OCEANOG affouillement *m*, chasse *f*, PAPER TECH dégraissage d'un feutre *m*, PETR affouillement

m, PROD ENG cleaning décapage *m*, dégraissage *m*, TEXTILES lavage à fond *m*, WATER SUPP chasse *f*, chasse d'eau *f*; ~ **agent** *n* CHEM dégraissant *m*; ~ **basin** *n* OCEANOG bassin de chasse *m*; ~ **liquid** *n* DETERGENTS lessive *f*; ~ **liquor** *n* DETERGENTS lessive *f*; ~ **powder** *n* DETERGENTS poudre à récurer *f*; ~ **soap** *n* DETERGENTS savon dégraisseur *m*; ~ **solution** *n* DETERGENTS liquide laveur *m*

SCPC abbr (single-channel per carrier) SPACE porteuse monovoie *f*, système à porteuse monovoie *m*, TELECOM porteuse monovoie *f*

SCR[1] abbr (silicon-controlled rectifier) ELEC ENG redresseur au silicium commandé *m*, thyristor au silicium *m*, PHYS redresseur au silicium commandé *m*, TELECOM thyristor au silicium *m*

SCR:[2] ~ **amplifier** *n* ELECTRON amplificateur à thyristor *m*; ~ **converter** *n* ELEC ENG convertisseur à thyristor *m*; ~ **crosspoint** *n* TELECOM point de connexion à thyristor *m*; ~ **preregulation** *n* ELEC ENG prérégulation par thyristors *f*; ~ **preregulator** *n* ELEC ENG prérégulateur à thyristors *m*; ~ **regulation** *n* ELEC ENG régulation par thyristors *f*; ~ **regulator** *n* ELEC ENG régulateur à thyristors *m*; ~ **trimmer transformer** *n* ELEC ENG transformateur de déclenchement de thyristor *m*

scram: ~ **rod** *n* NUCLEAR barre de compensation et d'arrêt d'urgence *f*, barre de compensation-sécurité *f*

scramble *vt* TELECOM embrouiller, TV coder, crypter, embrouiller

scrambler *n* SPACE communications, TELECOM embrouilleur *m*, TRANSP vélomoteur tout-terrain *m*, TV embrouilleur *m*; ~ **telephone** *n* MILIT brouilleur *m*

scrambling *n* MILIT brouillage *m*, TELECOM, TV of signal embrouillage *m*; ~ **control** *n* TELECOM gestion du brouillage *f*; ~ **motor cycle** *n* TRANSP vélomoteur tout-terrain *m*

scrammed: ~ **rod** *n* NUCLEAR barre d'arrêt d'urgence injectée *f*

scrap[1] *n* C&G déchets *m pl*, COAL TECH, MECH materials, METALL ferraille *f*, PROD ENG copeau *m*, mise au pilon *f*, mise au riblon *f*, mise à la ferraille *f*, rebut *m*, riblon *m*, sous-produit *m*, fragment *m*, morceau *m*, from foundry bocage *m*, débris de fonte *m*, déchets de fonderie *m pl*, scraps de fonderie *m pl*, vieilles fontes *f pl*, metal débris *m*, déchet *m*, déchets *m pl*, mitraille *f*, scraps *m pl*, débris *m*, déchet *m*, déchets *m pl*, mitraille *f*, scraps *m pl*, PROP MAT ferraille *f*; ~ **factor** *n* PROD ENG pourcentage de rebut *m*, taux de rebut *m*; ~ **iron** *n* PROD ENG débris de fer *m*, ferraille *f*, mitraille *f*, morceaux de ferraille *m pl*; ~ **material** *n* PACKAGING matériel rebuté *m*; ~ **metal** *n* PROD ENG débris métallique *m*, déchets métalliques *m pl*; ~ **process** *n* PROD ENG steel manufacture méthode par dilution *f*, système à chutes *m*; ~ **quantity** *n* PROD ENG quantité rebutée *f*; ~ **return** *n* C&G retour des déchets *m*; ~ **yard** *n* PROD ENG parc à ferraille *m*

scrap[2] *vt* MECH mettre à la ferraille, PROD ENG mettre au rebut

scrape *vt* CONST décaper, MAR POLL décaper, gratter, racler

scraped: ~ **surface freezer** *n* REFRIG congélateur à racleur *m*

scraper *n* COAL TECH couteau *m*, racleur *m*, CONST racloir *m*, scraper *m*, cabinet grattoir *m*, earthmoving décapeuse *f*, FOOD TECH racloir *m*, MAR POLL hand-held curette *f*, décapeuse *f*, gratteur *m*, grattoir *m*, raclette *f*, racleur *m*, MECH tool grattoir *m*, MECH ENG curette *f*,

grattoir *m*, raclette *f*, rognoir *m*, *tool* scraper *m*, MI-
NING *for cleaning out shothole* curette *f*, PAPER TECH
racloir *m*, PETR piston racleur *m*; ~ **board** *n* PRINT
papier procédé *m*; ~ **chain assembly** *n* MINING ensemble de chaînes à raclette *m*; ~ **chain conveyor** *n* MINING
convoyeur à raclette *m*; ~ **conveyor** *n* PROD ENG
convoyeur à palettes *m*, transporteur à palettes *m*,
transporteuse à palettes *f*

scraping *n* PROD ENG curage *m*, grattage *m*, raclage *m*; ~
plane *n* CONST rabot-racloir *m*; ~ **tools** *n pl* MINING
outils de curage *m pl*

scrapping: ~ **factor** *n* PROD ENG coefficient d'attrition *m*,
coefficient de majoration *m*, coefficient de rebut *m*,
taux de rebut *m*

scratch[1] *n* C&G griffe *f*, CINEMAT, P&R rayure *f*, PAPER
TECH strie *f*, PRINT brouillon *m*, griffure *f*, rayure *f*,
égratignure *f*, RECORDING accroc *m*; ~ **awl** *n* CONST
aiguille à tracer *f*, tracelet *m*, traceret *m*, traçoir *m*; ~
brush *n* CONST gratte-brosse *f*; ~ **file** *n* COMP, DP fichier
de travail *m*; ~ **filter** *n* RECORDING filtre antibruit *m*; ~
gage *n* (AmE), ~ **gauge** *n* (BrE) CONST trusquin de
côté *m*, trusquin à main *m*; ~ **pad** *n* COMP, DP bloc-
notes *m*; ~ **pad memory** *n* COMP mémoire de travail *f*; ~
resistance *n* P&R *surface property* résistance aux
rayures *f*; ~ **tape** *n* COMP, DP bande de manoeuvre *f*

scratch[2] *vt* TEXTILES charder

scratched: ~ **mold** *n* (AmE), ~ **mould** *n* (BrE) C&G moule
rayé *m*

scratching *n* TEXTILES chardage *m*

scree *n* GEOL éboulis *m*, GEOPHYS cailloutis *m*, talus *m*

screed: ~ **heater** *n* CONST chauffe-règle *m*; ~ **height** *n*
CONST hauteur de la règle *f*, profondeur de réglage *f*; ~
profile *n* CONST profil de règle *m*

screen[1] *n* CINEMAT trame *f*, écran *m*, COAL TECH crible *m*,
tamis *m*, COMP *display* écran *m*, *protection* blindage *m*,
CONST *for sieving aggregate* crible *m*, DP *display* écran
m, *protection* blindage *m*, ELECTRON écran *m*, GEOL
panneau *m*, HYDROL crible *m*, grille *f*, tamis *m*, MECH
grillage *m*, tamis *m*, écran *m*, MINING *of ore stamp*
tamis *m*, PAPER TECH classeur *m*, tamis *m*, PHYS écran
m, PRINT trame *f*, trame simili *f*, PROD ENG *safety* volet
m, *sieve* claie *f*, crible *m*, grille *f*, RECYCLING tamis *m*,
SAFETY volet *m*, SPACE écran *m*, TV écran *m*, *for isolating electronic components* blindage *m*; ~ **analysis** *n*
(AmE) *(cf granulometric analysis)* C&G, COAL TECH
analyse granulométrique *f*; ~ **angle** *n* PRINT angle de
trame *m*; ~ **bar** *n* CONST *rolled section* fer à barreaux de
grille *m*; ~ **brightness** *n* CINEMAT luminosité de l'écran
f; ~ **count** *n* PRINT décompte des lignes de trame *f*,
linéature *f*; ~ **curve** *n* PRINT courbe des trames *f*; ~
display *n* COMP affichage sur écran *m*; ~ **dump** *n* COMP
copie d'écran *f*, vidage d'écran *m*, DP copie d'écran *f*,
vidage d'écran *m*; ~ **effect** *n* TELECOM effet d'écran *m*; ~
factor *n* NUCLEAR facteur d'écran *m*; ~ **grid** *n* ELECTRON
grille-écran *f*; ~ **grid tube** *n* ELECTRON tube à grille-écran *m*; ~ **image** *n* COMP copie sur écran *f*, DP image
d'écran *f*; ~ **mask** *n* CINEMAT cache écran *m*; ~
painter *n* COMP programme de coloriage de l'écran *m*, DP
unité de coloriage de l'écran *f*; ~ **plate** *n* COAL TECH tôle
de criblage *f*, NUCLEAR tôle perforée *f*; ~ **printing** *n* C&G
impression au tamis de soie *f* (Bel), impression à
l'écran *f* (Fra); ~ **printing machine** *n* PACKAGING machine sérigraphique *f*; ~ **processing** *n* PRINT
traitement de l'écran *m*; ~ **ratio** *n* CINEMAT proportions
de l'écran *f pl*; ~ **resolution** *n* PRINT définition de
l'écran *f*, résolution de l'écran *f*; ~ **roller** *n* PRINT

rouleau tramé *m*; ~ **ruling** *n* PRINT définition de l'écran
f, linéature *f*; ~ **shape** *n* PRINT forme de l'alvéole du
rouleau anilox *f*; ~ **terminal** *n* TELECOM terminal à
écran *m*; ~ **test** *n* CINEMAT bout d'essai *m*, essai filmé
m; ~ **time** *n* CINEMAT durée de projection *f*; ~ **tint** *n*
PRINT fond tramé régulier *m*; ~ **varnish** *n* COATINGS
vernis pour sérigraphie *m*; ~ **washer** *n* PRINT dispositif
de lavage des tamis *m*

screen[2] *vt* CHEM tamiser, CINEMAT projeter, visionner,
COAL TECH cribler, CONST cribler, tamiser, MAR POLL
cribler, dégriller, filtrer, sasser, tamiser

screen-based *adj* COMP, DP à écran

screen-displayed *adj* PRINT qui s'affiche à l'écran

screened: ~ **aerial** *n* TV antenne blindée *f*; ~ **cable** *n*
COMP, ELEC câble blindé *m*, PHYS câble blindé *m*, câble
protégé *m*; ~ **coal** *n* COAL TECH charbon criblé *m*

screener *n* PAPER TECH épurateur *m*

screening *n* CONST criblage *m*, tamisage *m*, ELEC *electromagnetic field* écran *m*, MAR POLL criblage *m*,
dégrillage *m*, filtrage *m*, sassement *m*, tamisage *m*,
NUCLEAR tamisage *m*, PAPER TECH épuration *f*, PHYS
shielding blindage *m*, PROD ENG criblage *m*, passage au
crible *m*, passage à la claie *m*, RAD PHYS blindage *m*,
SPACE trame *f*, TV *of cable* blindage *m*, gainage *m*,
écrantage *m*; ~ **booth** *n* CINEMAT cabine de projection
f; ~ **box** *n* PROD ENG caisse de criblage *f*; ~ **constant** *n*
NUCLEAR constante d'effet d'écran *f*; ~ **effect** *n* ELEC
effet d'écran *m*; ~ **efficiency** *n* COAL TECH efficacité de
criblage *f*; ~ **indicator** *n (SI)* TELECOM indicateur de
contrôle *m*; ~ **inspection** *n* CONTROL, QUALITY
contrôle sélectif *m*; ~ **mesh** *n* COAL TECH maille de
tamisage *f*; ~ **number** *n* NUCLEAR constante d'effet
d'écran *f*; ~ **plant** *n* COAL TECH installation de criblage
f; ~ **room** *n* CINEMAT salle de projection *f*, salle de
vision *f*; ~ **surface** *n* COAL TECH surface criblante *f*; ~
test *n* QUALITY essai de sélection *m*, essai sélectif *m*,
SPACE essai de sélection *m*; ~ **time** *n* CINEMAT durée de
projection *f*

screenings *n pl* CHEM déchets de criblages *m pl*, COAL
TECH fins *m pl*, HYDROL détritus de criblage *m pl*,
PAPER TECH déchets d'épuration *m pl*

screenplay *n* CINEMAT découpage technique *m*, scénario *m*

screw[1] *n* MECH, MECH ENG vis *f*, NAUT hélice *f*, vis *f*, P&R
extruder, PAPER TECH, VEHICLES vis *f*; ~ **auger** *n* MECH
ENG tarière rubanée *f*, tarière torse *f*, tarière à double
spire *f*, tarière à tire-bouchon *f*, torse *f*; ~ **axis** *n*
CRYSTALL axe hélicoïdal *m*; ~ **base** *n* CINEMAT culot à
vis *m*, ELEC ENG *for lamps* douille à vis *f*; ~ **bear** *n* MECH
ENG poinçonneuse à main *f*, poinçonneuse à vis sim-
ple *f*; ~ **blank** *n* MECH ENG vis en blanc *f*; ~ **bolt** *n* MECH
ENG boulon à écrou *m*; ~ **box** *n* MECH ENG manchon à
vis *m*; ~ **brake** *n* MECH ENG, RAIL *vehicles*, VEHICLES
frein à vis *m*; ~ **brake with crank handle** *n* RAIL frein à
vis manivelle *m*; ~ **cap** *n* C&G capuchon vissé *m*, ELEC
ENG *of incandescent lamps* culot à vis *m*, PACKAGING
capsule à vis *f*; ~ **cap bottle** *n* PACKAGING bouteille
avec capsule à vis *f*; ~ **cap tooling** *n* MECH ENG outillage
pour couvercle fileté *m*; ~ **casing head** *n* MECH ENG tête
de tube à vis *f*; ~ **chuck** *n* MECH ENG mandrin à
queue-de-cochon *m*; ~ **clamp** *n* MECH ENG presse à vis
f; ~ **closure** *n* PACKAGING fermeture vissée *f*; ~ **compressor** *n* GAS TECH, MECH ENG compresseur à vis *m*; ~
contact *n* ELEC contact à vis *m*; ~ **conveyor** *n* MECH ENG
transporteur à vis *m*, PACKAGING transporteuse à vis
sans fin *f*, PAPER TECH transporteur à vis *m*, PROD ENG

convoyeur à vis sans fin *m*, transporteur à vis sans fin *m*, vis transporteuse *f*; ~ **coupling** *n* MECH ENG manchon à vis *m*; ~ **cutting** *n* MECH ENG filetage *m*; ~ **cutting lathe** *n* MECH ENG tour à fileter *m*; ~ **cutting reverse** *n* MECH ENG changement de marche pour fileter à droite et à gauche *m*; ~ **dislocation** *n* CRYSTALL, METALL, PROP MAT dislocation vis *f*; ~ **dog** *n* MECH ENG toc à vis *m*, *lathe* poupée à pompe *f*; ~ **drive** *n* P&R *extruder* entraînement de vis *m*; ~ **elevator** *n* CONST élévateur à vis sans fin *m*; ~ **extruder** *n* FOOD TECH *processing* extrudeur hélicoïdal *m*, extrudeur à vis *m*; ~ **eye** *n* CONST laceret *m*, piton *m*, piton à vis *m*; ~ **fan** *n* MINING vis pneumatique *f*; ~ **feed** *n* MECH ENG pression à vis *f*; ~ **ferrule** *n* MECH ENG manchon fileté *m*, manchon taraudé *m*; ~ **fixing** *n* MECH ENG fixation à vis *f*; ~ **gage** *n* (AmE), ~ **gauge** *n* (BrE) MECH ENG calibre de vérification des vis *m*, METR calibre fileté *m*; ~ **gear** *n* MECH ENG engrenage hélicoïdal *m*; ~ **gearing** *n* MECH ENG engrenage hélicoïdal *m*; ~ **hammer** *n* MECH ENG clé à marteau *f*; ~ **head** *n* MECH ENG tête de vis *f*; ~ **hook** *n* CONST crochet à vis *m*; ~ **jack** *n* MECH ENG vérin *m*, vérin à vis *m*; ~ **joint** *n* MECH ENG assemblage à vis *m*, joint à vis *m*; ~ **key** *n* MECH ENG clé à vis *f*; ~ **lid** *n* PACKAGING couvercle à vis *m*; ~ **lifting jack** *n* MECH ENG vérin *m*, vérin à vis *m*; ~ **locking device** *n* PACKAGING frein à vis *m*; ~ **lug** *n* PROD ENG cosse à vis *f*; ~ **machine** *n* MECH tour automatique *m*, tour à décolleter *m*, MECH ENG machine à tarauder *f*, taraudeuse *f*; ~ **mount** *n* CINEMAT monture à vis *f*; ~ **piece** *n* MECH ENG avisse *f*, pièce à vis *f*; ~ **pinch** *n* NUCLEAR striction hélicoïdale *f*; ~ **pitch** *n* MECH ENG pas de vis *m*; ~ **pitch gage** *n* (AmE), ~ **pitch gauge** *n* (BrE) MECH ENG jauge de pas *f*; ~ **plate** *n* MECH ENG filière *f*, filière plate *f*, filière simple *f*, filière à palette *f*, filière à truelle *f*, filière à cage *f*, filière à coussinets *f*, porte-filière *m*; ~ **plate stock** *n* MECH ENG porte-filière oblique *m*; ~ **plug** *n* CONST tampon à vis *m*; ~ **press** *n* MECH ENG, PAPER TECH presse à vis *f*; ~ **pulley** *n* CONST poulie de renvoi avec tige filetée *f*, renvoi avec tige filetée *m*; ~ **pump** *n* MAR POLL, PROD ENG pompe à vis *f*, TRANSP pompe hélice *f*, pompe à vis *f*; ~ **punching bear** *n* MECH ENG poinçonneuse à vis *f*, poinçonneuse à vis simple *f*; ~ **push starter** *n* AUTO démarreur à solénoïde *m*; ~ **reversing gear** *n* MECH ENG changement de marche à vis *m*; ~ **shoe** *n* CONST *for screw pile* sabot à vis *m*; ~ **socket** *n* MECH ENG douille filetée *f*, douille à vis *f*; ~ **stock** *n* MECH ENG filière *f*, filière à cage *f*, filière à coussinets *f*, porte-filière *m*; ~ **terminal** *n* CINEMAT, PROD ENG borne à vis *f*; ~ **thread** *n* MECH ENG filet de vis *m*, pas de vis *m*; ~ **thread gage** *n* (AmE), ~ **thread gauge** *n* (BrE) MECH ENG calibre de vérification des vis *m*, METR jauge pour filetage *f*; ~ **thread measuring cylinder** *n* METR cylindre de mesure de filetages *m*; ~ **thread profiles and tolerances** *n pl* MECH ENG profils et tolérances de filetage *m pl*; ~ **tightener** *n* MECH ENG tendeur à vis *m*; ~ **tool** *n* MECH ENG peigne *m*, peigne à fileter *m*; ~ **top** *n* PACKAGING couvercle à vis *m*; ~ **valve** *n* LAB EQUIP *fluids* robinet à vis *m*; ~ **wheel** *n* MECH ENG *gearing* roue hélicoïdale *f*; ~ **works** *n pl* PROD ENG visserie *f*; ~ **wrench** *n* MECH ENG clef à vis *f*, clé à molette *f*, clé à mâchoires mobiles *f*

screw[2] *vt* MECH visser, MECH ENG *fasten, press* serrer, visser, *thread, tap* fileter, tarauder

screw-and-socket: ~ **joint** *n* MECH ENG assemblage à enture à vis *m*

screw-down: ~ **cock** *n* CONST robinet à vis de pression

m; ~ **stopvalve** *n* CONST robinet d'arrêt à soupape *m*; ~ **valve** *n* CONST robinet à soupape *m*

screwdriver *n* MECH ENG, VEHICLES *tool* tournevis *m*; ~ **bit** *n* MECH ENG embout tournevis *m*, lame de tournevis pour vilebrequin *f*, tournevis au fût *m*, tournevis pour vilebrequin *m*; ~ **slot** *n* ELEC ENG fente tournevis *f*

screwed[1] *adj* MECH ENG, PROP MAT vissé

screwed:[2] ~ **and socketed bend** *n* MECH ENG *pipes* courbe filetée avec manchon *f*; ~ **fitting** *n* MECH ENG *pipes* raccord fileté *m*; ~ **hook** *n* SPRINGS boucle vissée dans les spires *f*, crochet vissé dans les spires *m*; ~ **joint** *n* NUCLEAR joint fileté *m*, raccord à vis *m*; ~ **pipe coupling** *n* MECH ENG raccord fileté pour tubes *m*; ~ **tip** *n* SPRINGS embout fileté vissé *m*

screw-head: ~ **file** *n* MECH ENG lime à dossière *f*, lime à fendre *f*, lime à losange *f*

screw-in: ~ **filter** *n* CINEMAT filtre à vis *m*

screwing *n* MECH ENG *fastening, pressing* serrage *m*, vissage *m*, *threading, tapping* filetage *m*, taraudage *m*, PETR TECH *pipe* vissage *m*; ~ **and tapping machine** *n* MECH ENG machine à tarauder *f*, taraudeuse *f*; ~ **chuck** *n* MECH ENG filière *f*, plateau porte-coussinets *m*, porte-coussinets *m*, porte-lunette *m*; ~ **device** *n* NUCLEAR *for drums* dispositif de vissage *m*; ~ **die** *n* MECH ENG coussinet *m*, filière *f*; ~ **head** *n* MECH ENG filière *f*, plateau porte-coussinets *m*, porte-coussinets *m*, porte-lunette *m*; ~ **in** *n* PETR TECH *pipes* vissage *m*; ~ **machine** *n* MECH ENG machine à tarauder *f*, taraudeuse *f*; ~ **up** *n* MECH ENG serrage *m*, vissage *m*, PETR TECH vissage *m*

screwing-out *n* PETR TECH *pipes* dévissage *m*

screw-on: ~ **lens cap** *n* PHOTO bouchon à vis *m*

screw-type: ~ **oil filter** *n* AUTO filtre à huile jetable *m*

scribe[1] *n* CINEMAT pointe sèche *f*; ~ **awl** *n* CONST *carpenter's* traceret *m*, traçoir *m*

scribe[2] *vti* CONST troussequiner, trusquiner

scriber *n* CONST *carpenter's* pointe de traçage *f*, traceret *m*, traçoir *m*, *of scribing block* pointe *f*, pointe de traçage *f*, ELECTRON *lasers* pointe à tracer *f*, MECH ENG *engineer's* aiguille à tracer *f*, pointe *f*, pointe à tracer *f*, *of centrebit* traçoir *m*

scribing *n* ELECTRON *with lasers* découpe *f*; ~ **awl** *n* CONST *carpenter's* traceret *m*, traçoir *m*; ~ **block** *n* MECH ENG *engineer's* troussequin *m*, trusquin *m*, trusquin à marbre *m*; ~ **gage** *n* (AmE), ~ **gauge** *n* (BrE) CONST *carpenter's* troussequin *m*, trusquin *m*, trusquin à pointe *m*; ~ **step** *n* ELECTRON étape de découpe *f*

scrim *n* CINEMAT diffuseur *m*, écran diffuseur *m*; ~ **screen** *n* TEXTILES canevas *m*

script *n* CINEMAT découpage technique *m*, scénario *m*, COMP, DP scénario *m*, PRINT scripte *f*; ~ **person** *n* CINEMAT secrétaire de plateau *m*; ~ **writer** *n* TV scénariste *m*

scroll:[1] ~ **bar** *n* COMP barre de défilement *f*, DP bande de défilement *f*; ~ **chuck** *n* MECH ENG mandrin à spirale *m*, plateau à rainures hélicoïdales *m*; ~ **clutch** *n* MECH ENG embrayage à enroulement *m*, embrayage à spirale *m*; ~ **saw** *n* MECH ENG sauteuse *f*, scie à chantourner *f*; ~ **shears** *n pl* MECH ENG *tool* cisailles chantourneuses *f pl*

scroll[2] *vi* COMP, DP défiler, faire défiler

scrolling *n* COMP, DP défilement *m*, PRINT défilement à l'écran *m*

scroop: ~ **finish** *n* COATINGS apprêt craquant *m*

SCR-regulated: ~ **power supply** *n* ELEC ENG alimentation à thyristors *f*

scrub: ~ **mark** *n* (BrE) *(cf rub)* C&G écrasure *f*

scrubber n CHEM TECH tour de lavage f, épurateur m, COAL TECH débourbeur m, laveur m, MINING laveur m, SPACE absorbeur-neutralisateur m; ~ **walls** n pl POLLUTION parois de séparateur f pl

scrubbing n CHEM TECH lavage m, épuration f, PETR TECH, POLLUTION lavage m, THERMOD gas lavage m, épuration f; ~ **soap** n DETERGENTS savon de récurage m

scuba n NAUT scaphandre autonome m; ~ **diving** n NAUT plongée sous-marine autonome f, PETR plongée autonome f; ~ **tank** n OCEANOG bloc-bouteilles m

scuff: ~ **mark** n C&G, TEXTILES éraflure f

scuffing n C&G éraflure f, PAPER TECH frottement m, TEXTILES éraflure f

scull[1] n C&G culot de poche m, NAUT aviron m, godille f, PROD ENG founding cul de poche m, fond de poche m

scull[2] vi NAUT godiller, ramer

Sculptor n ASTRON Atelier du Sculpteur m, Sculpteur m

scum n C&G drapeau m, CHEM mousse f, scorie f, écume f, COAL TECH, FOOD TECH, HYDROL écume f, PRINT mousse f, émulsion sale f; ~ **baffle** n HYDROL sewage pare-écume m

scumble n P&R paint peinture à faux bois f

scumming n PRINT émulsion sale f

scuppers n pl NAUT dalots m pl

scutcheon n (BrE) (cf escutcheon) CONST locksmithing entrée de serrure f, écusson m

scuttle vt NAUT ship saborder

Scutum n ASTRON Ecu m

SD abbr (signal distributor) TELECOM dégradation du signal f

SDH[1] abbr (synchronous digital hierarchy) TELECOM HNS (hiérarchie numérique synchrone)

SDH:[2] ~ **management network** n (SMN) TELECOM réseau de gestion SDH m; ~ **management subnetwork** n (SMS) TELECOM sous-réseau de gestion SDH m

S-distortion n TV distorsion en S f

SDLC abbr (synchronous data link control) COMP commande de transmission synchrone f, procédure de commande de transmission synchrone f

SDR abbr (system design review) SPACE revue de conception système f

SDU abbr (service data unit) TELECOM unité de données de service f

Se (selenium) CHEM Se (sélénium)

SE abbr (slurry explosive) MINING bouillie explosive f, explosif de chargement m, explosif en bouillie m

sea:[1] ~ **water-cooled** adj THERMOD refroidi par l'eau de mer

sea:[2] by ~ adv NAUT par mer, par voie de mer

sea:[3] ~ **anchor** n NAUT ancre flottante f; ~ **area** n NAUT parages m pl; ~ **bed** n CONST fond marin m, fonds marins m, FUELLESS, OCEANOG fond marin m, fonds marins m pl; ~ **bottom** n OCEANOG fond marin m, fonds marins m pl; ~ **breeze** n METEO brise de mer f, brise du large f; ~ **buoy** n NAUT navigation bouée extérieure f; ~ **canal** n OCEANOG canal interocéanique m, canal maritime m; ~ **carriage** n NAUT transport par mer m; ~ **carrier** n NAUT transporteur maritime m; ~ **chart** n TRANSP carte marine f; ~ **clutter** n NAUT radar retour de mer m, SPACE effet de mer m, TELECOM écho de vagues m; ~ **conditions** n pl NAUT conditions maritimes f pl; ~ **damage** n NAUT fortune de mer f; ~ **defence** n (BrE) METEO maritime protection contre la mer f; ~ **defense** n (AmE) see sea defence; ~ **dike** n (AmE), ~ **dyke** n (BrE) WATER SUPP digue maritime f;

~ **fleet** n TRANSP flotte de haute mer f; ~ **foam** n OCEANOG écume de mer f; ~ **grass bed** n OCEANOG verdière f; ~ **high** n OCEANOG colline abyssale f; ~ **ice** n NAUT glace en mer f; ~ **knoll** n OCEANOG colline abyssale f; ~ **lane** n NAUT couloir maritime m, OCEANOG couloir de navigation m, route maritime f; ~ **level** n CONST, FUELLESS, NAUT navigation, WATER SUPP niveau de la mer m; ~ **link** n NAUT liaison maritime f, route maritime f, voie maritime f; ~ **loch** n NAUT bras de mer m, fjord m; ~ **marsh** n OCEANOG marais maritime m; ~ **moat** n OCEANOG fossé m; ~ **noise** n OCEANOG bruit de la mer m; ~ **ranch** n OCEANOG enclos marin m, ferme marine f; ~ **ranching** n OCEANOG pacage en mer m, pacage marin m; ~ **route** n NAUT navigation route de mer f, trade route maritime f; ~ **salt** n FOOD TECH sel marin m; ~ **salt nucleus** n OCEANOG noyau de salinité m; ~ **salvage tug** n TRANSP remorqueur de sauvetage en mer m; ~ **scarp** n OCEANOG accore f, escarpement m; ~ **state** n NAUT état de la mer m; ~ **state spectrum** n OCEANOG spectre de la houle m; ~ **surface temperature** n NAUT température de la surface de la mer f; ~ **temperature** n NAUT température de la mer f; ~ **trade** n NAUT commerce maritime m; ~ **transport** n NAUT messageries maritimes f pl, transport maritime m; ~ **trial** n NAUT ship building essai à la mer m; ~ **tug** n NAUT, TRANSP remorqueur de haute mer m; ~ **vessel** n TRANSP navire de haute mer m; ~ **wall** n CONST, NAUT digue f; ~ **water** n NAUT, OCEANOG eau de mer f; ~ **water ice** n REFRIG glace d'eau de mer f; ~ **water in crude oil emulsion** n POLLUTION émulsion d'eau de mer dans du pétrole brut f; ~ **water interface** n HYDROL interface eau salée f; ~ **water intrusion** n WATER SUPP intrusion d'eau de mer f

Seabee: ~ **carrier** n TRANSP navire porte-barges Seabee m

seaboard n NAUT geography littoral m, OCEANOG bord m

seaborne[1] adj NAUT maritime, transporté par mer, TRANSP par voie maritime

seaborne:[2] ~ **trade** n NAUT commerce maritime m, transport maritime m

seacock n NAUT boat building prise d'eau à la mer f, sortie de coque f, vanne à passage direct f

sea-damaged adj NAUT avarié pendant le transport par mer, endommagé pendant le transport par mer

seafloor n OCEANOG fonds marins m pl; ~ **renewal** n OCEANOG renouvellement des fonds océaniques m; ~ **spreading** n GEOPHYS expansion océanique f, OCEANOG renouvellement des fonds océaniques m

seagoing: ~ **barge** n TRANSP barge transocéanique f; ~ **hovercraft** n TRANSP aéroglisseur marin m; ~ **vessel** n MAR POLL navire de haute mer m, navire océanique m, NAUT navire de mer m

seakeeping n TRANSP comportement en mer m; ~ **qualities** n pl NAUT qualités nautiques f pl, tenue à la mer f

seal[1] n C&G soudure f, ELEC protection joint d'étanchéité m, LAB EQUIP élément d'étanchéité m, MECH joint étanche m, MECH ENG for dynamic application joint d'étanchéité m, NAUT shipbuilding dispositif d'étanchéité m, PETR TECH étanchéité f; ~ **assembly** n NUCLEAR joint d'étanchéité m; ~ **block** n (AmE) (cf lipped cover tile) C&G brique couvre-goulotte avec bec f; ~ **coat** n CONST roads couche de scellement f, enduit de scellement m; ~ **gas** n NUCLEAR gaz d'arrêt m; ~ **unit** n NUCLEAR joint d'étanchéité m; ~ **of Viton** n PROD ENG joint d'étanchéité en Viton m; ~

water *n* NUCLEAR *of glanded pump* eau d'étanchéité *f*

seal[2] *vt* MINING coffrer, NAUT *shipbuilding* rendre étanche, sceller, PAPER TECH cacheter, PROD ENG boucher, obturer, sceller; **~ up** *vt* PROD ENG boucher, obturer, sceller

sealant *n* C&G adhésif *m*, CHEM agent d'étanchéité *m*, P&R mastic d'étanchéité *m*, PRINT produit scellant *m*, VEHICLES *body* produit d'étanchéité *m*; **~ polymer** *n* PETR TECH imperméabilisant *m*

sealed[1] *adj* MAR POLL scellé

sealed:[2] **~ battery** *n* (AmE) *(cf nonspill battery)* VEHICLES *electrical system* accumulateur inversible *m*; **~ beam unit** *n* AUTO *car* bloc optique *m*; **~ contact** *n* ELEC ENG contact scellé *m*; **~ cooling system** *n* AUTO système de refroidissement scellé *m*; **~ motor** *n* ELEC moteur hermétique *m*; **~ power factor** *n* PROD ENG facteur de puissance au maintien *m*; **~ quench furnace** *n* HEATING four de trempe scellé *m*; **~ reactor** *n* ELEC bobine d'inductance hermétique *f*; **~ rectifier** *n* ELEC ENG redresseur à cuve scellée *m*, redresseur à vide définitif *m*; **~ source** *n* NUCLEAR source scellée *f*; **~ switch contact** *n* PROD ENG contact à interrupteur scellé *m*; **~ transformer** *n* ELEC transformateur hermétique *m*; **~ wafer rotary switch** *n* ELEC ENG commutateur fermé *m*, commutateur à galette fermé *m*

sealer *n* COLOURS peinture isolante *f*, P&R *paint* peinture bouche-pores *f*

sealing *n* C&G soudure *f*, CONST *fixing* scellement *m*, PETR TECH, RAIL *vehicles* étanchéité *f*; **~ cap** *n* PACKAGING capsule verrou *f*; **~ compound** *n* CONST *joints* produit de scellement *m*; **~ edge** *n* C&G bord à sceller *m*; **~ machine** *n* PACKAGING machine à fermer *f*; **~ material** *n* NUCLEAR matériau pour scellement *m*; **~ paint** *n* COLOURS peinture hydrofuge *f*; **~ pliers** *n pl* MECH ENG pinces à plomber *f pl*; **~ plug** *n* MECH ENG tampon obturateur *m*; **~ ring** *n* AUTO *car* anneau d'étanchéité *m*, MECH ENG anneau d'étanchéité *m*, bague d'étanchéité *f*, PAPER TECH anneau d'étanchéité *m*, PROP MAT bague d'étanchéité *f*, VEHICLES joint annulaire *m*; **~ surface** *n* C&G surface de joint *f*; **~ tape** *n* PACKAGING, PAPER TECH ruban autocollant destiné à fermer les cartons *m*; **~ up** *n* CONST bouchage *m*, obturation *f*, scellage *m*; **~ weld** *n* NUCLEAR soudure d'étanchéité *f*

seam[1] *n* C&G couture *f*, COAL TECH couche *f*, MECH *welding* soudure *f*, MECH ENG *between parts* couture *f*, MINING veine *f*, PAPER TECH jonction *f*, *of machine wire* couture *f*, PRINT couture longue *f*, SPRINGS repli de laminage *m*; **~ line** *n* C&G corde mobile *f*; **~ roller** *n* MECH ENG *tool* rouleau à papier de tenture *m*; **~ sequence** *n* COAL TECH succession des couches *f*; **~ weld** *n* NUCLEAR soudure continue *f*; **~ welding wheel blank** *n* MECH ENG ébauche des molettes de soudage *f*; **~ work** *n* COAL TECH, MINING travaux en couche *m pl*; **~ working** *n* MINING travaux en couche *m pl*

seam[2] *vt* TEXTILES couture *f*, jonctionner

seamanship *n* NAUT art de la manoeuvre *m*, sens marin *m*, usages maritimes *m pl*

seamark *n* NAUT *navigation*, OCEANOG, SPACE amer *m*

seamarking *n* NAUT *navigation* balisage maritime *m*

seamed: ~ pipe *n* MECH ENG tuyau soudé *m*, tuyau à couture *m*

seaming *n* TEXTILES jonctionnement *m*

seamless[1] *adj* TEXTILES sans couture

seamless:[2] **~ pipe** *n* MECH ENG tuyau sans soudure *m*; **~ pressure vessel** *n* MECH ENG réservoir à pression sans

soudure *m*; **~ printing** *n* PRINT impression sans couture *f*, impression sans marge *f*; **~ rolled ring** *n* MECH ENG anneau laminé sans soudure *m*; **~ wrought copper tube** *n* MECH ENG tube sans soudure en cuivre corroyé *m*

seamount *n* GEOL guyot *m*, volcan sous-marin *m*, OCEANOG mont sous-marin *m*

seaplane *n* AERONAUT hydravion *m*; **~ base** *n* AERONAUT hydrobase *f*

seaport *n* NAUT port de mer *m*, port maritime *m*

seaquake *n* GEOPHYS tremblement de terre sous-marin *m*, OCEANOG séisme sous-marin *m*

search *n* COMP, DP, PATENTS recherche *f*; **~ and replace function** *n* COMP, DP fonction de recherche et remplacement *f*; **~ and rescue** *n* NAUT recherche et sauvetage *f*; **~ coil** *n* ELEC, ELEC ENG bobine exploratrice *f*, PHYS bobine détectrice *f*, TESTING bobine exploratrice *f*; **~ key** *n* COMP, DP clé de recherche *f*; **~ query** *n* COMP, DP demande de recherche *f*; **~ report** *n* PATENTS rapport de recherche *m*; **~ string** *n* PRINT chaîne de recherche *f*; **~ tree** *n* COMP, DP arbre de recherche *m*; **~ word** *n* COMP, DP mot de recherche *m*

searching *n* COMP, DP recherche *f*

searchlight *n* ELEC ENG, MILIT projecteur *m*

seascape *n* OCEANOG marine *f*

seashore: ~ fishing *n* OCEANOG pêche à pied *f*

seaside: ~ resort *n* MAR POLL station balnéaire *f*

season: ~ factor *n* PROD ENG facteur de saisonnalité *m*; **~ pattern code** *n* PROD ENG *for safety stock* fluctuation saisonnière *f*; **~ ticket holder** *n* RAIL abonné *m*

seasonal: ~ behavior *n* (AmE), **~ behaviour** *n* (BrE) PROD ENG saisonnalité *f*; **~ demand** *n* GAS TECH besoin saisonnier *m*; **~ index** *n* PROD ENG indice de saisonnalité *m*; **~ pattern** *n* PROD ENG fluctuation saisonnière *f*; **~ pattern code** *n* PROD ENG fluctuation saisonnière *f*

seasonality *n* PROD ENG saisonnalité *f*

seasoned: ~ timber *n* NAUT *boatbuilding* bois desséché *m*, bois séché à l'air *m*; **~ wood** *n* NAUT *boatbuilding* bois desséché *m*, bois séché à l'air *m*

seasoning *n* CONST *timber* dessiccation *f*

seat *n* C&G banquette *f*, CONST assiette *f*, HYDR EQUIP *of valve* siège *m*, MECH siège *m*, surface d'appui *f*, MECH ENG *support* chaise *f*, siège *m*, MINING *of mine* semelle *f*, NUCLEAR *part of valve*, PROD ENG siège *m*, SPRINGS *of spring* base *f*, portée *f*, siège *m*, TRANSP siège *m*, VEHICLES *interior* place *f*, siège *m*; **~ angle** *n* SPRINGS angle de bridage *m*; **~ back** *n* VEHICLES dossier *m*; **~ belt** *n* AERONAUT attache pilote *f*, ceinture de siège *f*, ceinture de sécurité *f*, SAFETY, TRANSP, VEHICLES *safety* ceinture de sécurité *f*; **~ belt attachment** *n* VEHICLES *safety* ancrage de la ceinture de sécurité *m*; **~ cushion** *n* VEHICLES coussin de siège *m*; **~ length** *n* SPRINGS longueur de bridage *f*; **~ of a slide-valve** *n* HYDR EQUIP table de distributeur *f*; **~ upholstery** *n* VEHICLES capitonnage de siège *m*, garnissage de siège *m*

seating *n* CONST assiette *f*, MECH ENG *support* chaise *f*, siège *m*, NUCLEAR siège *m*, PROD ENG *core print* porte-noyau *m*, portée *f*, portée de noyau *f*, portée de remmoulage *f*, SPRINGS portée *f*

seaward[1] *adj* NAUT *navigation* vers le large

seaward[2] *adv* NAUT *navigation* vers le large

seaward:[3] **~ defence boat** *n* NAUT *navy* vedette de défense côtière *f*, vedette de défense vers le large *f*

seaway *n* OCEANOG route maritime *f*

seaweed *n* MAR POLL algue *f*, goémon *m*

seaworthiness *n* MAR POLL navigabilité *f*, NAUT état de navigabilité *m*

seaworthy:[1] ~ *adj* NAUT en état de navigabilité, TRANSP en bon état de navigation

seaworthy:[2] ~ **packaging** *n* PACKAGING emballage pour transport maritime *m*

sebacic *adj* CHEM sébacique

SECAM[1] *abbr* TV SECAM, séquentiel couleur à mémoire *m*

SECAM:[2] ~ **system** *n* TV système SECAM *m*

secant[1] *adj* GEOM sécant

secant[2] *n* GEOM, sécante *f*

second:[1] ~ **anode** *adj* ELEC ENG de seconde anode; ~ **generation** *adj* COMP, DP de seconde génération; ~ **intermediate frequency** *adj (second IF amplifier)* E-LECTRON seconde fréquence intermédiaire

second[2] *n* ACOUSTICS seconde *f*, CONST *surveying* seconde d'angle *f*, METR seconde *f*, PHYS *of arc* seconde d'angle *f*, *time* seconde *f*; ~ **anode** *n* TV anode accélératrice *f*; ~ **channel frequency** *n* ELECTRON fréquence image *f*; ~ **condenser lens** *n* INSTRUMENT *microscope* lentille magnétique *f*; ~ **cut** *n* MECH ENG *files* taille demi-douce *f*, taille mi-douce *f*; ~ **deck** *n* NAUT *ship design* premier faux pont *m*; ~ **dog watch** *n* MILIT *naval* deuxième petit quart *m*; ~ **engineer** *n* NAUT *aboard ship* officier mécanicien en second *m*; ~ **gear** *n* AUTO *car* pignon de deuxième vitesse *m*; ~ **generation computer** *n* COMP, DP ordinateur de seconde génération *m*; ~ **generation copy** *n* CINEMAT copie de deuxième génération *f*; ~ **generation dupe** *n* CINEMAT contre-dupli *m*; ~ **hand** *n* MECH ENG *of watch* aiguille trotteuse *f*; ~ **harmonic** *n* ELECTRON deuxième harmonique *m*, harmonique 2 *m*; ~ **harmonic distortion** *n* ELECTRON distorsion par harmonique deux *f*; ~ **harmonic injection** *n* ELECTRON injection d'harmonique deux *f*; ~ **IF amplifier** *n* ELECTRON amplificateur à seconde fréquence intermédiaire *m*, ELECTRON second amplificateur à fréquence intermédiaire *m*; ~ **ionization potential** *n* PHYS potentiel de deuxième ionisation *m*; ~ **law of thermodynamics** *n* PHYS deuxième principe de la thermodynamique *m*; ~ **leaf** *n* SPRINGS lame sous-maîtresse *f*; ~ **local oscillator** *n* ELECTRON second oscillateur local *m*; ~ **moment of area** *n* MECH ENG *inertia* deuxième moment d'aire *m*; ~ **motion shaft** *n* MECH ENG arbre secondaire *m*, axe secondaire *m*; ~ **nearest neighbor** *n* (AmE), ~ **nearest neighbour** *n* (BrE) CRYSTALL second voisin *m*; ~ **order band-pass filter** *n* ELECTRON filtre passe-bande d'ordre 2 *m*, filtre passe-bande du second ordre *m*; ~ **order bandstop filter** *n* ELECTRON filtre coupe-bande du second ordre *m*; ~ **order filter** *n* ELECTRON filtre d'ordre 2 *m*, filtre du second ordre *m*; ~ **order high-pass filter** *n* ELECTRON filtre passe-haut d'ordre 2 *m*, filtre passe-haut du second ordre *m*; ~ **order low-pass filter** *n* ELECTRON filtre passe-bas d'ordre 2 *m*, filtre passe-bas du second ordre *m*; ~ **order prefilter** *n* ELECTRON préfiltre du second ordre *m*, préfiltre d'ordre deux *m*; ~ **order servo** *n* ELEC ENG système asservi du second ordre *m*; ~ **order transition** *n* PHYS transition du deuxième ordre *f*; ~ **proof** *n* PRINT révision *f*; ~ **quarter** *n* ASTRON deuxième quartier *m*; ~ **reducing firing** *n* C&G deuxième cuisson *f*; ~ **surface mirror** *n (SSM)* SPACE *spacecraft* miroir à couche secondaire *m*; ~ **tap** *n* MECH ENG second taraud *m*, taraud demi-conique *m*, taraud intermédiaire *m*; ~ **trace echo** *n* NAUT *radar* écho de deuxième balayage *m*, écho secondaire *m*; ~ **unit** *n* CINEMAT deuxième équipe *f*; ~ **window fiber** *n* (AmE),

~ **window fibre** *n* (BrE) OPT fibre à 113µm *f*

secondary[1] *adj* RAD PHYS secondaire

secondary:[2] ~ **acetate** *n* TEXTILES diacétate *m*; ~ **air** *n* AUTO, HEAT ENG air secondaire *m*; ~ **battery** *n* ELEC ENG batterie secondaire *f*, SPACE *spacecraft* accumulateur *m*, cellule *f*, TRANSP batterie secondaire *f*; ~ **blasting** *n* MINING tir secondaire *m*; ~ **brake system** *n* VEHICLES système de freinage de secours *m*; ~ **cell** *n* ELEC pile secondaire *f*, ELEC ENG accumulateur *m*, pile secondaire *f*, élément d'accumulateur *m*; ~ **center of disturbance** *n* (AmE) *see secondary centre of disturbance*; ~ **center tap** *n* (AmE) *see secondary centre tap*; ~ **centre of disturbance** *n* (BrE) WAVE PHYS *of wavefront* centre secondaire de perturbation *m*; ~ **centre tap** *n* (BrE) ELEC ENG point milieu du secondaire *m*, prise médiane au secondaire *f*; ~ **checkers** *n pl* C&G tas inférieur de l'empilage *m*; ~ **circuit** *n* ELEC ENG circuit de l'enroulement secondaire *m*, circuit secondaire *m*; ~ **coating** *n* OPT, TELECOM revêtement secondaire *m*; ~ **coil** *n* ELEC ENG, TESTING bobine secondaire *f*; ~ **collision** *n* TRANSP collision secondaire *f*; ~ **color** *n* (AmE), ~ **colour** *n* (BrE) COLOURS teinte mélangée *f*, PRINT couleur secondaire *f*; ~ **creep** *n* METALL fluage secondaire *m*; ~ **crusher** *n* COAL TECH concasseur secondaire *m*; ~ **cup** *n* AUTO coupelle d'étanchéité *f*; ~ **current** *n* ELEC *transformer*, ELEC ENG courant secondaire *m*; ~ **curvature** *n* C&G courbure secondaire *f*; ~ **duct** *n* AERONAUT *turbofan* conduit de dérivation *m*, conduit secondaire de dérivation *m*; ~ **electrochemical generator** *n* TRANSP générateur électrochimique secondaire *m*; ~ **electron** *n* ELECTRON, RAD PHYS électron secondaire *m*; ~ **element** *n* CHEM élément secondaire *m*; ~ **emission** *n* ELECTRON émission d'électrons secondaires *f*, émission secondaire *f*, PHYS émission secondaire *f*; ~ **emission multiplier** *n* TV multiplicateur d'électrons secondaires *m*; ~ **emission noise** *n* ELECTRON bruit d'émission secondaire *m*; ~ **emission ratio** *n* ELECTRON rendement d'émission secondaire *m*; ~ **emission target** *n* ELECTRON cible à émission secondaire *f*; ~ **emission tube** *n* ELECTRON tube à émission secondaire *m*; ~ **explosive** *n* MINING explosif de chargement *m*, explosif secondaire *m*; ~ **extinction** *n* CRYSTALL extinction secondaire *f*; ~ **fiber** *n* (AmE), ~ **fibre** *n* (BrE) PACKAGING fibre récupérée *f*; ~ **fuel cell** *n* TRANSP pile indirecte *f*; ~ **gas cap** *n* PETR chapeau de gaz secondaire *m*; ~ **grid emission** *n* ELECTRON émission secondaire par la grille *f*; ~ **grinding** *n* COAL TECH broyage secondaire *m*; ~ **headbox** *n* PAPER TECH caisse d'arrivée secondaire *f*; ~ **high explosive** *n* MINING explosif de chargement *m*, explosif secondaire *m*; ~ **index** *n* COMP, DP index secondaire *m*; ~ **inductance** *n* ELEC ENG inductance secondaire *f*; ~ **ionic emission** *n* TELECOM émission ionique secondaire *f*; ~ **ionization** *n* RAD PHYS ionisation secondaire *f*; ~ **ion mass spectrometry** *n (SIMS)* PHYS spectroscopie de masse aux ions secondaires *f*; ~ **line** *n* TRANSP ligne secondaire *f*; ~ **maxima** *n pl* OPT maxima secondaires *m pl*; ~ **memory** *n* COMP mémoire auxiliaire *f*, mémoire secondaire *f*; ~ **metal** *n* PROP MAT métal récupéré *m*; ~ **mirror** *n* INSTRUMENT miroir de déviation *m*; ~ **nozzle** *n* AERONAUT *engine* tuyère secondaire *f*; ~ **nuclear reaction** *n* NUCLEAR réaction nucléaire secondaire *f*; ~ **particle** *n* NUCLEAR particule secondaire *f*; ~ **piston** *n* AUTO piston secondaire *m*; ~ **porosity** *n* PETR porosité secondaire *f*; ~ **porosity index** *n (SPI)* PETR indice de porosité secondaire *m*; ~ **radiation** *n* RAD PHYS radiation secondaire *f*; **~ raw plastic material** *n* PROP MAT matière brute secondaire plastique *f*; **~ reactor** *n* NUCLEAR réacteur secondaire *m*; **~ recovery** *n* PETR, PETR TECH récupération secondaire *f*; **~ recrystallization** *n* METALL recristallisation secondaire *f*; **~ reflector** *n* SPACE réflecteur secondaire *m*; **~ refrigerant** *n* REFRIG frigorigène secondaire *m*; **~ relay** *n* ELEC relais indirect *m*; **~ resistance** *n* ELEC ENG résistance secondaire *f*; **~ road** *n* TRANSP route départementale *f*; **~ separation** *n* NUCLEAR *steam generator* séparation secondaire *f*; **~ settlement** *n* COAL TECH tassement secondaire *m*; **~ shutdown system** *n* NUCLEAR système d'arrêt complémentaire *m*; **~ side** *n* NUCLEAR *steam generator* côté secondaire *m*; **~ sleeve** *n* AUTO segment secondaire *m*; **~ source** *n* OPT source secondaire *f*; **~ standard** *n* PHYS étalon secondaire *m*; **~ still** *n* FOOD TECH *redistillation* appareil de redistillation *m*; **~ storage** *n* (AmE) *(cf secondary store)* COMP mémoire secondaire *f*; **~ store** *n* (BrE) *(cf secondary storage)* COMP mémoire secondaire *f*; **~ structure** *n* SPACE *spacecraft* structure secondaire *f*; **~ suspension** *n* TRANSP suspension secondaire *f*; **~ swelling** *n* NUCLEAR *of graphite* gonflement secondaire *m*; **~ tap** *n* ELEC ENG prise au secondaire *f*, prise sur l'enroulement *f*; **~ terminal** *n* ELEC ENG borne de secondaire *f*; **~ viewing tube** *n* INSTRUMENT microscope auxiliaire *m*; **~ voltage** *n* ELEC *transformer* tension induite *f*, tension secondaire *f*, ELEC ENG tension secondaire *f*; **~ wave** *n* PHYS *seismology* onde S *f*; **~ winding** *n* AUTO bobinage secondaire *m*, ELEC *transformer*, ELEC ENG, PHYS enroulement secondaire *m*; **~ X-ray radiation** *n* RAD PHYS rayonnement X secondaire *m*

second-order: **~ quantity** *n* GEOM quantité du second ordre *f*

seconds *n pl* TEXTILES rebuts *m pl*

second-tier: **~ trunk exchange area** *n* TELECOM zone de transit secondaire *f*

secret: **~ gutter** *n* CONST chéneau encaissé *m*

section *n* COMP section *f*, CONST *of road* tronçon *m*, DP section *f*, GEOL coupe *f*, GEOM section *f*, MECH ENG profil *m*, section *f*, *cut through bar* section *f*, échantillon *m*, *length* profil *m*, profilé *m*, *piece* coupon *m*, tronçon *m*, NAUT *shipbuilding* profilé *m*, section *f*, PETR section *f*, PETR TECH tronçon *m*, PRINT exemplaires *m pl*, *of book* cahier *m*, PROD ENG *of sectional boiler* élément *m*, *part* partie *f*, section *f*, RAIL canton *m*, TELECOM tronçon *m*, TEXTILES section *f*, WATER SUPP *of pipe* tronçon *m*; **~ adaptation** *n (SA)* TELECOM adaptation de section *f*; **~ drawing** *n* MECH ENG dessin de coupe *m*; **~ of maximum intensity of stress** *n* MECH ENG *materials* section dangereuse *f*; **~ mill** *n* PROD ENG *rolling* laminoir à profilés *m*; **~ overhead** *n (SOH)* TELECOM résidu de section *m*, surdébit de section *m*; **~ printing** *n* CINEMAT tirage de fil-à-fil *m*; **~ of uniform strength** *n* MECH ENG *materials* section d'égale résistance *f*; **~ warping** *n* TEXTILES ourdissage sectionnel *m*; **~ wire spring** *n* SPRINGS ressort à fil profilé *m*

sectional[1] *adj* GEOM sectionnel, MECH ENG *in sections* sectionnel, *of special section* profilé, *transportable* démontable, sectionné

sectional:[2] **~ beam** *n* TEXTILES *warp knitting* bobine sectionnelle *f*; **~ boiler** *n* HEATING chaudière sectionnelle *f*, PROD ENG chaudière sectionnelle *f*, chaudière à petits éléments *f*; **~ chart** *n* (AmE) *(cf aeronautical chart)* AERONAUT carte aéronautique *f*; **~ coldroom** *n* REFRIG *assembled on site* chambre froide préfabriquée

f; **~ curvature** *n* GEOM courbure sectionnelle *f*; **~ drawing** *n* MECH ENG *ship design* coupe *f*, vue en coupe *f*; **~ drive** *n* PAPER TECH commande sectionnelle *f*; **~ view** *n* MECH ENG vue en coupe *f*; **~ warping** *n* TEXTILES ourdissage sectionnel *m*; **~ warping machine** *n* TEXTILES ourdissoir sectionnel *m*; **~ warp sizing** *n* TEXTILES encollage de chaînes sectionnelles *m*; **~ warp slashing** *n* TEXTILES encollage de chaînes sectionnelles *m*

sectionalization *n* ELEC *supply network* sectionnement *m*

sectionalized: **~ busbar** *n* ELEC *supply* barre sectionnée *f*; **~ cross-bonding** *n* ELEC *shield bonding* permutation ternaire *f*

sectionalizing: **~ joint** *n* ELEC *cable* jonction de sectionnement *f*; **~ switch** *n* ELEC *supply network* sectionneur *m*

sectioning: **~ technique** *n* NUCLEAR *diffusion studies* méthode de sectionnement *f*

sector *n* COMP, CONST *of circle*, DP, GEOM, NAUT *of light*, PETR TECH secteur *m*; **~ gate** *n* FUELLESS *dams* vanne à secteur *f*; **~ gear** *n* AUTO secteur denté *m*, MECH ENG secteur crénelé *m*, secteur denté *m*, VEHICLES *steering* secteur denté *m*; **~ light** *n* NAUT *navigation* feu à secteur *m*; **~ scan** *n* MILIT *radar* balayage d'un secteur *m*; **~ shaft** *n* AUTO axe du secteur denté *m*; **~ shaped conductor** *n* ELEC *cable* âme sectorale *f*; **~ weir** *n* WATER SUPP barrage à segment *m*; **~ wheel** *n* MECH ENG secteur crénelé *m*, secteur denté *m*

secular[1] *adj* GEOPHYS séculaire

secular:[2] **~ acceleration** *n* ASTRON accélération séculaire *f*; **~ change** *n* GEOPHYS marche séculaire *f*, variation séculaire *f*; **~ equilibrium** *n* PHYS équilibre séculaire *m*; **~ variation** *n* ASTRON, GEOPHYS variation séculaire *f*

secure *vt* CONST ancrer, fixer, NAUT *mooring* amarrer

secured *adj* PROD ENG assujetti

security *n* COMP sécurité *f*, DP défense *f*, sécurité *f*, PROD ENG, SAFETY sécurité *f*; **~ audit** *n* TELECOM audit de sécurité *m*; **~ audit trail** *n* TELECOM journal d'audit de sécurité *m*; **~ bolt** *n* SAFETY verrou de sécurité *m*; **~ door** *n* SAFETY porte blindée *f*; **~ firm** *n* SAFETY société de surveillance *f*; **~ kernel** *n* COMP, DP noyau de sécurité *m*; **~ label** *n* TELECOM étiquette de sécurité *f*; **~ management information base** *n (SMIB)* TELECOM base d'informations de gestion de sécurité *f*; **~ officer** *n* SAFETY inspecteur chargé de la sécurité *m*; **~ paper** *n* PAPER TECH papier de sécurité *m*; **~ policy** *n* TELECOM politique de sécurité *f*; **~ service** *n* TELECOM service de sécurité *m*; **~ window** *n* SAFETY fenêtre blindée *f*

sedan *n* (AmE) *(cf saloon)* TRANSP *motor vehicles* berline *f*

sedentary[1] *adj* COAL TECH sédentaire

sedentary:[2] **~ fishery** *n* OCEANOG pêcherie sédentaire *f*

sediment *n* CHEM dépôt *m*, sédiment *m*, CHEM TECH dépôt *m*, résidu *m*, sédiment *m*, COAL TECH, PETR TECH, RECYCLING, WATER SUPP sédiment *m*; **~ break** *n* OCEANOG discontinuité sédimentaire *f*; **~ chamber** *n* AUTO chambre de sédimentation *f*; **~ discharge** *n* WATER SUPP débit solide *m*; **~ layer** *n* GAS TECH couche de sédiment *f*; **~ probe** *n* OCEANOG sondeur de sédiment *m*, sondeur de vase *m*; **~ sounder** *n* OCEANOG sondeur de sédiment *m*, sondeur de vase *m*; **~ space** *n* AUTO bac de sédimentation *m*

sedimentary: **~ basin** *n* GAS TECH, GEOL bassin sédimentaire *m*, PETR TECH bassin secondaire *m*; **~ deposit** *n* RECYCLING formation sédimentaire *f*; **~ environment** *n* GEOL milieu sédimentaire *m*; **~ model** *n* GAS TECH modèle sédimentaire *m*; **~ rock** *n* COAL TECH, PETR,

PETR TECH roche sédimentaire *f*, ~ **rock salt** *n* GAS TECH sel gemme sédimentaire *m*; ~ **sequence** *n* GEOL séquence sédimentaire *f*; ~ **soil** *n* COAL TECH sol sédimentaire *m*; ~ **structure** *n* GEOL figure sédimentaire *f*

sedimentation *n* CHEM, P&R *pigments, fillers*, PETR TECH, PHYS, POLLUTION, RECYCLING, WATER SUPP sédimentation *f*; ~ **analysis** *n* COAL TECH analyse par sédimentation *f*; ~ **basin** *n* CHEM TECH bassin de sédimentation *m*, bassin sédimentaire *m*, RECYCLING bassin de décantation *m*; ~ **break** *n* OCEANOG discontinuité sédimentaire *f*; ~ **pit** *n* CHEM TECH bassin de sédimentation *m*, bassin sédimentaire *m*; ~ **pond** *n* COAL TECH bassin de décantation *m*; ~ **potential** *n* CHEM TECH potentiel de sédimentation *m*; ~ **rate** *n* PETR TECH, PROP MAT, RECYCLING vitesse de sédimentation *f*; ~ **tank** *n* CHEM TECH bassin de sédimentation *m*, bassin sédimentaire *m*, RECYCLING bassin de décantation *m*, WATER SUPP bac de décantation *m*, tank à sédimentation *m*; ~ **test** *n* CONST essai de sédimentation *m*

sedimented *adj* CHEM TECH déposé par sédimentation

Seebeck: ~ **coefficient** *n* PHYS coefficient de Seebeck *m*; ~ **effect** *n* ELEC ENG *thermocouples*, PHYS effet de Seebeck *m*

seed *n* C&G point brillant *m*, point fin *m*; ~ **assembly** *n* NUCLEAR semence *f*; ~ **core reactor** *n* NUCLEAR réacteur à coeur à germes *m*; ~ **crystal** *n* CRYSTALL cristal germe *m*, germe cristallin *m*; ~ **element** *n* NUCLEAR *of reactor* semence *f*; ~ **lac** *n* COLOURS laque en grains *f*

seed-free[1] *adj* C&G fin

seed-free:[2] ~ **time** *n* C&G achèvement de l'affinage *m*

seeding *n* CHEM *of crystals*, NUCLEAR *X-ray crystallography* ensemencement *m*; ~ **potential** *n* C&G aptitude au bullage *f*

seedy: ~ **glass** *n* C&G verre piqué *m* (Bel), verre puceux *m* (Fra)

seeing *n* ASTRON vue *f*

seek:[1] ~ **area** *n* COMP, DP zone de recherche *f*; ~ **arm** *n* COMP, DP bras d'accès *m*; ~ **time** *n* COMP, DP temps de recherche *m*, OPT temps de positionnement *m*

seek[2] *vt* COMP, DP chercher, rechercher

seep *vi* CHEM s'infiltrer, suinter; ~ **through** *vi* TEXTILES s'infiltrer

seepage *n* CHEM infiltration *f*, suintement *m*, COAL TECH eau de pénétration *f*, GAS TECH suintement *m*, MAR POLL infiltration *f*, suintement *m*, WATER SUPP suintement *m*; ~ **water** *n* CHEM eau d'infiltration *f*

seesaw: ~ **motion** *n* MECH ENG mouvement basculaire *m*

seesawing *n* MECH ENG basculage *m*

see-through: ~ **mirror** *n* (AmE) *(cf two-way mirror)* C&G miroir semi-réfléchissant *m*; ~ **packaging** *n* PACKAGING emballage visuel *m*

Seger: ~ **cone** *n* C&G cône pyroscopique *m*

segment[1] *n* COMP, DP, GEOM, MECH ENG segment *m*, NUCLEAR *bearings* patin *m*; ~ **gear** *n* MECH ENG secteur crénelé *m*, secteur denté *m*; ~ **terminator** *n* TELECOM terminaison de segment *f*; ~ **type** *n* *(ST)* TELECOM type de segment *m*

segment[2] *vt* COMP, DP segmenter

segmental[1] *adj* GEOM segmentaire

segmental:[2] ~ **arch** *n* CONST *curve with flatter segment* arc bombé *m*, arc en segment de cercle *m*, *curve* arc surbaissé *m*, *for bridge with flatter segment* arche bombée *f*, arche en segment de cercle *f*, *for bridge arche* surbaissée *f*, *structure with flatter segment* voûte

bombée *f*, voûte en arc de cercle *f*, *structure* voûte surbaissée *f*; ~ **circular saw** *n* MECH ENG scie circulaire à segments rapportés *f*

segmentation *n* CHEM, COMP, DP segmentation *f*; ~ **and reassembly** *n* *(SAR)* TELECOM segmentation et réassemblage *f*; ~ **and reassembly sublayer** *n* TELECOM segmentation et réassemblage sous-couche *f*; ~ **permitted flag** *n* *(SPF)* TELECOM indicateur de segmentation permise *m*

segmented: ~ **approach path** *n* AERONAUT trajectoire d'approche segmentée *f*, trajectoire en ligne brisée *f*, trajectoire segmentée *f*; ~ **fuel rod** *n* NUCLEAR crayon segmenté *m*; ~ **multiprocessor system** *n* TELECOM système en répartition géographique *m*; ~ **pile** *n* COAL TECH pieu composé *m*; ~ **recording** *n* TV enregistrement fragmenté *m*; ~ **saw** *n* MECH ENG *for masonry stone* scie segmentée *f*; ~ **scanning** *n* TV balayage fragmenté *m*

Segrè: ~ **chart** *n* PART PHYS diagramme de Segrè *m*

segregation *n* C&G, CHEM, CONST *concrete mixing*, NUCLEAR *alloys*, PROP MAT ségrégation *f*

segue *n* RECORDING transition musicale *f*

seiche *n* FUELLESS *water level* seiche *f*, OCEANOG mascaret *m*, seiche *f*

seine *n* OCEANOG senne *f*; ~ **net** *n* NAUT *fishing* senne *f*; ~ **staff** *n* OCEANOG bourdon *m*

seiner *n* OCEANOG senneur *m*

seismic[1] *adj* CONST, GEOPHYS, PETR TECH sismique

seismic:[2] ~ **activity** *n* GEOL sismicité *f*; ~ **array** *n* GEOL dispositif de géophones *m*, ensemble de sismographes *m*, rangée de géophones *f*; ~ **borehole** *n* GEOPHYS trou de sondage sismique *m*; ~ **design** *n* CONST étude sismique *f*; ~ **engineering** *n* GEOPHYS génie sismique *m*; ~ **exploration** *n* COAL TECH, PETR TECH exploration sismique *f*; ~ **exploration method** *n* GEOPHYS exploration sismique *f*, recherche par méthode sismique *f*; ~ **focus** *n* GEOPHYS foyer *m*, foyer du séisme *m*, foyer du tremblement de terre *m*, hypocentre *m*, lieu de naissance du tremblement de terre *m*; ~ **mass** *n* GEOPHYS masse sismique *f*; ~ **path** *n* PETR TECH trajet sismique *m*; ~ **phenomena** *n pl* GEOPHYS phénomènes sismiques *m pl*; ~ **profile recorder** *n* WAVE PHYS enregistreur du profil sismique *m*; ~ **prospecting** *n* GEOPHYS recherche minière par secousses provoquées *f*; ~ **prospection** *n* GEOPHYS prospection sismique *f*; ~ **spectral analysis** *n* GEOPHYS analyse du spectre sismique *f*; ~ **station** *n* GEOPHYS station sismique *f*; ~ **survey** *n* CONST arpentage sismique *m*, prospection sismique *f*, GEOPHYS levé sismique *m*, PETR TECH campagne sismique *f*, levé sismique *m*, étude sismique *f*; ~ **velocity** *n* GEOL, PETR vitesse sismique *f*; ~ **wave** *n* GEOL onde sismique *f*, onde élastique *f*, GEOPHYS onde de séisme *f*, onde sismique *f*, PHYS, WAVE PHYS onde sismique *f*; ~ **wave trace** *n* GEOPHYS tracé des secousses *m*; ~ **zone** *n* GEOPHYS bande sismique *f*, zone de tremblements de terre *f*

seismicity *n* GEOPHYS, SPACE sismicité *f*

seismogenic *adj* GEOPHYS sismogénique

seismogram *n* PETR sismogramme *m*

seismograph *n* CONST, GAS TECH, PHYS sismographe *m*

seismological: ~ **map** *n* GEOPHYS carte sismique *f*

seismologist *n* GEOPHYS sismologiste *f*, sismologue *f*

seismology *n* GEOPHYS, PHYS sismologie *f*

seismometer *n* GEOPHYS sismographe *m*, sismographe horizontal *m*, sismomètre *m*

seismotectonics *n* GEOPHYS sismotectonique *f*

seize[1] *vt* NAUT amarrer, confisquer, saisir

seize[2] *vi* MECH ENG gripper, NUCLEAR *valve* bloquer, se coincer

seizing *n* AUTO grippage *m*, MECH ENG grippage *m*, grippement *m*, VEHICLES *bearing, piston* grippage *m*

seizure *n* NAUT *of ship* saisie *f*, TELECOM prise *f*

SELCAL *abbr (selective calling system)* TELECOM système d'appel sélectif *m*

select[1] *n* PRINT choix *m*

select[2] *vt* COMP, DP choisir, MINING *site for shaft* fixer

selected: ~ **chunks** *n pl* C&G verre demi-brut *m*; ~ **fill** *n* CONST *roads* couche de forme *f*; ~ **sizes** *n pl* MECH ENG *for bolts nuts* sélection de dimensions *f*

selecting *n* TELECOM invitation à recevoir *f*

selection *n* C&G choix *m*, COMP désignation *f*, sélection *f*, DP appel *m*, sélection *f*, désignation *f*; ~ **of arrivals** *n* GEOL pointé des arrivées *m*; ~ **information** *n* PROD ENG renseignements pour la sélection *m pl*; ~ **rule** *n* NUCLEAR loi de sélection *f*, règle de sélection *f*, PHYS règle de sélection *f*; ~ **stage** *n* TELECOM étage de sélection *m*

selective[1] *adj* PROP MAT sélectif

selective[2] ~ **calling** *n* TELECOM appel sélectif numérique *m*; ~ **calling system** *n (SELCAL)* TELECOM système d'appel sélectif *m*; ~ **catalytic reduction** *n* POLLUTION réduction catalytique sélective *f*; ~ **coating** *n* FUELLESS revêtement sélectif *m*; ~ **collection** *n* RECYCLING collecte sélective *f*; ~ **diffusion** *n* ELECTRON diffusion sélective *f*; ~ **diversion** *n* TRANSP *of traffic* déviation sélective *f*; ~ **dump** *n* COMP, DP vidage sélectif *m*; ~ **erasure** *n* COMP, DP effacement sélectif *m*; ~ **fading** *n* TELECOM évanouissement sélectif *m*; ~ **feedback** *n* ELECTRON contre-réaction sélective *f*; ~ **feedback amplifier** *n* ELECTRON amplificateur à contreréaction sélective *m*; ~ **field protection** *n* TELECOM protection sélective des champs *f*; ~ **quenching** *n* RAD PHYS *of ions* extinction sélective *f*; ~ **reducer** *n* PHOTO affaiblisseur sélectif *m*; ~ **reflection** *n* PHYS réflexion sélective *f*; ~ **sequential access** *n* COMP, DP accès séquentiel sélectif *m*; ~ **solvent** *n* CHEM, PETR TECH solvant sélectif *m*; ~ **surface** *n* FUELLESS surface sélective *f*; ~ **switch** *n* ELEC commutateur de sélection *m*; ~ **vehicle detector** *n* TRANSP *traffic* détecteur de classification des véhicules *m*; ~ **voltmeter** *n* ELEC voltmètre sélectif *m*

selectively-plated: ~ **contacts** *n pl* ELEC ENG contacts à placage sélectif *m pl*

selectivity *n* ELECTRON, PHYS sélectivité *f*; ~ **Q** *n* RECORDING facteur de pente *m*

selector *n* COMP, DP, ELEC ENG, TELECOM, VEHICLES *automatic transmission* sélecteur *m*; ~ **channel** *n* COMP, DP canal sélecteur *m*; ~ **lever** *n* AUTO, VEHICLES *automatic transmission* levier sélecteur *m*; ~ **relay** *n* ELEC ENG relais sélecteur *m*; ~ **switch** *n* CONTROL bouton tournant pour sélection *m*, commutateur de sélection *m*, commutateur pas à pas *m*, ELEC sélecteur en charge *m*, ELEC ENG commutateur *m*, ELECTRON, PROD ENG commutateur de sélection *m*

selenate *n* CHEM séléniate *m*

selenic *adj* CHEM sélénique

selenide *n* CHEM séléniure *m*

selenious *adj* CHEM sélénieux, sélénié

selenite *n* CHEM, MINERAL sélénite *m*

selenitic *adj* CHEM séléniteux

selenium *n (Se)* CHEM sélénium *m (Se)*; ~ **cell** *n* ELEC ENG, PHYS cellule au sélénium *f*; ~ **rectifier** *n* ELEC, ELEC ENG, PHYS redresseur au sélénium *m*; ~ **ruby glass** *n* C&G verre rubis au sélénium *m*

selenocyanate *n* CHEM sélénocyanate *m*

selenocyanic *adj* CHEM sélénocyanique

selenography *n* ASTRON sélénographie *f*

selenology *n* ASTRON sélénologie *f*

selenous *adj* CHEM sélénieux, sélénié

self-absorption *n* CHEM absorption propre *f*, RAD PHYS *of radiation* auto-absorption *f*

self-acting: ~ **brake** *n* VEHICLES frein automatique *m*; ~ **circular table** *n* MECH ENG *machine tool* table circulaire automatique *f*; ~ **feed** *n* MECH ENG pression automatique *f*; ~ **incline** *n* MECH ENG plan incliné automoteur *m*; ~ **injector** *n* MECH ENG injecteur à mise en marche automatique *m*; ~ **plane** *n* MECH ENG plan incliné automoteur *m*; ~ **regulator** *n* MECH ENG autorégulateur *m*, régulateur automatique *m*; ~ **sliding lathe** *n* MECH ENG *for surfacing, screw-cutting* tour parallèle à fileter charioter et surfacer *m*; ~ **switch** *n* ELEC ENG commutateur automatique *m*, commutateur conjoncteur *m*

self-adapting *adj* COMP, DP auto-adaptatif

self-adhering *adj* PROP MAT adhésif

self-adhesive: ~ **film** *n* PACKAGING film autocollant *m*; ~ **label** *n* PACKAGING étiquette autocollante *f*; ~ **laminated tape** *n* PACKAGING ruban autocollant laminé *m*; ~ **paper** *n* PACKAGING papier autocollant *m*; ~ **tape** *n* P&R bande adhésif *f*, ruban adhésif *m*, PACKAGING ruban autocollant *m*

self-adjusting[1] *adj* CONTROL auto-ajustable, autoréglable, avec calage automatique, à réglage automatique, autorégulé

self-adjusting[2] ~ **brake** *n* AUTO frein à rattrapage automatique de jeu *m*; ~ **clutch** *n* AUTO embrayage à rattrapage de jeu automatique *m*; ~ **floating weir** *n* MAR POLL barrage flottant autoréglable *m*, déversoir flottant autoréglable *m*, seuil flottant autoréglable *m*

self-adjustment *n* CONTROL autoréglage *m*, calage automatique *m*, réglage automatique *m*, TV autoréglage *m*

self-advancing: ~ **chock** *n* MINING pile de soutènement *f*

self-aligned: ~ **gate** *n* ELECTRON grille autoalignée *f*; ~ **transistor** *n* ELECTRON transistor à grille auto-alignée *m*

self-aligning: ~ **bearing** *n* MECH ENG coussinet à auto-alignement *m*, VEHICLES roulement à rotule *m*

self-balancing: ~ **switch** *n* ELEC ENG pont auto-équilibré *m*

self-bias *n* ELEC ENG polarisation automatique *f*

self-biased: ~ **tube** *n* ELECTRON tube à polarisation automatique *m*

self-blimped *adj* CINEMAT autosilencieux

self-canceling: ~ **steering column switch** *n* (AmE) *see self-cancelling steering column switch*; ~ **switch** *n* (AmE) *see self-cancelling switch*; ~ **turn signal switch** *n* (AmE) *see self-cancelling turn signal switch*

self-cancelling: ~ **steering column switch** *n* (BrE) ELEC *automotive* commutateur à rappel automatique *m*; ~ **switch** *n* (BrE) CONTROL interrupteur à rappel automatique *m*; ~ **turn signal switch** *n* (BrE) ELEC *automotive* commutateur à rappel automatique *m*

self-capacitance *n* ELEC *coil*, PHYS capacité propre *f*

self-centering: ~ **chuck** *n* (AmE) *see self-centring chuck*; ~ **die** *n* (AmE) *see self-centring die*; ~ **vise** *n* (AmE) *see self-centring vice*

self-centring: ~ **chuck** *n* (BrE) MECH ENG mandrin à serrage concentrique *m*; ~ **die** *n* (BrE) MECH ENG coussinet à rapprochement concentrique *m*; ~ **vice** *n* (BrE) MECH ENG étau à serrage concentrique *m*

self-checking: ~ **code** n *(cf error detecting code)* COMP, DP, ELECTRON code détecteur d'erreurs m

self-cleaning: ~ **air filter** n HEAT ENG filtre à air autonettoyant m

self-closing[1] *adj* CONTROL, PACKAGING autoserrant

self-closing:[2] ~ **cock** n (BrE) *(cf self-closing faucet)* CONST robinet se refermant automatiquement m, robinet à ressort m; ~ **door** n CONST porte automatique f; ~ **faucet** n (AmE) *(cf self-closing cock)* CONST robinet se refermant automatiquement m, robinet à ressort m

self-cocking: ~ **shutter** n PHOTO obturateur toujours armé m

self-color n (AmE), **self-colour** n (BrE) COLOURS teinte propre f

self-commutated: ~ **converter** n ELEC convertisseur à commutation automatique m

self-contained[1] *adj* PHYS autonome, SPACE *spacecraft* autonome, indépendant

self-contained:[2] ~ **accumulator** n HYDR EQUIP accumulateur autonome m; ~ **air conditioning unit** n REFRIG climatiseur monobloc m, conditionneur à air de type armoire m; ~ **countershaft** n MECH ENG renvoi adhérent m, renvoi de mouvement adhérent au bâti m; ~ **driving motion** n MECH ENG renvoi adhérent m, renvoi de mouvement adhérent au bâti m; ~ **navigational aid** n AERONAUT aide autonome à la navigation f; ~ **power steering system** n AUTO servodirection intégrée au boîtier f; ~ **pressure cable** n ELEC câble à pression sous gaine métallique m

self-controlling: ~ **system** n TV système autogérant m

self-coring: ~ **chisel** n CONST *wood-mortising* bédane à joues m

self-destruct n MILIT autodestructeur m

self-discharge n AUTO, ELEC ENG autodécharge f, SPACE *spacecraft* autodécharge f, décharge spontanée f; ~ **car** n (AmE) *(cf self-discharge wagon)* TRANSP wagon à déchargement automatique m; ~ **freight car** n (AmE) *(cf self-discharge goods wagon)* TRANSP wagon à déchargement automatique m; ~ **goods wagon** n (BrE) *(cf self-discharge freight car)* TRANSP wagon à déchargement automatique m; ~ **time constant** n ELEC ENG constante de temps d'autodécharge f; ~ **wagon** n (BrE) *(cf self-discharge car)* TRANSP wagon à déchargement automatique m

self-discharging: ~ **car** n (AmE) *(cf self-discharging wagon)* RAIL wagon autodéchargeable m; ~ **wagon** n (BrE) *(cf self-discharging car)* RAIL wagon autodéchargeable m; ~ **water bucket** n WATER SUPP cuffat à vidange automatique m

self-documenting *adj* COMP, DP autodocumentant

self-draining *adj* NAUT autovideur

self-drill: ~ **anchor** n CONST *building* cheville autoforeuse f

self-drive: ~ **taxi** n TRANSP taxi sans chauffeur m

self-dumping: ~ **bucket** n CONST benne à culbutage automatique f

self-erecting: ~ **screen** n PHOTO écran coffret automatique m

self-etching: ~ **primer** n COATINGS couche de fond au phosphate f, couche passivante à phosphate f

self-excitation n ELEC ENG, NUCLEAR auto-excitation f

self-excited: ~ **motor** n ELEC moteur excitateur m; ~ **oscillator** n ELECTRON oscillateur autoexcité m, oscillateur à autoexcitation m; ~ **power oscillator** n ELECTRON oscillateur de puissance autoexcité m, oscillateur de puissance à autoexcitation m

self-feeding: ~ **reamer** n MECH ENG alésoir à bout fileté pour l'amorçage m

self-firing n AUTO auto-allumage m

self-flux n PHYS flux propre m

self-generating: ~ **transducer** n ELEC ENG transducteur autogénérateur m

self-hardening n METALL autodurcissement m

self-healing n ELEC ENG autocicatrisation f; ~ **capacitor** n ELEC ENG condensateur autocicatrisant m; ~ **properties** n pl TEXTILES propriétés de resserrage de la maille f pl

self-heating n ELEC ENG auto-échauffement m, échauffement propre m; ~ **coefficient** n ELEC ENG coefficient d'auto-échauffement m

self-help: ~ **housing** n CONST *building* autoconstruction f

self-holding: ~ **taper** n MECH ENG *for tool shanks* cône à faible conicité m

self-identification n TELECOM auto-identification f

self-ignition n AUTO auto-allumage m

self-inductance n ELEC, PHYS inductance propre f; ~ **variation** n ELEC variation d'induction f

self-induction n AUTO auto-induction f, ELEC self-induction f, ELEC ENG auto-induction f, induction propre f, coefficient d'auto-induction m, coefficient d'induction propre m, inductance propre f, PHYS auto-induction f, self-induction f; ~ **current** n ELEC ENG courant d'auto-induction m

self-inflating *adj* MAR POLL autogonflant

self-inspection n QUALITY autocontrôle m

self-learning: ~ **machine** n COMP, DP machine d'auto-apprentissage f

self-lifting[1] *adj* PROD ENG à rappel

self-lifting:[2] ~ **pressure plate** n PROD ENG plaque de pression à rappel f; ~ **terminal clamp** n PROD ENG serre-fil terminal à rappel f

self-locking *adj* PACKAGING, VEHICLES autobloquant

self-loosening n NUCLEAR *bolts* desserrage spontané m

self-lubricating: ~ **bearing** n MECH ENG coussinet à graissage automatique m

self-luminosity n SPACE lueur propre f

self-noise n OCEANOG bruit propre m

self-opening: ~ **die head** n MECH ENG *of screwing machine* filière à déclenchement automatique f; ~ **screwing head** n MECH ENG *of screwing machine* filière à déclenchement automatique f

self-organizing: ~ **system** n COMP, DP système auto-organisateur m

self-orthogonal: ~ **convolutional coding** n TELECOM codage par convolution auto-orthogonal m

self-potential n GEOPHYS polarisation spontanée f; ~ **log** n GEOPHYS diagramme d'autopolarisation m, diagramme de polarisation spontanée m, PETR TECH diagraphie de polarisation spontanée f

self-powered *adj* ELEC ENG autonome

self-priming: ~ **dirty-water pump** n NUCLEAR pompe auto-amorçante à eau usée f; ~ **pump** n HYDR EQUIP pompe auto-amorçante f, VEHICLES *fuel* pompe auto-aspirante f

self-propelled[1] *adj* MAR POLL, NAUT *barge, dredger* automoteur, autopropulsé

self-propelled:[2] ~ **barge** n NAUT chaland automoteur m, péniche automotrice f; ~ **crane** n NUCLEAR grue automatique f; ~ **skimmer** n MAR POLL récupérateur autopropulsé m, écrémeur autopropulsé m; ~ **turret** n MILIT *of tank* tourelle à action automatique f

self-propulsion n SPACE autopropulsion f

self-purification n WATER SUPP auto-épuration f

self-reading: ~ staff n CONST *surveying* mire parlante f

self-registering: ~ apparatus n MECH ENG appareil enregistreur m, enregistreur m

self-regulating: ~ maintenance system n TRANSP système d'entretien autocontrôlé m

self-relative: ~ addressing n COMP adressage différentiel m, DP adressage autorelatif m

self-resetting: ~ loop n COMP, DP boucle autorestaurée f; **~ relay** n ELEC relais à réenclenchement m

self-righting[1] adj NAUT *lifeboat* inchavirable, à redressement automatique

self-righting:[2] **~ test** n NAUT *lifeboat* épreuve d'autoredressement f

self-sagging: ~ temperature n C&G température de fléchissement f

self-scattering n PHYS autodiffusion f

self-seal: ~ pocket envelope n PACKAGING pochette autocollante f

self-sealing[1] adj PACKAGING autocollant, SPACE *spacecraft* auto-obturant

self-sealing:[2] **~ pump** n PACKAGING pompe auto-étanchéifiante f

self-service n PACKAGING self-service m; **~ station** n TRANSP station libre-service f; **~ teller** n CONTROL guichet libre-service m

self-setting n CONTROL calage automatique m

self-shade n COLOURS teinture propre f

self-shielding adj PROD ENG autoprotecteur

self-starting: ~ synchronous motor n ELEC ENG moteur autosynchrone m

self-supporting: ~ partition n CONST *building* cloison en décharge f, cloison en porte-à-faux f; **~ rigid vehicle** n TRANSP véhicule autoportant rigide m

self-sustained: ~ discharge n ELEC ENG décharge autonome f

self-teach: ~ manual n PROD ENG manuel d'autoformation m

self-tensioning: ~ winch n NAUT *deck fittings* treuil à tension constante m

self-threading n CINEMAT chargement automatique m

self-timer n PHOTO déclencheur à retardement m

self-tipping: ~ car n (AmE) *(cf self-tipping wagon)* RAIL wagon à basculement automatique m; **~ wagon** n (BrE) *(cf self-tipping car)* RAIL wagon à basculement automatique m

self-tracking n ELECTRON autocentrage de la bande passante m, autocentrage m; **~ band-pass filter** n ELECTRON filtre passe-bande autocentré m

self-venting: ~ system n PACKAGING ventilation autonome f

self-vulcanization n P&R autovulcanisation f

sell: ~ by phr PACKAGING *date marking* à vendre avant le

sellaite n MINERAL sellaïte f

Sellers: ~ thread n MECH ENG pas américain système Sellers m

selsyn: ~ motor n CINEMAT moteur interlock m, moteur selsyn m, moteur à synchronisation automatique m

selvage n CONST *of lock* rebord m, tête de palastre f, têtière f, MINING *clay* lisière f, salbande f, salbande argileuse f, PAPER TECH, TEXTILES lisière f **~ cutting process** n TEXTILES processus de coupe des lisières m

selvedge n CONST rebord m, tête de palastre f, têtière f, MINING *clay* lisière f, salbande f, salbande argileuse f, PAPER TECH, TEXTILES lisière f

SEM abbr *(surface electron microscope)* INSTRUMENT microscope électronique à balayage de surface m

semantic: ~ analysis n COMP, DP analyse sémantique f

semantics n COMP, DP sémantique f

semaphore n COMP, DP sémaphore m; **~ signal** n CONTROL signal à bras m, sémaphore m

semaphoric: ~ program n (AmE), **~ programme** n (BrE) TRANSP *traffic* programme de signalisation m

semelin n MINERAL séméline f

semeline n MINERAL séméline f

SEMF abbr *(synchronous equipment management function)* TELECOM fonction de gestion d'équipement synchrone f

semiactive: ~ landing gear n AERONAUT train d'atterrissage semi-actif m

semiamphibious: ~ air cushion vehicle n TRANSP aéroglisseur semi-amphibie m; **~ hovercraft** n TRANSP aéroglisseur semi-amphibie m

semianthracite n COAL TECH houille anthraciteuse f

semiautomatic[1] adj MECH ENG semi-automatique

semiautomatic:[2] **~ labeling machine** n (AmE), **~ labelling machine** n (BrE) PACKAGING étiqueteuse semi-automatique f; **~ points switching** n RAIL aiguillage semi-automatique m; **~ pressing** n C&G pressage semi-automatique m; **~ system** n TELECOM système de commutation semi-automatique m, système semi-automatique m; **~ transmission** n VEHICLES boîte de vitesses semi-automatique f; **~ trunk working** n TELECOM exploitation semi-automatique interurbaine f

semibituminous[1] adj COAL TECH demi-gras

semibituminous:[2] **~ coal** n COAL TECH charbon demi-gras m

semibleached: ~ pulp n PAPER TECH pâte mi-blanchie f

semibrittle: ~ fracture n METALL rupture semi-fragile f

semicarbazide n CHEM semi-carbazide f

semicarbazone n CHEM semi-carbazone f

semichemical: ~ pulp n PAPER TECH pâte mi-chimique f

semicircle n CONST, GEOM demi-cercle m

semicircular: ~ arch n CONST *curve* arc plein cintre m, arc romain m, *for bridge* arche plein cintre f, *structure* voûte de plein cintre f, voûte en plein cintre f; **~ beta spectrograph** n NUCLEAR spectrographe semi-circulaire bêta m; **~ lens** n INSTRUMENT lentille demi-boule f

semiclassical: ~ approximation n NUCLEAR *scattering theory* approximation semi-classique f

semiconductor n COMP, ELECTRON, PHYS semi-conducteur m; **~ amplifier** n TELECOM amplificateur à semi-conducteurs m; **~ bolometer** n ASTRON, PHYS bolomètre à semi-conducteur m; **~ chip** n ELECTRON puce de semi-conducteur f; **~ component** n ELECTRON composant à semi-conducteur m, PROP MAT composant monolithique m, composant à semi-conducteur m; **~ contactor** n ELECTRON contacteur à semi-conducteur m; **~ crosspoint** n TELECOM point de connexion à semi-conducteur m; **~ crystal** n ELECTRON cristal semi-conducteur m; **~ device** n COMP dispositif à semi-conducteurs m; **~ diode** n COMP, ELECTRON diode à semi-conducteur f; **~ doping** n ELECTRON dopage des semi-conducteurs m; **~ fabrication** n ELECTRON fabrication de semi-conducteur f; **~ integrated circuit** n ELECTRON circuit intégré à semi-conducteur m; **~ laser** n ELECTRON, OPT, RAD PHYS, TELECOM laser à semi-conducteur m; **~ layer** n ELECTRON couche de semi-conducteur f, couche semi-conductrice f; **~ material** n ELECTRON corps semi-conducteur m, matériau semi-conducteur m; **~ memory** n COMP, ELEC ENG mémoire à semi-conducteurs f; **~ microphone** n RE-

CORDING microphone à semi-conducteur *m*; ~ **photo-detector** *n* ELECTRON photodétecteur à semi-conducteur *m*; ~ **rectifier** *n* ELEC, ELEC ENG redresseur à semi-conducteur *m*; ~ **relay** *n* ELEC ENG relais à semi-conducteur *m*; ~ **resistor** *n* ELEC ENG résistance à semi-conducteur *f*; ~ **single crystal** *n* ELECTRON monocristal de semi-conducteur *m*; ~ **substrate** *n* ELECTRON substrat en semi-conducteur *m*; ~ **switch** *n* ELEC ENG interrupteur à semi-conducteur *m*; ~ **switching device** *n* ELEC appareil de connexion à semi-conducteur *m*; ~ **technology** *n* ELECTRON technique des composants à semi-conducteur *f*; ~ **wafer** *n* ELECTRON plaquette en semi-conducteur *f*

semicontainer: ~ **ship** *n* TRANSP navire semi-porte conteneur *m*

semicontinuous: ~ **casting** *n* C&G coulée semi-continue *f*

semicustom[1] *adj* COMP, DP semi-personnalisé

semicustom:[2] ~ **chip** *n* ELECTRON puce semi-personnalisée *f*; ~ **circuit** *n* ELECTRON circuit semi-personnalisé *m*

semi-diesel: ~ **engine** *n* AUTO, MECH ENG moteur semi-diesel *m*

semidine *n* CHEM semidine *f*

semidirectional: ~ **microphone** *n* ACOUSTICS, RECORDING microphone semi-directionnel *m*

semidiurnal: ~ **tide** *n* NAUT, OCEANOG marée semi-diurne *f*; ~ **wave** *n* OCEANOG onde semi-diurne *f*

semielliptic: ~ **spring** *n* SPRINGS ressort semi-elliptique *m*

semienclosed: ~ **motor** *n* ELEC moteur demi-enfermé *m*

semifast: ~ **train** *n* (BrE) *(cf limited train)* RAIL train à desserte limitée *m*

semifinished *adj* PROD ENG semi-fini, semi-ouvré

semi-floating: ~ **axle** *n* AUTO arbre semi-porteur *m*, VEHICLES *rear axle* arbre semi-flottant *m*

semigantry: ~ **crane** *n* CONST grue à demi-portique *f*

semigelatin *n* MINING semi-gélatine dynamite *f*; ~ **dynamite** *n* MINING semi-gélatine dynamite *f*; ~ **explosive** *n* MINING semi-gélatine dynamite *f*

semihomogeneous: ~ **fuel element** *n* NUCLEAR élément combustible semi-homogène *m*

semihot: ~ **laboratory** *n* NUCLEAR laboratoire semi-chaud *m*

semi-impermeable: ~ **layer** *n* WATER SUPP couche semi-imperméable *f*

semi-infinite: ~ **crack** *n* NUCLEAR fissure semi-infinie *f*

semi-insulating: ~ **substrate** *n* ELECTRON substrat semi-isolant *m*

semimajor: ~ **axis** *n* SPACE demi-grand axe *m*

semimatt *adj* TEXTILES mi-mat

semimetal *n* CHEM demi-métal *m*

semimetallic *adj* CHEM demi-métallique

semipermanent: ~ **anticyclone** *n* METEO anticyclone semi-permanent *m*

semipermeable: ~ **membrane** *n* PHYS membrane semi-perméable *f*

semipermissive: ~ **stop signal** *n* RAIL disque rouge *m* (Fra)

semipolar *adj* CHEM semi-polaire

semiportable *adj* MECH ENG demi-fixe, mi-fixe, semi-fixe

semipositive: ~ **mold** *n* (AmE), ~ **mould** *n* (BrE) P&R *press* moule semi-positif *m*

semireflecting: ~ **mirror** *n* INSTRUMENT miroir semi-argenté *m*, miroir à argenture semi-transparente *m*; ~ **plate** *n* PHYS lame semi-réfléchissante *f*

semireinforcing: ~ **carbon black** *n* *(SRF carbon black)* P&R noir SRF *m*

semirigid: ~ **automatic coupling** *n* TRANSP attelage automatique semi-rigide *m*; ~ **delivery hose** *n* SAFETY *firefighting* tuyau de refoulement semi-rigide *m*

semirotary: ~ **actuator** *n* PROD ENG actionneur oscillant *m*; ~ **pump** *n* WATER SUPP pompe demi-rotative *f*, pompe semi-rotative *f*

semisilvered: ~ **mirror** *n* INSTRUMENT miroir semi-argenté *m*, miroir à argenture semi-transparente *m*

semiskimmed *adj* FOOD TECH demi-écrémé

semislipper: ~ **piston** *n* AUTO piston à jupe découpée *m*

semisolid: ~ **combustible waste** *n* POLLUTION déchets combustibles semi-solides *m pl*

semisubmersible: ~ **platform** *n* PETR plate-forme semi-submersible *f*; ~ **rig** *n* PETR TECH plate-forme semi-submersible *f*

semitone *n* ACOUSTICS demi-ton tempéré *m*, PHYS demi-ton *m*

semitraffic: ~ **actuated signal** *n* TRANSP feu commandé partiellement par les véhicules *m*

semitrailer *n* TRANSP *vehicles*, VEHICLES semi-remorque *f*; ~ **motor vehicle** *n* TRANSP tracteur de semi-remorque *m*; ~ **towing vehicle** *n* TRANSP tracteur de semi-remorque *m*; ~ **truck** *n* TRANSP tracteur de semi-remorque *m*

semitrailing: ~ **arm** *n* VEHICLES *rear axle* bras oblique *m*, triangle oblique *m*

semitransparent: ~ **color** *n* (AmE), ~ **colour** *n* (BrE) C&G couleur semi-transparente *f*; ~ **photocathode** *n* ELEC ENG photocathode semi-transparente *f*

semiverter *n* ELEC *circuit* circuit inverseur à semi-conducteurs *m*

senarmontite *n* MINERAL sénarmontite *f*

send *vt* COMP, DP envoyer, émettre; ~ **into space** *vt* SPACE *spacecraft* spatialiser

sender *n* TELECOM expéditeur *m*, émetteur *m*; ~ **identification** *n* TELECOM identification de l'expéditeur *f*

sender-receiver *n* COMP, DP émetteur-récepteur *m*

sending *n* COMP, DP émission *f*

sendout *n* GAS TECH débit *m*; ~ **rate** *n* GAS TECH débit de pointe *m*

senhouse: ~ **slip** *n* NAUT *deck fittings* bosse à échappement *f*

sennet *n* NAUT aiguillette *f*, tresse *f*

sense *n* COMP détection *f*, GEOL *of vector* sens *m*; ~ **amplifier** *n* ELECTRON amplificateur de lecture *m*

sensible: ~ **cooling effect** *n* REFRIG *of air* action refroidissante totale *f*; ~ **heat** *n* GEOPHYS, HEAT ENG, PHYS chaleur sensible *f*; ~ **heat ratio** *n* REFRIG rapport de chaleur sensible *m*

sensing *n* COMP, DP détection *f*, NUCLEAR captage *m*; ~ **electrode** *n* ELEC ENG électrode de mesure *f*; ~ **element** *n* ELECTRON élément sensible *m*, MAR POLL capteur *m*, détecteur *m*, sonde *f*, NUCLEAR capteur *m*; ~ **lead** *n* ELEC ENG fil de mesure *m*; ~ **relay** *n* ELEC ENG relais sensible *m*; ~ **resistor** *n* ELEC ENG résistance de détection *f*; ~ **switch** *n* ELEC ENG interrupteur à faible course *m*

sensitive: ~ **altimeter** *n* AERONAUT altimètre de précision *m*; ~ **energy** *n* GAS TECH énergie sensible *f*; ~ **friction drill** *n* MECH ENG machine à percer sensitive à plateaux de friction *f*; ~ **gang drill** *n* MECH ENG machine à percer sensitive multiple *f*; ~ **heat air cooler** *n* REFRIG refroidisseur d'air à chaleur sensible *m*; ~ **paper** *n* PHOTO papier sensible *m*

sensitivity *n* COAL TECH, COMP, DP, ELEC, ELEC ENG, MINING sensibilité *f*, OPT sensibilité *f*, sensibilité énergétique *f*, seuil de détection *m*, PHYS, RECORDING,

SPACE *communications*, TELECOM sensibilité *f*; **~ analysis** *n* PROD ENG analyse de sensibilité *f*; **~ to initiation** *n* MINING sensibilité à l'amorce *f*; **~ to light** *n* RAD PHYS sensibilité à la lumière *f*

sensitization *n* PHOTO sensibilisation *f*

sensitize *vt* CINEMAT, PHOTO sensibiliser

sensitized: **~ fluorescence** *n* RAD PHYS fluorescence sensibilisée *f*

sensitizer *n* CINEMAT, PRINT sensibilisateur *m*

sensitizing: **~ bath** *n* PHOTO bain sensibilisateur *m*

sensitometric: **~ curve** *n* ACOUSTICS courbe sensitométrique *f*, CINEMAT courbe caractéristique *f*, courbe sensitométrique *f*, ELECTRON courbe caractéristique *f*; **~ step wedge** *n* CINEMAT coin sensitométrique *m*

sensitometry *n* ACOUSTICS, CINEMAT sensitométrie *f*

sensor *n* AUTO, COMP, DP capteur *m*, ELECTRON capteur *m*, détecteur *m*, METEO, METR *of instrument*, NAUT, NUCLEAR capteur *m*, PHYS capteur *m*, détecteur *m*, sonde *f*, SPACE *communications* détecteur *m*, *spacecraft* capteur *m*, TELECOM capteur *m*, détecteur *m*, TESTING, VEHICLES *instruments* capteur *m*; **~ signal** *n* CONTROL, ELECTRON signal de capteur *m*; **~ system** *n* SPACE groupe-capteur *m*

sentence *n* COMP, DP *COBOL* phrase *f*

sentinel *n* COMP, DP sentinelle *f*, PRINT balise d'identification *f*, balise de codification *f*, balise de marquage *f*, sentinelle *f*

separability *n* NUCLEAR *diffractionometry* séparabilité *f*

separable *adj* CHEM séparable

separate:[1] **~ collection** *n* RECYCLING collecte sélective *f*; **~ excitation** *n* ELEC ENG excitation indépendante *f*, excitation séparée *f*; **~ excited dynamo** *n* ELEC ENG dynamo à excitation séparée *f*; **~ excited generator** *n* ELEC ENG génératrice à excitation séparée *f*; **~ lead cable** *n* ELEC câble armé multiple *m*; **~ sewerage system** *n* WATER SUPP réseau séparatif *m*, système séparatif d'assainissement *m*; **~ ventilation** *n* MINING aérage distinct *m*; **~ winding transformer** *n* ELEC transformateur à enroulements séparés *m*

separate[2] *vt* CHEM décanter, séparer, CHEM TECH *fluids* précipiter, séparer, *solids* cribler, trier, GAS TECH séparer; **~ by pressing** *vt* CHEM TECH faire sortir par pression; **~ out** *vt* CHEM séparer

separate[3] *vi* CHEM se séparer par précipitation; **~ as flocculent preparation** *vi* CHEM TECH se séparer en flocons; **~ out** *vi* CHEM se séparer par précipitation, CHEM TECH se séparer en dissociation, se séparer par précipitation

separated-braking: **~ circuits** *n pl* TRANSP double circuit de freinage *m*

separately: **~ excited motor** *n* ELEC moteur à excitation indépendante *m*; **~ lead-sheathed cable** *n* ELEC câble triplomb *m*

separating: **~ agent** *n* CHEM TECH agent de séparation *m*; **~ burette** *n* CHEM TECH burette de séparation *f*; **~ column** *n* CHEM TECH colonne à fractionner *f*; **~ funnel** *n* CHEM TECH entonnoir de décantation *m*, entonnoir de séparation *m*, LAB EQUIP *glassware* ampoule à décanter *f*; **~ power** *n* NUCLEAR pouvoir séparateur *m*; **~ rod** *n* TEXTILES baguette de séparation *f*

separation *n* CHEM dégagement *m*, séparation *f*, CHEM TECH décomposition *f*, COAL TECH séparation *f*, PETR TECH prétraitement *m*, séparation *f*, triage *m*, PHYS décollement *m*, PRINT sélection *f*, séparation *m*, SPACE *spacecraft*, TEXTILES séparation *f*; **~ by geometry** *n* NUCLEAR séparation géométrique *f*; **~ circuit** *n* TV

circuit de tri de signaux *m*; **~ density** *n* COAL TECH densité de séparation *f*; **~ effect** *n* CHEM TECH pouvoir séparateur *m*; **~ filter** *n* ELECTRON filtre de voie *m*, TV coupleur sélectif *m*; **~ funnel** *n* CHEM ampoule à décanter *f*, entonnoir à séparation *m*; **~ layer** *n* CHEM TECH couche de séparation *f*; **~ liquid** *n* CHEM TECH liquide séparateur *m*; **~ maneuver** *n* (AmE), **~ manoeuvre** *n* (BrE) SPACE *spacecraft* manoeuvre de séparation *f*; **~ master** *n* CINEMAT interpositif de sélection *m*; **~ mechanism** *n* SPACE mécanisme de séparation *m*; **~ motor** *n* SPACE *spacecraft* moteur de séparation *m*; **~ negative** *n* CINEMAT extraction monochrome *f*, négatif de sélection *m*; **~ positive** *n* CINEMAT positif de sélection *m*; **~ process** *n* CHEM TECH procédé de séparation *m*, technique de séparation *f*; **~ rocket** *n* SPACE *spacecraft* fusée de séparation *f*; **~ size** *n* CHEM TECH maille de séparation *f*

separative: **~ effort** *n* NUCLEAR pouvoir séparateur *m*

separator *n* CHEM TECH piège *m*, séparateur *m*, COAL TECH, COMP, CRYSTALL, DP, ELEC *cable* séparateur *m*, FOOD TECH écrémeuse *f*, MAR POLL séparateur *m*, MECH ENG *oil* dégraisseur *m*, déshuileur *m*, séparateur *m*, MINING séparateur *m*, trieur *m*, PETR, PROP MAT, TELECOM, WATER SUPP séparateur *m*; **~ funnel** *n* CHEM ampoule à décanter *f*, entonnoir à séparation *m*; **~ symbol** *n* COMP symbole séparateur *m*, DP symbole de séparation *m*

sepia: **~ toning** *n* PHOTO virage en sépia *m*

sepiolite *n* MINERAL sépiolite *f*

sepmag *n* CINEMAT positif double bande avec son magnétique *m*; **~ lock** *n* CINEMAT verrouillage double bande *m*

sepopt *n* CINEMAT positif double bande avec son optique *m*

septic: **~ sludge** *n* RECYCLING boues d'égout septique *f pl*, boues septiques *f pl*; **~ tank** *n* HYDROL *sewage* fosse septique *f*, fosse septique à compartiments *f*, RECYCLING, WATER SUPP fosse septique *f*

septivalent *adj* CHEM septivalent

septum *n* ELEC ENG *waveguides* diaphragme *m*

sequence *n* ACOUSTICS modulation musicale *f*, GEOL *of beds* ensemble *m*, faisceau *m*, séquence *f*, série *f*, MATH progression *f*, suite *f*; **~ check** *n* COMP, CONTROL, DP contrôle de séquence *m*; **~ control** *n* COMP mode séquentiel *m*, DP commande séquentielle *f*; **~ control register** *n* COMP compteur d'instructions *m*, registre de contrôle de séquence *m*, DP compteur d'instructions *m*, registre de contrôle de séquence *m*; **~ current transformer** *n* PROD ENG transformateur de courant séquentiel *m*; **~ number** *n* (*SN*) TELECOM numéro de séquence *m*; **~ number protection** *n* (*SNP*) TELECOM protection de numéro de séquence *f*; **~ relay** *n* ELEC ENG relais clignoteur *m*, relais à séquence *m*; **~ valve** *n* MECH ENG soupape de séquence *f*

sequencer *n* COMP séquenceur *m*, DP contrôleur de séquence *m*, séquenceur *m*, ELEC ENG, PROD ENG, TELECOM séquenceur *m*; **~ input** *n* PROD ENG entrée séquenceur *f*; **~ input instruction** *n* PROD ENG instruction de séquenceur sur entrées *f*; **~ instruction data form** *n* PROD ENG grille de saisie pour séquenceur *f*; **~ jump operation** *n* PROD ENG instruction de saut dans un séquenceur *f*; **~ load** *n* PROD ENG chargement séquenceur *m*; **~ output** *n* PROD ENG sortie séquenceur *f*; **~ output instruction** *n* PROD ENG instruction de séquenceur sur sorties *f*; **~ step instruction** *n* PROD ENG déroulement des pas de séquenceur *m*

sequencing n COMP, DP mise en séquence f, ELEC ENG séquencement m, TELECOM maintien en séquence m
sequential[1] adj COMP, DP séquentiel
sequential:[2] ~ **access** n COMP, DP accès séquentiel m; ~ **color with memory system** n (AmE), ~ **colour with memory system** n (BrE) TV standard système séquentiel à mémoire m; ~ **control** n CONTROL régulation en cascade f; ~ **decoding** n TELECOM décodage séquentiel m; ~ **file** n COMP, DP fichier séquentiel m; ~ **input/output** n (SIO) COMP entrée/sortie séquentielle f; ~ **interlace** n TV analyse entrelacée séquentielle f; ~ **numbering** n PRINT numérotation en séquence f; ~ **processing** n COMP traitement en séquence m, DP traitement séquentiel m; ~ **scanning** n TV analyse ligne par ligne non entrelacée f, balayage séquentiel m; ~ **search** n COMP, DP recherche séquentielle f; ~ **test** n TELECOM essai séquentiel m; ~ **tone coding** n TELECOM codage à tonalités séquentielles m
sequester vt CHEM complexer
sequestering: ~ **agent** adj CHEM complexant
sequestrene n CHEM sesquestrène m
serial[1] adj COMP série, DP séquentiel, série, PRINT, TELECOM en série
serial:[2] ~ **access** n COMP, DP accès séquentiel m; ~ **access device** n COMP dispositif à accès série m, DP unité à accès série f; ~ **access storage** n COMP mémoire à accès séquentiel f; ~ **adder** n COMP, DP, ELECTRON additionneur série m; ~ **analog-to-digital conversion** n (AmE) see serial analogue-to-digital conversion; ~ **analog-to-digital converter** n (AmE) see serial analogue-to-digital converter; ~ **analogue-to-digital conversion** n (BrE) CONST, ELECTRON conversion série f, numérisation série f; ~ **analogue-to-digital converter** n (BrE) CONST numériseur série m, ELECTRON convertisseur série m, numériseur série m; ~ **computer** n COMP ordinateur série m, DP calculateur sériel m; ~ **converter** n CONST convertisseur série m; ~ **digital output** n COMP, DP sortie numérique série f; ~ **digital signal** n ELECTRON signal numérique série m; ~ **form** n ELEC ENG forme série f; ~ **interface** n COMP, DP, PRINT, TELECOM interface série f; ~ **line** n ELEC ENG ligne de transmission en série f; ~ **memory** n ELEC ENG mémoire série f; ~ **number** n COMP numéro de série m, DP nombre ordinal m, numéro d'ordre m, ordinal m, MECH ENG, PATENTS numéro de série m, PHOTO numéro de fabrication m; ~ **operation** n COMP, DP opération séquentielle f; ~ **printer** n COMP imprimante sérielle f, PRINT imprimante en série f; ~ **processing** n COMP, DP traitement série m; ~ **programmable interface** n TELECOM interface série programmable f; ~ **programming** n COMP programmation série f, DP programmation séquentielle f; ~ **rudders** n pl AERONAUT aircraft gouvernes en série f pl; ~ **storage** n COMP mémoire série f; ~ **subtractor** n ELECTRON soustracteur série m; ~ **transfer** n COMP, DP transfert série m; ~ **transmission** n COMP, DP transfert série m; ~ **wiring** n PROD ENG câblage en série m
serialization n ELEC ENG sérialisation f
serialize vt COMP, DP sérialiser, ELEC ENG convertir de parallèle en série, sérialiser
serializer n ELEC ENG sérialiseur m
serial-parallel adj COMP, DP série-parallèle
serial-to-parallel: ~ **conversion** n ELEC ENG conversion de série en parallèle f, conversion série-parallèle f, parallélisation f; ~ **converter** n ELEC ENG convertisseur série-parallèle m, paralléliseur m

sericite n MINERAL séricite f; ~ **schist** n GEOL metamorphic rock séricito-schiste m
serie n CHEM of reactions caténaire f
series n COMP, DP, ELEC circuit, GEOL set of beds, MATH, MECH ENG of workstations série f; ~ **arrangement** n ELEC ENG branchement en série m, montage en série m; ~ **capacitance** n ELEC ENG capacité en série f; ~ **capacitor** n ELEC capaciteur série m, ELEC ENG condensateur monté en série m; ~ **circuit** n ELEC ENG, MINING, TELECOM circuit série m; ~ **coil** n ELEC bobine série f; ~ **collector resistance** n ELEC ENG résistance série du collecteur f; ~ **connection** n ELEC circuit montage en série m, ELEC ENG connexion en série f, couplage en série m, montage en série m, MINING branchement en série m, montage en série m, PHYS montage en série m; ~ **converter** n ELEC ENG convertisseur à inductance série m; ~ **DC motor** n (series direct current motor) ELEC ENG moteur série à courant continu m, moteur à courant continu à excitation série m; ~ **direct current motor** n (series DC motor) ELEC ENG moteur série à courant continu m, moteur à courant continu à excitation série m; ~ **dynamo** n ELEC ENG dynamo série f; ~ **excitation** n ELEC ENG excitation en série f; ~ **excited machine** n ELEC ENG machine à excitation en série f; ~ **feed** n ELEC ENG alimentation série f; ~ **feedback** n ELEC ENG contre-réaction série f; ~ **inductor** n ELEC inductance série f; ~ **input/output** n (SIO) COMP entrée/sortie série f; ~ **of links** n TELECOM connecting suite de passages f; ~ **motor** n ELEC moteur série m, ELEC ENG moteur série m, moteur à excitation série m; ~ **mounting** n ELEC circuit montage en série m; ~ **production** n NAUT shipbuilding construction en série f; ~ **reactance** n ELEC ENG réactance en série f; ~ **regulation** n ELEC ENG régulation série f; ~ **regulator** n ELEC ENG régulateur série m; ~ **resistance** n ELEC ENG rectifier junction résistance série f; ~ **resistor** n ELEC résistance série f; ~ **resonance** n ELEC ENG, PHYS résonance série f; ~ **resonant circuit** n ELEC ENG circuit résonnant série m; ~ **starter** n ELEC rhéostat-démarreur en série m; ~ **switch** n ELEC commutateur en série m, commutateur multiple m, commutateur à plusieurs directions m; ~ **transformer** n ELEC transformateur survolteur-dévolteur m; ~ **winding** n ELEC, ELEC ENG enroulement série m
series-connected[1] adj ELEC ENG, PHYS monté en série
series-connected:[2] ~ **resistance** n ELEC résistance en série f
series-parallel: ~ **circuit** n ELEC ENG circuit série-parallèle m, MINING circuit en séries parallèles m; ~ **switch** n ELEC ENG coupleur série-parallèle m
series-pass: ~ **power transistor** n ELECTRON transistor de puissance employé comme transistor ballast m; ~ **transistor** n ELECTRON transistor ballast m, transistor série m, transistor de régulation m
series-produced: ~ **power reactor** n NUCLEAR réacteur de puissance en série m;
series-regulated: ~ **power supply** n ELEC ENG alimentation régulée série f, alimentation à régulation série f
series-wound: ~ **dynamo** n ELEC generator dynamo en série f, ELEC ENG dynamo série f; ~ **machine** n ELEC generator machine à excitation en série f; ~ **motor** n ELEC, ELEC ENG moteur série m
serif n PRINT typeface empattement m
serigraphy n PRINT impression sérigraphique f, sérigraphie f
serotonin n CHEM entéromine f, sérotonine f

Serpens n ASTRON Serpent m

serpent: ~ **coil** n LAB EQUIP *distillation* serpentin m

serpentine n MINERAL serpentine f

serpentinization n FUELLESS serpentinisation f

serrated: ~ **lockwasher** n MECH ENG rondelle à denture extérieure f; ~ **pulse** n TV impulsion à crête fractionnée f

serration n MECH ENG denteluref; ~ **hackle** n C&G dents de requin f pl

serrodyne:[1] ~ **modulator** n ELECTRON modulateur dynamiseur m

serrodyne[2] vi ELECTRON dynamiser le signal

serve vt PROD ENG *boiler* chauffer

server n COMP, DP serveur m

service n COMP, DP, QUALITY service m, RAIL desserte f; ~ **access point** n *(SAP)* TELECOMpoint d'accès au service m; ~ **access point identifier** n *(SAPI)* TELECOM identificateur de point d'accès au réseau m; ~ **area** n AERONAUT *airport* bloc technique m, SPACE zone de service f; ~ **bit** n COMP, DP bit de service m; ~ **brake** n VEHICLES frein de service m; ~ **ceiling** n AERONAUT *aircraft* plafond d'utilisation m, plafond de service m, plafond pratique m, plafond utile m; ~ **cycle** n PROD ENG temps de cycle m; ~ **data unit** n *(SDU)* TELECOM unité de données de service f; ~ **gage** n (AmE), ~ **gauge** n (BrE) REFRIG manomètre de monteur m; ~ **layer** n TELECOM couche de services f; ~ **level** n PROD ENG niveau de service m; ~ **life** n COAL TECH, CONST durée de vie f, ELEC ENG durée de service f, durée de vie en service f, NUCLEAR durée de vie f, SPACE *spacecraft* vie opérationnelle f; ~ **line** n ELEC ENG branchement d'abonné m, ligne de service f; ~ **load** n REFRIG charge calorifique d'exploitation f, WATER SUPP charge utile f; ~ **mark** n PATENTS marque de service f; ~ **oscillator** n ELECTRON générateur HF m, hétérodyne m, oscillateur de service m; ~ **pistol** n MILIT revolver d'ordonnance m; ~ **program** n COMP, DP programme de service m; ~ **provider** n *(SP)* TELECOM fournisseur de service m, prestataire de service m; ~ **provider link** n *(SPL)* TELECOM liaison de prestataire de service f; ~ **road** n CONST voie de desserte f; ~ **station** n PROD ENG, TRANSP station-service f; ~ **steam** n NUCLEAR vapeur achetée au dedans f, vapeur de service f; ~ **string advice** n TELECOM avis de chaîne de service m; ~ **time** n PROD ENG durée d'utilisation f, TELECOM temps de service m; ~ **tools** n pl MECH ENG outils d'entretien et de dépannage m pl; ~ **trolley** n AERONAUT chariot de service à bord m; ~ **tunnel** n CONST tunnel de service m; ~ **vehicle** n TRANSP *aviation* véhicule d'entretien m; ~ **volume** n TRANSP débit de service m

serviceability n NUCLEAR *of fuel rod* disponibilité f

service-or-option: ~ **not available class** n TELECOM classe service-ou-option indisponible f; ~ **not implemented class** n TELECOM classe service-ou-option non mis en oeuvre f

servicer n AERONAUT oléoserveur m

services n pl PATENTS services m pl

serving n ELEC *cable* matelas extérieur m, TELECOM *of subscribers* desserte f; ~ **exchange** n TELECOM central serveur m, centre de rattachement m, commutateur de rattachement m

servo n CONTROL servomécanisme m, VEHICLES *brakes, steering, clutch* servo m;

servoaltimeter n AERONAUT altimètre asservi m

servoamplifier n CONTROL amplificateur automatique m, amplificateur de réglage m, ELECTRON amplificateur d'asservissement m

servo-assisted adj CONTROL assisté

servobrake n AUTO, TRANSP servofrein m

servocapstan n TV asservissement du cabestan m

servocomponent n CONTROL composant de réglage m

servocontrol n AERONAUT, CINEMAT, CONTROL, ELEC ENG, TRANSP servocommande f; ~ **mechanism** n CONTROL servocommande f

servo-controlled: ~ **tape mechanism** n TV mécanisme de bande asservi m

servocontroller n CONTROL régulateur par poursuite m

servodrive n CONTROL servomoteur m

servo-driven adj CONTROL asservi, à servomoteur

servofollower n CONTROL régulateur en cascade m

servogovernor n CONTROL régulateur par poursuite m

servohydraulic: ~ **test equipment** n MECH ENG moyens d'essais servo-hydrauliques m pl

servoloop n CINEMAT boucle d'asservissement f, circuit d'asservissement m, circuit de régularisation m, CONTROL boucle d'asservissement f, chaîne d'asservissement f, TV boucle d'asservissement f, circuit de régulation m; ~ **regulator** n CONTROL régulateur par poursuite f

servomechanism n COMP asservissement m, servomécanisme m, CONTROL servocommande f, DP mécanisme asservi m, servomécanisme m, ELEC ENG servomécanisme m, PHYS appareil d'asservissement m, servomécanisme m, TV servomécanisme m

servomodulator: ~ **valve** n AUTO soupape modulatrice de servo-piston f

servomotor n CONTROL moteur de commande m, moteur de positionnement m, servomoteur m, ELEC ENG, FUELLESS, NUCLEAR servomoteur m

servo-operated: ~ **valve** n REFRIG vanne télécommandée automatique f

servopositioner n CONTROL servopositionneur m

servostability n CONTROL stabilité d'un système asservi f

servostabilization n CONTROL stabilisation par asservissement f

servosystem n CONTROL système asservi m, système de commande en chaîne fermée m, SPACE *communications* système d'asservissement m, TV système asservi m; ~ **drift** n SPACE *communications* dérive de l'asservissement f

servo-unit n TRANSP servomoteur m

servovalve n CONTROL servosoupape f, MECH ENG servodistributeur m, PROD ENG servovanne f

servowheel n TV asservissement de disque de têtes m

servozoom n CINEMAT commande électronique de zoom f

SES abbr *(severely errored second)* NAUT *satellites*, TELECOM seconde gravement erronée f

sesquiterpenoid adj CHEM sesquiterpénique

sessile: ~ **dislocation** n CRYSTALL dislocation sessile f

session n COMP, DP session f; ~ **layer** n COMP, DP couche de session f; ~ **protocol** n *(SP)* TELECOM protocole de session m; ~ **protocol data unit** n *(SPDU)* TELECOM unité de données du protocole de session f

set[1] adj MECH ENG avoyé; ~ **solid** adj PRINT composé plein

set[2] n CINEMAT décor m, plateau m, COMP ensemble m, jeu m, CONST *in concrete* prise f, nail set chasse-clou m, chasse-pointe m, pousse-pointe m, *of pile* avant-pieu m, *rivet set* bouterolle f, chasse-rivet m, *street paving* pavé m, pavé en granit m, DP ensemble m, jeu m, ELEC ENG *of machines* groupe m, GEOL *of beds* ensemble m, faisceau *m*, série *f*, MATH ensemble *m*, MECH ENG *deformation* déformation *f*, *firmness* assiette *f*, *of instruments* trousse *f*, *of saw tooth* chasse *f*, voie *f*, *saws* tourne-à-gauche pour donner la voie aux scies *m*, *springs* affaissement *m*, flèche *f*, P&R déformation *f*, PRINT set *m*, TEXTILES ensemble *m*, WATER SUPP *pumps in mine* jeu *m*; ~ **of change wheels** *n* MECH ENG *for lathe* jeu de roues à fileter *m*, série de roues de filetage *f*, *geared machine* série de roues pour les variations de vitesse des avances *f*; ~ **of claims** *n* PATENTS jeu de revendications *m*; ~ **clamp** *n* CINEMAT mâchoire de fixation *f*, mâchoire étau *f*, pince universelle *f*; ~ **collar** *n* MECH ENG *for shafting* bague d'arrêt *f*, bague de butée *f*, collier d'arrêt *m*; ~ **of contacts** *n* ELEC jeu de contacts *m*; ~ **counter sensor** *n* PROD ENG détecteur de compteur de jeu *m*; ~ **of cutters** *n* PROD ENG *for emery wheel dresser* garniture de molettes *f*; ~ **of gears** *n* VEHICLES train d'engrenages *m*; ~ **grease cup** *n* MECH ENG graisseur à graisse consistante *m*; ~ **of instructions** *n* PROD ENG ensemble d'instructions *m*; ~ **key** *n* MECH ENG coin prisonnier *m*; ~ **of lenses** *n* CINEMAT série d'objectifs *f*, PHOTO jeu d'objectifs *m*; ~ **nut** *n* MECH ENG contre-écrou *m*; ~ **pin** *n* MECH ENG *binding* goupille de calage *f*, goupille à demeure *f*, *dowel pin* goujon *m*, goujon prisonnier *m*; ~ **point** *n* CHEM point de repère *m*; ~ **point accuracy** *n* NUCLEAR précision des points de consigne *f*; ~ **of points** *n* CONST, RAIL aiguillage *m*; ~ **pressure** *n* PROD ENG pression de tarage *f*; ~ **of rolls** *n* PAPER TECH ensemble de rouleaux *m*, PROD ENG *rolling mill* batterie de cylindres *f*, jeu de cylindres *m*, train de cylindres *m*, équipage de cylindres *m*; ~ **screw** *n* MECH ENG vis sans tête *f*; ~ **of shores** *n* CONST batterie d'étais *f*; ~ **of spare parts** *n* PROD ENG jeu de pièces de rechange *m*; ~ **of speeds** *n* MECH ENG gamme de vitesses *f*; ~ **square** *n* GEOM équerre à dessin *f*, MECH ENG équerre *f*; ~ **of supplementary lenses** *n* PHOTO trousse d'objectifs *f*; ~ **theory** *n* MATH théorie des ensembles *f*; ~ **of timber** *n* CONST cadre de boisage *m*; ~ **of tools** *n* MECH ENG assortiment d'outils *m*, boutique *f*, ensemble d'outils *m*, équipage d'outils *m*; ~ **of valves** *n* GAS TECH jeu de vannes *m*; ~ **versus reset** *n* PROD ENG état 1-0 *m*; ~ **of weights** *n* LAB EQUIP *analysis* jeu de poids *m*; ~ **of wells** *n* WATER SUPP batterie de puits *f*; ~ **of wheels** *n* VEHICLES train *m*; ~ **with stretcher piece** *n* CONST cadre avec tendard *m*

set³ *vt* CINEMAT *shutter* armer, COMP *counter* charger, *variable* fixer, CONST *cement* faire prise, *rivet* fixer à demeure, poser, *stake* planter, *place, put, fix, plant* fixer, fixer à demeure, planter, DP mettre à un, positionner, sélectionner, *counter* charger, *variable* fixer, MECH ENG *mount* monter, *saws* avoyer, donner de la voie à, refouler, *tools* affiler, doucir, OCEANOG *net* caler, PAPER TECH fixer, PRINT ajuster, composer, régler, caler, PROD ENG *bit* activer, mettre à zéro, monter; ~ **ablaze** *vt* THERMOD allumer, flamber, mettre le feu à; ~ **edgeways** *vt* CONST *boards* poser des planches de côté; ~ **fire to** *vt* THERMOD mettre le feu à; ~ **in motion** *vt* MECH ENG mettre en marche, mettre en mouvement, mettre en route, mettre en train; ~ **out** *vt* CONST *stone bed* disposer; ~ **over** *vt* MECH ENG désaxer, excentrer; ~ **to work** *vt* MECH ENG *machine* mettre en oeuvre; ~ **to zero** *vt* MECH ENG *instrument* ramener à zéro, remettre à zéro; ~ **up** *vt* CINEMAT installer, mettre en place, monter, COMP, DP établir, OCEANOG *net*, PAPER TECH *machine* monter, TELECOM *a call* établir, TV configurer, installer, régler, *studio, set, editing*

room monter

set⁴ *vi* ~ **in** *vi* NAUT *tide* commencer à monter; ~ **off an alarm** *vi* TELECOM déclencher une alarme; ~ **out** *vi* NAUT *tide* commencer à descendre, commencer à se retirer; ~ **over** *vi* MECH ENG s'excentrer; ~ **sail** *vi* NAUT appareiller, prendre la mer; ~ **a stone bed out** *vi* CONST *building* poser une pierre en délit; ~ **a stone in the sense of its natural bed** *vi* CONST *building* poser une pierre dans le sens de son lit de carrière

setback *n* CONST *wall* retraite *f*

set-off¹ *n* CONST *architecture* portée *f*, ressaut *m*, saillie *f*, PRINT décharge à l'impression *f*, maculage *m*

set-off² *vt* PRINT maculer

set-on: ~ **voltage-controlled oscillator** *n* ELECTRON VCO à fréquence instantanée *m*, oscillateur commandé en tension à fréquence instantanée *m*, oscillateur à régulation de tension à fréquence instantanée *m*

setscrew *n* MECH ENG vis de pression *f*, PROD ENG vis de blocage *f*

sett *n* CONST *street paving* pavé en granit *m*

setter: ~ **sight** *n* MILIT *artillery* servant de hausse *m*

setting *n* AERONAUT calage *m*, réglage *m*, CHEM TECH prise *f*, COAL TECH réglage *m*, CONST *landmarks* bornage *m*, pose *f*, *lines, cements* prise *f*, CRYSTALL montage *m*, MECH ENG *mounting* montage *m*, *mount* monture *f*, *teeth of saw* avoyage *m*, mise en voie *f*, refoulement des dents d'une scie *m*, *tools* affilage *m*, affilement *m*, doucissage *m*, OCEANOG *of net* armement *m*, PROD ENG *cores* renmoulage *m*; ~ **machine** *n* MECH ENG *band saw blades* machine à avoyer *f*; ~ **master** *n* MECH ENG *gauges* étalon de réglage *m*; ~ **out** *n* CONST *surveying* implantation *f*; ~ **rate** *n* C&G vitesse de figeage *f*; ~ **stick** *n* PRINT composteur *f*; ~ **time** *n* P&R temps de prise *m*; ~ **up** *n* CRYSTALL montage *m*, MECH ENG *of machine* ajustage d'une machine *m*, ajustement d'une machine *m*, montage *m*, établissement d'une machine *m*, PROD ENG *moulds* renmoulage *m*; ~ **up a telescope** *n* ASTRON réglage du télescope *m*

setting-in *n* C&G enfournement *n*

setting-over *n* MECH ENG désaxage *m*, excentration *f*

setting-up: ~ **machine** *n* PROD ENG *founding* machine à remouler *f*; ~ **partitions** *n* COMP, PROD ENG configuration des partitions *f*; ~ **pit** *n* PROD ENG *founding* fosse de remoulage *f*, fouille de remoulage *f*

settle:¹ ~ **mark** *n* C&G marque de remplissage *f*; ~ **ring** *n* C&G langue *f*

settle² *vt* CHEM TECH déposer, laisser rasseoir, laisser reposer, PROD ENG *dispute* lever, régler; ~ **on** *vt* CHEM TECH clarifier, fixer sur

settle³ *vi* CHEM TECH déposer son rassis, se déposer, sédimenter, COAL TECH sédimenter

settleable: ~ **solids** *n pl* HYDROL *sewage* matières en suspension décantables *f pl*

settled: ~ **apparent density** *n* CHEM TECH masse volumique apparente *f*; ~ **bed fast reactor** *n* NUCLEAR réacteur rapide à lit de boulets quasistatique *m*; ~ **sewage** *n* WATER SUPP eau usée déposée *f*; ~ **volume** *n* CHEM TECH volume après tassement *m*; ~ **weather** *n* NAUT temps beau-fixe *m*, temps fait *m*, temps fixe *m*, temps sûr *m*

settlement *n* COAL TECH, CONST tassement *m*; ~ **gage** *n* (AmE), ~ **gauge** *n* (BrE) COAL TECH capteur de tassement *m*; ~ **meter** *n* CHEM TECH tassomètre *m*; ~ **reference marker** *n* CHEM TECH indicateur de tassement *m*

settler: ~ **chamber** *n* NUCLEAR chambre de décantation *f*, décanteur *m*

settling *n* CHEM dépôt *m*, COAL TECH sédimentation *f*, CONST *of ground* tassement *m*, HYDROL décantation primaire *f*, PHYS décantation sédimentaire *f*, PROP MAT décantation *f*; ~ **basin** *n* CHEM TECH bassin de curage *m*, bassin à clarifier *m*, fosse de sédimentation *f*, COAL TECH bassin de décantation *m*, HYDROL bassin de dessablement *m*, bassin de tranquillisation *m*, chambre de tranquillisation *f*, *sewage* bassin de décantation *m*, MINING bassin de décantation *m*, WATER SUPP décanteur *m*; ~ **cistern** *n* CHEM TECH bassin de curage *m*, bassin à clarifier *m*, fosse de sédimentation *f*; ~ **cone** *n* CHEM TECH, COAL TECH cône de décantation *m*; ~ **cyclone** *n* CHEM TECH cyclone de séparation *m*; ~ **pit** *n* CHEM TECH tour de décantation pour fines *f*, CONST fosse de repos *f*, étang de décantation *m*; ~ **pond** *n* COAL TECH bassin de décantation *m*, bassin de décantation des boues *m*, bassin à stériles *m*; ~ **pool** *n* CHEM TECH bassin de curage *m*; ~ **reservoir** *n* CHEM TECH bassin à clarifier *m*; ~ **speed** *n* CHEM TECH vitesse de décantation *f*, vitesse de sédimentation *f*, COAL TECH vitesse de sédimentation *f*; ~ **sump** *n* CHEM TECH fosse de sédimentation *f*; ~ **tank** *n* CHEM TECH cône de décantation *m*, vase à clarifier *m*, COAL TECH bac de sédimentation *m*, décanteur *m*, HYDROL bassin de décantation *m*, clarificateur *m*, PETR TECH bac de décantation *m*; ~ **time** *n* CHEM TECH temps de dépôt *m*; ~ **tub** *n* CHEM TECH vase à clarifier *m*; ~ **vat** *n* CHEM TECH cuve à défécation *f*, vase à clarifier *m*

settlings *n pl* CHEM dépôts *m pl*, sédiment *m*

setup *n* COMP mise au point *f*, CONST *instrument* mise en station *f*, DP mise au point *f*, PROD ENG préparation *f*, réglage *m*, TV configuration *f*, installation *f*, montage *m*, réglage *m*; ~ **channel** *n* TELECOM voie d'établissement *f*; ~ **phase** *n* PROD ENG phase de préparation *f*; ~ **time** *n* COMP, DP temps de positionnement *m*, PROD ENG temps de mise en route *m*, temps de préparation *m*, temps de réglage *m*, TEXTILES temps de garnissage des machines *m*

set-valued: ~ **attribute** *n* TELECOM attribut à un ensemble de valeurs *m*

SEV *abbr (surface effect vehicle)* TRANSP véhicule à effet de sol *m*

seven-layer: ~ **reference model** *n* COMP, DP modèle de référence à sept couches *m*

seventh *n* ACOUSTICS septième *f*

severe: ~ **control** *n* CONTROL contrôle serré *m*

severely: ~ **errored second** *n (SES)* NAUT, TELECOM seconde gravement erronée *f*

severite *n* MINERAL sévérite *f*

sew *vt* TEXTILES coudre

sewage *n* HYDROL eau usée *f*, égouts *m pl*, RECYCLING, WATER SUPP eau d'égout *f*, eaux usées *f pl*; ~ **analysis** *n* WATER SUPP analyse des eaux usées *f*; ~ **disposal** *n* RECYCLING élimination des eaux d'égout *f*, évacuation des eaux d'égout *f*; ~ **disposal plant** *n* WATER SUPP installation de décharge des eaux résiduaires *f*; ~ **effluent** *n* RECYCLING effluent de l'eau d'égout *m*, WATER SUPP effluent des eaux usées *m*; ~ **farm** *n* RECYCLING, WATER SUPP champ d'épandage *m*; ~ **farming** *n* RECYCLING utilisation des eaux usées comme engrais *f*; ~ **gas** *n* GAS TECH gaz d'eaux résiduaires *m*, gaz de gadoues *m*, RECYCLING gaz d'égout *m*; ~ **pumping station** *n* HYDROL station de pompage des eaux usées *f*; ~ **sludge** *n* HYDROL traitement des eaux d'égout *m*, épuration *f*, RECYCLING boues d'égout *f pl*, WATER SUPP boues d'épuration *f pl*; ~ **treatment plant** *n* HYDROL installation d'assainissement *f*, station d'épuration des eaux usées *f*, usine d'assainissement *f*, RECYCLING station d'épuration des eaux usées *f*; ~ **waste** *n* RECYCLING eau d'égout *f*; ~ **waste water** *n* WATER SUPP eau usée domestique *f*; ~ **works** *n pl* HYDROL station d'épuration des eaux usées *f*, usine d'assainissement *f*

sewer *n* CONST, HYDROL égout *m*, RECYCLING canalisation d'évacuation *f*, égout *m*, WATER SUPP égout *m*; ~ **cleaning** *n* HYDROL, WATER SUPP curage des égouts *m*; ~ **network** *n* HYDROL réseau d'égouts *m*; ~ **system** *n* RECYCLING réseau d'assainissement *m*

sewerage *n* RECYCLING assainissement *m*, WATER SUPP canalisation *f*; ~ **system** *n* HYDROL installation d'assainissement *f*, RECYCLING réseau d'assainissement *m*

sewing *n* PRINT couture *f*; ~ **machine** *n* PRINT, TEXTILES machine à coudre *f*

sewn-in: ~ **label** *n* TEXTILES étiquette cousue sur le vêtement *f*

sexadecimal *adj* DP sexadécimal

Sextans *n* ASTRON Sextant *m*

sextant *n* NAUT sextant *m*, PHYS sextet *m*; ~ **altitude** *n* NAUT *navigation* hauteur instrumentale *f*

sextet *n* PHYS *spectroscopy* sextet *m*

seybertite *n* MINERAL seybertite *f*

Seyfert: ~ **galaxies** *n pl* ASTRON galaxies de Seyfert *f pl*

SF *abbr (signal fail)* TELECOM défaillance de signal *f*

SFET *abbr (synchronous frequency encoding technique)* TELECOM technique de codage à fréquence synchrone *f*

SFU *abbr (store-and-forward unit)* TELECOM unité d'enregistrement et de retransmission *f*

SGC *abbr (signalling grouping channel)* TELECOM canal de groupement de signalisation *m*

SGML *abbr (Standard Generalized Mark-up Language)* DP, PRINT SGML *(langage standard généralisé de balisage)*

shackle[1] *n* AUTO jumelle *f*, CONST *of padlock* anse *f*, branche *f*, MAR POLL, MECH *lifting gear* manille *f*, MECH ENG *ring, clasp* boucle *f*, NAUT manille *f*, SPRINGS *of leaf spring* chape *f*, VEHICLES *leaf spring* jumelle *f*, *towing device* attelage à boulon *m*; ~ **insulator** *n* ELEC ENG isolateur d'angle *m*

shackle[2] *vt* NAUT maniller

shade *n* C&G écran *m*, PHOTO ton *m*, PRINT teinte *f*, TEXTILES coloris *m*

shaded *adj* C&G dégradé, PRINT ombré

shaded-pole: ~ **motor** *n* ELEC moteur à bague de déphasage *m*, moteur à enroulement en court-circuit *m*, ELEC ENG moteur à spires Frager *m*

shading *n* P&R nuançage *m*, TV effet d'ombrage *m*; ~ **corrector** *n* TV signal compensateur d'ombrage *m*; ~ **paint** *n* COLOURS, P&R peinture antisolaire *f*; ~ **signal** *n* TV signal d'ombrage *m*

shading-off: ~ **pigment** *n* COLOURS pigment à nuancer *m*

shadow *n* CINEMAT, PHOTO, PRINT ombre *f*; ~ **area** *n* TV *reception* zone d'ombre *f*; ~ **detail** *n* PHOTO modelé dans les ombres; ~ **key** *n* CINEMAT incrustation avec ombre *f*; ~ **mask** *n* ELECTRON masque perforé *m*, TV masque d'ombre *m*; ~ **mask tube** *n* ELECTRON tube à masque *m*, tube à masque perforé *m*, TV tube à masque *m*; ~ **microscope** *n* INSTRUMENT microscope électronique à ombre *m*; ~ **wall** *n* C&G mur d'écran *m*

shadowgraph *n* C&G appareil à ombroscopie *m*

shadowing *n* TELECOM occultation *f*, TV masquage *m*

shaft *n* COAL TECH bac *m*, puits *m*, soute *f*, CONST *chimney stack* cheminée *f*, *of column* fût *m*, MAR POLL soute *f*, MECH arbre *m*, axe *m*, MECH ENG arbre *m*, arbre de transmission *m*, axe *m*, transmission *f*, *of hammer* manche *m*, MINING puits *m*, NAUT *propeller, engine* arbre *m*, VEHICLES *engine, transmission* arbre *m*, axe *m*; ~ **bearing** *n* MECH ENG palier de transmission *m*; ~ **bunker loading** *n* MINING chargement de silo de puits *m*; ~ **center height** *n* (AmE), ~ **centre height** *n* (AmE) MECH ENG hauteur de centre d'arbre *f*; ~ **collar** *n* MECH ENG collier d'arbre *m*, MINING orifice de puits *m*, *of mine shaft* cadre de superficie *m*; ~ **coupling** *n* ELEC ENG accouplement *m*, accouplement d'axes *m*, MECH ENG accouplement d'arbres *m*, manchon d'accouplement d'arbres *m*, manchon d'assemblage d'arbres *m*; ~ **deepening** *n* MINING approfondissement d'un puits *m*, réavalement d'un puits *m*; ~ **drive** *n* VEHICLES *transmission* commande par arbre *f*, entraînement par arbre *m*; ~ **furnace** *n* PROD ENG four à cuve *m*, four à manche *m*; ~ **in water-bearing ground** *n* WATER SUPP *excavation* avaleresse *f*; ~ **key** *n* MECH ENG cale d'arbre *f*, clavette d'arbre *f*, clavette de calage *f*; ~ **kiln** *n* COAL TECH four à cuve *m*; ~ **ladder** *n* WATER SUPP échelle de puits *f*; ~ **lap** *n* MECH ENG rodoir pour transmissions *m*; ~ **mine** *n* MINING mine exploitée par puits *f*; ~ **safety pillar** *n* MINING massif de protection de puits *m*, pilier de protection de puits *m*; ~ **spillway** *n* WATER SUPP déversoir de barrage *m*; ~ **step** *n* MECH ENG crapaudine *f*, palier de pied *m*

shafting *n* MECH ENG arbres *m pl*, arbres de transmissions *m pl*, transmission *f*; ~ **lathe** *n* MECH ENG tour pour arbres de transmission *m*

shaft-sinking: ~ **bar** *n* MINING affût pour fonçage de puits *m*

shake *n* CONST *timber* éclat *m*, MECH ENG *oscillatory movement* secousse *f*

shaker *n* LAB EQUIP agitateur secoueur *m*; ~ **conveyor** *n* PROD ENG transporteur-trembleur *m*

shaking *n* MECH ENG agitation *f*, secousse *f*, tremblement *m*; ~ **barrel** *n* PROD ENG *founding* tonneau dessableur *m*, tonneau à dessabler *m*; ~ **grate** *n* PROD ENG grille oscillante *f*, grille à barreaux mobiles *f*, grille à secousses *f*; ~ **machine** *n* PROD ENG *founding* tambour dessableur *m*, tonneau dessableur *m*; ~ **mill** *n* PROD ENG *founding* tambour dessableur *m*, tonneau dessableur *m*; ~ **motion** *n* MECH ENG mouvement à secousses *m*; ~ **screen** *n* PROD ENG crible à secousse *m*; ~ **table** *n* COAL TECH, PROD ENG table secoueuse *f*, table à secousses *f*; ~ **tray** *n* PROD ENG plateau à secousses *m*

shale *n* C&G argile schisteuse *f*, PETR argilite *f*, PETR TECH schiste *m*; ~ **base line** *n* PETR ligne de base des argiles *f*; ~ **density** *n* PETR TECH densité argile *f*; ~ **diapirism** *n* PETR TECH argilocinèse *f*; ~ **dome** *n* PETR TECH dôme d'argile *m*; ~ **shaker** *n* PETR tamis vibrant *m*, tamis vibratoire *m*, PETR TECH vibrateur *m*

shallow[1] *adj* C&G jeune, NAUT *water* peu profond

shallow[2] *n* OCEANOG haut-fond *m*, platain *m*, platin *m*; ~ **depression** *n* METEO faible dépression *f*; ~ **descent** *n* AERONAUT descente à pente faible *f*; ~ **draft** *n* NAUT *ship* faible tirant d'eau *m*; ~ **stabilization** *n* COAL TECH stabilisation superficielle *f*; ~ **water** *n* OCEANOG eau peu profonde *f*; ~ **water blackout** *n* OCEANOG rendez-vous syncopal *m*

shallowing-up: ~ **sequence** *n* GEOL *regressive* séquence de comblement *f*

shallows *n pl* GEOL, NAUT haut-fond *m*, petits fonds *m pl*, OCEANOG eau peu profonde *f*

shaly *adj* GEOL argileux, schisteux

shank *n* CONST *of key* branche *f*, tige *f*, *of rivet* fût *m*, MECH ENG *of bolt, nail* tige *f*, *of tool* queue *f*, PROD ENG *founding* poche avec armature à fourche *f*, poche à fourche *f*; ~ **ladle** *n* PROD ENG *founding* poche avec armature à fourche *f*, poche à fourche *f*

shape[1] *n* TEXTILES forme *f*; ~ **change** *n* METALL déformation *f*; ~ **cutting machine** *n* C&G machine de découpe à gabarit *f*; ~ **factor** *n* HEAT ENG *insulation* coefficient de forme *m*

shape[2] *vt* PROD ENG emboutir, façonner, modeler

shaped[1] *adj* MECH ENG annulaire

shaped:[2] ~ **beam** *n* ELECTRON faisceau mis en forme *m*; ~ **beam antenna** *n* SPACE *communications* antenne à faisceau conformé *f*, antenne à faisceau modelé *f*; ~ **beam tube** *n* ELECTRON tube à faisceau en forme *m*; ~ **bevel** *n* C&G biseau contourné *m*; ~ **conductor** *n* ELEC *cable* âme profilée *f*; ~ **pulse** *n* ELECTRON impulsion mise en forme *f*; ~ **reflector** *n* SPACE *communications* réflecteur conformé *m*

shaper *n* MECH étau-limeur *m*, PROD ENG emboutisseur *m*; ~ **tools** *n pl* MECH ENG outils d'étaux-limeurs *m pl*, outils de limeuses *m pl*

shaping *n* PROD ENG *stamping* emboutissage *m*; ~ **amplifier** *n* ELECTRON amplificateur de mise en forme *m*; ~ **block** *n* C&G mailloche *f*; ~ **machine** *n* MECH ENG limeuse *f*, étau-limeur *m*, *sheet metal* emboutisseuse *f*, emboutissoir *m*; ~ **network** *n* TV réseau conformateur *m*; ~ **planer** *n* MECH ENG limeuse *f*, étau-limeur *m*; ~ **tool** *n* C&G molette *f*

shard *n* GEOL *volcanic glass* éclat *m*

share *vt* COMP, DP partager

shared: ~ **file** *n* COMP, DP fichier partagé *m*; ~ **memory** *n* COMP mémoire commune *f*, mémoire partagée *f*; ~ **memory system** *n* COMP système à mémoire commune *m*, DP système à mémoire partagée *m*; ~ **service line** *n* TELECOM ligne partagée *f*

shareware *n* COMP, DP logiciel pour lequel une contribution volontaire est demandée *m*

sharing *n* COMP, DP partage *m*

sharp[1] *adj* CINEMAT net, piqué, MECH ENG *angle* vif, à vive arête, *edge, point* affûté, aigu, aiguisé, tranchant

sharp[2] *n* ACOUSTICS dièse *f*; ~ **curve** *n* GEOM courbe à petit rayon *f*; ~ **cutoff filter** *n* ELECTRON filtre à flancs raides *m*; ~ **cutoff tube** *n* ELECTRON tube à coude brusque *m*; ~ **edge** *n* C&G arête *f*, SPRINGS bord vif *m*, chant vif *m*; ~ **finish** *n* C&G vive arrête *f*; ~ **fire** *n* C&G feu court *m*; ~ **oil paint** *n* COLOURS peinture à la térébenthine *f*; ~ **pulse** *n* ELECTRON impulsion très courte *f*, impulsion très étroite *f*; ~ **ridges of steel** *n pl* PROD ENG stries d'acier à arêtes vives *f pl*; ~ **yield point** *n* METALL crochet de traction aigu *m*

sharp-crested: ~ **weir** *n* HYDR EQUIP déversoir à arête vive *m*, déversoir à crête mince *m*, déversoir à paroi *m*, WATER SUPP déversoir en mince paroi *m*

sharp-edged[1] *adj* MECH ENG *angle* vif, à vive arête

sharp-edged:[2] ~ **orifice** *n* HYDR EQUIP orifice percé dans une paroi mince *m*, orifice à bord vif *m*; ~ **tool** *n* MECH ENG outillage tranchant *m*

sharpen *vt* MECH ENG *tools* affûter, aiguiser, repasser, PRINT réduire la taille des points de

sharpened *adj* MECH ENG affûté

sharpener *n* MECH ENG *instrument* affiloir *m*, aiguisoir *m*, *machine* affûteuse *f*, machine à affûter *f*, *person* affûteur *m*, aiguiseur *m*

sharpening *n* MECH ENG affûtage *m*, aiguisage *m*, repassage *m*; ~ **machine** *n* MECH ENG, PAPER TECH affûteuse *f*, machine à affûter *f*; ~ **steel** *n* FOOD TECH *knives* fusil *m*, fusil à aiguiser *m*; ~ **wheel** *n* PROD ENG meule *f*, meule affûteuse *f*, meule à affûter *f*, meule à aiguiser *f*

sharpness *n* CINEMAT définition *f*, netteté *f*, GEOM *of angle* acuité *f*, MECH ENG *of cutting edge* acuité *f*, finesse *f*, PHOTO netteté *f*, PHYS *of resonance* acuité de résonance *f*, PRINT netteté *f*; ~ **control** *n* TV réglage de netteté *m*

shatter *n* MINING *ore* fragmentation *f*, morcellement *m*; ~ **cut** *n* MINING bouchon canadien *m*, bouchon parallèle *m*, bouchon à mines parallèles *m*, bouchon à trous parallèles *m*

shatterproof: ~ **glass** *n* TRANSP verre de sécurité *m*

shave: ~ **hook** *n* CONST grattoir triangulaire *m*, ébardoir *m*

shaving *n* CONST copeau *m*, rognure *f*

shavings *n pl* PAPER TECH rognures *f pl*

SHC *abbr (superhigh cube)* TRANSP SHC *(conteneur spécial hors-cotes)*

sheaf *n* PROD ENG faisceau *m*

shear[1] *n* GEOL, MECH *materials* cisaillement *m*, MECH ENG *materials* cisaillement *m*, glissement *m*, *metal* cisaille *f*, *shearing machine* cisailles *f pl*, machine à cisailler *f*, P&R *rheology* cisaillement *m*, PHYS cisaillement *m*, cission *f*; ~ **alignment** *n* C&G goutte de voûte *f*; ~ **blade** *n* C&G lame de ciseaux *f*, MECH ENG lame de cisailles *f*, lame à cisailler *f*; ~ **cut** *n* C&G coup de ciseaux *m*; ~ **cutter** *n* PRINT système de coupe irrégulière *m*; ~ **flow** *n* FLUID PHYS écoulement cisaillé *m*; ~ **flow instability** *n* FLUID PHYS instabilité des écoulements cisaillés *f*; ~ **folding** *n* GEOL plis en écailles *m pl*; ~ **force** *n* CONST effort tranchant *m*, MECH ENG force de cisaillement *f*; ~ **fracture** *n* METALL rupture de cisaillement *f*; ~ **layers** *n pl* FLUID PHYS *fluids* couches cisaillées *f pl*; ~ **legs** *n pl* CONST anches *f pl*, hanches *f pl*, bigue *f*, chèvre *f*; ~ **lip** *n* METALL lèvre de cisaillement *f*; ~ **mark** *n* C&G marque de ciseaux *f*; ~ **modulus** *n* COAL TECH, MECH ENG, PETR module de cisaillement *m*, PHYS *rigidity* coefficient de cisaillement *m*, module de cisaillement *m*, module de rigidité *m*; ~ **rate** *n* P&R vitesse de cisaillement *f*; ~ **resistance** *n* SPRINGS résistance au cisaillement *f*; ~ **spray** *n* C&G pulvérisation *f*; ~ **strain** *n* MECH ENG déformation due au cisaillement *f*, PHYS déformation due au cisaillement *f*, glissement unitaire *m*; ~ **strength** *n* COAL TECH, MECH *materials* résistance au cisaillement *f*, METALL intensité de cisaillement *f*, P&R, SPRINGS résistance au cisaillement *f*; ~ **stress** *n* CONST contrainte de cisaillement *f*, MECH ENG effort de cisaillement *m*, P&R contrainte de cisaillement *f*, PHYS contrainte de cisaillement *f*, tension de cisaillement *f*, SPRINGS contrainte de cisaillement *f*; ~ **test** *n* MECH ENG *for rivets* essai de cisaillement pour rivets *m*; ~ **wave** *n* ACOUSTICS onde rotationnelle *f*, onde équivolumique *f*, GEOL onde S *f*, onde transversale *f*; ~ **zone** *n* GEOL zone broyée *f*, zone cisaillée *f*

shear[2] *vt* MECH ENG *clip* cisailler, TEXTILES tondre

sheared: ~ **strip** *n* SPRINGS bande cisaillée *f*

shearer *n* MINING abatteuse à tambour *f*

shearer-high: ~ **pressure pump** *n* MINING pompe haute pression pour abatteuse à tambour *f*

shearing *n* GEOL, MECH ENG *act*, PROP MAT cisaillement *m*; ~ **and punching machine** *n* MECH ENG poinçonneuse-cisaille *f*; ~ **die** *n* MECH ENG *press tools* outillage de cisaillage pour presse *m*; ~ **displacement** *n* PROP MAT déplacement de cisaillement *m*; ~ **effect** *n* PAPER TECH cisaillement *m*; ~ **force** *n* PHYS, PROP MAT force de cisaillement *f*; ~ **machine** *n* COAL TECH rouilleuse *f*, MECH ENG cisailles *f pl*, machine à cisailler *f*, TEXTILES *for sheep* machine de tondage *f*, tondeuse *f*; ~ **pin** *n* PRINT goupille de sécurité *f*; ~ **strength** *n* MECH ENG résistance au cisaillement *f*; ~ **stress** *n* CONST effort de cisaillement *m*, MECH ENG effort de cisaillement *m*, effort tranchant *m*, travail au cisaillement *m*; ~ **tenacity** *n* MECH ENG résistance au cisaillement *f*

shearing-off *n* C&G rognage *m*

shear-jointed: ~ **telescope** *n* INSTRUMENT jumelles périscopiques *f pl*

shears *n pl* C&G ciseaux *m pl*, MECH *tools* cisaille *f*, MECH ENG *machine* machine à cisailler *f*, *of lathe* flasques *m pl*, *scissors* cisailles *f pl*, hachard *m*, TEXTILES ciseaux de couturière *m pl*, grands ciseaux *m pl*

sheath *n* ELEC *of cable* gaine *f*, ELEC ENG *of cable* enveloppe *f*, gaine extérieure *f*, MECH fourreau *m*, gaine *f*, manchon *m*, OPT enveloppe *f*, PROD ENG enveloppe *f*, gaine *f*; ~ **fold** *n* GEOL pli en fourreau *m*

sheathe *vt* ELEC ENG *cable* armer

sheathed: ~ **cable** *n* MECH ENG câble armé *m*; ~ **combination pliers** *n pl* MECH ENG *tool* pince universelle gainée *f*; ~ **deck** *n* NAUT *boatbuilding* pont doublé *m*; ~ **thermocouple** *n* NUCLEAR thermocouple gainé *m*

sheathing *n* PROD ENG *lagging* chemise *f*, enveloppe *f*, garniture *f*

sheave *n* MECH ENG bossage *m*, disque *m*, estomac *m*, moufle *m*, *for pitched chain* noix *f*, poulie à noix *f*, *grooved pulley* molette à gorge *f*, poulie à corde *f*, poulie à gorge *f*, roue à gorge *f*, *grooved pulley in pulley block* poulie *f*, poulie de moufle *f*, poulie mouflée *f*, rouet *m*, réa *f*, NAUT *fittings* réa *f*; ~ **block** *n* MECH ENG moufle *m*; ~ **pulley block** *n* MECH ENG moufle à poulies *m*

shed *n* CONST appentis *m*, baraque *f*, dépôt *m*, hangar *m*, TEXTILES *weaving* encroix *m*, foule *f*, pas *m*; ~ **roof** *n* CONST comble en dent de scie *m*, comble-shed *m*, shed *m*

sheen *n* MAR POLL reflet *m*, PROP MAT oeil d'une étoffe *m*, TEXTILES brillant *m*

sheep's: ~ **leap** *n* CONST saut de mouton *m*

sheepsfoot: ~ **roller** *n* CONST rouleau à pieds de mouton *m*

sheepshank *n* NAUT *knot* noeud de jambe de chien *m*

sheer[1] *adj* TEXTILES extra-fin, transparent

sheer[2] *n* NAUT *shipbuilding* tonture *f*; ~ **aft** *n* NAUT *ship design* tonture arrière *f*; ~ **draft** *n* NAUT *ship design* plan des formes *m*; ~ **drawing** *n* NAUT plan des formes *m*; ~ **forward** *n* NAUT *ship design* tonture avant *f*; ~ **line** *n* NAUT *boatbuilding* ligne de tonture *f*; ~ **plan** *n* NAUT *ship design* projection longitudinale *f*, élévation du plan des formes *f*

sheer:[3] ~ **off** *vi* NAUT *navigation* faire une embardée

sheerstrake *n* NAUT *boatbuilding* virure de carreau *f*

sheet:[1] ~ **fed** *adj* PRINT à feuilles; ~ **silicate-bearing** *adj* GEOL phylliteux

sheet[2] *n* MECH *materials* feuille *f*, tôle *f*, NAUT *rope, metal, sail* plaque *f*, voile *f*, écoute *f*, NUCLEAR *thick foil* lame *f*, tôle *f*, P&R feuille *f*, PAPER TECH feuille de papier *f*, PATENTS *of drawing* feuille *f*, PRINT feuille *f*, feuille de papier *f*, TEXTILES drap *m*; ~ **bend** *n* NAUT *knot* noeud d'écoute *m*; ~ **boiling** *n* NUCLEAR caléfaction *f*, ébullition par film *f*; ~ **calender** *n* PAPER TECH calandre à feuilles *f*; ~ **cutting machine** *n* PACKAGING cisaille pour feuilles *f*; ~ **feeder** *n* PRINT margeur à feuilles *m*; ~ **feeding** *n* COMP, DP alimentation feuille à feuille *f*; ~ **film** *n* PHOTO film grand format *m*; ~ **formation** *n* PAPER TECH formation *f*; ~ **gage** *n* (AmE), ~ **gauge** *n* (BrE) MECH ENG calibre d'épaisseur *m*, jauge pour tôle *f*, jauge pour tôle fine *f*; ~ **glass** *n* C&G verre à vitres *m*; ~ **iron gage** *n* (AmE), ~ **iron gauge** *n* (BrE) MECH ENG calibre d'épaisseur *m*, jauge pour tôle *f*, jauge pour tôle fine *f*; ~ **iron pipe** *n* CONST tuyau en tôle *m*; ~ **iron works** *n pl* PROD ENG tôlerie *f*; ~ **lead** *n* CONST plomb en feuilles *m*; ~ **lightning** *n* METEO éclair diffus *m*, éclair en nappes *m*; ~ **metal** *n* PROP MAT tôle *f*; ~ **metal punch** *n* MECH ENG *tool* emporte-pièce *m*; ~ **metal screw** *n* MECH ENG vis à tôle *f*; ~ **mill** *n* PROD ENG laminoir à tôles fines *m*; ~ **pile** *n* COAL TECH, CONST palplanche *f*; ~ **piling** *n* COAL TECH blindage *m*, CONST *wood* palplanches *f pl*, palplanches jointives *f pl*; ~ **resistance** *n* ELEC ENG résistance par carré *f*, résistivité en couche *f*; ~ **steel** *n* VEHICLES *body* tôle d'acier *f*; ~ **steel case** *n* PROD ENG boîtier en tôle d'acier *m*; ~ **of water** *n* HYDROL, OCEANOG plan d'eau *m*

sheet³ *vt* CONST *civil engineering* blinder

sheeted: ~ **car** *n* (AmE) *(cf sheeted wagon)* RAIL wagon à bâche *m*; ~ **wagon** *n* (BrE) *(cf sheeted car)* RAIL wagon à bâche *m*

sheeter *n* PRINT coupeuse en feuilles *f*, sortie à plat *f*

sheet-fed: ~ **carton printer** *n* PACKAGING machine à imprimer les cartons en feuilles *f*; ~ **machine** *n* PRINT machine à feuilles *f*

sheeting *n* CONST *civil engineering* blindage *m*, GEOL feuilletage *m*, foliation *m*, TEXTILES tissu de drap de lit *m*; ~ **pile** *n* CONST palplanche *f*

sheetwise: ~ **form** *n* (AmE), ~ **forme** *n* (BrE) PRINT imposition en feuille *f*

shelf *n* CONST *board* rayon *m*, tablette *f*, LAB EQUIP *furniture* étagère *f*, NAUT *geography* banc *m*, plate-forme *f*, OCEANOG bauquière *f*, haut-fond *m*; ~ **appeal** *n* PACKAGING emballage attrayant *m*; ~ **freezer** *n* REFRIG congélateur à étagères *m*; ~ **impact** *n* PACKAGING emballage attrayant *m*; ~ **life** *n* CINEMAT durée de conservation *f*, P&R durée de conservation *f*, durée limite de stockage *f*, PACKAGING durée de stockage *f*, PRINT durée de vie sur l'étagère *f*; ~ **life test** *n* PACKAGING contrôle de la durée de stockage *m*; ~ **space** *n* PACKAGING espace sur rayons *m*; ~ **stability** *n* PACKAGING stabilité de stockage *f*

shelfback *n* PRINT *bookbinding* dos du livre *m*

shell *n* C&G écaille *f*, COAL TECH virole *f*, MECH ENG *of crushing roll* anneau *m*, bague *f*, bandage *m*, *of pulley* chape *f*, MILIT obus *m*, NAUT *shipbuilding* bordé extérieur *m*, coque extérieure *f*, NUCLEAR *of heat exchanger, pressure vessel*, PAPER TECH virole *f*, PROD ENG *of boiler* corps cylindrique *m*, SPACE *spacecraft* coque *f*, enveloppe *f*; ~ **and auger** *n* MINING *boring* cuiller *f*, cuillère *f*; ~ **and coil condenser** *n* REFRIG condenseur à calandre et serpentin *m*; ~ **and tube evaporator** *n* REFRIG évaporateur à calandre et serpentin *m*; ~ **and tube heat exchanger** *n* NUCLEAR échangeur de chaleur tubulaire *m*, REFRIG échangeur thermique à calandre *m*; ~ **auger** *n* MINING *boring* cuiller *f*, cuillère *f*; ~ **breccia** *n* GEOL lumachelle *f*; ~ **burst** *n* MILIT éclat d'obus *m*; ~ **chuck** *n* MECH ENG mandrin à vis *m*; ~ **course** *n* NUCLEAR virole de corps *f*; ~ **drill** *n* MECH ENG foret creux *m*; ~ **end mill** *n* MECH ENG fraise cylindrique à deux tailles *f*; ~ **gimlet** *n* CONST vrille façon suisse *f*; ~ **ice** *n* REFRIG glace en tube *f*; ~

liner *n* COAL TECH blindage de virole *m*; ~ **mill** *n* MECH ENG *cutter* fraise creuse *f*; ~ **model** *n* NUCLEAR, PHYS modèle des couches *m*; ~ **molding resin** *n* (AmE), ~ **moulding resin** *n* (BrE) P&R résine pour moulage en coquilles *f*; ~ **plate** *n* PROD ENG *of barrel, boiler* virole *f*; ~ **plating** *n* NAUT *shipbuilding* bordé de coque *m*; ~ **reamer** *n* MECH ENG alésoir-fraise *m*; ~ **reamer with taper bore** *n* MECH ENG alésoir creux avec alésage conique *m*; ~ **section** *n* NUCLEAR virole de corps *f*; ~ **splinter** *n* MILIT éclat d'obus *m*; ~ **strength** *n* FOOD TECH *eggshell* solidité de coquille *f*

shellac¹ *n* COLOURS gomme laque *f*, laque *f*, CONST laque en feuilles *f*, laque en plaques *f*, laque en écailles *f*, laque plate *f*, ELEC *insulation* gomme laque *f*; ~ **varnish** *n* COATINGS vernis au shellac *m*, vernis à gomme-laque *m*

shellac² *vt* COATINGS enduire de gomme-laque, enduire de shellac

shellack *n* COLOURS gomme laque *f*

shelled *adj* FOOD TECH décortiqué, écossé

shellfish: ~ **basket** *n* OCEANOG bourriche *f*; ~ **culture** *n* OCEANOG conchyliculture *f*; ~ **farm** *n* OCEANOG ferme marine *f*, élevage de coquillages *m*; ~ **farmer** *n* OCEANOG conchyliculteur *m*

shell-on *adj* FOOD TECH *shellfish* entier

shell-type: ~ **boiler** *n* HEATING chaudière à bouilleur *f*; ~ **elbow** *n* MECH ENG *pipe fittings* coude en coquille *m*; ~ **motor** *n* ELEC moteur cuirassé *m*; ~ **transformer** *n* ELEC, ELEC ENG transformateur cuirassé *m*

shelly: ~ **limestone** *n* GEOL calcaire coquillier *m*, lumachelle *f*; ~ **sandstone** *n* GEOL grès coquillier *m*

shelter¹ *n* CONST abri *m*, caponnière *f*, lieu de refuge *m*, niche *f*, niche de refuge *f*, refuge *m*, retraite *f*, MILIT, NAUT *sailing*, SPACE *spacecraft* abri *m*, TRANSP abri *m*, aubette *f*

shelter² *vt* NAUT abriter

shelter³ *vi* NAUT *submarine* faire surface

shepherd: ~ **satellite** *n* ASTRON satellite berger *m*

SHF¹ *abbr (superhigh frequency)* ELECTRON supra-haute fréquence *f*

SHF:² ~ **signal generator** *n* ELECTRON générateur de signaux SHF *m*, générateur SHF *m*

shield¹ *n* CONST *tunnelling* bouclier *m*, *wooden screen, guard* volet *m*, DP blindage *m*, ELEC *cable* blindage *m*, écran de protection *m*, ELEC ENG *for lamp* blindage *m*, cuirasse *f*, LAB EQUIP *safety* protecteur *m*, NUCLEAR *of reactor* bouclier *m*, PROD ENG blindage *m*, écran métallique *m*, RECORDING blindage *m*, SPACE blindage *m*, bouclier *m*, écran *m*, TV *of cathode ray tube* cylindre de la cathode *m*; ~ **bonding** *n* ELEC *cable* connexions d'écrans *f pl*; ~ **cooling system** *n* NUCLEAR système de refroidissement du bouclier *m*; ~ **drain wire** *n* ELEC, PROD ENG fil de blindage *m*; ~ **support** *n* MINING soutènement avec bouclier *m*; ~ **tunneling** *n* (AmE), ~ **tunnelling** *n* (BrE) RAIL avancement horizontal au bouclier *m*, cheminement horizontal au bouclier *m*, procédé de bouclier *m*; ~ **volcano** *n* GEOL volcan bouclier *m*

shield² *vt* SPACE blinder, protéger

shield-driven: ~ **anchor** *n* CONST *building* expansion de douille par frappe *f*

shielded: ~ **cable** *n* ELEC, ELEC ENG câble blindé *m*, PHYS câble blindé *m*, câble protégé *m*, PROD ENG, RECORDING, TV câble blindé *m*; ~ **cable connection** *n* PROD ENG connexion à câbles blindés *f*; ~ **coffin** *n* NUCLEAR *flask* château de transport pour un seul assemblage combustible *m*; ~ **coil** *n* TESTING bobine protégée *f*; ~ **enclosure** *n* ELEC ENG enceinte blindée *f*; ~ **metal arc welding** *n* (*SMAW*) NUCLEAR soudage à l'arc avec électrode enrobée *m*; ~ **pair** *n* ELEC ENG paire blindée *f*; ~ **transformer** *n* ELEC ENG transformateur blindé *m*; ~ **transmission line** *n* ELEC ENG ligne blindée *f*; ~ **wire** *n* ELEC ENG fil blindé *m*

shielding *n* ELEC *cable* écran *m*, PHYS *screening*, RAD PHYS, RECORDING, SAFETY blindage *m*, SPACE blindage *m*, protection *f*; ~ **conductor** *n* ELEC *cable* conducteur de protection *m*, conducteur écran *m*; ~ **effect** *n* ELEC *electromagnetic field* effet d'écran *m*

shift[1] *n* (*cf tour*) COMP décalage *m*, déplacement *m*, DP décalage *m*, dérive *f*, NUCLEAR *spectroscopy* déplacement *m*, PETR TECH quart *m*, PROD ENG équipe *f*, PROP MAT déplacement de cisaillement *m*, SPACE *communications* brigade *f*, poste *m*, TV déphasage *m*, glissement de fréquence *m*, variation de phase *f*; ~ **character** *n* DP caractère de changement de code *m*; ~ **clock rate** *n* PROD ENG temporisation de décalage *f*; ~ **clock register** *n* PROD ENG temporisation de décalage *f*; ~ **of G** *n* NAUT *ship design* déplacement du centre de gravité *m*; ~ **in character** *n* COMP caractère de code normal *m*, caractère en-code *m*; ~ **left register** *n* PROD ENG registre à décalage à gauche *m*; ~ **pulse** *n* ELECTRON impulsion de décalage *f*; ~ **register** *n* COMP, DP, ELECTRON, PROD ENG, TELECOM registre à décalage *m*; ~ **right register** *n* PROD ENG registre à décalage à droite *m*; ~ **work** *n* PROD ENG travail posté *m*

shift[2] *vt* COMP, DP, PROD ENG décaler

shift[3] *vi* NAUT *cargo, wind* changer, désarrimer, riper, sauter, PROD ENG se déplacer

shift[4] *vti* TEXTILES changer de position

shifted: ~ **finish** *n* C&G bague décalée *f*

shift-in: ~ **character** *n* DP caractère de code normal *m*, caractère de passage en code normal *m*

shifting: ~ **link** *n* MECH ENG *link gear* coulisse mobile *f*; ~ **rod** *n* MECH ENG *valve gear* bielle de relevage *f*; ~ **spanner** *n* MECH ENG clé à molette *f*, clé à mâchoires mobiles *f*

shift-out: ~ **character** *n* COMP, DP caractère de code spécial *m*, caractère hors-code *m*, caractère de code spécial *m*, caractère de passage en code spécial *m*

shim *n* MECH *tools* cale d'épaisseur *f*, MECH ENG cale *f*, cale d'appui *f*, NUCLEAR barre de compensation et d'arrêt d'urgence *f*, barre de compensation-sécurité *f*, RAIL *for rail joint* fourrure *f*; ~ **assembly** *n* NUCLEAR assemblage d'arrêt d'urgence *m*; ~ **element** *n* NUCLEAR élément de compensation *m*; ~ **member** *n* NUCLEAR élément de compensation *m*; ~ **rod bank** *n* NUCLEAR grappe de compensation *f*; ~ **safety rod** *n* NUCLEAR barre de compensation et d'arrêt d'urgence *f*, barre de compensation-sécurité *f*

shimming *n* MECH ENG calage *m*

shimmy: ~ **damper** *n* AERONAUT *aircraft* amortisseur de shimmy *m*

shingle *n* CONST *wood tile* bardeau *m*, galet *m*, NAUT *beach, bank* galets *m pl*, PRINT bardeau *m*; ~ **bank** *n* OCEANOG poulier *m*; ~ **beach** *n* OCEANOG grève *f*; ~ **distance** *n* PRINT distance entre deux cahiers sortant de la rotative *f*, pas de la nappe *m*; ~ **spit** *n* OCEANOG *beach ridge* levée *f*

ship[1] *n* MAR POLL navire *m*, NAUT bateau *m*, bâtiment *m*, navire *m*, OCEANOG, TRANSP navire *m*; ~ **automation** *n* NAUT automatisation de navire *f*; ~ **broker** *n* NAUT courtier maritime *m*; ~ **canal** *n* NAUT, OCEANOG canal

maritime *m*; ~ **chandler** *n* NAUT approvisionneur de la marine *m*, fournisseur maritime *m*, avitailleur de navire *m*; ~ **chandling** *n* NAUT avitaillement *m*; ~ **designer** *n* NAUT architecte naval *m*, ingénieur en construction navale *m*; ~ **earth station** *n* NAUT station terrienne de navire *f*; ~ **girder** *n* NAUT *ship building* poutre-navire *f*; ~ **handling** *n* NAUT manoeuvre *f*; ~ **in ballast** *n* NAUT *trim* navire sur lest *m*; ~ **in distress** *n* NAUT navire en perdition *m*; ~ **loading** *n* NAUT *shipping* navire en charge *m*; ~ **model test tank** *n* NAUT *boatbuilding* bassin d'essai des carènes *m*; ~ **polling** *n* TELECOM interrogation des navires *f*; ~ **reporting system** *n* TELECOM système de comptes rendus des navires *m*; ~ **station identity** *n* TELECOM identité de station de navire *f*; ~ **station number** *n* TELECOM numéro de station de navire *m*

ship[2] *vt* NAUT charger, embarquer, enrôler, envoyer par voie de mer, expédier, *oars* border, rentrer, *water* embarquer

ship's: ~ **articles** *n pl* PETR TECH rôle d'équipage *m*; ~ **boat** *n* NAUT chaloupe *f*, embarcation de bord *f*; ~ **books** *n pl* NAUT livres de bord *m pl*; ~ **bottom** *n* NAUT fond du navire *m*; ~ **bottom paint** *n* COLOURS peinture sous-marine *f*; ~ **hands** *n pl* NAUT équipage *m*; ~ **log** *n* NAUT journal de bord *m*, livre de bord *m*; ~ **papers** *n pl* NAUT documents de bord *m pl*, papiers de bord *m pl*; ~ **passport** *n* NAUT permis de navigation *m*; ~ **position** *n* NAUT *navigation* position du navire *f*; ~ **protest** *n* NAUT *damage* déclaration d'avaries *f*; ~ **register** *n* NAUT certificat d'immatriculation *m*

shipboard: ~ **terminal** *n* NAUT, TELECOM terminal de bord *m*

ship-borne: ~ **Earth station** *n* SPACE *communications* station terrienne embarquée *f*; ~ **lighter** *n* TRANSP barge de navire *f*

shipbreaking *n* NAUT démolition du navire *f*

shipbuilder *n* NAUT constructeur de navires *m*

shipbuilding *n* NAUT construction navale *f*

shipload *n* NAUT cargaison *f*, chargement *m*

shipmaster *n* NAUT capitaine *m*

shipment *n* AERONAUT embarquement *m*, NAUT cargaison *f*, chargement *m*, embarquement *m*, expédition *f*, PROD ENG expédition *f*, livraison client *f*

shipowner *n* NAUT armateur *m*, propriétaire de navire *m*

shipped: ~ **quantity** *n* PROD ENG quantité expédiée *f*

shipper *n* NAUT affréteur *m*, chargeur *m*, expéditeur *m*

shipping *n* AERONAUT embarquement *m*, NAUT chargement *m*, embarquement *m*, expédition *f*, mise à bord *f*, navigation *f*, navires *m pl*, transports maritimes *m pl*, PROD ENG expédition *f*, livraison client *f*; ~ **agency** *n* NAUT agence maritime *f*; ~ **agent** *n* NAUT agent maritime *m*, commissionnaire chargeur *m*, commissionnaire expéditeur *m*; ~ **bill** *n* NAUT connaissement *m*; ~ **channel** *n* OCEANOG chenal de navigation *m*; ~ **charges** *n pl* NAUT frais d'expédition *m pl*; ~ **clerk** *n* NAUT expéditionnaire *m*; ~ **company** *n* NAUT compagnie de navigation *f*, compagnie maritime *f*, messageries maritimes *f pl*; ~ **corridor** *n* OCEANOG couloir de navigation *m*; ~ **documents** *n pl* NAUT documents d'expédition *m pl*, pièces d'embarquement *f pl*; ~ **intelligence** *n* NAUT mouvements des navires *m pl*, nouvelles maritimes *f pl*; ~ **lane** *n* NAUT route de navigation *f*; ~ **note** *n* NAUT note de chargement *f*, permis d'embarquement *m*; ~ **office** *n* NAUT bureau maritime *m*, inscription maritime *f*; ~ **order** *n* NAUT bon d'embarquement *m*; ~ **port** *n* NAUT port de chargement *m*; ~ **route** *n* NAUT route de navigation *f*; ~ **terms** *n pl* NAUT conditions du contrat de transport *f pl*; ~ **ton** *n* NAUT tonneau d'affrètement *m*; ~ **trade** *n* NAUT affaires maritimes *f pl*, commerce maritime *m*; ~ **weight** *n* NAUT poids embarqué *m*, PROD ENG poids d'expédition *m*

ship-to-ship: ~ **alerting** *n* TELECOM alerte navire-navire *f*
ship-to-shore: ~ **alerting** *n* TELECOM alerte navire-terre *f*; ~ **radio** *n* NAUT liaison radio navire-sol *f*
ship-type: ~ **rig** *n* NAUT, PETR, PFTR TECH navire de forage *m*
shipwright *n* NAUT charpentier de marine *m*, charpentier du bord *m*, constructeur de navires *m*
shipyard *n* NAUT chantier de constructions navales *m*, chantier maritime *m*, chantier naval *m*
shirt *n* PROD ENG *of furnace* chemise *f*
shirting *n* TEXTILES corsage *m*, tissu de chemiserie *m*
shive *n* PAPER TECH bûchette *f*
shoal *n* GEOL basse *f*, brisant *m*, haut-fond *m*, petit fond *m*, NAUT basse *f*, brisant *m*, haut-fond *m*, OCEANOG platain *m*, platin *m*, *of fish* banc *m*, *shallow, reef* basse *f*, haut-fond *m*, PROD ENG bas-fond *m*, haut-fond *m*
shoals *n pl* HYDROL, NAUT petits fonds *m pl*
shock *n* MECH ENG choc *m*, impact *m*, secousse *f*, PHYS choc *m*, collision *f*, SPACE secousse *f*; ~ **absorber** *n* AUTO *motor* amortisseur *m*, amortisseur de vibrations *m*, CONST amortisseur de chocs *m*, amortisseur *m*, ELEC amortisseur d'oscillations *m*, MECH *vehicles*, SPACE, VEHICLES *suspension* amortisseur *m*; ~ **and wear resistance** *n* MECH ENG résistance aux chocs et à l'usure *f*; ~ **chilling** *n* REFRIG réfrigération-choc *f*; ~ **excitation** *n* TELECOM excitation par choc *f*; ~ **mount** *n* SPACE *spacecraft* montage élastique *m*, silentbloc *m*; ~ **resistance** *n* P&R résistance aux chocs *f*; ~ **wave initiator** *n* SPACE *spacecraft* initiateur d'onde de choc *m*
shock-absorbing: ~ **body** *n* RAIL *vehicles* caisse antichoc *f*
Shockley: ~ **diode** *n* ELECTRON diode Shockley *f*; ~ **dislocation** *n* METALL dislocation Shockley *f*
shockproof[1] *adj* CINEMAT antichoc, PACKAGING résistant aux chocs
shockproof:[2] ~ **socket** *n* ELEC *safety* prise de sécurité *f*
shockwave *n* GEOPHYS onde de choc *f*, onde de choc de compression *f*, onde de propagation *f*, MINING onde de choc *f*, onde explosive *f*, PETR, PHYS, WAVE PHYS onde de choc *f*
shoddy-type: ~ **filling** *n* (AmE) *(cf shoddy-type weft)* TEXTILES filé de trame en produit de récupération *m*; ~ **weft** *n* (BrE) *(cf shoddy-type filling)* TEXTILES filé de trame en produit de récupération *m*
shoe *n* CONST *rain water* dauphin *m*, MECH *vehicles* mâchoire de frein *f*, MECH ENG sabot *m*, *of piston* patin *m*, semelle *f*, MINING *of ore stamp* sabot *m*, NUCLEAR, PROD ENG *of amalgamating pan* patin *m*, RAIL *vehicles* patin *m*, sabot *m*, semelle *f*, TV guide à dépression *m*, VEHICLES *brake* mâchoire *f*, sabot *m*, segment *m*; ~ **board** *n* PAPER TECH carton pour chaussures *m*; ~ **brake** *n* VEHICLES frein à mâchoire *m*; ~ **nog plate** *n* C&G ferrasse à pavés *f*
shoeing: ~ **bar** *n* CONST fer cavalier *m*
S-hook *n* MECH ENG S de suspension *m*, crochet en S *m*, esse *f*
shoot *vt* CINEMAT tourner, CONST bouter, chavirer, culbuter, déverser, *edge of board* dresser, planer, raboter, OCEANOG *net* caler

shooting *n* CINEMAT prises de vues *f pl*, tournage *m*; ~ **brake** *n* TRANSP break *m*; ~ **distance** *n* PHOTO distance de prise de vues *f*; ~ **needle** *n* MINING *blasting* aiguille *f*, épinglette *f*; ~ **range** *n* MILIT champ de tir *m*; ~ **ratio** *n* CINEMAT pellicule montée par rapport au métrage tournée *f*; ~ **script** *n* CINEMAT découpage technique *m*; ~ **star** *n* ASTRON étoile filante *f*; ~ **to playback** *n* CINEMAT tournage en playback *m*
shop *n* C&G place *f*, workers pause *f* (Bel), poste *m* (Fra), MECH, PROD ENG atelier *m*; ~ **arrival date** *n* PROD ENG date d'arrivée usine *f*; ~ **crane** *n* PROD ENG grue d'atelier *f*; ~ **date** *n* PROD ENG date en calendrier usine *f*, date usine *f*; ~ **floor** *n* PROD ENG atelier *m*; ~ **packet** *n* PROD ENG dossier de fabrication *m*; ~ **papers** *n pl* PROD ENG dossier atelier *m*; ~ **priming** *n* COATINGS couche d'impression à l'atelier *f*, primaire d'atelier *m*; ~ **receipt** *n* PROD ENG recette de fin de fabrication *f*, réception de fabrication *f*; ~ **traveler** *n* (AmE), ~ **traveller** *n* (BrE) PROD ENG pont roulant d'atelier *m*
shore[1] *n* CONST *building* butée *f*, étai *m*, étançon *m*, GEOL côte *f*, littoral *m*, rivage *m*, HYDROL côte *f*, MINING butte *f*, chandelle *f*, étai *m*, NAUT *geography, shipbuilding* accore *f*, bord *m*, côte *f*, littoral *m*, rivage *m*, OCEANOG bord *m*; ~ **end** *n* ELEC ENG câble d'atterrissage *m*; ~ **fisherman** *n* OCEANOG bassier *m*; ~ **leave** *n* NAUT permission à terre *f*; ~ **protection** *n* WATER SUPP protection des rivages *f*; ~ **reception facility** *n* MAR POLL installation de réception terrestre *f*
shore:[2] ~ **up** *vt* COAL TECH étayer, NAUT *ship* accorer, épontiller
Shore: ~ **hardness** *n* P&R dureté Shore *f*; ~ **hardness tester** *n* INSTRUMENT, LAB EQUIP duromètre Shore *m*
shoreline *n* C&G ligne d'eau *f*, HYDROL rive *f*, *of river* grève *f*, rivage *m*, rive *f*, MAR POLL côte *f*, NAUT *geography* littoral *m*, *mooring* amarre de poste *f*, OCEANOG trait de côte *m*; ~ **cleanup** *n* MAR POLL nettoyage du littoral *m*
shore-to-ship: ~ **alerting** *n* TELECOM alerte terre-navire *f*
shoreward[1] *adj* NAUT *navigation* vers la terre
shoreward[2] *adv* NAUT *navigation* vers la terre
shoring *n* CONST *props* buttes *f pl*, chandelles *f pl*, étais *m pl*, étançon *m*, *propping* étaiement *m*, étançonnement *m*, étayage *m*, étayement *m*; ~ **up** *n* COAL TECH étaiement *m*
short[1] *n* CINEMAT court métrage *m*, ELEC ENG court-circuit *m*; ~ **blast** *n* NAUT *sound signals* coup bref *m*; ~ **channel** *n* ELECTRON canal court *m*; ~ **channel MOS transistor** *n* ELECTRON transistor MOS à canal court *m*; ~ **circuit** *n* COMP, DP, ELEC, ELEC ENG, PHYS, TELECOM court-circuit *m*; ~ **circuit armature** *n* ELEC *generator, motor* induit à court-circuit *m*; ~ **circuit flux** *n* ACOUSTICS, TV flux de court-circuit *m*; ~ **circuit impedance** *n* ELEC *winding* impédance de court-circuit *f*, ELEC ENG impédance en court-circuit *f*; ~ **circuit interrupting current** *n* PROD ENG pouvoir de coupure en court-circuit *m*; ~ **circuit protection** *n* ELEC ENG, PROD ENG protection contre les courts-circuits *f*; ~ **circuit rotor** *n* ELEC *generator, motor* induit à court-circuit *m*; ~ **code dialing** *n* (AmE), ~ **code dialling** *n* (BrE) TELECOM composition abrégée *f*, numérotation abrégée *f*; ~ **distance transport** *n* TRANSP transport hectométrique *m*; ~ **end** *n* CINEMAT chute *f*; ~ **fibers** *n pl* (AmE), ~ **fibres** *n pl* (BrE) PROP MAT fibres courtes *f pl*; ~ **finish** *n* C&G mauvais poli *m*; ~ **flame burner** *n* HEAT ENG brûleur à courte flamme *m*; ~ **glass** *n* C&G verre court *m*; ~ **grain** *n* PRINT grain court *m*, sens

travers *m*; ~ **normal** *n* PETR petite normale *f*; ~ **pipe** *n* HYDR EQUIP ajutage cylindrique *m*, orifice percé dans une paroi épaisse *m*, tuyau court *m*; ~ **pitch** *n* CINEMAT pas court *m*, pas négatif *m*; ~ **pulse** *n* ELECTRON, NAUT *radar* impulsion courte *f*; ~ **run** *n* MECH ENG petite série *f*, PACKAGING fabrication en petite quantité *f*, PRINT tirage court *m*; ~ **stop** *n* CINEMAT bain d'arrêt *m*; ~ **takeoff and landing aircraft** *n* (*STOL aircraft*) AERONAUT, TRANSP avion à décollage et attérissage court *m* (*ADAC*); ~ **ton** *n* METR tonne courte *f*; ~ **vision segment** *n* C&G segment de près *m*; ~ **wave** *n* (*SW*) ELEC *radiation*, WAVE PHYS *radio* onde courte *f*; ~ **wavelength laser** *n* ELECTRON laser à courte longueur d'onde *m*; ~ **weight** *n* METR poids faible *m*, PACKAGING défaut de poids *m*

short[2] *vt* ELEC ENG court-circuiter, mettre en court-circuit; ~ **out** *vt* PROD ENG mettre en court-circuit

shortage *n* PROD ENG rupture de stock *f*

short-circuit *adj* PHYS, TELECOM court-circuit

short-circuited[1] *adj* PHYS court-circuit

short-circuited:[2] ~ **armature** *n* ELEC ENG induit en court-circuit *m*; ~ **slip ring rotor** *n* ELEC *generator, motor* induit en court-circuit à bagues collectrices *m*

short-circuiting: ~ **device** *n* ELEC appareil de court-circuit *m*

short-delay: ~ **detonator** *n* MINING amorce à microretard *f*, détonateur à microretard *m*; ~ **electric detonator** *n* MINING détonateur électrique à court retard *m*

shorted: ~ **output circuit** *n* PROD ENG circuit de sortie en court-circuit *m*; ~ **turn** *n* ELEC ENG spire en court-circuit *f*

shorten *vt* MILIT *range*, PAPER TECH raccourcir

shortening *n* FOOD TECH graisse *f*, matière grasse *f*, GEOL, PAPER TECH *of fibres* raccourcissement *m*

shortest-path: ~ **program** *n* (AmE), ~ **programme** *n* (BrE) TRANSP programme de plus courte distance *m*

shortest-route: ~ **program** *n* (AmE), ~ **programme** *n* (BrE) TRANSP *traffic* programme de recherche d'itinéraire *m*

short-focus: ~ **lens** *n* PHOTO objectif de courte focale *m*, objectif à court foyer *m*

short-haul: ~ **airliner** *n* TRANSP court courrier *m*; ~ **cable** *n* ELEC ENG câble à courte distance *f*; ~ **skidder** *n* TRANSP tracteur forestier *m*

shorting *n* ELEC ENG court-circuitage *m*, mise en court-circuit *f*; ~ **contact** *n* ELEC ENG contact de mise en court-circuit *m*, contact à chevauchement *m*; ~ **contact switch** *n* ELEC ENG commutateur à chevauchement *m*, commutateur à contacts à chevauchement *m*; ~ **switch** *n* ELEC ENG interrupteur de mise en court-circuit *m*

short-interaction: ~ **tube** *n* ELECTRON tube à interaction courte *m*

short-link: ~ **chain** *n* MECH ENG chaîne serrée *f*, chaîne à maillons courts *f*; ~ **chain cable** *n* MECH ENG chaîne-câble à mailles serrées *f*

short-lived: ~ **particles** *n pl* PART PHYS particules transitoires *f pl*; ~ **tornado** *n* METEO tornade éphémère *f*

short-neck: ~ **projection tube** *n* ELECTRON tube de projection court *m*, tube de projection à col court *m*

short-nose: ~ **pliers** *n pl* MECH ENG béguettes *f pl*, pinces à becs courts *f pl*

short-nosed: ~ **pliers** *n pl* MECH ENG béguettes *f pl*, pinces à becs courts *f pl*

short-oil: ~ **alkyd** *n* P&R *paint resin* alkyd court en huile

m; ~ **varnish** *n* COATINGS vernis faible *m*, vernis maigre *m*, COLOURS vernis court en huile *m*

short-pulsed: ~ **laser** *n* WAVE PHYS laser à impulsions courtes *m*

short-range: **very** ~ **attractive forces** *n pl* PART PHYS forces attractives de très courte portée *f pl*; ~ **order** *n* CRYSTALL, METALL ordre à courte distance *m*; ~ **particle** *n* NUCLEAR particule de faible parcours *f*, particule à court parcours *f*; ~ **radar** *n* MILIT radar à courte portée *m*

short-stroke: ~ **engine** *n* VEHICLES moteur à faible course *m*

short-term *n* PROD ENG court terme *m*; ~ **drift** *n* ELECTRON *oscillator* dérive à court terme *f*; ~ **frequency stability** *n* ELECTRON stabilité en fréquence à court terme *f*; ~ **protection** *n* ELEC ENG protection contre les surcharges de courte durée *f*

short-time: ~ **constant filter** *n* PROD ENG filtre à faible temps de réponse *m*; ~ **rating** *n* ELEC *equipment* service nominal temporaire *m*; ~ **test** *n* ELEC essai de courte durée *m*

short-wall: ~ **coal-cutting machine** *n* COAL TECH haveuse ripante *f*

shot:[1] **in** ~ *adv* CINEMAT dans le plan

shot[2] *n* CINEMAT plan *m*, prise de vue *f*, MILIT coup de feu *m*, MINING *blasting* coup *m*, coup de mine *m*, mine *f*, pétard *m*, PETR TECH tir *m*, PHOTO photo *f*, prise de vue *f*, vue *f*, tirage photographique *m*, PRINT instantané photogravure *m*, tirage photographique *m*; ~ **bag test** *n* C&G essai de choc au sac de lest *m*; ~ **boring** *n* MINING forage à la grenaille d'acier *m*, sondage à la grenaille d'acier *m*; ~ **breakdown** *n* CINEMAT dépouillement *m*; ~ **drill** *n* MINING sondeuse à grenaille d'acier *f*; ~ **drilling** *n* MINING forage à la grenaille d'acier *m*, sondage à la grenaille d'acier *m*, PETR TECH forage à la grenaille *m*; ~ **firer** *n* COAL TECH préposé au tir *m*, MINING boutefeu *m*; ~ **hole** *n* MINING chambre de mine *f*, mine *f*, trou de mine *m*; ~ **hole drilling** *n* PETR TECH forage sismique *m*; ~ **hole plug** *n* PETR TECH bouchon de forage sismique *m*; ~ **list** *n* CINEMAT liste de cadrages *f*, liste des plans tournés *f*; ~ **noise** *n* ELECTRON, OPT, PHYS, SPACE *communications*, TELECOM bruit de grenaille *m*; ~ **peening** *n* C&G grenaillage *m*

shot[3] *vt* PROD ENG *granules* grenailler

shot-blasting *n* CONST grenaillage *m*, préparation par jet d'abrasif *f*

shot-by-shot: ~ **firing** *n* MINING tir coup par coup *m*

shot-dye *vt* COLOURS teindre en effet changeant

shot-firing *n* MINING abattage par explosifs *m*, minage *m*, sautage *m*, tir de mines *m*, tirage de coups de mine *m*; ~ **circuit** *n* MINING circuit de tir *m*

shot-peened[1] *adj* SPRINGS grenaillé

shot-peened:[2] ~ **surface** *n* SPRINGS surface grenaillée *f*

shotting *n* MINING grenaillement *m*

shoulder *n* C&G épaule *f*, CONST *of road* accotement *m*, MECH ENG épaulement *m*, *of knife, chisel* embase *f*, SPRINGS *of spring* embase *f*; ~ **bed effect** *n* PETR effet d'épontes *m*; ~ **brace** *n* CINEMAT crosse d'épaule *f*; ~ **hole** *n* MINING *blasting* mine de dégraissage *f*; ~ **pad** *n* TEXTILES épaulette *f*; ~ **wing** *n* AERONAUT *aircraft* aile mi-haute *f*, aile semi-haute *f*

shouldered: ~ **tenon** *n* CONST tenon épaulé *m*

shovel[1] *n* CONST, MAR POLL pelle *f*; ~ **dredger** *n* NAUT pelle automatique *f*; ~ **work** *n* CONST pelletage *m*, travail à la pelle *m*

shovel[2] *vt* CONST pelleter, ramasser à la pelle, remuer à la pelle

shovelful *n* CONST pelletée *f*

show[1] *n* MINING *safety lamps* auréole *f*, PETR TECH indice *m*

show[2] *vt* SAFETY *on tag* afficher, indiquer; **~ in section** *vt* MECH ENG figurer en coupe

shower *n* CONST *of sparks* gerbe *f*, METEO averse *f*, grain *m*, PAPER TECH rinceur *m*; **~ screen** *n* C&G écran pare-douche *m*

showering: **~ arc transient** *n* PROD ENG courant transitoire en arc étincelant *m*

shrapnel *n* MILIT éclat d'obus *m*

shredded: **~ cullet** *n* (AmE) *(cf quenched cullet)* C&G calcin tiré à l'eau *m* (Fra), calcinures *f pl* (Bel)

shredder *n* PAPER TECH déchiqueteuse *f*

shredding: **~ machine** *n* PACKAGING déchiqueteuse *f*

shrimp: **~ boat** *n* NAUT, OCEANOG crevettier *m*

shrimper *n* OCEANOG bassier *m*, crevettier *m*

shrimping: **~ net** *n* OCEANOG haveneau *m*

shrink:[1] **~ capsule** *n* PACKAGING capsule rétractable *f*; **~ film** *n* PACKAGING feuille rétractile *f*, film plastique rétractile *m*, film thermorétractable *m*, THERMOD *heat shrinkable* pellicule thermorétractable *f*, pellicule thermorétrécissable *f*; **~ fit** *n* MECH emmanchement à chaud *m*; **~ flow line wrappers** *n pl* PACKAGING emballage thermorétractable pour travail en chaîne *m*; **~ head** *n* PROD ENG *founding* masselotte *f*; **~ overwrapping machine** *n* PACKAGING machine pour enveloppement thermorétractable *f*; **~ pack** *n* PACKAGING emballage thermorétractable *m*; **~ resistance** *n* TEXTILES résistance au retrait *f*; **~ rule** *n* PROD ENG *founding* mètre à retrait *m*; **~ sleeve** *n* PAPER TECH manchon rétractable *m*; **~ sleeve wrapping machine** *n* PACKAGING machine pour emballage en manchons thermorétractables *f*; **~ tubing** *n* PROD ENG gaine en plastique thermorétractable *f*, gaine thermorétractable *f*; **~ tunnel for sleeve sealing** *n* PACKAGING tunnel pour emballage thermorétractable de manchons *m*; **~ tunnel for sleeving** *n* PACKAGING tunnel thermorétractable pour manchons *m*; **~ wrap** *n* PACKAGING feuille rétractile *f*, film plastique rétractile *m*, THERMOD pellicule thermorétractable *f*, pellicule thermorétrécissable *f*; **~ wrapping** *n* PACKAGING emballage thermorétractable *m*

shrink[2] *vt* PAPER TECH, TEXTILES rétrécir; **~ on** *vt* PROD ENG emmancher à chaud

shrink[3] *vi* C&G s'amaigrir

shrinkable *adj* THERMOD *heat* thermorétractable, thermorétrécissable

shrinkage *n* C&G retrait *m*, CINEMAT contraction *f*, retrait *m*, rétrécissement *m*, CONST *of cement* retrait *m*, MECH ENG *shrinking on* serrage *m*, METALL contraction *f*, retrait *m*, P&R, PAPER TECH retrait *m*, PHYS contraction *f*, rétrécissement *m*, PROD ENG contraction *f*, retrait *m*, rétrécissement *m*, TELECOM rétrécissement *m*, TEXTILES contraction *f*, rétrécissement *m*; **~ allowance** *n* MECH ENG *showing on* serrage *m*; **~ crack** *n* CONST fissure de retrait *f*, GEOL fente de retrait *f*, PROD ENG *founding* tapure *f*; **~ cracking** *n* CONST fissuration de retrait *f*; **~ factor** *n* PROD ENG coefficient de rebut *m*, taux d'attrition *m*, taux de rebut *m*; **~ limit** *n* COAL TECH limite de retrait *f*; **~ on solidification** *n* PACKAGING rétraction au figeage *f*

shrinking *n* CONST contraction *f*, retrait *m*, rétrécissement *m*, PROD ENG emmanchement à chaud *m*, PROP MAT retassement *m*, TELECOM rétrécissement *m*; **~ and**

welding machine *n* MECH ENG machine à refouler et à souder *f*; **~ hammer** *n* MECH ENG *tool* marteau à rétreindre *m*; **~ on** *n* MECH ENG emmanchement à chaud *m*, frettage *m*, PROD ENG emmanchement à chaud *m*

shrinkproof: **~ finish** *n* COATINGS apprêt antiretrait *m*

shrink-wrapped: **~ pallet cover** *n* PACKAGING enveloppe thermorétractable pour palette *f*; **~ product** *n* PACKAGING produit avec emballage thermorétractable *m*

shroud *n* NAUT *rigging, standing* hauban *m*, SPACE virole conique *f*, *spacecraft* coiffe *f*; **~ ring** *n* AERONAUT *of turbine engine* anneau d'étanchéité *m*

shrouded[1] *adj* PROD ENG *terminal* protégé

shrouded:[2] **~ coupling** *n* MECH ENG manchon avec boulons à têtes noyées *m*, manchon à boulons noyés *m*; **~ cover screw** *n* PROD ENG vis de couvercle protégé *f*; **~ flange coupling** *n* MECH ENG manchon à plateaux à boulons noyés *m*; **~ gear** *n* MECH ENG engrenage gardé *m*, engrenage à joues *m*, roue épaulée *f*; **~ propeller** *n* AERONAUT, TRANSP hélice carénée *f*

shrouding: **~ gear** *n* MECH ENG engrenage gardé *m*, engrenage à joues *m*, roue épaulée *f*; **~ muff coupling** *n* MECH ENG manchon cylindrique avec boulons à têtes noyées *m*; **~ screw** *n* MECH ENG vis à pompe *f*

shuck *vt* OCEANOG *oysters* écailler

shunt[1] *adj* ELEC ENG en dérivation, en parallèle, PHYS monté en dérivation

shunt[2] *adv* ELECTRON en dérivation

shunt[3] *n* ELEC *resistor* résistance en dérivation *f*, shunt *m*, ELEC ENG, PHYS dérivation *f*, shunt *m*, RAIL *vehicles* dérivation *f*, RECORDING fondu *m*; **~ bar** *n* RAIL *vehicles* barre de shuntage *f*; **~ capacitance** *n* ELEC ENG capacité en parallèle *f*; **~ capacitor** *n* PHYS condensateur mis en parallèle *m*; **~ circuit** *n* ELEC ENG circuit en dérivation *m*; **~ coil** *n* ELEC ENG bobine en dérivation *f*; **~ controller** *n* RAIL combinateur de shuntage *m*; **~ current** *n* ELEC ENG courant dérivé *m*; **~ dynamo** *n* ELEC ENG dynamo shunt *f*; **~ excitation** *n* ELEC ENG excitation en dérivation *f*, excitation shunt *f*; **~ feed** *n* ELEC *supply*, ELEC ENG alimentation en parallèle *f*; **~ feedback** *n* ELEC ENG contre-réaction parallèle *f*; **~ motor** *n* ELEC moteur électrique shunt *m*, ELEC ENG moteur en dérivation *m*, moteur shunt *m*; **~ regulator** *n* ELEC ENG régulateur shunt *m*; **~ resistance** *n* ELEC ENG résistance en parallèle *f*; **~ resistor** *n* ELEC ENG résistance en dérivation *f*, résistance en parallèle *f*; **~ switch** *n* ELEC interrupteur shunt *m*; **~ trip** *n* PROD ENG déclenchement shunt *m*; **~ winding** *n* ELEC *motor* enroulement dérivé *m*, enroulement en dérivation *m*, ELEC ENG enroulement en dérivation *m*

shunt[4] *vt* ELEC ENG ponter, shunter, RAIL garer, manoeuvrer

shunter *n* RAIL *personnel* enrayeur *m* (Fra), *vehicles* agent de manoeuvre *m*, caleur *m*, sabotier *m* (Sui), TRANSP locomotive de manoeuvre *f*

shunting *n* RAIL, TRANSP manoeuvre *f*; **~ device** *n* ELEC *supply* dérivateur *m*; **~ engine** *n* (BrE) *(cf switch engine)* CONST, RAIL, TRANSP locomotive de manoeuvre *f*; **~ locomotive** *n* TRANSP locomotive de manoeuvre *f*; **~ on level tracks** *n* TRANSP débranchement en palier *m*; **~ siding** *n* TRANSP voie de triage *f*; **~ signal** *n* RAIL signal de manoeuvre *m*; **~ switch** *n* ELEC commutateur de dérivation *m*; **~ track** *n* RAIL, TRANSP voie de triage *f*; **~ winch** *n* CONST treuil de manoeuvre *m*; **~ yard** *n* RAIL chantier de manoeuvres *m*, installation de triage *f*, TRANSP gare de triage *f*

shunt-wound: ~ **dynamo** n ELEC ENG dynamo shunt f; ~ **motor** n ELEC ENG moteur en dérivation m, moteur shunt m

shut[1] n PROD ENG founding écluse f, WATER SUPP sluice gate bonde f, pale f, palle f, pelle f, vanne f

shut:[2] ~ **down** vt AERONAUT engine couper le contact, CONTROL interrompre, SPACE motor arrêter, couper; ~ **off** vt PROD ENG molten metal écluser, WATER SUPP water-bearing strata isoler, serrer; ~ **up** vt PROD ENG welding encoller

shutdown n C&G arrêt du four m, CONTROL interruption de fabrication f, NUCLEAR of reactor arrêt m, mise à l'arrêt f, SPACE spacecraft arrêt m, extinction f; ~ **amplifier** n CONTROL amplificateur du signal d'arrêt m; ~ **circuit** n ELEC ENG circuit de protection m; ~ **procedure** n SPACE spacecraft procédure d'arrêt du moteur f; ~ **sensor** n SPACE spacecraft détecteur d'arrêt moteur m

shut-in: ~ **pressure** n PETR pression statique f, PETR TECH pression en puits fermé f, pression statique f

shut-off n C&G pont m, WATER SUPP sluice gate bonde f, pale f, palle f, pelle f, vanne f; ~ **valve** n NAUT engine robinet d'arrêt m, PROD ENG vanne de coupure f

shutter n CINEMAT obturateur m, CONST volet m, HYDR EQUIP robinet d'arrêt m, vanne f, INSTRUMENT obturateur m, MINING of box regulator guichet m, PHOTO of camera obturateur m, PROD ENG of fan vanne f, safety volet m, SPACE spacecraft obturateur m, volet m; ~ **angle** n CINEMAT angle de l'obturateur m; ~ **blade** n CINEMAT, PHOTO pale d'obturateur f; ~ **blur** n CINEMAT flou d'obturateur m; ~ **release** n CINEMAT déclencheur m, PHOTO bouton de déclenchement d'obturateur m, gâchette de déclenchement f, déclencheur d'obturateur m; ~ **release button** n PHOTO bouton de déclenchement d'obturateur m, of camera déclencheur m; ~ **release cable** n CINEMAT déclencheur souple m; ~ **speed** n PHOTO temps d'obturation m; ~ **speed control** n PHOTO régleur de temps de pose m, régleur de vitesse m; ~ **speed setting** n PHOTO réglage de l'obturateur m; ~ **system** n SPACE spacecraft système à volets mobiles m; ~ **with B setting** n PHOTO obturateur fonctionnant à la pose m

shuttering n CONST for making concrete coffrage m

shutter-phasing: ~ **device** n CINEMAT dispositif de mise en phase de l'obturateur m

shutting: ~ **post** n CONST barreau de battement m, montant de battement m, poteau battant m; ~ **together** n PROD ENG welding encollage m

shutting-off n HYDR EQUIP steam arrêt m, fermeture f, WATER SUPP the water isolement m; ~ **water** n WATER SUPP in pipe fermeture de l'eau f

shutting-up n PROD ENG welding encollage m

shuttle n AERONAUT navette f, HYDR EQUIP navette f, tiroir m, SPACE spacecraft, TEXTILES, TRANSP navette f, TV défilement m, navette f; ~ **armature** n ELEC generator, motor induit en I m, induit en double T m; ~ **ferry** n NAUT navette f; ~ **haulage** n COAL TECH extraction en va-et-vient f; ~ **helicopter** n PETR TECH hélicoptère navette m; ~ **plate** n HYDR EQUIP opercule de vanne m, tablier de vanne m; ~ **search** n TV recherche avant arrière f; ~ **service** n AERONAUT, TRANSP service de navette m; ~ **spindle** n TEXTILES broche de navette f; ~ **tanker** n PETR TECH pétrolier-navette m; ~ **traffic** n TRANSP circulation en navette f; ~ **train** n CONST navette f; ~ **valve** n PROD ENG sélecteur de circuit m

Si CHEM (silicon), (silicium) Si (silicium)

SI[1] abbr METR (international system of units) SI (système international d'unités), TELECOM (screening indicator) indicateur de contrôle m

SI:[2] ~ **character** n COMP caractère de code normal m, DP caractère de code normal m, caractère de passage en code normal m; ~ **unit** n ELEC, PHYS unité SI f; ~ **units** n PHYS système international d'unités m

siberite n MINERAL sibérite f

sibilance n RECORDING sibilance f

siccative[1] adj THERMOD siccatif

siccative[2] n FOOD TECH siccatif m, THERMOD dessiccant m, siccatif m

side:[1] ~ **fit** adj MECH ENG centrage sur flancs

side[2] n CONST of roof pan m, GEOM of triangle, cube côté m, INSTRUMENT branche f, MECH ENG of lathe flasque m, MINING of mine level paroi latérale f, pied-droit m, OPT pit flanc m, PROD ENG of crab winch flasque m; ~ **bar** n CONST of ladder montant m, PROD ENG of roller chain flasque m; ~ **buffer screw coupling** n TRANSP attelage à vis et tampons latéraux m; ~ **car** n TRANSP side-car m; ~ **casting** n PROD ENG founding coulée à talon f; ~ **chain** n CHEM chaîne latérale f; ~ **channel** n OCEANOG faux chenal m; ~ **chisel** n CONST wood-turning biseau m, fermoir de tour nez rond m; ~ **circuit** n ELEC ENG circuit réel m; ~ **clearance** n MECH ENG jeu latéral m, gearing jeu entre les dents m; ~ **collision** n TRANSP collision de flanc f; ~ **construction** n NAUT shipbuilding construction des murailles f; ~ **cutting nippers** n pl MECH ENG pinces coupantes sur côté f pl; ~ **dump car** n (AmE) (cf side dump wagon) RAIL wagon à culbutage latéral m; ~ **dump wagon** n (BrE) (cf side dump car) RAIL wagon à culbutage latéral m; ~ **effect** n COMP, DP effet secondaire m; ~ **entry** n MINING galerie latérale f; ~ **finder** n CINEMAT viseur latéral m; ~ **frame** n PACKAGING of container cadre latéral m; ~ **frequency** n ELECTRON fréquence latérale f; ~ **gate** n PROD ENG founding chenal de coulée à talon m; ~ **gear** n AUTO satellite m, VEHICLES differential roue planétaire f; ~ **girder** n NAUT shipbuilding support latéral m; ~ **holes** n pl MINING blasting mines de mazières f pl; ~ **index** n PRINT répertoire encoché m; ~ **joint** n INSTRUMENT charnière f; ~ **lash** n MECH ENG jeu latéral m; ~ **lever press** n C&G presse à levier f; ~ **lobe** n ELECTRON, NAUT radar lobe secondaire m, PHYS aerial lobe latéral m, lobe secondaire m, SPACE communications lobe secondaire m; ~ **lobe cancellation** n ELECTRON suppression des lobes secondaires f, suppression des signaux reçus sur les lobes secondaires f; ~ **lock** n TV verrouillage sur fréquence latérale m; ~ **marker light** n (AmE) (cf sidelight) AUTO veilleuse f, VEHICLES feu de côté m, feu de position m, lampe de côté f, VEHICLES feu d'encombrement m; ~ **member** n VEHICLES chassis longeron m; ~ **mill** n MECH ENG cutter fraise de côté f; ~ **mirror** n VEHICLES rétroviseur extérieur m; ~ **note** n PRINT note marginale f; ~ **on collision** n TRANSP collision latérale f; ~ **panel** n PACKAGING, VEHICLES body panneau latéral m; ~ **plane** n CONST rabot à lumière de côté m; ~ **planing machine** n PROD ENG machine à raboter latérale f; ~ **plates** n pl PROD ENG for emery wheels plaques de serrage f pl, plateaux de serrage m pl, of roller chain flasque m; ~ **plating** n NAUT shipbuilding bordé de muraille m; ~ **play** n MECH ENG jeu latéral m; ~ **pocket** n C&G chambre à poussières f; ~ **product** n CHEM of reaction sous-produit m; ~ **pulley** n CONST hardware poulie de renvoi à plat f, renvoi à plat m; ~ **push rod** n PROD ENG tige à poussoir latéral f; ~ **rabbet plane** n

CONST guillaume de côté *m*; ~ **reaction** *n* CHEM sous-réaction *f*; ~ **register** *n* PRINT repérage latéral *m*; ~ **run** *n* PAPER TECH à-côté de fabrication *m*; ~ **stay bolt** *n* RAIL *vehicles* entretoise de parois latérales *f*; ~ **stoping** *n* MINING abattage conduit parallèlement à la descenderie *m*, abattage latéral *m*, abattage par gradins latéraux *m*; ~ **thrust** *n* ACOUSTICS poussée latérale *f*, FUELLESS poussée horizontale *f*, MECH ENG *machine tool* force centripète *f*; ~ **thruster** *n* NAUT propulseur latéral *m*; ~ **tool** *n* MECH ENG *lathe* outil de côté *m*; ~ **wiping** *n* ELEC ENG portée sur la tranche *f*

side:³ **this ~ up** *phr* PACKAGING *handling marking or label* haut *m*

side-and-face: ~ **milling cutter** *n* MECH ENG fraise à défoncer *f*, fraise à trois tailles *f*; ~ **milling cutter with plain** *n* MECH ENG fraise de trois tailles à alésage lisse *f*

sideband *n* COMP, DP, ELECTRON, PHYS, RECORDING, TELECOM, TV bande latérale *f*; ~ **alloy** *n* METALL alliage à satellites *m*; ~ **attenuation** *n* ELECTRON atténuation d'une bande latérale *f*; ~ **frequency** *n* ELECTRON fréquence d'une bande latérale *f*; ~ **interference** *n* ELECTRON interférence par bandes latérales *f*; ~ **suppression** *n* ELECTRON élimination d'une bande latérale *f*

side-by-side: ~ **cylinders** *n pl* MECH ENG cylindres placés côte à côte *m pl*

sidedraft: ~ **carburetor** *n* (AmE), ~ **carburettor** *n* (BrE) AUTO, VEHICLES carburateur horizontal *m*

sidegrooved: ~ **specimen** *n* METALL éprouvette à entailles latérales *f*

sidehill: ~ **cut** *n* CONST *excavation* déblai à flanc de coteau *m*

sidelight¹ *n* (BrE) *(cf side marker light)* AUTO veilleuse *f*, VEHICLES feu de côté *m*, feu de position *m*, lampe de côté *f*

sidelight² *vt* PHOTO éclairer de côté

sidelobe *n* ELECTRON lobe latéral *m*

side-mounted: ~ **terminal** *n* AUTO borne latérale *f*

side-push: ~ **roller** *n* PROD ENG poussoir latéral à galet *m*

sidereal¹ *adj* ASTRON sidéral

sidereal:² ~ **clock** *n* ASTRON horloge sidérale *f*; ~ **day** *n* ASTRON, PHYS jour sidéral *m*; ~ **period** *n* ASTRON période sidérale *f*; ~ **time** *n* ASTRON, SPACE temps sidéral *m*; ~ **year** *n* ASTRON, PHYS année sidérale *f*

siderite *n* ASTRON sidérite *f*, MINERAL sidérite *f*, sidérose *f*

sideritic: ~ **mudstone** *n* GEOL argile à sidérose *f*

sideromelane *n* PETR sidéromélane *f*

sideslip *n* PHYS dérapage *m*

sidetone *n* TELECOM effet local *m*

sidetrack: ~ **drilling** *n* PETR TECH forage dévié *m*

sidetracking *n* PETR TECH déviation de forage *f*

side-valve: ~ **engine** *n* AUTO moteur à soupapes latérales *m*

sidewalk *n* (AmE) *(cf pavement)* CONST trottoir *m*

sidewall *n* MINING paroi latérale *f*, parois *f pl*, WATER SUPP *of canal lock, of water wheel* bajoyer *m*, bas-joyer *m*; ~ **air cushion** *n* TRANSP *hovercraft* coussin à bulles d'air captives *m*; ~ **core** *n* PETR carotte latérale *f*, carottier latéral *m*; ~ **coring** *n* PETR carottage latéral *m*; ~ **hovercraft** *n* TRANSP aéroglisseur à parois latérales *m*; ~ **neutron log** *n* PETR diagramme neutron de paroi latérale *m*; ~ **pad** *n* PETR tampon latéral *m*; ~ **sampler** *n* PETR échantillonneur latéral *m*; ~ **with ventilation flaps** *n* TRANSP paroi latérale à claire-voie *f*

sidewall-coupled *adj* ELEC ENG *waveguides* couplé par le petit côté

sidewall-type: ~ **hovercraft** *n* TRANSP aéroglisseur à parois latérales *m*

sideways-looking: ~ **airborne radar** *n (SLAR)* MAR POLL radar aéroporté à balayage latéral *m*

sidewell: ~ **core** *n* PETR TECH carotte latérale *f*

side-wipe: ~ **contact** *n* ELEC ENG contact à portée sur la tranche *m*

siding *n* C&G mal centré, CONST *building* bardage *m*, *railway* voie de raccordement *f*, RAIL voie d'embranchement *f*, voie de raccordement *f*, *for splitting up trains* voie de débranchement *f*, TRANSP voie de garage *f*

sidings *n pl* RAIL faisceau *m*

siege: ~ **artillery** *n* MILIT artillerie de siège *f*

siemens *n* METR, PHYS siemens *m*

sieve¹ *n* COAL TECH sas *m*, tamis *m*, CONST crible *m*, passoire *f*, sas *m*, tamis *m*, HYDROL, LAB EQUIP, RECYCLING tamis *m*; ~ **analysis** *n* CHEM TECH analyse au tamis *f*, analyse par tamisage *f*, COAL TECH analyse granulométrique *f*, NUCLEAR contrôle de granulométrie par tamisage *m*, granulométrie *f*; ~ **bottom** *n* CHEM TECH fond à tamis *m*; ~ **classification** *n* CHEM TECH triage à tamis *m*; ~ **cloth** *n* CHEM TECH tissu filtrant *m*, tissu pour filtre *m*; ~ **diaphragm** *n* CHEM TECH fond à tamis *m*; ~ **drum** *n* CHEM TECH crible à tambour *m*, tambour tamiseur *m*; ~ **dryer** *n* CHEM TECH séchoir par tambours perforés *m*; ~ **fraction** *n* C&G fraction granulométrique *f*; ~ **frame** *n* CHEM TECH monture *f*; ~ **grate** *n* CHEM TECH grille de crible *f*, grille à barreaux *f*; ~ **jigger** *n* CHEM TECH bac de lavage *m*, bac laveur *m*; ~ **mesh** *n* COAL TECH maille *f*; ~ **netting** *n* CHEM TECH grillage du crible *m*, toile de tamisage *f*; ~ **plate** *n* CHEM TECH fond perforé *m*; ~ **set** *n* CHEM TECH jeu de tamis *m*, série de tamis *f*; ~ **shaker** *n* LAB EQUIP tamiseur *m*; ~ **table** *n* COAL TECH table secoueuse *f*; ~ **test** *n* CHEM TECH tamisage de contrôle *m*; ~ **tray** *n* CHEM TECH fond perforé *m*

sieve² *vt* CHEM TECH cribler, passer au crible, passer au tamis, tamiser, FOOD TECH bluter, passer au tamis, tamiser, HYDROL cribler, tamiser

sievert *n (Sv)* PHYS, RAD PHYS sievert *m (Sv)*

sieving *n* CHEM TECH tamisage *m*, CONST, MAR POLL criblage *m*, tamisage *m*, POLLUTION tamisage *m*; ~ **filter** *n* CHEM TECH filtre-tamis *m*; ~ **rate** *n* CHEM TECH capacité de tamisage *f*; ~ **residue** *n* CHEM TECH refus de criblage *m*

sift *vt* CONST cribler, tamiser, FOOD TECH bluter, passer au chinois, passer au tamis, tamiser, MAR POLL cribler

sifted: ~ **coal** *n* COAL TECH charbon criblé *m*

sifter *n* PROD ENG *founding* cribleuse *f*

sifting *n* CONST criblage *m*, tamisage *m*, PROD ENG criblage *m*, passage au tamis *m*, tamisage *m*

siftings *n pl* PROD ENG matières tamisées *f pl*, produits du tamisage *m pl*

sight¹ *n* CONST pinnule *f*, *aim, observation taken* coup *m*, coup de lunette *m*, visée *f*, INSTRUMENT mire *f*, viseur *m*, NAUT *navigation* visée *f*; ~ **bar** *n* NAUT *sextant* alidade *f*; ~ **distance** *n* CONST distance de dépassement *f*, TRANSP *traffic* distance de visibilité *f*; ~ **glass** *n* PETR TECH regard *m*, REFRIG *on cooler* vitre de visualisation *f*, voyant *m*; ~ **hole** *n* MECH ENG regard *m*, MILIT *on firearm* trou de visée *m*; ~ **rule** *n* CONST alidade *f*

sight² *vt* PHOTO *camera* viser

sighted: ~ **alidade** *n* CONST alidade à pinnules *f*; ~ **level** *n*

CONST niveau à pinnules *m*

sight-feed: **~ glass** *n* MECH ENG *lubricator* tube en verre de débit visible *m*; **~ lubricator** *n* MECH ENG graisseur à débit visible *m*; **~ needle valve** *n* MECH ENG pointeau de débit visible *m*

sighting *n* CONST visée *f*, MILIT *artillery* pointage *m*; **~ board** *n* CONST voyant *m*; **~ color** *n* (AmE), **~ colour** *n* (BrE) COLOURS couleur détectrice *f*; **~ line** *n* INSTRUMENT ligne de visée *f*, MILIT *of firearm* ligne de mire *f*; **~ mirror** *n* INSTRUMENT miroir *m*; **~ range** *n* MILIT portée de visée *f*; **~ telescope** *n* CONST lunette viseur *f*, INSTRUMENT lunette de pointage *f*

sights: **~ adjustment** *n* CONTROL alignement de hausse *m*

sigma: **~ bond** *n* CHEM *covalent bond* liaison sigma *f*; **~ particle** *n* PHYS particule sigma *f*; **~ pile** *n* NUCLEAR pile sigma *f*, réacteur sigma *m*

sign[1] *n* COMP, DP signe *m*, VEHICLES *road* panneau *m*; **~ bit** *n* COMP, DP bit de signe *m*; **~ digit** *n* COMP, DP bit de signe *m*; **~ language** *n* CONTROL langage par signes *m*

sign:[2] **~ off** *vi* COMP, DP sortir du système; **~ on** *vi* COMP entrer dans le système

signal[1] *n* ACOUSTICS, COMP, DP, ELECTRON, NAUT, PHYS signal *m*, RAIL panneau *m*, panneau-signal *m*, RECORDING, TV signal *m*; **~ agility** *n* ELECTRON sauts de fréquence du signal *m pl*; **~ amplitude** *n* ELECTRON amplitude du signal *f*; **~ analysis** *n* ELECTRON, TELECOM analyse de signaux *f*; **~ analyzer** *n* ELECTRON, RAD PHYS *atomic spectra*, TELECOM analyseur de signaux *m*; **~ arm** *n* CONTROL bras de signal *m*; **~ at danger** *n* RAIL *signalling* signal fermé *m*; **~ averaging** *n* ELECTRON moyennage de signaux *m*; **~ bandwidth** *n* ELECTRON largeur de bande du signal *f*; **~ beacon** *n* CONTROL fanal *m*; **~ bell** *n* CONTROL cloche d'avertissement *f*, sonnerie d'avertissement *f*; **~ book** *n* NAUT livre des signaux *m*; **~ box** *n* (BrE) (*cf signal tower, switch tower*) RAIL poste de commande *m*; **~ buried in noise** *n* ELECTRON signal noyé dans le bruit *m*; **~ circuit** *n* CONTROL circuit de commande *m*, circuit-pilote *m*; **~ clipping** *n* ELECTRON écrêtage du signal *m*; **~ comparator** *n* ELECTRON comparateur de signaux *m*, comparateur *m*; **~ comparison** *n* ELECTRON comparaison de signaux *f*; **~ complex** *n* TV ensemble des signaux *m*; **~ component** *n* ELECTRON composante du signal *f*; **~ compression** *n* TELECOM compression de signal *f*; **~ conditioning** *n* ELECTRON mise en forme de signaux *f*, PROD ENG mise en forme du signal *f*; **~ cone** *n* CONTROL cône des signaux *m*; **~ conversion** *n* TELECOM conversion de signaux *f*; **~ converter** *n* TELECOM convertisseur de signal *m*; **~ degradation** *n* TELECOM dégradation du signal *f*; **~ delay** *n* ELECTRON, TELECOM retard du signal *m*; **~ detection** *n* TELECOM détection de signal *f*; **~ detector** *n* TELECOM détecteur de signal *m*; **~ digitization** *n* ELECTRON numérisation de signaux *f*; **~ digitizer** *n* ELECTRON numériseur de signaux *m*; **~ distortion** *n* ELECTRON, TELECOM distorsion du signal *f*; **~ distributor** *n* (*SD*) TELECOM distributeur lent *m*; **~ edge** *n* ELECTRON flanc de signal *m*; **~ electrode** *n* ELECTRON électrode de signal *f*; **~ element timing** *n* TELECOM base de temps pour les éléments de signal *f*; **~ envelope** *n* TELECOM enveloppe de signal *f*; **~ expansion** *n* TELECOM extension de signal *f*; **~ extension** *n* TELECOM extension de signal *f*; **~ fail** *n* (*SF*) TELECOM défaillance de signal *f*; **~ flag** *n* CONTROL pavillon pour signaux *m*, NAUT pavillon alphabétique *m*, pavillon de signaux *m*; **~ frequency** *n* ELECTRON fréquence du signal *f*; **~ generation** *n* ELECTRON génération de si-

gnaux *f*; **~ generator** *n* ELECTRON, PHYS générateur de signaux *m*, TELECOM générateur de signal *m*; **~ generator calibration** *n* ELECTRON étalonnage de générateurs de signaux *m*; **~ glass** *n* C&G verre de signalisation *m*; **~ ground** *n* TELECOM terre de signalisation *f*; **~ identification plate** *n* RAIL plaque de repérage de signal *f*; **~ installation** *n* TRANSP installation de signalisation lumineuse *f*; **~ lamp** *n* CONTROL lampe de signal *f*, RAIL lanterne de queue *f*, lanterne de signal *f*; **~ level** *n* ELECTRON niveau du signal *m*, TELECOM niveau de signal *m*; **~ line** *n* ELEC ENG ligne de signaux *f*; **~ locker** *n* NAUT *flags* coffre à signaux *m*; **~ mast** *n* NAUT *ship building* mât de signaux *m*; **~ modeling** *n* (AmE), **~ modelling** *n* (BrE) ELECTRON modélisation de signaux *f*; **~ multiplexing** *n* ELECTRON multiplexage de signaux *m*; **~ phase** *n* ELECTRON phase du signal *f*; **~ plate** *n* ELECTRON plaque-signal *f*; **~ power** *n* ELECTRON puissance du signal *f*; **~ processing** *n* COMP, DP, ELECTRON, TELECOM traitement de signaux *m*; **~ processor** *n* (*SP*) ELECTRON processeur de signaux *m*, TELECOM dispositif de traitement des signaux *m*, unité de traitement de signaux *f*, TV dispositif de traitement de signal *m*, processeur de signal *m*; **~ pulse** *n* ELECTRON impulsion formant signal *f*; **~ quantization** *n* TELECOM quantification de signal *f*; **~ receiver** *n* TELECOM récepteur *m*, récepteur de signaux *m*; **~ regeneration** *n* ELECTRON régénération des signaux *f*; **~ regenerator** *n* ELECTRON régénérateur de signaux *m*; **~ restoration** *n* TELECOM rétablissement du signal *m*; **~ shaping** *n* COMP, DP mise en forme de signal *f*, ELECTRON mise en forme de signaux *f*; **~ simulation** *n* ELECTRON simulation de signaux *f*; **~ splitter** *n* TV répartiteur de signaux *m*, séparateur de signaux *m*; **~ station** *n* CONTROL station de signal *f*, NAUT sémaphore *m*; **~ strength** *n* CONTROL intensité du signal *f*, puissance reçue *f*; **~ structure** *n* RAIL nacelle de signal *f*, potence à signaux *f pl*; **~ synthesis** *n* ELECTRON synthèse de signaux *f*; **~ threshold** *n* TELECOM seuil de signal *m*; **~ tower** *n* (AmE) (*cf signal box*) RAIL poste de commande *m*; **~ transmission** *n* TELECOM émission de signal *f*; **~ weakening** *n* TELECOM dégradation du signal *f*

signal[2] *vt* ELECTRON signaler, émettre un signal

signal[3] *vti* NAUT signaler

signaling *n* (AmE), **signalling** *n* (BrE) COMP, DP signalisation *f*, NAUT signalisation *f*, timonerie *f*, SPACE *communications*, TELECOM signalisation *f* **~ channel** *n* (TELECOM canal sémaphore *m*; **~ connection control part** *n* TELECOM SSCS, sous-système de commande de connexion sémaphore *m*; **~ detector** *n* TELECOM détecteur de signalisation *m*; **~ device** *n* CONTROL signalisateur *m*; **~ distance** *n* TRANSP distance entre les signaux *f*; **~ flag** *n* CONTROL fanion-signal *m*; **~ generator** *n* ELEC ENG magnéto d'appel *f*; **~ grouping channel** *n* (*SGC*) TELECOM canal de groupement de signalisation *m*; **~ information** *n* TELECOM informations de signalisation *f pl*, messages de signalisation *m pl*; **~ lamp** *n* CONTROL lanterne-signal *f*; **~ lantern** *n* CONTROL lanterne-signal *f*; **~ network** *n* TELECOM signalisation *f*; **~ point** *n* (*SP*) TELECOM point sémaphore *m*; **~ protocol** *n* COMP, DP protocole d'échange de signaux *m*; **~ reliability** *n* TELECOM fiabilité de signalisation *f*; **~ system** *n* TELECOM système de signalisation *m*; **~ transfer point** *n* (*STP*) TELECOM point de transfert sémaphore *m*; **~ virtual channel** *n* (*SVC*) TELECOM canal virtuel de signalisation *m*, voie virtuelle de signalisation *f*; **~ wires** *n pl* RAIL câbles à signaux *m pl*

signal-operating: **~ rod** *n* RAIL tringle de manoeuvre de signal *f*

signal-processing: **~ chip** *n* ELECTRON puce de traitement de signaux *f*

signal-shaping: **~ filter** *n* TELECOM filtre de mise en forme du signal *m*

signal-to-noise: **~ ratio** *n (SNR)* ACOUSTICS, COMP, DP, ELECTRON, PETR, PHYS, RECORDING, TELECOM, TV rapport signal-bruit *m*

signature *n* COMP, DP signature *f*, PRINT cahier *m*; **~ number** *n* PRINT numéro du cahier *m*

signed: **~ magnitude representation** *n* COMP, DP représentation en valeur signée *f*

significance: **~ test** *n* COMP, DP test de signification *m*, MATH test de signifiance *m*

significant: **~ figure** *n* MATH chiffre significatif *m*; **~ figures** *n pl* MATH chiffres après la virgule *m pl*; **~ wave** *n* OCEANOG lame significative *f*, vague significative *f*

silage: **~ effluent** *n* HYDROL liquide d'ensilage *m*

silane *n* CHEM, P&R silane *m*

silence: **~ elimination** *n* TELECOM élimination de silence *f*

silencer *n* (BrE) ACOUSTICS amortisseur de bruit *m*, AUTO, *(cf muffler)* silencieux *m*, SAFETY *pipelines* amortisseur contre le bruit *m*, VEHICLES *(cf muffler) exhaust system* amortisseur de bruit *m*, pot d'échappement *m*, silencieux *m*

silent: **~ film** *n* CINEMAT film muet *m*; **~ print** *n* CINEMAT positif image seule *m*, positif muet *m*; **~ track** *n* CINEMAT silence modulé *m*

silhouetting *n* CINEMAT détourage *m*

silica *n* C&G, CHEM, ELECTRON, MINERAL, PHYS, PROP MAT silice *f*; **~ aerogel** *n* HEAT ENG silicagel *m*; **~ coating** *n* TELECOM revêtement silice *m*, revêtement de résine silicone *m*; **~ content** *n* MINING *of ore* teneur en silice *f*; **~ dust** *n* SAFETY poussière de silice cristalline *f*; **~ fiber** *n* (AmE), **~ fibre** *n* (BrE) HEAT ENG, OPT, TELECOM fibre de silice *f*; **~ gel** *n* CHEM *drying agent*, FOOD TECH gel de silice *m*, PACKAGING silicagel *m*, PROP MAT gel de silice *m*; **~ glass** *n* METALL verre de silice *m*; **~ scum** *n* C&G écume de silice *f*; **~ scum line** *n* (BrE) *(cf batch melting line)* C&G cordon de silice *m*

silicate *n* CHEM silicate *m*; **~ paint** *n* COATINGS couleur au verre soluble *f*, COLOURS peinture au verre *f*, peinture aux silicates *f*

silicates *n pl* PROP MAT silicates *m pl*

siliceous[1] *adj* CHEM siliceux

siliceous:[2] **~ nondetrital rock** *n* GEOL roche siliceuse non-détritique *f*; **~ sinter terrace** *n* GEOPHYS terrasse de travertin *f*

silicic: **~ acid** *n* CHEM acide silicique *m*

siliciclastic: **~ rock** *n* GEOL roche clastique terrigène *f*, roche silicoclastique *f*

silicide *n* CHEM siliciure *m*

silicium *n (Si)* CHEM silicium *m (Si)*

siliciuret *n* CHEM siliciure *m*

silicoborate *n* CHEM borosilicate *m*

silicofluoride *n* CHEM fluosilicate *m*

silicon *n (Si)* CHEM silicium *m (Si)*; **~ avalanche diode** *n* ELECTRON diode à avalanche au silicium *f*; **~ avalanche photodiode** *n* ELECTRON photodiode à avalanche au silicium *f*; **~ bipolar integrated circuit** *n* ELECTRON circuit intégré bipolaire au silicium *m*; **~ bipolar transistor** *n* ELECTRON transistor bipolaire au silicium *m*; **~ carbide** *n* ELEC ENG, PHYS carbure de silicium *m*; **~ carbide varistor** *n* ELEC ENG varistance au carbure de silicium *f*; **~ cell** *n* ELEC ENG, FUELLESS cellule au silicium *f*; **~ checkers** *n pl* RAD PHYS *particle detectors* damiers de silicium *m pl*; **~ chip** *n* COMP pastille de silicium *f*, puce *f*, DP puce de silicium *f*, ELEC pastille de silicium *f*, puce électronique *f*, ELECTRON puce de silicium *f*, RAD PHYS puce au silicium *f*; **~ counter** *n* RAD PHYS compteur au silicium *m*; **~ crystal** *n* ELECTRON cristal de silicium *m*; **~ crystal mixer** *n* ELECTRON mélangeur à cristal de silicium *m*; **~ detector** *n* ELECTRON détecteur au silicium *m*, photodétecteur au silicium *m*, RAD PHYS *particle scattering* détecteur au silicium *m*; **~ detector diode** *n* ELECTRON diode de détection au silicium *f*; **~ device** *n* ELEC ENG composant au silicium *m*; **~ diode** *n* ELEC *semiconductor*, ELECTRON diode au silicium *f*; **~ dioxide** *n* ELECTRON dioxyde de silicium *m*, PROP MAT dioxyde de silice *m*, dioxyde de silicium *m*; **~ dioxide layer** *n* ELECTRON couche d'oxyde de silicium *f*; **~ doping** *n* ELECTRON dopage du silicium *m*; **~ epitaxial layer** *n* ELECTRON couche épitaxiale de silicium *f*; **~ epitaxial planar transistor** *n* ELECTRON transistor planar épitaxial au silicium *m*; **~ FET** *n* ELECTRON transistor à effet de champ au silicium *m*; **~ foundry** *n* ELECTRON fonderie de silicium *f*; **~ gate** *n* ELECTRON grille en silicium *f*; **~ gate technology** *n* ELECTRON technique de la grille au silicium *f*; **~ gate transistor** *n* ELECTRON transistor à grille au silicium *m*; **~ junction diode** *n* ELECTRON diode à jonction au silicium *f*; **~ layer** *n* ELECTRON couche de silicium *f*; **~ microstrip detector telescope** *n* RAD PHYS télescope détecteur à microrubans de silicium *m*; **~ mixer diode** *n* ELECTRON diode mélangeuse au silicium *f*; **~ nitride** *n* ELECTRON nitrure de silicium *m*; **~ on sapphire** *n (SOS)* ELECTRON silicium sur saphir *m*; **~ oxide** *n* ELECTRON oxyde de silicium *m*; **~ photodiode** *n* ELECTRON photodiode au silicium *f*; **~ phototransistor** *n* ELECTRON phototransistor au silicium *m*; **~ rectifier** *n* ELEC, ELEC ENG, PHYS redresseur au silicium *m*; **~ sheet** *n* PROP MAT tôle au silicium *f*; **~ solar cell** *n* ELEC ENG cellule solaire au silicium *f*; **~ steel** *n* ELEC ENG acier au silicium *m*; **~ steel core** *n* ELEC ENG noyau en acier au silicium *m*; **~ steel lamination** *n* ELEC ENG tôle en acier au silicium *f*; **~ substrate** *n* ELECTRON substrat de silicium *m*; **~ wafer** *n* ELECTRON plaquette en silicium *f*

silicon-controlled: **~ rectifier** *n (SCR)* ELEC ENG redresseur au silicium commandé *m*, thyristor au silicium *m*, PHYS redresseur au silicium commandé *m*, TELECOM thyristor au silicium *m*; **~ rectifier crosspoint** *n* TELECOM point de connexion à thyristor *m*; **~ switch** *n* ELEC ENG interrupteur commandé au silicium *m*

silicone *n* CHEM, ELEC, ELEC ENG, P&R, PROP MAT silicone *f*; **~ cladding** *n* ELEC ENG gaine en caoutchouc aux silicones *f*; **~ compound** *n* NAUT mastic silicone *m*; **~ fluid** *n* ELEC *insulator* fluide silicone *m*; **~ rubber** *n* ELEC ENG *insulator* caoutchouc silicone *m*

siliconing *n* (BrE) *(cf siliconizing)* C&G siliconage *m*

silicon-integrated: **~ circuit** *n* ELECTRON circuit intégré au silicium *m*

silicon-intensifier: **~ target** *n* ELECTRON cible multiplicatrice au silicium *f*; **~ target camera tube** *n* ELECTRON tube analyseur à cible multiplicatrice au silicium *m*

siliconizing *n* (AmE) *(cf siliconing)* C&G siliconage *m*

silicophenyl *n* CHEM silicophényle *m*

silicotitanate *n* CHEM silicotitanate *m*

silicotungstate *n* CHEM silicotungstate *m*

silicotungstic *adj* CHEM silicotungstique
silk *n* C&G fibre longue *f*, TEXTILES soie *f*; ~ **spinning** *n* TEXTILES filature de soie *f*; ~ **yarn** *n* TEXTILES fil de soie *m*
silking *n* P&R *paint* soyage *m*
silk-like: ~ **handle** *n* TEXTILES toucher soyeux *m*
silk-screen *n* C&G écran de soie *m*; ~ **printing** *n* TEXTILES sérigraphie *f*; ~ **printing machine** *n* PACKAGING machine d'impression sérigraphique *f*
sill *n* CONST *at foot of structure* seuil *m*, traverse *f*, *of frame house, partition* sablière basse *f*, *up from ground, in doorway* appui *m*, HYDROL seuil *m*, MINING *of mine level* sole *f*, *timbering* semelle *f*, NAUT *port*, OCEANOG seuil *m*, PROD ENG *of ore stamp* seuil *m*, traverse de fondation *f*, WATER SUPP seuil *m*, *of canal lock* seuil *m*; ~ **block** *n* C&G brique de seuil *f*; ~ **piece** *n* MINING *timbering* semelle *f*, sole *f*; ~ **plate** *n* CONST *of plummer block* patin *m*, semelle *f*, PROD ENG *of fire door* pareringard *m*
sillimanite *n* MINERAL sillimanite *f*
silo *n* SPACE silo *m*; ~ **pressure** *n* COAL TECH pression de silo *f*
siloxane *n* CHEM siloxane *m*
SILP *abbr* *(single-in-line package)* COMP, DP boîtier à une rangée de broches *m*, ELECTRON boîtier SIP *m*, boîtier à une rangée de broches *m*
silt[1] *n* COAL TECH limon *m*, terrain limoneux *m*, GEOL aleurite *f*, silt *m*, HYDROL lais *m*, limon *m*, relais *m*, vase *f*, OCEANOG lais *m*, lais de la mer *m*, WATER SUPP limon *m*; ~ **discharge** *n* WATER SUPP débit solide *m*; ~ **field** *n* (BrE) *(cf grader waste pond)* C&G étang à boues *m*; ~ **plug** *n* OCEANOG bouchon vaseux *m*; ~ **storage space** *n* WATER SUPP retenue d'envasement *f*; ~ **trap** *n* WATER SUPP bac à boues *m*
silt:[2] ~ **up** *vt* HYDROL envaser
silt:[3] ~ **up** *vi* HYDROL s'envaser
silted: ~ **up** *adj* HYDROL envasé
silting *n* CHEM TECH envasement *m*, PROD ENG colmatage *m*, envasement *m*; ~ **up** *n* HYDROL envasement *m*
siltstone *n* GEOL aleuronite *f*, microgrès *m*
silver *n* *(Ag)* CHEM argent *m* *(Ag)*; ~ **battery** *n* ELEC ENG batterie à l'argent *f*; ~ **bromide** *n* CHEM bromure d'argent *m*; ~ **bromide collodion plate** *n* PHOTO plaque au collodiobromure d'argent *f*; ~ **bronze powder** *n* COLOURS pigment d'aluminium *m*; ~ **cadmium battery** *n* ELEC ENG batterie argent-cadmium *f*; ~ **cadmium cell** *n* ELEC ENG accumulateur argent-cadmium *m*; ~ **case tantalum capacitor** *n* ELEC ENG condensateur au tantale au boîtier en argent *m*; ~ **cell** *n* ELEC ENG accumulateur à l'argent *m*; ~ **chloride** *n* CHEM, ELEC ENG chlorure d'argent *m*; ~ **chloride emulsion** *n* PHOTO émulsion au chlorure d'argent *f*; ~ **coating** *n* PROP MAT argenture *f*; ~ **color** *n* (AmE), ~ **colour** *n* (BrE) COLOURS couleur argentée *f*; ~ **contact** *n* ELEC ENG contact en argent *m*; ~ **content** *n* PHOTO teneur en argent *f*; ~ **cyanide** *n* CHEM cyanure d'argent *m*; ~ **electrode** *n* LAB EQUIP *electrochemistry* électrode d'argent *f*; ~ **fluoride** *n* CHEM fluorure d'argent *m*; ~ **fog** *n* CINEMAT voile argentique *m*; ~ **frost** *n* METEO givre blanc *m*; ~ **glance** *n* CHEM argentite *f*, argyrite *f*, argyrose *f*; ~ **halide** *n* PHOTO halogénure d'argent *m*; ~ **halide emulsion** *n* PHOTO émulsion d'halogénures d'argent *f*; ~ **iodide** *n* PHOTO iodure d'argent *m*; ~ **lead ore** *n* MINING minerai de plomb argentifère *m*; ~ **mine** *n* MINING mine d'argent *f*; ~ **nitrate** *n* CHEM azotate d'argent *m*, nitrate d'argent *m*; ~ **oxide** *n* ELEC ENG

oxyde d'argent *m*; ~ **oxide battery** *n* ELEC ENG pile à l'oxyde d'argent *f*; ~ **oxide cell** *n* ELEC ENG pile à l'argent *f*, pile à l'oxyde d'argent *f*; ~ **oxide storage battery** *n* TRANSP accumulateur à oxyde d'argent *m*; ~ **plating** *n* PROD ENG argentage *m*, argenture *f*; ~ **recovery** *n* CINEMAT récupération de l'argent *f*; ~ **screen** *n* CINEMAT écran argenté *m*, écran métallisé *m*; ~ **selenide** *n* CHEM séléniure d'argent *m*; ~ **solder** *n* PROD ENG soudure d'argent *f*; ~ **staining** *n* C&G cémentation à l'argent *f*; ~ **zinc battery** *n* ELEC ENG batterie argent-zinc *f*; ~ **zinc cell** *n* ELEC ENG accumulateur argent-zinc *m*; ~ **zinc primary battery** *n* ELEC ENG batterie d'accumulateurs argent-zinc amorçables *f*; ~ **zinc primary cell** *n* ELEC ENG accumulateur argent-zinc amorçable *m*; ~ **zinc storage battery** *n* ELEC ENG batterie argent-zinc *f*, TRANSP accumulateur argent-zinc *m*; ~ **zinc storage cell** *n* ELEC ENG accumulateur argent-zinc *m*
silvered: ~ **mica capacitor** *n* ELEC ENG condensateur au mica argenté *m*; ~ **mirror** *n* INSTRUMENT miroir argenté *m*; ~ **reflector** *n* INSTRUMENT réflecteur argenté *m*
silvering *n* ACOUSTICS, C&G argenture *f*, PROD ENG argentage *m*, *mirrors* argenture *f*, tain *m*
silver-plated: ~ **contact** *n* ELEC ENG contact argenté *m*
silverware *n* FOOD TECH coutellerie *f*
sima *n* GEOPHYS couche intermédiaire *f*
SIMD: ~ **machine** *n* *(single-instruction multiple-data machine)* COMP machine de type SIMD *f*
similar: ~ **figures** *n pl* GEOM figures semblables *f pl*; ~ **fold** *n* GEOL pli semblable *m*; ~ **folding** *n* PETR pli semblable *m*
similarity *n* PATENTS similitude *f*
SIMM *abbr* *(single-in-line memory module)* COMP, DP module de mémoire à une rangée de broches *m*
simmer[1] *vt* CHEM *process* faire frémir
simmer[2] *vi* CHEM *process* frémir
simmer[3] *vti* FOOD TECH mijoter
simple: ~ **beam** *n* CONST poutre simple *f*; ~ **cubic lattice** *n* CRYSTALL réseau cubique simple *m*; ~ **expansion engine** *n* MECH ENG machine à détente simple *f*; ~ **fraction** *n* MATH fraction commune *f*; ~ **harmonic motion** *n* PHYS, WAVE PHYS mouvement harmonique simple *m*; ~ **hybrid circuit** *n* ELECTRON circuit hybride simple *m*; ~ **pendulum** *n* PHYS pendule simple *m*; ~ **rod cylinder** *n* PROD ENG vérin à simple tige *m*; ~ **shear stress** *n* METALL contrainte de cisaillement simple *f*
simple-packaged: ~ **crystal oscillator** *n* ELECTRON oscillateur à quartz non thermostaté *m*
simplex[1] *adj* COMP, DP, TELECOM simplex
simplex:[2] ~ **lap winding** *n* ELEC enroulement imbriqué parallèle *m*; ~ **operation** *n* COMP opération en mode simplex *f*, DP fonctionnement en mode simplex *m*
simplified: ~ **representation** *n* MECH ENG *of centre holes* représentation simplifiée *f*
simplify *vt* MATH simplifier
simply-supported *adj* CONST *beam, slab* posé sur appui simple, simplement appuyé
SIMS *abbr* *(secondary ion mass spectrometry)* PHYS spectroscopie de masse aux ions secondaires *f*
simulate *vt* COMP, DP simuler
simulated: ~ **event** *n* RAD PHYS événement simulé *m*; ~ **speech** *n* TELECOM parole artificielle *f*; ~ **watermark** *n* PAPER TECH faux filigrane *m*
simulation *n* COMP, DP, ELECTRON, GAS TECH, TESTING simulation *f*; ~ **language** *n* COMP langage de simulation *m*; ~ **program** *n* COMP, DP programme de simulation *m*; ~ **of traffic** *n* TRANSP simulation de la

circulation *f*

simulator *n* AERONAUT, COMP, DP, ELECTRON, TELECOM simulateur *m*

simulcast: ~ **broadcasting** *n* TV diffusion simultanée *f*

simultaneity *n* PHYS simultanéité *f*

simultaneous[1] *adj* COMP, DP simultané

simultaneous:[2] ~ **equation** *n* MATH équation équivalente *f*; ~ **firing** *n* MINING tir instantané *m*; ~ **shot firing** *n* MINING tir instantané *m*; ~ **system** *n* TRANSP *traffic control* système synchronisé *m*

sin *n (sine)* COMP, DP, GEOM, MATH sin *m (sinus)*

SINAD: ~ **ratio** *n* TELECOM rapport SINAD *m*

sinapic *adj* CHEM sinapique

sinapine *n* CHEM sinapine *f*

SINCGARS *abbr (single channel ground and airborne radio system)* MILIT système radio sol-air à voie simple *m*

sine *n (sin)* COMP, DP, GEOM *of angle*, MATH sinus *m (sin)*; ~ **bar** *n* METR barre de sinus *f*; ~ **center** *n* (AmE), ~ **centre** *n* (BrE) METR point de sinus *m*; ~ **curve** *n* MATH sinusoïde *f*; ~ **galvanometer** *n* ELEC galvanomètre du sinus *m*, PHYS boussole du sinus *f*, galvanomètre du sinus *m*; ~ **table** *n* GEOM table de sinus *f*, MECH *tools* plateau sinus *m*, METR table de sinus *f*; ~ **wave** *n* ACOUSTICS, ELEC, ELECTRON onde sinusoïdale *f*, PHYS sinusoïde *f*, WAVE PHYS, onde sinusoïdale *f*; ~ **wave convergence** *n* TV convergence par courant sinusoïdal *f*; ~ **wave modulation** *n* ELECTRON modulation par un signal sinusoïdal *f*; ~ **wave oscillator** *n* ELECTRON oscillateur harmonique *m*; ~ **wave tuning** *n* ELECTRON accord sinusoïdal *m*

singe *vt* TEXTILES flamber

singeing *n* TEXTILES flambage *m*; ~ **machine** *n* TEXTILES appareil de gazage *m*, machine de flambage *f*

singing *n* ELECTRON accrochage *m*, PETR pédalage *m*; ~ **point** *n* ELECTRON gain maximal d'un circuit *m*, limite d'accrochage *f*

single:[1] ~ **acoustic source** *n* ACOUSTICS source acoustique simple *f*; ~ **address** *n* COMP, DP adresse unique *f*; ~ **address instruction** *n* COMP, DP instruction à une adresse *f*; ~ **aisle aircraft** *n* AERONAUT avion à couloir unique *m*, avion à une seule travée *m*; ~ **and multilayer glass** *n* SAFETY glace Sécurit à une et à plusieurs couches de verre *f* (MD), glace Sécurit à une et à plusieurs plaques de verre *f* (MD); ~ **angle cutter** *n* MECH ENG fraise d'angle avec l'une des faces en bout *f*; ~ **angular cutter** *n* MECH ENG fraise d'angle avec l'une des faces en bout *f*; ~ **anode rectifier** *n* ELEC ENG redresseur monoanodique *m*; ~ **anode tube** *n* ELECTRON tube monoanodique *m*; ~ **bag** *n* PROD ENG poche simple *f*; ~ **balanced mixer** *n* ELECTRON mélangeur symétrique simple *m*; ~ **bar coach wrench** *n* MECH ENG clé anglaise simple à marteau *f*; ~ **bath developer** *n* PHOTO révélateur pour développement en bain unique *m*; ~ **bay enclosure** *n* PROD ENG armoire à baie unique *f*; ~ **beam cathode ray tube** *n* ELECTRON tube cathodique monofaisceau *m*; ~ **beam spectrophotometer** *n* RAD PHYS spectrophotomètre monofaisceau *m*; ~ **beam tube** *n* ELECTRON tube monofaisceau *m*; ~ **bituminous surface treatment** *n (SBST)* CONST revêtement monocouche *m*; ~ **blackwall hitch** *n* NAUT gueule-de-loup simple *f*; ~ **blade circular sawing machine** *n* MECH ENG machine à scier circulaire monolame *f*; ~ **blade shutter** *n* CINEMAT obturateur à pale unique *m*; ~ **blast circular bellows** *n pl* MECH ENG soufflet cylindrique à simple vent *m*; ~ **bolt clamping** *n*

PROD ENG fixation à boulon unique *f*; ~ **bond** *n* CHEM liaison simple *f*; ~ **break contact** *n* ELEC ENG contact à simple rupture *m*; ~ **buoy mooring** *n (SBM)* PETR TECH amarrage à point unique *m*, bouée monoposte *f*; ~ **camera extension** *n* PHOTO simple tirage de la chambre *m*; ~ **cascade control** *n* CONTROL régulation à cascade simple *f*; ~ **cascade regulation** *n* CONTROL régulation à cascade simple *f*; ~ **coil latching relay** *n* ELEC ENG relais à verrouillage sans enroulement de maintien *m*; ~ **conductor cable** *n* ELEC câble unipolaire *m*, câble à un conducteur *m*, ELEC ENG câble monoconducteur *m*, câble à un conducteur *m*; ~ **conductor wire** *n* PROD ENG fil à conducteur unique *m*; ~ **cord switchboard** *n* TELECOM tableau à monocordes *m*; ~ **core cable** *n* ELEC câble unipolaire *m*, câble à un conducteur *m*; ~ **crystal** *n* CRYSTALL, ELECTRON, PROP MAT monocristal *m*; ~ **crystal growth** *n* ELECTRON tirage de monocristaux *m*; ~ **crystal semiconductor** *n* ELECTRON semi-conducteur monocristallin *m*; ~ **cylinder engine** *n* MECH ENG machine à cylindre unique *f*, moteur monocylindrique *m*, moteur à un seul cylindre *m*; ~ **day tide** *n* NAUT marée diurne *f*; ~ **delivery** *n* PROD ENG livraison ponctuelle *f*, livraison unique *f*; ~ **diamond crossing with slips** *n* RAIL traversée jonction simple *f*; ~ **diffusion process** *n* ELECTRON procédé à simple diffusion *m*; ~ **digit dialing** *n* (AmE), ~ **digit dialling** *n* (BrE) TELECOM numérotation abrégée à un chiffre *f*; ~ **drive circuit** *n* ELEC ENG circuit à commande unique *m*; ~ **dry plate clutch** *n* AUTO embrayage monodisque à sec *m*; ~ **earth** *n* (BrE) *(cf single ground)* ELEC connection prise de terre simple *f*; ~ **effect evaporator** *n* FOOD TECH *machinery* évaporateur à effet simple *m*; ~ **element shipping cask** *n* NUCLEAR château de transport pour un seul assemblage combustible *m*; ~ **end sizing** *n* TEXTILES encollage du fil simple *m*; ~ **end tenoning machine** *n* MECH ENG tenoneuse simple *f*; ~ **escape peak** *n* RAD PHYS *gamma radiation* pic de premier échappement *m*; ~ **expansion engine** *n* MECH ENG machine à simple extension *f*; ~ **feeder** *n* ELEC *supply* ligne en antenne *f*; ~ **fiber cable** *n* (AmE) *see single fibre cable*; ~ **fiber line** *n* (AmE) *see single fibre line*; ~ **fibre cable** *n* (BrE) ELEC ENG câble monofibre *m*; ~ **fibre line** *n* (BrE) ELEC ENG ligne en câble monofibre *f*; ~ **flotation** *n* COAL TECH flottation simple *f*; ~ **flue boiler** *n* PROD ENG chaudière à tube-foyer *f*; ~ **frame** *n* CINEMAT image par image *f*; ~ **frame filming** *n* CINEMAT tournage image par image *m*; ~ **frequency laser** *n* TELECOM laser monofréquence *m*; ~ **frequency operation** *n* TELECOM fonctionnement à une seule fréquence *m*; ~ **gob feeding** *n* (BrE) *(cf single gob process)* C&G alimentation en simple paraison *f*; ~ **gob process** *n* (AmE) *(cf single gob feeding)* C&G alimentation en simple paraison *f*; ~ **gravity hoist** *n* PROD ENG balance sèche à simple effet *f*; ~ **grid tube** *n* ELECTRON tube à une seule grille *m*; ~ **ground** *n* (AmE) *(cf single earth)* ELEC *connection* prise de terre simple *f*; ~ **gun storage tube** *n* ELECTRON tube à mémoire monocanon *m*; ~ **head system** *n* PACKAGING *coding* système de codage simple *m*; ~ **heterojunction laser diode** *n* ELECTRON diode laser à simple hétérojonction *f*; ~ **impression mold** *n* (AmE), ~ **impression mould** *n* (BrE) MECH ENG moule à une empreinte *m*; ~ **inlet fan** *n* MECH ENG ventilateur à une seule ouïe *m*; ~ **jersey** *n* TEXTILES piqué simple *m*; ~ **jet injection nozzle** *n* AUTO injecteur à jet unique *m*, injecteur à un trou *m*; ~ **layer ceramic capacitor** *n* ELEC ENG condensateur céramique monocouche *m*; ~ **layer film** *n* CINEMAT pellicule monocouche *f*; ~ **leaf damper** *n* MECH ENG registre à organe mobile unique *m*, REFRIG registre à volet *m*; ~ **lens** *n* PHOTO objectif simple *m*; ~ **lens reflex camera** *n* *(SLR)* PHOTO appareil reflex mono-objectif *m*, reflex monoculaire *m*; ~ **level masking structure** *n* ELECTRON structure à simple niveau de masquage *f*; ~ **level polysilicon process** *n* ELECTRON procédé au polysilicium à simple couche *m*; ~ **level resonance** *n* NUCLEAR résonance de Briet et Wigner *f*, résonance à un niveau *f*; ~ **lift-lock** *n* HYDROL *canal* écluse à sas simple *f*; ~ **linear inductor motor** *n* *(SLIM)* TRANSP moteur linéaire à simple inducteur *m*; ~ **line diagram** *n* ELEC *supply network* schéma unifilaire *m*; ~ **line token** *n* RAIL bâton-pilote *m*, gage *m*, gage *m*; ~ **line working** *n* RAIL circulation à voie unique *f*; ~ **Matthew Walker** *n* NAUT *knot* noeud de ride simple *m*; ~ **notch joint** *n* CONST *carpentry* assemblage à entaille *m*, trave *f*; ~ **operation** *n* MECH ENG *for press tools* opération simple *f*; ~ **output power supply** *n* ELEC ENG alimentation monotension *f*; ~ **output switching power supply** *n* ELEC ENG alimentation à découpage monotension *f*; ~ **overlap** *n* MECH ENG agrafage simple *m*; ~ **overlap flexible metal hose** *n* MECH ENG tuyau métallique flexible à agrafage simple *m*; ~ **pair cable** *n* ELEC ENG câble à une paire *m*; ~ **parity check** *n* CONTROL contrôle simple de parité *m*; ~ **perforation film** *n* CINEMAT pellicule monoperf *f*; ~ **picture crank** *n* CINEMAT manivelle un-tour-une-image *f*; ~ **pilot instrument rating** *n* AERONAUT qualification de vol aux instruments monopilote *f*, qualification de volaux instruments pilote unique *f*; ~ **piston rod cylinder** *n* MECH ENG vérin à simple tige *m*; ~ **pitch roof** *n* CONST comble à un versant *m*, comble à une pente *m*, comble à une seule pente *m*;~ **plane iron** *n* CONST fer de rabot simple *m*; ~ **plate rudder** *n* NAUT gouvernail plat *m*; ~ **platform pallet** *n* TRANSP palette à un seul plancher *f*; ~ **ply board** *n* PAPER TECH carton un jet *m*; ~ **point bonding** *n* ELEC mise à la terre en un seul point *f*; ~ **point cutting tool** *n* MECH ENG outil de coupe à partie active unique *m*; ~ **portion** *n* FOOD TECH bouchée à la reine *f*; ~ **portion packaging machine** *n* PACKAGING machine d'emballage en portion unique *f*; ~ **precision** *n* COMP précision simple *f*, DP simple précision *f*; ~ **primary-type linear motor** *n* TRANSP moteur linéaire à simple inducteur *m*; ~ **processor common-control system** *n* TELECOM système monoprocesseur *m*; ~ **pulley drive** *n* MECH ENG commande par monopoulie *f*; ~ **pulley high-speed drilling machine** *n* MECH ENG machine à percer à grande vitesse à monopoulie *f*; ~ **pulse** *n* ELECTRON impulsion isolée *f*; ~ **pulse signal** *n* ELECTRON signal impulsionnel élémentaire *m*; ~ **rotor** *n* AERONAUT *helicopter* monorotor *m*; ~ **scan key** *n* PROD ENG touche de cycle unique *f*; ~ **screw ship** *n* NAUT navire à une hélice *m*; ~ **section filter** *n* ELECTRON filtre à une cellule *m*; ~ **segment message** *n* *(SSM)* TELECOM message à segment unique *m*, message à un seul segment *m*; ~ **server queue** *n* TELECOM file à un seul serveur *f*; ~ **shear** *n* MECH ENG *materials* cisaillement simple *m*; ~ **sheet thickness** *n* PAPER TECH épaisseur d'une feuille seule *f*; ~ **sideband** *n* ELECTRON, TELECOM, TV bande latérale unique *f*; ~ **sideband filter** *n* ELECTRON filtre de bande latérale unique *m*; ~ **sideband modulation** *n* ELECTRON modulation à bande latérale unique *f*; ~ **sideband modulator** *n* ELECTRON modulateur à bande latérale unique *m*; ~ **sideband signal** *n* ELECTRON signal à bande latérale unique *m*; ~ **sideband transmission** *n* PHYS, TV émission à bande latérale unique *f*; ~ **side claw** *n* CINEMAT griffe latérale unique *f*; ~ **size gravel aggregate** *n* CONST gravier de grosseur unique *m*; ~ **slot** *n* PROD ENG module simple *m*; ~ **slot module** *n* PROD ENG module simple *m*; ~ **speed counter motion** *n* MECH ENG renvoi de mouvement à simple vitesse *m*; ~ **spindle boring machine** *n* MECH ENG perceuse monobroche *f*; ~ **stage amplifier** *n* ELEC *electronics*, ELECTRON amplificateur à un étage *m*; ~ **stage compression** *n* REFRIG compression à un étage *f*; ~ **stage compressor** *n* HYDR EQUIP compresseur monocylindrique *m*, compresseur à simple effet *m*; ~ **stage pumping** *n* MINING épuisement en un seul jet *m*; ~ **stage turbine** *n* HYDR EQUIP turbine simple *f*; ~ **stamp mill** *n* PROD ENG *ore stamp* bocard à un pilon *m*; ~ **staple fiber yarn** *n* (AmE), ~ **staple fibre yarn** *n* (BrE) C&G filé de verranne *m*; ~ **start solid gear hob** *n* MECH ENG fraise mère monobloc à entrée *f*; ~ **station machine** *n* SPRINGS machine à poste unique *f*; ~ **step operation** *n* COMP, DP exécution pas à pas *f*; ~ **stroke lever** *n* PHOTO levier-gachette *m*; ~ **supply** *n* ELEC réseau simple *m*, ELEC ENG alimentation par une seule tension *f*; ~ **supply voltage** *n* ELEC ENG tension d'alimentation unique *f*; ~ **system** *n* CINEMAT prise de vues et enregistrement sonore sur la même bande *f*; ~ **tackle** *n* PROD ENG palan simple *m*; ~ **thickness sheet glass** *n* (BrE) *(cf single thickness window glass)* C&G verre simple *m*; ~ **thickness window glass** *n* (AmE) *(cf single thickness sheet glass)* C&G verre simple *m*; ~ **throw relay** *n* ELEC ENG relais non inverseur *m*; ~ **throw switch** *n* ELEC ENG interrupteur *m*, PHYS commutateur à une direction *m*; ~ **track line** *n* RAIL ligne à voie unique *f*; ~ **track recording** *n* RECORDING enregistrement à piste unique *m*; ~ **trip bottle** *n* C&G bouteille non récupérable *f*; ~ **turn encoder** *n* PROD ENG codeur simple tour *m*; ~ **user access** *n* COMP, DP accès monoutilisateur *m*; ~ **wall corrugated fibreboard** *n* PACKAGING carton ondulé à paroi simple *m*; ~ **wave rectification** *n* ELEC redressement demi-onde *m*; ~ **way modulator** *n* ELEC redresseur biphasé *m*; ~ **way rectifier** *n* ELEC redresseur biphasé *m*; ~ **weight paper** *n* PHOTO papier mince *m*; ~ **wire system** *n* ELEC système monoconducteur *m*

single:[2] ~ **up** *vi* NAUT *mooring line* dédoubler

single-acting: ~ **compressor** *n* REFRIG compresseur à simple effet *m*; ~ **servomotor** *n* FUELLESS servomoteur à simple effet *m*

single-channel:[1] ~ **per carrier** *adj* SPACE à une seule voie par porteuse

single-channel:[2] ~ **amplifier** *n* ELECTRON amplificateur monovoie *m*; ~ **ground and airborne radio system** *n* *(SINCGARS)* MILIT système radio sol-air à voie simple *m*; ~ **per carrier** *n* *(SCPC)* SPACE *communications* porteuse monovoie *f*, système à porteuse monovoie *m*, TELECOM porteuse monovoie *f*; ~ **protocol** *n* COMP protocole monovoie *m*, DP protocole univoie *m*

single-coated: ~ **paper** *n* PAPER TECH papier couché une fois *m*

single-cotton-covered *adj* *(SCC)* ELEC *conductor* guipé une couche coton

single-cut: ~ **file** *n* MECH ENG lime à simple taille *f*

singled: ~ **module** *n* PROD ENG module simple *m*

single-decked: ~ **pallet** *n* TRANSP palette à un seul plancher *f*; ~ **ship** *n* NAUT navire à un pont *m*

singled-ended: ~ **operation** *n* PROD ENG fonctionnement en sortie simple *m*

single-ended: ~ **amplifier** *n* ELECTRON amplificateur non-symétrique *m*; ~ **crystal mixer** *n* ELECTRON mélangeur à cristal non équilibré *m*; ~ **output** *n* ELEC ENG *of quadripole* sortie asymétrique *f*, sortie non équilibrée *f*; ~ **spanner** *n* (BrE) MECH ENG clé simple *f*, clé simple à fourche *f*; ~ **tube** *n* ELECTRON tube à grille au culot *m*, tube à sorties au culot *m*; ~ **wrench** *n* MECH ENG clé simple *f*, clé simple à fourche *f*

single-faced: ~ **pallet** *n* PACKAGING palette à simple planche *f*, TRANSP palette à simple face *f*

single-flanged: ~ **traveling wheel** *n* (AmE), ~ **travelling wheel** *n* (BrE) MECH ENG *of runner of overhead travelling crane* galet à une joue *m*

single-geared: ~ **lathe** *n* MECH ENG tour à simple harnais d'engrenage *m*

single-hull[1] *adj* NAUT *vessel* monocoque

single-hull:[2] ~ **ship** *n* TRANSP navire monocoque *m*

single-in-line: ~ **memory module** *n* (SIMM) COMP, DP module de mémoire à une rangée de broches *m*; ~ **package** *n* (SILP, SIP) COMP, DP, ELECTRON boîtier à une rangée de broches *m*

single-instruction: ~ **multiple-data machine** *n* (SIMD machine) COMP machine de type SIMD *f*; ~ **single-data machine** *n* (SISD machine) COMP machine de type SISD *f*

single-layer *adj* COATINGS seule couche, à couche unique

single-level: ~ **polysilicon process** *n* ELECTRON procédé poly I *m*

single-longitudinal: ~ **mode** *n* (SLM) TELECOM mode longitudinal unique *m*

single-mode: ~ **cable** *n* ELEC ENG câble monomode *m*; ~ **fiber** *n* (AmE), ~ **fibre** *n* (BrE) TELECOM fibre monomode *f*, fibre optique monomode *f*; ~ **optical fiber** *n* (AmE), ~ **optical fibre** *n* (BrE) ELEC ENG fibre monomode *f*, OPT fibre monomode *f*, fibre optique monomode *f*, fibre optique unimodale *f*, fibre unimodale *f*; ~ **optical integrated circuit** *n* ELECTRON circuit intégré optique monomode *m*

single-paper-covered *adj* (SPC) ELEC *conductor* guipé une couche papier

single-phase[1] *adj* ELEC *supply network*, ELEC ENG monophasé

single-phase:[2] ~ **bridge rectifier** *n* ELEC redresseur monophasé en pont *m*; ~ **current** *n* CINEMAT, ELEC ENG courant monophasé *m*; ~ **electric current** *n* CONST courant monophasé *m*; ~ **induction motor** *n* ELEC ENG moteur asynchrone monophasé *m*; ~ **machine** *n* ELEC ENG machine monophasée *f*; ~ **motor** *n* ELEC, ELEC ENG moteur monophasé *m*; ~ **supply** *n* ELEC, ELEC ENG alimentation monophasée *f*; ~ **transformer** *n* ELEC ENG transformateur monophasé *m*; ~ **winding** *n* ELEC ENG bobinage monophasé *m*, enroulement monophasé *m*

single-pole[1] *adj* ELEC *terminal*, TV unipolaire

single-pole:[2] ~ **double-throw** *n* (SPDT) ELEC, ELEC ENG à un contact inverseur; ~ **double-throw switch** *n* ELEC, ELEC ENG commutateur unipolaire *m*; ~ **single-throw relay** *n* (SPST relay) ELEC, ELEC ENG relais interrupteur unipolaire *m*; ~ **single-throw** *n* (SPST) ELEC, ELEC ENG à un contact interrupteur; ~ **single-throw switch** *n* (SPST switch) ELEC, ELEC ENG interrupteur unipolaire *m*; ~ **switch** *n* ELEC, ELEC ENG interrupteur unipolaire *m*

single-riveted: ~ **butt joint** *n* CONST rivure à un rang de rivets *f*; ~ **lap joint** *n* CONST rivure simple à recouvre-

ment *f*, rivure à un rang de rivets à clin *f*

single-rubber-covered *adj* (SRC) ELEC *conductor* guipé une couche caoutchouc

single-seated: ~ **valve** *n* HYDR EQUIP soupape à siège simple *f*

single-sided: ~ **disc** *n* (BrE) OPT disque monoface *m*; ~ **disk** *n* COMP disquette simple face *f*, DP disque simple face *m*, OPT disque monoface *m* ~ **distribution frame** *n* TELECOM répartiteur monoface *m*; ~ **printed circuit** *n* ELECTRON circuit imprimé simple face *m*

singlet *n* PHYS *spectroscopy* singulet *m*

single-threaded: ~ **screw** *n* MECH ENG vis à un filet *f*

singularity *n* ASTRON, PHYS singularité *f*

sinistral[1] *adj* GEOL sénestre

sinistral:[2] ~ **fault** *n* PETR faille senestre *f*

sink[1] *n* COMP, DP récepteur *m*, ELEC ENG récepteur de courant *m*, récepteur *m*, GEOL cuve d'effondrement *f*, HYDR EQUIP récepteur *m*, évacuation *f*, LAB EQUIP *services* évier *m*, METALL puits *m*, MINING bougniou *m*, puisard *m*, puisard de puits *m*, cône d'avancement *m*, POLLUTION piège *m*, puits *m*; ~ **trap** *n* HYDROL puisard *m*

sink[2] *vt* CONST *well* foncer

sink[3] *vi* MINING aréner, s'affaisser, s'enfoncer, se seller, se tasser, NAUT *boat* couler, sombrer

sinkage *n* NAUT *ship* enfoncement *m*, PRINT coulage *m*, descente *f*

sinker *n* FOOD TECH *milling* grain plongeur *m*, TEXTILES platine *f*; ~ **bar** *n* MINING *boring* barre de surcharge *f*, tige de surcharge *f*, TEXTILES barre de platines *f*

sinkhole *n* CONST puisard *m*, GEOL cratère d'effondrement *m*, MINING bouniou *m*, collecteur d'eau *m*, puisard *m*

sinking *n* MINING affaissement *m*, tassement *m*, creusage *m*, creusement *m*, foncement *m*, fonçage *m*, *shaft* excavation *f*, PROD ENG *casting* tassement *m*; ~ **agent** *n* MAR POLL agent coulant *m*, agent de coulage *m*, agent surfactant *m*, agent surfactif *m*, agent tensio-actif *m*; ~ **head** *n* PROD ENG *founding* masselotte *f*; ~ **point** *n* C&G point d'enfoncement *m*; ~ **trestle** *n* COAL TECH échafaudage de fonçage *m*

sinter[1] *n* GEOL travertin calcaire *m*, tuf *m*; ~ **inhibiter** *n* CHEM TECH inhibiteur de frittage *m*; ~ **terrace** *n* GEOPHYS terrasse de travertin *f*

sinter[2] *vt* CHEM *powder* fritter, CHEM TECH agglomérer par frittage, fritter

sinter[3] *vi* CHEM *powder* se fritter

sinter-activating *adj* CHEM TECH activant le frittage

sintered[1] *adj* CHEM TECH aggloméré, fritté, MECH *materials* fritté

sintered:[2] ~ **anode** *n* ELEC ENG anode frittée *f*; ~ **brake** *n* RAIL *vehicles* frein fritté *m*; ~ **density** *n* CHEM TECH masse volumique frittée *f*; ~ **density ratio** *n* CHEM TECH densité relative frittée *f*; ~ **glass** *n* C&G verre fritté *m*; ~ **glass filter crucible** *n* LAB EQUIP *filtration* creuset filtrant à plaque de verre fritté *m*; ~ **glass filter funnel** *n* LAB EQUIP *filtration* entonnoir filtrant à plaque de verre fritté *m*; ~ **metal material** *n* MECH ENG matériel métallique fritté *m*; ~ **refractory** *n* C&G réfractaire fritté *m*

sintering *n* C&G *of batch* frittage *m*, CHEM TECH agglomération *f*, frittage *m*, COAL TECH fluidisation *f*, HEATING, METALL, RAIL *vehicles*, TELECOM frittage *m*; ~ **and infiltration technique** *n* CHEM TECH technique de frittage et d'infiltration *f*; ~ **coal** *n* COAL TECH charbon d'agglomération *m*; ~ **furnace** *n* CHEM TECH cuve d'ag-

glomération *f*; ~ **heat** *n* CHEM TECH température de
frittage *f*; ~ **pallet** *n* CHEM TECH presse d'agglomération *f*; ~ **pan** *n* CHEM TECH presse d'agglomération *f*; ~
powder *n* CHEM TECH poudre frittée *f*; ~ **sand coal** *n*
COAL TECH charbon maigre sableux *m*; ~ **technique** *n*
CHEM TECH procédé de frittage *m*; ~ **time** *n* CHEM TECH
durée de frittage *f*; ~ **under pressure** *n* CHEM TECH
frittage sous pression *m*

sinter-inhibiting *adj* CHEM TECH inhibiteur de frittage
sinusoid *n* COMP, DP, GEOM, MATH sinusoïde *f*
sinusoidal[1] *adj* ELEC *wave* sinusoïdal
sinusoidal:[2] ~ **conditions** *n pl* ELEC ENG régime sinusoïdal *m*; ~ **current** *n* ELEC ENG, PHYS courant sinusoïdal
m; ~ **field** *n* ELEC ENG champ sinusoïdal *m*; ~ **function** *n*
ELEC ENG fonction sinusoïdale *f*; ~ **motion** *n* PHYS
mouvement sinusoïdal *m*; ~ **oscillation** *n* ELECTRON
oscillation sinusoïdale *f*; ~ **quantity** *n* ELEC ENG, ELECTRON grandeur sinusoïdale *f*; ~ **signal** *n* ELECTRON,
TELECOM signal sinusoïdal *m*; ~ **signal generator** *n*
ELECTRON générateur de signaux sinusoïdaux *m*; ~
voltage *n* ELEC ENG, PHYS tension sinusoïdale *f*; ~ **wave**
n (sine wave) WAVE PHYS onde sinusoïdale *f*
SIO *abbr* COMP *(sequential input/output)* entrée/sortie
séquentielle *f*, COMP *(series input/output)* entrée/sortie série *f*
SIP *abbr (single-in-line package)* COMP, DP boîtier à une
rangée de broches *m*, ELECTRON boîtier SIP *m*, boîtier
à une rangée de broches *m*
siphon *n* HYDROL, LAB EQUIP, PHYS siphon *m*; ~ **barrel** *n*
FUELLESS corps de siphon *m*; ~ **conduit** *n* HYDROL
siphon *m*; ~ **crest** *n* FUELLESS couronnement de siphon
m; ~ **spillway** *n* FUELLESS siphon à débordement *m*
siren *n* NAUT *navigation* sirène *f*, SAFETY *warning* sirène
d'alerte *f*
Sirius *n* ASTRON Sirius *m*
sisal *n* NAUT *ropes* sisal *m*; ~ **rope** *n* MECH ENG corde en
sisal *f*; ~ **wheel** *n* MECH ENG *polishing* disque en sisal *m*
sister: ~ **ship** *n* NAUT navire jumeau *m*
site:[1] **on** ~ *adj* CONST à pied d'oeuvre
site:[2] **on** ~ *adv* CONST sur le chantier, à pied d'oeuvre
site:[3] ~ **code** *n* PACKAGING code d'emplacement *m*; ~
concrete *n* CONST béton de chantier *m*, béton préparé
sur place *m*; ~ **criteria** *n pl* POLLUTION critères d'implantation *m pl*; ~ **diversity** *n* SPACE *communications*
diversité de site *f*; ~ **meeting** *n* CONST réunion de
chantier *f*; ~ **weld** *n* NUCLEAR soudure sur chantier *f*
site-delivered *adj* CONST à pied d'oeuvre
sitosterol *n* CHEM sitostérol *m*
six-channel: ~ **monitor** *n* INSTRUMENT moniteur à six
canaux *m*
six-fold: ~ **rotation axis** *n* CRYSTALL axe d'ordre six *m*
six-membered: ~ **ring** *n* CHEM *compound* cycle à six
éléments *m*, noyau hexagonal *m*, noyau à six éléments *m*
sixmo *n* PRINT in-six *m*
six-phase: ~ **current** *n* ELEC ENG courant hexaphasé *m*; ~
rectifier *n* ELEC ENG redresseur hexaphasé *m*
six-ply: ~ **belting** *n* PROD ENG courroies en six épaisseurs *f pl*, courroies à six plis *f pl*
sixteenmo *n* PRINT in-seize *m*
sixth *n* ACOUSTICS sixte *f*
six-tool: ~ **capstan** *n* MECH ENG *lathe* tourelle revolver
pour six outils *f*
sixty-four: ~ **kbps restricted bearer service** *n* TELECOM
ISDN service support à 64 kbit/s avec restriction *m*; ~
kbps restricted service *n* TELECOM *ISDN* service de

circuit commuté en canal B non transparent *m*; ~
kbps unrestricted service *n* TELECOM *ISDN* service
support à 64 kbit/s sans restriction *m*
size[1] *n* C&G ensimage *m*, CINEMAT *of film* format *m*,
COATINGS apprêt *m*, COLOURS apprêt *m*, colle *f*, P&R
glass fibre apprêt *m*, PAPER TECH colle *f*, format *m*,
PRINT dimension *f*, format *m*, PROD ENG *of fuse* calibre
m, TEXTILES *dimensions* taille *f*, *for fabric* colle *f*; ~
analysis *n* COAL TECH granulométrie *f*; ~ **bath** *n* TEXTILES bain d'encollage *m*; ~ **circulator unit** *n* TEXTILES
mécanisme pour circulation de colle *m*; ~ **color** *n*
(AmE), ~ **colour** *n* (BrE) COLOURS peinture gélatineuse *f*, peinture à la colle *f*; ~ **distribution** *n* COAL TECH
granulométrie *f*; ~ **fraction** *n* COAL TECH fraction granulométrique *f*; ~ **grading** *n* COAL TECH classement *m*,
granulométrie *f*; ~ **margin** *n* MECH ENG tolérance sur
les dimensions *f*; ~ **paint** *n* COLOURS peinture gélatineuse *f*; ~ **press** *n* PAPER TECH encolleuse *f*, presse
encolleuse *f*; ~ **reduction** *n* CHEM TECH broyage *m*,
comminution *f*, fragmentation *f*; ~ **roll** *n* PAPER TECH
cylindre de format *m*; ~ **tester** *n* PAPER TECH collagimètre *m*
size[2] *vt* COAL TECH calibrer, TEXTILES coller
size:[3] **be to** ~ *vi* CONST être de mesure
sized: ~ **ice** *n* REFRIG glace calibrée *f*; ~ **paper** *n* PAPER
TECH papier collé *m*; ~ **rolled flat iron** *n* METALL plat
laminé calibré *m*; ~ **warp** *n* TEXTILES chaîne encollée *f*
size-press: ~ **coating** *n* PAPER TECH couchage par presse
encolleuse *m*
size-press-coated: ~ **paper** *n* PAPER TECH papier couché
à la presse encolleuse *m*
sizer *n* MECH ENG classeur *m*, classeur-trieur *m*, classificateur *m*
sizing *n* C&G ensimage *m*, COAL TECH classement *m*,
classification *f*, COMP, DP dimensionnement *m*, MECH
ENG mise à dimensions *f*, PACKAGING encollage *m*,
PAPER TECH collage *m*, TEXTILES encollage *m*; ~ **agent** *n*
CHEM, COLOURS apprêt *m*, colle *f*, TEXTILES agent d'encollage *m*; ~ **machine** *n* TEXTILES *slasher* encolleuse *f*; ~
preparation *n* COLOURS apprêt *m*, colle *f*; ~ **screen** *n*
PROD ENG crible classeur *m*; ~ **tester** *n* PAPER TECH
collagimètre *m*
skate *n* PRINT patin à roulettes *m*
skatol *n* CHEM scatol *m*
skatole *n* CHEM scatol *m*
skatolecarboxylic *adj* CHEM scatolcarbonique
skatoxylsulphate *n* (BrE) CHEM scatoxylsulfate *m*
skatoxylsulphuric *adj* (BrE) CHEM scatoxylsulfurique
skatoxysulfate *n* (AmE) *see* skatoxylsulphate
skatoxysulfuric *adj* (AmE) *see* skatoxylsulphuric
skeg *n* NAUT *boatbuilding* aileron *m*
skeletal: ~ **coding** *n* COMP séquence paramétrable *f*, DP
programmation paramétrée *f*, séquence paramétrable *f*
skeleton *n* CONST *framework* carcasse *f*, châssis de charpente *m*, MECH ENG *framework* carcasse *f*; ~ **black** *n*
PRINT film noir *m*, squelette noir *m*; ~ **container** *n*
TRANSP conteneur à claire-voie *m*; ~ **girder** *n* CONST
poutre en treillis *f*, poutre évidée *f*, poutre à jour *f*,
poutrelle à croisillons *f*
skene: ~ **arch** *n* CONST *curve* arc surbaissé *m*, *structure*
voûte surbaissée *f*
sketch[1] *n* CONST croquis *m*
sketch[2] *vt* CONST croquer
skew *n* COMP obliquité *f*, CONST biais *m*, obliquité *f*, DP
effet d'obliquité *m*, PETR oblique *f*, TV enroulement en

biais de la bande *m*; ~ **block** *n* (AmE) *(cf skewback block)* C&G retombée de voûte *f*; ~ **bridge** *n* CONST pont biais *m*; ~ **error** *n* TV effet de store vénitien *m*; ~ **ray** *n* C&G rayon oblique *m*, OPT, TELECOM rayon non méridien *m*

skewback: ~ **block** *n* (BrE) *(cf skew block)* C&G retombée de voûte *f*

skewed: ~ **curve** *n* GEOM courbe de travers *f*

skewing *n* CONST biaisement *m*

skewness *n* GEOM biais *m*

skiatron *n* ELECTRON skiatron *m*

skid[1] *n* MECH patin *m*, TRANSP béquille *f*; ~ **base** *n* PACKAGING base de coulisse *f*; ~ **car** *n* TRANSP dérapeur *m*; ~ **pad** *n* VEHICLES piste de dérapage *f*; ~ **track** *n* CONST piste de glissance *f*, piste de patinage *f*; ~ **wire** *n* ELEC fil de glissement *m*

skid[2] *vi* AERONAUT déraper, PETR TECH *rig* riper, VEHICLES déraper, glisser

skidder *n* TRANSP skidder *m*

skidding *n* AERONAUT dérapage *m*; ~ **conditions** *n pl* TRANSP glissance *f*

skidproof *adj* CHEM antidérapant

skim[1] *n* PROD ENG écume *f*; ~ **bar** *n* C&G barre d'écrémage *f*; ~ **gate** *n* PROD ENG *founding* chambre d'épuration *f*; ~ **pocket** *n* (AmE) *(cf skimming pocket)* C&G niche d'écrémage *f*

skim[2] *vt* PROD ENG puiser à la cuiller, écrémer, écumer; ~ **off** *vt* POLLUTION écrémer, PROD ENG puiser à la cuiller, écrémer, écumer

skimmed: ~ **latex** *n* P&R latex pauvre *m*; ~ **milk cheese** *n* FOOD TECH fromage maigre *m*, fromage à 0 % de matière grasse *m*; ~ **milk powder** *n* FOOD TECH poudre de lait écrémé *f*

skimmer *n* C&G, MAR POLL, PETR TECH écrémeur *m*, POLLUTION récupérateur *m*, PROD ENG cuiller écumoire *f*, écrémoir *m*, écumoire *f*; ~ **block** *n* C&G bloc écrémeur *m*

skimming *n* C&G écrémage *m*, PROD ENG écrémage *m*, écumage *m*; ~ **barge** *n* MAR POLL chaland d'écrémage *m*, chaland récupérateur *m*, chaland écrémeur *m*; ~ **barrier** *n* MAR POLL barrage d'écrémage *m*, barrage récupérateur *m*, barrage écrémeur *m*; ~ **chamber** *n* PROD ENG *founding* chambre d'épuration *f*; ~ **head** *n* MAR POLL tête d'écrémage *f*; ~ **hole** *n* C&G trou d'écrémage *m*; ~ **ladle** *n* PROD ENG cuiller écumoire *f*, écrémoir *m*, écumoire *f*; ~ **pocket** *n* (BrE) *(cf skim pocket)* C&G niche d'écrémage *f*; ~ **rod** *n* C&G râble *m*

skimmings *n pl* C&G escramaisons *f pl*

skin[1] *n* AERONAUT *aircraft* peau *f*, revêtement *m*, COAL TECH manchon *m*, NAUT *shipbuilding* bordé *m*, P&R, PRINT peau *f*, SPACE revêtement *m*; ~ **blemish** *n* FOOD TECH défaut d'épiderme *m*, tache sur la peau *f*; ~ **blister** *n* C&G bouillon de surface *m*; ~ **cream** *n* SAFETY *protective* crème protectrice *f*; ~ **depth** *n* PHYS épaisseur de peau *f*, épaisseur de pénétration *f*; ~ **dive** *n* OCEANOG plongée en apnée *f*; ~ **diving** *n* OCEANOG plongée en apnée *f*; ~ **drying** *n* PROD ENG *founding* flambage *m*; ~ **effect** *n* AERONAUT effet pelliculaire *m*, ELEC effet de peau *m*, effet pelliculaire *m*, PETR colmatage des parois *m*, effet pariétal *m*, PHYS, TESTING effet de peau *m*; ~ **film** *n* PACKAGING film pour pelliplacage *m*; ~ **friction** *n* PHYS *fluid mechanics* frottement pariétal *m*; ~ **resistance** *n* COAL TECH résistance superficielle *f*

skin[2] *vt* OCEANOG *fish* écailler

skinning *n* PROD ENG *founding* décroûtage *m*

skinpack *n* PACKAGING pelliplacage *m*, PRINT emballage fin et souple comme une peau *m*

skin-to-skin: ~ **timbering** *n* MINING cadres jointifs *m pl*

skip[1] *n* COMP, DP saut *m*, MAR POLL benne *f*, TRANSP benne *f*, benne basculante *f*; ~ **car** *n* (AmE) *(cf skip wagon)* RAIL wagonnet *m*; ~ **distance** *n* WAVE PHYS *reflected radiowave* distance de saut *f*; ~ **extraction** *n* COAL TECH extraction par cuffat *f*; ~ **frame printing** *n* CINEMAT tirage en accéléré *m*; ~ **lorry** *n* MAR POLL, TRANSP camion benne *m*; ~ **truck** *n* TRANSP camion benne *m*; ~ **wagon** *n* (BrE) *(cf skip car)* RAIL wagonnet *m*

skip[2] *vt* PRINT sauter

skip:[3] ~ **frame** *vi* CINEMAT tirer une image sur deux

skip-winding: ~ **system** *n* MINING installation d'extraction par skip *f*

skirt *n* C&G chemise *f*, CONST, MAR POLL, MILIT *of rocket*, TRANSP *hovercraft* jupe *f*; ~ **board** *n* CONST *carpentry* filet d'embase *m*, plinthe *f*

skirting *n* CONST *carpentry* filet d'embase *m*, plinthe *f*; ~ **board** *n* (BrE) *(cf baseboard, mopboard)* CONST *carpentry* filet d'embase *m*, plinthe *f*

skiver *n* PRINT *bookbinding* mouton scié côté fleur *m*

skull *n* PROD ENG *founding* cul de poche *m*, fond de poche *m*

skutterudite *n* MINERAL skuttérudite *f*

sky: ~ **noise temperature** *n* SPACE *communications* température de bruit du ciel *f*; ~ **wave** *n* PHYS onde ionosphérique *f*

skybus *n* TRANSP skybus *m*

skylight *n* NAUT *deck equipment* claire-voie *f*

skylite *n* CINEMAT projecteur de 10 kw *m*, projecteur de 5 kw *m*

skypan *n* CINEMAT réflecteur parabolique de 5 kw *m*

SL: ~ **cable** *n* ELEC câble triplomb *m*

slab *n* C&G plateau *m*, COAL TECH semelle élargie *f*, CONST *of stone* dalle *f*, tranche *f*, *of timber* dosse *f*, flache *f*, PRINT marbre *m*; ~ **coil** *n* ELEC bobine plate *f*; ~ **interferometry** *n* OPT interférométrie axiale *f*, microscopie axiale interférentielle *f*, TELECOM interférométrie axiale *f*; ~ **pile** *n* NUCLEAR réacteur en forme d'une plaque infinie *m*; ~ **reactor** *n* NUCLEAR réacteur en forme d'une plaque infinie *m*; ~ **serifs** *n pl* PRINT empattement en forme de barre *m*; ~ **shears** *n pl* PROD ENG cisailles à brames *f pl*

slabber *n* PROD ENG *milling metal* fraiseuse genre raboteuse *f*

slabbing *n* PROD ENG tranchage *m*; ~ **mill** *n* PROD ENG *rolling* laminoir universel *m*; ~ **miller** *n* PROD ENG *milling metal* fraiseuse genre raboteuse *f*

slab-freezing: ~ **apparatus** *n* MECH ENG appareil frigorifique à plaques *m*

slack *n* MECH ENG *play* jeu *m*, MINING menu *m*, menu de houille *m*, NAUT *of rope, belt*, TELECOM *cable laying* mou *m*; ~ **coal** *n* COAL TECH menu brut *m*, MINING menu *m*, menu de houille *m*; ~ **heap** *n* MINING crassier *m*, terril *m*; ~ **length** *n* PROD ENG *of belt, transmission rope* brin conduit *m*, brin lâche *m*, brin mené *m*, brin mou *m*; ~ **portion** *n* PROD ENG *of belt, transmission rope* brin conduit *m*, brin lâche *m*, brin mené *m*, brin mou *m*; ~ **side** *n* PROD ENG *of belt, transmission rope* brin conduit *m*, brin lâche *m*, brin mené *m*, brin mou *m*; ~ **tide** *n* OCEANOG étale *m*, étale de courant *m*; ~ **time** *n* PROD ENG temps mort *m*; ~ **water** *n* HYDROL eau morte *f*, NAUT *navigation* mer étale *f*, étale du flot *m*, OCEANOG étale de courant *m*

slackening *n* MECH ENG ralentissement *m*, relâchement *m*

slacking *n* MECH ENG *of nut* desserrage *m*, PROD ENG *of blast furnace* refroidissement *m*

slag *n* C&G *spilled glass* piccadil *m*, COAL TECH fondant *m*, laitier *m*, CONST *welding*, HEAT ENG laitier *m*, METALL, PAPER TECH scorie *f*; ~ **dump** *n* PROD ENG crassier *m*, halde de scories *f*, remblai *m*; ~ **formation period** *n* PROD ENG *Bessemer process* période de scorification *f*, période des étincelles *f*; ~ **glass** *n* C&G verre de laitier *m*; ~ **heap** *n* MINING terril *m*, PROD ENG crassier *m*, halde de scories *f*, remblai *m*; ~ **pot** *n* PROD ENG poche à laitier *f*; ~ **tap furnace** *n* HEAT ENG foyer à cendres fondues *m*; ~ **tip** *n* PROD ENG crassier *m*, halde de scories *f*, remblai *m*; ~ **wool** *n* HEAT ENG laine minérale *f*

slag-free: ~ **refining** *n* PROP MAT affinage sans laitier *m*

slagging *n* PROP MAT décrassage *m*

slake *vi* CHEM éteindre de la chaux

slaked: ~ **lime** *n* CHEM, CONST, FOOD TECH chaux éteinte *f*

slam: ~ **tank** *n* PETR bac à boue *m*

slamming *n* NAUT *motion of boat* martèlement *m*, slamming *m*

slant *n* CONST inclinaison *f*, pente *f*, GEOM inclinaison *f*, PRINT inclinaison *f*, pente *f*; ~ **angle** *n* MILIT déclinaison *f*; ~ **course line** *n* AERONAUT *landing* alignement oblique *m*; ~ **fracture** *n* METALL rupture inclinée *f*; ~ **height** *n* GEOM *of right circular cone* hauteur d'inclinaison *f*; ~ **polarization** *n* ELEC ENG polarisation oblique *f*

slanted: ~ **letters** *n pl* PRINT italiques *m pl*

slanter: ~ **engine** *n* AUTO moteur incliné *m*

slanting *adj* CONST *oblique* oblique, *sloping* en pente, incliné

SLAR *abbr (sideways-looking airborne radar)* MAR POLL radar aéroporté à balayage latéral *m*

slash: ~ **print** *n* CINEMAT copie tirée en vitesse *f*

slasher: ~ **sizing** *n* TEXTILES encollage réunissage de bobines primaires *m*

slasher-dyed *adj* TEXTILES teint sur encolleuse

slat: ~ **dryer** *n* PAPER TECH sécheur à lattes *m*

slate *n* CINEMAT ardoise *f*, clap *m*, claquette *f*, CONST *thin sheet*, GEOL ardoise *f*; ~ **ax** *n* (AmE), ~ **axe** *n* (BrE) CONST hachette *f*, martelet *f*; ~ **industry** *n* MINING ardoiserie *f*; ~ **knife** *n* CONST rabattoir d'ardoisier *m*; ~ **lath** *n* CONST latte volige *f*, latte à ardoises *f*, volige *f*; ~ **nail** *n* MECH ENG clou ardoise *m*, clou de couvreur *m*; ~ **quarry** *n* MINING ardoisière *f*, carrière d'ardoise *f*; ~ **splitting** *n* CONST refente d'ardoises *f*

slate-foliated: ~ **lignite** *n* COAL TECH charbon lamelleux *m*

slater's: ~ **hammer** *n* CONST marteau à ardoise *m*

Slatis-Siegbahn: ~ **spectrometer** *n* NUCLEAR spectromètre Slätis-Siegbahn *m*

slaty: ~ **cleavage** *n* GEOL clivage ardoisier *m*

slave *n* COMP, DP esclave *m*; ~ **application** *n* COMP, DP application en mode asservi *f*; ~ **cylinder** *n* AUTO, VEHICLES *brakes, clutch* cylindre récepteur *m*; ~ **processor** *n* COMP processeur asservi *m*, processeur esclave *m*, DP processeur esclave *m*; ~ **relay** *n* ELEC relais séquentiel *m*; ~ **station** *n* COMP, DP station asservie *f*; ~ **unit** *n* TV dispositif d'asservissement *m*; ~ **videocassette recorder** *n* TV magnétoscope à cassette asservi *m*

slavelock *n* TV *transmitters* synchronisation d'émetteurs secondaires *f*

slaving *n* TV asservissement *m*, synchronisation externe *f*

SLC *abbr (subscriber line circuit)* TELECOM joncteur d'abonné *m*

SLD *abbr (superluminescent diode)* OPT, TELECOM DSL *(diode superluminescente)*

sledge[1] *n* CONST *stone breaking* masse *f*, massette *f*, têtu *m*

sledge[2] *vt* CONST battre à la masse

sledgehammer *n* CONST *stone breaking* masse *f*, massette *f*, têtu *m*

sleek[1] *adj* TEXTILES lisse

sleek[2] *n* C&G filasse *f*

sleeper *n* (BrE) *(cf tie, cross tie)* RAIL traverse *f*; ~ **bed** *n* (BrE) *(cf tie bed)* RAIL assiette des traverses *f*; ~ **screw** *n* (BrE) *(cf tie screw)* RAIL tirefond *m*; ~ **screwdriver** *n* (BrE) *(cf tie screwdriver)* RAIL tirefonneuse *f*; ~ **screw extractor** *n* (BrE) *(cf spike puller)* RAIL arrache-tirefond *m*

sleeper-adzing: ~ **machine** *n* (BrE) *(cf tie-adzing machine)* RAIL saboteuse de traverses *f*

sleeper-drilling: ~ **machine** *n* (BrE) *(cf tie drilling machine)* RAIL foreuse *f*

sleeping: ~ **car** *n* RAIL *vehicles* wagon lits *m*; ~ **car attendant** *n* RAIL accompagnateur de wagons-lit *m pl*

sleeve *n* C&G manchon *m*, MECH douille *f*, manchon *m*, MECH ENG manchon *m*, MILIT *of parachute* manchon de pliage *m*, PACKAGING manchon *m*, PRINT chaussette *f*, manchon *m*, PROD ENG gaine *f*; ~ **anchor** *n* CONST *building* cheville douille *f*; ~ **coupling** *n* MECH ENG accouplement à manchon *m*; ~ **ejector** *n* MECH ENG *diecasting die* éjecteur tubulaire *m*; ~ **joint** *n* MECH ENG assemblage à manchon *m*; ~ **nut** *n* MECH ENG manchon fileté *m*, manchon taraudé *m*; ~ **pattern** *n* HYDR EQUIP soupape d'équilibrage à manchon *f*; ~ **valve engine** *n* AUTO moteur sans soupape *m*; ~ **wrapping** *n* PRINT emballage sous manchon rétractable *m*

slenderness: ~ **ratio** *n* CONST coefficient d'élancement *m*, SPRINGS degré de subtilité *m*, rapport de sveltesse *m*

slew:[1] ~ **speed** *n* PROD ENG vitesse maximale de tenue mécanique *f*

slew[2] *vi* MECH pivoter

slewing *n* CONST *of crane* virage *m*; ~ **crane** *n* NUCLEAR grue pivotante *f*, grue à flèche *f*; ~ **gear** *n* NUCLEAR mécanisme vireur *m*, vireur *m*; ~ **rim** *n* MECH ENG *for bearings* couronne pivotante *f*; ~ **round** *n* CONST *of crane* virage *m*

slice *n* COMP, DP tranche *f*, GEOL copeau *m*, écaille *f*, PAPER TECH lèvre de la caisse de tête *f*; ~ **architecture** *n* COMP, DP architecture en tranches *f*; ~ **lip** *n* PAPER TECH lèvre de la caisse de tête *f*

slicing *n* PROD ENG décrassage *m*

slick *n* MAR POLL nappe *f*, PROD ENG *founding* lissoir *m*

slickenside *n* GEOL miroir de faille *m*

slicker *n* PROD ENG *founding* lissoir *m*

slide[1] *n* CINEMAT cliché de projection *m*, COAL TECH glissement *m*, éboulement *m*, HYDR EQUIP distributeur à tiroir *m*, tiroir *m*, LAB EQUIP *microscope* lame porte-objet *f*, MECH glissière *f*, MECH ENG coulisse *f*, coulisseau *m*, glissière *f*, tiroir *m*, *shear* cisaillement *m*, glissement *m*, PHOTO diapo *f*, diapositive *f*, *dark slide* châssis *m*, châssis négatif *m*, châssis porte-plaque *m*, PRINT diapositive *f*, glissière *f*, document transparent *m*; ~ **bar** *n* CINEMAT *of bellows, of matt box* glissière *f*, MECH ENG *piston crosshead* glissière *f*, glissière de crosse *f*, guide de la tête de piston *m*; ~ **bar carrier** *n*

MECH ENG *piston crosshead* tasseau de fixation des glissières *m*; ~ **block** *n* MECH ENG *of link valve motion* coulisseau *m*, *piston crosshead* tasseau de fixation des glissières *m*; ~ **box** *n* HYDR EQUIP *slide valve* boîte à vapeur *f*, chapelle de tiroir *f*, tiroir *m*, tiroir de distribution *m*, PHOTO coffret classeur pour diapos *m*; ~ **bridge** *n* ELEC ENG pont à corde *m*; ~ **caliper** *n* (AmE), ~ **calliper** *n* (BrE) SPRINGS pied à coulisse *m*; ~ **changer** *n* PHOTO *of projector* passe-vues va-et-vient *m*; ~ **control** *n* RECORDING réglage linéaire *m*; ~ **damper** *n* HEAT ENG registre à coulisses *m*, REFRIG registre à glissières *m*; ~ **duplication** *n* PHOTO reproduction de diapositives *f*; ~ **head** *n* MECH ENG *of lathe* support à chariot *m*; ~ **holder** *n* PHOTO châssis *m*, châssis négatif *m*, châssis porteplaque *m*; ~ **lathe** *n* MECH ENG tour à chariot *m*, tour à chariot *m*; ~ **motion film** *n* CINEMAT film réalisé par animation de diapositives *m*; ~ **pickup** *n* TV analyseur de diapositives *m*; ~ **potentiometer** *n* ELEC ENG potentiomètre à glissière *m*; ~ **projector** *n* PHOTO projecteur pour diapositives *m*; ~ **rest** *n* MECH ENG *of lathe* support à chariot *m*; ~ **rest tools** *n* MECH ENG *lathe* outils de chariotage *m pl*, outils à charioter *m pl*; ~ **rest turning tools** *n pl* MECH ENG *lathe* outils de chariotage *m pl*, outils à charioter *m pl*; ~ **rheostat** *n* ELEC *resistance* rhéostat à curseur *m*; ~ **rod** *n* HYDR EQUIP bielle de tiroir *f*, tige de tiroir *f*; ~ **rule** *n* COMP, DP règle à calculer *f*; ~ **scanner** *n* TV analyseur de diapositives *m*; ~ **switch** *n* CONTROL, ELEC interrupteur à coulisse *m*, ELEC ENG commutateur à glissière *m*, interrupteur à glissière *m*, inverseur à glissière *m*; ~ **throttle valve** *n* HYDR EQUIP régulateur à tiroir *m*, tiroir de freinage *m*; ~ **unit** *n* MECH ENG *for machine tools* table de déplacement rectiligne *f*; ~ **valve** *n* HYDR EQUIP distributeur *m*, distributeur à tiroir coulissant *m*, distributeur à tiroir rotatif *m*, distributeur à tiroir *m*, tiroir *m*, VEHICLES *of engine* soupape à coulisse *f*; ~ **valve gear** *n* HYDR EQUIP distribution à tiroir *f*; ~ **viewer** *n* PHOTO visionneuse pour diapositives *f*; ~ **wire bridge** *n* ELEC ENG pont de mesure à corde *m*

slide² *vi* MECH glisser, MECH ENG coulisser, glisser; ~ **back and forth** *vi* PROD ENG faire coulisser d'avant en arrière

slide-copying: ~ **attachment** *n* PHOTO adaptateur pour reproduction de diapositives *m*; ~ **device** *n* PHOTO dispositif de reproduction des diapositives *m*

slider *n* MECH ENG coulant *m*, curseur *m*, coulisse *f*, coulisseau *m*, glissière *f*, tiroir *m*; ~ **control** *n* CONTROL régulateur à coulisse *m*; ~ **control regulator** *n* CONTROL régulateur à coulisse *m*; ~ **crank** *n* MECH ENG manivelle-glisseur *f*

sliding *n* MECH ENG glissement *m*, *lathe work* chariotage longitudinal *m*, METALL glissement *m*; ~ **bolt** *n* MECH ENG verrou glissant *m*; ~ **bottom** *n* PACKAGING fond mobile *m*; ~ **caliper gage** *n* (AmE) *see sliding calliper gauge*; ~ **calipers** *n pl* (AmE) *see sliding callipers*; ~ **calliper gauge** *n* (BrE) MECH ENG calibre à coulisse *m*, compas à coulisse *m*, mesure à coulisse *f*, pied à coulisse *m*, équerre à coulisse *f*; ~ **callipers** *n pl* (BrE) MECH ENG calibre à coulisse *m*, compas à coulisse *m*, mesure à coulisse *f*, pied à coulisse *m*, équerre à coulisse *f*; ~ **contact** *n* ELEC ENG contact glissant *m*, PHYS curseur *m*; ~ **door** *n* CONST porte à coulisse *f*, porte à glissant *f*; ~ **filter drawer** *n* PHOTO tiroir porte-filtre *m*; ~ **fit** *n* MECH ajustage glissant *m*; ~ **formwork** *n* CONST coffrage glissant *m*, coffrage mobile *m*; ~ **fracture** *n* NUCLEAR rupture par glissement *f*, rupture à nerfs *f*; ~ **frequency** *n* TV fréquence glissante *f*; ~

friction *n* PHYS frottement par glissement *m*; ~ **friction coefficient** *n* PHYS coefficient de frottement par glissement *m*; ~ **gate** *n* CONST barrière roulante *f*; ~ **gear** *n* MECH ENG baladeur *m*, engrenages baladeurs *m pl*, VEHICLES baladeur *m*; ~ **gear starting motor** *n* ELEC démarreur à déplacement d'induit *m*; ~ **gear train** *n* MECH ENG train baladeur *m*; ~ **gear transmission** *n* AUTO boîte de vitesses à trains baladeurs *f*; ~ **headstock** *n* MECH ENG contre-pointe *f*, contre-poupée *f*, poupée courante *f*, poupée mobile *f*; ~ **lathe** *n* MECH ENG tour à charioter *m*; ~ **leg** *n* PHOTO *of tripod* branche coulissante *f*, branche à coulisse *f*; ~ **lid** *n* PACKAGING couvercle mobile *m*; ~ **load** *n* ELEC ENG charge réglable *f*; ~ **parallel vice** *n* (BrE) MECH ENG étau-tiroir *m*; ~ **parallel vise** *n* (AmE) *see sliding parallel vice* ~ **poppet** *n* MECH ENG contre-pointe *f*, contre-poupée *f*, poupée courante *f*, poupée mobile *f*; ~ **sash** *n* CONST *of window* châssis à guillotine *m*; ~ **scale** *n* PROD ENG *rate* échelle mobile *f*; ~ **shutter** *n* CONST *store door* porte glissante *f*, volet roulant *m*, MINING *of box regulator* guichet mobile *m*; ~ **sleeve** *n* AUTO crabot *m*; ~ **sluice gate** *n* FUELLESS *dams* vanne à coulisse *f*; ~ **surfacing and screw-cutting lathe** *n* MECH ENG tour parallèle à fileter charioter et surfacer *m*; ~ **switch** *n* ELEC ENG commutateur glissant *m*; ~ **tee socket wrench** *n* MECH ENG *tool* clé à béquille *f*; ~ **window** *n* CONST fenêtre glissante *f*, fenêtre roulante *f*

sliding-f-guide *n* RAIL guide de coulisseau *m*

sliding-frequency: ~ **generator** *n* RECORDING générateur de balayage de fréquence *m*

slim: ~ **hole** *n* PETR forage à faible diamètre *m*, PETR TECH forage en diamètre réduit *m*, forage à diamètre réduit *m*

SLIM *abbr (single linear inductor motor)* TRANSP moteur linéaire à simple inducteur *m*

slime *n* C&G boue *f*, COAL TECH boue *f*, schlamms *m*, HYDROL boue *f*, limon *m*, vase *f*, PAPER TECH dépôt dans les conduites *m*, REFRIG *on spoiled meat, fish* couche visqueuse *f*, WATER SUPP boue *f*, limon *m*, vase *f*

slimes *n* COAL TECH charbon limoneux *m*

sling *n* C&G bricole *f*, MAR POLL, NAUT élingue *f*, PROD ENG *chain sling* chaîne de suspension *f*; ~ **beam** *n* PROD ENG *foundry* balancier *m*; ~ **dog** *n* PROD ENG patte d'élingue *f*; ~ **hanger** *n* PROD ENG *shaft hanger* chaise en U *f*, chaise pendante à deux jambes *f*, chaise à deux jambages *f*; ~ **hygrometer** *n* REFRIG hygromètre fronde *m*; ~ **identification tag** *n* SAFETY plaque d'identification de l'élingue *f*; ~ **transport** *n* AERONAUT, MILIT *on helicopter* transport à l'élingue *m*

slingshot *n* SPACE *spacecraft* fronde *f*

slip¹ *n* AERONAUT *of propeller* glissement *m*, C&G barbotine *f*, CRYSTALL *defect* , ELEC *machine*, ELEC ENG glissement *m*, NAUT *boatbuilding, ropes* cale *f*, PAPER TECH lait de couche *m*, sauce de couchage *f*, PETR TECH coin grippeur *m*, PROP MAT glissement *m*; ~ **band** *n* CRYSTALL bande de glissement *f*; ~ **box** *n* MINING *in column pipe* boîte de dilatation *f*, boîte à plongeur *f*; ~ **case** *n* PACKAGING emboîtage *m*; ~ **casting** *n* C&G coulage en barbotine *m*; ~ **cast pot** *n* C&G pot coulé *m*; ~ **circle** *n* CONST, GEOL cercle de glissement *m*; ~ **cleavage** *n* GEOL clivage de crénulation *m*; ~ **cylinder** *n* METALL cylindre de glissement *m*; ~ **form** *n* CONST coffrage glissant *m*, coffrage mobile *m*; ~ **for taking up wear** *n* MECH ENG *machine tools* coin de rattrapage de jeu *m*; ~ **gage** *n* (AmE), ~ **gauge** *n* (BrE) METR calibre étalon *m*; ~ **jacket** *n* PROD ENG *for snap moulding* corbeille de coulée *f*; ~ **joint** *n* AUTO joint coulissant *m*, MECH ENG crémaillère *f*, joint de dilatation *m*; ~ **joint multigrip pliers** *n pl* MECH ENG *tool* pince réglable à crémaillère *f*; ~ **joint pliers** *n pl* MECH ENG *tool* pince motoriste *f*; ~ **kiln** *n* C&G caisse pour raffermir la barbotine *f*; ~ **line** *n* CRYSTALL ligne de glissement *f*; ~ **marking** *n* METALL trace de glissement *f*; ~ **plane** *n* CRYSTALL plan de glissement *m*; ~ **proof** *n* PRINT épreuve en placard *f*, épreuve en première *f*; ~ **rate** *n* PROP MAT vitesse de glissement *f*; ~ **ring** *n* ELEC *motor*, ELEC ENG, PHYS, VEHICLES *generator* bague collectrice *f*; ~ **road** *n* (BrE) *(cf access road)* TRANSP route d'accès *f*, voie d'accès *f*, voie de ralentissement *f*; ~ **road census** *n* (BrE) *(cf access road census)* TRANSP comptage des accès *m*; ~ **road control** *n* (BrE) *(cf access road control)* TRANSP régulation des accès *f*; ~ **road count** *n* (BrE) *(cf access road count)* TRANSP comptage des accès *m*; ~ **road metering** *n* (BrE) *(cf access road metering)* TRANSP régulation des rampes d'accès *f*; ~ **scar** *n* GEOL niche d'arrachement *f*; ~ **step height** *n* METALL hauteur de marche de glissement *f*; ~ **stone** *n* MECH ENG bâton rodoir *m*; ~ **surface** *n* COAL TECH surface de glissement *f*; ~ **transfer** *n* PROP MAT transfert du glissement *m*

slip² *vt* NAUT *boat building, ropes* choquer; ~ **one's cable** *vt* NAUT filer son câble par le bout

slip³ *vi* MECH ENG patiner; ~ **in** *vi* MECH ENG *fix or mount in* emmancher dans; ~ **into** *vi* MECH ENG *fix or mount in* emmancher dans

slip-on: ~ **sleeve** *n* PHOTO monture à friction *f*

slippage *n* CONST *earthworks* glissement *m*

slipper *n* MECH ENG *of piston crosshead* patin *m*, semelle *f*; ~ **block** *n* MECH ENG coulisseau *m*, *crosshead* crosse de piston *f*, crossette de piston *f*, tête de piston *f*

slipperiness *n* TRANSP glissance *f*

slipping *n* PROD ENG *of rolls of rolling mill* patinage *m*

slip-proof: ~ **finish** *n* COATINGS apprêt antiglisse *m*, apprêt antiglissant *m*

slip-resistant: ~ **sole** *n* SAFETY *protective footwear* semelle antidérapante *f*

slip-ring: ~ **induction motor** *n* ELEC ENG moteur asynchrone à bagues *m*; ~ **motor** *n* ELEC moteur à bagues *m*, moteur à bagues collectrices *m*; ~ **rotor** *n* ELEC *generator, motor* induit à bagues collectrices *m*

slips *n pl* PETR coins de retenue *m pl*

slipstream *n* AERONAUT *of propeller* remous *m*, souffle *m*, écoulement d'air *m*

slip-tongue: ~ **joint** *n* CONST assemblage à fausse languette *m*, assemblage à languette rapportée *f*

slipway *n* NAUT *shipbuilding, repair* cale *f*, chantier de construction *m*, slip *m*

slit¹ *n* PHOTO *of cassette* glissière *f*, PHYS, PROD ENG, SPACE fente *f*; ~ **diaphragm** *n* PHOTO diaphragme en fente *m*; ~ **mortise joint** *n* CONST assemblage à enfourchement *m*; ~ **rewind machine** *n* PACKAGING refendeuse-enrouleuse *f*; ~ **scanning** *n* TV balayage par fente *m*; ~ **shutter** *n* TV obturateur à fente *m*; ~ **system** *n* SPACE *communications* système à fentes *m*

slit² *vt* PACKAGING, PAPER TECH refendre

slits *n pl* WAVE PHYS *evenly spaced on stroboscope disc* fentes *f pl*

slitter *n* C&G choisisseuse *f*, PAPER TECH coupeuse en long *f*, PRINT molette de coupe *f*, refendeuse *f*; ~ **rewinder** *n* PAPER TECH bobineuse-refendeuse *f*

slitting *n* PACKAGING refente *f*, PAPER TECH refente *f*, refente d'une bobine *f*, tronçonnage d'une bobine *f*, PROD ENG fendage *m*; ~ **and printing machine** *n* PACKAGING refendeuse-imprimeuse *f*; ~ **and rewinding machine** *n* PACKAGING refendeuse-enrouleuse *f*; ~ **disc** *n* (BrE) C&G disque à trancher *m*; ~ **disk** *n* (AmE) *see slitting disc*; ~ **file** *n* MECH ENG lime à dossière *f*, lime à fendre *f*, lime à losange *f*; ~ **time** *n* PROD ENG ligne à refendre *f*

sliver *n* C&G mèche *f*, TEXTILES ruban *m*

SLM *abbr (single-longitudinal mode)* TELECOM mode longitudinal unique *m*

slogging: ~ **ring spanner** *n* (BrE) MECH ENG *tool* clé polygonale à frapper *f*; ~ **ring wrench** *n* MECH ENG *tool* clé polygonale à frapper *f*

sloop *n* NAUT aviso *m*, sloop *m*

slop: ~ **test** *n* CINEMAT bout d'essai *m*

slope *n* COAL TECH pente *f*, talus *m*, CONST penchant *m*, talus *m*, *downward* déclivité *f*, *of hill, slant, inclination* pente *f*, rampe *f*, *of hill* versant *m*, *of roof* rampant *m*, versant *m*, égout *m*, *upward* côte *f*, GEOM *surface* pente *f*, MINING fendue *f*, PHYS gradient *m*, pente *f*; ~ **current** *n* OCEANOG courant de pente *m*; ~ **failure** *n* COAL TECH rupture de talus *f*; ~ **level** *n* CONST *gradiometer* niveau de pente *m*; ~ **protection** *n* CONST protection de talus *f*; ~ **stability** *n* COAL TECH stabilité de talus *f*; ~ **toe** *n* COAL TECH pied de talus *m*; ~ **top** *n* COAL TECH sommet de talus *m*

sloshing *n* SPACE *spacecraft* ballottement de liquide *m*

slot *n* C&G fente de la débiteuse *f*, ELEC ENG *magnetic circuits* encoche *f*, *waveguides* fente *f*, MECH ENG encoche *f*, entaille *f*, fente *f*, mortaise *f*, rainure *f*, *in screw head* fente *f*, NUCLEAR *of gas generator rotor* rainure *f*, PRINT buse *f*, encoche *f*, orifice *m*, PROD ENG *for keying band* emplacement *m*, *for module* logement *m*, *on battery* lead encoche *f*, SPACE créneau *m*, TELECOM fente *f*, TV *in schedules* créneau *m*, tranche horaire *f*; ~ **antenna** *n* SPACE, TELECOM antenne à fente *f*; ~ **die** *n* PRINT buse d'alimentation sous pression *f*; ~ **diffuser** *n* REFRIG diffuseur linéaire *m*; ~ **drill** *n* MECH ENG fraise à rainurer *f*; ~ **feeding** *n* PRINT alimentation sous pression *f*, turbo-alimentation *f*; ~ **file** *n* MECH ENG fendante *f*; ~ **flap** *n* AERONAUT *of aircraft* volet à fente *m*; ~ **line** *n* PHYS ligne à fente *f*; ~ **lip** *n* C&G lèvre de la débiteuse *f*; ~ **machine** *n* MECH ENG distributeur automatique *m*; ~ **meter** *n* MECH ENG compteur à paiement préalable *m*; ~ **milling** *n* MECH ENG fraisage de rainures *m*; ~ **mortise joint** *n* CONST *carpentry* assemblage à enfourchement *m*

slot-drilling: ~ **machine** *n* MECH ENG rainureuse *f*

slotted¹ *adj* PROD ENG rainuré

slotted²: ~ **ALOHA system** *n* TELECOM système ALOHA crénelé *m*; ~ **armature** *n* ELEC *generator, motor* induit à encoches *m*, ELEC ENG induit denté *m*; ~ **box table** *n* MECH ENG *machine tool* table d'équerre à rainures *f*; ~ **cheese-head screw** *n* MECH ENG vis à métaux fendue à tête cylindrique *f*; ~ **clinch rivet** *n* CONST rivet bifurqué *m*; ~ **countersunk head tapping screw** *n* MECH ENG vis à tôle à tête fraisée fendue *f*; ~ **end notch** *n* SPRINGS *of leaf spring* encoche d'extrémité *f*; ~ **head fastener** *n* MECH ENG boulonnerie à tête fendue *f*; ~ **headless screw** *n* MECH ENG vis sans tête fendue *f*; ~ **head screw** *n* MECH ENG vis à tête fendue *f*; ~ **line** *n* ELEC ENG ligne de mesure *f*; ~ **line probe** *n* ELEC ENG sonde de ligne de mesure *f*; ~ **nut** *n* MECH ENG écrou à dents *m*, écrou à entailles *m*, écrou à rainures *m*; ~ **oil control ring** *n* AUTO segment racleur à fentes *m*; ~ **pan head tapping**

screw n MECH ENG vis à tôle à tête cylindrique large fendue f; ~ **rivet** n CONST rivet bifurqué m; ~ **round-head bolt** n MECH ENG boulon à tête ronde fendue m; ~ **screw** n MECH ENG vis à fente f; ~ **system** n TELECOM système crénelé m; ~ **table** n MECH ENG *machine tool* plateau à rainures m, table à rainures f, table à rainures de montage f; ~ **waveguide** n ELEC ENG guide d'ondes à fentes m, guide à fente m; ~ **wing** n AERONAUT aile à fente f

slotter n MECH ENG *metal working* machine à mortaises f, mortaiseuse f; ~ **tools** n pl MECH ENG outils de mortaiseuses m pl, outils à mortaiser m pl

slotting n MECH ENG encochement m, entaillage m, fendage m, mortaisage m, rainurage m; ~ **cutter** n MECH ENG fraise pour rainure f; ~ **file** n MECH ENG fendante f; ~ **machine** n MECH ENG machine à mortaiser f, mortaiseuse f; ~ **tool** n MECH ENG outil à rainures m, outil à mortaiser m

slough n C&G bac-baratte m

sloughed: ~ **yarn** n C&G fil éboulé m

sloughing: ~ **shale** n PETR argile mouvante f

slow:[1] ~ **ahead** adv NAUT *engine* en avant lente; ~ **astern** adv NAUT *engine* en arrière lente

slow:[2] ~ **combustion** n AUTO combustion lente f; ~ **freezing** n FOOD TECH, REFRIG congélation lente f; ~ **match** n MINING fusée à combustion lente f, mèche à combustion lente f; ~ **motion** n CINEMAT ralenti m; ~ **neutron** n PHYS neutron lent m; ~ **quenching** n METALL trempe lente f; ~ **sand filter** n HYDROL filtre lent m, WATER SUPP filtre lent au sable m; ~ **sand filtration** n WATER SUPP filtration lente sur sable f; ~ **train** n (BrE) *(cf local train, stopping train)* RAIL *vehicles* omnibus m, train omnibus m; ~ **wave** n ELEC ENG onde lente f

slow-acting: ~ **fuse** n PROD ENG fusible à action retardée m; ~ **relay** n ELEC relais à action lente m

slow-blow: ~ **fuse** n CINEMAT fusible à fusion lente m, ELEC fusible retardé m, fusible à action retardée m, PROD ENG fusible à fusion lente m

slow-break: ~ **switch** n CONTROL, ELEC interrupteur à rupture lente m

slow-burning: ~ **fuse** n MINING fusée à combustion lente f, mèche à combustion lente f, mèche de sûreté f, mèche lente f

slow-down: ~ **cylinder** n PRINT cylindre de ralentissement m

slowing: ~ **down** n NUCLEAR ralentissement des neutrons m

slowing-down: ~ **area** n NUCLEAR, PHYS aire de ralentissement f; ~ **density** n NUCLEAR, PHYS densité de ralentissement f; ~ **length** n NUCLEAR, PHYS longueur de ralentissement f; ~ **power** n NUCLEAR, PHYS pouvoir de ralentissement m

slowly: ~ **varying voltage** n ELEC ENG tension à variation lente f

slow-motion: ~ **adjusting screw** n MECH ENG vis de rappel pour le mouvement lent f; ~ **control knob** n INSTRUMENT bouton de réglage du mouvement lent m; ~ **disc** n (BrE) TV disque de ralenti m; ~ **disk** n (AmE) see *slow-motion disc*; ~ **screw** n MECH ENG vis à mouvement lent de rotation f

slow-moving: ~ **percentage** n PROD ENG seuil des taux de rotation faibles m

slow-operate: ~ **relay** n ELEC ENG relais temporisé au relâchement m

slow-running: ~ **diesel engine** n TRANSP moteur diesel lent m

slow-scan: ~ **television** n TELECOM télévision à balayage lent f; ~ **television system** n TV système de télévision à balayage lent m; ~ **videoconferencing** n TELECOM vidéoconférence à images fixes f

slow-setting: ~ **cement** n CONST ciment à prise lente m; ~ **glass** n C&G verre long m

slow-speed: ~ **compressor** n HYDR EQUIP compresseur lent m

slow-wave: ~ **structure** n ELEC ENG ligne à onde lente f, PHYS structure à retard f; ~ **tube** n ELECTRON tube hyperfréquence m, tube à onde lente m

SLR abbr *(single lens reflex camera)* PHOTO appareil reflex mono-objectif m

slub n TEXTILES bouton floche m

slubbing: ~ **frame** n TEXTILES banc à broches en gros m

slubbing-dyed adj TEXTILES teint en mèche

sludge n CHEM boue f, vase f, CONST boue f, FOOD TECH *machinery* boue f, bourbe f, vase f, HYDROL boue f, limon m, vase f, PROD ENG *ore dressing* boue f, schlamms m, slimes f pl, RECYCLING, REFRIG boue f, WATER SUPP boue f, vase f; ~ **bulking** n HYDROL *sewage* concentration des boues f, gonflement des boues m, épaississement des boues m, WATER SUPP gonflement des boues m; ~ **conditioning** n HYDROL *sewage*, WATER SUPP conditionnement des boues m; ~ **dewatering** n HYDROL *sewage* déshydratation des boues f; ~ **digestion** n HYDROL *sewage*, RECYCLING digestion des boues f; ~ **digestion gas** n HYDROL *sewage* gaz de digestion m; ~ **disposal** n WATER SUPP évacuation des boues f; ~ **formation test** n ELEC *transformer oil* essai de formation de boue m; ~ **gas** n RECYCLING biogaz m, gaz de digestion m; ~ **gulper** n RECYCLING camion de vidange des fosses septiques m; ~ **incineration** n WATER SUPP incinération des boues f; ~ **liquor** n HYDROL *sewage*, WATER SUPP liquide surnageant m; ~ **press** n HYDROL *sewage* presse à boues f; ~ **processing** n RECYCLING traitement des boues m; ~ **pump** n MINING *boring* cloche f, cloche de curage f, désensableur m, pompe à boue f, pompe à sable f, tube à sable m, tube-cuiller m; ~ **ripening** n WATER SUPP maturation des boues f; ~ **scraper** n HYDROL *sewage* racleur de boues m; ~ **stabilization** n HYDROL *sewage* stabilisation des boues f; ~ **thickening** n HYDROL concentration des boues f, épaississement des boues m, WATER SUPP épaississement des boues m

sludge-drying: ~ **bed** n HYDROL *sewage* lit de séchage des boues m

sludger n MINING *boring* cloche f, cloche de curage f, pompe à boue f, pompe à sable f, tube à sable m, tube-cuiller m

slug n C&G perle de verre f, COAL TECH cône m, ELEC ENG spire de silence f, HF *winding* noyau réglable m, *condensers* anode frittée f, *waveguides* sonde d'adaptation f, METR slug m; ~ **in neck** n C&G limace au col f; ~ **tuning** n ELEC ENG adaptation par sonde réglable f, *oscillating circuit* accord par noyau plongeur m, accord par noyau réglable m

slugged: ~ **bottom** n C&G fond en coin m

slugging n CHEM bouillonnage m, REFRIG coup de liquide m, SPRINGS ébauchage m

sluice n FUELLESS *dams* vanne f, MINING sluice m, NAUT *canal* pertuis m, vanne f, écluse f, RECYCLING vanne f, écluse f, WATER SUPP canal m, pertuis m, vanne f, écluse f; ~ **box** n WATER SUPP auge f

sluicegate n FUELLESS vanne f, NAUT *lock* écluse f, WATER SUPP vanne f

sluicevalve *n* WATER SUPP robinet-vanne *m*, vannelle *f*, vantelle *f*

sluiceway *n* WATER SUPP canal *m*

sluicing *n* WATER SUPP lavage aux sluices *m*

slump: ~ **cone** *n* CONST cône pour le slump-test *m*

slung: ~ **bucket** *n* MAR POLL cuve suspendue *f*; ~ **pump** *n* MINING pompe suspendue *f*, pompe volante *f*

slur *n* PRINT doublage par gain excessif du point *m*

slurry *n* C&G boue liquide *f*, COAL TECH pulpe *f*, schlamms *m*, DETERGENTS résidu *m*, FOOD TECH *machinery* bouillie *f*, crème *f*, MECH ENG boue *f*, liquide chargé *m*, MINING bouillie *f*, bouillie explosive *f*, explosif en bouillie *m*, PAPER TECH lait de couchage *m*, sauce de couchage *f*, RECYCLING purin *m*; ~ **explosive** *n (SE)* MINING bouillie explosive *f*, explosif de chargement *m*, explosif en bouillie *m*; ~ **pond** *n* COAL TECH bassin de décantation des boues *m*, bassin à boue *m*, bassin à schlamms *m*; ~ **pump** *n* MINING pompe à schlamms *f*; ~ **seal** *n* CONST scellement à coulis *m*; ~ **tanker** *n* TRANSP transporteur de minerai sous forme liquide *m*; ~ **trench wall** *n* COAL TECH paroi moulée *f*; ~ **trough** *n* PETR bac à boue *m*

slurry-blasting: ~ **agent** *n (SBA)* MINING bouillie explosive *f*, explosif de chargement *m*, explosif en bouillie *m*

slush *n* HYDROL bouillie neigeuse *f*, MINING remblai d'embouage *m*, REFRIG neige fondante *f*; ~ **ice** *n* REFRIG glace-neige mouillée *f*; ~ **molding** *n* (AmE), ~ **moulding** *n* (BrE) P&R *process* moulage des pâtes *m*, moulage par embouage *m*; ~ **propellant** *n* SPACE *propulsion* ergol en bouillie *m*; ~ **pump** *n* PETR TECH pompe de circulation *f*, pompe à boue *f*

slusher *n* MINING racleur *m*

slushing *n* PAPER TECH trituration *f*

Sm *(samarium)* CHEM Sm *(samarium)*

SM *abbr (synchronous multiplexer)* TELECOM multiplexeur synchrone *m*

SMAE *abbr (system management application entity)* TELECOM entité d'application de gestion de systèmes *f*

small *n* MINING charbon menu *m*, grésillon *m*, menu *m*, menu de houille *m*, grésillon *m*; ~ **angle prism** *n* PHYS prisme de petit angle *m*; ~ **angle scattering** *n* CRYSTALL diffusion aux petits angles *f*; ~ **arms** *n pl* MILIT armes portatives *f pl*; ~ **bar mill** *n* PROD ENG *rolling* petit laminoir *m*, petit train *m*, train de petits fers *m*; ~ **batch production** *n* MECH ENG fabrication de petits lots *f*; ~ **caps** *n pl* PRINT petites capitales *f pl*; ~ **coal** *n* COAL TECH charbon menu *m*, menu brut *m*, MINING charbon menu *m*, charbonnaille *f*, grésillon *m*, menu *m*, menu de houille *m*; ~ **coal without fines** *n* COAL TECH menu grenu *m*; ~ **end** *n* AUTO pied de bielle *m*, MECH ENG *connecting rod* petite tête *f*, pied *m*, VEHICLES *connecting rod* pied de bielle *m*; ~ **end bush** *n* AUTO bague de pied de bielle *f*, VEHICLES *connecting rod* bague de pied de bielle *f*, douille de pied de bielle *f*; ~ **parcels** *n pl* RAIL *vehicles* messageries *f pl*; ~ **signal** *n* ELECTRON petit signal *m*, signal de faible amplitude *m*; ~ **slam** *n* PETR petit schelem *m*; ~ **stream** *n* HYDROL ruisselet *m*; ~ **stuff** *n* NAUT *ropes* filin *m*; ~ **tip wagon** *n* (BrE) *(cf spoil car)* RAIL *vehicles* wagonnet *m*; ~ **tools** *n pl* MECH ENG petit outillage *m*; ~ **wall** *n* CONST muret *m*

Small: ~ **Magellanic Cloud** *n (cf Magellanic Clouds)* ASTRON petit nuage de Magellan *m*

small-gain: ~ **amplifier** *n* ELECTRON amplificateur à faible gain *m*

smalls *n pl* COAL TECH fines *f pl*

small-scale [1] *adj* GEOL à petite échelle, NAUT *chart* à petit point, à petite échelle

small-scale [2] ~ **integration** *n (SSI)* COMP intégration à petite échelle *f*, DP intégration à faible échelle *f*, ELECTRON intégration à petite échelle *f*

small-signal: ~ **amplification** *n* ELECTRON amplification de petits signaux *f*; ~ **amplifier** *n* ELECTRON amplificateur de petits signaux *m*; ~ **parameter** *n* ELECTRON paramètre pour signaux de faible amplitude *m*; ~ **transistor** *n* ELECTRON transistor pour petits signaux *m*

smaltite *n* MINERAL smaltite *f*

smaragdite *n* MINERAL smaragdite *f*

smart: ~ **bomb** *n* MILIT bombe guidée *f*; ~ **card** *n* COMP, DP carte à mémoire *f*; ~ **card reader** *n* TELECOM lecture de carte à mémoire *f*; ~ **shell** *n* MILIT obus guidé *m*; ~ **terminal** *n* COMP, DP terminal intelligent *m*; ~ **weapon** *n* MILIT arme intelligente *f*

SMAW *abbr (shielded metal arc welding)* NUCLEAR soudage à l'arc avec électrode enrobée *m*

SMC *abbr (surface-mounted component)* ELECTRON, TELECOM CMS *(composant monté en surface)*

SMDS *abbr (switched multimegabit data service)* TELECOM service commuté de données multimégabit *m*

smearing *n* PRINT maculage *m*, TV filage *m*

smectic: ~ **liquid crystals** *n pl* ELECTRON cristaux liquides smectiques *m pl*; ~ **phase** *n* CRYSTALL phase smectique *f*

smectite *n* CHEM argile smectique *f*, smectite *f*, terre à foulon *f*, COAL TECH, PETR TECH smectite *f*

smelt [1] *vt* PAPER TECH fondre

smelt [2] *vi* HEATING fondre

smelter *n* PROD ENG *person* fondeur *m*

smelting *n* COAL TECH fusion-réduction *f*, HEATING fonte *f*, PROP MAT fusion *f*; ~ **furnace** *n* ELEC ENG four de fusion *m*

SMF *abbr (submultiframe)* TELECOM sous-multitrame *m*

SMIB *abbr (security management information base)* TELECOM base d'informations de gestion de sécurité *f*

smith *n* CONST forgeron *m*, maréchal *m*, maréchal-ferrant *m*

Smith: ~ **chart** *n* PHYS diagramme de Smith *m*

smith's: ~ **pliers** *n pl* CONST tenaille à forger *f*

smithery *n* CONST assemblages de charpente en fer *m pl*

smithsonite *n* MINERAL smithsonite *f*

smithy *n* CONST atelier de forge *m*, atelier de forgeron *m*, atelier de maréchal ferrant *m*, forge *f*, maréchalerie *f*

SMN *abbr (SDH management network)* TELECOM réseau de gestion SDH *m*

smog *n* POLLUTION smog *m*

smoke *n* C&G traînées colorées *f pl*, HEAT ENG, POLLUTION, SAFETY *fumes* fumée *f*; ~ **alarm** *n* SAFETY alarme à la fumée *f*, alerte à la fumée *f*; ~ **and gas alarm installation** *n* SAFETY avertisseur de fumée et de gaz *m*; ~ **and heat exhaust installation** *n* SAFETY installation d'évacuation de fumée et de chaleur *f*; ~ **and heat extraction system** *n* SAFETY installation d'évacuation de fumée et de chaleur *f*; ~ **arch** *n* HEAT ENG boîte à fumée *f*; ~ **bomb** *n* MILIT bombe fumigène *f*; ~ **box** *n* CONST *of locomotive*, HEAT ENG, RAIL *vehicles* boîte à fumée *f*; ~ **candle** *n* CINEMAT fusée à fumée *f*; ~ **chart** *n* SAFETY *classification* graphique de fumée *m*, table des fumées *f*; ~ **control** *n* SAFETY contrôle des fumées *m*, désenfumage *m*; ~ **detector** *n* SAFETY détecteur de fumée *m*; ~ **gas desulfuration installation** *n* (AmE), ~ **gas desulphuration installation** *n* (BrE) SAFETY installation de désulfuration de gaz de fumée *f*; ~ **grenade** *n* MILIT grenade fumigène *f*; ~ **helmet** *n* SAFETY casque antifumée *m*, casque respiratoire *m*; ~ **mask** *n* AERONAUT masque antifumée *m*; ~ **protection door** *n* SAFETY porte d'isolation contre les fumées *f*; ~ **screen** *n* MILIT brouillard artificiel *m*, rideau de fumée *m*, rideau fumigène *m*; ~ **tube** *n* HEAT ENG tube de fumée *m*

smoked: ~ **glass** *n* C&G verre fumé *m*

smokeless[1] *adj* SAFETY sans fumée

smokeless:[2] ~ **fuel** *n* POLLUTION combustible non fumigène *m*; ~ **zone** *n* POLLUTION zone où les foyers ouverts sont interdits *f*

smokestack: ~ **first** *adv* RAIL *vehicles* tender en arrière

smoking *n* FOOD TECH boucanage *m*, fumage *m*, fumaison *f*

smoky: ~ **quartz** *n* MINERAL quartz enfumé *m*, quartz fumé *m*

smolder *vi* (AmE) *see* smoulder

smoldering: ~ **fire** *n* (AmE) *see* smouldering fire

smooth[1] *adj* PAPER TECH lisse

smooth:[2] ~ **blasting** *n* MINING tir périmétrique *m*; ~ **braking** *n* RAIL *vehicles* freinage sans à-coups *m*; ~ **core armature** *n* ELEC *generator, motor* induit lisse *m*; ~ **drift** *n* MECH ENG mandrin lisse *m*; ~ **finish** *n* PAPER TECH satinage *m*; ~ **grinding** *n* C&G doucissage *m*; ~ **operation** *n* PROD ENG fonctionnement sans à-coups *m*; ~ **plain packing** *n* C&G empilage en cheminées *m*; ~ **roller** *n* CONST cylindre lisse *m*, rouleau lisse *m*; ~ **traffic** *n* TELECOM trafic régularisé *m*; ~ **wall blasting** *n* MINING tir périmétrique *m*

smoothbore: ~ **gun** *n* MILIT fusil non rayé *m*

smoothed: ~ **edge** *n* C&G joint douci *m*

smoothing *n* C&G *of hollow glass* taille *f*, *of polished plate* savonnage *m*, COMP, DP, ELECTRON lissage *m*, PROD ENG lissage *m*, nivellement *m*; ~ **capacitor** *n* ELEC condensateur de filtrage *m*; ~ **choke** *n* ELEC inductor self de filtrage *f*, ELEC ENG bobine de lissage *f*; ~ **circuit** *n* ELEC circuit de lissage *m*; ~ **factor** *n* PROD ENG facteur de lissage *m*; ~ **factor for trend** *n* PROD ENG facteur de lissage de tendance *m*; ~ **filter** *n* ELECTRON filtre de lissage *m*; ~ **press** *n* PAPER TECH presse lisseuse *f*, presse offset *f*; ~ **resistor** *n* ELEC résistance de lissage *f*; ~ **roll** *n* PAPER TECH lisse *f*; ~ **roll coating** *n* PAPER TECH couchage par rouleaux lisseurs *m*

smoothness *n* PAPER TECH lissé *m*; ~ **tester** *n* PAPER TECH appareil de mesure du lissé *m*

smother *vt* THERMOD *fire* éteindre, étouffer

smoulder *vi* (BrE) THERMOD *fire* brûler lentement, couver

smouldering: ~ **fire** *n* (BrE) THERMOD feu couvant *m*

SMPTE: ~ **time code** *n* CINEMAT code horaire SMPTE *m*, TV code temporel SMPTE *m*

SMS *abbr* (*SDH management subnetwork*) TELECOM sous-réseau de gestion SDH *m*

smudge *n* PRINT saleté *f*, tache *f*

smudging *n* PRINT maculage *m*

Sn (*tin*) CHEM Sn (*étain*)

SN *abbr* TELECOM (*subscriber number*) numéro d'abonné *m*, TELECOM (*sequence number*) numéro de séquence *m*

SNA *abbr* (*systems network architecture*) COMP, DP architecture unifiée de réseau *f*

snag *n* TEXTILES accroc *m*

snake *n* C&G casse en long *f*

snaking *n* AERONAUT *aerodynamics* oscillation de lacet *f*,

C&G serpentage *m*; ~ **columns** *n pl* PRINT colonnes en serpent comportant des lézardes *f pl*

snap[1] *n* C&G croquage *m*; ~ **cap** *n* PACKAGING capsule à encliqueter *f*; ~ **hinge closure** *n* PACKAGING fermeture avec charnière à enclenchement *f*; ~ **lock** *n* PROD ENG dispositif de blocage à déclic *m*; ~ **perforation** *n* PRINT perforation destinée à céder sous la traction de la main *f*; ~ **shackle** *n* NAUT *fittings, rigging* manille rapide *f*, mousqueton *m*

snap[2] *vt* PROD ENG enclencher

snap-action[1] *adj* PROD ENG à rupture brusque

snap-action:[2] ~ **contact** *n* PROD ENG contact à déclic *m*, contact à rupture brusque *m*; ~ **switch** *n* ELEC ENG interrupteur à passage de point mort *m*; ~ **valve** *n* REFRIG vanne instantanée *f*

snap-gage *n* (AmE), **snap-gauge** *n* (BrE) METR calibre à mâchoires *m*

snap-in: ~ **socket** *n* ELEC ENG douille à encliqueter *f*; ~ **switch** *n* ELEC ENG interrupteur à encliqueter *m*

snap-off: ~ **closure** *n* PACKAGING fermeture à détente *f*; ~ **diode** *n* ELECTRON diode à coupure brusque *f*

snap-on[1] *adj* PROD ENG encliquetable, instantané

snap-on:[2] ~ **closure** *n* PACKAGING fermeture à encliquetage *f*; ~ **lid** *n* PACKAGING couvercle à enclenchement *m*

snap-out *n* PRINT technique de détachement de la feuille de son talon *f*

snapping *n* C&G croquage par cisaillement *m*

snappy: ~ **rubber** *n* P&R caoutchouc nerveux *m*

snapshot *n* COMP, DP instantané *m*; ~ **dump** *n* COMP, DP vidage à la demande *m*

snarl[1] *n* TEXTILES *twisted* fil vrillé *m*

snarl[2] *vt* TEXTILES emmêler

SNDCF *abbr* (*subnetwork dependent convergence function*) TELECOM fonction de convergence dépendant du sous-réseau *f*

Snell's: ~ **law** *n* PHYS loi de Descartes-Snell *f*

SNG *abbr* (*substitute natural gas, synthetic natural gas*) GAS TECH, PETR TECH GNS (*gaz naturel de synthèse*)

sniffer: ~ **device** *n* GAS TECH nez renifleur *m*

sniper *n* MILIT tireur embusqué *m*, tireur isolé *m*

snoot *n* CINEMAT coupe-flux cylindrique *m*

snorkel *n* CINEMAT périscope *m*, snorkel *m*, OCEANOG tuba *m*

snow[1] *n* ELECTRON, METEO, REFRIG, TV *on video or TV image* neige *f*; ~ **barrier** *n* CONST barrière pare-neige *f*; ~ **belt** *n* METEO région neigeuse *f*, zone neigeuse *f*; ~ **blower** *n* TRANSP chasse-neige rotatif *m*; ~ **cover** *n* METEO couverture neigeuse *f*, enneigement *m*; ~ **detector** *n* TRANSP détecteur de neige *m*; ~ **flurry** *n* METEO bourrasque de neige *f*, rafale de neige *f*; ~ **gun** *n* REFRIG canon à neige *m*; ~ **line** *n* METEO limite des neiges *f*, limite des neiges éternelles *f*; ~ **loading** *n* CONST surcharge neige *f*; ~ **machine** *n* CINEMAT canon à neige *m*; ~ **melt** *n* (AmE) (*cf snow water*) WATER SUPP eau de fonte *f*, eau de fusion *f*; ~ **storage** *n* HYDROL emmagasinement nival *m*; ~ **tire** *n* (AmE), ~ **tyre** *n* (BrE) VEHICLES pneu neige *m*; ~ **water** *n* (BrE) (*cf snow melt*) WATER SUPP eau de fonte *f*, eau de fusion *f*

snow[2] *vi* METEO neiger

snowdrift *n* METEO congère *f*

snowed: ~ **up** *adj* METEO enneigé

snowfall *n* METEO chute de neige *f*, nivosité *f*

snowflake: ~ **curve** *n* GEOM courbe en flocon de neige *f*; ~ **topology** *n* COMP, DP topologie en flocon de neige *f*

snow-ice *n* REFRIG glace-neige *f*

snowstorm n METEO tempête de neige f

snowy adj METEO neigeux, nival

SNP abbr (sequence number protection) TELECOM protection de numéro de séquence f

SNR abbr (signal-to-noise ratio) ACOUSTICS, COMP, DP, ELECTRON, PETR, PHYS, RECORDING, TELECOM, TV rapport signal-bruit m

snubber n MECH, SPACE spacecraft amortisseur m; ~ **capacitor** n ELEC ENG condensateur d'amortissement m; ~ **circuit** n ELEC ENG circuit d'amortissement m; ~ **resistor** n ELEC ENG résistance d'amortissement f

snubbing n PETR TECH curage m, descente sous pression f

SO: ~ **character** n (shift-out character) COMP caractère de code spécial m, caractère hors-code m, DP caractère de code spécial m

soak[1] vt C&G pot chambrer, FOOD TECH, PAPER TECH tremper, TEXTILES faire tremper, laisser tremper

soak[2] vi TEXTILES tremper

soaking n PAPER TECH, TEXTILES trempage m; ~ **pit** n C&G for optical glass cloche de refroidissement f, for cast glass four de braise m, WATER SUPP puits d'infiltration m

soaking-drying: ~ **cycle** n CONST cycle d'immersion-séchage m

soap n CHEM, TEXTILES savon m; ~ **and water solution** n SAFETY for leak detection in gas cylinders eau savonneuse f; ~ **mold** n (AmE), ~ **mould** n (BrE) MECH ENG moule pour la savonnerie m

soapstone n MINERAL pierre de savon f

societal: ~ **risk** n QUALITY risque social m

socket[1] n CINEMAT douille f, prise f, CONST of shovel douille f, ELEC connection prise de courant f, ELEC ENG for electric lamps douille f, ELECTRON fiche femelle f, prise de courant f, MECH douille f, logement m, MECH ENG bar hole of capstan logement de barre m, mortaise f, drill socket douille f, manchon m, of bit stock baril m, MINING culot m, PHYS fiche femelle f, prise de courant f, PROD ENG prise f, TV douille f; ~ **adaptor** n ELEC ENG for electronic tubes adaptateur de culot m, adaptateur de douille m; ~ **board** n ELEC ENG fond de panier m; ~ **bushed with gun metal** n MECH ENG assemblage à douille m; ~ **cap** n C&G capuchon en verre m; ~ **contact** n ELEC ENG contact femelle m; ~ **coupler** n ELEC connection prise femelle du prolongateur f; ~ **flange** n MECH ENG pipe fittings emboîtement à bride m; ~ **joint** n MECH raccord à emboîtement m, MECH ENG assemblage à douille m, ball-and-socket joint joint à calotte sphérique m, joint à genou m, joint à rotule m, joint à rotule sphérique f, jointure sphérique f, PAPER TECH joint sphérique m; ~ **outlet** n TELECOM prise f, prise enfichable f; ~ **pipe** n CONST conduite à emboîtement f, conduite à joints à emboîtements f, tuyau à emboîtement m; ~ **plug** n ELEC connection prise mâle du prolongateur f; ~ **punch** n PROD ENG découpoir m, emporte-pièce m; ~ **spanner** n (BrE) (cf socket wrench) MECH clé à douille f; ~ **with shrouded contacts** n ELEC connection prise à collet f; ~ **wrench** n MECH tools clé à douille f, MECH ENG clé à béquille f, clé à douille f

socket[2] vt CONST pipes emboîter

soda n C&G, CHEM, PAPER TECH soude f; ~ **acid fire extinguisher** n SAFETY extincteur d'incendie à acide carbonique m, extincteur d'incendie à neige carbonique m; ~ **ash** n CHEM cendre de soude f, DETERGENTS cristaux de soude m pl, soude calcinée f, PAPER TECH carbonate de soude m; ~ **lime** n CHEM chaux sodée f; ~ **niter** n (AmE), ~ **nitre** n (BrE) C&G nitrate de sodium m, MINERAL natronitre m; ~ **pulp** n PAPER TECH pâte à la soude f

soda-alum n CHEM alun de sodium m, alun de soude m

soda-chlorine: ~ **pulp** n PAPER TECH pâte au chlore f

sodalite n MINERAL, PROP MAT sodalite f

sodamide n CHEM amide de sodium m, amidure de sodium m

sodic adj CHEM, GEOL sodique

sodium n (Na) CHEM sodium m (Na); ~ **alginate** n FOOD TECH alginate de sodium m; ~ **bicarbonate** n CHEM, DETERGENTS, FOOD TECH bicarbonate de sodium m; ~ **borate** n CHEM borate de sodium m, borate de soude m; ~ **carbonate** n CHEM carbonate de soude m, DETERGENTS carbonate de sodium m, carbonate de soude m, PAPER TECH carbonate de soude m; ~ **caseinate** n FOOD TECH caséinate de sodium m; ~ **chloride** n CHEM, DETERGENTS chlorure de sodium m; ~ **D-line** n PHYS raie D du sodium f; ~ **hydroxide** n CHEM soude f, soude caustique f; ~ **lamp** n ELEC lighting lampe à sodium f; ~ **nitrate** n C&G nitrate de sodium m, CHEM azotate de sodium m, azotate de soude m, nitrate de sodium m, nitrate de soude m; ~ **polyphosphate** n FOOD TECH polyphosphate de sodium m; ~ **salt** n CHEM sel sodique m; ~ **sesquicarbonate** n DETERGENTS trona m, urao m; ~ **silicate** n DETERGENTS silicate de sodium m; ~ **sulfate** n (AmE) see sodium sulphate; ~ **sulfur storage battery** n (AmE) see sodium sulphur storage battery; ~ **sulphate** n (BrE) CHEM sulfate de sodium m, DETERGENTS sulfate neutre de sodium m; ~ **sulphur storage battery** n (BrE) TRANSP accumulateur sodium soufre m; ~ **thiosulfate** n (AmE), ~ **thiosulphate** n (BrE) CHEM hyposulfite de soude m, thiosulfate de sodium m

sodium-cooled: ~ **reactor** n NUCLEAR réacteur refroidi au sodium m; ~ **valve** n AUTO solénoïde m

sodium-vapor: ~ **lamp** n (AmE), **sodium-vapour lamp** n (BrE) CINEMAT lampe au sodium f, RAD PHYS lampe à vapeur de sodium f

soffit n CONST of arch douelle f, intrados m, underside of floor soffite m

soft: ~ **anneal** n THERMOD metals recuit complet m, recuit d'adoucissement m, recuit de coalescence m; ~ **annealing** n METALL recuit d'adoucissement m; ~ **brass solder** n PROD ENG brasure douce f, brasure tendre f; ~ **bromide paper** n PHOTO papier au bromure donnant doux m; ~ **coal** n COAL TECH charbon gras m, charbon tendre m; ~ **copy** n COMP image d'écran f, image vidéo f, DP image d'écran f, présentation visuelle f; ~ **cut** n CINEMAT fondu très court m; ~ **decision decoding** n TELECOM décodage à décision douce m, décodage à décision programmable m; ~ **developer** n PHOTO révélateur doux m; ~ **dot** n PRINT point imprécis m, point mou m; ~ **error** n COMP, DP erreur logicielle f; ~ **fail** n COMP panne douce f; ~ **fire** n C&G flamme molle f; ~ **focus** n CINEMAT flou, flou artistique m; ~ **fruit** n FOOD TECH fruits rouges m pl; ~ **glass** n C&G verre tendre m; ~ **grade** n PROD ENG emery wheels degré de dureté tendre m; ~ **ground** n CONST sol tendre m, terrain meuble m; ~ **hail** n METEO neige roulée f; ~ **handle** n TEXTILES toucher doux m; ~ **iron** n ELEC ENG, PHYS fer doux m; ~ **key** n COMP, DP touche programmable f; ~ **keyboard** n COMP, DP clavier programmable m; ~ **landing** n SPACE amarrage doux m, atterrissage doux m; ~ **light** n CINEMAT lumière douce f, lumière tamisée f; ~ **magnetic material** n ELEC ENG, PHYS matériau magnétique doux *m*; ~ **metal hammer** *n* PROD ENG marteau en métal tendre *m*; ~ **mock-up** *n* SPACE maquette d'agencement *f*; ~ **packing seal** *n* MECH ENG garniture à tresse *f*; ~ **porcelain** *n* C&G porcelaine tendre *f*; ~ **proof** *n* PRINT épreuve écran *f*; ~ **radiation** *n* RAD PHYS rayonnement mou *m*; ~ **return** *n* PRINT retour-chariot *m*; ~ **sectoring** *n* COMP, DP sectorisation logicielle *f*; ~ **snow** *n* METEO neige douce *f*; ~ **solder** *n* ELEC *connection* claire soudure *f*; ~ **soldering** *n* ELEC *connection*, PROD ENG *connection* brasage tendre *m*; ~ **source** *n* CINEMAT projecteur d'ambiance *m*; ~ **start** *n* PROD ENG mise en marche progressive *f*; ~ **superconductor** *n* ELECTRON supraconducteur de première espèce *m*; ~ **tissue** *n* PAPER TECH tissu ouaté *m*; ~ **tube** *n* ELECTRON tube à vide partiel *m*; ~ **water** *n* WATER SUPP eau douce *f*; ~ **wheel** *n* PROD ENG meule tendre *f*; ~ **X-ray** *n* PHYS, RAD PHYS rayon X mou *m*

soft-annealed *adj* SPRINGS recuit doux

soft-bound *adj* PRINT broché

soft-brazing: ~ **solder** *n* PROD ENG brasure douce *f*, brasure tendre *f*

soft-cover: ~ **binding** *n* PRINT reliure souple *f*

soften *vt* CONST *water* adoucir, PAPER TECH amollir

softener *n* P&R *additive* plastifiant *m*, TEXTILES adoucisseur *m*

softening *n* GAS TECH ramollissement *m*, PROP MAT adoucissement *m*; ~ **agent** *n* TEXTILES produit adoucissant *m*, produit assouplissant *m*; ~ **furnace** *n* C&G four de ramollissement *m*; ~ **point** *n* P&R, REFRIG, TEXTILES point de ramollissement *m*; ~ **range** *n* C&G intervalle de ramollissement *m*

soft-focus: ~ **lens** *n* CINEMAT lentille de flou *f*, INSTRUMENT lentille de flou *f*, lentille diffusante *f*, PHOTO bonnette diffusante *f*, lentille de flou *f*, objectif à flou artistique *m*

soft-iron: ~ **core** *n* ELEC ENG noyau de fer doux *m*

soft-sectored[1] *adj* COMP sectorisé par programme, DP à sectorisation logicielle

soft-sectored:[2] ~ **disk** *n* COMP disquette à secteurs définis par programme *f*, DP disquette à sectorisation logicielle *f*

soft-solder: ~ **alloy** *n* MECH ENG alliage de brasage tendre *m*

software *n* COMP, DP, ELEC logiciel *m*, PETR software *m*, PHYS, TV logiciel *m*; ~ **adaptation** *n* COMP, DP adaptation du logiciel *f*; ~ **configuration** *n* COMP, DP configuration logicielle *f*; ~ **design** *n* COMP, DP conception logicielle *f*; ~ **development** *n* COMP, DP développement de logiciel *m*; ~ **engineering** *n* COMP, DP ingénierie logicielle *f*; ~ **interrupt** *n* COMP, DP interruption programmée *f*; ~ **package** *n* COMP, DP, PHYS progiciel *m*; ~ **products** *n pl* TELECOM produits logiciels *m pl*; ~ **resources** *n pl* COMP, DP ressources logicielles *f pl*; ~ **tool** *n* COMP, DP outil logiciel *m*

softwood *n* CONST bois tendre *m*, NAUT bois doux *m*, PAPER TECH bois de résineux *m*; ~ **pulp** *n* PAPER TECH pâte de bois de résineux *f*

soggy *adj* PAPER TECH saturé d'eau

SOH *abbr* COMP *(start of header)*, DP *(start of header)* début *m*, TELECOM *(section overhead)* SDS *(surdébit de section)*

soil *n* COAL TECH, GEOPHYS sol *m*; ~ **exploration** *n* COAL TECH reconnaissance du sol *f*; ~ **freezing** *n* REFRIG gel du sol *m*; ~ **mechanics** *n* COAL TECH, CONST, GEOL mécanique des sols *f*; ~ **pipe** *n* WATER SUPP tuyau d'assainissement *m*; ~ **pollutants** *n pl* POLLUTION pol-luants des sols *m pl*; ~ **pollution** *n* POLLUTION pollution des sols *f*; ~ **pressure** *n* COAL TECH pression exercée sur le sol *f*; ~ **science** *n* COAL TECH, WATER SUPP pédologie *f*; ~ **skeleton** *n* COAL TECH squelette du sol *m*; ~ **stabilization** *n* CONST stabilisation des sols *f*; ~ **water** *n* WATER SUPP eau du sol *f*

soil-release: ~ **finish** *n* COATINGS apprêt antisalissant *m*

solanidine *n* CHEM solanidine *f*

solar[1] *adj* ASTRON *of sun*, CONST solaire

solar:[2] ~ **absorber** *n* SPACE *spacecraft* absorbeur solaire *m*; ~ **absorption coefficient** *n* FUELLESS coefficient d'absorption solaire *m*; ~ **absorptivity** *n* FUELLESS absorptivité solaire *f*; ~ **activity** *n* ASTRON, PHYS activité solaire *f*; ~ **altitude** *n* FUELLESS hauteur du soleil au-dessus de l'horizon *f*; ~ **altitude angle** *n* FUELLESS hauteur du soleil sur l'horizon *f*; ~ **apex** *n* ASTRON apex *m*; ~ **atmosphere** *n* ASTRON atmosphère du soleil *f*; ~ **azimuth** *n* FUELLESS azimut solaire *m*; ~ **battery** *n* FUELLESS batterie solaire *f*, TV batterie solaire *f*, pile solaire *f*; ~ **cell** *n* ASTRON pile solaire *f*, ELEC photopile *f*, pile solaire *f*, ELEC ENG, FUELLESS cellule solaire *f*, PHYS cellule solaire *f*, pile solaire *f*, RAD PHYS pile solaire *f*, SPACE *spacecraft*, TELECOM, THERMOD cellule solaire *f*; ~ **cell panel** *n* ELEC ENG panneau de cellules solaires *m*, panneau solaire *m*; ~ **collector** *n* CONST *building*, FUELLESS capteur solaire *m*, MECH ENG capteur solaire *m*, collecteur solaire *m*; ~ **concentrator** *n* FUELLESS concentrateur solaire *m*, INSTRUMENT miroir concentrateur *m*; ~ **constant** *n* ASTRON, FUELLESS, GEOPHYS, SPACE constante solaire *f*; ~ **control glass** *n* C&G vitrage solaire *m*; ~ **corona** *n* GEOPHYS couronne solaire *f*; ~ **cycle** *n* ASTRON, GEOPHYS cycle solaire *m*; ~ **day** *n* METR jour solaire *m*; ~ **distillation** *n* FUELLESS distillation solaire *f*; ~ **dynamics** *n* FUELLESS héliodynamique *f*; ~ **eclipse** *n* ASTRON éclipse du soleil *f*; ~ **electricity** *n* ELEC ENG électricité solaire *f*; ~ **electric power plant** *n* ELEC ENG centrale héliogénératrice *f*, centrale électrosolaire *f*; ~ **electric power station** *n* ELEC ENG centrale héliogénératrice *f*, centrale électrosolaire *f*, usine électrosolaire *f*; ~ **energy** *n* ASTRON, ELEC ENG, FUELLESS, PHYS énergie solaire *f*; ~ **energy conversion** *n* ELEC ENG conversion de l'énergie solaire *f*; ~ **engineering** *n* FUELLESS ingénierie solaire *f*; ~ **farm** *n* FUELLESS centrale solaire *f*; ~ **flare** *n* ASTRON facule solaire *f*, GEOPHYS, SPACE éruption solaire *f* ~ **furnace** *n* FUELLESS four solaire *m*; ~ **generator** *n* ELEC ENG générateur solaire *m*, héliogénérateur *m*, SPACE *spacecraft* générateur solaire *m*; ~ **granulation** *n* ASTRON granulation de la surface solaire *f*; ~ **heat** *n* FUELLESS chaleur solaire *f*; ~ **heating** *n* ASTRON chauffage solaire *m*; ~ **heating system** *n* FUELLESS chauffage solaire *m*; ~ **longitude** *n* ASTRON longitude solaire *f*; ~ **magnetic field** *n* ASTRON champ magnétique du soleil *m*, champ magnétique solaire *m*; ~ **mass** *n* ASTRON masse solaire *f*; ~ **mass black hole** *n* ASTRON trou noir d'une masse solaire *m*; ~ **panel** *n* ASTRON, FUELLESS, PHYS, SPACE *spacecraft*, TELECOM panneau solaire *m*; ~ **pond** *n* FUELLESS bassin solaire *m*; ~ **power** *n* PHYS énergie solaire *f*; ~ **power farm** *n* ELEC ENG ferme solaire *f*; ~ **proton** *n* GEOPHYS proton solaire *m*; ~ **radiation** *n* FUELLESS, GEOPHYS, POLLUTION, RAD PHYS rayonnement solaire *m*; ~ **radiation pressure** *n* SPACE *spacecraft* pression du rayonnement solaire *f*; ~ **sail** *n* SPACE *spacecraft* voile solaire *f*; ~ **sensor** *n* SPACE détecteur solaire *m*; ~ **storm** *n* GEOPHYS orage solaire *m*; ~ **system** *n* ASTRON système solaire *m*; ~ **technology**

n FUELLESS héliotechnique *f*; ~ **telescope** *n* INSTRU-MENT télescope solaire *m*; ~ **telescope tower** *n* INSTRUMENT tour de télescope solaire *f*; ~ **thermal conversion** *n* FUELLESS conversion thermodynamique de l'énergie solaire *f*, conversion thermodynamique du rayonnement solaire *f*; ~ **tide** *n* GEOPHYS marée atmosphérique solaire *f*; ~ **tower** *n* FUELLESS tour solaire *f*; ~ **water heater** *n* MECH ENG chauffe-eau solaire *m*; ~ **wind** *n* ASTRON, GEOPHYS, PHYS, SPACE vent solaire *m*; ~ **year** *n* ASTRON année solaire *f*

solarimeter *n* FUELLESS solarimètre *m*

solarization *n* CINEMAT, PHOTO solarisation *f*

solar-powered *adj* ELEC ENG hélioalimenté, à énergie solaire, FUELLESS alimenté par énergie solaire, à énergie solaire

solar-sail: ~ **propulsion** *n* SPACE propulsion à voile solaire *f*

solder[1] *n* ELEC ENG soudure à l'étain *f*; ~ **glass** *n* (AmE) *(cf intermediate sealing glass)* C&G verre intermédiaire *m*; ~ **joint** *n* PROD ENG joint de plomb *m*; ~ **tag** *n* PROD ENG cosse à souder *f*

solder[2] *vt* CONST braser, souder

solderable[1] *adj* PROD ENG soudable

solderable:[2] ~ **lacquer** *n* COATINGS vernis soudable *m*

soldered: ~ **fitting** *n* MECH ENG garniture soudée *f*; ~ **seam** *n* FOOD TECH *of can* soudure *f*; ~ **side** *n* TELECOM côté de soudure *m*

solderer *n* PROD ENG *person* soudeur *m*

soldering *n* CONST brasage *m*, brasement *m*, soudage *m*, PRINT soudure à l'étain *f*, PROD ENG soudage *m*, soudure *f*, PROP MAT soudage *m*; ~ **bit** *n* MECH ENG, PROD ENG fer à souder *m*; ~ **blowpipe** *n* CONST chalumeau braseur *m*, chalumeau soudage *m*; ~ **copper** *n* PROD ENG fer à souder *m*; ~ **flux** *n* ELEC *connections* flux décapant *m*, ELEC ENG flux à souder *m*; ~ **gun** *n* ELEC *connection* fer à souder *m*; ~ **iron** *n* CONST fer à braser *m*, fer à souder *m*, ELEC *connection*, PROD ENG fer à souder *m*; ~ **joint** *n* PROD ENG joint de plomb *m*

soldier-block *n* C&G bloc en palissade *m*

sole *n* CONST *of plane*, GEOL *of thrust* semelle *f*, MINING semelle *f*, *of mine level* sole *f*, PROD ENG *of furnace* sole *f*, *of plummer block* patin *m*, semelle *f*; ~ **inventor** *n* PATENTS seul inventeur *m*, unique inventeur *m*; ~ **piece** *n* CONST *building* couche *f*, couchis *m*, patin *m*, semelle *f*, sole *f*, MINING semelle *f*, sole *f*; ~ **plate** *n* CONST plaque d'assise *f*, plaque de base *f*, plaque de fondation *f*, semelle *f*, sole *f*, taque d'assise *f*, PROD ENG *of plummer block* patin *m*, semelle *f*, SPACE *spacecraft* semelle *f*

solenoid *n* ELEC *coil* solénoïde *m*, ELEC ENG *coil* solénoïde *m*, *electromagnet* électro-aimant à noyau-plongeur *m*, PHYS, PROD ENG, REFRIG solénoïde *m*, TV solénoïde *m*, électro-aimant *m*, VEHICLES *starter* solénoïde *m*; ~ **actuation** *n* ELEC ENG commande par électro-aimant à noyau-plongeur *f*; ~ **coil** *n* ELEC bobine solénoïde *f*, VEHICLES bobine d'électro-aimant *f*; ~ **relay** *n* ELEC, ELEC ENG relais à noyau plongeur *m*; ~ **stepper motor** *n* ELEC ENG moteur pas-à-pas à cliquet *m*; ~ **valve** *n* HYDR EQUIP électrodistributeur *m*, PROD ENG électrovanne *f*, REFRIG vanne à solénoïde *f*

solenoidal: ~ **field** *n* PHYS champ solénoïdal *m*

solenoid-operated: ~ **shut-off valve** *n* PROD ENG électrovanne de coupure *f*

solicited: ~ **information indicator** *n* TELECOM indicateur d'information demandée *m*

solid[1] *adj* CHEM solide, PROD ENG *wire* rigide, PROP MAT plein

solid[2] *n* CONST *ground* ferme *f*, terrain ferme *m*, GEOM *figure*, PHYS solide *m*, PRINT aplat *m*, PROD ENG masse *f*; ~ **aluminium capacitor** *n* (BrE) ELEC ENG condensateur à l'aluminium à électrolyte solide *m*; ~ **aluminum capacitor** *n* (AmE) *see solid aluminium capacitor*; ~ **angle** *n* GEOM angle polyèdre *m*, angle solide *m*, PHYS angle solide *m*; ~ **bifocals** *n pl* C&G verres bifocaux d'une seule pièce *m pl*; ~ **blank** *n* PROD ENG masse *f*; ~ **bloc** *n* PROD ENG monobloc *m*; ~ **board** *n* PAPER TECH carton homogène *m*; ~ **bond** *n* ELEC *shield bonding* connexion directe *f*; ~ **brick** *n* CONST brique pleine *f*; ~ **casting** *n* PROD ENG coulage plein *m*; ~ **color** *n* (AmE), ~ **colour** *n* (BrE) COLOURS teinte unie *f*; ~ **conductor** *n* ELEC *single wire cable conductor* âme massive *f*, ELEC ENG conducteur massif *m*; ~ **content** *n* PRINT teneur en produits solides *f*; ~ **cotter pin** *n* MECH ENG go upille pleine *f*; ~ **die** *n* MECH ENG *for engineer's die stock* lunette *f*, lunette à fileter *f*, lunette à tarauder *f*; ~ **dielectric** *n* ELEC ENG diélectrique solide *m*; ~ **die stock** *n* MECH ENG filière à coussinets-lunettes *f*, filière à lunettes *f*; ~ **electrolyte capacitor** *n* ELEC ENG condensateur à électrolyte solide *m*; ~ **exchanger** *n* COAL TECH échangeur solide *m*; ~ **expansion thermometer** *n* REFRIG thermomètre à dilatation solide *m*; ~ **fuel booster** *n* SPACE *spacecraft* moteur à poudre *m*; ~ **fuel heater** *n* MECH ENG réchauffeur à combustibles solides *m*; ~ **geometry** *n* GEOM géométrie dans l'espace *f*, géométrie à trois dimensions *f*; ~ **height** *n* SPRINGS hauteur à bloc *f*; ~ **hydrocarbons** *n pl* CHEM hydrocarbures solides *m pl*; ~ **ink density** *n* PRINT densité optique d'un aplat à 100% *f*; ~ **length** *n* SPRINGS longueur d'aplatissement *f*, longueur à spires jointives *f*, longueur à bloc *f*; ~ **letter** *n* PRINT *typeface* lettre pleine *f*; ~ **matter** *n* HYDROL *sewage* matière sèche *f*, résidu sec *m*; ~ **measure** *n* METR mesure de volume *f*; ~ **nuclear fuel** *n* NUCLEAR combustible solide *m*; ~ **object** *n* PROD ENG corps solide *m*; ~ **particles** *n pl* POLLUTION particules solides *f pl*; ~ **phase** *n* THERMOD phase solide *f*; ~ **pin** *n* MECH ENG goupille pleine *f*; ~ **piston** *n* HYDR EQUIP piston massif *m*, piston plein *m*, piston plongeur *m*; ~ **piston pump** *n* HYDR EQUIP pompe à piston plein *f*, pompe à plongeur *f*; ~ **position** *n* SPRINGS position solide *f*; ~ **propellant** *n* SPACE poudre *f*, *spacecraft* propergol solide *m*; ~ **propellant rocket** *n* SPACE *spacecraft* fusée à poudre *f*, propulseur à propergol solide *m*; ~ **propellant rocket engine** *n* MECH ENG moteur-fusée à propergol solide *m*; ~ **propellant system** *n* SPACE *spacecraft* filière à propulseurs solides *f*; ~ **pulley** *n* MECH ENG poulie en une pièce *f*; ~ **punch** *n* MECH ENG poinçon *m*; ~ **of revolution** *n* GEOM solide de révolution *m*; ~ **rotor** *n* ELEC *machine* rotor massif *m*; ~ **solution** *n* CHEM, CRYSTALL, GEOL solution solide *f*; ~ **spinning upper stage** *n* *(SSUS)* SPACE étage supérieur stabilisé par rotation *m*; ~ **synchrotransformer** *n* ELEC ENG synchrotransformateur *m*; ~ **tantalum capacitor** *n* ELEC ENG condensateur au tantale sec *m*, condensateur au tantale à électrolyte solide *m*; ~ **of uniform strength** *n* MECH ENG solide d'égale résistance *m*; ~ **waste** *n* POLLUTION déchets solides *m pl*; ~ **wire** *n* ELEC *conductor* fil plein *m*

solid-core-type: ~ **insulator** *n* ELEC ENG isolateur à fût massif *m*

solid-drawn: ~ **steel tube** *n* MECH ENG tube en acier étiré sans soudure *m*

solid-fuelled: ~ **rocket** *n* SPACE propulseur à propergol solide *m*

solidification *n* PHYS congélation *f*, solidification *f*, PROP MAT *of a melt* solidification *f*; **~ point** *n* REFRIG point de solidification *m*

solidified: **~ fat** *n* FOOD TECH graisse durcie *f*, graisse solidifiée *f*

solidifier *n* MAR POLL durcisseur *m*, gélifiant *m*

solidifying *n* METALL solidification *f*

solidity *n* AERONAUT *propeller* coefficient de plénitude *m*, FUELLESS solidité *f*

solid-liquid: **~ interface** *n* PROP MAT front de solidification *m*

solidly-earthed: **~ neutral system** *n* (BrE) *(cf solidly-grounded neutral system)* ELEC réseau à neutre directement à la terre *m*

solidly-grounded: **~ neutral system** *n* (AmE) *(cf solidly-earthed neutral system)* ELEC réseau à neutre directement à la terre *m*

solid-newel: **~ stair** *n* CONST escalier à noyau plein *m*, vis à noyau plein *f*

solids: **~ loading** *n* HYDROL charge solide *f*

solid-state[1] *adj* COMP à circuits intégrés, à semi-conducteurs, TV *relay* hermétique, transistorisé, à semi-conducteurs

solid-state[2] *n* DP, ELEC, ELECTRON, PART PHYS, RAD PHYS état solide *m*; **~ amplifier** *n* TELECOM amplificateur à semi-conducteurs *m*; **~ camera** *n* ELECTRON caméra sans tube *f*; **~ component** *n* PROD ENG élément à semi-conducteurs *m*; **~ controls** *n pl* PROD ENG commandes électroniques *f pl*, contrôles électroniques *m pl*; **~ detector** *n* RAD PHYS détecteur à état solide *m*; **~ device** *n* ELEC *component* appareil transistorisé *m*, ELECTRON dispositif transistorisé *m*, unité transistorisée *f*, PHYS, TELECOM dispositif à semi-conducteurs *m*; **~ effect** *n* NUCLEAR effet solide *m*; **~ electronics** *n* ELECTRON électronique de l'état solide *f*, électronique à semi-conducteurs *f*; **~ ignition** *n* AUTO allumage transistorisé sans rupteur *m*; **~ interlocking** *n* (BrE) *(SSI)* RAIL système d'enclenchement informatisé *m*; **~ laser** *n* ELECTRON laser à solide *m*; **~ maser** *n* ELECTRON maser à solide *m*; **~ memory** *n* ELEC ENG mémoire intégrée *f*; **~ module** *n* PROD ENG module électronique *m*; **~ motor controller** *n* PROD ENG démarreur statique *m*; **~ physics** *n* PART PHYS physique de l'état solide *f*, physique du solide *f*, PHYS physique de l'état solide *f*; **~ relay** *n* ELEC ENG relais statique *m*, relais à semi-conducteur *m*; **~ surge arrester** *n* ELEC ENG limiteur de surtension à semi-conducteur *m*

solidus *n* CHEM *phase diagram* solidus *m*

solifluction: **~ lobe** *n* GEOL loupe de glissement *f*, GEOPHYS effusion de boue *f*, épanchement de boue *m*; **~ tongue** *n* GEOPHYS effusion de boue *f*, épanchement de boue *m*

soling *n* P&R semelles *f pl*

solo: **~ flight time** *n* AERONAUT temps de vol en solo *m*

solstice *n* ASTRON, SPACE solstice *m*

solstitial: **~ period** *n* SPACE période de solstice *f*; **~ point** *n* ASTRON, SPACE point du solstice *m*

solubility *n* CHEM *of substance*, COAL TECH, P&R solubilité *f*; **~ product** *n* CHEM *of electrolyte* produit de solubilité *m*

soluble[1] *adj* CHEM, PETR TECH soluble

soluble:[2] **~ glass** *n* C&G, DETERGENTS verre soluble *m*; **~ sachet** *n* PACKAGING sachet soluble *m*

solute[1] *adj* CHEM dissous en solution

solute[2] *n* FOOD TECH soluté *m*, substance dissoute *f*,

PROP MAT soluté *m*; **~ phase** *n* PROP MAT phase du soluté *f*

solution *n* CHEM dissolution *f*, liqueur *f*, solution *f*, GEOM solution *f*; **~ annealing** *n* METALL recuit de mise en solution *m*; **~ gas drive** *n* PETR production par expansion de gaz dissous *f*, PETR TECH drainage par expansion de gaz dissous *m*; **~ gas-oil ratio** *n* PETR GOR de dissolution *m*; **~ mixer** *n* P&R *equipment* mélangeur dissolution *m*; **~ polymerization** *n* P&R polymérisation en solution *f*

solutizer *n* CHEM solubilisant *m*

solvate *n* CHEM solvate *m*

solvated *adj* CHEM solvatisé, solvaté

solvation *n* CHEM solvatation *f*, solvatisation *f*

Solvay's: **~ ammonia soda process** *n* DETERGENTS procédé de Solvay *m*; **~ process** *n* DETERGENTS procédé de Solvay *m*

solvency *n* CHEM solvabilité *f*

solvent *n* CHEM, CINEMAT dissolvant *m*, solvant *m*, COAL TECH solvant *m*, DETERGENTS diluant *m*, dissolvant *m*, solvant *m*, FOOD TECH dissolvant *m*, solvant *m*, METALL, P&R *raw material*, POLLUTION, TEXTILES solvant *m*; **~ dyeing** *n* COLOURS teinture avec addition de solvant *f*; **~ extraction** *n* FOOD TECH extraction par solvant *f*; **~ leaching** *n* COAL TECH lixiviation par solvant *f*; **~ recovery** *n* FOOD TECH, PRINT récupération du solvant *f*; **~ refining** *n* PETR TECH raffinage par solvants *m*; **~ welding** *n* P&R *process* soudage au solvant *m*

solvent-based: **~ ink** *n* PRINT encre à base de solvants *f*

solvent-coated: **~ paper** *n* PAPER TECH papier couché au solvant *m*

solventless *adj* PRINT sans solvant

SOM *abbr* (*start of message*) COMP, DP début de message *m*

Sommerfield: **~ number** *n* FUELLESS *tidal power* nombre de Sommerfield *m*

sonar *n* NAUT, OCEANOG, RAD PHYS sonar *m*; **~ hole** *n* OCEANOG puits de sonar *m*; **~ signal** *n* ELECTRON signal sonar *m*

sone *n* ACOUSTICS, PHYS sone *m*

sonic[1] *adj* PHYS sonique

sonic:[2] **~ boom** *n* AERONAUT bang supersonique *m*, PHYS bang supersonique *m*, détonation supersonique *f*, SAFETY bang supersonique *m*, *caused by supersonic aircraft* détonation supersonique *f*; **~ cleaner** *n* CINEMAT appareil de nettoyage aux ultrasons *m*; **~ depth finder** *n* MILIT sonar *m*; **~ detector** *n* TRANSP détecteur sonique *m*; **~ fatigue** *n* METALL fatigue sonique *f*; **~ log** *n* PETR diagramme sonique *m*, PETR TECH diagraphie sonique *f*

sonics *n* RECORDING science sonique *f*

sonometer *n* PHYS, WAVE PHYS sonomètre *m*

soot *n* C&G suie *f*

soot-and-whitewash: **~ print** *n* CINEMAT copie trop contrastée *f*

sorbent *n* CHEM agent absorbant *m*, MAR POLL absorbant *m*, sorbant *m*; **~ wick** *n* MAR POLL mèche absorbante *f*

sorbic: **~ acid** *n* CHEM acide sorbique *m*

sorbite *n* CHEM sorbite *f*

sorbitic: **~ structure** *n* SPRINGS structure sorbitique *f*

sorbitol *n* CHEM sorbitol *m*

sorbose *n* CHEM sorbose *m*

sorption *n* PROP MAT, WATER SUPP sorption *f*; **~ pump** *n* PHYS pompe à sorption *f* sort¹ *n* COMP, DP tri *m*; ~ **field** *n* COMP, DP champ de tri *m*; ~ **generator** *n* COMP, DP générateur de tri *m*; ~ **program** *n* COMP, DP programme de tri *m*

sort² *vt* COMP, DP trier, MINING scheider, PRINT trier; ~ **by color** *vt* (AmE) TEXTILES assortir à la couleur; ~ **by colour** *vt* (BrE) *see sort by color*; ~ **by hand** *vt* COAL TECH scheider; ~ **by shade** *vt* TEXTILES assortir à la couleur

sorter *n* C&G trieur *m*

sorting *n* C&G choix *m*, COAL TECH scheidage *m*, triage *m*, COMP, DP tri *m*, GEOL classement *m*, PAPER TECH, RAIL triage *m*; ~ **belt** *n* PROD ENG toile de triage *f*; ~ **line** *n* RAIL *vehicles* voie de triage *f*; ~ **machine** *n* PACKAGING trieuse *f*; ~ **siding** *n* RAIL *vehicles* chantier de triage *m*, voie de classement *f*

SOS *abbr (silicon on sapphire)* ELECTRON silicium sur saphir *m*

sound¹ *n* ACOUSTICS son *m*, NAUT *navigation* détroit *m*, OCEANOG détroit *m*, goulet *m*, PHYS, RECORDING son *m*; ~ **absorber** *n* ACOUSTICS matériau absorbant *m*; ~ **absorption** *n* ACOUSTICS absorption acoustique *f*, RECORDING absorption du son *f*; ~ **acceleration** *n* ACOUSTICS accélération acoustique *f*; ~ **acceleration level** *n* ACOUSTICS niveau d'accélération acoustique *m*; ~ **alarm radiation dosimeter** *n* RAD PHYS dosimètre sonore de radiation *m*; ~ **analyzer** *n* ACOUSTICS analyseur de son *m*; ~ **archive** *n* RECORDING sonothèque *f*; ~ **bars** *n pl* RECORDING *in picture* chenillards *f pl*; ~ **blanket** *n* RECORDING masque sonore *m*; ~ **boom** *n* RECORDING perche micro *f*, perche son *f*; ~ **boom man** *n* RECORDING perchman *m*; ~ **booth** *n* CINEMAT cabine de son *f*, cabine technique *f*, RECORDING cabine de prise de son *f*; ~ **broadcasting** *n* TELECOM radiodiffusion sonore *f*; ~ **broadcast transmitter** *n* TELECOM émetteur de radiodiffusion sonore *m*; ~ **camera** *n* CINEMAT caméra insonorisée *f*, caméra son *f*; ~ **carrier** *n* ELECTRON porteuse audio *f*, porteuse son *f*, RECORDING porteuse son *f*; ~ **channel** *n* OCEANOG chenal acoustique *m*, chenal sonore *m*, sonographe *m*, RECORDING, TV canal son *m*; ~ **code** *n* RECORDING indicatif sonore *m*; ~ **column** *n* ACOUSTICS colonne acoustique *f*, RECORDING colonne sonore *f*; ~ **console** *n* RECORDING console de mixage *f*, pupitre de mixage *m*, table de mixage *f*; ~ **control desk** *n* CINEMAT pupitre de mixage *m*; ~ **control room** *n* CINEMAT, RECORDING *film* régie de son *f*; ~ **detector** *n* MILIT détecteur de son *m*; ~ **diffuser** *n* RECORDING diffuseur de son *m*; ~ **direct positive** *n* CINEMAT son inversible *m*; ~ **dissolve** *n* RECORDING fondu sonore *m*; ~ **distortion** *n* RECORDING distorsion du son *f*; ~ **distribution** *n* RECORDING répartition sonore *f*; ~ **drum** *n* RECORDING tambour de lecture *m*; ~ **effects** *n pl* CINEMAT, RECORDING bruitages *m pl*, effets sonores *m pl*, TV bruitages *m pl*; ~ **energy** *n* ELEC ENG énergie acoustique *f*; ~ **energy density** *n* PHYS énergie volumique acoustique *f*; ~ **energy density level** *n* ACOUSTICS niveau de densité d'énergie *m*; ~ **energy flux** *n* PHYS flux d'énergie acoustique *m*, puissance acoustique *f*; ~ **equipment** *n* RECORDING matériel son *m*, équipement sonore *m*; ~ **exposure meter** *n* SAFETY sonomètre *m*; ~ **film head** *n* CINEMAT lecteur de son *m*; ~ **film lamp** *n* CINEMAT lampe excitatrice *f*, lampe phonique *f*; ~ **head** *n* TV tête sonore *f*; ~ **insulation** *n* ACOUSTICS isolement acoustique *m*, NAUT isolation phonique *f*, RECORDING insonorisation *f*, isolement sonore *m*, VEHICLES *body* isolation antibruit *f*; ~ **intensity** *n* ACOUSTICS, PHYS

intensité acoustique *f*; ~ **intensity level** *n* ACOUSTICS, PHYS niveau d'intensité acoustique *m*, RECORDING niveau d'intensité sonore *m*; ~ **isolation** *n* ACOUSTICS isolation acoustique *f*; ~ **level** *n* ACOUSTICS niveau sonore *m*; ~ **level meter** *n* ACOUSTICS sonomètre *m*, RECORDING mesureur du niveau sonore *m*, SAFETY indicateur du niveau sonore *m*, sonomètre *m*; ~ **locator** *n* ACOUSTICS appareil de repérage acoustique *m*; ~ **loop** *n* RECORDING boucle son *f*; ~ **modulation** *n* ACOUSTICS modulation *f*, RECORDING modulation sonore *f*; ~ **negative** *n* CINEMAT négatif son *m*; ~ **on sound** *n* RECORDING surimpression *f*; ~ **on vision** *n* TV son dans l'image *m*; ~ **path** *n* OCEANOG courbe des rayons sonores *f*; ~ **perspective** *n* RECORDING relief sonore *m*; ~ **positive** *n* CINEMAT positif son *m*; ~ **power** *n* ACOUSTICS *of source*, PHYS puissance acoustique *f*; ~ **power level** *n* ACOUSTICS, PHYS niveau de puissance acoustique *m*; ~ **pressure** *n* PHYS pression acoustique *f*, pression sonore *f*, POLLUTION pression acoustique *f*; ~ **pressure level** *n* ACOUSTICS, PHYS niveau de pression acoustique *m*, POLLUTION niveau sonore *m*; ~ **pressure spectrum** *n* POLLUTION spectre acoustique *m*; ~ **propagation** *n* RECORDING propagation du son *f*; ~ **pulse** *n* RECORDING top de synchronisation *m*; ~ **quality** *n* TELECOM qualité sonore *f*; ~ **ranging** *n* WAVE PHYS radar acoustique *m*, repérage par le son *m*; ~ **ray curve** *n* OCEANOG courbe des rayons sonores *f*; ~ **reader** *n* RECORDING lecteur de son *m*; ~ **recorder** *n* INSTRUMENT enregistreur phonographique *m*; ~ **recording** *n* CINEMAT, RECORDING enregistrement sonore *m*, TELECOM enregistrement du son *m*; ~ **recording system** *n* RECORDING système d'enregistrement sonore *m*; ~ **reduction index** *n* PHYS *sound transmission loss* indice d'affaiblissement acoustique *m*; ~ **reproduction system** *n* RECORDING système de reproduction sonore *m*; ~ **screen** *n* RECORDING écran sonore *m*; ~ **signal** *n* CONTROL signal phonique *m*, signal sonore *m*, ELECTRON signal sonore *m*, NAUT signal phonique *m*, RAIL *vehicles* signal sonore *m*, TELECOM signal acoustique *m*, signal sonore *m*; ~ **source** *n* ACOUSTICS source sonore *f*, POLLUTION source de bruit *f*; ~ **spectrograph** *n* ACOUSTICS spectrographe acoustique *m*; ~ **stage** *n* CINEMAT plateau insonorisé *m*, RECORDING plateau insonorisé *m*, scène sonore *f*; ~ **studio** *n* RECORDING studio son *m*; ~ **sync generator** *n* CINEMAT générateur de fréquence pilote *m*; ~ **system** *n* RECORDING équipement sonore *m*; ~ **take** *n* ACOUSTICS prise de son *f*, CINEMAT prise de vues avec son direct *f*; ~ **take desk** *n* ACOUSTICS pupitre de prise de son *m*; ~ **transfer** *n* CINEMAT repiquage *m*; ~ **transmission** *n* TELECOM transmission du son *f*

sound² *vt* NAUT *navigation*, OCEANOG sonder

sound-absorbent: ~ **ceiling** *n* SAFETY plafond insonorisant *m*; ~ **door** *n* SAFETY porte de protection contre les bruits *f*; ~ **foam panel** *n* SAFETY panneau antibruit en mousse *m*; ~ **wall** *n* SAFETY paroi antibruit *f*

sound-absorbing: ~ **machines** *n pl* SAFETY lutte antibruit *f*; ~ **material** *n* RECORDING matériel absorbant le son *m*

sound-deadening: ~ **paint** *n* COLOURS peinture antisonique *f*

sounder *n* NAUT *navigation* sondeur *m*

sounding *n* NAUT sondage *m*, OCEANOG brassiage *m*, sondage *m*, sonde *f*, PROD ENG sondage *m*; ~ **balloon** *n* METEO, SPACE ballon-sonde *m*; ~ **board** *n* WAVE PHYS table d'harmonie *f*; ~ **datum** *n* OCEANOG niveau de réduction des sondes *m*; ~ **datum level** *n* OCEANOG niveau de réduction des sondes *m*; ~ **lead** *n* NAUT plomb de sonde *m*, OCEANOG sonde *f*; ~ **lidar** *n* SPACE *spacecraft* lidar de sondage *m*; ~ **line** *n* NAUT ligne de sonde *f*, sonde *f*, OCEANOG profil de sonde *m*; ~ **pole** *n* NAUT *deck equipment* perche à sonder *f*, OCEANOG perche de sonde *f*; ~ **profile** *n* OCEANOG profil de sonde *m*; ~ **record** *n* COAL TECH rapport de sondage *m*; ~ **rocket** *n* MILIT, SPACE fusée-sonde *f*

soundings *n pl* NAUT *of sea bottom* fonds *m pl*

sound-insulated: ~ **door** *n* SAFETY porte isolée contre le bruit *f*

soundness *n* PROP MAT exactitude *f*, justesse *f*, validité *f*

soundproof: ~ **booth** *n* SAFETY cabine insonorisante *f*; ~ **capsule** *n* SAFETY capsule pour la protection de l'ouïe *f*; ~ **door** *n* SAFETY porte isolée contre le bruit *f*; ~ **hood** *n* SAFETY capot insonorisant *m*; ~ **insulating glass** *n* SAFETY verre isolant insonorisant *m*; ~ **plug** *n* SAFETY bouchon pour la protection de l'ouïe *m*; ~ **room** *n* RECORDING chambre insonorisée *f*; ~ **tiles** *n pl* SAFETY carreaux d'absorption acoustique *m pl*, tuiles insonorisantes *f pl*

soundproofed: ~ **booth** *n* RECORDING cabine insonorisée *f*

soundproofing *n* CINEMAT, SAFETY insonorisation *f*; ~ **material** *n* ACOUSTICS matériau insonore *m*

soundtrack *n* ACOUSTICS trace acoustique *f*, CINEMAT APHY, RECORDING piste sonore *f*, TV piste audio *f*, piste sonore *f*

soundwave *n* ACOUSTICS onde sonore *f*, PHYS onde acoustique *f*, onde sonore *f*, TELECOM onde acoustique *f*, onde sonore *f*, WAVE PHYS onde sonore *f*

souped-up *adj* (AmE) *(cf hotted-up)* VEHICLES *engine* gonflé

sour:[1] ~ **crude** *n* PETR TECH brut acide *m*; ~ **gas** *n* GAS TECH gaz acide *m*, PETR gaz corrosif *m*, PETR TECH gaz acide *m*

sour[2] *vt* PAPER TECH laver avec de l'eau acidulée

source *n* COMP, DP, ELEC ENG, ELECTRON source *f*, HYDR EQUIP alimentation *f*, HYDROL *of river* source *f*, *of water supply* provenance *f*, PHYS *of electromotive source* générateur *m*, *transistor electrode* source *f*; ~ **address** *n* COMP adresse émettrice *f*, DP adresse d'origine *f*, adresse source *f*, adresse émettrice *f*; ~ **area** *n* GEOL *of clastic material, magmas* région nourricière *f*, région source *f*, source *f*, POLLUTION région source *f*, région émettrice *f*; ~ **code** *n* COMP, DP code source *m*; ~ **contact** *n* ELEC ENG contact de source *m*; ~ **document** *n* COMP, DP document source *m*; ~ **impedance** *n* ELEC ENG impédance de la source *f*; ~ **language** *n* COMP langage source *m*; ~ **machine** *n* COMP ordinateur compilateur *m*, DP ordinateur de compilation *m*; ~ **power efficiency** *n* OPT, TELECOM rendement énergétique *m*; ~ **program** *n* COMP, DP programme source *m*; ~ **reactor** *n* NUCLEAR réacteur source *m*; ~ **region** *n* GEOL *of clastic material, magmas* région nourricière *f*, région source *f*, source *f*; ~ **rock** *n* GEOL, PETR, PETR TECH roche mère *f*

souse *n* OCEANOG marinade *f*

south[1] *adj* NAUT sud; ~ **by southeast** *adj* NAUT sud-quart-sud-est; ~ **by southwest** *adj* NAUT sud-quart-sud-ouest

south:[2] ~ **by southeast** *n* NAUT sud-quart-sud-est *m*; ~ **by southwest** *n* NAUT sud-quart-sud-ouest *m*; ~ **galactic pole** *n* ASTRON pôle sud galactique *m*; ~ **geomagnetic pole** *n* GEOPHYS pôle géomagnétique sud *m*; ~ **pole** *n* PHYS pôle sud *m*; ~ **seas** *n pl* OCEANOG mers du sud *f pl*;

~ **wind** *n* NAUT vent du sud *m*

southeast[1] *adj* NAUT sud-est; ~ **by east** *adj* NAUT sud-est-quart-est; ~ **by south** *adj* NAUT sud-est-quart-sud

southeast:[2] ~ **by east** *n* NAUT sud-est-quart-est *m*; ~ **by south** *n* NAUT sud-est-quart-sud *m*; ~ **wind** *n* NAUT vent du sud-est *m*

southeaster *n* NAUT sud-est *m*

southeasterly *adj* NAUT du sud-est

southeastwards *adv* NAUT vers le sud-est

southerly *adj* NAUT du sud

southern: ~ **latitude** *n* NAUT *navigation* latitude australe *f*

south-southeast[1] *adj* NAUT sud-sud-est

south-southeast[2] *n* NAUT sud-sud-est *m*

south-southwest[1] *adj* NAUT sud-sud-ouest

south-southwest[2] *n* NAUT sud-sud-ouest *m*, susuroît *m*

southwards *adv* NAUT vers le sud

southwest[1] *adj* NAUT sud-ouest; ~ **by south** *adj* NAUT sud-ouest-quart-sud; ~ **by west** *adj* NAUT sud-ouest-quart-ouest

southwest[2] *n* NAUT sud-ouest *m*; ~ **by south** *n* NAUT sud-ouest-quart-sud *m*; ~ **by west** *n* NAUT sud-ouest-quart-ouest *m*; ~ **wind** *n* NAUT vent du sud-ouest *m*

southwester *n* NAUT suroît *m*

southwesterly *adj* NAUT du sud-ouest

southwestwards *adv* NAUT vers le sud-ouest

sow *n* PROD ENG carcas *m*, cochon *m*, loup *m*, gueuse de mère *f*, mère *f*, mère-gueuse *f*, nourrice de gueuse *f*

Soxhlet: ~ **extraction equipment** *n* LAB EQUIP *glassware* extracteur Soxhlet *m*

soya *n* P&R soya *m*

Soyuz: ~ **craft** *n* SPACE *USSR* vaisseau Soyuz *m*

SP *abbr* COMP *(structured programming)*, DP *(structured programming)* PS *(programmation structurée)*, ELECTRON *(signal processor)* processeur de signaux *m*, TELECOM *(signalling point, signaling point)* point sémaphore *m*, TELECOM *(service provider)* prestataire de service *m*, TELECOM *(session protocol)* protocole de session *m*, TELECOM *(signal processor)* unité de traitement de signaux *f*, TV *(signal processor)* dispositif de traitement de signal *m*, processeur de signal *m*

space:[1] ~ **sick** *adj* SPACE atteint du mal de l'espace

space[2] *n* ASTRON, GEOM espace *m*, HYDR EQUIP *between piston and cylinder head* espace mort *m*, MECH ENG creux *m*, vide *m*, PHYS, SPACE espace *m*; ~ **age** *n* ASTRON, SPACE ère spatiale *f*; ~ **agency** *n* SPACE agence spatiale *f*; ~ **astronomy** *n* SPACE astronomie spatiale *f*; ~ **between rails** *n pl* RAIL entre-rails *m*; ~ **capsule** *n* SPACE capsule spatiale *f*; ~ **center** *n* (AmE), ~ **centre** *n* (BrE) SPACE centre spatial *m*; ~ **character** *n* COMP, DP caractère espace *m*, espace *m*; ~ **charge** *n* PHYS charge d'espace *f*, charge spatiale *f*; ~ **communications** *n pl* TELECOM télécommunications spatiales *f pl*; ~ **curve** *n* GEOM *helix* courbe dans l'espace *f*; ~ **detection and tracking system** *n (SPADATS)* MILIT système de surveillance d'espace et de poursuite *m*; ~ **division switching** *n* COMP, DP, TELECOM commutation spatiale *f*; ~ **engineering** *n* SPACE ingénierie spatiale *f*; ~ **flight** *n* SPACE vol spatial *m*; ~ **group** *n* CRYSTALL groupe d'espace *m*, groupe spatial *m*; ~ **heating** *n* GAS TECH chauffage des locaux *m*; ~ **laboratory** *n* ASTRON laboratoire spatial *m*; ~ **lattice** *n* CRYSTALL réseau d'espace *m*, réseau spatial *m*; ~ **launch** *n* SPACE lancement spatial *m*; ~ **observatory** *n* SPACE observatoire spatial *m*; ~ **occupied** *n* MECH ENG encombrement *m*; ~ **plane**

SPACE *spacecraft* avion spatial *m*; ~ **probe** *n* ASTRON, SPACE sonde spatiale *f*; ~ **program** *n* (AmE), ~ **programme** *n* (BrE) SPACE programme spatial *m*; ~ **qualification** *n* SPACE qualification pour usage spatial *f*; ~ **rendezvous** *n* SPACE rendez-vous spatial *m*; ~ **research** *n* SPACE recherche spatiale *f*; ~ **research service** *n* SPACE *communications* service de recherche spatiale *m*; ~ **rocket** *n* ASTRON fusée spatiale *f*; ~ **segment** *n* SPACE *communications* composante spatiale *f*, secteur spatial *m*; ~ **shot** *n* SPACE lancement spatial *m*; ~ **shuttle** *n* SPACE, TELECOM navette spatiale *f*; ~ **sickness** *n* SPACE mal de l'espace *m*; ~ **simulation chamber** *n* SPACE chambre de simulation spatiale *f*; ~ **stage** *n* TELECOM étage spatial *m*; ~ **station** *n* SPACE station spatiale *f*; ~ **step-out** *n* SPACE sortie dans l'espace *f*; ~ **switch** *n* TELECOM commutateur S *m*, commutateur spatial *m*; ~ **taken up** *n* MECH ENG encombrement *m*; ~ **technology** *n* TRANSP technologie spatiale *f*; ~ **telescope** *n* ASTRON télescope spatial *m*; ~ **tracking** *n* MILIT, SPACE poursuite spatiale *f*; ~ **tracking and data acquisition network** *n* (*STADAN*) MILIT réseau de poursuite et de saisie de données dans l'espace *m*; ~ **transportation system** *n* (*STS*) SPACE système de transport spatial *m*; ~ **travel** *n* SPACE voyage dans l'espace *m*; ~ **tug** *n* SPACE *spacecraft* remorqueur spatial 0Im; ~ **vehicle** *n* SPACE vaisseau spatial *m*; ~ **workshop** *n* SPACE atelier spatial *m*

spaceborne *adj* SPACE *spacecraft* spatioporté

space-bound *adj* SPACE en route vers l'espace, spatialisé

space-centered *adj* (AmE), **space-centred** *adj* (BrE) METALL centro-symétrique

spacecraft *n* ASTRON véhicule spatial *m*, SPACE astronef *m*, engin spatial *m*, spationef *m*, vaisseau spatial *m*, véhicule spatial *m*

spaced: ~ **division switching system** *n* TELECOM système de commutation spatiale *m*; ~ **division system** *n* TELECOM système spatial *m*; ~ **lathing** *n* MECH ENG lattage espacé *m*, lattis espacé *m*

spaced-out *adv* TELECOM espacé

spacelab *n* SPACE laboratoire spatial *m*

spacer *n* C&G intercalaire *m*, PROD ENG intercalaire *m*, *paper* entretoise *f*, SPACE entretoise *f*; ~ **block** *n* CONST *concrete works* cale en béton *f*, MECH ENG *injection mould* tasseau d'éjection *m*

space-saving *adj* PACKAGING à volume réduit

spaceship *n* SPACE astronef *m*, vaisseau spatial *m*

spacesuit *n* SPACE scaphandre spatial *m*

space-time *n* ASTRON, PHYS espace-temps *m*; ~ **continuum** *n* SPACE continuum espace-temps *m*; ~ **correlation** *n* TELECOM corrélation spatio-temporelle *f*

space-time-space *n* (*STS*) SPACE spatial-temporel-spatial *m* (*STS*); ~ **network** *n* TELECOM réseau STS *m*, réseau spatial-temporel-spatial *m*

spacewalk *n* SPACE marche dans l'espace *f*

spacing *n* AERONAUT *of aircraft* espacement *m*, CINEMAT amorce *f*, OPT espacement *m*, PHYS pas *m*, TRANSP espacement *m*; ~ **loss** *n* RECORDING perte de séparation *f*, TV perte par effet d'espacement tête-bande *f*

SPADATS *abbr (space detection and tracking system)* MILIT système de surveillance d'espace et de poursuite *m*

spade *n* CONST bêche *f*; ~ **lug** *n* PROD ENG cosse *f*; ~ **rudder** *n* NAUT gouvernail suspendu *m*

spalling *n* C&G écaillage *m*, CONST *of concrete, masonry* écaillement *m*, *of stone* taille brute *f*

span *n* AERONAUT *of wings* envergure *f*, CONST travée *f*, *of bridge, of arch* ouverture *f*, portée *f*, travée *f*, *of girder, roof* portée *f*, travée *f*, volant *m*, *of overhead travelling crane* portée *f*, METR *of measuring instrument* intervalle de mesure *m*, PHYS *of wing* envergure *f*; ~ **piece** *n* CONST *collar beam* entrait retroussé *m*, faux entrait *m*; ~ **pole** *n* ELEC *supply network* pylône de haubanage *m*, pylône à haubans *m*; ~ **roof** *n* CONST comble à deux longs pans *m*, comble à deux pentes *m*, comble à deux rampes *m*, comble à deux versants *m*, comble à deux égouts *m*

spandrel *n* CONST *architecture* hauteur du portail *f*, rein *m*, tympan *m*; ~ **glass** *n* C&G allège *f*

spaniolite *n* MINERAL spaniolite *f*

Spanish: ~ **burton** *n* NAUT *purchases* bredindin *m*

spanner *n* (BrE) *(cf wrench)* MECH clé *f*, MECH ENG clé *f*, clé de calibre *f*, clé fermée *f*, VEHICLES *tool* clé *f*; ~ **for hexagon nuts** *n* MECH ENG clé à six pans *f*

spar *n* AERONAUT *aircraft* longeron *m*, NAUT *boom, mast* épar *m*, PETR TECH stockage flottant *m*, SPACE *spacecraft* longeron *m*; ~ **buoy** *n* NAUT *navigation mark* bouée à espar *f*; ~ **deck** *n* NAUT pont léger *m*

spare: ~ **bulb** *n* PHOTO lampe de rechange *f*; ~ **ends** *n pl* TEXTILES fils de réserve *m pl*; ~ **line** *n* TELECOM ligne non attribuée *f*; ~ **number** *n* TELECOM numéro non attribué *m*; ~ **part** *n* MECH ENG pièce de rechange *f*, NAUT *after sales* pièce détachée *f*, VEHICLES pièce de rechange *f*, pièce détachée *f*; ~ **tire** *n* (AmE) *see spare tyre*; ~ **tools** *n pl* MECH ENG outils de rechange *m pl*; ~ **track** *n* COMP, DP piste de réserve *f*; ~ **tyre** *n* (BrE) AUTO roue de secours *f*, VEHICLES *car*, VEHICLES roue de secours *f*

spares *n pl* MECH ENG pièce de rechange *f*

sparge: ~ **pipe** *n* FOOD TECH *machinery* tuyau perforé *m*; ~ **ring cooler** *n* REFRIG refroidisseur à lait par collier d'aspersion *m*

sparging *n* CHEM barbotage *m*

spark[1] *n* AUTO étincelle *f*, C&G ligne de feu *f*, ELEC *relay*, ELEC ENG, PHYS étincelle *f*, PROD ENG flammèche *f*, étincelle *f*; ~ **absorber** *n* ELEC *relay* circuit d'absorption *m*; ~ **advance** *n* AERONAUT avance à l'allumage *f*; ~ **arrester** *n* ELEC *relay* éclateur pare-étincelles *m*; ~ **blowout** *n* ELEC *relay* éclateur pare-étincelles *m*; ~ **capacitor** *n* ELEC ENG condensateur pare-étincelles *m*; ~ **chamber** *n* ASTRON, PHYS chambre à étincelles *f*; ~ **coil** *n* ELEC ENG bobine d'allumage *f*; ~ **counter** *n* RAD PHYS compteur d'étincelles *m*; ~ **discharge** *n* PHYS décharge par étincelles *f*; ~ **erosion finish** *n* MECH ENG finition par électro-érosion *f*; ~ **extinguisher** *n* ELEC *relay* éclateur pare-étincelles *m*; ~ **fuse** *n* MINING amorce de tension *f*, amorce à étincelle *f*; ~ **gap** *n* ELEC *electrodes*, ELEC ENG, PHYS éclateur *m*; ~ **ignition** *n* AUTO, ELEC allumage commandé *m*; ~ **ignition engine** *n* MECH ENG moteur à bougie d'allumage *m*; ~ **machining** *n* MECH ENG usinage par étincelage *m*; ~ **plug** *n* AUTO, ELEC, VEHICLES *ignition* bougie *f*; ~ **plug body** *n* AUTO culot de bougie *m*; ~ **plug cable** *n* AUTO câble de bougie *m*; ~ **plug electrode** *n* AUTO électrode de bougie *f*; ~ **plug gap** *n* AUTO écartement des électrodes *m*; ~ **plug gasket** *n* AUTO joint de bougie *m*; ~ **plug hole** *n* AUTO trou de bougie *m*; ~ **plug point** *n* AUTO électrode de bougie *f*; ~ **plug shell** *n* AUTO culot de bougie *m*; ~ **plug terminal** *n* AUTO borne de bougie *f*; ~ **plug wire** *n* AUTO fil de bougie *m*; ~ **plug wrench** *n* MECH ENG *tool* clé à bougies *f*; ~ **quencher** *n* ELEC *relay* éclateur pare-étincelles *m*; ~ **quenching** *n* ELEC ENG étouffement d'étincelles *m*; ~ **recorder** *n* INSTRUMENT enregistreur à étincelles *m*; ~ **spectrum** *n* RAD PHYS spectre d'étincelles *m*; ~ **suppression** *n* ELEC ENG antiparasitage *m*, réduction des étincelles *f*; ~ **suppressor** *n* ELEC ENG antiparasite *m*, filtre antiparasite *m*, pare-étincelles *m*; ~ **timing** *n* AUTO point d'allumage *m*

spark[2] *vt* ELEC ENG émettre des étincelles

sparker *n* GEOPHYS étinceleur *m*

sparking *n* ELEC ENG jaillissement d'étincelles *m*, TV décharge disruptive *f*; ~ **distance** *n* ELEC ENG distance disruptive *f*

sparkling *n* PROD ENG scintillement *m*, étincellement *m*; ~ **heat** *n* PROD ENG blanc-soudant *m*, chaude blanc-soudant *f*, soudant *m*

spark-out: ~ **stop** *n* MINING arrêt d'étincelage *m*

spark-over: ~ **voltage** *n* ELEC *arc* tension d'éclatement *f*

sparks *n* CINEMAT électricien *m*

sparse: ~ **matrix** *n* COMP, DP matrice creuse *f*

spartalite *n* MINERAL spartalite *f*

spartein *n* CHEM spartéine *f*

spate *n* HYDROL *flood* crue *f*, *freshet* avalaison *f*, avalasse *f*

spatial: ~ **coherence** *n* PHYS, TELECOM cohérence spatiale *f*; ~ **distribution** *n* POLLUTION distribution géographique *f*, distribution spatiale *f*, répartition *f*; ~ **domain** *n* ELECTRON domaine spatial *m*; ~ **frequency** *n* ELEC ENG, PHYS fréquence spatiale *f*; ~ **modulation** *n* ELECTRON modulation spatiale *f*; ~ **pattern** *n* POLLUTION configuration spatiale *f*, profil spatial *m*, structure spatiale *f*; ~ **period** *n* ELECTRON période spatiale *f*; ~ **quantization** *n* PHYS quantification spatiale *f*; ~ **rendezvous** *n* SPACE rendez-vous spatial *m*; ~ **resolution** *n* POLLUTION résolution géographique *f*, résolution spatiale *f*; ~ **response** *n* ELECTRON réponse spatiale *f*; ~ **trend** *n* POLLUTION tendance géographique *f*, tendance spatiale *f*; ~ **variability** *n* POLLUTION variabilité spatiale *f*

spatter *n* CONST *welding* projection *f*; ~ **work** *n* MINING abattage hydraulique *m*, abattage à l'eau *m*, exploitation hydraulique *f*, hydrauliquage *m*, travail à l'eau *m*

spatula *n* LAB EQUIP spatule *f*

spawning: ~ **ground** *n* OCEANOG frayère *f*

SPC *abbr* ELEC *(single-paper-covered)* guipé une couche papier, TELECOM *(stored programme control, stored program control)* commande à programme enregistré *f*

SPDT[1] *abbr (single-pole double-throw)* ELEC, ELEC ENG à un contact inverseur

SPDT:[2] ~ **relay** ELEC, ELEC ENG relais SPDT *m*, relais inverseur unipolaire *m*, relais à simple contact inverseur *m*, relais à un contact inverseur *m*; ~ **switch** *n* ELEC ENG inverseur unipolaire *m*

SPDU *abbr (session protocol data unit)* TELECOM unité de données du protocole de session *f*

speaker: ~ **system** *n* RECORDING enceinte acoustique *f*

speaking: ~ **clock** *n* TELECOM horloge parlante *f*; ~ **rod** *n* CONST *surveying* mire parlante *f*

spear *n* WATER SUPP *pump rod* tige *f*, tige de pompe *f*; ~ **pyrites** *n* MINERAL marcassite *f*; ~ **rod** *n* MINING *of mine pump* maîtresse-tige *f*

spear-headed: ~ **railing** *n* CONST barreau à pique *m*

special: ~ **character** *n* COMP, DP caractère spécial *m*; ~ **edition** *n* PRINT numéro spécial *m*; ~ **effects** *n pl* CINEMAT effets spéciaux *m pl*, trucages *m pl*; ~ **effects bus** *n* TV voie d'effets *f*; ~ **effects department** *n* CINEMAT service trucages *m*; ~ **effects generator** *n* TV générateur d'effets spéciaux *m*, pupitre de trucages *m*;

~ **examination** *n* CONTROL contrôle particulier *m*; ~ **precautions** *n pl* SAFETY précautions spéciales *f pl*; ~ **purpose machine** *n* MECH ENG machine spéciale *f*; ~ **regulations** *n pl* SAFETY règlements spéciaux *m pl*; ~ **requirements** *n pl* MECH ENG applications particulières *f pl*; ~ **rubber-lining protecting against corrosion** *n* SAFETY gommes spéciales pour le revêtement anticorrosion *f pl*; ~ **sections** *n pl* MECH ENG fers spéciaux *m pl*; ~ **surface** *n* INSTRUMENT facette spéciale *f*; ~ **theory** *n* PHYS *of relativity* théorie de la relativité restreinte *f*; ~ **turnout** *n* RAIL branchement spécial *m*

specialized: ~ **cold store** *n* REFRIG entrepôt frigorifique spécialisé *m*; ~ **support group** *n* RAD PHYS *research development* groupe de soutien spécialisé *m*

special-purpose: ~ **computer** *n* COMP calculateur spécialisé *m*, DP ordinateur spécialisé *m*

specific[1] *adj* PHYS spécifique

specific:[2] ~ **absorption** *n* METEO absorption spécifique *f*; ~ **acoustic impedance** *n* ACOUSTICS, PHYS impédance acoustique spécifique *f*; ~ **activity** *n* PHYS activité spécifique *f*; ~ **adhesion** *n* P&R *adhesives* adhérence spécifique *f*; ~ **attenuation** *n* SPACE *communications* affaiblissement spécifique *m*; ~ **capacitance** *n* ELEC *condenser* capacité spécifique *f*; ~ **capacity** *n* FUELLESS *of well* capacité spécifique *f*; ~ **charge** *n* PART PHYS *of electron* charge spécifique *f*, PHYS *charge-mass ratio* charge massique *f*, charge spécifique *f*; ~ **conductance** *n* ELEC conductivité spécifique *f*; ~ **detectivity** *n* OPT, TELECOM détectivité spécifique *f*; ~ **efficiency** *n* ACOUSTICS efficacité intrinsèque *f*; ~ **emission** *n* ELEC ENG densité d'émission *f*; ~ **energy** *n* GAS TECH énergie spécifique *f*, PHYS énergie massique *f*, énergie spécifique *f*; ~ **enthalpy** *n* PHYS enthalpie massique *f*; ~ **entropy** *n* PHYS entropie massique *f*; ~ **Gibbs function** *n* PHYS enthalpie libre massique *f*; ~ **gravity** *n* NAUT *of sea water* densité *f*, P&R, PETR TECH poids spécifique *m*, PHYS densité *f*, TEXTILES densité *f*, poids spécifique *m*; ~ **gravity curve** *n* COAL TECH courbe densimétrique *f*; ~ **gravity fraction** *n* COAL TECH faction densimétrique *f*; ~ **heat** *n* HEAT ENG chaleur massique *f*, P&R chaleur spécifique *f*, PHYS, REFRIG chaleur massique *f*, SPACE *spacecraft*, THERMOD chaleur spécifique *f*; ~ **heat capacity** *n* PHYS capacité thermique massique *f*; ~ **heat capacity at constant pressure** *n* PHYS capacité thermique massique à pression constante *f*; ~ **heat capacity at constant volume** *n* PHYS capacité thermique massique à volume constant *f*; ~ **Helmholtz function** *n* PHYS énergie libre massique *f*; ~ **humidity** *n* METEO contenu en vapeur d'eau *m*, humidité spécifique *f*; ~ **impulse** *n* SPACE *spacecraft* impulsion spécifique *f*; ~ **index** *n* (AmE) *(cf bulking index)* PRINT bouffant *m*, indice de bouffant *m*, indice de main *m*; ~ **inductive capacity** *n* ELEC ENG pouvoir inducteur spécifique *m*, TV constante diélectrique *f*; ~ **internal energy** *n* PHYS énergie interne massique *f*; ~ **latent heat** *n* PHYS chaleur latente massique *f*; ~ **peak flow** *n* HYDROL débit spécifique de pointe *m*; ~ **power** *n* SPACE *spacecraft* puissance surfacique *f*; ~ **resistance** *n* ELEC résistance spécifique *f*, ELEC ENG résistance spécifique *f*, résistivité *f*; ~ **rotation** *n* PHYS pouvoir rotatoire *m*; ~ **speed** *n* FUELLESS vitesse spécifique *f*; ~ **stiffness** *n* SPACE *spacecraft* rigidité spécifique *f*; ~ **surface area** *n* P&R *pigment property* surface spécifique *f*; ~ **volume** *n* PHYS volume massique *m*, PRINT bouffant *m*, indice de bouffant *m*, indice de main *m*

specification *n* COMP, CONST, DP spécification *f*, NAUT caractéristique *f*, PATENTS fascicule *m*, mémoire descriptive *f*, PROD ENG cahier des charges *m*, SPRINGS cahier de charges *m*, TEXTILES spécification *f*, VEHICLES cahier des charges *m*; ~ **and description language** *n* TELECOM langage de description et de spécification *m*; ~ **change notice** *n (SCN)* TRANSP spécification de changement notifié *f*; ~ **of goods** *n* PATENTS liste des produits services *f*, liste des produits *f*; ~ **language** *n* COMP langage de spécification *m*; ~ **limits** *n pl* QUALITY limites de spécification *f pl*; ~ **of services** *n* PATENTS liste des produits services *f*; ~ **sheet** *n* PROD ENG cahier des charges *m*, TV fiche technique *f*, VEHICLES cahier des charges *m*

specifications *n pl* CONST cahier des charges *m*, devis descriptif *m*

specify *vt* SAFETY *details* préciser

specimen *n* CHEM exemplaire *m*, spécimen *m*, COAL TECH spécimen *m*, échantillon *m*, CRYSTALL échantillon *m*, MECH *materials* éprouvette *f*, P&R *test* spécimen *m*, échantillon *m*, PAPER TECH feuilles échantillons *f pl*; ~ **chamber** *n* INSTRUMENT sas *m*; ~ **holder** *n* NUCLEAR porte-échantillons *m*, porte-éprouvette *m*; ~ **insertion airlock** *n* INSTRUMENT orifice d'introduction de l'objet *m*; ~ **stage** *n* INSTRUMENT grille porte-objet *f*, platine *f*, porte-échantillons *m*

specking *n* C&G grains *m pl*

speckle[1] *n* PRINT impression grainée *f*, SPACE chatoiement *m*, spècle *m*, TEXTILES tacheture *f*; ~ **noise** *n* OPT bruit de tacheture *m*, TELECOM bruit de granulation *m*

speckle[2] *vt* TEXTILES moucheter

specks *n pl* PAPER TECH poivres dans le papier *m pl*

spectacle: ~ **frame** *n* INSTRUMENT monture *f*; ~ **glass** *n* C&G verre à lunettes *m*; ~ **lens** *n* INSTRUMENT verre de lunette *m*; ~ **magnifier** *n* INSTRUMENT loupes-lunettes *f pl*; ~ **plate** *n* MECH ENG support des glissières *m*

spectometry *n* GAS TECH spectrométrie *f*

spectral: ~ **analysis** *n* COMP, DP, PHYS, PROP MAT, TELECOM analyse spectrale *f*; ~ **bandwidth** *n* TELECOM largeur de bande spectrale *f*; ~ **characteristic** *n* ELECTRON caractéristique spectrale *f*, courbe de réponse spectrale *f*; ~ **colors** *n pl* (AmE), ~ **colours** *n pl* (BrE) RAD PHYS couleurs spectrales *f pl*; ~ **density** *n* ACOUSTICS, ELECTRON, PHYS densité spectrale *f*; ~ **emission** *n* PROP MAT émission spectrale *f*; ~ **emissivity** *n* PHYS émissivité spectrale *f*; ~ **energy distribution** *n* FUELLESS distribution spectrale d'énergie *f*, spectre d'énergie *m*; ~ **energy irradiance** *n* OPT éclairement énergétique spectrique *m*; ~ **irradiance** *n* OPT densité spectrale d'éclairement *f*, densité spectrale d'éclairement énergétique *f*, éclairement spectrique *m*, TELECOM densité spectrale d'éclairement *f*, densité spectrale d'éclairement énergétique *f*, éclairement spectrique *m*, éclairement spectrique *m*; ~ **line** *n* ASTRON *in spectra of stars* raie spectrale *f*, OPT raie *f*, raie spectrale *f*, PHYS raie du spectre *f*, RAD PHYS raie spectrale *f*, TELECOM raie *f*, raie spectrale *f*; ~ **line profile** *n* RAD PHYS profil de la raie spectrale *m*; ~ **line width** *n* OPT largeur de raie *f*, RAD PHYS, TELECOM largeur de la raie spectrale *f*; ~ **luminance** *n* PHYS luminance spectrale *f*; ~ **luminous efficiency** *n* PHYS efficacité lumineuse spectrale *f*; ~ **map** *n* SPACE carte spectraloïde *f*; ~ **occupancy** *n* TELECOM occupation du spectre *f*; ~ **pyranometer** *n* FUELLESS pyranomètre spectral *m*; ~ **radiance** *n* TELECOM densité spectrale de luminance *f*, densité spectrale de luminance énergétique *f*, luminance spectrique *f*, luminance énergétique

spectrique *f*; ~ **range** *n* PHYS intervalle spectral *m*; ~ **reflectance** *n* PHYS facteur spectral de réflexion *m*, réflectance spectrale *f*; ~ **responsivity** *n* TELECOM sensibilité spectrale *f*; ~ **sensibility** *n* OPT sensibilité spectrale *f*; ~ **sensitivity** *n* CINEMAT sensibilité spectrale *f*; ~ **terms** *n pl* PHYS termes spectraux *m pl*; ~ **transmittance** *n* PHYS transmittance spectrale *f*; ~ **type** *n* ASTRON classe spectrale *f*; ~ **width** *n* TELECOM largeur spectrale *f*; ~ **window** *n* OPT fenêtre spectrale *f*, TELECOM fenêtre *f*

spectrochemical *adj* CHEM, PROP MAT spectrochimique

spectrograph *n* PHYS, RAD PHYS spectrographe *m*

spectrographic: ~ **analysis** *n* PROP MAT, RAD PHYS analyse spectrographique *f*

spectroheliograph *n* ASTRON spectrohéliographe *m*

spectrohelioscope *n* ASTRON spectrohélioscope *m*

spectrometer *n* FUELLESS, GAS TECH, PHYS, PROP MAT, TELECOM, WAVE PHYS spectromètre *m*

spectrometric: ~ **analysis** *n* RAD PHYS analyse spectrale à lecture directe *f*, analyse spectrométrique *f*

spectrometry *n* PETR TECH, TELECOM spectrométrie *f*

spectrophotometer *n* PHYS spectrophotomètre *m*

spectrophotometry *n* PHYS spectrophotométrie *f*

spectroradiometer *n* FUELLESS spectroradiomètre *m*

spectroscope *n* PHYS, WAVE PHYS spectroscope *m*; ~ **collimator** *n* INSTRUMENT collimateur de spectroscope *m*

spectroscopy *n* CHEM, PHYS, RAD PHYS spectroscopie *f*

spectrum *n* ASTRON, CINEMAT, ELECTRON, PHYS spectre *m*, PROP MAT spectre diagramme *m*, RAD PHYS spectre *m*, *of background noise* plage *f*, RECORDING, SPACE spectre *m*; ~ **allocation** *n* NAUT *satellite communications* allotissement spectral *m*; ~ **analysis** *n* RAD PHYS analyse spectrale *f*; ~ **analyzer** *n* TELECOM analyseur de spectre *m*; ~ **projector** *n* RAD PHYS projecteur de spectres *m*; ~ **of turbulence** *n* FLUID PHYS spectre de la turbulence *m*

specular: ~ **density** *n* ACOUSTICS densité en lumière dirigée *f*; ~ **reflection** *n* CINEMAT, PHYS, TELECOM réflexion spéculaire *f*; ~ **reflection coeficient** *n* TELECOM coefficient de réflexion spéculaire *m*

speech: ~ **activity factor** *n* TELECOM facteur d'activité des signaux vocaux *m*; ~ **analysis** *n* TELECOM analyse de la parole *f*; ~ **audiogram** *n* ACOUSTICS audiogramme vocal *m*; ~ **audiometer** *n* ACOUSTICS audiomètre vocal *m*; ~ **audiometry** *n* ACOUSTICS audiométrie vocale *f*; ~ **channel** *n* COMP canal vocal *m*, DP canal à fréquence vocale *m*; ~ **chip** *n* COMP puce parole *f*, DP puce parole *f*, puce vocale *f*; ~ **circuit** *n* TELECOM circuit de parole *m*; ~ **clipper** *n* RECORDING écrêteur du signal de parole *m*; ~ **coding** *n* SPACE, TELECOM codage de la parole *m*; ~ **detection** *n* SPACE *communications* détection de parole *f*; ~ **detector** *n* TELECOM détecteur de parole *m*; ~ **encoding** *n* SPACE *communications*, TELECOM codage de la parole *m*; ~ **filter** *n* RECORDING filtre de parole *m*; ~ **generation** *n* TELECOM génération de parole *f*; ~ **interpolation** *n* SPACE *communications* concentration des conversations *f*; ~ **level** *n* RECORDING niveau de parole *m*; ~ **memory** *n* TELECOM mémoire de trame *f*, mémoire de parole *f*; ~ **module** *n* PROD ENG module à synthèse vocale *m*; ~ **path** *n* TELECOM trajet de conversation *m*; ~ **processing** *n* COMP, DP, TELECOM traitement de la parole *m*; ~ **production** *n* TELECOM production de la parole *f*; ~ **recognition** *n* COMP, DP reconnaissance de la parole *f*; ~ **scrambler** *n* TELECOM brouilleur de parole *m*; ~ **service** *n* TELECOM service de parole *m*, service de circuit commuté de parole *m*, service support CCBNT type parole *m*; ~ **signal** *n* TELECOM signal de parole *m*; ~ **synthesis** *n* COMP, DP, ELECTRON, TELECOM synthèse de la parole *f*; ~ **synthesizer** *n* COMP, DP synthétiseur de parole *m*; ~ **track** *n* RECORDING piste parole *f*

speech-data: ~ **network** *n* TELECOM réseau de parole-données *m*

speech-grade: ~ **private wire** *n* TELECOM liaison spécialisée tous usages *f*

speechware *n* COMP logiciel de reconnaissance de la parole *m*

speed:[1] **over** ~ *adv* PROD ENG en surrégime

speed[2] *n* MECH ENG débit de rouage *m*, PAPER TECH vitesse *f*, PHYS célérité *f*, vitesse *f*, TEXTILES, TRANSP vitesse *f*; ~ **brake** *n* TRANSP aérofrein *m*; ~ **cone** *n* MECH ENG cône *m*, cône de transmission *m*, cône de vitesse *m*, cône-poulie *m*, poire *f*, poulie étagée *f*, poulie à gradins *f*; ~ **control** *n* CONTROL régulation de vitesse *f*, ELEC *machine* réglage de vitesse *m*, régulation de vitesse *f*, TEXTILES contrôle de vitesse *m*; ~ **control device** *n* FUELLESS régulateur de vitesse *m*; ~ **controller** *n* MECH ENG contrôleur de vitesse *m*; ~ **counter** *n* MECH ENG compte-tours *m*, compteur de tours *m*; ~ **detector** *n* TRANSP détecteur de vitesse *m*; ~ **flow diagram** *n* TRANSP diagramme vitesse débit *m*; ~ **flow relationship** *n* TRANSP relation vitesse-débit *f*; ~ **governor** *n* MECH ENG régulateur de vitesse *m*, PAPER TECH réducteur de vitesse *m*; ~ **indicator** *n* MECH ENG tachymètre *m*, PAPER TECH indicateur de vitesse *m*; ~ **lathe** *n* MECH ENG tour avec poupée fixe à cône *m*, tour rapide *m*, tour à marche rapide *m*; ~ **of light** *n* PHYS célérité de la lumière *f*, WAVE PHYS vitesse de la lumière *f*; ~ **limit** *n* TRANSP limitation réglementaire de vitesse *f*, vitesse maximale permise *f*; ~ **limiter** *n* AUTO limiteur de vitesse *m*, régulateur *m*; ~ **over the ground** *n* NAUT *of ship* vitesse sur le fond *f*; ~ **pot** *n* PROD ENG potentiomètre de vitesse *m*; ~ **recorder** *n* INSTRUMENT, MECH ENG enregistreur de vitesse *m*, TEXTILES appareil enregistreur de vitesse *m*; ~ **recording tape** *n* RAIL bande Flaman *f*, bande tachygraphique *f*; ~ **reducer** *n* MECH ENG contrôleur de vitesse *m*, réducteur de vitesse *m*, PAPER TECH réducteur de vitesse *m*; ~ **regulation** *n* CONTROL régulation de vitesse *f*; ~ **regulator** *n* CONTROL régulateur de vitesse *m*; ~ **restriction** *n* TRANSP *vehicles* limitation de vitesse *f*; ~ **selector** *n* CINEMAT, RECORDING sélecteur de vitesse *m*; ~ **setting knob** *n* PHOTO bouton de réglage de temps de pose *m*, bouton de réglage de vitesse *m*; ~ **of sound** *n* PHYS célérité du son *f*, vitesse sonique *f*; ~ **switch** *n* PROD ENG interrupteur tachymétrique *m*; ~ **through the water** *n* NAUT *of ship* vitesse surface *f*; ~ **track** *n* REFRIG *for speed skating* anneau de vitesse *m*; ~ **trap** *n* TRANSP *traffic* détecteur de vitesse *m*; ~ **variation frequency** *n* ACOUSTICS fréquence de fluctuation *f*

speed:[3] ~ **up** *vt* PAPER TECH accélérer

speed-changing: ~ **device** *n* MECH ENG dispositif de changement de vitesse *m*; ~ **mechanism** *n* MECH ENG dispositif de changement de vitesse *m*

speed-checking: ~ **appliance** *n* MECH ENG appareil ralentisseur de vitesse *m*

speed-density: ~ **relationship** *n* TRANSP relation vitesse-densité *f*

speedometer *n* AUTO compteur de vitesse *m*, *of car* tachymètre *m*, NAUT *electronic equipment* indicateur de vitesse *m*, VEHICLES *accessory* compteur *m*, comp-

teur de vitesse *m*; ~ **cable** *n* AUTO *of car* flexible de tachymètre *m*; ~ **drive gear** *n* AUTO carré d'entraînement de cable de compteur de vitesse *m*, vis de commande de compteur de vitesse *f*

speed-volume: ~ **curve** *n* TRANSP courbe vitesse-débit *f*

spellcheck *vi* DP faire une vérification orthographique

spellchecker *n* DP contrôle orthographique *m*, programme de vérification orthographique *m*

spend: ~ **ground** *vi* MINING épuiser les chantiers d'abattage

spent[1] *adj* CHEM épuisé

spent:[2] ~ **acid** *n* DETERGENTS acide usagé *m*, TEXTILES acide de récupération *m*; ~ **capacity** *n* PROD ENG heures passées *f pl*, temps passé *m*; ~ **grinding sand** *n* C&G sable usé *m*

sperm: ~ **oil** *n* DETERGENTS huile d'ambre blanc *f*, huile de blanc de baleine *f*, huile de spermaceti *f*

spermaceti: ~ **oil** *n* DETERGENTS huile d'ambre blanc *f*, huile de blanc de baleine *f*, huile de spermaceti *f*

spermidine *n* CHEM spermidine *f*

spermin *n* CHEM spermine *f*

spermine *n* CHEM spermine *f*

sperrylite *n* MINERAL sperrylite *f*

spessartine *n* MINERAL spessartite *f*

spessartite *n* MINERAL spessartite *f*

SPF *abbr* (*segmentation permitted flag*) TELECOM indicateur de segmentation permise *m*

sphalerite *n* MINERAL sphalérite *f*

sphene *n* MINERAL sphène *m*

sphere *n* GEOM, PHYS, PROP MAT sphère *f*; ~ **gap** *n* ELEC ENG éclateur à sphères *m*; ~ **of reflection** *n* CRYSTALL sphère de réflexion *f*; ~ **wave** *n* ELEC ENG onde sphérique *f*

spherical[1] *adj* GEOM sphérique

spherical:[2] ~ **aberration** *n* ASTRON *of reflector telescope* aberration de sphéricité *f*, CINEMAT, PHOTO aberration sphérique *f*, PHYS *of reflector telescope* aberration de sphéricité *f*, TELECOM aberration sphérique *f*; ~ **antenna** *n* TELECOM antenne sphérique *f*; ~ **baffle** *n* RECORDING baffle sphérique *m*; ~ **burrs** *n pl* MECH ENG fraises-limes sphériques *f pl*; ~ **container** *n* TRANSP *of methane carrier* cuve sphérique *f*; ~ **coordinates** *n pl* PHYS coordonnées sphériques *f pl*; ~ **distortion** *n* CINEMAT distorsion sphérique *f*; ~ **geometry** *n* GEOM géométrie sphérique *f*; ~ **harmonic** *n* SPACE harmonique sphérique *m*; ~ **joint** *n* VEHICLES *steering* articulation sphérique *f*; ~ **lens** *n* CINEMAT objectif sphérique *m*, PHYS lentille sphérique *f*; ~ **mirror** *n* INSTRUMENT, LAB EQUIP, OPT, PHYS, TELECOM miroir sphérique *m*; ~ **plain bearing** *n* MECH ENG rotule lisse *f*; ~ **plain radial bearing** *n* MECH ENG rotule lisse à contact radial *f*; ~ **seat washer** *n* MECH ENG rondelle à siège sphérique *f*; ~ **sector** *n* GEOM secteur sphérique *m*; ~ **tank** *n* SPACE *spacecraft* réservoir sphérique *m*; ~ **triangle** *n* GEOM triangle sphérique *m*; ~ **wave** *n* ACOUSTICS, PHYS, WAVE phys onde sphérique *f*

sphericity *n* GEOM sphéricité *f*

spheroid *n* GEOM, PHYS sphéroïde *m*

spheroidal[1] *adj* GEOM sphéroïdal

spheroidal:[2] ~ **graphite** *n* MINERAL, PROP MAT graphite sphéroïdal *m*; ~ **graphite cast iron** *n* PROP MAT fonte à graphite sphéroïdal *f*

spherometer *n* PHYS sphéromètre *m*

spherosiderite *n* MINERAL sphérosidérite *f*

spherulite *n* GEOL sphérolite *m*, PETR sphérolithe *m*

spherulitic: ~ **texture** *n* GEOL, PROP MAT texture sphérolitíque *f*

sphingosine *n* CHEM sphingosine *f*

sphragidite *n* MINERAL sphragidite *f*

SPI *abbr (secondary porosity index)* PETR indice de porosité secondaire *m*

spicule *n* ASTRON spicule *f*

spider *n* C&G croisillon *m*, CINEMAT araignée *f*, triangle *m*, PETR araignée *f*, collier à coins *m*, croisillon *m*, étoile *f*, PROD ENG *for mould, core* armature *f*, *of amalgamating pan* curseur *m*, VEHICLES *universal joint* croisillon *m*; ~ **and slips** *n* MINING anneau de manoeuvre *m*; ~ **dolly** *n* CINEMAT chariot Elemack *m*, triangle sur roulettes *m*; ~ **unit** *n* AERONAUT *helicopter* tête du rotor *f*; ~ **wheel** *n* MECH ENG poulie à chicane *f*

spider-type: ~ **armature** *n* ELEC *generator, motor* induit à croisillons *m*

spigot *n* CONST *cock, faucet* robinet *m*, *plug of cock* clef *f*, *vent peg* fausset *m*; ~ **holder** *n* MECH ENG *die set* nez cylindrique pour pigeonneau *m*; ~ **joint** *n* CONST assemblage à emboîtement *m*, joint à emboîtement *m*

spigot-and-faucet: ~ **joint** *n* CONST assemblage à emboîtement *m*, joint à emboîtement *m*; ~ **joint pipes** *n pl* CONST assemblage à emboîtement *m*, joint à emboîtement *m*

spike *n* C&G picot fond *m*, CINEMAT pointe *f*, CONST broche *f*, crampon *m*, ELEC ENG pointe de tension *f*, MINING *quarrying* coin *m*, NUCLEAR semence *f*, TRANSP *aircraft* cône d'entrée d'air *m*, TV impulsion parasite *f*; ~ **driver** *n* RAIL tirefonneuse *f*; ~ **nail** *n* CONST broche *f*; ~ **puller** *n* (AmE) *(cf sleeper screw extractor)* RAIL arrache-tire-fond *m*

spile *n* CONST pieu *m*, pilot *m*

spiling *n* CONST *driving piles* pilotage *m*, *piles* pieux *m pl*, pilots *m pl*

spilite *n* PETR spilite *f*

spill *n* ELEC ENG redistribution des charges *f*, MAR POLL déversement *m*; ~ **light** *n* CINEMAT lumière parasite *f*

spillage *n* GAS TECH épandage *m*, PETR TECH, WATER SUPP déversement *m*

spillings *n pl* PROD ENG *iron founding* fuites de fonte *f pl*

spillover: ~ **loss** *n* SPACE *communications* perte par débordement *f*

spillway *n* CONST *dams*, FUELLESS *dams*, HYDROL déversoir *m*, WATER SUPP évacuateur *m*; ~ **canal** *n* HYDR EQUIP déversoir *m*; ~ **channel** *n* FUELLESS *dams* déversoir *m*

spilosite *n* PETR spilosite *f*

spin[1] *n* AERONAUT *manoeuvre* vrille *f*, PART PHYS *of proton, neutron*, PHYS, RAD PHYS spin *m*, SPACE rotation *f*; ~ **angular momentum** *n* PHYS moment cinétique de spin *m*; ~ **axis** *n* SPACE axe de rotation *m*; ~ **chiller** *n* REFRIG refroidisseur à tambour agitateur *m*, refroidisseur à tambour rotatif *m*; ~ **down** *n* SPACE *spacecraft* ralentissement de la rotation *m*; ~ **exchange** *n* NUCLEAR force d'échange de spin *f*; ~ **orbit coupling** *n* PHYS couplage spin-orbite *m*; ~ **quantum number** *n* PHYS nombre quantique de spin *m*; ~ **reversal transition** *n* PART PHYS transition avec inversion de spin *f*; ~ **rocket** *n* SPACE fusée de mise en rotation *f*; ~ **stabilization** *n* SPACE *communications* stabilisation par rotation *f*; ~ **temperature** *n* PHYS température de spin *f*; ~ **3/2** *n* PART PHYS spin 3/2 *m*; ~ **thruster** *n* SPACE *spacecraft* fusée de mise en rotation *f*, moteur de mise en rotation *m*; ~ **wave** *n* PHYS onde de spins *f*; ~ **wipe** *n* CINEMAT volet rotatif *m*

spin[2] *vt* TEXTILES filer

spin[3] *vi* SPACE tourner sur soi-même, être en rotation

spinasterol *n* CHEM spinastérol *m*

spindle *n* AUTO fusée *f*, C&G *in cutting of hollow glass* broche de machine *f*, *in glass fibre manufacture* tambour de bobinage *m*, CINEMAT axe *m*, MECH broche *f*, MECH ENG arbre *m*, axe *m*, broche *f*, mandrin *m*, *of capstan* mèche *f*, *of injector* aiguille *f*, aiguillede réglage *f*, *of roller* axe *m*, PAPER TECH axe *m*, PRINT axe *m*, PROD ENG axe *m*, *of rig for loam work* arbre à trousser *m*, TEXTILES canette *f*, VEHICLES *of wheel* fusée *f*; ~ **and sweep** *n* PROD ENG *rig for loam work* appareil à trousser *m*, trousseau *m*; ~ **arm** *n* AUTO levier de fusée *m*, PROD ENG *of rig for loam work* bras porte-profil *m*, trusquin porte-planche *m*; ~ **cam** *n* PROD ENG came des axes *f*; ~ **molding machine** *n* (AmE), ~ **moulding machine** *n* (BrE) CONST *wood working* machine à moulurer dite toupie *f*, toupilleuse *f*; ~ **nose** *n* MECH ENG nez de broche *m*, *lathe* nez du mandrin *m*; ~ **unit** *n* MECH ENG *machine tools* unité de broche d'usinage *f*

spindrift *n* HYDROL embrun courant *m*, poudrin *m*, poussière d'eau *f*; ~ **cloud** *n* METEO nuage en queue-de-chat *m*

spine *n* PRINT dos *m*

spinel *n* CHEM, MINERAL spinelle *m*; ~ **refractory** *n* C&G réfractaire de spinelle *m*

spinnaker *n* NAUT *sailing* spinnaker *m*; ~ **boom** *n* NAUT *spars* tangon *m*

spinner *n* AERONAUT *propeller* casserole d'hélice *f*, cône d'hélice *m*, C&G assiette *f*

spinning *n* C&G filage *m*; ~ **bodies** *n pl* FLUID PHYS *in fluid study* corps en rotation rapide *m*, corps tournant rapidement *m*; ~ **disc humidifier** *n* (BrE) REFRIG humidificateur à disque tournant *m*; ~ **disk humidifier** *n* (AmE) *see spinning disc humidifier*; ~ **line** *n* PETR TECH câble de vissage *m*; ~ **paper** *n* PAPER TECH papier à filer *m*; ~ **reserves** *n pl* FUELLESS *electrical motor* machine de réserve tournant à vide *f*; ~ **system** *n* TEXTILES système de filature *m*; ~ **of the wheel** *n* AUTO patinage d'une roue *m*; ~ **wheel** *n* TEXTILES rouet *m*; ~ **yarn** *n* TEXTILES fil à facettes *m*

spinodal: ~ **alloy** *n* PROP MAT alliage spinodal *m*; ~ **decomposition** *n* METALL décomposition spinodale *f*; ~ **instability** *n* PROP MAT transformation spinodale *f*

spin-up *n* SPACE *spacecraft* mise en rotation *f*

spiral[1] *adj* GEOM en spirale, spiroïdal, MECH ENG en hélice, en spirale, hélicoïde, spiraloïde, spiroïdal, à hélice, à spirale, spiral

spiral[2] *n* GEOM spirale *f*, MECH ENG hélice *f*, spirale *f*; ~ **antenna** *n* TELECOM antenne spirale *f*; ~ **arm** *n* ASTRON *of galaxy* bras spiral *m*; ~ **balance** *n* METR peson cylindrique *m*, peson à hélice *m*, peson à ressort *m*; ~ **bevel gearing** *n* AUTO couple conique à denture spirale *m*; ~ **bit** *n* PETR TECH trépan hélicoïdal *m*; ~ **casing** *n* PROD ENG *of turbine, centrifugal pump, fan* enveloppe en spirale *f*; ~ **chute** *n* MINING descenseur hélicoïdal *m*; ~ **classifier** *n* COAL TECH séparateur à hélice *m*; ~ **clutch** *n* MECH ENG embrayage à enroulement *m*, embrayage à spirale *m*; ~ **conveyor** *n* PROD ENG convoyeur à vis sans fin *m*, transporteur à vis sans fin *m*, vis transporteuse *f*; ~ **corkscrew** *n* TEXTILES fil chenillé *m*; ~ **dive** *n* AERONAUT piqué en spirale *m*, spirale engagée *f*; ~ **fracture** *n* C&G casse en spirale *f*; ~ **galaxy** *n* ASTRON galaxie spirale *f*; ~ **gear** *n* MECH ENG engrenage hélicoïdal *m*; ~ **gearing** *n* MECH ENG engrenage hélicoïdal *m*; ~ **glide** *n* AERONAUT descente en spirale *f*; ~ **milling cutter** *n* MECH ENG fraise à denture hélicoïdale *f*; ~ **ratchet**

screwdriver end *n* MECH ENG entraînement pour tournevis automatique *m*; ~ **runner bars** *n pl* C&G aubes *f pl*; ~ **spring** *n* MECH ENG ressort à boudin *m*, SPRINGS ressort spirale *m*; ~ **stairs** *n pl* CONST escalier en escargot *m*, escalier en limaçon *m*, escalier en spirale *m*, escalier en vis *m*, escalier hélicoïdal *m*, escalier tournant *m*; ~ **track** *n* OPT spire *f*; ~ **turbulence** *n* FLUID PHYS turbulence en spirale *f*; ~ **waveguide** *n* TELECOM guide d'ondes hélicoïdal *m*; ~ **wheel** *n* MECH ENG roue hélicoïdale *f*

spiral-coiled: ~ **spring** *n* MECH ENG ressort en spirale *m*

spirally: ~ **wound tube** *n* PACKAGING tube rubanné *m*

spiran *n* CHEM spiranne *m*

spirane *n* CHEM spiranne *m*

spire *n* MECH ENG spire *f*

spirit *n* CHEM alcool *m*, esprit *m*, essence *f*; ~ **duplicator copy paper** *n* PAPER TECH papier pour duplicateur à alcool *m*; ~ **gage** *n* (AmE), ~ **gauge** *n* (BrE) FOOD TECH pèse-alcool *m*; ~ **lacquer** *n* COLOURS vernis à l'alcool *m*, CONST laque alcoolique *f*; ~ **lamp** *n* LAB EQUIP *heating* lampe à alcool *f*; ~ **level** *n* CONST niveau à alcool *m*, niveau à bulle d'air *m*, METR niveau à bulle *m*; ~ **poise** *n* FOOD TECH *fermentation* alcoolomètre *m*; ~ **of turpentine** *n* CHEM essence de térébenthine *f*; ~ **varnish** *n* COLOURS vernis à l'alcool *m*

spit *n* HYDROL presqu'île *f*, OCEANOG barre littorale *f*, flèche littorale *f*, musoir *m*, éperon corallien *m*

SPITE *abbr (switching process interworking telephony event)* TELECOM événement téléphonique de traitement des opérations de commutation *m*

SPL *abbr (service provider link)* TELECOM liaison de prestataire de service *f*

splash *n* MINING paquet *m*; ~ **guard** *n* PROD ENG rabat-eau *m*; ~ **lubrication** *n* AUTO, RAIL graissage par barbotage *m*; ~ **lubrification** *n* REFRIG graissage par barbotage *m*; ~ **wing** *n* PROD ENG rabat-eau *m*

splashback *n* CONST revêtement *m*

splashboard *n* PROD ENG *for grinding wheel* rabat-eau *m*

splashdown *n* AERONAUT, SPACE amerrissage *m*

splasher *n* PROD ENG rabat-eau *m*

splashes *n pl* MINING *of ore* paquets *m pl*, taches *f pl*

splash-proof: ~ **vent cap** *n* AUTO bouchon anti-éclaboussure *m*

splat: ~ **cooling** *n* C&G hypertrempe *f*

splay *vi* CONST *window frame* s'ébraser

splayed: ~ **joint** *n* CONST assemblage en sifflet *m*, joint à sifflet *m*; ~ **miter joint** *n* (AmE), ~ **mitre joint** *n* (BrE) CONST assemblage à onglet en sifflet *m*

splice[1] *n* C&G épissure *f*, CINEMAT collure *f*, MECH collage mécanique *m*, NAUT *rope*, OPT épissure *f*, PAPER TECH collure *f*, PRINT collage de la bande neuve sur la bande finissante *m*, PROD ENG épissure *f*, TELECOM raccord *m*, épissure *f*, TV *mechanical* collage mécanique *m*; ~ **bar** *n* RAIL éclisse *f*; ~ **box** *n* ELEC *connection* boîte de jonction de câble *f*; ~ **joint** *n* CONST *scarf* enture *f*, RAIL éclisse *f*; ~ **loss** *n* TELECOM affaiblissement d'épissure *m*, perte d'épissure *f*

splice[2] *vt* CINEMAT coller, faire une collure, COMP *joint* coller, TELECOM épissurer, *cable* épissurer, TEXTILES épisser, TV faire une collure

spliced: ~ **rope** *n* NAUT câble épissé *m*

splicer *n* CINEMAT colleuse *f*, presse à coller *f*, TELECOM colleuse *f*; ~ **cable** *n* (AmE) TELECOM soudeur *m*, épisseur *m*

splicing *n* PAPER TECH raccordement *m*, TEXTILES épissage d'un fil cassé *m*; ~ **block** *n* CINEMAT gabarit de

collage *m*; ~ **cement** *n* CINEMAT colle à film *f*, pathéine *f*; ~ **table** *n* PRINT table de collage *f*, table de montage *f*; ~ **tape** *n* CINEMAT ruban adhésif *m*, scotch *m*

spline *n* MECH cannelure *f*, MECH ENG cannelure *f*, *feather key* clavette linguiforme *f*, languette *f*, SPACE cannelure *f*; ~ **and serration** *n* MECH ENG cannelure et dentelure *f*; ~ **gage** *n* (AmE), ~ **gauge** *n* (BrE) METR calibre à languette *m*; ~ **key** *n* NUCLEAR clavette parallèle *f*

splined *adj* MECH cannelé

splining: ~ **tool** *n* MECH ENG *slotting machine* outil à clavetage *m*

splinter *n* CONST écharde *f*, éclat *m*

splinters *n pl* C&G spliures *f pl*

splintery: ~ **fracture** *n* COAL TECH cassure à éclats *f*

split[1] *adj* C&G fendu

split[2] *n* C&G glaçure *f*, CONST *crack* fente *f*, éclat *m*, MINING dérivation *f*, *divided air current* courant partiel *m*, PRINT coupe délibérée *f*, PROD ENG fractionnement *m*, lot fractionné *m*, PROP MAT crevasse *f*; ~ **anode magnetron** *n* ELECTRON magnétron à anode en deux parties *m*; ~ **beam camera** *n* CINEMAT caméra à prisme diviseur *f*; ~ **beam cathode ray tube** *n* TV tube cathodique à faisceau divisé *m*; ~ **core box** *n* PROD ENG boîte à noyaux en deux parties *f*; ~ **die** *n* MECH ENG coussinet fendu *m*; ~ **field lens** *n* CINEMAT lentille bifocale *f*, lentille à double focale *f*; ~ **flap** *n* AERONAUT *aircraft* volet d'intrados *m*; ~ **housing** *n* AUTO pont à trompettes *m*, trompette de pont *f*, VEHICLES *rear axle assembly* pont à trompette *m*; ~ **image rangefinder** *n* PHOTO stigmomètre *m*; ~ **lens** *n* INSTRUMENT lentille fendue *f*; ~ **mold** *n* (AmE), ~ **mould** *n* (BrE) C&G moule ouvrant *m*, P&R moule à coins *m*; ~ **phase motor** *n* ELEC moteur à enroulement auxiliaire de démarrage *m*, ELEC ENG moteur à enroulement auxiliaire *m*; ~ **pin** *n* MECH ENG goupille fendue *f*; ~ **piston skirt** *n* AUTO jupe de piston fendue *f*; ~ **pole motor** *n* ELEC moteur à bague de déphasage *m*; ~ **pulley** *n* MECH ENG poulie en deux pièces *f*; ~ **railroad tie** *n* (AmE) *(cf split sleeper)* RAIL traverse crevassée *f*; ~ **reel** *n* CINEMAT bobine démontable *f*; ~ **ring** *n* MECH ENG bague fendue *f*; ~ **ring flare nut spanner** *n* (BrE) MECH ENG *tool* clé polygonale à tuyauterie *f*; ~ **ring flare nut wrench** *n* MECH ENG *tool* clé polygonale à tuyauterie *f*; ~ **rollers** *n pl* C&G roulettes de séparation *f pl*; ~ **screen** *n* CINEMAT multi-images *f*, polyptyque *m*, COMP, DP écran partagé *m*, écran partagé en régions *m*; ~ **sleeper** *n* (BrE) *(cf split railroad tie)* RAIL traverse crevassée *f*; ~ **spool** *n* CINEMAT bobine démontable *f*; ~ **stator variable capacitor** *n* ELEC ENG condensateur variable à rotor commun *m*; ~ **weld** *n* PROD ENG soudure à gueule-de-loup *f*; ~ **welding** *n* PROD ENG soudure à gueule-de-loup *f*

split[3] *vt* CONST *slate* refendre, MINING *air current* subdiviser, TEXTILES fendre; ~ **into thin sheets** *vt* CONST *slate* débiter en feuillets; ~ **in two** *vt* CONST *tree* refendre en deux; ~ **with wedges** *vt* CONST *wood* fendre avec des coins

split[4] *vi* CONST se fendre, se subdiviser, éclater, MECH ENG, RAIL crevasser, se crevasser

split-set: ~ **collar** *n* MECH ENG bague d'arrêt en deux pièces *f*

splitter *n* CINEMAT, COAL TECH diviseur *m*; ~ **box** *n* ELEC *cable accessory* boîte de séparation *f*

splitting *n* C&G *of the cylinder* fendage *m*, CONST fendage *m*, refente *f*, subdivision *f*, CRYSTALL *of crystal defects*,

PHYS *of multiplet* décomposition *f*, PROD ENG fractionnement *m*; ~ **ax** *n* (AmE), ~ **axe** *n* (BrE) CONST hache à fendre *f*; ~ **electrode** *n* TV électrode diviseuse de faisceau *f*

SPN *abbr (subscriber premises network)* TELECOM réseau d'installation d'abonnés *m*

spodumene *n* MINERAL spodumène *m*

spoil[1] *n* CONST *civil engineering*, RAIL déblai *m*; ~ **bank** *n* MINING halde *f*, halde de déblais *f*, halde de déchets *f*; ~ **car** *n* (AmE) *(cf small tip wagon)* RAIL wagonnet *m*; ~ **disposal** *n* CONST évacuation des déblais *f*; ~ **heap** *n* CONST *civil engineering* cavalier de déblais *m*, MINING crassier *m*, terril *m*, halde *f*, halde de déblais *f*, halde de déchets *f*; ~ **tip** *n* COAL TECH dépôt des schistes *m*; ~ **to waste** *n* CONST *roads* déblais mis en dépôt *m pl*

spoil[2] *vt* FOOD TECH gâter

spoiled: ~ **casting** *n* PROD ENG pièce manquée *f*, rebut *m*; ~ **negative** *n* PHOTO cliché manqué *m*

spoiler *n* AERONAUT *aircraft* déporteur *m*, spoiler *m*, TRANSP aileron *m*, bavette *f*, becquet *m*, déflecteur *m*, jupe *f*, volet *m*, *road vehicles* déporteur *m*, VEHICLES *body* becquet *m*

spoils *n pl* PRINT macules *f pl*

spoke *n* MECH ENG roue à rais *f*, roue à rayons *f*, VEHICLES roue à rayons *f*; ~ **wheel center** *n* (AmE), ~ **wheel centre** *n* (BrE) VEHICLES corps de roue à rayons *m*

spokeshave *n* CONST planchette *f*, racloir *m*, vastringue *f*

spondee *n* ACOUSTICS spondée *m*

sponge: ~ **bed** *n* GEOL spongolithe *m*; ~ **culture** *n* OCEANOG spongiculture *f*; ~ **lead** *n* AUTO plomb spongieux *m*

spongine *n* CHEM spongine *f*

spontaneous: ~ **brake application** *n* RAIL *vehicles* freinage de service *m*; ~ **breaking** *n* C&G pète *f*; ~ **combustion** *n* SAFETY combustion spontanée *f*; ~ **decay** *n* RAD PHYS *of radioactive element* désintégration spontanée *f*; ~ **emission** *n* ELECTRON, PHYS *of laser* émission spontanée *f*, RAD PHYS *of radiation* rayonnement spontané *m*, émission spontanée *f*, TELECOM émission spontanée *f*; ~ **excitation** *n* NUCLEAR auto-excitation *f*; ~ **fission** *n* PHYS, RAD PHYS fission spontanée *f*; ~ **fission probability** *n* RAD PHYS probabilité de fission spontanée *f*; ~ **ignition** *n* SPACE *spacecraft* inflammation spontanée *f*; ~ **log** *n* FUELLESS rapport spontané *m*; ~ **magnetization** *n* PHYS, RAD PHYS aimantation spontanée *f*; ~ **nucleation** *n* METALL germination spontanée *f*; ~ **potential log** *n* GEOPHYS diagramme de polarisation spontanée *m*, PETR TECH diagraphie de polarisation spontanée *f*; ~ **transitions** *n pl* RAD PHYS transitions spontanées *f pl*

spoofing *n* COMP duperie *f*, tromperie *f*, DP tentative de perturbation *f*, tentative de perturbation d'un système *f*, tromperie *f*; ~ **program** *n* DP programme espion *m*

spool[1] *n* ACOUSTICS, C&G bobine *f*, CINEMAT bobine *f*, dévidoir *m*, rouleau *m*, COMP, DP, PHOTO *of film* bobine *f*, PROD ENG tiroir *m*, RECORDING, TV bobine *f*; ~ **piece** *n* PETR manchette de raccordement *f*

spool[2] *vt* CINEMAT, TV enrouler

spooler *n* COMP, DP spooleur *m*

spooling *n* COMP spoolage *m*, DP traitement différé d'entrées-sorties *m*, PHOTO embobinage *m*, TV bobinage *m*

spoon: ~ **auger** *n* CONST laceret à cuiller *m*, tarière à cuiller *f*; ~ **bow** *n* NAUT *boatbuilding* avant en cuiller *m*,

étrave en cuiller *f*; ~ **dredge** *n* WATER SUPP drague à cuiller *f*; ~ **dredger** *n* WATER SUPP drague à cuiller *f*; ~ **sampler** *n* COAL TECH échantillonneur à curettes *m*

sports: ~ **finder** *n* PHOTO viseur sportif *m*

spot:[1] **on the** ~ *adj* CONST sur les lieux, sur place

spot[2] *n* CINEMAT projecteur à faisceau dirigé *m*, spot *m*, TRANSP point de poser *m*; ~ **beam** *n* SPACE *communications* faisceau étroit *m*, pinceau fin *m*; ~ **beam antenna** *n* SPACE *communications* antenne à faisceau étroit *f*, antenne à pinceau étroit *f*; ~ **beam coverage** *n* TELECOM couverture par faisceaux ponctuels *f*; ~ **color** *n* (AmE), ~ **colour** *n* (BrE) PRINT couleur d'accompagnement *f*; ~ **cooling** *n* REFRIG refroidissement localisé *m*; ~ **footing** *n* COAL TECH fondation isolée *f*; ~ **speed** *n* TRANSP vitesse instantanée *f*; ~ **train** *n* TRANSP train sauvage *m*, train spontané *m*; ~ **welding** *n* CONST soudage par résistance par points *m*, ELEC soudage par points *m*

spot[3] *vt* PHOTO retoucher

spotface: ~ **cutter** *n* MECH ENG foret-aléseur en bout *m*

spotlight *n* CINEMAT projecteur à faisceau dirigé *m*, spot *m*, ELEC *lighting* projecteur à faisceau concentré *m*, PHOTO projecteur spot *m*, projecteur à lentilles *m*, VEHICLES *lighting* projecteur à longue portée *m*

spotmeter *n* CINEMAT spotmètre *m*

spot-shape: ~ **corrector** *n* TV correction de la configuration du spot *f*

spotted: ~ **slate** *n* GEOL *contact metamorphic rock* schiste tacheté *m*

spotter: ~ **plane** *n* MAR POLL avion d'observation *m*, avion de repérage *m*, avion de réglage de tir *m*

spotting *n* PHOTO repiquage *m*; ~ **plate** *n* LAB EQUIP *analysis* plaque à godet *f*; ~ **tile** *n* LAB EQUIP *analysis* plaque à godet *f*

spout *n* C&G bec *m* (Bel), divergents à la réception *m pl* (Fra), *in rolling process* goulotte *f*, *of Owens machine* lèvre de coulée *f*, LAB EQUIP *glassware* bec *m*, METEO trombe *f*, PROD ENG dégorgeoir *m*, goulotte *f*, *of oil can* bec *m*, WATER SUPP *of pump* jet *m*; ~ **cover** *n* (AmE) *(cf cover tile)* C&G brique couvre-goulotte *f*; ~ **hole** *n* WATER SUPP *of pump* lumière *f*

spouting *n* HYDROL jaillissement *m*

spray[1] *n* FLUID PHYS pulvérisation *f*, HYDROL eau pulvérisée *f*, poussière d'eau *f*, pulvérin *m*, NAUT *of sea* embruns *m pl*, PROD ENG pulvérisateur *m*, vaporisateur *m*; ~ **aperture** *n* MAR POLL ouverture de jet *f*; ~ **boom** *n* MAR POLL rampe de pulvérisation *f*; ~ **cellulose paint** *n* COLOURS peinture cellulosique au pistolet *f*; ~ **chamber** *n* REFRIG chambre de pulvérisation *f*; ~ **coater** *n* PAPER TECH coucheuse par pulvérisation *f*; ~ **coating** *n* COATINGS revêtement par projection *m*, PRINT couchage par vaporisation *m*, enduction par vaporisation *f*; ~ **compressor** *n* PROD ENG compresseur à injection *m*, compresseur à injection d'eau *m*; ~ **condenser** *n* GAS TECH condenseur à jet *m*; ~ **cooling** *n* REFRIG refroidissement par aspersion *m*; ~ **cutter** *n* PAPER TECH coupe-feuilles hydraulique *m*; ~ **diffuser** *n* CHEM TECH pulvérisateur de liquide *m*; ~ **drag** *n* AERONAUT *at takeoff* traînée due aux projections *f*; ~ **drying** *n* DETERGENTS séchage par pulvérisation *m*; ~ **freezer** *n* REFRIG congélateur à aspersion *m*; ~ **freezing** *n* REFRIG congélation par pulvérisation *f*; ~ **gun** *n* MAR POLL diffuseur *m*, pistolet pulvérisateur *m*, pistolet à peinture *m*, pulvérisateur *m*; ~ **hood** *n* NAUT cabriolet *m*; ~ **irrigation** *n* HYDROL irrigation par aspersion *f*; ~ **pain-**

ting *n* CONST peinture au pistolet *f*; ~ **producer** *n* PROD ENG pulvérisateur *m*, vaporisateur *m*; ~ **tap** *n* MECH ENG robinet de pulvérisation *m*

spray² *vt* COLOURS peindre au pistolet, MAR POLL pulvériser, vaporiser, épandre, PAPER TECH pulvériser; ~ **down** *vt* CINEMAT mater; ~ **with shotcrete** *vt* CONST recouvrir d'une couche de béton appliquée par projection

spray-dried *adj* DETERGENTS séché par pulvérisation

sprayer *n* CHEM pulvérisateur *m*, vaporisateur *m*, PAPER TECH, PETR TECH pulvérisateur *m*; ~ **nozzle** *n* MECH ENG pistolet pulvérisateur *m*

spraying *n* HYDROL pulvérisation *f*; ~ **paint** *n* P&R peinture au pistolet *f*; ~ **screen** *n* COAL TECH crible de rinçage *m*

spraypath *n* MAR POLL trace de la pulvérisation *f*, trajectoire de pulvérisation *f*

spray-type: ~ **cooler** *n* REFRIG refroidisseur à pulvérisation *m*; ~ **evaporator** *n* REFRIG évaporateur à aspersion interne *m*

spread¹ *n* C&G élargissement du ruban *m*, COMP, DP dispersion *f*, étalement *m*, GAS TECH extension *f*, REFRIG *of air stream* étalement *m*, SPACE dispersion *f*, étalement *m*; ~ **roll** *n* PACKAGING, PAPER TECH rouleau déplisseur *m*; ~ **spectrum modulator** *n* ELECTRON modulateur à spectre étalé *m*, modulateur à étalement du spectre *m*; ~ **spectrum multiple access** *n* (*SSMA*) SPACE *communications* accès multiple par étalement du spectre *m* (*AMES*); ~ **spectrum signal** *n* ELECTRON, NAUT *satellite communications* signal à spectre étalé *m*

spread² *vt* PROD ENG *sand* répandre, WATER SUPP *jet of water* étaler

spread³ *vi* MAR POLL s'étaler, se répandre

spreader *n* CINEMAT araignée *f*, triangle *m*, MECH *lifting gear* palonnier *m*, écarteur *m*, MINING étrésillon *m*, PAPER TECH distributeur *m*, répartiteur *m*, TRANSP *loading, cranes* agrippeur *m*, palonnier *m*, *road making* répandeuse *f*; ~ **bar** *n* PAPER TECH barre déplisseuse *f*; ~ **jet** *n* WATER SUPP *for branch pipe* jet à éventail *m*; ~ **roll** *n* PAPER TECH rouleau brisé *m*

spreading *n* CHEM épandage *m*, MAR POLL épandage *m*, étalement *m*; ~ **field** *n* RECYCLING, WATER SUPP champ d'épandage *m*; ~ **lens** *n* INSTRUMENT lentille de redressement *f*; ~ **machine** *n* COATINGS enduiseuse *f*; ~ **rate** *n* GEOL *of ocean floor* taux d'expansion *m*, vitesse d'expansion *f*; ~ **table** *n* PROD ENG table d'épandage *f*

spreadsheet *n* COMP tableur électronique *m*, DP tableur *m*, PRINT tableau comptable *m*

spread-spectrum: ~ **modulation** *n* ELECTRON modulation avec étalement du spectre *f*, modulation à spectre étalé *f*, TELECOM modulation par étalement du spectre *f*

sprig *n* PROD ENG *moulder's nail* pointe de mouleur *f*; ~ **bolt** *n* CONST boulon de scellement à crans *m*, cheville barbelée *f*

spring¹ *n* CONST *of arch* naissance *f*, retombée *f*, HYDROL *of running water* source *f*, source vive *f*, *source* fontaine *f*, source *f*, MECH, MECH ENG *elastic body, device* ressort *m*, NAUT *mooring* garde montante *f*, PHYS, PROP MAT, VEHICLES ressort *m*; ~ **acid shock** *n* POLLUTION choc acide du printemps *m*, choc acide printanier *m*; ~ **adjusting caliper** *n* (AmE), ~ **adjusting calliper** *n* (BrE) METR compas d'épaisseur *m*; ~ **and toggle mechanism** *n* PROD ENG mécanisme à bascule et à ressort *m*; ~ **axis** *n* SPRINGS axe du ressort *m*; ~

balance *n* MECH ENG balance à ressort *f*, *for weighing* peson à hélice *m*, peson àressort *m*, PHYS balance à ressort *f*; ~ **band** *n* MECH ENG *for leaf spring* bride du ressort *f*; ~ **bolt** *n* CONST verrou à ressort *m*, *latch bolt of lock* demi-tour *m*, pêne à demi-tour *m*, pêne à ressort *m*, PROD ENG pêne à ressort *m*; ~ **buckle** *n* MECH ENG *for leaf-spring* bride du ressort *f*; ~ **bumper** *n* (AmE) (*cf spring damper*) RAIL *on wagon or coach* tampon sec *m*, tampon à ressort *m*; ~ **cage press** *n* C&G presse à cage à ressorts *f*; ~ **clip** *n* MECH ENG pince à ressort *f*; ~ **commutator** *n* ELEC *switch* commutateur à ressort *m*; ~ **cotter** *n* MECH ENG clavette fendue *f*; ~ **damper** *n* (BrE) (*cf spring bumper*) RAIL *on wagon or coach* tampon sec *m*, tampon à ressort *m*; ~ **dividers** *n pl* MECH ENG compas à ressort *m*; ~ **ejector** *n* MECH ENG poussoir à ressort *m*; ~ **end grinding** *n* SPRINGS meulage des extrémités de ressort *m*; ~ **equinox** *n see vernal equinox* ~ **forelock** *n* MECH ENG clavette fendue *f*; ~ **governor** *n* MECH ENG régulateur à ressort *m*; ~ **grease lubricator** *n* PROD ENG graisseur à compression *m*, graisseur à ressort *m*;~ **guide** *n* PROD ENG guide de ressort *m*; ~ **hanger pin** *n* CONST boulon de suspension *m*; ~ **head** *n* HYDROL source *f*; ~ **hook** *n* MECH ENG crochet de sûreté *m*, mousqueton *m*; ~ **index** *n* SPRINGS rapport d'enroulement *m*; ~ **jack** *n* ELEC ENG jack à ressort *m*; ~ **key** *n* MECH ENG clavette fendue *f*; ~ **latch** *n* PROD ENG loquet à ressort *m*; ~ **load** *n* SPRINGS charge du ressort *f*; ~ **load testing machine** *n* SPRINGS machine d'essai de charge de ressorts *f*; ~ **lock** *n* CONST serrure à bosse *f*, serrure à pêne à demi-tour *f*, serrure à ressort *f*; ~ **manometer** *n* PHYS manomètre à ressort *m*; ~ **materials** *n pl* SPRINGS matériaux de ressorts *m*; ~ **neap cycle** *n* FUELLESS *tides* cycle des marées de forts et faibles coefficients *m*; ~ **pitch** *n* SPRINGS pas de l'hélice *m*; ~ **power hammer** *n* PROD ENG marteau-pilon à ressort *m*; ~ **pressure plate** *n* CINEMAT planchette de pression à ressort *f*; ~ **rate** *n* SPRINGS raideur du ressort *f*; ~ **release device** *n* SPACE *spacecraft* ressorts de séparation *m pl*; ~ **retainer** *n* AUTO coupelle d'appui du ressort *f*; ~ **return force** *n* PROD ENG force de rappel à ressort *f*; ~ **return lever** *n* PROD ENG levier à rappel *m*; ~ **return switch** *n* ELEC interrupteur à ressort de rappel *m*; ~ **reverberation unit** *n* RECORDING chambre de réverbération à ressort *f*; ~ **seat** *n* AUTO siège du ressort *m*; ~ **stop** *n* MECH ENG *machine tool* butée à ressort *f*; ~ **subjected to bending** *n* MECH ENG ressort de flexion *m*; ~ **subjected to torsion** *n* MECH ENG ressort de torsion *m*; ~ **switch** *n* ELEC interrupteur à ressorts *m*; ~ **tab** *n* MECH ENG *machine tool* compensateur à ressort *m*; ~ **tape rule** *n* METEO *measuring* mesure roulante *f*, mesure à ruban *f*; ~ **tide** *n* (*cf neap tide*) FUELLESS marée de vive eau *f*, HYDROL grande marée *f*, marée de vive eau *f*, OCEANOG grande marée *f*; ~ **valve** *n* HYDR EQUIP clapet à ressort *m*, soupape à ressort *f*; ~ **washer** *n* MECH ENG rondelle élastique *f*, rondelle à ressort *f*; ~ **water** *n* HYDROL, WATER SUPP eau de source *f*; ~ **wire** *n* SPRINGS fil à ressort *m*; ~ **zone** *n* C&G point chaud *m*

spring² *vi* HYDROL *to rise from source* sourdre

spring-coiling: ~ **machine** *n* SPRINGS machine à enrouler les ressorts *f*

spring-drive: ~ **camera** *n* CINEMAT caméra à ressort *f*

springer *n* CONST *architecture* coussinet *m*, sommier *m*; ~ **stone** *n* CONST *architecture* coussinet *m*, sommier *m*

springiness *n* PROP MAT élasticité *f*

springing *n* CONST *architecture* coussinet *m*, sommier *m*,

MINING sautage en pochées *m*, sautage par mines pochées *m*, PROP MAT déjettement *m*; ~ **course** *n* CONST *of arch* assise de retombée *f*; ~ **line** *n* CONST *of arch* ligne des naissances *f*

spring-loaded[1] *adj* PROD ENG rappelé par ressort, à ressort

spring-loaded:[2] ~ **core** *n* MECH ENG *injection mould* noyau rapporté mobile *m*, P&R pièce rapportée mobile *f*; ~ **pressure relief valve** *n* REFRIG soupape de sûreté à ressort *f*; ~ **valve** *n* HYDR EQUIP soupape à ressort *f*

spring-mounted: ~ **pressure plate** *n* PHOTO presseur à ressort *m*

spring-tensioned: ~ **pressure lever** *n* PHOTO levier de pression à ressort *m*

sprinkle *vt* CHEM *dust* saupoudrer, WATER SUPP *water* arroser

sprinkled: ~ **edge** *n* PRINT tranche mouchetée *f*

sprinkler *n* CONST *for garden* arrosoir rotatif *m*, *for fire fighting* gicleur d'incendie *m*, SAFETY gicleur d'incendie *m*, *firefighting* appareil d'arrosage *m*, sprinkler *m*, WATER SUPP appareil d'arrosage *m*, arroseur *m*; ~ **and water spray fire-extinguishing installations** *n* SAFETY installation comportant des gicleurs et pulvérisateurs anti-incendie *f*

sprinkling *n* CHEM *dust* saupoudrage *m*, WATER SUPP *water* arrosage *m*, arrosement *m*

sprint: ~ **mission** *n* SPACE *spacecraft* mission express *f*, mission rapide *f*

sprite *n* COMP, DP motif programmé *m*

sprocket *n* AUTO roue dentée *f*, roue pignon *f*, CINEMAT tambour denté *m*, COMP, DP ergot *m*, PROD ENG pignon *m*, VEHICLES pignon à chaîne *m*; ~ **and chain timing** *n* AUTO distribution par chaîne et roues dentées *f*; ~ **chain** *n* MECH, MECH ENG chaîne Galle *f*; ~ **drive** *n* CINEMAT entraînement par tambour denté *m*; ~ **hole** *n* CINEMAT perforation *f*, COMP, DP perforation d'entraînement *f*, PHOTO perforation *f*; ~ **hole control track system** *n* RECORDING système à piste de contrôle sur les trous d'entraînement *m*; ~ **noise** *n* CINEMAT bruit des perforations *m*; ~ **tooth** *n* CINEMAT dent d'entraînement *f*; ~ **wheel** *n* MECH pignon à chaîne *m*, MECH ENG pignon de Galle *m*

sprue *n* P&R *moulding* carotte *f*, PROD ENG *metal left* jet *m*, *runner pin* broche de coulée *f*, coulée *f*; ~ **bush** *n* MECH ENG buse chambre chaude *f*, buse de moule chambre chaude *f*, *injection mould* raccord de buse plongeante *m*, P&R buse *f*; ~ **cutter** *n* PROD ENG coupe-coulées *m*, machine à couper les coulées *f*; ~ **ejector pin guide** *n* MECH ENG *injection mould* bague dévêtisseuse de carotte d'injection *f*; ~ **hole** *n* PROD ENG coulée *f*, jet de coulée *m*, trou de coulée *m*; ~ **opening** *n* P&R *injection moulding* ouverture de chargement *f*, ouverture de remplissage *f*; ~ **pin** *n* MECH ENG *diecasting die* diffuseur chambre chaude *m*; ~ **puller pin** *n* MECH ENG *injection mould* éjecteur de carotte d'injection par retenue *m*

sprung: ~ **gear** *n* VEHICLES *gearbox* engrenage à denture droite *m*; ~ **weight** *n* VEHICLES *body* élément suspendu *m*

SPST:[1] *abbr (single-pole single-throw)* ELEC, ELEC ENG à un contact interrupteur

SPST:[2] ~ **relay** *n (single-pole single-throw relay)* ELEC, ELEC ENG relais SPST *m*, relais à simple contact interrupteur *m*, relais à un contact interrupteur *m*; ~ **switch** *n (single-pole single-throw switch)* ELEC, ELEC ENG

interrupteur unipolaire *m*

spuce *n* PAPER TECH épicéa *m*

spud:[1] ~ **mud** *n* PETR TECH boue de démarrage *f*

spud:[2] ~ **in** *vt* PETR débuter

spudding:[1] ~ **in** *adv* PETR TECH en début de forage

spudding:[2] ~ **bit** *n* PETR TECH trépan bêche *m*, trépan d'attaque *m*, trépan de battage *m*; ~ **in** *n* PETR TECH début de forage *m*

spun: ~ **cable** *n* OPT câble assemblé *m*; ~ **concrete** *n* CONST béton filé *m*; ~ **glass** *n* C&G verre filé *m*; ~ **roving** *n* C&G stratifil bouclé *m*; ~ **yarn** *n* TEXTILES bitord *m*; ~ **yarn sizing** *n* TEXTILES encollage sur filé de fibre *m*; ~ **yarn winch** *n* TEXTILES moulinet à bitords *m*

spunbond *n* TEXTILES filé fondu non tissé *m*

spun-dyed *adj* TEXTILES teint dans la masse

spur *n* CONST *strut, brace* arc-boutant *m*, contrefiche *f*, entretoise *f*, éperon *m*, ELEC *system* dérivation *f*; ~ **chuck** *n* MECH ENG mandrin à trois pointes *m*; ~ **dike** *n* (AmE), ~ **dyke** *n* (BrE) OCEANOG épi *m*; ~ **gear** *n* MECH ENG roue droite *f*; ~ **line** *n* PETR TECH embranchement de conduite sous-marine *m*; ~ **tenon joint** *n* CONST enture à goujon *f*, enture à simple tenon *f*; ~ **wheel** *n* MECH ENG roue droite *f*

spur-geared: ~ **pulley block** *n* MECH ENG palan à engrenage droit *m*

spurious: ~ **emission level** *n* SPACE *communications* niveau des émissions parasites *m*; ~ **signal** *n* SPACE *communications* signal brouilleur *m*

spurt *n* SPACE *communications* impulsion vocale *f*

spurting: ~ **out** *n* HYDROL jaillissement *m*

sputter *vi* CHEM *liquid* éclabousser

sputtering *n* CHEM *of liquid* éclaboussage *m*, ELEC ENG pulvérisation cathodique *f*

spy: ~ **hole** *n* MECH ENG regard *m*

spyglass *n* INSTRUMENT lunette *f*, télescope *m*

squalane *n* CHEM squalane *m*

squalene *n* CHEM squalène *m*

squall *n* METEO bourrasque *f*, grain *m*, rafale *f*

square[1] *n* CONST carreau *m*, MECH ENG *drawing instrument* carré *m*, METR équerre *f*; ~ **back** *n* PRINT *bookbinding* dos carré *m*; ~ **bag** *n* PACKAGING *with gussets* sac carré *m*; ~ **ball lock retainer** *n* MECH ENG *die set* porte poinçon carré à bille *m*; ~ **bellows camera** *n* PHOTO chambre française à soufflet carré *f*; ~ **bit drive** *n* MECH ENG *tools* carré d'entraînement *m*; ~ **centimeter** *n* (AmE), ~ **centimetre** *n* (BrE) METR centimètre carré *m*; ~ **decimeter** *n* (AmE), ~ **decimetre** *n* (BrE) METR décimètre carré *m*; ~ **drift** *n* MECH ENG mandrin carré *m*; ~ **driftpin** *n* MECH ENG mandrin carré *m*; ~ **drive** *n* MECH ENG *tool* carré conducteur *m*; ~ **end** *n* SPRINGS bout droit *m*; ~ **file** *n* MECH ENG carreau *m*, carrelet *m*, lime carrée *f*; ~ **foot** *n* METR pied carré *m*; ~ **head** *n* CONST carré *m*; ~ **head screw** *n* MECH ENG vis à tête rectangulaire *f*; ~ **inch** *n* METR pouce carré *m*; ~ **joint** *n* CONST assemblage à plat *m*, assemblage à plat joint *m*, joint carré *m*, joint àplat *m*; ~ **loop** *n* ELEC ENG cycle rectangulaire *m*; ~ **loop ferrite** *n* ELEC ENG ferrite à cycle rectangulaire *f*; ~ **measure** *n* METR mesure de superficie *f*, mesure de surface *f*; ~ **meter** *n* (AmE), ~ **metre** *n* (BrE) METR mètre carré *m*; ~ **mile** *n* METR mille carré *m*; ~ **neck bolt** *n* MECH ENG vis à métaux à collet carré *f*; ~ **parallel keys** *n pl* MECH ENG clavettes parallèles carrées *f pl*; ~ **rabbet plane** *n* CONST guillaume de bout *m*, guillaume de fil *m*; ~ **root** *n* MATH racine carrée *f*; ~ **root and edge angles** *n pl* METR cornières à angles vifs *f pl*; ~ **ruler** *n* MECH ENG carrelet *m*, réglette *f*; ~

shank drill n MECH ENG foret à queue carrée m; ~ **thread** n MECH ENG of screw filet carré m; ~ **thread screw** n MECH ENG vis à filet carré f, vis à filet rectangulaire f, vis à pas carré f; ~ **thread tap** n MECH ENG taraud à filet carré m; ~ **timber** n CONST bois carré m; ~ **to roof** n CONST comble en dent de scie m, comble-shed m, shed m; ~ **transom stern** n NAUT boatbuilding arrière carré m; ~ **washer** n MECH ENG rondelle carrée f; ~ **wave** n ELECTRON onde carrée f, signal carré m, PHYS onde carrée f, onde rectangulaire f, signal carré m, signal rectangulaire m, RECORDING onde rectangulaire f; ~ **waveform** n TELECOM signal carré m; ~ **wave generation** n ELECTRON génération de signaux carrés f; ~ **wave generator** n ELECTRON, RECORDING générateur de signaux carrés m, TV générateur d'ondes rectangulaires m; ~ **wave voltage** n TV tension crénelée f; ~ **yard** n METR yard carré m

square[2] vt MATH élever au carré, PROD ENG carrer, dresser, équarrir

square:[3] **be ~** vi PROD ENG se carrer

squared: ~ **and ground end** n SPRINGS extrémité rapprochée et meulée f; ~ **end** n SPRINGS extrémité rapprochée f; ~ **timber** n CONST bois équarri m

square-edge: ~ **preparation** n CONST welding préparation d'un bord droit f

square-jointed: ~ **floor** n CONST plancher m

square-law[1] adj PHYS parabolique, quadratique

square-law:[2] ~ **detector** n ELEC ENG détecteur quadratique m

square-mouthed: ~ **rabbet** n CONST guillaume de bout m, guillaume de fil m

squareness n CONST équarrissage m, équarrissement m; ~ **cylinder** n METR cylindre d'équerrage m; ~ **tolerance** n SPRINGS tolérance de perpendicularité f

square-threaded: ~ **screw** n MECH ENG vis à filet carré f, vis à filet rectangulaire f, vis à pas carré f

squaring n CONST dressage m, équarrissage m, équarrissement m, PAPER TECH équerrage m; ~ **the circle** n GEOM quadrature du cercle f; ~ **circuit** n TV circuit conformateur m

squat n TRANSP ships accroupissement m

squawkbox n RECORDING interphone m

squealing n TELECOM accrochage m

squeegee[1] n C&G for optical glass colloir m, for enamelling raclette f, CINEMAT essoreuse f, raclette f, PHOTO raclette f, rouleau d'essorage m, PRINT, TEXTILES racle f

squeegee[2] vt PHOTO essorer

squeeze[1] n CINEMAT anamorphose f, compression f, MINING tassement m, PETR TECH cimentation sous pression f, esquichage m; ~ **roll** n PAPER TECH rouleau essoreur m; ~ **roll coater** n PAPER TECH coucheuse à rouleau essoreur f; ~ **roller** n PRINT rouleau d'essorage m; ~ **track** n RECORDING piste compressée f

squeeze[2] vt PAPER TECH essorer, PROD ENG presser; ~ **out** vt PROD ENG exprimer

squeeze[3] vi MINING mine roof charger, donner, tasser

squeezer n PROD ENG moulding machine machine à compression f

squeezing n MINING tassement m, PAPER TECH essorage par pression m; ~ **roller** n TEXTILES cylindre de pression m, rouleau exprimeur m

squelch n TELECOM silencieux m

squib n CONST fétu m, MINING amorce f, capsule f, mèche f, SPACE amorceur m, étoupille f

squid abbr (superconducting quantum interference de-

vice) PHYS squid (interféromètre quantique)

squirrel: ~ **cage** n ELEC ENG cage d'écureuil f; ~ **cage motor** n ELEC, ELEC ENG moteur en cage d'écureuil m, PROD ENG moteur d'écureuil m; ~ **cage rotor** n ELEC ENG rotor en cage d'écureuil m; ~ **cage winding** n ELEC ENG enroulement en cage d'écureuil m

squirt n PAPER TECH jet m; ~ **hose** n WATER SUPP tuyau d'arrosage m

squitter n NUCLEAR auto-excitation f

Sr (strontium) CHEM Sr (strontium)

SRAM abbr (static RAM) COMP RAM statique f

SRC abbr (single-rubber-covered) ELEC guipé une couche caoutchouc

SRD abbr (superradiant diode) OPT, TELECOM diode superluminescente f

SRF: ~ **carbon black** n (semireinforcing carbon black) P&R noir SRF m

SSB abbr (single sideband) TELECOM BLU (bande latérale unique)

SSC abbr (sudden storm commencement) SPACE début brusque d'orage magnétique m

S-shaped: ~ **hook** n MECH ENG S de suspension m, crochet en S m, esse f; ~ **spanner** n (BrE) (cf S-wrench) MECH ENG clé cintrée en S f, clé en S f

SSI abbr COMP (small-scale integration) intégration à petite échelle f, DP (small-scale integration) intégration à faible échelle f, ELECTRON (small-scale integration) intégration à petite échelle f, RAIL (solid-state interlocking) système d'enclenchement informatisé m

SSM abbr SPACE (second surface mirror) miroir à couche secondaire m, TELECOM (single segment message) message à segment unique m, message à un seul segment m

SSMA abbr (spread spectrum multiple access) SPACE communications AMES (accès multiple par étalement du spectre)

SSOG abbr (Satellite System Operation Guide) SPACE guide d'exploitation des liaisons par satellite m

SST abbr (supersonic transport) AERONAUT transport supersonique m

S-stage n TELECOM étage S m, étage spatial m

SSUS abbr (solid spinning upper stage) SPACE étage supérieur stabilisé par rotation m

ST abbr (segment type) TELECOM type de segment m

stab: ~ **stitching** n PRINT piqûre à plat f; ~ **terminal** n PROD ENG cosse à fiches f; ~ **termination** n PROD ENG branchement par cosses à fiches m

stabbing n PETR TECH guidage m, PRINT piqûre à plat f; ~ **board** n PETR TECH plate-forme de vissage f

stability n CHEM of compound, COAL TECH, COMP, DP, MINING, NAUT ship design, TELECOM stabilité f; ~ **curtain** n TRANSP rideau de stabilité m; ~ **curve** n NAUT ship design courbe de stabilité f; ~ **skirt** n TRANSP hovercraft jupe de stabilité f

stabilization n CHEM, COAL TECH, ELEC, GAS TECH, NAUT ship design, P&R process, QUALITY, REFRIG, SPACE communications stabilisation f; ~ **by low center of gravity** (AmE), ~ **by low centre of gravity** n (BrE) TRANSP stabilisation par position basse du centre de gravité f; ~ **device** n TRANSP dispositif de stabilisation m; ~ **rail** n TRANSP rail de stabilisation m; ~ **of rotation** n SPACE spacecraft stabilisation de la rotation f; ~ **time** n OPT temps de stabilisation m, PROP MAT temps de conditionnement m

stabilized[1] adj CHEM stabilisé

stabilized:[2] ~ **latex** *n* P&R latex stabilisé *m*; ~ **material** *n* CONST matériau stabilisé *m*; ~ **platform** *n* SPACE *spacecraft* plate-forme stabilisée *f*

stabilizer *n* AERONAUT *aircraft* stabilisateur *m*, C&G stabilisant *m*, CHEM stabilisant *m*, stabilisateur *m*, CINEMAT, COAL TECH, ELEC stabilisateur *m*, MILIT *guided missile* stabilisateur automatique *m*, NAUT *ship*, P&R *compounding ingredient*, PETR TECH, PHOTO stabilisateur *m*, TRANSP stabilisateur automatique *m*, VEHICLES *suspension* stabilisateur *m*; ~ **bar** *n* AUTO stabilisateur *m*, MECH, VEHICLES *suspension* barre stabilisatrice *f*

stabilizing: ~ **agent** *n* CHEM stabilisant *m*; ~ **bath** *n* CINEMAT bain stabilisateur *m*; ~ **fin** *n* NAUT empennage *m*; ~ **wheel** *n* TRANSP roue de stabilisation *f*; ~ **winding** *n* ELEC enroulement de stabilisation *m*

stabilotron *n* PHYS stabilotron *m*

stable[1] *adj* CHEM *compound* stable

stable:[2] ~ **air** *n* METEO air stable *m*; ~ **current** *n* OCEANOG courant établi *m*; ~ **emulsion** *n* PROP MAT émulsion stable *f*; ~ **equilibrium** *n* PHYS équilibre stable *m*; ~ **field** *n (cf disturbed field)* METEO champ stable *m*; ~ **flow** *n* TRANSP *of traffic* écoulement normal *m*; ~ **isotope** *n* PHYS isotope stable *m*; ~ **noise** *n* ACOUSTICS bruit stable *m*; ~ **state** *n* CONTROL état stable *m*

stable[3] *vt* RAIL *vehicles* garer

stable-to-light *adj* PACKAGING résistant à la lumière

stabling *n* RAIL garage *m*, *vehicles* remisage *m*

stachydrine *n* CHEM stachydrine *f*

stachyose *n* CHEM stachyose *m*

stack[1] *n* AERONAUT pile d'attente *f*, *of aircraft* ensemble *m*, C&G *of discs* carotte *f*, *of flat glass* pile *f*, COMP pile *f*, CONST *chimney* cheminée *f*, DP, PAPER TECH *of paper* pile *f*, PETR cheminée *f*, sommation *f*, somme *f*; ~ **architecture** *n* COMP, DP architecture de pile *f*; ~ **gas** *n* NUCLEAR gaz d'échappement *m*, gaz rejeté *m*; ~ **pipe** *n* CONST descente *f*, descente d'eau *f*, tuyau de descente *m*; ~ **plume** *n* C&G panache à la cheminée *m*

stack[2] *vt* COMP, CONST, DP empiler, PROD ENG empiler, entasser, mettre en tas; ~ **up** *vt* PAPER TECH empiler

stackable[1] *adj* PACKAGING, PROD ENG empilable

stackable:[2] ~ **container** *n* TRANSP conteneur gerbable *m*

stacked: ~ **dryer section** *n* PAPER TECH sécherie à cylindres sécheurs superposés *f*; ~ **heads** *n pl* TV têtes magnétiques empilées *f pl*; ~ **presses** *n pl* PAPER TECH presses étagées *f pl*

stacker *n* C&G chargeur d'arche *m*; ~ **arm** *n* C&G bras de mise à l'arche *m*

stacking *n* AERONAUT *air traffic control* échalonnage vertical *m*, C&G mise à l'arche *f*, *in warehouse* empilage *m*, COMP empilage *m*, CRYSTALL empilement *m*, DP empilage *m*, GEOM, PACKAGING empilement *m*, PAPER TECH empilage *m*, PRINT *of paper* gerbage *m*, PROD ENG empilage *m*, empilement *m*, entassement *m*, mise en tas *f*; ~ **box** *n* PACKAGING caisse d'empilage *f*; ~ **conveyor** *n* PACKAGING transporteur-gerbeur *m*; ~ **fault** *n* CRYSTALL défaut d'empilement *m*; ~ **height** *n* PACKAGING hauteur d'empilage *f*; ~ **pallet** *n* PACKAGING palette à montants *f*, TRANSP palette gerbable *f*; ~ **sequence** *n* CRYSTALL séquence d'empilement *f*; ~ **truck** *n* PACKAGING gerbeur *m*; ~ **up** *n* PACKAGING empilement *m*

STADAN *abbr (space tracking and data acquisition network)* MILIT réseau de poursuite et de saisie de données dans l'espace *m*

stadia: ~ **surveying** *n* CONST levé de plans au stadia *m*

stadiometer *n* CONST stadiomètre *m*

staff *n* CONST *surveyor's levelling rod* mire *f*, PROD ENG *puddler's rabble* crochet *m*, ringard *m*; ~ **holder** *n* CONST *person* porte-mire *m*; ~ **reading** *n* CONST *surveying* cote lue sur la mire *f*

staff-calling: ~ **installation** *n* SAFETY *radio operated* installation radio d'appel du personnel *f*

stage *n* CINEMAT plateau *m*, CONST *scaffold* échafaud *m*, échafaudage *m*, GEOL étage *m*, INSTRUMENT, LAB EQUIP *microscope* platine *f*, MINING jet *m*, travée *f*, étage *m*, *of ladderway* palier de repos *m*, plancher de repos *m*, PAPER TECH stade de fabrication *m*, PROD ENG opération *f*, passe *f*, stade *m*, étape *f*; ~ **base** *n* INSTRUMENT module porte-platine *m*, socle-support de la platine *m*; ~ **clip** *n* INSTRUMENT, LAB EQUIP *of microscope* valet de la platine *m*; ~ **compression** *n* PROD ENG *of air* compression compound *f*, compression étagée *f*; ~ **compressor** *n* MECH ENG *air* compresseur étagé *m*, PROD ENG compresseur compound *m*, compresseur étagé *m*; ~ **coupling** *n* ELEC ENG liaison entre étages *f*; ~ **efficiency** *n* ELECTRON rendement de l'étage *m*; ~ **integrator** *n* SPACE étagiste *m*; ~ **loader** *n* MINING répartiteur *m*; ~ **pumping** *n* MINING épuisement en répétitions *m*

staged *adj* PROP MAT étagé

staggered: ~ **air bar** *n* PRINT barre à air décalé en quinconce *f*; ~ **fin** *n* REFRIG ailette gaufrée *f*; ~ **heads** *n pl* RECORDING têtes décalées *f pl*, TV têtes magnétiques décalées *f pl*; ~ **locks** *n pl* HYDROL *canal* écluses jumelées décalées *f pl*; ~ **packing** *n* C&G empilage en dominos en simple chicane *m*

staggering *n* TV décalage *m*

stagger-tuned: ~ **amplifier** *n* ELECTRON amplificateur à circuits décalés *m*

staging *n* COMP transfert *m*, CONST échafaud *m*, échafaudage *m*, DP transfert *m*, PROD ENG réservation physique *f*

stagnant: ~ **area** *n* NUCLEAR région morte *f*, sillage dormant *m*; ~ **water** *n* HYDROL, WATER SUPP eau stagnante *f*

stagnation: ~ **point** *n* AERONAUT *aerodynamics* point d'arrêt *m*, point d'impact *m*, FLUID PHYS, PHYS point d'arrêt *m*; ~ **pressure** *n* FLUID PHYS pression d'arrêt *f*

stain[1] *n* PAPER TECH, QUALITY tache *f*

stain[2] *vt* CHEM colorer, COLOURS teindre, teinter, P&R *defect* tacher, PAPER TECH colorer, QUALITY tacher

stained: ~ **glass window** *n* C&G vitrail *m*

stainer *n* COLOURS teinturier *m*; ~ **pigment** *n* COLOURS pigment à nuancer *m*

staining *n* C&G cémentation *f*, ternissement *m*, CHEM coloration *f*; ~ **class** *n* C&G classe de durabilité *f*

stainless[1] *adj* METALL, PAPER TECH, PHOTO inoxydable

stainless:[2] ~ **steel** *n* PAPER TECH, PROP MAT, VEHICLES acier inoxydable *m*; ~ **steel beaker** *n* LAB EQUIP bécher en acier inoxydable *m*; ~ **steel dust** *n* COAL TECH poussière d'acier inoxydable *f*; ~ **steel tube** *n* MECH ENG tube en acier inoxydable *m*

stair *n* CONST escalier *m*, marche *f*; ~ **rod dislocation** *n* METALL dislocation tringle *f*

staircase *n* CONST cage d'escalier *f*, escalier *m*, passage d'escalier *m*, marche *f*, TV *shape of signal* escalier *m*; ~ **signal** *n* TV signal dégradé *m*

stairs *n pl* CONST marche *f*; ~ **interrupted by landings** *n pl* CONST escalier rompu en paliers *m*

stairway *n* CONST cage d'escalier *f*, escalier *m*, passage d'escalier *m*, marche *f*

stairwell *n* CONST cage d'escalier *f*

stake *n* CONST *stick, post* fiche *f*, jalon *m*, pieu *m*, *surveying* piquet *m*; ~ **net** *n* OCEANOG bas-parc *m*, haut-parc *m*

staking *n* CONST *surveying* jalonnement *m*, piquetage *m*

stalagmometer *n* PHYS stalagmomètre *m*

stale *adj* FOOD TECH éventé

staling *n* FOOD TECH rassissement *f*

stall¹ *n* AERONAUT *compressor, turbine engine* décollement *m*, *of aircraft* décrochage *m*, COAL TECH taille *f*, FUELLESS décrochage *m*, MINING chambre de grillage du minerai *f*; ~ **fence** *n* AERONAUT cloison de décrochage *f*; ~ **load** *n* PROD ENG charge provoquant un calage moteur *f*; ~ **road** *n* MINING allée de desserte *f*, galerie de desserte *f*, galerie desservant la taille *f*; ~ **warning device** *n* AERONAUT avertisseur de décrochage *m*

stall² *vt* VEHICLES *engine* caler

stall³ *vi* FUELLESS décrocher

stamp¹ *n* COAL TECH bocard *m*, PROD ENG bocard *m*, emboutisseuse *f*, emboutissoir *m*, estampeuse *f*, étampeuse *f*, pilon *m*; ~ **battery** *n* PROD ENG batterie de bocards *f*, batterie de pilons *f*; ~ **boss** *n* PROD ENG surcharge de pilon *f*, tête de pilon *f*; ~ **etching paste** *n* C&G pâte pour gravure au cachet *f*; ~ **guide** *n* PROD ENG guide de pilon *m*; ~ **head** *n* PROD ENG surcharge de pilon *f*, tête de pilon *f*; ~ **house** *n* MINING atelier des bocards *m*; ~ **mill** *n* PROD ENG bocard *m*, moulin à bocards *m*; ~ **milling** *n* PROD ENG bocardage *m*, broyage au bocard *m*; ~ **shoe** *n* PROD ENG sabot de pilon *m*; ~ **stem** *n* PROD ENG flèche de pilon *f*, tige du pilon *f*

stamp² *vt* PROD ENG bocarder, emboutir, estamper, étamper, frapper, poinçonner

stamped: ~ **bucket** *n* CONST godet embouti *m*

stamper *n* ACOUSTICS matrice de pressage *f*, OPT matrice de pressage *f*, PROD ENG *person* emboutisseur *m*, estampeur *m*, étampeur *m*

stamping *n* ELEC ENG tôle magnétique *f*, tôle magnétique découpée *f*, PRINT empreinte à la plaque *f*, estampage *m*, timbrage *m*, PROD ENG *branding* frappage *m*, poinçonnage *m*, *crushing* bocardage *m*, *sheet metal working* emboutissage *m*, estampage *m*, étampage *m*; ~ **machine** *n* PROD ENG *sheet metal working* emboutisseuse *f*, estampeuse *f*, étampeuse *f*; ~ **mill** *n* PROD ENG *for crushing ore* bocard *m*, moulin à bocards *m*; ~ **press** *n* PRINT presse à gaufrer *f*, PROD ENG *sheet metal working* emboutisseuse *f*, estampeuse *f*, étampeuse *f*; ~ **test** *n* PROD ENG *of metals* essai d'emboutissage *m*; ~ **varnish** *n* COATINGS vernis pour découpage *m*

stanchion *n* CONST *prop* étançon *m*, NAUT chandelier *m*, RAIL rancher *m*; ~ **deck fitting** *n* NAUT douille de chandelier *f*

stand¹ *n* CHEM support *m*, CINEMAT pied *m*, INSTRUMENT monture *f*, potence *f*, statif *m*, LAB EQUIP support *m*, VEHICLES *motorcycle* béquille *f*; ~ **on wheels** *n* PROD ENG socle à roulettes *m*; ~ **of pipe** *n* PETR TECH longueur de tige *f*; ~ **of tide** *n* NAUT étale de marée *m*, OCEANOG étale *m*; ~ **with rising table** *n* PROD ENG support en plateau à hauteur variable *m*

stand² *vt* PROD ENG *rough handling* résister; ~ **for** *vt* NAUT *navigation* gouverner sur

stand:³ ~ **inshore** *vi* NAUT *navigation* rallier la terre; ~ **to the north** *vi* NAUT *navigation* mettre le cap au nord

standage *n* MINING bouniou *m*, collecteur d'eau *m*, puisard *m*

stand-alone¹ *adj* COMP, DP autonome

stand-alone:² ~ **controller** *n* PROD ENG automate programmable indépendant *m*; ~ **exchange** *n* TELECOM central autonome *m*; ~ **system** *n* SPACE *communications* système indépendant *m*; ~ **unit** *n* PROD ENG unité indépendante *f*

standard¹ *adj* COMP, DP standard, MECH ENG au titre, classique, type, étalon, PHYS *statistics* étalon

standard² *n* COMP norme *f*, CONST *scaffold pole* baliveau *m*, perche *f*, échasse d'échafaud *f*, écoperche *f*, DP norme *f*, MECH ENG étalon *m*, *of rolling mill* cage *f*, colonne *f*, *upright support* affût *m*, pied *m*, support *m*, MINING chaise de sol *f*, PHYS norme *f*, standard *m*, étalon *m*, PRINT norme *f*, PROD ENG *for aerial ropeway* pylône *m*, *of power hammer* jambage *m*, *of planing machine* jumelle *f*, montant *m*, QUALITY, TELECOM, TV norme *f*; ~ **altimeter setting** *n* AERONAUT calage altimétrique standard *m*; ~ **ambient temperature** *n* REFRIG température ambiante normale *f*; ~ **atmosphere** *n* METEO atmosphère standard *f*; ~ **capacitor** *n* ELEC ENG condensateur étalon *m*; ~ **cell** *n* ELEC, ELEC ENG, PHYS pile étalon *f*; ~ **compass** *n* NAUT compas étalon *m*; ~ **container** *n* TRANSP conteneur normalisé *m*; ~ **control equipment** *n* PROD ENG équipement standard de commande *m*; ~ **deviation** *n* COMP, DP écart type *m*, ELECTRON écart quadratique moyen *m*, écart type *m*, MATH, PHYS, PROD ENG écart type *m*; ~ **gage** *n* (AmE) *see standard gauge*; ~ **gage film** *n* (AmE) *see standard gauge film*; ~ **gage railroad** *n* (AmE) *see standard gauge railway*; ~ **gauge** *n* (BrE) CONST écartement normal *m*, écartement standard *m*, MECH ENG *for measuring wire or drills* jauge étalon *f*, calibre de référence *m*, calibre étalon *m*, *template, former* gabarit type *m*, RAIL voie normale *f*, écartement normal *m*, écartement standard *m*; ~ **gauge film** *n* (BrE) CINEMAT film de format standard *m*; ~ **gauge railway** *n* (BrE) RAIL *track* chemin de fer à voie normale *m*; ~ **gray card** *n* (AmE), ~ **grey card** *n* (BrE) CINEMAT charte de gris normalisé *f*; ~ **ink** *n* PRINT encre normalisée *f*; ~ **interface** *n* COMP, DP interface standard *f*, TELECOM interface normalisée *f*; ~ **item** *n* PROD ENG article standard *m*; ~ **knob selector** *n* PROD ENG sélecteur à bouton standard *m*; ~ **leader** *n* CINEMAT amorce normalisée *f*; ~ **lens** *n* PHOTO objectif de focale normale *m*; ~ **light source** *n* ELEC ENG lampe étalon *f*; ~ **measure** *n* METR mesure étalon *f*; ~ **measuring signal** *n* TV signal type *m*; ~ **meter** *n* (AmE), ~ **metre** *n* (BrE) PHYS mètre-étalon *m*; ~ **microphone** *n* ACOUSTICS microphone étalon *m*, RECORDING microphone standard *m*; ~ **multigaging elements** *n pl* (AmE), ~ **multigauging elements** *n pl* (BrE) METR éléments standard de contrôles multiples *m pl*; ~ **nut** *n* MECH ENG écrou ordinaire *m*; ~ **ohm** *n* ELEC ohm étalon *m*; ~ **orifice** *n* HYDR EQUIP *in thin wall* orifice standard *m*; ~ **part** *n* MECH ENG élément normalisé *m*; ~ **pattern** *n* TV mire étalon *f*; ~ **pitch** *n* AERONAUT *of propeller* pas nominal *m*; ~ **pressure** *n* PETR pression normale *f*; ~ **of quality** *n* METR niveau de qualité *m*; ~ **rail gage** *n* (AmE), ~ **rail gauge** *n* (BrE) RAIL écartement standard *m*, écartement normal *m*; ~ **rating cycle** *n* REFRIG cycle de référence *m*; ~ **reference atmosphere** *n* MECH ENG atmosphère normale de référence *f*; ~ **reference intensity** *n* RECORDING intensité de référence standard *f*; ~ **sea water** *n* OCEANOG eau normale *f*; ~ **shape** *n* SPACE *spacecraft* profilé standard *m*; ~ **size** *n* PROD ENG dimension type *f*, grandeur normale *f*; ~ **solution** *n* CHEM liqueur titrée *f*, solution standard *f*; ~ **specification** *n* MECH ENG norme *f*, PROD ENG cahier des charges unifié *m*, spécification unifiée *f*; ~ **tape** *n* TV bande étalon *f*; ~ **temperature** *n* PETR température de référence *f*, PHYS température normale *f*; ~ **test piece** *n* PROD ENG éprouvette type *f*; ~ **time** *n* NAUT *navigation* heure du fuseau *f*, heure légale *f*, PROD ENG temps alloué *m*, temps standard *m*; ~ **tone** *n* RECORDING fréquence standard *f*; ~ **tone generator** *n* RECORDING générateur de fréquence standard *m*; ~ **track** *n* RAIL voie classique *f*; ~ **tuning frequency** *n* ACOUSTICS fréquence d'accord normale *f*; ~ **volume indicator** *n* RECORDING indicateur de volume standard *m*; ~ **weights** *n pl* METR poids étalons *m pl*

Standard: ~ **Generalized Mark-up Language** *n* (*SGML*) DP, PRINT langage standard généralisé de balisage *m* (*SGML*)

standardization *n* CHEM standardisation *f*, titrage *m*, COMP, DP, GAS TECH normalisation *f*, PHYS normalisation *f*, standardisation *f*, étalonnage *m*, QUALITY, TELECOM, TV normalisation *f*; ~ **of test methods** *n* MECH ENG unification des méthodes d'essai *f*

standardize *vt* CHEM standardiser, titrer, *solution* normaliser, MECH ENG, PROD ENG unifier, QUALITY normaliser

standardized: ~ **impact sound** *n* ACOUSTICS bruit de choc normalisé *m*; ~ **sound insulation** *n* ACOUSTICS isolement acoustique normalisé *m*; ~ **threshold hearing** *n* ACOUSTICS seuil normalisé d'audition *m*

standard-play: ~ **tape** *n* RECORDING bande de durée standard *f*

standards: ~ **conversion** *n* TV transcodage *m*; ~ **converter** *n* TV transcodeur *m*; ~ **selector** *n* TV sélecteur de normes *m*

stand-by[1] *adj* COMP en attente, en réserve, DP de secours, en attente, en double, en réserve, QUALITY de réserve, TELECOM de réserve, en redondance, en réserve; ~ **working** *adj* TELECOM de réserve, en redondance, en réserve

stand-by:[2] on ~ *adv* MAR POLL en attente

stand-by[3] *n* MILIT attente *f*, PROD ENG appareil de secours *m*, arrêt *m*, arrêt *m*; ~ **boat** *n* PETR TECH bateau d'intervention *m*; ~ **boiler** *n* HEAT ENG chaudière de réserve *f*; ~ **mode** *n* SPACE *spacecraft* mode d'attente *m*; ~ **processor** *n* TELECOM processeur de réserve *m*; ~ **pump** *n* PROD ENG pompe de secours *f*; ~ **set** *n* ELEC ENG groupe de secours *m*; ~ **supply** *n* ELEC réseau de réserve *m*; ~ **system** *n* TELECOM système en mode de secours *m*; ~ **time** *n* COMP, DP temps d'attente *m*; ~ **unit** *n* ELEC ENG groupe de secours *m*

standing:[1] ~ **by** *adj* PROD ENG de secours

standing:[2] ~ **block** *n* MECH ENG moufle fixe *m*, poulie fixe *f*, NAUT *fittings* poulie fixe *f*; ~ **bolt** *n* MECH ENG *stud bolt* boulon prisonnier *m*, goujon prisonnier *m*, prisonnier *m*; ~ **end** *n* MECH ENG *of tackle* dormant *m*; ~ **rigging** *n* NAUT gréement dormant *m*, manoeuvres courantes *f pl*; ~ **timber** *n* CONST bois en état *m*; ~ **vice** *n* (BrE) PROD ENG étau à table *m*; ~ **vise** *n* (AmE) *see standing vice*; ~ **water** *n* HYDROL eau dormante *f*, eau stagnante *f*; ~ **wave** *n* ACOUSTICS onde stationnaire *f*, ELEC ENG onde stationnaire *f*, système d'ondes stationnaires *m*, PHYS, RECORDING, TELECOM, WAVE PHYS onde stationnaire *f*

standing-wave: ~ **ratio** *n* (*SWR*) PHYS, TELECOM rapport d'ondes stationnaires *m* (*ROS*)

standpipe *n* PETR, PETR TECH colonne montante *f*

standstill *n* MECH ENG arrêt *m*

stand-up: ~ **capitals** *n pl* PRINT capitales dressées *f pl*

stannate *n* CHEM stannate *m*

stannic[1] *adj* CHEM stannique

stannic:[2] ~ **oxide** *n* CHEM oxyde stannique *m*

stannite *n* MINERAL stannite *f*

stannous *adj* CHEM stanneux

staple *n* CONST cavalier *m*, clou à deux pointes *m*, crampon *m*, crampon à deux pointes *m*, *lock staple* gâche *f*, FOOD TECH aliment de base *m*, nourriture de base *f*, MINING beurtia *m*, bure *m*, puits intérieur *m*, faux puits *m*, PACKAGING, PAPER TECH agrafe *f*, PROD ENG *stem chaplet* support simple *m*; ~ **fiber** *n* (AmE) *see staple fibre*; ~ **fiber yarn** *n* (AmE) *see staple fibre yarn*; ~ **fibre** *n* (BrE) C&G verranne *f*, TEXTILES bourre *f*; ~ **fibre yarn** *n* (BrE) TEXTILES filé *m*; ~ **food** *n* FOOD TECH aliment de base *m*, denrée principale *f*; ~ **length** *n* TEXTILES longueur de coupe *f*; ~ **pit** *n* MINING beurtia *m*, bure *m*, puits intérieur *m*, faux puits *m*; ~ **post** *n* WATER SUPP *of sluice gate* poteau de vanne *m*, potille *f*; ~ **remover** *n* MECH ENG *tool* outil à dégrafer *m*; ~ **shaft** *n* MINING beurtia *m*, puits intérieur *m*, faux puits *m*; ~ **tissue** *n* C&G voile *m*; ~ **vice** *n* (BrE) PROD ENG étau à pied *m*; ~ **vise** *n* (AmE) *see staple vice*

stapling *n* PRINT agrafage *m* ~ **equipment** *n* PACKAGING équipement d'agrafage *m*; ~ **machine** *n* PACKAGING agrafeuse *f*; ~ **pliers** *n pl* PACKAGING pinces pour agrafer *f pl*; ~ **wire** *n* PACKAGING fil pour agrafes *m*

star *n* COMP, DP étoile *f*, SPACE astre *m*; ~ **atlas** *n* ASTRON atlas des étoiles *m*, atlas stellaire *m*; ~ **bit** *n* MINING trépan à tranchant en croix *m*, PETR TECH trépan en croix *m*; ~ **catalog** *n* (AmE), ~ **catalogue** *n* (BrE) ASTRON catalogue d'étoiles *m*; ~ **chart** *n* NAUT carte des étoiles *f*; ~ **cluster** *n* ASTRON amas d'étoiles *m*; ~ **configuration** *n* TELECOM configuration en étoile *f*, interconnexion en étoile *f*; ~ **connection** *n* ELEC *transformer, reactor* connexion étoilée *f*, ELEC ENG montage en étoile *m*, PHYS connexion en étoile *f*, TELECOM connexion étoilée *f*; ~ **coupler** *n* OPT, TELECOM coupleur en étoile *m*; ~ **crack** *n* C&G amorce étoilée *f*; ~ **diagonal** *n* INSTRUMENT oculaire coudé *m*; ~ **distribution** *n* TELECOM distribution en étoile *f*; ~ **dyeing** *n* COLOURS teinture sur barre à tourniquet *f*; ~ **filter** *n* CINEMAT filtre étoile *m*; ~ **fracture** *n* C&G casse étoilée *f*; ~ **network** *n* COMP, DP réseau en étoile *m*, réseau étoilé *m*, SPACE *communications* réseau en étoile *m*, TELECOM réseau en étoile *m*, réseau étoilé *m*; ~ **quad** *n* ELEC ENG, PHYS *cable* quarte en étoile *f*; ~ **quadded cable** *n* ELEC ENG câble à quartes en étoile *m*; ~ **sensor** *n* SPACE détecteur stellaire *m*; ~ **structure** *n* TELECOM structure en étoile *f*; ~ **switch** *n* TELECOM commutateur en étoile *m*; ~ **topology** *n* COMP, DP topologie en étoile *f*; ~ **tracker** *n* SPACE suiveur stellaire *m*; ~ **transit detector** *n* SPACE détecteur de passage d'étoile *m*; ~ **voltage** *n* ELEC tension en étoile *f*, tension étoilée *f*; ~ **washer** *n* PROD ENG rondelle d'arrêt *f*

starboard *n* NAUT, SPACE *spacecraft* tribord *m*

starburst: ~ **galaxy** *n* ASTRON galaxie à flambée *f*

starch *n* CHEM *compound* amidon *m*, FOOD TECH amidon *m*, empois *m*, PAPER TECH amidon *m*, PRINT amidon *m*, fécule *f*, TEXTILES amidon *m*; ~ **paste** *n* PRINT colle d'amidon *f*, colle à froid *f*; ~ **slurry** *n* FOOD TECH empois d'amidon *m*

starchy *adj* CHEM amylacé, amyloïde, féculent, FOOD TECH amylacé

star-connected[1] *adj* TELECOM monté en étoile
star-connected:[2] ~ **armature** *n* ELEC *generator, motor* induit étoilé *m*
star-delta: ~ **connection** *n* ELEC ENG montage étoile-triangle *m*; ~ **starter** *n* ELEC *switch* commutateur étoile-triangle *m*, ELEC ENG démarreur étoile-triangle *m*; ~ **starting switch** *n* ELEC commutateur étoile-triangle *m*; ~ **switch** *n* ELEC ENG coupleur étoile-triangle *m*; ~ **transformation** *n* PHYS transformation étoile-triangle *f*
Stark: ~ **effect** *n* PHYS effet Stark *m*
starlight *n* ASTRON lumière des étoiles *f*
starred: ~ **roll** *n* PAPER TECH bobine détériorée aux extrémités *f*
star-star: ~ **connection** *n* ELEC connexion étoile-étoile *f*
start[1] *n* COMP, DP amorçage *m*, démarrage *m*, départ *m*, lancement *m*, TELECOM *of transmission* début *m*; ~ **address field** *n* PROD ENG adresse de début de zone *f*; ~ **bit** *n* COMP, DP bit de départ *m*; ~ **button** *n* CINEMAT bouton de mise en marche *m*, CONTROL bouton de démarrage *m*; ~ **element** *n* COMP signal de départ *m*, DP élément de départ *m*; ~ **fence** *n* PROD ENG bit de début *m*, bit de validation de début de zone *m*; ~ **of header** *n* (*SOH*) COMP, DP début *m*; ~ **mark** *n* CINEMAT marque de départ *f*, repère de départ *m*, TV repère de départ *m*; ~ **of message** *n* (*SOM*) COMP, DP début de message *m*; ~ **rung** *n* PROD ENG ligne de début *f*; ~ **statement** *n* PROD ENG instruction de début *f*; ~ **switch** *n* CONTROL interrupteur de démarrage *m*; ~ **of text** *n* (*STX*) COMP, DP début de texte *m*; ~ **time** *n* COMP heure de début *f*, DP instant de démarrage *m*, temps de démarrage *m*
start[2] *vt* C&G *cut* amorcer (Bel), étonner (Fra), COMP, DP amorcer, démarrer, lancer, MECH ENG faire démarrer, mettre en marche, mettre en route, mettre en train, *an injector* amorcer, PROD ENG *hole* amorcer; ~ **in operation** *vt* WATER SUPP *pump* allumer, amorcer; ~ **up** *vt* MECH ENG faire démarrer, mettre en marche, mettre en route, mettre en train
start:[3] ~ **the flow of water in a siphon** *vi* WATER SUPP amorcer un siphon
starter *n* AUTO démarreur *m*, CONTROL interrupteur de démarrage *m*, ELEC *motor* dispositif de démarrage *m*, ELEC *switch* interrupteur de démarrage *m*, starter *m*, ELEC ENG démarreur *m*, FOOD TECH *fermentation, baking* inoculum *m*, levain *m*, VEHICLES démarreur *m*, *engine component* démarreur *m*; ~ **bar** *n* CONST acier en attente *m*; ~ **battery** *n* ELEC, ELEC ENG batterie de démarrage *f*, TRANSP accumulateur de démarrage *m*; ~ **brush** *n* AUTO balai de démarreur *m*; ~ **button** *n* CONTROL bouton de démarrage *m*, VEHICLES *of engine* démarreur *m*; ~ **cable** *n* AUTO câble de démarreur *m*; ~ **collector ring** *n* AUTO collecteur de démarreur *m*; ~ **commutator** *n* AUTO collecteur de démarreur *m*; ~ **control** *n* AUTO commande de démarrage *f*, CONTROL contrôleur de démarrage *m*; ~ **drive assembly** *n* AUTO lanceur *m*; ~ **electrode** *n* ELEC ENG électrode auxiliaire *f*, électrode d'amorçage *f*; ~ **field coil** *n* AUTO inducteur de démarreur *m*; ~ **field winding** *n* AUTO inducteur de démarreur *m*; ~ **gear** *n* AUTO *of car* roue libre *f*, MECH ENG engrenage de démarrage *m*; ~ **jet** *n* AUTO gicleur de départ *m*; ~ **motor** *n* AUTO *of car*, ELEC ENG démarreur *m*, MECH ENG moteur de démarrage *m*, VEHICLES *of engine* démarreur *m*; ~ **motor pinion** *n* VEHICLES *of engine* pignon de démarreur *m*; ~ **pole shoe** *n* AUTO masse polaire de démarreur *f*; ~ **ring gear** *n* VEHICLES *of engine* couronne de démarreur *f*; ~ **slip ring** *n* AUTO

collecteur de démarreur *m*, VEHICLES *of engine* bague collectrice de démarreur *f*, collecteur de démarreur *m*
starting *n* MECH ENG amorçage *m*, commencement *m*, *of engine* démarrage *m*, mise en marche *f*, mise en route *f*, mise en train *f*, MINING *of clogged chute* déhourdage *m*, désancrage *m*; ~ **capacitor** *n* ELEC condensateur de démarrage *m*; ~ **changeover switch** *n* ELEC commutateur de démarrage *m*; ~ **crank** *n* VEHICLES *of engine* manivelle de démarreur *f*; ~ **device** *n* ELEC *motor* dispositif de démarrage *m*; ~ **down** *n* C&G écoulement avant relance *m*; ~ **friction** *n* MECH ENG frottement au départ *m*; ~ **gear** *n* MECH ENG appareil de démarrage *m*, appareil de mise en marche *m*, mise en train *f*, organe de mise en mouvement *m*; ~ **handle** *n* MECH ENG levier de mise en marche *m*, manette de mise en marche *f*; ~ **hum** *n* TV ronflement au démarrage *m*; ~ **jet** *n* AUTO gicleur de départ *m*; ~ **lever** *n* MECH ENG levier de mise en marche *m*, manette de mise en marche *f*; ~ **motor** *n* ELEC, MECH ENG moteur de démarrage *m*; ~ **point** *n* MECH ENG point de départ *m*; ~ **rheostat** *n* ELEC *resistance*, ELEC ENG rhéostat de démarrage *m*; ~ **torque** *n* MECH ENG, PROD ENG couple de démarrage *m*; ~ **transformer** *n* ELEC ENG transformateur de démarrage *m*
star-to-delta: ~ **conversion** *n* ELEC *connection* transformation étoile-triangle *f*; ~ **transformation** *n* ELEC *connection* transformation étoile-triangle *f*
startup *n* PAPER TECH mise en marche *f*; ~ **burner** *n* C&G alandier d'attrempage *m*; ~ **circuit** *n* TELECOM circuit de démarrage *m*; ~ **zero power test** *n* NUCLEAR essai à puissance nulle *m*
starvation *n* PRINT manque *m*
starved: ~ **gold** *n* C&G or transparent *m*
starving *n* REFRIG sous-alimentation *f*
starwheel *n* AUTO molette *f*, MECH ENG croisillon *m*, croisillon à poignées *m*
star-wired *adj* TELECOM câblé en étoile
stassfurtite *n* MINERAL stassfurtite *f*
stat *n* PRINT photocopie *f*, photostat *m*
state: ~ **of the art** *n* PATENTS état de la technique *m*, PROD ENG état des connaissances et des techniques *m*; ~ **diagram** *n* COMP, DP diagramme d'état *m*; ~ **equation** *n* PHYS équation d'état *f*; ~ **of equilibrium** *n* THERMOD état d'équilibre *m*; ~ **off** *n* ELEC ENG état bloqué *m*, état non conducteur *m*, état non passant *m*; ~ **on** *n* ELEC ENG état conducteur *m*, état de conduction *m*, état débloqué *m*, état passant *m* COMP, DP, NAUT *of weather* état *m*; ~ **of rest** *n* PHYS état de repos *m*; ~ **transition diagram** *n* TELECOM diagramme de transition d'état *m*
statement *n* COMP, DP, PROD ENG instruction *f*; ~ **label** *n* COMP étiquette d'instruction *f*, DP étiquette d'opérateur *f*
state-of-the-art: ~ **technique** *n* CONST technique de pointe *f*
stateroom *n* NAUT cabine de luxe *f*
static[1] *adj* COMP, DP, ELEC ENG statique
static[2] *n* ELEC ENG parasites électrostatiques *m pl*, RECORDING, TV parasites *m pl*; ~ **air cushion** *n* TRANSP coussin d'air statique *m*; ~ **allocation** *n* COMP affectation statique *f*, DP allocation statique *f*; ~ **balance** *n* MECH ENG *of grinding wheels* équilibrage statique *m*; ~ **balancer** *n* ELEC ENG bobine égalisatrice *f*; ~ **characteristic** *n* ELEC ENG caractéristique statique *f*; ~ **charge** *n* ELEC ENG charge statique *f*; ~ **conditions** *n pl* ELEC ENG régime statique *m*; ~ **converter** *n* ELEC, ELEC ENG,

SPACE *spacecraft* convertisseur statique *m*; ~ **correction** *n* PETR correction statique *f*; ~ **discharge head** *n* WATER SUPP hauteur de refoulement *f*; ~ **dump** *n* COMP, DP vidage statique *m*; ~ **electrical machine** *n* ELEC ENG machine électrique statique *f*; ~ **electric field** *n* ELEC ENG champ électrique statique *m*; ~ **electricity** *n* CONST, PROP MAT, TEXTILES électricité statique *f*; ~ **eliminator** *n* TEXTILES appareil antistatique *m*; ~ **error** *n* TV erreur statique de base de temps *f*; ~ **field** *n* ELEC ENG, TELECOM champ statique *m*; ~ **fluid level** *n* PETR niveau statique d'un fluide *m*; ~ **focus** *n* TV foyer statique *m*; ~ **friction** *n* MECH ENG frottement au départ *m*, PHYS frottement statique *m*; ~ **friction coefficient** *n* PHYS coefficient de frottement statique *m*; ~ **head** *n* HYDR EQUIP charge statique d'eau *f*, hauteur manométrique *f*, pression statique *f*, WATER SUPP hauteur *f*, hauteur d'élévation *f*, hauteur manométrique *f*; ~ **hovering** *n* TRANSP vol statique *m*; ~ **inverter** *n* ELEC ENG onduleur *m*, SPACE *spacecraft* inverseur statique *m*; ~ **lift** *n* WATER SUPP hauteur *f*, hauteur d'élévation *f*, hauteur manométrique *f*; ~ **mark** *n* CINEMAT effluves *f pl*; ~ **memory** *n* COMP, ELEC ENG mémoire statique *f*; ~ **on film** *n* PHOTO électrisation *f*; ~ **operation** *n* ELEC ENG fonctionnement statique *m*; ~ **pin** *n* MILIT *of parachute* broche de fermeture de câble automatique *f*; ~ **pressure** *n* ACOUSTICS, REFRIG pression statique *f*; ~ **RAM** *n* (*SRAM*) COMP RAM statique *f*; ~ **relay** *n* ELEC, TELECOM relais statique *m*; ~ **screen** *n* ELEC écran électrostatique *m*; ~ **stability** *n* AERONAUT *airworthiness* stabilité statique *f*; ~ **strain test** *n* MECH ENG épreuve statique à la déformation *f*; ~ **suction lift** *n* WATER SUPP hauteur d'aspiration *f*; ~ **test** *n* SPACE essai au point fixe *m*, essai statique *m*; ~ **thrust** *n* AERONAUT poussée au banc d'essai *f*, poussée au point fixe *f*, poussée statique *f*, MILIT poussée statique *f*; ~ **transformer** *n* ELEC ENG transformateur statique *m*; ~ **voltmeter** *n* ELEC voltmètre électrostatique *m*

statics *n* ELEC ENG, PHYS statique *f*

station *n* COMP, DP poste *m*, station *f*, ELEC ENG station *f*, usine *f*, SPACE position sur l'orbite *f*, TRANSP *(cf railroad depot)* gare *f*, station *f*; ~ **acquisition function** *n* SPACE *spacecraft* fonction de mise à poste *f*; ~ **area** *n* RAIL emprises de la gare *f pl*; ~ **barred** *n* TELECOM station interdite *f*; ~ **correction mode** *n* SPACE *spacecraft* mode de correction de poste *m*; ~ **coverage** *n* TV couverture d'un émetteur *f*; ~ **identification** *n* TV indicatif d'émetteur *m*; ~ **keeping** *n* SPACE *communications* maintien à poste *m*; ~ **keeping satellite** *n* SPACE *spacecraft* satellite maintenu à poste *m*; ~ **sync generator** *n* TV générateur de synchro général *m*; ~ **time** *n* TV heure de la station *f*; ~ **timing** *n* TV minutage des signaux *m*; ~ **wagon** *n* (AmE) *(cf estate car)* TRANSP familiale *f*

stationary: ~ **aerial wave** *n* WAVE PHYS onde aérienne stationnaire *f*; ~ **armature** *n* ELEC *generator, motor* induit fixe *m*, induit stationnaire *m*, ELEC ENG induit fixe *m*; ~ **blade** *n* HYDR EQUIP pale directrice *f*, pale fixe *f*; ~ **boiler** *n* PROD ENG chaudière fixe *f*, chaudière placée à demeure *f*; ~ **charger** *n* TRANSP chargeur à poste fixe *m*; ~ **contact** *n* PROD ENG contact fixe *m*; ~ **emission source** *n* POLLUTION source fixe *f*; ~ **field** *n* ELEC ENG champ stationnaire *m*; ~ **firefighting installation** *n* SAFETY poste d'incendie fixe *m*; ~ **front** *n* METEO front stationnaire *m*; ~ **hydraulic riveter** *n* (AmE), **hydraulic rivetter** *n* (BrE) PROD ENG machine à river hydraulique fixe *f*; ~ **light wave** *n* WAVE PHYS onde lumineuse stationnaire *f*; ~ **link** *n* MECH ENG *valve gear* coulisse fixe *f*; ~ **longitudinal wave** *n* WAVE PHYS onde longitudinale stationnaire *f*; ~ **orbit** *n* SPACE orbite stationnaire *f*; ~ **phase** *n* TELECOM phase stationnaire *f*; ~ **plate** *n* MECH ENG *machine tool* plateau fixe *m*; ~ **point** *n* SPACE position sur l'orbite *f*; ~ **portion** *n* PROD ENG partie fixe *f*; ~ **state** *n* PHYS, RAD PHYS, THERMOD état stationnaire *m*; ~ **traffic** *n* TRANSP circulation arrêtée *f*; ~ **transverse waves** *n pl* WAVE PHYS ondes transversales stationnaires *f pl*; ~ **vane** *n* HYDR EQUIP aube directrice *f*, aube fixe *f*; ~ **wave** *n* PHYS, TELECOM, WAVE PHYS onde stationnaire *f*; ~ **wave pattern** *n* WAVE PHYS figure d'onde stationnaire *f*

stations *n pl* NAUT *naval architecture* sections transversales *f pl*

statistic *n* MATH statistique *f*

statistical: ~ **analysis** *n* COMP, DP analyse statistique *f*; ~ **check** *n* METR contrôle statistique *m*; ~ **control by attributes** *n* TESTING contrôle statistique par attributs *m*; ~ **data** *n* COMP, DP données statistiques *f pl*; ~ **forecasting** *n* PROD ENG prévision statistique *f*; ~ **manufacturing quality control** *n* CONTROL contrôle statistique de la fabrication *m*; ~ **multiplexer** *n (statmux)* COMP, DP multiplexeur statistique *m*; ~ **physics** *n* PHYS physique statistique *f*; ~ **quality control** *n* CONTROL maîtrise statistique de la qualité *f*, régulation statistique des cotes *f*, QUALITY maîtrise statistique de la qualité *f*; ~ **sample of decay data** *n* RAD PHYS échantillon statistique des données de désintégrations *m*; ~ **tables** *n pl* QUALITY tables statistiques *f pl*; ~ **test** *n* TESTING essai statistique *m*

statistics *n* COMP, DP statistique *f*

statmux *n (statistical multiplexer)* COMP, DP multiplexeur statistique *m*

stator *n* AUTO, ELEC *machine*, ELEC ENG, PHYS stator *m*; ~ **coil** *n* ELEC ENG bobine du stator *f*, bobine statorique *f*; ~ **frame** *n* ELEC ENG carcasse de stator *f*; ~ **lamination** *n* ELEC ENG tôle du stator *f*; ~ **plate** *n* ELEC ENG lame du stator *f*, lame fixe *f*; ~ **rotor starter motor** *n* ELEC démarreur stator-rotor *m*; ~ **vane** *n* AERONAUT *compressor* aube de stator *f*, aube fixe de stator *f*; ~ **winding** *n* ELEC ENG bobinage du stator *m*, bobinage statorique *m*

status *n* COMP, DP état *m*; ~ **bar** *n* COMP, DP barre d'état *f*; ~ **character** *n* COMP, DP caractère d'état *m*; ~ **data** *n* TELECOM état *m*; ~ **indication** *n* TELECOM indication d'état *f*; ~ **indicator** *n* PROD ENG voyant d'état *m*; ~ **lamp** *n* TELECOM voyant d'occupation *m*; ~ **register** *n* COMP, DP registre d'état *m*; ~ **signal** *n* CONTROL signal d'état *m*; ~ **word** *n* COMP, DP mot d'état *m*

statute: ~ **law** *n* PATENTS loi *f*

statutory: ~ **regulations** *n pl* SAFETY règlements définis par un article de loi *m pl*

staunch *adj* PROD ENG étanche

staunchness *n* PROD ENG étanchéité *f*

staurolite *n* MINERAL staurotide *f*

staurotide *n* MINERAL staurotide *f*

stave *n* PROD ENG douve *f*

stay *n* CONST entretoise *f*, tirant *m*, prop étai *m*, NAUT *of standing rigging* étai *m*, PROD ENG *of foundry flask* barrette *f*, traverse *f*; ~ **block** *n* REFRIG entretoise *f*; ~ **bolt** *n* CONST entretoise *f*, tirant *m*; ~ **pole** *n* ELEC *overhead line* pylône de haubanage *m*, pylône à haubans *m*; ~ **rod** *n* CONST entretoise *f*, tirant *m*; ~ **tube** *n* PROD ENG *of boiler* tube-tirant *m*

staying *n* PROD ENG *stay bolting* entretoisage *m*, entretoisement *m*

stayput: ~ **agent** *n* CHEM épaississant *m*

stays: **in** ~ *adv* NAUT *sailing* vent debout

STD *abbr* *(BrE)* *(subscriber trunk dialling)* TELECOM interurbain automatique *m*, sélection à distance de l'abonné demandé *f*

Steadicam *n* (TM) CINEMAT Steadicam (MD) *m*

steadiness: ~ **test** *n* CINEMAT essai de fixité *m*

steady *n* MECH ENG *lathe* lunette *f*; ~ **approach** *n* AERONAUT approche en régime stabilisé *f*, approche stabilisée *f*; ~ **bearing** *n* NAUT *navigation* relèvement constant *m*; ~ **breeze** *n* NAUT brise établie *f*; ~ **current** *n* PHYS courant stationnaire *m*; ~ **flight** *n* AERONAUT vol en régime stabilisé *m*; ~ **flow** *n* AERONAUT *aerodynamics* écoulement permanent *m*, écoulement stabilisé *m*, FLUID PHYS écoulement permanent *m*, PHYS écoulement stationnaire *m*; ~ **noise** *n* ACOUSTICS bruit stable *m*; ~ **pin** *n* MECH ENG *shaft key* clavette de calage *f*, PROD ENG *core print* porte-noyau *m*, portée *f*, portée de noyau *f*, portée de remoulage *f*, *of moulding box* goujon *m*; ~ **rest** *n* MECH ENG *lathe* lunette *f*

steadying: ~ **pin** *n* SPRINGS étoquiau *m*

steady-state[1] *adj* PHYS en régime permanent, en régime stationnaire

steady-state[2] *n* CONTROL état permanent *m*, ELEC régime permanent *m*, état stationnaire *m*, ELEC ENG régime permanent *m*, régime établi *m*, PHYS régime permanent *m*, régime stationnaire *m*, TELECOM état d'équilibre *m*; ~ **condition** *n* ELEC ENG condition de régime permanent *f*, OPT répartition des modes à l'équilibre *f*, équilibre des modes *m*, TELECOM condition de régime permanent *f*, répartition des modes à l'équilibre *f*; ~ **creep** *n* METALL fluage stationnaire *m*; ~ **inversion** *n* RAD PHYS *laser production* inversion d'état continu *f*; ~ **launching conditions** *n pl* TELECOM conditions d'injections d'équilibre *f pl*; ~ **pressure** *n* MECH ENG pression en régime permanent *f*

stealthy *adj* MILIT furtif

steam:[1] **in** ~ *adj* MECH ENG en pression, sous pression; **under** ~ *adj* HYDR EQUIP, MECH ENG en pression, sous pression

steam[2] *n* FUELLESS, HEATING, HYDR EQUIP, PAPER TECH, PHYS, TEXTILES vapeur *f*, vapeur d'eau *f*; ~ **accumulator** *n* HYDR EQUIP, PAPER TECH accumulateur de vapeur *m*; ~ **admission** *n* HYDR EQUIP admission de vapeur *f*; ~ **balance** *n* ASTRON, HYDR EQUIP soupape de sûreté à contrepoids *f*; ~ **blowing** *n* C&G étirage par soufflage *m*; ~ **box** *n* HYDR EQUIP boîte de distribution de vapeur *f*, boîte à tiroir *f*, boîte à vapeur *f*, chambre de distribution *f*, chapelle de tiroir *f*; ~ **brake** *n* HYDR EQUIP frein à vapeur *m*; ~ **calender** *n* TEXTILES calandre à vapeur *f*; ~ **car** *n* TRANSP locomobile *f*, voiture à vapeur *f*; ~ **case** *n* HYDR EQUIP boîte de distribution de vapeur *f*, boîte à tiroir *f*, boîte à vapeur *f*, chambre de distribution *f*; ~ **chamber** *n* HYDR EQUIP boîte de distribution de vapeur *f*, boîte à tiroir *f*, boîte à vapeur *f*, chambre de distribution *f*, chapelle de tiroir *f*; ~ **chest** *n* HYDR EQUIP boîte de distribution de vapeur *f*, boîte à tiroir *f*, boîte à vapeur *f*, chambre de distribution *f*, chapelle de tiroir *f*; ~ **cleaning** *n* MAR POLL nettoyage à la vapeur *m*; ~ **cock** *n* HYDR EQUIP prise de vapeur *f*, robinet de prise de vapeur *m*, robinet de vapeur *m*; ~ **coil** *n* HEAT ENG serpentin à vapeur *m*; ~ **condenser** *n* PAPER TECH condensateur de vapeur *m*; ~ **cracking** *n* PETR TECH craquage à la vapeur d'eau *m*, vapocraquage *m*; ~ **cylinder** *n* HYDR EQUIP cylindre à vapeur *m*; ~ **cylinder casing** *n* HYDR EQUIP corps de

cylindre à vapeur *m*, enveloppe externe de cylindre à vapeur *f*; ~ **distillation** *n* CHEM *process* distillation à la vapeur *f*, CHEM TECH entraînement à la vapeur *m*; ~ **dome** *n* HYDR EQUIP dôme *m*, dôme à vapeur *m*, dôme de prise de vapeur *m*, réceptaclede vapeur *m*; ~ **dryer** *n* HYDR EQUIP appareil à sécher la vapeur *m*, dessiccateur de vapeur *m*, sécheur de vapeur *m*; ~ **dumping system** *n* NUCLEAR système de dérivation *m*; ~ **edge** *n* HYDR EQUIP *slide valve, cylinder port* bord d'attaque *m*; ~ **ejector** *n* HYDR EQUIP éjecteur à vapeur *m*; ~ **emission** *n* POLLUTION vapeurs *f pl*, évaporation *f*; ~ **engine** *n* AUTO moteur à vapeur *m*, HYDR EQUIP, MECH ENG machine à vapeur *f*, moteur à vapeur *m*, PHYS machine à vapeur *f*, TRANSP moteur à vapeur *m*; ~ **engineering** *n* MECH ENG ingénierie de la vapeur *f*; ~ **entraining** *n* CHEM TECH entraînement à la vapeur *m*; ~ **extraction** *n* FOOD TECH *processing machinery* extraction à la vapeur *f*; ~ **flowmeter** *n* PAPER TECH compteur de vapeur *m*; ~ **gage** *n* (AmE), ~ **gauge** *n* (BrE) HYDR EQUIP manomètre de pression de vapeur *m*, PHYS manomètre à vapeur *m*; ~ **generation** *n* NAUT *engine* production de vapeur *f*; ~ **generator** *n* HEATING générateur de vapeur *m*; ~ **governor** *n* HYDR EQUIP régulateur de débit de vapeur *m*; ~ **header** *n* PAPER TECH collecteur de vapeur *m*; ~ **heating** *n* CONST chauffage à vapeur *m*; ~ **heating jet** *n* MECH ENG tuyère pour réchauffeur à vapeur *f*; ~ **heating system** *n* HEATING installation de chauffage à vapeur *f*; ~ **hose** *n* HYDR EQUIP tuyauterie souple de vapeur *f*; ~ **humidifier** *n* REFRIG humidificateur à injection de vapeur *m*; ~ **injector** *n* HEAT ENG injecteur pompe à jet *m*; ~ **inlet** *n* HYDR EQUIP arrivée de vapeur *f*, orifice d'introduction de vapeur *m*; ~ **jacket** *n* HEAT ENG chemise à vapeur *f*, HYDR EQUIP chemise à vapeur *f*, enveloppe à vapeur *f*; ~ **jet** *n* GEOPHYS jet de vapeur *m*, HYDR EQUIP jet de vapeur *m*, projection de vapeur *f*; ~ **joint** *n* PAPER TECH joint d'amenée de vapeur *m*; ~ **lap** *n* HYDR EQUIP *slide valve* recouvrement à l'admission *m*, retard à l'admission *m*; ~ **loop** *n* HYDR EQUIP boucle de vapeur *f*; ~ **nozzle** *n* HYDR EQUIP *injector* ajutage à vapeur *m*, buse à vapeur *f*, tuyère à vapeur *f*; ~ **outlet** *n* HYDR EQUIP sortie de vapeur *f*, échappement de vapeur *m*; ~ **packing gland** *n* HYDR EQUIP garniture d'étanchéité d'un cylindre à vapeur *f*, presse-étoupe étanche à la vapeur *m*; ~ **pipe** *n* HYDR EQUIP canalisation de vapeur *f*, conduite de vapeur *f*, tuyau de vapeur *m*, tube de dégagement de vapeur *m*, tuyau d'évacuation de vapeur *m*; ~ **pipeline** *n* HYDR EQUIP canalisation de vapeur *f*; ~ **piston** *n* HYDR EQUIP piston à vapeur *m*; ~ **plant** *n* HEATING installation à vapeur *f*, MECH ENG installation de production de vapeur *f*; ~ **port** *n* HYDR EQUIP admission *f*, lumière d'admission *f*, lumière d'entrée *f*, orifice d'admission de vapeur *m*, orifice d'évacuation de vapeur *m*; ~ **power** *n* HYDR EQUIP force motrice de la vapeur *f*, énergie de la vapeur *f*; ~ **pressure** *n* HEATING, TEXTILES pression de la vapeur *f*; ~ **pressure gage** *n* (AmE), ~ **pressure gauge** *n* (BrE) CONTROL manomètre à vapeur *m*; ~ **pressure regulator** *n* CONTROL régulateur de pression de la vapeur *m*; ~ **quality** *n* HEAT ENG taux de vapeur sèche *m*, HYDR EQUIP titre en vapeur *m*; ~ **raising** *n* HYDR EQUIP montée en pression de la vapeur *f*, production de vapeur *f*; ~ **raising coal** *n* COAL TECH charbon à vapeur *m*; ~ **receiver** *n* MECH ENG réservoir de vapeur *m*; ~ **reforming** *n* PETR TECH vaporeformage *m*, PROP MAT réforming à la vapeur *m*; ~ **relief valve** *n* HYDR EQUIP détendeur de vapeur *m*; ~ **separator** *n* HYDR EQUIP dispositif séparant la vapeur de l'eau *m*, séparateur de vapeur *m*; ~ **space** *n* HYDR EQUIP *of boiler* chambre de vapeur d'une chaudière *f*, volume de vapeur d'une chaudière *m*; ~ **stop valve** *n* HYDR EQUIP robinet d'arrêt de vapeur *m*; ~ **stripper for wall paper** *n* ELEC ENG décolleuse de papier peint électrique *f*; ~ **superheater** *n* HEAT ENG surchauffeur de vapeur *m*; ~ **supply pipe** *n* HYDR EQUIP tuyauterie d'adduction de vapeur *f*; ~ **trap** *n* HEAT ENG séparateur d'eau de condensation *m*, HYDR EQUIP purgeur automatique *m*, MECH ENG purgeur de vapeur d'eau *m*, PAPER TECH purgeur de vapeur *m*, PETR TECH pot de purge *m*, purgeur *m*; ~ **turbine** *n* HEATING, HYDR EQUIP, NAUT *engine* turbine à vapeur *f*; ~ **valve** *n* HYDR EQUIP distributeur de vapeur *m*, tiroir à vapeur *m*, prise de vapeur *f*, robinet de prise de vapeur *m*, soupape d'admission de vapeur *f*, vanne d'admission de vapeur *f*, vanne de prise de vapeur *f*

steam³ *vt* FOOD TECH cuire à la vapeur, passer à la vapeur, TEXTILES passer à la vapeur; ~ **set** *vt* TEXTILES fixer à la vapeur

steam:⁴ ~ **distil** *vi* (BrE) CHEM distiller à la vapeur, extraire à la vapeur; ~ **distill** *vi* (AmE) *see steam distil*

steamboat *n* NAUT bateau à vapeur *m*, vapeur *m*

steam-boiler *n* HYDR EQUIP chaudière à vapeur *f*, générateur de vapeur *m*, THERMOD chaudière à vapeur *f*

steambus *n* TRANSP autobus à vapeur *m*

steamed *adj* NAUT *wood* ployé à la vapeur

steam-electric: ~ **generator** *n* ELEC ENG génératrice électrique à vapeur *f*; ~ **power plant** *n* ELEC ENG centrale thermique à vapeur *f*; ~ **power station** *n* ELEC ENG centrale thermique à vapeur *f*, usine d'énergie à vapeur *f*

steam-engine ~ **indicator** *n* HYDR EQUIP indicateur de pression de vapeur *m*, indicateur dynamométrique *m*

steamer *n* NAUT navire à vapeur *m*, vapeur *m*

steaming *n* PAPER TECH étuvage *m*; ~ **light** *n* NAUT feu de hune *m*

steam-laden: ~ **emission** *n* POLLUTION panache de fumée *m*

steamship *n* NAUT navire à vapeur *m*

steamtight *adj* HEAT ENG, HYDR EQUIP étanche à la vapeur

steamway *n* HYDR EQUIP tubulure de prise de vapeur *f*

stearate *n* CHEM stéarate *m*

stearic *adj* CHEM stéarique

stearin *n* CHEM stéarine *f*

stearyl *n* CHEM stéaryle *m*

steatite *n* MINERAL stéatite *f*

steel *n* MECH ENG acier *m*; ~ **alloy** *n* COAL TECH alliage d'acier *m*; ~ **alloy dust** *n* COAL TECH poussière d'acier allié *f*; ~ **ball hardness test** *n* MECH ENG essai de dureté à bille d'acier *m*; ~ **band chain** *n* CONST *land measuring* chaîne à ruban d'acier *f*; ~ **band strapping** *n* PACKAGING cerclage *m*; ~ **beam** *n* CONST poutre en acier *f*, poutre en fer *f*; ~ **belt lacing** *n* MECH ENG agrafes à griffes pour courroies *f pl*; ~ **bridge** *n* CONST pont métallique *m*; ~ **cable cutter** *n* MECH ENG *tool* coupe-câble acier *m*; ~ **casting** *n* NAUT *shipbuilding* moulage d'acier *m*; ~ **chimney** *n* CONST cheminée en acier *f*, cheminée en tôle *f*; ~ **construction** *n* CONST construction en acier *f*; ~ **cord conveyor belt** *n* MECH ENG courroie transporteuse à cables d'acier *f*; ~ **fixer** *n* CONST *person* ferrailleur *m*; ~ **fixing** *n* CONST mise en place de l'armature *f*; ~ **forms** *n pl* CONST coffrage en

acier *m*; ~ **furnace** *n* PROD ENG four de fabrication de l'acier *m*; ~ **locker** *n* LAB EQUIP *furniture* armoire en acier *f*; ~ **measuring tape** *n* METR roulette d'acier *f*, ruban d'acier *m*; ~ **pail** *n* PROD ENG bidon en acier *m*; ~ **pile** *n* COAL TECH pieu en acier *m*, CONST palplanche en acier *f*; ~ **platform** *n* PETR TECH plate-forme en acier *f*; ~ **reusable CKD container** *n* PACKAGING conteneur en acier pouvant être mis en pièces détachées *m*; ~ **section** *n* NAUT *shipbuilding* profilé *m*, profilé en métal *m*, PROP MAT profilé *m*; ~ **sheet** *n* PROP MAT feuille d'acier *f*, tôle d'acier *f*; ~ **softening** *n* PROP MAT adoucissement d'acier *m*; ~ **spring** *n* SPRINGS ressort d'acier *m*; ~ **straight edge** *n* METR règle plate de contrôle en acier *f*; ~ **tendon** *n* NUCLEAR membre de précontrainte *m*, tendon *m*; ~ **toecap** *n* SAFETY *protective footwear* bout renforcé *m*, bout renforcé en acier *m*; ~ **tool bit** *n* MECH ENG *high speed tool* barreau rectifié en acier *m*; ~ **vessel** *n* NAUT navire en acier *m*; ~ **weight** *n* PROP MAT masse d'acier *f*; ~ **wheel on steel rail system** *n* TRANSP système rail-roue *m*; ~ **wire** *n* NAUT câble d'acier *m*, câble métallique *m*

steel-colored *adj* (AmE), **steel-coloured** *adj* (BrE) COLOURS de couleur acier

steelwork *n* PROD ENG aciérie *f*

steelyard *n* PHYS balance romaine *f*

Steenbeck *n* CINEMAT *editing table* Steenbeck *m*

steep¹ *adj* C&G court

steep:² ~ **bevel** *n* C&G biseau assez tranché *m*; ~ **coast** *n* OCEANOG accore *m*; ~ **gradient** *n* CONST forte pente *f*, pente raide *f*, pente rapide *f*; ~ **road** *n* CONST chemin à forte pente *m*, route escarpée *f*; ~ **slope** *n* CONST forte pente *f*, pente raide *f*, pente rapide *f*; ~ **turn** *n* AERONAUT virage serré *m*; ~ **vein** *n* MINING dressant *m*

steep³ *vt* FOOD TECH faire macérer, TEXTILES tremper

steeple-head: ~ **rivet** *n* CONST rivet à tête conique *m*, rivet à tête en pointe de diamant *m*

steepness *n* CONST escarpement *m*, raideur *f*, OCEANOG cambrure *f*

steer:¹ ~ **angle** *n* VEHICLES angle de braquage *m*

steer² *vt* NAUT *boats* barrer, tenir la barre, *ships gouverner à un cap*, TRANSP voler à un cap, *car* conduire; ~ **clear of** *vt* NAUT *navigation* passer au large de; ~ **for** *vt* NAUT *navigation* gouverner sur

steerable: ~ **beam antenna** *n* TELECOM antenne orientable *f*; ~ **radio telescope** *n* ASTRON radiotélescope complètement orientable *m*

steered: ~ **wheel** *n* VEHICLES roue directrice *f*

steering *n* MILIT *of directional antenna* entraînement *m*, TELECOM pilotage *m*, VEHICLES direction *f*; ~ **angle** *n* NAUT angle de braquage *m*; ~ **arm** *n* AUTO levier de fusée *m*; ~ **axis inclination** *n* AUTO inclinaison du pivot *f*; ~ **axle** *n* VEHICLES *wheels* essieu de direction *m*; ~ **chain** *n* NAUT drosse *f*; ~ **circle** *n* VEHICLES braquage *m*, butée de direction *f*; ~ **column** *n* AUTO colonne de direction *f*, *car* axe de volant *m*, VEHICLES colonne de direction *f*; ~ **column lock** *n* VEHICLES serrure antivol sur la direction *f*; ~ **compass** *n* NAUT compas de route *m*; ~ **control wheel** *n* AERONAUT volant de direction *m*; ~ **gear** *n* AUTO direction *f*, VEHICLES mécanisme de direction *m*; ~ **gearbox** *n* AUTO boîtier de direction *m*, VEHICLES boîte de direction *f*; ~ **geometry** *n* AUTO géométrie du train avant *f*; ~ **head** *n* VEHICLES *of motorcycle* tête de direction *f*; ~ **idler arm** *n* AUTO *of car* levier de renvoi de direction *m*; ~ **knuckle** *n* AUTO pivot de fusée *m*, VEHICLES fusée d'essieu *f*; ~ **knuckle pin** *n* AUTO porte-fusée *m*; ~ **linkage** *n* AUTO timonerie de direction *f*; ~ **lock** *n* VEHICLES braquage *m*, butée de direction *f*; ~ **play** *n* VEHICLES jeu dans la direction *m*; ~ **rod** *n* AUTO *of car* bielle de direction *f*; ~ **shaft** *n* AUTO arbre de direction *m*; ~ **system** *n* AUTO direction *f*, NAUT appareil à gouverner *m*; ~ **wheel** *n* AUTO *of car* volant *m*, VEHICLES volant *m*, volant de direction *m*; ~ **wire** *n* NAUT *boatbuilding* drosse *f*

Stefan's: ~ **constant** *n* HEAT ENG constante de rayonnement *f*; ~ **law** *n* RAD PHYS loi de Stefan *f*

Stefan-Boltzmann: ~ **constant** *n* PHYS constante de Stefan-Boltzmann *f*; ~ **law** *n* PHYS, RAD PHYS loi de Stefan-Boltzmann *f*

steinmannite *n* MINERAL steinmannite *f*

Steinmetz: ~ **coefficient** *n* PHYS coefficient de Steinmetz *m*

Steinmetz's: ~ **law** *n* PHYS formule de Steinmetz *f*

stellar[1] *adj* ASTRON, SPACE stellaire

stellar:[2] ~ **association** *n* ASTRON association stellaire *f*; ~ **cannibalism** *n* ASTRON cannibalisme stellaire *m*; ~ **core** *n* ASTRON noyau d'étoile *m*; ~ **evolution** *n* ASTRON évolution stellaire *f*; ~ **guidance** *n* SPACE guidage stellaire *m*; ~ **navigation** *n* SPACE navigation stellaire *f*; ~ **nursery** *n* ASTRON nursery d'étoiles *f*; ~ **stream** *n* ASTRON courant d'étoiles *m*; ~ **wind** *n* ASTRON vent stellaire *m*

stellite: ~ **valve** *n* AUTO soupape stellitée *f*

stem[1] *n* C&G jambe *f*, CONST *of key* branche *f*, broche *f*, tige *f*, HYDR EQUIP *of slide valve* arbre de tiroir *m*, tige de tiroir *f*, *of valve* queue de soupape *f*, tige de soupape *f*, MECH ENG *of screw* tige *f*, NAUT *boatbuilding* proue *f*, étrave *f*, PHYS *of thermometer* tige *f*, WATER SUPP *of sluice gate* queue *f*, épée *f*; ~ **carrier** *n* C&G cueilleur de jambe *m*; ~ **fitting** *n* NAUT ferrure d'étrave *f*; ~ **flow** *n* POLLUTION eau d'écoulement *f*, ruissellement sur les troncs *m*, écoulement *m*, écoulement supercortical *m*; ~ **rake** *n* NAUT *ship design* élancement de l'étrave *m*

stem[2] *vt* MINING *blasting* bourrer

stemmer *n* MINING bourroir *m*

stemming *n* MINING bourrage *m*, bourre *f*; ~ **material** *n* MINING bourrage *m*, bourre *f*; ~ **rod** *n* MINING bourroir *m*; ~ **stick** *n* MINING bourroir *m*

stemware *n* C&G verre à pied *m*

stench: ~ **trap** *n* CONST *plumbing* coupe-odeur *f*, siphon *m*

stencil *n* C&G, PRINT, PROD ENG pochoir *m*; ~ **duplicator copy paper** *n* PAPER TECH papier pour duplicateur à stencil *m*; ~ **plate** *n* PROD ENG pochoir *m*; ~ **silk** *n* C&G typon *m*

stenter: ~ **frame** *n* TEXTILES rame élargisseuse *f*

step[1] *n* C&G amollisse *f*, COMP pas *m*, étape *f*, CONST *of ladder* barreau *m*, marche *f*, échelon *m*, *of stairway* marche *f*, *on monument* degré *m*, CRYSTALL *dislocation* gradin *m*, marche *f*, DP pas *m*, étape *f*, MECH ENG crapaudine *f*, palier de pied *m*, *of cone, cone pulley* gradin *m*, METALL marche *f*, PRINT plage d'une barre de contrôle *f*, plage de couleurs *f*, PROD ENG étape *f*, *of sequencer* pas *m*, RAIL *vehicles* marchepied *m*; ~ **bearing** *n* MECH ENG crapaudine *f*, palier de pied *m*; ~ **bit** *n* PETR TECH trépan à redans *m*; ~ **box** *n* MECH ENG crapaudine *f*, palier de pied *m*; ~ **completion bit** *n* PROD ENG bit de fin d'exécution *m*; ~ **cone** *n* MECH ENG cône *m*, cône de transmission *m*, cône de vitesse *m*, cône-poulie *m*, poire *f*, poulie étagée *f*, poulie à gradins *f*; ~ **cone drive** *n* MECH ENG commande par cône *f*; ~ **contact printer** *n* CINEMAT tireuse par contact image par image *f*; ~ **control** *n* CONTROL régulation par

paliers *f*; ~ **counter** *n* COMP compteur séquentiel *m*, DP compteur pas à pas *m*, compteur séquentiel *m*; ~ **data** *n* PROD ENG données relatives aux pas *f pl*; ~ **down ring** *n* CINEMAT bague intermédiaire *f*; ~ **down station** *n* ELEC *transformer* poste abaisseur *m*; ~ **drill** *n* MECH ENG *tool* foret étagé *m*; ~ **function** *n* COMP, DP, ELECTRON fonction en échelon *f*; ~ **function generator** *n* ELECTRON générateur de fonctions en échelon *m*; ~ **function response** *n* ELECTRON réponse à un échelon *f*; ~ **increment** *n* TEXTILES augmentation différentielle *f*; ~ **index fiber** *n* (AmE), ~ **index fibre** *n* (BrE) OPT fibre à saut d'indice *f*, PHYS fibre à saut d'indice *f*, fibre à échelon d'indice *f*, TELECOM fibre à saut d'indice *f*; ~ **index profile** *n* OPT profil d'indice à saut *m*, profil à saut d'indice *m*, TELECOM profil d'indice à saut *m*, profil à saut d'indice *m*; ~ **joint** *n* CONST assemblage à mi-bois *m*, coupe à mi-bois *f*, entaille à mi-bois *f*, MECH ENG assemblage à recouvrement *m*, joint à recouvrement *m*; ~ **lens** *n* CINEMAT lentille de Fresnel *f*; ~ **printing** *n* CINEMAT tirage image par image *m*; ~ **quenching** *n* SPRINGS trempe étagée *f*; ~ **recovery diode** *n* ELECTRON diode à coupure brusque *f*; ~ **regulation** *n* CONTROL régulation par paliers *f*; ~ **switch** *n* ELEC commutateur à gradins *m*, commutateur à plots *m*; ~ **tooth gear** *n* MECH ENG engrenage échelonné *m*, engrenage à denture croisée *m*; ~ **track system** *n* SPACE *communications* système de poursuite pas à pas *m*; ~ **transformer** *n* PROD ENG transformateur pas à pas *m*; ~ **wedge** *n* CINEMAT coin sensitométrique *m*, PHOTO coin photométrique *m*, PRINT barre de contrôle avec diverses plages *f*

step[2] *vt* NAUT *mast* arborer, mâter

step-and-repeat *n* PRINT report *m*

step-by-step: ~ **control** *n* ELEC *motor drive* dispositif de marche cran par cran *m*; ~ **system** *n* TELECOM système Strowger *m*, système pas à pas *m*

step-down: ~ **autotransformer** *n* ELEC ENG autotransformateur abaisseur de tension *m*; ~ **transformer** *n* ELEC transformateur abaisseur *m*, ELEC ENG transformateur abaisseur de tension *m*, PHYS, PROD ENG transformateur réducteur *m*

stephanite *n* MINERAL stéphanite *f*

step-hardened: ~ **wire** *n* SPRINGS fil trempé en étages *m*

step-in: ~ **effect** *n* PROD ENG pas en cours d'exécution *m*

stepladder *n* CONST marchepied *m*, échelle double *f*, SAFETY échelle marchepied *f*

stepless: ~ **control** *n* ELEC commande continue *f*

step-out: ~ **well** *n* PETR TECH puits d'extension *m*

stepped[1] *adj* MECH ENG disposé en gradins, en gradins, en échelons, échelonné, à gradins, à étages

stepped:[2] ~ **climb** *n* AERONAUT montée par paliers *f*; ~ **gear** *n* MECH ENG engrenage échelonné *m*, engrenage à denture croisée *m*; ~ **grate** *n* PROD ENG grille à gradins *f*, grille à étages *f*; ~ **roll** *n* MECH ENG cylindre à gradins *m*

stepper: ~ **controller** *n* PROD ENG contrôleur pas à pas *m*; ~ **motor** *n* CINEMAT, COMP *disk drive actuator*, DP *disk drive actuator* moteur pas-à-pas *m*, ELEC moteur fractionnaire *m*, ELEC ENG moteur pas-à-pas *m*

stepping *n* SPRINGS *of leaf springs* étagement *m*; ~ **motor** *n* ELEC moteur fractionnaire *m*; ~ **switch** *n* ELEC *relay* relais à cascade *m*, ELEC ENG commutateur pas à pas *m*, commutateur rotatif *m*

steps *n pl* CONST marchepied *m*, échelle double *f*

step-up: ~ **autotransformer** *n* ELEC ENG autotransformateur élévateur de tension *m*; ~ **station** *n* ELEC *transformer* poste élévateur *m*; ~ **transformer** *n* ELEC transformateur élévateur *m*, ELEC ENG transformateur élévateur de tension *m*, PHYS transformateur survolteur *m*, transformateur élévateur *m*, TV transformateur survolteur *m*

stepwise: ~ **refinement** *n* COMP, DP approximations successives *f pl*

steradian *n* ELECTRON, GEOM, PHYS stéradian *m*

stercorite *n* MINERAL stercorite *f*

stere *n* METR stère *m*

stereo[1] *adj* RECORDING stéréo

stereo:[2] ~ **decoder** *n* RECORDING décodeur stéréo *m*; ~ **effect** *n* RECORDING effet de stéréophonie *m*; ~ **headphones** *n pl* RECORDING casque stéréo *m*; ~ **recording** *n* RECORDING enregistrement stéréo *m*; ~ **seat** *n* RECORDING position optimale stéréo *f*; ~ **separation** *n* RECORDING séparation stéréo *f*; ~ **sound** *n* RECORDING audition stéréophonique *f*; ~ **subcarrier** *n* RECORDING sous-porteuse stéréo *f*; ~ **subchannel** *n* RECORDING canal supplémentaire stéréo *m*; ~ **tape recorder** *n* RECORDING magnétophone stéréo *m*; ~ **tape recording** *n* RECORDING enregistrement magnétique stéréo *m*; ~ **tuner** *n* RECORDING syntoniseur stéréo *m*; ~ **videocassette recorder** *n* TV magnétoscope stéréo à cassette *m*; ~ **viewer** *n* PHOTO binocle stéréoscopique *m*

stereochemistry *n* CHEM *of compounds* stéréochimie *f*

stereographic: ~ **projection** *n* CRYSTALL, METALL projection stéréographique *f*

stereoisomer *n* CHEM stéréo-isomère *m*

stereometric: ~ **camera** *n* INSTRUMENT appareil de stéréométrie *m*

stereomicroscope *n* LAB EQUIP stéréomicroscope *m*

stereophonic: ~ **decoder** *n* RECORDING décodeur stéréophonique *m*; ~ **microgroove** *n* RECORDING microsillon stéréophonique *m*; ~ **pick-up** *n* ACOUSTICS tête de lecture stéréophonique *f*; ~ **record** *n* RECORDING disque stéréophonique *m*; ~ **recording** *n* ACOUSTICS, RECORDING enregistrement stéréophonique *m*; ~ **reproduction** *n* RECORDING lecture stéréophonique *f*; ~ **sound** *n* RECORDING son stéréophonique *m*

stereophony *n* ACOUSTICS, RECORDING stéréophonie *f*

stereophotogrammetry *n* PROP MAT stéréophotogrammétrie *f*

stereoplate *n* PRINT cliché *m*

stereoscope *n* PHOTO stéréoscope *m*

stereoscopic: ~ **camera** *n* PHOTO appareil stéréoscopique *m*, chambre jumelée pour stéréophotographie *f*; ~ **film** *n* CINEMAT film en 3-D *m*, film en relief *m*, film en trois dimensions *m*, film stéréoscopique *m*; ~ **pair** *n* PHOTO couple stéréoscopique *m*

stereoscopy *n* PHOTO stéréoscopie *f*

stereotype: ~ **plate** *n* PRINT cliché *m*

stereovision *n* TV procédé stéréovision *m*

steric *adj* CHEM stérique

sterile[1] *adj* COAL TECH stérile

sterile:[2] ~ **dressing** *n* SAFETY *for wound treatment* pansement stérile *m*

sterilized *adj* FOOD TECH stérilisé

sterling: ~ **silver** *n* PROP MAT argent sterling *m*

stern *n* NAUT *of boat* arrière *m*, poupe *f*; ~ **flag** *n* NAUT pavillon de poupe *m*; ~ **frame** *n* NAUT *shipbuilding* cadre d'étambot *m*; ~ **light** *n* NAUT *navigation* feu arrière *m*, feu de poupe *m*; ~ **line** *n* NAUT *mooring* amarre debout de l'arrière *f*; ~ **post** *n* NAUT *shipbuilding* étambot *m*; ~ **pulpit** *n* NAUT *deck equipment* balcon arrière *m*; ~ **thruster** *n* NAUT propulseur arrière

m, propulseur de poupe *m*, propulseur latéral arrière *m*; ~ **tube** *n* NAUT *boatbuilding* tube d'étambot *m*

sternbergite *n* MINERAL sternbergite *f*

Stern-Gerlach: ~ **experiment** *n* PHYS expérience de Stern et Gerlach *f*

steroid *n* CHEM stéroïde *m*

sterol *n* CHEM stérol *m*

stevedore *n* NAUT arrimeur *m*, docker *m*, débardeur *m*

stevedore-type: ~ **pallet** *n* TRANSP palette à plancher débordant *f*

stibiconite *n* MINERAL stibiconite *f*

stibilite *n* MINERAL stibiconite *f*

stibious *adj* CHEM stibieux

stibium *n (Sb)* CHEM antimoine *m (Sb)*

stibnite *n* CHEM stibnite *f*, MINERAL stibine *f*

stick[1] *n* C&G bûche *f*, CONST *of timber* pièce *f*; ~ **lack** *n* COLOURS laque en masse *f*; ~ **of sulfur** *n* (AmE), ~ **of sulphur** *n* (BrE) CHEM soufre en bâton *m*

stick[2] *vt* CONST *joinery* adhérer, coller, pousser

stick[3] *vi* PROD ENG se gripper

sticking *n* C&G collage *m*, ELEC ENG collage *m*, *switch* tendance momostable *f*, PROD ENG adhérence *f*, adhésion *f*, collage *m*; ~ **contacts** *n pl* ELEC *relay* adhésion des contacts *f*, collage des contacts *m*; ~ **mark** *n* C&G collage *m*

sticking-up: ~ **iron** *n* (AmE) *(cf punty)* C&G pontil *m*

sticky[1] *adj* FOOD TECH, P&R poisseux, PAPER TECH adhésif

sticky:[2] ~ **clay** *n* PETR TECH argile collante *f*

stiff[1] *adj* TEXTILES raide

stiff:[2] ~ **finish** *n* TEXTILES finition raide *f*

stiffen *vt* TEXTILES *with starch* empeser

stiffener *n* MECH ENG pièce de renfort *f*, NAUT *shipbuilding* raidisseur *m*, renfort *m*, SPACE *spacecraft* raidisseur *m*, TEXTILES amidon *m*

stiffening *n* CONST entretoises *f pl*, liernes *f pl*, étrésillons *m pl*, MECH ENG, SPACE *spacecraft* raidissement *m*; ~ **dope** *n* COLOURS vernis de renforcement *m*; ~ **plate** *n* MECH ENG plaque de renfort *f*; ~ **varnish** *n* COLOURS vernis de renforcement *m*

stiffness *n* ACOUSTICS raideur *f*, MECH ENG raideur *f*, rigidité *f*, ténacité *f*, résistance à la flexion *f*, PAPER TECH rigidité *f*, PHYS raideur *f*, SPRINGS rigidité *f*, TEXTILES raideur *f*

stigmasterol *n* CHEM stigmastérol *m*

stigmatic: ~ **lens** *n* PHOTO objectif anastigmat *m*, objectif anastigmatique *m*, objectif stigmatique *m*

stilb *n* METR stilb *m*

stilbene *n* CHEM stilbène *m*

stilbite *n* MINERAL stilbite *f*

stile *n* CONST *of door, sash* montant *m*

still *n* CHEM TECH alambic *m*, appareil de distillation *m*, appareil distillatoire *m*, appareil à distiller *m*, matras *m*, FOOD TECH *fermentation* alambic *m*, appareil à distiller *m*, distillateur d'alcool *m*, LAB EQUIP *distillation* alambic *m*; ~ **air** *n* FUELLESS air calme *m*; ~ **camera** *n* PHOTO appareil photographique *m*; ~ **frame** *n* CINEMAT arrêt sur image *m*, image arrêtée *f*, image fixe *f*, TV image fixe *f*; ~ **shot** *n* CINEMAT plan fixe *m*; ~ **water** *n* FOOD TECH eau plate *f*, HYDROL eau calme *f*, eau dormante *f*, eau stagnante *f*, eau tranquille *f*, OCEANOG niveau d'équilibre *m*, WATER SUPP eau tranquille *f*

still-air: ~ **freezing** *n* REFRIG congélation sans circulation d'air *f*

stilling: ~ **basin** *n* HYDROL *spillway* bassin d'amortissement *m*

still-life: ~ **photography** *n* PHOTO photographie de nature morte *f*

stilpnomelane *n* MINERAL stilpnomélane *f*

stilted: ~ **arch** *n* CONST arc exhaussé *m*, arc surhaussé *m*, *for bridge* arche exhaussée *f*, arche surhaussée *f*, arche surélevée *f*, *structure* voûte exhaussée *f*, voûte surhaussée *f*, voûte surmontée *f*, voûte surélevée *f*

stimulate *vt* RAD PHYS *absorption of radiation* stimuler

stimulated: ~ **emission** *n* ELECTRON émission induite *f*, émission stimulée *f*, OPT, PHYS *laser*, RAD PHYS *of radiation*, TELECOM émission stimulée *f*

stimulation *n* PETR stimulation *f*

stinger *n* PETR rampe *f*, PETR TECH rampe de poste *f*, élinde flottante *f*

sting-out *n* C&G soufflard *m*

stink: ~ **trap** *n* CONST *plumbing* coupe-odeur *f*, siphon *m*

stippling *n* C&G pointillage *m*

stir *vt* CHEM *substance*, PAPER TECH agiter

stirrer *n* LAB EQUIP, P&R, PAPER TECH agitateur *m*; ~ **blade** *n* LAB EQUIP tige d'agitateur *f*

stirring *n* C&G guinandage *m*, CHEM *process* agitation *f*; ~ **rod** *n* CINEMAT agitateur *m*

stirrup *n* CONST fer de suspension *m*, étrier *m*, *reinforced concrete* cadre *m*, MECH ENG armature *f*, lien en fer à U *m*, étrier *m*; ~ **bolt** *n* MECH ENG armature *f*, lien en fer à U *m*, étrier *m*; ~ **hanger** *n* CINEMAT étrier *m*, MECH ENG appareil de suspension à étrier *m*; ~ **joint** *n* MECH ENG assemblage à étrier *m*; ~ **piece** *n* MECH ENG armature *f*, lien en fer à U *m*, étrier *m*; ~ **pump** *n* SAFETY *for water* pompe à main portative *f*; ~ **strap** *n* MECH ENG armature *f*, lien en fer à U *m*, étrier *m*

stirruped: ~ **concrete** *n* CONST béton fretté *m*

stitch[1] *n* TEXTILES maille *f*, point *m*, point de surjet *m*; ~ **detail** *n* TEXTILES détail de la maille *m*

stitch[2] *vt* TEXTILES coudre; ~ **down** *vt* TEXTILES rabattre

stitched[1] *adj* PRINT broché

stitched:[2] ~ **box** *n* PACKAGING boîte brochée *f*

stitching: ~ **wire** *n* PACKAGING fil à brocher *m*

STM *abbr* TELECOM (*synchronous transfer mode*) mode de transfert synchrone *m*, TELECOM (*synchronous transport module*) module de transport synchrone *m*

STM-n *abbr* (*synchronous transport module-n*) TELECOM module de transport synchrone-n *m*

STN *abbr* (*switched telephone network*) TELECOM RTC (*réseau téléphonique commuté*)

stochastic[1] *adj* COMP, DP, MATH *statistics* stochastique

stochastic:[2] ~ **cooling** *n* PART PHYS refroidissement stochastique *m*; ~ **loading** *n* METALL sollicitation stochastique *f*; ~ **model** *n* COMP, DP modèle stochastique *m*; ~ **process** *n* PHYS procédé stochastique *m*

stock *n* CINEMAT pellicule vierge *f*, MECH ENG *bit stock* vilebrequin *m*, *of plane* bois *m*, fût *m*, *screw stock, die stock* filière *f*, filière à cage *f*, filière à coussinets *f*, porte-filière *m*, MINING tuyau *m*, PAPER TECH pâte *f*, PETR TECH valeurs d'exploitation *f pl*, PROD ENG *charge of blast furnace* charge *f*; ~ **anchor** *n* NAUT ancre à jas *f*; ~ **and dies** *n* MECH ENG filière garnie *f*, filière garnie de coussinets *f*; ~ **at inspection** *n* PROD ENG stock au contrôle *m*; ~ **chest** *n* PAPER TECH cuvier à pâte *m*; ~ **coal** *n* COAL TECH charbon en parc *m*, charbon en stock *m*; ~ **control** *n* PROD ENG gestion des stocks *f*, RAIL groupe de répartition *m*; ~ **diameter** *n* TELECOM diamètre du stockage *m*; ~ **distributor** *n* PROD ENG *blast furnace* appareil de chargement distributeur *m*; ~ **indicator** *n* PROD ENG *blast furnace* bécasse *f*, tige de jaugeage *f*; ~ **inlet** *n* PAPER TECH arrivée de la pâte

sur machine *f*; ~ **issue status** *n* PROD ENG type de retrait de stock *m*; ~ **line** *n* PROD ENG *blast furnace* niveau de la charge *m*; ~ **location** *n* PROD ENG emplacement de stockage *m*; ~ **movements** *n pl* PROD ENG mouvements de stock *m pl*; ~ **on hand** *n* PROD ENG quantité en stock *f*, stock existant *m*, stock physique *m*; ~ **on order** *n* PROD ENG stock en cours d'approvisionnement *m*; ~ **preparation** *n* PAPER TECH préparation de la pâte *f*; ~ **receipt** *n* PROD ENG bordereau de réception *m*; ~ **record** *n* PROD ENG fiche de stock *f*, lettre de stock *f*; ~ **record card** *n* PROD ENG fiche de stock *f*; ~ **removal** *n* MECH ENG *machining* débit de copeaux *m*; ~ **sheets** *n pl* (AmE) (*cf stock sizes*) C&G mesures libres *f pl*; ~ **shortage** *n* PROD ENG rupture de stock *f*; ~ **shot** *n* CINEMAT prise de vue d'archive *f*; ~ **shot library** *n* CINEMAT archives cinématographiques *f pl*; ~ **sizes** *n pl* (BrE) (*cf stock sheets*) C&G mesures libres *f pl*; ~ **sizing** *n* PAPER TECH collage dans la pâte *m*; ~ **sound** *n* RECORDING son d'archives *m*; ~ **taking** *n* PROD ENG inventaire *m*; ~ **transaction** *n* PROD ENG ajustement de stock *m*; ~ **transfer** *n* PROD ENG transfert de stock *m*; ~ **turnover** *n* PROD ENG rotation des stocks *f*, taux de rotation des stocks *m*; ~ **unit** *n* PROD ENG unité de stockage *f*; ~ **valuation** *n* PROD ENG évaluation de stock *f*

stockade *n* HYDR EQUIP estacade *f*

stock-dyed *adj* TEXTILES teint en bourre

stocking *n* OCEANOG *with fish* empoissonnement *m*, *young fish* alevinage *m*

stockless: ~ **anchor** *n* NAUT ancre à pattes articulées *f*

stock-out *n* PROD ENG manquant *m*, stock en rupture *m*

stockpile[1] *n* CONST dépôt *m*; ~ **coal** *n* COAL TECH charbon en stock *m*

stockpile[2] *vt* CONST empiler, mettre en dépôt

stockpiled *adj* COAL TECH mise en décharge

stockyard *n* CONST parc à matières *m*; ~ **coal** *n* COAL TECH charbon en parc *m*

stoichiometric[1] *adj* CHEM, PROP MAT stoechiométrique

stoichiometric:[2] ~ **composition** *n* METALL composition stoechiométrique *f*; ~ **compound** *n* CRYSTALL composé stoechiométrique *m*

stoichiometry *n* CHEM stoechiométrie *f*

stoke:[1] ~ **hole** *n* PROD ENG enfer *m*, tisard *m*

stoke[2] *vt* PROD ENG approvisionner en combustible, chauffer, entretenir le feu de

stoker *n* PROD ENG *machine* chargeur mécanique *m*, foyer mécanique *m*, *person* chauffeur *m*

Stokes': ~ **law** *n* PHYS loi de Stokes *f*; ~ **theory** *n* FLUID PHYS théorie de Stokes *f*; ~ **velocity** *n* C&G vitesse de sédimentation *f*

stoking *n* PROD ENG chauffage *m*, chauffe *f*; ~ **door** *n* PROD ENG tisard *m*

STOL: ~ **aircraft** *n* (*short takeoff and landing aircraft*) AERONAUT, TRANSP ADAC (*avion à décollage et atterrissage court*)

stolzite *n* MINERAL stolzite *f*

stomach: ~ **cramps** *n pl* OCEANOG colique des scaphandriers *f*

stone[1] *n* METR *unit of weight* stone *m*, MINING *country rock* rocher *m*, *ore* mine *f*, minerai *m*, pierre de mine *f*; ~ **band** *n* COAL TECH banc stérile *m*, intercalation de roches *f*; ~ **bed** *n* COAL TECH couche de roche *f*; ~ **bolt** *n* MECH ENG boulon de scellement *m*; ~ **breaker** *n* CONST *machine* casse-pierre *m*, concasseur *m*; ~ **bridge** *n* CONST pont en pierre *m*; ~ **chippings** *n pl* CONST cailloux concassés *m pl*; ~ **coal** *n* MINING anthracite *m*; ~

crusher *n* CONST casse-pierre *m*, concasseur *m*; ~ **dresser** *n* CONST *person* tailleur de pierre *m*; ~ **dressing** *n* CONST taille des pierres *f*; ~ **drift** *n* COAL TECH galerie au rocher *f*, MINING bacnure *f*, bowette *f*, galerie au rocher *f*, travers-banc au rocher *m*, bouveau *m*, bovette *f*; ~ **dust** *n* COAL TECH poussière stérile *f*, poussière inerte *f*, MINING poussière incombustible *f*, pulvérin incombustible *m*, pulvérin rocheux *m*, pulvérin schisteux *m*; ~ **fruit** *n* FOOD TECH drupe *f*, fruit à noyau *m*; ~ **mill** *n* CONST concasseur *m*, moulin à meules *m*; ~ **oil** *n* COAL TECH huile de pierre *f*, PETR huile de pierre *f*, pétrole *m*; ~ **picking** *n* COAL TECH épierrage *m*; ~ **pit** *n* MINING carrière *f*; ~ **quarry** *n* MINING carrière *f*; ~ **spreader** *n* TRANSP épandeur-régleur-dameur *m*; ~ **tubbing** *n* COAL TECH cuvelage en maçonnerie *f*, MINING cuvelage en pierre *m*; ~ **wall** *n* COAL TECH faille *f*, CONST mur en pierre *m*; ~ **wedge** *n* CONST coin à pierre *m*, quille *f*

stone² *vt* (BrE) *(cf pit)* FOOD TECH dénoyauter

stoneman *n* COAL TECH bouveleur *m*, bowetteur *m*, mineur au rocher *m*

stonemason *n* CONST maçon *m*, tailleur de pierre *m*

stone-splitting: ~ **hammer** *n* COAL TECH marteau à trous de coins *m*

stoneware *n* C&G poterie de grès *f*

stonework *n* CONST maçonnage *m*, maçonnerie *f*

stoneworking *n* COAL TECH abattage de la roche *m*

stoning *n* C&G libération de pierres *f*

stony¹ *adj* CONST pierreux, rocailleux

stony:² ~ **bottom** *n* HYDROL *of river* fond pierreux *m*; ~ **ground** *n* CONST terrain pierreux *m*; ~ **meteorite** *n* ASTRON météorite pierreuse *f*

stop¹ *n* COMP arrêt *m*, stop *m*, CONST *for chamfer* arrêt *m*, DP arrêt *m*, stop *m*, MECH butée *f*, MECH ENG arrêt *m*, butée *f*, taquet *m*, PHOTO ouverture du diaphragme *f*, PHYS diaphragme *m*, TEXTILES arrêt *m*, VEHICLES butée *f*; ~ **bath** *n* CINEMAT, PHOTO bain d'arrêt *m*; ~ **belt** *n* C&G bourrelotte *f*; ~ **bit** *n* COMP bit d'arrêt *m*, DP bit d'arrêt *m*, bit de stop *m*; ~ **board** *n* RAIL guidon d'arrêt *m*; ~ **brake** *n* RAIL freinage d'immobilisation *m*; ~ **button** *n* CONTROL bouton d'arrêt *m*; ~ **button switch** *n* PROD ENG interrupteur d'arrêt *m*; ~ **code** *n* COMP, DP code d'arrêt *m*; ~ **collar** *n* MECH ENG bague d'arrêt *f*, bague de butée *f*, collier d'arrêt *m*; ~ **cylinder press** *n* PRINT presse en blanc *f*; ~ **element** *n* COMP, DP élément d'arrêt *m*; ~ **gap** *n* PROD ENG bouche-trou *m*; ~ **instruction** *n* COMP, DP instruction d'arrêt *f*; ~ **joint** *n* ELEC *cable* jonction à point d'arrêt *f*; ~ **key** *n* TV touche arrêt *f*; ~ **lamp** *n* VEHICLES *lighting* feu de freinage *m*, feu de stop *m*; ~ **light** *n* CONTROL feu de stop *m*, stop *m*; ~ **light switch** *n* AUTO *of car* contacteur de stop *m*; ~ **log weir** *n* WATER SUPP déversoir à poutrelles *m*; ~ **motion** *n* CINEMAT marche image par image *f*, MECH ENG *disengaging gear* débrayage *m*, TEXTILES mécanisme casse-fil *m*; ~ **motion on creel** *n* TEXTILES casse-fil sur cantre *m*; ~ **pin** *n* PHOTO butoir *m*; ~ **plank** *n* WATER SUPP *of dam, sluice gate* hausse *f*; ~ **plate** *n* PHOTO plaque de butée *f*; ~ **screw** *n* PHOTO, PROD ENG vis de butée *f*; ~ **signal disc shunting** *n* (BrE) RAIL disque d'arrêt *m* (Fra); ~ **signal disk shunting** *n* (AmE) *see stop signal disc shunting*; ~ **valve** *n* CONST robinet d'arrêt *m*, soupape d'arrêt *f*, HYDR EQUIP robinet, vanne d'arrêt *f*

stop² *vt* C&G *crack*, DP arrêter, PROD ENG aveugler, boucher, fermer, obturer, tamponner, étancher, TEXTILES arrêter, WATER SUPP *leak* aveugler, boucher,

tamponner, étancher; ~ **down** *vt* CINEMAT *diaphragm* diaphragmer, fermer l'objectif, PHOTO diaphragmer; ~ **a leak in** *vt* WATER SUPP aveugler; ~ **off** *vt* NAUT *hawser* bosser; ~ **up** *vt* NAUT boucher, PROD ENG *with plug* aveugler, boucher, fermer, obturer, tamponner, étancher; ~ **with putty** *vt* CONST *hole* mastiquer

stop:³ ~ **engines** *vi* NAUT stopper les machines

stop⁴ *vti* COMP, DP arrêter, stopper

stop-and-go: ~ **traffic** *n* TRANSP trafic discontinu *m*

stopclock *n* PHYS chronomètre à déclic *m*

stopcock *n* CONST robinet *m*, robinet d'arrêt *m*, robinet de fermeture *m*, LAB EQUIP robinet d'eau *m*, *fluid control* robinet d'arrêt *m*

stope¹ *n* MINING chantier *m*, chantier d'abatage *m*, chantier en gradins *m*, gradin *m*; ~ **face** *n* MINING front *m*, front d'abattage *m*, front d'attaque *m*, front de taille *m*; ~ **floor** *n* MINING sole du chantier *f*

stope² *vt* MINING abattre

stoped-out: ~ **workings** *n pl* MINING chantier épuisé *m*

stoping *n* MINING abattage *m*, abattage en gradins *m*, exploitation en gradins *f*; ~ **of the seam** *n* MINING dépècement *m*

stopover *n* AERONAUT arrêt en cours de route *m*, escale *f*, interruption de voyage *f*

stoppage *n* PROD ENG bouchage *m*, obturation *f*, occlusion *f*, engorgement *m*, obstruction *f*; ~ **for repairs** *n* PROD ENG arrêt pour procéder à des réparations *m*, arrêt pour réparations *m*

stopped: ~ **chamfer** *n* CONST *joinery* chanfrein arrêté *m*; ~ **lens** *n* PHYS lentille diaphragmée *f*

stopper *n* C&G couvercle *m* (Bel), portine *f* (Fra); ~ **knot** *n* NAUT noeud de bosse *m*

stoppered: ~ **bottle** *n* LAB EQUIP flacon bouché à rodage *m*; ~ **flask** *n* LAB EQUIP *glassware* fiole bouchée à rodage *f*; ~ **measuring cylinder** *n* LAB EQUIP *glassware* éprouvette bouchée *f*

stopping *n* C&G, CONST *for filling cracks* bouchage *m*, MECH ENG bouchage *m*, *of injector* désamorçage *m*, MINING arrêt-barrage *m*, barrage *m*, barrage d'arrêt *m*; ~ **knife** *n* CONST *putty knife* couteau à mastiquer *m*; ~ **marks** *n pl* TEXTILES marques d'arrêt *f pl*; ~ **potential** *n* PHYS contre-tension *f*, potentiel d'arrêt *m*; ~ **power** *n* PHYS *total linear* pouvoir d'arrêt *m*; ~ **sight distance** *n* TRANSP *traffic* distance de visibilité d'arrêt *f*; ~ **train** *n* (AmE) *(cf slow train)* RAIL *vehicles* omnibus *m*, train omnibus *m*

stopping-and-starting: ~ **gear** *n* MECH ENG appareil d'arrêt et de mise en marche *m*

stop-send: ~ **signal** *n* CONTROL signal d'arrêt d'émission *m*

stopwatch *n* PHYS chronomètre à déclic *m*

stopway *n* AERONAUT *runway* prolongement d'arrêt *m*, prolongement occasionnellement roulable *m*; ~ **light** *n* AERONAUT *runway* feu de prolongement d'arrêt *m*

storable: ~ **propellant** *n* SPACE *propulsion* ergol stockable *m*

storage *n* COMP *act* mise en mémoire *f*, COMP mémoire *f*, *act* mémorisation *f*, stockage *m*, DP mise en mémoire *f*, *act* mémorisation *f*, stockage *m*, MAR POLL, PHOTO *of photographic materials* stockage *m*, PRINT archivage *m*, stockage *m*, PROD ENG emmagasinage *m*, emmagasinement *m*, magasinage *m*, SAFETY emmagasinage *m*, *of dangerous materials* stockage *m* ~ **allocation** *n* COMP attribution de mémoire *f*, DP affectation mémoire *f*, allocation mémoire *f*, attribution de mémoire *f*; ~ **area** *n* CONST aire d'empilage *f*, aire de stockage *f*,

PRINT magasin *m*; ~ **basin** *n* FUELLESS réservoir de stockage *m*, HYDROL réservoir de retenue d'eau *m*; ~ **battery** *n* AUTO, ELEC *accumulator*, ELEC ENG batterie d'accumulateurs *f*, PHYS, TRANSP accumulateur *m*; ~ **canister** *n* NUCLEAR poubelle *f*; ~ **capacitor** *n* ELEC ENG condensateur de mémorisation *m*; ~ **capacity** *n* COMP capacité de mémoire *f*, WATER SUPP capacité de stockage *f*; ~ **cell** *n* ELEC ENG accumulateur *m*, élément d'accumulateur *m*, PRINT unité de stockage *f*, SPACE *spacecraft* accumulateur *m*, cellule *f*; ~ **configuration** *n* SPACE *spacecraft* configuration de stockage *f*; ~ **cupboard** *n* LAB EQUIP *furniture* armoire de stockage *f*; ~ **density** *n* COMP densité d'enregistrement *f*, DP densité de mémorisation *f*; ~ **device** *n* COMP dispositif de stockage *m*, mémoire *f*, DP mémoire *f*, unité de stockage *m*; ~ **durability** *n* PACKAGING durée d'emmagasinage *f*; ~ **effect** *n* ELEC ENG effet de la charge accumulée *m*; ~ **element** *n* COMP, DP élément de mémoire *m*, ELEC ENG élément de mémorisation *m*; ~ **entry** *n* COMP, DP entrée en mémoire *f*; ~ **facility** *n* MAR POLL capacité de stockage *f*, installation de stockage *f*, POLLUTION unité de stockage *f*; ~ **factor** *n* REFRIG taux de remplissage *m*; ~ **fragmentation** *n* COMP, DP fragmentation mémoire *f*; ~ **heater** *n* HEAT ENG radiateur à accumulation *m*; ~ **hierarchy** *n* COMP, DP hiérarchie de mémoire *f*; ~ **lake** *n* HYDROL lac de barrage *m*; ~ **level regulation** *n* WATER SUPP régularisation du niveau *f*; ~ **location** *n* COMP adresse de mémoire *f*, emplacement de mémoire *m*, DP emplacement de mémoire *m*, position de mémoire *f*; ~ **map** *n* COMP, DP carte de mémoire *f*; ~ **medium** *n* COMP, DP support de mémoire *m*; ~ **memory** *n* COMP mémoire *f*; ~ **mesh** *n* ELECTRON grille-mémoire *f*; ~ **oscilloscope** *n* PHYS oscilloscope à mémoire *m*; ~ **period** *n* PHOTO durée de conservation *f*; ~ **protection** *n* COMP, DP protection mémoire *f*; ~ **rack** *n* C&G chevalet *m*; ~ **requirement** *n* COMP besoins en mémoire *m pl*, DP mémoire nécessaire *f*; ~ **reservoir** *n* PROD ENG réservoir d'emmagasinage *m*; ~ **scheme** *n* FUELLESS *hydroelectric power* projet à réservoir *m*; ~ **screen** *n* ELECTRON écran à mémoire *m*; ~ **siding** *n* TRANSP voie de remisage *f*; ~ **space** *n* PACKAGING magasin *m*; ~ **tank** *n* PETR réservoir de stockage *m*, PETR TECH réservoir *m*, POLLUTION citerne de stockage *f*, PROD ENG citerne de stockage *f*, réservoir d'emmagasinage *m*, SPACE *spacecraft* réservoir de stockage *m*; ~ **temperature** *n* PROD ENG température de stockage *f*; ~ **time** *n* ELEC ENG *for dissipation of charge* temps de désaturation *m*, *of accumulated charge* temps de conservation *m*, *of data in memory* temps de conservation *m*, *of oscilloscope trace* temps de mémorisation *m*, *storage life* temps de stockage *m*; ~ **tube** *n* COMP, DP tube à mémoire *m*, ELECTRON tube cathodique à mémoire *m*, tube à mémoire *m*; ~ **unit** *n* PROD ENG unité de stockage *f*

store[1] *n* COMP, ELEC ENG mémoire *f*; ~ **and forward** *n* COMP, DP mémorisation et retransmission en différé *f*, mémorisation et retransmission *f*, PRINT *data processing* stockage et transfert des données sur disquettes *m*; ~ **bit** *n* PROD ENG bit de mémoire *m*

store[2] *vt* COAL TECH stocker, COMP, DP mémoriser, stocker, ELEC ENG mettre en mémoire, mémoriser, GAS TECH emmagasiner

store-and-forward: ~ **conversion facility** *n* TELECOM unité de conversion en différé *f*; ~ **facility** *n* TELECOM diffusion différée *f*, possibilité d'émission en différé *f*;

~ **switching center** *n* (AmE), ~ **switching centre** *n* (BrE) DP centre de commutation de messages *m*; ~ **switching network** *n* TELECOM réseau à commutation de messages *m*; ~ **transmission** *n* TELECOM transmission différée *f*; ~ **unit** *n* *(SFU)* TELECOM unité d'enregistrement et de retransmission *f*

stored: ~ **energy** *n* METALL, PHYS énergie emmagasinée *f*, RAD PHYS énergie accumulée *f*; ~ **program** *n* COMP, DP programme mémorisé *m*; ~ **program computer** *n* (AmE) *see stored programme computer*; ~ **program control** *n* (AmE) *see stored programme control*; ~ **program control exchange** *n* (AmE) *see stored programme control exchange*; ~ **program control PABX** *n* (AmE) *see stored programme control PABX*; ~ **programme computer** *n* TELECOM calculateur à programme enregistré *m*; ~ **programme control** *n* (BrE) *(SPC)* TELECOM commande à programme enregistré *f*; ~ **programme control exchange** *n* (BrE) TELECOM commutateur à programme enregistré *m*; ~ **programme control PABX** *n* (BrE) TELECOM autocommutateur privé à programme enregistré *m*; ~ **programme switching system** *n* (BrE) TELECOM système à programme enregistré *m*; ~ **program switching system** *n* (AmE) *see stored programme switching system*; ~ **up energy** *n* PROD ENG travail emmagasiné *m*, énergie emmagasinée *f*

storeman *n* PROD ENG magasinier *m*

storeroom *n* NAUT cambuse *f*, PACKAGING magasin *m*, PROD ENG dépôt *m*, magasin *m*

stores *n pl* PROD ENG magasin *m*; ~ **control** *n* PROD ENG gestion de magasin *f*

storing: ~ **shelf** *n* PACKAGING rayon de magasin *m*

storm *n* METEO tempête *f*; ~ **choke** *n* PETR TECH vanne de sécurité de fond *f*; ~ **drain** *n* CONST ouvrage d'assainissement *m*, égout pluvial *m*, HYDROL *sewage* égout pluvial *m*, RECYCLING égout d'évacuation des eaux pluviales *m*; ~ **sail** *n* NAUT trinquette *f*; ~ **sewage** *n* WATER SUPP eau usée pluviale *f*; ~ **sewer** *n* RECYCLING déversoir d'orage *m*; ~ **sewer system** *n* CONST réseau d'assainissement *m*; ~ **surge** *n* OCEANOG marée de tempête *f*, onde de tempête *f*, vague de tempête *f*; ~ **tide** *n* OCEANOG marée de tempête *f*, onde de tempête *f*, vague de tempête *f*; ~ **warning** *n* METEO, NAUT avis de tempête *m*; ~ **water** *n* COAL TECH eaux de pluie *f pl*, HYDROL eau pluviale *f*

stove[1] *n* PROD ENG étuve *f*; ~ **enamel** *n* COATINGS vernis-émail *m*, COLOURS laque au four *f*, émail au four *m*

stove:[2] ~ **enamel** *vt* COATINGS, COLOURS vernir au vernis à cuire, laquer à la laque à cuire, émailler au four

stoving *n* COATINGS séchage au four *m*, PROD ENG étuvage *m*, étuvement *m*; ~ **enamel varnish** *n* P&R *paint* vernis à cuire *m*, émail au four *m*; ~ **finish** *n* P&R *paint* peinture au four *f*

stow *vt* AERONAUT arrimer, MINING endiguer, remblayer, terrasser, NAUT arrimer, mettre à poste, SPACE *spacecraft* arrimer, loger

stowage *n* NAUT *of cargo*, SPACE arrimage *m*

stowing *n* MINING remblayage *m*; ~ **dirt** *n* COAL TECH remblai *m*; ~ **equipment** *n* MINING remblayeuse *f*; ~ **material** *n* COAL TECH matériau de remblai *m*; ~ **tool** *n* C&G pelle de poussage *f*

STP *abbr* PHYS *(standard temperature)* TPN *(température normale)*, TELECOM *(signalling transfer point, signaling transfer point)* point de transfert sémaphore *m*

straddle[1] *n* PRINT tête de rubrique *f*, têtière d'un tableau sur plusieurs colonnes *f*

straddle[2] *vt* PROD ENG faire chevaucher

straddling *n* MECH ENG chevauchement *m*

straight: ~ **chain** *n* CHEM *structure* chaîne droite *f*, chaîne non-ramifiée *f*; ~ **common crossing** *n* RAIL coeur de croisement droit *m*; ~ **engine** *n* MECH ENG moteur à cylindres en ligne *m*; ~ **fence** *n* MECH ENG *of saw bench* guide rectiligne *m*; ~ **flank gear** *n* MECH ENG engrenage à flancs rectilignes *m*; ~ **flight** *n* CONST *stairway* volée droite *f*; ~ **flight of stairs** *n* CONST escalier droit à une volée *m*, escalier à rampe droite *m*; ~ **hood** *n* PROD ENG couvercle plat *m*; ~ **joint** *n* ELEC *cable* jonction simple *f*, MECH ENG assemblage à plat *m*, assemblage à plat joint *m*, joint à plat *m*; ~ **line** *n* GEOM, PHYS droite *f*; ~ **negative** *n* PHOTO négatif d'origine *m*; ~ **packing** *n* C&G empilage en dominos droits *m*; ~ **pane hammer** *n* CONST marteau à panne en long *m*; ~ **peen hammer** *n* CONST marteau à panne en long *m*; ~ **pincers** *n pl* C&G crochet à trempe *m*; ~ **pressing** *n* C&G pressage simple *m*; ~ **run** *n* PRINT tirage avec sortie en nappe *m*; ~ **stem** *n* NAUT *boatbuilding* étrave droite *f*; ~ **tap** *n* MECH ENG taraud cylindrique *m*, taraud finisseur *m*, troisième taraud *m*; ~ **throat** *n* C&G gorge au niveau de la sole *f*; ~ **track** *n* RAIL voie en alignement *f*, voie en ligne droite *f*; ~ **turning** *n* MECH ENG *lathe work* cylindrage *m*

straightedge *n* C&G règle d'estimateur *f*, MECH ENG règle *f*, METR règle droite *f*

straighten *vt* CONST *alignment of road* rectifier, PROD ENG dresser, défausser, dégauchir, rectifier, *bent rod* redresser

straightener *n* MECH ENG banc de redressage *m*, banc à rectifier *m*, machine à redresser *f*

straightening *n* PROD ENG dressage *m*, dégauchissage *m*, dégauchissement *m*, rectification *f*, redressage *m*, *of buckled tubes* redressement *m*; ~ **machine** *n* MECH ENG banc de redressage *m*, banc à rectifier *m*, machine à redresser *f*

straight-faced: ~ **pulley** *n* MECH ENG poulie plate *f*

straight-flow: ~ **valve** *n* FUELLESS vanne à écoulement direct *f*

straight-fluted: ~ **drill** *n* MECH ENG foret à rainures droites *m*, mèche évidée *f*

straight-in: ~ **approach** *n* AERONAUT approche directe *f*, approche en ligne droite *f*, approche rectiligne *f*

straight-line: ~ **capacitance** *n* ELEC ENG variation linéaire de la capacité *f*; ~ **compressor** *n* PROD ENG compresseur monocylindrique simple *m*, compresseur à groupe unique de cylindres en tandem *m*; ~ **frequency** *n* ELEC ENG variation linéaire de la fréquence *f*; ~ **image reverser** *n* PRINT inverseur d'image *m*

straightness-measuring: ~ **instrument** *n* METR instrument de mesure de la droiture *m*

straight-nose: ~ **cock** *n* CONST robinet à bec droit *m*

straight-run: ~ **product** *n* PETR TECH produit de première distillation *m*

straight-shank: ~ **pins** *n* PRINT pointures droites *f pl*; ~ **twist drill** *n* MECH ENG foret hélicoïdal à queue cylindrique *m*

straight-sided: ~ **splines** *n pl* MECH ENG *for cylindrical shafts* flancs parallèles *f pl*

straight-through: ~ **can washer** *n* FOOD TECH *processing machinery* machine en continu à laver les bidons *f*; ~ **press** *n* PAPER TECH presse à passage direct *f*; ~ **traffic** *n* TRANSP courant direct *m*

straight-tooth: ~ **meshing gear** *n* AUTO pignon à denture

droite *m*; ~ **wheel** *n* MECH ENG roue à dents droites *f*, roue à denture droite *f*

strain[1] *n* C&G déformation *f*, GEOL contrainte *f*, déformation *f*, fatigue *f*, MECH *materials* déformation *f*, MECH ENG contrainte statique *f*, fatigue *f*, tension *f*, *produced by stress* déformation *f*, METALL déformation *f*, NAUT fatigue *f*, P&R, PHYS déformation *f*; ~ **disc** *n* (BrE) C&G disque étalon de recuisson *m*; ~ **disk** *n* (AmE) *see* strain disc; ~ **ellipsoid** *n* GEOL, MECH ENG ellipsoïde de déformation *m*; ~ **gage** *n* (AmE) *see* strain gauge; ~ **gage bridge** *n* (AmE) *see* strain gauge bridge; ~ **gage technique** *n* (AmE) *see* strain gauge technique; ~ **gauge** *n* CONST enregistreur de déformation *m*, ELEC ENG jauge d'extension *f*, LAB EQUIP instrument, MECH jauge de contrainte *f*, METR, OCEANOG tensiomètre *m*, P&R *test* jauge d'allongement *f*, jauge de contrainte *f*, PHYS extensomètre *m*, jauge d'allongement *f*, jauge extensométrique *f*; ~ **gauge bridge** *n* (BrE) ELEC ENG pont de jauges *m*; ~ **gauge technique** *n* (BrE) MECH ENG technique des jauges de déformation *f*; ~ **hardening** *n* METALL durcissement par déformation *m*, PROP MAT écrouissage *m*; ~ **modulus** *n* CONST module de déformation *m*; ~ **rate sensitivity exponent** *n* PROP MAT exposant de la sensibilité de la vitesse à la contrainte *m*; ~ **slip cleavage** *n* GEOL clivage par pli-fracture *m*; ~ **tensor** *n* PHYS tenseur de déformation *m*; ~ **viewer** *n* C&G polariscope *m*

strain[2] *vt* CHEM filtrer, MECH ENG charger

strainer *n* AUTO, GAS TECH crépine *f*, MECH ENG *stretcher* tendeur *m*, tenseur *m*, *wire stretcher* cric-tenseur *m*, raidisseur *m*, PETR TECH filtre *m*, PROD ENG filtre-tamis *m*, WATER SUPP *rose, snore piece of pump* aspirant *m*, crépine *f*, crépine d'aspiration *f*, grenouillère *f*, lanterne *f*, reniflard *m*, écumoire *f*; ~ **pump** *n* MAR POLL pompe à crépine *f*

strain-hardening: ~ **exponent** *n* PROP MAT exposant du durcissement par écrouissage *m*

strain-indicating: ~ **lacquer** *n* COATINGS vernis craquelant *m*

straining *n* CHEM filtrage *m*, filtration *f*; ~ **beam** *n* CONST entrait retroussé *m*, faux entrait *m*; ~ **chest** *n* PAPER TECH caisse d'égouttage *f*; ~ **piece** *n* CONST entrait retroussé *m*, faux entrait *m*; ~ **screw** *n* MECH ENG tendeur à vis *m*, vis de tension *f*; ~ **work** *n* COAL TECH exploitation par grandes tailles *f*

strait *n* OCEANOG détroit *m*

straits *n pl* NAUT *geography* pertuis *m*

strake *n* COAL TECH aire de lavoir *f*, NAUT *shipbuilding* lisse *f*, virure *f*, PROD ENG *of boiler* virole *f*; ~ **drum cam** *n* PROD ENG came à tambour à languettes *f*

strand *n* C&G fibre de base *f*, fil de base *m*, OCEANOG estran *m*, grève *f*, OPT toron *m*, PHYS *bundle of filaments* toron *m*, *single filament* brin *m*, monofilament *m*, PROD ENG brin *m*, toron *m*, SPACE toron *m*; ~ **break detector** *n* C&G casse-fil *m*

stranded[1] *adj* NAUT *navigation* échoué

stranded:[2] ~ **cable** *n* ELEC *conductor* câble toronné *m*, ELEC ENG câble à âme divisée *m*; ~ **conductor** *n* ELEC toron de câble *m*, âme câblée *f*, ELEC ENG conducteur divisé *m*; ~ **wire** *n* PROD ENG câble multibrins *m*, fil torsadé *m*, câble métallique *m*

stranding *n* NAUT échouage *m*; ~ **ground** *n* OCEANOG échouerie *f*

strange: ~ **quark** *n* PART PHYS, PHYS quark étrange *m*

strangeness *n* PHYS étrangeté *f*

strap *n* CONST armature *f*, armature de charpente *f*, lien *m*, lien en fer à U *m*, étrier *m*, *of double-strap gate hinge* bourdonnière *f*, *of strap hinge*, *butt-and-strap hinge* branche *f*, *of tackle block* estrope *f*, MECH ENG *of eccentric* bague *f*, collier *m*, *of end of connecting rod*, *side* rod chape *f*, chape de bielle *f*, étrier *m*, *strengthening strip*, *band* armature *f*, lien *m*, PAPER TECH, PHOTO courroie *f*, PROD ENG bride *f*, courroie *f*, lien *m*, sangle *f*, *butt strap*, *welt* bande de recouvrement *f*, couvre-joint *m*; ~ **bar** *n* MECH ENG barre de débrayage *f*; ~ **bolt** *n* CONST armature *f*, armature de charpente *f*, lien *m*, lien en fer à U *m*; ~ **brake** *n* MECH ENG frein à bande *m*, frein à enroulement *m*, frein à ruban *m*, frein à sangle *m*; ~ **clutch** *n* MECH ENG embrayage à ruban *m*; ~ **connecting rod end** *n* MECH ENG tête de bielle à chape *f*; ~ **fork** *n* MECH ENG fourche de débrayage *f*, fourche de manoeuvre de courroie *f*; ~ **hinge** *n* CONST couplet *m*, étrier *m*; ~ **rail** *n* RAIL rail méplat *m*; ~ **spanner** *n* (BrE) MECH ENG *tool* clé à sangle *f*; ~ **wrench** *n* MECH ENG *tool* clé à sangle *f*

S-trap *n* CONST *plumbing* siphon en S *m*

strapdown: ~ **equipment** *n* SPACE *spacecraft* matériel de bord *m*; ~ **inertial platform** *n* SPACE *spacecraft* plate-forme inertielle liée *f*; ~ **system** *n* SPACE *spacecraft* système lié *m*, système strapdown *m*

strapdown-mounted *adj* SPACE *spacecraft* lié, raccordé, relié

strap-end: ~ **connecting rod** *n* MECH ENG bielle avec tête à chape *f*, bielle à chape *f*

strap-on[1] *adj* SPACE *spacecraft* auxiliaire

strap-on:[2] ~ **booster** *n* SPACE *spacecraft* moteur latéral *m*, propulseur auxiliaire *m*, propulseur latéral *m*

strapping *n* PHYS *magnetron* strapage *m*; ~ **equipment** *n* PACKAGING équipement de cerclage *m*; ~ **machine** *n* PACKAGING cercleuse *f*; ~ **seal** *n* PACKAGING fermeture de cerclage *f*; ~ **steel** *n* PACKAGING feuillard pour cerclage *m*

strategic: ~ **missile** *n* MILIT missile stratégique *m*

stratification *n* COAL TECH, FUELLESS *of waters*, PETR stratification *f*

stratified[1] *adj* COAL TECH stratifié

stratified:[2] ~ **charge engine** *n* TRANSP moteur à charge stratifiée *m*; ~ **flow** *n* FLUID PHYS écoulement stratifié *m*; ~ **sampling** *n* COAL TECH, SAFETY échantillonnage stratifié *m*

stratify *vt* COAL TECH stratifier

stratigraphic: ~ **trap** *n* PETR TECH piège stratigraphique *m*

stratigraphy *n* COAL TECH stratigraphie *f*

stratocumulus *n* AERONAUT, METEO strato-cumulus *m*

stratosphere *n* METEO stratosphère *f*

stratospheric: ~ **balloon** *n* ASTRON ballon stratosphérique *m*

stratovolcano *n* GEOPHYS stratovolcan *m*

stratum *n* COAL TECH strate *f*

stratus *n* METEO stratus *m*; ~ **fractus** *n* METEO stratus fractus *m*

straw *n* PAPER TECH paille *f*; ~ **pulp** *n* PAPER TECH pâte de paille *f*; ~ **stem** *n* C&G jambe creuse *f*

strawboard *n* PACKAGING, PRINT carton paille *m*

stray[1] *adj* PHYS parasite

stray:[2] ~ **capacitance** *n* PHYS capacité parasite *f*; ~ **coupling** *n* ELEC ENG couplage parasite *m*; ~ **current** *n* ELEC ENG courant vagabond *m*; ~ **current corrosion** *n* ELEC ENG corrosion par courants vagabonds *f*; ~ **field** *n* ELEC *of machine*, *transformer* champ de dispersion *m*; ~ **light** *n* CINEMAT lumière parasite *f*; ~ **light filter** *n*

INSTRUMENT filtre optique encadrant *m*; ~ **oscillation** *n* PHYS oscillation parasite *f*; ~ **radiation** *n* RAD PHYS radiation parasite *f*

streak *n* MINING *of ore* bande *f*, PAPER TECH strie *f*, traînée *f*; ~ **camera** *n* CINEMAT caméra à fente *f*; ~ **image converter camera** *n* CINEMAT caméra à fente avec convertisseur d'image *f*

streaking *n* CINEMAT filage *m*, traînage *m*

streaklines *n pl* FLUID PHYS *cylinder moving through fluid* lignes d'émission *f pl*, stries *f pl*

stream[1] *n* COMP, DP flot *m*, flux *m*, suite *f*, FLUID PHYS courant *m*, HYDROL ruisseau *m*, ruisselet *m*, *of flowing water* cours d'eau *m*, *steady flow* filet *m*, jet *m*; ~ **bed** *n* HYDROL lit de cours d'eau *m*; ~ **function** *n* FLUID PHYS fonction de courant *f*; ~ **line** *n* FLUID PHYS ligne de courant *f*

stream[2] *vi* HYDROL *water* ruisseler; ~ **a warp** *vi* NAUT *in rough weather* filer une aussière

streamer *n* CINEMAT marque au crayon gras *f*, COMP dérouleur de bande *m*, dévideur *m*, DP dérouleur de bande *m*, lecteur de cartouche magnétique *m*, unité de sauvegarde sur cartouche magnétique *f*, PRINT lecteur et dérouleur de bande magnétique *m*, streamer *m*; ~ **chamber** *n* PART PHYS chambre à dards *f*, chambre à sillages lumineux *f*

streaming: ~ **tape drive** *n* COMP dérouleur de bande *m*, dévideur *m*, DP dérouleur de bande *m*, dévideur *m*, lecteur de cartouche magnétique *m*, unité de sauvegarde sur cartouche magnétique *f*

streamlet *n* HYDROL ruisselet *m*

streamline[1] *n* HYDROL *hydrodynamics* fil de l'eau *m*, PHYS ligne de courant *f*; ~ **pattern** *n* FLUID PHYS configuration des lignes de courant *f*

streamline[2] *vt* AUTO caréner

streamlined *adj* AERONAUT aérodynamique, fuselé, profilé, FLUID PHYS aérodynamique, PHYS arrondi, profilé, SPACE, VEHICLES *body* profilé

streamway *n* HYDROL chenal de cours d'eau *m*

street: ~ **cleaner** *n* TRANSP éboueuse *f*; ~ **cleaning lorry** *n* (BrE) TRANSP *(cf street cleaning truck)* balayeuse *f*; ~ **cleaning truck** *n* (AmE) *(cf street cleaning lorry)* TRANSP balayeuse *f*; ~ **signals** *n pl* CONTROL signalisation des rues *f*

streetcar *n* (AmE) *(cf tram)* TRANSP rame de tramway *f*, voiture de tramway *f*; ~ **stop** *n* (AmE) TRANSP arrêt de tramway *m*; ~ **track** *n* (AmE) TRANSP rail de tramway *m*

strength *n* CHEM *of acid* force *f*, *of solution* titre *m*, COAL TECH, GAS TECH résistance *f*, METALL résistance *f*, solidité *f*, MINING richesse *f*, *of explosive* puissance *f*, PAPER TECH force *f*, résistance *f*, PHYS *resistance* contrainte *f*, sollicitation *f*, PROD ENG *force*, *power* force *f*, puissance *f*, PROP MAT robustesse *f*, résistance *f*, TEXTILES résistance *f*

strengthen *vt* PROD ENG consolider

strengthened: ~ **passenger compartment** *n* TRANSP habitacle de sécurité *m*

strengthening *n* PROD ENG consolidation *f*, renforcement *m*, renforçage *m*

stress[1] *n* C&G contrainte *f*, COAL TECH tension *f*, CONST, GEOL contrainte *f*, effort *m*, MAR POLL tension *f*, MECH *materials* contrainte *f*, MECH ENG contrainte *f*, fatigue *f*, METALL contrainte *f*, NAUT *shipbuilding* effort *m*, P&R, PETR TECH contrainte *f*, PHYS contrainte *f*, sollicitation *f*, SPACE sollicitation *f*, SPRINGS contrainte *f*; ~ **analysis** *n* SPACE *spacecraft* analyse de contraintes *f*; ~

and strain analysis *n* MECH ENG analyse de contraintes et tensions *f*; **~ coating** *n* COATINGS vernis de vérification des contraintes *m*; **~ correction factor** *n* SPRINGS facteur de correction de la contrainte *m*, facteur de correction de flèche de la contrainte *m*; **~ expansion** *n* RAIL dilatation de contrainte *f*; **~ marks** *n pl* CINEMAT traces de serrage *f pl*; **~ relaxation** *n* C&G relaxation des contraintes *f*; **~ relief** *n* TESTING relaxation des contraintes *f*; **~ relieving** *n* HEATING traitement de relaxation *m*, SPRINGS stabilisation à chaud *f*; **~ tensor** *n* PHYS tenseur de contraintes *m*

stress[2] *vt* MECH ENG contraindre, PHYS solliciter; **~ relief** *vt* THERMOD *steel* faire un recuit

stressed: **~ zone** *n* C&G *around stone in glass* halo de contrainte *m*

stress-optical: **~ coefficient** *n* C&G coefficient de Brewster *m*

stress-relieving: **~ anneal** *n* THERMOD *metals* recuit d'élimination des tensions *m*, recuit de détente *m*

stress-strain: **~ curve** *n* P&R, PROP MAT courbe de contrainte-déformation *f*; **~ diagram** *n* NAUT *naval architecture* diagramme des contraintes-déformations *m*

stretch[1] *n* MECH ENG allongement *m*, P&R allongement *m*, élongation *f*, PAPER TECH allongement *m*; **~ at break** *n* PAPER TECH allongement à la rupture par traction *m*; **~ at breaking point** *n* PAPER TECH allongement à la rupture par traction *m*; **~ die** *n* MECH ENG *for forming* outillage d'étirage *m*; **~ film** *n* PACKAGING film étirable *m*; **~ length** *n* PAPER TECH allongement à la rupture par traction *m*; **~ modulus** *n* PETR module d'élasticité *m*; **~ roll** *n* PAPER TECH rouleau tendeur *m*; **~ thrust** *n* GEOL pli-faille *m*; **~ wrapping** *n* PACKAGING emballage étirable *m*, PRINT emballage sous manchon rétractable *m*; **~ of yarn in sizing** *n* TEXTILES allongement du fil à l'encollage *m*

stretch[2] *vt* PAPER TECH tendre, étirer, SPRINGS bander, TEXTILES tendre; **~ frame print** *vt* CINEMAT tirer les images plusieurs fois

stretchable *adj* PAPER TECH extensible

stretched: **~ aircraft** *n* AERONAUT avion allongé *m*

stretching *n* CHEM *of bond* étirage *m*, étirement *m*, CONST tension *f*, PAPER TECH étirage *m* **~ course** *n* CONST *masonry* assise de carreaux *f*, assise de panneresses *f*; **~ screw** *n* MECH ENG tendeur à vis *m*, vis de tension *f*; **~ zone** *n* TEXTILES zone de tension *f*

stretch-out: **~ operation** *n* PROD ENG exploitation en allongement de cycle *f*

stretchy *adj* TEXTILES extensible

striation *n* METALL strie *f*

strickle *n* PROD ENG *founding* gabarit *m*, trousse *f*; **~ board** *n* CONST planche *f*; **~ molding** *n* (AmE), **~ moulding** *n* (BrE) PROD ENG moulage au gabarit *m*, moulage au trousseau *m*

strickled: **~ casting** *n* PROD ENG pièce troussée *f*

Strickler's: **~ formula** *n* HYDROL formule de Strickler *f*

strickling *n* PROD ENG troussage *m*

strictly: **~ nonblocking network** *n* TELECOM réseau non blocable *m*

striding: **~ level** *n* MECH ENG niveau à bulle indépendant sur la lunette *m*, niveau à cheval *m*

strike[1] *n* MINING direction *f*, rencontre *f*, *of lode* direction *f*, *of vein* direction *f*; **~ aircraft** *n* MILIT avion d'appui sol *m*, avion de pénétration *m*; **~ drive** *n* MINING chassage *m*, chassante *f*, costière *f*, galerie chassante *f*, galerie d'allongement *f*, galerie de direc-

tion *f*, galerie en direction *f*; **~ gear** *n* MECH ENG débrayage *m*, débrayeur *m*, embrayeur *m*, passe-courroie *m*; **~ slip** *n* GEOL décrochement *m*, faille transversale *f*

strike[2] *vt* MINING atteindre, rencontrer, OCEANOG *fish* ferrer, PROD ENG araser

strike[3] *vi* CINEMAT *print* démonter un décor, tirer; **~ colors** *vi* (AmE), **~ colours** *vi* (BrE) NAUT *national flag* amener les couleurs, amener son pavillon, rentrer son pavillon

striker *n* MECH ENG *belt-striking gear* débrayage *m*, débrayeur *m*, embrayeur *m*, passe-courroie *m*; **~ spring** *n* MILIT *of firearm* ressort de percussion *m*

strike-slip: **~ movements** *n pl* GEOL *of plates* coulissage de plaques *m*, mouvements de coulissage *m pl*; **~ thrust** *n* GEOL décro-chevauchement *m*

striking *n* ELEC ENG *arc* amorçage *m*, ELECTRON *electro-deposition* dépôt d'une mince couche *m*; **~ the centering** *n* (AmE), **~ the centring** *n* (BrE) CONST *of arch* décintrage *m*, décintrement *m*; **~ gear** *n* MECH ENG *belt-striking gear* débrayage *m*, débrayeur *m*, embrayeur *m*, passe-courroie *m*; **~ plate** *n* CONST *locksmithing* gâche *f*; **~ post** *n* CONST poteau battant *m*

strimmer *n* CONST *gardening* désherbeuse électrique *f*

string *n* C&G filet *m* (Bel), fin *m* (Fra), COMP chaîne *f*, CONST limon *m*, DP chaîne *f*, GAS TECH *of pipes* train *m*, PETR TECH rame *f*, PRINT chaîne *f* **~ array** *n* DP tableau de caractères *m*; **~ board** *n* CONST limon *m*; **~ of casing** *n* CONST *well-sinking* colonne de tubage *f*, colonne de tubes *f*; **~ construction** *n* RAD PHYS *theoretical physics* construction de cordes *f*; **~ length** *n* COMP, DP longueur de chaîne *f*; **~ literal** *n* DP littéral chaîne *m*; **~ manipulation** *n* DP traitement de chaîne *m*; **~ operation** *n* DP opération sur chaîne *f*; **~ piece** *n* CONST limon *m*; **~ proof** *n* PRINT épreuve en placard *f*, épreuve en première *f*; **~ rod** *n* MECH ENG barre de renvoi *f*, tige de transmission *f*

stringer *n* CONST longeron *m*, longrine *f*, poutre de rive *f*, sommier *m*, *of roof truss* entrait *m*, tirant d'une ferme de comble *m*, *of stairway* limon *m*, MINING cordon *m*, crin *m*, filet *m*, veinule *f*, NAUT *boatbuilding* gouttière *f*, hiloire *f*, serre *f*, RAIL longrine *f*, SPACE *spacecraft* lisse *f*; **~ angle** *n* NAUT *shipbuilding* cornière de gouttière *f*; **~ head** *n* PETR première passe *f*

stringy: **~ knot** *n* C&G schlague *f*

strip[1] *n* AERONAUT bande d'atterrissage *f*, CONST feuillard de fer *m*, *of wood* languette *f*, tasseau *m*, PHOTO bande photographique *f*, PRINT lanière *f*, petite courroie *f*, *paper* bande étroite *f*, PROD ENG bornier *m*, strip bande *f*, *draught or draw taper* dépouille *f*; **~ chart recorder** *n* ELEC enregistreur à bande *m*, INSTRUMENT enregistreur sur bande *m*, enregistreur à papier déroulant *m*; **~ filling** *n* C&G enfournement en tapis sectionné *m*; **~ light** *n* CINEMAT rame de cyclorama *f*, unité au sol *f*; **~ line** *n* ELEC ENG ligne triplaque *f*, PHYS *transmission line* ligne à bande *f*; **~ log** *n* PETR log renseigné *m*; **~ mine** *n* MINING carrière exploitée en chassant *f*; **~ shim** *n* MECH ENG cale pelable *f*; **~ steel** *n* PROP MAT acier en bande *m*; **~ thickness** *n* PROP MAT épaisseur de feuillard *f*; **~ washer** *n* MECH ENG cale pelable *f*

strip[2] *vt* NUCLEAR appauvrir, PRINT *page* monter, PROD ENG arracher le filet de, *founding* décocher, démouler; **~ formwork** *vt* CONST décoffrer

stripe *n* CINEMAT piste magnétique *f*, DP piste *f*, TEXTILES fil flammé irrégulier *m*; **~ fabric** *n* TEXTILES tissu mille-raies *m*

striped[1] *adj* PAPER TECH rayé

striped:[2] **~ film** *n* CINEMAT pellicule avec piste couchée *f*, pellicule pistée *f*; **~ silvering** *n* C&G argenture en bandes *f*

stripiness: ~ in the warp *n* TEXTILES rayure en chaîne *f*

striping *n* RECORDING *of magnetic medium onto film* pistage *m*

stripper *n* COAL TECH séparateur *m*, PRINT dispositif de décollage *m*, décolleur *m*, dérouleur automatique *m*; **~ bush** *n* MECH ENG *injection mould* bague dévêtisseuse *f*; **~ plate** *n* MECH ENG *injection mould* plaque dévêtisseuse *f*

stripping *n* C&G descellage *m*, COAL TECH extraction *f*, MINING dépouillement du gîte *m*, PRINT décollage *m*, montage *m*, éjection des déchets *f*, PROD ENG décochage *m*, démoulage *m*, dépouillement *m*, PROP MAT *rolling mill* démoulage *m*; **~ column** *n* REFRIG colonne d'épuisement *f*; **~ machine** *n* PROD ENG *founding* machine démouleuse *f*; **~ pump** *n* MAR POLL pompe d'assèchement *f*

strippings *n pl* MINING morts-terrains de recouvrement *m pl*, terrains de couverture *m pl*, terrains de recouvrement *m pl*, terres de couverture *f pl*

strip-type: ~ detector *n* SPACE *spacecraft* détecteur à barrette *m*

strip-wound: ~ armature *n* ELEC *machine* enroulement en cuivre plat *m*; **~ flexible metal hose** *n* MECH ENG tuyau métallique flexible agrafé *m*

strobe: ~ light *n* CINEMAT lumière stroboscopique *f*, SPACE lumière stroboscopée *f*; **~ light projector** *n* SPACE projecteur stroboscopique *m*; **~ pulse** *n* TELECOM impulsion stroboscopique *f*

stroboscope *n* PHYS, WAVE PHYS stroboscope *m*

stroboscopic: ~ tape *n* RECORDING bande stroboscopique *f*

stroke *n* AUTO temps *m*, CONST *of piston*, HYDR EQUIP *of slide valve* course *f*, MECH ENG *of piston* battement *m*, coup *m*, course *f*, jeu *m*, levée *f*, NUCLEAR course *f*, levée *f*, PHYS course piston *f*, PRINT course de la balade *f*; **~ counter** *n* MECH ENG *machine tool* compteur de tours *m*; **~ of ram** *n* MECH ENG course du piston *f*; **~ of the walking beam** *n* MINING levée du levier de battage *f*

strong: ~ breeze *n* METEO bon frais *m*, vent frais *m*; **~ gale** *n* METEO forts coups de vent *m pl*; **~ interaction** *n* NUCLEAR, PHYS interaction forte *f*; **~ inversion** *n* ELECTRON forte inversion *f*; **~ nuclear force** *n* PART PHYS force nucléaire forte *f*; **~ solution** *n* CHEM solution forte *f*; **~ turbulent energy production** *n* FLUID PHYS forte production d'énergie turbulente *f*; **~ ultraviolet rays** *n pl* SAFETY fortes radiations ultraviolettes *f pl*

strontianite *n* MINERAL strontianite *f*

strontic *adj* CHEM strontique

strontium *n (Sr)* CHEM strontium *m (Sr)*; **~ chromate pigment** *n* COLOURS pigment au chromate de strontium *m*

strop *n* MECH ENG *of tackle block* estrope *f*

strophanthin *n* CHEM strophanthine *f*

Strowger: ~ system *n* TELECOM système Strowger *m*

struck *adj* CONST *loaded material* aplani

struck-up: ~ casting *n* PROD ENG pièce troussée *f*; **~ core** *n* PROD ENG *founding* noyau troussé *m*

structural[1] *adj* CONST structural

structural:[2] **~ analysis** *n* CONST calcul des ouvrages *m*, ingénierie *f*; **~ analysis software** *n* SPACE *spacecraft*

logiciel d'analyse de structures *m*; **~ dynamics** *n* MECH ENG dynamique structurale *f*; **~ effect** *n* CONST effet structural *m*; **~ fire protection** *n* SAFETY protection structurelle contre l'incendie *f*; **~ foam mold** *n* (AmE), **~ foam mould** *n* (BrE) MECH ENG moule en mousse *m*; **~ formula** *n* CHEM *of compound* formule de constitution *f*; **~ glass** *n* C&G moulages *m pl*; **~ iron** *n* CONST fer de construction *m*; **~ isomerism** *n* CHEM *of compound* isomérie structurale *f*; **~ map** *n* GEOL carte structurale *f*; **~ model** *n* SPACE maquette de structure *f*; **~ plastic** *n* PROP MAT plastique pour la construction *m*; **~ steel** *n* CONST acier de construction *m*; **~ tap** *n* PETR TECH piège structural *m*; **~ varnish** *n* COATINGS vernis à effet de structure *m*

structure *n* COMP structure *f*, CONST bâtisse *f*, construction *f*, structure *f*, *bridge, viaduct, tunnel* ouvrage *m*, DP, PHYS *of atom* structure *f*, RAIL ouvrage *m*; **~ contour map** *n* GEOL carte structurale de subsurface *f*; **~ factor** *n* CRYSTALL facteur de structure *m*; **~ index** *n* SPACE *spacecraft* indice de structure *m*; **~ of space time** *n* RAD PHYS structure de l'espace-temps *f*; **~ subsurface contour map** *n* GEOL carte structurale de subsurface *f*; **~ of turbulent flows** *n* FLUID PHYS structure des écoulements turbulents *f*

structured: ~ design *n* COMP, DP conception structurée *f*; **~ programming** *n (SP)* COMP, DP programmation structurée *f (PS)*; **~ type** *n* COMP, DP type structuré *m*

strut *n* AUTO jambe de force *f*, COAL TECH étai *m*, CONST arc-boutant *m*, boutée *f*, contrefiche *f*, bielle *f*, *between floor joists* entretoise *f*, lien *m*, lierne *f*, étrésillon *m*, *brace* entretoise *f*, étrésillon *m*, *raking strut placed across angle* aisselier *m*, *strength* of materials pièce chargée debout *f*, *timbering* force *f*, jambe de force *f*, MECH montant *m*, NAUT *boatbuilding* support *m*, PACKAGING étançon *m*, VEHICLES *body, engine* entretoise *f*

strut-action: ~ pawl motion *n* MECH ENG encliquetage à arc-boutement *m*, encliquetage à frottement *m*

strutting *n* CONST entretoises *f pl*, liernes *f pl*, étrésillons *m pl*, *act* entretoisement *m*, étrésillonnement *m*

struvite *n* MINERAL struvite *f*

STS *abbr* SPACE *(space-time-space)* STS *(spatial-temporel-spatial)*, SPACE *(space transportation system)* système de transport spatial *m*

stub *n* CONST tenon invisible *m*, *of bolt of tumbler lock* ergot *m*, mentonnet *m*, ELEC ENG adaptateur à ligne *m*, MECH ENG *short pin* goujon *m*, tourillon *m*, PHYS *waveguide* bras de réactance *m*, stub *m*; **~ axle** *n* VEHICLES *wheel* essieu à chapes *m*; **~ drill** *n* MECH ENG foret à queue cylindrique extra-court *m*; **~ end** *n* MECH ENG *of connecting rod* grosse tête *f*, tête *f*; **~ mortise** *n* CONST mortaise aveugle *f*; **~ tenon** *n* CONST tenon invisible *m*

stubborn: ~ ore *n* MINING minerai rebelle *m*, minerai réfractaire *m*

stubook *n* PRINT carnet à souches *m*

stuck: ~ shank *n* C&G jambe rapportée *f*

stud *n* AUTO, MECH goujon *m*, MECH ENG boulon prisonnier *m*, goujon *m*, goujon prisonnier *m*, prisonnier *m*, PROD ENG goujon *m*, support double *m*, VEHICLES goujon *m*; **~ bolt** *n* MECH ENG boulon prisonnier *m*, goujon *m*, goujon prisonnier *m*, prisonnier *m*; **~ chain** *n* MECH ENG chaîne à fuseau *f*, chaîne-Galle à fuseau *f*; **~ chaplet** *n* PROD ENG support double *m*; **~ coupling** *n* CONST *for pipes* nez de raccord *m*; **~ driver** *n* MECH ENG *tool* dégoujonneuse *f*; **~ extractor** *n* MECH ENG *tool*

extracteur de goujons cassés *m*; ~ **link** *n* CONST maille
étançonnée *f*, maille à étai *f*; ~ **mounting** *n* PROD ENG
montage à l'aide de goujons *m*; ~ **partition** *n* CONST
cloison à entretoise *f*; ~ **union** *n* CONST nez de raccord
m; ~ **welding** *n* CONST soudage des goujons *m*; ~
welding gun *n* CONST pistolet pour soudage des goujons *m*; ~ **wheel** *n* MECH ENG *gearing* roue
intermédiaire *f*, roue parasite *f*
studded: ~ **link cable chain** *n* CONST câble-chaîne à
mailles étançonnées *m*, câble-chaîne à étais *m*; ~ **tire** *n*
(AmE), ~ **tyre** *n* (BrE) VEHICLES pneu clouté *m*
studdles *n pl* MINING poteaux dans les angles *m pl*
studio *n* CINEMAT studio *m*; ~ **address system** *n* RECOR-
DING réseau d'ordres *m*; ~ **broadcast** *n* TV émission en
studio *f*; ~ **camera** *n* PHOTO caméra de studio *f*, chambre d'atelier *f*; ~ **control room** *n* TV régie *f*; ~ **facilities** *n*
pl TV moyens techniques studio *m pl*; ~ **lining** *n* RECOR-
DING revêtement interne de studio *m*; ~ **manager** *n* TV
régisseur de plateau *m*; ~ **monitor** *n* TV écran de
contrôle studio *m*; ~ **porcelain** *n* C&G porcelaine artistique *f*; ~ **pottery** *n* C&G poterie artistique *f*; ~ **work** *n*
PHOTO travail en studio *m*
stud-link: ~ **chain cable** *n* CONST câble-chaîne à mailles
étançonnées *m*, câble-chaîne à étais *m*
study *n* MECH ENG, RAD PHYS étude *f*
stuff[1] *n* COATINGS enduit des tanneurs *m*, PAPER TECH
pâte travaillée *f*, PROD ENG matière *f*, matériaux *m pl*;
~ **chest** *n* PAPER TECH cuvier de tête *m*; ~ **sizing** *n* PAPER
TECH collage dans la pâte *m*
stuff[2] *vt* TRANSP *containers* empoter
stuffing *n* PROD ENG *act* bourrage *m*, garnissage *m*,
rembourrage *m*, *material* garniture *f*, rembourrage *m*,
TELECOM bourrage *m*, TRANSP *of containers* empotage
m; ~ **box** *n* MECH ENG presse-étoupe *m*, PROD ENG boîte
à bourrage *f*, boîte à garniture *f*, boîte à étoupe *f*,
presse-garniture *m*, presse-étoupe *m*; ~ **box lid** *n* NU-
CLEAR bride *f*, collet *m*, couverture de la boîte à
étoupe *f*; ~ **character** *n* TELECOM caractère de bourrage
m; ~ **device** *n* TELECOM dispositif de bourrage *m*; ~ **digit**
n TELECOM chiffre de bourrage *m*, élément numérique
de bourrage *m*; ~ **rate** *n* TELECOM taux de bourrage *m*
stump *n* CONST *of bolt of tumbler lock* ergot *m*, mentonnet *m*
stun *vt* FOOD TECH *animal before slaughter* étourdir
stupefacient[1] *adj* CHEM stupéfiant
stupefacient[2] *n* CHEM stupéfiant *m*
S-twist *n* TEXTILES torsion S *f*
STX *abbr* (*start of text*) COMP, DP début de texte *m*
style[1] *n* TEXTILES *weave* armure *f*; ~ **attributes** *n pl* PRINT
attributs des feuilles de style *m pl*
style[2] *vt* TEXTILES *create* créer
styles *n pl* PRINT paramètres mémorisés gérant la composition *m pl*
styling *n* TEXTILES forme *f*
stylus *n* RECORDING aiguille *f*; ~ **crosstalk** *n* RECORDING
intermodulation d'aiguille *f*; ~ **force** *n* ACOUSTICS
force d'appui *f*; ~ **instrument** *n* INSTRUMENT instrument à palpeur *m*; ~ **recording instrument** *n*
INSTRUMENT enregistreur à pointe sèche *m*
styphnate *n* CHEM styphnate *m*, tricinate *m*, trinitroré-
sorcinate *m*
styphnic: ~ **acid** *n* CHEM acide styphnique *m*, trinitroré-
sorcine *f*
styracitol *n* CHEM styracine *f*
styramate *n* CHEM styramate *m*
styrene *n* CHEM styrol *m*, styrolène *m*, styrène *m*, PETR

TECH, PROP MAT styrène *m*; ~ **butadiene rubber** *n* P&R
caoutchouc au styrène butadiène *m*
Styrofoam *n* (TM) (AmE) P&R polystyrène expansé *m*,
PACKAGING polystyrène mousse *m*
styrolene *n* CHEM styrolène *m*
stythe *n* MINING acide carbonique *m*, pousse *f*, touffe *f*
sub: ~ **timer alarm** *n* LAB EQUIP réveil avertisseur *m*
SUB: ~ **character** *n* (*substitute character*) COMP, DP
caractère de substitution *m*
subacetate *n* CHEM sous-acétate *m*
subaddress *n* TELECOM *ISDN* sous-adresse *f*
subaddressing *n* TELECOM *ISDN* sous-adressage *m*
subambient: ~ **temperature flexibility test** *n* MECH ENG
essai de souplesse à température inférieure à l'ambiante *m*
subaqueous: ~ **pump** *n* WATER SUPP pompe pouvant
fonctionner noyée *f*
subatomic: ~ **particle** *n* PHYS particule subatomique *f*
sub-base *n* CONST fondation *f*, sous-couche *f*
sub-bottom: ~ **profiler** *n* OCEANOG sondeur de sédiment *m*, sondeur de vase *m*
subcarbonate *n* CHEM sous-carbonate *m*
subcarrier *n* SPACE *communications*, TV sous-porteuse *f*;
~ **component** *n* TV composante de la sous-porteuse *f*; ~
frequency *n* TELECOM fréquence de la sous-porteuse *f*,
TV fréquence sous-porteuse *f*; ~ **lock** *n* TV asservissement sous-porteuse *m*; ~ **modulation** *n* TV modulation
de sous-porteuse *f*; ~ **offset** *n* TV décalage de la sous-
porteuse de chrominance *m*; ~ **oscillator** *n* TV
générateur de la sous-porteuse *m*; ~ **phase** *n* TV phase
de sous-porteuse *f*; ~ **rectification** *n* TV redressement
du signal de chrominance *m*
subchannel *n* ELECTRON voie *f*
subchloride *n* CHEM sous-chlorure *m*
sub-Clos: ~ **network** *n* TELECOM réseau de Clos imparfait *m*
subcoating *n* COATINGS couche d'apprêt *f*
subcontracting *n* PROD ENG sous-traitance *f*; ~ **item** *n*
PROD ENG article sous-traité *m*
subcontractor *n* PROD ENG sous-traitant *m*
subcooled: ~ **boiling** *n* PROD ENG ébullition locale *f*
subcooler *n* REFRIG sous-refroidisseur *m*
subcritical: ~ **reaction** *n* RAD PHYS réaction sous-criti-
que *f*
subdirectory *n* COMP sous-répertoire *m*
subdominant[1] *adj* ACOUSTICS sous-dominant
subdominant[2] *n* ACOUSTICS sous-dominante *f*
subdrift *n* MINING coistresse *f*, costresse *f*, galerie costresse *f*
subduction *n* PETR TECH subduction *f*; ~ **zone** *n* PETR
TECH zone de subduction *f*
subdwarf *n* ASTRON *type of star* sous-naine *f*
suberate *n* CHEM subérate *m*
suberic *adj* CHEM subérique
suberification *n* CHEM subérification *f*
suberin *n* CHEM subérine *f*
suberone *n* CHEM subérone *f*
suberyl *n* CHEM subéryle *m*
suberylic *adj* CHEM subérylique
subframe *n* VEHICLES *body* cadre avant *m*
subgrade *n* RAIL plate-forme *f*, plate-forme de la voie *f*;
~ **reaction modulus** *n* COAL TECH module de réaction
du sol *m*
subharmonic[1] *adj* ACOUSTICS sous-harmonique
subharmonic[2] *n* ELECTRON harmonique inférieur *m*
subject: ~ **matter** *n* PATENTS objet *m*; ~ **under investiga-**

tion n MECH ENG question à l'étude f

subjective: ~ **camera** n CINEMAT caméra prenant la place de la personne f; ~ **loudness** n ACOUSTICS of sound intensité subjective f; ~ **test** n TELECOM essai subjectif m; ~ **tone** n ACOUSTICS ton subjectif m

subland: ~ **twist drill** n MECH ENG foret étagé m

sublayer n FLUID PHYS, TEXTILES sous-couche f

sublethal: ~ **effect** n POLLUTION effet sublétal m

sublevel n MINING sous-niveau m, sous-étage m, PHYS sous-niveau m

sublicence n (BrE) PATENTS sous-licence f

sublicense n (AmE) see sublicence

sublieutenant n NAUT navy enseigne de vaisseau m

sublimable adj CHEM sublimable

sublimate n CHEM sublimat m, sublime m, sublimé m, PETR TECH sublimé m

sublimation n CHEM, PHYS sublimation f

sublimatory n CHEM sublimatoire m

sublime vt CHEM sublimer

sublimed adj CHEM sublimé

sublot n PROD ENG sous-lot m

submachine: ~ **gun** n MILIT mitraillette f, pistolet-mitrailleur m

submarine: ~ **cable** n ELEC ENG, NAUT, OCEANOG, TELECOM câble sous-marin m; ~ **earthquake** n GEOPHYS tremblement de mer m; ~ **plateau** n OCEANOG plateau sous-marin m; ~ **relief** n OCEANOG topographie sous-marine f; ~ **slope** n OCEANOG talus m; ~ **tanker** n TRANSP pétrolier sous-marin m; ~ **topography** n OCEANOG topographie sous-marine f; ~ **valley** n OCEANOG vallée sous-marine f

submediant n ACOUSTICS sus-dominante f

submerge vt WATER SUPP noyer, submerger

submerged: ~ **arc welding** n CONST soudage à l'arc sous flux en poudre m, PROP MAT soudage sous flux électroconducteur m; ~ **bar** n HYDROL seuil m; ~ **combustion** n GAS TECH combustion submergée f; ~ **concrete** n CONST béton immergé m, béton sous-marin m; ~ **condenser** n REFRIG condenseur à immersion m; ~ **optical repeater** n TELECOM répéteur optique immergé m; ~ **orifice** n HYDR EQUIP orifice immergé m, orifice noyé m; ~ **pump** n WATER SUPP pompe pouvant fonctionner noyée f; ~ **repeater** n TELECOM répéteur immergé m; ~ **spring** n WATER SUPP source submergée f; ~ **turbine** n HYDR EQUIP turbine immergée f, turbine noyée f; ~ **weir** n HYDR EQUIP déversoir submergé m, déversoir à nappe noyée m

submergence n CHEM submersion f, OCEANOG ennoyage m

submersible n OCEANOG engin sous-marin m, submersible m, véhicule sous-marin m, PETR véhicule sous-marin m; ~ **platform** n PETR plate-forme immergée f, plate-forme submersible f; ~ **pump** n MINING pompe submersible f

submersion n CHEM submersion f

submicron: ~ **particulate airfilter** n SAFETY filtre contre les microparticules en suspension dans l'air m

submillimeter: ~ **astronomy** n (AmE), **submillimetre astronomy** n (BrE) ASTRON astronomie sub-millimétrique f

subminiature: ~ **camera** n PHOTO appareil photographique de microformat m; ~ **relay** n ELEC ENG relais subminiature m

submission: ~ **identifier** n TELECOM identificateur de dépôt m; ~ **time** n TELECOM temps de dépôt m

submit vt PATENTS soumettre

submultiframe n (SMF) TELECOM sous-multitrame m

submultiple n METR of unit of measurement sous-multiple m

submultiplex vt TELECOM sous-multiplexer

submunition n MILIT sous-munition f

subnetwork n TELECOM sous-réseau m; ~ **dependent convergence function** n (SNDCF) TELECOM fonction de convergence dépendant du sous-réseau f

subnitrate n CHEM sous-azotate m, sous-nitrate m

subnormal n GEOM sous-normal m; ~ **pressure** n PETR TECH pression de formation anormale négative f

subpopulation: ~ **collective dose** n POLLUTION équivalent de dose pour un sous-groupe m

subpreset: ~ **master** n TV commande de groupe préréglé f; ~ **switch** n TV commutateur de groupe préréglé m

subprogram n COMP, DP sous-programme m

subreflector n SPACE communications réflecteur secondaire m

subroutine n COMP, DP sous-programme m; ~ **call** n COMP, DP appel d'un sous-programme m; ~ **library** n COMP, DP bibliothèque de sous-programmes f

subsalt n CHEM sous-sel m

subsatellite: ~ **point** n SPACE point sous-satellite m

subscriber n COMP, DP, ELEC, TELECOM abonné m; ~ **calling rate** n TELECOM taux d'appel des abonnés m; ~ **line circuit** n (SLC) TELECOM joncteur d'abonné m; ~ **number** n (SN) TELECOM numéro d'abonné m; ~ **premises network** n (SPN) TELECOM réseau d'installation d'abonnés m; ~ **service** n TELECOM desserte des abonnés f, service aux abonnés m; ~ **trunk dialling** n (BrE) (STD, direct distance dialing) TELECOM interurbain automatique m, sélection à distance de l'abonné demandé f; ~ **trunk dialling access code** n (BrE) (cf direct distance dialing access code) TELECOM préfixe interurbain m

subscriber's: ~ **line** n TELECOM ligne d'abonné f, ligne de raccordement f, ligne de rattachement f, ligne téléphonique d'abonné f; ~ **meter** n TELECOM compteur de taxes d'abonné m, compteur de taxes m, compteur d'abonné m; ~ **private meter** n TELECOM compteur de taxes à domicile m, compteur à domicile m; ~ **store** n TELECOM fichier d'abonnés m

subscript n COMP indice inférieur m, DP indice m, PRINT caractères en indice m pl, chiffre en index m, indice m

subsea: ~ **completion** n PETR TECH complétion sous-marine f; ~ **well** n POLLUTION puits sous-marin m; ~ **wellhead** n PETR TECH tête de puits sous-marine f

subsequent: ~ **delivery** n PROD ENG reste à livrer m

subset n COMP, DP, MATH sous-ensemble m

subshell n PHYS atom sous-couche f

subside vi CONST ground s'affaisser, s'effondrer, HYDROL water baisser, se retirer

subsidence n CONST of building, mountain affaissement m, of surface affaissement m, cloche f, fondis m, fontis m, GEOL subsidence f, HYDROL effondrement m, of water level baisse d'une rivière f, décrue f, METEO subsidence f, MINING of roof affaissement m, effondrement m, tombée f, écrasée f, PETR TECH subsidence f, POLLUTION affaissement m, effondrement m, subsidence f, PROP MAT subsidence du fond f, RAIL affaissement m

subsident: ~ **basin** n PETR TECH bassin en subsidence m

subsoil: ~ **water** n WATER SUPP nappe souterraine f

subsonic: ~ **aircraft** n AERONAUT avion subsonique m; ~ **frequency** n RAD PHYS fréquence subsonique f

substage n MINING sous-étage m

substance *n* C&G épaisseur *f*, CHEM corps *m*, substance *f*, PAPER TECH grammage *m*
substandard[1] *adj* CHEM non conforme aux normes établies
substandard:[2] ~ **gage** *n* (AmE), ~ **gauge** *n* (BrE) CINEMAT format réduit *m*; ~ **ship** *n* TRANSP navire inférieur aux normes *m*
substation *n* CONST *electricity* poste *m*, poste de courant *m*, ELEC *supply network* poste *m*, ELEC ENG sous-centrale *f*, sous-station *f*, PROD ENG sous-station *f*; ~ **for frequency conversion** *n* ELEC *supply network* poste de conversion *m*, station de convertisseurs *f*
substituent *n* CHEM substituant *m*
substitute: ~ **character** *n* *(SUB character)* COMP, DP caractère de substitution *m*; ~ **natural gas** *n* *(SNG)* GAS TECH, PETR TECH gaz naturel de synthèse *m* *(GNS)*
substitution *n* CHEM substitution *f*, MATH changement *m*
substitutional: ~ **solid solution** *n* CRYSTALL solution solide de substitution *f*
substorm *n* GEOPHYS orage solaire *m*
substrate *n* COMP substrat *m*, P&R subjectile *m*, substrat *m*, PHYS substrat *m*, PRINT support d'impression *m*, PROP MAT support *m*, TELECOM substrat *m*
substratum *n* GEOL soubassement *m*, substratum *m*, PETR TECH substratum *m*
substring *n* COMP, DP sous-chaîne *f*
substructure *n* CONST souterrain *m*, substructure *f*, PETR TECH substructure *f*
subsulfate *n* (AmE), **subsulphate** *n* (BrE) CHEM sulfate basique *m*
subsurface: ~ **conditions** *n pl* PETR TECH conditions de sous-sol *f pl*; ~ **contour** *n* GEOL courbe de niveau *f*; ~ **current** *n* OCEANOG sous-courant *m*; ~ **erosion** *n* WATER SUPP érosion souterraine *f*; ~ **flow** *n* HYDROL écoulement de subsurface *m*, écoulement hypodermique *m*; ~ **geologist** *n* PETR TECH géologue de subsurface *m*; ~ **irrigation** *n* WATER SUPP irrigation en sous-sol *f*; ~ **zone** *n* OCEANOG subsurface *f*
subswitcher *n* TV présélecteur *m*
subsynchronous: ~ **satellite** *n* SPACE satellite sous-synchrone *m*
subsystem *n* COMP, DP, SPACE, TELECOM sous-système *m*
subtangent *n* GEOM sous-tangente *f*
subtask *n* COMP, DP sous-tâche *f*
subtend *vt* GEOM sous-tendre
subterranean: ~ **propagation** *n* TELECOM propagation souterraine *f*; ~ **river** *n* HYDROL rivière souterraine *f*; ~ **volcano** *n* GEOPHYS poche volcanique souterraine *f*; ~ **water** *n* WATER SUPP eau de subsurface *f*
subtitle[1] *n* CINEMAT sous-titre *m*
subtitle[2] *vt* CINEMAT sous-titrer
subtitler *n* TV sous-titreur *m*
subtitling *n* TV sous-titrage *m*
subtract *vt* COMP, DP, MATH soustraire
subtraction *n* COMP, DP, MATH soustraction *f*
subtractive: ~ **color printer** *n* (AmE), ~ **colour printer** *n* (BrE) CINEMAT tireuse soustractive *f*; ~ **method** *n* ELECTRON méthode soustractive *f*; ~ **primaries** *n pl* CINEMAT, TV couleurs primaires soustractives *f pl*; ~ **process** *n* CINEMAT procédé soustractif *m*; ~ **synthesis** *n* PHOTO mélange des couleurs par soustraction de lumière *m*
subtractor *n* COMP, DP soustracteur *m*
subtrahend *n* COMP diminuteur *m*, DP diminuteur *m*,

quantité à soustraire *f*, terme soustractif *m*
subtropical: ~ **anticyclone** *n* METEO anticyclone subtropical *m*; ~ **calms** *n pl* METEO, OCEANOG calmes subtropicaux *m pl*
subtype *n* COMP, DP sous-type *m*
suburban: ~ **traffic** *n* TRANSP trafic de banlieue *m*
subway *n* (AmE) *(cf underground)* RAIL métro *m*
successful: ~ **call** *n* TELECOM appel ayant abouti *m*
successfully: ~ **complete** *vt* CONST mener à bonne fin
successor: ~ **in title** *n* PATENTS ayant cause *m*
succinate *n* CHEM succinate *m*
succinic *adj* CHEM succinique
succinimide *n* CHEM succinimide *f*
succinite *n* MINERAL succinite *f*
succinyl *n* CHEM succinyle *m*
suck *vt* TEXTILES aspirer
suck-and-blow: ~ **process** *n* C&G procédé aspiré-soufflé *m*
sucker *n* INSTRUMENT ventouse de centrage *f*, MECH ENG aspirateur *m*, ventouse *f*, PRINT ventouse *f*; ~ **rod** *n* FUELLESS *of windmill pump* tige de pompage *f*, MECH ENG *of suction pump* tige de commande du piston *f*
sucrase *n* FOOD TECH invertase *f*, sucrase *f*
sucrate *n* CHEM sucrate *m*
suction *n* MECH aspiration *f*, MECH ENG aspiration *f*, succion *f*, PAPER TECH, REFRIG, TEXTILES aspiration *f*; ~ **accumulator** *n* REFRIG bouteille tampon *f*, vase tampon d'aspiration *f*; ~ **box** *n* MECH ENG chambre d'aspiration *f*, PAPER TECH caisse aspirante *f*; ~ **box cover** *n* PAPER TECH dessus de caisse aspirante *m*; ~ **carburetor** *n* (AmE), ~ **carburettor** *n* (BrE) AUTO carburateur à dépression *m*; ~ **chamber** *n* TRANSP chambre de sustentation *f*; ~ **circuit** *n* ELEC circuit d'absorption *m*; ~ **couch press** *n* PAPER TECH presse coucheuse aspirante *f*; ~ **couch roll** *n* PAPER TECH cylindre aspirant *m*; ~ **cover** *n* REFRIG couvercle d'aspiration *m*; ~ **dewatering** *n* TEXTILES déshydratation par aspiration *f*; ~ **dredge** *n* OCEANOG suceuse *f*, WATER SUPP drague aspirante *f*, drague suceuse *f*, drague à aspiration *f*, drague à succion *f*; ~ **dredger** *n* NAUT drague aspirante *f*, drague suceuse *f*, drague à succion *f*, TRANSP drague aspirante *f*, drague suceuse *f*; ~ **fan** *n* MECH ENG ventilateur aspirant *m*, ventilateur négatif *m*; ~ **feeding** *n* C&G alimentation par succion *f*; ~ **filter** *n* PROD ENG filtre d'aspiration *m*, WATER SUPP filtre d'aspiration *m*, filtre à vide *m*; ~ **gage** *n* (AmE) *see suction gauge*; ~ **gas producer** *n* PROD ENG gazogène à aspiration *m*; ~ **gauge** *n* (BrE) REFRIG manomètre d'aspiration *m*; ~ **head** *n* WATER SUPP hauteur d'aspiration *f*; ~ **hopper dredger** *n* NAUT drague suceuse porteuse *f*; ~ **hose** *n* SAFETY *firefighting equipment*, WATER SUPP tuyau d'aspiration *m*; ~ **hydroextraction** *n* TEXTILES déshydratation par aspiration *f*; ~ **lift** *n* WATER SUPP hauteur d'aspiration *f*; ~ **line** *n* PROD ENG canalisation d'aspiration *f*; ~ **line accumulator** *n* REFRIG accumulateur d'aspiration antibélier *m*, bouteille anticoup de liquide *f*; ~ **machine** *n* C&G machine à aspiration *f*; ~ **mold** *n* (AmE), ~ **mould** *n* (BrE) C&G moule aspirant *m*; ~ **mount** *n* CINEMAT monture à ventouse *f*; ~ **pipe** *n* HYDROL conduite d'aspiration *f*, NAUT *dredging* élinde *f*, TRANSP conduite d'aspiration *f*, WATER SUPP tubulure d'aspiration *f*, tuyau d'aspiration *m*; ~ **porosimeter** *n* PAPER TECH porosimètre à aspiration *m*; ~ **porosity tester** *n* PAPER TECH porosimètre à aspiration *m*; ~ **port** *n* PROD ENG orifice d'aspiration *m*; ~ **pump** *n* FOOD TECH

processing machinery pompe aspirante *f*, HYDR EQUIP pompe aspirante *f*, pompe suceuse *f*, TEXTILES pompe aspirante *f*, WATER SUPP machine aspirante *f*, pompe aspirante *f*, pompe suceuse *f*; ~ **ram** *n* PROD ENG bélier aspirateur *m*; ~ **roll** *n* PAPER TECH rouleau aspirant *m*; ~ **roll felt** *n* PAPER TECH feutre de rouleau aspirant *m*; ~ **strainer** *n* CHEM TECH entonnoir-filtre *m*, filtre de succion *m*, PROD ENG crépine d'aspiration *f*, REFRIG filtre d'aspiration *m*; ~ **tank** *n* HYDR EQUIP bâche d'aspiration *f*, réservoir d'aspiration *m*; ~ **temperature** *n* REFRIG température d'aspiration *f*; ~ **throttling valve** *n* AUTO soupape d'aspiration *f*; ~ **valve** *n* AUTO clapet d'aspiration *m*, HYDR EQUIP clapet d'aspiration *m*, clapet de pied d'aspiration *m*, REFRIG vanne d'aspiration *f*

suction-and-filter: ~ **installation** *n* SAFETY *for dust and chippings* installation d'aspiration et de filtration *f*
suction-suspended: ~ **vehicle** *n* TRANSP véhicule aéro-suspendu *m*
suction-type: ~ **governor** *n* AUTO régulateur à dépression *m*
sud-channel *n* MECH ENG *in machine tool table* rigole pour recevoir l'eau de savon *f*
sudden: ~ **contraction of cross section** *n* HYDR EQUIP diminution brusque de section *f*, rétrécissement brusque de section *m*; ~ **enlargement of cross section** *n* HYDR EQUIP augmentation brusque de section *f*, élargissement brusque de section *m*; ~ **short circuit test** *n* ELEC essai de court-circuit brusque *m*; ~ **storm commencement** *n (SSC)* SPACE début brusque d'orage magnétique *m*
sudden-grip: ~ **rotary bench vice** *n* (BrE) MECH ENG étau à base tournante pour établis à serrage instantané *m*; ~ **rotary bench vise** *n* (AmE) *see sudden-grip rotary bench vice*
suddenness: ~ **of conflagration** *n* SAFETY soudaineté de l'incendie *f*
suffer: ~ **damage** *vi* PATENTS subir un dommage; ~ **shipwreck** *vi* NAUT faire naufrage
suffix *n* COMP, DP suffixe *m*; ~ **notation** *n* COMP notation polonaise inversée *f*, notation suffixée *f*, DP notation polonaise inversée *f*, notation suffixée *f*
suffocation *n* SAFETY asphyxie *f*; ~ **by fumes** *n* SAFETY asphyxie due aux émissions de fumées *f*, asphyxie par les fumées *f*
sugar *n* C&G tache *f*, CHEM sucre *m*; ~ **dye** *n* COLOURS teinture pour caramel *f*; ~ **industry** *n* FOOD TECH industrie sucrière *f*; ~ **nucleus** *n* FOOD TECH cristal de sucre *m*
sugaring *n* FOOD TECH chaptalisation *f*, sucrage *m*
sugary: ~ **cut** *n* C&G mauvaise coupe *f*
suggested: ~ **order** *n* PROD ENG ordre suggéré *m*, proposition d'ordre *f*
suitable *n* PROD ENG *process* adapté
suitcase: ~ **board** *n* PAPER TECH carton pour valise *m*
suite *n* COMP, DP famille *f*, suite *f*, TELECOM *equipment* travée *f*; ~ **of switchboards** *n* TELECOM meuble *m*
suiting *n* TEXTILES tissu pour complet *m*
sulfa (AmE), **sulpha** (BrE): ~ **drug** *n* CHEM sulfamide *m*
sulfa-free (AmE), **sulpha-free** (BrE) *adj* CHEM *compound* exempt de soufre
sulfafurazole (AmE), **sulphafurazole** (BrE) *n* CHEM sulfafurazol *m*
sulfaguanidine (AmE), **sulphaguanidine** (BrE) *n* CHEM sulfaguanidine *f*
sulfamate (AmE), **sulphamate** (BrE) *n* CHEM sulfamate *m*

sulfamic (AmE), **sulphamic** (BrE)[1] *adj* CHEM sulfamique
sulfamic (AmE), **sulphamic** (BrE):[2] ~ **acid** *n* DETERGENTS acide sulfamique *m*
sulfamide (AmE), **sulphamide** (BrE) *n* CHEM sulfamide *m*
sulfanilamide (AmE), **sulphanilamide** (BrE) *n* CHEM sulfanilamide *f*
sulfanilate (AmE), **sulphanilate** (BrE) *n* CHEM sulfanilate *m*
sulfanilic (AmE), **sulphanilic** (BrE) *adj* CHEM sulfanilique
sulfapyridine (AmE), **sulphapyridine** (BrE) *n* CHEM sulfapyridine *f*
sulfarsenic (AmE), **sulpharsenic** (BrE) *adj* CHEM sulfarsénique
sulfarsenide (AmE), **sulpharsenide** (BrE) *n* CHEM sulfarséniure *m*
sulfate (AmE), **sulphate** (BrE) *n* CHEM, POLLUTION sulfate *m*; ~ **attack** *n* CONST attaque de sulfate *f*; ~ **of lime** *n* CHEM chaux sulfatée *f*, sulfate de chaux *m*; ~ **pulp** *n* PAPER TECH pâte au sulfate *f*
sulfated (AmE), **sulphated** (BrE): ~ **oil** *n* DETERGENTS huile sulfatée *f*
sulfathiazole (AmE), **sulphathiazole** (BrE) *n* CHEM sulfathiazole *m*
sulfatide (AmE), **sulphatide** (BrE) *n* CHEM sulfatide *m*
sulfation (AmE), **sulphation** (BrE) *n* DETERGENTS sulfatation *f*, sulforation *f*
sulfide (AmE), **sulphide** (BrE) *n* CHEM sulfure *m*; ~ **glass** *n* C&G verre de sulfure *m*; ~ **ore** *n* MINING minerai sulfuré *m*; ~ **soil** *n* COAL TECH sol de sulfure *m*; ~ **toning** *n* PHOTO virage par sulfuration *m*
sulfinic (AmE), **sulphinic** (BrE) *adj* CHEM sulfinique
sulfinyl (AmE), **sulphinyl** (BrE) *n* CHEM sulfinyle *m*
sulfite (AmE), **sulphite** (BrE) *n* CHEM sulfite *m*; ~ **pulp** *n* PAPER TECH pâte au bisulfite *f*
sulfochlorination (AmE), **sulphochlorination** (BrE) *n* DETERGENTS sulfochloration *f*
sulfolane (AmE), **sulpholane** (BrE) *n* CHEM, PETR TECH sulfolane *m*
sulfolene (AmE), **sulpholene** (BrE) *n* PETR TECH sulfolène *m*
sulfonamide (AmE), **sulphonamide** (BrE) *n* CHEM sulfamide *m*
sulfonate (AmE), **sulphonate** (BrE) *n* CHEM sulfonate *m*
sulfonated (AmE), **sulphonated** (BrE) *adj* CHEM sulfoné
sulfonation (AmE), **sulphonation** (BrE) *n* CHEM, DETERGENTS sulfonation *f*
sulfone (AmE), **sulphone** (BrE) *n* CHEM, DETERGENTS sulfone *m*
sulfonic (AmE), **sulphonic**[1] (BrE) *adj* CHEM sulfonique, sulfoné
sulfonic (AmE), **sulphonic**:[2] ~ **acid** *n* (BrE) PROP MAT acide sulfonique *m*
sulfonium (AmE), **sulphonium** (BrE) *n* CHEM sulfine *f*, sulphonium *m*
sulfonyl (AmE), **sulphonyl** (BrE) *n* CHEM sulfonyle *m*
sulfosalicylic (AmE), **sulphosalicylic** (BrE) *adj* CHEM sulfosalicylique
sulfur (AmE), **sulphur** (BrE) *n (S)* CHEM soufre *m (S)*; ~ **budget** *n* POLLUTION bilan du soufre *m*; ~ **chloride** *n* CHEM sulfochlorure *m*; ~ **compound** *n* GAS TECH composé soufré *m*; ~ **content** *n* PETR TECH teneur en soufre *f*; ~ **cycle** *n* POLLUTION cycle des composés soufrés *m*, cycle du soufre *m*; ~ **dioxide** *n* CHEM anhydride sulfureux *m*, oxyde sulfureux *m*, FOOD TECH dioxyde de

soufre *m*, POLLUTION anhydride sulfureux *m*, anhydride sulfurique *m*; ~ **dioxide reduction** *n* POLLUTION réduction des émissions de SO$_2$ *f*; ~ **oxide** *n* POLLUTION oxyde de soufre *m*; ~ **steam** *n* GAS TECH vapeur de soufre *m*; ~ **trioxide** *n* CHEM anhydride sulfurique *m*

sulfuration (AmE), **sulphuration** *(BrE)* *n* CHEM sulfuration *f*, sulfurisation *f*

sulfuretted (AmE), **sulphuretted** (BrE): ~ **hydrogen** *n* FOOD TECH hydrogène sulfuré *m*

sulfuric (AmE), **sulphuric** (BrE)[1] *adj* CHEM sulfurique

sulfuric (AmE), **sulphuric** (BrE):[2] ~ **acid** *n* CHEM acide sulfurique *m*, acide vitriolique *m*, vitriol *m*, DETERGENTS, POLLUTION acide sulfurique *m*; ~ **anhydride** *n* POLLUTION anhydride sulfurique *m*

sulfuring (AmE), **sulphuring** (BrE) *n* C&G soufrage *m*

sulfurization (AmE), **sulphurization** (BrE) *n* CHEM sulfuration *f*, sulfurisation *f*

sulfurize (AmE), **sulphurize** (BrE) *vt* CHEM sulfuriser

sulfurous (AmE), **sulphurous** (BrE)[1] *adj* CHEM sulfureux

sulfurous (AmE), **sulphurous** (BrE):[2] ~ **acid** *n* POLLUTION acide sulfureux *m*; ~ **combustibles** *n pl* POLLUTION combustibles sulfureux *m pl*

sulfuryl (AmE), **sulphfuryl** (BrE) *n* CHEM sulfuryle *m*

sulfydrate (AmE), **sulphydrate** (BrE) *n* CHEM sulfhydrate *m*

sulfydric (AmE), **sulphydric** (BrE) *adj* CHEM sulfhydrique

sullage *n* PROD ENG *founding* crasses *f pl*, scories *f pl* ~ **head** *n* PROD ENG masselotte *f*; ~ **piece** *n* PROD ENG masselotte *f*

sultam *n* CHEM sultame *f*

sultone *n* CHEM sultone *f*

sum *n* COMP, DP somme *f*, total *m*, MATH somme *f*

sum-and-difference: ~ **technique** *n* RECORDING *stereo broadcasting* technique de la somme et de la différence *f*

sumatrol *n* CHEM sumatrole *f*

summarize *vt* COMP, DP résumer

summary *n* COMP, DP, TELECOM résumé *m*; ~ **punch** *n* COMP, DP perforatrice récapitulative *f*; ~ **punching** *n* COMP, DP perforation récapitulative *f*; ~ **report** *n* PROD ENG état récapitulatif *m*

summation: ~ **hydrograph** *n* FUELLESS sommation hydrographique *f*

summer *n* CONST *building* poutre de plancher *f*; ~ **beam** *n* CONST *building* poutre de plancher *f*; ~ **load waterline** *n* NAUT *ship design* ligne d'eau à la flottaison d'été *f*; ~ **solstice** *n* ASTRON solstice d'été *m*; ~ **tree** *n* CONST *building* poutre de plancher *f*

summit: ~ **canal** *n* WATER SUPP *navigation* canal à bief de partage *m*, canal à point de partage *m*

sump *n* LAB EQUIP caniveau *m*, puisard *m*, MINING bougniou *m*, puisard de puits *m*, bouniou *m*, collecteur d'eau *m*, puisard *m*, PETR TECH, PROD ENG puisard *m*, VEHICLES *engine lubrication* carter d'huile *m*, WATER SUPP puisard *m*; ~ **guard** *n* VEHICLES *engine lubrication* pare-moteur *m*; ~ **man** *n* (BrE) CONST puisatier *m*; ~ **pump** *n* WATER SUPP puisard *m*; ~ **shaft** *n* MINING puits collecteur *m*, puits d'exhaure *m*, puits d'épuisement *m*

sump-type: ~ **lubrication** *n* VEHICLES *of engine* graissage à carter *m*

sun *n* ASTRON soleil *m*; ~ **gear** *n* AUTO planétaire *m*; ~ **gear control plate** *n* AUTO plateau de blocage *m*; ~ **gear lever collar** *n* (BrE) *(cf sun gearshift collar)* AUTO gorge du planétaire *f*; ~ **gear lock-out teeth** *n* AUTO denture de blocage du planétaire *f*; ~ **gearshift collar** *n*

(AmE) *(cf sun gear lever collar)* AUTO gorge du planétaire *f*; ~ **gun** *n* CINEMAT torche ciné *f*; ~ **interference** *n* SPACE *communications* brouillage solaire *m*; ~ **sensor** *n* GEOPHYS capteur solaire *m*, détecteur solaire *m*; ~ **tracker** *n* GEOPHYS pointeur solaire *m*; ~ **visor** *n* AUTO *of car* pare-soleil *m*, VEHICLES *accessory* écran anti-éblouissant *m*; ~ **vizor** *n* (AmE) *see sun visor*

sun's: ~ **atmosphere** *n* ASTRON atmosphère solaire *f*; ~ **color temperature** *n* (AmE), ~ **colour temperature** *n* (BrE) ASTRON température solaire par couleur *f*; ~ **magnetic field cycle** *n* ASTRON cycle du champ magnétique solaire *m*

sundial *n* ASTRON cadran solaire *m*

sun-dried: ~ **brick** *n* C&G, CONST brique crue *f*

sunfast *adj* COLOURS résistant à la lumière

S-universal: ~ **access** *n* TELECOM *ISDN* prise S *f*, prise universelle *f*; ~ **interface** *n* TELECOM *ISDN* serveur à accès multiples *m*; ~ **interface card** *n* TELECOM *ISDN* carte d'interface S *f*

sunk:[1] ~ **into the wall** *adj* CONST encastré dans le mur; ~ **up** *adj* CINEMAT synchronisé

sunk:[2] ~ **key** *n* MECH ENG clavette noyée *f*; ~ **mount** *n* PHOTO monture fourrée *f*, *of camera lens* monture rentrante *f*; ~ **setting** *n* PHOTO *of camera lens* monture rentrante *f*; ~ **well** *n* COAL TECH caisson *m*

sunken: ~ **rail** *n* RAIL rail noyé *m*; ~ **road** *n* CONST chemin creux *m*; ~ **track** *n* RAIL voie noyée *f*

sunlight: ~ **resistance** *n* P&R résistance à la lumière solaire *f*

sunroof *n* VEHICLES *body* toit ouvrant *m*

sunspot *n* ASTRON, GEOPHYS tache solaire *f*; ~ **cycle** *n* ASTRON, GEOPHYS cycle des taches solaires *m*; ~ **penumbra** *n* ASTRON pénombre d'une tache solaire *f*

sunstone *n* MINERAL pierre de soleil *f*

sun-synchronous: ~ **orbit** *n* SPACE orbite à ensoleillement constant *f*; ~ **satellite** *n* SPACE *spacecraft* satellite héliosynchrone *m*

super[1] *n* PRINT mousseline *f*; ~ **blanking pulse** *n* TV surimpression de suppression *f*; ~ **clean coal** *n* COAL TECH charbon extra pur *m*

super[2] *vt* CINEMAT surimpressionner

supercalender *n* PAPER TECH supercalandre *f*

supercalendered: ~ **paper** *n* PAPER TECH papier satiné *m*

supercalenderizing *n* PAPER TECH satinage *m*

supercargo *n* NAUT *merchant navy* subrécargue *m*

supercavitating: ~ **propeller** *n* TRANSP hélice à supercavitation *f*

supercharge *n* AERONAUT suralimentation *f*, surcompression *f*

supercharger *n* AUTO compresseur *m*, MECH compresseur de suralimentation *m*

supercharging *n* AUTO, RAIL *vehicles* suralimentation *f*

superchilling *n* REFRIG surréfrigération *f*

supercluster *n* ASTRON *of galaxies* superamas *m*

supercomputer *n* COMP supercalculateur *m*, DP superordinateur *m*

supercomputing *n* COMP, DP super-informatique *f*

superconducting: ~ **coil** *n* TRANSP bobine supraconductrice *f*; ~ **device** *n* ELECTRON dispositif à supraconduction *m*; ~ **magnet** *n* PART PHYS, TRANSP aimant supraconducteur *m*; ~ **magnet levitation** *n* TRANSP sustentation par aimant à supraconductivité *f*; ~ **memory** *n* COMP mémoire supraconductrice *f*

superconductive *adj* PROP MAT supraconducteur

superconductivity *n* COMP, DP supraconductivité *f*, ELEC *conductors* supraconduction *f*, supraconductivité *f*,

ELECTRON supraconduction *f*, PHYS supraconductibilité *f*, supraconductivité *f*, PROP MAT, RAD PHYS supraconductivité *f*
superconductor *n* ELEC, ELECTRON, PHYS, PROP MAT, TELECOM supraconducteur *m*; ~ **cable** *n* TELECOM câble supraconducteur *m*; ~ **line** *n* TELECOM ligne supraconductrice *f*
superconduting: ~ **quantum interference device** *n* (*squid*) PHYS interféromètre quantique *m* (*squid*)
supercooled[1] *adj* PHYS surfondu
supercooled:[2] ~ **cloud** *n* METEO nuage surfondu *m*; ~ **water** *n* HYDROL eau surfondue *f*
supercooling *n* CHEM TECH, METALL, PHYS surfusion *f*
supercritical: ~ **reaction** *n* RAD PHYS réaction supracritique *f*
superelevation *n* CONST surélévation *f*; ~ **of the outer rail** *n* TRANSP dévers *m*; ~ **of track** *n* RAIL dévers *m*, surhaussement *m*
superfinishing: ~ **honing stone** *n* MECH ENG pierre de superfinissage *f*; ~ **stone** *n* MECH ENG pierre de superfinissage *f*
superfluid *n* PHYS superfluide *m*
superfluidity *n* CHEM, PHYS superfluidité *f*
supergiant *n* ASTRON étoile supergéante *f*
supergranulation *n* ASTRON *of solar surface* supra-granulation *f*
supergroup *n* TELECOM groupe secondaire *m*
superheat[1] *n* REFRIG surchauffe *f*; ~ **assembly** *n* NUCLEAR *fuel element* élément combustible à eau bouillant-surchauffé *m*
superheat[2] *vt* HEAT ENG, HEATING surchauffer
superheated: ~ **steam** *n* HEAT ENG, HEATING, PHYS vapeur surchauffée *f*
superheater *n* HEAT ENG, HEATING surchauffeur *m*, PROD ENG surchauffeur *m*, surchauffeur de vapeur *m*; ~ **damper** *n* PROD ENG étouffoir de surchauffeur *m*; ~ **element** *n* PROD ENG élément surchauffeur *m*; ~ **header** *n* PROD ENG collecteur de surchauffeur *m*; ~ **heating surface** *n* PROD ENG surface de surchauffe *f*; ~ **manifold** *n* PROD ENG collecteur de surchauffeur *m*; ~ **pipe** *n* PROD ENG tube surchauffeur *m*; ~ **unit** *n* PROD ENG élément surchauffeur *m*
superheating *n* CHEM, METALL surchauffage *m*, PHYS surchauffe *f*, PROD ENG surchauffage *m*, surchauffe *f*
superheavy: ~ **nucleus** *n* PHYS noyau superlourd *m*
superhigh: ~ **cube** *n* (*SHC*) TRANSP *container* conteneur spécial hors-cotes *m* (*SHC*); ~ **frequency** *n* (*SHF*) ELECTRON supra-haute fréquence *f*
superhigh-speed: ~ **rail vehicle** *n* TRANSP véhicule pour voies ferrées super rapides *m*; ~ **traffic** *n* TRANSP transport ultrarapide *m*
superimpose *vt* TV superposer, surimpressionner
superimposed: ~ **interference** *n* TV transmodulation *f*
superinsulation *n* REFRIG surisolation *f*
superior: ~ **conjunction** *n* ASTRON conjonction supérieure *f*; ~ **planet** *n* ASTRON planète supérieure *f*
superlattice *n* CRYSTALL superréseau *m*, surstructure *f*
superluminal: ~ **velocity** *n* ASTRON, PHYS vitesse supérieure à celle de la lumière *f*
superluminescence *n* OPT, TELECOM superluminescence *f*
superluminescent: ~ **diode** *n* (*SLD*) OPT, TELECOM diode superluminescente *f* (*DSL*); ~ **LED** *n* TELECOM diode superluminescente *f*
supermini *n* COMP, DP supermini *m*
supernatant *adj* CHEM superposé, surnageant

supernova *n* ASTRON, SPACE supernova *f*; ~ **explosion** *n* ASTRON explosion de supernova *f*; ~ **remnant** *n* ASTRON rémanent de supernova *m*; ~ **residues** *n pl* ASTRON restes de supernova *m pl*
superoxygenate *vt* CHEM suroxygéner
superphosphate *n* CHEM superphosphate *m*; ~ **of lime** *n* CHEM superphosphate de chaux *m*
superplastic: ~ **ceramic material** *n* PROP MAT alliage métallique superplastique *m*; ~ **ceramics** *n pl* PROP MAT céramiques superplastiques *f pl*; ~ **flow** *n* PROP MAT écoulement superplastique *m*
superplasticity *n* PROP MAT superplasticité *f*
superplasticizer *n* CONST *concrete admixture* superplastifiant *m*
superradiance *n* OPT, TELECOM superluminescence *f*
superradiant: ~ **diode** *n* (*SRD*) OPT, TELECOM diode superluminescente *f*
super-refraction *n* SPACE *communications* supra-réfraction *f*
supersalt *n* CHEM sursel *m*
supersaturate *vt* CHEM sursaturer
supersaturated[1] *adj* POLLUTION sursaturé
supersaturated:[2] ~ **air** *n* METEO air sursaturé *m*; ~ **solution** *n* CHEM dissolution sursaturée *f*, solution sursaturée *f*
supersaturation *n* CHEM sursaturation *f*
superscript *n* COMP indice supérieur *m*, DP exposant *m*, PRINT chaîne *f*, exposant *m*
supersonic[1] *adj* WAVE PHYS ultrasonore
supersonic:[2] ~ **aircraft** *n* AERONAUT avion supersonique *m*; ~ **frequency** *n* RAD PHYS fréquence supersonique *f*; ~ **speed** *n* PHYS vitesse supersonique *f*; ~ **transport** *n* (*SST*) AERONAUT transport supersonique *m*
superspreader: ~ **roller** *n* PRINT rouleau d'enduction *m*
superstring *n* RAD PHYS superstring *m*, supracorde *f*
superstructure *n* CONST, NAUT *shipbuilding* superstructure *f*
supersymmetrical: ~ **particles** *n pl* RAD PHYS particules suprasymétriques *f pl*
supersync: ~ **signal** *n* TV signal de top de synchronisation *m*
supertanker *n* TRANSP superpétrolier *m*
supertonic *n* ACOUSTICS sus-tonique *f*
super-tweeter: ~ **loudspeaker** *n* RECORDING haut-parleur super-tweeter *m*
supertype *n* PRINT caractère de titrage *m*
supervision *n* TELECOM surveillance *f*
supervisor *n* COMP moniteur *m*, superviseur *m*, DP superviseur *m*, MAR POLL responsable *m*, superviseur *m*, SAFETY surveillant *m*; ~ **call** *n* (*SVC*) COMP, DP appel du superviseur *m*
supervisory: ~ **aid** *n* TELECOM outil de supervision *m*; ~ **announcement** *n* TELECOM message de contrôle *m*; ~ **message** *n* TELECOM message de supervision *m*; ~ **process** *n* PROD ENG processus de contrôle *m*; ~ **timer** *n* TELECOM temporisateur de supervision *m*; ~ **tone** *n* TELECOM message de contrôle *m*
supplement: ~ **to refrigeration** *n* REFRIG adjuvant au froid *m*
supplementary[1] *adj* PATENTS complémentaire
supplementary:[2] ~ **angle** *n* GEOM angle supplémentaire *m*; ~ **lens** *n* CINEMAT bonnette *f*, INSTRUMENT lentille additionnelle *f*, PHOTO lentille supplémentaire *f*; ~ **purification** *n* POLLUTION complément d'épuration *m*; ~ **service** *n* TELECOM *ISDN* service supplémentaire *m*
suppleness *n* PROP MAT souplesse *f*

supplied-air: ~ **breathing apparatus** n SAFETY appareil respiratoire avec alimentation d'air m

supplier n PROD ENG, QUALITY fournisseur m

supply[1] n ELEC *power*, GAS TECH alimentation f, GEOL apport m, WATER SUPP alimentation f, approvisionnement m; ~ **aircraft** n MILIT avion ravitailleur m; ~ **base** n PETR TECH point d'appui m; ~ **boat** n PETR bateau de ravitaillement m, PETR TECH navire de ravitaillement m, ravitailleur m; ~ **cable** n ELEC ENG câble secteur m, PROD ENG câble d'alimentation m; ~ **current** n (*cf mains current*) ELEC ENG courant d'alimentation m, ELEC ENG courant secteur m; ~ **lead** n (AmE) (*cf mains lead*) ELEC ENG conduite d'amenée de secteur f; ~ **line filter** n P&R *equipment* filtre sur conduite m; ~ **main** n ELEC ENG ligne d'alimentation f, ligne de réseau f, réseau de distribution m; ~ **network** n (AmE) (*cf mains*) ELEC réseau d'alimentation m, ELEC, ELEC ENG alimentation secteur f, réseau m, TV alimentation secteur f, WATER SUPP réseau de distribution m; ~ **pipe** n CONST conduite d'amenée f, tuyau d'amenée m; ~ **pump** n MAR POLL pompe d'alimentation f; ~ **reel** n CINEMAT, DP, TV bobine débitrice f; ~ **roll** n TV rouleau débiteur m; ~ **service** n ELEC *for consumer* branchement m; ~ **spool** n CINEMAT bobine débitrice f; ~ **tank** n AUTO réservoir d'expansion m; ~ **vessel** n NAUT *ship* navire ravitailleur m, PETR réservoir m; ~ **voltage** n ELEC tension du réseau f, ELEC ENG tension du secteur f, PHYS, PROD ENG tension d'alimentation f, TV tension du secteur f

supply[2] vt ELEC *power* alimenter, PHYS alimenter, amorcer, exciter; ~ **with** vt PROD ENG fournir de, pourvoir de

supplying n PROD ENG approvisionnement m, fourniture f

support[1] n COMP aide f, support m, CONST pied m, soutien m, étai m, *act* soutènement m, support m, *of arch* appui m, DP aide f, assistance f, prise en charge f, soutien m, support m, PAPER TECH soutien m; ~ **arm** n INSTRUMENT support de fixation m; ~ **boat** n NAUT bateau de soutien m; ~ **pier** n MINING montant m, pied-droit m; ~ **pillar** n MECH ENG *diecasting die* colonne entretoise f, MINING estau m, stock m, stot m, massif de protection m, montant m, pied-droit m; ~ **pillar bush** n MECH ENG *injection mould* bague à collerette centrale f; ~ **plate** n SPACE *spacecraft* plaque support f, platine f; ~ **program** n COMP logiciel d'aide à la programmation m, DP programme auxiliaire m; ~ **vehicle with non contact suspension** n TRANSP véhicule à sustentation sans contact m; ~ **vessel** n NAUT navire de servitude m, PETR navire d'assistance m, support flottant m, PETR TECH navire d'assistance m, navire de soutien m

support[2] vt COMP, DP aider, assister, MECH ENG appuyer, soutenir, supporter, tenir, PAPER TECH soutenir

supported[1] adj PROD ENG étayé

supported:[2] ~ **beam** n CONST poutre appuyée f; ~ **monorail** n TRANSP monorail supporté m

supporting n CONST soutènement m, support m; ~ **column** n RAIL support de la voie m; ~ **fork** n MINING clef de retenue f, tourne-à-gauche de support m; ~ **pillar** n MINING pilier de soutènement m; ~ **pylon** n ELEC *network* pylône porteur m; ~ **rail** n TRANSP rail de sustentation m; ~ **rope** n CONST câble porteur m; ~ **track** n TRANSP voie poutre f; ~ **wall** n CONST mur d'appui m, mur de soutien m

suppress vt COMP, DP supprimer

suppressed: ~ **carrier system** n TV système à suppres-

sion de porteuse m; ~ **carrier transmission** n ELECTRON transmission par onde porteuse supprimée f, transmission à suppression d'onde porteuse f; ~ **carrier transmitter** n ELECTRON émetteur à suppression de porteuse m

suppression n DP suppression f, ELEC ENG antiparasitage m, suppression f, TESTING suppression f; ~ **device** n PROD ENG dispositif antiparasite m; ~ **factor** n SPACE *communications* facteur de suppression m; ~ **grid** n ELEC ENG grille d'arrêt f, grille suppresseuse f

suppressor n ELEC *anti-interference* suppresseur m, ELEC ENG, ELECTRON antiparasite m, dispositif antiparasite m, PROD ENG antiparasite m, filtre antiparasite m, TELECOM suppresseur m; ~ **capacitor** n ELEC *anti-interference* suppresseur antiparasite m; ~ **choke** n ELEC *anti-interference* self antiparasite f; ~ **grid** n ELECTRON grille d'arrêt f, grille suppresseuse f

supratidal: ~ **deposits** n pl GEOL dépôts supratidaux m pl

surcharge n HYDROL *sewage* surcharge f; ~ **load** n COAL TECH charge additionnelle f

surcharged adj HYDROL surchargé

surd n MATH nombre irrationnel m

surf n OCEANOG ressac m

surface[1] adj MINING au jour, du jour, superficiel

surface[2] n GEOM, NAUT, PAPER TECH, PATENTS surface f, PHYS aire f, surface f, *separating two transparent media* dioptre m; ~ **acoustic wave** n (*SAW*) ELECTRON, TELECOM onde acoustique de surface f; ~ **acoustic wave device** n ELECTRON, TELECOM dispositif à ondes acoustiques de surface m; ~ **air supply** n OCEANOG narguilé m; ~ **application** n PAPER TECH enduction f; ~ **area** n POLLUTION *land, water* terrain m; ~ **auger** n MINING cuiller f, tarière à glaise f; ~ **bonding strength** n PAPER TECH arrachage m, résistance à l'arrachage f; ~ **boundary layer** n METEO couche limite de surface f; ~ **boundary level** n METEO couche limite atmosphérique f; ~ **burnishing facet** n ACOUSTICS facette de brunissage f; ~ **burst** n MILIT *nuclear warfare* explosion superficielle f; ~ **channel** n ELECTRON canal en surface m; ~ **charge** n ELEC *electrostatics*, PHYS charge superficielle f; ~ **charge density** n ELEC *electrostatics* densité de charge superficielle f, PHYS charge surfacique f, densité superficielle de charge f; ~ **color** n (AmE) *see surface colour*; ~ **coloring** n (AmE) *see surface colouring*; ~ **colour** n (BrE) COLOURS couleur propre f; ~ **colouring** n (BrE) PAPER TECH coloration en surface f; ~ **condenser** n PROD ENG *steam* condenseur par surface m, condenseur à surface m; ~ **conductance** n HEAT ENG conductance superficielle f; ~ **connection** n TELECOM connexion superficielle f; ~ **of contact** n MECH ENG surface de contact f; ~ **conveyance** n MINING transport à ciel ouvert m, transport à la surface m; ~ **cooling** n REFRIG refroidissement par surface d'écoulement m; ~ **corrosion** n TESTING corrosion de surface f; ~ **crack** n PROD ENG *in casting* gerçure f; ~ **current** n NAUT courant de surface m, TELECOM courant superficiel m; ~ **cut** n MINING fouille en surface f, tranchée f; ~ **damping** n RECORDING amortissement de surface m; ~ **defect** n QUALITY défaut de surface m, imperfection de surface f; ~ **dehumidifier** n REFRIG déshumidificateur à action de surface m; ~ **demand lifeline** n OCEANOG narguilé m; ~ **demarcation** n CONST bornage superficiel m, démarcation superficielle f; ~ **density** n ELEC ENG densité superficielle f; ~ **development** n PHOTO *of grain* développement superficiel m; ~ **discontinuities** n pl MECH ENG défauts de surface m pl; ~ **dressing** n

CONST enduit superficiel *m*; ~ **drive** *n* MINING fendue *f*; ~ **drive reel** *n* PAPER TECH enrouleuse à entraînement périphérique *f*; ~ **earthing connection** *n* (BrE) *(cf surface grounding connection)* ELEC prise de terre superficielle *f*; ~ **effect ship** *n* NAUT navire à effet de surface *m*; ~ **effect vehicle** *n (SEV)* TRANSP véhicule à effet de sol *m*; ~ **electron microscope** *n (SEM)* INSTRUMENT microscope électronique à balayage de surface *m*; ~ **energy** *n* PHYS énergie superficielle *f*; ~ **equipment** *n* MINING installation de surface *f*, matériel du jour *m*; ~ **erosion** *n* HYDROL érosion en surface *f*; ~ **finish** *n* PAPER TECH état de surface *m*, PRINT fini de surface *m*; ~ **finish microscope** *n* INSTRUMENT microscope pour l'étude de la couche superficielle des pièces *m*; ~ **float** *n* NAUT *research*, OCEANOG flotteur de surface *m*; ~ **gage** *n* (AmE), ~ **gauge** *n* (BrE) MECH *tools* trusquin *m*; ~ **geometry meter** *n* METR appareil de contrôle d'état de surface *m*; ~ **grinder** *n* MECH ENG machine à meuler les surfaces planes extérieures *f*, machine à rectifier les surfaces planes extérieures *f*; ~ **grinding** *n* MECH ENG rectification en plan *f*; ~ **grounding connection** *n* (AmE) *(cf surface earthing connection)* ELEC prise de terre superficielle *f*; ~ **hammering** *n* PROP MAT martelage d'une surface *m*; ~ **hardening** *n* METALL durcissement superficiel *m*; ~ **hardness** *n* MECH ENG dureté superficielle *f*; ~ **induction** *n* TV induction superficielle *f*; ~ **integral** *n* PHYS intégrale de surface *f*; ~ **layer** *n* MAR POLL couche superficielle *f*, OCEANOG couche superficielle d'eau chaude *f*; ~ **milling** *n* MECH ENG fraisage en plan *m*; ~ **milling machine** *n* MECH ENG fraiseuse à surface plane *f*; ~ **mining** *n* MINING exploitation au jour *f*, exploitation à ciel ouvert *f*; ~ **mirror** *n* INSTRUMENT miroir de surface *m*, miroir réfléchissant à la surface *m*; ~ **mounting** *n* COMP, DP, ELEC montage en surface *m*, ELECTRON montage en saillie *m*; ~ **noise** *n* ACOUSTICS, ELECTRON, RECORDING bruit de surface *m*; ~ **planer** *n* MECH ENG dégauchisseuse *f*, machine à dégauchir *f*; ~ **planing** *n* MECH ENG *woodworking* dégauchissage *m*, dégauchissement *m*; ~ **plate** *n* MECH *tools* marbre *m*, MECH ENG *engineer's* marbre *m*, marbre d'ajusteur *m*, marbre à dresser *m*, METR *for inspection and marking out in workshop* marbre de contrôle *m*; ~ **power** *n* GAS TECH puissance surfacique *f*; ~ **preparation** *n* CONST préparation de surface *f*; ~ **pressure chart** *n* METEO carte de surface isobare *f*; ~ **protection** *n* COATINGS revêtement protecteur *m*; ~ **protection film** *n* PACKAGING pellicule pour protéger la surface *f*; ~ **protection tape** *n* PACKAGING ruban pour protéger la surface *m*; ~ **rectification** *n* SPRINGS rectification extérieure *f*; ~ **resistance** *n* COAL TECH résistance superficielle *f*, HEAT ENG résistance de surface *f*, TESTING résistance superficielle *f*; ~ **resistivity** *n* ELEC ENG résistivité superficielle *f*; ~ **of revolution** *n* GEOM surface de révolution *f*; ~ **roughness** *n* CONST, MECH ENG rugosité de surface *f*; ~ **roughness standard** *n* METR rugosimètre *m*; ~ **rust** *n* CONST *on steel reinforcement* rouille superficielle *f*; ~ **sander** *n* MECH ENG *tool* surfaceuse-disqueuse *f*; ~ **search radar** *n* NAUT *navy* radar de veille surface *m*; ~ **sizing** *n* PAPER TECH collage en surface *m*; ~ **socket** *n* ELEC *connection* prise en saillie *f*, prise sur socle *f*; ~ **speed** *n* NAUT *submarine* vitesse en surface *f*; ~ **speed indicator** *n* MECH ENG compteur de vitesse linéaire *m*; ~ **storage** *n* HYDROL *water in lakes, ponds* stockage superficiel *m*; ~ **temperature limits** *n pl* SAFETY *for equipment* températures

maximales de la surface *f pl*; ~ **tension** *n* COAL TECH, CONST, P&R tension superficielle *f*, PHYS tensio-actif *m*, tension superficielle *f*; ~ **tension instabilities** *n pl* FLUID PHYS instabilités de tension superficielle *f pl*; ~ **tension meter** *n* LAB EQUIP *instrument* tensiomètre *m*; ~ **tension modifier** *n* MAR POLL modificateur de tension superficielle *m*; ~ **tension tank** *n* SPACE *spacecraft* réservoir à tension de surface *m*; ~ **texture** *n* MECH ENG *of product* état de surface *m*; ~ **texture measurement** *n* MECH ENG mesure des paramètres géométriques d'état de surface *f*; ~ **treatment** *n* C&G, PROP MAT traitement de surface *m*; ~ **ventilating fan** *n* MINING ventilateur *m*; ~ **ventilation chimney** *n* MINING cheminée d'aérage *f*; ~ **ventilation duct** *n* MINING cheminée d'aérage *f*; ~ **water** *n* COAL TECH eau de surface *f*, CONST eau superficielle *f*, HYDROL eau de ruissellement *f*, eau de surface *f*, eau superficielle *f*, OCEANOG, POLLUTION, WATER SUPP eau de surface *f*; ~ **water drainage** *n* CONST évacuation d'eaux superficielles *f*; ~ **water erosion** *n* COAL TECH érosion par l'eau de surface *f*; ~ **water layer** *n* COAL TECH couche d'eau superficielle *f*; ~ **water load** *n* HYDROL charge de ruissellement *f*; ~ **water management** *n* WATER SUPP gestion des eaux superficielles *f*; ~ **wave** *n* GEOPHYS onde de séisme *f*, onde sismique *f*, onde superficielle *f*, OCEANOG onde supérieure *f*, OPT onde de surface *f*; ~ **wind** *n* METEO vent de surface *m*; ~ **workers** *n pl* MINING ouvriers du jour *m pl*; ~ **working** *n* C&G surfaçage *m*

surface[3] *vt* MECH ENG dégauchir, TEXTILES calandrer
surface-active[1] *adj* CHEM tensio-actif
surface-active:[2] ~ **agent** *n* DETERGENTS agent actif de surface *m*, MAR POLL agent de surface *m*, agent surfactant *m*, agent surfactif *m*, agent tensio-actif *m*
surface-emitting: ~ **electroluminescent diode** *n* OPT DEL à émission frontale *f*, diode électroluminescente à émission frontale *f*; ~ **light-emitting diode** *n* TELECOM diode électroluminescente à émission par la surface *f*
surface-grinding: ~ **machine** *n* MECH ENG machine à meuler les surfaces planes extérieures *f*, machine à rectifier les surfaces planes extérieures *f*
surface-measuring: ~ **instrument** *n* METR instrument de mesure des surfaces *m*
surface-mounted: ~ **component** *n (SMC)* ELECTRON, TELECOM composant monté en surface *m (CMS)*; ~ **enclosure** *n* PROD ENG coffret pour montage en surface *m*; ~ **socket** *n* ELEC *connection* prise de montage en surface *f*
surface-piercing: ~ **craft** *n* TRANSP hydroptère à ailes en V *m*
surface-planing: ~ **machine** *n* MECH ENG dégauchisseuse *f*, machine à dégauchir *f*
surface-sized: ~ **paper** *n* PAPER TECH papier surfacé *m*, PRINT papier collé en surface *m*
surface-to-air: ~ **missile** *n (SAM)* MILIT engin sol-air *m*
surface-to-underwater: ~ **missile** *n* MILIT missile navire-sous-marin *m*
surface-written: ~ **videodisc** *n* (BrE) OPT vidéodisque à gravure superficielle *m*; ~ **videodisk** *n* (AmE) *see surface-written videodisc*
surfacing *n* CONST *civil engineering* empierrement *m*, MECH ENG dressage *m*, *lathe work* chariotage transversal *m*, planage *m*, surfaçage *m*, *wood working* dégauchissage *m*, dégauchissement *m* ~ **and boring lathe** *n* MECH ENG tour en l'air *m*, tour en l'air à plateau vertical *m*; ~ **motion** *n* MECH ENG *lathe work* mouvement de surfaçage *m*; ~ **of the road** *n* (AmE) *(cf*

surfacing of the track) RAIL nivellement de la voie *m*; ~ **sheet** *n* P&R *glass fibre* feuille de couverture *f*; ~ **of the track** *n* (BrE) *(cf surfacing of the road)* RAIL dressage en profil de la voie *m*, RAIL nivellement de la voie *m*

surfactant *n* CHEM surfactant *m*, tensio-actif *m*, COAL TECH agent tensio-actif *m*, DETERGENTS agent de surface *m*, agent tensio-actif *m*, tensio-actif *m*, FOOD TECH, MAR POLL agent tensio-actif *m*, P&R *additive* agent de surface *m*, agent tensio-actif *m*, PHYS tensio-actif *m*, POLLUTION agent de surface *m*, produit tensio-actif *m*; ~ **mud** *n* PETR TECH boue aux surfactants *f*

surfing *n* WAVE PHYS surf *m*

surge *n* AERONAUT *turbine engine* pompage *m*, ELEC *voltage* impulsion *f*, ELEC ENG surtension *f*, FLUID PHYS poussée *f*, poussée d'Archimède *f*, remontée de fluide *f*, PETR TECH pistonnage *m*, saute *f*, PROD ENG surpression *f*; ~ **absorber** *n* ELEC *transmission* parasurtenseur *m*; ~ **arrester** *n* ELEC *transmission* parasurtenseur *m*, ELEC ENG dispositif de protection contre les surtensions *m*, limiteur de surtension *m*; ~ **characteristic** *n* TV caractéristique de saut *f*, réponse au signal unité *f*; ~ **current** *n* PROD ENG courant de choc *m*; ~ **diverter** *n* ELEC *supply line* divertisseur de surtension *m*; ~ **generator** *n* ELEC générateur de tension d'impulsions *m*, NUCLEAR générateur de Marx *m*; ~ **impedance** *n* ELEC *cable* impédance caractéristique *f*; ~ **pressure** *n* PROD ENG surpression *f*; ~ **protection** *n* ELEC ENG protection contre les surtensions *f*; ~ **relay** *n* ELEC relais à maximum *m*; ~ **shaft** *n* FUELLESS, HYDROL cheminée d'équilibre *f*; ~ **suppressor** *n* PROD ENG antiparasite *m*; ~ **tank** *n* FUELLESS chambre d'équilibre *f*, chambre de compensation *f*, HYDROL *hydroelectric dams* cheminée d'équilibre *f*

surgical: ~ **microscope** *n* INSTRUMENT microscope chirurgical *m*

surplus: ~ **water** *n* WATER SUPP eau en excès *f*, excédent d'eau *m*, trop-plein *m*

surprint *n* PRINT repiquage *m*, surimpression *f*

surround: ~ **sound** *n* CINEMAT son tétraphonique *m*

surroundings *n pl* PHYS ambiance *f*, environnement *m*, milieu *m*

surveillance *n* QUALITY, SAFETY *of workers* surveillance *f*; ~ **approach radar rating** *n* AERONAUT qualification radar d'approche de surveillance *f*; ~ **balloon** *n* MILIT ballon de surveillance *m*; ~ **radar** *n* MILIT radar de veille *m*; ~ **satellite** *n* SPACE satellite de surveillance *m*

survey[1] *n* CONST *of public* étude *f*, *on Earth's surface* arpentage *m*, levé *m*, levé de plans *m*, *value litigation* expertise *f*, METR *quantity surveying* métrage *m*; ~ **diving bell** *n* OCEANOG tourelle d'observation *f*; ~ **traverse** *n* OCEANOG chemin de nivellement *m*

survey[2] *vt* MAR POLL relever un plan, surveiller, NAUT *ship, coast* faire l'expertise de l'état de, faire l'hydrographie de, hydrographier, inspecter

survey[3] *vi* MAR POLL procéder à une étude

surveying *n* CONST *of public works* étude *f*, *on Earth's surface* arpentage *m*, levé *m*, levé de plans *m*, METR *quantity surveying* métrage *m*, NAUT *ships, coast* hydrographie *f*, inspection *f*, visite *f*; ~ **aneroid barometer** *n* CONST baromètre anéroïde de nivellement *m*

surveyor *n* CONST inspecteur *m*, *of land* arpenteur *m*, *of public works* chercheur *m*, surveillant *m*, METR métreur *m*, NAUT *ships* commissaire d'avarie *m*, expert maritime *m*

surveyor's: ~ **chain** *n* CONST chaîne d'arpentage *f*, chaîne

d'arpenteur *f*; ~ **compass** *n* CONST boussole d'arpenteur *f*; ~ **dial** *n* CONST boussole d'arpenteur *f*; ~ **level** *n* CONST niveau à lunette *m*; ~ **tape** *n* CONST mesure à ruban d'arpenteur *f*, roulette d'arpenteur *f*; ~ **transit** *n* CONST théodolite à boussole *m*

survival: ~ **kit** *n* SPACE équipement de survie *m*; ~ **wind speed** *n* FUELLESS vitesse du vent résiduel *f*

susceptance *n* ELEC *reactance*, ELEC ENG, PHYS susceptance *f*

susceptibility *n* ELEC *reactance*, PHYS susceptibilité *f*

susceptible: ~ **of industrial application** *adj* PATENTS susceptible d'application industrielle

suspended[1] *adj* COMP, DP suspendu

suspended:[2] ~ **curtain wall** *n* C&G écran suspendu *m*; ~ **joint** *n* CONST *carpentry* assemblage suspendu *m*, joint à porte-à-faux *m*; ~ **lift** *n* MINING jeu volant *m*; ~ **liquid droplets** *n pl* POLLUTION gouttelettes liquides suspendues *f pl*; ~ **load** *n* HYDROL charge en suspension *f*; ~ **load trolley set** *n* RAIL *vehicles* wagon à basculement à becs *m*; ~ **monorail** *n* TRANSP monorail suspendu *m*; ~ **particle** *n* POLLUTION particule en suspension *f*; ~ **pump** *n* MINING pompe suspendue *f*, pompe volante *f*; ~ **scaffold** *n* CONST échafaudage suspendu *m*; ~ **set** *n* MINING jeu volant *m*; ~ **system** *n* TRANSP système suspendu *m*; ~ **vehicle system** *n* *(SVS)* TRANSP véhicule à suspension supérieure *m* *(VSS)*

suspension *n* CHEM, ELEC ENG, MECH ENG, MINING, P&R, PHYS suspension *f*; ~ **arm** *n* AUTO bras de suspension *m*; ~ **bridge** *n* CONST pont suspendu *m*; ~ **gear** *n* MINING dispositif de suspension *m*; ~ **hook** *n* MECH ENG crochet de suspension *m*; ~ **insulator** *n* ELEC ENG isolateur de suspension *m*; ~ **polymerization** *n* P&R *process* polymérisation en suspension *f*; ~ **rod** *n* RAIL *vehicles* tige de suspension *f*; ~ **of the rods** *n* MINING *boring* suspension de la sonde *f*; ~ **spring** *n* SPRINGS ressort de suspension *m*; ~ **stud** *n* MECH ENG *link motion* tourillon de suspension de la coulisse *m*; ~ **system** *n* AUTO suspension *f*; ~ **with linkages** *n* MECH ENG suspension articulée *f*

sustained: ~ **oscillation** *n* ELECTRON oscillation entretenue *f*

Sv *abbr (sievert)* PHYS, RAD PHYS Sv *(sievert)*

SVC *abbr* COMP *(supervisor call)*, DP *(supervisor call)* appel du superviseur *m*, TELECOM *(signalling virtual channel, signaling virtual channel)* canal virtuel de signalisation *m*, circuit virtuel commuté *m*, voie virtuelle de signalisation *f*

SVS *abbr (suspended vehicle system)* TRANSP VSS *(véhicule à suspension supérieure)*

SW *abbr (short wave)* ELEC, WAVE PHYS onde courte *f*

swab *n* PETR TECH pistonnage *m*, PROD ENG *moulder's* blaireau *m*; ~ **brush** *n* PROD ENG *moulder's* blaireau *m*

swabbing *n* C&G graissage du moule *m*, PETR pistonnage *m*

swage[1] *n* PROD ENG *casing swedge* redresse-tubes *m*, redresseur *m*, *for shaping metal* emboutisseuse *f*, emboutissoir *m*, suage *m*, étampe *f*, *saw set* tourne-à-gauche *m*; ~ **block** *n* PROD ENG tas-étampe *m*

swage[2] *vt* MECH ENG rétreindre

swaging *n* PROD ENG emboutissage *m*, estampage *m*, étampage *m*; ~ **die** *n* MECH ENG *for forming* outillage de matriçage de formage *m*

swallow: ~ **hole** *n* GEOL cratère d'effondrement *m*

swallow-tail: ~ **joint** *n* CONST assemblage à queue *m*, assemblage à queue d'aronde *m*, assemblage à queue d'hirondre *m*

swamp *n* WATER SUPP marais *m*

swampy: ~ **soil** n CONST sol marécageux m

swan: ~ **neck** n CINEMAT, CONST *plumbing*col de cygne m; ~ **neck cock** n CONST robinet à col de cygne m; ~ **neck fly press** n MECH ENG découpoir à col de cygne m; ~ **neck screw press** n MECH ENG découpoir à col de cygne m

swap:[1] ~ **bodies** n pl RAIL *vehicles* caisses mobiles f pl

swap[2] vt COMP, DP échanger

swap[3] vti COMP, DP permuter

swapping n COMP, DP permutation f, échange m

Sward: ~ **rocker hardness** n P&R *test, coatings* dureté Sward rocker f

swarf n PROD ENG *grit from grindstone* boue de meule f, *metal turnings* copeaux de métal m pl, riblon m

swash n NAUT *sea* clapotis m, OCEANOG jet de rive m; ~ **letter** n PRINT lettre ornée f

swatch n TEXTILES petit échantillon m; ~ **dyer** n COLOURS teinturier d'échantillons m; ~ **type** n PRINT caractères prétentieux m pl

swatching-out n PRINT technique de comparaison des épreuves progressives f

swath n MAR POLL trace f

S-wave n PHYS *seismology* onde S f

sway: ~ **stabilization** n TRANSP stabilisation latérale f

swaying n MECH ENG balancement m, oscillation f

sweat[1] n MINING exsudation f, PROP MAT ressuage m; ~ **cooling** n SPACE refroidissement par transpiration m; ~ **roll** n PAPER TECH cylindre refroidisseur m

sweat[2] vt FOOD TECH transsuder

sweating n PRINT condensation d'eau f, formation de gouttelettes d'eau f, perlage m, REFRIG condensation d'eau f; ~ **furnace** n PROD ENG four de liquidation m

sweat-type: ~ **expansion valve** n REFRIG détendeur à braser m

sweep[1] n ELECTRON balayage m, HYDROL *of river* boucle f, PETR TECH balayage m, PROD ENG *strickle* gabarit m, trousse f, SPACE balayage m, flèche f, TV analyse f; ~ **angle** n AERONAUT *airframe* angle de flèche m; ~ **antenna** n TELECOM antenne à balayage f; ~ **board** n PROD ENG *founding* planche à trousser f; ~ **circuit** n TV circuit de balayage linéaire m; ~ **frequency** n ELECTRON, TV fréquence de balayage f; ~ **gas** n MILIT *nuclear warfare* gaz nettoyant m; ~ **microscope** n TELECOM microscope à balayage m; ~ **mode** n ELECTRON mode de balayage m; ~ **molding** n (AmE), ~ **moulding** n (BrE) PROD ENG moulage au gabarit m, moulage au trousseau m

sweep[2] vt CONST *chimney* ramoner, PROD ENG *founding* trousser; ~ **up** vt PROD ENG *founding* trousser

sweeping n PROD ENG *strickling* troussage m; ~ **up** n PROD ENG *strickling* troussage m

sweepings n pl PROD ENG balayures f pl

sweet[1] adj CHEM doux, non grisouteux

sweet:[2] ~ **crude** n PETR TECH brut non-sulfuré m; ~ **gas** n PETR gaz non acide m; ~ **natural gas** n GAS TECH gaz non corrosif m

sweetened adj FOOD TECH sucré, édulcoré

sweetener n FOOD TECH édulcorant m

sweetening n PETR TECH adoucissement m, neutralisation f

swell[1] n FOOD TECH *can* bombage m, METEO *ocean* agitation f, NAUT *sea state*, OCEANOG houle f; ~ **abatement** n OCEANOG amortissement de la houle m

swell[2] vt TEXTILES gonfler

swell[3] vi PHYS gonfler

swelled: ~ **coking coal** n COAL TECH charbon à coke boursouflé m

swelling n P&R, TEXTILES gonflement m; ~ **clay** n PETR, PETR TECH argile gonflante f; ~ **soil** n COAL TECH sol expansible m

swell-resistant: ~ **finish** n COATINGS apprêt antigonflant m

swept: ~ **wing** n AERONAUT aile en flèche f, aile profilée f

swept-back: ~ **wing** n AERONAUT aile en flèche positive f, TRANSP voilure en flèche f

swept-up: ~ **casting** n PROD ENG pièce troussée f; ~ **core** n PROD ENG noyau troussé m

swift n TEXTILES dévidoir m

swimmer n FOOD TECH *milling* flotteur m, grain flottant m

swing[1] n MECH ENG diamètre maximum admis m, plus grand diamètre admissible m; ~ **arm** n PROD ENG bras extérieur m; ~ **axle** n AUTO essieu brisé m; ~ **of the bed** n MECH ENG diamètre admissible au-dessus du banc m, plus grand diamètre admis au-dessus du banc m; ~ **bob lever** n MECH ENG levier à contrepoids m; ~ **bolt coupling** n MECH ENG *pipe fitting* raccord à verrou bascule m; ~ **bridge** n CONST, NAUT *locks, inland waterways* pont tournant m; ~ **crane** n CONST grue pivotante f; ~ **door** n CONST porte tournante f, porte va-et-vient f; ~ **frame** n MECH ENG *of screw-cutting machine* cavalier m, lyre f, tête de cheval f; ~ **gate** n CONST barrière à pivot f, barrière à tournante f; ~ **in gap** n MECH ENG diamètre maximum admis dans le rompu m; ~ **nose crossing** n TRANSP croisement à coeur mobile m; ~ **over bed** n MECH ENG diamètre admissible au-dessus du banc m, plus grand diamètre admis au-dessus du banc m; ~ **over saddle** n MECH ENG diamètre admis au-dessus des chariots m, plus grand diamètre admis au-dessus des chariots m; ~ **radius** n PROD ENG rayon de dégagement m; ~ **of the rest** n MECH ENG diamètre admis au-dessus des chariots m, plus grand diamètre admisau-dessus des chariots m; ~ **sieve** n COAL TECH crible à bascule m, crible à manivelle m; ~ **stopper finish** n (BrE) *(cf wired stopper finish)* C&G bague percée f; ~ **ticket** n (BrE) PACKAGING étiquette volante f

swing[2] vt MECH ENG faire basculer

swing[3] vi MECH ENG basculer, PAPER TECH osciller

swing:[4] ~ **away** vti NAUT *ship* éviter

swing-by n SPACE *spacecraft* appui gravitationnel m, gravicélération f, gravidéviation f, relance f; ~ **effect** n SPACE gravicélération f, gravidéviation f

swing-in: ~ **filter** n PHOTO filtre escamotable m

swinging n C&G *of pipe* balancement m, MECH ENG balancement m, oscillation f, va-et-vient m; ~ **across the face** n WATER SUPP papillonnage m; ~ **back** n PHOTO dos pivotant m; ~ **brick** n C&G maillet m; ~ **choke** n ELEC ENG bobine saturable f; ~ **chute** n CONST couloir oscillant m, goulotte orientable f; ~ **crusher** n MECH ENG broyeur à pendule m; ~ **door** n CONST porte va-et-vient f; ~ **movement** n MECH ENG mouvement basculaire m, mouvement de bascule m; ~ **pit** n C&G longeage m; ~ **post** n CONST barreau de côtière m, montant de côtière m; ~ **round** n CONST *of crane* virage m; ~ **screen** n PROD ENG crible oscillant m; ~ **valve** n PROD ENG distributeur glissant à robinets m, distributeur oscillant m, distributeur tournant m, tiroir oscillant m, tiroir rotatif m, valve oscillante f

swing-jib: ~ **radial drill** n MECH ENG machine à percer radiale à potence f

swing-up: ~ **mirror** n PHOTO miroir déployable m

swipe: ~ **card** n TELECOM carte à mémoire f

swirl *n* FLUID PHYS taux de rotation *m*, tourbillon *m*, OCEANOG remous *m*

swirling: ~ **flow** *n* GAS TECH écoulement rotationnel *m*; ~ **injection** *n* GAS TECH injection tourbillonnaire *f*; ~ **stream** *n* GAS TECH écoulement tourbillonnaire *m*

swish: ~ **pan** *n* CINEMAT panoramique filé *m*

switch[1] *adj* ELEC ENG commutable; ~ **selectable** *adj* PROD ENG commutable

switch[2] *n* CINEMAT commutateur *m*, interrupteur *m*, rupteur *m*, sélecteur *m*, COMP aiguillage *m*, commutateur *m*, CONST aiguillage *m*, DP aiguillage *m*, bascule *f*, commutateur *m*, contact *m*, interrupteur *m*, inverseur *m*, ELEC *circuit* commutateur *m*, *circuit breaker* interrupteur *m*, ELEC ENG commutateur *m*, inverseur *m*, *branching* aiguillage *m*, branchement *m*, *change* changement *m*, *for making or breaking electric circuit* interrupteur *m*, PHYS commutateur *m*, interrupteur *m*, RAIL aiguille *f*, changement de voie *m*, RECORDING, TELECOM commutateur *m*, THERMOD interrupteur *m*, TV commutateur *m*, interrupteur *m*, sélecteur *m*; ~ **and crossing** *n* RAIL appareil de voie *m*; ~ **assembly** *n* PROD ENG ensemble d'interrupteurs *m*; ~ **blade** *n* RAIL lame d'aiguille *f*; ~ **body** *n* PROD ENG corps d'interrupteur *m*; ~ **box** *n* CINEMAT boîte de distribution *f*; ~ **button** *n* CONTROL bouton d'interrupteur *m*; ~ **clock** *n* ELEC commutateur à temps *m*, interrupteur horaire *m*; ~ **cock** *n* CONST robinet à trois eaux *m*, robinet à trois voies *m*; ~ **cover plate** *n* PROD ENG plaque de recouvrement des interrupteurs *f*; ~ **diamond** *n* RAIL pointe de coeur *f*; ~ **engine** *n* (AmE) *(cf shunting engine)* TRANSP locomotive de manoeuvre *f*; ~ **fuse** *n* ELEC ENG coupe-circuit sectionneur *m*; ~ **gears** *n pl* RAIL appareils de voie *m pl*; ~ **group assembly** *n* PROD ENG groupe de microcommutateurs *m*; ~ **handle** *n* ELEC ENG poignée d'interrupteur *f*; ~ **indicator** *n* PROD ENG indicateur de communication *m*, voyant d'état *m*; ~ **lever** *n* ELEC ENG levier d'interrupteur *m*, RAIL levier de manoeuvre des aiguilles *m*; ~ **lock** *n* TV asservissement de commutation *m*; ~ **panel** *n* NAUT tableau électrique *m*; ~ **relay** *n* ELEC relais de coupure *m*; ~ **signal** *n* CONTROL signal de commutation *m*; ~ **tongue** *n* RAIL lame d'aiguille *f*; ~ **tower** *n* (AmE) *(cf signal box)* RAIL poste de commande *m*; ~ **valve** *n* HYDR EQUIP distributeur à trois voies *m*, robinet à trois voies *m*

switch[3] *vt* COMP, DP, TELECOM commuter; ~ **in** *vt* ELEC ENG *close circuit* mettre en circuit; ~ **off** *vt* ELEC ENG mettre hors circuit, MECH ENG débrancher, TV débrancher, mettre hors circuit, éteindre; ~ **on** *vt* ELEC *apparatus* mettre sous tension, ELEC ENG mettre en circuit, TV allumer, brancher, mettre en circuit; ~ **to air** *vt* TV passer à l'antenne

switchable *adj* TV commutable

switchboard *n* ELEC ENG tableau de commutation *m*, tableau de distribution *m*, TELECOM commutateur manuel *m*, pupitre *m*, standard *m*, TV panneau de commande *m*, panneau de distribution *m*, pupitre de commande *m*, tableau de commutation *m*; ~ **operator** *n* (AmE) *(cf telephonist)* TELECOM standardiste *m*, TELECOM opérateur *m*; ~ **panel** *n* TELECOM panneau vertical *m*; ~ **plug** *n* TELECOM fiche téléphonique *f*

switched[1] *adj* TELECOM commuté

switched:[2] ~ **circuit** *n* TELECOM circuit commuté *m*; ~ **current** *n* ELEC courant commuté *m*; ~ **multimegabit data service** *n* (*SMDS*) TELECOM service commuté de données multimégabit *m*; ~ **network** *n* COMP, DP, ELEC ENG, TELECOM réseau commuté *m*; ~ **network layer** *n*

TELECOM couche commutée *f*; ~ **service** *n* TELECOM service commuté *m*; ~ **telephone network** *n* (*STN*) TELECOM réseau téléphonique commuté *m* (*RTC*); ~ **virtual circuit** *n* TELECOM circuit virtuel commuté *m*

switched-loop: ~ **console** *n* TELECOM poste d'opérateur de classe B *m*

switched-star: ~ **network** *n* TELECOM réseau en étoile commuté *m*

switcher *n* TRANSP locomotive de manoeuvre *f*, TV commutateur des signaux des têtes *m*, délangeur vidéo *m*

switchgear *n* ELEC appareillage de commutation *m*, appareillage de coupure *m*, appareillage électrique *m*, ELEC ENG appareillage de commutation *m*

switching *n* COMP, DP, ELEC ENG commutation *f*, RAIL manoeuvre *f*, SPACE *communications*, TELECOM commutation *f*; ~ **bar** *n* TV barre de commutation *f*; ~ **call-in-progress** *n* TELECOM commutation des appels en cours *f*, transfert entre les cellules *m*; ~ **center** *n* (AmE), ~ **centre** *n* (BrE) TELECOM centre de commutation *m*, TV centre nodal *m*; ~ **circuit** *n* ELEC ENG circuit de commutation *m*; ~ **delay** *n* TELECOM durée de sélection d'un commutateur *f*; ~ **device** *n* ELEC ENG, TELECOM dispositif de commutation *m*; ~ **diode** *n* ELECTRON, TELECOM diode de commutation *f*; ~ **equipment** *n* COMP autocommutateur *m*, DP équipement de commutation *m*; ~ **frequency** *n* PROD ENG fréquence de commutation *f*; ~ **in** *n* ELEC ENG mise en circuit *f*; ~ **loss** *n* ELEC ENG pertes de commutation *f pl*; ~ **matrix** *n* SPACE *communications*, TELECOM matrice de commutation *f*, TV grille de commutation *f*; ~ **multiplexer** *n* TELECOM multiplexeur aiguilleur *m*; ~ **mux** *n* TELECOM multiplexeur aiguilleur *m*; ~ **network** *n* ELEC ENG réseau de connexion *m*, TELECOM réseau de commutation *m*, réseau de connexion *m*; ~ **network complex** *n* TELECOM unité de connexion *f*; ~ **point** *n* TELECOM point de commutation *m*; ~ **power supply** *n* ELEC ENG alimentation à découpage *f*; ~ **process interworking telephony event** *n* (*SPITE*) TELECOM événement téléphonique de traitement des opérations de commutation *m*; ~ **processor** *n* TELECOM *data switching* processeur de commutation *m*; ~ **regulation** *n* ELEC ENG régulation par découpage *f*; ~ **regulator** *n* ELEC ENG régulateur à découpage *m*; ~ **sequence** *n* ELEC séquence de manoeuvres *f*; ~ **speed** *n* ELEC ENG vitesse de commutation *f*; ~ **stage** *n* TELECOM étage de commutation *m*; ~ **station** *n* ELEC *supply, distribution* poste de distribution *m*, station de commutation *f*, RAIL poste de sectionnement *m*; ~ **statistical multiplexer** *n* TELECOM multiplexeur aiguilleur *m*; ~ **substation** *n* ELEC ENG sous-station de sectionnement *f*; ~ **system** *n* TELECOM, TV système de commutation *m*; ~ **system processor** *n* TELECOM calculateur de commutation *m*; ~ **theory** *n* COMP, DP théorie de la commutation *f*; ~ **time** *n* ELEC ENG temps de commutation *m*; ~ **track** *n* (AmE) *(cf marshalling track)* RAIL voie de classement *f*; ~ **a train** *n* (AmE) RAIL aiguillage d'un train *m*; ~ **tube** *n* ELECTRON tube de commutation *m*; ~ **unit** *n* TELECOM commutateur *m*; ~ **yard** *n* (AmE) *(cf marshalling yard)* RAIL chantier de triage *m*, gare de triage *f*

switch-mode: ~ **power supply** *n* PROD ENG alimentation énergétique commutée *f*

switch-operating: ~ **handle** *n* PROD ENG poignée de commande du sectionneur *f*

switchpoint: ~ **light** *n* RAIL lanterne d'aiguille *f*

swivel *n* MECH émerillon *m*, MECH ENG rotule *f*, MINING

boring touret *m*, tête de sonde *f*, NAUT *fittings* émerillon *m*, PETR joint de rotation *m*, PETR TECH tête d'injection *f*, PROD ENG *of foundry flask* tourillon *m*; ~ **arm** *n* INSTRUMENT bras pivotant *m*; ~ **bearing motor** *n* ELEC moteur à balancier *m*; ~ **bearings** *n pl* MECH ENG palier à rotule *m*; ~ **block** *n* MECH ENG poulie à émerillon *f*; ~ **bridge** *n* CONST pont tournant *m*; ~ **hanger** *n* MECH ENG palier à rotule *m*; ~ **hook** *n* MECH ENG crochet tournant *m*, NAUT *rigging fittings* croc à émerillon *m*; ~ **joint** *n* MECH ENG joint à rotule *m*; ~ **loop** *n* SPRINGS *of spring coil* attache à élément inséré *f*; ~ **pipe connector** *n* MECH ENG embout à rotule *m*; ~ **plummer block** *n* MECH ENG palier à rotule *m*; ~ **range clockwise** *n* MECH ENG *machine tool* plage de pivotements sens horaire *f*; ~ **range counter clockwise** *n* MECH ENG plage de pivotements sens anti-horaire *f*; ~ **rod** *n* MINING *boring* tête de sonde *f*; ~ **slide rest** *n* MECH ENG support à chariot pivotant *m*; ~ **stirrup** *n* MECH ENG étrier à touret *m*; ~ **vice** *n* (BrE) MECH ENG étau tournant *m*, étau à base tournante *m*; ~ **vise** *n* (AmE) *see swivel vice*
swiveling: ~ **roof** *n* (AmE), **swivelling roof** *n* (BrE) TRANSP toit pivotant *m*
swivel-mounted: ~ **reflector** *n* PHOTO réflecteur orientable *m*
SWR *abbr (standing-wave ratio)* SPACE, TELECOM ROS *(rapport d'ondes stationnaires)*
S-wrench *n* (AmE) *(cf S-shaped spanner)* MECH ENG clé cintrée en S *f*, clé en S *f*
swung: ~ **baffle** *n* C&G marque de fond ébaucheur déportée *f*
syenite *n* CHEM syénite *f*
syllabic: ~ **companding** *n* TELECOM compression-extension syllabique *f*
syllable: ~ **articulation test** *n* TELECOM essai de netteté des syllabes *m*
sylvanite *n* MINERAL sylvanite *f*
sylvestrene *n* CHEM sylvestrène *m*
sylvine *n* MINERAL sylvite *f*
sylvinite *n* MINERAL sylvinite *f*
sylvite *n* MINERAL sylvite *f*
symbiotic: ~ **star** *n* ASTRON étoile symbiotique *f*
symbol *n* CHEM, DP symbole *m*; ~ **set** *n* DP jeu de symboles *m*; ~ **string** *n* DP chaîne de symboles *f*; ~ **table** *n* DP table de symboles *f*
symbolic: ~ **addressing** *n* COMP, DP adressage symbolique *m*; ~ **name** *n* COMP, DP nom symbolique *m*; ~ **processing** *n* COMP, DP traitement symbolique *m*
symmetric[1] *adj* COMP, DP, GEOM symétrique
symmetric:[2] ~ **matrix** *n* COMP, DP matrice symétrique *f*; ~ **pipe coupling** *n* MECH ENG raccord symétrique *m*; ~ **saddle shape** *n* GEOM *topology* selle symétrique *f*; ~ **wave function** *n* PHYS fonction d'onde symétrique *f*
symmetrical[1] *adj* CHEM, GEOM symétrique
symmetrical:[2] ~ **anastigmat** *n* PHOTO anastigmat symétrique *m*; ~ **arrangement** *n* ELEC ENG montage symétrique *m*; ~ **pair cable** *n* TELECOM câble à paires symétriques *m*; ~ **sound track** *n* ACOUSTICS trace acoustique symétrique *f*; ~ **time matrix** *n* TELECOM matrice temporelle symétrique *f*; ~ **transducer** *n* ELEC ENG transducteur symétrique *m*; ~ **trapezoidal screw thread** *n* MECH ENG filetage trapézoïdal symétrique *m*
symmetry *n* CHEM *of molecule*, GEOM symétrie *f*; ~ **elements** *n pl* CRYSTALL éléments de symétrie *m pl*
sympathetic: ~ **detonation** *n* MINING détonation par influence *f*, détonation par sympathie *f*; ~ **ink** *n* COLOURS encre sympathique *f*

SYN *abbr (synchronous idle character)* COMP, DP SYN *(caractère de synchronisation)*
synanthrose *n* CHEM lévuline *f*
sync:[1] **in** ~ *adj* CINEMAT synchrone, synchronisé, TV synchrone
sync:[2] ~ **amplifier** *n* TV ampli de synchronisation *m*; ~ **beep** *n* CINEMAT top de synchronisation *m*; ~ **blanking** *n* TV suppression de synchronisation *f*; ~ **cable** *n* CINEMAT câble de synchronisation *m*; ~ **feedback** *n* TV contre-réaction de synchronisation *f*; ~ **generator** *n* CINEMAT générateur de fréquence pilote *m*, TV générateur de synchro *m*; ~ **input** *n* TV entrée de la synchronisation *f*; ~ **line-up** *n* TV alignement des impulsions de synchronisation *m*; ~ **mark** *n* CINEMAT marque de synchronisation *f*; ~ **plop** *n* CINEMAT mille *m*; ~ **pulse** *n* CINEMAT signal de synchro *m*; ~ **pulse cable** *n* CINEMAT câble de synchronisation *m*, fil de synchro *m*; ~ **pulse generator** *n* CINEMAT générateur de synchro *m*, TV générateur d'impulsions de synchronisation *m*; ~ **separator** *n* TV séparateur des signaux de synchronisation *m*; ~ **tip frequency** *n* TV fréquence du fond de synchronisation *f*
sync[3] *vt* TV synchroniser
sync:[4] ~ **dailies** *vi* CINEMAT synchroniser les rushes
Synchro-Compur: ~ **shutter** *n* PHOTO obturateur Synchro-Compur *m*
synchrocyclotron *n* PHYS synchrocyclotron *m*
synchrolock *n* CINEMAT asservisseur *m*
synchromesh *n* AUTO synchro *m*; ~ **transmission** *n* AUTO boîte de vitesses synchronisées *f*
synchronisation: ~ **cable** *n* CINEMAT câble de synchronisation *m*
synchronism *n* ELECTRON, MECH ENG, RECORDING synchronisme *m*
synchronization *n* AUTO, COMP, DP, MECH ENG, RECORDING, SPACE *communications*, TELECOM synchronisation *f*, TRANSP *traffic lights* synchronisation des feux *f*; ~ **control** *n* CONTROL régulation de synchro *f*; ~ **loss** *n* TV perte de synchronisation *f*; ~ **network** *n* TELECOM réseau de synchronisation *m*; ~ **pulses** *n pl* TV impulsions de synchronisation *f pl*; ~ **transformer** *n* PROD ENG transformateur de synchronisation *m*; ~ **window** *n* SPACE *communications* fenêtre de synchronisation *f*
synchronize *vt* CINEMAT, TV synchroniser
synchronized: ~ **shooting** *n* CINEMAT tournage en synchrone *m*; ~ **transmission** *n* AUTO boîte de vitesses synchronisées *f*, boîte synchro *f*
synchronizer *n* AUTO synchro *m*, CINEMAT synchroniseuse *f*, COMP, DP, ELEC *machine* synchroniseur *m*, ELEC ENG synchronisateur *m*
synchronizing[1] *adj* ELEC *alternating current supplies* de synchronisation
synchronizing:[2] ~ **cone** *n* MECH ENG *machine tool* anneau de synchronisation *m*; ~ **relay** *n* ELEC relais synchronisé *m*
synchronous[1] *adj* COMP, DP, ELECTRON synchrone
synchronous:[2] ~ **alternator** *n* ELEC *generator* alternateur synchrone *m*; ~ **belt** *n* MECH ENG courroie synchrone *f*; ~ **belt drive** *n* MECH ENG transmission synchrone par courroies *f*; ~ **capacitor** *n* ELEC ENG condensateur synchrone *m*; ~ **circuit** *n* TELECOM circuit synchrone *m*; ~ **computer** *n* COMP calculateur synchrone *m*, DP ordinateur synchrone *m*; ~ **converter** *n* ELEC *alternating current supply* commutatrice *f*, ELEC ENG commutatrice *f*, convertisseur synchrone *m*; ~ **coupling** *n* ELEC

inductor accouplement synchrone *m*; ~ **data link control** *n (SDLC)* COMP commande de transmission synchrone *f*, procédure de commande de transmission synchrone *f*; ~ **detection** *n* ELECTRON démodulation cohérente *f*, détection synchrone *f*; ~ **digital hierarchy** *n (SDH)* TELECOM hiérarchie numérique synchrone *f (HNS)*; ~ **drive** *n* CINEMAT *motor*, TV entraînement synchrone *m*; ~ **electric clock** *n* ELEC horloge électrique synchrone *f*; ~ **equipment management function** *n (SEMF)* TELECOM fonction de gestion d'équipement synchrone *f*; ~ **frequency encoding technique** *n (SFET)* TELECOM technique de codage à fréquence synchrone *f*; ~ **generator** *n* ELEC alternateur synchrone *m*, ELEC ENG générateur synchrone *m*; ~ **idle character** *n (SYN)* COMP, DP caractère de synchronisation *m (SYN)*; ~ **induction motor** *n* ELEC, ELEC ENG moteur asynchrone synchronisé *m*; ~ **inverter** *n* ELEC ENG commutatrice inversée *f*, onduleur synchrone *m*; ~ **machine** *n* ELEC *generator* alternateur synchrone *m*, ELEC ENG machine synchrone *f*; ~ **modem** *n* ELECTRON modem synchrone *m*; ~ **motor** *n* CINEMAT, ELEC, ELEC ENG, PHYS, TRANSP moteur synchrone *m*; ~ **multiplexer** *n (SM)* TELECOM multiplexeur synchrone *m*; ~ **network** *n* DP réseau synchrone *m*; ~ **port** *n* TELECOM point d'accès synchrone *m*; ~ **satellite** *n* SPACE satellite synchrone *m*; ~ **sound** *n* RECORDING son synchrone *m*; ~ **speed** *n* ELEC, FUELLESS vitesse synchrone *f*; ~ **transfer mode** *n (STM)* TELECOM mode de transfert synchrone *m*; ~ **transmission** *n* COMP, DP, TELECOM transmission synchrone *f*; ~ **transport module** *n (STM)* TELECOM module de transport synchrone *m*; ~ **transport module-n** *n (STM-n)* TELECOM module de transport synchrone-n *m*; ~ **videodisc** *n* (BrE) OPT disque synchrone *m*, vidéodisque synchrone *m*; ~ **videodisk** *n* (AmE) *see synchronous videodisc*

synchrotron *n* PART PHYS, PHYS synchrotron *m* ~ **emission** *n* PHYS, RAD PHYS rayonnement synchrotron *m*; ~ **radiation** *n* ASTRON rayonnement synchrotron *m*

synclinal: ~ **axis** *n* MECH ENG axe synclinal *m*; ~ **flexure** *n* MECH ENG flexure synclinale *f*, pli synclinal *m*; ~ **fold** *n* MECH ENG flexure synclinale *f*, pli synclinal *m*

syncline *n* PETR TECH synclinal *m*

synclinorium *n* GEOL synclinorium *m*

syncword *n* TELECOM mot de synchronisation *m*

syneresis *n* CHEM *of liquid from gel*, FOOD TECH, P&R synérèse *f*

synergetic[1] *adj* CHEM *effect* synergique

synergetic:[2] ~ **effect** *n* POLLUTION effet synergique *m*; ~ **log** *n* PETR log d'interprétation géologique *m*

synergism *n* DETERGENTS synergie *f*; ~ **effect** *n* P&R synergie *f*

synergist *n* DETERGENTS agent augmentant la synergie *m*, synergiste *m*, FOOD TECH synergique *m*

synergistic[1] *adj* CHEM *effect* synergique

synergistic:[2] ~ **effect** *n* P&R synergie *f*

synergy *n* DETERGENTS synergie *f*

synform *n* GEOL synforme *f*

syngenite *n* MINERAL syngénite *f*

synodic: ~ **month** *n* ASTRON lunaison *f*, mois synodique *m*

synoptical: ~ **switchboard** *n* ELEC tableau synoptique *m*

synorogenic *adj* GEOL synorogénique

synschistous *adj* GEOL synschisteux

synsedimentary: ~ **fault** *n* (AmE) *(cf growth fault)* GEOL faille de croissance *f*, faille synsédimentaire *f*

syntactic[1] *adj* CHEM syntactique

syntactic:[2] ~ **analysis** *n* TELECOM analyse syntaxique *f*; ~ **analyzer** *n* TELECOM analyseur syntactique *m*

syntax *n* COMP, DP syntaxe *f*; ~ **analysis** *n* COMP, DP analyse syntaxique *f*; ~ **analyzer** *n* COMP, DP analyseur syntaxique *m*; ~ **error** *n* COMP, DP erreur de syntaxe *f*; ~ **identifier** *n* TELECOM identificateur de syntaxe *m*; ~ **version** *n* TELECOM version de syntaxe *f*

syntectonic *adj* GEOL syntectonique

synthesis *n* CHEM *of compound*, GAS TECH synthèse *f*

synthesized: ~ **local oscillator** *n* ELECTRON oscillateur local synthétisé *m*; ~ **oscillator** *n* ELECTRON oscillateur synthétisé *m*, oscillateur à fréquence synthétisée *m*; ~ **signal generator** *n* ELECTRON générateur synthétisé *m*, générateur de signaux synthétisés *m*

synthesizer *n* RECORDING, TELECOM synthétiseur *m*; ~ **settling time** *n* TELECOM temps d'acquisition de régime stable de synthétiseur *m*

synthetic[1] *adj* CHEM *compound* synthétique

synthetic:[2] ~ **adhesive** *n* PRINT adhésif synthétique *m*; ~ **crude** *n* PETR TECH brut de synthèse *m*, brut synthétique *m*; ~ **detergent** *n* DETERGENTS détergent synthétique *m*; ~ **elastomer** *n* PETR TECH élastomère synthétique *m*; ~ **enamel** *n* COLOURS laque synthétique *f*, peinture synthétique *f*; ~ **fault** *n* GEOL faille synthétique *f*; ~ **fiber** *n* (AmE), ~ **fibre** *n* (BrE) HEAT ENG, TEXTILES fibre synthétique *f*; ~ **flight trainer** *n* AERONAUT entraîneur synthétique de vol *m*; ~ **gas** *n* GAS TECH gaz synthétique *m*; ~ **gasoline** *n* AUTO essence synthétique *f*; ~ **latex** *n* P&R *latices* latex synthétique *m*; ~ **long-oil varnish** *n* COLOURS vernis synthétique long en huile *m*; ~ **membrane** *n* CONST membrane synthétique *f*; ~ **natural gas** *n (SNG)* GAS TECH, PETR TECH gaz naturel de synthèse *m (GNS)*; ~ **resin** *n* P&R, PETR TECH résine synthétique *f*, PROP MAT résine artificielle *f*; ~ **rubber** *n* P&R *elastomer*, PETR TECH caoutchouc synthétique *m*; ~ **silicate** *n* PROP MAT silicate synthétique *m*; ~ **size** *n* TEXTILES colle synthétique *f*; ~ **varnish** *n* COLOURS vernis synthétique *m*

synthol *n* CHEM synthol *m*

syntonin *n* CHEM syntonine *f*

syntonous: ~ **comma** *n* ACOUSTICS comma syntonique *m*

syringe *n* LAB EQUIP seringue *f*

syringic *adj* CHEM syringique

system *n* COMP système *m*, CONST *of wires, lines, pipes* réseau *m*, DP, GEOL, PROD ENG système *m*, TELECOM groupe quaternaire *m*, système *m*; ~ **configuration** *n* ELEC *supply network* architecture de réseau *f*, configuration d'un réseau *f*; ~ **crash** *n* COMP, DP écrasement système *m*; ~ **designer** *n* TELECOM responsable de la conception des systèmes *m*; ~ **design review** *n (SDR)* SPACE revue de conception système *f*; ~ **diagram** *n* ELEC *supply network* schéma d'un réseau *m*; ~ **disk** *n* COMP, DP disque système *m*; ~ **earth** *n* (BrE) *(cf system ground)* ELEC *connection* prise de terre du système *f*; ~ **expander module** *n* PROD ENG module d'extension du système *m*; ~ **generation** *n* COMP, DP génération de système *f*; ~ **ground** *n* (AmE) *(cf system earth)* ELEC *connection* prise de terre du système *f*; ~ **library** *n* PRINT bibliothèque système *f*; ~ **load** *n* TELECOM charge du système *f*; ~ **management application entity** *n (SMAE)* TELECOM entité d'application de gestion de systèmes *f*; ~ **management application entry** *n* TELECOM entité d'application de gestion *f*; ~ **operational diagram** *n* ELEC *supply network* schéma d'exploitation d'un réseau *m*; ~ **pattern** *n* ELEC *supply network* structure élémentaire d'un réseau *f*; ~ **of pipes** *n* CONST canalisation *f*, canalisation de tuyaux *f*, réseau de conduites *m*; ~ **pointer** *n* PROD ENG pointeur du système *m*; ~ **provider** *n* TELECOM fournisseur de systèmes *m*; ~ **of satellite navigation** *n* NAUT système de navigation par satellites *m*; ~ **of seals** *n* CONST *railway* système d'étanchéité *m*; ~ **security** *n* COMP, DP sécurité du système *f*; ~ **setup** *n* PROD ENG configuration du système *f*; ~ **of shoring** *n* CONST *building* batterie d'étais *f*; ~ **startup** *n* PROD ENG mise en service du système *f*; ~ **status menu** *n* PROD ENG menu des états du système *m*; ~ **stock** *n* PROD ENG stock comptable *m*; ~ **testing** *n* COMP, DP essai du système *m*; ~ **of tubing for conveying a liquid** *n* CONST réseau de tubes servant à transporter un liquide *m*; ~ **of units** *n* ELEC système de mesures *m*; ~ **with compulsory guidance by physical means** *n* TRANSP système à guidage par forme *m*; ~ **with endless transportation units** *n* TRANSP système sans fin *m*; ~ **with guidance by adhesion** *n* TRANSP système de guidage par adhérence *m*; ~ **with intermediate stops** *n* TRANSP système avec arrêts intermédiaires *m*; ~ **with transportation units of intermediate length** *n* TRANSP système avec unités de transport de longueur finie *m*

systematic: ~ **absence** *n* CRYSTALL absence systématique *f*, extinction systématique *f*; ~ **effects** *n pl* QUALITY effets systématiques *m pl*; ~ **error** *n* METR *in measuring system*, PHYS erreur systématique *f*; ~ **sampling** *n* COMP, DP échantillonnage systématique *m*; ~ **variations** *n pl* QUALITY variations systématiques *f pl*

systems: ~ **analysis** *n* COMP, DP analyse système *f*; ~ **engineering** *n* COMP systématique *f*, DP ingénierie des systèmes *f*; ~ **library** *n* COMP, DP bibliothèque système *f*; ~ **management** *n* TELECOM gestion des systèmes *f*; ~ **network architecture** *n* (*SNA*) COMP, DP architecture unifiée de réseau *f*; ~ **programming** *n* COMP, DP programmation système *f*; ~ **software** *n* COMP logiciel d'exploitation *m*, DP logiciel de base *m*

systolic: ~ **architecture** *n* TELECOM architecture systolique *f*; ~ **array** *n* COMP, DP tableau systolique *m*

syzygy *n* ASTRON, GEOM syzygie *f*

T

T *abbr* MECH ENG *(tee)* T *(té)* METR *(tera-)* T *(téra)* PHYS *(tesla)* T *(tesla)*

T/S: ~ **diagram** *n* OCEANOG diagramme T/S *m*, diagramme température-salinité *m*

Ta *(tantalum)* CHEM Ta *(tantale)*

TA *abbr (terminal adaptor)* TELECOM adaptateur de terminal *m*

tab[1] *n* COMP *marker* onglet *m*, COMP *(tabulation)* tabulation *f*, DP *marker* onglet *m*, DP *(tabulation)* tabulation *f*, MECH, PACKAGING patte *f*, PROD ENG patte *f*, tabulation *f*; ~ **card** *n* PRINT carte perforée *f*; ~ **form** *n* PRINT formulaire avec tableau *m*; ~ **stop** *n* PRINT taquet définissant un point d'un tableau *m*; ~ **washer** *n* MECH rondelle à languette *f*

tab[2] *vt* COMP, DP tabuler

TAB *abbr* COMP *(tabulator key)*, DP *(tabulator key)* touche de tabulation *f*, ELEC ENG *(tape automated bonding)* connexion sur bande *f*

Tabakin: ~ **potential** *n* NUCLEAR potentiel Tabakin *m*

Taber: ~ **abrasion** *n* P&R abrasion Taber *f*

tabergite *n* MINERAL tabergite *f*

table[1] *n* COAL TECH, COMP table *f*, CONST *of prices, values* barème *m*, DP table *f*, MECH ENG *of machine tool, moulding machine* plateau *m*, table *f*; ~ **canting to any angle** *n* MECH ENG table s'inclinant sous tout angle *f*; ~ **casting** *n* C&G coulée sur table *f*; ~ **editing machine** *n* CINEMAT table de montage horizontale *f*; ~ **lookup** *n* COMP, DP consultation de table *f*, interrogation de table *f*, recherche dans une table *f*, ~ **mike** *n* RECORDING micro de table *m*; ~ **search** *n* COMP, DP consultation de table *f*; ~ **top tripod** *n* CINEMAT pied de table *m*, trépied de table *m*; ~ **traverse speed** *n* MECH ENG *of machine tool* vitesse de déplacement de la table *f*; ~ **tripod** *n* PHOTO pied de table *m*; ~ **vice with clamp** *n* (BrE) MECH ENG étau à agrafes d'établi *m*, étau à griffes pour établi *m*; ~ **vise with clamp** *n* (AmE) *see table vice with clamp*; ~ **which can be raised or lowered** *n* MECH ENG plateau à hauteur variable *m*, table à hauteur variable *f*; ~ **with compound slides** *n* MECH ENG plateau à double coulisse *m*, table à double coulisse *f*; ~ **with top and side faces** *n* MECH ENG table à double équerre *f*; ~ **work surface** *n* MECH ENG *of machine tool* plan de travail de la table *m*

table[2] *vt* COAL TECH tabler

tablemount *n* OCEANOG guyot *m*

tablet *n* COMP, DP tablette *f*; ~ **bottle** *n* C&G pilulier *m*; ~ **sorting and inspection machine** *n* PACKAGING machine de triage et d'inspection pour pastilles *f*

tabular[1] *adj* COMP, DP tabulaire

tabular:[2] ~ **work** *n* PRINT tableautage *m*

tabulate *vt* COMP, DP tabuler

tabulating: ~ **card paper** *n* PAPER TECH papier pour cartes perforées *m*

tabulation *n (tab)* COMP, DP tabulation *f*

tabulator: ~ **key** *n (TAB)* COMP, DP touche de tabulation *f*

TAC *abbr (total allowable catch)* OCEANOG PMA *(prise maximale autorisée)*

tach: ~ **pulse** *n* TV impulsion de comptage *f*

tacheometer *n* CONST *surveying*, PHYS tachéomètre *m*

tacheometry *n* CONST *surveying* tachéométrie *f*

tachhydrite *n* MINERAL tachydrite *f*

tacho *n* PRINT tachymètre *m*

tachogenerator *n* MECH ENG générateur tachymétrique *m*

tachograph *n* CONTROL contrôlographe *m*, TRANSP tachygraphe *m*

tachometer *n (cf rev counter)* AUTO compte-tours *m*, CINEMAT tachymètre *m*, PHYS *speed measurement* cinémomètre *m*, tachymètre *m*, TV tachymètre *m*, VEHICLES *engine, accessory* compte-tours *m*; ~ **lock** *n* TV asservissement au compteur de défilement *m*

tachydrite *n* MINERAL tachydrite *f*

tachymeter *n* CONST *surveying*, PHYS tachéomètre *m*

tachyon *n* PHYS tachyon *m*

tack[1] *n* MECH ENG *type of nail* broquette *f*, NAUT *of sail* point d'amure *m*, *sailing* amure *f*, bord *m*, bordée *f*, PRINT poisseux *m*, tirant *m*; ~ **coat** *n* CONST enduit d'accrochage *m*; ~ **level** *n* PACKAGING degré d'adhésivité *m*; ~ **weld** *n* PROP MAT soudure provisionnelle *f*; ~ **welding** *n* MECH pointage *m*

tack[2] *vi* NAUT louvoyer, tirer des bords, virer de bord

tackifying: ~ **agent** *n* P&R *rubber, adhesives* agent collant *m*

tackiness *n* COATINGS adhésivité *f*, PROP MAT pouvoir collant *m*; ~ **agent** *n* CHEM additif d'adhésivité *m*

tacking *n* NAUT *sailing* louvoyage *m*

tackle *n* CONST palan *m*, poulie *f*, treuil d'extraction *m*, treuil de levage *m*, MECH *lifting gear* palan *m*, MECH ENG appareil *m*, engin *m*, NAUT *running rigging, lifting gear* palan *m*, PROD ENG palan *m*, *lifting gear, hoisting gear* appareil de levage *m*, engin de levage *m*, *shifting gear* agrès *m pl*; ~ **and fall** *n* PROD ENG palan *m*; ~ **block** *n* PROD ENG moufle *m*; ~ **fall** *n* PROD ENG courant de palan *m*; ~ **hook** *n* PROD ENG crochet de palan *m*; ~ **with hook block** *n* PROD ENG palan à croc *m*

tacky *adj* P&R *adhesives* collant, poisseux

tactical[1] *adj* MILIT *flight* tactique

tactical:[2] ~ **radius of action** *n* MILIT rayon d'action tactique *m*

tactile: ~ **feedback** *n* PROD ENG réaction tactile *f*

TACV *abbr (tracked air cushion vehicle)* TRANSP aéroglisseur guidé *m*

TADG *abbr (three-axis data generator)* SPACE centrale de référence de direction et d'attitude *f*

taffeta *n* TEXTILES taffetas *m*

taffrail *n* NAUT *boatbuilding* lisse de couronnement *f*

tag[1] *n* COMP, DP indicateur *m*, étiquette *f*, PRINT accroche *f*, étiquette *f*, TEXTILES étiquette *f*; ~ **image file format** *n* PRINT langage informatique de description d'image *m*

tag[2] *vt* COMP, DP, PROD ENG, TEXTILES étiqueter

tagboard *n* TEXTILES carton pour étiquettes *m*

tagged: ~ **atom** *n* NUCLEAR traceur *m*

tagging *n* TEXTILES étiquetage avec vignette attachée *m*

tail[1] *n* C&G queue de pierre larmée *f*, CINEMAT fin de bobine *f*, COMP fin *f*, queue *f*, CONST *of slate* chef de base *m*, DP fin *f*, queue *f*, ELECTRON queue *f*, PRINT blancs-de-pied *m pl*, queue *f*, TRANSPORT queue *f*, VEHICLES *of body* custode *f* ~ **assay** *n* NUCLEAR *of cascade* teneur de rejet *f*; ~ **bay** *n* WATER SUPP bief d'aval *m*, biez d'aval *m*; ~ **block** *n* PROD ENG *pulley* poulie à fouet *f*; ~ **box** *n* WATER SUPP *of sluices* boîte de queue *f*; ~ **disposal** *n* COAL TECH évacuation des résidus *f*; ~ **edge** *n* PRINT bord-queue *m*; ~ **elevator** *n* WATER SUPP élévateur en queue *m*; ~ **end** *n* PAPER TECH pointe pour engager la feuille *f*; ~ **fin** *n* AERONAUT dérive *f*, empennage vertical *m*, plan fixe vertical *m*; ~ **heaviness** *n* AERONAUT tendance à cabrer *f*; ~ **lamp** *n* VEHICLES feu arrière *m*; ~ **leader** *n* CINEMAT amorce de fin *f*; ~ **loading gate** *n* TRANSP porte de chargement *f*; ~ **miter sill** *n* (AmE), ~ **mitre sill** *n* (BrE) WATER SUPP *canal-lock* busc d'aval *m*; ~ **piston rod** *n* MECH ENG contre-tige de piston *f*, queue de piston *f*; ~ **propeller** *n* TRANSP hélice de queue *f*; ~ **pulley** *n* MECH ENG poulie de renvoi *f*; ~ **rotor** *n* AERONAUT *of helicopter* rotor anticouple *m*, TRANSP rotor de queue *m*; ~ **sheave** *n* PROD ENG poulie de renvoi *f*, poulie de retour *f*; ~ **shock wave** *n* AERONAUT front de choc arrière *m*; ~ **slate** *n* CINEMAT claquette de fin *f*; ~ **unit** *n* AERONAUT empennage *m*, empennage de queue *m*; ~ **vice** *n* (BrE) MECH ENG étau à main *m*, étau à queue *m*; ~ **vise** *n* (AmE) *see tail vice*; ~ **wheel** *n* AERONAUT roulette de queue *f*

tail² *vt* CONST *architecture* encastrer

tailback *n* TRANSP bouchon *m*

tailband *n* PRINT tranchefile inférieure *f*

tail-end: ~ **marker trackside detector** *n* RAIL point de contrôle de présence du signal de queue *m*; ~ **process** *n* NUCLEAR traitement final *m*

tail-first: ~ **configuration aircraft** *n* AERONAUT avion à voilure canard *m*

tailgate *n* CINEMAT partie projection d'une tireuse optique *f*, MECH *vehicles* hayon *m*, TRANSP ridelle arrière *f*, WATER SUPP *of canal lock* porte d'aval *f*

tailing: ~ **pond** *n* COAL TECH bassin à stériles *m*

tailings *n pl* COAL TECH résidu *m*, CONST rejet *m*, résidu *m*, résidu stérile *m*, tailings *m pl*, FOOD TECH *fermentation, milling* déchets d'orge *m pl*, déchets résiduels *m pl*, PAPER TECH déchets d'épuration *m pl*; ~ **area** *n* MINING chantier de dépôt *m*, chantier de versage *m*, dépôtdes déblais *m*, terris *m*; ~ **dam** *n* CONST arrêt-barrage des tailings *m*, barrage de retenue des tailings *m*, barrage pour retenir les tailings *m*; ~ **elevator** *n* CONST élévateur de tailings *m*

tail-lift: ~ **truck** *n* TRANSP camion à hayon élévateur *m*

tailor: ~ **made** *adj* PRINT sur mesure

tailout *adv* CINEMAT par la fin, à l'envers

tailpiece *n* CONST embout *m*, WATER SUPP *pump* aspirant *m*, crépine *f*, crépine d'aspiration *f*, grenouillère *f*, lanterne *f*, reniflard *m*

tailpin: ~ **thrust** *n* MECH ENG *of lathe* butée à l'arrière *f*

tailpipe *n* AUTO tuyau d'échappement *m*, CONST *of cock* tubulure *f*, VEHICLES *exhaust* tuyau arrière *m*, WATER SUPP *of pump* tubulure d'aspiration *f*; ~ **extension** *n* AUTO embout d'échappement *m*

tailplane *n* AERONAUT empennage horizontal *m*, plan fixe horizontal *m*

tailrace *n* WATER SUPP canal d'évacuation *m*, canal de décharge *m*, canal de fuite *m*, *of water mill* bief d'aval *m*, bief de fuite *m*, biez d'aval *m*; ~ **tunnel** *n* HYDROL *dams* galerie d'évacuation *f*, galerie de décharge *f*

tailrod *n* MECH ENG contre-tige *f*, queue *f*

tails *n pl* COAL TECH résidu *m*

tailskid *n* AERONAUT béquille arrière *f*, béquille de queue *f*, patin de queue *m*, sabot arrière *m*, sabot de queue *m*

tailsluice *n* WATER SUPP sluice de décharge *m*

tailspindle *n* MECH ENG *of lathe* arbre de la poupée mobile *m*

tailstock *n* MECH ENG *of lathe* contre-pointe *f*, contre-poupée *f*, poupée courante *f*, poupée mobile *f*

tailwater *n* FUELLESS, HYDR EQUIP eau d'aval *f*, HYDROL *dams* eau de fuite *f*, WATER SUPP eau d'aval *f*; ~ **level** *n* FUELLESS niveau de l'eau d'aval *m*

tailwind *n* (*cf headwind*) AERONAUT, METEO vent arrière *m*

taint *vt* FOOD TECH gâter

take¹ *n* CINEMAT *shot* prise *f*

take² *vt* PHYS *sample* faire un prélèvement, prélever; ~ **the burr off** *vt* MECH ENG *piece of metal* ébarber; ~ **the edge off** *vt* MECH ENG *chisel* émousser; ~ **in** *vt* MECH ENG *cramp* serrer; ~ **on** *vt* NAUT *hands* embaucher; ~ **on water** *vt* NAUT *ship* embarquer son eau, faire de l'eau; ~ **stock of** *vt* PROD ENG inventorier; ~ **the wire edge off** *vt* MECH ENG *chisel* émorfiler

take:³ ~ **a bearing** *vi* NAUT *navigation* effectuer un relèvement, faire le point; ~ **down scaffolding from a building** *vi* CONST déséchafauder un bâtiment; ~ **effect** *vi* MECH ENG prendre effet; ~ **off** *vi* AERONAUT décoller

take-about: ~ **chuck** *n* MECH ENG mandrin à toc *m*, plateau pousse-toc *m*, plateau à toc *m*, plateau-toc *m*

take-away: ~ **mechanism** *n* TEXTILES mécanisme d'entraînement *m*

take-down *n* C&G passage *m*

takeoff *n* AERONAUT décollage *m*; ~ **ability** *n* AERONAUT aptitude au décollage *f*; ~ **area** *n* AERONAUT aire de décollage *f*; ~ **distance available** *n* AERONAUT distance utilisable au décollage *f*; ~ **distance required** *n* AERONAUT distance nécessaire au décollage *f*; ~ **flight path** *n* AERONAUT trajectoire de décollage *f*; ~ **funnel** *n* AERONAUT trouée de décollage *f*; ~ **monitoring system** *n* AERONAUT dispositif de contrôle des décollages *m*; ~ **phase** *n* AERONAUT phase de décollage *f*; ~ **power rating** *n* AERONAUT puissance de décollage homologuée *f*; ~ **reel** *n* CINEMAT bobine débitrice *f*; ~ **run** *n* AERONAUT course *f*, distance de décollage *f*, longueur de décollage *f*, roulement au décollage *m*; ~ **speed** *n* AERONAUT vitesse de décollage *f*

takeout *n* C&G démoulage *m*, extracteur *m*; ~ **arm** *n* C&G bras d'extracteur *m*; ~ **with push-up** *n* C&G démoulage par poussoir *m* (Bel), démoulage par soupape *m* (Fra)

taker-in *n* C&G porteur à l'arche *m*

take-up *n* CINEMAT enroulement *m*, réembobinage *m*, MECH ENG tendeur *m*, TEXTILES *size* montée *f*; ~ **cassette** *n* PHOTO cassette réceptrice *f*; ~ **drum** *n* PHOTO *of camera* bobine réceptrice *f*; ~ **magazine** *n* CINEMAT magasin récepteur *m*; ~ **motion** *n* TEXTILES mécanisme d'enroulement *m*; ~ **reel** *n* CINEMAT, DP bobine réceptrice *f*; ~ **spool** *n* RECORDING, TV bobine réceptrice *f*; ~ **sprocket** *n* CINEMAT tambour d'enroulement *m*; ~ **system** *n* TEXTILES système d'enroulage du tissu *m*; ~ **unit** *n* PROD ENG banc de tirage à chenilles *m*

taking: ~ **lens** *n* PHOTO objectif de prise de vues *m*; ~ **out of wind** *n* CONST dégauchissage *m*, dégauchissement *m*; ~ **to pieces** *n* MECH ENG déconstruction *f*, démontage *m*; ~ **up play** *n* MECH ENG rattrapage du jeu *m*

taking-off: ~ **sheets hours** *n pl* PROD ENG liste des heures *f*; **~ sheets materials** *n pl* PROD ENG liste des matières *f*

TA-LB *abbr (B-ISDN terminal adaptor)* TELECOM adaptateur de terminal pour le RNIS-LB *m*

talc *n* C&G, MINERAL, PROP MAT talc *m*

talcking: ~ unit *n* PROD ENG *rubber* talqueur *m*

talkback *n* RECORDING interphone *m*; **~ circuit** *n* TV circuit d'ordres *m*; **~ microphone** *n* RECORDING micro d'intercom *m*

talking:[1] **~ road sign** *n* TRANSP panneau routier parlant-*m*

talking:[2] **to be ~ to** *vt* TELECOM être en communication avec

talk-listen: ~ switch *n* RECORDING commutateur ordre-écoute *m*

tall: ~ oil *n* CHEM tallol *m*, P&R *paint, raw material* huile de tall *f*

tallow *n* CHEM graisse *f*, TEXTILES suif *m*; **~ oil** *n* CHEM huile de suif *f*

tallowy *adj* FOOD TECH graisseux

tally *n* COMP *counter* unité de comptage *f*, *sum* total *m*, DP *counter* comptage *m*, OCEANOG *fish landed* écorage *m*, PROD ENG pointage des marchandises *m*; **~ light** *n* CINEMAT, TV voyant indicateur *m*

talonic *adj* CHEM talonique

talose *n* CHEM talose *m*

talus *n* GEOPHYS éboulis *m*

talweg *n see thalweg*

tamed: ~ frequency modulation *n* TELECOM modulation de fréquence asservie *f*

tamp *vt* MINING bourrer, PROD ENG bourrer, damer, pilonner, RAIL *ballast* damer

tamped: ~ carbon *n* CHEM fourreau de carbone *m*; **~ density** *n* P&R densité après damage *f*

tamper *n* MINING bourreuse *f*, bourroir *m*, PROD ENG *implement* batte à bourre *f*, bourroir *m*, *person* bourreur *m*

tamper-evident: ~ closure *n* PACKAGING fermeture inviolable *f*

tamperproof:[1] **~ closure** *n* PACKAGING fermeture inviolable *f*; **~ seal** *n* SAFETY scellé de sécurité *m*

tamperproof[2] *vt* PACKAGING rendre inviolable

tamping *n* CONST, MINING bourrage *m*, PROD ENG *material* bourrage *m*, bourre *f*; **~ clay** *n* C&G pisé *m*; **~ machine** *n* RAIL bourreuse *f*; **~ material** *n* MINING bourrage *m*, bourre *f*; **~ rod** *n* CONST *for slump test* acier de piquage *m*, MINING bourroir *m*; **~ stick** *n* MINING bourroir *m*

TAN *abbr (total acid number)* CHEM indice d'acidité *m*

tandem: ~ arrangement *n* ELEC ENG montage en cascade *m*; **~ axle** *n* VEHICLES *of truck* essieu en tandem *m*; **~ connection** *n* ELEC ENG couplage en série *m*, montage en série *m*, NUCLEAR connexion en cascade *f*; **~ exchange** *n* TELECOM commutateur de transit *m*; **~ generator** *n* PHYS accélérateur tandem *m*; **~ mirror fusion reactor** *n (TMR)* NUCLEAR réacteur à miroir tandem *m*; **~ rotor helicopter** *n* TRANSP hélicoptère à rotors en tandem *m*; **~ vibrating roller** *n* CONST compacteur vibrant en tandem *m*

tandem-mounted *adj* PROD ENG *contact blocks* monté en tandem

tang *n* MECH ENG *of file* queue *f*, soie *f*, *of knife, chisel* soie *f*

tangency *n* GEOM tangence *f*

tangent[1] *adj* GEOM tangent

tangent[2] *n* COMP, DP, GEOM *of angle* tangente *f*; **~ circle** *n* GEOM cercle tangent *m*; **~ equation** *n* GEOM équation de

la tangente *f*; **~ galvanometer** *n* ELEC galvanomètre à la tangente *m*, ELEC ENG boussole des tangentes *f*, galvanomètre à aimant mobile *m*, PHYS boussole des tangentes *f*; **~ key** *n* MECH ENG clavette tangentielle *f*; **~ plate** *n* MECH ENG *of screw-cutting lathe* cavalier *m*, lyre *f*, tête de cheval *f*; **~ radius dresser** *n* MECH ENG rhabilleur de rayon tangentiel *m*; **~ screw** *n* MECH ENG vis tangente *f*; **~ to the circle** *n* GEOM tangente au cercle *f*

tangential[1] *adj* GEOM, MECH, PHYS tangentiel

tangential:[2] **~ acceleration** *n* MECH, PHYS accélération tangentielle *f*; **~ arm** *n* RECORDING bras tangentiel *m*; **~ component** *n* PHYS composante tangentielle *f*; **~ control** *n* OPT asservissement tangentiel *m*; **~ diehead** *n* MECH ENG cage de filière tangentielle *f*; **~ distortion** *n* PROP MAT distorsion tangentielle *f*; **~ focal line** *n* PHYS focale tangentielle *f*; **~ force** *n* MECH ENG force tangentielle *f*; **~ keys and keyways** *n pl* MECH ENG clavetage par clavettes tangentielles *m*; **~ signal sensitivity** *n* PHYS sensibilité tangentielle *f*; **~ strain** *n* MECH ENG déformation tangentielle *f*; **~ stress** *n* MECH ENG, PROP MAT effort tangentiel *m*; **~ tectonics** *n pl* GEOL *structural geology* tectonique tangentielle *f*; **~ threading die** *n* MECH ENG coussinet de filière tangentiel *m*; **~ velocity** *n* FUELLESS vitesse tangentielle *f*

tangle: ~ net *n* OCEANOG folle *f*

tank *n* C&G bassin *m*, CONST citerne *f*, cuve *f*, GAS TECH caisson *m*, MECH citerne *f*, cuve *f*, réservoir *m*, MILIT char d'assaut *m*, NAUT *boatbuilding* réservoir *m*, PAPER TECH cuve *f*, PETR TECH, POLLUTION réservoir *m*, PROD ENG bâche *f*, citerne *f*, cuve *f*, réservoir *m*, REFRIG réservoir *m*, SPACE citerne *f*, cuve *f*, réservoir *m*, TRANSP, VEHICLES *for fuel, oil* réservoir *m*; **~ barge** *n* TRANSP chaland-citerne *m*, wagon citerne *m*; **~ block** *n* C&G bloc de cuve *m*; **~ bulldozer** *n* MILIT char-bulldozer *m*, tracteur-char *m*; **~ cap** *n* AUTO, MECH *vehicles*, VEHICLES *for fuel, oil* bouchon de réservoir *m*; **~ car** *n* MINES wagon réservoir *m*, MINING, RAIL *(cf tank wagon)* vehicles, TRANSP wagon citerne *m*; **~ container** *n* TRANSP conteneur citerne *m*; **~ developing** *n* CINEMAT développement en cuve *m*; **~ development** *n* PHOTO développement en cuves profondes *m*; **~ dozer** *n* MILIT tracteur-char *m*; **~ engine** *n* MINING locomotive-tender *f*, machine-tender *f*, RAIL locomotive-tender *f*; **~ furnace** *n* C&G four à bassin *m*; **~ hatch** *n* NAUT *of tanker* dôme de cuve *m*; **~ heater** *n* PHOTO réchauffeur pour cuve profonde *m*; **~ lining glass** *n* C&G verre pour revêtement de cuve *m*; **~ locomotive** *n* MINING locomotive-tender *f*, machine-tender *f*, RAIL locomotive-tender *f*; **~ neck** *n* C&G rétrécissement *m*; **~ semitrailer** *n* TRANSP semi-remorque citerne *f*; **~ storage** *n* PROD ENG emmagasinage en réservoirs *m*; **~ top** *n* NAUT *shipbuilding* plafond de ballast *m*; **~ top filter** *n* PROD ENG filtre de dessus du réservoir *m*; **~ truck** *n* TRANSP camion citerne *m*; **~ valve** *n* HYDR EQUIP soupape de réservoir *f*; **~ wagon** *n* (BrE) MINING, RAIL *(cf tank car)* vehicles, TRANSP wagon citerne *m*

tanker *n* MAR POLL, NAUT *type of ship* navire-citerne *m*, PETR TECH camion citerne *m*, pétrolier *m*, TRANSP *road* camion citerne *m*, *sea* pétrolier *m*, *ship* navire-citerne *m*, VEHICLES camion citerne *m*; **~ terminal** *n* TRANSP port pétrolier *m*; **~ truck** *n* CONST *railway truck* wagon citerne *m*, *road vehicle* camion citerne *m*

tannage *n* CHEM tannage *m*

tannate *n* CHEM tannate *m*

tannic *adj* CHEM tannique

tannin n CHEM tanin m, tannin m

tanning n CINEMAT tannage m

tantalate n CHEM tantalate m

tantalic adj CHEM tantalique

tantalite n MINERAL tantalite f

tantalum n (Ta) CHEM tantale m (Ta); ~ **anode** n ELEC ENG anode en tantale f; ~ **capacitor** n ELEC ENG condensateur au tantale m; ~ **foil capacitor** n ELEC ENG condensateur au tantale bobiné m; ~ **oxide** n ELEC ENG oxyde de tantale m; ~ **oxide capacitor** n ELEC ENG condensateur à l'oxyde de tantale m; ~ **slug** n ELEC ENG anode en tantale frittée f; ~ **slug capacitor** n ELEC ENG condensateur au tantale à anode frittée m; ~ **solid capacitor** n ELEC ENG condensateur au tantale à électrolyte solide m; ~ **wet capacitor** n ELEC ENG condensateur au tantale à électrolyte liquide m

tap[1] n (cf faucet) CONST robinet m, ELEC winding, ELEC ENG branchement m, prise f, LAB EQUIP robinet d'eau m, MECH tools, MECH ENG for cutting thread taraud m, PROD ENG metal from furnace coulée f; ~ **automated bonding** n ELEC ENG soudage sur bande m; ~ **bolt** n MECH ENG boulon taraudé m; ~ **change operation** n ELEC opération de changement de prises f; ~ **changer** n ELEC switch changeur de prises m, ELEC ENG commutateur à prises m; ~ **funnel** n LAB EQUIP glassware entonnoir à robinet m; ~ **holder** n MECH ENG porte-taraud m; ~ **hole** n PROD ENG of furnace coulée f, oeil m, trou de coulée m, trou de gueuse m; ~ **plate** n MECH ENG filière f, filière plate f, filière simple f, filière à palette f, filière à truelle f; ~ **position indicator** n ELEC tap changer indicateur de position de prise m; ~ **reseating tool** n MECH ENG outil pour rectifier les sièges de robinets m; ~ **selector** n ELEC sélecteur de prises m; ~ **switch** n ELEC commutateur à prises m; ~ **washer** n MECH ENG rondelle f; ~ **with crutch key** n CONST robinet à tête m; ~ **with metric thread** n MECH ENG taraud au pas métrique m; ~ **with square head** n MECH ENG robinet à carré m; ~ **with Whitworth thread** n MECH ENG taraud au pas Whitworth m; ~ **wrench** n MECH ENG tourne-à-gauche m

tap[2] vt C&G glass in melting furnace couler, COAL TECH soutirer, FOOD TECH fermentation mettre en perce, retirer, soutirer, MINING percer à, recouper, PHYS prélever, PROD ENG frapper, frapper un coup sur, draw off couler, draw off by diverting faire prise sur, faire une prise à, thread tarauder

tape[1] n C&G ruban m, COMP, DP bande f, ELEC insulation ruban m, recording bande f, MECH, P&R article, TEXTILES ruban m, TV boucle f; ~ **advance** n TV entraînement de la bande m; ~ **alignment guide** n TV galet de guidage de la bande m; ~ **automated bonding** n (TAB) ELEC ENG connexion sur bande f; ~ **backing** n RECORDING, TV dorsale f; ~ **base** n RECORDING support m, TV support de bande m; ~ **cartridge** n DP cartouche de bande f; ~ **cassette** n RECORDING cassette pour magnétoscope f; ~ **coating material** n RECORDING, TV enduit magnétique m; ~ **condenser** n TEXTILES condenseur à lanières m; ~ **control unit** n CONTROL contrôleur de dérouleurs m; ~ **copy** n DP copie sur bande f; ~ **counter** n RECORDING, TV compteur m; ~ **cupping** n RECORDING, TV courbure transversale de la bande f; ~ **curvature** n RECORDING, TV courbure de la bande f; ~ **deck** n ACOUSTICS platine de magnétophone f, COMP, DP dérouleur de bande magnétique m, RECORDING platine d'enregistrement f; ~ **drive** n COMP, DP entraînement de bande magnétique m, lecteur de

bande m, mécanisme d'entraînement de bande magnétique m, unité à bande magnétique f, RECORDING, TV entraînement de la bande m; ~ **dump** n COMP, DP vidage sur bande m; ~ **file** n COMP, DP fichier sur bande m; ~ **guide** n RECORDING, TV guide de bande m; ~ **header** n COMP, DP en-tête de bande m; ~ **input guide** n TV guide d'entrée de bande m; ~ **label** n COMP, DP étiquette de bande f; ~ **leader** n DP, TV amorce de bande f; ~ **length indicator** n TV indicateur de longueur de bande m; ~ **library** n COMP, DP bandothèque f, bibliothèque de bandes f; ~ **lifter** n TV écarteur de bande m; ~ **line** n METR double décamètre à ruban m, décamètre à ruban m; ~ **loop** n RECORDING boucle f, boucle de bande f, TV bande sans fin f; ~ **loop cassette** n TV chargeur à bande sans fin m; ~ **mark** n COMP marque de bande m, DP marque de bande f; ~ **measure** n MECH mètre à ruban m, METR mesure à ruban f, mètre à ruban m, in circular case roulette f, ruban m; ~ **moistening device** n PACKAGING dispositif d'humidification pour ruban m; ~ **neutral plane** n TV plan neutre de la bande m; ~ **output guide** n TV guide de sortie de bande m; ~ **oxide layer** n TV couche d'oxyde de bande f; ~ **player** n RECORDING lecteur de bande m; ~ **punch** n COMP, DP perforateur de bande m; ~ **reader** n DP lecteur de bande m; ~ **recorder** n ACOUSTICS, GEOPHYS, RECORDING magnétophone m; ~ **recording** n RECORDING enregistrement magnétique m; ~ **reel** n RECORDING bobine de bande f; ~ **reproducer** n COMP, DP reproducteur de bande m; ~ **roller** n RECORDING, TV galet d'entraînement de la bande m; ~ **run** n RECORDING, TV défilement de la bande m; ~ **scrape** n RECORDING flottement de ruban m; ~ **sealer** n PACKAGING fermeture avec ruban f; ~ **skip** n COMP, DP saut de bande m; ~ **slippage** n RECORDING, TV glissement de la bande m; ~ **speed** n ACOUSTICS, RECORDING vitesse de défilement f, TV vitesse de bande f, vitesse de défilement f; ~ **speed control** n TV sélecteur de vitesse m; ~ **spill** n RECORDING relâchement de ruban m; ~ **splice** n CINEMAT, RECORDING collure f; ~ **splicer** n CINEMAT colleuse à scotch f, RECORDING ciseau automatique m, réglette de montage f; ~ **streamer** n COMP streamer m; ~ **tension** n RECORDING, TV tension de la bande f; ~ **tension control** n RECORDING, TV réglage de la tension de la bande m; ~ **threading** n RECORDING chargement de la bande m; ~ **transport** n COMP, DP dérouleur de bande m, unité à bande magnétique f, RECORDING mécanisme d'entraînement de la bande m; ~ **transport geometry** n RECORDING schéma de chargement de la bande m; ~ **unit** n COMP, DP dérouleur de bande m, unité à bande magnétique f; ~ **width** n RECORDING largeur de bande f; ~ **wrap** n OPT rubanage m

tape[2] vi RECORDING, TV enregistrer sur bande

taped: ~ **closure** n PACKAGING fermeture avec ruban f; ~ **component** n ELEC ENG composant en bande m

tape-hanging: ~ **display reinforcement** n PACKAGING renforcement pour réclame suspendue par un ruban m

taper[1] n MECH conicité f, PROD ENG draw taper dépouille f; ~ **bend** n MECH ENG pipe fitting coude conique m; ~ **bevel** n C&G biseau diamant m; ~ **dowel** n MECH ENG goupille conique de positionnement f; ~ **dowel with extracting thread** n MECH ENG goupille conique de positionnement à trou taraudé f; ~ **key** n MECH ENG clavette inclinée f; ~ **keys and keyways** n pl MECH ENG clavetage par clavettes inclinées m; ~ **key with gib head**

n MECH ENG clavette inclinée avec talon *f*; **~ key without gib head** *n* MECH ENG clavette inclinée sans talon *f*; **~ pin** *n* MECH goupille conique *f*, MECH ENG goupille de position conique *f*; **~ pin with external thread** *n* MECH ENG goupille de position conique à longueur filetée *f*; **~ pin with internal thread** *n* MECH ENG goupille de position conique à trou taraudé *f*; **~ pipe** *n* MECH ENG tuyau conique *m*; **~ ratio** *n* AERONAUT *of helicopter* conicité *f*; **~ rolling bearings** *n pl* MECH ENG roulement à rouleaux coniques *m*; **~ sleeve** *n* MECH ENG douille de réduction *f*; **~ washer** *n* MECH ENG rondelle fuselée *f*

taper² *vt* SPRINGS amincir

tapered: **~ axle end** *n* AUTO portée conique *f*; **~ compression ring** *n* AUTO segment conique *m*; **~ end** *n* SPRINGS extrémité amincie *f*; **~ fiber** *n* (AmE), **~ fibre** *n* (BrE) OPT, TELECOM transition progressive de fibre optique *f*; **~ hub** *n* VEHICLES *of wheel* moyeu conique *m*; **~ loop** *n* SPRINGS anneau aminci *m*; **~ needle** *n* MECH ENG pointeau *m*; **~ pad** *n* C&G aiguille *f*; **~ roller bearing** *n* VEHICLES roulement à rouleaux coniques *m*; **~ section** *n* ELEC ENG transition *f*; **~ spring** *n* SPRINGS ressort forgé *m*, *leaf spring* ressort aminci *m*, ressort conique *m*; **~ stop bevel** *n* C&G biseau arrêté droit *m*; **~ transition** *n* OPT transition progressive *f*; **~ wing** *n* AERONAUT aile effilée *f*

tapering *n* MECH ENG effilement progressif *m*, SPRINGS amincissement *m*

tape-to-film: **~ transfer** *n* CINEMAT transfert de video sur pellicule *m*, TV kinescopage *m*

tape-wound: **~ core** *n* ELEC ENG tore en feuillard enroulé *m*

taphrogenesis *n* GEOL formation de rifts *f*, taphrogenèse *f*

tapiolite *n* MINERAL tapiolite *f*

tapout: **~ block** *n* C&G bouchon de coulée *m*

tapped: **~ coil** *n* ELEC ENG bobine à prise *f*; **~ control** *n* ELEC ENG potentiomètre à prises *m*; **~ delay** *n* ELECTRON retard échelonné *m*; **~ delay line** *n* ELECTRON ligne à retard à prises *f*; **~ fitting** *n* MECH ENG *pipe* raccord taraudé *m*; **~ hole** *n* PROD ENG trou taraudé *m*; **~ nut** *n* MECH ENG écrou taraudé *m*; **~ primary winding** *n* ELEC ENG enroulement primaire à prises *m*; **~ resistor** *n* ELEC ENG résistance à prises *f*; **~ secondary winding** *n* ELEC ENG enroulement secondaire à prises *m*; **~ substation** *n* ELEC *supply network* poste en dérivation *m*, poste en piquage *m*; **~ transformer** *n* ELEC, ELEC ENG transformateur à prises *m*; **~ winding** *n* ELEC ENG enroulement à prises *m*

tappet *n* AUTO poussoir de soupape *m*, MECH ENG mentonnet *m*, taquet *m*, VEHICLES *engine valve* poussoir *m*, taquet *m*; **~ adjuster** *n* MECH ENG *tool* clé de réglage des culbuteurs *f*; **~ stem** *n* AUTO tige de poussoir *f*; **~ valve drill** *n* CONST *rock drill* perforatrice à taquet *f*

tapping *n* C&G coulée du four *f*, ELEC *connection* branchement *m*, dérivation *f*, prise *f*, ELEC ENG prélèvement *m*, MECH ENG taraudage *m*, PHYS prélèvement *m*, PROP MAT *blast furnace* coulée *f*, WATER SUPP *to obtain water* captage de l'eau *m*; **~ bar** *n* PROD ENG *founding* pince de débouchage de trou de coulée *f*, périer *m*; **~ chuck** *n* MECH ENG mandrin porte-taraud *m*; **~ current** *n* ELEC *of winding* courant de prise *m*; **~ drill** *n* MECH ENG *for use prior to tapping screw threads* foret pour avant-trou de taraudage *m*; **~ duty** *n* ELEC régime de prise *m*; **~ factor** *n* ELEC facteur de prise *m*; **~ hole** *n* C&G trou de coulée *m*; **~ machine** *n* MECH ENG

machine à tarauder *f*, taraudeuse *f*; **~ the metal** *n* PROD ENG *cast iron* coulée de fonte *f*; **~ point** *n* ELEC ENG point de prélèvement *m*; **~ power** *n* ELEC *of winding* puissance de prise *f*; **~ quantities** *n pl* ELEC grandeurs de prises *f pl*; **~ range** *n* ELEC étendue de prises *f*; **~ screws thread** *n* MECH ENG filetage de vis à tôle *m*; **~ step** *n* ELEC échelon de réglage *m*; **~ streams** *n pl* WATER SUPP prises d'eau sur cours d'eau *f pl*; **~ water** *n* MINING percement aux eaux *m*, percée aux eaux *f*

tar¹ *n* CHEM bitume *m*, brai *m*, goudron *m*, CONST bitume *m*, goudron *m*, poix liquide *f*, NAUT, P&R *paint, raw material* goudron *m*; **~ ball** *n* MAR POLL aggloméré de goudron *m*, goudron *m*; **~ boiler** *n* CONST chaudière de bitumier *f*; **~ coating** *n* P&R *paint* peinture aux goudrons *f*; **~ dye** *n* COLOURS couleur de goudron *f*; **~ sand** *n* PETR TECH sable asphaltique *m*; **~ sprayer** *n* CONST goudronneuse *f*, machine arroseuse de goudron *f*; **~ sprinkler** *n* CONST goudronneuse *f*, machine arroseuse de goudron *f*

tar² *vt* NAUT goudronner

tare *n* PACKAGING, TEXTILES tare *f*; **~ weight** *n* PACKAGING poids à vide *m*

target *n* CONST *surveying* voyant *m*, PART PHYS cible *f*, SPACE cible *f*, objectif *m*, TV cible *f*; **~ burn-up** *n* NUCLEAR *of fuel* combustion massique cible *f*, niveau cible d'irradiation *m*; **~ computer** *n* COMP calculateur d'exécution *m*, DP ordinateur cible *m*, ordinateur d'exécution *m*; **~ designation laser** *n* ELECTRON laser marqueur de cible *m*; **~ detection** *n* PART PHYS détection de la cible *f*; **~ electrode** *n* ELEC ENG électrode de captage *f*, TV plaque à accumulation *f*; **~ illuminating laser** *n* ELECTRON laser illuminant la cible *m*, laser éclairant la cible *m*; **~ irradiation** *n* NUCLEAR combustion massique cible *f*, niveau cible d'irradiation *m*, PART PHYS irradiation d'une cible *f*; **~ layer** *n* TV couche de cible *f*; **~ levelling rod** *n* CONST *surveying* jalon-mire *m*, mire à voyant *f*; **~ levelling-staff** *n* CONST *surveying* jalon-mire *m*, mire à voyant *f*; **~ mesh** *n* TV gaze de cible *f*; **~ tug** *n* MILIT remorqueur de cible *m*

tariff *n* TELECOM tarif *m*; **~ structure** *n* TELECOM structure tarifaire *f*

tarmac *n* CONST tarmac *m*, tarmacadam *m*

tarmacadam *n* CONST tarmac *m*, tarmacadam *m*

tarnished *adj* PROP MAT mat

tarnishing *n* PROP MAT tarnissure *f*

tarpaper *n* PACKAGING papier goudronné *m*, PAPER TECH papier bitumé *m*

tarpaulin *n* CONST bâche *f*, prélart *m*, toile à bâches *f*, NAUT capot *m*; **~ covered container** *n* TRANSP conteneur bâché *m*

tarred: **~ brown paper** *n* PAPER TECH papier bitumé *m*, papier goudronné *m*; **~ felt** *n* CONST carton bitumé *m*; **~ rope** *n* NAUT cordage goudronné *m*

tarring *n* CONST bitumage *m*, goudronnage *m*

tartar *n* CHEM tartre *m*

tartaric¹ *adj* CHEM tartrique

tartaric:² **~ acid** *n* DETERGENTS acide tartrique *m*

tartrate *n* CHEM tartrate *m*

tartrated *adj* CHEM tartré

tartronic *adj* CHEM tartronique

tartronylurea *n* CHEM acide dialurique *m*, tartronylurée *f*

TAS *abbr (true air speed)* AERONAUT vitesse propre *f*

task *n* COMP, DP, QUALITY tâche *f*; **~ force** *n* NAUT *navy* force navale opérationnelle *f*, force navale tactique *f*, force opérationnelle *f*, force tactique *f*

tasmanite *n* MINERAL tasmanite *f*

taste: ~ **control** *n* WATER SUPP élimination des goûts *f*
tasting *n* FOOD TECH dégustation *f*, gustation *f*
tau: ~ **neutrino** *n* PART PHYS neutrino tau *m*, neutrino tauonique *m*; ~ **particle** *n* PART PHYS *heavy lepton* particule tau *f*
tauon *n* PHYS tauon *m*; ~ **neutrino** *n* PHYS neutrino tauique *m*
Taurids *n pl* ASTRON Taurides *f pl*
taurine *n* CHEM taurine *f*
tauriscite *n* MINERAL tauriscite *f*
taurocholate *n* CHEM taurocholate *m*
taurocholic *adj* CHEM taurocholique
Taurus *n* ASTRON Taureau *m*
tautomer *n* CHEM forme tautomère *f*
tautomerism *n* CHEM tautomérie *f*
tautomerization *n* CHEM tautomérisation *f*
taut-wire: ~ **angle indicator** *n* OCEANOG inclinomètre à câble tendu *m*; ~ **indicator** *n* OCEANOG inclinomètre à câble tendu *m*
taxi:[1] ~ **holding position** *n* AERONAUT point d'attente de circulation *m*; ~ **rank** *n* TRANSP station de taxi *f*; ~ **telephone** *n* TRANSP borne d'appel taxi *f*
taxi[2] *vi* AERONAUT rouler au sol
taxiing *n* AERONAUT circulation à la surface *f*
taxiway *n* AERONAUT *of airport* voie de circulation *f*; ~ **centerline light** *n* (AmE) *see taxiway centreline light*; ~ **centerline marking** *n* (AmE) *see taxiway centreline marking*; ~ **centreline light** *n* (BrE) AERONAUT feu axial de voie de circulation *m*; ~ **centreline marking** *n* (BrE) AERONAUT marque axiale de voie de circulation *f*; ~ **edge marker** *n* AERONAUT balise de bord de voie de circulation *f*; ~ **intersection marking** *n* AERONAUT marque d'intersection de voies de circulation *f*; ~ **light** *n* AERONAUT feu de voie de circulation *m*
Taylor: ~ **cone** *n* RAD PHYS cône Taylor *m*
taylorite *n* MINERAL taylorite *f*
Tb *(terbium)* CHEM Tb *(terbium)*
TBC *abbr (time-base corrector)* TV correcteur de base de temps *m*
T-beam *n* CONST poutre en T *f*, poutre en simple T *f*
TBF *abbr (traveling belt filter, travelling belt filter)* NUCLEAR filtre en ruban *m*
T-bolt *n (tee bolt)* MECH ENG boulon à T *m*, boulon à tête de marteau *f*
TBP[1] *abbr (tethered buoyant platform)* PETR TECH plateforme marine à câbles tendus *f*
TBP:[2] ~ **process** *n* NUCLEAR procédé TBP *m*
Tc *(technetium)* CHEM Tc *(technétium)*
TC *abbr (trunk code)* TELECOM indicatif interurbain *m*
TCE *abbr (transit connection element)* TELECOM élément de connexion de transit *m*
T-connection *n* MECH ENG té de raccordement *m*
T-core *n* CINEMAT noyau en plastique de 50 mm *m*
TCR *abbr (telemetry command and ranging subsystem)* SPACE TTL *(sous-système de télémesure télécommande et localisation)*
T-cramp *n* CONST *for stonework* agrafe à T *f*
TCRF *abbr (transit connection-related function)* TELECOM fonction liée à une connexion de transit *f*
TD *abbr (theoretical density)* NUCLEAR densité théorique *f*
TDC *abbr (top dead center, top dead centre)* AUTO, VEHICLES PMH *(point mort haut)*
TDF *abbr (trunk distribution frame)* TELECOM répartiteur de jonction *m*
TDI *abbr* P&R *(toluene diisocyanate)* diisocyanate de

toluène *m*, toluène diisocyanate *m*, TELECOM *(trade data interchange)* échange de données commerciales *m*
t-distribution *n* MATH loi de t *f*
TDM *abbr (time-division multiplexing)* COMP, DP, ELECTRON, PHYS, SPACE, TELECOM MRT *(multiplexage par répartition dans le temps)*
TDMA[1] *abbr (time-division multiple access)* DP, ELECTRON, SPACE, TELECOM AMRT *(accès multiple par répartition dans le temps)*
TDMA:[2] ~ **terminal** *n* SPACE *communications* terminal AMRT *m*
Te *(tellurium)* CHEM Te *(tellure)*
TE[1] *abbr (transverse electric)* OPT, TELECOM transversal électrique
TE:[2] ~ **mode** *n* OPT mode TE *m*, mode transversal électrique *m*, mode électrique *m*, mode électrique transversal *m*, TELECOM mode TE *m*, mode transversal électrique *m*, mode électrique transversal *m*
TE/TM: ~ **mode** *n* PHYS mode TE/TM *m*
teak *n* NAUT teck *m*
team *n* PROD ENG équipe *f*
tear[1] ~ C&G arraché *m*, P&R *test, fault*, PAPER TECH déchirement *m*, déchirure *f*; ~ **fault** *n* GEOL faille de déchirement *f*, faille décrochante *f*, fracture décrochante *f*; ~ **gas** *n* MILIT *chemical warfare* gaz lacrymogène *m*; ~ **grenade** *n* MILIT *chemical warfare* grenade lacrymogène *f*; ~ **initiation** *n* P&R *test, fault* amorçage du déchirement *m*; ~ **line** *n* PRINT ligne de perforations *f*; ~ **propagation** *n* P&R *test, fault* propagation du déchirement *f*; ~ **resistance** *n* P&R résistance au déchirement *f*; ~ **strength** *n* P&R résistance au déchirement *f*, PRINT, TEXTILES résistance à la déchirure *f*; ~ **strip** *n* PACKAGING bande d'arrachage *f*; ~ **tab lid** *n* PACKAGING couvercle avec patte d'arrachage *m*; ~ **tape** *n* PACKAGING ruban d'arrachage *m*
tear[2] *vt* P&R, PAPER TECH déchirer
teardown *n* PROD ENG démontage *m*
tearing *n* C&G crevasse *f*, PAPER TECH, TV *of image* déchirure *f*; ~ **test** *n* P&R essai de déchirement *m*; ~ **tester** *n* PAPER TECH déchiromètre *m*; ~ **wire** *n* PAPER TECH fil de coupage *m*
tear-off *n* PRINT épreuve prélevée par déchirement de la bande *f*; ~ **closure** *n* PACKAGING fermeture arrachable *f*; ~ **pack** *n* PACKAGING emballage arrachable *m*
teaser *n* C&G fondeur *m*
teat: ~ **screw** *n* MECH ENG vis à téton *f*
TEC *abbr (field-effect transistor)* DP transistor à effet de champ *m*
technetium *n (Tc)* CHEM technétium *m (Tc)*
technical: ~ **acknowledgement** *n* TELECOM accusé de réception technique *m*; ~ **breakdown** *n* TELECOM défaillance technique *f*; ~ **breakthrough** *n* PROD ENG percée technologique *f*; ~ **data management** *n* PROD ENG gestion des données techniques *f*; ~ **field** *n* PATENTS domaine technique *m*; ~ **instructions** *n pl* RAIL notice technique *f*; ~ **product documentation** *n* SAFETY documentation technique des produits *f*; ~ **regulation** *n* CONST règlement technique *m*; ~ **report** *n* TV fiche technique *f*; ~ **requirement** *n* METR prescription technique *f*; ~ **safety requirements** *n pl* SAFETY conditions requises techniques de sécurité *f pl*, prescriptions techniques de sécurité *f pl*; ~ **school** *n* PROD ENG école industrielle *f*; ~ **service** *n* MECH ENG service d'études techniques *m*; ~ **specification** *n* CONST spécification technique *f*; ~ **stop** *n* AERONAUT escale technique *f*; ~

viewpoint *n* TELECOM aspect technique *m*

Technical: ~ and Operational Control Center *n (TOCC)* SPACE *communications* Centre de contrôle technique et opérationnel *m*

technician *n* MECH ENG technicien *m*, MILIT artificier *m*, PROD ENG technicien *m*

technological: ~ restriction *n* SPACE contrainte technologique *f*

technology *n* MECH ENG technologie *f*

tectogenesis *n* PETR TECH tectogenèse *f*

tectonic[1] *adj* GEOL, PETR TECH tectonique

tectonic:[2] **~ map** *n* GEOL carte structurale *f*; **~ process** *n* PETR TECH phénomène tectonique *m*; **~ quake** *n* GEOPHYS tremblement tectonique *m*; **~ setting** *n* GEOL cadre tectonique *m*

tectonics *n pl* PETR TECH tectonique *f*

tee *n (T)* MECH ENG té *m (T)*; **~ bolt** *n (T-bolt)* MECH ENG boulon à T *m*, boulon à tête de marteau *m*; **~ coupler** *n* OPT, TELECOM coupleur en té *m*; **~ joint** *n* ELEC *cable* dérivation en té *f*; **~ socket wrench** *n* MECH ENG *tool* clé à béquille *f*

teem *vt* C&G couler, PROD ENG *founding* couler, jeter

teeming *n* PROD ENG *pouring* coulage *m*, coulée *f*, jet *m*; **~ pouch** *n* MECH ENG chasse-boulon *m*

tee-off: ~ substation *n* ELEC *supply network* poste en dérivation *m*, poste en piquage *m*

tee-piece: ~ union *n* CONST raccord à T *m*

teetered: ~ rotor *n* FUELLESS rotor balancé *m*

teeth *n pl* MECH ENG *of gear wheel* dents *f pl*, denture *f*, pleins *m pl*, *of saw, rack, file, fork* dents *f pl*

Teflon *n* (TM) CHEM téflon *m* (MD)

TEI *abbr (terminal end-point identifier)* TELECOM identificateur de point d'extrémité de terminal *m*

teintochemistry *n* COLOURS chimie de la teinture *f*

tektite *n* ASTRON tectite *m*

TE-LB *abbr (B-ISDN terminal equipment)* TELECOM équipement terminal pour le RNIS-LB *m*

telecast *vt* TV diffuser par la télévision, téléviser

telecine *n* TV télécinéma *m*; **~ chain** *n* CINEMAT chaîne de télécinéma *f*; **~ machine** *n* TV analyseur de film *m*, projecteur de télécinéma *m*, télécinéma *m*; **~ scan** *n* TV analyse par télécinéma *f*

telecommunications *n pl* COMP, DP, PHYS, TRANSP télécommunications *f pl*; **~ cable** *n* TELE, TELECOM câble de télécommunications *m*; **~ management network** *n (TMN)* TELECOM réseau de gestion des télécommunications *m (RGT)*; **~ network** *n* TELECOM réseau de télécommunication *m*; **~ operator** *n* TELECOM exploitant de télécommunications *m*

telecommuting *n* COMP télétravail *m*

teleconference *n* COMP, TELECOM téléconférence *f*

telecontrol *n* CONTROL télécommande *f*

teleconverter: ~ lens *n* CINEMAT multiplicateur de focale *m*

teledistribution *n* TV télédistribution *f*

teledynamic *adj* MECH ENG télédynamique

telegraph: ~ installation *n* TELECOM installation télégraphique *f*; **~ signal** *n* ELECTRON signal télégraphique *m*

teleinformatics *n* TELECOM téléinformatique *f*

telelens *n* PHOTO téléobjectif *m*

telemarketing *n* TELECOM télémarketing *m*

telematic[1] *adj* TELECOM télématique *f*

telematic:[2] **~ agent** *n (TLMA)* TELECOM agent télématique *m*

telematics *n* TELECOM télématique *f*

telemechanics *n* MECH ENG télémécanique *f*

telemechanism *n* MECH ENG télémécanisme *m*

telemeter *n* ELEC *measurement* appareil de télémesure *m*, MECH ENG, MILIT télémètre *m*

telemetrograph *n* MECH ENG télémétrographe *m*

telemetry *n* COMP, DP télémétrie *f*, ELEC *measurement* télémesure *f*, MECH ENG télémétrie *f*, MILIT, NUCLEAR, PHYS, SPACE *communications* télémesure *f*, TELECOM télémétrie *f*; **~ command and ranging subsystem** *n (TCR)* SPACE *communications* sous-système de télémesure télécommande et localisation *m (TTL)*

telephone: ~ answering machine *n* TELECOM répondeur *m*, répondeur téléphonique *m*, téléphone répondeur enregistreur *m*; **~ bell** *n* TELECOM sonnerie téléphonique *f*; **~ cable pair** *n* ELEC ENG paire de câble téléphonique *f*; **~ call** *n* TELECOM communication téléphonique *f*; **~ card** *n* TELECOM télécarte *f*; **~ conference** *n* TELECOM conférence téléphonique *f*; **~ directory** *n* TELECOM annuaire *m*, annuaire téléphonique *m*, répertoire *m*; **~ dugout** *n* MILIT abri de téléphone *m*; **~ earphone** *n* ACOUSTICS récepteur téléphonique *m*; **~ exchange** *n* TELECOM central téléphonique *m*, commutateur téléphonique *m*; **~ extension** *n* TELECOM extension *f*, poste *m*; **~ extension cable** *n* TELECOM prolongateur téléphonique *m*; **~ extension reel** *n* TELECOM enrouleur prolongateur téléphonique *m*; **~ frequency** *n* TELECOM fréquence téléphonique *f*; **~ induction coil** *n* ELEC ENG bobine d'induction *f*; **~ instrument** *n* TELECOM appareil téléphonique *m*, poste *m*; **~ kiosk** *n* TELECOM cabine téléphonique *f*, publiphone *m*; **~ line** *n* ELEC ENG ligne téléphonique *f*; **~ network** *n* TELECOM réseau téléphonique *m*; **~ number list** *n* TELECOM répertoire *m*; **~ operator** *n* (AmE) *(cf telephonist)* TELECOM opérateur *m*; **~ relay** *n* ELEC ENG relais téléphonique *m*; **~ switch** *n* ELEC ENG autocommutateur *m*; **~ switchboard** *n* TELECOM meuble téléphonique *m*, standard *m*; **~ switchgear** *n* ELEC ENG matériel de commutation téléphonique *m*; **~ terminal** *n* TELECOM terminal téléphonique *m*; **~ transmitter** *n* ACOUSTICS capsule téléphonique *f*; **~ user part** *n* TELECOM SSUT, sous-système utilisateur téléphonie *m*; **~ wire** *n* ELEC ENG fil téléphonique *m*

telephonist *n* (BrE) *(cf telephone operator)* TELECOM opératrice *f*, opérateur *m*, téléphoniste *m*

telephony *n* COMP, DP, PHYS téléphonie *f*

telephony-rated: ~ device *n* TELECOM périphérique téléphonique *m*

telephoto: ~ lens *n* CINEMAT objectif de longue focale *m*, téléobjectif *m*, objectif à longue focale *m*, PHOTO objectif de longue focale *m*, téléobjectif *m*, PHYS téléobjectif *m*

Telepoint *n* TELECOM Pointel *m*

teleprinter *n* (BrE) *(cf teletypewriter)* TELECOM téléimprimeur *m*, téléscripteur *m*

teleprocessing *n* DP télétraitement *m*

telerecorder *n* TV kinescope *m*

telerecording *n* CINEMAT, TV kinescopage *m*; **~ equipment** *n* INSTRUMENT enregistreur d'images *m*

telesales *n* TELECOM télévente *f*

telescope *n* ASTRON télescope *m*, INSTRUMENT lunette *f*, télescope *m*, NAUT longue-vue *f*, télescope *m*, SPACE télescope *m*; **~ focusing mechanism** *n* ASTRON système de mise au point du télescope *m*; **~ magnifier** *n* INSTRUMENT lunette d'observation *f*, lunette-loupe *f*; **~ mountings** *n pl* INSTRUMENT montures de télescope *f pl*; **~ mounts** *n pl* INSTRUMENT montures de télescope *f pl*; **~ objective** *n* INSTRUMENT lentille *f*

telescopic[1] *adj* MECH coulissant, télescopique
telescopic:[2] ~ **alidade** *n* INSTRUMENT alidade à lunette *f*;
~ **arm** *n* CINEMAT bras télescopique *m*; ~ **cylinder**
n MECH ENG cylindre télescopique *m*; ~ **erector arm** *n*
CONST bras érecteur télescopique *m*; ~ **forks** *n pl* VEHI-
CLES *motorcycle suspension* fourches télescopiques *f*
pl; ~ **guard** *n* SAFETY *used with planing machines* dispositif de sûreté télescopique *m*; ~ **jack** *n* MECH ENG vérin
télescopique *m*; ~ **joint** *n* MECH ENG joint télescopique
m; ~ **leg** *n* PHOTO *of tripod* branche coulissante *f*; ~
shock absorber *n* AUTO, VEHICLES *suspension* amortisseur hydraulique télescopique *m*; ~ **sight** *n*
INSTRUMENT lunette de visée *f*; ~ **spectacles** *n pl* INS-
TRUMENT lunette-loupe *f*, lunettes grossissantes *f pl*; ~
support *n* INSTRUMENT support télescopique *m*; ~
tripod *n* CINEMAT pied ajustable *m*; ~ **tube** *n* PHOTO
tube rentrant *m*
telescoping *n* MECH ENG télescopage *m*
Telescopium *n* ASTRON Télescope *m*
teleservice *n* TELECOM *ISDN* téléservice *m*
telesoftware *n* COMP, DP télogiciel *m*
teletex *n* COMP, DP télétex *m*
teletext *n* COMP, DP, TELECOM, TV télétexte *m*
teletype *n (TTY)* COMP téléscripteur *m*, téléscripteur
émetteur-récepteur à clavier *m*, DP téléscripteur *m*,
télétype *m*, TELECOM téléimprimeur *m*, télétype *m*
teletypesetting *n* PRINT composition à distance *f*
teletypewriter *n* (AmE) COMP, DP téléscripteur *m*, TELE-
COM téléimprimeur *m*, téléscripteur *m*
televise *vt* TV téléviser
television: ~ **broadcasting** *n* TELECOM diffusion de télévision *f*, télédiffusion *f*; ~ **broadcast satellite** *n* SPACE
communications satellite de télédiffusion *m*; ~ **cabinet**
n TV coffret de télévision *m*; ~ **cable** *n* ELEC ENG câble
de télévision *m*; ~ **camera** *n* ELECTRON caméra de
télévision *f*, PHYS caméra TV *f*, caméra de télévision *f*;
~ **camera tube** *n* ELECTRON tube analyseur *m*; ~ **film** *n*
TV téléfilm *m*; ~ **interference** *n* ELECTRON parasites de
télévision *m pl*; ~ **microscope** *n* INSTRUMENT microscope téléviseur *m*; ~ **picture tube** *n* ELECTRON
tube-image *m*; ~ **receiver** *n* ELECTRON récepteur de
télévision *m*, PHYS récepteur de télévision *m*, téléviseur *m*; ~ **relay** *n* ELEC ENG relais de télévision *m*; ~
rights *n pl* TV droits de diffusion *m pl*; ~ **set** *n* TV poste
de télévision *m*; ~ **signal** *n* ELECTRON signal de télévision *m*; ~ **standard** *n* TV norme de télévision *f*; ~
transmitter *n* TELECOM émetteur de télévision *m*; ~
viewer *n* TELECOM téléspectateur *m*
teleworking *n* TELECOM télétravail *m*
telewriter *n* TELECOM téléscripteur *m*
telewriting *n* TELECOM télé-écriture *f*
telex *n* COMP, DP, TELECOM télex *m*; ~ **access unit** *n*
TELECOM unité d'accès aux services télex *f*; ~ **exchange**
n TELECOM commutateur télex *m*; ~ **network identification code** *n* TELECOM CIRT, code d'identification de
réseau télex *m*; ~ **position** *n* TELECOM position télex *f*
telex-plus *n* TELECOM télex-plus *m*
telltale *n* MECH ENG *instrument* contrôleur *m*, PRINT
indication sur le contenu de la page *f*, titre courant *m*;
~ **lamp** *n* RAIL *vehicles* avertisseur lumineux *m*
tellurate *n* CHEM tellurate *m*
telluric[1] *adj* ASTRON, CHEM, FUELLESS tellurique
telluric:[2] ~ **ocher** *n* (AmE), ~ **ochre** *n* (BrE) MINERAL
tellurhydrique *m*, tellurite *f*; ~ **planet** *n* SPACE planète
tellurique *f*
telluride *n* CHEM tellurure *m*

tellurite *n* CHEM, MINERAL tellurite *f*
tellurium *n (Te)* CHEM tellure *m (Te)*; ~ **nitride** *n* ELEC
ENG nitrure de tellure *m*; ~ **nitride resistor** *n* ELEC ENG
résistance au nitrure de tellure *f*
tellurometer *n* CONST *surveying* telluromètre *m*
tellurous *adj* CHEM tellureux
TEM[1] *abbr (transverse electromagnetic)* ELEC ENG TEM
(électromagnétique transverse)
TEM:[2] ~ **mode** *n* OPT mode TEM *m*, mode électromagnétique *m*, mode électromagnétique transversal *m*,
TELECOM mode TEM *m*, mode électromagnétique
transversal *m*
temperament *n* ACOUSTICS tempérament *m*
temperate: ~ **zone** *n* METEO zone tempérée *f*
temperature PETR TECH, PHYS, REFRIG, TEXTILES, THER-
MOD température *f*; ~ **alarm** *n* PROD ENG alarme de
surchauffe *f*; ~ **balance** *n* THERMOD équilibre des températures *m*; ~ **coefficient** *n* ELEC ENG, THERMOD
coefficient de température *m*, TV coefficient de dilatation *m*; ~ **coefficient of capacitance** *n* ELEC ENG
coefficient de température de la capacité *m*; ~ **coefficient of resistance** *n* ELEC, ELEC ENG coefficient de
température de résistance *m*; ~ **compensation** *n* ELEC
ENG compensation de température *f*, ELECTRON compensation de température *f*, compensation thermique
f, THERMOD compensation de température *f*, compensation thermique *f*; ~ **control** *n* TEXTILES contrôle de
température *m*, THERMOD réglage de température *m*; ~
controller *n* CONTROL contrôleur de température *m*,
REFRIG régulateur de température *m*; ~ **control regulation** *n* SPACE régulation thermique *f*; ~ **curve** *n*
THERMOD courbe de température *f*; ~ **cycle** *n* THERMOD
cycle de température *m*; ~ **detector** *n* PROD ENG sonde
de température *f*; ~ **difference** *n* PHYS différence de
température *f*, THERMOD écart de température *m*; ~
drop *n* GAS TECH diminution de température *f*, THER-
MOD abaissement *m*, chute de température *f*; ~
equalization *n* THERMOD équilibre des températures *m*;
~ **equalizing** *n* THERMOD équilibrage des températures
m; ~ **factor** *n* CRYSTALL facteur de température *m*; ~
fluctuation *n* REFRIG fluctuation de température *f*; ~
gradient *n* HEATING, REFRIG, THERMOD gradient de
température *m*, gradient thermique *m*; ~ **inversion** *n*
POLLUTION, THERMOD *meteorology* inversion de température *f*; ~ **lag** *n* NUCLEAR temps de réponse en
température *m*, THERMOD inertie thermique *f*; ~ **log** *n*
FUELLESS rapport de température *m*, PETR enregistrement de température *m*; ~ **logging** *n* PETR TECH
diagraphie de température *f*; **over** ~ *n* THERMOD surchauffe *f*; ~ **probe** *n* THERMOD sonde de température *f*,
sonde thermique *f*; ~ **profile** *n* THERMOD profil des
températures *m*; ~ **raising** *n* PHYS élévation de la
température *f*; ~ **range** *n* PROP MAT plage de températures *f*, THERMOD domaine de températures *m*, plage
de températures *f*; ~ **ratio** *n* THERMOD rapport des températures *m*, rapport thermique *m*; ~ **recorder** *n* TEX-
TILES appareil enregistreur de température *m*; ~
regulator *n* CONTROL régulateur de température *m*,
thermorégulateur *m*, HEATING régulateur de température *m*, PROD ENG régulateur de température *m*,
régulateur thermique *m*; ~ **response** *n* ELEC ENG réponse en température *f*; ~ **rise** *n* PHYS hausse de

température *f*, élévation de la température *f*, POLLU-
TION échauffement *m*, THERMOD hausse de
température *f*, montée en température *f*; ~ **saturation**
n ELECTRON saturation de température *f*; ~ **scale** *n*
THERMOD échelle de température *f*; ~ **sending device** *n*
PROD ENG sonde de mesure de la température *f*; ~
sensor *n* AUTO sonde de température *f*, PROD ENG
capteur de température *m*, THERMOD détecteur de
température *m*, détecteur pyrométrique *m*; ~ **switch** *n*
PROD ENG contacteur thermique *m*, thermostat *m*; ~ **of**
touchable surfaces *n* SAFETY *of machinery* température des surfaces accessibles au toucher *f*; ~ **variation** *n*
REFRIG variation de température *f*; ~ **well logging** *n*
PETR TECH diagraphie de température *f*

temperature-compensated: ~ **crystal oscillator** *n* ELEC-
TRON oscillateur à quartz compensé en température
m, oscillateur à quartz à compensation thermique *m*;
~ **shadow mask mount** *n* TV support du masque compensé thermiquement *m*; ~ **Zener diode** *n* ELECTRON
diode Zener compensée en température *f*, diode de
référence de tension compensée en température *f*

temperature-compensating: ~ **capacitor** *n* ELEC ENG
condensateur de compensation thermique *m*; ~ **net-**
work *n* ELEC ENG réseau de compensation
thermique *m*

temperature-controlled[1] *adj* THERMOD à température
contrôlée

temperature-controlled:[2] ~ **crystal** *n* ELECTRON quartz
thermostaté *m*; ~ **crystal oscillator** *n* ELECTRON maître
oscillateur thermostaté *m*, oscillateur à quartz
thermostaté *m*, pilote thermostaté *m*; ~ **inspection**
room *n* MECH ENG salle d'inspection avec température
contrôlée *f*; ~ **switch** *n* ELEC ENG thermocontact *m*

temperature-dependent[1] *adj* THERMOD sujet à l'influence de la température

temperature-dependent:[2] ~ **resistor** *n* ELEC ENG résistance sensible à la température *f*

temperature-indicating: ~ **lacquer** *n* COATINGS vernis
pyrométrique *m*

temperature-monitoring: ~ **unit** *n* MINING surveillance de
la température *f*

temperature-related: ~ **failure** *n* ELEC ENG défaillance
due à la température *f*

temperature-salinity: ~ **diagram** *n* OCEANOG diagramme
température-salinité *m*

temperature-stable *adj* THERMOD stable à la chaleur,
thermostable

tempered[1] *adj* CRYSTALL, MECH *materials*, SPRINGS revenu

tempered:[2] ~ **glass** *n* C&G, TRANSP verre trempé *m*

tempering *n* CONST *concrete* humidification *f*, METALL,
NUCLEAR, SPRINGS revenu *m*

template *n* COMP, DP, ELEC *measurement, manufacture,*
etc, MECH gabarit *m*, MECH ENG calibre *m*, gabarit *m*,
patron *m*, NAUT *boatbuilding* gabarit *m*, PAPER TECH
calibre *m*, PETR TECH châssis de guidage *m*, plaque de
base *f*, PROD ENG *loam moulding* gabarit *m*, trousse *f*,
TEXTILES, VEHICLES *tool* gabarit *m*; ~ **command** *n* DP
commande de formatage *f*; ~ **drilling** *n* PETR base plate
temporaire *f*, forage au gabarit *m*, plaque de base
temporaire *f*

temple: ~ **spectacles** *n pl* INSTRUMENT lunettes à
branches *f pl*, lunettes à tempes *f pl*

templet *n see template*

tempo *n* ACOUSTICS mesure *f*, tempo *m*

temporal: ~ **coherence** *n* OPT, PHYS, TELECOM cohérence

temporelle *f*; ~ **fluctuation** *n* POLLUTION variation dans
le temps *f*; ~ **resolution** *n* POLLUTION, RAD PHYS résolution temporelle *f*; ~ **variation** *n* POLLUTION variation
temporelle *f*

temporally-coherent: ~ **beam** *n* ELECTRON faisceau à
cohérence temporelle *m*

temporary: ~ **bridge** *n* CONST pont provisoire *m*; ~ **dam** *n*
WATER SUPP barrage provisoire *m*; ~ **end instruction** *n*
PROD ENG instruction de fin temporaire *f*; ~ **file** *n*
COMP, DP fichier temporaire *m*; ~ **guide base** *n* PETR
plaque de base provisoire *f*, plaque de base temporaire *f*; ~ **load** *n* COAL TECH charge temporaire *f*; ~
memory *n* ELEC ENG mémoire intermédiaire *f*; ~ **regis-**
ter *n* COMP, DP registre intermédiaire *m*; ~ **road** *n*
CONST route provisoire *f*; ~ **set** *n* MECH ENG déformation momentanée *f*, déformation élastique *f*; ~
storage *n* COMP mémoire de transit *f*; ~ **stress** *n* C&G
contrainte temporaire *f*; ~ **threshold shift** *n* ACOUSTICS
déplacement temporaire de seuil *m*; ~ **works** *n pl*
CONST travaux provisoires *m pl*

tenacity *n* MECH ENG résistance *f*, ténacité *f*, TEXTILES
ténacité *f*

tendency: ~ **drive** *n* CINEMAT entraînement par friction
m; ~ **to reboil** *n* C&G aptitude au rebullage *f*

tender *n* MAR POLL avitailleur *m*, mazouteur *m*, NAUT
annexe *f*, navire annexe *m*, ravitailleur *m*, RAIL *vehi-*
cles tender *m*

tenderizer *n* FOOD TECH attendrisseur *m*, enzyme atten-
drissante *f*

tenderometer *n* FOOD TECH tendromètre *m*

tending: ~ **side** *n* PAPER TECH côté conducteur *m*

tendon *n* NUCLEAR *of prestressed concrete construction*
membre de précontrainte *m*, tendon *m*

tennantite *n* MINERAL tennantite *f*

tenner *n* CINEMAT projecteur de studio avec Fresnel de
10 kw *m*

tenon *n* CONST tenon *m*; ~ **drive** *n* MECH ENG *tools*
entraînement par tenon *m*; ~ **joint** *n* CONST assemblage
à tenon *m*, assemblage à tenon et à mortaise *m*; ~ **saw**
n CONST scie à dos *f*, scie à raccourcir *f*, scie à tenon *f*

tenoned: ~ **and housed joint** *n* CONST assemblage à
tenon *m*, assemblage à tenon et à mortaise *m*

tenoning: ~ **machine** *n* MECH ENG tenoneuse *f*

tenor *n* MECH ENG grade, MINING teneur *f*, titre *m*

tenorite *n* MINERAL ténorite *f*

ten-pole: ~ **filter** *n* ELECTRON filtre à dix pôles *m*

tensile[1] *adj* ELEC, MECH ENG extensible

tensile:[2] ~ **axis** *n* METALL axe de traction *m*; ~ **behavior** *n*
(AmE), ~ **behaviour** *n* (BrE) PROP MAT comportement
en traction *m*; ~ **ductility** *n* PROP MAT ductilité en
traction *f*; ~ **elongation** *n* PROP MAT élongation en
traction *f*; ~ **force** *n* MECH ENG force de traction *f*, PHYS
force de tension *f*, force de traction *f*; ~ **impact test** *n*
METALL essai de traction par choc *m*; ~ **length** *n* PAPER
TECH longueur de rupture *f*; ~ **strain** *n* MECH ENG
déformation due à la traction *f*, METALL déformation
de traction *f*; ~ **strength** *n* MECH *of materials* résistance
à la traction *f*, MECH ENG résistance à la rupture *f*,
résistance à la traction *f*, P&R résistance à la traction *f*,
PAPER TECH longueur de rupture *f*, résistance à la
rupture par traction *f*, PHYS résistance à la rupture par
traction *f*, résistance à la traction *f*, PROP MAT résistance *f*, TELECOM tenue à la traction *f*, TEXTILES
résistance à la traction *f*; ~ **strength tester** *n* PAPER
TECH dynamomètre *m*; ~ **stress** *n* MECH *materials*
contrainte de traction *f*, MECH ENG effort de traction

m, travail à l'extension *m*, travail à la traction *m*, METALL contrainte de traction *f*, PHYS contrainte de tension *f*, contrainte de traction *f*, SPRINGS contrainte de traction *f*; ~ **test** *n* MECH ENG essai à la traction *m*, METALL, PHYS, PROP MAT essai de traction *m*; ~ **tester** *n* P&R appareil de traction *m*; ~ **test piece** *n* MECH ENG éprouvette de traction *f*

tensiometer *n* OCEANOG tensiomètre *m*

tension *n* ELEC ENG tension *f*, MECH ENG *of spring* bande *f*, tension *f*, *strength of materials* traction *f*, METALL traction *f*, PHYS, TEXTILES tension *f*; ~ **arm** *n* COMP, DP bras de tension *m*; ~ **bar** *n* TEXTILES barre de tension *f*; ~ **block** *n* MECH ENG *counter-motion* renvoi tendeur *m*; ~ **control** *n* CONTROL contrôleur de tension *m*; ~ **device** *n* TEXTILES dispositif de tension *m*; ~ **efficiency** *n* ACOUSTICS efficacité en tension *f*; ~ **gash** *n* GEOL fente de tension *f*; ~ **member** *n* MAR POLL élément de tension *m*; ~ **piece** *n* MECH ENG tirant *m*; ~ **pulley** *n* MECH ENG galet tendeur *m*, poulie de tension *f*, rouleau de tension *m*; ~ **roller** *n* CINEMAT galet tendeur *m*, tendeur *m*, MECH ENG galet tendeur *m*, poulie de tension *f*, rouleau tendeur *m*, PAPER TECH rouleau tendeur *m*; ~ **screw** *n* MECH ENG vis de tension *f*; ~ **servo** *n* TV asservissement de tension *m*; ~ **side** *n* SPRINGS face tendue *f*; ~ **spring** *n* MECH ENG ressort de tension *m*; ~ **test bar** *n* SPRINGS éprouvette de traction *f*

tensioner *n* MECH ENG, PETR tensionneur *m*, TEXTILES dispositif de tension *m*, VEHICLES *chain* tendeur *m*

tensioning: ~ **bar** *n* PRINT *of plate, blanket* barre de serrage *f*

tensor *n* MATH tenseur *m*; ~ **calculus** *n* MATH calcul tensoriel *m*

tenterhook *n* CONST clou à crochet *m*

tentering *n* TEXTILES passage sur rame *m*

tephroite *n* MINERAL téphroïte *f*

tepid *adj* THERMOD tiède

tera- *pref (T)* METR téra-*(T)*

terabyte *n* OPT téraoctet *m*

terbium *n (Tb)* CHEM terbium *m (Tb)*

terchloride *n* CHEM trichlorure *m*

terebenthene *n* CHEM térébenthène *m*

terebic *adj* CHEM térébique

terephthalate *n* CHEM téréphtalate *m*

terephthalic *adj* CHEM théréphtalique

Tergal *n* (TM) P&R Tergal *m* (MD)

term *n* COMP, DP, MATH terme *m*; ~ **of patent** *n* PATENTS durée du brevet *f*

terminal *n* AERONAUT *airport* terminal *m*, AUTO borne *f*, COMP, DP terminal *m*, ELEC *connection*, ELEC ENG *connection* borne *f*, PETR TECH terminal *m*, PHYS *of battery* borne *f*, TELECOM borne *f*, poste de travail *m*, terminal *m*, TRANSP terminal *m*, VEHICLES *electrical system* borne *f*; ~ **adaptor** *n (TA)* TELECOM adaptateur de terminal *m*; ~ **aigrette** *n* GEOPHYS aigrette *f*; ~ **area** *n* AERONAUT *of airport* région terminale *f*; ~ **atom** *n* CHEM *of molecule* atome terminal *m*; ~ **barrier strip** *n* PROD ENG bornier de barrage *m*; ~ **block** *n* ELEC *connection* bloc de sorties *m*, répartiteur *m*, ELEC ENG bloc de connexion *m*, PROD ENG bornier *m*, VEHICLES *electrical system* bloc de connexion *m*; ~ **box** *n* ELEC *cable accessory* coffret d'extrémité *m*, ELEC ENG boîte de jonction *f*; ~ **call forwarding** *n* TELECOM renvoi du terminal *m*, renvoi temporaire du terminal *m*; ~ **capacity** *n* PROD ENG section maximale des câbles *f*; ~ **cover** *n* PROD ENG cache-borne *m*; ~ **coverplate** *n* PROD ENG couvercle de bornes *m*; ~ **crimper** *n* MECH ENG *tool*

pince à sertir les cosses *f*; ~ **designation** *n* PROD ENG désignation de borne *f*; ~ **device** *n* COMP, DP appareil terminal *m*; ~ **end-point identifier** *n (TEI)* TELECOM identificateur de point d'extrémité de terminal *m*; ~ **equipment** *n* TELECOM équipement terminal *m*; ~ **insulator** *n* ELEC ENG isolateur d'arrêt *m*; ~ **lug kit** *n* PROD ENG kit de cosses de raccordement *m*; ~ **marking** *n* PROD ENG inscription des bornes *f*; ~ **platform** *n* PETR TECH plate-forme terminale *f*; ~ **port** *n* COMP, DP port de périphérique *m*; ~ **screw** *n* PROD ENG vis de borne cruciforme *f*; ~ **server** *n* COMP, DP serveur de terminaux *m*; ~ **station** *n* TRANSP gare en cul-de-sac *f*; ~ **strip** *n* ELEC ENG barrette à bornes *f*, PROD ENG bornier *m*; ~ **strip module** *n* PROD ENG module à borniers *m*; ~ **subaddressing** *n* TELECOM *ISDN* sous-adressage des terminaux *m*; ~ **swing arm** *n* PROD ENG bras à bornes pivotant *m*; ~ **symbol** *n* COMP, DP symbole de terminaison *m*; ~ **tensioning screw** *n* PROD ENG vis de tension en bout *f*; ~ **tower** *n* ELEC *supply network* pylône d'arrêt *m*; ~ **velocity** *n* AERONAUT, PHYS, SPACE vitesse limite *f*

terminate *vi* TELECOM *of cable* aboutir

terminating *n* ELEC ENG bouclage *m*; ~ **element** *n* ELEC ENG élément dissipatif *m*; ~ **equipment** *n* TELECOM équipement terminal *m*; ~ **exchange** *n* TELECOM central d'arrivée *m*; ~ **impedance** *n* ELEC ENG impédance de bouclage *f*; ~ **junctor** *n* TELECOM joncteur d'arrivée *m*; ~ **resistor** *n* ELEC ENG résistance de bouclage *f*; ~ **stage** *n* TELECOM étage terminal *m*; ~ **traffic** *n* TELECOM trafic d'arrivée *m*, TRANSP trafic de destination *m*

termination *n* COMP, DP terminaison *f*, ELEC *cable connection* extrémité *f*, PROD ENG bornier *m*

terminator *n* ASTRON terminateur *m*, COMP, DP caractère d'arrêt *m*, caractère de fin *m*, PROD ENG connecteur de terminaison *m*

terms: ~ **of delivery** *n pl* PROD ENG conditions de livraison *f pl*; ~ **of the same degree** *n pl* MATH termes du même ordre *m pl*

ternary *adj* CHEM ternaire

ternitrate *n* CHEM ternitrate *m*

teroxide *n* CHEM trioxyde *m*

terpadiene *n* CHEM terpadiène *m*

terpene *n* CHEM *compound* terpène *m*

terpenic *adj* CHEM terpénique

terpin *n* CHEM terpinol *m*

terpinene *n* CHEM terpinène *m*

terpineol *n* CHEM terpinéol *m*

terpinol *n* CHEM terpine *f*, terpinol *m*

terpinolene *n* CHEM terpinolène *m*

terpolymer *n* CHEM, P&R ter-polymère *m*

terracotta *n* C&G terre cuite *f*; ~ **floor** *n* C&G dallage en terre cuite *m*

terrain *n* GEOL ensemble de formations *m*, terrain *m*

terramycin *n* CHEM terramycine *f*

terrane *n* GEOL terrane *m*

terraplane *n* TRANSP terraplane *m*

terrestrial[1] *adj* SPACE de Terre

terrestrial[2] ~ **crust** *n* SPACE croûte terrestre *f*, écorce terrestre *f*; ~ **magnetism** *n* GEOPHYS, PHYS magnétisme terrestre *m*; ~ **planet** *n* ASTRON planète tellurique *f*, planète terrestre *f*; ~ **station** *n* SPACE *communications* station de Terre *f*, station terrestre *f*; ~ **surface** *n* SPACE surface terrestre *f*, écorce terrestre *f*; ~ **telescope** *n* INSTRUMENT lunette terrestre *f*; ~ **tide** *n* OCEANOG marée terrestre *f*

terrigenous *adj* GEOL terrigène

territorial: ~ **waters** *n pl* OCEANOG eaux territoriales *f pl*
tert-butylbenzene *n* CHEM tertiobutylbenzène *m*
tertiary[1] *adj* GEOL tertiaire
tertiary:[2] ~ **creep** *n* METALL fluage tertiaire *m*; ~ **crushing** *n* COAL TECH concassage tertiaire *m*; ~ **fuel** *n* AUTO carburant tertiaire *m*; ~ **recovery** *n* PETR TECH récupération tertiaire *f*; ~ **recrystallization** *n* METALL recristallisation tertiaire *f*; ~ **winding** *n* ELEC *of transformer* enroulement tertiaire *m*
Tertiary: ~ **era** *n* PETR cénozoïque *m*, ère tertiaire *f*
tervalence *n* CHEM trivalence *f*
tervalent *adj* CHEM trivalent
Terylene *n* (TM) CHEM térylène *m* (MD), NAUT *sailcloth* Tergal *m* (MD)
tesla *n (T)* PHYS tesla *m (T)*
Tesla: ~ **coil** *n* ELEC ENG bobine de Tesla *f*
tesselite *n* MINERAL tessélite *f*
tessera *n* C&G carrelet pour mosaïque *m*
tesseral: ~ **harmonic** *n* SPACE harmonique tesseral *m*
test[1] *n* CHEM essai *m*, expérience *f*, épreuve *f*, COAL TECH essai *m*, COMP, DP essai *m*, test *m*, MECH essai *m*, épreuve *f*, METALL essai *m*, PHYS essai *m*, épreuve *f*, REFRIG, TESTING essai *m*, TEXTILES épreuve *f*; ~ **assembly** *n* NUCLEAR poste de mesure *m*; ~ **bar** *n* MECH ENG barreau d'essai *m*, coupon *m*, éprouvette *f*, PROP MAT barreau d'essai *m*; ~ **basin** *n* WATER SUPP bassin d'essai *m*; ~ **bay** *n* NUCLEAR banc d'essai *m*; ~ **bed** *n* COMP, DP, ELEC, MECH, SPACE banc d'essai *m*; ~ **bench** *n* MECH ENG, TELECOM banc d'essai *m*; ~ **board** *n* ELEC tableau de contrôle *m*; ~ **chart** *n* CINEMAT mire de réglage *f*; ~ **cock** *n* WATER SUPP robinet de hauteur d'eau *m*, robinet de jauge *m*; ~ **conditions** *n pl* PACKAGING, PROD ENG, PROP MAT, TESTING conditions d'essai *f pl*; ~ **continuous scan** *n* PROD ENG scrutation d'essai continue *f*; ~ **cube** *n* CONST *concrete* cube d'essai *m*, éprouvette *f*; ~ **customer** *n* TELECOM client pilote *m*; ~ **cylinder** *n* CONST cylindre d'épreuve *m*, éprouvette cylindrique *f*; ~ **data** *n pl* COMP données d'essai *f pl*, DP données d'essai *f pl*, données de test *f pl*, TESTING données d'essai *f pl*; ~ **equipment** *n* TESTING dispositif d'essai *m*; ~ **facility** *n* MECH ENG dispositif de démonstration *m*; ~ **firing** *n* SPACE essai de mise à fin *m*; ~ **flight** *n* AERONAUT, SPACE vol d'essai *m*; ~ **flume** *n* WATER SUPP canal d'essai *m*; ~ **for accuracy** *n* MECH ENG essai de précision *m*; ~ **frequency** *n* ELECTRON fréquence d'essai *f*; ~ **furnace** *n* PROD ENG fourneau d'essai *m*; ~ **ground** *n* VEHICLES terrain d'essai *m*; ~ **group** *n* TESTING groupe d'essais *m*; ~ **indicator** *n* TELECOM indicateur d'essai *m*; ~ **jack** *n* ELEC ENG douille de mesure *f*, NUCLEAR canon d'essai *m*, point de test *m*; **jig** *n* SPRINGS banc d'essai *m*; ~ **laboratory** *n* QUALITY laboratoire d'essai *m*; ~ **lead** *n* ELEC ENG cordon d'essai *m*; ~ **length** *n* SPRINGS longueur d'essai *f*; ~ **liner board** *n* PACKAGING couverture spéciale pour cartonnage *f*; ~ **load** *n* MECH ENG charge d'essai *f*, charge d'épreuve *f*; ~ **loading** *n* COAL TECH charge d'essai *f*; ~ **model** *n* TESTING modèle d'essai *m*; ~ **needle** *n* MECH ENG aiguille d'essai *f*, touchau *m*; ~ **oscillator** *n* ELECTRON hétérodyne de service *m*; ~ **paper** *n* CHEM papier à réactif *m*; ~ **pattern** *n* CINEMAT mire de réglage *f*, ELECTRON motif de contrôle *m*, *for use with logic analyzers* mire *f*, motif binaire de contrôle *m*, TV mire de réglage *f*; ~ **piece** *n* METALL échantillon *m*, PAPER TECH, PHYS, PROP MAT éprouvette *f*; ~ **piling** *n* COAL TECH battage d'essai de pieux *m*; ~ **pilot** *n* AERONAUT pilote d'essai *m*; ~ **pit** *n* COAL TECH puits d'essai *m*; ~

plate *n* C&G gabarit d'estimation *m*, HYDR EQUIP *of steam boiler* timbre *m*; ~ **point** *n* TELECOM point de test *m*; ~ **portion** *n* QUALITY prise d'essai *f*; ~ **position** *n* TELECOM poste d'essai *m*; ~ **pressure** *n* HYDR EQUIP surcharge d'épreuve *f*, REFRIG pression d'essai *f*; ~ **print** *n* PHOTO copie de contrôle *f*; ~ **procedures for braking systems** *n* MECH ENG procédure d'essai des systèmes de freinage *f*; ~ **prod** *n* ELEC ENG pointe de touche *f*; ~ **production** *n* PETR production d'essai *f*; ~ **program** *n* (AmE), ~ **programme** *n* (BrE) METR programme d'essais *m*; ~ **pump** *n* WATER SUPP pompe d'épreuve *f*; ~ **record** *n* ACOUSTICS disque de mesure *m*, RECORDING disque de test *m*, disque étalon *m*; ~ **reel** *n* CINEMAT bobine d'essai *f*; ~ **report** *n* COMP compte rendu d'essai *m*, rapport d'essai *m*, rapport de test *m*, DP compte rendu d'essai *m*, rapport d'essai *m*, rapport de test *m*; ~ **requirements** *n pl* PROD ENG impératifs des essais *m pl*, SAFETY, TESTING exigences pour les essais *f pl*; ~ **rig** *n* MECH ENG banc d'essai *m*, NUCLEAR poste de mesure *m*, SPACE banc d'essai *m*, montage d'essai *m*; ~ **rod** *n* PROD ENG *blast furnace gauge* bécasse *f*, tige de jaugeage *f*; ~ **room** *n* TELECOM salle d'essais et mesures *f*; ~ **run** *n* COMP, DP passage d'essai *m*, MECH ENG marche d'essai *f*; ~ **section** *n* CONST *roads* planche d'essai *f*, PHYS *wind tunnel* veine d'essai *f*; ~ **sheet** *n* CONTROL fiche de mesure *f*; ~ **shop** *n* MECH ENG atelier d'essai *m*; ~ **shot** *n* PHOTO photo de contrôle *f*; ~ **sieve** *n* MECH ENG tamis de contrôle *m*; ~ **sieving** *n* MECH ENG tamisage de contrôle *m*; ~ **signal** *n* ELECTRON signal d'essai *m*; ~ **signal generator** *n* ELECTRON générateur de signaux d'essai *m*; ~ **single scan** *n* PROD ENG scrutation unique d'essai *f*; ~ **specification** *n* SPACE *spacecraft* spécification d'essai *f*; ~ **specimen** *n* P&R témoin *m*, TESTING éprouvette d'essai *f*; ~ **speed** *n* TESTING vitesse d'essai *f*; ~ **stand** *n* NUCLEAR, SPACE banc d'essai *m*; ~ **strip** *n* CINEMAT essai image *m*, PHOTO bande essai *f*; ~ **switch** *n* ELEC ENG commutateur de mesure *m*; ~ **tape** *n* ACOUSTICS bande d'essai *f*, RECORDING, TV bande étalon *f*; ~ **terminal** *n* ELEC ENG borne de mesure *f*; ~ **track** *n* TRANSP ligne expérimentale *f*; ~ **train** *n* RAIL *vehicles* train-type *m*; ~ **transformer** *n* TELECOM transformateur de mesure *m*; ~ **transmission** *n* TV essai de transmission *m*; ~ **tube** *n* C&G, CHEM *equipment* éprouvette *f*, LAB EQUIP *glassware* tube à essai *m*, PROD ENG éprouvette *f*; ~ **tube holder** *n* LAB EQUIP pince pour tubes à essais *f*; ~ **tube rack** *n* LAB EQUIP *support* support de tubes à essai *m*; ~ **voltage** *n* ELEC tension d'essai *f*
test[2] *vt* CHEM essayer, expérimenter, vérifier, éprouver, DP contrôler, MECH ENG essayer, éprouver, TELECOM essayer, TESTING essayer, expérimenter; ~ **for bending and for compression** *vt* MECH ENG essayer au pliage et à la compression
test-data: ~ **generator** *n* COMP, DP générateur de données d'essai *m*, générateur de données *m*
tested:[1] ~ **first** *adj* TELECOM essayé en premier
tested:[2] ~ **chain** *n* MECH ENG chaîne éprouvée *f*
testing *n* CHEM essai *m*, essayage *m*, épreuve *f*, COAL TECH, COMP, DP, MECH ENG, QUALITY essai *m*; ~ **bed** *n* NUCLEAR banc d'essai *m*; ~ **drill** *n* MINING sonde de prospection *f*; ~ **flame** *n* MINING *for gas cap of safety lamps* auréole *f*; ~ **machine** *n* MECH ENG machine d'essai *f*; ~ **shop** *n* MECH ENG atelier d'essai *m*; ~ **tank** *n* NAUT *hull, model, engine* bassin d'essai *m*
tethered[1] *adj* SPACE *spacecraft* en laisse
tethered:[2] ~ **buoyant platform** *n (TBP)* PETR TECH plate-

forme marine à câbles tendus *f*; ~ **satellite** *n* SPACE
satellite en laisse *m*

Tethyan: ~ realm *n* GEOL Téthys *m*

Tethys: ~ Ocean *n* GEOL Téthys *m*

tetrabasic *adj* CHEM tétrabasique

tetrabromide *n* CHEM tétrabromure *m*

tetrabromoethane *n* CHEM tétrabrométhane *m*

tetrabromoethylene *n* CHEM tétrabrométhylène *m*

tetracarbonyl *n* CHEM tétracarbonyle *m*

tetrachlorethane *n* CHEM tétrachloréthane *m*

tetrachloride *n* CHEM tétrachlorure *m*

tetrachloroethane *n* CHEM tétrachloréthane *m*

tetrachloroethylene *n* CHEM tétrachloréthylène *m*

tetrachloromethane *n* CHEM tétrachlorométhane *m*

tetrachord *n* ACOUSTICS tétracorde *f*

tetradecanoic *adj* CHEM *acid* myristique

tetradymite *n* MINERAL tétradymite *f*

tetraethyl *n* CHEM tétraéthyle *m*; ~ **lead** *n* AUTO, CHEM
anti-knock additive plomb tétraéthyle *m*

tetragon *n* GEOM tétragone *m*

tetragonal[1] *adj* CRYSTALL quadratique

tetragonal:[2] ~ **system** *n* METALL système quadratique *m*,
système tétragonal *m*

tetrahedral *adj* CHEM *structure* tétraédrique, tétraèdre,
CRYSTALL tétraédrique, GEOM *rotation* tétraèdre

tetrahedrite *n* MINERAL tétraédrite *f*

tetrahedron *n* CRYSTALL, GEOM tétraèdre *m*

tetrahydride *n* CHEM hydrure *m*

tetrahydrobenzene *n* CHEM tétrahydrobenzène *m*

tetrahydroglyoxaline *n* CHEM tétrahydroglyoxaline *f*

tetrahydronaphthalene *n* CHEM tétrahydronaphtalène *m*, tétraline *f*

tetrahydroquinone *n* CHEM tétrahydroquinone *f*

tetrahydroxyquinone *n* CHEM tétrahydroxyquinone *f*

tetraiodofluorescein *n* CHEM tétraiodofluorescéine *f*

tetralin *n* CHEM tétrahydronaphtalène *m*, tétraline *f*

tetrameric *adj* CHEM tétramère

tetramethyl *adj* CHEM tétraméthyle

tetramethylene *n* CHEM tétraméthylène *m*

tetramine *n* CHEM tétramine *f*

tetranitrol *n* CHEM tétranitrol *m*

tetrapak *n* FOOD TECH carton *m*, tétrapack *m*

tetraphonic: ~ recording *n* ACOUSTICS enregistrement
tétraphonique *m*

tetrasulfide *n* (AmE), **tetrasulphide** *n* (BrE) CHEM tétra-
sulfide *m*

tetrathionic *adj* CHEM tétrathionique

tetratomicity *n* CHEM tétratomicité *f*

tetravalence *n* CHEM tétravalence *f*

tetravalency *n* CHEM tétravalence *f*

tetravalent *adj* CHEM tétravalent

tetrazene *n* CHEM tétrazène *m*

tetrazine *n* CHEM tétrazine *f*

tetrazole *n* CHEM tétrazole *m*

tetrode *n* ELECTRON, PHYS tétrode *f* ~ **transistor** *n* ELEC-
TRON transistor tétrode *m*; ~ **tube** *n* ELECTRON tube
tétrode *m*

tetrolic *adj* CHEM tétrolique

tetrose *n* CHEM tétrose *m*

tetroxide *n* CHEM tétroxyde *m*

tetryl *n* CHEM tétryl *m*

texasite *n* MINERAL texasite *f*

text *n* COMP, DP texte *m*; ~ **area** *n* PRINT zone réservée au
texte *f*; ~ **editing** *n* TELECOM contrôle des textes *m*; ~
editing function *n* DP fonction de traitement de texte *f*;
~ **editor** *n* COMP, DP, TELECOM éditeur de texte *m*; ~ **file**

n COMP, DP fichier texte *m*; ~ **formatter** *n* COMP, DP
formateur de texte *m*; ~ **greeking** *n* PRINT affichage à
l'écran du texte illisible *m*; ~ **label** *n* PRINT titre courant
m; ~ **mailbox** *n* TELECOM boîte à lettres *f*; ~ **processing**
n COMP, DP traitement de texte *m*; ~ **retrieval** *n* DP
recherche et extraction de texte *f*; ~ **stream** *n* PRINT
texte au kilomètre *m*

textile: ~ glass fiber *n* (AmE), ~ **glass fibre** *n* (BrE) C&G
fibre de verre textile *f*; ~ **labeling** *n* (AmE), ~ **labelling** *n*
(BrE) TEXTILES étiquetage textile *m*; ~ **reinforced hose**
n MECH ENG *hydraulic power* tuyau flexible à armature
textile *m*

textured: ~ carpet *n* TEXTILES tapis texturé *m*; ~ **paint** *n*
COLOURS peinture structurée *f*; ~ **vegetable protein** *n*
(TVP) FOOD TECH protéine végétale texturée *f*; ~ **yarn**
n C&G fil texturé *m*

TFA *abbr (transfer allowed)* TELECOM autorisation de
transfert *f*

TFC *abbr (controlled transfer)* TELECOM transfert sous
contrôle *m*

TFEL[1] *abbr (thin-film electroluminescence)* ELECTRON
électroluminescence à couches minces *f*

TFEL:[2] ~ **display technology** *n* ELECTRON technique d'affichage par électroluminescence à couches minces *f*,
technique des afficheurs électroluminescents à
couches minces *f*

T-flip-flop *n* ELECTRON bascule T *f*

TFP *abbr (transfer prohibited)* TELECOM transfert interdit *m*

TFR *abbr (transfer restricted)* TELECOM transfert restreint *m*

TG *abbr (transcoding gain)* TELECOM gain de transcodage *m*

TGA *abbr (thermogravimetric analyzer)* LAB EQUIP analyseur thermogravimétrique *m*

Th *(thorium)* CHEM Th *(thorium)*

thallic *adj* CHEM thallique

thallium *n (Tl)* CHEM thallium *m (Tl)*

thallous *adj* CHEM thalleux

thalweg *n* CONST, GEOL talweg *m*, thalweg *m*

thaw[1] *n* METEO dégel *m*; ~ **rigor** *n* REFRIG rigueur à la
décongélation *m*

thaw[2] *vt* FOOD TECH décongeler, METEO faire dégeler,
REFRIG décongeler, dégeler

thaw[3] *vi* FOOD TECH, METEO, REFRIG dégeler

thawing *n* REFRIG décongélation *f*; ~ **point** *n* CHEM point
de dégel *m*

T-head: ~ engine *n* AUTO moteur à soupapes bilatérales
m; ~ **valve train** *n* AUTO dispositif de commande des
soupapes latérales *m*

T-headed: ~ bolt *n* MECH ENG boulon à T *m*, boulon à
tête de marteau *m*

thebaine *n* CHEM thébaïne *f*

theft: ~ alarm installation *n* SAFETY installation d'alarme
antivol *f*; ~ **prevention device** *n* SAFETY dispositif antivol *m*

theine *n* CHEM théine *f*

thenardite *n* MINERAL thénardite *f*

theobromine *n* CHEM théobromine *f*

theodolite *n* CONST, INSTRUMENT théodolite *m*

theophylline *n* CHEM théophylline *f*

theorem *n* PHYS théorème *m*

theoretical[1] *adj* CHEM, PHYS théorique

theoretical:[2] ~ **chemistry** *n* CHEM chimie pure *f*; ~ **commercial dryness** *n* PAPER TECH *of pulp* siccité
commerciale théorique *f*; ~ **cutoff frequency** *n* ELEC-

TRON fréquence de coupure théorique *f*; ~ **density** *n* *(TD)* NUCLEAR densité théorique *f*, masse volumique théorique *f*; ~ **load value** *n* SPRINGS valeur théorique de charge *f*; ~ **solid load** *n* SPRINGS charge théorique à spires jointives *f*; ~ **work** *n* PHYS travaux théoriques *m pl*

theory *n* PHYS théorie *f*; ~ **of effective radius** *n* NUCLEAR théorie du rayon effectif *f*; ~ **of numbers** *n* MATH théorie des nombres *f*; ~ **of ordinals** *n* GEOM théorie des ordinaux *f*; ~ **of transcendental numbers** *n* MATH théorie des nombres transcendants *f*

thermal[1] *adj* PHYS, REFRIG, THERMOD thermal, thermique

thermal:[2] ~ **accommodation coefficient** *n* SPACE facteur d'accommodation thermique *m*; ~ **activation** *n* METALL activation thermique *f*; ~ **agitation** *n* ELEC ENG, METALL, PHYS agitation thermique *f*; ~ **ammeter** *n* ELEC ampèremètre thermique *m*; ~ **analysis** *n* CHEM, PROP MAT analyse thermique *f*, THERMOD analyse thermique *f*, thermoanalyse *f*; ~ **balance** *n* PROP MAT bilan thermique *m*, THERMOD bilan calorifique *m*, bilan thermique *m*; ~ **barrier** *n* C&G barrage thermique *m*, HEAT ENG, SPACE barrière thermique *f*, TRANSP mur de la chaleur *m*; ~ **battery** *n* ELEC ENG batterie thermoélectrique *f*; ~ **beam time-of-flight experiment** *n* RAD PHYS expérience de durée de trajectoire à faisceau thermique *f*; ~ **bimetallic overlay relay** *n* PROD ENG relais de protection thermique à bilames *m*; ~ **bimetallic overload relay** *n* PROD ENG relais de protection thermique à bilames *m*; ~ **blooming** *n* ELECTRON divergence thermique *f*; ~ **bonding** *n* THERMOD thermocollage *m*; ~ **breakdown** *n* ELECTRON claquage par emballement thermique *m*; ~ **bulb** *n* AUTO bulbe de détenteur *m*; ~ **capacitance** *n* FUELLESS capacitance thermique *f*; ~ **capacity** *n* HEAT ENG, THERMOD capacité thermique *f*; ~ **center** *n* (AmE), ~ **centre** *n* (BrE) REFRIG centre thermique *m*; ~ **characteristic** *n* TELECOM caractéristique thermique *f*; ~ **circuit breaker** *n* ELEC déclencheur thermique *m*, THERMOD *electricity* disjoncteur thermique *m*; ~ **column** *n* NUCLEAR colonne thermique *f*; ~ **component** *n* METALL composant thermique *m*; ~ **conductance** *n* HEAT ENG, PHYS conductance thermique *f*; ~ **conductibility** *n* THERMOD conductibilité calorifique *f*, conductibilité thermique *f*; ~ **conduction** *n* THERMOD conduction thermique *f*, transfert de chaleur *m*; ~ **conductivity** *n* CONST conductibilité thermique *f*, GAS TECH, HEAT ENG, P&R, PETR TECH, PHYS conductivité thermique *f*, THERMOD conductibilité calorifique *f*, conductibilité thermique *f*, conductivité calorifique *f*, conductivité thermique *f*; ~ **conductivity vacuum gage** *n* (AmE), ~ **conductivity vacuum gauge** *n* (BrE) REFRIG jauge thermique *f*, manomètre thermique *f*; ~ **conductor** *n* PROP MAT conducteur de chaleur *m*, conducteur thermique *m*; ~ **content** *n* THERMOD teneur calorifique *f*; ~ **contraction** *n* THERMOD *due to cold* contraction thermique *f*; ~ **control** *n* SPACE régulation thermique *f*, thermorégulation *f*; ~ **control paint** *n* COLOURS peinture thermo-chrome *f*; ~ **converter** *n* ELEC ENG convertisseur thermique *m*; ~ **converter reactor** *n* NUCLEAR réacteur convertisseur thermique *m*; ~ **cracking** *n* PETR TECH craquage thermique *m*; ~ **current** *n* METEO courant thermique *m*; ~ **cycle** *n* THERMOD cycle thermique *m*; ~ **cycling** *n* THERMOD oscillation thermique *f*; ~ **decomposition** *n* P&R, PROP MAT décomposition thermique *f*, THERMOD décomposition thermique *f*,

thermolyse *f*; ~ **delay switch** *n* CONTROL interrupteur à retard thermique *m*; ~ **diffusion** *n* THERMOD diffusion thermique *f*, thermodiffusion *f*; ~ **diffusion coefficient** *n* PHYS coefficient de diffusion thermique *m*; ~ **diffusion factor** *n* PHYS facteur de diffusion thermique *m*; ~ **diffusion process** *n* NUCLEAR procédé de diffusion thermique *m*; ~ **diffusion ratio** *n* PHYS rapport de diffusion thermique *m*; ~ **diffusivity** *n* HEAT ENG, PHYS, THERMOD diffusivité thermique *f*; ~ **diode** *n* ELECTRON caloduc *m*; ~ **discharge** *n* RECYCLING rejets thermiques *m pl*; ~ **dissociation** *n* THERMOD rendement thermique *m*; ~ **effect** *n* GAS TECH, HEAT ENG, PHYS, THERMOD effet thermique *m*; ~ **efficiency** *n* AUTO rendement thermique *m*, GAS TECH efficacité thermique *f*, HEAT ENG, PHYS, THERMOD rendement thermique *m*; ~ **electric power plant** *n* ELEC ENG centrale thermique *f*, usine thermique *f*; ~ **electric power station** *n* ELEC ENG centrale thermique *f*, usine thermique *f*; ~ **emission** *n* RAD PHYS *from incandescent solids* rayonnement thermique *m*; ~ **emissivity** *n* THERMOD émissivité thermique *f*; ~ **energy** *n* HEAT ENG, THERMOD énergie thermique *f*; ~ **energy storage system** *n* TRANSP accumulateur de chaleur *m*; ~ **engine** *n* THERMOD machine thermique *f*, moteur thermique *m*; ~ **equilibrium** *n* THERMOD équilibre thermique *m*, équilibre thermodynamique *m*; ~ **equivalent** *n* THERMOD équivalent mécanique de la chaleur *m*; ~ **etching** *n* METALL attaque thermique *f*; ~ **evaporation** *n* METALL évaporation thermique *f*; ~ **exchange** *n* GAS TECH échange thermique *m*; ~ **exhaust manifold reactor** *n* TRANSP réacteur thermique *m*; ~ **expansion** *n* P&R dilatation thermique *f*, expansion thermique *f*, PETR TECH expansion thermique *f*, PROP MAT, TELECOM, THERMOD *due to heat* dilatation thermique *f*; ~ **expansion coefficient** *n* MECH, PHYS, PROP MAT, THERMOD coefficient de dilatation thermique *m*; ~ **expansion joint** *n* THERMOD joint de dilatation thermique *m*; ~ **fatigue** *n* AERONAUT, SPACE, THERMOD *of metal* fatigue thermique *f*; ~ **fission factor** *n* PHYS facteur de fission thermique *m*; ~ **flash** *n* NUCLEAR flash thermique *m*, rayonnement thermique *m*; ~ **flow** *n* FLUID PHYS écoulement thermique *m*, PROP MAT flux thermique *m*; ~ **gradient** *n* HEATING, REFRIG, THERMOD *temperature* gradient de température *m*, gradient thermique *m*; ~ **gravimetric analysis** *n* THERMOD thermogravimétrie *f*; ~ **head** *n* THERMOD chute de potentiel thermique *f*; ~ **imager** *n* MILIT caméra thermique *f*; ~ **imaging** *n* MILIT, RAD PHYS, THERMOD thermographie *f*; ~ **imaging sight** *n* THERMOD *night sight* viseur thermoscopique *m*, viseur à imagerie thermique *m*; ~ **imaging tube** *n* ELECTRON tube analyseur infrarouge *m*; ~ **imbalance** *n* THERMOD déséquilibre thermique *m*; ~ **inertia** *n* GAS TECH, REFRIG, THERMOD *temperature lag* inertie thermique *f*; ~ **instability** *n* TELECOM, THERMOD instabilité thermique *f*; ~ **instrument** *n* INSTRUMENT instrument de mesure thermique *m*; ~ **insulation** *n* CONST isolation thermique *f*, HEAT ENG isolation thermique *f*, isolement thermique *m*, PROP MAT, RAIL isolation thermique *f*, THERMOD isolement calorifuge *m*; ~ **insulation coefficient** *n* PHYS coefficient d'isolation thermique *m*; ~ **insulation index** *n* THERMOD indice de calorifugeage *m*; ~ **jet engine** *n* AERONAUT thermopropulseur *m*; ~ **lagging** *n* THERMOD calorifugeage *m*; ~ **link** *n* THERMOD *fusible* liaison thermique *f*; ~ **load** *n* POLLUTION échauffement *m*; ~ **mass** *n* THERMOD masse thermique *f*; ~ **mixing** *n* NUCLEAR mélange thermique *m*; ~ **model** *n* SPACE *spacecraft* maquette thermique *f*; ~ **neutron** *n* NUCLEAR, PHYS, RAD PHYS *slow moving* neutron thermique *m*; ~ **neutron fission** *n* NUCLEAR fission thermique *f*; ~ **neutron nonleakage probability** *n* NUCLEAR probabilité de non-fuite d'un neutron thermique *f*; ~ **neutron yield** *n* NUCLEAR rendement des neutrons thermiques *m*; ~ **noise** *n* ELECTRON bruit thermique *m*, PHYS bruit d'agitation thermique *m*, SPACE *communications* bruit thermique *m*, souffle *m*; ~ **noise generator** *n* ELECTRON générateur de bruit thermique *m*; ~ **output** *n* MECH ENG puissance thermique *f*, THERMOD puissance thermique *f*, rendement thermique *m*; ~ **paper** *n* PRINT papier thermique *m*; ~ **pollution** *n* POLLUTION, THERMOD *of rivers* pollution thermique *f*; ~ **postcombustion** *n* TRANSP postcombustion thermique *f*; ~ **power** *n* THERMOD pouvoir calorifique *m*, puissance calorifique *f*; ~ **power plant** *n* NUCLEAR centrale thermique *f*; ~ **power station** *n* THERMOD centrale d'électricité thermique *f*, usine d'électricité thermique *f*; ~ **printer** *n* COMP imprimante thermique *f*; ~ **properties** *n pl* CONST propriétés thermiques *f pl*; ~ **property** *n* THERMOD caractéristique thermique *f*, propriété thermique *f*; ~ **protection** *n* SPACE protection thermique *f*; ~ **protection tile** *n* SPACE tuile *f*; ~ **radiation** *n* NUCLEAR flash thermique *m*, rayonnement thermique *m*, PHYS, THERMOD rayonnement thermique *m*; ~ **reactor** *n* RAD PHYS réacteur thermique *m*; ~ **reforming** *n* PETR TECH reformage thermique *m*; ~ **relay** *n* ELEC, ELEC ENG relais thermique *m*; ~ **relief** *n* PROD ENG décharge thermique *f*; ~ **resistance** *n* HEAT ENG, PHYS, THERMOD résistance thermique *f*; ~ **resistivity** *n* HEAT ENG résistivité thermique *f*, PHYS facteur d'utilisation thermique *m*; ~ **runaway** *n* ELECTRON emballement thermique *m*; ~ **screen** *n* SPACE écran thermique *m*; ~ **shield** *n* ELEC ENG, SPACE *spacecraft*, THERMOD bouclier thermique *m*; ~ **shock** *n* SPACE, THERMOD choc thermique *m*; ~ **shroud** *n* SPACE *spacecraft* bouclier thermique *m*; ~ **shutdown** *n* ELECTRON blocage thermique *m*; ~ **soaring** *n* THERMOD *of glider* vol en ascendance thermique *m*; ~ **spectrum** *n* THERMOD spectre thermique *m*; ~ **spraying** *n* COATINGS revêtement au pistolet à chaud *m*; ~ **spring** *n* HYDROL, THERMOD source thermale *f*; ~ **stability** *n* P&R stabilité thermique *f*; ~ **state equation** *n* THERMOD équation d'état thermique *f*; ~ **steam generator output** *n* NUCLEAR *of nuclear power station* puissance thermique du générateur de vapeur *f*; ~ **storage thermometer** *n* REFRIG thermomètre à stockage thermique *m*; ~ **stress** *n* PROP MAT, THERMOD contrainte thermique *f*; ~ **switch** *n* ELEC ENG thermocontact *m*; ~ **transfer** *n* GAS TECH transfert thermique *m*; ~ **transfer printer** *n* PACKAGING presse de transfert à chaud *f*; ~ **transmission** *n* HEAT ENG transmission thermique *f*; ~ **treatment** *n* PROP MAT traitement thermique *m*; ~ **tuning** *n* ELECTRON accord thermique *m*; ~ **utilization factor** *n* PHYS facteur d'utilisation thermique *m*; ~ **value** *n* THERMOD équivalent thermique *m*; ~ **water** *n* HYDROL eau thermale *f*; ~ **wrap** *n* OPT protection thermique *f*

thermalize *vt* CHEM thermaliser

thermally-induced: ~ **buoyancy** *n* POLLUTION flottation due au gradient thermique *f*

thermally-pumped: ~ **laser** *n* ELECTRON laser à pompage thermique *m*

thermic[1] *adj* THERMOD calorifique, thermique

thermic:[2] ~ **effect** *n* GAS TECH effet thermique *m*; ~

efficiency *n* GAS TECH efficacité thermique *f*; ~ **exchange** *n* GAS TECH échange thermique *m*; ~ **inertia** *n* GAS TECH inertie thermique *f*; ~ **lance** *n* THERMOD lance thermique *f*; ~ **plasma** *n* GAS TECH plasma thermique *m*; ~ **transfer** *n* GAS TECH transfert thermique *m*

thermion *n* THERMOD thermion *m*

thermionic[1] *adj* THERMOD thermionique

thermionic:[2] ~ **cathode** *n* ELEC ENG cathode à émission thermoélectrique *f*; ~ **conversion** *n* ELEC ENG, NUCLEAR conversion thermo-ionique *f*; ~ **converter** *n* ELEC ENG convertisseur thermo-ionique *m*; ~ **emission** *n* ELEC ENG, PHYS émission thermo-ionique *f*, émission thermoélectronique *f*, RAD PHYS émission thermo-ionique *f*; ~ **emission microscope** *n* INSTRUMENT microscope à émission thermoélectrique *m*; ~ **generator** *n* ELEC ENG générateur thermo-ionique *m*; ~ **rectification** *n* ELEC ENG redressement par effet thermoélectronique *m*; ~ **rectifier** *n* ELEC ENG redresseur thermo-ionique *m*; ~ **triode** *n* ELECTRON triode à cathode chaude *f*; ~ **tube** *n* ELEC tube thermo-ionique *m*, ELECTRON triode à cathode chaude *f*; ~ **valve** *n* ELEC tube thermo-ionique *m*, ELECTRON tube à cathode chaude *m*

thermistor *n* ELEC ENG résistance thermosensible *f*, thermistance *f*, PHYS, REFRIG, TELECOM thermistance *f*; ~ **bridge** *n* ELEC ENG pont de thermistances *m*; ~ **circuit** *n* PROD ENG circuit à thermistance *m*; ~ **control** *n* ELEC ENG commande par thermistances *f*; ~ **mount** *n* ELEC ENG support de thermistance *m*

thermit: ~ **welding** *n* CONST soudage aluminothermique *m*, soudage par aluminothermie *m*, RAIL soudage aluminothermique *m*

thermite *n* CHEM thermite *f*

thermoammeter *n* ELEC ampèremètre thermique *m*

thermoanalysis *n* CHEM analyse thermique *f*, THERMOD thermoanalyse *f*

thermobalance *n* CHEM thermobalance *f*

thermobank: ~ **defrosting** *n* REFRIG dégivrage par thermoaccumulateur *m*

thermobonding: ~ **fiber** *n* (AmE), ~ **fibre** *n* (BrE) TEXTILES fibre fusible *f*

thermochemical *adj* PROP MAT thermochimique

thermochemistry *n* CHEM thermochimie *f*

thermocline *n* OCEANOG thermocline *f*

thermocouple *n* ELEC *measurement* thermocouple *m*, ELEC ENG pince thermocouple *f*, LAB EQUIP *temperature measurement* thermocouple *m*, METALL couple thermoélectrique *m*, NUCLEAR, PETR TECH thermocouple *m*, PHYS couple thermoélectrique *m*, thermocouple *m*, THERMOD thermocouple *m*; ~ **converter** *n* ELEC ENG convertisseur à thermocouples *m*; ~ **expander** *n* PROD ENG unité d'extension à couple thermoélectrique *f*; ~ **input** *n* PROD ENG entrée à couple thermoélectrique *f*; ~ **instrument** *n* INSTRUMENT instrument de mesure thermoélectrique *m*; ~ **thermometer** *n* ELEC ENG thermomètre à thermocouples *m*

thermocurrent *n* NUCLEAR courant thermoélectrique *m*

thermodiffusion *n* THERMOD diffusion thermique *f*, thermodiffusion *f*

thermodynamic[1] *adj* PROP MAT, THERMOD thermodynamique

thermodynamic:[2] ~ **cycle** *n* HEATING cycle thermodynamique *m*; ~ **equation of state** *n* THERMOD équation thermodynamique d'état *f*; ~ **equilibrium** *n* SPACE *spacecraft* équilibre thermique *m*, équilibre thermodynamique *m*; **~ functions** *n pl* THERMOD fonctions thermodynamiques *f pl*; **~ laws** *n pl* THERMOD lois thermodynamiques *f pl*; **~ potential** *n* PHYS, THERMOD potentiel thermodynamique *m*; **~ probability** *n* PHYS, THERMOD probabilité thermodynamique *f*; **~ process** *n* THERMOD processus thermodynamique *m*; **~ system** *n* THERMOD système thermodynamique *m*; **~ temperature** *n* PHYS température thermodynamique *f*; **~ transformation** *n* THERMOD transformation thermodynamique *f*

thermodynamics *n* CHEM, CONST, PHYS thermodynamique *f*

thermoelastic: **~ distorsion** *n* SPACE *spacecraft* déformation thermoélastique *f*; **~ martensite** *n* METALL martensite thermoélastique *f*

thermoelectric[1] *adj* ELEC ENG, PHYS, THERMOD thermoélectrique

thermoelectric:[2] **~ conversion** *n* ELEC ENG conversion thermoélectrique *f*; **~ cooling** *n* REFRIG refroidissement thermoélectrique *m*; **~ effect** *n* ELEC *of circuit, temperature* effet thermoélectrique *m*; **~ generator** *n* ELEC ENG générateur thermoélectrique *m*; **~ power** *n* ELEC ENG, PHYS pouvoir thermoélectrique *m*

thermoelectrical *adj* ELEC ENG thermoélectrique

thermoelectricity *n* ELEC ENG, PHYS thermoélectricité *f*

thermoelectromotive: **~ force** *n* ELEC ENG force électromotrice d'origine thermique *f*

thermofixing *n* TEXTILES *in relation to dyeing* thermofixage *m*

thermoform: **~ machinery** *n* PACKAGING machine pour formage à chaud *f*

thermoforming[1] *adj* PAPER TECH thermocollable

thermoforming[2] *n* GAS TECH thermoformage *m*; **~ automatically from the reel** *n* PACKAGING thermoformage directement d'un rouleau *m*; **~ packaging system** *n* PACKAGING système d'emballage thermoformé *m*

thermograph *n* LAB EQUIP *temperature recorder* , NUCLEAR *temperature recorder*, PHYS thermographe *m*, THERMOD thermographe *m*, thermomètre enregistreur *m*

thermogravimetric: **~ analyzer** *n* *(TGA)* LAB EQUIP analyseur thermogravimétrique *m*

thermogravimetry *n* P&R thermogravimétrie *f*

thermohaline: **~ pumping** *n* OCEANOG succion thermohaline *f*

thermohygrograph *n* LAB EQUIP *temperature recorder* thermographe *m*

thermolecular *adj* CHEM trimoléculaire

thermoluminescence *n* PHYS, RAD PHYS, THERMOD thermoluminescence *f*

thermoluminescent[1] *adj* THERMOD thermoluminescent

thermoluminescent:[2] **~ dosimeter** *n* RAD PHYS dosimètre thermoluminescent *m*

thermolysis *n* THERMOD dissociation thermique *f*, thermolyse *f*

thermomagnetic *adj* THERMOD thermomagnétique

thermomagnetism *n* THERMOD thermomagnétisme *m*

thermomechanical: **~ effect** *n* THERMOD effet thermomécanique *m*; **~ pulp** *n* PAPER TECH pâte thermomécanique de copeaux *f*

thermometer *n* LAB EQUIP *instrument*, PHYS, REFRIG, THERMOD thermomètre *m*; **~ glass** *n* C&G verre pour thermomètres *m*

thermometric[1] *adj* THERMOD thermométrique

thermometric:[2] **~ depth** *n* OCEANOG profondeur thermométrique *f*

thermometry *n* PHYS, THERMOD thermométrie *f*

thermonatrite *n* MINERAL thermonatrite *f*

thermoneutrality *n* CHEM thermoneutralité *f*

thermonuclear: **~ combustion wave** *n* NUCLEAR onde de combustion thermonucléaire *f*; **~ power generation** *n* NUCLEAR production d'énergie par réaction thermonucléaire *f*; **~ reaction** *n* ASTRON, NUCLEAR, PHYS réaction thermonucléaire *f*

thermophone *n* ACOUSTICS thermophone *f*

thermophosphorescence *n* THERMOD thermoluminescence *f*

thermopile *n* ELEC ENG pile thermoélectrique *f*, thermopile *f*, PHYS, SPACE thermopile *f*

thermoplastic[1] *adj* MECH *materials*, NAUT *polyester construction*, P&R *plastics, rubbers, polymers*, PROP MAT, TEXTILES thermoplastique

thermoplastic[2] *n* NAUT *polyester construction* thermoplastique *m*; **~ components** *n pl* MECH ENG pièces composantes thermoplastiques *f pl*; **~ mold** *n* (AmE), **~ mould** *n* (BrE) MECH ENG moule pour thermoplastiques *m*; **~ position switch** *n* PROD ENG interrupteur de position avec boîtier thermoplastique *m*; **~ rubber** *n* P&R caoutchouc thermoplastique *m*

thermoplasticity *n* P&R thermoplasticité *f*

thermoregulator *n* CONTROL régulateur de température *m*, thermostat *m*

thermosealing *n* PRINT thermosoudage *m*

thermoset *adj* P&R *plastics, polymers* thermodurci

thermosetting[1] *adj* CHEM, MECH *materials*, P&R, THERMOD thermodurcissable

thermosetting:[2] **~ ink** *n* PRINT encre fixée à chaud *f*; **~ mold** *n* (AmE), **~ mould** *n* (BrE) MECH ENG moule pour thermoplastiques *m*

thermosiphon *n* FUELLESS thermosiphon *m*

thermosphere *n* GEOPHYS thermosphère *f*

thermostability *n* PROP MAT thermostabilité *f*

thermostable *adj* CHEM thermostable, PETR TECH thermorésistant, THERMOD thermostable

thermostat *n* AUTO, CONST, CONTROL, ELEC, HEATING, LAB EQUIP *temperature regulator*, PHYS, REFRIG, THERMOD, VEHICLES *cooling system* thermostat *m*; **~ control** *n* HEATING thermorégulation *f*; **~ well** *n* PROD ENG douille de protection pour sonde *f*

thermostatic[1] *adj* CONTROL, REFRIG, THERMOD thermostatique

thermostatic:[2] **~ element** *n* REFRIG élément thermostatique *m*; **~ expansion valve** *n* REFRIG détendeur thermostatique *m*; **~ valve** *n* MECH ENG vanne thermostatique *f*

thermostatically-controlled: **~ bath** *n* LAB EQUIP bain thermostaté *m*; **~ developing dish** *n* PHOTO cuvette de développement à thermostat *f*, cuvette à température constante *f*; **~ valve** *n* PROD ENG régulateur à commande thermostatique *m*, REFRIG vanne à commande thermostatique *f*

thermostatics *n* THERMOD thermostatique *f*

thermosteric: **~ anomaly** *n* OCEANOG anomalie thermostérique *f*

thermowell *n* PETR TECH puits thermométrique *m*

thesaurus *n* COMP, DP thesaurus *m*

Thévenin's: **~ theorem** *n* PHYS théorème de Thévenin *m*

thevetin *n* CHEM thévétine *f*

thial *n* CHEM thial *m*, thioaldéhyde *m*

thialdine *n* CHEM thialdine *f*

thiation *n* CHEM sulfuration *f*

thiazine *n* CHEM thiazine *f*

thiazole *n* CHEM thiazole *m*

thiazoline *n* CHEM thiazoline *f*

thick[1] *adj* CHEM *solution* féculent, visqueux, PAPER TECH épais

thick:[2] ~ **film** *n* ELECTRON couche épaisse *f*; ~ **oxide** *n* ELECTRON oxyde secondaire *m*; ~ **oxide metal gate MOS circuit** *n* ELECTRON circuit MOS à grille métallique et oxyde secondaire *m*; ~ **polished plate glass** *n* C&G dalle polie *f*; ~ **roughcast plate glass** *n* C&G dalle brute *f*; ~ **sheet glass** *n* (BrE) *(cf crystal sheet glass)* C&G verre épais *m*; ~ **space** *n* PRINT espace fort *m*; ~ **ware** *n* C&G grosse céramique *f*

thick-and-thin: ~ **yarn** *n* TEXTILES fil flammé *m*

thick-bedded *adj* GEOL à lits épais

thicken[1] *vt* CHEM TECH coaguler, épaissir; ~ **by boiling** *vt* CHEM TECH réduire par ébullition

thicken[2] *vi* CHEM TECH s'épaissir

thickened: ~ **slime** *n* COAL TECH schlamms épais *m*; ~ **slurry** *n* COAL TECH schlamms épais *m*

thickener *n* CHEM épaississeur *m*, CHEM TECH matière épaississante *f*, épaississeur *m*, COAL TECH épaississeur *m*, FOOD TECH épaississant *m*, épaississeur *m*, P&R *additive* épaississant *m*, PAPER TECH épaississeur *m*; ~ **drum** *n* CHEM TECH tambour épaississeur *m*; ~ **tank** *n* CHEM TECH épaississeur *m*

thickening *n* C&G refoulement en bourrelet *m*, COAL TECH épaississage *m*, FOOD TECH épaississant *m*, épaississement *m*; ~ **agent** *n* CHEM épaississeur *m*, DETERGENTS, FOOD TECH épaississant *m*; ~ **cone** *n* COAL TECH cône épaississeur *m*

thick-film: ~ **capacitor** *n* ELECTRON condensateur à couche épaisse *m*; ~ **conductor** *n* ELECTRON conducteur en couche épaisse *m*; ~ **device** *n* ELECTRON composant à couches épaisses *m*; ~ **electroluminescent display** *n* ELECTRON affichage par électroluminescence en couches épaisses *m*, afficheur électroluminescent à couches épaisses *m*; ~ **hybrid circuit** *n* ELECTRON circuit hybride à couches épaisses *m*; ~ **hybrid circuit substrate** *n* ELECTRON substrat de circuit hybride à couches épaisses *m*; ~ **material** *n* ELECTRON matériau pour couches épaisses *m*; ~ **resistor** *n* ELECTRON résistance à couche épaisse *f*; ~ **technology** *n* ELECTRON technique des couches épaisses *f*, SPACE *spacecraft* technologie des couches épaisses *f*

thick-layer: ~ **integrated circuit** *n* TELECOM circuit intégré à couche épaisse *m*

thickness *n* C&G épaisseur *f*, CHEM féculence *f*, viscosité *f*, MECH, P&R, PAPER TECH épaisseur *f*; ~ **calender** *n* PAPER TECH laminoir *m*; ~ **gage** *n* (AmE), ~ **gauge** *n* (BrE) C&G clé d'épaisseur *f*, LAB EQUIP, MECH *tools* jauge d'épaisseur *f*, MECH ENG calibre à lames *m*, jauge d'épaisseur *f*, PAPER TECH micromètre d'épaisseur *m*; ~ **of lines** *n* METR *on scale* épaisseur des traits *f*; ~ **of lining** *n* MECH ENG épaisseur de garniture *f*; ~ **loss** *n* TV perte par épaisseur de couche magnétique *f*; ~ **margin** *n* MECH ENG tolérance sur l'épaisseur *f*

thickness-chord: ~ **ratio** *n* AERONAUT *of aerofoil section* épaisseur relative *f*

thicknessing *n* MECH ENG mise d'épaisseur *f*, tirage d'épaisseur *m*

thick-seam: ~ **winning** *n* COAL TECH exploitation par grandes tailles *f*

thief: ~ **formation** *n* PETR formation absorbante *f*

thief-proof *adj* SAFETY antivol

Thiele: ~ **tube** *n* LAB EQUIP *melting point* tube de Thièle *m*

thimble *n* C&G guinand *m*, NAUT *fittings* cosse *f*, NUCLEAR chaussette *f*, doigt de gaut *m*, PROD ENG *boiler tube ferrule* bague *f*, virole *f*, *rope eyelet* cosse *f*

thin[1] *adj* PROD ENG faible, fin, mince, ténu

thin:[2] ~ **film** *n* ELECTRON couche mince *f*; ~ **lens** *n* PHYS lentille mince *f*; ~ **negative** *n* CINEMAT négatif sous-exposé *m*; ~ **paper** *n* PRINT papier léger *m*; ~ **print** *n* CINEMAT copie trop claire *f*; ~ **section** *n* CRYSTALL lame mince *f*; ~ **sheet glass** *n* C&G verre mince *m*; ~ **source** *n* NUCLEAR source mince *f*; ~ **space** *n* PRINT *typesetting* espace fin *m*; ~ **stock** *n* PAPER TECH pâte maigre *f*; ~ **taper key** *n* MECH ENG clavette inclinée mince *f*; ~ **ware** *n* C&G clairières *f pl*

thin[3] *vt* PROD ENG alléger, amaigrir, amenuiser, diminuer, réduire; ~ **down** *vt* PROD ENG *board* alléger, amenuiser, amincir, *plate* amincir; ~ **out** *vt* PROD ENG alléger, amaigrir, amenuiser, amincir, diminuer, réduire

thin-bedded *adj* GEOL finement stratifié, à lits minces

thindown *n* NUCLEAR dégradation *f*, perte *f*

thin-edged: ~ **weir** *n* HYDR EQUIP déversoir à arête vive *m*, déversoir à crête mince *m*, déversoir à paroi mince *m*

thin-film: ~ **capacitor** *n* ELEC condensateur à couches minces *m*; ~ **conductor** *n* ELECTRON conducteur en couches minces *m*; ~ **device** *n* ELECTRON composant à couches minces *m*; ~ **electroluminescence** *n* *(TFEL)* ELECTRON électroluminescence à couches minces *f*; ~ **hybrid circuit** *n* ELECTRON circuit hybride à couches minces *m*; ~ **hybrid circuit substrate** *n* ELECTRON substrat de circuit hybride à couches minces *m*; ~ **material** *n* ELECTRON matériau pour couches minces *m*; ~ **memory** *n* COMP, DP mémoire à couches minces *f*; ~ **optical waveguide** *n* OPT guide d'ondes optiques en couches minces *m*; ~ **resistor** *n* ELECTRON résistance à couches minces *f*; ~ **technology** *n* ELECTRON technique des couches minces *f*; ~ **transistor** *n* ELECTRON transistor à couches minces *m*; ~ **waveguide** *n* TELECOM guide d'ondes en couches minces *m*

T-hinge *n* CONST penture à T *f*

thin-layer: ~ **capacitor** *n* TELECOM condensateur à couches minces *m*; ~ **chromatography** *n* CHEM *(TLC) analysis* chromatographie sur couches minces *f*, LAB EQUIP *analysis* chromatographie à couches minces *f*

thinly-bedded *adj* GEOL finement stratifié

thinner *n* CHEM, COLOURS diluant *m*

thinners *n pl* PETR fluidifiants *m pl*

thinness *n* PROD ENG faible épaisseur *f*, finesse *f*, minceur *f*, ténuité *f*

thinning *n* CHEM dilution *f*, GEOL *of crust* amincissement *m*, PROD ENG amaigrissement *m*, amenuisement *m*, amincissement *m*; ~ **down** *n* PROD ENG amaigrissement *m*, amenuisement *m*, amincissement *m*; ~ **out** *n* PROD ENG amaigrissement *m*, amenuisement *m*, amincissement *m*

thin-ring: ~ **bearing** *n* MECH ENG roulement à anneau mince *m*

thin-spot: ~ **detector** *n* C&G détecteur de minces *m*

thin-walled[1] *adj* MECH ENG à parois minces

thin-walled:[2] ~ **cylinder** *n* MECH ENG cylindre à parois minces *m*; ~ **half-bearing** *n* MECH ENG demi-coussinet mince *m*; ~ **spherical shell** *n* MECH ENG coquille sphérique avec parois minces *f*

thio- *pref* CHEM thio-

thioacetic *adj* CHEM thioacétique

thioacid *n* CHEM sulfacide *m*, thioacide *m*

thioalcohol n CHEM mercaptan m, thioalcool m, thiol m
thioaldehyde n CHEM thial m, thioaldéhyde m
thioamide n CHEM thioamide m
thioarsenic adj CHEM sulfarsénique
thiocarbamide n CHEM thio-urée f, thiocarbamide f
thiocarbanilide n CHEM thiocarbanilide m
thiocarbonate n CHEM sulfocarbonate m, thiocarbonate m
thiocarbonic adj CHEM thiocarbonique
thiocyanate n CHEM sulfocyanate m, thiocyanate m
thiocyanic adj CHEM sulfocyanique, thiocyanique
thiodiphenylamine n CHEM thiodiphénylamine f
thioether n CHEM thioéther m
thioflavin n CHEM thioflavine f
thioglycolic adj CHEM thioglycolique
thioindamine n CHEM thiazine f, thio-indamine f
thioindigo n CHEM thio-indigo m
thioketone n CHEM thiocétone f
thiol n CHEM mercaptan m, thioalcool m, thiol m, FOOD TECH thioalcool m
thiolate n CHEM thiolate m
thionaphthene n CHEM thionaphtène m
thionate n CHEM thionate m
thionation n CHEM thionation f
thione n CHEM thiocétone f, thione m
thioneine n CHEM thionéine f
thionic adj CHEM soufré, thionique
thionine n CHEM thionine f
thionyl n CHEM thionyle m
thiopental n CHEM pentoxyde m, thiopental m
thiophene n CHEM thiofène m, thiophène m
thiophenol n CHEM phénylmercaptan m, thiophénol m
thiophosgene n CHEM thiophosgène m
thioplast n CHEM thiogomme f
thiosulfate n (AmE) see thiosulphate
thiosulfuric adj (AmE) see thiosulphuric
thiosulphate n (BrE) CHEM hyposulfite m, thiosulfate m
thiosulphuric adj (BrE) CHEM hyposulfureux, thiosulfurique
thiourea n CHEM thio-urée f
thioxanthone n CHEM thioxanthone m
thioxene n CHEM thioxène m
thiozene n CHEM ergothionéine f
third n ACOUSTICS tierce f, MATH troisième m ~ **deck** n NAUT ship design deuxième faux pont m; ~ **firing** n C&G troisième cuisson m; ~ **gear** n AUTO pignon de troisième vitesse m; ~ **generation** n COMP, DP troisième génération f; ~ **harmonic** n ELECTRON harmonique 3 m, troisième harmonique f; ~ **harmonic distortion** n ELECTRON distorsion par harmonique trois f; ~ **law of thermodynamics** n PHYS troisième principe de la thermodynamique m; ~ **party** n PATENTS tiers m; ~ **quarter** n ASTRON dernier quartier m; ~ **rail** n RAIL troisième rail m, TRANSP rail conducteur m; ~ **tap** n MECH ENG taraud cylindrique m, taraud finisseur m, troisième taraud m; ~ **wire system** n ELEC système à trois fils m
third-generation: ~ **computer** n COMP, DP ordinateur de troisième génération m
third-motion: ~ **shaft** n AUTO arbre secondaire m
third-order: ~ **active filter** n ELECTRON filtre actif du troisième ordre m; ~ **bandstop filter** n ELECTRON filtre coupe-bande du troisième ordre m; ~ **filter** n ELECTRON filtre d'ordre 3 m, filtre du troisième ordre m
third-party: ~ **warning tone** n TELECOM tonalité d'entrée d'un tiers f
thirsty adj PROP MAT avide d'eau

thirty-sixmo n PRINT in-trente-six m
thistle: ~ **funnel** n LAB EQUIP glassware entonnoir à tige m
thixotropic adj CHEM thixotrope, thixotropique, P&R, PHYS thixotrope
thixotropy n CHEM, COAL TECH, PETR, PHYS thixotropie f
tholoid: ~ **dome** n GEOL cumulo-dôme m, tholoïde m
thomsenolite n MINERAL thomsénolite f
Thomson: ~ **bridge** n ELEC pont de Thomson m; ~ **coefficient** n PHYS coefficient de Thomson m; ~ **cross-section** n PHYS section efficace de Thomson f; ~ **effect** n PHYS effet Thomson m; ~ **scattering** n PHYS diffusion de Thomson f
thomsonite n MINERAL thomsonite f
thoria n CHEM thorine f
thorianite n MINERAL thorianite f
thoriated: ~ **tungsten filament** n ELEC ENG cathode en tungstène thorié f
thoric adj CHEM thorique
thorite n MINERAL thorite f
thorium n (Th) CHEM thorium m (Th); ~ **fueled reactor** n (AmE), ~ **fuelled reactor** n (BrE) NUCLEAR réacteur à thorium m; ~ **series** n RAD PHYS famille du thorium f
thoroughfare n CONST passage m, voie f; ~ **hole** n CONST trou percé de part en part m, trou traversant la pièce de part en part m
thrasher n PAPER TECH batteur de feutre m
thrashing n COMP, DP emballement m
thread[1] n C&G filet m (Bel), fin m (Fra), MECH filet m, filetage m, MECH ENG filetage m, of nut filet m, worm projecting helical rib of screw filet m, pas m, MINING of ore filet m, veinule f, PAPER TECH fil m, PRINT fil m, filet m, PROD ENG filetage m, TEXTILES fil m; ~ **chaser** n MECH ENG peigne à fileter m; ~ **counter** n PAPER TECH compte-fils m; ~ **gage** n (AmE), ~ **gauge** n (BrE) MECH ENG calibre de vérification des vis m; ~ **grinding** n MECH ENG rectification des filetages f; ~ **insert** n MECH ENG douille filetée f; ~ **lead angle** n MECH ENG angle de pas de filet m; ~ **microscope** n INSTRUMENT microscope à fil m; ~ **milling cutter** n MECH ENG fraise à fileter f; ~ **pitch** n MECH ENG, VEHICLES pas de filetage m; ~ **pitch gage** n (AmE), ~ **pitch gauge** n (BrE) MECH ENG tool jauge de filetage f; ~ **restorer** n MECH ENG tool outil à restaurer les filets m; ~ **run-outs for fasteners** n pl MECH ENG filets incomplets pour éléments de fixation m pl; ~ **speed** n PROD ENG petite vitesse f; ~ **undercuts** n pl MECH ENG gorges de dégagement f pl
thread[2] vt CINEMAT, RECORDING machine with tape charger
thread[3] vi MECH ENG se visser, PRINT tape engager la bande, PROD ENG se visser
threadbare adj TEXTILES élimé
threaded[1] adj MECH fileté
threaded:[2] ~ **bolt** n VEHICLES boulon fileté m; ~ **bush** n MECH ENG bague filetée de guidage f; ~ **component** n MECH ENG composant fileté m; ~ **fastener** n MECH article de boulonnerie m, MECH ENG élément de fixation fileté m; ~ **fitting** n MECH ENG of pipe raccord fileté m; ~ **hole** n NUCLEAR in reactor pressure vessel trou taraudé m; ~ **joint** n NUCLEAR joint fileté m, raccord à vis m; ~ **nut** n MECH ENG écrou fileté m; ~ **plug end** n SPRINGS of spring coil attache à élément fileté f; ~ **tip** n SPRINGS embout fileté vissé m
threader n MECH ENG taraudeuse f
threading n MECH ENG filetage m; ~ **of paper** n PAPER TECH into machine engagement du papier m; ~ **path** n

CINEMAT parcours *m*; ~ **ring** *n* TELECOM tore *m*; ~ **slot** *n* CINEMAT fente de chargement *f*; ~ **tool** *n* MECH ENG *lathe* outil à fileter *m*

threading-in *n* PRINT *of tape into machine* engagement *m*

threat *n* COMP, DP menace *f*

three-address: ~ **instruction** *n* COMP, DP instruction à trois adresses *f*

three-axis: ~ **data generator** *n* *(TADG)* SPACE centrale de référence de direction et d'attitude *f*; ~ **gyro unit** *n* SPACE bloc de mesure gyrométrique tri-axiale *m*; ~ **indicator** *n* SPACE indicateur trois axes *m*; ~ **stabilization** *n* SPACE stabilisation sur trois axes *f*

three-beam: ~ **color picture tube** *n* (AmE), ~ **colour picture tube** *n* (BrE) ELECTRON tube-image couleur à trois faisceaux *m*

three-body: ~ **problem** *n* ASTRON problème des trois corps *m*

three-button: ~ **mouse** *n* COMP, DP souris à trois boutons *f*

three-cavity: ~ **klystron** *n* ELECTRON klystron à trois cavités *m*

three-centered: ~ **arch** *n* (AmE), **three-centred arch** *n* (BrE) CONST *curve* arc à trois centres *m*, *structure* voûte à trois centres *f*

three-circuit: ~ **nuclear power plant** *n* NUCLEAR centrale nucléaire à trois circuits *f*

three-color (AmE), **three-colour** (BrE): ~ **black** *n* PRINT noir de la trichromie *m*; ~ **map problem** *n* GEOM problème des cartes trichromatiques *m*; ~ **photography** *n* PHOTO photographie trichrome *f*; ~ **plate** *n* PHOTO plaque trichrome *f*; ~ **printing** *n* PRINT trichromie *f*; ~ **process** *n* CINEMAT procédé trichrome *m*

three-component: ~ **alloy** *n* METALL *ternary alloy* alliage ternaire *m*

three-conductor: ~ **cable** *n* ELEC ENG câble à trois conducteurs *m*

three-cone: ~ **bit** *n* PETR TECH trépan tricône *m*

three-cylinder: ~ **engine** *n* MECH ENG machine à trois cylindres *f*

three-D: ~ **log** *n* PETR diagraphie de densité variable *f*

three-dimensional[1] *adj* PHYS tridimensionnel, PROP MAT à trois dimensions; ~ **form working** *adj* MECH ENG travaillant avec formes tridimensionnelles

three-dimensional:[2] ~ **graphics** *n pl* DP graphique tridimensionnel *m*; ~ **image** *n* TELECOM image à trois dimensions *f*; ~ **integrated circuit** *n* ELECTRON circuit intégré tridimensionnel *m*; ~ **integration** *n* ELECTRON intégration tridimensionnelle *f*; ~ **machining** *n* MECH ENG usinage tridimensionnel *m*; ~ **manifold** *n* GEOM variété à trois dimensions *f*

three-electrode: ~ **tube** *n* ELECTRON tube à trois électrodes *m*

three-emulsion: ~ **film** *n* CINEMAT pellicule tripack *f*

three-fold: ~ **rotation axis** *n* CRYSTALL axe d'ordre trois *m*, axe ternaire *m*

three-grid: ~ **tube** *n* ELECTRON tube à trois grilles *m*

three-gun: ~ **color picture tube** *n* (AmE), ~ **colour picture tube** *n* (BrE) ELECTRON tube-image couleur à trois canons *m*

three-head: ~ **battery** *n* MINING batterie de trois pilons *f*, bocard à 3 pilons *m*

three-high: ~ **mill** *n* MECH ENG laminoir trio *m*, train trio *m*, trio *m*; ~ **rolls** *n pl* MECH ENG laminoir trio *m*, train trio *m*, trio *m*; ~ **train** *n* MECH ENG laminoir trio *m*, train trio *m*, trio *m*

three-hole: ~ **torus** *n* GEOM tore à trois trous *m*

three-in-one: ~ **stereo component system** *n* RECORDING chaîne compacte *f*

three-input: ~ **gate** *n* ELECTRON porte à trois entrées *f*; ~ **NAND gate** *n* ELECTRON porte NON-ET à trois entrées *f*

three-jaw: ~ **chuck** *n* MECH ENG mandrin à trois mâchoires *m*; ~ **concentric gripping chuck** *n* MECH ENG plateau à serrage concentrique à trois mors *m*, plateau à trois griffes concentriques *m*; ~ **steady** *n* MECH ENG *of lathe* lunette à trois touches réglables *f*; ~ **steady rest** *n* MECH ENG *of lathe* lunette à trois touches réglables *f*

three-layer: ~ **board** *n* PAPER TECH carton trois couches *m*; ~ **paper** *n* PAPER TECH papier trois couches *m*

three-leaf: ~ **spring** *n* SPRINGS ressort trilame *m*

three-lens: ~ **turret** *n* CINEMAT tourelle à trois objectifs *f*

three-level: ~ **laser** *n* ELECTRON laser à trois niveaux *m*; ~ **maser** *n* ELECTRON maser à trois niveaux *m*; ~ **signal** *n* ELECTRON signal à trois niveaux *m*

three-lift: ~ **cone pulley** *n* MECH ENG cône à trois gradins *m*, cône-poulie à trois étages *m*

three-month: ~ **characteristic flow rate** *n* HYDROL débit caractéristique de 3 mois *m*

three-necked: ~ **flask** *n* LAB EQUIP *glassware* ballon tricol *m*

three-part: ~ **flask** *n* PROD ENG *drag, cheek, cope* châssis à trois parties *m*; ~ **two-stroke engine** *n* AUTO moteur deux temps à trois lumières *m*

three-parted: ~ **box** *n* PROD ENG châssis à trois parties *m*

three-phase[1] *adj* ELEC *supply network* triphasé, ELEC ENG triphasé, à trois phases, PHYS triphasé

three-phase:[2] ~ **alternator** *n* ELEC *generator* alternateur à courant triphasé *m*; ~ **alternomotor** *n* TRANSP moteur triphasé *m*; ~ **balanced condition** *n* PROD ENG fonctionnement équilibré triphasé *m*; ~ **circuit** *n* TELECOM circuit triphasé *m*; ~ **current** *n* ELEC ENG courant triphasé *m*; ~ **current armature** *n* ELEC *of generator, motor* induit à courant triphasé *m*; ~ **earthing transformer** *n* (BrE) *(cf three-phase grounding transformer)* ELEC transformateur triphasé de mise à la terre *m*; ~ **four-wire system** *n* ELEC système triphasé à quatre fils *m*; ~ **generator** *n* ELEC générateur triphasé *m*; ~ **grounding transformer** *n* (AmE) *(cf three-phase earthing transformer)* ELEC transformateur triphasé de mise à la terre *m*; ~ **induction motor** *n* ELEC ENG moteur asynchrone triphasé *m*, TRANSP moteur triphasé *m*; ~ **machine** *n* ELEC ENG machine triphasée *f*; ~ **motor** *n* ELEC, ELEC ENG, PROD ENG moteur triphasé *m*; ~ **neutral reactor** *n* ELEC bobine d'inductance triphasée de mise à la terre *f*; ~ **rotor** *n* ELEC ENG rotor triphasé *m*; ~ **rotor winding** *n* ELEC ENG bobinage rotorique triphasé *m*; ~ **stator** *n* ELEC ENG stator triphasé *m*; ~ **stator winding** *n* ELEC ENG bobinage statorique triphasé *m*; ~ **stepper motor** *n* ELEC ENG moteur pas-à-pas à trois phases *m*; ~ **supply** *n* ELEC ENG alimentation triphasée *f*; ~ **supply network** *n* ELEC réseau triphasé *m*; ~ **synchronous motor** *n* ELEC ENG moteur synchrone triphasé *m*; ~ **system** *n* ELEC ENG réseau triphasé *m*; ~ **transformer** *n* ELEC transformateur triphasé *m*

three-piece: ~ **oil control ring** *n* AUTO segment racleur à trois pièces *m*; ~ **timber set** *n* MINING cadre ordinaire *m*

three-pin: ~ **socket** *n* ELEC *connection* prise tripolaire *f*

three-ply: ~ **wood** *n* CONST bois plaqué triplé *m*

three-point: ~ **bending** *n* METALL flexion en trois points *f*; ~ **bending specimen** *n* NUCLEAR éprouvette à fléchir à trois points *f*; ~ **landing** *n* AERONAUT atterrissage à trois points *m*; ~ **seat belt** *n* TRANSP ceinture de sécurité à trois points *f*; ~ **snap gage** *n* (AmE), ~ **snap gauge** *n* MECH ENG calibre-mâchoires à 3 points *m*; ~ **switch** *n* ELEC commutateur d'escalier *m*

three-pole: ~ **filter** *n* ELECTRON filtre à trois pôles *m*; ~ **switch** *n* ELEC ENG interrupteur tripolaire *m*

three-position: ~ **switch** *n* ELEC commutateur d'escalier *m*

three-pronged: ~ **chuck** *n* MECH ENG griffe *f*, mandrin à trois pointes *m*, mandrin à tulipe *m*

three-quarter: ~ **tone** *n* PRINT trame à 75% *f*

three-sheave: ~ **block** *n* MECH ENG moufle à trois poulies *m*, poulie triple *f*

three-sided: ~ **cutting machine** *n* PRINT massicot trilame *m*

three-slot: ~ **winding** *n* ELEC enroulement à trois rainures *m*

three-square: ~ **file** *n* MECH ENG lime tiers-point *f*, lime triangulaire *f*, lime trois-quarts *f*, tiers-point *m*, trois-carrés *m*, trois-quarts *m*

three-stage: ~ **amplifier** *n* ELECTRON amplificateur à trois étages *m*

three-stamp: ~ **mill** *n* MINING batterie de trois pilons *f*, bocard à 3 pilons *m*

three-state: ~ **gate** *n* ELECTRON porte à trois états *f*; ~ **logic** *n* ELECTRON logique à trois états *f*; ~ **output** *n* ELECTRON sortie à trois états *f*

three-step: ~ **cone pulley** *n* MECH ENG cône à trois gradins *m*, cône-poulie à trois étages *m*; ~ **relay** *n* ELEC relais à trois positions *m*

three-stranded: ~ **line** *n* NAUT cordage à quatre torons *m*

three-strip: ~ **camera** *n* CINEMAT caméra à trois bandes *f*; ~ **negative** *n* CINEMAT négatif à trois bandes *m*

three-threaded: ~ **screw** *n* MECH ENG vis à trois filets *f*

three-throw: ~ **crank** *n* MECH ENG manivelle triple *f*; ~ **crank shaft** *n* MECH ENG arbre à trois manivelles *m*; ~ **pump** *n* WATER SUPP pompe à trois corps *f*

three-to-em: ~ **space** *n* PRINT *typesetting* espace fort *m*

three-track: ~ **stereo** *n* RECORDING son stéréophonique à trois pistes *m*

three-tube: ~ **camera** *n* TV caméra tritube *f*

three-way[1] *adj* MECH à trois voies

three-way:[2] ~ **call** *n* TELECOM appel à trois *m*; ~ **cock** *n* CONST robinet à trois eaux *m*, robinet à trois voies *m*; ~ **conversation** *n* TELECOM conversation à trois *f*; ~ **process** *n* PRINT sélection indirecte *f*; ~ **switch** *n* ELEC commutateur d'escalier *m*, commutateur à trois positions *m*; ~ **system** *n* RECORDING *of loudspeaker* système à trois voies *m*; ~ **valve** *n* HYDR EQUIP distributeur à trois voies *m*, robinet à trois voies *m*

three-wheel: ~ **tube cutter** *n* MECH ENG coupe-tubes à trois molettes *m*

three-winding: ~ **transformer** *n* ELEC ENG transformateur à trois enroulements *m*

three-wire: ~ **current** *n* (AmE) *(cf three-wire mains)* ELEC ENG réseau à trois fils *m*; ~ **generator** *n* ELEC générateur à trois fils *m*; ~ **mains** *n pl* (BrE) *(cf three-wire current)* ELEC ENG réseau à trois fils *m*; ~ **system** *n* ELEC ENG système à trois fils *m*

three-zeros: ~ **anti-aliasing filter** *n* ELECTRON filtre anti-repliement de spectre à trois zéros *m*; ~ **filter** *n* ELECTRON filtre à trois zéros *m*

threose *n* CHEM thréose *m*

threshold[1] *n* ACOUSTICS, COMP, CONST *of door*, DP, ELECTRON seuil *m*, PHYS *of hearing* seuil *m*, *of pain* seuil de douleur *m*, SPACE seuil *m*; ~ **of audibility** *n* POLLUTION seuil d'audition *m*; ~ **audiometry** *n* SAFETY audiométrie liminaire *f*; ~ **current** *n* ELEC ENG, OPT *of laser diode*, RAD PHYS, TELECOM courant de seuil *m*; ~ **energy** *n* METALL énergie de seuil *f*; ~ **extension demodulator** *n* SPACE *communications*, TELECOM démodulateur à seuil amélioré *m*; ~ **frequency** *n* ELECTRON, PHYS, WAVE PHYS *of released electron* fréquence de seuil *f*; ~ **gate** *n* ELECTRON porte à seuil *f*; ~ **level** *n* PROD ENG seuil prédéterminé *m*; ~ **limit value** *n* *(TLV)* POLLUTION concentration maximale admissible *f*; ~ **limit value in the free environment** *n* POLLUTION concentration maximale admissible dans l'air ambiant *f*; ~ **operation** *n* COMP, DP opération de seuil *f*; ~ **signal** *n* ELECTRON signal minimal utilisable *m*; ~ **value** *n* ELECTRON valeur de seuil *f*; ~ **voltage** *n* ELEC ENG, TV tension de seuil *f*; ~ **wavelength** *n* ELECTRON longueur d'onde de seuil *f*

threshold[2] *vt* SPACE seuiller

thresholding *n* ELECTRON fixation d'un seuil *f*, SPACE seuillage *m*

throat *n* ACOUSTICS, C&G gorge *f*, CONST *of plane* lumière *f*, PROD ENG *of blast furnace* gueulard *m*, SPACE *nozzle of spacecraft* col *m*; ~ **cheek** *n* C&G longeron *m*; ~ **cover** *n* C&G ciel de gorge *m*; ~ **microphone** *n* ACOUSTICS, RECORDING laryngophone *m*

throttle[1] *n* AERONAUT *of aircraft* manette de gaz *f*, HYDR EQUIP modérateur *m*, registre de vapeur *m*, robinet de freinage *m*, régulateur *m*, étrangleur *m*, VEHICLES *of carburettor* papillon *m*, étrangleur *m*, SPACE *spacecraft* manette de gaz *f*; ~ **control lever** *n* AUTO levier de commande de papillons *m*; ~ **control rod** *n* AUTO tige de commande des gaz *f*; ~ **dashpot** *n* VEHICLES *of carburettor* amortisseur du papillon *m*; ~ **lever** *n* HYDR EQUIP levier de régulateur *m*; ~ **linkage** *n* VEHICLES *of carburettor* timonerie du papillon *f*; ~ **pintle nozzle** *n* AUTO injecteur à étranglement *m*; ~ **plate** *n* AUTO papillon de réglage *m*; ~ **pressure boost valve** *n* AUTO soupape d'amplification de pression de l'accélérateur *f*; ~ **reach rod** *n* HYDR EQUIP tringle de manoeuvre de régulateur *f*; ~ **rod** *n* HYDR EQUIP tringle de manoeuvre de régulateur *f*; ~ **slide** *n* VEHICLES *of carburettor* tiroir d'étranglement *m*; ~ **stem** *n* HYDR EQUIP tringle de manoeuvre de régulateur *f*; ~ **stop screw** *n* VEHICLES *of carburettor* vis du butée du papillon *f*; ~ **valve** *n* AUTO papillon des gaz *m*, COAL TECH vanne d'étranglement *f*, HYDR EQUIP papillon *m*, robinet de freinage *m*, vanne papillon *f*, MECH ENG soupape d'étranglement *f*, MINING soupape *f*, PROD ENG réducteur de débit *m*; ~ **valve switch** *n* AUTO contacteur de papillon d'air *m*

throttle:[2] ~ **back** *vi* AERONAUT réduire les gaz

throttling *n* MECH ENG serrage *m*, étranglement *m*, RAIL *vehicles, of steam* laminage de la vapeur *m*; ~ **device** *n* REFRIG obturateur *m*

through:[1] ~ **hardened** *adj* SPRINGS trempé à coeur

through:[2] ~ **band** *n* TRANSP *traffic control* bande de passage *f*; ~ **bolt** *n* CONST *building* cheville antiexpansion *f*, MECH ENG boulon libre *m*; ~ **bridge** *n* CONST pont à tablier inférieur *m*; ~ **hardening** *n* SPRINGS trempage à coeur *m*, trempe à coeur *f*; ~ **hardness** *n* SPRINGS dureté à coeur *f*; ~ **parcel service** *n* RAIL *vehicles* train de messageries direct *m*; ~ **station** *n* TRANSP gare directe *f*; ~ **traffic** *n* TRANSP trafic de transit *m*

through-binder *n* CONST *masonry* parpaing *m*

through-connection n TELECOM transfert m
through-deck: ~ **cable fitting** n NAUT passe-fil étanche m
throughfall n POLLUTION eau de pénétration par les frondaisons f
throughline n TELECOM ligne de transfert f
through-mortice n CONST mortaise passante f
throughput n COMP, DP débit m, PETR TECH capacité f, PROD ENG allure f, cadence f, débit m, flot m, flux m
through-rod: ~ **cylinder** n MECH ENG cylindre à tige de piston traversante m
through-stone n CONST *masonry* parpaing m
through-tenon n CONST tenon passant m
through-the-lens[1] adj CINEMAT à travers l'objectif
through-the-lens:[2] ~ **focusing** n CINEMAT mise au point à travers l'objectif f; ~ **meter** n CINEMAT cellule TTL f; ~ **reflex** n CINEMAT visée réflexe f
through-the-wall: ~ **air conditioning unit** n REFRIG climatiseur à encastrer m
throw[1] n CINEMAT *of projector* distance de projection f, MECH ENG *eccentricity* excentricité f; ~ **rod** n RAIL tringle de manoeuvre d'aiguille f
throw[2] vt C&G tourner; ~ **back into alignment** vt CONST *wall* pousser à l'alignement f; ~ **back to waste** vt CONST mettre au rebut f; ~ **into action** vt MECH ENG embrayer, engrener; ~ **into gear** vt MECH ENG embrayer, engrener; ~ **off** vt MECH ENG *belt* débrayer; ~ **off center** vt (AmE), ~ **off centre** vt (BrE) MECH ENG décentrer, désaxer, excentrer; ~ **on** vt MECH ENG *belt* embrayer une courroie; ~ **out of action** vt MECH ENG débrayer, désembrayer, désengrener; ~ **out of feed** vt MECH ENG débrayer; ~ **out of gear** vt MECH ENG débrayer
throw:[3] ~ **a bridge over a river** vi CONST jeter un pont sur une rivière, lancer un pont sur une rivière
throwaway n CINEMAT chute f; ~ **carbide drill** n MECH ENG foret avec plaquette à jeter en métal dur m; ~ **oil filter** n AUTO filtre à huile jetable m; ~ **tips** n pl MECH ENG *for tooling* plaquettes à jeter en métal dur f pl
thrower n C&G tourneur m
throwing n PETR TECH *chain* lancement m; ~ **wheel** n C&G tour de potier m
thrown: not to be ~ phr PACKAGING *handling marking or label* ne pas jeter
throw-out: ~ **bearing** n AUTO butée de débrayage f; ~ **bearing sleeve** n AUTO butée de débrayage f; ~ **fork pivot** n AUTO rotule de fourchette de débrayage f; ~ **fork strut** n AUTO plaquette de fourchette de débrayage f
thrust n AERONAUT poussée f, CONST *of arch* poussée f, *of ground* butée f, poussée f, MAR POLL butée f, poussée f, MECH ENG butée f, poussée f, palier de butée m, PHYS, PROD ENG poussée f, SPACE *spacecraft* poussée f; ~ **augmenter** n AERONAUT *of aircraft* augmentateur de poussée m; ~ **ball bearing** n MECH, MECH ENG butée à billes f; ~ **bearing** n FUELLESS palier de poussée m, MECH palier de butée m, MECH ENG butée f, palier de butée m, butée à l'arrière f, NAUT *of engine* palier de butée m; ~ **block** n MECH ENG butée f, palier de butée m, NAUT *of engine* bloc de butée m; ~ **chamber** n SPACE chambre de combustion f; ~ **coefficient** n SPACE facteur de poussée m; ~ **collar** n AUTO bague d'appui f, MECH ENG collet du palier de butée m, collier de butée m; ~ **cone** n SPACE cône central m; ~ **cutoff** n SPACE arrêt de poussée m, extinction commandée f; ~ **decay** n SPACE queue de poussée f; ~ **misalignment** n SPACE désalignement de la poussée m; ~ **modulation** n SPACE modulation de la poussée f; ~ **passing outside material**

n CONST *civil engineering* poussée au vide f; ~ **plate** n MECH ENG plaque de butée f; ~ **program** n (AmE), ~ **programme** n (BrE) SPACE programme de poussée m; ~ **reverser** n AERONAUT *of aircraft* inverseur de poussée m, TRANSP inverseur de jet m, inverseur de poussée m; ~ **subsystem** n SPACE groupe propulsif m; ~ **vector** n SPACE vecteur-poussée m; ~ **vector control** n (TVC) SPACE commande de contrôle de poussée f; ~ **washer** n AUTO anneau de butée m, rondelle d'appui f, MECH ENG, PROD ENG rondelle de butée f
thruster n SPACE propulseur m
thrusting n GEOL chevauchement m
thrust-to-mass: ~ **ratio** n SPACE rapport poussée-masse m, rapport poussée-poids m
thrust-to-weight: ~ **ratio** n SPACE rapport poussée-masse m, rapport poussée-poids m
thrust-vectoring: ~ **nozzle** n AERONAUT tuyère d'orientation f, tuyère de déflexion f, SPACE tuyère orientable f
thujane n CHEM thuyane m
thujene n CHEM thuyène m
thujone n CHEM thuyone f
thujyl: ~ **alcohol** n CHEM alcool thuylique m
thulite n MINERAL thulite f
thulium n (Tm) CHEM thulium m (Tm)
thumb: ~ **bolt** n MECH ENG boulon à oreilles m; ~ **latch** n CONST loquet à poucier m
thumbnut n MECH ENG papillon m, écrou papillon m, écrou à oreilles m
thumbscrew n MECH ENG vis ailée f, vis à oreilles f, vis moletée f
thumbwheel n CINEMAT molette f; ~ **setting** n PROD ENG positionnement du commutateur rotatif m; ~ **switch** n ELEC commutateur présélecteur à disque "multi-switch" m, PROD ENG commutateur rotatif m
thumper n PETR camion chute de poids m, thumper m
thunder[1] n METEO tonnerre m
thunder[2] vi METEO tonner
thunderbolt n METEO coup de foudre m
thunderclap n METEO coup de tonnerre m
thuringite n MINERAL thuringite f
thymol n CHEM thymol m
thymolphthalein n CHEM thymolphtaléine f
thyratron n CHEM, ELECTRON, PHYS thyratron m; ~ **inverter** n ELECTRON onduleur à thyratrons m
thyristor ELEC *electronics*, ELEC ENG, PHYS, TELECOM thyristor m; **off** ~ n ELECTRON thyristor à l'état bloqué m
thyristor-controlled: ~ **locomotive** n TRANSP locomotive à convertisseur statique f
thyronine n CHEM thyronine f
thyroxin n CHEM thyroxine f
thyroxine n CHEM thyroxine f
Ti (titanium) CHEM Ti (titane)
ticket: ~ **machine** n TRANSP distributeur automatique de billets m; ~ **number** n PROD ENG numéro de bon m; ~ **punch** n TRANSP poinçonneuse de contrôle f; ~ **slot machine** n TRANSP distributeur automatique de billets m
ticketing n PRINT fabrication de tickets f
tidal: ~ **basin** n FUELLESS bassin à flot m, OCEANOG bassin de marée m; ~ **bore** n OCEANOG barre f; ~ **capacity** n TRANSP *traffic control* capacité cyclique f; ~ **channel** n OCEANOG chenal de marée m; ~ **component** n OCEANOG composante de la marée f, onde de marée f, onde-marée f; ~ **corrections** n pl OCEANOG corrections de marée f pl; ~ **creek** n OCEANOG étier m; ~ **current** n FUELLESS,

NAUT, OCEANOG courant de marée *m*; ~ **delta** *n* OCEA-
NOG delta de marée *m*; ~ **dock** *n* NAUT bassin à marée
m; ~ **energy** *n* OCEANOG énergie des marées *f*, énergie
marémotrice *f*, PHYS énergie marémotrice *f*; ~ **epoch** *n*
OCEANOG situation de la marée *f*; ~ **fall** *n* NAUT, OCEA-
NOG baisse de la marée *f*; ~ **flow** *n* HYDROL flux de
marée *m*, TRANSP *traffic control* mise en circulation
alternée *f*, WATER SUPP écoulement de marée *m*; ~
force *n* ASTRON force de marée *f*; ~ **harbor** *n* (AmE),
harbour *n* (BrE) NAUT port à marée *m*; ~ **height** *n*
OCEANOG hauteur de la marée *f*; ~ **inlet** *n* OCEANOG
goulet de marée *m*; ~ **lock** *n* HYDROL écluse à marée *f*; ~
movement *n* FUELLESS mouvement de la marée *m*; ~
port *n* NAUT port à marée *m*; ~ **power** *n* FUELLESS
houille bleue *f*, PHYS énergie marémotrice *f*; ~ **power
plant** *n* ELEC ENG usine électrique marémotrice *f*; ~
power station *n* FUELLESS usine électrique marémotrice *f*, OCEANOG usine marémotrice *f*; ~ **prism** *n*
FUELLESS prisme de marée *m*; ~ **range** *n* FUELLESS,
GEOPHYS, HYDROL marnage *m*, NAUT amplitude de la
marée *f*, marnage *m*; ~ **scale** *n* OCEANOG échelle de
marée *f*; ~ **signature** *n* NAUT analyse des marées *f*; ~
stand *n* OCEANOG étale *m*; ~ **stream** *n* NAUT courant de
marée *m*; ~ **stream atlas** *n* NAUT atlas des courants *m*;
~ **wave** *n* GEOPHYS onde de marée *f*, raz de marée *m*,
tsunami *m*, NAUT *sea state* onde de marée *f*, raz de
marée *m*, vague de fond *f*, OCEANOG mascaret *m*, tsunami *m*

tide *n* FUELLESS, NAUT *sea*, OCEANOG marée *f*; ~ **chart** *n*
NAUT *navigation* charte des marées *f*; ~ **curve** *n* OCEA-
NOG courbe de marée *f*; ~ **duration** *n* OCEANOG durée de
la marée *f*; ~ **flat** *n* OCEANOG wad *m*; ~ **flow** *n* OCEANOG
flux *m*; ~ **gage** *n* (AmE) *see tide gauge*; ~ **gate** *n* NAUT
porte à flot *f*; ~ **gauge** *n* (BrE) FUELLESS maréomètre
m, GEOPHYS marégraphe *m*, marémètre *m*, OCEANOG
marégraphe *m*, échelle de marée *f*; ~ **level indicator** *n*
GEOPHYS échelle de marée *f*; ~ **mill** *n* FUELLESS moulin
marémoteur *m*, moulin à marée *m*; ~ **net** *n* OCEANOG
haut-parc *m*; ~ **phase** *n* OCEANOG situation de la marée
f; ~ **pole** *n* GEOPHYS marégraphe *m*, marémètre *m*,
échelle de marée *f*; ~ **race** *n* NAUT *of estuary* raz de
marée *m*; ~ **record** *n* GEOPHYS marégramme *m*; ~
recorder *n* OCEANOG marégraphe *m*, marémètre *m*; ~
scale *n* OCEANOG échelle de marée *f*; ~ **station** *n* OCEA-
NOG observatoire des marées *m*, station
d'enregistrement de la marée *f*; ~ **table** *n* NAUT *navigation* annuaire des marées *m*, indicateur des marées *m*,
OCEANOG annuaire des marées *m*

tidemark *n* GEOPHYS laisse de haute mer *f*, HYDROL laisse
de haute mer *f*, ligne des hautes eaux *f*, limite de la
marée *f*

tideway *n* NAUT fort du courant *m*

tie[1] *n* MECH ENG *flexible bond or fastening* attache *f*, lien
m, *tension member* tirant *m*, RAIL (AmE) *fixed equipment* traverse *f*; ~ **bar** *n* AERONAUT *helicopter* barre
d'ancrage *f*, CONST *of iron or steel roof truss* entrait *m*,
tirant d'une ferme de comble *m*, MECH ENG *tension
member* tirant *m*, RAIL *vehicles* entretoise *f*; ~ **beam** *n*
CONST *of wooden roof truss* entrait *m*, tirant d'une
ferme de comble *m*; ~ **bed** *n* (AmE) *(cf sleeper bed)*
RAIL assiette des traverses *f*; ~ **bolt** *n* MECH ENG *tension
member* tirant *m*; ~ **circuit interface** *n* TELECOM équipement de ligne de jonction *m* (Can), équipement de
ligne interautomatique *m*; ~ **coat** *n* COATINGS couche
adhésive *f*; ~ **line** *n* METALL conode *f*, droite de conjugaison *f*, TELECOM ligne de jonction *f*; ~ **plate** *n* NAUT

shipbuilding virure d'hiloire *f*, NUCLEAR *of fuel assembly* plaque support *f*; ~ **rod** *n* AUTO biellette de
direction *f*, C&G tirant *m*, CONST *of iron or steel roof
truss* entrait *m*, tirant d'une ferme de comble *m*, MECH,
MECH ENG *tension member*, NAUT *construction of engine* tirant *m*, PROD ENG *founding* armature *f*, VEHICLES
steering barre de connexion *f*, biellette de direction *f*;
~ **screw** *n* (AmE) *(cf sleeper screw)* RAIL tirefond *m*; ~
screwdriver *n* (AmE) *(cf sleeper screwdriver)* RAIL
tirefonneuse *f*; ~ **station** *n* (AmE) *(cf switching station)* RAIL poste de sectionnement *m*; ~ **wire** *n* ELEC
ENG fil de connexion *m*; ~ **wrap** *n* PROD ENG collier
d'attache *m*

tie:[2] ~ **up** *vt* NAUT amarrer

tie-adzing: ~ **machine** *n* (AmE) *(cf sleeper-adzing
machine)* RAIL saboteuse de traverses *f*

tieback *n* MECH ENG hauban *m*, TEXTILES embrasse *f*; ~
input *n* PROD ENG entrée de bouclage *f*

tied: ~ **letter** *n* PRINT ligature *f*

tie-down: ~ **point** *n* ELECTRON fréquence d'alignement *f*

tie-drilling: ~ **machine** *n* (AmE) *(cf sleeper drilling machine)* RAIL foreuse *f*

tie-in *n* PETR jonction *f*

tiemannite *n* MINERAL tiemannite *f*

ties: ~ **per inch** *n pl* PRINT perforations au pouce *f pl*

tiffanyite *n* MINERAL tiffanyite *f*

TIG: ~ **welding** *n (tungsten inert gas welding)* CONST
soudage TIG *m*

tiger's: ~ **eye** *n* MINERAL oeil-de-tigre *m*

tight: ~ **buffer** *n* OPT gainage serré *m*; ~ **buffering** *n* OPT
gainage serré *m*; ~ **coils** *n pl* SPRINGS spires serrées *f pl*;
~ **construction cable** *n* OPT câble à fibres enrobées *m*,
câble à structure serrée *m*; ~ **corner** *n* CONST coin étroit
m, courbe raide *f*; ~ **coupling** *n* ELEC ENG couplage
serré *m*, fort couplage *m*, PHYS couplage serré *m*; ~
editing *n* CINEMAT montage serré *m*; ~ **end** *n* TEXTILES
fil tirant en chaîne *m*; ~ **formation** *n* PETR formation
peu perméable *f*; ~ **framing** *n* CINEMAT cadrage serré
m; ~ **gravel** *n* CONST gravier serré *m*; ~ **hole** *n* PETR TECH
puits au secret *m*; ~ **inspection** *n* CONTROL contrôle
minutieux *m*, contrôle strict *m*; ~ **penetration** *n* NU-
CLEAR *pass-through* passage étanche *m*; ~ **pick** *n*
TEXTILES fil tirant en trame *m*; ~ **pulley** *n* PROD ENG
poulie fixe *f*; ~ **riveting** *n* CONST rivure étanche *f*; ~
selvage *n* TEXTILES lisière tendue *f*; ~ **selvedge** *n* TEX-
TILES lisière tendue *f*; ~ **spooling** *n* PHOTO bobinage à
spires serrées *m*; ~ **to gage** *n* (AmE), ~ **to gauge** *n* (BrE)
RAIL sous-écartement *m*; ~ **winder** *n* CINEMAT enrouleuse avec patin de serrage *f*

tightback: ~ **binding** *n* PRINT façonnage dos collé *m*

tighten *vt* MECH ENG *belt* raidir, roidir, serrer, tendre,
screw serrer; ~ **up hard** *vt* MECH ENG *screw* serrer à bloc

tightened: ~ **inspection** *n* CONTROL, QUALITY contrôle
renforcé *m*

tightener *n* MECH ENG tendeur *m*, tenseur *m*, PAPER TECH
tendeur *m*

tightening *n* MECH ENG raidissement *m*, serrage *m*, serrement *m*, tension *f*; ~ **cord** *n* MECH ENG corde de tension
f; ~ **pulley** *n* MECH ENG galet tendeur *m*, poulie de
tension *f*, rouleau de tension *m*; ~ **screw** *n* MECH ENG
vis de serrage *f*; ~ **wedge** *n* MECH ENG coin de serrage *m*

tight-jacketed: ~ **cable** *n* OPT câble à fibres enrobées *m*,
TELECOM câble à fibres enrobées *m*, câble à structure
serrée *m*

tightness *n* MECH ENG *of joint* herméticité *f*, étanchéité *f*,
RAIL *vehicles* étanchéité *f* - **test** *n* GAS TECH essai

d'étanchéité *m*

tiglic *adj* CHEM tiglique

tile[1] *n* C&G tuile *f*, CONST *for flooring, paving* carreau *m*, *for roofing* tuile *f*, SPACE *spacecraft* tuile *f*; ~ **burner** *n* C&G tuilier *m*; ~ **clay** *n* GEOL argile à tuiles *f*; ~ **cramp** *n* C&G crochet à tuiles *m*; ~ **cutter** *n* CONST *building* coupe-tuiles *m*; ~ **factory** *n* C&G tuilerie *f*; ~ **floor** *n* CONST carrelage *m*; ~ **flooring** *n* CONST carrelage *m*; ~ **kiln** *n* C&G tuilier *m*; ~ **maker** *n* C&G tuilier *m*; ~ **press** *n* C&G presse à carrelages *f*

tile:[2] ~ **the roof of a building** *vi* CONST poser des tuiles sur le comble d'un bâtiment

tiled: ~ **windows** *n pl* COMP fenêtres en mosaïque *f pl*, DP fenêtres juxtaposées *f pl*

tiler *n* C&G, CONST *person* tuilier *m*

tilery *n* C&G tuilerie *f*

tiling *n* C&G toiture en tuiles *f*

till *n* COAL TECH argile morainique *f*, moraine *f*

tiller *n* MINING *boring* manche de manoeuvre *m*, manivelle *f*, tourne-à-gauche *m*, tourne-à-gauche de manoeuvre *m*, NAUT *boatbuilding* barre franche *f*; ~ **axle** *n* NAUT *boatbuilding* axe de tête de mèche *m*; ~ **rope** *n* NAUT *boatbuilding* drosse *f*

tilt[1] *n* CINEMAT inclinaison *f*, panoramique vertical *m*, TV inclinaison *f*; ~ **bucket elevator** *n* TRANSP élévateur à godets oscillants *m*; ~ **container** *n* TRANSP conteneur à bâches *m*; ~ **control** *n* CINEMAT réglage d'inclinaison *m*; ~ **hammer** *n* PROD ENG marteau à bascule *m*, marteau à soulèvement *m*, martinet *m*; ~ **head** *n* PHOTO bascule sur rotule *f*; ~ **mixer** *n* TV tension de seuil *f*; ~ **shot** *n* CINEMAT plan avec mouvement vertical *m*; ~ **table** *n* C&G table de découpe basculante *f*

tilt[2] *vt* CINEMAT basculer, faire un panoramique vertical, incliner, pencher, TV faire un panoramique vertical; ~ **down** *vt* CINEMAT panoramiquer vers le bas

tilt[3] *vti* PRINT *font* italiser

tiltable: ~ **tower** *n* FUELLESS *wind power* tour basculante *f*

tiltainer *n* TRANSP conteneur à bâches *m*

tiltdozer *n* (BrE) TRANSP bouteur inclinable *m*

tilted: ~ **block** *n* GEOL bloc basculé *m*; ~ **shot** *n* CINEMAT plan oblique *m*

tilter *n* PROD ENG basculeur *m*, culbuteur *m*

tilting *n* PROD ENG *dumping* basculage *m*, culbutage *m*, déversement *m*; PHOTO plateau mobile *m*; ~ **basket** *n* NUCLEAR *for fuel assembly* cage de renversement *f*; ~ **body** *n* TRANSP benne basculante *f*; ~ **body coach** *n* TRANSP voiture à caisse inclinable *f*; ~ **car** *n* (AmE) *(cf tilting wagon)* TRANSP wagonnet verseur *m*; ~ **device** *n* NUCLEAR dispositif de déversement *m*; ~ **dozer** *n* TRANSP bouteur inclinable *m*; ~ **furnace** *n* HEATING four oscillant *m*; ~ **gate** *n* FUELLESS *dams*, HYDROL vanne basculante *f*; ~ **hammer** *n* PROD ENG marteau à bascule *m*, martinet *m*; ~ **head** *n* PHOTO *of enlarger* porte-cliché inclinable *m*; ~ **mold** *n* (AmE), ~ **mould** *n* (BrE) C&G moule basculant *m*; ~ **rotor helicopter** *n* TRANSP hélicoptère à rotors basculants *m*; ~ **skip** *n* TRANSP benne basculante *f*, wagonnet verseur *m*; ~ **table** *n* MECH ENG table inclinable *f*; ~ **wagon** *n* (BrE) *(cf tilting car)* TRANSP wagonnet verseur *m*

tiltmeter *n* GEOPHYS clinomètre *m*, pendage-mètre *m*

tilt-top: ~ **container** *n* TRANSP conteneur sans toit *m*, conteneur à toit ouvert *m*

tilt-type: ~ **semitrailer** *n* TRANSP savoyarde *f*

tilt-wing: ~ **plane** *n* AERONAUT avion à ailes inclinables *m*

timber[1] *n* CONST bois *m*, bois de charpente *m*, *suitable for conversion into market forms* bois d'oeuvre *m*, NAUT *shipbuilding* membre *m*, membrure *f*; ~ **bridge** *n* CONST pont en bois *m*; ~ **car** *n* (AmE) *(cf timber wagon)* RAIL wagon grumier *m*; ~ **dogs** *n pl* CONST *carpentry* clameaux *m pl*, clampe *f*, crampon *m*; ~ **frame** *n* CONST *for wall* pan de bois *m*, MINING *mine-timbering* cadre *m*, châssis *m*, châssis de mine *m*; ~ **framing** *n* CONST *for wall* pan de bois *m*; ~ **hitch** *n* NAUT *knot* noeud d'anguille *m*, noeud de bois *m*; ~ **jack** *n* CONST cric de charpentier *m*, viole *f*; ~ **raft** *n* CONST radeau de bois *m*, train de bois *m*; ~ **set** *n* MINING *mine-timbering* cadre *m*, châssis *m*, châssis de mine *m*; ~ **truss with iron bracing** *n* CONST ferme en bois à armature en fer *f*; ~ **wagon** *n* (BrE) *(cf timber car)* RAIL *vehicles* wagon grumier *m*

timber[2] *vt* CONST boiser, *to cut timber* couper du bois, faire du bois

timbered: ~ **shaft** *n* CONST puits boisé *m*

timbering *n* CONST boisage *m*

timber-splitting: ~ **wedge** *n* CONST coin à fendre le bois *m*

timberyard *n* CONST chantier de bois *m*, dépôt de bois *m*, MINING parc à bois *m*

timbre *n* ACOUSTICS, WAVE PHYS timbre *m*

time[1] *n* ACOUSTICS mesure *f*, temps *m*, COMP, DP temps *m*, ELECTRON durée *f*, instant *m*, temps *m*, PHYS *coordinate* temps *m*, *of event* instant *m*, *period* durée *f*, *series of events* période *f*, SPACE temps *m*; ~ **base** *n* ELECTRON, NUCLEAR *unit*, PHYS, PROD ENG, TELECOM, TV base de temps *f*; ~ **bomb** *n* MILIT bombe à retardement *f*; ~ **break** *n* GEOPHYS instant d'explosion *m*, instant zéro *m*; ~ **bucket** *n* PROD ENG période de base *f*, période de groupage *f*; ~ **card** *n* PROD ENG carte de pointage *f*, fiche de présence *f*; ~ **characteristic** *n* TELECOM caractéristique temporelle *f*; ~ **charter** *n* NAUT *transport* affrètement à temps *m*, PETR TECH affrètement à temps *m*, *petrol* charte d'affrètement à temps *f*; ~ **code** *n* CINEMAT code temporel *m*, RECORDING code temporel *m*, temps codé *m*, TV code temporel *m*; ~ **code editing** *n* CINEMAT, TV montage avec code temporel *m*; ~ **code generator** *n* CINEMAT, TV générateur de code temporel *m*; ~ **compression** *n* TELECOM compression temporelle *f*; ~ **constant** *n* ELEC *AC circuit*, PHYS constante de temps *f*; ~ **correlation** *n* TELECOM corrélation temporelle *f*; ~ **correlation analysis** *n* NUCLEAR analyse de corrélation par le temps *f*; ~ **delay** *n* ELEC retard *m*, ELECTRON, TELECOM temporisation *f*; ~ **dependent relay** *n* ELEC relais dépendant du temps *m*; ~ **derivative** *n* PHYS dérivée temporelle *f*; ~ **dilation** *n* PHYS dilatation des durées *f*; ~ **diversity reception** *n* TELECOM réception en diversité dans le temps *f*; ~ **division** *n* ELECTRON répartition dans le temps *f*; ~ **domain** *n* ELECTRON domaine temporel *m*; ~ **drift** *n* ELECTRON dérive temporelle *f*; ~ **equation** *n* ASTRON équation du temps *f*; ~ **exposure** *n* CINEMAT, PHOTO pose *f*; ~ **fence** *n* PROD ENG horizon de planification *m*; ~ **of flight velocity selector** *n* NUCLEAR sélecteur de vitesses à temps de vol *m*; ~ **frequency** *n* ELECTRON fréquence temporelle *f*; ~ **grenade** *n* MILIT grenade à retardement *f*; ~ **headway** *n* TRANSP *traffic control* intervalle entre véhicules *m*; ~ **indicator** *n* TRANSP *railways* indicateur des chemins de fer *m*; ~ **interval** *n* PROD ENG intervalle de temps *m*, période *f*; ~ **invariant signal** *n* ELECTRON signal constant *m*; ~ **jitter** *n* ELECTRON gigue temporelle *f*, instabilité temporelle *f*; ~ **key** *n* PROD ENG code unité de temps *m*; ~ **lag** *n* ELEC retard *m*; ~ **lag relay** *n* ELEC relais retardé *m*, relais à action différée *m*; ~ **lapse photography** *n* CINEMAT prise de vues image par image *f*, tournage d'un accéléré *m*; ~ **lapse survey** *n* TRANSP *traffic control* enquête par procédé aérocinématographique *f*; ~ **lapse videotape recorder** *n* PROD ENG magnétoscope de prise de vues image par image *m*; ~ **limit** *n* PATENTS délai *m*; ~ **marker** *n* ELECTRON marqueur de temps *m*; ~ **modulation** *n* ELECTRON modulation dans le temps *f*, modulation temporelle *f*; ~ **multiplex** *n* TV multiplex temporel *m*; ~ **multiplexing** *n* PHYS, TELECOM multiplexage temporel *m*; ~ **pattern control** *n* CONTROL régulation à programme *f*; ~ **period** *n* ELECTRON période temporelle *f*, PROD ENG période de base *f*, période de groupage *f*; ~ **per piece** *n* PROD ENG temps par pièce *m*, temps unitaire *m*; ~ **per unit** *n* PROD ENG temps par pièce *m*, temps unitaire *m*; ~ **phase** *n* PROD ENG échelonnement *m*; ~ **phased delivery** *n* PROD ENG livraison multiple *f*, livraison échelonnée *f*, livraison échéancée *f*; ~ **phasing** *n* PROD ENG cadencement *m*, échelonnement *m*; ~ **recorder** *n* INSTRUMENT enregistreur de temps *m*, PROD ENG *for registering employee's arrival and departure* appareil de pointage *m*, *watchman's clock* contrôleur de ronde *m*; ~ **recording** *n* PROD ENG pointage des temps *m*; ~ **resolved radiography** *n* NUCLEAR radiographie à résolution en temps *f*; ~ **response** *n* CONTROL comportement dans le temps *m*, fonction de temps *f*; ~ **series** *n* COMP série chronologique *f*, DP série temporelle *f*; ~ **setting knob** *n* CONTROL bouton de mise à l'heure *m*; ~ **sharing** *n* COMP, DP partage du temps *m*, temps partagé *m*, TELECOM partage du temps *m*; ~ **sheet** *n* PROD ENG feuille de présence *f*; ~ **shift** *n* ELECTRON décalage temporel *m*; ~ **signal** *n* ELECTRON, NAUT signal horaire *m*; ~ **slice** *n* COMP, DP tranche de temps *f*, ELECTRON intervalle de temps *m*; ~ **slicing** *n* COMP, DP allocation de temps *f*, découpage du temps *m*, ELECTRON découpage du temps *m*; ~ **slot** *n* ELECTRON tranche de temps *f*, SPACE créneau de temps *m*, intervalle de temps *m*, TELECOM créneau temporel *m*, intervalle de temps *m*, TV créneau temporel *m*; ~ **slot interchanger** *n (TSI)* TELECOM commutateur T *m*, commutateur temporel *m*; ~ **stage** *n (T-stage)* TELECOM étage temporel *m*; ~ **stamp** *n* TELECOM horodateur *m*; ~ **switch** *n* CINEMAT minuterie *f*, CONTROL interrupteur horaire *m*, interrupteur à minuterie *m*, ELEC interrupteur horaire *m*, ELEC ENG prise programmable *f*, programmateur *m*, TELECOM autocommutateur temporel *m*, commutateur temporel *m*; ~ **switching** *n* TELECOM commutation temporelle *f*; ~ **synthesis** *n* ELECTRON génération de retard *f*; ~ **synthesizer** *n* ELECTRON générateur de retard *m*; ~ **to manoeuvre** *n* NAUT *radar* délai de manoeuvre *m*; ~ **to rupture** *n* METALL durée de vie *f*; ~ **trace** *n* GEOPHYS tracé de l'heure *m*; ~ **trend** *n* POLLUTION tendance temporelle *f*; ~ **variant** *n* PETR temps variable *m*, variation de temps *f*; ~ **zone** *n* AERONAUT, NAUT fuseau horaire *m*

time² *vt* CINEMAT étalonner, ELECTRON cadencer, PROD ENG chronométrer

time-base: ~ **corrector** *n (TBC)* TV correcteur de base de temps *m*; ~ **error** *n* TV erreur de base de temps *f*, écart de base de temps *m*; ~ **error correction** *n* TV correction d'erreur de base de temps *f*; ~ **frequency** *n* ELEC *cathode ray tube* fréquence de balayage *f*; ~ **generator** *n* ELECTRON, TV générateur de base de temps *m*

time-based: ~ **function** *n* CONTROL fonction de temps *f*

time-consistent: ~ **busy hour** *n* TELECOM heure chargée moyenne *f*

timed: ~ **defrosting** *n* REFRIG dégivrage chronocommandé *m*; ~ **interval** *n* PROD ENG intervalle de temps *m*; ~ **print** *n* CINEMAT copie étalonnée *f*

time-delay: ~ **circuit** *n* ELECTRON circuit de temporisation *m*, circuit à retard *m*; ~ **distortion** *n* ELECTRON distorsion du temps de retard *f*; ~ **generation** *n* ELECTRON génération de retard *f*; ~ **position switch** *n* PROD ENG interrupteur de position temporisé *m*; ~ **relay** *n* ELEC relais retardé *m*, relais à action différée *m*, ELEC ENG relais retardé *m*; ~ **starter** *n* ELEC démarreur très lent *m*

time-dependent *adj* CONTROL en fonction du temps

time-division: ~ **demultiplexing** *n* ELECTRON démultiplexage temporel *m*; ~ **exchange** *n* TELECOM central temporel *m*; ~ **multiple access** *n* DP accès multiple par répartition dans le temps *m*, ELECTRON accès multiple temporel *m*, ELECTRON, SPACE *communications* accès multiple par répartition dans le temps *m*, TELECOM accès multiple temporel *m*, TELECOM accès multiple par répartition dans le temps *m*; ~ **multiplex** *n* TELECOM multiplex temporel *m*; ~ **multiplexed signals** *n pl* ELECTRON signaux multiplexés par répartition dans le temps *m pl*, signaux à multiplexage temporel *m pl*; ~ **multiplexer** *n* ELECTRON multiplexeur temporel *m*, multiplexeur à répartition dans le temps *m*; ~ **multiplexing** *n (TDM)* COMP, DP, ELECTRON multiplexage par répartition dans le temps *m*, multiplexage temporel *m*, PHYS multiplexage par partage du temps *m*, multiplexage par répartition dans le temps *m*, SPACE *communications* multiplexage par répartition en temps *m (MRT)*, TELECOM multiplexage dans le temps *m*, multiplexage par répartition dans le temps *m (MRT)*; ~ **network** *n* TELECOM réseau de connexion temporel *m*; ~ **switching** *n* COMP, DP commutation temporelle *f*, TELECOM commutation par répartition *f*, commutation temporelle *f*; ~ **switching system** *n* TELECOM système de commutation temporelle *m*, système temporel *m*; ~ **system** *n* TELECOM système de commutation temporelle *m*, système temporel *m*

time-domain: ~ **signal processing** *n* ELECTRON traitement de signaux dans le domaine temporel *m*, traitement temporel des signaux *m*

timed-phased: ~ **planning** *n* PROD ENG planification cadencée *f*, planification par période *f*, planification échelonnée *f*

time-driven *adj* PROD ENG déclenché par le temps

time-footage: ~ **calculator** *n* CINEMAT calculateur métrage-temps *m*

timekeeper *n* PROD ENG *person* contrôleur *m*, pointeur *m*

timekeeping *n* PROD ENG contrôle de présence *m*, pointage *m*

time-light: ~ **output curve** *n* PHOTO courbe de flux lumineux *f*

timeliness: ~ **rating** *n* PROD ENG note de respect des délais *f*

time-locking: ~ **relay** *n* ELEC relais à action différée *m*

time-of-flight: ~ **data analysis** *n* RAD PHYS *radioactivity experiments* analyse des données de temps de vol *f*

time-out¹ *n* COMP temps imparti *m*, DP dépassement du temps imparti *m*, TELECOM temporisation *f*; ~ **supervision** *n* TELECOM surveillance de temporisation *f*

time-out² *vi* PROD ENG dépasser

time-periodic: ~ **field** *n* ELEC ENG champ à périodicité temporelle *m*

timer *n* CINEMAT étalonneur *m*, COMP registre d'horloge *m*, CONTROL interrupteur horaire *m*, interrupteur à minuterie *m*, DP horloge *f*, registre d'horloge *m*, ELEC ENG minuterie *f*, LAB EQUIP chronomètre *m*, minuterie *f*, minuteur *m*, PHOTO compte temps *m*, PHYS chronomètre *m*, compteur horaire *m*, minuterie *f*, PROD ENG temporisateur *m*, REFRIG programmateur à horloge *m*, TELECOM temporisateur *m*; ~ **address** *n* PROD ENG adresse du temporisateur *f*; ~ **bit** *n* PROD ENG bit de temporisation *m*; ~ **clock bit** *n* PROD ENG bit d'horloge de temporisateur *m*; ~ **instruction** *n* PROD ENG instruction de temporisation *f*; ~ **reset** *n* PROD ENG remise à zéro du temporisateur *f*; ~ **rung** *n* PROD ENG ligne de temporisation *f*; ~ **status bit** *n* PROD ENG bit d'état du temporisateur *m*; ~ **timing bit** *n* PROD ENG bit de temporisation en cours *m*

time-related: ~ **failure** *n* ELEC ENG défaillance par vieillissement *f*

time-resolved: ~ **spectrum** *n* RAD PHYS spectre résolu dans le temps *m*

timer-off: ~ **delay** *n* PROD ENG temporisateur au repos *m*; ~ **done bit** *n* PROD ENG bit de fin de temporisation au déclenchement *m*

timer-on: ~ **delay** *n* PROD ENG temporisateur au travail *m*

time-series: ~ **analysis** *n* ELECTRON analyse de séries temporelles *f*

time-space: ~ **diagram** *n* TRANSP diagramme temps-distance *m*

time-space-time: ~ **network** *n* TELECOM réseau temporel-spatial-temporel *m*

time-tag *vt* TELECOM munir d'une étiquette

time-temperature: ~ **curve** *n* CINEMAT courbe temps-température *f*

time-temperature-tolerance *n* (*t-t-t*) REFRIG *of frozen food* tolérance temps-température *f*

time-variable: ~ **filtering** *n* GEOPHYS filtrage à temps variable *m*

time-varying: ~ **filter** *n* ELECTRON filtre à variation temporelle *m*; ~ **signal** *n* ELECTRON signal variant dans le temps *m*, signal à variation temporelle *m*

timing *n* AUTO distribution *f*, CINEMAT chronométrage *m*, étalonnage *m*, COMP synchronisation *f*, ELECTRON cadencement *m*, synchronisation *f*, TELECOM base de temps *f*, VEHICLES *ignition, valves* calage *m*, commande de l'avance *f*, distribution *f*; ~ **adjustment** *n* AUTO calage de la distribution *m*; ~ **analysis** *n* COMP, DP analyse temporelle *f*; ~ **angle** *n* VEHICLES *ignition* angle d'avance *m*, angle de calage *m*; ~ **belt** *n* MECH courroie crantée *f*, VEHICLES *of camshaft drive* courroie de distribution *f*; ~ **card** *n* CINEMAT fiche d'étalonnage *f*; ~ **chain** *n* AUTO chaîne de distribution *f*; ~ **cover** *n* AUTO carter de distribution *m*, couvercle de distribution *m*; ~ **diagram** *n* AUTO schéma de distribution *m*, COMP chronogramme *m*, DP chronogramme *m*, diagramme de temps *m*, PROD ENG diagramme séquentiel de comptage-décomptage *m*, schéma de temporisation *m*; ~ **drum** *n* C&G tambour de commande *m*; ~ **gear** *n* AUTO, VEHICLES *valve* pignon de distribution *m*; ~ **generator** *n* ELECTRON générateur de synchronisation *m*; ~ **line** *n* PETR ligne de comptage temps *f*, ligne de marquage *f*; ~ **mark** *n* AUTO repère de distribution *m*; ~ **pulse** *n* ELECTRON impulsion de cadencement *f*, TV impulsion de mar-

quage *f*; ~ **range** *n* PROD ENG gamme de temporisation *f*; ~ **signal** *n* ELECTRON signal d'horloge *m*, signal de synchronisation *m*; ~ **tape** *n* RECORDING bande d'étalonnage en temps *f*; ~ **track** *n* RECORDING bande rythmo *f*

timing-gear: ~ **housing** *n* AUTO carter de distribution *m*

tin *n* CHEM (*Sn*) étain *m* (*Sn*), PRINT boîte en fer blanc *f*; ~ **closing machine** *n* (BrE) (*cf can closing machine*) PACKAGING machine pour fermer les boîtes *f*; ~ **packing machine** *n* (BrE) (*cf can packing machine*) PACKAGING machine d'emballage de boîtes *f*; ~ **plate pail** *n* PROD ENG bidon en fer-blanc *m*; ~ **plate varnish** *n* COATINGS vernis pour fer-blanc *m*; ~ **plate worker** *n* PROD ENG ferblantier *m*; ~ **plate working** *n* PROD ENG ferblanterie *f*; ~ **pyrites** *n* MINERAL pyrite stannifère *f*, stannite *f*; ~ **stone** *n* MINERAL étain oxydé *m*; ~ **streak** *n* C&G traînée d'étain *f*; ~ **tack** *n* MECH ENG semence *f*

tincal *n* MINERAL tinkal *m*

tincalconite *n* MINERAL tincalconite *f*

tinctorial *adj* COLOURS tinctorial

tincture[1] *n* COLOURS teinture *f*; ~ **of iodine** *n* COLOURS teinture d'iode *f*

tincture[2] *vt* COLOURS teindre légèrement

tine *n* CONST *of fork* branche *f*, dent *f*

tin-filling: ~ **machine** *n* (BrE) (*cf can-filling machine*) PACKAGING machine pour remplir les boîtes *f*

tin-foiling: ~ **machine** *n* PACKAGING machine pour appliquer le papier métallisé *f*

tinge[1] *n* COLOURS teinte *f*

tinge[2] *vt* COLOURS teinter

tinman's: ~ **shears** *n pl* PROD ENG cisailles de ferblantier *f pl*; ~ **snips** *n pl* PROD ENG cisailles de ferblantier *f pl*

tinned[1] *adj* CHEM étamé, FOOD TECH en boîte, mis en boîte, mis en conserve

tinned:[2] ~ **conductor** *n* ELEC *cable* âme étamée *f*; ~ **food** *n* (BrE) (*cf canned food*) PACKAGING alimentation en boîte *f*; ~ **wire** *n* ELEC ENG fil étamé *m*

tinning *n* C&G, CONST, ELEC *of cable conductor* étamage *m*

tinnitus *n* ACOUSTICS tintement *m*

tinsel: ~ **conductor** *n* ELEC fil rosette *m*

tinsmith *n* PROD ENG *person* ferblantier *m*

tint[1] *n* C&G teinte légère *f*, COLOURS, PHOTO teinte *f*, PRINT fond tramé *m*, teinte *f*, fond tramé uniforme *m*, teinte *f*; ~ **plate** *n* C&G lame teinte sensible *f*

tint[2] *vt* COLOURS teinter

tinted[1] *adj* COLOURS teint légèrement

tinted:[2] ~ **base** *n* CINEMAT support teinté *m*; ~ **glass** *n* C&G verre teinté *m*; ~ **laminated glass** *n* C&G verre feuilleté coloré *m*

tinting *n* CINEMAT coloration *f*, P&R *paint* nuançage *m*, PRINT création d'une tonalité parasite *f*; ~ **strength** *n* PRINT intensité de la couleur *f*

tinware *n* PROD ENG objets en fer-blanc *m pl*

tin-zinc: ~ **finish** *n* COATINGS revêtement étain-zinc *m*

tip[1] *n* COAL TECH dépôt des schistes *m*, CONST *dumping ground* chantier de dépôt *m*, chantier de versage *m*, décharge *f*, dépôt des déblais *m*, CONST *tipping device* basculeur *m*, culbuteur *m*, verseur *m*, RECYCLING site de décharge *m*, SPRINGS embout *m*, TELECOM *wire* fil de pointe *m*; ~ **area** *n* (BrE) (*cf dump site*) MINING chantier de dépôt *m*, chantier de versage *m*, dépôt des déblais *m*, terris *m*; ~ **box car** *n* COAL TECH wagonnet à caisse basculante *m*; ~ **car** *n* (AmE) (*cf tip wagon*) RAIL wagonnet *m*; ~ **engagement** *n* TV pénétration des têtes *f*; ~ **heap** *n* (BrE) MINING crassier *m*, terril *m*; ~

height *n* TV dépassement des têtes *m*; ~ **loss** *n* FUELLESS tourbillons d'apex *m pl*, turbulences d'extrémité *f pl*, turbulences d'extrémité de pale *f pl*; ~ **penetration** *n* TV pénétration des têtes *f*; ~ **projection** *n* TV dépassement des têtes *m*; ~ **protrusion** *n* TV saillie de la pointe polaire *f*; ~ **sampler** *n* COAL TECH appareil de prise d'échantillons en bout *m*; ~ **speed ratio** *n* FUELLESS rapport de vitesse périphérique *m*; ~ **of switch tongue** *n* RAIL pointe d'aiguille *f*; ~ **wagon** *n* (BrE) *(cf tip car)* RAIL wagonnet *m*

tip[2] *vt* CONST abattre, chavirer, culbuter, faire basculer; ~ **on** *vt* PRINT rapporter, repiquer; ~ **up** *vt* CONST abattre, chavirer, culbuter, faire basculer

tip[3] *vi* CONST culbuter, se culbuter; ~ **up** *vi* CONST basculer, culbuter

tip[4] *vti* PROD ENG emboutir, ferrer

tip-on-form *n* PRINT formulaire avec bande adhésive sur le premier feuillet *m*

tipped:[1] ~ **in** *adj* PRINT rapporté

tipped:[2] ~ **crude** *n* PETR TECH *petrol* brut étêté *m*

tipper *n* (BrE) *(cf dump truck)* COAL TECH verseur *m*, CONST basculeur *m*, culbuteur *m*, verseur *m*, TRANSP culbuteur *m*

tipping *n* (BrE) *(cf dumping)* CONST basculement *m*, chavirement *m*, culbutage *m*, culbutement *m*, déversement *m*, versage *m*, POLLUTION décharge *f*, dépôt de déchets *m*, RECYCLING décharge *f*; ~ **bucket** *n* (BrE) *(cf dump bucket)* CONST benne basculante *f*, benne à bascule *f*; ~ **bucket conveyor** *n* TRANSP transporteur à godets basculants *m*; ~ **device** *n* CONST culbuteur *m*; ~ **mine car** *n* COAL TECH wagonnet à caisse basculante *m*; ~ **platform** *n* TRANSP pont de déversement *m*

tip-up: ~ **car** *n* (AmE) *(cf tip-up wagon)* RAIL *vehicles* wagon basculeur *m*; ~ **seat** *n* (BrE) *(cf folding seat)* VEHICLES strapontin *m*; ~ **wagon** *n* (BrE) *(cf tip-up car)* RAIL *vehicles* wagon basculeur *m*

tire *n* (AmE) *see* tyre

tissue *n* PAPER TECH ouate *f*; ~ **bank** *n* REFRIG banque de tissus *f*; ~ **machine** *n* PAPER TECH machine à ouate *f*; ~ **paper** *n* PACKAGING papier de soie *m*

tit *n* MECH ENG téton *m*; ~ **screw** *n* MECH ENG vis à téton *f*

titanate *n* CHEM titanate *m*

titanic[1] *adj* CHEM titanique

titanic:[2] ~ **acid** *n* CHEM acide titanique *m*

titanite *n* MINERAL titanite *f*

titanium *n (Ti)* CHEM titane *m (Ti)*; ~ **alloy** *n* SPACE alliage de titane *m*; ~ **dioxide** *n* P&R *pigment* dioxyde de titane *m*; ~ **forging** *n* SPACE pièce forgée en titane *f*; ~ **iron oxide** *n* MINERAL, PROP MAT ilménite *f*; ~ **nitride coating** *n* MECH ENG revêtement en nitrure de titane *m*; ~ **nitride hardening** *n* MECH ENG trempe de nitruration au titane *f*; ~ **oxide pigment** *n* COLOURS pigment à base d'oxyde de titane *m*

titanous *adj* CHEM titaneux

titanyl *n* CHEM titanyle *m*

title *n* CINEMAT, PATENTS *of invention*, PRINT titre *m*; ~ **card** *n* CINEMAT carton de générique *m*; ~ **keyer** *n* TV incrustateur de titres *m*, titreur *m*; ~ **page** *n* PRINT page de titre *f*; ~ **printer** *n* CINEMAT banc titre *m*

titles *n pl* CINEMAT générique *m*

titrate *vt* CHEM, COAL TECH titrer

titration *n* CHEM, COAL TECH titrage *m*, DETERGENTS analyse volumétrique *f*, titrage *m*

titrator *n* CHEM titrimètre *m*

titre *n* CHEM *analysis* titre *m*

titrimetry *n* CHEM *analysis* titrimétrie *f*

T-joint *n* CONST *plumbing* noeud d'empattement *m*, ELEC *cable* dérivation en té *f*

T-junction *n* CONST *roads* embranchement en T *m*

TKO *abbr (trunk offer)* TELECOM intervention ligne-réseau *f*

Tl *(thallium)* CHEM Tl *(thallium)*

TLC *abbr (thin-layer chromatography)* CHEM chromatographie sur couche mince *f*

TLMA *abbr (telematic agent)* TELECOM agent télématique *m*

TLV[1] *abbr (threshold limit value)* POLLUTION concentration maximale admissible *f*

TLV:[2] ~ **at place of work** *n* POLLUTION concentration maximale admissible *f*; ~ **in the free environment** *n* POLLUTION concentration maximale admissible dans l'air ambiant *f*

Tm *(thulium)* CHEM Tm *(thulium)*

TM[1] *abbr (transverse magnetic)* ELEC ENG, OPT, TELECOM magnétique transversal

TM:[2] ~ **mode** *n* OPT, TELECOM mode TM *m*, mode transversal magnétique *m*

TMN *abbr (telecommunications management network)* TELECOM RGT *(réseau de gestion des télécommunications)*

TMR *abbr (tandem mirror fusion reactor)* NUCLEAR réacteur à miroir tandem *m*

TMUX *abbr (transmultiplexer)* TELECOM transmultiplexeur *m*

T-network *n* ELEC ENG réseau atténuateur en T *m*, PHYS réseau en T *m*

to-and-fro *n* MECH ENG va-et-vient *m*

toboggan *n* SAFETY *aircraft* toboggan *m*

TOCC *abbr (Technical and Operational Control Center)* SPACE Centre de contrôle technique et opérationnel *m*

tocopherol *n* FOOD TECH tocophérol *m*

toe *n* CONST *of G cramp* patin *m*; ~ **board** *n* CONST *scaffolding* planche à pied *f*; ~ **region of characteristic curve** *n* PHOTO pied de la courbe *m*; ~ **weighting** *n* CONST *earthworks* lestage de talus *m*

toe-in *n* VEHICLES *of front wheels* pincement *m*, pincement positif *m*; ~ **angle** *n* AERONAUT *of runway lights* angle de convergence *m*

toe-out *n* VEHICLES *of front wheels* ouverture *f*, pincement négatif *m*

TOFC *abbr (trailer on flatcar)* TRANSP ferroutage *m*

toggle[1] *n* COAL TECH volet *m*, COMP, DP bascule *f*, NAUT cabillot d'amarrage *m*; ~ **on-off switch** *n* PROD ENG interrupteur marche-arrêt à bascule *m*; ~ **press** *n* C&G presse à genouillère *f*; ~ **selection** *n* PROD ENG sélection à bascule *f*; ~ **switch** *n* CINEMAT interrupteur basculant *m*, CONTROL commutateur à bascule *m*, interrupteur basculant *m*, ELEC interrupteur basculant *m*, interrupteur à jack *m*, ELEC ENG interrupteur à levier *m*

toggle[2] *vt* COMP, DP basculer, PROD ENG entre-basculer

tokamak *n* PHYS tokamak *m*

token *n* COMP, DP jeton *m*, PRINT *paper* demi-rame *f*; ~ **bus** *n* COMP, DP bus à jeton *m*; ~ **passing network** *n* COMP, DP réseau en anneau à jeton *m*; ~ **ring** *n* COMP anneau à jeton *m*

tolerable: ~ **gap** *n* TRANSP *between vehicles* écart acceptable *m*

tolerance *n* MECH tolérance *f*, MECH ENG limite *f*, tolérance *f*, METR limite *f*, PROP MAT, QUALITY, TEXTILES tolérance *f*; ~ **interval** *n* QUALITY intervalle de tolérance *m*; ~ **limit** *n* QUALITY limite de tolérance *f*; ~ **of**

parallelism *n* SPRINGS tolérance de parallélisme *f*

tolerancing *n* MECH ENG, PROD ENG tolérancement *m*

toll: **~ bridge** *n* CONST pont à péage *m*; **~ payment** *n* TRANSP télépéage *m*; **~ road** *n* CONST route à péage *f*; **~ switch** *n* TELECOM commutateur interurbain *m*

toll-free: **~ call** *n* (AmE) *(cf freephone call)* TELECOM appel gratuit *m*, appel sans frais *m* (Can); **~ number** *n* (AmE) *(cf freephone number)* TELECOM numéro d'appel sans frais *m* (Can), numéro vert *m* (Fra)

toluate *n* CHEM toluate *m*

toluene *n* CHEM toluol *m*, toluène *m*, DETERGENTS phénylméthane *m*, toluène *m*, P&R *solvent*, PETR TECH toluène *m*; **~ diisocyanate** *n (TDI)* P&R *curing agent* diisocyanate de toluène *m*, toluène diisocyanate *m*

toluic *adj* CHEM toluique

toluidine *n* CHEM toluidine *f*

toluldehyde *n* CHEM phénylacétaldéhyde *m*

tolunitrile *n* CHEM tolunitrile *m*

toluol *n* CHEM toluol *m*

toluquinoline *n* CHEM toluquinoléine *f*

toluyl *n* CHEM toluyle *m*

toluylene *n* CHEM toluylène *m*

tolyl *n* CHEM tolyle *m*

tolylene *adj* CHEM tolylénique

tomography *n* MECH ENG tomographie *f*

ton *n* METR *short, net* tonne *f*, tonne courte *f*, tonne forte *f*, tonne métrique *f*; **~ of displacement** *n* NAUT tonne de déplacement *f*

TON *abbr (type of number)* TELECOM type de numéro *m*

tonal: **~ gradation** *n* PHOTO gradation des teintes *f*; **~ inversion** *n* PRINT inversion des tonalités *f*; **~ note** *n* ACOUSTICS note tonale *f*; **~ value** *n* PHOTO valeur de gris *f*

tonalite *n* PETR tonalite *f*

tonality *n* COLOURS teinte *f*, RECORDING fréquence *f*, tonalité *f*

tone[1] *n* ACOUSTICS son *m*, son musical *m*, PHOTO ton *m*, PRINT teinte *f*, tonalité *f*, ton *m*, TELECOM tonalité *f*; **~ compression** *n* PRINT compression des tonalités *f*; **~ control** *n* CONTROL contrôle de tonalité *m*, RECORDING réglage de tonalité *m*; **~ control button** *n* CONTROL bouton de réglage de la tonalité *m*; **~ curve** *n* PRINT courbe des tonalités *f*; **~ disabler** *n* SPACE *communications* neutraliseur *m*; **~ generator** *n* ELECTRON générateur audiofréquence *m*, générateur de fréquences vocales *m*, RECORDING, TELECOM générateur de tonalité *m*; **~ pager** *n* TELECOM bip *m*; **~ pulse** *n* ELECTRON impulsion à fréquence vocale *f*; **~ reproduction** *n* PRINT reproduction fidèle de la tonalité *f*, RECORDING rendu des valeurs *m*; **~ scale** *n* PRINT échelle des tonalités *f*; **~ signal** *n* ELECTRON signal à fréquence vocale *m*; **~ signaling** *n* (AmE), **~ signalling** *n* (BrE) ELECTRON signalisation multifréquence *f*, signalisation par fréquences vocales *f*; **~ squelch system** *n* TELECOM silencieux à commande par tonalités *m*; **~ value** *n* PRINT tonalité *f*

tone[2] *vt* PRINT virer; **~ down** *vt* PRINT atténuer; **~ up** *vt* PRINT monter

tone-band: **~ frequency record** *n* RECORDING disque de fréquences à bande de tonalité *m*

toned: **~ print** *n* CINEMAT copie virée *f*

toner *n* PRINT toner *m*

tong: **~ line** *n* PETR TECH câble de clé *m*; **~ marks** *n pl* C&G marques de pinces *f pl*

tongs *n pl* CONST pinces *f pl*, pincettes *f pl*, tenaille *f*, tenailles *f pl*, PETR TECH clé de bocage *f*, clé à tiges *f*

tong-test: **~ instrument** *n* ELEC appareil de mesure à pince *m*

tongue *n* C&G *of burner* languette de brûleur *f*, CONST *carpentry* languette *f*, languette venue de bois *f*, MECH ENG *of scale* aiguille *f*, langue *f*, languette *f*, *tang of knife, of chisel, of file* soie *f*, TEXTILES languette *f*; **~ rotation** *n* NUCLEAR *of remote handling tool* rotation pince *f*; **~ weld** *n* PROD ENG soudure à gueule-de-loup *f*; **~ welding** *n* PROD ENG soudure à gueule-de-loup *f*

tongue-and-groove: **~ joint** *n* CONST assemblage à rainure et languette *m*, tenon à rainure et languette *m*

tongued-and-grooved: **~ joint** *n* CONST assemblage à rainure et languette *m*, tenon à rainure et languette *m*

tonguing: **~ iron** *n* CONST fer de bouvet double *m*; **~ plane** *n* CONST bouvet mâle *m*, bouvet à languette *m*, rabot à languette *m*

tonguing-and-grooving: **~ irons** *n pl* CONST fers à bouveter *m pl*; **~ machine** *n* CONST machine à faire les rainures et les languettes *f*; **~ planes** *n pl* CONST bouvet en deux morceaux *m*, coulisseur *m*

toning *n* CINEMAT, PHOTO virage *m*, PRINT mise au point de la couleur *f*; **~ bath** *n* CINEMAT, PHOTO bain de virage *m*

tonnage *n* METR tonnage *m*, NAUT jauge *f*, tonnage *m*

tonne *n* METR *metric* tonne *f*, tonne métrique *f*, PHYS tonne *f*

tonnes: **~ dead weight** *n pl* PETR TECH *of petrol* tonnes de port en lourd *f*

tool[1] *n* COMP, DP, MECH, MECH ENG, MINING outil *m*; **~ bar** *n* COMP, DP barre d'outils *f*; **~ belt and pouches** *n* MECH ENG ceinture et étuis pour outils *f*; **~ bit** *n* MECH ENG barreau traité *m*; **~ box** *n* MECH ENG *chest of tools* boîte à outils *f*, *of shaper, of planing machine* sabot *m*; **~ carriage** *n* MECH ENG *of machine tool* chariot porte-outil *m*; **~ changing system** *n* MECH ENG système de rechange d'outils *m*; **~ crib** *n* PROD ENG magasin d'outillage *m*; **~ grinder** *n* MECH ENG machine à affûter les outils *f*; **~ grinding** *n* MECH ENG affûtage d'outils *m*; **~ head** *n* MECH ENG *of shaping machine* tête porte-outil *f*; **~ holder** *n* MECH ENG porte-outil *m*; **~ life** *n* MECH ENG durée de vie d'un outil *f*; **~ post** *n* MECH ENG *of lathe, shaper, planer* étrier *m*; **~ pusher** *n* PETR contremaître de forage *m*, PETR TECH chef de chantier *m*; **~ ram** *n* MECH ENG *of slotting machine* coulisseau porte-outil *m*; **~ requisition** *n* PROD ENG bon d'outillage *m*, bon de sortie *m*; **~ rest** *n* MECH ENG support d'outil *m*; **~ sharpener** *n* MECH ENG *machine* machine à affûter les outils *f*; **~ sharpening** *n* MECH ENG affûtage d'outils *m*; **~ shed** *n* CONST baraque d'outils *f*; **~ slide** *n* MECH ENG *of slotting machine* coulisseau porte-outil *m*; **~ status** *n* DP barre d'état *f*; **~ trias** *n* MECH ENG essai d'outillage *m*

tool[2] *vt* PROD ENG *machine* travailler, usiner

tool-holding: **~ fixture** *n* MECH ENG *for machine centres* porte-outil *m*; **~ slide** *n* MECH ENG coulisseau porte-outils *m*

tooling *n* PROD ENG outillage *m*, *machining* usinage *m*; **~ allowance** *n* PROD ENG *founding allowance* surépaisseur pour usinage *f*

tool-kit *n* COMP, DP boîte à outils *f*

tool-life: **~ testing** *n* MECH ENG essai de durée de vie des outils *m*

toolmaker *n* MECH outilleur *m*, PROD ENG outilleur *m*, taillandier *m*

toolmaker's: **~ lathe** *n* MECH ENG tour d'outillage *m*; **~ microscope** *n* METR microscope d'atelier *m*

toolroom *n* MECH atelier d'outillage *m*

tools *n pl* C&G *with flat blades* pinces *f pl*, MECH ENG outillage *m*, outils *m pl*

tooth *n see groove*

toothed: ~ **drive belt** *n* MECH ENG courroie crantée *f*; ~ **rack** *n* NUCLEAR *of control rod drive* accouplement à dents crémaillère *m*; ~ **ring armature** *n* ELEC *of generator, motor* induit à dents *m*; ~ **sector** *n* MECH ENG secteur crénelé *m*, secteur denté *m*; ~ **segment** *n* MECH ENG secteur crénelé *m*, secteur denté *m*; ~ **wheel** *n* MECH ENG rouage *m*, roue d'engrenage *f*, roue dentée *f*, roue à dents *f*, PROD ENG roue crantée *f*

toothing *n* CONST *masonry* arrachement *m*, encaissement *m*, MECH ENG crénelage *m*, endentement *m*; ~ **plane** *n* CONST rabot denté *m*; ~ **stone** *n* CONST *masonry* attente *f*, harpe *f*, pierre d'arrachement *f*, pierre d'attente *f*

top[1] *n* PAPER TECH sommet *m*, PRINT réserve à l'acide *f*, TEXTILES *spinning* ruban *m*; ~ **and bottom clearance** *n* MECH ENG *gearing* jeu au fond des dents *m*; ~ **and bottom stapling** *n* PACKAGING agrafage supérieur et inférieur *m*; ~ **assembly** *n* FUELLESS assemblage supérieur *m*; ~ **blanket** *n* PRINT blanchet supérieur *m*; ~ **brass** *n* MECH ENG contre-coussinet *m*, coussinet supérieur *m*, demi-coussinet supérieur *m*; ~ **cap** *n* ELECTRON connexion de grille *f*; ~ **capacity** *n* PAPER TECH capacité de pointe maximum *f*; ~ **catch** *n* VEHICLES attache *f*; ~ **cementing plug** *n* PETR TECH bouchon de cimentation supérieur *m*; ~ **coat** *n* COLOURS couche de finition *f*, finition *f*, peinture de finition *f*; ~ **coat of paint** *n* P&R peinture définitive *f*; ~ **compression ring** *n* AUTO, VEHICLES *piston* segment de feu *m*; ~ **of convertible** *n* AUTO capote *f*; ~ **course of tank blocks** *n* C&G flottaison *f*; ~ **dead center** *n* (AmE), ~ **dead centre** *n* (BrE) *(TDC)* AUTO, VEHICLES *piston* point mort haut *m (PMH)*; ~ **of descent** *n* AERONAUT début de descente *m*; ~ **die** *n* PROD ENG *of power hammer* frappe *f*, frappe supérieure *f*, panne du pilon *f*; ~ **driving apparatus** *n* MECH ENG *of radial drilling machine* transmission supérieure *f*; ~ **dyeing** *n* COLOURS teinture en rubans de peigné *f*; ~ **fitting** *n* NUCLEAR *of fuel assembly* tête *f*; ~ **flange** *n* CONST *I-section beam* aile supérieure *f*; ~ **floor** *n* C&G recette *f*; ~ **gas** *n* GAS TECH gaz de gueulard *m*; ~ **hat** *n* CINEMAT trépied à branches courtes *m*; ~ **hole** *n* MINING mine de couronne *f*, trou de couronne *m*, trou de toit *m*; ~ **icing** *n* REFRIG glaçage direct sur le chargement *m*; ~ **layer** *n* TEXTILES canevas supérieur *m*; ~ **man** *n* C&G gazier *m*; ~ **mark** *n* NAUT *buoy* voyant *m*; ~ **pallet** *n* PROD ENG *of power hammer* frappe *f*, frappe supérieure *f*, panne du pilon *f*; ~ **part of flask** *n* PROD ENG *founding* chapeau de châssis *m*, dessus de châssis *m*; ~ **plate** *n* MECH ENG plaque supérieure *f*, plateau de dessus *m*, *of leafspring* maîtresse-feuille *f*, maîtresse-lame *f*, PROD ENG *founding* plaque de recouvrement *f*; ~ **plenum** *n* NUCLEAR plenum supérieur *m*; ~ **ply** *n* TEXTILES pli extérieur *m*; ~ **pouring** *n* PROD ENG *founding* coulée en chute directe *f*, coulée à la descente *f*; ~ **quark** *n* PART PHYS quark de sommet *m*, quark top *m*, PHYS quark top *m*; ~ **rail** *n* CONST *of door frame, sash frame* traverse du haut *f*; ~ **rake** *n* MECH ENG *of machine tool* angle de dégagement *m*; ~ **road** *n* MINING voie de tête *f*; ~ **roll** *n* MECH ENG *of rolling mill* cylindre du dessus *m*, cylindre mâle *m*, PAPER TECH rouleau supérieur *m*; ~ **rounding-tool** *n* MECH ENG dessus d'étampe *m*, étampe de dessus *f*; ~ **side** *n* PAPER TECH *of paper* côté grain du papier *m*; ~ **sizing** *n*

PRINT couchage de surface *m*; ~ **station** *n* TRANSP *of cableway* station supérieure *f*; ~ **of stroke** *n* MECH ENG *of piston* haut de course *m*; ~ **swage** *n* MECH ENG dessus d'étampe *m*, étampe de dessus *f*, étampe de dessus pour fers ronds *f*; ~ **tin** *n* (AmE) *(cf crater drip)* C&G goutte d'étain en cratère *f*

top:[2] ~ **up** *vt* SPACE ouiller

topaz *n* MINERAL topaze *f*

topazolite *n* MINERAL topazolite *f*

top-bottom: ~ **diffusion** *n* ELECTRON *of epitaxial impurities* diffusion par les deux faces *f*

top-down: ~ **construction** *n* CONST *tunnelling* construction de haut en bas *f*; ~ **methodology** *n* COMP, DP méthodologie descendante *f*

top-dyed *adj* TEXTILES teint en ruban

top-flame: ~ **furnace** *n* C&G four à brûleurs dans les pignons *m*

toplap *n* GEOL recouvrement en discordance angulaire *m*

topographer *n* CONST *person* topographe *m*

topographic: ~ **wave** *n* OCEANOG onde topographique *f*

topographical: ~ **survey** *n* CONST levé topographique *m*

topography *n* CONST topographie *f*

topological: ~ **property** *n* GEOM propriété topologique *f*

topologist *n* GEOM topologue *m*

topology *n* COMP, DP, GEOM topologie *f*

topping *n* FOOD TECH garniture *f*; ~ **charge** *n* ELEC ENG charge d'appoint *f*; ~ **cycle** *n* NUCLEAR cycle placé en amont *m*; ~ **lift** *n* NAUT *rigging, running* balancine *f*

top-road: ~ **bridge** *n* CONST pont à tablier supérieur *m*

topset: ~ **beds** *n pl* GEOL *delta-top facies* couches deltaïques peu profondes *f pl*

topsides *n pl* NAUT *shipbuilding* oeuvres mortes *f pl*

topsoil *n* COAL TECH couche arable *f*, terre arable *f*, CONST terre humus *f*, terre végétale *f*; ~ **stripping** *n* CONST décapage de terre végétale *m*

top-stabilized: ~ **rapid transit system** *n* TRANSP métro avec stabilisation au-dessus du véhicule *m*

top-to-bottom:[1] **from** ~ *adj* CONST de fond en comble

top-to-bottom:[2] **from** ~ *adv* CONST de fond en comble

torbernite *n* MINERAL torbernite *f*, torbérite *f*, NUCLEAR chalcolite *f*, torbernite *f*, uranophyllite *f*

torch *n* CONST *welding*, GAS TECH torche *f*, MECH chalumeau *m*; ~ **brazing** *n* CONST brasage aux gaz *m*; ~ **for MIG-MAG welding** *n* CONST torche pour soudage MIG-MAG *f*; ~ **for plasma welding** *n* CONST torche pour soudage plasma *f*; ~ **for TIG welding** *n* CONST torche pour soudage TIG *f*

torching *n* PROD ENG *founding* flambage *m*

tornado *n* METEO tornade *f*

toroid *n* ELEC *coil* enroulement toroïdal *m*, ELEC ENG, NUCLEAR bobine toroïdale *f*

toroidal: ~ **antenna** *n* TELECOM antenne toroïdale *f*; ~ **coil** *n* ELEC, NUCLEAR bobine toroïdale *f*; ~ **core** *n* ELEC ENG noyau torique *m*, noyau toroïdal *m*, NUCLEAR *of coil* noyau toroïdal *m*; ~ **electron gun** *n* TV canon électronique à faisceau toroïdal *m*; ~ **magnet** *n* PHYS aimant torique *m*; ~ **pinch effect** *n* NUCLEAR striction toroïdale *f*; ~ **sealing ring** *n* MECH ENG joint torique *m*; ~ **transformer** *n* ELEC ENG transformateur toroïdal *m*, transformateur à noyau toroïdal *m*

torpedo *n* MILIT, MINING *boring*, NAUT *navy*, P&R *extrusion press* torpille *f*, RAIL pétard *m*; ~ **boat** *n* MILIT vedette lance-torpilles *f*, NAUT *navy* torpilleur *m*; ~ **furrow** *n* MILIT sillage de torpille *m*; ~ **gunboat** *n* NAUT aviso-torpilleur *m*; ~ **launching tube** *n* MILIT tube lance-torpilles *m*; ~ **net** *n* MILIT filet pare-torpilles *m*; ~ **track** *n* MILIT sillage de torpille *m*

torque *n* ELEC ENG, MECH, MECH ENG, PETR TECH, PHYS, PROD ENG couple *m*, SPRINGS couple de torsion *m*, force de torsion *f*, VEHICLES *of engine* couple *m*; ~ **arm** *n* AUTO bielle de poussée *f*, VEHICLES *of wheel suspension* barre de poussée *f*, bielle de poussée *f*; ~ **ball** *n* AUTO rotule de joint de cardan *f*; ~ **converter** *n* AUTO convertisseur de couple *m*, MECH ENG *of hydraulic transmission* convertisseur hydraulique de couple *m*, VEHICLES *transmission* convertisseur de couple *m*; ~ **converter housing** *n* AUTO boîtier de convertisseur de couple *m*; ~ **link** *n* AERONAUT compas *m*, compas de train *m*; ~ **motor** *n* ELEC moteur vireur *m*; ~ **multiplier** *n* MECH ENG *tool* multiplicateur de couple *m*; ~ **nut** *n* PROD ENG écrou de serrage *m*; ~ **screwdriver** *n* MECH ENG *tool* tournevis dynanométrique *m*; ~ **spanner** *n* (BrE) *(cf torque wrench)* NUCLEAR, VEHICLES *tool* clé dynamométrique *f*; ~ **stabilizer** *n* AUTO barre de stabilisation *f*; ~ **tube** *n* AUTO tube de poussée *m*; ~ **tube drive** *n* VEHICLES transmission par tube de poussée *f*; ~ **wrench** *n* (AmE) *(cf torque spanner)* MECH ENG, NUCLEAR, VEHICLES *tool* clé dynamométrique *f*

torr *n* PHYS torr *m*

torrefaction *n* PROD ENG torréfaction *f*

torrefier *n* PROD ENG torréfacteur *m*

torrent *n* HYDROL gave *m*, ravine *f*, torrent *m*

torrential *adj* METEO torrentiel

torrid: ~ **zone** *n* *(cf equatorial zone)* METEO zone torride *f*

torsion *n* MECH ENG, METALL, PHYS, PROP MAT torsion *f*; ~ **balance** *n* GEOPHYS, MECH ENG, PHYS balance de torsion *f*; ~ **bar** *n* AUTO barre de torsion *f*; ~ **electrometer** *n* GEOPHYS électromètre de torsion *m*; ~ **meter** *n* INSTRUMENT, LAB EQUIP torsiomètre *m*; ~ **spring** *n* MECH ENG ressort de torsion *m*; ~ **string** *n* ELEC ENG fil de torsion *m*; ~ **test** *n* METALL essai de torsion *m*

torsional[1] *adj* MECH de torsion

torsional:[2] ~ **constant** *n* PHYS constante de torsion *f*; ~ **elasticity** *n* MECH ENG élasticité de torsion *f*; ~ **moment** *n* SPRINGS moment de torsion *m*; ~ **oscillation** *n* PHYS oscillation de torsion *f*; ~ **pendulum** *n* PHYS pendule de torsion *m*; ~ **strain** *n* MECH ENG déformation due à la torsion *f*, SPRINGS contrainte de torsion *f*; ~ **strength** *n* MECH ENG résistance à la torsion *f*; ~ **stress** *n* MECH ENG effort de torsion *m*; ~ **tear tester** *n* PAPER TECH torsiomètre *m*; ~ **tenacity** *n* MECH ENG résistance à la torsion *f*; ~ **test** *n* MECH ENG essai à la torsion *m*

torsion-spring: ~ **testing machine** *n* SPRINGS machine d'essai des ressorts de torsion *f*

torsion-string: ~ **galvanometer** *n* ELEC galvanomètre Einthoven *m*, galvanomètre à corde *m*

torulin *n* CHEM thiamine *f*

torus *n* ELEC *coil* enroulement toroïdal *m*, GEOM, RAD PHYS *nuclear fusion research* tore *m*

tosyl *n* CHEM tosyle *m*

total: ~ **absorption target** *n* RAD PHYS cible d'absorption totale *f*; ~ **acid number** *n* *(TAN)* CHEM indice d'acidité *m*; ~ **adherence train** *n* TRANSP train à adhérence totale *m*; ~ **allowable catch** *n* *(TAC)* OCEANOG prise maximale autorisée *f*, total autorisé de captures *m* *(PMA)*; ~ **angular momentum** *n* PHYS moment cinétique total *m*; ~ **angular momentum quantum number** *n* PHYS nombre quantique du moment cinétique total *m*; ~ **area** *n* CONST *of piece of ground* masse surface *f*, superficie totale *f*; ~ **atomic stopping power** *n* PHYS pouvoir d'arrêt atomique total *m*; ~ **authorized catch**

n OCEANOG prise maximale autorisée *f*; ~ **charge** *n* NUCLEAR *of reactor* charge totale de combustible *f*; ~ **coils** *n pl* SPRINGS spires totales *f pl*; ~ **configuration** *n* TELECOM interconnexion totale *f*; ~ **cooling effect** *n* REFRIG action refroidissante totale *f*; ~ **denier** *n* TEXTILES denier total *m*; ~ **deposition** *n* POLLUTION dépôt total *m*, retombées totales *f pl*; ~ **drag** *n* TRANSP traînée totale *f*; ~ **eclipse** *n* ASTRON éclipse totale *f*; ~ **energy density** *n* ACOUSTICS densité d'énergie totale *f*; ~ **evaporation** *n* HYDROL évaporation totale *f*, évapotranspiration *f*; ~ **float** *n* PROD ENG marge totale *f*; ~ **flow** *n* HYDROL *of nappe* débit globale *m*; ~ **height** *n* NUCLEAR *of reactor vessel including closure head* hauteur totale *f*; ~ **internal reflection** *n* C&G, WAVE PHYS réflexion interne totale *f*; ~ **inward leakage** *n* SAFETY *respiratory protective equipment* fuite totale intérieure *f*; ~ **lift** *n* TRANSP portance totale *f*; ~ **linear stopping power** *n* PHYS pouvoir d'arrêt linéique total *m*; ~ **line value** *n* PROD ENG pression maximale admissible *f*; ~ **losses** *n pl* ELEC pertes totales *f pl*, HYDROL évaporation totale *f*, évapotranspiration *f*; ~ **loss processing** *n* PRINT développement avec révélateur utilisable une seule fois *m*; ~ **loss refrigeration system** *n* REFRIG refroidissement à frigorigène perdu *m*; ~ **mass stopping power** *n* PHYS pouvoir d'arrêt massique total *m*; ~ **mean free path** *n* NUCLEAR *for all interactions* libre parcours moyen total *m*; ~ **oscillation amplitude** *n* ACOUSTICS amplitude totale d'oscillation *f*; ~ **permissible laden weight** *n* (BrE) *(cf total permissible loaded weight)* VEHICLES *regulations* PTAC, poids total autorisé en charge *m*; ~ **permissible loaded weight** *n* (AmE) *(cf total permissible laden weight)* VEHICLES *regulations* PTAC, poids total autorisé en charge *m*; ~ **permissible weight** *n* VEHICLES *regulations* PTMA, poids total maximal autorisé *m*; ~ **pitch** *n* MECH ENG *of screw* pas réel *m*; ~ **quality control** *n* PROD ENG gestion totale de la qualité *f*, QUALITY *(TQC)* maîtrise totale de la qualité *f*; ~ **quality management** *n* *(TQM)* QUALITY management total de la qualité *m*; ~ **radiation pyrometer** *n* PHYS pyromètre à rayonnement total *m*; ~ **radiator** *n* RAD PHYS radiateur intégral *m*; ~ **rate** *n* HYDROL *of nappe* débit globale *m*; ~ **reflection** *n* OPT, PHYS *internal*, TELECOM réflexion totale *f*; ~ **requirement** *n* PROD ENG impératifs globaux *m pl*; ~ **size** *n* METR effectif cumulé *m*; ~ **storage volume** *n* GAS TECH volume total stockable *m*; ~ **stress** *n* SPRINGS contrainte totale *f*; ~ **sulfur** *n* (AmE), ~ **sulphur** *n* (BrE) P&R *rubber, vulcanization* soufre total *m*; ~ **thickness test** *n* TESTING essai d'épaisseur totale *m*; ~ **turns** *n pl* SPRINGS spires totales *f pl*; ~ **width** *n* PAPER TECH largeur totale *f*

totally: ~ **enclosed headstock** *n* MECH ENG poupée blindée *f*; ~ **enclosed motor** *n* ELEC moteur fermé *m*

tote: ~ **box** *n* PACKAGING bac de manutention *m*

totem: ~ **pole arrangement** *n* ELECTRON *of amplifier with 2 bipolar transistors* montage en totem pôle *m*

touch:[1] ~ **contact switch** *n* ELEC commutateur à action fugitive *m*; ~ **needle** *n* MECH ENG aiguille d'essai *f*, touchau *m*; ~ **needle test** *n* MECH ENG essai au touchau *m*; ~ **screen** *n* COMP écran tactile *m*; ~ **switch** *n* ELEC ENG touche à effleurement *f*; ~ **trigger probe** *n* MECH ENG sonde à déclenchement par touches *f*

touch:[2] ~ **up** *vt* PRINT rehausser la couleur de, retoucher

touch:[3] ~ **bottom** *vi* NAUT *of ship* talonner; ~ **down** *vi* AERONAUT atterrir, SPACE *spacecraft* atterrir, se poser

touch-and-go: ~ **landing** *n* AERONAUT posé-décollé *m*

touchdown *n* AERONAUT point d'atterrissage *m*, point d'impact *m*, point de touché *m*, prise de contact *f*, SPACE atterrissage *m*, impact *m*; ~ **point** *n* SPACE point d'impact *m*; ~ **speed** *n* AERONAUT vitesse de toucher des roues *f*; ~ **zone** *n* AERONAUT zone de touché des roues *f*

touching: ~ **up** *n* C&G, PRINT retouche *f*

touchpad *n* COMP pavé tactile *m*, DP bloc de touches tactiles *m*

touch-sensitive: ~ **control** *n* DP commande sensible à l'effleurement *f*; ~ **screen** *n* COMP écran tactile *m*, DP écran sensitif *m*, écran tactile *m*

tough *adj* PACKAGING *tape* robuste

tough-brittle: ~ **transition** *n* METALL transition ductile-fragile *f*

toughened: ~ **glass** *n* C&G verre trempé *m*, CONST verre durci *m*, verre trempé *m*, TRANSP verre trempé *m*

toughness *n* MECH ENG résistance *f*, ténacité *f*, METALL ténacité *f*, NUCLEAR résilience *f*, P&R, PHYS, PROP MAT ténacité *f*, TEXTILES solidité *f*

tour *n* (AmE) *(cf shift)* PETR TECH quart *m*

tourmaline *n* MINERAL, PHYS tourmaline *f*

tow[1] *n* NAUT étoupe de chanvre *f*, PROD ENG *hemp or flax fibre* étoupe *f*, TEXTILES câble *m*; ~ **bar** *n* MECH *vehicles*, VEHICLES *trailer* barre de remorquage *f*; ~ **hook** *n* VEHICLES *trailer* crochet de remorquage *m*; ~ **net** *n* OCEANOG senne *f*; ~ **path** *n* CONST *on canal, river* banquette de halage *f*, chemin de halage *m*; ~ **rope** *n* NAUT câble de remorque *m*, remorque *f*; ~ **strap** *n* TRANSP sangle de remorquage *f*; ~ **train** *n* TRANSP convoi poussé *m*, convoi remorqué *m*; ~ **vehicle** *n* TRANSP véhicule tracteur *m*

tow[2] *vt* MAR POLL remorquer, NAUT haler, remorquer, touer, TRANSP remorquer; ~ **astern** *vt* NAUT remorquer en arbalète, remorquer en flèche

tow[3] *vi* NAUT prendre en remorque

towage *n* NAUT halage *m*, remorquage *m*, touage *m*; ~ **charges** *n* NAUT frais de remorquage *m pl*

towboat *n* TRANSP pousseur *m*

tow-dyed *adj* TEXTILES teint en câble

towed: ~ **convoy** *n* TRANSP convoi tracté *m*; ~ **instrument** *n* OCEANOG engin à câble *m*; ~ **submersible** *n* OCEANOG engin à câble *m*

tower *n* CONST *scaffolding* pylône *m*, *trellis post* pylône *m*, ELEC *supply network* pylône *m*, pyramide *f*; ~ **bolt** *n* CONST *locksmithing* verrou à la capucine *m*, verrou à platine *m*; ~ **crane** *n* CONST grue à colonne *f*, grue à tour *f*; ~ **door** *n* C&G porte de caisson *f*; ~ **section** *n* C&G caisson *m*; ~ **telescope** *n* INSTRUMENT télescope à tour *m*

towing *n* AERONAUT *of aircraft* tractage *m*, NAUT remorquage *m*, touage *m*, TRANSP tractage *m*; ~ **bracket** *n* VEHICLES *device* support de remorquage *m*; ~ **vehicle** *n* VEHICLES remorqueur *m*, tracteur *m*

towline *n* MAR POLL câble de remorque *m*, NAUT câble de remorque *m*, remorque *f*

town: ~ **gas** *n* GAS TECH, PETR TECH gaz de ville *m*; ~ **planning map** *n* CONST plan d'urbanisme *m*; ~ **water** *n* WATER SUPP eau de ville *f*

Townsend: ~ **discharge** *n* ELECTRON décharge de Townsend *f*

tow-to-top: ~ **converter** *n* TEXTILES convertisseur câble-ruban *m*

toxic[1] *adj* COAL TECH toxique, PETR TECH délétère, toxique, SAFETY toxique

toxic:[2] ~ **effect** *n* POLLUTION effet toxique *m*; ~ **effluent** *n* RECYCLING effluent toxique *m*; ~ **gases** *n pl* SAFETY gaz toxiques *m pl*; ~ **liquid** *n* SAFETY liquide toxique *m*; ~ **materials** *n pl* SAFETY matériaux toxiques *m pl*; ~ **substance** *n* SAFETY substance toxique *f*

toxicant *n* CHEM toxique *m*

toxicity *n* CHEM, MAR POLL, P&R, PETR TECH, SAFETY toxicité *f*

toxicology *n* SAFETY toxicologie *f*

toxin *n* QUALITY toxine *f*

toxisterol *n* CHEM toxistérol *m*

TP *abbr (transaction processing)* COMP, DP traitement de transactions *m*

TPDU *abbr (transport protocol data unit)* TELECOM unité de données du protocole de transport *f*

TPE *abbr (transmission path endpoint)* TELECOM extrémité de trajet de transmission *f*

T-peel: ~ **test** *n* P&R *for adhesives* essai de pelage angulaire *m*

TPI *abbr (tracks per inch)* COMP, DP, PRINT pistes par pouce *f pl*

T-piece *n* LAB EQUIP *connector* raccord de jonction en T *m*; ~ **union** *n* CONST raccord à T *m*

TQC *abbr (total quality control)* QUALITY maîtrise totale de la qualité *f*

TQM *abbr (total quality management)* QUALITY management total de la qualité *m*

TR[1] *abbr* ELECTRON *(transmit-receive)* émetteur-récepteur, TELECOM *(tributary)* affluent *m*

TR:[2] ~ **cell** *n* NAUT *radar* cellule TR *f*; ~ **tube** *n* ELECTRON tube TR *m*

trace[1] *n* COMP, DP trace *f*, ELEC ENG *conductor* ruban *m*, ELECTRON *on screen*, GAS TECH, PETR, PROP MAT trace *f*; ~ **analysis** *n* WATER SUPP *element* analyse en trace *f*; ~ **blanking** *n* ELECTRON suppression du faisceau *f*; ~ **element** *n* CHEM oligo-élément *m*, GEOL oligo-élément *m*, élément trace *m*, POLLUTION oligo-élément *m*; ~ **fossil** *n* GEOL indice d'activité biologique *m*; ~ **integration** *n* ELECTRON intégration de la trace *f*; ~ **intensification** *n* ELECTRON intensification de la trace *f*; ~ **interval** *n* TV durée de la ligne *f*; ~ **program** *n* COMP programme d'analyse *m*, DP programme de traçage *m*

trace[2] *vt* COMP, DP suivre à la trace, GEOM, GEOPHYS, MATH *curve* tracer, MECH ENG calquer

traceability *n* METR traçabilité *f*

traced: ~ **design** *n* PRINT calque *m*

tracer *n* C&G, MILIT traceur *m*, NUCLEAR indicateur isotopique *m*, traceur *m*, PETR traceur *m*; ~ **atom** *n* NUCLEAR traceur *m*; ~ **bullet** *n* MILIT balle traçante *f*; ~ **substance** *n* CHEM substance révélatrice *f*, substance traceur *f*

tracing *n* CINEMAT traçage *m*, MECH ENG *act* calquage *m*, tracement *m*, traçage *m*, PRINT calque *m*; ~ **distortion** *n* ACOUSTICS distorsion de contact *f*; ~ **paper** *n* MECH ENG papier à calquer *m*, papier-calque *m*

track[1] *n* ASTRON *of moon's shadow on Earth's surface* trajectoire *f*, AUTO voie *f*, CINEMAT canal d'enregistrement *m*, piste son *f*, rail *m*, *for dolly* rail *m*, COMP, DP piste *f*, MECH *vehicles* voie *f*, MECH ENG *of lathe* guidages *m pl*, NAUT *deck fitting* rail *m*, *of ship* sillage *m*, trajectoire *f*, NUCLEAR *in track detector* trace nucléaire *f*, OCEANOG *of ship* houache *f*, sillage *m*, OPT piste *f*, PROD ENG *for placing module in chassis* guide *m*, RAIL voie *f*, RECORDING piste *f*, TRANSP *railways* voie *f*, TV piste *f*; ~ **adjustment** *n* TV ajustage de piste *m*, réglage de piste *m*; ~ **allocation** *n* RAIL affectation de la voie *f*; ~ **and ballast renewal** *n* RAIL RVB; ~ **bed** *n* RAIL assiette de la voie *f*, plate-forme *f*, plate-forme de la voie *f*, plate-forme des terrassements *f*; ~ **cable** *n* TRANSP câble porteur *m*; ~ **channeler** *n* (AmE), ~ **channeller** *n* (BrE) MINING trancheuse montée sur rails *f*; ~ **chart** *n* NAUT *navigation* livre routier *m*; ~ **check** *n* CONTROL contrôle de piste *m*; ~ **circuit** *n* RAIL circuit de voie *m*; ~ **configuration** *n* TV géométrie des pistes *f*, répartition des pistes *f*;~ **connection** *n* RAIL jonction *f*, jonction de voies *f*; ~ **density** *n* OPT densité de pistes *f*; ~ **diagram** *n* RAIL panneau indicateur des voies *m*, plan des voies *m*;~ **gage** *n* (AmE), ~ **gauge** *n* (BrE) RAIL écartement des rails *m*; ~ **girder** *n* TRANSP poutre porteuse *f*; ~ **in service** *n* RAIL voie exploitée *f*; ~ **layer** *n* RAIL agent de la voie *m*; ~ **laying** *n* RAIL pose de rails *f*; ~ **magnet** *n* RAIL balise *f*; ~ **panel laying machine** *n* RAIL poseuse de panneaux de voie *f*, poseuse de travées de voie *f*; ~ **pitch** *n* DP entre-axe des pistes *m*, pas transversal *m*, OPT pas transversal *m*, RECORDING entre-axe des pistes *m*, pas de pistes *m*, TV entre-axe des pistes *m*; ~ **raising** *n* RAIL relèvement de la voie *m*; ~ **rod** *n* VEHICLES *steering* barre de connexion *f*, bielle de connexion *f*; ~ **roller** *n* MECH ENG *needle roller bearing* galet de came *m*; ~ **section** *n* RAIL tronçon de voie *m*; ~ **selector** *n* TV sélecteur de piste *m*; ~ **spacing** *n* RECORDING espace interpiste *m*; ~ **spreading** *n* RECORDING multiplication des pistes *f*; ~ **strip** *n* CONST *civil engineering* glissière de chenilles *f*; ~ **of totality** *n* ASTRON *of total eclipse of sun* trajectoire de totalité *f*; ~ **width** *n* RECORDING largeur de la piste *f*

track[2] *vi* CINEMAT faire un travelling

trackball *n* COMP, DP boule roulante *f*, trackball *m*

tracked: ~ **air cushion vehicle** *n* *(TACV)* TRANSP aéroglisseur guidé *m*; ~ **hovercraft** *n* TRANSP aéroglisseur guidé *m*; ~ **tractor** *n* CONST tracteur sur chenilles *m*, tractopelle *f*; ~ **vehicle** *n* VEHICLES véhicule à chenilles *m*

tracker *n* SPACE *technology* suiveur *m*; ~ **register** *n* NAUT *radar* calculateur de route *m*

track-guided: ~ **transport system** *n* TRANSP système de transport guidé *m*; ~ **vehicle** *n* TRANSP véhicule terrestre guidé *m*

tracking *n* AUTO géométrie du train *f*, ELEC *insulator fault* cheminement d'arc *m*, MILIT poursuite *f*, *of aircraft missile* pistage *m*, OCEANOG poursuite *f*, RECORDING centrage *m*, pistage *m*, SPACE poursuite *f*, TELECOM alignement *m*, *satellite* poursuite *f*, TRANSP *of helicopter* alignement des pales *m*, TV centrage de piste *m*, suivi de piste *m*; ~ **accuracy** *n* SPACE *communications* précision de poursuite *f*; ~ **antenna** *n* SPACE antenne de poursuite *f*; ~ **camera** *n* SPACE caméra de poursuite *f*; ~ **configuration** *n* RECORDING géométrie des pistes *f*, répartition des pistes *f*; ~ **control** *n* CONTROL contrôle de pistage *m*, TV régleur de centrage *m*; ~ **distortion** *n* RECORDING distorsion de centrage *f*; ~ **error** *n* METR *of measuring instrument* erreur de poursuite *f*, RECORDING erreur de pistage *f*, TELECOM erreur de poursuite *f*; ~ **filter** *n* ELECTRON filtre suiveur *m*; ~ **filter demodulator** *n* SPACE *communications* démodulateur à filtre asservi *m*; ~ **generator** *n* ELECTRON générateur asservi *m*, wobulateur *m*, TV générateur de signaux d'alignement *m*; ~ **local oscillator** *n* ELECTRON oscillateur local asservi *m*; ~ **mechanism** *n* OPT système de guidage *m*; ~ **oscillator** *n* ELECTRON oscillateur asservi *m*; ~ **radar** *n* SPACE radar de poursuite *m*; ~ **shot** *n* CINEMAT plan travelling *m*; ~ **station** *n* SPACE station de poursuite *f*; ~ **system** *n*

TELECOM système de poursuite *m*; ~ **telemetry and command** *n* *(TTC)* SPACE *communications* poursuite télémesure et télécommande *f* *(PTT)*

track-laying *n* CINEMAT préparation de bandes son pour mixage *f*, CONST *railway* pose des voies *f*; ~ **foreman** *n* RAIL chef de pose *m*

tracks: ~ **per inch** *n pl* *(TPI)* COMP, DP, PRINT pistes par pouce *f pl*

trackside: ~ **signaling** *n* (AmE), ~ **signalling** *n* (BrE) RAIL signalisation latérale *f*

traction *n* CONST traction *f*, MECH ENG tirage *m*, traction *f*, PRINT entraînement *m*, RAIL *vehicles* traction *f*; ~ **cable** *n* TRANSP câble tracteur *m*; ~ **differential** *n* AUTO différentiel autobloquant *m*; ~ **engine** *n* TRANSP véhicule tracteur *m*; ~ **locomotive** *n* RAIL *vehicles* locomotive de traction *f*; ~ **network** *n* ELEC *supply network* réseau de traction *m*; ~ **rope** *n* MECH ENG câble de tirage *m*, câble tracteur *m*, TRANSP câble tracteur *m*; ~ **supply-voltage changeover station** *n* RAIL gare commutable *f*

tractive: ~ **force** *n* METR force de traction *f*; ~ **unit** *n* TRANSP véhicule tracteur *m*

tractor *n* COMP, CONST, DP, TRANSP, VEHICLES tracteur *m*; ~ **feed** *n* PRINT tracteur à picots *m*; ~ **propeller** *n* AERONAUT hélice tractive *f*; ~ **unit** *n* TRANSP camion-tracteur *m*

tractor-trailer: ~ **truck** *n* (AmE) *(cf articulated lorry)* VEHICLES camion articulé *m*, camion semi-remorque *m*

trade: ~ **data interchange** *n* *(TDI)* TELECOM échange de données commerciales *m*; ~ **wind** *n* METEO alizé *m*, vent alizé *m*

trade-in *n* PROD ENG échange *m*

trademark *n* PATENTS, PROD ENG marque *f*, marque de fabrication *f*, marque de fabrique *f*

trading: ~ **name** *n* PATENTS nom commercial *m*; ~ **port** *n* NAUT port de commerce *m*

traditional: ~ **controls** *n pl* PROD ENG automatismes traditionnels *m pl*; ~ **telephone network** *n* TELECOM réseau téléphonique classique *m*

traffic *n* COMP, DP trafic *m*, TRANSP circulation *f*, trafic *m*, VEHICLES circulation *f*; ~ **analysis** *n* TELECOM analyse du trafic *f*; ~ **analysis detector** *n* TRANSP détecteur d'analyse de la circulation *m*; ~ **analyzer** *n* TRANSP analyseur de trafic *m*; ~ **assignment** *n* TRANSP affectation du trafic *f*; ~ **assignment model** *n* TRANSP modèle d'affectation du trafic *m*; ~ **assignment program** *n* (AmE), ~ **assignment programme** *n* (BrE) TRANSP programme d'affectation du trafic *m*; ~ **bollard** *n* CONTROL séparateur des courants de circulation *m*; ~ **burst** *n* SPACE *communication* salve de trafic *f*; ~ **carried** *n* TELECOM trafic écoulé *m*; ~ **census** *n* TRANSP comptage de trafic *m*; ~ **center** *n* (AmE), ~ **centre** *n* (BrE) TRANSP noeud de communication *m*; ~ **circle** *n* (AmE) *(cf roundabout)* CONST carrefour giratoire *m*, rond-point *m*; ~ **circuit** *n* TELECOM circuit de trafic *m*; ~ **computer** *n* TRANSP ordinateur de trafic *m*; ~ **concentration** *n* TRANSP densité du trafic *f*; ~ **conditions** *n pl* TRANSP conditions de trafic *f pl*; ~ **cone** *n* CONST cône avertisseur *m*; ~ **control** *n* CONTROL contrôle de la circulation *m*, TRANSP commande du trafic *f*; ~ **control installation** *n* TRANSP installation de régulation de la circulation *f*; ~ **control program** *n* (AmE), ~ **control programme** *n* (BrE) TRANSP programme de régulation de la circulation *m*; ~ **control signals** *n pl* CONTROL signalisation routière *f*; ~ **count**

n CONTROL comptage des mouvements *m*, TRANSP comptage de la circulation *m*; ~ **counter** *n* TRANSP compteur de trafic *m*; ~ **cuts** *n pl* TRANSP points de conflit *m pl*; ~ **demand** *n* TRANSP demande de trafic *f*; ~ **density** *n* TRANSP densité du trafic *f*; ~ **detector** *n* TRANSP détecteur de trafic *m*; ~ **distribution imbalance** *n* TELECOM déséquilibre du trafic *m*; ~ **division system** *n* TELECOM système en partage de trafic *m*; ~ **engineering** *n* TRANSP ingénierie de la circulation *f*; ~ **flow** *n* CONST circulation *f*, CONTROL intensité du trafic *f*, écoulement du trafic *m*, TELECOM flux du trafic *m*, écoulement du trafic *m*, TRANSP circulation *f*, débit de la circulation *m*; ~ **flow confidentiality** *n* TELECOM confidentialité du flux de données *f*; ~ **flow diagram** *n* TRANSP diagramme d'écoulement de la circulation *m*; ~ **forecast** *n* RAIL prévision de trafic *f*; ~ **forecasting** *n* TRANSP commande à temps fixe *f*; ~ **forecasting program** *n* (AmE), ~ **forecasting programme** *n* (BrE) TRANSP programme de prévision du trafic *m*; ~ **information** *n* TRANSP information routière *f*; ~ **information identification signal** *n* TRANSP signal d'identification de trafic *m*; ~ **island** *n* CONST îlot de canalisation *m*; ~ **jam** *n* TRANSP embouteillage *m*; ~ **lane** *n* NAUT *navigation* voie de circulation *f*, OCEANOG couloir de navigation *m*; ~ **load** *n* TELECOM, TRANSP charge de trafic *f*; ~ **load imbalance** *n* TELECOM déséquilibre du trafic *m*; ~ **management** *n* TRANSP plan de circulation *m*; ~ **network control** *n* TRANSP *traffic* commande zonale du trafic *f*; ~ **offered** *n* TELECOM trafic offert *m*; ~ **operator position** *n* TELECOM position de transit *f*; ~ **padding** *n* TELECOM bourrage *m*; ~ **parameter** *n* TRANSP paramètre de circulation *m*; ~ **queue** *n* (BrE) *(cf line of traffic, line of cars)* TRANSP file d'attente *f*; ~ **radio transmitter** *n* TRANSP émetteur de messages routiers *m*; ~ **region** *n* TRANSP région routière *f*; ~ **regulation system** *n* TRANSP système de régulation de la circulation *m*; ~ **routing program** *n* (AmE), ~ **routing programme** *n* (BrE) TRANSP programme de recherche d'itinéraire *m*; ~ **routing strategy** *n* TELECOM plan d'acheminement *m*; ~ **schedule** *n* RAIL plan de transport *m*; ~ **separation scheme** *n* NAUT *navigation* dispositif de séparation du trafic *m*; ~ **sign** *n* TRANSP panneau de signalisation *m*; ~ **signal** *n* ELECTRON signal de trafic *m*; ~ **signal controller** *n* CONTROL, TRANSP régulateur de signalisation *m*; ~ **signals** *n pl* CONTROL feu rouge *m*, feu tricolore de circulation *m*; ~ **signals program** *n* (AmE), ~ **signals programme** *n* (BrE) TRANSP programme de signalisation *m*; ~ **simulation** *n* TRANSP simulation de la circulation *f*; ~ **simulator** *n* TRANSP simulateur de circulation *m*; ~ **situation** *n* TRANSP situation de trafic *f*; ~ **stream** *n* TRANSP courant de circulation *m*; ~ **surveillance** *n* CONTROL surveillance du trafic *f*; ~ **survey** *n* TRANSP analyse de la circulation *f*; ~ **volume** *n* TRANSP débit *m*; ~ **volume meter** *n* TRANSP détecteur de débit *m*

traffic-actuated: ~ **signal** *n* TRANSP *traffic control* signal lumineux actionné par le trafic *m*

traffic-adjusted: ~ **controller** *n* TRANSP régulateur à commande par détection de trafic *m*

traffic-carrying: ~ **device** *n* TELECOM organe de trafic *m*

tragacanth *n* FOOD TECH gomme adragante *f*

trail *n* SPACE traînée *f*; ~ **dredging** *n* NAUT dragage à la traîne *m*

trail-edge: ~ **one-shot programing** *n* (AmE), ~ **one-shot programming** *n* (BrE) PROD ENG programmation d'impulsion sur front de descente *f*

trailer *n* *(cf bogie)* CONST, MECH *vehicles* remorque *f*, MECH ENG bogie *m*, RAIL *vehicles* remorque *f*, TRANSP caravane *f*, TRANSP remorque *f*, VEHICLES bogie *m*, VEHICLES caravane de camping *f*, remorque de camping *f*, remorque *f*; ~ **bogie** *n* (BrE) *(cf trailer car)* RAIL *vehicles* bogie porteur *m*; ~ **brake** *n* VEHICLES frein de remorque *m*; ~ **car** *n* (AmE) *(cf trailer bogie)* RAIL *vehicles* bogie porteur *m*; ~ **label** *n* COMP, DP label fin *m*; ~ **on flatcar** *n (TOFC)* TRANSP ferroutage *m*; ~ **record** *n* COMP, DP enregistrement de fin *m*; ~ **train** *n* TRANSP camion et remorque *m*; ~ **wagon** *n* (AmE) *(cf wagon car)* TRANSP wagonnet *m*

trailer-towing: ~ **machine** *n* TRANSP tracteur routier *m*

trailing:[1] ~ **edge** *adj* PROD ENG sur front de descente

trailing:[2] ~ **arm** *n* VEHICLES *of wheel suspension* bras oscillant longitudinal *m*; ~ **axle** *n* VEHICLES *of truck* essieu traîné *m*; ~ **cable** *n* ELEC ENG ligne de commande d'ascenseur *f*; ~ **edge** *n* AERONAUT *of wing* bord de fuite *m*, ELECTRON queue d'onde *f*, PHYS bord de fuite *m*, TV flanc arrière *m*; ~ **load** *n* TRANSP charge remorquée *f*; ~ **shoe** *n* VEHICLES *of brake* mâchoire tendue *f*, segment tendu *m*; ~ **vector** *n* AERONAUT *sonic boom* vecteur de fuite *m*; ~ **vortices** *n pl* FLUID PHYS tourbillons derrière des obstacles *m pl*

trailing-blade: ~ **coated paper** *n* PAPER TECH papier couché à lame traînante *m*; ~ **coating** *n* PAPER TECH couchage à lame traînante *m*

trailing-edge: ~ **flap** *n* AERONAUT volet de bord de fuite *m*; ~ **one-shot** *n* PROD ENG programmation d'impulsion sur front de descente *f*; ~ **video track** *n* TV bord de piste vidéo en amont *m*

train: ~ **about to depart** *n* RAIL train en partance *m*; ~ **of action** *n* MECH ENG *gearing* ligne de poussée *f*, ligne de pression *f*, normale commune des profils *f*, normale de contact *f*; ~ **of bubbles** *n* C&G fil bouillonneux *m*; ~ **connection** *n* RAIL correspondance *f*; ~ **consist** *n* (AmE) *(cf train formation)* RAIL composition du train *f*; ~ **crew** *n* RAIL *vehicles* personnel d'accompagnement *m*; ~ **describer** *n* RAIL suivi de train *m*; ~ **ferry** *n* NAUT bac transbordeur *m*, RAIL bac transbordeur *m*, navire transbordeur *m*; ~ **formation** *n* (BrE) *(cf train consist)* RAIL composition du train *f*; ~ **of gearing** *n* MECH ENG train d'engrenages *m*, équipage d'engrenages *m*; ~ **printer** *n* (BrE) *(cf chain printer)* COMP imprimante à chaîne *f*; ~ **rake** *n* RAIL *vehicles* rame *f*; ~ **of rolls** *n* MECH ENG batterie de cylindres *f*, jeu de cylindres *m*, train de cylindres *m*, équipage de cylindres *m*; ~ **service indicator** *n* RAIL pancarte *f*; ~ **set** *n* RAIL *vehicles* rame *f*; ~ **spacing** *n* RAIL distance *f*; ~ **supervision** *n* RAIL appareil d'annonce de trains *m*; ~ **supervision number** *n* RAIL suivi de train *m*; ~ **that cannot be split up** *n* RAIL *vehicles* train indéformable *m*

trainer *n* ELECTRON simulateur *m*

training *n* CONST *of personnel*, MECH ENG formation *f*; ~ **flight** *n* AERONAUT vol d'entraînement *m*; ~ **rack** *n* MILIT *artillery* circulaire de pointage *f*; ~ **reactor** *n* NUCLEAR réacteur d'entraînement *m*; ~ **scheme** *n* MECH ENG programme de formation *m*; ~ **ship** *n* NAUT navire-école *m*; ~ **wheel** *n* MILIT *artillery* volant de pointage en direction *m*

train-protecting: ~ **signal** *n* RAIL signal de protection de train *m*

train-through-the-lens: ~ **mask** *n* PROD ENG masque appris par la caméra *m*

trajectography *n* RAD PHYS *particle tracking*, SPACE trajectographie *f*

trajectory *n* AERONAUT trajectoire *m*, MILIT *of shell* courbe d'une trajectoire *f*, PHYS, SPACE trajectoire *f*

tram *n* (BrE) MINING *mine railways* berlaine *f*, berline *f*, wagonnet *m*, TRANSP voiture de tramway *f*; ~ **stop** *n* TRANSP arrêt de tramway *m*; ~ **system** *n* MINING installation de roulage *f*; ~ **track** *n* CONST voie de tram *f*

tramlines *n pl* PHOTO rayures parallèles *f pl*

trammel *n* C&G tournette *f*, MECH ENG *drawing* compas à verge *m*; ~ **net** *n* OCEANOG tramail *m*, trémail *m*

tramping *n* C&G marchage *m*, PROD ENG *founding, of sand* serrage *m*, serrage du sable *m*

tramway *n* (BrE) TRANSP tramway *m*; ~ **metro** *n* TRANSP semi-métro *m*; ~ **motor unit** *n* RAIL motrice de tramway *f*

trang: ~ **roll** *n* C&G contre-rouleau *m*

transaction *n* COMP, DP mouvement *m*, transaction *f*; ~ **capabilities application part** *n* TELECOM SSGT, sous-système de gestion des transactions *m*; ~ **file** *n* COMP fichier des mouvements *m*, DP fichier des transactions *m*; ~ **management software** *n* COMP, DP logiciel de gestion transactionnelle *m*; ~ **management subsystem** *n* TELECOM sous-système pour la gestion des transactions *m*; ~ **processing** *n* (*TP*) COMP, DP traitement de transactions *m*; ~ **record** *n* COMP, DP enregistrement mouvement *m*

transactional: ~ **set-header** *n* TELECOM en-tête d'ensemble transactionnel *m*

transceiver *n* DP, NAUT *radio*, TELECOM émetteur-récepteur *m*

transcendental *adj* MATH transcendent

transcoder *n* TELECOM, TV transcodeur *m*

transcoding *n* TELECOM transcodage *m*; ~ **gain** *n* (*TG*) TELECOM gain de transcodage *m*

transconductance *n* ELEC ENG conductance mutuelle *f*, transconductance *f*, PHYS transconductance *f*

transcontainer *n* TRANSP conteneur pour trafic d'outre-mer *m*, transconteneur *m*

transcribe *vt* COMP, DP transcrire

transcurrent: ~ **fault** *n* GEOL décrochement *m*; ~ **thrust** *n* GEOL décro-chevauchement *m*

transducer *n* ACOUSTICS, COMP, DP, ELEC, ELEC ENG, MECH ENG, PHYS, TELECOM, TESTING capteur *m*, transducteur *m*; ~ **efficiency** *n* ACOUSTICS efficacité d'un transducteur *f*; ~ **loss factor** *n* ACOUSTICS facteur de perte transductique *f*

transductor *n* ELEC ENG transducteur magnétique *m*, PHYS inductance saturable *f*, *saturable reactor* amplificateur magnétique *m*, transducteur *m*

transfer[1] *n* C&G décalcomanie *f*, COMP, DP, PATENTS transfert *m*, PRINT décalque *m*, report *m*, transfert *m*, SPACE *spacecraft* puisage *m*, remplissage *m*, transfert *m*, TELECOM transfert *m*; ~ **acoustic impedance** *n* ACOUSTICS impédance acoustique de transfert *f*; ~ **allowed** *n* (*TFA*) TELECOM autorisation de transfert *f*; ~ **button** *n* CONTROL bouton d'intercommunication *m*; ~ **characteristic** *n* ELECTRON, PHYS caractéristique de transfert *f*; ~ **charge call** *n* TELECOM appel en PCV *m*, appel à frais virés *m* (Can); ~ **die** *n* MECH ENG *press tools* outillage de transfert pour presses *m*; ~ **from tank** *n* SPACE puisage dans un réservoir *m*, remplissage *m*; ~ **function** *n* CONTROL, OPT, TELECOM fonction de transfert *f*; ~ **gate** *n* ELEC ENG porte de transfert *f*; ~ **glass** *n* C&G verre brut refroidi dans le pot *m*; ~ **impedance** *n* ELEC *network*, TELECOM impédance de transfert *f*; ~ **inefficiency** *n* ELEC ENG inefficacité de transfert *f*; ~ **of**

license *n* QUALITY cession de licence *f*; ~ **line** *n* MECH ENG ligne de transfert *f*; ~ **machine** *n* MECH machine de transfert *f*; ~ **of mass** *n* GAS TECH transfert de masse *m*; ~ **matrix** *n* PHYS *circuit theory* matrice de transfert *f*; ~ **mechanical impedance** *n* ACOUSTICS impédance mécanique de transfert *f*; ~ **mold** *n* (AmE) *see transfer mould*; ~ **molding** *n* (AmE) *see transfer moulding*; ~ **mould** *n* (BrE) MECH ENG *for rubber, for thermosetting* moule de transfert *m*; ~ **moulding** *n* (BrE) P&R *process* moulage par transfert *m*; ~ **orbit** *n* SPACE orbite de transfert *f*, transfert interorbital *m*; ~ **port** *n* NUCLEAR *of glove box* orifice d'accès *m*, VEHICLES *of two-stroke engine* lumière de transfert *f*; ~ **prohibited** *n* (*TFP*) TELECOM transfert interdit *m*; ~ **protocol** *n* COMP, DP protocole de transfert *m*; ~ **pump** *n* MAR POLL pompe de transfert *f*; ~ **rate** *n* COMP, DP vitesse de transfert *f*; ~ **ratio** *n* TV rapport de transfert *m*; ~ **reaction** *n* NUCLEAR réaction de transfert *f*; ~ **restricted** *n* (*TFR*) TELECOM transfert restreint *m*; ~ **stage** *n* SPACE étage de transfert *m*; ~ **station** *n* MINING station de transfert *f*; ~ **syntax** *n* TELECOM syntaxe de transfert *f*; ~ **tails** *n pl* TEXTILES rattaches *f pl*; ~ **track** *n* (AmE) (*cf transshipment track*) RAIL voie de transbordement *f*; ~ **tube** *n* PROD ENG tubulure transfert *f*

transfer[2] *vt* COMP, DP transférer, PRINT décalquer, RECORDING repiquer, transférer

transferred: ~ **electron diode** *n* ELECTRON diode à transfert d'électrons *f*

transfinite *adj* MATH transfini

transflective: ~ **back coating** *n* ELECTRON couche postérieure semi-transparente *f*; ~ **LCD** *n* ELECTRON afficheur à cristaux liquides à transflexion *m*

transform[1] *n* CHEM *of molecule* forme trans *f*, COMP, DP transformation *f*, MATH transformée *f*; ~ **fault** *n* GEOL faille transformante *f*

transform[2] *vt* COMP, DP transformer

transformation *n* ELEC ENG, PROP MAT transformation *f*; ~ **of electricity** *n* ELEC *supply network* transformation d'énergie électrique *f*; ~ **point** *n* C&G température de transformation *f*; ~ **process** *n* GAS TECH processus de transformation *m*; ~ **range** *n* C&G domaine de transformation *m*; ~ **rate** *n* POLLUTION taux de conversion *m*, taux de transformation *m*; ~ **temperature** *n* C&G température de transformation *f*

transformer *n* ELEC *AC/DC current*, ELEC ENG, PHYS, TELECOM transformateur *m*; ~ **core** *n* ELEC, ELEC ENG noyau de transformateur *m*; ~ **coupling** *n* ELEC couplage par transformateur *m*, ELEC ENG liaison par transformateur *f*; ~ **efficiency** *n* ELEC rendement d'un transformateur *m*; ~ **emf** *n* ELEC, PHYS force électromotrice de transformation *f*; ~ **hum** *n* RECORDING ronflement de transformateur *m*; ~ **isolation** *n* ELEC ENG isolement par transformateur *m*; ~ **loss** *n* ELEC ENG pertes dans un transformateur *f pl*; ~ **oil** *n* ELEC, ELEC ENG huile pour transformateur *f*; ~ **primary switching** *n* PROD ENG commutation de primaire de transformateurs *f*; ~ **secondary** *n* PROD ENG secondaire du transformateur *m*; ~ **substation** *n* ELEC *supply network* poste de transformation *m*, sous-station de transformation *f*, ELEC ENG sous-station de transformation *f*; ~ **tap** *n* ELEC ENG prise de transformateur *f*

transformerless: ~ **output stage** *n* RECORDING étage de sortie sans transformateur *m*; ~ **power supply** *n* ELEC *supply network* alimentation sans transformateur *f*

transformer-type: ~ **dual input** *n* PROD ENG entrée double à transformateur *f*

transfusion: ~ **bottle** _n_ C&G flacon pour transfusion _m_

transgranular: ~ **cracking** _n_ PROP MAT fissuration transgranulaire _f_

transgression _n_ GEOL transgression _f_

transient[1] _adj_ ELEC ENG, PHYS transitoire

transient[2] _n_ ELEC ENG transitoire _f_, PHYS phénomène transitoire _m_, PROD ENG pointe transitoire _f_, TELECOM clic _m_, pointe _f_, transitoire _f_; ~ **analysis** _n_ ELECTRON analyse des transitoires _f_; ~ **analyzer** _n_ ELECTRON analyseur de transitoires _m_; ~ **condition** _n_ ELEC, ELEC ENG régime transitoire _m_; ~ **creep** _n_ METALL fluage transitoire _m_; ~ **current** _n_ TRANSP _traffic_ courant transitoire _m_; ~ **distortion** _n_ RECORDING distorsion de transitoire _f_; ~ **equilibrium** _n_ PHYS équilibre transitoire _m_; ~ **error** _n_ COMP, DP erreur transitoire _f_; ~ **globule** _n_ PART PHYS globule éphémère _m_; ~ **oscillation** _n_ PHYS oscillation transitoire _f_; ~ **phase** _n_ METALL phase transitoire _f_; ~ **protection** _n_ PROD ENG protection contre les surintensités _f_; ~ **response** _n_ CONTROL réponse indicielle _f_, ELEC ENG réponse en régime transitoire _f_, réponse transitoire _f_, TV caractéristique de saut _f_, réponse au signal unité _f_; ~ **state** _n_ ELEC régime transitoire _m_; ~ **suppression** _n_ ELEC ENG élimination des transitoires _f_; ~ **suppressor** _n_ ELEC ENG suppresseur des transitoires _m_; ~ **voltage** _n_ ELEC tension transitoire _f_; ~ **voltage limitation** _n_ PROD ENG limitation des parasites transitoires _f_

transient-suppressed _adj_ PROD ENG antiparasite de façon transitoire

transistor COMP, DP, ELECTRON, PHYS transistor _m_; ~ **amplification** _n_ ELECTRON amplification par transistor _f_; ~ **amplifier** _n_ ELECTRON amplificateur à transistor _m_; ~ **base** _n_ ELECTRON, TELECOM base de transistor _f_; ~ **bias** _n_ ELECTRON polarisation d'un transistor _f_; ~ **characteristics** _n pl_ ELECTRON caractéristiques d'un transistor _f pl_; ~ **chip** _n_ ELECTRON puce de transistor _f_; ~ **collector** _n_ TELECOM collecteur de transistor _m_; ~ **control unit** _n_ AUTO bloc électronique _m_; ~ **emitter** _n_ TELECOM émetteur _m_; ~ **ignition unit** _n_ AUTO boîtier électronique _m_; ~ **modulator** _n_ ELECTRON modulateur à transistor _m_; **off** ~ _n_ ELECTRON transistor à l'état bloqué _m_; ~ **oscillator** _n_ ELECTRON oscillateur à transistor _m_; ~ **pair** _n_ ELECTRON paire de transistors _f_; ~ **power amplifier** _n_ ELECTRON amplificateur de puissance à transistor _m_; ~ **power gain** _n_ RECORDING gain en puissance du transistor _m_; ~ **saturation** _n_ ELECTRON saturation d'un transistor _f_

transistorized: ~ **ignition system** _n_ AUTO allumage transistorisé _m_; ~ **regulator** _n_ AUTO régulateur électronique _m_

transistor-transistor: ~ **logic** _n_ (_TTL_) COMP, DP logique transistor-transistor _f_, ELECTRON logique à transistor et transistors _f_

transit _n_ ASTRON _of Mercury and Venus_ passage _m_, CONST théodolite à lunette centrale _m_, théodolite à lunette centrée _m_, NAUT _navigation_ alignement _m_, NUCLEAR _of charged particle_ transit _m_; ~ **car** _n_ MINING berline de transport _f_; ~ **connection element** _n_ (_TCE_) TELECOM élément de connexion de transit _m_; ~ **connection-related function** _n_ (_TCRF_) TELECOM fonction liée à une connexion de transit _f_; ~ **exchange** _n_ TELECOM commutateur de transit _m_; ~ **passengers** _n pl_ TRANSP passagers en transit _m pl_; ~ **rub** _n_ C&G frôlure _f_; ~ **switching center** _n_ (AmE), ~ **switching centre** _n_ (BrE) TELECOM centre de transit _m_; ~ **telescope** _n_ ASTRON lunette méridienne _f_, INSTRUMENT

télescope réversible _m_; ~ **theodolite** _n_ CONST théodolite à lunette centrale _m_, théodolite à lunette centrée _m_; ~ **time** _n_ ELEC ENG, NUCLEAR _for charged particle_ temps de transit _m_, PETR temps de trajet _m_, temps de transit _m_, PHYS temps de transit _m_, PROD ENG temps de transfert _m_, temps de transit _m_, temps de transport _m_; ~ **traffic** _n_ TELECOM trafic de transit _m_; ~ **of Venus across the sun** _n_ ASTRON passage de Vénus d'un bord à l'autre du Soleil _m_

transition: ~ **contact** _n_ ELEC _of transformer_ contact de passage _m_; ~ **curve** _n_ CONST _surveying_ courbe de raccordement _f_; ~ **element** _n_ CHEM, PROP MAT élément de transition _m_; ~ **enthalpy** _n_ NUCLEAR enthalpie de transition _f_; ~ **impedance** _n_ ELEC _of resistor, reactance_ impédance de passage _f_; ~ **joint** _n_ ELEC _cable connection_ jonction mixte _f_; ~ **lake** _n_ POLLUTION lac en transition _m_; ~ **loss index** _n_ ACOUSTICS indice d'affaiblissement acoustique _m_; ~ **metal** _n_ METALL métal de transition _m_; ~ **point** _n_ NUCLEAR point de transition _m_, température de transition _f_; ~ **probability** _n_ PHYS probabilité de transition _f_; ~ **radiation detector** _n_ RAD PHYS détecteur à rayonnement de transition _m_; ~ **segment** _n_ AERONAUT _landing_ segment de transition _m_; ~ **temperature** _n_ METALL température de transition _f_, NUCLEAR point de transition _m_, température de transition _f_, PHYS, REFRIG température de transition _f_; ~ **to turbulence** _n_ FLUID PHYS transition de turbulence _f_; ~ **zone** _n_ PETR, PETR TECH zone de transition _f_

transitional: ~ **precipitate** _n_ METALL précipité de transition _m_

transit-time: ~ **device** _n_ ELEC ENG dispositif à temps de transit _m_; ~ **diode** _n_ ELECTRON diode à temps de transit _f_; ~ **reduction factor** _n_ PROD ENG facteur de réduction du temps de transit _m_; ~ **tube** _n_ SPACE tube à modulation de vitesse _m_

translate _vt_ COMP _image_, DP _image_ traduire, transcoder

translating: ~ **wheel** _n_ MECH ENG _screw-cutting lathe_ roue de correction _f_

translation _n_ COMP, DP traduction _f_, GEOM translation _f_, MECH ENG mouvement de translation _m_, translation _f_, PHYS _displacement_ translation _f_; ~ **on a drawing** _n_ PROD ENG déplacement sur un plan _m_; ~ **plane** _n_ CRYSTALL, METALL plan de translation _m_; ~ **speed** _n_ TRANSP vitesse de translation _f_; ~ **store** _n_ TELECOM mémoire de traduction _f_

translator _n_ COMP, DP, TELECOM traducteur _m_; ~ **station** _n_ TV émetteur relais _m_

translatory: ~ **motion** _n_ MECH ENG mouvement de translation _m_, translation _f_

transliterate _vt_ COMP, DP translittérer, translitérer

transliteration _n_ COMP, DP translittération _f_, translitération _f_

translucence _n_ PROP MAT, RAD PHYS translucidité _f_

translucency _n_ PROP MAT translucidité _f_

translucent[1] _adj_ CHEM translucide

translucent:[2] ~ **drawing paper** _n_ PAPER TECH papier-calque _m_; ~ **glass** _n_ C&G verre translucide _m_; ~ **medium** _n_ PHYS milieu translucide _m_; ~ **substance** _n_ RAD PHYS substance translucide _f_

transmission _n_ AUTO boîte de vitesse _f_, transmission _f_, COMP, DP transmission _f_, ELEC _of electricity_ transport d'énergie électrique _m_, _supply network_ transmission _f_, GAS TECH transport _m_, MECH, MECH ENG transmission _f_, PHYS transmission _f_, émission _f_, TELECOM envoi _m_, transmission _f_, TV transmission _f_, émission _f_, VEHICLES transmission _f_; ~ **attenuation** _n_ SPACE *communications* affaiblissement de transmission *m*; ~ **bearer** *n* TELECOM support de transmission *m*; ~ **belting** *n* PAPER TECH courroie de transmission *f*; ~ **block** *n* COMP, DP bloc de transmission *m*; ~ **breakdown** *n* TELECOM interruption de transmission *f*; ~ **bridge** *n* TELECOM pont d'alimentation *m*; ~ **bush chain** *n* MECH ENG chaîne de transmission à douilles *f*; ~ **channel** *n* COMP, DP, TELECOM voie de transmission *f*; ~ **characteristic** *n* TELECOM caractéristique de transmission *f*; ~ **copy** *n* PHYS *of sound* coefficient de transmission *m*; ~ **control** *n* COMP gestion de la transmission *f*, CONTROL contrôle de transmission *m*, DP commande de transmission *f*; ~ **convergence** *n* TELECOM convergence de transmission *f*, sous-couche de convergence de transmission *f*; ~ **convergence sublayer** *n* TELECOM sous-couche de convergence de transmission *f*; ~ **copy** *n* CINEMAT, TV copie d'antenne *f*; ~ **electron microscope** *n* ELECTRON, INSTRUMENT, LAB EQUIP, NUCLEAR, PHYS microscope électronique à transmission *m*, RAD PHYS microscope à rayons X *m*; ~ **electron microscopy** *n* RAD PHYS microscopie à électron de transmission *f*; ~ **of energy** *n* ELEC ENG transmission d'énergie *f*; ~ **error** *n* TELECOM erreur de transmission *f*; ~ **function** *n* NUCLEAR fonction de transmission *f*; ~ **gain** *n* ACOUSTICS gain de transmission *m*; ~ **gear** *n* MECH ENG organes de transmission *m pl*, transmission *f*, *intermediate toothed gearing* engrenage de transmission *m*; ~ **grating** *n* PHYS réseau par transmission *m*; ~ **highway** *n* TELECOM artère de transmission *f*; ~ **joint** *n* PROD ENG joint de transmission *m*; ~ **layer** *n* TELECOM couche réseau de transmission *f*; ~ **line** *n* CONST, ELEC ENG, ELECTRON, PHYS, TELECOM ligne de transmission *f*; ~ **line network** *n* ELEC *supply network* réseau aérien *m*; ~ **loss** *n* ACOUSTICS affaiblissement acoustique *m*, perte de transmission *f*, OPT affaiblissement de transmission *m*, SPACE perte de transmission *f*, TELECOM affaiblissement de transmission *m*, perte de transmission *f*; ~ **main** *n* PETR TECH canalisation *f*; ~ **medium** *n* COMP, DP, OPT support de transmission *m*; ~ **mode** *n* ELECTRON mode de transmission *m*, *for LCDs* mode par transmission *m*; ~ **network** *n* GAS TECH réseau de transport *m*, TELECOM réseau de transmission *m*; ~ **node** *n* TELECOM noeud de transmission *m*; ~ **overload** *n* TELECOM surcharge de transmission *f*; ~ **path** *n* TELECOM trajet de transmission *m*; ~ **path endpoint** *n* (*TPE*) TELECOM extrémité de trajet de transmission *f*; ~ **pinion** *n* AUTO pignon entraîneur *m*; ~ **priority code** *n* TELECOM code de priorité de la transmission *m*; ~ **quality** *n* TELECOM qualité de transmission *f*; ~ **rate** *n* ELEC ENG, PROD ENG vitesse de transmission *f*; ~ **ratio** *n* AUTO rapport de transmission *m*; ~ **recipient** *n* TELECOM destinataire *m*; ~ **reduction** *n* AUTO démultiplication *f*; ~ **requirements for ultraviolet filters** *n pl* SAFETY spécifications de transmission pour filtres ultraviolets *f pl*; ~ **rod** *n* MECH ENG barre de renvoi *f*, tige de transmission *f*; ~ **security** *n* COMP, DP sécurité de transmission *f*; ~ **sender** *n* TELECOM expéditeur *m*; ~ **sending** *n* TELECOM envoi *m*; ~ **shaft** *n* MECH ENG arbre de transmission *m*; ~ **spectrum** *n* NUCLEAR spectre de transmission *m*; ~ **speed** *n* COMP, DP, TELECOM vitesse de transmission *f*; ~ **system** *n* ELEC ENG système de transmission *m*; ~ **technique** *n* NUCLEAR *X-ray crystallography analysis*, TESTING méthode de transmission *f*, méthode par transmission *f*; ~ **tower** *n* ELEC *supply network* pylône de lignes électriques aériennes *m*; ~ **window** *n* OPT, TELECOM fenêtre

spectrale *f*, ~ **wire** *n* NAUT *boatbuilding, of rudder* drosse *f*

transmissive: ~ **disc** *n* (BrE) *see transparent disc*; ~ **disk** *n* (AmE) *see transmissive disc*; ~ **LCD** *n* ELEC ENG afficheur à cristaux liquides à transmission *m*, afficheur à transmission *m*

transmit:[1] ~ **antenna** *n* TELECOM antenne émettrice *f*; ~ **channel** *n* TELECOM canal d'émission *m*; ~ **fiber optic terminal device** *n* (AmE), ~ **fibre optic terminal device** *n* (BrE) TELECOM émetteur optique *m*; ~ **machine** *n* TELECOM *telex* machine émettrice *f*

transmit[2] *vt* COMP transmettre, émettre, DP, NAUT *radio* transmettre

transmit-receive *adj* (*TR*) ELECTRON émetteur-récepteur

transmittance *n* OPT facteur de transmission *m*, PHYS *transmission factor* facteur de transmission *m*, transmittance *f*, TELECOM facteur de transmission *m*, WAVE PHYS *transmission coefficient, reciprocal of opacity* transmittance *f*; ~ **density** *n* OPT densité optique par réflexion *f*

transmitted: ~ **beam** *n* PHYS faisceau transmis *m*; ~ **data** *n pl* TELECOM émission des données *f*; ~ **light** *n* PHOTO, RAD PHYS lumière transmise *f*; ~ **light microscope** *n* INSTRUMENT microscope à transmission *m*; ~ **light microscope with polarizer** *n* INSTRUMENT microscope à transmission de type Zeiss avec appareil polariseur *m*; ~ **wave** *n* PHYS onde transmise *f*

transmitter *n* NAUT *radio*, PHYS, SPACE *communications* émetteur *m*, TELECOM microphone *m*, microphone téléphonique *m*, émetteur *m*, TV poste émetteur *m*, émetteur *m*, WAVE PHYS *generates electromagnetic waves* émetteur *m*; ~ **failure** *n* TV panne d'émetteur *f*; ~ **identification signal** *n* TRANSP signal d'identification d'émetteur *m*; ~ **of motive power** *n* MECH ENG communicateur de mouvement puissance *m*; ~ **power** *n* TV puissance d'émetteur *f*; ~ **turn-on signal** *n* TELECOM signal de commande de mise en porteuse *m*; ~ **turn-on time** *n* TELECOM temps de montée de la porteuse *m*

transmitter-receiver *n* NAUT *radio*, TELECOM, TV émetteur-récepteur *m*

transmitting: ~ **aerial** *n* TV antenne d'émission *f*; ~ **aerial antenna** *n* PHYS antenne émettrice *f*; ~ **antenna** *n* TV antenne d'émission *f*; ~ **frequency** *n* TV fréquence d'émission *f*; ~ **microphone** *n* RECORDING micro-HF *m*, micro haute fréquence *m*

transmultiplexer *n* (*TMUX*) TELECOM transmultiplexeur *m*

transmutation *n* NUCLEAR, PHYS, RAD PHYS transmutation *f*

transom *n* CONST linteau *m*, sommier *m*, traverse *f*, NAUT *boatbuilding* tableau arrière *m*; ~ **plate** *n* NAUT *shipbuilding* tableau arrière *m*, tôle d'arcasse *f*; ~ **stern** *n* NAUT *boatbuilding* arrière à tableau *m*

transonic[1] *adj* AERONAUT, PHYS, TRANSP transsonique

transonic:[2] ~ **speed** *n* AERONAUT, PHYS, TRANSP vitesse transsonique *f*

transoral *adj* CINEMAT *screen* transonore

transparency *n* CINEMAT diapositive *f*, P&R *plastics, coatings* transparence *f*, PHOTO diapositive *f*, PRINT diapositive *f*, transparence *f*, ekta *m*, PROP MAT limpidité *f*

transparent[1] *adj* COMP, DP, TELECOM transparent

transparent:[2] ~ **antitamper cover** *n* PROD ENG capot transparent de plombage *m*; ~ **bearer service** *n* TELECOM service support terminal *m*; ~ **coating** *n* COATINGS enduit transparent *m*, revêtement transparent *m*; ~ **disc** *n* (BrE) OPT disque transparent *m*; ~ **disk** *n* (AmE) *see transparent disc*; ~ **enamel** *n* C&G émail transparent *m*; ~ **film** *n* PACKAGING film transparent *m*; ~ **glaze** *n* C&G glaçure transparente *f*; ~ **lacquer** *n* COLOURS vernis transparent *m*; ~ **medium** *n* PHYS milieu transparent *m*; ~ **overlay** *n* CINEMAT transparent superposable *m*; ~ **positive** *n* PRINT positif transparent *m*; ~ **substance** *n* RAD PHYS substance transparente *f*

transpiration: ~ **cooling** *n* GAS TECH, REFRIG refroidissement par transpiration *m*; ~ **of gases** *n* GAS TECH transpiration thermique des gaz *f*

transplutonium: ~ **element** *n* NUCLEAR élément transplutonien *m*

transponder *n* PHYS, SPACE *communications* répéteur *m*, transpondeur *m*, TELECOM répondeur *m*, répéteur *m*; ~ **beacon** *n* SPACE balise répondeuse *f*; ~ **system** *n* TELECOM système émetteur-récepteur *m*

transport[1] *n* COMP, DP transport *m*; ~ **and communications** *n pl* TRANSP transports et communications *m pl*; ~ **and communications aircraft** *n* AERONAUT avion de transport et de liaison *m*; ~ **and rescue helicopter** *n* TRANSP hélicoptère léger de transport et de secours *m*; ~ **by helicopter** *n* AERONAUT, NAUT, TRANSP héliportage *m*; ~ **capacity for solids** *n* HYDROL *of water course* capacité de débit solide *f*, capacité de transport *f*; ~ **glider** *n* MILIT planeur de transport *m*; ~ **helicopter** *n* TRANSP hélicoptère de transport *m*; ~ **in low-pressure tube** *n* TRANSP transport en tube à dépression *m*; ~ **layer** *n* DP *OSI* couche de transport *f*; ~ **mechanism** *n* TV mécanisme de transport *m*; ~ **model** *n* POLLUTION *of pollutant* modèle de transport *m*; ~ **protocol data unit** *n* (*TPDU*) TELECOM unité de données du protocole de transport *f*; ~ **service access point** *n* (*TSAP*) TELECOM point d'accès au service de transport *m*; ~ **under controlled temperature** *n* REFRIG transport sous contrôle de température *m*

transport[2] *vt* HYDROL *floating body* charrier, entraîner; ~ **by rail and road** *vt* TRANSP ferrouter

transportable[1] *adj* COMP, DP transportable

transportable:[2] ~ **Earth station** *n* SPACE *communications* station terrestre transportable *f*; ~ **gas container** *n* SAFETY bouteille à gaz transportable *f*; ~ **reactor** *n* NUCLEAR réacteur mobile *m*, réacteur transportable *m*

transportation *n* MINING *of personnel* translation *f*; ~ **safety** *n* SAFETY sûreté des transports *f*; ~ **source** *n* POLLUTION source mobile *f*; ~ **system** *n* CONST système de transport *m*; ~ **time** *n* PROD ENG temps de transfert *m*, temps de transit *m*

transporter *n* MECH ENG convoyeur *m*, transporteur *m*, transporteuse *f*

transposing: ~ **frame** *n* PHOTO *for printing stereo pairs* châssis inverseur *m*; ~ **instrument** *n* ACOUSTICS instrument de transposition *m*

transposition *n* ACOUSTICS, ELEC *of insulated cables* transposition *f*; ~ **tower** *n* ELEC *supply network* pylône de transposition *m*

transpressive *adj* GEOL décro-chevauchement *m*

transputer *n* COMP transordinateur *m*, DP transputer *m*

transship *vt* NAUT *passengers, cargo* changer, transborder

transshipment *n* NAUT, PETR TECH transbordement *m*; ~ **track** *n* (BrE) *(cf transfer track)* RAIL voie de transbordement *f*

transtainer *n* TRANSP pont roulant de chargement *m*; ~ **crane** *n* TRANSP *container loading* pont roulant de chargement *m*

transuranic[1] *adj* RAD PHYS transuranique

transuranic:[2] ~ **waste** *n* NUCLEAR déchets radioactifs contenant des transuraniens *m pl*

transversal *n* GEOM transversale *f*; ~ **filter** *n* ELECTRON, TELECOM filtre transversal *m*; ~ **filtering** *n* ELECTRON filtrage par filtre transversal *m*; ~ **scratch** *n* CINEMAT rayure transversale *f*

transverse[1] *adj* NAUT *ship design* latitudinal, transversal; ~ **electric** *adj* (*TE*) OPT, TELECOM transversal électrique; ~ **electromagnetic** *adj* (*TEM*) ELEC ENG électromagnétique transverse (*TEM*); ~ **magnetic** *adj* (*TM*) ELEC ENG, OPT, TELECOM magnétique transversal

transverse:[2] ~ **beam** *n* NAUT *shipbuilding* traverse *f*; ~ **bulkhead** *n* NAUT *ship design* cloison transversale *f*; ~ **chromatic aberration** *n* PHYS aberration chromatique transversale *f*; ~ **component** *n* PHYS composante transversale *f*; ~ **control arm** *n* VEHICLES *of wheel suspension* bras oscillant transversal *m*; ~ **current** *n* C&G courant transversal *m*; ~ **electric and magnetic wave** *n* PHYS *TEM wave* onde transversale électromagnétique *f*; ~ **electric mode** *n* OPT mode TE *m*, mode transversal électrique *m*, mode électrique *m*, mode électrique transversal *m*, TELECOM mode TE *m*, mode transversal électrique *m*, mode électrique transversal *m*; ~ **electric wave** *n* ELEC ENG, PHYS *TE wave*, TELECOM onde transversale électrique *f*; ~ **electromagnetic mode** *n* OPT mode TEM *m*, mode électromagnétique *m*, mode électromagnétique transversal *m*, TELECOM mode TEM *m*, mode électromagnétique transversal *m*; ~ **electromagnetic wave** *n* ELEC onde électromagnétique transversale *f*, ELEC ENG onde transversale électromagnétique *f*; ~ **energy distribution** *n* RAD PHYS distribution en énergie transversale *f*; ~ **engine** *n* AUTO, VEHICLES moteur horizontal *m*; ~ **framing** *n* NAUT *shipbuilding* construction transversale *f*, raidissage transversal *m*; ~ **interferometry** *n* OPT, TELECOM interférométrie transversale *f*; ~ **load** *n* SPRINGS charge transversale *f*; ~ **magnetic mode** *n* OPT, TELECOM mode TM *m*, mode transversal magnétique *m*; ~ **magnetic recording** *n* ACOUSTICS enregistrement magnétique transversal *m*; ~ **magnetic wave** *n* ELEC ENG, PHYS *TM wave* onde transversale magnétique *f*; ~ **magnification** *n* PHYS grandissement transversal *m*; ~ **member** *n* NAUT *shipbuilding* liaison transversale *f*; ~ **metacenter** *n* (AmE), ~ **metacentre** *n* (BrE) NAUT *ship design* métacentre latitudinal *m*, métacentre transversal *m*; ~ **offset loss** *n* OPT, TELECOM perte par décentrement transversal *f* ~ **recording** *n* RECORDING, TV enregistrement transversal *m*; ~ **scanning recorder** *n* TV magnétoscope à balayage transversal *m*; ~ **section** *n* NAUT *ship design* maître couple *m*, section transversale *f*, TELECOM section transversale *f*; ~ **slot** *n* TELECOM fente transversale *f*; ~ **spring** *n* RAIL ressort transversal *m*; ~ **stability** *n* NAUT *ship design* stabilité transversale *f*; ~ **wave** *n* ACOUSTICS, ELEC ENG, PHYS, TELECOM, WAVE PHYS onde transversale *f*

transverse-flux: ~ **linear motor** *n* TRANSP moteur linéaire à flux transversal *m*; ~ **machine** *n* TRANSP moteur linéaire à flux transversal *m*

tranverse: ~ **fracture** *n* C&G casse en travers *f*

trap[1] *n* CHEM TECH piège *m*, COMP déroutement *m*, interception *f*, CONST bascule *f*, trappe *f*, coupe-odeur *f*, siphon *m*, *plumbing* siphon *m*, CRYSTALL séparateur *m*, DP déroutement *m*, trappe *f*, GAS TECH, PETR, PETR TECH piège *m*, PROP MAT séparateur *m*, REFRIG piège *m*; ~ **door** *n* CONST trappe *f*; ~ **for vacuum pump** *n* LAB EQUIP piège-condenseur pour pompe à vide *m*

trap:[2] ~ **air** *vt* PROD ENG emmagasiner l'air

trapatt: ~ **diode** *n* *(trapped plasma avalanche transit-time diode)* PHYS diode Trapatt *f*

trapezium *n* GEOM trapèze *m*

Trapezium: ~ **Nebula** *n* ASTRON, SPACE nébuleuse du Trapèze *f*

trapezoid *n* GEOM trapézoïde *m*; ~ **arm-type suspension** *n* AUTO suspension par quadrilatères *f*

trapezoidal[1] *adj* GEOM trapézoïde

trapezoidal:[2] ~ **blade** *n* MECH ENG lame trapézoïdale *f*; ~ **distortion** *n* ELECTRON distorsion trapézoïdale *f*; ~ **thread** *n* MECH ENG filetage trapézoïdal *m*, *screws* filet trapézoïdal *m*

trapped: ~ **particle** *n* NUCLEAR particule piégée *f*; ~ **rail system** *n* MINING installation à guidage forcé *f*

trapping *n* PRINT accrochage de l'impression *m*, SAFETY accrochement *m*; ~ **site** *n* ELEC ENG piège à porteurs de charge *m*

traps *n pl* PRINT greffons *m pl*

trash *n* RECYCLING déchets *m pl*, TEXTILES second choix *m*; ~ **fish** *n* OCEANOG faux poisson *m*

travel[1] *n* MECH ENG *of carriage, valve* course *f*, NUCLEAR course *f*, levée *f*; ~ **follow-up** *n* AERONAUT détecteur de déplacement *m*; ~ **time** *n* GEOPHYS temps de trajet *m*, SPACE temps de propagation *m*

travel[2] *vi* WAVE PHYS se déplacer

traveler *n* (AmE) *see* traveller

traveling *n* (AmE) *see* travelling

traveling-field: ~ **motor** *n* (AmE) *see* travelling-field motor

traveling-gantry: ~ **crane** *n* (AmE) NAUT grue à portique *f*, PROD ENG grue roulante à portique *f*

traveling-wave (AmE) *see* travelling-wave

traveller *n* (BrE) MECH ENG *runner or slider* curseur *m*, PROD ENG *overhead crane* grue roulante *f*, pont roulant *m*

travelling *n* (BrE) PROD ENG *overhead travelling crane* translation *f*; ~ **apron** *n* (BrE) PROD ENG *conveyor belt* bande souple de transport *f*, courroie transporteuse *f*, toile transporteuse *f*; ~ **belt filter** *n* (BrE) *(TBF)* NUCLEAR filtre en ruban *m*; ~ **belt screen** *n* (BrE) PROD ENG tamis roulant *m*; ~ **block** *n* (BrE) PETR moufle mobile *m*, PETR TECH guignol *m*, moufle mobile *m*; ~ **cradle** *n* (BrE) CONST *building* échafaud volant *m*, échafaudage itinérant *m*, échafaudage volant *m*; ~ **crane** *n* (BrE) MECH pont roulant *m*, PROD ENG grue roulante *f*, pont roulant *m*; ~ **dolly** *n* (BrE) CINEMAT travelling de poursuite *m*; ~ **gantry** *n* (BrE) NAUT portique roulant *m*; ~ **gantry crane** *n* (BrE) NAUT grue à portique *f*; ~ **ladderway** *n* (BrE) CONST échelle mobile *f*, échelle mécanique *f*; ~ **matte** *n* (BrE) CINEMAT trucage par cache contre-cache *m*; ~ **microscope** *n* (BrE) LAB EQUIP *for length measurement* cathétomètre *m*; ~ **platform** *n* (BrE) CONST trottoir roulant *m*; ~ **pulley block** *n* (BrE) PROD ENG palan roulant *m*; ~ **runner** *n* (BrE) PROD ENG *of overhead crane, ropeway* chariot de roulement *m*, chariot roulant *m*, trolley *m*; ~ **staircase** *n* (BrE) CONST escalator *m*, escalier à marches mobiles *m*; ~ **stay** *n* (BrE) MECH ENG *of lathe* lunette à suivre *f*; ~ **table** *n* (BrE) MECH ENG *of rolling mill* conducteur de lingots *m*; ~ **trolley** *n* (BrE) PROD ENG *of overhead crane, ropeway* chariot de roulement

m, chariot roulant *m*, trolley *m*; ~ **wave** *n* (BrE) ACOUSTICS, ELECTRON, PHYS, TELECOM, WAVE PHYS onde progressive *f*; ~ **waveguide** *n* (BrE) TELECOM tube à onde progressive *m*; ~ **waveguide amplifier** *n* (BrE) TELECOM amplificateur à tubes à ondes progressives *m*; ~ **wheel** *n* (BrE) PROD ENG *for overhead travelling crane* galet de roulement *m*, roue de translation *f*

travelling-field: ~ **motor** *n* (BrE) TRANSP moteur à champ glissant *m*

travelling-gantry: ~ **crane** *n* (BrE) PROD ENG grue roulante à portique *f*

travelling-wave: ~ **acoustic amplifier** *n* (BrE) RECORDING amplificateur acoustique à ondes progressives *m*; ~ **aerial** *n* TELECOM, TV antenne à ondes progressives *f*; ~ **amplifier** *n* (BrE) TELECOM amplificateur à ondes progressives *m*; ~ **magnetron** *n* (BrE) ELECTRON magnétron *m*; ~ **maser** *n* (BrE) ELECTRON maser à ondes progressives *m*; ~ **motor** *n* (BrE) ELEC moteur à champ d'ondes progressives *m*; ~ **tube** *n* (BrE) *(TWT)* ELECTRON, PHYS, SPACE *communications*, TELECOM tube à onde progressive *m* *(TOP)*; ~ **tube amplifier** *n* (BrE) *(TWTA)* ELECTRON, SPACE *communications* amplificateur à tube à ondes progressives *m* *(ATOP)*

traverse *n* CONST *crosspiece, crossbar, transom* traverse *f*, *surveying* tracé polygonal *m*, MECH ENG *lathe work* chariotage *m*, *of drilling spindle* course verticale *f*, TEXTILES course *f*; ~ **feed** *n* MECH ENG *lathe work* avance *f*; ~ **motion bearing** *n* MECH ENG palier de déplacement latéral *m*; ~ **shaper** *n* MECH ENG étau-limeur à outil mobile *m*

traversing *n* PROD ENG *jenny of overhead travelling crane* translation *f*; ~ **jack** *n* MECH ENG vérin à chariot *m*; ~ **mechanism** *n* NUCLEAR *of thickness gauge* mécanisme de translation *m*

traversing-head: ~ **shaping machine** *n* MECH ENG étau-limeur à outil mobile *m*

travertine *n* FUELLESS travertin *m*

trawl[1] *n* NAUT, OCEANOG, TEXTILES chalut *m*; ~ **board** *n* OCEANOG panneau de chalut *m*; ~ **fishing** *n* OCEANOG chalutage *m*; ~ **net** *n* MAR POLL, NAUT *fishing*, OCEANOG chalut *m*; ~ **warp** *n* OCEANOG fune *f*; ~ **wing** *n* OCEANOG aile *f*

trawl[2] *vt* NAUT, OCEANOG chaluter

trawler *n* NAUT, OCEANOG chalutier *m*

trawling *n* OCEANOG chalutage *m*; ~ **and dredging gear** *n* OCEANOG arts traînants *m pl*

tray C&G tablette *f*, CHEM, LAB EQUIP plateau *m*, MECH ENG *under bed of lathe* bac *m*, réservoir *m*, PAPER TECH bacholle *f*, PHOTO cuvette *f*; ~ **bar** *n* (AmE) *(cf tray)* C&G tablette *f*; ~ **denesting filling and lidding machine** *n* PACKAGING machine de déboîtage de remplissage et de recouvrement de bac *f*; ~ **drying chamber** *n* REFRIG chambre de dessiccation à étagères *f*; ~ **erector** *n* PACKAGING formeuse de barquettes *f*; ~ **erector and loader** *n* PACKAGING embarqueteuse *f*; **in** ~ *n* PROD ENG corbeille arrivée *f*; ~ **packaging** *n* PACKAGING emballage en barquettes *m*; ~ **packing machine** *n* PACKAGING embarqueteuse *f*; ~ **sealer** *n* PACKAGING soudeuse de barquettes *f*

TRC: ~ **cathode ray pencil** *n* ELEC faisceau cathodique *m*

treacle *n* CHEM mélasse *f*

tread *n* AERONAUT *of landing gear* voie *f*, CONST *of girder* semelle *f*, table *f*, échelon *m*, *of step* foulée *f*, giron *m*, RAIL table de roulement *f*, *of wheel* bande de roulement *f*, TRANSP *of tyre* profil *m*, VEHICLES *tyre* bande de roulement *f*; ~ **depth gage** *n* (AmE), ~ **depth gauge** *n* (BrE) VEHICLES *tyre* jauge de profondeur de sculpture *f*; ~ **design** *n* VEHICLES *tyre* sculpture *f*

treadle *n* MECH ENG pédale *f*; ~ **brake valve** *n* AUTO, MECH ENG robinet de commande à pédale *m*; ~ **switch** *n* CONTROL interrupteur à commande au pied *m*, interrupteur à pédale *m*

treat *vt* COAL TECH traiter

treatment *n* CINEMAT scénario *m*, synopsis *m*, PETR TECH séparation *f*, traitement *m*, triage *m*, TEXTILES traitement *m*

treble[1] *adj* RECORDING aigu

treble[2] *n* RECORDING haut *m*; ~ **boost** *n* RECORDING renforcement des aigus *m*; ~ **compensation** *n* RECORDING compensation des aigus *f*; ~ **control** *n* RECORDING contrôle des aigus *m*; ~ **roll-off** *n* RECORDING filtrage des aigus *m*

treble-pass: ~ **boiler** *n* HEATING chaudière à trois passes *f*

tree *n* COMP, DP arborescence *f*, arbre *m*, MINING butte *f*, chandelle *f*, étai *m*, tuyau *m*; ~ **and branch network** *n* TELECOM réseau arborescent *m*, réseau en arbre *m*; ~ **distribution** *n* TELECOM distribution arborescente *f*; ~ **network** *n* COMP, DP, TELECOM réseau arborescent *m*; ~ **search** *n* COMP, DP recherche arborescente *f*, recherche hiérarchique *f*; ~ **structure** *n* COMP arborescence *f*, DP arborescence *f*, structure arborescente *f*, TELECOM structure en arbre *f*; ~ **topology** *n* COMP, DP topologie en arbre *f*

treed: ~ **system** *n* ELEC *supply network* réseau arborescent *m*

treeing *n* PRINT arborescence *f*

treenail *n* (AmE) *(cf trenail)* CONST cheville de bois *f*, trenail *m*

trefoil: ~ **formation** *n* ELEC *cable configuration* disposition en trèfle *f*

trehalose *n* CHEM tréhalose *f*

trellis *n* CONST treillage *m*, treillis *m*; ~ **post** *n* CONST fût-pylône *m*, pylône *m*; ~ **work** *n* CONST treillage *m*, treillis *m*

trembler *n* ELEC ENG trembleur *m*; ~ **bell** *n* ELEC sonnette à trembleur *f*

tremolite *n* MINERAL trémolite *f*

tremolo *n* ACOUSTICS trémolo *m*

tremorine *n* CHEM trémorine *f*

trenail *n* CONST cheville de bois *f*, trenail *m*

trench *n* COAL TECH fossé *m*, tranchée *f*, CONST fossé *m*, fouille *f*, saignée *f*, tranchée *f*, MAR POLL, MINING tranchée *f*, OCEANOG fosse *f*, fossé *m*, souille *f*, PETR tranchée *f*, PETR TECH fossé *m*; ~ **cutter** *n* CONST excavateur de tranchées *m*, trancheuse *f*; ~ **work** *n* CONST travaux en tranchées *m pl*

trenching *n* CONST creusement de fossés *m*, creusement de tranchées *m*, fouille *f*

trend *n* MINING *of lode* cours *m*, direction *f*, TEXTILES tendance *f*

trepanner *n* MECH ENG *tool* trépaneur *m*

T-rest *n* MECH ENG *lathe* support à éventail *m*

trestle *n* CONST cadre de puits *m*, chevalet *m*, tréteau *m*; ~ **bridge** *n* CONST pont de chevalets *m*, pont sur chevalets *m*, pont sur tréteaux *m*; ~ **car** *n* (AmE) *(cf trestle wagon)* RAIL *vehicles* wagon pupitre *m*; ~ **shore** *n* CONST *building* port de chevalement *m*; ~ **wagon** *n* (BrE) *(cf trestle car)* RAIL *vehicles* wagon pupitre *m*

triac *n* ELEC *thyristor*, ELEC ENG triac *m*

triacetate *n* TEXTILES triacétate *m*; ~ **base** *n* CINEMAT support triacétate *m*

triacetin *n* CHEM triacétine *f*

triacetonamin *n* CHEM triacétonamine *f*

triacetonamine *n* CHEM triacétonamine *f*

triacid *n* CHEM triacide *m*

triad *n* CHEM triade *f*

trial *n* COAL TECH programme d'essai *m*, NUCLEAR *of plant components*, TEXTILES essai *m*; ~ **and error calculation** *n* GEOM calcul par tâtonnement *m*; ~ **and error method** *n* CRYSTALL méthode essai-erreur *f*; ~ **cock** *n* WATER SUPP robinet de hauteur d'eau *m*, robinet de jauge *m*; ~ **composite print** *n* CINEMAT copie "O" standard *f*; ~ **frame** *n* INSTRUMENT monture sans verre *f*; ~ **run** *n* NUCLEAR *of boiler* course d'essai *f*, marche d'essai *f*; ~ **speed** *n* NAUT vitesse d'essai *f*; ~ **strip** *n* CONST *roads* planche d'essai *f*; ~ **structure** *n* CRYSTALL structure d'essai *f*

triamyl *n* CHEM triamyle *m*

triangle *n* GEOM triangle *m*; ~ **of forces** *n* CONST, PHYS triangle des forces *m*; ~ **test** *n* FOOD TECH méthode triangulaire *f*, test triangulaire *m*; ~ **testing** *n* FOOD TECH méthode triangulaire *f*

triangular[1] *adj* GEOM triangulaire

triangular:[2] ~ **arch** *n* CONST voûte triangulaire *f*, *curve described* arc triangulaire *m*; ~ **cam** *n* MECH ENG excentrique en triangle *m*, excentrique triangulaire *m*; ~ **matrix** *n* COMP, DP matrice triangulaire *f*

triangularity *n* C&G ovalisation *f*

triangulate *vt* GEOM trianguler

triangulation *n* CONST *surveying*, GEOM, METR, SPACE triangulation *f*; ~ **point** *n* CONST *surveying* point de triangulation *m*

Triangulum *n* ASTRON Triangle *m*; ~ **Australe** *n* ASTRON Triangle austral *m*

Triassic: ~ **period** *n* PETR TECH trias *m*

triaxial: ~ **pinch experiment** *n* NUCLEAR expérience de striction triaxiale *f*; ~ **state of stress** *n* METALL état de contrainte triaxial *m*; ~ **test** *n* CONST *roads* essai triaxial *m*

triazine: ~ **ring** *n* CHEM *structure* cycle triazinique *m*

triazoic *adj* CHEM azothydrique

triazole *n* CHEM triazole *m*

tribasic *adj* CHEM *acid* tribasique

tri-blade: ~ **cutting machine** *n* PRINT massicot trilame *m*

triboelectric *adj* TRANSP *detector* triboélectrique

triboelectricity *n* PHYS triboélectricité *f*

triboluminescence *n* PHYS triboluminescence *f*

tributary[1] *adj* HYDROL tributaire

tributary[2] *n* HYDROL, NAUT *geography, of river*, TELECOM affluent *m*; ~ **channel** *n* HYDROL cours d'eau affluent *m pl*, cours d'eau tributaire *m pl*; ~ **unit** *n* (*TU*) TELECOM unité d'affluents *f*; ~ **unit group** *n* (*TUG*) TELECOM groupe d'unité d'affluents *m*

tributyrin *n* CHEM tributyrine *f*

tricarballylic *adj* CHEM tricarballylique

trichite *n* PETR trichite *f*

trichlorethylene *n* CHEM, DETERGENTS trichloréthylène *m*

trichloride *n* CHEM trichlorure *m*

trichloroacetic *adj* CHEM trichloracétique

trichloroethylene *n* CHEM trichloréthylène *m*

trichroic *adj* PHYS trichroïque

trichroism *n* PHYS trichroïsme *m*

trichromatic *adj* INSTRUMENT *of filter* trichrome

trick: ~ **printer** *n* CINEMAT truca *f*

trickle: **~ charge** n CINEMAT charge d'appoint f, charge lente f, ELEC ENG charge lente f; **~ charger** n ELEC accumulator chargeur à régime lent m, ELEC ENG chargeur d'entretien m

trickling n HYDROL ruissellement m; **~ filter** n POLLUTION filtre bactérien m

triclinic[1] adj CHEM, CRYSTALL triclinique

triclinic:[2] **~ system** n METALL système triclinique m

tricone: **~ bit** n GAS TECH outil tricône m, PETR TECH trépan tricône m

tricosane n CHEM tricosane f

tricresol n CHEM tricrésol m

tricresyl n CHEM tricrésyle m

tricycle: **~ landing gear** n AERONAUT train d'atterrissage tricycle m

tricyclic adj CHEM tricyclique

tridimensional adj PROP MAT à trois dimensions

tridymite n MINERAL tridymite f

triester n CHEM triester m

triethanolamine n DETERGENTS triéthanolamine m

trifocal: **~ glass** n C&G verre à triple foyer m

trifurcating: **~ box** n ELEC cable accessory trifurcation f; **~ joint** n ELEC cable connection jonction tri-mono f

trifurcator n ELEC cable accessory trifurcation f

trig: **~ point** n CONST borne-signal f

trigatron n ELECTRON trigatron m

trigger[1] n CINEMAT déclencheur m, COMP bascule f, bascule électronique f, DP, ELEC circuit breaker déclencheur m, MECH ENG chien m, cliquet m, doigt m, détente f, gâchette f, MILIT of firearm détente f, gâchette f, PHOTO déclencheur m, gâchette f, PHYS trichroïsme m; **~ box** n AUTO module électronique m; **~ circuit** n ELEC, ELECTRON circuit de déclenchement m, PHYS bascule f, circuit de déclenchement m, TESTING circuit de déclenchement m; **~ contact** n AUTO, MECH ENG contact de déclenchement m; **~ diode** n ELECTRON diode de déclenchement f; **~ grip** n CINEMAT poignée à déclencheur f; **~ guard** n MILIT pontet m, sous-garde f; **~ pulse** n ELECTRON impulsion de déclenchement f; **~ relay** n PHOTO relais de déclenchement m; **~ release** n PHOTO of camera shutter déclenchement à doigt m; **~ wheel** n AUTO noyau synchroniseur m, tambour à écrans m

trigger[2] vt COMP, DP déclencher

trigger[3] vi MECH ENG se déclencher; **~ an alarm** vi TELECOM déclencher une alarme

triggering n COMP, DP déclenchement m; **~ circuit** n PHOTO circuit d'allumage m; **~ lead pulse** n TELECOM impulsion de déclenchement f; **~ pulse** n TV impulsion de déclenchement f; **~ systems** n pl RAD PHYS radiation activation systèmes de déclenchement m pl; **~ voltage** n TV tension de déclenchement f

triglyceride n CHEM, DETERGENTS triglycéride m

trigma n NUCLEAR trigma m

trigonal adj CRYSTALL rhomboédrique, trigonal

trigonometric adj GEOM trigonométrique

trigonometrical[1] adj GEOM trigonométrique

trigonometrical:[2] **~ functions** n pl GEOM fonctions trigonométriques f pl; **~ parallax** n ASTRON parallaxe trigonométrique f; **~ ratios** n pl GEOM proportions trigonométriques f pl

trigonometry n GEOM trigonométrie f

trihedral adj GEOM trièdre

trihedron n GEOM trièdre m

trihydrate n CHEM trihydrate m

trihydric adj CHEM trihydrique

trihydrol n CHEM trihydrol m

triiodide n CHEM triiodure m

trilateral n GEOM trilatéral m

trill n ACOUSTICS trille f

trim[1] n AERONAUT arrimage m, assiette f, équilibrage m, CINEMAT chute f, NAUT of boat, cargo arrimage m, assiette f, PAPER TECH rogne f, PRINT of margin découpe des marges f, finition f, rogne f, SPACE spacecraft arrimage m, attitude f, orientation f; **~ bin** n CINEMAT bac à chutes m, chutier m; **~ control** n AERONAUT commande de compensation f, commande de trim f, TRANSP aeroplanes contrôle d'assiette m; **~ controls** n pl AERONAUT commandes de compensateur de gouvernes f pl, commandes de trim f pl; **~ control switch** n AERONAUT interrupteur de commande électrique de compensation de régime m; **~ mark** n PRINT repère de rogne m; **~ removal** n PAPER TECH élimination des rognures de bordure f; **~ shower** n PAPER TECH rinceur de bordure m; **~ stability** n AERONAUT stabilité d'assiette f; **~ tab** n (AmE) (cf trimming tab) AERONAUT volet de compensation m, ELEC ENG languette d'ajustage f; **~ washer** n PROD ENG rondelle f

trim[2] vt AERONAUT arrimer, CINEMAT mettre un diffuseur sur, raccourcir, CONST carpentry corroyer, dresser, joist enchevêtrer, wood travailler, MECH finir, NAUT sailboat arrimer, border, PAPER TECH rogner, PRINT massicoter, rogner, ébarber, PROD ENG ébarber, to shear, shape parer, SPACE arrimer, spacecraft compenser, corriger; **~ off the burr from** vt PROD ENG ébarber; **~ off rough edges from** vt PROD ENG ébarber

trim[3] vi CINEMAT changer un charbon, NAUT établir les voiles

trimellitic adj CHEM trimellique, trimellitique

trimer n CHEM, P&R trimère m

trimerization n CHEM rognage de bords m

trimerize vt CHEM trimériser

trimesic adj CHEM trimésique

trimetallic adj PRINT plate trimétallique

trimethylbenzene n CHEM triméthylbenzène m

trimethylcarbinol n CHEM triméthylcarbinol m

trimethylene n CHEM triméthylène m

trimethylpyridine n CHEM triméthylpyridine f

trimmed:[1] **~ by the head** adj NAUT en différence négative, sur nez; **~ by the stern** adj NAUT en différence positive, sur cul

trimmed:[2] **~ end** n SPRINGS bout découpé m, extrémité découpée f; **~ joist** n CONST poutre secondaire f, solive boiteuse f, solive bâtarde f, solive d'enchevêtrure f; **~ size** n PACKAGING, PAPER TECH format fini m, PRINT format fini m, format rogné m

trimmed-off adj PROD ENG ébarbé

trimmer n CONST chevêtre m, MECH ENG for wood machine à trancher et dresser les bois en bout f, trancheuse pour le bois de bout f, MINING trou de côté m, PHOTO cisaille f, coupe-épreuves m; **~ beam** n CONST chevêtre m; **~ capacitor** n ELEC ENG condensateur ajustable m

trimming n AERONAUT compensation f, TEXTILES débordure f; **~ machine** n MECH ENG grinder machine à ébarber f, ébarbeuse f; **~ potentiometer** n ELEC resistor potentiomètre trimmer m, ELEC ENG potentiomètre ajustable m; **~ resolution** n ELEC ENG finesse d'ajustage f; **~ tab** n (BrE) (cf trim tab) AERONAUT volet de compensation m; **~ wheel** n MECH ENG meule à ébarber f

trimmings n pl PAPER TECH rognures f pl

trimolecular *adj* CHEM trimoléculaire
trimorphic *adj* CHEM trimorphe
trimorphism *n* CHEM trimorphisme *m*
trimorphous *adj* CHEM trimorphe
trimyristin *n* CHEM trimyristine *f*
trinitrate *n* CHEM trinitré *m*
trinitrated *adj* CHEM trinitré
trinitrin *n* CHEM trinitrine *f*
trinitrobenzene *n* CHEM trinitrobenzène *m*
trinitro-compound *n* CHEM trinitré *m*
trinitrocresol *n* CHEM trinitrocrésol *m*
trinitrophenol *n* CHEM trinitrophénol *m*
trinitrotoluene *n* CHEM trinitrotoluène *m*
trinomial *n* MATH trinôme *m*
triode *n* ELECTRON, PHYS triode *f*; ~ **action** *n* ELECTRON effet triode *m*; ~ **oscillator** *n* ELECTRON oscillateur à triode *m*; ~ **tube** *n* ELECTRON tube triode *m*
triode-hexode *n* ELECTRON triode-hexode *f*
triol *n* CHEM trialcool *m*, triol *m*
triolein *n* CHEM trioléine *f*
triose *n* CHEM triose *f*
trioxane *n* CHEM trioxyméthylène *m*
trioxide *n* CHEM trioxyde *m*
trioxymethylene *n* CHEM trioxyméthylène *m*
trioxypurine *n* CHEM acide urique *m*
trip[1] *n* MECH ENG déclenche *f*, déclenchement *m*, déclic *m*, modificateur instantané *m*, PETR TECH aller-retour *m*, manoeuvre *f*; ~ **amplifier** *n* CONTROL amplificateur du signal d'arrêt *m*; ~ **catch** *n* MECH ENG couteau de déclenche *m*; ~ **circuit** *n* ELEC circuit de déclenchement *m*; ~ **coil** *n* ELEC bobine de déclenchement *f*; ~ **contact** *n* PROD ENG contact de déclenchement *m*; ~ **counter** *n* (BrE) *(cf odometer)* VEHICLES *instrument* totalisateur partiel *m*; ~ **curve** *n* PROD ENG courbe des déclenchements *f*; ~ **device** *n* SAFETY dispositif à enclenchement *m*, déclic *m*; ~ **dog** *n* MECH ENG déclic *m*; ~ **gas** *n* PETR TECH bouchon d'ajout de tige *m*; ~ **gear** *n* ELEC *circuit breaker* déclencheur *m*, MECH ENG déclenche *f*, déclenchement *m*, déclic *m*, modificateur instantané *m*; ~ **guard** *n* SAFETY barrière à déclic *f*, garde de déclenche *f*; ~ **indicator** *n* CINEMAT indicateur de bourrage *m*; ~ **logic signal converter** *n* NUCLEAR dispositif terminal de déclenchement *m*; ~ **mileage indicator** *n* AUTO compteur journalier *m*, tachygraphe *m*; ~ **odometer** *n* (AmE) *(cf trip recorder)* AUTO tachygraphe *m*; ~ **pile driver** *n* CONST mouton à déclic *m*; ~ **recorder** *n* (BrE) *(cf trip odometer)* AUTO tachygraphe *m*; ~ **relay** *n* ELEC relais à action instantanée *m*, relais à action rapide *m*; ~ **scale** *n* PROD ENG échelle de réglage *f*; ~ **time** *n* PROD ENG temps de déclenchement *m*, TRANSP durée du trajet *f*; ~ **valve gear** *n* MECH ENG distribution à déclic *f*
trip[2] *vt* PHYS faire basculer; ~ **in** *vt* MECH ENG embrayer
trip[3] *vi* MECH ENG se déclencher; ~ **anchor** *vi* NAUT déraper
tripack: ~ **film** *n* PHOTO pellicule à trois couches *f*
tripalmitin *n* CHEM tripalmitine *f*
triparanol *n* CHEM triparanol *m*
trip-free[1] *adj* PROD ENG à déclenchement libre
trip-free:[2] ~ **release** *n* ELEC *circuit breaker* disjonction électrique indépendante *f*
triphane *n* MINERAL triphane *m*
triphase *adj* ELEC ENG triphasé
triphasic *adj* CHEM triphasique
triphenol *n* CHEM triphénol *m*
triphilic *adj* CHEM triphile
triphyline *n* MINERAL triphylite *f*

triphylite *n* MINERAL triphylite *f*
triplane *n* AERONAUT avion à trois plans *m*
triple: ~ **alpha process** *n* NUCLEAR réaction de Salpeter *f*; ~ **bond** *n* CHEM liaison triple *f*; ~ **junction** *n* METALL jonction triple *f*; ~ **ladder** *n* CONST *building* échelle à coulisses trois plans *f*; ~ **pack** *n* PACKAGING emballage triple *m*; ~ **point** *n* METALL, PHYS, THERMOD point triple *m*
triple-beam: ~ **coincidence spectrometer** *n* NUCLEAR spectromètre à coïncidence à trois faisceaux *m*
triple-cavity: ~ **mold** *n* (AmE), ~ **mould** *n* (BrE) C&G moule à triple cavité *m*
triple-core: ~ **cable** *n* ELEC câble à trois brins *m*, câble à trois conducteurs *m*
triple-expansion: ~ **engine** *n* NAUT machine à triple détente *f*
triple-standard *adj* TV tristandard
triplet *n* NUCLEAR *in spectrometry*, PHYS *spectroscopy* triplet *m*; ~ **lens** *n* PHOTO objectif à trois lentilles *m*, triplet *m*
triple-wall: ~ **corrugated board** *n* PACKAGING carton triplex *m*
triple-wound: ~ **transformer** *n* ELEC transformateur à trois enroulements *m*
triplex: ~ **board** *n* PAPER TECH carton trois couches *m*; ~ **engine** *n* MECH ENG machine à trois cylindres *f*
triplex-coated: ~ **particle** *n* NUCLEAR particule à triple enrobage *f*
triplite *n* MINERAL triplite *f*
tripod *n* CINEMAT, INSTRUMENT, LAB EQUIP *support* trépied *m*, MINING affût-trépied *m*, trépied *m*, PHOTO pied photographique *m*, trépied *m*, PROD ENG pied *m*, pied à trois branches *m*, trépied *m*; ~ **bush** *n* PHOTO écrou de pied *m*; ~ **extension** *n* PHOTO rallonge de trépied *f*; ~ **head** *n* CINEMAT tête de trépied *f*, PHOTO tête de pied *f*; ~ **leg** *n* CINEMAT branche de trépied *f*, PHOTO branche de pied *f*; ~ **screw** *n* CINEMAT vis de fixation pour tête de trépied *f*; ~ **stand** *n* PROD ENG pied à trois branches *m*, support à trois pieds *m*
tripolite *n* MINERAL tripolite *f*, PETR tripol *m*
tripper *n* MECH ENG dispositif de déclenchement *m*, déclenche *f*, déclic *m*
tripping *n* MECH ENG débrayage *m*, déclenche *f*, déclenchement *m*; ~ **advice** *n* PROD ENG dispositif de déclenchement *m*; ~ **bracket** *n* NAUT *shipbuilding* gousset de contreventement *m*; ~ **device** *n* MECH ENG dispositif de déclenchement *m*, déclenche *f*, déclic *m*; ~ **line** *n* NAUT orin *m*, OCEANOG vérine *f*; ~ **relay** *n* ELEC relais de détente *m*
tripropellant *n* SPACE tiergol *m*
triptane *n* CHEM triméthylbutane *m*, triptane *m*
triptych: ~ **screen** *n* CINEMAT triple écran *m*
TRISEC: ~ **ship** *n* TRANSP navire du type TRISEC *m*
trisection *n* GEOM *of angle* trisection *f*
trisnitrate *n* CHEM trisnitrate *m*
trisodium[1] *adj* CHEM trisodique
trisodium:[2] ~ **phosphate** *n* *(TSP)* DETERGENTS phosphate trisodique *m*
tri-square: ~ **file** *n* MECH ENG lime tiers-point *f*, lime triangulaire *f*, trois-carrés *m*
tristearin *n* CHEM tristéarine *f*
tristimulus: ~ **paint** *n* P&R peinture trichromatique *f*; ~ **signals** *n pl* TV signaux RVB *m pl*; ~ **values** *n pl* PHYS composantes trichromatiques *f pl*
trisubstituted *adj* CHEM trisubstitué
tritan *n* CHEM tritane *m*

trithionic *adj* CHEM trithionique
tritiated *adj* NUCLEAR tritié
triticin *n* CHEM triticine *f*
tritium *n* CHEM hydrogène hyperlourd *m*, tritium *m*, PHYS tritium *m*; **~ extraction** *n* NUCLEAR *of heavy water* détritiation *f*
tritoxide *n* CHEM tritoxyde *m*
triturate *vt* CHEM triturer
triturating *n* CHEM trituration *f*
triturator *n* MECH ENG triturateur *m*
trityl *n* CHEM trityle *m*
trivalence *n* CHEM trivalence *f*
trivalency *n* CHEM trivalence *f*
trivalent *adj* CHEM trivalent
trivial: **~ name** *n* CHEM *of element, compound* nom trivial *m*
trochoidal: **~ mass analyzer** *n* NUCLEAR spectromètre de masse cycloïdale *m*; **~ mass spectrometer** *n* NUCLEAR spectromètre de masse cycloïdale *m*
troctolite *n* PETR troctolite *f*
troctolyte *n* PETR troctolite *f*
troegerite *n* MINERAL troegérite *f*
trögerite *n* MINERAL troegérite *f*
troilite *n* MINERAL troïlite *f*
Trojan: **~ group** *n* ASTRON groupe des Troyens *m*, planètes troyennes *f pl*; **~ horse** *n* COMP, DP cheval de Troie *m*
troll *n* OCEANOG arts traînants *m pl*
troller *n* OCEANOG ligneur *m*
trolley *n* LAB EQUIP *furniture* chariot *m*, NUCLEAR *of refuelling machine* chariot *m*, treuil roulant *m*, PRINT boule du passage-papier *f*, galets d'entraînement *m pl*, PROD ENG chariot de roulement *m*, chariot roulant *m*, trolley *m*, TRANSP *public transport* trolley *m*
trolleybus *n* TRANSP trolleybus *m*
trolling: **~ fishing** *n* OCEANOG pêche à la traîne *f*
trommel *n* COAL TECH trommel *m*; **~ washer** *n* COAL TECH séparateur rotatif *m*
trona *n* MINERAL trona *m*
troop-carrying: **~ vehicle** *n* MILIT véhicule transporteur de troupes *m*
troopship *n* NAUT transport de troupes *m*
troostite *n* METALL, MINERAL troostite *f*
tropic *adj* CHEM *acid* tropique
tropical: **~ air** *n* METEO air tropical *m*; **~ calms** *n pl* METEO, OCEANOG calmes tropicaux *m pl*; **~ climate** *n* METEO climat tropical *m*; **~ cyclone** *n* METEO cyclone tropical *m*; **~ packaging** *n* PACKAGING emballage tropical *m*; **~ revolving storm** *n* METEO cyclone tropical *m*; **~ type** *n* NUCLEAR *of construction* type tropical *m*; **~ year** *n* ASTRON année tropique *f*
tropine *n* CHEM *compound* tropine *f*
tropopause *n* METEO tropopause *f*
troposphere *n* METEO, SPACE troposphère *f*
tropospheric: **~ scatter** *n* TELECOM diffusion troposphérique *f*
trotyl *n* CHEM tolite *f*, trinitrotoluène *m*
troubleshooter *n* MECH ENG spécialiste d'intervention *m*
trough *n* C&G *in manufacture of container glass* goulotte *f*, *in manufacture of rolled glass* récepteur *m*, CONST *building* auge *f*, GEOL fosse *f*, LAB EQUIP cuve *f*, *glassware* cuvette *f*, METEO creux barométrique *m*, creux dépressionnaire *m*, NAUT *swell*, OCEANOG creux *m*, PROD ENG auge *f*, bac *m*, baquet *m*, réservoir *m*; **~ compass** *n* PROD ENG déclinateur *m*, déclinatoire *m*; **~ conveyor** *n* PROD ENG convoyeur à palettes *m*, trans-

porteur à palettes *m*, transporteuse à palettes *f*; **~ cross-bedding** *n* GEOL stratification en feston *f*, stratification entrecroisée *f*; **~ gutter** *n* CONST *building* chéneau encaissé *m*, gouttière *f*; **~ lip** *n* C&G bord de goulotte *m*; **~ mixer** *n* C&G mélangeur à auge *m*; **~ washer** *n* MINING *ore-dressing* langelotte *m*
trowel *n* CONST truelle *f*
troy: **~ weight** *n* METR poids troy *m*
truck *n* (*cf cart*) AUTO camion *m*, CONST bogie *m*, MECH *vehicles* camion *m*, chariot *m*, MECH ENG bogie *m*, MINING wagonnet *m*, NAUT *of mast* pomme *f*, TRANSP, VEHICLES camion *m*, VEHICLES *trailer* bogie *m*; **~ bolster** *n* (AmE) (*cf bogie bolster*) RAIL *vehicles* traverse danseuse *f*; **~ car** *n* (AmE) (*cf truck wagon*) TRANSP wagon à déchargement *m*; **~ car with swiveling roof** *n* (AmE) (*cf bogie wagon with swivelling roof*) TRANSP wagon à bogies à toit pivotant *m*; **~ factor** *n* (AmE) TRANSP *traffic* facteur camions *m*; **~ open self-discharge car** *n* (AmE) (*cf bogie open self-discharge wagon*) TRANSP *railway* wagon ouvert autodéchargeur à bogies *m*; **~ pin** *n* (AmE) (*cf bogie pin*) VEHICLES *of trailer* pivot de bogie *m*; **~ pivot** *n* (AmE) (*cf bogie pivot*) VEHICLES *trailer* pivot de bogie *m*; **~ wagon** *n* (BrE) (*cf truck car*) TRANSP wagon à déchargement *m*
truck-to-truck: **~ handling** *n* TRANSP manutention horizontale *f*; **~ operation** *n* TRANSP poste de chargement *m*; **~ system** *n* TRANSP poste de chargement *m*
true:[1] **~ air speed** *n* (*TAS*) AERONAUT vitesse propre *f*; **~ anomaly** *n* ASTRON, SPACE anomalie vraie *f*; **~ course** *n* NAUT *navigation* cap vrai *m*; **~ density** *n* NUCLEAR densité théorique *f*, masse volumique théorique *f*; **~ fracture stress** *n* METALL contrainte réelle de rupture *f*; **~ half-width** *n* RAD PHYS *of spectral line* largeur vraie à mi-absorption *f*; **~ middlings** *n pl* COAL TECH mixtes de structure *m pl*, mixtes vrais *m pl*; **~ motion** *n* NAUT *radar* mouvement vrai *m*; **~ north** *n* NAUT *navigation* nord vrai *m*; **~ pitch** *n* MECH ENG *of screw* pas réel *m*; **~ strain** *n* METALL déformation réelle *f*; **~ stress** *n* METALL contrainte réelle *f*; **~ wind** *n* NAUT *navigation* vent vrai *m*
true[2] *vt* MECH ENG dresser, défausser, dégauchir, rectifier, redresser; **~ up** *vt* C&G réunir, MECH ENG dresser, défausser, dégauchir, rectifier, redresser
true-false: **~ check** *n* PROD ENG vérification vrai-faux *f*
true-to-false: **~ transition** *n* PROD ENG transition du vrai au faux *f*
truing *n* C&G ébauchage *m*; **~ wheel** *n* MECH ENG meule à rectifier *f*
truncate *vt* COMP tronquer, CONTROL interrompre, DP, GEOM tronquer
truncated: **~ cone** *n* GEOM tronc de cône *m*; **~ cone-abrasive sheet** *n* MECH ENG manchon abrasif tronconique *m*; **~ pyramid** *n* GEOM tronc de pyramide *m*; **~ test** *n* SPACE essai tronqué *m*
truncating *n* GEOM troncature *f*
truncation *n* COMP, DP, GEOM troncature *f*; **~ error** *n* COMP, DP erreur par troncature *f*
trunk *n* (AmE) AUTO (*cf boot*) coffre à bagages *m*, car coffre *m*, COMP, DP artère *f*, MINING ore-washing box caisse à débourber *f*, TELECOM circuit de jonction *m*, *exchange tie* joncteur *m*, *inter-switch tie* circuit de connexion *m*, TRANSP (*cf boot*) coffre à bagages *m*, VEHICLES (*cf boot*) *body* coffre *m*; **~ cable** *n* ELEC ENG, TELECOM câble interurbain *m*; **~ channel** *n* TELECOM canal interurbain *m*; **~ code** *n* (*TC*) TELECOM indicatif interurbain *m*; **~ distribution frame** *n* (*TDF*) TELECOM

répartiteur de jonction *m*; ~ **exchange** *n* TELECOM central interurbain *m*, centre interurbain *m*, commutateur interurbain *m*; ~ **feeder** *n* ELEC *supply* artère principale *f*, feeder principal *m*; ~ **handle** *n* (AmE) *(cf boot handle)* VEHICLES poignée du coffre *f*; ~ **lid** *n* (AmE) *(cf boot lid)* VEHICLES porte du coffre *f*; ~ **line** *n* ELEC *supply network* ligne principale *f*, PETR conduit principal *m*, RAIL ligne principale de chemin de fer *f*; ~ **line wiring** *n* PROD ENG câblage ligne principale *m*; ~ **main** *n* ELEC *supply* artère principale *f*, feeder principal *m*; ~ **network** *n* TELECOM réseau de transport *m*; ~ **offer** *n* *(TKO)* TELECOM intervention ligne-réseau *f*; ~ **piston engine** *n* NAUT moteur à pistons fourreaux *m*; ~ **switching** *n* TELECOM commutation de transit *f*; ~ **switching center** *n* (AmE), ~ **switching centre** *n* (BrE) TELECOM centre de transit *m*; ~ **switching exchange area** *n* TELECOM zone à autonomie d'acheminement *f*; ~ **system** *n* TELECOM relais commun *m*; ~ **transit exchange** *n* TELECOM CT, centre de transit *m*

trunked: ~ **dispatch system** *n* TELECOM système partagé du type "dispatching" *m*

trunking *n* ELEC ENG interconnexion des travées *f*, TELECOM partage *m*

trunnel *n* CONST cheville de bois *f*, trenail *m*

trunnion *n* COAL TECH, MECH, MECH ENG tourillon *m*, NUCLEAR *pin* appui à pivot *m*, pivot *m*, tourillon *m*, VEHICLES *universal joint* tourillon *m*

truss *n* CONST ferme *f*; ~ **bridge** *n* CONST pont en treillis *m*, pont à poutres armées *m*; ~ **rod** *n* CONST *building* tirant de ferme *m*

trussed: ~ **beam** *n* CONST poutre armée *f*, *underbraced type* poutre sous-bandée *f*; ~ **girder** *n* CONST poutre armée *f*; ~ **roof** *n* CONST comble sur fermes *m*; ~ **wooden beam** *n* CONST *underbraced* poutre en bois sous-bandée *f*

trussing *n* CONST armature *f*

trusted[1] *adj* DP sécurisé

trusted:[2] ~ **functionality** *n* TELECOM fonctionnalité de confiance *f*

truth: ~ **table** *n* COMP, DP table de vérité *f*

truxillic *adj* CHEM truxillique

truxilline *n* CHEM truxilline *f*

try:[1] ~ **cock** *n* WATER SUPP robinet de hauteur d'eau *m*, robinet de jauge *m*; ~ **plane** *n* CONST varlope *f*; ~ **square** *n* MECH ENG équerre à lame d'acier *f*

try[2] *vt* CONST *tenon in mortise* présenter, *to plane with plane* varloper; ~ **up** *vt* CONST *to plane with trying plane* varloper

trying: ~ **iron** *n* C&G cordeline *f*

trying-up: ~ **machine** *n* MECH ENG varlopeuse *f*

tryout: ~ **facility** *n* MECH ENG dispositif de démonstration *m*, dispositif des essais *m*; ~ **press** *n* MECH ENG presse d'essai *f*

tryptic *adj* CHEM tryptique

tryptomin *n* CHEM tryptomine *f*

tryptomine *n* CHEM tryptomine *f*

trysail *n* NAUT *sailing* voile de cape *f*

TS: ~ **network** *n* TELECOM structure TS *f*

TSAP *abbr (transport service access point)* TELECOM point d'accès au service de transport *m*

tscheffkinite *n* MINERAL tscheffkinite *f*

tschermakite *n* MINERAL tschermigite *f*

tschermigite *n* MINERAL tschermigite *f*

tschewkinite *n* MINERAL tscheffkinite *f*

T-section *n* ELECTRON cellule en T *f*

TSI *abbr (time slot interchanger)* TELECOM commuta-

teur T *m*, commutateur temporel *m*

T-slot *n* MECH ENG rainure en T *f*; ~ **cutter** *n* MECH ENG fraise pour rainure à T *f*

TSP *abbr (trisodium phosphate)* DETERGENTS phosphate trisodique *m*

T-square *n* MECH ENG té de dessin *m*, équerre en T *f*

T-stage *n* TELECOM étage T *m*, TELECOM étage temporel *m*

T-stop *n* CINEMAT ouverture photométrique *f*

tsunami *n* GEOPHYS onde de marée *f*, raz de marée *m*, tsunami *m*, OCEANOG tsunami *m*

TT: ~ **milk** *n* *(tuberculin-tested milk)* FOOD TECH lait certifié *m*, lait garanti *m*

T-tail *n* AERONAUT *aircraft* empennage en T *m*

T-Tauri: ~ **star** *n* ASTRON étoile T Tauri *f*

TTC *abbr (tracking telemetry and command)* SPACE *communications* PTT *(poursuite télémesure et télécommande)*

TTL[1] *abbr (transistor-transistor logic)* COMP, DP logique transistor-transistor *f*, ELECTRON logique à transistor et transistors *f*

TTL:[2] ~ **logic family** *n* ELECTRON famille logique TTL *f*

t-t-t *abbr (time-temperature-tolerance)* REFRIG *of frozen food* tolérance temps-température *f*

TTY *abbr (teletype)* COMP, DP téléscripteur *m*, télétype *m*, TELECOM téléimprimeur *m*, télétype *m*

TU *abbr (tributary unit)* TELECOM unité d'affluents *f*

tub[1] *n* MINING benne *f*, cuffat *m*, tonne *f*, berlaine *f*, berline *f*, wagonnet *m*, PACKAGING bac *m*, PROD ENG bac *m*, cuve *f*, tonneau *m*; ~ **controller** *n* MINING clichage *m*; ~ **wheel** *n* MECH ENG *emery cup wheel* meule à noyau rentrant *f*, meule-boisseau *f*

tub[2] *vt* MINING cuveler

tubbing *n* MINING *of mineshaft* cuvelage *m*, cuvellement *m*

tube *n* CONST tube *m*, *of lock* canon *m*, ELECTRON, LAB EQUIP, OPT *optical cable*, PHYS *of flow*, SPACE *communications* tube *m*, TEXTILES support de fil *m*; ~ **and fin radiator** *n* AUTO radiateur à tubes d'air *m*; ~ **bend** *n* MECH ENG coude de tube *m*; ~ **brush** *n* LAB EQUIP goupillon *m*, *cleaning* brosse à tubes *f*; ~ **bundle** *n* NUCLEAR *of steam generator* faisceau tubulaire *m*; ~ **center** *n* (AmE), ~ **centre** *n* (BrE) INSTRUMENT partie centrale du tube *f*; ~ **clip** *n* CONST pince pour tubes *f*; ~ **column** *n* CONST colonne de tubage *f*, colonne de tubes *f*; ~ **cutter** *n* LAB EQUIP, MECH ENG coupe-tubes *m*; ~ **expander** *n* CONST appareil à mandriner les tubes *m*, dilateur *m*, dudgeon *m*, extendeur *m*, mandrin à arrondir les tubes de chaudières *m*; ~ **filling and closing machine** *n* PACKAGING machine à remplir et à fermer les tubes *f*; ~ **gage** *n* (AmE), ~ **gauge** *n* (BrE) MECH ENG calibreur *m*; ~ **mill** *n* COAL TECH broyeur cylindrique *m*; ~ **neck** *n* TV col de tube *m*; ~ **nest** *n* NUCLEAR faisceau tubulaire *m*; ~ **paint** *n* COLOURS couleur en tube *f*; ~ **plate** *n* NUCLEAR *of steam generator* plaque tubulaire *f*; ~ **socket** *n* ELEC ENG support de tube *m*; ~ **thickness gage** *n* (AmE), ~ **thickness gauge** *n* (BrE) NUCLEAR indicateur d'épaisseur de tuyau *m*; ~ **train** *n* TRANSP train-tube *m*; ~ **transportation** *n* TRANSP transport de marchandises par conduites *m*; ~ **vehicle** *n* TRANSP transport en tube *m*; ~ **vehicle system** *n* *(TVS)* TRANSP transport en tube *m*; ~ **vice** *n* (BrE) MECH ENG étau à tubes *m*; ~ **vise** *n* (AmE) *see tube vice*; ~ **works** *n* PROD ENG tuyauterie *f*; ~ **wrench** *n* MECH ENG clé à fer creux *f*, clé à tubes *f*, serre-tubes *m*

tube-and-steel: ~ **drill** *n* MECH ENG *tool* foret conique *m*

tube-closing: ~ **machine** n PACKAGING machine à fermer les tubes f

tube-drawing: ~ **mandrel** n MECH ENG mandrin d'étirage de tubes m; ~ **press** n PROD ENG presse à étirer les tubes f

tube-holder n LAB EQUIP support porte-tube m

tubeless: ~ **tire** n (AmE), ~ **tyre** n (BrE) VEHICLES pneumatique sans chambre à air m

tuberculin-tested: ~ **milk** n (TT milk) FOOD TECH lait certifié m, lait garanti m

tuberin n CHEM tubérine f

tubes n pl FUELLESS flat plate collector tubes m pl

tube-scraper n PROD ENG raclette pour tubes de chaudière f

tube-screwing: ~ **machine** n MECH ENG machine à tarauder les tubes f

tube-type: ~ **heat exchanger** n MECH ENG échangeur thermique tubulaire m

tubing n CONST system of tubes tubage m, tubes m pl, tuyautage m, tuyauterie f, FUELLESS drilling colonne f, PETR tubing m; ~ **anchor** n PETR TECH ancrage de la colonne de protection m; ~ **glass** n C&G verre pour tubes m; ~ **hanger** n PETR suspension de tubing f

tubular[1] adj PROD ENG cylindrique

tubular:[2] ~ **air heater** n HEATING réchauffeur d'air tubulaire m; ~ **boiler** n FOOD TECH machinery, PROD ENG chaudière tubulaire f; ~ **carbon arc** n NUCLEAR arc tubulaire au carbone m; ~ **ceramic capacitor** n ELEC ENG condensateur céramique tubulaire m; ~ **cooler** n FOOD TECH machinery réfrigérant tubulaire m; ~ **dryer** n TEXTILES séchoir tubulaire m; ~ **frame** n VEHICLES of motorcycle châssis tubulaire m; ~ **furnace boiler** n HYDR EQUIP chaudière à foyer tubulaire f; ~ **lamp** n ELEC lampe tubulaire f; ~ **motor** n TRANSP moteur tubulaire m; ~ **radiator** n AUTO radiateur tubulaire m; ~ **scaffolding** n CONST échafaudage tubulaire m; ~ **sensor** n PROD ENG détecteur cylindrique m; ~ **slug** n NUCLEAR bloc tubulaire m; ~ **transportation** n TRANSP transport en tube m

Tucana n ASTRON Toucan m

Tuchel: ~ **connector** n CINEMAT fiche Tuchel f

tuck-in: ~ **closure** n PACKAGING fermeture rentrante f; ~ **flap** n PACKAGING volet rentrant m

tucking: ~ **blade** n PRINT lame engageante f; ~ **blades cylinder** n PRINT cylindre à lames engageantes m

tuckstone n C&G pièce de calage f

tue: ~ **iron** n PROD ENG tuyère f

tufa n CONST volcanic rock tuf m

tuff n PETR tuf m; ~ **deposit** n GEOL remblai de tuf m

tuft n TEXTILES touffe f

tufted: ~ **carpet** n TEXTILES tapis touffe m

tug n NAUT boat, PETR remorqueur m

TUG abbr (tributary-unit group) TELECOM groupe d'unité d'affluents m

tugboat n MAR POLL remorqueur m

tumble: ~ **dryer** n TEXTILES séchoir m, tambour m

tumblehome n NAUT ship building frégatage m

tumbler n CONST of lock gorge f, gorge mobile f, PROD ENG tambour dessableur m, tonneau dessableur m, tonneau à dessabler m; ~ **lock** n CONST serrure de sûreté à gorges mobiles f, serrure à gorge f; ~ **switch** n CONTROL commutateur à bascule m, interrupteur basculant m, interrupteur tumbler m, ELEC ENG interrupteur modèle tumbler m

tumbling n PROD ENG founding dessablage au tonneau m, PROP MAT metal finishing polissage au tonneau m; ~

barrel n PROD ENG tambour dessableur m, tonneau dessableur m, tonneau à dessabler m; ~ **box** n PROD ENG tambour dessableur m, tonneau dessableur m, tonneau à dessabler m; ~ **drum** n PROD ENG tambour dessableur m, tonneau dessableur m, tonneau à dessabler m; ~ **mill** n PROD ENG tambour dessableur m, tonneau dessableur m, tonneau à dessabler m; ~ **shaft** n MECH ENG if several cams on same shaft arbre des cames m, arbre à cames m, reverse shaft arbre de changement de marche m, arbre de relevage m

tumbuckle n CONST cric-tenseur m

tuna: ~ **boat** n OCEANOG thonier m

tunable: ~ **klystron** n SPACE klystron accordable m; ~ **magnetron** n ELECTRON magnétron accordable m; ~ **oscillator** n ELECTRON oscillateur accordable m

tune vt ELECTRON, TELECOM accorder, WAVE PHYS to frequency régler

tuned[1] adj RAD PHYS accordé, réglé

tuned:[2] ~ **amplifier** n ELECTRON amplificateur accordé m; ~ **circuit** n ELECTRON, PHYS circuit accordé m; ~ **filter** n ELECTRON filtre accordé m; ~ **impedance bond** n RAIL connection inductive accordée f; ~ **relay** n ELEC relais accordé m; ~ **transformer** n ELEC ENG transformateur accordé m

tuner n RECORDING syntoniseur m, TELECOM tuner m, TV dispositif d'accord m, syntoniseur m

tungstate n CHEM, PROP MAT tungstate m

tungsten n (W) CHEM tungstène m, wolfram m; ~ **carbide** n MECH ENG, PETR TECH carbure de tungstène m; ~ **filament** n ELEC of lamp filament au tungstène m; ~ **film** n CINEMAT pellicule lumière artificielle f, PRINT film au tungstène m, film couleur pour prise de vue en lumière artificielle m; ~ **inert gas welding** n (TIG welding) CONST soudage TIG m; ~ **lighting** n CINEMAT éclairage lumière artificielle m; ~ **spatter** n CONST welding projection de tungstène f

tungsten-carbide: ~ **grit hole saw** n MECH ENG tool trépan à concrétion carbure m; ~ **tipped turning and planing tools** n pl MECH ENG outils en carbure pour tours et raboteuses m pl; ~ **tooling** n MECH ENG outillage en métal dur m; ~ **wire-drawing die** n MECH ENG filière en métal dur pour le tréfilage de fils f

tungsten-rhenium: ~ **fibers** n pl (AmE), ~ **fibres** n pl (BrE) PROP MAT fibres de tungstène-rhénium f pl

tungsten-to-daylight n CINEMAT conversion de la lumière artificielle en lumière du jour f

tungstic adj CHEM tungstique

tungstosilicate n CHEM tungstosilicate m

tuning n ACOUSTICS accordage m, AUTO réglage moteur m, ELECTRON, NAUT of radar, radio accord m, TELECOM accord m, syntonisation f; ~ **capacitor** n ELEC ENG condensateur d'accord m; ~ **characteristics** n pl RAD PHYS of single-frequency laser caractéristiques de réglage f pl; ~ **circuit** n ELEC ENG, ELECTRON, TELECOM circuit d'accord m; ~ **coil** n MILIT army signals bobine d'accord f; ~ **dial** n RECORDING cadran d'ajustage des fréquences m; ~ **fork** n ACOUSTICS, PHYS, RECORDING, WAVE PHYS diapason m; ~ **indicator** n ELECTRON indicateur d'accord m; ~ **ranges** n pl RAD PHYS of laser dyes gammes de réglage f pl; ~ **screw** n ELEC ENG vis d'adaptation f, PHYS waveguide vis d'accord f; ~ **screwdriver** n MECH ENG tool tournevis de syntonisation m

tunnel n CONST souterrain m, tunnel m, FUELLESS hydroelectric power tunnel m, MINING galerie f, PRINT tunnel m, tunnel de séchage m, PROD ENG of blast furnace cuve *f*, vide *m*, REFRIG tunnel *m*; ~ **bar** *n* CONST *rock drill mounting* affût pour creusement de tunnels *m*; ~ **diode** *n* ELECTRON diode tunnel *f*, diode à effet tunnel *f*, PHYS diode tunnel *f*; ~ **effect** *n* ELECTRON effet tunnel *m*, PHYS, TRANSP effet de tunnel *m*; ~ **hardening** *n* REFRIG *for ice cream* durcissement en tunnel *m*; ~ **kiln** *n* HEATING *for ceramics* four à tunnel *m*; ~ **lehr** *n* C&G arche *f*; ~ **vault** *n* CONST voûte en berceau *f*

tunnel-boring: ~ **machine** *n* CONST tunnelier *m*

tunnel-diode: ~ **amplifier** *n* SPACE *communications* amplificateur à diode tunnel *m*

tunneling *n* (AmE), **tunnelling** *n* (BrE) CONST percement de tunnels *m*, ELECTRON franchissement par effet tunnel *m*, MINING chassage *m*, galerie de traçage *f*, percement *m*, percement de galeries de recherche *m*, percement de galeries en direction *m* ~ **machine** *n* (BrE) CONST machine à tunnels *f*, MINING machine de traçage *f*, machine à tracer les voies à travers les rochers *f*; ~ **ray** *n* (BrE) TELECOM rayon tunnel *m*; ~ **technique** *n* (BrE) CONST technique de percement *f*; ~ **work** *n* (BrE) CONST travaux de percement *m pl*

tunny: ~ **boat** *n* OCEANOG thonier *m*; ~ **net** *n* OCEANOG thonaire *m*

tup *n* PROD ENG *of pile-driver, drop-test machine* mouton *m*, *of power hammer* mouton *m*, pilon *m*; ~ **die** *n* PROD ENG *of power hammer* frappe *f*, frappe supérieure *f*, panne du pilon *f*; ~ **pallet** *n* PROD ENG *of power hammer* frappe *f*, frappe supérieure *f*, panne du pilon *f*

turbid: ~ **water** *n* POLLUTION boues *f pl*

turbidimeter *n* CHEM, OCEANOG turbidimètre *m*

turbidimetry *n* CHEM turbidimétrie *f*

turbidite *n* GEOL turbidite *m*

turbidity *n* CHEM féculence *f*, turbidité *f*, FUELLESS, HYDROL turbidité *f*; ~ **coefficient** *n* FUELLESS coefficient de turbidité *m*; ~ **current** *n* GEOL, OCEANOG courant de turbidité *m*; ~ **layer** *n* OCEANOG couche de turbidité *f*, couche néphéloïde *f*; ~ **meter** *n* LAB EQUIP *instrument, analysis*, OCEANOG turbidimètre *m*

turbine *n* AUTO, ELEC *generator*, FUELLESS, HYDR EQUIP, MECH, NAUT, VEHICLES *engine* turbine *f*; ~ **blade** *n* FUELLESS ailette de turbine *f*, MECH ENG pale de turbine *f*, NAUT ailette de turbine *f*, aube de turbine *f*; ~ **building** *n* NUCLEAR salle des machines *f*; ~ **bypass system** *n* NAUT système de dérivation *m*; ~ **casing** *n* NAUT enveloppe de turbine *f*; ~ **cooler** *n* REFRIG refroidisseur à tourniquet *m*; ~ **drilling** *n* PETR TECH turboforage *m*; ~ **efficiency** *n* FUELLESS rendement de turbine *m*; ~ **engine** *n* AERONAUT, AUTO turbomoteur *m*, NAUT machine à turbines *f*; ~ **fuel** *n* SPACE *technology* turbocombustible *m*; ~ **house** *n* NUCLEAR salle des machines *f*; ~ **meter** *n* GAS TECH compteur à turbine *m*; ~ **output** *n* FUELLESS rendement de turbine *m*; ~ **propulsion** *n* NAUT propulsion par turbines *f*; ~ **pump** *n* HYDR EQUIP pompe centrifuge *f*, turbopompe *f*; ~ **ring** *n* HYDR EQUIP couronne de turbine *f*; ~ **seating** *n* NAUT carlingage de turbine *m*; ~ **stop valve** *n* NUCLEAR vanne d'arrêt d'une turbine *f*; ~ **vessel** *n* NAUT navire à turbine *m*; ~ **wheel** *n* HYDR EQUIP rotor de turbine *m*, NAUT roue de turbine *f*; ~ **wheel with vanes** *n* HYDR EQUIP rotor de turbine *m*

turbine-engined: ~ **lorry** *n* (BrE) *(cf turbine-engined truck)* TRANSPORT camion à turbine *m*; ~ **truck** *n* (AmE) *(cf turbine-engined lorry)* TRANSP camion à turbine *m*

turbo-alternator *n* ELEC *generator*, ELEC ENG turbo-alternateur *m*

turbocharged: ~ **engine** *n* NAUT *diesel* moteur suralimenté *m*

turbocharger *n* MECH ENG turbocompresseur à suralimentation *m*, NAUT *engine* turbosoufflante *f*, VEHICLES *engine* turbocompresseur *m*

turbocharging *n* NAUT *of engine* suralimentation *f*

turbocompressor *n* NAUT turbocompresseur *m*

turbocruiser *n* TRANSP autocar à turbine *m*

turbodrill *n* PETR TECH trépan à turbine *m*, turboforeuse *f*

turbodrilling *n* PETR turboforage *m*

turboelectric *adj* TRANSP automotrice

turboexpander *n* REFRIG turbine de détente *f*, turbodétendeur *m*

turbofan *n* AERONAUT *engine* turbosoufflante *f*, TRANSP turboréacteur à double flux *m*, *aviation* réacteur à double flux *m*; ~ **engine** *n* MECH ENG turboréacteur à ventilateur *m*, THERMOD *bypass engine* turboréacteur à double flux *m*

turbogenerator *n* ELEC ENG turbo-alternateur *m*, turbogénérateur *m*, turbogénératrice *f*, PHYS turbo-alternateur *m*

turbojet *n* AERONAUT *engine*, TRANSP turboréacteur *m*; ~ **engine** *n* THERMOD turboréacteur *m*

turbomixer *n* PROD ENG *production* turbomélangeur *m*

turbomolecular *adj* MECH ENG *pump* turbomoléculaire

turboprop *n* AERONAUT turbopropulseur *m*

turbopropeller *n* AERONAUT turbopropulseur *m*

turbopump *n* NAUT, SPACE *spacecraft* turbopompe *f*, WATER SUPP pompe turbine *f*, turbopompe *f*

turbo-ramjet *n* TRANSP moteur à turbo-statoréacteur *m*

turboseparation *n* FOOD TECH *of product by air* séparation par turbine *f*, turboséparation *f*

turboshaft: ~ **engine** *n* THERMOD turbomachine *f*

turbo-stapler *n* TEXTILES turbo *m*

turbosupercharger *n* AUTO turbocompresseur *m*

turbo-top *n* TEXTILES ruban turbo *m*

turbotrain *n* TRANSP turbotrain *m*

turbulence *n* AUTO, FLUID PHYS, FUELLESS, METEO, SPACE turbulence *f*; ~ **chamber** *n* AUTO chambre de turbulence *f*; ~ **combustion chamber** *n* AUTO chambre de turbulence *f*

turbulence-generating: ~ **grid** *n* FLUID PHYS grille génératrice de turbulence *f*

turbulent[1] *adj* FLUID PHYS agité, turbulent, METEO turbulent

turbulent:[2] ~ **boundary layer** *n* FLUID PHYS couche limite turbulente *f*; ~ **diffusion** *n* NUCLEAR diffusion turbulente *f*; ~ **flow** *n* FLUID PHYS, PHYS écoulement turbulent *m*; ~ **layer** *n* METEO couche turbulente *f*; ~ **motion** *n* FLUID PHYS mouvement turbulent *m*; ~ **plug** *n* FLUID PHYS bouchon de turbulence *m*; ~ **reattachment** *n* FLUID PHYS recollement turbulent *m*; ~ **separation** *n* FLUID PHYS décollement turbulent *m*; ~ **spot** *n* FLUID PHYS bouffée turbulente *f*

turgite *n* MINERAL turgite *f*, turjite *f*

turgor *n* FOOD TECH turgescence *f*

Turing: ~ **machine** *n* COMP, DP machine de Turing *f*

turmeric *n* CHEM, FOOD TECH curcuma *m*

turn[1] *n* ELEC *winding* spire *f*, ELEC ENG *of wire in coil or winding* spire *f*, *rotation of axis* tour *m*, MECH ENG *revolution* révolution *f*, tour *m*, *wind or twist, post or core* spire *f*, tour *m*, tour de spire *m*, NAUT *of tide* renverse de la marée *f*, OCEANOG *of tide* renverse *f*, PHYS *of winding*, SPRINGS *of spring coil* tour *m*; ~ **bridge** *n* CONST pont tournant *m*; ~ **mold blowing** *n* (AmE), ~

mould blowing n (BrE) C&G procédé moulé-tourné m; ~ **pulley** n PROD ENG poulie de renvoi f, poulie de retour f; ~ **ratio** n ELEC transformer rapport de transformation m

turn[2] vt MECH ENG to shape on lathe cylindrer, tourner; ~ **full on** vt MECH ENG ouvrir en plein; ~ **off** vt AUTO engine arrêter, CINEMAT couper, débrancher, éteindre, ELEC ENG cut power supply arrêter, couper, mettre hors circuit, lamp éteindre, state annuler la conduction, bloquer, PROD ENG mettre à zéro, WATER SUPP couper, fermer; ~ **on** vt ELEC ENG connect power supply fermer le circuit, mettre en circuit, mettre en marche, mettre sous tension, lamp allumer, state mettre en conduction, PROD ENG mettre sous tension, mettre à un, WATER SUPP lâcher, ouvrir

turn[3] vi NAUT ship abattre, virer, SPACE virer; ~ **turtle** vi NAUT capoter

turn-and-bank: ~ **indicator** n (AmE) (cf bank-and-pitch indicator) AERONAUT indicateur d'inclinaison longitudinale et latérale m

turnapull: ~ **scraper** n CONST earthmoving equipment turnapull m

turnaround n AERONAUT demi-tour m, of aircraft rotation f; ~ **card** n PROD ENG carte aller-retour f, fiche aller-retour f; ~ **directive** n PROD ENG directive d'aller-retour f; ~ **document** n PROD ENG bon aller-retour m; ~ **time** n COMP temps d'inversion de ligne m, temps de retournement m, DP délai d'exécution m, temps d'inversion de ligne m, temps de retournement m, NUCLEAR of reprocessing plant temps de maintenance m, PROD ENG délai d'exécution m, RAIL crochet m, TELECOM temps d'inversion m; ~ **time at terminus** n RAIL vehicles battement au terminus m

turnbuckle n MECH ridoir m, MECH ENG lanterne f, lanterne de serrage f, NAUT rigging, OCEANOG ridoir m

turned-in-the-lathe adj; ~ **adj** MECH ENG tourné

turned:[2] ~ **rim** n (AmE) (cf reinforced rim) C&G bord de carafe m; ~ **washer** n MECH ENG rondelle tournée f

turned-and-bored: ~ **pulley** n PROD ENG poulie tournée et alésée f

turned-in-the-lathe adj MECH ENG tourné

turned-up: ~ **flange** n PROD ENG sheet-metal working collet rabattu m, collet tombé m

turner n C&G tourneur m; ~ **bar** n PRINT barre de retournement f

turning n CONST of crane virage m, MECH ENG crank shaft, lathe work tournage m; ~ **basin** n NAUT port bassin d'évitage m; ~ **between centers** n (AmE), ~ **between centres** n (BrE) MECH ENG tournage entre pointes m; ~ **bridge** n CONST pont tournant m; ~ **carrier** n MECH ENG doguin m, toc m, toc pour tourner m; ~ **circle** n NAUT shiphandling, VEHICLES courbe de giration f; ~ **diamonds** n pl MECH ENG diamants de tournage m pl; ~ **gear** n NAUT engine vireur m, NUCLEAR of turbine rotor mécanisme vireur m, vireur m; ~ **gouge** n MECH ENG gouge de tour f, gouge de tourneur f; ~ **knob** n CONTROL bouton tournant m; ~ **lathe** n MECH ENG tour m; ~ **mill** n MECH ENG tour en l'air à plateau horizontal m, tour à plateau horizontal m; ~ **moment** n MECH ENG moment d'un couple m; ~ **movements** n pl TRANSP débit directionnel m; ~ **on the face plate** n MECH ENG tournage en l'air m; ~ **point** n CONST surveying point perdu m; ~ **rest** n MECH ENG handrest of lathe support à main m, slide rest of lathe support à chariot m; ~ **saw** n MECH ENG scie à chantourner f; ~ **tool** n MECH ENG outil de tour m, outil pour

tours m, outil à tourner m; ~ **tool with carbide tip** n MECH ENG outil de tour à plaquette en carbures métalliques m; ~ **traffic** n TRANSP courant tournant m

turnings n pl COAL TECH copeaux de fraisage m pl, PROD ENG tournure f

turnkey n CONST civil engineering clé en main f; ~ **installation** n MECH ENG complete installation installation clef en main f; ~ **project** n MECH ENG ensemble clés en main m; ~ **system** n COMP, DP système clé en main m

turn-off n ELEC ENG cutting of power supply arrêt m, coupure de circuit f, mise hors circuit f, lamp extinction f, interruption f, transition to off state annulation de la conduction f, blocage m, interrompre, passage à l'état non conducteur m; ~ **pulse** n ELECTRON impulsion de blocage f, signal de blocage m, signal de coupure m; ~ **time** n ELEC ENG temps de blocage m

turn-on n CINEMAT brancher, ELEC ENG connection with power supply fermeture du circuit f, mise en circuit f, mise en marche f, mise sous tension f, lamp allumage m, transition to on state déblocage m, mise en conduction f, passage à l'état conducteur m; ~ **pulse** n ELECTRON impulsion de déblocage f, signal de branchement m, signal de déblocage m; ~ **time** n ELEC ENG, ELECTRON temps de déblocage m

turnout n CONST railway appareil m, roads zone de stationnement f, RAIL aiguille f, branchement m, changement de voie m, point d'évitement m, TEXTILES production f; ~ **on the curve** n RAIL branchement en courbe m

turnover n C&G retournement m, PROD ENG taux de rotation m, WATER SUPP of water renouvellement m

turnpin n CONST plumbing alésoir m

turns: ~ **per inch** n pl TEXTILES tours par pouce m pl; ~ **per meter** n pl (AmE), ~ **per metre** n (BrE) TEXTILES tours au mètre m pl; ~ **ratio** n AUTO, ELEC ENG, PHYS rapport de transformation m

turnscrew n MECH ENG of monkeywrench clef à molette f, clef à mâchoires mobiles f, of screwdriver tournevis m; ~ **bit** n MECH ENG lame de tournevis pour vilebrequin f

turntable n ACOUSTICS plateau m, AERONAUT airport carrousel m, MECH plateau tournant m, RECORDING tourne-disque m, TRANSP bridges couronne de pivotement f, rail plaque tournante f; ~ **feed** n PACKAGING alimentation avec plaque tournante f; ~ **wow** n RECORDING pleurage de tourne-disque m

turn-to-turn: ~ **winding** n ELEC enroulement fil à fil m

turpentine n CHEM, COLOURS, P&R paint, raw material, solvent térébenthine f; ~ **substitute** n COLOURS substitut de térébenthine m; ~ **varnish** n COATINGS vernis à l'essence m, COLOURS vernis à la térébenthine m

turquoise n MINERAL turquoise f

turret n CINEMAT, MECH tourelle f, MECH ENG of lathe porte-outil revolver m, revolver m, tourelle f, tourelle revolver f, MILIT of tank tourelle f; ~ **camera** n CINEMAT caméra à tourelle f; ~ **cap** n INSTRUMENT capuchon de protection m; ~ **gun** n MILIT canon à tourelle m; ~ **head** n MECH ENG of lathe porte-outil revolver m, revolver m, tourelle revolver f; ~ **lathe** n MECH ENG tour revolver m, MECH ENG tour avec porte-outil revolver m, tour avec tourelle revolver m, tour revolver m; ~ **slide** n MECH ENG chariot porte-tourelle m

turret-head: ~ **position switch** n PROD ENG interrupteur de position à tête à tourelle m

turtle n CINEMAT embase f; ~ **culture** n OCEANOG testudoculture f

tusk: ~ **tenon joint** n CONST assemblage à tenon avec

chaperon et renfort *m*, assemblage à tenon avec renfort *m*, assemblage à tenon renforcé *m*, assemblage à tenon de repos *m*

tutorial: **~ disk** *n* PROD ENG disque d'initiation *m*

tuyère *n* PROD ENG tuyère *f*; **~ nozzle** *n* PROD ENG bec de tuyère *m*

TV: **~ academy leader** *n* TV amorce télévision *f*; **~ bulb** *n* C&G ampoule de télévision *f*; **~ cutoff** *n* TV cadrage TV *m*

TVC *abbr (thrust vector control)* SPACE *spacecraft* commande de contrôle de poussée *f*

TVP *abbr (textured vegetable protein)* FOOD TECH protéine végétale texturée *f*

TVS *abbr (tube vehicle system)* TRANSP transport en tube *m*

tweel: **~ block** *n* C&G porte d'ouvreau *f*

tween: **~ deck** *n* NAUT *shipbuilding* entrepont *m*

tweeter *n* RECORDING haut-parleur d'aigus *m*, tweeter *m*

tweezers *n pl* C&G brucelles *f pl*, LAB EQUIP brucelles *f pl*, pince brucelles *f*

twelve: **~ ways back up** *n* PRINT impression tête-à-queue *f*

twelve-point: **~ recorder** *n* INSTRUMENT enregistreur à douze stylos *m*, enregistreur à douze traces *m*

twelve-row: **~ punched card** *n* DP carte perforée douze lignes *f*

twilight: **~ shot** *n* PHOTO prise de vue au crépuscule *f*

twill *n* TEXTILES sergé *m*

twin[1] *adj* PROP MAT conjugué

twin[2] *n* CRYSTALL, METALL, PROP MAT macle *f*; **~ bagging system** *n* PACKAGING système de remplissage jumelé pour sacs *m*; **~ boundary** *n* METALL joint de macles *m*; **~ cable** *n* ELEC ENG câble à paires symétriques *m*; **~ carburetor** *n* (AmE), **~ carburettor** *n* (BrE) AUTO carburateur double corps *m*; **~ cards** *n pl* TEXTILES bifil *m*; **~ cock** *n* WATER SUPP robinet à deux faces *m*; **~ ends** *n pl* TEXTILES deux fils parallèles *m pl*; **~ engine** *n* TRANSP moteur à deux cylindres *m*; **~ engines** *n pl* MECH ENG machines conjuguées *f pl*, machines jumelles *f pl*; **~ formation** *n* CRYSTALL hémitropie *f*, maclage *m*; **~ grinder** *n* C&G twin-douci *m*; **~ interlaced scanning** *n* TV analyse entrelacée double *f*; **~ lamella** *n* METALL lamelle maclée *f*; **~ magazine** *n* PHOTO chargeurs jumelés *m pl*; **~ pack** *n* PACKAGING emballage jumelé *m*; **~ paradox** *n* PHYS paradoxe des jumeaux *m*; **~ pole** *n* RAIL poteau jumelé *m*; **~ polisher** *n* C&G twin-poli *m*; **~ polishing** *n* C&G twin-poli *m*; **~ post** *n* RAIL poteau jumelé *m*; **~ projectors** *n pl* CINEMAT projecteurs jumelés *m pl*; **~ wheels** *n pl* AERONAUT roues en diabolo *f pl*, roues jumelées *f pl*

twin-barreled: **~ carburetor** *n* (AmE), **twin-barrelled carburettor** *n* (BrE) AUTO carburateur double corps *m*

twin-choke: **~ carburetor** *n* (AmE), **~ carburettor** *n* (BrE) AUTO carburateur double corps *m*

twin-cylinder: **~ engine** *n* MECH ENG machine bicylindrique *f*

twine *n* TEXTILES corde *f*

twin-engine: **~ jet aircraft** *n* AERONAUT biréacteur *m*

twin-engined *adj* AERONAUT, MECH ENG bimoteur

twin-ground: **~ plate** *n* C&G glace twinée *f*

twin-hull: **~ ship** *n* TRANSP catamaran *m*

twin-jet: **~ injection nozzle** *n* AUTO injecteur à deux trous *m*

twin-lens: **~ reflex** *n* PHOTO appareil reflex à deux objectifs *m*; **~ reflex camera** *n* PHOTO appareil à deux objectifs *m*

twin-line: **~ brake** *n* AUTO frein à double circuit *m*

twinned *adj* CRYSTALL maclé

twinning *n* CRYSTALL hémitropie *f*, METALL maclage *m*; **~ plane** *n* METALL plan de maclage *m*; **~ relationship** *n* PROP MAT relation de maclage *f*; **~ shear** *n* METALL cisaillement de maclage *m*; **~ system** *n* METALL système de maclage *m*

twin-piston: **~ engine** *n* AUTO moteur à double piston *m*

twin-reactor: **~ station** *n* NUCLEAR *nuclear power* centrale nucléaire à deux réacteurs *f*

twin-ribbon: **~ cable** *n* TRANSP câble à rubans jumelés *m*

twins *n pl* C&G billes doubles *f pl*

Twins *n pl* ASTRON Gémeaux *m pl*

twin-screw: **~ lathe** *n* MECH ENG tour ayant deux vis mères indépendantes et de pas différent *m*; **~ steamer** *n* NAUT navire à deux hélices *m*

twin-spindle: **~ lathe** *n* MECH ENG tour bibroche *m*

twin-stream: **~ collator** *n* PRINT assembleuse jumelée *f*

twin-T: **~ network** *n* ELEC ENG réseau en double T *m*

twin-tail: **~ unit** *n* AERONAUT *of aircraft* empennage double *m*

twin-track[1] *adj* RECORDING double piste

twin-track:[2] **~ recorder** *n* RECORDING magnétophone à double piste *m*

twin-wire: **~ board** *n* PAPER TECH carton double toile *m*; **~ paper** *n* PAPER TECH papier double toile *m*

T-wire *n* TELECOM fil-T *m*

twist[1] *n* NUCLEAR *of field lines*, PAPER TECH, TEXTILES torsion *f*; **~ disclination** *n* METALL disclinaison torse *f*; **~ drill** *n* MECH foret hélicoïdal *m*, MECH ENG foret hélicoïdal *m*, mèche hélicoïdale *f*; **~ drill grinder** *n* MECH ENG machine à affûter les forets hélicoïdaux *f*; **~ drill with parallel shank** *n* MECH ENG foret hélicoïdal à queue cylindrique *m*; **~ drill with straight shank** *n* MECH ENG foret hélicoïdal à queue cylindrique *m*; **~ drill with taper square shank** *n* MECH ENG foret hélicoïdal à queue carrée conique *m*; **~ factor** *n* TEXTILES coefficient de torsion *m*; **~ gimlet** *n* CONST vrille à torsade *f*; **~ grip** *n* VEHICLES *of motorcycle handlebar* poignée tournante *f*; **~ hand reamer** *n* MECH ENG alésoir à main en hélice *m*; **~ joint** *n* PROD ENG *of wires* joint par torsion *m*; **~ lock plug** *n* CINEMAT fiche verrouillable *f*; **~ tap** *n* MECH ENG taraud à rainures hélicoïdales *m*; **~ to release unit** *n* PROD ENG auxiliaire tourner pour relâcher *m*; **~ with shear** *n* NUCLEAR torsion avec cisaillement *f*

twist:[2] **~ to release** *phr* PROD ENG tourner pour relâcher

twisted:[1] **~ together** *adj* TELECOM torsadé

twisted:[2] **~ core** *n* TEXTILES fil d'âme tordu *m*; **~ pair** *n* COMP, DP, ELEC ENG, PROD ENG paire torsadée *f*; **~ waveguide** *n* ELEC ENG guide d'ondes torsadé *m*; **~ wire** *n* SPRINGS fil torsadé *m*

twisted-pair: **~ cable** *n* COMP câble bifilaire torsadé *m*, ELEC câble bifilaire torsadé *m*, câble à paires torsadées *m*, TELECOM câble à paires symétriques *m*; **~ flat cable** *n* ELEC ENG câble plat à paires torsadées *m*

twister *n* TEXTILES retordeuse *f*, TRANSP tortilleur *m*

twisting *n* C&G *of glass fibres* retordage *m*, *of tubes* vrillage *m*, FLUID PHYS *background vorticity*, MECH ENG torsion *f*; **~ closure** *n* PACKAGING fermeture à torsion *f*; **~ moment** *n* MECH ENG moment d'un couple *m*

twist-release *vt* PROD ENG tourner pour relâcher

twist-to-release: **~ pull unit** *n* PROD ENG auxiliaire tirer pour relâcher *m*; **~ push unit** *n* PROD ENG auxiliaire pousser pour relâcher *m*

two: **~ plies of a two-ply yarn** *n pl* TEXTILES deux bouts d'un fil retors *m pl*; ~ **stars surrounded by halos** *n pl* ASTRON deux étoiles entourées de halos *m pl*; ~ **teeth which engage completely** *n pl* MECH ENG deux dents qui sont complètement en prise *m pl*

two's: ~ **complement** *n* COMP, DP complément à deux *m*

two-address: ~ **instruction** *n* COMP, DP instruction à deux adresses *f*

two-bath: ~ **method** *n* NUCLEAR *of decontamination* méthode à deux bains *f*; ~ **processing** *n* PRINT développement en deux bains *m*; ~ **toning** *n* PHOTO virage en deux bains *m*

2B+D: ~ **arrangement** *n* TELECOM structure 2B+D *f*

two-button: ~ **mouse** *n* COMP, DP souris à deux boutons *f*

two-cell: ~ **capacitor** *n* ELEC condensateur double *m*

two-circle: ~ **instrument** *n* NUCLEAR *in X-ray crystallography* appareil à deux cercles *m*

two-circuit: ~ **ignition system** *n* AUTO allumage à double circuit *m*; ~ **nuclear power plant** *n* NUCLEAR centrale nucléaire à deux circuits *f*

two-color: ~ **press** *n* (AmE) *see two-colour press*; ~ **printing** *n* (AmE) *see two-colour printing*

two-colour: ~ **press** *n* (BrE) PRINT presse à deux couleurs *f*; ~ **printing** *n* (BrE) PRINT impression en deux couleurs *f*

two-contact: ~ **regulator** *n* AUTO régulateur à deux étages *m*

two-contacts: ~ **connector** *n* ELEC *capacitor* prise à deux fiches *f*

two-cylinder: ~ **press** *n* PRINT presse recto-verso *f*

two-dimensional *adj* COMP, DP, PHYS bidimensionnel

two-disc: ~ **clutch** *n* (BrE) AUTO embrayage bidisque *m*

two-disk: ~ **clutch** *n* (AmE) *see two-disc clutch*

two-electron: ~ **innermost shell** *n* NUCLEAR couche K *f*, couche à deux électrons *f*; ~ **problem** *n* NUCLEAR problème des deux électrons *m*

two-element: ~ **relay** *n* ELEC relais à deux circuits *m*

twofold: ~ **rotation axis** *n* CRYSTALL axe binaire *m*, axe d'ordre deux *m*; ~ **screw axis** *n* CRYSTALL axe binaire hélicoïdal *m*

two-frequency: ~ **channeling plan** *n* (AmE), ~ **channelling plan** *n* (BrE) TELECOM plan de disposition des voies à deux fréquences *m*; ~ **operation automatic repeater mode** *n* TELECOM fonctionnement à deux fréquences avec relais automatique *m*; ~ **operation non-repeater mode** *n* TELECOM fonctionnement à deux fréquences sans relais *m*; ~ **relay system** *n* TELECOM système de relais à deux fréquences *m*; ~ **simplex** *n* TELECOM simplex à deux fréquences *m*

two-high: ~ **mill** *n* PROD ENG laminoir duo *m*, train duo *m*; ~ **rolls** *n pl* PROD ENG duo *m*, laminoir duo *m*, train duo *m*; ~ **train** *n* PROD ENG duo *m*, laminoir duo *m*, train duo *m*

two-hole: ~ **torus** *n* GEOM tore à deux trous *m*

two-layer: ~ **board** *n* PAPER TECH carton deux couches *m*; ~ **paper** *n* PAPER TECH papier deux couches *m*

two-leg: ~ **puller** *n* MECH ENG *tool* extracteur 2 griffes *m*

two-nucleon: ~ **system** *n* NUCLEAR système à deux nucléons *m*

two-on: ~ **signatures** *n pl* PRINT cahiers sortant 2 à 2 *m pl*

two-pack: ~ **primer** *n* P&R *paint* peinture primaire réactive *f*

two-part: ~ **screw plate** *n* MECH ENG filière double *f*

two-phase[1] *adj* ELEC *AC supply* à deux phases, ELEC ENG biphase, diphasé, à deux phases

two-phase:[2] ~ **alternator** *n* ELEC *generator* alternateur diphasé *m*; ~ **carburetor** *n* (AmE), ~ **carburettor** *n*

(BrE) AUTO carburateur à étages *m*; ~ **controller** *n* TRANSP *traffic control* régulateur biphase *m*; ~ **cooling** *n* NUCLEAR refroidissement diphasique *m*; ~ **current** *n* ELEC ENG courant diphasé *m*; ~ **flow** *n* REFRIG écoulement diaphasique *m*; ~ **machine** *n* ELEC ENG machine diphasée *f*; ~ **motor** *n* ELEC moteur diphasé *m*, ELEC ENG moteur asynchrone diphasé *m*, moteur diphasé *m*; ~ **network** *n* ELEC *supply* réseau diphasé *m*; ~ **reactor** *n* NUCLEAR réacteur diphasique *m*, réacteur à deux phases *m*; ~ **rotor** *n* ELEC rotor diphasé *m*; ~ **rotor winding** *n* ELEC ENG bobinage rotorique diphasé *m*; ~ **stator** *n* ELEC ENG stator diphasé *m*; ~ **stator winding** *n* ELEC ENG bobinage statorique diphasé *m*; ~ **system** *n* ELEC *network* système diphasé *m*, ELEC ENG réseau diphasé *m*

two-piece: ~ **connector** *n* ELEC ENG connecteur en deux parties *m*; ~ **drive shaft** *n* AUTO arbre de transmission à relais *m*; ~ **propeller shaft** *n* AUTO arbre de transmission à relais *m*

two-pin: ~ **plug** *n* ELEC ENG fiche polaire *f*

two-plate: ~ **clutch** *n* AUTO embrayage bidisque *m*

two-plus-one: ~ **address instruction** *n* COMP, DP instruction à deux adresses plus une *f*

two-pole: ~ **motor** *n* ELEC moteur bipolaire *m*; ~ **switch** *n* ELEC ENG interrupteur bipolaire *m*; ~ **system** *n* ELEC *of machine* système bipolaire *m*

two-polymer: ~ **adhesive** *n* PROP MAT colle à base de deux polymères *f*

two-port: ~ **network** *n* ELEC ENG réseau à deux accès *m*

two-revolution: ~ **press** *n* PRINT presse à double révolution *f*

two-roll: ~ **system** *n* PRINT système à doubles rouleaux *m*

two-seat: ~ **aircraft** *n* AERONAUT biplace *m*

two-side: ~ **colored board** *n* (AmE) *see two-side coloured board*; ~ **colored paper** *n* (AmE) *see two-side coloured paper*; ~ **coloured board** *n* (BrE) PAPER TECH carton coloré deux faces *m*; ~ **coloured paper** *n* (BrE) PAPER TECH papier coloré deux faces *m*

two-sided[1] *adj* PROP MAT à deux faces

two-sided:[2] ~ **disc** *n* (BrE) OPT disque double face *m*; ~ **disk** *n* (AmE) *see two-sided disc*

two-sidedness *n* PAPER TECH *of paper* double face *f*, envers *m*

two-slot: ~ **module** *n* PROD ENG module à deux emplacements *m*

two-space: ~ **compression** *n* MECH ENG *of air* compression en deux étages *f*

two-speed: ~ **counter motion** *n* MECH ENG renvoi de mouvement à double vitesse *m*; ~ **filling** *n* PACKAGING remplissage à deux vitesses *m*; ~ **final drive** *n* AUTO couple à deux rapports *m*, réduction finale à double rapport *f*

two-stage: ~ **controller** *n* CONTROL régulateur à deux niveaux *m*; ~ **fuel filter** *n* AUTO filtre à combustible double *m*; ~ **regulator** *n* CONTROL régulateur à deux niveaux *m*; ~ **relay** *n* ELEC relais à deux paliers *m*, relais à deux seuils *m*

two-state: ~ **register** *n* TELECOM registre à deux états *m*

two-step: ~ **cone** *n* PROD ENG bipoulie *f*; ~ **cone pulley** *n* PROD ENG bipoulie *f*

two-stream: ~ **instability** *n* NUCLEAR instabilité de double faisceau *f*

two-stroke: ~ **engine** *n* AUTO, MECH, MECH ENG, NAUT *diesel*, TRANSP, VEHICLES moteur à deux temps *m*; ~ **oil** *n* AUTO huile pour moteurs 2 temps *f*

two-system: ~ **contact breaker** *n* AUTO rupteur double *m*

two-table: ~ **machine** *n* C&G machine à deux plateaux *f*

two-tanged: ~ **file** *n* MECH ENG lime à deux queues *f*, lime à deux soies *f*

two-terminal: ~ **network** *n* PHYS *quadripole* dipôle électrocinétique *m*

two-throw: ~ **crank shaft** *n* MECH ENG arbre à deux manivelles *m*

two-tone: ~ **dyeing** *n* COLOURS teinture en deux tons *f*

two-way: ~ **cock** *n* WATER SUPP robinet à deux eaux *m*, robinet à deux voies *m*; ~ **damper valve** *n* AUTO, MECH ENG soupape d'amortissement à deux voies *f*; ~ **feed** *n* ELEC *supply* alimentation bilatérale *f*; ~ **finned cooler** *n* REFRIG refroidisseur à air à double écartement d'ailettes *m*; ~ **mirror** *n* (BrE) *(cf see-through mirror)* C&G miroir semi-réfléchissant *m*; ~ **pallet** *n* TRANSP palette à deux entrées *f*; ~ **restrictor** *n* PROD ENG restricteur à deux voies *m*; ~ **road** *n* CONST route à deux voies *f*; ~ **switch** *n* CONTROL interrupteur à deux directions *m*, ELEC interrupteur va-et-vient *m*, interrupteur à deux directions *m*; ~ **tap** *n* LAB EQUIP *glassware* robinet à deux voies *m*

two-wheel: ~ **grinding machine** *n* MECH ENG machine à meuler double *f*

two-wire: ~ **circuit** *n* COMP, DP, ELEC circuit à deux fils *m*; ~ **crosspoint** *n* TELECOM point de connexion à deux fils *m*; ~ **delta network** *n* ELEC *supply* réseau en delta *m*; ~ **network** *n* ELEC *supply* réseau à deux fils *m*; ~ **switch** *n* TELECOM commutateur à deux fils *m*; ~ **switching system** *n* TELECOM commutateur à deux fils *m*; ~ **system** *n* ELEC *supply network* réseau à deux fils *m*, ELEC ENG système bifilaire *m*, système à deux fils *m*, TELECOM commutateur à deux fils *m*

TWT[1] *abbr (traveling-wave tube, travelling-wave tube)* ELECTRON, PHYS, SPACE, TELECOM TOP *(tube à onde progressive)*

TWT:[2] ~ **amplifier** *n* ELECTRON amplificateur à TOP *m*; ~ **transfer coefficient** *n* SPACE *communications* coefficient de réflectivité *m*

TWTA *abbr (traveling-wave tube amplifier, travelling-wave tube amplifier)* ELECTRON, SPACE ATOP *(amplificateur à tube à onde progressive)*

TX *abbr (transmission)* TV transmission *f*

tying: ~ **closure** *n* PACKAGING fermeture nouée *f*

Tyler: ~ **mount** *n* CINEMAT système antivibratoire

Tyler *m*

tymp *n* PROD ENG *of blast furnace* tympe *f*

tympan *n* PRINT tympan *m*

tympanus *n* HYDR EQUIP tympan *m*

Tyndall: ~ **effect** *n* PHYS effet Tyndall *m*

type[1] *n* COAL TECH *of pile, soil*, COMP, DP type *m*; ~ **approval** *n* GAS TECH estampillage *m*, QUALITY homologation de type *f*, SPACE homologation *f*; ~ **color** *n* (AmE), ~ **colour** *n* (BrE) PRINT couleur du caractère *f*; ~ **family** *n* PRINT famille de caractères *f*, jeu de caractères *m*; ~ **height** *n* PRINT hauteur du caractère *f*, hauteur typographique *f*; ~ **of number** *n* *(TON)* TELECOM type de numéro *m*; ~ **plate** *n* PRINT marbre *m*; ~ **section** *n* GEOL stratotype *m*; ~ **size** *n* PRINT corps de caractère *m*, *of typeface* corps *m*; ~ **test** *n* AERONAUT *turbine engines* essai d'homologation de type *m*

type[2] *vt* COMP, DP taper

typeface *n* DP dessin de caractère *m*, oeil de caractère *m*, PRINT caractère *m*, oeil de caractère *m*

type-M: ~ **carcinotron** *n* PHYS *M-type oscillators* carcinotron de type M *m*

typescript: ~ **proof** *n* PRINT document dactylographié *m*

typesetter *n* PRINT compositeur *m*

typesetting *n* PRINT composition typographique *f*; ~ **machine** *n* PRINT machine à composer *f*

typewriter: ~ **face** *n* PRINT caractères à machine à écrire *m pl*; ~ **paper** *n* PAPER TECH papier pour machine à écrire *m*

typewritten *adj* PATENTS dactylographié

typhoon *n* METEO typhon *m*

typo *n* PRINT compositeur typographique *m*

typographic: ~ **point** *n* PRINT point typographique *m*

typography *n* PRINT typographie *f*

tyre *n* (BrE) RAIL *vehicles* bandage *m*, TRANSP, VEHICLES pneu *m*; ~ **groove** *n* (BrE) RAIL *vehicles* congé de bandage *m*; ~ **pressure gauge** *n* (BrE) CONTROL contrôleur de pression des pneus *m*, vérificateur de pression des pneus *m*; ~ **profile** *n* (BrE) RAIL *vehicles* profil de bandage *m*; ~ **reinforcement** *n* (BrE) TEXTILES renfort pneumatique *m*; ~ **tread** *n* (BrE) P&R *rubber* bande de roulement *f*; ~ **yarn** *n* (BrE) TEXTILES fil de pneu *m*

tyrosamine *n* CHEM tyrosamine *f*

tyrosine *n* CHEM tyrosine *f*

U

U *(uranium)* CHEM U *(uranium)*

UA *abbr* COMP *(user area)*, zone de l'utilisateur *f* DP *(user area)* zone de l'utilisateur *f*, TELECOM *(user agent)* agent d'usager *m*, agent utilisateur *m*

UAS *abbr (unavailable second)* TELECOM seconde d'indisponibilité *f*

UAT *abbr (unavailable time)* TELECOM temps d'indisponibilité *m*

UAX *abbr (unit automatic exchange)* TELECOM central automatique de localité *m*

ubitron *n* ELECTRON ubitron *m*

U-bolt *n* CONST lien en fer à U *m*, étrier *m*, NAUT *boatbuilding* boulon étrier *m*, étrier *m*, VEHICLES *suspension, leaf spring* bride centrale *f*

UFO *abbr (unidentified flying object)* ASTRON, SPACE OVNI *(objet volant non identifié)*

UHF[1] *abbr (ultrahigh frequency)* ELECTRON, TELECOM, TV, WAVE PHYS UHF *(ultrahaute fréquence)*

UHF:[2] **~ broadcasting** *n* TV diffusion à ondes décimétriques *f*; **~ converter** *n* TV convertisseur de fréquence UHF *m*; **~ signal** *n* ELECTRON signal UHF *m*; **~ signal generator** *n* ELECTRON générateur UHF *m*, générateur de signaux UHF *m*; **~ tuner** *n* TV syntoniseur UHF *m*

UHT *abbr (ultra heat treated)* FOOD TECH UHT *(longue-conservation)*

Uhuru: **~ satellite** *n* ASTRON satellite Uhuru *m*

UI *abbr* TELECOM *(unnumbered information)* information non numérotée *f*, TELECOM *(unit interval)* intervalle unitaire *m*

UIC: **~ leaflet** *n* RAIL fiche UIC *f*

UIH: **~ control field** *n* TELECOM champ de commande UIH *m*

UITS *abbr (unacknowledged information transfer service)* TELECOM service de transfert d'informations sans accusé de réception *m*

UK: **~ Infrared Telescope** *n (UKIRT)* ASTRON télescope infrarouge du Royaume-Uni *m (UKIRT)*

UKIRT *abbr (UK Infrared Telescope)* ASTRON UKIRT *(télescope infrarouge du Royaume-Uni)*

ULCC *abbr (ultralarge crude carrier)* PETR TECH UGPB *(ultragros porteur de brut)*

ulcer *n* CINEMAT cache projetable *m*

ulexine *n* CHEM cytisine *f*, uléxine *f*

ulexite *n* MINERAL ulexite *f*

ullage *n* CHEM *of container* creux *m*, FOOD TECH vidange *f*, vide *m*, MECH volume libre *m*, PETR TECH *of container* creux *m*, SPACE *spacecraft* ouillage *m*, remplissage à niveau constant *m*, volume libre *m*, volume mort *m*, volume résiduel *m*

ullmannite *n* MINERAL ullmannite *f*

ulmic *adj* CHEM ulmique

ulmin *n* CHEM ulmine *f*

ulmous *adj* CHEM ulmique

ultimate: **~ bending strength** *n* MECH ENG résistance à la rupture par flexion *f*; **~ burn-up** *n* NUCLEAR combustion massique finale *f*; **~ crushing strength** *n* MECH ENG résistance à la rupture par compression *f*; **~ elongation** *n* P&R allongement à la rupture *m*; **~ heat sink** *n*

NUCLEAR source froide d'ultime secours *f*; **~ installation** *n* NUCLEAR installation complète *f*; **~ load** *n* COAL TECH charge de rupture *f*; **~ magnification** *n* METALL grossissement ultime *m*; **~ recovery** *n* PETR récupération finale *f*; **~ shear strength** *n* MECH ENG résistance limite au cisaillement *f*; **~ strength** *n* CONST résistance à la rupture *f*, MECH ENG résistance extrême *f*, résistance limite *f*, résistance à la rupture *f*, ténacité extrême *f*; **~ stress** *n* MECH ENG contrainte de rupture *f*, SPRINGS contrainte finale *f*; **~ tensile strength** *n* MECH *materials* résistance à la rupture *f*, MECH ENG résistance à la rupture par traction *f*, METALL résistance ultime à la traction *f*, P&R résistance à la rupture *f*; **~ tensile stress** *n* NUCLEAR résistance à la rupture par traction *f*; **~ vacuum** *n* THERMOD vide limite *m*; **~ waste disposal** *n* NUCLEAR entreposage définitif *m*, stockage définitif *m*

ultra: **~ heat treated** *adj (UHT)* FOOD TECH longue-conservation *(UHT)*

ultrabasic: **~ rock** *n* GEOL roche ultrabasique *f*

ultracentrifugation *n* CHEM, NUCLEAR ultracentrifugation *f*

ultracentrifuge *n* CHEM ultracentrifugeur *m*, LAB EQUIP *separation* centrifugeur à supra vitesse *m*, NUCLEAR, PHYS ultracentrifugeuse *f*; **~ enrichment plant** *n* NUCLEAR usine d'enrichissement à ultracentrifugation *f*

ultrachemical *adj* CHEM ultrachimique

ultrachromatography *n* CHEM ultrachromatographie *f*

ultracold: **~ neutron** *n* NUCLEAR neutron ultrafroid *m*

ultrafilter *n* CHEM ultrafiltre *m*

ultrafiltrate *n* CHEM ultrafiltratum *m*

ultrafiltration *n* CHEM, CHEM TECH ultrafiltration *f*

ultrafine: **~ focus** *n* NUCLEAR *of X-ray tube* foyer ultrafin *m*

ultrahigh: **~ accuracy weighing** *n* PACKAGING pesage à très grande exactitude *m*; **~ frequency** *n (UHF)* ELECTRON, TELECOM, TV, WAVE PHYS ultrahaute fréquence *f (UHF)*; **~ frequency thawing** *n* REFRIG décongélation par hyperfréquence *f*; **~ speed photography** *n* CINEMAT prise de vue à très grande vitesse *f*; **~ speed traffic** *n* TRANSP transport ultrarapide *m*; **~ temperature** *n* FOOD TECH ultrahaute température *f*; **~ temperature reactor** *n* NUCLEAR réacteur à ultra haute température *m*; **~ vacuum** *n* PHYS vide secondaire *m*, vide très poussé *m*, REFRIG vide très poussé *m*

ultralarge: **~ crude carrier** *n (ULCC)* PETR TECH ultragros porteur de brut *m (UGPB)*; **~ scale integration circuit** *n* TELECOM circuit ULSI *m*

ultralight: **~ alloy** *n* SPACE alliage ultra-léger *m*

ultramafic: **~ rock** *n* GEOL roche ultrabasique *f*, roche ultramafique *f*

ultramafite *n* GEOL roche ultrabasique *f*

ultramarine *n* CHEM outremer *m*; **~ pigment** *n* COLOURS pigment d'outremer *m*

ultramicroanalysis *n* NUCLEAR ultramicroanalyse *f*

ultramicroscope *n* CHEM ultramicroscope *m*

ultramicroscopic *adj* CHEM ultramicroscopique

ultramicroscopy *n* CHEM ultramicroscopie *f*

ultramylonite *n* GEOL ultramylonite *f*

ultrapasteurization *n* THERMOD upérisation *f*

ultrarapid: ~ **reaction** *n* CHEM réaction ultrarapide *f*

ultrashort: ~ **wave radar** *n* MILIT radar à ondes ultracourtes *m*; ~ **waves** *n pl* WAVE PHYS ondes ultracourtes *f pl*

ultrasmall *adj* PROD ENG hyper petit, ultracompact

ultrasonic: ~ **bath** *n* LAB EQUIP *cleaning* bain à ultrasons *m*; ~ **cleaning** *n* AERONAUT, CINEMAT, RECORDING, TV nettoyage par ultrasons *m*; ~ **detector** *n* TRANSP détecteur à ultrasons *m*; ~ **engineering** *n* MECH ENG ingénierie ultrasonique *f*; ~ **examination** *n* MECH, NUCLEAR, PROP MAT examen aux ultrasons *m*; ~ **frequency** *n* ACOUSTICS, PHYS, RAD PHYS fréquence ultrasonique *f*; ~ **fuel atomizer** *n* TRANSP atomiseur de combustible à ultrasons *m*; ~ **generator** *n* RAD PHYS générateur ultrasonique *m*; ~ **hazards** *n pl* SAFETY dangers des ultrasons *m pl*; ~ **inspection** *n* SPRINGS essai aux ultrasons *m*, WAVE PHYS contrôle aux ultrasons *m*; ~ **machining** *n* NUCLEAR, RAD PHYS usinage par ultrasons *m*; ~ **probe** *n* CONST palpeur à ultrasons *m*, RAIL palpeur de contrôle ultrasonore *m*; ~ **radar** *n* RAD PHYS radar ultrasonique *m*; ~ **sealing** *n* THERMOD soudage par ultrasons *m*, soudage ultrasonique *m*; ~ **sounding** *n* WAVE PHYS sondage par ultrasons *m*; ~ **testing** *n* CONTROL, NUCLEAR, PROP MAT, TESTING essai aux ultrasons *m*; ~ **waves** *n pl* WAVE PHYS ondes ultrasonores *f pl*; ~ **welding** *n* P&R *process*, THERMOD soudage par ultrasons *m*

ultrasonics *n* WAVE PHYS science des ultrasons *f*, ultrasons *f pl*

ultrasound *n* ACOUSTICS, PHYS, RAD PHYS ultrason *m*; ~ **generator** *n* LAB EQUIP sonificateur *m*; ~ **meter** *n* GAS TECH compteur à ultrason *m*; ~ **scan** *n* RAD PHYS échographie *f*

ultratrace *n* CHEM *analysis* ultramicroanalyse *f*

ultravacuum *n* THERMOD ultravide *f*

ultraviolet[1] *adj (UV)* OPT ultraviolet *(UV)*

ultraviolet[2] *n* OPT rayonnement ultraviolet *m*, SPACE ultraviolet *m*; ~ **astronomy** *n* ASTRON astronomie dans l'ultraviolet *f*; ~ **catastrophe** *n* PHYS catastrophe ultraviolet *f*; ~ **erasing** *n* COMP, DP effacement par ultraviolet *m*; ~ **filter** *n* CINEMAT filtre ultraviolet *m*, PHOTO filtre antiultraviolet *m*, SAFETY filtre ultraviolet *m*; ~ **lamp** *n* LAB EQUIP lampe-UV *f*; ~ **light** *n* P&R *physics*, RAD PHYS lumière ultraviolette *f*; ~ **microscope** *n* RAD PHYS microscope à ultraviolet *m*; ~ **mirror** *n* RAD PHYS miroir ultraviolet *m*; ~ **photography** *n* RAD PHYS photographie ultraviolette *f*; ~ **photon** *n* PART PHYS photon UV *m*, photon ultraviolet *m*; ~ **radiation** *n* FUELLESS radiation ultraviolette *f*, GEOPHYS lumière noire *f*, PHYS, POLLUTION rayonnement ultraviolet *m*, RAD PHYS radiation ultraviolette *f*, SPACE rayonnement ultraviolet *m* ~ **ray** *n* WAVE PHYS rayon ultraviolet *m*; ~ **spectrophotometry** *n* CHEM *analysis* spectrophotométrie dans l'ultraviolet *f*

ultraviolet-visible: ~ **spectrophotometer** *n* LAB EQUIP *analysis* spectrophotomètre à UV-visible *m*

U-magnet *n* MECH ENG aimant en fer à cheval *m*

umbellic *adj* CHEM ombellique

umbilical[1] *adj* GEOL *paleontology* ombilical

umbilical[2] *n* OCEANOG ombilical *m*; ~ **cable** *n* SPACE câble ombilical *m*; ~ **connector** *n* SPACE connecteur ombilical *m*; ~ **mast** *n* SPACE mât ombilical *m*

umbra *n* PHYS ombre pure *f*

umbrella *n* CINEMAT réflecteur parapluie *m*; ~ **reflector**

antenna *n* SPACE antenne à réflecteur en parapluie *f*; ~ **roof** *n* CONST comble avec avant-toit *m*

umbrella-type: ~ **alternator** *n* ELEC *generator* alternateur en cloche *m*

Umklapp: ~ **process** *n* NUCLEAR processus Umklapp *m*

UNA: ~ **segment** *n* TELECOM segment UNA *m*

unable: ~ **to comply** *adj* TELECOM pas en mesure de se conformer

unacceptable: ~ **quality** *n* TELECOM qualité intolérable *f*

unacknowledged: ~ **information transfer service** *n (UITS)* TELECOM service de transfert d'informations sans accusé de réception *m*

unalloyed: ~ **steel** *n* SPRINGS acier non allié *m*

unaltered *adj* GEOL frais, non altéré

unamplified *adj* TELECOM *circuit* non amplifié

unannealed *adj* PROP MAT *glass* non-recuit

unanswered: ~ **call** *n* TELECOM appel resté sans réponse *m*, appel sans réponse *m*

unary[1] *adj* COMP, DP unaire

unary:[2] ~ **operation** *n* COMP, DP opération unaire *f*

unattended[1] *adj* SPACE télésurveillé

unattended:[2] ~ **exchange** *n* TELECOM centrale non surveillée *f*; ~ **operation** *n* COMP, DP exploitation sans surveillance *f*, fonctionnement automatique *m*, fonctionnement sans surveillance *m*

unauthorized: ~ **operation** *n* PROD ENG intervention non autorisée *f*

unavailability: ~ **time** *n* NUCLEAR temps d'indisponibilité *m*

unavailable[1] *adj* QUALITY indisponible

unavailable:[2] ~ **second** *n (UAS)* TELECOM seconde d'indisponibilité *f*; ~ **time** *n (UAT)* TELECOM temps d'indisponibilité *m*

UNB: ~ **segment** *n* TELECOM segment UNB *m*

unbaked *adj* THERMOD *brick* cru, non cuit

unbalance *n* MECH balourd *m*, défaut d'équilibrage *m*, déséquilibre *m*, MECH ENG balourd *m*, déséquilibre *m*

unbalanced[1] *adj* ELEC déséquilibré, SPACE *communications* dissymétrique

unbalanced:[2] ~ **channel** *n* RECORDING voie mal modulée *f*; ~ **filter** *n* RECORDING filtre dissymétrique *m*; ~ **input** *n* ELEC ENG entrée asymétrique *f*; ~ **line** *n* ELEC ENG ligne non équilibrée *f*; ~ **operation normal response mode class** *n (UNC)* TELECOM classe d'exploitation asymétrique en mode réponse normal *f*; ~ **output** *n* ELEC ENG sortie asymétrique *f*, SPACE *communications* sortie dissymétrique *f*; ~ **rudder** *n* NAUT gouvernail non compensé *m*; ~ **system** *n* TELECOM système non équilibré *m*; ~ **three-phase system** *n* ELEC *AC system* système triphasé déséquilibré *m*

unbiased[1] *adj* COMP, DP non polarisé

unbiased:[2] ~ **polarized relay** *n* ELEC relais à direction *m*

unblanking *n* ELECTRON déblocage du faisceau *m*; ~ **circuit** *n* TV circuit d'annulation de la suppression *m*; ~ **pulses** *n pl* TV impulsions d'annulation *f pl*

unbleached: ~ **mechanical pulp board** *n* PAPER TECH carton de pâte mécanique brune *m*; ~ **pulp** *n* PAPER TECH pâte écrue *f*

unbolt *vt* NUCLEAR déboulonner

unbolting *n* MECH ENG déboulonnage *m*, déboulonnement *m*

unbonded: ~ **skin** *n* SPACE *spacecraft* peau décollée *f*

unbound: ~ **mode** *n* OPT, TELECOM mode non lié *m*

unbroken: ~ **ore** *n* MINING minerai en place *m*, minerai non abattu *m*

unburned *adj* NUCLEAR *uranium* non épuisé

unburnt: ~ brick n THERMOD adobe m, brique séchée au soleil f

UNC abbr MECH ENG (unified coarse thread) systems of threads filetage unifié gros m, TELECOM (unbalanced operation normal response mode class) classe d'exploitation asymétrique en mode réponse normal f

uncanned: ~ fuel element n NUCLEAR élément combustible nu m

uncapping n MECH ENG découronnement m

uncased: ~ hole n PETR sondage non-tubé m

uncemented: ~ lens n CINEMAT objectif à lentilles non collées m

uncertainty n COMP, DP incertitude f; ~ of measurement n METR incertitude de mesure f; ~ principle n PHYS principe d'incertitude m

uncharged adj ELEC non chargé, RAD PHYS neutre

unclamp vt MECH ENG débrider

unclocked: ~ flip-flop n ELECTRON bascule asynchrone f

unclutch vt AUTO, MECH ENG débrayer

uncoated: ~ fuel particle n NUCLEAR particule non enrobée f

uncoded adj TELECOM en clair

uncollided: ~ neutron n NUCLEAR neutron vierge m

uncombined adj CHEM non-combiné

uncommitted: ~ transistor n ELECTRON transistor non connecté m

unconditional[1] adj COMP, DP inconditionnel

unconditional:[2] ~ branch n COMP, DP branchement inconditionnel m; ~ end rung n PROD ENG ligne de fin inconditionnelle f; ~ jump n COMP, DP saut inconditionnel m

unconditionally adv PROD ENG en permanence

unconfined: ~ ground water n COAL TECH nappe libre f; ~ water n WATER SUPP eau libre f

unconformity n PETR TECH geology discordance f; ~ trap n PETR TECH formation of hydrocarbons piège par discordance m

uncontrolled: ~ dump site n RECYCLING décharge sauvage f

uncorking: ~ machine n PACKAGING débouchonneuse f

uncorrected: ~ lens n CINEMAT objectif non corrigé m; ~ result n METR résultat brut m; ~ stress n SPRINGS contrainte non corrigée f

uncouple vt RAIL cars, coaches, wagons découpler, décrocher, dételer

uncoupling n NUCLEAR of control rod découplage m, RAIL dételage m, SPACE découplage m; ~ rods n MINING boring désassemblage des rallonges m

uncured[1] adj P&R plastics, rubber non-durci, non-polymérisé, non-vulcanisé

uncured:[2] ~ mat n C&G feutre non polymérisé m

uncut: ~ length n TELECOM longueur non coupée f; ~ pile n TEXTILES poil non coupé m

undecane n CHEM undécane m

undecanoic adj CHEM undécanoïque

undecomposed adj CHEM indécomposé

undecorated: ~ dislocation n METALL dislocation non décorée f

undecylinic adj CHEM undécylénique

undefined: ~ error n COMP, DP erreur non définie f; ~ key n COMP, DP touche non attribuée f, touche non définie f; ~ statement n COMP, DP instruction indéfinie f

underbead: ~ crack n NUCLEAR fissure sous cordon f

underbody n VEHICLES dessous de carrosserie m; ~ protection n VEHICLES produit d'étanchéité de dessous de carrosserie m

underbridge n CONST pont à tablier inférieur m

underbunching n ELECTRON fonctionnement en soustension n

undercarriage n AERONAUT, SPACE spacecraft train d'atterrissage m, TRANSP lorries, trucks béquilles à roues f pl

undercoat n CHEM sous-couche f, COATINGS vernissage de fond m, COLOURS apprêt m, sous-couche f, CONST painting sous-couche f, VEHICLES body produit d'étanchéité de dessous de carrosserie m

undercoating n COATINGS couche de base f

under-color: ~ removal n (AmE), under-colour removal n (BrE) PRINT retrait des sous-couleurs m

undercompacted[1] adj PETR sous-compacté

undercompacted:[2] ~ zone n GEOL, PETR zone sous-compactée f

undercompaction n PETR sous-compaction f

under-crank vt CINEMAT tourner à une vitesse inférieure à la normale

undercurrent n FUELLESS courant sous-marin m, NAUT sea state contre-courant sous-marin m, ressac m, OCEANOG sous-courant m, PROD ENG sous-intensité f, WATER SUPP sluices courant dérivé m; ~ relay n ELEC relais de courant m, relais à minimum m

undercut n C&G creux m, MECH ENG incomplete thread filet décolleté m, PRINT creux du cylindre m

undercutting: ~ saw n MECH ENG scie d'entre-lames f

underdevelop vt PHOTO sous-développer

underdeveloped adj CINEMAT sous-développé, PRINT insuffisamment développé

underdriven adj MECH ENG à commande par le bas

underexpose vt CINEMAT, PHOTO sous-exposer

underexposed[1] adj PRINT sous-exposé

underexposed:[2] ~ picture n PHOTO cliché sous-exposé m

underexposure n PHOTO sous-exposition f

underfishing n OCEANOG sous-exploitation f

underfloor: ~ condenser n NUCLEAR below turbine condenseur en sous-sol m; ~ engine n AUTO moteur plat m; ~ heating n ELEC plancher chauffant m, HEAT ENG chauffage par le sol m, THERMOD chauffage par plancher chauffant m; ~ ventilation n REFRIG ventilation sous plancher f

underflow n COAL TECH sous-verse f, COMP, DP dépassement de capacité inférieur m, dépassement négatif m, dépassement négatif de capacité m, OCEANOG courant de fond m, courant profond m, WATER SUPP sluices courant dérivé m

underframe n MECH ENG châssis m, infrastructure f, NUCLEAR of reactor coolant pump châssis m, support m, RAIL vehicles châssis m

undergage: ~ hole n (AmE), undergauge hole n (BrE) PETR trou sous-calibré m

underglaze: ~ painting n COLOURS peinture sous émail f

undergoing: ~ repairs phr CONST en réparation

undergrade: ~ bridge n CONST pont à tablier supérieur m

underground[1] adj GAS TECH sous-sol, MINING au fond

underground[2] n (BrE) RAIL (cf subway) métro m; ~ bus n TRANSP autobus souterrain m; ~ cable n ELEC supply network câble souterrain m, ligne souterraine f, ELEC ENG câble souterrain m; ~ cable railway n TRANSP funiculaire souterrain m; ~ cabling n CONST réseau de câbles souterrains m; ~ chamber n TELECOM chambre souterraine f; ~ drainage n WATER SUPP drainage profond m; ~ exploration n GAS TECH exploration du sous-sol f; ~ flow n HYDROL écoulement souterrain m, stream courant d'eau souterrain m; ~ gasification n

THERMOD gazéification souterraine *f*; ~ **line** *n* ELEC ENG, TELECOM ligne souterraine *f*; ~ **mine** *n* MINING mine souterraine *f*; ~ **nappe** *n* HYDROL nappe souterraine *f*; ~ **operation** *n* MINING exploitation souterraine *f*; ~ **river** *n* HYDROL rivière souterraine *f*; ~ **storage** *n* GAS TECH stockage souterrain *m*, THERMOD stockage en cavité souterraine *m*, stockage souterrain *m*, WATER SUPP stockage souterrain *m*; ~ **storage system** *n* GAS TECH réservoir souterrain *m*; ~ **tramway** *n* TRANSP semi-métro *m*; ~ **trolleybus** *n* TRANSP trolleybus souterrain *m*; ~ **waste disposal** *n* WATER SUPP rejet souterrain *m*; ~ **water** *n* HYDROL, POLLUTION eau souterraine *f*; ~ **working** *n* MINING exploitation au fond *f*, exploitation souterraine *f*

undergrounded: ~ **system** *n* PROD ENG système flottant *m*

underhung: ~ **rudder** *n* NAUT gouvernail suspendu *m*

underlap *n* TV rétrécissement de la ligne *m*

underline *vt* PRINT souligner

underliner *n* PAPER TECH demi-intérieur *m*

underload *n* NUCLEAR charge incomplète *f*, sous-charge *f*; ~ **relay** *n* ELEC relais à minimum *m*

underlying[1] *adj* GEOL sous-jacent

underlying:[2] ~ **rock** *n* GEOL soubassement *m*, substratum *m*

undermanned *adj* PROD ENG, TRANSP à court de personnel

undermine *vt* MINING miner, saper

undermining *n* CONST affouillement *m*, sapement *m*

undermoderated: ~ **blanket** *n* NUCLEAR *of breeder* couche fertile sous-modérée *f*

undermodulation *n* ELECTRON modulation insuffisante *f*, sous-modulation *f*, RECORDING sous-modulation *f*

underpass *n* CONST passage inférieur *m*, RAIL passage inférieur *m*, passage souterrain *m*

underpinning *n* CONST bétonnage *m*, reprise en sous-oeuvre *f*

underpressure *n* MECH ENG sous-pression *f*

underrange *n* PROD ENG dépassement inférieur *m*

underreaming *n* MINING élargissement *m*

underrun: ~ **bar** *n* VEHICLES *body* dispositif antiencastrement *m*; ~ **bumper** *n* VEHICLES dispositif antiencastrement *m*; ~ **guard** *n* VEHICLES dispositif antiencastrement *m*

undersaturated *adj* GEOL non-saturé, sous-saturé

undersaturation *n* METALL sous-saturation *f*

undersea[1] *adj* NAUT sous-marin

undersea:[2] ~ **habitat** *n* OCEANOG habitat sous-marin *m*, maison sous la mer *f*; ~ **pipeline** *n* TRANSP conduite sous-marine *f*

underseal *n* (BrE) *(cf undercoat)* VEHICLES *body* produit d'étanchéité de dessous de carrosserie *m*

undersensitized *adv* PRINT insuffisamment sensibilisé

underset *n* OCEANOG ressac *m*

undershoot[1] *n* AERONAUT atterrissage trop court *m*, ELECTRON dépassement négatif *m*

undershoot[2] *vi* ELECTRON présenter un dépassement négatif, présenter une sous-modulation

undersize *n* COAL TECH déclassé inférieur *m*, passant *m*, passé *m*

undersoil *n* MINING sous-sol *m*

understeer *n* VEHICLES *steering* sous-virage *m*

underswing *n* TV sous-oscillation *f*

underthrust *n* GEOL sous-charriage *m*

undertitration *n* CHEM sous-titrage *m*, titrage par défaut *m*

undertow *n* NAUT *sea* contre-courant de fond *m*, OCEANOG ressac *m*

undervoltage *n* PROD ENG sous-tension *f*

underwashing *n* OCEANOG affouillement *m*

underwater: ~ **acoustics** *n* OCEANOG acoustique sous-marine *f*; ~ **camera** *n* PHOTO appareil sous-marin *m*; ~ **cutting blowpipe** *n* CONST chalumeau coupeur sous l'eau *m*; ~ **fishing** *n* OCEANOG chasse sous-marine *f*; ~ **habitat** *n* OCEANOG habitat sous-marin *m*; ~ **housing** *n* CINEMAT caisson étanche *m*, PHOTO boîtier étanche *m*; ~ **hull** *n* NAUT *ship design* oeuvres vives *f pl*; ~ **photography** *n* PHOTO photographie sous-marine *f*; ~ **propagation** *n* TELECOM propagation sous-marine *f*; ~ **reactor** *n* NUCLEAR réacteur sous eau *m*; ~ **shot** *n* CINEMAT plan tourné sous l'eau *m*; ~ **vehicle** *n* OCEANOG, PETR véhicule sous-marin *m*; ~ **welding** *n* PETR, THERMOD soudage sous l'eau *m*

underwriter *n* NAUT *marine insurance* assureur maritime *m*

underwriting *n* NAUT *marine insurance* assurance maritime *f*

undetected: ~ **failure time** *n* NUCLEAR temps de défaillance non détectée *m*

undiluted *adj* CHEM non dilué

undipped *adj* TEXTILES *fabric* non adhérisé

undissociated *adj* METALL *dislocation* non dissocié

undistorted *adj* ELECTRON non déformé

undisturbed: ~ **sample** *n* COAL TECH échantillon intact *m*

undoped *adj* PROP MAT *semiconductors* non dopé

unducted: ~ **fan** *n* AERONAUT *engine* soufflante non-carénée *f*

undulating *adj* TELECOM *surface* ondulé

undyed *adj* TEXTILES écru

unenriched *adj* NUCLEAR *uranium* non enrichi

uneven: ~ **running** *n* RAIL *vehicles* instabilité de marche *f*; ~ **temper** *n* C&G trempe irrégulière *f*

unexpected: ~ **braking** *n* RAIL *vehicles* freinage intempestif *m*

unexploded: ~ **bomb** *n* MILIT bombe non-explosée *f*

unexposed: ~ **film** *n* CINEMAT pellicule vierge *f*, PHOTO film vierge *m*

UNF *abbr (unified fine thread)* MECH ENG *system of threads* filetage unifié fin *m*

unfavored: ~ **transition** *n* (AmE), **unfavoured transition** *n* (BrE) NUCLEAR transition non favorisée *f*

unfenced *adj* CONST non-clos

unfill *n* ACOUSTICS manque d'impression *m*

unfinished *adj* COATINGS *paper*, PAPER TECH *paper* sans apprêt

unfired[1] *adj* THERMOD *ceramics* non cuit, vert

unfired:[2] ~ **pot** *n* C&G pot cru *m*; ~ **tube** *n* ELECTRON tube non amorcé *m*

unfissioned *adj* NUCLEAR *fuel* non-fissionné

unfit: ~ **for human consumption** *phr* FOOD TECH impropre à la consommation humaine, non comestible

unflavored *adj* (AmE), **unflavoured** *adj* (BrE) FOOD TECH nature

unfolding *n* NUCLEAR *of spectrum* déconvolution *f*

unfordable *adj* HYDROL inguéable

unforeseen: ~ **interruption** *n* TELECOM interruption imprévisible *f*

unfurlable *adj* SPACE *of antenna* déroulable, TELECOM *of antenna* déployable

ungated: ~ **spillway** *n* HYDROL *dams* déversoir libre *m*

unglazed *adj* CHEM poreux

ungraduated *adj* CHEM *of beaker* non gradué, sans graduations

UNH: ~ **segment** *n* TELECOM segment UNH *m*

unhook *vt* TELECOM décrocher

unhooking *n* MECH ENG décrochage *m*, décrochement *m*

UNI *abbr (user-network interface)* TELECOM interface usager-réseau *f*

uniaxial *adj* CRYSTALL uniaxe

uniconductor: ~ **waveguide** *n* ELEC ENG guide d'ondes à un conducteur *m*

unidentified: ~ **flying object** *n (UFO)* ASTRON, SPACE objet volant non identifié *m (OVNI)*

unidirectional[1] *adj* ACOUSTICS *microphone*, ELEC *current*, ELEC ENG, RECORDING *microphone* unidirectionnel, TELECOM unidirectionnel, unilatéral

unidirectional:[2] ~ **transducer** *n* ELEC ENG transducteur non réversible *m*

unified[1] *adj* COMP *architecture*, DP *architecture*, SPACE *propulsion* unifié

unified:[2] ~ **bolt** *n* MECH ENG boulon à filetage *m*; ~ **coarse thread** *n (UNC)* MECH ENG filetage unifié gros *m*; ~ **fine thread** *n (UNF)* MECH ENG filetage unifié fin *m*; ~ **screw thread** *n* MECH ENG filetage unifié *m*

unifilar: ~ **suspension** *n* ELEC suspension unifilaire *f*

unifining *n* CHEM procédé de désulfuration catalytique *m*

uniflex: ~ **tray** *n* CHEM plateau de barbotage *m*

uniflow: ~ **compressor** *n* REFRIG compresseur à équicourant *m*

uniform[1] *adj* CHEM homogène, régulier

uniform:[2] ~ **acceleration** *n* PAPER TECH accélération uniforme *f*; ~ **corrosion** *n* METALL corrosion uniforme *f*; ~ **field** *n* PHYS champ uniforme *m*; ~ **flow** *n* HYDROL écoulement uniforme *m*; ~ **layer winding** *n* ELEC enroulement fil à fil *m*; ~ **line** *n* ELEC ENG ligne uniforme *f*; ~ **motion** *n* PHYS mouvement uniforme *m*

uniform-index: ~ **fiber** (AmE), ~ **fibre** (BrE) OPT fibre à gradient linéaire *f*; ~ **profile fiber** (AmE), ~ **profile fibre** (BrE) OPT fibre à gradient linéaire *f*

uniformity: ~ **coefficient** *n* COAL TECH coefficient d'uniformité *m*

unijunction: ~ **transistor** *n* ELECTRON transistor unijonction *m*

unilateral: ~ **track** *n* ACOUSTICS trace unilatérale *f*

uninflammability *n* PROP MAT ininflammabilité *f*

uninflammable[1] *adj* PROP MAT ininflammable

uninflammable:[2] ~ **coal** *n* COAL TECH charbon maigre *m*

uninstrumented: ~ **fuel assembly** *n* NUCLEAR assemblage combustible non-instrumenté *m*

unintended: ~ **actuation** *n* PROD ENG actionnement intempestif *m*

uninterrupted: ~ **duty** *n* ELEC *equipment* service ininterrompu *m*; ~ **flow** *n* TRANSP écoulement continu *m*

union *n* CONST raccord *m*, *pipe coupling* raccordement *m*, union *f*, DP union *f*, PRINT *rotatives* joint *m*, syndicat *m*; ~ **cloth** *n* TEXTILES tissu métis *m*; ~ **cock** *n* CONST *with or without tail pipe* raccord *m*; ~ **elbow** *n* CONST coude de raccord *m*, raccord coudé *m*; ~ **screw** *n* MECH ENG tendeur à vis *m*, vis de tension *f*; ~ **T** *n* CONST raccord à T *m*

uniphase *adj* ELEC *conductor* uniphasé, ELEC ENG monophasé

unipod *n* CINEMAT monopied *m*

unipolar[1] *adj* COMP, DP unipolaire, ELEC *dynamo*, *generator*, ELEC ENG, ELECTRON *transistor*, NUCLEAR *arc* unipolaire

unipolar:[2] ~ **integrated circuit** *n* ELECTRON circuit intégré unipolaire *m*

unipole: ~ **antenna** *n* TELECOM antenne unipolaire *f*

unipotential[1] *adj* ELEC ENG *cathode* équipotentiel

unipotential:[2] ~ **lens** *n* NUCLEAR lentille unipotentielle *f*

unique: ~ **I/O location addressing** *n* PROD ENG adressage unique de l'emplacement des E/S *m*; ~ **word** *n (UW)* SPACE *communications* mot particulier *m*; ~ **word detection** *n* SPACE *communications* détection de mot unique *f*

uniselector *n* ELEC ENG commutateur rotatif *m*, sélecteur rotatif *m*

unison *n* ACOUSTICS unisson *m*

unit *n* CHEM *of compound* motif *m*, unité *f*, CINEMAT équipe *f*, COMP organe *m*, unité *f*, élément *m*, DP unité *f*, élément *m*, ELEC, GEOL *informal subdivision* unité *f*, NUCLEAR *turbine, boiler of nuclear power plant* bloc *m*, tranche *f*, unité *f*, PHYS unité *f*, PRINT groupe imprimant *m*, TELECOM unité *f*, VEHICLES groupe *m*; ~ **of absorbed dose** *n* RAD PHYS unité de dose absorbée *f*; ~ **of area** *n* METR unité d'aire *f*, unité de surface *f*; ~ **automatic exchange** *n (UAX)* TELECOM central automatique de localité *m*; ~ **auxilliary transformer** *n* NUCLEAR transformateur auxiliaire du bloc *m*; ~ **capacity** *n* NUCLEAR puissance unitaire *f*; ~ **cell** *n* CRYSTALL, NUCLEAR *of reactor* cellule élémentaire *f*; ~ **cell parameters** *n pl* CRYSTALL paramètres de maille *m pl*; ~ **conductance** *n* THERMOD thermoconductivité unitaire *f*; ~ **construction body** *n* VEHICLES caisse autoporteuse *f*, caisse à châssis intégré *f*, carrosserie autoporteuse *f*; ~ **of energy** *n* THERMOD unité d'énergie *f*; ~ **of entropy** *n* THERMOD unité d'entropie *f*; ~ **of exposure** *n* RAD PHYS unité de l'exposition *f*; ~ **of fishing effort** *n* OCEANOG unité d'effort de pêche *f*; ~ **of force** *n* MECH ENG unité de force *f*; ~ **heater** *n* THERMOD *stand-alone heater* aérotherme *m*; ~ **housing** *n* REFRIG chaise grillage *f*; ~ **impulse function** *n* CONTROL fonction d'impulsion mathématique *f*, fonction unitaire *f*; ~ **interval** *n (UI)* TELECOM intervalle unitaire *m*; ~ **of length** *n* METR unité de longueur *f*; ~ **load vertical conveyor** *n* PROD ENG monte-charge en continu *m*; ~ **magnetic pole** *n* PETR pôle magnétique *m*; ~ **of measurement** *n* METR, PETR TECH unité de mesure *f*; ~ **output** *n* NUCLEAR *of nuclear power unit* puissance unitaire *f*; ~ **pack** *n* PACKAGING conditionnement par unité *m*; ~ **separative power** *n* NUCLEAR *one stage* travail de séparation unitaire *m*; ~ **string** *n* COMP, DP chaîne unitaire *f*; ~ **supervisor** *n* PROD ENG responsable d'atelier *m*; ~ **thrust** *n* SPACE *spacecraft* poussée unitaire *f*; ~ **time** *n* PROD ENG temps unitaire *m*; ~ **vector** *n* PHYS vecteur unitaire *m*; ~ **weight** *n* COAL TECH poids spécifique *m*

unit-dose: ~ **container** *n* PACKAGING récipient-dose *m*; ~ **packet** *n* (AmE) *(cf unit-dose sachet)* PACKAGING sachet à dosage simple *m*; ~ **sachet** *n* (BrE) *(cf unit-dose packet)* PACKAGING sachet à dosage simple *m*

unite *vi* CHEM s'unir, se combiner, PROP MAT s'unir

united: ~ **injector** *n* AUTO injecteur pompe *m*

unitization *n* PETR TECH *commerce, licence blocks* pooling *m*

unitized: ~ **body** *n* VEHICLES caisse autoporteuse *f*

unit-type: ~ **cable** *n* OPT câble en faisceaux *m*

unity *n* PATENTS *of European patent* unicité *f*; ~ **gain** *n* ELECTRON gain d'unité *m*; ~ **gain amplifier** *n* ELECTRON amplificateur à gain unité *m*; ~ **of invention** *n* PATENTS unité d'invention *f*

univalence *n* CHEM monovalence *f*

univalent *adj* CHEM monovalent, univalent

universal: ~ **bridge** *n* ELEC *measurement* pont universel *m*; ~ **centering apparatus** *n* (AmE), ~ **centring apparatus** *n* (BrE) INSTRUMENT focomètre universel *m*; ~ **character set** *n* DP jeu universel des caractères *m*; ~ **condenser** *n* INSTRUMENT condenseur universel *m*; ~ **developing tank** *n* PHOTO cuve universelle *f*; ~ **grinder** *n* C&G machine universelle à tailler *f*; ~ **grinding** *n* PROD ENG rectification universelle *f*; ~ **inverter controller** *n* CONTROL contrôleur inverseur universel *m*; ~ **jack** *n* AUTO *car maintenance* vérin universel *m*; ~ **joint** *n* AUTO *car* cardan de roue *m*, MECH joint à croisillon *m*, joint à rotule *m*, MECH ENG charnière universelle *f*, genou de Cardan *m*, joint brisé *m*, joint de Cardan *m*, joint hollandais *m*, joint universel *m*, VEHICLES *transmission* joint universel *m*; ~ **leader** *n* CINEMAT amorce passe-partout *f*; ~ **level protractor** *n* METR rapporteur universel *m*; ~ **manipulator** *n* NUCLEAR télémanipulateur universel *m*; ~ **milling machine** *n* MECH ENG fraiseuse universelle *f*, machine à fraiser universelle *f*; ~ **motion** *n* FLUID PHYS mouvement universel *m*; ~ **motor** *n* ELEC, ELEC ENG moteur universel *m*; ~ **number** *n* TELECOM numéro universel *m*; ~ **ripper-loader** *n* MINING abatteuse-chargeuse universelle *f*; ~ **set** *n* COMP référentiel *m*, DP jeu universel *m*, référentiel *m*, MATH *set theory* univers *m*; ~ **shears** *n pl* MECH ENG *tool* cisailles universelles *f*; ~ **shunt** *n* ELEC *resistance* shunt universel *m*; ~ **stage** *n* CRYSTALL platine universelle *f*, INSTRUMENT platine rotative universelle *f*; ~ **switch** *n* TELECOM commutateur universel *m*; ~ **time coordinated** *n* (*UTC*) TELECOM heure TU *f*, heure universelle *f*, temps universel coordonné *m*; ~ **tool-and-cutter sharpener** *n* MECH ENG machine à affûter universelle *f*; ~ **viewfinder** *n* PHOTO viseur multiformat *m*; ~ **wide-field microscope** *n* INSTRUMENT microscope universel à grand champ *m*

Universal: ~ **Time** *n* (*UT*) ASTRON *sidereal*, SPACE *measures* temps universel *m* (*TU*)

universe *n* ASTRON univers *m*

unkeying *n* MECH ENG décalage *m*, décoincement *m*

unknown: ~ **message** *n* TELECOM message inconnu *m*

unladen *adj* MAR POLL lège, sans cargaison

unlatch: ~ **instruction** *n* PROD ENG instruction de déverrouillage *f*; ~ **rung** *n* PROD ENG ligne de sortie déverrouillée *f*

unlatching *n* NUCLEAR découplage *m*

unleaded: ~ **gas** *n* (AmE) *(cf unleaded petrol)* PETR TECH, POLLUTION, VEHICLES *fuel* essence sans plomb *f*; ~ **gasoline** *n* (AmE) *(cf unleaded petrol)* PETR TECH, POLLUTION, VEHICLES *fuel* essence sans plomb *f*; ~ **petrol** *n* (BrE) *(cf unleaded gasoline)* PETR TECH, POLLUTION, VEHICLES *fuel* essence sans plomb *f*

unleavened: ~ **bread** *n* FOOD TECH pain azyme *m*

unlike: ~ **poles** *n pl* ELEC *magnetism*, PHYS pôles de nom contraire *m pl*

unlined *adj* CHEM sans garnissage

unload:[1] ~ **file** *n* PROD ENG fichier des travaux réalisés *m*

unload[2] *vt* COMP, DP, MAR POLL, MILIT *firearm* décharger, NAUT *cargo* débarder, décharger

unloaded[1] *adj* CINEMAT non chargé, SPRINGS sans charge

unloaded:[2] ~ **cable** *n* TELECOM câble non chargé *m*, câble non pupinisé *m*

unloader *n* REFRIG dispositif de délestage *m*

unloading *n* METALL décharge *f*, PHYS déchargement *m*; ~ **the cage** *n* MINING décagement *m*, déchargement de

la cage *m*; ~ **rod** *n* NUCLEAR tige de démontage *f*; ~ **valve** *n* MECH ENG soupape de décharge *f*

unlock *vt* CINEMAT déverrouiller, MILIT *artillery* déculasser

unlocking *n* COMP, DP déverrouillage *m*

unmake *vt* MECH ENG *joint* défaire, démonter

unmaking *n* MINING *of rod joints* démontage *m*

unmanned[1] *adj* SPACE *spacecraft* automatique, non habité, sans pilote

unmanned:[2] ~ **exchange** *n* TELECOM centrale non surveillée *f*; ~ **lander** *n* SPACE *spacecraft* module d'atterrissage automatique *m*; ~ **landing stage** *n* SPACE module d'atterrissage automatique *m*; ~ **passing point** *n* RAIL point d'évitement sans personnel *m*; ~ **submersible** *n* OCEANOG robot sous-marin *m*; ~ **turnout** *n* RAIL point d'évitement sans personnel *m*

unmarried: ~ **sound** *n* CINEMAT son seul *m*, son séparé *m*

unmask *vt* MILIT *artillery* démasquer

unmesh *vt* OCEANOG démailler

unmoderated: ~ **fission neutron** *n* NUCLEAR neutron de fission non modéré *m*

unmodulated[1] *adj* SPACE *communications* non modulé

unmodulated:[2] ~ **track** *n* RECORDING silence modulé *m*

unmoor *vti* NAUT *ship* démarrer

unmooring *n* NAUT démarrage *m*

unnavigable *adj* HYDROL innavigable

unnumbered: ~ **information** *n* (*UI*) TELECOM information non numérotée *f*

unordered: ~ **tree** *n* COMP, DP arbre non-ordonné *m*

unoriented *adj* GEOL *texture* non orienté

unoxidizable *adj* CHEM inoxydable

unoxidized *adj* CHEM inoxyde

unpack *vt* COMP, DP décomprimer, décondenser, étendre

unpacked *adj* COMP, DP non condensé

unpaired *adj* CHEM *electron* libre, PHYS *electron* célibataire

unperforated *adj* TELECOM *tape* non perforé

unperturbed: ~ **orbit** *n* SPACE orbite non perturbée *f*

unpinning *n* METALL désancrage *m*

unplanned[1] *adj* PROD ENG aléatoire, imprévu, non planifié, *work* non prévu

unplanned:[2] ~ **maintenance** *n* QUALITY maintenance imprévue *f*

unplasticized[1] *adj* P&R non plastifié

unplasticized:[2] ~ **polyvinyl chloride** *n* P&R chlorure de polyvinyle non plastifié *m*, polyvinylchlorure non plastifié *m*

unplug *vt* ELEC *connection*, TELECOM, TV débrancher

unpolled: ~ **mode** *n* PROD ENG mode non interrogé *m*

unpressurized: ~ **line** *n* NUCLEAR *pipe* conduite sans pression *f*

unproved: ~ **area** *n* CONST zone non-reconnue *f*

unramming *n* MINING débourrage *m*

unravel *vt* OCEANOG démailler

unrectified: ~ **AC** *n* ELEC *supply network* courant alternatif brut *m*

unrefined *adj* FOOD TECH non-raffiné

unregistered: ~ **mark** *n* PATENTS marque non déposée *f*

unregulated: ~ **bus system** *n* SPACE *spacecraft* système à barre non régulée *m*; ~ **input** *n* PROD ENG alimentation non stabilisée *f*; ~ **voltage** *n* ELEC ENG tension non régulée *f*

unrestricted: ~ **bearer service** *n* TELECOM *ISDN* service support sans restriction *m*; ~ **digital data ratio** *n* TELECOM rapport de données numériques sans restriction *m*; ~ **information transfer service** *n* TELECOM *ISDN* service de transfert sans restriction *m*; ~ **service** *n* TELECOM *ISDN* service sans restriction *m*

unrevealed: ~ **failure** *n* QUALITY défaillance non révélée *f*

unrig *vt* NAUT *mast, crane* dégréer

unrigging *n* NAUT *mast, crane* dégréement *m*

unsafe: ~ **act** *n* SAFETY acte dangereux pour la sécurité *m*, conduite dangereuse *f*; ~ **conditions** *n* pl SAFETY régime dangereux *m*; ~ **environmental conditions** *n* pl SAFETY conditions ambiantes dangereuses *f pl*

unsaturable *adj* CHEM insaturable

unsaturate *n* CHEM insaturé *m*

unsaturated[1] *adj* CHEM insaturé, non saturé, FOOD TECH *fat*, P&R *polyester*, PETR TECH *hydrocarbon* non-saturé

unsaturated:[2] ~ **carbon-to-carbon bond** *n* PETR TECH liaison non saturée entre carbones *f*; ~ **completely stable layer** *n* METEO couche absolument stable non saturée *f*; ~ **zone water** *n* HYDROL eau vadose *f*

unscheduled: ~ **withdrawal** *n* NUCLEAR *of control rod* extraction non planifiée *f*

unscramble *vt* TV débrouiller, décoder, décrypter

unscrambler *n* TV décodeur *m*, désembrouilleur *m*

unscreened: ~ **coal** *n* COAL TECH charbon tout-venant *m*

unscrew *vt* NUCLEAR dévisser

unscrewing *n* MECH ENG dévissage *m*; ~ **bush** *n* MECH ENG écrou de réglage *m*; ~ **core** *n* MECH ENG *injection mould* noyau de vis à crémaillère *m*; ~ **parts mold** *n* (AmE), ~ **parts mould** *n* (BrE) MECH ENG moule à pièces dévissables *m*; ~ **pipe** *n* PETR TECH *drilling* dévissage *m*

unseaworthy *adj* NAUT *ship* en mauvais état de navigabilité

unsettled *adj* METEO variable

unsewn *adj* PRINT *binding* sans couture

unshielded: ~ **source** *n* NUCLEAR source non blindée *f*

unship *vt* NAUT *cargo* débarquer

unshrinkable *adj* PAPER TECH irrétrécissable

unsized *adj* PAPER TECH non collé, sans colle

unslaked *adj* CHEM *lime* anhydre, non éteint

unsoldering *n* MECH ENG dessoudure *f*

unsplit: ~ **bush** *n* MECH ENG coussinet non fendu *m*

unsplittable *adj* RAIL *of train* indéformable

unspoilt: ~ **land** *n* POLLUTION sol naturel *m*, sol sans perturbation artificielle *m*, zone intacte *f*

unspool *vt* PHOTO dérouler

unsprung: ~ **weight** *n* VEHICLES *wheels, tyres, brakes* élément non suspendu *m*

unsqueeze *vt* CINEMAT désanamorphoser

unstable[1] *adj* ELEC, PHYS instable

unstable:[2] ~ **air** *n* METEO air instable *m*; ~ **equilibrium** *n* PHYS équilibre instable *m*; ~ **flow** *n* FLUID PHYS écoulement instable *m*, écoulement instationnaire *m*, TRANSP *traffic* écoulement instable *m*; ~ **fracture** *n* METALL rupture instable *f*; ~ **nucleus** *n* PART PHYS noyau instable *m*; ~ **state** *n* CONTROL état instable *m*

unsteady: ~ **flow** *n* NUCLEAR écoulement irrégulier *m*

unstep *vt* NAUT *mast* démâter

unstick: ~ **speed** *n* AERONAUT vitesse au lever des roues *f*, vitesse de décollage *f*

unstop *vt* CONST *pipe* déboucher

unstuff *vt* TRANSP *container* dépoter

unstuffing *n* TRANSP *container* dépotage *m*

unsulfonated: ~ **matter** *n* (AmE), **unsulphonated matter** *n* (BrE) DETERGENTS insulfoné *m*

unsupercharged: ~ **engine** *n* AUTO moteur atmosphérique *m*

unsupported: ~ **beam** *n* CONST *strength of materials*

poutre en porte-à-faux *f*; ~ **shrink wrapping** *n* PACKAGING emballage sous film thermorétractable sans support *m*

unsymmetrical: ~ **arrangement** *n* ELEC ENG montage non symétrique *m*

untapped *adj* ELEC *coil* sans prises

unthread *vt* CINEMAT décharger

untreated[1] *adj* HYDROL *water* brut

untreated:[2] ~ **sewage** *n* HYDROL boue fraîche *f*, effluent brut *m*; ~ **small** *n* COAL TECH menu brut *m*, menu de houille brut *m*

untrimmed: ~ **machine width** *n* PAPER TECH largeur non rognée de la machine *f*; ~ **size** *n* PAPER TECH format brut *m*

untrussed: ~ **roof** *n* CONST comble sans ferme *m*

untwisting *n* MECH ENG détorsion *f*

unvulcanized *adj* THERMOD non vulcanisé

unwanted: ~ **emission** *n* TELECOM émission brouilleuse *f*

unwashed[1] *adj* COAL TECH brut, *coal* cru

unwashed:[2] ~ **small** *n* COAL TECH menu brut *m*

unweighted *adj* RECORDING *noise level* non-pondéré

unwind *vt* CINEMAT débobiner, dérouler, PHOTO dérouler

unwinder *n* TEXTILES dérouleur *m*

unwinding *n* MECH ENG déroulement *m*, RAIL *cable* décommettage *m*; ~ **machine** *n* PACKAGING dérouleuse *f*

U0$_2$: ~ **fuel** *n* NUCLEAR combustible d'U0$_2$ *m*, combustible de bioxyde *m*; ~ **pellet** *n* NUCLEAR pastille d'U0$_2$ *f*, pastille de bioxyde d'uranium *f*

U0$_2$-Gd$_2$-0$_3$: ~ **pellet** *n* (*urania-gadolinia pellet*) NUCLEAR pastille de bioxyde d'uranium-oxyde de gadolinium *f*

up: ~ **and lower transistor switch** *n* PROD ENG transistor haut et bas *m*; ~ **count** *n* PROD ENG comptage *m*; ~ **counter** *n* ELECTRON compteur additif *m*, compteur progressif *m*, PROD ENG compteur *m*; ~ **counter rung** *n* PROD ENG ligne de compteur incrémentiel *f*; ~ **quark** *n* PART PHYS quark haut *m*, PHYS quark up *m*

up-and-down: ~ **motion** *n* MECH ENG mouvement ascendant et descendant *m*

upconverter *n* TELECOM changeur élévateur de fréquence *m*

update[1] *n* COMP actualisation *f*, mise à jour *f*, DP actualisation *f*, mise à jour *f*

update[2] *vt* COMP, DP actualiser, mettre à jour, MECH ENG mettre à jour

updating *n* COMP *of files*, TELECOM mise à jour *f*

updip[1] *adv* GEOL en amont-pendage

updip[2] *n* GEOL, PETR TECH amont-pendage *m*

up-down: ~ **counter** *n* ELECTRON compteur bidirectionnel *m*, compteur-décompteur *m*, PROD ENG compteur-décompteur *m*

updraft *adj* (AmE), **updraught** *adj* (BrE) AUTO *carburettor* vertical

updraw: ~ **process** *n* C&G procédé d'étirage vertical par le haut *m*

upender *n* NUCLEAR dispositif de déversement *m*

uperization *n* FOOD TECH *machinery* upérisation *f*

upfaulted: ~ **block** *n* GEOL compartiment relevé *m*

upflow *n* NUCLEAR courant montant *m*

upgrade *n* COMP extension *f*, CONST rampe *f*, DP extension *f*, mise à niveau *f*

upgradeable *adj* COMP évolutif

upgrading *n* CHEM amélioration *f*, COAL TECH valorisation *f* uphand: ~ welding n MECH soudage en montant m

uphill adj CONST ardu, montant

upholstery n TEXTILES tissu d'ameublement m, VEHICLES seats garnissage m

upkeep n PROD ENG entretien m

uplift n FLUID PHYS ascendance f, remontée f, GEOL structural geology soulèvement m, surrection f, METEO, THERMOD ascendance f

uplink n SPACE communications liaison montante f; ~ block n TELECOM bloc de liaison montante m; ~ frequency n SPACE communications fréquence de la liaison montante f; ~ transmission phase n TELECOM phase de transport f

upper[1] adj GEOL supérieur

upper:[2] ~ annealing temperature n C&G température supérieure de recuit f; ~ bainite n METALL bainite supérieure f; ~ ball joint n MECH ENG rotule de direction supérieure f; ~ case n PRINT majuscule f; ~ containment pool n NUCLEAR piscine supérieure f; ~ control limit n QUALITY limite supérieure de contrôle f; ~ core n NUCLEAR guide structure internes supérieurs m pl; ~ culmination n ASTRON culmination supérieure f; ~ deck n NAUT pont supérieur m; ~ end fitting n NUCLEAR tête f; ~ end plug n NUCLEAR of fuel can bouchon supérieur m; ~ grid n NUCLEAR grille supérieure f; ~ internals n pl NUCLEAR assembly internes supérieurs m pl; ~ ionosphere n TELECOM ionosphère supérieure f; ~ limit n TELECOM limite supérieure f; ~ limit of ozone layer n METEO limite supérieure de l'ozonosphère f; ~ millstone n FOOD TECH milling meule courante f, meule tournante f, molette f; ~ part n HYDROL of river amont m, cours supérieur m, haut m; ~ plenum n NUCLEAR plenum supérieur m; ~ roll n MECH ENG rolling mill cylindre du dessus m, cylindre mâle m; ~ sheet n PRINT feuille de dessus f; ~ shell assembly n NUCLEAR of steam generator above reactor floor virole supérieure f; ~ side n PRINT côté supérieur m; ~ sideband n (USB) ELECTRON, TELECOM bande latérale supérieure f; ~ stage n SPACE étage supérieur m; ~ storage basin n FUELLESS réservoir de stockage supérieur m; ~ subfield n TELECOM sous-champ supérieur m; ~ surface n AERONAUT of wing, PHYS of wing extrados m; ~ tie plate n NUCLEAR of fuel assembly plaque support supérieure f; ~ wind n METEO vent de haute altitude m, vent de haute atmosphère m; ~ works n pl NAUT ship design oeuvres mortes f pl

upright n CONST of ladder montant m, MECH ENG of planing machine jumelle f, post montant m, pied-droit m, MINING montant m, RAIL rancher m; ~ fold n GEOL pli droit m; ~ freezer n REFRIG congélateur vertical m; ~ radiator n AUTO radiateur à débit vertical m; ~ shaft n MECH ENG arbre de transmission verticale m

uprighter n C&G releveur m

uprise n GEOL of magma montée f, venue f

uprush n OCEANOG jet de rive m

upset: ~ welding n THERMOD butt welding soudage en bout par résistance m

upsetting-press n MECH ENG presse à refouler f

upside: ~ down slate n CINEMAT clap à l'envers m, claquette de fin f

upstream[1] adj CONST, FLUID PHYS, FUELLESS, HYDROL, NAUT river, PHYS, TRANSP, TV d'amont

upstream[2] adv FLUID PHYS, FUELLESS, GAS TECH, NAUT river, SPACE en amont

upstream:[3] ~ fairing n REFRIG carénage amont m; ~ head n FUELLESS colonne d'eau en amont f; ~ resistance n PROD ENG résistance au débit en amont f; ~ wake n FLUID PHYS sillage amont m

upstream-downstream: ~ symmetry n FLUID PHYS symétrie amont-aval f

upstroke n AUTO, MECH ENG, VEHICLES engine, piston course ascendante f; ~ press n P&R moulding presse ascendante f

upsurge n HYDROL ressaut hydraulique m

uptake n TEXTILES of dye montée f, WATER SUPP réception f; ~ crown n (AmE) (cf port crown) C&G voûte de brûleur f

upthrust n PHYS poussée f, fluid poussée d'Archimède f

upthrusted: ~ wedge n GEOL structural geology pincée tectonique f, écaille tectonique f

uptime n COMP temps de bon fonctionnement m, DP temps utilisable m

upturned: ~ eye n SPRINGS of leaf spring oeil droit m

U-Pu: ~ cycle n NUCLEAR cycle d'uranium-plutonium m

upward:[1] ~ compatible adj COMP, DP à compatibilité ascendante

upward:[2] ~ compatibility n COMP compatibilité vers le haut f, DP compatibilité ascendante f; ~ current classifier n COAL TECH classeur à courant ascendant m; ~ drilling n C&G érosion remontante f; ~ flow n NUCLEAR courant montant m; ~ heave n NUCLEAR of the ground élévation f

upwarp n GEOL bombement m

upwash n AERONAUT airworthiness déflexion vers le haut f

upwelling n OCEANOG remontée d'eau f

upwind adv NAUT sailing contre le vent

uralite n MINERAL ouralite f

uramido adj CHEM uraminé

uranate n CHEM uranate m

urania-gadolinia: ~ pellet n (UO2-Gd2-O3 pellet) NUCLEAR pastille de bioxyde d'uranium-oxyde de gadolinium f

uranic[1] adj CHEM uranique

uranic:[2] ~ fluoride n NUCLEAR hexafluorure d'uranium m

uranide n CHEM uranide m

uraninite n MINERAL uraninite f

uranium n (U) CHEM uranium m (U); ~ aluminide fuel n NUCLEAR combustible aluminure d'uranium m; ~ black n NUCLEAR noir d'uranium m, petchblende f, pechblende f; ~ compound n NUCLEAR composé d'uranium m; ~ concentrate n NUCLEAR concentré uranifère m; ~ conversion plant n NUCLEAR installation de conversion d'uranium f; ~ dicarbide n NUCLEAR bicarbure d'uranium m; ~ dioxide fuel n NUCLEAR combustible d'U02 m, combustible de bioxyde m; ~ dioxide pellet n NUCLEAR pastille d'U02 f, pastille de bioxyde d'uranium f; ~ free from its daughters n NUCLEAR uranium frais m; ~ fuel element n NUCLEAR élément combustible en uranium m; ~ galena n NUCLEAR U-galène f; ~ heavy water reactor n NUCLEAR réacteur à uranium-eau lourde m; ~ hexafluoride n NUCLEAR hexafluorure d'uranium m; ~ ingot n NUCLEAR lingot d'uranium m; ~ isotope separation plant n NUCLEAR usine de séparation isotopique d'uranium f; ~ milling n NUCLEAR broyage des minéraux d'uranium m; ~ nucleus n NUCLEAR noyau d'uranium m; ~ oxide n CHEM oxyde d'uranium m, urane m; ~ preconcentrate n NUCLEAR préconcentré d'uranium m; ~ reactor n NUCLEAR réacteur pile à uranium m; ~ refining n NUCLEAR affinage d'uranium *m*; ~ **scrap** *n* NUCLEAR rebut d'uranium *m*; ~ **slug** *n* NUCLEAR bloc d'uranium *m*

uranium-bearing[1] *adj* CHEM, RAD PHYS uranifère

uranium-bearing:[2] ~ **mineral** *n* NUCLEAR minéral uranifère *m*

uranium-plutonium: ~ **cycle** *n* NUCLEAR cycle d'uranium-plutonium *m*

uranous *adj* CHEM uraneux

uranyl *n* CHEM uranyle *m*

urazole *n* CHEM urazol *m*

urban: ~ **and regional metropolitan railroad** *n* (AmE), ~ **and regional metropolitan railway** *n* (BrE) TRANSP métro urbain et régional *m*; ~ **catchment** *n* WATER SUPP bassin urbain *m*; ~ **cycle** *n* VEHICLES *driving* cycle de conduite urbaine *m*; ~ **electric vehicle** *n* TRANSP véhicule électrique urbain *m*; ~ **network** *n* TELECOM réseau urbain *m*; ~ **traffic** *n* TRANSP trafic urbain *m*; ~ **water management** *n* WATER SUPP gestion des eaux urbaines *f*

urea *n* CHEM carbamide *m*, urée *f*, DETERGENTS urée *f*; ~ **resin** *n* PROP MAT résine d'urée *f*

urea-formaldehyde: ~ **resin** *n* ELEC *insulation* résine urée-formaldéhyde *f*, P&R résine urée-formol *f*

ureal *adj* CHEM uréique

ureic *adj* CHEM uréique

ureide *n* CHEM uréide *m*

ureido- *pref* CHEM uréido-

ureotelic *adj* CHEM uréotélique

urethane *n* CHEM uréthane *m*; ~ **buffer** *n* MECH ENG *die set* ressort uréthane *m*

uric *adj* CHEM urique

uridine *n* CHEM uridine *f*

urobilinogen *n* CHEM urobilinogène *m*

uronic *adj* CHEM uronique

uropterin *n* CHEM uroptérine *f*

urotropin *n* CHEM urotropine *f*

urotropine *n* CHEM urotropine *f*

uroxanic *adj* CHEM uroxanique

Ursa: ~ **Major** *n* ASTRON Grande Ourse *f*; ~ **Minor** *n* ASTRON Petite Ourse *f*

US: ~ **standard thread** *n* MECH ENG pas américain système Sellers *m*

usable[1] *adj* POLLUTION *byproducts, waste products*, PROD ENG utilisable

usable:[2] ~ **memory** *n* COMP, DP mémoire utilisable *f*

USB *abbr* (*upper sideband*) ELECTRON, TELECOM bande latérale supérieure *f*

use[1] *n* PATENTS mise en oeuvre *f*, *of mark* usage *m*

use:[2] ~ **by date** *phr* PACKAGING *indication on packaging* utiliser avant la date; ~ **no hooks** *phr* PACKAGING *handling marking or label* défense d'utiliser des crochets

used *adj* POLLUTION *oil* usagé

useful: ~ **heat** *n* HEAT ENG chaleur utile *f*; ~ **rain** *n* METEO pluie utile *f*; ~ **refrigerating effect** *n* REFRIG action frigorifique utile *f*, puissance frigorifique utile *f*; ~ **satellite load** *n* SPACE charge utile d'un satellite *f*; ~ **surface** *n* MECH ENG surface utile *f*; ~ **working range** *n* TRANSP rayon d'action par charge *m*

user:[1] ~ **friendly** *adj* COMP, DP convivial, orienté opérateur

user[2] *n* COMP, DP, SAFETY *person* utilisateur *m*, TELECOM usager *m*; ~ **access** *n* TELECOM accès d'usager *m*; ~ **agent** *n* (*UA*) TELECOM agent d'usager *m*, agent utilisateur *m*; ~ **area** *n* (*UA*) COMP, DP zone de l'utilisateur *f*; ~ **group** *n* COMP, DP groupe d'utilisateurs *m*; ~ **guide** *n* TELECOM manuel de l'utilisateur *m*; ~ **interface** *n* COMP, DP, TELECOM interface utilisateur *f*; ~ **manual** *n* COMP, DP manuel de l'utilisateur *m*; ~ **name** *n* COMP, DP nom de l'utilisateur *m*; ~ **operating environment** *n* COMP, DP configuration de l'utilisateur *f*; ~ **query** *n* COMP interrogation d'utilisateur *f*, DP interrogation de l'utilisateur *f*

user-defined *adj* COMP, DP défini par l'utilisateur

user-network: ~ **interface** *n* (*UNI*) TELECOM interface usager-réseau *f*

user-signaling: ~ **bearer service** *n* (AmE), **user-signalling bearer service** *n* (BrE) TELECOM service support de signalisation d'usager *m*

user-to-user: ~ **indicator** *n* TELECOM indicateur de signalisation d'usager à usager *m*; ~ **information** *n* (*UUI*) TELECOM information d'usager à usager *f*, mini-message *m*; ~ **information message** *n* TELECOM message d'information d'usager à usager *m*; ~ **signaling** *n* (AmE), ~ **signalling** *n* (BrE) (*UUS*) TELECOM signalisation d'usager à usager *f*

use-surface *n* COATINGS couche d'usage *f*

U-shaped: ~ **base plate** *n* MECH ENG *for drilling machine* pied à fourche *m*; ~ **track girder** *n* TRANSP poutre en forme de T inversé *f*

UT *abbr* (*Universal Time*) ASTRON, SPACE TU (*temps universel*)

UTC *abbr* (*universal time coordinated*) TELECOM temps universel coordonné *m*

utensil *n* CONST, PROD ENG ustensile *m*

utilities *n pl* COMP programmes utilitaires *m pl*, PETR TECH services généraux *m pl*

utility[1] *adj* PROD ENG utilitaire, TRANSP de servitude, utilitaire

utility[2] *n* PROD ENG auxiliaire *m*, service *m*, utilitaire *m*, SPACE *spacecraft* servitude *f*, TRANSP utilitaire *m*; ~ **certificate** *n* PATENTS certificat d'utilité *m*; ~ **knife** *n* MECH ENG *tool* couteau universel *m*; ~ **model** *n* PATENTS modèle d'utilité *m*; ~ **program** *n* COMP, DP programme utilitaire *m*; ~ **satellite** *n* SPACE *communications* satellite polyvalent *m*; ~ **vehicle** *n* MILIT, VEHICLES voiture tout usage *f*

utilization: ~ **curve** *n* FUELLESS courbe d'utilisation *f*, graphe d'utilisation *m*

U-tube *n* LAB EQUIP *glassware* tube en U *m*

U-type: ~ **engine** *n* AUTO moteur à cylindres parallèles *m*

UUI *abbr* (*user-to-user information*) TELECOM information d'usager à usager *f*

UUS *abbr* (*user-to-user signaling, user-to-user signalling*) TELECOM signalisation d'usager à usager *f*

UV *abbr* (*ultraviolet*) OPT, SPACE UV (*ultraviolet*)

UV-absorbing *adj* C&G *glass* anti-UV

uvarovite *n* MINERAL ouvarovite *f*, uvarovite *f*

uvitic *adj* CHEM uvitique

UV-transmitting *adj* C&G *glass* transparent aux UV

UW *abbr* (*unique word*) SPACE *communications* mot particulier *m*

U-wrap *n* TV enroulement en U *m*

V

V^1 *abbr (volt)* METR V *(volt)*

V^2 *(vanadium)* CHEM V *(vanadium)*

V8: **~ engine** *n* AUTO moteur V8 *m*

V4: **~ engine** *n* AUTO moteur V4 *m*

V1 *abbr (decision speed)* AERONAUT V1 *(vitesse de décision)*

V6: **~ engine** *n* AUTO moteur V6 *m*

vacancy *n* CRYSTALL *defect*, METALL lacune *f*; **~ absorbing jog** *n* METALL cran absorbeur de lacunes *m*; **~ diffusion** *n* METALL diffusion des lacunes *f*, diffusion par un mécanisme lacunaire *f*; **~ disc** *n* (BrE) METALL disque de lacunes *m*; **~ disk** *n* (AmE) *see vacancy disc*; **~ emitting jog** *n* METALL cran émetteur de lacunes *m*

vacciniin *n* CHEM vacciniine *f*

vacuum:^{1} **~ encapsulated** *adj* ELEC ENG encapsulé sous vide; **under ~** *adj* PHYS, PROD ENG sous vide PHYS à vide

vacuum^2 *n* AUTO dépression *f*, CHEM *distillation and other processes* vide *m*, MECH dépression *f*, vide *m*, PAPER TECH vide *m*, PETR TECH dépression *f*, vide *m*, PHYS, PROP MAT, REFRIG, SPACE, TEXTILES, TV vide *m*; **~ advance mechanism** *n* AUTO, VEHICLES *ignition* avance automatique à dépression *f*; **~ air pump** *n* FOOD TECH pompe à vide *f*; **~ arc** *n* ELEC ENG arc dans le vide *m*; **~ arc furnace** *n* HEATING four à arc sous vide *m*; **~ blowing** *n* C&G soufflage par le vide *m*; **~ box** *n* PAPER TECH caisse aspirante *f*; **~ brake** *n* MECH ENG, RAIL *vehicles*, VEHICLES frein à dépression *m*, frein à vide *m*; **~ brazing** *n* CONST brasage sous vide *m*; **~ bubble** *n* C&G bouillon de retassure *m*; **~ capacitor** *n* ELEC ENG condensateur à vide *m*; **~ capstan** *n* RECORDING, TV cabestan à dépression *m*; **~ casting** *n* NUCLEAR coulée sous vide *f*; **~ chamber** *n* TV chambre à dépression *f*; **~ check valve** *n* AUTO clapet de retenue *m*; **~ cleaner for dusts hazardous to health** *n* SAFETY aspirateur de poussières dangereuses pour la santé *m*; **~ cleaner for industrial purposes** *n* SAFETY aspirateur pour usages industriels *m*; **~ contact element** *n* PROD ENG élément à contact sous vide *m*; **~ contact plate process** *n* FOOD TECH séchage à plaques sous vide *m*; **~ cooling** *n* REFRIG refroidissement par le vide *m*; **~ deposition** *n* ELECTRON dépôt sous vide *m*; **~ desiccator** *n* HEATING, LAB EQUIP dessiccateur à vide *m*; **~ diode** *n* ELECTRON diode à vide *f*; **~ discharge** *n* ELEC ENG décharge dans le vide *f*; **~ distillation** *n* CHEM distillation dans le vide *f*, CHEM TECH, FOOD TECH *fermentation* distillation sous vide *f*, PHYS distillation dans le vide *f*; **~ dryer** *n* COAL TECH sécheur à vide *m*, FOOD TECH séchoir sous vide *m*, étuve à vide *f*; **~ drying** *n* FOOD TECH séchage sous vide *m*; **~ drying cabinet** *n* MECH ENG armoire de séchage sous vide *f*; **~ drying oven** *n* FOOD TECH four à sécher sous vide *m*; **~ engineering** *n* MECH ENG ingénierie du vide *f*; **~ equipment** *n* MECH ENG matériel pour vide élevé *m*; **~ evaporator** *n* FOOD TECH évaporateur sous vide *m*; **~ factor** *n* NUCLEAR facteur de vide *m*; **~ filling** *n* FOOD TECH *machine process* remplissage sous vide *m*; **~ film transport system** *n* PACKAGING système de transport pour film sous vide *m*; **~ filter** *n* COAL TECH filtre sous vide *m*, filtre à vide *m*; **~ filtration** *n* COAL TECH, FOOD TECH, LAB EQUIP filtration sous vide *f*; **~ flask** *n* C&G bouteille isolante *f*, LAB EQUIP fiole à vide *f*; **~ forming** *n* P&R *process* formage sous vide *m*; **~ frame** *n* PRINT châssis pneumatique *m*; **~ freeze dryer** *n* PACKAGING machine pour lyophilisation sous vide *f*; **~ fuel pump** *n* AUTO pompe à essence à dépression *f*; **~ furnace** *n* MECH ENG four à vide *m*; **~ gage** *n* (AmE), **~ gauge** *n* (BrE) FOOD TECH indicateur de vide *m*, manomètre *m*, INSTRUMENT indicateur du vide *m*, MECH ENG manomètre à vide *m*, PETR TECH vacuomètre *m*, PHYS jauge à vide *f*, PROD ENG, REFRIG jauge à vide *f*, manomètre à vide *m*; **~ grating spectrograph** *n* WAVE PHYS spectrographe à réseau sous vide *m*; **~ guide** *n* TV guide à dépression *m*; **~ guide system** *n* RECORDING guide-bande à effet de vide *m*, TV conformateur pneumatique *m*; **~ heatsealer** *n* PACKAGING thermosoudeuse sous vide *f*; **~ heat treatment** *n* METALL traitement thermique sous vide *m*; **~ hose** *n* MECH ENG flexible à dépression *m*; **~ insulation** *n* ELEC ENG isolement par le vide *m*, MECH ENG isolement sous vide *m*; **~ jacket** *n* NUCLEAR *of calorimeter* enceinte vide *f*; **~ manifold** *n* INSTRUMENT canalisation de pompage *f*; **~ melting** *n* METALL fusion sous vide *f*; **~ metallization** *n* ELECTRON métallisation sous vide *f*; **~ metallizing** *n* C&G métallisation sous vide *f*; **~ mold** *n* (AmE), **~ mould** *n* (BrE) MECH ENG moule sous vide *m*; **~ oven** *n* LAB EQUIP étuve à vide *f*; **~ pack** *n* PACKAGING conditionnement sous vide *m*; **~ packaging machine** *n* PACKAGING emballeuse sous vide *f*; **~ packaging tool** *n* MECH ENG outil pour emballage à vide *m*; **~ pan** *n* LAB EQUIP cuve à vide *f*; **~ phototube** *n* ELECTRON phototube à vide *m*; **~ polarization** *n* NUCLEAR *free* polarisation polarisation du vide *f*; **~ pump** *n* FOOD TECH, LAB EQUIP, MAR POLL, MECH ENG, PHYS pompe à vide *f*; **~ seal** *n* MECH ENG scellage à vide *m*; **~ shelf dryer** *n* FOOD TECH armoire à déshydrater sous vide *f*, armoire à sécher sous vide *f*; **~ sintering** *n* METALL frittage sous vide *m*; **~ suspension** *n* TRANSP sustentation à dépression dynamique *f*; **~ switch** *n* ELEC *circuit breaker* interrupteur à vide *m*; **~ tanker** *n* MAR POLL tonne à lisier *f*; **~ technology** *n* MECH ENG technique du vide *m*; **~ test** *n* REFRIG essai sous vide *m*; **~ thermoforming machine** *n* PACKAGING thermoformeuse sous vide *f*; **~ thrust** *n* SPACE *spacecraft* poussée dans le vide *f*; **~ triode** *n* ELECTRON triode à vide *f*; **~ truck** *n* MAR POLL camion d'assainissement *m*; **~ tube** *n* COMP, DP, ELECTRON, PHYS tube à vide *m*, TV lampe à vide *m*, tube à vide *m*; **~ tube amplification** *n* ELECTRON amplification par tube *f*; **~ tube amplifier** *n* ELECTRON amplificateur à tube *m*, amplificateur à tube électronique *m*; **~ tube modulator** *n* ELECTRON modulateur à tube *m*, modulateur à tube électronique *m*; **~ tube oscillator** *n* ELECTRON oscillateur à tube *m*, oscillateur à tube électronique *m*; **~ ultraviolet** *n* SPACE ultraviolet lointain *m*; **~ unit** *n* MAR POLL groupe à vide *m*, pompe à vide *f*, élément à vide *m*; **~ valve** *n* AUTO, VEHICLES *cooling system* soupape de dépression *f*

vacuum-assisted: **~ power brake** *n* AUTO frein assisté par servofrein à dépression *m*

vacuum-closing: ~ **machine** *n* PACKAGING machine pour fermeture sous vide *f*

vacuum-coated: ~ **film** *n* COATINGS couche mince déposée sous vide *f*

vacuum-deposited: ~ **film** *n* ELECTRON couche déposée sous vide *f*

vacuum-filling: ~ **machine** *n* PACKAGING machine pour le remplissage sous vide *f*

vacuum-formed: ~ **package** *n* PACKAGING emballage formé sous vide *m*

vacuum-forming: ~ **mold** *n* (AmE), ~ **mould** *n* (BrE) MECH ENG moule pour formage sous vide *m*

vacuum-insulated *adj* ELEC ENG isolé par le vide

vacuum-packed *adj* FOOD TECH conditionné sous-vide, emballé sous vide, PACKAGING emballé sous vide

vacuum-sealing: ~ **machine** *n* PACKAGING machine pour fermeture sous vide *f*

VAD *abbr* (*vapor phase axial deposition, vapour phase axial deposition*) OPT, TELECOM DAV (*dépôt axial en phase vapeur*)

vadose: ~ **water** *n* WATER SUPP eau vadose *f*

valence *n* METALL, PHYS valence *f*; ~ **band** *n* PHYS bande de valence *f*; ~ **electron** *n* METALL, PHYS électron de valence *m*; ~ **electron concentration** *n* NUCLEAR concentration des électrons liants *f*; ~ **state** *n* NUCLEAR état de valence *m*

valency *n* CHEM valence *f*

valentinite *n* MINERAL valentinite *f*

valeramide *n* CHEM valéramide *m*

valerate *n* CHEM valérate *m*

valeric *adj* CHEM valérique

valeryl *n* CHEM valéryle *m*

valerylene *n* CHEM valérylène *m*

valid: ~ **signal** *n* CONTROL signal valable *m*

validate *vt* COMP, DP valider

validation *n* COMP, DP, QUALITY validation *f*

validity *n* PATENTS, TELECOM validité *f*; ~ **check** *n* COMP, CONTROL, DP, TELECOM contrôle de validité *m*; ~ **period** *n* CONST *of tenders* délai d'option *m*

valley *n* CONST *architecture* noue *f*; ~ **breeze** *n* METEO brise de vallée *f*; ~ **station** *n* TRANSP *cableways* station inférieure *f*

valuable: ~ **element** *n* NUCLEAR *in spent fuel* élément utilisable *m*

value *n* REFRIG *air conditioning* soupape *f*, TELECOM valeur *f*; ~ **added** *n* MECH ENG *of tolerance, laid down in performance* valeur ajoutée directe *f*; ~ **analysis** *n* PROD ENG analyse de la valeur *f*

value-added: ~ **network** *n* (*VAN*) COMP, DP, TELECOM réseau à valeur ajoutée *m* (*RVA*); ~ **services** *n pl* TELECOM services à valeur ajoutée *m pl*

valve *n* AUTO soupape *f*, CONST robinet *m*, soupape *f*, ELECTRON tube électronique *m*, HYDR EQUIP clapet *m*, distributeur *m*, soupape *f*, valve *f*, *conical seat* siège conique *m*, HYDROL, LAB EQUIP vanne *f*, MAR POLL soupape *f*, vanne *f*, MECH robinet *m*, soupape *f*, vanne *f*, MECH ENG valve *f*, MINING clapet *m*, NUCLEAR soupape *f*, vanne *f*, PETR TECH *in refinery* clapet *m*, robinet *m*, soupape *f*, vanne *f*, PHYS *mechanical* clapet *m*, soupape *f*, vanne *f*, *vacuum tube* lampe *f*, tube *m*, REFRIG, SPACE vanne *f*, VEHICLES *in engine* soupape *f*, *of tyre* valve *f*; ~ **adaptor gasket** *n* REFRIG joint de raccord de vanne *m*; ~ **body** *n* MECH ENG corps de vanne *m*, MECH ENG corps de vanne *m*; ~ **cage** *n* PETR TECH boîte à soupape *f*; ~ **cap** *n* VEHICLES *of tyre* bouchon de

valve *m*; ~ **chamber** *n* HYDROL chapelle à clapet *f*, chapelle à soupape *f*; ~ **chest** *n* HYDR EQUIP boîte de distribution *f*, boîte à vapeur *f*, chambre de distribution *f*, boîte à clapet *f*, boîte à soupape *f*, PETR TECH boîte à soupape *f*; ~ **clearance** *n* AUTO, MECH ENG jeu des soupapes *m*; ~ **cock** *n* HYDR EQUIP robinet d'isolation de soupape *m*; ~ **control** *n* AUTO commande à soupapes *f*; ~ **disc** *n* (BrE) AUTO tête de soupape *f*; ~ **disk** *n* (AmE) *see valve disc*; ~ **eccentric** *n* HYDR EQUIP came *f*, excentrique *m*; ~ **face** *n* VEHICLES *in engine* face de soupape *f*, portée de soupape *f*; ~ **flap** *n* NUCLEAR clapet de soupape *m*; ~ **flutter** *n* REFRIG battement d'un clapet *m*; ~ **gear** *n* HYDR EQUIP dispositif de commande *m*, dispositif de commande de tiroir *m*, distributeur de vapeur *m*, distribution *f*, mécanisme de commande *m*, VEHICLES *engine* commande des soupapes *f*; ~ **gear mechanism** *n* AUTO mécanisme de distribution *m*; ~ **guide** *n* AUTO, HYDR EQUIP, VEHICLES *in engine* guide de soupape *m*; ~ **head** *n* AUTO tête de soupape *f*; ~ **lap** *n* AUTO chevauchement des soupapes *m*; ~ **lifter** *n* VEHICLES *in engine* poussoir de soupape *m*; ~ **mating surface** *n* AUTO portée de soupape *f*; ~ **motion** *n* HYDR EQUIP *distribution of expansion class* appareil de distribution de vapeur *m*, distribution *f*, *of link class* dispositif de commande *m*; ~ **off** *n* NUCLEAR clavette d'une soupape *f*, fermeture d'une vanne *f*; ~ **outlet** *n* MECH ENG sortie de robinet *f*; ~ **push rod** *n* AUTO tige de poussoir *f*; ~ **rod** *n* HYDR EQUIP queue de soupape *f*, tige de soupape *f*, *slide valve* bielle de tiroir *f*, RAIL *vehicles* tige de soupape *f*; ~ **rotator** *n* AUTO, VEHICLES *in engine* rotateur de soupape *m*; ~ **seat** *n* AUTO siège de soupape *m*, HYDR EQUIP siège de clapet *m*, *slide valve* glace de cylindre *f*, glace de distribution *f*, glace de tiroir *f*, VEHICLES *in engine* siège de soupape *m*; ~ **setting** *n* AUTO réglage des soupapes *m*; ~ **shaft** *n* AUTO tige de soupape *f*; ~ **shaft seal** *n* AUTO joint d'étanchéité de soupape *m*; ~ **spindle** *n* HYDR EQUIP queue de soupape *f*, tige de soupape *f*; ~ **spool grinding** *n* PROD ENG rectification des clapets à boisseau *f*; ~ **spring** *n* AUTO, VEHICLES *in engine* ressort de soupape *m*; ~ **spring steel** *n* SPRINGS acier pour ressorts de soupape *m*; ~ **spring washer** *n* HYDR EQUIP coupelle *f*; ~ **stem** *n* HYDR EQUIP queue de soupape *f*, tige de soupape *f*, VEHICLES *in engine* tige de soupape *f*; ~ **tappet** *n* AUTO, HYDR EQUIP poussoir de soupape *m*; ~ **train** *n* VEHICLES *of engine* commande des soupapes *f*; ~ **travel** *n* HYDR EQUIP course du clapet *f*, course du tiroir *f*; ~ **yoke** *n* MECH ENG bâti de soupape *m*

valveless: ~ **engine** *n* AUTO moteur sans soupapes *m*

valve-timing: ~ **diagram** *n* AUTO diagramme de distribution *m*

valving: ~ **out** *n* NUCLEAR clavette d'une soupape *f*, fermeture d'une vanne *f*

Van: ~ **Allen radiation belt** *n* ASTRON, GEOPHYS, PHYS, RAD PHYS ceinture de rayonnements de Van Allen *f*; ~ **de Graaff generator** *n* ELEC générateur électrostatique *m*, ELEC ENG, PHYS générateur de Van de Graaff *m*; ~ **der Waals bond** *n* CRYSTALL liaison de Van der Waals *f*; ~ **der Waals equation** *n* PHYS équation de Van der Waals *f*; ~ **der Waals radius** *n* PHYS rayon de Van der Waals *m*

VAN *abbr* (*value-added network*) COMP, DP, TELECOM RVA (*réseau à valeur ajoutée*)

vanadate *n* CHEM vanadate *m*

vanadic *adj* CHEM vanadique

vanadiferous *adj* CHEM vanadifère

vanadinite n MINERAL vanadinite f
vanadiolite n MINERAL vanadiolite f
vanadite n CHEM vanadite m
vanadium n (V) CHEM vanadium m (V)
vanadous adj CHEM vanadeux
vanadyl n CHEM vanadyle m
vane n AERONAUT of turbine engine aube f, CONST sight-vane pinnule f, target voyant m, HYDR EQUIP of turbine pale f, MECH of turbine aube f, palette f, MECH ENG of turbine aube f, palette f, of ventilating fan aile f, ailette f, PROD ENG aube f, palette f; ~ **axial fan** n REFRIG ventilateur axial à aubage directeur m; ~ **circuit breaker** n RAIL on points interrupteur à vanne m; ~ **pump** n PROD ENG pompe rotative à palettes f, WATER SUPP pompe rotative à ailettes f, pompe rotative à palettes f; ~ **velocity** n FUELLESS vitesse d'aube f; ~ **wattmeter** n ELEC wattmètre à palette m
vane-type: ~ **anode** n ELEC ENG anode cloisonnée f; ~ **relay** n ELEC relais à palette m
vanish vi PHYS annuler
vanishing: ~ **point** n GEOM point de fuite m
vanity: ~ **mirror** n VEHICLES accessory miroir de courtoisie m
vapor n (AmE) see vapour
vapor-catching: ~ **cone cap** n (AmE) see vapour-catching cone cap
vapor-expanded adj (AmE) see vapour-expanded
vapor-grown adj (AmE) see vapour-grown
vaporization n AUTO vaporisation f, CHEM TECH vaporisation f, évaporation f, GAS TECH, PHYS vaporisation f ~ **dish** n CHEM TECH cuvette d'évaporation f, cuvette de vaporisation f
vaporize[1] vt CHEM gazéifier, vaporiser, liquid vaporiser, CHEM TECH, THERMOD vaporiser, évaporer
vaporize[2] vi CHEM liquid se vaporiser
vaporized adj THERMOD vaporisé, évaporé
vaporizer n CHEM vaporisateur m, CHEM TECH pulvérisateur de liquide m, THERMOD vaporiseur m, évaporateur m
vaporizing: ~ **burner** n THERMOD brûleur à vaporisation m
vaporous adj CHEM vaporeux
vapor-proof adj (AmE) see vapour-proof
Vapotron n ELECTRON Vapotron m
vapour n (BrE) CHEM, METALL, POLLUTION, THERMOD vapeur f ~ **bath** n (BrE) CHEM TECH bain de vapeur m; ~ **bubble** n (BrE) CHEM TECH bulle de vapeur f; ~ **compression** n (BrE) CHEM TECH compression de la vapeur f; ~ **compression cycle** n (BrE) THERMOD cycle de Carnot inverse m; ~ **condensation** n (BrE) NUCLEAR condensation des vapeurs f; ~ **density** n (BrE) CHEM, PHYS, THERMOD densité de vapeur f; ~ **deposited layer** n (BrE) CHEM TECH couche obtenue par condensation de vapeur f; ~ **deposition** n (BrE) C&G dépôt par évaporation m, ELECTRON dépôt en phase vapeur m, évaporation sous vide f, THERMOD of metals métallisation sous vide f; ~ **deposition technique** n (BrE) CHEM TECH technique de métallisation sous vide f; ~ **discharge lamp** n (BrE) THERMOD lampe à vapeur f; ~ **dispersion** n (BrE) GAS TECH dispersion de vapeur f; ~ **generator** n (BrE) NUCLEAR générateur de vapeur m; ~ **jet refrigerating cycle** n (BrE) REFRIG cycle de réfrigération à éjection de vapeur m; ~ **lock** n (BrE) AUTO, TRANSP bouchon de vapeur m; ~ **permeability** n (BrE) HEAT ENG, THERMOD perméabilité à la vapeur f; ~ **permeance** n (BrE) HEAT ENG perméance à la vapeur f;

~ **phase** n (BrE) CHEM TECH, THERMOD phase vapeur f; ~ **phase axial deposition** n (BrE) (VAD) OPT, TELECOM dépôt axial en phase vapeur m (DAV); ~ **phase chemical deposition** n (BrE) TELECOM dépôt chimique en phase vapeur m; ~ **phase epitaxy** n (BrE) CHEM TECH, ELECTRON épitaxie en phase vapeur f; ~ **phase grown epitaxial layer** n (BrE) ELECTRON couche épitaxiale en phase vapeur f; ~ **phase nitration** n (BrE) CHEM TECH nitration en phase vapeur f; ~ **phase reaction** n (BrE) ELECTRON réaction en phase vapeur f; ~ **phase verneuil method** n (BrE) OPT procédé verneuil au plasma m; ~ **pressure** n (BrE) HEATING pression de la vapeur f, PETR TECH tension de vapeur f, PHYS, REFRIG pression de la vapeur f; ~ **pressure thermometer** n (BrE) REFRIG thermomètre à tension de vapeur m; ~ **quenching** n (BrE) METALL trempe à la vapeur f; ~ **resistance** n (BrE) HEAT ENG résistance à la vapeur f; ~ **resistivity** n (BrE) HEAT ENG résistivité à la vapeur f; ~ **return line** n (BrE) AUTO canalisation de retour des vapeurs f; ~ **state** n (BrE) CHEM TECH état de vapeur m; ~ **trap** n (BrE) CHEM TECH baffle m, chicane f, piège à vapeur m
vapour-catching: ~ **cone cap** n (BrE) CHEM TECH baffle à chapeau m
vapour-expanded adj (BrE) CHEM TECH expansé sous forme de vapeur
vapour-grown adj (BrE) CHEM TECH cristallisé en phase vapeur
vapour-proof adj (BrE) SAFETY étanche aux vapeurs
varactor n ELECTRON diode varicap f; ~ **chip** n ELECTRON puce de diode varicap f; ~ **diode** n PHYS diode varactor f, TV diode à capacité variable f, varicap f; ~ **tuning** n ELECTRON accord par diode varicap m
varactor-tuned: ~ **oscillator** n ELECTRON oscillateur accordé par diode varicap m, oscillateur à diode varicap m
variable[1] adj MATH variable
variable[2] n COMP, DP, MATH variable f; ~ **amplitude recording** n ACOUSTICS enregistrement à amplitude variable m; ~ **amplitude test** n METALL essai sous amplitude variable m; ~ **aperture shutter** n CINEMAT obturateur à ouverture variable m; ~ **area recording** n TV enregistrement à densité variable m; ~ **area soundtrack** n RECORDING piste RCA f, piste son à densité fixe f; ~ **attenuation** n ELECTRON atténuation variable f; ~ **attenuator** n CONTROL régulateur variable d'affaiblissement m, ELECTRON atténuateur variable m; ~ **audio level** n RECORDING niveau audio instable m; ~ **bit rate** n (VBR) TELECOM débit binaire variable m (DBV); ~ **capacitor** n ELEC, ELEC ENG condensateur variable m, PHYS condensateur réglable m, condensateur variable m; ~ **capacitor section** n ELEC ENG cage de condensateur variable f; ~ **capicitance diode** n TV diode à capacité variable f; ~ **carrier modulation** n ELECTRON modulation à taux constant f; ~ **coaxial attenuator** n ELECTRON atténuateur coaxial variable m; ~ **delay** n TELECOM retard variable m; ~ **delivery pump** n PROD ENG pompe à débit variable f; ~ **density recording** n ACOUSTICS enregistrement à densité variable m; ~ **density soundtrack** n RECORDING piste Western Electric f, piste son à densité variable f; ~ **density track** n TV piste à densité variable f; ~ **discharge pump** n MECH ENG pompe à débit réglable f, pompe à débit variable f; ~ **displacement motor** n PROD ENG moteur à cylindrée variable m; ~ **field** n COMP, DP, ELEC ENG champ variable m; ~ **flow** n

HYDROL écoulement varié *m*; ~ **focal length** *n* PHOTO focale variable *f*; ~ **focus reflector** *n* PHOTO réflecteur à foyer réglable *m*; ~ **frequency oscillator** *n* ELECTRON oscillateur à fréquence variable *m*; ~ **gain amplifier** *n* ELECTRON amplificateur à gain variable *m*; ~ **geometry aircraft** *n* AERONAUT avion à flèche variable *m*, avion à géométrie variable *m*; ~ **geometry inlet** *n* TRANSP entrée d'air variable *f*, prise d'air variable *f*; ~ **geometry intake** *n* TRANSP entrée d'air variable *f*, prise d'air variable *f*; ~ **geometry skirt** *n* TRANSP jupe à géométrie variable *f*; ~ **inductance** *n* ELEC, ELEC ENG inductance variable *f*; ~ **length** *n* COMP, DP longueur variable *f*; ~ **length code** *n* TELECOM code à longueur variable *m*; ~ **length record** *n* COMP, DP enregistrement de longueur variable *m*; ~ **message sign** *n* TRANSP *traffic control* signal routier variable *m*; ~ **microwave attenuator** *n* ELECTRON atténuateur hyperfréquence *m*; ~ **mixture** *n* AUTO mélange à dosage variable *m*; ~ **moment of inertia model** *n* NUCLEAR *nuclear model* modèle du moment d'inertie variable *m*; ~ **mu tube** *n* ELECTRON tube à pente variable *m*; ~ **name** *n* COMP, DP nom de variable *m*; ~ **persistence** *n* ELECTRON persistance variable *f*, rémanence variable *f*; ~ **persistence storage** *n* ELECTRON mémorisation à persistance variable *f*; ~ **persistence storage tube** *n* ELECTRON tube à mémoire à persistance variable *m*, tube à persistance variable *m*; ~ **pitch** *n* REFRIG inclinaison variable *f*, SPRINGS pas variable *m*; ~ **pitch air propeller** *n* TRANSP hélice aérienne à pas variable *f*; ~ **pitch inlet vanes** *n pl* NUCLEAR *of centrifugal pump, turbocompressor* aubes d'admission variables *f pl*; ~ **pitch propeller** *n* AERONAUT, MAR POLL, NAUT hélice à pas variable *f*; ~ **point representation** *n* COMP, DP représentation en virgule variable *f*; ~ **quantity** *n* ELEC ENG grandeur variable *f*; ~ **range marker** *n* NAUT *radar* cercle de distance variable *m*; ~ **ratio transformer** *n* ELEC ENG transformateur à enroulement mobile *m*; ~ **reluctance motor** *n* TRANSP moteur à réluctance variable *m*; ~ **reluctance stepper motor** *n* ELEC ENG moteur pas-à-pas à réluctance *m*; ~ **resistance** *n* ELEC ENG résistance variable *f*; ~ **resistor** *n* ELEC, ELEC ENG, PHYS résistance variable *f*; ~ **route sign** *n* TRANSP panneau indicateur variable *m*; ~ **shutter** *n* CINEMAT obturateur variable *m*; ~ **slope delta modulation** *n* SPACE *communications* modulation delta à pente asservie *f*; ~ **slow motion** *n* TV dispositif de ralenti variable *m*; ~ **space** *n* PRINT espace justifiante *m*; ~ **speed camera** *n* CINEMAT caméra à vitesse variable *f*; ~ **speed control** *n* TV dispositif de réglage de vitesse *m*; ~ **speed conveyor belt** *n* TRANSP bande transporteuse à vitesse variable *f*; ~ **speed drive** *n* MECH ENG transmission à vitesse variable *f*; ~ **speed message sign** *n* TRANSP *traffic control* signal à limitation de vitesse variable *m*; ~ **speed motor** *n* ELEC ENG moteur à vitesse variable *m*; ~ **speed scanning** *n* TV balayage à vitesse rapide *m*; ~ **star** *n* ASTRON étoile variable *f*; ~ **transformer** *n* ELEC ENG transformateur variable *m*; ~ **valve timing** *n* TRANSP distribution à programme variable *f*; ~ **velocity** *n* MECH ENG vitesse variée *f*; ~ **venturi carburetor** *n* (AmE), ~ **venturi carburettor** *n* (BrE) AUTO carburateur à diffuseur variable *m*; ~ **voltage generator** *n* ELEC dynamo pilote *f*; ~ **width soundtrack** *n* RECORDING piste son à densité constante *f*; ~ **word length computer** *n* COMP, DP ordinateur à mots de longueur variable *m*

variamine *n* CHEM variamine *f*

variance *n* COMP, DP, MATH *statistics*, PHYS variance *f*

variate *n* CHEM variable *f*

variation *n* GEOPHYS déclinaison magnétique *f*, MECH ENG changement *m*, variation *f*, écart *m*, NAUT déclinaison *f*; ~ **compass** *n* GEOPHYS boussole de déclinaison *f*, compas de variation *m*; ~ **order** *n* CONST avenant *m*, ordre architectonique *m*, ordre de change *m*

variational: ~ **calculus** *n* MATH calcul des variations *m*

varicolored *adj* (AmE), **varicoloured** *adj* (BrE) COLOURS de couleurs différentes

varied: ~ **pitchblende** *n* NUCLEAR noir d'uranium *m*, petchblende *f*

variegated: ~ **copper ore** *n* MINERAL érubescite *f*

varifocal: ~ **lens** *n* CINEMAT objectif à distance focale variable *m*

variocoupler *n* ELEC ENG variocoupleur *m*

variometer *n* ELEC ENG variomètre *m*

variscite *n* MINERAL variscite *f*

varistance *n* ELEC ENG résistance non linéaire *f*, varistance *f*

varistor *n* ELEC *resistor* varistor *f*, PHYS, PROD ENG varistance *f*

varnish[1] *n* CHEM, *m*, COATINGS, COLOURS, CONST, ELEC *insulation,P&R coating*, PRINT laque vernis *fm*; ~ **maker** *n* COATINGS vernisseur *m*; ~ **maker's naphtha** *n* COATINGS ligroïne *f*, éther de pétrole *m*; ~ **paint** *n* COATINGS, COLOURS peinture laquée *f*; ~ **run** *n* COATINGS coulure de peinture *f*, coulure de vernis *f*; ~ **tear** *n* COATINGS coulure de peinture *f*, coulure de vernis *f*; ~ **tit** *n* COATINGS coulure de peinture *f*, coulure de vernis *f*

varnish[2] *vt* COATINGS enduire de vernis, vernir, vernisser, COLOURS vernir

varnished *adj* COATINGS enduit de vernis, verni

varnisher *n* COATINGS vernisseur *m*

varnishing *n* COATINGS vernissage *m*, COLOURS laquage *m*, CONST vernissage *m*, PRINT pelliculage *m*, vernissage *m*, PROD ENG vernissage *m*; ~ **machine** *n* COATINGS machine à vernir *f*, vernisseuse *f*

varve *n* GEOL varve *f*

varying: ~ **loading** *n* METALL sollicitation variable *f*

vasopressin *n* CHEM vasopressine *f*

vat *n* CHEM, FOOD TECH, PAPER TECH cuve *f*, PROD ENG bac *m*, cuve *f*, TEXTILES cuve *f*; ~ **dye** *n* TEXTILES colorant de cuve *m*; ~ **dyeing** *n* COLOURS teinture aux colorants de cuve *f*; ~ **lined board** *n* PROD ENG carton doublé à la cuve *m*; ~ **machine** *n* PAPER TECH machine à onduler *f*

vault *n* CINEMAT local de stockage de films *m*, CONST *architecture* voûte *f*, *cellar* cave *f*

vauquelinite *n* MINERAL vauquelinite *f*

Vauxhall: ~ **bevel** *n* C&G biseau antique *m*

V-belt *n* AUTO, MECH, MECH ENG, PROD ENG, VEHICLES *cooling system* courroie trapézoïdale *f*; ~ **drive** *n* MECH ENG transmission à courroie trapézoïdale *f*; ~ **speed transmission** *n* MECH ENG transmission mécanique à courroie trapézoïdale *f*; ~ **tension** *n* MECH ENG tension de courroie trapézoïdale *f*

V-belting *n* TEXTILES courroie de transmission *f*

V-block *n* MECH ENG *draughtsman's* V, V de mécanicien *m*, cale en V *f*, support en V pour le traçage *m*, METR cale en V *f*

V-bob *n* MECH ENG balancier d'équerre *m*, varlet *m*

VBR *abbr* (*variable bit rate*) TELECOM DBV (*débit binaire variable*)

V-C: ~ **ratio** *n* (*volume capacity ratio*) TRANSP rapport débit-capacité *m*

VC *abbr* (*virtual channel*) TELECOM canal virtuel *m*, voie virtuelle *f*

VCC *abbr* (*virtual channel connection*) TELECOM connexion de canal virtuel *f*, connexion de voie virtuelle *f*

VCCE *abbr* (*virtual channel connection endpoint*) TELECOM extrémité de connexion de canal virtuel *f*

VCF *abbr* (*video command freeze-picture request*) TELECOM commande vidéo de demande de gel de l'image *f*

VCI *abbr* (*virtual channel identifier*) TELECOM identificateur de canal virtuel *m*, identificateur de voie virtuelle *m*

VC-n *abbr* (*virtual container-n*) TELECOM conteneur virtuel-n *m*

VCO *abbr* (*voltage-controlled oscillator*) ELECTRON, SPACE, TELECOM oscillateur commandé en tension *m*

V-connection *n* ELEC connexion en V *f*

VCS *abbr* (*virtual-circuit switch*) TELECOM CCV (*commutateur de circuits virtuels*)

VCU *abbr* (*video command fast-update request*) TELECOM commande vidéo de demande de rafraîchissement rapide *f*

V-cut *n* MINING bouchon en V *m*, bouchon-charrue *m*

V-cylinder: ~ **engine** *n* MECH ENG moteur à cylindres en V *m*

VDA *abbr* (*video distribution amplifier*) TV amplificateur de distribution vidéo *m*

VDU[1] *abbr* (*visual display unit*) COMP, DP, TELECOM, TV console de visualisation *f*, écran de visualisation *m*

VDU:[2] ~ **operator** *n* PROD ENG opérateur de clavier-écran *m*

vector *n* COMP, DP, ELEC *electromagnetism*, ELEC ENG, GEOM, MATH, PHYS, SPACE vecteur *m*; ~ **coupling** *n* RAD PHYS *electron orbits* couplage vectoriel *m*; ~ **field** *n* ELEC *electromagnetism*, ELEC ENG champ vectoriel *m*; ~ **graphics** *n* COMP, DP graphique vectoriel *m*; ~ **group** *n* ELEC *transformer* groupe de couplage *m*; ~ **model** *n* PHYS *of atom* modèle vectoriel *m*; ~ **network analysis** *n* ELEC ENG analyse vectorielle des réseaux *f*; ~ **network analyzer** *n* ELEC ENG analyseur vectoriel de réseaux *m*; ~ **potential** *n* ELEC ENG, PHYS potentiel vecteur *m*; ~ **processing** *n* COMP, DP traitement vectoriel *m*; ~ **product** *n* PHYS produit vectoriel *m*; ~ **scan cathode ray tube** *n* ELECTRON tube cathodique à balayage cavalier *m*; ~ **scan electron beam lithography** *n* ELECTRON gravure par faisceau d'électrons à balayage cavalier *f*, gravure à balayage cavalier *f*; ~ **scanning** *n* ELECTRON balayage cavalier *m*

vectored[1] *adj* SPACE *of spacecraft* vectorisé

vectored:[2] ~ **interrupt** *n* COMP, DP interruption vectorisée *f*; ~ **thrust** *n* SPACE *of spacecraft* poussée vectorielle *f*; ~ **thrust engine** *n* SPACE *of spacecraft* moteur à poussée vectorielle *m*

vectorial *adj* GEOM, PHYS vectoriel

vector-scanned: ~ **beam** *n* ELECTRON faisceau à balayage cavalier *m*

vectorscope *n* TV vecteurscope *m*

veer *vi* NAUT *wind* tourner, virer; ~ **aft** *vi* NAUT *wind* adonner; ~ **forward** *vi* NAUT *wind* refuser; ~ **off course** *vi* NAUT *ship* dévier de la route

vegetable: ~ **fat** *n* FOOD TECH graisse végétale *f*; ~ **glue** *n* PROD ENG colle végétale *f*; ~ **oil** *n* FOOD TECH huile végétale *f*; ~ **parchment** *n* PAPER TECH papier sulfurisé *m*, PROD ENG papier sulfurisé *m*, parchemin végétal *m*; ~ **protein** *n* FOOD TECH protéine végétale *f*; ~ **size** *n*

COLOURS colle végétale *f*

vehicle *n* CHEM, MECH véhicule *m*, PRINT liant de l'encre *m*, liant du carbone *m*, SPACE, TRANSP véhicule *m*; ~ **characteristic detector** *n* TRANSP détecteur des caractéristiques des véhicules *m*; ~ **extension period** *n* TRANSP *traffic control* durée de prolongation *f*; ~ **ferry** *n* TRANSP bac à voitures *m*; ~ **intercept survey** *n* TRANSP enquête papillons *f*; ~ **location subsystem** *n* TELECOM sous-système de localisation des véhicules *m*; ~ **ramp** *n* TRANSP rampe d'accès *f*; ~ **tagging** *n* TRANSP système d'identification *m*; ~ **tanker** *n* TRANSP camion citerne *m*

vehicle-actuated: ~ **control** *n* TRANSP commande adaptative *f*; ~ **signalization** *n* TRANSP commande adaptative des signaux *f*; ~ **traffic signals** *n* TRANSP commande adaptative des signaux *f*

vehicle-mounted: ~ **short primary linear motor** *n* TRANSP moteur linéaire à inducteur *m*

vehicular: ~ **flow at peak hour** *n* TRANSP débit à l'heure de pointe *m*

veil *n* CINEMAT *on emulsion or film* voile *m*

Veil: ~ **Nebula** *n* ASTRON, SPACE nébuleuse de Veil *f*, nébuleuse de la Dentelle du Cygne *f*

vein *n* CONST *in wood, marble*, MINING veine *f*; ~ **wall** *n* GEOL éponte *f*

veined: ~ **board** *n* PAPER TECH carton chiné *m*; ~ **paper** *n* PAPER TECH papier chiné *m*

veinlet *n* GEOL filonnet *m*

Veitch: ~ **diagram** *n* COMP, DP diagramme de Veitch *m*

Vela *n* ASTRON Voiles *f pl*

vellum: ~ **finish** *n* PROD ENG fini vélin *m*

velocimeter *n* PHYS vélocimètre *m*

velocimetry *n* PHYS vélocimétrie *f*

velocity *n* ACOUSTICS, ELECTRON vitesse *f*, HYDROL *flow of a current* dérive *f*, vitesse *f*, MECH, MECH ENG vitesse *f*, PHYS vitesse *f*, vélocité *f*, WAVE PHYS *of sound, waves* vitesse *f*; ~ **banding** *n* TV bande de décalage vitesse *f*, vitesse *f*; ~ **coefficient** *n* FUELLESS coefficient de vitesse *m*; ~ **control servo** *n* TV régulateur de vitesse asservie *m*; ~ **of detonation** *n* (*VOD*) MINING vitesse de détonation *f*; ~ **diagram** *n* FUELLESS diagramme des vitesses *m*, MECH ENG graphique de répartition des vitesses *m*; ~ **error** *n* TV erreur de vitesse de têtes *f*; ~ **error compensator** *n* TV compensateur d'erreur de vitesse de têtes *m*; ~ **of flow** *n* COAL TECH, HYDROL, REFRIG vitesse d'écoulement *f*; ~ **fluctuation** *n* FLUID PHYS variation de vitesse *f*; ~ **head** *n* HYDR EQUIP vitesse acquise *f*; ~ **increment** *n* SPACE incrément de vitesse *m*; ~ **inversion** *n* PETR inversion de vitesse *f*; ~ **loss** *n* NUCLEAR perte hydraulique *f*; ~ **microphone** *n* ACOUSTICS microphone à vitesse *m*, RECORDING microphone à ruban *m*; ~ **modulation** *n* ELECTRON, PHYS, TV modulation de vitesse *f*; ~ **potential** *n* FUELLESS potentiel de vitesse *m*; ~ **profile** *n* PHYS profil de vitesse *m*; ~ **resonance** *n* PHYS résonance de vitesse *f*; ~ **of sound** *n* ACOUSTICS, WAVE PHYS vitesse du son *f*; ~ **stage turbine** *n* HYDR EQUIP turbine à étages de vitesse *f*

velocity-depth: ~ **curve** *n* PETR TECH *seismic survey* courbe vitesses-profondeur *f*

velocity-modulated: ~ **amplifier** *n* ELECTRON amplificateur à modulation de vitesse *m*; ~ **beam** *n* ELECTRON faisceau modulé en vitesse *m*; ~ **oscillator** *n* ELECTRON oscillateur à modulation de vitesse *m*; ~ **tube** *n* ELECTRON tube hyperfréquence *m*, tube à modulation de vitesse *m*

velvet *n* TEXTILES velours *m*; ~ **light trap** *n* PHOTO garni-

ture en velours *f*; ~ **trap** *n* CINEMAT garniture de
velours *f*

venasquite *n* MINERAL venasquite *f*

vendor: ~ **scheduler** *n* PROD ENG acheteur *m*

veneer *n* CONST feuille de placage *f*; ~ **board** *n* PROD ENG
carton plaqué bois *m*; ~ **splicing machine** *n* MECH ENG
machine à jointer les placages *f*

veneering *n* CONST placage *m*; ~ **press** *n* MECH ENG presse
à plaquer *f*

Venera: ~ **space probe** *n* ASTRON sonde spatiale Venera *f*

venetian: ~ **blind effect** *n* TV effet de persiennes *m*, effet
de store vénitien *m*

V-engine *n* AUTO, NAUT moteur en V *m*

Venn: ~ **diagram** *n* COMP, DP diagramme de Venn *m*,
MATH diagramme d'Euler-Venn *m*

vent *n* C&G évent *m*, CONST *air hole* aspirail *m*, conduit
d'air *m*, ouverture de ventilation *f*, soupirail *m*, trou
d'évent *m*, évent *m*, GEOL *volcanic* cheminée *f*, évent
m, LAB EQUIP prise d'air *f*, MECH évent *m*, NUCLEAR
mise à l'air *f*, ouverture de ventilation *f*, purge de l'air
f, soutirage *m*, P&R évent *m*, PROD ENG *of mould* trou
d'air *m*, SPACE évent *m*; ~ **hole** *n* CONST aspirail *m*,
soupirail *m*, trou d'évent *m*, évent *m*, PROD ENG trou
d'air *m*, SPACE évent *m*; ~ **nozzle** *n* NUCLEAR *of tank*
tubulure d'échappement *f*; ~ **peg** *n* CONST fausset *m*; ~
pipe *n* CONST cheminée de ventilation *f*, tube de ventilation *m*, ventilateur *m*, NUCLEAR *of pressure
suppression system* tube de condensation *m*; ~ **plug** *n*
CONST fausset *m*; ~ **window** *n* AERONAUT déflecteur de
porte avant *m*

vented: ~ **fuel assembly** *n* NUCLEAR assemblage combustible ventilé *m*; ~ **fuel rod** *n* NUCLEAR crayon
combustible ventilé *m*

ventiduct *n* CONST ventouse *f*

ventilate *vt* COAL TECH aérer, SAFETY, THERMOD aérer,
ventiler; ~ **gas-filled workings** *vt* MINING assainir un
chantier contaminé

ventilated[1] *adj* SAFETY ventilé, THERMOD aéré, ventilé

ventilated:[2] ~ **fan** *n* REFRIG ventilateur ventilé *m*; ~ **fros-
ter** *n* REFRIG évaporateur ventilé *m*; ~ **motor** *n* ELEC
moteur ventilé *m*; ~ **nappe** *n* WATER SUPP nappe aérée
f; ~ **propeller** *n* TRANSP hélice ventilée *f*; ~ **tank crew
helmet** *n* MILIT casque ventilé pour équipage de char
m; ~ **vehicle** *n* REFRIG véhicule aéré *m*

ventilating *n* CONST aérage *m*, ventilation *f*; ~ **door** *n*
CONST porte d'aérage *f*; ~ **fan** *n* CONST, MINING *above-
ground* ventilateur *m*

ventilation *n* COAL TECH aération *f*, CONST aérage *m*,
ventilation *f*, HEATING ventilation *f*, MINING aérage *m*,
aération *f*, ventilation *f*, NAUT aération *f*, ventilation *f*,
REFRIG ventilation *f*, SAFETY aérage *m*, aération *f*,
ventilation *f*, THERMOD aération *f*, ventilation *f*, VEHI-
CLES *of engine, interior* ventilation *f*; ~ **breakdown** *n*
COAL TECH arrêt de l'aérage *m*, panne d'aérage *f*; ~
control *n* CONTROL contrôle d'aérage *m*; ~ **door** *n*
MINING porte d'aérage *f*, porte à guichet *f*; ~ **door
openers** *n pl* SAFETY ouvre-portes d'aération *f pl*,
ouvre-portes de ventilation *f pl*; ~ **drive** *n* MINING
tunnel airage *m*, galerie d'aérage *f*, voie d'air *f*; ~ **duct** *n*
CONST *tunnelling* conduite de ventilation *f*; ~ **ducting** *n*
MINING canalisation d'aérage *f*; ~ **loss** *n* HEATING perte
par la ventilation *f*; ~ **pipe** *n* MINING tuyau d'aération
m, tuyau de ventilation *m*; ~ **shaft** *n* MINING puits
d'aérage *m*, puits de ventilation *m*

ventilator *n* CONST ventilateur *m*, NAUT *deck equipment*
dorade *f*, manche à air *f*, ventilateur *m*, PAPER TECH,

REFRIG aérateur *m*, SAFETY ventilateur *m*; ~ **cowl** *n*
NAUT *deck fitting* pavillon de manche à air *m*; ~ **socket**
n NAUT embase pour manche à air *f*

ventimeter *n* NAUT ventimètre *m*

venting *n* NUCLEAR *of air from pipe* mise à l'air *f*, purge
de l'air *f*, soutirage *m*

venturi *n* AUTO diffuseur *m*, VEHICLES *carburettor* buse
d'air *f*, diffuseur *m*; ~ **effect** *n* METEO effet venturi *m*; ~
meter *n* PHYS tube de venturi *m*; ~ **nozzle** *n* MECH
convergent-divergent *m*; ~ **scrubber** *n* COAL TECH laveur venturi *m*, POLLUTION séparateur laveur *m*; ~
sludge *n* COAL TECH boue du venturi *f*; ~ **tube** *n* MECH
ENG venturi *m*, PHYS tube de venturi *m*, VEHICLES
venturi *m*

Venturi-Parshall: ~ **flume** *n* HYDROL canal Venturi-
Parshall *m*

veratramine *n* CHEM vératramine *f*

veratric *adj* CHEM vératrique

veratrine *n* CHEM vératrine *f*

veratrol *n* CHEM vératrol *m*, vératrole *m*

verbena: ~ **oil** *n* CHEM essence de verveine *f*

verdigris *n* CHEM vert-de-gris *m*

verification *n* COMP, DP, MECH ENG *by means of limit
gauge* vérification *f*; ~ **testing** *n* QUALITY essai de
vérification *m*

verifier *n* COMP, DP vérificatrice *f*

verify *vt* COMP vérifier, CONTROL contrôler, vérifier, DP
vérifier

vermiculite *n* HEAT ENG, MINERAL, REFRIG *insulant* vermiculite *f*

vernal: ~ **equinox** *n* ASTRON, SPACE équinoxe vernal *m*; ~
point *n* ASTRON, SPACE point gamma *m*, point vernal *m*

vernier *n* MECH, MECH ENG, METR *scale* vernier *m*; ~
caliper *n* (AmE), ~ **calliper** *n* (BrE) METEO, MECH,
METR, PHYS pied à coulisse à vernier *m*; ~ **depth gage** *n*
(AmE), ~ **depth gauge** *n* (BrE) METR trusquin de
profondeur à vernier *m*; ~ **height gage** *n* (AmE), ~
height gauge *n* (BrE) METR trusquin de hauteur à
vernier *m*; ~ **knob** *n* CONTROL bouton à vernier *m*; ~
motor *n* SPACE *on spacecraft* moteur vernier *m*; ~
potentiometer *n* ELEC potentiomètre vernier *m*; ~
scale *n* MECH ENG échelle à vernier *f*

veronal *n* CHEM véronal *m*

versals *n pl* PRINT lettrine habillée *f*

versene *n* CHEM versène *m*

version *n* COMP, DP, PROD ENG version *f*

verso *n* PRINT verso *m*

vertex *n* CRYSTALL, GEOM, PHYS, TELECOM sommet *m*; ~
angle *n* PRINT, TELECOM angle au sommet de l'alvéole
m; ~ **feed** *n* TELECOM alimentation axiale *f*; ~ **plate** *n*
TELECOM *of an aerial reflector* cache sommet *m*; ~
refractionometer *n* INSTRUMENT fronto-focomètre *m*

vertical[1] *adj* GEOM opposé, vertical

vertical:[2] ~ **alignment** *n* CONST alignement vertical *m*; ~
amplifier *n* ELECTRON amplificateur vertical *m*; ~ **amplifier bandwidth** *n* ELECTRON bande passante de
l'amplificateur vertical *f*; ~ **amplifier dynamic range** *n*
ELECTRON dynamique de l'amplificateur vertical *f*; ~
amplifier input *n* ELECTRON entrée de l'amplificateur
vertical *f*; ~ **amplifier output** *n* ELECTRON sortie de
l'amplificateur vertical *f*; ~ **amplitude** *n* TV amplitude
verticale *f*; ~ **amplitude control** *n* TV réglage de l'amplitude verticale *m*; ~ **and horizontal form fill seal
machine** *n* PACKAGING machine verticale et horizontale pour former remplir et fermer *f*; ~ **angles** *n pl*
GEOM angles opposés *m pl*; ~ **ascent** *n* ASTRON, SPACE

ascension droite *f*; ~ **axis** *n* MATH axe des ordonnées *m*, axe des y *m*, axe vertical *m*; ~ **axis wind turbine** *n* FUELLESS turbine éolienne à axe vertical *f*; ~ **bipolar transistor** *n* ELECTRON transistor bipolaire vertical *m*; ~ **blanking** *n* COMP, DP, ELECTRON suppression de trame *f*, TV suppression de trame *f*, suppression verticale *f*; ~ **blanking interval** *n* TV intervalle de suppression de trame *m*, intervalle de suppression verticale *m*; ~ **blanking pulse** *n* TV impulsion de suppression de trame *f*; ~ **burning test** *n* TESTING essai de combustion verticale *m*; ~ **cartoner** *n* PACKAGING encartonneuse verticale *f*; ~ **centering** (AmE) *see* vertical centring; ~ **centering control** *n* (AmE) *see* vertical centring control; ~ **centring** *n* ELECTRON cadrage vertical *m*; ~ **centring control** *n* (BrE) TV réglage de décentrement vertical *m*; ~ **clamp** *n* INSTRUMENT vis de blocage du mouvement en site *f*; ~ **component** *n* PHYS composante verticale *f*; ~ **control** *n* CINEMAT réglage de la hauteur de l'image *m*, OPT asservissement vertical *m*; ~ **convergence** *n* ELECTRON convergence radiale *f*; ~ **curve radius** *n* CONST *road alignment* rayon de raccordement vertical *m*; ~ **cylinder-grinding machine** *n* MECH ENG machine à rectifier en l'air les surfaces cylindriques *f*; ~ **deflecting plates** *n pl* PHYS plaques de déviation verticale *f pl*; ~ **deflection** *n* ELECTRON déviation verticale *f*, TV déviation de la trame *f*, déviation verticale *f*; ~ **deflection coil** *n* ELEC ENG bobine de déviation verticale *f*; ~ **deflection plate** *n* ELECTRON plaque de déviation verticale *f*; ~ **digester** *n* PROD ENG lessiveur vertical *m*; ~ **dispersion** *n* POLLUTION dispersion verticale *f*; ~ **drainage** *n* COAL TECH drainage vertical *m*; ~ **engine** *n* AUTO, VEHICLES moteur vertical *m*; ~ **field effect transistor** *n* ELECTRON transistor à effet de champ vertical *m*; ~ **format** *n* COMP, DP format vertical *m*; ~ **gyro** *n* SPACE *on spacecraft*, TRANSP gyroscope vertical *m*; ~ **handsaw** *n* MECH ENG *machine tool* scie à ruban verticale *f*; ~ **hold** *n* CONTROL commande de synchronisation verticale *f*; ~ **hold button** *n* CONTROL bouton de commande de synchronisme vertical *m*; ~ **hold control** *n* TV réglage de la synchronisation de trame *m*; ~ **hole** *n* MINING trou de mine vertical *m*; ~ **illumination** *n* INSTRUMENT éclairage incident *m*; ~ **interval** *n* TV intervalle de trame *m*, intervalle vertical *m*; ~ **interval test signal** *n* TV signal d'essai entre trames *m*; ~ **lever** *n* PROD ENG poignée à action verticale *f*; ~ **lime kiln** *n* HEATING four à chaux vertical *m*; ~ **linearity control** *n* TV réglage de la linéarité de trame *m*; ~ **lock** *n* TV asservissement vertical *m*; ~ **milling attachment** *n* MECH ENG appareil à fraiser verticalement *m*; ~ **MOS transistor** *n* ELECTRON transistor MOS vertical *m*; ~ **output stage** *n* ELECTRON étage de sortie de la base de temps trames *m*, étage de sortie trames *m*; ~ **parity** *n* COMP, DP parité verticale *f*; ~ **plan** *n* GEOM plan vertical *m*; ~ **pneumatic pick longwall face** *n* MINING taille en dressant à marteaux-piqueurs *f*; ~ **polarization** *n* ELEC ENG, PHYS, TELECOM polarisation verticale *f*; ~ **power MOS transistor** *n* ELECTRON transistor MOS de puissance verticale *m*; ~ **rabbit** *n* NUCLEAR tube pneumatique vertical *m*; ~ **recording** *n* ACOUSTICS enregistrement vertical *m*; ~ **redundancy check** *n* (*VRC*) COMP, DP contrôle par redondance verticale *m*; ~ **reference unit** *n* SPACE *of spacecraft* centrale de référence de verticale *f*; ~ **scanning** *n* TV balayage vertical *m*; ~ **section** *n* CONST *of building* section *f*; ~ **seismic profile** *n* (*VSP*) PETR TECH profil sismique vertical *m* (*PSV*); ~ **seismo-**

graph *n* GEOPHYS sismographe vertical *m*; ~ **separation** *n* PROD ENG distance verticale *f*; ~ **shaft** *n* MINING puits vertical *m*; ~ **shaft furnace** *n* HEATING fourneau à cuve *m*; ~ **shaft Pelton Wheel** *n* FUELLESS roue Pelton à arbre vertical *f*; ~ **shore** *n* CONST chandelle *f*, étai vertical *m*; ~ **spacing** *n* PROD ENG espacement vertical *m*; ~ **speed indicator** *n* AERONAUT, SPACE *of spacecraft* variomètre *m*; ~ **stability** *n* TRANSP stabilité verticale *f*; ~ **surface-type broaching machine** *n* MECH ENG machine verticale à brocher les extérieurs *f*; ~ **sweep** *n* ELECTRON balayage des trames *m*, balayage vertical *m*; ~ **sync pulse** *n* TV signal de synchronisation de trame *m*; ~ **tabulation** *n* (*VT*) COMP, DP tabulation verticale *f*; ~ **takeoff** *n* MILIT décollage vertical *m*; ~ **takeoff and landing** *n* TRANSP décollage et atterrissage verticaux *m*; ~ **takeoff and landing aircraft** *n* (*VTOL aircraft*) AERONAUT avion à décollage et atterrissage verticaux *m* (*ADAV*); ~ **tangent screw** *n* INSTRUMENT vis de rappel du mouvement en site *f*; ~ **temperature gradient** *n* METEO gradient vertical de température *m*; ~ **throw** *n* GEOL rejet vertical *m*; ~ **tracking angle error** *n* ACOUSTICS erreur de piste verticale *f*; ~ **tracking force** *n* RECORDING force d'appui de la pointe de lecture *f*; ~ **vacuum sealer** *n* PACKAGING machine pour fermeture verticale sous vide *f*; ~ **water flow** *n* TEXTILES écoulement vertical de l'eau *m*; ~ **wipe** *n* CINEMAT volet vertical *m*

verticality: ~ **tolerance** *n* C&G tolérance de verticalité *f*

vertical-type: ~ **evaporator** *n* REFRIG évaporateur à tubes verticaux *m*

vervein: ~ **oil** *n* CHEM essence de verveine *f*

Very: ~ **Large Array** *n* (*VLA*) ASTRON *of dishes to form radio telescope* très grand réseau d'antennes *m* (*VLA*); ~ **Long Baseline Array** *n* (*VLBA*) ASTRON réseau d'antennes à très longue ligne de base *m* (*VLBA*); ~ **pistol** *n* NAUT *signal* pistolet lance-fusée *m*

vesicular *adj* GEOL vésiculeux

vessel *n* LAB EQUIP récipient *m*, MAR POLL navire *m*, NAUT bâtiment *m*, navire *m*, vaisseau *m*, OCEANOG navire *m*, PAPER TECH vaisseau *m*, PHYS récipient *m*, vase *m*, TEXTILES récipient *m*, TRANSP navire *m*; ~ **equipment** *n* OCEANOG gréement *m*; ~ **location** *n* NAUT *by satellite navigation* localisation du navire *f*; ~ **traffic services** *n pl* NAUT services de trafic des navires *m pl*

vestibule *n* HEATING *furnace* foyer *m*, RAIL vestibule d'accès *m*

vestigial: ~ **sideband** *n* ELECTRON bande latérale atténuée *f*, TELECOM, TV bande latérale restante *f*; ~ **sideband filter** *n* ELECTRON filtre de bande *m*; ~ **sideband signal** *n* ELECTRON signal à bande latérale atténuée *m*

vesuvianite *n* MINERAL vésuvianite *f*

vesuvin *n* CHEM brun de Bismark *m*, vésuvine *f*

VF *abbr* (*voice frequency*) ELECTRON, RAD PHYS, TELECOM fréquence vocale *f*

V-foil: ~ **craft** *n* TRANSP hydroptère à ailes en V *m*

V-gage *n* (AmE), **V-gauge** *n* C&G clé d'épaisseur *f*

V-gear *n* MECH ENG engrenage hélicoïdal double *m*, engrenage à chevrons *m*

V-groove *n* ELECTRON *transistors*, MECH ENG rainure en V *f*; ~ **clutch** *n* MECH ENG embrayage à coins *m*; ~ **etching** *n* ELECTRON *transistors* gravure de la rainure en V *f*

VHD *abbr* (*video high-density disc*) OPT disque VHD *m* (*disque électrostatique*)

VHF[1] *abbr* (*very high-frequency*) ELECTRON, SPACE, TE-

LECOM, TV, WAVE PHYS VHF *(très haute fréquence)*

VHF:[2] **~ and UHF tuner** *n* TV sélecteur d'ondes métriques et décimétriques *m*; **~ frequency band** *n* TV bande de fréquence VHF *f*; **~ omnidirectional radio range** *n* *(VOR)* AERONAUT radiophare omnidirectionnel VHF *m*; **~ radio telephone** *n* NAUT radiotéléphone VHF *m*; **~ signal** *n* ELECTRON signal VHF *m*; **~ signal generator** *n* ELECTRON générateur VHF *m*, générateur de signaux VHF *m*

VHFO *abbr (very high-frequency omnirange)* TRANSP radiophare omnidirectionnel VHF *m*

VHS *abbr (video home system)* TV système VHS *m*

VHS-C: **~ system** *n (video home system-compact)* TV système VHS-C *m*

VI[1] *abbr (volume indicator)* RECORDING vumètre *m*

VI:[2] **~ meter** *n (volume indicator meter)* TV vumètre *m*

VIA *abbr (video indicate active)* TELECOM indication vidéo active *f*

viable: **~ bacterium** *n* WATER SUPP bactérie revivifiable *f*

viaduct *n* CONST pont viaduc *m*, viaduc *m*

vial *n* C&G fiole *f*, CHEM fiole *f*, flacon *m*, LAB EQUIP *glassware* fiole *f*

vibrate *vt* CONST *concrete placing* vibrer

vibrated: **~ concrete** *n* CONST béton vibré *m*

vibrating: **~ ball mill** *n* LAB EQUIP *grinding equipment* broyeur vibrant à billes *m*; **~ contact regulator** *n* CONTROL régulateur à contacts vibrants *m*; **~ feeder** *n* PROD ENG alimentateur vibrant *m*; **~ feeders and conveyors** *n pl* MECH ENG distributeurs et transporteurs vibrants *m pl*; **~ grizzly** *n* COAL TECH grille vibrante *f*; **~ reed frequency meter** *n* ELEC ENG fréquencemètre à lames vibrantes *m*; **~ rod mill** *n* COAL TECH broyeur vibrant à barre *m*; **~ roller** *n* CONST compacteur à cylindre vibrant *m*, rouleau vibrant *m*, vibro-compacteur *m*; **~ sample magnetometer** *n* NUCLEAR magnétomètre à échantillon vibrant *m*; **~ screen** *n* CHEM tamis à secousses *m*, COAL TECH crible vibrant *m*, vibrocrible *m*; **~ sheepsfoot roller** *n* CONST pied de mouton vibrant *m*; **~ stirrer** *n* LAB EQUIP agitateur vibrant *m*; **~ string** *n* PHYS corde vibrante *f*; **~ system** *n* WAVE PHYS *causing waves* système vibrant *m*; **~ table** *n* C&G table vibrante *f*, COAL TECH table secoueuse *f*, table à secousses *f*

vibration *n* MECH, METALL vibration *f*, PHYS mouvement oscillatoire *m*, oscillation *f*, vibration *f*, PRINT, SAFETY vibration *f*; **~ analysis** *n* MECH analyse vibratoire *f*; **~ and shock pick-up** *n* MECH ENG capteur de vibrations et de chocs *m*; **~ conveyor** *n* FOOD TECH transporteur à vibrations *m*; **~ damper** *n* AERONAUT, MECH ENG, REFRIG, VEHICLES *in engine* amortisseur de vibrations *m*; **~ damper and shock absorber** *n* SAFETY amortisseur de vibrations et de chocs *m*; **~ galvanometer** *n* ELEC galvanomètre à vibrations *m*, PHYS galvanomètre de résonance *m*, galvanomètre à vibrations *m*; **~ generator** *n* SPACE *on spacecraft* générateur de vibrations *m*, pot vibrant *m*; **~ hazards** *n pl* SAFETY dangers des vibrations *m pl*; **~ isolator** *n* GEOPHYS isolateur de vibration *m*; **~ measurer** *n* INSTRUMENT instrument de mesure des vibrations *m*; **~ recorder** *n* INSTRUMENT enregistreur des vibrations *m*; **~ severity** *n* SAFETY intensité vibratoire *f*; **~ test** *n* AERONAUT essai de vibration *m*, CONTROL contrôle de vibration *m*, METR, TESTING essai de vibration *m*

vibrational: **~ energy** *n* NUCLEAR *of molecule* énergie de vibration *f*; **~ entropy** *n* METALL entropie de vibration *f*; **~ quantum number** *n* PHYS nombre quantique d'os-

cillations *m*, nombre quantique de vibrations *m*; **~ spectrum** *n* PHYS spectre des vibrations *m*

vibration-rotation: **~ spectrum** *n* PHYS spectre de vibration-rotation *m*

vibrato *n* ACOUSTICS vibrato *m*

vibrator *n* CONST *concreting equipment*, ELEC ENG vibreur *m*, PRINT table d'encrage *f*, table de mouillage *f*, SPACE générateur de vibrations *m*

vibratory: **~ feeder** *n* MECH bol vibrant *m*, PACKAGING alimentation vibratoire *f*; **~ hopper** *n* PACKAGING trémie vibratoire *f*; **~ sifter** *n* PACKAGING tamis à châssis vibrant *m*

vibrocompaction *n* NUCLEAR vibrocompaction *f*, vibrotassement *m*

vibroseis *n* PETR vibroseis *m*

vice *n* (BrE) MECH *tools*, MECH ENG étau *m*; **~ bench** *n* (BrE) PROD ENG établi roulant pour étaux *m*, étau roulant *m*; **~ cap** *n* (BrE) MECH ENG *of soft metal* mordache *f*, *of wood* bois à limer *m*, entibois *m*, estibois *m*; **~ clamp** *n* (BrE) MECH ENG *of soft metal* bois à limer *m*, mordache *f*, *of wood* entibois *m*, mordache *f*; **~ grips** *n pl* (BrE) MECH ENG pince-étau *f*; **~ jaw** *n* (BrE) MECH ENG *of soft metal* bois à limer *m*, mordache *f*, *of wood* entibois *m*, mordache *f*; **~ jaws** *n pl* (BrE) PRINT mâchoires *f pl*; **~ plate** *n* (BrE) MECH ENG *drilling machine* plateau-étau *m*, étau-plateau *m*; **~ press** *n* (BrE) MECH ENG presse à vis *f*; **~ sliding between parallel bars** *n* (BrE) MECH ENG *drilling machine* étau à barres parallèles *m*; **~ with clamp** *n* (BrE) MECH ENG étau à agrafes *m*, étau à griffes *m*; **~ with detachable jaws** *n* (BrE) MECH ENG étau à mâchoires rapportées *m*; **~ with inserted jaws** *n* (BrE) MECH ENG étau à mâchoires rapportées *m*; **~ with protected screw** *n* (BrE) MECH ENG étau à vis cachée *m*

vicidity *n* CHEM élevée *f*

vicinal *adj* CHEM vicinal

Vickers: **~ hardness testing machine** *n* MECH ENG machine d'essais de dureté Vickers *f*

video *n* COMP, DP, TELECOM, TV vidéo *f*; **~ amplification** *n* ELECTRON amplification vidéo *f*; **~ amplifier** *n* ELECTRON, PHYS, TV amplificateur vidéo *m*; **~ assist** *n* CINEMAT reprise vidéo *f*; **~ bandwidth** *n* COMP, DP, TV largeur de bande vidéo *f*; **~ cable** *n* ELEC ENG câble vidéo *m*; **~ carrier** *n* TV porteuse vidéo *f*; **~ channel** *n* TV canal vidéo *m*, voie vidéo *f*; **~ check** *n* CONTROL contrôle d'image *m*; **~ color analyser** *n* (AmE), **~ colour analyser** *n* (BrE) CINEMAT machine à étalonner à lecture vidéo *f*; **~ command fast-update request** *n* *(VCU)* TELECOM commande vidéo de demande de rafraîchissement rapide *f*; **~ command freeze-picture request** *n* *(VCF)* TELECOM commande vidéo de demande de gel de l'image *f*; **~ confidence head** *n* TV tête de vérification d'enregistrement *f*; **~ control room** *n* TV régie image *f*; **~ display** *n* COMP moniteur vidéo *m*, écran *m*; **~ display unit** *n* *(VDU)* TV console de visualisation *f*, visu *m*; **~ distribution amplifier** *n* *(VDA)* TV amplificateur de distribution vidéo *m*; **~ feedback circuit** *n* TV circuit de retour vidéo *m*; **~ frequency** *n* ELECTRON fréquence vidéo *f*, PHYS, TELECOM, TV vidéofréquence *f*; **~ frequency converter** *n* TV transcodeur vidéo *m*; **~ head** *n* TV tête vidéo *f*; **~ head alignment** *n* TV réglage de la tête vidéo *m*; **~ head assembly** *n* TV bloc de têtes vidéo *m*; **~ head optimizer** *n* TV optimiseur de têtes vidéo *m*; **~ high-density disc** *n* (BrE) *(VHD)* OPT disque électrostatique *m* *(disque VHD)*; **~ high-density disk** *n* (AmE) *see video high-*

density disc; ~ **home system** *n (VHS)* TV système VHS *m*; ~ **home system-compact** *n (VHS-C system)* TV système VHS-C *m*; ~ **indicate active** *n (VIA)* TELECOM indication vidéo active *f*; ~ **indicate ready-to-activate** *n (VIR)* TELECOM indication vidéo prête à être activée *f*; ~ **indicate suppressed** *n (VIS)* TELECOM indication vidéo supprimée *f*; ~ **input** *n* TV entrée vidéo *f*; ~ **level** *n* TV niveau vidéo *m*; ~ **level indicator** *n* TV indicateur du niveau vidéo *m*; ~ **long play** *n (VLP)* OPT disque vidéo longue durée *m*; ~ **loop** *n* TELECOM boucle vidéo *f*; ~ **monitoring** *n* CONTROL contrôle d'image *m*; ~ **output** *n* TV sortie vidéo *f*; ~ **phase reversal** *n* TV inversion de polarité vidéo *f*; ~ **pre-emphasis** *n* TV préaccentuation vidéo *f*; ~ **projector** *n* TV projecteur vidéo *m*; ~ **record current** *n* TV courant d'enregistrement vidéo *m*; ~ **recorder** *n* TV magnétoscope *m*; ~ **recording** *n* TELECOM enregistrement vidéo *m*; ~ **signal** *n* ELECTRON, PHYS, SPACE *communications*, TELECOM signal vidéo *m*, TV signal d'image complet *m*, signal vidéo *m*; ~ **signal pulse** *n* TV impulsion vidéo *f*; ~ **signal with blanking** *n* TV signal vision à suppression *m*; ~ **switch** *n* TELECOM commutateur vidéo *m*; ~ **switching matrix** *n* TV grille de commutation vidéo *f*; ~ **synthesizer** *n* TV synthétiseur vidéo *m*; ~ **terminal** *n* COMP, DP terminal vidéo *m*; ~ **track** *n* TV piste image *f*, piste vidéo *f*; ~ **transmission** *n* TELECOM vidéotransmission *f*

videocassette *n* TV vidéocassette *f*; ~ **recorder** *n* TV magnétoscope à cassette *m*

videoclip *n* TV vidéoclip *m*

videoconference *n* SPACE, TELECOM visioconférence *f*

videodisc *n* OPT, TV vidéodisque *m*; ~ **player** (BrE) OPT, TV lecteur de vidéodisque *m*; ~ **recording** *n* (BrE) TV enregistrement sur vidéodisque *m*; ~ **system** *n* (BrE) OPT système de vidéodisque *m*

videodisk *n* (AmE) *see videodisc*

videography *n* COMP, DP, TELECOM vidéographie *f*

videophone *n* TELECOM visiophone *m* ~ **switching system** *n* TELECOM autocommutateur visiophonique *m*

videotape *n* PHYS bande magnétoscopique *f*, TELECOM, TV bande vidéo *f*; ~ **dubbing** *n* TV repiquage vidéo *m*; ~ **facilities** *n pl* TV moyens techniques vidéo *m pl*; ~ **library** *n* TV vidéothèque *f*; ~ **player** *n* TV magnétoscope de lecture *m*; ~ **recorder** *n (VTR)* TV magnétoscope *m*

videotaping *n* TV enregistrement vidéo *m*

videotex *n* COMP, DP, TELECOM vidéographie interactive *f*, vidéotex *m*; ~ **gateway** *n* TELECOM point d'accès vidéotex *m*; ~ **PAD** *n* TELECOM vidéo PAD *f*; ~ **server** *n* TELECOM serveur vidéotex *m*

videoware *n* TV programme vidéo *m*

vidicon *n* ELECTRON vidicon *m*; ~ **camera** *n* TV caméra à tube vidicon *f*; ~ **tube** *n* ELECTRON tube vidicon *m*

view *vt* CINEMAT *film* visionner

viewdata: ~ **terminal** *n* TV terminal de vidéotex *m*

viewer *n* TV téléspectateur *m*

viewfinder *n* CINEMAT, PHOTO *camera*, SPACE *on spacecraft* viseur *m*; ~ **eyepiece** *n* CINEMAT oculaire de viseur *m*, PHOTO fenêtre de viseur *f*, *of camera* oculaire de visée *m*; ~ **with hood** *n* PHOTO viseur à capuchon *m*

viewing *n* PRINT observation *f*, visualisation *f*; ~ **chamber** *n* INSTRUMENT chambre d'observation *f*; ~ **lens** *n* ASTRON lentille de visée *f*, PHOTO objectif de visée *m*; ~ **magnifier** *n* PHOTO loupe de visée *f*; ~ **port** *n* SPACE *on spacecraft* hublot d'observation *m*; ~ **theatre** *n* CINEMAT salle de projection *f*, salle de vision *f*; ~ **transformation** *n* COMP, DP transformation fenêtre

clôture *f*; ~ **window** *n* COMP, DP fenêtre de visualisation *f*, INSTRUMENT fenêtre d'observation *f*

vigilance: ~ **device** *n* RAIL dispositif de vigilance *m*

Vigneron-Dahl: ~ **trawl** *n* OCEANOG VD, Vigneron-Dahl *m*

vignette *n* CINEMAT cache *m*, masque *m*, PRINT fond tramé en dégradé *m*, vignette *f*

vignetting *n* CINEMAT effet de cache *m*, effet de masque *m*, vignettage *m*, PHOTO diaphragmation en oeil de chat *f*

Viking: ~ **lander** *n* ASTRON atterrisseur Viking *m*; ~ **orbiter** *n* ASTRON orbiteur Viking *m*

VI-meter *n* ACOUSTICS, RECORDING VU-mètre *f*

vinic *adj* CHEM vinique

Vinten: ~ **crane** *n* CINEMAT grue Vinten *f*

vinyl *n* CHEM vinyle *m*; ~ **acetate** *n* PROP MAT acétate de vinyle *m*; ~ **lacquer** *n* CONST laque vinylique *f*

vinylacetylene *n* CHEM vinylacétylène *m*

vinylation *n* CHEM vinylation *f*

vinylbenzene *n* CHEM vinylbenzène *m*

vinyl-coated: ~ **fin** *n* REFRIG ailette protégée par vinyle *f*

vinylidene *n* CHEM vinylidène *m*

vinylite *n* CHEM vinylite *f*

vinylog *n* CHEM vinylogue *m*

vinylogous *adj* CHEM vinylogue

vinylpyridine *n* CHEM vinylpyridine *f*

viocid *n* CHEM chlorure de méthylrosalinium *m*

violent: ~ **boiling** *n* NUCLEAR ébullition violente *f*

violet: ~ **square signal** *n* RAIL carré violet *m*

violuric *adj* CHEM violurique

VIR *abbr (video indicate ready-to-activate)* TELECOM indication vidéo prête à être activée *f*

virgin[1] *adj* COMP, DP vierge

virgin:[2] ~ **medium** *n* COMP, DP support vierge *m*; ~ **neutron** *n* NUCLEAR neutron vierge *m*

Virgo *n* ASTRON Vierge *f*; ~ **supercluster** *n* ASTRON super-amas de galaxies de la Vierge *m*

virial: ~ **theorem** *n* PHYS théorème du viriel *m*

viridine *n* CHEM viridine *f*

virtual[1] *adj* COMP, DP virtuel

virtual:[2] ~ **call service** *n* COMP, DP service de communication virtuelle *m*; ~ **channel** *n (VC)* TELECOM canal virtuel *m*, voie virtuelle *f*; ~ **channel connection** *n (CRF, VCC)* TELECOM connexion de canal virtuel *f*, connexion de voie virtuelle *f*; ~ **channel connection endpoint** *n (VCCE)* TELECOM extrémité de connexion de canal virtuel *f*; ~ **channel connection-related function** *n* TELECOM fonction liée à la connexion sur les VC *f*; ~ **channel identifier** *n (VCI)* TELECOM identificateur de canal virtuel *m*, identificateur de voie virtuelle *m*; ~ **charged particle** *n* PART PHYS particule virtuelle chargée *f*; ~ **circuit** *n* COMP, DP, TELECOM circuit virtuel *m*; ~ **connection** *n* COMP, DP connexion virtuelle *f*; ~ **container** *n* TELECOM CTV, conteneur virtuel *m*; ~ **container-n** *n (VC-n)* TELECOM conteneur virtuel-n *m*; ~ **image** *n* CINEMAT, PHOTO, PHYS, WAVE PHYS image virtuelle *f*; ~ **machine** *n* COMP, DP machine virtuelle *f*; ~ **memory** *n* COMP mémoire virtuelle *f*; ~ **memory system** *n (VMS)* COMP, DP système à mémoire virtuelle *m*; ~ **neutral particle** *n* PART PHYS particule virtuelle neutre *f*; ~ **object** *n* PHYS objet virtuel *m*; ~ **particle** *n* PART PHYS particule virtuelle *f*; ~ **path** *n (VP)* TELECOM conduit virtuel *m*, trajet virtuel *m*; ~ **path connection** *n (VPC)* TELECOM connexion de conduit virtuel *f*, connexion de trajet virtuel *f*; ~ **path connection endpoint** *n (VPCE)* TELECOM extrémité de connexion de trajet virtuel *f*; ~ **path connection-related function** *n (CRF)* TELECOM fonction liée à la connexion sur les VP *f*; ~ **path identifier** *n (VPI)* TELECOM identificateur de conduit virtuel *m*, identificateur de trajet virtuel *m*; ~ **reality** *n* COMP réalité virtuelle *f*; ~ **sound source** *n* ACOUSTICS source sonore virtuelle *f*; ~ **storage** *n* COMP mémoire virtuelle *f*; ~ **terminal** *n (VT)* COMP, DP terminal virtuel *m*

virtual-circuit: ~ **bearer service** *n* TELECOM service support de circuit virtuel *m*; ~ **switch** *n (VCS)* TELECOM commutateur de circuits virtuels *m (CCV)*; ~ **switching node** *n* TELECOM centre de commutation en mode virtuel *m*

virus *n* COMP, DP virus *m*

VIS *abbr (video indicate suppressed)* TELECOM indication vidéo supprimée *f*

visbreaker *n* PETR TECH viscoréducteur *m*

viscid *adj* CHEM, FLUID PHYS gluant, visqueux

viscidity *n* CHEM, FLUID PHYS viscosité *f*

viscin *n* CHEM viscine *f*

viscoelasticity *n* P&R visco-élasticité *f*

viscometer *n* CHEM TECH, FLUID PHYS, LAB EQUIP *instrument*, P&R *instrument*, PETR TECH, PHYS viscomètre *m*, viscosimètre *m*

viscoplastic *adj* GAS TECH, PROP MAT *polycrystal* viscoplastique

viscose *n* CHEM viscose *f*; ~ **fiber** *n* (AmE), ~ **fibre** *n* (BrE) PROD ENG fibre de viscose *f*; ~ **pulp** *n* PROD ENG pâte de viscose *f*

viscosimeter *n* CHEM TECH, FLUID PHYS, LAB EQUIP *instrument*, P&R *instrument*, PETR TECH, PHYS viscomètre *m*, viscosimètre *m*

viscosity *n* CHEM, COAL TECH, FLUID PHYS, GAS TECH, P&R, PETR, PETR TECH, PHYS, PROPmat, THERMOD viscosité *f*; ~ **coefficient** *n* FLUID PHYS, THERMOD coefficient de viscosité *m*; ~ **index** *n* FLUID PHYS, PETR TECH *of petrol*, THERMOD, VEHICLES *of oil* indice de viscosité *m*; ~ **index improver** *n* PETR TECH améliorant d'indice de viscosité *m*

viscosity-gravity: ~ **constant** *n* THERMOD constante viscosité-gravité *f*

viscosity-temperature: ~ **characteristics** *n pl* THERMOD tenue à la viscosité-température *f*; ~ **coefficient** *n* THERMOD coefficient viscosité-température *m*

viscostatic *adj* CHEM viscostatique

viscous[1] *adj* CHEM, FLUID PHYS, FOOD TECH, PHYS visqueux

viscous:[2] ~ **action** *n* FLUID PHYS effet de la viscosité *m*; ~ **clutch** *n* VEHICLES *transmission* viscocoupleur *m*; ~ **damping** *n* MECH amortissement visqueux *m*; ~ **flow** *n* FOOD TECH, METALL, NUCLEAR, PHYS écoulement visqueux *m*; ~ **flow equation** *n* FLUID PHYS équation des écoulements visqueux *f*; ~ **force** *n* FLUID PHYS force de viscosité *f*; ~ **incompressible flow** *n* FLUID PHYS écoulement visqueux incompressible *m*; ~ **stress** *n* FLUID PHYS contrainte visqueuse *f*

vise *n* (AmE) *see* vice

visibility *n* METEO, NAUT, PHYS visibilité *f* ~ **distance** *n* TRANSP distance de visibilité *f*; ~ **distance measuring equipment** *n* TRANSP équipement de mesure de la distance de visibilité *m*

visible: ~ **grains** *n pl* GEOL *sedimentology, mineralogy* éléments figurés *m pl*, éléments visibles à l'oeil nu *m pl*; ~ **horizon** *n* NAUT *celestial navigation* horizon visuel *m*; ~ **light** *n* OPT, TELECOM visible *m*, WAVE PHYS ondes lumineuses *f pl*; ~ **radiation** *n* OPT lumière *f*, rayonnement visible *m*, SPACE, TELECOM rayonnement visible *m*; ~ **region** *n* PHYS champ visible *m*; ~ **signal** *n* CONTROL signal visible *m*; ~ **spectrum** *n* PHYS spectre visible *m*; ~ **stars** *n pl* ASTRON étoiles visibles *f pl*

vision: ~ **carrier** *n* TV porteuse image *f*; ~ **clap** *n* CINEMAT claquette image *f*; ~ **control room** *n* TV régie image *f*; ~ **mixer** *n* TV mélangeur vidéo *m*, pupitre de régie image *m*

visor *n* SAFETY *eye shield* pare-soleil *m*, *face shield* visière *f*

visual:[1] ~ **exempted** *adj* AERONAUT à vue exempté

visual:[2] ~ **alarm** *n* TELECOM alarme visuelle *f*; ~ **approach** *n* AERONAUT approche visuelle *f*; ~ **binary** *n* ASTRON étoile binaire visuelle *f*; ~ **carded packaging** *n* PACKAGING présentation sous carte *f*; ~ **display unit** *n* VDU COMP, DP, PHYS, TELECOM, TV console de visualisation *f*, écran de visualisation *m*; ~ **inspection** *n* CONTROL contrôle visuel *m*, METR examen visuel *m*; ~ **leak test** *n* REFRIG contrôle visuel d'étanchéité *m*; ~ **magnitude** *n* ASTRON magnitude visuelle *f*; ~ **pack** *n* PACKAGING emballage transparent sur carton *m*; ~ **range meter** *n* INSTRUMENT instrument à mesurer la visibilité *m*; ~ **signal** *n* CONTROL signal optique *m*; ~ **threshold of illumination** *n* AERONAUT seuil visuel de l'éclairement lumineux *m*

visual-audible: ~ **signal** *n* COMP, DP signal opto-acoustique *m*

visualization *n* COMP, DP visualisation *f*

vital: ~ **stain** *n* COLOURS teinture vitale *f*

vitellin *n* CHEM vitelline *f*

Viterbi: ~ **decoding** *n* TELECOM décodage de Viterbi *m*

vitrea: ~ **cutter** *n* C&G règle de découpe automatique *f*

vitreous[1] *adj* CHEM hyalin, vitreux

vitreous:[2] ~ **enamel** *n* C&G, COATINGS émail vitrifié *m*; ~ **enamel label** *n* C&G étiquette vitrifiée *f*; ~ **silica** *n* C&G silice vitreuse *f*, OPT silice fondue *f*, silice vitreuse *f*, TELECOM silice vitreuse *f*; ~ **state** *n* C&G état vitreux *m*

vitric: ~ **tuff** *n* GEOL *fine-grained lithified ash* cinérite *f*

vitrifiable: ~ **colors** *n pl* (AmE), ~ **colours** *n pl* (BrE) C&G couleurs vitrifiables *f pl*

vitrification *n* CHEM vitrification *f*

vitrify *vt* COATINGS vitrifier

vitriol *n* CHEM acide sulfurique *m*, acide vitriolique *m*, vitriol *m*

vitriolic: ~ **acid** *n* CHEM acide sulfurique *m*, acide vitriolique *m*, vitriol *m*

vitriolization *n* CHEM vitriolisation *f*

vivianite *n* MINERAL vivianite *f*

vizor *n* see visor

VLA *abbr (Very Large Array)* ASTRON VLA *(très grand réseau d'antennes)*

VLBA *abbr (Very Long Baseline Array)* ASTRON VLBA *(réseau d'antennes à très longue ligne de base)*

VLCC *abbr (very large crude carrier)* PETR TECH TGTB *(très gros transporteur de brut)*

VLP *abbr (video long play)* OPT disque vidéo longue durée *m*

VLSI[1] *abbr (very large-scale integration)* COMP, DP, ELECTRON, TELECOM intégration à très grande échelle *f*

VLSI:[2] ~ **chip** *n* COMP, DP puce VLSI *f*; ~ **circuit** *n* TELECOM circuit VLSI *m*, circuit à très grande intégration *m*

VMOS: ~ **transistor** *n* ELECTRON transistor VMOS *m*

VMS *abbr (virtual memory system)* COMP, DP système à mémoire virtuelle *m*

vocal: ~ **frequency** *n* PHYS, RECORDING, TELECOM fréquence vocale *f*

vocoder *n* COMP vocodeur *m*, DP synthétiseur vocal *m*, RECORDING codeur à fréquences vocales *m*, synthétiseur de parole *m*, TELECOM codeur à fréquences vocales *m*

vocoding *n* TELECOM codage de la voix *m*

VOD *abbr (velocity of detonation)* MINING vitesse de détonation *f*

vogesite *n* (AmE), **vogesyte** *n* (BrE) PETR vogésite *f*

voice *n* COMP, DP voix *f* ~ **activation** *n* TELECOM commande par la voix *f*; ~ **amplifier** *n* TELECOM amplificateur téléphonique *m*; ~ **annotation** *n* TELECOM annotation vocale *f*; ~ **channel** *n* COMP, DP, TELECOM voie téléphonique *f*; ~ **coder** *n* TELECOM vocodeur *m*; ~ **control** *n* TELECOM commande par la voix *f*; ~ **detector** *n* SPACE *communications* détecteur de parole *m*; ~ **dialler** *n* TELECOM composeur vocal *m*; ~ **dialling** *n* TELECOM numérotation par commande vocale *f*; ~ **digitization** *n* TELECOM numérisation des signaux vocaux *f*; ~ **frequency** *n (VF)* ELECTRON, RAD PHYS, TELECOM fréquence vocale *f*; ~ **grade** *n* TELECOM *circuit* qualité téléphonique *f*; ~ **level test** *n* RECORDING essai de niveau pour la voix *m*; ~ **mail** *n* TELECOM audiomessagerie *f*; ~ **mailbox** *n* TELECOM boîte à lettres vocale *f*, boîte vocale *f*; ~ **message processor** *n* TELECOM serveur de messagerie vocale *m*; ~ **messaging** *n* TELECOM messagerie vocale *f*; ~ **network** *n* TELECOM réseau téléphonique *m*; ~ **operation** *n* CONTROL commande vocale *f*; ~ **output** *n* COMP, DP sortie vocale *f*; ~ **privacy** *n* TELECOM secret des conversations *m*; ~ **recognition** *n* TELECOM reconnaissance de la parole *f*; ~ **recognizer** *n* TELECOM unité de reconnaissance de la parole *f*; ~ **recorder** *n* SPACE *on spacecraft* enregistreur de conversations *m*; ~ **response** *n* ELECTRON, TELECOM réponse vocale *f*; ~ **response unit** *n* TELECOM unité à réponse vocale *f*; ~ **sensor** *n* SPACE *communications* détection de parole *f*; ~ **signal** *n* CONTROL signal vocal *m*; ~ **track** *n* RECORDING piste parole *f*

voice-activated *adj* TELECOM commandé par fréquence vocale

voice-band *n* COMP bande téléphonique *f*, DP bande audio *f*, canal téléphonique *m*, voie téléphonique *f*, TELECOM bande téléphonique *f*, bande vocale *f*; ~ **data detector** *n* TELECOM détecteur de données à fréquence vocale *m*; ~ **data ratio** *n* TELECOM rapport de données dans la bande des fréquences vocales *m*

voice-controlled: ~ **operation** *n* TELECOM commutation à commande vocale *f*

voice-data: ~ **entry** *n* COMP, DP entrée vocale de données *f*; ~ **packet switch** *n* TELECOM commutateur de paquets téléphonie-données *m*

voice-operated[1] *adj* CONTROL commandé par la voix, à commande vocale

voice-operated:[2] ~ **relay** *n* TELECOM commutation à commande vocale *f*; ~ **switch** *n* TELECOM commutateur commandé par la voix *m*; ~ **switching** *n* TELECOM commutation à commande vocale *f*

voice-switched *adj* TELECOM commuté par la voix

voice-switching: ~ **equipment** *n* TELECOM appareil à commutation vocale *m*

void *n* C&G retassure *f*, CHEM bulle *f*, vide *m*, COAL TECH pore *m*, vide *m*, METALL cavité *f*, P&R *defect* bulle *f*, PROP MAT cavité *f*; ~ **coalescence** *n* METALL coalescence des cavités *f*; ~ **formation** *n* METALL, PROP MAT formation de cavités *f*; ~ **growth** *n* METALL croissance des cavités *f*; ~ **ratio** *n* COAL TECH indice des vides *m*,

PROD ENG rapport de vide *m*; ~ **volume** *n* TEXTILES volume de vide *m*

voile *n* TEXTILES voile *f*

Volans *n* ASTRON Poisson Volant *m*

volatile[1] *adj* CHEM gazéifiable, volatil, DP, P&R, TEXTILES volatil

volatile[2] *n* GEOL gaz *m*, substance volatile *f*; ~ **body** *n* COAL TECH corps volatil *m*; ~ **memory** *n* COMP, ELEC ENG mémoire non rémanente *f*, mémoire volatile *f*

volatility *n* CHEM, METALL, P&R, PROP MAT, TEXTILES volatilité *f*

volatilization *n* CHEM subtilisation *f*, volatilisation *f*

volatilize[1] *vt* CHEM volatiliser, évaporer

volatilize[2] *vi* CHEM se volatiliser, TEXTILES s'évaporer

volborthite *n* MINERAL volborthite *f*

volcanic[1] *adj* GEOL, PETR volcanique

volcanic:[2] ~ **cinders** *n pl* GEOL cendres volcaniques *f pl*, scorie *f*; ~ **cone** *n* GEOPHYS cône volcanique *m*; ~ **ejecta** *n pl* GEOL projections volcaniques *f pl*; ~ **ejectamenta** *n pl* GEOL projections volcaniques *f pl*; ~ **quake** *n* GEOPHYS tremblement volcanique *m*; ~ **vent** *n* GEOL canal d'éruption *m*, cheminée volcanique *f*, OCEANOG évent volcanique *m*

volcanism *n* ASTRON, GEOL volcanisme *m*

volley *n* MILIT salve *f*, *of firearm* décharge *f*

volt *n* ELEC, ELEC ENG, METR, PHYS volt *m*

voltage *n* ELEC, ELEC ENG, PHYS, TELECOM, VEHICLES *electrical system, ignition* tension *f*, voltage *m*; ~ **amplification** *n* ELECTRON amplification de tension *f*; ~ **amplifier** *n* ELECTRON amplificateur de tension *m*; ~ **antinode** *n* ELEC ENG ventre de tension *m*; ~ **balance** *n* ELEC équilibre de la tension *m*; ~ **comparator** *n* ELEC ENG comparateur de tension *m*; ~ **comparison** *n* ELEC ENG comparaison de tension *f*; ~ **control** *n* ELEC réglage de tension *m*; ~ **difference** *n* ELEC différence de potentiel *f*; ~ **divider** *n* ELEC, ELEC ENG, PHYS, TELECOM diviseur de tension *m*, TV diviseur de tension *m*, potentiomètre *m*; ~ **doubler** *n* ELEC *rectifier circuit* doubleur de tension *m*; ~ **drop** *n* ELEC chute de tension *f*, ELEC ENG chute de tension *f*, perte de tension *f*, PHYS, PROD ENG chute de tension *f*; ~ **dropping resistor** *n* ELEC ENG résistance chutrice *f*; ~ **feedback** *n* ELEC ENG contre-réaction de tension *f*; ~ **fluctuation** *n* ELEC *supply* fluctuation de tension *f*; ~ **gain** *n* ELEC ENG gain de tension *m*; ~ **generator** *n* PHYS générateur de tension *m*; ~ **gradient** *n* ELEC gradient de tension *m*; ~ **indicator** *n* ELEC ENG indicateur de tension *m*; ~ **jump** *n* ELEC saut de tension *m*; ~ **level** *n* PROD ENG niveau de tension *m*; ~ **limiter** *n* ELEC limiteur de tension *m*; ~ **loss** *n* ELEC chute de tension *f*; ~ **multiplier** *n* ELEC *rectifier circuit*, ELEC ENG multiplicateur de tension *m*; ~ **polarity** *n* ELEC ENG polarité de la tension *f*; ~ **pulse** *n* ELEC impulsion de tension *f*; ~ **reference** *n* ELEC ENG référence de tension *f*; ~ **reference diode** *n* ELECTRON diode de référence de tension *f*; ~ **reference tube** *n* ELEC ENG tube de référence de tension *m*; ~ **regulation** *n* ELEC ENG régulation de tension *f*; ~ **regulator** *n* AUTO, COMP régulateur de tension *m*, CONTROL régulateur conjoncteur-disjoncteur *m*, régulateur de tension *m*, DP, ELEC, ELEC ENG, PROD ENG, TV, VEHICLES *electrical system* régulateur de tension *m*; ~ **regulator diode** *n* ELECTRON diode régulatrice de tension *f*; ~ **regulator tube** *n* ELEC ENG tube stabilisateur de tension *m*; ~ **relay** *n* ELEC ENG relais de tension *m*; ~ **selector** *n* ELEC ENG sélecteur de tension *m*; ~ **source** *n* ELEC ENG, PHYS source de tension *f*; ~ **spike** *n* ELEC ENG pointe de tension *f*; ~ **stabilizer** *n* ELEC ENG stabilisateur de tension *m*; ~ **stabilizer tube** *n* ELEC ENG tube stabilisateur de tension *m*; ~ **standing-wave ratio** *n* *(VSWR)* PHYS rapport d'ondes stationnaires *m* *(ROS)*; ~ **step** *n* PHYS marche de tension *f*, saut de potentiel *m*, saut de tension *m*, échelon de tension *m*; ~ **surge** *n* ELEC ENG onde de tension *f*, TELECOM surtension *f*; ~ **tester screwdriver** *n* MECH ENG tournevis détecteur de tension *m*; ~ **to earth** *n* (BrE) *(cf voltage to ground)* ELEC ENG tension par rapport à la masse *f*, tension par rapport à la terre *f*; ~ **to ground** *n* (AmE) *(cf voltage to earth)* ELEC ENG tension par rapport à la masse *f*, tension par rapport à la terre *f*; ~ **transformer** *n* ELEC, ELEC ENG transformateur de tension *m*

voltage-controlled: ~ **capacitor** *n* ELEC ENG condensateur commandé en tension *m*; ~ **input** *n* ELEC ENG entrée commandée en tension *f*; ~ **oscillator** *n* *(VCO)* ELECTRON, SPACE *communications*, TELECOM oscillateur commandé en tension *m*, oscillateur à régulation de tension *m*

voltage-current: ~ **characteristic** *n* ELEC ENG caractéristique tension-courant *f*

voltage-dependent: ~ **resistor** *n* ELEC ENG résistance sensible à la tension *f*

voltage-regulated: ~ **power supply** *n* ELEC ENG alimentation régulée en tension *f*

voltage-regulating: ~ **transformer** *n* ELEC ENG transformateur régulateur de tension *m*

voltage-stabilized: ~ **power supply** *n* ELEC alimentation stabilisée *f*

voltage-to-frequency: ~ **conversion** *n* ELEC ENG conversion tension-fréquence *f*; ~ **converter** *n* ELEC ENG convertisseur tension-fréquence *m*

voltaic: ~ **cell** *n* ELEC pile galvanique *f*; ~ **pile** *n* ELEC ENG pile voltaïque *f*

voltameter *n* (BrE) CHEM, ELEC ENG, PHYS voltmètre *m*

voltammeter *n* (AmE) *see* voltameter

Volterra: ~ **dislocation** *n* METALL dislocation de Volterra *f*

voltmeter *n* ELEC, ELEC ENG, PHYS voltmètre *m*

volume *n* ACOUSTICS volume *m*, volume sonore *m*, CHEM, COMP, DP, GEOM, MATH volume *m*, NAUT *of tank* cubage *m*, PHYS, RECORDING, TEXTILES volume *m*; ~ **capacity ratio** *n* *(V-C ratio)* TRANSP rapport débit-capacité *m*; ~ **change** *n* METALL changement de volume *m*; ~ **charge density** *n* PHYS densité volumique de charge *f*; ~ **compression** *n* ELECTRON *microphone signals* compression de la dynamique *f*; ~ **compressor** *n* RECORDING compresseur de volume *m*; ~ **control** *n* CONTROL bouton de réglage du volume *m*, RECORDING contrôle de volume *m*; ~ **density relationship** *n* TRANSP relation débit-densité *f*; ~ **diffusion** *n* METALL diffusion de volume *f*, diffusion volumique *f*; ~ **dosing** *n* PACKAGING dosage volumétrique *m*; ~ **emission and absorption coefficient** *n* RAD PHYS coefficient du volume d'émission et d'absorption *m*; ~ **equalizer** *n* RECORDING atténuateur *m*; ~ **expansion coefficient** *n* PHYS coefficient de dilatation volumique *m*; ~ **filling** *n* PACKAGING remplissage volumétrique *m*; ~ **flow rate** *n* REFRIG débit volume *m*; ~ **fraction** *n* METALL fraction volumique *f*, *of particles* fraction volumétrique *f*, PROP MAT fraction volumique *f*; ~ **indicator** *n* RECORDING vumètre *m*; ~ **indicator meter** *n* TV vumètre *m*; ~ **integral** *n* PHYS intégrale de volume *f*; ~ **label** *n* COMP, DP étiquette de volume *f*; ~ **range** *n* RECORDING étendue de volume *f*; ~ **rate** *n* PHYS *of flow* débit volumique

m; ~ **resistivity** *n* ELEC ENG résistivité volumique *f*, TESTING résistivité volumique *f*, résistivité volumique électrique *f*; ~ **of rotation** *n* GEOM volume de révolution *m*; ~ **size factor** *n* METALL facteur de taille volumétrique *m*; ~ **unit** *n* ACOUSTICS unité de volume *f*; ~ **velocity** *n* ACOUSTICS *across surface element* flux de vitesse acoustique *m*

volume-limiting: ~ **amplifier** *n* ELECTRON régulateur de niveau *m*

volumeter *n* ACOUSTICS volumètre *f*

volumetric[1] *adj* METALL *equation*, PROP MAT volumétrique

volumetric:[2] ~ **analysis** *n* TESTING analyse volumétrique *f*, titration *f*; ~ **efficiency** *n* AUTO rendement volumétrique *m*, ELEC ENG efficacité volumique *f*, FUELLESS rendement volumétrique *m*; ~ **filling unit** *n* PACKAGING remplisseuse volumétrique *f*; ~ **flask** *n* LAB EQUIP *glassware, analysis* fiole jaugée *f*; ~ **strain** *n* MECH ENG déformation volumétrique *f*

volumic: ~ **power** *n* GAS TECH puissance volumique *f*

volute: ~ **casing** *n* AUTO carter en spirale *m*, carter en volute *m*; ~ **chamber** *n* WATER SUPP *of centrifugal pump* canal collecteur *m*; ~ **spring** *n* MECH ENG ressort en volute *m*

volutin *n* CHEM volutine *f*

vomicine *n* CHEM vomicine *f*

von: ~ **Neumann machine** *n* COMP, DP machine de von Neumann *f*

VOR *abbr* *(VHF omnidirectional radio range)* AERONAUT radiophare omnidirectionnel VHF *m*

vortex *n* COAL TECH, FLUID PHYS, MECH *hydraulics* METEO, PHYS, SPACE tourbillon *m*, vortex *m*; ~ **effect** *n* GAS TECH effet vortex *m*; ~ **generator** *n* TRANSP générateur de tourbillons *m*; ~ **meter** *n* GAS TECH compteur à vortex *m*; ~ **skimmer** *n* MAR POLL récupérateur à vortex *m*, écrémeur à vortex *m*; ~ **street** *n* FLUID PHYS *flow pattern* rue de tourbillons *f*

vorticity *n* FLUID PHYS rotationnel *m*, vorticité *m*, METEO circulation tourbillonaire *f*, PHYS rotationnel *m*; ~ **diffusion** *n* FLUID PHYS *thermal conductivity* vortex de diffusion *m*; ~ **equation** *n* FLUID PHYS équation de vorticité *f*

votator *n* FOOD TECH votator *m*

voussoir *n* CONST *archstone* claveau *m*, clef de voûte *f*, vousseau *m*, voussoir *m*

voyage: ~ **charter** *n* NAUT, PETR TECH *commerce* affrètement au voyage *m*

Voyager: ~ **space probe** *n* ASTRON sonde d'espace Voyager *f*

VP *abbr* *(virtual path)* TELECOM conduit virtuel *m*, trajet virtuel *m*

VPC *abbr* *(virtual path connection)* TELECOM connexion de conduit virtuel *f*, connexion de trajet virtuel *f*

VPCE *abbr* *(virtual path connection endpoint)* TELECOM extrémité de connexion de trajet virtuel *f*

VPI *abbr* *(virtual path identifier)* TELECOM identificateur de conduit virtuel *m*, identificateur de trajet virtuel *m*

V-pulley *n* MECH ENG poulie à corde *f*

VRC *abbr* *(vertical redundancy check)* COMP, DP contrôle par redondance verticale *m*

V-shaped[1] *adj* MECH ENG en forme de V

V-shaped:[2] ~ **antenna** *n* TELECOM antenne en V *f*; ~ **cylinders** *n pl* AUTO cylindres en V *m pl*; ~ **notch** *n* NUCLEAR entaille en V *f*

VSI *abbr* *(vertical speed indicator)* SPACE variomètre *m*

VSP *abbr* *(vertical seismic profile)* PETR TECH PSV *(pro-*

fil sismique vertical)

VSWR *abbr (voltage standing-wave ratio)* SPACE *communications* ROS *(rapport d'ondes stationnaires)*

VT *abbr* COMP *(vertical tabulation)* tabulation verticale *f*, COMP *(virtual terminal)* terminal virtuel *m*, DP *(vertical tabulation)* tabulation verticale *f*, DP *(virtual terminal)* terminal virtuel *m*

V-tail *n* AERONAUT *of aircraft* empennage papillon *m*

V-threaded: ~ **screw** *n* MECH, MECH ENG vis à filet triangulaire *f*

VTOL: ~ **aircraft** *n (vertical takeoff and landing aircraft)* AERONAUT ADAV *(avion à décollage et atterrissage verticaux)*

VTR *abbr (videotape recorder)* TV magnétoscope *m*

V-type: ~ **engine** *n* VEHICLES moteur à cylindres en V *m*

vug *n* GEOL géode *f*, vacuole *f*

vuggy *adj* GEOL, PETR TECH *ground* vacuolaire

vughy *adj* GEOL, PETR TECH *ground* vacuolaire

vugular *adj* GEOL, PETR TECH *ground* vacuolaire

vulcanicity *n* GEOPHYS volcanisme *m*

vulcanite *n* CHEM vulcanite *f*, ELEC *insulation* caoutchouc vulcanisé *m*, P&R *rubber* vulcanite *f*, ébonite *f*

vulcanization *n* CHEM, P&R *rubber*, THERMOD vulcanisation *f*

vulcanize *vt* THERMOD vulcaniser

vulcanized[1] *adj* THERMOD vulcanisé

vulcanized:[2] ~ **fiber disk** *n* (AmE), ~ **fibre disc** *n* (BrE) MECH ENG *abrasives* disque abrasif en fibre vulcanisée *m*

Vulpecula *n* ASTRON Petit Renard *m*

W

W[1] *abbr (watt)* ELEC, ELEC ENG, METR, PHYS W *(watt)*
W[2] *(tungsten)* CHEM W *(tungstène)*
wacke *n* GEOL wackestone *m*
wackestone *n* GEOL wackestone *m*
wad[1] *n* MINERAL wad *m*, TEXTILES ouate *f*; **~ of cotton wool** *n* TEXTILES tampon d'ouate *m*; **~ punch** *n* MECH ENG *tool* découpe-joints *m*
wad[2] *vt* TEXTILES ouatiner
wadding *n* CHEM tampon d'ouate *m*, PACKAGING rembourrage *m*, PAPER TECH ouate *f*, TEXTILES nappe pour ouatinage *f*, ouate *f*, rembourrage *m*
wadi *n* HYDROL *valley* oued *m*
wafer *n* COMP tranche de silicium *f*, DP, ELEC ENG *plate in commutators* galette *f*, ELECTRON *semiconductors* plaquette *f*, puce *f*; **~ distortion** *n* ELECTRON *semiconductors* déformation des plaquettes *f*; **~ fabrication** *n* ELECTRON *semiconductors* fabrication de plaquettes *f*; **~ mask** *n* ELECTRON *semiconductors* masque à plaquette *m*; **~ processing** *n* ELECTRON *semiconductors* traitement des plaquettes *m*; **~ scale integration** *n* COMP intégration à l'échelle d'une tranche *f*, DP intégration sur plaquette *f*, ELECTRON intégration sur plaquette *f*, intégration à l'échelle d'une tranche *f*; **~ switch** *n* CONTROL interrupteur rotatif à gaufres *m*, ELEC ENG commutateur à galette *m*, inverseur à galette *m*; **~ yield** *n* ELECTRON rendement des plaquettes *m*
wagnerite *n* MINERAL wagnérite *f*
wagon *n* (BrE) *(cf car)* COAL TECH, MINING wagonnet *m*, RAIL *especially goods* wagon *m*, TRANSP chariot *m*, TRANSP *railways* wagon *m*; **~ car** *n* (BrE) *(cf trailer wagon)* TRANSP wagonnet *m*; **~ for internal yard use** *n* (BrE) *(cf car for internal yard use)* RAIL *vehicles* wagon de brouettage *m*; **~ hoist** *n* (BrE) *(cf car elevator)* RAIL monte-wagon *m*; **~ lift** *n* (BrE) *(cf car elevator)* RAIL *vehicles* monte-wagon *m*; **~ shed** *n* (BrE) *(cf car shed)* RAIL dépôt de wagons *m*; **~ vault** *n* CONST *architecture* voûte en berceau *f*
wagonload *n* (BrE) *(cf carload)* TRANSP charge complète *f*
waist *n* TEXTILES taille *f*; **~ dart** *n* TEXTILES pince de taille *f*
waistband *n* TEXTILES hausse de ceinture *f*
waistline *n* TEXTILES taille *f*
waistsize *n* TEXTILES tissu de taille *m*
wait: ~ loop *n* COMP, DP boucle d'attente *f*; **~ state** *n* COMP, DP état d'attente *m*
waiting: ~ call *n* TELECOM appel en attente *m*; **~ on weather** *n* (*WOW*) PETR TECH attente mauvaise *f*
waiving *n* PATENTS renonciation *f*
wake *n* FLUID PHYS, MAR POLL, NAUT *of ship*, OCEANOG *of ship*, PHYS *turbulent flow* sillage *m*; **~ area** *n* NUCLEAR région morte *f*, sillage dormant *m*; **~ intensity** *n* FLUID PHYS intensité du sillage *f*; **~ space** *n* NUCLEAR région morte *f*, sillage dormant *m*; **~ turbulence** *n* AERONAUT turbulence de sillage *f*
walchowite *n* MINERAL walchowite *f*
Walden: ~ inversion *n* CHEM *optical inversion* inversion de Walden *f*
wale *n* COAL TECH lisse *f*, TEXTILES colonne *f*

waling *n* COAL TECH cavalier *m*, CONST moisage *m*
walk: ~ down *n* COMP, DP perte cumulative *f*
walkaround: ~ inspection *n* SPACE *spacecraft* inspection externe *f*
walk-in: ~ freezer *n* REFRIG chambre de congélation *f*
walking: ~ beam *n* MECH ENG balancier *m*, MINING *boring* balancier de battage *m*, bascule de battage *f*, levier de battage *m*; **~ dragline excavator** *n* CONST *civil engineering* dragline sur patins *f*; **~ line** *n* CONST *stair-building* ligne d'emmarchement *f*, ligne defoulée *f*, ligne de giron *f*
walkway *n* CONST passerelle *f*, trottoir *m*, MECH, SPACE *spacecraft* passerelle *f*
wall[1] *n* CONST *building* mur *m*, muraille *f*, paroi *f*, FLUID PHYS paroi *f*, MINING *of a mine level* mur *m*, parement *m*, paroi *f*, éponte *f*, paroi latérale *f*, pied-droit *m*, PROD ENG *of cylinder, boiler* paroi *f*, *of furnace* mortmur *m*, paroi *f*; **~ attachment** *n* FLUID PHYS adhérence à la paroi *f*; **~ bearing** *n* MINING *for shafting* palier mural *m*; **~ box** *n* CONST boule à mur *f*, niche murale *f*; **~ brace** *n* CINEMAT écharpe *f*; **~ bracket** *n* CONST console murale *f*, MINING *shafting* chaise console *f*, chaise-applique *f*, palier à potence *m*, TELECOM support mural *m*; **~ coil** *n* REFRIG *of condenser* élément mural *m*; **~ crane** *n* CONST grue d'applique *f*, grue murale *f*, grue à potence *f*, grue à potence murale *f*; **~ cupboard** *n* LAB EQUIP *furniture* placard suspendu *m*; **~ effect** *n* COAL TECH effet de paroi *m*; **~ fitting** *n* CONST montage mural *m*; **~ holdfast** *n* CONST clou à crochet *m*, clou à patte *m*, crochet mural *m*; **~ lamp** *n* ELEC *lighting* lanterne murale *f*; **~ losses** *n pl* REFRIG *of heat through walls* déperditions calorifiques de paroi *f pl*; **~ mount enclosure assembly** *n* PROD ENG coffret à montage mural *m*; **~ outlet** *n* ELEC *connection* prise murale *f*; **~ paint** *n* COLOURS revêtement mural *m*; **~ piece** *n* CONST *shoring* couchis *m*; **~ plate** *n* CONST lambourde *f*, *roof plate* contreplaqué *m*, plate-forme *f*, poutre sablière *f*, sablière *f*, sablière de comble *f*, semelle *f*; **~ socket** *n* ELEC *connection* prise murale *f*; **~ string** *n* CONST *stair-building* contre-limon *m*, faux limon *m*; **~ thickness gaging** *n* (AmE), **~ thickness gauging** *n* (BrE) NUCLEAR mesure de l'épaisseur de paroi *f*
wall[2] *vt* MINING murailler, murer; **~ in** *vt* MINING murailler, murer; **~ up** *vt* MINING murailler, murer
walled: ~ enclosure *n* CONST clôture murée *f*, enclos muré *m*
wall-entrance: ~ insulator *n* ELEC ENG isolateur d'entrée *m*
wallet-type: ~ envelope *n* PACKAGING enveloppe portefeuille *f*
walling *n* CONST murage *m*, muraillement *m*; **~ scaffold** *n* MINING palier *m*, plancher volant *m*, échafaudage volant *m*; **~ stage** *n* MINING palier *m*, plancher volant *m*, échafaudage volant *m*
wallpaper: ~ base *n* PAPER TECH papier support pour tenture *m*
walnut: ~ oil *n* FOOD TECH huile de noix *f*
wand *n* COMP, DP baguette *f*, PRINT baguette *f*, crayon *m*,

stylo *m*; ~ **scanner** *n* COMP, DP crayon-lecteur *m*

wane *n* CONST *bevelled edge of board cut from log* flache *f*

Wankel: ~ **engine** *n* AUTO moteur rotatif Wankel *m*, MECH ENG moteur Wankel *m*, THERMOD moteur Wankel *m*, moteur rotatif Wankel *m*, TRANSP moteur Wankel *m*, VEHICLES moteur Wankel *m*, moteur rotatif Wankel *m*

wanted: ~ **emission** *n* TELECOM émission utile *f*; ~ **signal** *n* ELECTRON signal utile *m*

wanted-to-unwanted: ~ **carrier power ratio** *n* TELECOM rapport de puissance porteuse utile-porteuse brouilleuse *m*

wap *n* SPRINGS bobine élémentaire *f*

warble *n* ACOUSTICS ton hululé *m*, TELECOM hululement *m*

ward *n* CONST *of lock* garde *f*, garniture *f*

warded: ~ **lock** *n* CONST serrure à garnitures *f*

warding: ~ **file** *n* MECH ENG lime à bouter *f*, lime à garnir *f*

Ward-Leonard: ~ **set** *n* ELEC ENG groupe convertisseur Ward-Leonard *m*

wardroom *n* (BrE) NAUT *Royal Navy* carré *m*

ware: ~ **pusher** *n* C&G bras-poussoir *m*

warehouse *n* NAUT entrepôt *m*, PROD ENG entrepôt *m*, magasin *m*; ~ **delivery** *n* PROD ENG livraison magasin *f*, transfert en magasin *m*; ~ **management** *n* PROD ENG gestion de magasin *f*; ~ **order** *n* PROD ENG ordre de transfert en magasin *m*; ~ **price** *n* PROD ENG prix magasin *m*

warehouseman *n* PROD ENG magasinier *m*

warehousing *n* PROD ENG emmagasinage *m*, emmagasinement *m*, entreposage *m*, gestion de magasin *f*; ~ **charges** *n pl* PROD ENG coût de stockage *m*

warfarin *n* CHEM warfarine *f*

warm:[1] ~ **air heating system** *n* HEATING installation de chauffage à air chaud *f*; ~ **air stream** *n* METEO courant d'air chaud *m*; ~ **cloud** *n* METEO nuage chaud *m*; ~ **front** *n (cf cold front)* METEO front chaud *m*; ~ **laboratory** *n* NUCLEAR *low activity* laboratoire semi-chaud *m*; ~ **layer** *n* METEO couche chaude *f*; ~ **start** *n* COMP, DP démarrage à chaud *m*

warm:[2] ~ **up** *vt* THERMOD *engine* échauffer

warming: ~ **room** *n* REFRIG salle de réchauffage *f*

warming-in *n* C&G réchauffage *m*; ~ **hole** *n* C&G boucassin *m*

warmth *n* THERMOD chaleur douce *f*

warm-up: ~ **time** *n* THERMOD durée de préchauffage *f*, temps de mise en fonctionnement *m*

warm-water: ~ **sphere** *n* OCEANOG couche superficielle d'eau chaude *f*

warning *n* PROD ENG avertissement *m*; ~ **bell** *n* SAFETY avertisseur sonore *m*, sonnerie d'alarme *f*; ~ **button** *n* CONTROL bouton-poussoir d'avertissement *m*; ~ **color** *n* (AmE), ~ **colour** *n* (BrE) COLOURS couleur de signalisation *f*, couleur tranchante *f*; ~ **distance** *n* RAIL distance d'avertissement *f*; ~ **label** *n* SAFETY plaquette d'avertissement *f*; ~ **light** *n* AERONAUT voyant lumineux *m*, CONTROL signal avertisseur lumineux *m*, ELEC ENG alarme lumineuse *f*, SAFETY feu d'avertissement *m*; ~ **message** *n* TRANSP message d'avertissement *m*; ~ **sign** *n* CONST panneau avertisseur *m*, CONTROL, RAIL avertisseur optique *m*, SAFETY signe d'avertissement *m*, signe d'alerte *m*; ~ **signal** *n* CONTROL signal avertisseur *m*, signal d'avertissement *m*, NAUT, PROD ENG signal avertisseur *m*; ~ **triangle** *n* SAFETY triangle d'avertissement *m*

warp[1] *n* ACOUSTICS voile *m*, C&G *of optical glass* boitage

m, NAUT *towing* aussière de halage *f*, haussière de déhalage *f*, PAPER TECH, TEXTILES chaîne *f*, chaîne d'un tissu *f*; ~ **beam** *n* TEXTILES ensouple d'ourdissage *f*; ~ **breakage** *n* PROD ENG rupture du fil de chaîne *f*; ~ **dyeing** *n* COLOURS teinture sur chaîne *f*; ~ **knitting** *n* TEXTILES tricotage chaîne *m*; ~ **setting** *n* TEXTILES compte de la chaîne *m*; ~ **stop motion** *n* TEXTILES casse-fil de chaîne *m*; ~ **yarn** *n* PAPER TECH fil de chaîne *m*

warp[2] *vt* NAUT *ship* haler, touer, touer avec point fixe, TEXTILES ourdir

warpage *n* C&G gauchissement *m*

warped[1] *adj* MECH faussé, gauchi

warped:[2] ~ **finish** *n* C&G bague retombée *f*; ~ **sheet** *n* (BrE) *(cf bow and warp)* C&G tôle *f*; ~ **surface** *n* SPRINGS surface gauche *f*; ~ **timber** *n* CONST bois déjeté *m*, bois déversé *m*, bois gauchi *m*, bois voilé *m*

warper *n* TEXTILES ourdissoir *m*

warping *n* CONST *of wood* déjettement *m*, déversement *m*, gauchissement *m*, voilure *f*, PRINT *book binding* déformation *f*, PROD ENG *of castings* déformation *f*, flexion *f*, gauchissement *m*, RAIL *of a wheel* gauchissement *m*, TEXTILES ourdissage *m*; ~ **creel** *n* TEXTILES cantre *m*; ~ **drum** *n* NAUT *deck fittings* poupée *f*, tambour *m*; ~ **head** *n* NAUT *winch* poupée *f*, TEXTILES peigne d'ourdissage *m*

warp-knitting: ~ **machine** *n* TEXTILES métier chaîne *m*

warrant *vt* PROD ENG *guarantee* garantir

warranty *n* PROD ENG garantie *f*

Warren: ~ **engine** *n* TRANSP moteur Warren *m*

warship *n* MILIT navire de guerre *m*, NAUT *navy* navire de guerre *m*, vaisseau de guerre *m*

wash[1] *n* CHEM lavage *m*, CINEMAT lavage *m*, rinçage *m*, CONST *of window* jet d'eau *m*, MECH ENG *watercolour drawing* lavis *m*; ~ **boring** *n* COAL TECH forage par injection *m*, PETR TECH forage à injection *m*; ~ **bottle** *n* CHEM, LAB EQUIP pissette *f*; ~ **house** *n* PROD ENG atelier de lavage *m*, laverie *f*; ~ **primer** *n* COATINGS couche de fond au phosphate *f*, couche passivante à phosphate *f*, P&R *paint* couche d'accrochage primaire *f*; ~ **tank** *n* PHOTO cuve de lavage *f*

wash[2] *vt* CHEM laver, éliminer par lavage, MINING *gold from plates* récolter, PAPER TECH, TEXTILES laver; ~ **away** *vt* CHEM TECH entraîner au lavage, HYDROL charrier, emporter, entraîner; ~ **with hot water** *vt* MAR POLL laver à l'eau chaude

washability *n* PAPER TECH, TEXTILES lavabilité *f*

washable *adj* PAPER TECH lavable

wash-and-wear *adj* TEXTILES repassage superflu

washback *n* NUCLEAR *in underwater cratering* éjecta *m pl*

washboard *n* C&G fripé *m* (Bel), fripées *f pl*, CONST *skirting* plinthe *f*

washboards *n pl* NAUT *boat building* panneau de descente *m*, porte d'entrée *f*, RAIL pancarte *f*

washed[1] *adj* PRINT délavé, imprécis; ~ **out** *adj* CINEMAT délavé; ~ **overboard** *adj* NAUT enlevé par une vague

washed:[2] ~ **and squashed consumer waste carton** *n* PACKAGING carton récupéré lavé et comprimé *m*; ~ **small** *n* COAL TECH menu lavé *m*

washer *n* CHEM TECH appareil de lavage *m*, laveur *m*, COAL TECH laveur *m*, CONST, MECH ENG *perforated* disc rondelle *f*, PROD ENG *washing machine* laveur *m*, lavoir *m*, SPRINGS rondelle *f*, TEXTILES laveur *m*, VEHICLES *glazing* lave-glace *m*, *screw, bolt* rondelle *f*; ~ **cutter** *n* MECH ENG compas à lame tranchante *m*, coupe-cercle m, coupe-rondelle m; ~ **for tapered guide pillar** n MECH ENG rondelle de blocage pour colonne conique f

washery n MINING lavoir m

washing n C&G fluage m, CHEM TECH lavage m, PRINT lavage m, rinçage m, PROD ENG, TEXTILES lavage m; ~ **adjuvant** n DETERGENTS produit lessiviel m; ~ **agent** n DETERGENTS agent de lavage m, produit de lavage m; ~ **auxiliary** n DETERGENTS produit lessiviel m; ~ **bath** n DETERGENTS bain détergent m; ~ **column** n CHEM TECH tour de lavage f; ~ **drum** n PAPER TECH tambour laveur m; ~ **facilities** n pl TEXTILES lavabilité f; ~ **instructions** n pl TEXTILES instructions de lavage f pl; ~ **machine** n PROD ENG laveur m, laveur mécanique m, lavoir m, TEXTILES machine à laver f; ~ **out** n CHEM TECH enlèvement par lavage m, lavage m; ~ **plant** n PROD ENG appareils de lavage m pl; ~ **powder** n DETERGENTS lessive en poudre f; ~ **powder slurry** n DETERGENTS résidu de détergents m; ~ **soda** n CHEM soude en cristaux f; ~ **tower** n CHEM TECH tour de lavage f; ~ **tube** n LAB EQUIP glassware tube laveur m

washings n pl CHEM TECH eau de lavage f, eau à laver f, PROD ENG produits de lavage m pl, produits lavés m pl

washout n POLLUTION lavage m, lessivage m, lessivage atmosphérique m, washout atmosphérique m, RAIL of embankment fixed equipment ravinement de remblai m; ~ **hole** n PROD ENG boiler regard de lavage m, trou de bras m, trou de sel m, trou à main m; ~ **plug** n PROD ENG bouchon de lavage m, tampon de lavage m; ~ **rate** n POLLUTION taux d'élimination m, taux de lavage m

washover n PETR lessivage m, surforage m; ~ **string** n PETR TECH drilling colonne de surforage f

washup n PAPER TECH, PRINT lavage m

wasp-waisted: ~ **tank** n C&G four en taille de guêpe m

wastage n NUCLEAR of tubes usure f, PROD ENG loss déperdition f, gaspillage m, perte f, RECYCLING gaspillage m

waste[1] n C&G déchets m pl, FOOD TECH déchets m pl, résidu m, MINING déchets m pl, rebuts m pl, stériles m pl, PAPER TECH, POLLUTION product déchets m pl, PROD ENG déblais m pl, déchets m pl, rebuts m pl, stériles m pl, loss déperdition f, gaspillage m, perte f, RECYCLING, TEXTILES déchets m pl; ~ **canister** n NUCLEAR for ultimate storage poubelle f; ~ **cock** n CONST robinet de purge m, robinet purgeur m; ~ **collection** n RECYCLING collecte f, ramassage m; ~ **condensate pump** n NUCLEAR pompe de réservoir d'eau traitée f; ~ **disposal** n RECYCLING élimination des déchets f, évacuation des déchets f, WATER SUPP évacuation des déchets f; ~ **drive** n MINING bowette f; ~ **drum** n NUCLEAR for transportation or storage fût m; ~ **dump** n MINING halde f, halde de déblais f, halde de déchets f, tas de rejets m, RECYCLING décharge f, dépôt m, décharge de déchets f, dépôt de déchets m; ~ **energy** n THERMOD énergie gaspillée f; ~ **of energy** n THERMOD gaspillage d'énergie m; ~ **evaporator** n NUCLEAR liquid évaporateur des déchets liquides m; ~ **extraction system** n PACKAGING système d'extraction des déchets m; ~ **gas** n CHEM gaz d'échappement m, GAS TECH gaz brûlé m, gaz de récupération m, NUCLEAR gaz d'échappement m, gaz rejeté m, POLLUTION effluent gazeux m, gaz d'échappement m; ~ **gases** n PROD ENG of furnace flammes perdues f pl, gaz perdus m pl; ~ **gas heat** n THERMOD chaleur des gaz brûlés f; ~ **gas heat recovery** n THERMOD recirculation recirculation des gaz brûlés f; ~ **ground** n MINING déblais de mine m pl, déchets m pl, rebuts m pl, stériles m pl; ~ **heap** n CONST halde de

déblais f, halde de déchets f, tas de déchets f, tas de déchets m, RECYCLING tas de déblais m, tas de déchets m; ~ **heat** n HEAT ENG, NUCLEAR, POLLUTION, THERMOD chaleur perdue f; ~ **heat boiler** n HEAT ENG, THERMOD chaudière chauffée par chaleur perdue f; ~ **heat recovery** n THERMOD récupération de la chaleur perdue f, récupération thermique f; ~ **management** n RECYCLING gestion des déchets f; ~ **outlet** n NUCLEAR of irradiated fuel processing plant émissaire de rejet m; ~ **paper** n PAPER TECH, RECYCLING vieux papiers m pl; ~ **paper contraries** n PAPER TECH matières indésirables contenues dans les vieux papiers f; ~ **pipe** n CONST trop-plein m, tuyau d'écoulement du trop-plein m; ~ **processing** n RECYCLING traitement des déchets m, transformation des déchets f; ~ **product** n PROD ENG déchet m, RECYCLING déchet m, effluent m; ~ **recycling** n RECYCLING recyclage des déchets m; ~ **rock** n MINING déblais de mine m pl, déchets m pl, stériles m pl; ~ **sheets** n pl PRINT gâche f, passe f; ~ **sorting** n RECYCLING tri des déchets m; ~ **space** n HYDR EQUIP in steam cylinder espace mort m; ~ **treatment** n RECYCLING traitement des déchets m; ~ **treatment plant** n RECYCLING station de traitement des déchets f, usine de traitement des déchets f

waste[2] vt PROD ENG, RECYCLING gaspiller

wastewater n CHEM eau usée f, COAL TECH effluent m, CONST trop-plein m, HYDROL sewage eau d'égout f, eau résiduelle f, eau usée f, POLLUTION eau résiduaire f, eau usée f, RECYCLING eau usée f, WATER SUPP eau résiduaire f, eau usée f; ~ **disposal** n RECYCLING vidange des eaux usées f; ~ **outfall** n WATER SUPP dégorgeoir des eaux résiduaires m; ~ **purification** n WATER SUPP épuration des eaux résiduaires f; ~ **recycling operation** n NUCLEAR recyclage des eaux résiduaires m; ~ **tank** n SPACE réservoir d'eaux usées m; ~ **treatment** n HYDROL, POLLUTION, RECYCLING traitement des eaux usées m; ~ **treatment plant** n RECYCLING station d'épuration des eaux usées f

watch:[1] **on** ~ adj NAUT sailing de quart

watch:[2] ~ **casing** n MECH ENG boîtier de montre m; ~ **glass** n LAB EQUIP verre de montre m; ~ **screw plate** n MECH ENG very fine pitch filière de bijouterie f

watchdog: ~ **applications** n pl DP applications de surveillance f pl; ~ **timer** n COMP chien de garde m, horloge de surveillance m, DP horloge chien de garde f, horloge de surveillance f, PROD ENG horloge chien de garde m; ~ **timer set valve** n PROD ENG valeur établie sur l'horloge chien de garde f

watchman's: ~ **clock** n PROD ENG contrôleur de ronde m

watchtower n MILIT tour de guet f

water:[1]

~ a ~ **absorption** n TESTING absorption d'eau f; ~ **absorption capacity** n WATER SUPP absorptivité f, capacité d'absorption d'eau f; ~ **accumulator** n NUCLEAR of hydraulic control rod drive réservoir d'eau m; ~ **adit** n WATER SUPP galerie d'assèchement f, galerie d'écoulement f, galerie de drainage f, voie d'écoulement f; ~ **analysis kit** n LAB EQUIP trousse d'analyse d'eau f; ~ **authority** n WATER SUPP autorités de gestion des eaux f pl;

~ b ~ **balance** n HYDROL nappe, NAUT bilan d'eau m; ~ **barrier** n MINING prevent propagation of coal dust arrêt-barrage d'eau m; ~ **base mud** n PETR TECH drilling boue à base d'eau f; ~ **bath** n CHEM, LAB EQUIP heating bain-marie m; ~ **bath evaporator** n NUCLEAR évaporateur à bain-marie m; ~ **box** n C&G boîte à eau f;

~ budget n WATER SUPP bilan hydraulique m; **~ butt** n CONST tonneau à eau m;

~ c – **can** n PROD ENG fontaine d'arrosage f; **~ carriage** n NAUT water transport transport par eau m; **~ catchment** n WATER SUPP captage de l'eau m; **~ channel** n COAL TECH kermet m; **~ chiller** n REFRIG refroidisseur à eau m; **~ clearance** n OCEANOG brassiage m; **~ cock** n CONST robinet hydraulique m, robinet pour conduite d'eau m, robinet pour eau m; **~ conditioning** n WATER SUPP conditionnement de l'eau m; **~ conditioning process** n NUCLEAR traitement des eaux m; **~ conservation** n HYDROL conservation des eaux f; **~ container** n TEXTILES bidon à eau m; **~ content** n COAL TECH, CONST teneur en eau f, GAS TECH degré d'humidité m, METEO contenu en vapeur d'eau m, OPT, PHYS teneur en eau f; **~ curtain** n MINING to prevent propagation of coal dust arrêt-barrage d'eau m;

~ d – **decomposition under irradiation** n NUCLEAR décomposition de l'eau sous rayonnement f, radiolyse d'eau f; **~ deficiency** n WATER SUPP déficit hydrique m; **~ defrosting** n REFRIG dégivrage par aspersion d'eau m; **~ delivery** n WATER SUPP adduction d'eau f; **~ distribution** n CONST, WATER SUPP distribution d'eau f; **~ doctor** n PROD ENG docteur à eau m; **~ drain cock** n WATER SUPP robinet de vidange d'eau m; **~ drive** n PETR, PETR TECH poussée d'eau f;

~ e – **electrolysis** n NUCLEAR for tritium separation électrolyse de l'eau f; **~ enamel** n COLOURS peinture à l'eau brillante f; **~ equivalent** n PHYS valeur en eau f, équivalent en eau m; **~ erosion** n HYDROL érosion due à l'eau f, érosion par la pluie f; **~ extraction structure** n CONST ouvrage de captage d'eau m;

~ f – **fall height** n HYDR EQUIP chute d'eau f, hauteur de chute f; **~ feed** n PROD ENG for drill alimentation d'eau f; **~ filter** n NAUT, WATER SUPP filtre à eau m; **~ finish** n PAPER TECH apprêt à l'eau m, calandrage humide m; **~ finishing** n PAPER TECH apprêt à l'eau m, calandrage humide m; **~ fire extinguisher** n SAFETY extincteur d'incendie à eau m; **~ fitting** n WATER SUPP raccord à circulation d'eau m; **~ flooding** n PETR injection d'eau f; **~ flow rate** n HEATING débit d'eau m;

~ g – **gage** n (AmE) see water gauge; **~ gap** n NUCLEAR between fuel assemblies in BWR core veine d'eau f; **~ gas** n GAS TECH gaz à l'eau m; **~ gate** n WATER SUPP gate valve robinet-vanne m, gate for controlling flow of water vanne f, vannelle f, vantelle f; **~ gauge** n (BrE) WATER SUPP échelle de l'étiage f, for determining level of water in river indicateur de niveau d'eau m; **~ glass** n C&G, DETERGENTS verre soluble m; **~ gradient pressure** n TEXTILES variation de pression d'eau f;

~ h – **hammer** n FLUID PHYS, PETR TECH coup de bélier m; **~ hardness** n WATER SUPP dureté de l'eau f; **~ heater** n LAB EQUIP chauffe-eau m; **~ hose** n MINING flexible d'eau m; **~ hydrant** n WATER SUPP bouche d'eau f, hydrante m;

~ i – **indicator** n WATER SUPP indicateur de niveau d'eau m; **~ inflow** n WATER SUPP coup d'eau m, venue d'eau f; **~ ingress** n NUCLEAR into repository or reactor core entrée d'eau f; **~ inhibition** n TEXTILES absorption d'eau f; **~ injection** n PETR TECH wells injection d'eau f; **~ injection compressor** n HYDR EQUIP compresseur à injection d'eau m; **~ inlet** n REFRIG entrée d'eau m, WATER SUPP orifice d'introduction d'eau m; **~ intake** n CONST, FUELLESS, HYDROL prise d'eau f; **~ irruption** n WATER SUPP venue d'eau f;

~ j – **jacket** n AUTO chemise d'eau f, PROD ENG che-

mise d'eau f, chemise à circulation d'eau f, enveloppe d'eau f, THERMOD, VEHICLES cooling system chemise d'eau f; **~ jet** n WATER SUPP jet d'eau m; **~ jet propulsion** n TRANSP propulsion par jet d'eau f;

~ k – **knock out** n PETR TECH séparateur d'eau m;

~ l – **lacquer** n COLOURS peinture à l'eau brillante f; **~ law** n WATER SUPP législation des eaux f; **~ leakage alarm** n MINING alarme pour fuite d'eau f; **~ level** n CHEM, WATER SUPP instrument niveau d'eau m; **~ level indicator** n WATER SUPP indicateur de niveau d'eau m; **~ line** n CONST canalisation d'eau f, MAR POLL, NAUT of ship, TRANSP ships ligne de flottaison f; **~ lines** n pl NAUT naval architecture lignes d'eau f pl, sections horizontales f pl; **~ logging** n NUCLEAR pénétration d'eau dans un élément combustible f;

~ m – **main** n WATER SUPP conduite de distribution d'eau f, conduite principale d'eau f; **~ meter** n TEXTILES compteur d'eau m, WATER SUPP compteur à eau m;

~ o – **outlet** n REFRIG sortie d'eau f, WATER SUPP orifice de sortie d'eau m, sortie de l'eau f; **~ outlet port** n WATER SUPP orifice de sortie d'eau m, sortie de l'eau f;

~ p – **permeability** n P&R perméabilité à l'eau f; **~ pipe** n PROD ENG tuyau de prise d'eau m, WATER SUPP for conveying water conduite d'eau f, tuyau d'eau m; **~ plug** n WATER SUPP bouche d'eau f, hydrante m; **~ pollutant** n POLLUTION polluant des eaux m; **~ pollution** n HYDROL, POLLUTION pollution des eaux f, WATER SUPP contamination des eaux f, pollution des eaux f; **~ port** n PROD ENG orifice d'eau m; **~ power** n FUELLESS houille blanche f, énergie hydroélectrique f, TEXTILES, THERMOD énergie hydraulique f, WATER SUPP force hydraulique f, houille blanche f; **~ power station** n ELEC ENG centrale hydroélectrique f, installation de force motrice hydraulique f; **~ pressure** n CONST, HEATING, TEXTILES pression de l'eau f, WATER SUPP charge d'eau f, pression de l'eau f; **~ pressure regulator** n CONTROL régulateur de pression d'eau m; **~ propeller** n (BrE) (cf water screw) TRANSP hélice marine f; **~ pulverizing** n WATER SUPP pulvérisation d'eau f; **~ pump** n AUTO, VEHICLES cooling system pompe à eau f; **~ pump housing** n VEHICLES cooling system corps de pompe à eau m; **~ purification** n CHEM TECH clarification de l'eau f, purification de l'eau f, épuration de l'eau f, WATER SUPP épuration des eaux f; **~ purification filter** n CHEM TECH filtre clarificateur m; **~ purifier** n TEXTILES épurateur d'eau m;

~ q – **quality** n FUELLESS, HYDROL, POLLUTION, WATER SUPP qualité de l'eau f; **~ quality monitoring** n WATER SUPP auscultation de qualité de l'eau f; **~ quenching** n METALL trempe à l'eau f;

~ r – **radiolysis** n NUCLEAR décomposition de l'eau sous rayonnement f, radiolyse d'eau f; **~ ratio** n COAL TECH teneur en eau f; **~ repellant coat** n COATINGS enduit hydrofuge m; **~ repellency** n COATINGS hydrophobicité f; **~ reservoir** n MINING réservoir d'eau m; **~ resource development project** n HYDROL projet d'aménagement hydraulique m; **~ resources study** n HYDROL appraisal étude des ressources en eau f; **~ retention** n HYDROL, WATER SUPP rétention de l'eau f; **~ ring** n MINING in mine shaft gargouille f;

~ s – **sampler** n LAB EQUIP échantillonneur d'eau m; **~ saturation** n PETR saturation d'eau f, saturation en eau f; **~ screw** n (AmE) (cf water propeller) TRANSP hélice marine f; **~ slurry** n NUCLEAR suspension aqueuse *f*; ~ **softener** *n* CHEM TECH, CONST, PAPER TECH, PRINT, TEXTILES adoucisseur d'eau *m*; ~ **softening** *n* CHEM TECH adoucissement d'eau *m*; ~ **spray system** *n* NUCLEAR système d'aspersion *m*; ~ **stain** *n* COLOURS teinture à l'eau *f*; ~ **storage coefficient** *n* HYDROL coefficient d'emmagasinement *m*; ~ **strainer** *n* RAIL *vehicles* crépine *f*; ~ **string** *n* PETR TECH colonne de fermeture d'eau *f*; ~ **supplier** *n* POLLUTION distributeur d'eau *m*; ~ **supply** *n* HYDROL, PROD ENG, TEXTILES alimentation en eau *f*, WATER SUPP *system* distribution d'eau *f*, service des eaux *m*; ~ **supply pipe** *n* WATER SUPP conduite d'amenée d'eau *f*, tuyau d'amenée d'eau *m*; ~ **suspension** *n* NUCLEAR suspension aqueuse *f*; ~ **swivel** *n* MINING touret hydraulique *m*; ~ **system** *n* HYDROL réseau hydrographique *m*, NAUT circuit d'eau *m*;

■ **t** ~ **table** *n* GEOL nappe phréatique *f*, HYDROL nappe phréatique *f*, nappe souterraine *f*, niveau hydrostatique *m*, PETR TECH nappe phréatique *f*; ~ **table fluctuation** *n* HYDROL fluctuation de la nappe phréatique *f*; ~ **tank** *n* NAUT cale à eau *f*, réservoir à eau *m*, RAIL *vehicles* soute à eau *f*, WATER SUPP bâche à eau *f*, citerne *f*, réservoir à eau *m*; ~ **tanker** *n* CONST camion citerne *m*; ~ **tap** *n* LAB EQUIP *services* robinet d'eau *m*; ~ **temperature gage** *n* (AmE), ~ **temperature gauge** *n* (BrE) AUTO *car* indicateur de température de l'eau *m*; ~ **thermostat** *n* THERMOD thermostat mouillé *m*; ~ **tower** *n* CONST, HYDROL, MINING château d'eau *m*; ~ **transport** *n* NAUT transport par voie d'eau *m*; ~ **treatment** *n* CHEM TECH traitement des eaux *m*, épuration des eaux *f*, COAL TECH traitement des eaux *m*, HYDROL traitement des eaux *m*, épuration des eaux *f*, NUCLEAR traitement des eaux *m*; ~ **treatment plant** *n* CONST usine de potabilisation *f*, HYDROL usine d'épuration de l'eau *f*, WATER SUPP station de traitement de l'eau *f*; ~ **truck** *n* CONST camion citerne *m*; ~ **tube** *n* AUTO, HEAT ENG tube d'eau *m*; ~ **tube boiler** *n* HEAT ENG chaudière aquatubulaire *f*, chaudière à tubes d'eau *f*, HEATING chaudière sectionnelle aquatubulaire *f*; ~ **turbine** *n* FUELLESS turbine hydraulique *f*, THERMOD turbine hydraulique *f*, turbine à eau *f*;

■ **u** ~ **under pressure** *n* WATER SUPP eau sous pression *f*;

■ **v** ~ **valve** *n* CONST robinet de prise d'eau *m*; ~ **vapor barrier** *n* (AmE) *see water vapour barrier*; ~ **vapor condensation test** *n* (AmE) *see water vapour condensation test*; ~ **vapour barrier** *n* (BrE) PACKAGING barrière pour la buée *f*; ~ **vapour condensation test** *n* (BrE) MECH ENG *refrigerated cabinets* essai de condensation de vapeur d'eau *m*;

■ **w** ~ **wheel** *n* TEXTILES roue hydraulique *f*

water² *vt* CHEM diluer, CONST arroser, WATER SUPP alimenter en eau

water³ *vi* WATER SUPP faire de l'eau

Water: ~ **Carrier** *n* ASTRON Verseau *m*

water-activated: ~ **battery** *n* ELEC ENG pile amorçable à l'eau *f*

waterage *n* NAUT *water transport* batelage *m*, droits de batelage *m pl*, prix de transport par eau *m*, transport par eau *m*

water-based: ~ **backing adhesive** *n* PACKAGING colle d'emballage à base d'eau *f*; ~ **paint** *n* CONST peinture à base d'eau *f*

water-bearing¹ *adj* HYDROL, PROP MAT aquifère

water-bearing:² ~ **stratum** *n* HYDROL couche perméable *f*, strate perméable *f*, WATER SUPP couche

aquifère *f*

waterborne *adj* HYDROL charrié par l'eau, transporté par l'eau

water-carrying: ~ **capacity** *n* TEXTILES capacité de transport d'eau *f*

water-cement: ~ **ratio** *n* CONST rapport eau-ciment *m*

water-cleansing: ~ **plant** *n* MINING station d'épuration *f*, station de traitement d'eau *f*

water-cool *vt* CHEM refroidir par l'eau

water-cooled¹ *adj* GAS TECH refroidi par l'eau, PROD ENG refroidi par l'eau, à refroidissement d'eau, TEXTILES à refroidissement par eau

water-cooled:² ~ **air conditioning unit** *n* REFRIG climatiseur à condenseur à l'eau *m*; ~ **condenser** *n* HEAT ENG condenseur refroidi par l'eau *m*; ~ **engine** *n* AUTO, VEHICLES moteur à refroidissement par l'eau *m*; ~ **furnace** *n* HEATING *marine boilers* four à refroidissement l'eau *m*; ~ **heat trap** *n* CINEMAT cuvette de refroidissement par l'eau *f*; ~ **reactor** *n* NUCLEAR réacteur refroidi à l'eau *m*; ~ **retort** *n* HEATING cornue à refroidissement à l'eau *f*; ~ **system** *n* MECH ENG système à refroidissement par l'eau *m*; ~ **transformer** *n* ELEC transformateur à refroidissement par l'eau *m*; ~ **tube** *n* ELECTRON tube à refroidissement par l'eau *m*

water-cooling *n* AUTO, PROP MAT, TEXTILES refroidissement par eau *m*; ~ **cascade** *n* MECH ENG *diecasting die* refroidissement type fontaine *m*

watercourse *n* CONST *drain* cours d'eau *m*, drain *m*, HYDROL *stream, canal*, POLLUTION cours d'eau *m*

water-eroded *adj* HYDROL érodé par l'eau

waterfall *n* HYDROL cascade *f*, chute *f*, saut *m*; ~ **head** *n* HYDROL chute d'eau *f*

water-finished¹ *adj* PAPER TECH calandré humide, calandré à l'eau

water-finished:² ~ **board** *n* PAPER TECH carton calandré humide *m*; ~ **carton** *n* PAPER TECH carton calandré humide *m*; ~ **paper** *n* PAPER TECH, PRINT papier calandré humide *m*

water-free¹ *adj* CHEM, TEXTILES anhydre

water-free² *n* POLLUTION eau exclue *f*

waterfront *n* NAUT façade maritime *f*

watergel: ~ **explosive** *n* MINING bouillie *f*, bouillie explosive *f*

waterglass *n* CHEM silicate de potasse *m*; ~ **color** *n* (AmE), ~ **colour** *n* (BrE) couleur au verre soluble

water-hardened *adj* THERMOD *metals* trempé à l'eau

waterleaf: ~ **paper** *n* PAPER TECH papier absorbant *m*

waterless *adj* DETERGENTS anhydre, sans eau

waterlogged *adj* HYDROL sursaturé, NAUT *of ship* entre deux eaux, plein d'eau

waterman *n* NAUT *water transport* batelier *m*, marinier *m*

watermark *n* C&G brunissage *m*, CINEMAT trace de séchage *f*, PAPER TECH, PRINT filigrane *m*; ~ **roll** *n* PAPER TECH rouleau filigraneur *m*

water-oil: ~ **ratio** *n* (*WOR*) PETR rapport eau-pétrole *m*

waterplane *n* NAUT *naval architecture* section horizontale *f*, surface de la flottaison *f*

waterproof¹ *adj* P&R, PAPER TECH imperméable, PROP MAT imbrifuge, TEXTILES imperméable

waterproof:² ~ **abrasive paper** *n* MECH ENG abrasif sur support papier imperméable *m*; ~ **coating** *n* COATINGS enduit imperméable à l'eau *m*, enduit étanche à l'eau *m*; ~ **paint** *n* COATINGS peinture hydrofuge *f*; ~ **painting** *n* COATINGS peinture hydrofuge *f*; ~ **sealed camera** *n* PHOTO appareil étanche *m*; ~ **sheet** *n* TEXTILES alaise *f*;

~ tissue *n* COATINGS tissu enduit imperméable *m*

waterproof[3] *vt* COATINGS hydrofuger, imperméabiliser

waterproofing *n* COATINGS imperméabilisation *f*, CONST imperméabilisation à l'eau *f*, étanchéisation *f*, TEXTILES imperméabilisation *f*; **~ agent** *n* COATINGS imperméabilisant *m*; **~ salts** *n pl* COATINGS sels hydrofuges *m pl*

water-propelled: **~ hovercraft** *n* TRANSP aéroglisseur à propulsion marine *m*

water-regulating: **~ valve** *n* REFRIG vanne de modération de débit d'eau *f*

water-repellent[1] *adj* COATINGS hydrofuge, hydrophobe, repousseur d'eau, PROP MAT, TEXTILES hydrofuge

water-repellent:[2] **~ finish** *n* TEXTILES apprêt hydrofuge *m*; **~ finishing** *n* COATINGS imperméabilisation *f*; **~ impregnation means** *n pl* COATINGS agent hydrofuge *m*

water-resistant *adj* PACKAGING, TEXTILES résistant à l'eau

water-resisting *adj* PROP MAT hydrofuge

waters *n pl* NAUT *geography* parages *m pl*

watershed *n* HYDROL aire d'alimentation *f*, ligne de faîte *f*, ligne de partage *f*, ligne de partage des eaux *f*, WATER SUPP aire d'alimentation *f*, ligne de partage des eaux *f*

water-soluble[1] *adj* CHEM, FOOD TECH hydrosoluble, TEXTILES soluble dans l'eau

water-soluble:[2] **~ flux** *n* CONST *welding* flux hydrosoluble *m*

waterspout *n* METEO trombe marine *f*, NAUT *sea-state* trombe d'eau *f*, OCEANOG trombe *f*

watertight[1] *adj* CONST imperméable à l'eau, étanche à l'eau, HEAT ENG, NAUT, PACKAGING, PHYS étanche à l'eau, PROP MAT imperméable à l'eau, TEXTILES étanche à l'eau

watertight:[2] **~ caprock** *n* GAS TECH roche imperméable *f*; **~ socket outlet** *n* ELEC *connection* prise femelle étanche à l'eau *f*

watertightness *n* CONST étanchéité à l'eau *f*

water-use: **~ efficiency** *n* HYDROL efficacité d'utilisation de l'eau *f*

waterwall *n* OCEANOG coup de mer *m*

waterway *n* HYDROL, NAUT voie navigable *f*, WATER SUPP tube de raccordement d'eau *m*

waterworks *n* HYDROL station hydraulique *f*, usine hydraulique *f*

watery *adj* PROP MAT aquatique, aqueux

watt *n* (*W*) ELEC, ELEC ENG, METR, PHYS watt *m* (*W*)

Watt's: **~ fission spectrum** *n* NUCLEAR spectre de fission de Watt *m*

wattage *n* ELEC ENG consommation en watts *f*, PHYS wattage *m*, wattage physique *m*

watt-hour *n* ELEC, ELEC ENG, PHYS wattheure *f*; **~ meter** *n* PHYS wattheuremètre *m*

wattless[1] *adj* ELEC *alternating current* déwatté, réactif

wattless:[2] **~ component** *n* ELEC *alternating current*, ELEC ENG composante déwattée *f*, composante réactive *f*; **~ current** *n* ELEC *alternating current*, ELEC ENG courant déwatté *m*, courant réactif *m*

wattmeter *n* ELEC, PHYS wattmètre *m*

wave *n* ACOUSTICS, ELEC *electromagnetic*, ELEC ENG onde *f*, NAUT *sea state* lame *f*, onde *f*, vague *f*, PHYS, TELECOM, WAVE PHYS onde *f*, marine vague *f*, on beach rouleau *m*; **~ amplification** *n* TELECOM amplification d'onde *f*; **~ amplitude** *n* OCEANOG amplitude d'une vague *f*, amplitude de la houle *f*; **~ analyzer** *n* ELECTRON analyseur d'ondes *m*; **~ base** *n* OCEANOG niveau de base des vagues *m*; **~ coherence** *n* TELECOM cohérence d'onde *f*; **~ coupling** *n* TELECOM couplage d'ondes *m*; **~ crest** *n* FUELLESS, OCEANOG crête d'une vague *f*; **~ damper** *n* OCEANOG amortisseur *m*; **~ damping** *n* OCEANOG amortissement de la houle *m*; **~ decay** *n* OCEANOG amortissement de la houle *m*; **~ delta** *n* PETR delta de tempête *m*, lessivage *m*; **~ diffraction** *n* TELECOM diffraction d'onde *f*; **~ dispersion** *n* TELECOM dispersion d'onde *f*; **~ drag** *n* TRANSP traînée d'onde *f*; **~ duct** *n* ELEC ENG couche-piège *f*; **~ energy** *n* OCEANOG énergie de la houle *f*, énergie marémotrice *f*, WAVE PHYS énergie ondulatoire *f*; **~ equation** *n* PHYS, RAD PHYS équation d'onde *f*; **~ filter** *n* WAVE PHYS filtre à ondes *m*; **~ frequency** *n* RAD PHYS fréquence d'ondulation *f*; **~ function** *n* PHYS, WAVE PHYS fonction d'onde *f*; **~ generation** *n* TELECOM génération d'ondes *f*; **~ generator** *n* WAVE PHYS générateur d'ondes *m*; **~ group** *n* PHYS groupe d'ondes *m*; **~ height** *n* FUELLESS hauteur des vagues *f*, NAUT *sea state* hauteur de la houle *f*, OCEANOG hauteur de la houle *f*, hauteur des vagues *f*; **~ interference** *n* TELECOM interférence d'onde *f*; **~ maker** *n* NAUT *ship or boat design* volet batteur *m*; **~ mechanics** *n* CHEM *electronic theory*, ELEC ENG, WAVE PHYS mécanique ondulatoire *f*; **~ momentum per metre of crest** *n* FUELLESS énergie cinétique de vague par mètre de crête *f*; **~ motion** *n* WAVE PHYS mouvement ondulatoire *m*; **~ number** *n* ACOUSTICS, CHEM *of radiation*, WAVE PHYS nombre d'onde *m*; **~ optics** *n* OPT optique ondulatoire *f*, optique physique *f*, TELECOM optique ondulatoire *f*; **~ packet** *n* PHYS paquet d'ondes *m*; **~ particle duality** *n* PHYS dualité onde-corpuscule *f*, WAVE PHYS dualité onde-particule *f*; **~ period** *n* NAUT *ship or boat design* période de vague *f*; **~ physics** *n* PHYS physique ondulatoire *f*; **~ polarization** *n* TELECOM polarisation des ondes *f*; **~ power** *n* FUELLESS houille bleue *f*, WAVE PHYS puissance ondulatoire *f*; **~ propagation** *n* FUELLESS propagation des vagues *f*, PHYS propagation des ondes *f*; **~ propagation direction** *n* OCEANOG orthogonales de houle *f pl*; **~ propagation speed** *n* WAVE PHYS vitesse de propagation de l'onde *f*; **~ recorder** *n* OCEANOG houlographe *m*; **~ refraction diagram** *n* NAUT *ship design* plan de réfraction des vagues *m*, OCEANOG plan de vagues *m*; **~ resistance** *n* NAUT *ship or boat design* résistance de vague *f*; **~ shadowing effect** *n* TELECOM effet d'écran des vagues *m*; **~ spectrum** *n* OCEANOG spectre de la houle *m*, WAVE PHYS spectre d'ondes *m*; **~ surface** *n* ELEC ENG, PHYS surface d'onde *f*; **~ theory of light** *n* WAVE PHYS théorie ondulatoire de la lumière *f*; **~ train** *n* ACOUSTICS, PHYS, WAVEPHYS train d'ondes *m*; **~ transmission** *n* TELECOM transmission d'ondes *f*; **~ trough level** *n* OCEANOG niveau de base des vagues *m*; **~ vector** *n* ELEC ENG vecteur de propagation *m*, PHYS vecteur d'onde *m*; **~ velocity** *n* OCEANOG célérité des vagues *f*, force des vagues *f*, vitesse des vagues *f*, WAVE PHYS vitesse des ondes *f*; **~ zone** *n* RAD PHYS zone d'onde *f*

waveband *n* NAUT *radio*, RAD PHYS gamme d'ondes *f*, WAVE PHYS bande de fréquences *f*; **~ switching** *n* TV commutation de gammes d'ondes *f*

wave-cut: **~ bench** *n* OCEANOG trottoir *m*

waved: **~ washer** *n* SPRINGS rondelle ondulée *f*

waveform *n* COMP, DP, ELEC *alternating current*, ELEC ENG, PHYS, WAVE PHYS forme d'onde *f*; **~ error** *n* WAVE

PHYS déviation de la forme d'onde *f*; ~ **monitor** *n* TV oscilloscope de contrôle *m*, oscilloscope de profil *m*; ~ **synthesis** *n* ELECTRON *signal generation* synthèse de signaux *f*

wavefront *n* ACOUSTICS front d'onde *m*, surface d'onde *f*, ELEC ENG front d'onde *m*, OPT surface d'onde *f*, PETR, PHYS front d'onde *m*, TELECOM surface d'onde *f*, WAVE PHYS front d'onde *m*; ~ **array** *n* COMP, DP matrice à vague *f*

wave-generating: ~ **area** *n* OCEANOG aire de génération de la houle *f*; ~ **test tank** *n* NAUT *ship, boat design* bassin d'essai générateur de vagues *m*

waveguide *n* ELEC ENG, NAUT *radar*, PHYS, TELECOM, WAVE PHYS guide d'ondes *m*; ~ **antenna** *n* TELECOM antenne à guide d'ondes *f*; ~ **component** *n* ELEC ENG composant en guide d'ondes *m*; ~ **coupling** *n* ELEC ENG raccordement de guide d'ondes *m*; ~ **dispersion** *n* OPT dispersion de guidage d'ondes *f*, dispersion de guide d'ondes *f*, TELECOM dispersion de guidage d'ondes *f*, dispersion de guide d'ondes *f*; ~ **filter** *n* ELECTRON filtre en guide d'ondes *m*; ~ **fixed load** *n* ELEC ENG charge fixe en guide d'ondes *f*; ~ **isolator** *n* ELEC ENG isolateur en guide d'ondes *m*; ~ **load** *n* ELEC ENG charge en guide d'ondes *f*; ~ **mode** *n* TELECOM mode du guide d'ondes *m*; ~ **phase shifter** *n* ELEC ENG, NUCLEAR déphaseur en guide d'ondes *m*; ~ **plunger** *n* ELEC ENG piston de guide d'ondes *m*; ~ **section** *n* ELEC ENG tronçon de guide d'ondes *m*; ~ **sliding load** *n* ELEC ENG charge réglable en guide d'ondes *f*; ~ **slotted section** *n* ELEC ENG tronçon de mesure en guide d'ondes *m*; ~ **transformer** *n* ELEC ENG adaptateur à lame quart d'onde *m*; ~ **transition** *n* ELEC ENG transition de guides d'ondes *f*

wavelength *n* ACOUSTICS, CHEM *of radiation*, ELEC, ELECTRON, METALL, OPT, PETR, PHYS, TELECOM, WAVE PHYS longueur d'onde *f*; ~ **dispersive double X-ray spectrometer** *n* *(WDX)* NUCLEAR double spectromètre à rayons-X *m*; ~ **division multiplexing** *n* *(WDM)* TELECOM multiplexage en longueur d'onde *m*, multiplexage par répartition en longueur d'onde *m*, multiplexage spectral *m*; ~ **division switch** *n* TELECOM commutateur en longueur d'onde *m*; ~ **fluctuation** *n* OPT fluctuation de longueur d'onde *f*; ~ **multiplexing** *n* OPT multiplexage en longueur d'onde *m*; ~ **switching** *n* TELECOM commutation à longueur d'onde *f*

wavelet *n* WAVE PHYS ondelette *f*, vaguelette *f*

wave-like *adj* PART PHYS ondulatoire

wavellite *n* MINERAL wavellite *f*

wavemeter *n* NAUT ondomètre *m*, PHYS, WAVE PHYS ondemètre *m*

wave-propagating: ~ **accelerator** *n* RAD PHYS accélérateur à propagation d'ondes *m*

waviness *n* PAPER TECH gondolage *m*

wavy[1] *adj* C&G ondulé

wavy[2] ~ **cord** *n* C&G sirop *m*

wax[1] *n* PRINT cire *f*; ~ **content** *n* REFRIG teneur en paraffine *f*; ~ **impregnation** *n* PRINT paraffinage *m*; ~ **laminating** *n* PRINT encirage à la cire *m*, enduction à la cire *f*, pelliculage *m*; ~ **master** *n* RECORDING master gravure vinyle *m*; ~ **paper** *n* PACKAGING, PRINT papier paraffiné *m*; ~ **resist** *n* C&G enduit protecteur *m*

wax[2] *vt* COATINGS enduire de cire

waxed: ~ **board** *n* PAPER TECH carton paraffiné *m*

waxing *n* CINEMAT paraffinage *m*; ~ **machine** *n* CINEMAT appareil à paraffiner *m*

way:[1] **under** ~ *adv* NAUT *sailing* en route

way[2] *n* CHEM voie *f*, CONST *method* méthode *f*, procédé

m, voie *f*, *path* chemin *m*, route *f*, NAUT *of a ship*, OCEANOG *ship speed* erre *f*, PROD ENG méthode *f*, procédé *m*; ~ **of carrying out the invention** *n* PATENTS manière d'exécuter l'invention *f*, mode de réalisation de l'invention *m*; ~ **freight train** *n* (AmE) *(cf pick-up goods train)* RAIL *vehicles* train collecteur *m*; ~ **out** *n* CONST sortie *f*; ~ **point** *n* NAUT *navigation* point intermédiaire *m*

Way: ~ **and Works Department** *n* (BrE) RAIL section de l'equipement *f*

waybill *n* NAUT feuille de route *f*, lettre de transport maritime *f*

Wb *abbr* *(weber)* METR, PHYS Wb *(weber)*

WDM *abbr* *(wavelength division multiplexing)* TELECOM MRL *(multiplexage par répartition en longueur d'onde)*

WDX *abbr* *(wavelength dispersive double X-ray spectrometer)* NUCLEAR double spectromètre à rayons X *m*

weak: ~ **coupling** *n* NUCLEAR couplage faible *m*, couplage normal *m*; ~ **force** *n* PART PHYS force faible *f*; ~ **interaction** *n* PHYS *nuclear* interaction faible *f*; ~ **inversion** *n* ELECTRON *MOS transistors* faible inversion *f*; ~ **positron transition** *n* NUCLEAR transition positronique faible *f*

weakly-guiding: ~ **fiber** *n* (AmE), ~ **fibre** *n* (BrE) TELECOM fibre à guidage faible *f*

weapons: ~ **system** *n* MILIT système d'armes *m*

wear:[1] ~ **resistant** *adj* PACKAGING résistant à l'usure

wear[2] *n* GAS TECH érosion *f*, MAR POLL, MECH, MECH ENG, PAPER TECH, PROP MAT, TEXTILES usure *f*; ~ **and tear** *n* MECH ENG usure *f*, usure normale *f*, TEXTILES usure détérioration *f*; ~ **bushing** *n* PETR bague d'usure *f*; ~ **limit** *n* MECH ENG limite d'usure *f*; ~ **pad** *n* MECH ENG plaquette d'usure *f*; ~ **part** *n* MECH ENG pièce d'usure *f*; ~ **plate** *n* MECH ENG plaque de friction *f*, plaque de frottement *f*; ~ **rate** *n* CONST taux d'usure *m*; ~ **resistance** *n* PROP MAT, TEXTILES résistance à l'usure *f*; ~ **strip** *n* MECH ENG cale d'usure *f*

wear[3] *vt* MECH ENG, PROP MAT user, TEXTILES faire de l'usage; ~ **down** *vt* MECH ENG user; ~ **off** *vt* MECH ENG user; ~ **out** *vt* MECH ENG, TEXTILES user

wear[4] *vi* NAUT *ship round* virer vent arrière

wearer: ~ **trial** *n* TEXTILES essai au porter *m*

wearing *n* MECH ENG usure *f*; ~ **course** *n* CONST couche de roulement *f*; ~ **detail** *n* NUCLEAR élément d'usure *m*; ~ **element** *n* NUCLEAR élément d'usure *m*; ~ **part** *n* COAL TECH, GAS TECH pièce d'usure *f*; ~ **parts of a machine** *n pl* MECH ENG parties frottantes d'une machine *f pl*; ~ **plate** *n* MECH ENG plaque de friction *f*, plaque de frottement *f*; ~ **surface** *n* MECH ENG surface de frottement *f*, surface frottante *f*, TEXTILES surface d'usure *f*

wear-out: ~ **defect** *n* NUCLEAR *of fuel element* défaut dû à l'usure *m*; ~ **failure** *n* ELEC ENG défaillance due à l'usure *f*; ~ **failure period** *n* QUALITY période de défaillance par usure *f*

wear-resistant: ~ **coating** *n* COATINGS couche anti-usure *f*, couche résistante à l'usure *f*

weather:[1] ~ **balloon** *n* METEO ballon-sonde *m*; ~ **bureau** *n* METEO bureau météorologique *m*, service météorologique *m*; ~ **chart** *n* METEO carte météo *f*, carte météorologique *f*; ~ **forecast** *n* METEO prévision du temps *f*, prévision météo *f*, prévision météorologique *f*, METR prévision météo *f*, prévision météorologique *f*, SPACE prévision météo *f*; ~ **helm** *n* NAUT *sailing* barre au vent *f*; ~ **map** *n* NAUT carte météorologique *f*; ~ **pattern** *n* SPACE situation météorologique *f*; ~ **report** *n*

METEO, NAUT bulletin météo *m*, bulletin météorologique *m*, prévision météorologique *f*, SPACE bulletin météorologique *m*; ~ **routing** *n* NAUT routage météorologique *m*; ~ **ship** *n* METEO, NAUT navire météorologique *m*, navire-météo *m*; ~ **side** *n* NAUT bord du vent *m*; ~ **station** *n* METEO, NAUT, SPACE observatoire météorologique *m*, station météorologique *f*; ~ **station cabinet** *n* NAUT boîtier de plate-forme météorologique *m*; ~ **system** *n* METEO système météorologique *m*; ~ **warning** *n* METEO, NAUT alerte météorologique *f*; ~ **watch** *n* METEO, SPACE veille météorologique *f*; ~ **window** *n* PETR TECH fenêtre météorologique *f*

weather[2] *vt* CONST biaiser, taluter, GEOL altérer, désagréger

weather[3] *vi* CONST s'altérer par l'atmosphère, se désagréger par les intempéries; ~ **a squall** *vi* NAUT *sailing* essuyer un grain; ~ **a storm** *vi* NAUT *sailing* étaler une tempête

weather-beaten *adj* NAUT battu par la tempête, battu par les vents

weather-bound *adj* NAUT *of ship* retenu par le mauvais temps

weathered: ~ **oil** *n* MAR POLL hydrocarbure vieilli *m*, pétrole altéré *m*

weathering *n* COAL TECH désagrégation par les intempéries *f*, CONST désagrégation par les intempéries *f*, effritement par les agents atmosphériques *m*, effritement par les intempéries *m*, GEOL altération due aux intempéries *f*, MAR POLL altération *f*, dégradation *f*, P&R exposition aux intempéries *f*, *coatings* exposition aux intempéries *f*, PETR zone altérée *f*, PROP MAT désagrégation par les intempéries *f*, détérioration due aux intempéries *f*, TEXTILES altération due aux intempéries *f*; ~ **agencies** *n pl* PROP MAT agents d'intempérisme *m pl*; ~ **resistance** *n* CONST résistance aux intempéries *f*

weatherproof[1] *adj* PAPER TECH résistant aux intempéries, SAFETY protégé contre les intempéries, résistant aux intempéries

weatherproof:[2] ~ **clothing** *n* SAFETY vêtements à l'épreuve des intempéries *m pl*; ~ **paint** *n* COLOURS peinture résistant aux intempéries *f*

weave[1] *n* TEXTILES *of a fabric* armure *f*

weave[2] *vt* TEXTILES tisser

weaver's: ~ **beam** *n* TEXTILES ensouple au tissage *f*

weaving *n* TEXTILES tissage *m*, TRANSP entrecroisement *m*; ~ **factor** *n* TRANSP facteur d'entrecroisement *m*; ~ **maneuver** *n* (AmE), ~ **manoeuvre** *n* (BrE) TRANSP manoeuvre d'entrecroisement *f*

web *n* AERONAUT *of spar* âme *f*, CONST *of girder, T iron* âme *f*, *of key* panneton *m*, MECH *of beam* âme *f*, MECH ENG *of crank* bras *m*, corps *m*, PAPER TECH bande *f*, feuille continue *f*, PRINT bande *f*, TEXTILES voile de carde *f*, VEHICLES *crankshaft* toile *f*; ~ **break** *n* PRINT casse de bande *f*; ~ **break detectors** *n pl* PRINT détecteurs de casse *m pl*; ~ **frame** *n* NAUT *shipbuilding*, OCEANOG porque *f*; ~ **guide** *n* PRINT guide-bande *m*; ~ **into festoon** *n* PRINT dispositif d'entrée de la bande dans le feston *m*; ~ **lead** *n* PRINT passage papier *m*; ~ **offset press** *n* PRINT rotative offset *f*; ~ **path** *n* PRINT passage papier *m*; ~ **press** *n* PRINT rotative *f*; ~ **severer** *n* PRINT dispositif de section de la bande *m*, herse *f*; ~ **width** *n* PRINT laize *f*, largeur de bande *f*

webbing *n* MAR POLL sangle *f*, OCEANOG alèze *f*, TEXTILES courroie *f*

webbing-in *n* PRINT engagement de la bande *m*

weber *n* ELEC, ELEC ENG, METR, PHYS weber *m*

web-fed: ~ **offset rotary press** *n* PRINT rotative offset *f*

websterite *n* MINERAL websterite *f*

web-turning: ~ **device** *n* PRINT dispositif de retournement de la bande *m*

web-up *n* PRINT organisation du passage papier *f*

wedge[1] *n* CONST cale *f*, clavette *f*, coin *m*, MECH coin *m*, MECH ENG cale *f*, coin *m*, MINING *quarrying* coin *m*, PRINT barre de contrôle *f*, code-barre *m*, coin *m*; ~ **brake** *n* MECH ENG *braking systems* frein par coinçage *m*; ~ **crack** *n* METALL fissure en coin *f*; ~ **cut** *n* MINING bouchon convergent *m*; ~ **densitometer** *n* PHOTO densitomètre à coin gris *m*; ~ **disclination** *n* METALL disclinaison coincée *f*; ~ **key** *n* SPRINGS *of leaf spring* coin *m*; ~ **print** *n* CINEMAT sensitogramme *m*

wedge[2] *vt* MECH bloquer, caler, coincer, MECH ENG coincer

wedge:[3] ~ **out** *vi* GEOL se terminer en biseau

wedged: ~ **mortise-and-tenon joint** *n* CONST assemblage à tenon mortaise et cale *m*

wedge-type: ~ **combustion chamber** *n* AUTO chambre de combustion en coin *f*; ~ **fracture** *n* METALL rupture en coin *f*

wedging *n* MECH ENG coincement *m*, coinçage *m*

weed-killing: ~ **train** *n* RAIL train de désherbage chimique *m*, train désherbeur *m*, groupe désherbeur *m*

week: ~ **utilization** *n* PROD ENG utilisation hebdomadaire *f*

weephole *n* CONST barbacane *f*, trou d'écoulement *m*

weever *n* OCEANOG vive *f*

weft *n* PAPER TECH, SPACE, TEXTILES *of fabric* trame *f*; ~ **break** *n* TEXTILES cassé en trame *f*; ~ **density** *n* TEXTILES réduction en trame *f*; ~ **stop motion** *n* TEXTILES casse du fil de trame *f*; ~ **yarn** *n* PAPER TECH fil de trame *m*

weft-knitted: ~ **fabric** *n* TEXTILES tricot sans trame *m*

Wehnelt: ~ **cylinder** *n* INSTRUMENT, PHYS *electrode* électrode de Wehnelt *f*

weigh:[1] ~ **bridge** *n* CONST pont à bascule *m*

weigh[2] *vt* NAUT *anchor* appareiller, lever, PROD ENG peser; ~ **down** *vt* CONST *a floor by overloading* effondrer, surcharger

weighing *n* PAPER TECH pesage *m*; ~ **and punnet filling** *n* PACKAGING pesage et remplissage de barquettes *m*; ~ **boat** *n* LAB EQUIP nacelle de pesée *f*; ~ **bottle** *n* CHEM flacon à peser *m*, flacon à tare *m*, LAB EQUIP flacon à tare *m*; ~ **dish** *n* LAB EQUIP coupelle de pesée *f*; ~ **machine** *n* PRINT balance *f*, machine à peser *f*, PROD ENG bascule *f*; ~ **scale** *n* METR balance *f*

weight *n* METR mesure de poids *f*, mesure pondérale *f*, pesanteur *f*, poids *m*, PAPER TECH, PHYS poids *m*, PRINT graisse *f*, poids *m*; ~ **belt** *n* OCEANOG ceinture de lest *f*; ~ **of face** *n* PRINT graisse de caractère *f*; ~ **feeding** *n* PROD ENG alimentation massique *f*; ~ **filling machine** *n* PACKAGING doseuse par poids *f*; ~ **fraction** *n* NUCLEAR fraction massique *f*, teneur en masse *f*; ~ **governor** *n* CONTROL régulateur à poids *m*; ~ **on bit** *n* (*WOB*) PETR TECH poids sur l'outil *m*; ~ **optimization** *n* SPACE *spacecraft* optimisation de la masse *f*; ~ **penetration test** *n* COAL TECH essai statique de charge *m*; ~ **range** *n* PAPER TECH gamme de poids *f*; ~ **strength** *n* (*WS*) MINING coefficient d'utilisation pratique *m* (*CUP*), puissance au mortier balistique *f* (*PMB*); ~ **of type** *n* PRINT graisse de caractère *f*; ~ **unit** *n* METR unité de poids *f*

weighted: ~ **average** *n* PROD ENG moyenne pondérée *f*; ~

noise level indicator *n* POLLUTION indice d'évaluation du bruit *m*; **~ signal-to-noise ratio** *n* RECORDING rapport signal-bruit pondéré *m*

weighting *n* COMP, DP pondération *f*; **~ factor** *n* SPACE *communications* facteur de pondération *m*; **~ material** *n* PETR matières denses *f*, matériaux denses *m pl*, équipement de pesage *m*

weightlessness *n* PHYS agravité *f*, apesanteur *f*, SPACE apesanteur *f*

weights *n pl* METR poids *m pl*, série de poids *f*; **~ and measures** *n pl* METR poids et mesures *m pl*

weir *n* C&G déversoir *m*, FUELLESS barrage mobile *m*, HYDR EQUIP déversoir *m*, déversoir de jaugeage *m*, HYDROL déversoir *m*, WATER SUPP barrage mobile *m*, *dam* barrage *m*, *waste weir* déversoir *m*, trop-plein *m*; **~ bed** *n* OCEANOG parc *m*; **~ boom** *n* MAR POLL barrage à déversoir *m*; **~ skimmer** *n* MAR POLL récupérateur à déversoir *m*, récupérateur à seuil *m*, écrémeur à déversoir *m*, écrémeur à seuil *m*, POLLUTION récupérateur à déversoir *m*; **~ with vortex skimmer** *n* MAR POLL écrémeur à effet de vortex *m*

Weiss: **~ domain** *n* PHYS domaine de Weiss *m*

Weissenberg: **~ camera** *n* CRYSTALL chambre de Weissenberg *f*

weld[1] *n* METALL, NUCLEAR, PROD ENG, THERMOD soudure *f*; **~ metal** *n* METALL métal de soudure *m*; **~ overlay cladding** *n* NUCLEAR revêtement *m*; **~ region** *n* NUCLEAR région de soudure *f*; **~ strength check** *n* PROD ENG contrôle de résistance à la soudure *m*

weld[2] *vt* MECH, PAPER TECH, THERMOD souder

weldability *n* MECH ENG, METALL, PROP MAT soudabilité *f*; **~ test** *n* TESTING essai de soudabilité *m*

weld-deposited: **~ cladding** *n* NUCLEAR revêtement *m*

welded[1] *adj* PROD ENG, THERMOD soudé

welded:[2] **~ body seam** *n* PACKAGING bord soudé *m*; **~ buckle** *n* SPRINGS bride soudée *f*; **~ collar** *n* MECH ENG *pipe fitting* collet à souder *m*; **~ fitting** *n* MECH ENG monture soudée *f*; **~ seam** *n* PAPER TECH couture soudée *f*; **~ tuff** *n* GEOL dépôt pyroclastique soudé *m*

welder *n* MECH, SAFETY soudeur *m*

welder's: **~ goggles** *n pl* INSTRUMENT lunettes de soudure *f pl*; **~ hand shield** *n* SAFETY écran de soudeur *m*; **~ hood** *n* SAFETY casque de soudeur *m*; **~ protective curtain** *n* SAFETY rideau de protection pour soudeurs *m*; **~ safety helmet** *n* SAFETY casque de sécurité pour soudeurs *m*; **~ shield** *n* SAFETY bouclier de soudeur *m*

welding *n* C&G soudure *f*, MECH ENG, P&R *process* soudage *m*, PROD ENG, SAFETY soudage *m*, soudure *f*, THERMOD soudage *m*; **~ blowpipe** *n* CONST chalumeau soudeur *m*; **~ circuit** *n* CONST circuit de soudage *m*; **~ cycle** *n* CONST cycle de soudage *m*; **~ electrode** *n* PROP MAT électrode de soudage *f*; **~ handshield** *n* CONST masque à main *m*; **~ helmet** *n pl* CONST casque de soudeur *m*, masque à serre-tête *m*, SAFETY casque de soudeur *m*; **~ machine** *n* PROD ENG machine à souder *f*; **~ procedure** *n* CONST mode opératoire de soudage *m*; **~ process** *n* CONST procédé de soudage *m*; **~ program** *n* (AmE), **~ programme** *n* (BrE) CONST programme de soudage *m*; **~ protection** *n* SAFETY protection pendant le soudage *f*; **~ seam** *n* NUCLEAR cordon de soudabilité *m*, soudure *f*; **~ sequence** *n* CONST séquence de soudage *f*; **~ smoke extraction system** *n* SAFETY système d'évacuation des fumées de soudage *m*; **~ station** *n* PETR poste de soudage *m*; **~ steel wire** *n* PROP MAT fil d'acier pour électrodes de soudure *m*; **~ tables with vacuum apparatus** *n pl* SAFETY tables à soudure avec

aspirateur *f pl*; **~ torch** *n* THERMOD chalumeau *m*; **~ transformer** *n* ELEC ENG transformateur de soudage *m*; **~ wire** *n* CONST baguette *f*

weldless *adj* PROD ENG sans soudure

weldment *n* MECH *welding* assemblage soudé *m*

well *n* CONST jour *m*, jour de l'escalier *m*, HYDROL, PETR puits *m*, PETR TECH forage *m*, puits *m*, sondage *m*, trou *m*; **~ bore** *n* PETR TECH forage *m*, puits *m*, sondage *m*, trou *m*; **~ casing** *n* COAL TECH tuyau de fonçage *m*, FUELLESS *geothermal* anneau de puits *m*; **~ drill hole** *n* COAL TECH forage profond *m*; **~ log** *n* GEOPHYS diagramme de puits *m*; **~ logging** *n* FUELLESS radiocarottage *m*, GEOL diagraphie de forage *f*, GEOPHYS diagraphie du trou de sondage *f*, PETR TECH *drilling, prospecting* diagraphie de forage *f*; **~ logging equipment** *n* NUCLEAR équipement de carottage *m*; **~ potential** *n* PETR capacité de production d'un puits *f*; **~ sinking** *n* FUELLESS construction de puits *f*; **~ wagon** *n* (BrE) *(cf depressed deck car)* RAIL *vehicles* wagon kangourou *m*, wagon à évidement central *m*

wellhead *n* FUELLESS, GAS TECH, PETR tête de puits *f*, PETR TECH tête d'éruption *f*, tête de production *f*, tête de puits *f*; **~ equipment** *n* PETR équipement de tête de puits *m*; **~ pressure** *n* FUELLESS, PETR pression en tête de puits *f*; **~ temperature** *n* FUELLESS température en tête de puits *f*; **~ valve** *n* FUELLESS vanne de tête de puits *f*

well-known: **~ mark** *n* PATENTS marque notoire *f*

well-moderated core *n* NUCLEAR *of breeder reactor* coeur bien modéré *m*

well-plugging: **~ block** *n* GAS TECH bloc d'obturation de puits *m*

well-pump: **~ switch** *n* CONTROL interrupteur à pompe de puits *m*

well-sorted: **~ grains** *n pl* GEOL grains bien classés *m pl*

well-type: **~ planchet** *n* NUCLEAR *for radioactive assay* coupelle creuse *f*

welt *n* PROD ENG bande de recouvrement *f*, couvre-joint *m*, fourrure *f*

welted: **~ joint** *n* PROD ENG assemblage à couvre-joints *m*

wernerite *n* MINERAL avernérite *f*, wernérite *f*

west *adj* NAUT de l'ouest

Westcott: **~ model** *n* NUCLEAR *for calculating effective thermal cross section* modèle de Westcott *m*

westerlies *n pl* METEO vents de l'ouest *m pl*, OCEANOG quarantièmes rugissants *m pl*

westerly *adj* NAUT d'ouest

Weston: **~ standard cell** *n* ELEC pile étalon Weston *f*, ELEC ENG pile Weston *f*, pile étalon Weston *f*, pile étalon au cadmium *f*

westwards *adv* NAUT vers l'ouest, à l'ouest

wet[1] *adj* PAPER TECH, TEXTILES humide, THERMOD mouillé; **~ on wet** *adj* P&R *paint application* mouillé sur mouillé

wet:[2] **~ acidic fallout** *n* POLLUTION dépôt acide humide *m*, retombées acides humides *f pl*; **~ and dry polishing** *n* C&G travail à la séchée *m*; **~ ashing** *n* NUCLEAR obtention de cendres humides *f*; **~ assay** *n* CHEM essai par voie humide *m*, COAL TECH analyse par voie humide *f*; **~ break** *n* PAPER TECH casse *f*; **~ broke** *n* PAPER TECH cassés humides *m pl*; **~ bulb temperature** *n* HEAT ENG température au thermomètre mouillé *f*; **~ bulb thermometer** *n* REFRIG thermomètre mouillé *m*, thermomètre à boule mouillée *m*, THERMOD thermomètre mouillé *m*, thermomètre à boule mouillée *m*, thermomètre à réservoir mouillé *m*; **~ cell** *n* ELEC ENG pile à électrolyte liquide *f*; ~ **chamber** *n* OCEANOG caisson humide *m*; ~ **compression** *n* REFRIG fonctionnement en régime humide *m*, marche en régime humide *f*; ~ **creping** *n* PAPER TECH crêpage humide *m*; ~ **cylinder liner** *n* AUTO chemise humide *f*; ~ **deposition** *n* POLLUTION dépôt humide *m*, retombées humides *f pl*; ~ **desulfurization process** *n* (AmE), ~ **desulphurization process** *n* (BrE) POLLUTION processus de désulfuration humide *m*; ~ **dock** *n* NAUT dock flottant *m*; ~ **dust removal installation** *n* SAFETY installation de dépoussiérage à l'humidité *f*; ~ **end** *n* CINEMAT partie au noir *f*, partie humide *f*, PAPER TECH partie humide *f*; ~ **fog** *n* METEO brouillard mouillant *m*; ~ **gas** *n* GAS TECH gaz riche *m*, PETR, PHYS gaz humide *m*; ~ **gate** *n* CINEMAT tirage humide *m*, tirage par immersion *m*; ~ **gate printer** *n* CINEMAT tireuse par immersion *f*; ~ **glue label** *n* PACKAGING étiquette à encoller *f*; ~ **grinding** *n* COAL TECH broyage humide *m*, SPRINGS meulage à l'eau *m*; ~ **hole** *n* MINING trou humide *m*; ~ **machine** *n* PAPER TECH presse-pâte *m*; ~ **natural gas** *n* PETR TECH gaz humide *m*, gaz riche *m*; ~ **paint** *n* CONST peinture fraîche *f*, peinture mouillée *f*; ~ **period** *n* POLLUTION période de précipitation *f*, période humide *f*; ~ **polishing** *n* C&G travail humide *m*, PROD ENG polissage humide *m*; ~ **precipitation** *n* POLLUTION précipitations humides *f pl*; ~ **press** *n* PAPER TECH presse humide *f*; ~ **press roll** *n* PAPER TECH rouleau de presse humide *m*; ~ **pulp** *n* PAPER TECH pâte humide *f*; ~ **radome** *n* TELECOM radome humide *m*; ~ **reaction** *n* CHEM réaction par voie humide *f*; ~ **reed relay** *n* CONTROL contact basculant à mercure *m*, interrupteur basculant à mercure *m*; ~ **rot** *n* CONST *timber* carie humide *f*; ~ **screening** *n* COAL TECH criblage à l'eau *m*; ~ **scrubber** *n* POLLUTION dépoussiéreur humide *m*, séparateur humide *m*; ~ **standpipe** *n* CONST *building* colonne en charge *f*; ~ **steam** *n* FUELLESS vapeur humide *f*; ~ **stock** *n* PAPER TECH pâte grasse *f*; ~ **strength** *n* P&R résistance à l'humidité *f*, résistance à l'état humide *f*, PAPER TECH résistance à l'état humide *f*; ~ **strength paper** *n* PAPER TECH papier résistant à l'état humide *m*; ~ **strength retention** *n* PAPER TECH indice de résistance à l'état humide *m*; ~ **track** *n* PRINT tirant de la colle *m*; ~ **treatment** *n* COAL TECH traitement à l'eau *m*, MECH ENG traitement par voie humide *m*, traitement à l'eau *m*; ~ **tree** *n* PETR TECH tête d'éruption en pleine eau *f*

wet[3] *vt* CHEM humecter, mouiller, PHYS humidifier, mouiller

wet-air: ~ **filter** *n* HEAT ENG filtre à air perdu *m*

wet-aluminium: ~ **capacitor** *n* (BrE) ELEC ENG condensateur électrochimique *m*, condensateur à l'aluminium à électrolyte liquide *m*

wet-aluminum: ~ **capacitor** *n* (AmE) *see wet- aluminium capacitor*

wet-collodion: ~ **process** *n* PHOTO, PRINT procédé au collodion humide *m*

wet-dry: ~ **processing treatment** *n* TEXTILES traitement mouillé ou à sec *m*

wet-plate: ~ **process** *n* PRINT procédé au collodion humide *m*

wet-slug: ~ **tantalum capacitor** *n* ELEC ENG condensateur au tantale à anode frittée et électrolyte gélifiée *m*, condensateur au tantale à électrolyte gélifiée *m*

wetsuit *n* NAUT tenue de plongée *f*, combinaison de plongée *f*, OCEANOG combinaison de plongée *f*, habit de plongée *m*, vêtement de plongée *m*, PETR scaphandre *m*

wettability *n* P&R *adhesives*, PETR mouillabilité *f*

wetted: ~ **pad evaporative cooler** *n* REFRIG refroidisseur à tampon humide *m*; ~ **surface** *n* NAUT *ship design* surface immergée *f*

wetting[1] *adj* CHEM mouillant

wetting[2] *n* CHEM, MECH ENG humidification *f*, mouillage *m*, mouillement *m*; ~ **agent** *n* C&G agent mouillant *m*, CHEM agent mouillant *m*, tensio-actif *m*, CINEMAT, FOOD TECH, MAR POLL agent mouillant *m*, P&R *additive* agent de surface *m*, mouillant *m*, PHOTO mouillant *m*, PHYS, PRINT, TEXTILES agent mouillant *m*; ~ **of dry material** *n* TEXTILES mouillage à sec *m*

wetting-off: ~ **iron** *n* (BrE) *(cf crack-off iron)* C&G fer à détacher *m*

wet-type: ~ **cooler** *n* REFRIG refroidisseur de type humide *m*

whale: ~ **boat** *n* OCEANOG baleinière *f*; ~ **factory ship** *n* OCEANOG navire baleinier *m*

whaler *n* OCEANOG baleinier *m*, navire baleinier *m*

whaling: ~ **ship** *n* OCEANOG baleinier *m*, navire baleinier *m*

wharf *n* NAUT appontement *m*, débarcadère *m*, embarcadère *m*, quai *m*

what: ~ **you see is what you get** *n* *(WYSIWYG)* COMP, DP tel vu tel imprimé, vu- imprimé *(WYSIWYG)*

wheatmeal *n* FOOD TECH farine grossière *f*

Wheatstone: ~ **bridge** *n* ELEC, ELEC ENG, PHYS pont de Wheatstone *m*

wheel *n* MECH ENG roulette *f*, *grinding wheel* meule *f*, *hand wheel* volant *m*, *pulley* poulie *f*, roue *f*, volant *m*, *small metal roller, runner* galet *m*, galet mécanique *m*, roue *f*, NAUT *boat building* barre à roue *f*, PROD ENG *of fan* tourniquet *m*, *of turbine* couronne mobile *f*, roue mobile *f*, TRANSP, VEHICLES roue *f*; ~ **alignment** *n* TRANSP alignement des roues *m*; ~ **and axle drive** *n* TRANSP rail réducteur d'essieu monté *m*; ~ **bearing** *n* VEHICLES roulement de roue *m*; ~ **bond** *n* RAIL *vehicles* connexion de roue *f*; ~ **carriage** *n* MECH ENG *grinding machine* chariot porte-meule *m*; ~ **clearance** *n* RAIL *vehicles* jeu de roues *m*; ~ **cover** *n* VEHICLES chapeau de roue *m*, enjoliveur de roue *m*; ~ **crank** *n* MECH ENG coude circulaire *m*, manivelle à plateau *f*, plateau-manivelle *m*; ~ **cylinder** *n* AUTO cylindre récepteur *m*; ~ **dresser** *n* MECH ENG décrasse-meule *m*, rhabilleur pour meules *m*; ~ **flange** *n* RAIL *vehicles* boudin de roue *m*, VEHICLES bord de roue *m*, rebord de roue *m*; ~ **flange lubricant** *n* RAIL *vehicles* lubrifiant de boudin *m*; ~ **flange rollers** *n pl* MECH ENG galets à boudins *m pl*; ~ **guard** *n* MECH ENG carter *m*, carter d'engrenage *m*, couvre-engrenages *m*, couvre-roue *m*, SAFETY *machine tools* capot couvre-meule *m*; ~ **head** *n* PROD ENG *for mounting on emery wheel* porte-meule *m*; ~ **house** *n* NAUT timonerie *f*; ~ **load** *n* CONST charge par roue *f*; ~ **nut** *n* (BrE) *(cf lug nut)* AUTO *car* écrou de roue *m*; ~ **nut cross brace** *n* MECH ENG *tool* clé en croix *f*; ~ **ore** *n* MINERAL bournonite *f*; ~ **slide** *n* PROD ENG glissière des roues *f*; ~ **slide mark** *n* RAIL *track* crapaud de patinage *m*; ~ **slip** *n* AUTO patinage *m*; ~ **slip mark on rails** *n* RAIL *track* crapaud de patinage *m*; ~ **spindle** *n* MECH ENG *grinding machine* arbre porte-meule *m*; ~ **spindle speed** *n* MECH ENG *machine tool* vitesse de meule *f*; ~ **suspension lever** *n* AUTO bras porte fusée *m*; ~ **swarf** *n* PROD ENG boue de meule *f*; ~ **tooth** *n* MECH ENG dent d'engrenage *f*; ~ **train** *n* MECH ENG train de roues *m*; ~ **web** *n* RAIL *vehicles* flasque de roue *m*; ~ **well** *n* AERONAUT *landing gear* case de train *f*, logement de train *m*, logement des roues *m*, puits de roue *m*; ~ **which engages a worm** *n* MECH ENG roue qui engrène une vis sans fin *f*

wheelbarrow *n* CONST, TRANSP brouette *f*

wheelbase *n* AERONAUT, VEHICLES empattement *m*

wheeled: ~ **carriage** *n* MILIT *of gun* affût à roues *m*; ~ **glass cutter** *n* C&G *tool* coupe-verre à molette *m*

wheelfeed: ~ **increment range** *n* MECH ENG *machine tool* plage d'incréments d'avance *f*

wheels-up: ~ **landing** *n* AERONAUT atterrissage sur le ventre *m*, atterrissage train rentré *m*

whetstone *n* PROD ENG affiloire *f*, pierre à aiguiser *f*

whetting *n* PROD ENG repassage *m*

whewellite *n* MINERAL whewellite *f*

whey *n* FOOD TECH lactosérum *m*, petit-lait *m*; ~ **concentrate** *n* FOOD TECH concentré de petit-lait *m*, concentré de protéines de lactosérum *m*; ~ **powder** *n* FOOD TECH poudre de petit-lait *f*

whip: ~ **aerial** *n* NAUT antenne fouet *f*; ~ **antenna** *n* NAUT *radio*, SPACE antenne fouet *f*; ~ **gin** *n* MECH ENG poulie à chape croisée *f*; ~ **pan** *n* CINEMAT pano filé *m*

whiplash: ~ **effect** *n* TRANSP coup du lapin *m*

whipper *n* PAPER TECH batteur de feutre *m*

whipping *n* NAUT *ropes* surliure *f*, NUCLEAR fouettement *m*

whipstock *n* PETR TECH *drilling* sifflet de déviation *m*

whirler *n* C&G assiette *f*

whirling: ~ **of shafts** *n* MECH ENG tourbillonnement des arbres *m*

whirlpool *n* HYDROL tourbillon *m*, vortex *m*

Whirlpool: ~ **galaxy** *n* ASTRON galaxie des Chiens de Chasse *f*

whirlwind *n* METEO, NAUT tourbillon de vent *m*

whisker *n* CRYSTALL fil monocristallin *m*, trichite *f*, ELECTRON *point-contact diodes* pointe de contact *f*, METALL monocristal sans dislocations *m*, monocristal whisker *m*, whisker *m*, PROP MAT monocristal sans dislocations *m*, monocristal whisker *m*; ~ **strength** *n* PROP MAT résistance mécanique des trichites *f*; ~ **toughening** *n* PROP MAT durcissement par trichites *m*

whistle *n* ELECTRON sifflet *m*; ~ **buoy** *n* NAUT *navigation marks, sound signal* bouée sonore à sifflet *f*

whistling *n* RECORDING sifflement *m*

white: ~ **arsenic** *n* C&G anhydride arsénieux *m*; ~ **balance** *n* TV balance des blancs *f*; ~ **caps** *n* OCEANOG écume *f*; ~ **clip** *n* TV écrêteur du blanc *m*; ~ **compression** *n* TV compression du blanc *f*; ~ **dwarf** *n* ASTRON *type of small star* naine blanche *f*; ~ **frost** *n* METEO gelée blanche *f*; ~ **heat** *n* THERMOD blanc soudant *m*, chaleur blanche *f*, chaude blanche *f*, rouge blanc *m*; ~ **horses** *pl* OCEANOG écume *f*; ~ **ice** *n* REFRIG glace opaque *f*; ~ **iron pyrites** *n* MINERAL pyrite blanche *f*; ~ **lead** *n* CHEM céruse *f*; ~ **leader** *n* CINEMAT amorce blanche *f*; ~ **level** *n* TV niveau de blanc *m*; ~ **light** *n* PHYS, PRINT lumière blanche *f*; ~ **limiter** *n* TV écrêteur du blanc *m*; ~ **lined board** *n* PACKAGING carton blanc avec revêtement *m*; ~ **metal packing** *n* RAIL *vehicles* garniture en métal blanc *f*; ~ **mica** *n* P&R *raw material* mica moscovite *m*; ~ **noise** *n* ACOUSTICS, COMP, DP, ELECTRON, PHYS, RECORDING, SPACE, TELECOM bruit blanc *m*; ~ **noise generator** *n* ELECTRON générateur de bruit blanc *m*; ~ **noise signal** *n* ELECTRON signal de bruit blanc *m*; ~ **noise source** *n* ELECTRON source de bruit blanc *f*; ~ **peak** *n* TV crête du blanc *f*; ~ **phosphate opal** *n* C&G verre laiteux au phosphate *m*; ~ **photocopy** *n* PRINT photocopie blanche *f*; ~ **pigment** *n* COLOURS pigment

blanc *m*; ~ **pigmented powder** *n* COLOURS pigment blanc en poudre *m*; ~ **product** *n* MAR POLL produit blanc *m*; ~ **radiation** *n* RAD PHYS radiation blanche *f*, rayonnement à spectre uniforme *m*; ~ **reference** *n* TV blanc de référence *m*; ~ **room** *n* SPACE salle blanche *f*; ~ **saturation** *n* TV saturation du blanc *f*; ~ **signal frequency** *n* CONTROL fréquence du blanc *f*; ~ **size** *n* COLOURS colle blanche *f*; ~ **squall** *n* OCEANOG grain blanc *m*; ~ **vinegar** *n* FOOD TECH acide acétique *m*

white-hot *adj* THERMOD incandescent, porté à blanc, *condition* chauffé à blanc

white-level: ~ **frequency** *n* TV fréquence du niveau de blanc *f*

white-light: ~ **fringe** *n* PHYS frange de lumière blanche *f*

whiteness *n* PAPER TECH blancheur *f*

white-out *n* METEO blanc dehors *m*, temps laiteux *m*

whitewash[1] *n* CHEM badigeon *m*, COATINGS enduit à la chaux *m*, COLOURS peinture à la chaux *f*, CONST blanc de chaux *m*, lait de chaux *m*; ~ **brush** *n* COLOURS brosse à badigeon *f*, pinceau à badigeon *m*, queue de morue *f*

whitewash[2] *vt* COLOURS badigeonner à la chaux, chauler

whitewashing *n* CONST blanchiment *m*, blanchiment à la chaux *m*

whiting *n* CHEM carbonate de chaux *m*

whitneyite *n* MINERAL whitneyite *f*

Whitworth: ~ **screw thread** *n* MECH ENG filetage Whitworth *m*, filetage normal anglais *m*, pas Whitworth *m*; ~ **thread** *n* MECH ENG filetage Whitworth *m*, filetage normal anglais *m*, pas Whitworth *m*

who-are-you *phr* (*WRU*) TELECOM qui êtes-vous

whole: ~ **food** *n* FOOD TECH produit naturel *m*; ~ **piece** *n* TEXTILES pièce entière *f*; ~ **rock analysis** *n* PETR analyse de roche totale *f*; ~ **rock isochrone** *n* GEOL isochrone roches totales *f*; ~ **tone** *n* ACOUSTICS ton *m*

wholesale: ~ **supplier** *n* PROD ENG revendeur en gros *m*

wholesome: ~ **water** *n* WATER SUPP eau saine *f*

wick *n* SPACE *spacecraft* mèche *f*

wicket: ~ **wall** *n* C&G devanture *f*

wide:[1] ~ **open** *adv* CINEMAT à pleine ouverture

wide:[2] ~ **aperture lens** *n* CINEMAT objectif à grande ouverture *m*; ~ **area network** *n* PRINT réseau de transmission de données à longues distances *m*; ~ **area system** *n* TELECOM système desservant des zones étendues *m*; ~ **band** *n* COMP, TELECOM bande large *f*; ~ **band amplification** *n* ELECTRON amplification à large bande *f*; ~ **band amplifier** *n* ELECTRON amplificateur à large bande *m*; ~ **band antenna** *n* SPACE antenne à large bande *f*; ~ **band axis** *n* TV axe *m*; ~ **band band-pass filter** *n* (*cf wide band high-pass filter*) ELECTRON filtre passe-bande à large bande *m*; ~ **band beams** *n pl* RAD PHYS *emission* faisceaux à bande large *m pl*; ~ **band circuit** *n* TELECOM circuit à large bande *m*; ~ **band filter** *n* ELECTRON filtre à large bande *m*; ~ **band filtering** *n* ELECTRON filtrage à large bande *m*; ~ **band high-pass filter** *n* (*cf wide band band-pass filter*) ELECTRON filtre passe-haut à large bande *m*; ~ **band integrated services digital network** *n* TELECOM réseau numérique avec intégration des services à large bande *m*; ~ **band interference** *n* ELECTRON parasites à large bande *m pl*; ~ **band ISDN** *n* TELECOM RNIS à large bande *m*; ~ **band low-pass filter** *n* ELECTRON filtre passe-bas à large bande *m*; ~ **band measurement** *n* ELECTRON mesure à large bande *f*; ~ **band modem** *n* ELECTRON modem à large bande *m*; ~ **band modulation** *n* ELECTRON modulation à large bande *f*; ~ **band noise** *n* ELECTRON, TELECOM bruit à large bande *m*; ~ **band pipette** *n* CHEM pipette à bord large f; ~ **band power amplifier** n ELEC-TRON amplificateur de puissance à large bande m; ~ **band receiver** n TELECOM récepteur à large bande m; ~ **band signal** n ELECTRON, TELECOM signal à large bande m; ~ **band switching network** n TELECOM réseau de connexion à large bande m; ~ **band transmission** n TELECOM transmission à large bande f; ~ **band tube** n ELECTRON tube hyperfréquence m, tube à large bande m; ~ **band tunable oscillator** n ELECTRON oscillateur accordable à large bande m; ~ **shot** n CINEMAT plan d'ensemble m, plan large m; ~ **to gage** n (AmE), ~ **to gauge** n (BrE) RAIL track surécartement m

wide-angle: ~ **converter** n PHOTO bonnette positive convergente f; ~ **instrument** n INSTRUMENT instrument grand-angulaire m, instrument à grand angle m; ~ **lens** n CINEMAT grand angulaire m, objectif grand angulaire m, PHOTO objectif panoramique m, objectif à grand angle m; ~ **scattering** n NUCLEAR diffusion aux grands angles f

wideband adj TELECOM bande large

wide-bodied: ~ **aircraft** n AERONAUT, TRANSP avion gros porteur m

wide-body: ~ **aircraft** n AERONAUT, TRANSP avion gros porteur m

wide-bore: ~ **tube** n LAB EQUIP glassware tube de forte section m

wide-field: ~ **metallurgical microscope** n INSTRUMENT microscope de métallographie à grand champ m; ~ **stereo microscope** n INSTRUMENT microscope stéréoscopique à grand champ m

wide-mouth: ~ **bottle** n LAB EQUIP container flacon à col large m, glassware flacon à large ouverture m; ~ **containers** n pl C&G verrerie d'emballage à col large f; ~ **neck** n PACKAGING goulot large m

wide-necked: ~ **flask** n LAB EQUIP glassware ballon à col large m

wide-screen: ~ **picture** n CINEMAT image panoramique f

Widmannstätten: ~ **figure** n ASTRON figure de Widmannstätten f; ~ **plate** n METALL plaque de Widmannstätten f; ~ **structure** n METALL structure de Widmannstätten f

widow n PRINT isolation en bas de page f, veuve f

width n COMP, DP largeur f, PAPER TECH laize f, largeur f, PRINT chasse f, TEXTILES largeur f; ~ **adjustment** n CONTROL réglage de la largeur m; ~ **of blade** n SAFETY largeur de lame f; ~ **choke** n TV bobine d'ajustage de la largeur de l'image f; ~ **coding** n ELECTRON pulse-width modulation codage par modulation de largeur m; ~ **in reed** n TEXTILES largeur au peigne f; ~ **jitter** n ELECTRON gigue de largeur f, instabilité de largeur f; ~ **of splitting** n METALL largeur de fendage f

Wiedemann-Franz: ~ **law** n PHYS loi de Wiedemann et Franz f

Wien: ~ **bridge** n ELECTRON, PHYS pont de Wien m; ~ **bridge oscillator** n ELECTRON oscillateur à pont de Wien m; ~ **displacement law** n PHYS loi de déplacement de Wien f; ~ **law** n PHYS loi de Wien f

Wigner: ~ **effect** n PHYS effet Wigner m

wig-wag: ~ **signal** n RAIL signal wig-wag m

wild: ~ **camera** n CINEMAT caméra non synchrone f; ~ **formation** n PAPER TECH épair irrégulier m; ~ **look-through** n PAPER TECH épair irrégulier m; ~ **motor** n CINEMAT moteur asynchrone m, moteur non synchrone m; ~ **recording** n RECORDING enregistrement non synchrone m; ~ **shot** n CINEMAT plan tourné en muet m; ~ **track** n CINEMAT son non synchrone m; ~ **well** n PETR TECH forage en éruption non contrôlée m

wildcard: ~ **character** n COMP, DP caractère générique m

wildcat: ~ **drilling** n PETR TECH forage d'exploration m, forage de recherche m; ~ **well** n PETR puits d'exploration m, puits de recherche m, puits de sondage m

willemite n MINERAL willémite f

williamsite n MINERAL williamsite f

Willison: ~ **coupling** n TRANSP attelage Willison m

Wilson: ~ **cloud chamber** n PART PHYS detection of ionized particles, PHYS chambre de Wilson f, chambre à brouillard f

wiluite n MINERAL wiluite f

Wimshurst: ~ **machine** n ELEC ENG machine de Wimshurst f

winch[1] n CONST cranked handle manivelle f, windlass treuil m, MAR POLL manivelle f, treuil m, NAUT deck fittings treuil m, winch m, TEXTILES barque f; ~ **drum** n NAUT deck fittings tambour de treuil m, OCEANOG touret m

winch:[2] ~ **into helicopter** vt AERONAUT, NAUT air-sea rescue, TRANSP hélitreuiller

Winchester: ~ **disk** n COMP, DP disque Winchester m

wind:[1] **off the** ~ adv NAUT sailing aux allures portantes

wind[2] n METEO vent m, TEXTILES croisure du fil sur le support f; ~ **and sea state capability handling** n TRANSP tenue à la mer et au vent f; ~ **arrow** n METEO on wind chart flèche de vent f; ~ **bore** n WATER SUPP of pump aspirant m, crépine f, crépine d'aspiration f, grenouillère f, lanterne f, reniflard m; ~ **brace** n CONST building contrevent m; ~ **bracing** n CONST poutre de contreventement f; ~ **break** n METEO brise-vent m; ~ **chart** n METEO, NAUT navigation carte des vents f; ~ **conditions** n pl METEO régime des vents m; ~ **cone** n AERONAUT manche à air f, manche à vent f; ~ **direction** n AERONAUT, METEO, NAUT direction du vent f; ~ **dispersion** n GAS TECH, POLLUTION dispersion par le vent f; ~ **energy** n FUELLESS, PHYS énergie éolienne f; ~ **erosion** n GEOL érosion éolienne f; ~ **gage** n (AmE), ~ **gauge** n (BrE) FUELLESS tidal power anémomètre m; ~ **inclination meter** n METEO anémoclinomètre m; ~ **machine** n CINEMAT machine à produire du vent f; ~ **power** n FUELLESS, METEO, PHYS énergie éolienne f; ~ **pressure** n METEO poussée du vent f, pression du vent f; ~ **recorder** n METEO anémomètre enregistreur m; ~ **resistance** n FLUID PHYS résistance due au vent f; ~ **rose** n FUELLESS, METEO rose des vents f; ~ **sail** n NAUT manche à vent f; ~ **sensor** n METEO, NAUT anémomètre m; ~ **shaft** n METEO hampe de vent f; ~ **shear** n METEO cisaillement de vent m; ~ **sock** n AERONAUT manche à air f, manche à vent f; ~ **speed** n FUELLESS, METEO vitesse du vent f; ~ **speed barb** n METEO on wind chart barbule f; ~ **stress** n OCEANOG tension du vent f; ~ **stress sea** n OCEANOG mer du vent f; ~ **telltale** n NAUT girouette f; ~ **tunnel** n AERONAUT soufflerie f, CONST tunnel à vent m, PHYS, SPACE soufflerie f; ~ **tunnel balance** n AERONAUT balance aérodynamique f, balance de soufflerie f; ~ **tunnel test** n SPACE spacecraft, TESTING essai en soufflerie m; ~ **turbine** n FUELLESS turbine éolienne f, MECH ENG turbine à vent f; ~ **turbine fan** n REFRIG ventilateur à turbine éolienne m; ~ **turbine generator** n FUELLESS turbine aérogénérateur f; ~ **velocity** n FUELLESS, METEO vitesse du vent f; ~ **velocity cubed** n FUELLESS cube de la vitesse du vent m, vitesse du vent au cube f

wind[3] vt CINEMAT enrouler, MECH ENG put onto spool bobiner, dévider, enrouler, PAPER TECH bobiner, PHYS enrouler, TEXTILES bobiner; ~ **off a cord rolled round a**

drum *vt* MECH ENG détourner une corde roulée sur un tambour; ~ **up** *vt* MECH ENG *coil spring* monter, remonter

wind[4] *vi* CONST *warp* gauchir, se gauchir, MECH ENG *coil* s'enrouler, se dévider

windage: ~ **adjustment screw** *n* INSTRUMENT vis de réglage latéral *f*; ~ **losses** *n pl* ELEC pertes par la ventilation *f pl*

wind-driven: ~ **generator** *n* ELEC ENG génératrice pour énergie éolienne *f*; ~ **sea** *n* OCEANOG mer du vent *f*

wind-electric: ~ **power station** *n* ELEC ENG centrale éolienne *f*

winder *n* C&G bobinoir *m*, CONST marche dansante *f*, marche gironnée *f*, marche rayonnante *f*, marche tournante *f*, PAPER TECH bobineuse *f*, enrouleuse *f*; ~ **house** *n* MINING salle de la machine *f*

wind-eroded *adj* METEO érodé par le vent

winding *n* CONST *warping* gauchissement *m*, ELEC *motor, generator* bobinage *m*, enroulement *m*, ELEC ENG enroulement *m*, MECH ENG enroulement *m*, *coiling* bobinage *m*, enroulage *m*, enroulement *m*, PAPER TECH bobinage *m*, PHYS enroulement *m*, VEHICLES *generator* armature *f*; ~ **and fanning** *n* PRINT effet d'élargissement et d'aplatissement *m*; ~ **capacitance** *n* ELEC *coil* capacité de bobine *f*, ELEC ENG capacité de l'enroulement *f*; ~ **direction** *n* SPRINGS sens d'enroulement *m*; ~ **drum** *n* PAPER TECH rouleau porteur *m*; ~ **engine** *n* MINING machine d'extraction *f*, moteur d'extraction *m*; ~ **inset** *n* MINING chambre d'accrochage *f*; ~ **insulation** *n* ELEC *coil* isolation d'enroulement *f*; ~ **machine** *n* CINEMAT bobineuse *f*, enrouleuse *f*, PACKAGING enrouleuse *f*; ~ **mechanism** *n* VEHICLES lève-glace *m*; ~ **motion** *n* MECH ENG mouvement d'enroulement *m*, mouvement enrouleur *m*; ~ **off** *n* PAPER TECH débobinage *m*; ~ **pitch** *n* ELEC *coil* pas d'enroulement *m*; ~ **process** *n* PROD ENG, TEXTILES bobinage *m*; ~ **ratio** *n* ELEC *transformer* rapport de transformation *m*; ~ **RTD** *n* PROD ENG PTC pour enroulement *m*; ~ **shaft** *n* MINING puits d'extraction *m*, puits de travail *m*; ~ **tackle** *n* NAUT caliorne *m*; ~ **tension** *n* CINEMAT tension d'enroulement *f*; ~ **tower** *n* MINING tour d'extraction *f*

winding-on: ~ **machine** *n* PACKAGING enrouleuse *f*

windlass *n* CONST treuil *m*, NAUT *deck equipment* guindeau *m*

windmill: ~ **pump** *n* FUELLESS pompe éolienne *f*; ~ **torque** *n* AERONAUT couple en autorotation *m*

windmilling: ~ **propeller** *n* AERONAUT hélice en moulinet *f*; ~ **restart** *n* AERONAUT remise en marche en moulinet *f*

window *n* COMP fenêtre *f*, CONST *architecture* croisée *f*, fenêtre *f*, DP, MECH ENG *of vernier* fenêtre *f*, NAUT *boat building* hublot *m*, PRINT *within text* fenêtre *f*, réserve *f*, VEHICLES *body* fenêtre *f*, vitre *f*; ~ **air conditioning unit** *n* REFRIG climatiseur de fenêtre *m*, conditionneur à air de type fenêtre *m*; ~ **bar** *n* CONST barre d'appui *f*, barrière *f*, barre de fermeture *f*, barre de treillis *f*, barreau de fenêtre *m*, croisillon à treillis enfer *m*, petit bois *m*, petit bois en fer *m*; ~ **catch** *n* CONST crampon de fermeture *m*; ~ **clipping** *n* COMP, DP détourage de fenêtre *m*; ~ **crank** *n* (AmE) *(cf window regulator)* VEHICLES *body* lève-glace *m*; ~ **fastener** *n* CONST crampon de fermeture *m*; ~ **filter** *n* ELECTRON filtre à bande étroite accordable *m*; ~ **frame** *n* CONST bâti de croisée *m*, bâti dormant *m*, châssis de fenêtre *m*, châssis dormant *m*, dormant *m*, dormant de fenêtre *m*, VEHICLES *body* cadre de fenêtre *m*, cadre de vitre *m*; ~ **glass**

n CONST verre à vitres *m*; ~ **opening** *n* CONST baie de fenêtre *f*, ouverture de fenêtre *f*; ~ **packaging** *n* PACKAGING emballage à fenêtre *m*; ~ **rabbet** *n* CONST feuillure *f*; ~ **regulator** *n* (BrE) *(cf window crank)* VEHICLES *body* lève-glace *m*; ~ **sash** *n* CONST cadre de fenêtre *m*, châssis de fenêtre *m*, châssis mobile *m*; ~ **seal** *n* VEHICLES *body* joint d'étanchéité de vitre *m*; ~ **transformation** *n* COMP, DP transformation fenêtre clôture *f*; ~ **winder** *n* AUTO *car* manivelle lève-glace *f*, remonte-glace *m*

windowing *n* COMP, DP fenêtrage *m*

windowsill *n* CONST appui de fenêtre *m*

wind-powered: ~ **generator** *n* ELEC génératrice éolienne *f*

wind-rode *adj* NAUT *mooring* évité au vent

windscreen *n* (BrE) *(cf windshield)* C&G, RAIL *vehicles* pare-brise *m*, RECORDING bonnette paravent *f*, SPACE, VEHICLES *body* pare-brise *m*; ~ **washer** *n* (BrE) *(cf windshield washer)* VEHICLES *accessory* lave-glace de pare-brise *m*; ~ **washer jet** *n* (BrE) *(cf windshield washer jet)* AUTO gicleur *m*; ~ **wiper** *n* (BrE) *(cf windshield wiper)* VEHICLES *accessory* essuie-glace *m*

windshield *n* (AmE) *(cf windscreen)* C&G, RAIL *vehicles* pare-brise *m*, RECORDING bonnette paravent *f*, SPACE, VEHICLES *body* pare-brise *m*; ~ **washer** *n* (AmE) *(cf windscreen washer)* VEHICLES *accessory* lave-glace de pare-brise *m*; ~ **washer jet** *n* (AmE) *(cf windscreen washer jet)* AUTO gicleur *m*; ~ **wiper** *n* (AmE) *(cf windscreen wiper)* VEHICLES *accessory* essuie-glace *m*

wind-unwind: ~ **equipment** *n* PACKAGING équipement d'enroulement et de déroulement *m*

wind-up *n* TEXTILES enroulage du tissu *m*; ~ **apparatus** *n* TEXTILES rouloir *m*

windward[1] *adj* METEO, NAUT *navigation* au vent

windward[2] *adv* NAUT *navigation* au vent

windward:[3] *n* CONST côté du vent *m*

wine: ~ **tanker** *n* NAUT pinardier *m*

wing *n* CONST *of building* aile *f*, MECH ENG *of thumbscrew* aile *f*, oreille *f*, OCEANOG, PHYS aile *f*, VEHICLES *body* aile *f*, garde-boue *m*; ~ **bar light** *n* AERONAUT feu de barre de flanc *m*; ~ **base** *n* MECH ENG *for slide units* bâti latéral *m*; ~ **bolt** *n* MECH ENG boulon à oreilles *m*; ~ **compasses** *n pl* MECH ENG compas quart de cercle *m*; ~ **end** *n* OCEANOG aile de seine *f*, aile de senne *f*; ~ **fillet** *n* TRANSP raccordement d'aile *m*; ~ **flap** *n* TRANSP volet hypersustentateur *m*; ~ **lever knob** *n* PROD ENG bouton à levier à ailette *m*; ~ **loading** *n* AERONAUT charge alaire *f*; ~ **nut** *n* (BrE) MECH ENG, VEHICLES écrou à oreilles *m*; ~ **pallet with projecting deck** *n* TRANSP palette à plancher débordant *f*; ~ **rail** *n* RAIL patte de lièvre *f*; ~ **root** *n* AERONAUT encastrement d'aile *m*, *aircraft* emplanture *f*; ~ **screw** *n* MECH ENG vis ailée *f*, vis à oreilles *f*; ~ **slot** *n* AERONAUT *aircraft* fente d'aile *f*; ~ **span** *n* TRANSP *aircraft* envergure *f*; ~ **tank** *n* AERONAUT réservoir d'aile *m*; ~ **tip** *n* AERONAUT saumon *m*, saumon de voilure *m*, *aircraft* extrémité d'aile *f*; ~ **tip vortex** *n* AERONAUT tourbillon d'extrémité d'aile *m*

winged: ~ **screw** *n* MECH ENG vis ailée *f*, vis à oreilles *f*

wingwall *n* CONST mur en aile *m*

winnowing *n* GEOL vannage *m*

Winston: ~ **collector** *n* FUELLESS capteur Winston *m*

winter: ~ **solstice** *n* ASTRON solstice d'hiver *m*; ~ **storage** *n* NAUT *of boat* hivernage *m*

winterization *n* REFRIG *cooling of edible oils* frigélisation *f*

winterize *vt* AUTO hiverniser, CHEM démargariner, CINE-

MAT lubrifier pour le froid

winze *n* MINING descenderie *f*

wipe[1] *n* CINEMAT volet *m*, MECH ENG came *f*, virgule *f*, TV enchaînement *m*, fondu enchaîné *m*; ~ **joint** *n* CONST noeud de soudure *m*, soudure à noeud *f*

wipe[2] *vt* CONST *joint* ébarber; ~ **off** *vt* CINEMAT fermer par un volet; ~ **on** *vt* CINEMAT ouvrir par un volet

wiped: ~ **joint** *n* CONST noeud de soudure *m*, soudure à noeud *f*

wiper *n* MECH ENG came *f*, virgule *f*, VEHICLES *accessory* essuie-glace *m*; ~ **arm** *n* VEHICLES *accessory* bras d'essuie-glace *m*; ~ **blade** *n* VEHICLES *accessory* balai d'essuie-glace *m*; ~ **shaft** *n* MECH ENG arbre des cames *m*, arbre à cames *m*

wiping *n* PRINT action de la racle sur un rouleau *f*, essuyage *m*

wire[1] *n* ELEC ENG fil *m*, PAPER TECH toile *f*; ~ **aerial** *n* TELECOM antenne à fil *f*; ~ **bag tie** *n* PACKAGING fil d'attache pour sac *m*; ~ **bonding** *n* ELEC ENG soudage des connexions *m*; ~ **brush** *n* PROD ENG *iron* brosse en fil de fer *f*; ~ **bundle** *n* ELEC ENG faisceau de fils *m*; ~ **cloth** *n* PAPER TECH, PROD ENG toile métallique *f*; ~ **cloth screen** *n* PROD ENG crible en toile métallique *m*; ~ **coating machine** *n* PROD ENG machine à enrober les fils *f*; ~ **core** *n* ELEC ENG noyau en fils *m*; ~ **diameter** *n* SPRINGS diamètre du fil *m*; ~ **dragging** *n* OCEANOG dragage hydrographique *m*; ~ **drawing** *n* PROD ENG filetage *m*, tirage *m*, tréfilage *f*, étirage *m*, REFRIG laminage *m*; ~ **edge** *n* MECH ENG *tool-sharpening* bavure *f*, morfil *m*, morflat *m*; ~ **enamel** *n* COATINGS vernis pour fils *m*; ~ **end** *n* ELEC ENG bout de fil *m*, extrémité d'un fil *f*, PAPER TECH table de fabrication *f*; ~ **erosion** *n* MECH ENG *machining* érosion par fil *f*; ~ **fence** *n* CONST clôture en fil de fer *f*; ~ **frame** *n* PAPER TECH bâti de toile *m*; ~ **fuse** *n* ELEC fil fusible *m*; ~ **gage** *n* (AmE), ~ **gauge** *n* (BrE) METR jauge pour fil métallique *f*; ~ **gauze** *n* LAB EQUIP *heating, support* treillis métallique *m*, PROD ENG gaze métallique *f*, toile métallique *f*; ~ **guard** *n* PROD ENG cage en fil de fer *f*, grille de protection en fil de fer *f*, protecteur en fil de fer *m*; ~ **guide** *n* C&G guide-fil *m*, PAPER TECH guide-toile *m*; ~ **mark** *n* PAPER TECH, PRINT marque de toile *f*; ~ **mesh** *n* C&G treillis métallique *m*, P&R *equipment* fil tressé *m*; ~ **mesh reinforcement** *n* C&G renforcement par armature métallique *m*, CONST armature de treillis métallique *f*, grillage métallique *m*; ~ **mesh target** *n* RAD PHYS cible à fils *f*; ~ **mill** *n* MECH ENG *rolling* train de machine *m*, train de serpentage *m*, train à serpenter *m*; ~ **netting** *n* CONST grillage *m*, réseau en fil métallique *m*, treillis métallique *m*; ~ **pair** *n* ELEC ENG paire de fils *f*; ~ **recorder** *n* RECORDING enregistreur sur fil d'acier *m*; ~ **reinforced hose** *n* MECH ENG tuyau flexible renforcé par des fils métalliques *m*, P&R tuyau renforcé de fils métalliques *m*; ~ **roll** *n* PAPER TECH rouleau de toile *m*; ~ **rope** *n* PROD ENG câble métallique *m*; ~ **screen** *n* PROD ENG crible de fil de fer *m*, crible en toile métallique *m*, gaze métallique *f*; ~ **side** *n* PAPER TECH côté envers d'un papier *m*, PRINT côté toile *m*; ~ **sieve** *n* PROD ENG crible de fil de fer *m*, crible en toile métallique *m*, gaze métallique *f*; ~ **spark machine** *n* MECH ENG machine à électro-érosion *f*; ~ **stacking machine** *n* PACKAGING machine pour empiler les fils *f*; ~ **staple** *n* CONST cavalier *m*, clou à deux pointes *m*; ~ **steel race ball bearing** *n* MECH ENG roulement à billes en fil d'acier *m*; ~ **strainer** *n* CONST cric-tenseur *m*, raidisseur *m*, RAIL tendeur *m*; ~ **strapping equipment** *n* PACKA-

GING équipement de cerclage avec fil *m*; ~ **stretcher** *n* CONST cric-tenseur *m*, raidisseur *m*, PAPER TECH tendeur de toile *m*; ~ **stripping pliers** *n pl* MECH ENG pince à dénuder *f*; ~ **wear** *n* PRINT usure provenant de la tôle mécanique *f*; ~ **wheel** *n* VEHICLES roue à rayons *f*; ~ **wobble stick head** *n* PROD ENG tête à tige à ressort en fil métallique *f*; ~ **works** *n* PROD ENG tréfilerie *f*; ~ **wrapping** *n* ELEC ENG connexion par enroulement *f*

wire[2] *vt* TV câbler

wired: ~ **broadcasting** *n* TV télédistribution *f*; ~ **cast glass** *n* C&G verre de sécurité armé *m*; ~ **safety glass** *n* C&G verre de sécurité armé *m*; ~ **stopper finish** *n* (AmE) *(cf swing stopper finish)* C&G bague percée *f*

wired-logic: ~ **system** *n* TELECOM système à logique câblée *m*

wired-program: ~ **control system** *n* (AmE), **wired-programme control system** *n* *(WPC system)* TELECOM système à programme câblé *m*

wire-drag: ~ **survey** *n* OCEANOG dragage hydrographique *m*

wiredrawer *n* PROD ENG *person* agréyeur *m*, tréfileur *m*

wiredrawing: ~ **bench** *n* PROD ENG argue *f*, banc de tréfilerie *m*, étireur *m*; ~ **die** *n* MECH ENG filière de tréfilage de fils métalliques *f*

wire-drive: ~ **roll** *n* PAPER TECH rouleau d'entraînement de toile *m*

wireframe: ~ **representation** *n* COMP, DP représentation fil de fer *f*

wire-guide: ~ **roll** *n* PAPER TECH rouleau guide-toile *m*

wireless: ~ **headset** *n* RECORDING microphone HF mains libres *m*, microphone haute fréquence mains libres *m*; ~ **hearing aid receiver** *n* TELECOM récepteur de prothèse auditive sans fil *m*; ~ **infrared headphones** *n pl* RECORDING casque à infrarouges *m*; ~ **microphone** *n* MILIT microphone émetteur *m*; ~ **remote control** *n* CINEMAT commande à distance sans fil *f*; ~ **telephony** *n* TELECOM radiophonie *f*

wireline: ~ **log** *n* PETR TECH *drilling, prospecting* diagraphie différée *f*

wire-return: ~ **roll** *n* PAPER TECH rouleau de retour de toile *m*

wire-rope: ~ **clamp** *n* PROD ENG manchon-bride *m*, serre-câble *m*; ~ **sling** *n* SAFETY élingue à câble métallique *f*

wire-tray *n* PAPER TECH bacholle *f*

wire-wound: ~ **armature** *n* ELEC *generator, motor* induit à enroulement *m*, induit à fils *m*; ~ **coil** *n* ELEC enroulement à bobines *m*; ~ **core** *n* ELEC *transformer* noyau en fil *m*; ~ **potentiometer** *n* ELEC potentiomètre bobiné *m*; ~ **resistor** *n* ELEC résistance en fil bobiné *f*, ELEC ENG, PHYS résistance bobinée *f*

wire-wove: ~ **screen** *n* PROD ENG crible en toile métallique *m*

wire-wrap *n* MECH ENG connexion enroulée *f*

wiring *n* ELEC *connection* câblage *m*, montage *m*, pose de ligne *f*, ELEC ENG, SPACE câblage *m*; ~ **arm** *n* PROD ENG bras de câblage *m*, bras pivotant *m*; ~ **configuration** *n* PROD ENG configuration de câblage *f*; ~ **diagram** *n* AUTO schéma de câblage *m*, ELEC plan de câblage *m*, schéma de câblage *m*, TELECOM schéma de câblage *m*; ~ **duct** *n* PROD ENG goulotte pour câble *f*, goulotte pour fil *f*; ~ **error** *n* PROD ENG erreur de câblage *f*; ~ **harness** *n* SPACE *spacecraft* harnais de câbles *m*; ~ **terminal** *n* PROD ENG borne de branchement électrique *f*

witch: ~ **mirror** *n* C&G sorcière *f*

withamite *n* MINERAL withamite *f*
withdrawal: ~ **current** *n* (AmE) *(cf pull current)* C&G courant de tirée *m*
withdrawing: ~ **pins** *n pl* PRINT pointures *f pl*
withered *adj* FOOD TECH défraîchi, flétri
witherite *n* MINERAL withérite *f*
within: **to** ~ **an arbitrary constant** *adv* PHYS à une constante arbitraire près
within-plate *adj* GEOL *tectonic setting* intraplaque
without:[1] ~ **finish** *adj* PAPER TECH non apprêté
without:[2] ~ **interacting** *adv* RAD PHYS sans interagir
withstand: ~ **current** *n* PROD ENG courant temporaire admissible *m*; ~ **impulse** *n* PROD ENG pointe de tension admissible *f*; ~ **impulse voltage** *n* PROD ENG pointe de tension admissible *f*; ~ **voltage** *n* ELEC *installation* tension de tenue *f*; ~ **voltage test** *n* ELEC *installation* essai de tension de tenue *m*
wittichenite *n* MINERAL wittichite *f*, wittichénite *f*
WOB *abbr (weight on bit)* PETR TECH poids sur l'outil *m*
wobble[1] *n* SPACE mouvement de lacet *m*, oscillation *f*; ~ **stick head** *n* PROD ENG tête à tige à ressort *f*; ~ **stick operating head** *n* PROD ENG tête à tige à ressort *f*; ~ **stick position stick** *n* PROD ENG interrupteur de position à tige à ressort *m*
wobble[2] *vi* AERONAUT vaciller, SPACE osciller, vaciller
wobbulation *n* ELECTRON vobulation *f*
wobbulator *n* ELECTRON vobulateur *m*
woehlerite *n* MINERAL wöhlérite *f*
wöhlerite *n* MINERAL wöhlérite *f*
Wolf: ~ **number** *n* ASTRON nombre de Wolf *m*
wolfram *n* CHEM tungstène *m*, wolfram *m*
wolframic *adj* CHEM tungstique
wolframite *n* CHEM, MINERAL wolframite *f*
wolfsbergite *n* MINERAL wolfsbergite *f*
wollastonite *n* MINERAL wollastonite *f*
wood: ~ **alcohol** *n* THERMOD alcool de bois *m*; ~ **bit** *n* MECH ENG *tool* mèche à bois *f*; ~ **brick** *n* CONST brique de bois *f*; ~ **charcoal** *n* CHEM, COAL TECH charbon de bois *m*; ~ **coal** *n* COAL TECH charbon de bois *m*; ~ **defect** *n* QUALITY défaut inhérent au bois *m*; ~ **flour** *n* P&R *filler* farine de bois *f*; ~ **lagging** *n* HYDR EQUIP isolation thermique en bois *f*; ~ **paint** *n* COLOURS peinture pour bois *f*; ~ **paper** *n* PAPER TECH, PRINT papier avec bois *m*; ~ **preservative** *n* CONST *preventive* traitement préventif pour bois *m*; ~ **primer** *n* COATINGS couche d'impression pour bois *f*; ~ **pulp** *n* PACKAGING cellulose technique *f*; ~ **reinforcements** *n pl* NAUT *as in GRP for deck fittings* bois noyés *m pl*; ~ **rosin** *n* P&R *raw material* colophane *f*; ~ **saw** *n* CONST buck saw scie à bûches *f*; ~ **screw** *n* CONST vis à bois *f*; ~ **shavings** *n pl* CONST copeaux de bois *m pl*; ~ **stain** *n* COLOURS lasure *f*, peinture pour bois *f*, teinture pour bois *f*; ~ **suitable for building** *n* CONST bois propre à la construction *m*; ~ **tin** *n* MINERAL étain de bois *m*; ~ **wool** *n* PACKAGING fibre de bois *f*
WOOD *abbr (write-once optical disk)* DP DON *(disque optique non effaçable)*
Wood's: ~ **glass** *n* C&G verre pour lampe de Wood *m*
woodchip: ~ **wall covering** *n* COATINGS papier peint ingrain *m*; ~ **wallpaper** *n* COATINGS papier peint ingrain *m*
wooden: ~ **cradle** *n* PROD ENG bâti en bois *m*; ~ **dunnage** *n* PROD ENG plancher en bois *m*; ~ **pile** *n* COAL TECH pieu en bois *m*; ~ **plug** *n* NAUT *boat building* matrice *f*; ~ **sleeper** *n* (BrE) *(cf wooden tie)* CONST *railway* traverse bois *f*; ~ **tie** *n* (AmE) *(cf wooden sleeper)* CONST

railway traverse bois *f*
woodfree[1] *adj* PACKAGING sans cellulose
woodfree:[2] ~ **paper** *n* PAPER TECH papier sans bois *m*
woodpulp *n* PAPER TECH pâte de bois *f*
woodruff: ~ **keys and keyways** *n pl* MECH ENG clavetage par clavettes disques *m*
Woodruff: ~ **cutter** *n* MECH ENG fraise demi-lune *f*; ~ **key** *n* VEHICLES clavette disque *f*
woods *n pl* C&G fers à lames de bois *m pl*
woodsawing: ~ **circular saw blade** *n* MECH ENG *tool* lame de scie circulaire à bois *f*
wood-turning: ~ **lathe** *n* CONST tour à bois *m*; ~ **tools** *n pl* CONST outils de tourneur sur bois *m pl*
woodtypes *n pl* PRINT caractères sur bois *m pl*
woodwork *n* CONST boiserie *f*
woodworking: ~ **machinery hazard** *n* SAFETY risque dû aux machines à bois *m*
woody *adj* PAPER TECH ligneux
woofer *n* RECORDING woofer *m*
wool *n* C&G fibre courte *f*, PAPER TECH, TEXTILES laine *f*; ~ **counts** *n pl* TEXTILES comptes lainiers *m pl*; ~ **merchant** *n* TEXTILES négociant en lainages *m*
woolen *adj* PAPER TECH laineux
woollen: ~ **dyer** *n* COLOURS teinturier en laine *m*; ~ **spinning** *n* TEXTILES filature de laine cardée *f*
woolliness *n* TEXTILES caractère laineux *m*
woolly *adj* TEXTILES laineux
woolpack *n* TEXTILES ballot de laine *m*
WOR *abbr (water-oil ratio)* PETR rapport eau-pétrole *m*
word:[1] ~ **oriented** *adj* COMP, DP orienté mot
word[2] *n* COMP, DP mot *m*; ~ **address field** *n* PROD ENG champ de l'adresse du mot *m*; ~ **delimiter** *n* COMP, DP délimiteur de mot *m*; ~ **generation** *n* ELECTRON génération de mots *f*; ~ **generator** *n* ELECTRON générateur de mots *m*; ~ **length** *n* COMP, DP longueur de mot *f*; ~ **processing** *n (WP)* COMP, DP traitement de texte *m (TdT)*; ~ **processor** *n* COMP machine de traitement de texte *f*, DP traitement de texte *m*; ~ **size** *n* COMP, DP longueur de mot *f*; ~ **time** *n* COMP, DP temps de transfert d'un mot *m*; ~ **usage** *n* PROD ENG nombre de mots utilisés *m*; ~ **wrap** *n* COMP, DP passage automatique à la ligne *m*, PRINT enroulement du texte *m*, passage automatique à la ligne *m*
wordage *n* PRINT calibrage *m*, estimation du nombre de mots dans un texte *f*
word-and-device: ~ **mark** *n* PATENTS marque combinée *f*
words: ~ **per second** *n pl* PRINT mots à la seconde *m pl*
work[1] *n* PHYS, PROD ENG travail *m*; ~ **area** *n* COMP, DP zone de travail *f*; ~ **assembly** *n* PROD ENG coordination du travail *f*, ordonnancement *m*; ~ **barge** *n* PETR TECH *offshore* barge de travail *f*; ~ **boots** *n pl* SAFETY chaussures de travail *f pl*; ~ **center** *n* (AmE) *see work centre*; ~ **center utilization** *n* (AmE) *see work centre utilization*; ~ **centre** *n* (BrE) PROD ENG centre de charge *m*; ~ **centre utilization** *n* (BrE) PROD ENG utilisation du poste de charge *f*; ~ **file** *n* COMP, DP fichier de travail *m*; ~ **function** *n* ELEC ENG travail d'extraction *m*, travail de sortie *m*, énergie d'extraction *f*, PHYS travail d'extraction *m*; ~ **handling** *n* PACKAGING manutention *f*; ~ **hardened state** *n* SPRINGS état écroui *m*; ~ **hardening** *n* CRYSTALL durcissement à froid *m*, écrouissage *m*, MECH *materials*, METALL, SPRINGS écrouissage *m*; ~ **load** *n* TEXTILES charge de travail *f*; ~ **mark** *n* PATENTS marque dénominative *f*, marque verbale *f*; ~ **order** *n* PROD ENG ordre de fabrication *m*; ~ **plate** *n* MECH ENG *of machine* plateau porte-pièce *m*, table porte-pièces *f*;

~ **print** n CINEMAT copie de travail f; ~ **rest blade** n MECH ENG *for centreless grinding* lame de support f; ~ **safety** n SAFETY sécurité au travail f; ~ **softening** n METALL adoucissement par déformation m; ~ **station** n COMP, DP, MECH ENG, PACKAGING, PROD ENG poste de travail m; ~ **surface** n PROD ENG plan de travail m; ~ **traffic** n TRANSP trafic professionnel m

work[2] vt MECH ENG ouvrer, travailler, PATENTS mettre en oeuvre

work:[3] ~ **against the grain** vi CONST *wood* prendre contre le fil, travailler à contre-fil; ~ **to full capacity** vi MECH ENG *engine* travailler à plein rendement, travailler à pleine charge; ~ **loose** vi MECH ENG *keying* prendre du jeu; ~ **with tripod** vi PHOTO travailler sur pied; ~ **underground** vi CONST travailler en sous-sol

workability n C&G ouvrabilité f, CONST *concrete* maniabilité f, MINING exploitabilité f

workable adj CONST maniable, MINING exploitable

work-and-whirl n PRINT impression ailes de moulin f

workbench n INSTRUMENT table de travail f; ~ **unit** n PROD ENG *production* établi d'outillage m

workday n CONST jour de travail m

worked: ~ **thickness** n COAL TECH *coal seam* ouverture f

worked-out: ~ **lode** n MINING filon épuisé m; ~ **vein** n MINING filon épuisé m

workholding: ~ **fixed table** n MECH ENG *machine tools* taque porte-pièce f; ~ **pallet** n MECH ENG *machine tools* palette porte-pièce f

working[1] n MECH ENG *action* fonctionnement m, jeu m, marche f, roulement m, PATENTS usage m, PROD ENG *of furnace* allure f, marche f; ~ **area** n COMP, DP zone de travail f; ~ **beam** n MECH ENG balancier m; ~ **channel** n TELECOM voie de trafic f; ~ **clothes** n pl CONST, TEXTILES vêtements de travail m pl; ~ **conditions** n pl PROD ENG, SAFETY *environment* conditions de travail f pl; ~ **current relay** n ELEC relais actionné par le courant de travail m; ~ **cycle** n AUTO cycle de fonctionnement m; ~ **deflection** n SPRINGS flèche de travail f; ~ **depth of tooth** n MECH ENG *gearing* hauteur de la dent f; ~ **distance** n METALL distance à travailler f; ~ **end** n C&G avant-bassin m; ~ **face** n MINING front d'abattage m, front d'attaque m, front de taille m; ~ **gloves** n pl SAFETY gants de travail m pl; ~ **hours counter** n SAFETY compteur d'heures de travail m; ~ **length** n SPRINGS longueur en place f; ~ **life** n C&G campagne f, PHOTO *of solution* limite d'emploi f; ~ **load** n MECH ENG charge de travail f, charge pratique f; ~ **mechanism** n MECH ENG mécanisme d'action m; ~ **mine** n MINING mine en activité f; ~ **on blown post** n C&G travail sur poste soufflé m; ~ **part** n MECH ENG partie ouvrière f, partie travaillante f, NUCLEAR élément d'usure m; ~ **platform** n C&G plancher de travail m, CONST plate-forme de travail f; ~ **range** n C&G domaine de travail m; ~ **section** n PHYS *wind tunnel* veine f; ~ **speed** n MECH ENG vitesse de régime f, vitesse de travail f; ~ **standard** n PHYS étalon de travail m; ~ **storage** n COMP mémoire de travail f; ~ **stress** n METALL contrainte appliquée f, SPRINGS taux de travail m; ~ **temperature** n C&G température de travail f; ~ **time percentage** n PROD ENG temps de travail quotidien m; ~ **title** n CINEMAT titre provisoire m; ~ **vacuum** n RAIL *vehicles* dépression de régime f; ~ **voltage** n ELEC tension de fonctionnement f

working:[2] **in ~ order** phr MECH ENG en état de fonctionner, PROD ENG en exploitation normale

work-in-hand n PROD ENG travail en main m, travail en progrès m, travaux en main m pl

work-in-progress n PROD ENG travail en main m, travail en progrès m, travaux en main m pl; ~ **by employee** n PROD ENG en-cours par employé m; ~ **control** n PROD ENG gestion de l'en-cours de fabrication f

workmanship n PROD ENG façon f, main-d'oeuvre f, travail m

workover n PETR TECH *drilling* reconditionnement m; ~ **barge** n PETR TECH *drilling, offshore* barge de reconditionnement f

workpiece n MECH pièce à usiner f

workplace n SAFETY lieu de travail m; ~ **regulations** n pl SAFETY règlements relatifs aux lieux de travail m pl

works n pl PROD ENG atelier m, usine f; ~ **in progress** n pl PROD ENG travaux en progrès m pl; ~ **recording clock** n SAFETY pendule enregistreuse f

workshop n MECH, PROD ENG atelier m, RAIL atelier de réparation de wagons m, SAFETY atelier m

world: ~ **line** n ASTRON ligne du monde f

worldwide: ~ **communications** n pl TELECOM télécommunications à l'échelle du globe f pl; ~ **network** n TELECOM *communications* réseau mondial m

worm n LAB EQUIP *still* serpentin m, MECH vis sans fin f, MECH ENG *screw thread* filet m; ~ **gear** n MECH, MECH ENG, NAUT engrenage à vis sans fin m; ~ **gear final drive** n AUTO couple à vis sans fin m, réduction finale à vis sans fin f; ~ **gearing** n MECH ENG engrenage à vis sans fin m; ~ **rack** n MECH ENG crémaillère à vis sans fin f; ~ **roll** n PAPER TECH rouleau spiralé m; ~ **screw** n MECH ENG *wad hook* tire-bourre m; ~ **wheel** n MECH ENG roue à vis sans fin f

WORM abbr *(write-once read many times)* OPT disque inscriptible une seule fois m

worm-drive: ~ **clamp** n MECH ENG *hose clip* bride de serrage à vis sans fin f

worn[1] adj MECH abîmé, usé

worn:[2] ~ **bit** n PETR TECH *drilling* trépan usé m; ~ **tools** n pl SAFETY outils usés m pl

worn-out adj TEXTILES usé

worsted: ~ **spinning** n TEXTILES filature de laine peignée f

wort n FOOD TECH *brewing* moût m; ~ **cooler** n REFRIG refroidisseur à moût m

wound[1] adj SPRINGS enroulé; ~ **onto the beam** adj TEXTILES enroulé sur ensouple

wound:[2] ~ **rotor** n ELEC ENG rotor bobiné m; ~ **rotor induction motor** n ELEC ENG moteur asynchrone à rotor bobiné m, moteur à bagues m; ~ **rotor motor** n ELEC ENG moteur à rotor bobiné m; ~ **stator** n ELEC ENG stator bobiné m; ~ **stator motor** n ELEC ENG moteur à stator bobiné m

wove n PAPER TECH vélin m; ~ **paper** n PAPER TECH, PRINT papier vélin m

woven: ~ **carpet** n TEXTILES tapis tissé m; ~ **fabric** n TEXTILES nappe tissée f, tissu chaîne et trame m

wow n ACOUSTICS, RECORDING, TV pleurage m; ~ **and flutter** n RECORDING fluctuation de vitesse f, pleurage et scintillement m, TV fluctuations de vitesse f, pleurage et scintillement m

WOW abbr *(waiting on weather)* PETR TECH attente mauvaise f

WP abbr *(word processing)* COMP, DP TdT *(traitement de texte)*

W-particle n PART PHYS, PHYS particule W f

WPC: ~ **system** n *(wired-programme control system)* TELECOM système à programme câblé m

wrap vt MECH ENG *coil* enrouler, PAPER TECH, TEXTILES emballer

wraparound *n* COMP, DP bouclage *m*, PACKAGING enveloppe *f*, PRINT enroulement du papier autour des cylindres lors d'une casse *m*, manchon d'emballage *m*; ~ **evaporator** *n* REFRIG évaporateur enveloppant *m*; ~ **label** *n* PACKAGING étiquette enveloppante *f*; ~ **plate** *n* PRINT plaque enveloppante *f*; ~ **sleeving machine** *n* PACKAGING enveloppeuse pour manchons *f*; ~ **tray** *n* PACKAGING barquette wrap-around *f*

wrapped: ~ **overlay** *n* PRINT surimpression par enroulement électronique *f*; ~ **yarn** *n* TEXTILES fil guipé *m*

wrapper *n* PACKAGING, TEXTILES emballeur *m*; ~ **fiber** *n* (AmE), ~ **fibre** *n* (BrE) TEXTILES fibre de guipage *f*

wrapping *n* MECH ENG *coiling* enroulement *m*, PAPER TECH emballage *m*, PRINT emballage de bobine *m*, PROD ENG, TEXTILES emballage *m*; ~ **machine** *n* PACKAGING machine enveloppeuse *f*; ~ **paper** *n* PAPER TECH papier d'emballage *m*; ~ **tissue** *n* PAPER TECH papier mousseline *m*

Wratten: ~ **filter** *n* CINEMAT filtre Wratten *m*

wreath *vt* CONST *carpentry* débillarder, entrelacer

wreck *n* NAUT *navigation, danger* épave *f*

wrecked: be ~ *vi* NAUT *navigation* faire naufrage

wrecker *n* MILIT dépanneuse lourde *f*, véhicule lourd de dépannage *m*, TRANSP véhicule lourd de dépannage *m*

wrecking: ~ **crane** *n* (AmE) *see heavy breakdown crane*

wrench *n* (AmE) *(cf spanner)* MECH *tools* clef *f*, clé *f*, MECH ENG clé de calibre *f*, clé fermée *f*, VEHICLES *tool* clef *f*, clé *f* ~ **fault** *n* GEOL cisaillement *m*, faille verticale de décrochement *f*, décrochement *m*

wring *vt* MAR POLL déformer, essorer, forcer, tordre, PAPER TECH, TEXTILES essorer

wringer *n* POLLUTION essoreuse *f*; ~ **roll** *n* PAPER TECH foulon *m*, rouleau de foulon *m*, rouleau essoreur *m*

wringing *n* PAPER TECH essorage par torsion *m*

wrinkle *n* PAPER TECH faux pli *m*; ~ **paint** *n* COATINGS vernis ridé *m*, COLOURS vernis craqueleur *m*, P&R peinture givrée *f*

wrinkled: ~ **rim** *n* C&G bord ridé *m*

wrinkle-resistant: ~ **finish** *n* COATINGS apprêt antifroisse *m*

wrinkling *n* CINEMAT réticulation *f*, tuilage *m*

wrist: ~ **pin** *n* (AmE) *see gudgeon pin*; ~ **protector** *n* SAFETY protecteur de poignets *m*

writable: ~ **optical disc** *n* (BrE) OPT disque optique inscriptible *m*; ~ **optical disk** *n* (AmE) *see writable optical disc*

write[1] *n* COMP, DP écriture *f* ~ **error** *n* COMP, DP erreur d'écriture *f*; ~ **head** *n* COMP, DP tête d'écriture *f*; ~ **instruction** *n* COMP, DP instruction d'écriture *f*; ~ **permit ring** *n* COMP, DP anneau d'autorisation d'écriture *m*; ~ **protect** *n* COMP protection contre l'écriture *f*, DP protection en écriture *f*; ~ **protection** *n* COMP, DP protection en écriture *f*; ~ **pulse** *n* COMP, DP impulsion

d'écriture *f*; ~ **ring** *n* COMP, DP anneau d'écriture *m*; ~ **time** *n* COMP, DP, ELEC ENG *magnetic media* temps d'écriture *m*

write[2] *vt* COMP, DP écrire

write-once: ~ **data disc** *n* (BrE) OPT disque optique numérique inscriptible une seule fois *m*, disque optique numérique non effaçable *m*, DON inscriptible une seule fois *m*; ~ **data disk** *n* (AmE) *see write-once data disc*; ~ **disc** *n* (BrE) OPT disque optique numérique non effaçable *m*; ~ **disk** *n* (BrE) COMP disque optique numérique inscriptible *m*, disque optique numérique non effaçable *m*, DP, OPT disque optique numérique non effaçable *m* ~ **medium** *n* OPT support non effaçable *m*; ~ **optical disk** *n* *(WOOD)* DP disque optique non effaçable *m*, disque optique non réinscriptible *m*; ~ **optical medium** *n* OPT support optique inscriptible une seule fois *m*; ~ **optical storage** *n* OPT mémoire optique inscriptible une seule fois *f*; ~ **read many times** *n* COMP, OPT disque inscriptible une seule fois *m*

write-protect: ~ **notch** *n* COMP, DP encoche de protection écriture *f*

write-through: ~ **capability** *n* ELECTRON possibilité de surimpression *f*

writing: ~ **gun** *n* ELECTRON canon d'inscription *m*, *storage tubes* canon d'écriture *m*; ~ **speed** *n* ELECTRON vitesse d'inscription *f*, *storage tubes* vitesse d'écriture *f*; ~ **time** *n* ELECTRON temps de gravure *m*

written: ~ **policy statement on health and safety** *n* SAFETY document écrit réglementant la sûreté *m*; ~ **state** *n* ELECTRON *storage tubes* état écrit *m*

wrong: ~ **capacity** *n* C&G mauvaise contenance *f*; ~ **color rendering** *n* (AmE), ~ **colour rendering** *n* (BrE) PRINT mauvais rendu des couleurs *m*; ~ **direction running** *n* RAIL circulation à contre-voie *f*; ~ **number** *n* TELECOM faux numéro *m*

wrought[1] *adj* MECH *materials* forgé

wrought:[2] ~ **iron** *n* CONST fer ductile *m*, fer forgé *m*

wrought-copper: ~ **alloy for plain bearings** *n* MECH ENG alliage de cuivre corroyé pour paliers lisses *m*

WRU *abbr (who-are-you)* TELECOM qui êtes-vous

WS *abbr (weight strength)* MINING CUP *(coefficient d'utilisation pratique)*, PMB *(puissance au mortier balistique)*

W-type: ~ **engine** *n* AUTO moteur en W *m*

wulfenite *n* MINERAL wulfénite *f*

wurtzite *n* MINERAL wurtzite *f*

wye: ~ **connection** *n* ELEC *transformer-reactor* connexion étoile *f*

Wylie: ~ **relationship** *n* PETR rapport de Wylie *m*, relation de Wylie *f*

WYSIWYG *abbr (what you see is what you get)* COMP, DP WYSIWYG *(tel vu tel imprimé, vu- imprimé)*

X

XALS *abbr (extended application layer structure)*
TELECOM structure en couches d'application étendue *f*

xanthate *n* CHEM xanthate *m*

xanthein *n* CHEM xanthogène *m*, xanthéine *f*

xanthene *n* CHEM xanthène *m*

xanthic *adj* CHEM xanthique

xanthine *n* CHEM xanthine *f*

xanthocreatinine *n* CHEM xanthocréatine *f*

xanthogenic *adj* CHEM xanthogénique

xanthone *n* CHEM xanthone *f*

xanthophyllite *n* MINERAL xanthophyllite *f*

xanthoproteic *adj* CHEM xanthoprotéique

xanthosine *n* CHEM xanthosine *f*

xanthotoxin *n* CHEM xanthotoxine *f*

xanthous *adj* CHEM jaune

xanthoxylin *n* CHEM xanthoxyline *f*

xanthydrol *n* CHEM xanthydrol *m*

xanthyl *n* CHEM xanthyle *m*

x-arm: ~ machine *n* C&G machine à x têtes *f*

x-axis *n* CONST axe X *m*, MATH axe des abscisses *m*, axe des x *m*, PHYS axe des l'abscisses *m*, axe des x *m*, TV axe des x *m*

X-band *n* ELECTRON bande X *f*; **~ magnetrons** *n pl* ELECTRON magnétron en bande X *m*; **~ traveling-wave tube** *n* (AmE), **~ travelling-wave tube** *n* (BrE) ELECTRON TOP en bande X *m*, tube à onde progressive en bande X *m*; **~ TWT** *n* ELECTRON tube à onde progressive en bande X *m*

X-body: ~ decaying into two jets *n* RAD PHYS corps X désintégrant en deux jets *m*

X-box *n* PRINT case à cocher *f*

x-coordinate *n* PHYS *abscissa* abscisse *f*

x-deflection *n* TV déviation x *f*

Xe *(xenon)* CHEM Xe *(xénon)*

X-emitter *n* NUCLEAR émetteur X *m*

xenocryst *n* GEOL xénocristal *m*

xenolith *n* GEOL enclave *f*, xénolite *f*

xenomorphic *adj* GEOL xénomorphe

xenon *n (Xe)* CHEM xénon *m (Xe)*; **~ arc lamp** *n* CINEMAT lampe à arc de xénon *f*; **~ arc projector** *n* CINEMAT appareil de projection à lampe au xénon *m*; **~ buildup** *n* NUCLEAR *after shutdown* empoisonnement xénon *m*; **~ chloride** *n* ELECTRON chlorure de xénon *m*; **~ chloride laser** *n* ELECTRON laser au chlorure de xénon *m*; **~ poisoning reactivity** *n* NUCLEAR réactivité de l'empoisonnement xénon *f*; **~ poisoning effect** *n* NUCLEAR effet xénon d'empoisonnement *m*; **~ print** *n* CINEMAT copie étalonnée pour projection à 5400 K *f*

xenotime *n* MINERAL xénotime *f*

xerography *n* COMP, DP, ELEC, ELECTRON, GAS TECH xérographie *f*

X-height *n* PRINT hauteur de l'oeil du caractère *f*

xi: ~ particle *n* PHYS particule xi *f*

XLR: ~ connector *n* CINEMAT fiche Cannon *f* (MD), TV fiche Cannon *f* (MD), fiche XLR *f*

XM: ~ synchronized shutter *n* PHOTO obturateur avec double synchronisation pour flash *m*

X-plate *n* TV électrode de déviation horizontale *f*

X-radiograph *n* PHOTO radiographie *f*

X-ray[1] *n* ELEC, ELECTRON, METALL, PHYS, SPACE, WAVE PHYS rayon X *m*; **~ absorption** *n* RAD PHYS absorption de rayons X *f*; **~ absorption analysis** *n* RAD PHYS analyse par absorption de rayons X *f*; **~ absorption spectrum** *n* NUCLEAR, PHYS spectre d'absorption X *m*; **~ amplifier tube** *n* INSTRUMENT tube intensificateur d'images de rayons X *m*; **~ analysis** *n* INSTRUMENT, RAD PHYS analyse à rayons X *f*; **~ apparatus** *n* INSTRUMENT appareil radiographique *m*, appareil à rayons X *m*, équipement à rayons X *m*; **~ astronomy** *n* ASTRON astronomie à rayons X *f*; **~ background radiation** *n* RAD PHYS bruit de fond de rayonnement X *m*; **~ beam** *n* ELECTRON faisceau de rayons X *m*; **~ camera** *n* NUCLEAR chambre de diffraction X *f*, RAD PHYS appareil photo à rayons X *m*; **~ cartridge** *n* INSTRUMENT cassette radiographique *f*; **~ cinematography** *n* CINEMAT cinéradiographie *f*; **~ coloration** *n* (AmE), **~ colouration** *n* (BrE) NUCLEAR coloration due aux rayons X *f*; **~ control room** *n* INSTRUMENT salle de commande de radiographie *f*; **~ crystallography** *n* RAD PHYS radiocristallographie *f*; **~ diagnostics** *n pl* INSTRUMENT diagnostic aux rayons X *m*; **~ diagram** *n* INSTRUMENT diagramme de diffraction des rayons X *m*; **~ diffraction** *n* CRYSTALL, ELECTRON, METALL, SPACE, WAVE PHYS diffraction des rayons X *f*; **~ diffraction analysis** *n* RAD PHYS analyse par diffraction à rayons X *f*; **~ diffraction camera** *n* NUCLEAR chambre de diffraction X *f*; **~ diffraction pattern** *n* CRYSTALL, INSTRUMENT diagramme de diffraction des rayons X *m*; **~ diffractometer** *n* CRYSTALL diffractomètre des rayons X *m*, INSTRUMENT spectrographe à rayons X *m*, RAD PHYS diffractomètre des rayons X *m*; **~ dosimeter** *n* INSTRUMENT dosimètre à rayons X *m*; **~ emitting binary stars** *n pl* ASTRON étoiles binaires émettant des rayons X *f pl*; **~ escape peak** *n* RAD PHYS *in X-ray spectrum* pic de fuite des rayons X *m*; **~ examination** *n* CONTROL, MECH examen aux rayons X *m*; **~ examination table** *n* INSTRUMENT table d'examen radiologique *f*; **~ film** *n* INSTRUMENT roentgen-film *m*; **~ flash** *n* INSTRUMENT éclair de rayons X *m*; **~ fluorescence** *n* RAD PHYS *secondary radiation* fluorescence X *f*; **~ fluorescence analysis** *n* RAD PHYS analyse de fluorescence de rayonnement X *f*; **~ gate** *n* INSTRUMENT fenêtre du tube X *f*; **~ head** *n* INSTRUMENT tête de radiographie *f*; **~ image** *n* INSTRUMENT radiographie *f*; **~ image amplifier** *n* INSTRUMENT feuille à intensifier les radiographies *f*; **~ inspection** *n* NUCLEAR essai aux rayons X *m*, examen aux rayons X *m*, inspectiona à rayons X *f*, SPACE *spacecraft* contrôle radiographique *m*, inspection radiographique *f*; **~ irradiation** *n* NUCLEAR irradiation aux rayons X *f*; **~ laser** *n* ELECTRON, NUCLEAR, RAD PHYS laser à rayons X *m*; **~ lithography** *n* ELECTRON gravure aux rayons X *f*; **~ luminescence** *n* NUCLEAR luminescence aux rayons X *f*; **~ mask** *n* ELECTRON masque pour rayons X *m*; **~ metallography** *n* NUCLEAR métallographie par rayons X *f*, RAD PHYS radiométallographie *f*; **~ microscope** *n* NUCLEAR, RAD

PHYS microscope à rayons X *m*; ~ **microstructure investigation** *n* NUCLEAR examen de la microstructure par rayons X *m*, étude de la microstructure par rayons X *f*; ~ **photoelectron spectroscopy** *n* PHYS spectroscopie de photo-électrique X *f*; ~ **photoelectron spectroscopy** *n* CHEM *analysis* spectroscopie photo-électrique X *f*; ~ **photoelectron spectrum** *n* NUCLEAR spectre photoélectronique *m*; ~ **photograph** *n* INSTRUMENT, RAD PHYS radiographe *m*; ~ **photography** *n* INSTRUMENT radiographie *f*; ~ **photon** *n* NUCLEAR photon de rayonnement X *m*; ~ **powder camera** *n* NUCLEAR chambre de Debye-Scherrer *f*; ~ **powder diffractometer** *n* NUCLEAR diffractomètre à rayons X pour les substances pulvérulentes *m*; ~ **protective glass** *n* C&G, INSTRUMENT, SAFETY verre de protection contre les rayons X *m*; ~ **protective glasses** *n pl* INSTRUMENT lunettes de sûreté *f pl*, lunettes protectrices *f pl*; ~ **proximity printing** *n* ELECTRON gravure en proximité aux rayons X *f*; ~ **pulsar** *n* ASTRON pulsar à rayons X *m*; ~ **pulse** *n* ELECTRON impulsion de rayon X *f*; ~ **quantum** *n* NUCLEAR photon de rayonnement X *m*; ~ **radiation** *n* RAD PHYS rayonnement X *m*; ~ **reflection** *n* RAD PHYS réflexion des rayons X *f*; ~ **resist** *n* ELECTRON résist pour rayons X *m*, résist à rayons X *m*; ~ **scattering** *n* CRYSTALL diffusion des rayons X *f*; ~ **source** *n* ASTRON source à rayons X *f*, NUCLEAR *other than cosmic* source de rayons X *f*; ~ **spectrograph** *n* INSTRUMENT spectrographe à rayons X *m*, RAD PHYS radiospectrographe *m*; ~ **spectrography** *n* NUCLEAR spectrographie à rayons X *f*; ~ **spectrometer** *n* RAD PHYS radiospectromètre *m*; ~ **spectrometry** *n* NUCLEAR spectrométrie à rayons X *f*; ~ **spectroscopy** *n* NUCLEAR spectroscopie à rayons X *f*; ~ **spectrum** *n* RAD PHYS spectre des rayons X *m*; ~ **station** *n* PETR poste à rayon X *m*, station à rayons X *f*; ~ **telescope** *n* ASTRON télescope à rayons X *m*; ~ **testing** *n* NUCLEAR essai aux rayons X *m*, examen aux rayons X *m*, inspectionaux rayons X *f*; ~ **topogram** *n* CRYSTALL topogramme à rayons X *m*; ~ **topography** *n* METALL topographie aux rayons X *f*; ~ **transformer** *n* INSTRUMENT transformateur pour radiographie *m*; ~ **tube** *n* CRYSTALL, ELECTRON tube à rayons X *m*, INSTRUMENT générateur de rayons X *m*, tube radiogène *m*, tube à rayons X *m*, RAD PHYS tube à rayons X *m*; ~ **tube stand** *n* INSTRUMENT porte-ampoule *m*, support du tube à rayons X *m*; ~ **unit** *n* INSTRUMENT service de radiologie *m*; ~ **yield** *n* NUCLEAR rendement des rayons X *m*

X-ray[2] *vt* INSTRUMENT radiographier

X-type: ~ **engine** *n* AUTO moteur en X *m*

X-Y: ~ **alignment** *n* TV centrage de faisceau *m*; ~ **plotter** *n* SPACE traceur de courbes *m*; ~ **recorder** *n* ELEC, SPACE enregistreur X-Y *m*

xylanthite *n* CHEM xylanthite *f*

xylene *n* CHEM diméthylbenzène *m*, xylène *m*, DETERGENTS, P&R *solvent*, PETR TECH xylène *m*

xylenethiol *n* CHEM xylènethiol *m*

xylenol *n* CHEM xylénol *m*

xylidine *n* CHEM xylidine *m*

xylite *n* CHEM xylite *f*

xylitol *n* CHEM, FOOD TECH xylitol *m*

xylograph *n* PRINT bois gravé *m*

xylol *n* CHEM xylol *m*

xylonite *n* P&R xylonite *f*

xylose *n* CHEM xylose *m*

xylotile *n* MINERAL xylotile *m*

xylyl *n* CHEM xylyle *m*

xylylene *n* CHEM xylylène *m*

Y

Y *(yttrium)* CHEM Y *(yttrium)*

YAG[1] *abbr (yttrium aluminium garnet, yttrium aluminum garnet)* ELECTRON YAG *(grenat d'yttrium et d'aluminium)*

YAG:[2] ~ **laser** *n* ELECTRON laser YAG *m*

Yagi: ~ **antenna** *n* SPACE *communications*, TELECOM antenne Yagi *f*

yankee: ~ **cylinder** *n* PROD ENG cylindre frictionneur *m*, cylindre yankee *m*; ~ **dryer** *n* PAPER TECH sécherie monocylindrique *f*, sécheur frictionneur *m*

yapp: ~ **binding** *n* PRINT reliure à la Hollandaise *f*; ~ **edges** *n pl* PRINT reliure souple *f*

yard *n* CONST *storage ground* chantier *m*, dépôt *m*, parc *m*, METR yard *m*; ~ **good knitters** *n pl* TEXTILES tricoteurs au mètre *m pl*

yardage *n* METR cubage *m*, TEXTILES métrage *m*

yardarm *n* NAUT bout de vergue *m*

yardstick *n* TEXTILES mesure *f*, étalon *m*

yarn *n* C&G fil *m*, P&R *product* fil *m*, fil textile *m*, PAPER TECH fil textile *m*, TEXTILES fil *m*; ~ **applicator** *n* C&G fileur *m*; ~ **carrier** *n* TEXTILES transporteur de fil *m*; ~ **carrier assembly** *n* TEXTILES système de transport de fil *m*; ~ **dyeing** *n* TEXTILES teinture en fil *f*; ~ **end** *n* TEXTILES bout de fil *m*; ~ **feed control** *n* TEXTILES contrôle de l'alimentation du fil *m*; ~ **roll** *n* TEXTILES ensouple dérouleuse *f*

yarn-dye *vt* TEXTILES teindre avant tissage

yaw[1] *n* AERONAUT, FUELLESS lacet *m*, PHYS, SPACE *spacecraft* embardée *f*, lacet *m*; ~ **adjustment** *n* FUELLESS réglage de lacet *m*; ~ **angle** *n* SPACE *spacecraft*, TRANSP angle de lacet *m*; ~ **axis** *n* AERONAUT, SPACE *spacecraft* axe de lacet *m*; ~ **control** *n* FUELLESS contrôle de lacet *m*; ~ **rate** *n* SPACE *spacecraft* taux de lacet *m*, vitesse de lacet *f*

yaw[2] *vi* FUELLESS faire des lacets, NAUT faire une embardée, SPACE *spacecraft* faire un mouvement de lacet, faire une embardée

yawing *n* PHYS lacet *m*; ~ **moment** *n* AERONAUT, FUELLESS moment de lacet *m*

yawl *n* NAUT yawl *m*

y-axis *n* CONST axe des y *m*, MATH axe des ordonnées *m*, axe des y *m*, axe vertical *m*, PHYS axe de l'ordonnée *m*, axe des y *m*, TV *vertical axis* axe des y *m*

Yb *(ytterbium)* CHEM Yb *(ytterbium)*

y-branch *n* CONST culotte *f*

y-cable *n* RECORDING, TV connecteur en Y *m*

Y-connection *n* ELEC *transformer, reactor* connexion étoile *f*, ELEC ENG montage en étoile *m*, PHYS connexion en étoile *f*

y-coordinate *n* PHYS ordonnée *f*

y-coupler *n* OPT, TELECOM coupleur en Y *m*

y-deflection *n* TV déviation y *f*

y-delta: ~ **starter** *n* ELEC *switch* commutateur étoile triangle *m*; ~ **starting switch** *n* ELEC commutateur étoile triangle *m*

year: all ~ **air conditioning** *n* REFRIG climatisation toutes saisons *f*

yeast: ~ **extract** *n* FOOD TECH concentré de levure *m*, extrait de levure *m*

yellow:[1] ~ **cake** *n* NUCLEAR concentré uranifère *m*; ~ **filter layer** *n* PRINT couche filtrante jaune *f*; ~ **flag** *n* NAUT pavillon de quarantaine *m*; ~ **strawpaper** *n* PAPER TECH papier pure paille *m*; ~ **straw pulp** *n* PAPER TECH pâte de paille lessivée *f*

yellow[2] *vt* TEXTILES jaunir

yellowing *n* PAPER TECH *of paper* jaunissement *m*

yellowness *n* TEXTILES couleur jaune *f*

yield[1] *n* CHEM rendement *m*, COAL TECH débit *m*, rendement *m*, COMP, DP, ELECTRON rendement *m*, FUELLESS débit *m*, GAS TECH rendement *m*, MINING production *f*, rendement *m*, NUCLEAR, PAPER TECH rendement *m*, PETR TECH débit *m*, rendement *m*, PROD ENG débit *m*, production *f*, produit *m*, rendement *m*, récolte *f*, TEXTILES production *f*, rendement *m*; ~ **point** *n* METALL crochet *m*, NUCLEAR limite élastique *f*, PHYS limite d'écoulement *f*, PROP MAT limite d'allongement *f*, SPRINGS limite élastique *f*; ~ **strength** *n* MECH *materials*, METALL, NUCLEAR *limit* limite élastique *f*, P&R résistance à l'allongement *f*; ~ **stress** *n* PHYS contrainte d'écoulement *f*, PROP MAT effort de tension *m*

yield[2] *vt* TEXTILES produire

yield[3] *vi* MECH ENG fléchir

yielding *n* METALL flexion *f*, NUCLEAR *in metals* fluage *m*, fluage plastique *m*

YIG[1] *abbr (yttrium iron garnet)* ELECTRON YIG *(grenat d'yttrium ferreux)*

YIG:[2] ~ **band pass filter** *n* ELECTRON filtre passe-bande YIG *m*; ~ **filter** *n* ELECTRON filtre à YIG *m*; ~ **tuned oscillator** *n* ELECTRON oscillateur à YIG *m*; ~ **tuned transistor oscillator** *n* ELECTRON oscillateur à transistor à YIG *m*; ~ **tuning** *n* ELECTRON accord par YIG *m*, accord par cristal YIG *m*

y-joint *n* ELEC *cable connection* dérivation en Y *f*, dérivation tangente *f*

y-lead *n* RECORDING, TV connecteur en Y *m*

Y-level *n* CONST *surveying* niveau à lunette *m*

Y-network *n* PHYS réseau en Y *m*

yoke *n* CHEM tube collecteur *m*, MECH ENG joug *m*, NUCLEAR *of magnet* bague *f*, culasse *f*, PHYS *of magnet* culasse *f*, VEHICLES *universal joint* fourche *f*, mâchoire *f*; ~ **coil** *n* ELEC bobine de déviation *f*

yoked: ~ **coil** *n* TESTING bobine à culasse *f*

young: ~ **river** *n* HYDROL rivière au stade de jeunesse *f*

Young's: ~ **modulus** *n* COAL TECH, METALL, P&R, PETR, PETR TECH *of elasticity*, PHYS module de Young *m*; ~ **slits** *n pl* PHYS fentes de Young *f pl*

Y-parameter *n* ELECTRON paramètre Y *m*

Y-piece *n* LAB EQUIP raccord de jonction en Y *m*

yrast: ~ **radiation** *n* NUCLEAR rayonnement yrast *m*

Y-signal *n* *(luminance signal)* TV signal de luminance *m*

ytterbia *n* CHEM ytterbine *f*

ytterbium *n* *(Yb)* CHEM ytterbium *m* *(Yb)*

yttria *n* CHEM yttria *m*

yttrite *n* MINERAL yttrite *f*

yttrium *n* *(Y)* CHEM yttrium *m* *(Y)*; ~ **aluminium garnet** *n* (BrE) *(YAG)* ELECTRON grenat d'yttrium et d'aluminium *m (YAG)*; ~ **aluminum garnet** *n* (AmE) *see yttrium aluminium garnet*; ~ **iron garnet** *n (YIG)* ELECTRON grenat d'yttrium ferreux *m (YIG)*

yttrocerite *n* CHEM, MINERAL yttrocérite *f*

yttrocolumbite *n* NUCLEAR *uranium mineral* yttrocolumbite *f*

yttrogummite *n* NUCLEAR yttrogummite *f*

yttrotantalite *n* MINERAL yttrotantalite *f*

yttrotitanite *n* MINERAL yttrotitanite *f*

Yukawa: ~ **potential** *n* PHYS potentiel de Yukawa *m*; ~ **well** *n* NUCLEAR puits de Yukawa *m*

Z

Z *abbr (proton number)* PART PHYS Z *(nombre de protons)*

zapon: ~ **foil** *n* NUCLEAR feuille zapon *f*; ~ **lacquer** *n* COATINGS, NUCLEAR vernis zapon *m*

zaratite *n* MINERAL zaratite *f*

z-axis *n* PHYS axe des z *m*

Z-boson *n* PHYS boson Z *m*

z-coordinate *n* PHYS Z *m*, cote Z *f*

z-direction: ~ **tensile strength** *n* PROD ENG résistance à la rupture par traction dans la direction z *f*

zeaxanthin *n* CHEM zéaxanthine *f*

Zeeman: ~ **component** *n* PHYS composante Zeeman *f*; ~ **effect** *n* NUCLEAR, PHYS effet Zeeman *m*

zein *n* CHEM, P&R zéine *f*

Zeiss: ~ **system transmitted light microscope with polarizer** *n* INSTRUMENT microscope à transmission de type Zeiss avec appareil polariseur *m*

Zener: ~ **breakdown** *n* ELECTRON claquage par effet Zener *m*; ~ **diode** *n* ELECTRON, PHYS, TELECOM diode de Zener *f*; ~ **effect** *n* ELECTRON effet Zener *m*; ~ **voltage** *n* PHYS tension de Zener *f*

Zener-Hollomon: ~ **parameter** *n* METALL paramètre de Zener-Hollomon *m*

zenith *n* ASTRON, NAUT *celestial navigation*, SPACE zénith *m*; ~ **angle** *n* FUELLESS angle zénithal *m*; ~ **carburetor** *n* (AmE), ~ **carburettor** *n* AUTO carburateur compensé *m*, carburateur zénith *m*; ~ **distance** *n* ASTRON, SPACE distance zénithale *f*; ~ **point** *n* ASTRON, SPACE point zénithal *m*; ~ **reduction** *n* SPACE réduction au zénith *f*; ~ **telescope** *n* INSTRUMENT lunette zénithale *f*, SPACE télescope zénithal *m*

zenithal: ~ **hourly rate** *n* ASTRON taux horaire au zénith *m*

zeolite *n* CHEM *mineral*, DETERGENTS, MINERAL, PROP MAT zéolite *f*

zephyr *n* METEO zéphyr *m*

zero[1] *n* CHEM zéro *m*, MATH nul *m*, zéro *m*, METR *of measuring instrument* zéro *m*; ~ **address instruction** *n* COMP, DP instruction sans adresse *f*; ~ **adjustment** *n* NUCLEAR réglage du zéro *m*; ~ **anode** *n* ELEC ENG anode zéro *f*; ~ **band** *n* NUCLEAR *in electron spectrum* bande zéro *f*; ~ **beat** *n* TV battement nul *m*; ~ **capacitance** *n* ELEC ENG capacité résiduelle *f*; ~ **carrier** *n* TV porteuse zéro *f*; ~ **conductor** *n* ELEC ENG conducteur neutre *m*; ~ **creep** *n* METALL fluage nul *m*; ~ **crossing** *n* ELEC ENG passage par zéro *m*; ~ **current** *n* ELEC ENG courant nul *m*; ~ **current turn off** *n* ELEC ENG ouverture du circuit au zéro du courant *f*; ~ **degrees** *n* THERMOD température de zéro *f*; ~ **displacement** *n* C&G déplacement du zéro *m*; ~ **energy level** *n* NUCLEAR niveau d'énergie zéro *m*; ~ **energy reactor** *n* NUCLEAR réacteur pile de puissance nulle *m*; ~ **frame** *n* CINEMAT image de départ *f*; ~ **gravity** *n* SPACE apesanteur *f*; ~ **impedance source** *n* ELEC ENG source à impédance nulle *f*; ~ **insertion force connector** *n* ELECTRON connecteur à effort nul *m*; ~ **level** *n* CINEMAT, RECORDING niveau de référence *m*; ~ **lift angle** *n* AERONAUT incidence de portance nulle *f*; ~ **loss circuit** *n* TELECOM circuit sans perte *m*; ~ **luminance** *n* TV luminance zéro *f*; ~ **luminance plane** *n* TV plan de luminance zéro *m*; ~ **neutron-absorption cross section** *n* NUCLEAR section d'absorption zéro de neutrons *f*; ~ **pitch propeller** *n* MAR POLL hélice à pas nul *f*; ~ **point energy** *n* PHYS énergie au zéro absolu *f*, énergie de point zéro *f*, RAD PHYS *in quantum electrodynamics* énergie à point zéro *f*; ~ **point fluctuations** *n pl* RAD PHYS fluctuations à point zéro *f pl*; ~ **power factor test** *n* ELEC essai à facteur de puissance nul *m*; ~ **power reactor** *n* NUCLEAR réacteur pile de puissance nulle *m*; ~ **power test** *n* NUCLEAR essai à puissance nulle *m*; ~ **pressure gradient** *n* FLUID PHYS *boundary layers* gradient de pression nul *m*; ~ **sequence impedance** *n* ELEC *polyphase winding* impédance homopolaire *f*; ~ **setting** *n* NUCLEAR *point* réglage du zéro *m*; ~ **span tensile strength** *n* PROD ENG résistance à la rupture par traction "zero span" *f*; ~ **suppression** *n* COMP, DP suppression des zéros *f*; ~ **thermostat** *n* CONTROL thermostat de zéro *m*; ~ **twist** *n* TEXTILES torsion nulle *f*; ~ **volt adjustment** *n* TV mise à tension zéro *f*, réglage de zéro *m*; ~ **voltage** *n* ELEC, ELEC ENG tension nulle *f*; ~ **voltage switching** *n* ELEC ENG commutation au zéro de la tension *f*

zero[2] *vt* CHEM, CINEMAT remettre à zéro, CONTROL mettre au point zéro, mettre à zéro, RECORDING, TESTING *instrument*, TV remettre à zéro; ~ **fill** *vt* COMP, DP remplir de zéros; ~ **reset** *vt* CONTROL mettre au point zéro, mettre à zéro

zero-crossing: ~ **switching** *n* ELEC ENG commutation au passage par zéro *f*

zero-g *n* SPACE apesanteur *f*

zeroize *vt* COMP, DP remplir de zéros

zeroth: ~ **law** *n* PHYS, THERMOD principe zéro *m*

zerovalent *adj* CHEM nullivalent

zeunerite *n* MINERAL zeunérite *f*

z-fold *n* PRINT pli zigzag *m*

z-height *n* PRINT oeil de la lettre *m*

Ziegler: ~ **alcohol** *n* DETERGENTS alcool de Ziegler *m*; ~ **catalyst** *n* CHEM catalyseur de Ziegler *m*

zietrisikite *n* CHEM zietrisikite *f*

zigzag: ~ **connection** *n* ELEC *transformer, reactor* connexion en zigzag *f*; ~ **dislocation** *n* METALL dislocation en zigzag *f*; ~ **fold** *n* GEOL pli en accordéon *m*, PRINT pli paravent *m*; ~ **rule** *n* (AmE) *(cf jointed rule)* CONST règle articulée *f*

zinc[1] *n* (Zn) CHEM zinc *m* (Zn); ~ **battery** *n* ELEC ENG pile au zinc *f*; ~ **blende** *n* CHEM *mineral* blende *f*, blende de zinc *f*, sphalérite *f*, MINERAL blende de zinc *f*; ~ **chloride** *n* ELEC ENG chlorure de zinc *m*; ~ **chloride cell** *n* ELEC ENG pile au chlorure de zinc *f*; ~ **chromate pigment** *n* COLOURS pigment au chromate de zinc *m*; ~ **coating** *n* COATINGS couche de zinc *f*, galvanisation *f*, zingage *m*, P&R *paint* peinture en zinc *f*; ~ **condensation** *n* COAL TECH condensation du zinc *f*; ~ **dust pigment** *n* COLOURS pigment de poudre de zinc *m*; ~ **oxide** *n* ELEC ENG oxyde de zinc *m*; ~ **oxide varistor** *n* ELEC ENG varistor à l'oxyde de zinc *f*; ~ **plate** *n* PRINT plaque *f*; ~ **vapor** *n* (AmE), ~ **vapour** *n* (BrE) COAL TECH vapeur de zinc *f*; ~ **wire** *n* ELEC ENG fil de zinc *m*, fil galvanisé *m*

zinc² *vt* CONST galvaniser, zinguer

zinc-air: **~ storage battery** *n* TRANSP accumulateur zinc-air *m*

zincate *n* CHEM zincate *m*

zinc-carbon: **~ cell** *n* ELEC ENG pile charbon-zinc *f*

zinc-coated *adj* COATINGS galvanisé

zincic *adj* CHEM zincique

zincite *n* MINERAL zincite *f*

zinckenite *n* MINERAL zinckénite *f*

zincking *n* CHEM galvanisation *f*, zingage *m*

zincky *adj* CHEM zincifère, zingueux

zinc-manganese: **~ dioxide cell** *n* ELEC ENG pile au bioxyde de manganèse *f*

zincoid *adj* CHEM zincide

zincon *n* CHEM zincon *m*

zinconize *n* MINERAL zinconite *f*

zincosite *n* MINERAL zincosite *f*

zincous *adj* CHEM zingueux

zinc-silver: **~ cell** *n* ELEC ENG pile au chlorure d'argent *f*; **~ oxide cell** *n* ELEC ENG pile à l'oxyde d'argent *f*

zingiberene *n* CHEM zingibérène *m*

zinkosite *n* MINERAL zincosite *f*

zinnwaldite *n* MINERAL zinnwaldite *f*

zip:¹ **~ fastener** *n* (BrE) TEXTILES fermeture éclair *f*; **~ lock bag** *n* PACKAGING sachet à fermeture par pression et glissière *m*; **~ pan** *n* CINEMAT panoramique filé *m*

zip² *vt* (BrE) TEXTILES fermer avec une fermeture éclair; **~ in** *vt* TEXTILES *lining* agrafer avec une fermeture éclair

zip-a-tone *n* PRINT trames mécaniques *f pl*

zipper *vt* (AmE) *see zip*

zircaloy *n* NUCLEAR zircaloy *m* **~ cladding** *n* NUCLEAR gaine en zircalloy *f*; **~ hull** *n* NUCLEAR coque en zircaloy *f*

zircon *n* C&G, MINERAL, PROP MAT zircon *m*; **~ refractory** *n* C&G réfractaire de zircon *m*

zirconate *n* CHEM zirconate *m*

zirconia *n* C&G, CHEM zircone *f*; **~ refractory** *n* C&G réfractaire de zircone *m*

zirconia-alumina: **~ composite** *n* PROP MAT composite zircone-alumine *m*

zirconic *adj* CHEM zirconique

zirconifluoride *n* CHEM zirconifluorure *m*

zirconium *n* (Zr) CHEM zirconium *m* (Zr); **~ base alloy** *n* NUCLEAR alliage à base de zirconium *m*, zircaloy *m*; **~ sponge** *n* NUCLEAR éponge de zirconium *f*

zirconyl *n* CHEM zirconyle *m*

Zn (zinc) CHEM Zn (zinc)

zodiac *n* ASTRON zodiaque *m*

zodiacal: **~ band** *n* ASTRON bande zodiacale *f*; **~ cloud** *n* ASTRON nuage zodiacal *m*; **~ dust** *n* ASTRON poussière zodiacale *f*; **~ light** *n* ASTRON lumière zodiacale *f*

zoisite *n* MINERAL zoïsite *f*

zonal: **~ harmonic** *n* SPACE harmonique zonal *m*; **~ soil** *n* COAL TECH sol à couches alternées *m*

zonation *n* GEOL *of metamorphic terrain* zonéographie *f*

zone *n* COMP, CRYSTALL *reciprocal lattice* zone *f*, DP groupe de caractères *m*, zone *f*, GEOL *subdivision of stage* zone *f*; **~ air conditioning unit** *n* REFRIG climatiseur de zone *m*, conditionneur à air de zone *m*; **~ axis** *n* CRYSTALL axe de zone *m*; **~ formation** *n* METALL formation de zones *f*; **~ melting** *n* METALL fusion en zones *f*, NUCLEAR fusion de zone *f*; **~ of petroleum accumulation** *n* PETR TECH zone d'accumulation pétrolière *f*; **~ refining** *n* CRYSTALL raffinage zonal *m*, METALL purification par fusion en zones *f*; **~ of saturation** *n* HYDROL zone de saturation *f*; **~ of silence** *n* RECORDING zone anacoustique *f*, zone de silence *f*; **~ test** *n* PROD ENG mesure du pouvoir absorbant *f*; **~ time** *n* NAUT temps civil du fuseau *m*; **~ toughening** *n* C&G trempe différenciée *f*

zoned: **~ fuel loading** *n* NUCLEAR chargement par zones *m*; **~ lens** *n* INSTRUMENT lentille de Fresnel *f*

zone-toughened: **~ glass** *n* C&G verre à trempe différenciée *m*

zoning *n* GEOL *of a mineral* zonation *f*, PRINT *computer output* impression de zones *f*, *of document* définition des zones *f*; **~ plan** *n* WATER SUPP plan d'occupation du sol *m*

zoogenic: **~ rock** *n* PETR roche zoogène *f*

zoom¹ *n* CINEMAT APHY, COMP, DP zoom *m*, PHOTO objectif zoom *m*, zoom *m*, PRINT effet d'agrandissement *m*, zoom *m*; **~ in** *n* COMP, DP zoom avant *m*; **~ lens** *n* CINEMAT objectif zoom *m*, objectif à distance focale variable *f*, zoom *m*, INSTRUMENT lentille à focale variable *f*, objectif zoom *m*, objectif à focale *m*, PHOTO objectif zoom *m*, objectif à focale variable *m*, zoom *m*; **~ lever** *n* CINEMAT levier de zoom *m*, TV commande de zoom *f*, levier de zoom *m*; **~ out** *n* COMP, DP zoom arrière *m*; **~ range** *n* CINEMAT gamme des focales *f*; **~ ring** *n* CINEMAT bague de réglage du zoom *f*; **~ stereo-microscope** *n* INSTRUMENT microscope stéréoscopique équipé d'un zoom *m*; **~ viewfinder** *n* CINEMAT viseur multifocal *m*

zoom² *vt* CINEMAT faire un travelling optique, zoomer, PHOTO zoomer

zooming *n* COMP, DP effet de zoom *m*, variation d'échelle *f*

zoosterol *n* CHEM zoostérol *m*

zootaxic *adj* CHEM zootaxique

zootaxy *n* CHEM zootaxie *f*

zooxanthine *n* CHEM zooxanthine *f*

zorgite *n* MINERAL zorgite *f*

Z-parameters *n pl* ELECTRON paramètres Z *m pl*

Z-particle *n* PART PHYS particule Z *f*, PHYS boson Z *m*

Zr (zirconium) CHEM Zr (zirconium)

Z-twist *n* TEXTILES torsion Z *f*

zunyite *n* MINERAL zunyite *f*

zwitter: **~ ion** *n* CHEM ion hybride *m*

zymase *n* CHEM zymase *f*

zymic *adj* CHEM zymique

zymin *n* CHEM zymine *f*

zymohydrolysis *n* CHEM zymohydrolyse *f*

Abréviations/
Abbreviations

A *abbr (amp, ampere)* ELEC, ELEC ENG, METR, PHYS A *(ampère)*

AAL *abbr (ATM adaptation layer)* TELECOM couche d'adaptation AAL *f*

AAL-PCI *abbr (AAL protocol control information)* TELECOM information de contrôle du protocole AAL *f*

AAL-SDU *abbr (AAL service data unit)* TELECOM unité de données de service AAL *f*

AARE *abbr (A-associate response)* TELECOM réponse A-associate *f*

AC *abbr (alternating current)* ELEC, ELEC ENG, ELECTRON, PHYS, RECORDING, TELECOM, TV CA *(courant alternatif)*

ACC *abbr* CONTROL *(adaptive control constraint)* commande ACC *f (contrainte de commande adaptative)*, TV *(automatic chrominance control)* CAC *(contrôle automatique de chrominance)*

ACD *abbr (automatic call distributor)* TELECOM distributeur automatique d'appels *m*

ACE *abbr (access connection element)* TELECOM élément de connexion d'accès *m*

ACI *abbr (automatic car identification)* TRANSP identification automatique des wagons *f*

ACK *abbr (acknowledgement)* COMP, DP, TELECOM AR *(accusé de réception)*

ACO *abbr (adaptive control optimization)* CONTROL optimisation de la commande adaptative *f*

ACSE *abbr (association control service element)* TELECOM élément de service de commande d'association *m*, élément de service de contrôle d'association *m*

ACU *abbr (automatic calling unit)* COMP, DP EAA *(équipement d'appel automatique)*

ACV *abbr (air cushion vehicle)* TRANSP véhicule à coussin d'air *m*

ADC *abbr* COMP *(analog-to-digital converter)*, ELECTRON *(analog-to-digital converter, analogue-to-digital converter)*, PHYS *(analogue-to-digital converter, analog-to-digital converter)*, TELECOM *(analog-to-digital converter, analogue-to-digital converter)* CAN *(convertisseur analogique-numérique)*

ADD *abbr (address prompt)* TELECOM incitation d'adressage *f*

ADF *abbr (automatic direction finding)* AERONAUT, TELECOM radiogoniométrie automatique *f*

ADP *abbr (automatic data processing)* COMP traitement automatique de données *m*

ADPCM *abbr (adaptive differential pulse code modulation)* TELECOM MICDA *(modulation par impulsion et codage différentiel adaptatifs)*

ADT *abbr (average daily traffic)* TRANSP débit journalier moyen *m*

AE *abbr (application entry)* TELECOM entité d'application *f*

AES *abbr (Auger electron spectroscopy)* PHYS spectroscopie électronique Auger *f*

AF *abbr (audio frequency)* ACOUSTICS, ELECTRON, RECORDING, TELECOM, WAVE PHYS audiofréquence *f*, fréquence audible *f*

AFC *abbr (automatic frequency control)* CONTROL, ELEC, ELECTRON, PHYS, PROD ENG, RECORDING, TELECOM, TV CAF *(contrôle automatique de fréquence)*

AFD *abbr (accelerated freeze-drying)* FOOD TECH lyophilisation accélérée *f*

AFI *abbr (authority and format identifier)* TELECOM identificateur d'autorité et de format *m*

AFV *abbr (armoured fighting vehicle, armored fighting vehicle)* MILIT véhicule blindé de combat *m*

AGC *abbr (automatic gain control)* CONTROL CAG *(contrôle automatique de gain)*, ELECTRON CAG *(commande automatique de gain)*, GEOPHYS CAG *(contrôle automatique de gain)*, RECORDING réglage automatique du gain *m*, TELECOM CAG *(commande automatique de gain)*

AGE *abbr (allyl glycidyl ether)* P&R éther allylglycidique *m*

AI *abbr* COMP *(artificial intelligence)*, TELECOM *(artificial intelligence)* IA *(intelligence artificielle)*, TELECOM *(articulation index)* IN *(indice de netteté)*

AIA *abbr (audio indicate active)* TELECOM indication audio active *f*

AIM *abbr (audio indicate muted)* TELECOM indication audio muette *f*

AIR *abbr (air injection reactor)* TRANSP réacteur à injection d'air *m*

AIS *abbr (alarm indication signal)* TELECOM SIA *(signal d'indication d'alarme)*, SNA *(signal de neutralisation d'alarme)*

AITS *abbr (acknowledged information transfer service)* TELECOM service de transfert d'informations avec accusé de réception *m*

AL *abbr (access link)* TELECOM liaison d'accès *f*

ALDP *abbr (axial plasma deposition)* TELECOM déposition axiale *f*

ALS *abbr* TELECOM *(automatic laser shutdown)* coupure automatique du laser *f*, TELECOM *(application layer structure)* structure en couches d'application *f*

ALU *abbr (arithmetic and logic unit)* COMP ULA *(unité arithmétique et logique)*

AM *abbr (amplitude modulation)* COMP, ELECTRON, RECORDING, TV MA *(modulation d'amplitude)*

AMI *abbr (alternate mark inversion)* TELECOM signal bipolaire alternant *m*

ANC *abbr (acid neutralizing capacity)* POLLUTION CNA *(capacité de neutralisation des acides)*, PNA *(potentiel de neutralisation de l'acide)*

ANFO *abbr (ammonium nitrate fuel oil)* MINING nitrate d'ammonium et fuel-oil *m*, nitrate-fioul *m*, nitrate-fuel *m*, nitrate-huile *m*

ANOVA *abbr (analysis of variance)* COMP analyse de la variance *f*

ANPN *abbr (army navy performance number system)* TRANSP *fuel rating octane* système ANPN *m*

ANSI *abbr (American National Standards Institute)* TELECOM ANSI *(Institut Américain de Normalisation)*

AOCS *abbr (attitude and orbit control system)* SPACE système de commande d'attitude et d'orbite *m*

AOQ *abbr (average outgoing quality)* QUALITY QMAC *(qualité moyenne après contrôle)*

APC *abbr (automatic phase control)* ELECTRON, TV contrôle automatique de phase *m*

APD *abbr* ELECTRON *(avalanche photodiode)* photodiode à avalanche *f*, OPT *(avalanche photodiode)* photodiode à avalanche *f*, TELECOM *(amplitude probability distribution)* distribution de probabilité des amplitudes *f*, répartition de probabilité des amplitudes *f*, TELECOM *(avalanche photodiode)* photodiode à avalanche *f*

APDU *abbr (application protocol data unit)* TELECOM unité de données du protocole d'application *f*

APS *abbr (automatic protection switching)* TELECOM commutation automatique sur liaison de réserve *f*, commutation de protection automatique *f*

APT *abbr* COMP *(automatic programming tool)* programme de commande automatique *m*, RAIL *(advanced passenger train)* TGV *(train expérimental à grande vitesse)*

AQL *abbr (acceptable quality level)* QUALITY NQA *(niveau de qualité acceptable)*

ARMA *abbr (autoregressive moving average)* COMP moyenne mobile autorégressive *f*

ARPA *abbr (automatic radar plotting aid)* NAUT *radar* aide de pointage radar automatique *f*

ASC *abbr (automatic sequence control)* CONTROL contrôle automatique à séquence *m*, vérification automatique *f*

ASCII *abbr (American Standard Code for Information Interchange)* COMP, DP, PRINT ASCII

ASE *abbr* TELECOM *(application service element)* élément de service d'application *m*, TRANSP *(automatic stabilization equipment)* stabilisateur automatique *m*, système de stabilisation artificielle *m*

ASIC *abbr (application-specific integrated circuit)* COMP circuit spécifique à une application *m*

ASN1 *abbr (abstract syntax notation one)* TELECOM notation de syntaxe abstraite numéro un *f*

ASO *abbr (application service object)* TELECOM objet de service d'application *m*

ASR *abbr (automatic send-receive)* COMP téléimprimeur émetteur-récepteur *m*, DP appareil émetteur-récepteur *m*, émetteur-récepteur automatique *m*

ATC *abbr* RAIL *(automatic train control)* contrôle automatique des trains *m*, TRANSP *(air traffic control)* contrôle du trafic aérien *m*

ATDM *abbr (asynchronous time division multiplexing)* TELECOM multiplexage temporel asynchrone *m*

ATE *abbr (automatic test equipment)* COMP matériel de test automatique *m*

ATK *abbr (aviation turbine kerosene)* PETR TECH carburéacteur *m*

ATM *abbr* COMP *(automatic teller machine)* guichet automatique de banque *m*, OPT *(alternative test method)* optical fibres méthode de mesure de remplacement *f*, TELECOM *(Asynchronous Transfer Mode)* TTA *(Transfert Temporel Asynchrone)*

ATM-SDU *abbr (ATM service data unit)* TELECOM unité de données de service ATM *f*

ATO *abbr (automatic train operation)* TRANSP commande automatique des trains *f*

ATOMIC *abbr (automatic train operation by mini computer)* RAIL conduite automatique des trains par mini-ordinateur *f*

ATP *abbr* (BrE) *(automatic train protection)* RAIL PAT *(protection automatique de trains)*

AU *abbr* ASTRON *(astronomical unit, astronomic unit)* UA *(unité astronomique)*, COMP *(arithmetic unit)* unité arithmétique *f*, TELECOM *(administrative unit)* UAD *(unité administrative)*, TELECOM *(access unit)* unité d'accès *f*

AUW *abbr (all-up weight)* TRANSP poids total en charge *m*

AVC *abbr (automatic volume control)* CONTROL, ELEC ENG, OPT, PHYS CAV *(commande automatique de volume)*

AVI *abbr (automatic vehicle identification)* TRANSP identification automatique des véhicules *f*

AVL *abbr (automatic vehicle location)* TELECOM localisation automatique des véhicules *f*

AWT *abbr (acid well treatment)* PETR TECH acidification *f*

AWU *abbr (atomic weight unit)* NUCLEAR UPA *(unité de poids atomique)*

b *abbr (barn)* PART PHYS b *(barn)*

B&W *abbr (black and white)* PRINT noir et blanc *m*

B3ZS *abbr (bipolar code with three-zero substitution)* TELECOM code bipolaire avec substitution de trois zéros *m*

BASIC *abbr (beginner's all-purpose symbolic instruction code)* COMP, DP BASIC

BAW *abbr (bulk acoustic wave)* ELEC ENG onde acoustique en volume *f*

BBD *abbr (bucket brigade device)* ELEC ENG, TELECOM dispositif de transfert à la chaîne *m*

BC *abbr* PETR TECH *(bit change)* drilling changement d'outil *m*, TELECOM *(bearer channel)* voie porteuse *f*, voie support *f*, TELECOM *(broadcast)* émission *f*

BCD *abbr (binary-coded decimal)* COMP DCB *(décimal codé binaire)*

BCU *abbr (big close up)* CINEMAT très gros plan *m*

BDC *abbr (bottom dead center, bottom dead centre)* MECH PMB *(point mort bas)*

BECN *abbr (backward explicit congestion notification)* TELECOM notification d'encombrement explicite émise vers l'arrière *f*

bemf *abbr* ELEC ENG *(back electromotive force, back emf)*, ELECTR *(back emf, back electromotive force)*, PHYS *(back electromotive force, back emf)* fcém *(force contre-électromotrice)*

BER *abbr (binary error rate, bit error rate)* COMP, ELECTRON, TELECOM TEB *(taux d'erreurs binaires, taux d'erreurs sur les bits)*

BFA *abbr (basic frame alignment)* TELECOM verrouillage de trame de base *m*

BFO *abbr (beat frequency oscillator)* TELECOM oscillateur à battements *m*

BG *abbr (background gas)* PETR TECH *while drilling* fond gazeux *m*

BHA *abbr* FOOD TECH *(butylated hydroxyanisole)* BHA *m (hydroxyanisol butylé)*, PETR TECH *(bottom-*

hole assembly) bas de garniture *m*

BHP *abbr (brake horsepower)* MECH ENG, PROD ENG cheval effectif *m*, puissance au frein en chevaux *f*, puissance effective en chevaux *f*, puissance en chevaux-vapeur effectifs *f*, TRANSP puissance au frein *f*

BHT *abbr (butylated hydroxytoluene)* FOOD TECH BHT *(hydroxytoluène butylé)*

BIP *abbr (bit interleaved parity)* TELECOM parité d'entrelacement des bits *f*

BIP-8 *abbr (bit interleaved parity 8, bit interleaved parity order 8)* TELECOM parité 8 à entrelacement de bits *f*, parité entrelacée bit d'ordre 8 *f*

BIP-X *abbr (bit interleaved parity-X)* TELECOM parité X à entrelacement de bits *f*

B-ISDN *abbr (broadband integrated services digital network, broadband ISDN)* TELECOM RNIS-LB *(réseau numérique avec intégration des services à large bande)*; **~ PBX** *abbr* TELECOM autocommutateur privé pour le RNIS-LB *m*

BISYNC *abbr (binary synchronous communication)* COMP transmission binaire synchrone *f*

BOC *abbr (Bell operating company)* (TM) TELECOM compagnie opératrice Bell *f* (MD)

BOD *abbr (biochemical oxygen demand)* FOOD TECH, HYDROL *sewage*, PETR TECH, POLLUTION DBO *(demande biologique d'oxygène)*

BOE *abbr (barrel oil equivalent)* PETR TECH baril équivalent pétrole *m*

BOM *abbr (beginning of message)* COMP, TELECOM début de message *m*

BOP *abbr (blowout preventer)* CONTROL, GAS TECH, OCEANOG, PETR, PETR TECH BOP *(bloc obturateur de puits)*

BOT *abbr (beginning of tape)* COMP, DP début de bande *m*

BPF *abbr (band-pass filter)* COMP, DP, ELEC, ELECTRON, PHYS, RECORDING, TELECOM, TV FPB *(filtre passe-bande)*

BPS *abbr (bits per second)* COMP BPS *(bits par seconde)*

BPSK *abbr (binary phase shift keying)* TELECOM MDPB *(modulation par déplacement de phase bivalente)*

Bq *abbr (becquerel)* METR, PHYS, RAD PHYS Bq *(becquerel)*

BRA *abbr (basic rate access)* TELECOM accès au débit de base *m*

BS *abbr (backspace)* COMP caractère espace arrière *m*, espace arrière *m*

BSC *abbr (binary synchronous communication)* COMP transmission binaire synchrone *f*

BSP *abbr (British Standard parallel pipe thread)* MECH ENG filetage cylindrique de tuyauterie à norme britannique *m*

BSPT *abbr (British Standard pipe thread)* MECH ENG filetage conique de tuyauterie à norme britannique *m*

BSS *abbr (British Standards Specification)* MECH ENG norme britannique *f*

BSVC *abbr (broadcast signalling virtual channel, broadcast signaling virtual channel)* TELECOM voie virtuelle diffusée de signalisation *f*

BT *abbr (both justified)* PRINT justifié à droite et à gauche

BThU *abbr (British thermal unit)* METR calorie Britannique *f*

BTU *abbr (British thermal unit)* METR calorie Britannique *f*

BU *abbr (base unit)* TELECOM coeur de chaîne *m*

BWO *abbr (backward wave oscillator)* TELECOM OOR *(oscillateur à ondes rétrogrades)*

BWR *abbr (boiling water reactor)* PHYS réacteur à eau bouillante *m*

c *abbr (centi-)* METR c *(centi-)*

C *abbr (coulomb)* ELEC, ELEC ENG *(coulomb)* C *(coulomb)*, METR *(Celsius)* C *(Celsius)*, METR *(centigrade)* C *(centigrade)*, METR *(coulomb)*, PHYS *(coulomb)* C *(coulomb)*

CAD *abbr (computer-aided design)* COMP, ELEC, MECH, PRINT, PROD ENG, TELECOM CAO *(conception assistée par ordinateur)*

CADCAM *abbr (computer-aided design and manufacturing)* COMP, PROD ENG CFAO *(conception et fabrication assistées par ordinateur)*

CAI *abbr (computer-assisted instruction)* COMP IAO *(instruction assistée par ordinateur)*

CAL *abbr (computer-assisted learning)* COMP EAO *(enseignement assisté par ordinateur)*

CAM *abbr (computer-aided manufacturing)* COMP, ELEC, TELECOM FAO *(fabrication assistée par ordinateur)*

CAMC *abbr (customer access maintenance centre, customer access maintenance center)* TELECOM centre de maintenance des accès client *m*

CAP *abbr (controlled atmosphere packaging)* PACKAGING conditionnement sous atmosphère contrôlée *m*

CARM *abbr (chemical agent resisting material)* MILIT matériel résistant aux produits chimiques *m*

CARS *abbr (coherent anti-Stokes Raman scattering)* PHYS DRASC *(diffusion Raman anti-Stokes cohérente)*

CAS *abbr (channel-associated signalling, channel-associated signaling)* TELECOM signalisation canal par canal *f*

CASE *abbr (computer-aided software engineering)* COMP ingénierie logicielle assistée par ordinateur *f*

CAT *abbr (computer-aided testing)* COMP vérification assistée par ordinateur *f*

CAV *abbr (constant angular velocity)* COMP, OPT vitesse angulaire constante *f*

CAW *abbr (channel address word)* COMP mot d'adresse de canal *m*

CB *abbr (citizen's band)* TELECOM bande de fréquence banalisée *f*, bande de fréquence publique *f*

CBDS *abbr (connectionless broadband data service)* TELECOM service de données à haut débit en mode non connecté *m*

CBL *abbr (cement bond log)* PETR TECH diagraphie d'adhésivité *f*, diagraphie d'adhésivité du ciment *f*

CBO *abbr (continuous bit stream oriented)* TELECOM train de bits en continu *m*

CBR *abbr (California Bearing Ratio)* CONST essai de poinçonnement *m*

Cc *abbr (cirrocumulus)* METEO Cc *(cirro-cumulus)*

CC *abbr* TELECOM *(control channel)* canal de commande *m*, TELECOM *(connect confirm)* confirmation de connexion *f*, TELECOM *(country code)* indicatif du pays *m*, TELECOM *(call control)* traitement d'appel *m*

CCA *abbr (call control agent)* TELECOM agent de traitement d'appel *m*

CCD *abbr (charge-coupled device)* ASTRON, COMP, ELEC ENG, ELECTRON, PHYS, TELECOM, TV CCD *(dispositif à couplage de charge)*

CCIR *abbr (International Radio Consultative Commit-*

tee) TELECOM CCIR *(Comité consultatif international des radiocommunications)*

CCITT *abbr (International Telegraph and Telephone Consultative Committee)* TELECOM CCITT *(Comité consultatif international télégraphique et téléphonique)*

CCTV *abbr (closed-circuit television)* TV télévision en circuit fermé *f*

CCU *abbr (camera control unit)* TV dispositif de réglage de caméra *m*, téléréglage de caméra *m*, voie de caméra *f*

cd *abbr (candela)* ELEC ENG, METR, OPT, PHYS cd *(candela)*

CD *abbr* COMP *(compact disk)* disque audionumérique *m*, disque compact *m*, COMP *(collision detection)* détection de collisions *f*, DP *(compact disk)* disque compact *m*, DP *(collision detection)* détection de collisions *f*, ELECTRON *(carrier detect)* détection de porteuse *f*, OPT *(compact disc, compact disk)*, RECORDING *(compact disc, compact disk)* disque compact *m*, TELECOM *(collision detection)* détection de collisions *f*, TELECOM *(carrier detect)* détection de porteuse *f*

CDF *abbr* MATH *(cumulative distribution function)* fonction de répartition *f*, TELECOM *(combined distribution frame)* répartiteur mixte *m*

CD-I *abbr (compact disc-interactive, compact disk-interactive)* OPT disque compact interactif *m*

CDLI *abbr (called line identification)* TELECOM identification de la ligne du demandé *f*

CDM *abbr* TELECOM *(code-division multiplexing)* MRC *(multiplexage par répartition de code)*, TELECOM *(companded delta modulation)* modulation delta avec compression-extension *f*

CDMA *abbr (code-division multiple access)* SPACE communications AMRC *(accès multiple par répartition en code)*

CDO *abbr* TELECOM *(community dial office)* central automatique local *m*, TELECOM *(connect data overflow)* débordement de données de connexion *m*

CDR *abbr* SPACE *(critical design review)* revue critique de définition *f*, TELECOM *(call data recording, call detail recording)* enregistrement des données d'appels *m*

CD-ROM *abbr* COMP *(compact disk-read only memory)*, DP *(compact disk-read only memory)*, OPT *(compact disk-read only memory, compact disc-read only memory)* CD-ROM *(disque compact ROM)*

CDU *abbr (crude distillation unit)* PETR TECH unité de distillation au brut *f*

CE *abbr* TELECOM *(common equipment)* matériel commun *m*, organe commun *m*, TELECOM *(channel equipment)* matériel de canaux *m*, matériel de voies *m*, équipement de canaux *m*, TELECOM *(connection element)* élément de connexion *m*

CEB *abbr (consecutive error block)* TELECOM bloc erroné consécutif *m*

CEC *abbr (cation exchange capacity)* GEOL, PETR TECH, POLLUTION CEC *(capacité d'échange cationique)*

cemf *abbr (counter-electromotive force, counter emf)* ELEC ENG, ELECTR, PHYS fcém *(force contre-électromotrice)*

CEQ *abbr (customer equipment)* TELECOM équipement d'usager *m*

CERN *abbr (European Organization for Nuclear Research)* PART PHYS CERN *(Conseil européen pour la recherche nucléaire)*

CF *abbr (control function)* TELECOM fonction de commande *f*

CFC *abbr (chlorofluorocarbon)* PACKAGING, POLLUTION CFC *(hydrocarbure chlorofluoré)*

CG *abbr (connection gas)* PETR TECH bouchon d'ajout de tige *m*

CGA *abbr* COMP *(colour graphics adaptor, color graphics adaptor)* carte graphique couleur *f*, TELECOM *(carrier group alarm)* alarme de groupe de voies *f*

CGS abbr (centimetre-gramme-second, centimeter-gram-second) METR CGS *(centimètre-gramme-seconde)*

Ci *abbr* METEO *(cirrus)* Ci *(cirrus)*, PHYS *(curie)*, RAD PHYS *(curie)* curie *m*

CI *abbr* TELECOM *(conversation impossible)* conversation impossible *f*, TELECOM *(concatenation indication)* indication de concaténation *f*

CID *abbr* TELECOM *(charge injection device)* dispositif à injection de charge *m*, TELECOM *(consecutive identical digits)* symboles identiques consécutifs *m pl*

CIF *abbr (cost insurance freight)* PROD ENG coût assurance fret *m*

CIM *abbr (computer-integrated manufacturing)* COMP productique intégrée *f*

CIME *abbr (customer installation maintenance entities)* TELECOM entité de maintenance d'installation de client *f*

CIP *abbr (cleaning in place)* FOOD TECH *food-processing machinery* nettoyage en place *m*

CIR *abbr* TELECOM *(committed information rate)* débit d'information garanti *m*, TELECOM *(carrier-to-interface ratio)* rapport porteuse/brouillage *m*

CISC *abbr (complex instruction set computer)* COMP ordinateur à jeu d'instructions complexe *m*

CL *abbr (connectionless)* TELECOM en mode non connecté, sans connexion

CLCP *abbr (connectionless convergence protocol)* TELECOM protocole de convergence du mode non connecté *m*

CLI *abbr (calling line identification)* TELECOM ILA *(identification de ligne appelante)*

CLID *abbr (calling line identification display, CLIP)* TELECOM PILA *(présentation de l'identification de la ligne appelante)*

CLIR *abbr (calling line identification restriction)* TELECOM RILA *(restriction de l'identification de la ligne appelante)*

CLLM *abbr (consolidated link-layer management message)* TELECOM message de gestion de couche liaison consolidé *m*

CLNP *abbr (connectionless network layer protocol)* TELECOM protocole de couche réseau sans connexion *m*

CLNS *abbr (connectionless network layer service)* TELECOM service de couche réseau sans connexion *m*

CLP *abbr (cell loss priority)* TELECOM priorité de perte de cellule *f*

CLS *abbr (connectionless server)* TELECOM serveur en mode non connecté *m*

CLSF *abbr (connectionless service function)* TELECOM fonction de service sans connexion *f*

CLV *abbr (constant linear velocity)* COMP, OPT vitesse linéaire constante *f*

CM *abbr* COMP *(configuration management)*, DP *(configuration management)* contrôle de configuration *m*,

TELECOM *(conditionally mandatory)* PO *(partiellement obligatoire),* TELECOM *(connection matrix)* matrice de connexion *f*

CMB *abbr (CRC message bloc)* TELECOM bloc de messages pour le contrôle du CRC *m*

CMC *abbr* DETERGENTS *(carboxymethyl cellulose),* FOOD TECH *(carboxymethyl cellulose),* P&R *(carboxymethyl cellulose)* carboxyméthylcellulose *f,* TELECOM *(call modification completed message)* MAE *(message de modification d'appel effectuée)*

CMI *abbr (coded mark inversion)* TELECOM code CMI *m*

CMIP *abbr (common management information protocol)* TELECOM protocole commun d'information de gestion *m*

CMIPM *abbr (common management information protocol machine)* TELECOM machine du protocole commun de transfert d'informations de gestion *f*

CMIS *abbr (common management information service)* TELECOM service commun d'information de gestion *m,* service commun de transfert d'informations de gestion *m*

CMISE *abbr (common management information service element)* TELECOM élément de service commun d'information de gestion *m,* élément de service commun de transfert d'informations de gestion *m*

CMOS *abbr (compatible metal-oxide semiconductor)* COMP MOS complémentaire *m,* semi-conducteur à oxyde métallique complémentaire *m*

CMR *abbr (call modification request message)* TELECOM MAD *(demande de modification d'appel)*

CMRJ *abbr (call modification reject message)* TELECOM MAR *(message de refus de modification d'appel)*

C-n *abbr (container-n)* TELECOM conteneur-n *m*

CN *abbr (customer network)* TELECOM réseau client *m*

COD *abbr (chemical oxygen demand)* CHEM, HYDROL, POLLUTION DCO *(demande chimique d'oxygène)*

COLI *abbr (connected line identification)* TELECOM identification de la ligne connectée *f*

COLP *abbr (connected line identification presentation)* TELECOM PILC *(présentation de l'identification de la ligne connectée)*

COLR *abbr (connected line identification restriction)* TELECOM RILC *(restriction de l'identification de la ligne connectée)*

COM *abbr* COMP *(computer output on microfilm)* sortie ordinateur sur microfilm *f,* TELECOM *(continuation of message)* suite de message *f*

COMSAT *abbr (communications satellite)* NAUT satellite de communication *m*

CON *abbr (concentrator)* TELECOM concentrateur *m*

CONP *abbr (connection-oriented network layer protocol)* TELECOM protocole de couche réseau en mode connexion *m*

CONS *abbr (connection-oriented mode network service)* TELECOM service de réseau avec connexion *m*

cot *abbr (cotangent)* CONST cot *(cotangente)*

COW *abbr (crude oil washing)* PETR TECH lavage au brut des citernes *m*

CP *abbr (call processor)* TELECOM processeur de traitement des appels *m*

CPI *abbr* PRINT *(characters per inch)* caractères par pouce *m pl,* TELECOM *(computer-PBX interface)* interface PABX-serveur *f*

CPM *abbr (critical path method)* COMP méthode du chemin critique *f*

CPS *abbr (characters per second)* COMP, PRINT CPS *(caractères par seconde)*

CPSK *abbr (coherent phase shift keying)* TELECOM MDPC *(modulation par déplacement de phase cohérente)*

CPU *abbr (central processing unit)* COMP, DP, TELECOM UC *(unité centrale)*

CPVC *abbr (critical pigment volume concentration)* COATINGS *paint* CVCP *(concentration volumique critique de pigment)*

CQM *abbr (circuit group query message)* TELECOM IGD *(message d'interrogation de groupe de circuits)*

CQR *abbr (circuit group query response message)* TELECOM IGR *(message de réponse à une interrogation de groupe de circuits)*

CR *abbr* COMP *(carriage return)* caractère de retour chariot *m,* retour de chariot *m,* TELECOM *(call register)* compteur d'appels *m,* registre d'appels *m,* TELECOM *(connection request)* demande de connexion *f*

CRC *abbr* CONTROL *(cyclic redundancy check),* ELECTRON *(cyclic redundancy check)* CRC *(contrôle de redondance cyclique),* PRINT *(camera-ready copy)* copie prête à la reproduction *f,* document prêt *m,* TELECOM *(communications research centre)* centre de recherche sur les communications *m*

CRF *abbr* TELECOM *(connection-related function)* fonction liée à la connexion *f,* TELECOM *(virtual channel connection)* fonction liée à la connexion sur les VC *f,* TELECOM *(virtual path connection-related function)* fonction liée à la connexion sur les VP *f*

CRT *abbr (cathode ray tube)* COMP, ELEC, ELECTRON, PRINT, SAFETY, TV TRC *(tube à rayons cathodiques)*

Cs *abbr (cirrostratus)* METEO Cs *(cirro-stratus)*

CS *abbr* COMP *(circuit switching),* DP *(circuit switching),* ELECTRON *(circuit switching)* commutation de circuits *f,* TELECOM *(calls per second)* appels par seconde *m pl,* TELECOM *(communication services)* services de communication *m pl,* TELECOM *(convergence sublayer)* sous-couche de convergence *f*

CSI *abbr* TELECOM *(called subscriber identification)* identification de l'abonné demandé *f,* *(called station identity)* identité de la station demandée *f*

CSM *abbr* COMP *(command and control system)* système de commande et contrôle *m,* SPACE *(command and service module)* module de commande et de service *m*

CSMA *abbr (carrier sense multiple access)* TELECOM CSMA *(accès multiple par détection de porteuse)*

CSMA-CD *abbr (carrier sense multiple access with collision detection)* COMP, DP, ELECTRON CSMA-CD *(accès multiple par détection de porteuse avec détection de collision)*

CSN *abbr (Canadian Switched Network)* TELECOM RCC *(réseau commuté canadien)*

CSPDU *abbr (convergence sublayer protocol data unit)* TELECOM unité de données du protocole de la sous-couche convergence *f*

ct *abbr (continuous thread)* PACKAGING vis préfiletée *f*

CT *abbr* ELEC *(center tap, centre tap)* prise médiane *f,* TELECOM *(container)* conteneur *m,* TELECOM *(control terminal)* terminal de commande *m*

CTCSS *abbr (continuous tone controlled squelch system)* TELECOM dispositif silencieux à commande par tonalité *m,* silencieux de sous-porteuse *m*

CTD *abbr* ELEC ENG *(charge transfer device),* PHYS *(charge transfer device),* SPACE *(charge transfer device),* TELECOM *(charge transfer device)* DTC *(dispositif à transfert de charges)*, TELECOM *(conditionally toll denied)* blocage partiel de l'accès à l'interurbain *m*

CTS *abbr (container transport ship)* TRANSP navire porte-conteneurs *m*

Cu *abbr (cumulus)* METEO Cu *(cumulus)*

CUE *abbr (catch per unit effort)* OCEANOG CPUE *(prise par unité d'effort)*

CUG *abbr (closed user group)* COMP, DP, TELECOM GFU *(groupe fermé d'usagers)*

CV *abbr (code violation)* TELECOM violation de code *f*

CVD *abbr (chemical vapor deposition, chemical vapour deposition)* ELECTRON, OPT, TELECOM DCV *(dépôt chimique en phase vapeur)*

CVS *abbr (constant volume sampling)* POLLUTION échantillonnage à volume constant *m*

CW *abbr* ELEC ENG *(clockwise)* dans le sens horaire, ELEC ENG *(continuous wave)* onde entretenue *f*, TELECOM *(call waiting)* appel en instance *m*, WAVE PHYS *(continuous wave)* onde entretenue *f*

CWR *abbr (continuous welded rail)* RAIL LRS *(long rail soudé)*

d *abbr (deci)* METR déci

da *abbr (deca-)* METR da *(déca)*

DAC *abbr* COMP *(digital-to-analog converter)*, ELECTRON *(digital-to-analog converter, digital-to-analogue converter)*, TV *(digital-to-analog converter, digital-to-analogue converter)* CNA *(convertisseur numérique-analogique)*

DAO *abbr (deasphalted oil)* PETR TECH huile désasphaltée *f*

DAT *abbr* COMP *(digital audio tape)* bande audio-numérique *f*, COMP *(dynamic address translation)* traduction dynamique d'adresse *f*, RECORDING *(digital audio tape)* cassette numérique *f*

dB *abbr (decibel)* ACOUSTICS, PHYS, POLLUTION, RAD PHYS, RECORDING dB *(décibel)*

DBA *abbr (database administrator)* COMP, DP administrateur de base de données *m*

DBM *abbr* COMP *(database management)*, DP *(database management)* GBD *(gestion de base de données)*, ELECTRON *(double-balanced mixer)* mélangeur symétrique double *m*

DBMS *abbr (database management system)* COMP, DP, TELECOM SGBD *(système de gestion de bases de données)*

DBS *abbr (direct broadcasting satellite)* TELECOM satellite de transmission en direct *m*

DBST *abbr (double bituminous surface treatment)* CONST revêtement bicouche *m*

DC *abbr* COMP *(device control)*, DP *(device control)* gestion des périphériques *f*, ELEC ENG *(direct current)* CC *(courant continu)*, ELEC ENG *(directional coupler)* coupleur directif *m*, ELECTRON *(direct current)*, PROD ENG *(direct current)*, RAIL *(direct current)*, RECORDING *(direct current)*, TELECOM *(direct current)*, TV *(direct current)* CC *(courant continu)*

DCC *abbr* ELEC *(double-cotton-covered)* guipé au coton double, TELECOM *(data communication channel)* canal de communication de données *m*, canal de transmission de données *m*, voie de données *f*, TELECOM *(data collection centre, data collection center)* centre de collecte de données *m*

DCD *abbr (data carrier detect)* TELECOM détection de porteuse de données *f*

DCE *abbr* TELECOM *(data circuit terminal equipment)* ETCD *(équipement terminal de circuit de données)*, TELECOM *(data communications equipment)* installation de transmission de données *f*

DCME *abbr (digital circuit multiplication equipment)* TELECOM EMCN *(équipement de multiplication de circuit numérique)*

DCMG *abbr (digital circuit multiplication gain)* TELECOM GMCN *(gain de l'équipement de multiplication de circuit numérique)*

DCMS *abbr (digital circuit multiplication system)* TELECOM SMCN *(système de multiplication de circuit numérique)*

DCP *abbr (data collection platform)* SPACE plate-forme de collecte de données *f*

DCS *abbr* TELECOM *(defined context set)* ensemble des contextes définis *m*, TELECOM *(digital command signal)* signal de commande numérique *m*

DDC *abbr (direct digital control)* COMP, DP commande numérique directe *f*

DDD *abbr* (AmE) *(direct distance dialing)* TELECOM automatique interurbain *m* (Fra), interurbain automatique *m* (Can), sélection à distance de l'abonné demandé *f*

DDE *abbr (direct data entry)* COMP, DP entrée directe de données *f*

DDI *abbr* (BrE) *(direct dialling in)* TELECOM accès directe à l'arrivée *f*, selection directe à un poste *f*

DDL *abbr (data description language)* COMP langage de description de données *m*

DDP *abbr (distributed data processing)* COMP informatique distribuée *f*

DEL *abbr (delete character)* COMP, DP caractère de suppression *m*

DF *abbr (direction finding)* TELECOM goniométrie *f*, radiogoniométrie *f*

DID *abbr* (AmE) *(direct inward dialing)* TELECOM accès directe à l'arrivée *m*, sélection directe à un poste *f*

DIN *abbr (Deutsche Industrienorm)* MECH ENG DIN *(Deutsche Industrienorm)*

DIP *abbr (dual-in-line package)* COMP, DP, ELEC ENG boîtier DIP *m*, boîtier à deux rangées de broches *m*

DIS *abbr (draft international standard)* TELECOM projet de norme internationale *m*

DIT *abbr (directory information tree)* TELECOM arbre d'information d'annuaire *m*

DL *abbr* TELECOM *(data link)* liaison de données *f*, TELECOM *(direct line)* ligne directe *f*, ligne privée *f*

DLC *abbr* TELECOM *(data link control)* commande de liaison de données *f*, TELECOM *(data link connection)* connexion pour liaison de données *f*

DLCI *abbr (data link connection identifier)* TELECOM identificateur de connexion de liaison consolidée *m*

DLE *abbr (data link escape)* COMP, DP échappement en transmission *m*, échappement à la transmission *m*

DLS *abbr (data link service)* TELECOM service de liaison de données *m*

DM *abbr* COMP *(data management)* gestion de données *f*, COMP *(delta modulation)* modulation delta *f*, DP *(data memory)* mémoire de données *f*, DP, TELECOM *(data management)* gestion de données *f*, TELECOM *(degraded minute)* minute dégradée *f*, TELECOM *(digital multiplexer)* multiplexeur numérique *m*

DMA *abbr (direct memory access)* COMP accès direct à la mémoire *m*

DME *abbr (distance-measuring equipment)* AERONAUT

interrogateur de distance *m*, équipement DME *m*

DML *abbr (data manipulation language)* COMP langage de manipulation de données *m*

DMM *abbr (direct metal mastering)* PROD ENG, RECORDING gravure directe sur métal *f*

DMNSC *abbr (digital main network switching centre)* TELECOM centre de commutation numérique du réseau principal *m*

DN *abbr* TELECOM *(directory number)* numéro d'appel *m*, TELECOM *(destination network)* réseau de destination *m*, TELECOM *(digital network)* réseau numérique *m*

DNA *abbr (deoxyribonucleic acid)* CHEM ADN *(acide désoxyribonucléique)*

DNIC *abbr (data network identification code)* TELECOM CIRD *(code d'identification de réseau de données)*

DO *abbr (dissolved oxygen)* POLLUTION OD *(oxygène dissous)*

DOD *abbr (direct outward dialing, direct outward dialling)* TELECOM accès direct au réseau *m*, prise directe du réseau *f*

DOM *abbr (digestible organic matter)* RECYCLING MOD *(matière organique digestible)*

DOS *abbr (disk operating system)* COMP, DP DOS *(système d'exploitation à disque)*

DP *abbr* COMP *(data processing)*, DP *(data processing)*, ELECTRON *(data processing)* TD *(traitement de données)*, ELECTRON *(differential phase)* phase différentielle *f*, GEOL *(datum plane)* surface de référence *f*, TELECOM *(data processing)* TD *(traitement de données)*, TELECOM *(dial impulse)* impulsion décimale *f*, TELECOM *(detailed procedure)* procédure détaillée *f*

DPC *abbr (data processing centre, data processing center)* DP centre de traitement d'information *m*, centre de traitement de données *m*, centre informatique *m*, TELECOM centre de traitement de données *m*

DPCM *abbr (differential pulse code modulation)* ELECTRON modulation PCM différentielle *f*, modulation différentielle par impulsions codées *f*

DPDT *abbr (double-pole double-throw)* ELEC, ELEC ENG bipolaire double course *f*, bipolaire à deux directions *f*

DPL *abbr (distribution primary link)* TELECOM liaison primaire pour les services de distribution *f*

DPRC *abbr (double-pure-rubber-covered)* ELEC guipé deux couches caoutchouc

DPS *abbr (double-pole switch)* ELEC interrupteur bipolaire *m*

DPSK *abbr (differential phase-shift keying)* ELECTRON modulation DPSK *f*, modulation par déplacement de phase différentielle *f*

DPSS *abbr (double-pole snap switch)* ELEC commutateur bipolaire à bascule *m*

DPST *abbr (double-pole single-throw switch)* ELEC ENG contact à deux directions *m*, interrupteur bipolaire à une direction *m*

DRAM *abbr (dynamic random access memory)* COMP, DP mémoire dynamique *f*

DRAW *abbr (direct read after write)* OPT contrôle en cours d'enregistrement *m*

DRS *abbr* SPACE *(digital radio system)* faisceau hertzien numérique *m*, SPACE *(data relay satellite)* satellite relais de données *m*

DS *abbr* COMP *(data store)* mémoire de données *f*, PRINT *(drive side)* côté commande *m*, TELECOM *(digital sec-tion)* section numérique *f*, TELECOM *(direct sequence)* séquence directe *f*

DSC *abbr (digital selective calling)* TELECOM appel sélectif numérique *m*

DSE *abbr* COMP *(data switching exchange)* centre de commutation de données *m*, TELECOM *(data switching exchange)* centre de commutation de données *m*, commutateur de données *m*, TELECOM *(digital switching element)* organe de commutation automatique *m*

DSI *abbr* TELECOM *(digital speech interpolation)* CNC *(concentration numérique des conversations)*, TELECOM *(data set identifier)* identificateur de modem *m*, TELECOM *(display station interface)* interface de poste d'affichage *m*

DSL *abbr (deep scattering layer)* OCEANOG couche diffusante profonde *f*

DSP *abbr* ELECTRON *(digital signal processing)* traitement numérique de signaux *m*, TELECOM *(domain-specific part)* partie spécifique du domaine *f*

DSR *abbr (data set ready)* COMP, TELECOM modem prêt *m*, poste de données prêt *m*

DST *abbr (drill stem test)* PETR TECH essai de formation *m*

DTA *abbr (differential thermal analysis)* CONST, P&R, POLLUTION, THERMOD ATD *(analyse thermique différentielle)*

DTE *abbr (data terminal equipment)* AERONAUT, COMP, TELECOM ETD, ETTD *(équipement terminal de données)*

DTI *abbr (digital trunk interface)* TELECOM module multiplex numérique *m*

DTL *abbr (diode-transistor logic)* COMP, ELECTRON logique à diodes et transistors *f*

D-to-A *abbr (digital-to-analog, digital-to-analogue)* TV numérique-analogique

DTP *abbr (desktop publishing)* COMP, DP, PRINT PAO *(publication assistée par ordinateur)*

DVE *abbr (digital video effects)* TV effets spéciaux *m pl*, effets spéciaux numériques *m pl*

DVTR *abbr (digital videotape recorder)* TV magnétoscope numérique *m*

DWT *abbr (deep well thermometer)* PETR thermomètre de fond *m*

DXC *abbr* TELECOM *(digital cross-connect)* brasseur-répartiteur numérique *m*, TELECOM *(digital cross-connect equipment)* équipement multiplexeur-aiguilleur numérique *m*

E *abbr (exa-)* METR E *(exa-)*

EA *abbr (external access equipment)* TELECOM équipement d'accès externe *m*

EAF *abbr (electric arc furnace)* COAL TECH four à arc électrique *m*

EB *abbr* COMP *(electron beam)*, ELEC *(electron beam)* microscope faisceau électronique *m*, ELECTRON *(electron beam)* faisceau d'électrons *m*, METALL *(electron beam)* faisceau électronique *m*, NUCLEAR *(electron beam)*, PART PHYS *(electron beam)* faisceau d'électrons *m*, TELECOM *(erroneous block)* bloc erroné *m*, TELECOM *(electron beam)*, TV *(electron beam)* faisceau électronique *m*, WAVE PHYS *(electron beam)* faisceau d'électrons *m*

EBC *abbr (electron beam curing)* PRINT réticulage *m*, séchage de surface par bombardement d'électrons *m*, séchage de surface par faisceau d'électrons *m*

EBCDIC *abbr (extended binary coded decimal inter-change code)* COMP, DP, ELECTRON code EBCDIC *m (code* décimal codé binaire étendu)

EBCS *abbr (European barge carrier system)* TRANSP système EBCS *m*

EBS *abbr (electron-bombarded semiconductor)* ELEC-TRON triode EBS *f*, triode à cible *f*

ECC *abbr* COMP *(error correcting code)*, DP *(error correcting code)*, ELECTRON *(error correcting code)*, SPACE *(error correcting code)* communications code correcteur d'erreurs *m*, TELECOM *(embedded control channel)* canal de commande intégré *m*, TELECOM *(error correcting code)* code correcteur d'erreurs *m*

ECD *abbr* PETR TECH *(equivalent circulating density) drilling* densité équivalente de circulation *f*, TELECOM *(error control device)* dispositif de protection contre les erreurs *m*

ECL *abbr (emitter-coupled logic)* COMP, ELECTRON logique ECL *f*, logique à couplage par émetteurs *f*

ECN *abbr (explicit congestion notification)* TELECOM notification d'encombrement explicite *f*

EDAX *abbr (energy dispersive analysis by X-rays)* CHEM système de microanalyse par dispersion en énergie *m*

EDI *abbr* TELECOM *(electronic document interchange)*, *(electronic data interchange)* EDI *(échange de données informatisées)*

EDI-AU *abbr (EDI access unit)* TELECOM unité d'accès EDI *f*

EDIM *abbr (EDI message)* TELECOM message EDI *m*

EDIME *abbr (EDI messaging environment)* TELECOM environnement de messagerie EDI *m*

EDIMG *abbr (EDI messaging)* TELECOM messagerie EDI *f*

EDI-MS *abbr (EDI message store)* TELECOM mémoire de messages EDI *f*

EDIMS *abbr (EDI messaging system)* TELECOM système de messagerie EDI *m*

EDIN *abbr (EDI notification)* TELECOM notification EDI *f*

EDI-UA *abbr (EDI user agent)* TELECOM agent d'usager EDI *m*, agent d'utilisateur EDI *m*

EDM *abbr (electrodischarge machining)* MECH ENG usinage par électro-érosion *m*, PROD ENG électro-érosion *f*

EDP *abbr (electronic data processing)* COMP informatique *f*, traitement électronique de données *m*, DP, ELECTRON informatique *f*

EDTA *abbr (ethylenediamino tetra-acetic acid)* DETER-GENTS acide éthylène-diamino-tétracétique *m*

EDTV *abbr (extended definition television)* TV télévision à définition améliorée *f*

E-E *abbr* TV *(electronic-to-electronic)* direct modulateur-démodulateur, vidéo-sur-vidéo, TV *(electronic editing)* montage électronique *m*

EEROM *abbr (electrically erasable ROM)* COMP, DP ROM effaçable électriquement *f*, mémoire morte effaçable électriquement *f*

EFA *abbr (essential fatty acid)* FOOD TECH acide gras essentiel *m*

EFT *abbr (electronic funds transfer)* TELECOM transfert électronique de fonds *m*

EFTPOS *abbr (electronic funds transfer at point of sale)* TELECOM transfert électronique de fonds au point de vente *m*

EFTS *abbr (electronic funds transfer system)* COMP système de télépaiement *m*, virement électronique *m*

EGA *abbr (enhanced graphics adaptator)* COMP *card*

EGA *(adaptateur graphique couleur)*

EHT *abbr (extra high tension)* ELECTRON, TV THT *(très haute tension)*

EIRP *abbr (equivalent isotropically-radiated power)* SPACE *communications* PIRE *(puissance isotrope rayonnée équivalente)*

EIT *abbr (encoded information type)* TELECOM type d'informations codées *m*, type de codage *m*

EL *abbr (elevated line)* TRANSP métro aérien *m*

ELED *abbr (edge-emitting light-emitting diode)* OPT diode électroluminescente à émission longitudinale *f*, TELECOM diode électroluminescente à émission par la tranche *f*

ELSBM *abbr (exposed location single-buoy mooring)* PETR TECH amarrage à point unique *m*, bouée d'amarrage à point unique *f*, bouée monoposte *f*

ELT *abbr (emergency locator transmitter)* TELECOM radiobalise de détresse *f*, émetteur de localisation d'urgence *m*

EM *abbr* COMP *(electronic mail, E-mail)* courrier électronique *m*, messagerie électronique *f*, COMP *(end of medium)* fin de support *f*, DP *(electronic mail, E-mail)*, ELECTRON *(electronic mail, E-mail)*, TELECOM *(electronic mail, E-mail)* courrier électronique *m*, messagerie électronique *f*

emf *abbr (electromotive force)* ELEC, ELEC ENG, PHYS fém *(force électromotrice)*

EMI *abbr* COMP *(electromagnetic interference)* interférence électromagnétique *f*, PROD ENG *(electromagnetic induction)* induction électromagnétique *f*, SPACE *(electromagnetic interference)* perturbation électromagnétique *f*

EMS *abbr* COMP *(expanded memory specification)* norme EMS *f (spécification de mémoire étendue)*, TELECOM *(electronic message system)* système de commutation électronique de messages *m*, système de messagerie électronique *m*

EMW *abbr (Equivalent Mud Weight)* PETR TECH *drilling* DBE *(densité de boue équivalente)*

ENG *abbr (electronic news gathering)* TV journalisme électronique *m*, production vidéo en reportage *f*

ENQ *abbr (enquiry character)* COMP caractère d'interrogation *m*

E-O *abbr (electrical-optical)* TELECOM électrique-optique

EOB *abbr (end of block)* COMP fin de bloc *f*

EOC *abbr* TELECOM *(embedded operations channel)* canal d'exploitation intégré *m*, TELECOM *(end of communication)* fin de communication *m*

EOD *abbr (end of data)* COMP, DP fin de données *f*

EOF *abbr (end of file)* COMP fin de fichier *f*

EOJ *abbr (end of job)* COMP fin de travail *f*

EOM *abbr (end of message)* COMP, TELECOM fin de message *f*

EOT *abbr* COMP, DP *(end of tape)* fin de bande *m*, COMP, DP *(end of transmission)* fin de transmission *f*, TELE-COM *(end of transaction)* fin de transaction *f*

EOW *abbr (engineering order wire)* TELECOM ligne d'ordre technique *f*

EP *abbr* GEOPHYS *(equilibrium potential)* potentiel d'équilibre *m*, TELECOM *(erroneous period)* période erronée *f*

EPIRB *abbr (emergency position-indicating radio beacon)* NAUT, TELECOM radiobalise de localisation de sinistre *f*

EPOS *abbr (electronic point of sale)* COMP point de

vente électronique *m*

EPROM *abbr (erasable PROM)* COMP PROM effaçable *f*

ERP *abbr (effective radiated power)* TELECOM puissance apparente rayonnée *f*

ERRA *abbr* (BrE) *(European Recycling and Recovery Association)* PACKAGING Association européenne pour le recyclage et la récupération *f*

ES *abbr* COMP *(echo suppressor)*, DP *(echo suppressor)*, ELECTRON *(echo suppressor)*, SPACE *(echo suppressor)* suppresseur d'écho *m*, TELECOM *(errored second)* seconde avec erreur *f*, TELECOM *(echo suppressor)* suppresseur d'écho *m*

ESA *abbr (European Space Agency)* ASTRON, SPACE ASE *(Agence spatiale européenne)*

ESC *abbr (escape, escape key)* COMP, DP ESC *(échappement)*

ESCA *abbr (electron spectroscopy for chemical analysis)* CHEM spectroscopie électronique pour analyses chimiques *f*

ESI *abbr (equivalent step index)* TELECOM indice à saut équivalent *m*

ESP *abbr (electrostatic precipitator)* POLLUTION dépoussiéreur électrique *m*, précipitateur électrostatique *m*, séparateur électrique *m*, électrofiltre *m*

ESR *abbr (electron spin resonance)* PART PHYS résonance de spin électronique *f*, PHYS résonance de spin électronique *f*, résonance magnétique électronique *f*

ESS *abbr (electronic switching system)* TELECOM système de commutation électronique *m*

ESV *abbr (experimental safety vehicle)* TRANSP voiture expérimentale de sécurité *f*

ET *abbr (exchange termination)* TELECOM terminaison de commutateur *f*

ETA *abbr (estimated time of arrival)* AERONAUT, NAUT navigation HPA *(heure prévue d'arrivée)*

ETB *abbr (end of transmission block)* COMP, DP fin de bloc de transmission *f*

E-to-E *abbr (electronic-to-electronic)* TV direct modulateur-démodulateur, vidéo-sur-vidéo

ETS *abbr (European Telecommunication Standard)* TELECOM Norme de Télécommunication Européenne *f*

ETSI *abbr (European Telecommunication Standardization Institute)* TELECOM Institut Européen de Normalisation des Télécommunications *m*

ETX *abbr (end of text)* COMP, DP fin de texte *f*

eV *abbr (electronvolt)* ELECTRON, METR, PART PHYS, PHYS eV *(électron-volt)*

EVA *abbr (ethylene vinyl acetate)* P&R éthylène-acétate de vinyle *m*

EW *abbr (electronic warfare)* ELECTRON guerre électronique *f*

EX *abbr (extinction ratio)* TELECOM taux d'extinction *m*

f *abbr (femto-)* METR f *(femto-)*

F *abbr (farad)* METR F *(farad)*

FAA *abbr (facility accepted message)* TELECOM SUAC *(message d'acceptation de service supplémentaire)*

FACR *abbr (first article configuration review)* SPACE revue de conformité du premier article *f*

FAR *abbr (facility request message)* TELECOM SUDM *(message de demande de service supplémentaire)*

FAS *abbr* TELECOM *(flexible access switch)* commutateur à accès flexible *m*, TELECOM *(frame alignment signal)* signal de verrouillage de trame *m*

FAXIF *abbr (facsimile interworking function)* TELECOM fonction d'interfonctionnement télécopie *f*

FCC *abbr (face-centered cubic, face-centred cubic)* CHEM, CRYSTALL CFC *(cubique à faces centrées)*

FDAU *abbr (flight data acquisition unit)* AERONAUT boîtier d'acquisition de données de vol *m*

FDDI *abbr (fiber-distributed data interface, fibre-distributed data interface)* TELECOM interface de données avec distribution par fibre *f*

FDHM *abbr (full-duration half-maximum)* OPT *pulse*, TELECOM durée à mi-crête *f*

FDM *abbr (frequency-division multiplexing)* COMP MPF *(multiplexage par partage des fréquences)*, MRF *(multiplexage par répartition en fréquence)*, ELECTRON MRF *(multiplexage par répartition en fréquence)*, PHYS MA *(multiplexage analogique)*, MPF *(multiplexage par partage des fréquences)*, MRF *(multiplexage par répartition en fréquence)*, TELECOM MRF *(multiplexage par répartition en fréquence)*

FDMA *abbr (frequency-division multiple access)* SPACE, TELECOM AMRF *(accès multiple à répartition en fréquence)*

FDR *abbr (final design review)* SPACE RDF *(revue de définition finale)*

FDX *abbr (full-duplex)* COMP duplex intégral

FE *abbr* TELECOM *(format effector)* caractère de mise en page *f*, TELECOM *(functional entity)* entité fonctionnelle *f*

FEA *abbr (functional entity action)* TELECOM action d'entité fonctionnelle *f*

FEBE *abbr (far-end block error)* TELECOM erreur de bloc à l'extrémité distante *f*

FEC *abbr (forward error correction)* COMP correction d'erreurs sans voie de retour *f*

FECN *abbr (forward explicit congestion notification)* TELECOM notification d'encombrement explicite émise vers l'avant *f*

FEP *abbr (front-end processor)* COMP processeur frontal *m*

FERF *abbr (far-end receive failure)* TELECOM défaut en réception à l'extrémité distante *m*, dérangement de réception à l'extrémité *m*

FET *abbr (field-effect transistor)* COMP, ELECTRON, OPT, PHYS TEC *(transistor à effet de champ)*

FF *abbr (form feed)* COMP, PRINT alimentation en papier *f*, avance-papier *m*

FFT *abbr (fast Fourier transform)* COMP, ELECTRON transformation de Fourier rapide *f*

FIFO *abbr (first-in first-out)* COMP, DP PEPS *(premier entré premier sorti)*

FIR *abbr (finite impulse response)* ELECTRON réponse impulsionnelle finie *f*

FITE *abbr (forward interworking telephony event)* TELECOM événement téléphonique d'interfonctionnement vers l'avant *m*

FLS *abbr* TELECOM *(frame loss second)* seconde avec perte de trame *f*, TELECOM *(free line signal)* signal d'inoccupation *m*

FM *abbr (frequency modulation)* COMP, ELEC, ELECTRON, PHYS, RECORDING, TELECOM, TV, WAVE PHYS MF *(modulation de fréquence)*

FMBS *abbr (frame-mode bearer service)* TELECOM service support en mode trame *m*

FOB *abbr (free on board)* NAUT *commerce, shipping*

FOB *(franco à bord)*

FoE *abbr (Friends of the Earth)* POLLUTION Amis de la Terre *m pl*

FOF *abbr (freeze-out fraction)* TELECOM fraction de gel *f*

FPC *abbr (fish protein concentrate)* OCEANOG CPP *(concentré de protéines de poisson)*

FPLA *abbr (field programmable logic array)* COMP, DP réseau à logique programmable par l'utilisateur *m*

FPP *abbr (floating point processor)* COMP, DP processeur en virgule flottante *m*

FPS *abbr (fast packet switch)* TELECOM commutateur de paquets rapide *m*

FRC *abbr (fault reception centre, fault reception center)* TELECOM service de dépannage *m*

FRJ *abbr (facility rejected message)* TELECOM SURF *(message de refus de service supplémentaire)*

FRP *abbr (fast-reservation protocol)* TELECOM protocole de réservation rapide *m*

FRR *abbr (flight readiness review)* SPACE RAV *(revue d'aptitude au vol)*

FSK *abbr (frequency shift keying)* COMP, DP, ELECTRON, TELECOM, TV MDF *(modulation par déplacement de fréquence)*

FSR *abbr (flowable solids reactor)* NUCLEAR réacteur à suspension solide *m*

FSS *abbr (fixed satellite service)* SPACE service fixe par satellite *m*

FTAMSE *abbr (file transfer access and manipulation service element)* TELECOM élément de service de l'accès aux transfert et manipulation *m*

FTTB *abbr (fiber to the building, fibre to the building)* TELECOM fibre jusqu'à l'immeuble *f*

FTTC *abbr (fiber to the kerb, fibre to the kerb)* TELECOM fibre jusqu'au trottoir *f*

FTTH *abbr (fiber to the home, fibre to the home)* TELECOM fibre jusqu'au logement *f*

FTTO *abbr (fibre to the office, fiber to the office)* TELECOM fibre jusqu'au bureau *f*

FU *abbr (functional unit)* TELECOM unité fonctionnelle *f*

FWF *abbr (first window fibre, first window fiber)* OPT fibre à 0,85mm *f*

FWHM *abbr (full-width half-maximum)* OPT largeur à mi-crête *f*, étendue à mi-crête *f*

FX *abbr (effects)* TV trucages *m pl*

G *abbr (giga-)* METR G *(giga-)*

GA *abbr (go ahead)* TELECOM invitation à continuer *f*

GCBR *abbr (gas-cooled breeder reactor)* NUCLEAR réacteur surrégénérateur refroidi au gaz *m*

GCR *abbr (group code recording)* COMP enregistrement par codage de groupe *m*, enregistrement par groupe *m*

GEM *abbr (ground effect machine)* TRANSP véhicule à effet de sol *m*

GFC *abbr (generic flow control)* TELECOM contrôle de flux générique *m*

GIGO *abbr (garbage-in/garbage-out)* COMP rebut à l'entrée et à la sortie *m*

GMAT *abbr (Greenwich Mean Astronomical Time)* ASTRON temps sidéral moyen de Greenwich *m*

GMDSS *abbr (Global Marine Distress and Safety System)* NAUT *sea rescue* SMDSM *(système mondial de détresse et de sécurité en mer)*

GMSK *abbr (Gaussian-filtered minimum shift keying)* TELECOM modulation à déplacement minimal à filtre gaussien *f*

GMT *abbr (Greenwich Mean Time)* PHYS, SPACE TMG *(Temps Moyen de Greenwich)*

GOR *abbr (gas-to-oil ratio)* PETR rapport gaz-pétrole *m*, PETR TECH proportion gaz-huile *f*

GP *abbr (Guinier-Preston zone)* CRYSTALL zone Guinier-Preston *f*

GPU *abbr (ground power unit)* AERONAUT groupe auxiliaire au sol *m*, groupe de démarrage au sol *m*

GRP *abbr (glass reinforced polyester)* MECH polyester armé *m*, NAUT *(glass refined plastic) boatbuilding material* matière plastique armée de fibre de verre *f*

GS *abbr (group separator)* COMP séparateur de groupes *m*, DP bande de protection *f*

GSC *abbr (group switching centre, group switching center)* TELECOM centre de transit *m*, commutateur à autonomie d'acheminement *m*

G-T *abbr (gain-to-noise temperature ratio)* SPACE quality factor G-T *(rapport gain-température de bruit)*

GUT *abbr (grand unified theory)* PART PHYS, PHYS théorie de grande unification *f*

GVW *abbr (gross vehicle weight)* VEHICLES PTC *(poids total en charge)*, PTM *(poids total maximum)*

Gy *abbr (gray)* METR, PHYS Gy *(gray)*

h *abbr (hecto-)* METR h *(hecto-)*

H *abbr (henry)* ELEC, ELEC ENG, METR, PHYS H *(henry)*

HASAWA *abbr (BrE) (Health and Safety at Work Act)* SAFETY avis d'interdiction *m*

HC *abbr (high cube container)* TRANSP HC *(conteneur hors-cotes)*

HCF *abbr (highest common factor)* MATH PGCD *(plus grand commun diviseur)*

hcp *abbr (hexagonal close-packed structure)* CRYSTALL structure hexagonale compacte *f*

HD *abbr (heavy-duty oil)* PETR TECH huile à haute tenue *f*

HDB2 *abbr (high-density bipolar of order 2 code)* TELECOM code bipolaire à haute densité d'ordre 2 *m*

HDLC *abbr (high-level data link control)* COMP, DP, TELECOM commande de liaison de données à haut niveau *f*, procédure de liaison de données à haut niveau *f* procédure HDLC *f*

HDPE *abbr (high-density polyethylene)* PACKAGING polyéthylène à haute densité *m*

HDTV *abbr (high definition television)* TELECOM, TV TVHD *(télévision à haute définition)*

HDX *abbr (half duplex)* COMP semi-duplex

HEC *abbr (header error control)* TELECOM contrôle d'erreur d'en-tête *m*, contrôle d'erreur sur l'en-tête *m*

HF *abbr (high-frequency)* AERONAUT, ELEC, ELEC ENG, ELECTRON HF *(haute fréquence)*

HGV *abbr (heavy goods vehicle)* TRANSP poids lourd *m*

HHSV *abbr (high hypothetical speed vehicle)* TRANSP véhicule à grande vitesse hypothétique *m*

HLLV *abbr (heavy-lift launch vehicle)* SPACE lanceur lourd *m*

HOOD *abbr (hierarchical object-oriented design)* COMP, DP conception hiérarchique orientée objet *f*

hp *abbr (horsepower)* AUTO cheval vapeur *m*, puissance en chevaux *f*

HPA *abbr (higher-order path adaptation)* TELECOM adaptation de conduit d'ordre supérieur *f*

HPC *abbr (higher-order path connection)* TELECOM connexion de conduit d'ordre supérieur *f*

HPLC *abbr (high-pressure liquid chromatography)* CHEM, FOOD TECH, LAB EQUIP, POLLUTION CLHP *(chromatographie liquide à haute pression)*

HPT *abbr (higher-order path termination)* TELECOM terminaison de conduit d'ordre supérieur *f*

HR *abbr (high resistance)* TELECOM haute résistance *f*

HST *abbr (high-speed train)* RAIL TGV *(train expérimental à grande vitesse)*

HT *abbr* COMP, DP *(horizontal tabulation)* tabulation horizontale *f*, ELEC *(high-tension)*, ELEC ENG *(high-tension)*, PHYS *(high-tension)* HT *(haute tension)*

HTST *abbr (high-temperature short time)* FOOD TECH pasteurisation HTST *f*

HUD *abbr (head-up display)* INSTRUMENT collimateur de pilotage *m*

HV *abbr (high-voltage)* ELEC, ELECTROTEC, PHYS HT *(haute tension)*

HVL *abbr (half value layer)* NUCLEAR, PHYS CDA *(couche de demi-atténuation)*

HWOST *abbr (high water ordinary spring tide)* FUELLESS plus hautes eaux des grandes marées ordinaires *f pl*

Hz *abbr (hertz)* ELEC, ELEC ENG, METR, PETR, PHYS, TV Hz *(hertz)*

I/F *abbr (interface)* TELECOM interface *f*

I/O *abbr (input/output)* COMP, PROD ENG E/S *(entrée/sortie)*

IAGC *abbr (instantaneous automatic gain control)* CONTROL régulateur automatique de niveau *m*

IAS *abbr (immediate access store)* COMP mémoire à accès immédiat *f*

IAT *abbr (International Atomic Time)* ASTRON TAI *(Temps Atomique International)*

IAVC *abbr (instantaneous automatic volume control)* CONTROL régulateur automatique de niveau *m*

IBG *abbr (interblock gap)* COMP espace entre blocs *m*

IC *abbr (integrated circuit)* COMP, ELEC, ELECTRON, PHYS, TELECOM, TV CI *(circuit intégré)*

ICB *abbr (incoming calls barred)* TELECOM interdiction des appels à l'arrivée *f*

ID *abbr* COMP *(identification)*, DP *(identification)* ID *(identification)*, MECH *(inner diameter, inside diameter)* diamètre intérieur *m*, TELECOM *(identifier)* identificateur *m*

IDD *abbr (International Direct Dialing)* TELECOM Automatique International *m*

IDDD *abbr (International Direct Distance Dialing)* TELECOM Automatique International *m*

IDF *abbr (intermediate distribution frame)* TELECOM RI *(répartiteur intermédiaire)*

IDI *abbr (initial domain identifier)* TELECOM IDI *(identificateur du domaine initial)*

IDN *abbr (integrated digital network)* TELECOM RNI *(réseau numérique intégré)*

IDP *abbr* DP *(integrated data processing)* traitement intégré de l'information *m*, traitement intégré des données *m*, TELECOM *(initial domain part)* partie du domaine initial *f*

IDSE *abbr (international data switching exchange)* TELECOM centre international de commutation de données *m*

IDT *abbr (interdigital transducer)* TELECOM transducteur interdigital *m*

IF *abbr (intermediate frequency)* ELECTRON, TELECOM FI *(fréquence intermédiaire)*

IFM *abbr (instantaneous frequency measurement)* ELEC-

TRON mesure de fréquence instantanée *f*

IFRB *abbr (International Frequency Registration Board)* SPACE *communications* Comité international d'enregistrement des fréquences *m*

IFU *abbr (interworking functional unit)* TELECOM unité fonctionnelle d'interfonctionnement *f*

IG *abbr (interpolation gain)* TELECOM gain de concentration *m*

IGFET *abbr (insulated gate FET)* ELECTRON TEC à grille isolée *m*

IGN *abbr (international gateway node)* TELECOM NTI *(noeud de transit international)*

IHS *abbr (integrated home system)* COMP domotique *f*

IIR *abbr (infinite impulse response)* ELECTRON réponse impulsionnelle infinie *f*, TELECOM réponse infinie à une impulsion *f*

I²L *abbr (integrated injection logic)* ELECTRON I²L *(logique intégrée à injection)*

ILD *abbr (injection laser diode)* OPT diode laser *f*, laser à injection *m*, laser à semi-conducteur *m*, TELECOM laser à injection *m*

ILS *abbr (instrument landing system)* AERONAUT système d'atterrissage aux instruments *m*, système d'atterrissage radiogoniométrique *m*, SPACE, TRANSP système d'atterrissage aux instruments *m*

IM *abbr* TELECOM *(intermodulation product)* produit d'intermodulation *m*, TELECOM *(interface module)* unité de raccordement *f*

IMA *abbr (input message acknowledgment)* TELECOM accusé de réception de message d'entrée *m*

IMO *abbr (International Maritime Organization)* NAUT OMI *(Organisation Maritime Internationale)*

IMP *abbr* ASTRON *(interplanetary monitoring platform)* plate-forme d'observation interplanétaire *f*, TELECOM *(interface message processor)* serveur de message *m*

Ind *abbr (indication)* TELECOM indication *f*

INF *abbr (information message)* TELECOM message d'information *m*

INR *abbr (information request message)* TELECOM IND *(message de demande d'information)*

INTTR *abbr (international transit exchange)* TELECOM commutateur de transit international *m*

IOC *abbr (integrated optical circuit)* OPT, TELECOM circuit d'optique intégré *m*, circuit intégré optique *m*

IOP *abbr (input/output processor)* COMP processeur d'entrée/sortie *m*

IOS *abbr* COMP *(integrated office system)* bureautique intégrée *f*, système BI *m*, SPACE *(Intelsat Operations Center)* Centre d'exploitation intelsat *m*

IP *abbr* COMP *(input processor)* processeur d'entrée *m*, COMP *(information processing)*, DP *(information processing)*, ELECTRON *(information processing)* traitement de l'information *m*

IPA *abbr* DETERGENTS *(isopropyl acid)* alcool isopropylique *m*, isopropanol *m*, PRINT *(isopropylic alcohol)* alcool isopropylique *m*

IPL *abbr* COMP *(initial program load)* programme de chargement initial *m*, TELECOM *(interactive primary link)* liaison primaire pour services interactifs *f*

IPS *abbr (inches per second)* COMP, RECORDING PPS *(pouces par seconde)*

IR *abbr* COMP *(information retrieval)*, DP *(information retrieval)* recherche documentaire *f*, OPT *(infrared)*, PHYS *(infrared)*, RAD PHYS *(infrared)* IR *(infrarouge)*

IRAS *abbr (infrared astronomical satellite)* ASTRON

IRAS *(satellite astronomique infrarouge)*

IRP *abbr (internal reference point)* TELECOM point de référence interne *m*

IRPTC *abbr (International Register of Potentially Toxic Chemicals)* POLLUTION RISCPT *(Registre international des substances potentiellement toxiques)*

IRS *abbr* POLLUTION *(international referral system)* système international de référence *m*, TELECOM *(information reference system)* SRI *(système de référence intermédiare)*, TELECOM *(information receiver station)* station de réception d'informations *f*

IS *abbr* COMP *(information system)* système informatique *m*, COMP *(information separator)* séparateur *m*, TELECOM *(intermediate system)* système intermédiaire *m*

ISC *abbr (international switching center, international switching centre)* TELECOM centre de commutation international *m*

ISCP *abbr (international signalling control part, international signaling control part)* TELECOM sous-système de contrôle de signalisation *m*

ISCPAE *abbr (ISCP application entity)* TELECOM entité d'application ISCP *f*

ISD *abbr (International Subscriber Dialling)* TELECOM Automatique International *m*

ISDN *abbr (integrated services digital network)* TELECOM RNIS *(réseau numérique à intégration des services)*

ISE *abbr (ion selective electrode)* LAB EQUIP electrochemistry électrode sélective *f*

ISO *abbr (International Standards Organization)* MECH ENG, TELECOM ISO *(Organisation internationale de normalisation)*

ISR *abbr (information storage and retrieval)* COMP, DP stockage-restitution des données *m*

IT *abbr* COMP *(information technology)* informatique *f*, TELECOM *(intermediate trunk)* canal interurbain intermédiaire *m*, TELECOM *(information technology)* informatique *f*, télématique *f*, TELECOM *(information type)* type d'information *m*

ITD *abbr (input transaction accepted for delivery)* TELECOM acceptation pour remise *f*

ITR *abbr (input transaction rejected)* TELECOM rejet de transaction d'entrée *m*

ITT *abbr (integrated transit time)* PETR TECH *seismic survey* intégration du temps de trajet *f*

IUE *abbr (International Ultraviolet Explorer Satellite)* ASTRON Satellite Explorer pour l'étude en ultraviolet *m*

IUS *abbr (Inertial Upper Stage)* SPACE étage supérieur inertiel *m*

IVPO *abbr (inside vapour phase oxidation, inside vapor phase oxidation)* TELECOM dépôt en phase vapeur interne *m*

IWP *abbr (interworking protocol)* TELECOM protocole d'interfonctionnement *m*

J *abbr (joule)* ELEC, FOOD TECH, MECH, METR, PHYS, THERMOD J *(joule)*

JATO *abbr (jet assisted takeoff)* TRANSP décollage assisté *m*

JCL *abbr (job control language)* COMP langage de contrôle des travaux *m*

JDF *abbr (junction distribution frame)* TELECOM répartiteur de jonction *m*

JET *abbr (Joint European Torus)* NUCLEAR, RAD PHYS

JET *(tore européen conjoint)*; **~ Tokamac** *abbr* NUCLEAR, RAD PHYS JET Tokamac *m*

JIT *abbr (just-in-time)* TEXTILES juste à temps *m*

k *abbr (kilo-)* METR k *(kilo-)*

K *abbr (kelvin)* METR, PHYS, THERMOD K *(kelvin)*

kb *abbr (kilobyte)* COMP, DP ko *(kilo-octet)*

Kcal *abbr (kilocalorie)* FOOD TECH Kcal *(kilocalorie)*

kCi *abbr (kilocurie)* CHEM kCi *(kilocurie)*

keV *abbr (kilo-electronvolt)* CHEM keV *(kilo-électronvolt)*

kg *abbr (kilogramme)* METR kg *(kilogramme)*

kHz *abbr (kilohertz)* ELEC kilohertz *m*

km *abbr (kilometre)* METR km *(kilomètre)*

kn *abbr (kilonem)* CHEM kn *(kilonème)*

KRL *abbr (knowledge representation language)* COMP langage de représentation des connaissances *m*

KSR *abbr (keyboard send-receive)* COMP émetteur-récepteur à clavier *m*

kV *abbr (kilovolt)* ELEC ENG kV *(kilovolt)*

kW *abbr (kilowatt)* ELEC, ELEC ENG kW *(kilowatt)*

KWIC *abbr (keyword in context)* COMP, DP mot-clé en contexte *m*

KWOC *abbr (keyword out of context)* COMP, DP mot-clé hors contexte *m*

l *abbr (litre, liter)* METR l *(litre)*

LADR *abbr (linear-accelerator-driven reactor)* NUCLEAR réacteur d'accélérateur linéaire *m*

LAN *abbr (local area network)* COMP, DP, TELECOM RLE *(réseau local d'entreprise)*

LAP *abbr (line access protocol)* TELECOM protocole d'accès de ligne *m*

LASER *abbr (light amplification by stimulated emission of radiation)* RAD PHYS amplification de la lumière par rayonnement stimulé *f*

LAW *abbr (light anti-armour weapon)* MILIT lance portable antichar *f*

LCA *abbr* TELECOM *(loopback command "audio loop request")* commande de boucle "demande de boucle audio" *f*, TELECOM *(local calling area)* zone locale *f*

LCD *abbr (liquid crystal display)* COMP, DP, ELEC, ELECTRON affichage à cristaux liquides *m*, écran à cristaux liquides *m*, MATH *(least common denominator, lowest common denominator)* PPCMD *(plus petit commun multiple des dénominateurs)*, PHYS *(liquid crystal display)* affichage à cristaux liquides *m*, écran à cristaux liquides *m*, TELECOM *(loopback command "digital loop request")* commande de boucle "demande de boucle numérique" *f*, TV *(liquid crystal display)* affichage à cristaux liquides *m*, écran à cristaux liquides *m*

LCM *abbr (least common multiple, lowest common multiple)* COMP, MATH PPCM *(plus petit commun multiple)*

LCO *abbr (loopback command off)* TELECOM commande d'ouverture de boucle *f*

LCV *abbr (loopback command "video loop request")* TELECOM commande de boucle "demande de boucle vidéo" *f*

LD *abbr (lethal dose)* PHYS, POLLUTION DL *(dose létale)*

LD50 *abbr (median lethal dose)* NUCLEAR, POLLUTION, RAD PHYS, SAFETY DL50 *(dose létale médiane)*

LDF *abbr (light distillate feedstock)* PETR TECH distillat de tête *m*

LE *abbr (local exchange)* TELECOM commutateur

local *m*

LEAR *abbr (low-energy antiproton ring)* PART PHYS LEAR *(anneau d'antiprotons de basse énergie)*

LED *abbr (light-emitting diode)* COMP, DP, ELEC, ELECTRON, OPT, PHYS, RAD PHYS, TELECOM, TV DEL *(diode électroluminescente)*

LEP *abbr (large electron-positron collider)* PARTp h y s LEP *(grand collisionneur électron-positron)*

LF *abbr* COMP *(line feed),* DP *(line feed)* changement de ligne *m,* saute de ligne *m,* ELEC *(low-frequency) wave,* ELEC ENG *(low-frequency),* ELECTRON *(low-frequency)* BF *(basse fréquence),* PRINT *(line feed)* changement de ligne *m,* saut de ligne *m,* RAD PHYS *(low-frequency)* TELECOM *(low-frequency)* LF *(basse fréquence),* TELECOM *(line feed) telegraphy* changement de ligne *m,* saut de ligne *m,* TELECOM *(line finder)* chercheur de ligne *m*

LFA *abbr (loss of frame alignment)* TELECOM PVT *(perte de verrouillage de trame)*

LFC *abbr (local function capabilities)* TELECOM capacité fonctionnelle locale *f*

LHC *abbr (large hadron collider)* PART PHYS *being developed at CERN* grand collisionneur de hadrons *m*

LHCP *abbr (left-hand circular polarization)* SPACE polarisation circulaire gauche *f*

LI *abbr (length indicator)* TELECOM indicateur de longueur *m*

LIFO *abbr (last-in first-out)* COMP, DP, PROD ENG dernier entré premier sorti *m*

LISP *abbr (list processing language)* COMP langage de traitement de listes *m*

LLC *abbr* TELECOM *(line load control)* CCL *(contrôle de charge de ligne),* TELECOM *(logical link control)* commande de liaison logique *f*

LLV *abbr (lunar logistics vehicle)* SPACE véhicule logistique lunaire *m*

lm *abbr (lumen)* METR lm *(lumen)*

LME *abbr* TELECOM *(layer management entity)* entité de gestion de couche *f,* TELECOM *(line module equipment)* matériel de modules de lignes *m*

LMS *abbr (land mobile station)* TELECOM station mobile terrestre *f*

LNA *abbr* ELECTRON *(low-noise amplifier),* SPACE *(low-noise amplifier) communications,* TELECOM *(low-noise amplifier)* amplificateur à faible bruit *m,* TELECOM *(launch numerical aperture)* ouverture numérique d'injection *f*

LNG *abbr* GAS TECH *(liquefied natural gas),* PETR TECH *(liquefied natural gas),* THERMOD *(liquid natural gas)* GNL *(gaz naturel liquéfié)*

LO *abbr (local oscillator)* TELECOM oscillateur local *m*

LOF *abbr (loss of frame)* TELECOM perte de trame *f*

L-OM *abbr (laser-optic memory)* OPT mémoire à lecture par laser *f*

LOM *abbr (loss of multiframe)* TELECOM perte de multitrame *f*

LOP *abbr (loss of pointer)* TELECOM perte de pointeur *f*

LOS *abbr (loss of signal)* TELECOM perte de signal *f*

LOT *abbr (leak-off test)* PETR TECH essai de pression *m,* test d'injectivité *m*

LPA *abbr (lower-order path adaptation)* TELECOM adaptation de conduit d'ordre inférieur *f*

LPC *abbr* TELECOM *(linear predicting coding)* codage prédictif linéaire *m,* TELECOM *(lower-order path connection)* connexion de conduit d'ordre inférieur *f*

LPDT *abbr (low-power distress transmitter)* TELECOM

émetteur de détresse de faible puissance *m*

LPG *abbr* GAS TECH *(liquefied petroleum gas),* HEAT ENG *(liquefied petroleum gas),* PETR TECH *(liquefied petroleum gas),* THERMOD *(liquid petroleum gas),* TRANSP *(liquefied petroleum gas)* GPL *(gaz de pétrole liquéfié)*

LPM *abbr (lines per minute)* COMP, DP LPM *(lignes par minute)*

LPT *abbr (lower-order path termination)* TELECOM terminaison de conduit d'ordre inférieur *f*

LQ *abbr (letter quality)* COMP, PRINT qualité courrier *f*

LRC *abbr (longitudinal redundancy check)* COMP contrôle par redondance longitudinale *m*

LRE *abbr (low rate encoding)* TELECOM codage à débit réduit *m,* codage à faible débit *m*

LRT *abbr (light rail transport)* RAIL *vehicles* métro léger *m*

LRU *abbr (line replaceable unit)* ELEC ENG unité remplaçable en ligne *f*

LSB *abbr* COMP *(least significant bit)* bit de plus faible poids *m,* bit de poids faible *m,* ELECTRON *(lower sideband)* bande latérale inférieure *f,* PROD ENG *(least significant bit)* bit de poids le plus faible *m,* TELECOM *(lower sideband)* bande latérale inférieure *f*

LSD *abbr (least significant digit)* COMP chiffre de poids le plus faible *m*

LSI *abbr (large-scale integration)* COMP, DP, ELECTRON, NAUT, PHYS, TELECOM LSI *(intégration à grande échelle)*

LT *abbr (line termination)* PRINT, TELECOM terminaison de ligne *f*

LTE *abbr (line termination equipment)* COMP équipement de terminaison de ligne *m*

LUF *abbr (lowest usable frequency)* SPACE fréquence minimale utilisable *f*

LUT *abbr (local user terminal)* TELECOM station terminale d'usager local *f*

LV *abbr* ELEC *(low-voltage),* ELEC ENG *(low-voltage)* basse tension *f,* OPT *(laser vision)* laservision *f,* TELECOM *(low-voltage)* basse tension *f*

LWHR *abbr (light water hybrid reactor)* NUCLEAR réacteur hybride à eau légère *m*

lx *abbr (lux)* METR lx *(lux)*

m *abbr (milli-)* METR m *(milli-)*

M *abbr (mega-)* METR M *(méga-)*

mA *abbr (milliampere)* ELEC, ELEC ENG mA *(milliampère)*

MA *abbr (medium adaptor)* TELECOM adaptateur de support *m*

MAC *abbr* AERONAUT *(mean aerodynamic chord)* CAM *(corde aérodynamique moyenne),* POLLUTION *(maximum allowable concentration)* concentration maximale admissible *f,* TELECOM *(medium access control)* commande d'accès au support *f,* contrôle d'accès au média *m*

MAF *abbr (management applications function)* TELECOM fonction d'application de gestion *f*

MAN *abbr (metropolitan area network)* TELECOM réseau de zone urbaine *m*

MAP *abbr (modified atmosphere packaging)* PRINT emballage en atmosphère modifiée *m*

Mb *abbr (megabyte)* COMP, DP Mo *(méga-octet)*

MC *abbr (master change)* TRANSP spécification de changement notifié *f*

MCA *abbr (multipoint command assign token)* TELECOM

commande multipoint d'assignation de jeton *f*

MCC *abbr (multipoint command conference)* TELECOM commande multipoint de conférence *f*

MCD *abbr (maintenance cell description)* TELECOM description de cellule de maintenance *f*

MCF *abbr (message communication function)* TELECOM fonction de communication de messages *f*

MCFD *abbr (millions of cubic feet per day)* PETR TECH *unit of volume in prospecting, production* millions de pieds cubes par jour *m pl*

MCN *abbr (multipoint command negating MCS)* TELECOM commande multipoint de neutralisation de MCS *f*

MCR *abbr* PROD ENG *(master control reset)* contrôle relais maître *m*, TELECOM *(multipoint command release token)* commande multipoint de libération de jeton *f*, TV *(master control room)* régie centrale *f*

MCS *abbr (multipoint command symmetrical data transmission)* TELECOM commande multipoint de transmission symétrique des données *f*

MCT *abbr (multipoint command token claim)* TELECOM commande multipoint de demande de jeton *f*

MCV *abbr (multipoint command visualization forcing)* TELECOM commande multipoint d'imposition de visualisation *f*

MD *abbr* TELECOM *(mediation device)* dispositif de médiation *m*, équipement de médiation *m*, TELECOM *(management domain)* domaine de gestion *m*

MDF *abbr (main distribution frame)* TELECOM répartiteur d'entrée *m*

MDI *abbr (diphenylmethane diisocyanate)* P&R *curing agent* diisocyanate de diphénylméthane *m*

MDR *abbr (memory data register)* COMP, DP registre mémoire de données *m*

MEFP *abbr (minimum error-free pad)* TELECOM période minimale sans erreur *f*

MESFET *abbr (metal semiconductor field effect transistor)* ELECTRON transistor MESFET *m*

MF *abbr* ELEC *(modulation frequency) alternating current* fréquence de modulation *f*, ELEC ENG *(medium frequency)* moyenne fréquence *f*, ELECTRON *(modulation frequency)* fréquence de modulation *f*, TELECOM *(mediation function)* fonction de médiation *f*, TELECOM *(multiple frequency)* fréquence multiple *f*

MFA *abbr (multiframe alignment)* TELECOM verrouillage de multitrame *m*

mfd *abbr (manufactured)* PROP MAT manufacturé

mg *abbr (milligram, milligramme)* METR mg *(milligramme)*

MGD *abbr (magnetogasdynamics)* NUCLEAR magnétodynamique des gaz *f*

MH *abbr (message handling)* TELECOM messagerie *f*

MHD *abbr (magnetohydrodynamic)* ELEC ENG, GEOPHYS, SPACE MHD *(magnétohydrodynamique)*

MHS *abbr (message handling system)* TELECOM messagerie *f*, système de messagerie *m*

MIB *abbr (management information base)* TELECOM base d'informations de gestion *f*, base de données de gestion *f*

MIC *abbr* ELECTRON *(microwave integrated circuit)* circuit hybride hyperfréquence *m*, PHYS *(microwave integrated circuit)* circuit intégré micro-onde *m*, TELECOM *(marked idle channel)* repérage des voies au repos *m*

MICR *abbr (magnetic ink character recognition)* COMP, DP RMC *(reconnaissance magnétiques de caractères)*

MIL *abbr (multipoint indication loop)* TELECOM indication multipoint de boucle *f*

MIMD *abbr (multiple-instruction multiple-data)* COMP, DP MIMD *(multiflux d'instruction-multiflux de données)*

MIPS *abbr (millions of instructions per second)* COMP, DP, PRINT MIPS *(millions d'instructions par seconde)*

MIS *abbr* COMP *(management information system)*, DP *(management information system)* SIG *(système intégré de gestion)*, TELECOM *(multipoint indication secondary status)* indication multipoint d'état secondaire *f*

MISD *abbr (multiple-instruction single-data)* COMP, DP MISD *(multiflux d'instruction-monoflux de donnés)*

MIV *abbr (multipoint indication visualization)* TELECOM indication multipoint de visualisation *f*

MIZ *abbr (multipoint indication zero communication)* TELECOM indication multipoint de non-communication *f*

MLD *abbr (mean lethal dose)* NUCLEAIRE, POLLUTION, RAD PHYS, SAFETY DLM *(dose létale moyenne)*

MLM *abbr (multilongitudinal modes)* TELECOM MLM *(modes longitudinaux multiples)*

MLS *abbr (microwave landing system)* AERONAUT système d'atterrissage hyperfréquences *m*

mm *abbr (millimeter, millimetre)* METR mm *(millimètre)*

mmf *abbr (magnetomotive force)* ELEC, PHYS fmm *(force magnétomotrice)*

MMI *abbr (man-machine interface)* COMP, DP, SPACE *spacecraft* interface homme-machine *f*

MMIC *abbr (monolithic microwave integrated circuit)* PHYS circuit intégré monolithique micro-ondes *m*

MO *abbr (managed object)* TELECOM objet géré *m*

MOC *abbr (managed object class)* TELECOM classe d'objet géré *f*

mol *abbr (mole)* CHEM, METR, PHYS mol *(môle)*

MOL *abbr (manned orbiting laboratory)* SPACE laboratoire orbital habité *m*

MOS *abbr* COMP *(metal-oxide semiconductor)* MOS *(semi-conducteur à oxyde métallique)*, TELECOM *(mean opinion score)* note moyenne d'opinion *f*

MOTIS *abbr (message-oriented text interchange system)* TELECOM système d'échange de textes en mode message *m*

mpg *abbr (miles per gallon)* TRANSP milles par gallon *m pl*

MRTIE *abbr (maximum relative time interval error)* TELECOM erreur relative maximum d'intervalle de temps *f*

ms *abbr (millisecond)* COMP, DP ms *(milliseconde)*

MS *abbr* ELECTRON *(main station)* PP *(poste principal)*, PRINT *(mobile station)*, SPACE *(mobile station)* station mobile *f*, TELECOM *(message store)* mémoire de messages *f*, TELECOM *(multiplex section)* section de multiplexage *f*, TELECOM *(mobile station)* station mobile *f*

MSB *abbr (most significant bit)* COMP, PROD ENG, TELECOM bit de poids fort *m*

MSC *abbr* TELECOM *(maritime switching centre, maritime switching center)* centre de commutation maritime *m*, TELECOM *(mobile switching centre, mobile switching center)* centre de commutation mobile *m*

MSD *abbr (most significant digit)* COMP, DP chiffre de poids fort *m*, chiffre le plus significatif *m*, PROD ENG chiffre de poids fort *m*

MSE *abbr (mean square error)* COMP, DP, MATH erreur quadratique moyenne *f*

MSG *abbr (monosodium glutamate)* FOOD TECH glutamate de sodium *m*, glutamate monosodique *m*

MSI *abbr (medium-scale integration)* COMP, DP, ELECTRON, TELECOM intégration à moyenne échelle *f*

MSK *abbr (minimum-shift keying)* ELECTRON modulation à déplacement minimal *f*, TELECOM manipulation par déplacement minimal *f*

MSN *abbr (multiple-subscriber number)* TELECOM numéro d'abonné multiple *m*

MSP *abbr* TELECOM *(maintenance service provider)* prestataire de service de maintenance *m*, TELECOM *(multiplex section protection)* protection de section de multiplexage *f*

MST *abbr (multiplex section termination)* TELECOM terminaison de section de multiplexage *f*

MSU *abbr (message signal unit)* TELECOM trame sémaphore de message *f*

MT *abbr (message transfer)* TELECOM transfert de messages *m*

MTA *abbr (message transfer agent)* TELECOM agent de transfert de messages *m*

MTBF *abbr (mean time between failures)* COMP, DP, MÈCH, QUALITY, SPACE MTBF *(moyenne de temps de bon fonctionnement)*

MTBR *abbr (mean time between removals)* SPACE temps moyen entre réparations *m*

MTIE *abbr (maximum time interval error)* TELECOM erreur maximum d'intervalle de temps *f*

MTL *abbr (merged transistor logic)* ELECTRON logique à transistors fusionnés *f*

MTPI *abbr (multiplexer timing physical interface)* TELECOM interface physique de rythme de multiplexeur *f*

MTR *abbr (materials testing reactor)* NUCLEAR réacteur d'essais de matériaux *m*

MTS *abbr* TELECOM *(mobile telephone service)* SRM *(service radiotéléphonique mobile)*, TELECOM *(multiplexer timing source)* source de rythme de multiplexeur *f*, TELECOM *(message transfer system)* système de transfert de messages *m*

MTTF *abbr (mean time to failure)* QUALITY durée moyenne avant défaillance *f*

MTTR *abbr (mean time to repair)* COMP, DP, ELEC ENG temps moyen de réparation *m*, MECH, SPACE durée moyenne de réparation *f*

MUF *abbr (maximum usable frequency)* ELEC ENG fréquence maximale utilisable *f*

mV *abbr (millivolt)* ELEC, ELEC ENG mV *(millivolt)*

mW *abbr (milliwatt)* ELEC mW *(milliwatt)*

MW *abbr* ELEC *(megawatt)* MW *(mégawatt)*, ELEC *(medium wave)*, WAVE PHYS *(medium wave)* onde moyenne *f*

MWD *abbr (measurements while drilling)* PETR TECH mesures en cours de forage *f pl*

Mx *abbr (maxwell)* ELEC ENG Mx *(maxwell)*

n *abbr (nano-)* METR n *(nano-)*

N *abbr (newton)* ELEC, METR, PHYS N *(newton)*

NA *abbr (numerical aperture)* OPT ouverture numérique *f*

NAD *abbr (noise amplitude distribution)* TELECOM distribution d'amplitude de bruit *f*

NAK *abbr (negative acknowledgement)* COMP, DP accusé de réception négatif *m*

NASA *abbr (National Aeronautics and Space Administration)* SPACE NASA *(Agence nationale de l'aéronautique et de l'espace)*

NATM *abbr (New Austrian Tunnelling Method)* CONST nouvelle méthode autrichienne de percement des tunnels *f*

NBFM *abbr (narrow band frequency modulation)* ELECTRON, TELECOM modulation de fréquence à bande étroite *f*

NBPSK *abbr (narrow band phase shift keying)* TELECOM manipulation par déplacement de phase à bande étroite *f*

NBVM *abbr (narrow band voice modulation)* TELECOM modulation vocale à bande étroite *f*

NC *abbr (numerical control)* CONTROL, MECH ENG, PROD ENG CN *(commande numérique)*

NCC *abbr (network control centre, network control center)* TELECOM centre de gestion *m*, centre de gestion de réseau *m*

NCR *abbr (network control room)* TV régie de continuité *f*, régie finale *f*

NCS *abbr (network coordination station)* SPACE station de coordination du réseau *f*

NDC *abbr (national destination code)* TELECOM code national de destination *m*, indicatif national de destination *m*

NDF *abbr (new data flag)* TELECOM fanion de nouvelles données *m*, indicateur de nouvelles données *m*

NDM *abbr (normal disconnected mode)* TELECOM mode normal déconnecté *m*

NDN *abbr (nondelivery notification)* TELECOM notification de non-remise *f*

NDR *abbr (normalized drilling rate)* PETR TECH vitesse d'avancement normalisée *f*

NDT *abbr (nondestructive testing)* SPACE essai non destructif *m*

NE *abbr (network element)* TELECOM élément de réseau *m*

NEF *abbr (network element function)* TELECOM fonction d'élément de réseau *f*

NEP *abbr (noise equivalent power)* OPT, TELECOM PEB *(puissance équivalente de bruit)*

NGL *abbr (natural gas liquid)* GAS TECH, PETR TECH LGN *(liquide de gaz naturel)*

NID *abbr (national identification digit)* TELECOM chiffre d'identification de nationalité *m*

NLQ *abbr (near letter quality)* COMP, DP qualité pseudo-courrier *f*

NLR *abbr (network layer relay)* TELECOM relais de couche réseau *m*

NM-ASE *abbr (network management application service element)* TELECOM élément de service d'application pour la gestion de réseau *m*

NMC *abbr (network management center, network management centre)* TELECOM centre de gestion de réseau *m*

NMR *abbr (nuclear magnetic resonance)* CHEM, PETR TECH, PHYS, RAD PHYS RMN *(résonance magnétique nucléaire)*

NN *abbr* TELECOM *(negative notification)* notification négative *f*, TELECOM *(national number)* numéro national *m*

NNE *abbr (non-SDH network element)* TELECOM élément de réseau non SDH *m*

NNI *abbr (network node interface)* TELECOM interface de noeuds de réseau *f*

NOMC *abbr (network operators maintenance channel)* TELECOM canal de maintenance des exploitants de réseau *m*

NOS *abbr (network operating system)* COMP système d'exploitation de réseau *m*

NP *abbr (network performance)* TELECOM performance du réseau *f*

NPDU *abbr (network protocol data unit)* TELECOM unité de données du protocole de réseau *f*

NPI *abbr* TELECOM *(numbering plan identification)* identification du plan de numérotage *f*, TELECOM *(null pointer indication)* indication de pointeur zéro *f*

NPT *abbr (National Pipe Taper)* MECH ENG filetage conique de tuyauterie à norme américaine *m*

NRM *abbr (normal response mode)* TELECOM mode normal de réponse *m*

NRZ *abbr (nonreturn to zero)* TELECOM non retour à zéro

NRZI *abbr (nonreturn to zero inverted)* TELECOM non retour à zéro inversé

Ns *abbr (nimbostratus)* METEO Ns *(nimbo-stratus)*

NS *abbr (network service)* TELECOM service de réseau *m*

NSAP *abbr (network service access point)* TELECOM point d'accès au service de réseau *m*

NSN *abbr (national significant number)* TELECOM numéro national significatif *m*

NT *abbr (network termination)* TELECOM terminaison de réseau *f*

NT1-LB *abbr (B-ISDN network termination 1)* TELECOM terminaison de réseau 1 pour le RNIS-LB *f*

NT2-LB *abbr (B-ISDN network termination 2)* TELECOM terminaison de réseau 2 pour le RNIS-LB *f*

NTE *abbr (network terminal equipment)* TELECOM équipement terminal de réseau *m*

NT-LB *abbr (B-ISDN network termination)* TELECOM terminaison de réseau pour le RNIS-LB *f*

NU *abbr (national use)* TELECOM usage national *m*

NUC *abbr (not under command)* NAUT shiphandling pas maître de sa commande, pas maître de sa manoeuvre

NUL *abbr (null character)* COMP, DP caractère nul *m*, nul *m*

NVT *abbr (network virtual terminal)* COMP, DP terminal virtuel de réseau *m*

OA *abbr* COMP *(office automation)* bureautique *f*, TELECOM *(overflow accept)* acceptation de débordement *f*

OAM *abbr (operations and maintenance)* TELECOM exploitation et maintenance *f*

OAMC *abbr (operation administration and maintenance centre, operation administration and maintance center)* TELECOM centre de gestion d'exploitation et de maintenance *m*

OAMP *abbr (operation, administration, maintenance and provisioning)* TELECOM exploitation, administration, maintenance et mise en service *f*

OB *abbr (outside broadcast)* TV émission transmise de l'extérieur *f*

OBO *abbr (ore-bulk-oil)* PETR TECH minerai-vrac-pétrole *m*

OCB *abbr (outgoing calls barred)* TELECOM interdiction des appels au départ *f*

OCR *abbr* COMP *(optical character recognition)* ROC *(reconnaissance optique des caractères)*, COMP *(optical character reader)* lecteur optique de caractères *m*, DP *(optical character recognition)* ROC *(reconnaissance optique des caractères)*, DP *(optical character reader)* lecteur optique de caractères *m*, PRINT *(optical character recognition)* ROC *(reconnaissance optique des caractères)*, PRINT *(optical character reader)* lecteur optique de caractères *m*

OD *abbr* HYDROL *(oxygen deficit)* déficit d'oxygène *m*, MECH *(outside diameter)*, MECH ENG *(outside diameter)* diamètre extérieur *m*

ODAS *abbr (Ocean Data Acquisition System, Oceanic Data Acquisition* System*)* OCEANOG SADO *(Système d'acquisition de données océaniques)*

ODP *abbr (open distribution processing)* TELECOM traitement à distribution ouverte *m*

O-E *abbr (optical-electrical)* TELECOM optique-électrique

OFF *abbr (optical flexibility frame)* TELECOM répartiteur optique *m*

OFS *abbr (out-of-frame second)* TELECOM seconde de perte du verrouillage de trame *f*

OHA *abbr (overhead access)* TELECOM accès au surdébit *m*, accès aux octets de surdébit *m*

OHC *abbr (overhead camshaft)* AUTO, MECH, VEHICLES arbre à cames en tête *m*

OLRT *abbr (on-line real-time)* COMP, DP temps réel en ligne

OMR *abbr (optical mark reading)* COMP, DP lecture optique de marques *f*

OMS *abbr (orbital maneuvring system, orbital manoeuvring system)* SPACE système de manoeuvre en orbite *m*

ON *abbr (octane number)* PETR TECH indice d'octane *m*

ONP *abbr (open network provision)* TELECOM provision de réseau ouvert *f*

ONR *abbr (octane number rating)* AUTO indice d'octane *m*

OO *abbr (oil-ore carrier)* NAUT, TRANSP minéralier-pétrolier *m*

OOD *abbr (object-oriented design)* COMP, DP COO *(conception orientée objet)*

OPC *abbr (originating point code)* TELECOM code du point d'origine *m*

OPEC *abbr (Organization of Petroleum Exporting Countries)* PETR TECH OPEP *(Organisation des pays exportateurs de pétrole)*

OR *abbr (operational research, operations research)* COMP, DP RO *(recherche opérationnelle)*

ORL *abbr (optical return loss)* TELECOM affaiblissement d'adaptation optique *m*

OS *abbr (operating system)* COMP, TELECOM système d'exploitation *m*

OSA *abbr (open systems architecture)* TELECOM architecture de systèmes ouverts *f*

OSC *abbr* MAR POLL *(on-scene commander)* commandant des opérations sur le terrain *m*, TELECOM *(on-scene communications)* communications sur place *f pl*

OSD *abbr (optical scanning device)* TV analyseur optique *m*

OSF *abbr (operating system function)* TELECOM fonction de système d'exploitation *f*

OSI *abbr (open systems interconnection)* COMP, DP, TELECOM ISO *(interconnexion de systèmes ouverts)*

OSN *abbr (optical switching network)* TELECOM réseau de connexion optique *m*

OSR *abbr (optical solar reflector)* SPACE spacecraft réflecteur solaire optique *m*

OTDR *abbr (optical time domain reflectometry)* OPT

réflectométrie optique dans le domaine temporel *f*, technique de rétrodiffusion *f*, TELECOM réflectométrie optique dans le domaine temporel *f*

OTSG *abbr (once-through steam generator)* NUCLEAR générateur de vapeur à passage unique *m*

OTTO *abbr (once-through-then-out)* NUCLEAR cycle à sortir après passage unique *m*

OTV *abbr (orbital transfer vehicle)* SPACE véhicule de transfert interorbital *m*, véhicule de transfert orbital *m*

p *abbr* METR *(peta-)* p *(peta-)*, METR *(pico-)* p *(pico-)*

Pa *abbr (pascal)* METR, PETR TECH, PHYS Pa *(pascal)*

PA *abbr (power amplifier)* TELECOM amplificateur de puissance *m*

PABX *abbr (private automatic branch exchange)* TELECOM autocommutateur privé *m*

PAD *abbr (packet assembler-disassembler)* COMP, DP, TELECOM assembleur-désassembleur de paquets *m*

PAL *abbr* COMP *(programmable array logic)*, DP *(programmable array logic)* circuit logique programmable *m*, TV *(phase alternation line)* ligne d'alternance de phase *f*, système PAL *m*

PAM *abbr* COMP, DP, ELECTRON, SPACE, TELECOM *(pulse amplitude modulation)* MIA *(modulation d'impulsions en amplitude)*, TELECOM *(pass-along message)* message à faire passer *m*

PAN *abbr (peroxoacetylnitrate)* POLLUTION PAN *(peroxoacétylnitrate)*

PAX *abbr (private automatic exchange)* TELECOM central automatique privé *m*

PBX *abbr (private branch exchange)* TELECOM autocommutateur privé *m*, commutateur téléphonique privé *m*

PBXIS-LB *abbr* TELECOM autocommutateur privé pour le RNIS-LB *m*

PC *abbr* COMP *(printed circuit)* CI *(circuit imprimé)*, COMP *(personal computer)* OP *(ordinateur personnel)*, DP *(printed circuit)* CI *(circuit imprimé)*, DP *(personal computer)* OP *(ordinateur personnel)*, ELECTRON *(printed circuit)*, PHYS *(printed circuit)*, TELECOM *(printed circuit)*, TV *(printed circuit)* CI *(circuit imprimé)*

PCB *abbr (printed circuit board)* COMP, DP, ELEC, ELECTRON, TELECOM carte de circuit imprimé *f*

PCI *abbr (pattern correspondence index)* TELECOM indice de correspondence spectrale *f*

PCM *abbr (pulse code modulation)* COMP, DP, ELECTRON, PHYS, RAD PHYS, SPACE, TV MIC *(modulation par impulsion codée)*

PCS *abbr (plastic-clad silica)* OPT, TELECOM silice gratinée de plastique *f*

PCT *abbr (peak cladding temperature)* NUCLEAR température maximale de la gaine *f*

PCU *abbr (passenger car unit)* TRANSP UVP *(unité de voiture particulière)*

PCV *abbr (positive crankcase ventilation)* AUTO recyclage des gaz de carter *m*

PCVD *abbr (plasma-activated chemical vapor deposition, plasma-activated chemical vapour deposition)* ELECTRON procédé de dépôt chimique en phase vapeur activé au plasma *m*

pd *abbr (potential difference)* PHYS ddp *(différence de potentiel)*

PD *abbr* TELECOM *(protocol discriminator)* DP *(discriminateur de protocole)*, TELECOM *(physical delivery)* remise physique *f*

PDAU *abbr (physical delivery access unit)* TELECOM unité d'accès au service de remise physique *f*

PDF *abbr (probability density function)* MATH fonction de densité de probabilité *f*

PDH *abbr (plesiochronous digital hierarchy)* TELECOM hiérarchie numérique plésiochrone *f*

PDM *abbr (pulse duration modulation)* ELECTRON, SPACE MID *(modulation par impulsions de durée)*

PDN *abbr (public data network)* COMP, DP réseau public de données *m*, réseau public de transmission de données *m*

PDR *abbr* ELEC *(power directional relay)* relais directionnel de puissance *m*, SPACE *(preliminary design review)* revue de définition préliminaire *f*

PDS *abbr (physical delivery system)* TELECOM système de remise physique *m*

PDU *abbr (protocol data unit)* TELECOM unité de données du protocole *f*

PE *abbr* COMP *(phase encoding)*, DP *(phase encoding)* enregistrement en modulation de phase *m*, TELECOM *(protocol emulator)* émulateur de protocol *m*

PEC *abbr (photoelectric cell)* PHYS, RAD PHYS, SPACE, TV cellule photoélectrique *f*

PERT *abbr (program evaluation and review technique)* CONTROL, PROD ENG méthode du planning PERT *f*

PFM *abbr (pulse frequency modulation)* COMP, DP, ELECTRON modulation de fréquence d'impulsion *f*

PFR *abbr (power fail restart)* COMP, DP redémarrage automatique *m*

pH *abbr (potential of hydrogen)* CHEM pH *(potentiel hydrogène)*

PhC *abbr (physical connection)* TELECOM connexion physique *f*

PHF *abbr (peak hour factor)* TRANSP traffic control facteur de pointe *m*

PhS *abbr (physical service)* TELECOM service physique *m*

PI *abbr* TELECOM *(presentation indicator)* indicateur de présentation *m*, TELECOM *(physical interface)* interface physique *f*

PICS *abbr (protocol implementation conformance statement)* TELECOM déclaration de conformité de mise en oeuvre du protocole *f*

PIT *abbr (programable interval timer, programmable interval timer)* ELECTRON temporisateur programmable *m*

PJC *abbr (pointer justification count)* TELECOM compte de justification de pointeur *m*

PJE *abbr (pointer justification event)* TELECOM événement de justification de pointeur *m*

PL *abbr (primary link)* TELECOM liaison primaire *f*

PLA *abbr* COMP *(programable logic array, programmable logic array)* réseau logique programmable *m*, COMP *(programmed logic array)* réseau à logique programmée *m*, DP *(programable logic array, programmable logic array)* réseau logique programmable *m*, DP *(programmed logic array)* réseau à logique programmée *m*

PLL *abbr (phase-locked loop)* ELECTRON boucle à blocage de phase *f*, boucle à phase asservie *f*, SPACE, TELECOM, TV boucle à verrouillage de phase *f*

PLO *abbr (phase-locked oscillator)* ELECTRON oscillateur asservi en phase *m*

PL-OAM *abbr (physical layer operations and maintenance)* TELECOM cellule OAM de la couche physique *f*, cellule OAM de la physique *f*

PLS *abbr (physical layer service)* TELECOM service de la couche physique *m*

PM *abbr (phase modulation)* COMP, DP, ELECTRON, PHYS, RECORDING, TELECOM, TV MP *(modulation de phase)*

PMBX *abbr (private manual branch exchange)* TELECOM commutateur privé manuel *m*

PN *abbr (positive notification)* TELECOM notification positive *f*

PNP *abbr (private numbering plan)* TELECOM PNP *(plan de numérotage privé)*

PNX *abbr (private network exchange)* TELECOM commutateur de réseau privé *m*

POH *abbr (path overhead)* TELECOM préfixe de conduit *m*, résidu de trajet *m*

POM *abbr (polyoxymethylene)* P&R polyoxyméthylène *m*

PON *abbr (passive optical network)* TELECOM réseau optique passif *m*

POS *abbr (point of sale)* COMP, DP point de vente *m*

pp *abbr (pages)* PRINT pages *f pl*

PP *abbr (peripheral processor)* TELECOM calculateur périphérique *m*

PPDU *abbr (presentation protocol data unit)* TELECOM unité de données du protocole de présentation *f*

PPM *abbr* CHEM *(parts-per-million)* parties par million *f pl*, COMP *(pages per minute)*, DP *(pages per minute)* pages par minute *f pl*, ELECTRON *(pulse position modulation)* modulation de position d'impulsion *f*, SPACE *(pulse position modulation)* modulation d'impulsion en position *f*

pps *abbr (pulses per second)* TELECOM impulsions par seconde *f pl*

PRA *abbr (primary rate access)* TELECOM accès au débit primaire *m*

PRBS *abbr (pseudorandom binary sequence)* TELECOM séquence binaire pseudoaléatoire *f*

PRF *abbr (pulse repetition frequency)* COMP, DP fréquence de répétition des impulsions *f*, ELECTRON fréquence de récurrence des impulsions *f*, fréquence de répétition des impulsions *f*, TELECOM fréquence de répétition des impulsions *f*

PRM *abbr (protocol reference model)* TELECOM modèle de référence de protocole *m*

PRMD *abbr (private management domain)* TELECOM domaine de gestion privé *m*

PROM *abbr (programable read-only memory, programmable read-only memory)* COMP, DP PROM *(ROM programmable)*

PRT *abbr (personal rapid transport)* TRANSP transport en commun personnalisé *m*

PS *abbr (packet switch)* ELEC, TELECOM commutateur de paquets *m*

PSA *abbr (particle size analyzer)* NUCLEAR granulomètre *m*

PSE *abbr (packet switching exchange)* TELECOM centre de commutation de paquets *m*

psi *abbr (pounds per square inch)* METR, PETR TECH livres par pouce carré *f pl*

PSK *abbr (phase shift keying)* COMP, DP, ELECTRON, SPACE MDP *(modulation par déplacement de phase)*

PSN *abbr* COMP *(packet-switched network)*, DP *(packet-switched network)* réseau de commutation par paquets *m*, TELECOM *(packet switching node)* noeud à commutation de paquets *m*, TELECOM *(packet-switched network)* réseau de commutation par paquets *m*, TELECOM *(public switched network)* réseau public commuté *m*

PSTN *abbr (public switched telephone network)* TELECOM réseau téléphonique public commuté *m*

PSW *abbr (program status word)* COMP, DP mot d'état du programme *m*

PTC *abbr* INSTRUMENT *(parabolic trough conveyor)* miroir cylindro-parabolique avec foyer tubulaire *m*, SPACE *(passive thermal control)* régulation thermique passive *f*

PU *abbr (protocol unit)* TELECOM unité de protocole *f*

PV *abbr (parameter value)* TELECOM valeur de paramètre *f*

PVC *abbr* COMP *(permanent virtual circuit)* circuit virtuel permanent *m*, CONST *(polyvinyl chloride)* PVC *(polyvinylchlorure)*, DP *(permanent virtual circuit)* circuit virtuel permanent *m*, ELEC ENG *(polyvinyl chloride)*, P&R *(polyvinyl chloride)*, PROP MAT *(polyvinyl chloride)* PVC *(polyvinylchlorure)*, TELECOM *(permanent virtual circuit)* circuit virtuel permanent *m*

PVP *abbr (polyvinylpyrrolidone)* DETERGENTS polyvinylpyrrolidone *m*

PW *abbr (private wire)* TELECOM liaison spécialisée *f*

PWM *abbr (pulse width modulation)* SPACE modulation d'impulsions en largeur *f*

QA *abbr (quality assurance)* MECH assurance de la qualité *f*

QAM *abbr (quadrature amplitude modulation)* COMP, DP, ELECTRON, TELECOM *(quadrature amplitude modulation)* MAQ *(modulation d'amplitude en quadrature)*

QC *abbr (quality control)* QUALITY maîtrise de la qualité *f*

QL *abbr (query language)* COMP, DP langage d'interrogation *m*

QOS *abbr (quality of service)* TELECOM qualité de service *f*

QPSK *abbr (quadriphase shift keying, quaternary phase-shift keying)* ELECTRON, TELECOM MDPQ *(modulation par déplacement de phase quadrivalente)*

QSG *abbr (quasi-stellar galaxy)* SPACE galaxie quasi-stellaire *f*

QSO *abbr (quasi-stellar object)* ASTRON, SPACE objet quasi-stellaire *m*

QSS *abbr (quasi-stellar radio source)* SPACE quasar *m*

QUIP *abbr (quad-in-line package)* ELECTRON boîtier à quatre rangées de broches *m*

R *abbr (roentgen)* RAD PHYS roentgen *m*

RAI *abbr (remote alarm indication)* TELECOM indication d'alarme distante *f*

RAM *abbr (random access memory)* COMP, DP, ELECTRON MEV *(mémoire vive)*

RAU *abbr (remote acquisition unit)* CONTROL unité d'acquisition décentralisée *f*

RBT *abbr (remote batch terminal)* COMP, DP terminal de télétraitement *m*

RC *abbr* ELEC ENG *(resistance-capacitance)*, ELECTRON *(resistance-capacitance)* RC *(résistance-capacité)*, SPACE *(rate of climb)* vitesse ascensionnelle *f*

RCU *abbr (remote concentration unit)* TELECOM concentrateur satellite numérique *m*

RDB *abbr (relational database)* COMP, DP, TELECOM

BDR *(base de données relationnelles)*

RDF *abbr (radio direction finder)* AERONAUT radiogoniomètre *m*, NAUT *navigation* radiogonio *m*, radiogoniomètre *m*

RDR *abbr (reflection density reference)* PRINT densité de référence d'un document opaque *f*

Re *abbr (Reynolds number)* FLUID PHYS Re *(nombre de Reynolds)*

REL *abbr (release message)* TELECOM LIB *(message de libération)*

RES *abbr (reserved field)* TELECOM champ réservé *m*

RF *abbr (radio frequency)* ELEC ENG, ELECTRON, RECORDING, TELECOM, TRANSP, TV RF *(radiofréquence)*

RGB *abbr (red green blue)* COMP, DP, TV RVB *(rouge vert bleu)*

RISC *abbr (reduced instruction set computer)* COMP, DP ordinateur RISC *m*, ordinateur à jeu d'instructions réduit *m*

RJE *abbr (remote job entry)* COMP, DP soumission des travaux à distance *f*

RMS *abbr (root mean square)* CONST, ELECTRON, MATH, TELECOM valeur quadratique moyenne *f*

RO *abbr (remote operations)* TELECOM opérations distantes *f pl*

ROM *abbr (read-only memory)* COMP, DP, ELEC ENG, ELECTRON ROM, mémoire fixe *f*, mémoire morte *f*

ROP *abbr (rate of penetration)* PETR TECH taux de pénétration *m*

ROS *abbr (residual oil saturation)* PETR saturation en huile résiduelle *f*

ROSE *abbr (remote operation service element)* TELECOM élément de service d'opération distante *m*

RP *abbr (regional processor)* TELECOM processeur régional *m*

RS *abbr* COMP, DP *(record separator)* séparateur d'articles *m*, séparateur d'enregistrements *m*, TELECOM *(regenerator section)* section de régénération *f*

RST *abbr (regenerator section termination)* TELECOM terminaison de section de régénération *f*

RSU *abbr (remote switching unit)* TELECOM centre satellite *m*

RT *abbr (radar tracking)* TRANSP localisation par radar *f*

RTC *abbr (road tank car)* TRANSP camion citerne *m*

RTG *abbr (regenerator timing generator)* TELECOM générateur de rythme de régénérateur *m*

RTM *abbr (reference test method)* OPT méthode de mesure de remplacement *f*, TELECOM méthode de mesure de référence *f*

RTS *abbr* RAIL *(rapid transit system)* système de transport rapide *m*, TELECOM *(reliable transfer server)* serveur de transfert fiable *m*

RU *abbr (remote unit)* TELECOM unité distante *f*

s *abbr (second)* METR s *(second)*

S *abbr (siemens)* METR S *(siemens)*

SA *abbr (section adaptation)* TELECOM adaptation de section *f*

SAM *abbr (surface-to-air missile)* MILIT engin sol-air *m*

SAMSARS *abbr (satellite-aided maritime search and rescue system)* TELECOM système de recherche et de sauvetage maritimes par satellite *m*

SAP *abbr (service access point)* TELECOM point d'accès au service *m*

SAPI *abbr (service access point identifier)* TELECOM identificateur de point d'accès au réseau *m*

SAR *abbr (segmentation and reassembly)* TELECOM segmentation et réassemblage *f*

SAW *abbr (surface acoustic wave)* ELECTRON, TELECOM onde acoustique de surface *f*

SBA *abbr (slurry-blasting agent)* MINING bouillie explosive *f*, explosif de chargement *m*, explosif en bouillie *m*

SBM *abbr (single buoy mooring)* PETR TECH amarrage à point unique *m*

SBST *abbr (single bituminous surface treatment)* CONST revêtement monocouche *m*

SCC *abbr (single-cotton-covered)* ELEC guipé d'une couche coton

SCN *abbr (specification change notice)* TRANSP spécification de changement notifié *f*

SCPC *abbr (single channel per carrier)* SPACE porteuse monovoie *f*, système à porteuse monovoie *m*, TELECOM porteuse monovoie *f*

SCR *abbr (silicon-controlled rectifier)* ELEC ENG redresseur au silicium commandé *m*, thyristor au silicium *m*, PHYS redresseur au silicium commandé *m*, TELECOM thyristor au silicium *m*

SD *abbr (signal distributor)* TELECOM dégradation du signal *f*

SDH *abbr (synchronous digital hierarchy)* TELECOM HNS *(hiérarchie numérique synchrone)*

SDLC *abbr (synchronous data link control)* COMP procédure de commande de transmission synchrone *f*, DP commande de transmission synchrone *f*

SDR *abbr (system design review)* SPACE revue de conception système *f*

SDU *abbr (service data unit)* TELECOM unité de données de service *f*

SE *abbr (slurry explosive)* MINING bouillie explosive *f*, explosif de chargement *m*, explosif en bouillie *m*

SECAM *abbr* TV SECAM, séquentiel couleur à mémoire *m*

SELCAL *abbr (selective calling system)* TELECOM système d'appel sélectif *m*

SEM *abbr (surface electron microscope)* INSTRUMENT microscope électronique à balayage de surface *m*

SEMF *abbr (synchronous equipment management function)* TELECOM fonction de gestion d'équipement synchrone *f*

SES *abbr (severely errored second)* NAUT *satellites*, TELECOM seconde gravement erronée *f*

SEV *abbr (surface effect vehicle)* TRANSP véhicule à effet de sol *m*

SF *abbr (signal fail)* TELECOM défaillance de signal *f*

SFET *abbr (synchronous frequency encoding technique)* TELECOM technique de codage à fréquence synchrone *f*

SFU *abbr (store-and-forward unit)* TELECOM unité d'enregistrement et de retransmission *f*

SGC *abbr (signalling grouping channel)* TELECOM canal de groupement de signalisation *m*

SGML *abbr (Standard Generalized Mark-up Language)* DP, PRINT SGML *(langage standard généralisé de balisage)*

SHC *abbr (superhigh cube)* TRANSP SHC *(conteneur spécial hors-cotes)*

SHF *abbr (superhigh frequency)* ELECTRON supra-haute fréquence *f*

SI *abbr* METR *(international system of units)* SI *(système international d'unités)*, TELECOM *(screening indicator)* indicateur de contrôle *m*

SILP *abbr (single-in-line package)* COMP, DP boîtier à une rangée de broches *m*, ELECTRON boîtier SIP *m*, boîtier à une rangée de broches *m*

SIMM *abbr (single-in-line memory module)* COMP, DP module de mémoire à une rangée de broches *m*

SIMS *abbr (secondary ion mass spectrometry)* PHYS spectroscopie de masse aux ions secondaires *f*

SINCGARS *abbr (single channel ground and airborne radio system)* MILIT système radio sol-air à voie simple *m*

SIO *abbr* COMP *(sequential input/output)* entrée/sortie séquentielle *f*, COMP *(series input/output)* entrée/sortie série *f*

SIP *abbr (single-in-line package)* COMP, DP boîtier à une rangée de broches *m*, ELECTRON boîtier SIP *m*, boîtier à une rangée de broches *m*

SLAR *abbr (sideways-looking airborne radar)* MAR POLL radar aéroporté à balayage latéral *m*

SLC *abbr (subscriber line circuit)* TELECOM joncteur d'abonné *m*

SLD *abbr (superluminescent diode)* OPT, TELECOM DSL *(diode superluminescente)*

SLIM *abbr (single linear inductor motor)* TRANSP moteur linéaire à simple inducteur *m*

SLM *abbr (single-longitudinal mode)* TELECOM mode longitudinal unique *m*

SLR *abbr (single lens reflex camera)* PHOTO appareil reflex mono-objectif *m*

SM *abbr (synchronous multiplexer)* TELECOM multiplexeur synchrone *m*

SMAE *abbr (system management application entity)* TELECOM entité d'application de gestion de systèmes *f*

SMAW *abbr (shielded metal arc welding)* NUCLEAR soudage à l'arc avec électrode enrobée *m*

SMC *abbr (surface-mounted component)* ELECTRON, TELECOM CMS *(composant monté en surface)*

SMDS *abbr (switched multimegabit data service)* TELECOM service commuté de données multimégabit *m*

SMF *abbr (submultiframe)* TELECOM sous-multitrame *m*

SMIB *abbr (security management information base)* TELECOM base d'informations de gestion de sécurité *f*

SMN *abbr (SDH management network)* TELECOM réseau de gestion SDH *m*

SMS *abbr (SDH management subnetwork)* TELECOM sous-réseau de gestion SDH *m*

SN *abbr* TELECOM *(subscriber number)* numéro d'abonné *m*, TELECOM *(sequence number)* numéro de séquence *m*

SNA *abbr (systems network architecture)* COMP, DP architecture unifiée de réseau *f*

SNDCF *abbr (subnetwork dependent convergence function)* TELECOM fonction de convergence dépendant du sous-réseau *f*

SNG *abbr (substitute natural gas, synthetic natural gas)* GAS TECH, PETR TECH GNS *(gaz naturel de synthèse)*

SNP *abbr (sequence number protection)* TELECOM protection de numéro de séquence *f*

SNR *abbr (signal-to-noise ratio)* ACOUSTICS, COMP, DP, ELECTRON, PETR, PHYS, RECORDING, TELECOM, TV rapport signal-bruit *m*

SOH *abbr* COMP *(start of header)*, DP *(start of header)* début *m*, TELECOM *(section overhead)* SDS *(surdébit de section)*

SOM *abbr (start of message)* COMP, DP début de message *m*

SOS *abbr (silicon on sapphire)* ELECTRON silicium sur saphir *m*

SP *abbr* COMP *(structured programming)*, DP *(structured programming)* PS *(programmation structurée)*, ELECTRON *(signal processor)* processeur de signaux *m*, TELECOM *(signalling point, signaling point)* point sémaphore *m*, TELECOM *(service provider)* prestataire de service *m*, TELECOM *(session protocol)* protocole de session *m*, TELECOM *(signal processor)* unité de traitement de signaux *f*, TV *(signal processor)* dispositif de traitement de signal *m*, processeur de signal *m*

SPADATS *abbr (space detection and tracking system)* MILIT système de surveillance d'espace et de poursuite *m*

SPC *abbr* ELEC *(single-paper-covered)* guipé une couche papier, TELECOM *(stored programme control, stored program control)* commande à programme enregistré *f*

SPDT *abbr (single-pole double-throw)* ELEC, ELEC ENG à un contact inverseur

SPDU *abbr (session protocol data unit)* TELECOM unité de données du protocole de session *f*

SPF *abbr (segmentation permitted flag)* TELECOM indicateur de segmentation permise *m*

SPI *abbr (secondary porosity index)* PETR indice de porosité secondaire *m*

SPITE *abbr (switching process interworking telephony event)* TELECOM événement téléphonique de traitement des opérations de commutation *m*

SPL *abbr (service provider link)* TELECOM liaison de prestataire de service *f*

SPN *abbr (subscriber premises network)* TELECOM réseau d'installation d'abonnés *m*

SPST *abbr (single-pole single-throw)* ELEC, ELEC ENG à un contact interrupteur

squid *abbr (superconduting quantum interference device)* PHYS squid *(interféromètre quantique)*

SRAM *abbr (static RAM)* COMP RAM statique *f*

SRC *abbr (single-rubber-covered)* ELEC guipé une couche caoutchouc

SRD *abbr (superradiant diode)* OPT, TELECOM diode superluminescente *f*

SSB *abbr (single sideband)* TELECOM BLU *(bande latérale unique)*

SSC *abbr (sudden storm commencement)* SPACE début brusque d'orage magnétique *m*

SSI *abbr* COMP *(small-scale integration)* intégration à petite échelle *f*, DP *(small-scale integration)* intégration à faible échelle *f*, ELECTRON *(small-scale integration)* intégration à petite échelle *f*, RAIL *(solid-state interlocking)* système d'enclenchement informatisé *m*

SSM *abbr* SPACE *(second surface mirror)* miroir à couche secondaire *m*, TELECOM *(single segment message)* message à segment unique *m*, message à un seul segment *m*

SSMA *abbr (spread spectrum multiple access)* SPACE communications AMES *(accès multiple par étalement du spectre)*

SSOG *abbr (Satellite System Operation Guide)* SPACE guide d'exploitation des liaisons par satellite *m*

SST *abbr (supersonic transport)* AERONAUT transport supersonique *m*

SSUS *abbr (solid spinning upper stage)* SPACE étage supérieur stabilisé par rotation *m*

ST *abbr (segment type)* TELECOM type de segment *m*

STADAN *abbr (space tracking and data acquisition network)* MILIT réseau de poursuite et de saisie de données dans l'espace *m*

STD *abbr* (BrE) *(subscriber trunk dialling)* TELECOM interurbain automatique *m*, sélection à distance de l'abonné demandé *f*

STM *abbr* TELECOM *(synchronous transfer mode)* mode de transfert synchrone *m*, TELECOM *(synchronous transport module)* module de transport synchrone *m*

STM-n *abbr (synchronous transport module-n)* TELECOM module de transport synchrone-n *m*

STN *abbr (switched telephone network)* TELECOM RTC *(réseau téléphonique commuté)*

STP *abbr* PHYS *(standard temperature)* TPN *(température normale)*, TELECOM *(signalling transfer point, signaling transfer point)* point de transfert sémaphore *m*

STS *abbr* SPACE *(space-time-space)* STS *(spatial-temporel-spatial)*, SPACE *(space transportation system)* système de transport spatial *m*

STX *abbr (start of text)* COMP, DP début de texte *m*

Sv *abbr (sievert)* PHYS, RAD PHYS Sv *(sievert)*

SVC *abbr* COMP *(supervisor call)*, DP *(supervisor call)* appel du superviseur *m*, TELECOM *(signalling virtual channel, signaling virtual channel)* canal virtuel de signalisation *m*, circuit virtuel commuté *m*, voie virtuelle de signalisation *f*

SVS *abbr (suspended vehicle system)* TRANSP VSS *(véhicule à suspension supérieure)*

SW *abbr (short wave)* ELEC, WAVE PHYS onde courte *f*

SWR *abbr (standing-wave ratio)* SPACE, TELECOM ROS *(rapport d'ondes stationnaires)*

SYN *abbr (synchronous idle character)* COMP, DP SYN *(caractère de synchronisation)*

T *abbr* MECH ENG *(tee)* T *(té)*, METR *(tera-)* T *(téra-)*, PHYS *(tesla)* T *(tesla)*

TA *abbr (terminal adaptor)* TELECOM adapteur de terminal *m*

TAB *abbr* COMP *(tabulator key)*, DP *(tabulator key)* touche de tabulation *f*, ELEC ENG *(tape automated bonding)* connexion sur bande *f*

TAC *abbr (total allowable catch)* OCEANOG PMA *(prise maximale autorisée)*

TACV *abbr (tracked air cushion vehicle)* TRANSP aéroglisseur guidé *m*

TADG *abbr (three-axis data generator)* SPACE centrale de référence de direction et d'attitude *f*

TA-LB *abbr (B-ISDN terminal adaptor)* TELECOM adaptateur de terminal pour le RNIS-LB *m*

TAN *abbr (total acid number)* CHEM indice d'acidité *m*

TAS *abbr (true air speed)* AERONAUT vitesse propre *f*

TBF *abbr (traveling belt filter, travelling belt filter)* NUCLEAR filtre en ruban *m*

TBP *abbr (tethered buoyant platform)* PETR TECH plate-forme marine à câbles tendus *f*

TC *abbr (trunk code)* TELECOM indicatif interurbain *m*

TCE *abbr (transit connection element)* TELECOM élément de connexion de transit *m*

TCR *abbr (telemetry command and ranging subsystem)* SPACE TTL *(sous-système de télémesure, télécommande et localisation)*

TCRF *abbr (transit connection-related function)* TELECOM fonction liée à une connexion de transit *f*

TDC *abbr (top dead center, top dead centre)* AUTO, VEHICLES PMH *(point mort haut)*

TDF *abbr (trunk distribution frame)* TELECOM répartiteur de jonction *m*

TDI *abbr* P&R *(toluene diisocyanate)* diisocyanate de toluène *m*, toluène diisocyanate *m*, TELECOM *(trade data interchange)* échange de données commerciales *m*

TDM *abbr (time-division multiplexing)* COMP, DP, ELECTRON, PHYS, SPACE, TELECOM MRT *(multiplexage par répartition dans le temps)*

TDMA *abbr (time-division multiple access)* DP, ELECTRON, SPACE, TELECOM AMRT *(accès multiple par répartition dans le temps)*

TE *abbr (transverse electric)* OPT, TELECOM transversal électrique

TEC *abbr (field-effect transistor)* DP transistor à effet de champ *m*

TEI *abbr (terminal end-point identifier)* TELECOM identificateur de point d'extrémité de terminal *m*

TE-LB *abbr (B-ISDN terminal equipment)* TELECOM équipement terminal pour le RNIS-LB *m*

TEM *abbr (transverse electromagnetic)* ELEC ENG TEM *(électromagnétique transverse)*

TFA *abbr (transfer allowed)* TELECOM autorisation de transfert *f*

TFC *abbr (controlled transfer)* TELECOM transfert sous contrôle *m*

TFEL *abbr (thin-film electroluminescence)* ELECTRON électroluminescence à couches minces *f*

TFP *abbr (transfer prohibited)* TELECOM transfert interdit *m*

TFR *abbr (transfer restricted)* TELECOM transfert restreint *m*

TG *abbr (transcoding gain)* TELECOM gain de transcodage *m*

TGA *abbr (thermogravimetric analyzer)* LAB EQUIP analyseur thermogravimétrique *m*

TKO *abbr (trunk offer)* TELECOM intervention ligne-réseau *f*

TLC *abbr (thin-layer chromatography)* CHEM chromatographie sur couche mince *f*

TLMA *abbr (telematic agent)* TELECOM agent télématique *m*

TLV *abbr (threshold limit value)* POLLUTION concentration maximale admissible *f*

TM *abbr (transverse magnetic)* ELEC ENG, OPT, TELECOM magnétique transversal

TMN *abbr (telecommunications management network)* TELECOM RGT *(réseau de gestion des télécommunications)*

TMR *abbr (tandem mirror fusion reactor)* NUCLEAR réacteur à miroir tandem *m*

TMUX *abbr (transmultiplexer)* TELECOM transmultiplexeur *m*

TOCC *abbr (Technical and Operational Control Center)* SPACE Centre de contrôle technique et opérationnel *m*

TOFC *abbr (trailer on flatcar)* TRANSP ferroutage *m*

TON *abbr (type of number)* TELECOM type de numéro *m*

TP *abbr (transaction processing)* COMP, DP traitement de transactions *m*

TPDU *abbr (transport protocol data unit)* TELECOM unité de données du protocole de transport *f*

TPE *abbr (transmission path endpoint)* TELECOM extrémité de trajet de transmission *f*

TPI *abbr (tracks per inch)* COMP, DP, PRINT pistes par pouce *f pl*

TQC *abbr (total quality control)* QUALITY maîtrise totale de la qualité *f*

TQM *abbr (total quality management)* QUALITY management total de la qualité *m*

TR *abbr* ELECTRON *(transmit-receive)* émetteur-récepteur, TELECOM *(tributary)* affluent *m*

TSAP *abbr (transport service access point)* TELECOM point d'accès au service de transport *m*

TSI *abbr (time slot interchanger)* TELECOM commutateur T *m*, commutateur temporel *m*

TSP *abbr (trisodium phosphate)* DETERGENTS phosphate trisodique *m*

TTC *abbr (tracking telemetry and command)* SPACE *communications* PTT *(poursuite télémesure et télécommande)*

TTL *abbr (transistor-transistor logic)* COMP, DP logique transistor-transistor *f*, ELECTRON logique à transistor et transistors *f*

t-t-t *abbr (time-temperature-tolerance)* REFRIG *of frozen food* tolérance temps-température *f*

TTY *abbr (teletype)* COMP, DP téléscripteur *m*, télétype *m*, TELECOM téléimprimeur *m*, télétype *m*

TU *abbr (tributary unit)* TELECOM unité d'affluents *f*

TUG *abbr (tributary-unit group)* TELECOM groupe d'unité d'affluents *m*

TVC *abbr (thrust vector control)* SPACE *spacecraft* commande de contrôle de poussée *f*

TVP *abbr (textured vegetable protein)* FOOD TECH protéine végétale texturée *f*

TVS *abbr (tube vehicle system)* TRANSP transport en tube *m*

TWT *abbr (traveling-wave tube, travelling-wave tube)* ELECTRON, PHYS, SPACE, TELECOM TOP *(tube à onde progressive)*

TWTA *abbr (traveling-wave tube amplifier, travelling-wave tube amplifier)* ELECTRON, SPACE ATOP *(amplificateur à tube à onde progressive)*

TX *abbr (transmission)* TV transmission *f*

UA *abbr* COMP *(user area)*, DP *(user area)* zone de l'utilisateur *f*, TELECOM *(user agent)* agent d'usager *m*, agent utilisateur *m*

UAS *abbr (unavailable second)* TELECOM seconde d'indisponibilité *f*

UAT *abbr (unavailable time)* TELECOM temps d'indisponibilité *m*

UAX *abbr (unit automatic exchange)* TELECOM central automatique de localité *m*

UFO *abbr (unidentified flying object)* ASTRON, SPACE OVNI *(objet volant non identifié)*

UHF *abbr (ultrahigh frequency)* ELECTRON, TELECOM, TV, WAVE PHYS UHF *(ultrahaute fréquence)*

UHT *abbr (ultra heat treated)* FOOD TECH UHT *(longue-conservation)*

UI *abbr* TELECOM *(unnumbered information)* information non numérotée *f*, TELECOM *(unit interval)* intervalle unitaire *m*

UITS *abbr (unacknowledged information transfer service)* TELECOM service de transfert d'informations sans accusé de réception *m*

UKIRT *abbr (UK Infrared Telescope)* ASTRON UKIRT *(télescope infrarouge du Royaume-Uni)*

ULCC *abbr (ultralarge crude carrier)* PETR TECH UGPB *(ultragros porteur de brut)*

UNC *abbr* MECH ENG *(unified coarse thread)* systems of threads filetage unifié gros *m*, TELECOM *(unbalanced operation normal response mode class)* classe d'exploitation asymétrique en mode réponse normal *f*

UNF *abbr (unified fine thread)* MECH ENG *system of threads* filetage unifié fin *m*

UNI *abbr (user-network interface)* TELECOM interface usager-réseau *f*

USB *abbr (upper sideband)* ELECTRON, TELECOM bande latérale supérieure *f*

UT *abbr (Universal Time)* ASTRON, SPACE TU *(temps universel)*

UTC *abbr (universal time coordinated)* TELECOM temps universel coordonné *m*

UUI *abbr (user-to-user information)* TELECOM information d'usager à usager *f*

UUS *abbr (user-to-user signaling, user-to-user signalling)* TELECOM signalisation d'usager à usager *f*

UV *abbr (ultraviolet)* OPT, SPACE UV *(ultraviolet)*

UW *abbr (unique word)* SPACE *communications* mot particulier *m*

V *abbr (volt)* METR V *(volt)*

V1 *abbr (decision speed)* AERONAUT V1 *(vitesse de décision)*

VAD *abbr (vapor phase axial deposition, vapour phase axial deposition)* OPT, TELECOM DAV *(dépôt axial en phase vapeur)*

VAN *abbr (value-added network)* COMP, DP, TELECOM RVA *(réseau à valeur ajoutée)*

VBR *abbr (variable bit rate)* TELECOM DBV *(débit binaire variable)*

VC *abbr (virtual channel)* TELECOM canal virtuel *m*, voie virtuelle *f*

VCC *abbr (virtual channel connection)* TELECOM connexion de canal virtuel *f*, connexion de voie virtuelle *f*

VCCE *abbr (virtual channel connection endpoint)* TELECOM extrémité de connexion de canal virtuel *f*

VCF *abbr (video command freeze-picture request)* TELECOM commande vidéo de demande de gel de l'image *f*

VCI *abbr (virtual channel identifier)* TELECOM identificateur de canal virtuel *m*, identificateur de voie virtuelle *m*

VC-n *abbr (virtual container-n)* TELECOM conteneur virtuel-n *m*

VCO *abbr (voltage-controlled oscillator)* ELECTRON, SPACE, TELECOM oscillateur commandé en tension *m*

VCS *abbr (virtual-circuit switch)* TELECOM CCV *(commutateur de circuits virtuels)*

VCU *abbr (video command fast-update request)* TELECOM commande vidéo de demande de rafraîchissement rapide *f*

VDA *abbr (video distribution amplifier)* TV amplificateur de distribution vidéo *m*

VDU *abbr (visual display unit)* COMP, DP, TELECOM, TV, console de visualisation *f*, écran de visualisation *m*

VF *abbr (voice frequency)* ELECTRON, RAD PHYS, TELECOM fréquence vocale *f*

VHD *abbr (video high-density disc)* OPT disque VHD *m* *(disque électrostatique)*

VHF *abbr (very high-frequency)* ELECTRON, SPACE, TELECOM, TV, WAVE PHYS VHF *(très haute fréquence)*

VHFO *abbr (very high-frequency omnirange)* TRANSP radiophare omnidirectionnel VHF *m*

VHS *abbr (video home system)* TV système VHS *m*

VI *abbr (volume indicator)* RECORDING vumètre *m*

VIA *abbr (video indicate active)* TELECOM indication vidéo active *f*

VIR *abbr (video indicate ready-to-activate)* TELECOM indication vidéo prête à être activée *f*

VIS *abbr (video indicate suppressed)* TELECOM indication vidéo supprimée *f*

VLA *abbr (Very Large Array)* ASTRON VLA *(très grand réseau d'antennes)*

VLBA *abbr (Very Long Baseline Array)* ASTRON VLBA *(réseau d'antennes à très longue ligne de base)*

VLCC *abbr (very large crude carrier)* PETR TECH TGTB *(très gros transporteur de brut)*

VLP *abbr (video long play)* OPT disque vidéo longue durée *m*

VLSI *abbr (very large-scale integration)* COMP, DP, ELECTRON, TELECOM intégration à très grande échelle *f*

VMS *abbr (virtual memory system)* COMP, DP système à mémoire virtuelle *m*

VOD *abbr (velocity of detonation)* MINING vitesse de détonation *f*

VOR *abbr (VHF omnidirectional radio range)* AERONAUT radiophare omnidirectionnel VHF *m*

VP *abbr (virtual path)* TELECOM conduit virtuel *m*, trajet virtuel *m*

VPC *abbr (virtual path connection)* TELECOM connexion de conduit virtuel *f*, connexion de trajet virtuel *f*

VPCE *abbr (virtual path connection endpoint)* TELECOM extrémité de connexion de trajet virtuel *f*

VPI *abbr (virtual path identifier)* TELECOM identificateur de conduit virtuel *m*, identificateur de trajet virtuel *m*

VRC *abbr (vertical redundancy check)* COMP, DP contrôle par redondance verticale *m*

VSI *abbr (vertical speed indicator)* SPACE variomètre *m*

VSP *abbr (vertical seismic profile)* PETR TECH PSV *(profil sismique vertical)*

VSWR *abbr (voltage standing-wave ratio)* SPACE communications ROS *(rapport d'ondes stationnaires)*

VT *abbr* COMP *(vertical tabulation)* tabulation verticale *f*, COMP *(virtual terminal)* terminal virtuel *m*, DP *(vertical tabulation)* tabulation verticale *f*, DP *(virtual terminal)* terminal virtuel *m*

VTR *abbr (video tape recorder)* TV magnétoscope *m*

W *abbr (watt)* ELEC, ELEC ENG, METR, PHYS W *(watt)*

Wb *abbr (weber)* METR, PHYS Wb *(weber)*

WDM *abbr (wavelength division multiplexing)* TELECOM MRL *(multiplexage par répartition en longueur d'onde)*

WDX *abbr (wavelength dispersive double X-ray spectrometer)* NUCLEAR double spectromètre à rayons X *m*

WOB *abbr (weight on bit)* PETR TECH poids sur l'outil *m*

WOOD *abbr (write-once optical disk)* DP DON *(disque optique non effaçable)*

WOR *abbr (water-oil ratio)* PETR rapport eau-pétrole *m*

WORM *abbr (write-once read many times)* OPT disque inscriptible une seule fois *m*

WOW *abbr (waiting on weather)* PETR TECH attente mauvaise *f*

WP *abbr (word processing)* COMP, DP TdT *(traitement de texte)*

WRU *abbr (who-are-you)* TELECOM qui êtes-vous

WS *abbr (weight strength)* MINING CUP *(coefficient d'utilisation pratique)* PMB *(puissance au mortier balistique)*

WYSIWYG *abbr (what you see is what you get)* COMP, DP WYSIWYG *(tel vu tel imprimé, vu-imprimé)*

XALS *abbr (extended application layer structure)* TELECOM structure en couches d'application étendue *f*

YAG *abbr (yttrium aluminium garnet, yttrium aluminum garnet)* ELECTRON YAG *(grenat d'yttrium et d'aluminium)*

YIG *abbr (yttrium iron garnet)* ELECTRON YIG *(grenat d'yttrium ferreux)*

Z *abbr (proton number)* PART PHYS Z *(nombre de protons)*

Tables de conversion/ Conversion tables

1 Longueur / Length

		mètre *metre*	pouce *inch*	pied *foot*	yard *yard*	rod *rod*	mile *mile*
1 mètre *metre*	=	1	39,37	3,281	1,093	0,1988	$6,214 \times 10^{-4}$
1 pouce *inch*	=	$2,54 \times 10^{-2}$	1	0,083	0,02778	$5,050 \times 10^{-3}$	$1,578 \times 10^{-5}$
1 pied *foot*	=	0,3048	12	1	0,3333	0,0606	$1,894 \times 10^{-4}$
1 yard *yard*	=	0,9144	36	3	1	0,1818	$5,682 \times 10^{-4}$
1 rod *rod*	=	5,029	198	16,5	5,5	1	$3,125 \times 10^{-3}$
1 mile *mile*	=	1609	63360	5280	1760	320	1

1 yard standard légal = 0,914 398 41 mètre / 1 imperial standard yard = 0.914 398 41 metre
1 yard (scientifique) = 0,9144 mètre (exactement) / 1 yard (scientific) = 0.9144 metre (exact)
1 yard US = 0,914 401 83 mètre / 1 US yard = 0.914 401 83 metre
1 mile marin anglais = 6080 pieds = 1853,18 mètres / 1 English nautical mile = 6080 ft = 1853.18 metres
1 mile marin international = 1852 mètres = 6076,12 pieds / 1 international nautical mile = 1852 metres = 6076.12 ft

2 Superficie / Area

		mètre^2 *sq. metre*	pouce^2 *sq. inch*	pied^2 *sq. foot*	yard^2 *sq. yard*	acre *acre*	mile^2 *sq. mile*
1 mètre^2 *sq. metre*	=	1	1550	10,76	1,196	$2,471 \times 10^{-4}$	$3,861 \times 10^{-7}$
1 pouce^2 *sq. inch*	=	$6,452 \times 10^{-4}$	1	$6,944 \times 10^{-3}$	$7,716 \times 10^{-4}$	$1,594 \times 10^{-7}$	$2,491 \times 10^{-10}$
1 pied^2 *sq. foot*	=	0,0929	144	1	0,1111	$2,296 \times 10^{-5}$	$3,587 \times 10^{-8}$
1 yard^2 *sq. yard*	=	0,8361	1296	9	1	$2,066 \times 10^{-4}$	$3,228 \times 10^{-7}$
1 acre *acre*	=	$4,047 \times 10^{3}$	$6,273 \times 10^{6}$	$4,355 \times 10^{4}$	4840	1	$1,563 \times 10^{-3}$
1 mile^2 *sq. mile*	=	$259,0 \times 10^{4}$	$4,015 \times 10^{9}$	$2,788 \times 10^{7}$	$3,098 \times 10^{6}$	640	1

1 are = 100 mètres carrés = 0,01 hectare / 1 are = 100 sq. metres = 0.01 hectare
1 millimètre circulaire   = $5,067 \times 10^{-10}$ mètres carrés / 1 circular mil = 5.067×10^{-10} sq. metre
                           = $7,854 \times 10^{-7}$ pouces carrés /   = 7.854×10^{-7} sq. in
1 acre (légal) = 0,4047 hectare / 1 acre (statute) = 0.4047 hectare

3 Volume / Volume

		mètre cube *cubic metre*	pouce cube *cubic inch*	pied cube *cubic foot*	gallon UK *UK gallon*	gallon US *US gallon*
1 mètre cube *cubic metre*	=	1	$6,102 \times 10^{4}$	35,31	220,0	264,2
1 pouce cube *cubic in*	=	$1,639 \times 10^{-5}$	1	$5,787 \times 10^{-4}$	$3,605 \times 10^{-3}$	$4,329 \times 10^{-3}$
1 pied cube *cubic ft*	=	$2,832 \times 10^{-2}$	1728	1	6,229	7,480
1 gallon UK* *UK gallon*	=	$4,546 \times 10^{-3}$	277,4	0,1605	1	1,201
1 gallon US† *US gallon*	=	$3,785 \times 10^{-3}$	231,0	0,1337	0,8327	1

* volume de 10 lb d'eau à 62 ° F / volume of 10 lb of water at 62 ° F
† volume de 8,328 28 lb d'eau à 60 ° F / volume of 8.328 28 lb of water at 60 ° F
1 mètre cube = 999,972 litres / 1 cubic metre = 999.972 litres
1 acre pied = 271 328 gallons UK = 1233 mètres cube / 1 acre foot = 271 328 UK gallons = 1233 cubic metres

jusqu'en 1976 le litre était égal à 1000,028 cm^3 (volume de 1 kg d'eau à la masse volumique maximale) mais il a été depuis redéfini à 1000 cm^3 exactement

until 1976 the litre was equal to 1000.028 cm^3 (the volume of 1 kg of water at maximum density) but then it was revalued to be 1000 cm^3 exactly

4 Angle / Angle

		degré *degree*	minute *minute*	seconde *second*	radian *radian*	tour *revolution*
1 degré *degree*	=	1	60	3600	$1{,}745 \times 10^{-2}$	$2{,}778 \times 10^{-3}$
1 minute *minute*	=	$1{,}677 \times 10^{-2}$	1	60	$2{,}909 \times 10^{-4}$	$4{,}630 \times 10^{-5}$
1 seconde *second*	=	$2{,}778 \times 10^{-4}$	$1{,}667 \times 10{-2}$	1	$4{,}848 \times 10^{-6}$	$7{,}716 \times 10^{-7}$
1 radian *radian*	=	57,30	3438	$2{,}063 \times 10^{5}$	1	0,1592
1 tour *revolution*	=	360	$2{,}16 \times 10^{4}$	$1{,}296 \times 10^{6}$	6,283	1

1 millième (d'artillerie) = 10^{-3} radian / 1 mil = 10^{-3} radian

5 Temps / Time

		année *year*	jour (solaire moyen) *solar day*	heure *hour*	minute *minute*	seconde *second*
1 année *year*	=	1	365,24*	$8{,}766 \times 10^{3}$	$5{,}259 \times 10^{5}$	$3{,}156 \times 10^{7}$
1 jour (solaire moyen) *solar day*	=	$2{,}738 \times 10^{-3}$	1	24	1440	$8{,}640 \times 10^{4}$
1 heure *hour*	=	$1{,}141 \times 10^{-4}$	$4{,}167 \times 10^{-2}$	1	60	3600
1 minute *minute*	=	$1{,}901 \times 10^{-6}$	$6{,}944 \times 10^{-4}$	$1{,}667 \times 10^{-2}$	1	60
1 seconde *second*	=	$3{,}169 \times 10^{-8}$	$1{,}157 \times 10^{-5}$	$2{,}778 \times 10^{-4}$	$1{,}667 \times 10^{-2}$	1

1 année = 366,24 jours sidéraux / 1 year = 366.24 sidereal days
1 jour sidéral = 86 164,090 6 secondes / 1 sidereal day = 86 164.090 6 seconds
*chiffre exact =365,242 192 64 en l'an 2000 A.D. / exact figure = 365.242 192 64 in A.D. 2000

6 Masse / Mass

		kilogramme *kilogram*	livre *pound*	slug *slug*	slug métrique *metric slug*	tonne UK *UK ton*	tonne US *US ton*	u
1 kilogramme *kilogram*	=	1	2,205	$6,852 \times 10^{-2}$	0,1020	$9,842 \times 10^{-4}$	$11,02 \times 10^{-4}$	$6,024 \times 10^{26}$
1 livre *pound*	=	0,4536	1	$3,108 \times 10^{-2}$	$4,625 \times 10^{-2}$	$4,464 \times 10^{-4}$	$5,000 \times 10^{-4}$	$2,732 \times 10^{26}$
1 slug *slug*	=	14,59	32,17	1	1,488	$1,436 \times 10^{-2}$	$1,609 \times 10^{-2}$	$8,789 \times 10^{27}$
1 slug métrique *metric slug*	=	9,806	21,62	0,6720	1	$9,652 \times 10^{-3}$	$1,081 \times 10^{-2}$	$5,907 \times 10^{27}$
1 tonne UK *UK ton*	=	1016	2240	69,62	103,6	1	1,12	$6,121 \times 10^{29}$
1 tonne US *US ton*	=	907,2	2000	62,16	92,51	0,8929	1	$5,465 \times 10^{29}$
1 u	=	$1,660 \times 10^{-27}$	$3,660 \times 10^{-27}$	$1,137 \times 10^{-28}$	$1,693 \times 10^{-28}$	$1,634 \times 10^{-30}$	$1,829 \times 10^{-30}$	1

1 livre standard légale = 0,453 592 338 kilogramme / 1 imperial standard pound = 0.453 592 338 kilogram
1 livre US = 0,453 592 427 7 kilogramme / 1 US pound = 0.453 592 427 7 kilogram
1 livre internationale = 0,453 592 37 kilogramme / 1 international pound = 0.453 592 37 kilogram
1 tonne = 10^3 kilogramme / 1 tonne = 10^3 kilograms
1 livre troy = 0,373 242 kilogramme / 1 troy pound = 0.373 242 kilogram

7 Force / Force

		dyne *dyne*	newton *newton*	livre poids *pound force*	poundal *poundal*	*gramme poids *gram force*
1 dyne *dyne*	=	1	10^{-5}	$2,248 \times 10^{-6}$	$7,233 \times 10^{-5}$	$1,020 \times 10^{-3}$
1 newton *newton*	=	10^5	1	0,2248	7,233	102,0
1 livre poids *pound force*	=	$4,448 \times 10^5$	4,448	1	32,17	453,6
1 poundal *poundal*	=	$1,383 \times 10^4$	0,1383	$3,108 \times 10^{-2}$	1	14,10
1 gramme poids *gram force*	=	980,7	$980,7 \times 10^{-5}$	$2,205 \times 10^{-3}$	$7,093 \times 10^{-2}$	1

* unité non légal en France / not recognized officially in France

8 Puissance / Power

		Btu/h *Btu per hr*	livre pied/s *ft lb s^{-1}*	kilogramme mètre/s *kg metre s^{-1}*	calorie/s *cal s^{-1}*	*cheval- vapeur *HP*	watt *watt*
1 Btu par heure *Btu per hour*	=	1	0,2161	$2,987 \times 10^{-2}$	$6,999 \times 10^{-2}$	$3,929 \times 10^{-4}$	0,2931
1 livre pied par seconde *ft lb per second*	=	4,628	1	0,1383	0,3239	$1,818 \times 10^{-3}$	1,356
1 kilogramme mètre par seconde *kg metre per second*	=	33,47	7,233	1	2,343	$1,315 \times 10^{-2}$	9,807
1 calorie par seconde *cal per second*	=	14,29	3,087	$4,268 \times 10^{-1}$	1	$5,613 \times 10^{-3}$	4,187
1 cheval-vapeur *HP*	=	2545	550	76,04	178,2	1	745,7
1 watt *watt*	=	3,413	0,7376	0,1020	0,2388	$1,341 \times 10^{-3}$	1

1 watt international = 1,000 19 watt absolu / 1 international watt = 1.000 19 absolute watt
* unité non légal en France / not recognized officially in France

9 Energie, travail, chaleur / Energy, work, heat

		Btu *Btu*	joule *joule*	livre pied *ft lb*	cm⁻¹ *cm⁻¹*	**calorie *cal*	kilowattheure *kW h*	électron volt *electron volt*	kilogramme* *kg*	u*
1 Btu *Btu*	=	1	$1,055 \times 10^{3}$	778,2	$5,312 \times 10^{25}$	252	$2,930 \times 10^{-4}$	$6,585 \times 10^{21}$	$1,174 \times 10^{-14}$	$7,074 \times 10^{12}$
1 joule *joule*	=	$9,481 \times 10^{-4}$	1	$7,376 \times 10^{-1}$	$5,035 \times 10^{22}$	$2,389 \times 10^{-1}$	$2,778 \times 10^{-7}$	$6,242 \times 10^{18}$	$1,113 \times 10^{-17}$	$6,705 \times 10^{9}$
1 livre pied *ft lb*	=	$1,285 \times 10^{-3}$	1,356	1	$6,828 \times 10^{22}$	$3,239 \times 10^{-1}$	$3,766 \times 10^{-7}$	$8,464 \times 10^{18}$	$1,507 \times 10^{-17}$	$9,092 \times 10^{9}$
1 cm⁻¹ *cm⁻¹*	=	$1,883 \times 10^{-26}$	$1,986 \times 10^{-23}$	$1,465 \times 10^{-23}$	1	$4,745 \times 10^{-24}$	$5,517 \times 10^{-30}$	$1,240 \times 10^{-4}$	$2,210 \times 10^{-40}$	$1,332 \times 10^{-13}$
1 calorie 15°C *cal 15°C*	=	$3,968 \times 10^{-3}$	4,187	3,088	$2,108 \times 10^{23}$	1	$1,163 \times 10^{-6}$	$2,613 \times 10^{19}$	$4,659 \times 10^{-17}$	$2,807 \times 10^{10}$
1 kilowattheure *kW h*	=	3412	$3,600 \times 10^{6}$	$2,655 \times 10^{6}$	$1,813 \times 10^{29}$	$8,598 \times 10^{5}$	1	$2,247 \times 10^{25}$	$4,007 \times 10^{-11}$	$2,414 \times 10^{16}$
1 électron volt *electron volt*	=	$1,519 \times 10^{-22}$	$1,602 \times 10^{-19}$	$1,182 \times 10^{-19}$	$8,066 \times 10^{3}$	$3,827 \times 10^{-20}$	$4,450 \times 10^{-26}$	1	$1,783 \times 10^{-36}$	$1,074 \times 10^{-9}$
1 kilogramme* *kg*	=	$8,521 \times 10^{13}$	$8,987 \times 10^{16}$	$6,629 \times 10^{16}$	$4,525 \times 10^{39}$	$2,147 \times 10^{16}$	$2,497 \times 10^{10}$	$5,610 \times 10^{35}$	1	$6,025 \times 10^{2}$
1 u*	=	$1,415 \times 10^{-13}$	$1,492 \times 10^{-10}$	$1,100 \times 10^{-10}$	$7,513 \times 10^{12}$	$3,564 \times 10^{-11}$	$4,145 \times 10^{-17}$	$9,31 \times 10^{8}$	$1,660 \times 10^{-27}$	1

* à partir du rapport énergie–masse $E = mc^2$ / from the mass–energy relationship $E = mc^2$

* *unité non légal en France / not recognized officially in France*

** *calorie / cal*

10 Pression / Pressure

		atmosphère normale standard atmosphere	kg poids cm⁻² kg force cm⁻²	dyne cm⁻² dyne cm⁻²	pascal pascal	livre poids pouce⁻² pound force in⁻²	livre poids pied⁻² pound force ft⁻²	millibar millibar	*torr torr	pouce Hg barométrique barometric in. Hg
1 atmosphère normale standard atmosphere	=	1	1,033	$1,013 \times 10^6$	$1,013 \times 10^5$	14,70	2116	1013	760	29,92
1 kg poids cm⁻² kg force cm⁻²	=	0,9678	1	$9,804 \times 10^5$	$9,804 \times 10^4$	14,22	2048	980,7	735,6	28,96
1 dyne cm⁻² dyne cm⁻²	=	$9,869 \times 10^{-7}$	$10,20 \times 10^{-7}$	1	0,1	$14,50 \times 10^{-6}$	$2,089 \times 10^{-3}$	10^{-3}	$750,1 \times 10^{-6}$	$29,53 \times 10^{-6}$
1 pascal pascal	=	$9,869 \times 10^{-6}$	$10,20 \times 10^{-6}$	10	1	$14,50 \times 10^{-5}$	$2,089 \times 10^{-2}$	10^{-2}	$750,1 \times 10^{-5}$	$29,53 \times 10^{-5}$
1 livre poids pouce⁻² pound force in⁻²	=	$6,805 \times 10^{-2}$	$7,031 \times 10^{-2}$	$6,895 \times 10^4$	$6,895 \times 10^3$	1	144	68,95	51,71	2,036
1 livre poids pied⁻² pound force ft⁻²	=	$4,725 \times 10^{-4}$	$4,882 \times 10^{-4}$	478,8	47,88	$6,944 \times 10^{-3}$	1	$47,88 \times 10^{-2}$	0,3591	$14,14 \times 10^{-3}$
1 millibar millibar	=	$0,9869 \times 10^{-3}$	$1,020 \times 10^{-3}$	10^3	10^2	$14,50 \times 10^{-3}$	2,089	1	0,7500	$29,53 \times 10^{-3}$
1 torr torr	=	$1,316 \times 10^{-3}$	$1,360 \times 10^{-3}$	$1,333 \times 10^2$	$1,333 \times 10^3$	$1,934 \times 10^{-2}$	2,784	1,333	1	$3,937 \times 10^{-2}$
1 pouce Hg barométrique barometric in. Hg	=	$3,342 \times 10^{-2}$	$3,453 \times 10^{-2}$	$3,386 \times 10^4$	$3,386 \times 10^3$	$4,912 \times 10^{-1}$	70,73	33,87	25,40	1

1 torr = 1 millimètre de mercure conventionnel à une masse volumique de 13,5951 g cm⁻³ à 0° C et pour une accélération due à la pesanteur de 980,665 cm/s⁻²

1/ torr = 1 barometric mmHg density 13.5951 g cm⁻³ at 0° C and acceleration due to gravity 980.665 cm/s⁻².

* le torr est une unité non légal en France / the torr is not recognized officially in France

1 dyne cm⁻² = 1 barad / 1 dyne cm⁻² = 1 barad

11 Flux magnétique / Magnetic flux

		*maxwell *maxwell*	kiloline *kiloline*	weber *weber*
1 maxwell (1 ligne) *maxwell (1 line)*	=	1	10^{-3}	10^{-8}
1 kiloline *kiloline*	=	10^3	1	10^{-5}
1 weber *weber*	=	10^8	10^5	1

*unité non légal en France / not recognized officially in France

12 Densité de flux magnétique / Magnetic flux density

		*gauss *gauss*	weber m^{-2} (tesla) *weber m^{-2} (tesla)*	gamma *gamma*	maxwell cm^{-2} *maxwell cm^{-2}*
1 gauss (ligne cm^{-2}) *gauss (line cm^{-2})*	=	1	10^{-4}	10^5	1
1 weber m^{-2} (tesla) *weber m^{-2} (tesla)*	=	10^4	1	10^9	10^4
1 gamma *gamma*	=	10^{-5}	10^{-9}	1	10^{-5}
1 maxwell cm^{-2} *maxwell cm^{-2}*	=	1	$10-4$	10^5	1

*unité non légal en France / not recognized officially in France

13 Force magnétomotrice / Magnetomotive force

		abampère tour *abamp turn*	ampère tour *amp turn*	*gilbert *gilbert*
1 abampère tour *abampere turn*	=	1	10	12,57
1 ampère tour *ampere turn*	=	10^{-1}	1	1,257
1 gilbert *gilbert*	=	$7,958 \times 10^{-2}$	0,7958	1

*unité non légal en France / not recognized officially in France

14 Intensité de champ magnétique / Magnetic field strength

		ampère tour cm^{-1} *amp turn cm^{-1}*	ampère tour m^{-1} *amp turn m^{-1}*	*oersted *oersted*
1 ampère tour cm^{-1} *amp turn cm^{-1}*	=	1	10^2	1,257
1 ampère tour m^{-1} *amp turn m^{-1}*	=	10^{-2}	1	$1,257 \times 10^{-2}$
1 oersted *oersted*	=	0,7958	79,58	1

*unité non légal en France / not recognized officially in France

15 Eclairement lumineux / Illumination

		lux *lux*	*phot *phot*	bougie pied *foot-candle*
1 lux $(1 m\, m^{-2})$ *lux ($1 m\, m^{-2}$)*	=	1	10^{-4}	$9,29 \times 10^{-2}$
1 phot $(1 m\, cm^{-2})$ *phot ($1 m\, cm^{-2}$)*	=	10^4	1	929
1 bougie pied $(1 m\, pied^{-2})$ *foot-candle ($1 m\, ft^{-2}$)*	=	10,76	$10,76 \times 10^{-4}$	1

*unité non légal en France / not recognized officially in France

16 Luminance lumineuse/Luminance

		*nit *nit*	*stilb *stilb*	candela pied^{-2} *cd ft^{-2}*	apostilb *apostilb*	*lambert *lambert*	lambert pied *foot-lambert*
1 nit (candela m^{-2}) *nit (cd m^{-2})*	=	1	10^{-4}	$9{,}29 \times 10^{-2}$	π	$\pi \times 10^{-4}$	0,292
1 stilb (candela cm^{-2}) *stilb* *(cd cm^{-2})*	=	10^4	1	929	$\pi \times 10^4$	π	2920
candela (pied^{-2}) *1 cd ft^{-2}*	=	10,76	$1{,}076 \times 10{-}3$	1	33,8	$3{,}38 \times 10^{-3}$	π
1 apostilb (1m m^{-2}) *apostilb* *(1m m^{-2})*	=	$1/\pi$	$1/(\pi \times 10^4)$	$2{,}96 \times 10^{-2}$	1	10^{-4}	$9{,}29 \times 10^{-2}$
1 lambert (1m cm^{-2}) *lambert* *(1m cm^{-2})*	=	$1/(\pi \times 10^{-4})$	$1/\pi$	296	10^4	1	929
1 lambert pied *ou* bougie pied équivalent *foot* *lambert* or *equivalent foot* *candle*	=	3,43	$3{,}43 \times 10^{-4}$	$1/\pi$	10,76	$1{,}076 \times 10^{-3}$	1

intensité lumineuse de la candela = 98,1% de celle de la bougie internationale
luminous intensity of candela = 98.1% that of international candle
1 lumen = flux lumineux émis par dans l'angle solide de
1 stéradian par une source ayant une intensité lumineuse de
1 candela
1 lumen = flux emitted by 1 candela into unit solid angle
*unité non légal en France / not recognized officially in France

Eléments chimiques/Chemical elements

Symbole/Symbol	Element	Elément	Numéro atomique/ Atomic number
Ac	Actinium	Actinium	89
Ag	Silver	Argent	47
Al	Aluminium	Aluminium	13
Am	Americium	Américium	95
Ar	Argon	Argon	18
As	Arsenic	Arsenic	33
At	Astatine	Astate	85
Au	Gold	Or	79
B	Boron	Bore	5
Ba	Barium	Baryum	56
Be	Beryllium	Béryllium	4
Bi	Bismuth	Bismuth	83
Bk	Berkelium	Berkélium	97
Br	Bromine	Brome	35
C	Carbon	Carbone	6
Ca	Calcium	Calcium	20
Cd	Cadmium	Cadmium	48
Ce	Cerium	Cérium	58
Cf	Californium	Californium	98
Cl	Chlorine	Chlore	17
Cm	Curium	Curium	96
Co	Cobalt	Cobalt	27
Cr	Chromium	Chrome	24
Cs	Caesium	Césium	55
Cu	Copper	Cuivre	29
Dy	Dysprosium	Dysprosium	66
Er	Erbium	Erbium	68
Es	Einsteinium	Einsteinium	99
Eu	Europium	Europium	63
F	Fluorine	Fluor	9
Fe	Iron	Fer	26
Fm	Fermium	Fermium	100
Fr	Francium	Francium	87
Ga	Gallium	Gallium	31
Gd	Gadolinium	Gadolinium	64
H	Hydrogen	Hydrogène	1
He	Helium	Hélium	2
Hf	Hafnium	Hafnium	72
Hg	Mercury	Mercure	80
Ho	Holmium	Holmium	67
I	Iodine	Iodine	53
In	Indium	Indium	49
Ir	Iridium	Iridium	77
K	Potassium	Potassium	19

Kr	Krypton	Krypton	36
La	Lanthanum	Lanthane	57
Li	Lithium	Lithium	3
Lr	Lawrencium	Lawrençium	103
Lu	Lutetium	Lutétium	71
Md	Mendelevium	Mendelévium	101
Mg	Magnesium	Magnésium	12
Mn	Manganese	Manganèse	25
Mo	Molybdenum	Molybdène	42
N	Nitrogen	Azote	7
Na	Sodium	Sodium	11
Nb	Niobium	Niobium	41
Nd	Neodymium	Néodyme	60
Ne	Neon	Néon	10
Ni	Nickel	Nickel	28
No	Nobelium	Nobélium	102
Np	Neptunium	Neptunium	93
O	Oxygen	Oxygène	8
Os	Osmium	Osmium	76
P	Phosphorus	Phosphore	15
Pa	Proctactinium	Proctactinium	91
Pb	Lead	Plomb	82
Pd	Palladium	Palladium	46
Pm	Promethium	Prométhium	61
Po	Polonium	Polonium	84
Pr	Praseodymium	Praséodyme	59
Pt	Platinum	Platine	78
Ra	Radium	Radium	88
Rb	Rubudium	Rubudium	37
Re	Rhenium	Rhénium	75
Rh	Rhodium	Rhodium	45
Rn	Radon	Radon	86
Ru	Ruthenium	Ruthénium	44
S	Sulphur	Soufre	16
Sb	Antimony	Antimoine	51
Sc	Scandium	Scandium	21
Se	Selenium	Sélénium	34
Si	Silicon	Silicium	14
Sm	Samarium	Samarium	62
Sn	Tin	Etain	50
Sr	Strontium	Strontium	38
Ta	Tantalum	Tantale	73
Tb	Terbium	Terbium	65
Tc	Technetium	Technétium	43
Te	Tellurium	Tellure	52
Th	Thorium	Thorium	90
Ti	Titanium	Titane	22
Tl	Thallium	Thallium	81
Tm	Thulium	Thulium	69
U	Uranium	Uranium	92
V	Vanadium	Vanadium	23
W	Tungsten	Tungstène	74
Xe	Xenon	Xénon	54
Y	Yttrium	Yttrium	39

Yb	Ytterbium	Ytterbium	70
Zn	Zinc	Zinc	30
Zr	Zirconium	Zirconium	40